〕—

MICHAELIS

DICIONÁRIO ILUSTRADO

VOLUME II

PORTUGUÊS-INGLÊS

MICHAELIS

ILLUSTRATED DICTIONARY

VOLUME II

PORTUGUESE-ENGLISH

MICHAELIS

DICIONÁRIO ILUSTRADO

Volume II
PORTUGUÊS-INGLÊS

Amplo vocabulário moderno
Frases idiomáticas • Grande número de pranchas
com mais de 4.000 referências

Seção Lexicográfica
das Edições Melhoramentos

Orientação de
FRANZ WIMMER

Ilustrações redesenhadas por
WILSON MARIOTTI

MELHORAMENTOS

MICHAELIS

ILLUSTRATED DICTIONARY

Volume II
PORTUGUESE-ENGLISH

Comprehensive modern vocabulary
Idiomatic phrases • Numerous plates with
more than 4,000 conceptions

The Lexicographic Staff
of Edições Melhoramentos

Direction of
FRANZ WIMMER

Renewed drawings by
WILSON MARIOTTI

**É proibida a venda
desta edição
em Portugal**

MELHORAMENTOS

Atendimento ao consumidor:
Caixa Postal 2547 – CEP 01065-970 – São Paulo – SP – Brasil

Edição: 59 58 57 56
Ano: 200 99 98

NE-V

ISBN: 85-06-01598-7

Impresso no Brasil

DO PINHEIRO AO LIVRO, UMA REALIZAÇÃO MELHORAMENTOS

ÍNDICE

TABLE OF CONTENTS

PREFÁCIO

O sucesso dos dicionários MICHAELIS tem sido motivo de orgulho da Melhoramentos. Há décadas esta linha de dicionários, líderes no mercado, tem sido constantemente atualizada e acrescida de novos volumes.

Ao ser lançada mais esta edição do MICHAELIS — Dicionário Ilustrado Inglês/Português, cabe aqui fazer breve retrospecto desta obra.

Assim, o dicionário Michaelis Inglês-Português, de autoria da lexicógrafa alemã Henriette Michaelis, foi publicado pela primeira vez em 1893, alguns anos após a autora ter publicado o importante dicionário Alemão-Português. Na ocasião da 1.ª edição a autora contou com a valiosa colaboração de sua irmã Carolina Michaelis de Vasconcelos, figura de destaque nas letras portuguesas, a qual, com seus profundos conhecimentos da língua de sua pátria adotiva, muito contribuíra para fazer do referido dicionário uma obra na qual filólogos e estudantes pudessem encontrar um guia seguro para seus trabalhos científicos e literários.

É evidente que um dicionário, para manter todo o seu valor e eficiência, precisa sempre estar em contato com a língua viva. Entretanto, após algumas revisões durante as primeiras décadas da sua existência, o Dicionário Michaelis deixou de registrar as modificações ocorridas nas línguas portuguesa e inglesa. Nestas circunstâncias é natural que a obra se tornasse cada vez mais desatualizada e, em muitos pontos, anacrônica. Impunha-se sua revisão, trabalho de enorme vulto, demandando longo tempo e a colaboração de especialistas. O trabalho deveria, para alcançar sua finalidade, estender-se à estrutura da obra e ao confronto, palavra por palavra, com a terminologia viva e atual.

Na década de 1950 a Melhoramentos lançou-se com arrojo a esse empreendimento. A reestruturação da obra ficou a cargo do Prof. Fritz Pietzschke que, entre seus colaboradores, contou com a participação dos Srs. Franz Wimmer, Gustavo Lohnefink, José Curado, Lothar Fritsch e Hans Rzeppa. Após vários anos de trabalho foi publicado, em dezembro de 1957, o volume Inglês-Português, seguido quatro anos depois pelo volume Português-Inglês. Neste segundo volume os trabalhos iniciados sob a orientação do Prof. Fritz Pietzschke tiveram prosseguimento e ficaram a cargo de Franz Wimmer, que contou com a valiosa participação de Franz Schmidt, José Curado, Lothar Fritsch, Milly Herting, Oswaldo A. Virgílio, Germano Discher, Anita Mangels, Vilma Klusemann Plaas, Heinke e Hans Mitteldorf.

Em 1983 os dois volumes — o Inglês/Português e o Português/Inglês — passaram por extensa revisão e atualização efetuada pelo Sr. Franz Wimmer, com a colaboração do Sr. Ottokar Hanns Hoeldtke. Assim, o volume Inglês-Português passou a conter cerca de 68.000 verbetes e o volume Português-Inglês mais de 78.000 verbetes.

Oferece esta obra uma série de inovações de caráter formal, umas quanto ao aspecto gráfico, outras quanto à nova e eficiente concepção da tarefa funcional da parte ilustrativa.

As magníficas pranchas apresentadas, que reúnem cerca de 4.000 ilustrações, possuem excelente função prática na elucidação de inúmeros pormenores, os quais, de outra forma, seria quase impossível esclarecer.

Além do objetivo propriamente informativo, as pranchas possuem alta finalidade didática, pois facilitam a fixação e ampliação do vocabulário, estabelecendo, ainda, um grupo de palavras organicamente relacionadas entre si, por força do assunto de que tratam.

A fim de fazer do MICHAELIS — Dicionário Ilustrado um instrumento eficiente de trabalho para o estudioso, no volume Inglês-Português foi incluída a transcrição fonética para o inglês, optando-se pelo sistema da Associação Fonética Internacional.

Procurando-se, ainda, dar aos MICHAELIS — Dicionários Ilustrados alto valor universal e prático, fizeram-se os seguintes acréscimos de informações úteis:

1. conjugação dos verbos irregulares em inglês.
2. conjugação dos verbos regulares e irregulares em português.
3. relação dos nomes próprios em inglês com pronúncia figurada.
4. tabela de conversão de pesos e medidas anglo-americanas para o sistema decimal.
5. siglas e abreviaturas mais usadas.

Assim, os editores têm certeza de que no MICHAELIS — Dicionário Ilustrado tanto o leitor comum quanto o estudioso, dos mais variados campos da atividade humana, encontrarão um instrumento eficiente e atualizado.

Contudo, quaisquer sugestões serão sempre bem-vindas.

EDIÇÕES MELHORAMENTOS

VIII

PREFACE

Melhoramentos is proud of its success with the MICHAELIS dictionaries. For many years this line of dictionaries, leaders on the market, have constantly been actualized and increased by new items.

When launching this further edition of the MICHAELIS — Illustrated Dictionary English/Portuguese, a short retrospect is interesting.

Thus the Michaelis dictionary English Portuguese by the German Lexicographer Henriette Michaelis was first published in 1893 a few years after the author had published the important German Portuguese dictionary. On occasion of the 1st edition the author had the assistance of her sister Carolina Michaelis de Vasconcelos, a notable figure of Portuguese letters, who thanks to her thorough knowledge of the language spoken in her adoptive country had greatly contributed to make said dictionary a sure guide for scientific and literary work.

Evidently a dictionary must be kept up-to-date to maintain its efficiency, it must always be in contact with the living language. However, after a few revisions during the first years of its existence, the dictionary did not take up the changes that had happened in the Portuguese and English languages, becoming obsolete at several points. A complete revision became necessary, demanding much time and the cooperation of specialists. In order to reach its purpose it was necessary to change completely the structure of the dictionary and to include a word by word confrontation with the actualized terminology of the present life.

About 1950 Melhoramentos boldly started the enterprise; Prof. Fritz Pietzschke was entrusted with giving the dictionary a new structure, assisted by Messrs. Franz Wimmer, Gustavo Lohnefink, José Curado, Lothar Fritsch and Hans Rzeppa. After several years the volume English Portuguese was published during December 1957. The volume Portuguese English followed 4 years later. The work commenced under Prof. Fritz Pietzschke, was continued and finished under Mr. Franz Wimmer with the assistance of Messrs. Franz Schmidt, José Curado, Lothar Fritsch, Oswaldo A. Virgílio, Germano Discher, Hans Mitteldorf, Misses Milly Herting, Anita Mangels, Vilma Klusemann Plaas and Heinke Mitteldorf.

In 1983 the two volumes English Portuguese and Portuguese English are submitted to a thorough revision and actualization by Mr. Franz Wimmer with the assistance of Mr. Ottokar Hanns Hoeldtke. In this way the volume English Portuguese reaches about 68.000 entries and the volume Portuguese English attains 78.000 entries.

This work offers a number of formal innovations, both graphically as well as in view of the efficient and most helpful illustrations. The excellent pictures with about 4,000 illustrations explain countless details otherwise difficult to show. Aside from the informative purpose, the pictures are highly didactic as they help to remember and retain groups of words belonging together and pertaining to the same subject.

In order to make the MICHAELIS Illustrated Dictionary an efficient tool for the student the volume English-Portuguese includes the phonetics of the International Phonetic Association.

Besides, to increase the practical and universal value of the MICHAE-LIS — Illustrated Dictionary, the following useful indications were included:

1. irregular English verbs
2. irregular Portuguese verbs (conjugated)
3. list of English proper names (with pronunciation)
4. list of English weights and measures with their equivalents in the metric system
5. list of the most used abbreviations

So the editors are sure that in the MICHAELIS — Illustrated Dictionary both common reader and the students of the various fields of human activities will find a useful and up-to-date instrument.

However any further suggestions will always be welcome.

EDIÇÕES MELHORAMENTOS

X

ORGANIZAÇÃO DO DICIONÁRIO

1. A entrada

a) a entrada, as frases e as locuções são impressas em negrito; o texto em inglês aparece em letras comuns;

b) os nomes próprios, com raras exceções, aparecem apenas quando assumem sentido de nomes comuns, p. ex.:
maria-rendeira;

c) as palavras compostas com hífen são colocadas como entradas novas na ordem alfabética, p. ex.:
amora-preta forma entrada própria, ficando entre as entradas **amoralizar** e **amorar;**

d) algumas variantes ortográficas são apresentadas depois da entrada, entre parênteses como em:
desacobardar v. (also **desacovardar**);

e) as palavras menos usadas aparecem como entrada e remetem às mais usadas:
deplumar v. = **depenar;**

f) variantes que não interrompem a ordem alfabética aparecem justapostas: **dálmata, dalmatense.**

2. A categoria gramatical

a) quando houver mais de uma categoria gramatical, estas são separadas por duplo traço vertical | |, na seguinte ordem: substantivo, verbo, adjetivo, advérbio, etc., usando-se as abreviaturas: s., v., adj., adv., etc.;

b) nos substantivos é indicado o gênero, m. = masculino, f. = feminino, m. + f. = palavra com dois gêneros, p. ex.:
dentista;

c) nos verbos, em vez das indicações de transitivo ou intransitivo, são dados exemplos que esclarecem a regência do verbo;

d) a preposição "to" antecede o infinitivo dos verbos em inglês nas diferentes acepções, p. ex.:
dirigir v. 1. to direct: a) govern, rule, command, superintend, head, boss, preside. b) regulate, control. c) manage, dispose, manipulate,

administer. d) order, prescribe, instruct. e) tend, point toward, aim. f) (mus.) act as a director or conductor. g) superscribe, address, dedicate. 2. to conduct, guide, lead, drive, steer, pilot. 3. ~-se: a) to address o. s. to, apply to. b) to be directed.

e) a preposição ''to'' também é colocada nos casos em que sua omissão poderia causar dúvidas, p. ex.:
to cross the styx, to die.

3. O plural
Somente os plurais irregulares são indicados em negrito, entre parênteses, dando-se apenas o final do vocábulo, p. ex.: **abalável** (pl. **-áveis**; **abanão** pl. **-ões**).

4. A tradução
a) a tradução inglesa, na medida do possível, fornece o equivalente ao português e quando não existir é substituída por uma definição, p. ex.: **serpentina** s. f. branched candlestick, cane with three triangularly disposed candles at the top of it, used on the Saturday of the Holy Week;

b) as diversas acepções de uma entrada são separadas umas das outras por algarismos. Os sinônimos, reunidos sob um algarismo, são separados por vírgulas. Às vezes, para maior clareza numa série de definições, usa-se o ponto-e-vírgula;

c) em geral os algarismos indicam a freqüência das acepções, de modo que a palavra mais usada precede a menos usada;

d) entradas com versão inglesa de grande semelhança lingüística, que englobam as mesmas acepções do português, são anotadas assim: **devoção** s. f. (pl.**-ões**) devotion: 1. adoration, cult, religious fervour, godliness, religion. 2. dedication, attachment, adherence. 3. fidelity, constancy. 4. affection, devotedness. 5. attention;

e) entradas que incluem outras acepções, além da versão inglesa, são anotadas como a seguir:
abater v. 1. to abate: a) lower. b) reduce, discount, deduct. c) lessen, decrease, diminish. d) throw down, pull down. e) cut down, fell. .f) prostrate. g) humiliate, humble, abase. 2. to fall. 3. to kill, slaughter (cattle). 4. to weaken, debilitate, enfeeble. 5. to make lean, grow thin. 6. to despond. 7. to shoot down (plane). 8. (naut.) to drive (or fall) to leeward. 9. ~-se: a) to sink in, fall in, subside. b) to abase o. s., prostrate o. s.;

f) o til (~) nas frases ou locuções substitui por inteiro a entrada, p. ex.:
agora adv., **de ~ em diante** (= **de agora em diante**);

g) o hífen (-) substitui a parte básica da entrada, p. ex.:
antigo adj., **-amente** adv. (= **antigamente**).

5. Ilustrações

A indicação da prancha ilustrativa é feita entre parênteses quando houver uma ilustração do objeto ou pormenor em questão, p. ex.:
acima adv. above, up (plate P 18).

6. Frases e locuções

Na fraseologia os exemplos aparecem com as entradas em primeiro lugar, depois aqueles precedidos por outras palavras, p. ex.:
abaixo: ~ **e acima** (= abaixo e acima), **ela canta** ~ **do tom** (= ela canta abaixo do tom).

ARRANGEMENT OF THE DICTIONARY

1. The entry

a) the entry, phrases and locutions are printed in boldface, the English text in common type;

b) proper names, with rare exceptions, appear only when employed as common nouns, e.g.:
maria-rendeira;

c) the hyphenated compound words constitute independent entries in alphabetical order, e.g.:
amora-preta appears between
amoralizar and **amorar;**

d) some orthographic variants are printed in parenthesis after the entry, as in:
desacobardar v. (also **desacovardar**);

e) the entry of a less used word refers to the more used one, e.g.:
deplumar v. = **depenar;**

f) variants are printed side by side when the alphabetical order is not interrupted:
dálmata, dalmatense.

2. The grammatical classification

a) when more than one grammatical class appears, these are separated by two vertical bars || in the following order: substantive (noun), verb, adjective, adverb, etc., indicated by: s., v., adj., adv., etc.;

b) the gender of the substantive is indicated by: m. = masculine, f. = feminine, m. + f. = both masculine and feminine, e. g.:
dentista;

c) after the verbs the indications transitive or intransitive are omitted as there generally are examples explaining the proper use of the verbs;

d) the preposition "to" precedes the infinitive of the English verbs, before the different meanings, e.g.:
dirigir v. 1. to direct: a) govern, rule, command, superintend, head,

boss, preside. b) regulate, control. c) manage, dispose, manipulate, administer. d) order, prescribe, instruct. e) tend, point toward, aim. f) (mus.) act as a director or conductor. g) superscribe, address, dedicate. 2. to conduct, guide, lead, drive, steer, pilot. 3. ~-se: a) to address o. s. to, apply to. b) to be directed;

e) the preposition "to" also appears whenever omission may cause doubt, e.g.: to cross the styx, to die.

3. The plural

Only the irregular plural is indicated in parenthesis, printed in boldface, showing only the final part of the entry, e. g.: **abalável** (pl. -**áveis**; **abanão** pl. -**ões**).

4. The translation

a) the English translation, whenever possible, shows the Portuguese equivalent or is substituted by a definition, e. g.:
serpentina s. f. branched candlestick, cane with three triangularly disposed candles at the top of it, used on the Saturday of the Holy Week;

b) the different basic meanings of a word are separated by numbers. The synonims within each group are separated by commas. Sometimes after a series of definitions the semicolon is used;

c) generally the numbers indicate the frequency of the meaning, so that the more often used word appears before the less used;

d) entries with a very similar English translation including the same meanings of the Portuguese word are indicated in this way:
devoção s. f. (pl. ~**ões**) devotion: 1. adoration, cult, religious fervour, godliness, religion. 2. dedication, attachment, adherence. 3. fidelity, constancy. 4. affection, devotedness. 5. attention;

e) entries with further meanings than those of the English translation, are indicated as follows:
abater v. 1. to abate: a) lower. b) reduce, discount, deduct. c) lessen, decrease, diminish. d) throw down, pull down. e) cut down, fell. f) prostrate. g) humiliate, humble, abase. 2. to fall. 3. to kill, slaughter (cattle). 4. to weaken, debilitate, enfeeble. 5. to make lean, grow thin. 6. to despond. 7. to shoot down (plane). 8. (naut.) to drive (or fall), to leeward. 9. ~ **se:** a) to sink in, fall in, subside. b) to abase o. s., prostrate o. s.;

f) the tilde (~) in phrases and locutions substitutes the entry, e. g.:
agora adv., de ~ **em diante** (= **de agora em diante**);

g) the dash (-) only substitutes the main part of the entry, e. g.:
antigo adj., -**amente** adv. (= **antigamente**).

5. Illustrations

The illustrative plate is indicated in parenthesis, when there is an illustration of the object or detail in question, e. g.:

acima adv. above, up (plate P 18).

6. Phrases and locutions

In the phraseology first appear the examples beginning with the entry, then those preceded by other words, e. g.:

abaixo: ~ e acima (= abaixo e acima), ela canta ~ do tom (= ela canta abaixo do tom).

Índice alfabético, em português, das pranchas ilustrativas

Alphabetical list of the illustrations (Portuguese titles)

Índice alfabético, em inglês, das pranchas ilustrativas
Alphabetical list of the illustrations (English titles)

VERBOS VERBS

1ª CONJUGAÇÃO (1st group, ending in ar)

MODELO DE VERBO REGULAR (Example of the regular form)

Infinitivo impessoal / Impersonal Infinitive: louvar

	Presente / Present	Pretérito imperfeito / Imperfect	Pretérito perfeito / Preterite	Pretérito mais-que-perfeito / Pluperfect	Futuro do presente / Future	Futuro do pretérito / Conditional
eu	louvo	louvava	louvei	louvara	louvarei	louvaria
tu	louvas	louvavas	louvaste	louvaras	louvarás	louvarias
ele	louva	louvava	louvou	louvara	louvará	louvaria
nós	louvamos	louvávamos	louvamos	louváramos	louvaremos	louvaríamos
vós	louvais	louváveis	louvastes	louváreis	louvareis	louvaríeis
eles	louvam	louvavam	louvaram	louvaram	louvarão	louvariam

MODELOS DE VERBOS IRREGULARES (Examples of Irregular forms)

adequar

	Presente / Present	Pretérito imperfeito / Imperfect	Pretérito perfeito / Preterite	Pretérito mais-que-perfeito / Pluperfect	Futuro do presente / Future	Futuro do pretérito / Conditional
eu	—	adequava	adequei	adequara	adequarei	adequaria
tu	—	adequavas	adequaste	adequaras	adequarás	adequarias
ele	—	adequava	adequou	adequara	adequará	adequaria
nós	adequamos	adequávamos	adequamos	adequáramos	adequaremos	adequaríamos
vós	adequais	adequáveis	adequastes	adequáreis	adequareis	adequaríeis
eles	—	adequavam	adequaram	adequaram	adequarão	adequariam

aguar

	Presente / Present	Pretérito imperfeito / Imperfect	Pretérito perfeito / Preterite	Pretérito mais-que-perfeito / Pluperfect	Futuro do presente / Future	Futuro do pretérito / Conditional
eu	águo	aguava	agüei	aguara	aguarei	aguaria
tu	águas	aguavas	aguaste	aguaras	aguarás	aguarias
ele	água	aguava	aguou	aguara	aguará	aguaria
nós	aguamos	aguávamos	aguamos	aguáramos	aguaremos	aguaríamos
vós	aguais	aguáveis	aguastes	aguáreis	aguareis	aguaríeis
eles	águam	aguavam	aguaram	aguaram	aguarão	aguariam

ansiar

	Presente / Present	Pretérito imperfeito / Imperfect	Pretérito perfeito / Preterite	Pretérito mais-que-perfeito / Pluperfect	Futuro do presente / Future	Futuro do pretérito / Conditional
eu	anseio	ansiava	ansiei	ansiara	ansiarei	ansiaria
tu	anseias	ansiavas	ansiaste	ansiaras	ansiarás	ansiarias
ele	anseia	ansiava	ansiou	ansiara	ansiará	ansiaria
nós	ansiamos	ansiávamos	ansiamos	ansiáramos	ansiaremos	ansiaríamos
vós	ansiais	ansiáveis	ansiastes	ansiáreis	ansiareis	ansiaríeis
eles	anseiam	ansiavam	ansiaram	ansiaram	ansiarão	ansiariam

antiquar

	Presente / Present	Pretérito imperfeito / Imperfect	Pretérito perfeito / Preterite	Pretérito mais-que-perfeito / Pluperfect	Futuro do presente / Future	Futuro do pretérito / Conditional
eu	—	antiquava	antiqüei	antiquara	antiquarei	antiquaria
tu	—	antiquavas	antiquaste	antiquaras	antiquarás	antiquarias
ele	—	antiquava	antiquou	antiquara	antiquará	antiquaria
nós	antiquamos	antiquávamos	antiquamos	antiquáramos	antiquaremos	antiquaríamos
vós	antiquais	antiquáveis	antiquastes	antiquáreis	antiquareis	antiquaríeis
eles	—	antiquavam	antiquaram	antiquaram	antiquarão	antiquariam

Presente / Present	Subjuntivo (Subjunctive) Pretérito Imperfeito / Imperfect	Futuro Imperfeito / Future	Imperativo / Imperative	Gerúndio / Gerund	Particípio Past Participle
louve	louvasse	louvar		louvando	louvado
louves	louvasses	louvares	louva		
louve	louvasse	louvar			
louvemos	louvássemos	louvarmos			
louveis	louvásseis	louvardes	louvai		
louvem	louvassem	louvarem			
LACKING	adequasse	adequar		adequando	adequado
	adequasses	adequares	—		
	adequasse	adequar			
	adequássemos	adequarmos			
	adequásseis	adequardes	adequai		
	adequassem	adequarem			
águe	aguasse	aguar		aguando	aguado
águes	aguasses	aguares	água		
águe	aguasse	aguar			
aguemos	aguássemos	aguarmos			
agueis	aguásseis	aguardes	aguai		
águem	aguassem	aguarem			
anseie	ansiasse	ansiar		ansiando	ansiado
anseies	ansiasses	ansiares	anseia		
anseie	ansiasse	ansiar			
ansiemos	ansiássemos	ansiarmos			
ansieis	ansiásseis	ansiardes	ansiai		
anseiem	ansiassem	ansiarem			
LACKING	antiquasse	antiquar		antiquando	antiquado
	antiquasses	antiquares	—		
	antiquasse	antiquar			
	antiquássemos	antiquarmos			
	antiquásseis	antiquardes	antiquai		
	antiquassem	antiquarem			

Indicativo (Indicative)

Infinito Impessoal / Impersonal infinitive	Presente / Present	Pretérito Imperfeito / Imperfect	Pretérito perfeito / Preterite	Pretérito mais-que-perfeito / Pluperfect	Futuro do presente / Future	Futuro do pretérito / Conditional
apaziguar	eu apaziguo tu apaziguas ele apazigua nós apaziguamos vós apaziguais eles apaziguam	apaziguava apaziguavas apaziguava apaziguávamos apaziguáveis apaziguavam	apaziguei apaziguaste apaziguou apaziguamos apaziguastes apaziguaram	apaziguara apaziguaras apaziguara apaziguáramos apaziguáreis apaziguaram	apaziguarei apaziguarás apaziguará apaziguaremos apaziguareis apaziguarão	apaziguaria apaziguarias apaziguaria apaziguaríamos apaziguaríeis apaziguariam
apiedar	eu me apiedo tu te apiedas ele se apieda nós nos apiedamos vós vos apiedais eles se apiedam	apiedava apiedavas apiedava apiedávamos apiedáveis apiedavam	apiedei apiedaste apiedou apiedamos apiedastes apiedaram	apiedara apiedaras apiedara apiedáramos apiedáreis apiedaram	apiedarei apiedarás apiedará apiedaremos apiedareis apiedarão	apiedaria apiedarias apiedaria apiedaríamos apiedaríeis apiedariam
dar	eu dou tu dás ele dá nós damos vós dais eles dão	dava davas dava dávamos dáveis davam	dei deste deu demos destes deram	dera deras dera déramos déreis deram	darei darás dará daremos dareis darão	daria darias daria daríamos daríeis dariam
estar	eu estou tu estás ele está nós estamos vós estais eles estão	estava estavas estava estávamos estáveis estavam	estive estiveste esteve estivemos estivestes estiveram	estivera estiveras estivera estivéramos estivéreis estiveram	estarei estarás estará estaremos estareis estarão	estaria estarias estaria estaríamos estaríeis estariam
ficar	eu fico tu ficas ele fica nós ficamos vós ficais eles ficam	ficava ficavas ficava ficávamos ficáveis ficavam	fiquei ficaste ficou ficamos ficastes ficaram	ficara ficaras ficara ficáramos ficáreis ficaram	ficarei ficarás ficará ficaremos ficareis ficarão	ficaria ficarias ficaria ficaríamos ficaríeis ficariam
mobiliar	eu mobílio tu mobílias ele mobília nós mobiliamos vós mobiliais eles mobíliam	mobiliava mobiliavas mobiliava mobiliávamos mobiliáveis mobiliavam	mobiliei mobiliaste mobiliou mobiliamos mobiliastes mobiliaram	mobiliara mobiliaras mobiliara mobiliáramos mobiliáreis mobiliaram	mobiliarei mobiliarás mobiliará mobiliaremos mobiliareis mobiliarão	mobiliaria mobiliarias mobiliaria mobiliaríamos mobiliaríeis mobiliariam

	Subjuntivo (Subjunctive)			Imperativo Imperative	Gerúndio Gerund	Particípio Past Participle
	Presente Present	Pretérito Imperfeito Imperfect	Futuro Imperfeito Future			
apazigúe apazigúes apazigúe apaziguemos apaziguéis apazigúem		apaziguasse apaziguasses apaziguasse apaziguássemos apaziguásseis apaziguassem	apaziguar apaziguares apaziguar apaziguarmos apaziguardes apaziguarem	**apazigua** apaziguai	apaziguando	apaziguado
apiade apiades apiade apiademos apiadeis apiadem		apiedasse apiedasses apiedasse apiedássemos apiedásseis apiedassem	apiedar apiedares apiedar apiedarmos apiedardes apiedarem	**apiada** apiedai	apiedando	apiedado
dê dês dê demos deis deem		desse desses desse déssemos désseis dessem	der deres der dermos derdes derem	**dá** dai	dando	dado
esteja estejas esteja estejamos estejais estejam		estivesse estivesses estivesse estivéssemos estivésseis estivessem	estiver estiveres estiver estivermos estiverdes estiverem	**está** estai	estando	estado
fique fiques fique fiquemos fiqueis fiquem		ficasse ficasses ficasse ficássemos ficásseis ficassem	ficar ficares ficar ficarmos ficardes ficarem	fica ficai	ficando	ficado
mobilie mobilies mobilie mobiliemos mobilieis mobiliem		mobiliasse mobiliasses mobiliasse mobiliássemos mobiliásseis mobiliassem	mobiliar mobiliares mobiliar mobiliarmos mobiliardes mobiliarem	**mobilia** mobiliai	mobiliando	mobiliado

Indicativo (Indicative)

Infinitivo impessoal / Infinitive	Presente / Present	Pretérito Imperfeito / Imperfect	Pretérito perfeito / Preterite	Pretérito mais-que-perfeito / Pluperfect	Futuro do presente / Future	Futuro do pretérito / Conditional
moscar	eu musco tu muscas ele musca nós moscamos vós moscais eles muscam	moscava moscavas moscava moscávamos moscáveis moscavam	mosquei moscaste moscou moscamos moscastes moscaram	moscara moscaras moscara moscáramos moscaram	moscarei moscarás moscará moscaremos moscareis moscarão	moscaria moscarias moscaria moscaríamos moscaríeis moscariam
obliquar	eu obliquo tu obliquas ele obliqua nós obliquamos vós obliquais eles obliquam	obliquava obliquavas obliquava obliquávamos obliquáveis obliquavam	obliquei obliquaste obliquou obliquamos obliquastes obliquaram	obliquara obliquaras obliquara obliquáramos obliquáreis obliquaram	obliquarei obliquarás obliquará obliquaremos obliquareis obliquarão	obliquaria obliquarias obliquaria obliquaríamos obliquaríeis obliquariam
saudar	eu saúdo tu saúdas ele saúda nós saudamos vós saudais eles saúdam	saudava saudavas saudava saudávamos saudáveis saudavam	saudei saudaste saudou saudamos saudastes saudaram	saudara saudaras saudara saudáramos saudáreis saudaram	saudarei saudarás saudará saudareis saudarão	saudaria saudarias saudaria saudaríamos saudaríeis saudariam

Subjuntivo (Subjunctive)

Presente / Present	Pretérito Imperfeito / Imperfect	Futuro Imperfeito / Future	Imperativo / Imperative	Gerúndio / Gerund	Particípio / Past Participle
musque musques musque musquemos musqueis musquem	moscasse moscasses moscasse moscássemos moscásseis moscassem	moscar moscares moscar moscarmos moscardes moscarem	musca moscai	moscando	moscado
oblique obliques oblique obliquemos obliqueis obliquem	obliquasse obliquasses obliquasse obliquássemos obliquásseis obliquassem	obliquar obliquares obliquar obliquarmos obliquardes obliquarem	obliqua obliquai	obliquando	obliquado
saúde saúdes saúde saudemos saudeis saúdem	saudasse saudasses saudasse saudássemos saudásseis saudassem	saudar saudares saudar saudarmos saudardes saudarem	saúda saudai	saudando	saudado

2.ª CONJUGAÇÃO (2nd group, ending in er and or)

Infinitivo impessoal / Impersonal infinitive	Presente / Present	Pretérito imperfeito / Imperfect	Pretérito perfeito / Preterite	Pretérito mais-que-perfeito / Pluperfect	Futuro do presente / Future	Futuro do pretérito / Conditional
			Indicativo (Indicative)			

MODELO DE VERBO REGULAR TERMINADO EM ER (Example of the regular form ending in er)

vender	Presente	Pretérito imperfeito	Pretérito perfeito	Pretérito mais-que-perfeito	Futuro do presente	Futuro do pretérito
eu	vendo	vendia	vendi	vendera	venderei	venderia
tu	vendes	vendias	vendeste	venderas	venderás	venderias
ele	vende	vendia	vendeu	vendera	venderá	venderia
nós	vendemos	vendíamos	vendemos	vendêramos	venderemos	venderíamos
vós	vendeis	vendíeis	vendestes	vendêreis	vendereis	venderíeis
eles	vendem	vendiam	venderam	venderam	venderão	venderiam

MODELOS DE VERBOS IRREGULARES TERMINADOS EM ER (Examples of irregular forms ending in er)

aprazer-se	Presente	Pretérito imperfeito	Pretérito perfeito	Pretérito mais-que-perfeito	Futuro do presente	Futuro do pretérito
eu me	aprazo	aprazia	aprouve	aprouvera	aprazerei	aprazeria
tu te	aprazes	aprazias	aprouveste	aprouveras	aprazerás	aprazerias
ele se	apraz	aprazia	aprouve	aprouvera	aprazerá	aprazeria
nós nos	aprazemos	aprazíamos	aprouvemos	aprouvéramos	aprazeremos	aprazeríamos
vós vos	aprazeis	aprazíeis	aprouvestes	aprouvéreis	aprazereis	aprazeríeis
eles se	aprazem	apraziam	aprouveram	aprouveram	aprazerão	aprazeriam

comprazer-se	Presente	Pretérito imperfeito	Pretérito perfeito	Pretérito mais-que-perfeito	Futuro do presente	Futuro do pretérito
eu me	comprazo	comprazia	comprazi	comprazera	comprazerei	comprazeria
tu te	comprazes	comprazias	comprazeste	comprazeras	comprazerás	comprazerias
ele se	compraz	comprazia	comprazeu	comprazera	comprazerá	comprazeria
nós nos	comprazemos	comprazíamos	comprazemos	comprazêramos	comprazeremos	comprazeríamos
vós vos	comprazeis	comprazíeis	comprazestes	comprazêreis	comprazereis	comprazeríeis
eles se	comprazem	compraziam	comprazeram	comprazeram	comprazerão	comprazeriam

or (Pretérito perfeito / Pretérito mais-que-perfeito):

	Pretérito perfeito	Pretérito mais-que-perfeito
	comprouve	comprouvera
	comprouveste	comprouveras
	comprouve	comprouvera
	comprouvemos	comprouvéramos
	comprouvestes	comprouvéreis
	comprouveram	comprouveram

caber	Presente	Pretérito imperfeito	Pretérito perfeito	Pretérito mais-que-perfeito	Futuro do presente	Futuro do pretérito
eu	caibo	cabia	coube	coubera	caberei	caberia
tu	cabes	cabias	coubeste	couberas	caberás	caberias
ele	cabe	cabia	coube	coubera	caberá	caberia
nós	cabemos	cabíamos	coubemos	coubéramos	caberemos	caberíamos
vós	cabeis	cabíeis	coubestes	coubéreis	cabereis	caberíeis
eles	cabem	cabiam	couberam	couberam	caberão	caberiam

Subjuntivo (Subjunctive)

Presente / Present	Pretérito Imperfeito / Imperfect	Futuro Imperfeito / Future	Imperativo / Imperative	Gerúndio / Gerund	Particípio Past Participle
venda vendas venda vendamos vendais vendam	vendesse vendesses vendesse vendêssemos vendêsseis vendessem	vender venderes vender vendermos venderdes venderem	vende vendei	vendendo	vendido
apraza aprazas apraza aprazamos aprazais aprazam	aprouvesse aprouvesses aprouvesse aprouvéssemos aprouvésseis aprouvessem	aprouver aprouveres aprouver aprouvermos aprouverdes aprouverem	apraze aprazei	aprazendo	aprazido
compraza comprazas compraza comprazamos comprazais comprazam	comprazesse comprazesses comprazesse comprazêssemos comprazêsseis comprazessem or comprouvesse comprouvesses comprouvesse comprouvéssemos comprouvésseis comprouvessem	comprazer comprazeres comprazer comprazermos comprazerdes comprazerem or comprouver comprouveres comprouver comprouvermos comprouverdes comprouverem	compraze comprazei	comprazendo	comprazido
caiba caibas caiba caibamos caibais caibam	coubesse coubesses coubesse coubéssemos coubésseis coubessem	couber couberes couber coubermos couberdes couberem	LACKING	cabendo	cabido

Infinitivo impessoal / Infinitive	Presente / Present	Indicativo (Indicative)				
		Pretérito imperfeito / Imperfect	Pretérito perfeito / Preterite	Pretérito mais-que-perfeito / Pluperfect	Futuro do presente / Future	Futuro do pretérito / Conditional
crer	eu creio	cria	cri	crera	crerei	creria
	tu crês	crias	creste	creras	crerás	crerias
	ele crê	cria	creu	crera	crerá	creria
	nós cremos	críamos	cremos	crêramos	creremos	creríamos
	vós credes	críeis	crestes	crêreis	crereis	creríeis
	eles crêem	criam	creram	creram	crerão	creriam
dizer	eu digo	dizia	disse	dissera	direi	diria
	tu dizes	dizias	disseste	disseras	dirás	dirias
	ele diz	dizia	disse	dissera	dirá	diria
	nós dizemos	dizíamos	dissemos	disséramos	diremos	diríamos
	vós dizeis	dizíeis	dissestes	disséreis	direis	diríeis
	eles dizem	diziam	disseram	disseram	dirão	diriam
esquecer	eu esqueço	esquecia	esqueci	esquecera	esquecerei	esqueceria
	tu esqueces	esquecias	esqueceste	esqueceras	esquecerás	esquecerias
	ele esquece	esquecia	esqueceu	esquecera	esquecerá	esqueceria
	nós esquecemos	esquecíamos	esquecemos	esquecêramos	esqueceremos	esqueceríamos
	vós esqueceis	esquecíeis	esquecestes	esquecêreis	esquecereis	esqueceríeis
	eles esquecem	esqueciam	esqueceram	esqueceram	esquecerão	esqueceriam
fazer	eu faço	fazia	fiz	fizera	farei	faria
	tu fazes	fazias	fizeste	fizeras	farás	farias
	ele faz	fazia	fez	fizera	fará	faria
	nós fazemos	fazíamos	fizemos	fizéramos	faremos	faríamos
	vós fazeis	fazíeis	fizestes	fizéreis	fareis	faríeis
	eles fazem	faziam	fizeram	fizeram	farão	fariam
haver	eu hei	havia	houve	houvera	haverei	haveria
	tu hás	havias	houveste	houveras	haverás	haverias
	ele há	havia	houve	houvera	haverá	haveria
	nós havemos	havíamos	houvemos	houvéramos	haveremos	haveríamos
	vós haveis	havíeis	houvestes	houvéreis	havereis	haveríeis
	eles hão	haviam	houveram	houveram	haverão	haveriam
ler	eu leio	lia	li	lera	lerei	leria
	tu lês	lias	leste	leras	lerás	lerias
	ele lê	lia	leu	lera	lerá	leria
	nós lemos	líamos	lemos	lêramos	leremos	leríamos
	vós ledes	líeis	lestes	lêreis	lereis	leríeis
	eles leem	liam	leram	leram	lerão	leriam

Presente / Present	Subjuntivo (Subjunctive) Pretérito Imperfeito / Imperfect	Futuro Imperfeito / Future	Imperativo / Imperative	Gerúndio / Gerund	Particípio Passado / Past Participle
creia creias creia creiamos creiais creiam	cresse cresses cresse crêssemos crêsseis cressem	crer creres crer crermos crerdes crerem	crê crede	crendo	crido
diga digas diga digamos digais digam	dissesse dissesses dissesse disséssemos dissésseis dissessem	disser disseres disser dissermos disserdes disserem	dize dizei	dizendo	dito
esqueça esqueças esqueça esqueçamos esqueçais esqueçam	esquecesse esquecesses esquecesse esquecêssemos esquecêsseis esquecessem	esquecer esqueceres esquecer esquecermos esquecerdes esquecerem	esquece esquecei	esquecendo	esquecido
faça faças faça façamos façais façam	fizesse fizesses fizesse fizéssemos fizésseis fizessem	fizer fizeres fizer fizermos fizerdes fizerem	faze fazei	fazendo	feito
haja hajas haja hajamos hajais hajam	houvesse houvesses houvesse houvéssemos houvésseis houvessem	houver houveres houver houvermos houverdes houverem	há havei	havendo	havido
leia leias leia leiamos leiais leiam	lesse lesses lesse lêssemos lêsseis lessem	ler leres ler lermos lerdes lerem	lê lede	lendo	lido

Infinitivo impessoal / Impersonal Infinitive	Presente / Present	Indicativo (Indicative) Pretérito imperfeito / Imperfect	Pretérito perfeito / Preterite	Pretérito mais-que-perfeito / Pluperfect	Futuro do presente / Future	Futuro do pretérito / Conditional
moer						
eu	moo	moía	moí	moera	moerei	moeria
tu	móis	moías	moeste	moeras	moerás	moerias
ele	mói	moía	moeu	moera	moerá	moeria
nós	moemos	moíamos	moemos	moêramos	moeremos	moeríamos
vós	moeis	moíeis	moestes	moêreis	moereis	moeríeis
eles	moem	moíam	moeram	moeram	moerão	moeriam
perder						
eu	perco	perdia	perdi	perdera	perderei	perderia
tu	perdes	perdias	perdeste	perderas	perderás	perderias
ele	perde	perdia	perdeu	perdera	perderá	perderia
nós	perdemos	perdíamos	perdemos	perdêramos	perderemos	perderíamos
vós	perdeis	perdíeis	perdestes	perdêreis	perdereis	perderíeis
eles	perdem	perdiam	perderam	perderam	perderão	perderiam
poder						
eu	posso	podia	pude	pudera	poderei	poderia
tu	podes	podias	pudeste	puderas	poderás	poderias
ele	pode	podia	pôde	pudera	poderá	poderia
nós	podemos	podíamos	pudemos	pudéramos	poderemos	poderíamos
vós	podeis	podíeis	pudestes	pudéreis	podereis	poderíeis
eles	podem	podiam	puderam	puderam	poderão	poderiam
prazer						
eu	—	—	—	—	—	—
tu	—	—	—	—	—	—
ele	praz	prazia	prouve	prouvera	prazerá	prazeria
nós	—	—	—	—	—	—
vós	—	—	—	—	—	—
eles	—	—	—	—	—	—
prover						
eu	provejo	provia	provi	provera	proverei	proveria
tu	provês	provias	proveste	proveras	proverás	proverias
ele	provê	provia	proveu	provera	proverá	proveria
nós	provemos	províamos	provemos	provêramos	proveremos	proveríamos
vós	provedes	províeis	provestes	provêreis	provereis	proveríeis
eles	proveem	proviam	proveram	proveram	proverão	proveriam
querer						
eu	quero	queria	quis	quisera	quererei	quereria
tu	queres	querias	quiseste	quiseras	quererás	quererias
ele	quer	queria	quis	quisera	quererá	quereria
nós	queremos	queríamos	quisemos	quiséramos	quereremos	quereríamos
vós	quereis	queríeis	quisestes	quiséreis	querereis	quereríeis
eles	querem	queriam	quiseram	quiseram	quererão	quereriam

Subjuntivo (Subjunctive)

Presente / Present	Pretérito Imperfeito / Imperfect	Futuro Imperfeito / Future	Imperativo / Imperative	Gerúndio / Gerund	Particípio / Past Participle
moa	moesse	moer		moendo	**moído**
moas	moesses	moeres	**mói**		
moa	moesse	moer	moei		
moamos	moêssemos	moermos			
moais	moêsseis	moerdes			
moam	moessem	moerem			
perca	perdesse	perder		perdendo	perdido
percas	perdesses	perderes	perde		
perca	perdesse	perder	perdei		
percamos	perdêssemos	perdermos			
percais	perdêsseis	perderdes			
percam	perdessem	perderem			
possa	pudesse	puder	LACKING	podendo	podido
possa	pudesses	puderes			
possa	pudesse	puder			
possamos	pudéssemos	pudermos			
possais	pudésseis	puderdes			
possam	pudessem	puderem			
—	—	—	LACKING	prazendo	prazido
—	—	—			
praza	prouvesse	prouver			
—	—	—			
—	—	—			
—	—	—			
proveja	provesse	prover		provendo	provido
provejas	provesses	proveres	**provê**		
proveja	provesse	prover	**provede**		
provejamos	provêssemos	provermos			
provejais	provêsseis	proverdes			
provejam	provessem	proverem			
queira	**quisesse**	**quiser**	LACKING	querendo	querido
queiras	**quisesses**	**quiseres**			
queira	**quisesse**	**quiser**			
queiramos	**quiséssemos**	**quisermos**			
queirais	**quisésseis**	**quiserdes**			
queiram	**quisessem**	**quiserem**			

Infinitivo impessoal / Impersonal infinitive		Presente / Present	Pretérito imperfeito / Imperfect	Indicativo (Indicative) Pretérito perfeito / Preterite	Pretérito mais-que-perfeito / Pluperfect	Futuro do presente / Future	Futuro do pretérito / Conditional
reaver	eu	—	reavia	reouve	reouvera	reaverei	reaveria
	tu	—	reavias	reouveste	reouveras	reaverás	reaverias
	ele	—	reavia	reouve	reouvera	reaverá	reaveria
	nós	reavemos	reavíamos	reouvemos	reouvéramos	reaveremos	reaveríamos
	vós	reaveis	reavíeis	reouvestes	reouvéreis	reavereis	reaveríeis
	eles	—	reaviam	reouveram	reouveram	reaverão	reaveriam
requerer	eu	requeiro	requeria	requeri	requerera	requererei	requereria
	tu	requeres	requerias	requereste	requereras	requererás	requererias
	ele	requer	requeria	requereu	requerera	requererá	requereria
	nós	requeremos	requeríamos	requeremos	requerêramos	requereremos	requereríamos
	vós	requereis	requeríeis	requerestes	requerêreis	requerereis	requereríeis
	eles	requerem	requeriam	requereram	requereram	requererão	requereriam
saber	eu	sei	sabia	soube	soubera	saberei	saberia
	tu	sabes	sabias	soubeste	souberas	saberás	saberias
	ele	sabe	sabia	soube	soubera	saberá	saberia
	nós	sabemos	sabíamos	soubemos	soubéramos	saberemos	saberíamos
	vós	sabeis	sabíeis	soubestes	soubéreis	sabereis	saberíeis
	eles	sabem	sabiam	souberam	souberam	saberão	saberiam
ser	eu	sou	era	fui	fora	serei	seria
	tu	és	eras	foste	foras	serás	serias
	ele	é	era	foi	fora	será	seria
	nós	somos	éramos	fomos	foramos	seremos	seríamos
	vós	sois	éreis	fostes	foreis	sereis	seríeis
	eles	são	eram	foram	foram	serão	seriam
ter	eu	tenho	tinha	tive	tivera	terei	teria
	tu	tens	tinhas	tiveste	tiveras	terás	terias
	ele	tem	tinha	teve	tivera	terá	teria
	nós	temos	tínhamos	tivemos	tivéramos	teremos	teríamos
	vós	tendes	tínheis	tivestes	tivéreis	tereis	teríeis
	eles	têm	tinham	tiveram	tiveram	terão	teriam
trazer	eu	trago	trazia	trouxe	trouxera	trarei	traria
	tu	trazes	trazias	trouxeste	trouxeras	trarás	trarias
	ele	traz	trazia	trouxe	trouxera	trará	traria
	nós	trazemos	trazíamos	trouxemos	trouxéramos	traremos	traríamos
	vós	trazeis	trazíeis	trouxestes	trouxéreis	trareis	traríeis
	eles	trazem	traziam	trouxeram	trouxeram	trarão	trariam

Subjuntivo (Subjunctive)			Imperativo	Gerúndio	Particípio
Presente Present	**Pretérito imperfeito** Imperfect	**Futuro imperfeito** Future	Imperative	Gerund	Past Participle
LACKING	reouvesse	reouver	—	reavendo	reavido
	reouvesses	reouveres	reavei		
	reouvesse	reouver			
	reouvéssemos	reouvermos			
	reouvésseis	reouverdes			
	reouvessem	reouverem			
requeira	requeresse	requerer	LACKING	requerendo	requerido
requeiras	requeresses	requereres			
requeira	requeresse	requerer			
requeiramos	requerêssemos	requerermos			
requeirais	requerêsseis	requererdes			
requeiram	requeressem	requererem			
saiba	soubesse	souber	sabe	sabendo	sabido
saibas	soubesses	souberes	sabei		
saiba	soubesse	souber			
saibamos	soubéssemos	soubermos			
saibais	soubésseis	souberdes			
saibam	soubessem	souberem			
seja	fosse	for	sê	sendo	sido
sejas	fosses	fores	sede		
seja	fosse	for			
sejamos	fôssemos	formos			
sejais	fôsseis	fordes			
sejam	fossem	forem			
tenha	tivesse	tiver	tem	tendo	tido
tenhas	tivesses	tiveres	tende		
tenha	tivesse	tiver			
tenhamos	tivéssemos	tivermos			
tenhais	tivésseis	tiverdes			
tenham	tivessem	tiverem			
traga	trouxesse	trouxer	traze	trazendo	trazido
tragas	trouxesses	trouxeres	trazei		
traga	trouxesse	trouxer			
tragamos	trouxéssemos	trouxermos			
tragais	trouxésseis	trouxerdes			
tragam	trouxessem	trouxerem			

Infinitivo impessoal Impersonal infinitive	Presente Present	Pretérito imperfeito Imperfect	Pretérito perfeito Preterite	Pretérito mais-que-perfeito Pluperfect	Futuro do presente Future	Futuro do pretérito Conditional
			Indicativo (Indicative)			
valer	eu **valho**	valia	vali	valera	valerei	valeria
	tu **vales**	valias	valeste	valeras	valerás	valerias
	ele **vale**	valia	valeu	valera	valerá	valeria
	nós **valemos**	valíamos	valemos	valêramos	valeremos	valeríamos
	vós **valeis**	valíeis	valestes	valêreis	valereis	valeríeis
	eles **valem**	valiam	valeram	valeram	valerão	valeriam
ver	eu **vejo**	via	vi	**vira**	verei	veria
	tu **vês**	vias	**viste**	**viras**	verás	verias
	ele **vê**	via	**viu**	**vira**	verá	veria
	nós **vemos**	víamos	**vimos**	**víramos**	veremos	veríamos
	vós **vedes**	víeis	**vistes**	**víreis**	vereis	veríeis
	eles **vêem**	viam	**viram**	**viram**	verão	veriam

MODELO DE VERBOS IRREGULARES TERMINADOS EM ÔR E OR (Examples of irregular forms ending in ôr and or)

Infinitivo impessoal Impersonal infinitive	Presente Present	Pretérito imperfeito Imperfect	Pretérito perfeito Preterite	Pretérito mais-que-perfeito Pluperfect	Futuro do presente Future	Futuro do pretérito Conditional
pôr	eu **ponho**	punha	pus	pusera	porei	poria
	tu **pões**	punhas	puseste	puseras	porás	porias
	ele **põe**	punha	pôs	pusera	porá	poria
	nós **pomos**	púnhamos	pusemos	puséramos	poremos	poríamos
	vós **pondes**	púnheis	pusestes	puséreis	poreis	poríeis
	eles **põem**	punham	puseram	puseram	porão	poriam

Subjuntivo (Subjunctive)			Imperativo	Gerúndio	Particípio
Presente Present	**Pretérito imperfeito** Imperfect	**Futuro imperfeito** Future	Imperative	Gerund	Past Participle
valha	valesse	valer		valendo	valido
valhas	valesses	valeres	vale		
valha	valesse	valer			
valhamos	valêssemos	valermos			
valhais	valésseis	valerdes	valei		
valham	valessem	valerem			
veja	visse	vir		vendo	**visto**
vejas	visses	vires	**vê**		
veja	visse	vir			
vejamos	víssemos	virmos			
vejais	vísseis	virdes	**vede**		
vejam	vissem	virem			
ponha	pusesse	puser		pondo	**posto**
ponhas	pusesses	puseres	**põe**		
ponha	pusesse	puser			
ponhamos	puséssemos	pusermos			
ponhais	pusésseis	puserdes	**ponde**		
ponham	pusessem	puserem			

3.ª CONJUGAÇÃO (3rd group, ending in ir)

Infinitivo impessoal / Impersonal infinitive	Presente / Present		Indicativo (Indicative) Pretérito Imperfeito / Imperfect	Pretérito perfeito / Preterite	Pretérito mais-que-perfeito / Pluperfect	Futuro do presente / Future	Futuro do pretérito / Conditional

MODELO DE VERBO REGULAR (Example of the regular form)

partir	eu	parto	partia	parti	partira	partirei	partiria
	tu	partes	partias	partiste	partiras	partirás	partirias
	ele	parte	partia	partiu	partira	partirá	partiria
	nós	partimos	partíamos	partimos	partíramos	partiremos	partiríamos
	vós	partis	partíeis	partistes	partíreis	partireis	partiríeis
	eles	partem	partiam	partiram	partiram	partirão	partiriam

MODELOS DE VERBOS IRREGULARES (Examples of irregular forms)

abolir	eu	—	abolia	aboli	abolira	abolirei	aboliria
	tu	aboles	abolias	aboliste	aboliras	abolirás	abolirias
	ele	abole	abolia	aboliu	abolira	abolirá	aboliria
	nós	abolimos	abolíamos	abolimos	abolíramos	aboliremos	aboliríamos
	vós	abolis	abolíeis	abolistes	abolíreis	abolireis	aboliríeis
	eles	abolem	aboliam	aboliram	aboliram	abolirão	aboliriam

acudir	eu	acudo	acudia	acudi	acudira	acudirei	acudiria
	tu	acodes	acudias	acudiste	acudiras	acudirás	acudirias
	ele	acode	acudia	acudiu	acudira	acudirá	acudiria
	nós	acudimos	acudíamos	acudimos	acudíramos	acudiremos	acudiríamos
	vós	acudis	acudíeis	acudistes	acudíreis	acudireis	acudiríeis
	eles	acodem	acudiam	acudiram	acudiram	acudirão	acudiriam

aderir	eu	adiro	aderia	aderi	aderira	aderirei	aderiria
	tu	aderes	aderias	aderiste	aderiras	aderirás	aderirias
	ele	adere	aderia	aderiu	aderira	aderirá	aderiria
	nós	aderimos	aderíamos	aderimos	aderíramos	aderiremos	aderiríamos
	vós	aderis	aderíeis	aderistes	aderíreis	aderireis	aderiríeis
	eles	aderem	aderiam	aderiram	aderiram	aderirão	adeririam

agredir	eu	agrido	agredia	agredi	agredira	agredirei	agrediria
	tu	agrides	agredias	agrediste	agrediras	agredirás	agredirias
	ele	agride	agredia	agrediu	agredira	agredirá	agrediria
	nós	agredimos	agredíamos	agredimos	agredíramos	agrediremos	agrediríamos
	vós	agredis	agredíeis	agredistes	agredíreis	agredireis	agrediríeis
	eles	agridem	agrediam	agrediram	agrediram	agredirão	agrediriam

Subjuntivo (Subjunctive)			Imperativo	Gerúndio	Particípio
Presente Present	**Pretérito imperfeito** Imperfect	**Futuro imperfeito** Future	Imperative	Gerund	Past Participle
parta partas parta **partamos** partais partam	partisse **partisses** partisse **partíssemos** **partísseis** partissem	partir partires **partir** **partirmos** **partirdes** partirem	parte parti	partindo	**partido**
LACKING	abolisse abolisses abolisse abolissemos abolisseis abolissem	abolir abolires abolir abolirmos abolirdes abolirem	abole aboli	abolindo	abolido
acuda acudas acuda acudamos acudais acudam	acudisse acudisses acudisse acudissemos acudisseis acudissem	acudir acudires acudir acudirmos acudirdes acudirem	**acode** acudi	acudindo	acudido
adira adiras adira **adiramos** adirais adiram	aderisse aderisses aderisse aderissemos aderisseis aderissem	aderir aderires aderir aderirmos aderirdes aderirem	adere aderi	aderindo	aderido
agrida agridas agrida **agridamos** agridais agridam	agredisse agredisses agredisse agredissemos agredisseis agredissem	agredir agredires agredir agredirmos agredirdes agredirem	**agride** agredi	agredindo	agredido

		Presente / Present	Pretérito imperfeito / Imperfect	Pretérito perfeito / Preterite	Indicativo (Indicative) Pretérito mais-que-perfeito / Pluperfect	Futuro do presente / Future	Futuro do pretérito / Conditional
argüir	eu	**arguo**	argüia	argüi	argüira	argüirei	argüiria
	tu	**argüis**	argüias	argüiste	argüiras	argüirás	argüirias
	ele	**argüi**	argüia	argüiu	argüira	argüirá	argüiria
	nós	argüimos	argüíamos	argüimos	argüíramos	argüiremos	argüiríamos
	vós	argüis	argüíeis	argüistes	argüíreis	argüireis	argüiríeis
	eles	**argüem**	argüiam	argüiram	argüirma	argüirão	argüiriam
atrair	eu	**atraio**	**atraía**	**atraí**	**atraíra**	atrairei	atrairia
	tu	**atrais**	**atraías**	**atraíste**	**atraíras**	atrairás	atrairias
	ele	**atrai**	**atraía**	atraiu	**atraíra**	atrairá	atrairia
	nós	**atraímos**	atraíamos	**atraímos**	atraíramos	atrairemos	atrairíamos
	vós	**atraís**	atraíeis	**atraístes**	atraíreis	atraireis	atrairíeis
	eles	atraem	**atraíam**	**atraíram**	**atraíram**	atrairão	atrairiam
cerzir	eu	**cirzo**	cerzia	cerzi	cerzira	cerzirei	cerziria
	tu	**cirzes**	cerzias	cerziste	cerziras	cerzirás	cerzirias
	ele	**cirze**	cerzia	cerziu	cerzira	cerzirá	cerziria
	nós	cerzimos	cerzíamos	cerzimos	cerzíramos	cerziremos	cerziríamos
	vós	cerzis	cerzíeis	cerzistes	cerzíreis	cerzireis	cerziríeis
	eles	cerzem	cerziam	cerziram	cerziram	cerzirão	cerziriam
cobrir	eu	**cubro**	cobria	cobri	cobria	cobrirei	cobriria
	tu	cobres	cobrias	cobriste	cobrias	cobrirás	cobririas
	ele	cobre	cobria	cobriu	cobrira	cobrirá	cobriria
	nós	cobrimos	cobríamos	cobrimos	cobríramos	cobriremos	cobriríamos
	vós	cobris	cobríeis	cobristes	cobríreis	cobrireis	cobriríeis
	eles	cobrem	cobriam	cobriram	cobriram	cobrirão	cobririam
conduzir	eu	conduzo	conduzia	conduzi	conduzira	conduzirei	conduziria
	tu	conduzes	conduzias	conduziste	conduziras	conduzirás	conduzirias
	ele	**conduz**	conduzia	conduziu	conduzira	conduzirá	conduziria
	nós	conduzimos	conduzíamos	conduzimos	conduzíramos	conduziremos	conduziríamos
	vós	conduzis	conduzíeis	conduzistes	conduzíreis	conduzireis	conduziríeis
	eles	conduzem	conduziam	conduziram	conduziram	conduzirão	conduziriam
construir	eu	construo	**construía**	**construí**	**construíra**	construirei	construiria
	tu	**construis**	**construías**	**construíste**	**construíras**	construirás	construirias
	ele	**construi**	**construía**	construiu	**construíra**	construirá	construiria
	nós	**construímos**	construíamos	**construímos**	construíramos	construiremos	construiríamos
	vós	**construís**	construíeis	**construístes**	construíreis	construireis	construiríeis
	eles	**construem**	**construíam**	**construíram**	**construíram**	construirão	construiriam

or

		Presente / Present
	eu	construo
	tu	**constróis**
	ele	**constrói**
	nós	**construímos**
	vós	**construís**
	eles	**constroem**

Subjuntivo (Subjunctive)

Presente / Present	Pretérito imperfeito / Imperfect	Futuro imperfeito / Future	Imperativo / Imperative	Gerúndio / Gerund	Particípio Past Participle
argua	argüisse	argüir		argüindo	argüido
arguas	argüisses	argüires	**argüi**		
argua	argüisse	argüir			
arguamos	argüíssemos	argüirmos			
arguais	argüísseis	argüirdes	argüi		
arguam	argüissem	argüirem			
atraia	atraísse	atrair		atraindo	**atraído**
atraias	**atraísses**	**atraíres**	**atrai**		
atraia	**atraísse**	atrair			
atraíamos	atraíssemos	atrairmos			
atraíais	atraísseis	atrairdes	**atrai**		
atraíam	**atraíssem**	**atraírem**			
cirza	cerzisse	cerzir		cerzindo	cerzido
cirzas	cerzisses	cerzires	**cirze**		
cirza	cerzisse	cerzir			
cirzamos	cerzíssemos	cerzirmos			
cirzais	cerzísseis	cerzirdes	cerzi		
cirzam	cerzissem	cerzirem			
cubra	cobrisse	cobrir		cobrindo	**coberto**
cubras	cobrisses	cobrires	cobre		
cubra	cobrisse	cobrir			
cubramos	cobríssemos	cobrirmos			
cubrais	cobrísseis	cobrirdes	cobri		
cubram	cobrissem	cobrirem			
conduza	conduzisse	conduzir		conduzindo	conduzido
conduzas	conduzisses	conduzires	conduze		
conduza	conduzisse	conduzir			
conduzamos	conduzíssemos	conduzirmos			
conduzais	conduzísseis	conduzirdes	conduzi		
conduzam	conduzissem	conduzirem			
construa	**construísse**	construir		construindo	**construído**
construas	**construísses**	**construíres**	**construí**		
construa	**construísse**	construir			
construamos	construíssemos	construirmos			
construais	construísseis	construirdes	**construí**		
construam	**construíssem**	**construírem**			

or

constrói

construí

Infinitivo impessoal / Impersonal infinitive		Presente / Present	Pretérito imperfeito / Imperfect	Pretérito perfeito / Preterite	Pretérito mais-que-perfeito / Pluperfect	Futuro do presente / Future	Futuro do pretérito / Conditional
despedir	eu	**despeço**	despedia	despedi	despedira	despedirei	despediria
	tu	despedes	despedias	despediste	despediras	despedirás	despedirias
	ele	despede	despedia	despediu	despedira	despedirá	despediria
	nós	despedimos	despedíamos	despedimos	despedíramos	despediremos	despediríamos
	vós	despedis	despedíeis	despedistes	despedíreis	despedireis	despediríeis
	eles	despedem	despediam	despediram	despediram	despedirão	despediriam
despir	eu	**dispo**	despia	despi	despira	despirei	despiria
	tu	despes	despias	despiste	despiras	despirás	despirias
	ele	despe	despia	despiu	despira	despirá	despiria
	nós	despimos	despíamos	despimos	despíramos	despiremos	despiríamos
	vós	despis	despíeis	despistes	despíreis	despireis	despiríeis
	eles	despem	despiam	despiram	despiram	despirão	dispiriam
dormir	eu	**durmo**	dormia	dormi	dormira	dormirei	dormiria
	tu	dormes	dormias	dormiste	dormiras	dormirás	dormirias
	ele	dorme	dormia	dormiu	dormira	dormirá	dormiria
	nós	dormimos	dormíamos	dormimos	dormíramos	dormiremos	dormiríamos
	vós	dormis	dormíeis	dormistes	dormíreis	dormireis	dormiríeis
	eles	dormem	dormiam	dormiram	dormiram	dormirão	dormiriam
erigir	eu	**erijo**	erigia	erigi	erigira	erigirei	erigiria
	tu	eriges	erigias	erigiste	erigiras	erigirás	erigirias
	ele	erige	erigia	erigiu	erigira	erigirá	erigiria
	nós	erigimos	erigíamos	erigimos	erigíramos	erigiremos	erigiríamos
	vós	erigis	erigíeis	erigistes	erigíreis	erigireis	erigiríeis
	eles	erigem	erigiam	erigiram	erigiram	erigirão	erigiriam
falir	eu	—	falia	fali	falira	falirei	faliria
	tu	—	falias	faliste	faliras	falirás	falirias
	ele	—	falia	faliu	falira	falirá	faliria
	nós	falimos	falíamos	falimos	falíramos	faliremos	faliríamos
	vós	falis	falíeis	falistes	falíreis	falireis	faliríeis
	eles	—	faliam	faliram	faliram	falirão	faliriam
frigir	eu	**frijo**	frigia	frigi	frigira	frigirei	frigiria
	tu	**freges**	frigias	frigiste	frigiras	frigirás	frigirias
	ele	**frege**	frigia	frigiu	frigira	frigirá	frigiria
	nós	frigimos	frigíamos	frigimos	frigíramos	frigiremos	frigiríamos
	vós	frigis	frigíeis	frigistes	frigíreis	frigireis	frigiríeis
	eles	**fregem**	frigiam	frigiram	frigiram	frigirão	frigiriam

Indicativo (Indicative)

Presente / Present	Subjuntivo (Subjunctive)		Imperativo / Imperative	Gerúndio / Gerund	Particípio / Past Participle
	Pretérito imperfeito / Imperfect	Futuro imperfeito / Future			
despeça despeças **despeça** **despeçamos** despeçais **despeçam**	despedisse despedisses despedisse despedíssemos despedísseis despedissem	despedir despedires despedir despedirmos despedirdes despedirem	despede despedi	despedindo	despedido
dispa dispas **dispa** **dispamos** dispais **dispam**	despisse despisses despisse despíssemos despísseis despissem	despir despires despir despirmos despirdes despirem	despe despi	despindo	despido
durma durmas **durma** **durmamos** durmais **durmam**	dormisse dormisses dormisse dormíssemos dormísseis dormissem	dormir dormires dormir dormirmos dormirdes dormirem	dorme dormi	dormindo	dormido
erija erijas **erija** **erijamos** erijais **erijam**	erigisse erigisses erigisse erigíssemos erigísseis erigissem	erigir erigires erigir erigirmos erigirdes erigirem	erige erigi	erigindo	erigido or **ereto**
LACKING	falisse falisses falisse falíssemos falísseis falissem	falir falires falir falirmos falirdes falirem	— fali	falindo	falido
frija frijas **frija** **frijamos** frijais **frijam**	frigisse frigisses frigisse frigíssemos frigísseis frigissem	frigir frigires frigir frigirmos frigirdes frigirem	**frege** frigi	frigindo	frigido or **frito**

Indicativo (Indicative)

instruir

	Presente / Present	Pretérito imperfeito / Imperfect	Pretérito perfeito / Preterite	Pretérito mais-que-perfeito / Pluperfect	Futuro do presente / Future	Futuro do pretérito / Conditional
eu	instruo	instruía	instruí	instruíra	instruirei	instruiria
tu	instruis	instruías	instruíste	instruíras	instruirás	instruirias
ele	instrui	instruía	instruiu	instruíra	instruirá	instruiria
nós	instruímos	instruíamos	instruímos	instruíramos	instruiremos	instruiríamos
vós	instruís	instruíeis	instruístes	instruíreis	instruireis	instruiríeis
eles	instruem	instruíam	instruíram	instruíram	instruirão	instruiriam

ir

	Presente / Present	Pretérito imperfeito / Imperfect	Pretérito perfeito / Preterite	Pretérito mais-que-perfeito / Pluperfect	Futuro do presente / Future	Futuro do pretérito / Conditional
eu	vou	ia	fui	fora	irei	iria
tu	vais	ias	foste	foras	irás	irias
ele	vai	ia	foi	fora	irá	iria
nós	vamos	íamos	fomos	fôramos	iremos	iríamos
vós	ides	íeis	fostes	fôreis	ireis	iríeis
eles	vão	iam	foram	foram	irão	iriam

luzir

	Presente / Present	Pretérito imperfeito / Imperfect	Pretérito perfeito / Preterite	Pretérito mais-que-perfeito / Pluperfect	Futuro do presente / Future	Futuro do pretérito / Conditional
eu	—	—	—	—	—	—
tu	—	—	—	—	—	—
ele	luz	luzia	luziu	luzira	luzirá	luziria
nós	—	—	—	—	—	—
vós	—	—	—	—	—	—
eles	luzem	luziam	luziram	luziram	luzirão	luziriam

medir

	Presente / Present	Pretérito imperfeito / Imperfect	Pretérito perfeito / Preterite	Pretérito mais-que-perfeito / Pluperfect	Futuro do presente / Future	Futuro do pretérito / Conditional
eu	meço	media	medi	medira	medirei	mediria
tu	medes	medias	mediste	mediras	medirás	medirias
ele	mede	media	mediu	medira	medirá	mediria
nós	medimos	medíamos	medimos	medíramos	mediremos	mediríamos
vós	medis	medíeis	medistes	medíreis	medireis	mediríeis
eles	medem	mediam	mediram	mediram	medirão	mediriam

ouvir

	Presente / Present	Pretérito imperfeito / Imperfect	Pretérito perfeito / Preterite	Pretérito mais-que-perfeito / Pluperfect	Futuro do presente / Future	Futuro do pretérito / Conditional
eu	ouço	ouvia	ouvi	ouvira	ouvirei	ouviria
tu	ouves	ouvias	ouviste	ouviras	ouvirás	ouvirias
ele	ouve	ouvia	ouviu	ouvira	ouvirá	ouviria
nós	ouvimos	ouvíamos	ouvimos	ouvíramos	ouviremos	ouviríamos
vós	ouvis	ouvíeis	ouvistes	ouvíreis	ouvireis	ouviríeis
eles	ouvem	ouviam	ouviram	ouviram	ouvirão	ouviriam

or

	Presente / Present
eu	oiço
tu	ouves
ele	ouve
nós	ouvimos
vós	ouvis
eles	ouvem

Subjuntivo (Subjunctive)			Imperativo Imperative	Gerúndio Gerund	Particípio Past Participle
Presente Present	**Pretérito imperfeito** Imperfect	**Futuro imperfeito** Future			
instrua	instruísse	instruir	**instrui**	instruindo	**instruído**
instruas	instruísses	**instruíres**			
instrua	instruísse	instruir	**instruí**		
instruamos	instruíssemos	instruirmos			
instruais	instruísseis	instruírdes			
instruam	instruíssem	**instruírem**			
vá	fosse	**for**	**vai**	indo	ido
vás	fosses	**fores**			
vá	fosse	**for**	**ide**		
vamos	**fôssemos**	**formos**			
vades	**fôsseis**	**fordes**			
vão	fossem	**forem**			
LACKING	—	—	LACKING	luzindo	luzido
	luzisse	luzir			
	—	—			
	—	—			
	—	—			
	luzissem	luzirem			
meça	medisse	medir	mede	medindo	medido
meças	medisses	medires			
meça	medisse	medir	medi		
meçamos	medíssemos	medirmos			
meçais	medísseis	medirdes			
meçam	medissem	medirem			
ouça	ouvisse	ouvir	**ouça**	ouvindo	ouvido
ouças	ouvisses	ouvires			
ouça	ouvisse	ouvir	ouvi		
ouçamos	ouvíssemos	ouvirmos			
ouçais	ouvísseis	ouvirdes	or		
ouçam	ouvissem	ouvirem			
or			**oiça**		
oiça					
oiças			ouvi		
oiça					
oiçamos					
oiçais					
oiçam					

Infinitivo impessoal / impersonal infinitive		Presente / Present	Pretérito imperfeito / Imperfect	Pretérito perfeito / Preterite	Pretérito mais-que-perfeito / Pluperfect	Futuro do presente / Future	Futuro do pretérito / Conditional
				Indicativo (Indicative)			
pedir	eu	peço	pedia	pedi	pedira	pedirei	pediria
	tu	pedes	pedias	pediste	pediras	pedirás	pedirias
	ele	pede	pedia	pediu	pedira	pedirá	pediria
	nós	pedimos	pedíamos	pedimos	pedíramos	pediremos	pediríamos
	vós	pedis	pedíeis	pedistes	pedíreis	pedireis	pediríeis
	eles	pedem	pediam	pediram	pediram	pedirão	pediriam
polir	eu	pulo	polia	poli	polira	polirei	poliria
	tu	poles	polias	poliste	poliras	polirás	polirias
	ele	pule	polia	poliu	polira	polirá	poliria
	nós	polimos	políamos	polimos	políramos	poliremos	poliríamos
	vós	polis	políeis	polistes	políreis	polireis	poliríeis
	eles	pulem	poliam	poliram	poliram	polirão	poliriam
restituir	eu	restituo	restituía	restituí	restituíra	restituirei	restituiria
	tu	restituis	restituías	restituíste	restituíras	restituirás	restituirias
	ele	restitui	restituía	restituiu	restituíra	restituirá	restituiria
	nós	restituímos	restituíamos	restituímos	restituíramos	restituiremos	restituiríamos
	vós	restituís	restituíeis	restituístes	restituíreis	restituireis	restituiríeis
	eles	restituem	restituíam	restituíram	restituíram	restituirão	restituiriam
rir	eu	rio	ria	ri	rira	rirei	riria
	tu	ris	rias	riste	riras	rirás	ririas
	ele	ri	ria	riu	rira	rirá	riria
	nós	rimos	ríamos	rimos	ríramos	riremos	riríamos
	vós	rides	ríeis	ristes	ríreis	rireis	riríeis
	eles	riem	riam	riram	riram	rirão	ririam
sair	eu	saio	saía	saí	saíra	sairei	sairia
	tu	sais	saías	saíste	saíras	sairás	sairias
	ele	sai	saía	saiu	saíra	sairá	sairia
	nós	saímos	saíamos	saímos	saíramos	sairemos	sairíamos
	vós	saís	saíeis	saístes	saíreis	saireis	sairíeis
	eles	saem	saíam	saíram	saíram	sairão	sairiam
sortir	eu	surto	sortia	sorti	sortira	sortirei	sortiria
	tu	surtes	sortias	sortiste	sortiras	sortirás	sortirias
	ele	surte	sortia	sortiu	sortira	sortirá	sortiria
	nós	sortimos	sortíamos	sortimos	sortíramos	sortiremos	sortiríamos
	vós	sortis	sortíeis	sortistes	sortíreis	sortireis	sortiríeis
	eles	surtem	sortiam	sortiram	sortiram	sortirão	sortiriam

| Subjuntivo (Subjunctive) | | | Imperativo Imperative | Gerúndio Gerund | Particípio Past Participle |
Presente Present	Pretérito imperfeito Imperfect	Futuro imperfeito Future			
peça peças peça peçamos peçais peçam	pedisse pedisses pedisse pedíssemos pedísseis pedissem	pedir pedires pedir pedirmos pedirdes pedirem	pede pedi	pedindo	pedido
pula pulas pula pulamos pulais pulam	polisse polisses polisse políssemos polísseis polissem	polir polires polir polirmos polirdes polirem	**pule** poli	polindo	polido
restitua restituas restitua restituamos restituais restituam	**restituísse restituísses restituísse restituíssemos restituísseis restituíssem**	restituir **restituíres** restituir restituirmos restituirdes **restituírem**	**restitui** **restitui**	restituindo	**restituído**
ria rias ria riamos riais riam	risse risses risse ríssemos rísseis rissem	rir rires rir rirmos rirdes rirem	**ri** **ride**	rindo	rido
saia saias saia saiamos saiais saiam	saísse saísses saísse **saíssemos** **saísseis** saíssem	sair **saíres** sair sairmos sairdes **saírem**	**sai** **sai**	saindo	**saído**
surta surtas surta surtamos surtais surtam	sortisse sortisses sortisse sortíssemos sortísseis sortissem	sortir sortires sortir sortirmos sortirdes sortirem	**surte** sorti	sortindo	sortido

Indicativo (Indicative)

Infinitivo impessoal / Impersonal infinitive	Presente / Present	Pretérito imperfeito / Imperfect	Pretérito perfeito / Preterite	Pretérito mais-que-perfeito / Pluperfect	Futuro do presente / Future	Futuro do pretérito / Conditional
tossir	eu **tusso**	tossia	tossi	tossira	tossirei	tossiria
	tu **tosses**	tossias	tossiste	tossiras	tossirás	tossirias
	ele **tosse**	tossia	tossiu	tossira	tossirá	tossiria
	nós tossimos	tossíamos	tossimos	tossíramos	tossiremos	tossiríamos
	vós tossis	tossíeis	tossistes	tossíreis	tossireis	tossiríeis
	eles **tossem**	tossiam	tossiram	tossiram	tossirão	tossiriam
urgir	eu —	—	—	—	—	—
	tu —	—	—	—	—	—
	ele **urge**	urgia	urgiu	urgira	urgirá	urgiria
	nós —	—	—	—	—	—
	vós —	—	—	—	—	—
	eles **urgem**	urgiam	urgiram	urgiram	urgirão	urgiriam
vir	eu **venho**	vinha	**vim**	**viera**	virei	viria
	tu **vens**	vinhas	**vieste**	**vieras**	virás	virias
	ele **vem**	vinha	**veio**	**viera**	virá	viria
	nós vimos	vínhamos	**viemos**	**viéramos**	viremos	viríamos
	vós **vindes**	vínheis	**viestes**	**viéreis**	vireis	viríeis
	eles **vêm**	vinham	**vieram**	**vieram**	virão	viriam

Subjuntivo (Subjunctive)

	Presente / Present	Pretérito imperfeito / Imperfect	Futuro imperfeito / Future	Imperativo / Imperative	Gerúndio / Gerund	Particípio / Past Participle
	tussa	tossisse	tossir		tossindo	tossido
	tussas	tossisses	tossires	tosse		
	tussa	tossisse	tossir			
	tussamos	tossíssemos	tossirmos			
	tussais	tossísseis	tossirdes	tossi		
	tussam	tossissem	tossirem			
	—	—	—		urgindo	urgido
	—	urgisse	urgir	LACKING		
	—	—	—			
	LACKING	—	—			
	—	—	—			
	—	urgissem	urgirem			
	venha	viesse	vier		vindo	**vindo**
	venhas	viesses	vieres	**vem**		
	venha	viesse	vier			
	venhamos	viéssemos	viermos			
	venhais	viésseis	vierdes	**vinde**		
	venham	viessem	vierem			

Pesos e Medidas / Weights and Measures

Medidas de Comprimento / Linear Measures

1 milímetro (mm)	0,001 m	0.03937 in.
1 centímetro (cm)	0,01 m	0.3937 in.
1 decímetro (dm)	0,1 m	3.937 in.
1 metro (m)	100 cm	39.37 in.
1 quilômetro (km)	1.000 m	0.62137 mi.
1 miriâmetro (Mm)	10.000 m (10 km)	6.2137 mi.

Medidas de Superfície / Square Measures

1 milímetro quadrado (mm²)	0,000001 m²	0.00155 sq. in.
1 centímetro quadrado (cm²)	0,0001 m²	0.155 sq. in.
1 decímetro quadrado (dm²)	0,01 m²	15.50 sq. in.
1 metro quadrado (m²)	0,01 are	1.1960 sq. yd.
1 are (a)	100 m²	119.6 sq. yd.
1 hectare (ha)	100 ares	2.471 acres
1 quilômetro quadrado (km²)	10.000 ares	247.104 acres

Medidas de Volume / Cubic Measures

1 milímetro cúbico (mm³)	0,000000001 m³	0,000061 cu. in.
1 centímetro cúbico (cm³)	0,000001 m³	0.0610 cu. in.
1 decímetro cúbico (dm³)	0,001 m³ (1 litro)	61.023 cu. yd.
1 metro cúbico (m³)	1.000 dm³ (1.000 litros)	1.308 cu. yd.

Pesos Comerciais / Avoirdupois Weights

1 quilate métrico	0,2 g	3.09 gr.
1 miligrama (mg)	0,001 g	0.0154 gr.
1 centigrama (cg)	0,01 g	0.154 gr.
1 decigrama (dg)	0,1 g	1.543 gr.
1 grama (g)	0,001 kg	15.432 gr.
1 decagrama (dag)	10 g	0.352 oz.
1 quilograma (kg)	1.000 g	2.204 lb.
1 arroba métrica	15 kg	33.07 lb.
1 quintal métrico (q)	100 kg	220.4 lb.
1 tonelada (t)	1.000 kg	2,204 lb.

Medidas de Capacidade / Measures of Capacity

1 centilitro (cl)	0,01 l	Br.:	0.352 fluid ounce
		Am.:	0.338 fluid ounce
1 decilitro (dl)	0,1 l		6.1025 cu. in.
1 litro (l)	1 dm³		61.025 cu. in.
1 decalitro (dal)	10 l		610.25 cu. in.
1 hectolitro (hl)	100 l	Br.:	22 gallons
		Am.:	26.418 gallons
1 quilolitro (kl)	1.000 l		35.315 cu. ft.

Medidas Antigas / Ancient Measures

Medidas Itinerárias / Itinerary Measures

1 milha brasileira	2.200 m		1.36 mi.
1 milha portuguesa	2.066 m		1.28 mi.
1 milha marítima (nó)	1.852 m		1,013 fathoms
1 légua brasileira	6.600 m		4.10 mi.
1 légua portuguesa	6.200 m		3.85 mi.
1 légua marítima	5.555 m		3 nautical miles

Medidas de comprimento / Linear measures

1 ponto	0,2 mm		0.007874 in.
1 linha	2,3 mm		0.09 in.
1 polegada	2,75 cm		1.08 in.
1 palmo	22 cm		8.66 in.
1 pé	33 cm		1.08 ft.
1 côvado	66 cm		25.98 in.
1 vara	1,10 m		43.31 in.
1 braça	2,20 m		86.62 in.

Medidas de superfície / Square measures

1 braça quadrada	4,84 m^2		5.7886 sq. yd.
1 alqueire (N. Braz.)	27.225 m^2		32,560 sq. yd.
1 alqueire (Minas, Rio, Goiás)	48.400 m^2		57,886 sq. yd.
1 alqueire paulista	24.200 m^2		28,943 sq. yd.

Pesos / Weights

1 quilate	199 mg		3.07 gr.
1 onça	28,691 g		1.012 oz.
1 libra	459,5 g		1.013 lb.
1 arroba	14,689 kg		32.38 lb.
1 quintal	58,758 kg		129.50 lb.
1 tonelada	793,238 kg		1,748.70 lb.

Abreviaturas explicativas usadas nos verbetes

Abreviations used in the entries

abbr.	abbreviation of	fenc.	fencing
abs.	absolute	fig.	figurative(ly)
adj.	adjective	folkl.	folklore
adv.	adverb, adverbial	form.	formerly
aeron.	aeronautics	fort.	fortification
agric.	agriculture	Fr.	French, France
agron.	agronomy	ftb.	football
anat.	anatomy	Gall.	Gallicism
anthr.	anthropology	gard.	gardening
ant.	antiquated, antiquity	geogr.	geography
arch.	archaic	geol.	geology
archaeol.	archaeology	geom.	geometry
archit.	architecture	geneal.	genealogy
arith.	arithmetic	geophys.	geophysics
astr.	astronomy	Germ.	German(y)
augm.	augmentative	gram.	grammar
bact.	bacteriology	Gr.	Greek, Greece
B.C.	before Christ	gym.	gymnastics
bib.	biblical	her.	heraldry
biochem.	biochemistry	hist.	history
biol.	biology	horse.	horsemanship
bot.	botany	hort.	horticulture
box.	boxing	hum.	humorous(ly)
Braz.	Brazil(ian)	hunt.	hunting
carp.	carpentry	ichth.	ichthyology
chem.	chemistry	indef.	indefinite
cin.	cinema	ind.	industry
coll.	colloquial	inf.	infinitive
com.	commerce	ins.	insurance
conj.	conjunction	interj.	interjection
constr.	construction	Ir.	Irish, Ireland
contr.	contraction	ironic.	ironically
cryst.	crystallography	It.	Italian, Italy
cul.	culinary	jur.	jurisprudence
def.	definite	L.	Latin
dent.	dentistry	lit.	literature
depr.	depreciative	loc.	local
dial.	dialectal	log.	logic
dim.	diminutive	mach.	machinery
dipl.	diplomacy	m.	masculine
eccl.	ecclesiastical	math.	mathematics
econ.	economy	mech.	mechanics
e.g.	for instance	med.	medicine
electr.	electricity	met.	metallurgy
embriol.	embriology	meteor.	meteorology
Engl.	English, England	mil.	military
engr.	engraving	min.	mineralogy, mining
ent.	entomology	mot.	motoring
esp.	especially	mus.	music
ethn.	ethnology	myth.	mythology
etym.	etymology	N.	North(ern)
euphem.	euphemistic	naut.	nautical
exam.	examination	N.E.	Northeastern
fam.	familiar	nucl. eng.	nuclear engineering
f.	feminine	obs.	obsolete

opt.	optics	rhet.	rhetoric
ornith.	ornithology	S.	South
o. s.	oneself	s.	substantive
paint.	painting	scient.	scientific
pal.	palaeontology	Scot.	Scotch, Scotland
parl.	parliamentary	sculp.	sculpture
path.	pathology	sg.	singular
p.	person, personal	sl.	slang
petrog.	petrography	s. o.	someone
pharm.	pharmacology	Span.	Spanish
phil.	philology	s. th.	something
philos.	philosophy	stat.	statistics
phon.	phonetics	suf.	suffix
phot.	photography	sup.	superlative
phys.	physics	surg.	surgery
physiol.	physiology	surv.	surveying
pl.	plural	swim.	swimming
poet.	poetry, poetical	tail.	tailoring
pol.	politics, political	tech.	technical
pop.	popular	telegr.	telegraphy
Port.	Portuguese, Portugal	teleph.	telephony
p. p.	past participle	ten.	tennis
pref.	prefix	theat.	theatre
prep.	preposition	theol.	theology
Presb.	Presbyterian	topogr.	topography
pres. p.	present participle	T V	television
pron.	pronoun	typogr.	typography
pros.	prosody	U. S. A.	United States of
prov.	provincialism		America
psych.	psychology	v.	verb
rail.	railroad, railway	vet.	veterinary
†	rare(ly used)	vulg.	vulgar
R. C.	Roman Catholic	weav.	weaving
rel.	religion	zool.	zoology

A

A, a s. m. the first letter of the Portuguese alphabet.
a def. art. f. (pl. **as**) the.
  a mãe the mother. **as mães** the mothers.
a pers. pron. f. (pl. **as** them) her, it.
  vendo-a(s) seeing her (them).
a demonstr. pron. f. that, the one.
a prep. according to, after, against, at, by, from, in, of, on, till, to, towards, under, upon, with, within. **a custo** with difficulty. **a leste** towards the east, east of. **a partir desse dia** from that day on. **a meu ver** in my opinion. **a pouca distância** within a short distance. **a pé** on foot. **a que horas?** at what time? **a seu gosto** according to his (her) taste. **a seu modo** after his way. **a título** on the basis of. **cheirar a rosas** to smell of roses. **encostar a uma parede** to lean against a wall. **irei a Londres** I shall go to London. **passo a passo** step by step.
à contraction of the prep. **a** with the art. or pron. **a**. **à agulha** with the needle. **à sua chegada** upon her arrival. **à direita** on the right. **sair ~ francesa** to take a French leave. **à hora marcada** at the appointed time. **à pressa** in haste. **às onças** by the ounce. **irei à França** I shall go to France.
aba s. f. 1. brim (hat), rim (plate C 5). 2. coattail (plate R 7). 3. skirt (saddle) (plate S 2). 4. edge. 5. border. 6. bank, side (river). 7. eaves (pl.) (roof). 8. flap (envelope) (plate C 10), (fig.) protection. 9. outskirts. 10. foot (mountain).
  ~ de cantoneira web (or leg) of an angle iron. **~ do ferro T** flange of a tee iron. **de ~ larga** broad brimmed.
ababadar v. 1. to flounce. 2. to pleat, make pleats.
ababelado adj. confused, untidy, in a mess.
ababelar v. to confuse, mix up, disorder.
abacá s. m. 1. Manil(l)a hemp plant. 2. fibre of the Manil(l)a hemp plant.
abacamartado adj. like a blunderbuss.
abaçanado adj. (also **abacinado**) dark-complexioned, swarthy, sunburnt.
abaçanar v. 1. to darken. 2. to tan, bronze.
abacate s. m. (bot.) avocado-pear, alligator-pear.
abacateiro s. m. avocado-pear tree.
abacaxi s. m. 1. (bot.) pineapple (Ananas sativus). 2. (Braz., sl.) confused state of things. 3. (Braz., sl.) anything hard to handle. 4. (N. E. Braz.) bad, clumsy dancer.
abacelar v. 1. to plant young vines. 2. to graft. 3. to heap up earth round about a plant.
abacharelar-se v. 1. to graduate as a bachelor. 2. to live or act as a holder of a bachelor's degree.
abacial adj. m. + f. (pl. -ais) abbatial.
abaciar v. to shape into a basin.
abacinar v. 1. = **abaçanar**. 2. **~-se** to become dark, lose brilliancy.
abacisco s. m. (archit.) 1. ceramic, cement or brick floor tile. 2. mosaic-tiled floor.
abacista s. m. abacist.
ábaco s. m. abacus: 1. counting frame or table. 2. (archit.) uppermost division of a capital.
abactor s. m. cattle thief.
abada (I) s. f. lot, great quantity.
abada (II) s. f. 1. female rhinoceros. 2. her horn.
abadado s. m. 1. dignity of an abbot. 2. tenure of an abbot. ‖ adj. having an abbot.
abadágio s. m. 1. a parish priest's meal, formerly provided by his parishioners. 2. an abbey's benefice.
abadalado adj. shaped like a bell-clapper.

abadar v. (also **abadiar**) 1. to introduce an abbot to his parish. 2. to provide with an abbot or parish priest.
abade s. m. abbot.
abadengo adj. abbatial, belonging to an abbot or his jurisdiction.
abadengos s. m. pl. the real estate of an abbey.
abadernas s. f. pl. (naut.) hooks to hitch ropes to.
abadesco adj. proper or relating to an abbot.
abadessa (ê) s. f. 1. abbess. 2. matron, elderly lady.
abadessado s. m. 1. dignity of an abbess. 2. tenure of an abbess. 3. festival of her election.
abadessar v. to act as an abbess.
abadia s. f. (also **abadado, abadiado** m.) 1. abbey (building and community of monks or nuns), monastery. 2. parish and its benefice (Port.).
abado adj. large-brimmed.
abaetado adj. baizelike, hairy.
abaetar v. 1. to cover with baize. 2. to wrap up (in woollies). 3. **~-se** to clothe (o. s.) well. 4. to manufacture baizelike cloth.
abafadela s. f. 1. short-windedness. 2. a sudden stifling.
abafadiço adj. (also **abafante**) 1. not aired, not ventilated, sultry, stifling, smouldry, choking. 2. (fig.) ill-tempered, cross.
  calor ~ sultriness, suffocating heat.
abafado adj. 1. well-covered. 2. sultry, sweltry. 3. (fig.) hidden, kept secret, hushed up. 4. oppressed. 5. restrained, restricted, checked. 6. dissimulated. 7. (Braz.) opposed, annoyed. 8. (Braz.) very busy.
abafador s. m. 1. (mus.) damper. 2. cosy, cozy (padded covering for a teapot). 3. (Braz., sl.) pilferer. ‖ adj. sultry, stifling, smouldry.
abafamento s. m. (also **abafação** f.) 1. choking, checking, suffocation, oppression, smothering. 2. short-breathedness. 3. (Braz.) unlawful retaining of an object or money; stealing.
abafante adj. m. + f. stifling, suffocating.
abafar (I) v. 1. to choke. 2. to smother. 3. to suffocate. 4. to asphyxiate. 5. to stifle. 6. to dissimulate. 7. to hold back or retain (unlawfully), steal. 8. to hush up, keep concealed, hide. 9. (mus.) to damp. 10. to cloth, wrap up, keep o. s. warm. 11. to cover well, overlay. 12. (Braz.) to succumb. 13. (Braz.) to dominate.
  ~ as velas (naut.) to lower the sails. **~ a terra** to harrow or break the clods after the first ploughing. **~ os rumores** to hush up rumours.
abafar (II) s. m. = **albafar**.
abafarete s. m. 1. choking, smothering. 2. stoppage, arrest, act of stopping the course of s. th. 3. hushing up.
abafo s. m. 1. muffler, warming cloth. 2. kindness, endearment.
abagualado adj. 1. shy (esp. of animals). 2. rough, rude, uncivil.
abagualar-se v. to become shy (said of animals, also: wild and free).
abagunçado adj. = **bagunçado**.
abagunçar v. = **bagunçar**.
abaianado adj. (Braz.) like a **baiano** (native of Bahia).
abainhar v. (tail.) to hem (plate P 15).
abairramento s. m. division into wards, districts or quarters.
abairrar v. to divide into wards, districts or quarters.
abaiucar v. to transform into a low gin-shop.

abaixador s. m. depressor, abater, person who or thing which lowers.

abaixa-língua s. m. (pl. **abaixa-línguas**) (surg.) tongue depressor.

abaixamento s. m. (also **abaixadela** f.) 1. lowering, bringing or letting down, sinking. 2. abatement, diminishing, diminution. 3. falling of prices. 4. humiliation. 5. depression.

abaixante s. m. depressor, abater, person who or thing which lowers. || adj. m. + f. 1. lowering, sinking. 2. falling. 3. humiliating.

abaixar v. 1. to lower. 2. to let or bring down. 3. to diminish, lessen, shorten. 4. to decrease, decline, fall. 5. to check, abate. 6. to depress. 7. to weaken. 8. to humiliate, humble, come down. 9. **~-se:** a) to humble o. s. b) to stoop down.
~ a crista a alguém to take s. o. down a peg. **~ a cortina** (theat.) to ring down the curtain.

abaixa-voz s. m. (pl. **abaixa-vozes**) canopy covering a pulpit.

abaixo adv. down, under, inferior, below. || interj. down!
~ e acima up and down. **~ mencionado** undermentioned, mentioned below. **ela canta ~ do tom** she sings flat.

abaixo-assinado s. m. (pl. **abaixo-assinados**) 1. application with the signature of several petitioners. 2. subscription.
fazer um ~ ao presidente to make an application to the president.

abajoujamento s. m. 1. flattery. 2. infatuation.

abajoujar-se v. 1. to be or pretend to be foolish. 2. to become infatuated. 3. to be conceited.

abajur s. m. (also **quebra-luz**) 1. lamp shade. 2. bedside lamp (plate D 4).

abalada s. f. 1. direction the game takes when stirred or started. 2. direction of a flight of birds. 3. hasty departure, decamping. 4. (fam.) shedaddle.
estar de ~ to be about to leave.

abalado adj. 1. shaky, loose. 2. (fig.) moved, touched. || **-amente** adv. hastily, hurriedly.

abalador adj. 1. causing vibrations, shaking or trembling. 2. impressive. 3. moving, touching.

abalamento s. m. (also **abaladura** f.) 1. shake or shock that causes a weakening. 2. affection, sympathy. 3. agitation. 4. fuss, mess. 5. change of mind. 6. urging. 7. hasty marching. 8. flight. 9. loss of countenance.

abalançamento s. m. 1. start, spring, swing, sudden motion. 2. balance, control of accounts.

abalançar v. 1. to balance: a) weigh. b) control the accounts. 2. to counterpoise. 3. to urge, thrust on, stir. 4. to swing. 5. to see-saw. 6. to wag. 7. to venture, dare. 8. **~-se a** to throw o. s. upon, venture upon.

abalar v. 1. to weaken by shaking. 2. to shake, jog. 3. to make tremble. 4. to move, touch, affect. 5. to agitate, stir. 6. to meddle, mess, confuse. 7. to cause a change of mind. 8. to confound, shock. 9. to urge, stir up. 10. to march off or depart hastily. 11. to flight, run away, decamp. 12. to lose countenance.
~ a saúde to affect one's health. **~ o crédito, a reputação** to shake the credit, the reputation. **a notícia abalou a cidade** the news shook the city. **o incidente abalou-o muito** the incident was a great blow to him.

abalaustrado adj. 1. provided with balusters. 2. in form of balusters.

abalaustramento s. m. supplying or furnishing with balusters.

abalaustrar v. 1. to supply or provide with balusters, rail. 2. to shape like a baluster.

abalável adj. m. + f. (pl. **-áveis**) 1. shak(e)able. 2. liable to be agitated, sensitive.

abaldeirado, abaldeiro adj. = **albardeiro**.

abalizado adj. 1. very competent, authoritative. 2. distinguished, notable. 3. marked out by bounds or buoys. 4. measured.

abalizador s. m. 1. surveyor. 2. person that sets up marks. 3. stake (for surveying).

abalizar v. 1. to mark out by bounds or buoys. 2. to beacon. 3. to survey or measure land. 4. to show, indicate, trace. 5. to attain distinction, excellence or renown.

abalo s. m. (also **abalada** f., **abalamento** m.) 1. commotion, disturbance. 2. shock. 3. grief, trouble of mind. 4. earthquake.
dar (fazer) ~ a alg. to give s. o. a push, impress a person. **causar ~** to affect.

abaloar v. to give the shape of a balloon.

abalofado adj. 1. puffed up, swollen. 2. presumptuous, pretentious, arrogant.

abalofar v. 1. to swell, puff up. 2. to become presumptuous, pretentious or arrogant.

abalonado adj. 1. like a balloon. 2. swollen, tumefied. 3. puffed up.

abaloso adj. 1. (Braz.) heavy and tossing (gait of a horse). 2. shaking, trembling, lacking firmness and stability. 3. troublesome, disagreeable.

abalroação, abalroada, abalroadela s. f., **abalroamento** m. 1. onset, assault. 2. collision (vehicles). 3. (naut.) grappling, boarding, grapnel.

abalroar v. 1. to board (a ship with grappling irons). 2. to assault, attack or invest against. 3. to run into, collide.

abalsar v. to put into the must-tub.

abaluartamento s. m. fortification by means of bulwarks or bastions.

abaluartar v. 1. to fortify with bulwarks or bastions. 2. to give the form of bulwarks or bastions. 3. **~-se** to entrench o. s.

abâmea s. f. (bot.) bog-asphodel.

abanação s. f. (also **abanamento** m., **abanadura, abanadela** f.) fanning, winnowing (of corn).

abanadela s. f. agitation, jolting, tossing.

abanado adj. 1. ventilated, fanned. 2. agitated, moving to and fro. 3. heedless, reckless. 4. (coll.) sick. 5. valetudinarian.

abanador s. m. 1. fan. 2. fanner, winnower.

abana-moscas s. m., sg. + pl. 1. fly-flap. 2. (fig.) something trifling.

abananado adj. 1. like banana. 2. soft, mild. 3. foolish. 4. confused, confounded, stupefied. 5. sullen.

abananar v. 1. (fig.) to grow stupid. 2. to bewilder, confound, confuse.

abanante adj. m. + f. fanning.

abanão s. m. (pl. **-ões**) (coll.) 1. intensive fanning. 2. jolt, jerk.

abanar (I) v. 1. to cool by fanning, fan. 2. to agitate, move to and fro. 3. to shake, jolt, toss. 4. to dissuade. 5. to tremble. 6. to winnow. 7. **~-se** to cool o. s. with a fan. 8. to air.
~ as árvores to shake the trees. **~ as moscas** to drive the flies away. **~ o lume** to fan the fire. **as árvores abanavam ao sabor do vento** the trees bowed in the wind. **vir com as mãos abanando** to come empty-handed.

abanar (II) v. (Braz., sl.) to pilfer.

abancar v. 1. to sit down (at table on a bench). 2. to group or arrange around a table.

abandado adj. gathered in bands, flocks, etc. (of animals).

abandalhação s. f. (pl. **-ões**) (also **abandalhamento** m.) debasement, degradation, vileness.

abandalhado adj. 1. debased, degraded, vilified. 2. demoralized. 3. roguish.
abandalhar v. 1. to debase, degrade, vilify. 2. to play the fop, be ridiculous.
abandar (I) v. 1. to gather in bands or flocks. 2. (coll.) to join a political party.
abandar (II) v. 1. to provide with sides, borders, etc. (see **banda**). 2. to separate, put aside. 3. to give as a share or portion.
abandear v. = **abandar** (I), **bandear**.
abandeirado adj. = **embandeirado**.
abandeirar v. = **embandeirar**.
abandejado adj. like a tray.
abandejar v. 1. to give to s. th. the shape of a tray. 2. to winnow with a tray.
abandidar-se v. (Braz.) to become a bandit.
abandoar-se v. = **abandar** (I).
abandonado adj. 1. abandoned. 2. forlorn, forsaken, helpless. 3. alone, friendless. 4. disregarded, despised. ‖ **-amente** adv. in abandon, at random.
abandonador s. m. a person who abandons.
abandonar v. 1. to abandon, relinquish. 2. to forsake. 3. to disregard, discard. 4. to leave, renounce, quit. 5. to let go. 6. to back down from. 7. to fall away. 8. **~-se:** a) to despair, let oneself go, give oneself up. b) to indulge in, addict o. s. to a vice.
~ uma ação judicial to drop a lawsuit. **~ um amigo (em apuros)** to let down a friend (in need), to throw a friend overboard. **~ o avião em vôo, i. e., saltar de pára-quedas** to bail out. **~ a caça** to give up the chase. **~ uma idéia** to discard, abandon an idea. **~ o jogo** to give up gambling. **~ uma linha aérea** to give up an air line. **~ o país** to abandon one's country. **~ o trabalho** to stop work, quit, leave. **~ tudo** to drop everything. **o campo ficou abandonado** the land fell out of cultivation.
abandonatário s. m. one who acquired abandoned rights or things.
abandonável adj. m. + f. (pl. **-áveis**) that may or should be abandoned.
abandono s. m. (also **abandonamento**) 1. abandonment, abandoning, forsaking. 2. forlornness. 3. helplessness, destitution. 4. disregard. 5. defection, dereliction.
~ de um direito abandonment of a right. **~ do emprego** the abandonment of one's job. **~ do trabalho** stoppage (or cessation) of work. **~ aos seguradores** abandonment (relinquishment or surrender) to the underwriters. **ao ~** abandoned, neglected.
abanicar v. to fan with an **abanico**.
abanico s. m. (**abaninho, abanozinho**) 1. small fan. 2. **~s** witty sayings.
abano s. m. 1. fire-fan, ventilator. 2. shake. 3. fly-flap. **fruta de ~** ripe fruit that falls easily, windfall.
abantesma s. m. + f. ghost, spectre.
abanto s. m. frightened bull (in bullfighting).
abaquetado adj. like a drum-stick.
abaquetar v. to shape like a drum-stick.
abar v. to provide with a brim, flap, skirt, etc. (see **aba**).
abaratar v. 1. to make or sell cheaper. 2. to reduce, fall (price). 3. to have in less regard, cheapen.
abarbado adj. 1. overloaded (with work). 2. embarrassed, troubled. 3. very close, touching.
~ com a morte face to face with death.
abarbar v. 1. to draw nigh, come near. 2. to beard, face, meet face to face. 3. to equal. 4. to overload, overburden. 5. to embarrass. 6. **~-se** to cluster (bees).
abarbarado adj. (Braz.) 1. terrible. 2. daring. 3. heedless. 4. rude, rough.
abarbarar-se v. (Braz.) 1. to acquire savage or barbarous habits. 2. to act daringly or heedlessly.

abarbarizar v. = **barbarizar**.
abarbelar v. to fasten with a curb or curb chain.
abarbilhar v. 1. to muzzle. 2. (fig.) to hinder, obstruct.
abarca s. f. 1. simple sandal. 2. ill-shaped or badly made footwear.
abarcador s. m. 1. grasper, clasper. 2. (fig.) monopolizer, monopolist, forestaller.
abarcamento s. m. 1. monopoly. 2. environment, enclosing, inclusion.
abarcante adj. m. + f. 1. monopolizing. 2. encircling, enclosing, including.
abarcar v. 1. to monopolize. 2. to environ, encircle, enclose, include. 3. to comprise, comprehend. 4. to reach. 5. to grasp, clasp. 6. to obtain, get. 7. to embrace. 8. to understand.
~ a lua com a joeira to deny what is evident. **quem muito abarca, pouco aperta** grasp all, lose all. **querer ~ o céu com as mãos** to cry for the moon.
abaritonado adj. similar to or nearly baritone.
abaritonar v. 1. to adapt the voice to that of a baritone. 2. to become a baritone.
abarracado adj. like a barrack.
abarracamento s. m. barrack(s), encampment, camp, camping.
abarracar v. 1. to camp, encamp, pitch up tents. 2. **~-se** to lodge in barracks, tents or huts. 3. to make similar to a barrack or tent. 4. to be standing in a corner with a woman and keep talking with her.
abarrancar v. 1. to form or cause gullies, gorges, or ravines. 2. to hit against or fall down a slope or bank. 3. to run into an obstacle.
abarregar-se v. to live in concubinage.
abarreirar v. 1. to surround with barriers. 2. to entrench.
abarretar(-se) v. to put on a cap.
abarrotamento s. m. fulness, overfilling, repletion, cramming.
abarrotar v. 1. to overfill. 2. to overload. 3. to overcrowd. 4. to cover or support with rafters or beams. 5. to glut, satiate.
abarticular adj. m. + f. (med.) not affecting the joints (rheumatism).
abas s. f. pl. surroundings, neighbo(u)rhood.
abasbacar v. = **embasbacar**.
abascanto s. m. talisman against witchcraft or evil. ‖ adj. having the properties of a talisman.
abasia s. f. (med.) abasia.
abastado adj. rich, wealthy, well off. ‖ **-amente** adv. abundantly, largely.
bem ~ on easy street, well-to-do.
abastamento s. m. 1. act of supplying. 2. abundant supply. 3. abundance.
abastança s. f. 1. abundance, plenty, plenteousness, sufficiency. 2. riches, wealth, easy circumstances. **viver na ~** to be well off, rich, in easy circumstances.
abastar v. 1. to supply, cater, provide or store with, furnish. 2. to suffice, be sufficient or enough.
abastardado adj. degenerate.
abastardamento s. m. degeneration (through bastardy), bastardization.
abastardar v. 1. to degenerate or cause degeneration. 2. to adulterate, falsify. 3. to corrupt.
abastecedor s. m. 1. supplier, caterer, provider. 2. victualler. ‖ adj. supplying, catering, providing.
abastecer v. to supply, provide or store with, furnish, cater.
~ um mercado to supply a market. **~-se de** to

provide o. s. with. ~ **um navio** to victual a ship. ~ **de víveres** to supply with provisions.
abastecido adj. supplied, provided with, abundant.
abastecimento s. m. 1. supply, provision. 2. supplying, provisioning. 3. (aeron.) refuel(l)ing. 4. (naut.) victualling.
~ **de água** water supply. ~ **de um avião** refuel(l)ing of a plane. ~ **de um navio** victualling of a ship. **navio de** ~ victualling ship.
abastoso adj. 1. abundant. 2. plentiful, full, filled. 3. rich.
abatatado adj. 1. potatolike. 2. broad, wide. 3. coarse, thick.
nariz ~ bulbous nose.
abatatar v. 1. to shape like a potato. 2. to widen, broaden. 3. (Braz.): a) to abate, diminish. b) to demoralize, abase. c) to grieve, sadden.
abate s. m. 1. discount, abatement, reduction. 2. lessening, decrease. 3. slaughter, killing (cattle). 4. felling (trees).
abatedor s. m. abater, reducer.
abatedouro s. m. slaughterhouse.
abater v. 1. to abate: a) lower. b) reduce, discount, deduct. c) lessen, decrease, diminish. d) throw down, pull down. e) cut down, fell. f) prostrate. g) humiliate, humble, abase. 2. to fall. 3. to kill, slaughter (cattle). 4. to weaken, debilitate, enfeeble. 5. to make lean, grow thin. 6. to despond. 7. to shoot down (plane). 8. (naut.) to drive (or fall) to leeward. 9. ~**-se:** a) to sink in, fall in, subside. b) to abase o. s., prostrate o. s.
~ **a árvore** to fell the tree. ~ **as armas** to surrender. ~ **o avião** to shoot down the plane. ~ **a bandeira** 1. to strike the flag. 2. to dip the flag. ~ **as cristas de alguém** to bring someone down a peg or two. ~ **os olhos** to cast down one's eyes. ~ **do valor total** to discount from the total value.
abatido adj. 1. abated: a) prostrated. b) humiliated, humbled, abased. c) diminished, reduced (price). 2. exhausted, fatigued. 3. disheartened, discouraged. 4. cut down, felled. 5. killed, slaughtered.
abatimento s. m. 1. abatement: a) lessening, diminishing, decrease. b) reduction, discount. 2. low spirits, dejectedness. 3. humbleness, submissiveness. 4. abasement. 5. decay. 6. weakness. 7. cutting down, felling (trees, woods). 8. collapse, falling in (building).
~ **de espírito** low spirits. ~ **de preço** price reduction. ~ **por avaria** allowance for average.
abatina s. f. = **batina**.
abatinar v. to put on, dress a cassock.
abatis s. m. 1. (mil.) abatis, rampart made of logs. 2. (cul.) gibblets (as of a chicken).
abatocar v. to bung.
abatumado adj. 1. = **abetumado**. 2. tough, stodgy, heavy and insufficiently risen (bread).
abatumar v. to become compact and heavy (bread, due to insufficient leavening).
abaulado adj. convex, bulged, arched, incurvated.
abaulador adj. incurvating, arching.
abaulamento s. m. 1. camber of the street, permitting the water to run off. 2. incurvation, arching, bulging. 3. convexity, bulge. 4. sloping, curving.
abaular v. to incurve, arch, bulge, vault.
abaxial adj. m. + f. (pl. **-ais**) abaxial, out of the line of the axis.
abdicação s. f. (pl. **-ões**) abdication, renunciation.
abdicador s. m. (f. ~**a**, **-triz**) (also **abdicante** m. + f.) abdicator, renouncer, resigner.
abdicar v. 1. to abdicate, resign, renounce. 2. to give up or over. 3. to relinquish, leave, abandon, desist.

~ **em** to resign in favour of. ~ **a pátria** to emigrate, go into exile.
abdicativo, abdicatório adj. abdicative, relative to abdication.
abdicável adj. m. + f. (pl. **-áveis**) abdicable.
abdome, abdômen s. m. (anat.) abdomen.
abdominal adj. m. + f. (pl. **-ais**) (anat.) abdominal.
abdominoscopia s. f. (med.) abdominal examination with the endoscope.
abdominoso adj. abdominous, abdominal.
abdução s. f. (pl. **-ões**) abduction.
abducente adj. m. + f. abducent.
abdutor s. m. abductor. ‖ adj. abducent.
abduzir v. 1. to abduct. 2. to abduce, take away.
abeatar v. 1. to become devout (sincerely or affectedly). 2. to become sanctimonious.
abeberado adj. 1. quenched (thirst). 2. watered (animals). 3. soaked, imbibed, steeped.
abeberar v. 1. to give to drink, water. 2. ~**-se** to imbibe, soak, steep.
abecar v. (Braz.) to grab by the collar, attack.
abecedária s. f. (bot.) Pará cress, alphabet plant.
abecedário s. m. 1. abecedary, alphabet. 2. primer, spellingbook. ‖ adj. in alphabetic order, alphabeted.
abecedense s. m. + f. a native from or dweller of the ABC region of São Paulo (Santo André, São Bernardo do Campo and São Caetano do Sul). ‖ adj. m. + f. born or living in that region.
abegão s. m. (pl. **-ões**) (f. **abegoa**) 1. farm hand. 2. overseer of a farm.
abegoaria s. f. 1. barn, stable, shed. 2. farmwork.
abeirante adj. m. + f. near, close, bordering.
abeirar v. 1. to border. 2. to approximate, approach, draw or come near.
abelha s. f. (ent.) bee, honey bee (also ~**-do-reino**) (plate A 11).
~ **obreira** worker bee (plate A 11). **enxame de** ~**s** swarm of bees. **zumbido das** ~**s** hum of the bees.
abelha-africana s. f. (pl. **abelhas-africanas**) (Braz.) African bee(s) (Apis mellifera adamsoni).
abelha-da-terra s. f. (pl. **abelhas-da-terra**) (ent.) any kind of bees nesting in the earth.
abelha-mestra s. f. (pl. **abelhas-mestras**) queen bee.
abelha-mosquito s. f. (pl. **abelhas-mosquitos**) (Braz., ent.) mosquito bee.
abelhão s. m. (pl. **-ões**) (ent.) 1. drone. 2. (Braz.) bumble-bee.
abelharuco s. m. (ornith., also **abelheiro**) bee-eater.
abelheira s. f. 1. beehive. 2. (bot.) bee orchis.
abelheiro s. m. 1. bee-keeper. 2. (ornith.) bee-eater.
abelhuco s. m. = **abelharuco**.
abelhudice s. f. 1. indiscretion, curiosity, interference, meddlesomeness. 2. impudence, boldness. 3. hastiness, fussiness.
abelhudo adj. 1. curious, indiscreet. 2. interfering, meddlesome. 3. impudent, bold. 4. hasty, busy.
abelidar-se v. to become blear-eyed.
abemolado adj. 1. (mus.) flat. 2. soft, sweet. 3. effeminate.
abemolar v. 1. (mus.) to set or mark with a flat. 2. to soften, ease, smooth. 3. to lessen, abate.
abençoador s. m. quack doctor, who cures with prayers or charms. ‖ adj. blessing or protecting.
abençoador s. m. (f. **abençoadeira**) 1. blesser. 2. wellwisher. ‖ adj. blessing.
abençoante adj. m. + f. = **abençoador**.
abençoar, abendiçoar v. 1. to bless, give blessings. 2. to consecrate. 3. to wish well. 4. to protect, make happy or prosperous, benefit, favour.
abentérico adj. abenteric, located without the intestines.

aberém s. m. (pl. **-éns**) (Braz.) a sort of cake made of maize or rice flour.
aberração s. f. (pl. **-ões**) 1. aberration (also astr.). 2. deviation. 3. organic anomaly. 4. temporary mental disorder, aberrance (from truth or memory (etc.). ~ **da refrangibilidade** colour aberration. ~ **planetária** planetary aberration. ~ **intelectual** aberration of intellect.
aberrante adj. m. + f. aberrant.
aberrar v. 1. to deviate. 2. to become different or strange.
aberrativo, aberratório adj. aberrant, indicating aberration.
aberta s. f. 1. opening, gap, hole. 2. rainless days in winter, spell of fine weather. 3. opening or break in the clouds. 4. pause, break, coffee--break. 5. (Braz.) clearing, forest glade. 6. (fig.) opportunity. 7. solution (of a problem). **aproveitar uma** ~ to make hay while the sun shines.
abertão s. m. (pl. **-ões**) large clearing.
abertas s. f. pl. blanks: blank spaces left in a document to be filled in or completed later, or serving as divisions of a manuscript.
aberto s. m. opening, aperture. ‖ adj. 1. open, opened (plate Q). 2. exposed. 3. frank, open-hearted, sincere. 4. broad, wide, 5. clear: a) evident. b) free. c) bright. ‖ **-amente** adv. openly.
~ **ao público, ao tráfego** open to the public, traffic. **mar** ~ open sea. **ter os olhos** ~**s** to have one's eyes open, be on the watch. **de braços** ~**s** with open arms, heartily. **deixar em** ~ to leave open, unconcluded, unfinished. **conta aberta** (com.) open account. **de boca aberta** open-mouthed, stunned. **falar abertamente** to speak openly, frankly.
abertura s. f. 1. opening: a) act of opening, laying open. b) crevice, gap, hole. c) (also opt.) aperture. d) loophole. e) inauguration. f) (mus.) overture. 2. sincerity, candour.
~ **do parlamento** opening of the parliament. ~ **das hostilidades** outbreak of hostilities. ~ **de conta corrente** opening of a current account. ~ **de crédito** opening of credit. ~ **oficial de um testamento** opening or reading of a will, sealing of the probate of a will.
abesana s. f. 1. yoke of oxen. 2. the first furrow the plow makes.
abesantado adj. (arch.) adorned with bezants.
abesantar v. (arch.) to decorate with bezants.
abespinhado adj. irritable, excitable. ‖ **-amente** adv. irritably, excitably.
abespinhamento s. m. irritability, excitability, angriness.
abespinhar-(se) v. to get irritated, become angry, fly into a passion.
abestalhado adj. (Braz.) foolish, silly, imbecile.
abeta s. f. dim. of **aba.**
abeto s. m. (bot.) fir, abies.
abetumado adj. 1. bituminized. 2. covered with bitumen. 3. sorrowful, sad. 4. tough, stodgy, heavy (bread).
abetumador s. m. 1. bituminizer. 2. calker, caulker.
abetumar v. 1. to bituminize. 2. to calk, caulk.
abevacuação s. f. (pl. **-ões**) incomplete evacuation.
abexim s. m. + f. (pl. **-ins**) (also **abissínio**) Abyssinian. ‖ adj. Abyssinian.
abezerrado adj. calf-like, calvish.
abibe s. m. (ornith.) lapwing.
abibliotecar v. to keep or arrange in a library.
abicadoiro, abicadouro s. m. (naut.) natural or habitual landing-place or beaching point.
abicar v. 1. to arrive, approach. 2. (naut.) to land, beach, bring a ship to the coast or shore. 3.

(naut.) to drop or cast the anchor (with the prow touching the shore). 4. to put a point on, sharpen.
abichar v. 1. to get, obtain advantage. 2. (Braz.) to be infested with worms (the wound of an animal). 3. (Braz.) to spoil, decay because of insect larvae (fruits).
abichornado adj. (Braz.) 1. weary, annoyed. 2. discouraged, dispirited. 3. vexed. 4. ashamed. 5. frightened, cowardly. 6. (fig.) done with.
abichornar v. (Braz.) to weary, discourage, etc.
abieiro s. m. star apple-tree.
abietáceas s. f. pl. (bot.) Pinnaceae, trees of the genus Abies: balsam fir, silver fir.
abietina s. f. abietin(e), coniferin(e).
abietino adj. abietic, firlike.
abigeato s. m. (jur.) cattle-theft.
abintestado adj. 1. intestate. 2. leaving a void will.
abioceno s. m. a lifeless place.
abiogênese s. f. abiogenesis.
abiogenético adj. (biol.) abiogenetic.
abiose s. f. (med.) abiosis.
abiótico adj. (med.) abiotic.
abioto s. m. (bot.) hemlock.
abiotrofia s. f. (path.) abiotrophy.
abiotrófico adj. (path.) abiothrophic.
abirritação s. f. (pl. **-ões**) weakness, debility, asthenia.
abirritante adj. m. + f. weakening, debilitating.
abirritativo adj. (path.) that causes prostration or lack of motor reaction.
abiscoitado adj. 1. like a biscuit or cracker. 2. accomplished. 3. gained, achieved.
abiscoitar v. 1. to bake like a biscuit. 2. to get, obtain. 3. (Braz.) to gain, profit by.
abismado adj. 1. thrown or fallen into an abyss. 2. (fig.) stupefied, shocked. 3. lost in meditation.
abismal adj. m. + f. (pl. **-ais**) abysmal, unfathomable, abyssal.
abismamento s. m. 1. a fall into an abyss (also fig.). 2. great surprise or shock.
abismar v. 1. to throw or fall into an abyss. 2. to stun, stupefy, shock, surprise greatly. 3. to lose o. s. 4. to meditate, dwell in thought.
abismo s. m. (also **abisso**) 1. abyss. 2. vortex. 3. precipice. 4. any immensity.
abismoso adj. 1. with many abysses. 2. surrounded by abysses.
abissal adj. m. + f. (pl. **-ais**) (also **abismal**) abyssal.
abissínio s. m. + adj. = **abexim.**
abita s. f. (naut.) bitt, riding bitt.
abitar v. (naut.) to bitt.
abitolar v. 1. to gauge. 2. to measure with a gauge, render uniform in shape or size.
abjeção s. f. (pl. **-ões**) abjection, debasement, vileness, infamy.
abjeto adj. abject, vile, base, contemptible, low. ‖ **-amente** adv. abjectly, vilely, contemptibly.
abjudicação s. f. (pl. **-ões**) (jur.) abjudication, dispossession.
abjudicador, abjudicante s. m. one who abjudges. ‖ adj. relating to abjudgement.
abjudicar v. (jur.) to abjudge, dispossess by legal means.
abjugar v. 1. to take off the yoke. 2. to liberate, free.
abjunção s. f. (pl. **-ões**) separation.
abjungir v. to separte, part.
abjuração s. f. (pl. **-ões**) abjuration.
abjurador s. m. **abjurante** m. + f. abjurer. ‖ adj. abjuratory, abjuring.
abjurar v. to abjure, renounce, retract.
abjuratório adj. abjuratory.

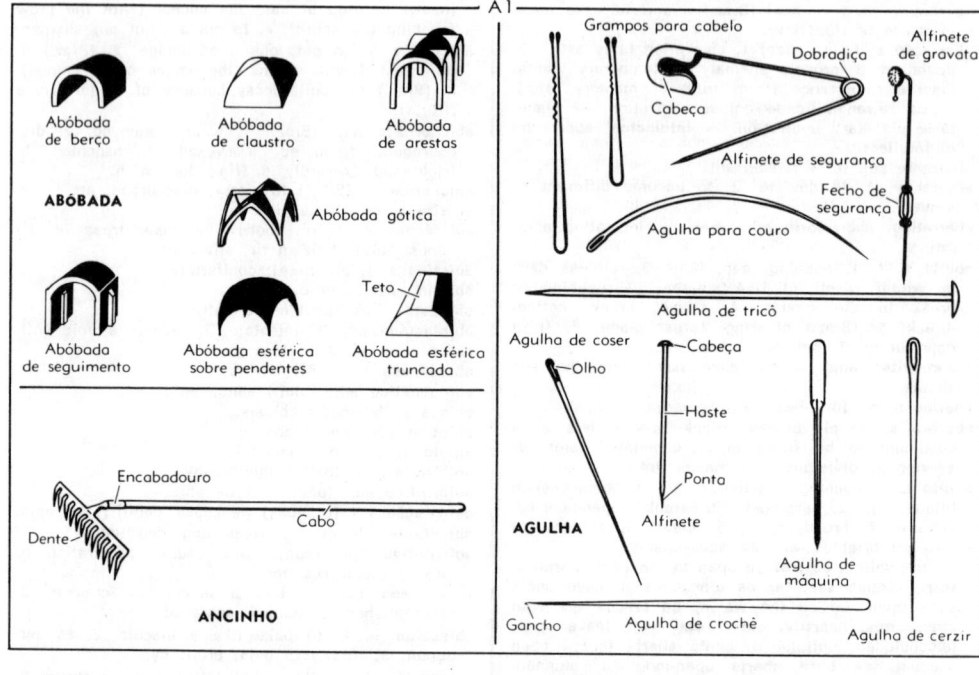

A 1

ablação s. f. (pl. -ões) 1. ablation. 2. taking by force. 3. (surg.) excision (of a tumour, etc.). 4. (gram.) aphaeresis.

ablactação s. f. (pl. -ões) ablactation, weaning.

ablactar v. to ablactate, wean.

ablaqueação s. f. (pl. -ões) ablaqueation: laying bare of tree roots.

ablaquear, ablaquecer v. 1. to lay bare roots of trees. 2. to loose, loosen.

ablativo s. m. (gram.) the ablative case. ‖ adj. ablative.

fazer ~ de viagem to take to one's heels.

ablator s. m. (vet.) ablator: instrument for castration. ‖ adj. extractive.

abléfaro adj. ablepharous.

ablegação s. f. (pl. -ões) proscription, banishment.

ablegar v. to proscribe, banish.

ablepsia s. f. 1. (med.) loss or lack of vision, blindness. 2. (fig.) loss of intellectual faculties.

ablução s. f. (pl. -ões) ablution, washing.

os árabes executam as suas -ões diárias the Arabs perform their daily ablutions.

abluente s. m. abluent. ‖ adj. m. + f. abluent.

abluir v. 1. to purify. 2. to wash, cleanse.

ablutor s. m. purifier or washer.

abmigração s. f. (ornith.) abmigration.

abnegação s. f. (pl. -ões) abnegation, self-denial, self-forgetfulness, unselfishness.

ato de ~ self-sacrifice.

abnegado s. m. unselfish person. ‖ adj. unselfish, self-forgetful.

abnegar v. to abnegate, renounce, deny (anything) to o. s.

abnegativo adj. unselfish, abnegative.

abneto s. m. (also trineto or tetraneto) great-great-grandson.

abnodar v. to cut the knots from trees.

abnormalidade s. f. = anormalidade.

abóbada s. f. arch, vault: arched roof, ceiling, space or passage (plate A 1).

~ celeste the roof of heaven. ~ cilíndrica, ~ de berço barrel-vault. ~ de arestas groined vault, crossvault(ing) ~ ogival gothic vault (plate A 1). ~ palatina the palate, the roof of the mouth. fechar a ~ 1. to put the key-stone to a vault. 2. (fig.) to finish a work, to give the finishing touch. fecho ou chave da ~ key-stone of a vault.

abobadado adj. 1. vaulted, arched. 2. shaped like a cupola or dome.

abobadar v. 1. to cover with a vault, cupola or dome. 2. to vault, arch.

abobadilha s. f. 1. small vault. 2. jack-arch.

abobado adj. (also abobalhado, abobarrado) 1. foolish, silly. 2. senseless, crazy.

ele é um pouco ~ he is somewhat wanting.

abobar v. 1. to become silly. 2. to act or simulate the fool.

abóbora s. f. 1. (bot.) pumpkin. 2. (fig.) softy, slouch. 3. fat woman.

~ -porqueira (bot.) melon pumpkin.

abóbora-carneira s. f. (pl. abóboras-carneiras) (bot.) calabash, bottlegourd.

abóboras-d'água s. f. (pl. abóboras-d'água) = abobrinha.

aboboral s. m. (pl. -ais) pumpkin-field, gourd-field.

abóbora-menina s. f. (pl. abóboras-meninas) (bot.) hubbard squash, winter squash, giant gourd.

aboborar v. 1. to ripen (also fig.). 2. to keep in bed, be confined to one's bed.

aboboreira s. f. name of several plants of the family Cucurbitaceae, such as the pumpkin or gourd.

abobrinha s. f. (also abóbora-d'água) (Braz.) summer squash.

abocadura s. f. 1. embrasure, loophole. 2. catching, snapping (with the mouth).

abocamento s. m. 1. catching or snapping with the mouth. 2. meeting of two mouths, channels, ducts, etc. 3. talk, conversation, conference. 4. (med.) inosculation. 5. (anat.) anastomosis.

aboçamento s. m. (naut.) lashing, use of stoppers.

abocanhar (I) v. (also **aboquejar**) 1. to bite, bite off. 2. (Braz.) to snap, catch with the mouth. 3. to slander, defame. 4. to get hold of by unfair means. 5. to misspeak a foreign language. **homem de má língua que abocanha toda gente** a foulmouthed, slanderous man. **o cachorro tentou ~ minha perna** the dog snapped at my leg.

abocanhar (II) v. to show an opening or break (clouds).

abocar v. 1. to snap, catch with the mouth. 2. to meet with, arrive at. 3. to disembogue, enter, run into. 4. to direct, aim, point. 5. (med.) to inosculate. 6. (physiol.) to anastomose. **~ o estreito** to enter the strait. **~ a artilharia** to point the guns.

aboçar v. (naut.) to stopper, lash.

abocetado adj. oval or round, orbicular.

abocetar v. 1. to give the form of a small box usually round or oval. 2. to keep in such a box.

abochornado adj. 1. warm, hot. 2. stifling, sultry.

abochornar v. to become stifling, sultry (weather).

abodegação s. f. (pl. **-ões**) (Braz.) 1. weariness, disgustedness. 2. affliction, trouble, worriment.

abodegado adj. 1. weary, disgusted. 2. dirty, sloven.

abodegar v. to afflict, worry, vex.

aboiar (I) v. 1. to buoy : a) float. b) furnish or mark with buoys. 2. to moor to a buoy.

aboiar (II) v. (Braz.) 1. to sing to the oxen. 2. to guide a herd of oxen by singing monotonous, sad songs. 3. to work with oxen.

aboio s. m. (Braz., also **abiviado**) sad song by which the cowboys guide herds of oxen.

aboiz s. m. (pl. **aboízes**) snares.

abojar v. (Braz.) to catch, seize or grasp.

abolachado adj. like a biscuit or cracker.

abolachar v. to shape like a biscuit or cracker.

abolado (I) adj. ball-like, spherical.

abolado (II) adj. 1. crumpled, crushed, wrinkled. 2. bruised, injured. 3. cake-like.

abolar (I) v. to ball: form or gather into a ball.

abolar (II) v. 1. to crush, crumple. 2. to shape like a cake. 3. to bruise, injure.

abolçar v. (also **bolçar**) 1. to throw out, throw away. 2. to vomit.

aboleimado adj. 1. coarse. 2. foolish, silly. 3. flat.

aboleimar v. 1. to flatten. 2. to frighten, stupefy. 3. to coarsen. 4. **~-se** to become foolish.

aboletamento s. m. (mil.) billeting, quartering.

aboletar v. 1. (mil.) to billet, quarter (soldiers). 2. to lodge.

abolição s. f. (pl. **-ões**, also **abolimento**) 1. abolition, abolishment. 2. abrogation, revocation. 3. annulment, cancellation.

abolicionismo s. m. abolitionism.

abolicionista s. m. + f. abolitionist. ‖ adj. of or referring to abolitionism.

abolido adj. abolished, cancelled.

abolimento s. m. = **abolição.**

abolinar v. to sail close to the wind.

abolir v. 1. to abolish, abrogate, revoke. 2. to annul, cancel, extinguish. 3. to do away with, suppress.

abolorecer v. to mould, moulder, become musty.

abolorecimento s. m. 1. moulding, act or fact of becoming mouldy. 2. mould, mouldiness.

abolsado adj. 1. puckered. 2. purse-shaped.

abolsar v. 1. to pucker, bag. 2. to be or become pocket-shaped.

abomaso s. m. abomasum: the fourth or true stomach of ruminating animals.

abombachado adj. (Braz.) wide-breeched trousers.

abombado adj. (Braz.) 1. (of animals) tired, worn out. 2. out of breath, panting for breath. 3. (fig.) overworked.

abombador s. m. (Braz.) a poor rider who tires his horse.

abombamento s. m. (Braz.) stopping, refusal to go on because of fatigue (horse).

abombar v. 1. to exhaust (a horse) through incompetence or excessive heat. 2. to stop (the horse) because of heat or exhaustion.

abominação s. f. (pl. **-ões**) abomination, detestation, execration, abhorrence.

abominador s. m. abominator. ‖ adj. abominable.

abominar v. 1. to abominate, loathe, abhor, detest, hate. 2. to feel disgust or repulsion.

abominável adj. m. + f. (pl. **-áveis**; also **abominando**, **abominoso**) abominable, detestable, loathsome, repulsive. ‖ **-avelmente** adv. abominably, repulsively, detestably.

abonação s. f. (pl. **-ões**) (also **abonamento**) 1. bail, guarantee. 2. security, warranty, guaranty.

abonado adj. 1. (Braz.) well-off, wealthy, rich. 2. trustworthy. 3. having credit. **uma testemunha abonada** a trustworthy witness.

abonador s. m. warrantor, warranter, guarantor.

abonançar v. 1. to calm, appease, quiet. 2. to clear up (weather), become calm (sea).

abonar v. 1. to declare good or true. 2. to bail. 3. to stand security, stand surety for, answer for. 4. to guarantee, warrant. 5. to sanction. 6. to advance (money). 7. **~-se de** to boast of. **a construção foi abonada por vários arquitetos** the building was declared safe by several architects. **abonou-lhe uma grande soma** he advanced him a large sum. **ele se abona de rico** he boasts of his riches.

abonatório adj. warranting, guaranteeing.

abonável adj. m. + f. (pl. **-áveis**) 1. warrantable, guaranteed. 2. bailable.

abonecado adj. foppish, affected, dandylike, doll-like.

abonecar v. 1. to dress foppishly. 2. to make doll-like.

abono s. m. 1. advance-money, bonus. 2. surplus. 3. remuneration. 4. corroboration. 5. approval, praise. 6. (Braz.) manure. 7. warranty. **ele falou em seu ~** he spoke in his behalf. **~ de família** family allowance.

aboquejar v. = **abocanhar** (I).

aboral adj. m. + f. (pl. **-ais**) away or remote from the mouth, distant.

aborbulhar v. 1. to form or grow into a pimple or boil, pustulate. 2. to bubble, become filled with bubbles.

abordador s. m. (naut.) 1. boarder. 2. boarding vessel. ‖ adj. boarding.

abordagem s. f. (pl. **-ens**) (also **abordada**) 1. boarding: a) a going aboard a ship. b) colliding or running foul of. c) attack on a ship. 2. approximation, approach. 3. (naut.) landing. 4. touch.

abordar v. 1. (naut.) to board: a) attack. b) run foul of. 2. to approach, accost. 3. to go aboard. 4. (naut.) to land. 5. to touch. 6. to broach. **~ um navio inimigo** to lay a ship aboard. **~ um assunto** to broach a subject.

abordável adj. m. + f. (pl. **-áveis**) 1. that may be boarded. 2. accessible.

abordo (ô) s. m. 1. boarding (of a ship). 2. landing. **de fácil ~** of easy access.

abordoar v. 1. to flog, spank. 2. to lean on, rest against. 3. to depend, rely. 4. **~-se** to prop o. s. on a staff.

aborígine adj. m. + f. aboriginal.
aborígines s. m. pl. 1. indigenes, natives (pl.). 2. aborigines (pl.).
aborletar v. to tassel.
abornalar v. = **embornalar**.
aborrascar v. 1. to become stormy, tempestuous. 2. to threaten with storm.
aborrecedor s. m. bore, dull or tiresome person. ‖ adj. boring, tiresome, tedious.
aborrecer v. (also **aborrir**) 1. to bore, displease, disgust, weary, tire. 2. to cause or feel aversion for. 3. to loathe, detest, abhor. 4. to nauseate. 5. ~-se to become disgusted, weary, tired, feel dull. **isto me aborrece muito** this displeases me very much, I am sick of it. **aborrece-me a vida** I am tired of life.
aborrecido adj. 1. disgusted, displeased, weary, tired, bored, annoyed. 2. disgusting, wearisome, tiresome, tedious. 3. detested, hated. 4. odious. ‖ **-amente** adv. 1. disgustedly, wearily. 2. odiously.
~ **da vida** weary of life. **conversa aborrecida** tiresome talk. **estar horrivelmente aborrecido** to be bored to death. **eu estou** ~ **com o seu comportamento** I am vexed by your (his, her, their) behaviour.
aborrecimento s. m. (also **aborrimento**) 1. disgust, annoyance, nuisance. 2. weariness, tediousness. 3. hatred, detestation. 4. aversion.
que ~! what a nuisance! **ser causa de** ~ **para alguém** to be a thorn in one's side (flesh).
aborrecível adj. m. + f. (pl. **-íveis**) 1. disgusting, annoying. 2. tiresome, wearisome, boring, tedious. 3. hateful, detestable, odious.
aborregado adj. 1. lamblike. 2. (geol., glaciers) with smooth, round fronts.
aborrido adj. 1. very disgusting or annoying. 2. sorrowful, peevish, melancholic, gloomy. 3. angry. ‖ **-amente** adv. 1. disgustingly, annoyingly. 2. gloomily, peevishly. 3. angrily.
abortado adj. aborted.
abortamento s. m. = **aborto**.
abortar v. 1. to abort, miscarry. 2. to fail, be unsuccessful. 3. to hinder, check, make unsuccessful.
abortício adj. abortive: born prematurely.
abortífero adj. abortive: causing abortion.
abortivo s. m. abortive: drug causing abortion. ‖ adj. abortive: 1. causing abortion. 2. imperfectly formed or developed. ‖ **-amente** adv. abortively.
aborto (ô) s. m. (also **abortamento**) 1. abortion: a) (med.) miscarriage. b) imperfect or immature product, something that has failed to develop properly. 2. (fig.) monstrosity, monster. 3. something extraordinary, extraordinary phenomenon.
aboscar v. 1. to receive, get. 2. to obtain, acquire.
abossadura s. f. = **bossagem**.
abostelar v. to pustulate, form pimples, become blotchy.
abotecar v. (Braz.) to catch, grasp, grip.
aboticado adj. (Braz.) 1. wide-opened, staring. 2. goggle-eyed, bulging.
aboticar v. (Braz.) to exaggerate.
abotinado adj. boot-shaped.
abotinar v. to shape like a boot, give the form of a boot.
abotoação s. f. (pl. **-ões**, bot.) budding.
abotoadeira s. f. also **abotoador** m.) 1. buttonhook. 2. buttonmaker or sewer.
abotoado (I) adj. buttoned.
abotoado (II) adj. (bot.) budded.
abotoador s. m. (also **abotoadeira** f.) 1. buttonhook. 2. buttoner: one who buttons.
abotoadura s. f. 1. set of buttons. 2. buttoning.
~**s para camisa** wrist-studs (pl.) (plate J 3).

abotoar (I) v. 1. to button, button oneself up. 2. to appropriate unrightfully, pinch. 3. to invest upon s. o.
eles abotoaram-se com a quantia de they pinched the amount of.
abotoar (II) v. 1. to bud. 2. to appear, show up.
abotocado adj. = **abatocado**.
abotocar v. = **abatocar**.
aboubado adj. (med.) covered with skin tumours.
aboubar-se v. to be covered with tumours (skin).
abra s. f. 1. bay, creek. 2. anchorage.
abraâmico adj. Abrahamic.
abracadabra s. m. 1. abracadabra (a cabalistic word). 2. superstition. 3. unintelligible terms or expressions.
abracadabrante, abracadábrico adj. 1. extraordinary. 2. mysterious, magic.
abraçadeira s. f. (tech.) 1. cramp, brace, clamp, locking collar. 2. (naut.) hank.
abraçador s. m. embracer. ‖ adj. embracing.
abraçamento s. m. embrace, embracing.
abraçante s. + adj.; m. + f. = **abraçador**.
abraçar v. 1. to embrace: a) hug. b) encircle, encompass, surround. c) comprise, include, contain. d) adopt, follow. e) accept. f) interlace, twine round. 2. ~-se to embrace each other.
~ **o cristianismo** to embrace Christianity. **abraçaram-no** they fell on his neck. **ele abraçou a criança** he strained the child to his heart, he clasped the child in his arms. **ele abraçou uma profissão intelectual** he entered a learned profession. **querer abraçar o céu e a terra com as mãos** to want the impossible.
abraço s. m. 1. embrace, embracing, embracement, hug. 2. clasp. 3. tendril.
~ **de tamanduá** (Braz.) disloyalty, treachery. **com um grande** ~ **de seu amigo...** (conclusion of a letter) I remain affectionately, yours... **dar um** ~ to embrace, give a hug.
abrandamento s. m. softening, mitigation, appeasement, relenting.
abrandar v. (also **abrandecer, embrandecer**) 1. to mitigate, milden, assuage. 2. to soften, mollify. 3. to appease, soothe. 4. to subside. 5. to calm, calm down. 6. to allay: a) tranquilize. b) relent. c) decrease, lessen. 7. to drop (wind). 8. to ease off or up.
~ **a dor** to soothe the pain. ~ **a marcha** to slow down (the speed). ~ (or **baixar**) **a voz** to lower one's voice. **a chuva abrandou o tempo** the weather has grown mild after the rain. **o vento abrandou** the wind has dropped.
abrangente adj. m. + f. including, comprehending, reaching.
abranger v. 1. to embrace, enclose. 2. to comprise, include. 3. to comprehend, contain. 4. to reach. 5. to be enough, suffice. 6. to understand, perceive.
~ **o sentido** to understand the meaning. **até onde a vista abrange** as far as the eyes can reach. **o estudo abrange muitas matérias** the study embraces many subjects.
abraquia s. f. (anat.) abrachia: absence of arms.
abrasado adj. 1. burnt. 2. burning, on fire, inflamed, ardent (also fig.). 3. red, blushing. ‖ **-amente** adv. ardently (also fig.).
abrasador, abrasante adj. 1. burning, scorching. 2. glowing, blazing. 3. ardent, fervent, eager.
o vento ~ **do deserto** the scorching wind of the desert. **um céu** ~ a glowing sky.
abrasamento s. m. 1. fire, violent burning, conflagration. 2. (fig.) enthusiasm.
abrasão s. f. 1. abrasion. 2. (geol.) marine abrasion or erosion.

abrasar v. 1. to fire, burn, consume by fire. 2. to scorch, singe, dry up. 3. to heat greatly, to overheat. 4. to glow. 5. to devastate, ravage, lay waste. 6. to kindle, inflame (also fig.). 7. to enthuse (fam.), fill with enthusiasm, enrapture. 8. ~-se: a) to be on fire. b) to be inflamed with passion.

abraseado adj. (also **esbraseado**) red-hot, glowing, like embers.

abrasear v. (also **esbrasear**) 1. to make red-hot. 2. to reduce to embers. 3. to colour like ember.

abrasileirado adj. Brazilianized: 1. appearing Brazilian. 2. similar to Brazilians in features, manners and idiomatic peculiarities.

abrasileiramento s. m. 1. adoption of Brazilian ways and manners. 2. becoming a Brazilian.

abrasileirar v. (also **abrasilianar**) 1. to adopt Brazilian ways and manners. 2. to become Brazilian.

abrasivo s. m. (tech.) abrasive, abrading agent.

abrasonar v. 1. to bestow a coat of arms. 2. to put a coat of arms on.

abre s. m. (Braz., also **cachaça** f.) liquor, brandy.

abre-boca s. m. (pl. **abre-bocas**) (vet.) gag (plate C 12).

abre-ilhós s. m. sg. + pl. bodkin, punch.

abrejar v. 1. to swamp, become swampy. 2. to abound.

abrejeirado adj. waggish, mischievous.

abrenhar v. (also **embrenhar**) to penetrate or hide in brushwood or in a thicket.

abrenunciação s. f. (pl. -ões) renunciation, renouncement.

abrenunciar v. 1. to renounce. 2. to reject, repel.

abrenúncio interj. God forbid! away! far be it from me!

ab-reptício adj. 1. possessed. 2. impassioned, excited. 3. enraptured.

abretanhado adj. similar to the linen cloth called **bretanha**.

abreu s. m. (Braz.) a sort of wild bee.

abreugrafia s. f. = **roentgenfotografia**.

abreviação s. f. (pl. -ões) 1. abbreviation. 2. shortening. 3. reduction. 4. abridgement. 5. anticipation. 6. precipitation.

abreviado adj. 1. abbreviated, shortened. 2. reduced. 3. abridged, condensed. 4. for short. || **-amente** adv. in an abbreviated form or manner, summarily, briefly.

abreviador s. m. abbreviator, shortener.

abreviamento s. m. abbreviation, abridg(e)ment.

abreviar v. 1. to abbreviate. 2. to curtail. 3. to shorten, abridge. 4. to reduce. 5. to summarize. 6. to anticipate. 7. to precipitate.
para ~ to be short, to make a long story short, to put it in a few words.

abreviativo adj. abbreviative, shortening, reducing.

abreviatura s. f. 1. abbreviation (also gram.). 2. shortening.

abricó, abricote s. m. apricot.

abricoteiro s. m. apricot-tree.

abrideira s. f. 1. (tech.) willow: machine for cleaning wool. 2. liquor, brandy.

abridela s. f. act of opening (mouth, eyes).

abridor s. m. 1. opener. 2. engraver. 3. tool for engraving or opening.

abrigada s. f. (also **abrigadouro** m.) 1. shelter, cover. 2. refuge, protection.

abrigado adj. sheltered, well-covered or protected.

abrigador s. m. protector, shelterer. || adj. sheltering, protecting.

abrigar v. 1. to shelter, protect. 2. to exempt, free from. 3. to cover, hide, conceal. 4. ~-se to take shelter.
~-se da chuva to take shelter from the rain.

abrigo s. m. 1. shelter. 2. guard, protection. 3. cover, covering. 4. refuge, asylum.
~ **antiaéreo** air-raid shelter. ~ **noturno** night shelter. ~ **de tráfego** traffic island. **ao** ~ **da noite** under the cover of, or favoured by darkness. **ao** ~ **da terra** landlocked. **ofereci-lhe** ~ I gave him shelter. **procurar** ~ to seek refuge. **sem** ~ without roof.

abril s. m. 1. April. 2. (fig.) youth, innocence.
1.º de abril All Fools' Day.

abrilada s. f. 1. event that happens in or occurred during April. 2. revolt of Lisbon in 1824. 3. (Braz.) revolution of Pernambuco in 1832.

abrilhantar v. 1. to brighten, embellish, enliven. 2. to extol, emphasize. 3. to polish.

abrilino adj. = **aprilino**.

abrimento s. m. (also **abertura** f.) act or fact of opening.

abrir v. 1. to open (set, tear, cut, dig, or break open). 2. to break up. 3. to unlock. 4. to uncover. 5. to unfasten, untie. 6. to unbutton. 7. to unfold, lay open. 8. to make an incision, cleave. 9. to pierce. 10. to bore. 11. to broach. 12. to found, establish. 13. to initiate, begin. 14. to inaugurate. 15. to engrave. 16. to register. 17. to blow, blossom, bloom. 18. (Braz.) to go, leave, depart. 19. (Braz.) to flee. 20. to clear up (weather).
~ **o apetite** to sharpen or whet the appetite. ~ **a audiência** to open the court (or session). ~ **as asas** to spread the wings. ~ **um barril de vinho** to broach a cask of wine. ~ **uma conta** to open a current account. ~ **caminho** 1. to open or clear the way, make way. 2. to force one's way. 3. (fig.) to break the ice. ~ **uma filial** to open a branch office or plant. **ele abriu o caminho na multidão** he shouldered his way through the crowd. ~ **a campanha** to open (or begin) the campaign. ~ **uma conta corrente** to open an account. ~ **o concerto** (ê) to strike up. ~ **o coração** (fig.) to open one's heart. ~ **as cortinas** to draw back the curtains. ~ **um crédito** to open a credit. ~ **uma estrada** to open a road. ~ **falência** to go bankrupt. ~ **peixe** to gut fish. ~ **à força** to wedge open. ~ **loja** to set up (or open) a shop. ~ **mão de alguma coisa** (fig.) to give up, renounce s. th. ~**-os olhos** (fig.) to be careful. ~ **os olhos a alguém** (fig.) to undeceive a person. ~ **um poço** to sink a well. ~**-se** (**porta**) to swing open. ~**-se repentinamente** to fly open. ~ **a torneira da água** to turn on the water-tap. **ele se abriu comigo** he bared his soul to me, he confided himself to me. **não** ~ **a boca** to keep one's mouth shut. **num** ~ **e fechar de olhos** in the twinkling of an eye.

abrocadado, abrocado adj. brocade-like.

abrochado adj. (Braz.) very busy.

abrochador s. m. button-hook, clasp. || adj. clasping, that clasps.

abrochadura s. f. clasping, clasp.

abrochar v. 1. to clasp, fasten with a clasp, brooch or crotchet. 2. to tighten up, button up. 3. (Braz.) to overwork, be busy.

ab-rogação s. f. (pl. -ões), **abrogamento** m. abrogation, repeal, abolishment.

ab-rogador s. m. abrogator, repealer, abolisher.

ab-rogar v. 1. to abrogate, repeal, abolish. 2. to cancel, annul.

ab-rogativo, ab-rogatório adj. abrogative, abrogatory.

abrolhado adj. 1. buddy, blossomy. 2. thorny, bristly.

abrolhador adj. 1. budding. 2. bristling.

abrolhar v. 1. to bud, blossom, bloom. 2. to become thorny, bristly. 3. to produce, bring forth. 4. to cause, originate. 5. to germinate. 6. to appear.

abrolho (ô) s. m. 1. caltrop: a) (bot.) a kind of thistle. b) (mil.) crow's foot (obstacle made of iron spikes). 2. prickling thorns. 3. abrolhos pl.: a) reefs: dangerous underwater rocks. b) difficulties, annoyances. ~ terrestre thistle, land caltrop. ~ aquático water caltrop.

abrolhoso adj. 1. thorny, full of thorns or caltrops. 2. (fig.) full of difficulties or annoyances.

abronzar v. to found bronze, to produce bronze (copper and tin).

abronzear v. to bronze.

abroquelado adj. like a buckler.

abroquelar v. 1. to protect (or cover) with a buckler. 2. to shield, defend, protect.

abrotar v. = brotar.

abrótea (I) s. f. (bot.) branched asphodel, daffodil, silverod, king's spear.

abrótea (II) s. f. (icht.) ling.

abrumar v. 1. to fog: a) fill or cover with fog. b) to darken, dim, blur. 2. to become or make apprehensive. 3. to sadden.

abrunheiro s. m. (bot.) blackthorn (tree), damson.

abrunho s. m. sloe, wild plum.

abrupção s. f. (pl. -ões) (surg.) abruption, transverse fracture.

abruptela s. f. cleared land (for cultivation).

abrupto adj. 1. abrupt: a) very steep, almost vertical. b) unexpected, sudden. c) disconnected. 2. (fig.) rough, rude. || -amente adv. 1. abruptly. 2. (fig.) rudely.

rochedo ~ steep cliff. falar de modo ~ to jerk out, talk rudely or abruptly.

abrutado, abrutalhado adj. 1. brutal, brutish. 2. rude, coarse.

abrutalhar v. (also abrutar, abrutecer, embrutecer) 1. to brutify. 2. to coarsen.

abrutamento s. m. = brutalidade.

abrutar, abrutecer v. 1. to make brutal. 2. to treat brutally. 3. to become like a brute.

absceder v. 1. to form an abscess. 2. to suppurate.

abscesso s. m. (med.) abscess.

abscidar v. to become separated, disconnected.

abscisão s. f. abscission.

abscissa s. f. (geom.) abscissa, absciss.

absconder v. to abscond, hide, conceal, disguise.

abscôndito adj. hidden, concealed.

absconso adj. hidden, secret.

absenteísmo s. m. 1. (Braz.) abstention from voting. 2. = absentismo.

absenteísta s. m. + f. 1. absentee. 2. (Braz.) person who abstains from voting. || adj. absentee, that abstains from voting, non-voting.

absentismo s. m. absenteeism: 1. absentee administration of an estate, factory, etc. 2. an employee's repeated absence from work.

absidal adj. m. + f. (pl. -ais) apsidal.

abside s. f. 1. (archit.) apse. 2. (astr.) apsis. 3. reliquary.

absintado adj. 1. absinthic, containing absinth. 2. bitter. 3. (fig.) tormented, afflicted.

absintina s. f. absinthine.

absintismo s. m. (med.) absinthism.

absinto s. m. (bot., also absíntio) 1. absinth: common wormwood. 2. liquor flavoured with wormwood.

absogra s. f. grandmother of a father- or mother-in-law.

absogro s. m. grandfather of a father-in-law or mother-in-law.

absolto adj. ausolved, pardoned.

absolução s. f. = absolvição.

absolutamente adv. 1. absolutely. 2. completely, unconditionally, unrestrictedly. 3. wholly, entirely, altogether, quite. 4. positively. 5. by all means.

6. imperiously. 7. at all. ~ o melhor far and away the best. ~ nada nothing whatever, nothing at all. eu não sabia ~ o que fazer I simply did not know what to do. não se importam ~ com isto they do not care a twopence for it.

absolutismo s. m. (hist.) absolutism.

absolutista s. m. + f. absolutist. || adj. m. + f. absolutistic.

absoluto adj. absolute: 1. unrestricted, unlimited, unconditional, (philos.) unconditioned. 2. total, complete, entire. 3. perfect. 4. real, actual. 5. positive. 6. not to be contested. 7. only, unique. 8. independent. 9. imperious, haughty. 10. arbitrary. 11. pure, free from mixture. 12. absolved. confiança absoluta absolute trust. umidade absoluta absolute humidity. senti absoluta certeza I was just sure of it. imperador absoluto absolute ruler. em ~ not at all.

absolutório adj. absolutory. sentença absolutória (jur.) acquittal.

absolver v. 1. to absolve. 2. to clear, acquit. 3. to isent, exempt, discharge, dispense, free. 4. to forgive, pardon, remit. 5. to exonerate. 6. ~-se to make excuses, to excuse o. s. os jurados absolveram-no the jury acquitted him. pode absolvê-lo disso? can you acquit him of that?

absolvição s. f. (pl. -ões) absolution: 1. pardoning, forgiving of sins. 2. acquittal, discharge. uma ~ a verdict of acquittal.

absolvido adj. absolved, pardoned, acquitted.

absonar v. 1. to produce dissonance. 2. to discord, diverge.

ábsono adj. absonant, dissonant, discordant.

absorção s. f. (pl. -ões) (also absorvimento m.) 1. absorption. 2. engrossment of mind.

absorto adj. 1. absorbed, deep in thought. 2. enraptured. ~ em êxtase wrapped up in ecstasy. ~ em reflexão in a brown study. ele estava ~ com o seu trabalho he was full of his subject.

absorvedor s. m. (also absorvente) 1. absorber. 2. absorbent. || adj. absorbing, absorbent.

absorvedouro s. m. = sorvedouro.

absorvência s. f. absorbency, absorbancy.

absorvente s. m. absorbent. || adj. m. + f. 1. absorbing, absorbent. 2. attractive. 3. dominating.

absorver v. 1. to absorb. 2. to consume. 3. to assimilate. 4. to take in, suck up. 5 to imbibe. 6. to swallow. 7. to captivate, enthral. 8. to fill with enthusiasm, enrapture, carry away. 9. ~-se em become wrapt (or absorbed) in. ~ a umidade to absorb the moisture. estar absorvido em (por) to be wrapped up in. absorvido self-absorbed. o líquido está sendo absorvido the liquid is sinking in, is being soaked up.

absorvimento s. m. = absorção.

absorvível adj. m. + f. (pl. -íveis) absorbable.

abstemia s. f. abstemiousness.

abstêmio adj. 1. abstemious. 2. teetotal.

abstenção s. f. (pl. -ões) abstenticn.

abstencionismo s. m. abstentionism.

abstencionista s. m. + f. abstentionist: one who abstains from voting. || adj. abstentious.

abster v. 1. to abstain, forbear. 2. to restrain, refrain. 3. to deprive oneself. 4. not to interfere. eu me abstive de empregar violência I withheld myself from violence. ~-se de votar to abstain from voting.

abstergente s. m. abstergent, cleansing agent. || adj. m. + f. abstergent.

absterger v. to absterge, cleanse.

abstersão s. f. (pl. -ões) abstersion, cleansing.

abstersivo s. m. abstergent. ‖ adj. abstersive, abstergent, cleansing.
absterso adj. clean, cleansed, absterged.
abstido adj. 1. abstinent. 2. suppressed.
abstinência s. f. 1. abstinence, temperance, sobriety. 2. forbearance, abstemiousness. 3. fasting.
abstinente s. m. + f. abstainer. ‖ adj. abstinent, temperate, moderate, sober, forbearing.
abstração s. f. (pl. -ões) (also **abstraimento** m.) 1. abstraction, absorption of mind. 2. distraction, absence of mind. 3. retiredness.
~ **de espírito** distraction, absence of mind. **fazer** ~ **de** to abstract.
abstracionismo s. m. (fine arts, phil.) abstractionism.
abstracionista s. m. + f. abstractionist: an artist producing abstract paintings.
abstrair v. 1. to abstract: a) consider separately. b) separate. 2. ~-se to become absorbed in thought. 3. ~-se to distract oneself from.
ele abstraiu sua atenção do trabalho he abstracted his attention from the work. **ele abstraiu-se em sua lição** he concentrated himself on his lesson.
abstrativo adj. abstractive.
abstrato s. m. abstract. ‖ adj. abstract: 1. abstracted. 2. separated, isolated. 3. absent-minded, lost in thought.
abstrator s. m. abtracter, person tending to abstraction.
abstruso adj. 1. abstruse. 2. confused, intricate. 3. obscure. 4. hard to understand, unintelligible. ‖ -**amente** adv. 1. abstrusely. 2. confusedly. 3. unintelligibly.
absurdo s. m. **absurdez, absurdeza, absurdidade** f. absurdity, folly, nonsense. ‖ adj. absurd, nonsensical, unreasonable.
abugalhado adj. wide-open (eyes).
abugalhar v. (also **esbugalhar**) to open the eyes widely, stare.
abugrado adj. similar to or descended from the Brazilian Bugres.
abular v. to seal with a bull (or with lead).
abulia s. f. (med.) abulia: lack or loss of will power.
abúlico adj. (med.) abulic.
abundância s. f. 1. abundance, plenty, plentifulness, copiousness. 2. wealth, riches.
em ~ abundantly. **nunca** ~ **fez mal** store is no sore. **viver na** ~ to live in plenty, live on the fat of the land.
abundante adj. m. + f. (also **abundoso**) 1. abundant, plentiful, copious. 2. abounding in, rich in. ‖ ~**mente** adv. abundantly, plentifully, copiously.
abundar v. 1. to abound (in), be rich in, be well supplied with. 2. to run or flock to, come in abundantly. 3. to agree to.
este córrego abunda em trutas this brook is alive with trout.
abunhadio s. m. bondage, serfdom.
abunhado s. m. Indian held in serfdom (being no slave).
abunhar v. 1. to live in bondage. 2. (fig.) to live parsimoniously.
aburacar v. 1. to make holes in. 2. to pierce, perforate.
aburelado adj. very coarse (cloth), like sackcloth.
aburelar v. to manufacture sackcloth.
aburguesado adj. bourgeois.
aburguesar v. to make or become bourgeois.
abusado adj. 1. abused, taken advantage of. 2. tiresome, wearisome. 3. meddlesome.
abusador s. m. abuser. ‖ adj. abusive.
abusão s. f. (pl. -ões) 1. abuse. 2. mistake, error. 3. fabrication, fib. 4. superstition. 5. (rhet.) catachresis: misuse or strained use of words.

abusar v. 1. to abuse, misuse, treat badly. 2. to delude, deceive. 3. to go beyond limits or measure. 4. to cause damage or harm. 5. to insult. 6. to affront, revile. 7. to annoy, bore. 8. (Braz.) to make or get roguish. 9. to belittle. 10. (fig.) to sicken. 11. to violate.
~ **do álcool** to overindulge in spirits. ~ **da autoridade** to abuse one's authority. ~ **da confiança** to abuse the confidence. ~ **da paciência de alguém** to wear out someone's patience. **ele abusou da bondade da minha tia** he trespassed on my aunt's kindness.
abusivo adj. abusive. ‖ -**amente** adv. abusively.
abuso s. m. 1. abuse. 2. misuse. 3. overuse. 4. contravention. 5. roguery. 6. annoyance, disgust, nuisance. 7. abhorrence. 8. reviling.
~ **de álcool** abuse of spirits. ~ **de confiança** breach of trust. **um** ~ **manifesto** a crying abuse.
abutilão, abutilo s. m. (bot.) abutilon.
abutre s. m. (ornith.) vulture. 2. (fig.) bad or cruel individual.
abutreiro s. m. a vulture hunter.
abutua s. f. (bot.) common name of several plants of the family Menispermaceae.
abuzinar v. 1. to hoot, toot, sound the horn. 2. to make a loud noise. 3. to speak in a loud voice. 4. to importune.
aca s. m. (Braz.) bad smell, stench.
aça s. m. + f. bright-complexioned mulatto. ‖ adj. albinic.
acabaçado adj. gourdlike in taste or form.
acabaçar v. to shape like a gourd.
acabadiço adj. sickly, feeble.
acabado adj. 1. finished, accomplished. 2. ready, complete. 3. excellent, well-wrought, perfect. 4. worn, used, consumed. 5. worn-out, exhausted. 6. debilitated, impaired, aged. ‖ -**amente** adv. perfectly, completely, wholly.
e está ~ (**o assunto**) and there it stands, and no more of that. **produto** ~ finished product. **meio** ~ semi-manufactured.
acabador s. m. finisher.
acabadote adj. (coll.) 1. shaky, decrepit, ramshackle. 2. aged, wonky.
acabamento s. m. 1. finishing, completion. 2. final touch. 3. end, conclusion. 4. accomplishment. 5. death. 6. extinction.
~ **à lima murça** fine finishing. ~ **do prazo** expiration of the term. ~ **ao esmeril** finishing polish. ~ **esmerado** perfect finish.
acabanar v. 1. to give the form of a hut to. 2. to pull or turn down (a hat or hat-brim).
acaba-novenas s. m. sg. + pl. (Braz.) rowdy, rogue, hooligan.
acabar v. to finish: 1. end, terminate. 2. conclude, complete. 3. accomplish, achieve. 4. cease, come to an end. 5. be over. 6. decease, die. 7. consume. 8. extinguish. 9. give the final touch.
~ **bem** (**mal**) to end well (badly), to have a good (bad) end. ~ **com alguém** 1. to have done with s. o. 2. to kill s. o. ~ **com alguma coisa** to put an end to a thing. ~ **por** (**com, em**) **fazer** ~ **fazendo** to end by doing. ~ **em ponta** to taper. ~ **a sua tarefa** to accomplish one's task. ~ **um trabalho** to finish, give the final touch to a work. **acabarei com ele para sempre** I will have nothing to do with him any more. **acabo de ver o meu amigo** I have just seen my friend. **acabou em casamento** it ended in marriage. **acabou em nada** it ended in nothing. **acabou que ele se decidiu** it ended in his deciding. **acabou-se** it is all over, it is up. **acabou-se!** that will do!, call it a day! **ainda bem que já acabou** I am glad it is over.

como **acabará tudo isto?** how will it all turn out? **é coisa de nunca** ~ it never comes to an end. **ele acabou comendo o bolo** he ended by eating the cake. **estar acabando** to come to an end. **nossa farinha está acabando** we are running short of flour. **os bobos nunca acabam** there is a sucker born every minute. **um nunca** ~ **de...** an unending... (ceaseless).

acabelado adj. hairy.

acabelar v. to form a growth of hair.

acaboclado adj. (Braz.) 1. having Indian-white half-breed characteristics. 2. like a peasant. 3. rustic, rural. 4. churlish, boorish (see **caboclo**).

acaboclar v. Braz.) 1. to give the appearance of a **caboclo** or Indian-white half-breed to. 2. to become rustic, boorish.

acabralhado adj. (Braz.) of mixed breed (said of a person having one mulatto and one Negro parent).

acabramar v. to tie one foot of an ox to his body so that he cannot injure the person treating him.

acabramo s. m. halter or tether used for the above purpose.

acabrunhado adj. 1. downcast, sad, distressed. 2. melancholic. 3. feeble, weak. 4. ashamed, humiliated. ‖ **-amente** adv. 1. feebly. 2. melancholically.

acabrunhador adj. (also **acabrunhante**) distressing, grieving.

acabrunhamento s. m. distress, oppressiveness.

acabrunhar v. 1. to oppress. 2. to cast or weigh down. 3. to lessen, enfeeble. 4. to afflict. 5. to grieve, sadden. 6. to harm. 7. to humiliate, humble. 8. ~-**se** to lose courage, become dispirited.

acaburro s. m., ad. = **zaburro**.

acaçá s. m. (Braz.) 1. sort of cake made of maizena and rice. 2. refreshment of fermented rice or maize. 3. strong perfume. 4. intoxicant. 5. (fig.) attraction, allurement.

açacalado adj. 1. polished, burnished. 2. shining.

açacalador s. m. burnisher.

açacaladura s. f. burnishing.

açacalar v. 1. to polish, burnish. 2. (fig.) to improve.

acaçapado adj. (also **acachapado**). 1. like a rabbit. 2. cowered, crouched. 3. shrunk, hunched up. 4. close to the ground.

acaçapador s. m. one who or that which lowers, flattens, etc.

acaçapar v. (also **acachapar**) 1. to diminish, lower. 2. to flatten, squash. 3. ~-**se** to cower, squat, crouch, shrink.

~-**se com medo** to shrink trembling with fear.

acachapamento s. m. 1. diminishing, lowering. 2. flattening, squashing.

acachar v. 1. to hide, conceal. 2. = **acaçapar**.

acachoar v. 1. to bubble. 2. to surge. 3. to foam, froth.

acácia s. f. (bot.) acacia.

acacianismo s. m. (Braz.) ridiculously sententious word, expression or phrase with little or no meaning.

acaciano adj. (Braz.) 1. sententious. 2. ridiculously conventional and meaningless.

acacifar v. to put in a box or drawer.

acácio s. m. 1. (Braz.) stuffed shirt: a typically pompous and bombastic fool or nitwit. 2. dunce, simpleton.

açacu s. m. (also **açacuzeiro**) sand-box tree.

acaculado adj. (Braz.) over-full.

acacular v. (Braz.) to fill to excess.

acadeirar-se v. to take a seat, sit down.

academia s. f. 1. academy: a) college, high school, university. b) society of learned men, authors, artists, etc. 2. student's association.

Academia das Ciências Academy of Sciences. **Academia das Belas-Artes** Academy of Fine Arts.

acadêmia s. f. 1. plaster model (painting). 2. academy figure.

academial adj. m. + f. (pl. **-ais**) academic.

academiar v. to speak or act academically.

academicismo s. m. academicism.

acadêmico s. m. 1. academician. 2. student of a high school. ‖ adj. academic, academical. ‖ **-amente** adv. academically.

academismo s. m. academism.

academista s. m. + f. 1. academician. 2. student or member of a school for recreative activities.

acafajestado adj. 1. low, dirty (character), vulgar. 2. roguish. ‖ **-amente** adv. roguishly.

acafajestar-se v. 1. to become vile. 2. to become roguish. 3. to abase o. s.

açafata s. f. lady-in-waiting, lady of the queen's wardrobe.

açafate s. m. wicker basket without handle.

acafelado adj. 1. plastered. 2. (fig.) dissimulated. 3. hidden, concealed.

acafelador s. m. plasterer.

acafeladura s. f., **acafelamento** s. m. plastering.

acafelar v. 1. to plaster. 2. (fig.) to hide, conceal.

acafetado adj. coffee-coloured.

acafetar v. to colour like coffee.

acafobado adj. (also **afobado**) 1. hurried, hasty. 2. busy, bustling. 3. confused, embarrassed.

acafobar v. 1. to hurry on, hasten. 2. to busy, bustle. 3. to confuse, embarrass.

açafrão s. m. 1. (bot., also **açaflor**) saffron, crocus. 2. (chem.) saffron.

açafroa s. f. (bot.) safflower.

açafroado adj. 1. saffron-coloured. 2. seasoned with saffron.

açafroal s. m. (pl. **-ais**) saffron field.

açafroar v. 1. to colour with saffron. 2. to season with saffron.

açafroeiro s. f. (bot.) 1. Indian saffron. 2. tree of sadness.

açaí s. m. (bot.) cabbage-palm.

acaiçarado adj. 1. like a peasant (see **caiçara**). 2. rustic, rural. 3. churlish, boorish. 4. of low birth.

acaiçarar-se v. 1. to become a peasant. 2. to become rustic, churlish, boorish.

açaimar v. (also **açamar**) 1. to muzzle. 2. to repress, restrain. 3. to tame, domesticate.

açaimo s. m. 1. muzzle. 2. nosepiece. 3. gag.

acaipirado adj. 1. boorish, churlish. 2. shy, bashful.

acaipirar-se v. 1. to become churlish or boorish. 2. acquire the habits and the mode of speech of the country folks.

acairelado adj. piped or bound (edge of garment).

acairelador s. m. one who applies piping or binding. ‖ adj. that pipes or binds.

acairelar v. to pipe, bind, adorn or trim.

açaizeiro s. m. (Braz., bot.) cabbage-palm.

acajadado adj. 1. beaten (with a stick). 2. crooked like a shepherd's staff.

acajadar v. to beat (esp. with a crook or shepherd's staff).

acajipado adj. (pop.) deformed.

acaju s. m. acajou: 1. cashew-tree or its fruit. 2. mahogany, Spanish cedar or its timber.

acajucica s. f. resin of the cashew-tree.

acalcanhado adj. 1. trodden, trampled, stepped on. 2. vexed, annoyed. 3. humiliated, humbled. 4. worn by use (heel).

acalcanhamento s. m. 1. treading or trampling with the heel. 2. vexation, annoyance. 3. humiliation. 4. a wearing down at the heels.

acalcanhar v. 1. to tread or trample with the heels. 2. to vex, annoy. 3. to humiliate, humble. 4. to wear down at the heels.

acalcar v. to compress, trample down, tread upon.

acalculia s f. (path.) inability to make even simple arithmetical calculations.

acalentador adj. 1. lulling. 2. soothing.

acalentar v. (also **acalantar**) 1. to lull or rock to sleep. 2. to soothe, comfort. 3. to caress, fondle, pet. 4. to flatter.

acalento s. m (also **acalanto**) 1. lulling, rocking to sleep. 2. soothing, comfort. 3. caressing, fondling, petting. 4. flattery.

acálice, acalicino adj. (bot.) acalycine, having no calyx.

acalmação s. f. (pl. **-ões**) 1. act of calming, soothing. 2. calmness, tranquility.

acalmado adj. soothed, made calm, appeased.

acalmar v. to calm: 1. pacify, appease. 2. quiet, silence, still, hush. 3. alleviate, soothe, assuage, soften. 4. moderate. 5. tranquilize. 6. ~-se grow or fall calm, smooth, settle, sober or calm down. **acalme-se** set your mind at rest. **acalmou sua ira** his anger passed (off). **o vento acalma** the wind abates.

acalmia s. f. lull, pause.

acalorado adj. 1. agitated, excited, inflamed, lively, heated. 2. vehement, impetuous. 3. passionate.

acalorar v. 1. to heat, warm. 2. to agitate, excite, inflame.

acamado adj. lying in bed, abed. **estar** ~ to stay in bed.

acamamento s. m. 1. confinement to bed. 2. stratification, layering. 3. flattening of grain stalks by wind.

acamar v. 1. to arrange in layers. 2. to put on the ground or other surface. 3. to fall ill, have to stay in bed. 4. to lie in bed. 5. to lay (corn). 6. to fall down, drop.

açamar v. = **açaimar**.

acamaradar v. to join in fellowship, associate with, befriend.

acâmato adj. robust, sturdy.

açambarcador s. m. monopolist, monopolizer, forestaller.

açambarcamento s. m. (also **açambarcação** f.) monopolization, monopoly.

açambarcar v. to monopolize, forestall.

acambetado adj. (also **cambeta, cambaio, cambado**) bandy-legged.

acambetar v. (also **cambetar**) to limp, hobble.

acamboar v. to crook, bend, make or become awry.

acambulhado adj. helter-skelter, confused.

acambulhar v. 1. to put in a helter-skelter way. 2. to arrange in layers, disorder.

açamo s. m. = **açaimo**.

açamoucado s. m. 1. bad use of materials, resulting in an artless, unsafe construction. 2. helter-skelter work.

acampado adj. camping, encamped.

acampainhado adj. bell-like.

acampamento s. m. camp, encampment, camping. ~ **de escoteiros** a boy scouts camp. **levantar** ~ to break up a camp, abandon a camp.

acampar v. to camp, encamp, live or settle in a camp.

acampsia s. f. (med.) acampsia.

acamurçado adj. chamoislike.

acamurçar v. to give a chamoislike surface.

acamutanga s. f. (Braz., ornith.) amazon (parrot).

acanalado adj. channelled, grooved, furrowed, fluted.

acanalador s. m. person who or thing that makes channels, etc. ‖ adj. making channels, grooves, or furrows.

acanaladura s. f. channel, groove, flute, furrow.

acanalar v. to channel, groove, furrow, flute, chamfer.

acanalhado adj. roguish, rascally.

acanalhador s. m. one who or that which makes roguish. ‖ adj. causing roguishness.

acanalhamento s. m. act or fact of becoming a rogue or scoundrel.

acanalhar v. to make roguish, become a rogue or scoundrel.

acanaveado adj. 1. tortured by having needlelike pieces of bamboo pierced under the nails. 2. emaciated, feeble.

acanaveadura s. f. 1. torturing by piercing needlelike pieces of bamboo under the nails. 2. emaciation.

acanavear v. 1. to torture by piercing needlelike pieces of bamboo under the nails. 2. to emaciate, enfeeble.

acancelado adj. (bot.) cancellous, cancellate.

acancelar v. to form or install a gate or barrier (as at a railway crossing).

acanelado adj. = **acanalado**.

acanelar v. 1. to give cinnamon colour to. 2. to flavour or besprinkle with cinnamon. 3. = **acanalar**.

acangaceirado adj. characteristic of, behaving like the N.E. Braz. outlaws.

acangatara s. m. 1. plume of feathers. 2. an Indian's headdress.

acanguçu s. m. (Braz., also **onça pintada, jaguar**) (zool.) jaguar.

acangulado adj. provided with projecting teeth like the triggerfish.

acanhado adj. 1. timid, bashful, awkward, shy. 2. tight, narrow, close. 3. mean, stingy, miserly. **eu me sinto acanhado aqui** I do not feel at ease here. **o espaço é muito acanhado** there is not enough space, it is too narrow.

acanhador s. m. person or thing that causes timidity, tightness, etc. ‖ adj. causing timidity, tightness, etc.

acanhamento s. m. (also **acanho**) 1. timidity, bashfulness, awkwardness, shyness. 2. tightness, narrowness. 3. stinginess, meanness.

acanhar v. 1. to check the development of, choke. 2. to restrict. 3. to lessen. 4. to ashame. 5. to intimidate. 6. to depress, cause low spirits. 7. to make or become tight, narrow. 8. ~-se to be ashamed, shy, timid. 9. ~-se to be afraid, frightened, get discouraged. **a falta de chuva acanhou o milho** the lack of rain delayed the growth of the corn.

acanhoar v. 1. to fire a cannon against. 2. to bombard, cannonade.

acanoado adj. warped lengthwise (boards).

acanoar v. to shape like a canoe.

acanônico adj. contrary to canon-law.

acanonista s. m. + f. transgressor of canon-law.

acantáceo adj. (bot.) acanthaceous.

acanto s. m. (bot.) acanthus, bear's-breech, brank-ursine.

acantoado adj. 1. put or thrown in a corner. 2. occult. 3. neglected. 4. wrapt up in o. s., living apart.

acantoar v. 1. to put or throw in a corner. 2. to hide, conceal. 3. to separate, put aside. 4. to flee from society, to become wrapt up in o. s.

acantocarpo adj. (bot.) acanthocarpous.

acantocéfalo s. m. (zool.) acanthocephalan, a parasitic worm found in the intestines of vertebrates. ‖ adj. belonging or pertaining to the Acanthocephala class.

acantólise s. f. (path.) acantholysis, atrophy and separation of the derma or corium layer of the skin.

acantonado adj. divided into cantons, cantoned.

acantonamento s. m. cantonment, military camp.

acantonar v. to canton, allot quarters.

acantose s. f. (med.) acanthosis.

acanular v. to shape like a cannula or tube.

ação s. f. (pl. -ões) action: 1. movement, activity. 2. act. 3. deed. 4. feat. 5. way of acting. 6. event. 7. (milit.) operation, engagement, battle. 8. (lit.) theme, subject. 9. (rhet.) elocution, gesture. 10. proceeding, lawsuit. 11. (com.) share. 12. energy. 13. influence.
~ de graças thanksgiving. ~ de sociedade bancária (com.) bank share. ~ judicial (jur.) lawsuit. ~ liberada (com.) fully paid-up share. ~ não liberada (com.) partially paid-up share. ~ nominativa (com.) nominal share of stock. ~ ordinária (com.) share of common stock. ~ penal criminal procedure. ~ preferencial (com.) preference (or preferential) share. ~ primitiva (com.) original share. ~ real (jur.) real action. ~ retardada delayed action, time-lag action. em ~ resultante de on the strength of, by virtue of. entrar em ~ to come into operation. homem de ~ man of action. intentar uma ~ em juízo (jur.) to bring an action against s. o. liberdade de ~ liberty of action. pôr em ~ to put in practice. o conto se ressente de falta de ~ the story lacks action. uma má ~ a wicked deed.

acapachar v. 1. to humiliate, humble. 2. (fig.) to crush. 3. to demoralize.

acapangar-se v. to become or act like a hired assassin.

acapelar v. 1. to shape like a hood. 2. to hood. 3. to submerge. 4. to sink, founder. 5. ~-se to roughen (sea).

acapitular v. 1. to chapter. 2. (eccl.) to reprimand in presence of the chapter.

acapna s. f. dry wood that does not smoke.

acapnia s. f. (med.) acapnia.

acapno adj. (referring to honey) obtained without driving the bees out of the beehive by means of smoke.

acapoeirar-se v. (Braz.) to become a rogue or scoundrel.

acapu s. m. (Braz., bot.) acapu, partridgewood.

acará (I) s. m. (Braz.) dish made of beans and palm oil.

acará (II) s. m. (Braz.) 1. (ichth.) popular name of several fishes of the Cichlidae family, the most common being the Geophagus brasiliensis. 2. (zool.) great white heron.

acará-bandeira s. m. (pl. acarás-bandeiras) (Braz., ichth.) scalare.

acará-cascudo s. m. (pl. acarás-cascudos) (Braz., ichth.) chanchito.

acarajé s. m. an Afro-Bahian delicacy of kidney bean paste fried in dendê palm oil.

acarapicu s. m. (Braz., ichth.) silver jenny.

acarapinhar v. = encarapinhar.

acarapixuna s. m. (Braz., ichth.) chocolate cichlid.

acarar v. = encarar.

acaratimbó s. m. (Braz., ornith.) Amazon heron.

acaratinga s. m. (Braz., ornith.) American egret.

acardia s. f. (path.) acardia.

acardíaco adj. (path.) acardiac.

acardiotrofia s. f. (path.) atrophy of the cardiac muscle.

acardumar-se v. to shoal (fish).

acareação s. f. (pl. -ões), acareamento m, confronting or confrontation of witnesses.

acarear v. 1. to contrast one thing with another, compare. 2. to confront (witnesses).

acariciador s. m. fondler, caresser. ‖ adj. (also acariciativo) fondling, caressing.

acariciar v. 1. to caress, fondle. 2. to pet. 3. to cherish, foster. 4. to maintain, nourish.

acariçoba s. f. (Braz., bot.) water navelwort.

acaridar v. 1. to treat with kindness or charity. 2. ~-se to feel pity for, commiserate.

acarídeos s. m. pl. (zool.) acaridae (pl.), mites (pl.).

acarinhar v. 1. to caress, fondle. 2. to treat with kindness. 3. to pet.

acarino s. m. = acarídeo.

acarneirado adj. sheeplike.

ácaro s. m. (zool.) acarid.

acarofobia s. f. (path.) fear of contracting scabies.

acárpico, acarpo adj. (bot.) acarpous.

acarraçado adj. sticking to like a tick.

acarrado adj. 1. moveless. 2. resting in the shade (cattle).

acarradouro s. m. shady place where the cattle rests.

acarrancar v. to frown, scowl, glower.

acarrapatado adj. 1. ticklike. 2. slow like a tick.

acarrar (I) v. 1. to stop moving. 2. to rest in a shady place (cattle). 3. to keep close together in order to protect itself from the sun (cattle). 4. to rest, have one's siesta.

acarrar (II) v. to cart.

acarrear v. (also carrear, acarretar) 1. to cart, transport in a cart. 2. to occasion, cause.
~ (ou acarretar) dificuldades to cause (or bring about) difficulties.

acarreio s. m. (also acarretadura, acarretamento) 1. carting, cartage. 2. causing, occasioning.

acarretado adj. provided with a carriage (gun).

acarretador s. m. carter, waggoner, carrier.

acarretadura s. f. acarretamento s. m. = acarreio.

acarretar v. = acarrear.

acartonado adj. like cardboard.

acartonar v. to make like cardboard.

acasacado adj. coatlike.

acasalamento s. m. 1. mating, coupling. 2. joining, bringing together. 3. equalling, matching.

acasalar v. 1. to mate, couple. 2. to join, bring together. 3. to equal, match.

acasear v. (also casear) to make buttonholes.

acaso s. m. chance, hazard, fortune, luck. ‖ adv. by chance, perhaps, incidentally.
sofrer os ~s da fortuna to bear the chances of fortune. ao ~ at random. deixei-o ao ~ I left it to chance. por ~ by chance, perchance. nada foi deixado ao ~ nothing was left to chance.

acastanhado adj. brownish, chestnut-coloured.

acastanhar v. to give a brownish or chestnut-colour to.

acastelado adj. 1. fortified with or protected by castles. 2. castle-like. 3. castellated.

acastelamento s. m. 1. act or effect of fortifying or building defenses. 2. adoption of a defensive attitude.

acastelar v. 1. to fortify or protect with castles. 2. to build like a castle. 3. to fortify. 4. ~-se to be on one's guard, be cautious.

acastelhanado adj. 1. after the Castilian (or Spanish) way. 2. sympathizing with the Castilians (or Spaniards).

acastelhanar v. 1. to give a Castilian (or Spanish) appearance (or style) to. 2. to make Castilian (or Spanish).

acasulado adj. 1. husk-shaped. 2. cocoon-shaped.

acasular v. to shape like a husk (or cocoon).

acatado adj. respected, esteemed. ‖ -amente adv. respectfully, in a respectful manner.

acataléctico, acatalético adj. acatalectic.
acatalepsia s. f. 1. (med.) acatalepsia. 2. (philos.) acatalepsy.
acataléptico adj. acataleptic.
acatamento s. m. regard, respect, reverence, deference.
acatar v. 1. to respect, venerate, regard, honour, revere. 2. to follow, obey, 3. to fulfil, observe. ~ **uma ordem** to observe, obey an order.
acatarrado, acatarroado adj. (also **encatarrado, encatarroado**) catarrhal.
acatarroar-se v. to be troubled with a cold.
acatassolado adj. 1. shot, shot-coloured. 2. woven like camlet.
acatável adj. m. + f. (pl. **-veis**) respectable, deserving deference.
acatingado (I) adj. (Braz.) foul, fetid, stinking.
acatingado (II) adj. covered with brushwood or underbrush (see **caatinga**).
acatitado (adj. dandy, dandyish.
acatólico s. m. non-catholic. || adj. non-catholic.
acatruzar v. to vex, annoy, molest.
acauã s. m. + f. (Braz., ornith.) laughing falcon.
acaudilhar v. 1. to command like a caudilho. 2. to command, lead, direct a political party or faction.
acaule adj. m. + f. (bot.) acaulous.
acaulescência s. f. (bot.) acaulescence.
acautelado adj. 1. cautious, careful, prudent. 2. cunning, astute, sagacious. || **-amente** adv. 1. cautiously, carefully. 2. cunningly, sagaciously.
acautelador adj. 1. warning. 2. precautional. 3. protective, defensive.
acautelamento s. m. 1. act or effect of warning or cautioning. 2. taking of precautions, guarding against.
acautelar v. 1. to warn, forewarn, caution. 2. to avoid, shun. 3. to watch. 4. to protect, guard, safeguard. 5. ~**-se** to be careful, to beware. 6. ~**-se** to be on watch (or guard).
começamos a ~**-nos dele** we began to be on guard against him. **acautelem-se com os batedores de carteiras!** beware of pickpockets!
acavalado adj. 1. superimposed one on the other. 2. (Braz.) very large.
acavalamento s. m. act of covering a mare.
acavalar v. 1. to cover a mare. 2. (fig.) to superimpose one on the other.
acavaleirado adj. 1. placed in a superior or leading position. 2. haughty.
acavaleirar v. 1. to place in a superior or leading position. 2. to heap up.
acavaletado adj. crooked, aquiline (nose).
acebolado adj. (cul.) seasoned or covered with onions.
acebolar v. (cul.) to season, spice or cover with onions.
aceca s. f. = **acéquia**.
acedares s. m. pl. fishing net (for sardines).
acedência s. f. assent, agreement, accordance.
acedente s. m. + f. assentient, assenter. || adj. assentient, complying.
aceder v. 1. to accede: a) conform, comply with. b) acquiesce, consent. c) assent, agree. 2. to add. ~ **a um pedido** to comply with a request. **eles** ~**am ao convite** they accepted the invitation.
acedia s. f. (also **acídia**) 1. apathy. 2. melancholy. 3. slackness.
acefálico, acéfalo adj. (path.) 1. acephalous, headless. 2. without chief or leader.
aceimar v. = **açaimar**.
aceiração s. f., **aceiramento** m. (met.) steeling, casehardening, steel-facing or -plating.

aceirar (I) v. to steel, steel-face, acirate.
aceirar (II) v. 1. to make a clearing around a wood. 2. to divide or distribute uncultivated land. 3. to surround, encircle. 4. to observe, lurk, spy. 5. to look longingly at, covet.
aceiro (I) s. m. steelworker. || adj. 1. made of steel. 2. like steel.
aceiro (II) s. m. 1. clearing around a wood (to prevent the spreading of fire). 2. (Braz.) resting place from which the underwood has been removed by fire. 3. (Braz.) a clearing on both sides of a fence to avoid its destruction by fire.
aceitação s. f. (pl. **-ões**), **aceitamento** m.) 1. acceptance, acceptation, reception. 2. approval, approbation. 3. applause. 4. consideration.
a ~ **de seu cargo ou sua dignidade** the assumption of his rank. **a** ~ **das mercadorias** the acceptance of the goods. **ter** ~ to meet with approval, to be well received.
aceitador s. m. 1. accepter, acceptor. 2. endorser. || adj. accepting, approving.
aceitante s. m. + f. (com.) acceptor, receiver. || adj. accepting, acceptant, receiving.
aceitar v. 1. (also com.) to accept. 2. to receive, take. 3. to admit, acknowledge. 4. to consent, permit, approve.
~ **de boa-fé** to take on trust. ~ **um convite** to accept an invitation. ~ **um desafio** to take up the glove, to accept the challenge. ~ **o inevitável** 1. to accept the inevitable. 2. (coll., USA.) to face the music. ~ **uma letra** to accept a bill. ~ **a responsabilidade** to take upon oneself, to assume the responsibility. **aceite! (diga que sim)** say the word! **ela aceita serviço de costura** she takes in sewing. **ele aceitou a proposta** he agreed to the proposal. **ele não aceita conselhos** you can't tell him a thing. **queira** ~ **a expressão de minha mais alta consideração** 1. accept the assurance of my highest consideration. 2. (conclusion of a letter) Yours faithfully.
aceitável adj. m. + f. (pl. **-áveis**) acceptable, agreeable.
aceite s. m. (com.) acceptance. || adj. = **aceito**.
apresentar para ~ to present for acceptance. **por falta de** ~ for non-acceptance.
aceito adj. 1. accepted, admitted. 2. received.
aceleirar v. to store in a barn or granary.
aceleração s. f. (pl. **-ões**) (also **aceleramento** m.) 1. acceleration, increase in speed. 2. speed. ~ **negativa** deceleration, retardation.
acelerado adj. accelerated, sped-up, quick. || **-amente** adv. hastily, quickly, in a hurry.
a passo ~ at a quick step or pace, (mil.) in forced march.
acelerador s. m. (tech., math.) accelerator. || adj. accelerating.
pisar no ~ (sl.) to step on the gas.
acelerar v. 1. to accelerate. 2. to press, push on. 3. to speed up, hasten, quicken. 4. (mot.) to put on speed. 5. ~**-se** to gather speed.
~ **a execução dos trabalhos** to speed up, push on the work. **ele acelerou a velocidade** he raised the velocity.
acelga s. f. (bot.) Swiss chard.
acelomado adj. (zool.) acoelomate, lacking a true coelom or body cavity.
acém s. m. (pl. **-éns**) the forerib, middle rib (or chuck rib) of an ox (plate G 1).
acenamento s. m. = **aceno**.
acenar v. 1. to beckon. 2. to provoke. 3. to call to attention.
~ **com a mão** to wave one's hand. **eu lhe acenei que podia ir embora** I waved him away or off.

nós lhe acenamos um adeus we waved him farewell.

acendalha s. f. 1. chip, chippings, parings. 2. anything to make fire with.

acendedor s. m. 1. lighter, igniter. 2. cigarette lighter.

acender v. 1. to light, ignite. 2. to kindle, set on fire. 3. to switch on (light). 4. (fig.) to fill with enthusiasm, excite, inflame. 5. to animate. 6. to enrapture. 7. to irritate, provoke. 8. ~-se: a) to be or become lighted. b) to catch fire. c) to deflagrate. d) to be or become inflamed. ~ a vela to light the candle. ~ a luz to switch on the light. ~ um fósforo to light or strike a match. ~ um lume, fogo to light a fire. isto bastará para ~ a guerra that will be sufficient to unleash the war.

acendimento s. m. (also **acensão**) 1. act or fact of lighting, ignition. 2. kindling, setting of fire. 3. (fig.) inflammation. ~ das lâmpadas lighting of the lamps.

acendível adj. m. + f. (pl. -íveis) 1. that may be lighted. 2. inflammable, combustible, ignitable.

acendrar v. 1. to clean with ash. 2. (fig.) to purify. 3. to refine (metals).

aceno s. m. (also **acenamento**) 1. nodding. 2. calling or invitation. 3. wink. eles me chamaram à parte com um aceno they called me aside with a wave.

acenoso adj. (bot.) curved at the upper end, hanging down, bowed, bent.

acento s. m. accent: 1. emphasis given to a syllable or word. 2. a mark to indicate this. 3. characteristic manner of pronunciation. ~s grave, agudo e circunflexo grave (`), acute (´) and circumflex (^) accents. ~ tônico stress. ~ secundário secondary accent. pôr ~ em to put the accent on. põe-se o ~ no i, assinala-se com o ~ o i the accent must be put on the i.

acentuação s. f. (pl. -ões) accentuation, accent. ~ gráfica marking with accents.

acentuado adj. 1. accentuated, pronounced. 2. (fig.) evident, outstanding, emphasized.

acentuar v. 1. to accentuate, accent, pronounce. 2. (fig.) to emphasize, stress, make stand out.

acepção s. f. (pl. -ões) 1. acceptation (of a word). 2. meaning, sense. 3. signification. 4. (obs.) preference. ~ primitiva, ~ original basic (or original) meaning. na verdadeira ~ do termo in the true sense of the term.

acepilhado adj. 1. smoothed off. 2. polished. 3. improved, perfected.

acepilhador s. m. (carp.) 1. planer. 2. plane.

acepilhadura s. f. 1. planing. 2. ~(s) shavings, parings.

acepilhar v. 1. to plane wood and metals. 2. to pare, cut off. 3. to polish. 4. to improve, perfect. 5. to civilize.

acepipe s. m. dainty, delicacy, titbit.

acepipeiro s. m. dainty feeder, dainty person. ele é um ~ he has a sweet tooth.

aceptilação s. f. (pl. -ões) formal acknowledg(e)ment of receipt by creditor (with or without payment).

acéquia s. f. 1. irrigation ditch, trench. 2. gutter, drain. 3. dam, weir. ~ de moinho mill-race.

aceração s. f. (pl. -ões) 1. steeling, tempering iron with steel. 2. sharpening, whetting. 3. stimulation.

acerácea s. f. (bot.) specimen of the maple family.

aceráceo (adj.) (bot.) of or referring to acer (or maple).

acerado adj. 1. steeled. 2. that hurts very much. 3. exacerbated. 4. excited. 5. sharpened.

acerador s. m. cutler. || adj. 1. steeling. 2. sharpening.

aceragem s. f. (pl. -ens) 1. steeling, case-hardening. 2. sharpening, whetting. 3. cutlery.

acerante adj. m. + f. qualified for steeling.

acerar v. 1. to steel, steel-face, coat with steel. 2. to sharpen, whet. 3. to excite, stimulate. 4. to make painful, pungent. 5. to refine.

aceratose s. f. (med.) lack or shrinking of corneal tissue.

acerbar v. 1. to acerbate. 2. to embitter. 3. to exacerbate, irritate. 4. to be or become severe, rude or cruel. 5. to afflict, distress.

acerbidade s. f. acerbity: 1. harshness. 2. severity. 3. sharpness of taste.

acerbo adj. 1. acerb. 2. bitter. 3. tart. 4. harsh, rough. 5. severe. 6. cruel, fierce. || -amente adv. 1. bitterly. 2. fiercely. 3. rigorously, severely.

acerca adv. 1. near, about, circa. 2. almost. || prep. concerning, regarding, as for, as to, as regards. falamos ~ disso we talked about that.

acercar v. 1. to surround, enclose. 2. ~-se to approach, draw (or come) near.

acerejado adj. cherry-coloured.

acerejar v. to burnish, give cherry colour to.

aceria (I) s. f. steel mill, steel works.

aceria (II) s. f. 1. sudden or inopportune occurrence. 2. (med.) untimely appearance of a sympton or premature growth of an organ.

ácero adj. (of insects or molluscs) having no horns, antennae or tentacles.

aceroso adj. (bot.) needle-shaped (plate F 5).

acerotosia s. f. (zool.) hornlessness (of ruminants).

acerra s. f. vessel containing perfume.

acérrimo adj. 1. excessively acid or bitter. 2. tenacious, obstinate, persistent.

acertado adj. 1. right, correct. 2. proper, fit. 3. judicious, wise. || -amente adv. rightly, properly.

acertador s. m. 1. one who guesses right. 2. (Braz.) rough-rider. ~ da loteria lottery winner.

acertamento s. m. 1. setting right, adjustment. 2. accuracy of aim.

acertar v. 1. to make or set right, adjust, regulate, arrange, settle, harmonize. 2. to find out, conjecture right. 3. to succeed, prosper. 4. to be or act judiciously. 5. to break (horse). 6. to hit (target, mark), hit upon. 7. to happen, come to pass. ~ com to find out, to be lucky (or successful). ~ em cheio to hit the nail on the head. ~ (ou dar) ~no alvo to hit the mark or target. ~ as contas to balance (or settle) accounts. ~ um relógio to regulate or set a watch.

acerto s. m. 1. hit, lucky hit. 2. judg(e)ment, prudence. 3. skill, adroitness. falar com ~ to speak to the point. isto foi feito com ~ this was done with discretion and cleverness. de ~, por ~ perchance.

acervar v. 1. to accumulate, amass (assets). 2. to take inventory, determine the value of.

acervejado adj. 1. tasting of beer. 2. fond of beer.

acervo s. m. 1. heap, pile. 2. a great many, lot. 3. total assets.

acérvulo s. m. little heap or pile.

acescência s. f. 1. acrescence, acetosity. 2. bitterness, sourness.

acescento adj. 1. acescent. 2. bitter, sour.

aceso adj. 1. lighted, lit, kindled, burning. 2. inflamed, excited, vehement, violent. 3. switched on (light). estar ~ to burn. ~ em greedy of.

acessão s. f. accession.

acessibilidade s. f. accessibility.

acessional adj. m. + f. (pl. -ais) accessional.

acessível adj. m. + f. (pl. -eis) 1. accessible, approachable. 2. attainable. 3. tractable. 4. communicative.
o pico da montanha é ~ the summit of the mountain is accessible. ~ à razão amenable to reason.
acessivo adj. accessory, adjuvant, increased.
acesso s. m. 1. access, admittance, admission, entrance. 2. approach, approximation. 3. accessibility. 4. promotion, accession, rise in rank or dignity. 5. fit, paroxism. 6. commotion.
~ de choro crying fit. ~ de tosse fit of coughing. um ~ de emoção an access of emotion. um ~ de febre an attack of fever, shivering, ague. de difícil ~ difficult of access. de fácil ~ easy of access, of easy access. eles tinham ~ livre ao jardim they had the run of the garden.
acessório s. m. 1. accessory. 2. complement, appendage. 3. increase, addition. 4. ~s pl. fittings, accessories (plates F 6, M 4). 5. (gram.) attribute. ‖ adj. 1. accessory. 2. additional. 3. secondary.
~s do vestuário clothing requisites. ~s de um automóvel accessories of a motorcar.
acessual adj. m. + f. (pl. -ais) by access.
acetabuliforme adj. m. + f. acetabuliform.
acetábulo s. m. (anat.) acetabulum.
acetar v. = azedar.
acetato s. m. (chem.) acetate.
acéter s. m. (pl. -eres) mug.
acético adj. acetic, acetous.
acetificação s. f. acetification, acetifying.
acetificar v. to acetify.
acetileno s. m. acetylene.
acetímetro s. m. (also acetômetro) acetimeter.
acetinado adj. satiny, silky.
papel ~ satin-paper, tissue paper.
acetinar v. 1. to satin, satinize, make satinlike. 2. to calender. 3. to smooth.
acetol s. m. (pl. -óis) (chem.) acetol.
acetomel s. m. (pl. -éis) acetomel, oxymel.
acetona s. f. (chem.) acetone.
acetonemia s. f. (med.) acetonemia.
acetonúria s. f. acetonuria.
acetoso adj. acetous, related to vinegar.
acevadar v. to feed with barley.
acevar v. (also cevar) 1. to fatten, feed up. 2. to glut. 3. to become glutted.
acha (I) s. f. billet, log.
acha (II) s. f. battle-axe.
achacadiço adj. sickly, valetudinarian, feeble, of poor health.
achacado adj. sickly, of poor health.
achacar v. 1. to crab, carp at. 2. to ill-treat, be unkind. 3. to steal by threatening, rob. 4. to fall ill, become sick. 5. to impute, ascribe, accuse.
achacoso adj. ailing, sickly.
achada (I) s. f. finding, find, discovery.
achada (II) s. f. (geogr.) table-land, plateau.
achadão s. m. (pl. -ões) 1. good deal, bargain. 2. lucky acquisition. 3. shelter, protection. 4. extra earnings.
achadiço adj. easily found.
achado s. m. 1. finding: a) act of finding. b) thing found, find. 2. invention, discovery. 3. good bargain. um verdadeiro ~ a real find. não se dar por ~ to pretend ignorance.
achador s. m. 1. finder. 2. inventor. ‖ adj. that finds.
achadouro s. m. 1. finding place. 2. (Braz.) place of prehistoric findings.
achamalotado adj. like camlet.
achamboado adj. (also achambonado) 1. coarse, rough, crude. 2. of bad make. 3. inelegant. 4. badly dressed.

achamboar v. (also achambonar) to make or become coarse, rough or crude.
achambonado adj. = achamboado.
achamento s. m. (also achado) finding, find, discovery.
achamorrado adj. (Braz.) 1. shorn, clipped, very short (hair). 2. flattened. 3. flat and broad (nose).
achanado adj. levelled, evened, smoothed.
achanar v. 1. to even, level, smooth, make plain. 2. to pacify, appease. 3. to vanquish, surmount.
achaparrado adj. 1. squat, thick-set. 2. gnarled, knobby (wood), like a young cork oak.
achaparrar v. to broaden, with little increase in height.
achaque s. m. 1. ailment, habitual indisposition, illness. 2. vice. 3. excuse, pretext, pretense. 4. imputation, complaint.
saber do ~ da vinha to know the weak side of a person.
achaquilho s. m. dim. of achaque, ailment of no serious character.
achar (I) v. 1. to find, meet, meet with, hit on, come across. 2. to find out, discover. 3. to invent, contrive, devise. 4. to verify. 5. to understand. 6. to comprehend. 7. to suppose, think, believe, judge. 8. to consider. 9. ~-se: a) to be, find o. s.; feel. b) to be met with, be found. c) to turn up.
~ por acaso (coll.) to stumble upon. ~ o caminho de to find one's way to. acho difícil acreditar I find it hard to believe. ~ conveniente to find or think (it) advisable. ~ um emprego to get a situation. ~ erros to find mistakes. ~ em ordem to find in order. ~-se em (des)ordem to be in (dis)order. ~-se nas boas graças de to find favour with. ~-se em grandes dificuldades to be in great difficulties. ~-se mal to be mal (at ease). ~-se presente to be present. ~-se em situação crítica to be in a tight spot. ~-se à venda to be on sale. achei o que queria I am suited. acho conveniente dizer it would be as well to say. acho que o melhor é... I think it best to... eu acho que não I do not think so. eu acho que sim I think so. eu me acho bem aqui I feel fine here. dificilmente achará coisa melhor you will hardly find s. th. better, you may go farther and fare worse. que acha do livro? what do you think of the book? você acha? do you think so?
achar (II) s. m. (India) a sort of pickled roots, fruits or herbs.
acharoado adj. coated, varnished (with Japanese or Chinese lacquer).
acharoamento s. m. japanning, varnishing.
acharoar v. to japan, varnish.
achatadela s. f. (also achatadura f., achatamento m.) 1. squashing, flattening. 2. crushing. 3. (fig.) thrashing.
achatado adj. 1. flattened, flat. 2. crushed, squashed.
achatar v. 1. to flatten, squash. 2. to crush. 3. to humble, humiliate. 4. to defeat, subdue. 5. to defeat by an argument, gain a dispute. 6. to haul s. o. over the coals, take s. o. to task.
achavascado adj. rude, rough, unpolished.
achavascar v. 1. to do negligently, bungle. 2. to work (or cut) out roughly. 3. ~-se to become rough, rude, boorish.
achega s. f. (also achego m.) 1. supplement. 2. help, assistance, subsidy. 3. ~s (pl.) building material(s). 4. heap (potatoes).
achegadeira s. f. procuress.
achegado s. m. relation, kinsman. ‖ adj. close, near.
achegador s. m. procurer, panderer.
achegamento s. m. 1. approach. 2. proximity, nearness. 3. approximation.

acheganças s. f. pl. 1. = **achegas**. 2. belongings.
achegar v. 1. to arrange, adjust. 2. to approximate, near, bring (or put) nearer. 3. ~-se to approach, draw nearer. 4. ~-se: a) to take shelter, refuge. b) to make o. s. comfortable.
achego s. m. 1. close fit, union. 2. snug protection or shelter. 3. unforeseen profit.
achém s. m. (pl. -éns) Chinese balance.
achibantado adj. boastful, braggart. ‖ -amente adv. boastfully, braggingly.
achibantar v. to make or become boastful.
achicar v. 1. (naut.) to bail, scoop out (water). 2. to drain, dry.
achichelar v. (Braz.) to flatten, squash.
achinado adj. Chineselike.
achincalhação s. f. (pl. -ões) (also **achincalhamento**, **achincalhe** m.) 1. ridicule. 2. mock, mockery, scoff. 3. abasement, humiliation, degrading.
achincalhador s. m. 1. ridiculer. 2. scoffer. 3. person who humiliates or degrades. ‖ adj. ridiculous, absurd, unworthy, degrading.
achincalhar v. 1. to ridicule. 2. to jest, mock, scoff at. 3. to abuse, lower, humble, degrade.
achinelar v. 1. to give the form of a slipper to. 2. to wear down at the heels.
achinesado adj. Chineselike.
achinesar v. (also **achinar**) 1. to give a Chinese appearance (or expression) to. 2. to acquire Chinese ways and manners.
achoar v. to tread, step upon.
achocalhado adj. 1. provided with a cowbell. 2. like a cowbell. 3. spread out (news), divulged, made known.
achocalhar v. 1. to give the form of a cowbell to. 2. to spread, make known or divulged.
achumbado adj. leaden, lead-coloured.
achumbar v. 1. to lead. 2. to make similar to lead.
acica s. f. (Braz., pop.) pocket.
acicatar v. 1. to spur (horse). 2. (fig.) to stimulate, incite, urge.
acicate s. m. 1. spur with one point only. 2. stimulus, incitement.
aciclia s. f. (med.) movelessness of fluids of the physiological system.
acíclico adj. non-cyclic, non-cyclical; (chem., ecology) acyclic.
aciculado, acicular adj. acicular, aciculated, needle--shaped.
acidação s. f. (pl. -ões) acidification.
acidade s. f. = **acidez**.
acidar v. to acidify.
acidável adj. m. + f. (pl. -áveis) acidifiable.
acidência s. f. accidentalness, fortuitousness, casualty.
acidentação s. f. (pl. -ões) 1. unevenness, roughness, inequality (ground). 2. (mus.) accidental.
acidentado s. m. casualty: victim of an accident. ‖ adj. 1. uneven, rough, irregular, broken (ground) (plate Q). 2. that suffered an accident, killed, damaged, injured. 3. (mus.) changed by an accidental.
vida acidentada agitated, eventful, checkered life (having ups and downs).
acidental adj. m. + f. (pl. -ais) (also **acidentário**) accidental, unexpected, casual, fortuitous, occasional, eventual. ‖ ~mente adv. accidentally, unexpectedly, casually, eventually.
ele morreu ~mente he died in an accident.
acidentar v. 1. to cause an accident. 2. (mus.) to change a note by an accidental. 3. to change, alter. 4. ~-se to become irregular; to suffer an accident.
acidentável adj. m. + f. (pl. -áveis) liable to become uneven (ground).

acidente s. m. 1. accident: a) misfortune, mishap, disaster, casualty. b) chance. c) unevenness, roughness (ground). d) (gram.) inflexion, accidence. 2. (med.) fit, access, stroke. 3. (mus.) accidental.
~ **de automóvel** motor accident. ~ **de aviação** flying (or) air accident. ~ **de tráfego** road accident. ~ **do (no) trabalho** industrial accident, accident of work. ~**s do terreno** (topogr.) irregularities of ground. ~ **ferroviário** railway accident. ~ **marítimo** sea accident. **por** ~ by chance. **morte por** ~ accidental death. **seguro contra** ~**s** accident insurance. **sofrer um** ~ to meet with an accident.
acidez s. f. (also **acidade, azedia**) acidity, sourness, ionic acidity.
~ **do estômago** gastric acidity.
acídia s. f. 1. acedia, depression, low spirits, downheartedness. 2. laziness, slackness.
acidífero adj. acidiferous, acidic, acid-forming.
acidificação s. f. acidification, acidifying, acidation.
acidificante adj. m. + f. acidifying.
acidificar v. (also **acidular**) to acidify.
acidimetria s. f. acidimetry.
acidímetro s. m. acidimeter, acidometer.
acidioso adj. 1. depressed, downhearted. 2. lazy, slack.
ácido s. m. acid. ‖ adj. acid, sour, tart.
~ **azótico** nitric acid. ~ **clorídrico** hydrochloric acid. ~ **fênico** carbolic acid. ~ **láctico** lactic acid. ~ **muriático** soldering spirit. ~ **sulfúrico** sulphuric acid.
acidófilo adj. acidophile.
acidose s. m. (med.) acidosis.
acidótico, acidósico adj. acidotic.
acidrado adj. citronlike.
acidrar v. to make like cider, give the flavour or colour of cider to.
acidulação s. f. (pl. -ões) acidification.
acidulado adj. acidified, acidulated.
acidulante adj. m. + f. acidifying.
acidular v. to acidify.
acídulo adj. acidulous.
aciganado adj. gipsylike.
aciganar-se v. to gipsify.
acilia s. f. loss or absence of eyelashes.
acima adv. above, up (plate P 18).
~ **(abaixo) da média** above (below) the average. ~ **de** 1. above. 2. beyond. 3. over. ~ **de tudo** above all things, above all, first of all. ~ **do nível do mar** above sea level. ~ **do solo** above ground, overground. ~ **dos cinqüenta** on the wrong side of fifty. ~ **mencionado** above mentioned. **como** ~ as above. **mais** ~ higher up. **pela rua** ~ up the street.
acincho s. m. (also **cincho**) cheese-press, cheese--mould.
acinesia s. f. 1. immovability. 2. (med.) paralysis.
acinético, acinésio adj. 1. contrary to movement, immovable. 2. (med.) paralysing.
acingir v. = **cingir**.
ácino s. m. (bot.) acinus.
acinoso adj. acinous.
acinte s. m. 1. spite, malice, ill will. 2. provocation. ‖ adv. purposefully, intentionally.
por ~ out of spite, purposefully, intentionally. **fazer** ~**s** to banter, provoke.
acintoso adj. purposeful, spiteful, malicious. ‖ adv. purposefully, spitefully, maliciously.
acinzado adj. grayish.
acinzamento s. m. colouring gray.
acinzar v. to make or paint gray.
acinzentado adj. (also **griséu**) grayish, ash-coloured.
acionado s. m. gestures (pl.) (of an actor or speaker), gesticulation. ‖ p. p. driven, operated, actuated.

acionador s. m. person or thing that sets in motion, mover, driver (plate F 8). ‖ adj. driving, operating.

acional adj. m. + f. (pl. -ais) acting, actional.

acionar v. 1. to put in (or to) action. 2. to sue at law. 3. (com.) to incorporate, to form a stock company. 4. to gesticulate. 5. to set in motion, to drive, operate, work.

acionário s. m. (also acionista) shareholder.

acionável adj. m. + f. (pl. -áveis) that may be put to action or set in motion.

acionista s. m. + f. shareholder, stockholder.

acipitrino adj. accipitrine, accipitral: of or referring to birds of prey.

acipreste s. m. (also cipreste) (bot.) cypress.

acirandar v. (also cirandar) to screen, winnow, sift.

acirologia s. f. acyrology, bad diction.

acirrado adj. 1. intransigent, uncompromising. 2. stubborn. 3. obstinate. 4. irritated, angry. 5. incited, set on (dogs).

acirramento s. m. irritation, incitement.

acirrante adj. m. + f. 1. irritating, inciting. 2. prickling. 3. piquant.

acirrar v. 1. to irritate. 2. to incite, instigate. 3. to stimulate. 4. ~-se to get irritated, angry.

acismo s. m. (rhet.) accismus: affected refusal.

acistia s. f. acystia: absence of the bladder.

acitara s. f. 1. covering. 2. saddle-cloth. 3. veil (used in church).

acitrinado adj. lemon-coloured.

aclamação s. f. (pl. -ões) 1. acclamation, shout of approval, applause, cheers (pl.). 2. (rhet.) sententious phrase summing up a reasoning.

por ~ by acclamation. as aclamações do povo the acclamations of the crowd.

aclamado adj. = proclamado.

aclamador s. m., aclamante m. + f. applauder. ‖ adj. applauding.

aclamar v. 1. to acclaim, applaud. 2. to cheer, shout in approval. 3. to elect by acclamation, proclaim, hail.

aclamativo, aclamatório adj. acclamatory.

aclaração s. f. (pl. -ões) 1. clearing, brightening. 2. explanation, elucidation. 3. = aclaramento.

aclarado adj. 1. cleared. 2. explained.

aclarador adj. 1. clearing, brightening. 2. explanatory.

aclaramento s. m. 1. = aclaração. 2. grade or intensity of illumination.

aclarar v. 1. to clear, make clear. 2. to brighten, clarify. 3. to elucidate, explain. 4. to purify. 5. to clean. 6. to clear up, uncloud. 7. to sensitize. 8. to make distinct. 9. ~-se to become clear.

~ uma dúvida to clear up a doubt.

aclaustrado adj. cloisterlike.

aclavado adj. club-shaped, claviform.

aclidiano, áclido adj. (zool.) acleidian, without clavicles.

aclimação s. f. (also aclimamento m., aclimatação, aclimatização f.) acclimation, acclimatization, acclimatation.

aclimado adj. acclimatized, acclimated.

aclimador s. m. acclimatizer. ‖ adj. acclimatizing.

aclimar, aclimatar, aclimatizar v. 1. to acclimatize, acclimate. 2. ~-se to get accustomed, habituated to.

aclimável adj. m. + f. (pl. -áveis) acclimatable, acclimatizable.

aclive s. m. acclivity, ascent, slope. ‖ adj. m. + f. acclivitous.

aclorofilado adj. without chlorophyll.

acme s. m. acme, opex, culmination, perfection.

acne s. f. (med.) acne.

aço (I) s. m. 1. steel. 2. (fig.) steellike hardness and strength. 3. amalgam (for silvering mirrors). 4. (fig.) power, hardness, flexibility.

~ fino fine steel. ~ fundido cast steel. ~ homogêneo ingot steel, homogeneous steel. ~ temperado hardened steel. artigos de ~ steelwares. blindado com ~ steel-clad, steel-plated. capacete de ~ steel helmet. cor de ~ steel-blue. gravura em ~ steel-engraving. limalha de ~ steel-filings. palha de ~ steel-wool. usina de ~ steelworks.

aço (II) s. m. = aça.

aço (III) s. m. (S. Braz., sl.) white rum.

acoar v. (Braz.) to bark.

acobardado adj. cowardly, faint-hearted.

acobardamento s. m. (also acovardamento) cowardice, pusillanimity, discouragement.

acobardar v. 1. to dishearten, discourage, intimidate, despond. 2. ~-se to become faint-hearted, be discouraged.

acobertado adj. 1. protected, shielded. 2. concealed, disguised. 3. well-clothed. ‖ -amente adv. 1. protectingly. 2. disguisedly.

acobertar v. 1. .to cover. 2. to cloak. 3. to hide, conceal, dissimulate, disguise, dissemble. 4. to protect, shield. 5. to caparison, dress a horse in caparison.

acobilhar v. 1. to be hospitable to. 2. to clothe or shelter. 3. to cover the fire with ashes.

acobrear v. to colour like copper.

acocação s. f. (pl. -ões) (Braz.) 1. endearment, kindness. 2. caress, petting.

acocar v. (Braz.) to endear, caress, pet.

acochado adj. 1. lying in bed, abed, (fig.) sick. 2. tight, narrow. 3. overfull, crowded.

acochar v. 1. to compact in layers. 2. to tighten. 3. to press together. 4. (Braz.) to hasten, urge on. 5. to twist (a rope). 6. ~-se to squat. 7. ~-se to crouch, stoop down.

acocho s. m. 1. compacting, compression, tightening, pressing. 2. hastening. 3. twisting (of a rope).

acóclide adj. m. + f. (zool.) shell-less (mollusk).

acocorado adj. squatted, squatting.

acocoramento s. m. squatting.

acocorar(-se) v. 1. to squat. 2. to crouch.

açodado adj. 1. hasty, hurried. 2. diligent, industrious. ‖ -amente adv. 1. hastily, hurriedly. 2. diligently, industriously.

açodamento s. m. 1. urging, urge, acceleration. 2. haste, hurry, speed.

açodar v. 1. to urge, haste, speed. 2. to incite, instigate, stimulate. 3. ~-se to make haste, run.

acofiar v. (also cofiar) to smooth, stroke out (beard or hair).

acognosia s. f. (med.) 1. knowledge of therapeutical, surgical and medical means. 2. pharmacognosy, the science dealing with materia medica.

acogulado adj. overfull, overfilled.

acogular v. to overfill, pack, cram, pile or heap up.

açoiaba s. f. (Braz.) Indian headdress.

acoimador s. m. punisher, person who fines; reproacher, censurer. ‖ adj. punishing, fining, reproachful, censuring.

acoimamento s. m. punishment, fine, reproach, censure.

acoimar v. 1. to punish, fine, reproach, censure. 2. ~-se to accuse o. s., recognize one's guilt.

acoirelamento s. m. (also acourelamento) division into coirelas (land-measure, about 220 × 22 meters).

acoirelar v. (also acourelar) to divide land into coirelas (about 220 × 22 meters).

açoita-cavalos s. m., sg. + pl. (Braz.) tree of the family Tiliaceae.

acoitador s. m. (also **acoutador**) shelterer, protector. ‖ adj. sheltering, protecting.

açoitador s. m. (also **açoutador**) whipper, lasher, beater. ‖ adj. whipping, lashing, beating.

açoitamento s. m. (also **açoutamento**) whipping, lashing, beating.

acoitar v. (also **acoutar**) to shelter, protect.

açoitar v. (also **açoutar**) 1. to whip, lash. 2. to beat, flog. 3. to scourge, fustigate. 4. ~-se to discipline oneself.

açoitado pela tempestade storm-beaten.

açoite s. m. (also **açoute**) 1. whip, lash, scourge. 2. whipping, lashing, scourging. 3. a clap or slap (on a child's back).

açoiteira s. f. (also **açouteira**, Braz.) 1. end of the rein, used to lash the horse. 2. short horsewhip.

acola s. f. (formerly) delicacy made of chocolate and maize flour.

acolá adv. there, yonder, thither, to that place. ~ **adiante** over there. **cá e ~** here and there.

acolchetar v. 1. to fasten with hook and eyes. 2. to clasp, hook, fasten. 3. to be attached or fastened to.

acolchoadinho s. m. 1. checkered woollen cloth. 2. fine thin cloth with interwoven patterns or designs.

acolchoado s. m. 1. wadding, padding, stuffing, upholstery (plate C 4). 2. cloth woven like a (ornamental) bedspread. 3. (Braz.) quilt (plate C 7). ‖ adj. 1. wadded, padded, stuffed. 2. woven like a bedspread.

acolchoador s. m. wadder, padder. ‖ adj. wadding, padding.

acolchoamento s. m. wadding, padding, quilting.

acolchoar v. 1. to wad, pad, quilt. 2. to weave (or sew) like a bedspread.

acoletado adj. like a waistcoat.

acoletar v. 1. to give the form of a waistcoat to. 2. to put on a waistcoat.

acolhedor s. m. welcomer; one who receives or shelters. ‖ adj. welcoming, sheltering.

acolher v. 1. to welcome, receive. 2. to shelter, lodge, house. 3. (fig.) to protect. 4. to admit. 5. to listen to, lend an ear, give heed to. 6. to have in mind. 7. ~-se to take shelter or refuge.

acolherar v. 1. to leash, hitch up together, ~-yoke. 2. to couple, unite.

acolhida s. f. **acolhimento** s. m. 1. reception, welcome. 2. shelter, refuge.

ter bom acolhimento (boa acolhida) to be well received, to meet with a favourable reception.

acolia s. f. (med.) acholia.

acólico adj. (med.) acholic.

acolitado s. m. (also **acolitato**) one of the lower orders of the Roman Catholic Church. ‖ adj. 1. assisted, attended. 2. accompanied.

acolitar v. 1. to assist, attend. 2. to accompany.

acólito s. m. acolyte: 1. (R. C. Church): a) a priest's attendant at mass. b) person ordained to the fourth of the minor orders. 2. assistant, helper.

acologia s. f. pharmacognosy.

acomadrar-se v. 1. to become a godmother. 2. to get acquainted or familiar with.

acometedor s. m. aggressor, assailant, provoker. ‖ adj. 1. attacking, assailing. 2. provoking. 3. enterprising, bold.

acometer v. 1. to attack, assault, assail. 2. to provoke, hostilize. 3. to undertake, attempt. 4. to rush, run a risk.

ela acometeu-me com injúrias she flew out at me. **fui acometido de** I was taken with.

acometida s. f., **acometimento** m. 1. attack, onset, assault. 2. attempt. 3. enterprise, undertaking. 4. fit, access (disease).

acometível adj. m. + f. (pl. **-íveis**) assailable.

acomia s. f. (also **calvície**) baldness.

acomodação s. f. (pl. **-ões**) (also **acomodamento** m.) 1. accomodation. 2. arrangement, agreement. 3. room, lodging. 4. adaptation. 5. (com.) settlement. ~ **para gente** accomodation for people.

acomodadiço adj. (also **acomodatício, acomodável**) 1. easy to be settled or accomodated. 2. adjustable, adaptable. 3. condescending, yielding, compromising.

acomodado adj. 1. accomodated. 2. settled. 3. adjusted. 4. quiet, calm. 5. well installed. 6. reasonably cheap. ‖ **-amente** adv. 1. accomodatingly. 2. opportunely.

acomodar v. 1. to accomodate, put in order, arrange. 2. to make easy or comfortable. 3. ~-se: a) to make o. s. comfortable. b) to conform o. s., submit. c) to be suitable. 4. to settle, harmonize, conciliate, reconcile. 5. to employ, place. 6. to adapt, make fit. 7. to retire to one's room. 8. to make suitable, proper, adequate. 9. to lodge.

~-se **às circunstâncias** to accomodate o. s. to circumstances, set one's sail to every wind.

acomodável adj. m. + f. (pl. **-áveis**) suitable, adaptable, adjustable, capable of being arranged.

acômodo adj. (obs.) 1. opportune. 2. apt.

acompadrar v. 1. to become a godfather. 2. (fig.) to become familiar.

acompanhadeira s. f. (woman) companion, follower or attendant.

acompanhador s. m. companion, follower or attendant. ‖ adj. accompanying, attendant.

acompanhamento s. m. 1. retinue, attendance, train, suite. 2. accompanying, waiting on. 3. (mus.) accompaniment.

~ **fúnebre** funeral train.

acompanhante s. m. + f. companion, follower or attendant. ‖ adj. accompanying, attendant.

acompanhar v. 1. to accompany: a) come or go along with. b) escort. c) follow. d) wait on, attend. e) (mus.) execute an accompaniment. 2. to watch, observe. 3. to have the same ideas. 4. to join, unite, ally. 5. to sort, match. 6. ~-se to have as one's attendance or company.

~ **alguém até à porta** to show s. o. out. ~ **uma canção ao piano** to accompany a song on the piano. ~ **o naipe** to follow the suit. ~**am o meu passo** they kept up with me. **acompanhá-lo-ei para casa** I'll see you home. **acompanhá-lo-ei um pouco** I will go a little way with him. **acompanhamo-la até o trem** let us see her off. **ela acompanha a moda** she follows the fashion. **ele acompanhou-a a casa** he took her home. **estava acompanhado de circunstâncias dolorosas** it was attended by painful circumstances. **não acompanhamos a moda** we have not taken up with fashion. **o que é que acompanha isto?** what goes with it?

acompleicionado adj. complexioned.

acompridar v. to elongate, lengthen, prolong.

acomunar-se v. (also **mancomunar-se**) to agree mutually, act in concert.

aconchado adj. 1. conchate, shell-shaped. 2. (archit.) conchal: fitted to the outer roof (ceiling).

aconchavador s. m. (Braz.) person who hires farm hands.

aconchavar v. (Braz.) 1. to put the hollow hand behind the ear in order to hear better. 2. to shape like a shell.

aconchegado adj. 1 near, close. 2. cosy, comfortable.

aconchegar v. 1. to approximate, bring or draw near. 2. to unite. 3. to shelter. 4. to make comfortable, cosy. 5. ~-se to snuggle together.

aconchego s. m. 1. lodging, shelter. 2. comfort, comfortableness. 3. warmth, snugness, coziness. 4. help, assistance.
acondicionação s. f. (pl. -ões) 1. = acondicionamento. 2. caution, watchfulness, lookout.
acondicionado adj. 1. packed. 2. disposed, conditioned.
~ **em caixas** packed in cases. **mal** ~ 1. badly packed, in a bad state. 2. ill-humoured.
acondicionador s. m. 1. packer. 2. conditioning apparatus.
acondicionamento s. m. 1. packing (of goods, commodities). 2. conditioning. 3. preservation. 4. adaptation. 5. accomodation, arrangement.
~ **de ar** air-conditioning.
acondicionar v. 1. to condition. 2. to pack (goods, commodities), box. 3. to place suitably or adequately. 4. to preserve. 5. to adapt, accomodate, arrange.
acôndilo adj. (anat.) acondyle.
acondroplasia s. f. (med.) achondroplasia.
aconfeitado adj. like sweetmeat or comfit.
aconfeitar v. to make like comfit or sweetmeat.
aconfradar v. 1. to become a colleague, a fellow member. 2. to flock together.
aconitato s. m. (chem.) aconitate.
aconiteia s. f. plant similar to wolf's bane.
aconítico adj. (chem.) aconitic.
aconitina s. f. (chem.) aconitine.
acônito s. m. (bot.) aconite, wolf's bane.
aconselhado adj. prudent, judicious, wise. || -amente adv. prudently, judiciously, wisely.
bem (mal) ~ well- (ill-)advised.
aconselhador s. m. advisor, counsellor.
aconselhamento s. m. counselling: 1. (psych.) way of assistance to solve behavio(u)ral disarrangements. 2. act of effect of counselling.
aconselhar v. 1. to advise. 2. to counsel. 3. to persuade. 4. ~-se to take advice, consult.
~-**se com o travesseiro** to sleep over. **eu o aconselho a ...** my advice to you is ... ~-**se com o advogado** to consult the lawyer.
aconselhável adj. m. + f. (pl. -áveis) advisable.
seria ~ **que ele viesse** it would be well for him to come.
aconsoantado adj. 1. consonantal. 2. rhymed, agreeing in sound.
aconsoantar v. 1. to make consonant, bring in accord. 2. to rhyme.
acontecer v. to happen, take place, come about, occur, come to pass.
aconteça o que ~ 1. come what may. 2. whatever may happen. **aconteceu eu estar aí** I happened to be there. **isto acontece muitas vezes** it happens oftentimes, is often the way. **isto não acontecerá mais** this won't occur again. **nunca se sabe o que acontecerá** there's no telling what may happen. **são coisas que acontecem** such things happen, that's what happens.
acontecido s. m. = acontecimento. || adj. past, done, bygone.
acontecimento s. m. 1. occurrence, happening, incident, event. 2. sensation.
~**s imprevistos** unforeseen or unexpected events.
~ **sem precedentes** unheard-of (or unprecedented) event.
acôntio s. m. small arrow, dart.
acontista s. m. darter, person who throws a dart.
acôo s. m. (Braz.) barking.
acoplamento s. m. (mot. and radio) coupling.
acoplar v. to join, couple, connect, hook up.
acoquinar v. (Braz.) 1. to intimidate, frighten. 2. to disquiet, trouble, make uneasy.

açor s. m. (pl. açores) (ornith.) goshawk.
acoraçoador s. m. = acoroçoador.
açorado adj. greedy, avid.
açorar v. 1. to rouse (or excite) a great desire. 2. to show greediness for. 3. to provoke, tempt.
acorçoar s. m. = acoroçoar.
acorcundado adj. somewhat hunchbacked.
açorda s. f. 1. bread panada. 2. (fig.) weakling. || adj. (fig.) weak, frightened.
acordado adj. 1. awake. 2. alert, watchful. 3. agreed, determined. 4. (mus.) tuned in, harmonious. 5. in mind, in memory. || -amente adv. unanimously.
ficar ~ 1. to stay awake. 2. to be in agreement.
estou, fico acordado I wake.
acordamento s. m. awaking.
acordante adj. m. + f. 1. accordant, agreeing. 2. harmonious, harmonic.
acórdão s. m. (pl. acórdãos) (jur.) sentence, judgement.
acordar v. 1. to wake up, awake, awaken. 2. to rouse, stir up. 3. to agree upon, harmonize. 4. to resolve. 5. to remember, recollect. 6. to put to action. 7. to be in a certain state. 8. to grant. 9. ~-se to come to an agreement.
ele não acordou a horas he overslept himself. **estar acordado** to be awake. **eu acordei às sete horas** I woke up at seven o'clock. **ele acordou** he woke up. **ele o acordou** he woke him up. **acorda!** 1. wake up! 2. snap out of it!
acorde s. m. (mus.) chord, accord, harmony. || adj. 1. (mus.) accordant, consonant. 2. concordant, conformable, agreeing.
acordeão s. m. (pl. -ões) (mus.) (Braz., also harmônica, sanfona) accordion.
acordina s. f. chiming watch or clock.
acordo (I) s. m. Italian musical instrument with twelve or fifteen strings.
acordo (II) s. m. (pl. acordos) 1. agreement, harmony. 2. accord, accordance. 3. treaty, pact. 4. conciliation. 5. convention. 6. settlement. 7. care, caution. 8. use of the senses.
~ **baseado na boa-fé e cavalheirismo** gentleman's agreement. **um** ~ **secreto** a secret understanding. **agimos perfeitamente de** ~ **com** we acted in perfect unison with. **chegar a um** ~ to come to terms. **chegaram a um** ~ **com** they came to an agreement (or understanding) with. **de** ~! it's agreed! **de** ~ **com o contrato** under the contract. **de** ~ **com** in accordance with. **de mútuo** ~ by mutual agreement. **eles agiram de** ~ **com a lei** they kept within the law. **entrar em** ~ to enter into an agreement. **está de** ~ **com** it is in keeping with. **estar de** ~ **com** to be in accordance with. **estar de** ~ **com alguma coisa** to agree to s. th. **exatamente de** ~ in strict conformity. **fazer um** ~ to make a deal. **não dar** ~ **de si** to show no sign of life. **não puderam chegar a um** ~ they came to no terms. **ter pronto** ~ to be quickwitted. (coll.) to be quick on the trigger. **vivo de** ~ **com as minhas possibilidades** I live within my income. **você precisa trabalhar de** ~ you must work according(ly). (properly).
acori s. m. blue coral.
acoria (I) s. f. (med.) acoria: insatiable hunger, craving desire for food.
acoria (II) s. f. (med.) acorea: absence of the pupil of the eye.
açorianismo s. m. linguistic peculiarity of the Azores.
açoriano s. m. (also açoreano) Azorian. || adj. (also açórico) Azorian.
acornado adj. hornlike.
acornar v to shape like a horn.

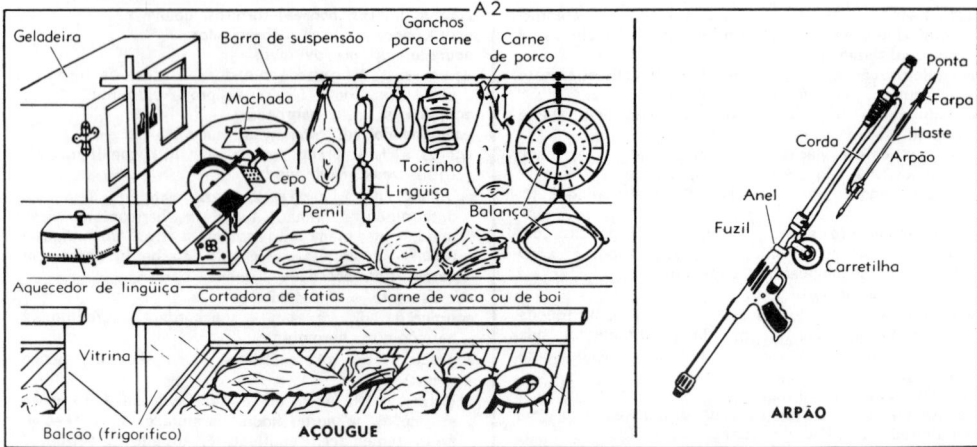

— A 2 —

Geladeira   Barra de suspensão   Ganchos para carne   Carne de porco

Machada

Cepo

Toicinho

Linguiça

Pernil

Balança

Aquecedor de linguiça   Cortadora de fatias   Carne de vaca ou de boi

Vitrina

Balcão (frigorífico)   **AÇOUGUE**

Ponta

Farpa

Corda

Haste

Anel

Arpão

Fuzil

Carretilha

ARPÃO

---

acoroçoado adj. (also **acoraçoado, acorçoado**) encouraged, animated, hopeful.

acoroçoador s. m. (also **acoraçoador, acorçoador**) encourager, animator, stimulator.

acoroçoamento s. m. (also **acoraçoamento, acorçoamento**) encouragement, stimulus.

acoroçoar v. (also **acoraçoar, acorçoar**) to encourage, animate, stimulate.

acorrentamento s. m. chaining, fettering.

acorrentar v. 1. to chain. 2. to fetter. 3. to enslave.

acorrer v. 1. to run to help, assist, succour. 2. to come in haste. 3. to prevent. 4. to put (or set) right. 5. to take shelter.

eles acorreram a ele they flocked to him.

acorrilhar v. 1. to corner: put or drive into a corner. 2. to enclose, shut in. 3. to put aside.

acorrimento s. m. (also **acorro**) 1. assistance, aid, help, succour. 2. coming in haste.

acortinar v. to curtain: provide with a curtain.

acoruchar v. to shape like a pinnacle or spire.

acosmismo s. m. (philos.) acosmism.

acossa s. f. 1. pursuit, close pursuit. 2. weariness, trouble. 3. harassment, torment.

acossador s. m. 1. pursuer. 2. troubler. 3. harasser. ‖ adj. pursuing, troubling, harassing.

acossamento s. m. 1. pursuit, close pursuit, chase. 2. torment. 3. punishment. 4. annoyance.

acossar v. 1. to pursue, chase. 2. to vex, torment, annoy. 3. to punish.

~ alguém to drive someone hard.

acostado s. m. dependent, person who lives at somebody else's expense. ‖ adj. (also **encostado**) leaning or resting against.

acostamento s. m. highway shoulder.

acostar v. 1. (also **encostar**) to lean against, touch, border. 2. to prop, uphold. 3. (naut.): a) to run or keep close to the shore. b) to run ashore, land, come alongside. 4. to accost. 5. to agree, consent. 6. to look for help. 7. to retire, go to bed.

acostável adj. m. + f. (pl. **-áveis**) appropriate for ships coming alongside (quay or pier).

acosto s. m. = **encosto**.

acostumado adj. 1. accustomed, used, customary. 2. habituated, wont (only pred.), wonted (only attr.). 3. inured. ‖ **-amente** adv. customarily.

bem (mal) ~ 1. properly (unproperly) brought up. 2. well accustomed. **nós estamos ~s a andar** we are wont to go. **ele não está ~ a isto** he is unaccustomed to it.

acostumar v. 1. to accustom, habituate, inure (to). 2. to familiarize a p. with s. th. 3. **~-se a** to accustom o. s. to, to get accustomed (or used) to. **acostumamo-nos facilmente a este modo de vida** we took kindly to this way of life. **~-se a alguma coisa** to become seasoned, get used to something.

açoteado adj. terraced, provided with a terrace.

açotéia s. f. terrace, belvedere.

acotiar v. 1. to use (frequently). 2. to frequent. 3. to be assiduous, persistent.

acotilédone adj. m. + f. (bot. also **acotiledôneo, acotilédono**) acotyledonous.

acotoar v. to cover with down or fluff.

acotonar v. to cover with fine soft hair.

acotovelador s. m. shover, pusher, person who uses his elbows. ‖ adj. elbowing, shoving, pushing.

acotoveladura s. f. thrust or blow with the elbow.

acotovelamento s. m. elbowing, jostling.

acotovelar v. 1. to elbow, thrust with the elbow. 2. to push, shove. 3. to provoke. 4. to touch (with the elbow). 5. to meet, be near each other.

acoturnar v. to shape like a cothurnus or buskin, to put on buskins.

açougada s. f. (also **açougaria**) 1. clamour, shouting, hallooing. 2. row, uproar, bustle.

açougue s. m. 1. butchery, butcher shop (plate A 2). 2. slaughterhouse, shamble(s) 3. (also fig.) slaughtering. 4. abundance of meat.

açougueiro s. m. butcher.

acoutador s. m., **acoutar** v. = **açoitador, açoitar**.

açoutador, açoutamento, açoute s. m., **açoutar** v. = **açoitador, açoitamento, açoite, açoitar**.

acovar v. 1. to make holes or caves in. 2. = **encovar**.

acovardamento s. m., **acovardar** v. = **acobardamento, acobardar**.

acovilhar v. = **acobilhar**.

acracia s. f. acracy: lack of government.

acrania s. f. acrania: total or partial absence of the skull.

acrânio adj. acranial.

acraniota s. m. (zool.) Acrania (Cephalocorda). ‖ adj. m. + f. acraniote.

acrasia s. f. unconventional or disorderly conduct, intemperance.

ácrata s. m. + f. person sympathizing with acracy. ‖ adj. (also **acrático**) referring to acracy.

acratismo s. m. system based upon acracy.

acravar v. 1. to sink or drive in, plug into. 2. to inter. 3. to nail, pierce with nails. 4. to soak up, be soaked in. 5. to sink in the mud or mire.

acre (I) adj. m. + f. (abs., sup. acríssimo, acérrimo) 1. acre, acrid, sharp, biting, tart, acrimonious. 2. (fig.) mordant, biting, nasty, rude. ‖ ‖ ~mente adv. acridly.

acre (II) s. m. acre: measure of land.

acreano s. m. (Braz. also acriano) native or inhabitant of the State of Acre, Brazil. ‖ adj. of or referring to the State of Acre, Brazil.

acreditado adj. 1. credited, accredited. 2. having credentials.

acreditador s. m. creditor, warrantor. ‖ adj. crediting, accrediting.

acreditar v. 1. to credit: give, obtain or open credit. 2. to bail, warrant, sanction. 3. to give credentials to. 4. to believe, believe in, trust in. 5. ~-se to make o. s. respected.
~ em Deus to believe in God. acreditaria você que...? should you believe that...? acreditou-se que eu tivesse estado lá I was thought to have been there. ele acredita no efeito de seu banho diário he swears by his daily bath. estou inclinado a ~ que... 1. I am inclined to believe that. 2. I should say that. eu também o acredito I believe so, too. você pode ~-me you can take it from me.

acreditável adj. m. + f. (pl. -áveis) believable, creditable.

acre-doce adj. m. + f. (pl. acre-doces) = agridoce.

acredor s. m. (also credor) creditor.

acrescentador s. m. increaser, enlarger. ‖ adj. increasing, augmenting.

acrescentamento s. m. 1. increase, addition. 2. enlargement, augmentation.

acrescentar v. 1. to add. 2. increase, enlarge. 3. to raise (salary). 4. to stretch (a dish). 5. ~-se to increase.
ela acrescentou a sopa com água she "stretched" the soup. vamos ~ a palavra "it" let us add the word "it". "E isto é verdade", acrescentou ele "And that's a fact", he added.

acrescentável adj. m. + f. (pl. -áveis) addable, capable of being added.

acrescente s. m. 1. = acrescentamento. 2. (pop.) wig. ‖ adj. m. + f. 1. (bot.) developing after fecundation. 2. increasing, enlarging.

acrescer v. 1. to add, increase. 2. to supervene. 3. to grow.

acrescido s. m. addition, increase. ‖ adj. increased, added.

acrescimento s. m. (also acrescência f.) addition, increase, augmentation.

acréscimo s. m. 1. = acrescimento. 2. intermittent fever. 3. (math.) increment, difference.
~ de temperatura raise in temperature. ~ da função, ~ da variável dependente (math.) increment of the function. cobra-se um ~ pela música music is an extra.

acriançado adj. 1. childish. 2. childlike.

acriançar-se v. to behave or become childish (or childlike).

acribologia s. f. severity and precision of style.

acridão, acridez, acrimônia, acritude s. f. acridity, acridness, bitterness.

acridiano, acrídio s. m. (zool.) locust, grasshopper. ‖ adj. of or referring to locusts.

acridofagia s. f. practice of eating locusts.

acridófago s. m. locust-eater. ‖ adj. locust-eating.

acridogenose s. f. plant disease caused by locusts.

acrílico s. m. (chem.) acrylic resin or plastic: generic designation of polymers derived from acrylic aldehyde. ‖ adj. (chem.) acrylic, pertaining to or derived from acrylic acid.

acrimônia s. f. 1. = acridão. 2. (fig.) harshness, asperity.

acrimonioso adj. acrimonious.

acrioulado adj. like a Creole, or adopting his ways.

acrisia s. f. (med.) acrisia.

acrisolado adj. refined, purified.

acrisolador s. m. purifier. ‖ adj. purifying.

acrisolar v. 1. to purify, refine (esp. metals). 2. to test, examine. 3. to chasten (or purify) o. s. submitting to trials.

acrítico adj. 1. uncritical. 2. (med.) acritical.

acro adj. 1. brittle, fragile. 2. severe, hard.

acroama s. m. 1. acroama, harmonious speech or song. 2. (Roman hist.) instrumental music, musical performance or play.

acroamático adj. 1. acroamatic. 2. agreeable to the ear.

acroase s. m. impossibility of understanding without explanations.

acroático adj. uncomprehensible without explanation.

acrobacia s. f. 1. acrobatics, acrobacy, acrobatism. 2. (aeron.) trick flying.
~ aérea aerial acrobatics.

acrobata, acróbata s. m. + f. 1. acrobat. 2. tightrope walker. 3. tumbler.
~ contorcionista contortionist.

acrobático adj. acrobatic, acrobatical. ‖ -aticamente adv. acrobatically.

acrobatismo s. m. acrobatism.

acrocarpo adj. (bot.) acrocarpous.

acrocefalia s. f. (med.) acrocephalia, acrocephaly.

acrocefálico adj. (med.) acrocephalic, acrocephalous.

acrocéfalo s. m. (med.) 1. acrocephalia. 2. acrocephalic. ‖ adj. acrocephalic.

acroceráunio adj. Acroceraunian.

acrodinia s. f. (med.) acrodynia, acrodyny.

acrofobia s. f. (med.) acrophobia: morbid fear of high places.

acroíta s. f. colourless tourmalin(e).

acrólito s. m. acrolith. ‖ adj. acrolithic.

acromania s. f. (med.) total madness.

acromático adj. (opt. and biol.) achromatic.

acromatismo s. m. achromatism.

acromatização s. f. (pl. -ões) achromatization.

acromatizado adj. achromatized.

acromatizar v. to achromatize, deprive of colour.

acromatopsia s. f. (med.) achromatopsy, colour blindness.

acromegalia s. f. (med.) acromegaly.

acromia s. f. (med.) achromia, achroma.

acromial adj. m. + f. (pl. -ais) (anat.) acromial.

acrômio s. m. (anat.) acromion.

acromo adj. achromous, achromic, colourless.

acrônico adj. (astr.) acronych(al).

acropatia s. f. (path.) acropathy.

acropódio s. m. acropodium, pedestal.

acrópole s. f. acropolis.

acrossofia s. f. divine wisdom.

acrossomo s. m. (path.) acrosome: the apex of the spermatozoon in relation to the nucleus.

acróstico s. m. acrostic.

acrostólio s. m. acrostolium.

acrotarso s. m. (ornith.) acrotarsium: the instep of a bird's foot.

acrotério s. m. (archit.) acroter, acroterium, acroterion.

acrotismo (I) s. m. (med.) acrotism.

acrotismo (II) s. m. transcendent philosophy.

actínia s. f. (zool.) sea anemone, actinia.

actínico adj. actinic.

actínio s. m. (chem.) actinium.

actinismo s. m. actinism.

actinólito s. m. (also actinoto) (min.) actinolite.

actinomancia s. f. divination by the radiation of the stars.

24   actinomante — acurar

actinomante s. m. + f. diviner who interprets the radiation of stars.
actinomântico adj. of or referring to the divination through stars.
actinometria s. f. actinometry.
actinomicose, actinomicetose s. f. (med.) actinomycosis.
actinomorfo adj. actinomorphous.
actinoto s. m. (also **actinólito**) (min.) actinolite.
açu adj. m. + f. (Braz.) large, big, great.
acuação s. f. (pl. -ões) (Braz.) 1. chasing or cornering of game. 2. hunting down (game, enemies).
acuado adj. (Braz.) 1. reared, pranced, stopped, restive, balky (horse). 2. cornered, encircled, hard pressed (game). 3. embarrassed, perplexed, in a tight spot. 4. concealed, hidden (game).
acuador adj. (Braz.) rearing, prancing, balky, refusing to go on (horse).
acuamento s. m. 1. recoiling, contraction (before leaping). 2. retrogression, retrocession. 3. (Braz.) rearing, prancing, stopping, balking (horse). 4. perplexity. 5. (Braz.) abandonment of a person in need. 6. rounding up (game), esp. surrounding and harassing with hounds. 7. hiding, concealing (esp. game). 8. cornering, (fig.) checking. 9. humiliating retreat.
acuar v. 1. to recoil, contract, cower (before leaping). 2. to retrogress, retrocede. 3. (Braz.) to rear, prance, stop, refuse to go on (horse). 4. to stop or shrink back because of fear. 5. to become perplexed. 6. to abandon, drop, leave a person in a tight spot. 7. to round up, chase down (game) esp. with hounds. 8. to hide, conceal (esp. game). 9. to corner, (fig.) check, leave no way out.
acúbito s. m. (hist.) accubitum.
açúcar s. m. 1. sugar. 2. (chem.) saccharose. 3. (fig.) sweetness, flattering.
~ **cristal** granulated (or crystallized) sugar. ~ **de beterraba** beetroot sugar. ~ **de cana** cane sugar. ~ **refinado** refined or loaf-sugar. ~ **em pó** sifted (or powder(ed)) sugar. ~ **em tabletes** lump-sugar, cube sugar. ~ **mascavado ou em rama** raw (or brown) sugar. ~ **pilé** crushed sugar. **coberto de** ~ sugar-coated. **engenho de** ~ (usina) sugar mill. **pão de** ~ sugar loaf. ~ **dos diabéticos** saccharin(e).
açucarado adj. 1. sugary, sugared. 2. sweet. 3. mellifluous.
açucarar v. 1. to sugar, sweeten with sugar. 2. to become sugary.
açúcar-cande s. m. (also **alfênico**) sugar-candy.
açucareiro s. m. 1. sugar basin, sugar bowl, sugarcaster (plate M 8). 2. sugar refiner. 3. sugar dealer. ‖ adj. of or referring to sugar and its production.
açucena s. f. 1. (bot.) white lily (Lilium candidum). 2. (Braz.) socket of a candlestick.
açucenal s. m. (pl. -ais) plantation of lilies.
acucular v. = **acogular**.
açudador adj. damming (watercourse).
açudagem s. f. (pl. -ens) **açudamento** m. damming of watercourse.
açudar v. 1. (Braz.) to dam up, embank. 2. to build dams or embankments.
açude s. m. 1. dam, weir, sluice. 2. (Braz.) marginal land of a river used for cultivation when the level of the water sinks.
~ **de comportas** sluice weir. ~ **de abater** shutter dam. ~ **de armadilha** bear-trap dam.
acudir v. 1. to run to help, help, succour, assist. 2. to have recourse (to). 3. to resort, appeal. 4. to attend. 5. to report, present o. s. 6. to obey. 7. to throng to, flock to. 8. to occur, come to one's mind. 9. to reply, answer readily, retort. ~ **a quem chame** to answer a call. ~ **a quem**

manda to obey an order. ~ **por alguém** to take someone's side. **acudam!** help! help! **acodem a ele de todas as partes** they flock to him from all sides. **o navio acode ao leme** the ship answers the helm readily.
acuera s. f. (Braz.) extinct or abandoned things.
acúfeno s. m. (med.) tinnitus: a buzzing or ringing in the ears.
acuidade s. f. 1. acuity, sharpness, keenness. 2. perspicacity, acuteness. 3. cunning, craft. 4. delicacy, sensibility.
açulador s. m. instigator. ‖ adj. instigative.
açulamento s. m. (also **açulo**) 1. instigation. 2. setting on (of dogs). 3. provocation.
açular v. 1. to instigate. 2. (dogs) to set on (to). 3. to provoke, excite.
aculeado adj. aculeate, aculeated.
aculear v. to provide with stings, prickles, etc.
aculeiforme adj. m. + f. aculeiform: like a sting, princkle or thorn.
acúleo s. m. 1. (bot., zool.) aculeum: sting, princkle or thorn. 2. (fig.) stimulus, incentive.
açulo s. m. = **açulamento**.
aculturação s. f. (pl. -ões) cultural adaptation (to a new environment).
aculturado adj. cultured, cultivated.
açumagrar v. to dye with sumac(h).
açumagre s. m. (also **sumagre**) (bot.) sumac(h).
acumatanga s. f. (also **acamutanga**) (Braz.) Amazon, Amazon parrot.
acume s. m. (also **acúmen**, pl. **acumens** or **acúmenes**) 1. top, summit, height. 2. sharpness. 3. acuteness.
acumetria s. f. (med.) audiometry, measurement of hearing acuity with the audiometer.
acuminado adj. 1. acuminate, pointed. 2. (bot.) acuminated.
acuminar v. to acuminate, render sharp or pointed, sharpen.
acumpliciar v. to become an accomplice, make an accomplice of.
acumulação s. f. (pl. -ões) 1. accumulation, storage. 2. heap, pile. 3. concentration of functions or economic power. 4. formation of cumulus clouds. ~ **de calor** heat storage. ~ **de gente** crowds (of people). ~ **(ou depósito) litoral** (geol.) shore deposit.
acumulado adj. accumulated, increased. ‖ -**amente** adv. accumulatedly.
acumulador s. m. 1. (also electr.) accumulator. 2. (electr.) battery, storage battery. ‖ adj. accumulative, accumulating.
acumular v. 1. to accumulate, amass. 2. to heap, pile up. 3. to collect, gather. 4. to fill (to excess), agglomerate. 5. ~-**se** to become accumulated, increase, accrue. ~ **crime a crime** to add crime upon crime.
acumulativo adj. accumulative. ‖ -**vamente** adv. accumulatively.
acumulável adj. m. + f. (pl. -áveis) accumulatable, accumulative. ‖ -**avelmente** adv. accumulatively.
acúmulo s. m. (also **acumulação**) accumulation.
acunhar v. 1. to wedge (up). 2. to fasten with a wedge. 3. to protect.
acunhear v. to shape like a wedge.
acuo s. m. (Braz.) = **acuação**.
acuômetro, acúmetro s. m. (med.) acoumeter.
acupremir v. (med.) to acupress.
acupressão, acupressura s. f. (med.) acupressure.
acupuntura, acupunctura s. f. (med.) acupuncture.
acupunturar, acupuncturar v. (med.) to acupuncture.
acurado adj. accurate, exact. ‖ -**amente** adv. accurately, exactly.
acurar v. to perfect, improve, polish, finish.

acurativo adj. (gram., referring to certain verbs) modifying the action of the main verb, e. g. "tornar" a ver.

acurralar v. to pen (up), corral.

acurtar v. (also **encurtar**) 1. to shorten. 2. to lessen, diminish. 3. to abridge.

acurvado adj. (also **curvo**) curved, arched, crooked, bent.

acurvamento s. m. curving, arching, bending.

acurvar v. 1. to curve, bend, incurvate, round. 2. to yield, give up, cede, submit. 3. to succumb. 4. ~**-se** to stoop down.

acurvilhar v. to kneel, fall on the knees (horse).

acusabilidade s. f. accusability.

acusação s. f. (pl. **-ões**) (also **acusamento** m.) 1. accusation, charge, impeachment, indictment. 2. prosecutor. 3. prosecution. 4. notification. 5. spontaneous confession. 6. acknowledgement of receipt. ~ **escrita** bill of indictment. **a** ~ **não me atinge** the accusation does not affect (or touch) me; (coll.) my withers are unwrung. **estar sob** ~ to be under an accusation.

acusado s. m. 1. accused, offender, defendant. 2. a children's game of hide and seek. ‖ adj. accused (of **de**), charged (with **de**).

acusador s. m. (also **acusante** m. + f.) plaintiff, accuser. ‖ adj. accusing, charging.

acusar v. 1. to accuse, charge with, make a charge against, indict, impeach, arraign. 2. to reveal, expose. 3. to show, indicate. 4. ~**-se** to accuse oneself, confess. 5. to acknowledge (the receipt of goods). 6. to qualify. ~ **a recepção de** to acknowledge the receipt of. ~ **alguém de** to tax s. o. with, to bring an accusation against. **não devo ser acusado disto** I am not to be taxed with it.

acusativo s. m. (gram.) accusative. ‖ adj. accusative, accusatorial, accusatory, accusing.

acusatório adj. accusatorial. ‖ **-oriamente** adv. accusatorially.

acusável adj. m. + f. (pl. **-áveis**) accusable, impeachable, censurable.

acusma s. m. acousma.

acústica s. f. acoustics.

acústico adj. acoustic(al). **galeria** **-a** (archit.) whispering-gallery. **nervo** ~ auditory nerve. **tubo** ~ ear-trumpet.

acuta s. f. (math.) 1. (also **salta-regra**) bevel, bevel square, bevel-rule. 2. square.

acutangulado, acutangular, acutângulo adj. (math.) acute-angled.

acutelado adj. chopperlike.

acutenáculo s. m. (surg.) needle-holder, needle-carrier.

acuticaudado adj. (zool.) sharp-tailed.

acuticórneo adj. (zool.) provided with tapering antennae.

acutifólio adj. (bot.) acuminated, acutifoliate.

acutilador s. m. slasher. ‖ adj. slashing.

acutilamento s. m. slashing.

acutilar v. to slash, gash.

acutipum s. m. (pl. **-uns**) small Brazilian monkey.

acutirrostro adj. (zool.) having a rostriform or beak--shaped head.

adáctilo, adátilo adj. (zool.) adactylous: without fingers or toes.

adaga s. f. dagger.

adagada s. f. stab or thrust with a dagger.

adage s. m. (Braz., colloq.) 1. usefulness, serviceableness, aptitude. 2. courage, valour.

adagial adj. m. + f. (pl. **-ais**) 1. proverbial. 2. (mus.) adagio.

adagiar v. to quote adages, proverbs.

adagiário s. m. collection of adages or proverbs.

adágio (I) s. m. adage, proverb, saying.

adágio (II) s. m. (mus.) adagio.

adagueiro s. m. young stag.

adail s. m. (pl. **adaís**) (hist.) 1. commander, guide, leader. 2. sentry, outpost.

adamado adj. 1. womanlike, effeminate. 2. light, sweet (wine).

adamantino adj. adamantine, hard, diamondlike.

adamar(-se) v. to behave or act effeminately.

adamascado adj. 1. damask, damasked. 2. tasting like apricot. **linho** ~ linen damask.

adamascar v. to damask.

adamasquinado adj. damascened, damaskeened.

adâmico adj. 1. Adamic, Adamical. 2. primitive, simple.

adamita s. m. + f. Adamite.

adamítico adj. Adamitic, Adamitical.

Adão s. m. Adam. **em trajes de** ~ in the altogether, stripped to the buff.

adaptabilidade s. f. adaptability, adaptiveness.

adaptação s. f. (pl. **-ões**) 1. (also lit., theat.) adaptation, 2. (tech.) fitting, matching. ~ **ao clima** acclimatization. ~ **à luz** bright adaptation. ~ **à obscuridade** dark adaptation. ~ **de impedância** impedance matching.

adaptado adj. 1. adapted. 2. suitable, fit. ‖ **-amente** adv. suitably. ~ **de um conto de Andersen** adapted from Andersen.

adaptador s. m. 1. adapter. 2. (tech.) connector, connecting piece. ‖ adj. adapting. ~ **cônico** (tech.) taper adapter.

adaptar v. 1. to adapt, adjust, suit. 2. to apply. 3. to conform. 4. (tech.) to fit. 5. ~**-se** to adapt or accustom o. s. to. ~**-se perfeitamente** to fit like a glove. ~**-se aos tempos** to trim with the time. **adaptaram-se a meu passo** they came up with me. **adapte à ação as suas palavras** suit the action to the word. **ele adaptou-se às circunstâncias** he adapted himself to circumstances. **ele tem que** ~**-se às suas possibilidades** he must cut his suit according to his cloth. **estas peças adaptam-se uma à outra** these pieces fit together. **isto não se adapta às minhas intenções** that does not enter into my plans.

adaptável adj. m. + f. (pl. **-áveis**) adaptable, suitable.

adarga s. f. (hist.) oval leather shield, target, buckler.

adargueiro s. m. (hist.) 1. targeteer, soldier armed with an oval leather shield. 2. target maker, person who makes oval leather shields.

adarme s. m. 1. (hist. Braz., and Port.) ancient weight = 1.793g. 2. calibre of a shotgun bullet. 3. (fig.) insignificance. **por** ~**s** niggardly.

adarvar v. (fort.) to provide with battlements or a passage along the battlement.

adarve s. m. battlement, parapet.

adastra s. f. (tech.) triblet, hand anvil.

adastragem s. f. (pl. **-ens**) straightening, redressing or correcting with a triblet or hand anvil.

adastrar v. to straighten, redress or correct with a triblet or hand anvil.

adefagia s. f. (med.) insatiable appetite, voracity.

adega s. f. 1. cellar. 2. wine cellar.

adegar v. 1. to keep in a cellar. 2. to drink too much (wine).

adegueiro s. m. cellarer, butler.

adejar v. 1. to flutter, flit, flicker, flap with the wings. 2. to hover. 3. to agitate.

adejo (I) s. m. 1. flutter, fluttering, flicker, flickering, flapping with the wings. 2. agitation.

adejo (II) s. m. (N. Braz.) stray horse.
adeleiro s. m. (also **adelo, ferro-velho, merca-tudo**) 1. dealer in old clothes. 2. second-hand dealer. 3. scrap iron dealer, junk dealer.
adelfa s. f. (also **espirradeira**) (bot.) oleander.
adelfal s. m. (pl. **-ais**) oleander plantation.
adelfia s. f. (bot.) adelphia.
adelfo adj. (bot.) adelphous.
adelgaçado adj. 1. thin, slender. 2. thinned, pointed. 3. tapered. 4. narrow. 5. worn-out, impaired by use. ‖ **-amente** adv. 1. thinly, slenderly. 2. pointedly. 3. narrowly.
adelgaçador s. m. person, thing or machine that makes s. th. thin, pointed or narrow. ‖ adj. thinning, pointing, narrowing.
adelgaçamento s. m. 1. thinning. 2. tapering, pointing, narrowing. 3. diminishing. 4. decrease. 5. wearing out. 6. paring or cutting off. 7. emaciation. 8. (naut.) clearing up, brightening (weather).
adelgaçar v. 1. to thin, make thin. 2. to taper, point. 3. to diminish. 4. to rarefy, dilute. 5. to get thin, grow lean. 6. to pare (or cut) off. 7. to emaciate. 8. (naut.) to clear up, brighten. 9. ~-se to become thin, etc.
adelgadar v. less used synonym for **adelgaçar**.
ademanes s. m. pl. 1. affectation. 2. affected manners. 3. foppery.
~ **de ternura** billing and cooing, display of affection (U. S. A., sl.) ballyhoo.
ademão s. m. (Braz., coll. **demão** f.) help, assistance.
adenção s. f. (pl. **-ões**) ademption, revocation of a will or donation etc.
adenda s. f. addendum.
adenia s. f. (med.) adenia.
adenina s. f. (chem.) adenine.
adenite s. f. (med.) 1. adenitis. 2. (rare) inflammation of a gland.
adenóide adj. m. + f. (path.) (obs.) adenoid.
adenoma s. m. (path.) adenoma: a tumour originating in a gland.
adensamento s. m. 1. densification. 2. (archit.) stirring of concrete to make it fill out the forms.
adensar v. 1. to densify. 2. to condense, compact, thicken. 3. (Braz.) ~-se to join in a crowd, crowd together. 4. ~-se to darken, become clouded.
adentado adj. 1. toothed. 2. indented.
adentar v. (also **dentar**) 1. to tooth, provide with teeth. 2. to indent, notch.
adentrar v. 1. to enter, penetrate into. 2. to intern, confine oneself to (a place).
adentro adv. 1. inwards, inwardly, interiorly. 2. indoors.
meteu-se pelo mato ~ he made his way into the woods. **terra** ~ inland. **de portas** ~ within the house.
adepto s. m. adept, follower, adherent.
adequação s. f. (pl. **-ões**) 1. adaptation, adjustment, accommodation. 2. proportionment. 3. appropriation. 4. adequacy, fitness, suitability. 5. adequateness.
adequado adj. adequate, fit, suitable, appropriate, proper. ‖ **-amente** adv. adequately, fitly, suitably, appropriately, properly.
adequar v. 1. to adjust, adapt, accommodate. 2. to proportion. 3. to appropriate. 4. to fit, make fit, suit.
adereçamento s. m. 1. adornment, decoration. 2. the act of attiring. 3. trimming up.
adereçar (I) v. 1. to adorn, decorate. 2. to attire. 3. to trim up.
adereçar (II) v. (also **endereçar**) to address.
aderecista s. m. + f. 1. decorator. 2. (theat.) property man.

adereço (I) s. m. 1. finery, jewellery, jewelry. 2. ornaments, trimmings, decorations. 3. (theat.) properties, stage properties (plate P 2). 4. harness.
adereço (II) s. m. (also **endereço**) address.
aderência s. f. 1. adherence. 2. adhesion. 3. (fig.) agreement, consent, assent. 4. = **adesão**. 5. attachment (plate F 5). 6. (med.) accretion, adhesion, deformity.
aderente s. m. + f. adherent, follower. ‖ adj. adherent, sticking, clinging.
estar ~, **ser** ~ to adhere, stick (to).
adergar v. (coll.) 1. to happen, chance. 2. to come in handy, hit on (upon) opportunely. 3. = **adregar**.
aderir v. 1. to adhere. 2. to approve, agree. 3. to join, unite. 4. to stick to (or together). 5. to apply.
~ **ao catolicismo** to go over to Rome. ~ **a um partido** to adhere to a party. ~ **à sua opinião** to stick to one's point.
adernado adj. 1. (naut.) heeling over, careened. 2. (Braz.) upset, overturned. 3. (fig.) down, downhearted.
adernar v. 1. (naut.) to heel over, careen, have a list. 2. to tilt, incline (for pouring out).
~ **a bombordo** (**estibordo**) to heel to port (starboard).
aderno s. m. (bot.) privet.
adesão s. f. (pl. **-ões**) 1. adhesion, adherence, enrolment. 2. agreement. 3. aproval, approbation. **a sua** ~ **aos princípios** his adherence to the principles.
adesismo s. m. tendency of adapting o. s. to new situations, opportunism (esp. in politics).
adesista s. m. + f. one who easily adapts himself to a new situation, opportunist. ‖ adj. opportunistic.
adesividade s. f. adhesiveness.
adesivo s. m. (also **emplastro** ~) sticking plaster, adhesive tape or bandage. ‖ adj. adhesive, sticking, holding fast.
adestrado adj. dextrous, skilled. ‖ **-amente** adv. dextrously.
adestrador s. m. instructor, teacher, trainer, coach. ‖ adj. instructive, teaching, training, coaching.
adestramento s. m. (also **adestração** f.) instruction, teaching, training, exercise, (horse) break-in.
adestrar v. 1. to instruct, teach. 2. to train, exercise, coach. 3. to drill, (horse) break in. 4. ~-se to exercise oneself, become skilled.
adestro adj. spare, in reserve (horse).
adeus s. m. 1. good-bye, farewell, adieu. 2. end. ‖ interj. good-bye, bye-bye, farewell, adieu, so-long!
dizer ~ 1. to say good-bye. 2. to take one's leave. ~, **até a vista** good-bye, see you again. ~ **para sempre** forever. **dizer** ~ 1. to say good-bye. 2. to take one's leave. **o último** ~ the last farewell.
adeusar v. (also **endeusar**) 1. to deify. 2. (fig.) to ecstasize, enrapture.
adeusinho interj. cheerio!
adevão s. m. (pl. **-ões**) (Braz.) 1. contention. 2. fight. 3. quarrel. 4. disorder.
adiáfano adj. opaque, impenetrable to sight.
adiáforo adj. adiaphorous.
adiamantado adj. diamondlike, adamantine.
adiamantar v. to make brilliant, brighten, shine s. th.
adiamantino adj. (also **adamantino**) adamantine.
adiamento s. m. 1. adjournment, postponement, delay, procrastination. 2. failure (in an examination).
adiantado (I) adj. 1. advanced. 2. forwarded. 3. meddlesome, interfering. 4. indiscreet. 5. unpolite, inconsiderate. 6. boastful. ‖ ~ or **-amente** adv. in advance, beforehand.
~ **na idade** elderly. **dinheiro** ~ advanced money. **este homem tem-se** ~ **muito** this man has gone too far. **o menino está bem** ~ **nos estudos** the boy

is well ahead in his studies. **a obra está muito ~a** the work made considerable progress. **pagar ~ to** pay in advance, to prepay. **meu relógio está ~** my watch is fast.
adiantado (II) s. m. (hist.) governor of a province.
adiantamento s. m. 1. advancement, advancing. 2. progress. 3. improvement. 4. anticipation. 5. acceleration, speeding up. 6. advance, advance payment, loan, subsistence money.
adiantar v. 1. to advance: a) move forward. b) pay in advance. c) go in front or ahead. 2. to accelerate, speed up, hasten. 3. to credit. 4. to progress, improve. 5. to anticipate. 6. to say beforehand. 7. to help s. o. on, help to advance. 8. **~-se:** a) (Braz.) to become (too) familiar, take liberties, exceed o. s., go too far. b) (watch) to be fast, gain. **~ o cabedal** to increase one's fortune. **~ o relógio** to put the clock on. **~-se nos anos** to grow older. **isto não adianta** that is no good. **não lhe adiantaria escrever** it would not pay him to write.
adiante adv. 1. before. 2. in front, ahead (of). 3. onward(s), forward(s). 4. in the first place (instance). 5. later on. 6. farther on, further. ‖ interj. go on! **ir (passar) ~** to go on (pass on). **levar ~** to urge on. **passar ~ de** to pass (get) ahead of. **mais ~** 1. later on. 2. farther on. **como ~ indicado** as indicated (in a text) below. **veremos pelo tempo ~** we shall see it in the days to come (in the course of time).
adiapneustia s. f. (med.) adiaphoretic: preventive perspiration.
adiar v. 1. to adjourn, postpone. 2. to delay, procrastinate, while off, defer, put off. 3. to reject (an examinee). **~ a sessão** to adjourn the meeting. **ele foi adiado no exame** he failed in the examination, (sl.) he was ploughed (or plucked). **o parlamento foi adiado** the parliament is up. **o que está adiado não está acabado** forbearance is not acquittance.
adiável adj. m. + f. (pl. **-áveis**) delayable.
adição s. f. (pl. **-ões**) 1. (also **adicionamento** m., **adicionação** f.) 1. addition. 2. sum. 3. acceptance of an inheritance. 4. increase. 5. bill (in a restaurant or café). 6. postscript, supplement, appendix.
adicionado adj. 1. added. 2. increased. 3. (Braz.) ailing or injured (horse).
adicionador s. m. adder: one who adds, machine for adding. ‖ adj. adding.
adicional s. m. + f. (pl. **-ais**) extra, supplement. ‖ adj. m. + f. additional, extra, supplementary. **parágrafo ~** subsequent clause. **pagamento ~** supplemental payment. **fornecimento ~** subsequent delivery.
adicionar v. 1. to add. 2. (Braz.) to cause a chronic illness (horse).
adicionável adj. m. + f. (pl. **-áveis**) addable, addible.
adícto adj. addicted, affectionate, inclined, dedicated, devoted.
adido s. m. attaché. **~ aeronáutico** air attaché. **~ cultural** cultural attaché. **~ da imprensa** press attaché. **~ militar** military attaché. **~ naval** naval attaché.
adietar v. to diet, keep to a diet.
adimplemento s. m. performance or completion of a contract.
adimplente adj. m. + f. (jur.) duly complying with contractual obligations.
adimplir v. to comply with, perform, complete (a contract).
adinamia s. f. (med.) adynamia, atony.
adinâmico, adínamo adj. adynamic, weak, feeble.
adinheirado adj. (also **endinheirado**) well-off, well-to-do, wealthy, moneyed.

ádipe s. f., **ádipo** m. fat (of animals).
adipocera s. f. (med.) adipocere.
adipoma s. m. (med.) lipoma.
adipose s. f. (med.) adiposis, obesity.
adiposidade s. f. 1. adiposity. 2. adiposis.
adiposo adj. adipous, adipose, fatty.
adipsia s. f. adipsia: absence of thirst.
adir (I) v. to come into possession (of an inheritance).
adir (II) v. 1. to add. 2. to join. 3. to aggregate.
aditamento s. m. additament: 1. addition. 2. thing added, supplement. **em ~** in addition (to).
aditar (I) v. to make happy, bless.
aditar (II) v. 1. to add. 2. to increase. 3. to make an additament.
aditício adj. added, additional, supplemental.
aditivo s. m. (math.) minuend. ‖ adj. additive, that is to be added.
ádito s. m. 1. adit. 2. entrance. 3. approximation. 4. access, admission. 5. (hist.) secret chamber of a temple.
adivinha (I) s. f. (also **adivinhação** f.) 1. riddle, puzzle, enigma. 2. prophecy, prediction, vaticination. 3. presentiment, foreboding. **~ acertada** lucky guess.
adivinha (II) s. f. (also **adivinhadeira, adivinhadora, adivinhoa**) fortune-teller, soothsayer.
adivinhador s. m. (also **adivinhadeiro, adivinhão, adivinho**) guesser.
adivinhar v. 1. to prophecy, predict, vaticinate, foretell, soothsay. 2. to decipher, unriddle, find out, conjecture right. 3. to guess, divine. 4. to have a presentiment, forbode. **adivinhei a intenção dele** I made a guess at his purpose. **adivinhou!** guessed!
adjacência s. f. 1. adjacency. 2. neighbourhood. 3. contiguity, proximity.
adjacente adj. m. + f. 1. adjacent, adjoining. 2. neighbouring. 3. contiguous.
adjazer v. to be adjacent, contiguous, neighbouring.
adjeção s. f. (pl. **-ões**) 1. adjection. 2. addition.
adjetivação s. f. (pl. **-ões**) (also **adjetivamento** m.) 1. formation or use of adjectives. 2. qualification. 3. adaptation, conformation, concordance.
adjetivado adj. 1. formed into or used as an adjective. 2. accompanied by an adjective.
adjetival adj. m. + f. (pl. **-ais**) adjectival.
adjetivamento s. m. = **adjetivação.**
adjetivar v. 1. to qualify. 2. to accompany as an adjective. 3. to use as an adjective. 4. to adapt, conform. 5. to accord, harmonize.
adjetivo s. m. (gram.) adjective. ‖ adj. 1. (gram.) adjective. 2. (also **adjeto**) additional, added, joined.
adjudicação s. f. (pl. **-ões**) adjudication, award, decree.
adjudicador s. m. adjudicator. ‖ adj. adjudicative.
adjudicar v. 1. to adjudicate, adjudge, award. 2. **~-se** to assume, arrogate. **~ ao maior oferente** to award to the highest bidder.
adjudicatário s. m. one to whom s. th. is awarded by adjudication.
adjudicativo, adjudicatório adj. adjudicative.
adjunção s. f. (pl. **-ões**) adjunction, addition.
adjunto s. m. 1. adjunct, assistant. 2. aggregate. ‖ adj. 1. joined, annexed. 2. contiguous. 3. associated. 4. (gram.) adjunctive. **médico ~** medical assistant, assistant surgeon.
adjuração s. f. (pl. **-ões**) adjuration, adjuring.
adjurador s. m. adjurer, adjuror. ‖ adj. adjuratory.
adjurar v. 1. to adjure, entreat, ask earnestly. 2. (also **esconjurar**) to conjure, exorcise.
adjutor s. m. assistant, helper.

adjutorar v. to assist, help, aid.
adjutório s. m. 1. assistance, help, aid. 2. (med.) enema.
adjuvante adj. m. + f. assisting, assistant, helpful, adjuvant.
adligar v. (bot.) to adhere to the host by means of suckers or appendages.
adminiculante adj. m. + f. (also adminicular) 1. adminicular: assistant, helpful, subsidiary. 2. (obs.) ornamental (medals).
adminicular v. to give aid, assist, further.
adminículo s. m. adminicle: 1. assistance, help. 2. support, protection. 3. subsidiary. 4. (law) corroborative or explanatory proof. 5. (obs.) an ornament surrounding the figure on a coin or medal.
administração s. f. (pl. -ões) administration: 1. management, government. 2. direction, control. 3. directorship, person or persons who control or manage, executive(s). 4. administration office, head office. 5. giving out, applying, application (medicine). 6. ministration (sacraments).
~ das alfândegas board of customs. ~ das finanças exchequer. ~ de trânsito transit administration. ~ do aeroporto airport authorities. ~ das estradas de ferro railway board.
administrador s. m. administrator, manager, executive, director. ‖ adj. administrative, executive, managerial.
~ de fazenda manager of an estate, farm bailiff. ~ gerente managing director.
administradora s. f. administratress.
administrante adj. m. + f. administrant.
administrar v. to administer: 1. manage, direct, conduct, control. 2. (med.) dispense. 3. supply, apply, give. 4. govern, administrate.
~ remédios to give medicine to s. o. ~ uma propriedade to manage an estate.
administrativista s. m. specialist in administrative law.
administrativo adj. administrative. ‖ -amente adv. administratively.
admirabilidade s. f. admirableness.
admiração s. f. (pl. -ões) 1. admiration. 2. strangeness, wonder, wondering. 3. surprise, astonishment. 4. fright, shock.
isto não me causa ~ that does not astonish me. ponto de ~ exclamation mark. ela causava ~ a todos she commanded everybody's admiration.
admirado adj. 1. admired. 2. astonished, amazed, surprised.
admirador s. m. 1. admirer. 2. lover. ‖ adj. admiring.
admirando adj. admirable: worth admiring.
admirar v. 1. to admire. 2. to esteem, appreciate. 3. to cause admiration or strangeness. 4. to surprise, astonish. 5. ~se to wonder, be surprised, astonished, perplexed.
não é de ~ it is not astonishing. não me admiro de I am quite unamazed. não devíamos ~-nos se ... we should not wonder if ... não é de ~ se ... it is not to be wondered at if ... não é de ~ que no wonder that. eu não me admiro disso I do not wonder at it. ele se admira de você não ter escrito he wonders (that) you have not written. é de ~ it's a wonder.
admirativo adj. admiring, demanding admiration, feeling admiration. ‖ -amente adv. admiringly.
admirável adj. m. + f. (pl. -áveis) admirable: 1. wonderful, excellent. 2. worth admiring.
~ mundo novo wonderful new world.
admissão s. f. 1. admission: a) admittance. b) (tech.) inlet, intake (plate E 10). 2. (Braz.) preparatory course for the admission to the gymnasium.
~ máxima (tech.) maximum cut-off. curso de ~

preparatory course for the gymnasium. exame de ~ entrance examination. jóia de ~ (U. S. A.) initiation fee. livre ~ open door. sua ~ como sócio do clube his admission to the club. tubo de ~ (mot.) induction manifold.
admissibilidade s. f. admissibility.
admissível adj. m. + f. (pl. -íveis) admissible.
carga ~ (tech.) permissible load. tolerância ~ (tech.) permissible tolerance.
admistão s. f. (pl. -ões) admixture, mixture.
admitido adj. 1. admitted. 2. esteemed, regarded. 3. accepted. 4. permitted.
ele foi ~ como advogado no foro he was called to the bar.
admitir v. 1. to admit. 2. to let in. 3. to adopt. 4. to acknowledge. 5. to accept. 6. to receive. 7. to agree. 8. to allow, permit, tolerate, concede. 9. to confess. 10. to have room for.
~ em casa to take into one's house. ~ demora to admit of delay. ~ um empregado to engage an employee. eu o admito I acknowledge it. admito a sua razão quanto a isto I allow that you are right in that. não admito que se faça uma coisa dessas I won't stand for it, I won't have it, I can't let a thing like that happen. não posso ~ a idéia I cannot entertain the idea. é preciso ~ que it must be owned that.
admoestação s. f. (pl. -ões) 1. admonition, reproof, reprehension. 2. monition, warning.
admoestador s. m. admonisher, reprover, warner. ‖ adj. admonitory, reproving, reprehensive, warning.
admoestar v. to admonish, reprove, reprehend, reprimand, warn.
admoestatório adj. admonitory, admonitive, reprehensive.
admonição s. f. (pl. -ões) admonition, warning, reprehension.
admonitor s. m. 1. admonisher. 2. Jesuit novice. ‖ adj. admonitory, reprehensive.
admonitório s. m. = admoestação. ‖ adj. admonitory.
adnata s. f. (anat.) adnata.
adnominação s. f. (pl. -ões) (gram.) paronymy.
adnominal adj. m. + f. (pl. -ais) paronomastic, referring to similarity of words in different languages.
adnotação s. f. (pl. -ões) 1. annotation. 2. (R. C. Church) rescript: pontifical reply to a petition by simply signing it.
adnumeração s. f. (pl. -ões) (obs.) enumeration.
adnumerar v. (obs.) to enumerate.
ado s. m. (Braz.) toasted maize seasoned with oil from the fruit of the African oil palm (dendê).
adoba s. f. (ant.) cuff, shackle.
adobar v. to make adobes (sun-dried bricks).
adobe (I) s. m. (also adoba) adobe: sun-dried brick.
adobe (II) s. m. (Port., prov.) = adubo.
adoçado adj. sweetened, sugared, smoothed over.
adoçamento s. m. 1. sweetening. 2. softening, relief. 3. (archit): a) cannelure. b) concave mouldings of an architrave.
adoçante s. m. assuaging medicament. ‖ adj. m + f. sweetening.
adoção s. f. (pl. -ões) adoption.
adoçar v. 1. to sweeten. 2. to soften, assuage, attenuate. 3. to facilitate. 4. to smooth.
~ a boca de alguém to butter a p. up. ~ as cores to soften the colours. ~ a pílula to sugar the pill.
adocicado adj. sweetened, sweetish.
adocicar v. 1. to sweeten. 2. to soften, assuage, attenuate. 3. to become mellifluous. 4. to denote or show affectation.
~ as palavras to flute.
adoecer v. 1. to become (or fall) sick or ill, be taken ill, sicken. 2. to make sick.

adoecido adj. sick, ill.
adoecimento s. m. falling ill.
adoentado adj. indisposed, sickish, sickly, ailing.
estar (ou andar) ~ to be ailing, (fam.) be out of sorts.
adoentar v. to sicken: make or become sickish, ailing.
adoestar v. (also **doestar**) to insult, offend, affront.
adoidado adj. (also **adoudado, adoidarrado, adoudarrado**) 1. heedless, rash, foolish, inconsiderate, imprudent. 2. crazy, mad.
adoidar v. (also **adoudar**) to madden, make or become crazy.
adolescência s. f. adolescence, adolescency.
adolescente s. m. + f. adolescent. ‖ adj. adolescent, youthful, juvenile.
adolescer v. to adolesce, advance from childhood to maturity.
adomado adj. (coll.) 1. tamed, domesticated. 2. habituated, accustomed. 3. resigned.
adomar-se v. (Braz., coll.) 1. to get used (or accustomed) to. 2. to resign, submit quietly.
adomingado adj. Sundaylike.
adomingar-se v. to put on Sunday clothes.
adonar-se v. (Braz.) to appropriate s. th. by astuteness or unfair means.
adonde adv. (ant. or pop.) = **aonde, onde.** ‖ (Braz.) interj. why! impossible! out of question!
adônico, adônio adj. adonic (verse).
Adônis s. m. 1. (myth.) Adonis. 2. very beautiful young man. 3. dandy, beau, fop. 4. (bot.) Adonis, pheasant's eye.
adonisar v. 1. to make dandylike, foppish. 2. to embellish, decorate. 3. ~-**se** to become dandylike, foppish, embellished.
a-do-ó s. f. (pl. **as-do-ó**) (Braz., sl.) liquor, rum.
adoperar v. 1. to employ, use. 2. to manufacture.
adoração s. f. (pl. **-ões**) 1. adoration, veneration, worship, devotion. 2. devoted love.
é a minha ~ it is one and all with me. **ele tem grande** ~ **por sua arte** he worships his art.
adorado (I) adj. 1. adored, venerated, worshipped. 2. beloved.
adorado (II) adj. (obs.) 1. ailing, sick. 2. hurtful.
adorador s. m. 1. adorer, worshipper. 2. lover. ‖ adj. adoring, worshipping.
adorar v. 1. to adore, venerate, worship. 2. to love (or like) extremely.
~ **a Deus** to worship God. **eu adoro chocolate** (coll.) I simply adore chocolate.
adorativo adj. adorable, adorant, adoring.
adorável adj. m. + f. (pl. **-áveis**) 1. adorable. 2. charming, enchanting. ‖ **-avelmente** adv. adorably, charmingly.
adorbital s. m. (pl. **-ais**) (anat.) adorbital. ‖ adj. m. + f. adorbital.
adormecedor s. m. soporific. ‖ adj. that causes sleep, soporific.
adormecer v. (also **adormentar, adormir**) 1. to put to sleep, lull asleep. 2. to fall asleep, to nod off. 3. to soothe, assuage. 4. to stop moving. 5. (fig.) to be careless.
estar adormecido to be asleep.
adormecido adj. (also **adormido**). 1. asleep. 2. careless, negligent.
completamente ~ dead asleep, fast asleep. **a bela adormecida** the sleeping beauty.
adormecimento s. m. 1. falling asleep. 2. drowsiness. 3. numbness. 4. (fig.) negligence, carelessness.
adormentador s. m. = **adormecedor.** ‖ adj. 1. = **adormecedor.** 2. causing numbness. 3. quieting.

adormentar v. 1. to fall asleep, make sleep. 2. to anesthetize. 3. to cease action, lose conciousness.
adornado adj. adorned. ‖ **-amente** adv. adornedly.
adornamento s. m. 1. adornment. 2. (also **adorno**) ornament.
adornar v. 1. to adorn, attire, dress, array, embellish, ornament, deck. 2. to garnish. 3. ~-**se** to adorn o. s.
adorno s. m. adornment, attire, ornament, decking, decoration, embellishment. 2. garnishment.
adotante adj. m. + f. adoptive, adopting.
adotar v. 1. to adopt. 2. to accept. 3. to use. 4. to resolve. 5. to follow, embrace. 6. to affiliate.
~ **como base** to take (or accept) as a basis. ~ **medidas enérgicas** to take energetic steps (measures), to take strong line. ~ **uma criança** to adopt a child. ~ **medidas de precaução** to take precautions.
adotável adj. m. + f. (pl. **-áveis**) adoptable.
adotivo adj. adoptive.
pai, filho ~ adoptive father, son.
adoutrinar v. (also **doutrinar**) to indoctrinate.
adquirente s. m. + f. acquirer. ‖ adj. acquiring.
adquirição s. f. (pl. **-ões**) (also **aquisição**) acquirement, acquisiton.
adquirido adj. acquired, purchased, taken possession of.
adquiridor s. m. acquirer. ‖ adj. acquiring.
adquiridos s. m. pl. properties obtained through marriage.
adquirir v. 1. to acquire. 2. to get, obtain. 3. to come into possession of. 4. to attain. 5. to contract, catch.
~ **altura** (aeron.) to get height. ~ **reputação** to become renowned. ~ **velocidade** to gain speed. ~ **um nome, fama** to get a good name, (coll.) come to the front. ~ **uma doença** to catch a disease. ~ **força de lei** to become law, pass into law. ~ **prática (no serviço)** to work oneself into. **adquira bons hábitos enquanto for jovem** form good habits while you are young.
adquirível adj. m. + f. (pl. **-íveis**) acquirable.
adquisição s. f. = **aquisição.**
adrede adv. purposely, intentionally.
adregar v. 1. to chance, happen by chance, coincide. 2. to come much to the purpose. 3. to meet by chance.
adrenalina s. f. (pharm.) adrenalin.
adriático adj. Adriatic: of or referring to the Adriatic Sea and its surroundings.
adriça s. f. (also **driça**) halyard, halliard.
a meia ~ at half-mast, (U. S. A.) at half-staff.
adriçar v. to raise by means of a halyard.
adro s. m. churchyard.
ad-rogação s. f. (pl. **-ões**) adoption, affiliation.
ad-rogar v. to adopt, affiliate.
adscrever v. 1. to add (in writing), make a postscript. 2. to register, inscribe.
adscrição s. f. (pl. **-ões**) addition to something written, postscript.
adscriticio adj. (also **adstrito**, hist.) adscript: attached to the soil (said of a serf).
adsorção s. f. (chem., phys.) adsorption: fixing of the molecules of a substance on the surface of another substance.
adsorvente adj. (chem., phys.) adsorbent, capable of adsorbing.
adsorver v. (chem., phys.) to adsorb.
adstrição s. f. (pl. **-ões**) 1. (also med.) astriction, contraction (stomach). 2. action of an astringent.
adstringência s. f. (med.) astringency.
adstringente s. m. (also med. **adstringitivo, adstringivo, adstritivo**) astringent. ‖ adj. m. + f. astringent.

adstringir v. 1. (also med.) to astringe. 2. to compel, coerce, constrain, 3. to limit, confine.

adstrito adj. 1. (also med.) astricted. 2. tight. 3. contracted. ~ **a** dependent on.

adua s. f. 1. pack of hounds. 2. (hist.) calling to war. 3. (hist.) obligatory work (repairing castles etc.). 4. compulsory enlistment. 5. running, rushing. 6. herd. 7. tax for exemption of compulsory enlistment. 8. sharing of irrigation water among neighbours (also **aduagem**). 9. work tax.

aduana s. f. 1. (also **alfândega**) custom-house. 2. customs, custom-duties. 3. Christian quarter in a Moorish country.

aduanar. v. to clear (at a custom-house).

aduaneiro s. m. tidewaiter, custom-house officer. ‖ adj. of or referring to customs or to the custom--house.

aduar (I) v. to share irrigation water among neighbours.

aduar (II) s. m. Moorish encampment.

adubação s. f. (pl. -ões) (also **adubagem**) 1. manuring, fertilization. 2. seasoning.

adubador s. m. manurer. ‖ adj. manuring.

adubar v. 1. to season, flavour. 2. to tan, dress. 3. to repair (ships). 4. (agric.) to manure, fertilize. 5. to decorate, embellish (report, story).

adubo s. m. (also but obs. **adúbio**) 1. seasoning, seasoner, flavouring. 2. spices, condiment. 3. manure, fertilizer, compost. 4. dressing (material). ~ **artificial** artificial fertilizer. ~ **animal** manure of animal origin. ~ **composto** mixed manure, compost. ~ **para correias** (tech.) belt composition. ~ **vegetal** vegetable manure.

adução s. f. (pl. -ões) adduction. ~ **de água** delivery of the water. ~ **dos fios** leading in of the wires. ~ **por carro e cremalheira** (tech.) rack carriage feed.

aduchas s. f. pl. coils of a cable.

aducir v. to make (metals) flexible.

aduela s. f. 1. stave (of a barrel) (plate B 4). 2. (archit.) intrados. 3. a sort of clapboard. 4. opening of the gun worm. **ter uma ~ a menos** to be crazy, have a screw loose.

aduelagem s. f. (pl. -ens) making or applying staves, intrados or clapboards.

adufa s. f. 1. lattice. 2. dam, weir. 3. flood-gate, sluice, penstock. 4. crusher in an olive oil press.

adufada s. f. beat of the timbrel.

adufar (I) v. to provide with lattices.

adufar (II) v. to beat the timbrel.

adufe s. m. (also **adufo**) timbrel (square-formed).·

adufeiro s. m. 1. manufacture of (square-formed) timbrels. 2. timbrel-player.

adufo s. m. adobe: sun-dried brick.

adulação s. f. (pl. -ões) 1. flattery, coaxing, adulation. 2. cajolery. 3. wheedling, cringing, fawning.

adulador s. m. (also **adulão, aduloso**) 1. flatterer, coaxer, adulator. 2. cajoler, fawner, toady. ‖ adj. (also **aduloso**) flattering, coaxing, cajoling, fawning, cringing. ~ **servil** servile flatterer, (U.S.A., sl.) apple polisher.

adular v. 1. to flatter, coax, adulate. 2. to cajole. 3. to wheedle, cringe, fawn. ~ **servilmente** to polish apples.

adulária s. f. (geol.) adularia: a variety of orthoclase, e. g. moonstone.

adulativo, adulatório adj. adulatory, flattering.

adulçorar v. (also **adoçar**) 1. to sweeten. 2. to soften, attenuate.

aduloso s. m. + adj. = **adulador**.

adúltera s. f. adulteress.

adulteração s. f. (pl. -ões) 1. adulteration, falsification. 2. corruption.

adulterado adj. 1. adulterated, falsified. 2. corrupt. **ele apresentou um relatório ~** he gave a garbled account.

adulterador s. m. 1. adulterator, falsifier. 2. corrupter. 3. adulterer. ‖ adj. 1. adulterating, falsifying. 2. corrupting. 3. adulterous.

adulterar v. 1. to adulterate, falsify. 2. to corrupt. 3. to counterfeit. 4. to commit adultery.

adulterinidade s. f. spuriousness, illegitimacy.

adulterino adj. 1. adulterine, spurious. 2. falsified, counterfeit.

adultério s. m. adultery.

adulterioso, adulteroso adj. adulterous.

adúltero s. m. adulterer. ‖ adj. 1. adulterous. 2. adulterated, falsified.

adulteroso adj. 1. adulterine, illegitimate. 2. of or involving adultery. 3. prone to adultery.

adulto s. m. adult, grown-up person. ‖ adj. adult, grown-up.

adumbrar v. 1. to adumbrate. 2. to shadow. 2. to sketch, outline. 4. to foreshadow. 5. to symbolize. 6. to cloud, darken.

adunação s. f. (pl. -ões) (also **adunamento** m.) 1. assemblage, union. 2. incorporation. 3. congregation. 4. subordination.

adunar v. 1. to assemble, join. 2. to incorporate. 3. to congregate. 4. to subordinate.

aduncar v. to crook, bend, curve.

aduncidade s. f. crookedness, crooked shape.

aduncirrostro adj. unciform, hook-shaped.

adunco adj. crooked, bent, curved, unciform.

adurar v. (obs. and coll. = **durar**) to last, hold out.

adurência s. f. 1. causticity. 2. piquancy, burning taste.

adurente s. m. (med.) caustic. ‖ adj. m. + f. (also **adustivo**) caustic, burning.

adurir v. (med.) to apply cauteries, cauterize.

adustão s. f. (pl. -ões) 1. cauterization 2. scorching.

adustível. m. + f. (pl. -íveis) (also **combustível**) combustible.

adusto adj. 1. adust, scorched. 2. ardent, fiery, hot.

adutor s. m. 1. adducer, exposer. 2. water main. 3. (anat.) adductor. ‖ adj. expository, adducible.

aduzir v. 1. to adduce, expose, show, bring forward. 2. to conduct, bring or lead to. ~ **escapatórias** to allege evasions (or empty excuses). ~ **razões** to allege motives.

adveniente adj. m. + f. 1. coming after. 2. happened. 3. added.

adventício s. m. (also **ádvena**) 1. foreigner, stranger, alien. 2. intruder. ‖ adj. 1. alien, foreign, extraneous. 2. casual, accidental, eventual.

adventismo s. m. Adventism.

adventista s. m. + f. Adventist.

advento s. m. 1. coming, arrival, approach. 2. institution. 3. beginning. 4. Advent: the season before Christmas.

adverbial adj. m. + f. (pl. -ais) (gram.) adverbial. ‖ ~**mente** adv. adverbially.

adverbialidade s. f. (gram.) adverbial quality.

adverbializar v. (gram.) to adverbialize, change into an adverb.

adverbiar v. (gram.) to use or employ adverbially.

advérbio s. m. (gram.) adverb.

adversão s. f. (pl. -ões). 1. opposition. 2. warning.

adversar v. 1. to oppose, counteract. 2. to contest, fight against.

adversário s. m. 1. adversary, opponent, antagonist. 2. enemy. ‖ adj. 1. adverse, opposing, antagonistic. 2. inimical.

adversativo adj. 1. (gram.) adversative. 2. opposite. **conjunção adversativa** adversative conjunction.

adversidade s. f. adversity, misfortune, distress, ill--luck.
as ~s da vida fret and fume of life.

adverso adj. 1. adverse, contrary, opposed. 2. unhappy, unlucky.
lances ~s da fortuna adverse fate. **ser ~ a** to be against. **sorte adversa** ill-luck.

advertência s. f. (also **advertimento**) 1. warning. 2. rebuke, admonition, censure. 3. remark, reference. 4. caution, care.
ele fez um sinal de ~ com o dedo he wagged his finger (at a p.). **que isto sirva de ~ para você** let this be a warning to you.

advertido adj. 1. attentive, watchful. 2. cautious. 3. discreet, judicious. 4. warned, advised. ‖ **-amente** adv. 1. attentively. 2. cautiously. 3. judiciously. 4. knowingly.
mal ~ rash, inconsiderate.

advertimento s. m. admonition, warning.

advertir v. 1. to warn, give notice, caution, advise. 2. to admonish, rebuke.
advirto-lhe que... I warn you that. **ela o advertiu de que seria melhor não fazê-lo** she warned him better not to do it. **advertimo-lo em tempo** we gave him fair warning of it.

advincular adj. m. + f. 1. dependent. 2. connected, linked.

advindo p. p. of **advir**.

advir v. 1. to happen, come upon, befall, occur. 2. to follow, succeed, supervene. 3. to add, increase.

advocacia s. f. (also **advocatura, advogacia**) advocacy, advocateship, attorneyship.

advocatório adj. = **avocatório**.

advogado s. m. 1. advocate, lawyer, barrister. 2. attorney. 3. (depr.) limb of the law. 4. (Scottish) writer to the signet. 5. protector, patron, intercessor. **~ de defesa** the counsel for the defence. **~ substituto** outer barrister.

advogar v. 1. to act as a lawyer. 2. to plead a cause (at court). 3. to defend. 4. to patronize. 5. to advocate. 6. to intercede.
~ no Foro to be at the bar. **ele advogou que** he took the view that. **ele advogou a importação de trigo** he advocated the importation of wheat.

aedo s. m. 1. (hist.) Greek popular singer. 2. poet.

aeração, aragem s. f. (pl. **-ões, -ens**) aeration, airing, ventilation.

aeremoto s. m. = **aeromoto**.

aerênquima s. m. (bot.) aerenchyma.

aéreo adj. 1. aerial. 2. living in the air. 3. airlike. 4. of or pertaining to the air. 5. air-borne. 6. imaginary. 7. relating to aircraft. 8. vain. 9. futile, trifling.
estar ~ to be in the clouds. **ataque ~** air raid. **guerra aérea** war in the air, aerial warfare. **por via aérea** by air, by airmail. **navegação aérea** air navigation.

aeríola adj. m. + f. living in the air.

aerífero adj. aeriferous, air-conducting.

aerificação s. f. (pl. **-ões**) (also **aerização**) aerification.

aerificar v. (also **aerizar**) to aerify.

aeriforme adj. m.+ f. aeriform, gaseous, gasiform.

aerívoro adj. feeding on air.

aerização s. f. (pl. **-ões**) aerification.

aerizar v. to aerify.

aerobata, aeróbata s. m. + f. person who performs aerobatics.

aeróbio s. m. an aerobic organism. ‖ adj. aerobic.

aeroclube s. m. aeroclub.

aerocolia s. f. (med.) intestinal tumefaction.

aerodinâmica s. f. aerodynamics.

aerodinâmico adj. aerodynamic, aerodynamical.

aeródromo s. m. aerodrome, airdrome, airport, airfield.
~ civil civil aerodrome. **~ marítimo** water aerodrome. **~ flutuante** floating air base.

aeroduto s. m. vent or air-duct.

aeroespacial adj. m. + f. aerospacial, aerospatial.

aeroelasticidade s. f. (phys.) aeroelasticity.

aerofagia s. f. (med.) aerophagy.

aerófago s. m. aerophagist.

aerófano adj. diaphanous.

aerófito adj. (also **epífito**, bot.) epiphytic, epiphytous.

aerofobia s. f. aerophobia.

aerófobo s. m. aerophobe. ‖ adj. aerophobe.

aerofone s. m. (also **aerofono**) 1. (mus.) steam organ. 2. air communications phone.

aerofotografia s. f. aerial photography.

aerofotogrametria s. f. aerophotogrammetry.

aerofotogramétrico adj. aerophotogrammetric.

aerognosia s. f. aerognosy.

aerognóstico adj. aerologic, aerological.

aerografia s. f. aerography.

aerográfico adj. aerographic.

aerógrafo s. m. 1. aerographer. 2. (graphic arts) airbrush, spraying apparatus.

aerograma s. m. (also **radiograma**) aerogram, radiogram (message).

aeróide adj. m. + f. airlike.

aerólito s. m. (also **meteorólito**) 1. aerolite, aerolith. 2. meteorite. 3. shooting star.

aerologia s. f. aerology.

aerológico adj. aerologic, aerological.

aeromancia s. f. aeromancy.

aeromante s. m. + f. aeromancer.

aeromântico adj. aeromantic.

aerometria s. f. aerometry.

aerométrico adj. aerometric.

aerômetro s. m. aerometer.

aeromoço s. m. flight steward (f. **aeromoça** flight stewardess).

aeromodelismo s. m. model aeronautics.

aeromodelo s. m. model aircraft.

aeromoto s. m. 1. violent air shock. 2. storm, thunderstorm.

aeronauta s. m. + f. aeronaut; balloonist.

aeronáutica s. f. 1. aeronautics. 2. aviation.

aeronáutico adj. aeronautical.

aeronave s. f. aircraft, airship (plate A 3).

aeroplano s. m. airplane (plate A 3).
~ propulsor pusher airplane. **~ trator** tractor airplane.

aeroporto s. m. airport.
~ civil civil airport. **~ comercial** commercial airport.

aeroposta s. f. air mail.

aeroscópio s. m. aeroscope.

aerosfera s. f. atmosphere.

aerossol s. m. (pl. **-óis**) aerosol: 1. (chem., phys.) a coloidal solution. 2. a liquid substance under pressure in a container, to be used by spraying. 3. the container.

aerostação s. f. aerostation.

aeróstata s. m. + f. (air)balloonist.

aerostática s. f. aerostatics.

aerostático adj. aerostatic, aerostatical.

aeróstato s. m. airship, balloon.
~ cativo captive balloon, (sl.) sausage, blimp, kite balloon. **~ livre** free balloon.

aerotecnia s. f. technical aeronautics.

aerotécnico adj. aerotechnical.

aerotelúrico adj. referring to air currents and other aerial phenomena.

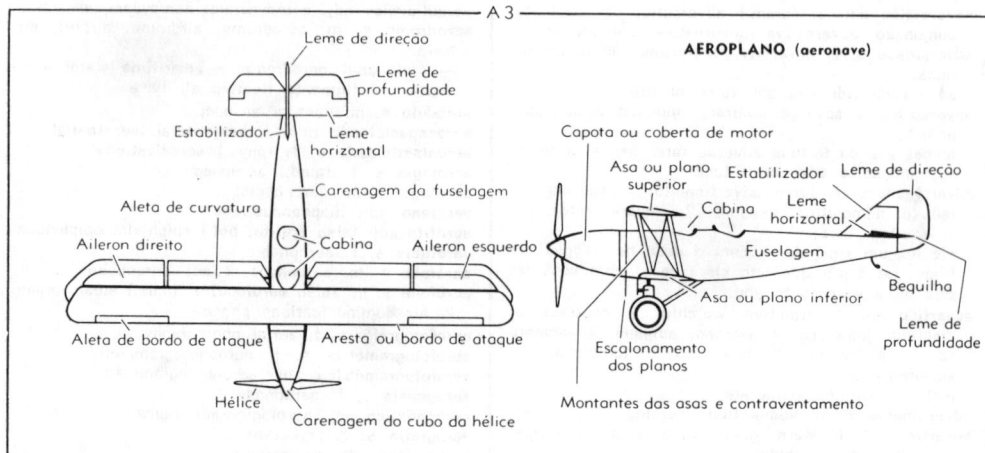

——————————— A 3 ———————————

Leme de direção
Leme de profundidade
Estabilizador
Leme horizontal
Carenagem da fuselagem
Aleta de curvatura
Aileron direito
Cabina
Aileron esquerdo
Aleta de bordo de ataque
Aresta ou bordo de ataque
Hélice
Carenagem do cubo da hélice

AEROPLANO (aeronave)
Capota ou coberta de motor
Asa ou plano superior
Estabilizador
Leme de direção
Cabina
Leme horizontal
Fuselagem
Bequilha
Asa ou plano inferior
Leme de profundidade
Escalonamento dos planos
Montantes das asas e contraventamento

aeroterapêutica s. f. aerotherapeutics, aerotherapy.
aeroterrestre adj. m. + f. air-ground.
aerotransportado adj. airborne, transported by air.
aerotransportadora s. f. air transport company.
aerotransportar v. to transport by air.
aerotransporte s. m. transportation by air.
aerotropismo s. m. aerotropism.
aerovia s. f. airway.
aeroviário s. m. person employed in the air service. ‖ adj. of or referring to air service or transport.
aerozoário s. m. 1. animal that needs air to live. 2. (zool.) vertebrate.
afã s. m. 1. anxiety, eager desire, eagerness. 2. solicitude. 3. great care. 4. great effort, toil. 5. ado. com ~ strenuously.
afabilidade s. f. affability, affableness, politeness, kindness, gentleness, courtesy.
afacia s. f. (med.) aphacia, aphakia.
afadigador s. m. tiresome person or thing. ‖ adj. tiring.
afadigar v. 1. to tire, fatigue. 2. to pursue, chase. 3. to worry, vex, bore, tease. 4. ~-se to tire o. s., toil and moil.
afadigoso adj. 1. tiring. fatiguing. 2. pursuing. 3. vexing. boring. 4. toilsome, laborious.
afadistado adj. ruffianlike, rough, violent.
afadistar v. to become a ruffian, behave like a ruffian, be rough, violent.
afagador s. m. caresser, fondler, flatterer. ‖ adj. (also **afagante** m. + f.) caressing, fondling.
afagamento s. m. caressing, comforting, fondling.
afagar v. 1. to caress, fondle, pet, comfort, stroke. 2. to nourish, cherish (ideal), think of with pleasure. 3. to smooth, pare, cut off or even.
afago s. m. 1. caress, allurement. 2. friendly reception.
afagoso adj. 1. amiable, affable. 2. flattering.
afaimado adj. (also **esfomeado**) hungry, famishing.
afaimar v. to starve, famish.
afalado adj. said of animals that obey when spoken to.
afalar v. to speak to animals to make them work.
afalcoado adj. falconlike.
afalcoar v. (fig.) to instigate.
afaluado adj. (Braz.) 1. hasty. 2. tired. 3. laborious. 4. very busy. 5. breathless.
afamado adj. 1. famous. 2. notable, remarkable. 3. distinguished. 4. celebrated. 5. notorious, ill-

-famed. ‖ **-amente** adv. remarkably, notoriously. **mal** ~ ill-famed, ill-reputed.
afamar v. 1. to fame, make famous or renowned. 2. to obtain fame, become famous. 3. ~-se to win a high reputation.
afamilhado adj. 1. prolific, blessed with many children. 2 (Braz.) having a family. 3. married. 4. living in concubinage.
afamilhar-se v. (Braz.) 1. to have many children. 2. to form a large family.
afanar v. 1. to strive (for, after). 2. to obtain laboriously. 3. (Braz., coll.) to pilfer, steal. 4. to work hard, toil. 5. to tire, get tired. 6. ~-se (em) to labour (at a th.)
afandangado adj. like a fandango.
afano s. m. 1. fetching, getting. 2. pilfering. 3. hard work, toil. 4. = **afã**.
afanoso adj. 1. toilsome. 2. laborious. 3. anxious, eager.
afaquear v. (also **esfaquear**) to knife, stab.
afarar-se v. to find the scent (dog), to be on the scent.
afasia s. f. (med., also **afemia**) 1. aphasia: loss of speech. 2. word-blindness.
afásico adj. (med.) aphasiac, aphasic.
afastado adj. 1. remote, distant, far off. 2. apart (plate Q). 3. removed. 4. secluded. 5. retired. ‖ **-amente** adv. 1. secludedly, retiredly, 2. (U.S.A., coll.) away back.
~ **da cidade** down from town. ~ **do caminho** off (from) the road. ~ **do serviço** 1. retired from work. 2. temporarily suspended from the service. **estar** ~ **to be out of things. manter-se** ~ **de** (fig.) to steer clear of. **ele manteve-se** ~ he made himself scarce, **muito** ~ far off. **parente** ~ a distant relative. **no ponto mais** ~ at farthest, at the farthest. **primo** ~ far-away cousin.
afastador s. m. remover ‖ adj. removing.
afastamento s. m. 1. removal, dismissal. 2. seclusion, retirement. 3. separation. 4. distance, remoteness. 5. spacing.
~ **angular** angular pitch. ~ **dos pólos de um campo** field pitch. ~ **polar** polar pitch. ~ **das rodas** wheel-gauge.
afastar v. 1. to remove, separate. 2. to dismiss. 3. to repel, reject. 4. to deviate, avert. 5. to withdraw. 6. to retire, seclude.
~ **(barco) da costa** (naut.) to shove off. ~ **uma suspeita** to remove a suspicion. ~-**se** to stand back.

~-se de (naut.) to stand off from. ele afastou as dificuldades he smoothed away the difficulties. ele afastou-se numa fúria he went away enraged, he flung away in a rage. ele afastou-se de nossa companhia he withdrew himself from our company. eles afastaram-no, liquidaram-no (mataram-no) they put him out of the way (killed him). nós nos afastamos we removed ourselves.

afatiar v. 1. to slice. 2. to slash, gash.

afavecos s. m. (Braz.) 1. clothes in use. 2. travelling preparations.

afável adj. m. + f. (pl. -áveis) 1. affable, civil, polite, courteous. 2. complaisant, pleasant-spoken, fair-spoken.

afaxinar v. to clean, cleanse.

afazendado adj. landed, owing much land.

afazendar-se v. 1. to acquire much land, become a landowner. 2. to become rich.

afazer v. 1. to habituate. 2. to accustom. 3. ~-se to habituate o. s. to or get accustomed to.

afazeres s. m. pl. (also quefazer, quefazeres) work, business, occupation, affairs.

afeamento s. m. 1. misrepresentation. 2. disfigurement, defacement.

afear v. (also desfear, enfear) 1. to disfigure, deface, mar. 2. to misrepresent, exaggerate.

~ a reputação de alguém to mar someone's reputation.

afecção, afeção s. f. (pl. -ões) (med.) 1. affection. 2. disease.

afegã, afegane s. m. + f. (also afegão m.) Afghan. || adj. (also afegânico) Afghan.

afeição s. f. (pl. -ões) (also afeto) affection, love, friendly feeling, inclination.

tomar ~ por to become fond of.

afeiçoado s. m. friend, lover, amateur, enthusiast, fan. || adj. affectionate, loving, enthusiastic, adept, given to. || -amente adv. affectionately, enthusiastically.

um ~ de boa leitura a friend of good reading. sou-lhe sinceramente ~ I am sincerely attached to him.

afeiçoador s. m. shaper, fashioner, former. || adj. shaping, forming.

afeiçoamento s. m. endearment, affection, inclination.

afeiçoar (I) v. 1. to shape, form, mould, fashion. 2. to adapt, make appropriate.

afeiçoar (II) v. 1. to captivate, charm. 2. ~-se to take a fancy to, love, feel inclined towards. ~-se por to take kindly to.

afeito (I) adj. accustomed to, habituated, used to.

afeito (II) s. m. (obs.) = afeto.

afelear v. to embitter, add bitterness to.

afélio s. m. (astr.) aphelion.

afemia s. f. (med.) aphasia, loss of speech.

afeminação s. f. (also efeminação) effeminacy.

afeminado adj. (also efeminado) effeminate.

afeminar v. (also efeminar) to make or become effeminate.

aferente adj. m. + f. afferent.

aférese s. f. (gram.) aphaeresis.

aferético adj. (gram.) aphaeretic.

aferição s. f. (pl. -ões) (also aferimento) 1. gauging, calibrating. 2. checking, collation. 3. confrontation, comparison. 4. standardization. 5. indication of gauging, calibrating.

aferido s. m. mill-race. || adj. 1. gauged, calibrated. 2. checked, collated, standardized.

aferidor s. m. 1. gauger. 2. standard (of weights and measures). 3. surveyor of weights and measures. || adj. gauging, calibrating.

aferir v. 1. to gauge, calibrate. 2. to check, collate. 3. to confront, compare. 4. to standardize.

rate. 6. to show or indicate that the gauging, calibrating etc. has been done.

aferível adj. m. + f. (pl. -íveis) gaugeable.

aferrado adj. insistent, persistent, pertinacious, obstinate, stubborn. || -amente adv. insistently, obstinately, stubbornly.

aferrar v. 1. to graple, lay hold of, hold fast, grip, grasp. 2. to anchor. 3. to harpoon. 4. to concentrate on. 5. to persist in, insist on. 6. to hold or stick fast to.

aferretoador s. m. (also aferroador) brander. || adj. branding.

aferretoar v. (also aferroar) 1. to sting, prick. 2. to spur. 3. (fig.) to incite.

aferro s. m. 1. attachment, concentration. 2. assiduity, tenacity. 3. obstinacy, stubbornness.

aferroar v. = aferretoar.

aferrolhador s. m. 1. jailer: person who shuts up or imprisons. 2. hoarder.

aferrolhar v. (also ferrolhar) 1. to bolt (up.) 2. to imprison. 3. to shut up, keep carefully. 4. to hoard.

aferventação s. f. (pl. -ões) 1. parboiling, half-boiling. 2. (Braz.) speed up. 3. (coll.) excitement. 4. restlessness.

aferventado s. m. (Braz.) meat or fish boiled with vegetables and potatoes. || adj. 1. parboiled, half-boiled. 2. (Braz.) impatient, restless.

aferventar v. 1. to parboil. 2. (Braz., pop.) to hasten. 3. ~-se (N. Braz.) to become excited.

afervorar v. 1. to inflame, fill with enthusiasm. 2. to stimulate. 3. to effervesce. 4. ~-se to be zealous. 5. to fly into a passion.

afervorizar v. to fill with enthusiasm, inflame.

afestoado adj. festooned.

afestoar v. 1. to festoon. 2. to garland.

afetação s. f. (pl. -ões) 1. affectation. 2. affection (of an organ). 3. pedantism. 4. presumption. 5. vanity. 6. finicalness.

afetado adj. 1. affected: a) unnatural. b) sick. 2. presumptive. 3. vain, conceited. || -amente adv. affectedly.

conversa afetada stilted conversation. falar afetadamente to talk tall.

afetante adj. m. + f. affecting.

afetar v. to affect: 1. pretend to have or feel, feign, simulate. 2. attack (as a disease). 3. behave or act presumptively.

afetividade s. f. affectivity, capacity to be affective, affection, tenderness.

afetivo adj. 1. affective. 2. dedicated, devoted.

afeto s. m. 1. = afeição. 2. friendship. 3. sympathy. 4. passion. || adj. 1. affectionate 2. friendly. 3. charged or entrusted with. 4. submitted to. 5. pending.

afetuoso adj. affectionate, kind, affable, complaisant.

afiação s. f. (pl. -ões) (also afiamento) 1. sharpening, whetting (said also of animals' teeth or claws). grinding. 2. vexation, irritation. 3. improvement, perfection.

afiado adj. 1. sharpened, whetted. 2. sharp (plate Q). 3. sharp-edged.

~ contra alguém irritated about, angry with. bem ~ sharp-ground.

afiador s. m. grinder: person or thing that grinds.

afiambrado adj. 1. high and thin (said of the heel of a shoe). 2. excessively affected in dressing, foppish. 3. (Braz.) prepared with or like ham.

afiambrar v. 1. (Braz.) to prepare meat like ham. 2. ~-se to dress in an excessively affected manner.

afiançado s. m. warrantee. || adj. 1. warranted, bailed. 2. guaranteed. 3. assured.

afiançador s. m. warranter, bailsman. || adj. 1. warrating, bailing. 2. assuring.

afiançar v. 1. to warrant, bail, guarantee. 2. to answer for, be responsible for. 3. to assure, asseverate. 4. to find sureties, stand security.

afiar v. 1. to sharpen, whet (said also of animals' teeth and claws), grind (plate C 16). 2. to vex, irritate. 3. to improve, perfect.
~ **a língua** to be about to abuse somebody. ~ **com alguém** to attack someone. **pedra de** ~ grindstone.

aficionado s. m. = **afeiçoado**.

afidalgado adj. 1. distinguished, noble. 2. peered, raised to nobility. 3. not used to work.

afidalgamento s. m. 1. raising to nobility. 2. nobility. 3. nobleness.

afidalgar v. 1. to raise to nobility. 2. to give the appearance of nobility. 3. ~-**se**: a) to become a noble. b) to lose the habit of work.

afidio s. m. (zool.) aphid; plant-louse.

afiguração s. f. (pl. -**ões**) 1. representation, configuration. 2. imagination, supposition. 3. whim, fancy.

afigurar v. 1. to figure, represent. 2. to imagine. 3. to seem, appear.
ele é um homem bem afigurado he is a good-looking chap (man).

afigurativo adj. figurative.

afilado adj. 1. gauged, calibrated, standardized. 2. delicate, fine. 3. thin. 4. tapered, pointed. 5. set (dogs).

afilador s. m. 1. surveyor of weights and measures. 2. person who sets on dogs. 3. person who or thing that tapers.

afilamento s. m. 1. gauging, calibration, standardization. 2. setting on of dogs. 3. tapering.

afilar (I) v. (also **aferir**) to gauge, calibrate, standardize.

afilar (II) v. 1. to taper, make pointed. 2. to sharpen. 3. (naut.) to turn windwards. 4. ~-**se** to taper off.

afilar (III) v. to set on dogs.

afilhada s. f. god-daughter.

afilhadagem s. f. (pl. -**ens**) protection.

afilhadismo s. m. nepotism.

afilhado s. m. 1. godson. 2. protégé.

afilhar (I) v. 1. to produce offspring. 2. to bud, germinate.

afilhar (II) v. (also **afilar**) to set on dogs.

afiliação s. f. (pl. -**ões**) 1. affiliation. 2. connection.

afiliar v. to affiliate, incorporate, join.

afilo adj. (bot.) leafless.

afim s. m. (pl. -**ins**) kinsman, kinswoman, relative. ‖ adj. m. + f. similar, alike.

afinação s. f. (pl. -**ões**) (also **afinamento**) 1. refinement, improvement, finishing touch. 2. (mus.): a) tuning. b) sound, tone. 3. refining (metals). 4. offense. 5. irritation. 6. tapering.

afinado adj. 1. (mus.) tuned in or up, in tune. 2. finished. 3. fined, refined. 4. irritated, vexed. 5. (Braz.) combined, joined, conjoined.

afinagem s. f. refining (metals).

afinal adv. finally, at last, after all.
~ **de contas** after all.

afinar v. 1. to fine, make fine. 2. to refine. 3. to taper. 4. to tune in or up, put in tune. 5 to offend, vex. 6. to agree, harmonize. 7. ~-**se**: a) to become fine or thin. b) to taper off.

afincado adj. 1. persistent, tenacious. 2. persevering. ‖ -**amente** adv. persistently, perseveringly, stubbornly.
olhar -amente to stare at.

afincamento s. m. (also **afinco**) 1. attachment, assiduity, tenacity. 2. insistence. 3. obstinacy, stubbornness.

afincar v. 1. to drive in (like a stake). 2. to stick stubbornly to. 3. to insist. 4. to spit, pierce.

afinco s. m. attachment, assiduity, tenacity.

afinidade s. f. affinity: 1. relation. 2. relationship. 3. degree of attraction. 4. resemblance, likeness. 5. conformity. 6. (biol., chem.) attractive force.
~ **eletiva** elective affinity. **parentes por** ~ in-laws.

afirmação s. f. (pl. -**ões**) affirmation, assertion.
uma ~ **confirmada por fatos** a claim fortified by facts.

afirmador s. m. (also **afirmante** m. + f.) affirmer. ‖ adj. affirmative.

afirmar v. 1. to affirm, asseverate, maintain, assert. 2. to say. 3. to confirm, ratify. 4. to prove. 5. to firm, make firm, fasten, fix. 6. to look closely.
~ **com juramento** to confirm with an oath. **afirmo-lhe que** I can tell you. ~-**se de alguma coisa** to make oneself sure of a thing.

afirmativa s. f. affirmative.

afirmativo adj. affirmative. ‖ -**amente** adv. affirmatively.

afirmável adj. m. + f. (pl. -**áveis**) affirmable.

afistulado adj. fistulous.

afistular-(se) v. to grow into a fistula, become fistulous.

afitamento s. m. 1. infantile indigestion, diarrhea. 2. (Braz.) act of casting an evil eye.

afitar (I) v. (also **enfitar**) to ribbon, adorn with ribbons.

afitar (II) v. (also **fitar**) to look at closely, gaze at.

afitar (III) v. 1. (obs.) to cause diarrhea. 2. (Braz.) to cast an evil eye at.

afito s. m. 1. indigestion. 2. diarrhea. 3. (Braz.) evil eye.

afivelado, adj. buckled.

afivelar v. 1. to buckle, hold or fasten with a buckle. 2. to hold, fasten.

afixação s. f. (pl. -**ões**) 1. affixture. 2. (gram.) the use of affixes.

afixar v. 1. to fix, fasten, make firm or fast. 2. to post, fasten (a notice) where it can be seen.

afixo s. m. (gram.) affix.

aflamengado adj. Flemish, after the Flemish fashion.

aflante adj. m. + f. 1. breathing. 2. breathless, panting. 3. puffing.

aflar v. 1. to breathe. 2. to blow, puff. 3. (fig.) to inspire. 4. to move in the wind.

aflato s. m. 1. blowing, puff of air. 2. breath. 3. respiration.

aflautado adj. 1. flutelike (in tone or shape). 2. shrill.

aflautar v. 1. to shape like a flute. 2. to sound like a flute.

aflechado adj. (also **afrechado**) 1. arrowlike. 2. wounded by an arrow.

aflechar v. (also **afrechar**) 1. to shape like an arrow. 2. to wound with an arrow.

afleimar-(se) v. (also **afreimar-se, afuleimar-se**) 1. to become impacient, bored, vexed. 2. to quarrel.

afleumar v. 1. to make phlegmatic, dull. 2. (Braz.) to inflame, become sore or swollen. 3. to form an abscess.

aflição s. f. (pl. -**ões**) 1. affliction, trouble, grief, anguish, distress. 2. agony, anxiety, torment.
~ **espiritual** anguish of mind.

afligidor s. m. afflicter. ‖ adj. (also **aflitivo**) afflicting.

afligimento s. m. affliction: act or fact of afflicting.

afligir v. 1. to afflict, trouble, distress, grieve. 2. to torment. 3. to devastate, ravage. 4. ~-**se** to be afflicted.
a consciência o afligiu his conscience smote him. **não se aflija por isso** don't worry about it. **que te aflige?** what's on your mind?

aflitivo adj. (also afligente, afligidor) afflicting, af flictive, grievous.

aflito adj. afflicted, distressed, grieved, worried, sick at heart.

deixar alguém ~ to keep s. o. on tenterhooks.

aflogístico adj. aphlogistic, flameless, burning without flame.

afloração s. f. (pl. -ões) (also afloramento m.) 1. levelling. 2. emergence. 3. showup, appearance. 4. outcrop.

aflorar v. 1. to level, bring to the same level. 2. to emerge. 3. to show up, appear. 4. to crop out.

afluência s. f. 1. affluence. 2. abundance, copiousness. 3. concourse, crowd. 4. confluence, conflux. ~ de palavras fluidity of expression.

afluente s. m. tributary (stream). ‖ adj. m. + f. 1. affluent, confluent. 2. tributary (stream).

afluir v. 1. to flow to, flow in, stream towards. 2. to flock, pour or crowd in. 3. to abound.

o sangue afluiu-lhe ao rosto the blood flushed to her cheeks.

afluxo s. m. 1. afflux (also med.). 2. affluence.

afobação s. f. (pl. -ões) (Braz., also afobamento m.) 1. hurry, bustle, haste. 2. embarrassment. 3. fatigue.

afobado adj. (Braz., also acafobado) 1. very busy, in a haste. 2. embarrassed. 3. tired, fatigued.

afobar v. (Braz.) 1. to hurry, bustle. 2. to embarrass.

afocinhamento s. m. 1. blow or stroke with the snout. 2. rooting or digging with the snout. 3. fall on the nose. 4. (fig.) dive.

afocinhar v. 1. to strike at with the snout. 2. to root, dig with the snout. 3. to fall on the nose. 4. (fig.) to dive. 5. to succumb.

afofado adj. 1. disaggregate. 2. spongy. 3. (fig.) vainglorious.

afofamento s. m. 1. disaggregation. 2. sponginess. 3. vainglory.

afofar v. 1. to disaggregate. 2. to make spongy. 3. to make proud, puff up.

afogadela s. f. 1. (also afogadilho) haste, hurry, precipitation. 2. suffocation, asphyxia.

afogadiço adj. 1. susceptible to suffocation. 2. suffocating. 3. stifling, airless.

afogadilho s. m. 1. haste, hurry. 2. precipitation.

obra feita de ~ thing done in haste.

afogado s. m. a drowned person. ‖ adj. 1. drowned. 2. asphyxiated. 3. watered, soaked. 4. suffocated, stifled. 5. high-necked (dress).

morrer ~ to be drowned.

afogador s. m. 1. choker (person or thing). 2. necklace, collar. 3. (mot.) throttle. ‖ adj. suffocating, stifling.

afogadura s. f., afogamento s. m. 1. drowning. 2. suffocation.

afogar v. 1. to suffocate, asphyxiate. 2. to stifle. 3. to check or hinder the development. 4. to submerge. 5. to drown. 6. to soak, imbibe. 7. to overflow, inundate. 8. to forget. 9. (mot.) to throttle.

afogo s. m. 1. suffocation. 2. affliction, trouble. 3. oppression. 4. haste, speed. 5. culmination, auge.

afogueado adj. 1. submitted or exposed to great heat. 2. cooked or baked very much. 3. inflamed. 4. ardent. 5. affronted.

afogueamento s. m. 1. heating. 2. burning. 3. blushing. 4. animation.

afoguear v. 1. to heat, submit to great heat or fire. 2. to burn. 3. to blush or flush, make blush or flush. 4. to animate, excite. 5. to get animated or excited.

afoiçado adj. (also afouçado) scythelike.

afoitar v. (also afoutar) 1. to encourage, animate, make bold. 2. to incite. 3. ~-se to venture, dare, affront.

afoiteza s. f. (also afouteza) 1. courage, fearlessness. 2. intrepidity, audacity, affrontery.

afoito adj. (also afouto, valentão) 1. fearless, courageous. 2. bold, daring.

afolar s. m. (also folar) easter gift or present. ‖ v. to bellow: blow air (in a fire) with a bellows.

afolhado adj. 1. submitted to crop rotation. 2. rubricated and numbered (book).

afolhamento s. m. (also rotação f.) rotation of crops.

afolhar s. m. rotation of crops. ‖ v. 1. to rotate (crops). 2. to leaf, to shoot out leaves.

afonia s. f. aphonia, loss of voice.

afônico, áfono, afono adj. aphonic, voiceless.

afora adv. 1. except. 2. save. 3. excepting, with exception of. 4. besides.

aforador s. m. leaser: person who gives or takes a lease on.

aforamento s. m. (also aforação f.) act or fact of leasing: taking or giving a lease.

aforar (I) v. 1. to lease: give or take a lease on. 2. to grant certain privileges. 3. ~-se to arrogate to o. s.

aforar (II) v. (Braz.) to except, exclude.

aforçurado adj. 1. hasty. 2. rushed.

aforçuramento s. m. 1. hastiness, speediness. 2. haste, speed.

aforçurar v. 1. to make haste, speed up. 2. ~-se to be overhasty, act precipitately.

aforia s. f. (path.) 1. aplasia, defective development of an organ or tissue. 2. sterility, impotence, agenesis.

aforismático adj. aphoristic.

aforismo s. m. aphorism, maxim.

aforista s. m. + f. aphorist.

aforístico adj. aphoristic.

aformoseador s. m. beautifier, embellisher. ‖ adj. beautifying, embellishing.

aformoseamento s. m. 1. beautification, embellishment. 2. ornamentation.

aformosear, aformosentar v. (also formosear) 1. to beautify, embellish. 2. to adorn, decorate, ornament. 3. ~-se to beautify, adorn o. s.

aforquilhado adj. forked.

aforquilhar v. to fork: 1. shape or form like a fork. 2. divide into branches. 3. hold with a fork.

aforrado adj. 1. free, cleared. 2. hasty, speedy.

aforramento s. m. 1. lining (providing with an inside layer). 2. padding, stuffing. 3. turning or tucking up (sleeve). 4. clearance, clearing. 5. saving, putting aside. 6. buying of freedom (slave).

aforrar v. 1. to line, put a layer inside of. 2. to pad, stuff. 3. to turn or tuck up. 4. to free, clear. 5. to save, put aside. 6. to take off the coat or jacket. 7. to obtain or buy the freedom.

aforro s. m. 1. = aforramento. 2. economizing, economy.

afortalezado adj. fortified, provided with castles.

afortalezamento s. m. 1. fortification, a fortified place. 2. a providing with forts or fortified places.

afortalezar v. 1. to provide with forts or fortified places, fortify. 2. to build like a fort. 3. to confirm. 4. ~-se: a) to get strength. b) to protect o. s.

afortunar v. 1. to make happy or lucky. 2. to enrich.

afracar v. = enfraquecer to weaken.

afrancesado adj. 1. Frenchified, after the French style or manner. 2. (coll.) disloyal, false.

afrancesar v. 1. to Frenchify. 2. to acquire French manners.

afrasia s. f. 1. (path.) aphrasia. 2. dumbness, speechlessness.

afrechado adj. = **aflechado.**

afrechar v. = **aflechar.**

afreguesado adj. 1. having customers. 2. rather frequented, sought after. 3. prospering (shop). **uma loja bem -a** a well frequented shop.

afreguesar v. 1. to get a customer, make a customer of. 2. ~-**se:** a) to become a customer. b) to agree.

afrentar v. 1. = **enfrentar.** 2. to confine. 3. to vex, exasperate. 4. ~-**se** to become afflicted, distressed.

afrescalhado adj. (Braz., sl.) effeminate, prissy.

afresco (ê) s. m. (also **fresco**) fresco (painting).

afretamento s. m. chartering, charter party.

afretar v. (also **fretar**) to freight, charter.

áfrica s. f. feat, deed, prowess.
julgou ter feito uma grande ~ he thought he had done a great deed. **meter uma lança em África** to do something extraordinary.

africanas s. f. pl. golden ear-rings (similar to those used by the Africans).

africânder s. m. + f. Afrikaner: a white South African native.

africâner s. m. Afrikaans, Cape Dutch, Taal: the language of the Afrikaners.

africanismo s. m. 1. Africanism. 2. word of African origin.

africanista s. m. + f. 1. Africanist. 2. explorer of Africa or person who travels in Africa.

africanizar v. to Africanize.

africano s. m. 1. African: native of or person living in Africa. ‖ adj. African.

africanologia s. f. study about Africa or the Africans.

africanologista s. m. + f., **africanólogo** s. m. person who studies Africa or the Africans.

áfrico s. m. 1. African: inhabitant of Africa. 2. southeastern wind. ‖ adj. (also **afro, africano**) African.

afrodisia s. f. aphrodisia.

afrodisíaco s. m. aphrodisiac. ‖ adj. aphrodisiac.

afrodita s. f. (bot.) cryptogam. ‖ adj. m. + f. cryptogamic.

afro-negro adj. (pl. **afro-negros**) of or referring to African Negroes.

afronta s. f. affront, insult, offence, reviling, violence, injury, assault.

afrontação s. f. (pl. **-ões**) dyspnea, shortness of breath.

afrontado adj. 1. affronted, insulted, offended. 2. suffocated. 3. importuned, annoyed. 4. tired, exhausted. 5. panting, gasping. 6. = **abombado.**

afrontador s. m. 1. affronter, insulter, offender. 2. importuner, annoyer. 3. person who or thing that tires or exhausts. ‖ adj. 1. affronting. 2. importunate.

afrontamento s. m. 1. affront, insult, offence. 2. suffocation, stifling. 3. annoyance. 4. exhaustion. 5. pant, puff, hard breath. 6. confrontation (of witnesses).

afrontar v. 1. to affront, insult, offend. 2. to suffocate, stifle. 3. to importune, annoy, vex. 4. to tire, exhaust. 5. to pant, gasp. 6. = **abombar.** 7. to confront (witnesses). 8. to face (danger).

afrontoso adj. 1. offensive, insulting, ignominious, abusive. 2. stifling, suffocating.

afrouxamento s. m. (also less used **afroixamento**) 1. slackening. 2. loosening. 3. relaxing. 4. release. 5. widening. 6. moderation.

afrouxar v. (also less used **afroixar**) 1. to slacken, relax. 2. to loosen. 3. to release. 4. to slow down. 5. to widen. 6. to make or become faint-hearted. 7. to discourage. 8. to moderate, diminish. 9. (Braz.): a) to augment the grazing grounds. b) to let the cattle run free. 10. to lose strength, weaken. 11. to ease off or up.

afrouxelado adj. (also less used **afroixelado**) 1. downed, covered with down. 2. soft.

afrouxelar v. (also less used **afroixelar**) 1. to soften, give a downlike softness to. 2. to down, cover with down.

afrutado adj. fruited, bearing fruit, fruitful.

afrutar v. to bear fruit, fruit.

afta s. f. aphtha, thrush.

aftoso adj. aphthous.

afuazado adj. (Braz.) 1. frightened, scared. 2. angry, vexed.

afugentador s. m. chaser. ‖ adj. 1. chasing. 2. removing. 3. repelling.

afugentamento s. m. 1. chase, chasing away. 2. removal. 3. repellence.

afugentar v. 1. to chase away, put to flight, scare away. 2. to repel, reject. 3. to frighten.

afuleimação s. f. (pl. **-ões**) (Braz.) quarrel, altercation.

afuleimado adj. (Braz., also **valentão**) quarrelsome.

afuleimar-se v. = **afleimar-se.**

afumado adj. (also **defumado, esfumado**) 1. smoked: a) smoke-dried. b) smoke-stained. 2. darkened.

afumadura s. f. 1. smoking, smoke-drying. 2. darkening.

afumar v. (also **defumar, esfumar**) 1. to smoke, smoke-dry. 2. to get a smoky taste. 3. to darken. 4. (obs.) to cultivate and live on a land.

afundado adj. 1. sunk, submerged. 2. excavated, deepened, lowered. 3. sad, discouraged, depressed, afflicted.

afundamento s. m. 1. sinking. 2. depression, low place.

afundar v. 1. (~-**se**) to sink. 2. to founder, go under, submerge. 3. to deepen. 4. to examine thoroughly. 5. to dig or hollow out. 6. to disappear, get lost. 7. (Braz.) to repeat over and over. 8. (fig.) to swim like a rock.

afundir v. 1. to sink, go under, submerge. 2. to disappear, vanish.

afunilado adj. funnelled, funnel-shaped, infundibuliform.

afunilar v. 1. to shape like a funnel. 2. to narrow. 3. ~-**se** to take the shape of a funnel.

afurá s. m. (Braz.) a refreshment made of fermented rice.

afuroado adj. 1. ferreted, hunted with ferrets. 2. searched carefully.

afuroador s. m. 1. person who hunts with ferrets. 2. searcher, investigator.

afuroar v. to ferret: 1. hunt with ferrets. 2. search, investigate, find out.

afusado adj. spindle-shaped.

afusal s. m. (pl. **-ais**) quantity woven with one spindle of thread.

afusão s. m. (pl. **-ões**) affusion: 1. pouring liquid upon (baptism). 2. (med.) pouring water or other liquid upon, as a form of treatment.

afusar v. 1. to shape like a spindle. 2. to thin. 3. to taper.

afustuado adj. shafted.

afutricar v. (Braz.) 1. to patch, make hastily or badly. 2. to pester, vex. 3. to cheapen.

afuzilar (v. (less used form of **fuzilar**) to shoot down.

agachada s. f. (Braz.) 1. assault, sudden attack. 2. a slowing down (said of a running animal). 3. provocation to start a discussion on a disagreeable subject. 4. joke. 5. enterprise, venture, feat, prowess.

agachados s. m. pl. (Braz.) 1. reverences. 2. courtesies. 3. flattering. ‖ **agachado** adj. 1. crouched, squatted, cowered. 2. humiliated.

agachamento s. m. 1. crouching, squatting, cowering. 2. humiliation. 3. surrender, giving in. 4. (Braz.) start, beginning.

agachar-se v. 1. to crouch, squat, cower. 2. to humiliate o. s. 3. to surrender. 4. (Braz.) to start, begin. 5. to lie low.

agacho s. m. crouch.

agadanhado adj. (also **agatanhado**) 1. clawed, scratched. 2. like an iron rake.

agadanhador s. m. 1. scratcher: person who or thing that scratches. 2. raker. 3. pilferer.

agadanhar v. 1. to rake. 2. (also **agatanhar**) to scratch, claw. 3. to pilfer.

agafanhar v. 1. to gaff, spear. 2. (also **agatanhar**) to claw, scratch).

agafita s. f. (min.) agaphite, oriental turquoise.

agaiatado adj. 1. naughty, mischievous. 2. roguish.

agaiatar-se v. to behave naughtily, mischievously, boyishly or roguishly.

agaitado adj. like a mouth-organ or reed in shape or tune.

agalactação, agalactia s. f. (med. + vet.) agalactia.

agaláctico adj. (med. + vet.) agalactic, relative to nonlactation in mammals.

agalanado adj. (also **engalanado**) adorned, trimmed, embellished.

agalonar v. (also **engalanar**) to adorn, trim, embellish.

agalegado adj. impolite, uncivil, rustic, rude, ill-bred.

agalegar(-se) v. to make (or become) uncivil, impolite, rustic or ill-bred.

agalgar v. 1. to grow similar to a greyhound. 2. to grind with a mill-stone.

agalhado adj. branched, that has branches.

agalhar v. to branch, put out branches.

agalhas s. f. pl. (Braz.) 1. knavery, trickery, deceit. 2. bragging, boasting.

agalhudo adj. 1. diligent, hard-working. 2. strong, hardy. 3. audacious, daring.

agalinhar-se v. (Braz., coll.) 1. to humiliate o. s. 2. to bow, shrink back, act cowardly. 3. to be (too) easygoing (said of women in regard to men).

agaloado s. m. lacing. || adj. laced.

agaloadura s. m. lacing: 1. trimming, braid. 2. act or fact of braiding, lacing.

agaloar v. (also **galonar**) to lace, braid.

ágamo s. m. (zool.) agama. || adj. (bot.) agamous.

agamogênese s. f. (biol.) agamogenesis.

agapanto s. m. (bot.) African lily, African tulip, loveflower.

ágape s. m. agape: 1. love-feast common among the early Christians. 2. banquet.

agapeta s. f. (hist.) agapetae: among the early Christians, virgins who lived in community, without vows.

agareno s. m. 1. (bib.) descendant of Agar. 2. Ismaelite. 3. Arab. || adj. 1. Ismaelitish. 2. Arab, Arabian.

agaricácea s. f. (bot.) Agaricaceae: any of the gill fungy.

agaricáceo adj. (bot.) agaricaceous.

agárico s. m. (bot.) agaric.

agarnachar v. to gown, invest with a gown.

agarotado adj. 1. naughty, mischievous. 2. troublesome, turbulent. 3. boyish.

agarotar-se v. to become boyish.

agarração s. f. (pl. -ões) seizing, holding, catching.

agarrotadeiras s. f. pl. saliency made under the hoof of a horse to avoid sliding.

agarradiço adj. 1. clinging. 2. adhesive, adherent. 3. adhering, clinging to.

agarrado s. m. (Braz.) ravine, gulch. || adj. 1. stingy, avaricious, miserly. 2. caught, held firmly or tightly. 3. clinging or sticking to.

ser ~ a alguém to be an inseparable friend of, to stick to.

agarrador s. m. 1. catcher, seizer. 2. (Braz.) horseman who maintains himself firmly in the saddle on a bucking horse. || adj. catching, seizing.

agarramento s. m. 1. seizing, holding, catching. 2. stinginess, miserliness, avariciousness. 3. close relation, constant keeping or sticking together.

agarranado adj. (Braz.) 1. like a pony. 2. knavish, dishonest, roguish.

agarrante adj. m. + f. 1. catching, seizing, holding. 2. (her.) said of a bird holding its prey.

agarrar v. 1. to catch, seize. 2. to clasp, grasp, grip, tighten on. 3. to lay hold of. 4. to hold (firmly). 5. to take. 6. to come to or take a decision. **~ e segurar firmemente** to lay fast. **~-se com unhas e dentes** to stick obstinately to. **ele agarrou e partiu** he made up his mind to leave and did so. **ele agarrou a idéia** he snapped at the idea.

agarrochar v. 1. to wound with a goad. 2. to goad, incite, urge on. 3. to torment, afflict.

agarrotar v. (also **garrotar**) to garrote, strangle.

agarruchado adj. tightened (packsaddle).

agarruchar v. to tighten, firm.

agarrunchar v. (naut.) to make fast by means of cringles.

agasalhadeiro adj. (also **agasalhador**) 1. hospitable, serviceable, obliging, kind. 2. sheltering.

agasalhado adj. 1. sheltered, covered. 2. lodged. 3. cosy, comfortable. 4. stifling.

agasalhador s. m. shelterer, host, entertainer. || adj. (also **agasalhadeiro**) 1. hospitable, obliging, kind. 2. sheltering.

agasalhar v. 1. to shelter, give shelter to, lodge, house. 2. to warm. 3. to protect. 4. to receive kindly. 5. **~-se**: a) to retire. b) to keep o. s. warm, snuggle up. c) to shelter, take shelter. **agasalhei-me bem** I wrapped myself up.

agasalho s. m. 1. shelter. 2. kind reception, welcome, hospitality. 3. lodging. 4. warm clothing.

agastadiço adj. 1. irritable. 2. irascible.

agastado adj. 1. irritated, vexed. 2. bored, annoyed. 3. sorrowful, distressed.

agastamento s. m. 1. annoyance. 2. irritation, vexation, anger. 3. offense. 4. rage, infuriation.

agastar v. 1. to annoy. 2. to irritate, vex, anger. 3. **~-se**: a) to take offense, feel hurt. b) enrage, infuriate.

agastria s. f. 1. (med.) congenital or surgical absence of the stomach. 2. (zool.) absence of vestiges of the intestinal duct.

agástrico adj. agastric.

agastura s. f. 1. indisposition. 2. want of or desire for food.

ágata s. f. agate.

agatanhado adj. clawed, scratched.

agatanhadura s. f., **agatanhamento** m. scratching, clawing.

agatanhar v. 1. to scratch, claw, hurt with the claws. 2. **~-se** to scratch o. s., hurt o. s. by scratching.

agateado adj. (Braz.) 1. catlike (colour of the eyes). 2. blueish.

agáteo adj. striped like an agate.

agatífero adj. containing agate.

agatinhar v. to climb with difficulties.

agatóide adj. m. + f. 1. benign. 2. good-natured.

agatunado adj. 1. thievish. 2. good-natured.

agaturrar v. (Braz.) 1. to seize, catch, hold. 2. to capture, arrest.

agauchado adj. (Braz.) Gaucholike.

agauchar-se v. (Braz.) to acquire Gaucho habits.

agave s. f. (bot.) agave.

agavelar v. (also **engavelar**) to bind in sheaves, bundle.

agazuado adj. like a picklock's tool.

agência s. f. 1. agency. 2. activity, action. 3. exertion, diligency, industriousness. 4. an agent's commission. 5. business office. 6. branch office. 7. way of living. ~ **bancária** bank agency. ~ **funerária** funeral parlour. ~ **de empregos** employment agency. ~ **de informação** intelligence office, information bureau. ~ **de navegação** shipping office. ~ **de publicidade** advertising agency.

agenciação s. f. (pl. **-ões**) business or activity of an agent or agency.

agenciadeira s. f. procuress. ‖ adj. diligent, industrious, hard-working.

agenciador s. m. 1. agent, representative. 2. negotiator, mediator. ‖ adj. 1. carrying on the activity or business of an agency or agent. 2. active, hard-working, diligent, zealous.

agenciar v. 1. to negotiate. 2. to work as an agent or representative. 3. to further. 4. to exert o. s., be diligent. 5. to try hard to find or obtain.

agencioso adj. active, diligent, zealous.

agenda s. f. agenda, notebook.

agenesia s. f. (med.) agenesia.

agenésico adj. (med.) agenesic.

agente s. m. + f. agent. ‖ adj. m. + f. agent, acting. ~ **de câmbios** stock-broker. ~ **de conservação de alimentos** food-preservative. ~ **de seguros marítimos** underwriter. ~ **marítimo** shipping agent.

agerasia s. f. (med.) agerasia.

agermanar v. 1. († **~-se**) to fraternize. 2. to make equal. 3. to associate, join, unite.

ageusia, ageustia s. f. (med.) ageusia, ageustia: loss of taste.

agigantado adj. 1. enormous, gigantic. 2. herculeous. ‖ **-amente** adv. gigantically.

agigantamento s. m. gigantic increase or propositionment, assumption of enormousness.

agigantar v. 1. to give gigantic proportions to, make gigantic. 2. to enlarge greatly, augment enormously, assume gigantic proportions.

ágil adj. m. + f. (pl. **-eis**) 1. agile, nimble, quick. 2. quick on the pins, light-foot, light-footed, light-heeled. ‖ **agilmente** adv. 1. nimbly. 2. light-footedly.

agilidade s. f. 1. agility, nimbleness, quickness, liveliness, vivacity. 2. light-footedness.

ágio s. m. (com.) agio.

agiota s. m. + f. 1. jobber, stock-jobber. 2. usurer, money-lender, loan-shark. 3. egoist. ‖ adj. 1. jobbing. 2. usurious.

agiotagem s. f. 1. (com.) agiotage, stock-jobbing. 2. usury: lending of money at an unlawful rate of interest.

agiotar v. 1. (com.): a) to job, work as a stock-jobber. b) to advance with an agio. 2. to speculate.

agir v. 1. (also jur.) to act, proceed. 2. to act as an agent. 3. to operate. 4. to take action. ~ **com cautela** to play safe. ~ **de acordo com** to act up to. ~ **corretamente** 1. to play fair. 2. to play the game. ~ **para com (uma pessoa)** to act by. ~ **sobre** 1. to tell on. 2. to strike on. **ele agiu no momento oportuno** he stepped in just in time. **aja com delicadeza** act gently, apply a soft pedal.

agirafado adj. like a giraffe (tall and slender).

agironado adj. (her.) provided with triangles.

agitação s. f. (pl. **-ões**) (also **agitamento** m.) 1. agitation. 2. perturbation, trouble. 3. conflict. 4. insurrection. 5. discussion.

agitadiço adj. easily agitated, agitable.

agitado adj. 1. agitated, excited. 2. perturbated, confused, bewildered. 3. troubled, disquieted. 4. turbulent. ‖ **-amente** adv. 1. excitedly. 2. confusedly. 3. turbulently. **mar** ~ rough sea. **meu sangue estava** ~ my blood was up. **tempos** **~s** stirring times.

agitador s. m. agitator. ‖ adj. agitating.

agitante adj. m. + f. agitating.

agitar v. 1. to agitate. 2. to shake (up). 3. to shock. 4. to excite, disturb. 5. to move, touch. 6. to perturb, disconcert. 7. to discuss violently. 8. to riot, revolt, rebel. 9. to give rise to. 10. to bring into discussion. 11. **~-se** to be anxious.

agitável adj. m. +f. (pl. **-áveis**) 1. agitable. 2. excitable.

aglaia s. f. plant of the family Meliaceae.

áglifo s. m. (zool.) aglyphodont, snake of the family Colubridae. ‖ adj. of or referring to this snake.

aglomeração s. f. (pl. **-ões**) 1. agglomeration, gathering. 2. mass, heap.

aglomerado s. m. 1. artificial marble made of stone and cement. 2. mortar of cement and road metal. 3. (geol.) agglomerate. ‖ adj. 1. agglomerated. 2. massed up, heaped.

aglomerante adj. m. + f. agglomerative.

aglomerar v. 1. to agglomerate. 2. to accumulate. 3. to join, assemble.

aglomerato s. m. (geol.) agglomerate: heterogeneous rock of volcanic origin.

aglosso adj. 1. tongueless. 2. barbarous (speaking).

aglutição s. f. (med.) aphagia, aglutition.

aglutinação s. f. (pl. **-ões**) (also **aglutinamento** m.) agglutination.

aglutinado adj. (also bot.) agglutinated.

aglutinante adj. m. + f. (also bot.) agglutinant.

aglutinar v. 1. to agglutinate. 2. to unite, join (also phil.). 3. to glue together.

aglutinativo adj. (also **aglutinante**) agglutinative (also phil.).

aglutinável adj. m. + f. (pl. **-áveis**) agglutinative.

aglutinidade s. f. agglutinability.

agnação s. f. (pl. **-ões**) (also **agnatia**) agnation.

agnado s. m. (also **agnato**) agnate.

agnatício, agnático adj. agnatic.

ágnatos s. m. pl. agnates.

agnelina s. f. 1. agneline. 2. lamb's wool.

agnome s. m. 1. agnomen. 2. nickname.

agnominação s. f. (pl. **-ões**) agnomination.

agnosticismo s. m. agnosticism.

agnóstico adj. agnostic.

ágnus-dei s. m. (pl. **ágnus-deis**) a wax medallion stamped with the figure of a lamb, representative of Christ, blessed by the Pope and worn as a protection against evils and danger.

agogô (s. m. (Braz.) musical instrument of African origin.

agoirar, agoiro, etc. = **agourar, agouro,** etc.

agolpear v. = **golpear.**

agomar v. to bud, germinate.

agomia s. f. 1. simitar, scimitar. 2. dagger.

agomiada s. f. a stroke or slash with a scimitar.

agomil s. m. old form of **gomil**: jug.

agomilado adj. juglike.

agonais s. f. pl. (hist.) Roman festivity to honour Janus.

agonfíase, agonfose s. f. (med.) agomphiasis: looseness of the teeth.

agongorado adj. bombastic (style).

agongorar v. to write in a bombastic style.

agonia s. f. (also **agoniação**) 1. agony. 2. pangs of death. 3. extreme anguish, grief, trouble, suffering. 4. nausea, disgust. 5. (Braz.) haste, hurry. **nas vascas da** ~ in death-struggle.

agoniadina s. f. (chem.) agoniadin, plumieride.
agoniado adj. 1. agonizing. 2. uneasy. 3. anxious. 4. distressed, afflicted.
sinto-me ~ I feel ill.
agoniador adj. 1. that causes agony. 2. distressing.
agoniar v. 1. to agonize. 2. to afflict, distress, worry. 3. to nauseate, sicken. 4. to disgust. 5. to be or feel uneasy.
agoniei-me I feel (felt) ill.
agônico adj. (med.) agonizing, of or referring to agony.
agonística s. f. agonistics.
agonístico adj. agonistic.
agonizado adj. agonized, agonizing.
agonizante s. m. + f. agonizing, dying person. ‖ adj. agonizing, dying.
agonizar v. 1. to agonize. 2. to afflict, distress, worry, penalize. 3. to struggle with death, be dying. 4. to come to an end.
ágono adj. agonic.
agonóteta s. m. (hist.) agonotheta.
agora adv. 1. now, at the present time, by this time. 2. however. ‖ conj. but.
~ **é a vez dela** now it is her turn, now she has her innings. ~ **mesmo** only just now, just now. ~ **ou nunca** now or never. **até** ~ up till now. **de** ~ **em diante** from now on. **e** ~? well then? **justamente** ~ now of all times.
ágora s. f. agora: place of assembly, esp. the market place in an ancient Greek city.
agorafobia s. f. (med.) agoraphobia: morbid dread of crossing open spaces.
agorentar v. = aguarentar.
agorinha adv. (Braz., also **agora-agora**) 1. just now. 2. this minute. 3. a few moments ago.
agostiniano s. m. Augustinian: member of an Augustinian order. ‖ adj. Augustinian.
agosto s. m. August: the eighth month of the year.
agoural adj. m. + f. (pl. **-ais**) (**agoiral**) of or referring to an omen, foreboding, ominous.
agourar v. (also **agoirar**) 1. to omen, forebode, presage, augur. 2. to foretell, foresee, predict. 3. to conjecture, surmise.
agoureiro s. m. (also **agoireiro**) foreboder, presager. ‖ adj. 1. foreboding, auguring. 2. ill-omened, unlucky.
agourentar v. (also **agoirentar**) to portend, presage evil.
agourento adj. (also **agoirento**) foreboding.
agouro s. m. (also **agoiro**) omen, foreboding, prediction, presage.
agra s. f. field, tilled land.
agraciação s. f. (pl. **-ões**) 1. endowment. 2. bestowal. 3. grace. 4. award.
agraciado adj. 1. honoured, graced. 2. (also **engraçado**) graceful, elegant.
agraciador s. m. 1. honourer. 2. awarder. 3. bestower (of a title, insignia, honour).
agraciar v. 1. to grace. 2. to reward, recompense, honour. 3. to bestow with a title, insignia, etc. 4. to consider (as being).
ele foi agraciado com a Ordem do Mérito he was awarded the Order of Merit.
agraço s. m. (also **agraz**) 1. unripe grape. 2. verjuice. 3. (fig.) youth, vigour.
agradar (I) v. 1. to please. 2. to be pleased with. 3. to be agreeable. 4. to content, satisfy. 5. to cause a good impression. 6. to take a liking to. 7. (Braz.) to pet, caress.
como agradou a peça? how did the play go off?
a peça agrada the play acts well. **de modo a** ~ to pleasure. **ele procura agradá-la** he endeavours to please her, (U. S. A., coll.) he shines up to her.

ela não me agrada I don't like her, she is not for my turn. **ele agradou a todos** he pleased everybody. **isto não me agrada** I do not like the look of it. **isto me agrada** this is to my taste, strikes my fancy.
agradar (II) v. (also **gradar**) to harrow (land).
agradável adj. m. + f. (pl. **-áveis**) (abs. sup. **agradabilíssimo**) agreeable, pleasant, pleasing, well-pleasing. ‖ **agradavelmente** adv. pleasantly, agreeably.
~ **para** agreeable to. **apenas para lhe ser** ~ only to please you. **estou em circunstâncias agradáveis** I am in agreeable circumstances, (U. S. A., sl.) I am sitting pretty. **pouco** ~ rather unpleasant.
agradecer v. to thank, show or express gratitude, return thanks.
agradeço a sua delicadeza I thank you for your kind attention. **agradeço muito** I thank you kindly, I thank you very much. **agradeço e retribuo cordialmente vivos votos de prosperidade** heartiest thanks for your good wishes which I return most cordially. **agradeço da mesma forma** thank you just the same. **agradecendo-lhe antecipadamente** thanking you in anticipation. **não tem de que agradecer** don't mention it.
agradecido adj. grateful, thankful, obliged. ‖ **-amente** adv. gratefully, thankfully.
~! thanks! **fico-lhe muito** ~ I am much obliged to you. **mal** ~ ungrateful.
agradecimento s. m. thanks, thankfulness, gratefulness.
como ~ **a** in thanks for. **dar** ~**s** to return thanks. **receber** ~**s** to receive thanks.
agradecível adj. m. + f. (pl. **-íveis**) thankworthy.
agrado s. m. 1. pleasure, contentment, delight, satisfaction. 2. kindness, affability, courtesy. 3. (Braz.) tenderness, endearment, caress.
com ~ friendly, willingly, with pleasure. **isto não foi de meu** ~ that did not please me at all. **se for de seu** ~ if it is all right with you.
agrafia s. f. (med.) agraphia: inability to write.
agráfico adj. (med.) agraphic.
agrafo s. m. (surg.) wound clip.
ágrafo adj. 1. unwritten. 2. that can not be written.
agramatismo s. m. (med.) agrammatism: syntactical aphasia.
agranelar v. to collect or store in a barn or corn-loft.
agranizar v. to cover with hail.
agranulocitose s. f. (med.) agranulocytosis.
agrar v. 1. to clear (land for cultivation). 2. to till.
agrário adj. agrarian.
agraudar v. 1. to increase, enlarge, augment. 2. to grow.
agravação s. f. (pl. **-ões**) (also **agravamento** m.) aggravation.
agravado s. m. person who suffered a wrong or injury. ‖ adj. 1. (med.) aggravated, worsened. 2. (jur.) wronged, injured.
agravador s. m. aggravator. ‖ adj. aggravating.
agravamento s. m. (also **agravação** f.) aggravation.
agravante s. 1. f. aggravating circumstance, culpability. 2. m. + f. aggravator. ‖ adj. m. + f. (also **agravativo**) aggravating, aggravative.
agravar v. 1. to aggravate. 2. to make heavy or heavier. 3. to worsen. 4. to oppress. 5. to molest. 6. to offend. 7. (med.) to inflame. 8. to exacerbate. 9. (jur.) to lodge an appeal.
ele ainda agrava o prejuízo pela injúria he adds insult to injury.
agravável adj. m. + f. (pl. **-áveis**) susceptible to aggravation.
agravo s. m. 1. offense, loss, damage, injury. 2. (jur.) appeal. 3. complaint.
agraz s. m. = agraço.

agre adj. m. + f. (also **acre, agro**) 1. sour. 2. bitter. 3. acre.

agredido s. m. person who suffered an aggression.

agredir v. 1. to attack, assault, aggress. 2. to strike, beat. 3. to provoke.

agrediram-me they attacked me, (coll.) walked into me.

agregação s. f. (pl. **-ões**) 1. aggregation. 2. association. 3. agglomeration.

agregado s. m. 1. aggregation, assemblage, reunion. 2. (Braz.) servant living in the house and belonging to the household. ‖ adj. 1. aggregate(d), reunited. 2. adjoined, annexed, conjunct, joined.

agregar v. 1. to aggregate. 2. to join, annex, associate. 3. to add, increase. 4. to heap, accumulate.

agregativo adj. aggregative.

agremiação s. f. (pl. **-ões**) 1. association, fellowship, confederation. 2. reunion, assemblage.

agremiar v. 1. to associate. 2. to reunite, assemble.

agressão s. f. (pl. **-ões**) 1. aggression. 2. wound, injury. 3. blow, stroke. 4. attack, assault (and battery). 5. provocation. 6. insult. 7. offense.

agressividade s. f. aggressiveness.

agressivo adj. 1. aggressive, offensive. 2. ill-conditioned. 3. injurious. 4. provocative.

agressor s. m. aggressor. ‖ adj. aggressive.

agreste s. m. (Braz.) dry area in the north-east. ‖ adj. m. + f. 1. rural. 2. wild, sylvan. 3. rustic. 4. rough, crude. 5. rude, impolite.

agrestia, agrestidade s. f. 1. rurality. 2. roughness, crudeness, rusticity. 3. rudeness, impoliteness.

agrião (I) s. m. (bot.) water-cress.

agrião (II) s. m. (pl. **-ões**) (vet.) unhurting tumour on the hock of quadrupeds, as the horse.

agrião-do-pará s. m. (pl. **agriões-do-pará**) Pará-cress, alphabet plant.

agrícola s. m. agriculturist. ‖ adj. m. + f. agricultural.

agricultar v. 1. to till, cultivate, farm. 2. to work as a farmer.

agricultável adj. m. + f. (pl. **-áveis**) tillable, farmable, arable.

agricultor s. m. agriculturist, farmer. ‖ adj. agricultural, agriculturing.

agricultura s. f. 1. agriculture, farming, husbandry. 2. tillage, ploughing, cultivation.

agridoce adj. m. + f. (also **agro-doce, acre-doce**) sour-sweet, between sweet and sour.

agrilhoamento s. m. 1. chaining, fettering. 2. (fig.) restraint, control.

agrilhoar v. 1. to chain, fetter, shackle. 2. to put in irons. 3. (fig.) to constrain, coerce. 4. to catch, arrest. 5. to associate.

agrimar-se v. 1. to enrage, get mad. 2. to be overpowered by superstitious awe.

agrimensar v. to survey (a tract of land).

agrimensor s. m. surveyor.

agrimensura s. f. (also **agrimensão**) 1. geodesy, art and science of surveying. 2. surveying, land-surveying.

agrimônia (I) s. f. (bot.) agrimony.

agrimônia (II) s. f. = **acrimônia**.

agrinaldar v. (also **engrinaldar**) 1. to garland. 2. to festoon.

agriófago s. m. agriophagist, animal that feeds on wild animals. ‖ adj. feeding on wild animals.

agripa s. f. child born with the feet first.

agripene adj. m. + f. fanlike (said of birds's tails).

agrisalhado adj. greyish.

agrisalhar v. to make or become grey or greyish.

agro (I) s. m. (obs.) 1. field, ground, meadow. 2. tilled land.

agro (II) adj. (also **acre, agre,** abs. sup. **agérrimo, agríssimo**) 1. rough, uneven 2. acrid, sour, bitter.

agrografia s. f. treatise on agriculture.

agrográfico adj. of or referring to a treatise on agriculture.

agrologia s. f. agrology: geological aspect of agronomy.

agrológico adj. agrological: of or referring to agronomy, esp. its geological aspect.

agrólogo s. m. expert in agrology.

agromancia s. f. divination by judging the look of fields.

agromania s. f. agromania: passion for farming.

agromaníaco adj. crazy about farming.

agromante s. m. + f. person who divines by the look of fields.

agromântico adj. of or referring to the divination by the look of the fields.

agronomando s. m. (Braz.) person graduating in agriculture.

agronometria s. f. agronometry: calculation of the agricultural possibilities of a piece of land.

agronométrico adj. agronometric, agronometrical: of or referring to the calculation of the agricultural possibilities.

agronomia s. f. agronomy, agronomics.

agronômico adj. agronomic(al), agricultural.

agrônomo s. m. agronomist, agriculturist.

agropecuária s. f. combined agriculture and stock raising.

agror s. m. acridity.

agrostografia s. f. agrostography: a description of grasses.

agrostográfico adj. agrostographic.

agrostologia s. f. agrostology: the branch of botany treating of the grasses.

agrostológico adj. agrostologic.

agrostólogo s. m. agrostologist.

agrovila s. f. (Braz., neol.) an organized farm settlement, providing community services, aiding to open up new territories.

agrumar-se v. to form into grumes or clots.

agrumelar v. to curdle, coagulate, thicken, clot.

agrumetar v. (naut.) to hire ship boys, cabin-boys.

agrumular v. to curdle, coagulate, thicken, clot.

agrupação s. f. (pl. **-ões**) grouping.

agrupamento s. m. 1. grouping. 2. assembly, gathering. 3. group.

agrupar v. 1. to group, form (into) a group. 2. ~-se to cluster, gather. 3. to arrange, classify.
~ **em famílias** to group in families.

agrura s. f. 1. acrity. 2. coarseness, roughness. 3. harshness, asperity. 4. displeasure, nuisance. 5. bitterness, acerbity.

água s. f. 1. water. 2. any liquid that suggests water: a) saliva, tears, wine. b) cosmetic waters. 3. a body of water: sea, lake, river. 4. rain (water). 5. slope, slanted pane of a roof. 6. talent, ability. 7. drunkenness. 8. ~s waters (medicinal springs). 9. the limpidity of a precious stone.
~ **abaixo** down the river. ~ **acima** (arriba) up the river. ~ **benta** holy water. ~ **de chuva** rain water. ~ **doce** fresh water. **de** ~ **doce** fresh-water. ~ **férrea** chalybeate. ~ **gelada** iced water. ~ **mineral** mineral water. ~ **mole em pedra dura tanto dá até que fura** constant dripping wears the stone. ~ **oxigenada** peroxide of hydrogen. ~ **que passarinho não bebe** brandy, rum. ~ **salgada** salt water. ~s **mortas** neap tide. ~s **quietas são profundas** still waters run deep. ~s **vivas** spring tides. ~ **termal** thermal water, hot mineral water. ~ **viva** running water. **à flor d'**~ between wind and water, awash. **afogar-se em pouca** ~ to fret at trifles, be over-hasty. **até debaixo da** - anyway. **buscar** - **no cesto** to carry water in a sieve, do useless work.

claro como ~ as clear as clear can be. com ~s passadas não mói o moinho let bygones be bygones. como ~ like water, abundant. cozinhar em ~ fria to delay, procrastinate. dar ~ a um cavalo to water a horse. dar ~ pela barba to cause trouble. dar em ~ de bacalhau to fail, show no results. deitar ~ na fervura to pour oil in troubled waters. entre a cruz e a ~ benta in a sad dilemma. fazer ~ (naut.) to spring a leak. fazer estação de ~s to take (or drink) the waters. gato escaldado da ~ fria tem medo the burnt child fears the fire. ir por ~ abaixo to go down the stream. ir-(se) por ~ abaixo 1. to be lost. 2. to lose everything. isto faz vir ~ à boca that makes your mouth water. lançar um navio à ~ to launch a ship. levar ~ ao mar to take coals to Newcastle. linha divisória de ~ watershed. na ~, no mar on the water. negócio de ~ arriba a tough job. pescar em ~s turvas to fish in foul or troubled waters. por que cargas de ~? by what right? saber levar ~ a seu moinho to know how to bring grist to one's mill. ser à prova de ~ to be waterproof, hold water.

aguaça s. f. 1. torrent, rushing stream of water. 2. impetuous current. 3. (fig.) plenty.

aguaçal s. m. (pl. -ais) 1. puddle of standing water. 2. swamp, marsh, bog.

aguaceira s. f. watery humour, saliva.

aguaceirada s. f. (Braz.) repeated rain showers.

aguaceiro s. m. 1. (also manga d'água) a shower of rain. 2. reverse, hindrance, drawback. 3. nuisance, aversion. 4. blast of wind, gust, wind, squall. ~ branco (Braz.) sudden storm without rain.

aguacento adj. 1. watery, waterish. 2. plashy, marshy.

aguada s. f. 1. (naut.): a) watering. b) watering place. c) water supply. 2. bookbinder's glue. 3. aquarelle, water-colour. 4. well, river or any water source on a farm. fazer ~ (naut.) to take up fresh water.

água-de-briga s. f. (pl. águas-de-briga) (Braz., sl.) rum.

água-de-cheiro s. f. (pl. águas-de-cheiro) scented water, extract.

água-de-coco s. f. (pl. águas-de-coco) (Braz.) coconut milk, the juice of green coconuts.

água-de-colônia s. f. Cologne water.

aguadeiro s. m. 1. water seller. 2. water distributor.

aguadilha s. f. 1. lymph. 2. serosity. 3. humour similar to water.

aguado adj. 1. frustrated, failed. 2. imperfect, defective. 3. with the hair standing on end. 4. founderous. 5. (Braz.) with little sugar (coffee, tea). 6. watered, watery.

aguador s. m. 1. waterer. 2. watering can.

água-emendada s. f. (pl. águas-emendadas) (Braz.) common source or outlet of two or more rivers belonging to different basins.

água-flórida s. f. (pl. águas-flóridas) sort of perfume.

água-forte s. f. (pl. águas-fortes) aqua-fortis, an etching.

água-fortista s. m. + f. (pl. águas-fortistas) aquafortist.

água-furtada s. f. (pl. águas-furtadas) garret, attic, loft.

aguagem s. f. (pl. -ens) 1. agitation, roughness (sea). 2. race (of water), tiderace. 3. wake, backwater. 4. dilution (with water). 5. watering.

água-mãe s. f. mother-water, mother liquor, mother liquid.

água-marinha s. f. (pl. águas-marinhas) aquamarine.

água-mel s. f. (pl. águas-méis) (also hidromel) hydromel.

aguamento s. m. (vet.) foundering.

água-morna s. m. + f. (pl. águas-mornas) (fam.) 1. softy. 2. slowcoach.

aguapé (I) s. f. 1. after wine. 2. light wine.

aguapé (II) s. m. (bot.) pond lily.

aguapezal s. m. (pl. -ais) (Braz.) expanse of water covered with pond lilies.

água-que-gato-não-bebe, água-que-passarinho-não-bebe s. f. (pl. águas-que-gato-não-bebe, águas-que-passarinho-não-bebe) (Braz., sl.) rum.

aguar v. 1. to dilute, mix with water. 2. to water. 3. to sprinkle, besprinkle. 4. to stop, check, disturb (fun, pleasure), throw a wet blanket on. 5. to long for. 6. to frustrate. 7. to be foundered (horse).

aguarapondá s. f. (bot.) bastard vervain.

aguaraquiá s. m. (bot., Braz.) nightshade.

aguarda s. f. expectation: act or fact of expecting.

aguardador s. m. expectant.

aguardamento s. m. 1. expectation: act of expecting, awaiting. 2. watching. 3. respecting. 4. courting. 5. spying, lurking.

aguardar v. 1. to expect. 2. to await, wait for. 3. to observe: a) watch. b) spy, peep, lurk. c) respect. 4. to court.
aguardando as suas prezadas notícias (correspondence) looking forward to your good news. ele o aguardou pacientemente he patiently waited for it, (U. S. A., sl.) he sweated it out.

aguardentado adj. 1. mixed with brandy. 2. drunken with brandy.

aguardentar v. to mix with brandy.

aguardente s. f. 1. brandy, aqua-vitae. 2. (U. S. A.) firewater.
~ de cana-de-açúcar (cachaça) rum. ~ de cereais whisky, corn spirit. ~ ordinária tangle-foot.

aguardenteiro s. m. 1. distiller or vender of brandy. 2. drunkard, person given to drinking.

água-redonda s. f. (pl. águas-redondas) (Braz.) lake, small lake, pool.

água-régia s. f. (pl. águas-régias) aqua regia.

aguarela s. f. (also aquarela) 1. aquarelle. 2. colour diluted in water, water-colour.

aguarelar v. to paint in water-colours.

aguarelista s. m. + f. (also aquarelista) aquarellist.

aguarentador s. m. 1. that cuts or pares around. 2. blemisher, slanderer.

aguarentar v. 1. to cut or pare all round. 2. to clip, cut short. 3. to curtail. 4. to murmur about. 5. to blemish, slander. 6. to disparage, depreciate. 7. to make sultry, tasteless. 8. to water.

aguarrás s. f. essence of turpentine, turpentine.

águas-iguais s. f. pl. (Braz.) the tides of the 4th day after new or full moon.

águas-mestras s. f. pl. trapeziform roof.

água-só s. m. (pl. águas-sós) snipe, bird of the genus Capela (Capela undulata gigantea).

águas-pegadas s. f. pl. (Braz.) tides of the 4th day after the first and last quarter of the moon.

águas-puladeiras s. f. pl. (Braz.) torrent, wild or rapid flow of water.

água-suja s. f. (pl. águas-sujas) (Braz.) 1. (coll.) gossip, chat, small talk. 2. noise, uproar, bustle. 3. admonition, scolding. 4. intrigue, plot.

aguatal s. f. (pl. -ais) (Braz.) insipid water.

aguateiro s. m. (Braz.) 1. animal that carries water or pulls a water cart. 2. worthless horse. 3. odd-jobber on a farm, kept rather for indulgence.

água-viva s. f. (pl. águas-vivas) (ichth.) medusa, jelly-fish.

aguaxado adj. 1. water-soaked. 2. said of a horse unable to travel long distances due to lack of exercise and overfattening.

aguazil s. m. (pl. -is) (hist.) 1. bailiff. 2. a minor clerk of a court of justice.

aguçadeira s. f. 1. f. of aguçador. 2. grindstone. 3. (fig.) stimulation, instigation.

aguçado adj. 1. sharp, sharpened, whetted. 2. pointed, spiked.

aguçador s. m. 1. grinder, sharpener, whetter. 2. stimulant. ‖ adj. 1. grinding, whetting. 2. stimulant, stimulative.

aguçadura s. f. 1. grinding, sharpening, whetting. 2. edge. 3. tapering, thinning.

aguçar v. 1. to grind, sharpen, whet. 2. to taper, point. 3. to excite, stimulate. 4. to make keen. 5. to hasten, accelerate. 6. to sneak away. ~ **os ouvidos** to prick (or perk) up the ears. ~ **uma vara** to whittle at a stick. ~ **o apetite** to whet one's appetite.

aguço s. m. sharp, edged or pointed object.

agude s. f. (also **agúdia**, ent.) winged ant.

agudez(a) s. f. 1. sharpness. 2. intenseness, acuteness. 3. keenness, cunning, perspicacity. 4. ability, capacity. 5. pointedness.

agudo s. m. (mus.) sharp. ‖ adj. 1. pointed. 2. sharpened. 3. thin. 4. keen, acute. 5. quick-witted, subtle. 6. intense. 7. vexed. 8. exasperate. 9. (mus.) sharp. 10 (gram.) stressed on the last syllable.

agüeira s. f. water furrow (for irrigation).

agüeiro s. m. 1. = **agüeira**. 2. gutter, eaves.

agüentador s. m. supporter, person or thing bearing the weight of something. ‖ adj. supporting, sustaining.

agüentar v. 1. to support, bear. 2. to bear the weight of, hold. 3. to equilibrate, balance. 4. to maintain. 5. to resist, sustain. 6. to suffer, endure. 7. to stand. 8. to tolerate. ~ **as conseqüências** to endure the consequences, (U. S. A., sl.) stand the racket. ~ **e mostrar cara alegre** to grin and bear it. ~ **o tempo** (naut.) to ride out the weather. ~ **o temporal** to stand the storm. **agüenta!** stick it out! **ele agüenta firme** he keeps a stiff upper lip. **ele não agüenta o tranco** (Braz., sl.) he is not up to it. **ele agüenta muito** he can stand a lot. **ele não agüentou** he couldn't take it. **não o agüento mais** I can't stand (or stick) it any longer. **ninguém agüenta a sua estupidez** there is no standing her stupidity.

aguerrear v. 1. to accustom to war. 2. to get accustomed to battles. 3. = **aguerrir**.

aguerrido adj. 1. accustomed to war. 2. courageous, brave.

aguerrilhar v. 1. to form or convert into guerillas. 2. to enlist or join in a guerrilla.

aguerrir v. 1. to accustom to war. 2. to accustom to hardship. 3. to make valorous, brave. 4. to exercise o. s. in arms and warfare.

águia s. f. 1. (ornith.) eagle. 2. picture of an eagle as an emblem or insignia. 3. (U. S. A.) gold coin of the value of ten dollars. 4. (astr.) **Aguia** Eagle: constellation of Aquilla. 5. genius, very intelligent person. 6. m. (Braz.) rogue, deceitful person. ~ **nova** eaglet. ~ **pescadora** fish-hawk. **olhos de** ~ piercing eyes. **pedra de** ~ eagle-stone. **ele é** ~ (Braz.) he is sly. **a Águia de Haia** the Hague Eagle: a nickname given to the Brazilian statesman Ruy Barbosa.

aguieiro s. m. cross-piece of timber, brace.

aguieta s. f. eaglet.

águila s. f. (bot.) aloeswood.

aguilhada s. f. (Braz.; also **picana, pereiro, guiada**) goad. ~ **de terra** former agrarian measure.

aguilhão s. m. (pl. **-ões**) 1. iron point of a goad. 2. sting of insects. 3. spur, incentive. 4. suffering.

aguilhó s. m. former hairdressing or head attire of women.

aguilhoada, aguilhoadela s. f. sting or prod with a goad.

aguilhoador s. m. person who goads, goad. ‖ adj. goading.

aguilhoamento s. m. goading, pricking, incitation, incitement.

aguilhoar v. 1. to goad, princk, spur. 2. (fig.) to incite, stir up, urge on.

aguilhoeiro s. m. goad-maker or seller.

aguitarrado adj. guitarlike in shape or sound.

agulha s. f. 1. needle (plate A 1, 5, P 15). 2. pointer, hand of a watch. 3. steel pointer of a compass or electric machinery. 4. phonograph needle. 5. injection needle. 6. (railway) switch point (plates E 12, V 4). 7. firing pin of a gun. 8. obelisk. 9. peak of a mountain (plate M 11). 10. spire. 11. piquancy of certain wines. 12. business of a seamstress. 13. (ichth.) needlefish, hornfish. 14. (archit.) iron for testing the soil. 15. junction point of the shoulder blades of animals (plate G 1). ~ **de alcolcheiro** square needle. ~ **de cerzir** darning-needle (plate A 1). ~ **de coser** sewing needle (plates A 1, 5). ~ **de crochê** crochet hook (plate A 1). ~ **de máquina** machine needle (plates A 1, 5). ~ **de marear** mariner's needle, sea compass. ~ **de meia** knitting needle. ~ **de pastor** (bot.) shepherd's needle. ~ **de tricô** knitting needle (plate A 1). ~ **ferrugenta** (fig.) meddler. **procurar** ~ **em palheiro** to look for a needle in a haystack. **trabalho de** ~ needlework.

agulhada s. f. 1. needle prick. 2. needleful.

agulhão s. m. (pl. **-ões**) 1. large needle. 2. (ichth.) needlefish.

agulhão-bandeira s. m. (pl. **agulhões-bandeira**) (Braz., ichth.) volador.

agulhar v. 1. to prick with a needle. 2. to goad. 3. to vex. 4. to torture.

agulheado adj. needle-shaped.

agulheiro s. m. 1. needle-case. 2. needlemaker. 3. switchman, switcher (railway). 4. scaffolding hole. 5. a deep and narrow cleft. 6. flowoff, discharge (water).

agulheta s. f. 1. tag, aglet, aiglet. 2. nozzle, jet-pipe. 3. stay-lace. 4. bodkin: a large-eyed blunt needle for drawing tape etc. through a loop or hem.

agulheteiro s. m. manufacturer of tags, aiglets or needles.

aguti s. m. (zool.) agouti.

agutiguepe s. f. (Braz., also **araruta**) arrowroot.

agutipuru s. m. (Braz., also **acutipuru, serelepe**) (zool). a tropical squirrel.

ah interj. ah! oh!

ah, que pena! oh, what a pity!

ai s. m. groan, moan. ‖ interj. ah! alas! woe! ~ **dele** woe betide him. ~ **de mim** woe is me. ~ **dos vencidos** woe to the vanquished. **dar** ~**s** to groan, lament. **num** ~ instantly, suddenly.

aí (I) s. m. (zool., Braz., also **preguiça**) three-toed sloth.

aí (II) adv. 1. there, in that place. 2. in this respect. 3. (Braz.) in that moment. ‖ interj. of applause or cheer: splendid! good! fine!. ~ **é que o carpinteiro fez a porta** there is the door the carpenter made. ~ **mesmo** in that very place, right there. ~, **rapaz, muito bem!** there, my boy, fine! ~ **tens** there you are. **ele vem** ~ there he comes.

aia s. f. 1. chambermaid. 2. nursemaid.

aiaçá s. f. (Braz.) name of several fresh-water turtles.

aiaia s. f. (Braz.) 1. plaything, toy (for babies). 2. children's dress.

aiar v. (also **guaiar**) to moan, wail, lament, groan.

aibi s. m. (Braz.) brook (esp. one flowing into the ocean).

aicuna interj. (Braz.) denoting surprise, anger: gosh! darn!

ai-jesus s. m. sg. + pl. favourite, darling. ‖ interj. denoting grief or surprise: dear me! good gracious!

aijulata s. f. (Braz.) a sort of loincloth (of an Indian).

ailanticultura s. f. plantation and cultivation of ailantus.

ailantina s. f. ailantine.

ailanto s. m. (bot.) ailantus, ailanto.

aileron s. m. (tech., aeron.) aileron (plate A 3).

aimará s. m. (Braz.) cotton tunic interwoven with feathers.

aí-mirim s. m. (pl. **aís-mirins**) (Braz., zool. also **preguiça-pequena**) two-toed sloth.

aimoré (I) s. m. + f. (Braz.) member of the Aimoré tribe. ‖ adj. of or referring to the Aimorés.

aimoré (II) s. m. (Braz.) an Amazonian monkey.

ainda adv. 1. still, yet. 2. again. 3. further, more. ~ **agora** just now. ~ **assim** nevertheless, for all that, even so. ~ **bem** fortunately. ~ **está dormindo?** are you still asleep? ~ **há tempo** there is yet time, yet time serves. ~ **maior** still bigger. ~ **mais** still more, yet more, moreover. ~ **mais essa!** and now (still) that! ~ **menos** still less. ~ **nunca** never yet. ~ **que** though, although. ~ **que esteja ausente** even though I am absent. ~ **uma vez** once more. **indagarei** ~ I shall inquire further. **não,** ~ **não** no, not (as) yet. **posso mencionar** ~ I may further mention. **vale a pena tentar,** ~ **que falhemos** it is worth attempting, though we may fail.

ainhum s. m. (med.) ainhum, spontaneous dactylolysis.

aino s. m. Ainu. ‖ adj. Ainu.

aio s. m. 1. preceptor, tutor. 2. valet de chambre. 3. chamberlain. 4. squire to a knight.

aló s. m. (Braz.) gamebag made from the fibre of a thistle.

aipi, aipim s. m. (Braz., bot., also **uaipi, mandioca-doce, macaxeira**) sweet cassava.

aipo s. m. (bot.) celery.

aipo-do-banhado s. m. (pl. **aipos-do-banhado**) (bot. also **botão-de-ouro**) amaranth.

airado adj. 1. airy. 2. distracted. 3. idle, sluggish. 4. (Braz.) having a cold. 5. light-minded. 6. slovenly, disorderly.

vida -a disorderly, loose life or way of living.

airão s. m. (pl. **-ões;** ant.) ornament of precious stones forming a bunch of flowers.

airar v. (Braz.) to take some fresh air, refresh o. s.

aire s. m. futility, futileness.

airi s. f. a Brazilian palm tree.

airosidade s. f. 1. slenderness, gracefulness. 2. kindness, affability. 3. elegance, distinguished bearing. 4. honourableness. 5. decorousness.

airoso adj. 1. slender, graceful. 2. kind, affable. 3. elegant. 4. honourable. 5. decorous.

aiuara-aiuara s. f. (pl. **aiuara-aiuaras**) (Braz., also **mãe-d'água**) a sort of mermaid, goddess of rivers and lakes.

aiúba s. f. (Braz.) tree of the family Lauraceae (Aydendron permalle), found in the Amazon forest.

aiurujuba s. m. name the Brazilian natives gave to the French invaders.

aíve adj. m. + f. (Braz.) 1. bad, evil. 2. insignificant. 3. useless. 4. ailing. 5. wretched.

aivado s. m. (Braz.) entrance (to a beehive).

aivão s. m. (pl. **-ões**) (ornith.) 1. martin. 2. pheasant.

aiveca s. f. earth-board or mould-board of a plough (plate C 13).

aizoácea s. f. Aizoaceae: a family of herbs and shrubs.

aizoáceo adj. (bot.) aizoaceous.

ajaezado adj. in full harness, trimmed up (horse).

ajaezar v. 1. to harness. 2. to trim. 3. to adorn.

ajajá s. f. (Braz., ornith.) roseate spoonbill.

ajanotado adj. dandyish, foppish, vain (in dress or show).

ajanotar v. 1. to dress in a dandyish, foppish style. 2. to act dandylike or foppishly. 3. to put on one's Sunday best.

ajantarado s. m. a (single) substantial Sunday meal. ‖ adj. dinnerlike, copious.

ajardinado adj. gardenlike.

ajardinamento s. m. 1. gardening. 2. landscape-gardening. 3. formation into a garden.

ajardinar v. 1. to make or form into a garden. 2. to garden.

ajeitar v. 1. to arrange, dispose. 2. to accomodate, adapt, fit. 3. to proportion, manage. 4. to show ability for. 5. ~-se to accomodate or adapt o. s. easily.

~-se **de acordo com as necessidades** to make both ends meet.

ajesuitado adj. Jesuitlike.

ajesuitar v. 1. to make a Jesuit out of. 2. to become a Jesuit.

ajirauzado adj. (Braz.) 1. disposed in the way or form of an estrade. 2. like an estrade or platform.

ajoanetado adj. 1. having an (over)large knuckle-bone (great toe). 2. knucklelike.

ajoelhação s. f. (pl. **-ões**) genuflection, kneel.

ajoelhado adj. 1. kneeling. 2. (fig.) humiliated, humbled.

ajoelhar v. 1. (~-se) to kneel, kneel down. 2. to put (down) on the knees.

ele ajoelhou-se he went to his knees.

ajorcado adj. adorned, dressed up, trimmed (used exclusively in the contrary sense, preceded by the adverb **mal**): **mal ajorcado** of bad make-up, badly dressed.

ajornalado adj. hired by the day.

ajornalar v. to hire by the day.

ajoujado adj. leashed, coupled.

ajoujamento s. m. 1. leashing. 2. coupling, union. 3. (over)loading, burdening. 4. oppression.

ajoujar v. 1. to leash. 2. to couple, unite, join. 3. to (over)load, burden. 4. to oppress. 5. to give way, cede, yield (under pressure or weight).

ajoujo s. m. 1. leash, couple. 2. violent union. 3. (Braz.) strip of leather fastened at the horns of two oxen, to keep them together. 4. (Braz.) outrigger.

ajuaga s. f. tumour on a horse's hoof.

ajuba s. f. tree of the laurel family.

ajuda s. f. 1. help (act or fact of helping), assistance, support, aid, succour, relief. 2. favour. 3. enema, clyster. 4. sort of federal tax. 5. (Braz.) alcaline ingredient used to eliminate the acids from the sugar cane extract.

~ **de custo** an (extra) allowance (as for a traveller or salesman). **com a** ~ **de Deus** by God's help. **sem** ~ by yourself, without help.

ajudador s. m. assistant, aid, help(er). ‖ adj. assistant, aiding, helpful.

ajudadouro s. m. (also **ajudadoiro**) assistance, help, aid, relief, succour.

ajudância s. f. (Braz.) assistantship.

ajudante s. m. + f. (Port., also f. **ajudanta**) 1. assistant, helper, aid. 2. acolyte.

~ **de campo** aide-de-camp. ~ **de cozinha** kitchen boy, kitchen-maid.

ajudar v. 1. to help, aid, assist, succour, relieve, support, give or lend a hand, lend assistance. 2. to favour, facilitate. 3. to collaborate. 4. to be

useful. 5. (~-se): a) to prevail oneself of. b) to help each other.
~ à missa to serve at mass. ~ a passar (por uma dificuldade) to help over. ~ a subir to help up. ajude-me give me a hand. ajuda-te que Deus te ajudará God helps those, who help themselves. eles os ajudaram na mudança they settled them in. eles ajudaram-no a levantar-se they helped him to his feet.

ajudengado adj. having Jewish ways and manners.

ajudengar v. to transmit or acquire Jewish ways and manners, judaize.

ajudeuzado adj. (also **ajudengado**) Jewish in ways and manners.

ajuizado adj. reasonable, discreet, wise, judicious.

ajuizador s. m. estimator, judger, arbiter. ‖ adj. estimative, judicial, arbitrational.

ajuizar v. 1. to judge. 2. to form an opinion. 3. to estimate. 4. to suppose, believe. 5. to bring before the court. 6. to make a subject of (legal) dispute. 7. (~-se): a) to believe oneself to be..., consider oneself to be... b) to become sensible. 8. to make (a person) sensible.

ajuizável adj. m. + f. (pl. -áveis) 1. judgeable. 2. estimable. 3. (law) triable.

ajular v. (Braz.) 1. to turn leewards. 2. to draw backwards.

ajulata s. f. (also **aijulata**) a sort of loin-cloth used by the Braz. Indians.

ajumentado adj. donkeyish, donkeylike.

ajunta s. f. (also **junção**) 1. junction, connexion, joint. 2. confluence. 3. reunion.

ajuntadeira s. f. woman who assembles and sews uppers (of shoes).

ajuntado adj. 1. together. 2. close. 3. congregated. 4. added. 5. united.

ajuntador s. m. 1. collector, assembler. 2. fisher who closes the net below the water. ‖ adj. collecting, assembling.

ajuntadouro s. m. (also **ajuntadoiro**) place where rain-water gathers.

ajuntamento s. m. 1. reunion, meeting, assembly. 2. crowd, throng. 3. mixture.

ajuntar v. 1. to gather. 2. to accumulate. 3. to compile. 4. to add. 5. to collect, assemble, fit and join together, unite. 6. to ally, confederate. 7. to treasure, lay up, save. 8. ~-se: a) to meet, crowd. b) to unite, join.
~ dinheiro to hoard money. ~ o dia com a noite to prolong something throughout the night.

ajuntável adj. m. + f. (pl. -áveis) assemblable, joinable, uniteable.

ajuntoura s. f. (also **ajuntoira**) (building) header.

ajupe interj. (Braz.) expression used to urge on horses.

ajuramentado adj. sworn, bound by an oath.

ajuramentar v. 1. to swear. 2. to bind (or ~-se be bound) by an oath.

ajuru s. m. (Braz.) 1. plant of the rose family. 2. (ornith.) amazon with a red border on its wing.

ajuruaçu s. m. (Braz., ornith.) mealy amazon.

ajurucatinga s. m. (Braz., ornith. also **ajurucuruca**) Amazonian bird whose wings are green on their upper side.

ajustado s. m. thing that has been adjusted. ‖ adj. 1. agreed upon, settled, combined. 2. adjusted. 3. proportional. 4. suitable, fit. 5. fitting close (dress). com as velas -as in sailing trim. homem ~ a sober man.

ajustador s. m. adjuster, fitter (plate B 13).
~ de condutores de vapor steam-fitter.

ajustagem s. f. (pl. -ens) (Braz.) adjustment, regulation (said of machines) (plates B 13, M 9).

ajustamento s. m. 1. adjustment, adjusting. 2. adaptation. 3. arrangement, disposition. 4. settlement (of accounts). 5. reconciliation. 6. agreement, contract. 7. convention, covenant.
~ de precisão fine-fit.

ajustar v. 1. to adjust, regulate, order, dispose. 2. to accord. 3. to adapt. 4. to fit, suit. 5. to fit a thing to another. 6. to join closely. 7. to complete. 8. to stipulate. 9. to make an agreement. 10. to contract. 11. to hire. 12. to come to terms. 13. to settle (accounts). 14. (~-se) to adapt, conform or accommodate o. s.
~ a to piece on. ~-se bem ao corpo to fit closely (as a dress). ajustei a conta com ele I am even with him. ela tem contas a ~ com você she has a bone to pick with you. ele tem contas a ~ com ela he has a crow to pluck with her.

ajustável adj. m. + f. (pl. -áveis) 1. adjustable. 2. adaptable. 3. appliable. 4. that can be settled.
quilha ~, quilha corrediça sliding-keel, drop keel.

ajuste s. m. 1. = **ajustamento**. 2. agreement, understanding, (com)pact. 3. settlement (accounts or questions).
fazer ~ de contas to play out. conforme ao nosso ~ in conformity to our agreement.

ajustura s. f. little cavity of a horseshoe to make it fit better.

ajusturar v. to make a cavity in a horseshoe for better fit.

ajutório s. m. (Braz., also **adjutório**) help, aid, assistance.

al (I) pron. (obs.) 1. another thing. 2. everything else. 3. more, still more.

Al (II) (chem.) Al: symbol for aluminium.

ala s. f. 1. line, row, file. 2. guard, breastwork, railing. 3. wing (bird, insect, building, army). 4. half a battalion.
pôr em ~s to set in ranks.

alá adv. (obs. and. coll.) there.

alabama s. m. 1. big brilliant, but of low quality. 2. travelling salesman. 3. runner for gambling-houses, tout, touter. 4. (ent.) cotton leafworm, the larva of the Alabama argillacea (also **curuquerê**).

alabamba s. f. (Braz.) type of paper kite.

alabanda s. f. (min.) black marble.

alabandina s. f. (also **rubi-negro**) almandine, almandite.

alabarar v. 1. to roast. 2. to burn, destroy.

alabarda s. f. halberd.

alabardada s. f. stroke or beat with a halberd.

alabardeiro s. m. 1. halberdier. 2. archer, bowman.

alabardino adj. halberd-shaped (plate F 5).

alabastrino adj. 1. alabastrine. 2. white, snow-white.

alabastrita s. f. (min.) alabastrite.

alabastro s. m. alabaster.

alabirintado adj. 1. labyrinthine, labyrinthian. 2. labyrinthiform. 3. (fig.) tortuous, confused.

alabregado adj. 1. rustic, churlish. 2. coarse, crude.

alacaiado adj. showing ways and manners of a lackey, servile.

alacoado adj. rubicund, reddish, rosy.

alacrado, alacreado adj. lac-coloured.

alacranado adj. (Braz.) 1. rough, uneven. 2. sore, full of wounds (animal).

álacre adj. m. + f. 1. alacritous, happy, gay. 2. enthusiastic.

alacridade s. f. 1. alacrity, happiness, gayness. 2. vigour. 3. enthusiasm.

aladeirado s. m. (Braz.) hilly, uneven ground. ‖ adj. hilly, full of declivities, sloping.

alado adj. winged.

aladroado adj. 1. thievish. 2. stealing. 3. fraudulent (weight).

aladroar v. to cheat, defraud, retain or diminish fraudulently.

alagação s. f. (pl. **-ões**) 1. overflow, inundation, flood. 2. (Braz.) periodic inundation of the lands bordering on the Amazon river.

alagadeira s. f. spendthrift, prodigal woman. ‖ adj. prodigal.

ela é uma ~ she is a spendthrift.

alagadeiro (I) s. m. spendthrift, prodigal (man). ‖ adj. prodigal.

alagadeiro (II) s. m. bog, marsh, swamp.

alagadiceiro adj. pasturing or grazing on boggy ground.

alagadiço adj. 1. subject to be overflowed. 2. drenched, wet. 3. swampish, marshy, paludal.

alagado adj. 1. full of water, waterlogged. 2. drenched, soaked. 3. swampy, marshy.

alagador s. m. flooder, inundator. ‖ adj. flooding, invading.

alagamar s. m. small bay.

alagamento s. m. 1. overflow, inundation. 2. foundering.

alagar v. 1. to inundate, overflow, flood. 2. to form a pond or saltwater puddles. 3. to fill or cover with any liquid. 4. to invade. 5. (obs.) to dissipate, squander. 6. to shipwreck, founder.

alagartado adj. 1. like a lizard, lizard-coloured. 2. (fig.) asleep.

alagartixado adj. (zool.) geckolike, similar to a gecko.

alagoa s. f. (also **lagoa**) pond, lagoon.

alagoano s. m. (Braz.) native or inhabitant of Alagoas. ‖ adj. of or referring to Alagoas.

alagoinha s. f. (Braz.) small pond or pool formed by occasional water sources (as from receding flood water).

alagoso adj. swampish, marshy, boggy.

alagostado adj. lobsterlike (colour).

alalá s. m. (Braz.) newspaper commentary with the purpose to give a sensational touch to an occurrence.

alalia s. f. (med.) alalia: lack of ability to talk.

alamanda s. f. (bot.) yellow bell.

alamar s. m. (pl. ~**es**) gold braiding, galloon, lace, braid.

alamarado adj. laced, gold-braided, gallooned.

alambari s. m. (Braz., also **lambari**) name of several freshwater fish (Tetragnopterus argenteus).

alambazado adj. 1. corpulent. 2. awkward. 3. rustic, churlish. 4. savage. 5. gluttonous.

alambazar-se v. 1. to grow clumsy, corpulent, awkward. 2. to eat very much, cram o. s. with. 3. to become a glutton.

alambicado adj. 1. presumptuous, arrogant. 2. affected, conceited. 3. embellished or made up exaggeratedly. 4. distilled.

alambicar v. 1. to distil. 2. to make affected, presumptuous, arrogant. 3. to embellish exaggeratedly. 4. to refine, polish (style, language). 5. ~**-se** to become affected.

alambique s. m. 1. still. 2. alembic.

alambiqueiro s. m. distiller, person who works with a still or alembic.

alambor s. m. stronger or thicker base of a wall, scarp.

alamborado adj. having a stronger or thicker base (wall).

alamborar v. 1. to thicken or make stronger at the base (wall). 2. to slope. 3. to give a convex form to. 4. to make crooked.

alambra s. f. 1. (bot.) black poplar. 2. resin it yields.

alambrado s. m. (also **aramado**) wire fence. ‖ adj. provided with a wire fence.

alambrador s. m. manufacturer of wires (for fences).

alambrar v. to fence in (with wire fence).

alambre s. m. 1. amber. 2. (fig.) sly fox, cunning fellow.

alambreado adj. amber, yellowish-brown.

alameda (ê) s. f. 1. lane, alley, avenue (plate E 14). 2. grove. 3. park. 4. poplar grove.

alamedado adj. planted or provided with poplars.

alamedar v. to provide with poplars (lane, alley, park), transform into an alley.

alamia s. f. piece of a horse's harness.

alamiré s. m. diapason (standard of pitch).

dar o ~ 1. to give the signal to start. 2. to indicate the tune. 3. to lead, direct. **dar um** ~ to give a hint.

álamo s. m. (bot.) poplar.

~ **branco** white poplar. ~ **preto** black poplar. **ser como a folha do** ~ to be fickle.

alâmpada s. f. (also **lâmpada**) lamp.

alanceado adj. distressed, harrowed, mortified.

alanceador s. m. 1. lancer. 2. (fig.) harrower. ‖ adj. 1. lancing, piercing. 2. (fig.) harrowing, distressing.

alanceamento s. m. 1. wounding with a lance or spear. 2. affliction, distress. 3. stimulation, stimulus.

alancear v. 1. to lance. 2. to distress, harrow, afflict. 3. to stimulate.

alandeado adj. glandiform, acorn-shaped.

alandro s. m. (bot., also **loendro**) oleander.

alanguidar-se v. 1. to become languid. 2. to languish, pine away.

alanhado adj. wounded, slashed, full of cuts, knifed.

alanhador s. m. slasher, cutter, person who knifes. ‖ adj. slashing, cutting, knifing.

alanhar v. 1. to wound, cut, knife, slash. 2. to disembowel, gut. 3. to oppress. 4. ~**-se** to exhaust one's forces.

~ **o peixe** to eviscerate or draw a fish.

alanita s. f. (also **ortita**) allanite (orthite).

alano s. m. (also **alão**) mastiff, bulldog.

alanos s. m. pl. (hist.) Scythians.

alanterna s. f. (also **lanterna**) lantern.

alantíase s. f. (path.) botulism, poisoning due to eating improperly canned foods.

alantóide s. m. (anat.) allantois.

alantoidiano s. m. (zool.) allantoidian.

alantotóxico s. m. allantotoxic: toxic formed in sausages.

alanzoador s. m. idle talker, boaster, chatterbox.

alanzoar v. 1. to talk idle. 2. to talk monotonously. 3. to boast. 4. to chatter, gossip.

alão s. m. (pl. **-ões**), (also **álamo**) headstone of a wall.

alapado adj. hidden, squatted, crouched.

alapar v. 1. to hide (esp. in a cave). 2. to squat, crouch. 3. = **alapardar-se**.

alapardado adj. squatted, crouched, hidden.

alapardar-se v. to hide o. s., cover, squat, crouch.

alapoado adj. 1. like a Lapp. 2. churlish, uncivil.

alaque s. m. (archit., also **plinto**) plinth.

alar (I) adj. 1. wing-shaped. 2. of or referring to wing.

alar (II) v. to set in rows or ranks.

alar (III) v. to heave, hoist, haul. 2. to lift.

alar (IV) v. 1. to provide with wings, form into wings. 2. to cause to fly. 3. to rise, ascend. 4. to soar, take to flight. 5. to exalt o. s.

alar (V) v. (sl.) 1. to go, leave. 2. to live (along).

alar (VI) v. (Braz.) to urge on, speed up.

alaranjado s. m. orange (colour). ‖ adj. orange: like an orange in shape or colour.

alarar v. to hang out (clothes) in the house or near the fireplace.

alardar (I) v. (also **alardear**) to make a show, show off, boast.

alardar (II) v. (also **lardear**) to lard, interlard.

alarde s. m. 1. ostentation, vainglory. 2. pomp, state, grandeur. 3. vanity, vainness.
fazer ~ to make a noise. **fazer** ~ **de** to make a parade of.

alardeadeira s. f. ostentatious woman.

alardeador s. m. boaster, ostentatious man. ‖ adj. boastful, ostentatious.

alardear v. to boast, bluster; to flaunt; to show off.

alardo s. m. 1. muster: a) review. b) troops available or ready for action. c) muster-roll or list of such troops. 2. show-off, boasting, ostentation.

alares s. m. pl. bird net (to catch partridges).

alargador s. m. 1. (tech.) counterbore, broach, reamer. 2. widener. ‖ adj. widening.

alargamento s. m. 1. widening. 2. enlargement, extension. 3. dilatation, expansion.

alargar v. 1. to widen. 2. to dilate. 3. to spread out. 4. to slacken, relax. 5. to augment, amplify, enlarge. 6. to develop, evolve. 7. to prolong, extend, stretch. 8. to spend a lot of money.
~ **a bolsa** to give (money), pay, spend. ~ **a língua** to speak without restraint. ~ **a mão** to go too far. ~ **o passo** to go faster. ~ **as rédeas** to give reins. ~-**se com alguém** to impart a secret.

alarido s. m. (less used **alarida** f.) 1. clamour, row, uproar. 2. vociferation. 3. complaint, crying, weeping.

alarifaço adj. (Braz.) (sup. of **alarife**) 1. lively, quick on the pins. 2. roguish.

alarifagem s. f. (Braz.) 1. expertise, skill, ability. 2. shrewdness, astuteness. 3. fraud, trickery, slyness, cunning.

alarife s. m. 1. architect. 2. (constr.) foreman.

alarma s. m. (less used **alarme**) 1. alarm, warning of danger. 2. signal. 3. shock. 4. row, vociferation. 5. tumult, confusion.
~ **aéreo** air-alarm, air-alert. ~ **de incêndio** fire alarm (plate R 8). ~ **falso** false alarm. **não dê** ~ **falso** don't cry wolf.

alarmante adj. m. + f. alarming, frightening.
notícias ~s scare news.

alarmar v. 1. to alarm. 2. to frighten. 3. to trouble, disturb. 4. ~-**se** to become frightened.

alarme s. m. = **alarma**.

alarmista s. m. + f. alarmist. ‖ adj. alarming.

alarvado adj. churlish, rustic, rough.

alarvaria s. f. 1. churlishness, rusticity. 2. brutality. 3. gluttony.

alarve s. m. + f. 1. churl, brute. 2. glutton. 3. m. (obs.) Bedouin. ‖ adj. m. + f. 1. churlish, brute. 2. gluttonous.

alarvia s. f. a crowd of brutes.

alastramento s. m. spreading, expansion, diffusion.

alastrante adj. m. + f. spreading, expanding, diffusing.

alastrar v. 1. to ballast, stow. 2. to spread out. 3. to diffuse. 4. to scatter. 5. to shed, pour. 6. to widen gradually. 7. to fill, cover.

alastrim s. m. (med.) alastrim, milk pox.

alatinado adj. Latinized.

alatinar v. to Latinize.

alatoar v. to provide with brass strips or inlay.

alaudado adj. lute-shaped.

alaúde (I) s. m. (mus.) lute.

alaúde (II) s. m. Portuguese (tunny-) fishing boat.

alavanca s. f. 1. lever, handspike (plates B 4, 15, C 15, M 2, 5, 12, 13). 2. (fig.) means. 3. collector (tramway). 4. handle, crank (plate B 15).
~ **de inversão de marcha** reversing lever (plate B 15). ~ **manual de entrelinha** line space lever (typewriter).

alavercar v. 1. to humble, bring down, humiliate. 2. ~-**se** to stoop, subject o. s. to.

alazão s. m. (also **lazão**, pl. **-ões**, f. **-zã**). sorrel (horse). ‖ adj. sorrel.

alazarado adj. 1. lazarlike, full of wounds. 2. indebted.

alazeirado adj. 1. hungry, starving, miserable. 2. leprous.

alba s. f. alba: former Provençal lyric poetry.

albacora s. f. (ichth.) germon.

albafar s. m. 1. perfume. 2. incense.

albanês s. m. (pl. **-eses**) (also **albano**) Albanian. ‖ adj. Albanian.

albanesa s. f. 1. f. of **albanês**. 2. (bot.) white anemone.

albano s. m. native or inhabitant of Alba Longa (Italy). ‖ adj. of or referring to Alba Longa.

albarda s. f. 1. packsaddle, sumpter saddle. 2. badly or poorly made jacket or coat. 3. oppression. 4. vexation.
nem de sela, nem de ~ by no means.

albardado adj. 1. said of a particular colouring of an ox or bull. 2. provided with a packsaddle.

albardão s. m. (pl. **-ões**) 1. large packsaddle. 2. improved form of packsaddle for riding too. 3. (Braz.) chain of mountains and valleys. 4. raised border of rivers or lakes.

albardar v. 1. to put a packsaddle on, to saddle. 2. to oppress. 3. to crumb (for frying or baking). 4. to cheat, deceit. 5. (coll.) to dress badly. 6. (coll.) to make hastily and badly, bungle, patch.

albardeira s. f. (bot.) wild rose.

albardeiro s. m. 1. saddler. 2. (coll.) unskillful tailor, botcher. ‖ adj. (also **abaldeiro, abaldeirado**) imperfect, unskilful. 2. lying, untruthful, cheating.

albardilha s. f. 1. a small packsaddle. 2. trap for falcons.

albarela s. f. eatable mushroom.

albarrã (I) s. f. (bot.) wild onion.

albarrã (II) s. f. (hist.) tower of a fort, fortification or castle, barbican.

albarrada s. f. 1. (hist.) stone wall without mortar. 2. flowerpot. 3. a sort of mug.

albatroz s. m. (ornith.) albatross.

albente adj. m. + f. (also **alvejante**) whitening.

alberca s. f. drain for excess water, drainage channel.

albergado adj. lodged, housed, sheltered.

albergador s. m. host, person who receives another in his house, gives lodge or shelter. ‖ adj. lodging, housing, sheltering.

albergagem s. f. (hist.) right to lodging or shelter.

albergamento s. m. lodging, sheltering, housing.

albergar v. 1. to lodge, shelter, receive. 2. to contain. 3. ~-**se** to lodge, take shelter or refuge.

albergaria s. f. 1. inn, hostelry, lodging-house. 2. asylum. 3. lodging agreement.

albergue s. m. 1. inn, hostelry, lodging-house. 2. lodging. 3. asylum. 4. hospice. 5. shelter. 6. den.

albergueiro s. m. host, innkeeper.

albescente adj. m. + f. fading, whitening.

albicante adj. m. + f. whitish.

albicastrense s. m. native or inhabitant of Castelo Branco (Portuguese city). ‖ adj. m. + f. of or referring to Castelo Branco.

albicaule adj. m. + f. (bot.) white-stemmed.

albicole adj. m. + f. white-necked.

álbido adj. 1. almost white, whitish. 2. cream.

albificação s. f. (pl. **-ões**) whitening, blanching, bleaching.

albiflor adj. m. + f. white-blossomed.

albigense s. m. + f. (hist.) Albigense. ‖ adj. Albigensian.

albina s. f. (bot.) yellow alder.

albínia s. f., **albinismo** m. albinism.

albinismo s. m. albinism, lack of normal pigmentation.

albino s. m. albino. ‖ adj. albinic.
albirrosado adj. pale-pink.
albirrostro adj. 1. white-beaked. 2. white-snouted.
albistelado adj. (Braz.) having white spots (ox).
albita s. f. (min) feldspar, albite.
albogue, alboque s. m. shepherd's horn.
albor s. m. = alvor.
alborcar v. to exchange, barter, trade, permute.
albornoz s. m. burnous.
alboroque s. m. meal served to celebrate the conclusion of a contract or agreement.
alborotar v. = alvoroçar.
alborque s. m. (also troca) barter, exchange.
albricoque s. m. (also, less used abricoque) apricot (fruit).
albricoqueiro s. m. (also, less used abricoqueiro) apricot (-tree).
albufeira s. f. 1. lagoon (of sea water), shallow lake. 2. residual water of olives.
albugem s. f. (pl. -ens) (less used form albugo m., med.) albugo, leucoma.
albuginado adj. (med., also albugíneo, albuginoso) albugineous.
albugínea s. f. (anat.) albuginea.
álbum s. m. (pl. álbuns) album.
~ para recortes scrapbook.
albume, albúmen s. m. albumen.
albumina s. f. (chem.) albumin.
albuminado adj. albuminous, albuminose.
albuminato s. m. (chem.) albuminate.
albuminiforme adj. m. + f. (chem.) albuminiform.
albuminóide s. m. (chem.) albuminoid. ‖ adj. m. + f. albuminoidal.
albuminoso adj. albuminous.
albuminúria, albuminuria s. f. (path.) albuminuria.
albuminúrico s. m. albuminuric: person suffering from albuminuria. ‖ adj. albuminuric.
alburno s. m. (bot.) alburnum, sapwood, splintwood.
alça (I) s. f. 1. ring, eye, loop. 2. handle, holder, ear (plate S 3). 3. (a pair of) braces. 4. strap (of slip, apron, etc.) (plate R 6). 5. notch (of the rearsight) (gun). 6. present, gift. 7. appellation. 8. leather piece or pad a shoemaker uses on his last.
~ de bolsa de viagem bag clasp.
alça (II) interj. used when heaving: heave!
alcaçaria s. f. 1. tannery, tan-yard. 2. shop street. 3. lodging. 4. (hist.) place where Moors and Jews where allowed to buy and sell.
alcácer s. m. (also alcáçar) 1. fortress. 2. castle. 3. palace. 4. sumptuous residence.
alcacereno s. m., alcacerense s. m. + f. native or inhabitant of Alcacer. ‖ adj. of or referring to Alcacer.
alcachinado adj. 1. curved, bent. 2. hunchbacked.
alcachinar v. 1. to curve, bend, bow. 2. to be distressed. 3. to shrink, contract. 4. to stoop down.
alcachofra (ô) s. f. (bot) artichoke.
alcachofrado s. m. artichoke-patterned embroidery. ‖ adj. artichoke-patterned.
alcachofral s. m. (pl. -ais) artichoke plantation.
alcachofrar v. 1. to pattern like an artichoke. 2. to rug. 3. to embroider with embossments.
alcáçova s. f. 1. fortress. 2. (hist.) castle (also naut.).
alcaçuz s. m. liquorice or licorice (plant and root).
alçada s. f. 1. competence. 2. jurisdiction. 3. sphere of influence. 4. (hist. + law) visiting court.
é da sua ~ it is in your way. estar debaixo da ~ de alguém to be under someone's jurisdiction or sphere of influence. isto é da minha ~ that comes within my scope. não é da minha ~ it is no matter of mine.
alcadafe, alcadefe s. m. a barkeeper's vessel (either for measure or receiving the overmeasure).

alçado s. m. 1. elevation, upright projection. 2. (typogr.) dry-room. ‖ adj. 1. lifted, raised, heaved. 2. (Braz.) runaway (cattle or domestic animal).
alçador s. m. lifter, raiser, heaver.
alçadura s. f. lifting, raising, heaving.
alçagem s. f. hanging up (printed sheets for drying).
alcagüetar v. to denounce, accuse (a criminal), reveal a crime.
alcagüete s. m. 1. telltale, stool pigeon, informer. 2. (Braz., thief's sl.) alarm watch.
alcaidaria s. f. position or dignity of an alcaide.
alcaide s. m. 1. alcaide, alcayde. 2. (Braz.): a) old and useless thing. b) unsellable goods, remainders. c) ugly or old person. d) bad horse.
alcaidessa s. f. (also alcaidina) 1. an alcaide's wife. 2. a female alcaide.
alcaiota s. f. of alcaiote = alcoviteiro.
alcalescência s. f. alkalescence.
alcalescente adj. m. + f. alkalescent.
álcali s. m. alkali.
alcalificante adj. m. + f. alkalifying.
alcalificar v. to alkalify.
alcalimetria s. f. alkalimetry.
alcalimétrico adj. alkalimetric(al).
alcalímetro s. m. alkalimeter.
alcalinar, alcalinizar, alcalizar v. to alkalize.
alcalinismo s. m. excessive use of alkalis or its effect.
alcalinização, alcalização s. f. (pl. -ões) alkalization.
alcalinizar v. (also alcalinar) to alkalize.
alcalino adj. alkaline.
alcalóide s. m. alkaloid.
alcaloideu adj. (f. -éia) alkaloid.
alçamento s. m. 1. (typogr.) raising (of the printed sheets). 2. hoisting, heaving.
alcamonia s. f. (also alcomonia) sweet made of syrup and manioc flour.
alcançadiço adj. easily reached.
alcançado adj. 1. in arrears. 2. obtained. 3. attained.
alcançador s. m. 1. attainer. 2. obtainer. ‖ adj. 1. attaining. 2. obtaining.
alcançadura s. f. bruise or gall on the hoofs caused by interfering.
alcançamento s. m. 1. reaching, attainment. 2. obtainment.
alcançar v. †. to reach, attain. 2. to carry (gun). 3. to obtain, get, succeed. 4. to catch. 5. to catch up. 6. to extend, stretch out. 7. to touch. 8. to understand, perceive, conceive. 9. to suffice. 10. to follow (in short intervals), recur. 11. to find out the reach or extent of.
alcançar um resultado to obtain a result. alcançaram a vitória they achieved victory, carried the day. alcança números de sete algarismos it runs into seven figures. alcancei o meu objetivo I've secured my object, I gained my end. sua vista alcança longe his eyes reach very far. tudo quanto a vista alcança as far as the eye reaches. a água alcançou o ponto de ebulição the water is at the boiling point.
alcançável adj. m. + f. (pl. -áveis) 1. reachable, attainable. 2. gettable, get-at-able. 3. understandable, conceivable.
alcance s. m. (also less used alcanço) 1. reach (sight, mind, gun), wideness of range. 2. range (gun). 3. reach, overtaking. 4. track, trail, pursuit. 5. obtainment, attainment. 6. intelligence, understanding, comprehension. 7. value, importance. 8. defalcation, fraud.
~ visual range of vision. ao ~ da mão within arm's reach. ao ~ da voz (do ouvido) within call (hearing). ao ~ do tiro within gunshot. ao ~ de todos easy, comprehensible. ao ~ dos raios within

the verges of the rays. **ao meu** ~ within my grasp. **de grande** ~ long range. **fora de** ~ out of one's reach. **não está ao meu** ~ it is not within my reach. **farão tudo o que estiver ao seu** ~ they will do all in their power. **ir no** ~ **de** to follow closely. **ter outro** ~ to aim at something else. **um homem de grande** ~ a man of consequence.
alcancilhos s. m. pl. a sort of (riding) tournament.
alcândor s. m. 1. summit, top, pinnacle. 2. = **alcândora.**
alcândora s. f. a hawk's or falcon's perch or roost.
alcandorado adj. 1. roosted or perched high up. 2. high up. 3. (fig.) exalted, sublime.
alcandorar-se v. 1. to roost. 2. to place o. s. high up. 3. to raise, elevate o. s. 4. to sublimate, sublime. 5. to boast, be proud of.
alcanfor s. m., **alcânfora** f. (also **cânfora**) camphor.
alcânfora s. f. = **cânfora.**
alcanforar v. = **canforar.**
alcanforeira s. f. (also **canforeira**) camphor tree.
alcantil s. m. (pl. **-is**) 1. slope, declivity, precipice, crag. 2. pinnacle, summit.
alcantilada s. f. chain of mountains, crags.
alcantilado adj. 1. craggy. 2. pinnacled.
alcantilar v. to cut steep down, to scarp. 2. to rise steeply.
alcantiloso adj. 1. craggy, cragged. 2. pinnacled.
alcanzia s. f. 1. (also **alcancia**) pot full of flowers or other small tokens (or ash) formerly thrown at knights during tournaments. 2. (hist.) a sort of earthen grenade. 3. earthenware money-box.
alcanziada s. f. throwing of **alcanzias.**
alçapão s. m. (pl. **-ões**) 1. trap-door (plate P 2). (fig.) snare, device, trap. 3. fly or flap of trousers.
alcaparra s. f. (bot.) caper: 1. the shrub (also **alcaparreira**). 2. its buds.
alcaparrado adj. 1. seasoned with capers. 2. (fig.) a) sharpened (appetite). b) appetizing. c) cheerful.
alcaparral s. m. (pl. **-ais**) growth or field of capers.
alcaparreira-cheirosa s. f. (pl. **alcaparreiras-cheirosas**) mustard shrub.
alcaparreiro s. m. seller of capers.
alça-pé s. m. (pl. **alça-pés**) 1. snare (for catching birds). 2. trip (to throw down a man). 3. (fig.) trick, snare, fraud.
alçaprema s. f. 1. crowbar, heaver pole (plate G 2). 2. dentist's forceps.
alçapremar v. 1. to lift with a crowbar. 2. to oppress.
alçar v. 1. to raise. 2. to lift, elevate. 3. to edify. 4. to exalt, praise. 5. to heave. 6. to hoist (sails). 7. to collect (printed sheets for binding). 8. to plough up. 9. to nominate, elect. 10. to acclaim. 11. to stand out, overtop. 12. to pride oneself on. 13. (Braz.) to go astray, abscond (cattle). 14. (~-se) to rebel, rise against.
alcaravão s. m. (pl. **-ões**) (ornith.) European bittern.
alcaravia s. f. (bot.) caraway seeds.
alcaraviz s. m. (pl. **~es**) tuyère (of a smithy) (plate A 6).
alcarrada s. f. the movements of a bird of prey when it catches its victim.
alcatear v. to flock together, form a pack or gang.
alcatéia s. f. 1. pack of wolves. 2. herd (of wild animals). 3. gang (of criminals).
estar de ~ to lurk, be on the lurk.
alcatifa s. f. 1. carpet. 2. sward.
alcatifado adj. 1. covered with a carpet or carpets. 2. swarded.
alcatifar v. 1. to carpet, cover with carpets. 2. to cover with swards or turf.
alcatifeiro s. m. carpetmaker or manufacturer.
alcatira s. f. (bot.) tragacanth.
alcatra s. f. (also **alcatra**) rump (beef).

alcatrão s. m. 1. tar. 2. pitch.
alcatrate s. m. (naut.) plank-sheer, gunwale.
alcatraz (I) s. m. (pl. **~es**) 1. frigate bird, man-of-war bird. 2. designation of several kinds of pelicans.
alcatraz (II) s. m. (pl. **~es**) (coll.) bonesetter.
alcatreiro adj. (coll.) big-rumped.
alcatroado adj. tarred.
cartão ~ tarboard. **macadame** ~ tar macadam.
alcatroamento s. m. tarring.
alcatroar v. 1. to tar. 2. to asphalt.
alcatroeiro s. m. 1. tar maker. 2. tar seller.
alcatruz s. m. (pl. **~es**) bucket (of a noria).
alcatruzado adj. 1. curved, bent, arched, bulged. 2. awkward, clumsy.
alcatruzar v. 1. to shape like a bucket. 2. to provide with buckets. 3. to bend, curve, arch, bulge. 4. to raise and lower. 5. to bow (old age).
alcavala s. f. 1. tax. 2. excise tax, fiscal extorsion. 3. (fig.) roguery, rascality. 4. (obs.) company, band, gang. 5. (obs.) rushing, running.
alcavaleiro s. m. (hist.) 1. taxator, tax-renter. 2. tax assessor. 3. tollman, tax-collector.
alce (I) s. m. (zool.) moose, elk.
alce (II) s. m. (Braz.) bridling, raising or lifting of the horse by means of the bridles.
alce (III) s. m. (Braz.) 1. rest. 2. truce. 3. improvement (health). 4. fattening. 5. slowing down (a horse) to spare its forces.
alceamento s. m. raising, lifting, hoisting.
alcear v. 1. to heave, lift. 2. to bear the weight (said of a block used for lifting heavy objects). 3. to provide with loops, handles, straps, etc. (see **alça**). 4. to collect (printed) sheets for binding.
alcedinídeo s. m. bird of the genus Alcedo, e. g. kingfisher, halcyon.
alcicorne adj. m. + f. antlered like a moose.
alcionário s. m. (zool.) alcyonarian.
alcíone s. f. 1. (astr. also **alciona** f.) Alcyon: brightest star, in the Pleiades. 2. (ornith. also **alcião, alcíon** m., **alcíona** f.) halcyon: kingfisher.
alciôneo, alciônico adj. halcyon: 1. of or referring to the halcyon (the kingfisher). 2. peaceful, pleasant, agreeable.
alcmânio adj. Alcmanian (verse).
alcobaça s. m. big (coloured) handkerchief used by persons who snuff.
alcobacense s. m. + f. native or inhabitant of Alcobaça. ‖ adj. of or referring to Alcobaça (city or monastery).
alcoceifa s. f. (obs.) 1. brothel, bawdy-house. 2. district containing many brothels, (U.S.A.) red-light district.
alcofa (ô) (I) s. f. flat basket with handles.
alcofa (ô) (II) s. m. + f. pander.
alcofar v. to pander.
alcomonia s. f. = **alcamonia.**
álcool s. m. (pl. **-ois**) 1. alcohol. 2. spirit(s).
lâmpada a ~ spirit-lamp.
alcoolato s. m. (chem.) alcoholate.
alcoólatra s. m. + f. alcoholic, drunkard. ‖ adj. alcoholic; suffering from the excessive use of alcoholic liquors.
alcoolatura s. f. alcoholature, alcoholic tincture.
alcoólico s. m. alcoholic, drunkard. ‖ adj. alcoholic: containing, of or referring to alcohol.
bebidas alcoólicas spirituous liquors.
alcoolismo s. m. alcoholism: 1. morbid consequence of overindulgence in alcoholic liquors. 2. the state of being affected by alcohol.
alcoolista s. m. + f. alcoholic, drunkard.
alcoolização s. f. (pl. **-ões**) alcoholization.

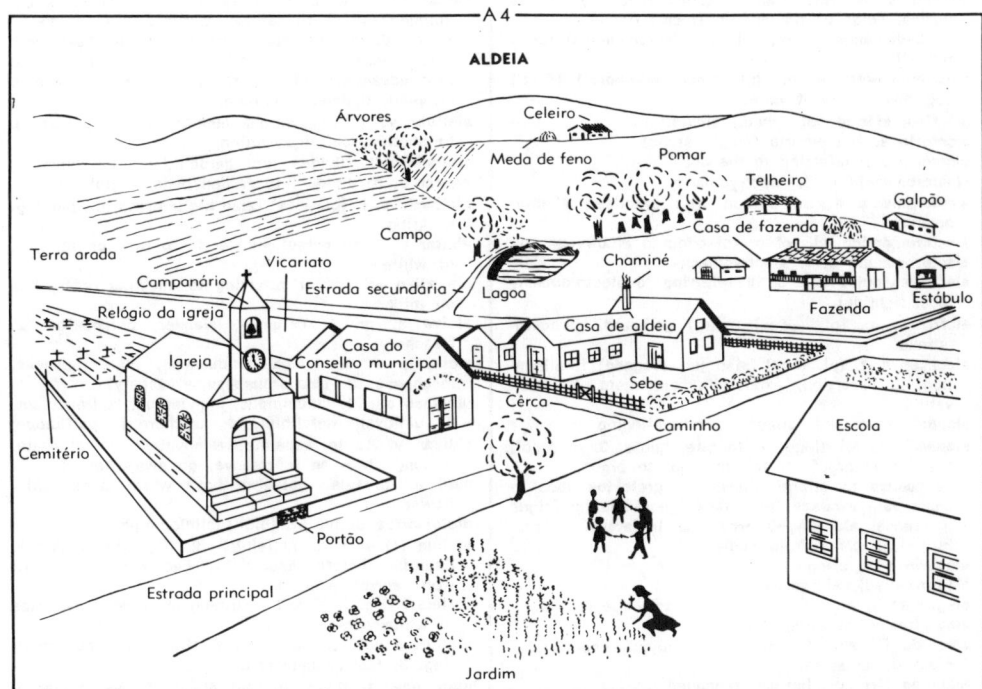

A 4

ALDEIA

Árvores — Celeiro — Meda de feno — Pomar — Telheiro — Galpão — Campo — Casa de fazenda — Terra arada — Vicariato — Chaminé — Campanário — Estrada secundária — Lagoa — Estábulo — Relógio da igreja — Casa de aldeia — Fazenda — Igreja — Casa do Conselho municipal — Sebe — Cêrca — Caminho — Escola — Cemitério — Portão — Estrada principal — Jardim

alcoolizado adj. drunk, intoxicated, in liquor.
alcoolizar v. 1. to alcoholize. 2. to intoxicate.
alcoolômetro, alcoômetro s. m. alcoholometer.
alcoranista s. m. + f. 1. Alcoranist. 2. Alcoran expert. ‖ adj. 1. Alcoranic. 2. expert in the Alcoran.
alcorão s. m. 1. Alcoran, Koran. 2. Mohammedanism.
alcorca s. f. furrow, drainage-channel.
alcorça s. f., **alcorce** m. sugar-icing, sugar-coating.
alcorcova s. f. 1. (also **corcova**) hump. 2. ditch. 3. hedge, hedgerow.
alcorcovar v. 1. to ditch. 2. to hedge.
alcorque s. m. (hist.) high (thick-soled) shoe for women.
alconce s. m. (also **alcoice, prostíbulo**) brothel.
alconceiro s. m. (also **alcoiceiro**) 1. bawd, brothel keeper. 2. person who frequents brothels.
alcova s. f. 1. alcove (plate C 7). 2. hiding-place.
alcovista s. m. mash, masher, wolf.
alcovitagem s. f. (pl. **-ens**) 1. panderism. 2. intrigue. 3. telltale, gossip.
alcovitar v. 1. to pander, bawd. 2. to intrigue, plot. 3. to tell tales, blab, gossip.
alcoviteira s. f. (also **alcoveta, alcaiota**) panderess.
alcoviteirice s. f. (also **alcovitice**) 1. panderism. 2. procuring, pimping. 3. seduction, allurement. 4. gossip, tittle-tattle.
alcoviteiro s. m. (also **alcoveto, alcaiote**) 1. panderer, pimp. 2. telltale, gossiper. 3. intriguer.
alcunha s. f. nickname.
alcunhar v. to nickname.
aldagrante s. m. (Braz.) 1. rogue, swindler. 2. vagabond, good-for-nothing.
aldeado adj. 1. arranged in villages. 2. settled with villages.
aldeamento s. m. 1. division into villages. 2. (Braz.) Indian settlement, directed by a missionary or

lay authority. 3. (Braz.) quarters for convicts on Fernando Noronha.
aldeão s. m. (pl. **aldeãos, aldeões, aldeães;** f. **aldeã**) 1. countryman, peasant. 2. villager. ‖ adj. 1. of or referring to a village. 2. born in a village. 3. rustic, rural.
aldear v. 1. to divide into villages. 2. to populate (forming villages). 3. to join or unite in(to) one village only.
aldebarã s. f. (astr.) Aldebaran.
aldeia s. f. 1. village (plates A 4, P 17). 2. (Braz.): a) Indian settlement. b) any one of the huts or houses of an Indian settlement. c) cluster of houses of soldiers' families around barracks.
estar na ~ e não ver as casas to see no trees because of the wood.
aldeído s. m. (chem.) aldehyde.
aldeola, aldeota s. f. hamlet.
aldino adj. (typogr.) Aldine: pertaining or relating to the Italian printer Aldo Manuzio (1450-1515).
aldrabas s. f. pl. (Braz.) leather leggings used by the natives.
aldrava s. f. (also **aldraba**) 1. latch. 2. (door) knocker. 3. door handle.
aldravada s. f. rap at the door with the knocker.
aldravado adj. patched: made hastily and poorly.
aldravão s. m. (pl. **-ões**) 1. big latch, door handle or knocker. 2. swindler, liar, rogue. 3. patcher, botcher.
aldravar v. 1. to latch. 2. to patch: make hastily or poorly. 3. to rap (at the door with a knocker). 4. to talk confusedly. 5. to lie a lot.
aldravice s. f. roguery, swindle, fraud, big lie.
álea s. f. (also **aléia**) alley, walk.
alealdar v. (also **lealdar**) to legalize.
aleatório adj. aleatory, contingent, fortuitous, casual.
alecítico adj. (biol., also **alécito**) alecithal.

alecrim s. m. (pl. **-ins**) 1. (bot.) rosemary. 2. its leaves, twigs or flowers. 3. .(tech.) timber.

alecrim-do-campo s. m. (pl. **alecrins-do-campo**) (bot.) romerillo.

alecrim-do-norte s. m. (pl. **alecrins-do-norte**) (Braz.) bog myrtle, sweet gale.

aléctico, alético adj. (med.) alexic.

alectória s. f. alectoria (magic stone).

alectório adj. referring to the cock.

alectoromancia s. f. alectryomancy.

alectoromante s. m. person who practised alectryomancy.

alectoromântico adj. of or referring to alectryomancy.

alectoromaquia s. f. alectryomachy.

alectoromáquico adj. of or referring to alectryomachy (cock-fighting).

alefriz s. m. (pl. **~ões**) (naut.) garboard, garboard-strake.

alegação s. f. (pl. **-ões**) (also jur. **alegado**) 1. allegation. 2. assertion, exposition, statement. 3. motivation.

alegante s. m. + f. alleger. ‖ adj. alleging.

alegar v. 1. to allege. 2. to cite, quote. 3. to proof, present as proof. 4. to plead. 5. to argue. **~ doença** to allege illness. **~ pretextos vãos** to make vain excuses. **ele alega ignorância** he feigns ignorance. **ele alegou provir da Inglaterra** he professed to come from England.

alegoria s. f. allegory.

alegórico adj. allegoric(al).

alegorista s. m. + f. allegorist. ‖ adj. allegoristic.

alegorizar v. to allegorize.

alegrado (I) adj. 1. happy, gay, joyful, cheerful. 2. pleased, satisfied.

alegrado (II) adj. (surg.) trepanned.

alegrador s. m. cheerer, animator. ‖ adj. cheering, animating.

alegramento s. m less used form of **alegria**.

alegrão s. m. (pl. **-ões**) 1. great joy. 2. merry fellow.

alegrar (I) v. 1. to make happy, rejoice, gladden, cheer. 2. to embellish. 3. to intoxicate slightly (with drinks). 4. **~-se** to be or become happy, gay.

alegrar (II) v. (surg.) to trepan.

alegrativo adj. cheering, cheerful, animating.

alegre (I) adj. m. + f. 1. happy, gay, cheerful, light-hearted, light-spirited. 2. (also **alegrete, tocado**) slightly intoxicated, tipsy. 3. lively (colours). 4. pleased, satisfied. **~ como um passarinho** as merry as a cricket (or grig), gay as a lark.

alegre (II) s. m. (Braz.) tool used: 1. to incise lactiferous trees. 2. to make wooden spoons or ladles.

alegrete (I) s. m. (flower) bed.

alegrete (Ii) adj. m. + f. 1. rather gay. 2. a bit tipsy.

alegreto s. m. (mus.) allegretto. ‖ adj. (mus.) allegretto: light, graceful and moderately fast in tempo.

alegria s. f. 1. joy, gladness, cheerfulness, happiness, gayness, mirth. 2. satisfaction. 3. pleasure, delight. 4. Mexican tree of the family Liliaceae. **ele pulou de ~** he lept for joy.

alegro s. m. (mus.) allegro. ‖ adv. allegro.

aléia s. f. 1. alley. 2. row of shrubs or trees.

aleijada s. f. 1. f. form of **aleijado**: cripple. 2. (Braz.) variety of sugar-cane.

aleijado s. m. cripple. ‖ adj. 1. crippled, disabled, maimed, game. 2. lame. **uma perna aleijada** a game leg.

aleijamento s. m. 1. crippling, maiming. 2. = **aleijão**.

aleijão s. m. (pl. **-ões**) 1. physical deformity. 2. weak-mindedness.

aleijar v. 1. to cause physical deformity or weak-mindedness. 2. to deform, mutilate, cripple, maim. 3. to disfigure, alter, corrupt. 4. to hurt very much (feeling). 5. to sell for a high price. 6. to take advantage (of a person). 7. **~-se** to become crippled, maimed, mutilated.

aleiloar v. 1. to auction, auctioneer. 2. to put up to auction, sell by auction.

aleirado adj. divided into garden beds or fields.

aleirar v. to divide into garden beds or fields.

aleitação s. f. (pl. **-ões**) (also **aleitamento** m.) nursing, suckling.

aleitar v. 1. to nurse, suckle. 2. to feed on milk. 3. to whiten.

aleitativo adj. of or referring to suckling or feeding on milk.

aleive s. m. 1. calumny, slander, defamation. 2. treachery.

aleivosia s. f. 1. calumniousness, slanderousness, meanness. 2. trecherousness, treachery.

aleivoso adj. 1. calumnious, slanderous. 2. fraudulent. 3. disloyal, unfaithful. 4. trecherous, perfidious.

aleixar v. 1. to separate, remove. 2. to elongate, prolong. 3. **~-se** to remove, go away, leave.

aleli s. m. (also **goiveiro**, bot.) white stock, gillyflower.

alelomorfos s. m. pl. (biol.) allelomorph.

aleluia (I) s. f. 1. hallelujah. 2. (fig.) happiness. 3. Saturday berofe Easter. 4. Eastertide. 5. (bot.) wood sorrel, shamrock.

aleluia (II) s. f. (Braz.) swarming of (winged) termites or white ants.

aleluítico adj. 1. laudatory. 2. (fig.) welcome, greeting. 3. festive celebrating.

além adv. 1. there, in that place. 2. over there. 3. farther on. 4. on the other side, beyond. 5. far. 6. farther. 7. over and above. 8. besides. **~ de** 1. yonder. 2. over and above. **~ de (do) que** besides. **~ de sessenta** over, above or beyond sixty, on the thither side of sixty. **~ disto**. 1. add to that. 2. on the back of that. 3. besides, moreover. **~ do que** in addition (to). **o ~, além-mundo** the future life. **isso está ~ de minhas forças** that surpasses my possibilities. **para ~ de** over and above, more than. **passar ~ de** to pass over.

alemânico adj. 1. Alamanic, Alemanic. 2. German, Germanic.

alemanismo s. m. 1. Alamanic trait or feature. 2. Germanism.

alemanizar v. 1. to Germanize, germanize. 2. **~-se** to acquire German habits.

alemão s. m. (pl. **-ães**; f. **-ã**) German: 1. native or inhabitant of Germany. 2. German language.' ‖ adj. German. **ele falou mal o ~** he spoke bad German.

além-mar s. m. oversea country, territories, etc. ‖ adj. + adv. oversea(s).

alemoado adj. (Braz.) Germanlike, Germanized.

alemoar(-se) v. Braz.) = **alemanizar(-se)**.

alentado adj. 1. courageous, brave. 2. diligent, hard-working. 3. corpulent, stout. 4.' large, voluminous. 5. abundant. 6. good. 7. succulent, juicy.

alentador s. m. 1. encourager, animator, cheerer. 2. nourisher. ‖ adj. 1. encouraging, animating, cheering. 2. nourishing.

alentar v. 1. to encourage, animate, cheer. 2. to nourish. 3. to breathe, take one's breath, recover o. s. 4. to cheer up, take a heart. 5. to get excited.

alentecer v. to slow (down).

alentejano s. m. native or inhabitant of Alentejo (Portuguese town). ‖ adj. of or referring to Alentejo.

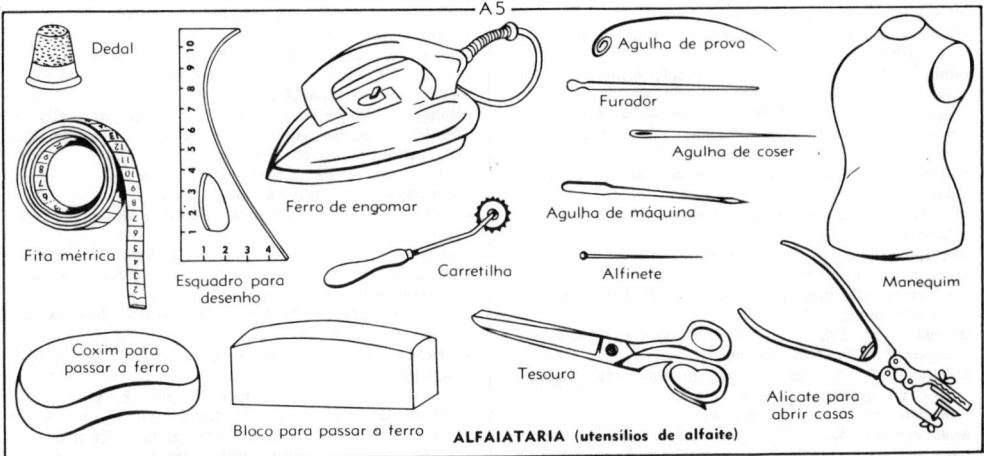

— A 5 —

Dedal

Ferro de engomar

Fita métrica

Esquadro para desenho

Carretilha

Coxim para passar a ferro

Bloco para passar o ferro

Agulha de prova

Furador

Agulha de coser

Agulha de máquina

Alfinete

Tesoura

Manequim

Alicate para abrir casas

ALFAIATARIA (utensilios de alfaite)

alento s. m. 1. breath. 2. respiration. 3. courage. 4. diligence, effort. 5. food, nourishment. 6. enthusiasm. 7. ~s pl. nostrils (horse).
dar ~ to encourage.

áleo adj. (her.) winged.

aleonado adj. 1. that has the colour of a lion, tawny. 2. fulvous, reddish-yellow.

alepidoto s. m. (ichth.) alepidote. || adj. alepidote.

alepocéfalo s. m. (ichth.) alepicephalous.

alequeado adj. fanlike, fan-shaped (bot.), flabelliform.

alergênio s. m. (immunology) allergen.

alergia s. f. allergy.

alérgico adj. allergic.

alerta s. m. 1. alert. 2. watchfulness. || adv. alert. || interj. attention!
dar ~ to give (sound) alarm.

alertar v. 1. to alert, give alarm. 2. ~-se to be watchful, be on the lookout.

alesado adj. (Braz., less used form of lesado) prejudiced, wronged, etc.

alestar v. 1. to make or become nimble. 2. to disembarrass.

aleta s. f. 1. (little) room. 2. (tech.) wing. 3. (anat.) wing of the nose.
~ de curvatura (aeron.) camber flap (plate A 3).
~ de bordo de ataque (aeron.) auto-slot (plate A 3).

aletargado adj. inert, lethargic.

alético adj. (med., also aléctico) alexic, alexinic.

aletologia s. f. (philos.) alethiology.

aletradar-se v. to become learned or lettered.

aletria s. f. vermicelli.

aletriado adj. like vermicelli.

aleuromancia s. f. aleuromancy.

aleuromante s. m. + f. person who practises aleuromancy.

aleuromântico adj. aleuromantic.

aleurômetro s. m. aleurometer.

aleurona s. f. aleuron(e)

alevadouro s. m. (also alevadoiro) wooden lever to raise the (mill)stone in a (horse-)mill.

alevantadiço adj. seditious, turbulent, riotous.

alevantar v. (also levantar) to lift, raise, etc.

alevante s. m. 1. = levantamento. 2. mutiny, rebellion. 3. plant of the family Labiatae.

alevedar v. (less used form of levedar) to leaven, ferment.

alevim s. m. (pl. -ins) fry, young fish.

alexandrinismo s. m. Alexandrine peculiarity.

alexandrino (I) adj. Alexandrine, Alexandrian: of or referring to Alexander the Great.

alexandrino (II) s. m. Alexandrine, Alexandrian: native or inhabitant of Alexandria. || adj. Alexandrine: of or referring to Alexandria.

alexandrino (III) s. m. (poetry) Alexandrine. || adj. Alexandrine.

alexandrita s. f. (min.) alexandrite.

alexia s. f. (path.) alexia.

aleziriado adj. boggy, marshy, swampy.

alfa (I) s. m. alpha: 1. first letter of the Greek and Syrian alphabet. 2. (fig.) beginning. 3. chief star in any constellation.
~ e ômega alpha and omega, the beginning and the end.

alfa (II) s. f. (Port.) 1. boundary or landmark between private and common lands. 2. boundary, frontier. 3. furrow for sowing.

alfa (III) s. f. (Port.) 1. flame. 2. rosy colour of the cheeks.

alfa (IV) s. m. mullah priest of the Mahomedan Senegalese Negroes.

alfabetação s. f. (also alfabetização f., alfabetamento m.) alphabetization, alphabetizing.

alfabetado adj. alphabetical, in alphabetical order.

alfabetador s. m. alphabetizer.

alfabetar v. to alphabetize, put in alphabetical order.

alfabetário adj. alphabetic(al), of or referring to the alphabet.

alfabético adj. alphfabetic(al): 1. of or referring to the alphabet. 2. in alphabetical order.

alfabetismo s. m. literacy, the ability to read and write.

alfabetização s. f. making literate, teaching to read and write.

alfabetizado s. m. literate: person who can read and write. || adj. literate: able to read and write.

alfabetizar v. to teach to read and write.

alfabeto s. m. 1. alphabet: a) letters or signs forming an alphabet. b) first notions, elementary principles 2. any conventional series.

alfaçal s. m. (pl. -ais) lettuce plantation.

alface s.-f. (bot.) lettuce.
fresco como uma ~ fresh as a daisy.

alfacinha s. f. 1. dim. of alface 2. m. + f. (playful) nickname of Lisbon natives (because of their fondness for lettuce). || adj. (playful) of or referring to Lisbon natives.

alfafa s. f. (bot., also luzerna) alfalfa, lucern(e).

alfafal s. m. (pl. -ais) alfalfa plantation.
alfageme s. m. (obs.) 1. sword cutler. 2. armourer. 3. barber.
alfaia s. f. 1. domestic implement, furniture, tableware. 2. adornment, ornament, decoration. 3. jewel, gem. 4. silver plate or tray. 5. agricultural implement. 6. (church) vestments, garments, clerical robes.
alfaiar v. 1. to adorn, embellish, beautify. 2. to furnish, fit up (house).
alfaiata s. f. seamstress, tailoress, dressmaker.
alfaiatar v. to tailor, sew.
alfaiataria s. f. tailor's workshop.
alfaiate s. m. tailor.
  ~ remendão patcher, botcher. utensílios de ~ a tailor's utensils (plate A 5).
alfame s. m. (hist.) 1. Jewish quarters or districts. 2. asylum, shelter, refuge.
alfândega s. f. 1. (also aduana) customhouse, customs. 2. (fig.) uproarious, noisy place.
  direitos da ~ custom-duties.
alfandegagem s. f. (pl. -ens) (also alfandegamento) 1. fixing, collection or payment of customs. 2. storage in the customhouse.
alfandegar v. 1. to fix, collect or pay customs, clear goods. 2. to store in the customhouse.
alfandegário adj. (also alfandegar m. + f.) of or referring to customs.
alfandegueiro s. m. customhouse officer. || adj. of or referring to customs.
alfanjada s. f. stroke or cut with a scimitar or cutlass.
alfanje s. m. cutlass or scimitar.
alfanumérico adj. alphameric, alphanumeric: referring to a code system combining letters of the alphabet and numbers.
alfaque s. m. 1. reef, rock. 2. (quick)sand-bank. 3. whirlpool, swirling water. 4. dangerous depression in a bathing place.
alfaqui s. m. fakir, fakeer.
alfaraz s. m. (pl. ~es) 1. Arabian horse trained for war. 2. skilled horseman.
alfario adj. said of a playful and neighing horse.
alfarrábio s. m. (depr.) old or second-hand book.
alfarrabista s. m. + f. 1. second-hand bookseller. 2. collector of second-hand books.
alfarrabístico adj. of or referring to second-hand books.
alfarricoque s. m. insignificant person.
alfarroba (ô) s. f. (bot.) carob, locust bean.
alfarrobal s. m. (bot. pl. -ais) plantation of carob-trees.
alfarrobar v. to rub (fishing lines) with carob.
alfarrobeira s. f. (bot.) carob, locust-tree.
alfavaca s. f. (bot.) basil.
alfavaca-cheirosa s. f. (pl. alfavacas-cheirosas) (bot.) sweet basil.
alfavaca-de-cobra s. f. (pl. alfavacas-de-cobra) (bot.) pellitory.
alfazema s. f. (bot.) lavender.
  óleo de ~ spike oil.
alfazemar v. to perfume with lavender.
alfeça s. f. (tech.) 1. die holder. 2. block or plate under a die. 3. stripper (for freeing a punch). 4. bolster.
alfeire s. m. 1. flock of young female sheep. 2. pigsty, pigpen.
alfeireiro s. m. shepherd (of young female sheep).
alfeizar s. m. (pl. ~es) strecher (of a frame-saw) (plate S 2).
alféloa s. f. 1. sugar-coating, icing. 2. confectionery, sweetmeats.
alfeloeiro s. m. confectioner.

alfena s. f. (bot., also alfeneiro) privet.
alfenado adj. privet-coloured.
alfenar v. 1. to dye with privet berries. 2. to embellish, adorn. 3. to effeminate.
alfênico s. m. candy(-sugar).
alfenide s. m. alfenide (alloy of nickel and silver).
alfenim s. m. (pl. -ins) 1. confectionery, sweetmeats. 2. dainty or touchy person.
  ele é um ~ he is a touchy fellow.
alfeninado adj. delicate, effeminate.
alfeninar-se v. to become fragile, touchy, effeminate.
alferça s. f. alferce s. m. 1. pick(-axe). 2. mattock.
alferes s. m. sg. + pl. 1. (hist.) second lieutenant 2. standard-bearer, ensign.
alfim adv. (preferable forms are: afinal, finalmente), finally, at the end.
alfinetada s. f. 1. pin-prick, pin-stich. 2. sudden strong pain.
alfinetar v. 1. to prick with a pin. 2. to pin on, fasten with pins. 3. to shape like a pin. 4. to criticize harshly. 5. to satirize. 6. to epigrammatize. 7. to hurt with words, chaff, tease.
alfinete (ê) (I) s. m. 1. pin (plate A 1, 5). 2. tiepin. 3. ~s pl. pin money.
  ~ de gravata tiepin (plate A 1). ~ de peito brooch. ~ de segurança safety-pin (plate A 1). não vale um ~ it is not worth anything.
alfinete (ê) (II) s. m. (bot.) red spur valerian.
alfineteira s. f. 1. pincushion. 2. pincase.
alfitete s. m. 1. dough containing eggs, sugar, butter or bacon. 2. big pie or pastry.
alfobre s. m. (also alfofre). 1. seedling nursery (plate F 4) 2. hotbed. 3. garden-bed between two furrows of water.
  ~ florestal young tree nursery (plate F 4).
alfombra s. f. 1. carpet. 2. swardy or turfy land. 3. lawn.
alfombrado adj. 1. covered with carpets. 2. lawny. 3. swardy, mossy.
alfombrar v. 1. to carpet. 2. to sward, sod, moss.
alfonsia s. f. (also alforra) mildew.
alfonsim s. m. (pl. -ins) silver coin formely used in Portugal.
alforjada s. f. 1. bagful. 2. contents of a bag. 3. great many of several things. 4. huge bag entirely filled.
alforjar v. 1. to bag, put in a bag or sack. 2. to collect (taxes) 3. to put into one's pocket or purse. 4. to stuff one's pockets.
alforje s. m. 1. bag or sack with two pouches. 2. saddle-bag. 3. knapsack, travelling bag. 4. contents or capacity of a bag or saddle-bag.
  ir de ~ to carry but small provision on a journey.
alforra (ô) s. f. (also alfonsia) mildew.
alforrar v. to mildew.
alforreca s. f. (zool., also água-viva) medusa, jellyfish.
alforria s. f. 1. enfranchisement, release from slavery. 2. libertation.
  dar carta de ~ to set free, to give liberty to a slave.
alforriado adj. enfranchised, freed.
alforriar v. 1. to enfranchise, free. 2. to ransom, redeem, liberate. 3. ~-se to liberate o. s.
alfredo s. m. simple lamp whithout chimney or glass.
alfridária s. f. (astr.) alfridary.
alfurja s. f. (pop. form alfuja; obs.) 1. back yard or court. 2. narrow street, back street (where rubbish and dirt was thrown), slum. 3. dung heap. 4. pigsty. 5. dirty room or dwelling. 6. cave, den.
alga s. f. seaweed, alga.

algáceo adj. algal, algoid.
algaço s. m. seaweed thrown on the beach.
algália (I) s. f. (med.) catheter, probe.
algália (II) s. f. 1. (zool.) musk deer. 2. musk (secretion). 3. civet: a) (zool.) civet cat. b) its musky secretion.
algaliar v. (med.) to catheterize, to probe.
~ **a bexiga** to probe the bladder.
algar s. m. 1. gully, gorge formed by a stream of water. 2. den, cavern, 3. precipice.
algaravia s. f. (also **algravia**) 1. Arabic (language). 2. similar way of speaking 3. confusion of voices. 4. gibberish.
algaraviada s. f. (also **algraviada**) 1. confusion of voices. 2. vociferation, clamour, shouting.
algaraviar v. (also **algraviar**) 1. to gibber. 2. to write confusedly. 3. to express in Arabic.
~ **uma língua** to bungle a language.
algaraviz s. m. tuyère, twyer.
algarismo s. m. 1. cipher, figure, numeral. 2. number.
algarobeira s. f., **algarobo** s. m. (bot.) mesquite.
algarvio s. m. (also **algarviense** m. + f.) native or ihabitant of Algarve (Port. city). ‖ adj. (also **algarviense** m. + f.) 1. of or referring to Algarve. 2. (fig.) talkative.
algazarra s. f. 1. clamour, bawling, shouting, racket. 2. mutiny, insubordination. 3. tumult, hubbub.
fazer ~ to make a racket.
algazarrar v. to clamour.
álgebra s. f. algebra.
algébrico adj. algebraic(al).
algebrista s. m. + f. 1. algebraist, algebrist. 2. (obs.) bone-setter.
algebrizar v. to employ algebraic formulae and processes.
algema s. f. 1. manacles, shackles, handcuffs. 2. fetter(s). 3. (fig.) oppression.
algemar v. 1. to shackle. 2. to fetter. 3. (fig.) to oppress, dominate. 4. (fig.) to coerce, compel.
algente adj. m. + f. 1. very cold, glacial. 2. algid, frozen.
algeroz s. m. gutter (pipe), eaves.
algia s. f. (med.) pain.
algibe s. m. cistern.
algibebe s. m. person who makes or sells ready-made clothes or slops, slop-seller.
loja de ~ slop-shop.
algibeira s. f. pocket (plate R 7).
andar de mãos na ~ to (go) idle. **ciência de** ~ smattering. **saiu (pagou) de sua** ~ it was (paid) out of his pocket. **dinheiro para** ~ pocket-money.
algidez s. f. algidity, coldness.
álgido adj. 1. algid, very cold. 2. chilling, causing shivers.
algirão s. m. (pl. **-ões**) mouth of a fishing-net or trap.
algo s. m. 1. fortune, riches, goods, wealth. 2. rich, well-off person. ‖ adv. somewhat, a bit. a little. ‖ pron. something, anything.
~ **cansativo** somewhat tiresome. ~ **de belo** something beautiful. **homem de** ~ rich, wealthy man. **nisto há** ~ **de certo** there is somewhat in it.
algodão s. m. cotton: 1. the soft, white fibre. 2. the plant that produces it. 3. cloth made of cotton thread. 4. (med.) wadding.
~ **de vidro** spun glass. ~ **em rama, em lã** cotton-wool, raw cotton. ~ **estampado** printed cotton. ~ **hidrófilo** (med.) cotton-wool. **fio de** ~ cotton thread. **pólvora de** ~ cotton powder.
algodão-doce s. m. (pl. **algodões-doces**) (Braz.) cotton candy (a fluffy confection).
algodão-pólvora s. m. (pl. **algodões-pólvora**) guncotton.

algodãozinho s. m. (Braz.) cheap (or coarse) cotton cloth.
algodoal s. m. (pl. **-ais**) cotton plantation.
algodoar v. 1. to line with cotton. 2. to make similar to cotton.
algodoaria s. f. (also **cotonaria**) cotton mill.
algodoeiro s. m. 1. cotton, cotton-plant. 2. cotton spinner (manufacturer). ‖ adj. cotton: of or referring to cotton.
algodoim s. m. (pl. **-ins**) coarse cotton cloth (coarser than **algodãozinho**).
algofilia s. f. (med.) algophilia, algophily.
algófilo s. m. (med.) algophilist.
algofobia s. f. (med.) algophobia.
algófobo s. m. (med.) person suffering from algophobia. ‖ adj. algophobic.
algóide adj. m. + f. algoid.
algolagnia s. f. (med.) algolagnia, algolagny: pleasure in suffering or inflicting pain.
algologia s. f. (bot.) algology.
algológico adj. (bot.) algological.
algologista s. m. + f. (bot.) algologist.
algor s. m. 1. extreme cold. 2. chill, feeling of cold.
algoritmo s. m. (math.) algorithm, algorism.
algoso adj. algous.
algóstase s. f. (med.) algiostasis.
algoz s. m. (pl. ~**es**) 1. executioner, hangman. 2. torturer. 3. cruel person, monster, brute.
algozar v. 1. to be cruel, treat cruelly. 2. torment, martyrize.
algozaria s. f. cruelty, barbarity.
algoz-das-árvores s. m. (pl. **algozes-das-árvores**) (bot.) climbing bittersweet.
algrafia s. f. algraphy: printing from aluminium plates.
algravia s. f. = **algaravia**.
alguazil s. m. = **aguazil**.
alguém indef. pron. 1. somebody, someone. 2. anybody, anyone. 3. someone or other. 4. important person.
comer pela mão de ~ to feed out of someone's hand. **dar em** ~ to beat s. o., (sl.) to let the sawdust out of s. o. **ele é** ~? is he anybody? **está** ~ **à porta?** is there anybody at the door? **há** ~ **aí?** is there anybody?
alguergar v. to mosaic: decorate with mosaics.
alguergue s. m. mosaic: 1. small piece of stone. 2. inlaid work.
alguidar s. m. earthen or metal vessel or bowl.
alguidarada s. f. contents of an **alguidar**.
algum indef adj. (pl. **-uns**; f. **-ma**; pl. **-mas**) 1. some. 2. any. 3. **-uns** pl. some, a few, several.
~ **dia** some day. ~ **tempo atrás** some time ago. ~**as das minhas coisas** a few of my things. **alguns cigarros** a cigarette or two, several cigarettes. **alguns deles** several of them. **alguns estrangeiros isolados** a sprinkling of foreigners. **alguns homens** one or two men. **alguns poucos hóspedes** some few guests. **alguns quinhentos** about five hundred. **alguns vieram, outros foram** some came, others went. **depois de** ~ **tempo** after some time. **de forma** ~**a** by no means. **em** ~ **lugar** someplace. **ele vale** ~**a coisa?** is he any good? **não dispondo de tempo** ~ not having any time. **ele tem** ~**as noções de francês** he has a smattering of French.
algures adv. somewhere, in some place.
alhada s. f. 1. quantity of garlic. 2. garlic(ky) stew. 3. (fig.) intrigue. 4. mess, muddle.
alhal (I) s. m. (pl. **-ais**) garlic plantation.
alhal (II) s. m. (pl. **-ais**) (Port.) place in the kitchen for firewood.
alhanar v. 1. to soften, give a friendly touch to. 2. to make even, level. 3. to devastate. lay waste, lay

in ruins. 4. to resolve, decide. 5. ~-se to humble, humiliate o. s.

alhas adj. f. pl. only used in:

palhas ~ 1. dry garlic leaves. 2. (pop.) trifles.

alheabilidade s. f. alienability.

alheação s. f. (pl. -ões) (also **alheamento, alienação**) alienation.

alheado adj. 1. enraptured, ecstasized. 2. absent-minded, distracted, lost in thought. 3. crazy, mad. foolish.

alheador s. m. person or thing that maddens, enraptures, etc.

alheamento s. m. 1. alienation. 2. ecstasy.

alhear v. 1. to alienate, transfer property or ownership. 2. to deprive, dispossess. 3. to ecstasize, enrapture. 4. to hallucinate, bewilder, madden. 5. to disconcert, disquiet. 6. to indispose, estrange. 7. to separate, remove. 8. to renounce. 9. to lose. 10. ~-se to be enraptured, enchanted, ecstatic, lost in thought, etc.

alheatório adj. alienating, enrapturing, etc.

alheável adj. m. + f. (pl. -áveis) (also **alienável**) alienable.

alheio s. m. another's or alien property. ‖ adj. 1. strange. 2. foreign, alien. 3. improper. 4. distant. 5. contrary. 6. deprived. 7. exempt from. 8. distracted, lost in thought. 9. mad, crazy. 10. alienated.

~ **de si** absorbed, lost in thought. **ser quieto é** ~ **à natureza de um menino** sitting still is foreign to a boy's nature.

alheira s. f. 1. (bot.) yellow rocket. 2. sausage prepared with yellow rocket.

alheiro s. m. garlic seller, dealer in garlic.

alheta (I) s. f. (naut.) quarter, buttocks of a ship.

alheta (II) s. f. track, trail.

ir na ~ **de alguém** to follow someone's track; pursue, chase.

alheta (III) s. f. (Port., bot.) entire, undivided bulb or head of garlic.

alho s. m. 1. garlic. 2. (fig.) smart fellow, sly fox. ~-**dourado** (bot.) lily, moly. ~-**porro** (bot.) leek. **cabeça de** ~ **chocho** distracted person, daydreamer. **dente de** ~ clove or bulb of garlic. **misturar** ~**s com bugalhos** to make a mess, confuse utterly.

alhures adv. elsewhere, somewhere else.

ali adv. 1. there, in that place. 2. then, at that time.

até ~ as far as there. **d**~ **a dois dias** two days hence. **o que há** ~? what is up there? **por** ~ 1. that way. 2. thereabout.

aliáceo adj. (bot.) alliaceous.

aliado s. m. ally. ‖ adj. allied, associated.

aliadofilia s. f. sympathies for or affinity with the Allies.

aliadófilo s. m. sympathizer or adherent of the Allies. ‖ adj. pro-Allies.

aliadofobia s. f. aversion toward the Allies.

aliadófobo s. m. person adverse to the Allies. ‖ adj. having aversion to the Allies.

aliança s. f. (less used **aliagem**) 1. alliance: a) confederacy, confederation. b) association, connexion, connection. c) league. d) union. 2. wedding ring (plate J 3).

em ~ **com** in league with. **fazer** ~ **com** to ally or associate with.

aliar v. 1. to ally. 2. to join, unite. 3. to combine. 4. to harmonize. 5. to connect. 6. to confederate. 7. to group. 8. to coadunate. 9. to unite by marriage. 10. to alloy (metals). 11. ~-se to enter into an alliance.

~-**se a** to make or form an alliance with. ~**am-se a ele contra mim** they united with him against me.

aliás adv. 1. else, otherwise. 2. besides, on the other hand. 3. by the way. 4. respectively.

~, **estava bem certo** it was quite certain, though.

aliável adj. m. + f. (pl. -áveis) alliable, etc.

aliazar s. m. (pl. ~**es**) marshy, muddy river island.

alibambar v. (Braz.) to fetter, chain.

álibi s. m. (jur.) alibi.

alíbil adj. m. + f. (pl. -eis) alible, nourishing.

alibilidade s. f. alibility.

alicaído adj. 1. dro(o)p-winged. 2. depressed, discouraged. 3. faint, feeble.

alicali s. m. spiritual guide of Negro Moslems in Brazil.

alicantina s. f. 1. astuteness, shrewdness. 2. craft, trickishness. 3. fraud, deceit.

alicantinador, alicantineiro s. m. cheat(er), trickster, crafty or astute fellow.

alicate s. m. (a pair of) pliers, pincers, nippers; wire cutter (plate A 8).

~ **de cutícula** cuticle pliers.

~ **para abrir casas** (tail.) buttonhole punch (plate A 5). ~ **para lacrar** sealing pliers.

alicerçador s. m. 1. founder. 2. foundation, basis. ‖ adj. foundational.

alicerçar v. 1. to lay the foundation. 2. to found, base. 3. to cement. 4. to consolidate.

alicerce s. m. foundation, base, basis (also fig.) (plate A 7).

a casa estremeceu até os ~**s** the house rocked to its foundation. **lançar os** ~**s** to lay the foundation.

aliciação s. f. (pl. -ões) (also **aliciamento** m.) 1. seduction, allurement, enticement. 2. procurement. 3. subornation. 4. provocation. 5 (Braz.) unloyal recruting of labour.

aliciador s. m 1 tempter, enticer, seducer. 2. (Braz.) unloyal labour recruiter. ‖ adj. (also **alicinate, aliciente**) enticing, alluring, seductive.

aliciar v. 1. to allure, bait, attract. 2. to seduce, tempt. 3. to provoke. 4. to suborn. 5. (Braz.) to recruit labour unloyaly.

aliciente s. m. temptation, seduction. ‖ adj. m. + f. (also **aliciador**) enticing, alluring, seductive.

alicorne s. m. (Braz., ornith; also **anhuma**) horned screamer.

alidada, alidade s. f. alidad(e).

alienabilidade s. f. alienability.

alienação s. f. (pl. -ões) 1. alienation: a) transfer of ownership. b) estrangement. 2. ecstasy, ravishment. 3. madness, insanity.

alienado s. m. lunatic, madman. ‖ adj. 1. alienated. 2. ceded, transferred. 3. enraptured. 4. insane, mad, mentally affected.

alienador s. m. alienator: 1. transferrer. 2. person or thing that maddens. ‖ adj. maddening.

alienante s. m. + f. alienator. ‖ adj. alienating.

alienar v. 1. to alienate, cede, transfer. 2. to indispose, estrange, set at variance. 3. to hallucinate. 4. to madden. 5. to separate. 6. to deviate.

alienatório s. m. (jur.) alienee.

alienável adj. m. + f. (pl. -áveis) (also **alienatório**) alienable.

alienígena s. m. + f. alien, foreigner. ‖ adj. alien, foreign.

alienista s. m. + f. alienist, specialist in mental diseases. ‖ adj. of or referring to an alienist.

alifafe (I) m. wind-gall: soft tumour on the fetlock of a horse.

alifafe (II) s. m. 1. bed-spread. 2. quilt. 3. blanket.

alifático adj. (chem.) aliphatic, referring to open-chain or non-cyclic organic compounds.

alífero adj. winged.

aliforme adj. m. + f. (also **ansiforme**) aliform.

aligátor s. m. (pl. **aligatores**) (zool.) alligator.
aligeirar v. 1. to hasten, make haste, speed up. 2. to lighten, ease. 3. to mitigate, assuage, alleviate. 4. to lessen, moderate.
alígero adj. 1. winged. 2. (poet.) quick, swift.
alijamento s. m. (also **alijação** f., pl. **-ões**) 1. jettison, throwing overboard. 2. riddance. 3. act of throwing, jetting.
alijar v. 1. to jettison. 2. to lighten, ease. 3. to get rid of. 4. to throw, cast.
 ~ carga to jettison cargo.
alimária s. f. 1. animal, beast. 2. brute. 3. stupid fellow.
alimentação s. f. (pl. **-ões**) 1. alimentation, nourishment. 2. food. 3. feed, feeding (machine). 4. supplies, provisions.
 água de ~ feed water. **aparelho de ~** (tech.) feeding arrangement.
alimentador s. m. feeder (plate C 16). ‖ adj. feeding.
alimentar (I) v. 1. to feed: a) nourish. b ‖ supply with material (machine, etc.). 2. to preserve. 3. to maintain. 4. to support, sustain. 5. to provide. **mal alimentado** underfed. **~ ódios** to harbour grudges. **~ uma esperança** to hold out hopes for.
alimentar (II) adj. m. + f. alimentary: 1. nutritious, nourishing. 2. of or referring to food.
alimentício adj. alimentary, alimentative, nutritive, nourishing.
 indústria -a provision industry.
alimento s. m. 1. food, victuals. 2. maintenance. 3. provisions, supply. 4. subsistence, support. 5. alimony. 6. allowance. 7. (tech.) feed(ing).
 ~s de poupança stimulants, as alcohol, coffee, etc.
alimentoso adj. alimentary, alimentative, nutritive, nourishing.
alimpa s. f. cleaning, cropping, lapping, weeding.
alimpadeira s. f. 1. charwoman. 2. **~s** pl. bees that prepare the working place for the others.
alimpador s. m. cleaner (person or tool), weeder.
alimpadura s. f. 1. (also **alimpamento** m.) cleaning. 2. residues, remainders. 3. chaff.
alimpar v. (also **limpar**) 1. to clean, cleanse, rinse, 2. to purify, refine. 3. (fam.) to steal.
alindado adj. embellished, adorned, ornamented.
alindamento s. m. (also **alinde**) embellishment, adornment, ornament.
alindar v. to embellish, beautify, adorn, ornament.
alínea s. f. 1. paragraph. 2. break.
alinegro adj. black-winged.
alingüetado adj. tongue-shaped.
alinhado adj. 1. ali(g)ned, lined up. 2. carefully or elegantly dressed.
alinhador s. m. ali(g)ner.
alinhamento s. m. 1. ali(g)nment. 2. arrangement. 3. ranging. 4. rectification. 5. (fig.) elegance.
alinhar v. 1. to ali(g)n, range, line up. 2. to dress up, spruce.
alinhavar v. 1. to baste, tack (sewing). 2. to prepare. 3. to patch, make hastily or badly. 4. to delineate. 5. (fig.) to scribble, scrawl.
alinhavo s. m. 1. bastings, tack. 2. basting. 3. sketch, outline.
alinho s. m. 1. lining up, ranging. 2. plumb(-line). 3. refinement. 4. cleanliness, niceness, neatness. 5. order, care. 6. decency. 7. ornament, decoration.
alípede adj. m. + f. wing-footed.
alipina s. f. (med.) alypin: an anesthetic derived from opium.
alipotente adj. m. + f. strong-winged.
alíquota adj. f. aliquot.
 cinco é uma parte ~ de quinze five is an aliquot part of fifteen.

alisado s. m. (Braz., also **aliseu, alísio**) trade wind. ‖ adj. 1. smoothened, sleek. 2. plain, level. 3. softened. 4. monsoonal.
alisar v. 1. to make plane, smooth (out.) 2. to level, equal. 3. to round off, bevel. 4. to comb. 5. to wear down or away. 6. to relent, calm, soften. 7. to sweeten. 8. to unwrinkle, unplait, face down. 9. (Braz.) to show mercy, forbear to punish.
 ~ a lanugem to lay the nap of a cloth.
alisboetar v. to become a Lisbonian.
alísio s. m. trade wind. ‖ adj. trade (wind).
alisma s. f. (bot.) alisma.
alismatácea s. f. plant of the plantain family.
alistabilidade s. f. possibility of being enlisted.
alistamento s. m. 1. enlistment, recruitment. 2. enrol(l)ment.
 no rol do ~ (mil.) on the strength.
alistando s. m. person being enlisted.
alistão s. m. (pl. **-ões**) squared stone (stonemasonry).
alistar v. 1. to enlist, recruit. 2. to list, enrol. 3. to inventory.
 ~-se no exército to join the ranks. **ele alistou-se** he signed up. **ele alistou-se no serviço militar** he took on the service. **ele alistou-se, entrou na marinha** he entered the navy.
alistável adj. m. + f. (pl. **-áveis**) liable to enrolling, subject to enlistment, fit for service.
alistridente adj. m. + f. (poet.) that makes a noise with its wings.
aliteração s. f. (pl. **-ões**), **aliteramento** m. alliteration.
aliterar v. to alliterate.
aliteratado adj. having or showing airs of a literate.
aliteratar-se v. to assume airs or ways of a literate.
alitúrgico adj. non-liturgical.
aliviação s. f. (pl. **-ões**) also **alívio, aliviamento** m.) 1. ease, comfort, relief, alleviation. 2. soothing, assuagement. 3. lightening, lessening. 4. repose, rest. 5. consolation.
aliviado adj. eased, relieved, soothed, etc.
aliviador s. m. alleviator, soother, assuager, comforter. ‖ adj. alleviating, soothing, assuaging, comforting.
aliviar v. 1. to alleviate, assuage, mitigate. 2. to lighten. 3. to ease. 4. to lessen, diminish. 5. to soften. 6. to comfort. 7. to tranquilize, calm down. 8. to isent, exempt, release from duty, dispense. 9. to slack(en).
 ~ o luto to put on half-mourning. **~ saudades** to still one's longing.
alívio s. m. 1. alleviation, softening, relief, ease. 2. lightening. 3. consolation.
alizaba s. f. wide-sleeved Moorish tunic.
alizar s. m. 1. lining a door-frame as window-frame (plate P 10). 2. wainscot, wainscot(t)ing. 3. skirting(-board). 4. wash-board. 5. broom bin.
alizarina s. f. alizarin(e), modder red.
aljafra s. f. pouch of a drag-net or trawl-net.
aljava s. f. (also **carcás, fáretra**) quiver: case to hold arrows.
aljazar s. m. 1. (also **alizar**) marshy or muddy river island. 2. island in the sea.
aljôfar s. m. (pl. **~es**) (also **aljofre**) 1. seed-pearl. 2. dew. 3. tears.
aljofarar v. (also **aljofrar**) 1. to cover with tears. 2. to cover with dew. 3. to decorate with pearls.
aljuba s. f. wide garment used by Moorish women.
aljube s. m. 1. (dark) prison, jail. 2. den, cavern. 3. prison for clergymen.
aljubeiro s. m. (obs.) gaoler, jailer.
aljubeta s. f. m. 1. dim. of **aljuba**. 2. gown, robe, former clothing that reached down to the heels.
aljubeteiro s. m. maker of **aljubas**, gown maker (wide Moorish garments).

alma s. f. 1. soul: a) the spiritual part of a person, the inner man. b) moral faculties. c) spirit, temper, nature. d) courage, animation, enthusiasm. e) heart, life. f) the moving spirit, propelling force, leadership. g) disembodied spirit. h) person, inhabitant. .2 (gun) bore. 3. (tech.) core. 4. sound post (violin). 5. web (of a beam or girder). 6. button-mould. 7. (bellows) valve. 8. (anat.) plantar arch (foot). 9. stick around which plug tobacco is wound. ~ **do outro mundo** spectre, ghost. ~ **do padeiro** hollow in the bread. **abrir a sua** ~ to make a clean breast. **dar a** ~ **a Deus** to give up the ghost. **dar vida e** ~ **por** to do all one can. **de** ~ **e coração** with heart and soul. **nenhuma** ~ not a soul. **pela minha** ~ upon my soul. **sem** ~ heartless, unscrupulous. **uma boa** ~ a good soul.

almácega s. f. receptacle for water (from a noria or rain).

almácego s. m. (Braz.) = **alfobre**.

almaço s. m. type or size of a writing paper. ‖ adj. of or referring to that paper.

alma-de-mestre s. m. (pl. **almas-de-mestre**) (ornith.) Wilson's petrel.

almádena s. f. minaret.

almadia s. f. almadia: long and narrow Indian or African boat.

almadrava s. f. 1. netting or net for catching tunny. 2. tunny fishing. 3. fishing ground for tunny.

almagrar v. 1. to rubricate: a) colour or redden with ochre. b) furnish with a rubric or rubrics. 2. to mark, signalize.

almagre s. m. (also **almagra, almagro**) 1. red ochre. 2. rubric. 3. (fig.) plebeian blood.

almainha s. f. 1. fenced garden. 2. small landed property, suburban week-end place.

almajarra s. f., **almajarrar** v. = **almanjarra, almanjarrar**.

almalho s. m. bullock, a young bull.

almanaque s. m. 1. almanac. 2. calendar.

almandina s. f. (min.) almandine.

almanjarra s. f. 1. hands or bars of a capstan or whim. 2. broad wooden scraper. 3. colossal, huge man. 4. enormous thing.

almanjarrar v. to scrape (with a broad wooden scraper).

almarado adj. 1. said of oxen or bulls with differently coloured circles around the eyes. 2. having reddish or blueish hair on several spots of the head (horses, cattle).

almargeado adj. 1. grassy, covered with grass and herbage for cattle. 2. abandoned, empty (ground).

almargeal s. m. (pl. -ais) 1. marshy, swampy ground (for pasture). 2. (fig.) meadow.

almargem s. m. (pl. -ens) (also less used **dimarge**) 1. herbage for cattle. 2. pasture, grazing. 3. meadow.

almargio adj. 1. thrown away, rubbish. 2. pasturing.

almécega s. f. 1. gum mastic. 2. adhesive.

almecegar v. 1. to dye with mastic. 2. to apply mastic.

almecegueira s. f. mastic (tree).

almeia (I) s. f. female dancer of India.

almeia (II) s. f. French balsam of oriental origin.

almeida s. f. (naut.) 1. counter. 2. helm port.

almeirão s. m. (pl. -ões) (bot.) wild chicory.

almejante adj. m. + f. longing, wistful, desirous.

almejar v. 1. to long for, desire ardently. 2. to be dying, agonize. 3. to crave, covet. ~ **alguma coisa** 1. to pant after. 2. to aspire, long for s. th. **almejaram a fama** they wooed fame. **ele almeja um casamento rico** he aims at a rich marriage. **ele não almeja aquilo** he is undesirous of it.

almejável adj. m. + f. ardently desired, wished for, yearned.

almejo s. m. craving desire or longing for.

almenara s. f. (obs.) signal fire on the walls or towers of castles.

alminha s. f. 1. dim. of **alma**. 2. person.

almiranta s. f. (naut.) admiral-ship.

almirantado s. m. 1. admiralship: dignity of an admiral. 2. admiralty. 3. naval staff.

almirante s. m. 1. admiral. 2. admiral-ship, flagship. 3. (zool.) admiral shell. 4. (obs.) a sort of woman's headdress. 5. (ent.) red admiral. 6. variety of pear. **ele quer um** ~ **suíço** he cries for the moon.

almíscar s. m. musk: 1. substance obtained from the musk deer. 2. (bot.) storax.

almiscarado adj. perfumed with musk.

almiscarar v. to perfume with musk.

almiscareira s. f. (bot.) stork's-bill, geranium.

almiscareiro s. m. (zool.) musk deer.

almo adj. 1. (poet.): a) creative. b) fostering. 2. good, benign. 3. adorable, venerable.

almoçadeira s. f. large (soup) cup used at breakfast and lunch.

almocadém s. m. (obs.) 1. captain of infantry. 2. commanding officer, captain. 3. chief.

almocafre s. m. a miner's pickaxe.

almoçar v. 1. to breakfast. 2. to lunch.

almocávar s. m. (obs., also **almocábar**) Moors' cemetery.

almoço (ô) s. m. (pl. **almoços**) 1. breakfast. 2. lunch. 3. food taken at these meals. 4. (fig.) first occurrence of the day. ~ **bravo** (over)late breakfast or lunch. ~ **de garfo** luncheon. ~ **manso** breakfast or lunch in time. **o** ~ **está pronto?** is breakfast ready?

almocrevar v. 1. to transport on muleback. 2. to work as a muleteer.

almocrevaria s. f. 1. trade or work of a mule-driver. 2. (obs.) the taxes assessed on this trade.

almocreve s. m. 1. mule-driver, muleteer. 2. transporter, carter. 3. porter, carrier.

almoeda s. f. auction, public sale. **pôr uma coisa em** ~ to sell something by auction.

almoedar v. 1. to auction. 2. to offer for sale.

almofaça s. f. currycomb (horses) (plate C 12).

almofaçadura s. f. act of grooming with a currycomb.

almofaçar v. to currycomb, groom.

almofacilha s. f. protective tow (flax or the like) around a horse's curb.

almofada s. f. 1. cushion, pillow (plate D 4). 2. panel (plates A 13, P 10). 3. pad. 4. (typogr.) liner, lining, padding. ~ **da porta** door panel. ~ **elétrica** warming pad. ~ **para carimbo** ink pad. ~ **pneumática** air cushion.

almofadado adj. 1. cushioned, provided with cushions. 2. panel(l)ed. 3. padded. 4. lined.

almofadão s. m. 1. large cushion. 2. large wood or stone panel. 3. (ornith.) mass of dorsal feathers of certain birds, partially covering the tail; undertail coverts.

almofadar v. 1. to cushion, provide with cushions. 2. to panel. 3. to pad. 4. to line, put a layer on.

almofadinha s. m. 1. m. (Braz.) fop, dandy. 2. f.: a) dim. of **almofada**. b) compress; plédget. ~ **para alfinetes** pincushion.

almofadismo s. m. (Braz.) 1. effeminate elegance. 2. foppishness, dandyism.

almofariz s. m. 1. mortar. 2. pestle.

almofate s. m. awl, bodkin, sort of punch.

almofeira s. f. 1. black liquid that runs out of olive bins. 2. olive water.

almofreixar v. to put into a large travelling trunk.

almofreixe s. m. (large) travelling trunk.

almofrez s. m. (also almofate) awl, bodkin.
almogaure, almogávar, almograve s. m. (hist.) guerilla who fought the Moors.
almogavaria s. f. (obs., hist.) 1. troop of soldiers, guerillas, who fought the Moors by surprise attacks. 2. such an attack.
almojávena s. f. sort of small cheese tart.
almolina s. f. (children's game) blind-man's-buff.
almôndega s. f. (cul.) meatball.
almorávida, almorávide s. m. + f. (hist.) members of a religious and political Moorish sect in Spain.
almorreimas s. m. pl. (pop.) hemorrhoids.
almotaçar v. (obs.) 1. to examine and fix the price of (esp. victuals). 2. to regulate, adjust.
almotaçaria s. f. (obs.) 1. position of a price-fixer (esp. victuals). 2. price-fixing of victuals.
almotacé, almotacel s. m. (obs.) price-fixer (esp. for victuals) and inspector of weights and measures.
almotolia s. f. oil-can: 1. (obs.) oil cruse, can for holding oil. 2. oil feeder, oiler (plate M 1).
almoxarifado s. m. 1. warehouse, storehouse. 2. supervision and treasury of the royal domains.
almoxarife s. m. 1. storekeeper, warehouse keeper. 2. superintendent of the royal domains. 3. (obs.) tax-collector. 4. royal treasurer.
almuadem s. m. (pl. -ens) (better than muezim; also almuédão) muezzin.
almudada s. f., almude m. 1. almud(e): a grain measure of about 32 litres. 2. land into which such a measure has been sown.
almudar v. to measure by almudes (32 litres).
almude s. m. almud(e): former liquid measure equivalent to about 32 litres.
alna s. f. ell: former linear measure (about 66 cm.).
alno s. m. (bot.) scholarly form of amieiro: alder, elder.
alô interj. hullo! hallo! hello!
aló adv. windward!
alobrógico adj. (fig.) rustic, rough.
alóbrogo s. m. (fig.) rustic fellow, churl.
alocar v. 1. to allocate, assign. 2. to place in a specific position in a series. 3. to allot (funds) to a specific purpose.
alocroísmo s. m. allochroism.
alocromia s. f. (med.) allochromatism.
alocrômico, alocromático adj. allochromatic.
alóctone s. m. 1. inhabitant of a country not that of origin. 2. (geol.) allochthon. || adj. 1. not originating in country of residence or where found. 2. (geol.) allochthonous.
alocução s. f. (pl. -ões) address, speech, allocution.
alodial adj. m. + f. (pl. -ais) allodial.
alodialidade s. f. 1. allodium, free tenure. 2. exemption from charges.
alódio s. m. (obs.) allod, allodium, freehold, freeland.
aloendro s. m. (bot., also espirradeira) oleander.
aloés s. m. (bot.) aloe. 2. aloes: bitter drug made from aloe leaves.
aloético adj. aloetic.
aloetina s. f. (chem.) aloin, aloetin: medicinal aloetic solution.
aloftalmia s. f. (med.) allophthalmia.
aloftálmico adj. (med.) allophthalmic.
alogamia s. f. allogamy, cross-fertilization in plants.
alógamo adj. (bot.) allogamous.
alógeno adj. allogeneous.
alogia s. f. alogy, nonsense.
alogiano s. m. (rel.) Alogian.
alogismo s. m. (philos.) paralogism: 1. argument or conclusion not based on principles of valid reasoning, midway between logical and illogical. 2. paralogical thinking.

alogonia s. f. (gen., biol.) differing periods of reaching maturity by individuals of same species.
aloína s. f. (chem.) aloin.
aloinado adj. like aloes, aloid.
aloirado adj. (also alourado) blondish, blond.
aloite s. m. (Braz.) fight, contest, quarrel.
alojação s. f. (pl. -ões), (also alojamento, alogo m.) 1. lodging, lodgement. 2. shelter. 3. accommodation. 4. dwelling, habitation. 5. (mil.) billeting, quartering, quarters, barracks. 6. (tech.): a) housing. b) bearing.
alojar (I) v. 1. to take up or introduce (goods, commodities) in a shop. 2. to receive, shelter, lodge, house. 3. to dwell, take lodgings. 4. to store, warehouse. 5. (mil.) to billet, quarter, camp. 6. (tech.) to embed.
alojar (II) v. (Braz., sl.) to vomit.
alojo (ô) (I) s. m. (Port., prov.) = alojamento, alojação.
alojo (ô) (II) s. m. (Braz., sl.) vomit.
alombado adj. 1. bowed, arched, bent. 2. crooked (from tiredness or from an ailment). 3. (Braz.) lazy, indolent. 4. indisposed or unwilling to work. 5. sleepy, drowsy.
alombamento s. m. 1. rounding, bending, arching. 2. hipshot beating. 3. operation of rounding books.
alombar v. 1. to round, bend, arch. 2. to beat s. o. hipshot, break the back. 3. to round the backs of books.
alomorfia s. f. 1. allomorphism. 2. metamorphosis.
alomórfico adj. allomorphic.
alomorfismo s. m. 1. allomorphism. 2. paramorphism.
alonga s. f. 1. (chem.) adapter. 2. (obs.) supplement. 3. border, margin, verge.
alongado adj. 1. lengthened, prolonged, elongated. 2. away, far off, distant. 3. (Braz.) runaway (said of cattle).
alongador s. m. lengthener, prolonger. || adj. lengthening, prolonging.
alongamento s. m. 1. prolongation, extension, expansion, elongation. 2. removal. 3. delay, procrastination.
alongar v. 1. to prolongate, extend, lengthen, elongate. 2. to expand, dilate. 3. to remove. 4. to look about or into the distance, survey.
alônimo s. m. 1. allonym, name of another person assumed by an author. 2. work published under another name.
alopata, alópata s. m. + f. (med.) allopath.
alopatia s. f. (med.) allopathy.
alopático adj. (med., also enantiopático, heteropático) allopathic.
alopecia s. f. (med.) alopecia: baldness.
alopécico s. m. (also alopático) person suffering from alopecia. || adj. alopecic, referring to alopecia.
alópia s. f. thin and corrugated shell.
aloprado adj. (Braz.) 1. restless, uneasy. 2. foolish, mad.
aloprar v. (Braz., sl.) 1. to become crazy. 2. to become very upset, agitated.
aloquete s. m. 1. padlock. 2. bolt, slide bar.
alor s. m. 1. stimulus, incentive. 2. impetus, impulse. 3. movement, stately progress.
alosna s. f. (bot., also losna) wormwood.
alotador s. m. (Braz.) stud-horse, stallion.
alotar v. 1. to allot, divide into lots. 2. (Braz.) to keep the mares of a group together. 3. to round up cattle and get it accustomed to the herd.
alote s. m. (naut.) small cable (for heaving).
alotriomórfico adj. (also xenomórfico) xenomorphic.
alotropia s. f. (chem.) allotropy.
alotrópico adj. (chem.) allotropic.

alótropo s. m. word of equal etymology. ‖ adj. (chem.) allotropic.

aloucado adj. 1. tending to madness. 2. that seems to be mad, deranged, somewhat crazy, foolish.

aloucamento s. m. maddening.

aloucar v. to behave like mad.

alourar v. (also **aloirar**) 1. to make fair (blond) or the like. 2. to brown, roast.

alousar v. (also **aloisar**) to slate, cover with slates.

alpaca s. f. 1. alpaca: a) (zool.) variety of llama. b) its wool. c) cloth made of alpaca wool. 2. alpak(k)a, German silver (alloy).

alparavaz s. m. (obs.) 1. fringe. 2. valance.

alparcata s. f. (also **alpargata, alpercata**) sandal or sandallike footwear, a sort of espadrille.

alparcateiro s. m. (also **alpargateiro, alparqueiro, alpercateiro**) manufacturer of sandals (see **alparcata**).

alpargataria s. f. 1. sandal factory. 2. sandal shop.

alpedo adv. (Braz.) in vain.

alpendrada s. f. large shed or porch.

alpendrado s. m. = **alpendrada**. ‖ adj. like a shed or porch.

alpendrar v. to provide with a shed or porch, or build in such a way.

alpendre s. m. 1. shed, porch. 2. lean-to, penthouse.

alpense adj. m. + f. Alpine.

alperche, alperce s. m. a sort of large apricot.

alperc(h)eiro s. m. (bot.) apricot tree.

alpestre adj. m. + f. 1. alpine, mountainous. 2. Alpine. 3. alpestrine, growing on mountains, alpigene. 4. (fig.) wild, rocky, steep.

alpícola s. m. + f. inhabitant of the Alps. ‖ adj. Alpine (referring to inhabitants).

alpinismo s. m. Alpinism, mountaineering, mountain climbing.

alpinista s. m. + f. Alpinist, mountaineer. ‖ adj. m. + f. (also **alpico**) of or referring to Alpinism.

alpino s. m. (mil.) Alpino, mountain soldier. ‖ adj. 1. Alpine: of or referring to the Alps. 2. alpestrine, growing on Alps.

alpista s. f., **alpiste** m. 1. (bot.) canary grass. 2. its seed: canary seed.

alpondras s. f. pl. stepping-stones (in a brook).

alporama s. m. panoramic picture of the Alps.

alporca s. f. 1. = **alporque**. 2. (med.) scrofula.

alporcar v. (bot.) to layer, set or plant layers.

alporque s. m. (bot.) layering.

alporquento adj. 1. (bot.) layered, that has layers, covered with layers. 2. (med.) scrofulous.

alquebrado adj. 1. weak, feeble, bowed down. 2. worn out. 3. (naut.) cambered.

alquebramento s. m. (also **alquebre**) 1. weakening, debilitation. 2. weakness, tiredness. 3. exhaustion. 4. (naut.) camber, warping.

alquebrar v. 1. to weaken, debilitate. 2. to break. 3. to crook, bend or stoop down. 4. to surrender, give up. 5. (naut.) to camber, bend, become broken-backed.

alqueiramento s. m. measuring or division in **alqueires**.

alqueirão s. m. (pl. **-ões**) one **alqueire** of wheat.

alqueirar v. to measure by **alqueires**.

alqueire s. m. 1. measure of contents = 13.8 litres, (Port.: 8.4 litres). 2. (Braz.) land measure = 48,400 m² in Minas Gerais, Rio de Janeiro and Goiás; 27,225 m² in the Northern States; 24,200 m² in São Paulo. 3. land into which one measure of 13.8 litres seed has been sown.

alqueivar v. (agric.) to fallow, lay up.

alqueive s. m. fallow. 1. ploughed and unseeded land. 2. the ploughing of land without seeding.

alquequenje, alquequenque s. m. (bot.) alkekengi: ground cherry (Physalis alkekengi).

alquermes s. m. (pharm.) alkermes.

alquifa s. f., **alquifu** m. (also **alquifol**, pl. **-óis**) (min.) alquifou.

alquilador s. m. (horse) hirer.

alquilar v. to hire (esp. horse, mules).

alquilaria s. f. 1. place where horses are hired out. 2. hiring contract (esp. for transport on horseback). 3. profession or business of hiring out horses.

alquilé, alquiler s. m. 1. horse hirer. 2. hire or price agreed upon.

alquime s. m. 1. tombac, tombak. 2. pinchbeck.

alquimia s. f. alchemy.

alquimiar v. to practise alchemy.

alquímico adj. alchemic(al).

alquimista s. m. alchemist.

alquitara s. f. a sort of alembic without condensing coil.

alrotar v. 1. to clamour, shout (many voices). 2. to beg for alms loudly and insistently.

alrotaria s. f. (obs.) 1. uproar, clamour, row. 2. raillery, mockery.

alsaciano s. m. Alsatian. ‖ adj. Alsatian.

alta s. f. 1. raising, rise, boom. 2. increase, augmentation. 3. leave, discharge (-paper or ticket). 4. high life or society. 5. nobility. 6. delay. 7. stop, stoppage. 8. (obs.) former dance. ‖ adj. f. of **alto**: high. ~ **do hospital** discharge from hospital. ~ **noite** high night. ~ **pressão** high pressure. **a ~ do custo de vida** the increase of the costs of living. **em ~** on the rise. **sofrer uma ~** to be increased (prices).

alta-fidelidade s. f. (pl. **altas-fidelidades**) high fidelity: 1. the electronic reproduction of sound with minimal distortion. 2. sound equipment employing high fidelity techniques.

altaico adj. Altaic, Altaian.

altamado adj. of all sorts and qualities (cloths).

altamisa s. f. (Braz., bot., also **artemísia**) artemisia.

altanadice s. f. 1. frivolousness. 2. rashness, inconsiderateness. 3. haughtiness, arrogance.

altanado s. m. 1. (sl.) judge. 2. haughty or arrogant person. ‖ adj. 1. haughty, arrogant. 2. soaring, high-flying (bird of prey, also fig.). 3. frivolous. 4. rash, inconsiderate.

altanar v. 1. to make haughty or arrogant. 2. to behave with pride. 3. to soar. 4. to get excited about.

altanaria s. f. 1. haughtiness, arrogance. 2. soaring birds of game. 3. hawking.

altaneiro adj. 1. soaring. 2. raising very much, high up. 3. haughty, arrogant. 4. in high spirits, wanton.

altar s. m. 1. altar, Lord's table. 2. (fig.) cult. 3. (fig.) veneration. 4. (astr.) Altar. ~ **dedicado à Virgem Maria** Lady-altar. **levar ao ~** to lead to the altar, marry.

altaragem s. f. (pl. **-ens**) (obs.) 1. offerings placed on the altar. 2. fees due to a priest for altar services. 3. offerings destined for a requiem.

altareiro s. m. 1. person with a propensity for church services. 2. bigot. 3. devotee. 4. formerly person who kept the altar clean.

altarista s. m. canon in charge of the high altar (Vatican).

altar-mor s. m. (pl. **altares-mores**) high altar.

alta-roda s. f. (pl. **altas-rodas**) high society.

alta-tensão s. f. (pl. **altas-tensões**) 1. (electr.) high voltage. 2. (radiotech.) the voltage fed to the plate of a vacuum tube.

alteador s. m. raiser, lifter. ‖ adj. raising, lifting.

alteamento s. m. raising (also archit.: wall, building) lifting.

altear v. 1. to raise, make higher. 2. to increase, augment. 3. to lift. 4. to grow, enlarge. 5. **~-se** a) to become higher or taller. b) to elevate o. s.

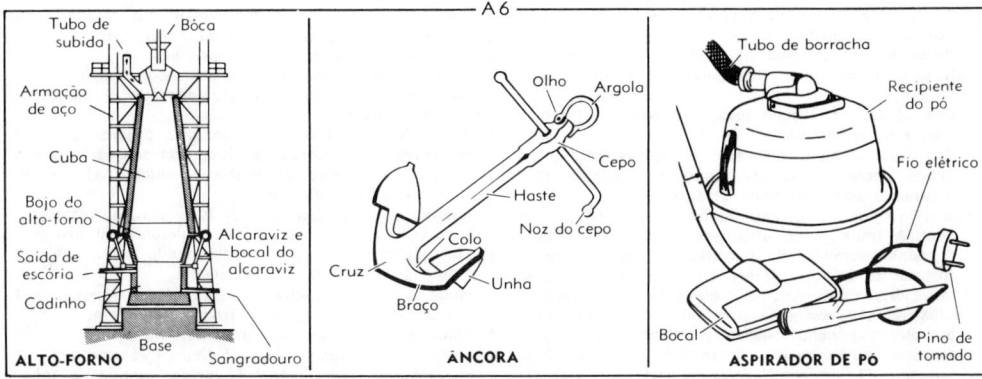

ALTO-FORNO: Tubo de subida, Bôca, Armação de aço, Cuba, Bojo do alto-forno, Alcaraviz e bocal do alcaraviz, Saída de escória, Cadinho, Base, Sangradouro

ÂNCORA: Olho, Argola, Cepo, Haste, Noz do cepo, Colo, Cruz, Unha, Braço

ASPIRADOR DE PÓ: Tubo de borracha, Recipiente do pó, Fio elétrico, Bocal, Pino de tomada

altéia s. f. (bot.) marsh-mallow.
alterabilidade s. f. alterability, changeability, changeableness.
alteração s. f. (pl. -ões) 1. alteration, change, modification. 2. degeneration, destruction, ruin. 3. decomposition, decay. 4. uneasiness, unquietude. 5. disturbance, perturbation. 6. altercation, dispute. 7. falsification. 8. indignation, vexation.
~ da moeda (de)valuation (currency). ~ da voz breaking of the voice. ~ dos preços fluctuation of prices. sem ~ changeless.
alterado adj. 1. changed. 2. upset, angry. 3. uneasy, unquiet. 4. revolted.
alterador s. m. 1. changer. 2. upsetter. 3. vexer. 4. cheat. ‖ adj. (also alterante) 1. changing, altering. 2. disturbing, disquieting, vexatious. 3. upsetting, revolting.
alterar v. 1. to change, modify, alter. 2. to perturbate, disturb, frighten. 3. to decompose, spoil. 4. to falsify. 5. to disfigure. 6. to corrupt. 7. to excite. 8. to agitate. 9. to cause a tumult. 10. to vex, annoy. 11. (obs.) to cause thirst. 12. ~-se to get excited, upset or revolted.
isto altera o caso that makes a difference. ele alterou o balanço he falsified the account. (coll.) he cooked accounts.
alterativo adj. alterative.
alterável adj. m. + f. (pl. -áveis) changeable, alterable, modifiable.
altercação s. f. (pl. -ões) altercation, (loud) dispute, quarrel.
altercador s. m. person who altercates; wrangler, quarrel(l)er, disputer, arguer. ‖ adj. quarrelsome.
altercar v. 1. to altercate, discuss noisily. 2. to dispute, quarrel, wrangle. 3. to debate.
alternação s. f. (pl. -ões) alternation, regular interchange.
alternado adj. alternate(d), by turns, alternative. ‖ -amente adv. alternately, alternatively.
claro e escuro -amente light and dark by turns.
alternador s. m. alternator (dynamo or generator), alternating current generator. ‖ adj. alternative, alternating.
alternância s. f. 1. alternation. 2. (electr.) reversal(s). 3. rotation of crops (soil). 4. stratification, position in layers.
alternante adj. m. + f. alternating, alternant.
alternar v. 1. to alternate. 2. to happen or cause to happen in turns. 3. to interchange. 4. to reverse. 5. to come about, appear. 6. (agric.) to rotate crops. 7. ~-se to alter, change, vary.

alternativa s. f. 1. alternative, choice between two things which exclude each other. 2. alternation, change.
não há outra ~ there is no remedy (but). não há outra ~ a não ser retirar-se you have no choice but to go.
alternativo adj. alternate(d), alternative: 1. by turns, periodic, intermittent. 2. every second. ‖ -amente adv. alternatedly, alternatively.
fazer alguma coisa por turno ou -amente to take turns about.
alternifIóreo adj. (bot.) alterniflorous.
alternifólio adj. (bot.) alternifoliate.
alternípede adj. m. + f. (zool.) alternipede.
alterno adj. alternate(d), periodic.
ângulos ~s alternate angles.
alteroso adj. 1. very high, tall. 2. imperious, haughty. 3. majestic, magnificent, grand. 4. (naut.) high-boarded, high-decked. 5. stormy (sea).
alteza s. f. 1. highness, loftiness. 2. elevation. 3. greatness, sublimity. 4. (title) Alteza Highness.
Sua Alteza Real His or Her Royal Highness.
altibaixos s. m. pl. 1. unevenness of the ground. 2. ups and downs of life, adversities, misfortunes. 3. favourable and unfavourable qualities.
alticolúnio adj. high-columned.
alticomo adj. (bot.) alti-comose, alticomous.
alticornígero adj. long-horned.
altiloqüência s. f. altiloquence: 1. elevation or sublimity of expression or speech. 2. pompous language.
altiloqüente adj. m. + f., altíloquo m. altiloquent, elevated or sublime in style or expression, high-sounding, pompous.
altimetria s. f. altimetry: science of measuring altitudes.
altímetro s. m. altimeter.
altimurado adj. (poet.) high-walled, having lofty walls.
altiplano s. m., altiplanura f. elevated plain, plateau.
altipotente adj. m. + f. very powerful.
altirrostro adj. (zool.) high-beaked, alti-rostrate.
Altíssimo s. m. The Almighty, God. ‖ altíssimo adj. abs. sup. highest.
altissonante adj. m. + f., altíssono m. 1. altisonant, loud (voiced). 2. highfalutin(g), pompous.
altista (I) s. m. + f. (mus.) violist.
altista (II) s. m. (com.) bull, boom speculator. ‖ adj. speculative, of or referring to speculators or price manipulators.
altitonante adj. m. + f. 1. (poet.) altitonant: thundering in the heights. 2. clamorous, noisy.

altitude s. f. altitude: 1. the vertical height above sea level. 2. elevation or high place. 3. height. 4. (astr.) elevation of a star above the horizon.

altitúdico adj. altitudinal.

altívago adj. (poet.) soaring, high up, high flown.

altivar v. 1. to elevate, heighten. 2. to make proud or haughty.

altivez(a) s. f. 1. haughtiness, arrogance. 2. pride. 3. magnanimity, nobility.

altivo adj. 1. high, elevated. 2. self-reliant, courageous, noble. 3. haughty, arrogant, high-stomached. ‖ -**amente** adv. haughtily, arrogantly.

alto (I) s. m. 1. height. 2. heaven. 3. government seat. 4. (mus.) alto: a) singer. b) althorn. c) viola. 5. peak, summit. 6. elevation. 7. the upper or remoter part (e. g. river). ‖ adj. 1. high, elevated, tall, lofty (plate Q). 2. excellent, magnificent. 3. illustrious, renowned, distinguished. 4. important. 5. bold, courageous, noble. 6. superior. 7. haughty, arrogant. 8. excessive. 9. remote. 10. loud, high-pitched. 11. profound, deep (silent).
~ **dia** plain day. ~-**forno** blast-furnace (plate A 6). o ~ **Amazonas** the upper Amazonas. **os** ~**s da casa** the upper part of a house, (second) floor, floor above the ground floor. -**a noite** deep in the night. -**a pressão** high pressure. **a -a sociedade** the high society. -**a traição** high treason. **clamar em** ~**s brados** to shout at the top of one's voice. **em** ~ **grau** to a great degree. **em** ~-**mar** on the high seas. **fale mais** ~ speak louder, speak up. **no** ~ on high. **no** ~ **do céu** up in the sky. **no ponto mais** ~ **da maré** at full of the tide. **passar por** ~ to pass over superficially. **sempre mais** ~ up and up. **a vida tem seus** ~**s e baixos** life has its ups and downs.

alto (II) s. m. stopping, halting. ‖ interj. stop! halt! **fazer** ~ to stop.

alto-cúmulo s. m. (pl. **altos-cúmulos**) (meteor.) altocumulus, a rounded pebble-like cloud formation.

alto-e-maio, **alto-e-mau** adv. at random, at hap-hazard.

alto-estrato s. m. (pl. **altos-estratos**) (meteor.) altostratus, an extended cloud formation.

alto-falante s. m. (pl. **alto-falantes**) loudspeaker.

alto-mar s. m. (pl. **altos-mares**) (naut.) deep sea, high seas: 1. offshore waters. 2. open waters of an ocean. 3. sea outside limits of a national territorial jurisdiction.

altoplano s. m. (also **planalto**) elevated plain, plateau.

altor s. m. (physiol.) the nutritive part of a substance. ‖ adj. (f. **altriz**) nutritive.

alto-relevo s. m. (pl. **altos-relevos**) high-relief, alto-relievo.

altruísmo s. m. 1. altruism, unselfishness. 2. abnegation. 3. philanthropy.

altruísta s. m. + f. altruist. ‖ adj. altruistic(al).

altruístico adj. altruistic(al).

altura s. f. 1. height (plate A 12, T 6). 2. altitude. 3. top, summit. 4. size. 5. elevation, eminence. 6. time, period. 7. climax. 8. degree, point. 9. grandeur. 10. greatness, loftiness.
~ **dinâmica** height of velocity. **à** ~ **das exigências** up to the mark. **até a** ~ **de** as high as. **a certa** ~ at a certain point, suddenly. **em que** ~ **está o seu trabalho?** how far has your work developed? **estar à** ~ **de** to be a match for, to cope with, to be equal to. **ele se sentiu à** ~ **do caso** he felt up to his subject. **mostrar-se à** ~ to approve oneself. **na** ~ **de** abreast of. **na** ~ **de Plymouth** off Plymouth. **nessa** ~ at that time. **palavras à** ~ **do tempo** words worthy of the time. **que** ~ **tem você?** how tall are you? **salto de (em)** ~ high jump. **uma** ~ **vertiginosa** a giddy height.

aluá s. m. (Braz.) refrigerant made of fermented rice flour or maize.

aluamento s. m. 1. (naut.) curved cut of the lower side of a mainsail. 2. (zool.) rut(ting). 3. folly, foolishness. 4. crazyness, madness.

aluar v. (naut.) to cut in a half-moon shape.

alucinação s. f. (pl. -**ões**) **alucinamento** m. hallucination, delusion.

alucinado adj. hallucinated, deluded, possessed, crazy.

alucinador s. m. person or thing that causes hallucination. ‖ adj. (also **alucinatório, alucinante**) hallucinatory, hallucinating.

alucinar v. 1. to hallucinate. 2. to delude, befool, infatuate. 3. to be or to fall desperately in love.

alucinógeno s. m. hallucinogen. ‖ adj. hallucinatory.

alucinose s. f. (med.) hallucinosis.

alude s. m. avalanche: a mass of ice, snow, earth and rock crashing down from a mountain.

aludir v. to allude, hint, mention, refer to.

alufá s. m. (Braz.) priest of Negro Mahometans.

alugação s. f. (pl. -**ões**) 1. hiring, renting. 2. (obs.) rent.

alugado s. m. (Braz.) hired diamond miner or washer. ‖ adj. p. p. of **alugar**: hired, rented, let.

alugador s. m. hirer, renter, person who lets.
~ **de carros** jobmaster.

alugamento s. m. hiring, renting, letting.

alugar v. 1. to hire (out), rent, let, lease. 2. to hackney out (horses, cars).
para ~ on hire, for rent. ~ **quartos** to let rooms. **aluga-se** (advertisement) to let.

aluguel s. m. (pl. -**éis**) (also less used **aluguer**) 1. letting, hiring (out), lease. 2. rent.
~ **de casa** house rent. **carro de** ~ a public cab, taxi. **casa de** ~ tenement house. **cavalo de** ~ a job horse, hackney horse. \

aluição s. f. (pl. -**ões**) (also **aluimento**) 1. shaking. 2. ruin, destruction, collapse. 3. sagging of the ground, landslide.

aluído adj. loose, shaky, tumble-down, ramshackle.

aluidor adj. ruinous, destructive.

aluir v. 1. to shake, tremble. 2. to threaten ruin or collapse. 3. to ruin, collapse. 4. to fall, come down, give way, crash. 5. to sink in or down.

álula s. f. winglet.

alumbrado s. m. Alumbrado: one of a sect of Illuminati. ‖ adj. illuminated, enlightened, inspired.

alumbrador adj. illuminated, enlightening, inspiring.

alumbramento s. m. 1. illumination, enlightenment, inspiration. 2. (rel.) illuminism.

alumbrar v. to enlighten, illuminate, inspire.

alume s. m. (also ~**n**, pl. ~**ns**, **alúmenes**) (min.) alum.

alumiação s. f. (pl. -**ões**) (also **alumiamento**) illumination (also fig.), enlightenment.

alumiado adj. 1. illuminated. 2. bright, luminous.

alumiador s. m. 1. illuminator. 2. enlightener, instructor. 3. device for lighting. ‖ adj. 1. illuminatory. 2. enlightening. 3. resplendent, bright.

alumiar v. 1. to illuminate. 2. to enlighten, instruct. 3. light up.

alumina s. f. (chem.) alumina, aluminium oxide.

aluminação s. f. mixing with alum, alum-making.

aluminagem s. f. (pl. -**ens**) (phot.) aluming, steeping in a solution of alum.

aluminar (I) v. (phot.) to aluminate, steep in alum water.

aluminar (II) v. obs. form of **alumiar**.

aluminato s. m. (chem.) aluminate.

alumínico adj. aluminic, aluminous.

aluminífero adj. aluminiferous.

alumínio s. m. aluminium.

aluminita s. f. (min.) aluminite.

aluna s. f. pupil, schoolgirl.

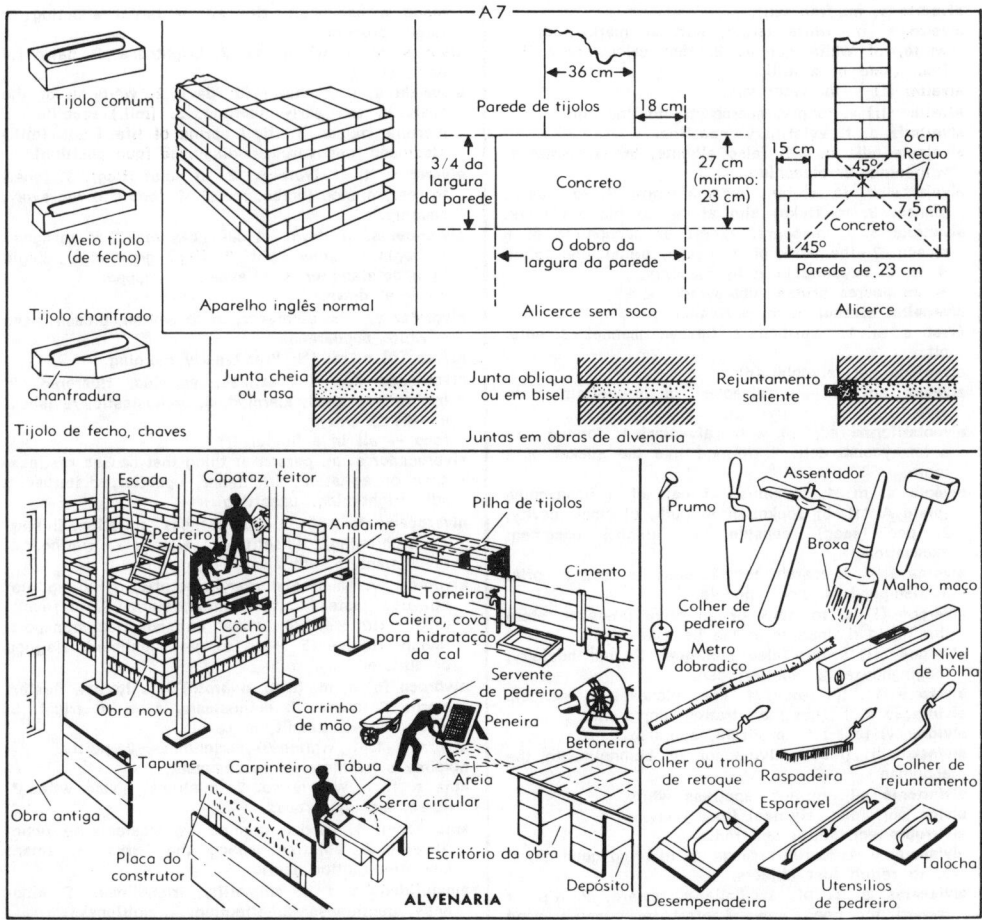

— A 7 —

Tijolo comum

Meio tijolo (de fecho)

Tijolo chanfrado

Chanfradura

Tijolo de fecho, chaves

Aparelho inglês normal

Parede de tijolos 18 cm
36 cm
3/4 da largura da parede
Concreto
27 cm (mínimo: 23 cm)
O dobro da largura da parede
Alicerce sem soco

15 cm — 6 cm Recuo
45°
Concreto 7,5 cm
45°
Parede de 23 cm
Alicerce

Junta cheia ou rasa
Junta obliqua ou em bisel
Rejuntamento saliente
Juntas em obras de alvenaria

Escada | Capataz, feitor
Pedreiro
Andaime
Pilha de tijolos
Cimento
Torneira
Caieira, cova para hidratação da cal
Côcho
Servente de pedreiro
Obra nova
Carrinho de mão
Peneira
Betoneira
Tapume
Carpinteiro | Tábua
Areia
Serra circular
Obra antiga
Placa do construtor
Escritório da obra
Depósito
ALVENARIA

Prumo
Assentador
Broxa
Malho, maço
Colher de pedreiro
Metro dobradiço
Nível de bôlha
Colher ou trolha de retoque
Raspadeira
Colher de rejuntamento
Esparavel
Desempenadeira
Talocha
Utensílios de pedreiro

alunissagem s. f. (astron.) moonfall, moon-landing.
alunissar v. (astron.) to land on the moon.
aluno s. m. 1. pupil, schoolboy. 2. scholar, follower, disciple. 3. apprentice. 4. foster son.
~ **de escola primária** lower boy.
alusão s. f. (pl. -ões) allusion, hint, reference.
~ **desvelada** broad hint. **fazer** ~ **a** to aim at.
alusivo adj. allusive, hinting. ‖ **-amente** adv. alusively.
tornar-se ~ to become personal.
aluvai interj. (N. Braz.) stop! stay!
aluvial adj. m. + f. (pl. -ais), **aluviano** m. alluvial.
aluvião s. f. (pl. -ões) 1. (geol.) alluvium, alluvion. 2. inundation, deluge. 3. torrent, stream. 4. (fig.) great quantity or number. 5. (geol.) sedimentary deposit.
alva s. f. 1. down, daybreak, aurora. 2. (rel.) alb (plate P 5). 3. (anat.) sclera (white of the eye). 4. (obs.) a sort of tunic worn by sentenced criminals on their way to execution. 5. name of a troubadour song. 6. (Port.) a variety of grapes.
alvação adj. (pl. -ões) (f. -çã) said of spotless white cattle.
alvacento adj. (also **alvadio**) 1. whitish. 2. light grey.
alvado s. m. 1. entrance or opening to a beehive (plate A 11). 2. eye or socket of a tool. 3. alveolus (tooth).

alvaiadado adj. painted with white lead.
alvaiadar v. to apply white lead to, paint with white lead.
alvaiade s. m. (chem.) white lead, ceruse.
~ **de zinco** white zinc, snow white.
alvanel s. m. (pl. -éis) (also **alvaner, alvanéu**) 1. bricklayer, brick mason. 2. (obs.) botcher, patcher.
alvar adj. m. + f. 1. whitish. 2. stupid, foolish, silly. 3. coarse, crude. 4. candid, simple.
alvará s. m. permit, charter, warrant, letters patent.
alvaraz(o) s. m. 1. (med.) white leprosy. 2. (vet.) horse pustules.
alvarenga s. f. (Braz., naut.) lighter.
alvarengueiro s. m. owner or one of the crew of a lighter.
alvarinho s. m. 1. (Port.) a sort of grapes. 2. (vet.) harmless pocks of sheep and goats. 3. (Port., pop.) scatter-brain.
alvarrã s. f. = **albarrã**.
alvazir, alvazil s. m. (pl. -is) (obs.) 1. governor. 2. judge. 3. member of a town council.
alveador s. m. whitewasher (painter).
alveamento s. m. whitewash(ing) (paint).
alvear v. to whitewash (paint).
alveário s. m. 1. beehive. 2. apiary. 3. auricle: external ear.

alvedrio s. m. free will.

alveiro s. m. white target, butt or mark. ‖ adj. 1. white, of white colour. 2. that grinds only fine flour (said of a mill).

alveitar (I) s. m. veterinary.

alveitar (II) v. to pry, search, try to find out.

alveitaria s. f. veterinary medicine.

alvejante adj. m. + f. (also **albente, branquejante**) 1. whitening. 2. bleaching.

alvejar v. 1. to whiten, become white. 2. to bleach, blanch. 3. to (take) aim at. 4. to hit the mark.

alvenaria s. f. masonry: 1. art or occupation of a mason. 2. the work of a mason, bricklaying (plate A 7). 3. anything built by masonry.
~ **de pedras brutas** rubblework.

alveneiro, alvenel s. m. = **alvanel.**

álveo s. m. 1. river-bed. 2. furrow, channel. 3. hole, pit.

alveolado adj. alveolate(d).

alveolar adj. m. + f. alveolar: of or pertaining to alveoli.

alveolariforme adj. m. + f. ‖ alveolar: 1. formed like a honeycomb cell. 2. formed like the socket of a tooth.

alvéolo s. m. 1. alveolus: a) cell of a honeycomb (plate A 11). b) socket of a tooth. c) small cavity. 2. pod (seed), capsule. 3. (archit.) basement excavation.

alverca s. f. 1. marsh, fen. 2. pond to feed a noria. 3. fish-pond. 4. pool, puddle.

alvergue (I) s. m. tank of an olive press to store the liquid drained from the bagasse.

alvergue (II) s. m. (also **albergue**) 1. inn, hostelry, lodginghouse. 2. shelter, den.

alvião s. m. (pl. -**ões**) 1. hoe, pickaxe. 2. mattock.

alvidração s. f. (obs.) arbitration, appraising.

alvidrar v. (obs.) to arbitrate, appraise.

alvíneo adj. (med.) alvine, of or belonging to the abdomen.

alvinitente adj. m. + f. spotless white.

alvino adj. (also **alvíneo**) (med.) alvine.

alvirrubro adj. white and red.

alvissarar v. 1. to run errands. 2. to bring good news. 3. to return lost objects.

alvíssaras s. f. pl. 1. finder's reward. 2. tip or reward for good news. ‖ interj. announcing good news.

alvissareiro s. m. 1. person who asks for or who gives tips or rewards (as for good news, devolution of lost objects, etc.). 2. bearer of good news. 3. person who watched for the appearance of ships and brought the good news to the owner; ship announcer. ‖ adj. auspicious.

alvitana s. f. 1. large narrow-meshed fish-net. 2. sweep-net. 3. trammel-net (outside).

alvitórax adj. m. + f., sg. + pl. said of an animal that has a white thorax.

alvitrador s. m. proposer, arbitrator. ‖ adj. arbitral, arbitrary, proposing.

alvitramento s. m. act or method of suggesting, proposing.

alvitrar v. 1. to suggest, propose, offer. 2. (obs.) to arbitrate.

alvitre s. m. 1. reminder, hint. 2. proposal, suggestion. 3. opinion, judg(e)ment. 4. (obs.) arbitration. 5. news, information.

alvitreiro s. m. 1. proposer, suggester. 2. kibitzer, unasked for advisor. 3. newsmonger.

alvo s. m. 1. white. 2. target, aim. 3. purpose, object, design, intent, end. 4. the white of the eye. ‖ adj. 1. white. 2. pure. 3. clear, limpid.
~ **actínico** fluorescent screen. **dar no** ~ to hit the target. **errar o** ~ to miss the mark. **errei o** ~ I

made a bad shot. **tiro ao** ~ target shooting or target practice.

alvor s. m. 1. whiteness. 2. brightness. 3. dawn (of day), aurora.

alvorada s. f. 1. dawn (of day). 2. warbling of the birds in the early morning. 3. (mil.) reveille. 4. morning music. 5. (fig.) spring of life. ‖ adj. (mil.) disclosed, uncovered, undisguised (gun position).

alvorar v. 1. = **alvorecer.** 2. to hoist (flag). 3. (obs.) to rear, prance (horse, mule). 4. (pop.) to run away, decamp.

alvorecer s. m. dawn (of day), daybreak. ‖ v. to dawn: 1. begin to grow light. 2. (fig.) grow clear, begin to understand or see, awake. 3. appear.
ao ~ at dawn.

alvorejar v. 1. = **alvorecer.** 2. to whiten, bleach, have a white appearance.

alvoro (ô) s. m. (N. Braz.) early morning.

alvoroçado adj. 1. restless, agitated, flustered. 2. frightened, upset, alarmed. 3. enthusiastic, ravished. 4. (Braz.) crazy.
todo ~ all in a fluster.

alvoroçador s. m. person or thing that causes restlessness or agitation, frightener, upsetter, disturber. ‖ adj. frightening, upsetting.

alvoroçamento s. m. 1. restlessness, agitation, fluster. 2. frigh(tening), upset(ting), alarm. 3. rioting. 4. ravishment. 5. entusiasm, rejoicing.

alvoroçar v. (also **alvorotar, alborotar**) 1. to agitate, stir up, fluster. 2. to frighten, alarm. 3. to revolt, rebel, riot. 4. to make enthusiastic, transport, ravish, rejoice. 5. ~-**se** to get frightened, alarmed or agitated.

alvoroço (ô) s. m. (also **alvoroto**) 1. agitation, fluster, alarm. 2. haste. 3. enthusiasm. 4. start, fright. 5. noise, brawl, tumult. 6. revolt.

alvura s. f. 1. whiteness, brightness. 2. purity.

alxaima s. f. Moorish encampment.

ama s. f. 1. wet nurse. 2. mistress, house wife. 3. nursemaid, governess.

amã s. m. 1. pardon granted by Moslems to unbelievers. 2. ablution among the Turks. 3. aman: Levantine cotton fabric.

amabilidade s. f. 1. amiability, friendliness. 2. kindness, gentleness. 3. affection. 4. politeness.
isto é a sua maior ~ this is his nearest approach to friendliness.

amacacado adj. 1. monkeyish, apish. 2. small, reduced.

amaçarocado adj. like a full spindle or corn-cob.

amaçarocar v. to shape like a (full) spindle or corn-cob.

amachorrada adj. (Braz.) sterile she-animal.

amachorrar v. (Braz.) to become sterile (she-animal).

amachucado adj. 1. crumpled, wrinkled. 2. (fig.) despondent, distressed.
ficar ~ **com alguma coisa** to take s. th. to heart.

amachucar v. 1. to crumple, wrinkle. 2. to distress, dishearten. 3. to worry, grief.

amaciado adj. soft, supple.

amaciar v. 1. to smooth, soften. 2. to soothe, ease. 3. to appease, calm, tranquilize.

amada s. f. sweetheart, mistress fiancée, girl friend, lady-love.

amadeirado adj. imitating wood, woodlike, ligniform.

amadeirar v. 1. to colour like wood, imitate wood. 2. to plank, timber (building).

ama-de-leite s. f. (pl. **amas-de-leite**) wet nurse.

amado s. m. sweetheart, lover, beau. ‖ adj. loved, beloved.

amador s. m. 1. lover. 2. fan. 3. amateur.

amadorismo s. m. 1. fondness, fancy, hobby. 2. amateurism, amateurship.

amadorista s. m. + f. 1. amateur. 2. person who favours amateurism. ‖ adj. m. + f. amateurish, favouring amateurism.

amadorrar v. = **amodorrar**.

amadrinhado adj. gregarious: said of animals (esp. horses or mules) that keep together.

amadrinhador s. m. 1. tamer of horses, asses or mules. 2. horse tamer's helper.

amadrinhar v. 1. to join a bull to an ox in order to get him used to work. 2. to yoke a horse and a mare. 3. to accustom mules, horses or asses to follow the leader, called **madrinha** (the leading mare).

amadurado adj. (also **maduro**) ripe(ned).

amaduramento s. m. ripening, ripeness.

amadurar, amadurecer v. to ripen: 1. grow ripe, bring to ripeness. 2. come to a head, attain ripeness. 3. mature, bring to maturity.

amadurecido adj. (also **maduro, amadurado**) ripe(ned), matured.

amadurecimento s. m. (also **amaduramento**) 1. ripening, maturation. 2. ripeness, matureness.

amagar v. (S. Braz.) to throw or bunt the body forward when riding on a horse to give impulse to the animal.

âmago s. m. 1. (bot.) pith or heart, pulp. 2. core: a) the central or innermost part of anything. b) the heart of timber. c) the central meaning, essence, the soul of.

ele foi ferido até o ~ he was cut to the quick.

âmago-furado s. m. (pl. **âmagos-furados**) (Braz.) disease of the tobacco-plant.

amagotado adj. in heaps, quantities, crowds.

amagotar v. to heap, crowd, accumulate in piles.

amainar v. 1. (naut.) to strike (sails). 2. to appease, compose. 3. to calm down, lull. 4. to settle, abate. 5. to diminish, lessen, relent.

amaldiçoado s. m. cursed person. ‖ adj. cursed, execrated, damned.

amaldiçoador s. m. curser. ‖ adj. cursing, execrable, damnable.

amaldiçoar v. 1. to curse, execrate, damn. 2. to abhor, detest, loathe. 3. to blaspheme.

amaleitado adj. suffering from malarial fever.

amálgama s. m. + f. 1. amalgam. 2. (min.) native alloy of mercury and silver. 3. mixture. 4. (fig.) mingle-mangle.

amalgamação s. f. (pl. **-ões**) 1. amalgamation. 2. mixture. 3. (fig.) confusion. 4. process of gold and silver mining.

amalgamador s. m. amalgamator. ‖ adj. amalgamative.

amalgamar v. 1. to amalgamate. 2. to mix, blend. 3. to join, unite. 4. to mingle, confound.

amalgâmico adj. amalgamative, amalgamate.

amalhar v. (also pop. **amalhoar**) 1. to drive in or home, pen in (cattle), fold (sheep). 2. to shelter. 3. to track down (beasts). 4. (fig.) to corner. 5. to lead or direct the right way. 6. to entangle, ensnare. 7. ~-se to withdraw.

amalocar v. (Braz.) to put, shelter or live in an Indian hut; to den.

amaltado adj. in gangs, troops or bands; mobbed.

amaltar v. to gang, troop, mob, form bands.

amalucado adj. 1. slightly crazy, queer. 2. silly, foolish. 3. maniac.

amalucar v. to turn crazy.

amame adj. m. + f. said of a two-coloured (black and white) horse.

amamentação s. f. (pl. **-ões**) lactation, nursing, breast feeding.

amamentadora s. f. woman who gives suck, wet nurse. ‖ adj. giving suck to, for suck.

amamentar v. 1. to suckle, give to suck, nurse. 2. to nourish, feed.

amancebado s. m. lover, man who keeps a woman. ‖ adj. concubinary.

amancebamento s. m. concubinage.

amancebar-se v. 1. to live in concubinage. 2. (fig.) to get used to some vice.

amanchar-se v. to lay in a slough (said of boars).

amaneirado adj. 1. affected, presumptuous. 2. pompous. 3. shoddy, trashy. 4. finical.

amaneiramento s. m. airs; affectation, artificiality, insincerity.

amaneirar v. 1. to make affected, cause affection in. 2. to make shoddy or trashy. 3. ~-se to become affected.

amanequinar v. to paint or sculpture roughly or artlessly.

amanhã s. m. 1. tomorrow. 2. (fig.) time to come, future. ‖ adv. tomorrow.

~ ou depois later. de ~ a oito dias tomorrow week. de hoje para ~ 1. from one day to the other. 2. from one moment to the other. deixar para ~ to leave for tomorrow. depois de ~ the day after tomorrow.

amanhação s. f. (pl. **-ões**) 1. tillage, cultivation. 2. dressing.

amanhado adj. 1. tilled, cultivated. 2. dressed. 3. arranged.

amanhador s. m. 1. tiller, cultivator. 2. dresser (food) 3. arranger. ‖ adj. 1. tilling, cultivating. 2. dressing.

amanhar v. 1. to till, cultivate, prepare. 2. to arrange, dispose. 3. to obtain, attain, succeed. 4. to prepare, dress (meat or fowl). 5. ~-se: a) to dress o. s. b) to adapt, adjust o. s., settle.

amanhecente adj. m. + f. dawning.

amanhecer v. m. dawn, break of the day. ‖ v. 1. to dawn, grow day. 2. to rise (sun). 3. to appear or come in the early morning. 4. to awake (also fig.). ao ~ at dawn. ele amanheceu tarde (fig.) he was caught napping. nós amanhecemos no Rio we arrived in Rio at dawn (or in the morning).

amanhecido adj. 1. dawned. 2. old, of yesterday. pão ~ old bread, yesterday's bread.

amanhecimento s. m. (rare) dawn(ing).

amanho s. m. 1. tilling, tillage. 2. arrangement, disposition. 3. neatness, good order. 4. ~s pl. tools, implements, esp. for farmwork.

amaninhador s. m. (fig.) causing sterility, stagnancy, barrenness.

amaninhar v. (fig.) to sterilize, cause barrenness.

amanonsiado (adj. (S. Braz.) said of a tamed horse that has not been ridden.

amanonsiador s. m. horse tamer who breaks in horses without riding them.

amanonsiar v. to tame horses without riding them.

amansadela s. f. taming or breaking of a horse.

amansador s. m. tamer.

amansamento s. m. taming, domestication, breaking.

amansar v. 1. to tame, domesticate, break in. 2. to mitigate, assuage, soften. 3. to appease, pacify. 4. to moderate, calm, quiet down. 5. to grow, rear, graft. 6. to till, cultivate.

amansia s. f. taming of a bull.

amantar v. to cover with a cloak.

amante s. m. 1. lover, boy friend. 2. (naut.) hoisting rope or chain. 3. f. paramour, mistress, sweetheart; (sl.) jam tart, concubine. ‖ adj. m. + f. 1. loving, in love. 2. fond of.

ele é ~ de boa música he is fond of good music. ser ~ da paz to be peaceful.

amanteigado s. m. (Braz.) cake of flour and eggs. ‖ adj. 1. like butter, buttery. 2. anointed or besmeared with butter. 3. (fig.) soft, delicate.

amanteigar v. to make buttery, give the colour or taste of butter to.

amantelar v. to fortify, wall in.

amantético adj. 1. passionate, in love. 2. affectionate, kind. 3. fond of, indulgent.

amantilhar v. 1. (naut.) to top. 2. to have sexual intercourse with. 3. (sl.) to involve, catch. 4. to live in concubinage.

amantilho s. m. (naut.) lift, yard rope, halyard (plate B 10).

amanuensado s. m. office or position of an amanuensis or scribe.

amanuense s. m. + f. amanuensis, scribe.

amapá s. m. amapa (tree).

amar v. 1. to love, be in love. 2. to like, adore, be fond of. 3. to worship. 4. (obs.) to choose, want. 5. ~-se to love each other.
fazer-se ~ to make o. s. dear.

amáraco s. m. (bot.) sweet marjoram.

amarado adj. 1. full of water. 2. inundated. 3. (fig.) mournful. 4. offshore.

amaragem s. f. (pl. -ens) (aeron.) alighting on water, sea landing.

amaranto s. m. (bot.) purplewood.

amarar v. 1. (naut.) to put to sea. 2. (aeron.) to alight on water. 3. to become full of water, be flooded. 4. to be grieved.

amarasmear v. to become apathic.

amarelado adj. yellowish, tending towards yellow.

amarelão s. m. (path.) ancylostomiasis: hookworm disease.

amarelar, amarelecer, amarelejar v. 1. to yellow. 2. to fade, lose colour.

amarelecimento s. m. act or fact of turning yellow.

amarelento adj. 1. yellowish. 2. pale. 3. faded. 4. (Braz.) affected by the hookworm disease.

amarelidão, amarelidez s. f. 1. yellowness. 2. paleness.

amarelinha s. f. 1. (bot.) black-eyed susan. 2. hopscotch.

amarelo s. m. 1. yellow (colour). 2. (Braz.) person suffering from hookworm disease. 3. (Braz.) pale person. ‖ adj. 1. yellow. 2. pale. 3. faded. 4. forced (smile).
~ mineral patent yellow. ~ pálido primrose. ela me lançou um sorriso ~ her mouth twitched in a half-hearted smile. ficar mais ~ do que cera to become pale as death.

amarescente adj. m. + f. that bitters, causing bitterness.

amarfalhar, amarfanhar v. 1. to crumple, wrinkle. 2. to ill-treat.

amargado adj. 1. rendered bitter. 2. painful. 3. harsh, severe.

amargar v. 1. to embitter: a) make or become bitter or acrid. b) be grievous or cause grief; distress. 2. to pay dear for. 3. to have a bitter taste.

amargo s. m. 1. bitter (quality or taste). 2. (Braz.) tea without sugar. 3. (Braz.) ~s pl. bitter remedies. ‖ adj. bitter: 1. acrid, acrimonious. 2. distressing, painful, sad. 3. hard to bear. 4. harsh, severe (complaints, words).
até o ~ fim to the bitter end.

amargor s. m. bitterness, bitter taste.

amargoseira s. f. (bot.) pride of China.

amargoso adj. 1. = amargo. 2. (Braz., pop.) brave, daring.

amargura s. f. bitterness: 1. acridity, acrimoniousness. 2. distress, grief, sorrow, affliction.

as ~s da vida the seamy side of life. uma taça de ~ a bitter cup.

amargurado adj. distressed, grieved, sorrowful, afflicted.

amargurar v. 1. to cause grief or sorrow; afflict, distress. 2. to embitter.

amaricado adj. effeminate, womanish, unmanly.

amaricar-se v. to become effeminate, womanish.

amaridar v. (fig.) to be intimate with a person.

amarídeo adj. (pharm.) designation of a bitter thing.

amarilha s. f. cachexy (of beasts).

amarilho s. m. (Braz., med.) bandage, dressing.

amarílico adj. of or pertaining to the yellow fever.

amarinhar v. 1. to man a ship, furnish with men, equip. 2. to command a ship. 3. to enlist as a sailor.

amario adj. (S. Braz.) referring to a bay horse with white mane and tail.

amariolar-se v. 1. to turn a coward. 2. to get roguish.

amaro adj. (obs., poet.) bitter.

amarotar-se v. to become roguish or naughty.

amarra s. f. 1. (nau.t) cable, chain cable; hawser. 2. (fig.) support, protection, aid.
picar a ~ to cut the cables. estar sobre a ~ to ride at anchor. estar a duas ~s (fig.) to be on the safe side, have two irons in the fire.

amarração s. f. (pl. -ões). 1. fastening, tying, lashing. 2. mooring, moorage, anchorage. 3. (Braz. fig.) amorous entanglement.

amarrado s. m. 1. parcel, bundle. 2. fag(g)ot. 3. dense growth of creepers or climbers. ‖ adj. 1. fastened, bound, stringed, tied. 2. (naut.) moored. 3. compromised. 4. apprehensive, cautious. 5. (Braz.): a) shy, embarrassed. b) (fam.) married.

amarrador s. m. 1. (Braz.) master of a float (jangada). 2. person who or thing that fastens, ties, moors. ‖ adj. fastening, binding, mooring.

amarradouro s. m. berth, moorings.

amarrar v. 1. to moor, fash, anchor. 2. to bind, fasten, tie (down) (also fig.). 3. to chain. 4. (Braz.) to bet, wager. 5. to close, come to an agreement. 6. to stop, stay, halt (said of a hound that tracks down the game) (also fig.). 7. ~-se a) (fig.) to take shelter or protection. b) to attach o. s. to. c) to compromise, commit o. s. d) (Braz., fam.) to marry.
~ o cavalo a um poste to tie up the horse to a pole. ~ o pacote to tie up the parcel. amarrei o meu sapato I tied up my shoe. ela amarrou-o firmemente (fig.) she entangled him entirely. quer ~ 100 cruzeiros? bet a 100 cruzeiros?

amarreta s. f. dim. of amarra.

amarrilho s. m. twine, (pack) thread.

amarroado adj. 1. downcast, discouraged, spiritless, melancholic. 2. (obs.) obstinate.

amarroamento s. m. 1. discouragement, downheartedness, melancholy. 2. hammering (with a sledgehammer).

amarroar v. 1. to be discouraged, downhearted, spiritless. 2. to beat with a sledgehammer.

amarronzado adj. (Braz.) chestnut brown, tending towards brown, brownish.

amarroquinado adj. like Morocco leather.

amarroquinar v. to make like Morocco leather.

amarrotado adj. 1. wrinkled, crumpled. 2. hurt.

amarrotar v. 1. to crumple, rumple. 2. to wrinkle, ruffle. 3. to ripple. 4. to reprimand, abate, bring down. 5. to disconcert, discompose. 6. to outargue. 7. to beat, thresh. 8. to lose luster, become dull.

amartelado adj. 1. conquered, brought down, abated. 2. inclined, fond of.

amartelar v. 1. to hammer, beat. 2. to shape by hammering. 3. to pester. 4. to discuss, argue. 5. to conquer, abate, be victorious.

amarugem s. f. (pl. -ens) (also Port. amarujo) slightly bitter taste, moderate bitterness.

amarujar v. 1. to taste slightly bitter. 2. to become somewhat bitter.

amarujento adj. tasting or becoming somewhat bitter.

amarulento adj. very bitter, full of bitterness.

amarulhar v. 1. (sea) to become billowy. 2. to become noisy.

amarume s. m. 1. bitter taste, bitterness. 2. affliction.

ama-seca s. f. (pl. amas-secas) dry nurse, baby sitter.

amásia s. f. mistress, concubine.

amasiar-se v. to take a mistress, live in concubinage.

amasio s. m. concubinage.

amásio s. m. lover, man who keeps a woman.

amassa-barro s. m. (pl. amassa-barros) (Braz., ornith., also joão-de-barro) ovenbird.

amassadeira s. f. 1. kneader: woman who kneads. 2. kneading trough (plate P 1). 3. kneading machine.

amassadela s. f. 1. kneading. 2. crushing, bruising.

amassado adj. 1. squashed, crushed, flattened. 2. battered, bruised.

amassador s. m. 1. kneading trough (dough, mortar). 2. kneading machine. 3. kneader: person who kneads (dough, mortar).

amassadouro s. m. (also amassadoiro) kneading-trough or board.

amassadura s. f. 1. (also amassamento m.): a) kneading or working up. b) bump, blow. c) squash, crush. 2. ovenful, batch.

amassar v. 1. to knead, mix (dough, mortar). 2. to thrash, beat. 3. to squash, crush. 4. to crumple, wrinkle. 5. to depress, dishearten. 6. ~-se to become pasty.

amassaria s. f. 1. bakery. 2. kneading-trough.

amassilho s. m. 1. quantity of flour to be kneaded. 2. kneading machine. 3. heap (of things or reasons).

amastozoário s. m. (zool.) Amasta (pl.): nippleless mammals.

amatalar v. to cover with sores (draught or pack animal).

amatalotar v. 1. to enlist as a sailor. 2. to associate with a ship-chandler.

amatilhar v. 1. to pack (hounds). 2. to join, associate with.

amatividade s. f. amativeness.

amatório adj. amatory, erotic.

amatronar v. 1. to assume airs of a matron. 2. to age, grow old (said of a woman). 3. to become corpulent, grow stout.

amatular-se v. to associate with populace or rabble.

amatungado adj. (Braz.) apparently bad (horse).

amatutar-se v. to become boorish, rustic.

amaurose s. f. (med.) amaurosis: loss of sight.

amaurótico s. m. person suffering from amaurosis. || adj. amaurotic.

amaurotizar v. to cause amaurosis.

amável adj. m. + f. (pl. -áveis) 1. amiable, kind, lovable. 2. friendly, courteous, polite. || amavelmente adv. amiably, kindly, courteously, politely.
o senhor é muito ~ you are most kind. quão ~ de sua parte how nice of you. pouco ~ unkind.

amavios s. m. pl. 1. love potion, philtre. 2. means of seduction. 3. charms: a) incantations. b) allurements.

amavioso adj. 1. seductive, alluring. 2. gentle, delicate. 3. amiable.

amaxofobia s. f. amaxophobia, sensation of fear when riding a car.

amaxófobo s. m. amaxophobe.

amazelado adj. 1. full of sores (pack or draught animal). 2. (fig.) unclean, impure.

amazelar v. to cover with sores.

amazia s. f. (zool.) absence of nipples in certain mammals (Amasta).

amazona s. f. 1. Amazon: legendary female warrior. 2. sturdy manlike woman, virago. 3. horsewoman. 4. habit: riding costume of a lady.

amazonense s. m. + f. Amazonian: native or inhabitant of Amazonas (Braz. state). || (also amazônico, amazônio) adj. Amazonian.

ambages s. m. pl. ambage: 1. circumlocution., 2. subterfuge, evasion. 3. roundabout ways.

ambaíba s. f. (Braz., bot.) trumpetwood.

âmbar s. m. amber.
~ amarelo yellow amber. ~ gris ambergris.

ambárico adj. (also ambarino) amber.

ambarina s. f. (chem.) ambrein.

ambarizar v. to amber: 1. perfume with ambergris. 2. colour like amber.

ambição s. f. (pl. -ões) ambition, eager desire.
ter -ões to fly high.

ambicionar v. to pursue ambitiously, strive after, desire eagerly, hanker after.

ambicioso s. m. (also, less used ambicioneiro) ambitious person. || adj. ambitious, desirous of, high-flying, of great pretension.

ambidestria s. f., ambidestrismo m. ambidexterity, ambidextrousness.

ambidestro adj. ambidextrous.

ambiência s. f. ambiance, environment, atmosphere.

ambientar v. 1. (fig.) to form an atmosphere, favourable conditions. 2. to adapt, accustom to an environment. 3. ~-se to adapt o. s. or get used to an environment.

ambiente s. m. environment: 1. surrounding, ambiance. 2. circle, sphere, atmosphere. || adj. m. + f. ambient, surrounding, environmental.

ambiesquerdo adj. awkward, clumsy, unskil(l)ful.

ambígeno adj. hybrid, ambigenous.

ambigüidade s. f. 1. ambiguity, ambiguousness. 2. amphibology. 3. uncertainness, doubtfulness.

ambíguo adj. 1. ambiguous. 2. doubtful, dubious, uncertain. 3. equivocal. 4. hesitating. || ambiguamente adv. ambiguously, dubiously.
ser ~ to carry two faces.

ambilátero adj.: bifacial, having two faces, fronts or façades or two opposing surfaces.

ambíparo adj. (bot.) ambiparous.

ambisséxuo adj. bisexual.

âmbito s. m. 1. ambit, circuit, circumference. 2. extent, scope. 3. sphere or field of action. 4. precinct, bounds.

ambivalência s. f. ambivalence, simultaneously conflicting feelings or thoughts about some person, object or idea.

ambivalente adj. m. + f. ambivalent.

ambívio s. m. 1. road crossing. 2. crossway, cross-road(s).

amblígono adj. obtuse-angled.

amblíope, amblíope s. m. person suffering from amblyopia (weak-sightedness).

ambliopia s. f. (med.) amblyopia, weak-sightedness.

amblíópico adj. (med.) amblyopic.

amblose s. f. (also aborto) amblosis: abortion, miscarriage.

amblótico s. m. (med.) amblotic: abortive medicine. adj. amblotic, abortive, abortifacient.

amboré s. m. (Braz., ichth.) tetard.

ambos adj., pron. both.
em ~ os lados on either side.

ambre s. m. (also âmbar) amber.

ambreada s. f. artificial amber.

ambreado adj. 1. perfumed with amber. 2. of the colour of amber.

ambrear v. 1. to perfume with amber, aromatize. 2. to colour like amber.

ambreta s. f. (bot.) abelmosk.

ambrósia s. f. ambrosia: 1. food and drink of gods. 2. anything delicious in taste. 3. (Braz.) sweet of milk, sugar and eggs. 4. (bot.) ragweed.
ambrosíaco adj. 1. ambrosial. 2. delicious, fragrant.
ambrosiano adj. (hist.) Ambrosian: of, pertaining to or instituted by St. Ambrose.
canto ~ Ambrosian chant.
ambrosnato s. m. (Braz.) a sort of cream.
âmbula s. f. (rel.) ampulla.
ambulacrário adj. (zool.) ambulacral.
ambulacro s. m. 1. (zool.) ambulacrum: ambulacral sucker. 2. plantation of trees in regular rows.
ambulância s. f. ambulance: 1. field-hospital. 2. a vehicle to transport sick or wounded. 3. mail van.
ambulante adj. m. + f. moving, ambulatory, ambulant. **companhia ~ de artistas** strolling company. **vendedor** ~ hawker, peddler.
ambular v. to stroll, amble, meander, saunter.
ambulativo adj. 1. ambulatory, ambulant. 2. roving, wandering, vagrant. 3. movable, moving. 4. unsteady.
ambulatório s. m. 1. (med.) (poli)clinic. 2. ambulatory. ‖ adj. ambulatory, movable.
ambustão s. f. (med.) ambustion, cauterization.
ameaça s. f. 1. threat, menace. 2. foreboding.
fazer ~**s** to threaten.
ameaçado s. m. threatened person. ‖ adj. threatened.
ameaçador s. m. threatener. ‖ adj. threatening, menacing.
tempo ~ **(de chuva)** threatening weather.
ameaçante adj. m. + f. threatening, menacing.
ameaçar v. to threaten, menace: 1. menace with punishment, frighten. 2. give a forewarning. 3. be a sign of evil or harm. 4. expose to danger, jeopardize. 5. be or come near. 6. be about to happen. ~ **a** to threaten to. **ameaça chover** it looks like rain, the weather threatens rain. **eles foram ameaçados com demissão** they were threatened with dismissal. **um perigo está ameaçando** a danger threatens.
ameaço s. m. 1. threat, menace. 2. omen, foreboding presage.
ameado adj. provided with battlements.
amealhado adj. 1. saved, economized. 2. divided into small shares or portions.
amealhador s. m. 1. bargainer, haggler. 2. niggard, miser.
amealhar v. 1. to bargain, haggle. 2. to be parsimonious. 3. to save, economize. 4. to divide into small shares or portions.
amear v. 1. to provide with battlements. 2. to divide, halve.
ameba s. f. (zool.) am(o)eba.
amebiano adj. (zool.) am(o)eban.
amebíase s. f. (med.) am(o)ebiasis.
amébico adj. (zool.) am(o)ebic.
amedrontado adj. frightened, afraid, fearful, scared. **ficar** ~ to stand in awe of.
amedrontador s. m. frightener, intimidator, scarer. ‖ adj. frightening, scaring.
amedrontamento s. m. frightening, scaring, fear.
amedrontar v. 1. to frighten, scare, alarm. 2. ~**-se** to be afraid.
ameia s. f. battlement.
ameigado adj. 1. fondled, caressed. 2. appeased, calmed.
ameigador s. m. 1. fondler, caresser. 2. appeaser. ‖ adj. 1. fondling, caressing. 2. appeasing.
ameigar v. to fondle, caress, pet, cherish, appease.
amêijoa s. f. (also obs. and pop.: **ameij(e)a** eatable mussel, cockle.
ameijoada s. f. 1. cockle stew. 2. pasture ground, fold. 3. night spent in carousing or working.

levar o gado à ~ to lead the cattle to pasture at night.
ameijoar v. 1. to fold, confine (sheep) in a fold. 2. to pen, shut in a pen. 3. to go or be driven to the pasture ground during the night. 4. to retire.
ameixa, amêixoa s. f. 1. plum. 2. (pop.) bullet. ~ **seca** prune.
ameixal s. m. (pl. **-ais**) (also **ameixial, ameixoal**) plum tree orchard.
ameixeira s. f. plum tree.
amelaçar v. 1. to colour like sirup or molasses. 2. to make sirup or molasses of. 3. to make or cause to be affected.
amelado adj. honey-coloured.
ameloado adj. melonlike (in shape, colour or taste).
amelopia s. f. (med.) decrease or partial loss of vision.
amelroado adj. like the blackbird: black.
amém s. m. amen. ‖ interj. amen! **dar o** ~ to agree, consent. **em menos de um** ~ in a wink. **dizer** ~ **a tudo** to comply with everything.
amência s. f. = demência.
amêndoa s. f. 1. almond. 2. any seed contained in a kernel. 3. Easter present. 4. (petrog.) cavity filled with secondary minerals. ~**s em casca** shell almonds. ~ **torrada** crisp almond.
amendoada s. f. 1. emulsion of almonds, milk of sweet almonds, orgeat. 2. almond cake.
amendoado adj. 1. similar to almonds. 2. made with almonds.
amendoal s. m. (pl. **-ais**) almond plantation.
amendoeira s. f. (bot.) almond tree.
amendoim s. m. (pl. **-ins**) peanut, groundnut, earth nut. **manteiga de** ~ peanut butter. **óleo de** ~ peanut oil.
amenia s. f. (path.) = **amenorréia**.
amenidade s. f. 1. amenity, pleasantness, delightfulness. 2. serenity, cheerfulness. 3. gracefulness.
ameninado adj. 1. childish, childlike, boyish. 2. weak, feeble.
ameninar(-se) v. 1. to become or act childish. 2. to rejuvenate, rejuvenize.
amenista s. m. + f. 1. person who agrees, says yes and amen to everything. 2. condescending person.
amenizado adj. softened, eased, soothed, appeased.
amenizador s. m. softener, easer, soother, appeaser. ‖ adj. softening, easing, soothing, appeasing.
amenizar v. to soften, ease, soothe, appease.
ameno adj. (also **amenoso**) 1. suave, bland, mild. 2. agreeable. 3. delicate. 4. delicious, pleasant. 5. affable, courteous.
amenorréia s. f. (path.) amenorrhoea, amenorrhea, abnormal absence or suppression of menstruation.
amenta s. f. 1. remembrance, reminiscence. 2. prayer for the dead. 3. conjuration.
amentador s. m. 1. reminder. 2. person who prays for the dead. 3. conjurer.
amentar v. 1. (obs.) to deprive of reason. 2. to remind, remember. 3. to pray for the dead. 4. to tie down with leather straps. 5. to conjure.
amente adj. m. + f. (obs.) insane.
amentífero adj. (bot.) amentiferous.
amentiforme adj. m. + f. (bot.) amentiform.
amentilho s. m. (bot.) ament.
amerceador s. m. pardoner, compassionate person, pitier.
amerceamento s. m. 1. pity, compassion. 2. pardon.
amercear v. 1. to pardon. 2. ~**-se** to pity, partake of someone's suffering, be sorry for.
América s. f. (Braz., sl.) 1. something big, great, extraordinary. 2. good bargains.
americana s. f. small, light, four-wheeled carriage.

americanada s. f. typical American action or way of proceeding.

americanismo s. m. Americanism: 1. attachment to the U. S. A. 2. an American custom or characteristic. 3. peculiarity of American English.

americanista s. m. + f. Americanist: 1. follower of Americanism, sympathizer of American ways and manners. 2. scholar devoted to the study of subjects specially relating to America.

americanização s. f. (pl. **-ões**) Americanization.

americanizar v. to Americanize.

americano s. m. 1. American: native or inhabitant of America (especially U. S. A.). 2. coarse cotton cloth. ‖ adj. American.

ameríndio s. m. American Indian.

amerissagem s. f. (pl. **-ens**) (aeron.) alighting on the water.

amerissar v. (aeron.) to alight on the water.

amesend(r)ar-se v. 1. to sit down (comfortably) at table. 2. to make o. s. comfortable.

amesquinhado adj. 1. depreciated, disparaged. 2. humbled, humiliated. 3. wretched. 4. closefisted, avaricious, miserly.

amesquinhador s. m. 1. depreciator. 2. humbler. 3. miser. ‖ adj. 1. depreciative. 2. humiliatory.

amesquinhamento s. m. 1. depreciation. 2. humiliation. 3. wretchedness. 4. closefistedness, miserliness.

amesquinhar v. 1. to depreciate, disparage. 2. to humble, humiliate. 3. to pester. 4. to be avaricious.

amestrado adj. 1. trained, instructed. 2. domesticated.

amestrador s. m. 1. rough-rider. 2. trainer. ‖ adj. instructing, instructive, training.

amestramento s. m. training, instruction, teaching, domestication.

amestrar v. 1. to instruct, teach, train. 2. to break in (horse), domesticate. 3. **~-se** to exercise o. s., practise, learn.

ametade s. f. (less used form of **metade**) half, moiety.

ametalar v. 1. to adorn with metal. 2. to mix with metal, alloy. 3. to give the appearance of metal to.

ametista s. m. (min.) amethyst.

ametístico adj. 1. amethystlike. 2. amethystine.

ametria s. f. lack of measure.

ametropia s. f. (med.) ametropia (myopia, astigmatism).

amétropo, amétrope s. m. person suffering from ametropia.

amezinhador s. m. naturopath: person who treats or cures with household medicines.

amezinhar v. to treat or heal with household medicines.

amial s. m. (pl. **-ais**) alder grove.

amianto s. m. amianthus: fine silky asbestos.

amiastenia s. f. (path.) muscular asthenia, loss or lack of strength, sensation of tiredness, prostration.

amical adj. m. + f. (pl. **-ais**) amicable, friendly.

amicícia s. f. (rare) friendship.

amicto s. m. (rel.) amice: part of a priest's vestment at mass (plate P 5).

amículo s. m. small dress or veil, sort of mantilla.

amida s. f. (chem.) amide.

amideria s. f. (Braz.) amide factory.

amidina s. f. (chem.) amidin(e).

amido, âmido, s. m. starch, amylum.

~ de arroz rice starch.

amidoado adj. starchy, containing starch.

amieiral s. m. (pl. **-ais**) (bot.) alder grove.

amieiro s. m. (bot.) alder (tree), common alder.

amielia s. f. congenital lack of the medulla.

amiélico adj. (biol.) amielinic, non-medullated (nerve fibers).

amiga s. f. 1. female friend. 2. mistress, concubine.

amigação s. f. (pl. **-ões**) act or fact of befriending.

amigaço s. m. (also **amigalhaço, amigalhão**) (frequently used depreciatively) great friend.

amigado adj. living in concubinage.

viver ~ to live in tally.

amigar v. 1. to make friends with, befriend. 2. to take a mistress. 3. **~-se** to become friends.

amigável adj. m. + f. (pl. **-áveis**) friendly, amicable, amiable.

amí(g)dala s. f. (anat.) tonsil, amygdala.

ami(g)dálico adj. (anat.) tonsilar.

ami(g)dalina s. f. (chem.) amygdalin.

ami(g)dalino adj. (chem.) amygdaline.

ami(g)dalite s. f. (med.) amygdalitis, tonsillitis: inflammation of the tonsils.

ami(g)dalóide adj. m. + f. amygdaloid(al).

amigo s. m. 1. friend. 2. lover, man who keeps a woman. 3. protector. ‖ adj. friendly, ami(c)able, favourable, kind, fond of.

~ do peito bosom friend. **Am.º e Sr.** (in letters) 1. sir. 2. Dear Sir. **~ íntimo** close friend. **Am.ºˢ e Srs.** (in letters) Dear Sirs; Gentlemen. **~ leitor** dear reader. **~s, ~s, negócios à parte** gentlemen, business is business! **~s de tempos prósperos** fair-weather friends. **ele é ~ de boa música** he is fond of good music. **eles são ~s muito íntimos** they are very intimate friends, (fam.) they are thick as thieves, they are chums. **ele tem cara de poucos ~s** he has an unfriendly look. **estamos entre ~s** we are among friends. **meu caro ~** my dear fellow. **o ~ se conhece na hora do aperto** a friend in need is a friend indeed. **que ~ da onça você é!** a fine friend you are! **tornar-se ~ de** to make friends with. **um ~ necessário** a friend in need. **um escoteiro é ~ de todos** a scout is a friend of all. **velho ~** old friend, (fam.) old crony, old egg, (Engl., fam.) old chap. **você conquistou um ~** you have made a friend.

amigo-da-onça, amigo-urso s. m. (pl. **amigos-da-onça, amigos-ursos**), (Braz.) false friend.

amigueiro adj. friendly, amiable, attentive, obliging.

amiláceo adj. amylaceous.

amílase s. f. (biochem.) amylase.

amilhado adj. (Braz.) said of an animal fed with maize.

amilhar v. (Braz.) 1. to feed with maize. 2. to include maize in the ration.

amimado adj. 1. fondled, petted, caressed. 2. spoilt.

amimador s. m. fondler, caresser, dandler.

amimalhar v. to coddle, spoil.

amimar v. 1. to fondle, caress, pet, pamper, dandle. 2. to spoil (child).

amimia s. f. (med.) amimia, loss or lack of ability to mimic.

amina s. f. (chem.) amine.

amineirar v. (Braz.) to give the appearance of proceeding from Minas Gerais.

aminguar v. to diminish, run short of.

aminoácido s. m. (chem.) aminoacid.

amiostenia s. f. (med.) amyosthenia.

amiostênico adj. (med.) amyosthenic.

amiotrofia s. f. (med.) amyotrophia, amyotrophy, atrophy of a muscle.

amir s. m. emir, emeer: Turkish title of dignity.

amiseração s. f. (pl. **-ões**) pitying, compassion, commiseration.

amiserar-se v. 1. to have, take pity (up)on, feel sorry for. 2. to lament over, wail.

amissão s. f. (pl. **-ões**) loss.

amissível adj. m. + f. (pl. **-íveis**) susceptible to be lost.

amistar v. 1. to make a friend of. 2. **~-se** to reconcile o. s.

amistoso adj. friendly, amicable, well-meaning, well-intentioned.
ter relações -as com alguém to be on familiar terms with s. o. **um entendimento** ~ an amicable understanding.
amisular v. (archit.) to bracket: provide with or place on brackets.
amitose s. f. (biol.) amitosis.
amiudado adj. frequent, repeated.
-as vezes frequently, very often.
amiudar v. 1. to do, happen or occur frequently. 2. to crow (cock) at the break of the day. 3. to be very precise about, be punctilious.
amiúde adv. repeated, frequent, often.
amizade s. f. 1. friendship, amity, affection. 2. amiableness, friendliness, benevolence.
fazer ~ to make friends. **fiz** ~ **com ele** I have contracted a friendship with him. **tenho** ~ **com ela** I am friends with her.
amnésia, amnesia s. f. (med.) amnesia: loss of memory.
amnesiar v. (med.) to cause amnesia.
amnésico adj. (med.) amnesic.
amnéstico adj. (med.) causing amnesia.
âmnio s. m. (anat.) amnion.
amniota s. m. (zool.) Amniota, amniote.
amniótico adj. (anat.) amniotic.
amo s. m. 1. master. 2. master of the house, father of the family, husband. 3. owner, proprietor. 4. boss, chief.
amocambado adj. (Braz.) hidden, fugitive.
amocambamento s. m. (Braz.) 1. hiding in the woods (said of fugitive slaves and stray cattle). 2. hiding, concealing. 3. withdrawal, retiring, seclusion.
amocambar v. (Braz.) 1. to shelter or take refuge in the woods (said of fugitive slaves or stray cattle). 2. to withdraw, retire, seclude.
amochar-se v. 1. to withdraw, retire, seclude. 2. to take shelter, hide.
amodernar v. to modernize.
amódita s. m. + f. plant or animal living in or on sand. ‖ adj. ammodytoid: said of animals or plants living in or on sand.
amodorrar v. 1. to make drowsy, lull to sleep. 2. to become sleepy. 3. to doze. 4. to lethargize.
amoedação s. f. coinage, mintage.
amoedar v. 1. to coin, mint. 2. (fig.) to turn into cash. 3. to admit. 4. to adopt.
amoedável adj. m. + f. (pl. **-áveis**) coinable; that can or may be minted.
amofinação s. f. (pl. **-ões**) 1. vexation. 2. affliction. 3. worry(ing). 4. grief.
amofinado adj. 1. vexed. 2. afflicted. 3. worried. 4. grieved.
amofinador s. m. 1. vexer. 2. afflicter, tormentor. 3. worrier. 4. griever.
amofinar v. 1. to vex, irritate. 2. to afflict. 3. to worry. 4. to grieve.
amofumbar v. (Braz.) to hide.
amoitar(-se) v. (Braz.) to hide o. s.
amojada adj. (Braz.) swelled (said of animals about to bring forth young).
amojar v. to swell, fill or be filled with milk (said of the breasts or the udder).
amojo (ô) s. m. swelling or hardening of the udder or breasts with milk.
amolação s. f. (pl. **-ões**) (also **amoladura, amoladela**) 1. grinding, whetting, sharpening. 2. (fig.) vexation, affliction, worry, nuisance, pestering.
amoladeira s. f. whetstone, grindstone.
amolado adj. 1. sharpened, whetted. 2. (fig.) vexed, worried, annoyed, bored. 3. (fig.) first-rate, excellent.

amolador s. m. 1. sharpener, whetter, grinder. 2. tormentor, pesterer, vexer. ‖ adj. pestering, annoying, vexatious.
~ **ambulante** itinerant knife grinder.
amolante s. m. + f. = **amolador** ‖ adj. = **amolador**.
amolar v. 1. to whet, grind, sharpen. 2. to vex, pester, annoy, harass, importune, bother. 3. to mislead, deceive. 4. to think, ponder, brood. 5. to suffer a loss or punishment. 6. to cause to withdraw.
~**am a sua paciência** they wearied him. **não me amole!** leave me alone; don't push; don't be a nuisance!
amoldado adj. 1. moulded. 2. used to, wonted.
amoldar v. 1. to mould, shape, frame, form. 2. to adjust, adapt. 3. ~**-se** to get used to.
amoldável adj. m. + f. (pl. **-áveis**) 1. mouldable. 2. adjustable, adaptable.
amolecado adj. 1. rascally, roguish, knavish. 2. mischievous.
amolecar v. 1. to ill-treat, treat unbecomingly. 2. to ridicularize. 3. to lower, degrade. 4. (Braz.) to turn a street Arab, become mischievous.
amolecedor s. m. mollifier ‖ adj. mollifying.
amolecer v. (also **amolentar**) 1. to mollify, soften. 2. to soak. 3. to weaken. 4. to move, touch, affect. 5. to effeminate.
amolecido adj. 1. mollified, softened. 2. weakened. 3. soaked. 4. moved, touched.
amolecimento s. m. 1. mollification, softening. 2. weakening. 3. soaking.
~ **cerebral** encephalomalacia, softening of the brain.
amolegar v. 1. to touch, feel, handle. 2. to crush, crash.
amolentamento s. m. 1. = **amolecimento**. 2. enervation.
amolentar v. 1. = **amolecer**. 2. to enervate.
amolestar v. (also **molestar**) to molest.
amolgação s. f. (pl. **-ões**) (also **amolgadela, amolgadura**) 1. crushing, squashing. 2. beating, bruising. 3. surrender. 4. abatement, subdual. 5. imposition. 6. shock.
amolgar v. 1. to crush, crash, squash. 2. to beat, bruise. 3. to surrender, yeld. 4. to abate, subdue. 5. to impose, force. 6. to shock. 7. to harass.
amolgável adj. m. + f. (pl. **-áveis**) that can or may be crushed, squashed, beaten, subdued, forced, etc.
amônia s. f. (chem.) ammonia.
amoniacado adj. (also **amoniacal**) (pl. **-ais**) (chem.) ammoniacal.
amoníaco s. m. (chem.) ammonia, volatile alkali.
solução de goma -a gum ammoniac.
amônio s. m. (chem.) ammonium.
amonite s. f. (pal.) ammonite, snakestone.
amonômetro s. m. (chem.) ammonia meter.
amontado adj. (Braz.) said of a domestic stray animal that ran wild again.
amontanhar v. 1. to rise like a mountain. 2. to accumulate, heap up.
amontar v. 1. to heap, shape like a heap. 2. to go or allow to go up a hill or mountain. 3. to run away and run wild again (domestic animals). 4. to amount to, total. 5. to appear, show up.
os prejuízos amontam em dez mil cruzeiros the losses amount to ten thousand cruzeiros.
amontoa, amontoação s. f. (pl. ~**s, -ões**) (agric.) moulding up, earthing up.
amontoado s. m. heap, mass, pile. ‖ adj. heaped up, piled up.
é um ~ **de mentiras** it is a heap of lies.
amontoador s. m. heaper: person who or machine that heaps or piles up.
amontoamento s. m. 1. heaping or piling up. 2. heap, pile.

amontoar v. 1. to heap or pile up. 2. to accumulate. 3. to amass, gather. 4. to hoard. 5. (agric.) to earth up.
~ **brasa sobre a cabeça de** to heap coals of fire on the head of.
amonturar v. to heap up dung.
amor s. m. (pl. **amores**) 1. love, affection, attachment, devotion, fondness. 2. passion, enthusiasm. 3. friendship. 4. object of love. 5. sweetheart. 6. love-affair, amour. 7. **Amor**: Cupid. 8. (obs.) favour, grace. 9. darling, lovely person or thing.
~ **maternal** mother's love. **casamento por** ~ **love** match. **o** ~ **à paz** the will to peace. **pelo** ~ **de Deus!** for goodness' sake! **perdido de** ~ lovelorn. **por** ~ out of love. **por** ~ **à pátria** for love of one's country. **por** ~ **à paz** for the sake of peace. **sem** ~ loveless. **ter amores com alguém** to be in love with s. o. **trabalho feito por** ~ **à arte** labour of love. **que** ~**!** what a darling! how charming! how delightful!
amora s. f. mulberry (plate B 1).
amorado adj. 1. mulberry-coloured. 2. in love.
amoral adj. m. + f. (pl. **-ais**) amoral.
amoralismo s. m. amoralism.
amoralista s. m. + f. amoralist, an amoral person. ‖ adj. m. + f. amoralistic.
amoralizar v. to deprive of moral.
amora-preta s. f. (pl. **amoras-pretas**) (bot.) blackberry (plate B 1).
amorar v. (obs.) 1. to scare or frighten away. 2. to hide. 3. to withdraw, abscond.
amorativo adj. lovable, worth of love.
amorável adj. m. + f. (pl. **-áveis**) 1. loving, affectionate, fond. 2. lovable. 3. lovely. 4. gentle, affable.
amor-crescido s. m. (pl. **amores-crescidos**) (bot.) sunflower.
amordaçamento s. m. gagging (also fig.).
amordaçar v. to gag: 1. thrust a gag in the mouth. 2. (fig.) shut the mouth of, hinder to speak or express freely.
amoreira s. f. (bot.) mulberry tree.
amoreiral s. m. (pl. **-ais**) mulberry tree grove.
amorenado adj. rather dark complexioned, tawny.
amorenar v. to become tawny, tan.
amorfia s. f. amorphousness, shapelessness.
amorfo adj. amorphous: 1. shapeless. 2. (chem.) uncrystallized.
amorico s. m. flirt.
amorífero adj. causing or provoking love.
amoriscado adj. loverly.
amoriscar-se v. to fall in love.
amormado adj. (vet.) glandered.
amornado adj. lukewarm.
amornar, amornecer v. to warm up, make lukewarm.
amorosa s. f. (obs., mus.) aria played on a string instrument.
amorosidade s. f. 1. lovingness, affectionateness, fondness. 2. gentleness. 3. mildness. 4. smoothness. 5. softness.
amoroso s. m. (theat.) lead, lover. ‖ adj. 1. loving, affectionate, fond. 2. gentle, affable, kind. 3. mild. 4. smooth. 5. soft.
amor-perfeito s.m. (pl. **amores-perfeitos**) (bot.) (wild) pansy.
amor-perfeito-do-mato s. m. (pl. **amores-perfeitos-do-mato**) (bot.) pansy orchid.
amor-próprio s. m. 1. self-love. 2. self-respect.
amorreado adj. hilly, having many hills or rounded elevations.
amorrinhar-se v. 1. (vet.) to be attacked by murrain. 2. to weaken, enfeeble.
amorsegar v. (also **morsegar**) to bite off, tear off with the teeth.

amortalhadeira s. f. woman who shrouds corpses for burial; layer-out.
amortalhado adj. shrouded, dressed for the grave.
amortalhador s. m. man who shrouds corpses for burial. ‖ adj. fit for shrouding.
amortalhamento s. m. shrouding.
amortalhar v. 1. to shroud, dress for burial. 2. to dress in sackcloth (for penitence).
amortecedor s. m. 1. (mech., mot., aeron.) shock absorber. 2. damper. ‖ adj. 1. shock-absorbing. 2. damping.
amortecer v. 1. to deaden. 2. to debilitate, weaken, lessen. 3. to soften, mitigate, diminish. 4. to benumb, grow torpid. 5. to dampen (sound). 6. to dim (light). 7. to absorb (shock).
amortecido adj. 1. deadened. 2. debilitated, weakened. 3. softened. 4. benumbed. 5. dampened (sound). 6. dimmed (light).
amortecimento s. m. 1. deadening. 2. debilitation, weakening, diminishing. 3. mitigation. 4. torpidity. 5. dampening (sound). 6. dimming (light).
amortiçar v. 1. to deaden, dull, discourage. 2. ~**-se:** a) to be about to go out, be dying (fire, embers). b) to become dull, spiritless or discouraged.
amortização s. f. (pl. **-ões**) amortization, paying off, discharge of debts, wipe-out.
~ **da dívida pública** redemption of the public debt. **fundo de** ~ sinking fund.
amortizar v. (com.) to amortize, pay off, discharge. ~ **por depreciação** to write off.
amortizável adj. m. + f. (pl. **-áveis**) amortizable.
amorudo adj. (Braz., vulg.) in love, passionate.
amossar v. 1. to crush, crumple, bump. 2. to blunt, fissure, notch.
amostado adj. mustlike, tasting like must (unfermented fruit or grape juice).
amostardado adj. spiced or prepared with mustard.
amostra s. f. 1. sample. 2. specimen. 3. pattern. 4. sign, indication. 5. proof. 6. exposition. 7. (mil.) review.
~ **grátis** free sample. ~ **sem valor** sample of no value. ~**s de perfuração** (min.) sampling of drill cutting. **cartão de** ~ sample card. **como** ~ **sem valor** by sample post. **conforme** ~ according to sample. **livro de** ~**s** specimen book. **pipeta para tirar** ~**s** sampling pipe. **sala com exposição de** ~**s** sample room.
amostradiço adj. 1. showy, exhibitive, ostentatious. 2. (obs.) said of a fisher's apprentice.
amostragem s. f. sampling: 1. act or process of taking a sample. 2. (stat.) selection of elements of a whole population as a sample.
amostrar v. (also **mostrar**) to show.
amostrinha s. f. (dim. of **amostra**) sample.
amota s. f. (also **moto**) 1. dike, dam, mound. 2. earthing up.
amotar v. 1. to mound, dike, dam. 2. to earth up.
amotinação s. f. (pl. **-ões**) (also **amotinamento**) 1. mutiny, insurrection, rebellion, revolt, sedition. 2. tumult, uproar. 3. instigation.
amotinado adj. 1. revolted, mutinying, insurgent, up in arms. 2. tumultuous. 3. instigated.
amotinador s. m. 1. rebel, mutineer, instigator, insurgent. 2. brawler. ‖ adj. rebellious, mutinous, insurgent, seditious.
amotinar v. 1. to rebel, revolt, mutiny, instigate. 2. to brawl, clamour, agitate.
amotinável adj. m. + f. (pl. **-áveis**) rebellious, susceptible of revolt.
amoucado adj. 1. rather deaf, hard of hearing. 2. servile, submissive, cringing.
amoucar v. 1. to become deaf, hard of hearing; to deafen. 2. to toady, adopt a servile attitude. 3.

to humble o. s. before superiors. 4. to become angry, desperate.

amouco s. m. 1. servile or submissive person. 2. (India) person who swears to die for his master. ‖ adj. 1. voted to death. 2. desperate.

amouriscado adj. (also **amoiriscado**) Moorish.

amouriscar v. (also **amoiriscar**) to give a Moorish appearance to.

amouxar v. (Braz.) to hoard, amass, treasure, store up.

amover v. 1. to remove. 2. to dispossess.

amovibilidade s. f. 1. transferability. 2. transistoriness (not of lifelong character).

amovível adj. m. + f. (pl. **-íveis**) 1. transferable, removable. 2. transitory, not lifelong.

amoxamar v. 1. to dry like fish. 2. to emaciate.

amparado adj. 1. supported. 2. sustained. 3. protected.

amparador s. m. 1. supporter, sustainer. 2. protector. ‖ adj. 1. supporting. 2. sustaining. 3. protecting.

amparar v. 1. to support. 2. to prop. 3. to sustain. 4. to protect, favour, assist. 5. to patrocine. 6. **~-se** to take refuge with; have recourse to, resort to.

amparo s. m. 1. support. 2. protection, shelter, assistance, aid, help, relief. 3. prop. **em ~** for support. **sem ~** helpless.

ampelito s. m. (min.) ampelite.

ampelografia s. f. ampelography: description or treatise on vineyards.

ampelográfico adj. of or pertaining to the scientific description of vineyards.

ampelógrafo s. m. person who writes scientifically about vineyards.

ampelologia s. f. principles and theories about the cultivation of vineyards.

ampelológico adj. concerning the cultivation of vineyards.

amperagem s. f. (pl. **-ens**) (electr.) current intensity, amperage.

ampère s. m. (electr.) ampere.

amperímetro, amperômetro s. m. (electr.) ammeter.

ampletivo, amplexátil adj. (bot.) amplectant: said of the vegetal organ embracing completely another organ.

amplexicaule adj. m. + f. (bot.) amplexicaul (plate F 5).

amplexifloro adj. (bot.) amplexiflorous.

amplexifólio adj. (bot.) amplexifoliate.

amplexo s. m. embracement.

ampliação s. f. (pl. **-ões**) (also phot.) amplification, enlargement.

ampliado adj. (also phot.) amplified, enlarged, increased.

edição revista e ampliada enlarged and revised edition.

ampliador s. m. (also phot.) amplifier, enlarger. ‖ adj. amplifying, increasing.

ampliar v. 1. (also phot.) to amplify, enlarge, increase, augment. 2. to prorogate.

ampliatiforme adj. m. + f. of great proportions, large-sized.

ampliativo adj. ampliative, enlarging.

amplificar v. 1. (also phot. and radio) to amplify, enlarged or augmented.

amplidão s. f. (pl. **-ões**) 1. amplitude, ampleness. 2. wideness, largeness, extensiveness. 3. space (boundlessness).

amplificação s. f. (pl. **-ões**) 1. (also phot. and radio) amplification, enlargement. 2. (rhet.) emphasis.

amplificador s. m. (also phot. and radio) amplifier, amplificator. ‖ adj. amplifying.

amplificar v. 1. (also phot. and radio) amplify, enlarge, increase, widen. 2. to prorogate.

amplificativo adj. amplifying, amplificatory.

amplificável adj. m. + f. (pl. **-áveis**) (also phot. and radio) amplifiable.

amplitude s. f. 1. amplitude. 2. largeness, wideness. 3. vastness. 4. abundance.

amplo adj. 1. ample. 2. wide, extensive. 3. spacious, vast. 4. large-scale.

uma educação ampla a general education. de amplas conseqüências far-reaching (consequences).

ampola s. f. = **empola**: 1. vesicle, blister. 2. (med.) ampoule, vial. 3. raising of the ground.

ampulheta s. f. log glass, sand-glass, hour-glass (plate R 4).

amputação s. f. (pl. **-ões**) (med.) amputation.

amputado adj. amputated, mutilated, crippled.

amputador s. m. amputator. ‖ adj. amputative.

amputar v. 1. to amputate, cut off. 2. to mutilate. 3. to reduce, restrict, curtail.

amuado adj. 1. surly, angry. 2. sulky, sullen. 3. dead, improductive (capital).

estar ~ to be sulky, take the pet.

amuamento s. m. 1. surliness. 2. sulkiness. 3. obstinateness. 4. improductivity (capital).

amuar v. 1. to make sullen, disgust, vex, annoy. 2. to take a pet, be sulky, sullen or surly; to pout. 3. to insist, be obstinate. 4. not to come to ripeness.

amulatado adj. mulattolike.

amulatar-se v. to become dark or tawny like a mulatto.

amulético adj. amuletic, fetishistic.

amuleto s. m. amulet, fetish, talisman.

amulherado adj. (also **amulherengado**) effeminate.

amulherar-se v. (also **amulherengar-se**) to effeminate.

amumiado adj. 1. like a mummy. 2. mummified. 3. skinny, emaciated.

amumiar v. to mummify, emaciate, get skinny.

amundiçado adj. 1. dirty. 2. ill-bred, uneducated. 3. of bad behaviour.

amunhecar v. (Braz.) 1. to weaken, grow weak (forelimbs of a horse). 2. to fall. 3. to tire, get tired. 4. to run away, avoid fight, shun. 5. to despond.

amunhegado adj. (Braz.) weakened, debilitated.

amuniciamento s. m. (mil.) munitioning.

amuniciar v. (mil.) to munition: provide with munitions.

amuo s. m. 1. ill humour, sulkiness, sullenness. 2. pouting. 3. irascibility.

amura s. f. (naut.) tack, main tack.

amurada s. f. 1. (naut.) main rail. 2. wall.

amurado adj. 1. (naut.) tacked to the right or left main rail. 2. walled in.

amuralhar, amurar v. to wall in.

amurar v. (naut.) to tack.

amurchecer-se v. (also **emurchecer, murchar;** obs.) to fade, wither.

amusia s. f. (med.) amusia: loss of ability to follow or appreciate music.

anã s. f. woman dwarf.

anabatismo s. m. (rel.) Anabaptism.

anabatista s. m. + f. (rel.) Anabaptist. ‖ adj. Anabaptist.

anabenodá(c)tilo adj. (zool.) having toes to climb with.

anabiose s. f. (bot.) anabiosis: recovery after suspended animation.

anabólico adj. (biol., physiol.) anabolic.

anabolismo s. m. (biol., physiol.) anabolism.

anabrose s. f. (med.) anabrosis.

anabrótico adj. (med.) anabrotic.

anacã, anacá s. m. (ornith.) hawk parrot.

anacâmptico adj. anacamptic.

anaçar v. to mix, stir up (liquids).

anacarado adj. nacreous, reddish.

anacardiácea s. f. (bot.) a specimen of the family Anacardiaceae.
anacatártico adj. (med.) anacathartic, expectorant.
anacefaleose s. f. anacephaliosis: recapitulation.
anacenose s. f. (rhet.) anacoenosis: appeal to one's opponent for his opinion on the debated point.
anacíclico adj. (poet.) readable from left to right and right to left.
anáclase s. f. (poet., optics, med.) anaclasis.
anaclisia s. f. (med.) anaclisis, decubitus.
anacolia s. f. (med.) lack of bile secretion.
anacolutia s. f., **anacoluto** m. (gram.) anacoluthon.
anacoreta s. m. 1. anchorite, anchoret, hermit, recluse. 2. unsociable person.
anacorético adj. anchoritic(al).
anacreôntica s. f. Anacreontic (poem).
anacreôntico adj. Anacreontic.
anacrônico adj. anachron(ist)ic.
anacronismo s. m. anachronism.
anacronizar v. 1. to anachronize: commit an error of chronology. 2. to become anachronistical.
anacrústico adj. (mus.) anacrustic.
anadel s. m. (obs.) (pl. **-éis**) captain, commander.
anadelaria s. f. (obs.) captainship, commandership.
anadiplose s. f. (rhet.) anadiplosis.
anaeróbio s. m. (biol.) anaerobe. ‖ anaerobic.
anafa s. f. (bot.) melilot.
anafado adj. well-fed, fat, glossy (animals; by extension also man).
anafaia s. f. the first silk thread spun by the silk worm.
anafar v. 1. to feed on melilots. 2. to comb, smooth. 3. to fatten, feed well.
anáfase s. f. (biol.) anaphase.
anáfega s. f. (also **jujuba**) jujube fruit.
anafil (I) s. m. (pl. **-is**) Moorish trumpet.
anafil (II) adj. said of a variety of corn.
anafilá(c)tico adj. (med.) anaphylactic.
anafila(c)tizar v. (med.) to cause anaphylaxis.
anafilaxia s. f. (med.) anaphylaxis.
anafileiro s. m. Moorish trumpet blower.
anafonese s. f. exercise to improve the voice; crying.
anáfora s. f. (rhet.) anaphora.
anafórico adj. (rhet.) anaphoric(al).
anaforismo s. m. (rhet.) excessive use of anaphora.
anafrodisia s. f. (med.) anaphrodisia.
anafrodisíaco adj. (med.) anaphrodisiac.
anafrodita s. m. + f. (med.) anaphroditous person. ‖ adj. anaphroditous.
anafrodítico adj. (biol.) anaphroditic.
anagênese s. f. (physiol.) anagenesis.
anáglifo s. m. anaglyph: basso-relievo, enchased work.
anagliptografia s. f. anaglyptography: embossed letter writing for the blind.
anagliptográfico adj. anaglyptographic.
anagnosta s. m. anagnost(es).
anagogia s. f. (rel.) anagoge: 1. elevation of the soul. 2. mystic sense of the Bible.
anagógico adj. (rel.) anagogic(al).
anagrama s. m. anagram.
anagramático adj. anagrammatic(al).
anagramatismo s. m. anagrammatism.
anagramatizar v. to anagrammatize.
anágua s. f. (also **saia de baixo**) petticoat, slip.
anais s. m. pl. annals: 1. historical records, chronicals. 2. periodical.
anaiuri s. f. (zool.) an Amazon turtle.
anajá s. m. (bot.) inaja.
anal (I) adj. (anat.) anal.
anal (II) s. m. (pl. **anais**) (rel.) mass said regularly for a year. ‖ adj. m. + f. yearly, annual.
analcita s. m. (min.) analcite.
analecto s. m. analecta, collectanea.

analector s. m. author of a collectanea.
analema s. m. (astr.) analemma.
analemático adj. (astr.) analemmatic.
analepse, analepsia s. f. (med.) analepsis, recovery, convalescence.
analéptica s. f. (med.) branch of hygiene dealing with convalescence.
analéptico adj. (med.) restaurative, analeptic.
analfabético adj. said of languages that have no alphabet.
analfabetismo s. m. analphabetism: lack of rudimentary instruction.
analfabeto s. m. analphabete: person who lacks rudimentary instruction. ‖ adj. analphabete, letterless.
analgesia s. f. (med.) analgesia, analgesis.
analgésico, analgético adj. (med.) analgesic.
analgia s. f. (med.) analgia, analgesia.
análgico adj. (med.) analgesic.
analisador s. m. 1. analyser, analyst. 2. critical person. ‖ adj. 1. analysing. 2. critical.
analisar v. to analyse: 1. (gram., chem.) separate (s. th.) into its elements. 2. study the facts.
analisável adj. m. + f. (pl. **-áveis**) analysable.
análise s. f. analysis: 1. a separation of a thing or substance into its elements. 2. study of facts, examination, investigation.
~ **clínica** clinical analysis. ~ **espe(c)tral** spectrum analysis.
analista s. m. + f. 1. analyst. 2. algebraist. 3. writer of annals.
~ **legal** public analyst.
analítico adj. analytic(al). ‖ **analiticamente** adv. analytically.
analogia s. f. analogy: 1. conformity, likeness, similarity. 2. relation. 3. comparison.
analógico adj. analogic(al). ‖ adv. analogically.
analogismo s. m. analogism.
analogista s. m. + f. analogist.
analogístico adj. analogistic.
análogo adj. analogous, resembling, similar.
anambé s. m. (Braz., ornith.) cotinga.
anamês s. m. **anamita** m. + f. Annamese: 1. native or inhabitant of Annam. 2. the Annamese language. ‖ adj. Annamese.
anamnese, anamnésia, anamnesia s. f. anemnesis: 1. a recalling to mind. 2. (med.) the history of a disease.
anamnés(t)ico adj. anamnestic.
anamniota s. m. + f. (zool.) Anamniota. ‖ adj. anamniotic.
anamorfose s.f. anamorphosis: 1. distorted image. 2. the art of representing such an image. 3. change or degeneration of certain plants.
anamorfótico adj. (opt.) anamorphous, distorted.
ananás, ananaseiro s. m. pine-apple plant.
anandrio adj. (bot.) anandrous.
anani s. m. (Braz., bot.) hog gum tree.
ananicado adj. 1. dwarfish. 2. wretched, mean, base.
ananicar v. 1. to dwarf. 2. to make or become wretched, mean, base.
ananico, anano adj. 1. dwarflike. 2. small.
ananismo s. m. underdevelopment of a plant.
anão s. m. (pl. **anões**) (f. **anã**) dwarf. ‖ adj. 1. dwarfish. 2. small.
anapéstico adj. (poet.) anapaestic(al).
anapesto s. m. (poet.) anapaest.
anaplas(t)ia s. f. (med.) anaplasty: plastic surgery.
anaplás(t)ico adj. (med.) anaplastic.
anaptixe s. f. (gram.) anaptyxis.
anarcotina s. f. anarcotine: pure narcotine.
anarmônico adj. (mus.) inharmonic.
anarquia s. f. anarchy: 1. absence of government or law. 2. disorder, confusion.

anárquico adj. anarchic(al): 1. instigating an anarchy. 2. confuse, chaotic.

anarquismo s. m. anarchism.

anarquista s. m. + f. anarchist. ‖ adj. anarchistic.

anarquização s. f. the turning into or becoming an anarchy.

anarquizador s. m. person who anarchizes, anarchist. ‖ adj. anarchizing, anarchistic.

anarquizar v. to anarchize: 1. reduce to anarchy. 2. to cause confusion and disorder.

anartria s. f. (med.) anarthria.

anartro adj. (gram.) anarthrous.

anasarca s. f. (vet.) anasarca.

anasarcado adj. (vet.) anasarcous.

anastático adj. (typogr.) anastatic.

anastigmático adj. (opt.) anastigmatic, not astigmatic (lenses).

anastomosar v. (anat.) to anastomose.

anastomose s. f. (anat.) anastomosis.

anastomótico adj. (anat.) anastomotic.

anástrofe s. f. (rhet.) anastrophe.

anata s. f. (obs.) tax paid on a benefice.

anatado adj. creamy, like cream.

anatar v. to cream: 1. cover with cream. 2. become like cream.

anateirado adj. covered with slime or soft mud (after the overflowing of a river).

anateirar v. to cover with slime or soft mud (said of an overflowing river).

anátema s. m. anathema: 1. (rel.) excommunication. 2. imprecation, malediction. 3. cursed person or thing. ‖ adj. m. + f. 1. (rel.) excommunicated. 2. (rel.) reprobate. 3. cursed, damned.

anatematismo s. m. (rel.) anathematism: 1. (rel.) condemnatory bull. 2. imprecation.

anatematização s. f. anathematization.

anatematizador s. m. anathematizer.

anatematizar v. 1. to anathematize. 2. to curse, damn. 3. to condemn, reprove. 4. to banish, exclude.

anatídeos s. m. pl. (zool.) Anatidae: family of birds including ducks, geese, swans.

anatista s. m. (obs.) clerk who registered the taxes on benefices.

anatocismo s. m. anatocism, compound interest.

anatomia s. f. 1. anatomy: a) science of the structure of animals or plants; morphology. b) dissection, dissecting. 2. (fig.) careful examination or analysis.

anatômico s. m., anatomista m. + f. anatomist. ‖ adj. anatomic(al). ‖ -amente adv. anatomically.

anatomização s. f. anatomization.

anatomizar v. to anatomize: 1. dissect. 2. examine carefully, analyse.

anatomopatologia s. f. (med.) pathological anatomy.

anatomopatológico adj. (med.) anatomopathologic(al).

anatoxina s. f. (med.) anatoxin.

anátropo adj. (bot.) anatropous.

anavalhado adj. 1. razor-shaped. 2. sharp, whetted. 3. cut or wounded with a razor; knifed.

anavalhar v. 1. to cut or wound with a razor; knife. 2. to shape like a razor (blade).

ana-velha s. f. (pl. anas-velhas) (Braz., ornith.) green heron.

anca s. f. 1. buttock. 2. haunch, hind quarters (plate C 12). 3. croup, rump. 4. hip (plate G 1). 5. seat, backside, posterior. 6. (naut.) stern.

não dar ~ not to allow to ride pillion or behind.

ancado adj. hipshot.

ancestral adj. m. + f. (pl. -ais) 1. ancestral. 2. very old.

ancestralidade s. m. ancestry.

ancestre s. m. ancestor.

anchietano adj. referrind to Anchieta, the Jesuit missionary in Brazil (XVI century).

anchietina s. f. (bot. and med.) anchietin(e).

ancho adj. 1. broad, wide. 2. ample. 3. haughty, conceited, arrogant.

anchova, enchova s. f. (ichth.) anchovy.

anchura s. f. width, breadth.

anciã s. f. venerable old woman.

anciania, ancianidade s. f. 1. old age. 2. ancientness, ancient(r)y. 3. antiquity.

ancião s. m. (pl. -ãos, -ães, -ões) venerable old man. ‖ adj. ancient, old.

ancila s. f. 1. ancilla: woman slave or female servant. 2. support, subsidy.

ancilar adj. m. + f. ancillary.

anciloglossia s. f. (med.) adherence of the tongue to the bottom of the mouth through the lingual bridle.

ancilostomíase s. f. (med.) ancylostomiasis: hookworm disease.

ancilóstomo s. m. (zool.) ancylostome: parasitical hookworm.

ancilótomo s. m. any curved cutting tool.

ancinhar v. to rake (scrape together with a rake).

ancinho s. m. rake (plates A 1, J 2, P 6, S 1).

anco s. m. a crooked firth or inlet.

ancôneo s. m. (anat.) anconad muscle.

anconeu adj. (anat.) pertaining to the anconad muscle.

âncora s. f. 1. anchor of a ship or watch (plates A 6, R 4). 2. (fig.) refuge, shelter, support. 3. symbol of hope. 4. (parts of an anchor: argola ring; cepo stock; haste shank; bico bill; pata fluke or palm; braço arm; cruz crown).

~ flutuante sea anchor. ~ grande sheet anchor. ~ leve stream anchor. cabos de ~ stock-tackle. lançar a ~ to drop anchor. levantar a ~ to weigh anchor.

ancoração s. f. (pl. -ões) anchoring.

ancoradouro s. m. (also ancoradoiro) anchorage, anchor-ground, lay-by.

ancoragem s. f. (pl. -ens) anchorage: 1. money for anchoring, harbour dues. 2. act or fact of anchoring. 3. anchor-ground.

ancorar v. 1. to anchor, cast anchor, ride at anchor 2. (fig.) to fix, fasten, solidify. 3. (fig.) to ground, base upon.

ancoreta s. f. 1. dim. of âncora; also ancorete or ancorote: small anchor. 2. breaker: small, flat barrel.

ancudo adj. having large buttocks, haunches or hips.

anda interj. come! come on!

andá-açu s. m. (pl. andás-açus) (Braz.) anda-assu. a medicinal tree.

andaço s. m. 1. contagious or epidemic disease. 2. contagion, infection.

andada s. f. 1. act or fact of going; walk. 2. long walk or way. 3. errand.

andadeira(s) s. f. (pl.) leading-strings.

não precisar de ~ to know what to do. ser levado em ~ to be in leading-strings.

andadeiro adj. 1. light-footed. 2. that walks much.

andado adj. covered (distance), passed or travelled over.

andador s. m. 1. errand-boy, messenger. 2. collector of alms (of a confraternity). 3. good walker. ‖ adj. light-footed.

andadoria s. f. occupation of messenger or collector of alms.

andadura s. f. gait: 1. manner of walking. 2. pace of a horse (plate C 12).

andaimada s. f. (archit., also andaimaria) scaffolding.

andaimar v. 1. (archit.) to provide with a scaffold. 2. (fig.) to puzzle out, contrive.

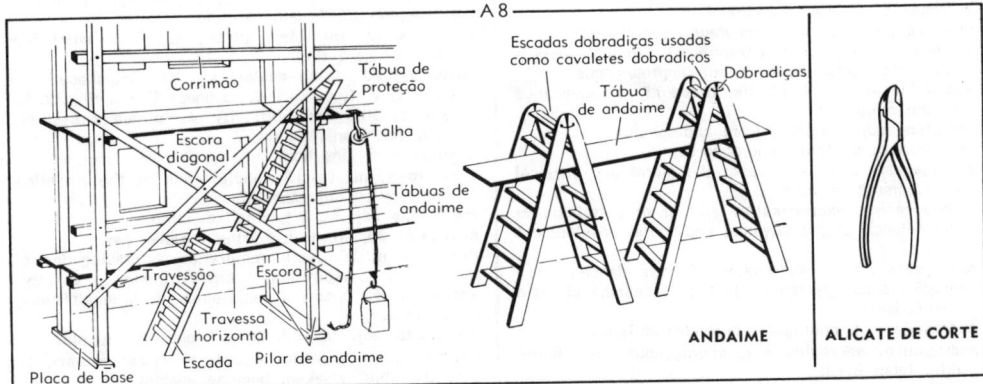

A 8

Corrimão / Tábua de proteção / Escora diagonal / Talha / Tábuas de andaime / Travessão / Escora / Travessa horizontal / Escada / Pilar de andaime / Placa de base

Escadas dobradiças usadas como cavaletes dobradiços / Tábua de andaime / Dobradiças

ANDAIME | ALICATE DE CORTE

andaime, andaimo s. m. (archit.) scaffold(ing) (plates A 8, T 5).

andaina s. f. (also **andana**) 1. row, rank, line. 2. set or suit of clothes. 3. set of sails. 4. a sort of fishing-boat.

andaluz s. m. Andalusian: native or inhabitant of Andalusia (Spain). ‖ adj. Andalusian.

andamento s. m. 1. process, proceeding, course. 2. gait, pacing. 3. speed. 4. (mus.) time, measure. ~ **natural das coisas** course of nature. **em ~** in process.

andança s. f. 1. gait: a) manner of walking. b) pace of a horse. 2. (coll.) labour, toil, work, struggle.

andante s. m. 1. (mus.) andante. 2. passer-by. ‖ adj. m. + f. 1. walking, going (also her.) 2. errant. 3. wandering, roving. ‖ adv. (mus.) andante.

andantesco adj. 1. pertaining to medieval cavalry. 2. gentlemanly, chivalrous.

andantino s. m. (mus.) andantino. ‖ adv. andantino.

andar s. m. 1. gait: a) manner of walking. b) pace of a horse. 2. floor, story. 3. flat, level bank of a river. 4. speed, velocity. ‖ v. 1. to go, walk, wander. 2. to drive, ride, sail. 3. to travel over. 4. to move. 5. to function, work. 6. to proceed, act. 7. to pass (time). 8. to live, be, feel. 9. to have sexual intercourse.

~ **desesperado** to be desperate. ~ **a esmo** to poke off. ~ **à toa** to gad about. ~ **desajeitadamente** to barge along. ~ **com rodeios** to beat about the bush. ~ **a pé** to walk, go on foot, ride a shank's mare. ~ **de bicicleta** to cycle, ride on a bicycle. ~ **de modo afetado** to walk Spanish. ~ **depressa** to hasten, spank along. ~ **mal de dinheiro** to be short of money. ~ **mal de saúde** to be unhealthy. ~ **para lá e para cá** to go about, go to and fro. ~ **térreo** ground floor, (U. S. A.) first floor. **anda!** go on! get going! come along! **andamos pela cidade** we walked about the town. **aprender a ficar em pé ou ~** to learn to stand upright or to walk. **com o ~ dos tempos** in the course of time. **como andam as coisas** as things go. **diz-me com quem andas e dir-te-ei quem és** tell me your company and I will tell you your character. **ele anda bem a pé** he is a good walker. **ele anda com ela** (sl.) he's square-pushing with her. **ele andava de muletas** he went on crutches. **ele andou pelo mundo** he has been around. **ele andou armado** he carried arms. **gosto de ~ a pé** I walk on foot by choice. **ir andando** to walk along. **leve-me ao ~ térreo** take me down to the ground floor, please. **o maior salafrário que andar por aí** the greatest rascal going. **o negócio não anda** the business is doing badly, there is

no go in the show. **os navios andam com todas as velas desfraldadas** the ships carry all sails.

andaresco s. m. (Braz.) small ugly animal (esp. horse). ‖ adj. quick-paced but uncomfortable to ride on (horse).

andarengo adj. (also **andejo**) 1. wandering, roving. 2. quick-footed, light-footed.

andarilho s. m. 1. person who walks much, good walker. 2. messenger; errand-boy. 3. (obs.) footman, lackay. 4. person in charge of collecting fallen objects in the arena after a bullfight.

andarivel s. m. (pl. **ivéis**) one of the stakes used to mark off the tracks in a horse race.

andas s. f. pl. 1. stilts. 2. (obs.) a sort of litter or sedan-chair. 3. bier or poles upon which a bier is borne.

andável adj. m. + f. (pl. **-áveis**) that may be walked or reached on foot.

andeiro adj. that walks well.

andejar v. 1. to rove, wander, be unsteady. 2. to walk much, to go frequently away from home.

andejo adj. rambling, wandering, roving.

andesita s. f., **andesito** m. (min.) andesite.

andícola s. m. + f. inhabitant of the Andes. ‖ adj. living or growing in the Andes.

andilhas s. f. pl. supporting frame for a woman's saddle.

andino adj. Andean.

andirá s. m. (Braz., zool.) bat.

andirapuampé s. m. (bot.) bignonaceous plant.

andiroba s. f. (Braz., bot.) crab-tree.

ândito s. m. 1. footpath, sidewalk. 2. path around a building.

andó adj. f. (Braz.) said of a goateelike beard.

andóbia s. f. stone upon which the millstone turns.

andor s. m. 1. a sort of bier, wooden framework to carry statues in a procession. 2. (hist.) litter, sedan-chair. 3. stilts.

andorinha s. f. 1. (ornith.) swallow. 2. (Braz.) furniture van or truck. 3. steam launch. 4. ambulant dressmaker.

rabo-de-~ (archit.) swallowtail. **uma andorinha só não faz verão** one swallow does not make a summer.

andorinha-do-mar s. f. (pl. **andorinhas-do-mar**) (ornith.) royal tern.

andorinha-do-mato s. f. (pl. **andorinhas-do-mato**) (Braz., ornith.) smaller swallow-wing.

andorinhão s. m. (pl. **-ões**) (ornith.) swift.

andorinho s. m. 1. a little swallow. 2. (naut.) stirrup.

andrajo s. m. rag, tatter.

andrajoso adj. tattered, ragged, torn.

andrequicé s. m. (Braz., bot.) river grass.
androceu s. m. (bot.) androecium.
androfagia s. f. (also **antropofagia**) cannibalism.
andrófago s. m. (also **antropófago**) cannibal; person who eats human flesh. ‖ adj. androphagous.
androfobia s. f. androphobia: dread of or repugnance to the male sex.
andrófobo adj. suffering from androphobia.
andróforo s. m. (bot.) androphore.
androgenesia s. f. science of the moral and physical development of man.
androgenésico, androgenético adj. of or pertaining to the science of the physical and moral development of man.
androgenesia s. f. succession of male descendants.
androgênico adj. pertaining to the succession of male descendants.
androginia s. f. androgyny, hermaphroditism.
androgínico, andrógino adj. androgynous, hermaphroditic (also bot.).
andróide s. m. 1. android. 2. puppet (also fig.).
andrólatra s. m. + f. worship(p)er of a human being as a deity.
androlatria s. f. worship of a deified human being.
andrologia s. f. 1. science of man and his ailments. 2. (med.) study of venereal diseases of males.
andrológico adj. of or pertaining to the study of venereal diseases of males.
andromania s. f. (med.) andromania, nymphomania.
andrômeda s. f. 1. Andromeda: a boreal constellation. 2. andromeda: a shrub of the family Ericaceae.
androplasma s. m. (biol.) protoplasm of the male gamete.
androsperma s. m. (genetics, biol.) gamete produced by the heterogametic individual that determines the male sex of the offspring.
androsterona s. m. (chem.) androsterone, a male sex hormone.
andu s. m. (Braz., bot.) pigeon pea.
andurrial s. m. 1. solitary wayless place. 2. (pl. -ais) dirty public places.
anecúmeno s. m. (geogr.) an uninhabitable area. ‖ (geogr.) relating to such an area.
anediar v. 1. to make shiny, polish. 2. to smooth. 3. to fatten.
anedota s. f. 1. anecdote. 2. joke.
anedotário s. m. collection of anecdotes.
anedótico adj. anecdotic.
anedotista s. m. + f. anecdotist.
anedotizar v. 1. to give the form of an anecdote to. 2. to tell anecdotes.
anegar v. 1. to flood, inundate. 2. to drown. 3. to submerge.
anegrado adj. 1. somewhat black. 2. negroid.
anegrar v. 1. to blacken, darken. 2. to become black, dark.
anegrejar v. to blacken, darken.
anegriscado adj. blackish, dark.
aneiro adj. 1. subject to the vicissitudes of the seasons. 2. uncertain, eventual. 3. bearing fruit every second year.
anejo adj. one year old.
anel s. m. (pl. **anéis**) 1. ring (plates F 3, G 4, J 3, M 3). 2. circle. 3. link (chain). 4. lock of hair. ~ **de casamento** wedding-ring. ~ **de guarnição**, ~ **de gaxeta** (tech.) packing-ring. ~ **do cabelo** curl of hair. ~ **de segmento** (tech.) piston-ring. ~ **sinete** seal-ring, signet-ring (plate J 3).
anelação s. f. (pl. **-ões**) 1. longing, craving. 2. a hanking after. 3. heavy or quick breath, shortness of breath, panting.
anelado (I) adj. 1. curled, curly. 2. ringlike, circular.
anelado (II) s. m. (zool.) annelid: one of the Annelida.

anelante adj. m. + f. 1. longing, craving; eager for. 2. gasping for breath, panting.
anelão s. m. (pl. **-ões**) (Braz., augm. of **anel**) big silver or gold ring.
anelar (I) adj. (also **anular**) annular, ring-shaped.
anelar (II) v. 1. to curl. 2. to shape like a ring. 3. to pant, breathe with difficulty. 4. to desire eagerly, crave for, hanker after.
aneleira s. f. ring box.
anelídeo s. m. (zool.) annelid: one of the Annelida (ringworm). ‖ adj. annelid.
aneliforme adj. m. + f. ringlike, circular.
anelípede adj. m. = f. having circular paws.
anélito s. m. 1. breath, respiration. 2. craving desire.
anelo s. m. 1. aspiration. 2. craving desire. 3. anxiety.
anemia s. f. (med.) 1. an(a)emia. 2. greensickness, chlorosis.
anemiante adj. m. = f. (med.) causing anemia.
anemiar v. (also **anemizar**). 1. to cause anemia. 2. to enfeeble, weaken, become anemic.
anêmico adj. 1. (med.) anemic. 2. bloodless. 3. weak, feeble. 4. pale, colourless (also fig.).
anemófilo adj. (bot.) anemophilous.
anemografia s. f. anemography: description of the winds.
anemográfico adj. anemographic.
anemógrafo s. m. 1. anemograph. 2. expert of anemography.
anemologia s. f. anemology: the science of the winds.
anemológico adj. anemological.
anemólogo s. m. specialist in anemology.
anemometria s. f. anemometry.
anemométrico adj. anemometrical.
anemômetro s. m. anemometer, wind-gauge.
anêmona s. f. (bot.) anemone, wind-flower.
anêmona-dos-bosques s. f. (pl. **anêmonas-dos-bosques**) (bot.) wood anemone.
anemoscopia s. f. study of the directions of winds.
anemoscópico adj. pertaining to the study of the directions of winds.
anemoscópio s. m. anemoscope.
anencefalia s. f. (med.) anencephaly.
anencéfalo s. m. anencephalic monster. ‖ adj. anencephalic.
anepigrafia s. f. unepigraphous quality.
anepigráfico adj. unepigraphous.
anequim s. m. (pl. **-ins**) (Braz., ichth.) man-eater.
aneróide s. m. aneroid barometer. ‖ adj. m. + f. aneroid.
anestesia s. f. 1. (med.) an(a)esthesia. 2. insensibility.
anestesiador s. m. an(a)esthetist.
anestesiante adj. m. + f. an(a)esthetic.
anestesiar v. to an(a)esthetize.
anestésico, anestético s. m. (med.) an(a)esthetic.‖adj. an(a)esthetic.
anete s. m. 1. (naut.) anchor ring. 2. small brass ring.
aneto s. m. (bot.) dill.
aneurina s. f. aneurin: vitamina B_1.
aneurisma s. f. (path.) aneurism.
aneurismal adj. m. + f. (path.) aneurismal.
aneurismático adj. (path.) aneurismatic.
anexação s. f. (pl. **-ões**) annexation.
anexado adj. annexed.
anexador s. m. person who or machine that annexes. ‖ adj. annexing, joining.
anexar v. to annex, join, attach.
anexim s. m. (pl. **-ins**) saying, adage, proverb.
anexionismo s. m. doctrine or principle of annexing small states to their larger neighbours of similar language, etc.
anexionista s. m. + f. annex(at)ionist. ‖ adj. annexational.

anexite s. f. (med.) adnexitis: inflammation of the adnexa of the uterus.
anexo s. m. 1. something attached or annexed; appurtenance. 2. appendage. 3. supplementary building, outbulding.
anfíbio s. m. 1. amphibian (animal or plant). 2. (fig.) person who maintains opposite opinions. ‖ adj. amphibious (also bot. and zool.).
anfibiografia s. f. description of amphibia.
anfibiótico s. m. fragments of petrified amphibia.
anfibiologia s. f. (zool.) amphibiology.
anfibiológico adj. amphibiological.
anfibólio s. m. (min.) amphibole.
anfibologia s. f. (gram.) amphibology.
anfibológico adj. amphibological, dubious.
anfibologista s. m. + f. amphibologist. ‖ adj. amphibologic, ambiguous.
anfibolóide adj. m. + f. amphiboloid.
anfíbraco s. m. (poet.) amphibrachus: a foot of three syllables.
anfictião, anfictíone s. m. (pl. **-ões,** ~**s**) (hist.) amphictyon.
anfictionia s. f. (hist.) amphictyony.
anfictiônico adj. (hist.) amphictyonic.
anfígena adj. (bot.) amphigen.
anfigênio s. m. (min.) leucite, amphigene.
anfiguri s. m. amphigory: meaningless rigmarole.
anfigúrico adj. (also **anfigurítico**) amphigoric: meaningless.
anfigurismo s. m. amphigoric quality.
anfimixia s. f. (biol.) amphimixis.
anfioxo s. m. (zool.) amphioxus: any lancelet.
anfípode s. m. (zool.) amphipod. ‖ adj. m. + f. amphipod.
anfisbena s. f. 1. (zool.) amphisbaena. 2. (her.) two-headed snake.
anfíscios s. m. pl. amphiscians: the inhabitants of the tropics.
anfísdromo adj. (naut.) that can land with the prow or the stern.
anfiteatral adj. m. + f. (pl. **-ais**) (also **anfiteátrico**) amphitheatric(al).
anfiteatro s. m. 1. amphiteatre. 2. construction or landscape suggesting an amphitheatre.
anfitrião s. m. (pl. **-ões**) (f. **anfitrioa**) amphitryon, host.
anfitrite s. f. 1. (myth.) goddess of the sea. 2. amphitrite: a genus of marine worms. 3. (fig.) the sea.
anfítropo adj. (bot.) amphitropous.
ânfora s. f. amphora.
anforal adj. m. + f. (pl. **-ais**) amphoral.
anforicidade s. f. amphoricity.
anfórico adj. amphoric.
anfótero adj. amphoteric (also chem.).
anfractuosidade s. f. anfractuousness.
anfractuoso adj. anfractuous: 1. full of turnings and windings. 2. roundabout.
angária s. f. hire of beasts of burden.
angariação s. f. (pl. **-ões**) (also **angariamento** m.) 1. enlistment, engagement, enrolment, recruitment. 2. allurement, enticement. 3. attainment, getting.
angariador s. m. 1. recruiter, engager, canvasser. 2. allurer, enticer. 3. collector. ‖ adj. 1. recruiting, canvassing. 2. alluring, enticing. 3. collecting.
angariar v. 1. to recruit, engage, canvass. 2. to allure, entice. 3. to collect, obtain.
angarilha s. f. wicker (of wicker bottles and other such vessels).
angatecô s. m. (N. Braz.) fright, shock.
angaturama s. m. (Braz.) protective spirit of the (Mura) Indians.
angélica s. f. (bot.): a) garden angelica. b) tuberose. 2. (eccl.) angelic hymn. 3. former instrument with ten keys and seventeen strings.

angélico adj. (also **angelical, angelino**) angelic(al): pure, heavenly, beautiful.
angelim s. m. (pl. **-ins**) Brazilian hardwood tree.
angelim-amarelo, angelim-araroba s. m. (pl. **angelins-amarelos, angelins-araroba**) araroba.
angelita s. m. + f. (rel.) angelist.
angelitude s. f. (Braz.) angelicalness.
angelizar v. to angelicize: render angelic.
angelólatra s. m. + f. follower of angelolatry, worshipper of angels.
angelolatria s. f. angelolatry: worship of angels.
angelologia s. f. angelology.
angelológico adj. angelologic(al).
ângelus s. m. (rel.) Angelus.
angevino s. m. Angevin(e): native or inhabitant of Anjou (France).
angialgia s. f. (med.) angialgia.
angiálgico adj. (med.) angialgic(al).
angical s. m. (pl. **-ais**) angico grove.
angico s. m. angico: tree of the family Mimoseaceae.
angiectasia s. f. (med.) angiectasia, angiectasis.
angiectásico adj. (med.) of, pertaining to or suffering from angiectasia.
angiite s. f. (med.) angiitis.
angina s. f. (med.) angina.
~ **do peito** angina pectoris.
anginoso adj. (med.) anginous.
angiografia s. f. (med.) angiography.
angiográfico adj. (med.) angiographic.
angiologia s. f. (ant.) angiology.
angiológico adj. (anat.) of or referring to angiology.
angioma s. m. (med.) angioma.
angiopatia s. f. (path.) general designation of the diseases of the blood and lymph vessels.
angiose s. f. (med.) angiosis.
angiospermia s. f. (bot.) angiospermy.
angiospermo s. m. (bot.) angiosperm.
anglicanismo s. m. Anglicanism.
anglicano s. m. Anglican. ‖ adj. Anglican.
anglicismo s. m. Anglicism: typically English quality or trait.
anglicizar v. (also **anglizar**) to Anglicize (also anglicize).
ânglico adj. English.
anglo s. m. (hist.) Angle. ‖ adj. English.
anglo-americano s. m. (pl. **anglo-americanos**) Anglo-American. ‖ adj. Anglo-American.
anglofilia s. f. admiration for England and English things.
anglófilo s. m. Anglophile. ‖ adj. fond of England or English things.
anglofobia s. f. Anglophobia.
anglófobo adj. Anglophobic.
anglomania s. f. Anglomania.
anglomaníaco s. m. Anglomaniac.
anglo-normando s. m. (pl. **anglo-normandos**) (hist.) Anglo-Norman. ‖ adj. Anglo-Norman.
anglo-saxão s. m. (pl. **anglo-saxões**) (also **anglo-saxônio**) (pl. **anglo-saxônios**) Anglo-Saxon. ‖ adj. Anglo-Saxon.
Angola s. m. + f. 1. native or inhabitant of Angola. 2. black, Negro. ‖ adj. of or pertaining to Angola.
angolinha s. f. (Braz.) guinea-fowl.
angorá s. m. + f. Angora: designation of an Angora cat, goat or rabbit. ‖ adj. m. + f. 1. of Angora (breed.). 2. of or pertaining to Angora.
angra s. f. bay, creek.
angrense s. m. + f. native or inhabitant of Angra. (Azores). ‖ adj. of or pertaining to Angra.
angu s. m. (Braz.) 1. manioc flour or maize boiled in water and salt. 2. (coll., also **angu-de-caroço**, pl. **angus-de-caroço**) mess, bad outcome. 3. intrigue, plot, machination. 4. quarrel, strife.

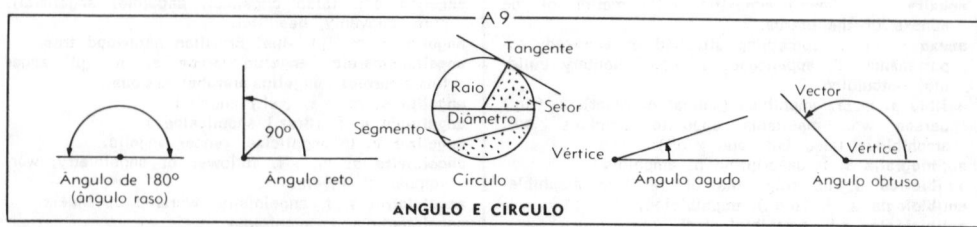

Ângulo de 180° (ângulo raso) — Ângulo reto — Círculo — Ângulo agudo — Ângulo obtuso

ÂNGULO E CÍRCULO

angüicida adj. m. + f. snake-killing.
angüífero adj. 1. snake breeding. 2. full of snakes.
angüiforme adj. m. + f. anguiform.
angüípede adj. m. + f. (zool.) anguiped(e).
angüite s. f. (N. Braz.) dish of: herbs, shrimps, fishes, pepper, and oil.
angulado adj. 1. angulate, angled. 2. crooked (street). 3. cornered. 4. (fig.) bony.
angular v. to form an angle. ‖ adj. m. + f. 1. angular. 2. cornered.
 afastamento ~ **das manivelas** (tech.) angle between cranks. **pedra** ~ corner stone. **velocidade** ~ (phys.) angular velocity.
angularidade s. f. angularity.
angulário s. m. square, angulimeter.
angulete s. m. 1. dim. of **ângulo.** 2. right-angled cutting.
angulicolo adj. crooknecked.
angulirrostro adj. (zool.) angulirostrous.
ângulo s. m. 1. angle (plate A 9). 2. corner. 3. nook.
 ~ **adjacente** adjacent angle. ~ **agudo** acute angle. ~ **de cone** angle of taper. ~ **de deslocamento** angle of displacement. ~ **de divergência** angle of joint. ~ **de incidência** angle of incidence. ~ **de meia volta** straight angle. ~ **de reflexão** angle of reflection. ~ **exterior** exterior angle. ~ **facial** facial angle. ~ **obtuso** obtuse angle. ~ **reto** right angle. ~ **visual** visual angle. ~**s verticalmente opostos** vertical angles. **em** ~ **reto** at right angles.
anguloso adj. 1. angulate, angular. 2. angled. 3. cornered. 4. (fig.) bony.
angurriado adj. (S. Braz.) 1. annoyed, distressed. 2. sad.
angústia s. f. 1. narrowness. 2. briefness. 3. anguish, affliction. 4. annoyance, displeasure. 5. anxiety, distress, agony.
 ~ **mortal** pangs of death.
angustiado adj. 1. afflicted, distressed. 2. annoyed. **um rosto** ~ a face of woe.
angustiador adj. **angustiante** m. + f. afflictive, distressing, annoying.
angustiar v. 1. to afflict, torment, distress, annoy. 2. ~**-se** to feel anguish, be distressed.
angustidentado adj. having narrow teeth.
angustifoliado adj. (bot.) angustifoliate.
angustioso adj. afflicting, tormenting, distressing, annoying.
angustipene adj. m. + f. (ornith.) having narrow wings.
angustirrostro adj. (ornith.) angustirostrate.
angusto adj. angust, narrow, tight.
angustura s. f. 1. narrowness, straightness, tightness. 2. narrow passage. 3. opening of a river. 4. (med., bot.) angostura.
anguzada s. f. (N. Braz.) 1. mingle-mangle, mixture. 2. confusion. 3. intrigue, gossip. 4. boisterous or tumultuous reunion.
anguzô s. m. (Braz.) a mixture of **angu** and **angüite.**
anhanga, anhangá s. m. (Braz.) 1. evil spirit. 2. devil (in Tupi language).

anhangüera, anhanguera s. m. (Braz.) 1. evil spirit. 2. the personified devil. 3. resolute, daring person. ‖ adj. bold, daring, determined.
anho s. m. lamb.
anhoto adj. (Braz.) slow.
anhuma s. f. (Braz., ornith.) horned screamer.
anhumapoca s. m. (Braz., ornith.) crested screamer.
aniagem s. m. (pl. -ens) burlap, sacking, sackcloth.
anichar v. 1. to niche, place in a niche. 2. to place (a person) in a lucrative position. 3. to squat, crouch. 4. to fix, settle, take root. 5. to hide.
anidrido, anídrido s. m. anhydride.
 ~ **arsênico** arsenic anhydride. ~ **carbônico** carbon dioxide. ~ **sulfuroso** sulphur dioxide.
anidrita s. f. (min.) anhydrite.
anidro adj. (chem.) anhydrous.
anidrose s. f. (med.) anhydrosis: deficiency of perspiration.
anielado adj. enamel(l)ed.
anielagem s. f. (pl. -ens) enamel(l)ing.
anielar v. to enamel.
anil s. m. 1. anil, indigo. 2. indigo plant. ‖ adj. m. + f. 1. blue. 2. anile, senile.
anilado adj. 1. dyed with indigo. 2. bluish.
anilar v. to dye with indigo, dye with a dark blue colour.
anileira s. f. indigo tree.
anilha s. f. ring, washer.
anilho s. m. 1. ring, eye, loop. 2. swivel. 3. (S. Braz.) guide belt (horses, etc.).
anilina s. f. aniline.
animação s. f. (pl. -ões) 1. animation. 2. liveliness. 3. enthusiasm. 4. activity, agitation.
animado adj. 1. animated. 2. encouraged. 3. lively, brisk. 4. high-spirited.
 ~ **pelo desejo de agradar** prompted by the desire to please. **ele está** ~ he is in high spirits.
animador s. m. 1. animator. 2. encourager. ‖ adj. animating, encouraging.
animadversão s. f. (pl. -ões) 1. animadversion, criticism, reproach. 2. punishment. 3. hatred.
animal s. m. (pl. -ais) 1. animal. 2. (Braz.) horse, mule. 3. (fig.) brute, brutal person. ‖ adj. m. + f. 1. animal. 2. material. 3. carnal.
 ~ **carnívoro** carnivorous animal, carnivore (plate R 2).
animalaço, animalão s. m. (pl. -s, -ões) 1. augm. of **animal.** 2. enormous brute. 3. (S. Braz.) good horse.
animalada s. f. (S. Braz.) a great number of horses, mules, etc.
animálculo s. m. animalcule: microscopic animal.
animalejo s. m. 1. dim. of **animal:** little animal. 2. stupid person.
animalesco adj. 1. animal, referring to animals. 2. brutal, bestial. 3. animalistic.
animália s. f. (also **alimária**) dumb, irrational animal, beast.
animalidade s. f. animality: the phenomena of animal life.

animalismo s. m. animalism: condition of the animal.
animalista s. m. + f. painter or sculptor of animals.
animalização s. f. (pl. **-ões**) animalization: 1. conversion into an animal substance. 2. brutalization.
animalizar v. to animalize: 1. to convert into an animal substance, make into an animal. 2. to brutalize.
animante adj. m. + f. 1. animating. 2. heartening, encouraging. 3. inspiring. 4. life-giving.
animar v. 1. to animate, encourage, stimulate, boost, embolden, cheer up, forward, fortify, brighten, spirit up. 2. **~-se** to take heart or courage.
~-se a fazer alguma coisa to dare, to resolve to do anything. **preciso animá-lo** I must humour him up. **você precisa animar-se** you must gather yourself together.
animável adj. m. + f. (pl. **-áveis**) animable; capable of being animated.
anime s. f. gum anime; copal.
animicida s. m. + f. (theol.) person who kills the soul.
anímico adj. pertaining to the soul.
animismo s. m. animism: 1. philosophical system of the animists. 2. the attribution of a living soul to inanimate objects.
animista s. m. + f. (philos.) animist: person who maintains, that the soul is the only cause of life. ‖ adj. animistic.
ânimo s. m. 1. animation, vitality. 2. life, soul. 3. spirit, heart. 4. courage, boldness. 5. intention, purpose, attention, thought.
ânimo! interj: courage! go on! come on! cheer up! **grandeza de ~** greatness of soul. **fraqueza de ~** faintheartedness. **não tivemos ~ para** we could not prevail ourselves to. **temos de manter o ~** we must keep the flag flying. **recobrar o ~** to recollect o. s. **perder o ~** to be discouraged. **sem ~** weakhearted.
animosidade s. f. 1. animosity, animus, aversion, dislike, ill will. 2. courage, boldness, valour, heart.
animoso adj. brave, stout, valiant, courageous, resolute, (abs. superl. **-osíssimo**).
aninado adj. 1. snugly wrapped up. 2. lulled to sleep.
aninar v. to rock to sleep; to lull to sleep (as by singing lullabies).
aninga s. f. (bot.) a philodendron (P. speciosum).
aningaçu s. f. plant of the arum family.
aningaíba s. f. = **aninga**.
aningal s. m. (pl. **-ais**) a place abounding in **aningas**.
aningapara s. f. (bot.) 1. the variable tuftroot. 2. the poisonous seguin tuftroot.
aninhar v. 1. to put in a nest. 2. to shelter, harbour, lodge, protect. 3. **~-se**: a) to nestle, build a nest; to take shelter. b) to snuggle up (as in a bed or in a blanket), cuddle up. c) (fam.) to go to bed.
aniodol s. m. (pharm.) an antiseptic.
aníon s. m. (also **anionte**) (phys., chem.) anion.
aniqui s. f. (biol.) an Amazonian ant.
aniquilação s. f. (pl. **-ões**) 1. annihilation. 2. extinction, destruction.
aniquilado adj. 1. annihilated, extinguished, destroyed. 2. (fig.) ruined, defeated.
~ pelo pavor awe-stricken.
aniquilador s. m. annihilator, destroyer; annuller. ‖ adj. annihilating; crushing; destructive.
aniquilamento s. m. 1. annihilation, extermination. 2. obliteration; abolition. 3. extinction.
aniquilar v. 1. to annihilate, extinguish, destroy utterly. 2. to obliterate. 3. to bring or turn to nothing. 4. to annul. 5. to checkmate, wreck. 6. **~-se**: a) to run to ruin. b) to eat humble pie. **~ totalmente** to put to rout.
aniquilável adj. m. + f. (pl. **-áveis**) erasable, destroyable.

aniria s. f. (also **aniridia**) (med.) congenital absence or defect of the iris.
anis s. m. (bot.) anise, aniseed (Pimpinella anisum). **óleo de ~** anise oil, aniseed oil.
anisanto adj. (bot.) anisanthous: having varying flowers.
anisar v. to anisate, cover or flavour with anise.
anis-doce s. m. (pl. **anises-doces**) (bot.) fennel.
anis-estrelado s. m. (pl. **anises-estrelados**) (bot., also **badiana**) the Japanese star anis tree.
aniseta s. f. (also **anisete** m.) anisette (liqueur).
anisina s. f. (also **anisidina**) (chem.) anisidin(e).
anisocéfalo adj. referring to plants whose flowers form distinct capitula.
anisocoria s. f. (med.) anisocoria.
anisofilia s. f. (bot.) quality of being anisophyllous.
anisogamia s. f. (biol.) anisogamia.
anisomelia s. f. (med.) anisomelia: inequality between normally equal members.
anisopia s. f. (med.) anisopia: inequality of vision in the two eyes.
anistia s. f. amnesty, general pardon, act of oblivion.
anistiar v. to grant amnesty to, pardon.
anistórico adj. in contradiction to history.
anisúria, anisuria s. f. (med.) anisuria: alternating oliguria and polyuria.
aniversariante s. m. + f. person having a birthday. ‖ adj. referring to a birthday.
aniversariar v. to have (celebrate) one's birthday.
aniversário s. m. anniversary, birthday. ‖ adj. anniversary.
~ de casamento wedding anniversary. **~ natalício** birthday.
anixi s. m. (Braz.) fine debris floating on the surface of the Amazonian rivers.
anixo s. m. (naut.) an S hook, attached to a cable.
anjinho s. m. 1. dim. of **anjo**: angel. 2. small child, dead or alive; innocent. 3. thumbscrew.
ir para os ~s to die.
anjo s. m. 1. angel. 2. a cherubic child or adult. 3. girl dressed as an angel (in a procession). 4. (fig.) very kind person.
~ da guarda guardian angel. **salto de ~** swan dive. **cara de ~** charming face. **seja um ~ e ajude-me** be an angel and help me.
anjo-mau s. m. (pl. **anjos-maus**) (Braz.) a species of mosquito whose sting hurts.
anjuvino s. m. Angevine; native or inhabitant of Anjou (France).
ano s. m. 1. year. 2. **~s** (pl.) birthday.
~ bissexto leap year. **~ -bom** New Year's day. **~ civil** calendar year. **~ fiscal** fiscal year. **~ lunar** lunar year. **~ escolar, ~ letivo** school year. **~ luz** light-year. **~ -novo** new year. **~ Santo** jubilee year. **~ a ~** year by year. **~s atrás** years ago. **de ~ a ~** from year's end to year's end. **muitos ~s a fio** many a long year. **fazer ~s** to have one's birthday. **o ~ todo** the whole year. **feliz ~ novo** happy New Year! **meio ~** half a year. **todo ~** every year. **um ~ antes** a year before. **quantos ~s tem você** how old are you? **dia do ~ bom** New Year's day. **durante o ~ todo** all the year around. **exatamente um ~** a year and a day. **entrado em ~s** advanced in years. **quarto de ~** a quarter of a year. **quadra do ~** season of the year. **no próximo ~** next year. **dar os bons ~s** to wish a happy New Year. **de dois em dois ~s** every other year. **ele fez seus ~s de serviço** he has served his time. **deve fazer um ~** it must be about a year. **no começo deste ~** on the threshold of this year. **o peso dos ~s** the burden of the years. **uma vez por ~** once a year.

ano-base s. m. (pl. **anos-bases**) (stat.) basis-year.
anodia s. f. (med.) mania to say obscenities.
anodinia s. f. (med.) anodynia; insensibility.
anódino adj. 1. anodyne, anodic. 2. assuaging, softening.
remédios ~s anodynes, paregorics.
ânodo s. m. (also **anódio**) (electr.) anode.
anodonte adj. m. + f. edentate, toothless, without teeth.
anodontia s. f. (med.) anodontia, absence of the teeth.
anófele s. m. the malaria carrying mosquitoes of the genus Anopheles.
anoftalmia s. f. (med.) anophthalmia: congenital absence of the eyes.
anogueirado adj. of the colour of the walnut wood.
anogueirar v. to give the colour of the walnut wood.
anoitecer (I) s. m. nightfall.
ao ~ at nightfall.
anoitecer (II) v. (also **anoutecer**) to darken, grow dark, grow night.
anoiteceu rapidamente rapidly it grew night.
anojadiço adj. 1. sickening, nauseating. 2. tiresome. 3. irascible; disposed to anger.
anojado adj. 1. nauseated, sick. 2. displeased. 3. sad, wearied, tired. 4. in mourning.
anojador adj. 1. nauseating, wearisome 2. loathsome, tiresome, troublesome; dull. 3. sad.
anojamento s. m. 1. nausea. 2. mourning. 3. sorrow, grief.
anojar v. 1. to nauseate. 2. to disgust, displease, weary, tire. 3. to vex, annoy, trouble, make angry. 4. to be tiresome, be tedious. 5. ~-se: a) to be weary or tired. b) to mourn, put on mourning. c) to become sorrowful.
~-se da vida to be sick or weary of life.
anojoso adj. nauseous, disgusting.
anóleno adj. armless.
ano-luz s. m. (pl. **anos-luz**) (astr.) light-year.
anomalia s. f. anomaly: 1. irregularity, abnormality, freak, deviation from rule. 2. (astr.) apparent inequality in the motion of the planets; angular distance of a planet from its perihelion or perigee.
~ média (astr.) mean anomaly. **~ verdadeira** (astr.) true anomaly.
anomalifloro adj. (bot.) having irregular flowers.
anomalípede adj. m. + f. anomaliped: having irregular feet, syndactylous.
anomalístico adj. (astr.) anomalistic.
ano ~ anomalistical or periodical year.
anômalo adj. anomalous, irregular, abnormal, anomalistic, aberrant; extra.
exceção -a (jur.) dilatory and peremptory exception.
anomia s. f. anomie, anomy: 1. lack of laws or standards regulating organization. 2. collapse of the social structure governing any society. 3. alienation arising therefrom. 4. personal disorganization with unsocial behaviour.
anominação s. f. (pl. -ões) alteration of a word to change its sense.
anomocarpo adj. (bot.) anomocarpous: having irrregular fruits.
anomocéfalo adj. anomocephalous: having an irregular head.
anonácea s. f. (bot.) specimen of the Annonaceae (the custard-apple family).
anonáceo adj. (bot.) annonaceous.
anonadar v. (Braz.) to reduce to nothing, bring down, diminish.
anonário adj. referring to food.
anônfalo adj. (med.) having no navel.
anonimato s. m. anonymity.
anonímia s. f. anonymousness, anonymity.

anônimo s. m. anonym; person who retains anonymity. ‖ adj. anonymous, nameless, unnamed.
sociedade -a joint-stock company, corporation.
ano-novo s. m. (pl. **anos-novos**) new year.
anopsia s. f. (med.) anopsia, blindness.
anoque s. m. tannery, place where hides are tanned.
anorexia s. f. (med.) anorexia; inappetency, loathing of food.
anorgânico adj. inorganic.
anormal s. m. + f. (pl. **-ais**). abnormal person. ‖ adj. 1. abnormal, anomalous, irregular, unnatural. 2. mentally defective. ‖ **~mente** adv. abnormally, unnaturally.
anormalidade s. f. abnormality; anomaly.
anorquia s. f. (med.) anorchia, anorchism.
anorrinco adj. (zool.) noseless.
anortita s. f. (min.) anorthite.
anoruegado adj. cold, shadowy (slope, hillside).
anosidade s. f. old age.
anosmia s. f. (med.) anosmia: loss of the sense of smell.
anoso adj. aged, well on in years, old.
anosteozoário s. m. boneless animal. ‖ adj. boneless (animal).
anotação s. f. (pl. **-ões**) 1. annotation, notation, note. 2. comment; remark, observation. 3. record, entry. 4. **-ões** pl. commentary.
~ breve jotting. **~ de bens** a list or inventory of goods attached or distrained.
anotador s. m. 1. noter, marker, annotator. 2. writer of notes, commenter, recorder. ‖ adj. annotating.
anotar v. 1. to annotate, (en)register, record, write down. 2. to note, remark, observe. 3. to pencil, mark. 4. to comment on.
~ apressadamente to jot down, clap down. **~ por escrito** to commit to paper.
anovelar v. (also **enovelar**) to wind into a ball (yarn).
anquilosar v. to ankylose.
anquinhas s. f. pl. 1. pannier (of a skirt). 2. puffings, paddings; dress improver.
ansa s. f. (also **asa**) 1. wing. 2. (fig.) pretext, pretense.
anseio s. m. 1. longing, craving, yearning. 2. wistfulness, wish. 3. anxiety; disquietude, trouble.
anseriformes s. m. pl. (zool.) the Anseriformes: birds comprising ducks, geese, swans, mergansers and the screamers. ‖ **anseriforme** adj. m. + f. pertaining to the Anseriformes.
anserina s. f. (bot.) silverweed, wild tansy, pigweed.
anserino adj. (zool.) anserine, resembling a goose.
pele -a goose-skin, goose-flesh.
ânsia s. f. 1. anguish, anxiety, anxiousness. 2. trouble, pain, sorrow, grief. 3. agony. 4. ardent desire, longing, eagerness. 5. **~s** pl. nausea.
com ~s eagerly, anxiously. **estar com ~s** to be qualmish, feel sick. **as ~s da morte** the pangs of death. **~ pelo poder** craving for power.
ansiado adj. 1. yearned for. 2. qualmish.
ansiar v. 1. to crave, desire earnestly, hanker, covet, aspire, yearn, long, pine. 2. to cause anguish, make uneasy, strike with fear, alarm. 3. to be anxious, worry about. 4. **~-se** to fret about.
~ por to pine for, hanker after.
ansiedade s. f. 1. anxiety, worry, apprehension, disquietude, fear, concernment. 2. anguish, longing, craving, yearning, eagerness. 3. (fig.) vehemence, wildness.
ansiforme adj. m. + f. aliform; shaped like the handle of a basket or of a jug.
ansioso adj. 1. anxious. 2. careworn, uneasy. 3. eager longing for, hankering after, desirous. 4. impatient, solicitous, ardent. ‖ **-amente** adv. anxiously, ardently, wishfully.

~ **de curiosidade** tense with inquisitiveness. **estou ~ por** I am anxious about. **estou ~ de agir corretamente** I am anxious to do right. **estou ~ para fazê-lo** I am aching to do it. **deixar alguém ~** to keep s. o. in suspense, on tenterhooks. **estou muito ~ para saber** I am very keen to know.

anspeçada s. m. military rank of a private first class; lance-corporal.

anta (I) s. f. 1. prehistoric stone monument, dolmen. 2. (archit.) anta.

anta (II) s. f. 1. (Braz. zool.) tapir. 2. (Braz., sl.) inexperienced football player.

cor de ~ buff colour.

antado adj. buff-coloured.

antagônico adj. antagonistic, opposing, adverse, opposite, contrary, opponent, conflictive, adversative. || **-amente** adv. antagonistically, contrarily, oppositely.

antagonismo s. m. antagonism, opposition, incompatibility, opponency, contrariness; conflict.

antagonista s. m. + f. antagonist, adversary, opponent, competitor, enemy, rival, opposer. || adj. antagonistic, adversative.

músculo ~ muscle of an opposite situation or contrary quality.

antalgia s. f. absence of pain.

antálgico adj. (med.) painless, without pain.

antanáclase s. f. (rhet.) antanaclasis: repetition of the same word in another sense.

antanagoge s. f. (rhet.) antanagoge.

antanho adv. last year; in bygone times.

tempos de ~ bygone days; the good old days.

antão adv. (ant., pop., also **então**) then, at that time; in that case.

Antares s. m. (astr.) Antares: scorpion's heart, a fixed star of the first magnitude.

antarquismo s. m. antarchism.

antarquista s. m. + f. antarchist. || adj. antarchistic.

antártico adj. antarctic, southern.

antaxuré s. f. (zool.) the Andean tapir (Tapirus roulinii).

ante adv. (ant.) before. || prep. 1. before, in the face of, in the presence of. 2. in view of.

ele falou ~ a multidão he spoke before the crowd. **pé ~ pé** slowly.

anteâmbulo s. m. preface.

anteambulone s. m. Roman slave who fought the way for his master.

anteato s. m. (theat.) introductory piece; curtain raiser; short representation preceeding the main performance.

anteaurora s. f. antedawn.

anteavante s. f. (naut.) foredeck.

anteboca s. f. fore-part of the mouth.

antebraço s. m. (anat.) forearm, underarm, antebrachium (plate C 18).

antebraquial ajd. m. + f. (pl. **-ais**) antebrachial: referring to the forearm.

antecâmara s. f. vestibule, lobby, foreroom, waiting room, antechamber, anteroom.

fazer ~ 1. to wait in the antechamber. 2. (fam.) to dance attendance on a person.

antecanto s. m. (mus.) refrain, burden, chorus.

antecedência s. f. 1. antecedence, priority, precedence. 2. **~s** pl. the facts occurred before.

com ~ in advance, early, beforehand. **com três meses de ~** three months ahead of time.

antecedente s. m. (gram.) antecedent: 1. a word, phrase or clause referred to by a pronoun. 2. (math.) the first term of a ratio. || adj. m. + f. antecedent, preceding, foregoing, before, previous,

prior, precedential, anterior, prevenient. || **~mente** adv. antecedently.

sem ~s unprecedented.

anteceder v. 1. to antecede, precede (in time or place). 2. to anticipate, forego. 3. (fig.) to surpass.

antecessor s. m. antecessor, predecessor, foregoer.

antecipação s. f. (pl. **-ões**) 1. anticipation: a) act or fact of being anticipated. b) expectation; forestalling. c) forethought, prescience. 2. advance, earliness; prospect, forehandedness. 3. foretaste.

com uma semana de ~ one week ahead of time.

antecipado adj. 1. anticipated, beforehand, in advance. 2. premature, anticipative. || **-amente** adv. beforehand, ahead, previously, immaturely.

conhecimento ~ foreknowledge. **pagamento ~** advance payment. **o fim ~** the untimely end.

antecipador adj. anticipative, anticipatory, prevenient, anticipant.

antecipar v. 1. to anticipate: a) do or use in advance; b) forestall. c) take up beforehand or before the time. d) expect, experience beforehand. 2. to advance (time or date), antedate, predate. 3. **~-se** to do or happen earlier or beforehand.

~ alguém em alguma coisa to anticipate s. o., steal a march on s. o. **~ os agradecimentos** to thank in advance.

antecipo s. m. (S. Braz.) advance payment.

antecor s. m. (vet.) tumor on the breast of horses.

antecoro s. m. (archit.) antechoir.

antecos s. m. pl. antiscii, antiscians.

antedata s. f. antedate, older date.

antedatar v. to antedate, predate.

antediluviano adj. antediluvian: existing before the deluge; very old.

antedizer v. to predict; foretell; forestall.

anteduna s. f. foredune, an upwind barrier or sand fence stabilizing a dune.

anteface s. m. veil (to cover the face), mask.

anteferir v. to prefer.

antefirma s. f. usual final phrase of compliments at the end of a letter; letter ending.

antefixas s. f. pl. (archit.) antefixes. || adj. antefixal.

antefosso s. m. (fort.) fore ditch.

antegostar v. to foretaste, experience beforehand the pleasures of.

antegosto (ô) s. m. foretaste, prospect of what is to come.

antegozar v. to foretaste.

antegozo (ô) s. m. foretaste, a beforehand experience, prospect, ideal.

anteguarda s. f. 1. vanguard. 2. forefront.

ante-histórico adj. (pl. **ante-históricos**) prehistoric.

anteiro s. m. (Braz.) hound trained to hunt tapirs.

antelação s. f. (pl. **-ões**) 1. preference. 2. antecedence, previousness.

antélice s. f. (anat.) antihelix.

antélio s. m. (meteor.) anthelion.

antelmíntico s. m. (med.) anthelmintic: remedy that destroys intestinal worms. || adj. anthelmintic.

antelóquio s. m. preface, introduction; prologue.

antelucano adj. done before daylight.

antemanhã s. f. dawn, predawn. || adv. before daylight, predawn.

antemão adv. beforehand.

de ~ previously, in advance, from the jump. **fazer de ~** to anticipate. **isso já se sabia de ~** it was a foregone conclusion.

antemeridiano adj. antemeridian, before noon.

antemurado adj. 1. encompassed with walls. 2. (fig.) protected.

antemural adj. m. + f. (pl. **-ais**) (fort.) referring to a barbican or rampart.

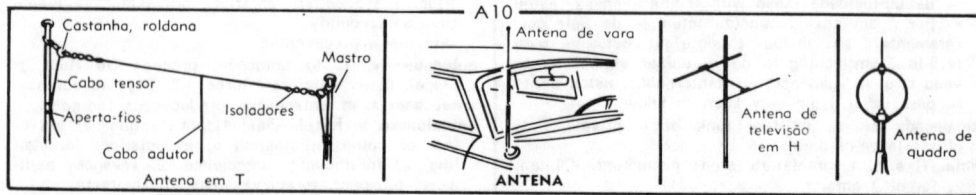

antemurar v. (fort.) 1. to provide with a barbican, an outer wall or rampart. 2. (fig.) to defend, protect.

antemuro s. m. (fort.) barbican; avant-mure; outside wall; rampart.

antena s. f. (radio) 1. antenna: a) radio, television aerial (plates A 10, V 3). b) (zool.) feeler, tentacle. 2. (naut.) yard, sail-yard. ~ de quadro frame aerial. ~ exterior external aerial. ~ muda dummy aerial. ~ dirigida beam aerial, beam antenna.

antenado adj. provided with antennae, tentaculate, tentacled.

antenal s. m. (pl. -ais) (zool.) the wandering albatross. ‖ adj. m. + f. antennal.

antenome s. m. 1. Christian name, first name. 2. title of rank, nobility or the like.

antênula s. f. (zool.) short feeler, antennule.

antenupcial adj. m. + f. (pl. -ais) antenuptial, pre-nuptial.

anteocupação s. f. (pl. -ões) preoccupation, prepossession.

anteocupar v. to preoccupy, occupy beforehand.

anteolhos s. m. pl. blinkers, blinds (of a horse's harness).

anteontem adv. (on) the day before yesterday.

antepagar, v. to pay in advance, pay ahead of time.

antepaixão s. f. (pl. -ões) (obs.) prejudice, bias.

antepara s. f. 1. (naut.) bulkhead. 2. (also anteparo) screen.

anteparar v. 1. to screen, shield, fence, defend, secure, shelter, protect. 2. to hinder, check, stop. 3. to stop short. 4. ~-se to be on the lookout, be on one's guard.

anteparo s. m. 1. rampart, fence, intrenchment. 2. any screen, shield or protection (plate L 1). 3. precaution. 4. (mach.) baffle plate.

anteparto s. m. characteristic symptoms or period immediately before parturition.

antepassado s. m. 1. forefather, ancestor, forerunner, predecessor. 2. ~s pl. ancestors, forefathers. ‖ adj. 1. former, anterior, past, expired. 2. foregone, bygone.

antepassar v. to precede, happen before.

antepeitoral adj. m. + f. (pl. -ais) belonging to the front part of the breast.

antepenúltimo adj. antepenult, the last but two.

antepor v. 1. to set, put or place before or ahead. 2. to prefer, give preference to, like better. ~ como prefixo to prefix.

anteporta s. f. 1. outer door. 2. double door. 3. screen.

anteportaria s. f. porch.

anteporto s. m. safe anchorage for ships near the harbour.

anteposição s. f. (pl. -ões) 1. anteposition. 2. preference.

antepositivo adj. put in advance.

antepredicamentais s. f. pl. preliminary questions or matters.

anteprimeiro adj. preceding the first, preliminary.

anteprojeto s. m. 1. project, plan, preliminary sketch. 2. rough calculation, estimate.

antera s. f. anther: pollen-bearing organ of a plant.

anterídio s. m. (bot.) antheridium. ‖ adj. antheridial.

anterior adj. m. + f. 1. anterior, former, foregoing, prior, earlier. 2. fore, front, in front, set before, foremost. 3. antecedent, aforetime. ‖ ~mente adv. hitherto, previously, before, anteriorly. no caso ~ in the former case. as observações ~es the above remarks.

anterioridade s. f. 1. anteriority, anteriorness. 2. priority, precedency. 3. preference.

ântero-dorsal adj. m. + f. (pl. ântero-dorsais) (anat.) antedorsal, predorsal.

ântero-exterior adj. m. + f. (pl. ântero-exteriores) (anat.) anteroexternal.

ântero-lateral adj. m. + f. (pl. ântero-laterais) (anat.) anterolateral.

ante-rosto s. m. (pl. ante-rostos) title page of a book.

anterozóide s. m. (bot.) antherozoid.

antes adv. 1. before, formerly, previously. 2. sooner. 3. ahead. 4. aforetime. 5. rather, better. ~ de previous to. ~ de tudo first of all, above all. ~ de Cristo before Christ. ~ disto ere this. ~ do meio-dia ante meridiem. ~ pelo contrário rather the contrary. ~ dum ano inside of a year. ~ do tempo anticipate. ~ pouco do que nada half a loaf is better than no bread. ~ de partir before departing. ~ que cases vê o que fazes look before you leap. ~ só do que mal acompanhado better alone than in bad company. ~ tarde do que nunca better late than never. quanto ~ melhor the sooner the better. pouco ~ short before. eu quisera ~ ficar aqui do que ir I would rather stay here than go. o quanto ~ as soon as possible.

ante-sala s. f. (pl. ante-salas) 1. antechamber, ante-cabinet. 2. waiting-room.

antese s. f. (bot.) anthesis, expansion of a flower, blooming.

antetempo adv. 1. too soon, ahead of time. 2. early, untimely.

antever v. to foresee. ~ o destino to foresee the destiny.

anteversão s. f. (med.) anteversion; inversion of the matrix.

antevéspera s. f. the day before the eve.

antevidência s. f. 1. foresight. 2. forethought.

antevisão s. f. foresight.

antevocálico adj. antevocalic, prevocalic, placed before a vowel.

anti prep. a Greek preposition which, in composition, signifies contrary.

antiabortivo s. m. antiabortive substance or measure. ‖ adj. antiabortive.

antiácido s. m. antacid.

antiaéreo adj. antiaircraft.

antialcoólico adj. antialcoholic.

antiamarílico adj. (med.) preventing yellow fever, antimalarial.

antiamericanismo s. m. anti-Americanism.

antiaristocrata s. m. + f. antiaristocrat. ‖ adj. anti-aristocratic.

antiartrítico adj. (med.) antiarthritic; good against the gout.

antiasmático adj. antiasthmatic.
antibiótico s. m. antibiotics, antibiotic drug.
antibotrópico adj. said of the antivenom serum against bites of snakes of the genus Bothrops (**jaracuçu, urutu,** etc.)
antibrasileiro adj. anti-Brazilian.
anticefalálgico adj. anticephalalgic.
anticéptico or **anticético** adj. antiskeptical.
anticiclone s. m. (meteor.) anticyclone.
anticiclônico adj. anticyclonic.
anticívico adj. anticivic.
anticlerical s. m. + f. (pl. **-ais**) anticlerical person. ‖ adj. anticlerical.
anticlericalismo s. m. anticlericalism.
anticlímax s. m. anticlimax.
anticlinal s. f. (pl. **-ais**) anticline. ‖ adj. m. + f. anticlinal.
anticloro s. m. (chem.) antichlor.
anticomania s. f. mania for antiquities.
anticomercial adj. m. + f. (pl. **-ais**) anticommercial; against the interests of the commerce.
anticoncepção s. f. (med.) contraception, prevention of pregnancy.
anticoncepcional adj. m. + f. (pl. **-ais**) contraceptive. **meio** ~ contraceptive.
anticonstitucional adj. m. + f. (pl. **-ais**) anticonstitutional.
anticorpo s. m. (chem., med.) antibody, antitoxin.
anticorrosivo adj. anticorrosive.
anticrepúsculo s. m. anticrepuscule.
anticrese s. f. (law) antichresis.
anticresista s. m. + f. (jur.) antichretic creditor.
anticrético adj. antichretic.
anticristão s. m. (pl. **-ãos**) antichristian. ‖ adj. antichristian.
anticristo s. m. Antichrist.
anticronismo s. m. error in dates.
anticrotálico adj. anticrotalic; effective against the bites of a rattlesnake.
antictone s. m. (also **antipoda**) antipode.
antidemocrata s. m. + f. antidemocrat.
antidemocrático adj. antidemocratic(al).
antiderrapante adj. m. + f. antiskid, nonskid. **proteção** ~ nonskid device. **correntes** ~**s** skid-chains. **pneus** ~**s** nonskid tyres.
antidetonante s. m. (tech.) antiknock. ‖ adj. m. + f. antiknock.
antidiabético adj. (med.) antidiabetic.
antidiftérico adj. (med.) antidiphtheric.
antidínico adj. (med.) against giddiness.
antidivorcista s. m. + f. person who is against divorce. ‖ adj. antidivorce.
antidogmático adj. antidogmatic.
antidotismo s. m. use or abuse of antidotes.
antídoto s. m. (med.) antidote, counterpoison, preservative, corrective.
antidramático adj. antidrãmatical.
antiemético adj. (med.) antiemetic.
antiepiléptico adj. (med.) antiepileptic.
antiespasmódico s. m. antispasmodic (agent). ‖ adj. antispasmodic.
antiestabelecimento s. m. (pol.) antiestablishment.
antiestatismo s. m. antistatism.
antiestético adj. antiaesthetic.
antievangélico adj. (rel.) antievangelic(al).
antievolucionista s. m. + f. antievolutionist. ‖ adj. antievolutionist.
antifaz s. m. (also **anteface**) veil (to cover the face).
antifebril adj. m. + f. (pl. **-is**) antifebrile; against fever; febrifugal.
antifen s. m. (pl. **antifens, antifenes**) sign of the proofreader to indicate separation of words which are connected by mistake.

antiferromagnetismo s. m. (phys.) antiferromagnetism.
antifermentescível adj. m. + f. (pl. **-íveis**) antifermentative.
antifermento s. m. antiferment.
antiferruginoso adj. antirust.
antifilosófico adj. antiphilosophic(al).
antifísico adj. antiphysical.
antiflatulento adj. (med.) antiflatulent.
antiflogístico adj. (med.) antiphlogistic.
antífona s. f. (mus.) 1. antiphon. 2. invitatory. 3. anthem.
antifonário s. m. antiphonary.
antifonia s. f. (mus.) antiphony.
antifônico adj. antiphonic.
antifrancês adj. anti-French.
antifrase s. f. (rhet.) antiphrasis.
antifricção s. f. (pl. **-ões**) antifriction metal. **metal de** ~ Babbit metal. **mancal** ~ sliding bearing.
antigaláctico adj. antigalactic.
antigalha s. f. 1. lumber, trash, trumpery. 2. curio. 3. antique.
antigelante s. m. antifreeze.
antigênico adj. antigenic.
antígeno s. m. (med.) antigen.
antigermânico adj. anti-German.
antigo adj. 1. ancient, old, olden. 2. antique. 3. quondam. 4. archaic, old-fashioned, antiquated. 5. once, one-time; secular, former, aforetime, early, bygone, erstwhile, oldtime, pre-existing. ‖ **-amente** adv. formerly, in former days, anciently, in days of old, of old, aforetime, heretofore, erstwhile. **os** ~**s** the ancient. **mais** ~ older. **objetos** ~**s** antiquities. **meu** ~ **professor** my quondam teacher. **um** ~ **aluno** a sometime pupil. **à moda -a** antiquely, old-fashioned. **de tempos** ~**s** of old.
antigório s. m. coarse enamel, glazing.
antigorita s. f. (min.) antigorite.
antigotoso adj. (med.) antipodagric, against gout or arthritis.
antigovernamental adj. m. + f. (pl. **-ais**) contrary to government.
antigramatical adj. m. + f. (pl. **-ais**) antigrammatical.
antígrafo s. m. a sign to distinguish the words we make notes about.
antigualha s. f. 1. antiquity. 2. old stuff.
antiguidade s. f. 1. antiquity, antique, antiquities, oldness. 2. ancientry, ancients. 3. hoar. 4. primitiveness. 5. seniority (as in an employment). **adaptar à Antiguidade** to antiquate. **história da Antiguidade** ancient history. **loja de** ~**s** curiosity shop. **os povos da Antiguidade** the ancients. **costumes e vida na Antiguidade** antiquities. **estudo ou gosto por** ~**s** antiquarianism.
antiguíssimo adj. = **antiqüíssimo.**
anti-helmíntico adj. (pl. **anti-helmínticos**) (med.) antihelminthic.
anti-hemorrágico adj. (pl. **anti-hemorrágicos**) (med.) antihemorrhagic.
anti-hidrofóbico adj. (pl. **anti-hidrofóbicos**) (med.) antihydrophobic.
anti-higiênico adj. (pl. **anti-higiênicos**) 1. antihygienic. 2. unsanitary.
anti-histérico adj. (pl. **anti-histéricos**) antihysteric.
anti-histórico adj. (pl. **anti-históricos**) antihistoric, antihistorical.
anti-humano adj. (pl. **anti-humanos**) antihuman.
antiictérico adj. (med.) anti-icteric.
antiinflamatório adj. (med.) antiphlogistic.
antílabe s. f. brief sentence.
antilêmico adj. (med.) antiloimic.
antiletárgico adj. antilethargic.

antilhano s. m. Antillean: native or inhabitant of the Antilles.
Antilhas s. f. pl. Antilles.
antiliberal adj. m. + f. (pl. **-ais**) antiliberal.
antilogaritmo s. m. (math.) antilogarithm.
antilogia s. f. antilogy: contradiction of ideas.
antilógico adj. antilogical: against logic.
antílope s. m. (zool.) 1. antelope. 2. steenbok.
antimalárico (adj. antimalarial.
antimatéria s. f. (phys.) antimatter.
antimedical adj. m. + f. (pl. **-ais**) antimedical.
antimeridiano s. m. (astr.) that part of the celestial sphere below the horizon.
antimilitar adj. m. + f. antimilitary.
antimilitarismo s. m. antimilitarism.
antimilitarista s. m. + f. antimilitarist. ‖ adj. antimilitarist.
antimíssil adj. m. + f. (pl. **-eis**) antimissile.
antimoda s. f. (stat.) the value of the abscissa in a probability curve.
antimonarquista s. m. + antimonarchist. ‖ adj. antimonarchical.
antimonial adj. m. + f. (pl. **-ais**) antimonial.
antimoniato s. m. (chem.) antimoniate.
antimônico adj. (chem.) antimonic.
antimonífero adj. antimoniferous.
antimonilo s. m. (chem.) antimonyl.
antimônio s. m. (chem.) 1. antimony. 2. stibium.
~ **cru** native antimony. ~ **diaforético** diaphoretic antimony. ~ **metálico** pure antimony. ~ **sulfurado** sulphuret of antimony. ~ **tartarizado** tartrated antimony, tartar emetic.
antimonioso adj. antimonious.
antimonióxido s. m. (chem.) antimony oxide.
antimoral adj. m. + f. (pl. **-ais**) 1. antimoral, immoral. 2. wicked. 3. licentious.
antinacional adj. m. + f. (pl. **-ais**) antinational.
antinarcótico adj. antinarcotic.
antinatural adj. m. + f. unnatural.
antinefrítico adj. (med.) antinephritic.
antineurálgico adj. (med.) antineuralgic.
antinodo s. m. (phys.) antinode.
antinomia s. f. antinomy: 1. a contradiction between two laws. 2. a paradox.
antinômico adj. antinomical: contrasting; paradox; contrary to law.
antinomismo s. m. (philos.) antinomianism.
antinupcial adj. m. + f. (pl. **-ais**) opposed to marriage.
antiofídico adj. antidotal (against snake bites).
antioxidante s. m. antioxidant. ‖ adj. antioxidant.
antipapa s. m. antipope; false pope.
antipapado s. m. jurisdiction of the antipope.
antipapismo s. m. antipapism.
antipapista s. m. + f. antipapist; a person opposed to the pope. ‖ adj. of or referring to antipapism.
antiparalelo s. m. (geom.) antiparallel (line). ‖ adj. antiparallel.
antiparástase s. f. (rhet.) counterproof.
antipartícula s. f. (nuch. plys.) antiparticle.
antipatia s. f. 1. antipathy, aversion, averseness, dislike. 2. disrelish, repugnance, repugnancy. 3. reluctance, contrariety.
causar ~ to cause aversion.
antipático adj. 1. antipathetic(al), averse. 2. obnoxious, repugnant. 3. dislikable, unsympathetic. 4. opposite. ‖ **antipaticamente** adj. antipathetically.
antipatizar v. 1. to dislike. 2. to feel antipathy against, disrelish, bear ill will.
antipatriota s. m. + f. unpatriotic person. ‖ adj. unpatriotic.
antipatriótico adj. unpatriotic: against the interest of one's native country.

antipedagógico adj. contrary to the precepts of pedagogy.
antiperiódico s. m. (med.) antiperiodic. ‖ adj. antiperiodic.
antiperistáltico adj. (med.) antiperistaltic.
antiperístase s. f. antiperistasis.
antipestoso adj. (med.) antibubonic.
antipirético adj. (med.) antipyretic; febrifuge, antifebrile.
antipirina s. f. (med.) antipyrine.
antipleurítico adj. (med.) antipleuritic; efficacious against pleurisy.
antipneumônico s. m. (med.) remedy against diseases of the lungs.
antípodas s. m. pl. 1. antipodes, persons living on the opposite side of the globe. 2. (fig.) opposite, contrary, antipoda. ‖ **antípoda** adj. m. + f. antipodal.
antipódico adj. antipodean.
antipodismo s. m. quality or situation of an antipode.
antipolítico adj. antipolitical.
antipestoso adj. (med.) antibubonic.
antiptose s. f. (gram.) antiptosis: the putting of one case for another.
antipútrido adj. antiputrid, against putrefaction.
antiquado adj. 1. antiquated, antique, old, outmoded, outdate, passé, out of date, obsolete. 2. old-fashioned, antediluvian, archaic, ancient. 3. old-fogey, unfashionable, fossil, corny, crusted. 4. slow. ‖ **-amente** adv. antiquely, anciently, fustily.
tornar ~ to outmode.
antiqualha s. f. = **antigalha**.
antiquar v. 1. to antiquate. 2. to outdate, abolish. 3. to render antique, become antiquated. 4. ~**-se** to fall in disuse, become obsolete.
~ **a linguagem** to imitate the language of the ancients.
antiquário s. m. 1. antiquary; antiquarian. 2. archaist. 3. secondhand bookseller. ‖ adj. antiquarian.
antiquíssimo or **antiguíssimo** adj. (abs. superl. of **antigo**) most ancient.
anti-rábico adj. (pl. **anti-rábicos**) (med.) 1. antihydrophobic. 2. antirabic.
anti-republicano adj. (pl. **anti-republicanos**) antirepublican.
anti-revisionismo s. m. (pl. **anti-revisionismos**) antirevisionism.
anti-revisionista s. m. + f. (pl. **anti-revisionistas**) antirevisionist. ‖ adj. contrary to revision.
anti-revolucionário adj. (pl. **anti-revolucionários**) antirevolutionary.
anti-sátira s. f. (pl. **anti-sátiras**) satyrical refutation of a satyre.
anti-semita s. m. + f. (pl. **anti-semitas**) anti-Semite.
anti-semítico adj. (pl. **anti-semíticos**) anti-Semitic.
anti-sepsia s. f. (pl. **anti-sepsias**) antisepsis.
anti-séptico s. m. (pl. **anti-sépticos**) antiseptic. ‖ adj. antiseptic.
anti-sifilítico adj. (pl. **anti-sifilíticos**) (med.) antisyphilitic.
anti-social adj. m. + f. (pl. **anti-sociais**) antisocial, unsocial.
anti-soro s. m. (pl. **anti-soros**) (med.) antiserum.
antispase s. f. (med.) antispasis, revulsion.
antispástico adj. (med.) antispasmodic.
antispasto s. m. antispast.
antiste s. m. (rel., also **antistite**) bishop, priest; cleric.
antístrofe s. f. 1. (mus.) antistrophe. 2. (gram.) inversion.
antistrumático adj. antiscrofulous, against scrofula.
antítese s. f. 1. antithesis. 2. contraposition. 3. opposition.

antitetânico adj. (med.) antitetanic.
antitético adj. antithetic.
antítipo s. m. antitype; figure representing another figure.
antitóxico s. m. (med.) antidote. ‖ adj. antitoxic.
antitoxina s. f. (med.) antitoxin; antivenin.
antítrago s. m. (anat.) antitragus.
antitrinitário adj. (rel.) anti-Trinitarian.
antivariólico adj. (med.) antivariolous, against smallpox.
antivenéreo adj. (med.) antivenereal.
antiverminoso adj. vermifuge.
antizímico adj. antizymic.
antódio s. m. (bot.) anthodium.
antófago adj. anthophagous.
antófilo adj. (zool.) anthophilous.
antófitos s. m. pl. (bot.) Anthophyta, the division comprising the flowering plants.
antogênese s. f. anthogenesis: flower formation.
antografia s. f. description of flowers.
antojadiço adj. capricious, whimsical.
antojar v. (also antolhar) 1. to long for, lust after. 2. to covet. 3. to imagine, fancy. 4. ~-se to offer to the sight.
antojo (ô) (I) s. m. (pl. antojos) (also antolho pl. antolhos) 1. mental image. 2. fancy. 3. mind. 4. desire. 5. whim. 6. a pregnant woman's longing.
antojo (ô) (II) s. m. (pl. antojos) disgust, nausea.
antolhos s. m. pl. eyeflaps, blinkers, blinders, blinds (plates A 12, C 12).
antologia s. f. 1. anthology. 2. florilegium. 3. analects.
antologiar v. to anthologize.
antológico adj. anthological.
antologista s.m. + f. anthologist.
antomania s. f. anthomania, passion for flowers.
antomaníaco adj. referring to anthomania.
antonímia s. f. (gram.) antonymy: quality of being antonym or application of antonyms.
antônimo s. m. (gram.) antonym. ‖ adj. antonymous.
antonomásia s. f. antonomasia; substitution of the proper name for another name; nickname; surname.
antoplastia s. f. (med. also anaplastia) plastic surgery.
antorismo s. m. (rhet.) substitution of a word for another better one.
antotaxia s. f. (bot.) anthotaxy.
antozoário s. m. (zool.) anthozoan.
antracemia s. f. (med.) 1. carbon monoxide poisoning. 2. presence of this gas in the blood.
antraceno s. m. (chem.) anthracene.
antracífero adj. anthraciferous.
antracite s. f. anthracite, stone coal.
antracóide adj. m. + f. 1. (med.) anthracoid. 2. coal--coloured.
antracomancia s. f. ancient divination by examining burning coal.
antracose s. f. (med.) anthracosis: miner's malady.
antranilato s. m. (chem.) anthranilate.
antranol s. m. (chem.) anthranol.
antraz s. m. (med. + vet.) anthrax.
~ maligno carbuncle.
antrecambado adj. 1. variegated. 2. mixed. 3. jumbled.
antrite s. f. (path.) inflammation of an antrum (= antro 1).
antro s. m. 1. (anat.) antrum. 2. antre, cave, sty. 3. den. 4. hole, dive, lair. 5. gambling hell.
~ de fumadores opium joint, opium den. o ~ do leão the lion's den. ~ mastóide (anat.) mastoid foramen (plate C 17).
antrol s. m. (chem.) anthrol.
antropagogia s. f. social pedagogy; civics.

antropocêntrico adj. anthropocentric: said of a philosophical system wherein the human being is the center of the universe.
antropocentrismo s. m. anthropocentrism.
antropocentrista s. m. + f. adherent of the anthropocentrism.
antropócoro s. m. (bot.) anthropochore. ‖ adj. (bot.) anthropochorous.
antropofagia s. f. anthropophagy: cannibalism.
antropófago s. m. anthropophagite, cannibal. ‖ adj. anthropophagous, man-eating.
antropofobia s. f. anthropophobia.
antropófobo s. m. misanthrope. ‖ adj. misanthropic.
antropogenia s. f. anthropogenesis; anthropogeny.
antropogênico adj. anthropogenetic.
antropogeografia s. f. anthropogeography (human geography).
antropografia s. f. anthropography; anatomical description of the human body.
antropográfico adj. referring to anthropography.
antropóide s. m. anthropoid ape. ‖ adj. m. + f. anthropoidal.
antropólatra s. m. + f. anthropolater. ‖ adj. anthropolatric.
antropolatria s. f. anthropolatry: adoration of a human being.
antropolátrico adj. anthropolatric.
antropologia s. f. anthropology.
antropológico adj. anthropological.
antropologista s.m. + f. antropólogo m. anthropologist.
antropomagnetismo s. m. anthropomagnetism.
antropomancia s. f. art of divination by examining the human viscera.
antropometria s. f. anthropometry; science of the dimensions and measurements of the human body.
antropômetro s. m. anthropometer.
antropomorfismo s. m. anthropomorphism: attribution of a human form to God.
antropomorfista s. m. + f. anthropomorphist: adherent of anthropomorphism.
antropomorfo s. m. (zool.) one of the Anthropomorpha. ‖ adj. anthropomorphic(al).
antroponomia s. f. anthroponomy.
antroponômico adj. anthroponomical.
antropopatia s. f. anthropopathy: attribution of human feelings to a divinity or to animals or objects.
antropopiteco s. m. Anthropopithecus.
antropossociologia s. f. anthroposociology.
antropossociológico adj. referring to anthroposociology.
antropossofia s. f. (philos.) anthroposophy: knowledge of the spiritual human being and his spiritual world.
antropossófico adj. anthroposophical.
antropossomatologia s. f. study of the structure of the human body.
antropoteísmo s. m. anthropotheism: deification of humanity.
antropotomia s. f. anthropotomy: anatomy of the human body.
antrotomia s. f. (surg.) antrostomy, antrotomy, the operation of opening an antrum.
antúrio s. m. (bot.) anthurium.
anu s. m. (Braz.) = anum.
ânua s. f. (obs.) yearly report.
anual adj. m. + f. (pl. -ais) 1. annual, yearly. 2. etesian; once a year. ‖ -mente adv. annually, per annum, yearly.
anuário s. m. yearly publication, yearbook, directory.
anuência s. f. 1. approvement, approval. 2. acquiescence. 3. consent. 4. placet.
anuente s. m. + f. person who consents, acquiesces. ‖ adj. consenting, assenting.

anuidade s. f. (also **anualidade**) annuity, yearly payment or rent.

~ **perpétua** perpetuity. **título de** ~s annuity bond.

anuir v. 1. to assent, approve, agree, consent, acquiesce. 2. to adhere. 3. to temporize.

anuitário adj. amortizing (a debt) with annuities.

anujá s. m. (Braz., also **cachorro-de-padre**) a freshwater catfish (Trachycoristes galeatus).

anulabilidade s. f. defeasibility, voidableness.

anulação s. f. (pl. **-ões**) 1. annulment, nullification, cancellation, invalidation. 2. rescission, repeal. 3. revokement, voidance. 4. (jur.) cassation; circumduction; abatement. 5. abrogation; disaffirmation. 6. abolition.

anulado adj. cancel(l)ed, null and void.

anulador s. m. canceller, nullifier, annuller. || adj. nullifying.

anulamento s. m. annulment; avoidance; effacement.

anulante adj. m. + f. (also **anulativo**) nullifying.

anular (I) adj. m. + f. annular, ring-shaped, hoop-shaped.

dedo ~ ring-finger.

anular (II) v. 1. to annul, make void, nullify, cancel, disannul, undo, unmake. 2. to destroy, annihilate. 3. to negate, disaffirm, recall. 4. to supersede, suppress, abolish, efface, dissolve; neutralize.

~ **um voto** to annul a vote. **ele não pode** ~ **sua assinatura** he cannot go back on his signature.

anulatório adj. (jur.) nullifying.

anulável adj. m. + f. (pl. **-áveis**) 1. cancellable, defeasible, voidable. 2. annullable, abolishable. 3. abrogable. 4. effaciable.

ânulo s. m. (archit.) annulet.

anuloso adj. annulated, annular, ringed, ring-shaped, formed of rings.

anum s. m. (pl. **-uns**) (Braz., zool., also **anu** or **anuguaçu**) the common ani of the family Crotophaga as the **anum-branco, anum-do-brejo, anum-do-campo, anum-peixe.**

anunciação s. f. (pl. **-ões**) 1. (also **anunciada**) annunciation, announcement. 2. (rel.) Lady day; Annunciation.

anunciador s. m. 1. annunciator, announcer. 2. toastmaster || adj. annunciating.

anunciante s. m. + f. announcer, advertiser. || adj. advertising.

anunciar v. 1. to announce, annunciate, advertise. 2. to make known, promulgate, proclaim. 3. to foretell, prophesy. 4. (fig.) to signify, presage.

~ **o início ou o fim de uma irradiação** (radio) to sign on (off). ~ **nos jornais** to advertise in the papers. **o casamento foi -do** the banns were called.

anunciativo adj. annunciatory.

anúncio s. m. 1. advertisement, announcement, notice. 2. bill. 3. insertion.

~ **berrante** a puff. ~ **classificado** classified advertisement, (U. S. A., coll.) want ad. ~ **de imprensa** press advertisement. ~ **de rádio** radio advertisement. ~ **luminoso** electric sign. ~s **de colocação e empregos** advertisement for positions. **procurar por meio de** ~ to advertise for.

anuncista s. m. + f. (typogr.) adman, admaker: a compositor who sets advertisements.

anunguaçu s. m. (zool., also **anum**) the greater ani (Crotophaga major).

anurese s. f. (med.) anuresis.

anúria, anuria s. f. (med.) anuria.

anuro s. m. (zool.) anuran, salientian, batrachian. || adj. anurous, having no tail.

ânus s. m., sg. + pl (anat.) anus.

anuviado adj. clouded, overcast.

anuviar v. 1. to grow cloudy, becloud, cloud. 2. to darken, shadow. 3. (fig.) to become unhappy.

anverso s. m. obverse; the side of a coin on which the head is impressed.

anzol s. m. (pl. **-óis**) 1. fishhook, hook, angle (plate P 9). 2. (fig.) bait; snare; trick.

cair no ~ to let o. s. be caught. **pescar com** ~ to angle.

anzol-de-lontra s. m. (pl. **anzóis-de-lontra**) (bot.) a climber of the nightshade family.

anzolado adj. 1. formed like a (fish)hook. 2. (Braz.) lean, skinny, emaciated.

anzolar v. to hook, form like a hook.

anzoleiro s. m. manufacturer of or trader in fishhooks.

ao contraction of the prep. **a** and the article **o**: in the, for the, at the, to the, by the, etc.

~ **amanhecer** at dawn. ~ **andar** in going. ~ **brincar** playing. ~ **certo** certainly, for sure. ~ **correr do dia (da noite)** during the day (the night). ~ **fim de tudo** at the end of all. ~ **inverso** inversely. ~ **invés de** instead of. ~ **lado de** near of, close to. ~ **máximo** at the utmost. ~ **menos** at least. ~ **pé da letra** literally, word by word. ~ **que se diz** as it is reported. ~ **que eu saiba** for all that I know. ~ **redor** roundabout. ~ **romper do dia** at daybreak. ~ **terminarem as aulas** at the end of the lessons. ~ **todo** all in all. **ela sorriu** ~ **fazê-lo** she smiled as she did it.

aonde adv. where, whither; wherever.

aonde! interj. of surprise: why, really!? ~ **você vai?** where are you going to. ~ **você for!** wherever you go! ~ **ele foi levar o livro?** whither did he take the book?

aoristo s. m. (gram.) aorist.

aorta s. m. (anat.) aorta; the largest artery in the body.

aortectasia s. f. (med.) dilation of the aorta.

aórtico adj. aortic, aortal.

aortite s. f. (med.) inflammation of the aorta.

aortoclasia s. f. (also **aortoclastia**, med.) aortoclasia, hernia of the aorta.

apá s. m. 1. (Braz.) shovel, spade. 2. (bot.) wallaba tree (Eperua falcata, also called **espadeira** f.).

apacamã s. m. (Braz.) an Amazonian fish.

apacanim s. m. (pl. **-ins**) (Braz.) a hawk eagle; crested eagle.

apache s. m. 1. (U. S. A.) Apache: member of an Indian tribe. 2. apache: Parisian criminal, gangster; explorer of women.

apachismo s. m. crime or deed peculiar to an apache.

apachorrar-se v. to become idle, sluggish, apathetic.

apadrinhador s. m. protector, supporter, patronizer, backer. || adj. supporting, sponsoring, favouring.

apadrinhamento s. m. act or fact of sponsoring, protecting.

apadrinhar v. 1. to be a godfather to. 2. to protect, support, back, patronize, favour. 3. ~-**se** to ask for another's protection.

apadroar v. to protect, support, sponsor.

apagado adj. 1. extinguished, extinct, without fire or light, put out. 2. dark, dim, unlit. 3. erased, wiped out, illisible. 4. faint, vague. 5. colourless, tintless. 6. (fig.) quiet, modest.

uma pessoa -a a person of no consequence.

apagador s. m. 1. extinguisher (person). 2. dampener, quencher, eraser. || adj. extinguishing.

~ **de vela** candle extinguisher.

apaga-fenóis s. m. pl. (also **apaga-fenóis** or **apaga-penóis**) (naut.) cables to furl the topsails.

apagamento s. m. extinguishment, extinction; quenching; suppression; erasure, rasing, blotting or rubbing out, deletion.

apaga-pó s. m. (pl. **apaga-pós**) (Braz.) drizzle, mizzle.

apagar v. 1. to extinguish, quench, damp. 2. to smother, blot, sponge, dele, delete. 3. to expurge, abolish. 4. to scratch out, scrape out, wipe out, efface, deface, erase. 5. to snuff out, pop out, switch off (light). 6. (fig.) to calm, appease. 7. to fade. 8. ~-se to die away, go out, become extinguished; weaken.
~ **com os pés** to tread out. ~ **com sopros** to blow out.

apagável adj. m. + f. (pl. -áveis) erasable.

ápage interj. away! go! get out! be gone!

apagma s. f. (med.) dislocation of a bone.

apagogia s. f. apagogy, demonstration of a proposition by the falsity of a contrary proposition.

apaiari s. m. (ichth.) a cichlid (Hydrogonus ocellatus).

apaideguado adj. (N. Braz., pop.) very large.

apainelado s. m. panel-work. || adj. panelled.

apainelamento s. m. panelling.

apainelar v. 1. to panel. 2. to inlay.

apaiolar v. to put in a barn or shed.

apaisanado adj. having manners of or dressed like a civilian.

apaisanar v. to behave or dress like a civilian.

apaixonado s. m. 1. lover. 2. enthusiast. || adj. 1. enamoured, passionate, impassioned, impassionate, flaming, amorous, passion-ridden, lovesick, infatuated. 2. (fig.) fiery, fervent, fervid, burning, hot, spoony. 3. enthusiastic. || -amente adv. passionately, enthusiastically.
~ **por livros** crazy about books. **estar ~ por alguém** to be over head and ears enamoured of s. o., in love with s. o. **ela o ama -amente** she is passionately fond of him.

apaixonar v. 1. to impassion, infatuate, enamour; smite; inspire; exalt. 2. to grieve. 3. ~-se to fall in love, lose one's heart to.
ele apaixonou-se com a morte do irmão he grieved over his brother's death. **ele apaixonou-se por ela** he fell in love with her.

apaixonável adj. m. + f. (pl. -áveis) capable of falling in love.

apajear v. 1. to page. 2. to attend upon. 3. to work as a nursemaid.

apalaçado adj. palacelike.

apalaçar v. to give the aspect or form of a palace to.

apalacianado adj. courtly (manners).

apalacianar v. to give courtly manners to.

apaladar v. to give a good taste to, to give savour.

apalancar (I) v. to barricade.

apalancar (II) v. to erect platforms as bandstands or the like.

apalancar (III) v. to dig, break or turn up.

apalancar (IV) v. to oscillate, swing, sway.

apalavrado adj. adjusted, agreed upon.

apalavramento s. m. agreement, promise.

apalavrar v. 1. to bespeak, adjust, agree upon; conform by word; oblige, obligate. 2. ~-se to engage o. s.
~ **para casar** to betroth.

apalazador s. m. (N. Braz.) worker who sews the shoe uppers.

apalazar v. (N. Braz.) to stitch, sew the shoe uppers.

apaleador s. m. cudgeller; person who beats, belabours with a stick.

apaleamento s. m. cudgelling, thrashing: act or fact of beating (with a stick).

apalear v. 1. to cudgel; beat; belabour. 2. to dry-beat.

apalermado adj. imbecile, meaningless, inane, silly, backward.

apalermar-se v. to become silly, behave like an imbecile, to grow foolish.

apalhaçado adj. clownish, foolish, ridiculous.

apalmado adj. (her.) showing a hand with exposed palm (escutcheon).

apalpação s. f. (pl.-ões) (also **apalpadela** f., **apalpamento**, **apalpo** m.) 1. palpation: act or fact of touching. 2. (med.) percussion.
andar às apalpadelas to grope one's way.

apalpadeira s. f. woman in charge of the inspection of women suspected of contraband.

apalpadela s. f. the act of groping, touching, feeling.

apalpador s. m. 1. feeler, fingerer; groper. 2. (mach.) a feeler gauge. || adj. contacting, feeling, groping.

apalpão s. m. (pl. -ões) crude touch or fumbling.

apalpar v. 1. to touch, feel, palp, palpate. 2. to finger, fumble, handle. 3. to grope one's way. 4. to sound, sift, pump. 5. to molest.
~ **o caminho para a porta** to grope one's way towards the door. ~ **a situação** to sound the situation. ~ **o terreno** to proceed cautiously.

apanágio s. m. apanage, appanage: 1. lands or office assigned for the maintenance of a royal home. 2. a natural endowment.

apandado adj. full, inflated, swollen (as sails).

apandilhar v. 1. to swindle, cheat (as at cards). 2. to join a fraudulent scheme.

apanha, apanhação s. f. (pl. ~s, -ões) (also **apanhadura**) act of harvesting, gathering (the crop).

apanhadeira s. f. 1. woman who picks or harvests fruits; gleaner (woman). 2. dustpan.

apanhadiço adj. easily collected, picked up or harvested.

apanhado s. m. 1. resumé, summary, abstract. 2. fold, tuck (of a dress). || adj. caught, held fast, picked, gathered.

apanhador s. m. 1. harvester, picker, gatherer. 2. (Braz.) coffee cherry picker.

apanhamento s. m. 1. harvesting, gathering. 2. = **apanhado**.

apanha-moscas s. m., sg. + pl. 1. fly-trap. 2. (bot.) Venus's fly-trap.

apanhar v. 1. to pick, pick out, pluck. 2. to gather, harvest. 3. to clutch, grip, seize, swoop, whisk, snap, snatch. 4. to catch (as a ball). 5. to capture. 6. to catch red-handed. 7. to tuck up, fold. 8. to get a sound beating. 9. to lose a game. 10. to ensnare, entrap. 11. to reach, overreach, catch up with.
~ **a caça** to retrieve. ~ **alguém numa mentira** to catch one in a lie. ~ **com laço** to lasso. ~ **com o bico** to peck. ~ **flores** to pick flowers. ~ **no ar** to learn by hearsay, pick up a rumor. ~ **numa armadilha** to ensnare, insnare. ~ **numa cilada** to entrap. ~ **o sentido** to understand. ~ **passageiros** to pick up passengers. ~ **uma doença** to contract a disease. ~ **um resfriado** to catch a cold. **a criança foi apanhada em flagrante com o pote de doce na mão** the child was surprised with the jam pot in his hands. **ele foi apanhado pelo trem** he was run over by the train.

apanho s. m. = **apanha**.

apaniguado s. m. sectarian, follower; protegé.

apaniguar v. to protect, to favour, sustain.

apantomancia s. f. fortune-telling, divination based on interpreting things seen unexpectedly.

apantomante s. m. + f. practiser of **apantomancia**.

apantufado adj. slipper-shaped.

apantufar v. to pad on slippers.

apapá s. m. (Braz.) a herringlike freshwater fish of the Amazon river.

apaparicar v. 1. to nibble at. 2. to caress, fondle.

apar s. m. (also **apara**, zool.) apar, the three-banded armadillo.

apara s. f. 1. chip, scrap, snip, snippet, shred. 2. ~s pl. chippings, clippings, parings; shavings, kindling; leftovers.

~ **de charuto** cigar tip. ~s **de furagem** borings.

aparabolar v. to present in the form of a parable.

aparadeira s. f. an unskilled midwife.

aparadela s. f. paring; smoothing.

aparado s. m. (Braz.) abrupt ending of a mountain range. ‖ adj. clipped, pared, trimmed.

não ~ 1. untrimmed. 2. unopened (books).

aparador s. m. 1. parer, cropper. 2. parrier. 3. dresser, sideboard. 4. dumb waiter.

~ **de óleo** drip-pan.

aparafusar v. (also **parafusar**) to bolt, fasten with a screw.

aparagem s. f. 1. the act of clipping, trimming, cutting of, paring. 2. the act of receiving or catching (cuttings, a ball, etc.).

aparamentar v. 1. to adorn, ornament, decorate. 2. to vest, dress ecclesiastical vestments.

aparar v. 1. to clip, trim, cut, crop, part; chip. 2. to prune; lop. 3. to turn; pare; whittle. 4. to plane off; smoothen; polish (also fig.). 5. to sharpen (pencil). 6. to parry (blow); to ward off. 7. to tolerate, bear. 8. to coax, adulate. 9. to catch (ball).

~ **a cauda de um animal** to dock (horse). ~ **as unhas** to pare the nails.

aparas s. f. pl. parings, trimmings, scraps, chips.

aparatar v. to adorn, bedeck, trim, embellish, decorate.

aparato s. m. display, grandeur, pomp, state, swank, ostentation, pageant.

exibir grande ~ to make a great display.

aparatoso adj. 1. sumptuous, ostentatious, showy, swanky, purple. 2. magnificent. ‖ **-amente** adv. ostentatiously.

aparceirar v. 1. to admit s. o. as a partner. 2. ~-**se** to enter into a society, become a member or partner.

aparcelado (I) adj. arranged in parcels, parts or shares.

aparcelado (II) adj. full of reefs (sea).

aparcelamento s. m. parcel(l)ing: division into parcels or shares.

aparcelar v. to parcel: separate, divide in parcels, bits, parts, shares.

aparecente adj. m. + f. beginning to apear.

aparecer v. 1. to appear, show up, turn up, show one's face. 2. to come to sight, emerge. 3. to begin. 4. to arise. 5. to peer out. 6. to occur; happen. 7. to supervene; dawn; exude.

~ **inesperadamente** to appear, turn up unexpectedly; fall in upon. **apareceu uma nova edição** a new edition has come out. **ele estava aparecendo** he was forthcoming. **finalmente você torna a aparecer** do you put in an appearance at last! **há tempo que você não aparece!** you are making yourself very scarce; you are quite a stranger! **nunca mais apareça aqui!** never show your face again! **o livro perdido não apareceu mais** the lost book has not turned up again. **quem não aparece se esquece** out of sight, out of mind.

aparecido adj. appeared, emerged.

aparecimento s. m. emersion, emergence, appearing, appearance, uprising, forthcoming; apparition.

aparelhado adj. 1. prepared, ready; arranged, disposed; apt, fit. 2. harnessed (horse). 3. plained off, smoothened.

cavalo bem ~ a well-harnessed horse.

aparelhador s. m. construction foreman; rigger, fitter, preparer.

aparelhagem s. f. (pl. **-ens**) 1. implements, tools, equipments. 2. act of planing (wood). 3. a complex of tackles, gears.

aparelhamento s. m. 1. equipment, apparatus. 2. outfit. 3. rig; fig. 4. caparison.

aparelhar v. 1. to equip, fit, outfit, furnish. 2. to prepare. 3. to prime, trim. 4. to dress. 5. to finish (lumber). 6. to rough-hew, cut (stone) 7. to harness (horse). 8. to put to sea.

aparelhável adj. m. + f. (pl. **-áveis**) that can be equipped, prepared.

aparelho s. m. 1. equipment, arrangement, preparation. 2. apparatus, device, implement, gadget; tool, instrument. 3. block and pulley. 4. (naut.) rigging. 5. harness (horse). 6. fishing implements. 7. service, set of dishes, plates. 8. bandage; dressing. 9. (Braz.) telephone.

~ **de alimentação** (tech.) feeding arrangement. ~ **de barbear** safety-razor (plate B 7). ~ **de chá** tea-service. ~ **de pedras** (constr.) stone bond (plate A 7). ~ **digestivo** (anat.) digestive system. ~ **para desinfetar** deodorizer. ~ **telefônico** telephone receiver. ~ **transmissor** radio transmitting set. ~ **visual** (anat.) sight organs. **ele está no** ~ he is on the telephone.

aparência s. f. 1. appearance, aspect. 2. semblance. 3. likelihood, likeness. 4. shape, cast, form, seeming.

~ **enganosa** false appearance, feint. ~ **estranha** strange appearance, sight. ~ **exterior** (fig.) outward appearance. **as** ~**s enganam** appearances are deceptive. **com ele tudo é** ~ he puts up a big front. **de boa** ~ good-looking, well-favoured. **ele é de má** ~ he is ill-favoured, not much of a looker. **eles tentam salvar as** ~**s** they try to keep up appearances. **julgar pela** ~ to judge from outward appearances, by the outside. **sob a** ~ **de santo** under the cloak of sanctity.

aparentado adj. 1. connected, kin, agnate, related. 2. allied.

não ~ unrelated. **a compaixão é -a ao amor** pity is akin to love.

aparentar (I) v. to become related by marriage, to establish kinship, be united by kindred.

aparentar (II) v. 1. to pretend, to make look like, give the appearance of, to feign; to simulate, to affect. 2. to have the appearance of.

~ **indiferença** to affect indifference. **ele não aparenta a sua idade** he does not show his age.

aparente adj. m. + f. 1. apparent, that gives the appearance of, seeming. 2. semblable, evident, manifest, obvious. ‖ ~**mente** adv. apparently, seemingly.

~**mente bom** well-seeming. **apenas** ~**mente** in name only.

aparição s. f. (pl. **-ões**) 1. appearance, apparition, revenant. 2. vision, sight. 3. origin.

aparo s. m. 1. act or fact of clipping, cropping, paring. 2. pen point, nib.

aparoquiado adj. that turned parochial.

aparoquiar-se v. to turn o. s. parochial, settle in a parish.

aparrado adj. 1. like a grapevine leaf. 2. squat, stocky, chunky, dumpy.

aparreirado adj. fenced in with vines.

aparreirar v. 1. to surround or cover with vines. 2. to plant vines.

aparta s. f. (ant.) partition, diving, division.

apartação, apartada s. f. (pl. **-ões**) 1. separation. 2. (Braz.) act of putting aside cattle.

apartado adj. 1. astray, deviate, out of the way. 2. separated, secluded. 3. distant, far-away, at a great distance. ‖ **-amente** adv. separately.

apartador s. m. separator, person who or thing that separates. ‖ adj. separating, dividing.

apartamento (I) s. m. separation, division.

apartamento (II) s. m. flat (England), apartment (USA). **prédio de ~s** tenement house.

apartar v. 1. to separate, part, divide, seclude. 2. to alienate, estrange. 3. to discriminate. 4. to disjoin. 5. to reserve, set aside. 6. **~-se:** a) to get away from, move away from. b) to divorce. c) to straggle. d) to detach, estrange, retire. **~ o grão da palha** (also fig.) to separate the tares from the wheat. **~ uma briga** to settle a quarrel, to separate the quarrelers. **~-se do assunto principal** to digress.

aparte (I) s. m. incidental remark; an aside.

aparte (II) s. m. (Braz.) = **apartação.**

apartear v. to interrupt an orator or speaker.

apartista s. m. + f. interrupter, person used to interrupt another's talk, especially a speaker. ‖ adj. interrupting (a speaker).

aparvalhado adj. stupid, foolish, idiotical; confused, bewildered, puzzled.

aparvalhamento s. m. act or fact of confusing, puzzling; bewilderment.

aparvalhar v. to make a fool of, to confuse, confound, puzzle.

aparvoado adj. stupid, foolish.

aparvoar v. to become stupid, idiotic.

apascentador s. m. herdsman, cattle herder.

apascentamento s. m. pasturing, herding. **direito de ~** pasturage.

apascentar v. 1. to take to pasture, to herd, feed. 2. (fig.): a) to doctrinate. b) to be a sight to the eyes. 3. **~-se** to delight in, revel in, take pleasure in.

apassamanado adj. adorned with passementeries, laced, braided.

apassamanar v. to lace, braid, adorn with passementeries.

apassionar v. (ant.) = **apaixonar.**

apassivação s. f. (pl. **-ões**) act or fact of changing to the passive.

apassivado adj. (gram.) used in the passive.

apassivador adj. (gram., also **apassivante** m. + f.) rendering passive.

apassivamento s. m. act or fact of changing to the passive.

apassivar v. 1. (gram.) to change to the passive. 2. **~-se** to become passive.

apastorar v. to pasture, herd.

apatacado adj. (Braz.) having plenty of **patacas** (silver coins); rich.

apatetado adj. 1. demented (person). 2. foolish, simple, dazed, doltish, doting.

apatetamento s. m. foolishness, foolish behaviour.

apatetar v. to make foolish, silly, to besot.

apatia s. f. apathy: insensibility, indifference, indolence.

apático adj. 1. apathetic, torpid. 2. cool; indifferent. ‖ **apaticamente** adv. apathetically, lethargically.

apatifar v. 1. to make a rogue of. 2. **~-se** to become despicable, scurvy, be a rascal.

apatita s. f. (min.) apatite.

apatizar v. to turn apathetic, indifferent.

apátrida s. m. + f. war refugee, displaced person.

apatronar v. (Braz.) to lasso, catch with a lasso (cattle).

apaulado adj. marshy, paludous, fenny, moorish.

apaular v. to transform in marshland, tideland, render marshy.

apaulistado adj. like a **paulista,** like a native of the State of São Paulo.

apavesar v. (also **empavesar**) to deck out.

apavonar v. (also **empavonar**) to fill with pride, to cock, strut.

apavorado adj. panic-stricken, panic-driven, terrified, appalled.

apavorador adj. fearful, terrifying, appalling.

apavoramento s. m. act or fact of appalling, dismaying.

apavorante adj. m. + f. **apavorador.**

apavorar v. to frighten, terrify, appal, horrify, shock, dismay.

apazeiro s. m. (bot.) wallaba (Eperua falcata).

apaziguado adj. pacified, appeased, calmed. ‖ **-amente** adv. peaceably.

apaziguador s. m. peacemaker, mollifier, appeaser, pacificator. ‖ adj. peacemaking.

apaziguamento s. m. peacemaking, placation, appeasement, pacification.

apaziguante adj. m. + f. appeasing, pacifying. ‖ **~mente** adv. appeasingly.

apaziguar v. 1. to pacify, appease, reconcile. 2. to calm, quiet, mollify. 3. to disarm; settle. 4. to placate. 5. to accommodate. 6. **~-se** to subside, calm down.

apé s. m. (Braz.) victoria regia, royal water lily.

apê s. m. (Braz.) plant of the family Araceae.

apeadeira s. f. horse-block used to mount a horse.

apeadeiro s. m. casual railroad stop.

apealar v. (Braz.) to rope, lasso.

apeamento s. m. act or fact of dismounting (horse).

apeanhado adj. like a pedestal (as of a cross).

apear v. 1. to put or help down (as from a car or cart). 2. to deprive of; depose; discharge, dismiss. 3. to dismount (from a horse). 4. to alight from. 5. to put up at (as at a hotel), to pass or stay for the night.

apecu s. m. (Braz.) a crown of sand formed by the sea.

apecuitá s. m. (Braz.) Indian paddle.

apeçonhar v. to poison.

apedantado adj. pedantic, priggish.

apedantar v. to turn pedantic.

apedeuta s. m. + f., **apedeuto** m. ignorant, unlearned person.

apedeutismo s. m. ignorance.

apedicelado adj. (bot.) pedicellate.

apedido s. m. (Braz., journalism) 1. statement published with full responsibility of its author. 2. letter to the editor.

apedrar v. 1. to stone, throw stones. 2. to enchase, mount, set with precious stones. 3. to ornament. 4. to harden.

apedregulhar v. to gravel: cover with crushed gravel.

apedrejado adj. hurt by stones, stoned, lapidated.

apedrejador s. m. lapidator.

apedrejamento s. m. stoning, lapidation.

apedrejar v. 1. to stone, lapidate. 2. to pepper. 3. (fig.) to insult, offend; abuse of, upbraid.

apegação s. f. (pl. **-ões**) 1. sympathy, attachment. 2. (obs., jur.) seizing.

apegadiço adj. 1. sticky, viscous. 2. becoming easily attached; making friends easily. 3. sticking to a person, run after a person.

apegado adj. 1. stuck or fastened to. 2. neighbouring. 3. attached, affectionate.

apegar (I) v. 1. to attach, infect, transmit by contagion. 2. **~-se:** a) to stick, adhere, cleave, cling to. b) to take hold of, grasp; to dedicate o. s. c) to insist stubbornly upon. d) to be very fond of, become rather attached to. e) to become entangled.

apegar (II) v. to sink, submerge.

apego (ê) s. m. 1. affection, strong attachment, fondness. 2. adherence, adhesion. 3. obstinacy, insistence. 4. beam of a plough.

apeguilho s. m. dim. of **apego.**

apeíba s. f. (Braz.) plant of the family Tiliaceae.

apeiragem s. f. (pl. **-ens**) 1. yoke (for oxen). 2. farm implements.

apeirar v. to yoke to an oxcart.

apeiro s. m. farm implements, including harnesses and tools.

apejar-se v. (also **pejar-se**) to fill, encumber.

apelação s. f. (pl. **-ões**) **apelamento** m. 1. appeal, appelation. 2. recourse, resort. 3. (fig.) expedient, shift. 4. act of calling.
sem ~ without appeal or resource.

apelado s. m. (jur.) appellee, one against whom an appeal is taken. ‖ adj. appealed.

apelante s. m. + f. appellant, appealer. ‖ adj. appealing.

apelar v. 1. to appeal, solicit, plead. 2. to retrace (as a lawsuit). 3. to ask or cry for help or assistance. 4. ~-se to have the name of.
~ **de uma corte inferior para uma superior** to appeal from an inferior to a superior court. ~ **para a humanidade** to appeal to humanity. ~ **solenemente** to conjure.

apelativo adj. (gram.) appellative. ‖ **-amente** adv. appellatively.

apelatório adj. of or referring to an appeal(er).

apelável adj. m. + f. (pl. **-áveis**) appealable.

apelidação s. f. (pl. **-ões**) imposition of a name, cognomination.

apelidar v. to cognominate, nickname; name, denominate.

apelido s. m. 1. surname, byname, family name, cognomen. 2. nickname, epithet. 3. denomination.

apelintrado adj. rough-mannered, vulgar.

apelo (ê) s. m. 1. appellation, appeal, plea. 2. call (as for assistance). 3. invocation.
fazer um ~ to make a plea.

apenar v. to impose a fine on; to embargo.

apenas adv. 1. scarcely, hardly. 2. only, merely, barely, (nothing) but, alone. 3. just.
~ **uma gota de água no oceano** but a drop in a bucket. **diga-me** ~ just tell me. **se é** ~ **isso** if it is only that. **você** ~ **tinha saído, quando** you had scarcely left, when.

apenável adj. m. + f. punishable.

apender v. (also **apensar**) to annex, append.

apêndice s. m. (also anat., zool.) 1. appendix. 2. supplement, appendage (plate F 5). 3. annexment, addendum.

apendiceado adj. provided with an appendix or annexment.

apendicectomia s. f. (med.) appendicectomia.

apendiciforme adj. m. + f. appendiciform: having the form of an appendix.

apendicite s. f. (med.) appendicitis: inflammation of the appendix.

apendiculado adj. (bot.) that ends in an appendix.

apendicular adj. (anat., zool.) appendicular.

apendículo s. m. appendicle.

apendoamento s. m. act of flagging, decoration with flags.

apendoar v. 1. to provide with pennants, flags. 2. to grow tassels (maize).

apenedado adj. rocky, stony; craggy, cliffy.

apenhado adj. rocky, full of cliffs.

apenhascado adj. rocky, craggy, cliffy, having the form of a massive rock.

apeninsulado adj. having the form of a peninsula.

apensamento s. m. act of appending, annexing a document.

apensar v. to join, add, append, annex.

apenso s. m. enclosure, thing annexed. ‖ adj. joined, enclosed, attached, annexed, appended, appendant.

apepinar v. to ridicule, deride, laugh at, scoff, mock.

apepsia s. f. (med.) apepsia, indigestion.

apéptico adj. referring to apepsia.

apequenado adj. 1. smallish, low. 2. modest.

apequenar v. 1. to make smaller, diminish. 2. to depress; lower; debase.

aperado adj. (Braz.) 1. harnessed, dressed up (horse). 2. (fig.) well-dressed.

aperaltado adj. dandyish, foppish.

aperaltar, aperalvilhar v. 1. to give manners of a dandy. 2. ~-se to become a dandy.

aperana s. f. (Braz.) plant of the family Gencianaceae, a floating heart.

aperar v. 1. to harness, dress up (horse). 2. ~-se (fig.) to dress o. s. well.

aperceber v. 1. to prepare, fit, adapt. 2. to warn, inform, notify. 3. to prevent, prelude. 4. to perceive, understand. 5. to distinguish. 6. to provide. 7. ~-se to feel, become aware of.

apercebimento s. m. 1. preparation; adaptation. 2. perception. 3. precaution. 4. supply. 5. warning, preventing.

apercepção s. f. (pl. **-ões**) 1. (psych.) apperception. 2. clear perception of an object. 3. intuition, insight.

aperceptibilidade s. f. perceptibility, perceivableness.

aperceptível adj. m. + f. (pl. **-íveis**) perceptible, perceivable. ‖ **aperceptivelmente** adv. perceptively.

apereá s. m. (Braz., zool., also **preá**) cavy.

aperema s. m. (Braz.) turtle of the family Testudinideae.

aperfeiçoado adj. improved, polished, ameliorated.

aperfeiçoador s. m. improver, perfecter, meliorater, completer, accomplisher, finisher. ‖ adj. ameliorant, perfective, improving.

aperfeiçoamento s. m. perfection, improvement; progress; melioration, betterment, amendment.
curso de ~ refresher course.

aperfeiçoar v. 1. to improve on (upon), to perfect, meliorate, better, amend, complete. 2. to polish, finish, refine. 3. to elaborate. 4. ~-se to improve in.

aperfeiçoável adj. m. + f. (pl. **-áveis**) ameliorable, perfectible, amendable.

apergaminhado adj. parchmentlike.

apergaminhar v. to parchmentize.

aperiente adj. m. + f. (also **aperitivo**) aperitive.

aperiódico adj. (electr. + phys.) aperiodic.

aperispérmico adj. (bot.) aperispermic, having no perisperm.

aperitivo s. m. aperitif; short drink; appetizer; ‖ adj. aperitive, stimulating the appetite.

apero (ê) s. m. (pl. **aperos**) (Braz.) harness, trappings (horse).

aperolar v. to give a pearly shape or colour.

aperrar v. to cock (a firearm).

aperreação s. f. (pl. **-ões**) (also **aperreamento, aperreio** m.) 1. act or fact of cocking (a firearm). 2. (Braz.): a) pressure, difficulty. b) vexation.

aperreado adj. 1. oppressed. 2. living or being in financial difficulties. 3. (Braz.) thin or weak. 4. dreary, sad. 5. vexed.

aperreador s. m. cause of torment or oppression. ‖ adj. oppressive, harassing; tormentous.

aperrear v. 1. to chase or pursue with dogs. 2. to harass, vex. 3. to check, curb. 4. to cock (a gun).

apertadela s. f. squeeze: act or fact of squeezing, compressing.

apertado s. m. (Braz.) defile, narrow pass, gorge. ‖ adj. 1. narrow. 2. compressed. 3. scarce. 4. hurried, hasty. 5. (Braz.) close, stuffy. 6. oppressive. 7. severe. 8. rigorous, strict. 9. in financial difficulties.

apertador s. m. tightener; buckle; clincher, clamp; bodice. ‖ adj. tightening.

apertadouro s. m. 1. place where one tightens. 2. belt, band, girth or the like used for tightening; bodice.

aperta-nervos s. m., sg. + pl. (typogr.) band nippers.

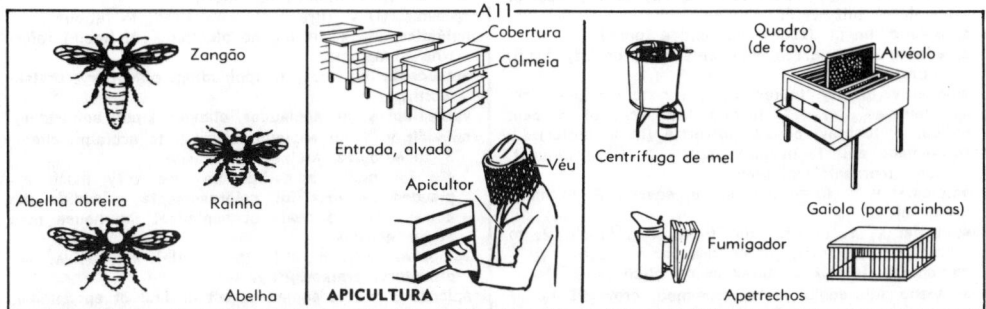

Zangão · Cobertura · Colmeia · Quadro (de favo) · Alvéolo · Entrada, alvado · Apicultor · Véu · Centrífuga de mel · Abelha obreira · Rainha · Gaiola (para rainhas) · Fumigador · Abelha · **APICULTURA** · Apetrechos · A 11

apertão s. m. (pl. **-ões**) 1. a strong pressure or squeeze. 2. a lot of people, a crowd.
um ~ de gente an enormous crowd.

apertar v. 1. to compress, squeeze, press; pinch. 2. to straiten, narrow, tighten; confine, limit, constrict, restrict, restrain; diminish; shorten, abbreviate. 3. to hold fast, grasp, seize. 4. to afflict, grieve, distress. 5. to hurry, hasten, expedite, speed, push on. 6. to insist. 7. (Braz.) to bind, tie, join. 8. **~-se:** a) to worry. b) to crowd.
~ a bolsa, ~ as despesas to restrict expenses. **~ a mão** to shake hands. **~ o cinto** (fig.) to tighten one's belt. **~ o passo** to double one's pace. **~ um parafuso** to tighten a screw. **apertamo-lo até confessar** we screwed it out of him. **cada um sabe onde lhe aperta o sapato** everyone knows where the shoe pinches. **o calor está -ando** the heat is increasing.

aperta-ruão s. m. (pl. **aperta-ruões**) (Braz.) name of a plant of the family Piperaceae.

apertinente adj. m. + f. conciliatory.

aperto (ê) s. m. (pl. **apertos**) (also **apertura**) 1. squeeze. 2. pressure, stress. 3. tightness, straitness, narrowness. 4. haste, dispatch, speed, hurry. 5. crowd, throng. 6. jam, distress, pinch, scrape, trouble, dilemma. 7. narrow passage. 8. need. 9. penury, destitution. 10. affliction. 11. austerity, exigence, exigency.
dei-lhe um ~ de mão I shook hands with him, I gave his hand a wring. **na hora do ~ todo o mundo fugiu** when trouble started, everyone ran away. **estar em ~** to be in great straits. **estou num ~** I am in a fix, up a tree. **ele está em ~s financeiros** he is hard up for money.

aperuação s. f. (Braz.) a looking on from the outside (game, play).

aperuar v. (Braz.) to look on (at a game or something else) from the outside.

apesar de prepositional locution: in spite (of), despite, although, notwithstanding, though.
~ de ele estar resfriado in spite of his cold. **~ de todos os seus defeitos, ainda gostamos dele** for all his faults we like him still. **~ de ver o perigo, ele ficou** though he saw the danger, he stayed. **~ de tudo** after all, for all that, all the same. **~ de treinar muito, não melhorou** he is none the better for his hard training.

apesarar v. to become sorry, sorrowful, to sadden.

apesentar v. to become heavy or weighty.

apessoado adj. good-looking, well-shaped.

apestanado adj. having eyelashes.

apestar v. (also **empestar**) to infect with pest, to plague.

apetalifloro adj. (bot.) having flowers without corolla.

apétalo adj. (bot.) apetalous.

apetecedor adj. appetizing, desiring.

apetecer v. 1. to have an appetite for. 2. to desire, hunger for. 3. to suit, gratify, please.
não me apetece comida alguma no meat relishes with me. **não me apetece o trabalho hoje** I do not feel like working to-day.

apetecível adj. m. + f. (pl. **-íveis**) 1. desirable, tempting. 2. suitable.

apetência s. f. (also **apetite**) appetency, appetite.

apetente adj. m. + f. appetizing, desirable, appreciable.

apetitar v. 1. to appetize. 2. to arouse a desire for.

apetite s. m. 1. appetite, volition to eat, hunger, appetence. 2. desire, lust, craving for.
falta de ~ inappetence. **perder o ~** to lose one's appetite.

apetitivo adj. appetitive, appetizing.

apetitoso adj. appetizing, lickerish, savoury, desirable. ‖ **-amente** adv. appetizingly.

apetrechar v. to equip, provide, supply, fit out.

apetrecho s. m. supplies, equipments, provisions, fixings, outfit, implements, appliances (plate A 11).
~ de pesca fishing tackle.

apezinhar v. = **espezinhar.**

apiabar v. (Braz.) to lend money (gambling).

apiançado adj. (Braz., pop., also **asmático**) asthmatic.

apiançar v. (Braz., pop.) to crave for, desire ardently.

apiari s. m. (Braz.) a certain fresh-water fish.

apiário s. m. apiary. ‖ adj. apiarian.

apiastro s. m. (bot., also **erva-cidreira**) lemon balm; garden balm; balm mint; bee balm.

apicaçar v. (also **espicaçar**) to prick, sting; spur, goad.

apicado adj. apical: having an apex; topped.

apical adj. m. + f. (pl. **-ais**) that ends in an apex, apical. ‖ **~mente** adv. apically.

ápice s. m. 1. apex, vertex, top, summit (plates A 12, E 1, F 5). 2. (fig.) pink; climax.

apichar-se v. (Braz.) to become frightened, scared.

apicida adj. m. + f. causing the death of bees.

apicifloro adj. (bot.) having terminal flowers.

apiciforme adj. m. + f. having the form of an apex or a top.

apicoado (I) adj. pared down roughly.

apicoado (II) adj. (Braz.) vertical, cut vertically.

apicoar v. to pare down as with a chisel or an axe.

apícola s. m. + f. apiarist. ‖ adj. apiculate, apicultural.

apicuí s. m. (Braz., also **rola-cabocla**) talpacoti: a small wild dove (Chamaepelia talpacoti).

apiculado adj. ending in a sharp point, apiculate.

apículo s. m. (also **apícula** f.) sharp point, apiculus.

apicultor s. m. apiculturist, beekeeper, apiarist (plate A 11).

apicultura s. f. apiculture, beekeeping (plate A 11)

apicum s. m. (pl. **-uns**) (also **apicu**) (Braz.) bog or marsh of salt water.

apídeos s. m. pl. (zool.) the Apidae (bees).

apiedador s. m. person who feels sorry or pity. ‖ adj. feeling sorry for.

apiedar v. to pity, to feel sorry for, to condole with.

apiforme adj. m. + f. having the form of a bee.

apiloar v. to bray, pound, pulverize (in a mortar).

apimentado adj. 1. peppery, spicy. 2. (fig.) piquant, sharp, mordant; malicious.

apimentar v. 1. to pepper, spice, season. 2. to make piquant.

apincelar v. 1. to give the form of a brush. 2. to paint with a brush; to whitewash; to daub.

apinchar v. (Braz.) to throw away; pitch.

apinhado adj. agglomerate, crammed, crowded.
~ **de gente** crowded with people.

apinhar, apinhoar v. 1. to pile up, heap up; agglomerate; to fill, fill up, to overcrowd. 2. ~-**se to** cluster, form into a bunch, stick close together, crowd together.

apióide adj. m. + f. 1. unsullied, pure, clean. 2. (med.) not purulent.

apiol s. m. (chem.) apiole; parsley camphor.

apipado adj. pipe-shaped, barrel-shaped.

apipar v. to give the shape of a pipe or barrel to.

apirético adj. (med.) apyretic: having fever.

apirexia s. f. (med.) apyrexia: cessation of fever.

ápiro adj. apyrous: resistant to fire.

apisoamento s. m. 1. act or fact of fulling or milling cloth. 2. act or fact of tramping.

apisoar v. 1. to full or mill cloth. 2. to tramp (soil, earth).

apisteiro s. m. vase or cup to give soup to a sick person.

apisto s. m. 1. substantial soup for sick persons. 2. (fig.) comfort.

apitar v. 1. to whistle. 2. to blow the whistle. 3. to toot. 4. (Braz., pop.) to die. 5. (Braz., ftb.) to referee.

apito s. m. whistle: 1. the instrument. 2. the sound.
~ **a vapor** steam whistle.

apívoro adj. apivorous: eating bees.

aplacação s. f. (pl. **-ões**) placation, soothing, appeasement.

aplacador s. m. placater; pacifier. ‖ adj. appeasing, soothing.

aplacar v. 1. to placate. 2. to tranquilize, quiet. 3. to render serene, calm. 4. to soften, appease, mitigate, assuage. 5. to pacify. 6. ~-**se** to calm down.

aplacável adj. m. + f. (pl. **-áveis**) appeasable, placable, propitiable.

aplainado adj. 1. (carp.) planed. 2. level, even, smooth.

aplainador s. m. (carp.) planer. ‖ adj. smoothing, levelling.

aplainamento s. m. 1. (carp.) planing. 2. smoothing, grading, flattening, levelling.

aplainar v. 1. to plane off (with a carpenter's plane). 2. to level, smooth, grade; even, flatten. 3. to remove difficulties, clear the way, facilitate.

aplanado adj. = **aplainado** 2.

aplanador s. m. 1. level(l)er, equalizer. 2. (fig.) smoother, facilitater. 3. (tech.) flattener, set hammer.

aplanamento s. m. (also **aplanação** f.) 1. levelling, equalization. 2. removal of difficulties, disembarrassment.

aplanar v. 1. to level, equalize. 2. to remove difficulties, disembarrass, facilitate.

aplasia s. f. (med.) aplasia.

aplastado (I) adj. (naut.) unfurled, flying (flags or sails).

aplastado (II) adj. (Braz.) tired, worn out.

aplastar (I) v. (naut.) to unfurl.

aplastar (II) v. (Braz.) to grow tired; to fatigue.

aplástico adj. 1. having no plasticity. 2. (med.) referring to aplasia.

aplaudente adj. m. + f. applauding, plauditory, praiseworthy.

aplaudidor s. m. applauder, clapper. ‖ adj. applauding.

aplaudir v. 1. to applaud, clap. 2. to acclaim, cheer. 3. to eulogize, praise, extol, laud.
ele foi muito aplaudido he was very much applauded. **a atriz foi calorosamente aplaudida** the actress evoked peals of applause, the house rose at the actress.

aplausível adj. m. + f. (pl. **-íveis**) applausive, approbatory, praiseworthy.

aplauso s. m. 1. applause, act or fact of applauding; acclamation, cheering. 2. laudation, praise, approval.
receber ~**s** (theat.) to get applause.

aplebear-se v. to acquire manners of a plebeian.

aplestia s. f. insatiable appetite.

aplicabilidade s. f. applicability, applicableness; relevancy, relevance; workability.

aplicação s. f. (pl. **-ões**) 1. application. 2. adaptation; accommodation, suiting. 3. appointment; utilization, usage, destiny. 4. diligence, attention, perseverance and concentration in studying. 5. (Braz.) a) laces, lacework. b) a sort of embroidery.

aplicado adj. 1. applied, employed, used for. 2. apposed. 3. diligent, hard-working; attentive.
bem ~ well-applied, well-employed, well-directed.

aplicante s. m. + f. applier. ‖ adj. applicant, applicatory.

aplicar v. 1. to apply, put into practice. 2. to prescribe (a remedy). 3. to adapt, appose. 4. to superpose. 5. to employ. 6. to inflict. 7. to attribute, impute, adjudge. 8. to impose. 9. to destine, appoint. 10. to accommodate. 11. to suit, fit. 12. to put, set, place. 13. to consecrate, dedicate. 14. ~-**se**: a) to be applied to. b) to exert o. s., be diligent.
~ **água** to apply water. ~ **com algodão** (med.) to apply with cotton-wool, to swab. ~ **força bruta** to use violence, slug it out. ~ **mal** to misapply. ~ **métodos comerciais** to use commercial methods, commercialize. ~ **o bom senso** to resource to sound judgement. ~ **o ouvido** to listen carefully. ~ **sanguessugas** to leech. ~ **um remédio** to administer a medicine. ~-**se com vigor** to exert o. s., lay out. **isto não se aplica ao caso** that does not suit the case. **isto também se aplica a você** that goes for you too.

aplicável adj. m. + f. (pl. **-áveis**; also **aplicativo**) applicable, applicative, applicatory, exercisable; adaptable; apposable.

aplique s. m. (Fr.) appliqué; a decoration or ornamental application on a wall surface; a wall sconce.

aplúvio s. m. accumulation of detritus transported by rainwater.

apnéia s. f. (med.) apnea, apnoea.

apnéico adj. apneal, referring to apnea.

apo s. m. plow beam (plate C 13).

Apocalipse s. m. 1. Apocalypse. 2. (fig.) incomprehensible language.

apocalíptico, apocalítico adj. 1. apocalyptic, referring to the Apocalypse. 2. (fig.) difficult to understand; obscure.

apocatástase s. f. (astr.) periodical revolution of a star.

apocináceas s. f. pl. (bot.) the Apocynaceae.

apocopado adj. (gram.) having the last letter or syllable suppressed by apocope.

apocopar v. (gram.) to apocopate.

apócope s. f. (gram.) apocope: omission of the last letter or syllable.

apócrifo adj. apocryphal.

apodador s. m. punster, jester, banterer, joker, scoffer, derider. ‖ adj. playful, mocking, jeering, derisive.

apodar v. 1. to jest; taunt. 2. to deride; call names. 3. to nickname, dub. 4. to stigmatize: 5. to qualify. 6. to compare. 7. to assimilate. 8. to esteem, to guess by sight.
apodaram-nos com ovelhas they compared us with sheep.

ápode adj. m. + f. apodal; without feet.

apodengado adj. (also podenga) like a harrier or rabbit hound.

apoderar-se v. to take possession, possess; to grabble, appropriate, seize, take hold of.
~ de to catch hold of. ~ de alguma coisa to seize upon. ~ do dinheiro to seize the money. o pavor apoderou-se dele he was seized by awe.

apodia s. f. devoidness of feet.

apodíctico, apodítico adj. apodictical, evident, clear, convincing, incontestable.

apodioxe s. f. (rhet.) (also apodixe) apodixis.

apodo s. m. (pl. apodos) 1. ridiculous comparison. 2. banter, derision. 3. mockery. 4. cognomen, nickame.

apódose s. f. (gram.) apodosis.

apodrecer v. (also ~-se, apodrentar) 1. to corrupt, to spoil morally. 2. to putrefy, decompose, rot, canker.

apodrecido adj. rotten, putrefied.

apodrecimento s. m. 1. putrefaction, organical decomposition. 2. (fig.) corruption, perversion.

apodrido adj. 1. beginning to decay. 2. spoiled, putrefied.

apodrir v. to start to rot, putrefy or decompose.

apoético adj. 1. antipoetic, opposed to poetry. 2. unpoetic.

apófige s. f. (archit.) apophyge.

apófise s. f. (anat.) apophysis: eminence of a bone
~ espinhosa apophyseal process of the spine. ~ estilóide (anat.) styloid process (plate C 17).

apofisiário adj. referring to apophysis.

apofonia s. f. (gram.) apophony, (German) ablaut.

apogamia s. f. (biol.) apogamy, apomixis.

apogeu s. m. apogee: 1. the greatest distance of the moon from the earth. 2. (fig.) the highest degree or point, peak of glory.
em seu ~ at his zenith. no ~ da mocidade in the hey-day of youth.

apogístico adj. apogeal, apogean, referring to the apogee.

apográfico adj. referring to an apograph.

apógrafo s. m. reproduction, copy of a piece of writing, apograph, transcript.

apoiado s. m. applause, acclamation, shout of approval. ‖ adj. 1. supported, backed, upborne. 2. approved. 3. reclining. ‖ interj. very good!

apoiar v. 1. to support. 2. to stay, sustain, prop, uphold. 3. to make firm. 4. to carry, hold. 5. to favour, patronize, back; justify, confirm, encourage, enshield. 6. to applaud, acclaim, aprove. 7. to stick to. 8. ~-se (sobre, em, ao, à) to rest, lean (on, against); rely, depend on.
~ alguém num empreendimento to aid s. o. in a thing. ~ com almofada to bolster. ~ com consolo to bracket. ~ devidamente to give convenient support. ~-se à parede to lean against the wall.

apoio s. m. 1. base, basis, foundation; support, prop, stay, rest, backing (plates D 1, V 1). 2. protection, help, aid, patronage. 3. sustenance, stand-by; strength. 4. applause. 5. (archit.) supporter, support (plate P 14). 6. (moral) grip. 7. (fig.) anchorage, anchor.
barra de ~ stay bar. um forte ~ a strong support. sem ~ unprotected, in the air.

apojado adj. intumesced with a liquid (breasts with milk).

apojadura s. f. apojamento m., abundance of milk in the breasts or udder.

apojar v. to fill, swell, intumesce (as the breast or the udder).

apojatura s. f. (mus.) appoggiatura, a grace-note.

apojitaguara s. f. (Braz.) a tree of the family Rutaceae.

apojo (ô) s. m. (Braz.) aftermilk, strippings.

apolainado adj. having the form of leggings, puttees or gaiters.

apoldrado adj. having a colt (mare).
égua -a a mare that has a colt.

apolegar v. 1. to hurt or crumble with the fingers. 2. (anat.) to macerate.

apolentador s. m. person who feeds or fattens with polenta (Italian porridge).

apolentar v. to fatten (animals) with polenta (Italian porridge).

apólice s. f. policy, bond, stock, share.
~ de seguro insurance policy. ~s vinculadas trustee stock.

apolíneo, apolínico adj. Apolline, Apollonian: referring to or resembling Apollo.

apólise s. f. apolysis: final part of the Greek mass, corresponding to the "Ite, missa est" (Roman).

apolítico adj. nonpolitical, strange to politics.

apologal adj. m. + f. (pl. -ais) apologal: containing apologues, referring to apologues.

apologético adj. apologetic(al); excusatory, deprecatory, explanatory.

apologia s. f. apologismo m. 1. apology; discourse, speech to justify or defend. 2. encomium, high praise; eulogy.

apologista s. m. + f. apologist. ‖ adj. of or referring to an apologist.

apologizar v. 1. to defend or justify. 2. to apologize.

apólogo s. m. apologue, fiction, moral allegory.

apoltronar-se (I) v. to make o. s. comfortable in an armchair.

apoltronar-se (II) v. to become a coward, behave like a poltroon.

apolvilhar v. (also polvilhar) to powder dust.

apombocado adj. (Braz.) foolish, silly.

apomorfina s. f. (chem.) apomorphine.

aponeurologia s. f. (anat.) aponeurology.

aponeurose s. f. (anat.) aponeurosis.

aponeurótico adj. (anat.) aponeurotic.

aponogetonácea s. f. plant of the monocotyledonous. family.

apontado adj. 1. pointed, having a, or ending in a point. 2. indicated, noted.
não ~ unpointed.

apontador (I) s. m. 1. one who points or makes points (as of instruments). 2. (Braz.) pencil sharpener.

apontador (II) s. m. recorder, timekeeper.

apontamento s. m. 1. notice, annotation, note, entry. 2. sketch; jotting. 3. indication, reference.
caderno de ~s notebook. tomar ~s to take notes, make notes of.

apontar (I) v. 1. to point, sharpen. 2. to rise, appear, emerge (moon).

apontar (II) v. 1. to indicate, show; to mark, label. 2. to mention, speak of. 3. to cite, summon. 4. to allege, affirm. 5. to adduce, bring forward. 6. to register, make notes of. 7. to indicate, point at with the finger. 8. to designate. 9. to point out, point to. 10. to aim, take one's aim. 11. to prompt (actors).
~ alguém to point the finger at s. o. ~ os erros to show the mistakes. ~ para to point towards, aim at. ~ uma arma to point, level a gun. ~ uma letra

de câmbio to note a foreign bill. **ao ~ do dia** at daybreak.

apontável adj. m. + f. (pl. **-áveis**) 1. that can be pointed. 2. that can be shown.

apontoado adj. stitched or sewn together.

apontoar v. 1. to stitch, baste, sew. 2. to indicate, show, point out.

apopléctico, apoplético adj. 1. apoplectic(al), referring to apoplexy. 2. angry, excited.

apoplexia s. f. (med.) apoplexy, stroke.

apoquentação s. f. (pl. **-ões**) chagrin, trouble, bother, affliction, vexation; act or fact of worrying.

apoquentado adj. 1. afflicted, upset, troubled. 2. (fig.) tormented, tortured.

apoquentador s. m. 1. person who annoys; vexer, botherer, importuner. 2. cause of annoyance. ‖ adj. importunate; annoying; vexatious, irritating; impertinent.

apoquentar v. (also pop. **aporrinhar**) 1. to vex, annoy, torment, harry, pester. 2. to oppress; scourge. 3. to afflict, grieve, distress. 4. **~ -se** to get worried, upset.

ele apoquentou minha paciência he was trying my pacience. **não comece a me ~** don't get on my nerves.

apor v. 1. to put together or above. 2. to appose; affix, append. 3. to attach, enclose.

aporia s. f. aporia: hesitation, simulated doubt of an orator in the midst of a speech.

aporismar(-se) v. (also **apostemar**) to corrupt, spoil; putrefy, fester.

áporo s. m. 1. a hemipterous insect. 2. difficult problem.

aporreado adj. 1. belaboured, drubbed, beaten. 2. (fig.) bothered, pestered, vexed. 3. (Braz.) untamed or unruly (horse).

aporreamento s. m. 1. cudgel(l)ing, spanking, belabouring. 2. imperfect taming or training of a horse. 3. unruliness or viciousness of a horse on account of imperfect training.

aporrear v. 1. to belabour, drub, beat. 2. (fig.) to vex, annoy. 3. (S. Braz.) to break in a horse imperfectly. 4. to become vicious (horse) due to poor training.

aporrinhação s. f. (pl. **-ões**), **aporrinhamento** m. (pop.) annoyance, worry, vexation, disgust.

aportada s. f. (ant.) **aportamento** m. 1. (naut.) arrival at a port, a coming to anchor. 2. (fig.) arrival, entrance.

aportar v. 1. (naut.) to enter a port, arrive at a port, call at a port, cast anchor. 2. to take or carry something to a place. 3. to shore.

o navio aporta em Santos the ship calls at Santos.

aportelado adj. having a pass (between mountains).

aportilhar v. 1. to provide with loopholes. 2. to provide with embrasures.

aportuguesado adj. after the Portuguese fashion, the Portuguese way.

aportuguesamento s. m. act or fact of giving or taking Portuguese characteristics.

aportuguesar v. to give Portuguese characteristics to, render Portuguese in form or shape (esp. language).

eles aportuguesaram-se they took Portuguese ways and habits.

aportuguesável adj. m. + f. (pl. **-áveis**) susceptible to take Portuguese forms, ways, manners.

após adv. after, thereafter, behind. ‖ prep. after, behind.

~ isso thereon, thereafter, thereupon. **~ o recebimento** when received, upon receipt. **dia ~ dia** day after day. **logo ~** subsequently to. **um ~ o outro** one after another. **a vida ~ a morte** afterlife.

aposentado s. m. pensioner. ‖ adj. retired; emeritus.

aposentador s. m. 1. one who provides for retirement. 2. (obs.) person in charge of providing lodgings for the pensioners.

aposentadoria s. f., **aposentamento** m. (also **aposentação** f.) 1. old age pension; retirement; superannuation. 2. (obs.) lodgings.

caixa de ~ superannuation fund. **idade para ~** retirement age. **contribuição para a ~** superannuation money. **direito à ~** right to a pension.

aposentar v. 1. to receive as a guest, to lodge, give lodging to. 2. to pension off. 3. **~-se**: a) to retire from employment, to superannuate. b) to take lodgings, to room with, stay with.

ele foi aposentado he was pensioned off.

aposento s. m. 1. residence, dwelling, domicile. 2. apartment. 3. room. 4. shelter, lodgement.

aposição s. f. apposition: 1. (gram.) juxtaposition of a word beside another, as an attribute. 2. act of apposing, putting together.

aposiopese s. f. (rhet.) aposiopesis: intentional interruption in the midst of a phrase.

aposítico adj. (med.) apositic: causing loss of appetite.

apósito s. m. apposite: external remedy. ‖ adj. 1. fit, suitable, appropriate. 2. apposed.

apossar v. 1. to put in possession of. 2. **~-se** to take possession of; (S. Braz., also **apossear-se**; obs., **apossuir-se**) seize control of, take over.

apossínclise s. f. (gram.) insertion of a word between the verb and the unaccented pronoun. **a flor que lhe eu mandei** instead of **a flor que eu lhe mandei**.

aposta s. f. 1. wager, bet, betting. 2. stake, thing or amount wagered.

eu aceitei a ~ I took up the bet. **quanto vale a ~?** what will you bet? name your wager!

apostado adj. 1. wagered. 2. decided, determined, resolved. 3. resolute.

apostador s. m. better, backer, betting man. ‖ adj. betting.

apostar v. 1. to bet, make a bet, wager, lay a wager; to risk, game, play; stake; to sustain. 2. to be convinced of the victory of. 3. (ant.) to prepare, put in order.

~ em to lay one's bet on, to wager on, back. **~ no totalizador** to totalize: bet in a parimutual. **~ todo o seu dinheiro em** to bet one's shirt on. **~ dez cruzeiros num cavalo** to lay ten cruzeiros on a horse. **quanto quer ~?** what will you bet? **eu aposto que você não sabe fazê-lo!** I defy you to do it! **perder na ~** to bet away.

apóstase s. f. (med.) apostasis.

apostasia s. f. apostasy; lapse, renunciation.

apostásia s. f. a kind of orquids.

apóstata s. m. + f. apostate; renegade. ‖ adj. apostate, apostatical.

apostatar v. 1. to apostatize, revolt; desert, leave. 2. to change religion or party.

apostema s. m. (med.) aposteme, abscess, fester.

apostemar v. 1. to corrupt; putrefy. 2. to infect, form an abscess, fester. 3. to spoil.

apostemático adj. (also **apostemoso**) of or referring to an aposteme.

apostemeira s. f. (Braz.) a lot of apostemes.

apostemeiro s. m. (ant.) lancet to open abscesses.

apostila s. f. apostil(le), postil: addition or annotation to a script, supplementary note to an official diploma; comment; rider; postscript; marginal note.

apostilador s. m. person who makes apostilles, comments.

apostilar v. to write apostilles to, to make marginal notes; to annotate; to emend.

apostilha s. f. 1. mimeographed or typewritten texts for pupils (when books on that particular subject are not available). 2. (ant.) calumny, slander.
aposto (ô) s. m. (pl. apostos) (gram.) appositive. ‖ adj. (f. aposta, pl. apostas) adj. apposed, appositive.
apostolado s. m. 1. apostleship, apostolate. 2. a group of apostles. 3. propaganda of a doctrine.
apostolar v. (also apostolizar) 1. to preach. 2. to evangelize.
apostolicidade s. f. apostolicity, apostolicism; apostolic character; conformity with the doctrine of the apostles.
apostólico s. m. (ant.) the pope. ‖ adj. m. + f., (pl. -ais) (also apostolical) 1. apostolic(al); proceeding from the apostles. 2. papal.
apóstolo s. m. apostle: each of the twelve disciples of Christ.
apostrofar (I) v. (rhet.) to apostrophize; to direct, interrupt with apostrophes.
apostrofar (II) v. to insert apostrophes in a writing.
apóstrofe s. f. (rhet.) apostrophe: interruption.
apóstrofo s. m. (gram.) apostrophe (mark).
apostura (I) s. f. (naut.) riders.
apostura (II) s. f. carriage, deportment, bearing, politeness.
apotegma s. m. apothegm; aphorism; proverb.
apotegmático adj. apothegmatic(al).
apotegmatismo s. m. the use of apothegms.
apótema s. m. (math.) apothem.
apoteosar v. to apotheosize, exalt, deify, glorify.
apoteose s. f. apotheosis, deification, glorification.
apoteótico adj. 1. referring to an apotheosis. 2. (fig.) very eulogizing.
apótese s. f. (med.) apothesis: setting of a fractured bone (limb).
apótomo s. m. apotome: 1. (mus.) interval between two tones. 2. (math.) the difference between two imponderable quantities.
apotrar-se v. (S. Braz.) 1. to become skittish (horse). 2. to get angry.
apoucado adj. 1. faint-hearted, timid. 2. mean, stingy. 3. poorly developed, stunted. 4. belittled. 5. imbecilic.
apoucador s. m. person who lessens, diminishes. ‖ adj. belittling.
apoucamento s. m. 1. diminution; lessening. 2. humiliation. 3. meanness. 4. deficiency of energy.
apoucar v. 1. to reduce; diminish. 2. to belittle, minify; depreciate; disdain; to give little value to; to curtail. 3. ~-se to belittle o. s., undervalue o. s.
apoutar v. to cast stones (poutas) instead of an anchor to hinder small boats to be carried away.
apózema s. f. apozem, decoction of herbs, roots.
apragatar, aparagatar v. (Braz., pop.) to flatten, squash; crush.
apraxia s. f. (med.) apraxia.
aprazador s. m. person who fixes a respite; assigner, summoner; convener.
aprazamento s. m. act or fact of giving a respite; assignation appointment, a convening, summons, citation.
aprazar v. to convene, summon, cite, mark a day or an hour (as for a reunion); to convoke; designate; adjourn.
aprazer v. 1. to gratify, please. 2. ~-se to content o. s.; to be pleased.
apraz-me convidá-lo I am pleased to invite you.
aprazibilidade s. f. pleasantness, affability; kindness.
aprazimento s. m. liking, delight, contentment, pleasure, consentment.
aprazível adj. m. + f. (pl. -íveis) that pleases or delights, pleasant, delightful; diverting, amusing; said of a place with a beautiful view.

apre interj. fie! away! the devil!
apreçador s. m. 1. person who determines the price; appraiser, esteemer. 2. person who asks for or inquires prices. 3. bargainer.
apreçamento s. m. act or fact of esteeming or setting a price; pricing, appraisal.
apreçar v. 1. to price, determine the price of. 2. to ask for or determine prices. 3. to appraise, rate, esteem. 4. to barter, bargain, haggle.
apreciação s. f. (pl. -ões) 1. appreciation. 2. rating, valuation. 3. concept, idea. 4. recognition, esteem. 5. opinion. 6. analysis.
apreciador s. m. appraiser, appreciator.
apreciar v. 1. to appreciate. 2. to rate, compute, value; to estimate; to judge. 3. to admire, recognize the value of. 4. to esteem.
ele aprecia música he has a taste for music.
apreciativo adj. appreciating, appreciative.
apreciável adj. m. + f. (pl. -áveis) appreciable, deserving regard; considerable, remarkable. ‖ apreciavelmente adv. appreciably.
apreço (ê) s. m. 1. valuation, estimation. 2. deference, regard, esteem. 3. consideration.
o assunto em ~ the matter in question. temo-lo em grande ~ we think much of him. ter em ~ appreciate very much.
apreendedor s. m. apprehender, person who apprehends. ‖ adj. apprehending.
apreender v. 1. to make apprehension of, apprehend: a) arrest. b. confiscate, sequester. c) understand, perceive. d) fear (as death), dread. 2. to think hard, muse, ponder, brood. 3. to impound; carry off, capture; take, seize, catch.
apreensão s. f. 1. apprehension: a) act or fact of apprehending. b) arrest. c) seizure, capture; (law) attachment. d) understanding, conceiving. e) distrust as to the future. 2. pondering, brooding.
de fácil ~ easy to be understood.
apreensibilidade s. f. apprehensiveness, apprehensibility.
apreensível adj. m. + f. (pl. -íveis) apprehensible, that can be apprehended.
apreensivo adj. apprehensive, fearful; uneasy; jumpy, afraid.
apreensor s. m. apprehender, capturer. ‖ adj. that apprehends.
apreensório adj. that serves to apprehend; that serves to arrest.
aprefixar v. to prefix (words).
apregoado adj. divulged; proclaimed; well-known.
apregoador s. m. crier, proclaimer. ‖ adj. proclaiming, divulging.
apregoar v. 1. to announce by a crier, proclaim, make known, divulge. 2. to puff, boom, ballyhoo. 3. to publish the banns.
apremer v. 1. to press, compress. 2. to oppress.
aprender v. 1. to learn, study. 2. to come to know. ~ de cor to learn by heart, by rote, (coll.) get by heart. ~ por experiência própria (fig.) to learn from experience, (coll.) go through the mill. os meninos aprenderam a ler the boys were taught reading. por experiência se aprende experience teaches, experience is a sure guide.
aprendiz s. m. (pl. -izes) apprentice, novice, beginner. ~ de escritório office boy. trabalho de ~ prentice work. servir como ~ to serve one's articles.
aprendizado s. m., aprendizagem f. (pl. ~s, -ens) 1. apprenticeship, apprenticement. 2. (Braz.) trade school.
apresador s. m. person who apprehends, capturer. ‖ adj. apprehensible.
apresamento s. m. apprehension, act or fact of seizure, capture.

apresar v. 1. (also naut.) to capture. 2. to seize, apprehend. 3. to seize, grip, grab, clutch.

apresbiterar-se v. to take orders of a presbyter.

apresentação s. f. (pl. **-ões**) 1. presentation. 2. introduction. 3. letter of introduction. 4. bearing; personal appearance. 5. the getup, make-up (as of a merchandise). 6. suggestion. 7. showing (as of documents).
contra ~ (com.) on demand, on presentation. **de má** ~ of bad appearance. **festa da** ~ **de Nossa Senhora** the feast of the presentation of our Lady in the Temple.

apresentador s. m. person who presents or introduces. ‖ adj. presenting.

apresentante s. m. + f. bearer of a bill or a draft; presenter.

apresentar v. 1. to present: a) introduce. b) show. c) display. d) expose, exhibit. e) submit for consideration; propose. 2. to suggest, recommend, advise. 3. to announce. 4. **~-se**: a) to show up. b) to occur, come to mind. c) to seem, appear. ~ **o seu alibi** to establish one's alibi. ~ **um argumento** to put forward an argument. ~ **armas!** present arms! ~ **desculpas** to apologize. ~ **novamente** to re-present. ~ **seu pedido de demissão** to ask for one's leave, quit one's job. ~ **uma queixa** to enter an action, go to law. ~ **uma petição** to present, prefer a petition. ~ **um projeto de lei** to introduce a bill. **apreser 'amo-lo como candidato** we proposed him as a candidate. **o documento foi apresentado para assinatura** the document was submitted for signature. **novas dificuldades apresentaram-se** new difficulties arose. **como a ocasião se apresenta** as occasion offers. **uma vista estranha apresenta-se aos olhos** a strange sight greets the eyes.

apresentável adj. m. + f. (pl. **-áveis**) presentable; good-looking.

apresilhar v. to provide or secure with a cleat, to fasten with or as with a buckle or loop.

apressado adj. in a hurry, hurried; ready; hasty, speedy, quick; diligent; expeditious; precipitate; urgent. ‖ **-amente** adv. hastily.

apressador adj. speeding up, urging on.

apressar v. 1. to speed up, accelerate, hurry, quicken, make haste. 2. to stimulate, instigate, urge on, incite, insist with, to press. 3. to do with celerity. **~-se** to bustle, make haste; get moving. ~ **o passo** to quicken one's steps. **acho bom ~-nos** we should better make haste, we should get moving. **apressa-te!** hurry up! make haste! **ele não se apressa** he takes his time.

apresso (ê) s. m. (ant.) 1. tough situation, pinch. 2. haste, hurry.

apressurado adj. hurried, quick, speedy, hasty.

apressuramento s. m. precipitation; diligence; celerity, speed.

apressurar v. 1. to hurry, speed, hasten; press, urge. 2. **~-se**: a) to get ready with precipitation. b) to make haste.

aprestador s. m. person who makes ready; preparer.

aprestamento s. m. preparation, preparative, disposition; perceiving.

aprestar v. 1. to prepare, make ready. 2. to perceive. 3. to equip, furnish.

apresto s. m. 1. preparation, preparatory, preparative. 2. (mil.) equipment, equipage. 3. **~s** (pl.): a) furnishings. b) tools, implements. c) apparel.

aprilino adj. (also **abrilino**) Apriline: referring to April (month).

aprimorado adj. refined, excellent, fine, perfect, elegant; nicely made or performed; well done.

aprimoramento s. m. refinement: act or process of refining; the state of being refined; elegance of taste, manners, language; perfection, elaboration.

aprimorar v. to perfect, improve, ameliorate, refine, bring to perfection, accomplish.

apriorismo s. m. apriorism: a priori reasoning.

apriorista s. m. + f. apriorist: follower of a priori reasoning.

apriorístico adj. aprioristic, referring to apriorisms.

aprisco s. m. 1. sheepfold; pen. 2. shack, hut, shanty. 3. cave, den.

aprisionado adj. captive: 1. incarcerated, imprisoned, confined. 2. (fig.) captivated, charmed.

aprisionador s. m. imprisoner, captivator. ‖ adj. captive.

aprisionamento s. m. imprisonment, capture.

aprisionar v. 1. to take a person prisoner; to lead captive. 2. to arrest, imprison, put in jail. 3. to capture.

aproamento s. m. act or fact of steering towards, heading for, directing to (harbour, land).

aproar v. (also **aproejar**) to steer, turn the prow of a ship towards.

aprobativo, aprobatório adj. approbative, approbatory, approving. ‖ **-amente** adv. approvingly.

aproche s. m. 1. (fort., obs.) approaches. 2. **~s** pl. assaults, onslaughts.

aprofundamento s. m. 1. deepening: act or fact of making or getting deeper. 2. (fig.) a plunging into, an engrossing in; absorption, engrossment, serious study.

aprofundar v. (also **profundar**) 1. to deepen, make deeper: sink or drive down or in. 2. also **~-se**, (fig.) to make a profound study of; to plunge into; examine carefully, fathom.
~-se em to steep o. s. in.

aprontamento s. m. (also **apronto**) act of making or getting ready; preparation; finishing.

aprontar v. 1. to prepare, make or get ready. 2. to put in order. 3. to fit out, equip. 4. to finish. 5. **~-se** to prepare o. s., get o. s. ready. ~ **o navio para combate** to clear decks. **ele apronta o tear** he gaits the loom. **preciso aprontar-me** I must get ready.

apropinquação s. f. (pl. **-ões**) (also **aproximação**) approximation; act or fact of getting closer to, coming nearer to.

apropinquar v. (also **aproximar**) to approximate, approach, come nearer to.

apropositado adj. appropriate, opportune, seasonable; pertinent; convenient. ‖ **-amente** adv. opportunely. **isto me vem muito -amente** it suits me perfectly. **mal** ~ untimely.

apropositar v. 1. to say or do to the purpose; to do at a proper time. 2. to accommodate things. 3. **~-se**: a) to adapt o. s. to circumstances. b) to come in handy.

apropriabilidade s. f. appropriateness.

apropriação s. f. 1. appropriation; arrogation; assumption; 2. accommodation, adaptation, adjustment. ~ **indébita** undue appropriation.

apropriado adj. 1. appropriate, proper, adequate, suitable, applicable, fit. 2. convenient, useful. 3. likely; opportune, apt. ‖ **-amente** adv. adequately; suitably, applicably.
bem ~ well-suited. **é** ~ **para ela** it is proper for her. **este clima é** ~ **para mim** this climate is congenial to me. **em tempo** ~ at a suitable time; opportunely. **estar** ~ **para** to be suitable for.

apropriador s. m. appropriator ‖ adj. appropriative.

apropriar v. 1. to appropriate. 2. to make suitable, adapt. 3. to accommodate. 4. to apportion. 5. **~-se**:

a) to arrogate; assume; take; confiscate. b) to be suitable for.
apropriaram-se do dinheiro they misappropriated the money, they took the money.
apropriável adj. m. + f. (pl. **-áveis**) appropriable.
aprosexia s. f. (med.) aprosexia: impossibility of concentration or paying attention.
aprovação s. f. (pl. **-ões**) 1. approval, approbation, agreement, consent. 2. appreciation, acceptance. 3. ratification, sanction, enactment; allowance. 4. (fig.) sympathy, applause.
~ **da construção** building test. ~ **em exame** passing in an examination.
aprovado adj. approved; accredited, sanctioned.
~**!** agreed! right! **ela foi aprovada em inglês** she passed in English. **ele foi ~ no exame** he has passed, got through; he has been successful in his examination.
aprovador s. m. approver; consenter; acknowledger. ‖ adj. approving; favourable.
aprovar v. 1. to approve, approbe of, approbate. 2. validate, ratify, accept, sanction, confirm, vote, pass. 3. to consent, allow, to stand for. 4. to enact, adopt. 5. to hold true, good. 6. to applaud; sympathize with.
~ **um aluno** to pass a pupil in an examination. ~ **uma demanda** to find a true bill. ~ **uma lei** to pass a law. **a moção foi aprovada** the ayes have it.
aprovativo adj. = **aprobativo**.
aprovável adj. m. + f. (pl. **-áveis**) approvable; passable; praiseworthy.
aproveitado adj. 1. utilized, put to use. 2. useful, profitable. 3. economic, frugal; sparing, saving. 4. diligent (pupil).
aproveitador s. m. 1. person who takes advantage of, who turns things to good account; winner. 2. hanger-on. 3. enjoyer. 4. profitteer. ‖ adj. using, enjoying.
aproveitamento s. m. 1. utilization, good use. 2. profit. 3. advantage. 4. improvement. 5. exploitation.
aproveitante adj. m. + f. taking advantage of, making the best of.
aproveitar v. 1. to use to advantage, make good use of, put to good use, make the best of, to profit. 2. to utilize, use. 3. to exploit. 4. to capitalize, improve. 5. to profiteer. 6. ~**-se (de)** to avail o. s. (of), take advantage (of).
~ **a oportunidade** to avail o. s. of an opportunity; make hay while the sun shines. ~ **bem a oportunidade** to make the most of the opportunity. ~**-se de alguma coisa** to avail o. s. of a thing. ~**-se dos conhecimentos de alguém** to take advantage of someone's knowledge, suck the brains of s. o. **ela se aproveitou de mim** she took advantage of me; made a convenience of me. **ele aproveitou com a mudança** he won with the change. **ele aproveitou-o com vantagem** he turned it to account. **eles aproveitaram-se da sua bondade** they imposed upon his good nature.
aproveitável adj. m. + f. (pl. **-áveis**) profitable, useful, usable, utilizable; serviceable; well enough; exploitable.
aprovisionador s. m. supplier, provisioner. ‖ adj. supplying.
aprovisionamento s. m. supply of provisions, victualling; provisioning; purveyance.
aprovisionar v. 1. to provision, provide with food, supply, victual. 2. ~**-se:** a) to stock. b) to lay in stores.
aproximação s. f. (pl. **-ões**) 1. approximation, approach; a coming on; forthcoming. 2. close estimate.

aproximado adj. approximate, close. ‖ **-amente** adv. approximately, almost, about, nearly, circa.
aproximar v. 1. to approximate, bring near, cause to approach; colligate. 2. ~**-se** to come near or close to, to reach, approach, accost.
~**-se da cidade** to approach the town. **aproximai!** come here!, up! **aproxima-se à loucura** it comes close to madness. **eu me aproximei dele** I walked up to him. **não se aproxime de mim!** don't come near me! **nós nos aproximamos a uma milha da cidade** we came within a mile of the town. **um temporal está se aproximando** a thunderstorm threatens. **você conseguirá aproximar-se dele?** will you be able to approach him? can you get at him?
aproximativo adj. approximative; close to.
aprumado adj. 1. erect, perfectly vertical, upright. 2. (fig.) correct, honest (person). 3. (Braz.): a) in good financial situation. b) healthy. c) well-dressd.
aprumar v. 1. to put in an upright position, erect. 2. (fig.) to render haughty. 3. ~**-se** a) to mend one's condition of life. b) to become healthy. c) to become haughty.
aprumo s. m. 1. vertical position, uprightness. 2. hauteur, arrogance, haughtiness. 3. correctness.
apside s. f. 1. (astr.) apse, apsis. 2. (archit.) vault; choir (of a church).
apterigoto s. m. apterygotous insect: apterous (wingless) insect without a metamorphosis.
aptério s. m. Greek building without columns.
áptero adj. (zool.) apterous: wingless.
aptidão s. f. (pl. **-ões**) (also **aptitude**) aptness, aptitude, ability, capability, acquirement, capacity, knack; talent, qualification, competence.
~ **física** physical fitness. **não tenho aptidões para isso** my talent does not run this way. **possuir a ~ necessária** to have the necessary ability; have got what it takes. **ter ~ para o estudo** to be good at learning.
aptigmático adj. (geol.) without folds or wrinkles.
apto adj. 1. able, capable, qualified, apt, fit. 2. adroit. 3. idoneous.
~ **para o serviço militar** fit for military service; effective. ~ **para o trabalho** able, fit for work. **estar** ~ to be able.
apuado adj. 1. pricked, stung or pierced all over. 2. sharp-pointed (like a needle).
apuamento s. m. 1. act or fact of boring with an auger. 2. torture by piercing, stinging, pricking.
apuar v. 1. to bore with an auger. 2. to torture, especially with pointed instruments.
apuava adj. m. + f. (Braz.) startled, frightened (horse).
apuirana s. f. (Braz.) tree of the family Loganiaceae (Strychnos rouhamon).
apunhalado adj. stabbed or killed with a dagger or dirk.
apunhalar v. 1. to stab or kill with a dagger, to poniard. 2. (fig.) to offend with words; to hurt the feelings of s. o.; to betray. 3. ~**-se** to kill o. s. with a dagger.
apunhar v. (also **empunhar**) 1. to grasp or hold by the handle (as a sword). 2. to beat with the fists.
apupada s. f. derision, mockery, jeers; hissing, hooting.
apupar v. to scoff, jeer, boo, sneer; to hoot, whoop, hiss.
apupo s. m. 1. hoot, jeer, boo. 2. street riot, tumult.
apuração s. f. (pl. **-ões**) 1. examination, verification. 2. purifying; refinement; purification. 3. improvement. 4. result, income (as at a box office).
~ **de votos** poll.
apurado adj. refined, select, choice; elegant, fine; accurate, exact. ‖ **-amente** adv. carefully, exactly.

apurador s. m. refiner; purifier; selecter; examiner, checker. ‖ adj. purifying, refining.

apuramento s. m. (also **apuração** f.) 1. purification, refinement. 2. inquiry, examination. 3. settlement, settling of accounts. 4. counting. 5. earnings, proceeds.

apurar v. 1. to perfect, improve. 2. to clean, cleanse, purify, refine. 3. to choose, select, pick out. 4. to verify, investigate, try to find out, search into, to sift. 5. to straighten (a matter) out, to square, settle. 6. to try one's passion. 7. to settle accounts, balance. 8. to give an elegant appearance to. 9. to amass, collect (money) by selling. 10. ∼-**se**: a) to improve, become improved. b) to be purified, grow finer or purer.
∼ **contas** to settle accounts. ∼ **as mercadorias** to sell goods at the highest price. ∼ **os danos** to determine the damages. **é preciso** ∼ **a verdade** we must find out the truth. **não apuramos nada** 1. we had no (or no good) returns. 2. we did not find out anything.

apurativo adj. (also **depurativo**) purifying, cleansing; (med.) depurative.

apuro s. m. 1. act or fact of purifying, purification. 2. precision, accuracy, refinedness. 3. act of counting, checking, selecting; selection. 4. carefulness in dressing or speaking. 5. the sum entered (as at a box office). 6. plight, tight corner; distress. **deixar em** ∼**s** to leave in the lurch. **estamos no mesmo** ∼ we are in the same boat. **estar em** ∼**s** to be in distress, hard up, (coll.) in a fix, a tight corner. **num** ∼ **tremendo** in great straights, in a pretty predicament. **vestir-se com** ∼ to be neat in dress. **você vai meter-se em** ∼**s** you will get into trouble.

apurpurado adj. 1. of a purple colour. 2. covered with purple.

apuruí s. m. (Braz.) common name of four trees of the family Rubiaceae.

aquadrilhamento s. m. a gathering in crowds, armed gangs or bands.

aquadrilhar v. 1. to enlist or form a gang or band. 2. ∼-**se** to flock, gather in crowds.

aquaforte s. f. = **água-forte.**

aquafortista s. m. + f. **água-fortista.**

aqualouco s. m. (Braz.) acrobatic water clown.

aquarela s. f. (also **aguarela**) aquarelle, water colour (paint or picture).

aquarelar v. to make, paint aquarelles; to paint in water colours.

aquário (**l**) s. m. 1. aquarium: deposit of water to keep living fishes or water plants in; fish bowl. 2. (astr.) Aquarius.

aquartalado adj. thick-set (horse).

aquartelado adj. lodged in barracks or quarters; quartered, billeted.

aquartelamento s. m. act or fact of providing with lodgements or quarters; (mil.) billeting.

aquartelar v. (mil.) 1. to lodge in barracks; to quarter, billet; to canton. 2. ∼-**se** to take quarters. 3. (her.) to quarter.

aquartilhar v. to measure, gauge or sell in **quartilhos** (0.665 l).

aquático s. m. (Braz.) person who frequents spas (health-resorts with mineral springs.) ‖ adj. (also **aquátil** adj. m. + f. (pl.-**áteis**) aquatic; living in the water.
esportes -**áteis** aquatics. **plantas** -**áteis** water plants.

aquatinta s. f. aquatint, etching with aqua fortis, imitating drawings with India ink or water colours.

aquatintista s. m. + f. aquatintist.

aquavia s. f. waterway, canal.

aquebrantar v. (also **quebrantar**) to break (down); bruise; hurt.

aquecedor s. m. warmer, heater, radiator. ‖ adj. heating, warming.
∼ **a gás** gas geyser (plate B 3). ∼ **de ar** air heater. ∼ **de lingüiça** sausage heater (plate A 2). ∼ **elétrico** electric heater. ∼ **para cama** bedpan, warming pan.

aquecer v. 1. to make or become warm or hot; heat, warm. 2. (fig.) to get angry; to excite.
∼ **demais** to overheat. **aqueça-se!** interj. warm yourself! (coll.) take a warming. **aqueci os pés** I warmed my feet; (coll.) I toasted my toes. **tenho de** ∼ **levemente a água** I must take the chill off the water. **você precisa** ∼**-se** you must warm yourself; (coll.) have a warm.

aquecimento s. m. 1. heating, warming, calefaction. 2. (fig.) irritation.
∼ **central** central heating.

aquecível adj. m. + f. (pl. -**íveis**) 1. heatable, warmable. 2. (fig.) irritable.

aquedar v. 1. to quiet down, calm down. 2. ∼-**se** tranquilize.

aqueduto s. m. aqueduct: an artificial channel.

aquela adj. and pron. (f. form of **aquele**) 1. that (one), the one. 2. ∼**s** pl. those.
∼ **mulher** that woman. **esta casa é nova,** ∼ **é velha** this house is new, that one is old. **sem mais** ∼ without ceremony.

àquela contr. of the prep. **a** and the f. adj. or f. demonstrative pron. **aquela** to that; the one.
dei o livro ∼ **moça** I gave the book to that girl.

aquelar v. 1. to arrange, set in order; to do, make. 2. to find out.

aquele (**ê**) adj. + pron. 1. that, that one; the former. 2. ∼**s** pl. those.
∼ **livro é bom** that book is good. ∼ **que** he who, he that. **desde** ∼ **tempo** from thenceforward. **esse ou** ∼ this or that. **não quero este, quero** ∼ I do not want this one, I want that one. **Pedro e Paulo pintam; este** (Paulo) **pinta bem; aquele** (Pedro) **pinta muito bem** Peter and Paul paint; the latter (Paul) paints well; the former (Peter) paints very well.

àquele contr. of the prep. **a** and the adj. or demonstrative pron. **aquele** to that, to that one.
dê o livro ∼ **rapaz, não a este** give the book to that boy, not to this one.

aqueloutro contr. of the adj. or pron. **aquele + outro** that other one.

aquém adv. 1. on this side. 2. inferiorly, beneath, below. 3. less. ‖ prep. this side.
∼ **de suas possibilidades reais** below his real possibilities. **de aquém e de além** from this side and from that. **fica** ∼ **do que esperávamos** it is beneath our expectations.

aquém-mar s. m. the lands on this side of the ocean. ‖ adv. on this side of the ocean.

aquênio s. m. (bot.) achene, achaene.

aquentamento s. m. act or fact of warming, heating.

aquentar v. 1. to warm, heat, chafe. 2. to animate; excite, irritate. 3. ∼-**se.** a) to become warm or hot. b) (fig.) to become excited.

áqueo adj. aqueous, watery.

aquerenciadeira s. f. (S. Braz.) bell mare joined with another animal which is to get used to a place.

aquerenciado adj. (S. Braz.) said of an animal accustomed to a certain place or to live with other animals.

aquerenciador adj. (S. Braz.) said of good pastures that attract animals.

aquerenciar v. (S. Braz.) 1. to accustom (esp. an animal) to a certain place (not of its origin). 2. ∼-**se** to become used to a certain place.

aqueronteu, aquerôntico adj. Acherontic: referring to Acheron, one of the rivers of the infernal region.

aqui adv. here, herein, in this, on this place, at this occasion. ~ **dentro** in here. ~ **estou** here I am. ~ **mesmo** right here. **até** ~ 1. up till now. 2. up to this point, hereabout.

aqüícola s. m. + f. aquicolous animal. ‖ adj. aquicolous: living in the water.

aqüicultura s. f. aquiculture.

aqui-del-rei interj. (obs.) help, help! police!

aquiescência s. f. acquiescence, act of consenting, assent, accession, compliance.

aquiescente adj. m. + f. aquiescent.

aquiescer v. to acquiesce, consent, permit, assent; agree, yeld.

aquietação s. f. (pl. **-ões**) act or fact of appeasing, quieting; pacification; allayment; tranquility.

aquietador s. m. appeaser; quieter; person who or thing that appeases. ‖ adj. appeasing, calming, quieting.

aquietar v. 1. to appease, quiet, pacify, calm, allay; lull. 2. to grow quiet, to grow less violent. 3. ~**-se** to be quiet or appeased.

aqüífero adj. aquiferous; bearing or yielding water.

aqüifoliácea s. f. (bot.) a holly.

aquilão s. m. (poet.) the north wind.

aquilatador s. m. 1. assayer; appraiser (as of gold). 2. valuer. 3. improver, ameliorator.

aquilatar v. 1. to determine or examine the carat or fineness of gold. 2. to appraise, assay. 3. to appreciate the value of. 4. to improve.

aquilégia s. f. aquilegia: an ornamental plant of the genus Ranunculus; a columbine.

aquileu ad. (f. **-léia**) (anat.) referring to the Achilles' tendon.

aquilhado adj. 1. having a keel, furnished with a keel (boat). 2. (bot.) keeled, carinated.

aquilia (I) s. f. (med.) achylia.

aquilia (II) s. f. absense of lips.

aquilino adj. aquiline: hawked (nose). **olho** ~ eagle eye.

aquilo demonstrative pron. that. ~ **é melhor** that is better. ~ **é homem?** (depr.) that's a man? **por** ~ therefore, for (all) that.

àquilo contr. of the prep. **a** and the demonstrative pron. **aquilo** thereto, to that.

áquilo s. m. = **aquilão**.

aquilombado adj. (Braz., hist.) runaway and sheltered in a **quilombo** (hiding-place of fugitive Negroes).

aquilombar v. (Braz., hist.) to gather in a hiding-place (runaway slaves).

aquilonal adj. m. + f. (pl. **-ais**) (also **aquilonar** m. + f. **aquilônio**) northerly, coming from the north.

aquilotado adj. (Braz., pop.) in the habit of, used to.

aquilotar-se v. (Braz., pop.) to be in the habit of.

aquinhoado s. m. person who received his share. ‖ adj. portioned.

aquinhoador s. m. sharer; apportioner. ‖ adj. distributing, apportioning.

aquinhoamento s. m. apportionment, allotment, assignation; admeasurement.

aquinhoar v. to portion, share out, divide into shares; assess, assign, admeasure, allot.

aquiqui s. m. (Braz.) inferior Indian brandy of maize.

aquiritivo adj. 1. that may be acquired. 2. aquisitive.

aquisição s. f. (pl. **-ões**) 1. acquisition, acquirement; acquest; buy, purchase. 2. act or fact of acquiring. 3. the acquired thing.

aquisitivo adj. acquisitive. **capacidade -a** purchasing power.

aquistar v. (obs.) to acquire, gain, obtain.

aquosidade s. f. aqueousness, waterishness, wateriness.

aquoso adj. aqueous, waterish; serous.

ar s. m. air: 1. atmosphere. 2. breath. 3. breeze, wind. 4. (radio) ether. 5. climate. 6. aspect, look, appearance. 7. bearing, behaviour. 8. (Braz.) paralysis. ~ **comprimido** compressed air. ~ **fresco** fresh air. ~ **seco** dry air. **andar com a cabeça no** ~ to be scatter-brained. **ao** ~ **livre** out of doors. **apanhar as coisas no** ~ to understand readily. **bolha de** ~ air bubble. **bomba de** ~ air pump. **câmara-de-ar** (mot.) inner tube (tyre). **com** ~ **condicionado** air-conditioned. **corrente de** ~ draught, current of air. **dar-se** ~**es de** 1. to pretend to be. 2. to ride the high horse. **está no** ~ it is undecided yet. **a estação de rádio saiu do** ~ the studio is no longer on the ether. **falta de** ~ shortness of breath. **fazer castelos no** ~ to build air castles. **feito no** ~ done headlessly. **há algo no** ~ (fig.) there is s. th. in the wind. **ir aos** ~**es** 1. to be blown up. 2. (fig.) to explode. **tem** ~**es de mentira** it looks like a lie. **tomar** ~ to draw breath. **você nem deu o** ~ **de sua graça** you did not even show up.

ara (I) s. f. 1. sacrificial altar. 2. Ara; Altar: a southern constellation.

ara (II) interj. (Braz.) oh! why! now!

ará s. m. 1. macaw: a Brazilian parrot. 2. (bot.) common caladium.

arabaiana s. f. (Braz., ichth., also **olho-de-vidro**) amber jack, yellowtail.

árabe s. m. + f. 1. Arab, Arabian. 2. m. Arabic. ‖ adj. Arabic; Arabian.

arabescar v. to adorn with arabesques.

arabesco (ê) s. m. arabesque; scroll; flourish. ‖ adj. in the Arabian fashion.

arabi s. m. (also **rabino**) rabbi.

arábico s. m. (also **arábio**) Arabic: the Arabic language. ‖ adj. (also **arábigo**) Arabic, Arabian.

arabina s. f. (chem.) arabin; arabic acid.

arabinose s. f. (chem.) arabinose.

arabismo s. m. Arabicism, Arabism: Arabian expression or phrase.

arabista s. m. + f. Arabist; expert of the Arabian language.

arabizar v. to Arabize, to give an Arabian form; to study the Arabic language or culture.

arabóia s. f. (Braz.) a rat snake.

arabutã s. m. (Braz., also **pau-brasil**, bot.) Brazilwood.

araca s. f. arrack (rice-brandy).

araçá s. m. any Brazilian guava (Psidium littorale). ‖ adj. having yellow hair with black markings (a steer).

araçá-da-praia s. m. (pl. **araçás-da-praia**) (Braz., bot., (also **araçás-de-coroa**) strawberry guava.

araçaeiro s. m. (also **araçazeiro**) the Brazilian guava.

araçá-felpudo s. m. (pl. **araçás-felpudos**) tree of the family Myrtaceae.

araçaí s. m. (Braz., bot.) Brazilian guava.

aracambé s. m. (Braz.) a kind of a wild dog.

aracanga s. m. (Braz., also **papagaio**) parrot.

araçanga s. f. (Braz.) little cudgel used to kill hooked fish with.

aracangüira s. m. (Braz.) the threadfish (Alectis ciliaris).

aração s. f. (pl. **-ões**) 1. plowing. 2. (Braz.): a) devouring, gulping down, greedy eating. b) excessive hunger.

aracapuri s. m. (Braz.) small fish of the Amazonian region.

araçari s. m. (Braz.) any of the toucans of the genus Pteroglossus.

araçari-banana s. m. (pl. **araçaris-banana**) (Braz.) the saffron-coloured aracari.

araçari-de-minhoca s. m. (pl. **araçaris-de-minhoca**) (Braz.) the black-necked aracari.

aracatu s. m. (N. Braz.) day with steady weather.

araçazada s. f. (Braz.) candy made of the fruits of the strawberry guava.

araçazal s. m. (pl araçazais) (Braz.) plot of ground planted with Brazilian guavas (Psidium littorale).

araçazeiro s. m. (also araçareiro) the Brazilian guava.

arácea s. f. any plant of the family Araceae.

aráceo adj. (bot.) aroid, aroideous.

aracnídeo s. m. arachnid: any of the Arachnida (spiders, scorpions).

aracnóide s. f. (anat.) arachnoid: a thin membrane lying between the dura and pia mater.

aracnóideo adj. (anat.) arachnoid.

aracnoidite s. f. (med.) arachnoiditis: inflammation of the arachnoid.

aracnologia s. f. arachnology: study of the spiders.

aracnológico ad. arachnological: of or referring to arachnology.

araçóia s. f. (Braz.) belt of feathers used by Indian women.

araçuaiava s. m. (Braz., also sabiacica) the blue-bellied parrot.

aracuão s. m. (pl. -ões) (Braz., ornith.) the large-tailed squirrel cuckoo.

aracu-branco s. m. (pl. aracus-brancos) (Braz.) a fresh-water fish (Leporinus affinis Gunther).

aracuí s. m. (bot., also angelim-de-folha-larga) the Brazilian andira.

arada s. f. 1. tilled grounds, ploughed soil. 2. ploughing.

arado (I) s. m. plough, plow.
    timão do ~ plough-beam, plow beam. não é aí que o ~ pega (fig.) it is not here that the shoe pinches.

arado (II) adj. (Braz.) hungry, famished.

arador s. m. ploughman, plougher, plower.

aradura s. f. 1. ploughing, plowing, tilling. 2. ploughed land.

aragem s. f. (pl. -ens) 1. whiff; breath of air; gentle wind or breeze. 2. (pop.) opportunity; occasion.

aragonês s. m. Aragonese: native or inhabitant of Aragon (Spain). ‖ adj. Aragonese.

aragonita s. f. (min.) aragonite.

araguaguá s. m. (Braz., also peixe-serra) sawfish.

araguaí s. m. (Braz., ornith.) any of various small macaws.

araguari s. m. (Braz., ornith.) a kind of a macaw.

araguirá s. m. (Braz.) one of the Fringillidae.

aralha s. f. heifer (two years old).

araliácea s. f. (bot.) the Araliaceae.

aramá, aramã s. m. (Braz., also borá-boi) a black, wild bee (Melipon heideri Fièse).

aramaçá, aramaçã s. m. (Braz., ichth.) an Amazonian flounder.

aramado s. m. (Braz., also alambrado) wire fence. ‖ adj. enclosed with a wire fence.

aramador s. m. (Braz.) manufacturer of wire netting.

aramagem s. f. (pl. -ens) (Braz.) wire grating, wire netting, chicken wire, wire lattice.

aramaico s. m. Aramaean, Aramean. ‖ adj. Aramaean, Aramean.

aramandaia s. m. (Braz., ent.) snout beetle.

aramar v. (Braz.) 1. to manufacture wire. 2. to enclose, fence with wire.

arame s. m. 1. wire. 2. (fam.) money.
    ~ de amarração binding wire. ~ de cobre copper wire. ~ estirado drawn wire. ~ farpado barbed wire. calibrador de ~ wire gauge. cerca de ~ wire fence. escova de ~ wire brush. ir aos ~s (fig.) to explode. pêlo de ~ wire-haired (terrier).

arameiro s. m. person who works with wire or in the wire industry.

aramifício s. m. (Braz.) wireworks.

aramina s. f. (Braz.) the textile fiber of the cocklebur.

aramista s. m. + f. wire-dancer, rope-walker, funambulist.

aramudo adj. (Braz., fam.) 1. full of wire. 2. having much money (rich).

arancim s. m. (pl. -ins) (Braz., also iraxim) a stingless bee.

arandela s. f. 1. socket of a candlestick. 2. lamp holder. 3. wall .bracket. 4. sword hilt. 5. bracket sconce; prolonger. 6. (Braz.) an earthenware ring--shaped vase, filled with water and put around plants to protect them from ants.

araneídeo s. m. specimen of the Araneida: a spider.

araneífero adj. having spider webs.

araneiforme adj. m. + f. araneiform: like a spider.

aranha s. f. 1. (zool. + tech.) spider. 2. various things having the form of or suggesting a spider: a) a dogcart, a light carriage. b) penny-farthing bicycle (plate B 11). c). (naut.) crowfoot. d) (tech.) central or radial distributing heater. e) (fig.) slowcoach. f) (bot.) glory lily. g) (ichth.) weever.
    ~-caranguejeira (zool.) bird-catching spider. ~ de maca hammock clew. ~ do linho black widow spider. estar em palpos de ~ (pop.) to be in a very difficult position. teia de ~ cobweb.

aranhaçu s. f. (Braz., also aranha-caranguejeira) bird--catching spider.

aranha-do-mar s. f. (pl. aranhas-do-mar) (Braz.) sea spider; crawfish; starfish.

aranhar v. (Braz.) to go or move slowly (like a spider), to be in no hurry.

aranhento adj. proper of spiders; spidery; full of spiders.

aranhiço s. m. 1. a small spider. 2. (fig.) weakly person. 3. ~s pl. the ribs of an ogival vault.

aranhol s. m. (pl. -óis) (also aranheiro) 1. a spider's nest or hole. 2. (Braz.) fishing net. 3. net for catching birds.

aranhoso adj. similar to a spider or a' spider's web.

aranzel s. m. (pl. -éis) 1. long and tiresome series of things in a story, rigmarole, boring long-winded talk. 2. (obs.) roll, register.

arão s. m. (also jarro, bot.) any of various aroids, arum, priest's hood.

arapabaca s. f. pinkroot: name of various plants of the family Loganiaceae.

arapaçu s. m. (Braz., ornith.) tree creeper.

arapapá s. m. (Braz.) boatbill: bird of the family Dendrocolaptidae.

arapoca s. f. (Braz.) name of various trees of the family Rutaceae.

araponga s. f. (Braz.) 1. (ornith.) bellbird, campanero. 2. a person with a shrill voice or person who speaks very loud.

araponguinha s. f. (Braz., ornith.) 1. the crested sharpbill. 2. the inquisitive tityra.

araponguira s. f. (Braz.) bird of the family Cotingidae (Tityra cayana brasiliensis).

arapuá, arapuã s. f. (Braz.) 1. a bee (Trigona ruficus). 2. disheveled hair.

arapuar-se v. (Braz.) to become angry.

arapuca s. f. (Braz.) 1. a bird-trap shaped like a pyramid. 2. (fig.): a) an old ramshackle house. b) pitfall, snare, trap. 3. (Braz., pop.) a gyp-joint.
    cair na ~ to fall into the trap.

arapuê s. m. (Braz.) tree of the dogbane family.

arapuru s. m. (Braz.) name of various songless birds of the Amazonian region.

arar v. 1. to plow, till. 2. (poet.) to navigate.

arara s. f. 1. macaw, a Brazilian parrot. 2. (Braz., fam.) a lie, fib, false rumour. 3. m. + f. fool, nincompoop.
    ficar uma ~ (Braz., pop.) to become very angry.

araracanga s. f. (also ararapiranga) (Braz., ornith.) the red and the blue macaw.

araracangaçu s. m. (also tracajá) a fresh-water turtle (Amazon).

ararambóia s. f. (Braz.) snake of the Amazonian region.

araratucupé, araratucupi s. f. (Braz.) tree of the family Mimosaceae, a nitta tree.

araraúna s. f. (Braz.) a kind of a macaw of blue colour.

arara-vermelha s. f. (pl. araras-vermelhas) red macaw.

arariba s. f. (also aréua) timber tree of the genus Sickingia, tree with dark-red wood.

arariba s. f. (Braz.) a porcupine pod tree (Centrolobium tomentosum).

ararinha s. f. (Braz) a macaw.

araroba s. f. 1. (bot.) araroba. 2. Goa powder.

araruama s. m. (Braz.) = caipira.

araruna s. f. (Braz.) = araraúna.

araruta s. f. arrowroot: 1. the plant. 2. the starch it yelds.

arataca s. f. (Braz.) trap for wild animals.

arataciú s. f. (Braz.) plant of the family Euphorbiaceae.

arataiaçu s. m. (also arapapá) (ornith.) boatbill.

aratanha s. f. (Braz.) a small cow.

araticum s. m. (pl. -uns) (also araticu, araticunzeiro, araticuzeiro) any of various shrubs and small trees of the custard-apple family.

aratinga s. f. (Braz.) any green parakeet.

aratório adj. pertaining to a plough.

aratriforme adj. m. + f. ploughlike, plowlike.

aratu s. m. (Braz.) a small crab of squarish forms.

arauatu s. m. (Braz.) Amazonian monkey.

araucária s. f. (bot.) araucaria: the Brazilian pine. ~ da Austrália (bot.) Bunya-Bunya.

arauiri s. m. (Braz.) a fresh-water fish (Chalecinus auritus).

arauto s. m. (ant.) herald; public crier, town-crier, proclaimer; harbinger.

arável adj. m. + f. (pl. -áveis) arable; tillable, ploughable, plowable.

aravela s. f. plough handle, plow handle, plow-staff.

aravia s. f. gibberish.

araxá s. m. (also planalto) (Braz.) tableland.

arazóia s. f. (Braz., also araçóia) Indian belt made of feathers.

arbim s. m. (pl. -ins) coarse woollen cloth worn formerly for mourning.

arbitração s. f. (pl. -ões) arbitration, arbiter's sentence.

arbitrador s. m. arbitrator, umpire, arbiter, referee. || adj. arbitrating.

arbitragem s. f. (pl. -ens) arbitration, arbitrament, umpirage.

~ de câmbio arbitrage. ~ de títulos (com.) arbitration of exchange. sujeito à ~ arbitrable. comissão de ~ arbitration committee.

arbitral adj. m. + f. (pl. -ais) arbitrational, arbitrary, by umpire.

arbitramento s. m. arbitrament, decision of an arbiter, umpirage, compromise.

arbitrar v. 1. to arbitrate, decide, regulate by way of arbitration. 2. to umpire, mediate, award. 3. to rate, estimate, determine.

~ um jogo de futebol to referee a soccer game.

arbitrariedade s. f. arbitrariness, wilfulness.

arbitrário adj. arbitrary, despotic, left to a man's choice; by or of arbiters; discretionary; masterful. || arbitrariamente adv. wantonly, arbitrarily, despotically.

arbitrativo adj. arbitrative, arbitrable, arbitrational.

direito e poder ~ arbitrament.

arbítrio s. m. will, discretion, judgement, choice, expedient; disposal, decision, award; arbitration, umpirage.

livre ~ free will. ao ~ de at one's pleasure or discretion.

arbitrista s. m. + f. contriver, planner, projector.

árbitro s. m. 1. arbiter, umpire, arbitrator, judge, judger, referee, awarder, adjudicator. 2. master, overman. 3. judgement, criterion.

~ de futebol referee of a soccer game. baseado em decisão de ~ arbitrary. decidir como ~ to arbitrate. decisão ou julgamento dos ~s arbitration. decisão de ~ arbitrator's award.

arbóreo adj. arboreal, arboreous, arborous.

arborescência s. f. (also arvorecência) arborescence.

arborescente adj. m. + f. (bot., also arvorecente) arborescent, arboreous; dendriform, dendritic, dendritical. || ~mente adv. arborescently.

arborescer v. (also arvorecer) to grow into a tree.

arboreto s. m. arboretum.

arborícola adj. m. + f. (zool.) arboricole, living on trees.

arboricultor s. m. arboriculturist.

arboricultura s. f. arboriculture.

arboriforme adj. m. + f. dendriform, tree-shaped.

arborista s. m. + f. arboriculturist.

arborização s. f. (pl. -ões) 1. arborization, tree planting, forestation. 2. treelike ramification of certain minerals.

arborizado adj. arboreous, arbored, arboreal, forested, woody, timbered.

arborizar v. to plant with trees, to forest.

arbúsculo s. m. a small tree, shrub.

arbústeo adj. shrubby.

arbustiforme adj. m. + f. like a shrub.

arbustivo adj. like undershrub, shrubby.

arbusto s. m. shrub, bush, underbrush.

arca s. f. 1. ark, chest, coffer, trunk, large box. 2. treasure. 3. chest, thorax.

~ da aliança ark of the covenant. ~ de Noé Noah's Ark. as ~s do tesouro, as ~s da nação the nation's coffers. ~ da bomba (naut.) pump well. ~ do pão bread bin. lutar ~ por ~ com alguém to single out one's enemy. não ser de ~s encouradas to be plain-spoken. na ~ aberta o justo peca an open door will tempt a saint.

arcabouço s. m. 1. framework. 2. skeleton, carcass. 3. a person's chest or breast.

arcabuz s. m. (pl. ~es) (hist.) harquebus, hackbut, arquebuse, handgun.

arcabuzada s. f. (hist.) musket-shot or series of musket-shots.

arcabuzamento s. m. (hist.) discharge, volley of muskets.

arcabuzar v. (hist.) to shoot, kill by shooting (with a musket).

arcabuzaria s. f. (hist.) 1. corps of musketeers or riflemen. 2. discharge or volley of muskets.

arcabuzeiro s. m. (hist.) 1. gunsmith. 2. harquebusier, musketeer, rifleman.

arcada s. f. 1. arcade, arched vault, arch, range of arches. 2. (mus.) bow: a stroke with the bow over the strings. 3. ~s pl. heavings: movement of the chest when a person gasps for breath.

~ zigomática (anat.) zygomatic arch.

árcade s. m. + f. Arcadian: 1. native or inhabitant of Arcadia in Greece. 2. (hist.) member of the Arcadia, an ancient Roman literary academy.|| adj. 1. Arcadian: of Arcadia in Greece. 2. referring to the style of the members of the literary academy Arcadia.

arcádico adj. arcadic: relating to the literary academy Arcadia.

A 12

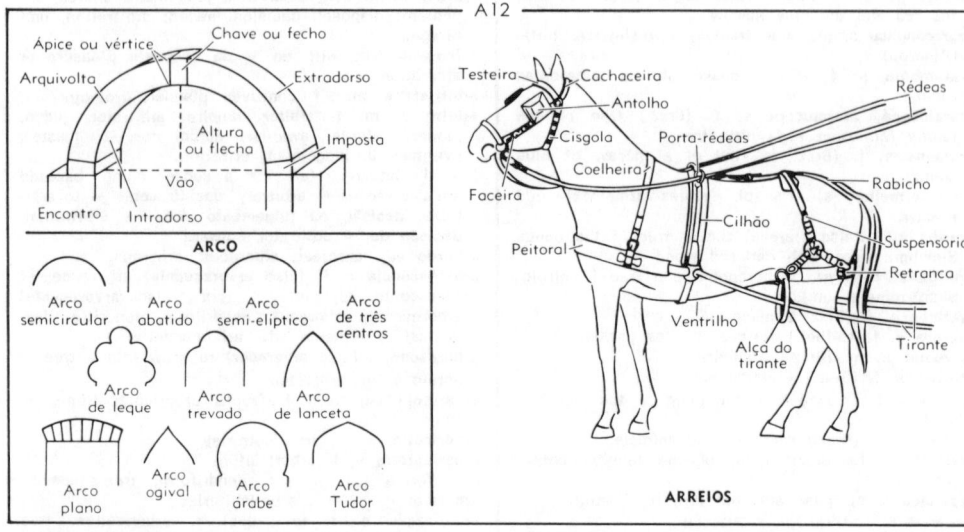

Ápice ou vértice — Chave ou fecho — Extradorso — Arquivolta — Altura ou flecha — Imposta — Vão — Encontro — Intradorso

ARCO

Arco semicircular — Arco abatido — Arco semi-elíptico — Arco de três centros

Arco de leque — Arco trevado — Arco de lanceta

Arco plano — Arco ogival — Arco árabe — Arco Tudor

Testeira — Cachaceira — Antolho — Cisgola — Porta-rédeas — Coelheira — Rédeas — Rabicho — Faceira — Cilhão — Peitoral — Suspensório — Retranca — Ventrilho — Alça do tirante — Tirante

ARREIOS

arcado adj. arched, curved, bowed.
arcadura s. f. curvature, bow, bend, curved line.
arcaico adj. archaic, disused, antique, obsolete.
arcaísmo s. m. archaism: 1. archaic expression or word. 2. use of obsolete words or expressions. **usar ~s** to archaize.
arcaísta s. m. + f. archaist. ‖ adj. archaistic. ‖ **arcaisticamente** adv. archaically, antiquely.
arcaizar v. to archaize, use archaisms.
arcal s. m. (pl. **-ais**) (bot.) a rockrose.
arcangélico adj. archangelic, archangelical.
arcanjo s. m. archangel.
arcano s. m. arcanum, secret, mystery. ‖ adj. arcane, secret, concealed, hidden, mysterious.
arção s. m. pommel, saddle-bow.
arcar (I) v. 1. to bend, curve, arch, bow. 2. to hoop barrels.
arcar (II) v. to struggle, grapple (**com** with). **~ com dificuldades** to cope with difficulties. **~ com a responsabilidade** to assume the responsibility, (coll.) face the music. **bem posso ~ com as despesas de um táxi** I can well afford to take a taxi.
arcaria s. f. the arches which support a building; range of arches.
arcatura s. f. (archit.) ornamental imitation of arcades on a façade.
arcaz s. m. (pl. **~es**) great chest.
arcebispado s. m. archbishopric, archdiocese, archiepiscopate.
arcebispal adj. m. + f. (pl. **-ais**) archiepiscopal.
arcebispo s. m. archbishop, hierarch.
arcediagado s. m. archdeaconate, archdeaconship, archdeaconry.
arcediago s. m. archdeacon.
arcete s. m. stone saw.
archa s. f. halberd.
archeiro s. m. halberdier; soldier armed with a halberd.
archete (I) s. m. small chest or ark.
archete (II) s. m. arched ornament.
archotada s. f. torch-light procession.
archote s. m. torch, torch-light, flambeau; link. **luz de ~** torch-light. **portador de ~** torch-bearer, torcher.
arcífero adj. armed with an arc.

arciforme adj. m. + f. shaped like a bow, bowed.
arciprestado s. m. archpresbytery.
arciprestal adj. m. + f. (pl. **-ais**) belonging to an archpriest.
arcipreste s. m. archpriest, chief priest.
arco s. m. 1. (also geom.) arc. 2. (archit.): a) arch (plates A 12, P 14). b) squinch. 3. (also weapon and mus.) bow. 4. hoop (plate B 4). 5. (soccer) goal. **~ abatido** segmental arch (plate A 12). **~ alveolar** alveolus, alveoli. **~ árabe** horseshoe arch (plate A 12). **~ campanulado** reversed ogee arch. **~ de descarga** (archit.) relieving arch. **~ de lanceta** lancet arch (plate A 12). **~ de leque** fan arch (plate A 12). **~ diastáltico** (physiol.) reflex arch. **~ do pé** arch of the foot. **~ de pua** fly-drill, brace for holding a boring bit (plates F 8, M 4). **~ de serra** hack-saw frame. **~ de três centros** three-centered arch (plate A 12). **~ de triunfo** triumphal arch. **~ elíptico** elliptical arch. **~ ogival** ogival arch (plate A 12). **~ plano** flat arch (plate A 12). **~ trilobado** three-lobed arch. **abrir o ~** to run away. **~ trevado** trefoil arch (plate A 12). **cobrir com um ~** to over-arch. **colocar ~s** to hoop. **solda pelo ~ voltaico** electrical arch welding.
arcobotante s. m. flying buttress, pier.
arco-da-aliança s. m. (pl. **arcos-da-aliança**) rainbow.
arco-da-chuva s. m. (pl. **arcos-da-chuva**) rainbow.
arco-da-velha s. m. (pl. **arcos-da-velha**) (pop.) rainbow. **fazer, dizer coisas do ~** to make wondrous things, tell big stories.
arco-de-deus s. m. (pl. **arcos-de-deus**) rainbow.
arco-de-pipa s. m. (pl. **arcos-de-pipa**) 1. barrel hoop (plate B 4). 2. a cocaine tree.
arco-íris s. m., sg. + pl. rainbow.
arcontado s. m. archonship.
arconte s. m. (Greek hist.) archon, one of the chief magistrates of Athens.
arcote s. m. taper, link (torch).
arctação s. f. (pl. **-ões**) (med.) arctation, arctitude.
arctos s. m. pl. (astr.) Ursa Maior, the Greater Bear.
Arcturo s. m. (astr.) Arcturus, a fixed star in the constellation Boötes.
arcual adj. m. + f. (pl. **-ais**) arched, bowed.
ar-de-dia s. m. (pl. **ares-de-dia**) (N. Braz.) sunrise or sunset.

árdego adj. 1. fiery, ardent, vehement, passionate, easily provoked. 2. eager, sedulous. 3. painful, difficult.

Ardeídeos s. m. pl. (ornith.) the herons (Ardeidae).

ardência s. f. 1. ardency, fervency. 2. burning, glow, gleam. 3. zeal, eagerness. 4. violence.

ardente adj. m. + f. 1. ardent: a) vehement, fervent, strong, longing. b) fiery, ablaze, afire, flagrant, blazing, torrid. c) intense, violent, eager. 2. impassionate, devoted, devout. 3. hasty, unruly. 4. fierce, forward. ‖ **-mente** adv. ardently.
câmara ~ death chamber. **desejo** ~ violent desire. **lágrimas** ~**s** scalding tears.

ardentia s. f. 1. gleam, glow. 2. burning heat. 3. phosphorescence of the sea.

ardentoso adj. stinging like nettles.

arder v. 1. to burn, flame, blaze, smoulder, glow. 2. to shine, glisten, glitter. 3. to smart. 4. to rage. 5. to sting. 6. to fire, deflagrate. 7. (fig.) to burn up, waste, spoil. 8. to long, wish earnestly.
~ **de vontade de** to burn with desire for, be eager about. ~ **em cólera** to boil with rage. ~ **em febre** to have a burning fever. ~ **por** to desire ardently.

ar-de-vento s. m. (pl. **ares-de-vento**) paralysis, stupor, transe, lethargy.

ardidez, ardideza s. f. courage, bravery, boldness; eargerness, dauntlessness.

ardido (I) s. m. (Braz.) a slight infection of the skin.
‖ adj. 1. burned, burnt. 2. burning. 3. sharp, strong. 4. spoilt, rancid.
um gosto ~ a rancid taste.

ardido (II) adj. courageous, brave, bold.

ardil s. m. (pl. **-is**) 1. cunning, slyness, craftiness, trickiness. 2. trick, artifice. 3. stratagem, craft, contrivance. 4. snare, trap. 5. fetch. 6. dodgery, doubling, elusion.

ardileza s. f. cunning, trickery, stratagem, contrivance, slyness, craftiness, guilefulness.

ardiloso adj. 1. cunning, artful, crafty, subtle, elusive, captious, guileful, astute, ambidextrous, wily, tricky. 2. fraudulent, underhand, fallacious, crooked, obreptitious. ‖ **-amente** adv. cunningly, ambidextrously, artfully, fraudulently.

ardimento (I) s. m. ardency, fervour, ardour.

ardimento (III) s. m. boldness, courage.

ardísia s. f. (bot.) some of the Mirsinaceae.

ardor s. m. 1. ardour. 2. heat, burning, hotness. 3. eagerness, passion. 4. zeal. 5. briskness, sprightliness, liveliness. 6. boldness, courage, fierceness, wildness. 7. itching, pricking (skin). 8. acridness.
no ~ **da batalha** in the heat of battle.

ardoroso adj. 1. ardent, fervent, fervid. 2. zealous. ‖ **-amente** adv. fervently, zealously.

ardósia s. f. (geol.) slate.
lápis de ~ slate-pencil. **pedreira de** ~ slate quarry.

ardosieira s. f. slate-quarry.

ardoso adj. pungent, piquant.

arduidade s. f. arduousness.

ardume s. m. (Braz.) pungency, piquancy.

árduo adj. 1. arduous, difficult, laborious, strenuous. 2. hard, tough. 3. troublesome, painful. ‖ **arduamente** adv. arduously, painfully.
é uma tarefa -a it is hard work. **ganhar arduamente o seu pão** to work hard for one's living.

are s. m. are: metric land measure equal to 119.6 square yards.

aré s. m. + f. (Braz.) Indian belonging to the Tupi-Guarani tribe.

área s. f. area: 1. surface. 2. ground. 3. space. 4. yard, inner court. 5. areaway. 6. sector, region. 7. range, radius.
~ **de circulação (de um jornal)** circulation area (of a paper). ~ **cultivada** infield. ~ **de gol** (ftb.) goal area (plate F 9). ~ **de penal** penalty area (plate F 9). ~ **drenada** drainage-area.

areação s. f. (pl. **-ões**) covering with sand.

areado (I) adj. 1. cleaned or covered with sand. 2. (S. Braz.) pennyless.
açúcar ~ powdered sugar.

areado (II) adj. bewildered, dazed, astonished, stupefied.

areal s. m. (pl. **-ais**) beach, sand dune; sandy plain; sand pit.

areão s. m. (pl. **-ões**) (Braz.) large **areal**.

arear v. 1. to sand, clean or scour with sand. 2. to be dazed, be taken aback, be at a loss. 3. to refine (sugar).

areca s. f. 1. any areca palm; esp. the betel nut palm. 2. its fruit.

arecal s. m. (pl. **-ais**) grove of areca palms.

arecíneo adj. (bot.) belonging to or related with the areca palm.

arecuná s. m. + f. (Braz.) Indian belonging to the Caraíbas tribe.

areeiro s. m. 1. sand-box (plate P 6). 2. sand pit. 3. person who transports or sells sand.

areento adj. sanded, sandy, sabulous, gravelly.

arefação s. f. (med.) arefaction.

areia s. f. 1. sand, grit (plates A 7, P 6), gravel. 2. (coll.) nonsense, foolishness. 3. m. sand (colour). ‖ adj. sandy (colour).
~ **de construção** building sand (plate A 7). ~ **de fundição** foundry sand. ~ **lavada** river sand. ~ **movediça** quicksand, drift sand (plate C 19). ~ **dos rins ou da bexiga** gravel. **baixio de** ~ sandy shoal. **banco de** ~ sandbank. **banho de** ~ sand bath. **caixa de** ~ sand-box. **edificar sobre** ~ to build on sand. **jacto de** ~ sand-blast. **jogar** ~ **nos olhos de alguém** to throw dust in a person's eyes, to deceive.

areia-engolideira s. f. (pl. **areias-engolideiras**) (Braz.) slough, marshy place, mire.

areia-manteiga s. f. (pl. **areias-manteiga**) marshy river-side.

areia-preta s. f. (pl. **areias-pretas**) 1. titanium minerals. 2. (pop.) snuff.

areias-gordas s. f. pl. 1. rich sandy loam. 2. (pop.) hell.

areísco adj. sandy.

areiúsca s. f. (Braz.) sandy earth.

arejado adj. aired, ventilated.

arejamento s. m. 1. airing, ventilation. 2. (Braz.) a certain disease of horses and mules.

arejar v. 1. to air, expose to the air, weather. 2. to ventilate, aerate. 3. to take airing. 4. to wither, dry up (fruit).
~ **uma sala** to air a room.

arejo s. m. airing, ventilation.

arena s. f. 1. arena: a) fighting area of a Roman circus. b) lists. c) scene of action. 2. sand.
~ **para touradas** bull ring. ~ **de torneio** barrier.

arená s. m. (Braz.) ruffian, braggart; bad man.

arenáceo adj. arenaceous, gravelly, sandy.

arenado adj. sand-covered, sandy.

arenal s. m. (pl. **-ais**) + **areal**.

arenária s. f. (bot.) one of the sandworts (Arenaria).

arenário adj. inhabiting the sand.

arenato s. m. (min.) arenaceous quartz. ‖ adj. arenaceous.

arenga s. f. 1. harangue; prose, tirade, screed, spigot; preachment, long tedious speech. 2. ~**s** pl. quarrel, dispute, discussion, debate.

arengada s. f. (Braz.) endless talk, tirade.

arenga-de-mulher s. f. (pl. **arengas-de-mulher**) (Braz.) a palm tree.

arengador s. m. (also **arengueiro**) haranguer, speechmaker; soap box orator; windbag.

arengar v. 1. to harangue, declaim, prattle, gossip. 2. (Braz.) to be swittish (horse). 3. to argue, dispute, altercate.

arenícola s. m. + f. (zool.) a sandworm. ‖ (zool.) arenicolous.

arenífero adj. arenaceous, arenose.

areniforme adj. m. + f. sandlike, arenaceous.

arenito s. m. (Braz.) sandstone, grit (plate M 10).

arenoso adj. (also **areoso**) sandy, gravelly, gritty, arenaceous.

pedra -a sandstone, freestone. **terreno** ~ sandy soil.

arenque s. m. herring; anchovy.

~ **defumado** red herring. ~ **salgado** bloater, kipper.

arensar s. m. a swan's voice or song. ‖ v. to sing (swan).

aréola s. f. 1. areola, areole. 2. aureole. 3. garden bed.

areolado adj. areolate, areolar.

areometria s. f. hydrometry, areometry.

areométrico adj. hydrometric.

areômetro s. m. (phys.) hydrometer, areometer.

areopagita s. m. (Greek hist.) areopagite; member of the Areopagus.

areópago s. m. (Greek hist.) Areopagus; Athenian tribunal.

areotectônica s. f. (mil. + fort.) strategy of attacking and defending fortifications.

arequeira s. f. = **areca**.

ares s. m. pl. 1. climate. 2. airs, appearances, manners, ways.

aresta s. f. 1. edge, corner. 2. brim, border. 3. (geom.) edge: intersecting line. 4. small portion, trifle. 5. headless nail, as a shoe tack. 6. ridge, crest, peak. 7. (archit.) arris, groin. 8. (bot.) awn (of corn). **achar** ~**s nos olhos dos outros** to see the faults of others. **polir as** ~**s** to smooth the rough edges (also fig.). **ter** ~**s nos olhos** not to see well.

aresteiro s. m. judge who bases his judgements on previous judgements and sentences and not on laws.

arestim s. m. (pl. **-ins**) (vet.) the scratches.

aresto s. m. 1. judgement, sentence, decree, legal decision, sentence based upon a precedent. 2. (fig.) solution.

arestoso adj. awned; angular, having edges.

arestudo adj. 1 = **arestoso**. 2. rough, coarse (as linen).

aretologia s. f. ethics, a treatise on moral or virtue.

aretológico adj. ethical.

aréu adj. puzzled, bewildered; hesitant.

arfada, arfadura, arfagem s. f. 1. (naut.) rolling, pitching. 2. palpitation. 3. panting.

arfante adj. m. + f. 1. gasping, heaving. 2. (naut.) pitching, rolling.

arfar v. 1. to heave. 2. to gasp, breathe with difficulty, pant, to palpitate, throb. 3. (naut.) to pitch, roll.

~ **de cansaço** to pant from exhaustion. ~ **sobre a amarra** to pitch at anchor.

argali s. m. (zool.) the argali, an Asiatic wild sheep.

argamandel s. m. (pl. **-éis**) (pop.) blunderer: fumbler; tatterdemalion, ragamuffin.

argamassa s. f. mortar, building cement, daub, pug, bond.

~ **de gesso** plaster of Paris. ~ **gorda** mortar with more lime than sand. ~ **líquida** grout. ~ **magra** mortar with more sand than lime.

argamassador s. m. plasterer, person who makes or applies mortar or plaster.

argamassar v. 1. to plaster, mortar, pug. 2. to stir, knead, mix (as mortar).

arganaz s. m. (pl. **-es**) (zool.) field-mouse, dormouse, a woodrat; (coll.) very tall man.

ele dorme como um ~ he sleeps like a dormouse.

arganel s. m. (pl. **-éis**) small iron hoop.

arganéu s. m. (naut., obs.) 1. a sort of ring which serves to push a cannon backwards and forwards. 2. ringbolt.

argau s. m. pipette, wine tester.

argel adj. m. + f. (pl. **-éis**) 1. having white hind feet (horse). 2. (N. Braz.): a) awkward. b) slovenly.

argelino s. m. Algerian: native or inhabitant of Algeria. ‖ adj. Algerian.

argemona s. f. (bot.) the Mexican prickly poppy.

argentado adj. argentine, silvered, silvery.

argentador s. m. silverer, silver plater. ‖ adj. silvered, silver-plated.

argentão s. m. German silver, white metal.

argentar v. (also **arguentear**) to silver; to silver-plate.

argentaria s. f. table silverware; garniture or embroidery of silver.

argentário s. m. 1. a rich, well off man. 2. buffet or cupboard for the silverware.

argênteo adj. silvery, bright as silver; argentine.

argentífero adj. silvery, bearing or containing silver, argentous.

argentino (I) adj. argentine, silvery.

som ~ clear sound. **voz -a** a clear voice.

argentino (II) s. m. Argentinean, native or inhabitant of Argentina. ‖ adj. Argentinean.

argentita s. f. (min.) argentite.

argento s. m. (obs.) silver.

salso ~ (poet.) the sea.

argento-vivo s. m. (pl. **argentos-vivos**) quicksilver, mercury.

argila s. f. argil, potter's earth (plate. M 10).

~ **em bruto** rough clay. ~ **em obra** burned clay. ~ **friável** bole. ~ **ocrosa** iron clay. ~ **para manilhas** pipe clay. ~ **plástica** plastic clay. ~ **refratária** fire clay. ~ **xistosa** argillite.

argiláceo adj. (also **argiloso**) argillaceous, clayish.

argileira s. f. clay pit.

argilífero adj. (geol.) argilliferous.

argiliforme adj. m. + f. (petrog.) argilloid, like clay.

argilóide adj. m. + f. similar to clay, clayey, clayish.

arginase s. f. a liver enzyme that decomposes arginine.

argirântemo adj. argyranthem, having silvery flowers (plants).

argírico adj. silvery, argyric; bright or clear as silver.

argirofilo adj. (bot.) argyrophyl, having white argentic leaves.

argivo s. m. Argive, Greek. ‖ adj. Argive.

argo s. m. 1. (astr.) Argo, a constellation in the Southern Hemisphere. 2. (Greek myth.) Argo, ship used by the Argonauts.

argola s. f. 1. ring (plates A 6, M 1, R 4), hoop; link. 2. door knocker. 3. collar (dog) 4. ~**s** pl.: a) earrings. b) (gym.) rings (plates G 3, P 6). 5. pillory. **jogo da** ~ (also **argolinha**) running at the ring, a children's game.

argolaço s. m. (S. Braz.) (also **argolada** s. f.) 1. large ring. 2. a stroke at the door with the knocker.

argolado adj. provided with rings.

argolão s. m. (pl. **-ões**) a large and massive ring.

argolar v. 1. to fasten with rings. 2. to provide with rings. 3. to adorn with rings.

argoleiro s. m. person who makes or sells metal rings.

argolinha s. f. 1. a small ring. 2. pastry used in soups. 3. small biscuits, cookies.

argonaço adj. irritated; impertinent.

argonauta s. m. (Greek myth.) 1. Argonaut. 2. (fig.) a daring navigator. 3. (zool.) the paper nautilus.

argonáutico adj. Argonautic.

argônio s. m. (chem.) argon.

Argos s. m. 1. Argus. 2. (fig.) an Argus-eyed person. a smart person.

argúcia s. f. 1. astuteness, craftiness, captiousness, shrewdness. 2. smartness. 3. subtlety, cavil, quirk. 4. witticism.

arguciar v. to proceed with subtleness, to argue cleverly or astutely.

argucioso adj. subtle, crafty, sophistical, shrewd, artful; witty.

argueireiro adj. 1. petty, paltry. 2. hairsplitting. 3. subtle.

argueiro s. m. straw, mote, trifle, a nothing, insignificance, petty fault.

de um ~ fazer um cavaleiro to make mountains out of mole-hills.

argüente s. m. + f. arguer, ranter, opponent, disputant. ‖ adj. arguing, argumenting.

argüição s. m. (pl. -ões) 1. arguing. 2. argument, argumentation. 3. (school) oral: an examination.

argüidor s. m. 1. arguer. 2. blamer, reprover, accuser.

argüir v. 1. to accuse, reprove, reprehend, condemn, impugn. 2. to reveal, disclose. 3. to argue: a) gather, conclude, infer. b) discuss, debate.

~ por to blame for. ~-se de to accuse o. s. of.

argüitivo adj. conclusive, demonstrative; accusatory.

argüível adj. m. + f. (pl. -íveis) accusable; censurable; discussable.

argumentação s. f. (pl. -ões) 1. argumentation, reasoning. 2. dispute, debate. 3. controversy.

argumentador s. m. arguer; argumentator; disputer, wrangler, mooter.

argumentante s. m. + f. mooter; arguer. ‖ adj. disputatious, arguing.

argumentar v. 1. to argue: a) dispute, debate. b) deduce, conclude, infer. 2. to plead. 3. to urge. 4. to moot, remonstrate.

~ com alguém to dispute with s. o. ~ insistentemente to argue pertinaciously, (coll.) argufy.

argumentativo adj. argumentative, disputatious.

argumento s. m. argument: 1. argumentation, reason. 2. contention, contestation. 3. subject, topic. 4. summary.

~ convincente sound argument, a clincher. ~ esmagador a smashing argument. ~ sutil (fig.) cobweb. isto não serve como ~ that is no argument.

arguto adj. 1. subtle, quick-witted, shrewd, cunning, astute, acute. 2. sharp, shrill, loud, high-pitched.

ariá s. f. (Braz.) a plant of the arrowroot family.

ária (I) s. f. aria: air, song, tune, melody.

ária (II) s. m. + f. Aryan.

ariacó s. m. (zool.) the spot snapper.

arianismo s. m. Aryanism, Arianism: the doctrine of Arius.

ariano (I) s. m. a folloyer of Aryanism.

ariano (II) adj. Aryan, Arian.

aricuí s. f. (bot. also aricuri) the aricury palm (it yelds a useful fiber).

aricungo s. m. (S. Braz.) jade, worthless horse.

aricuriroba s. f. (Braz., bot.) the aricury palm.

aridez s. f. aridity, aridness, dryness. 2. drought 3. barrenness. 4. (fig.) dullness.

árido adj. 1. arid, dry, desert, withered. 2. sterile. 3. barren. 4. (fig.) insipid, washy.

áries s. f. (astr.) Aries: the ram (sign of the zodiac).

arieta s. f. (dim. of ária) arietta, little song.

aríete s. m. (mil., hist.) 1. battering ram. 2. hydraulic ram.

arigbóia s. f. (Braz., zool.) an anaconda.

arigó s. m. (Braz.) rustic, boor.

arilado adj. (bot.) arillate, provided with a seed-coat.

arilo s. m. (bot.) aril, seed-coat, integument.

arimaru s. f. (Braz., bot.) one of the Loganiaceae (Strychnos cogens).

arimbá s. m. (Braz.) a glazed clay jar.

arinque s. m. cable of the anchor buoy (of a ship).

arinta s. f. (also arinto) a variety of white grapes.

arioso s. m. (mus.) arioso.

aripar v. to dig and sift the sand in search of pearls.

aripeiro s. m. person who sifts sand in search for pearls.

aripo s. m. sifting of sand to the purpose of finding pearls.

ariramba s. f. (Braz., ornith.) one of the kingfishers.

ariramba-da-mata-virgem s. f. (pl. arirambas-da-mata--virgem) (ornith.) a jacamar.

ariramba-miudinha s. f. (pl. ariarambas-miudinhas) (also ariramba-pequena, martim-pescador-pequeno) (ornith.) the green kingfisher.

ariranha s. f. a Brazilian otter (Pteroneura brasiliensis).

ariri s. f. = aricuí.

arísaro s. m. (bot.) aron, arum.

ariscar v. to frighten, scare.

arisco s. m. (N. Braz.) a type of fertile sandy soil. ‖ adj. 1. sandy. 2. skittish, shy. 3. distrustful. 4. sulky, wild, rough. 5. austere.

aristado adj. (bot., also aristoso) aristate, provided with one or more awns.

aristarco s. m. Aristarch; a severe critic.

aristiforme adj. m. + f. beardlike, shaped like an awn.

aristocracia s. f. 1. aristocracy, nobility. 2. distinction, superiority.

aristocrata s. m. + f. aristocrat, patrician, noble. ‖ adj. aristocratic(al).

~ rural a country gentleman.

aristocrático adj. aristocratic, aristocratical; noble, distinguished. ‖ aristocraticamente adv. aristocratically.

aristocratismo s. m. aristocratic principles or manners.

aristocratizar v. 1. to render aristocratic. 2. ~-se to become an aristocrat.

aristodemocracia s. f. aristodemocracy.

aristodemocrata s. m. + f. aristodemocrat.

aristolóquia s. f. (bot.) one of the Aristolochiaceae. (birthwort family).

aristoloquiáceo adj. (bot.) aristolochiaceous.

aristotélico adj. Aristotelian, Aristotelic: of or pertaining to Aristoteles.

aristotelismo s. m. Aristotelianism.

aritencéfalo s. m. (anthrop.) cranial capacity of over 1,450 cm³. ‖ adj. descriptive of such a capacity.

aritmética s. f. arithmetic.

aritmético s. m. arithmetician. ‖ adj. arithmetic, arithmetical. ‖ aritmeticamente adv. arithmetically.

aritmografia s. f. arithmography.

aritmográfico adj. arithmographic.

aritmógrafo s. m. arithmograph.

aritmomancia s. f. (also aritmancia) arithhmomancy: divination by means of numbers.

aritmomania s. f. (med.) arithmomania.

aritmômetro s. m. calculating machine.

arlequim s. m. (pl. -ins) 1. harlequin. 2. (ornith.) a sort of nightingale. 3. braggart, bully. 4. (Braz.) a character in the popular farce bumba-meu-boi. 5. (ent.) harlequin beetle (Acrocinus longimanus).

arlequinada s. f. harlequinade; farce.

arlequinal adj. m. + f. (pl. -ais) of or pertaining to a harlequin.

arlequíneo adj. multicoloured (animals).

arma s. f. 1. weapon, arm. 2. power, might. 3. resource, expedient. 4. ~s pl.: a) arms, weapons, armour. b) armed forces. c) coat of arms.

~ branca (mil.) cold steel. ~ de caça hunting weapon. ~ de fogo firearm. ~ de longo alcance long range gun. ~s ao ombro! shoulder arms! apresentar ~s! present arms! às ~s! to arms! depor as ~s to lay down arms. estar em ~s to be up in

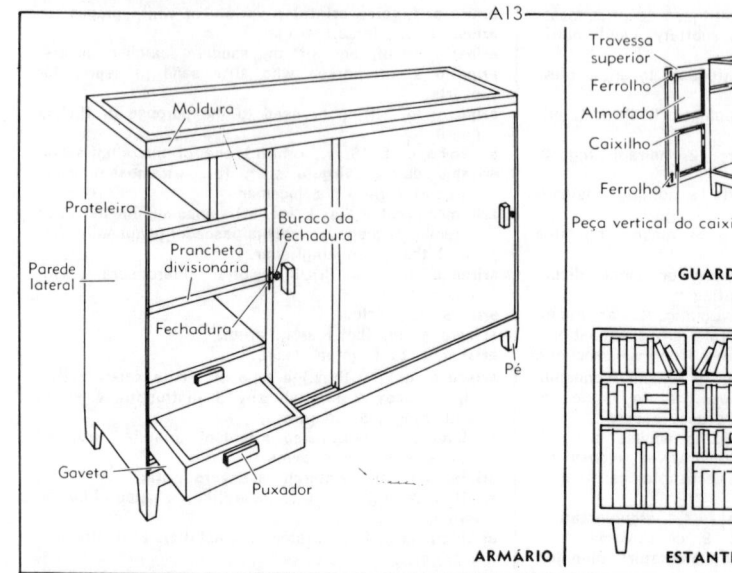

—A13—

ARMÁRIO

GUARDA-ROUPA

ESTANTE PARA LIVROS

arms. **homem de** ~s man-at-arms. **mestre de** ~s fencing master. **passar pelas** ~s to shoot to death or to be shot to death. **pegar em** ~s to take up arms. **praça de** ~s military training ground. **seguir as** ~s to bear arms, be a soldier. **suspensão de** ~s a truce.

armação s. f. (pl. **-ões**) 1. arming. 2. equipment, outfit. 3. frame, framework, easel (plates F 6, M 1). 4. timberwork, structure. 5. (naut.) gear, tackle. 6. furniture, tapestry, carpets. 7. (mil., biol.) armature. 8. casement, setting. 9. (Braz.) low rain-clouds. ~ **de concreto** (archit.) reforced concrete structure. ~ **de cama** bedstead (plate C 7). ~ **de veado ou de boi** horns of stags or oxen (plate A 14). ~ **de janela** window frame. ~ **de pescaria** fishing tackle.

armada s. f. 1. armada, fleet, navy. 2. (also fig.) snare. 3. (Braz.) spectre. 4. feat, prowess.

armadilha (I) s. f. 1. snare, gin. 2. net, pitfall, trick, cheat, swindle.
armar ~s to set traps. **cair na** ~ to fall into the trap.

armadilha (II) s. f. (obs.) a flotilla.

armado adj. 1. armed, harnessed. 2. supplied with, equipped. 3. forewarned. 4. ready, prepared. 5. adorned.
~ **de ponto em branco** armed from top to toe. **à mão -a** by force of arms. **chapéu** ~ cocked hat.

armador s. m. 1. shipowner. 2. person who arms or fits out. 3. trapper. 4. hook of a hammock. 5. undertaker, mortician. 6. church decorator.

armadouras s. f. (also **armadoiras**) shores, props to support a ship (when out of the water).

armadura s. f. 1. armour, suit of armour, mail. 2. armament, arms, weapons. 3. (tech.); a) armature (also electr.) (plate C 9). b) shielding, plating. c) casing. d) framework. e) frame of a plough (plate C 13). 4. weapon: an animal's horns, teeth, claws. ~ **de malhas de ferro** chain-mail. **proteger com** ~ to armour.

armamentismo s. m. belief in and policy of military strength.

armamentista s. m. + f. adherent of a policy of military strength.

armamento s. m. 1. armament, weapons. 2. arming. 3. accoutrements. 4. (naut.) gunnage.
~ **de um soldado** the weapons of a soldier.

armando s. m. remedy to excite the appetite of horses.

armão s. m. (pl. **-ões**) 1. futchel (of a wagon). 2. (mil.) limber, gun-carriage.

armar v. 1. to arm, put in arms, supply with armament. 2. to equip. 3. to outfit. 4. to prepare, rig (up), dispose. 5. to mount, fix, fit or arrange, furnish (as a room or shop), to cock (a trigger). 6. to frame. 7. (naut.) to commission. 8. to scheme, plot, breed, hatch, brew. 9. to fortify. 10. ~**-se** to arm o. s., get ready or prepared for war.
~ **baionetas** to fix baionets. ~ **barracas** to pitch tents. ~ **castelos no ar** to build castles in the air. ~ **uma armadilha** to set a trap. ~ **uma briga** to start a quarrel. ~ **uma cilada** to lay a snare or an ambush. ~ **uma traição** to plot a conspiracy. ~**-se contra** to get ready against something. ~**-se de paciência** to arm o. s. with patience.

armaria s. f. 1. arsenal, armoury. 2. arms or coat of arms.

armarinheiro s. m. (Braz.) haberdasher.

armarinho s. m. 1. small cupboard, cabinet (plate D 4). 2. (Braz.) haberdashery, a haberdasher's shop: shop of small wares, notion store.

armário s. m. cupboard (plate A 13), buffet, case, locker, press, cabinet.
~ **de pão** breadbox (plate C 20). ~ **de remédios** medicine chest. ~ **de roupa** press; linen (clothes) closet. ~ **para livros** bookcase. ~ **para louça** china closet. ~**s de parede** wall cabinets (plate C 20).

armazém s. m. (pl. **-éns**) 1. store, shop. 2. warehouse, magazine, storehouse, depot (plate E 12).
~ **alfandegário** bonded store (plate P 16). ~ **de atacado** wholesale warehouse. ~ **de secos e molhados** (also **mercearia**) grocery store.

armazenado adj. stored, laid up, warehoused.
a colheita foi ~**a** the crops were gathered in.

armazenagem s. f. (pl. **-ens**) 1. storage, warehousing. 2. warehouse charges. 3. demurrage charges. 4. hoarding.

armazenar v. 1. to store, lay up. 2. to stockpile. 3. to garner. 4. to harvest.
~ em caixa to bin. **~ em celeiro** to cellar. **~ em excesso** to overstore.
armazenário s. m. (N. Braz.) 1. dealer in sugar or cotton. 2. owner of a warehouse of sugar or cotton.
armazeneiro s. m. (S. Braz.) storekeeper, owner of a warehouse.
armazenista s. m. (Braz.) person who is in charge of a store, warehouse.
armeiro s. m. 1. armourer. 2. gunsmith, gunman. 3. armoury.
armela s. f. an iron or wooden staple for a lock or bolt.
armelina s. f. (also **pele de ~**) ermine fur.
armelino s. m. (zool.) ermine, a sort of weasel. ‖ adj. ermined, adorned with ermine.
armênico, armênio s. m. Armenian, native or inhabitant of Armenia. ‖ adj. Armenian: of or referring to Armenia.
armental adj. m. + f. (pl. **-ais**) referring to a herd of cattle.
armento s. m. herd of cattle.
armentoso adj. abounding in cattle or herds.
arméu s. m. (also **armo**) a distaff full of yarn, linen or flax.
armezim s. m. (pl. **-ins**) a kind of Bengal taffeta.
armífero s. m. (obs.) a soldier. ‖ adj. armigerous: bearing arms or weapons.
armila s. f. 1. = **armela**. 2. (archit.) annulet, torus. 3. bracelet. 4. (astr.) armil.
armilar adj. m. + f. 1. armillary. 2. consisting of rings.
esfera ~ (astr.) armillary sphere.
armilheiro s. m. small firmer, ripping chisel.
armim s. m. (pl. **-ins**) (also **armino**) white or black spots close to a horse's hoof.
arminado adj. having spots near the hoofs.
arminhado adj. ermined.
arminho s. m. 1. ermine: a) the animal. b) its fur. 2. (fig.) whiteness. 3. **~s** pl. titles of nobility, position or rank.
armipotente adj. m. + f. 1. armipotent, powerful. 2. (poet.) valiant, mighty.
armissono adj. (poet.) brandishing arms.
armista s. m. + f. armourist: person skilled in heraldry.
armistício s. m. armistice, truce, suspension of hostilities.
armolão s. m. (pl. **-ões**) (Braz., bot.) spinach.
armoriado adj. armorial.
armorial s. m. (pl. **-ais**) book on armoury, heraldry. ‖ adj. m. + f. armorial.
armoriar v. to furnish or provide with heraldic arms.
armoricano s. m. (also **armórico**) Armorican, inhabitant of ancient Brittany. ‖ adj. Armoric.
arnado, arnedo, arneiro s. m. barren sandy ground.
arnela s. f. stump, snag of a tooth.
arnês s. m. (pl. **arneses**) 1. (also hist., mil.) harness. 2. (hist.) armour, coat of mail. 3. (fig.) protection.
arsenar v. 1. to harness. 2. to protect with or to put on an armour.
arnica s. f. (bot.) 1. mountain arnica. 2. the tincture it yields.
aro (I) s. m. 1. iron or wooden hoop. 2. environs, adjacent parts. 3. rim of a wheel (plates B 11, R 2). 4. (tech.) disk. 5. door-frame, window-frame. 6. flange.
~ do farol (mot.) head lamp glass rim. **~ do volante** rim of flywheel.
aro (II) s. m. (bot., also **arão**) arum.
aroeira s. f. (Braz.) the California pepper tree.

aroeira-da-praia s. f. (pl. **aroeiras-da-praia**) (Braz., bot.) the lentisk pistache.
aroeira-de-bugre s. f. (pl. **aroeiras-de-bugre**) (Braz.) plant of the sumac or cashew family.
aroeira-do-campo s. f. (pl. **aroeiras-do-campo**) (Braz., bot.) one of the Anacardiaceae (Schinus weinmanniaefolia).
aroeira-do-rio-grande s. f. (pl. **aroeiras-do-rio-grande**) (Braz.) the pinkberry pepper tree.
arolio s. m. (zool.) arolium.
aroma s. m. (also **arômata** m., **aromaticidade** f.) 1. aroma. 2. perfume, fragrance. 3. bouquet; flavour. 4. smell, scent, odour.
aromal adj. m. + f. (pl. **-ais**) aromatic, fragrant.
aromático adj. 1. aromatical. 2. balsamic. 3. flavoured. 4. odoriferous, spicy. ‖ **aromaticamente** adv. aromatically; balsamically.
aromatização s. f. (pl. **-ões**) aromatization.
aromatizador s. m. aromatiser, flavourer. ‖ adj. aromatizing, flavourous.
aromatizante adj. m. + f. aromatizing, flavouring.
aromatizar v. 1. to aromatize. 2. to scent. 3. to flavour. 4. to perfume.
arpado adj. barbed.
arpão s. m. (pl. **-ões**) 1. harpoon (plate A 2). 2. gaff. 3. fish-gig. 4. eelspear.
~ de lenhadores peavey.
arpar, arpear v. (also **arpoar**) 1. to harpoon. 2. to grapple. 3. to spear. 4. (fig.) to seduce.
arpejar v. (mus.) to arpeggiate.
arpejo s. m. (mus.) arpeggio, a striking of notes in rapid succession.
arpéu s. m. (mar.) 1. grapnel, grappling iron. 2. small harpoon. 3. **~s** pl. (coll.) paws, claws, nails.
arpista adj. m. + f. (Braz.) 1. distrustful. 2. fearful. 3. skittish. 4. cautious.
arpoação s. f. 1. harpooning. 2. grappling.
arpoador s. m. harpooner.
arpoar v. 1. to harpoon; to spear or impale with a harpoon. 2. to seduce, to hook.
arpoeira s. f. 1. rope tied to a harpoon. 2. iron head of a harpoon.
arqueação s. f. (pl. **-ões**) (also **arqueio** m.) 1. arching: a) vaulting. b) bending. 2. curvature. 3. gauging of the cubic content of a ship, barrel.
arqueado adj. 1. arch-shaped, arched, bent, round. 2. gauged (as to its cubic contents).
arqueador s. m. 1. person who arches, bends. 2. (naut.) gauger.
arqueadura s. f. (also **arqueamento** m.) 1. incurvation, incurvature, curvature. 2. camber. 3. warp. 4. vault. 5. sag.
arqueano s. m. (geol.) the Archean period. ‖ adj. Archean, Archaean.
arquear v. to arch. 2. to vault, bow, curve. 3. to warp. 4. to gage, gauge, measure (as the dimensions of a ship or the capacity of a cask). 5. **~-se** to become curved.
~ as sobrancelhas to frown.
arqueiro (I) s. m. 1. archer. 2. (Braz., also **goleiro**) goalkeeper (soccer).
arqueiro (II) s. m. chest maker.
arquejante adj. m. + f. 1. panting, gasping. 2. out of breath, wheezy.
arquejar (I) v. 1. to puff, blow, pant. 2. to labour, gasp for breath, wheeze.
arquejar (II) v. = **arquear**.
arquejo s. m. (also **arquejamento**) 1. panting. 2. shortness of breath. 3. gasp. 4. asthma.
arqueografia s. f. archaeography.
arqueográfico adj. archaeographical.
arqueologia s. f. archaeology, antiquarianism.
arqueológico adj. archaeologic.

arqueólogo s. m. archaeologist, antiquary.
arqueta s. f. 1. a small chest or safe. 2. a poor-box. 3. box of a hawker or ped(d)ler.
arquete (I) s. m. (mus.) little bow, arch.
arquete (II) s. m. burial urn.
arquétipo s. m. archetype, prototype. ‖ adj. archetypical, prototypic.
arquiabade s. m. archabbot, the superior of a monastery.
arquiabadia s. f. archabbey, the principal monastery of a region.
arquiavô s. m. **arquiavó** f. (pl. **arquiavós** or **arquiavôs**) great-great-grandfather (a remote ancestor).
arquibancada s. f. (Braz.) tiers of seats or benches as in a stadium.
arquibanco s. m. bench with a drawer below the seat.
arquiclavo s. m. the regent or superior of a church or monastery.
arquidiácono s. m. archdeacon.
arquidiocesano adj. archdiocesan.
arquidiocese s. f. archdiocese.
arquiducado s. m. archduchy.
arquiduque s. m. archduke.
arquiduquesa s. f. archduchess.
arquiepiscopado s. m. 1. archiepiscopate. 2. archbishopric.
arquiepiscopal adj. m. + f. (pl. **-ais**) archiepiscopal.
arquilho s. m. ring or hoop either of wood or metal.
arquimilionário s. m. multimillionaire.
arquimosteiro s. m. the main monastery of an order.
arquipélago s. m. archipelago.
arquitetar v. 1. to build, construct, exercise the profession of an architect. 2. to project, plan. 3. to conceive. 4. to scheme.
arquiteto s. m. 1. architect; master builder. 2. creator, founder.
arquitetônico adj. architectonic(al).
arquitetura s. f. (also **arquitetônica**) 1. architectonics, architecture. 2. (fig.): a) plan, project. b) form, shape.
arquitetural adj. m. + f. (pl. **-ais**) architectural. ‖ **-mente** adv. architecturally.
arquitravada s. f. (archit.) friezeless moulding.
arquitravado adj. (archit.) friezeless.
arquitrave s. f. architrave; principal beam of a structure, epistyle (plate P 10).
arquivamento s. m. filing (as of papers).
arquivar v. 1. to collect documents and other papers in archives, file. 2. to shelve. 3. to record; register. ~ **um assunto** (coll.) to quit, forget about a thing. ~ **uma correspondência** to file a letter.
arquivista s. m. + f. 1. archivist, filing clerk. 2. registrar. 3. recorder.
arquivística s. f. technique of filing or recording.
arquivo s. m. 1. archive, a place where records are kept, file. 2. register. 3. filing department. 4. index book.
~ **do Estado** office of public records, chancery. **ficha de** ~ index card. **no** ~ on file.
arquivolta s. f. (archit.) archivolt, ring (plate A 12).
arrabalde s. m. suburbs, environs, outskirts, adjacency. **rumo aos** ~s uptown.
arrabaldeiro adj. living in adjacent parts of a town.
arrabil s. m. (pl. **-is**) a rebec(k), musical instrument like a small fiddle.
arrabileiro s. m. person who plays on a rebec(k).
arrabujar-se v. to become ill-humoured.
arraçar v. to improve the livestock by crossbreeding with superior animals.
arracimado adj. grapelike, having the form of grapes, clustery.
arracimar-se v. to take the form of grapes, bunches, clusters.

arraçoamento s. m. division into rations.
arraçoar v. 1. to divide into rations. 2. to allow or give a ration to.
arraia (I) s. f. (ichth. also **raia**) 1. ray, skate, any of the elasmobranch fishes. 2. (Braz.) a small paper kite.
arraia (II) s. f. border, frontier.
arraia (III) s. f. (also **arraia-miúda**) the populace, masses.
arraiada s. f. sunrise; dawn.
arraiado adj. striped.
arraia-elétrica s. f. (pl. **arraias-elétricas**) the electric ray (Narcine brasiliensis).
arraial s. m. (pl. **-iais**) 1. camp, camping ground. 2. country festivity. 3. hamlet. 4. small village.
arraialesco adj. of or referring to: 1. a camp or bivouac. 2. a rural festivity. 3. a hamlet.
arraia-mijona s. f. (pl. **arraias-mijonas**) (Braz.) a paper kite with a string of flags.
arraia-miúda s. f. (pl. **arraias-miúdas**) the populace, masses.
arraiano s. m. frontiersman, borderer. ‖ adj. living at the border, in the neighborhood.
arraiar v. 1. to shine, to cast forth beams and rays. 2. (also **raiar**) to rise (sun).
arraia-viola s. f. (pl. **arraias-viola**) guitar-fish.
arraieira s. f. fishing net, especially to catch rays.
arraieiro s. m. (N. Braz.) ray fisher.
arraigada s. f. 1. root of the tongue. 2. ~s pl. (naut.) ropes of the mast.
arraigado adj. 1. deep-rooted. 2. radicated. 3. inveterate, old. 4. incarnate. 5. ingrain.
arraigar v. 1. to root, take root, irradicate. 2. to grow. 3. ~-**se**: a) to become inveterate or incurable. b) to settle, fix definite residence.
arrais s. m., sg. + pl. 1. master of a boat (usually coastal). 2. (fig.) guide, conductor.
arralentar v. 1. to delute, make thinner, watery (as coffee or soup). 2. to pare down (by cutting or chiseling).
arramalhar v. (also **ramalhar**) 1. to hide below twigs. 2. to struggle in the net; flounder (fish) 3. to rustle. 4. ~-**se** to come close to.
arramar v. to spread, ramify, branch out (tree).
arrampado s. m. (Braz.) slope, declivity.
arrampadouro s. m. (also **arrampadoiro**) 1. sloping ground, hill-side. 2. fallow field.
arranca s. f. 1. = **arrancada**. 2. (Braz.) harvesting of the cassava (**mandioca**).
arrancada s. f. 1. pull, jolt, jerk. 2. plucking, pulling up. 3. ready start (as of an engine), quick getaway. 4. dash. 5. soaring, swing, outleap. 6. cleared land (of stumps, shrubs or the like).
~ **final** (sport) final heat. **de uma só** ~ at a stretch. **fugir de** ~ to take to one's heels.
arrancador s. m. puller, jerker.
arrancadura s. f. (also **arrancadela**, **arrancamento** m.) act of pulling out, an uprooting.
arranca-estrepe s. m. (pl. **arranca-estrepes**) (bot.) the barbifruit pavonia (Pavonia spinifex).
arranca-milho s. m. (pl. **arranca-milhos**) (ornith.) the chopi grackle.
arrancar v. 1. to pull or tear away violently; to pluck out. 2. to force, wrench or wrest from, to snatch away. 3. to root up, to uproot. 4. to start rapidly and with force (as an engine). 5. to leave suddenly, abruptly; run away; withdraw. 6. to extort. 7. to expectorate, retch, agonize. 8. to extract.
~ **contra alguém** to fly at a person. ~ **um dente** to pull a tooth. ~ **da espada** to draw the sword. ~ **um grito** to let out a cry (as of pain or rage). ~ **à morte** to snatch from death. ~ **o motor** to start the motor. ~ **um prego** to pull out a nail. ~

um **segredo** to force or drag out a secret from a person. ~ **um suspiro** to fetch a sigh. ~ **o vôo** to take off (airplane). **o ~ da boiada** the stampede of a herd of oxen. **arranque-o da cama!** rout him out of bed!

arranca-rabo s. m. (pl. **arranca-rabos**) (Braz., pop.) shindy, brawl, melee, quarrel; scuffle, dog-fight.

arranca-sonda s. m. (pl. **arranca-sondas**) (min.) instrument to pull out jammed boring tools.

arranca-toco s. m. (pl. **arranca-tocos**) 1. (Braz., pop.) a neurasthenic. 2. (N. Braz.) shindy, melee.

arranca-tocos s. m., sg. + pl. (Braz.) 1. bully, ruffian. 2. strong, resistant cloth. 3. (also **destocador**) stump puller.

arranchação s. f. (pl. **-ões**) (Braz., pop.) 1. home, dwelling. 2. temporary domicile.

arranchamento s. m. (Braz.) a group of huts or cottages.

arranchar v. 1. to lodge, harbour. 2. to assemble in a group of huts or cottages. 3. (mil.) to mess, take meals with a mess. 4. to make a cottage for temporary use; to establish o. s. temporarily.

arranco s. m. 1. sudden pull, yank, lug, jerk. 2. sudden start, spurt. 3. rooting up. 4. flight, soaring up (bird). 5. **~s pl.**: a) convulsion, gasps. b) retchings. c) rattling in the throat.
aos ~s by jerks. **os ~s da morte** the pangs of death. **dar os últimos ~s** to die.

arrancorar-se v. to become rancorous.

arranha-céu s. m. (pl. **arranha-céus**) skyscraper, building with many stories.

arranhador s. m. 1. scratcher, scraper. 2. bad musician.

arranhadura s. f., **arranhão** m. (pl. **~s, -ões**) a scratch; light wound.

arranhar v. 1. to scratch, graze, scrabble. 2. to scrape (on a musical instrument). 3. to mangle, bungle. 4. **~-se** to suffer a slight wound. 5. to speak imperfectly (a language), to lead a miserable life.

arranjadeiro adj. methodical; careful; neat.

arranjado adj. (Braz.) arranged; almost wealthy; well off, prosperous.
estou bem ~ (coll.) I am done for.

arranjamento s. m. 1. arrangement, arranging. 2. disposal, composition, conformation. 3. agreement.

arranjar v. 1. to arrange: a) provide for. b) set in order. c) adjust, settle. d) dispose. e) accommodate, compromise. f) manage. g) tidy. 2. to obtain, get, wangle. 3. **~-se** to know how to take care of o. s. **~ dinheiro** to raise money. **~ o assunto** to straighten out affairs. **~ uma colocação** to find a job. **~-se na vida** to make a good living, to do nicely. **arranje-me um carro** find me a taxi. **arranje-se de acordo com suas possibilidades** cut your coat according to your cloth. **deixe, que eu arranjo tudo** leave it to me, I settle matters for you. **ele que se arranje** let that be his problem. **isso há de arranjar-se** it will dry straight, turn out well.

arranjo s. m. 1. arrangement, settling. 2. fixing. 3. disposition. 4. solution. 5. good order. 6. repair(ing). 7. make-up plot. 8. **~s** pl. arrangements.

arranque s. m. 1. sudden start. 2. (sport) push, thrust, spurt. 3. (archit.) springer of an arch. 4. (mot.) starter, self-starter.
~ elétrico electric starter.

arrapazado adj. boyish, childish. || **-amente** adv. boyishly.

arraposar-se v. 1. to be astute and cunning like a fox. 2. to curl up to sleep.

arras s. f. pl. 1. earnest-money, handsel. 2. pledge, token. 3. jointure. 4. dowry. 5. superiority. 6. handicap.

arrás s. m. Arras tapestry.

arrasado adj. 1. levelled, laid even, demolished, razed. 2. knocked down. 3. crushed.
as casas foram ~s the houses were made even with the ground. **olhos ~s em lágrimas** eyes swimming in tears.

arrasador s. m. 1. demolisher, destroyer. 2. a strickle. || adj. (also **arrasante** m. + f.) crushing, ruining, demolishing.
argumento ~ a shattering argument.

arrasadura s. f., **arrasamento** m. 1. a levelling with the ground, demolition, razing; overthrow. 2. striking the overmeasure of corn.

arrasar v. 1. to demolish. 2. to lay even with the ground. 3. to level. 4. to raze. 5. to strike corn. 6. (fig.) to crush; ruin utterly; humiliate, humble. 7. **~-se** to humble o. s., come down a peg or two. **~ com alguém** (fig.) to tear someone to pieces. **arrasaram a fortaleza** they dismantled the fort. **os olhos arrasaram-se-lhe de lágrimas** her eyes swam in tears.

arrastadeiro adj. dragging, trailing.
plantas -as (bot.) trailers.

arrastadiço adj. 1. easily dragged. 2. (fig.) easily influenced.

arrastado adj. 1. dragged, dragging. 2. laggard. 3. miserable, wretched. 4. tired, fatigued. || **-amente** adv. scantily, poorly, miserably.
andar ~ (fig.) to live poorly. **a nação foi -a à guerra** the country was plunged into war.

arrastador s. m. (N. Braz.) a rough footpath through the forest.

arrastadura s. f., **arrastamento** m. act or fact of dragging.

arrastão s. m. (pl. **-ões**) 1. wrench, jerk; dragging, trailing. 2. (bot.) sucker. 3. fishing net, trawl. 4. (Braz.) the taking in of the fishing net.
ir no ~ (Braz., pop.) to be easily influenced. **levar de ~** to drag, draw along (as in a net).

arrasta-pé s. m. (pl. **arrasta-pés**) (Braz., pop.) (also **bate-chinela, gafieira**) 1. a dance, a ball party; (U. S. A.) hop. 2. a low quality ball.

arrastar v. 1. to drag, draw. 2. to pull. 3. to induce into, to plunge. 4. to trail, crawl. 5. (chem., phys.) to entrain. 6. **~-se** to grovel, lug, creep, move slowly and with difficulty.
~ a asa (coll.) to court, make love. **~ a vida** (fig.) to vegetate, be hard up. **~ a voz** to drawl. **~ na lama** to drag a person's name or reputation in the mud. **~ os pés** 1. to trollop. 2. (coll.) to dance. **~ rodopiando** to whirl. **rede de ~** draw-net, sweep-net.

arrasto s. m. 1. trailing. 2. a haul. 3. trawl, dragnet. 4. a transport of logs out of the woods. 5. (N. Braz.) shallow place in a river. 6. decay.

arrátel s. m. (pl. **-eis**) a former Portuguese unit of weight, corresponding to about 16 ounces.

arratelar v. to weigh or sell by pounds.

arrazoado (I) s. m. 1. (jur.) pleading, plea, reason, defence. 2. empty talk.

arrazoado (II) adj. 1. rational, reasonable, fit, just. 2. moderate. || **-amente** adv. reasonably; conveniently.

arrazoador s. m. 1. pleader (in court); orator. 2. arguer, reasoner. 3. talker, chatterbox. || adj. reasoning, arguing.

arrazoamento s. m. 1. reasoning. 2. argument. 3. discourse. 4. judgement.

arrazoar v. to plead, defend. 2. to reason, argue, discuss, discourse, dispute. 3. to talk idly. 4. to sing an improvised song at the guitar. 5. **~-se** to yield to reason.
~ o feito to take up the plea.

arre (interj.) 1. dammit! yah! 2. gee up! giddap! (to urge on horses)

arreação s. f. (pl. -ões) (also **arreamento**) tapping of a rubber tree.
arreado adj. harnessed.
arreador s. m. 1. harnesser. 2. mule-driver, muleteer.
arreamento s. m. 1. furniture of a house. 2. act or fact of harnessing. 3. household goods or trappings.
arrear v. 1. to harness. 2. to array. 3. to dress, adorn. 4. to furnish, provide with furniture, equip. 5. ~-se: a) to provide o. s. with furniture. b) to adorn o. s. c) to boast.
~ **as velas** to strike sail. ~ **a bandeira** to strike the flag.
arreata s. f. (also **reata, reate**) halter or rope of a halter.
arreatadura s. f. 1. cordage. 2. act or fact of fastening with ropes. 3. mooring cables.
arreatar v. 1. to secure with ropes or cables. 2. to tie horses or mules to the packsaddle of the animal that goes in front. 3. (naut.) to woold.
arrebanhador s. m. herder, shepherd. ‖ adj. herding.
arrebanhar v. 1. to herd. 2. to assemble or bring together. 3. (fig.) to scrape together. 4. ~-se to gather, flock.
~ **eleitores** to round up voters.
arrebatado adj. 1. vehement, quick-tempered, passionate. 2. overhasty, rash. 3. rapt, ecstatic. 4. hot-headed, impetuous, violent. 5. enraptured. 6. furious. ‖ -**amente** adv. rashly.
arrebatador s. m. ravisher; person who or thing that ravishes. ‖ adj. (also **arrebatante** m. + f.) ravishing, charming, overpowering.
arrebatamento s. m. 1. ecstasy, trance, ravishing. 2. fit of anger, furiousness. 3. rashness, impetuosity, hastiness, precipitation. 4. enthusiasm, overjoy. 5. passion. 6. snatching.
arrebatar v. 1. to snatch, grab. 2. to take by force. 3. to rash, rape. 4. to enchant. 5. to enrapture, entrance, delight. 6. to transport. 7. ~-se to fly into a passion; to enrage.
~ **a audiência** to hold the stage. **a morte arrebatou-o de nós** death took him away from us.
arrebém s. m. (pl. -éns) (naut.) a cable or rope.
arrebenta-boi s. m. (pl. **arrebenta-bois**) (bot.) the harebell or bluebell.
arrebentação s. f. (pl. -ões) 1. breaking of the waves; roaring of the surf. 2. (coll.) lack of money.
arrebenta-cavalo s. m. (pl. **arrebenta-cavalos**) (Braz.) a plant of the nightshade family.
arrebentadiço adj. easily torn or broken.
arrebentado adj. (also **rebentado**) 1. torn; broken. 2. ruined; penniless. 3. worn out, dog-tired, beaten up.
arrebentamento s. m. tearing, parting; burst, bursting; dissilience.
arrebenta-pedra s. f. (pl. **arrebenta-pedras**) (Braz.) (also **quebra-pedra, erva-pombinha** and **saxífraga**) plant of the spurge family.
arrebentar v. 1. to tear; burst, break, crush, dash to pieces; explode; rift. 2. to wish eagerly, to long for. 3. (bot.) to bud; branch.
~ **de inveja** to pop with envy. ~ **de riso** to split one's sides with laughing. ~ **um pneu** to blow out a tire. **o ~ das ondas** the breaking of the waves. **arrebentou uma guerra** a war broke out. **meus ouvidos estão arrebentando** my ears split.
arrebento s. m. = **rebento**.
arrebicado adj. ridiculously made up, dolled.
arrebicar v. 1. to overdress. 2. to bedizen. 3. ~-se to rig o. s. out, to smarten, use exaggerate make-up.
arrebique s. m. 1. face make-up. 2. finery, full dress, fard; 3. frippery. 4. affected style. 5. embellishment. 6. trifles, vagaries.

arrebitado adj. 1. snub, retroussé, turned up. 2. (Braz., fig.) ill-tempered. 3. smart. 4. pretentious, insolent, bold.
nariz ~ snub nose.
arrebitamento s. m. 1. raising, turning up. 2. (fig.) haughtiness, pride.
arrebitar v. 1. to turn up, raise, lift. 2. to clinch (a nail), to rivet. 3. to cock (a hat). 4. ~-se to grow proud, become angry.
arrebita-rabo s. f. (pl. **arrebita-rabos**) the Brazilian mockingbird.
arrebite s. m. rivet.
arrebito s. m. 1. upturn, raising. 2. clinched nail. 3. (fig.) insolence, haughtiness.
arrebol s. m. (pl. -óis) afterglow; aurora, redness of the clouds at sunrise or sunset.
arrebolar (I) v. to round, give a round form.
arrebolar (II) v. to make red, give the colour of the sunset.
arre-burrinho s. m. (pl. **arre-burrinhos**) 1. see-saw, swing. 2. (fam.) butt (of jokes), anyone's drudge.
arrecabe s. m. rope of the drawnet.
arrecadação s. f. (pl. -ões) 1. magazine, deposit, depository. 2. collection of taxes, exaction. 3. gathering, levying. 4. prison, custody.
arrecadado adj. 1. exact, diligent, careful. 2. saving, economic, frugal. 3. in custody.
arrecadador s. m. exactor, collector, tax-collector.
arrecadamento s. m. 1. (tax) collecting. 2. safe-keeping. 3. attainment.
arrecadar v. 1. to collect duties or taxes. 2. to deposit, take care of, lay up. 3. to levy, exact, demand. 4. to secure. 5. to take into custody.
arrecadas s. f. pl. earrings; ornaments.
arrecear v. = **recear**.
arrecuas s. f. pl. used in the adverbial locution: **às** ~ backwards.
arreda interj. back with you! go away! get back! out of the way!
arredado adj. 1. withdrawn. 2. removed. 3. put back. 4. distant.
arredamento s. m. removing, removal, withdrawal, putting aside.
arredar v. 1. to remove, withdraw. 2. to pull, draw back, put or push aside. 3. to leave off. 4. to cause to give up (purpose). 5. to overcome, surpass. ~-se **de** to withdraw or turn from; to go back, retrocede.
arredável adj. m. + f. (pl. -áveis) that may be set aside, removable.
arre-diabo s. m. (pl. **arre-diabos**) (Braz., bot., also **urtiga-de-mamão**) spurge nettle.
arredio adj. 1. withdrawn, far off. 2. lonesome, apart 3. retired, unsociable. 4. strayed, wild (animals). 5. aloof.
arredondado adj. 1. round, roundish. 2. (bot.) rotundate. 3. (tech.) cambered.
arredondamento s. m. roundness, rounding off.
arredondar v. 1. to make round, to round. 2. to sphere. 3. to circularize.
~ **a conta** to make a round sum. ~ **cifras** to round out figures.
arredor adj. adjacent, near, close by. ‖ adv. around, about.
arredores s. m. pl. 1. environs, environment. 2. surroundings, outskirts. 3. adjacency, vicinage, precinct.
nos ~s **da cidade** in the outskirts of the city.
arrefeçado adj. (fig.) degraded, abased, diminished.
arrefeçar v. 1. to abate, to lower (the prices), to sell under the price. 2. (fig.) to degrade. 3. to reduce, diminish.

arrefecedor adj. growing indifferent; diminishing.

arrefecer v. 1. to cool, chill. 2. to allay. 3. to become less intense, moderate. 4. to grow indifferent. 5. to grow cold.

~ **no zelo** to cool down (enthusiasm).

arrefecido adj. cooled, cooled off.

arrefecimento s. m. 1. cooling (off). 2. (fig.) relenting, moderation, slackness, carelessness. 3. refrigeration.

arrefentado adj. somewhat cold.

arrefentar v. to cool, to make cold.

arregaçada s. f. 1. lapful. 2. a lot. 3. tucking up (as of a sleeve).

arregaçar v. 1. to tuck up, pin up, roll up (as trousers, skirts, sleeves). 2. to truss. 3. to draw up (as lips).

arregaço s. m. (Braz.) conflict; violent discussion.

arregalado adj. wide-open (eyes).

ele ficou de olhos ~s his eyes widened.

arregalar v. to open one's eyes wide, stare or gaze at.

arreganhar v. 1. to grin, laugh. 2. to snarl, bare the teeth as in anger. 3. to sneer, mock. 4. to split, open (fruit).

~**-se de frio** to be shivering with cold.

arreganho s. m. 1. snar(ling). 2. grinning, grin. 3. courage, boldness. 4. haughtiness. 5. martial, ferocious appearance.

arregimentação s. f. (pl. **-ões**) regimentation.

arregimentar v. to regiment, to form into regiments or troops.

arreglar v. (S. Braz.) 1. to adjust things, to settle, combine. 2. to put in order.

arreglo s. m. (Braz.) 1. settlement. 2. (theat.) adaptation of a play.

arregoar v. 1. to furrow, channel, trench. 2. to crack, split, gape.

arreio s. m. 1. saddlery, harness, gear (plate A 12). 2. array; ornament.

sacudir os ~s (S. Braz., fig.) to revolt against something.

arreitar v. 1. to excite lust in. 2. ~**-se** to feel lust for.

arrejeitar v. to throw to a distance.

arrelhada s. f. scraper to clean the plough.

arrelia s. f. 1. tease. 2. aversion, vexation. 3. bad omen.

que ~! what a nuisance!

arreliado adj. (Braz., pop.) 1. quarrelsome; insolent. 2. disgusting.

arreliante adj. m. + f. annoying.

arreliar v. 1. to tease, upset. 2. to vex. 3. to annoy, bother, pester. 4. ~**-se** to grow angry.

não se arrelie! keep your temper! **não me arrelie!** don't try my temper!

arreliento adj. teasing, irritating; vexatious, disgusting.

arrelvar v. to sod, become covered with grass.

arremangar v. 1. to pull or tuck up the sleeves. 2. to threaten with the lifted arm. 3. ~**-se** to get ready.

arremansar-se v. to stagnate or flow countercurrentwise along the river-side.

arrematação s. f. (pl. **-ões**) (also **rematação**) 1. public sale, auction. 2. outbidding. 3. finishing, final touch.

~ **judicial** forced sale.

arrematador s. m. the highest bidder at an auction. ‖ adj. outbidding.

arrematante s. m. + f., adj. m. + f. ≐ **arrematador**.

arrematar (I) v. 1. to finish up. 2. to give the final touch to. 3. to accomplish. 4. to hoe, weed (maize). 5. ~**-se** to be finished, settled.

arrematar (II) v. 1. to buy or sell at auctions, to sell to the highest bidder. 2. to damn; yell, shout.

arremate s. m. (also **remate**) 1. = **arrematação**. 2. end, conclusion. 3. peak. 4. knot, fastening of a seam.

arremedador s. m. mocker, counterfeiter, imitator, mimic.

arremedar v. 1. to imitate, impersonate. 2. to ape, mimic, mock. 3. to parody. 4. to counterfeit. 5. to resemble, come near to.

arremedilho s. m. (theat.) short, witty show in a popular mould; farce.

arremedo (ê) s. m. 1. imitation, mimicry. 2. dissembling. 3. disguise, pretence. 4. counterfeitment.

~**s de guerra** mock fights.

arremessado adj. heedless, reckless, careless.

arremessador s. m. thrower, hurler, darter. ‖ adj. throwing.

arremessão s. m. (pl. **-ões**) 1. dart, javelin, missile. 2. act of throwing, flinging.

arremessar v. 1. to fling, dart, throw, hurl, cast. 2. to jaculate, bolt. 3. (tech.) to launch, expel. 4. ~**-se** to throw o. s. on; to run or rush headlong into, to dash.

~ **novas tropas contra o inimigo** to throw new troops into the battle. ~**-se em negócio perigoso** to embark upon a dangerous enterprise.

arremesso (ê) s. m. (**arremessamento**) 1. act or fact of throwing, rushing. 2. throw, thrust. 3. fling; push; yerk, pull. 4. impetus. 5. audacity, boldness. 6. attack, onset, assault. 7. threat.

~ **de poeta** poetical genius. **arma de** ~ missile weapon. **fazer** ~**s de** to make much fun about.

arremetedor s. m. 1. aggressor, assaulter, attacker. 2. thrower, hurler. ‖ adj. aggressive.

arremetente adj. m. + f. aggressive, assaulting, on the onset.

arremeter v. 1. to assail, invade. 2. to attack, assault, charge. 3. to rush violently upon. 4. to incite, provoke. 5. to throw, hurl.

arremetida s. f. (also **arremetedura** f., **arremetimento** m.) 1. attack, onset, onslaught, assault, swoop, dash, sally. 2. thrust. 3. daring action.

arreminação s. f. act or fact of flying into a passion.

arreminado adj. furious, angry.

arreminar-se v. (pop.) to fly into a passion, threaten.

arrendado (I) adj. rented, tenemental, leased.

arrendado (II) adj. laced, trimmed with lace.

arrendado (III) adj. (also **redrado**) hoed and weeded (as vines or maize).

arrendador s. m. lessor, landlord, letter, hirer, renter. ‖ adj. leasing.

arrendamento s. m. (also **arrendação** f.) renting tenure, lease, tenantry, hire.

~ **de feudos** crown lease. ~ **e empréstimo** lend-lease. ~ **vitalício** life tenancy. **contrato de** ~ a lease contract. **dar em** ~ to let out on lease.

arrendar (I) v. to let, rent, lease, hire.

~ **uma fazenda** to rent a farm. **arrenda-se** (Braz., **aluga-se**) **uma casa** a house to let.

arrendar (II) v. (also **redrar**) to hoe and weed vines.

arrendar (III) v. to trim with lace.

arrendar (IV) v. to harness, use to harness (horse).

arrendatário s. m. tenant, renter, leaseholder, lessee.

~ **de fazenda** tenant farmer.

arrendável adj. m. + f. (pl. **-áveis**) rentable, leasable, demisable.

arrendilhado adj. (also **rendilhado**) laced.

arrenegação s. f. (pl. **-ões**) (also **arrenego** m.) 1. apostasy. 2. fury, anger.

arrenegada s. f. ombre, a sort of game of cards.

arrenegado s. m. (Braz., pop.) devil. ‖ adj. 1. renegade, apostate. 2. angry, upset.

arrenegar v. (also **renegar**) 1. to forswear, abjure. 2. to renounce, deny. 3. to detest, abhor, loathe. 4. to execrate, curse. 5. to get mad, angry, upset.

arrepanhado adj. 1. shrivelled, wrinkled. 2. (fig.) avaricious, close-fisted, greedy, niggard.

arrepanhar v. 1. to fold, tuck. 2. to wrinkle, crumple. 3. to take, catch, seize eagerly, gripe, snatch. 4. to steal. 5. to hoard, amass.

arrepelação s. f. (pl. **-ões**) (also **arrepelada** f., **arrepelamento**, **arrepelão** m.) 1. tugging, plucking up (hair, feathers, etc.). 2. pulling, tearing one's hair. 3. tug, violent pull. 4. dishevelment. 5. lament.

arrepelador adj. pulling violently, esp. one's hair.

arrepelar v. 1. to pull out hair or feathers, to tug, twitch. 2. **~-se:** a) to pull one's hair or beard. b) to complain, lament.

arrepender-se v. 1. to repent, be sorry for, regret. 2. to rue. 3. to change one's mind.

   ainda haverão de ~ disso they will live to rue it. **o tempo está se arrependendo** the weather is changing (threatening rain). **você vai ~ disto** you will be sorry for it.

arrependido adj. regretful, penitent, rueful, remorseful, repenting, sorry. ‖ **-amente** adv. ruefully, regretfully.

arrependimento s. m. 1. regret. 2. penitence, repentance. 3. rue, compunction. 4. change of mind. 5. sorrow, remorsefulness.

arrepia-cabelo (I) adv. against the grain, the wrong way.

arrepia-cabelo (II) s. m. (pl. **arrepia-cabelos**) sullen, stand-offish person.

arrepiado adj. 1. standing on end (hair), horrent. 2. hispid, bristly. 3. unkempt. 4. terrified, creepy.

arrepiadura s. f. (also **arrepiamento** m.) act of bristling.

arrepiante adj. m. + f. (also **arrepiador** m.) 1. bristly, upstanding. 2. horrid, terrible.

arrepiar v. 1. to ruffle, to fluff up (hair, feathers), bristle, roughen. 2. to make one's hair stand on end. 3. to frighten, to fill with horror. 4. to make one's flesh creep. 5. to make one's blood run cold. 6. to comb or brush against the hair. 7. **~-se** to shudder, dither, to shiver with cold or fear.

   ~ caminho, a carreira 1. to retrace one's way. 2. to retract.

arrepio s. m. 1. shiver, chill, shudder, creep. 2. horror. 3. (fig.) goose-flesh.

   ao ~ against the hair or grain, the wrong way.

arrepolhado adj. 1. like a cabbage head. 2. (pop.) short and thick, stout. 3. wrapped up in clothes.

arrepolhar v. 1. to take the form of a cabbage. 2. to become puffed up.

arrepsia s. f. hesitation; irresolution.

arrestado s. m. (jur.) person under an attachment. ‖ adj. under an embargo, seized for debt.

arrestante s. m. + f. (jur.) arrester, distrainer, person who requests an embargo.

arrestar v. 1. to apprehend, arrest, seize, confiscate, distress. 2. to attach. 3. to put under distraint.

arresto s. m. (jur.) 1. arrest, seizure, escheat, confiscation. 2. attachment, arrestment.

arretar v. to stop; force to turn back.

arrevesado adj. 1. intricate, obscure. 2. difficult, complicated, crack-jaw.

arrevesar v. (also **revesar**) I. to reverse. 2. to turn upside down or inside out. 3. to make obscure. 4. to alterate the meaning of text, words.

arrevessado s. m. 1. vomit; that which is vomited. 2. (fig.) error, howler.

arrevessar v. 1. to vomit. 2. to detest, hate. 3. to breathe out, breathe one's last. 4. **~-se** to become rough (sea).

arrevesso (ê) adj. twisted.

arriação s. f. (pl. **-ões**) act of dropping, lowering, striking (flag, sails), putting down (burden).

arriar v. 1. to break down, collapse. 2. to lose strength or courage, give up. 3. to lay or put down. 4. to surrender. 5. to drop, lower, strike (flag, sails). 6. to veer, haul.

arriaria s. f. a harness maker's or saddler's trade or workshop.

arriba (I) s. f. = **riba**.

arriba (II) adv. upward, above, up. ‖ interj. up! onward!

   ~ de upwards of. **água ~** upstream. **negócio de água ~** thorny business.

arribaçã s. f. (Braz.) = **avante**.

arribação s. f. (pl. **-ões**) 1. arrival, landing (in a port). 2. (Braz.) a dish made of rice, beans and dried pigeons.

   ave de ~ bird of passage, migratory bird.

arribada s. f. 1. arrival, landing, coming or putting into a harbour. 2. convalescence.

arribadiço adj. 1. migratory (birds). 2. (fig.) intruding; vagrant, roving.

arribana s. f. a thatched shed to take cattle in.

arribanceirado adj. having steep riverbanks.

arribar v. 1. to land, put into harbour. 2. to be forced into a harbour by stormy weather. 3. (naut.) to be driven out of one's course. 4. to attain the top of. 5. to attain one's aim. 6. to depart; to run away. 7. (fig.) to recover, to get well.

arribe s. m. (Braz., also **arribação**) 1. arrival. 2. importation.

arriçado adj. (naut.) tied up with cords.

arriçar (I) v. (naut.) to reef, lash.

arriçar (II) v. (also **eriçar**) 1. to bristle. 2. to stand on end (hair).

arriçar (III) v. (also **enrijar**) to stiffen, toughen.

arrida s. f. (naut.) lanyard, laniards.

arridar v. (naut.) to fasten with lanyards.

arrieiro s. m. muleteer.

arriel s. m. (pl. **-éis**) 1. earrings formerly used. 2. gold bar. 3. lever used by diggers.

arrife s. m. = **recife**.

arrijar v. = **enrijar, enrijecer**.

arrimadiço adj. 1. sponging. 2. (fig.) parasitical.

arrimador s. m. 1. supporter. 2. prop. 3. rhymer.

arrimar v. 1. to support. 2. to lean against, to prop. 3. to rhyme; put in order. 4. (fig.) to protect. 5. **~-se** to resource to; rely or depend upon.

   ~ os pés à parede to carry one's point against reason. **~-se à sua opinião** to be stubborn. **~ os ombros** (fig.) to be hard at work.

arrimo s. m. 1. support, prop; help, stand-by, protection. 2. (fig.) anchorage.

arriós s. m. (pl. **-oses**) missile of a cross-bow.

arriosca s. f. trap, fraud, hoax, stratagem, deceit, trick.

arriscado adj. 1. risky, daring, dangerous. 2. scabrous, perilous, hazardous. 3. delicate, speculative, adventurous. 4. rash. ‖ **-amente** adv. dangerously; venturesomely; jeopardously.

   é ~ demais there is too much at stake. **situação -a** hazardous situation, touch-and-go.

arriscar v. 1. to risk, dare. 2. to gamble, hazard, endanger, peril, venture, expose. 3. **~-se** to expose o. s. to risks or dangers.

   ~ sua sorte to try one's luck. **~ sua vida** to risk one's life, take one's life into one's hands. **~-se a perder** to run the risk of losing. **quem não arrisca, não petisca** nothing ventured, nothing gained.

arrispidar-se v. to become rispid, unsociable.

arritmia s. f. (path.) arrhythmia.

arrítmico adj. arrhythmical, rhythmless.

arrivismo s. m. arrivism: practice of resourcing to all means in order to succeed in life.
arrivista s. m. + f. arrivist, climber, parvenu, upstart, pusher.
arrizo adj. (bot.) arrhizal, rootless.
arrizotônico adj. said of verbal forms which have not stressed their root vowel.
arro s. m. mud, clay.
arroba (ô) s. f. arroba, measure of weight, equivalent to about 15 kg.
arrobação s. f. (pl. -ões) **arrobamento** m. weighing by arrobas.
arrobar (I) v. 1. to weigh by arrobas. 2. (fig.) to make an offhand appraisal.
arrobar (II) v. to ravish, ecstasize, ecstasy.
arrobe (ô) s. m. 1. sodden wine. 2. rob, fruitjuice.
arrobustar v. 1. to strengthen, invigorate. 2. ~-se to become strong.
arrocado adj. formed like a distaff.
arrochada s. f. blow with a cudgel.
arrochado adj. 1. very tight or compressed. 2. (fig.) difficult, hard to manage.
arrochador s. m. a severe and exacting person. ‖ adj. tight, compressed.
arrochadura s. f. act or fact of tightening by twisting as with a tightening stick.
arrochar v. 1. to tighten or compress as with a tightening stick. 2. to compress, cram, fill to excess. 3. to be severe in treating one's subordinates. 4. to cause difficulties.
arrocheiro s. m. muleteer.
arrocho (ô) s. m. 1. tightening stick used to tighten ropes. 2. (naut.) ropes with knots at their end. 3. cudgel. 4. garrote. 5. difficulty, rub. 6. (N. Braz.) small machine to express manioc pulp.
arrocinador s. m. (S. Braz.) horse-breaker.
arrocinar v. (S. Braz.) to break in (horses).
arrodelar v. to arm or cover with a shield or buckler.
arrofo s. m. hole in a trammel or dragnet.
arrogação s. f. (pl. -ões) 1. arrogation; usurpation. 2. adoption.
arrogador s. m. arrogator; usurper. ‖ adj. arrogating; usurping.
arrogância s. f. (also **arrogo** m.) arrogance, presumption, pride, overbearingness, haughtiness, loftiness.
arrogante adj. m. + f. arrogant, superior, self-assertive, disdainful, presumptuous, cocky, haughty, insolent; saucy. ‖ **-mente** adv. arrogantly, uppishly, pridefully.
arrogar v. 1. to arrogate, usurp, claim. 2. ~-se to arrogate to o. s.
~-**se muita sabedoria** to pretend to be a scholar.
arroio s. m. arroyo, rivulet, beck, brook.
arrojadiço adj. 1. for throwing; missile, easy to be flung. 2. fearless, audacious. 3. inconsiderate, rash.
arrojadita s. f. (min.) arrojadite.
arrojado adj. 1. bold, rash. 2. daring, fearless, courageous. 3. enterprising, venturous, keen. 4. (N. Braz.) progressive, active. ‖ **-amente** adv. boldly, enterprisingly, venturously.
arrojador s. m. person who throws, flings, hurls.
arrojadura s. f. = **arrochadura**.
arrojamento s. m. 1. boldness, audacity. 2. act of dragging, throwing.
arrojão s. m. (pl. -ões) wrench, violent push.
arrojar v. to fling, throw violently. 2. to drag. 3. to reject, repel, repulse. 4. ~-**se**: a) to rush in or upon, precipitate o. s. b) to creep along, crawl. c) to do or say rashly.
~-**se à luta** to throw o. s. into the battle. ~-**se num negócio arriscado** to embark in a dangerous enterprise.

arrojo (ô) s. m. 1. boldness, audacity, daring, venturousness, fearlessness. 2. derring-do. 3. impudence. 4. ostentation. 5. (pop.) animation, liveliness. 6. act of hurling.
~**s de mar** stranded goods.
arrolador s. m. 1. person who makes an inventory (as of an estate). 2. person who or machine that enrols.
arrolamento s. m. enrolment; register, roll; inventory.
arrolar (I) v. 1. to enroll, inscribe. 2. to list, make a list of.
~ **bens** to make an inventory of an estate.
arrolar (II) v. to roll up.
arrolar (III) v. to lull asleep (a child).
arrolhador (I) s. m. bottle corker.
arrolhador (II) s. m. 1. (S. Braz.) weakling, coward. 2. (Braz.) intimidator, person who frightens others to silence. 3. worker who strips leaves from mate shrubs. ‖ adj. (S. Braz.) weak, timid, easily silenced.
arrolhamento (I) s. m. corkage.
arrolhamento (II) s. m. (S. Braz.) operation of stripping leaves from mate shrubs.
arrolhar (I) v. 1. to cork, put corks on bottles. 2. (Braz.) to intimidate, frighten to silence. 3. to defeat. 4. to hold one's tong cowardly, fly in defeat.
arrolhar (II) v. (S. Braz.) 1. to round up horses, mules. 2. to strip the leaves from mate shrubs.
arrolo (ô) s. m. lullaby, cradlesong.
arromançar v. (also **romancear**) 1. to romanticize. 2. to translate into the vernacular.
arromba s. f. a loud and lively guitar song.
festa de ~ a great, wonderful party.
arrombada s. f. 1. break, burst, opening, gap (as in the sides of a ship). 2. a forced entry.
arrombado adj. forced open, broken up; lucky.
arrombador s. m. housebreaker, burglar. ‖ adj. breaking in, forcing.
~ **de cofres** safecracker. ~ **escala-muros** cat burglar.
arrombamento s. m. 1. breaking in, inbreak; forced entry. 2. housebreaking, burglary.
arrombar v. 1. to break into. 2. to burst, force, wrench open. 3. to crack open (a safe). 4. (fig.) to humble, humiliate, crush.
~ **portas abertas** to flog a willing horse.
arrosetado adj. (bot.) rosettelike.
arrostar v. 1. to face, confront, front. 2. to defy, brave, outbrave. 3. ~-**se** to expose o. s.
arrotador s. m. 1. belcher. 2. (fig.) boaster, braggart, swaggerer.
arrotar v. 1. to belch. 2. to boast, swagger.
arroteado adj. 1. cultivated (as land). 2. rudimentarily instructed.
arroteador s. m. person who improves, cultivates land.
arroteamento s. m. 1. cultivation of land. 2. rudimentary instruction.
arrotear v. 1. to cultivate land, till, grub. 2. to educate, teach rudimentarily.
arrotéia s. f. recently cultivated land, newly ploughed ground.
arroto (ô) s. m. (pl. **arrotos**) eructation, belch.
arroubamento s. m. ecstasy, rapture, ravishment, transport.
arroubar v. 1. to ravish, enrapture, transport. 2. ~-**se** to fall into ecstasy.
arroubo s. m. 1. ravishment. 2. delirium, trance. 3. flight, verve. 4. ecstasy, rapture.
~ **temperamental** outburst of temper, blowout.
falar com ~ to speak passionately, gush.
arroupar v. = **enroupar**.

arroxado adj. (also **arroxeado**) violet, purplish, violaceous.

arroxar, arroxear v. to become purplish, make violaceous.

arroz s. m. rice.

arrozal s. m. (pl. **-ais**) (also **arrozeira** f.) rice field, rice paddy.

arrozalva s. f. (Braz.) rice flour.

arroz-de-cuxá s. m. (Braz.) a dish of cooked rice, mixed with **cuxá**.

arroz-de-festa s. m. (Braz., pop.) person fond of parties.

arroz-de-função s. m. (Braz.) a dessert made of rice and cinnamon.

arroz-doce, arroz-de-leite s. m. rice milk, rice pudding.

arroz-doce-de-pagode s. m. (Braz., pop.) person to be met with at all feasts, amusement seeker.

arrozeiro s. m. 1. rice grower. 2. rice merchant. 3. rice field. ‖ adj. 1. fond of rice. 2. (Braz.) referring to rice.

arruá adj. (Braz.) 1. skittish. 2. intractable. 3. wild, rough. 4. peevish, mean, wicked.

arruaça s. f. 1. uproar, street riot, tumult. 2. rush, crowd.

arruação s. f. (pl. **-ões**) squaring, dividing into streets, street layout.

arruaçar v. to row, kick up a row, to riot (in the streets).

arruaceiro s. m. 1. street rioter. 2. rowdy, mobber, hoodlum. ‖ adj. rioting in the streets, rowdyish.

arruado s. m. (N. Braz., also **arruamento**) a row of houses built along a road.

arruador s. m. 1. street loafer, idler, sluggard, vagrant. 2. person who plans street layouts.

arruamento s. m. 1. arrangement of streets, dividing in streets. 2. a series of similar shops in one street. 3. row or range of buildings in a street.

arruar (I) v. 1. to divide into or provide with streets. 2. to align streets. 3. to loaf, to bum around.

arruar (II) v. to grunt like a wild boar, to moo.

arrubé s. m. (N. Braz.) oil extracted from a manioc.

arruçado adj. greyish.

arruçar v. to become grey.

arruda s. f. (bot.) rue, herb grace (Ruta graveolens).

arruda-dos-muros s. f. (pl. **arrudas-dos-muros**) (Braz., bot.) the wall rue.

arrudão s. m. (pl. **-ões**) a species of rue.

arruela s. f. (tech.) washer (ring of iron), roundel (plate P 4).

~ **de aperto, de fecho,** ~ **de pressão** lock washer. ~ **de rebitagem** hole mending washer (plate R 1). ~ **elástica** spring washer, spacing washer.

arruelado adj. provided with washers.

arrufadiço adj. touchy, peevish.

arrufar v. 1. to make angry, to irritate, vex. 2. to ruffle. 3. ~-**se** to become irritated, take offence, to sulk.

arrufianado adj. rowdyish, having a ruffian's manners.

arrufo s. m. 1. ill-humour. 2. tout, tiff. 3. pouting, resentment. 4. pique. 5. livers' quarrel.

arrugado adj., **arrugadura** s. f., **arrugamento** m., **arrugar** v. = **enrugado, enrugamento, enrugar**.

arrúgia s. f. drain of a mine.

arruído s. m. noise, tumult, brawl, stir, uproar.

arruinação s. f. (pl. **-ões**) ruin, ruination.

arruinado adj. 1. ruined, decayed, broken-down, destroyed. 2. spoiled. 3. bankrupt.

arruinador s. m. person who or thing that ruins; dilapidator, desolator. ‖ adj. ruinous, destructive.

arruinamento s. m. 1. ruin. 2. unrepair.

arruinar v. 1. to ruin. 2. to destroy, devastate, lay waste. 3. to blight. 4. to spoil. 5. (fig.) to under-

mine. 6. ~-**se:** a) to ruin o. s. b) to go broke. c) to decay.

arruivado, arruivascado adj. reddish (esp. hair).

arrular, arrulhar v. 1. to lull asleep. 2. to coo (as doves). 3. to speak gently and lovingly.

arrulho, arrulo s. m. 1. lullaby; a lulling asleep. 2. cooing. 3. endearments.

arrumação s. f. (pl. **-ões**) (also **arrumo**) 1. arrangement, putting in order. 2. placing, disposal, disposition. 3. clearing up. 4. (naut.) stowing, trim. 5. shipment. 6. geographical position. 7. situation, employment. 8. (com.) entry. 9. roguery, swindling.

arrumadeira s. f. 1. (Braz.) housemaid. 2. a good housekeeper (woman).

arrumadela s. f. (also **arrumação**) a quick clearing up.

arrumador s. m. 1. person who disposes, sets in order, arranges. 2. (naut.) stower. 3. usher; (theat.) attendant. 4. manservant.

arrumar v. 1. to arrange, dispose, set in order. 2. to settle, tidy up. 3. to pack. 4. (naut.): a) to stow. b) to steer the course. 5. to put aside. 6. to place, employ. 7. ~-**se** to feather one's nest; to do nicely; obtain a job; get married.

~ **a casa** to do the house. ~ **as malas** to pack one's bags. ~ **emprego** to obtain an employment. **ele arrumou tudo** (Braz.) he managed everything.

arrunhar v. to smoothen the sides of a sole (shoe).

arsenal s. m. (pl. **-ais**) arsenal, repository of provisions and munition.

~ **de armas** armoury. ~ **de guerra** army arsenal. ~ **da marinha** navy yard, dockyard.

arseniado adj. (chem.) combined with arsenic, arseniureted.

arseniato s. m. (chem.) arsenate.

arsenical adj. m. + f. (pl. **-ais**) arsenic.

arsênico s. m. (chem.) arsenic.

arsênio s. m. (chem.) arsine.

arsenioso adj. (chem.) arsenious.

ársis s. f. (mus.) arsis: the unaccented part of the measure.

arsonvalização s. f. (pl. **-ões**) (med.) arsonvalization.

artanita s. f. (also **violeta-dos-alpes, pão-de-porco**) sowbread; an ointment made from the sowbread.

arte s. f. 1. art. 2. skill, craft. 3. workmanship, trade, profession. 4. a book on art or workmanship. 5. cunning artifice, trickiness. 6. (Braz.) mischief, prank. 7. ~**s** s. f. pl. a net for catching pilchards or sardels.

~ **culinária** culinary art. ~ **dramática** dramatic art. ~ **mágica** black magic, necromancy. ~ **mecânica** craft, handicraft. ~**s e ofícios** arts and crafts. ~**s liberais** liberal arts. **com** ~ artistically, artificial, ingenious, **conhecer a sua** ~ to be a handy man with one's tools. **ele tem** ~**s de fazê-lo** is well able to do it. **falta de** ~ artlessness. **imitação de** ~ artiness. **obra de** ~ work of art. masterpiece. **pôr um fim às** ~**s de alguém** (fig.) to put a stop to a person's arts.

artefato s. m. 1. workmanship; artifact; petard. 2. produce, product, manufacture, make.

~**s de borracha** rubber goods.

arte-final s. f. (pl. **artes-finais**) (typogr.) the finished drawing, ready for graphic reproduction.

arteirice s. f. 1. craft, cunning, artifice, stratagem. 2. trickishness, artifice. 3. mischief, childish trick, prank, naughtiness.

arteiro adj. 1. crafty, wily. 2. draughty, sly, cunning, deceitful. 3. (Braz.) mischievous, naughty, plotful.

artelho s. m. (anat.) ankle, anklebone.

artemão s. m. (pl. **-ões**) (naut.) mizen, mizzen: a fore-and-aft sail.

artemísia s. f. (also **artemigem, artemija,** bot.) artemisia, mugwort, oriental wormwood.

artemísia-da-praia s. f. (pl. **artemísias-da-praia**) (bot.) sea ragweed.

artéria s. f. artery: 1. (anat.) blood vessel. 2. a main channel; highway.
~ **de tráfego** arterial highway.

arterial adj. m. + f. (pl. **-ais**) arterial. || ~**mente** adv. arterially.

arterialização s. f. (pl. **-ões**) (physiol.) arterialization.

arterializar v. to arterialize.

arteriografia s. f. 1. (anat.) description of the arteries. 2. (med.) arteriography.

arteriográfico adj. arteriographic.

arteríola s. f. arteriole.

arteriologia s. f. (med.) arteriology: a treatise on the arterial system.

arteriológico adj. arteriologic.

arteriosclerose s. f. (med.) arteriosclerosis: a thickening of the walls of the arteries.

arterioscleroso adj. (med.) arteriosclerotic.

arterioso adj. (physiol.) arterious, arterial.

arteriotomia s. f. (surg.) arteriotomy: an opening of an artery for bleeding.

arterite s. f. (med.) arteritis: inflammation of an artery.

artesa s. f. (ant.) kneading-trough.

artesanato s. m. workmanship; industrial arts.

artesão (I) s. m. (pl. **-ões**) artisan, craftsman.
~ **itinerante** tramper.

artesão (II) s. m. (pl. **-ões**) (archit.) panel, coffer, vaulted roof or its painting.

artesiano adj. artesian.
poço ~ artesian well.

artesoar, artesoinar v. (archit.) to ornament ceilings or vaults as with panels or paintings.

ártico adj. (geogr.) arctic.

articulação (I) s. f. (pl. **-ões**) (anat., biol., bot., zool. and mech.) articulation; joint; link (plates B 13, J 3, M 9).
~**axial** axial hinge, joint of axis (plate J 3). ~ **com pino** pin joint. ~ **da anca** hip joint (plate C 12). ~ **de pivô** bolted joint. ~ **de rótula** ball and socket joint (plate J 3). ~ **em forquilha** forked joint (plate J 3). ~ **esférica** whirl-bone. ~ **trocóide** a trochoid joint, a pivot joint.

articulação (II) s. f. (pl. **-ões**) articulation: pronunciation, enunciation.

articulação (III) s. f. (pl. **-ões**) (jur.) division into articles or paragraphs; enunciation of things article by article.

articulação (IV) s. f. (pl. **-ões**) (N. Braz.) controversy, dispute.

articulado (I) s. m. (jur.) a well founded, paragraphed or articled exposition.

articulado (II) s. m. specimen of the Articulata (pl.), Cuvier's name for the third sub-kingdom of animals, such as insects, crustaceans, centipedes and worms. || adj. articulate.

articulante s. m. + f. a person who writes articles, news-writer. || adj. articulate, distinct.

articular (I) adj. m. + f. articular.

articular (II) v. 1. to articulate, join by articulation; to link. 2. ~**-se** to become linked or joined.

articular (III) v. to pronounce, enunciate.

articular (IV) v. 1. (jur.) to found on paragraphs or articles. 2. to set down in articles, write articles about.

articular (V) v. (N. Braz., coll.) to argue, debate.

articulável adj. m. + f. (pl. **-áveis**) capable of being articulated.

articulista s. m. + f. newspaper writer, gazetteer.

artículo s. m. 1. article as of a contract. 2. (anat.) joint, knuckle, articulation. 3. (bot.) knot, inter-

node. 4. (zool.) the segment of the appendix of the Arthropoda.

articuloso adj. articulated.

artífice s. m. + f. 1. artificer, artisan. 2. craftsman. 3. artist. 4. (fig.) author, inventor.

artificial adj. m. + f. (pl. **-ais**) 1. artificial, artful. 2. unnatural, synthetic. 3. fictitious. 4. false. || ~**mente** adv. artificially, fictitiously.

artificialidade s. f. (also **artificialismo** m.) 1. artificiality, artificialness. 2. fictitiousness. 3. affectation.

artificializar v. to artificialize.

artificiar v. 1. to make or contrive skillfully. 2. to improve. 3. to scheme, machinate.

artifício s. m. 1. artifice, skilful making. 2. work of art. 3. ability, practice. 4. elaborateness, inventiveness. 5. art, cunning; fraud, deceit, machinism.
~ **de cálculo** a mathematical shortcut. **fogos de** ~ fireworks.

artificioso adj. 1. skilful, artful. 2. clever. 3. cunning, fraudulent, crafty. || **-amente** adv. skilfully; craftily.

artigo s. m. article: 1. commodity, product. 2. chapter, portion of writing. 3. clause as of a contract. 4. a literary composition (as for a newspaper). 5. (gram.) the definite and indefinite articles "the, a, an" in English with their Portuguese correspondents: o, a, um, uma.
~ **de fé** article of faith. ~ **definido** (gram.) definite article. ~ **de fundo** leading article in a newspaper. ~ **indefinido** (gram.) indefinite article. ~**s de consumo** consumer goods. ~**s de exportação** exports. ~**s de importação** imports. ~**s de luxo** luxury goods, items. ~**s de primeira necessidade** essential commodities.

artiguelho s. m. 1. an insignificant article. 2. an aggressive or slanderous article in a newspaper.

artilhamento s. m. gunnage, mounting of or protection with guns.

artilhar v. to furnish with artillery, supply with guns.

artilharia s. f. 1. artillery (men and guns). 2. gunnery.
~ **antiaérea** anti-aircraft artillery. ~ **costal** coast artillery. ~ **de campanha** field artillery. ~ **ligeira** light artillery. ~ **montada** horse artillery. ~ **pesada** heavy artillery. **peça de** ~ a cannon.

artilheiro s. m. 1. artillerist; gunner, cannoneer. 2. (Braz.) center forward (association football).

artimanha s. f. 1. artifice, trick, fetch. 2. quirk.

artinha s. f. (Braz.) handbook.

artiodáctilo adj. (zool., also **artiodátilo**) artiodactyl.

artista s. m. + f. artist: 1. person who executes his work with great skill; artisan. 2. person who practises one of the fine arts. 3. (theat. + cin.) actor. || adj. 1. artistic. 2. cunning.

artístico adj. artistic(al). || **artisticamente** adv. artistically.

artófago adj. bread-eating; fond of bread.

artola s. f. (Braz.) handbarrow.

artólatra s. m. + f. a person who likes very much to eat bread.

artolátrico adj. preference for bread.

artralgia s. f. (med.) arthralgia.

artrálgico adj. arthralgic.

artrite s. f. (med.) arthritis.

artrítico adj. arthritic.

artritismo s. m. arthritism.

artrobactéria s. f. (biol.) Arthrobacter, a genus of soil bacteria.

artropatia s. f. (med.) arthropathy.

artrópode s. m. (zool.) an arthropod (insects, arachnids, crustaceans).

artrose s. f. (anat.) arthrosis.

artrósporo, artrospório s. m. (biol., bot.) arthrospore.

aru s. m. (Braz.) an Amazonian frog.

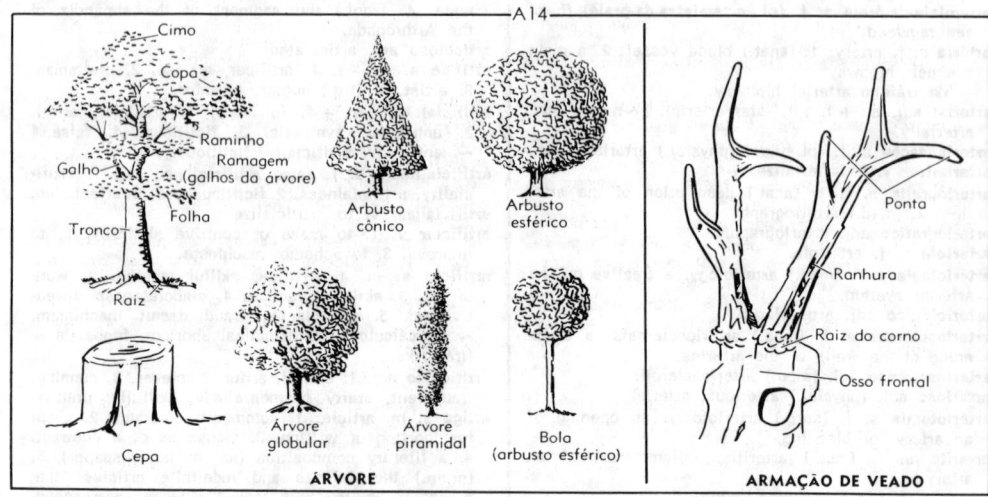

—A14—

ÁRVORE

Cimo
Copa
Raminho
Ramagem
(galhos da árvore)
Galho
Folha
Tronco
Raiz
Cepa

Arbusto
cônico

Arbusto
esférico

Árvore
globular

Árvore
piramidal

Bola
(arbusto esférico)

ARMAÇÃO DE VEADO

Ponta
Ranhura
Raiz do corno
Osso frontal

aruá s. m. (also arurá) 1. Brazilian amphibious mol-lusc. 2. cayman. ‖ adj. (Braz.) m. + f. ill-natured.

aruaná s. m. (also barrigudinho) (Braz.) a large river fish (Osteoglossum bicirrhosum).

aruaque s. m. family of languages of several tribes of Northern Brazil.

arubé s. m. (N. Braz., also arubê) a condiment made of manioc, salt, pepper, garlic and fish sauce.

aruega s. f. (Braz., pop.) cold drizzle accompanied by fog.

árula s. f. a small altar.

arumã s. m. (Braz., bot.) aririte.

arumará s. m. (Braz.) bird of the family icteridae.

arumarana s. f. (Braz., bot.) a thalia (Thalia geni-culata).

arumbava s. m. (Braz.) 1. sponger, parasite. 2. adu-lator, fawner. ‖ adj. flattering, fawning.

arunco s. m. (bot., also barba-de-cabra, barba-de--bode) the sylvan goatsbeard.

arundináceo adj. arundinaceous: of or like reeds.

arundíneo adj. made of reed.

arundinoso adj. arundineous, arundiferous: reedy, bearing reeds.

arupanado adj. (N. Braz.) irritated; unreasoning; restless.

arúspice s. m. haruspex, soothsayer.

aruspicino adj. haruspicy; the oracle of a haruspex.

arvais s. m. pl. (hist.) priests of Ceres.

arval s. m. (pl. -ais) tilled ground. ‖ adj. m. + f. per-taining to fields.

arvelas s. f. pl. (naut.) rings used to hold dowel pins in place.

arvense adj. m. + f. growing on tilled ground.

arvícola s. m. + f., arvicultor countryman, country-woman; agriculturist. ‖ adj. arvicoline, living in the country.

arvicultura s. f. arviculture, agriculture.

arvoado adj. giddy, dizzy, dazed, amazed, dumb-founded.

arvoamento s. m. giddiness, amazement, dizziness.

arvoar v. 1. to make giddy, dizzy. 2. ~-se to be amazed, dizzy.

arvorado s. m. (mil.) a soldier with the privileges of a corporal. ‖ adj. 1. set upright. 2. provided with masts. 3. lifted, raised, hoisted, displayed (flag).

arvoragem s. f. act or effect of: 1. lifting, raising, hoisting. 2. planting with trees.

arvorar v. 1. to hoist colours, raise, lift the flag. 2. to unfurl. 3. to set up. 4. to provide with masts. 5. to plant with trees. 6. to escape, run, decamp. 7. ~-se to arrogate, ascribe to o. s., usurpate.
~ a bandeira to hoist the flag. ~-se em enten-dido to pretend to be an expert.

árvore s. f. arbor: 1. (bot.) tree (plate A 4, A 14). 2. mast. 3. (mech.) axle, shaft, spindle (plate E 2).
~ de direção steering column. (plate B 11). ~ do eixo axle-tree (plate C 15). ~ da hélice propeller shaft (plate L 2). ~ de natal christmas-tree. ~ genealógica family tree, genealogical table. ~ glo-bular globular tree (plate A 14). ~ piramidal pyramidal tree (plate A 14). tal ~ tal fruto like father, like son.

arvorecer v. = arborescer.

árvore-da-borracha s. f. (pl. árvores-da-borracha) Pará rubber tree.

árvore-da-goma-elástica s. f. (pl. árvores-da-goma--elástica) the India rubber ficus.

árvore-da-preguiça s. f. (pl. árvores-da-preguiça) (Braz.) the shieldleaf pumpwood or the trumpet tree.

árvore-da-vida s. f. (pl. árvores-da-vida) eastern arborvitae.

árvore-de-são-sebastião s. f. (pl. árvores-de-são-sebas-tião) (Braz., also coroa-de-cristo) the malabar tree euphorbia.

arvoredo s. m. 1. a grove of trees, stand (plate F 4). 2. the masts of a ship.

árvore-do-papel-de-arroz s. f. (pl. árvores-do-papel-de-arroz) the rice-paper plant.

árvore-dos-pagodes s. f. (pl. árvores-dos-pagodes) Japanese pagoda tree.

árvore-mãe s. f. (pl. árvores-mães) seed tree, left standing for reforestation.

arvorejar v. 1. to cover with trees. 2. ~-se to become covered with trees.

arvoreta s. f. a small tree.

árvore-triste s. f. (pl. árvores-tristes) (also ~-da-noite) night jasmine.

arxar v. to clean vines of weeds.

arzola s. f. (bot.) spiny burweed.

as (I) f. pl. form of the def. art. a the.

as (II) f. pl. form of the pers. pron. a those, them. eu ~ vi I saw them.
as (III) f. pl. form of the demonstrative pron. a the ones.
ás s. m. 1. ace (cards, aeron.). 2. (fig.) big gun; star. ~ de copas ace of hearts (plate B 5).
às contraction of the prep. a + pl. of the f. article as to the, at the, etc.
~ armas! to arms! ~ avessas 1. backwards. 2. inside out. ~ boas com on good terms with. ~ cegas blindly. ~ dezenas by tens. ~ escondidas, escuras 1. clandestinely. 2. In the dark. ~ expensas de at the expense of. ~ mil maravilhas marvelously well. ~ ordens de at the disposal of. ~ portas da morte at death's door. ~ pressas hurriedly. ~ vésperas de on the eve of. ~ vezes sometimes, at times.
asa s. f. 1. (ornith., aeron.) wing (plate A 3). 2. lobe. 3. fin. 4. handle. 5. (Braz., soccer) wing. ~ do nariz side, wing of the nose. arrastar a ~ a to court. bater ~s (pop.) to flee, run away, escape, decamp. cortar as ~s de alguém (fig.) to clip a person's wings. ter ~s nos pés (fig.) to have wings on the feet.
asa-branca s. f. (pl. asas-brancas) (Braz.) = pomba-trocaz.
asa-de-papagaio s. f. (pl. asas-de-papagaio) (Braz., bot., also poinsetia) a poinsettia.
asa-de-telha s. f. (pl. asas-de-telha) bird of the family Icteridae.
asado s. m. a vase with ears. || adj. winged.
asafia s. f. (med.) erroneous and indistinct articulation of words.
asa-negra s. m. + f. (pl. asas-negras) a hoodoo: thing that or person who always brings bad luck.
asar v. to furnish with wings.
asbestino adj. asbestine.
asbesto s. m. (min.) asbestos.
asca s. f. 1. aversion, repugnance, abhorrence. 2. offensive odor, bad smelling.
ascágrafo s. m. (geophysics) apparatus for transmitting data on polar auroras.
ascárida s. f. (also lombriga) any nematode of the genus Ascaridae (parasites in human intestines).
ascarídeo s. m. specimen of the Ascaridae, family of nematode worms. || adj. referring to the Ascaridae.
ascaridíase s. f. (med.) ascaridiasis, ascariasis.
ascendência s. f. 1. ascendancy, ancestry, genealogy. 2. ascending line. 3. superiority; influence; power.
ascendente s. m. 1. (also astr.) ascendant. 2. ancestor. 3. horoscope. 4. influence, power. || adj. m + f. ascendant, rising, increasing.
ascender v. to ascend, rise, climb. ~ a to come to, mount to (as prices, costs). ~ ao poder to take over the power.
ascensão s. f. (pl. -ões) (also ascendimento, ascenso m.) 1. ascension, ascent, rising. 2. promotion. 3. the ascent of Christ to heaven. 4. Ascension Day. ~ oblíqua (astr.) oblique ascension. ~ reta (astr.) right ascension.
ascensional adj. m. + f. (pl. -ais) (astr.) ascensional.
ascensionário adj. ascensive.
ascensionista s. m. + f. (Braz.) 1. person fond of climbing mountains. 2. baloonist.
ascensor s. m. lift; elevator.
ascensorista s. m. + f. (Braz.) lift boy; elevator operator.
ascese s. f. ascesis, asceticism; spiritual exercise of devotion, religious meditation and self-denial.
asceta s. m. + f. ascetic.
ascetério s. m. monastery; a place for meditation.
asceticismo s. m. (also ascetismo) asceticism.
ascético adj. ascetic, self-denying.

ascídia s. f. (bot.) ascidium.
ascidiado adj. (bot.) ascidiate.
áscios s. m. pl. ascians (inhabitants of the torrid zone).
ascite s. f. (med.) ascites: dropsy of the abdomen.
ascítico s. m. person suffering from ascites. || adj. ascitical.
asclepiadácea s. f. (bot.) specimen of the Asclepiadaceae, the milkweed family; swallowort.
asclepiadáceo adj. asclepiadaceous: referring to the milkweed family.
asco (I) s. m. loathing, aversion, disgust, repugnance. dá ~ it is sickening. ter ~ a to feel sick with.
asco (II) s. m. (bot.) ascus.
ascoma s. f. 1. (bot.) ascoma. 2. piece of leather on oars or paddles as a protection against friction.
ascomiceto s. m. (bot.) an ascomycete.
ascórbico adj. (chem.) ascorbic: referring to the vitamin C.
ascorosidade, ascosidade s. f. = asquerosidade.
ascoroso, ascoso adj. = asqueroso.
ascotorácicos s. m. pl. (zool.) Ascothoracica, an order of hermaphrodite barnacles that parasite the black coral.
áscua s. f. 1. ember, a burning coal of fire. 2. (fig.) the glance of an enraged person.
ascuma s. f. a small javelin.
ascumada s. f. a blow with a javelin.
ascuna, ascunha s. f. = ascuma.
aselha s. f. 1. a little wing. 2. tab, tag, bootstrap, pulling (plate B 16).
asfaltador s. m. asphalter.
asfaltar v. to cover with asphalt.
asfalto s. m. asphalt.
asfixia s. f. (med., physiol.) asphyxia.
asfixiador adj. asphyxiating.
asfixiante adj. m. + f. (also asfíxico, asfixioso m.) stifling, suffocating, asphyxiating.
asfixiar v. to asphyxiate, suffocate, stifle.
asiano s. m. Asian. || adj. Asian.
asiaticismo s. m. Asiaticism: word or expression of Asiatic origin.
asiático s. m. an Asiatic. || adj. 1. Asiatic. 2. (fig.) luxurious; indolent; prolix; bombastic. || asiaticamente adv. asiatically.
asiatismo s. m. pompous, prolix style.
asilado s. m. inmate of an asylum. || adj. living in an asylum.
asilar v. 1. to shelter, give shelter, asylum, refuge. 2. ~-se to take shelter, refuge; to go into an asylum.
asilo (I) s. m. asylum; refuge, place of refuge, retreat; haven, shelter; sanctuary. ~ de órfãos orphanage. ~ dos velhos home for old people, (U. S. A.) old folks' home. ~ para doentes mentais insane asylum.
asilo (II) s. m. (ent.) robber fly.
asimina s. f. (bot.) pawpaw, custard-apple.
asinha (I) s. f. a small wing.
asinha (II) adv. rapidly, hurriedly.
asinino adj. (also asinal m. + f. pl. -ais, asinário m.) 1. asinine, asslike. 2. stupid; brutal, beastlike.
asir v. to catch, to seize, take hold of.
asma s. f. (med.) asthma: chronic shortness of breath.
asmático s. m. (also asmento) asthmathic person. || adj. 1. asthmathic: characterized by asthma. 2. narrow-chested. || asmaticamente adv. asthmatically. cavalo ~ wind-broken horse.
asmo adj. (pop., also ázimo) unleavened.
asmodeu s. m. (Jewish demonology) Asmodeus.
asna s. f. 1. a she-donkey. 2. (constr.) roof truss in form of a triangle. 3. (her.) chevron.
asnada s. f. 1. a drove of asses or donkeys. 2. stupidity, blunder, asinity.

asnal adj. m. + f. (pl. **-ais**) = **asinino.**

asnamento s. m. (also **asnaria** f.) trusses or framework of a roof.

asnaria s. f. drove of donkeys.

asnático adj. foolish, idiotic, stupid, asinine.

asnear v. 1. to behave foolishly, to say or make stupid things. 2. to behave arroganthly, haughtily.

asneira s. f. (also **asnice, asnidade**) 1. foolishness, stupidity, silliness, folly, daftness. 2. nonsense, blunder, bad mistake.

asneirada s. f. a big blunder, nonsense, absurdity.

asneirão s. m. a big ass, fool, idiot.

asneirar v. (Braz.) to say or do absurdities, make an ass of o. s.

asneirento adj. stupid, foolish, nonsensical.

asneiro s. m. (also **asnal**) ass driver, donkey driver. ‖ adj. asslike, mulelike.

asneirola s. f. 1. an obscenity. 2. an ambiguous, vulgar expression or statement.

asnice s. f. = **asneira.**

asnil adj. m. + f. (pl. **-is**) = **asinino.**

asno s. m. 1. ass, donkey. 2. stupid, ignorant person; a fool.

   como ~ diante de palácio dumbfounded. **ficar com cara de ~** to meet with a rebuff, be disappointed.

aspa s. f. 1. St. Andrew's cross (X). 2. **~s** pl. inverted commas (" "), quotation marks. 3. horns. 4. vanes, arms of a windmill.

   estar de ~s tortas (S. Braz., pop.) to be ill-humoured, in a bad temper. **fincar as ~s** to fall head over.

aspaço s. m. (Braz.) a thrust with horns.

aspado adj. (gram.) placed between inverted commas. (fig.) plagued, vexed.

aspar (I) v. 1. to place between inverted commas. 2. to vex, mortify.

aspar (II) v. to expurge, erase, eliminate.

asparagina s. f. (chem.) asparagine.

asparagolita s. f. (min.) asparagolite.

aspargo s. m. (bot.) asparagus.

aspas s. f. pl. quotation marks.

aspe, aspa s. m. (Braz.) vane (of a water mill).

aspear v. to quote; to set off by quotation marks.

aspecto s. m. (also **aspeto**) 1. aspect, look, appearance, form, shape (plate R 4). 2. point of view, prospect. 3. feature, face. 4. exterior. 5. vision, view. 6. configuration.

   ~ de doente sickly appearance. **de bom ~** good-looking. **isto dá outro ~ ao assunto** that puts another complexion on the matter. **por todos os ~s** in every sense. **todas as questões têm dois ~s** there are two sides to every question.

asperejar v. (S. Braz., also **asprejar**) to treat someone harshly, to reprehend rudely.

aspereza s. f. 1. asperity, roughness, rispidness. 2. rudeness, severeness, abruptness, harshness.

asperges s. m. (eccl.) 1. Asperges. 2. an aspergillum.

aspergiliforme adj. m. + f. (bot.) aspergilliform.

aspergilo s. m. 1. (bot.) an aspergilliform organ. 2. (zool.) a genus of mollusks.

aspergilose s. f. (med.) aspergillosis.

aspergir v. (also **asperger, aspersar**) to sprinkle, asperse.

asperidade, asperidão s. f. = **aspereza.**

asperifólio adj. (bot.) asperifoliate.

aspermatismo s. m. (med.) aspermatism.

aspermia s. f. 1. (bot.) seedlessness. 2. (med.) aspermatism.

aspermo adj. seedless.

áspero adj. 1. rough. 2. coarse, rude, crude. 3. rugged, uneven. 4. grating. 5. biting, sharp. 6. unpleasant. 7. acid, sour (wine). 8. (fig.) harsh, rigorous, austere, severe. ‖ **asperamente** adv. roughly, harshly, austerely.

aspérrimo, asperíssimo (absolute sup. of **áspero**) most rough.

aspersão s. f. (pl. **-ões**) (also **aspergimento** m.) 1. aspersion. 2. sprinkling.

asperso adj. aspersed, besprinkled.

aspersório s. m. aspergillum, aspersorium.

aspérula s. f. (bot.) woodruff.

áspide s. m. + f. an Old World snake (Vipera aspis).

aspidospermo s. m. (bot.) quebracho.

aspiração s. f. (pl. **-ões**) 1. breathing. 2. aspiration, longing, yearning. 3. (gram.) aspiration. 4. a pause in music. 5. (tech.) suction.

aspirado adj. 1. inhaled. 2. (phon.) aspirate.

aspirador s. m. aspirator, exhaustor. ‖ adj. aspirating. **~ de pó** vacuum cleaner (plate A 6).

aspirância s. f. an aspiring to something.

aspirante s. m. + f. aspirant, candidate, one who aspires. ‖ adj. aspiring, drawing up by suction (as a pump).

   ~ a oficial officer candidate. **~ de marinha** midshipman. **bomba ~** sucking pump.

aspirar v. 1. (phon.) to aspirate. 2. to breathe in, to inhale (air, smoke). 3. to aspire to, be a candidate, to aim at, covet, desire.

aspirativo adj. (phon.) aspirate, aspirated.

aspirina s. f. (pharm.) aspirin.

asplênio s. m. (bot.) a genus of spleenworts.

áspero adj. (bot.) without spores.

asprejar v. (S. Braz., pop.) = **asperejar.**

aspudo s. m. (S. Braz.) cuckold. ‖ adj. having big horns, cuckoldy.

asquerosidade s. f. (also **ascosidade**) loathsomeness, aversion, dislike.

asqueroso adj. (also **ascoroso**) loathsome, nasty, nauseous, sickening, detestable. ‖ **-amente** adv. disgustingly.

assacadilha s. f. false imputation, slander.

assacador s. m. slanderer, imputer. ‖ adj. imputing, slanderous.

assacar v. to impute, slander, backbite.

assacate s. m. tallow extracted from the mesentery of slaughtered cattle.

assadeira s. f. 1. woman who roasts and sells chestnuts, peanuts. 2. roasting or baking pan (plate C 20). 3. flat cake tin (plate D 3).

assado s. m. 1. a roast (meat). 2. **~s** pl. difficulty, rub. ‖ adj. 1. roasted, baked. 2. (N. Braz., fig.) angry. 3. in a tight corner.

   ~ demais overdone. **~ de vitela** roast veal. **assim ou ~** by hook or by crook. **frango ~** roast chicken. **nem assim, nem ~** neither this way nor that. **pouco ~** underdone.

assador s. m. (also **assadeiro**) 1. roaster. 2. Dutch oven. 3. (S. Braz.) (roasting) spit, broach. **~ elétrico** electric roaster.

assadura s. f. 1. roasting, baking. 2. a piece of meat for roasting. 3. gall, blister, irritation.

assa-fétida s. f. (pl. **assa-fétidas**) (bot.) asafetida.

assalariado s. m. 1. employee; person who receives a salary. 2. retainer. 3. henchman. ‖ adj. employed, on the pay roll.

assalariador s. m. employer.

assalariamento s. m. employment on a salary basis.

assalariar v. 1. to engage, employ, to take in pay; to fee 2. to subsidize. 3. to bribe. 4. **~-se** to take an employment, work for a salary.

assa-leitão s. m. (pl. **assa-leitões**) (Braz., bot.) a hardwood tree.

assalmonado adj. salmonlike.

assaloiado adj. rude, boorish.

assaltada s. f. assault, attack, onslaught.

assaltador s. m. assailant; burglar; waylayer. || adj. assailing, assaulting.

assaltante s. m. + f., adj. = **assaltador**.

assaltar, assaltear v. 1. to assault, attack, charge, storm. 2. to ambush, take by surprise. 3. to set or fall upon.

assalto s. m. 1. assault, attack, onset. 2. (mil.) charge. 3. round (boxing). 4. temptation. ~ **a mão armada** holdup. ~ **de esgrima** assault at arms. **carro de** ~ armoured car. **tomar de** ~ (mil. fig.) to take by storm.

assalvado adj. (bot.) infundibuliform, funnel-shaped.

assana s. f. asana, posture, manner of sitting (in yoga practices).

assanhaço s. m. (Braz.) = **sanhaço**.

assanhadiço adj. irascible, irritable.

assanhado adj. 1. excited, furious. 2. (Braz.): a) restless; b) erotic. c) philandering, flirtatious.

assanhamento s. m. (also **assanho** m., **sanha** f.) anger, fury, wrath.

assanhar v. 1. to provoke, enrage, anger. 2. ~-**se** to get angry, become furious, rage.

assar v. 1. to roast; bake; grill. 2. ~-**se** to be roasted. ~ **no espeto** to roast on a spit, barbecue. ~ **no forno** to bake. ~-**se ao sol** to sunburn.

assaranzar, azaranzar v. (Braz., also **zaranzar**) to loiter.

assarapantado adj. 1. frightened. 2. confused, disconcerted, upset.

assarapantar v. 1. to frighten. 2. to upset. 3. to confuse, confound, disconcert. 4. ~-**se** to be perplexed, disconcerted.

assaria s. f. a sort of grapes.

assarilhado adj. verticillate.

assassinado adj. assassinated, murdered, killed.

assassinar v. to murder: 1. assassinate. kill. 2. (coll.) execute (music) or speak (language) badly.

assassinato s. m. (also **assassinamento, assassínio**) assassination, murder, homicide.

assassino s. m. (also **assassinador**) assassin, murderer, killer. || adj. murderous.

assaz adv. enough, sufficiently; tolerably.

assazonado adj. (also **sazonado**) ripe.

asseado adj. 1. clean, neat, proper, trim, spruce. 2. (S. Braz.) elegant, beautiful (esp. horses). || -**amente** adv. neat, dapperly, trimly.

assear v. 1. to adorn, trim up. 2. to clean. 3. ~-**se** to dress properly or be properly dressed, to be spruce.

assecla s. m. + f. follower, partisan, sectarian.

assecuratório adj. (Braz.) assuring.

assedadeira s. f. female flax-dresser or flax-comber.

assedagem s. f. (pl. -**ens**) combing, hackling (flax).

assedar v. 1. to ripple, hackle, comb (flax). 2. to make smooth as silk.

assedentado adj. thirsty.

assediador s. m. 1. besieger. 2. (fig.) bore. || adj. 1. besieging. 2. (fig.) boring.

assediante adj. m. + f. 1. besieging. 2. (fig.) boring.

assediar v. 1. to besiege. 2. to ply, importune, molest, inconvenience, annoy.

assédio s. m. 1. siege. 2. insistence, importunement, molestation, beseechingness.

asseguração s. f. (pl. -**ões**) (also **segurança**) 1. security, safety. 2. assurance. 3. reliance.

assegurado adj. (also **segurado**) 1. insured. 2. assured. 3. secure. || -**amente** adv. assuredly.

assegurador s. m. 1. assurer. 2. insurer. || adj. 1. assuring. 2. reassuring.

assegurar v. 1. to assert, affirm; guarantee. 2. to assure, make sure (of). 3. to insure, secure. 4. ~-**se** to verify, check, make sure, ascertain.

asseio s. m. 1. cleanliness, neatness, spruceness. 2. decency. 3. dapperness, perfection. **falta de** ~ untidiness.

asselar v. (also **selar**) 1. to stamp, put stamps on (as for mailing). 2. to seal. 3. to legalize. 4. to confirm. 5. to consider.

asselvajado adj. savage. wild, rough, brutal, uncultivated. || -**amente** adv. savagely, coarsely.

asselvajamento s. m. savageness, rudeness, bluntness.

asselvajar v. 1. to make savage, wild, rude. 2. ~-**se** to become savage, brutalize, take coarse manners.

assembléia s. f. 1. assembly meeting, gathering. 2 congregation. 3. (bot.) purple candytuft. ~ **constituinte** constitutional convention. ~ **eclesiástica** council. ~ **legislativa** legislative assembly, parliament, congress.

assemelhação s. f. (pl. -**ões**) assimilation.

assemelhar v. 1. to assimilate. 2. to liken to. 3. to parallel, compare. 4. -**se** to be similar to. **assemelha-se-me** it seems to me.

assenhoreamento s. m. a taking into possession, appropriation, seizure; act of domineering; conquering.

assenhorear v. 1. to master, domineer. 2. ~-**se** to take possession (of); to conquer.

assenso s. m. = **assentimento**.

assentada s. f. 1. session of a board of inquiry. 2. sitting. 3. (Braz.) sudden stop (horse). 4. (N. Braz.) a level area on a hill or mountain. **ler um livro de uma** ~ to read a book at one sitting.

assentado s. m. (N. Braz.) = **assentada**. || adj. 1. seated. 2. steady, firm. 3. resolved, decided, agreed upon, settled. **palavras bem** ~**as** a wise and firm speech.

assentador s. m. 1. recorder. 2. razor-strop. 3. bricklayer. 4. machine fitter.

assentamento s. m. 1. a seating, sitting down. 2. a putting into place. 3. entry, recording, registry, enrollment. 4. foundation, base. 5. agreement, settlement, accord. ~ **de casas** homes built on the same groundplot. ~ **de trilhos** tracklaying.

assentar v. 1. to seat (**em** on). 2. to place. 3. to base. 4. to lay. 5. to settle: a) fix, establish. b) stipulate. c) decide. d) secure. e) clear of dregs, clarify. f) calm down. 6. to agree upon. 7. to consent. 8. to assure. 9. to deem, suppose. 10. to note down, register, record. 11. to fit well (dress), be becoming, show up well. 12 .~-**se** sit down. ~ **um acordo** to make an agreement upon the terms of. ~ **uma bofetada na cara** to give one a box on the ear. ~ **o fio da navalha** to strop a razor. ~**a mão** 1. to beat, thresh, spank. 2. to develop skill. ~ **pazes** to make (one's) peace. ~ **o pé** to take a firm standing; to resist. ~ **pedras, tijolos** to lay (with) bricks or stones. ~ **pedras preciosas** to set jewels. ~ **a primeira pedra de uma casa** to lay the foundations of a house. ~ **praça** (mil.) to enlist. ~ **no rol** to enlist, enrol. ~ **sua vivenda** to fix one's abode. **azul assenta bem sobre branco** blue shows up well on white.

assente (I) adj. m. + f. 1. firm, solid. 2. established, decided. 3. settled. 4. placed or based upon. **bem** ~ deep-rooted.

assente (II) s. m. (Braz.) a plateau, tableland.

assentimento s. m. assent, consent, permission.

assentir v. 1. to assent, agree, acquiesce, consent.

assento s. m. 1. a seat (plate B 2, C 2, L 2, P 19). 2. a place to sit. 3. (aeron.) cockpit. 4. base; bottom; fundament. 5. sediment. 6. (anat.) seat (place C 18). 7. dwelling, abode. 8. good judgement, reasonableness. 9. tranquility, rest. 10. agreement.

11. bookkeeping entry, record. 12. (Braz.) a plateau, tableland.

~ **corrediço** (naut.) sliding seat (plate B 9). ~ **de dobrar** tip-up seat, flap-up seat (plate C 2). ~ **estofado** upholstered seat (plate V 1).

assenzalar v. to give the aspect of a slave house to.

assépalo adj. (bot.) without sepals.

assepsia s. f. asepsis.

asséptico adj. aseptic. ‖ **assepticamente** adv. aseptically.

asserção s. f. (pl. -ões) assertion; affirmation; allegation.

asserenar v. = **serenar.**

assertivo s. m. assertion. ‖ adj. (also **assertório**) assertive.

asserto s. m. assertion.

assertor s. m. (obs.) assertor: defender.

assertório adj. assertive.

assessor s. m. assessor, adviser, counsellor.

~ **técnico** technical adviser.

assessoramento s. m. counselling, assistance.

assessorial adj. m. + f. (pl. -ais) (also **assessório** m.) assessorial.

assessorar v. to counsel, assist, advise.

assessoria s. f. 1. = **assessoramento.** 2. advisory committee or group. 3. independent office or organization providing technical assistance.

assestar v. 1. to aim, point out, level; to regulate, adjust. 2. to discharge, fire.

~ **um telescópio** to point a telescope.

assesto s. m. aim, act of aiming, levelling or pointing a gun.

assetar, assetear v. 1. to wound or kill with arrows. 2. to attack; annoy.

asseteador s. m. archer.

assevandijamento s. m. degradation, debasement.

assevandijar v. to humble, debase, degrade.

asseveração s. f. (pl. -ões) asseveration, affirmation, averment, assurance.

asseverador s. m. asserter, affirmer. ‖ adj. asserting, affirmative.

asseverar v. 1. to asseverate, assure, assert, affirm, aver. 2. to certify. 3. to allege.

asseverativo adj. assertory, affirmative.

assexo, assexuado, assexual adj. asexual; non-sexual.

assialia s. f. (med.) assialia, aptyalism.

assidrar v. (also **acidrar**) to flavour with cider.

assiduidade s. f. assiduity, assiduousness, diligence.

assíduo adj. assiduous, sedulous, diligent, constant. ‖ **assiduamente** adv. assiduously.

assim adv. thus, so; in this manner, like this, like that, then, consequently, therefore.

~ **assim** so so, more or less. ~ **como** as well as, just as, such as. ~ **é que vocês trabalham?** is this your way to work? ~ **mesmo** exactly like that; notwithstanding; even so. ~ **ou assado** in this way or that, in any case, by hook or by crook. ~ **que** as soon as. ~ **seja!** be it so! **e** ~ **por diante** and so on, and so forth. **ainda** ~ even so. **como** ~? how come? **mesmo** ~ nevertheless. **não é** ~? isn't that so? **por** ~ **dizer** so to speak. **sendo** ~ in such case, in this case. **tanto** ~ so that.

assimetria s. f. asymmetry.

assimétrico adj. asymmetric(al); unbalanced, proportionless. ‖ **assimetricamente** adv. asymmetrically.

assimilabilidade s. f. assimilability.

assimilação s. f. (pl. -ões) 1. assimilation: a) act or process of assimilating. b) (physiol.) anabolism. 2. absorption.

assimilador s. m. assimilator. ‖ adj. assimilative.

assimilar v. 1. to assimilate: a) make similar. b) incorporate. c) absorb. d) compare. 2. ~-**se** to become similar.

assimilativo adj. (also **assimilador**) assimilative.

assimilável adj. m. + f. (pl. -áveis) assimilable.

assimilhar v. = **assemelhar.**

assinação s. f. (pl. -ões) 1. signature, act of signing. 2. notification. 3. citation, summons. 4. consignment.

assinado s. m. signed document. ‖ adj. 1. signed. 2. subscribed.

~ **e selado** under hand and seal. **o abaixo** ~ the undersigned, **um abaixo-** ~ a petition signed by many persons.

assinalado adj. 1. signalized, marked. 2. branded. 3. signal, outstanding, remarkable. 4. appointed. 5. famous, illustrious.

assinalador s. m. marker. ‖ adj. marking.

assinalamento s. m. (also **assinalação** f.). 1. signalment. 2. earmark (of cattle).

assinalar v. 1. to mark, provide with a mark, distinguish, set off. 2. to mark with an earmark (cattle). 3. to signalize. 4. to designate, determine. 5. to become famous, distinguish o. s.

~ **com ponto de interrogação** to query, mark with an interrogation point.

assinalativo adj. 1. marking. 2. designative.

assinalável adj. m. + f. (pl. -áveis) 1. assignable. 2. remarkable.

assinante s. m. + f. 1. subscriber (to a newspaper or periodical). 2. signatory.

assinapse s. f. biol. asynapsis, faulty pairing of homollogous chromosomes in meiosis.

assinar v. 1. to sign, underwrite. 2. to subscribe. 3. to mark out, note. 4. to approve. 5. to assign. 6. to designate, appoint, specify. 7. to pledge. 8. ~-**se** to sign one's name.

~ **em branco** to sign in blank. ~ **o ponto** to sign the attendance sheet. ~ **uma carta** to sign a letter. ~ **termo** to fix or limit time. ~ **um jornal** to subscribe a newspaper.

assinatura s. f. 1. signature. 2. subscription. 3. (theat.) season ticket.

reconhecer uma ~ to witness a signature. **tomar** ~ (Braz., coll.) to pick on someone.

assinável adj. m. + f. (pl. -áveis) assignable; that can be signed.

assíndese s. f. (biol.) = **assinapse.**

assíndeto s. m. (rhet.) asyndeton.

assinargia s. f. asynergia.

assíntota, assimptota s. f. (geom.) asymptote.

assintótico, assimptótico adj. asymptotic.

assírio s. m. Assyrian. ‖ adj. Assyrian.

assiriologia s. f. Assyriology.

assiriologista s. m. + f. Assyriologist.

assisado adj. prudent, wise.

assísmico adj. (geol.) aseismic, free or almost free from earthquakes.

assistência s. f. 1. presence, atendance (gathering). 2. audience, auditory. 3. assistance, aid, relief, protection, help. 4. (Braz.) first aid, first-aid station. 5. (mil.) support. 6. assiduity. 7. residence.

~ **à infância** child welfare work. ~ **hospitalar** hospitalization. ~ **judiciária** free legal aid. ~ **médica** medical assistance. ~ **religiosa** ministerial office. ~ **social** social welfare work.

assistente s. m. + f. 1. assistant, helper. 2. right hand. 3. acolyte. 4. spectator, looker-on. 5. (Braz.) midwife, accoucheuse. ‖ adj. assisting; auxiliary.

médico ~ attending physician.

assistida adj. f. attended by a midwife.

assistido adj. helped, attended, aided.

assistir v. 1. to attend. 2. to be present at. 3. to watch (a game, a play). 4. to live at a certain place. 5. to assist, aid, help. 6. to stand by, wait upon. 7. to minister. 8. to comfort, nurse. 9. to favour.

assistolia s. f. (physiol) asystole.

assitia s. f. (med.) asitia.

assoalhado (I) adj. 1. exposed to the sun. 2. (fig.) divulged.

assoalhado (II) adj. floored, having a wooden floor.

assoalhador s. m. 1. floor layer. 2. newsmonger; tale-bearer, blabber.

assoalhadura s. f. (also **assoalhamento**) 1. exposure to the sun. 2. laying of a floor (boarding). 3. (fig.) divulging, exposing, tale-bearing, blabbing.

assoalhar (I) v. 1. to expose to the sun. 2. (fig.) to divulge, to spread about, tell tales or secrets, to blab. 3. to brag, put on airs, show off, to blow one's own horn.

assoalhar (II) v. to lay a wood floor.

assoalho s. m. = **soalho**.

assoante s. f. assonant words. ‖ adj. m. + f. assonant.

assoar(-se) v. to wipe or blow one's nose.

assoberbado adj. 1. supercilious, arrogant, lofty, self-important. 2. overloaded with work. 3. rich in.

assoberbamento s. m. 1. a treating with contempt, overbearing, haughtiness. 2. an overloading with work.

assoberbante adj. m. + f. (also **assoberbador** m.) overbearing, contemptuous.

assoberbar v. 1. to treat with disdain. 2. to dominate, domineer. 3. to humiliate. 4. to threaten. 5. to overwhelm, overload with work. 6. ~-se to act superciliously.

assobiada s. f. whistling; hissing; hooting.

assobiadeira s. f. (ornith.) pidgeon; wood-wren.

assobiado adj. 1. whistled. 2. jeered or hissed at; hooted.

assobiador s. m. 1. whistler. 2. (Braz.) a bird (Tijuca nigra).

assobiante adj. m. + f. whistling.

assobiar v. 1. to whistle. 2. to hiss, hoot, to give the bird.

assobio s. m. 1. whistle: a) the instrument. b) the sound. c) whistling, act of whistling. 2. hiss; shrill sound.

não vale um ~ it is not worth a penny.

assobradado adj. two-story, two-storied (house).

assobradar v. (also **ensobradar**) 1. to build with two or more stories or floors. 2. lay the floor, to board, plank.

associação s. f. (pl. **-ões**) association; community, society. partnership, conjunction, guild.

~ **beneficente** welfare agency. ~ **comercial, industrial** Chamber of Commerce; Board of Trade. ~ **Cristã de Moços** Y. M. C. A. Young Men's Christian Association. ~ **religiosa** congregation.

associacionismo s. m. (psych.) associationism.

associado s. m. associate, partner. ‖ adj. associated, allied.

associar(-se) v. 1. to associate with, to join, unite. 2. to form into a society, enter into partnership with, affiliate. 3. to accompany. 4. to cooperate. 5. to colligate.

~ **idéias** to link ideas. ~-**se a um tratado** to enter a treaty.

associativo adj. 1. associative. 2. sociable.

espírito ~ social-mindedness. **propriedade -a** (math.) association law. **vida -a** society (club) activities.

assolação s. f. (pl. **-ões**) (also **assolamento** m.) devastation, ruin, desolation, ravage.

assolador s. m. devastator, waster, destroyer, ravage. ‖ adj. ravaging, destructive, desolate.

assolapador s. m. (also **solapador**) sapper, subverter. ‖ adj. sapping, undermining.

assolapar v. = **solapar**.

assolar v. to desolate, devastate, destroy, ravage, to lay waste.

assoldadar v. 1. to hire for wages. 2. ~-**se** to hire o. s. out for wages.

assoleado adj. (S. Braz.) sick or tired (animal) on account of overwork or too much heat or sun.

assoleamento s. m. (S. Braz.) fatigue due to excessive work in great heat (animal).

assolear v. (S. Braz.) to tire, fatigue excessively (animal) due to prolonged walking or work in great heat.

assomada s. f. 1. top, summit. 2. watchtower. 3. appearing. 4. fit of rage.

~ **do século** dawn of the century.

assomadiço adj. irascible.

assomado adj. 1. irascible, rash, overhasty. 2. (Braz.) skittish, easily frightened.

assomar v. 1. to mount or ascend to the top. 2. to loom. 3. to emerge. 4. to appear at a high place. 5. to get tipsy. 6. to vex, irritate. 7. to become angry, fly into a passion. 8. to show up in public.

assombração s. f. (pl. **-ões**) (Braz.) 1. terror, awe. 2. spook, apparition, phantom.

no castelo há ~ the castle is haunted.

assombradiço adj. easily frightened; timorous.

assombrado adj. 1. shadowy, somber. 2. haunted, spooky. 3. terrified, thunderstruck, dismayed, aghast, disconcerted. ‖ -**amente** adv. amazedly.

casa mal -a haunted house. **fiquei** ~ I was quite disconcerted.

assombramento s. m. 1. dismay, consternation, perplexity, astonishment. 2. great surprise. 3. fear, terror, awe, dread. 4. shading, darkening.

assombra-pau s. m. (pl. **assombra-paus**) (Braz.) = **cangaceiro**.

assombrar v. 1. to shade, shadow, darken. 2. to terrify, awe, frighten, scare. 3. to amaze, dismay, perplex. 4. to startle. 5. ~-**se** to be surprised, perplexed, awe-stricken.

assombreamento s. m. shading (picture).

assombrear v. = **sombrear**.

assombro s. m. 1. astonishment, surprise. 2. admiration, wonder. 3. fright, terror, dread. 4. marvel(l)ous or startling thing.

foi um ~! it was quite a spectacle.

assombroso adj. 1. amazing. 2. terrific, dreadful. 3. prodigious, wonderful.

assomo s. m. 1. appearance. 2. dawn. 3. sign, mark. 4. irritation.

~ **de raiva** fit of anger.

assonância s. f. assonance.

assonante adj. m. + f. (also **assoante**) assonant.

assonorentado adj. sleepy, drowsy.

assonsado adj. (Braz., pop.) foolish, stupid.

assonsar v. (Braz.) 1. to become slightly tired (a horse). 2. to break a journey briefly to rest (a horse).

assopradela s. f. 1. blowing. 2. blow.

assoprado adj. 1. blown. 2. (fig.) blown up, vain.

assoprador s. m. 1. blower. 2. prompter, instigator, setter-on.

assopradura s. f., **assopramento, assopro** m., **assoprar** v. = **sopro, soprar**.

assoreamento s. m. a silting up, an accumulation of sand.

assorear v. to silt up.

assossegar v. = **sossegar**.

assovelado adj. (bot.) subulate, of the shape of an awl.
folhas -as subulated leaves. **voz -a** falsetto.
assovelar v. 1. to prick with an awl. 2. (fig.) to tease, vex.
assoviada s. f., **assoviadeira** s. f., **assoviado** adj = **assobiada**, **assobiadeira**, **assobiado**.
assoviar v. = **assobiar.**
assovinar v. 1. to sting with an awl. 2. to tease, vex 3. ~-**se** to become sordid, stingy.
assovio s. m. = **assobio.**
assuã s. f. (Braz.) = **suã.**
assuada s. f. 1. gang, mob. 2. riot. 3. uproar. 4. vociferation, tumult, rout, hurly-burly.
entrar com ~ to rush in by force.
assuar v. to jeer at; to boo, hiss.
assubstantivar v. (gram.) to turn into a substantive.
assumir v. 1. to assume. 2. to take over. 3. to shoulder, take upon o. s. 4. to enter upon or accede to an office. 5. to arrogate.
~ **o comando** to take over the command. ~ **a responsabilidade** to assume, shoulder the responsibility. ~ **o risco** to take the risk.
assunção s. f. (pl. **-ões**) (also **assumpção**) 1. assumption. 2. promotion. 3. (theol.) Assumption: a bodily taking up into heaven.
~ **de Nossa Senhora** the Assumption of our Blessed Lady.
assungar v. (Braz., also **sungar**) 1. to lift. 2. to snuffle instead of cleaning the nose.
assuntar v. (Braz.) 1. to pay attention to, give heed to. 2. to reflect upon. 3. to notice, observe.
assuntível adj. m. + f. (pl. **-íveis**) (also **assumptível**) assumable,. admissible, allowable.
assuntivo adj. assumptive.
assunto s. m. 1. topic, subject, theme. 2. affair, matter, proposition, concernment. 3. plot, argument.
~ **de dinheiro** a money matter. ~**s familiares** family affairs. **conhecer o** ~ to know one's subject. **fugir ao** ~ to stray from the subject. **limitar-se ao** ~ to keep to the point. **liquidar o** ~ to settle the case. **resolver um** ~ **amigavelmente** to settle a matter amicably (out of court). **isso não tem nada de ver com o** ~ that has nothing to do with the question. **um** ~ **de negócio** a matter of business. **um** ~ **importante** a matter of moment.
assurgente adj. m. + f. emerging.
assustadiço adj. easily frightened; skittish.
assustado (I) adj. 1. frightened, afraid. 2. timid, timorous, fearful.
assustado (II) s. m. (Braz.) an improvised dance party.
assustador s. m. person who frightens, alarms, startles. ‖ adj. frightening, alarming, startling.
não se assuste! don't be afraid.
assustar v. 1. to frighten. 2. to startle, alarm. 3. to terrify, make afraid. 4. ~-**se** to become afraid, startled.
assustoso adj. frightening.
astasia s. f. (med.) astasia.
astático adj. astatic.
asteca s. m. + f. (also **azteca**) Aztec. ‖ adj. Aztec, Aztecan.
asteísmo s. m. (rhet.) asteism.
astenia s. f. (med.) asthenia.
astênico adj. (med.) asthenic, weak.
astenopia s. f. (path.) asthenopia: weakness or rapid tiring of the eyes.
astéria (I) s. f. (cryst.) asterism.
astéria (II) s. f. starfish; star sapphire.
asteriscos s. m. pl. asterisk, star.
asterismo s. m. asterism, constellation.

asternal adj. m. + f. (pl. **-ais**) (anat.) asternal.
asteróide s. m. asteroid: 1. a minor planet. 2. a starfish. ‖ adj. m. + f. asteroidal.
astigmático adj. astigmatic.
astigmatismo s. m. (opt. + med.) astigmatism: a defect of the eye causing imperfect vision.
astilbe s. m. plant. of the genus Saxifraga.
astilha s. f. 1. (also **hastilha**) rod, shaft. 2. (also **lasca, estilhaço**) splinter.
astracã s. m. astrakhan: 1. the curled fur of lambs. 2. the Persian lamb.
astrágalo s. m. 1. (archit.) astragal. 2. (anat.) astragalus, talus, anklebone. 3. (bot.) milk-vetch, wild licorice.
astral adj. m. + f. (pl. **-ais**) astral, sideral, starry.
astropéia s. f. (bot.) scarlet dombeya.
astréia s. f. 1. (astr.) Virgo. 2. certain star corals. 3. (fig.) justice, peace.
ástreo adj. (also **ástrico, astral**) starry.
astrígero adj. (poet.) astriferous, starred.
astro s. m. star: 1. heavenly body. 2. celebrity, luminary, famous person.
~ **do dia** sun. ~ **da noite** moon. ~ **da tela** a movie star.
astrofísica s. f. astrophysics.
astrofobia s. f. (med.) astrophobia.
astrófobo s. m. (med.) a person who suffers from astrophobia.
astrógrafo s. m. (astr.) astrograph.
astróide adj. m. + f. star-shaped.
astrolábio s. m. astrolabe: instrument formely used to determine the position of heavenly bodies.
astrólatra s. m. + f. astrolater.
astrologia s. f. astrology: the (supposed) influence of the stars on the destiny of man.
astrológico adj. astrologic(al).
astrólogo s. m. astrologer.
astromancia s. f. astromancy: art of divining by means of the stars.
astrometria s. f. astrometry.
astronauta s. m. + f. (USA) astronaut. (USSR) cosmonaut.
astronáutica s. f. astronautics.
astronave s. f. spacecraft, spaceship.
astronomia s. f. astronomy: science of the heavenly bodies or a treatise thereon.
astronômico adj. astronomic: 1. pertaining to astronomy. 2. (fig.) exaggerate, fantastic.
um preço ~ a startling price.
astrônomo s. m. + f. astronomer.
astroscopia s. f. astroscopy.
astroscópio s. m. astroscope.
astroso adj. ill-starred, unlucky.
astúcia s. f. 1. astuteness, subtlety. 2. sagacity, cunning, craft, artfulness. 3. deceit, trick, guile.
astuciar v. to contrive, plot, to plan astutely.
astucioso adj. (also **astuto**) astute, cunning, shrewd, crafty, guileful, artful, shifting, foxy. ‖ **-amente** adv. astutely, trickishly, shiftingly.
asturiano s. m. Asturian: native or inhabitant of Asturias (Spain). ‖ adj. Asturian.
ata (I) s. f. 1. record, register, writing. 2. ~**s** pl. proccedings, minutes (as of a meeting or conference).
~ **de parlamento** act of Parliament.
ata (II) s. f. 1. (N. Braz., also **pinha, fruta-do-conde, condessa**) a sugar apple. 2. (zool.) any leaf-cutting ant, including the sauva, found all over Brazil.
atá adv. (Braz.) word used in the expression:
ao ~ aimlessly.
atabacado adj. tobacco-coloured.

atabafado adj. (also abafado) 1. well-covered. 2. protected, sheltered. 3. (fig.) concealed, secret; forgoten.

um negócio ~ a thing forgotten or buried in disregard.

atabafador s. m. (also abafador) a person who conceals, hushes or suppresses. ‖ adj. concealing, hushing, suppressing.

atabafar v. (also abafar) 1. to cover well. 2. (fig.): a) to suppress, keep secret; to hush; to conceal. b) to steal.

atabal s. m. (pl. -ais), atabale m. (also timbale) attabal, kettledrum.

atabaleiro s. m. kettledrummer.

atabalhoado adj. 1. topsy-turvy, disorderly, confused. 2. precipitate. 3. inconsiderate, rash.

atabalhoamento s. m. 1. helter-skelter, confusion. 2. senseless or precipitate way of speaking or acting.

atabalhoar v. 1. to act or speak senselessly or in a precipitate way. 2. to botch, bungle, make badly and hastily. 3. to flounder, embarrass. 4. to confuse, stun. 5. ~-se to become embarrassed, bewildered.

atabaque s. m. a kind of drum used in Asia and Africa.

atabernado adj. (also atavernado) tavernlike.

atabernar v. (also atavernar) 1. to sell in a tavern. 2. to retail. 3. to frequent taverns.

atabular v. (Braz.) 1. to hurry, make haste. 2. to wrangle. 3. to be incoherent in speech, talk nonsense.

ataca s. f. (also atacador m.) lace, staylace.

atacadista s. m. + f. wholesaler, wholesale merchant. ‖ adj. m. + f. wholesale.

atacado adj. 1. attacked. 2. laced, attached, tied.

comércio de ~ wholesale business. por ~ wholesale.

atacador s. m. 1. attacker. 2. lace, staylace, shoelace, shoestring (plate E 9). 3. ramrod.

atacadura s. f. fastening, lacing.

atacamita s. f. (min.) atacamite.

atacante s. m. + f. 1. aggressor, assailant. 2. lineman (soccer game). ‖ adj. 1. assailant, attacking. 2. offensive, insulting.

atacar v. 1. to attack, assault, seize. 2. to have a go at. 3. to lace (as shoes), tie up. 4. to impugn, insult. 5. to ram (a gun with a ramrod). 6. to corrode.

atacável adj. m. + f. assailable, open to attack.

atacoar v. 1. to botch. 2. to heel (shoes).

atada s. f. atado m. bundle, fag(g)ot, sheaf; parcel, packet.

atado adj. 1. tied, bound. 2. hampered, hindered. 3. timid; irresolute. 4. awkward, clumsy.

~ à cama confined to bed.

atador s. m. person who or thing that binds; binder.

atadura s. f. 1. tie, band, ligature, string, anything to tie with. 2. (surg.) bandage, fillet, fascia. 3. link. 4. union.

~ de emergência (mil.) field-dressing.

atafal s. m. (pl. -ais) crupper (of a saddle or harness).

atafona s. f. 1. hand-mill. 2. horse-mill. 3. water-mill.

atafoneiro s. m. miller of a horse-mill.

atafular-se v. to dress up, become a dandy.

atafulhado adj. 1. replete. 2. satiate, excessively full.

atafulhamento s. m. filling to excess; cramming, stuffing.

atafulhar v. 1. to cram, stuff. 2. to glut. 3. to devour greedily.

ataganhar v. 1. to afflict, torment. 2. to strangle, throttle.

atalaia s. m. + f. 1. sentinel. 2. f. watchtower. 3. (N. Braz.) the highest spot of a mountain; point of lookout. 4. m. watchman.

ficar de ~, de sobreaviso to be on the lookout.

atalaiar v. 1. to stand sentry. 2. to protect, guard. 3. to lurk, spy. 4. to watch, observe. 5. (also ~-se) to be on the watch, be cautious or careful.

ataléia s. f. (Braz.) a genus of palms.

atalhada s. f. a cut through the woods as a barrier against fire; firebreak.

atalhador s. m. 1. person who obstructs, checks, stops. 2. (obs. + mil.) scout.

atalhamento s. m. 1. hindrance, obstacle, obstruction; check, stop. 2. (mil.) enbankment, fortification.

atalhar v. 1. to block, hinder, obstruct. 2. to stop, check, intercept. 3. to impede, prevent. 4. to shorten, sum up. 5. to interrupt, cut short. 6. to short-cut. 7. to embarrass, puzzle, perplex, intimidate. 8. ~-se: a) to coagulate (milk). b) to become puzzled, perplexed.

atalho s. m. 1. bypath, sideway. 2. resourcing to a shortcut (also fig.). 3. shourtcut. 4. obstacle, obstruction, hindrance, impediment. 5. stop, check. 6. abridgement.

não há ~ sem trabalho no gain without pain.

tomar pelo ~ (also fig.) to take the shortest way.

atamancar v. to bungle, dabble, botch, tinker.

atamarado adj. that has the colour of a date (tâmara).

atambeirado adj. (S. Braz.) half-tamed (bovine cattle).

atambor s. m. (bot.) betel.

atamento s. m. 1. (obs.) tying, binding; ligament. 2. (fig.) shyness.

ataná s. f. (Braz.) a leguminous plant of the family Caesalpiniaceae (Dimorphandra macrostachya).

atanado s. m. tan, tanbark, tanned leather, tanned hide.

atanar v. to tan (leather, hides).

atanazar v. = atenazar.

atangará s. m. (Braz., also tangará) the long-tailed manakin.

atangaratinga s. m. (Braz., ornith.; also rendeira) the white-bearded manakin.

ataperado adj. abandoned or in ruins.

ataperar v. (Braz.) to transform into a ghost town, reduce to ruins, abandon.

atapetar v. to carpet, cover with carpets, upholster, tapestry.

atapu s. m. (N. Braz.) a large shell used by fishermen as a sort of horn.

atapulhar v. 1. to plug, stop with a plug. 2. to cork. 3. to stuff (the stomach).

ataque s. m. 1. attack, assault, onset, onslaught, aggression. 2. offensive, charge. 3. hit, thrust. 4. (mil.) shock, drive. 5. fit, stroke, seizure (of sickness).

~ aéreo air raid. ~ cardíaco cardiac attack. ~ de cólera fit of rage. ~ de surpresa ambushment. ~ epiléptico epileptic fit. ~ simulado (mil.) feint. ~ violento onslaught.

atar (I) v. 1. to tie, fasten, lace, bind. 2. to dress, bandage (wound). 3. (fig.) to hinder, fetter, stop. 4. to tighten (bonds of friendship). 5. to link, couple. 6. to attach, establish, form. 7. ~-se: a) to be irresolute. b) to bind o. s. c) to addict o. s. to. d) to entangle o. s.

~ um embrulho to bind up a parcel. ao ~ das feridas (fig.) when it is too late. não ~ nem desatar to leave (problems) without solution.

atar (II) s. m. Indian perfume made of flowers, esp. rose oil.

atarantação s. f. (pl. -ões) confusion, bewilderment, embarassment, perturbation.

atarantado adj. perplexed, confused, bewildered, disconcerted.

atarantar v. 1. to perplex, puzzle, disconcert, bewilder, embarrass, confuse. 2. ~-**se** to be at a loss, be disconcerted, become confused.

ataraú s. m. (Braz.) 1. fury, rage. 2. frenzy, excitement. 3. impertinence, insolence.

ataraxia s. f. ataraxia, stoicism, impassiveness, ataraxy.

atarefado adj. very busy, excessively occupied, engaged, active.

eu ando muito ~ I am overexerted.

atarefamento s. m. (over)burdening with work, overexertion.

atarefar v. 1. to overexert, (over)burden or overload with work. 2. ~-**se** to be diligent, be very busy, occupied, active.

ataroucado adj. fatuous, foolish, stupid.

estilo ~ affected style.

ataroucar v. 1. to turn stupid. 2. ~-**se** to grow stupid, dote.

atarracado adj. short and stout, thickset, stocky, blocky, squat(ty).

atarracar v. 1. to forge (horseshoes and horseshoe nails), to hammer. 2. to jam, sandwich. 3. to fasten with wedges. 4. to puzzle, embarrass, disconcert; vex.

~ **a ferradura** to finish a horseshoe.

atarraxado adj. fastened with a screw, bolt, wedge or the like.

atarraxar v. (also **tarraxar**) to screw together, bolt, fasten with bolts, to rivet, to wedge.

atartarugado adj. having the colour and shape of a turtle.

atas s. f. pl. 1. (jur.) legal or juridical records. 2. minutes of a meeting.

atascadeiro s. m. (also **atasqueiro**) marshy place, quagmire, puddle.

atascal s. m. (pl. -ais) (Braz.) mudhole, quagmire.

atascar v. 1. to stick in the mire. 2. to bog down. 3. (fig.) to sink, degrade, debase o. s.

atassalhador s. m. tearer, render, person who lacerates; calumniator.

atassalhadura s. f. tearing, rending.

atassalhar v. 1. to cut, tear or rend to pieces. 2. to calumniate, disbelieve, slander, backbite.

ataúba s. f. (Braz.) musk-tree, musk-wood.

ataúde s. m. 1. coffin, bier. 2. tomb, tombstone.

atauxiar v. (also **tauxiar**) to inlay.

atavanado adj. black or chestnut with white spots (horse).

atavernado adj. (also **atabernado**) tavernlike.

atavernar v. = **atabernar**.

ataviador s. m. adorner, trimmer.

ataviamento s. m. 1. ornament, rigging, array. 2. spruceness.

ataviar v. 1. to trim, rig up, array, embellish, adorn. 2. to prank, caparison. 3. to spruce up. 4. ~-**se** to dress, attire, make o. s. fine.

atávico adj. (biol.) atavistic.

atavio s. m. 1. attire, ornament, dressing up, caparison. 2. ~-**s** pl. fineries, accoutrements.

atavismo s. m. (biol.) atavism, retroversion.

ataxia s. f. (path.) ataxia: inability to co-ordinate muscular movements.

atáxico adj. (path.) ataxic.

atazanar v. (pop.) = **atenazar**.

até prep. till, until, by, up to, up till. ‖ adv. thus, even, likewise, not only, but also.

~ **agora** up till now, hitherto, as yet. ~ **a volta** until your return. ~ **amanhã** until tomorrow. ~ **aqui, muito bem** so far so good. ~ **aqui, e nem um passo a mais** so far and no farther. ~ **às**

últimas to the very last. ~ **breve** see you soon. ~ **depois**, ~ **já**, ~ **a vista** see you later. ~ **então** till then. ~ **logo** so long, good-bye. ~ **Londres** as far as London, up to London. ~ **Londres confirmou a notícia** even London confirmed the news. ~ **não poder mais** to the limit of one's capacity. ~ **o máximo** to the utmost. ~ **novo aviso** until further notice. ~ **onde?** how far? ~ **quando?** until when? ~ **quanto?** up to how much? ~ **que** until, till. ~ **que enfim** at last. ~ **tanto** so much. **ainda há muito tempo** ~ **lá** it is a long time yet. **ele disse** ~ **que não viria** he even said he would not come. **talvez seria** ~ **mais prudente** not that it might not be wiser.

ateador s. m. 1. incendiary. 2. instigator. ‖ adj. promoting quarrels.

atear v. 1. to set fire, light, kindle, inflame; fan, stir, poke. 2. to excite, foment, arouse. 3. to provoke, stir up, set on. 4. ~-**se:** a) to take fire, burst into flame. b) to become excited. c) to spread.

atecnia (I) s. f. lack of technique, artlessness.

atecnia (II) s. f. (med.) sterility, barrenness.

atecos s. m. pl. (zool.) Athecae, a suborder of Testudinata, comprising the **tartaruga-de-couro** (the marine leatherback, Dermochelys coriacea), the largest existing sea turtle.

atediar v. 1. to tire, disgust, weary, bore. 2. ~-**se** to become tedious, tired, weary, bored.

ateira s. f. (Braz.) the sugar apple, its fruits are the **ata** or **fruta-do-conde.**

ateísmo s. m. atheism, godlessness.

ateísta s. m. + f. atheist: person who does not believe in God.

ateístico adj. atheistic(al).

atelanas s. f. pl. (hist.) satiric pieces, performed in the Roman theaters.

atelectasia s. f. (path.) atelectasis.

atelépode adj. m. + f. (zool.) lacking any digit.

Áteles s. m. pl. (zool.) Ateles, a genus of cebid monkeys from the American continent, comprising the **coatá** (spider monkey).

atelhamento s. m. (N. Braz.) tiling of a roof.

atelhar v. (N. Braz.) to tile a roof.

ateliê s. m. atelier, studio.

atelocardia s. f. (path.) incomplete development of the heart.

atelomielia s. f. (path.) incomplete development of the medulla.

atemorizador s. m. person who or thing that frightens, intimidates. ‖ adj. (also **atemorizante**) alarming, frightening.

atemorizar v. 1. to intimidate, scare, daunt. 2. to frighten, terrify. 3. ~-**se:** a) to be intimidated. b) to become frightened, be terrified (of).

atempado adj. (S. Braz.) sickish.

atempar v. to postpone, put off.

atenazamento s. m. 1. molestation, vexation. 2. torture.

atenazar v. 1. to grip as with pincers. 2. to tire, molest. 3. to afflict. 4. (fig.) to torture.

atença s. f. attachedness, devotedness, fondness of.

estar às ~**s** to rely upon something or somebody.

atenção s. f. (pl. -ões) 1. attention, concentration. 2. care, carefulness. 3. watchfulness, vigilance. 4. respect, regard, politeness, complaisance, kindness; courtesy, heedfulness, gallantry. 5. application, study. ‖ interj. watch out!

chamar a ~ **para** 1. to direct a person's attention to. 2. to upbraid. **dar** ~ **a** to give (take, pay) attention, heed to. **em** ~ **a seu pedido** in compliance with your request. **falta de** ~ 1. inattention. 2. crossness, heedlessness. **prestar** ~ to pay attention, lend an ear. **tratar com** ~ to be courteous with.

atencioso adj. 1. attentive. 2. respectful, considerate. 3. polite, gallant, courteous; kind. 4. mindful, regardful. 5. complaisant. 6. vigilant, assiduous. ‖ -**amente** adv. respectfully; considerably; assiduously.

atendente s. m. + f. (Braz.) nurse's aid, orderly.

atender v. to attend: 1. consider, mind. 2. give an ear, pay attention, listen. 3. heed, observe, regard, follow. 4. care for. 5. serve. 6. be in attendance. 7. wait for, expect. ~ **a** 1. to pay attention to, heed. 2. to take care of. ~ **a campainha, o telefone** to answer the bell, a telephone call. ~ **um pedido** to comply with a request. **atendendo às circunstâncias** in view of the circumstances. **estar pronto para** ~ to be ready at call. **ninguém me atendeu** nobody let me in (home).

atendível adj. m. + f. (pl. -**íveis**) attendable, worthy of being noticed, deserving consideration.

ateneu s. m. 1. athenaeum. 2. a non-official school. 3. academy.

ateniense s. m. + f. Athenian: native or inhabitant of Athens. ‖ adj. Athenian.

atenorado adj. tenorlike.

atenorar v. (mus.) to set in tenor.

atenrar v. to make tender.

atentado s. m. 1. attempted assassination, criminal assault. 2. outrage.

atentar (I) v. 1. to attend, observe; to take into consideration, consider, give heed, give thought to, mind. 2. to be attentive. 3. to look into a matter. ~ **para** to look at. **é preciso** ~ **a...** you must have in mind that... **não** ~ **a** to disregard.

atentar (II) v. to attempt (against). ~ **contra a vida de alguém** to attempt against a person's life.

atentar (III) v. 1. (pop.) to try, venture. 2. (Braz., pop.) to provoke, irritate.

atentatório adj. offensive, criminal, heinous, outrageous, shameless.

atentivo adj. attentive.

atento adj. 1. attentive: a) thoughtful, heedful, mindful. b) polite, kind, respectful, obliging. 2. alert, observant, sharp. 3. careful. 4. diligent. ‖ -**amente** adv. attentively, closely. **ficar** ~ **ao trabalho** to mind one's work.

atenuação s. f. (pl. -**ões**) attenuation, lessening, diminishing, tapering.

atenuado adj. attenuated, weakened.

atenuador adj. attenuating.

atenuante adj. m. + f. attenuating; attenuant; mitigating. **circunstâncias** ~**s** attenuating circumstances.

atenuar v. 1. to attenuate: a) extenuate. b) make thin or slender. c) weaken. d) lessen, diminish. e) dilute; reduce. f) mitigate, ease. 2. to taper. 3. to commute. **o tempo** ~**á a sua dor** time will dull the edge of his pain. **a idade juvenil atenua a culpa** youth lessens guilt.

ater v. 1. to stop, detain. 2. to hold on for support.

atérmano adj. (phys.) athermanous, athermic, impervious to heat.

atermar v. to put a limit to, fix a certain date.

atermasia s. f. (med.) athermasia.

atermia s. f. 1. (phys.) adiathermancy. 2. (med.) absense of heat.

atérmico adj. (also **atérmano**) athermic.

ateroma s. m. (path.) atheroma.

aterosclerose s. f. (path.) atherosclerosis.

aterrado s. m. 1. a filling up with earth, levelling. 2. (Braz.) a piece of solid ground in a swamp. ‖ adj. 1. frightened, startled, awe-stricken, aghast.

2. filled up with earth, levelled. 3. landed (airplane).

aterrador adj. awe-inspiring, frightful, frightening, appalling.

aterragem s. f. (pl. -**ens**) (also **aterrissagem**) 1. landing (aircraft). 2. a filling up with earth; levelling.

aterraplanar, aterraplenar v. = **terraplenar.**

aterrar (I) v. 1. to frighten, terrify, appal, horrify. 2. to puzzle, startle, astound. 3. ~-**se** to become frightened, awe-stricken.

aterrar (II) v. to fill (in) or cover with earth, level.

aterrar (III) v. to land (aircraft).

aterrissagem s. f. (pl. -**ens**) (Braz., also **aterragem**) landing (aircraft).

aterrissar v. (Braz., also **aterrar**) to land (aircraft).

aterrizar v. 1. = **aterrissar, aterrar.** 2. to fill or cover with earth.

aterro (ê) s. m. 1. place filled up with earth, embankment, earthwork. 2. earth, or anything else used to fill up a place.

aterroada s. f. (N. Braz.) 1. cattle hoofprints on swampy ground. 2. anthill.

aterrorizador adj. m., **aterrorizante** m. + f. frightful, terrifying, appalling.

aterrorizar v. 1. to terrify, horrify, dismay, frighten; to appal. 2. ~-**se** to be horrified, shocked.

atesar v. to stretch, stiffen.

atestação s. f. (pl. -**ões**) 1. attestation. 2. attest. 3. testification.

atestado (I) s. m. certificate, certification, credential, testimonial, attestation. ‖ adj. certified. ~ **de boa conduta** testimonial to a person's character. ~ **de óbito** death certificate. ~ **de saúde** health certificate.

atestado (II) adj. filled to the top, brimful.

atestador s. m. certifier, attestor; testimony, witness. ‖ adj. attestant, certifying, attesting.

atestante s. m. + f. attestant: person who signs or authenticates certificates. ‖ adj. m. + f. attesting, attestive.

atestar (I) v. 1. to attest, vouch, witness. 2. to bear withness, certify.

atestar (II) v. to fill to the top, cram, stuff.

atestatório adj. attestant, attesting, certifying.

atesto s. m. making up to the original volume to compensate for evaporation loss (wine).

ateu s. m. (fem. **atéia**) atheist, a godless person. ‖ adj. atheistic, godless, ungodly.

atiçador s. m. 1. instigator, fomenter, plotter. 2. poker, stoking iron, fire hook (plate P 1). ‖ adj. inciting, provoking, instigating, fomenting.

atiçamento s. m. 1. instigation, provocation. 2. stirring up of the fire, poking.

aticar v. (S. Braz.) to find, run across.

atiçar v. 1. to poke, rake or stir up a fire. 2. to instigate, foment, incite. 3. ~-**se** to get angry, become irritated. ~ **discórdias** to foment discord, to add fuel to the fire.

aticismo s. m. atticism: elegance of language.

ático s. m. (archit.) attic: a low story above an entablature. ‖ adj. Attic: of or pertaining to Attica (Greece).

atiçoar v. to burn with firebrands.

atiçu s. m. basket used by the Nambiquara Indians.

atigrado adj. spotted or speckled like a tiger.

atijolado adj. (Braz.) paved with bricks.

atijolar v. (Braz.) to pave with bricks.

atilado adj. 1. elegant, fine, refined. 2. conscientious, scrupulous. 3. sensible, judicious, understanding, reasonable. 4. witty, ingenious, clever. ‖ -**amente** adv. scrupulously; sensibly; refinedly, elegantly.

atilamento s. m. 1. punctuality, accuracy, perfection. 2. diligence. 3. prudence; discretion.

atilar v. 1. to execute with care. 2. to improve, meliorate, perfect. 3. to refine. 4. ~-se to become smart, quick, nimble.

atilho s. m. 1. small tie, string, lace, band. 2. (Braz.) a bundle of maize spikes.

não tem ~ nem vincilho it is good for nothing.

atimia s. f. (med.) athymia: melancholy, depression.

átimo s. m. (Braz.) instant, moment.

num ~ in an instant.

atinado adj. 1. cautious, heedful, prudent, discreet. 2. reasonable, wise. 3. intelligent, smart, shrewd, clever.

atinar v. 1. to guess right. 2. to discover, find out, hit upon. 3. to succeed. 4. to remember.

não posso ~ com o motivo do seu silêncio I cannot make out your silence.

atincal s. m. (min., also **tincal**) borax.

atinência s. f. reference.

atinente adj. m. + f. referent, relative.

atinga s. f. (ichth.) a Brazilian sea fish (Chilomycterus atinga) akin to the globefish.

atingaçu, atinguaçu s. m., **atingaú** f. (Braz., ornith.) squirrel cuckoo.

atingir v. 1. to reach. 2. to attain. 3. to arrive at. 4. to touch. 5. to conceive, grasp, understand. 6. to affect, concern.

~ a maioridade to come of age. **~ o cume, o ponto alto** to reach the top, the climax. **ele foi atingido pela bola** he was hit by the ball. **isto não me atinge** this does not affect me. **o rebanho atinge 800 cabeças de ovelhas** the herd amounts to 800 sheep.

atingível adj. m. + f. (pl. **-íveis**) 1. attainable. 2. touchable. 3. conceivable.

atino s. m. 1. guess: act or fact of guessing (right). 2. a hit, hitting upon, catching on. 3. = **tino**.

atintamento s. m. (typogr.) inking, colouring.

atintar v. (typogr.) to ink a form.

atípico adj. atypic(al).

atiplar v. (mus.) to put or set in soprano.

atirada s. f. throw, hurl, cast: act or fact of throwing, hurling, casting.

atiradeira s. f. (Braz., also **estilingue**) slingshot.

atiradiço adj. (fam.) adventurous, daring, given to amorous adventures.

atirado adj. (Braz.) 1. bold, daring; brave, intrepid. 2. given to amorous affairs; impudent. 3. thrown, hurled.

atirador s. m. 1. shooter, rifleman. 2. marksman, sharpshooter. 3. soldier. ‖ adj. shooting.

atiramento s. m. 1. shooting. 2. casting. 3. throwing.

atirar v. 1. to shoot, fire, rifle, discharge a firearm. 2. to throw violently; to hurl, fling, cast, pitch. 3. ~-se (contra, em) to throw o. s. (against, in, into).

~ a esmo to shoot at random. **~ a cabeça para trás** to fling back one's head. **~ bem** to be a good shot. **~ ao chão** to throw to the ground. **~ contra** to shoot at. **~ longe** to carry far. **~ para longe** to throw far away. **~ para o lado** to fling aside. **~ lama em alguém** (fig.) to fling mud at s. o. **~ pedras** to fling stones. **~ de volta** to throw back. **~-se aos pés de alguém** to throw o. s. at a person's feet. **ele atirou uma flecha no pássaro** he sent an arrow after the bird. **o cavalo atirou coices** the horse kicked. **o touro atirou o cachorro para o ar** the bull tossed the dog.

atiriba s. f. (Braz., also **ateréua**, bot.) manbarklak.

atitar v. 1. to shriek, squawk, scream (birds). 2. to yell. 3. to hiss.

atito s. m. 1. squawk, scream (birds). 2. shrill sound; yell. 3. hiss.

atitude s. f. 1. attitude: a) posture, pose. b) position, disposition. 2. aspect, expression; air, mood.

~ evasiva evasiveness. **~s grosseiras** coarse manners. **eles alteraram a sua ~** they changed their attitude, changed front. **sua ~ foi muito arrogante** he (she, they) rode the high horse. **tomar uma ~** to assume an attitude. **uma ~ amigável** a friendly attitude.

ativa s. f. 1. (gram.) active: the active voice. 2. active service.

ativação s. f. (pl. **-ões**) activation: act or fact of activating, actuating.

ativante s. m. activator, accelerator. ‖ adj. m. + f. activating, accelerating.

ativar v. 1. to activate, actuate, bring into action, push. 2. ~-se to become active.

atividade s. f. activity, energy, alacrity, function, initiative, vigo(u)r, agency, quickness, pursuit, industriousness, business, action, vivacity.

~s literárias literary pursuits. **em plena ~** in full activity, in full play, swing. **manter(-se) em ~** to keep astir, (fig.) to keep the pot boiling.

ativismo s. m. activism.

ativista s. m. + f. an active person. ‖ adj. active, favouring activism.

ativo adj. active, busy, brisk, enterprising, expeditious, energetic(al), alive, alert, pushful, efficient, up-and-coming, up-and-doing, dynamic(al), vivacious, vivid. ‖ -**amente** adv. actively, busily, efficiently, energetically, vividly, vivaciously.

~s e passivos (com.) assets and liabilities. **demasiadamente ~** overactive. **exército ~, permanente** military establishment, standing army, regular army.

atlante s. m. 1. atlas: image of a man supporting a sphere or globe. 2. a strong man. 3. (fig.) pillar, support.

atlântico s. m. Atlantic Ocean. ‖ adj. Atlantic: 1. of or referring to an atlas. 2. of or referring to the Atlantic Ocean.

atlas s. m. atlas: 1. collection of maps in the form of a book. 2. (anat.) the first vertebra of the neck.

atleta s. m. + f. 1. athlete. 2. daring person.

atlético adj. athletic: 1. referring to athletes. 2. (fig.) vigorous, strong.

atletismo s. m. athletics: the practice of physical exercises.

atmidômetro, atmômetro s. m. instrument to measure evaporation.

atmosfera s. f. atmosphere: 1. the air around the earth. 2. the pressure of the earth's atmosphere. 3. (fig.) climate, environment.

atmosférico adj. atmospheric(al).

ato s. m. 1. act: a) performing of a function; doing, action. b) instrument, deed; part of a play. 2. thesis; final examination.

~ contínuo immediately. **~ de agressão** aggression. **Atos dos Apóstolos** the Acts of the Apostles. **fazer ~ de presença** to pay just a very short visit. **um mau ~** an ill, bad turn.

à-toa adj. m. + f. 1. worthless. 2. useless, void.

atoada s. f. (ant., also **atoarda**) rumour, hearsay, false rumour.

atoalhado s. m. table-cloth, linen. ‖ adj. 1. like a table-cloth (texture). 2. covered with a table-cloth or linen.

atoalhar v. 1. to cover with a table-cloth or linen. 2. (by extension) to cover.

atoamente adv. (Braz.) uselessly, without consideration, inconsiderately.

atoar v. 1. to tow, haul, drag. 2. to buck, jib, refuse to move on (animal).

atoarda s. f. vague news, rumor, hearsay.
atocaiar v. (Braz.) 1. to waylay. 2. to stalk (game). 3. to spy on.
atochado adj. 1. jammed, tight, fixed. 2. overful, crammed.
atochador s. m. 1. tool to fix, press or tighten something. 2. person who performs this operation. ‖ adj. fixing, pressing, tightening.
atochar v. 1. to fill up, stuff. 2. to clog, obstruct. 3. to put between splints; to fix, wedge, press, pack in. 4. to force into. 5. to crowd in.
atocho s. m. 1. wooden wedge; chock. 2. act of fastening with a wedge.
atocia s. f. (med.) atocia: sterility in the female.
atoicinhado adj. (also **atoucinhado**) larded, lardy, like pork fat.
atol s. m. (pl. **atóis**) atoll.
atoladiço adj. miry, muddy.
atolado (I) adj. mired, to be stuck in the mire, bogged down.
atolado (II) adj. foolish, idiotic; simple.
atolador s. m. mudhole. ‖ adj. that mires in, bogs down.
atolambar v. to turn or become foolish or simple.
atolar (I) v. 1. to stick in the dirt, mud or mire; to bog, stall. 2. to put into difficulties, embarrass; muddle, mismanage. 3. ~-se: a) to poach, to get stuck in the mud. b) to degenerate, be dissolute. ~ no lodo to bemire; get stuck; degenerate. ~-se na lama to stick fast in the mud.
atolar (II) v. to become foolish.
atoleimado adj. (also **atolambado**) stupid, simple, foolish.
atoleimar v. 1. to make stupid, to besot. 2. ~-se to become stupid; to play the fool.
atoleiro s. m. (also **atoladouro**, **atoledo**) 1. marshy place, slough, puddle, mire. 2. lurch, plunge; embarrassment, difficulty; mess, pickle. 3. immorality, degradation.
tirar-se da lama e meter-se em ~ to jump from the frying-pan into the fire.
atomatar v. 1. to shame. 2. to confuse. 3. to mash, squash (as a tomato).
atombar v. to enroll, list; to annotate, register.
atômico adj. atomic, referring to the atom.
bomba -a atomic bomb. **energia -a** atomic energy. **número** ~ atomic number. **peso** ~ atomic weight.
atomismo s. m. (philos.) atomism: atomical philosophy or theory.
atomista s. m. + f. (philos.) atomist: adherent of atomism. ‖ adj. (also **atomístico**) atomistic.
atomizador s. m. sprayer, pulverizer.
atomizar v. to atomize, reduce to atoms; pulverize; spray.
átomo s. m. 1. atom. 2. corpuscle, least mote. 3. (fig.) thing of no consequence.
atonal adj. m. + f. (pl. **-ais**) (mus.) atonal.
atonalidade s. f. (mus.) atonality.
atonalismo s. m. (mus.) atonalism, atonality.
atonelado adj. having the form of a tun or large cask.
atonia s. f. (med.) atony: slackness, weakness, debility.
atônico (I) adj. atonic: (med.) referring to atony.
atônico (II) adj. (gram.) unaccented.
atonismo s. m. (ancient Egypt) the worship of Aten, or "solar disk".
atônito adj. 1. aghast, stupefied, perplexed. 2. astonished, amazed, surprised. 3. startled.
átono adj. (gram.) atonic.
atontar v. 1. to make dizzy, to bewilder, fluster. 2. to stupify, besot.
atopetar v. 1. to haul to the top (of a mast). 2. (Braz.) to fill, fill up, fill full, cram.

atopia s. f. (med.) atopy.
atópico adj. 1. (med.) atopic. 2. displaced.
ator s. m. (pl. **atores**) 1. (theat., cinema) star, actor, artist, performer, player. 2. (fig.): a) imitator, simulator. b) participant.
~ **principal** leading man. ~ **de televisão** telecaster.
atora s. f. (Braz.) piece of timber; log.
atorácico adj. without thorax.
atorar (I) v. 1. to saw wood into logs or timber. 2. to divide into two, to halve.
atorar (II) v. to go away.
atorçalado adj. laced with silk galloons, provided with silk cords.
atorçalar v. to lace with silk galloons, provide with silk cord.
atorçoar v. to grind grossly as oatmeal; to crush, crunch.
atordoado adj. 1. stunned, stupefied. 2. giddy, dizzy; vertiginous; swimming. 3. thunderstruck, thunderstricken. 4. heedless, inconsiderate. ‖ -**amente** adv. giddily; heedlessly.
atordoador adj. (also **atordoante** m. + f.) stunnning, stupefying, confounding.
um barulho ~ a thundering, stupefying noise.
atordoamento s. m. 1. loss of consciousness. 2. stunning, stun, daze, giddiness; obfuscation. 3. stupefaction. 4. heedlessness.
atordoar v. 1. to stun, stupefy, consternate, puzzle, unhinge, dizzy, confuse, daze, bewilder. 2. to overnoise, deafen.
atormentação s. f. (pl. **-ões**) torment, racket, anguish, affliction, trouble.
atormentadiço adj. easily tormented or afflicted; worrisome.
atormentado adj. tormented; troubled; tortured; pinched, pained, afflicted.
~ **pela consciência** stung with remorse. **estou** ~ **com dores de cabeça** I am troubled with headache.
atormentador s. m. tormentor, fretter; worrier, tantalizer, harrower, plaguer. ‖ adj. tormenting. vexatious, worrisome, afflictive, tantalizing.
atormentar (I) v. to torture, torment, afflict; worry, harrass; excruciate, trouble, aggrieve, fret, vex; pinch, sting, prick; bedevil, tantalize, victimize. ~-se bother, worry, be afflicted.
atormentar (II) v. = **adormentar**.
atormentativo adj. tormenting, vexatious, worrisome.
atossicar v. (Braz.) to give a bad piece of advice, to instigate to act badly, mislead.
atoucado adj. 1. toquelike, like a bonnet or hood. 2. hooded.
atóxico adj. non-poisonous, poisonless, innocuous.
atrabile, **atrabilis** s. f. atrabilis, black choler; black bile, melancholy.
atrabiliário, **atrabilioso** adj. 1. atrabilious, atrabiliar, melancholic(al), hypochondriacal. 2. bilious, choleric, angry, ill-tempered.
atracação s. f. (pl. **-ões**) (also **atracadela**) 1. grappling, docking, boarding, mooring. 2. approach. 3. scuffle, dog-fight.
atracador s. m. mooring line, seizing, lashing, hawser.
atracadouro s. m. moorings, mooring place, berth.
atracão s. m. (pl. **-ões**) 1. collision, thrust, push, shock. 2. impertinence.
atração s. f. (pl. **-ões**) attraction: 1. act or fact of attracting. 2. magnetization. 3. affinity. 4. tendency, interest. 5. engagingness, winsomeness; allurement.
~ **elétrica** electrical attraction. ~ **sexual** sex appeal. **exercer uma** ~ to exert an attraction. **força de** ~ (phys.) attractive power. **peça de grande** ~ (theat.) stock piece.

atracar v. 1. (naut.) to come alongside, moor; .asi, seize; tie up, make fast. 2. to approach (a woman). 3. ~-se to come to grips, to scuffle.
atraca! interj. come alongside!
atraente adj. m. + f. attracting, attractive: 1. magnetic(al). 2. engaging, fascinating, engrossing, catching, captivating, lovely, winning. 3. appealing, interresting. 4. alluring, tempting, seductive. ‖ ~mente adv. captivatingly, winsomely.
muito ~ very attractive, fascinating. **não** ~ unpossessing, unlovely.
atrafegar-se v. to overwork o. s., to have too much to do, to overburden o. s. with responsibilities.
atraiçoado adj. 1. betrayed. 2. treacherous, perfidious. ‖ -amente adv. treacherously.
atraiçoador s. m. traitor, betrayer. ‖ adj. traitorous, treacherous.
atraiçoar v. 1. to betray, deceive, double-cross. 2. to delude, mislead. 3. to play foul. 4. to be unfaithful to, brake the faith. 5. to forsake, let down. 6. ~-se to reveal o. s.
atraimento s. m. = **atração.**
atrair v. to attract: 1. captivate. 2. magnetize. 3. draw, pull (to o. s.). 4. engross, enlist. 5. appeal, interest. 6. allure, lure. 7. fascinate.
ela atraiu um grande público she drew a large public. **o livro não me atrai mais** the book has lost all interest for me. **o seu modo de viver não me atrai** your way of living does not attract me.
atrancamento s. m. act or fact of barring, bolting, locking up.
atrancar v. (also **trancar**) 1. to bar, bolt, lock up. 2. ~-se to intrench, barricade o. s.
atranqueirado adj. provided with stockades, trenches.
atranqueirar v. to close (street or road) with stakes or a barrier.
atrapachar v. (Braz. also **atravancar**) to clog, obstruct.
atrapalhação s. f. (pl. -ões) 1. confusion, disorder, mix-up, muddle. 2. perplexity, embarrassment, fluster, flurry. 3. disturbance, impediment.
atrapalhado adj. 1. confused, confounded. 2. perplexed, puzzled. 3. mixed up, jumbled. 4. addle, higgledy-piggledy, flustered. 5. fumbling.
atrapalhador s. m. 1. person who is easily disconcerted. 2. person who causes confusion.
atrapalhar v. 1. to confuse, upset, perturb, disorder, confound, embarrass, make a mess of, mix up. 2. ~-se to get mixed up, become confused, to flounder.
atrapalho s. m. (Braz.) confusion or embarrassment (especially financial).
atrás adv. 1. behind, back, after. 2. before, ago. 3. (naut.) astern, aback.
~ **da casa** at the back of the house. ~ **de** back of, after, behind (plate P 18). ~ **do palco** backstage. ~ **de que anda você?** what are ou after? **anos** ~ years ago. **o cão corre** ~ **dele** the dog is after him. **deixamo-los** ~ we surpassed them. **estar de pé** ~ **com alguém** to mistrust a person. **ele estava** ~ **de mim** he was at my back. **ele não fica** ~ **de ninguém** he is inferior to none. **não ficamos** ~ we are equal to them. **eu não vou** ~ **dele** I do not mind him, do not listen to him. **voltar com a palavra** ~ to retract o. s., not to keep one's word.
atrasado adj. 1. backward, retrograde, belated, tardy, behindhanded, behind, late. 2. retarded (growth). 3. overdue, back. 4. slow (watch). 5. antiquated. **aluguel** ~ arrears in rent. **uma criança** ~**a** a backward child. **ela chegou** ~**a à mesa** she was tardy for dinner. **navio** ~ overdue (ship). **número** ~ back number. **seu relógio está** ~ your watch is slow.
atrasador s. m. delayer, retarder, person who retards or delays. ‖ adj. delaying.

atrasar v. 1. tu set back (watch). 2. to delay, retard, defer, postpone, put off. 3. to hinder, impede, lose time. 4. to be slow (clock or watch). 5. ~-se: a) to stay or fall behind. b) to get in arrears (payments). c) to be late.
atraso s. m. (also **atrasamento**) 1. delay. 2. retardation. 3. tardiness, lateness, late attendance, latecoming. 4. slowness, backwardness. 5. retrogression. 6. (fig.) rudeness. 7. (com.) arrear.
ele costuma pagar com ~ he is of slow payment. **dívidas em** ~ arrearage. **você atrasou-se** you were late.
atratividade s. f. attractiveness.
atrativo s. m. attraction, appeal, draw, zest, loadstone, pull; charm. ‖ adj. attractive; comely, enticing, sporty, charming, graceful, inviting, winning, catchy, engaging.
ela tem modos ~**s** she has winning manners.
atravancador s. m. encumbrance, impediment. ‖ adj. encumbering, impeding.
atravancamento s. m. (also **atravanco**) act or fact of obstructing, obstruction.
atravancar v. 1. to cluttter, encumber, embarrass. 2. to obstruct, block up, bar. 3. to impede, hinder.
através adv. transverse(ly), through, over, cross, across, athwart.
~ **de** through, by, across, from one side to the other, in the midst, among. ~ **dos campos** across or over the fields. ~ **da cidade** cross-town, through the town. ~ **dos séculos** throughout the centuries, down the ages.
atravessadeiro s. m. (S. Braz.) short cut, bypath.
atravessadiço adj. opposing, irksome; contrary to reason; thwarting.
atravessado s. m. (N. Braz.) watchdog. ‖ adj. 1. crossed. 2. laid across. 3. athwart, oblique, slanting. 4. stuck or thrust through; pierced. 5. unruly. 6. (fig.) perfidious, false, malevolent. 7. crossbred (animals). ‖ -amente adv. across, thwart, athwart.
andar ~ **com alguém** to bear a person a grudge. **ele fez cara -a** he made a wry face. **olhar com olhos** ~**s** to look askew upon.
atravessador s. m. 1. person who or thing that crosses. 2. profiteer, commodity monopolist.
atravessadouro s. m. 1. right of way across unowned property. 2. crossing.
atravessamento s. m. (typogr.) strike-through.
atravessar v. 1. to cross (over), pass over, traverse, transverse, overpass, travel across, transit. 2. to thwart, forestall, impede, hinder, block. 3. to lay across. 4. to get stuck, as in a tube. 5. to perforate, transfix, pierce. 6. to buy in great quantities for retailing and profiteering purposes.
~ **a cavalo** to cross on horseback, ride through. ~ **a cidade a pé** to walk through the town. ~ **correndo** to run through. **atravessamos um tempo difícil** we are going through hard times. **cuidado ao** ~ **a rua!** be careful when you cross the street. **ele atravessou meus planos** he frustrated my plans, he spiked my guns. **o rio nos atravessou o caminho** the river checked our way. **uma espinha atravessou-se-lhe na garganta** he got a fishbone across in his throat.
atravincado adj. secure.
atravincar v. to hold fast, to grip.
atreguar v. 1. to declare a truce. 2. to give a rest. 3. to relieve.
atreito adj. given to, accustomed to, used to, inclined to.
~ **à bebida** given to drink.
atrelar v. 1. to harness. 2. to leash, lead in a leash. 3. to link. 4. to yoke; hitch to. 5. to seduce. 6. ~-se to cling or stick to somebody.

atremar v. 1. to proceed correctly, accurately. 2. to reason with good judgement and skill. 3. to discover by reasoning for guesswork.

atrepsia s. f. (med.) athrepsia.

atresia s. f. (med.) atresia.

atrever-se v. 1. to dare, adventure, venture, brave. 2. to be bold, saucy.
~ **a alguma coisa** to risk, try s. th. **atreva-se!** you just try! **como se atreveu a fazer isto?** how did you dare to do so? **Pedro atreveu-se com Paulo** Peter picked up a quarrel with Paul.

atrevidaço, atrevidão s. m. (pl. -ões) insolent, daring person. ‖ adj. very bold or saucy; impertinent.

atrevido s. m. a daring, bold, forward person. ‖ adj. 1. daring, bold, bold-faced, cheeky. 2. inconsiderate. 3. pushing. 4. insolent, malapert, wanton, saucy. ‖ **-amente** adv. daringly, boldly, wantonly, pertly.
ser ~ (at school, coll.) to have an edge on.

atrevimento s. m. 1. dare, daring, daringness. 2. boldness, recklessness. 3. insolence, pertness, cool-cheek; sauciness.
ele tem o ~ **de fazer isso** he has the conscience to do that. **seu** ~ **me confunde** his (her) assurance baffles me. **que** ~! what a cheek!

atribuição s. f. (pl. -ões) attribution: 1. act or fact of attributing. 2. -ões pl. ascription; duty, assignment; right, prerogative; power.

atribuidor s. m. attributor, attributer, person who attributes.

atribuir v. 1. to attribute, impute to, ascribe to, assign to. 2. to relate. 3. to confer, bestow.
~ **a culpa a outrem** to lay the blame to another's door. **não atribuo importância àquilo** I attach no importance to that. **foi-lhe atribuída uma função** he was assigned a function. **a constituição atribui-lhe esta prerrogativa** the constitution assures him this privilege. **o crime está sendo atribuído a ela** the crime is being laid to her.

atribuível adj. m. + f. (pl. -íveis) attributable, ascribable.

atribulação s. f. (pl. -ões) tribulation, suffering, affliction.

atribulado adj. afflicted, troubled; painful, grievous.

atribulador s. m. person who afficts, distresses. ‖ adj. distressing.

atribular v. 1. to afflict, trouble, vex, grieve. 2. ~-se to be afflicted, distressed.

atribulativo adj. that causes affliction or distress.

atributivo adj. attributive.

atributo s. m. attribute: 1. peculiar quality; characteristic. 2. predicate. 3. symbol, emblem. 4. (gram.) apposition, attributive word or phrase.

atrição s. f. (pl. -ões) attrition: 1. friction. 2. (rel.) penitence, compunction.

atricaude adj. m. + f. (zool.) having a black tail.

atrigado adj. wheat-coloured.

atrigueirado adj. almost brunet.

atril s. m. (pl. -is) lectern, reading desk.

atrimarginar v. to provide with a mourning border (letter, envelope).

átrio s. m. atrium: 1. vestibule; courtyard, porch; living-room. 2. (anat.) chamber of the heart.

atrioventricular adj. m. + f. atrioventricular, auriculoventricular.

atrípede adj. m. + f. (zool.) black-footed.

atriquia s. f. (med.) atrichia: hairlessness.

atritar v. 1. to irritate, torment, annoy. 2. to create or cause friction.

atrito s. m. 1. attrition, friction, rubbing. 2. misunderstanding, difference, dissension. 3. ~s pl. difficulties. ‖ adj. repentant, penitent, contrite.
provocar ~s to cause trouble. **sem** ~ frictionless.

atriz s. f. (pl. ~es) 1. actress, star, player. 2 (fig.) hypocritical woman.
~ **de comédias** comedienne. ~ **substituta** double. ~ **trágica** tragedienne. **ela vai ser atriz** she goes on the stage.

atro adj. atrous, black, dark; (fig.) dismal, tenebrous, ill-omened.

atroada s. f. loud noise; roar, peal.

atroado adj. (Braz.) 1. loud and fast talking. 2. unjudicious.

atroador adj. (also **atroante** m. + f.) deafening, roaring, thundering.

atroamento s. m. 1. thunder-clap. 2. a stunnning with a great noise or shock. 3. lack of good or sound judgement.

atroar v. 1. to thunder, make a great noise, roar. 2. to stun, stupefy, terrify.

atrocidade s. f. atrocity, cruelty, inhumanity, fierceness, fellness, flagitiousness.

atrofia s. f. atrophy.

atrofiado adj. atrophic; scrubby, stunted.

atrofiador adj. (also **atrofiante**) atrophying.

atrofiamento s. m. atrophy, wasting away.

atrofiar v. to atrophy, grow weak, waste away.

atrófico adj. atrophic.

atrombetado adj. trumpetlike.

atrôo s. m. act of thundering, making noise.

átropa s. f. (bot.) belladonna.

atropar v. (mil.) 1. to provide with troops. 2. to enlist.

atropelação s. f. (pl. -ões) (also **atropelamento, atropelo** m.) 1. act or fact of running over, trampling, knocking down. 2. confusion, tumult.

atropelado adj. run over, knocked down (by a car).

atropelador s. m. trampler; person who runs over, knocks down. ‖ adj. (also **atropelante** m. + f.) that runs over, tramples.

atropelar v. 1. to step on or tread on, to trample. 2. to tread under foot (also fig.). 3. to overrun, overturn. 4. to push, press, shove. 5. to jostle, thrust aside. 6. to squash. 7. to smash. 8. (fig.) to outrage. 9. ~-se: a) to swarm, troop. b) to crowd together. c) to do things in a hurry.

atropilhar v. to form a drove, flock (horses).

atropina s. f. 1. (chem., pharm.) atropine, atropin. 2. (bot.) belladonna.

atróptero adj. (ornith.) black-winged.

atropurpúreo adj. dark-red in colour.

atroz adj. m. + f. (pl. ~es) atrocious, heinous, cruel, fierce, merciless, enormous; excruciating (pain). ‖ ~**mente** adv. atrociously.

atuação s. f. (pl. -ões) act or fact of actuating, actuation, performance.

atual adj. m. + f. (pl. -ais) actual: 1. at this moment, now existing, present(-day), current. 2. real, absolute. 3. of immediate interest. ‖ ~**mente** adv. nowadays, now, currently, modernly.
a ~ **situação** the present situation. **ser de interesse** ~ to be of topical interest. **o problema não é** ~ the problem is of no immediate interest.

atualidade s. f. 1. the present, the present time or situation. 2. opportunity. 3. ~s pl. information, news.
~s **cinematográficas** newsreel.

atualização s. f. (pl. -ões) act or fact of bringing up to date, modernization.

atualizado adj. up-to-date.

atualizar v. to modernize, bring up to date.

atuante adj. m. + f. that is in action, acting.

atuar (I) v. to address familiarly with **tu** (thou).

atuar (II) v. 1. to actuate, bring or put into action, give activity to. 2. to function, operate, act, do. **ele atuou como juiz** he refereed. **ele atuou energicamente** he acted energetically, he went it strong.

atuária s. f. actuarial science.
atuário s. m. 1. actuary. 2. (Braz.) employee of an insurance company.
atuável adj. m. + f. (pl. -áveis) dirigible; docile, manageable.
atubibar v. (Braz.) to beset, harass.
atucanado adj. (ornith.) similar to a toucan.
atucanar v. 1. (Braz.) to peck, strike with the beak. 2. (fig.) to beset, harass, cavil.
atueira s. f. net to catch tunny.
atufar v. 1. to fill, full. 2. to dive; plunge; penetrate.
atulhamento s. m. (also **atulho**) a filling or heaping up; a blocking up, jam.
atulhar v. 1. to fill or heap up. 2. to block, obstruct; jam. 3. to overcrowd.
atum s. m. (pl. -uns) (ichth.) tunny, tuna.
atumultuador s. m. person who causes a tumult, rioter. ‖ adj. riotous, tumultuous.
atumultuar v. to cause a tumult, to riot.
atuneiro s. m. (naut.) tuna clipper. ‖ adj. (naut.) relating to the tuna clipper.
atuosidade s. f. diligence, activity, assiduousness.
atuoso adj. active, very diligent, assiduous.
aturá s. m. (Braz.) a cylindrical basket which the Indians carry on the back; it is held by a strap across the forehead.
aturado adj. constant, persistent, continued, continual.
aturador s. m. person who endures, tolerates; sufferer. ‖ adj. suffering, enduring.
aturar v. 1. to support: a) suffer, endure; tolerate, bear, abide. b) sustain, bear the stress of. 2. to last.
aquilo não atura muito that will not last long. **ele atura tudo** he puts up with everything. (coll.) lets them step all over him. **eu não aturaria isto** I wouldn't stand this, take it from anybody. **não aturo contradições** I cannot abide contradictions. **o barco não aturou a tempestade** the boat did not put up against the storm.
aturável adj. m. + f. (pl. -áveis) supportable, endurable; tolerable.
aturdido adj. dizzy, stunned; perturbed, bewildered, confounded, amazed, perplexed, stupefied.
aturdimento s. m. (also **atordoamento**) stunning, stupefaction, bewilderment; dizziness, giddiness.
aturdir v. 1. to stun, din, daze, bewilder, amaze, surprise. 2. to confound, confuse. 3. to fluster. 4. to deafen. 5. to intimidate, frighten (away).
aturiá s. m. (Braz.) 1. (ornith.) hoatzin stinkbird. 2. (bot.) bindoree. 3. (also **cigana**) gypsy woman.
auaduri s. m. (Braz., also **abiurana**) a tree of the genus Lucuma.
audácia s. f. audacity, audaciousness, fearlessness, daring; rashness, forwardness, presumption, boldness, confidence.
ele teve a ~ de dizer he had the confidence to say.
audacioso adj. (also **audaz**) audacious, daring, fearless, adventurous; bold, insolent. ‖ **-amente** adv. boldly, fearlessly.
audibilidade s. f. audibility.
audição s. f. (pl. -ões) audition, reception, hearing; recital; (mus.) performance.
audiência s. f. 1. audience: a) audition. b) listeners, hearers, assembly of spectators. 2. reception of persons who want an interview. 3. hearing of a cause, court session.
~ judicial judgement. **dar ~ to** give audience. **eles foram recebidos em ~** they were admitted; they were given an audience. **julgar em ~ to** sit in judgement.
audiente adj. m. + f. (rare) that hears.
audimudez s. f. congenital muteness.

áudio s. m. audio: 1. (electronics) sound. 2. (Television) indication of the descriptive part of a sound (in a script).
audio- combining form meaning sound, e.g. **audiofreqüência**, **audiograma** and **audiovisual**.
audiofreqüência s. f. (phys.) audiofrequency.
audiograma s. m. audiogram: a graph that indicates the relation between audibility and frequency.
audiovisual adj. m. + f. audiovisual.
auditivo adj. auditive, auditory.
auditor s. m. 1. auditor, hearer, listener. 2. assessor provost; judge.
auditoria s. f. office of an auditor.
auditório s. m. 1. audience, listeners, hearers, spectators; attendance. 2. auditorium. 3. (radio) studio.
audível adj. m. + f. (pl. -íveis) audible, hearable.
auferir v. 1. to gain, profit, make profits. 2. to pocket, rake, reap. 3. to receive, get, obtain.
auferível adj. m. + f. (pl. -íveis) that can be profited, earned, obtained, received.
auge s. m. summit, height, the highest point, acme; pinnacle; peak; culmination; top; apogee, zenith; the highest degree; hey-day.
no ~ at its height, at the highest pitch. **no ~ da fama** at the zenith of one's fame. **no ~ de sua felicidade** on the height of one's felicity; on the crest of the wave. **no ~ do desespero** in the depth of dispair. **o movimento alcançou seu ~** the movement reached its culmination.
augita s. f. (min.) augite.
augural adj. m. + f. (pl. -ais) augural.
augurar v. to augur, predict, forebode, presage, presignify, portend, betide, omen.
áugure s. m. augurer, fortune-teller.
augúrio s. m. augury; foretoken; preapprehension; presage; foreboding, omen; portent.
augustinismo s. m. Augustinism: the philosophical doctrines of St. Augustine.
augusto adj. august, kindly, majestic, royal, venerable.
auiba s. f. (Braz., bot.) xylosma: common name of two trees of the family Flacourtiaceae (Xylosma benthami and Xylosma digynum).
aula s. f. 1. class (room). 2. lecture, lessons.
~ de natação swimming lesson. **dar ~s** to teach, give lessons. **dou-lhe aulas particulares** he coaches with me. **ter ~s** to take lessons.
aulete s. m. (hist.) Greek flute-player.
aulética s. f. art of flute-playing (among the Greeks and Romans).
aulétride, auletriz s. f. (hist.) female flute-player.
áulico s. m. courtier. ‖ adj. courtly, pertaining to the court.
aulido s. m. cry or howling of animals, yell(ing).
aulista s. m. + f. student, scholar, collegian, pupil.
aulo s. m. aulos: Greek name of the flute.
aumentação s. f. 1. = **aumento**. 2. (rhet.) a series of propositions of increasing importance.
aumentador s. m. augmenter, one who or that which augments, enlarges; amplifier. ‖ adj. augmentative; enhancive.
aumentar v. 1. to augment, enlarge, amplify, increase. 2. to grow, develop. 3. to add to. 4. to multiply. 5. to mount, rise, raise. 6. to extend. 7. to intensify, aggravate. 8. to enhance. 9. to greaten.
~ o salário to raise the salary. **aumentando ainda mais as dívidas** increasing debts still further. **isso aumenta as nossas dificuldades** that adds to our difficulties. **uma lente que aumenta muito** a powerful magnifying lens.
aumentativar v. to use too many augmentatives (words).

aumentativo s. m. (gram.) augmentative: an augmentative word. ‖ adj. augmentative.

aumentável adj. m. + f. (pl. **-áveis**) augmentable, increasable.

aumento s. m. (also **aumentação** f., pl. **-ões**) 1. augmentation, enlarging, enlargement, amplification. 2. increase, development, growth, expansion, enhancement. 3. addition, accrescence. 4. rise, raise. ~ **de preço** rise in (of) prices. ~ **de sonoridade** (mus.) swell. **vidro de** ~ magnifying glass.

aunar v. to unite, join into one.

aura s. f. 1. zephyr, breeze, gentle wind, breath of air. 2. (fig.) renown, fame.

áureo adj. (also **áurico**) 1. aureate, golden, shining like gold, brilliant. 2. (fig.) magnificent, valuable, precious.

auréola s. f. aureole; nimbus; halation, glory.

aureolar (I) adj. m. + f. having the forms of an aureole, halo-shaped.

aureolar (II) v. to halo, surround or adorn with a halo; glorify.

auribranco adj. golden-white in colour.

auricídia s. f. thirst for gold.

auricolor adj. m. + f. having the colour of gold, golden-coloured.

auricomo adj. having golden hair.

auricórneo adj. (zool.) having yellow or golden-coloured antennae.

auricrinito adj. (poet.) having a golden braid of hair.

aurícula s. f. (anat., zool., bot.) 1. auricle: a) the projecting part of the external ear. b) atrium: any of the two chambers of the heart. c) an ear-shaped appendage of leaves. 2. (bot.) bear's ear, auricula. ~ **do coração** atrium, atria.

auriculado adj. auriculate(d).

auricular adj. m. + f. auricular: of or referring to the hearing system or the ears.
confissão ~ auricular confession.

auriculiforme adj. m. + f. having the form of an ear.

auriculoso adj. (zool. + bot.) auriculate, auriculated, auricled.

aurífero adj. auriferous: containing or producing gold.

aurificação s. f. (pl. **-ões**) (dent.) filling or stopping made with gold.

aurífice s. m. goldsmith.

aurífico adj. aurific; auriferous; golden.

auriflama s. f. oriflamme, auriflamb, St. Denis' purple standard; flag.

auriforme adj. m. + f. auriform, ear-shaped.

aurifulgente adj. m. + f. shining like gold.

auriga s. f. 1. coachman. 2. (astr.) Auriga (a constellation).

auriginoso adj. (also **auricolor**) golden-coloured.

aurilavrado adj. carved in gold.

auriluzir v. to shine like gold.

auripurpúreo adj. gold and purple-coloured.

aurirrosado, aurirróseo adj. rose and golden-coloured.

auriverde adj. m. + f. green and golden; green and yellow.
o pendão ~ the Brazilian flag.

aurívoro adj. 1. (poet.) that devours gold. 2. (fig.) dissipating.

aurogástreo adj. (zool.) said of animals with a yellowish belly.

auroque s. m. (zool.) aurochs; bison.

aurora s. f. 1. aurora: a) daybreak, dawn. b) begin, start. 2. youth. 3. an ornamental tree.
~ **boreal** aurora borealis. **cor de** ~ pink colour.

auroral, auroreal adj. m. + f. (pl. **-ais**) auroral.

aurorescer v. to dawn, begin to grow light.

ausculta, auscultação s. f. (pl. **-ões**) (med.) auscultation; stethoscopy.

auscultador s. m. 1. (med.) auscultator, stethoscopist. 2. (med.) auscultator, stethoscope. 3. earphone, telephone receiver. 4. listener. ‖ adj. listening; auscultating.

auscultar v. 1. to stethoscope, auscultate: sound out, examine with the stethoscope. 2. to try to find out, inquire.

ausência s. f. 1. absence, nonappearance, nonattendance. 2. privation. 3. ~s pl. remarks about one who is not present.
brilhar por sua ~ to be conspicuous by one's absence. **fazer boas ou más** ~s **de alguém** to speak fair or ill of an absent person. **período de** ~ absent-time.

ausentar-se v. to absent o. s., go away; depart.

ausente s. m. + f. absentee. ‖ adj. absent, away, departed, out, gone, lacking, missing.
~ **com licença** (mil.) absent with leave. **ele está** ~ he is not present; he is absent from home, (fam.) he is not in. **estar** ~ **sem motivo** to be absent without a motive; (U. S. A.) to play hooky. **os** ~s **nunca têm razão** the absent party is always to blame. **pessoa** ~ absentee.

auso s. m. (ant., also **ousio**) daring, boldness, audacity.

áuspice s. m. augurer; arupex, soothsayer.

auspiciar v. to augur, promise, prognosticate.

auspício s. m. (also **augúrio**) 1. auspice. 2. augury. 3. (fig.) a) promise; counsel, advice. b) patronage. **sob os** ~s **de** under the auspices of.

auspicioso adj. auspicious, of good augury, fortunate, promising, propitious. ‖ **-amente** adv. auspiciously, rosily, fortunately.

austenita s. f. (chem.) austenite, a solid solution of carbon in gamma iron.

austereza, austeridade s. f. austerity, austereness, severity, strictness, rigour.

austero adj. severe, austere, rigorous, rigid, strict, grave, stern, harsh. ‖ **-amente** adv. austerely.

austral adj. m. + f. (pl. **-ais**) austral, southern, meridional.

austríaco s. m. Austrian; native or inhabitant of Austria. ‖ adj. Austrian.

austrífero adj. bringing rain from the south.

austro s. m. south (wind), Auster.

autarquia s. f. autharchy: absolute sovereignty, autocracy.

autárquico adj. autarchic(al), autonomous; referring to an autarchy.

autêntica s. f. (also eccl.) attest of authenticity.

autenticação s. f. (pl. **-ões**) authentication; legalization, seal.

autenticado adj. authentic, legalized, approved.

autenticar v. to make authentic, authenticate, legalize, seal, approbate.

autenticidade s. f. authenticity; legality, legitimateness.

autêntico adj. authentic(al), of good authority, legitimate, genuine, real, true, veritable. ‖ **-amente** adv. authentically, veritably.

autígeno s. m. (geol.) authigenic mineral particle. ‖ adj. (geol.) authigenous, authigenous.

autismo s. m. (med.) autism.

autista s. m. + f. autist. ‖ adj. autistic.

auto (I) s. m. 1. solemnity, public and solemn act. 2. document, writ, deed. 3. act of a play; formerly a short dramatic piece. 4. ~s pl. papers, documents; records of a lawsuit, minute of a case.
levantar ~s **de** to make the minutes.

auto (II) s. m. abbr. of **automóvel**: motor-car.

auto (III) s. m. (Braz.) moment, instant.

auto-acusação s. f. (pl. **auto-acusações**) (jur.) self--accusation.

auto-admiração s. f. (pl. auto-admirações) self-admiration, narcissism.

auto-afirmação s. f. (pl. auto-afirmações) (psych.) self-affirmation.

auto-agressão s. f. (pl. auto-agressões) (psych.) self-aggression.

auto-análise s. f. (pl. auto-análises) (psychanalysis) self-analysis.

autobiografia s. f. autobiography, memoir.

autobiográfico adj. autobiographic(al). || autobiograficamente adv. autobiographically.

autobiógrafo s. m. autobiographer.

autocarga s. f. (Braz.) truck.

autocarro s. m. (Port.) omnibus.

autocéfalo adj. governed by itself.

autoclave s. f. autoclave; sterilizer.

autoclínica s. f. study of the illness made by the patient himself.

autocópia s. f. an autocopist copy.

autocopiar v. to copy with an autocopist; manifold.

autocopista s. m. autocopist: a manifolding apparatus.

autocracia s. f. autocracy: absolute authority.

autocrata s. m. + f. autocrat, despot.

autocrático adj. autocratic(al). || autocraticamente adv. autocratically.

autocrítica s. f. self-criticism.

autóctone s. m. autochthon. || adj. autochthonal, autochthonous.

auto-de-fé s. m. (pl. autos-de-fé) (inquisition) auto-da-fé.

autodefesa s. f. self-defense.

autodidata s. m. + f. self-taught person. || adj. self-taught.

autodidaxia s. f. self-instruction.

autodomínio s. m. self-control.

autódromo s. m. autodrome, motordrome.

auto-erotismo s. m. (pl. auto-erotismos) (psych.) autoerotism, autoeroticism.

auto-estrada s. f. (pl. auto-estradas) arterial road, motor road, auto highway.

autófago s. m. referring to autophagia; self-devouring.

autofecundação, autofertilização s. f. (pl. -ões) (med., also autogamia) self-fertilization, self-fertility.

autofilia s. f. (med.) self-love.

autogamia s. f. (biol.) autogamy: sel-fertilization, self-fertility.

autógamo adj. autogamous.

autógeno adj. autogenous.

autogiro s. m. autogiro, autogyro.

autografar v. to autograph.

autografia s. f. autography.

autográfico adj. autographic(al).

autógrafo s. m. autograph. || adj. autographic.

auto-indução s. f. (pl. auto-induções) (phys.) self-induction,

autólatra s. m. + f. person with exaggerated self-love.

autolatria s. f. self-worship.

autólise s. f. (biochem.) autolysis.

autolotação s. m. (pl. -ões) (Braz., more used lotação) a jitney bus.

automático adj. automatic, automatous; self-acting, self-service, mechanical. || automaticamente adv. automatically, mechanically.

alimentação -a automatic feed. canhão ~ automatic gun. controle ~ (radio) automatic volume control. registrador ~ (mach.) telltale. tear ~ power loom.

automatismo s. m. automatism.

automatizar v. to automatize.

autômato s. m. 1. automaton, robot. 2. self-operating automatic machine or instrument. 3. (fig.) person incapable of proper action.

automedonte s. m. skilful charioteer.

autometamorfismo s. m. self-metamorphism.

automobilismo s. m. 1. automobilism, motoring. 2. racing (of motor cars).

automobilista s. m.+f. automobilist, motorist.

automobilístico adj. referring to automobilism or motor-cars.

automorfismo s. m. (geol.) idiomorphism.

automotriz s. m. rail motor, shuttle car. || adj. f. self-propelling, automotive.

automóvel s. m. (pl. -áveis) automobile, motor-car, car. || adj. m. + f. self-moved, self-propelling, automotive.

~ de corrida racing car, racer. ~ pequeno small car. ~ de praça taxi.

autônimo (adj. (lit.) signed by its author.

autonomia s. f. autonomy, self-government.

autonômico adj. autonomous, autonomic.

autonomista s. m. + f. autonomist.

autônomo adj. autonomous, independent, autonomic.

auto-ônibus s. m., sg. + pl. (also and more used ônibus m.) autobus, motor-bus, omnibus.

autopeça s. f. spare part or component for motor vehicles.

autoplastia s. f. (surg.) autoplasty.

autópsia, autopsia s. f. autopsy: post mortem examination; coroner's inquest, necropsy.

autopsiar v. to make an autopsy.

autor s. m. (pl. -es) 1. author: a) writer, composer, penman. b) creator, inventor, maker. 2. originator, cause. 3. plaintiff.

o ~ do crime the criminal. ~ de sua fortuna the framer of one's own fortune. ~ de livros writer. ~ de peças teatrais playwright.

autora s. f. authoress.

auto-radiografia s. f. (pl. auto-radiografias) (nucl. phys.) auto-radiograph.

autoral adj. m. + f. (pl. -ais) authorial.

autorama s. m. miniature racetrack for toy cars.

auto-retrato s. m. (pl. auto-retratos) self-portrait.

autoria s. f. 1. authorship; paternity. 2. responsibility.

chamar à ~ to call to account.

autoridade s. f. authority: 1. legal power, power to command and act. 2. person or (~s pl.) group of persons invested with power and authority. 3. jurisdiction. 4. an expert. 5. headship. 6. influence, prestige.

dar ~ to invest with authority. ele é uma ~ no assunto he is an authority on this matter. eu tenho ~ (para isso) I am in authority. fazer valer a sua ~ to speak a decisive word. precisamos dirigir-nos às ~s we must apply to the authorities.

autoritário adj. authoritarian, authoritative, imperative, dogmatic, magisterial, commanding, peremptory. || autoritariamente adv. peremptorily.

autoritarismo s. m. authoritarianism.

autorização s. f. (pl. -ões) authorization, permission, permit, sanction, warranty, allowance.

fi-lo com ~ especial de meu pai I did it by my father's special permission.

autorizado adj. 1. authorized, approved, permitted. 2. official, regular, commissioned. 3. credible, trustworthy. || -amente adv. authentically, officially.

edição -a authorized edition. estar ~ de to have authority to. não ~ unwarranted. você está ~ a falar you are permitted to speak.

autorizar v. 1. to authorize; permit, allow, sanction, approve, commission, approbate, entitle, warrant, empower; accredit; certificate, legalize. 2. ~-se to justify o. s.

autorizável adj. m. + f. (pl. -áveis) authorizable, warrantable, permissible.

autos s. m. pl. orderly file of documents concerning a legal process.

auto-suficiente adj. m. + f. (pl. **auto-suficientes**) self--sufficient, independent.

auto-serviço s. m. (pl. **auto-serviços**) self-service.

auto-sugestão s. f. (pl. **auto-sugestões**) self-suggestion, autosuggestion.

autotélico adj. (philos.) autotelic.

autotipia s. f. (typogr.) autotype: half-tone photo-engraving.

autotonia s. f. (zool.) autotomy.

autotransformador s. m. (electronics) autotransformer.

autotrem s. m. (pl. **-ens**) train van (plate V 3).

autotrófico adj. (bot., biol.) autotrophic.

autovia s. f. motor highway.

autuação s. f. (pl. **-ões**) 1. collection (the act) of the documents and papers for a lawsuit. 2. a deposition, recording, making minutes.

autuar v. to deposit, record, make minutes of.

autunal adj. m. + f. (pl. **-ais**) (also **autonal**) autumnal.

autunita s. f. (min. also **uranita**) uranite.

autuparana s. f. (Braz., also **quina-da-serra**) tree of the family Rubiaceae.

auxese s. f. (rhet.) auxesis: exaggeration.

auxiliador s. m. auxiliary, helper, assistant, supporter, forwarder, stand-by. ‖ adj. auxiliar(y), supporting.

auxiliar (I) s. m. assistant, adjudant, secondary, ally. ‖ adj. m. + f. auxiliary; helpful.
~ **de escritório** office clerk. **estrada** ~ subsidiary road. **verbo** ~ auxiliary verb.

auxiliar (II) v. to help, aid, lend a hand, assist, avail back up, support; facilitate; to subvene, subsidize; favour.
~ **a uma pessoa necessitada** to help an indigent person. **auxiliaram-no** he was helped. **desejo auxi-liá-lo** I mean to favour him. **ele auxiliou-me** he helped me, gave me a lift.

auxiliário s. m. (Braz.) plan for instalment payments. ‖ adj. that helps, aids.

auxílio s. m. help, aid, succour, assistance, backing, support; recourse; subsidy.
chamar por ~ to cry for help. **conceder** ~ to lend one's aid and assistance. **com seu** ~ with your support. **consegui-o sem o seu** ~ I succeeded without his help. **corremos em seu** ~ we rushed to his help **ela representa um grande** ~ **para nós** she is a great help to us. **prestar** ~ **a alguém** to give aid to a person. **sem** ~ aidless.

auxina s. f. (bot.) auxin.

auxômetro s. m. (opt.) instrument to measure the magnifying power of lenses.

avacalhação s. f. (pl. **-ões**) (also **avacalhamento** m.) (Braz.) demoralization, negligence.

avacalhado adj. demoralized; run down; messy.

avacalhar v. 1. to demoralize, depress, lower. 2. ~-**se** to become demoralized, run down, messy; to turn a coward.

aval s. m. (pl. ~**es**) aval, surety bond; collateral security.

avaladar v. to surround with a trench or rampart.

avalancha s. f. **avalanche** m. 1. avalanche. 2. (fig.) deluge, lawine.
~ **de neve** avalanche, snow-slip. ~ **de palavras** avalanche of words.

avalentoar-se v. (Braz.) 1. to become a ruffian, tough or braggart. 2. to refuse to obey.

avaliação s. f. (pl. **-ões**) 1. valuation, estimate, estimation, appraisal, appraisement, survey, appreciation. 2. consideration, esteem.
~ **baixa** undervaluation. ~ **excessiva** overestimate.

avaliado adj. appraised, rated, valued, estimated; considered, esteemed.
bem (**mal**) ~ well (bad) rated.

avaliador s. m. appraiser, prizer, valuator, averager, estimator, rater.

avaliar v. 1. to evaluate, appraise, prize, value, valuate, estimate, rate. 2. to take stock. 3. to judge, consider, esteem.
~ **de antemão** to prejudge. ~ **em demasia** to overestimate. ~ **novamente** reassess. ~ **o prejuízo** em to lay the loss at.

avaliável adj. m. + f. (pl. **-áveis**) that can be appraised, valued; estimable, assayable, ratable.

avalista s. m. + f. (com.) surety (of bonds or bills).

avalizado s. m. endorsee. ‖ adj. guaranteed by endorsement.

avalizar v. to guarantee, vouch for bonds or shares.

avaluador s. m., **avaluar** v. (ant., pop) = **avaliador**; **avaliar**.

avança s. m. (Braz., pop.) gate crasher, uninvited guest.

avançada s. f. 1. assault, attack. 2. charge, onslaught, advance.
às ~**s** by intermittent advances, step by step.

avançado adj. advanced, onward, well on.
o dia já está ~ the day is far spent. **em hora** ~**a** at such an hour of the night. **de idade** ~**a** far on in years, well up in years. **mais** ~ farther. **opiniões** **-as** forward opinions. **em posição** ~**a** ahead.

avançador s. m. (Braz., pop.) unfaithful depository of money; pilferer. ‖ adj. that advances, attacks.

avançamento s. m. 1. advance, act or fact of going onward, forward, far; progress. 2. (archit.) projection or overhang.

avançar v. 1. to attack. 2. to go, bring or put forward, ahead; to make go on, push on, march forward, proceed. 3. to exceed, transcend. 4. to expose. 5. to winnow. 6. to get along; gain. 7. to forge ahead, press on. 8. to progress, better, improve. 9. to promote. 10. (archit.) to be projecting, stand out. 11. ~-**se** to come close, draw near; go too far.
~ **contra alguém** to go for s. o. ~ **lentamente** to inch. **ele avançou ao sinal** (transit) he disregarded the yellow traffic light, he shot the amber.

avanço s. m. 1. advance: a) advancement. b) progress, progression. c) improvement. d) advance money. 2. onward march. 3. profit. 4. (tech.) feed.
~ **automático** automatic advance or feed. ~ **da ignição** advance ignition. **embreagem de** ~ feed clutch. **engrenagem de** ~ feeder gear. **fuso de** ~ feed spindle.

avania s. f. humiliation.

avantajado adj. 1. advantageous, profitable. 2. superior, better. 3. endowed, able.

avantajar v. 1. to ameliorate, make better, improve. 2. (also ~-**se**) to have advantage over, to surpass in, be superior, exceed, excel, outstrip.

avante adv. forward, onward, forth, along. ‖ interj. go it! go ahead! here goes!
de ora ~ from now on. **ela vai** ~ (fig.) she is doing nicely. **levar** ~ to push. **levar um trabalho** ~ to carry on a job.

avantesma s. m. + f. phantasm, ghost, spectre.

avaqueirado adj. having the manners of a cowboy.

avará s. m. (Braz.) a palm tree (Astrocaryum segregatum).

avarandado s. m. building with a veranda. ‖ adj. verandaed.

avarandar v. (archit.) to provide with a porch, veranda.

avaremotemo s. m. (Braz.) avaremotemo (tree).

avarento s. m. (also **avaro**) miser, niggard, money-grubber, flay-flint, penny pincher, close file; churl; hog-grubber. ‖ adj. avaricious, niggardly, stingy, iron-fisted, hard, tight, churlish.

avareza s. f. 1. miserliness, avarice, avidity, avariciousness, niggardliness. 2. (fig.) cheese-paring; jealousy.

avaria s. f. 1. average, damage. 2. breakdown (car). 3. engine failure.

~ **grossa, comum** general average. ~ **simples** partial average. **indenizar uma** ~ to make good an average.

avariado adj. averaged, damaged, impaired; injured.

avariar v. 1. to cause average, damage. 2. to fail, break down. 3. to impair, spoil. 4. ~**-se** to become damaged or spoilt, suffer average.

avariose s. f. (med.) syphilis.

avaro s. m. = **avarento**.

avascular adj. m. + f. (anat., bot.) having no vessels.

avassalador s. m. person or thing that vassalizes, conqueror, subduer, dominator, oppressor. ‖ adj. vassalazing, overwhelming, overpowering.

avassalamento s. m. 1. act of vassalizing. 2. vassalage, vassality.

avassalante adj. m. + f. vassalizing.

avassalar v. 1. to vassal, vassalize, subdue, subject, dominate, oppress. 2. to captivate; seduce. 3. ~**-se** to vassalize o. s., become a vassal.

avatar s. m. (India) avatar: incarnation of a God.

ave (I) s. f. bird, fowl.

~ **andadora** (ornith.) walker. ~ **aquática** water bird. ~ **cacarejadora** cackler. ~ **doméstica** chicken. ~ **migratória** visitant, bird of passage. ~ **de rapina** bird of prey. **filhote de** ~ peeper.

ave (II) interj. ave!

aveado adj. mad, hairbrained, lunatic.

aveal s. m. (pl. -**ais**) field of oats.

ave-do-paraíso s. f. (pl. **aves-do-paraíso**) paradise bird.

aveia s. f. oat, oats; flaked oats; groats.

~ **amarela** yellow oat grass. ~ **brava, doida** (bot.) wild oats. ~ **estéril** animal oat, fly oat, hygrometric oat. ~ **silvestre** oat grass. **sopa de** ~ oatmeal soup, brose.

avejão s. m. (pl. -**ões**) (also **fantasma**) 1. phantasm, phantom, ghost. 2. ugly man.

avelã s. f. hazelnut, filbert.

avelal s. m. = **avelanal**.

avelanado adj. hazelnut-coloured, hazel(ly), light brown.

avelanal s. m. (pl. -**ais**) (also **avelal**) grove of hazels, plantation of hazels.

avelaneira s. f. (also **aveleira, avelãzeira, aveleeira** f., **aveleiral** m.) hazel (shrub).

avelar (I) s. m. = **avelanal**.

avelar (II) v. 1. to wrinkle, shrivel. 2. to be strong in old age.

avelhacado adj. rather scoundrelly, crooked.

avelhado, avelhentado adj. (also **avelhantado**) oldish, grown old, elderly, aged.

avelhantador adj. (also **avelhentador**) that makes old.

avelhantar, avelhentar v. 1. to make old. 2. (also ~**-se**) to grow old, antiquated, become old- fashioned.

avelórios s. m. pl. (also **velórios, vidrilhos**) 1. small beads of glass to make necklaces or strings for the arms. 2. (fig.) wares of small value; trifles.

avelós s. m. (bot.) aveloz.

aveludado adj. velvet, velvety.

aveludar v. to give the appearance of velvet to (textiles).

ave-maria s. f. (pl. **ave-marias**) Ave Mary; Hail Mary: 1. the first words of the salutation to the blessed Virgin. 2. (R. C. Church) a prayer to the Virgin. 3. (ecl.) angelus. 4. one of the small beads of a rosary.

avena s. f. 1. (poet.) reed-pipe; shepherd's pipe. 2. (bot.) oat, oats.

avenaína s. f. avenin.

avenca s. f. (bot.) maidenhair, silver fern, serpent fern.

avença s. f. 1. adjustment, agreement. 2. settlement among litigants. 3. lump sum; payment for a certain work during a certain period.

estar de boas ~**s com** to be on good terms with. **mais vale má** ~ **do que boa sentença** better come to an agreement than to go to the law.

avençal s. m. (pl. -**ais**) person who works under a certain agreement (**avença**).

avençar-se v. to come to an agreement, make a settlement upon a rent to be paid in corn, oil, etc.

avenida s. f. avenue; alley, parkway, esplanade.

aventador s. m. (N. E. Braz.) a wooden estrade to separate sugar loaves from their moulds.

avental s. m. (pl. -**ais**) apron, pinafore (plate R 6); smock, smock-frock.

aventar v. 1. to winnow. 2. to hurl, fling. 3. to air, expose to the air. 4. to raise, pose (a question). 5. to suggest (an idea); suspect. 6. to say, speak (one's mind), enunciate. 7. to scent, smell. 8. to guess, forebode. 9. to split (a board that is being sawed). 10. (N. E. Braz.) to separate (sugar loaves from their moulds).

aventura s. f. 1. adventure, venture. 2. hazard, risk, hazardous enterprise or exploit. 3. experience. 4. amorous intrigue, love affair.

procurar ~**s** to seek adventures.

aventurado adj. adventurous; bold, daring; hazardous.

aventurar v. 1. to risk, venture, chance, hazard, run the hazard, jeopard. 2. ~**-se** to enterprise, attempt, adventure, to have a fling at, dare, take one's chance.

~**-se na vida** to try one's luck in life. **não me aventuro a isto** I do not dare it.

aventureiro s. m. adventurer, venturer, soldier of fortune. ‖ adj. venturesome, venturous, dangerous. ‖ -**amente** adv. venturously.

espírito ~ venturous spirit.

aventurina s. f. (min.) aventurin(e).

aventuroso adj. adventurous, adventuresome, venturesome, dangerous, risky.

averbação s. f. (pl. -**ões**) **averbamento** m. legal registration, legalization, protocolling, marginal note (document, contract).

averbar v. 1. to protocol, annotate, note, register, legalize, sign or annotate on the margin (contracts, documents). 2. (gram.) to use as a verb. 3. to label, accuse of.

avergalhar v. to beat with a whip.

avergar v. (also **vergar**) to bend, curve, crook.

avergoar v. to lash, wale, weale.

averiguação s. f. (pl. -**ões**) inquiry, investigation, ascertainment, finding, making out the truth.

averiguado adj. proved, ascertained. ‖ -**amente** adv. provedly.

averiguador s. m. indagator, investigator, examiner. ‖ adj. investigating, searching, indagating, examining.

averiguar v. 1. to inquire, investigate, verify, indagate, examine; ascertain, view, explore; determine. 2. ~**-se** to find out, make sure.

averiguável adj. m. + f. (pl. -**áveis**) examinable, ascertainable. checkable, investigable, determinable, verifiable.

avermelhado adj. reddish, russety, refuscent, rubicund.

ter um tom ~ to have a reddish tint.

avermelhamento s. m. reddening: act or fact of making red.

avermelhar v. 1. to redden, turn or make red, encrimson, vermilion; sanguine; blush. 2. ~-se to redden, grow red.

avernal adj. m. + f. (pl. -ais) (also **avernoso, averno**) avernal; infernal.

averno s. m. avernus, inferno, hell.

averroísmo s. m. (philos.) Averroism: the doctrine of Averroes.

aversão s. f. (pl. -ões) aversion, averseness, hatred; antipathy; repulse; repellence, distaste, repugnance. ~ **irresistível** thrill of dislike. **causar** ~ to be loathsome. **ter** ~ **contra** to have an aversion to.

averso adj. (also **adverso**) averse, reluctant, antipathetic(al).

averter v. to divert, deflect, turn aside from its course.

avessada s. f. the thong of leather to tie the hawk with (to the perch).

avessado adj. done contrariwise, made the wrong way round.

avessar v. to do things the wrong way round, contrariwise.

avessas s. f. pl. opposite things, the wrong way, contraries. **às** ~ upside down, inside out, the wrong way round. **sair às** ~ to fall flat.

avessia s. f. oppositeness, contrariness.

avesso (ê) s. m. 1. contrary, opposite, reverse, back, converse. 2. the wrong side. 3. (fig.) the seamy side. || adj. 1. opposite, converse. 2. cross, crossgrained, intoward. **ao** ~ the wrong side out, the wrong way.

avesta s. m. (phitos.) the Avesta.

avestruz s. m. + f. (pl. ~es) 1. (ornith.) ostrich; emu. 2. (Braz.) an odd person, queer fellow.

avestruzeiro s. m. (Braz.) person (or horse) trained to catch ostriches.

avexação s. f., **avexado** adj., **avexar** v. = **vexação** s. f. **vexado** adj., **vexar** v.

avezado adj. customary, habitual; used to.

avezar (I) v. 1. to habituate, accustom. 2. ~-se to get used to.

avezar (II) v. to posses, own.

aviação s. f. (pl. -ões) aviation; flying. ~ **civil** civil aviation. **campo de** ~ airfield, aerodrome.

aviadado adj. (Braz., sl.) effeminate, queer.

aviado s. m. (Braz.) commercial agent. || adj. hurried, hasty, quick; unencumbered, untrammeled; dispatched. **estamos bem** ~**s!** we are in a nice plight!

aviador (I) s. m. (Braz.) supplier, person who supplies merchandises; forwarder, dispatcher.

aviador (II) s. m. aviator, flyer, aeronaut; (coll.) birdman.

aviamento s. m. 1. act or fact of dispatching, forwarding or supplying with merchandises. 2. the merchandise dispatched. 3. dispatch; execution; making, finishing. 4. course, progress (in business transactions). 5. ~**s** pl.: a) tools, implements, accessories. b) notions (as for a dress).

avião s. m. (pl. -ões) aeroplane, airplane, plane, flying machine. ~ **biplano** biplane. ~ **de bombardeio** bomber. ~ **de caça** pursuit plane, chaser. ~ **de combate** battleplane. ~ **foguete** rocket plane. ~ **fumigador** agricultural or crop-dusting airplane. ~ **de guerra** war plane. ~ **a jato** jet plane. ~ **de pasageiros** air liner. ~ **para transporte de tropas** troop plane. ~ **de treino** training plane. **pilotar um** ~ to fly an aeroplane. **viajar de** ~ to travel by plane, fly.

aviar v. 1. to dispatch, expedit, ship, put on the way; make ready. 2. to execute. 3. to supply. 4. to attend, serve. 5. (med.) to prescribe. 6. to get rid of, kill. 7. ~-se to make haste, get ready. ~ **com presteza** to dispatch in time. ~ **uma receita** to dispense, put up a prescription.

aviário (I) s. m. aviary, vivarium for birds; hen yard, volery.

aviário (II) adj. avian, aviary, referring to birds.

aviatório adj. aviatic, aviatorial, aerial.

aviceptologia s. f. bird trapping.

avícola s. m. + f. poultry farmer; bird fancier. || adj. avian.

avícula s. f. dim. of **ave** little bird, any small bird.

avicular adj. m. + f. referring to birds.

aviculário s. m. birdseller, fowler.

avicultor s. m. (also **avícola**) aviculturist, breeder, poultry raiser; fancier of birds.

avicultura s. f. aviculture; poultry raising.

avidez s. f. avidity, greediness, impatience, rapacity, wistfulness.

ávido adj. avid, eager, grasping, greedy, covetous, desirous of, edacious, ravenous, voracious. || **avidamente** adv. avidly, eagerly, ravenously, voraciously, graspingly. **demasiado** ~ overgreedy, overeager. **estar** ~ **de** to thirst after.

avieirado adj. (Braz.) adorned with shells.

avifauna s. f. (zool.) avifauna.

avigoramento s. m. invigoration: act or fact of invigorating.

avigorar v. to invigorate, fortify, strengthen; consolidate; make firm.

ávila s. f. (bot.) the large, fleshy fruit of a cucurbitaceous plant (Fevilea trilobata).

avilanado adj. rustic; ruffian; villainous.

avilanar-se v. to become a rustic, ruffian, villain.

avilar v. = **aviltar**.

aviltado adj. abased, degraded, contemptible, vilified; humiliated, humbled.

aviltador s. m. degrader, defiler. || adj. = **aviltante**.

aviltamento s. m. (also **aviltação** f.) abasement, abjection, contempt, disgrace, dishonour; degradation, vilification, defilement.

aviltante adj. m. + f. (also **aviltoso** m.) degrading, debasing, disgraceful, shameful.

aviltar v. 1. to abase, debase, disgrace, defile, vilify, depress, demean, decry, dishonour, profane; degrade, descend. 2. ~-se to dishonour, abase, bemoan o. s., to grow contemptible.

avinagrado adj. 1. somewhat sour, sourish. 2. (fig.) ill-natured, preevish, irritable.

avinagrar v. 1. to mix with (or steep in) vinegar. 2. ~-se to become irritated, peevish, cross.

avindo adj. harmonized, agreed upon, agreeing. **bem** ~ in harmony. **mal** ~ discordant.

avindor s. m. mediator; arbiter. || adj. mediative, mediating.

avinhado s. m. (zool.) = **curió**. || adj. 1. winy, winelike. 2. (also **aquilotado**) given to drinking.

avinhar v. 1. to mix with (or steep in) wine. 2. to give the savour of wine to. 3. to make drunk. 4. ~-se to get drunk.

avio s. m. = **aviamento**.

aviolado (I) adj. having the form of a guitar.

aviolado (II) adj. made of violets; violet.

avir v. 1. to adjust, combine, conciliate, harmonize, accommodate, compose. 2. ~-se to get along with, come to an agreement.

avisado adj. 1. discreet, prudent. 2. advised, warned. 3. sensible, wise, sage, judicious. || **-amente** adv. prudently.

avisador s. m. 1. warner; informer, notifier. 2. warning. ‖ adj. informing, informative, warning.

avisar v. 1. to give notice, advise, let know, inform, acquaint, notify. 2. to advertise. 3. to warn, forewarn. 4. to admonish, caution. 5. ~-**se** to consider or think of, reflect upon, to be well advised, be careful.

aviso s. m. (also **avisamento**) 1. aviso: a) notice, advice, communication, information. b) a dispatch boat. 2. circular. 3. warning. 4. tip, hint. 5. opinion. 6. admonition. 7. caution, prudence. ~ **prévio** the notice to quit. ~ **de saque** information of draft. **até novo** ~ until further notice. **conforme** ~ as per advice. **ficar de** ~ to be on the alert. **quadro de** ~ notice board.

avistar v. 1. to see from a distance, come in sight of, behold, sight, see, distinguish. 2. to discover, espy, descry. 3. ~-**se**: a) to meet casually. b) to have a meeting or an interview. ~ **terra** to come in sight of land. **chegamos a avistá-lo** we got a sight of it.

avistável adj. m. + f. (pl. -**áveis**) visible; that can be sighted.

avitaminose s. f. (med.) avitaminosis: vitamin deficiency.

avito adj. ancestral, proceeding from ancestors.

avitualhamento s. m. victualling: act or fact of providing with victuals.

avitualhar v. to victual: supply with provisions.

aviú s. m. (Braz.) a kind of a shrimp or prawn.

avivador s. m. burnisher.

avivamento s. m. enlivenment, revival, invigoration.

avivar v. to give life to, revive, awake, vivify, enliven, inflame, encourage, kindle, stir up, invigorate, animate, quicken; to recover spirits.

aviventação s. f. (pl. -**ões**) reanimation, revival, rousing, revivification.

aviventador s. m. reviver, revivifier, animator, encourager, inspirer. ‖ adj. animating, encouraging.

aviventar v. 1. to revive, revivify. 2. to animate, reanimate. 3. to enliven, encourage, cheer. 4. to strengthen, invigorate. 5. ~-**se** to come to life.

avizinhação s. f. (pl. -**ões**) approach, approximation.

avizinhar v. 1. to approach, approximate, to bring or draw near, put near of. 2. to border, adjoin, touch; be close to. 3. ~-**se** to come near, be near or contiguous.

avo s. m. word used together with the denominator of a fraction, as $^1/_{13}$ **um treze avos** one thirteenth.

avô s. m. grandfather.

avó s. f. grandmother; granny, grannie, grandma.

avoaçar v. 1. to rouse, frighten. 2. to flap or clap the wings, flutter, flitter, flit.

avoado adj. (Braz.) 1. dizzy, giddy. 2. senseless, crackbrained. 3. trickish, tricky.

avoador adj. (Braz.) scoundrelly, crooked, trickish.

avoamento s. m. (archit.) the rise of an arch.

avoante s. m. (Braz., also **pomba-de-arribação, arribação, arribaçã, ribaçã, rabação**) the Paraguayan eared dove.

avoar v. (pop.) = **voar.**

avocação s. f. (pl. -**ões**) (jur.) the taking away of a lawsuit from one jurisdiction to a higher court.

avocar v. 1. (jur.) to appeal to a higher court. 2. to attract. 3. to arrogate, claim. 4. to distract.

avocatório adj. avocatory.

avocatura s. f. 1. (jur.) appeal. 2. arrogation, claiming. 3. attraction. 4. distraction.

avocável adj. m. + f. (pl. -**áveis**) appealable.

avoejar v. to flit, flutter, flicker, flap, flitter.

avoengo adj. proceeding from the ancestors, ancestral.

avoengueiro adj. for or from the ancestors· ancestral.

avolumar(-se) v. to augment, increase the volume of; enlarge, make or become bigger; take much space, swell. **o trabalho vem se avolumando** work is increasing.

à-vontade s. m. (pl. **à-vontades**) a natural, easy, unembarrassed attitude.

avós s. m. pl. grandparents, forefathers, ancestors.

avosar v. (Braz.) to address as **vós** (you, second person plural).

avoezar v. to acclaim, applaud, call out loudly.

avulsão s. f. (pl. -**ões**) 1. avulsion, violent extraction. 2. sudden start, jerk.

avulso adj. 1. pulled out, torn off. 2. detached, unconnected. 3. odd. 4. single. **notícias -as** doubtful news. **artigos** ~**s** sundry articles. **somas -as** sundry amounts.

avultação s. f. (pl. -**ões**) resemblance, likeness, similarity.

avultado adj. (also **avultoso**) bulky, voluminous, big, large; considerable. **-as quantias** considerable sums.

avultante adj. m. + f. augmenting, increasing.

avultar v. 1. to increase, augment, make bigger, greater or thicker, enlarge. 2. to amplify, exaggerate. 3. to emphasize. ~ **sobre** to excel.

avuncular adj. m. + f. avuncular: of or pertaining to an uncle.

axada s. m. Asarh: the fourth month of the Hindu calendar.

axadrezado adj. checked, checkered.

axadrezar v. (also **enxadrezar**) to checker.

axe s. m. (also **eixo**) axle, axis.

axial adj. m. + f. (pl. -**ais**) axial: referring to, having the form of, or serving as an axle.

axicarado adj. having the form of a coffee cup.

axicarar v. to shape like a coffee cup.

axículo s. m. a small axle.

axifero adj. axled, axised.

axiforme adj. m. + f. axiform.

áxil adj. m. + f. (pl. **áxeis**) (bot.) axile.

axila s. f. 1. (anat.) axilla, armpit (place C 18). 2. (bot.) axil.

axilar adj. m. + f. axillar(y).

áxilo adj. producing no wood (plant).

axilose s. f. excessive perspiration of the armpits.

axinomancia s. f. axinomancy.

axilogia s. f. (philos.) axiology.

axioma s. m. axiom: a common self-evident principle; maxim.

axiomático adj. axiomatic, self-evident.

axiônimo s. m. expression of reverence: Sir, Doctor, Majesty, etc.

axipeto adj. (phys.) inclined towards the axis.

áxis s. m. axis: 1. axle. 2. (anat.) the second cervical vertebra. 3. (zool.) axis deer.

axóide s. m. (anat.) axis: the second cervical vertebra. ‖ adj. m. + f. 1. axoid: pertaining to the axis vertebra. 2. axiform.

axolotle s. m. (zool.) axolotl: larval salamander.

axônio s. m. (anat.) axon.

axorca s. f. in Asia, a ring for the arms or legs.

axuá s. f. (Braz.) tree of the family Humiriaceae.

az (I) s. m. squadron; wing of an army; rank, row, line, tier.

az (II) s. m. (chem.) symbol of **azoto**, azote, former name for nitrogen.

azabumbado adj. 1. astonished. 2. frightened. 3. crumpled. 4. bruised. 5. beaten like a drum.

azabumbar v. to confound, muddle, rattle, confuse.

azado adj. 1. adroit, able, dexterous. 2. opportune; proper. 3. comfortable.

azáfama s. f. great haste, hurry, hurry-scurry, flurry, bustle, whirl, fuss.

azafamado adj. hasty, busy, bustling, in great hurry.

azafamar v. 1. to hasten, hurry, press, urge. 2. ~-**se** to be very busy; to fluster.

azagaia s. f. assagai: a small spear.

azagaiada s. f. thurst with an assagai.

azagaiar v. to wound or kill with an assagai.

azálea s. f. azalea: a genus of flowering shrubs.

azamboar v. 1. to stun, daze, bewilder, cause to be giddy or dizzy. 2. to make insipid.

azambujal s. m. (pl. -**ais**) field of oleasters, growth of wild olive trees.

azambujeiro, azambujo s. m. a wild olive tree.

azangar v. (Braz.) to molest, annoy; irritate.

azar (I) s. m. 1. misfortune, bad luck, mischance, mishap, hard luck. 2. chance, hazard.
  ~ **no jogo** ill run at play. **ele está com** ~ (coll.) it is hard lines for him. **ter** ~ to be down on one's luck. **trazer** ~ **a alguém** to bring bad luck upon a person. **jogo de** ~ game of chance.

azar (II) v. 1. to give occasion to, offer an opportunity for, to cause. 2. to come in handy.

azarado s. m. (Braz.) ill-starred fellow, lame duck. ‖ adj. unfortunate, unlucky, luckless, ill-starred.

azaranzado adj. (Braz.) 1. clumsy, blundering. 2. bewildered, confused.

azaranzar v. (Braz.) 1. to get mixed up, blunder, be at a loss. 2. to be giddy, dizzy.

azarão s. m. (S. Braz.) a racehorse with little chances to win.

azarar v. (Braz.) to cause misfortune to, bring bad luck.

azarcão s. m. (also **zarcão**) red oxid of lead.

azarento adj. (also **azarado**) ill-starred.

azebrar v. 1. to become verdigrised. 2. to become covered with aloe.

azebre (ê) s. m. 1. verdigris. 2. (bot.) aloe.

azebuado adj. (Braz.) zebulike, half-blooded (zebu cattle).

azeda (ê) s. f. (bot., also **azedeira**) wood sorrel, dock.
  ~ **romana** French sorrel. **sal de** ~ (chem.) sorrel salt.

azedado adj. 1. sourish, acid. 2. (fig.) angry.

azedador s. m. 1. irritating person or thing. 2. acidifying agent. ‖ adj. 1. souring, causing sourness. 2. irritating, vexatious.

azedamento s. m. 1. acidification. 2. sourness. 3. irritation, crossness, crabbedness.

azedar v. 1. to acidify, sour, make or become sour. 2. to coagulate, curdle. 3. to exacerbate, irritate, embitter. 4. ~-**se** to turn sour.

azedete, azedote adj. m. + f. 1. acidulous: somewhat sour. 2. acrimony, harshness, bitterness, peevishness.

azedia s. f. 1. sourness, tartness, acidity. 2. acrimony, irritation, exasperation.

azedinha s. f. several plants of the families Poligonaceae, Oxalidaceae and Begoniaceae; wood sorrel; the creeping oxalis.

azedo (ê) s. m. sourness, acidity, acidness. ‖ adj. 1. sour, tart, tartish, sharp, acid. 2. rough, harsh, crabbed, peevish, morose.

azedume s. m. (also **azedia** f.) 1. sourness, tartness, acidity, acidness. 2. acrimony, harshness, bitterness, peevishness.

azeirado adj. 1. sour. 2. acrimonious, mordant.

azeitada s. f. big portion of olive oil.

azeitado adj. oily; full of oil.

azeitão s. m. (Braz.) oil of the castor-bean. ‖ adj. black-coloured (of cattle).

azeitar v. 1. to oil, smear with oil, season with oil. 2. to grease, lubricate. 3. (Braz., pop.) to court, pay one's addresses to a lady.

azeite s. m. 1. olive-oil. 2. every vegetable or animal oil.
  ~ **de coco** palm-oil. ~ **doce** (Braz.) olive-ol. **beber** ~ (Braz.) to be smart. **deitar** ~ **no fogo** to add fuel to the fire.

azeite-de-cheiro, azeite-de-dendê s. m. (pl. **azeites--de-cheiro, azeites-de-dendê**) oil from the African oilpalm, grown in Brazil.

azeiteira (I) s. f. (also **azeiteiro** m.) cruet, oil-can.

azeiteira (II) s. f. (Braz., pop.) coquette, flirt. ‖ adj. coquettish, flirtatious.

azeiteiro (I) s. m. oilman, oil merchant or manufacturer.

azeiteiro (II) s. m. (Braz., pop.) 1. ruffian, hooligan. 2. ladies man.

azeiteiro (III) adj. oily, oil: of or pertaining to oil.

azeitinho s. m. (Braz.) castor-oil.

azeitona s. f. olive: fruit of the olive tree.

azeitona-da-terra s. f. (pl. **azeitonas-da-terra**) (Braz.) plant of the family Litraceae (Cuphea pseudovaccinium).

azeitonado adj. olive-coloured.

azeitonar v. 1. to give or acquire the colour of an olive. 2. to add olives to.

azeitoneira s. f. 1. plate for olives, vessel to hold olives. 2. (Port.) olive tree.

azeitoneiro s. m. 1. seller of olives. 2. plate for olives.

azemeleiro s. m. caretaker of pack animals.

azêmola s. f. 1. beast of burden, pack animal. 2. (fig.) stupid person.

azenha s. f. water-mill.

azeótropo s. m. (phys., chem.) azeotrope.

azerado adj. steel-coloured.

azerar v. (also **acerar**) 1. to acierate. 2. to give the colour of steel to.

azereiro s. m. (bot.) Portuguese laurel cherry.

azevém s. m. (pl. -**éns**) rye-grass.

azevichado adj. jet-black, deep black.

azeviche s. m. 1. jet, bituminous coal, pitch coal. 2. something very black.
  negro como ~ as black as jet.

azevieiro s. m. 1. libertine. 2. smart fellow. ‖ adj. 1. clever, smart. 2. crafty, deceitful. 3. lewd.

azevim s. m. (pl. -**ins**) **azevinho** (bot.) holly; ilex.

azia s. f. (also **pirose;** med.) pyrosis: heartburn, water-brash, sour stomach.

aziago adj. inauspicious; ill-fated, unlucky, unhappy.
  dia ~ an unlucky day.

aziar s. m. barnacles: 1. twitch (to restrain a horse) (plate C 12). 2. (fig.) tormenting instrument.

ázigo adj. azygous, odd, unpaired.

azigoto s. m. (biol.) azygote.

ázimo adj. azymous, unleavened; without ferment (bread).

azimutal adj. m. + f. (pl. -**ais**) azimuthal, referring to azimuth.

azimute s. m. (astr.) azimuth.

azinha s. f. acorn; the fruit of the holm-oak.

azinhaga s. f. narrow path or passage, lane.

azinhal s. m. (pl. -**ais**) a grove of holm-oaks.

azinhavrar v. to become tarnished, covered with verdigris.

azinhavre s. m. (also **azebre**) verdigris.

azinheira s. f., **azinheiro** m. (bot.) holm-oak.

azinhoso adj. abounding in holm-oaks.

aziumado adj. 1. full of sourness or bitterness. 2. (fig.) irritated.

aziumar v. 1. to render sour, cause bitterness. 2. (fig.) to irritate.

aziúme s. m. 1. sourness. 2. (fig.) irritation.

azo s. m. 1. occasion, opportunity. 2. reason. 3. pretext, pretence. 4. means, way to perform anything. **dar ~ a** to make possible, cause. **por ~ de** thanks to.

azoado adj. 1. stunned, dizzy. 2. perturbed, upset, bothered. 3. bored, annoyed.

azoamento s. m. 1. act of stunning, bothering. 2. unpleasant feeling of annoyance, displeasure.

azoar v. 1. to stun, stupefy. 2. to annoy, bother. 3. **~-se** to grow angry.

azóico adj. (geol.) azoic.

azoinado adj. 1. giddy, dizzy. 2. perturbed.

azoinante adj. m. + f. irksome, wearisome.

azoinar v. 1. to stun with noise. 2. to molest, trouble, importune.

azombado adj. (Braz.) uneasy, worried; concerned, anxious.

azonal adj. m. + f. azonal, not divided into zones (soil).

azoratado adj. giddy, dizzy, stunned, dazed.

azoratar v. (also **azoretar**) 1. to make dizzy, fluster; bewilder. 2. to hebetate. 3. to irritate.

azoretado adj. (Braz.) = **azoratado;** angry, furious.

azoretar v. = **azoratar.**

azorragada s. f. blow with a whip.

azorragamento s. m. whipping, punishment with a scourge.

azorragar v. to scourge, flagellate, flog.

azorrague s. m. 1. scourge, whip. 2. (fig.) punishment; plague.

azorrar v. to face courageously or in defiance.

azotado adj. (chem.) containing azote or nitrogen; azotic, nitrogenous.

azotar v. to azotize, nitrogenize, nitrogenate.

azotato s. m. (chem.) nitrate.

azotemia s. f. (path.) azotemia.

azotêmico adj. referring to azotemia.

azoto (ô), **azote** s. m. (chem.) azote: former name for nitrogen.

azotúria s. f. (path.) azoturia.

azotúrico adj. (med.) referring to azoturia.

azougado adj. 1. alive, lively, restless, turbulent. 2. very clever, smart. 3. (Braz.) irritable.

azougar v. 1. to mix with or add mercury to. 2. to tin, line, foliate looking-glasses. 3. to enliven. 4. to pester, annoy. 5. to wither.

azougue s. m. 1. quicksilver, mercury 2. (fig.) a very lively, vivacious or smart person.

azougue-do-campo s. m. (pl. **azougues-do-campo**) (bot.) Jamaica ironwood.

azougue-dos-pobres s. m. (pl. **azougues-dos-pobres**) a medicinal plant of the family Cucurbitaceae (Will brandia hibiscoides).

azucrim s. m. (pl. **-ins**) (Braz.) 1. an imp. 2. importunate, troublesome person.

azucrinante adj. m. + f. (Braz.) annoying, importunate, troublesome.

azucrinar v. (Braz., also **apoquentar**) to worry, plague, annoy (lamenting or crying for something).

azul s. m. (pl. **-uis**) 1. blue (colour). 2. (fig.) the sky, firmament. || adj. m. + f. blue, cyanic, azure. **~ acinzentado** slate blue, grayish blue. **~ claro, ~ pálido** pale blue. **~ de cobalto** cobalt blue. **~ escuro, ~ imperial, ~ real** royal blue, indigo. **~ esmalte** powder blue, zaffre. **~ esverdeado** turquoise. **~ mineral** (min.) azurite. **~ ultramarino** ultramarine. **corante ~** saxe blue. **tudo ~!** (fig.) everything is allrigth, rosy!.

azuladinha s. f. (Braz., pop.) rum, booze.

azulado adj. of blue colour, steel-blue, bluish, blueish.

azulador adj. m. 1. one who or that which imparts a blue colour. 2. a fugitive, an escapee. || adj. imparting a blue colour.

azulão s. m. (pl. **-ões**) (Braz.) common name of various blue birds (esp. the **papa-arroz**) of the family Fringilideae.

azulão-bóia s. f. (pl. **azulões-bóia**) name of two tree snakes of the genus Leptophis.

azular v. 1. to blue, make or turn blue, to azure. 2. **~-se** to run away, make o. s. scarce.

azul-celeste, azul-do-céu s. m. (also **azul-fino, azul-pombinho**) sky-blue colour, azure. || adj. sky-blue, azure.

azulear, azulecer v. 1. to dye blue, give a blue tint to. 2. **~-se** to become blue(ish).

azulego adj. (Braz.) 1. bluish, blueish. 2. piebald (coat of a horse).

azulejador, azulejista, s. m. tile setter, tilemaker.

azulejar (I) v. to set tiles.

azulejar (II) v. 1. to turn blue. 2. to have a blue tint.

azulejo s. m. glazed tile; Dutch tile; floor tile; wall tile.

azul-ferrete s. m. mazarine, electric blue. || adj. m. + f., sg. + pl. mazarine, deep blue.

azulinho s. m. (Braz., ornith.) a grosbeak.

azulino s. m. a thrush of Cayenne. || adj. blue-coloured, blue, bluish.

azulóio s. m. violet blue. || adj. violet-blue.

azulona s. f. (Braz., ornith.) a bluish-gray tinamou (Tinamus tao).

azul-turquesa s. m. + adj. m. + f., sg. + pl. = **azul-ferrete.**

azumbrado adj. humped; crooked.

azumbrar v. to become crooked, stooped, humped.

azumbre s. m. a Spanish liquid measure of about 2 or 3 liters.

azurado s. m. a printed background hatching (in documents). || adj. azure, of the heraldic colour blue.

azurrador s. m. brayer. || adj. braying.

azurrar v. (also **zurrar**) to bray.

B

B, b s. m. second letter of the Portuguese alphabet. ‖ adj. second, "b", immediately following the first.
parágrafo ~ paragraph B, second paragraph.
bá, babá s. f. (Braz.) 1. pet name given by children to their nurses. 2. wet or dry nurse.
Baal p. n. Baal, supreme deity of ancient Phoenician peoples.
baba s. f. 1. saliva, slaver, slobber. 2. lather. 3. spittle, spit. 4. drivel. 5. (fig.) spite, insult.
~ **do caracol** slime of the snail.
babá (I) s. m. cake made of flour, milk and eggs.
babá (II) s. m. (Braz.) = **pai-de-santo.**
babá (III) s. f. (Braz.) baby sitter.
bababi s. m. (Braz.) conflict, trouble.
babaca (I) s. f. (Braz., vulg.) vulva.
babaca (II) s. m.+f. (Braz., sl.) fool, stupid, imbecile.
babaça s. m. + f. (Braz.) twin (brother or sister).
babaçu s. m. (Braz., bot.) babassu.
babaçual, babaçuzal s. m. (pl. **-ais**) (Braz.) forest of babassu palms.
baba-de-boi s. f. (pl. **babas-de-boi**) (bot.) pindo palm.
baba-de-moça s. f. (pl. **babas-de-moça**) (Braz.) candy of sugar, syrup, cocojuice and egg yolk.
babadinho adj. 1. wanting extremely, very fond of. 2. punctilious. 3. excessive, impassioned.
babado (I) adj. 1. slavered, slobbered, full of slime. 2. (coll.) in love, fond of, keen on.
andar ~ **por alguém** to be in love with, be crazy about.
babado (II) s. m. 1. (Braz.) flounce (tail.) 2. frill. 3. lappet.
babador s. m. 1. (also **babadouro, babadoiro**) bib, slobbering bib, napkin, feeder (plate R 6). 2. (also **barbela**) curb.
babal s. m. (pl. **-ais**) (Braz.) an Indian's loin-cloth.
babão s. m. (pl. **-ões**) (f. **babona**) 1. slobberer, drivel(l)er, a slavering child. 2. nitwit, idiot, silly talker. ‖ adj. 1. slobbering, slavering. 2. foolish. 3. doting upon, fond of.
babaquara s. m. + f. (Braz.) silly, great fool.
babar v. 1. to slaver, slobber, dribble, drivel, beslaver, smear with saliva or spittle. 2. (fig.) to stammer, lisp. 3. ~**se por** to be desperately in love with, infatuated with, crazy about.
~**se por uma mulher** to be madly in love with a woman. "**todo por você me babo**" (Castilho) I am madly in love with you.
babaré, babaréu s. m. 1. bawling, clamour, hubbub, row. 2. alarm, warning cry.
babatar v. (Braz.) 1. to grope, fumble. 2. to try to find out cautiously.
babau! (I) interj. gone!, it's all up!
babau (II) s. m. (Braz.) personage of the popular farce "**bumba-meu-boi**".
babeira s. f. chinplece of a medieval helmet.
babeiro s. m. = **babador.**
babel s. f. 1. (bib.) city and tower of Babel. 2. (fig.): a) confusion of languages. b) hubbub, tumult.
ouvimos uma ~ **de vozes** we heard a Babel of voices. **uma** ~ **de línguas** a Babel of tongues.
babélico adj. (also **babelesco**) 1. concerning Babel, Babylonian. 2. confused, disordered.
babésia s. f. babesia, a protozoan of the genus Babesia.
Babilônia s. f. 1. Babylon, Babel. 2. babel, confusion, disorder.
houve uma ~ **completa** there was a complete mess or babel.

babilônico s. m. Babylonian. ‖ adj. Babylonian, Babylonic.
babismo s. m. (rel.) Babism, Babiism, Babi.
babosa s. f. 1. (bot.) aloe. 2. seafish of the family Gobiidae.
babosa-branca s. f. (pl. **babosas-brancas**) a shrub of the family Boraginaceae.
baboseira, babosice s. f. 1. folly, nonsense, blunder, footle, piffle. 2. slobber.
ele fala ~**s** he talks nonsense.
baboso s. m. 1. slobberer, dribbler, driveler. 2. stammerer. 3. passionate lover. 4. fool, simpleton. ‖ adj. 1. slavering, slobbery. 2. in love. 3. silly, stupid. 4. uxorious.
babu s. m. babu, baboo: Hindu title equivalent to Mr., Sir., or Esq.
babucha s. f. babouche, baboosh.
babugem s. f. (pl. **-ens**) 1. slaver. 2. foam, spray. 3. rests of food, leavings, residues (pl.). 4. trifle, bagatelle. 5. (Braz.) new shoots (pl.) that appear after the first spring rains.
à ~ **da água** on the surface of the water.
babuíno s. m. (zool.) baboon.
babujar v. 1. to drivel, dirty with slaver. 2. to cajole, adulate, fawn upon. 3. to corrupt. 4. to dirty o. s. with slaver or food. 5. to gather or eat shellfish. 6. to eat daintily (for lack of appetite or other reasons).
babunha s. f. (also **coqueiro** ~) Brazilian palm tree.
bacaba s. f. (bot.) bacaba, a palm tree of the genus Oenocarpus.
bacáceo ad. (bot.) berried, like a berry, of a berry.
bacada s. f. (Braz.) shock caused (to a vehicle) by an unevenness of the ground.
bacafuzada s. f. (Braz.) 1. confusion. 2. mess. 3. disorder.
bacafuzar v. (Braz.) to confuse, disorder.
bacalaureato s. m. = **bacharelado.**
bacalhau s. m. 1. cod, codfish. 2. (Braz.) a whip of twisted leather. 3. (fig.) a very lean person. 4. (sl.) servant of a circus. 5. (Braz.) emergency stuffing of a punctured tyre.
~ **curado** dun-fish. ~**de porta de venda** extremely lean person. ~ **novo** codling. ~ **seco,** ~ **salgado** stockfish, dried cod. **meter o** ~ **em** (Braz.) to slander, defame. **óleo de fígado de** ~ cod-liver oil. **para quem é** ~ **basta** for a disrespected person it will do. **tudo ficou em águas de** ~ it came to nothing.
bacalhoada s. f. 1. dish of codfish. 2. (Braz., hist.) whipping, beating.
bacalhoeiro (I) s. m. codfish retailer.
bacalhoeiro (II) s. m. codfisher (vessel).
bacalhoeiro (III) adj. 1. fond of cod. 2. smelling like cod. 3. dirty. 4. rude. 5. talkative.
bacamartada s. f. (hist.) shot fired from a blunderbuss.
bacamarte s. m. 1. blunderbuss, harquebus. 2. (sl.) anything unavailable or inefficient. 3. good-for-nothing.
bacana adj. m. + f. (sl.) good, splendid, excellent, beautiful, posh.
bacanal s. f. (pl. **-ais**) bacchanals, bacchanalia (pl.): 1. feast in honour of Bacchus. 2. orgies (pl.). 3. drinking-party or -bout. 4. revel. 5. debauch. ‖ adj. bacchanal, bacchanalian, orgiastic, licentious.
bacano s. m. (sl.) wealthy man, man of means.

bacante s. f. 1. bacchant, priest(ess) of Bacchus. 2. maenad. 3. dissolute woman. 4. (ent.) a butterfly (Papilio dejanira).

bacântico adj. 1. bacchantic, bacchanal. 2. concerning bacchants. 3. orgiastic, dissolute, maenadic.

bacará (I) s. m. baccara(t): a kind of game of cards.

bacará (II) s. m. Baccarat glass.

bacaraí s. m. a dead cow's fetus.

baceira s. f. (vet.) anthrax.

baceiro adj. of, pertaining to or located in the spleen.

bacelada s. f. newly planted vineyard.

bacelar v. to plant young vines.

baceleiro s. m. vine-dresser.

bacelo (ê) s. m. 1. twig or shoot of vine ready for planting or grafting. 2. newly planted vine.

bacento adj. dull, dim, tarnished.

bacharel s. m. (pl. **-éis**) 1. (also **bacharelado**) bachelor. 2. alumnus, alumni. 3. prattler, chatterbox.
~ **em humanidades** Bachelor of Arts.

bacharela s. f. 1. female bachelor or graduate. 2. talkative woman, gossip. 3. wiseacre.

bacharelada s. f. (also **bacharelice**) 1. silly, dull or pretentious discourse. 2. tedious chitchat, idle words or talk.

bacharelado s. m. (also **bacharelato**) 1. bachelorship. degree of bachelor, baccalaureate, bachelorhood. 2. alumnus, alumni. 3. the entire series of studies leading to a bachelor degree. ‖ p. p. of **bacharelar.**

bacharelando s. m. one who takes his degree (of bachelor), inceptor.

bacharelar v. 1. take one's degree (of bachelor). 2 to prattle, chatter, talk too much or digressively, prate.
ele bacharelou-se em direito he took the degree of bachelor of laws.

bacharelesco adj. of or pertaining to a bachelor.

bacharelismo s. m. 1. = **bacharelado.** 2. (Braz.) predominance of college or university graduates in public administration.

bacia s. f. 1. basin, wash-basin (plate V 2); lavabo. 2. barber's basin. 3. frying-pan, baking tin. 4. tray. 5. pot, chamber pot. 6. bowl, bowl of a watercloset (plate P 19). 7. (eccl.) plate for collecting the offertory. 8. (geol.) a) basin, surface depression, valley. b) watershed, drainage-basin, drainage area, draw. 9. scale pan or bowl. 10. (met.) casting pit. 11. fire pan. 12. circular pond in a garden. 13. inland port, inner harbour (plate P 16). 14. (anat.) pelvis, hip, hip-bone, innominate bone. 15. coffer of a canal lock. 16. cock-pit (enclosed place for cock-fights). 17. a hatter's block of form.
~ **fluvial** drainage-basin. ~ **hidrográfica** hydrological basin, catchment area. ~ **marítima** drainage area whose waters flow into an inland sea. ~ **para lavar louça** dish pan. **comprar na** ~ **das almas** (Braz. pop.) to buy very cheap.

baciada s. f. basinful.

bacial adj. m. + f. (pl. **-ais**) of, pertaining to, or related to a basin (see **bacia**).

bacífero adj. (bot.) bacciferous, bearing berries. berried, cocciferous, baccate.

baciforme ad. m. + f. bacciform, baccate.

bacilar adj. m. + f. (also **bacilário**) 1. bacillary. bacilliform. 2. (bact.) produced by or resembling bacilli.

bacilários s. m. pl. (zool.) the family of Infusoria.

bacilemia s. f. (path.) bacillemia, bacteremia.

bacilicida adj. m. + f. bacillicide.

baciliforme adj. m. + f. bacilliform, rod-shaped, bacillary.

bacilo s. m. (biol.) bacillus, bacterium.

bacilose s. f. (med.) bacillosis.

bacineta s. f. small basin, basinet.

bacinete s. m. (med.) 1. pelvis of the kidney, renal pelvis. 2. (hist.) basinet.

bacio s. m. 1. chamber pot, urinal. 2. (obs.) big, flat plate resembling a tray.

bacívoro adj. (zool.) baccivorous, subsisting on berries.

back s. m. (Engl.) backhand (ten.).

baco (I) s. m. (Braz.) wooden box for diamond washing.

baco (II) adj. reddish yellow (cattle).

baço s. m. 1. spleen, milt. 2. (med.) rose-rash of babies, roseola. 3. (Port.) mole: spot on the skin. ‖ adj. 1. dark brown, copper-coloured. 2. tarnished, dim, wan. 3. dull, dim-sighted.
doente do ~ sick of the spleen.

baco-baco s. m. (onom.) pit-a-pat: sound made by trotting horses.

baconiano adj. Baconian, of or pertaining to Francis Bacon or his works.

baconista s. m. + f. Baconian, follower of Bacon.

bácora s. f. of **bácoro.**

bacorá s. f. (Braz., zool.) false coral snake.

bacorejar v. 1. to guess, forebode, foresee, to have a presentiment (or misgiving). 2. to peep, lurk, spy. 3. to wait for, await.
o seu coração parecia ~ **desgraças** his mind misgave him.

bacorejo s. m. (coll.) presentiment (of luck).

bacorim s. m. (pl. **-ins**) (Braz.) = **bacorinho.**

bacorinha s. f. 1. top-hat of hard felt. 2. (Braz.) package or small trunk with the belongings of railroad or sugar-mill workers.

bacorinho s. m. diminutive of **bácoro.**

bácoro s. m. piglet, pigling, suckling pig, farrow. piggy.
~ **que deixa de mamar** weanling piglet.

bacorote s. m. yearling pig.

bactéria s. f. 1‖ bacterium (pl. bacteria). 2. bacillus (pl. bacilli), microbe.

bacteriano adj. bacterial.

bactericida s. m. bactericide. ‖ adj. m. + f. bactericidal: destructive to bacteria.

bacteriemia s. f. (path.) bacteremia.

bacterina s. f. (med.) bacterin, bacterial vaccine.

bacteriofagia s. f. (biol.) bacteriophagy.

bacteriófago s. m. bacteriophage.

bacteriólise s. f. (med.) bacteriolysis.

bacteriologia s. f. bacteriology.

bacteriológico adj. bacteriologic, bacteriological.

bacteriólogo s. m., **bacteriologista** m. + f. bacteriologist.

bacteriopurpurina s. f. (biol.) bacteriopurpurin.

bacterioscopia s. f. bacterioscopy.

bacteriostase s. f. (biol.) bacteriostasis.

bacteróide adj. bacteroid.

bactriano s. m. (hist.) Bactrian. ‖ adj. Bactrian.

bacu s. m. (Braz.) 1. freshwater fish of the family Doradidae (also **vacu** or **pacu**). 2. (Braz.) pot-bellied person.

bacucu s. m. 1. eatable mollusk of the Brazilian coast. 2. (Braz., colloq.) fisherman of the beach.

bacuçu s. m. (coll., Braz.) canoe made of one trunk the sides of which are heightened.

baculiforme adj. m. + f. baculiform, rod-shaped.

báculo s. m. 1. staff, stick, rod. 2. (a bishop's) crosier (plate P 5) (also ~ **pastoral**).
~ **de peregrino** pilgrim's staff.

baculômetro s. m. graduated measuring rod for field surveys.

baculometria s. f. method of measuring with graduated rods or sticks.

bacumixá. s. m. tall Brazilian tree of the family Sapotaceae.

bacupari s. m. (Braz., bot.) bakupari, a guttiferous tree (Rheedia brasiliensis).

bacu-pedra s. m. (pl. **bacus-pedra**) (Braz.) freshwater fish of the family Doradidae.

bacurau s. m. (Braz.) 1. common name of the birds of the family Caprimulgidae. 2. nickname of Negroes. 3. one who goes out only at night.

bacuri s. m. bacury: a tropical South-American timber tree.

badalação s. f. (Braz., pop.) flattery; apple polishing; flattering praise.

badalada s. f. clang of a bell, stroke of the clapper of a church-bell, toll.

ouvimos as ~s fúnebres we heard the tolling of the funeral bell.

badaladal s. m. (pl. -ais) continuous ringing, tinkling or peal of bells.

badalão s. m. (pl. -ões) talkative or foolish individual, prattler.

badalar v. (also **badalejar**) 1. to ring, peal, toll, tinkle. 2. to set bells clanging. 3. to strike, sound with a stroke. 4. to blab, hint, or talk indiscreetly, imply.

~ tristemente to toll.

badaleira s. f. 1. ring or eyelet which holds the clapper of a bell. 2. talkative woman, prattler.

badalejar s. 1. = **badalar**. 2. to chatter (of teeth, with cold or fear).

ele badalejava his teeth chattered.

badalo s. m. 1. clapper, bell-clapper, tongue of a bell (plates C 9, S 3). 2. (Port.) fool. 3. (coll.) tongue. 4. (sl.) flattery, wheedling.

correr o ~, dar o ~ to talk too much, prattle.

badame s. m. (also **badamo**) chisel (for stone or wood) (plate E 9, F 2, M 4).

badameco s. m. 1. (ant.) satchel, school bag. 2. (fig.) lad, youth, prig. 3. fop, popinjay.

badana s. f. 1. lean, old ewe. 2. meat of an old ewe. 3. drooping, flabby skin. 4. (coll.) fin. 5. soft leather put over the saddle. 6. man of no consequence, fool.

badanal s. m. (pl. -ais) 1. (coll.) confusion, disorder, muddle. 2. great haste, precipitance. 3. mess, complication.

badejo s. m. name of several fishes of the family Serranidae. ‖ adj. (Braz., coll.) 1. great, huge. 2. showy. 3. beautiful. 4. extraordinary.

badeleíta s. f. (min.) baddeleyite.

badelsita s. f. a mineral consisting of zirconium oxyde.

baderna (I) s. f. = **abadernas**.

baderna (II) s. f. 1. (Braz.) gang of youths, group of vagrants. 2. high-jinks, frolics. 3. (fam.) spree. 4. conflict, rumpus, riot, quarrel.

badernar v. 1. to frolic, feast. 2. to belong to a gang of youths or vagrants. 3. to lead an idle life, play truant, loiter.

badernista s. m. + f. (Braz.) rowdy, brawler, ruffian. ‖ adj. 1. frolicsome. 2. disorderly, rowdy.

badó s. m. + f. (Braz.) simpleton, stupid or gullible person. ‖ adj. silly, foolish, gullible.

badofe s. m. (Braz.) dish of shrimps, palm-oil, etc.

badorar v. (pop.) to eat greedily, devour, gobble up.

badulaque s. m. 1. hash made of lights, pluck, or liver. 2. (fig.) trifle, insignificance. 3. stocky man. 4. trash, rubbish. 5. cosmetic.

baé s. m. + f. (Braz.) 1. variety of short-legged, fat pigs. 2. (fig.) short, stout person. ‖ adj. 1. concerning the above mentioned variety of pigs. 2. (fig.) stout, stocky.

baeco adj. (Braz.) stout, stocky, thickset.

baeta s. f. 1. coarse, shaggy fabric made of wool. baize. 2. m. (Braz., hist.) nickname for natives of Minas Gerais.

baetal adj. (pl. -ais) made of baize, wooly, coarse.

baetão s. m. (pl. -ões) 1. heavy or thick baize. 2. (Braz.) woo(l)len coverlet.

baetilha s. f. (also **baetinha**) 1. fine baize, flannel. 2. flannelette, cotton flannel. 3. linsey-woolsey. ~ de lã duffel.

baetóideos s. m. pl. (ent.) insects of the order Ephemoptera.

bafa s. m. (Braz., sl.) confusion, uproar, bustle, clamour.

bafafá s. m. (Braz., sl.) altercation, quarrel, strife, barney. 2. bustle, uproar, tumult.

bafagem s. f. (pl. -ens) 1. light breath of air, gentle wind, breeze. 2. (fig.) inspiration, incentive, stimulus. 3. expiration, exhalation.

bafejado adj. 1. protetecd, favoured. 2. breathed on. 3. pampered, coddled. 4. inspired, stimulated, animated.

o menino, ~ pela sorte, escapou ileso favoured by his good luck the boy escaped unhurt.

bafejador s. m. 1. one who breathes at (or on), whiffer. 2. protector. 3. inspirer. 4. pamperer, spoiler. ‖ adj. 1. breathing, exhaling. 2. shielding. 3. inspiring. 4. pampering.

bafejar v. 1. to warm (by breathing on). 2. to favour, protect. 3. to inspire, stimulate. 4. to breathe, blow softly, gasp. 5. to caress, pet. 6. to whiff, whiffle. 7. to fan.

a menina bafejou as pontas dos seus dedos the girl breathed on her fingertips. bafejado pelas palavras do seu mestre stimulated by his teacher's words. o vento bafejava as folhas tenras the wind fondled the tender leaves.

bafejo s. m. 1. puff of wind, breath, slight breeze, whiff, air, waft. 2. enthusiasm. 3. favour, assistance, help. 4. stroke of good luck.

bafio s. m. 1. mouldy or musty smell, fetid odour, stench, frowziness, frowst, fustiness. 2. mould.

esta água cheira a ~ this water has a mouldy odour. esta carne tem ~ this meat has a faint smell.

bafo s. m. 1. air breathed out, breath, respiration, exhalation, perspiration. 2. (fig.) favour (granted), help. 3. soft and warm puff of wind, waft. 4. shelter, cover. 5. inspiration.

ele sentiu um ~ de vento no rosto he felt a gentle breeze in his face.

bafômetro s. m. breath analyzer.

baforada s. f. 1. expiration, breathing out, breath, respiration whiff, puff. 2. puff of smoke (from a cigar or cigarette). 3. offensive breath. 4. bravado, bluff. 5. fuss, great bustle.

dar ~s (em cachimbo) to whiff away. ele deu uma ~ em seu cachimbo he took a whiff at his pipe.

baforar v. 1. to exhale, breathe forth, blow. 2. to expel (odour, breath, smoke), whiff. 3. to belch. 4. to boast, brag.

baforda s. f. (anat.) 1. a kind of a short lance, javelin. 2. insult, affront.

baforeira s. f. caprifig, wild fig-tree.

bafuge s. m. (Braz., pop.) gentle intermittent wind.

baga s. f. 1. berry or berrylike fruit (plate B 1). 2. drop. 3. drop of sweat. 4. (Braz.) castor-oil seed.

bagaçada s. f. 1. heap of husks. 2. stack of chopped wood. 3. heap of trash or garbage. 4. (fig.) trifle, thing of little value or importance. 5. (fig.) empty talk, prattle.

bagaceira s. f. 1. heap of husks, husk-pit. 2. open place or covered yard for keeping bagasse. 3. rest, remainder, residue. 4. rubbish, waste, stuff. 5. sugar-cane brandy. 6. brandy made of husks of

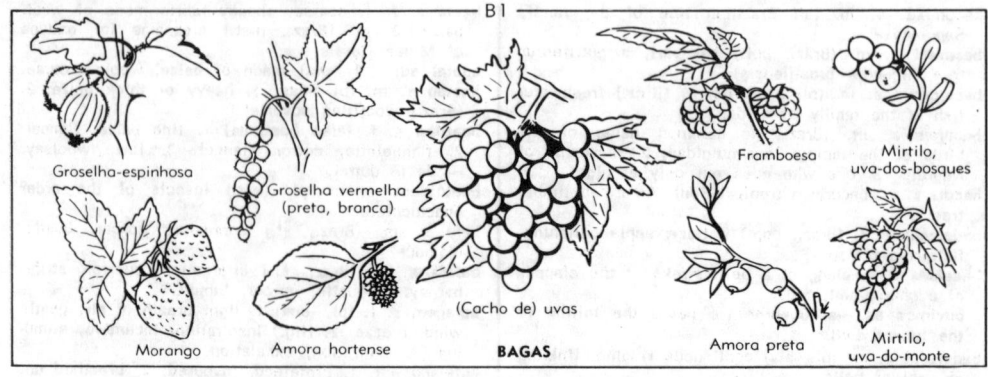

B1

Groselha-espinhosa

Groselha vermelha (preta, branca)

Framboesa

Mirtilo, uva-dos-bosques

(Cacho de) uvas

Morango

Amora hortense

BAGAS

Amora preta

Mirtilo, uva-do-monte

grapes. 7. stack of logs. 8. vulgar people, mob, rabble. 9. (fig.) empty talk, chatter. 10. (teath., sl.) bad play or acting.

bagaceiro s. m. 1. workman who removes the husks. 2. husk-pit or heap. 3. felon or stupid fellow. ‖ adj. 1. feeding on husks (animal). 2. vulgar, common.

bagaço s. m. 1. bagasse (crushed sugar-cane), marc. 2. husks of grapes after crushing. 3. old prostitute. 4. amusement, entertainment, dancing.
~ **da cana-de-açúcar** cane-trash. ~ **de cevada** grains. **um** ~ entirely down person.

bagada s. f. 1. big tear-drop. 2. a lot of berries.

bagageira s. f. 1. portage, cost of carriage. 2. bluish--gray, lentiform pebble of titanium dioxide. 3. baggage cart, luggage-van.

bagageiro s. m. 1. railway employee in charge of the luggage-van. 2. insectivorous bird of the family Tyrannidae. 3. race-horse that comes in last, also-ran. 4. (mil.) orderly, batman. 5. (railway) luggage-van. ‖ adj. 1. carrying luggage. 2. tardy, lagging in (race-horse). 3. associating with vulgar people.

bagagem s. f. (pl. **-ens**) 1. baggage, luggage, lug (plate E 13). 2. (mil.) equipage, outfit, impedimenta. 3. (mil.) fatigue clothes. 4. (fig.) complete works, literary baggage (of an author). 5. traps, plunder. 6. swag. 7. vulgar people, rabble, mob.
~ **transportada gratuitamente** free baggage. **chegar na** ~ to arrive last. **depósito de** ~ left-luggage office, cloak-room. **despachar** ~ to book (register) luggage. **despacho de** ~ luggage office. **posso mandar registrar minha** ~? can I have my luggage registered?

bagajudo s. m. (Braz.) coarse gravel. ‖ adj. of or like coarse gravel.

bagalhão s. m. (pl. **-ões**) big berry.

bagalhoça s. f. (sl.) money, cash, brass.

bagana s. f. 1. cigarette or cigar end. 2. cigar. 3. (Braz.) flat cake, tortilla. 4. bad food, unappetizing dish. 5. worthless thing, rubbish.

baganha s. f. 1. hull of seed. 2. epidermis, cuticle.

bagarote s. m. (sl.) one Cruzeiro bank-note (usually in pl.).
custa dez ~**s** it costs ten Cruzeiros.

bagatela s. f. bagatelle: 1. trifle, fleabite, fiddlestick, straw. 2. game similar to billiards.
isto e é uma ~ (sl.) that's a fleabite.

bagateleiro s. m. 1. trifler, fusser. 2. punctilious person. 3. piddler, potterer, hair-splitter. ‖ adj. 1. trifling, insignificant. 2. punctilious, fussy.

bagauri s. m. (Braz.) = **baguari**.

bagaxa s. f. prostitute. ‖ adj. lewd, base, lascivious, obscene.

bage s. f. (Braz. also **bagem**) = **vagem**.

bagear v. (also **bajar**) to pod, produce pods.

bago s. m. 1. each fruit of a bunch of grapes or any grapelike fruit, berry, acinus. 2. (sl.) testicle(s). 3. (coll.) money, paper-money, banknote. 4. grain of shot.
~ **de uvas** grape. ~ **do loureiro** bayberry.

bagoado adj. grapelike, in clusters, berrylike.

bagralhão s. m. (pl. **-ões**) (Braz.) freshwater fish of Maranhão.

bagre s. m. 1. common name of several freshwater and salt-water fishes of the family Siluridae. 2. sheatfish, catfish.

baguinho s. m. (Braz., naut., sl.) occasional stevedore substitute.

baguá s. m. (Braz.) a variety of mongrel dogs.

baguaçu s. f. (Braz.) plant of the family Palmaceae.

bagual s. m. (pl. **-ais**) (also **baguá**) 1. untamed colt. 2. colt recently broken and still unruly. 3. horse that turned wild again, stray horse. ‖ adj. 1. untamed, savage, unruly. 2. unsociable, reserved, unfriendly.

bagualada s. f. 1. herd of half-tamed foals and colts. 2. (fig.) rudeness, coarseness, brutality.

bagualão s. m. (pl. **-ões**) horse, recently broken and still unreliable, bronco.

baguari s. m. (ornith.) heron (Ardeo cocoi). ‖ adj. m. + f. slow, sluggish, dull, slothful.

baguear v. to hold an animal's testicles for castration.

bagueta s. f. clock (stocking).
com ~ clocked.

bagulhado, bagulhento, bagulhoso adj. full of (stones, kernels) seeds.

bagulheiro s. m. (Braz., sl.) receiver of stolen goods.

bagulho s. m. 1. grapestone, grain, kernel. 2. (Braz.) duster fixed on a long stick. 3. worthless pieces of furniture, trash.

bagunça s. f. (Braz.) 1. machine for the removal of earth. 2. (sl.) disorder, confusion. 3. noisy feasting, high jinks, frolics, hoity-toity.
era uma ~ **danada** it was a terrible hoity-toity. **fazer** ~ to start a quarrel, do a bit of skylarking.

bagunçada s. f. 1. (Braz., sl.) merrymaking, spree, fun. 2. = **bagunça**.

baguncear v. to provoke disorder, feast noisily, cause confusion.

bagunceiro s.m. 1. disorderly or careless person. 2. hooligan, rowdy. ‖ adj. 1. disorderly. 2. noisy, rowdy.

bah! interj. exclamation expressing surprise, astonishment, fright or fear.

baia s. f. stall, box, bail (stable) (plate E 11).

baía s. f. 1. bay (of a sea, lake or river), inlet, embayment, voe, gulf, bight (plate C 19). 2.

drainage canal. 3. lagoon, small lake communicating with a river.

baiacu s. m. (Braz.) 1. (ichth.) globefish, puffer. 2. (ornith.) oyster-catcher. 3. short and fat person.

baiagu s. m. (also **bejaqui**, ornith.) oyster-catcher.

baiana s. f. 1. girl or woman native of Bahia. 2. caparison, saddle-cloth. -

baianada s. f. 1. imposture, fraud, deceit. 2. boasting, bragging, exaggeration. 3. (S. Braz.) poor horsemanship. 4. group of people from Bahia.

baianca s. f. (Braz.) uneven ground between ditches.

baiano s. m. (also **baiense** m. + f.) 1. inhabitant or native of Bahia. 2. poor horseman. 3. (Braz.) infantryman, foot soldier. 4. (S. Braz.) rustic, peasant, agricultural labourer. 5. inhabitant of Brazilian wild lands. 6. cattle raised in the wilderness.

baião s. m. (pl. -ões) (Braz.) folk music and dance.

baiar v. (Braz.) to dance.

baila (I) s. f. = **bailado**, **baile.**

baila (II) s. f. = **balha.**
trazer à ~ to bring upon the carpet (on the tapis), to broach. vir à ~ to come up for discussion.

bailadeira s. f. 1. female dancer. 2. ballet girl, ballerina, figurante.

bailado s. m. 1. (theat.) interlude of ballet, divertissement. 2. ballet, choreography. 3. any artistic dancing. 4. ball, social dancing.

bailador s. m. 1. dancer. 2. figurant, ballet artist.

bailão s. m. (pl. -ões) 1. man fond of dancing, dancing enthusiast. 2. singer or player of **fados** (Port. popular songs).

bailar v. 1. to dance. 2. to perform a ballet. 3. to leap, jump. 4. (fig.) to tremble, oscillate. 5. to float.
uma lágrima bailava na sua pálpebra a tear trembled on her eyelid.

bailarico s. m. 1. popular ball. 2. improvised dance reunion.

bailarina s. f. dancer, ballet-dancer, figurante, chorus girl.

bailarino, **bailarim** s. m. 1. ballet dancer, dance artist, figurant, dancer. 2. (fig.) waddler, person moving as on tiptoe.

bailariqueiro s. m. dance enthusiast or habitué.

baile s. m. 1. festive dance reunion, ball, function, dance. 2. hooting, hissing, derisive shouting or stamping. 3. (sl.) brawl, noisy conflict, quarrel.
~ de corte state-ball. ~ de máscara, ~ à fantasia fancy dress ball, masked ball. ~ estudantil promenade. ~ que termina à meia-noite Cinderella dance. dar um ~ (fig.) to provoke s. o., play s. o. a nasty trick. ela deu um ~ she gave a ball. ele o ofendeu e o ~ começou he offended him and the brawl started. o príncipe abriu o ~ the prince opened the ball.

bailéu s. m. 1. cradle, a painter's cradle, scaffold. 2. (naut.): a) forecastle, aftcastle, quarterdeck. b) gangway. c) orlop deck. d) (sailors' sl.) gaol, jail, prison.

bailiado s. m. bailiwick.

bailio s. m. (ant.) 1. chief commander of ancient knightly orders. 2. provincial chief magistrate, bailiff, officer.

bailomania s. f. dancing mania.

bainha s. f. 1. sheath, scabbard, case, casing. 2. hem, border, tuck, seaming, edge, edging, margin of a garment (plate P 15). 3. (bot.) vagina; sheathing part of some leaf bases (plate F 5). 4. (zool.) sheath of the penis (plate C 12). 5. drum of a micrometer gauge (plate M 9}.
~ de calça cuff (plate R 6) ~ de cobre para juntas copper jointing sleeve. ~ de proteção protecting sheath. ~ dobrada lapped seam (plate P 15). ~

dobrada e sobrecosida run and fell seam (plate P 15). ela costura a ~ do vestido she sews the hem of the dress. ele não mais coube nas ~s he nearly burst with pride. ponha a espada na ~! sheathe your sword.

bainha-de-espada s. f. (pl. **bainhas-de-espada**) (Braz.) forest tree of the family Moraceae.

bainhar v. 1. to sheathe, hem. 2. to make a sheath or a border.

bainheiro s. m. sheath- or scabbard-maker.

baio s. m. 1. bay dun (horse). 2. cigarette made of husks of maize. 3. (Port.) stomach of animals, maw. || adj. 1. bay, reddish brown (speaking of horses, cattle, dogs). 2. swarthy, of dark complexion. ~-castanho chestnut. ~-claro light-bay. ~-escuro dark-bay.

baionesa s. f. a brown apple with a pleasing scent. || adj. of or referring to this apple.

baioneta s. f. (mil.) bayonet, side-arm.
~ calada fixed bayonet. fecho de ~ bayonet joint. suporte a ~ bayonet lamp-holder (plate L 1).

baionetada s. f. thrust with the bayonet.

baioneta-espanhola s. f. (pl. **baionetas-espanholas**) (bot.) Spanish-bayonet.

baionetar v. to bayonet.

baiquara s. f. (Braz.) rustic, peasant, boor.

bairã s. m. Bairam: Mohammedan festivals held after Ramadan (Easter).

bairari s. m. a species of pigeon.

bairrismo s. m. 1. localism, local patriotism, sectionalism, provincialism. 2. (fig.) narrowness (of mind or conceptions).

bairrista s. m. + f. 1. inhabitant of a certain district (country or city). 2. defender of local interests. 3. regionalist, local patriot, person who places local interests above national ones. || adj. 1. regional, local. 2. narrow-minded.

bairro s. m. district: 1. ward, precinct, quarter. 2. portion of a country or state, region.
~ de bordéis red-light district. ~ jardim garden suburb. ~ operário workmen quarter. ~ residencial residential quarter, suburb, (U. S. A.) uptown. ~s de lata slums (pl.).

baita adj. 1. (Braz.) very tall, large or great, enormous. 2. famous. 3. courageous. 4. good, nice.

baitaca s. f. 1. (Braz., ornith.) a kind of parrot. 2. prattler, chatterbox, gossip.

baitarra s. m. (Braz.) 1. tall and strong fellow, bloke. 2. sharper, swindler, crook.

baiúca s. f. 1. canteen, paltry wine-shop, pub. 2. any run-down and dirty tavern. 3. dump.

baiuqueiro s. m. 1. habitué of a tavern, bar or pub. 2. canteen-keeper, tavern-keeper.

baixa s. f. 1. depression, hollow, basin. 2. decrease, reduction, stringency, slump, break (in price or value). 3. decadence, decline, decay, hardpan. 4. lowland, valley, flat country, plain. 5. shoal, shallow waters. 6. regularly inundated land. 7. (law) cancellation of the bill of indictment. 8. expiration of a ship's charter-contract. 9. dismissal, discharge (from military service or office). 10. release (from hospital). 11. release-ticket, discharge-paper. 12. casualty. 13. (meteor.) depression, trough.
~ de terreno depression. ~ no mercado depression. a parte mais ~ the bottom. ela falou em voz ~ she spoke under her breath. ele deu ~ ao soldado he released the soldier from duty, he discharged the soldier. há ~ no preço do trigo the wheat (price) falls. houve uma ~ de temperatura there was a decrease of temperature. jogar na ~ da Bolsa to speculate on (with) the fall of the stock-exchange. luz ~ town light (of a motorcar). máquina de ~

rotação low-speed engine. **pessoa** ~ (fig.) a rat. **o relatório anunciou uma** ~ **do câmbio** the report showed a fall of exchange (rate or agio). **o soldado deu** ~ the soldier left service. **uma** ~ **considerável dos preços** a considerable abatement or fall in prices.

baixada s. f. 1. slope, declivity. 2. marshland, boggy land, swale, holm, bottoms. 3. plain between mountains, valley. 4. lowland, depression, hollow. 5. ravine, gully. 6. (radio) aerial connexion. 7. sinking.
~ **de capim** humid grassland.

baixadão s. m. (pl. **-ões**) vast lowland, big plain.

baixa-falésia s. f. (pl. **baixas-falésias**) (geol.) protective rocky blocks at the foot of a cliff.

baixa-mar s. f. (pl. **baixa-mares**) low-tide, ebb.

baixamente adv. lowly, basely, shamefully.

baixão s. m. (pl. **-ões**) (mus.) kind of bassoon, contra--bassoon (wind instrument).

baixar v. 1. to lower, let (send, bring) down. 2. to shorten, make or become shorter. 3. to incline, stoop, droop. 4. to step or go down, pass from a higher to a lower place, turn down, come down. 5. to lessen, diminish, abate, ebb, subside, decrease, decline. 6. to look down, cast down (eyes). 7. to bow, bend (the head, knees, etc.). 8. to reduce, humble, abase, degrade, humiliate, subdue. 9. (mus.) to sing or play in a lower tone, or more softly. 10. to travel down-stream (on a river-boat). 11. to set, sink below the horizon (sun, stars). 12. to issue (orders). 13. to return to inferior authorities or departments for further revision. 14. (law) to return to a lower court. 15. to throw a horse or cattle (as for branding). 16. to fall, slump. 17. ~**-se:** a) to bow, bend, stoop. b) to humble, humiliate o. s.
~ **o rádio** to tune down the radio. **baixei rapidamente as escadas** I came rapidly downstairs. **ela baixou a bainha** she shortened the hemline. **ela baixou os olhos** she cast down her eyes. **ele baixou os preços** he reduced the prices. **ele baixou-se e pediu perdão** he humiliated himself and asked for pardon. **eles** ~**am a bandeira** they struck the colours. **a enchente vai baixando** the flood abates, is abating. **o menino baixou a cabeça** the boy inclined his head, ducked his head. **o ministro baixou um ofício** the minister issued a decree. **sua influência baixou muito** his influence diminished considerably. **O Supremo Tribunal baixou os autos à primeira instância** the Supreme Court of Appeal returned the pleading to the (Court of the) first instance. **a temperatura baixou** the temperature fell.

baixate s. m. a cooper's tool.

baixeira s. f. (Braz.) first cotton harvest of the year.

baixeiro s. m. saddle-cloth. || adj. 1. underlying, underlaid (referring to covers lying under a saddle or under the mattress of a cot). 2. short-legged, stumpy (horse). 3. ambling (horse).

baixela s. f. table-ware, table-set (plates, cups, silver, china, cutlery).

baixete s. m. 1. a cooper's bench. 2. a cooper's tool.

baixeza s. f. 1. low position or situation, lowness. 2. inferiority in rank or quality. 3. baseness, meanness, wickedness, low-mindedness, wretchedness, hoggishness, dirt(iness), flatness, vileness. 4. indignity.

baixia s. f. 1. shallowness. 2. = **baixio**.

baixinho adv. 1. in a low voice or tone, under one's breath, soft. 2. secretly, stealthily.

baixio s. m. 1. sand-bank, shelf, shoal, sands (pl.), shallow, flat, ford. 2. reef, ledge, cay (also key). 3. (fig.) danger, difficulty. 4. river-turn, river-bay.

baixista s. m. + f. (com.) 1. stock exchange operator who speculates on (with) the fall of prices. 2. bearish speculator, bear. || adj. bear.

baixo s. m. 1. inferior or lower part (plate Q). 2. (naut.) part of the hull under the waterline. 3. sand-ridge or shoal which emerges at low-tide. 4. (mus.): a) low tone or note. b) bass. c) bass string or instrument. d) flat. 5. amble, ambling pace or gait. 6. = **baixio. 7.** ~**s** pl.: a) depression, hollow. b) skirt or lower part of a mountain. c) ground-floor. d) difficulty, danger, misfortune. || adj. (abs. superl. **baixíssimo, ínfimo**) 1. low (plate Q). 2. shallow, shoal. 3. inferior. 4. (mus.) low, deep, grave, bass. 5. almost soundless, hard to hear or understand. 6. cheap, inexpensive. 7. poor, destitute (quality, value, etc.). 8. ordinary, mediocre, small. 9. vulgar, mean, vile, base. 10. (Braz.) incapable, unfit. 11. stumpy, strong-set, short, tubby. || adv. 1. lowly, in a law place or position. 2. (mus.) gravely, in a low tone or pitch. 3. softly, whisperingly.
-a pressão low pressure. **de tom** ~ low-pitched. **ela o pôs** ~ she humiliated him. **ele é** ~ he is low-minded. **ele é de nascença -a** he is of low birth. **ele está muito em**~ he is badly off. **ele fez mão baixa** he stole. **ele usou linguagem de** ~ **calão** he used bad language. **ele vendeu a carne por** ~ **do balcão** he sold the meat underhand. **ele vendeu por preço** ~ he sold for a cheap price. **eles falaram** ~ they spoke softly. **é uma máquina de baixa rotação** it is a slow speed machine. **eu vou para** ~ I go downstairs. **gente baixa** mob. **um homem** ~ a short man. **o menino ficou por** ~ the boy was overcome. **o primeiro período do** ~**-império** the first period of the Lower Empire (Roman hist.) **o quadro é de** ~ **valor** the picture is of small value. **os** ~**s da casa** the ground-floor of the house. **o mais** ~ the undermost. **por** ~ underneath, under (plate P 18).

baixo-relevo s. m. (pl. **baixos-relevos**) (arts) bas-relief. low-relief.

baixote s. m. basset, dachshund (plate C 3). || adj. somewhat low or short (usually said of people). ~ **de pêlo comprido** Sussex spaniel.

baixo-ventre s. m. (pl. **baixos-ventres**) (colloq.) lower part of the abdominal cavity.

baixura s. f. 1. = **baixeza**. 2. depression, esp. tract of land under water- or sea-level. 3. hollow, valley. 4. decrease.

bajar v. (bot.) to pod, produce pods.

bajerê s. m. (Braz., Mato Grosso) tip, hint (as to the localization of diamonds).

bajesto s. m. (Braz.) trifle, trash.

bajogar v. (Braz., Maranhão) 1. to throw, fling, toss, eject. 2. to throw away.

bajoujar v. 1. to flatter, adulate, fawn upon. 2. to fondle.
ele era o filho mais bajoujado do casal he was the couple's most pampered son.

bajoujice s. f. 1. flattery, adulation. 2. silliness, tomfoolery.

bajoujo s. m. 1. ridiculous flatterer. 2. love-sick swain. 3. silly person. || adj. silly, (fam.) namby-pamby.

bajulação s. f. (pl. **-ões**) (also **bajulice**) flattery, fawning, adulation, cajoling, sawder.

bajulador s. m. flatterer, adulator, wheedler, coaxer, foot-licker. || adj. coaxing, slimy, soapy, fawning, servile.
ser ~ **de alguém** to suck up to someone.

bajular v. 1. to flatter, compliment a person upon a thing. 2. to adulate, fawn upon, cringe. 3. (coll.) to butter, soft-soap, bow and scrape.

bala s. f. 1. bullet, missile, shot, ball, slug, lead. 2. cannon ball, projectile, shell. 3. bale, package, paper- or hempsack. 4. paper measure corresponding to 32 reams. 5. bonbon, sweet(meat). ~ blindada jacketed bullet. ~ contra tosse cough--drop. ~ de alta velocidade high speed bullet. ~ de canhão round shot, cannon ball, pill. ~ de leite toffee, toffy. ~ de papel bale of 10 reams of paper. ~ incendiária incendiary bullet. ~ traçadora tracer bullet. aço à prova de ~ shot-proof steel. ele agiu como uma ~ he acted swift as lightning. ferir à ~ to pip. uma ~ sem força a spent bullet.

balabrega s. m. 1. mimic, mime, mimicker. 2. charlatan, mountebank.

balaço s. m. (less used form balázio) 1. large ball. 2. gunshot, cannon-shot.

balacobaco adj. m. used in do ~: excellent.

balada s. f. 1. ballad, lay. 2. (mus.) ballade. 3. (hist.) popular poem which recounts legendary events.

baladeira s. f. sling, catapult.

baladesco adj. balladic.

baladista s. m. + f. ballad-writer.

balado s. m. = balido.

balador (I) s. m. (bot.) Malacca bean, marking nut.

balador (II) adj. bleating, lowing.

balafo s. m. West African marimba.

balaiada s. f. (Braz., hist.) rebellion of the "balaios" (Maranhão, 1838-1840).

balaieiro (I) s. m. 1. manufacturer of wicker-baskets, panniers, or hampers. 2. costermonger, hawker of fruit or vegetables.

balaieiro (II) s. m. harpooner (of whales).

balaio (I) s. m. 1. hamper, basket made of straw, palm-leaf ribs, lianas and the like. 2. (S. Braz.) ancient dance (a kind of fandango).

balaio (II) s. m. partisan of the Maranhão insurrection (Braz. 1838-1840).

balalaica s. f. balalaika, Russian guitar.

balame s. m. a lot of bullets, missiles.

balamento s. m. (N. Braz.) folk song which recounts important events of the region.

balança s. f. 1. balance, scales, pair of scales, weighing-machine. 2. ponderation, consideration. 3. equilibrium, equipoise, steadiness. 4. parallel, confrontation. 5. the Scales, Libra (zodiacal constellation). 6. scales: emblem of justice.
~ automática automatic weighing apparatus (plate A 2). ~ de caixa box scale. ~ decimal decimal balance. ~ de cozinha kitchen scale. ~ de ensaio assay balance. ~ de molas spring balance. ~ de mostrador dial balance. ~ de plataforma weighbridge, platform scale. ~ de precisão analytical balance. ~ de travessão beam balance. ~ registradora recording balance. ~ romana 1. Roman balance. 2. Danish balance. 3. steelyard. cursor da ~ jockey weight. estar em ~ to be irresolute. fazer pender a ~ to turn the scale. fiel ou língua da ~ needle or tongue of the balance. gancho da ~ cheeks of the balance. pesar na ~ to make one's influence felt (upon a question or decision). pôr em ~ todas as palavras to weigh every word carefully. prato da ~ scale of the balance. travessão da ~ scale beam.

balançar v. (also balancear) 1. to balance, counterbalance, equilibrate. 2. to swing, oscillate, fluctuate, rock, waggle. 3. to examine, compare, ponder, poise. 4. to compensate, make equivalent. 5. (com.) to balance accounts. 6. to weigh, ascertain the weight. 7. to hesitate, be irresolute, teeter.
~ bem os motivos to ponder the motives carefully. ~ uma criança no berço to cradle a child. ~ uma criança no joelho to dandle a child. a criança

começou a ~-se na cadeira the child began to rock with the chair. eles ~am a conta corrente they settled the current account. a firma balançou-se com uma perda the firm closed with a loss. o lucro não balança com os grandes esforços the profit does not compensate for the great efforts.

balancê s. m. 1. screw-press, coining-press or die stamp. 2. one of the movements of the quadrille (square dance).

balanceado adj. (Braz.) 1. foolish, somewhat crazy. 2. (com.) nearly bankrupt, (fam.) broke. 3. balanced. não ~ uneven.

balanceamento s. m. 1. swinging, oscillation, rocking, seesaw. 2. counterbalancing.

balancear v. = balançar.

balanceio s. m. balancing, rocking, swing.
condensador de ~ (radio) trimmer.

balanceiro (I) s. m. 1. (mech.) rokshaft, rocking lever, beam. 2. = balancim. 3. weigher. 4. (naut.) outrigger.

balanceiro (II) s. m. person who weighs goods in a warehouse or sugar cane in a factory.

balancete s. m. (com.) 1. trial, intermediate or interim balance, balance sheet. 2. summary of an annual balance.

balancia s. f. pop. form for melancia.

balancim s. m. (pl. -ins) 1. = balanceiro. 2. (mech.) rocker arm, bascule, valve rocker, yoke, balance arbour. 3. gate made of vertical lattice held together by horizontal wires. 4. main swing-tree, swing-bar or swing-tree (of a cart). 5. balance of a watch.

balancista s. m. (also balanceador). 1. surveyer of weights and measures, keeper of public scales. 2. weigher.

balanço (I) s. m. (bot.) darnel (weed).

balanço (II) s. m. 1. swinging, oscillation, fluctuation. 2. swing see-saw, sway, teeter (plate P 6). 3. shaking, tossing, rocking. 4. rolling (ship). 5. alteration, revolt, agitation. 6. (com.) balance (accounts), cash--balance, balance-sheet. 7. (fig.) examination, ponderation.
~ anual balance. ~ de caixa balance in cash. ~ de comprovação (verificação) trial balance. ~ de navio rolling of a ship, tumble. ~ térmico heat balance. agüentar-se no ~ to overcome difficulties. comprimento de ~ (arch.) length of overhang. dar ~ 1. to settle an account. 2. to account for, give or render an account of a thing. 3. (theat., sl.) to control whether the actors know their rôles. ele fez o ~ he struck a balance. estar em ~ to be in suspense, be irresolute. fazer ~ to take stock. livro de ~ balance book.

balanço-d'água s. m. (pl. balanços-d'água) (bot.) water-balance.

balandra s. f. one-masted sailing ship.

balandrão s. m. (pl. -ões) (Braz.) boaster, browbeater, bully.

balandrau s. m. 1. gown worn by some religious fraternities. 2. (Braz.) overcoat. 3 (fig.) shapeless or disproportionate body.

balandronada s. f. boasting, swaggering, bluff.

balangandã s. m. 1. jewelry, trinkets worn by women in Bahia. 2. fandangle, fangle, frippery, frill.

balanífero adj. (bot.) balaniferous.

balanite (I) s. f. balanite: a kind of precious stone.

balanite (II) s. f. (med.) balanitis: inflammation of the glans of the penis.

balanoglosso s. m. (zool.) Balanoglossus.

balanóide adj. m. + f. glandiform, glanduliform.

balanquear v. (Braz.) to boast, brag.

balante adj. m. + f. bleating, bellowing.

balão s. m. (pl. **-ões**) 1. aerostat, balloon. 2. paper balloon, toy balloon. 3. (chem.) glass flask, matrass. 4. bell-shaped skirt, balloon skirt. 5. lamp globe. 6. fib, false report, lie, twister. 7. log-pile for charcoal burning. 8. bladder. ~ **cativo** captive balloon. ~ **de barragem** (mil.) barrage (or kite) balloon. ~ **de gás** gas bag. ~ **de sondagem**, ~**-sonda** registering balloon. ~ **dirigível** dirigible. ~ **livre** free balloon. ~ **papagaio** sausage balloon. **ele até empregou** ~ **de oxigênio** (coll.) he did everything in his power to fend off (a disaster, inconveniences). **pneu** ~ balloon tire.

balão-de-ensaio s. m. (pl. **balões-de-ensaio**) 1. trial balloon. 2. (fig.) project or scheme announced in order to test the public opinion, feeler. **eles soltaram um** ~ they tested the possibilities, they probed the terrain, they flew a kite.

balar v. 1. to bleat, (of cattle) to low, bellow. 2. (fam.) to baa. **o gado balava nos currais** the cattle was bleating in the corrals.

balastraca s. f. 1. (Braz.) ancient coin of 400 réis. 2. Argentine and Uruguayan copper coin.

balastragem s. f. (pl. **-ens**) ballasting.

balastrar v. to ballast: 1. steady, stabilize or fill with ballast. 2. prepare a roadbed or railway track with broken stone or gravel.

balastro s. m. sand, gravel, broken stone, road metal.

balata s. f. balata, bully-tree. **resina de** ~ balata gum.

balateiro s. m. balata-gum gatherer.

balaustrada s. f. railing, breast-work, hand-rail, balustrade, parapet, banisters, balusters (plates E 7, 13).

balaustrar v. to furnish with banisters.

balaústre s. m. 1. (archit.) baluster (plate E 7). 2. rail post, banister. 3. grip-rail, handrail (on vehicles, ships, etc.). 4. small wooden pillars of chair-backs. 5. (archit.) bolster of a Ionic capital. ~ **da popa** (naut.) taffrail.

balaxe s. m. (min.) spinel. ‖ adj. of or related to the spinel.

balázio s. m. 1. large ball. 2. gunshot, cannon-shot.

balbado s. m. furbelow.

balbo adj. (also **gago**) stammering.

balbuciação s. f. (pl. **-ões**) stuttering, stammering, babbling.

balbuciante ad. m. + f. stammering, stuttering.

balbuciar v. 1. to stammer, stutter. 2. to utter with hesitation, babble, falter, talk in a confused manner. **ele balbuciava uma desculpa** he stammered an apology.

balbúcie, balbuciência s. f. speech defect or difficulty, logopathy.

balbucio s. m. 1. = **balbuciação**. 2. (fig.) attempt, trial, essay.

balbúrdia s. f. 1. disorder, disarrangement, confusion, tumult, messiness, hoity-toity, rumpus. 2. shouting, clamour. **fizeram uma** ~ **terrível** they made a hell of a row. **que** ~**!** what a mess!

balburdiar v. 1. to upset, disorder, confuse. 2. to clamour, cause tumult. 3. to mingle, mix. 4. to confound, embarrass, disconcert.

balça s. f. 1. thick forest. 2. thicket, underbrush. 3. (pl.) copse bushes, shrubs. 4. fence, paling.

balcânico adj. Balkan, Balkanic.

Bálcãs prop. n. os ~ the Balkans. **nos** ~ in the Balkans.

balcão s. m. (pl.-ões) (arch.) 1. balcony, projecting alcove or terrace, oriel. 2. (shop) counter, show counter (plate A 2). 3. (theat.) projecting gallery, dress-circle. ~ **de bar** bar (plate R 5). ~ **de primeira ordem** dress-circle (plate T 3). ~ **de segunda ordem** upper circle (plate T 3).

balcedo s. m. 1. thicket, thick forest. 2. (Amazonas) large floating mass of vegetation. 3. swamp, fen, marsh.

balceiro adj. 1. of, pertaining to or related to thickets. 2. wild, sylvan, silvan. **ele possuía um bom cão** ~ he had a good hunting-dog.

balconista s. m. + f. 1. shop assistant. 2. m. salesman, shopman, clerk. 3. f. saleswoman, saleslady, shoppy, lady-clerk.

balda s. f. 1. imperfection, foible, failing. 2. craze, mania. 3. (cards) renounce.

baldada s. f. pailful.

baldado adj. 1. useless, ineffectual, inefficient. 2. unsuccessful, failing. 3. frustrate, vain, to no effect, effectless, fruitless. ~ **em sua esperança, ele voltou** disappointed in his hopes he came back. **todos os seus esforços foram** ~**s** all (his) their efforts were in vain.

baldão (I) s. m. (pl. **-ões**) 1. encounter with fate. 2. misfortune, mishap, adversity. 3. useless effort or work. 4. offence, affront, insult. 5. billow, huge wave, breakers (pl.). **de** ~ impetuously.

baldão (II) s. m. (pl. **-ões**) idler, sluggard, lazybones. ‖ adj. idle, lazy.

baldaquim s. m. baldachin.

baldaquinado adj. of, pertaining to, or resembling a baldachin.

baldar v. 1. to frustrate, disappoint, thwart (a person's hopes or designs). 2. to toil in vain, lose one's labour, waste one's efforts. 3. to be inefficient. 4. (cards) to discard, cast off from the hand. 5. ~**-se** to be disappointed. ~ **a esperança de alguém** to thwart a person's hopes. ~ **o seu dinheiro** to squander one's money. ~**am-se as suas ameaças** his threats were in vain. **baldei-me dos ouros** (cards) I discarded the diamonds. **o tempo baldou completamente** the weather changed completely.

balde s. m. 1. pail, bucket, scuttle (plates E 11, P 6, 12, V 2). 2. dust-bin. 3. tub, vat. 4. grab or bucket of a dredge. 5. (Braz.) dam, dike. 6. a kind of paper-kite. ~ **de madeira** kit. ~ **de madeira para ordenha** trug.

baldeação s. f. (pl. **-ões**) 1. transfusion, decantation. 2. transshipment, transfer of goods from one ship or conveyance to another. 3. washing up of a ship's deck. 4. (railway) change, connection, connexion, (U. S. A., transfer). 5. small strip of land surrounding a saltern.

baldeador s. m. bailer.

baldear v. 1. to decant, transfuse, bail. 2. to transship, change (passengers, luggage, goods). 3. to swing, rock, roll (like a ship). 4. to transfer, pass from one place to another. 5. to throw up, vomit. 6. to throw, fling. 7. ~**-se:** a) to rush in or upon, fling o. s. b) to cross over the other side. **os índios baldeavam da ilha para a terra** the Indians crossed from the island to the mainland. **os marujos** ~**am o convés** the sailors washed the deck. **temos de** ~ **em São Paulo** we have to change trains in São Paulo.

baldio s. m. 1. unused plot of land. 2. uncultivated or barren land, wasteland. ‖ adj. 1. uncultivated, barren, fallow. 2. frustrate, purposeless. 3. naked.

baldo adj. 1. deficient, lacking, wanting, devoid. 2. useless, purposeless. 3. (cards) wanting a suit.
estar ou ficar ~ ao naipe (fam.) to be penniless.
baldoar v. 1. to offend, affront, insult. 2. to cry, shout, clamour. 3. to vociferate.
sem vergonha ~am nomes ilustres they shamelessly insulted distinguished persons.
baldoso (I) adj. unruly, vicious (esp. of horses).
baldoso (II) adj. useless, ineffectual, fruitless, trying in vain.
baldrame s. m. (Braz.) foundation, basement.
baldréu s. m. kid-leather for gloves.
baldroca s. f. (pop.) cheat, imposture, fraud.
andar com ~s to swindle, cheat.
baldrocar v. to trick, swindle, defraud.
balduína s. f. (Braz., pop.) locomotive, engine.
balé s. m. ballet.
baleação s. f. (pl. -ões) whaling.
baleado adj. shot: wounded with a shot.
balear v. (Braz.) to wound with a shot.
ele baleou o amigo he shot at his friend.
baleárico adj. Balearic: of, pertaining to or related to the Balearic Isles.
baleato, baleote s. m. (zool.) whale-calf.
baleeira s. f. whaleboat, whaleship, whaler.
baleeiro s. m. 1. whale-fisher, whaler, whaleman. 2. harpooner. 3. = **baleeira**. ‖ adj. of, pertaining to or related to whales.
baleia s. f. 1. (zool.) whale, spouter. 2. (astr.) equatorial constellation, the Whale, the Cetus. 3. whalebone, whale fin. 4. (Braz., pop.) something impressive in size. 5. a fat woman.
~ azul (zool.) blue whale, sulphur-bottom. **~ branca** (zool.) bowhead, Greenland whale, right whale, sea-canary. **~ verdadeira** (zool.) southern right whale. **barba de ~** whale fins. **óleo de ~** whale-oil, train-oil. **caça ou pesca de ~** whaling, whale-fishing.
baleiro s. m. (Braz.) street-vendor selling candy.
balela s. f. 1. false report, unfounded rumour. 2. lie, fib.
balema s. f. (naut.) rope by which the halyard is fastened to the yard.
balenídeos s. m. pl. (zool.) Balaenidae.
balenopterídeos s. m. pl. (zool.) Balaenopteridae.
balestilha s. f. 1. (naut.) cross-staff: instrument formerly used at sea for taking the altitude. 2. (vet.) lancet for bleeding.
balestra s. f. (hist. mil.) 1. ballista: machine for throwing stones. 2. cross-bow.
balestreiro s. m. (fort.) machicolation.
balha (I) s. f. 1. enumeration, mention. 2. talk, rumour.
andar na ~, estar na ~ to be often mentioned or quoted. **chamar à ~** to provoke. **trazer à ~** to broach, bring s. th. on the tapis. **vir à ~** (or **baila**) 1. to appear opportunely. 2. to come up for discussion.
balha (II) s. f. 1. (hist.) division of a tilt-yard. 2. tilting place, lists.
balido s. m. 1. bleat of a sheep or lamb; boa. 2. complaint of the parish against the vicar.
balim s. m. (pl. -ins) 1. little bullet, pellet. 2. (Braz.) large-sized grain of shot.
balinês s. m. Balinese. ‖ adj. Balinese.
balir v. = **balar**.
balista s. f. 1. (mil., hist.) ballista: engine for hurling stones, arrows, etc. 2. cross-bow. 3. triggerfish, filefish.
balística s. f. ballistics.
balístico adj. ballistic.
balistídeos s. m. pl. (ichth.) Balistidae.

baliza s. f. 1. mark, land-mark, sign, boundary stone or mark. 2. delimitation, boundary, limit. 3. indication-sign, traffic signal. 4. guide-post, finger-post, direction-indicator. 5. buoy, sea-mark, beacon, floating beacon. 6. (nav. construction) square frames, midship framework. 7. stake, terminus, tee. 8. tree left standing when cutting down a forest. 9. (Braz.) drum major(ette). 10. side ruler (printing). 11. parking of a motorcar between two stakes. 12. (swimming pool) starting-block. 13. (swimming competition) lane.
~ da fuselagem (aeron.) transverse frame of the fuselage. **~ de enchimento** (nav. construction) filling timber. **~ luminosa** light beacon.
balizado adj. marked, provided with signals, sign-posts, buoys, etc.
balizador s. m. 1. person who installs signals or buoys; marker. 2. mark, sign, signal.
balizagem s. f. (pl. -ens), **balizamento** m. installation of signposts or signals, buoyage, marking, demarcation (of boundaries).
balizar v. 1. to put up signs, signals, buoys, marks. 2. to delimit, limit, set bounds for. 3. to estimate, appraise, calculate the size or value of. 4. to set apart, separate, distinguish.
ele balizou as horas de lazer he limited (or restricted) his leisure time. **eles ~am o canal** they buoyed the channel. **os garimpeiros ~am os seus lotes** the gold-diggers staked their claims.
balmázio s. m. round-head(ed) tack.
balneação s. f. (pl. -ões) balneation, bathing.
balnear (I) adj. m. + f. balneal.
balnear (II) v. to bathe, go to a (seaside) health-resort, take the waters.
balneário s. m. 1. health-resort, watering-place, balneary. 2. bathing establishment, bathhouse. ‖ adj. balneal, balneary.
balneatório adj. balneary, balneal.
balneável adj. m. + f. (pl. -áveis) proper for bathing, suitable for taking the waters.
balneologia s. f. balneology: science of the therapeutic effects of bathing and the use of mineral waters.
balneoterapia s. f. (med.) balneotherapy.
balneoterápico adj. (med.) balneotherapeutic.
balofice s. f. 1. vacuity, emptiness, hollowness. 2. deceit, fraud.
balofo adj. 1. puffy, spongy, voluminous but light, without consistency, flabby, flaccid. 2. superficial, exaggerated. 3. fraudulent, deceitful. 4. adipose, fat.
balona s. f. 1. jabot. 2. shirt-collar the flap of which covers the shoulder.
balonete s. m. (aeron.) ballonet(te).
balordo s. m. 1. blockhead, duffer. 2. dirty fellow. ‖ adj. dirty, filthy.
balote s. m. 1. = **balim**. 2. bundle, bale (of cotton).
balouçamento s. m. rocking, shaking, swinging.
balouçante adj. waggly.
balouçar v. 1. to balance, swing, rock to and fro. 2. to toss. 3. to dangle, pendulate. 4. to labour (ships). 5. **~-se** to bob.
balouço s. m. (also **baloiço**) 1. swinging, shaking, rocking. 2. oscillation, vibration, quiver. 3. swing, seesaw.
balroa s. f. grapnel, grappling hook.
balroar v. = **abalroar**.
balsa s. f. 1. husks of grapes. 2. mash-tub or mash-vat. 3. (thorny) thicket, briar, bushes (pl.). 4. cask to keep cured meat in. 5. (hist.) standard or banner of the Templars. 6. (Braz.) crude rubber transported in form of rafts. 7. float, raft, balsa, wherry,

ferry-boat. 8. wicker case for a glass-vessel. 9. (bot.) balsa, cork-tree.

viajar em ~ to raft.

balsamadina s. f. (bot.) vegetable gland secreting an aroma.

balsamar v. 1. to extract or distill balsam. 2. to aromaitze, perfume, scent. 3. to alleviate, soothe, mitigate.

as flores ~am um perfume agradável the flowers exhaled an agreeable perfume.

balsâmico adj. 1. balsamic, containing balsam, balmy. 2. aromatic, fragrant. ‖ **-amente** adv. balsamically, balmily.

balsamífero adj. balsamiferous.

balsâmina s. f. 1. balsam. 2. garden-balsam, balsamine: ornamental plant of the family Balsaminaceae.

balsamináceo adj. balsaminaceous.

balsâmina-de-purga s. f. (pl. **balsâminas-de-purga**) (bot.) balsam-apple.

balsâmina-do-mato s. f. (pl. **balsâminas-do-mato**) (bot.) touch-me-not.

balsamita s. f. (bot.) cat-mint, alecost, costmary.

balsamizar v. 1. to perfume, make fragrant, aromatize. 2. to alleviate, soothe. 3. to comfort, cure.

bálsamo s. m. 1. balsam, balm: a) aromatic and resinous substance of certain plants. b) any preparation of balsamic qualities, salve, unction. c) plant that yields balsam. d) perfume, fragrance. 2. (fig.) allevation, relief, comfort.

bálsamo-de-tolu s. m. (pl. **bálsamos-de-tolu**) Tolu balsam.

bálsamo-do-peru s. m. (pl. **bálsamos-do-peru**) Peru(vian) balsam.

bálsamo-tranqüilo s. m. (pl. **bálsamos-tranqüilos**) an infusion of narcotic plants in olive oil, for friction.

balsão s. m. (pl. **-ões**) (hist.) 1. banner, standard, flag. 2. banner of the Templars.

balsar v. (sl.) to bark.

balseira s. f. (Braz.) inferior sugar-cane.

balseiro (I) s. m. 1. mash-tub, mash-vat. 2. = **balseira**.

balseiro (II) s. m. 1. waterman, ferryman, wherryman. 2. rafter, raftsman. ‖ adj. of, pertaining to, or living on a ferry.

balso (I) s. m. rope, cable, mooring rope.

baltar adj. wild, fruitless (vines).

cepa ~ wild or fruitless vine.

báltico adj. Baltic.

baluarte s. m. 1. fortress, stronghold, bulwark, fortification. 2. bastion. 3. (fig.) shelter, refuge. 4. support, stay, prop.

baluda s. f. (also **bocuda**) large-bore gun.

baludo adj. (Braz.) rich, wealthy.

balurdo s. m. big screw pressing down the stone of an oil-press.

balustrino s. m. pair of compasses for drawing small circles.

balzaquiana s. f. (Braz.) woman about 30 years. ‖ adj. of or referring to such a woman.

balzaquiano adj. of or referring to Balzac.

bamba (I) s. f. (also **bambúrrio**) 1. unexpected gain at a game. 2. unexpected piece of good luck. 3. chance.

bamba (II) s. m. 1. expert. 2. bigwig. 3. m. + f. (Braz., sl.) bully, rowdy. ‖ adj. m. + f. braggart, boastful, rowdy.

bambá s. m. 1. oil-lees, dregs (from nuts of the African oil palm). 2. Negro dance. 3. game of cards. 4. disorder, confusion. 5. any dance that ends in disorder. 6. (S. Braz.) a game played by cattle herders with four halves of peach-stones.

bambaleadura s. f., **bambaleamento** m. oscillation, swinging or rocking movement, wavering, dangle.

bambaleante adj. m. + f. swinging, rocking, reeling.

bambalear v. 1. to swing, oscillate. 2. to waggle, waddle, wobble, dangle. 3. to be unstable or insecure.

a criança bambaleava no balanço the child swung up and down on the swing.

bambalhão adj. (pl. **-ões**) (f. **-ona**) 1. slack. 2. weak, languid. 3. undecided, irresolute. 4. lazy, indolent.

bambalhona s. f. slut, slattern.

bambambã s. m. (Braz.) = **bamba** (II).

bambão s. m. (pl. **-ões**) 1. plant of the family Solanaceae and its edible fruit. 2. swing. 3. core of the jack (fruit of the jaca- or jack-tree). 4. slack cord.

a ~ (coll.) 1. in large quantities. 2. extraordinarily.

bambaquerê s. m. 1. = **bambá** (2.). 2. disorder, confusion. 3. country dance also called **fandango**.

bambar v. 1. to weaken, enfeeble. 2. to slacken, loosen.

bambaré s. m. 1. clamour, loud bawling, screaming. 2. brawl, noisy quarrel or confusion.

bambê s. m. narrow strip of brake which delimits and separates different plots.

bambear v. 1. to weaken, enfeeble. 2. to slacken, make or become less taut. 3. (fig.) to vacillate, falter.

bambeza s. f. 1. slackness. 2. weariness, lassitude. 3. weakness. 4. floppiness.

bambinar v. to flutter, dangle, wave (in the wind).

bambinela s. f. window curtain, portière.

bambo adj. 1. slack, loose, not tight, not taut. 2. feeble, weak, weary, tired. 3. undecided, irresolute. 4. floppy.

ficar ~ (fam.) to become disconcerted or confused, get into a tight spot.

bambochar v. (Braz.) to lark, go on a spree.

bambochata s. f. 1. painting that represents a revelry. 2. spree, lark. 3. orgy. 4. extravagance.

bambolê s. m. hula hoop.

bamboleadura s. f., **bamboleamento** s. m. = **bamboleadura**, **bamboleamento**.

bamboleante adj. (also **bambaleante**) 1. swinging. 2. dangling.

bambolear v. = **bambalear**.

bamboleio s. m. 1. swinging, wagging, oscillation. 2. flounce.

bambolim s. m. (pl. **-ins**) lambrequin, drapery covering the upper part of window curtains or portières.

bambolina s. f. (theat.) flies (pl.), drape border which covers the side-scenes and the stage ceiling.

bamboré s. m. 1. plant of the family Solanaceae. 2. its edible fruit.

bambu s. m. (bot.) bamboo. 2. bamboo-cane or bamboo-stick.

bambuada s. f. (also **bambucada**) a blow or stroke with a bamboo.

bambual s. m. (pl. **-ais**) (also **bambuzal**) bamboo thicket, bamboo plantation, bamboo grave, cane-brake.

bambu-balde s. m. (pl. **bambus-balde**) (bot.) giant bamboo.

bambucada s. f. a blow or stroke with a bamboo cane.

bambu-dourado s. m. (pl. **bambus-dourados**) (bot.) yellow bamboo.

bambueira s. f. bamboo: 1. plant. 2. shoot.

bamburral s. m. (pl. **-ais**) 1. grove of holm-oaks. 2. bamboo thicket. 3. marshy pasture ground.

bambúrrar v. (prospecting) to make an unexpected fortune or find a valuable stone.

bambúrrice s. f. encounter with good luck or fortune.

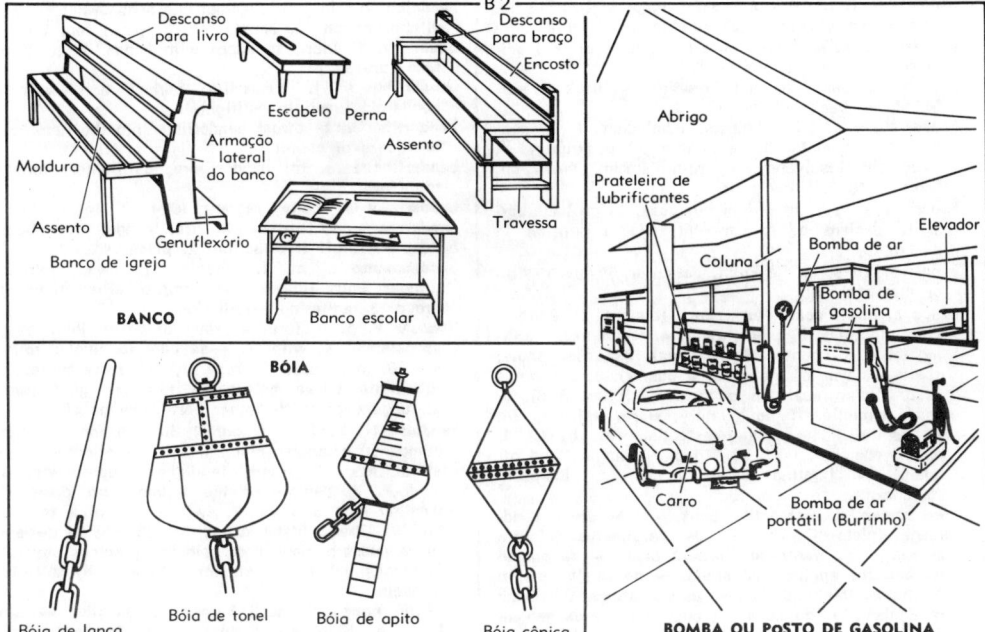

BANCO — BÓIA — BOMBA OU POSTO DE GASOLINA

bambúrrio s. m. (also **bamburro**) 1. unexpected gain, piece of good luck, lucky hit, fluke. 2. chance, hazard, casual event.

bamburrista s. m. + f. person favoured by good luck, lucky fellow or chap.

bamburro s. m. forest, thicket, copse.

bambuzinho s. m. 1. (dim. of **bambu**) a little bamboo. 2. (bot.) asparagus fern.

banal adj. m. + f (pl. **-ais**) 1. banal, trite, common, trivial, vulgar. 2. (ant.) feudatory. ‖ **~mente** adv. trivially, vulgarly, commonly, tritely, banally.

banalidade s. f. banality, triviality, vulgarity, bagatelle, commonplaceness, triteness.

banalizar v. to vulgarize, make or become common, trite, or ordinary.

banana s. f. 1. banana: a) tropical plant. b) its edible fruit. 2. (Braz., sl.) a certain obscene gesture. 3. m. weakling, ninny, coward, stupid fellow. **a preço de ~** dirt-cheap.

bananada s. f. jam of bananas in consistent form.

banana-d'água s. f. (pl. **bananas-d'água**) (bot.) = **bananeira-anã**.

banana-do-brejo s. f. (pl. **bananas-do-brejo**) (bot.) ceriman.

bananal, bananeiral s. m. (pl. **-ais**) banana grove or plantation.

banana-maçã s. f. (pl. **bananas-maçã**) (Braz., bot.) a variety of small and tasty bananas.

bananeira s. f. (bot.) banana plant. **~ que já deu cacho** (coll.) person from whom nothing more is expected. **plantar ~** (Braz. coll. gym.) to make a handstand.

bananeira-anã s. f. (pl. **bananeiras-anãs**) (bot.; also: **bananeira nanica**) dwarf banana.

bananeirinha s. f. common name for several tropical herbs of the Canna family.

bananeiro s. m. person who sells bananas.

bananicultor s. m. banana planter.

bananinha s. f. 1. dim. of banana. 2. cooky in the form of bananas.

bananosa s. f. (Braz., sl.) embarrassment.

bananose s. f. banana flour.

banazola, bananzola s. m. + f. 1. weakling, wash-out. 2. good-for-nothing, simpleton, mug, duffer, bonehead.

banca s. f. 1. table, writing-table, desk, bureau. 2. bureau, business office. 3. a lawyer's office and profession. 4. board of examiners, bench of court. 5. game of hazard. 6. stake(s) in gambling, pool. 7. (Braz.) dinner-table. 8. newspaper stall, (U. S. A.) newsstand. 9. (Port.) tripod. **~ de examinadores** examining board. **~ de feirante** market-stall. **~ de jornais** newsstand. **~ dos jurados** jury-box. **~ de livros** bookstall. **abafar a ~** to overcome all opponents, to gain a complete victory. **abrir** or **pôr a ~** to establish a lawyer's office. **levar a ~ à glória**. 1. to sweep the stakes. 2. to be successful all the way along. **ele quebrou a ~** he broke the bank.

bancada s. f. 1. row of seats, group of benches. 2. persons seated on benches. 3. (parl.) group of representatives of a state or political party who sit together in Congress or Senate. 4. workbench. **~ de escaler** thwart. **~ de prova** (tech.) testing bench. **~ do torno** lathe bed. **~ geral** unreserved seats in a stadium or circus.

bancal s. m. (pl. **-ais**) 1. cloth to cover a bench, bench cloth, bench carpet. 2. (tech.) pillowblock, plummer, plummerblock.

bancar v. 1. to keep the bank (in gambling), hold the stakes. 2. to pretend to be, dissimulate, sham, play. **~ o cavalheiro** to play the gentleman. **~ o mandão** to lord it. **~ o palhaço** to make a fool of o. s. **deixe de ~ o grã-fino!** (coll.) don't give yourself airs! **ele banca o importante** he puts on airs; **ele bancou o jogo** he kept the bank.

bancaria s. f. 1. rows or great number of benches. 2. interference of Roman bankers in papal bulls.

bancário s. m. employee of a bank, bank clerk. ‖ adj. of or concerning banks. **conta -a** bank account. **crédito** ~ bank credit. **feriado** ~ bank holiday.

bancarrota s. f. 1. bankruptcy, insolvency. 2. suspension of payments. 3. declaration of bankruptcy. 4. fraudulent insolvency. 5. ruin, smash, smash-up. **fazer** ~ to turn bankrupt.

bancarrotear v. 1. to fail in business, to go bankrupt. 2. to declare o. s. bankrupt, file a petition in bankruptcy.

bancarroteiro s. m. bankrupt, defaulter, insolvent firm or merchant.

banco s. m. 1. seat, pew, bench (plate B 2). 2. footstool, footrest. 3. piano stool. 4. workbench, working table. 5. counter. 6. sand-bank, bar, reef, shoal, shelf. 7. layer of stone (in a quarry). 8. a rower's seat, sliding seat (in a rowboat) (plate B 8). 9. seat, domicile. 10. ambulatory, ward, infirmary (in a hospital). 11. banking establishment, bank. 12. privy, chamber pot. 13. (geol.) alluvial land or island. 14. floating iceblocks, drift-ice, ice-pack. 15. cockpit.
~ **comercial** mercantile bank. ~ **de areia** sand-bank (plate C 19). ~ **de carpinteiro** joiner's bench. ~ **de desconto** discount bank. ~ **de ensaio de motores** engine test stand. ~ **de igreja** pew in a church (plate B 2). ~ **da Inglaterra** the Bank of England. ~ **de nuvens** cloud bank. ~ **de sangue** blood bank. ~ **das testemunhas** witness-box. ~ **emissor** bank of issue. **ainda hei de vê-lo no** ~ **dos réus** I wish to see him in the (prisioner's) dock. **ela está no** ~ **da paciência** she suffers with patience. **filial de** ~ branch bank.

banco-d'água s. m. (pl. **bancos-d'água**) (Braz.) small waterfall, cascade.

banco de fusos s. m. (tech.) jack-frame.

bancroftíase, bancroftose s. f. (med.) bancroftosis.

banda (I) s. f. 1. side, flank. 2. shore, bank. 3. (her.) diagonal stripe in an escutcheon. 4. band, strip, stripe. 5. trimming, border (on a dress). 6. officer's belt, waistband, shoulder-belt. 7. scarf, sash. 8. band of musicians, streetband. 9. simultaneous discharge of guns, broadside. 10. backside, rear. 11. party. 12. zone, part. 13. beam.
~ **marcial** brass band. ~ **de frequência**, ~ **de onda** (radio) frequency range, band of wave length. ~ **de rodagem** tread (of a tire). ~ **transportadora** endless belt. **à** ~ inclined. **à maneira de** ~ scarf-wise. **comer da** ~ **podre** to do strenuous work, endure hardships. **da outra** ~ on the other side. **dar a** ~ to career (ship). **desta** ~ on this side. **ele correu para estas** ~**s** he ran this way, in this direction. **ficar de cara à** ~ to be taken aback. **mandar à outra** ~ to throw s. o. out. **pôr de** ~ 1. to lay aside, save. 2. to abandon. **sair de** ~ (Braz.) to take o. s. off. **ter** ~ to career (ship). **três por** ~ three on each side. **um navio que tem muita** ~ a ship careening to her bearings. **de** ~ **a** ~ through (and through).

banda (II) s. f. = **bando**.

banda (III) s. f. fabric woven by the natives of Portuguese Guinea.

bandada s. f. flight (flock) of birds.

bandado adj. (her.) banded, striped.

bandagem s. f. (pl. **-ens**) 1. (surg.) dressing, bandaging, ligature. 2. compress.
~ **de roda** tyre, tire.

bandalheira, bandalhice s. f. mean action, ridiculous, uncouth or improper proceeding, shabby trick.

bandalho s. m. 1. ragamuffin, scoundrel, scamp, villain, rascal. 2. shred, rag. 3. (ant.) fop, dandy.

bandar v. 1. (her.) to adorn with bands. 2. to trim, face (dresses).

bandarilha s. f. banderilla: barbed dart with a banderole (used in bullfights).

bandarilhar v. to thrust banderillas into the neck and shoulders of a bull.

bandarilheiro s. m. banderillero, bullfighter, torero, toreador.

bandarra s. f. loafer, vagrant, idler.

bandarrear v. to lead an idle life, lounge, hang about.

bandas s. f. pl. 1. direction. 2. place, site.

bandeamento s. m. 1. grouping, groupage, joining, joinder, entry (into a club, etc.). 2. alliance, union, group. 3. agitation, oscillation.

bandear v. 1. to form a group or party, join, gang, associate o. s. with. 2. ~**-se com** to cluster round s. o. 3. to consider or regard (from every angle). 4. to agitate, shake, balance. 5. to cross, go beyond. 6. to go over to the other party, change sides.

bandeira (I) s. f. 1. colour(s), flag, banner, ensign, standard, labarum (plate L 2). 2. reflector of a street lamp. 3. (archit.) fan-light. 4. upper wing of a door. 5. panicle of the Indian corn plant. 6. weather-vane or cock. 7. switch-lever of a taximeter. 8. (Braz., hist.) expedition (to the hinterland in conquest of new land, gold and precious stones). 9. (zool.) a kind of anteater with a bushy tail. 10. transom.
~ **de armador** (naut.) burgee, house flag. ~ **dos E. U. A.** Stars and Stripes. ~ **de janela** transom (plate J 1). ~ **de parlamentar** flag of truce. ~ **de partida** (naut.) blue-peter. ~ **de quarentena** (naut.) quarantine flag. ~ **nacional** national flag (plate L 2). ~ **negra** the black or pirate flag, Jolly Roger black jack. ~**s de sinais** signal flags. **arriar a** ~ 1. to strike the colours. 2. (fig.) to yield, acknowledge a defeat. **arvorar, içar a** ~ to hoist the flag. **arvorar a** ~ **a meio-pau** to hoist the flag at half-mast, (E. U. A.) haul the flag to half-staff. **baixaram a** ~ they lowered their colours. **com** ~**s desfraldadas** with flying colours. **cobrir com a** ~ **da misericórdia** to cover up, conceal under the cloak of charity. **comunicar por meio de** ~**s** to flagwag. **desfile de** ~**s** trooping of the colours. **mostrar a** ~ **branca** to show the white flag. **rir às** ~**s despregadas** to have a good laugh. **saudar com a** ~ to dip the flag. **virar a** ~ to change sides.

bandeira (II) s. m. (also **bandeirista**) (railway) signalman, signaller.

bandeirada s. f. basic fare indicated by taximeters.

bandeirante s. m. (Braz., hist.) member of the expeditions called **bandeiras** (see **bandeira I,** 8.) ‖ adj. of, pertaining to or related to the **bandeiras**.

bandeirar v. (Braz.) 1. to take part in a campaign or expedition. 2. (hist.) to chase or capture Indians.

bandeireiro s. m. manufacturer or seller of flags and standards.

bandeirinha s. f. 1. (dim. of **bandeira**) little flag, streamer, pennant. 2. (mus.) hook (plate N 1). 3. s. m.: a) (fig.) political busybody. b) (ftb., ten.) linesman, touch judge.

bandeirismo, bandeirantismo s. m. (Braz.) the history and principles of expeditions, called **bandeiras**.

bandeirista s. m. 1. = **bandeirante**. 2. = **bandeira** (II).

bandeirístico adj. referring to the **bandeiras**.

bandeiro adj. 1. seditious, insurgent. 2. fickle, inconstant, unreliable. 3. partial, prejudiced, unjust.

bandeirola s. f. 1. (banderol(e), streamer, signal-flag. 2. fringed banderol of a trumpet. 3. standard, gonfalon. 4. little flag, pennant, pennon. 5. (surv.) surveyor's pole.

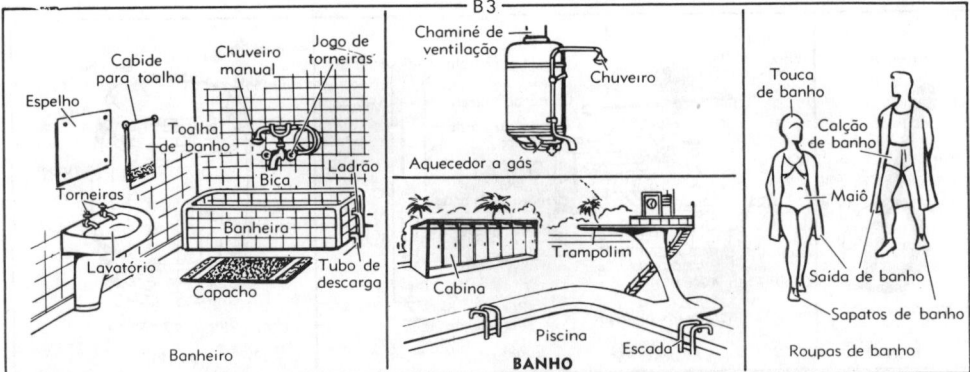

B3

Espelho · Cabide para toalha · Chuveiro manual · Jogo de torneiras · Chaminé de ventilação · Chuveiro · Touca de banho

Toalha de banho · Bica · Ladrão · Aquecedor a gás · Calção de banho

Torneiras · Banheira · Maiô

Lavatório · Capacho · Tubo de descarga · Cabina · Trampolim · Saída de banho · Sapatos de banho

Banheiro · Piscina · Escada · Roupas de banho

BANHO

---

bandeirologia s. f. study of the history of the **bandeiras (bandeira I,** 8).

bandeja s. f. 1. tray, salver, board (plate R 5). 2. winnowing-fan. 3. (naut.) kid, a sailor's mess tub. ~ **para banho revelador** developing tray (plate F 6). ~ **para chá** tea-tray.

bandejar v. to winnow (wheat, rye, etc.).

bandeta s. f. strip of metal.

bandidaço s. m. (augm. of **bandido**) bandit, dangerous outlaw.

bandido s. m. 1. bandit, outlaw, brigand, gangster. 2. robber, highwayman.

banditismo s. m. (also **bandidismo**) 1. brigandism, bringandage, ruffianism. 2. banditry, robbery.

bando s. m. 1. party, group, faction. 2. multitude, crowd. 3. gang, mob, group of mobsters or criminals. 4. group of soldiers or guerrillamen. 5. flock, band, flight, herd. 6. proclamation. ~ **de meninas** a bevy of girls. ~ **de perdizes** a flock or flight of partridges. **tomar ~ por alguém** to side with someone. **tomar** or **fazer ~ por si** to lead a faction or party. **eles vêm em ~s** they come in flocks (or floods).

bandó s. m. coiffure lying close on either side of the forehead.

bandola (I) s. f. 1. shoulder-belt, cartridge-belt. 2. (naut.) emergency sail.

bandola (II) s. f. (mus.) a kind of big mandolin.

bandoleira s. f. 1. bandoleer, bandolier, shoulder-belt, baldric. 2. rifle strap, gun sling.

bandoleirismo s. m. 1. life and ways of a bandit. 2. brigandism, brigandage.

bandoleiro s. m. 1. bandit, brigand, outlaw. 2. stray dog. 3. inconstant lover, fickle person. 4. sharper, rogue. ‖ adj. 1. inconstant, fickle. 2. idle, lazy. 3. vagrant, wayward. 4. stray (cattle).

bandoleta s. f. (mus.) small mandolin.

bandolim s. m. (pl. **-ins**) (mus.) mandolin.

bandolina s. f. bandoline (pomade for hairdressing).

bandolinista s. m. + f. mandolin player.

bandônion, bandônio s. m. (mus.) bandonion, large concertina.

bandoria s. f. (ant.) 1. group of rioters, mutineers or insurgents. 2. rebellion, insurrection.

bandulho s. m. (hum.) pounch, belly. **encher o ~** to fill the belly.

bandurra s. f. (mus.) bandore (kind of guitar with a short finger board).

bandurrear v. 1. to play the bandore. 2. (fig.) to idle, lounge. 3. (fig.) to frolic, make merry.

bandurrilha, bandurrinha s. f. 1. (mus.) small kind of bandore. 2. (fig.) vagrant, scamp.

bandurrista s. m. + f. bandore player.

banga (I) s. f. (Braz.) hut, hovel, cabin.

banga (II) interj. (ironic or depr.) there! that is that!

bangalafumenga s. m. (pl. **bangalafumengas**) (Braz., coll.) unimportant person, Jack Sauce, Jack Sprat.

bangalô s. m. bungalow.

bangue, bango s. m. 1. (bot.) Indian hemp. 2. its leaves, chewed by Indians as stimulant.

bangüê s. m. 1. litter, bier, stretcher. 2. handbarrow. 3. liana-made handbarrow (to transport husks of sugar-cane). 4. tile-paved drain (sugar mill). 5. furnace and boiling pans (sugar mill). 6. sugar-cane plantation and sugar mill (collectively). 7. leather-covered sedan chair. 8. leather trough used for washing and curing raw hides.

bangue-bangue s. m. (pl. **bangue-bangues**) 1. (cin.) Western. 2. riot, shooting.

bangueiro s. m. 1. (Braz.) person intoxicated from **bangue**. 2. (fig.) drunkard, boozer.

bangüeiro s. m. (Braz.) mash-master: man who prepares the juice of sugar-cane.

banguela, benguela s. m. + f. (also **banguelo** m.) 1. (Braz.) toothless or gap-toothed person 2. (fig.) stammerer, stutterer. ‖ adj. 1. gap-toothed. 2. stammering, stuttering.

banguelê s. m. (Braz.) 1. disorder, row, brawl. 2. revolt, insurrection, mutiny.

bangüezeiro s. m., **bangüezista** m. + f. proprietor of a sugar-cane plantation with sugar-mill.

banguina s. f. (N. Braz.) mare.

bangula s. f. (Braz.) fisherboat.

bangulê s. m. (Braz.) Negro dance.

banha s. f. 1. lard, fat, drippings. 2. pomatum, pomade. 3. adulation, flattery.

banhadal s. m. marshland, extensive swamp.

banhado s. m. marsh, swamp, bog.

banhar v. 1. to bathe, take a bath, wash. 2. to inundate, flood, cover (with water or any other liquid). 3. to wet, moisten. 4. to flow or run along (the banks, or shore). 5. (poet.) to lave. 6. to sprinkle water. 7. to soak, imbibe. 8. to dip, plunge, submerge. 9. (fig.) to envelop. ~ **em pranto** to dissolve in tears. **a criança estava banhada em lágrimas** the child was drowned in tears. **ele banhava-se em água-de-rosas** he was entranced in his bliss. **ele está banhado de suor** he is in a bath of perspiration. **um rio banha o sopé da colina** a river washes the foot of the hill. **o sol banhava a paisagem em raios dourados** the sun imbued the landscape with golden rays.

B 4

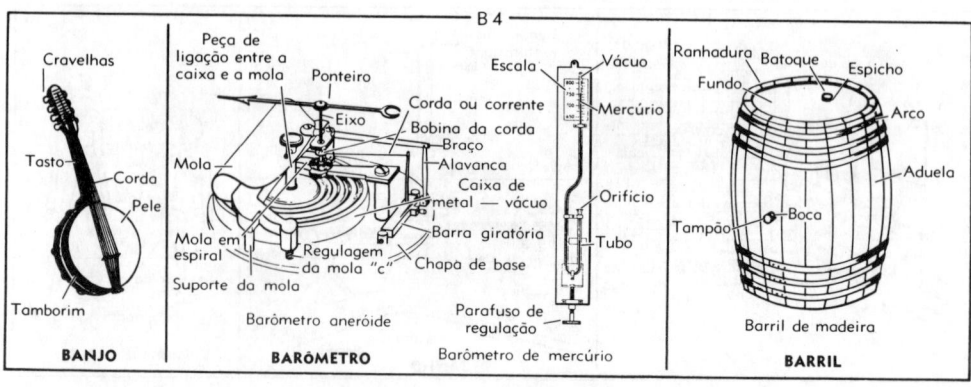

Cravelhas · Tasto · Corda · Pele · Tamborim · **BANJO**

Peça de ligação entre a caixa e a mola · Ponteiro · Eixo · Mola · Mola em espiral · Regulagem da mola "c" · Suporte da mola · Barômetro aneróide · **BARÔMETRO**

Escala · Vácuo · Corda ou corrente · Mercúrio · Bobina da corda · Braço · Alavanca · Caixa de metal — vácuo · Orifício · Barra giratória · Tubo · Chapa de base · Parafuso de regulação · Barômetro de mercúrio

Ranhadura · Batoque · Espicho · Fundo · Arco · Aduela · Tampão · Boca · Barril de madeira · **BARRIL**

---

banheira s. f. 1. female bathing attendant. 2. bath-tub, bath. 3. (phot.) developing tray.

banheiro s. m. 1. bathing attendant. 2. bath-keeper. 3. bath-tub (plate B 3). 4. bathroom, bath, lavatory, washroom (plate B 3). 5. closet, toilet.

banhista (I) s. m. + f. 1. bather, visitor of a seaside resort or a watering-place (plate P 17). 2. bathing attendant.

banhista (II) s. m. + f. (fig.) flatterer, adulator.

banho (I) s. m. 1. bathing, bath, bathe (plate B 3). 2. bathing place, health- or seaside-resort, bathroom. 3. water or any other medium for bathing. 4. (chem.) vessel used for immersion. 5. ~s pl. therapeutic baths. 6. English military order. ~ de ar air bath. ~ de areia sand bath. ~ de assento hip-bath. ~ de chuveiro showerbath. ~ de cobrear copper(ing) bath. ~ de decapagem pickling bath. ~ de imersão dip, tub. ~ de lama mud bath. ~ de mar bathe. ~ de sol sun-bath. ~ de vapor steam bath. ~ turco Turkish bath. **acidente de** ~ bathing fatality. **calção de** ~ bathing drawers. **Cavaleiros do Banho** Knights of the Bath. **roupa de** ~ bathing costume. **vá tomar ~!** (coll.) leave me alone! go to hell!

banho (II) s. m. (usually in pl., esp. in Braz.) banns. **correr os** ~s to ask (call, publish) the banns.

banho (III) s. m. 1. prison. 2. galley (punishment).

banho-da-igreja s. m. (pl. **banhos-da-igreja**) (Braz., fam.) marriage, wedlock.

banho-maria s. m. (pl. **banhos-maria**) (cul., chem.) water-bath.

banido s. m. exile, outlaw, outcast. ‖ adj. banished, outlawed, excluded.

banimento s. m. 1. banishment, exile, expatriation. 2. proscription. 3. expulsion.

banir v. 1. to banish, expatriate, exile. 2. to outlaw, proscribe. 3. to expel, eliminate, exclude, expulse.

banível adj. (pl. **-íveis**) subject to or deserving banishment.

banja s. f. cardsharping, swindle (at gambling).

banjista s. m. + f. cardsharper, gambling cheat. ‖ adj. swindling, fraudulent (at cards or gambling).

banjo s. m. (mus.) banjo (plate B 4).

banjoísta s. m. + f. banjo player, banjoist.

banqueiro s. m. 1. banker, bank manager or director. 2. (gambling) keeper of the bank, dealer, croupier. 3. rich man, capitalist, financier. 4. exchanger. 5. (Braz.) night stoker in a cane-sugar mill. 6. a butcher's chopping block or bench.

banqueta s. f. 1. little bench, footstool (plate D 4). 2. row of candlesticks and the crucifix of an altar; the shelf on which they stand. 3. (fort.) banquette (platform along the inside of a parapet). 4. sidewalk.

banquete s. m. banquet, cerimonious feast, sumptuous dinner. **o** ~ **sagrado** the Lord's supper. **dar um** ~ to banquet.

banqueteador s. m. banqueter.

banquetear v. 1. to banquet, junket. 2. to feast, regale. 3. to spend a lot of money for festivities, food or drinks. ~ **alguém** to give a banquet in honour of s. o.

banquinho s. m. little bench, footstool, cricket, stool (plate C 2).

banquisa s. f. pack-ice, floe.

banto s. m. (ethn.) Bantu. ‖ adj. Bantu.

banza s. f. (coll.) small guitar, viola.

banzado adj. 1. surprised, astonished, amazed. 2. disappointed, disconcerted, perturbed. **ficar** ~ to be beside o. s., to be struck dumb (with).

banzar v. 1. to frighten, scare. 2. to surprise, amaze. 3. to disappoint, disconcert. 4. to ponder, meditate, brood.

banzativo adj. pensive, pondering, meditative.

banzé s. m. (pop.) 1. noise, brawl, disorder. 2. popular festival, tumultuous feast.

banzear v. 1. to balance, move to and fro, shake, toss. 2. to be choppy (sea).

banzeiro s. m. 1. heavy swell. 2. strong wind. 3. (Braz.) breakers (breaking waves). 4. tumult, agitation. ‖ adj. 1. choppy (sea). 2. drawn (game, play). 3. sad, melancholic. 4. tipsy, unsteady, staggering.

banzo s. m. 1. deadly melancholy of African Negroes. 2. day-dreaming. ‖ adj. (Braz.) 1. sad, sorrowful. 2. depressed, dejected. 3. pensive, pondering. 4. surprised.

banzos s. m. pl. 1. the sidepieces of a ladder (plate E 6). 2. sideboards of an embroidering frame. 3. stretcher handles.

baobá s. m. (bot.) baobab, monkey-bread.

baonesa, baionesa s. f. a sort of big sweet apple. ‖ adj. of or pertaining to this sort of apples.

baquara s. m. + f. cunning, shrewd person. ‖ adj. clever, cunning, shrewd.

baque s. m. 1. thud. 2. fall, tumble, collision. 3. sudden disaster, break-down, collapse. 4. distrust, suspicion, misgiving. 5. (Braz.) moment, instant.

baquear v. 1. to fall (esp. noisily), thud. 2. to ruin o. s., fail. 3. to convince s. o. 4. to fling o. s. down, prostrate o. s.

baquelita s. f. bakelite.

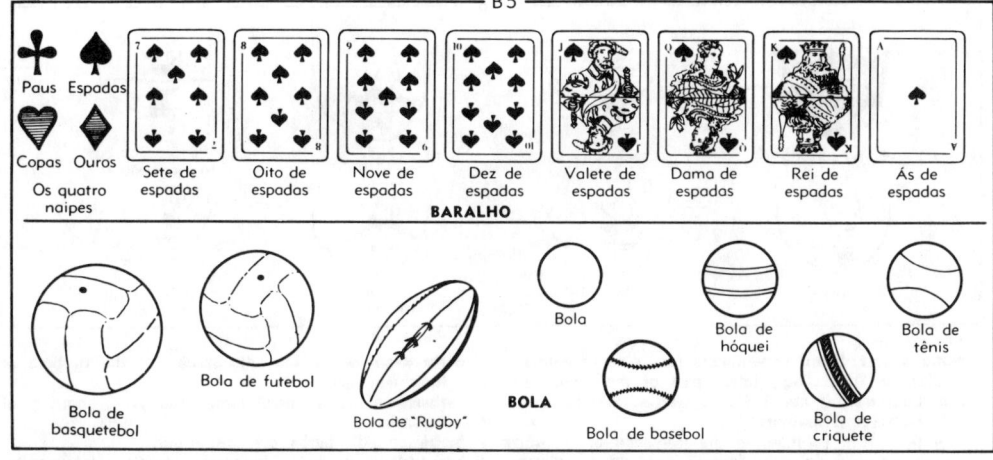

B 5

Paus — Espadas — Copas — Ouros — Os quatro naipes — Sete de espadas — Oito de espadas — Nove de espadas — Dez de espadas — Valete de espadas — Dama de espadas — Rei de espadas — Ás de espadas

BARALHO

Bola de basquetebol — Bola de futebol — Bola de "Rugby" — Bola — Bola de baseból — Bola de hóquei — Bola de criquete — Bola de tênis

BOLA

baquerubu s. m. tree of the family Leguminosae.
baqueta (ê) s. f. 1. drum-stick. 2. rib (U. S. A.) or spoke of a sunshade.
baquetar, baquetear v. to drum, beat the drum.
báquico adj. 1. Bacchic, Bacchical. 2. bacchantic, bacchanal(ian), orgiastic.
baquio s. m. (poet.) bacchius: metrical foot of one short and two long syllables.
baquiqui s. m. (Braz., zool.) eatable mollusc.
baquista s. m. + f. drunkard, tippler, reveller. || adj. drunk, tipsy, revelling, orgiastic.
baquité s. m. (Braz.) a kind of basket (of lianes or bamboo).
bar s. m. 1. bar, counter. 2. bar-room, tap-room, beer-shop, ale-house, (U. S. A.) soloon (plate R 5).
baraço s. m. 1. string, cord, tape. 2. halter.
estar com o ~ na garganta to be pressed, forced. por ~ forcedly. por um abraço dar um ~ to pay with ingratitude.
barafunda s. f. 1. throng, crowd, multitude. 2. noise, clamour. 3. tumult, disorder, confusion. 4. mess, hodgepodge. 5. nonplus. 6. ~s pl. kind of lacework.
barafustar v. 1. to enter by force, burst in. 2. to meddle, interfere. 3. to move about excitedly, struggle with feet and hands, quiver.
baragnose s. f. (path.) baragnosis.
barajuba s. f. forest tree (Amazon region).
baralha s. f. 1. (cards) pack of cards. 2. clamour, confusion. 3. intrigue. 4. (horse) single foot.
jogar com toda a ~ to set all wheels agoing. meter alguém na ~ to kipper s. o.
baralhada s. f. 1. disorder, confusion, tumult. 2. = barafunda.
baralhador s. m. 1. horse going in the single foot pace. 2. shuffler (of cards). 3. disturber, entangler.
baralhamento s. m. 1. shuffle, shuffling of cards. 2. confusion, disorder. 3. entanglement. 4. ambling pace.
baralhar v. 1. to shuffle (cards). 2. to disorder, disturb, confuse. 3. to confound, entangle. 4. to ride in the baralha pace. 5. ~-se to become confused or embarrassed.
~ uma proposta to reject a proposal. ele baralhou as cartas he shuffled the cards. eles ~am o negócio they made the matter intricate. eles ~am as suas pretensões they crossed them in their designs.
baralho s. m. pack of playing cards (plate B 5).

barambaz s. m. (fam.) anything hanging down like drapery or a valance.
barandar s. m. outrigger.
barangandá s. m. = balangandá.
barão s. m. (pl. -ões) 1. baron. 2. (ant.) distinguished person, feudal lord. 3. variety of cotton. 4. banneret.
barata (I) s. f. 1. (ent.) cockroach, black beetle. 2. (mot., also **baratinha**) convertible coupé seating two persons. 3. (Braz.) albino.
barata (II) s. f. churn.
barata-d'água s. f. (pl. **baratas-d'água**) (ent.) aquatic bug of the family Belostomatidae.
barata-de-sacristia s. f. (pl. **baratas-de-sacristia**) (pop.) devote; old, devote churchgoer (esp. woman).
baratar v. (ant.) to destroy.
barataria s. f. 1. gift offered with a view to an advantageous recompense. 2. barratry. 3. (com.) speculation, barter.
barateamento, baratelo s. m. fall of (in) prices.
baratear v. 1. to sell at a low price or at an under-price. 2. to undervalue, underestimate, despise. 3. to grant or concede easily. 4 to become cheaper, depreciate, lower, cheapen.
o leite barateou milk is down
barateiro s. m. 1. merchant who sells cheap. 2. spoiler of the market, underseller. 3. street vendor. || adj. moderate in price, cheap.
barateza s. f. cheapness, inexpensiveness, moderateness.
baratinado adj. (Braz., sl.) embarrassed, perplexed, confused.
baratinar v. to embarrass, perplex, confuse.
baratinha s. f. (Braz.) 1. (bot.) forest tree (Cassia fastuosa Wild.). 2. (zool.) wood-louse, sow-bug. 3. (mot.) convertible coupé for two persons.
barato s. m. 1. card-money. 2. percentage the croupier pays the owner of a gambling house. 3. concession, favour, benefit. 4. easiness, readiness. || adj. cheap. || adv. cheaply, at a low price.
dar de ~ to grant, admit readily. fazer bem ~ to sell under price. pôr a vida a ~ to risk one's life. valer ~ to be cheap.
baratômetro s. m. thermometer used in butter-making.
barátrico adj. abysmal, precipiced.
báratro s. m. 1. precipice, abyss. 2. (fig.) hell.
baraúna s. f. (Braz.) brauna, tree of the family Caesalpiniaceae.

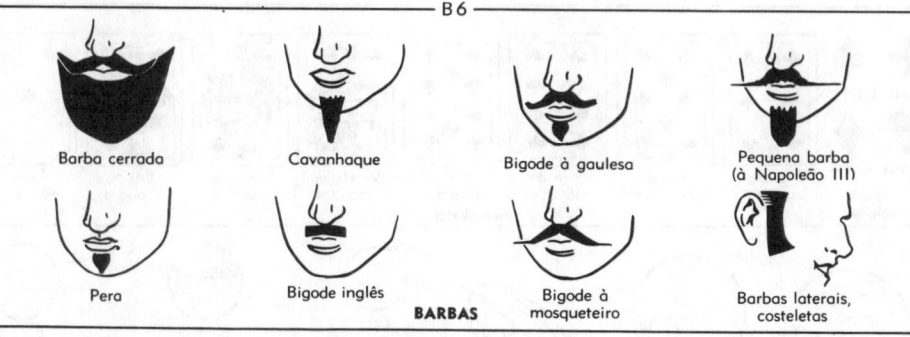

— B 6 —

Barba cerrada   Cavanhaque   Bigode à gaulesa   Pequena barba (à Napoleão III)

Pera   Bigode inglês   Bigode à mosqueteiro   Barbas laterais, costeletas

BARBAS

barba s. f. 1. beard or whiskers (pl., also of animals) (plate B 6). 2. (fig.) lower part of the face, chin. 3. barb awn (plate E 9). 4. wattle. 5. whalebone. 6. barb (of a feather).
~ a ~ face to face, in the presence of. ~ **curta** stubbles. ~**s de gato** feelers. ~**s de pena** bane, web. **à ~** in the presence of (somebody). **à custa da longa** ~ (to get s. th.) without working, at father's expense. **com** ~**s grisalhas** grey-bearded. **cortei a** ~ **dele** I shaved off his beard. **estojo de** ~ shaving set. **fazer** ~ **medrosa** to show fear. **fazer tremer a** ~ **a alguém** to intimidate, dispirit somebody. **fui fazer a** ~ I got shaved. **navalha de** ~ razor. **pincel de** ~ shaving brush. **por favor, faça-me a** ~ give me a shave, please. **sabão para** ~ shaving stick or soap. **sem** ~ smooth-faced. **ter a** ~ **tesa** to resist, withstand.
barba-azul s. m. (pl. **barbas-azuis** or **barba-azuis**) Bluebeard.
barbacã s. f. (fort.) barbican (outer defensive work).
barbaças, barbacena s. m. long-bearded man, long-beard, greybeard.
barbaçudo adj. thickly bearded.
barbada s. f. 1. lower lip of a horse. 2. (turf, sport) walk-over, easy victory.
barba-de-baleia s. f. (pl. **barbas-de-baleia**) 1. whalebone. 2. (Braz., naut.) small sail on the bowsprit.
barba-de-bode, barba-de-cabra s. m. (pl. **barbas-de--bode, barbas-de-cabra**) 1. man with a goatee beard. 2. f. (bot.) goat's-beard.
barba-de-pau s. m. (pl. **barbas-de-pau**) (bot.) long-moss, Florida moss.
barbadiano s. m. Barbadian, a native or inhabitant of Barbados. || adj. Barbadian.
barbadinho s. m. 1. (pop.) (bearded) Franciscan monk. 2. fresh-water fish of the family Loricariidae. 3. = **quiabo bravo.**
barbado (I) adj. 1. bearded, whiskered, barbed. 2. barbate (also bot.).
barbado (II) s. m. 1. wine twig, new roots. 2. fresh-water fish of the family Siluridae.
barbado (III) s. m. + f. (Braz.) member of an Indian tribe of Mato Grosso. || adj. of or pertaining to this tribe.
barbalhada s. f. thick beard.
bárbalho s. m. rootlet, rootling, radicle.
barbalhoste adj. 1. downy bearded, fluffy. 2. (pop.) frail, disregarded, weakly. 3. insignificant, trifling.
barbante s. m. (pack)thread, twine, string.
barbaquim s. m. (pl. **-ins**) brace and bit, bit brace.
barbar v. 1. to beard, begin to have a beard. 2. to begin to strike rootlets.
bárbara (I) s. f. powder-room.
bárbara (II) s. f. (logic) barbara.

barbaresco, barbarisco adj. Berber, of the Berbers or their language.
barbaria s. f. 1. barbarism, cruelty. 2. hordes of barbarians.
barbárico adj. barbaric, rude, cruel.
barbaridade s. f. 1. barbarity, cruelty, inhumanity. 2. (fig.) gross mistake, inaptitude, absurdness, absurdity.
ele diz ~**s** he talks nonsense.
barbárie s. f. barbarity, inhumanity.
barbarismo s. m. barbarism: 1. incorrect use of words or phrases. 2. foreign words used in the vernacular. 3. savagery, cruelty, barbarity, barbarousness.
barbarizar v. 1. to barbarize. 2. to become or make barbarous, brutalize. 3. to treat brutally. 4. to corrupt the language, use barbarisms.
~ **os costumes** to corrupt morals.
bárbaro s. m. 1. barbarian. 2. ~**s** pl. (hist.) invaders of the Roman empire, coming from the north. || adj. barbarous, uncivilized, rude, coarse, rough, brutal, savage. || **barbaramente** adv. barbarously, savagely.
barbarolexia s. f. (rhet.) 1. a compound of a vernacular word together with a foreign word. 2. wrong pronunciation of foreign words.
barbarrão s. m. (pl. **-ões**) long-bearded man.
barba-ruiva s. m. (pl. **barbas-ruivas**) (Braz.) goblin, forest sprite.
barbasco s. m. (bot.) 1. great mullein. 2. golden cudweed, goldenlocks.
barbata s. f. toothless part of a horse's mouth where the bit sits.
barbatana s. f. fin (of a fish), whalebone, baleen, flipper.
~ **anal, caudal e dorsal** anal, caudal and dorsal fin (plate P 7). ~ **de espartilho** busk. ~ **peitoral** pectoral fin (plate P 7). ~ **pélvica** pelvic fin (plate P 7). ~ **pequena** pinnule. **pôr** ~**s** to bone.
barbatão s. m. (pl. **-ões**) wildling, stray cattle, grown wild.
barbato s. m. long-bearded lay brother. || adj. bearded.
barbeação (pl. **-ões**), **barbeadura** s. f. shave, shaving (plate B 7).
barbeado adj. shaven, shaved.
bem ~ clean or smooth shaven. **não** ~ unshaved.
barbeador s. m. shaver. ~ **elétrico** electric shaver.
barbear v. 1. to shave. 2. ~**se** to shave o. s. **aparelho para** ~ shaver. **jogo completo para** ~ shaving kit. **pincel para** ~ shaving brush. **por** ~ unshaved.
barbearia s. f. barber's shop, barbershop.
barbechar v. 1. to plough untilled or idle land. 2. to fallow.
barbecho s. m. (agric.) 1. fallow: ploughing, harrowing, breaking, without seeding. 2. fallow ground.

B 7

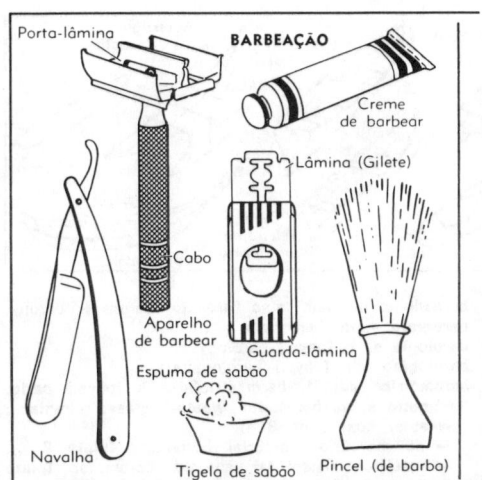

BARBEAÇÃO

Porta-lâmina
Creme de barbear
Lâmina (Gilete)
Cabo
Aparelho de barbear
Guarda-lâmina
Espuma de sabão
Navalha
Tigela de sabão
Pincel (de barba)

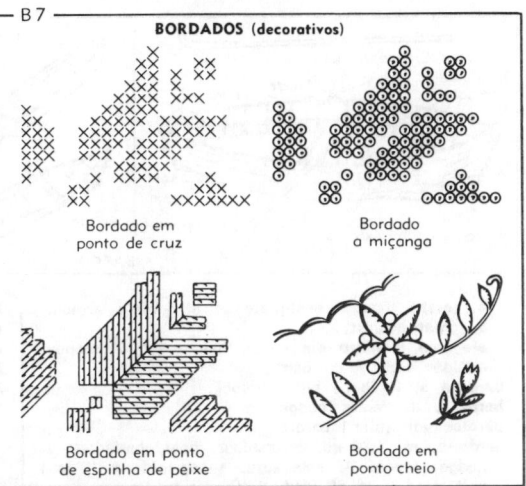

BORDADOS (decorativos)

Bordado em ponto de cruz
Bordado a miçanga
Bordado em ponto de espinha de peixe
Bordado em ponto cheio

barbeiragem s. f. (pl. -ens) (Braz., pop.) bad driving (motorcar, etc.).

barbeiro s. m. 1. barber, shaver. 2. (fig.) sharp, cutting wind. 3. bristle shearer. 4. (ent.) barbeiro: bug which transmits the trypanosome causing Chagas' disease. 5. (ichth.) surgeonfish, barberfish, tang. 6. unskilful person. 7. (pop.) inexperienced or bad driver. 8. unsuccessful hunter.

barbeirola s. m. clumsy barber.

barbeito s. m. 1. = **barbecho.** 2. earth mound or furrow (to delimit farms).

barbela s. f. 1. dewlap (plate G 1). 2. double chin. 3. curb of a bridle, curb chain (plate C 12). 4. barb (of a crochet needle, fishhook, etc.).

barbelões s. m. pl. tumours or folds under the tongue of a horse or cow.

barbete s. m. (mil.) barbette, gun platform.

barbialçado adj. bristling (beard), erected.

barbiana s. f. (Braz., sl.) a gangster's mistress.

barbicacho s. m. 1. halter. 2. (fig.) obstacle, impediment, embarrassment. 3. hat-guard, cheekstrap. 4. subordination, subjection. 5. main or principal condition (in business dealings).
pôr o ~ a alguém to hamper somebody, keep somebody under control.

barbicas, barbichas s. m., sg. + pl. 1. beardless man. 2. (fig.) insignificant person.

barbicha s. f. little or downy beard.

barbífero adj. bearded, whiskered.

barbiforme adj. beard-shaped.

barbilhão s. m. (pl. -ões) 1. wattle (poultry). 2. barbel (fish).

barbilho 1. muzzle (cover or straps). 2. flock silk, waste silk. 3. impediment, check, obstacle. 4. barb(el). 5. wattle.

barbilongo adj. long-bearded.

barbilouro adj. blond-bearded.

barbinegro adj. black-bearded.

barbino s. m. (Braz., bot.) 1. broom sedge. 2. long moss.

barbirrostro adj. having bristles on the beak or bill.

barbirruivo adj. 1. red-bearded. 2. red-feathered.

barbital s. m. (chem.) barbital.

barbiteso adj. 1. stiff-bearded. 2. (fig.) strong, resistant.

barbiturato s. m. (chem.) barbiturate.

barbitúrico adj. (chem.) barbituric.

barbitúrio s. m. (chem.) barbiture.

barbiturizar v. to treat with barbiturate: to give a soporific drug (to a race-horse).

barbo s. m. (ichth.) barbel.

barbotina s. f. (bot.) wormwood seeds.

barbudo s. m. 1. (Braz., ichth.) barbudo. 2. (ornith.) puffbird. 3. full-bearded man. ‖ adj. bearded.

bárbulas s. f. pl. barbule: lateral filament of a barb (feather).

barbuzano s. m. (bot.) ironwood (Esenbeckia leiocarpa.)

barca s. f. 1. flatboat, barge, lighter (plate B 8). 2. (naut.) log. 3. (astr.) Great Bear, Ursa Major.
~ de São Pedro the Catholic Church. **levar a ~ a bom porto** to handle s. th. skilfully, bring s. th. to a good end. **passar na ~ de Caronte** to cross the Styx, to die.

barça s. f. straw cover or lining (to protect earthenware, china, glass).

barcaça s. f. 1. barge, large bark. 2. coaster, lighter. **~ de bombeiros** fire-boat.

barcacinha s. f. (dim. of **barcaça**) small barge.

barcada s. f. boatload, boatful.

barcagem s. f. (pl. -ens) 1. freight, freightage. 2. fare, ferriage.

barcana s. f. (geog.) barchan.

barcarola s. f. (mus.) barcaro(l)le.

barcerio s. m. maker or seller of straw covers or linings for bottles, china, etc.

barco s. m. boat, bark, ship (plates B 8, 9, P 17).
~ a motor powerboat. **~ a remo** rowboat. **~ a vapor** steamship. **~ a vela** sailing ship (plate B 10). **~ costeiro** coaster, coasting vessel. **~ de assalto** storm-boat. **~ de corridas** race-boat. **~ de motor de popa** outboard-motor boat (plate L 2). **~ de passagem** ferryboat. **~ de passagem (para comboios ferroviários)** railway ferry, ferry-bridge. **~ de passeio** pleasure boat (plate L 2). **~ de pesca** fishing-boat. **~ de transporte** freighter, cargo boat. **~ desmontável** (sport) folding-boat. **~ farol** lightship. **~ salva-vidas** life-boat (plate P 17). **aguentar o ~** to face the situation. **deixar ~s e redes** to abandon house and home. **por aqui não faz o ~ água** that is not the worst of it.

barcola s. f. (usually **~s** pl.) (naut.) coamings (of the hatches).

barda s. f. 1. fence, wicker fence, hedge. 2. palling, partition. 3. plank, thick board (used as prop).

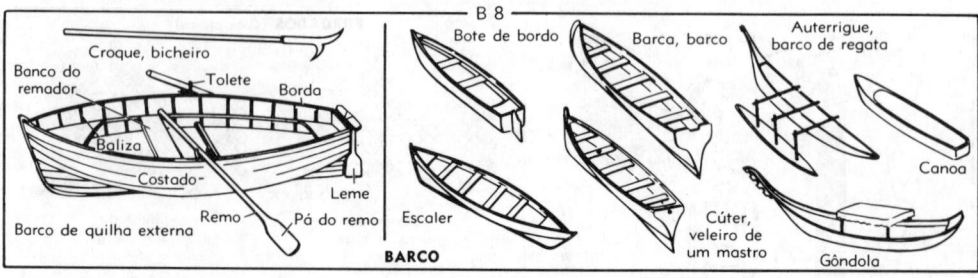

— B 8 —

Bote de bordo — Barca, barco — Auterrigue, barco de regata

Banco do remador — Croque, bicheiro — Tolete — Borda

Baliza — Costado — Remo — Pá do remo — Leme

Barco de quilha externa — Escaler — Cúter, veleiro de um mastro — Canoa — Gôndola

BARCO

4. (hist.) bard: breast-plate of a horse's armour. 5. great quantity.
ele tem dinheiro em ~ he has a lot of money. **equipar com ~** to bard.
bardana s. f. (bot.) bur, burdock.
bardar v. to fence (hedge) in.
bárdico adj. (hist.) bardic.
bardo s. m. 1. bard, troubadour, poet, balladist. 2. hedge, fence. 3. enclosure, sheep-fold. 4. (Port.) cultivated tract of land. 5. (hort.) trellis.
barestesia s. f. (med.) baresthesia.
bareta s. f. (archit.) half-round moulding.
barga s. f. 1. straw-hut, thatched cot. 2. a kind of fishing net.
bargado adj. (Braz.) 1. clever, cunning, shrewd. 2. deceitful, cheating, tricky.
barganha s. f. 1. barter, exchange. 2. (pop.) swindle, cheat, trick.
barganhar v. 1. to barter, negotiate. 2. to trade. 3. to cheat, swindle.
barganhista s. m. + f. 1. barterer, trader, dealer. 2. double-dealer, swindler.
bargantaria s. f. villainy, trickery, debauchery.
bargante s. m. (also **bragante**) 1. vagabond, vagrant. 2. rowdy, ruffian. 3. swindler, cheat.
bargantear v. (also **bragantear**) 1. to ramble, roam. 2. to loaf, idle. 3. to go about as a vagabond or tramp.
bária s. f. (phys.) bar.
bárico adj. (chem.) baric.
barifonia s. f. (med.) baryphonia, hoarseness, huskiness.
barigui s. m. (ent.) a kind of gnat.
barilha s. f. (bot.) kali, glasswort.
barimetria s. f. (phys.) barymetry.
barimétrico adj. (phys.) barymetric.
bário s. m. (chem.) barium.
bárion s. m. (nucl. phys.) baryon.
bariri s. m. (Braz.) rapids (pl.), swift current.
baririço s. m. (Braz., bot.) jalap.
barita s. f. (chem.) baryta, barium monoxide.
baritina, baritita s. f. (min.) heavy spar, barytes.
barítono s. m. barytone, baritone.
barjuleta s. f. leather bag or knapsack, purse.
barlaventeador adj. (naut.) against the wind, in the wind's eye (sailing or cruising), weatherly.
barlaventear v. (naut.) 1. to tack: sail against the wind, ply to the windward. 2. to sail in the lee of another vessel or island.
barlavento s. m. (naut.) luff, weather side (of a ship), windward, weatherboard.
conseguimos o lado a ~ we got the windward of the ship. **para ~** aweather.
barn s. m. (nucl. phys.) barn.
barnabé s. m. (Braz., pop.) public functionary or officer of lower classification.
barnabita s. m. Barnabite: priest of the order of "The Regular Clerks of St. Paul".

baroado s. m. (ant., also **baronato**) baronage, barony.
barógrafo s. m. barograph.
barologia s. f. (phys.) barology.
barológico adj. (phys.) barologic(al).
barométrico adj. 1. barometric(al). 2. (phys.) baric.
barômetro s. m. barometer, weather glass, rain-glass, weather box (plate B 4).
~ de mercúrio mercurial barometer (plate B 4). **~ metálico (aneróide)** aneroid barometer (plate B 4). **~ de Torricelli** cup barometer.
barometrografia s. f. barometrography.
barometrógrafo s. m. barometrograph.
baronato s. m. baronage, barony.
baronesa s. f. 1. baroness. 2. (Braz., bot.) water hyacinth. 3. (Braz.): a) = **cachaça**. b) **~s** pl. ear-rings.
baronete s. m. baronet (title of an English nobleman next below a baron and above a knight).
baronia s. f. barony, baronage.
baronial adj. m. + f. (pl. **-ais**) baronial.
barosânemo s. m. (phys.) anemometer, wind gauge.
baroscópio s. m. (phys.) baroscope.
barostato s. m. (phys.) barostat.
barqueira s. f. 1. wife of a ferryman. 2. woman who handles a ferryboat. 3. fishing-line with several hooks.
barqueiro s. m. boatman, ferryman, bargee, waterman.
barquejar v. 1. to govern a boat. 2. to go by boat, go boating.
barqueta s. f. small boat, barge, sloop.
barquilha s. f. (naut.) log, common log (also **barquinha**).
deitar a ~ to heave the log. **carretel da ~** reel of the log.
barquilho s. m. wafer.
barquinha s. f. 1. (naut.) log, common log. 2. small boat. 3. (aeron.) nacelle, basket (of a balloon or airship). 4. cradlelike small coffin.
salvar-se numa ~ to escape by a hair's breadth, have a narrow escape.
barquinho s. m. cockle-boat.
barra (I) s. f. 1. bar, iron bar, metal-rod, bloom. 2. bullion, ingot (of gold or silver) (plates A 2, C 11, G 3). 3. piece of wood, billet. 4. (naut.) bar of the capstan, stay-bar. 5. (print.) press-jack, sliding bar of a printing press. 6. trimming, hem (of a skirt or frock). 7. border, fringe. 8. bedstead, cot. 9. bar of a harbour entrance. 10. sandbank, sands. 11. skirting board. 12. cake of soap. 13. (gym.) horizontal bar. **~s** pl. parallel bars. 14. (her.) bendlet, bend. 15. (Braz.) bank of heavy clouds near the horizon at sunset. 16. bar of a horses's hoof (plate C 9). 17. **~s** pl. (Braz.) sunset glow, aurora. 18. prisioner's base or bar (children's game). 19. (mus.) bar. 20. fid, stick, rod. 21. rail. 22. spindle. 23. spar. 24. edging.
~ de acoplamento coupling rod. **~ de alimentação (de avanço)** feed-bar. **~ de apoio** stay-bar. **~ de**

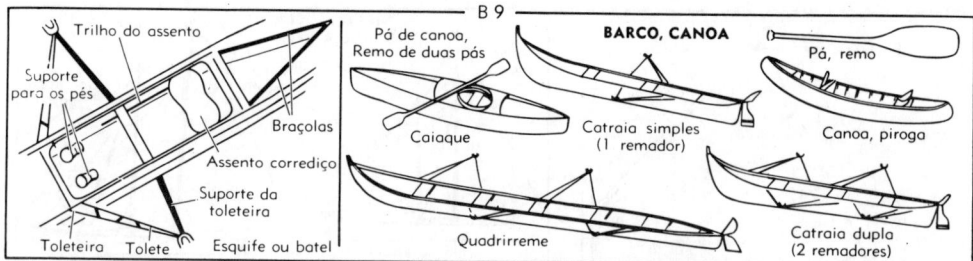

B 9

Trilho do assento
Suporte para os pés
Braçolas
Assento corrediço
Suporte da toleteira
Toleteira   Tolete   Esquife ou batel

Pá de canoa, Remo de duas pás
Caiaque

BARCO, CANOA

Catraia simples (1 remador)
Quadrirreme

Pá, remo

Canoa, piroga

Catraia dupla (2 remadores)

contato conducting pole (plate B 15). ~ **de espaços** space-bar (typewriter) (plate M 2). ~ **de grelha** fire-bar, grate-bar. ~ **do leme** (naut.) tiller. ~ **de ligação** connecting rod. ~ **de tração** draw-bar (plate C 15), sliding head (plate C 13). ~ **do tribunal** witness-box, (E. U. A.) witness-chair. ~ **de vestido** dress-trimming. ~ **fixa** horizontal bar (plates G 3, P 6). **~-manteiga** (game) chevy, chivy, chivvy. ~ **principal do arado** share beam. **~s paralelas** (gym.) parallel bars. **uma ~ de sabão** a cake of soap. **botar a ~ mais além** to work (or do) more than others, to outdo others. **de ~ a ~** all through, all the way from one end to the other. **estirar a ~** (fig.) to work hard, strive. **forma para fundir ~s** ingot-mould.

barra (II) s. m. (coll.) big shot, important person.

barraca s. f. 1. stall, tent, hut, barrack. 2. shelter, cover. 3. shed. 4. (Braz., fam.) big umbrella. 5. (Braz.) commercial firm, dealing specially in hides, leather, wool and similar products of rural industries. ~ **de lona** tent. ~ **de madeira** timber-lined shed. **estaca para ~** tent-peg. **ele montou sua ~** he pitched his tent.

barracamento s. m. camp (of barracks or tents).

barracão s. m. (pl. **-ões**) 1. large barrack or tent. 2. penthouse, shed (plate C 11). 3. awning. 4. trade post. 5. (Braz.) small store-room(s) near the market-place.

barracento, barrento adj. argillaceous, clayish.

barraco s. m. (Braz., Rio de Janeiro) hut, cottage.

barraconista s. m. (N. Braz.) proprietor of a cottage or barrack.

barracuda s. f. (Braz., ichth.) barracuda.

barradela s. f. 1. plastering, coating (walls). 2. (Braz.) obstruction, frustration. **ele deu-me uma ~** he cheated me.

barrado (I) s. m. (her.) coloured field covered with metal bars. ‖ adj. 1. striped. 2. barred.

barrado (II) adj. covered with clay or mud.

barragem s. f. (pl. **-ens**) 1. crawl, weir (for fish). 2. barrier, palisade, stockade. 3. dam, storage dam, stop wall, barrage. **fogo de ~ (de artilharia)** rolling barrage.

barral s. m. (pl. **-ais**) 1. clayish soil, clay-ground. 2. loam-pit, clay-pit.

barra-limpa s. m. + f. (pl. **barras-limpas**) a good and friendly person. ‖ adj. of or relating to such a person.

barramaque s. m. valuable antique fabric (brocade, tapestry, etc.).

barramento s. m. 1. wooden planks of a bedstead (supporting the mattress). 2. (mech.) slide bars (of a lathe).

barranceira s. f. steep bank (of a river).

barranco s. m. (also **barranca** f.) 1. rut, groove. 2. hollow, gully, gorge, ravine. 3. precipice, abrupt declivity, bank (plate C 8). 4. obstacle. 5. high and steep bank (of a river). 6. (N. Braz.) floating grass island. 7. (fig.) difficulty, impediment, bottle-neck. 8. (fig.) misfortune. **conseguir uma coisa aos trancos e ~s** to obtain something under great difficulties, by fits and starts. **meter-se em ~s** to let o. s. in for a lot of trouble.

barrancoso adj. full of ravines, declivous, gullied, rutted.

barranheira s. f. loam-pit.

barranqueira s. f. 1. (Braz.) steep bank (of a river). 2. precipice, steep slope.

barranqueiro s. m. 1. (Braz.) inhabitant of the banks of the São Francisco river. 2. riverside dweller.

barrão s. m. (pl. **-ões**) 1. boar. 2. lout, boor, rustic.

barra-pesada s. m. + f. (pl. **barras-pesadas)** 1. awful individual. 2. a serious problem or nut to crack.

barraqueiro s. m. 1. proprietor of a hut, barrack, tent or stand. 2. retailer, vendor (in the stall of a market or fair). 3. swimming master.

barraquim (pl. **-ins**) **barraquinha** s. f. dim. of **barraca.**

barraquista s. m. proprietor of a Manihot (cassava or manioc) plantation.

barrar (I) v. also **barrear**) 1. to clay. 2. to plug, daub with clay. 3. to cover (with any soft claylike matter); spread (butter).

barrar (II) v. 1. to cross or pierce with bars. 2. to cast metal bars. 3. to hem, border, trim (dress, cloth). 4. to hamper, hinder, obstruct. 5. (her.) to trim an escutcheon with bars. **ela barrou o vestido com fitas de ouro** she trimmed the dress with gold laces.

barrasco (I) s. m. young boar.

barrasco (II) s. m. rustic, boor, simpleton.

barra-suporte s. f. (pl. **barras-suporte**) fid.

barregã s. f. concubine.

barregana s. f. barracan: 1. a coarse camlet. 2. a mantle made from that fabric.

barregão s. m. (pl. **-ões**) (also **barregueiro**) man living in concubinage.

barregar v. 1. to shout, scream. 2. to cry out, bawl.

barreguice s. f. concubinage.

barreio s. m. (Braz.) pasture (on a loamy saliferous ground).

barreira s. f. 1. loam-pit, clayey soil, clay-bottom, clay-pit. 2. palisade, stockade, barricade. 3. trench, ditch, bank, dike, mound. 4. obstacle, hindrance, barrier, rail, bar (plate E 13). 5. bounds, limit. 6. target, mark. 7. gate, gatehouse, tollhouse, turnpike, level-crossing gate (plate V 4). 8. (hist.) tilt-yard, lists. 9. (Braz.) erosion gap, cave, hollow (caused by waves). 10. escarpment, scarp. 11. (sport) hurdle. 12. traverse. 13. screen. ~ **alfandegária** tariff wall. ~ **racial** colour line, colour bar. **corrida com (sobre) ~s** hurdle-race, hurdling. **corredor de ~** hurdler. **disputar corrida sobre ~s** to hurdle. **ele saltou as ~s** (fig.) he went too far, he went beyond limits.

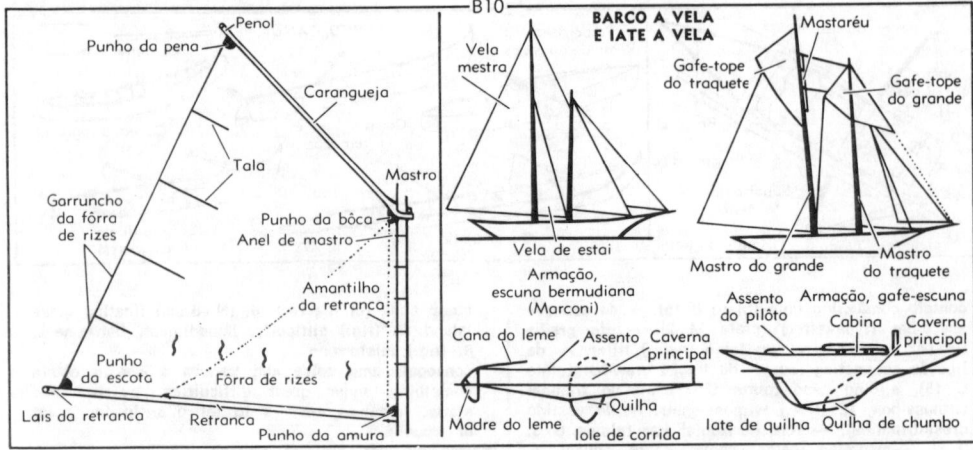

barreirar v. 1. to fence in, enclose with posts and stakes. 2. to entrench, surround with trenches, barricade, bar.

barreiro s. m. 1. clay-pit, loam-pit, brick-yard. 2. saliferous, nitrous marshland. 3. marsh, swamp, bog. 4. cover or look-out (a hiding place) for tapir hunters. 5. (ornith.) ovenbird.

barrela s. f. 1. lye. 2. wash. 3. (pop.) a restoring of a person's good reputation. 4. (coll.) deceit, swindle. dia de ~ washing day. meter na ~ to send to the washing.

barreleiro s. m. 1. lye ashes. 2. wicker basket (to prepare lye). ‖ adj. of or relative to the lye basket.

barrenhão s. m. (pl. -ões) earthen bowl, basin.

barrento adj. 1. loamy, clayey, full of clay, muddy. 2. clay-coloured, clayish, mellow, turbid.

barreta s. f. 1. little bar (of metal). 2. little bar, mole or jetty. 3. = barrete.

barretada s. f. capping, taking off or lifting the hat. dar ~s com o chapéu alheio to do favours at another's expense.

barrete s. m. 1. cap, barret, toque. 2. (eccl.) biretta (plate P 5). 3. (fort.) bonnet, outwork. 4. (bot.). European spindle tree. 5. (zool.) reticulum, the second stomach of ruminants.
~ de advogado, ~ de dormir biggin. ~ de bobo ou de bufão coxcomb, fool's cap. ~ doutoral cap. ~ frígio Phrygian cap. ~ mágico wishing cap. ~ turco tarboosh. homem de muitos ~s a sharper, swindler.

barretear v. to cast bars (of gold).

barreteiro s. m. cap-maker, cap-seller.

barretina s. f. 1. military cap, shako, busby, bearskin. 2. (obs.) lady's hat.

barrica s. f. barrel, keg, cask, tub.

barricada s. f. barricade, stockade.

barricão s. m. (pl. -ões) big barrel.
ela ficou no ~ she remained single, she did not find a husband.

barricar v. to barricade, entrench.

barrido s. m. = barrito.

barriga s. f. 1. abdominal cavity. 2. stomach, belly (plate C 12). 3. paunch, potbelly. 4. pregnancy. 5. (fig.) any salience or prominence. 6. bulge, swelling. 7. (Braz.) false report (of the papers), newspaper hoax.
~ da perna calf of the leg (plate C 18). doeu-lhe a ~ de riso he shook his sides with laughing. dor de ~ belly-ache. ele me alvejou na ~ he hit me in the wind. encher a ~ to fill one's belly. encher

a ~ de corvo to die (speaking of animals). estar com a ~ dando hora to be very hungry. estar com a ~ no espinhaço 1. to be very lean or spare. 2. to be hungry. estar com a ~ para o ar to be idle. fazer ~ to bulge out. o jornal levou ~ the journal published a hoax.

barrigada s. f. 1. bellyful. 2. repletion, satiety, over-eating. 3. (Braz., pop.) pregnancy. 4. entrails (of newly slaughtered cattle). 5. (swim. sl.) belly buster.
dar uma ~ (swim. sl.) to gutter. tomar ~s de riso to roar with laughter.

barriga-d'água s. f. (pl. barrigas-d'água) (med.) ascites, dropsy of the abdomen.

barrigal adj. m. + f. (pl. -ais) of or relative to the belly, bellied.

barrigão s. m. (pl. -ões) 1. big paunch, potbelly. 2. (coll.) corporation.

barriga-verde s. m. + f. (pl. barrigas-verdes) (Braz.) nickname of the natives of Santa Catarina.

barriguda s. f. 1. (bot.) barriguda. 2. (N. Braz.) pregnant woman. ‖ adj. pregnant.

barrigudinho s. m. (dim. of barrigudo) designation of several small viviparous freshwater fishes of the family Cyprinodontidae. ‖ adj. bellied.

barrigudo s. m. lagothrix: prehensile-tailed monkey. ‖ adj. (also barrigana, barriganha) stout, corpulent, obese.

barrigueira s. f. 1. bellyband, girth (harness). 2. beef or leather from the belly region. 3. pregnancy. ‖ adj. pregnant, gravid, with young.

barril s. m. (pl. -is) barrel, cask, wooden keg, coop (plates B 4, C 11).
cerveja do ~ draught beer, beer on draught. ele é um ~ de chope he is as big as a tub. do ~ on tap.

barrilada s. f. 1. contents of a barrel, barrelful. 2. (pop.) disorder, prank, mischievous trick.

barrileira s. f. lye-vat, leaching-vat or dissolving-vat.

barrilete s. m. 1. holdfast, clamp. 2. small barrel, firkin. 3. barrel: case holding the mainspring of a watch or clock. 4. (anat.) tympanic cavity. 5. (carp.) bench screw.

barrilha s. f. kelp, calcined ashes of saltwort, soda, barilla.

barrilheira s. f. (bot.) saltwort.

barrilinho, barrilzinho s. m. small barrel, rundlet.

barriqueiro s. m. cooper.

barriquinha s. f. (Braz.) well coated with planks.

barrir v. (defective verb used in the third person) to trumpet (elephant).

barrisco s. m. loamy soil.
barrista (I) s. m. + f. 1. clay or loam worker. 2. mud waller. 3. clay moulder or modeller.
barrista (II) s. m. + f. gymnast on the horizontal bar or the parallel bars.
barrito s. m. an elephant's cry, bellow (of bulls).
barro s. m. 1. clay, potter's earth, kaolin. 2. loam, mud. 3. mud cottage. 4. (fig.) trifle, trivial affair. 5. ~s pl. pimples (pl.).
~ **de oleiro** argil, plastic clay. **artefato de** ~ earthenware. **de** ~ clayey. **feito de** ~ earthen. **panela de** ~ pipkin. **ter pés de barro** to have feet of clay.
barroar v. (hunt.) to put the dog again on the right scent.
barroca s. f. 1. gutter made by a water-flood, rut. 2. clay mound. 3. gully, crag, slope. 4. grotto, cave.
barrocada s. f., **barrocal** m. (pl. **barrocais**) place full of ruts, crags or caves.
barrocão s. m. (pl. **-ões**) huge gutter or crag.
barroco (I) s. m. 1. = **barroca**. 2. small rock.
barroco (II) s. m. cylindrical or irregular pearl.
barroco (III) s. m. (archit., arts, literat.) baroque style. ‖ adj. 1. of or related to the baroque style. 2. baroque, quaint, extravagant, irregular.
barroqueira s. f. glen, deep gorge.
barroso adj. 1. clayish, loamy. 2. full of clay. 3. covered with pimples. 4. (Braz.) flaxen or clayish coloured cattle or horses.
barrotar v. (also **barrotear**) 1. to support, prop up (with joists or rafters). 2. to set (or put) up spars, joists, rafters or beams.
barrote s. m. rafter, spar, beam, joist, jack rafter, sleeper (plate A 7).
barrotim s. m. (pl. **-ins**) small rafter, beam or spar.
barrufar v. (sl.) 1. to sprinkle, besprinkle. 2. to bedew, bedabble.
barrufo s. m. (sl.) sprinkling, drizzle.
barruma s. f. (pop. form of **verruma**) gimlet, bolt auger, bit, drill.
barruntar v. 1. to suspect, doubt, mistrust. 2. to forebode, portend.
barrunto s. m. foreboding.
bartedouro s. m. (naut.) scoop, skeet.
barulhada, **barulheira** s. f. uproar, racket, clamour, noise, hubbub, noisiness.
barulhar v. 1. to disarrange, disorder. 2. to revolt, stir up, excite. 3. to confuse, mix up. 4. ~**-se:** a) to err, be wrong. b) to confound, be or become confused.
barulheiro adj. noisy, uproarious, tumultuous, disorderly.
barulhento adj. 1. loud, noisy, uproarious. 2. tumultuous, disorderly, turbulent. 3. excited, agitated.
barulho s. m. 1. noise, uproar, clamour. 2. tumult, disturbance. 3. revolt, quarrel, brawl. 4. confusion, medley.
armar ~ to raise hell, (U. S. A.) raise Cain. **comprar** ~ to be meddlesome, poke one's nose in other people's concerns. **fazer** ~ to make a noise, (fig.) boast, (U. S. A.) whoop it up. **fazer um** ~ **dos diabos** to raise the roof. **quando o** ~ **começa** (fig.) when the balloon goes up. **ser do** ~ (coll.) to be excellent, firstclass. **ele é um craque do** ~ he is a football crack.
barulhoso adj. noisy.
barúria s. f. (med.) wine with above normal density.
basal adj. m. + f. (pl. **-ais**) basal, basic.
metabolismo ~ (med.) basal metabolism.
basáltico adj. basaltic.
basaltiforme adj. basaltiform, basaltic.
basalto s. m. 1. (min.) basalt. 2. (geol.) whin.
basaltóide adj. basaltoid, basaltiform.

basanita s. f. (min.) basanite, touchstone, Lydian stone.
basbaque s. m. 1. booby, jackanapes. 2. driveller, gaper, mope. 3. (Braz.) fisherman who looks out for the shoals before throwing the net.
basbaquice s. f. silliness, foolishness.
basco s. m. Basque: 1. one of a people inhabiting the Pyrenees. 2. their language. ‖ adj. Basque.
tambor ~ (mus.) tambourine with bells.
báscula s. f. 1. bascule. 2. decimal balance or weighing machine, platform-scale. 3. rocking movement.
carro de ~ dump waggon (car).
basculador s. m. dumping mechanism (car, truck, etc.).
basculante adj. dumping, inclinable, tilting.
vagão ~ side tip (dumping) waggon.
bascular v. to tip.
basculhadeira s. f. charwoman.
basculhadela s. f. dusting, cleaning.
basculhador s. m. cleaner, sweeper.
basculho s. m. (also **vasculho**) 1. broom or dusting brush with a long stick (to sweep walls and ceilings). 2. rubbish, dirt, dust.
básculo s. m. 1. bascule, rocker, swipe-beam, spring-bar, swing-bar. 2. a kind of drawbridge.
base s. f. 1. base: a) basis. b) foot, bottom (plates B 12, T 4). c) fundamental principle. d) principal element. e) essential part. f) (archit.) plinth, pedestal. g) foundation (plate A 6). h) groundwork. i) starting place. j) (mil.) place from which an army operates or from which supplies are obtained, headquarters. k) (math.) number on which a system of calculation depends. l) (geom.) ground-line, base line. m) (chem.) compound capable of reacting with acids to form salts. n) (anat., bot., zool.) part of an organ by which it is attached to a more central structure of an organism, attachment (plate F 5). 2. (mus.) keynote. 3. (geol.) noncrystalline interstitial rock, magma. 4. root of a tooth. 5. support. 6. corner-stone, keystone. 7. bed. 8. seat. 9. substrate, substratum.
~ **aérea** air base. ~ **das rodas** (mot.) wheel-base (plate E 1). ~ **do divisor** index base. ~ **da rosca** bottom of thread. ~ **de uma taxa** (com. math.) quotient of 360 divided by that rate. ~ **naval** naval station. **cone de** ~ (tech.) pitch cone. **ficar sem** ~ to be without foundation. **indústria de** ~ key industry, basic industry. **na** ~ **de** taking as a basis. **na** ~ **de comissões** on commission basis. **não ter** ~ to be without foundation.
baseado (I) adj. 1. firm, set, steadfast. 2. well--founded, established. 3. experienced, competent. 4. self-conscious, self-reliant. 5. sagacious, shrewd.
baseado (II) s. m. 1. a sort of hemp. 2. narcotic drug made from hemp.
baseamento s. m. foundation.
basear v. 1. to base: a) form, make or serve as a base. b) found, establish. 2. to put on a base or basis. 3. ~**-se** to be based, rest, rely on, found.
essa amizade baseia-se no respeito mútuo this friendship is based on mutual respect. **um argumento baseado em fatos** an argument based on facts. **a história baseia-se em fatos** the story is grounded in fact.
basebol s. m. baseball.
baselácea s. f. herb of the family Basellaceae.
basicidade s. f. (chem.) basicity.
básico adj. basic, fundamental, principal, essential.
‖ **basicamente** adv. basically, essentially.
os fatos ~**s da natureza** the ultimate facts of nature.
basidade s. f. (chem.) the amount of protons an acid can release in solution.

basídio s. m. (bot.) basidium (pl. basidia).
basidiomicete s. m. (bot.) basidiomycete.
basificação s. f. (pl. -ões) (chem.) basification, conversion into a base.
basificar v. (chem.) to basify.
basifixo adj. basifixed, attached or fixed by the base.
basilar adj. 1. basic, fundamental. 2. principal, essential. 3. (anat.) basilar.
basílica s. f. 1. basilica, principal or patriarchal church. 2. shrine, reliquary. 3. (hist.) royal palace. 4. law court. 5. (anat.) basilic vein.
basilicão s. m. basilicon, basilicon ointment.
basilisco s. m. 1. basilisk: a) cockatrice. b) (mil.) ancient piece of artillery. 2. name of several tropical American lizards.
basinérveo adj. (bot.) basinerved, basal-nerved.
básio s. m. (anat.) basion.
basiofobia s. f. morbid fear or incapacity of walking.
basioglosso s. m. (anat.) basioglossus.
basiótribo s. m. (med.) basiotribe.
basófilo adj. (bot.) basophil(e), basophilic.
basônimo s. m. (bot.) basonym.
basquetebol s. m. (sport) basketball.
basqueteira s. f. (Braz.) shoe for playing basket-ball.
basquine s. m. short coat for ladies.
basset s. m. (Fr.) basset (plate C 3).
bassorina s. f. (chem.) bassorin, tragacanth.
bassoura s. f. (ant., pop. = vassoura) broom.
basta (I) s. f. 1. quilting stitch. 2. trimming to cover the stitches (on mattresses, etc.). 3. dresstrimming.
basta (II) interj. enough!, that's enough!, stop! that will do!, shut up!
bastante adj. m. + f. 1. enough, sufficient. 2. satisfactory. ‖ adv. sufficiently, satisfactorily.
~ amplo plenty large. ~ comprido long enough, rather long. ~ ruim rather bad. ~ tempo a great while. as suas opiniões divergem ~ their views differ widely. divertimo-nos ~ we had a good time. ele é ~ homem para defender-se he is man enough to defend himself. é o ~ it will do. festejar ~ to make a whoopee.
bastão s. m. (pl. -ões) 1. staff, stick. 2. baton. 3. truncheon. 4. walking stick, cane. 5. (archit.) round moulding.
~ de esquiar ski-stick (plate G 4). ~ de marechal marshal's staff. empunhar o ~ to command, lead. lançar o ~ no meio da contenda to interfere in order to stop a quarrel. meter o ~ 'to give a good thrashing.
bastão-de-são-josé s. m. (pl. bastões-de-são-josé) (bot.) trumpet lily.
bastar v. 1. to be enough, be sufficient, suffice. 2. to satisfy, have the required quality or ability. 3. ~-se: a) to be self-sufficient, content o. s. with. b) to be self-conceited.
basta de palavras! no more words! basta-me saber it is enough for me to know. basta que mo diga! you have but to tell me. dois bastam two are enough. para que você o tenha, ~ pedi-lo! it's yours for the asking. ~, chega com isto! there is an end of it! dar o basta 1. to put an end to conversation, nuisance, etc.). 2. to dismiss an employee.
bastardear v. = abastardar.
bastardia s. f. 1. bastardy. 2. spurious or bastard branch of a family. 3. degeneration, degeneracy.
bastardinho s. m. (typogr.) type in size between bastard and cursive characters.
bastardo s. m. 1. bastard, illegitimate child, love--child. 2. a kind of sweet, black grapes. 3. handwriting of unusual, or nonstandard form, size or shape. 4. (typogr.) bastard type. 5. (naut.) parrel

rope. ‖ adj. 1. spurious, illegitimate. 2. degenerate, spoiled. 3. altered, changed. 4. half-bred.
bastear v. 1. to quilt a mattress. 2. to make quilted work.
bastecer v. = abastecer.
basteirado adj. marked by packsaddle sores.
basteirar v. to cause saddlesores (on mules, horses, etc.).
basteiras s. f. pl. saddlesore, saddle-gall.
bastiães s. m. pl. gold or silver relief work, featuring animals.
bastião s. m. pl. -ães, -ões) 1. (fort.) bastion. 2. (Goa, Portuguese India) old silver coin.
bastida s. f. 1. paling, palisade. 2. ditch. 3. lathwork. 4. (hist.) assault carriage, montelet.
bastidão s. f. (pl. -ões) 1. thickness, density. 2. multitude, crowd. 3. fullness, plenty.
bastidor s. m. 1. embroidery frame, tambour frame. 2. (theat.) side-scene(s), wing of a scene, side-wing (plate P 2). 3. (fig.) intimacy, familiarity, confidence (e. g. in politics).
por detrás dos ~es behind the scene or curtain, secretly. recolher-se aos ~es to retire (from public life, business activities), to quit (the stage).
bastilha s. f. 1. (hist.) defensive tower, fortress. 2. Bastilha the Bastille: formerly a state prison in Paris.
bastimento s. m. (also abastecimento) provisions (pl.), military supplies (pl.) of all kinds.
basto (I) s. m. (cards) ace of clubs.
basto (II) adj. 1. thick, dense, compact. 2. (fig.) numerous, abundant.
bastonada s. f. 1. bastinado, bastonade. 2. blow with a stick or cudgel, cudgelling.
bastonar v. to bastinado.
bastonário s. m. mace bearer, beadle, verger.
bastonete s. m. 1. short stick, rod. 2. rhabdoidal bacillus.
bastos s. m. pl. (S. Braz.) 1. saddle pads. 2. rustic sheepskin saddle.
bata s. f. 1. (ant.) dressing gown, gown. 2. overall, smock, smock-frock, frock. 3. (sl.) hand, paw.
batacaço s. m. (S. Braz.) an outsider's victory at horse races.
batalha s. f. 1. battle, combat, action, engagement (with the enemy). 2. conflict, fight. 3. (fig.) contest, strife. 4. dispute, head argument. 5. game at cards. 6. (paint.) battle-piece. 7. (bot.) forest tree of the laurel family.
~ naval naval battle. campo de ~ battle-field. cavalo de ~ battle-horse. fazer cavalo de ~ to offer as the strongest argument and insist upon it. dar ~ to engage (in) or give battle. ganhar a ~ to win the battle. ordem de ~ battle array. perder a ~ 1. to lose the battle. 2. (fig.) to lose the day. pôr o exército em ordem de ~ to array the army for battle. tocar à ~ to sound the charge.
batalhação s. f. (pl. -ões) 1. strife, discord. 2. perseverance, obstinacy, tenacity of purpose.
batalhador s. m. 1. champion, defender (of a cause, principle, party). 2. fighter, disputer. ‖ adj. fighting.
batalhante adj. m. + f. 1. (her.) rampant. 2. fighting, offensive.
batalhão s. m. (pl. -ões) battalion.
batalhar v. 1. to fight, engage in battle. 2. to combat, contend, struggle. 3. to persist, insist on. 4. to argue, debate, discuss.
batalheira s. f. (Braz.) dry, nearly barren soil.
batará s. m. (ornith.) ant shrike. ‖ adj. black, yellow or red speckled (rooster).
bataréu, botaréu s. m. (archit.) buttress.
bataria s. f. 1. hubbub, racket, noise. 2. idle talk, gossip.

batata s. f. 1. potato. 2. common name of several saltwater fishes of the family Scaridae. 3. (pop.) big nose, potato-nose. 4. (pop.) large biceps. 5. solecism. 6. nonsense, blunder. ~s fritas fried potatoes. fécula de ~s potato starch. morder a ~ to have some drink. na ~! exactly, precisely! purê de ~s mashed potatoes. vá plantar ~s! don't worry (annoy) me!, go to hell!

batatada s. f. 1. great quantity of potatoes. 2. sweetmeat made with potatoes. 3. (Braz., pop.) a succession of blunders.

batata-de-purga s. f. (pl. **batatas-de-purga**) (bot.) jalap.

batata-doce s. f. (pl. **batatas-doces**) sweet potato, yam.

batatal s. m. (pl. -**ais**) (also **batateiral**) potato field.

batatarana s. f. (bot.) 1. seaside bean. 2. morning--glory.

batateira s. f. potato plant.

batateiro s. m. (bot.) = **batateira**. ‖ adj. 1. liking potatoes. 2. foolish. 3. faltering, failing (pronunciation).

batatinha s. f. (also **batata-inglesa**) 1. small potato 2. (bot.): a) white potato. b) contrayerva.

batatuda adj. said of a prominent biceps (leg).

batávico adj. Batavian, Dutch.

batavo s. m. Dutchman, Batavian. ‖ adj. Batavian.

bate s. m. (baseball) willow.

bateada s. f. contents of a **bateia** (a wooden bowl).

bateador s. m. panner, gold-washer.

batear v. to wash gold in a pan.

bate-bate s. m. 1. rattling, clattering. 2. drink made of sugar-cane brandy, sugar and lemon.

bate-boca s. m. (pl. **bate-bocas**) 1. bawling, shouting, clamour. 2. quarrel, dispute between women, altercation.

bate-bola s. m. (pl. **bate-bolas**) football played by boys or for mere amusement.

bate-chinela s. m. (pl. **bate-chinelas**) (also **bate-coxa**) (N. Braz.) popular dancing party or ball.

bate-coxa s. m. (pl. **bate-coxas**) (sl.) dance, ball.

bate-cu s. m. (pl. **bate-cus**) (sl., vulg.) 1. thud, thump (on the behind). 2. blow with the flat hand on the buttocks.

batedeira s. f. 1. churn, butter vat. 2. kneading--machine, dough mixer. 3. (vet.) hog cholera, swine pest. 4. (med.) intermittent fever, malaria. ~ de ovos egg whisk. ~ elétrica electric mixer (plate C 20).

batedor s. m. 1. beater: a) person or device for beating. b) (hunt.) one who beats up game. 2. knocker (on a door). 3. coiner, minter (of hard coin). 4. explorer, scout, rural or forest guard. 5. grain washer and grinder (instrument used in starch production). 6. forerunner, precursor, harbinger (also fig.). 7. (Braz.) carnauba wax gatherer. 8. special flail for threshing corn. 9. (N. Braz.) overgrazed, poor pastures. 10. (N. Braz.) cattle's track to their watering place. 11. (N. Braz.) place where cattle harassed by flies use to hide. 12. bat. 13. batter, batsman, hitter. 14. rammer. 15. pulp engine, rag-breaker (papermaking). ~ de campo scout. ~ de carteiras pickpocket. ~ de ouro gold beater. ~ de ovos egg beater, egg whisk (plates C 20, D 3). ~ de roupas clothes beater. ~ de tapetes carpet-beater. ~es precederam a carruagem do rei forerunners (mounted guards) preceded the king's carriage. cuidado! ~es de carteiras beware of pickpockets!

batedouro s. m. (also **batedoiro**) 1. beating stone (used by washerwomen). 2. beating place (for cleaning rugs, carpets, etc.).

batedura (I), **batedela** s. f. 1. batting, beating. 2. clapping, knocking, thrashing. ~ de algodão cotton batting. ~ de manteiga churning.

batedura (II) s. f. forge-scale.

bateeiro s. m. (Braz.) gold-washer, panner, man who works with the **bateia**.

bate-enxuga s. m., sg. + pl. (Braz., fam.) 1. clothes worn every day, the only clothes. 2. any object constantly used.

bate-estacas s. m., sg. + pl. pile-driver, pile-rammer

bate-folha s. m. (pl. **bate-folhas**) 1. tinsmith, tinker. 2. plumber. 3. gold or silver beater.

bátega s. f. 1. old-fashioned metal basin. 2. contents of such a basin. 3. sudden shower, rainstorm. 4. ~s pl. (mus.) cymbals.

bateia s. f. wooden bowl for gold- or diamond--washing.

bateira s. m. small flat-bottomed riverboat. água ~ shallow water of a rice paddy.

batel s. m. (pl. **batéis**) canoe, small bark, skiff (plate B 9).

batelada s. f. 1. cargo of a bark, boat-load. 2. great number of things.

batelão s. m. (pl. -**ões**) 1. barge. 2. (N. Braz.) small canoe, punt.

bateleiro s. m. ferryman, master of a river boat.

batente s. m. 1. rabbet of a door or window, door--post, sash. 2. door-knocker, latch. 3. wing or leaf of a folding-door. 4. doorstop, catch. 5. shoreline where the sea breaks. 6. (Braz., pop.) hard work, drudging labour. 7. (tech.) arrestment, arrest(er). backstop (plate T 4).

bate-orelha s. m. (pl. **bate-orelhas**) (pop.) ass, dolt, dullard, stupid.

bate-papo s. m. (pl. **bate-papos**) friendly conversation, cosy chat, small talk.

bate-pau s. m. (pl. **bate-paus**) (Braz.) citizen serving in a rural police force.

bate-pé s. m. (pl. **bate-pés**) 1. tap-dancing. 2. rustic dance.

bate-prego s. m. (pl. **bate-pregos**) (Braz.) the sound of hammering as a signal to begin or stop working.

bater v. 1. to beat, strike, thrash, hammer, cudgel. 2. to stir, mix, agitate, shake violently. 3. to knock about, explore, investigate. 4. (mil.) to open fire, cannonade. 5. to defeat, vanquish, conquer. 6. to fight, combat, struggle. 7. to coin, mint. 8. to flutter, flap (the wings). 9. to kick, stamp, clap (the hands), applaud. 10. (Braz., pop.) to steal. 11. (Braz.) to diminish the volume of. 12. to sound, resound, strike (the hour). 13. to strike against an obstacle, knock against, collide. 14. (Braz.) to arrive at, get to, come to a place by chance. 15. to palpitate, pant, pound. ~ a bola (golf) to tee off. ~ à porta to knock or rap at the door. ~ as botas (coll.) to snuff out (to die). ~ boca (Braz.) to squabble. ~ com a cabeça na parede to knock one's head against the wall. ~ com a mão na mesa to tap the hand on the table. ~ contra to knock, strike against. ~ em alguém to strike at or beat s. o. ~ em retirada to beat a (hasty) retreat. ~am-lhe os dentes de frio his teeth chattered with cold. ~-se em duelo to fight a duel. aí é que bate o ponto that is the salient (main) point. a porta bateu bang went the door. a ave bateu as asas the bird flapped its wings. ele bate sempre na mesma tecla he is always harping on the same string. ele bateu os calcanhares he clicked his heels. ele bateu um instantâneo de mim he made a snapshot of me. eles ~am-se bem they put up a good fight. ele foi ~ num lugar ermo he happened to come to a desolated spot. **estão a** ~ there is a knock at the door. **o sol bate na parede** the sun shines on the wall. **os amigos** ~**am palmas** the friends clapped their hands, applauded. **vale a pena** ~**-se por isso** it's worth fighting for.

bateria s. f. 1. (mil.) battery, emplacement where artillery is mounted, two or more pieces of artillery. 2. basic unit of field artillery. 3. (naut.) broadside of a warship. 4. (electr.) dry or storage battery, accumulator, pile. 5. whole set of kitchen utensils (pans, pots, etc.). 6. (fig.) attack, assault. 7. (Braz.) succession of fireworks. 8. set of percussion instruments of an orchestra.
descobrir as ~**s** to disclose one's real intentions.

batial adj. (geol.) bathyal, deep-sea.

batibarba s. f. 1. gentle tap on the chin, chuck. 2. sharp reprimand, severe rebuke. 3. = **bate-boca**.

batição s. f. (pl. **-ões**) (Braz.) catching of fish or turtles by beating the water.

batida s. f. 1. beat, stroke, tap. 2. (fig.) rebuke, reprimand. 3. (hunt.) battue. 4. (mil.) scouting, reconnoitering. 5. (Braz.) razzia, police raid. 6. (Braz.) drink made of brandy, lemon, sugar or honey. 7. eggnog. 8. (Braz.) track or trail in the wilderness.
~ **de asa** wing-stroke. ~ **de leite** milk-shake. **dar uma** ~ (fig.) to rebuke, blame. **de** ~ in a hurry. **a polícia deu uma** ~ **na favela** the police raided the slum. ~ **do coração** heartbeat.

batidácea s. f. plant of the family Batidaceae.

batidáceo adj. (bot.) batidaceous.

batido s. m. 1. = **batida**. 2. = **batimento**. ‖ adj. 1. beaten, hit. 2. defeated, routed. 3. worn out, threadbare. 4. hammered out, coined, wrought. 5. (fig.) commonplace, ordinary, vulgar. 6. rutly (road).

batimento s. m. 1. act of beating, beat, throb. 2. collision, shock, impact. 3. (mus.) interference of sounds (producing increased intensity, silence or beats).

batimetria s. f. = **batometria**.

batímetro s. m. = **batômetro**.

batina s. f. (eccl.) cassock, long outer garment.

batinga s. f. Brazilian tree of the myrtle family.

batiputá s. m. Brazilian shrub of the family Ochnaceae.

batiscafo s. m. bathyscaphe, bathyscaph.

batisfera s. f. bathysphere.

batismal adj. m. + f. (pl. **-ais**) baptismal, fontal.
pia ~ baptismal font.

batismo s. m. 1. baptism, christening. 2. act or ceremony of baptizing. 3. (fig.) purification, initiation. 4. (pop.) adulteration of wine, milk, etc. (by adding water).
~ **de fogo** baptism of fire. **certidão de** ~ certificate of baptism.

batisseia s. f. bad or clumsy horseman.

batista (I) s. f. cambric, batiste.

batista (II) s. m. 1. baptizer. 2. **Batista** John the Baptist.

batista (III) s. m. + f. Baptist: member of a Christian denomination. ‖ adj. Baptist.

batistério s. m. 1. baptist(e)ry. 2. (Braz., pop.) certificate of baptism.

batizado s. m. 1. = **batizamento**. 2. baptized child (or person).

batizamento s. m. 1. baptism, religious ceremony. 2. christening feast.

batizando s. m. 1. infant (or person) to be christened, candidate for christening. 2. godchild.

batizante s. m. + f. 1. godfather, godmother. 2. baptizer.

batizar v. 1. to baptize, christen. 2. (pop.) to nickname. 3. (pop.) to water, adulterate, dilute (wine, milk). 4. to name, denominate.
~ **sinos** to consecrate church bells. ~ **por imersão** to dip.

bato s. m. a children's play (with five pebbles).

batoca s. f. a strain of grapes.

batocaço s. m. stroke with the spur or gaff (of a game-cock).

batocada s. f. (N. Braz.) 1. heavy loss, great damage. 2. unexpected and heavy expenses.

batocar v. to bung: close a bunghole.

batocromo s. m. (chem.) bathochrome.

batografia s. f. bathography.

batográfico adj. bathographic.

batólito s. m. (geol.) batholith, batholite.

batologia s. f. battology: needless repetition in speech or writing.

batológico adj. battological.

batom s. m. lipstick.

batometria s. f. bathymetry: method of measuring the depth of the sea.

batométrico adj. bathymetric.

batômetro s. m. bathymeter, bathometer: instrument for sounding depths.

batoque s. m. 1. bunghole. 2. bung, stopper. 3. thickset man, short and stout fellow. 4. brandmark on cattle.

batoqueira s. f. 1. bunghole. 2. track, trace, trail (through the thicket).

batota s. f. 1. false play, double-dealing, cheating, trick (at cards or gambling). 2. gambling house. 3. game of hazard.
casa de ~ gambling house, gambling hell. **fazer** ~ to cheat, trick.

batotar, batotear v. 1. to cheat at cards or gambling. 2. to defraud, deceive.

batoteiro s. m. 1. gambler, sharper, cheat at cards or gambling. 2. defrauder, cheater.

batracóide adj. (zool.) batrachoid.

batráquios s. m. pl. (zool., also **batrácios**) Batrachia, Amphibia (pl.).

batucada s. f. music and rhythm of Afro-Brazilian dances.

batucador s. m. mediocre pianist.

batucajé s. m. (N. Braz.) regional Negro dance.

batucar v. 1. to hammer, drum. 2. to dance the **batuque**. 3. to play badly on the piano.

batuera, batueira s. f. corn cob.

batumado adj. curly, woolly (hair of Negroes).

batume s. m. separation wall of clay or wax in a hive.

batuque s. m. (Braz.) 1. hammering, drumming, noisiness. 2. generic designation of Afro-Brazilian Negro dances. 3. Negro ball.

batuqueiro s. m. (Braz.) 1. frequenter, habitué of **batuques**. 2. fan of Negro dances. 3. bird of the family Fringillidae.

batuta s. f. 1. a conductor's baton, wand. 2. m. + f. intelligent, sagacious or courageous person. ‖ adj. m. + f. (Braz.) 1. intelligent, sagacious. 2. notable, remarkable. 3. agile, lively. 4. brave, courageous.
ter a ~ **na mão** to command, lead, direct.

batuvira s. m. (zool.) tapir.

baú s. m. travelling box, trunk, chest, locker.
não ser ~ **de ninguém** not to pledge o. s. to secrecy.

baud s. m. (data processing) baud.

baudelairiano adj. of or relative to the French poet Baudelaire.

bauleiro s. m. manufacturer of trunks or tin boxes, trunk maker.

baúna s. f. (ichth.) dog snapper.
baunilha s. f. vanilla: 1. the plant. 2. the flavoring extract.
baunilhão s. m. (pl. -ões) (bot.) vanillon.
bauxita s. f. (min.) bauxite.
bávaro s. m. Bavarian. ‖ adj. Bavarian.
baxá s. m. pasha, pacha.
baxalato s. m. pashalik.
bazar s. m. 1. oriental market, market place. 2. bazaar, fancy fair. 3. shop or stand for the sale of fancy wares. 4. jumble sale. 5. warehouse, store.
bazareiro s. m. bazaar merchant, trader.
bazé s. m. tobacco of inferior quality.
bazófia s. f. 1. vanity, haughtiness, pride. 2. boast, swaggèr. 3. a stew made of leftovers.
bazofiador s. m. boaster, braggart. ‖ adj. boastful, vauting.
bazofiar v. to boast, brag, swagger.
bazófio s. m. boaster, braggart. ‖ adj. boasting, swaggering, ostentatious.
bazuca s. f. (mil.) bazooka.
bazulaque s. m. 1. liver ragout or stew. 2. viscera. 3. badly cooked food. 4. trifles. 5. cosmetic. 6. fat and short man. 7. (Braz.) sweetmeat of grated coconut and honey.
B.C.G. s. m. (med.) B.C.G. vaccine (against tuberculosis).
bdelômetro s. m. (med.) bdelometer.
bê-a-bá s. m. 1. the A B C, alphabeth. 2. fundamentals (pl.).
  ele não sabe o ~ he is an illiterate person, a fool.
beata (I) s. f. 1. pious woman, bigot. 2. sanctimonious woman, hypocrite. 3. beatified woman.
beata (II) s. f. (pop.) fag-end (of a cigarette).
beatão s. m. (pl. -ões) sanctimonious man, hypocrite.
beataria s. f. group of pious or sanctimonious people.
beateiro s. m. one who has relations with pious people. ‖ adj. religious, pious.
beatério s. m. 1. pious people. 2. their religious practices. 3. bigotry, hypocrisy.
beatice s. f. bigotry, sanctimoniousness.
beatificação s. f. (pl. -ões) beatification.
beatificado adj. beatified, blessed, canonized.
beatificador s. m. beatifying consistory, beatifier. ‖ adj. beatifying, beatific.
beatificar v. to beatify.
beatífico adj. blessed, beatific(al).
beatinha s. f. 1. dim. of beata. 2. scorpaena (salt-water fish).
beatismo s. m. religionism.
beatíssimo adj. obs. superl. of beato 1. most beatific, most blessed. 2. Beatíssimo Your Holiness: correct form of addressing the Holy Father.
beatitude s. f. 1. beatitude, blessedness, supreme happiness, bliss. 2. form of addressing the Pope.
beato s. m. 1. beatified man. 2. pious person. 3. bigot. ‖ adj. 1. happy devout, exceedingly pious. 2. fanatic. 3. hypocritical.
beatorro s. m. = beatão.
bebaça, bebaço s. m. (sl., N. Braz.) = beberrão.
bêbado s. m. drunk(ard). ‖ adj. drunk, intoxicated, tipsy.
bebê s. m. baby, babe.
bebedeira s. f. 1. spree, drinking bout. 2. drunkenness, intoxication, inebriety.
  dado a ~s given to drinking. cozer a ~ (fam.) to sleep away or off the drunkenness, sleep o. s. sober.
bebedice s. f. dipsomania, inebriety.
bêbedo s. m. 1. drunk(ard). 2. scoundrel. ‖ adj. drunk, tipsy, intoxicated, tight, fogged, groggy.
  ~ como um cacho blind drunk. completamente ~

dead drunk, tight as a drum, stewed to the gills.
  estar ~ to be top-heavy.
bebedor s. m. + adj. = beberrão.
bebedouro s. m. 1. well, drinking fountain, drinking place (plate E 13). 2. drinking vessel, vase of a fountain, basin. 3. watering place, horse pound or pond.
bebeerina s. f. = beberina.
beber v. 1. to drink, take a drink, imbibe, swallow. 2. to spend or squander money on drinks. 3. to be given to drinking, be fond of the bottle, booze. 4. to absorb, sip, sap. 5. (fig.) to assimilate easily (knowledge, wisdom).
  ~ azeite (fig.) to be very lively or clever. ~ do fino to be well-informed. ~ um ovo to sip up an egg. ~ os ventos por alguém to be nuts on s. o., be potty on s. o. bebemos à sua saúde we drank your health, your toast. desta água eu não bebo that won't happen to me, I never should do that. ele bebe muito he drinks hard, (deep). ele bebeu (tomou) um trago he crooked an elbow.
bêbera s. f. a fig that ripens early.
beberagem s. f. (pl. -ens) 1. (pharm.) decoction, infusion. 2. stale or disagreeable water. 3. watered bran, swill. 4. drinks, potion, drench.
beberar v. to quench the thirst.
bebereira s. f. (also bêbera) fig-tree.
beberes (ê) s. m. pl. liquors, drinks (pl.).
beberete s. m. 1. appetizer (drink), apéritif, cocktail. 2. coktail party.
bebericação s. f. (pl. -ões) 1. drinking. 2. draught, sip, pull.
bebericador s. m. sipper, tippler, drunkard. ‖ adj. given to drink, sipping.
bebericar v. 1. to sip, kiss the cup, drink little by little (but continuously). 2. to booze.
beberina s. f. (chem.) bebeerin(e): amorphous alkaloid from the bark of the bebeeru tree.
beberrão s. m. (pl. -ões) (f. -ona; also beberraz, beberrote) drunkard, tippler, hard drinker, boozer. ‖ adj. addicted to drink, bibacious.
  ele é tido como ~ he is said to be a drunkard.
beberrica s. m. easy drinker, sipper.
beberricação s. f., beberricador m. + adj., beberricar v. = bebericação, bebericador, bebericar.
beberronia s. f. 1. spree, drinking bout. 2. group of heavy drinkers.
beberu s. m. (bot., also bebeeru) bebeeru: a large lauraceous tree.
bebes s. m. pl. (also beberes) drinks, beverages.
  os comes e ~ foodstuff and drinks.
bebida s. f. 1. drink, beverage, potion. 2. act of drinking. 3. (N. Braz.) watering place (for domestic or wild animal). 4. = bebedouro.
  ~ efervescente pop. ~ entorpecente dope. estimulante cordial. ~ falsificada hocus. ~s alcoólicas alcoholic drinks, spirits. dado à ~ addicted to drink. encher-se de ~ to swill, exceder-se em ~s to overdrink o. s.
bebido adj. 1. drunk, drunken, tipsy. 2. quenched, satisfied (thirst).
bebível adj. m. + f. (pl. -íveis) drinkable, potable.
beca s. f. 1. a magistrat's gown, long robe, toga. 2. (fig.) magistracy. 3. (Braz., pop.) suit of clothes. 4. m. magistrate.
beça (Braz.) used only in the adverbial locution à ~ in great quantities, numerously.
bechamel s. m. (pl. bechaméis) bechamel, bechamel sauce.
beco s. m. lane, alley.
  ~ sem saída 1. blind alley. 2. tight spot, serious trouble, deadlock. desocupar o ~ to clear, leave, vacate.

bedame s. m. (also **badame**) mortise chisel (plates F 2, M 4).

bedel s. m. (pl. **bedéis**) 1. beadle, school attendant. 2. janitor. 3. mace. 4. bumble.

bedelhar v. 1. to interfere, meddle, intrude. 2. to chat, prattle.

bedelho s. m. 1. door latch, night latch, bolt of a lock. 2. boy, lad, urchin. 3. little trump. **meter o ~** to poke one's nose into everything.

bedelia s. f. office of a beadle.

bedém s. m. (pl. **-éns**) Moorish tunic, raincape or tunic made of rush.

beduíno, beduí, beduim s. m. Bedouin, Arab.

bege adj. m. + f. beige, pale brown.

begônia s. f. (bot.) begonia.

begoniácea s. f. (bot.) any plant of the family Begoniaceae.

beguaba, beguava s. m. molusc of the familly Donacidae.

beguina s. f. 1. Beguine: member of a certain religious sisterhood. 2. devout or sanctimonious woman.

beguinaria s. f. monastic (penitent) life.

beguino s. m. Beguin: 1. mendicant friar, devout person, penitent. 2. Beghard.

begume s. f. begum: Mohammedan lady of high rank.

behaviorismo s. m. (psych.) behaviourism.

bei s. m. bey: governor of a Turkish city or district.

beiça s. f. pout. **fazer ~** to pout, look sullen.

beiçada s. f. 1. lips of animals. 2. blubber lip, thick and hanging lip.

beicinho s. m. small lip. **fazer ~** to pout, mope. **ela fez ~** she pursed her lips.

beiço s. m. 1. lip (plate C 2). 2. rim, salience. **~ rachado** hare-lip. **~s de uma ferida** lips of a wound. **de ~** (sl.) for a kiss (or song). without payment. **lamber os ~s** to lick one's chops, show satisfaction after a good meal. **levar alguém pelo ~** to lead by the nose, to turn s. o. round one's little finger. **morder os ~s** to bite one's lips.

beiçola, beiçoca s. f. (also **beiçorra**) 1. big. pouting lip, blubber lip. 2. m. + f. person with pouting or blubber lips.

beiçolada s. f. (Braz., pop.) slap on the lips or in the face (with the flat hand).

beiçudo s. m. man with pouting lips. || adj. blubber- -lipped, thick-lipped.

beija s. f. religious ceremony of kissing sacred images or statues.

beijado adj. kissed, covered with kisses. **de mão beijada** gratuitous, free. **aceitarei de mão beijada** I'll accept that with (the greatest) pleasure.

beijador s. m. kisser, man fond of kissing. || adj. kissing, fond of kissing.

beija-flor s. m. (pl. **beija-flores**) (ornith.) humming-bird, colibri.

beija-mão s. m. (pl. **beija-mãos**) kissing of the hand, kissing a sovereign's hand (at levee or royal reception). **ele deu-lhe um ~** he kissed her hand.

beija-pé s. m. (pl. **beija-pés**) kissing the foot, ceremony of kissing the Pope's toe.

beijar v. 1. to kiss, caress. 2. to touch lightly, oscula-te. 3. **~-se** to kiss each other.

beijinho s. m. 1. light or little kiss. 2. (fig.) the best of a thing: quintessence, prime, cream.

beijo s. m. kiss, osculation, (arch.) buss. **~ ligeiro** peck. **atirar um ~** to throw a kiss. **dar um ~ no copo** to take a few drops of wine. **o ~ de Judas** a Judas kiss, treacherous kiss.

beijoca s. f. (coll.) hearty kiss, (arch.) buss, smack.

beijocador s. m. a hearty kisser. || adj. given to or fond of kissing.

beijocar v. to kiss, kiss frequently and heartily, exchange kisses, smack.

beijo-de-frade s. m. (pl. **beijos-de-frade**) (Braz., bot.) garden balsam.

beijo-de-moça s. m. (pl. **beijos-de-moça**) candy of eggs and sugar.

beijoeiro s. m. (bot.) = **benjoeiro**.

beijo-frio s. m. (pl. **beijos-frios**) a kind of ice-cream with a covering of chocolate.

beijoim s. m. = **benjoim**.

beijoqueiro adj. caressing, fond of kissing.

beiju, beijuaçu s. m. tapioca cake.

beijucaba s. f. kind of wasp (Apoica pallida Oliv.).

beijueira s. f. woman who bakes tapioca cakes.

beijupirá s. m. (Braz.) sergeant fish.

beilhó s. m. + f. (cul.) wafer with pumpkim filling.

beira s. f. 1. bank, edge, shore. 2. rim, brim. 3. proximity, verge, border (plates C 8, T 5). 4. ledge, brink. 5. eaves (pl.). **~s do telhado** house eaves. **à ~ de um abismo** 1. on the edge of a precipice. 2. on the verge of a catastrophe. **à ~ do caminho** on the roadside. **à ~ da miséria** on the verge of starvation. **che-gar(-se) à ~ do** to approach. **estar à ~ da morte** to be on the brink of the grave, near one's death. **estar à ~ da ruína** to be nearly ruined, to be on one's last legs. **fica à ~ d'água** it is on the water-side. **medida cheia até a ~** struck measure. **não ter eira nem ~** to have neither house nor home.

beirada s. f. 1. = **beira**. 2. margin, border. 3. eaves of a roof. 4. (coll., Braz.) suburbs, surroundings, environs.

beiradear v. 1. to walk along (a water edge or river bank). 2. to coast, skirt, circuit.

beiradeiro s. m. (Braz.) 1. riverside dweller. 2. merchant, caterer living near a railway track. 3. forester dwelling in the neighbourhood of rural settlements.

beirado, beiral s. m. (pl. **-s, -ais**) eaves edge of a roof, weatherboard (plate T 5).

beira-mar s. f. 1. seashore, strand. 2. coast, littoral. || adj. coastal, littoral, near the seashore, seaboard. **à ~** on the coast, at the seaside.

beirante adj. bordering, verging, limiting.

beirão s. m. (pl. **-ões**) (also **beirense**; f. **beiroa, beirã**) native or inhabitant of Beira (Portugal). || adj. of or relative to the province of Beira.

beirar v. 1. to walk or run along the border of. 2. to be situated near the border of. 3. to confine with, border upon, limit. 4. to face, be opposite to. 5. **~-se** to come near, approximate (amount). **beirando os 40 anos** on the right side of forty.

beisebol s. m. baseball. **quadra de ~** (U.S.A.) diamond, baseball playing field.

bejaqui s. f. (Braz., ornith.) = **baiagu**.

beje s. m. (Braz., folklore) the twins, in popular worship (African origin: Cosmas and Damian; Crispin and Crispinian).

bel adj. poet. abbr. of **belo**: beautiful, fair, fine. **ele está a seu ~** he proceeds according to his own will. **a seu ~-prazer** to his heart's content.

bela s. f. beauty, beautiful woman. **~ adormecida** sleeping beauty.

beladona s. f. (bot.) belladona, deadly nightshade, banewort.

bela-emília s. f. (pl. **belas-emílias**) (bot. also **jas-mim-azul**) leadwort.

belas-artes s. f. pl. the fine (plastic, visual) arts. **academia das ~** academy of arts.

belas-letras s. f. pl. literature, belles-lettres.

belatriz adj. (poet.) martial, valiant, bellicose, belligerent.

belbute s. m. cotton velvet, velveteen.

~ **de riscas** striped cotton velvet.

belbutina s. f. fine velvet, cord, fustian, velveteen.

belchior s. m. (Braz.) 1. dealer in secondhand goods. 2. scrap-iron merchant, junk seller.

beldade s. f. beauty, belle.

beldosa s. f. (S. Braz.) red paving brick.

beldroega s. f. (bot.) purslane.

beldroegas s. m., sg. + pl. (pop.) 1. simpleton, idiot, imbecile. 2. scamp, good-for-nothing.

beleguim s. m. (pl. -ins) police agent, bailiff's official, apparitor.

belemnite s. m. belemnite: fossil shell.

belendengue s. m. (Braz.) mounted frontier guard.

beletrista s. m. + f. belletrist, connoisseur of literature, man of letters.

beletrística s. f. belles-lettres, belletristic literature.

beletrístico adj. belletristic.

beleza s. f. 1. beauty, gracefulness, handsomeness, good looks. 2. beautiful person, animal, or thing. **destituído de** ~ ill-favoured. **dizer** ~s to talk gracefully, talk civilities. **salão de** ~ beauty parlour, beauty shop. **seu jardim é uma** ~ your garden makes a fine show. **uma** ~ **de criança** a picture of a child. **uma** ~ **sem senão** a perfect beauty.

belezinha s. f. creeping plant of the family Thymelaeaceae.

belfa s. f. fleshy excrescence below the head of some gallinaceans.

belfarinheiro s. m. hawker, pedlar.

belfo adj. with a drooping (hanging) hunderlip.

belfudo adj. blubber-lipped.

belga (I) s. m. + f. Belgian, native or inhabitant of Belgium. ‖ adj. Belgian.

belga (II) s. m. (Braz.) big hanging lamp.

belho s. m. door-latch, bolt of a lock.

beliche s. m. 1. (mar., aeron.) sleeping berth, bunk. 2. cabin.

~ **de proa** fore cabin. **equipar com** ~ to berth.

bélico adj. 1. warlike, bellicose. 2. martial. ‖ **belicamente** adv. in a warlike manner, bellicosely.

equipamento ~ armament.

belicosidade s. f. bellicosity, warlikeness.

belicoso adj. 1. warlike, bellicose, pugnacious. 2. quarrelsome, litigious. 3. intent on or provoking conflict. 4. accustomed to war.

belicuete s. m. (Braz.) dungeon, narrow construction, badly illuminated and ventillated, used mostly as storage space.

belida s. f. (med.) nebula, slight cloudlike opacity of the córnea.

beligerância s. f. belligerance, belligerency.

beligerante adj. m. + f. belligerent, pugnacious, contentious.

não ~ non-belligerent.

belígero adj. bellicose, martial, military.

belipotente adj. m. + f. powerful at war, ready for war.

beliquete s. m. lumber-room.

belisária s. f. money which a lucky gambler hands over to his partner who lost all his money.

belisário s. m. (Braz.) ancient 50 reis nickel coin. ‖ adj. (obs.) poor, unfortunate.

beliscado adj. 1. pinched, nipped. 2. somewhat irritated, excited. 3. stimulated, incited.

beliscadura s. f. (also **belisco** m.) pinch(ing), nippling, scratch.

beliscão s. m. (pl. -ões) squeeze, pinch(ing), nip.

dar um ~ to give someone a pinch.

beliscar v. 1. to pinch, squeeze, nip with the fingers. 2. to touch slightly. 3. to wound superficially, scratch. 4. to stimulate, incite. 5. to nettle, annoy, vex. 6. to eat daintily, take a very small portion.

belíssimo abs. superl. of **belo** adj. very fair, most or perfectly beautiful.

beliz s. m. high-spirited, intelligent or clever person. ‖ adj. m. + f. clever, shrewd, cunning, devilish.

belo s. m. 1. beautifulness, fairness. 2. perfection. 3. sublimeness, exaltation. ‖ adj. 1. beautiful, fair, fine. 2. handsome, graceful. 3. harmonious, melodious. 4. agreeable, pleasant, mild. 5. kind, good, generous. ‖ **-amente** adv. 1. beautifully, finely, fairly. 2. perfectly, very well. ‖ interj. well, very well.

ela é bela como um sonho she is a perfect dream. **uma bela casa** a fine house. **um** ~ **dia** some fine day, once. **belas palavras não enchem a barriga** fine words butter no parsnips. **uma bela embrulhada** a pretty mess. **o** ~ **sexo** the fair sex.

belona s. f. Bellona: Roman goddess of war.

belonave s. f. (Braz.) man-of-war, warship.

belostomatídeos s. m. pl. (ent.) Belostomatidae: family of predaceous water bugs.

bel-prazer s. m. free will, desire, pleasure, liking, discretion.

a seu ~ off-hand, to one's liking, to one's heart's content.

beltrano, beltrão s. m. Mr. So-and-So.

ele brigou com fulano e beltrano he quarreled with everybody. **quem ama beltrão, ama o seu cão** love me, love my dog.

beluário s. m. tamer of wild beasts.

beluíno adj. 1. of or relative to wild animals. 2. beastly, savage, monstrous.

belvedere, belveder, belver s. m. belvedere: terrace commanding a fine view.

belzebu s. m. Beelzebub, prince of demons, devil.

bem s. m. (pl. **bens**) 1. the good, goodness, happiness, blessing virtue. 2. benefit, advantage, satisfaction. 3. object of love, darling. 4. **bens** pl.: a) landed property, real estate, immovables. b) property, possession, personal estate. ‖ adv. 1. well, very, right. 2. conveniently. 3. affectionately. 4. healthfully, salutarily. ‖ interj. well!, so! ‖ **se** ~ **que** conj. though, although, albeit.

~, ~! well, well! ~ **adiantado** well on. ~ **assim seja** so be it. ~ **avisado** well-advised. ~ **condimentado** highly spiced. ~ **conhecido** well-known. ~ **dirigido** well-conducted. ~, **e daí?** well, and what of all this? ~ **educado** well-bred, well-behaved. ~ **está o que** ~ **acaba** all's well that ends well. ~ **longe** very far. ~ **mais** much more. ~ **merecido** well deserved. ~ **no alto** far up, well up. ~ **nutrido** well-fed. ~ **pago** highly paid. ~ **pensado** well-thought. ~ **pouco** very little. ~ **relacionado** well-connected. ~ **reputado** well-reputed. ~ **satisfeito** well-pleased. ~ **tratado** well-groomed, well-kept. **a** ~ **de** on account of. **com todos os bens** with bag and baggage. **de idade** ~ **avançada** well on in years. **ele é** ~ **capaz de** he is well able of. **ele não está** ~ **hoje** he is not up to much to-day. **ele vai** ~ he is doing nicely, he is thriving. **eles estão** ~ **de vida** they are well off. **é para seu próprio** ~ it's for your own profit. ...**e poderia** ~ **ser** and well it might be. **está** ~ all right. **estamos** ~ **com eles** we are on good terms with them. **eu estou** ~ **(de saúde)** I am quite all right. **eu me sinto tão** ~ **como o peixe na água** I feel as fresh as a daisy. **fizeram** ~ **em ir embora** they did well to go. **meu** ~! darling, sweetheart, sugar! **muito** ~ very well. **para o** ~ **de** for the good of. **passe** ~! so long, good-bye! **por** ~ willingly, by fair means. **pois** ~ well then. **por** ~ **ou por mal** willy-nilly, compulsory. **uma força para o** ~ **a** power for good. **uma mudança para o** ~ **a** turn for the good. **você ~ entende o que eu quero dizer** you know well enough what I mean.

bem-acabado adj. (pl. **bem-acabados**) well finished, finished, finished with perfection.

bem-afortunado adj. (pl. **bem-afortunados**) happy, prosperous.

bem-amado s. m. (pl. **bem-amados**) lover, sweetheart, darling. ‖ adj. darling, dear, beloved.

bem-aventurado s. m. (pl. **bem-aventurados**) blessed person, saint. ‖ adj. blessed, very fortunate, lucky. ‖ **-amente** adv. blissfully, blessedly.

bem-aventurança s. f. (pl. **bem-aventuranças**) 1. bliss, blessedness. 2. heavenly happiness, exalted joy. 3. good luck fortune.

bem-aventurar v. to make happy, cause heavenly joy or happiness, bless.

bem-avindo adj. (pl. **bem-avindos**) amicable, friendly, peaceable, conciliatory, conciliated.

bembé s. m. (Braz., ent.) punkie, punky.

bem-bom s. m. 1. comfort, ease, convenience. 2. free will or determination.
estar no seu ~ at one's ease or discretion.

bem-casado s. m. (pl. **bem-casados**) (cul.) sort of cooky (cookie).

bem-casados s. m. pl. (bot.) water milfoil.

bem-criado adj. (pl. **bem-criados**) 1. well-educated, well-bred, polite, affable. 2. well-fed, fat (domestic animals).

bem-de-fala s. m. simple and sympathetic manner of speech, unpretentious language.

bem-encarado adj. well-featured.

bem-estar s. m. comfort, welfare, well-being, satisfaction, ease, wealth.

bem-fadado adj. (pl. **bem-fadados**) happy, fortunate, lucky.

bem-fadar v. to predict good fortune.

bem-falante adj. m. + f. (pl. **bem-falantes**) 1. eloquent, speaking fluently. 2. discrete, judicious.

bem-fazer s. m. charity, charitableness, generosity. ‖ v. to do good to, show kindness or generosity, benefit.

bem-humorado adj. (pl. **bem-humorados**) good-humo(u)red.

bem-me-quer s. m. (pl. **bem-me-queres**) (bot.) daisy, ox-eye, daisy.

bem-nascido adj. (pl. **bem-nascidos**, also **bem-nado** pl. **bem-nados**) well-borne, noble.

bemol s. m. (pl. **bemóis**) (mus.) flat (plate N 1).

bem-ouvido adj. (pl. **bem-ouvidos**) 1. obedient, submissive. 2. docile, compliant.

bem-parecido adj. (pl. **bem-parecidos**) good-looking, nice, atractive.

bem-posto adj. (pl. **bem-postos**) 1. elegant, well--dressed. 2. graceful, tactful.

bem-querer s. m. = **benquerença**. ‖ v. 1. to like, love, wish well. 2. to like or love each other.

bem-te-vi s. m. (pl. **bem-te-vis**) (ornith.) tyrant flycatcher.

bem-te-vizinho s. m. (pl. **bem-te-vizinhos**) (ornith.) a smaller species of flycatcher.

bem-vindo adj. (pl. **bem-vindos**) welcome, willingly received or admitted, pleasing.
seja ~ a nossa casa! welcome home!

bem-visto adj. (pl. **bem-vistos**) well-beloved, welcome, appreciated.

bênção s. f. (formerly **benção**; pl. **-ãos**) 1. act or ceremony of blessing. 2. divine grace. 3. blessing, benediction.
~ da mesa grace before meals.

bênção-de-deus s. f. (pl. **bênçãos-de-deus**) (bot.) 1. Brazilian abutilon. 2. redvein abutilon (both belonging to the family Malvaceae).

bençoairo, bençoário s. m. (obs.) inventory, esp. of properties bequeathed to the Church.

Bendengó s. m. 1. a famous Brazilian aerolith (on view in the National Museum of Rio de Janeiro). 2. **bendengó** uncommon occurrence.

bendenguê s. m. Afro-Brazilian Negro songs, music and dance.

bendito s. m. a prayer beginning with the word **bendito** (= blessed). ‖ adj. blessed, praised.
~ seja benedicite.

bendizente adj. m. + f. praising, laudatory.

bendizer v. 1. to bless, praise. 2. to laud, glorify.

Beneditino s. m. Benedictine. ‖ adj. Benedictine.
os ~s the Black Friars.

benedito s. m. (Braz., ornith.) a species of woodpecker.

benefe s. f. (bot.) hedge violet.

beneficência s. f. 1. beneficence, charity. 2. act or practice of charity, well-doing. 3. philanthropy.
obra de ~ social social welfare work.

beneficente adj. 1. beneficent, charitable, beneficial. 2. kind, well-doing.
obra ~ benefaction. **caixa ~** provident society.

beneficiação s. f. (pl. **-ões**) (also **beneficiamento**) betterment, improvement, amelioration, reform, benefaction.

beneficiado s. m. beneficiary, grantee, incumbent. ‖ adj. 1. beneficial. 2. processed.

beneficiador s. m. benefactor. ‖ adj. beneficent, beneficial, advantageous.

beneficial adj. m. + f. (pl. **-ais**) beneficial, relative to ecclesiastical benefits.

beneficiar v. 1. to benefit, be beneficial to. 2. to improve, better. 3. to repair, overhaul. 4. to increase the value, quantity or quality of agricultural or industrial products by improvements. 5. to process. 6. (Braz.) to castrate or brand animals. 7. to bestow upon the church.
~ o algodão to core and clean cotton.

beneficiário s. m. beneficiary, payee, foundationer, gainer. ‖ adj. beneficiary.
~ de uma promessa (jur.) promisee. **~ de uma anuidade** annuitant.

beneficiável adj. (pl. **-áveis**) susceptible to be beneficed, beneficial, beneficent.

benefício s. m. 1. service, labour (for the benefit of another), beneficence, benefaction. 2. good, benefit, favour, mercy. 3. advantage, gain, profit, behoof, avail. 4. church living, church preferment. 5. beneficial performance (theatre, concert, etc.). 6. improvement, amelioration. 7. benefice, boon, privilege. 8. usefulness. 9. blessing.
~ líquido net profit. **em ~ das vítimas** for the benefit of the victims. **~ espiritual** edification.

benéfico adj. 1. beneficial, benefic, beneficent, useful, salutary. 2. kind, helpful, charitable. 3. profitable. ‖ **beneficamente** adv. 1. beneficially, advantageously. 2. kindly.

benemerência s. f. 1. merit, meritoriousness. 2. benefaction. 3. reputability, reputableness.

benemerente adj. m. + f. 1. meritorious, well-deserving. 2. merited.

benemérito s. m. 1. meritorious person. 2. benefactor. ‖ adj. 1. well-deserving, worthy. 2. meritorious. 3. illustrious, distinguished.

beneplácito s. m. 1. consent, approval. 2. permission, licence. 3. approbation, sanction. 4. satisfaction.

benesse s. f. 1. altarage, altar dues. 2. emolument, gain, profit.

benevolência s. f. 1. benevolence, goodwill, amity, friendship, amicability. 2. complaisance, affability. 3. esteem, respect.
consegui a ~ dele I found favour in his eyes.

benevolente, benévolo adj. benevolent, kind, charitable, benign. ‖ **benevolamente** adv. with benevolence, benevolently, kindly, charitably.

benfazejo adj. wholesome, beneficent, beneficial, charitable.

benfeitor s. m. 1. benefactor, well-doer, amender. 2. improver. ‖ adj. beneficial.

benfeitora s. f. benefactress.

benfeitoria s. f. 1. improvement, betterment, melioration. 2. benefit, profit.

benfeitorizar v. to improve, ameliorate.

bengala s. f. 1. walking-stick, cane, staff (plate G 4). 2. bengaline.

bengalada s. f. stroke(s) with a cane.

bengaleiro s. m. 1. cane-maker, cane-seller. 2. cane and wardrobe keeper (in a theater, concert-hall, etc.). 3. hat-and-umbrella-stand. 4. dealer in Bengali products.

bengali s. Bengali: 1. m. + f. native or inhabitant of Bengal. 2. m. the language. ‖ adj. Bengali: of or pertaining to Bengal.

bengo s. m. (Braz.) 1. alley, lane, narrow street. 2. ill-frequented locality. 3. lowest type of shop.

benguela s. m. + f. = **banguela.**

benignidade s. f. 1. benignity, benevolence. 2. kindness, complaisance. 3. mildness, innocuousness.

benigno adj. 1. kind, benign, benevolent. 2. mild, gentle. 3. favourable, advantageous. 4. (med.) benign, not malignant. ‖ **-amente** adv. benignly, kindly, mildly, forgiving.

beniquê s. m. (surg.) metallic probe used in catheteric widening of the urethra.

benjamim s. m. (pl. **-ins**) 1. favourite or darling son (usually the youngest). 2. the youngest member of a group, society or club. 3. (electr.) socket or plug for two or three lamps.

benjoeiro s. m. benzoin-tree, benjamin, spicebush.

benjoim s. m. 1. benzoin, benjamin, balsamic resin. 2. (Braz.) a species of bees.

benodáctilo, benodátilo adj. (zool.) digitigrade.

benquerença s. f. = **afeto.**

benquerente adj. m. + f. benevolent, kind, charitable.

benquistar v. 1. to make sympathetic or lovable. 2. to conciliate, gain the goodwill of, win over. 3. to endear o. s., win the esteem or friendship of.

benquisto adj. beloved, esteemed, respected, well-beloved.

~ **com o chefe** on good terms with the boss. **você não é ~ aqui** you are not wanted here.

bens s. pl. see **bem** 4.

~ **confiscados** or **devolutos** escheat. ~ **imóveis** real estate. ~ **naufragados** jetsam. **com todos os** ~ with bag and baggage.

bentererê s. m. (Braz.) bird of the family Dendrocolaptidae.

bentinho s. m. scapular.

bento s. m. 1. Benedictine monk. 2. (pop.) quack. 3. old-fashioned piece of furniture. ‖ adj. (also **ben-zido**) sacred, consecrated, holy.

água-benta holy water.

bentos s. m. pl. fauna and flora of the sea bottom.

benzaldeído s. m. (chem.) benzaldehyde.

benzamida s. f. (chem.) benzamide.

benzedeira s. f. 1. female faith healer or quack. 2. witch, sorceress.

benzedeiro s. m. (also **benzilhão**) 1. faith healer, quack. 2. witch doctor, sorcerer.

benzedura s. f. 1. act of blessing, benediction. 2. conjuration.

benzeno s. m. (chem.) benzene, benzol.

benzer v. 1. to bless, pronounce one's blessing upon a person. 2. to consecrate, ordain. 3. to make happy. 4. to make the sign of the cross. 5. to

surprise, amaze. 6. to conjure. 7. ~**-se** to cross o. s.

benzidina s. f. (chem.) benzidine.

benzina s. f. benzine, gasolene, gasoline.

benzinho-amor s. m. (Braz.) (mus., dance) a kind of fandango.

benzoato s. m. (chem.) benzoate.

benzóico adj. (chem.) benzoic.

benzoína s. f. (chem.) benzoin.

benzol s. m. benzol, benzene.

beócio s. m. Boeotian. ‖ adj. 1. Boeotian. 2. dull, stupid, simple.

bequadro s. m. (mus.) natural: sign used to cancel the effect of a preceding sharp or flat.

beque (I) s. m. 1. (naut.) prow, head of a ship. 2. (pop.) beak, nose. 3. (ftb.) back (plate F 9).

beque (II) s. m. tree of the family Acanthaceae.

bequilha s. f. (aeron.) tail-skid (plate A 3).

berbequim s. m. (pl. **ins**) breast drill, brace, bit brace (plate F 1).

berbere s. m. + f. (also **sambaqui** m.) kitchen-midden: ancient deposits of oyster shells, conches, kitchen waste, bones and skeletons, bearing evidence of prehistoric life in American coastal regions.

berçar v. to lull to sleep.

berçário s. m. baby ward of a maternity hospital, day nursery, nursery.

berço s. m. 1. cradle, bassinet. 2. (archit.) section of a barrel-vault. 3. (mar.) stocks, slips (pl.) for launching ships. 4. birthplace, home, fatherland. 5. infancy, origin, provenience. 6. (Braz.) inkpad. 7. (Braz.) rocking blotter (plate E 2). 8. enclosure of a grave. 9. (mech.) bearer. 10. (typogr.) carriage. ~ **da máquina** (phot.) camera mount. ~ **de lança-mento (de navios)** launching cradle. **balançar no berço** to cradle. **colocar no** ~ to crib. **desde o** ~ from the cradle. **nascer em** ~ **de ouro** to be born from rich parents. **ter** ~ to have a rich, famous, noble origin.

bereba s. f. (also: **pereba, bereva**) abscess, itch.

bereberê s. m. (Braz., pop.) a nobody, (fig.) cipher.

berenguendém s. m. = **balangandã.**

bereré s. m. (Braz.) 1. noise, clamour, revolt. 2. fish of the Amazon (Acara festivus).

bergamota s. f. (bot.) 1. bergamot. 2. water mint, fish mint. 3. (Braz.) mandarin, a variety of orange. 4. perfume extracted from bergamot plants.

bergantim s. m. (pl. **-ins**) (naut.) brigantine, brig.

beribá s. m. (also **berivá**) horse purchaser or trader.

beribéri s. m. (med.) beriberi.

beribérico adj. beriberic.

berilino adj. (min.) berylline.

berílio s. m. (chem.) beryllium, glucinum.

berilo s. m. (min.) beryl.

berimbau s. m. jew's harp.

pensar que ~ **é gaita** to be easily mistaken.

berinjela s. f. aubergine, egg-plant, mad apple.

beririçó s. m. (Braz., pop.) plant of the family Tridaceae.

berjaçote s. m. a kind of fig with a red pulp.

berlinda s. f. 1. (hist.) berlin: two-seated covered carriage. 2. movable reliquary. 3. a certain game of forfeits.

estar na ~ to be the center of general attention.

berlinense s. m. + f., **berlinês** m. Berliner: native or inhabitant of Berlin. ‖ adj. of or relative to Berlin.
berliques s. m. pl. only used in the expression ~ **e berloques** jugglery, tricks.
berloque s. m. watch trinket, small jewell or decorative object, fandangle, pendant, charm.
berma s. f. berm(e), small footpath on a rampart or dam.
bermuda s. f. Bermuda shorts.
bernarda (I) s. f. (coll.) revolt, riot, tumult, uproar.
bernarda (II) s. f. (bot.) a variety of pear.
bernardice s. f. folly, imbecility, stupidity, nonsense.
bernardo s. m. Bernardine, Cistercian monk. ‖ adj. (fig.) stupid and gluttonous.
cão-de-são ~ Saint Bernard dog.
berne s. m. larva of the botfly Dermatobia hominis, which penetrates the skin of animals and men.
bernento adj. infested with **bernes**.
bernês s. m. Bernese: native or inhabitant of Bern. ‖ adj. Bernese.
bernicida s. m. special insecticide used for exterminating **bernes**, botflies, etc.
beroba s. f. (Braz., pop.) mare.
beróideos s. m. pl. (zool.) Beroida: an order of ctenophores.
berôncio s. m. shy, withdrawn and distrustful person.
beronha s. f. (Braz.) stable fly.
berquélio s. m. (chem.) berkelium.
berra s. f. rut, heat (esp. of deer and cattle).
estar na ~ to be in fashion, be the topic of conversation.
berraçada s. f. = **berreiro**.
berrador s. m. bleater, bellower, crier, brawler, shouter, yeller, howler. ‖ adj. bleating, bellowing, crying.
berrante s. m. (Braz., sl.) revolver, gun. ‖ adj. m. + f. 1. crying, shouting, harsh, vociferous, loud. 2. showy, striking, glaring.
cores ~s flashy (glaring) colours.
berrar v. 1. to cry, shout. 2. to roar, howl. 3. to bellow, bleat. 4. (Braz., pop.) to be of Negro or mulatto descent. 5. to vociferate, clamour. 6. to invoke, call forth insistently.
~ **nos ouvidos de alguém** to din into a person's ears.
berregar v. 1. to shout, scream. 2. to cry insistently. 3. to bleat, bellow, low.
berrego (ê) s. m. 1. shouting, bellowing or bleating. 2. outcry, scream. 3. howling, roaring.
berreiro s. m. 1. frequent screams, yowl. 2. clamour, bawling, vociferation. 3. noisy weeping or crying.
berro s. m. 1. the cry of animals: lowing, howl, bellow, bleat, shriek, etc. 2. shout, clamour. 3. roar. 4 = **berne**. 5. (ent.) warble-fly, bot-fly. 6. (bot.) monkey flower.
bertalha s. f. (bot.) Malabar nightshade.
bertoldice s. f. stupidity, blunder, folly, nonsense.
beruanha s. f. (Braz., ent.) stable fly.
berzabum s. m. (pl. -uns) (Braz.) 1. clamour, shouting. 2. conflict, tumult. 3. brawl, fight.
besantado adj. (her.) covered with bezants.
besantar v. (her.) to adorn (an escutcheon) with golden disks.
besante s. m. 1. bezant: an ancient gold coin, solidus. 2. (her.) disk resembling a gold coin (on an escutcheon).
besigue s. m. (cards) bezique.
besouragem, **besoiragem** s. f. (pl. -ens) 1. intrigue, scheme. 2. plot.
besoural adj. m. + f. (pl. -ais) 1. beetlelike. 2. coleopteral, coleopterous.
besouro, **besoiro** s. m. 1. beetle: any coleopterous insect. 2. (ent.) May-bug. 3. (Braz.) splinter from

the burrs of a bit, drill or chisel. 4. (Braz.) seeds of the castor-oil plant. 5. (electr.) buzzer.
bespa s. f. (also **vespa**) wasp.
besta s. f. crossbow, arbalest.
besta (ê) s. f. 1. quadruped, mare, mule, jenny ass. 2. beast of burden. 3. brutish fellow. 4. m. + f. (fig.) simpleton, fool, blockhead, duffer. ‖ adj. m. + f. stupid, silly, simple.
~ **de carga** beast of burden, pack animal. ~ **de sela** saddle horse. (fam.) mount. **fazer-se de** ~ to play the fool.
besta-fera s. m. + f. (pl. **bestas-feras**) 1. beast of prey, wild animal. 2. (fig.) brute, cruel or savage person.
bestalhão s. m. (pl. -ões) (f. **bestalhona**) 1. fool, blockhead. 2. duffer, lout, dolt. ‖ adj. silly, stupid, foolish.
bestar v. 1. to act foolishly, talk nonsense. 2. to roam about, idle away, loaf.
bestarel s. m. (pl. **bestaréis**) (Braz., sl.) depr. form of **bacharel**.
besteira s. f. (also **bestagem**, **bestice**) 1. nonsense, absurdity. 2. foolishness, stupidity. 3. ingenuousness.
besteiro s. m. 1. cross-browman, arbalester. 2. cross-bow maker.
besteria s. f. troop of cross-bowmen.
béstia s. f. (Braz., sl.) burlesque speech, farcical talk.
bestiaga s. f. 1. worthless, miserable beast. 2. (fig.) fool, blockhead, duffer.
bestiagem s. f. (pl. -ens) any group of beasts (of burden).
bestial adj. m. + f. (pl. -ais) 1. bestial, beastly. ferine. 2. brutish, irrational. 3. (fig.) stupid. 4. (fig.) crude, rough, common. 5. (fig.) beastly, brutal. ‖ ~mente adv. bestially, brutishly.
bestialidade s. f. 1. bestiality, brutality, atrocity, beastliness, doggishness. 2. stupidity.
bestialização s. f. (pl. -ões) brutalization.
bestializar v. 1. to bestialize, brutalize. 2. to stupefy, make stupid.
bestialógico s. m. burlesque, nonsensical discourse. ‖ adj. 1. foolish, silly. 2. bombastic, pretentious.
bestiário s. m. bestiary: 1. (Rom, hist.) one who fought with beasts in the amphiteatre. 2. (Middle Ages) treatise on beasts and their habits. ‖ adj. bestial, brutish.
bestidade s. f. 1. bestiality, beastliness. 2. nonsensical saying, platitude.
bestificação s. f. (pl. -ões) brutalization.
bestificante adj. m. + f. bestializing, stupefying.
bestificar v. 1. to bestialize, brutalize. 2. to make stupid or irrational. 3. to amaze, bewilder, confound.
bestilha, balestilha s. f. 1. (naut.) cross-staff. 2. (vet.) fleam.
bestunto s. m. 1. (hum., coll.) noddle, pate. 2. weakness of mind, dullness, stupidity, narrowness.
besuntadela s. f. 1. anointment. 2. besmearing or begriming.
besuntão s. m. (pl. -ões) (f. **besuntona**) dirty fellow.
besuntar v. 1. to anoint. 2. to grease, smear. 3. to soil, besmear.
beta s. f. beta: the second letter of the Greek alphabet.
partícula ~ (nucl. phys.) beta particle.
beta (ê) s. f. 1. stripe of a contrasting colour (in textile fabrics, plumage, furs). 2. (min.) metal vein. 3. longish stain. 4. (naut.) any cordage of a boat not especially designated. 5. (Braz.) deep excavation in auriferous rock.
ser de estrela e ~ (coll.) to be very cunning. **ver-se em** ~s to be in difficulties, be in hot water.

betaemissor s. m. (nucl. phys.) a nuclide that disintegrates releasing beta particles.
betaína s. f. (chem.) betain(e).
betão s. m. (pl. -ões) concrete.
~ **vazado** poured concrete.
betar v. 1. to stripe, make stripe-patterned. 2. to blend colours. 3. to suit, agree, match, harmonize.
betatron s. m. (phys.) betatron.
bétel, bétele, bétere s. m. (bot.) betel palm, betel.
beterraba, betarraba, s. f. (bot.) beet, beetroot, red beet, sugar beet.
beterrabal s. m. (pl. -ais) beetroot field.
betesga s. f. 1. narrow lane, alley. 2. blind alley. 3. dark corridor.
betilho s. m. halter, muzzle (for oxen).
betonada s. f. portion of concrete produced in one operation by the mixer.
betonar v. to concrete: 1. mix or form concrete. 2. cover with concrete, cement.
betoneira s. f. concrete mixer (machine) (plate A 7).
betônica s. f. purple or wood betony.
betu s. m. mollusc of the family Olivideae.
bétula s. f. (bot.) birch, white birch.
 feito de ~ birchen.
betuláceo adj. (bot.) betulaceous.
betulíneo adj. (bot.) birch(en).
betumar v. 1. to bituminize, asphalt. 2. to prepare or treat with bitumen. 3. to putty, cement.
betume s. m. 1. bitumen, asphalt, mineral pitch. 2. putty.
betuminífero adj. bituminiferous.
betuminoso adj. bituminous, asphaltic, tarry.
bexiga s. f. 1. (anat.) vesica, bladder, gall-bladder, urinary bladder. 2. air-bladder, swim-bladder, poke (of fishes). 3. tube (for toothpaste, oilpaint, etc.). 4. ~s pl. (sometimes also sg., med.) variola, small-pox. 5. pock-mark(s).
 ~ **irritada** nervous bladder. ~**s doidas** chicken-pox, varicella. **com** ~ bladdery. **fazer-se** ~**s** to crack jokes. **pedir** ~ to show the white flag. **sinal deixado por** ~ pockmark.
bexigada s. f. 1. blow with a pig's bladder filled with air. 2. a quantity of bladders.
bexigar v. 1. to jest, joke. 2. to jeer, scoff.
bexigoso, bexiguento adj. pock-marked, pitted (with pustule scars).
bezerra s. f. 1. (zool.) heifer. 2. calfskin.
 pensar na morte da ~ to be distracted or day-dreaming.
bezerrão s. m. (pl. -ões) 1. big calf. 2. tall and fat boy.
bezerro s. m. 1. bull-calf, male calf, bossy. 2. calfskin, calf-leather. 3. (zool.) young manatee.
 ~ **de ouro** mammon, riches.
bezoar (I) s. m. (med.) bezoar, antidote.
bezoar (II) v. to bleat (like goats).
bi s. m. (Braz. fam.) one billion (speaking of money).
biaba s. f. 1. affray, scuffle, brawl. 2. stroke with a stick.
bialado adj. 1. two-winged. 2. dipterous.
biango s. m. hut, hovel, cottage, shack.
biangulado, biangular adj. biangular, two-angled.
biaribu s. m. (Braz.) Indian way of cooking game or fish in hot earth holes.
biaristado adj. (bot., zool.) biaristate.
biarticulado adj. (bot., zool.) biarticulate, two-jointed.
bias s. m., sg. + pl. bias.
biatatá s. m. (pop., also **boitatá**) ignis fatuus, will-o'-the-wisp.
biatômico adj. (chem.) biatomic, diatomic.
biaxial adj. m. + f. (pl. -ais) (optics, chem.) biaxial.
biaxífero adj. (bot.) biaxial.
bibásico adj. (chem.) bibasic, dibasic.

bibe s. m. pinafore, bib. little apron for children.
bibelô s. m. 1. trinket, bibelot. 2. fancy jewellery. 3. trifles (pl.). 4. (coll.) pretty-pretty.
biberão s. m. (pl. -ões) biberon: sucking-bottle, feeding bottle or nursing bottle.
bibi (I) s. f. American palm tree.
bibi (II) s. f. bibi: 1. lady. 2. Mohammedan princess.
bibiano s. m. (ornith.) parakeet, paroquet.
bibiru s. m. (Braz., bot.) bibiri, bebeeru, greenheart.
bíblia s. f. 1. **Bíblia**: the Bible, the Holy Scriptures, the Book. 2. (fig.) a valuable or important work of literature. 3. m. (Braz., sl.) Protestant.
bibliátrica s. f. the art of restoring books.
biblicismo s. m. biblicism.
biblicista s. m. + f. biblicist.
bíblico adj. biblic(al), scriptural. ‖ **biblicamente** adv. biblically.
bibliocanto s. m. a bracket used as a book support.
biblioclasta s. m. + f. biblioclast: destroyer or mutilator of books.
biblioclepta s. m. + f. biblioklept.
bibliófago s. m. bibliophagist. ‖ adj. bibliophagic.
bibliofilia s. f. bibliophily, bibliophilism.
bibliófilo s. m. 1. bibliophile, booklover, bibliophilist. 2. book collector, book hunter.
bibliofobia s. f. bibliophobia, dislike of books.
bibliófobo s. m. bibliophobe, hater of books.
bibliografia s. f. bibliophaghy: 1. history or description of books. 2. notice regarding authors and (or) their works. 3. newspaper column announcing recent publications. 4. reference list (at the end of a book).
bibliográfico adj. bibliographic(al). ‖ **bibliograficamente** adv. bibliographically.
bibliógrafo s. m. bibliographer.
bibliólatra s. m. bibliolater.
bibliolatria s. f. bibliolatry: 1. worship of books. 2. excessive reverence for the letter of the Bible.
bibliologia s. f. bibliology.
bibliólogo s. m. bibliologist.
bibliomancia s. f. bibliomancy: divination by books.
bibliomania s. f. bibliomania.
bibliomaníaco adj. bibliomaniac.
bibliômano s. m. bibliomane.
bibliomante s. m. + f. practicer of bibliomancy.
bibliomântico adj. of, pertaining to or related to bibliomancy.
bibliônimo s. m. collective designation of books of universal importance (Bible, Iliad, Odyssey, Koran, etc.).
bibliopirataria s. f. book publishing piracy.
bibliopola s. m. bibliopole, bibliopolist, bookseller (esp. of rare or curious books).
biblioteca s. f. 1. library: a) a collection of books. b) room or building where a collection of books is kept. 2. bookstand, bookcase, bookshelf. 3. stack.
 ~ **circulante** circulating library. ~ **viva** (fig.) a very learned person. ~ **pública** public library, free library.
bibliotecário s. m. librarian, bibliothecary.
bibliotecnia s. f. know-how in book production (material, size, quality).
biblioteconomia s. f. bibliotheconomy: the science of organizing and managing libraries.
biblista s. m. + f. bibli(ci)st, scholar of the Bible.
biboca s. f. 1. crevice, crack. 2. hole, hollow. 3. cave, grotto. 4. gully, gorge, ravine. 5. straw hut, hovel.
bibocal s. m. (pl. -ais), **biboqueira** f. gullied and creviced place.
bibocão s. m. (pl. -ões) valley gorge, large and deep ravine.
biboqueira s. f. (Braz.) rugged tract of land.
bíbulo adj. absorbent, absorptive, blotting.

bica s. f. 1. conduit, pipe, gutter pipe, spout (plate B 3). 2. eaves, waterspout. 3. (tech.) tap, cock. 4. springlet, fountain. 5. (Braz., coll.) a great number of good marks (justified or not) at an examination. 6. a certain type of bread. ~ **dos olhos** lachrymal duct. **em** ~ gushing out. **correr em** ~ to flow abundantly. **suor em** ~ dropping sweat. **estar à** ~ (fig.) to be on the brink of, very near. **ele está na** ~ **para chefe** he is on the point of becoming a boss.

bicada (I) s. f. 1. peck, thrust (with the bill or beak), pecking (of birds). 2. beakful. 3. edge of a forest. 4. spur of a mountain. 5. (Braz., coll.) sip of brandy. 6. ~s pl. brushwood. **dar** ~s **em** to pick at, beak. **marca de** ~ peck.

bicada (II) s. f. 1. (Braz., coll.) big tube. 2. eaves, gutter.

bicado (I) adj. (her.) bicolour (when a bird's beak differs in colour from its body).

bicado (II) adj. (Braz., pop.) tipsy.

bical adj. m. + f. (pl. **-ais**) beaked, beaklike.

bicame s. m. (Braz.) 1. system of conduits or gutter pipes, eaves. 2. planking of a river-bed or channel.

bicameral adj. m. + f. (pl. **-ais**) bicameral.

bicanca s. f. 1. proboscis, big nose. 2. (Braz., sport) football boots. 3. m. big-nosed fellow.

bicão s. m. (coll.) freeloader.

bicapsular adj. m. + f. bicapsular.

bicar (I) v. to peck, strike with the beak or bill.

bicar (II) v. (Braz., coll.) to tipple, get tipsy.

bicarbonado adj. bicarbonated.

bicarbonato s. m. (chem.) bicarbonate, acid carbonate. ~ **de sódio** saleratus (U. S. A.), bicarbonate of soda, baking soda, effervescent powder.

bicaria s. f. (Braz., sl.) 1. boastful display, ostentation. 2. dissimulation, pretence.

bicaudado adj. bicaudal, bicaudate.

bicéfalo adj. bicephalous, bicephalic.

bicelular adj. m. + f. (biol.) bicellular.

bicentenário s. m. bicentennial, bicentenary. ‖ adj. bicentennial, bicentenary.

bíceps s. m., sg. + pl. 1. (anat.) biceps, bicipital muscle. 2. (fig., sl.) physical strength, vigour.

bicha s. f. 1. (zool.) collective designation of snakes, worms and similarly formed reptiles. 2. leech. 3. dance figure (double-rows of pairs). 4. queue: a long line of people. 5. (hist.) body of troops. 6. (fam.) angry or scolding woman. 7. (mar.) revenue cutter (for customs control). 8. stripes, gold lace (on uniforms). 9. toy snake, toy lizard. 10. cobra, viper. 11. ear-rings. 12. (fireworks) cracker, pin wheel. 13. (sl.) yellow fever. 14. (Braz.) pipe coil on distilling apparatus (in sugar mills). ~ **amarela** (ent.) cutworm. ~ **de rabear** (fireworks) cracker. ~ **de sangrar** leech. ~ **solitária** (ent.) tapeworm, taenia. **estar com uma** ~ to be furious. **meter-se na** ~ to line up. **fazer** ~ to wait in line, (E. U. A.) line up. **fazer** ~s to play mischievous tricks. **ver se as** ~s **pegam** to watch for good results.

bichado adj. wormy, worm-eaten, maggoty.

bichador s. m. (S. Braz.) wooden spatula to clean vermin boils on cattle.

bichanado adj. whispered.

bichanar v. 1. to whisper, speak softly. 2. to murmur, speak in a low voice. 3. to confide: tell as a secret.

bichancrice s. f. affectation, act of making ridiculous or amorous gestures.

bichancros s. m. pl. 1. ridiculous or amorous gestures. 2. fright, sudden terror.

bichano s. m. (pop.) kitten, pussy.

bichão s. m. (pl. **-ões**) 1. topper, stunner, (U. S. A., fam.) jim-dandy. 2. strong or stout man.

bichar v. 1. to become wormy, worm-eaten. 2. to be subject to infestation by vermin. 3. (Braz.) to make money.

bicharé s. m. (Braz.) 1. coarse wool (used for ponchos). 2. poncho or blanket made of such wool.

bicharada s. f. 1. a lot of animals, animals collectively. 2. vermin. 3. (fig.) multitude, crowd.

bicharedo s. m. (Braz.) plague of insects, vermination.

bicharia s. f. 1. = **bicharada**. 2. (fig.) crowd, multitude, throng of people. 3. vermin.

bicharoco s. m. large, repulsive or loathsome animal.

bicheira s. f. boil, furuncle, wound full of worms (on the skin of animals).

bicheiro s. m. 1. leech glass. 2. hook, fish-hook (plate B 8). 3. boat-hook. 4. ticket-vendor of a sort of lottery, banker of this lottery. ‖ adj. 1. living on worms. 2. (fig.) pedantic, punctilious. 3. experienced, skilled.

bichento adj. 1. wormy, verminous. 2. (Braz.) bowlegged.

bichices s. f. pl. (coll.) caresses, endearment.

bicho s. m. 1. any animal, excepting fowl and fish. 2. worm, vermin. 3. ugly, repulsive or unsociable person, ugly customer. 4. expert, skilful or intelligent person. 5. novice. 6. (coll.) fleas, lice. 7. furuncle, boil. 8. (Braz., coll.) daring fellow. ~ **da cozinha** (pop.) scullion, kitchen help. ~ **da madeira** wood-worm. ~ **da terra** earthworm. ~ **de sete cabeças** something very difficult. ~ **que rói na consciência** the sting of conscience, remorse. ~ **ruim não morre** ill weeds grow apace. **ela é um** ~ **de concha** she is a shy person. **ele é um grande** ~ he is a cunning fellow. **ele virou** ~ he became furious and aggressive. **eles foram matar o** ~ they had a drink. **este livro está cheio de** ~s this book is worm-eaten. **fazer de alguma coisa um** ~ **de sete cabeças** to exaggerate, make a mountain out of a molehill. **jogo do** ~ (Braz.) forbidden kind of lottery. **mal do** ~ (med.) infestation by tapeworms. **sem** ~ wormless.

bicho-barbeiro s. m. (pl. **bichos-barbeiros**) barbeiro, a bug which transmits the trypanosome, causing Chagas' disease.

bichoca s. f. 1. (pop.) earthworm. 2. little phlegmon, boil, furuncle.

bicho-cabeludo s. m. (pl. **bichos-cabeludos**) (zool.) caterpillar of an American moth (family Magalopygidae).

bicho-careta s. m. (pl. **bichos-careta**) (fig.) cipher.

bicho-carpinteiro s. m. (pl. **bichos-carpinteiros**), (ent.) woodworm. **ter o** ~ to be fidgety.

bichoco adj. 1. paltry, useless (horse). 2. wormy, worm-eaten.

bicho-da-seda s. m. (pl. **bichos-da-seda**), (ent.) silkworm.

bicho-da-terra s. m. (pl. **bichos-da-terra**) (Braz.) cricket.

bicho-de-cesto s. m. (pl. **bichos-de-cesto**), (ent.) bagworm.

bicho-de-coco s. m. (pl. **bichos-de-coco**) 1. larva of insects (esp. Pachymerus nucleorum) that infest coconuts and coconut palm. 2. (Braz., fig.) a cautious, taciturn fellow.

bicho-de-conta s. m. (pl. **bichos-de-conta**), (ent.) sow bug, wood louse, slater.

bicho-de-frade s. m. (pl. **bichos-de-frade**), (ent.) barbeiro, barber bug.

bicho-de-pé s. m. (pl. **bichos-de-pé**), (ent.) chigo(e), jigger.

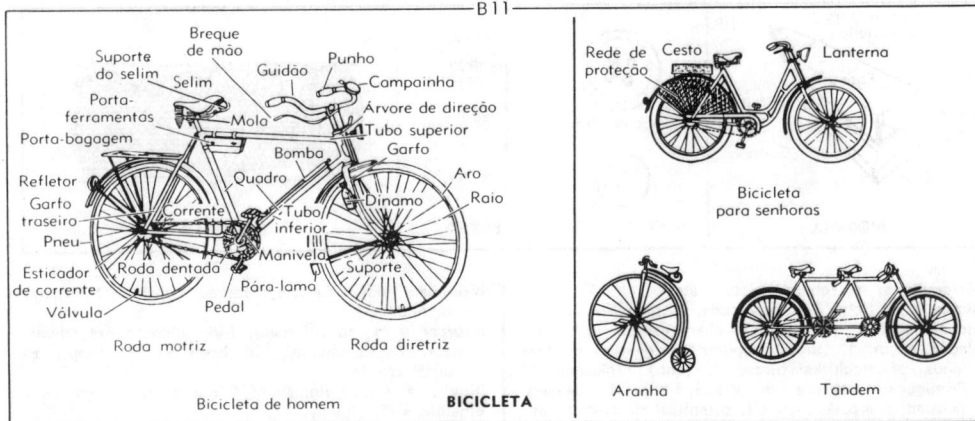

——B 11——

Bicicleta de homem   **BICICLETA**

Suporte do selim — Breque de mão — Selim — Guidão — Punho — Campainha — Árvore de direção — Tubo superior — Garfo — Aro — Raio — Dínamo — Tubo inferior — Manivela — Suporte — Pára-lama — Pedal — Roda dentada — Esticador de corrente — Válvula — Pneu — Garfo traseiro — Refletor — Quadro — Corrente — Bomba — Mola — Porta-bagagem — Porta-ferramentas — Roda motriz — Roda diretriz

Rede de proteção — Cesto — Lanterna — Bicicleta para senhoras — Aranha — Tandem

bicho-do-mato s. m. (pl. **bichos-do-mato**) (Braz., also **bicho-da-concha**) 1. shy, solitary person, recluse. 2. queer fellow. 3. wild beast.

bicho-gordo s. m. (pl. **bichos-gordos**), (pop.) fat larva (sometimes used as bait for fishing).

bicho-papão s. m. (pl. **bichos-papões**) bugbear, bugaboo, children's scare, scarebabe, ogre, rawhead. **ele é o ~ da aldeia** (fig.) he is the bogeyman of the village.

bicho preguiça s. m. (zool.) sloth.

bichoso adj. wormy, worm-eaten.

bicicleta s. f. bicycle, bike, (U. S. A.) wheel (plate B 11). **~ de corrida** racing-bicycle. **~ para transportes** carrier-cycle. **andar de ~** to ride on a bicycle, cycle.

biciclo s. m. velocipede (old-fashioned bicycle with a bigger front wheel).

bicipital adj. m. + f. (pl. **-ais**) bicipital.

bicípete s. m. bicipital muscle, biceps. ‖ adj. bicipitous, two-headed.

bicloreto s. m. (chem.) bichloride.

bico (I) s. m. 1. beak, bill, pecker, peak. 2. (pop.) poultry. 3. anything resembling a beak or bill: point, sharp end, spout, snout, prow, nose, lip (plates B 12, C 16, G 4). 4. nib of a pen. 5. (coll.) human mouth. 6. drunkenness. 7. (Port.) kiss. 8. small change, one milreis or cruzeiro. 9. needle-point lace. 10. (gambling) the lowest cards in the play. 11. small gains, casual earnings. 12. insignificant debt. 13. burner, nozzle, jet. 14. **~s:** pl. a) rest, remainder, residue. b) trifles. ‖ interj. hush! mum! be silent!.

~ cruzado crossbeak. **~ de Bunsen** Bunsen burner. **~ de candeia** lamp burner. **~ de mamadeira** nipple. **~-de-pena** in the expression: **desenho a ~-de-pena** pen-and-ink drawing. **~ do peito** nipple, teat. **~ grossudo** (ornith.) grosbeak. **acudir ao ~ de pena** to flash upon one's mind at writing. **abrir o ~** 1. to delate. 2. (Braz., ftb. sl.) to be tired and to play badly. **calar o ~** to be quiet, hold one's mouth, keep a secret. **com ~ dentado** tooth-billed. **criar ~** to become proud or haughty. **é ~ ou cabeça?** heads or tails? **ele é um pássaro de ~ amarelo** he is a very cunning fellow. **em forma de ~** beaked. **estar sobre o ~ do pé** to stand on tip-toe. **isso é o ~ da obra** (fig.) this is the hurdle to be cleared. **isso traz água no ~** there is something at the bottom of this. **jogar com pau de dois ~s** to hunt with the hounds and run with the hare. **levar al-**

guém no ~ to lead someone up the garden. **meter no ~** to blab out, divulge a secret. **meter o ~ em** to meddle, poke one's nose in. **molhar o ~** to wet one's whistle. **pegar no ~ da chaleira** (Braz.) to flatter, coax. **pôr-se nos ~s dos pés** to offer resistence, get angry. **ser bom de ~** to have a well-oiled tongue. **ter ~** to be complicated or difficult.

bico (II) s. m. (Buddhism) mendicant monk, dervish.

bicó adj. m. + f. (Braz.) tailless.

bico-branco, bico-blanco s. m. (pl. **bicos-brancos**) white nose (of a horse). ‖ adj. white-nosed.

bico-de-brasa s. m. (pl. **bicos-de-brasa**) (Braz., ornith.) nunbird.

bico-de-furo s. m. (pl. **bicos-de-furo**) fringilline singing bird (Oryzoborus angolensis).

bico-de-gavião s. m. (pl. **bicos-de-gavião**) (Braz.) identifying mark (cut into the ears of cattle).

bico-de-jaca s. m. (pl. **bicos-de-jaca**) glassware with prismatic embossments resembling the horny epicarp of the jackfruit.

bico-de-obra s. m. (pl. **bicos-de-obra**) (Braz.) difficult task, difficulty.

bico-de-papagaio s. m. (pl. **bicos-de-papagaio**) 1. hawk-nose. 2. plant of the family Cactaceae. 3. (path.) a painful osteophyte on the backbone.

bico-de-pato s. m. (pl. **bicos-de-pato**) 1. plant of the family Leguminosae. 2. plow with a flat symmetric share.

bico-de-proa s. m. (pl. **bicos-de-proa**) (Braz.) bow and stern of a fishing raft.

bico-de-veludo s. m. (pl. **bicos-de-veludo**) bird of the family Tangaridae.

bicolor adj. m. + f. two-coloured, bicolour(ed).

bico-miúdo s. m. (pl. **bicos-miúdos**) (ornith.) painted snipe.

bicôncavo adj. biconcave, concave-concave.

bicônico adj. biconic(al).

biconjugado adj. (bot.) biconjugate, bigeminate.

biconvexo adj. biconvex, convex-convex.

bico-pimenta s. m. (pl. **bicos-pimenta**) bird of the family Fringillidae.

bico-rasteiro s. m. (pl. **bicos-rasteiros**) (ornith.) 1. black skimmer. 2. American snipe, Wilson's snipe. 3. solitary sand piper.

bico-revolto s. m. (pl. **bicos-revoltos**) bird with a bent-up bill (Himantopus melanurus Vieill.).

bicorne adj. bicorn, bicornuate, bicornous.

bicos s. m. pl. (Braz.) left-overs; small portions.

bicota s. f. loud kiss, smack, buss.

bicotar v. to kiss with a smack.

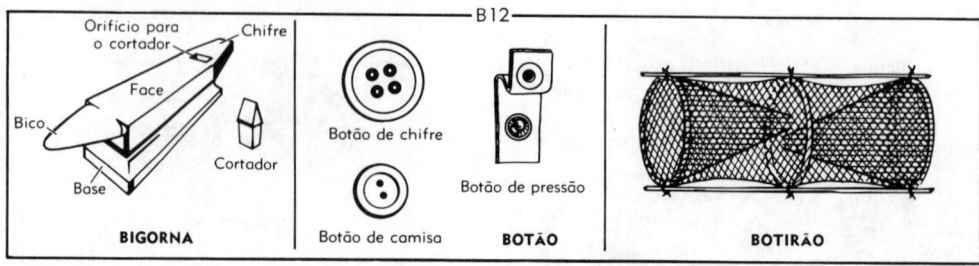

Orifício para o cortador — Chifre — Face — Bico — Cortador — Base — **BIGORNA**

Botão de chifre — **Botão de camisa** — Botão de pressão — **BOTÃO**

B 12

BOTIRÃO

bicromato s. m. (chem.) bichromate.
bicuda s. f. (ichth.) 1. barracuda. 2. picudilla.
bicudez s. f. 1. pointedness, sharpness. 2. difficulty.
bicudo s. m. 1. (Braz.) popular designation of five kinds of finchlike birds. 2. (ant.) nickname of Portuguese settlers in Brazil. ‖ adj. 1. beaked, pointed, sharp. 2. difficult, complicated. 3. dejected, dispirited, angry.
bicudo-encarnado s. m. (pl. **bicudos-encarnados**) (ornith.) scarlet tanager.
bicuíba s. f. (also **bicuibeira**) (Braz., bot.) 1. becuiba (tree). 2. becuiba nut.
bicúspide adj. m. + f. biscupid(ate).
bidê, bidé s. m. 1. bidet: a kind of sitz-bath. 2. (Braz., pop.) bedside or night table.
bidentado, bidenteado adj. bidentate, bidenticulate (plate F 5).
bidigitado adj. bidigitate: 1. (zool.) two-fingered. 2. (bot.) biconjugate.
bidó s. m. (N. Braz.) manioc cake.
bidoque s. m. (Braz.) eddy, whirlpool.
bíduo s. m. space of two days.
biebdomanário adj. biweekly.
biela s. m. (tech.) connecting or coupling rod, pitman, piston rod.
bienal adj. m. + f. (pl. **-ais**) biennial. ‖ **~mente** adv. biennially.
biênio s. m. biennium: period of two years.
biestável adj. m. + f. (electr.) bistable.
bifada (I) s. f. (pop.) many beefsteaks.
bifada (II) s. f. 1. foul smell. 2. offensive breath.
bifar v. 1. to pilfer, steal. 2. to cheat.
bifário adj. bifarious.
bifásico adj. double-phase.
bife s. m. 1. steak, beefsteak. 2. (coll. or ironic.) an Englishman. 3. (Braz., sl.) cut caused by shaving. ‖ adj. anglicized.
~ a cavalo beefsteak with a fried egg on it. **~ a pé** beefsteak with eggs and potatoes.
bifendido adj. bifid(ate), two-cleft.
bífero adj. biferous: fruiting or flowering biannually.
bifesteque s. m. beefsteak.
bífido adj. bifid(ate), two-cleft, forked.
bifilar adj. bifilar, two-threaded.
biflagelado adj. (biol.) biflagellate.
biflexo adj. biflex, bent in two directions, having two bends.
bifloro adj. (bot.) biflorate, biflorous.
bifocal adj. m. + f. (pl. **-ais**) bifocal.
bifoliado, bifólio adj. (bot.) bifoliate, two-leaved.
bífore adj. two-winged (doors).
biforme adj. m. + f. 1. biform, having two forms. 2. (fig.) ambiguous, equivocal.
bifronte adj. m. + f. 1. bifront(al). 2. treacherous, false. 3. fickle, unreliable.
bifurcação s. f. (pl. **-ões**) bifurcation, fork, parting, divarication, dichotomy.
ponto de ~ point of bifurcation, point of forking.

bifurcado adj. furcate, forked, forky, bifurcate, crotched.
bifurcar v. 1. to bifurcate, fork, dichotomize, divaricate. 2. to divide into branches. 3. (pop.) to mount astride.
biga s. f. (hist.) Roman or Greek chariot, biga.
bigamia s. f. bigamy.
em ~ bigamously.
bígamo s. m. bigamist. ‖ adj. bigamous, bigamistic.
bigêmeo adj. (bot.) bigeminate(d).
bigênero adj. bigeneric.
bigênito adj. twice begotten.
biglanduloso adj. biglandular.
bigle s. m. beagle: short-legged dog for hunting hares.
bignônia s. f. (bot.) bignonia.
bignoniáceas s. f. pl. (bot.) Bignoniaceae, the trumpet creeper family.
bigode (I) s. m. 1. moustache (plate B 6). 2. game of cards. 3. (pop.) correction, admonition. 4. (print.) vignette, ornament (on the title page). 5. (naut.) bow spray. 6. fringillaceous bird.
dar um ~ to play s. o. a trick. **~ de rato, gato**, etc. wiskers.
bigode (II) s. m. canary bird of Angola.
bigodear v. 1. to deceive, trick. 2. to cheat, swindle. 3. to fool someone.
bigode-de-arame s. m. (pl. **bigodes-de-arame**) man with a handle-bar moustache.
bigode-de-gato s. m. (pl. **bigodes-de-gato**) (electronics) cat whisker.
bigodeira s. f. 1. thick moustache. 2. a horse brush.
bigodeiro s. m. (Braz., ornith.) = **bigode 6.**
bigorna s. f. 1. anvil (plates B 12, M 9). 2. (anat.) incus.
entre a ~ e o martelo. 1. between two fires. 2. in great difficulties. **o tronco da ~** the stock of the anvil.
bigorrilha(s) s. m. 1. scoundrel, rotter. 2. weakling.
bigota s. f. (naut.) dead-eye.
bigotismo s. m. 1. bigotry. 2. falsehood, hypocrisy. 3. knavery, villainy.
bigu s. m. (also **carona**) clandestine travelling (without paying, esp. in busses, trams, etc.).
biguá s. f. (ornith.) cormorant.
biguancha s. f. (also **piguancha**) (Braz.) peasant strumpet, wench.
biguano adj. (also **biguane** m. + f.) great, big, large.
biguar v. (Braz.) to dive for diamonds (in rivers).
biguatinga s. f. (Braz., ornith.) darter, American snakebird.
bigúmeo adj. two-edged, ancipital, ancipitous.
biju s. m. (Braz., also **beiju**) manioc cake.
bijugado adj. (bot.) bijugate, bijugous.
bíjugo adj. drawn by two horses.
bijuí s. f. (ent.) a kind of honey-bee.
bijungarias s. f. pl. (Braz.) food, dish, delicacy.
bijuteria s. f. 1. bijouterie, trinkets, small jewels. 2. children's toys, trifles.

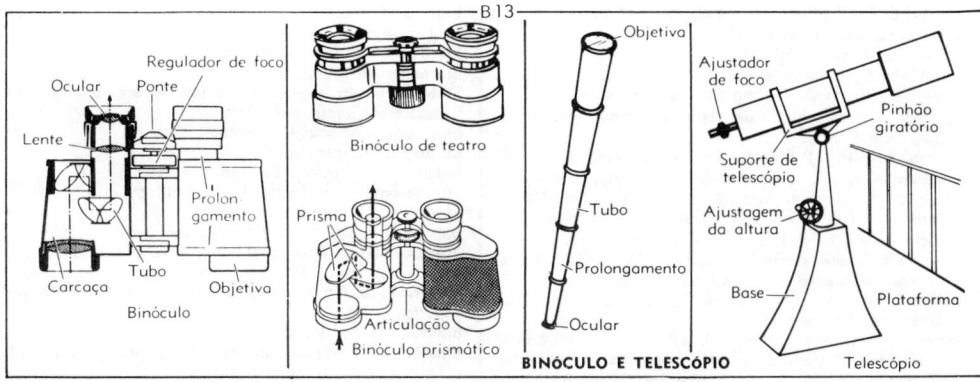

B 13

Ocular — Regulador de foco — Ponte — Lente — Prolongamento — Tubo — Carcaça — Objetiva — Binóculo

Binóculo de teatro

Prisma — Articulação — Binóculo prismático

Objetiva — Tubo — Prolongamento — Ocular

Ajustador de foco — Pinhão giratório — Suporte de telescópio — Ajustagem da altura — Base — Plataforma

BINÓCULO E TELESCÓPIO Telescópio

bil s. m. Portuguese form of the English word "bill": proposed law.
bilabiado adj. bilabiate, two-lipped.
bilabial adj. m. + f. (pl. **-ais**) bilabial.
bilaminado adj. bilaminate(d).
bilaterado adj. (bot.) bisymmetrical.
bilateral adj. m. + f. (pl. **-ais**) bilateral.
bilatérios s. m. pl. (zool.) Bilateria.
bilbaíno s. m. native or inhabitant of Bilbao. ‖ adj. of, pertaining to or relative to Bilbao (Spanish town).
bilbode s. m. fusillade.
   fogo de ~ continuous discharge of numerous rifles.
bilboquê s. m. bilboquet (children's wooden toy).
bile s. f. = **bilis**.
bilha s. f. pitcher, earthen pot with a narrow neck, monkey jar (plate R 5).
bilhão s. m. (pl. **-ões**) billion (in Braz. and U. S. A. with 9 zeroes; in Germany and England with 12 zeroes).
bilhar s. m. billiards, billiard-table, billiard-room or house.
   bolas de ~ ivories.
bilharda s. f. (also **bilha**) tip-cat (a boy's game, played with two bats and a little stick).
bilhardar (I) v. to hit a ball twice or cause two balls to strike together (at billiards).
bilhardar (II) v. 1. to play tipcat. 2. (pop.) to roam, loaf, idle away time.
bilhardeiro s. m. 1. billiardist. 2. (pop.) loafer, meddlesome fellow. 3. onlooker, spectator.
bilharista s. m. + f. billiardist, billiard player.
bilhete s. m. 1. note, billet, short letter, notice. 2. ticket (admission, railway, lottery, etc.).
   ~ **com direito a baldeação** transfer ticket. ~ **de assinatura de estradas de ferro** commutation ticket. ~ **de entrada,** ~ **de ingresso** admission ticket, card. ~ **de excursão** excursion ticket. ~ **de ida e volta** return ticket, (U. S. A.) round-trip ticket. ~ **de loteria** lottery ticket. ~ **do Tesouro** Treasury bill, exchequer bill. ~ **gratuito** pass. **comprar um** ~ to take a ticket. **escreva-me um** ~ drop me a line. **ele recebeu o** ~ **azul** he was fired, he was discharged from his position, he got the kick. **tirar** ~ to book.
bilheteira s. f. 1. card tray. 2. pocket-book, purse. 3. female box-office clerk.
bilheteiro s. m. box-office clerk, agent.
bilhete-postal s. m. (pl. **bilhetes-postais**) postcard.
   ~ **ilustrado** picture postcard.
bilheteria s. f. booking-office, box-office or ticket--office (plate E 13).

bilhostre s. m. 1. (depr.) foreigner, stranger. 2. intruder. 3. rascal, scoundrel.
bilião s. m. = **bilhão**.
biliar adj. biliary, bilious.
   vias ~**es** biliary canal, hepatic duct.
biliário adj. bilious, biliary.
biligulado adj. biligulate.
bilimbi(m) s. m. (bot.) bilimbi.
bilinear adj. m. + f. bilinear.
bilíngüe adj. m. + f. 1. bilingual. 2. double-tongued.
bilionário s. m. billionaire, multimillionaire.
biliosidade s. f. biliousness.
bilioso adj. 1. bilious. 2. choleric, ill-tempered.
bilirrubina s. f. (biochem.) bilirubin.
bilis s. f., sg. + pl. 1. (anat.) bile, gall. 2. (fig.) choler, ill humour. 3. hypochondria.
biliteral adj. m. + f. (pl. **-ais**) (also **bilítero** m.) biliteral.
biliverdina s. f. (biochem.) biliverdin.
bilobado adj. bilobed, bilobate(d), bilobular.
bilocular adj. m. + f. bilocular, biloculate.
bilontra s. m. 1. rascal, scoundrel. 2. (Braz.): a) flirter. b) habitué of brothels.
bilontragem s. f. (pl. **-ens**) roguery, knavery, cheating.
bilontrar v. 1. to swindle, cheat. 2. to lead a licentious life.
bilosca s. f. marbles (children's game).
biloto s. m. excrescence, wart, verruca.
bilrar v. to make lace.
bilreira s. f. (ornith.) bearded manakin.
bilro s. m. 1. bobin. 2. dwarf, weakling, molly. 3. ~**s** pl. (bot.) Peruvian swamp lily.
   renda de ~ bone-lace. **trabalho de** ~ tatting.
biltra s. f. slut, slattern.
biltre s. m. rascal, scoundrel, rogue, ruffian.
bimaculado adj. bimaculate(d).
bímano s. m. 1. bimane, human beings. 2. ~**s** pl. bimana. ‖ adj. bimanous, two-handed.
bímare adj. m. + f. bimarine, between two seas.
bimarginado adj. bimarginate.
bimba s. f. 1. (sl.) thigh. 2. (Braz., sl.) (little) penis.
bimbalhada s. f. tolling or tinkling of many bells.
bimbalhar v. to toll, tinkle, ring (bells).
bimba-n'água s. f. (N. Braz.) net fishing in a lagoon.
bimbarra s. f. (dim.: **bimbarreta**) big wooden lever, handspoke.
bimembre adj. m. + f. composed of two limbs or members.
bimensal adj. m. + f. (pl. **-ais**) bimensal, bimonthly, semimonthly: twice a month.
bimestral adj. m. + f. (pl. **-ais**) bimestrial, bimonthly: 1. lasting two months. 2. occurring every two months.

bimestre s. m. bimester: a two months' period.
bimetálico adj. bimetallic.
bimetalismo s. m. bimetalism.
bimilênio s. m. bimillenium.
bimo adj. biennial, lasting for two years.
bimotor s. m. vehicle or plane with two motors. ‖ adj. twin-engined.
binada adj. (bot.) binate, double, growing in pairs.
binagem s. f. (pl. -ens) method of silk spinning.
binar v. 1. to spin silk. 2. to till a second time (newly broken ground). 3. to say mass twice a day.
binário s. m. (tech.) couple. ‖ adj. binary, dual.
~ de arranque starting torque. ~ de torção turning torque. compasso ~ (mus.) two-four time.
binerval adj. m. + f. (pl. -ais) (also binérveo m.) binervate, two-nerved.
binga s. f. (Braz.) 1. horn. 2. tobacco box or snuff-box made of horn. 3. gravel. 4. popular designation of hummingbirds. 5. crude gasoline lamp. 6. primitive cigarette lighter (as used by caboclos).
bingo s. m. bingo: game of chance.
binoculado adj. binocular, binoculate.
binocular (I) adj. m. + f. binoculate, binocular.
binocular (II), binoculizar v. to focalize with binocles or a binocular instrument, to look through binoculars.
binóculo s. m. binocle, binocular, field-glass, opera glass (plate B 13).
binominal adj. m. + f. (pl. -ais) binomial, binominal, binominous.
binômino adj. binomial, binominous.
binômio s. m. binomial.
bínubo adj. married twice, remarried.
binucleado adj. binucleate(d), binuclear.
bioastronáutica s. f. bioastronautics.
biobibliografia s. f. biobibliography.
biobjetivo adj. (gram.) having two objects (verb).
biocenose s. f. (biol.) biocoenosis.
bioco s. m. 1. hood, veil, mantilla. 2. (fig.) prudery, false modesty.
biodinâmica s. f. biodynamics.
biodinâmico adj. biodynamic(al).
biófago adj. (biol.) biophagous.
biofobia s. f. (med.) biophobia: morbid fear of life.
biofóbico adj. (med.) biophobic.
biogênese s. f. biogenesis, biogeny.
biogenésico, biogenético adj. biogenetic.
biografar v. to biographize, write a biography.
biografia s. f. biography.
biográfico adj. biographic(al).
biógrafo s. m. biographer.
biólito s. m. (petrog.) biolith, an organic sedimentary rock.
biologia s. f. biology.
biológico adj. biologic(al). ‖ biologicamente adv. biologically.
biologista s. m. + f., biólogo m. biologist.
biombo s. m. 1. folding screen, screen. 2. partition wall, blind.
~ corrediço sliding panel.
biometria s. f. (biol.) biometry.
biométrico adj. biometric(al).
biongo s. m. 1. little shop, tavern. 2. straw hut, hovel. 3. hiding-place.
bionomia s. f. bionomics.
biopse, biopsia s. f. (med.) biopsy.
bioquice s. f. primness, hypocrisy.
bioquímica s. f. biochemistry, biochemics.
bioquímico adj. biochemical.
biosofia s. f. biosofy.
biossatélite s. m. (astronautics) biosatellite.
biostática s. f. (biol.) biostatics.

biota s. f. (biol.) biota: characteristic flora and fauna of a region.
biotaxia s. f. (biol.) biotaxy, taxonomy.
biotáxico adj. biotaxic.
biotério s. m. vivarium: place where animals for laboratory tests are kept.
biótico adj. biotic(al), biologic.
biotina s. f. (biochem.) biotin.
biotipo s. m. (biol.) biotype.
biotipologia s. f. biotypology, typology.
biotita s. f. (min.) biotite.
bioxalato s. m. (chem.) binoxalate.
bióxido s. m. (chem.) dioxide, binoxide.
bíparo adj. (bot., zool.) biparous.
bipartição s. f. (pl. -ões) bipartition: division into two parts.
bipartido adj. bipartite.
bipartir v. 1. to divide into two parts, divide into halves. 2. to bifurcate, fork.
bipatente adj. m. + f. open on two sides.
bipedal adj. m. + f. (pl. -ais) bipedal, two-footed.
bípede s. m. biped, two-footed animal.
bipene (I) adj. m. + f. bipennate, two-winged.
bipene (II) s. f. double-edged hatchet.
bipétalo adj. (bot.) bipetalous.
bipinulado adj. (bot.) bipinnate(d), decompound (plate F 5).
biplano s. m. (aeron.) biplane.
biplume adj. m. + f. two-winged, bipennate(d).
bipolar adj. m. + f. bipolar.
bipolaridade s. f. bipolarity.
bipolo s. m. (electr.) bipin terminal.
biquadrado adj. biquadratic.
biquara s. f. (Braz., ichth.) common or white grunt.
biqueira s. f. 1. finishing part or ornament of a building. 2. ferrule, tip of a cane or umbrella. 3. spout, gutter, drip. 4. toe cap (plate B 16). 5. iron tack (to protect the tip of a sole). 6. muzzle (cover over an animal's head to keep it from eating). 7. (S. Braz.) cigarette-holder.
biqueiro (I) adj. (pop.) fastidious.
biqueiro (II) s. m. (Braz., sl.) low class ball.
biquinho s. m. (dim. of bico) little beak or bill.
fazer ~ to pout, be sulky.
biquíni s. m. bikini: bathing suit.
biraia s. f. (Braz.) strumpet, slut.
birbante s. m. rascal, scoundrel.
biriba (I) s. m. m. + f. (Braz.) 1. rustic, yokel. 2. horse driver, muleteer. ‖ adj. sly, distrustful.
biriba (II) s. f. (Braz.) 1. young mare. 2. cudgel.
biribá s. m. fruit of the biriba tree.
biribarana s. f. (Braz.) forest tree of the family Annonaceae.
biribazeiro s. m. (Braz., bot.) biriba tree.
biribiri s. m. (Braz.) freshwater fish (Leporinus nigro-taeniatus).
biricera s. f. (Braz.) trifle.
birita s. f. (Braz.) any alcoholic drink.
tomar uma ~ to have a drink (esp. of white rum).
birmã, birmane s. m. + f., birmanês m. Burmese, Burman.
biró s. m. morsel, bit.
birola s. f. (Braz.) a kind of cotton fabric.
biroró s. m. (Braz.) manioc cake.
birosca s. f. (Braz.) marbles.
birote s. m. knot of a woman's head-dress, bun.
birra s. m. 1. obstinacy, stubbornness. 2. (fig.) whim, freak. 3. crib-biting. 4. beer. 5. (N. Braz.) hemp.
estar com a ~ to be obstinate. ter ~ to crib (horse).
birrada s. f. a blow with a cudgel or club.
birrar v. to be or become stubborn, to persevere.
birrefra(c)ção s. f. (pl. -ões) (opt.) birefringence.

birrefringente adj. m. + f. (opt.) birefringent.
birrelativo adj. (gram.) bi-relative.
birreme s. f. 1. (hist.) bireme: a Roman galley with two banks of oars. 2. two-oared boat for one oarsman.
birrento adj. stubborn, obstinate, mad.
birro s. m. 1. scarlet hat, cardinal's cap. 2. (ornith.) popular name of two birds (Leuconerpes candidus Otto and Hirundinea bellicosa Vieill.). 3. heavy and large cane or walking stick, cudgel.
birrostrado adj. birostrate(d).
biru s. f. snake of the family Colubridae.
biru-manso s. m. (pl. birus-mansos) (bot.) achira.
biruta s. f. (aeron.) wind sleeve, wind sock.
bis adv. bis, again, twice. ‖ interj. once more! encore! da capo!
pedir ~ to encore.
bisaco s. m. 1. bag, foddersack. 2. knapsack, haversack.
bisagra s. f. hinge.
bisalho s. m. 1. (ant.) little bag or pouch for jewels. 2. ~s pl. cheap jewellery, glass beads or trinkets.
bisanual adj. m. + f. (pl. -ais) biennial.
bisão s. m. (pl. -ões) (zool.) bison.
bisar v. 1. to repeat, do or play once more, encore, 2. to call for a repetition (song or music).
bisarma s. f. 1. a kind of halberd, two-edged battle-axe. 2. (fig.) a stout person, a very bulky thing.
bisarrona s. f. (pop.) variation of bujarrona.
bisavô s. m. great-grandfather.
bisavó s. f. great-grandmother.
bisbilhotar v. 1. to (make) intrigue(s), scheme, complicate. 2. to chatter, gossip. 3. to whisper, speak covertly. 4. to examine, investigate. 5. to poke.
bisbilhoteiro s. m. intriguer, tell-tale, gossiper.
bisbilhotice s. f. 1. intrigue, machination, scheme. 2. gossip, chitchat.
bisbórria s. m. ridiculous man, wretch, vile, or miserable person.
bisca s. f. 1. game of cards. 2. (coll.) scoff, a sharp word, sarcastic criticism. 3. hypocrite, bad sort, rascal, scoundrel. 4. (Port. sl.) flea.
ele é uma boa ~ he is a rogue, a scoundrel.
biscaia s. f. (S. Braz.) slut, slattern, harlot.
biscainho s. m. Basque: 1. native or inhabitant of Biscay (Spain). 2. Biscayan dialect. ‖ adj. Biscayan, Basque.
biscaio s. m. (S. Braz.) machete: large, heavy knife.
biscate s. m. 1. odd job, casual earnings. 2. casual work, chore, char(e).
fazer ~s to job.
biscateador, biscateiro s. m. (Braz.) odd-jobber, roustabout.
biscatear v. to do odd jobs, char.
biscato s. m. 1. morsel. 2. beakful (birds).
biscoitar, biscoutar v. to bake or make like biscuits.
biscoiteira, biscouteira s. f. biscuit tray or plate.
biscoiteiro s. m. biscuit maker or seller.
biscoito, biscouto s. m. 1. biscuit, sugar bread, scone, tea-cake, shortcake, rusk, cracker. 2. (fam.) slap in the face.
~ de marinheiro ship-biscuit, hard tack. ~ em forma de colher sponge finger. fazer ~ para viagem to get ready for the last trip (to die).
bisegre s. m. (shoemaker's) burnishing stick.
bisel s. m. (pl. biséis) 1. bevelled edge of a mirror, chamfer, bevel, bezel. 2. intersecting line, edge. 3. (print.) footstick, sidestick. 4. mounting (of a precious stone).
biselar v. to bevel, chamfer.
bisesdrúxulo adj. accented on the fourth syllable (counting from the last, e. g.: conferíamo-lo).
bismutal adj. m. + f. (pl. -ais) bismuthal.

bismútico adj. (chem.) bismuthic.
bismuto s. m. (chem.) bismuth.
bismutoso adj. bismuthous.
bisnaga s. f. 1. tube (for toothpaste, vaseline, etc.). 2. squirt (to spurt perfume during carnival).
bisnagada s. f. squirting, sprinkling.
bisnaga-das-searas s. f. (pl. bisnagas-das-searas) (bot.) bishop's-weed, Spanish toothpick.
bisnagar v. to squirt, sprinkle, spurt.
bisnau adj. malicious, spiteful.
pássaro ~ rogue, rascal.
bisneta s. f. great-granddaughter.
bisneto s. m. great-grandson.
bisonharia, bisonhice s. f. 1. awkwardness, shyness. 2. ignorance, lack of experience.
bisonho s. m. inexperienced recruit, new hand, tenderfoot, freshman. ‖ adj. 1. shy, awkward. 2. clumsy, inexperienced, verdant, callow, raw, fresh.
bispado s. m. (eccl.) bishopric: 1. see, diocese. 2. episcopal dignity, episcopacy, episcopate.
bispal adj. m. + f. (pl. -ais) episcopal.
bispar v. 1. to act as a bishop. 2. to discover at a distance, perceive, catch sight of. 3. to spy, observe. 4. (sl.) to steal. 5. to escape, bolt.
bispo s. m. 1. (eccl. and chess) bishop (plates P 5, X). 2. pontiff. 3. mitrelike uropygium of some birds. 4. burnt food (esp. meat).
~s e arcebispos lords spiritual. deixar entrar o ~ (cul.) to burn the food. para o ~ useless, worthless. queixar-se ao ~ to find nobody to whom one may complain of s. th. ter ~ (cul., fam.) to be burnt. trabalhar para o ~ to work without pay, for a song.
bispote s. m. chamber pot.
bisse(c)ção s. f. (pl. -ões) bisection, division into two (equal) parts.
bissemanal adj. m. + f. (pl. -ais) twice weekly, semi-weekly.
bissemanário s. m. biweekly periodical (newspaper or magazine). ‖ adj. biweekly.
bisserrilhado adj. (bot.) biserrate.
bisse(c)tor adj. (geom.) bisectional.
bisse(c)triz s. f. (geom.) bisector, bisectrix, line of an angle.
bissexto s. m. intercalary day (February 29th) in a leap-year. ‖ adj. (also bissêxtil m. + f.) 1. bissextile. 2. of small productivity (with respect to writers and poets).
ano ~ leap-year, bissextile.
bissexual adj. m. + f. (pl. -ais) (also bissexo) bisexed, bisexual, hermaphroditic.
bissexualidade s. f. bisexuality, bisexualism.
bissílabo adj. (gram.) disyllabic.
bisso s. m. byssus: 1. valuable fabric of the ancients. 2. (zool.) a tuft of filaments, beard.
bissulcado adj. bisulcate.
bissulfato s. m. (chem.) bisulphate.
bissulfeto (ê) s. m. bisulfide.
bissultor s. m. (Braz.) double avenger.
bistorta s. f. (bot.) bistort(a), snake-weed.
bistrado adj. swarthy, dark, brown.
bistre s. m. bister, bistre.
bisturi s. m. bistoury, scalpel, catling.
bisturi-do-mato s. m. (pl. bisturis-do-mato) a kind of orchid (Cytopodium punctatum).
bita s. f. stamp, rammer (for gravel(l)ing, ballasting).
bitácula s. f. 1. binnacle, binnacle box or stand. 2. (sl.) nose.
levar nas ~s to get slaps in the face.
bitartarato s. m. (chem.) bitartrate.
bitesga s. f. = betesga.
bitola s. f. 1. gauge, standard measure, tread, width of the track (plate E 1). 2. norm, pattern. 3.

railway gauge. 4. (naut.) thickness of a cable. 5. (fig.) rule of life, maxim. ~ **estreita** narrow railway gauge. ~ **normal** (de **estrada de ferro**) standard gauge. **chegar à** ~ to come up to standard. **governar-se pela própria** ~ to do a thing guided by one's own knowledge. **medir tudo pela mesma** ~ to treat all alike, make no difference.

bitolar v. to gauge: 1. establish a norm or standard. 2. appraise, estimate. 3. measure, mark out.

bitransitivo adj. (gram.) bitransitive.

bitributação s. f. double taxation.

bitu s. m. (Braz.) popular folksong.

biunívoco adj. bi-reciprocal.

biurá, biuri s. m. (bot.) Job's tears.

bivacar v. to bivouac, camp.

bivalência s. f. bivalence, bivalency.

bivalente adj. m. + f. bivalent, divalent.

bivalve adj. bivalve(d), bivalvular.

bivaque s. m. 1. bivouac, encampment, camp. 2. bivouacking troops.

biviário adj. bivious.

bívio s. m. parting of a road, fork, bifurcation.

bixácea s. f. Bixaceae: a family of tropical shrubs.

bizantinismo s. m. Byzantinism.

bizantino s. m. Byzantine: native or inhabitant of Byzantium. ‖ adj. Byzantine, Byzantian.

bizarraço adj. 1. elegant, fair, graceful. 2. extravagant, eccentric.

bizarrear v. 1. to act gallantly or extravagantly. 2. to give o. s. airs. 3. to boast, brag.

bizarria s. f. 1. gracefulness, elegance. 2. gentleness, generosity. 3. gallantry, bravery. 4. pride, honour. 5. arrogance, extravagance.

bizarrice s. f. ostentation, arrogance.

bizarro adj. 1. gentle, generous, noble. 2. elegant, graceful, comely. 3. brave, gallant. 4. arrogant, extravagant. 5. boasting, boastful.

blablablá s. m. (Braz., sl.) blab, chatter.

blandícia, blandície s. f. 1. meakness, mildness, gentleness. 2. caress, endearment. 3. flattery, blandishment.

blandicioso adj. 1. gentle, caressing. 2. flattering.

blandífluo adj. flowing softly.

blandíloquo adj. blandíloqu(i)ous, soft-spoken, smooth-tongued.

blasfemador s. m. blasphemer, curser, swearer. ‖ adj. blasphemous.

blasfemar v. 1. to blaspheme, profane, damn, sweâr, curse. 2. to speak evil of, defame, slander.

blasfematório adj. blasphemous, profane.

blasfêmia s. f. 1. blasphemy, impiety, profanity. 2. imprecation, cursing, swearing, malediction, irreverence, sacrilege.

blasfemo adj. blasphemous, impious, profane.

blasonador s. m. boaster, bragger. ‖ adj. boasting, (fig.) windy.

blasonar v. 1. to boast, brag. 2. to show off, display. 3. (her.) to blazon, emblazon: describe heraldic or armorial bearings. 4. to pride or praise oneself. 5. to proclaim, make known. ~ **de** to set up for. **ele blasona** he blows his own trumpet.

blasonaria s. f. 1. ostentation, display. 2. blazonry, blazoning.

blasônico adj. of, pertaining to or relative to blazonry.

blastema s. m. (biol., bot.) blastema.

blasto s. m. 1. germ. 2. (bot.) plumule.

blastobasídeos s. m. pl. (ent.) a family of lepidopterous insects.

blastocarpo adj. (bot.) blastocarpous.

blastoderma, blastoderme s. m. (embriol.) blastoderm.

blastodérmico adj. blastodermic.

blastogênese s. f. (biol.) blastogenesis.

blastoma s. m. (med.) blastoma, neoplasm.

blastômero s. m. (embriol.) blastomere.

blastomicose s. f. blastomycosis.

blástula s. f. (embriol.) blastula.

blatária s. f. (bot.) mullein, mullen.

blatários s. m. pl. (ent.) Blattaria: cockroaches.

blateração s. f. (pl. -ões) blatancy, blatant voice.

blaterar v. to bleat, cry (like a camel).

blau s. m. (her.) blue colour (of escutcheons). ‖ adj. (her.) blue.

blefador s. m. four-flusher.

blefar v. 1. to bluff, trick. 2. to dupe, delude, (U. S. A.) four-flush. 3. to cheat, swindle.

blefarite s. f. (med.) blepharitis.

blefe s. m. bluff, thimblerig.

blefista s. m. + f. bluffer, thimblerigger. ‖ adj. bluffing.

blemômetro s. m. instrument used for measuring the explosion intensity (firearm).

blenda s. f. (min.) blende, mock lead, black jack.

blenorragia, blenorréia s. f. (med.) blennorhea, gonorrhea.

blenorrágico adj. (med.) blennorrhagic, gonorrheal.

blesidese s. f. mispronunciation (voiced pronunciation of voiceless consonants).

bleso adj. of or relative to the mispronunciation of consonants.

blindado adj. armour-clad, armoured, steel-plated, mail-clad, mailed.

blindagem s. f. (pl. -ens) 1. screening. 2. shield, blindage, plating, armature, armour. 3. casing. ~ **de aço** steel armour. ~ **de metal** metal shield.

blindar v. 1. to armour, plate, case in steel. 2. to coat, cover, protect (with steel plates). 3. to fill (up).

blocausse s. m. blockhouse (also mil.).

bloco s. m. 1. block, log of wood, pig of iron, heavy piece of earth or stone (plate A 13). 2. writing pad, date block, memoranda tablet (plate E 2). 3. bloc: a political group (e. g.: farm bloc). 4. (Braz.) carnivalesque group of dancers. ~ **de cilindro** (tec.) cylinder block. ~ **de decomposição** (geol.) boulder. ~ **de desenho** drawing block or pad. ~ **de papel** block, writing pad, tablet. ~ **errático** (geol.) erratic block or rock. **como um** ~ blocky. **em** ~ in the lump. **ele comprou a mercadoria em** ~ he bought the merchandise wholesale. **eles apareceram em** ~ they appeared in closed ranks. **formar um** ~ to block. **um** ~ **de casas** a block.

bloco-diagrama s. m. (pl. **blocos-diagramas**) block diagram.

bloqueado adj. blocked, obstructed, embarrassed.

bloqueador s. m. blocker, blockader. ‖ adj. blocking, blockading.

bloqueante adj. m. + f. blockading.

bloquear v. 1. to block up, blockade. 2. to block, obstruct, bar, stop, spike, stuff, jam, foul. 3. to besiege. 4. to attack. ~ **uma conta** to block an account.

bloqueio s. m. 1. blockade, siege. 2. blockage. 3. obstruction, obstacle, stoppage, bolting.

bloquista s. m. + f. (typogr.) a person who binds vouchers, paper-blocks, etc.

blusa s. f. 1. blouse (plate R 6). 2. smock (of a workman). 3. (U. S. A.) shirtwaist. 4. jumper. 5. a sailor's frock.

blusão s. m. (pl. -ões) windbreaker (sports jacket), blouse, slop.

boa (I) s. f. (zool.) boa: a genus of nonvenomous snakes.

boa (II) s. f. (jur.) real or landed estates (or property), immovables. ‖ adj. 1. f. of **bom**. 2. (sl.) sexy. ~ **conduta** propriety of conduct. ~ **viagem!** have a nice trip! **dar as** ~**s noites** to say good night. **de** ~ **família** well-born. **dei-lhe** ~**s palavras** I spoke him fair. **desejar** ~ **viagem** to bid God--speed. **é boa!** indeed!, you don't mean it. **ele tem** ~ **vida** he is on easy street. **ele tem uma** ~ **índole** he has an equal temper. **em** ~**s graças** in great favour. **escapar de** ~ to have a narrow escape. **esta é** ~ 1. this is a fine thing indeed. 2. that's a good one. **estar de** ~ **saúde** to enjoy good health. **estar em** ~**s condições físicas** (sport) to be in good form. **estar metido em** ~**s** to be in a tight spot. **lapso de** ~ **conduta** fall from grace. **levar** ~ **vida** to be flushed. **pregar uma** ~ **a alguém** to make a fool of a person. **uma** ~ **peça!** a pretty trick. **uma** ~ **piada** not a bad joke.

boá s. m. boa (scarf worn around a woman's neck).

boal s. m. (pl. **-ais**) a variety of white, sweet grapes.

boana s. f. 1. thin board, deal. 2. plated metal. 3. shoal of little fish.

boa-noite s. f. (pl. **boas-noites**) moonflower (Ipomoea bona-nox).

boa-nova s. f. (pl. **boas-novas**) 1. white butterfly. 2. good news. 3. evangel.

boa-pinta s. m. + f. (pl. **boas-pintas**) (Braz., pop.) a Beau Brummell, dandy. ‖ adj. m. + f. good-looking; elegant, dady.

Boas-festas s. f. pl. Merry Christmas.

boas-noites s. f. pl. (bot.) Madagascar periwinkle.

boas-vindas s. f. pl. welcome. **demos-lhe as** ~ we bade him welcome. **deram-lhe cordiais** ~ they gave him a kind welcome. **ela deu as** ~ **a ele** she made him welcome.

boatar v. to spread false reports, to rumour.

boa-tarde s. f. (pl. **boas-tardes**) (bot.) periwinkle.

boataria s. f. false reports, rumours.

boate s. f. night-club.

boateiro s. m. rumourmonger, rumourer, scandalmonger, alarmist, retailer.

boato s. m. 1. rumour, report. 2. common talk, hearsay. 3. fib, falsehood. ~ **falso** canard. ~**s estão correndo por aí** rumours are about, it is in the air. **corre o** ~ the rumour is afloat, rumour has it. **correu o** ~ **de boca em boca** the rumour spread from mouth to mouth. **o** ~ **circulou pela cidade** the rumour made the round of the town. **espalhar** ~**s** to spread rumours.

boava s. m. + f. (Braz., coll.) 1. foreigner, alien. 2. Portuguese (immigrant).

boa-vida s. m. + f. (pl. **boas-vidas**) idler, easygoing fellow, lazybones.

boazuda s. f. (Braz., sl.) a sexy woman. ‖ adj. sexy (of a woman).

boba (ô) (I) s. f. (med.) = **bouba**.

boba (ô) (II) s. f. silly (woman or girl).

bobagem s. f. (pl. **-ens**) (also **bobice**) 1. foolery, buffoonery. 2. folly, stupidity, nonsense, trash, (fig.) eye-wash, (fig.) moonshine. ‖ interj fudge! bosh! **eles falaram -ens** they talked nonsense, they talked wild. **ora, que** ~**!** that's stuff and nonsense! fiddlesticks!

bobalhão s. m. (pl. **-ões**) (f. **-ona**) fool, blockhead, dunce, ridiculous fellow.

bobeada s. f. a silly move, a blunder.

bob(e)ar v. 1. to play the fool, behave like a buffoon. 2. to jest, joke, banter. 3. to talk nonsense.

bobéia s. f. 1. folly, silliness. 2. foolery, clownishness. 3. crumb (of bread).

bobiciada s. f. a lot of nonsense, foolery, clownishness.

bobina s. f. 1. bobbin. 2. spool, reel (plate M 2). 3. (electr.) coil, winding.

~ **de choque** ou **reatância** choking coil, impedance coil. ~ **de sintonização** tuning coil. ~ **"favo de mel"** honeycomb coil. ~ **de tensão** pressure coil.

bobinadeira, bobinador s. m. (tech.) winding frame, reeler, winder (plate M 1).

bobinar v. to wind, coil, reel.

bobinete s. m. net lace, bobbinet.

bobo (ô) s. m. 1. half-wit, fool, imbecile, saphead, dunce. 2. buffoon, clown, mimic. 3. (Braz., ornith.) manx shearwater. 4. (hist.) court-jester. ‖ adj. foolish, silly, numskulled, soft, gaga, simple, boobyish, mad, imbecile, weak. ~**!** you silly! **dia dos** ~ April fools' day. **ele é um** ~ he is light in the head. **ele é um** ~ **reconhecido** he is an allowed fool, he is an arrant dunce. **ele não é** ~ he knows the time of the day. **ele não é tão** ~ **como parece** he is not so green as cabbage-looking. **fazer alguém de** ~ to befool, bosh s. o. **fazer papel de** ~ to play the fool. **não seja** ~**!** don't be stupid!

bobó s. m. 1. (Braz.) African dish prepared with beans, bananas, manioc, and coconut oil. 2. (S. Braz.) = **bobo**.

boboca s. m. + f. (Braz.) a great fool or silly. ‖ adj. stupid, silly.

boca (ô) s. f. 1. mouth (plate C 18). 2. (sl.) clapper, whistle, grub-trap. 3. muzzle, jaw (plates P 13, T 1). 4. throat, gullet. 5. opening, vent, throat (plate A 6). 6. passage, entrance. 7. beak. ~ **de carregamento** kiln hole. ~ **da chave** jaw of a wrench (plate P 4). ~ **do estômago** the pit of the stomach. ~ **de mina** bank. ~ **do navio** beam: breadth of a ship. ~ **do palco** apron stage. ~ **da peça** muzzle of a cannon. ~ **das pernas das calças** (tail.) opening of a trouser-leg. ~ **do rio** mouth of the river. ~ **de riso** smiling looks. ~ **do vulcão** crater. ~ **torta** splay mouth. **a** ~ **não admite fiador** the belly has no ears. **à** ~ **da noite** at nightfall, in the dusk, in the evening. **abrir a** ~ to open the mouth, talk. **abrir tamanha** ~ to show unrestrained admiration. **adoçar a** ~ to coax, cajole somebody. **andar nas** ~**s do mundo** to be in bad repute. **botar a** ~ **no mundo** to set up a great fuss. **cair na** ~ **do lobo** to fall into a trap. **cale a** ~**!** hold your tongue! cut the cackle! hold your jaw! shut up! **de** ~ **dura** hardmouthed. **de** ~ **em** ~ from mouth to mouth, to be spread about. **da mão à** ~ **se perde a sopa** there's many a slip twixt the cup and the lip. **de sua própria** ~ from his own lips. **você me deixa com água na** ~ you make my mouth water. **dizer à** ~ **pequena** to tell in a whisper. **dizer de** ~ **cheia** to talk freely. **dizer o que vem à** ~ to call a spade a spade. **encher a** ~ **de uma coisa** to talk too big (or too much) about a thing. **estar com a** ~ **doce** to be fastidious, be pampered. **estar com a** ~ **seca** to miss a drink. **ficar de** ~ **aberta** to gape in wonder. **minha** ~ **é um botão** (also ironically) I am silent as a grave. **pagar à** ~ **do cofre** to pay cash. **pegar com a** ~ **na botija** to catch in the very act, catch red-handed. **pela mesma** ~ unanimously. **pôr a** ~ **em alguém** to slander somebody. **tapamos-lhe a** ~ we stopped his mouth. **tapar a** ~ **de alguém** to stop a person's tongue. **ele não tem** ~ **para dizer não** he does not know to give a refusal. **ter a** ~ **suja** to use foul language. **ter sete** ~**s a sustentar** to have seven mouths to feed.

boça s. f. (naut.) stopper, lashing. ~ **de mezena** (naut.) throat brail of the mizen. ~ **da lancha** (naut.) guess'-rope (also guest-rope) of a launch. ~ **das unhas** (naut.) shank-painter.

boca-aberta s. m. + f. (pl. **bocas-abertas**) 1. gaper, starer. 2. booby, dunce.

bocaça s. f. wide or big mouth, jaws (pl.).

bocada s. f. 1. (fishing) aperture of a trawling net or trammel. 2. bite, biting. 3. mouthful. 4. gulp, draught.

boca-de-barro s. m. (pl. **bocas-de-barro**) (Braz.) a kind of tropical honey-bees (Melipona pallida).

boca-de-cano s. f. (pl. **bocas-de-cano**) (Braz., sl.) lucrative business, bargain.

boca-de-dragão s. f. (pl. **bocas-de-dragão**) (bot.) dragon's-mouth orchid.

boca-de-fogo s. m. (pl. **bocas-de-fogo**) 1. cannon, piece of artillery. 2. salt-water fish (family Haemulonidae).

boca-de-fumo s. f. (pl. **bocas-de-fumo**) (Braz., sl.) a drug market spot.

boca-de-leão s. f. (pl. **bocas-de-leão**) (bot.) snapdragon, lion's mouth.

boca-de-lobo s. f. (pl. **bocas-de-lobo**) 1. gully-hole. 2. = **boca-de-leão**.

boca-de-sapo s. f. (pl. **bocas-de-sapo**) (Braz.) 1. = **boca-de-barro**. 2. (bot.) gentianwort.

boca-de-sino s. m. (pl. **bocas-de-sino**) blunderbuss.

bocadinho s. m. little bit, morsel.

há ~ not long ago, just now.

bocado s. m. 1. a mouthful, piece, bit. 2. morsel, slice, small portion. 3. bit, bar, cannon-bit, cannon. 4. little while.

~ **sem osso** (coll.) gains without much pains. **aos** ~**s** little by little. **ele comeu um** ~ he ate a wee bit. **ele é um amigo de bons** ~**s** he is fond of a good dish. **há** ~ recently, a short time ago. **levantar-se da mesa com o** ~ **na boca** to be a hasty eater. **ele o vendeu por um** ~ **de pão** he sold it for a mere song.

bocadura s. f. mouth or muzzle of a cannon.

bocagem s. f. (pl. **-ens**) 1. idle talk, prattle, verbiage. 2. obscenity, foul language. 3. curse, imprecation.

bocagiano adj. of or referring to Bocage (Port. poet).

bocaina s. f. (Braz.) 1. mountain gorge. 2. valley, basin. 3. gully, ravine. 4. channel, mouth (river).

bocaiúva s. f. macaw tree.

bocal s. m. (pl. **-ais**) 1. mouth of a flask, vase, etc. 2. hole of a candlestick. 3. brim or brink of a well. 4. mouthpiece of a phone, nipple, nozzle (of a wind instrument) (plates M 9; R 2; T 4). 5. muzzle (for oxen). 6. (tech.) nozzle, jet, beak (plates A 6; F. 3; T 6). 7. cuff (of a sleeve). 8. curb-bit (plate C 12).

~ **de descarga** discharger. ~ **do ejetor** ejector nozzle. ~ **de escapamento** exhaust trimble. ~ **de injeção de ar** blast nozzle. ~ **de mangueira** hose nipple.

boçal s. m. (pl. **-ais**) (Braz., hist.) newly arrived Negro slave. ‖ adj. m. + f. 1. stupid, rude. 2. recently arrived (of African Negro slaves).

boçalidade s. f. stupidity, ignorance.

boca-lisa s. f. (pl. **bocas-lisas**) (Braz., ichth.) a species of catfish.

bocanho s. m. (meteor.) blue spot in the overcast sky.

boca-preta s. m. (pl. **bocas-pretas**) (zool.) squirrel monkey.

bocar v. (also **abocar**) 1. to catch, snatch, take up. 2. to pick up.

boçardas s. f. pl. (naut.) breasthook, crutch.

bocarra s. f. wide or big mouth.

bocaxim s. m. (pl. **-ins**) buckram.

bocejador s. m. yawner, gaper. ‖ adj. yawning, gaping.

bocejar v. to gape, yawn.

bocejo s. m. yawn(ing), gaping, gape(s).

o último ~ the last gasp.

bocel s. m. (pl. **bocéis**) (archit.) 1. tore, torus. 2. a fluted moulding.

bocelão s. m. (pl. **-ões**) (archit.) big torus.

bocelar v. to adorn with or form like a tore.

bocelino s. m. thinnest part of a column at the capital.

boceta s. f. 1. little box of wood or pasteboard. 2. snuff-box. 3. (Braz.) fishing-tackle. 4. (vulg.) vulva. ~ **de Pandora** Pandora's box.

bocete s. m. 1. nailhead. 2. breastplate of a cuirass.

boceteira s. f. (N. Braz.) female street vendor (who shows her wares in **bocetas**).

bocha s. m. (Braz.) 1. boccie, bocce: game of bowls. 2. wooden ball used in it.

boche s. m. (S. Braz.) great quantity.

a ~ in great quantity, abundantly.

bochecha s. f. 1. cheek, jowl (plate C 18). 2. anything resembling a cheek. 3. (naut.) sny, snying.

com uma ~ **de água** with little trouble, easily. **dizer nas** ~**s de alguém** to tell to one's face. **entrar de** ~ to enter without paying (a ticket).

bochechada s. f. 1. slap on the cheeks. 2. mouthful.

bochecha-de-velho s. f. (pl. **bochechas-de-velho**) (Braz.) tropical shrub of the family Hippocrateaceae.

bochechão s. m. (pl. **-ões**) hard slap on the cheeks.

bochechar v. 1. to fill or clean the mouth with a liquid. 2. to rinse the mouth.

bochecho s. m. 1. mouthful. 2. rinsing of the mouth. 3. small quantity of a liquid.

bochechudo s. m. round-cheeked person. ‖ adj. chubby, blub-cheeked, apple-cheeked, cheeky, fubsy.

bochinchada s. f. (Braz., sl.) 1. row, brawl. 2. provocation of a conflict.

bochinche s. m. (S. Braz., sl.) 1. row, conflict. 2. mobbish dancing party.

bochincheiro s. m. 1. rowdy, rough, hooligan. 2. one who frequents vulgar dancing parties. ‖ adj. rowdy, rough.

bochornal adj. m. + f. (pl. **-ais**) 1. very hot and dry, sultry, stuffy. 2. breathless.

bochorno s. m. 1. sweltry air, hot wind. 2. sultriness, oppressive heat, stuffiness. 3. breathlessness.

bócio s. m. (med.) goitre, goiter, struma.

bocó (I) s. m. (Braz.) little hole in the earth (for playing marbles).

bocó (II) s. m. saddle-bag, pouch (of undressed leather).

bocó (III) s. (Braz., pop.) goof, simpleton, fool. ‖ adj. goofy, foolish, silly.

bocório s. m. (Braz.) 1. clamour, vociferation. 2. heated discussion. 3. (sl.) scoundrel. 4. scolding.

boçoroca s. f. ravine, gully.

bocuba s. f. (Braz., bot.) becuíba.

bocuda s. f. (Braz.) musket, rifle.

boda s. f. 1. wedding feast, dinner or banquet. 2. wedding, nuptials, marriage.

~**s de prata** silver wedding. ~**s de ouro** golden wedding. ~**s de diamante** diamond wedding.

bodalha s. f. farrow, young pig.

bode s. m. 1. he-goat, buck-goat, billy-goat. 2. goatskin (to carry liquids in). 3. little money pouch or box. 4. provisions, victuals. 5. (fig.) a grown-up man. 6. (Braz., sl.) mulatto.

~ **expiatório** scapegoat, fall guy, whipping-boy. **é bom ter um** ~ **expiatório** it's nice to have a peg to hang things on. **ele está de** ~ **amarelo** he is very angry. **pintar o** ~ to raise hell.

bodeco s. m. (Braz., Amazonas, ichth.) arapaíma.

bodega s. f. 1. wine-cellar, canteen. 2. (coll.) coarse food. 3. a filthy house. 4. (Braz., sl.) useless or unserviceable object. 5. trash, garbage.

bodegueiro, bodegão (pl. **-ões**) s. m. 1. proprietor of a wine cellar, tavern-keeper, tapster. 2. dirty or negligent fellow, also botcher.

bodeguim s. m. (pl. **-ins**) (Braz.) wild or mountain goat, wild billy-goat.

bodejar v. 1. to bleat, blather. 2. to stammer, stutter.
bodejo s. m. bleat, cry of a sheep or goat.
bodelha s. f., **bodelho** m. (bot.) 1. sea oak. 2. seaweed.
bode-preto s. m. (pl. **bodes-pretos**) (Braz., coll.) devil.
bodiano, bodião (I) s. m. (ichth.) a kind of perch.
bodião (II) s. m. (pl. -ões) (N. Braz.) fool, booby, boaster.
bodinho s. m. (ichth.) smooth dogfish, switch-tail.
bodionice s. f. bombastic trope, senseless figure of speech.
bodiônico adj. 1. bombastic, high-flown. 2. senseless, absurd.
bodo s. m. distribution of food and money to paupers on high days or holidays.
bodocada s. f. 1. the shooting and throwing of clay-pigeons. 2. (fig.) scoff, sharp critic, reproach.
bodoque s. m. 1. trap: apparatus for throwing clay-pigeons. 2. sling.
bodoqueiro s. m. clay-pigeon shooter, clay-pellet thrower.
bodoso adj. (Braz.) dirty, filthy.
bodum s. m. (pl. -uns) 1. rank smell, rancidity. 2. offensive odour (of he-goats).
boêmia s. f. 1. folly, dissipation. 2. loafing, vagrancy. 3. Bohemianism.
boêmio (I) s. m. 1. Bohemian. 2. language of the Bohemians. ‖ adj. 1. Bohemian. 2. knockabout.
boêmio (II) s. m. 1. gipsy. 2. (ant.) short cloak. 3. idler, loafer, vagrant. ‖ adj. idle, vagrant, careless, light-headed.
bôer s. m. + f. Boer. ‖ adj. Boer.
bofar v. 1. to throw out from the lungs, exhale. 2. to gush, spout out, spurt. 3. to belch, buster, boast.
bofe s. m. 1. the lungs, lights. 2. (fig.) character, temper, disposition. 3. pluck, heart, liver and lungs of animals. 4. frill(ing) (plate R 6). 5. (Braz., sl.) unattractive woman, slut.
   bonitos ~s de camisa beautiful shirt frills. **botar os ~s pela boca** to make every effort, strain one's forces, be tired out. **ele é um homem de ~s lavados** he is an ingenious man. **homens de bons ~s** good-natured men. **homens de maus ~ ill-disposed**, hard-hearted men. **mostrar os ~s to** speak frankly.
bofetada s. f. 1. box on the ear, slap in the face, flap, cuff, chopper. 2. (fig.) insult, injury.
   ela lhe deu uma ~ she pasted him one.
bofetão s. m. (pl. -ões) 1. facer, hard blow in the face. 2. (fig.) severe reproach. 3. (Braz.) theft.
bofete s. m. a light slap in the face.
bofetear v. to slap in the face, beat on the cheek, box on the ear.
boga s. f. (ichth.) boce.
bogari(m) s. m. (Braz., bot.) Arabian jasmine.
bogó s. m. (Braz.) leather pail.
boi s. m. 1. ox, bull, bullock. 2. any bovine. 3. (Braz.) rustic shelter, bower. 4. (Braz.) boat-hook. 5. covering of a canoe.
   ~ carreiro, ~ de cambão draught-ox. **~ na linha** an unexpected or additional difficulty. **~ silvestre** wild ox. **carro de ~s** oxcart. **colocar o carro diante dos ~s** to put the cart before the oxen. **ele comeu um ~** he ate too much. **junta de ~s** oxteam. **olhar como ~ para palácio** to stare like a stuck pig, look unappreciatively at something, to think s. th. unimportant. **olho de ~** dormer-window, skylight. **a passo de ~** to go at a snail's gallop or pace. **pé de ~** considerate, heedful. **tirar o ~ da linha** to remove difficulties. **pegar o ~ pelo chifre** to tackle a task with energy. **vá amolar o ~!** stop pestering.
bói s. m. office-boy, messenger.

bóia s. f. 1. buoy: a) seamark (plates B 2, C 19, P 16). b) lifebuoy. 2. dolphin, mooring spar. 3. float, ball (for level regulation in a tank). 4. floater (of a fishing line or net). 5. (Braz.) meal, food, provisions, grub. 6. (Braz.) remnants, unsold merchandise.
   ~ cônica nun-buoy (plate B 2). **~ de amarração** dolphin. **~ de apito** whistling buoy (plate B 2). **~ de salvação** lifebuoy. **~ luminosa** light buoy. **~ sino** bell buoy. **deitar as ~s** to sound somebody out. **pôr ~ na rede** to cork a fishing net. **não ver ~** 1. to obtain nothing. 2. to be unhappy.
boiaçu s. f. (Braz., Amazonas) a water-nymph.
boiada, boiama s. f. herd of oxen, drove.
boiadão s. m. (pl. -ões) big herd of cattle.
boiadeiro s. m. 1. cattle drover, herdsman, cowboy. 2. foreman on a cattle ranch. 3. cattle dealer.
boiador, boiadouro s. m. (Braz., Amazonas) tortoise grounds of a river.
boiante adj. m. + f. buoyant, floating.
boião s. m. (pl. -ões) big-bellied pot with two handles, jar.
boiar v. 1. to connect with a buoy, set afloat. 2. to float, buoy, be afloat, drift. 3. to fluctuate, waver, oscillate. 4. to swim on the surface. 5. (fig.) to hesitate. 6. (Braz.) to eat, dine. 7. (Braz.) to remain unsold, be left over.
   a ~ awash.
boi-bumbá s. m. (Braz.) = **boi-surubi(m)**.
boiceira s. f. tow, flax refuse.
boicininga s. f. (zool.) rattlesnake.
boi-com-folhagens s. m. (pl. **bois-com-folhagens**) (Braz.) beefsteak with lettuce salad.
boicorá s. f. (zool.) coral-snake.
boi-corneta s. m. (pl. **bois-cornetas**) 1. one-horned ox. 2. (fig.) brawler, squabbler, rowdy. 3. turbulent or noisy person.
boicotagem s. f. (pl. -ens) (also **boicote** m.) boycottage.
boicot(e)ar v. 1. to boycott. 2. to coerce, repress, restrict.
boi-de-cova s. m. (pl. **bois-de-cova**) (Braz.) cooperative work, mutual help at harvest, etc.
boieira (I) s. f. herdswoman, cowherdess.
boieira (II) s. f. 1. (astr.) morning star. 2. (ornith.) wagtail.
boieiro s. m. cowboy, cattle drover, herdsman.
boi-espácio, boi-espaço s. m. (pl. **bois-espácio, bois-espaço**) longhorn, longhorn cattle.
boi-gordo s. m. (pl. **bois-gordos**) (bot.) cassia rugosa.
boina s. f. cap, bonnet, beret (plate R 6).
boioçu s. m. (zool.) anaconda.
boiota s. f. (Braz., coll.) 1. backward person, idiot. 2. (med.) hypertrophy of the testicles.
boiote s. m. 1. yearling calf, young ox. 2. castrated bull-calf.
boiquatiara s. f. (Braz., zool.) a viper of the family Crotalidae.
boirel s. m. (pl. -éis) a small cork float.
boi-surubi(m) s. m. (N. Braz.) dramatic folk-ballet.
boitatá s. m. 1. will-o'-the-wisp. 2. tutelar spirit of home and fields. 3. a furious bull. 4. bogey, bugbear.
boiúna s. f. (Braz., pop.) 1. a water-nymph. 2. a haunted ship. 3. a big cobra.
boiúno adj. bovine.
boi-vivo s. m. (pl. **bois-vivos**) (Braz.) a stew made of ox testicles.
boiz s. f. snare, trap for small game (esp. birds), springe.
bojador, bojamento s. m. cornice, ledge, moulding. ‖ adj. jutting, salient.
bojante adj. m. + f. jutting, salient, prominent.

bojar v. 1. to swell, bulge, cockle. 2. to puff up, jut out. 3. to be salient or jutting out.

bojarda s. f. a sort of pear.

bojo (ô) s. m. 1. salience, bulge, bowl. 2. big belly, paunch. 3. any swelling, projecture. ~ **de alto-forno** bosh (plate A 6). ~ **de barril** bilge. ~ **da garrafa** belly of the bottle. ~ **de navio** belly of the ship. **ele é um homem de grande** ~ he is a very kind-hearted (or generous) man. **ele tem** ~ **para suportá-lo** he is able to bear it patiently. **fazer** ~ to belly, bilge.

bojobi s. m. (Braz., zool.) boa constrictor.

bojudo adj. 1. round, prominent, bulgy, baggy. 2. big-bellied, pot-bellied.

bojuí s. f. (Braz., ent.) a species of bees.

bola s. f. 1. ball, globe, sphere, bowl, round (plates A 14, B 5, P 6). 2. (pop.) head, wits, think-box. 3. stout or rotund person. 4. (Braz.) joke, crack, witty saying. 5. (Braz.) poisoned meatballs (to kill stray dogs). 6. cob. 7. ~s pl.: a) balls of coal and clay to keep the heat in the oven. b) bolas (weapon). ~ **ao cesto** basketball. ~ **de bilhar** billiard ball. ~ **de futebol** football, (joc.) pigskin (plate B 5). ~ **de sabão** soap-bubble. ~ **de tênis** tennis ball (plate B 5). **comer a** ~ to allow o. s. to be bribed, be bribed. **dar** ~ · to accept the attentions of an admirer. **ele não é certo da** ~ or **ele sofre da** ~ he is not quite right in the upper story. **jogar à** ~ to play ninepins. **jogar uma** ~ to bowl. **ela é redonda como uma** ~ she is a rotund woman. **martelo de** ~ stretching hammer. **trocar as** ~s to err, make a mistake. **virado da** ~ (Braz., fam.) dotty, cracked.

bolacha s. f. 1. biscuit, cracker, cookies, snap (plate D 3). 2. (pop.) box on the ear, slap on the cheek. **ele tem uma cara de** ~ he has a pug-face. ~ **doce,** ~ **para o chá** tea-cake.

bolacha-quebrada s. f. (pl. **bolachas-quebradas**) trifle, thing of little value or importance.

bolacheiro (I) s. m. biscuit baker, maker or vendor.

bolacheiro (II), **bolachudo** adj. chubby-cheeked, bloated (face).

bolaço s. m. (S. Braz.) a blow with bolas.

bolada s. f. 1. a hit with a bowl, (foot)ball, etc. 2. chase of a cannon. 3. opportunity, occasion. 4. (gambling) pool, stake, jack-pot. 5. lot of money. 6. embezzlement. **nesta** ~ **conseguiu o intento** on this occasion he attained his aim. **ele ganhou a** ~ 1. he swept the stakes. 2. he hit the jack-pot. **uma boa** ~ (pop.) a pretty penny.

bola-de-neve s. m. (pl. **bolas-de-neve**) (bot.) cranberry tree; guelder rose, snowball.

bolaina s. f. plant of the family Sterculiaceae.

bolandas s. f. pl. 1. reproach, abusive language. 2. misfortune. 3. haste, bustle. **andar em** ~ 1. to hasten. 2. to be dead tired, stumble along.

bolandeira s. f. 1. main wheel of a sugar-mill. 2. (Braz.) cotton gin. 3. (Braz.) wheel of a manioc-mill. 4. printer's galley, letter-board.

bolão s. m. (pl. **-ões**) 1. big ball. 2. any round or roundish mass (plastics, dough, etc.).

bolapé s. m. deep ford.

bolar (I) adj. m. + f. spherical, globular.

bolar (II) v. 1. to hit with a ball. 2. to hit, hit the target. 3. to succeed, be successful (in business, sports, etc.). 4. (sport) to lead off.

bolas s. m. + f. 1. scamp, a good-for-nothing. 2. dunce, stupid. ‖ interj. you don't say so! is it possible! **ora** ~! nuts! that's absurd! nonsense!

bolbífero adj. (bot.) bulbiferous, bulbous.

bolbiforme adj. m. + f. (bot.) bulbiform.

bolbilho s. m. little bulb.

bolbo s. m. bulb, bulbeous root.

bolboso adj. (bot.) bulbous, bulbiform, bulbaceous.

bolçado s. m. curdled milk brought up by babies.

bolçar v. to bring up or vomit milk (babies).

bolchevique s. m. + f. bolshevik, bolshevist, communist.

bolchevismo s. m. bolshevism, communism.

bolchevista s. m. + f. bolshevist, communist. ‖ adj. bolshevist(ic), communistic.

bolchevizar v. to bolshevize.

boldo s. m. boldo, boldu: shrub belonging to the family Monimiaceae.

boldrié s. m. baldric, shoulder-belt, sling.

boleadeiras s. f. pl. bola(s), hurl balls.

boleado adj. 1. turned (in a lathe), roundish. 2. (pop.) crazy, cracked, mad.

boleador s. m. bola thrower, Gaucho skilled in the use of bolas.

boleamento s. m. (also **boleio**) 1. turning, rounding off, camber. 2. improvement, perfection. 3. throwing of the bolas.

bolear v. 1. to round, turn (in a lathe). 2. to shape into a ball. 3. to improve, perfect. 4. to hurl the bola, picket animals. 5. (fig.) to captivate, enchant. 6. to drive a coach.

bole-bole s. m. (pl. **bole-boles**) (bot.) quaking-grass.

boleeiro s. m. coachman, driver.

boléia s. f. 1. trace bar (of a carriage). 2. coach-box, carriage box, driving-seat (plate C 15).

boleima s. f. 1. simple cake. 2. m. + f. simpleton, booby.

bolero s. m. bolero: 1. a Spanish dance and accompanying music. 2. a kind of short jacket.

boleta (ê) s. f. = **bolota**.

boletim s. m. (pl. **-ins**) bulletin: 1. short notice, short advertising announcement. 2. official report, school report, authorized statement. 3. military routine publication. 4. periodical publication. 5. (U. S. A.) bill, dodger. ~ **comercial** commercial news. ~ **meteorológico** weather-forecast. ~ **das cotações cambiais** exchange list.

boletineiro s. m. 1. author of bulletins. 2. bulletin distributor, messenger.

boleto (ê) s. m. 1. (mil.) soldier's billet. 2. Boletus: a genus of mushrooms some species of which are poisonous. 3. fetlock joint (plate C 12).

boléu s. m. 1. fall, tumble. 2. jolt, jerk. 3. thud.

bolha (ô) s. f. 1. blister, pimple, vesicle, blain, bleb, blotch. 2. bubble, globule of gas in a liquid. 3. blowhole. ~ **de sabão** soap-bubble. **cheio de** ~s blebby. **criar** ~s to raise blisters, blister.

bolhante adj. m. + f. 1. bubbling, bubbly. 2. frothy, foamy.

bolhar v. 1. to blister, affect by blistering. 2. to bubble. 3. to foam, froth.

bolhelho s. m. 1. grimy sweat (from dirty hands). 2. a kind of cake.

bolhoso adj. 1. bubbly, bubbling, blistered. 2. foamy, frothy.

boliche s. m. 1. poolroom, gambling house. 2. inn, tavern. 3. boliche: (Spanish) bowls. **jogo de** ~ skittles, (U. S. A.) tenpins. **pista de** ~ skittle alley. **jogar** ~ to bowl.

bolich(e)ar v. to peddle, hawk.

bolicheiro s. m. 1. tavern keeper, proprietor of a gambling joint. 2. peddler, hawker.

bólide s. f. bolide, meteor, aerolite, falling star.

bolina s. f. 1. (naut.) bowline, centre-board, bilge keel. 2. (also **bolinador**) masher (sl.).

~ **de sotavento** lee-bowline. **nó de** ~ bowline knot. **largar as** ~**s** to veer the bowlines. **navegar à** ~ **cerrada** to sail near the wind.

bolinar v. (naut.) 1. to haul up the bowline. 2. to sail close to the wind.

bolineiro adj. (naut.) sailing close to the wind, weatherly.

bolinete s. m. 1. (naut.) capstan, windlass. 2. wooden bucket for gold washing.

bolinha (I) s. f. 1. little ball. 2. marble. 3. taw. 4. pellet. 5. dumpling.

bolinha (II) s. f. (Braz., sl.) a psychedelic pill.

bolinho s. m. little cake, biscuit, cooky, cookie, wafer, waffle (plate D 3).

bolita s. f. 1. marbles. 2. children's game played with marbles.

boliviano s. m. Bolivian. || adj. Bolivian.

bolo (ô) (I) s. m. 1. cake (plate D 3). 2. dumpling. 3. (pop.) stroke on the palm of the hand with a ruler. 4. fishing-net sinker made of a baked clayball.

~ **de claras** angel cake. ~ **de frutas** cobbler. ~ **de casamento** bride cake.

bolo (ô) (II) s. m. pool, stake, pot, jack-pot, kitty. **levantar o** ~ to sweep the stakes. **dar o** ~ to break a promise, engagement or agreement. **dar** ~ **em alguém** (Braz.) to know more than s. o. else. **dar um** ~ to embezzle.

bolo-armênio s. m. (pl. **bolos-armênios**) bole: soft, unctuous clay.

bolo-de-fermento s. m. (pl. **bolos-de-fermento**) (cul.) barmbrack.

bolo-de-rolo s. m. (pl. **bolos-de-rolo**) (Braz.) roly-poly.

bolômetro s. m. (physics) bolometer.

bolônio s. m. simpleton, ignorant fellow, rustic. || adj. ignorant, boorish.

bolo-podre s. m. (pl. **bolos-podres**) (Braz., pop.) raised cake.

bolor s. m. 1. mould, mildew, mustiness, frowziness, fustiness, rust. 2. (fig.) old age. 3. decay. 4. musty smell.

pedra movediça não cria ~ a rolling stone never gathers moss.

bolorecer v. to mould, gather mould, become musty.

bolorência s. f. 1. mouldiness, mustiness. 2. (fig.) old age, decadence. 3. musty smell.

bolorento adj. 1. mouldy, musty, frowzy, rusty. 2. (fig.) old, decrepit. 3. foul, smelly, fusty.

bolota s. f. 1. acorn. 2. any acorn-shaped adornment, tuft, tassel. 3. oak-apple, oak-gall.

bolotada s. f. a lot of acorns.

bolotal s. m. (pl. **-ais**) oak forest.

bolsa (ô) s. f. 1. purse, small bag, pouch. 2. money contained in a purse. 3. burse, carry-all, satchel, pocket, poke. 4. a lady's handbag (plate R 6). 5. scholarship, studentship. 6. exchange, stock exchange, stock market. 7. (geol.) pocket: cavity containing minerals. 8. saddlebag. 9. m. cashier, treasurer, purser (of a corporation). 10. (anat.) cyst, bursa. 11. (mech.) pod. 12. socket (of a pipe) (plate C 1).

~ **de água quente** hot-water bottle. ~ **de ar** air pocket, air-hole. ~ **de câmbio** stock exchange. ~ **de cereais** corn-exchange. ~ **de estudos** scholarship, studentship, exhibition. ~ **de valores** stock exchange, stock market. ~ **de viagem** Gladstone bag, travelling bag, grip. **andar a** ~ **seca** to be short of money, have an empty purse. **ele abre a** ~ he spends freely. **cortador ou ladrão de** ~**s (batedor de carteira)** pickpocket. **fazer** ~ **comum** to pay from a common purse. **fechar a** ~ to stop spending. **puxar pela** ~ to spend a lot of money. **ter a** ~ **bem provida** to have a well-filled pocket.

bolsa-de-pastor s. f. (pl. **bolsas-de-pastor**) (bot.) shepherd's purse, capsella.

bolsar v. 1. to wrinkle, pucker, crumple. 2. to swell, inflate.

bolseiro s. m. 1. purse maker or purse seller. 2. treasurer. 3. student who holds a scholarship.

bolsinha s. f. vanity bag.

bolsinho s. m. 1. little pocket, fob (plate R 7). 2. pocket-money, small change.

bolsista s. m. + f. 1. stock exchange operator, stockbroker, stock-speculator. 2. exhibitioner: a student who receives an allowance. || adj. 1. of, pertaining to or relative to the stock exchange. 2. receiving an allowance.

bolso s. m. 1. pocket, fob (plates R 6, 7). 2. belly of a sail. 3. crease, wrinkle (in a garment).

~ **interno do paletó** breast-pocket. ~ **de vestido** placket. **edição de** ~ pocket edition. **lanterna de** ~ pocket lamp. **livro de** ~ pocketbook. **pôr no** ~ to pocket, place into one's pocket. **provido de** ~**s** pocketed. **relógio de** ~ pocket watch. **do tamanho de um** ~ pocket-size(d). **ter no** ~ to have in pocket.

bom s. m. (pl. **bons**) 1. good, goodness. 2. a good, kindhearted man. 3. a good thing. || adj. (f. **boa**; comp. **melhor**, superl. **o melhor**, abs. superl. **boníssimo**) 1. good, well, well-made, fine, right. 2. sufficient, satisfactory. 3. favourable, beneficial, fair. 4. kind, benevolent, charitable. 5. useful, advantageous, profitable. 6. reliable, strict. 7. proper, becoming. 8. safe, secure. 9. perfect, complete. 10. large, ample. 11. pretty. 12. fit. 13. (sl.) spanking, canny. || interj. splendid! that's nice (fine, well, swell, etc.)!

~ **acolhimento** welcome. ~ **comportamento** correct manners. ~-**dia** good morning. ~ **gênio** good nature. ~ **humor** high spirits. ~ **para a saúde** wholesome. ~ **senso** sound sense. ~ **tempo** fine weather. **a** ~ **tempo** opportunely. **achar** ~ to approve. **ano** ~ New Year. **um** ~ **ano** a good year. **boa-noite** good night. **boa-tarde** good afternoon. **boas palavras** fair words. **de** ~ **aspecto** well-favoured, well-seeming. **de** ~ **grado o faria se pudesse** I would fain do it, if I could. **o** ~ **negócio** (sl.) the correct card. **os bons tempos de antigamente** the piping times of yore. **ele é** ~ **companheiro** he is good company. **isto é** ~ **para você** this is good for you. **o melhor é inimigo do** ~ I leave well alone. **ele escapou de boa** he had a narrow escape. **esta comida tem** ~ **aspecto** this food looks good. **estar** ~ to be in good health. **ela está longe de ter** ~ **aspecto** she looks far from well. **o tempo está** ~ the weather is fair. **não estou** ~ **hoje** I feel indisposed today. **ele fez uma boa a alguém** he played a trick on s. o. **ela meteu-se em boas** she brought herself into troubles. **eles não sabem o que é** ~ they have no experience at all. **ser um** ~ **esgrimista** to be great at fencing. **tudo ficará** ~ all will be well. **vir às boas** to come to terms (after a fight, brawl, etc.).

bomba s. f. 1. (mil.) shell, bomb. 2. (tech.) any pump, siphon, suction-pipe; supercharger (plate B 14). 3. (railway) buffer, bumper. 4. (archit.) span or well of a staircase. 5. (cul.) éclair, puff, sweet pastry (plate D 3). 6. unexpected event, surprise. 7. (Braz.) plough, plow, flunk: failure in an examination.

~ **alimentadora** feed pump. ~ **a nora**, ~ **a rosário** paternoster pump, chain pump. ~ **arrasa-quarteirão** blockbuster. ~ **aspirante premente** double action pump. ~ **atômica** atomic bomb, city buster. ~ **de ação retardada** delayed action bomb. ~ **de alta potência** armour piercing bomb. ~ **de ar** air-

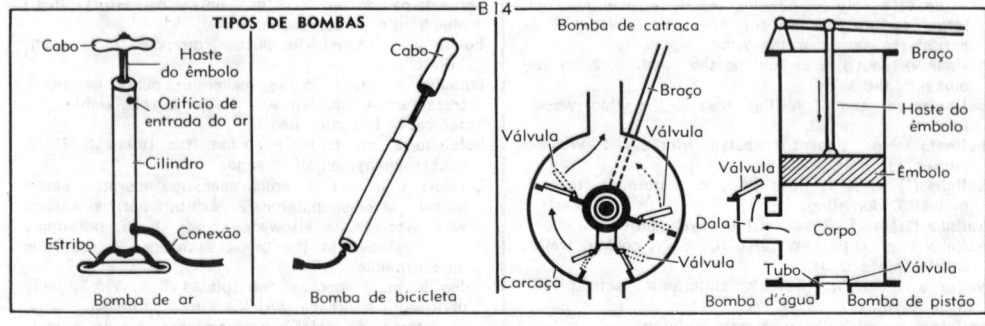

TIPOS DE BOMBAS — B 14

Bomba de ar — Bomba de bicicleta — Bomba de catraca — Bomba d'água — Bomba de pistão

-pump. ~ **de elevação** lift pump. ~ **de êmbolo** piston pump. ~ **de gasolina** petrol pump, filling-station, (U. S. A.) gasoline pump (plate B 2). ~ **de hidrogênio** fusion bomb. ~ **de incêndio** fire-engine. ~ **de mão** hand pump. ~ **de profundidade** depth bomb. ~ **falhada** blind shell, dud. ~ **de recalque** pressure pump. ~ **de vácuo** vacuum pump. ~ **incendiária** incendiary bomb, flare-bomb. ~ **premente** force pump. ~ **rotativa** rotary pump. ~ **voadora** robot bomb, flying bomb, buzz-bomb. **cair como uma** ~ to come off like a bomb shell. **casa de** ~ pump house. **corpo de** ~ pump barrel. **ele levou** ~ he was plucked (rejected at an examination). **não leve** ~! don't take a plough! **manivela de** ~ pump handle. **à prova de** ~**s** shellproof.
bombachas s. f. pl. 1. wide breeches, sailor's breeches. 2. long wide trousers closed or buttoned at the ankles. 3. knickerbockers.
bombacho s. m. little pump.
bombada s. f. 1. deceit, trick. 2. damage, loss.
bomba-d'água s. f. (pl. **bombas-d'água**) torrential rain, violent downpour.
bomba-foguete s. f. (pl. **bombas-foguetes**) antisubmarine rocket bomb.
bomba-granada s. f. (pl. **bombas-granadas**) depth charge, depth bomb.
bombão s. m. (pl. **-ões**) plant of the family Solanaceae.
bombarda s. f. 1. bombard, mortar, cannon. 2. barge, pontoon. 3. gunboat.
bombardada s. f. cannon-shot, shot of a mortar piece.
bombardão s. m. (pl. **-ões**) (mus.) bass, bassoon, bombardon.
bombardeador s. m. bombardier, bombarder. ‖ adj. bombarding.
bombardeamento s. m. bombardment, shelling, bombing.
bombardear v. to bombard, bomb, cannon, cannonade, shell, batter, strafe.
bombardeio s. m. bombardment, shelling, bombing.
bombardeiro s. m. 1. bombardier, bombarder, gunner. 2. master of a gunboat. 3. bomber (aircraft). ~ **a jacto** jet fighter. ~ **de mergulho** dive bomber.
bombardino s. m. (mus.) bombardon.
bomba-relógio s. f. (pl. **bombas-relógios**) time bomb.
bombástico adj. 1. noisy, clamorous. 2. pompous, magnificent. 3. (fig.) bombastic(al), highflown, inflated, puffy, mouthy, swollen, ranting. 4. extravagant, pretentious. ‖ adv. rantingly, noisily, bombastically, etc.
usar linguagem -a to rant.
bombazina s. f. 1. bombazine, bombasine. 2. corded velveteen.
bombeação s. f. (pl. **-ões**) 1. bombardment, throwing of shells. 2. (pop.) failure, flunk (in an examination).

bombeado adj. bombarded, bombed.
bombeador s. m. 1. bombardier, bombarder, bomber. 2. severe teacher (who flunks students).
bombeamento s. m. 1. bombardment, shelling. 2. (Braz., pop.) failure, reprovation, flunk (at examinations).
bombear v. 1. to bombard, throw bombs on, shell. 2. to pluck (a candidate). 3. to reject, flunk (at an examination). 4. (Braz.) to spy upon, weep an eye on, observe. 5. to pump.
bombeiro s. m. 1. fireman, hoseman. 2. drummer. 3. plumber.
corpo de ~**s** fire brigade. **posto de** ~**s** fire station.
bombicídeos s. m. pl. (ent.) Bombycidae.
bombídeos s. m. pl. (ent.) Bombidae: the bumblebee family.
bombilha s. f. (S. Braz.) sucker, sucking-tube (used esp. for mate).
bombinha s. f. (fire)cracker.
bombo s. m. big drum, bass drum.
bom-bocado s. m. (pl. **bons-bocados**) sweetmeat of sugar, yolk, coconut milk and ground peanuts.
bombom s. m. (pl. **bombons**) bonbon, fondant, sweet, candy, sweetmeat.
bombona s. f. gas-holder.
bombonaça s. f. (bot.) jipijapa.
bombordo s. m. (naut.) larboard, portside, the left side of a ship.
a ~ aport.
bom-é s. m. (pl. **bom-és**) (Braz., ornith.) cacique.
bom-moço s. m. (pl. **bons-moços**) (ironic.) hypocrite, deceiver, pretender.
bomôncia s. f. (bot.) creeper of the family Apocynaceae.
bom-tom s. m. 1. politeness, civility, correct manners. 2. fashionableness. 3. fashion.
pessoa de ~ fashionable person.
bonachão, bonacheirão s. m. (pl. **-ões**) (f. **-ona**) good-natured, kind-hearted person, honest fellow. ‖ adj. kind, friendly, indulgent.
bonacheirice s. f. kindness, good-nature, indulgence.
bonaerense s. m. + f. (also **portenho**) native or inhabitant of Buenos Aires. ‖ adj. of or relative to Buenos Aires.
bonança s. f. 1. calm, fair weather (at sea). 2. calmness, tranquil(l)ity, peace, lull. 3. (fig.) prosperity. ‖ adj. 1. calm, still. 2. quiet, peaceful. 3. (fig.) favourable.
passar a vida em ~ to spend a quiet and happy life.
bonançar v. 1. to be calm (sea). 2. to become calm, clear up (weather).
bonançoso adj. 1. quiet, still, calm, peaceful. 2. (fig.) happy, favourable.

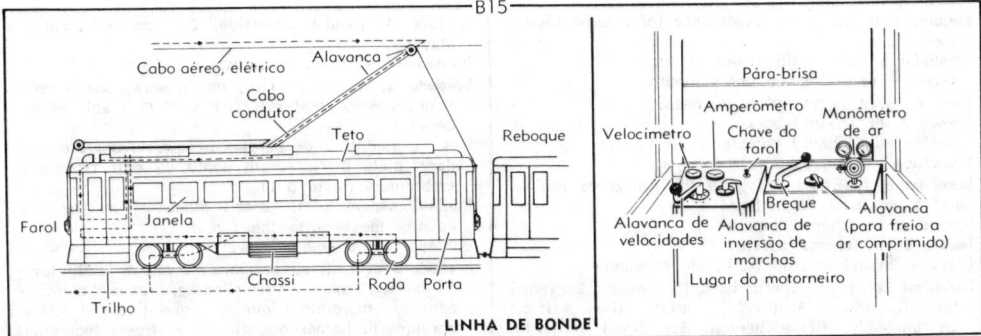

LINHA DE BONDE

bona-xira s. f. (pl. **bonas-xiras**) (Braz.) 1. a rich or bountiful table. 2. good food, rich repast.

bondade s. f. 1. goodness, kindness, kindliness, affableness, affability, amiability. 2. benevolence, charitableness. 3. mildness, tender-heartedness, humanity. 4. (N. Braz.) pride, arrogance.
a ~ de uma terra (fig.) the fruitfulness of a country. ela é a ~ em pessoa she is kindness herself. ele é um homem rico mas sem ~ he is a rich but unkind man. tenha a ~ de... be kind enough, be so kind as to.

bonde s. m. (Braz.) 1. streetcar, (U. S. A.) trolley (car) (plate B 15). 2. (sl.) trick, deceit, swindle.
comprar ~ to fall into a trap, make a bad bargain. nós pegamos o ~ errado we got hold of the wrong end of the stick.

bondoso adj. (also **bondadoso** but rare). 1. amiable, good-natured, kindhearted. 2. benevolent, charitable, gentle, generous, humane, forgiving. 3. (Braz., pop.) proud, arrogant. 4. kind, mild, boon, nice, decent. ‖ **-amente** adv. kindly, mildly, etc.

bonduque s. m. (bot.) bonduc, nicker tree.

boné s. m. cap, bonnet, skull cap, headgear, kepi, headpiece (plate R 6).

boneca s. f. 1. doll, toy, baby. 2. a neat doll-like woman. 3. (fig.) puppet, poppet. 4. (tech.) poppet head, tail stock (of a lathe). 5. pad for polishing.
teatro de ~s puppet-show, (Engl.) Punch and Judy (show).

bonecada s. f. a lot of dolls.

boneco s. m. 1. puppet, marionette, doll. 2. toy figures or animals. 3. (fig.) fop, conceited silly man. 4. (typog.) dummy. 5. manikin.
~ de engonço jumping jack. ele é um ~ de engonço he is a stuffed shirt.

boné-de-bispo, boné-quadrado s. m. (pl. **bonés-de--bispo, bonés-quadrados**) (bot.) botong.

bonete s. m. 1. cap, bonnet. 2. barret.

bonete (ê) s. m. (naut.) bonnet, an additional jib-sail.

bongar v. (Braz., pop.) 1. to pick, gather carefully. 2. to seek, look for.

bonicos s. m. pl. manure, animal excreta, dung.

bonificação s. f. (pl. **-ões**) 1. allowance, money grant, privilege, bonus. 2. improvement.

bonificar v. 1. to improve, better. 2. to make an allowance, grant money or privileges.

bonifrate s. m. prig, fop, stuffed shirt.

bonina s. f. 1. (bot.) daisy, marvel of Peru, four--o'clock. 2. (Braz., bot.) Madagascar periwinkle.

boninal s. m. (pl. **-ais**) field of daisies.

bonita s. f. pastry of manioc, sugar and pepper.

bonitaço adj. very pretty, very beautiful.

bonitete adj. m. + f. = **bonitote**.

boniteza s. f. beauty, prettiness.

bonitinha s. f. (Braz., pop.) infectious conjunctivitis (inflammation of the eyelids).

bonito (I) s. m. a noble action. ‖ adj. 1. pretty, handsome, beautiful, nice, beautious, cute, bonny, trig, nifty. 2. good, kind, noble. 3. (ironic.) reprehensible, bad.
palavras -as não enchem barriga the belly is not filled with fine words. uma -a senhora a fine woman. uma carinha -a a pretty face.

bonito (II) s. m. 1. (ichth.): a) victorfish, oceanic bonito. b) little tunny. 2. shaving basin. 3. any toy (children's language). 4. (ornith.) a species of tanager.

bonitote adj. m. + f. quite nice, rather pretty.

bonomia s. f. 1. goodness, kindness. 2. straightforwardness, integrity. 3. credulity, gullibility.

bonotom s. m. (Braz.) aromatic resin, copal (from tropical American timber trees).

bons-dias s. m. sg. + pl. (bot.) 1. hedge bindweed. 2. morning-glory.

bônus s. m., sg. + pl. bonus, bond, paper, premium, privilege.
~ do tesouro exchequer bond.

bonzão adj. (pl. **-ões**) (Braz., pop.) very good, splendid.

bonzinho adj. (dim. of **bom**) good, well-behaved.
seja ~ e vá buscar meu livro be a pet and fetch me my book.

bonzo s. m. 1. Buddhist priest, bonze. 2. (fig.) hypocrite, charlatan.

bonzó s. m. (Braz.) share of a lottery ticket, raffle ticket.

boqueada s. f. 1. yawn(ing), gaping. 2. agony. 3. short-windedness.

boquear v. 1. to yawn, gape. 2. to gasp (for breath). 3. to agonize.

boqueira s. f. (vulg.) chappy lip corner(s).

boqueirão s. m. (pl. **-ões**) 1. big mouth, wide opening. 2. estuary, gulf, mouth of a channel or river. 3. abyss, gully. 4. large cave or hollow.

boquejadura s. f. (also **boquejo** m.) 1. gape, gaping, yawn. 2. muttering, stammer. 3. murmur, whisper (ing).

boquejar v. 1. to gape, yawn. 2. to murmur, whisper. 3. to mutter, stammer.

boquelho s. m. vent-hole of an oven.

boquete s. m. opening or entrance to a narrow pass between two mountains.

boquiaberto adj. 1. open-mouthed, agape, gaping. 2. staring. 3. dumbfounded, amazed, stunned. ‖ adv. **-amente** gapingly.

boquiabrir v. 1. to stand gaping about. 2. to open the mouth in wonder. 3. to dumbfound, stun.

boquilha s. f. 1. (also **piteira**) 1. cigar-holder, cigarette--holder. 2. mouthpiece (of a pipe) (plate F 7). 3. (carp.) rabbet, embrasure of a door or window.

boquim s. m. (pl. **-ins**) mouthpiece (of a wind instrument).

boquinha s. f. 1. little mouth. 2. kiss.
  fazer ~ to pucker up one's mouth.

borá s. m. a variety of honey-bees.

borace s. m. (chem.) borax.

borácico adj. (chem.) boracic.

boracita s. f. (min.) boracite.

borajuba s. f. (Braz.) timber of the Amazonas region.

boral s. m. (nucl. eng.) boral.

borano s. m. (chem.) borane.

borato s. m. (chem.) borate.

bórax s. m. (chem.) borax, borate of sodium.

borboleta s. f. 1. (ent.) butterfly, moth. 2. (bot.) butterfly flower. 3. (ichth.) butterfly fish. 4 (fig.) an unsteady, fickle person. 5. (Braz.) turnstile, wicket. 6. (Braz.) fastener of drop windows. 7. wing nut. 8. bow tie.

borboleta-da-couve s. f. (pl. **borboletas-da-couve**) (ent.) cabbage butterfly.

borboleteador, borboleteante adj. 1. flitting, fluttering. 2. (fig.) unsteady, fickle. 3. musing, meditating.

borboleteamento s. m. 1. flitting, fluttering. 2. meditation, imagination. 3. (fig.) fickleness.

borboletear v. 1. to flutter, flit, flirt about. 2. to muse, meditate. 3. (fig.) to be unsteady, be fickle.

borboletice s. f. 1. caprice, capriciousness. 2. dream, fancy. 3. fickleness.

borborismo, borborigmo s. m. intestinal gurgle or rumble.

borboró adj. m. + f. stammering, stuttering.

borbotão s. m. (pl. **-ões**) 1. gush(ing), jet, spout, flash. 2. bubbling up (of boiling water, etc.).
  ~ **de vento** a squall, a blast of wind. **o sangue rebentou em** ~**ões** the blood spurted out.

borbotar v. 1. to bubble, boil. 2. to gush, flush, flow. 3. (fig.) to talk or act effusively. 4. to bud, form buds.

borbulha s. f. 1. pimple (on the skin), pustule, quat, rash, carbuncle, acne. 2. bud, shoot (of a plant). 3. bubble, burble (of boiling water). 4. (fig.) stain, spot, flaw, defect.

borbulhação s. f. (pl. **-ões**) popple.

borbulhagem s. f. (pl. **-ens**) a lot of bubbles or pimples.

borbulhante s. f. (Braz., sl.) sugar-cane brandy. || adj. m. + f. bubbling, bubbly.

borbulhão s. m. (pl. **-ões**) 1. a large bubble or pimple. 2. a big bud.

borbulhar v. 1. to germinate, sprout, burd. 2. to burble, gurgle, popple, wallop, sparkle, bubble up. 3. to gush or spurt out. 4. (fig.) to talk or act effusively.

borbulhento adj. 1. pimpled, pimplous. 2. bubbling, bubbly.

borbulhoso adj. 1. full of bubbles, bubbly. 2. pimply, pimpled.

borcar v. 1. to turn upside down. 2. to empty, dump. 3. to throw up, vomit.

borco (ô) s. m. used only in the adverbial locution:
  de ~ upside-down.

dar de ~ (ship) to capsize. **virar de** ~ to tilt, turn over. **ficar de** ~ to become sick.

borda s. f. 1. border, edging, list, rim, edge, skirt (plates C 5, 10, M 2, S 3). 2. margin, fringe. 3. extremity. 4. bank, brink, brim, verge. 5. shore, strand. 6. hem, flap. 7. outskirt. 8. skirting-board. 9. (naut.) gunwale (plate B 8).
  ~ **chanfrada** bezel. ~ **do chapéu** hatbrim. ~ **do mar** seaside, seashore. ~ **do tapete** webbing. **à** ~ abreast, alongside. **dar** ~ (naut.) to heel over.

bordada s. f. 1. (naut.) tack, stretch, change of course by tacking. 2. board, shipboard. 3. border,

brink. 4. (naut.) broadside. 5. side. 6. (naut.) a staysail.

bordadeira s. f. embroideress.

bordado s. m. embroidery, needlework, needle-point, tambour work (plates B 7, P 5, R 6). || adj. embroidered.
  ~ **de contas** or **de pérolas** beadwork, pearl embroidery (plate B 7). ~ **em ponto de cruz** cross-stich embroidery (plate B 7).

borda-do-campo s. f. (Braz.) place where the open country meets with the forest.

bordador s. m. embroiderer.

bordadura s. f. (also **bordamento** m.) 1. embroidery. 2. border, margin. 3. clipping, retrenchment. 4. adorned margin, trimming, garniture. 5. (her.) bordure. 6. border bed (hort.) 7. frame mouldings. 8. false board of a canoe. 9. (mus.) figurate counterpoint.

bordagem s. f. (pl. **-ens**) (naut.) side planks of a ship.

bordaleiro s. m. a sheep with crisp or curly wool. || adj. crisp, curly.

bordalengo adj. 1. coarse, unrefined. 2. ignorant, stupid.

bordalesa s. f. (also **calda bordalesa**) (hort.) Bordeaux mixture: a fungicide made of copper sulphate, lime and water.

bordalo s. m. freshwater fish of the family Cyprinidae.

bordão s. m. (pl. **-ões**) 1. (mus.) bass-string, bourdon. 2. stick, staff. 3. (fig.) help, aid, assistence, support. 4. word or (idiomatic) phrase often used.
  ~ **ferrado** pikestaff.

bordão-de-velho s. m. (pl. **bordões-de-velho**) (bot.) avaremotemo.

bordar v. 1. to embroider. 2. to hem. 3. to garnish. 4. to border, edge. 5. (fig.) to embellish a speech or story. 6. (Port.) to accept boarders or (paying) guests.
  ~ **com ponto de cruz** to cross-stitch. **aldeias bordam as margens do rio** villages lie along the river.

bordejar, bordear v. 1. (naut.) to tack, cruise. 2. (naut.) to beat close to or against the wind. 3. to stagger. 4. to march, border. 5. to outskirt.

bordejo s. m. (naut.) 1. tack, a laveering close to or against the wind. 2. cruising.

bordel s. m. (pl. **-éis**) brothel, bawdy-house.

bordeleiro, bordelengo s. m. frequenter of brothels.

bordelês s. m. native or inhabitant of Bordeaux (France). || adj. of, pertaining to or relative to Bordeaux.

borderô s. m. (com.) bordereau.

bordo s. m. 1. (naut.) tack. 2. board of a ship, shipside. 3. course of a ship. 4. border, margin, edge, flange (plate F 5). 5. (fig.) temper, humour, disposition of mind.
  ~ **chanfrado** bevel-edged. ~ **livre** freeboard. ~ **plantar** bearing surface (plate C 9). **a** ~ on board, aboard ship. **a** ~ **do "Eagle"** on board the "Eagle". **ir a** ~ to go on board. **meter a** ~ to take aboard. **posto a** ~ free on board (abbr. F. O. B.). **todos a** ~**!** all aboard! **aos** ~**s** staggering (drunk). **bote de** ~ jolly-boat. **dar ou fazer um** ~ to tack a ship. **de alto** ~ 1. high (vessel). 2. (fig.) huge. **fazer** ~**s curtos** to sail windwards by small boards. **virar de** ~ 1. to change the course. 2. (fig.) to draw or go back.

bordo (ô) s. m. (bot.) silver or soft maple.

bordoada s. f. 1. stroke, knock. 2. blow with a cudgel.
  dar ~**s de cego** to strike out blindly (at random). **surra a** ~**s** clubbing.

bordoeira s. f. 1. brawl, row, quarrel. 2. thrashing, spanking.

boré s. m. (Braz.) Indians' trumpet.

boreal adj. m. + f. (pl. **-ais**) boreal, northern, northerly, septentrional.
aurora ~ northern lights.
bóreas s. m. 1. (Greek myth.) Boreas: the god of the north wind. 2. (poet.) north wind.
boreste s. m. (naut.) starboard.
todo a ~! hard at (or to) starboard!
borgonhês, borguinhão s. m. Burgundian: native of Burgundy. ‖ adj. Burgundian.
boricado adj. (chem.) boricated.
bórico adj. (chem.) boric, boracic.
borjaca s. f. 1. a tinker's bag (for tools). 2. a long and wide frock-coat.
borla s. f. 1. tuft, tassel. 2. academic cap, mortar-board. 3. truck of a flagstaff. 4. a tropical sterculiaceous tree (Dombeya tiliacea). 5. bullion. 6. pompon.
~ **de espada** sword knot. **tomar a** ~ to qualify o. s. for lecturing (university). **de** ~ gratuitous, for nothing.
borleta s. f. a little tuft or tassel.
bornal s. m. (pl. **-ais**) 1. fodder sack, feed-bag. 2. provision sack. 3. packsack.
borne s. m. 1. (electr.) terminal, wire clamp, binding screw. 2. (bot.) alburnum.
bornear v. to take aim at, level a gun or cannon.
borneio s. m. 1. the act of turning around, levelling or training a gun, cannon, etc. 2. (hist.) lance.
borneira s. f. millstone of black siliceous rock.
borneiro adj. ground (with a millstone).
bornita s. f. (chem.) bornite.
boro s. m. (chem.) boron.
boró s. m. 1 counter, token coin, fish (at cards). 2. (pop.) money. 3. hot (stolen) goods.
boroa s. f. = **broa**.
borocotó s. m. 1. (Braz.) rough or uneven ground. 2. ravine, gully.
borocoxô s. m. + f. (Braz., sl.) a sluggish person. ‖ adj. sluggish.
boroeiro adj. 1. living on maize bread. 2. (fig.) rude, uncouth, boorish.
bororé s. m. (Braz.) arrow poison used by Indians.
bororó s. m. (zool.) pampean deer.
borquilho s. m. bandy-legged person. ‖ adj. bandy-legged, bow-legged.
borra (ô) s. f. 1. lees, dregs, grounds, tiltings, bottom, sludge, mother, waste. 2. feculence, faeces. 3. waste wool, silk refuse. 4. (fig.) mob, rabble.
~ **de chá** tea-leaves. **de** ~ worthless, trashy.
borra-botas s. m., sg. + pl. 1. an unskilled boot-black. 2. (fig.) rascal, scoundrel, good-for-nothing.
borraçal s. m. (pl. **-ais**) marsh, moor.
borraceiro s. m. drizzle, drizzling rain. ‖ adj. 1. rainy, drizzling. 2. full of dregs, not clear.
borracha s. f. 1. rubber, india-rubber. 2. eraser. 3. caoutchouc. 4. leather sack, leather bottle. 5. rubber bottle, enema apparatus (rubber syringe).
~ **esponjosa** or **espuma de** ~ foam rubber. ~ **para apagar tinta** Ink eraser. ~ **sintética** synthetic rubber.
borrachada s. f. 1. administering of an enema (with a rubber syringe). 2. a blow with a rubber hose or stick.
borrachão s. m. (pl. **-ões**) (pop.) drunkard.
borracheira s. f. 1. drunkenness, intoxication. 2. rudeness, coarseness. 3. nonsense, blunder. 4. poor or bungled work, botch.
borracheiro s. m. 1. (Braz.) latex collector. 2. tyre fitter or vulcanizer.
borrachífero adj. laticiferous.
borracho s. m. 1. drunkard, sot. 2. young pigeon. ‖ adj. drunk, tipsy.
borrachudo s. m. (ent.) black fly, buffalo gnat. ‖ adj. full, round.

borrada s. f. filth, dirt, uncleanliness. 2. improper or indecorous action. 3. nonsense, stupidity.
borradela s. f. 1. blur, blot, blemish. 2. crude layer of paint. 3. = **borrão**.
borrado adj. blurry, splotchy, spotty, smudgy.
borrador s. m. 1. (com.) blotter, rough journal, roughbook, waste-book, pad. 2. bad painter, dauber. 3. poor writer.
borradura s. f. 1. blur, blot. 2. erasure. 3. blotting out. 4. rough painting (of a house), daub.
borragem s. f. (pl. **-ens**) (bot.) borage, bee-bread.
borragem-do-campo s. f. (pl. **borragens-do-campo**) (bot.) heliotrope.
borraina s. f. saddle pad.
borralha s. f. 1. embers, (hot) ashes. 2. = **borralho**.
borralhara s. f. (ornith.) ant shrike.
borralheira s. f. fireside, ashpan.
gata ~ Cinderella.
borralheiro s. m. stay-at-home, friend of the fireside. ‖ adj. fond of the fireside, homely.
borralhento adj. ash-coloured, ashen.
borralho s. m. 1. embers, hot ashes. 2. (fig.) home. 3. fireside, fireplace. ‖ adj. ash-coloured.
borrão s. m. (pl. **-ões**) 1. blot, stain, blemish, dot, spatter, spot, smudge, splodge. 2. sketch, rough draft, outline. 3. (com.) blotter, rough journal. 4. discredit, dishonour. 5. indecent action. 6. daub.
caderno de ~ waste-book.
borrar v. 1. to stain, besmear, dirty, bedaub, slubber, blur, splodge, spot, smudge. 2. to paint clumsily, unskil(l)fully. 3. to erase, wipe out. 4. to strike out, dash. 5. to defecate, void (excrement). 6. to scrawl, scribble.
borrasca s. f. 1. tempest, thunderstorm, storm of rain. 2. squall, hurricane. 3. (fig.) vexation, disappointment. 4. (fig.) fit of anger, rage.
borrascoso adj. 1. stormy, tempestuous. 2. squally. 3. (fig.) furious, violent, rough. 4. foul.
borratão s. m. (pl. **-ões**) big ink blot.
borra-tintas s. m. + f. sg. + pl. 1. unskilled painter. 2. any botcher or patcher.
borrega (ê) s. f. ewe lamb, yearling sheep.
borregã s. f. wool of a male lamb.
borregada s. f. flock of lambs.
borregagem s. f. (pl. **-ens**) herd of sheep, flock of lambs.
borregar v. to bleat.
borrego (ê) s. m. 1. male lamb (not older than a year). 2. calm or peaceful person.
borregueiro s. m. shepherd, herdsman of lambs.
borreguice s. f. indolence, stupidity.
borrelho s. m. (ornith.) ring plover.
borrento adj. dreggy, dreggish, full of lees.
borriçar v. to drizzle, mizzle.
borriço s. m. drizzle, drizzling rain.
borrifadela s. f. spatter.
borrifador s. m. watering can, sprinkler.
~ **de perfumes** perfume sprayer.
borrifar v. 1. to (be)sprinkle, asperse, spray, (be)dabble, perfuse. 2. to bedew. 3. to damp, moisten. 4. to drizzle, drop. 5. to dash.
borrifo s. m. 1. sprinkling. 2. drizzle, drizzling rain. 3. spray. 4. aspersion.
borriscada s. f. = **borrasca**.
borrisco s. m. heavy shower, downpour of rain.
borro (ô) s. m. ram (between one and two years).
borrusquê s. m. (Braz.) I. O. U. Issued by businessmen in the XIX centruy, in lieu of money change.
bortalá s. m. veil or hood to frighten children.
borzeguim s. m. (pl. **-ins**) buskin, high laced boot.
bosboque s. m. (zool.) bushbuck, boschbok.
boscagem s. f. (pl. **-ens**) boscage, grove, wood, thicket.

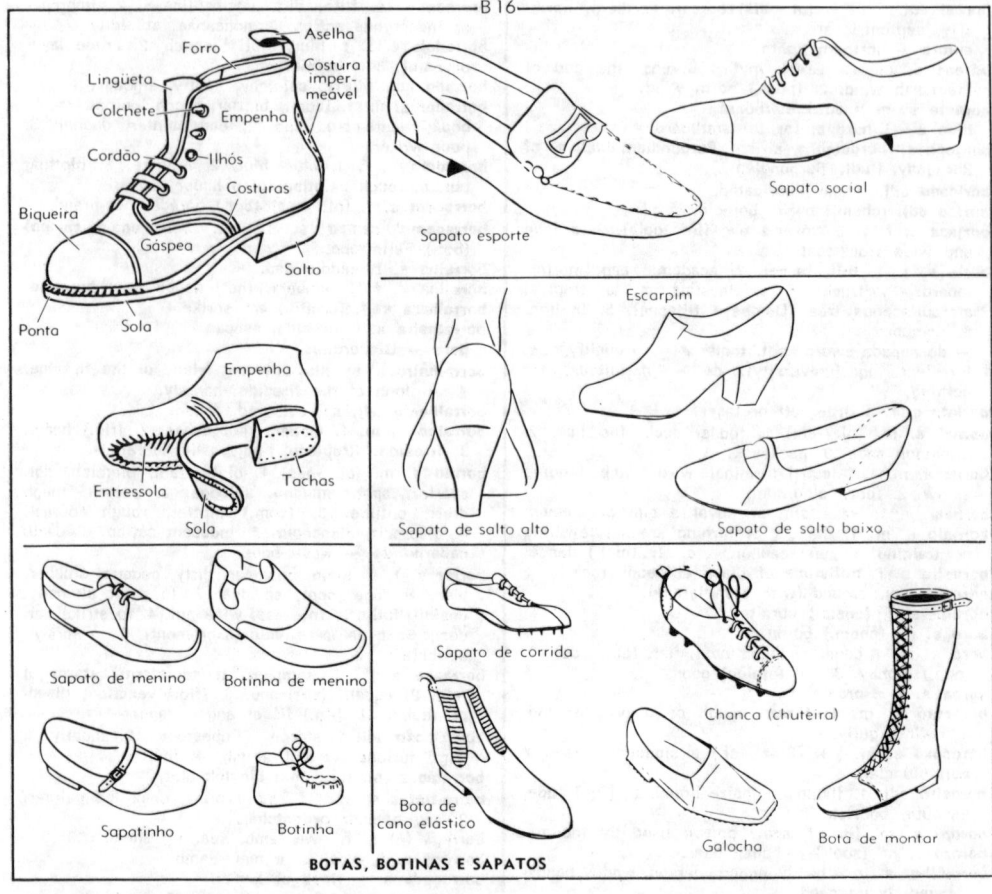

B 16

Aselha · Forro · Costura imper-meável · Lingüeta · Colchete · Empenha · Cordão · Ilhós · Biqueira · Costuras · Gáspea · Salto · Ponta · Sola

Sapato esporte · Sapato social

Empenha · Entressola · Tachas · Sola

Escarpim · Sapato de salto alto · Sapato de salto baixo

Sapato de menino · Botinha de menino · Sapato de corrida · Chanca (chuteira)

Sapatinho · Botinha · Bota de cano elástico · Galocha · Bota de montar

BOTAS, BOTINAS E SAPATOS

boscarejo adj. referring to or living in woods or thickets.

boscoso adj. woody.

bosniano s. m. Bosnian: native or inhabitant of Bosnia. ‖ adj. Bosnian.

bóson s. m. (nucl. phys.) boson.

bosque s. m. 1. wood, forest. 2. thicket, grove, coppice, copse (plate F 4).

sem ~s woodless.

bosquejar v. 1. to sketch, outline. 2. to delineate, draft, diagram, trace. 3. to summarize, resume.

bosquejo s. m. 1. outline, sketch, design. 2. delineation, diagram. 3. general plan, project.

bosquete s. m. grove, thicket, bosket, bosquet.

bosquímano s. m. Bushman.

bossa s. f. 1. swelling, bump, bruise, boil. 2. protuberance, hump, lump, bulge, hunch. 3. knoll, knob, elevation. 4. aptitude, talent, vocation, calling. 5. (naut.) stopper. 6. (mech., bot., zool.) boss.

bossagem s. f. (pl. **-ens**) boss(age), projecting part.

bossa-nova s. f. (Braz., pop.) bossa nova. ‖ adj. bossa nova.

ele é cantor ~ he is a bossa nova singer.

bosta s. f. 1. cow dropping, cow dung. 2. turd excrement.

bosta-de-cabra s. f. (pl. **bostas-de-cabra**) (Braz.) diamond-bearing pebble.

bostal s. m. (pl. **-ais**) (Port.) cattle pen.

bosteiro s. m. (also **escaravelho**) (ent.) tumblebug.

bostela s. f. blister, pimple, pustule.

bostelento adj. pustulous, pimply.

bóston s. m. boston: 1. game at cards. 2. (mus.) form of waltz.

bóstrix s. m. (bot.) bostryx.

bota (I) s. f. 1. boot (plates B 16, R 6). 2. barrel, tub. 3. leather bag or bottle. 4. wine-cask. 5. (Braz., pop.) difficulty, obstacle. 6. poor painting or drawing.

~ de cano comprido top-boot. **~s de cano curto** bluchers. **~s de abotoar** button-boots. **~s de borracha** rubber boots, waders, gum boots (plate B 16). **~s de montaria** riding boots, jack-boots (plates B 16, R 7). **meter as ~s em** to criticize somebody severely. **arranjar um par de ~s a alguém** to get a p. into trouble. **bater as ~, bater a ~** to kick the bucket, die. **cano de ~** leg of a boot. **não sei como ele vai descalçar aquela ~** I don't know how he will get out of that scrape. **onde Judas perdeu as ~s** in a far-away, impassable place.

bota (II) s. f. (pop.) fib, petty lie.

botada s. f. 1. blow or stroke with a boot. 2. (fig.) aggression, attack. 3. (Braz.) start of cane-crushing in a sugar-mill.

bota-fogo s. m. (pl. **bota-fogos**) 1. (mil.) linstock, portfire. 2. (mil.) gunner. 3. (fig.) fire-brand, rioter.

bota-fora s. m., sg. + pl. 1. departure. 2. launching (of a ship). 3. send-off party, farewell party.
botalós s. m. pl. (naut.) 1. three-pronged grappling hook. 2. boom, spar.
botânica s. f. botany.
livro de ~ botany (book).
botânico s. m. botanist, herbalist. ‖ adj. botanic(al).
botanomancia s. f. divination or fortune-telling using plants.
botão s. m. (pl. **-ões**) 1. bud, flower-bud, gemmule. 2. wart, verruca. 3. metal knob, stud, boss. 4. button (plates B 12; C 11; L 3; M 2, 3; R 4, 6; V 5). 5. cauterizing iron. 6. (fig.) person or thing not yet mature. 7. (Braz.) traces of diamond-bearing rock.
~ **de campainha** bell-button. ~ **de colarinho** collar stud. ~ **de contato** (electr.) contact button, push--button (plate M 5). ~ **de partida**, ~ **de arranque** (mot.) starter button, starter switch (plate V 3). ~ **de pressão** 1. patent-fastener, press-fastener (plate B 12). 2. press button, push button (plate T 4). ~ **de punho de camisa** wrist-stud, sleeve-link. ~ **de rosa** rose-bud. **carregar no** ~ to press the button. **casa do** ~ buttonhole. **conversar com seus botões** to talk to o. s.
botão-de-farda s. m. (pl. **botões-de-farda**) (bot.) amaranth, love-lies-bleeding.
botão-de-ouro s. m. (pl. **botões-de-ouro**) (bot.) 1. Anthony's turnip. 2. yellow-eyed grass. 3. meadow crowfoot. 4. lesser celandine.
botar v. 1. to throw, cast, fling. 2. to revoke, repel, repulse. 3. ~**-se:** a) to throw or fling o. s. b) to dare, venture. c) to leave, depart. 4. to bud, flower, fructify. 5. to protrude, swell, jut out. 6. (Braz.) to start the crushing of sugar-cane (in a mill). 7. to pour out.
~**am-no para fora** they threw him out, they turned him out of doors. ~ **o navio ao mar** to launch a ship. **boto o crime para aquele homem** I lay the crime to that man's charge.
botara s. f. (Braz.) snare, trap.
botaréu s. m. (archit.) abutment, counterfort, buttress, pier, prop, arch of a vault.
bota-sela s. m. (pl. **bota-selas**) (mil.) boot and saddle, signal to saddle.
tocar à ~ to sound to horse.
bote (I) s. m. 1. boat, skiff. 2. jolly-boat, long-boat, dingey, dinghy (plate B 8).
~ **de bordo** jolly-boat. ~ **a remo** rowboat. ~ **de borracha** rubber boat. ~ **de recreio** pleasure-boat.
bote (II) s. m. 1. (fencing) cut, stab, thrust, blow, lunge. 2. assault, attack.
de um ~ 1. at once. 2. with one blow or cut.
boteco s. m. (Braz.) 1. stall, booth. 2. tavern, bar, barrel house, jerry-shop. 3. (pop.) eyeball.
boteiro s. m. 1. boatman, bargeman, bargee. 2. boatbuilder.
botelha s. f. 1. bottle, flask. 2. wine contained in a bottle.
botelharia s. f. wine-cellar, cellarage.
botelheiro s. m. butler.
botelho s. m. ancient measure for corn.
botequim s. m. (pl. **-ins**) 1. tavern, bar, pub(lic), taphouse, alehouse, dram shop. 2. coffee-house.
botequineiro s. m. tavern keeper, bar-keeper, proprietor of a bar or coffee-house.
botica s. f. 1. druggist's or apothecary's shop, pharmacy, dispensary. 2. (obs.) retail shop.
boticada s. f. remedy, medicine, drug.
boticão s. m. (pl. **-ões**) tooth forceps, tooth pincers.
boticária s. f. 1. apothecary's wife. 2. female pharmacist.
boticário s. m. apothecary, pharmacist, chemist.

botija s. f. stone jug, jar, flask.
~ **de água quente** hot-water bottle. **com a boca na** ~ in the very deed.
botijão s. m. (pl. **-ões**) cylinder: steel vessel for holding compressed gas.
botim s. m. (pl. **-ins**) half-boot.
botina s. f. (plate B 16) small boot, half-boot, lady's boot, bottine, gaiter.
botiqueiro s. m. shopkeeper, merchant.
botirão s. m. (pl. **-ões**) wicker net used for lamprey fishing, fish trap (plate B 12).
boto (ô) (I) s. m. hindu monk.
boto (ô) (II) s. m. 1. (zool.) bouto (river dolphin). 2. dolphin (family Iniidae). 3. any bulky thing. ‖ adj. 1. dull: a) blunt. b) apathetic. 2. set on edge (teeth).
botoado s. m. (ichth.) a variety of catfish.
botoaria s. f. button factory.
botocar v. (Braz., pop.) to jump out, go out.
botocudismo s. m. (Braz.) savageness, savagery, barbarity.
botocudo s. m. (Braz.) Botocudo: an Indian of a Tapuyan tribe. ‖ adj. of or relative to this tribe.
botoeira s. f. 1. button hole (plate R 7). 2. (woman) button maker.
botoeiro s. m. button maker or button manufacturer.
botoque s. m. (Braz) pierced stone worn esp. by Botocudos in the earlobes and underlips.
Botrídio s. m. (bot.) Botrydium: a genus of algae.
botrióide adj. m. + f. botryoid(al).
botulismo s. m. (med., vet.) botulism: any poisoning by the toxin of the Bacillus botulinus.
bouba s. f. 1. (med.): a) buba(s). b) bubo. 2. (vet.) roup.
boubento s. m. 1. (med.) buboed. 2. (vet.) roupy.
bouça s. f. (also **boiça**) uncultivated fallow land, pasture.
bouçar v. (also **boiçar**) to break or clear (uncultivated) land.
bournonita s. f. (min.) bournonite.
bovarismo s. m. bovarysm: domination by a romantic conception of o. s.
bovídeo s. m. bovid, bovine animal. ‖ adj. bovid, bovine.
bovino s. m. bovine, bullock. ‖ adj. bovine: of or resembling oxen, cattle, vaccine.
bovinocultor s. m. cattle breeder, stock-farmer.
bovinotecnia s. f. science and technique of cattle breeding, animal husbandry.
boxador s. m. (sport) boxer.
boxe s. m. 1. boxing, pugilism, knuckles. 2. knuckle--duster. 3. stall (in a horse stable).
luta a curta distância no ~ infighting.
boxeador s. m. pugilist, (sl.) pug.
boxear v. to box.
boxer s. m. boxer (dog).
boximane s. m. + f. Bushman, Bushwoman. ‖ adj. of or relative to the Bushmen or women.
boxista s. m. (sport) boxer.
bozerra s. f. (Braz.) 1. dung, fecal matter. 2. (fig.) lazybones.
bozó s. m. (Braz.) game of dice.
brabanção s. m. (pl. **-ões**) (f. **-ona**) native of Brabant (Belgium). ‖ adj. Brabantine.
brabeza, brabura, brabo = **braveza, bravura, bravo**.
braça s. f. 1. ancient measure of length. 2. fathom. 3. brace.
braçada s. f. 1. armful, as much as the arms can seize. 2. (swimming) crawl stroke.
~ **em nado de costas** (swimming) backstroke.
braçadeira s. f. 1. leather handle (of a shield). 2. band of a rifle. 3. curtain loop or ring. 4. armrest

or elbow rest. 5. drum-spanner. 6. wirst-strap. 7. brace, band, clamp.

~ **para tubos** pipe-clip, pipe-saddle (plate E 3).

braçagem s. f. (pl. **-ens**) 1. manual work. 2. money earned by manual work.

bracaiá s. m. a kind of wild cat.

bracajá s. m. (Braz., zool.) a kind of tortoise.

braçal (I) s. m. (pl. **-ais**) bracer, brassard, protective armour for the arms.

braçal (II) adj. m. + f. (pl. **-ais**) 1. of, pertaining to or relative to the arm. 2. brachial, manual, by the strength of the arms. 3. (fig.) material, corporeal.

bracamarte s. m. two-handed sword.

braçaria s. f. the art of throwing darts, lances, etc.

bracatinga s. f. I. leguminous tree of the genus Mimosa. 2. open thicket.

braceador adj. (horse) moving the front legs widely apart.

braceagem s. f. (pl. **-ens**) 1. coinage, mintage. 2. right of coinage. 3. (naut.) bracing of the sails, rigging.

bracear v. 1. (naut.) to brace the sails. 2. to move the arms. 3. (fig.) to struggle, take much pains, fight. 4. (horses) to move the front legs in lateral direction. 5. to swim with strong movements of the arms.

braceiro s. m. hand, manual labourer, workman. ‖ adj. 1. strong-armed. 2. brachial.

bracejador adj. 1. moving, stirring (the arms). 2. gesticulating, gesticulatory.

bracejamento s. m. (also **bracejo**) 1. movement of the arms. 2. gesticulation. 3. (fig.) diffusion, dissemination. 4. germination. 5. rankness, luxuriant growth.

bracejar v. 1. to move the arms. 2. to take much pains, struggle, fight. 3. to gesticulate, flounce. 4. to become excited. 5. to germinate, sprout, branch out.

braceleira s. f. bracer, protective armour for the arms.

bracelete s. m. 1. bracelet, armlet, bangle, wristlet, circlet (plate J 3). 2. (ironic.) handcuff.

braco s. m. hound.

braço s. m. 1. arm: a) part of the human body (plates C 12, 18). b) forelimb of an animal (plate G 1). c) anything resembling an arm in use or shape (arm of a chair, sea, etc.) (plates A 6, B 14, M 1). d) power, might, courage. 2. manual labourer, hand, workman. 3. tentacles. 4. branch (river), bough (tree), tendril (vine). 5. (fig.) strength, work. 6. ~**s** pl. (naut.) braces, shrouds. 7. (violin) neck, (guitar) finger board (plates G 2, V 5). 8. (mech.) tappet, strut, bracket, stay (plates B 4, D 2, R 4). 9. offshoot.

~ **da balança** scale beam. ~ **da bomba** drawbeam. ~ **de manivela** crank arm, web (plate E 2). ~ **de mar** inlet, gulf. ~ **de mar ou de rio** horn, arm. ~ **de rio** reach, branch of a river. ~ **de semáforo** signal arm (plates E 12, V 4). ~ **de terra** neck of land. ~ **direito**, esquerdo right, left arm. ~ **real** royal power. **os** ~**s de uma cadeira** the elbow rests of a chair. **à força de** ~ by the strength of arms. **andar em** ~**s** to keep company with. **apoiar-se ao** ~ **de alguém** to take s. o.'s arm. **de** ~ **dado** arm in arm. **não dar o** ~ **a torcer** not to be willing to give in, refuse to be trifled with. **deixar alguém a** ~**s com** 1. to leave s. o. alone with. 2. to fob off s. th. on a p. **deixar cair os** ~**s** to lose courage (one's nerve). **ele é o meu** ~ **direito** he is my right hand. **estar com os** ~**s cruzados** 1. to be or stand with arms across. 2. to refuse any assistance. **receber alguém com** ~**s abertos** to receive somebody with open arms. **sem** ~ armless. **ver-se a** ~**s com**

uma coisa to have to tackle a problem. **vir a** ~**s com alguém** to come to blows with somebody.

braço-de-ferro s. m. (pl. **braços-de-ferro**) energetic, authoritative person, strong man.

ele é o ~ **de sua organização** he is the strong man of their organization.

braço-de-mono s. m. (pl. **braços-de-mono**) plant of the nightshade family.

braçolas s. f. pl. (naut.) combing, coaming (plate B 10).

Braconídeos s. m. pl. (ent.) Braconidae: a large family of minute insects.

bráctea s. f. (bot.) bract.

bracteado adj. (bot.) bracteate.

bracteal adj. m. + f. (pl. **-ais**) (bot.) bracteal.

bractéola s. f. (bot.) bractlet, bracteole.

bracteolado adj. (bot.) bracteolate.

braçudo adj. strong-armed, brawny, sinewy.

bradado s. m. 1. cry, shout, scream. 2. (mus. Passion Week) liturgical hymn containing the words of Pontius Pilatus.

bradador s. m., **bradante** m. + f. bawler, crier. ‖ adj. bawling, shouting.

bradal s. m. (pl. **-ais**) (carp.) bradawl.

bradar v. 1. to cry, call, hollo, shout, bawl. 2. to scream, yell, roar. 3. to cry for help, clamour, vociferate. 4. to demand, claim. 5. to cry out in protest, object, inveigh against.

que brada ao céu crying to heaven.

bradejar v. to cry, shout, yell, scream.

bradicardia s. f. (med.) bradycardia.

bradicardíaco adj. (med.) bradycardiac(al).

bradifasia s. f. (med.) bradyphasia.

bradipepsia s. f. (med.) bradypepsy.

bradípode s. m. (zool.) bradypod, sloth.

Bradipodídeos s. m. pl. (zool.) Bradypodidae: the sloth family.

brado s. m. 1. cry, shout, scream. 2. exclamation, acclamation, call. 3. clamour, roar. 4. complaint, protest, objection.

~ **de guerra** cry of war. **dar** ~ to become famous, win notoriety.

brafoneira s. f. brassart, armour for the upper arm.

braga s. f. 1. shackle (for the ankles), fetters. 2. palisade, rampart. 3. ~**s** pl. short and wide breeches.

bragada s. f. 1. part of the leg covered by shackles. 2. veins of the leg where horses are bled.

bragado adj. dappled, spotted, speckled (horses, cattle, etc.).

bragadura s. f. dapple, spottiness.

bragal s. m. (pl. **-ais**) (body-)linen, bed-clothes.

bragante s. m. = **bargante**.

bragantear v. = **bargantear**.

bragantino s. m. (also **bragançano, braganção, bragancês**) 1. native or inhabitant of Bragança. 2. member of the former reigning dynasty of Portugal and Brazil. ‖ adj. of, pertaining to or relative to Bragança.

bragas s. f. pl. 1. short and wide trousers. 2. long pants, drawers.

bragueiro s. m. 1. hernial truss or bandage. 2. swaddles, clouts. 3. (naut.) hawser.

braguês s. m. = **bracarense**.

braguilha s. f. slit of trousers.

braille s. m. Braille, braille: system of writing and printing for blind people.

bralha (I) s. f. Buddhistic pagoda.

bralha (II) s. f. (Braz.) easy trot (of a horse).

bralhar v. to trot, ride at a trot.

brama s. f. rut, lust, heat.

bramadeiro s. m. place where deer gather during rutting time.

bramador s. m., **bramante** m. + f. roarer (deer in heat). ‖ adj. roaring, rutting.

brâmane, brâmine s. m. + f. Brahmin, Brahman. ‖ adj. Brahmanic.

bramanismo s. m. Brahmanism.

bramar v. 1. to roar, bellow, howl. 2. to shout, cry. 3. to get angry, upset or vexed. 4. to be enraged, rave. 5. to clamour for or against.

bramido s. m. 1. roar, bellow, howling yell (animals, storm, sea). 2. thundering, clangour.

bramidor s. m. roarer, yeller. ‖ adj. roaring.

bramir v. 1. to roar, bellow. 2. to yell, scream, howl, rumble, bell. 3. to cry out, vociferate, clamour. 4. to reverberate, resound.

bramoso adj. 1. roaring, thundering, howling. 2. (fig.) furious, tempestuous, violent.

branca (I) s. f. 1. white hair. 2. (hist.) a silver coin. 3. rum.

branca (II) s. f. shackle, fetter.

brancacento adj. whitish, light grey, hoar.

Branca-de-neve prop. n. Snow-White (fairy tale).

brancagem s. f. (pl. **-ens**) (obs.) tax on retail sales of bread and meat.

brancão s. m. (pl. **-ões**) (Braz.) a wicked white (man).

brancarana s. f. light-coloured mulatto girl or woman.

brancar(r)ão s. m. (pl. **-ões**) light-coloured mulatto. ‖ adj. light brown.

branca-ursina s. f. (pl. **brancas-ursinas**) (bot.) 1. bear's-breech, brank-ursine, sea holly. 2. cow parsnip, hogweed.

branco s. m. 1. white colour, whiteness. 2. a white person. 3. sclerotic, white of the eye. 4. blank, gap. 5. (hist.) silver coin. 6. (bot.) alburnum, sapwood. ‖ adj. 1. white, light. 2. clear, bright. 3. white-haired, fair, hoar(y). 4. blank. 5. (fig.) pure, innocent.

~ **como a neve** snow-white. ~ **como uma mortalha** as white as a sheet. ~ **de chumbo** white lead. ~ **do olho** white of the eye. **armas -as** cold steel. **bandeira -a** white flag. **bilhete de loteria em** ~ blank in the lottery. **crédito (cheque) em** ~ blank credit (blank acceptance). **calor** ~ white heat. **ter carta -a** to be given free hand. **em** ~ unwritten, blank. **de cabelos** ~**s** white-haired, wintry (fig.). **deixar em** ~ 1. to leave a blank in writing. 2. not to fill in, (E. U. A.) or out. **de pele -a** white--skinned. **de ponto em** ~ well-dressed, well-groomed. **ele é um livro em** ~ he is a blank sheet. **ele passou a noite em** ~ he has not had a wink of sleep. **escrava -a** white slave. **espaço em** ~ blank. **ficar** ~ **to bleach. molho** ~ white sauce. **pão** ~ white bread. **roupa -a** under-wear. **sair em** ~ to draw a blank. **tráfego de escravas -as** white slave trade. **verso** ~ blankverse. **vestido de** ~ dressed in white.

branco-da-baía s. m. (pl. **brancos-da-baía**) (ironic.) mulatto.

brancura s. f. white, whiteness, hoar, hoariness, blankness.

brandal s. m. (pl. **-ais**) (naut.) shrouds, backstay.

brandalhão adj. (pl. **-ões**) (f. **brandalhona**) 1. very mild or gentle, soft. 2. (fig.) indolent, lazy.

brandão s. m. (pl. **-ões**) 1. torch, flambeau. 2. long candle.

brandíloquo adj. soft-spoken, gentle-tongued.

brandimento s. m. 1. brandishing. 2. shaking, swinging. 3. vibration, oscillation. 4. nodding, waving.

brandir v. 1. to brandish, flourish, wield. 2. to shake, swing, wave. 3. to nod. 4. to vibrate, oscillate.

~ **uma espada** to brandish a sword.

brando adj. 1. tender, soft, mild, bland, light, temperate. 2. flexible, lithe. 3. smooth, sleek. 4. (fig.) gentle, kind. 5. quiet. 6. meek. 7. emollient, relent-

ing, lenient. ‖ **-amente** adv. 1. tenderly, softly, gently, quietly. 2. by flattery.

brandura s. f. 1. softness, tenderness, mildness, lightness. 2. docility, blandness, gentleness, kindness, smoothness. 3. indulgence, affability, clemency. 4. moderation. 5. leniency, amenity. 6. meekness. 7. (Port.): a) fine rain, drizzle. b) dew.

branqueação (pl. **-ões**), **branqueadura** s. f., **branqueamento** m. 1. bleaching, whitening. 2. whitewashing. 3. cleaning. 4. purification.

branqueador s. m. bleacher, blancher, whitener, whitewasher. ‖ adj. bleaching.

branquear v. 1. to whiten: make or become white. 2. to bleach, blanch. 3. to whitewash. 4. to wash, clean. 5. to purify: make or become pure. 6. to daub. 7. to decolorate.

~ **ao sol** to sun.

branquearia s. f. bleachery: bleaching yard or ground.

branquejante adj. m. + f. bleaching, decolorant, canescent.

branquejar v. 1. to whiten, bleach. 2. to appear, grow or look white.

brânquia s. f. (zool.) gill, branchia.

branquiado adj. branchiate.

branquial adj. m. + f. (pl. **-ais**) branchial.

brânquias s. f. pl. (zool.) gills.

branquicento adj. whitish, light grey.

branquidade s. f. 1. whiteness. 2. (fig.) pureness. 3. (fig.) pureness of blood, nobility.

branquidão s. f. (pl. **-ões**) whiteness, white colour.

branquiópode s. m. (zool.) branchiopod.

braquia s. f. breve: curved mark (◡) put over a vowel or syllable to show that it is short.

braquial adj. m. + f. (pl. **-ais**) brachial.

braquicefalia s. f. (anat.) brachycephaly.

braquicéfalo s. m. (anat.) brachycephal (person). ‖ adj. brachycephalic, brachycephalous.

braquidá(c)tilo adj. brachydactylous.

braquídeo adj. brachial, arm-shaped.

braquiélitro adj. brachyelytral.

braquiópodes s. m. pl. (zool.) brachiopods: marine animals of the phyllum Brachiopoda.

braquióptero s. m. brachypterous bird or insect. ‖ adj. brachypterous.

braquiúro s. m. (zool.) any brachyuran crustacean, the true crabs. ‖ adj. brachyuran.

brasa s. f. 1. live or burning coal. 2. incandescence, ember, cinder. 3. (fig.) ardour, zeal. 4. (fig.) anxiety, anguish. 5. (fig.) anger, wrath, passion.

em ~ red-hot, ardent. **estar sentado sobre** ~**s** to be on thorns, (U. S. A.) to be on the anxious seat, to be on tenter-hooks. **pisar em** ~**s** to be on pins and needles. 4. **pôr em** ~ to incandesce, cause to glow. **puxar a** ~ **para sua sardinha** to seek one's own advantage, bring grist to one's mill.

brasa-escondida s. f. (pl. **brasas-escondidas**) (Braz., pop.) hypocrite.

brasão s. m. (pl. **-ões**) 1. arm, armorial bearings, cognizance, coat of arms, escutcheon. 2. blazonry. 3. (fig.) honour, glory , distinction. 4. hatchment.

dourar o ~ to marry a rich woman of low birth.

brasa-viva s. f. (pl. **brasas-vivas**) shrub of the myrtle family (Calyptranthes grandifolia).

braseiro s. m. (also **braseira** f.) 1. brazier, chafing dish. 2. fire-pan, little stove. 3. ashes, fire remains.

brasido s. m. 1. embers, live coals. 2. intense heat.

Brasil s. m. 1. Brazil. 2. brazil-wood. 3. m. + f. (hist.) Brazilian Indian.

brasilaçu s. m. (also **brasilete, brasileto**) (bot.) brasiletto.

brasileira s. f. 1. Brazilian woman or girl. 2. (Braz., sl.) rum. 3. ~**s** pl. (pop.) a sweetmeat.

brasileirice s. f. Brazilian idiom.

brasileirismo s. m. 1. Brazilian mannerism. 2. distinctive Brazilian character. 3. love for Brazil.

brasileiro s. m. (also **brasiliano**) Brazilian: native or inhabitant of Brazil. ‖ adj. Brazilian.

brasiliana s. f. collection of books, publications, essays and studies concerning Brazil.

brasílico adj. of, pertaining to or relative to Brazilian Indians.

brasilidade s. f. 1. characteristics of the Brazilian people. 2. Brazilian mannerism. 3. love for Brazil.

brasiliense s. m. + f. Brasilian: native or inhabitant of Brasília, the capital of Brazil. ‖ adj. m. + f. Brasilian.

brasilina s. f. (chem.) brazilin.

brasílio adj. Brazilian.

brasilita s. f. (min.) brazilite.

brasilografia, brasilologia s. f. brazilography, brazilology.

brasilográfico, brasilológico adj. brazilographic, brazilologic.

brasilógrafo, brasilólogo s. m. brazilographer.

brasino adj. glowing red, red-brown, rusty-coloured.

brasonar v. 1. to adorn with a coat of arms. 2. to brag, boast.

Brassolídeos s. m. pl. (ent.) Brassolidae: a family of butterflies.

brasume s. m. 1. ardour, fervour, zeal. 2. flame-colour, colour of ember.

bravata s. f. 1. bravado, defiance, challenge, bravura. 2. vainglory, boastfulness. 3. (fig.) panache.

bravateador, bravateiro s. m. 1. bravo, bravado. 2. swaggerer, bully, boaster. ‖ adj. boastful, swaggering.

bravatear v. 1. to defy, provoke, challenge. 2. to boast, bully. 3. to threaten, menace. 4. to show bravado. 5. to extol o. s.

bravejar v. 1. to rage, fume, roar. 2. to vociferate, shout, clamour. 3. to be excited or irritated.

braveza s. f. 1. ferocity, savagery. 2. rage, fury, wrath. 3. courage, valour. 4. impetuosity, boisterousness.

bravio s. m. uncultivated ground, wild country. ‖ adj. 1. wild, savage, ferocious. 2. feral, fierce, farouche. 3. ungovernable, unruly. 4. wicked. 5. rough, rustic, rude, rugged. 6. untilled, uncultivated, barren.

bravo s. m. a brave, courageous, daring man. ‖ adj. 1. brave, valiant, courageous, stout-hearted, gallant, valorous. 2. daring, bold, fierce, rampant. 3. wild, savage, ferocious. 4. furious, impetuous. 5. tempestuous. 6. unusual, rare. 7. exalted. 8. magnificent, excellent (also ironic.). 9. swaggering, boastful, snappish. 10. desolate. ‖ interj. bravo!, very well! ‖ **-amente** adv. bravely.

ele ficou ~ he got into his stride, became angry. **o mar está ~** the sea is rough.

bravura s. f. 1. bravery, courage, prowess, exploit, derring-do. 2. boldness, daring. 3. valour, valiantness, pluckiness. 4. gallantry, chivalry.

breado adj. 1. tarry, covered with pitch. 2. soiled, dirty.

breadura s. f. tarring, pitching.

brear v. 1. to pitch, tar. 2. (naut.) to pay a ship. 3. to soil, dirty.

breca s. f. cramp.

levado da ~ mischievous, devilish, naughty. **vai-te com a ~!** get out of here! **com a ~!** dash it all!

brecar v. (Braz.) 1. to brake, put on the brake or lock, apply the drag. 2. to stop, halt.

brecha s. f. 1. breach, gap, rent, fissure, chasm, burst. 2. wound, sore. 3. rupture, break (also mil.). 4. void. 5. (geol.) breccia. 6. (fig.) damage, prejudice.

~ de falha (geol.) fault (plate M 10). **bater em ~** to batter a breach in a wall. **entrar na ~** to step into the breach. **estar na ~** to fight in the front lines.

brechão s. m. (pl. **-ões**) river gorge, defile, canyon.

bredinho s. m. (Braz., bot.) samphire, saltweed.

bredo s. m. (bot.) prince's feather.

bredo-verdadeiro s. m. (pl. **bredos-verdadeiros**) (bot.) tumbleweed.

bregma s. f. (anat.) bregma, sinciput.

bregmático, brégmico adj. (anat.) bregmatic.

brejal, brejão s. m. (pl. **-ais, -ões**) (Braz.) big swamp, marsh or bog.

brejaúva, brejaúba s. f. tucuma: any of several Brazilian palm trees of the genus Astrocaryum.

brejeira s. f. (Braz., sl.) chewing tobacco.

brejeirada s. f. (also **brejeirice**) 1. knavish trick, waggery, archness, rowdyism. 2. cant of rogues. 3. gang of rogues.

brejeiral adj. m. + f. (pl. **-ais**) roguish, knavish, rascally.

brejeirar v. 1. to swindle, cheat. 2. to play a roguish trick. 3. to roam the streets, rove, loaf, idle.

brejeiro s. m. 1. loafer, tramp, rover, vagrant. 2. blackguard, rascal, scoundrel. ‖ adj. 1. malicious, spiteful. 2. shameless. 3. vagrant, lazy. 4. inhospitable.

brejento, adj. marshy, swampish, swampy, boggy.

brejo s. m. 1. swamp, bog, fen, slough, slash, morass, marsh, moor. 2. thicket, underbrush. 3. (pop.) cold and windy place. 4. heath, moorland, wasteland.

brejoso adj. marshy, swampish, swampy, boggy.

brelho s. m. pebble, fragments of bricks or tiles.

brema s. f. (ichth.) bream.

brenha s. f. 1. thicket, brake, dense wood, brushwood. 2. (fig.) confusion, complication.

brenhoso adj. brushy, bushy, woody.

breque s. m. 1. brake, break: wagonette (carriage). 2. (Braz.) brake (check).

~ de mão hand-brake (plate B 11, 15).

brequista s. m. brake(s)man.

bretanha s. f. fine cloth of linen or cotton.

bretão s. m. (pl. **-ões**) (f. **bretã**) Breton: 1. native or inhabitant of Brittany (or Bretagne). 2. language spoken in Brittany. ‖ adj. Breton.

brete s. m. 1. snare, trap. 2. (fig.) deceit, trick.

brete (ê) s. m. cattle pass(ageway).

breu s. m. 1. pitch, tar. 2. colophony, rosin. 3. (Braz.) bumboat, dinghy.

escuro como ~ pitch-dark.

breve (I) s. f. (mus.) breve (plate N 1). 2. abbreviation, abridgment. 3. short syllable, short vowel. ‖ adj. m. + f. 1. short, brief. 2. rapid, quick. 3. concise, laconic, compact. 4. prompt. ‖ adv. soon, before long. ‖ **~mente** adv. 1. shortly, briefly. 2. speedily. 3. concisely.

em ~ at an early date, soon, early, ere long. **dentro em ~** in the near future, before long. **seja ~!** cut it short, be brief! make it short and sweet! **o mais ~ possível** as soon (or brief) as possible. **até ~!** see you again soon!

breve (II) s. m. 1. brief: papal document, letter. 2. (Braz.) scapular (badge).

brevê s. m. (aeron.) a pilot's diploma (Fr. **brevet**).

brevetar v. (aeron., mil.) to brevet: 1. confer a rank by brevet. 2. graduate as aviator.

breviário s. m. 1. breviary. 2. (fig.) favourite book or reading matter. 3. abridgment, abbreviation. 4. synopsis, summary.

ler pelo mesmo ~ to think the same way.

brevicauda adj. m. + f. (zool.) brevicaudate, short-tailed.

brevidade s. f. 1. brevity, shortness. 2. conciseness, briefness. 3. haste, speed.
com a possível ~ at your earliest convenience.
brevifloro adj. (bot.) breviflorate.
brevifoliado adj. (bot.) brevifoliate.
brevípede adj. m. + f. breviped.
brevipene adj. m. + f. (ornith.) brevipennate, short--winged.
brevirrostro adj. (zool.) brevirostral.
brevista s. m. drafter of an apostolic brief.
brial s. m. (pl. **-ais**) 1. lady's tunic. 2. (hist.) tunic worn esp. over the armour.
brica s. f. (her.) square on the right side of an escutcheon indicating the ancestry of second sons.
bricabraque s. m. 1. antique or curiosity shop, bric-a--brac shop. 2. lumber: useless things.
bricabraquista s. m. + f. dealer in bric-a-brac, antique dealer.
briche s. m. a coarse woollen cloth (made in Portugal).
brida s. f. bridle, rein, guider.
correr a toda a ~ to run at full speed. **ter a** ~ **curta** to hold in the reins. **a toda** ~ at full gallop, as fast as possible.
bridão s. m. (pl. **-ões**) snaffle, snaffle-bit, bridoon, check-rein (plate C 12).
bridar v. 1. to bridle: a) put a bridle on. b) restrain. c) repress, curb, check. 2. (fig.) to govern.
bridge s. m. (cards) bridge.
briga s. f. 1. strife, quarrel, broil. 2. fighting, brawl(ing), row, scrimmage, scrummage, scrap, tussle. 3. dispute, bust-up, set-to. 4. bicker, dissension, contention, altercation, variance, wrangle.
~ **de galo** cock-fight(ing), spar. **homem de** ~ brawler. **procurar** ~ **com** to pick a quarrel with. **você vai ter** ~ **com ele** you will get into hot water with him.
brigada s. f. (mil.) brigade.
~ **de ensalos** testing crew.
brigadeiro s. m. 1. brigadier (-general). 2. (Braz.) air force general.
brigador s. m. 1. quarreler, brawler. 2. game-cock. ‖ adj. quarreling, quarrelsome.
brigalhada s. f. prolonged quarrel or discord.
brigalhão s. m. (pl. **-ões**) brawler, rowdy.
brigandina s. f. (hist.) brigandine: tightly fitting coat of body armour.
brigante adj. m. + f. quarreling, quarrelsome, pugnacious, contentious.
brigantino s. m. = **bragantino**.
brigão s. m. (pl. **-ões**) (f. **-ona**) brawler, rowdy, rough, ruffian, bully, quarreler. ‖ adj. quarrelsome, rowdy, ruffian(ly), pugnacious, fighting.
brigar v. 1. to quarrel, dispute. 2. to fight, combat, battle, grapple, wrestle, row, scrimmage, scrap, scuffle. 3. to disagree, altercate. 4. to discord, clash, argue.
~ **por dá cá aquela palha** to dispute about nothing.
brigue s. m. (naut.) brig, ketch.
briguela s. m. (Braz., fig.) puppet.
briguento s. m. wrangler, scuffler. ‖ adj. quarrelsome, rowdy, ruffian(ly), cantankerous, termagant, scrappy.
brilhância s. f. (opt.) luminance.
brilhante s. m. brilliant, diamond of a particular cut. ‖ adj. 1. brilliant, bright, radiant, sparkling, beamy, dazzling, lustrous. 2. magnificent, illustrious, splendid; (sl.) corking, crack. 3. shining, sparkling. 4. successful. ‖ ~**mente** adv. brilliantly, magnificently, illustriously, etc.
brilhantina s. f. 1. brilliantine, pomade. 2. (bot.) roseroot.

brilhantismo s. m. 1. brilliancy, splendour. 2. magnificence, grandeur, illustriousness. 3. brightness, radiance.
brilhar v. 1. to shine, glitter, sparkle, scintillate, star, flash, beacon, spangle. 2. (fig.) to distinguish o. s. 3. to excel. 4. to display, show off.
ela brilhou pela ausência she was conspicuous by her absence. **seus olhos** ~**am de alegria** his (her) eyes sparkled with joy.
brilho s. m. 1. brightness, brilliancy, radiance, blaze, luminosity, shininess. 2. splendour, splendidness, magnitude, magnificence. 3. lustre. 4. pomp. 5. (fig.) vivacity. 6. celebrity. 7. scintillation (of styles, colours, etc.). 8. polish, polishedness, burnish.
sem ~ blind, lustreless. **falso** ~ tawdriness.
brilhoso adj. (Braz., pop.) 1. brilliant, radiant, splendid. 2. bright, lustrous.
brim s. m. single canvas, sailcloth, drill.
brinça s. f. (bot.) brimstonewart, sow-fennel, hog's--fennel.
brincadeira s. f. 1. entertainment, fun, children's play, game, sport. 2. merrymaking, bantering. frolicsomeness, skylarking. 3. joke, jest, prank, monkeyshine, hoax. 4. festive family reunion.
de ~ in joke, in jest. **dito por** ~ said for fun. **ele não pode deixar de fazer uma** ~ he cannot resist playing a joke. **eles não gostam de** ~ they stand no trick. **nada de** ~ joking apart. **não é** ~ **(de criança)** it is serious, it is no joke, no fun! **por** ~ for the fun of it. **que** ~! what a game! **saiu-lhe cara a** ~ he had to face the music. **sem** ~! seriously now! **topar uma** ~ to take a joke.
brincado s. m. 1. beautiful ornament, decoration, trimming. 2. embroidery, needlework. ‖ adj. trimmed with lace, ornamented, embellished.
brincador, brincalhão (pl. **-ões**) s. m. jester, sport, wag, droll, joker, wit, toyer, merry fellow. ‖ adj. funny, frolicsome, cheerful, playful, larky, frisky, roguish.
brincar v. 1. to play, dally, toy. 2. to frolic, gambol, caper. 3. to play pranks. 4. to entertain, amuse, divert. 5. to mock, jest, fun, fool. 6. to trifle, twiddle. 7. to flirt, fondle. 8. to adorn, embellish. 9. to lace.
~ **com** to play with. ~ **com o fogo** to play with fire. ~ **de esconder** to play at hid-and-seek, (fam.) at peek-aboo. **com disposição para** ~ in wild spirits. **com ele não se brinca** he stand no nonsense. **eu estava brincando** I was only making fun. **isto não é para** ~ this is no jesting matter. **quando o gato está longe, os ratos brincam** when the cat is away, the mice will play. **quarto de** ~ playroom.
brinco s. m. 1. ear-ring, drop, pendant (plate J 3). 2. toy, plaything. 3. jest, joke, sport. 4. something very neat, clean or delicate. 5. ~**s** ear-rings, ear--drops.
ser um ~ to be very clean, nice, or beautiful.
brinco-de-princesa s. m. (pl. **brincos-de-princesa**) (bot.) fuchsia.
brindar v. 1. to drink to a person's health, propose a p.'s health, toast. 2. to present, make a gift. 3. to grant, pledge, allow. 4. to give as premium or reward. 5. to pledge to someone. 6. to punish.
~ **à saúde de alguém** to drink (propose) to a p.'s health. ~ **a vontade** to allure, entice. ~**-se mutuamente** to toast each other. **ele nos brindou com um livro** he presented us with a book. **eu o brindei** I raised my glass to him.
brinde s. m. 1. toast, wish of health. 2. present, gift, token, souvenir. 3. pledge.
fazer ~ to drink (propose) to a person's health.
brinjela s. f. = **berinjela**.

brinquedo s. m. 1. toy, plaything. 2. joke, jest, fun. 3. dancing party. 4. merrymaking. 5. sport.
~ **de sela** leap-frog. **loja de** ~**s** toyshop.
brinquinharia s. f. 1. toy factory or works. 2. toyshop or trade.
brio s. m. 1. sense of dignity or honour, valour, manliness. 2. self-respect, self-reliance, character, pride. 3. generosity, liberality. 4. courage, mettlesomeness. 5. elegance, gracefulness.
abater os ~**s de alguém** to break one's pride, take one down a peg or two. **cheio de** ~ mettlesome, lively. **homem de** ~ man of mettle.
brioche s. f. brioche: a light roll made of yeast dough, eggs and butter.
briófito s. m. (bot.) bryophite.
briol s. m. (pl. -óis) 1. (naut.) brails, buntliness. 2. (pop.) wine.
briologia s. f. (bot.) bryology.
briológico adj. (bot.) bryologic(al).
briologista s. m. + f. bryologist.
briônia s. f. (bot.) devil's turnip, commom bryony.
briosa s. f. (the proud one): 1. nickname of the former Brazilian National Guard. 2. nickname of the Military Police. 3. brass band.
brioso adj. 1. proud, honour-loving, self-sure, self--reliant. 2. lively, sprightly, 3. energetic. 4. brave, courageous, knightly, chivalrous. 5. liberal. 6. elegant, graceful. || **-amente** adv. 1. proudly. 2. generously, liberally. 3. bravely, courageously. 4. gracefully, elegantly.
brioteca s. f. (bot.) a duly-classified moss collection.
briozoário s. m. (zool.) bryozoon, bryozoum.
brique s. m. (Braz.) bric-a-brac.
briquete (ê) s. m. briquette, patent fuel.
briquitar v. (Braz., pop) 1. to strive, endeavour. struggle. 2. to toil, exert, slave. 3. to pain, trouble (oneself).
brisa s. f. breeze; light, fresh wind, breath(ing), whiff, air, cat's paw, sea-breeze.
~ **terrestre** land-breeze. **estar na** ~ to have not a farthing. **batido pela** ~ airy. **sem** ~ airless.
brístol s. m. Bristol cloth.
brita s. f. broken stones, pebble, flintstone.
britadeira s. f. 1. stone crusher (machine). 2. f. of **britador:** a female stone crusher.
britado adj. broken, crushed.
britador s. m. 1. breaker, crusher, stonebreaker. 2. stamp, stamping mill.
britamento s. m. (also **britagem** f.) breaking, crushing, trituration.
Britânia s. f. 1. Britannia. 2. Britannia metal.
britânico s. m. British, Englishman. || adj. Britannic, British, English.
britar v. 1. to break, crush, spall, stamp (stone, ore). 2. (fig.) to confuse, embarrass. 3. to grind, triturate. 4. to break in, force open. 5. to annul.
brives s. m. pl. (naut.) reef-tackle.
brizomancia s. f. oneuromancy: divination by dreams.
brizomante s. m. + f. oneurocritic: interpreter of dreams.
brizomântico adj. oneurocritical.
broa s. f. 1. bread of maize, rice and whipped eggs, pone. 2. (pop.) fat woman. 3. loaf-shaped Christmas cake.
broca s. f. 1. bit, drill, auger, gimlet, boring machine (plate F 1). 2. mandrel. 3. chisel. 4. flaw (in metal). 5. (Braz., ent.) woodborer, fruit-tree borer.
~ **de dentista** burr(-drill) (plate D 1). ~ **de romã** rose countersink bit (plate F 8). ~ **de três pontas** centre bit (plates F 8, M 4). ~ **para arco de pua** auger bit (plate M 4).
brocadilho s. m. brocatel(le).
brocado s. m. brocade.

broca-do-café s. f. (pl. **brocas-do-café**) (ent.) coffee borer (Hypothenemus hampei Ferrari).
brocador s. m. (Braz., pop.) wood-cutter.
brocagem s. f. (pl. -ens) boring.
brocal s. m. (pl. -ais) (hist.) iron edging around an escutcheon.
brocar v. 1. to bore, drill, perforate, wimble. 2. to sift, winnow (coffee). 3. to cut brushwood or underbrush.
brocardo s. m. proverb, maxim, adage.
brocatel s. m. (pl. -éis) brocatel(le), damasklike fabric, tinsel.
brocatelo s. m. brocatello: a sort of spotted marble.
brocha s. f. 1. tack, boss, little nail (plate P 15). 2. peg, trunnion. 3. leather strips to tie the oxen to the yoke.
brochado adj. in paper cover, paper back stitched, sewed (books).
brochador s. m. (book) stitcher or sewer.
brochagem s. f. (pl. -ens) stitching or sewing of books.
brochar v. to stitch or sew books or pamphlets.
broche s. m. 1. brooch, locket (plate J 3). 2. ornamental clasp, pin, breast-pin, agrafe.
brochote s. m. (Braz.) boy, lad, youngster.
brochura s. f. 1. brochure, pamphlet, booklet, chapbook. 2. the art of stitching books. 3. any book in paper cover.
broco (ô) adj. (N. Braz.) 1. short-horned (cattle). 2. crazy, foolish.
brocojó s. m. (Braz.) a kind of cake.
brócolos s. m. pl. (bot.) broccoli: variety of cabbage resembling the cauliflower.
bródio s. m. 1. banquet, feast. 2. revelry, carousing, racket. 3. alms-soup.
brodista s. m. + f. banqueteer, revel(l)er. 2. merrymaker. 3. almsman, almsfolk.
broeiro s. m. 1. maizebread vendor. 2. one who likes to eat maizebread. 3. (fig.) rustic, boor.
brolho (ô) s. m. (bot.) young shoot.
broma s. f. 1. inner edge of the horseshoe into which the hoof fits. 2. (S. Braz.) jest, prank. 3. ship's worm, teredo. 4. m. + f. fool, boor. || adj. m. + f. 1. coarse, rough. 2. inferior in quality.
bromado s. m. = **brumado**.
bromar v. 1. to corrode, waste away. 2. to destroy, spoil, deteriorate. 3. to degenerate, ruin o. s. 4. to pervert, corrupt. 5. (chem.) to brominate. 6. to be unsuccessful.
bromato s. m. (chem.) bromate.
bromatologia s. f. bromatology.
bromatológico adj. bromatologic.
bromatólogo s. m. bromatologist.
bromeliácea s. f. any plant of the pineapple (Bromeliaceae) family.
bromeliáceo adj. (bot.) bromeliaceous.
brometo s. m. (chem.) bromide.
brômico adj. (chem.) bromic.
bromídrico adj. bromidic(al).
bróm(i)o s. m. (chem.) bromine.
bromofórmio s. m. (chem.) bromoform.
bromureto s. m. (chem.) bromide.
bronca s. f. (school sl.) scolding, reprimand.
dar uma ~ to give a person a good scolding. **levar uma** ~ (school sl.) to be blown up, reprimanded.
bronco s. m. dullar, dunce. || adj. 1. dull, blunt. 2. rude, rough. 3. coarse, crude. 4. common, impolite, ill-mannered. 5. stupid, foolish, dull-brained, slow--witted, purblind, barren.
broncoscopia s. f. (med.) bronchoscopy.
broncoscópio s. m. (med.) bronchoscope.
broncotomia s. f. (med.) bronchotomy.
broncótomo s. m. bronchotome: surgical instrument used for bronchotomies.

brongo s. m. (N. Braz.) funnel-shaped cave or grotto.
bronquial adj. m. + f. (pl. -ais) bronchial.
bronquice s. f. stupidity, foolishness.
brônquico adj. bronchial.
brônquio s. m. (anat.) bronchial tube, bronchus.
bronquíolo s. m. (anat.) bronchiole.
bronquite s. f. (med.) bronchitis.
bronzagem s. f., **bronzeamento** m. bronzing, brazing.
bronze s. m. 1. bronze: a) alloy of copper and tin. b) a similar alloy of copper with zinc or other metals, brass. c) (art.) sculpture, medal, etc. of bronze. 2. gun metal, piece of artillery. 3. bell. 4. ancient coin. 5. (fig.) hardness, insensibility. ~ **de canhão** admiralty alloy. ~ **de canhões** gun metal. ~ **fundido** bronze casting. **de** ~ brazen. **céu de** ~ a brazen sky. **gravado em** ~ engraved upon brass.
bronzeado adj. 1. bronzed, covered or adorned with bronze. 2. bronzy. 3. sunburnt. tanned, weather-beaten.
bronzeador s. m. bronzer.
bronzear v. to bronze: 1. paint in, colour, cover or adorn with bronze. 2. become brown, make brown, tan, burn, darken.
brônzeo adj. bronzy, brazen.
bronzita s. f. (min.) bronzite.
bronzista s. m. + f. bronzer worker in bronze.
brookita s. f. (min.) brookite.
broque s. m. (tech.) tuyere.
broqueado adj. 1. worm-eaten, wormy, vermiculated. 2. ulcerated. 3. fistulous.
broqueamento s. m. boring.
broquear v. to drill, bore, pierce, perforate.
broquel s. m. (pl. -éis) buckler, shield.
broquelar v. to shield, protect.
broqueleiro s. m. (hist.) 1. maker of bucklers. 2. buckler-bearer.
broquento adj. 1. full of sores, ulcerated. 2. corroded, worm-eaten.
broslar v. = **bordar.**
brossa s. f. 1. printer's brush. 2. horse brush.
brota s. f. spring, fountain.
brotamento s. m. 1. budding, sprouting. 2. launching, casting.
brotar v. 1. to produce, bring forth, bear, issue, grow. 2. to originate, arise. 3. to expel, eject. 4. to express, declare. 5. to bud, germinate, sprout, shoot forth. 6. to appear, burst or break out. 7. to flow, stream, spring up, spout. 8. (N. Braz.) to boast of intrepidity. ~ **injúrias contra** to inveigh against, revile a person. ~ **queixas** to utter complaints. **as águas ~am do solo** waters sprang from the earth. **as batatas ~am** the potatoes have grown out. **lágrimas ~am de seus olhos** tears welled up to her eyes.
brote s. m. (Braz.) biscuit.
brotinho s. m. (Braz. sl.) (fig.) flapper, girl in her teens, (U.S.A.) bobby-soxer, chicken.
broto (ô) s. m. (Braz.) 1. budding, sprouting. 2. bud, shoot, sprout, burgeon, runner, eye, sucker, twig, tiller, sprig. 3. (Braz., sl.) = **brotinho.**
brotoeja s. f. (med.) sudamen, vesicular eruption.
broxa s. f. a painter's brush, stock brush (plates A 7, E 8, P 12).
broxante s. m. house painter, whitewasher.
broxar v. to whithewash, paint with a big brush.
broziado adj. affected by **brózio.**
brózio s. m. (N. E. Braz.) dry rot: a plant disease.
bruaca s. f. (Braz.) 1. a rawhide travelling bag used on horseback. 2. leather bag.
bruaqueiro s. m. 1. sumpter. 2. marketer, marketman.
brucelose s. f. (med.) brucellosis, undulant fever.
brucina s. f. (pharm.) brucin(e).

brucita s. f. (min.) brucite.
bruços s. m. pl. only used in the adverbial locution: **de** ~ lying face downwards. **beber de** ~ to drink lying flat on the ground. **atirar-se de** ~ to throw o. s. headlong down.
bruega s. f. 1. shower, drizzle. 2. (pop.) row, tumult.
brugalheira s. f. bare, stony ground, barren land.
brujarara s. f. (ornith.) ant shrike.
brulho s. m. olive husks.
brulate s. m. fire-ship.
bruma s. f. 1. thick fog, mist, haze, vapour, cloud. 2. (fig.) uncertainty, mystery.
brumaceiro adj. foggy, misty, hazy.
brumado s. m. dense thicket, coppice.
brumal adj. m. + f. (pl. -ais) 1. foggy, misty. 2. sad, sorrowful. 3. shady, dusky.
brumário s. m. Brumaire: second month of the French Revolutionary calendar (Oct. 22 to Nov. 21).
brumbrum adj. m. + f. (pl. -uns) gibberish, jabbering.
brumoso adj. foggy, misty, hazy.
brunido adj. 1. burnished, polished. 2. glittering, shiny. 3. ironed, starched.
brunidor s. m. 1. burnisher, furbisher. 2. polisher (person). 3. burnishing-stick.
brunidura s. f. burnishing, polishing, metal spinning.
brunir v. 1. to polish, burnish, furbish. 2. to iron, starch. 3. to make brilliant or shiny, scour. 4. (fig.) to perfect, improve.
bruno adj. 1. brown, dark. 2. (fig.) unfortunate.
brusca s. f. (bot.) butcher's broom, knee-holly.
brusco adj. 1. dark, cloudy (weather). 2. rough, harsh, curt, sharp, blunt. 3. impetuous, precipited. 4. abrupt, brusque. 5. unforeseen, unexpected. || -amente adv. abruptly, brusquely, curtly, smack. **sua maneira -a** his abrupt manner. **levantar-se -amente** to start up.
brusquidão s. f. (pl. -ões) brusqueness, harshness, abruptness.
brussa s. f. = **brossa.**
bruta word used in the adv. locution: **à** ~: violently, exceedingly, excessively.
brutal adj. m. + f. (pl. -ais) 1. brutal, brutish, cruel, bestial, savage, feral, barbarous. 2. rough, ruffian, tough, rowdy, uncivil, coarse. 3. violent, impetuous. || ~**mente** adv. brutally, beastly, violently, etc.
brutalidade s. f. (also **bruteza, brutidade, brutidão**) 1. brutality, brutishness, atrocity, wildness, bestiality, savagery, barbarity, beastliness. 2. violence, impetuosity. 3. rudeness, impoliteness.
brutalizar v. 1. to brutalize, make stupid or brutish, bestialize. 2. to become brutal, grow stupid.
brutamontes s. m. brute, rough, stupid, boor, yahoo, lummox, animal.
brutesco s. m. grotesque artistic representation of animals and wild life. || adj. 1. rough, coarse. 2. ridiculous, grotesque. 3. raw, natural, savage.
brutificador adj. brutalizing.
brutificar v. to make or become brutish or stupid.
bruto s. m. 1. animal, beast. 2. brute, inhuman person. || adj. 1. rude, rough, coarse. 2. inert, dull. 3. raw, unmanufactured, unrefined, unfinished. 4. uncivil, uncouth, ungracious, ungentle, uncultivated, rustic, unpolished. 5. violent, ferocious. 6. brutish, savage. 7. complete, without deduction. **em** ~ in the rough, row. **diamante** ~ rough diamond. **pedra bruta** unhewn stone. **peso** ~ gross weight. **força bruta** brute force.
bruxa s. f. witch, sorceress, enchantress, hag, hellcat, harridan.
bruxaria s. f. (also **bruxedo** m.) witchery, diablerie, baffler, witching, witchcraft, sorcery.
bruxear v. to practise witchcraft.

bruxismo s. m. (med.) bruxism, bruxomania: the (unconscious) habit of grinding the teeth.
bruxo s. m. sorcerer, wizard, conjurer, baffler.
bruxuleante adj. m. + f. 1. flickering, flaring scintillating, wavering. 2. extinguishing, going out (fire).
bruxulear v. to flicker, waver, bicker, scintillate weakly, burn fitfully, go out (light, fire).
bruxuleio s. m. flicker(ing) waver(ing).
Btu s. m. (phys.) Btu: abbr. of British termal unit.
búbalo s. m. (zool.) 1. bubalus: an African bovid. 2. bubalis, bubal(e): the northern hartebeest (Alcelaphus boselaphus).
bubão s. m. (pl. -ões), (med.) bubo, adenitis, swelling of the groin.
bubônica s. f. (med.) bubonic plague.
bubônico adj. bubonic.
bubonocele s. f. (med.) inguinal rupture.
bubu s. m. (Braz.) a kind of blouse for women.
bubuia s. f. (Braz.) 1. floatation. 2. anything that floats (esp. along with the current).
de ~ floating.
bubuiar v. to float, drift (in the current).
bubuituba s. f. (Braz.) buoy, float.
bucal adj. m. + f. (pl. -ais) buccal.
buçal s. m. (pl. -ais) (Braz.) 1. head-harness, headgear. 2. feed bag. 3. halter(-rope).
buçalar v. (also **embuçalar**) to put a harness or halter on.
bucaneiro s. m. 1. buccaneer, freebooter. 2. buffalo hunter. 3. rifle used for buffalo hunting.
bucéfalo s. m. (hist.) Bucephalus: 1. the war-horse of Alexander the Great. 2. (fig.) a high-spirited horse. 3. (pop.) any riding horse. 4. a worn-out horse.
bucelário adj. like a little mouth.
bucentauro s. m. (hist.) bucentaur: Venetian state barge.
bucha s. f. 1. wad(ding). 2. (tech.) bush (plate F 1). 3. (tech.) sleeve. 4. plug, stopper, bung. 5. burnisher. 6. hunk of bread, mouthful, morsel, bite. 7. (non-nutritive) filling food. 8. annoyance, inconvenience. 9. cheat, fraud, fake. 10. (Braz., bot.) dishcloth gourd.
~ cônica taper sleeve. **~ de arma de fogo** tampion. **~ de bronze** bronze bushing. **~ de fundo** bush of stuffing-box. **agüentar com a ~** to make an unpleasant experience. **aturar a ~** to swallow the pill. **tomar uma ~** to be cheated.
buchada s. f. 1. entrails. 2. mouthful, bit. 3. (fig.) overeating, repletion. 4. wad(ding). 5. (fig.) annoyance, inconvenience. 6. damage, loss.
buchar v. to bush.
bucheiro s. m. (pop.) habitual drinker.
buchela s. f. a goldsmith's pincers.
bucho s. m. 1. craw, crop. 2. stomach. 3. paunch, belly. 4. (Braz.) prostitute.
despejar o ~ to unburden one's heart. **tirar do ~ de alguém** to get out of s. o.
bucho-de-piaba, bucho-furado s. m. (pl. **buchos-de-piaba, buchos-furados**) (Braz., pop.) indiscrete person.
buchudo adj. paunchy, pot-bellied.
bucinador s. m. (anat.) buccinator: masticatory muscle, masseter. || adj. masseteric.
bucle s. m. (also **bucre**) curl, ringlet (hair) .
buco s. m. 1. belly of a ship. 2. bulge. 3. capacity. 4. width of a ship.
bucofacial adj. buccofacial.
bucomaxilar adj. buccomaxillary.
buço s. m. fluff, first growth of a beard.
bucólica s. f. eclogue, bucolic poem, pastoral.
bucólico adj. 1. bucolic, pastoral. 2. (fig.) simple, innocent. 3. graceful, elegant.

bucolismo s. m. 1. bucolic poetry. 2. inclination or preference for this type of poetry.
bucolista s. m. + f. bucolic: a pastoral poet.
bucolizar v. 1. to give a bucolic character to, make idyllic. 2. to write idyllic poetry.
Buconídeos s. m. pl. (ornith.) Bucconiade, the puffbird family.
bucrânio s. m. a bullock's skull.
buçu s. f. (bot.) bussu (a low palm).
bucuva s. m. + f. fool, simpleton.
budapestense s. m. + f. (also **budapestino** m.) native or inhabitant of Budapest. || adj. of, pertaining to or relative to this city.
búdico adj. Buddhistic.
budismo s. m. Buddhism.
budista s. m. + f. Buddhist. || adj. (also **budístico**) Buddhist(ic).
bué s. m. (Braz., pop.) bawling, crying (of children).
bueiro s. m. 1. sewer, drainpipe, gutter, gully (plate R 8). 2. dike, channel, watercourse. 3. air gate, breathing hole, man-hole (plate E 10). 4. factory chimney. 5. (naut.) limber.
buenacho, buenaço adj. (Braz.) 1. very well, good. 2. splendid. 3. kind, generous.
buena-dicha s. f. fortune, good luck.
ler a ~ to tell one's fortune.
buenairense s. m. + f. native or inhabitant of Buenos Aires. || adj. of, pertaining to or relative to Buenos Aires.
bufa s. f. (vulg.) fart, wind.
bufa-de-lobo s. f. (pl. **bufas-de-lobo**) (bot.) puffball.
bufador s. m. (Braz., pop.) 1. braggart, boaster. 2. blowhole, spiracle (as a whale). || adj. blowing, expelling (air, gas, water, etc.), snorting.
búfaga s. f. (ornith.) beefeater, oxpecker.
bufalino adj. of, pertaining to or relative to buffaloes.
búfalo s. m. (zool.) buffalo, bison.
~ da Índia water buffalo.
bufante adj. m. + f. luffy, loose-fitting (blouse, skirt).
bufão s. m. (pl. -ões) (f. -ona) 1. braggart, boaster. 2. (hist.) jester, fool, buffoon, droll, mime.
bufar v. (also **bufir**) 1. to blow, puff. 2. to breathe hard, snuff, snort. 3. to get mad, grow furious. 4. to brag, boast.
bufarinhar v. to peddle.
bufarinhas s. f. pl. 1. baubles, trifles, knick-knacks. 2. pedlary.
bufarinheiro s. m. peddler, hawker.
bufete s. m. 1. buffet: a) sideboard. b) cupboard, dresser (plate R 5). c) canteen, bar for refreshments (in railway stations, clubs, etc.) (plate E 13). 2. an engineer's kit for field work.
bufido s. m. sound of puffs, whiffs, blasts of air, etc.
bufo s. m. 1. puff, whiff, blast. 2. (ornith.) eagle owl. 3. (fig.) miser, niggard. 4. buffoon. 5. (Port.) spy, informer. || adj. burlesque, comical.
bufonaria s. f. buffoonery, drollery, jesting.
bufonear v. to play the buffoon, jest, be full of beans, joke, be funny.
Bufonídeos s. m. pl. (zool.) Bufonidae, the toad family.
buftalmia s. f. (med.) buphtalmia.
bugalho s. m. 1. gall-nut, oak-apple, oak-gall. 2. eyeball.
bugalhudo adj. 1. glandiform, like a gall-apple. 2. goggle-eyed.
buganvília s. f. (bot.) bougainvillaea.
bugia s. f. 1. she-ape, she-monkey. 2. wax candle. 3. candle-stick, candle-holder. 4. (surg.) urethro-probe.
bugiar v. 1. to ape, mimic, imitate. 2. to drive piles into.

bugiaria s. f. 1. mimicry, imitation, aping. 2. grimace. 3. trifles, knick-knacks, toys.

bugiganga s. f. 1. (ant.) monkey's dance or hopping. 2. ~s pl. trifles, knick-knacks, gewgaws. 3. peddlery, truck, trumpery, stuff, frippery, rummage. 4. (fishery) sweeping net.

loja de ~s swagg-shop. **toda a** ~ the whole bag of tricks.

bugio s. m. 1. ape, monkey, simian. 2. pile-driver.

buglossa s. f. (bot.) bugloss, oxtongue.

buglossa-menor s. f. (pl. **buglossas-menores**) (bot.) small, wild or field bugloss.

bugra s. f. of **bugre**.

bugrada s. f. (Braz.) a group or band of Indians.

bugraria s. f. (Braz.) 1. band of Indians. 2. region inhabited by Indians.

bugre s. m. (Braz.) 1. Indian, savage, aborigine. 2. (S. Braz.) civilized Indian. 3. (fig.) brute. 4. (fig.) treacherous, untrustworthy person.

bugreiro s. m. (Braz.) tracker or persecutor of Indians.

bugrinho s. m. (Braz.) Indian boy or lad.

bugrismo s. m. (Braz.) Indian ancestry.

búgula s. f. (bot.) bugle.

buído adj. worn out, used up.

buinho s. m. (Braz.) willow (tree).

buir v. to polish, smooth down.

buítra s. f. (obs.) guide-shelf of a printing press.

buiuçu s. m. (Braz., bot.) campanilla.

bujamé s. m. 1. wind instrument of African natives. 2. (Braz.) son of a mulatto and a Negress.

bujão s. m. (pl. **-ões**) 1. plug, stopper, stopple. 2. dowel, peg. 3. little wedge, quoin.

~ **de contato** contact plug. ~ **de gás** liquid gas container (for home use). ~ **postiço** dummy plug.

bujarrona s. f. 1. (naut.) jib, jib-sail. 2. (fig.) affront, insult, outrage. 3. (Braz.) kite.

estai da ~ jib-stay. **pau de** ~ jib-boom.

bula s. f. 1. bull, sealed papal letter, papal or imperial edict. 2. printed instructions for the use of medicines. 3. ~s pl. capacity, qualification.

bular v. to seal with a bull.

bulário s. m. 1. bullary, collection of papal bulls. 2. papal clerk (copyist of bulls).

bulático adj. of or referring to a bull (papal letter or edict).

bulbar adj. m. + f. bulbar, bulbaceous.

bulbífero adj. (also **bulbiloso**) bulbous, bulbiferous.

bulbo s. m. 1. (seed-)bulb, bulbous root. 2. (anat.) medulla oblongata.

~ **piloso** (anat.) hair-bulb.

bulbul s. m. (pl. **-uis**) (ornith.) bulbul.

bulcão s. m. (pl. **-ões**) 1. thick fog, heavy mist. 2. dark storm-cloud, cloud of smoke.

buldogue s. m. bulldog (plate C 3).

bule s. m. teapot (plate M 8).

abafador para o ~ **de chá** tea cosy.

bulevar s. m. boulevard.

búlgaro s. m. Bulgarian: 1. native or inhabitant of Bulgaria. 2. the language. ‖ adj. Bulgarian.

bulha s. f. 1. noise, din. 2. clamour, shouting, uproar. ruffle, fracas, rough-house, stirabout. 3. confusion, tumult, pother, bustle, fuss(iness), ado, bother. 4. ruction, fray. 5. revolt, mutiny.

às ~s at variance, quarreling. **sem** ~ **nem matinada** silently, secretly.

bulhão s. m. (pl. **-ões**) (also **bulhento**) 1. rowdy, brawler. 2. quarrelsome person, squabbler. ‖ adj. quarrelsome, rowdy.

bulhar v. 1. to make a noise, shout. 2. to fight, quarrel, squabble. 3. to revolt, rebel.

bulharaça s. f. infernal noise, din, row.

bulício s. m. 1. murmur, whisper. 2. rumour. 3. agitation, unrest. 4. mutiny, revolt.

buliçoso adj. 1. restless. 2. noisy, turbulent, uproarious, effervescent. 3. active, lively, sprightly. 4. fidgety.

bulideiro adj. 1. stirring, active, bustling. 2. restless, excited.

bulímico adj. bulimi(a)c.

bulimia s. f. (med.) bulimia, bulimy, insatiable hunger.

bulinete s. m. (Braz.) race, open water channel (to make the diamond-bearing sand settle).

bulir v. 1. to agitate, move slightly. 2. to change one's position, stir. 3. to pulsate, throb. 4. to touch, handle lightly, meddle, fidget. 5. to move about. 6. to banter.

bulista s. m. (hist.) curial registerer of bulls.

bululu s. m. (N. Braz.) air bubles (indicating the presence of big fishes or turtles).

bumba s. m. (Braz., pop.) (large) drum. ‖ interj. puff! flop! splash! bang! bang-off! wumph!

bumba-meu-boi s. m. (Braz.) popular dramatic show.

bumbar v. 1. to slap, bang. 2. to beat soundly.

bumbo s. m. (Braz., pop.) big drum.

bumbum s. m. (pl. **-uns**) 1. beat of the drum, clang, clangour. 2. sound of the big drum.

bumerangue s. m. boomerang.

bunda (I) s. f. (Braz., sl.) backside, bum, posterior, buttock, breech.

bunda (II) s. f. Mbundu: a Bantu language of Angolan Negroes.

bundá s. m. (Braz.) old furniture or household implements.

bundo s. m. (also **quimbundo**) 1. Mbundu: a Bantu language of Angolan Negroes. 2. any Negro dialect. 3. Angolan Negro. 4. lingo, jargon. 5. (ornith.) gambo goose, spur-winged goose.

bunho s. m. (bot.) river bulrush, mat rush.

buprestídeo s. m. (ent.) buprestid: beetle of the family Buprestidae. ‖ adj. buprestidi(an).

buque s. m. jolly-boat, cutter.

buquê s. m. 1. bouquet, bunch of flowers, nosegay, posy. 2. buttonhole, corsage. 3. fragrance, cromo (of wine).

buquê-de-noiva s. m. (pl. **buquês-de-noiva**) (bot.) 1. ocean spray, arrow-wood. 2. Italian May. 3. queen of the prairie. 4. meadow sweet.

buraca (I) s. f. big hole or gap, hollow or cave.

buraca (II) s. f. (Braz.) leather sack used by mule and cattle drovers.

buracada, buracama s. f. 1. lots of holes in a road. 2. rough, uneven tract of land.

buraçanga s. f. 1. wooden bat, stick. 2. club, cudgel.

buraco s. m. 1. hole, gap, hollow. 2. cavity, cave, gully. 3. orifice, aperture, bore, boring, ventage. 4. (bot., zool.) foramen. 5. hovel, den, pit. 6. loophole, creephole. 7. (fig.) disappointment, trouble, embarrassment. 8. (Braz.) a certain game of cards.

~ **de bicho** wormhole. ~ **de fechadura** keyhole (plate A 13, F 1, P 10). **ele arranjou um** ~ he obtained a lucrative position. **não cabe no** ~ **de um dente** that is really an insignificant matter. **ai, que** ~! oh, what a mess! **tapar um** ~ to pay a debt. **tapar** ~s to mend carelessly and superficially.

buraco-soturno s. m. (pl. **buracos-soturnos**) grotto, cave, cavern.

buranhém s. m. (pl. **-éns**) Brazilian forest tree (family Sapotaceae).

buraqueira s. f. 1. bad, uneven road or tract of land. 2. steep, precipitous slope. 3. (Braz.) solitary, far-off place.

buraqueiro s. m. uneven ground, holey tract of land.

burara s. f. (Braz.) ⚹. branches of fallen trees barring the way. 2. small cacao(-tree) plantation. 3. small farm. 4. muddy place in a cacao plantation.

burarema s. f. (Braz.) any timber tree.
burato s. m. a lacelike textile fabric.
burbom s. m. (Braz.) Bourbon-coffee: a variety of coffee shrub (Coffea bourbonica).
burburejar v. to bubble, simmer, gurgle.
burburinhar v. 1. to murmur, simmer, purl. 2. to rustle, quiver. 3. to clamour, shout, make a noise. 4. to kick up a row, fight, brawl.
burburinho s. m. 1. murmur(ing), purl, simmer. 2. rustling, ripple. 3. shouting, vociferation, clamour, noise. 4. tumult, row, brawl. 5. disorder, confusion.
burdo adj. coarse, rough, of bad quality.
buré s. m. porridge of green Indian corn.
burel s. m. (pl. **-éis**) 1. burel: coarse woollen cloth, russet. 2. a nun's or friar's habit. 3. (fig.) sorrow, grief, mourning.
   cobrir-se de ~ to wear mourning.
burela s. f. (her.) stripe in an escutcheon.
burelado adj. (her.) horizontally striped (the breadth of the stripes being equal to their distance).
bureling s. f. woollen cloth, somewhat finer than a **burel**.
bureva s. f. (Braz.) freshwater fish (Glanidium albescens).
burgalhão s. m. (pl. **-ões**) deposit of shell limestone, shell marl.
burgalhau s. m. pebble.
bargau, burgó s. m. rubble, gravel.
burgaudina s. f. mother-of-pearl extracted from shell banks.
burgo s. m. 1. borough, burgh, market town. 2. village, hamlet. 3. palace, manor house. 4. monastery, convent. 5. suburb, outskirts of a city. 6. rubble, pebble.
burgomestre s. m. mayor, burgomaster.
burgrave s. m. burgrave, commander of a castle or fortified town.
burguês s. m. 1. burgher. 2. citizen, bourgeois, burgess, villager. 3. a cautious methodical person, snob. 4. rich. ‖ adj. burgeois.
burguesia s. f. 1. bourgeoisie, middle class, commons. 2. burghership.
buri s. m. (bot.) Brazilian palm tree.
buril s. m. (pl. **-is**) 1. burin, graver, an engraver's chisel. 2. (fig.) an engraver's style. 3. (astr.) Sculptor: a southern constellation.
   ~ **triangular** claw bar, parting tool, burr chisel.
burilada s. f. a stroke with the burin.
burilador s. m. engraver, carver, graver. ‖ adj. engraving.
burilagem s. f. (pl. **-ens**) (filat.) net, network.
burilar v. 1. to chisel, carve, engrave. 2. to perfect, adorn (a sentence). 3. (tech.) to bulge. 4. (fig.) to impress deeply (mind).
   para lhe ~ **na memória estas verdades** to engrave these truths in your memory.
burindangas s. f. pl. trifles, knickknacks, gewgaws.
Burinídeos s. m. pl. (ornith.) Burhinidae, the stone curlew family.
buriqui, buriquim s. m. (Braz.) monkey, ape.
buriti, muritizeiro s. m. (bot.) Brazilian wine-palm.
buritizada s. f. sweetmeat of the buriti fruit.
buritizal s. m. (pl. **-ais**) grove of buriti palms.
burjaca s. f. 1. a tinsmith's satchel. 2. long and wide coat or jacket.
buria s. f. (also **burlaria**) 1. jest, joke, humbuggery. 2. trick, prank, jugglery. 3. cheat, deceit, fraud, (sl.) shave, fiddle, flim-flam, bob.
   fazer ~ **de alguém** to make sport of s. o. **ele não é homem de** ~ he is not a man to be trifled with.
burlado adj. 1. cheated, deceived, duped. 2. scoffed, mocked.

burlador, burlão s. m. 1. joker, jester. 2. tricker, sharper, cheater, swindler. ‖ adj. 1. joking. 2. cheating.
burladora s. f. (bot.) thorn apple.
burlar v. 1. to jest, joke. 2. to fool, tease a person, play a trick. 3. to cheat, dupe, deceit, swindle. 4. to disappoint, frustrate. 5. to juggle.
   não me deixo ~ I am not to be swindled. **eles me** ~**am em vinte cruzeiros** they swindled me out of twenty cruzeiros. **ele os burlou deveras** he really sold them a pup.
burlequeador s. m. (S. Braz.) tramp, vagrant, vagabond.
burlequear v. 1. to tramp, roam about. 2. to loaf, loiter.
burlesco adj. 1. burlesque. 2. comical, jocose, farcical, ludicrous. 3. ridiculous, grotesque, caricatural. 4. mocking, sneering. ‖ **-amente** adv. burlesquely, comically, jocosely, grotesquely.
burlesquear v. 1. to burlesque. 2. to talk funny. 3. to act in a jocose way. 4. to play the buffoon.
burleta s. f. (theat.) 1. burlesque. 2. farce (with music).
burlista s. m. + f. 1. joker, jester. 2. trickster, swindler, sharper. ‖ adj. joking, cheating.
burloso adj. 1. cheating, fraudulent. 2. scoffing, mocking. 3. comical, funny, jocose.
burmaniáceo adj. (bot.) burmanniaceous.
burneira adj. juicy, sappy (grapes).
burnus(s) s. m. burnous: hooded cloak worn by Arabs.
burocracia s. f. bureaucracy, officialism, red-tape, bumbledom, officialdom.
burocracial adj. m. + f. (pl. **-ais**) bureaucratic(al).
burocracismo s. m. bureaucratism.
burocrata s. m. + f. 1. (pop.) jack-in-office, red-tapist. 2. (rare) bureaucrat, offical of a bureau.
burocrático adj. 1. bureaucratic(al). 2. formal, rigid, narrow-minded, red-tape. ‖ **burocraticamente** adv. bureaucratically.
burocratizar v. to give s. th. a bureaucratic character or form.
burra s. f. 1. she-ass, she-mule, jenny-ass. 2. strong-box, safe, coffer. 3. (naut.) miz(z)en rope.
burrada, burragem (pl. **-ens**) s. f. 1. drove of asses. 2. foolish act, nonsense, blunder.
burrama s. f. a lot of asses or mules.
burrão s. m. (pl. **-ões**) big ass or donkey (also fig.).
burrego s. m. dolt, fool, silly person. ‖ adj. foolish, stupid.
burrica s. f. dim. of **burra**.
burricada s. f. 1. drove of asses, lot donkeys. 2. foolish act, nonsense, blunder.
burrical adj. m. + f. (pl. **-ais**) foolish, stupid, asinine.
burrice s. f. (also **burriquice**) 1. stupidity, foolishness, nonsense, blunder. 2. dullness, sulkiness.
burrico s. m. little ass, young donkey.
burrificar v. to become stupid or brutish.
burrinha s. f. 1. dim. of **burra**. 2. (N. Braz.) a kind of raft.
burrinho s. m. 1. little ass, young donkey. 2. (tech.): a) donkey pump. b) duplex pump. c) portable air pump (plate B 2). (ent.) meloid.
burriqueiro s. m. 1. donkey driver, muleteer. 2. person who hires or lets donkeys.
burro s. m. 1. ass, donkey, mule, jackass, moke, burro, dickey. 2. sawing jack, sawhorse. 3. stupid, fool, saphead, cuddy. 4. crib: translations of classics for students. 5. children's game at cards. 6. (naut.) ropes of the miz(z)en yard. 7. (tech.) donkey engine. ‖ adj. stupid, foolish.
   ~ **de carga** (fig.) Joe Soap, (mil.) drudge. **ela é o** ~ **de carga da família** she is the drudge in the family. ~ **de mato** wild ass, onager. ~ **velho não aprende línguas** an old dog will not

learn new tricks. **cabeça de** ~ blockhead. **daqui até lá morre o** ~ **ou o tocador** it's a long way to Tipperary. **dar com os** ~**s n'água** to meet with disappointment, end in failure. **deixe-o em paz, ele está com o** ~ **(emburrado)** leave him alone, he is pouting today. **ele tem dinheiro pra** ~ **(Braz.) (sl.)** he has heaps of money, he rolls in riches. **pensando morreu o** ~ he who thinks too much, loses his time. **é mais fácil um** ~ **voar** sooner the heavens would fall. **ele trabalha como um** ~ he works like a nailer. **usar** ~ to crib.

burserácea s. f. plant of the torchwood family (Burseraceae).

burseráceo adj. (bot.) burseraceous.

bursite s. f. (path.) bursitis.

buruçanga s. f. (Braz.) club or mallet (to stun caught fish).

burundanga s. f. 1. confused din of voices, gibberish. 2. medley, confusion, mess. 3. badly prepared or dirty food.

burumdum s. m. (pl. **-uns**) (Braz.) a passionate hunter.

buruso s. m. residues of fruit, husks of grapes, grapeskins.

busano s. m. (Braz.) a marblelike cretaceous soil stone, used in building.

busca s. f. 1. search(ing) 2. inquiry, quest. 3. investigation, examination, research, rummage. 4. tracker, liner. 5. pursuit, fetch, raid, hunt. ‖ interj. take him! get it! (setting the dogs at). ~ **de falhas** fault testing. **andar em** ~ **de alguém** to inquire after somebody. **em** ~ **de fortuna** in pursuit of wealth.

buscado adj. forced, affected, stiff, formal.

buscador s. m. searcher, investigator, seeker, tracker. ‖ adj. searching, investigatory. ~ **de ensaio** testing spike.

buscante s. m. + f. beater, game beater.

busca-pé s. m. (pl. **busca-pés**) firecracker, serpent (firework), squib.

buscar v. 1. to search, seek, look for. 2. to inquire, quest. 3. to investigate, examine. 4. to go for, fetch, hunt. 5. to try to obtain, try to acquire. 6. to track down, trace. 7. to appeal to, resort to. 8. to collect. 9. to summon one's strength, pull o. s. together. ~ **agulha em palheiro** to look for a needle in a bundle of hay. ~ **brigas** to ruffle. ~ **desculpas** to use lame excuses. ~ **o seu proveito** to mind one's own interest. ~ **rodeios** to beat about the bush. ~ **a vida** to work for one's bread and cheese. **ir** ~ to fetch. **posso vir buscá-lo?** may I come for you? **vá buscá-lo!** go and get it! **vá** ~ **uma cadeira!** go and fetch a chair!

busca-vidas s. m., sg. + pl. 1. industrious person. 2. (naut.) creeper.

busilhão s. m. (pl. **-ões**) 1. heap of dirty linen or clothes. 2. dunghill, rubbish heap. 3. badly dressed person.

busílis s. m., sg. + pl. rub, difficulty, flaw, hitch, main point. **aí é que está o** ~ there's the rub (of it). **onde está o** ~? where is the hitch?

bússola s. f. 1. magnetic needle, (mariner's) compass. 2. (fig.) guide, direction. 3. (astr.) Circinus, the Compasses: a small southern constellation. **desvio da** ~ compass variation. ~ **de observação** bearing compass. ~ **de inclinação** dipping compass. ~ **giratória** gyro-compass.

bussolar v. (fig.) to guide, lead.

busto s. m. bust: 1. torso, sculpture representing the upper part of the human body (plate E 9). 2. half-length portrait, kit-cat portrait. 3. a woman's bust, bosom.

bustuário s. m. 1. sculptor, bust-maker. 2. (hist.) gladiators who fought near funeral piles.

butadieno s. m. (chem.) butadiene.

butano s. m. (chem.) butane.

butara s. f. (Braz.) trap for wild beasts.

butargas s. f. pl. (Braz., Amazonas) pickled fish-eggs.

buteiro s. m. (Braz.) jobbing tailor, botcher.

butelo (I) s. m. (Braz.) big objects, voluminous thing.

butelo (II) (ê) s. m. (Port.) hog's tail sausage.

buteno s. m. (chem.) butene.

butiá, butiazeiro s. m. (Braz., bot.) name of several species of coco-palms.

butiatuba s. f., **butiazal** m. coco palm grove.

butileno s. m. (chem.) butylene.

butílico adj. (chem.) butylic. **álcool** ~ butyl alcohol, butanol.

butilo s. m. (chem.) butyl.

bútio s. m. 1. (ornith.) buzzard. 2. (fig.) blockhead, dunce. 3. airvent. 4. conduit, pipe.

butiráceo adj. butyraceous.

butirada s. f. butter cake.

butirato s. m. (chem.) buthyrate.

butirina s. f. (chem.) butyrin.

butirômetro s. m. butyrometer: instrument for determining the amount of fat in milk.

butomáceas s. f. pl. (bot.) Butomaceae, a family of aquatic and marsh herbs.

bútomo s. m. (bot.) flowering rush.

butuca s. f. (Braz.) 1. (also **mutuca**) (ent.) gadfly, breeze. 2. spur. 3. (fig.) stimulus.

butucada s. f. (Braz.) 1. sting of a gadfly. 2. prick with a spur. 3. (fig.) stimulus, incitement.

butucar v. 1. to sting, prick. 2. (fig.) to stimulate, incite.

butucari s. m. + f. (Braz.) Indian of the Jacuí river. ‖ adj. of, pertaining to or relative to this tribe.

butucum s. m. (pl. **-uns**) (Braz.) bag worn by means of a shoulder-belt.

buva s. f. (Braz.) plant of the thistle family.

buvar s. m. (Braz.) rocker blotter.

buxácea s. f. plant of the box family (Buxaceae).

buxáceo adj. (bot.) buxaceous.

buxina s. f. (chem.) buxine.

buxo, buxeiro s. m. 1. (bot.) box tree, box. 2. boxwood.

búxulo s. m. bearberry.

buzarate s. m. 1. corpulent man. 2. boaster, braggart. ‖ adj. 1. boastful. 2. silly, foolish.

buzegar v. to squall, blow.

buziar v. to sound or blow the trumpet.

buzina s. f. 1. horn, trumpet, bugle. 2. megaphone, hooter, tooter. 3. (astr.) little Bear (Ursa Minor). 4. nave of a wheel. 5. (naut.) hawser port. ‖ adj. (Braz.) angry, vexed, upset. ~ **de cerração** (naut.) fog-horn. ~ **de automóvel** horn, **ficar** ~ to get angry.

buzinação s. f. (pl. **-ões**) horn blowing, tooting (also fig.).

buzinar v. 1. to sound a horn, blow a trumpet, hoot, toot, honk. 2. to insist importunely, repeat endlessly. 3. (sl.) to talk nonsense.

buzinote s. m. spout of a pipe, drainpipe (of balconies or terraces).

búzio s. m. 1. (zool.) music shell. 2. horn, trumpet, cornet. 3. (pearl) diver, submarine fisher. ‖ adj. 1. sulky, sullen. 2. unclear, dim.

buzo s. m. (Braz.) popular game played with disks of orange peels, corn grains, etc.

buzugo s. m. (Braz.) bungled work, any badly finished thing.

byroniano, byrônico adj. (also **baironiano**) 1. Byronic. 2. imitating Byron.

C

C, c s. m. 1. the third letter of the Portuguese alphabet. 2. (mus.) formerly the keynote of the major musical scale (replaced in Brazil and Portugal by **Dó**). 3. (mus., when placed after the clef) common measure, common time. 4. (math.) a third known quantity. 5. one hundred in Roman numerals. 6. (chem.) abbr. and symbol of carbon. 7. (electr.) abbr. of coulomb. ‖ adj. third in class, group or order.

ca conj. (arch.) that, than, why.

cá adv. 1. here, in this place. 2. hither, to this place. 3. between ourselves, between us. 4. to us. 5. to me.
~ **e lá** hither and thither, here and there. ~ **e lá, más fadas há** bad people may be found anywhere. ~ **entre nós, eu lhe digo que** confidentially I tell you that. **andar para** ~ **e para lá** to go about, up and down. **de** ~ from this side. **de** ~ **e de lá** from both sides. **de 1950 para** ~ since 1950. **dê** ~ **o livro!** give me that book! **diga-me,** ~ **doutor, como...** say, doctor, how... **dize-me** ~**!** well now, tell me! **de cinco anos para** ~ it is five years since. **para** ~ **e para lá** hither and thither. **venha** ~**, já!** come here immediately!

cã (I) s. f. (almost always **cãs** pl.) white hair, white locks.

cã (II) s. m. khan: a title of Eastern dignitaries.

cã (III) adj. f. (arch.) (f. of **cão** II) white-haired, hoary.

caá s. m. + f. (Braz.) 1. herb, plant. 2. the maté tea plant. 3. maté, Paraguay tea. 4. concoction of maté.

caaba s. f. Kaaba, Kaabeh, a small stone building in the courtyard of the Great Mosque of Mecca.

caabopoxi s. f. (Braz.) creeping plant of the family Convolvulaceae (Ipomoea malvaeioides).

caacambuí s. m. (Braz., bot.) an euphorbia.

caacuí s. f. (Braz.) a new leaf of the maté plant.

caaetê s. m. (Braz.) the rarely flooded plains of the Amazon forest.

caaguaçu s. m. (S. Braz., bot.) an acaulescent herb of the genus Eriocaulon.

caaingá s. f. (Braz.) tree of the mimosa family (Pithecolobium sanguineum).

caajaçara s. f. (Braz.) climbing plant of the family Euphorbiaceae (Dalechampia brasiliensis).

caamembeca s. f. (Braz.) plant of the milkwort family (Polygala spectabilis).

caaobi s. m. (N. Braz.) evergreen woodland, jungle.

caapi s. m. (Braz., bot.) caapi (Banisteria caapi).

caapiá s. m. (Braz.) herb of the mulberry family (Dorstenia multiformis).

caapitiú s. m. (Braz.) common name of two plants of the boldo family (Siparuna guyanensis, Siparuna mollicoma).

caapomonga s. f. (Braz., bot.) leadwort.

caapora s. m. + f. (N. Braz.) backwoodsman, ranger, small planter.

caapuã s. m. (Braz.) a clump of trees in an open plain, coppice.

caarina s. f. (Braz.) cassava root, manioc.

caatiguá s. m. (Braz.) plant of the mahogany family (Trichilia caatigoa).

caatinga s. f. (Braz.) 1. a stunted sparse forest. 2. region covered with brushwood. 3. plant of the family Bignoniaceae, a trumpet bush (Tecoma caatinga).

caavurana s. f. (N. Braz.) a bad-smelling solanaceous shrub (Solanum caavurana).

caba s. f. (ent.) any of the social wasps.

cabaça (I) s. f. 1. (bot.) bottle gourd. 2. a drinking vessel made from the shell of this plant, calabash.

cabaça (II) s. m. (Braz.) 1. the second born of twins. 2. simpleton, dunce. 3. feeble-minded person.

caba-caçadeira s. f. (pl. **cabas-caçadeiras**) (Braz.) a wasp of the family Pompilidae.

cabaçada s. f. a gourdful.

cabaceiro s. m. (bot.) 1. calabash tree (Crescentia cujete). 2. bottle gourd, common gourd.

cabaceiro-amargoso s. m. (pf. **cabaceiros-amargosos**) (Braz., bot.) calabash gourd.

cabacinha s. f. 1. a small gourd. 2. (bot.) egg gourd, orange gourd.

cabacinha-do-campo s. f. (pl. **cabacinhas-do-campo**) (Braz., bot.) eugenia.

cabacinho s. m. (Braz.) medicinal herb of the family Cucurbitaceae (Momordica bucha).

cabaço s. m. 1. bottle gourd, calabash (tree or fruit). 2. drinking vessel made from the shell of this plant. 3. (ichth.) swallow fish, sapphirine gurnard.

cabaçudo s. m. (Braz.) a naive person. ‖ adj. naive, simple.

cabaia s. f. a tunic or blouse with wide sleeves.

cabal adj. m. + f. (pl. **-ais**) 1. complete, whole. 2. full. 3. perfect, accomplished. 4. just, exact. ‖ ~**mente** adv. completely, perfectly, exactly.

cabala s. f. 1. cabala: a) (hist.) mystical interpretation of the Scriptures among Jewish rabbis. b) occult theosophy, occult science. 2. cabal: a) intrigue, plot. b) machinations. c) clique, conspirators, camarilla.

cabalagem s. f. caballing, clique.

cabalar v. 1. to cabal. 2. to plot, intrigue. 3. to form a cabal. 4. to solicit votes, canvass.

cabaleta s. f. (mus.) cabaletta, short lively song or melodious instrumental composition.

cabalino adj. (poet.) of or referring to Pegasus.

cabalista s. m. + f. 1. cabalist, master of occult sciences. 2. plotter, intriguer. 3. astrologer.

cabalístico adj. 1. cabalistic(al): of or referring to occultism or magic. 2. secret, occult. 3. mysterious, enigmatical. 4. obscure. ‖ **cabalisticamente** adv. cabalistically, mysteriously.

cabana s. f. 1. hut, shack. 2. cottage, cabin. 3. hovel. 4. cote, cot, cot-house.

cabanada s. m. (Braz., hist.) popular designation of the insurrection which broke out in Pernambuco in 1832.

cabanagem s. f. (pl. **-ens**), (Braz.) 1. brutal or bestial act. 2. savagery, cruelty, atrocity. 3. popular designation of the seditious movement which broke out in Pará in 1835.

cabaneiro (I) s. m. 1. man who lives in a cottage, cottager. 2. a poor man, destitute hut-dweller.

cabaneiro (II) s. m. a large wicker basket.

cabanha s. f. (S. Braz., Span. cabaña) cattle-breeding ranch.

cabano s. m. 1. a large wicker basket. 2. (Braz., hist.) name given collectively to the followers of a political faction in Pernambuco (1830). 3. (Braz., zool.) a large bat (Plecoctus andira). ‖ adj. 1. having horizontal or drooping horns (oxen). 2. (S. Braz.) having drooping ears (said of horses).

cabaré s. m. cabaret, honky-tonk.

cabatã s. f. (Braz.) a species of bees.

cabaú s. m. (N. Braz.) honey-coloured viscid sirup which drains from sugar in the process of its manufacture.

cabaz s. m. 1. frail, pannier, hamper. 2. a metal box used for food transportation.

cabazada s. f. 1. the contents of a frail or hamper. 2. (fig.) a large amount, lots.

cabazeiro s. m. a frail or pannier maker.

cabe (I) s. m. distance between two balls (at an outdoor game similar to cricket).

cabe (II) s. m. (Braz.) man's coat.

cabear v. to whisk or flap violently with the tail (said of horses when bitten by insects).

cabeça s. f. 1. head (plates C 18, G 1). 2. poll: the part of the head covered with hair, scalp. 3. intelligence, sagacity. 4. discernment, judgment. 5. judicious and intelligent person. 6. principal town of a district, province or country, capital. 7. each individual or animal as a unit of computation. 8. the upper end of anything. 9. the leading group of a cortege or procession. 10. the title or heading of a chapter. 11. the top or foliaged part of a plant. 12. the rounded end of a bone. 13. heading, headline. 14. top, summit. 15. chief, leader. 16. ringleader. 17. captain. 18. (mus.) head of a note (plate N 1). ~ **de alfinete** pinhead (plate A 1). ~ **de cabrestante** (mech.) trundle-head. ~ **de culatra** (mil.) bolt-head. ~ **de êmbolo** pistonhead. ~ **de flecha** arrow-head. ~ **de martelo** hammer-head (plate M 5). ~ **de página** headline. ~ **de papoula** (bot.) poppyhead. ~ **de parafuso** bolt-head (plate P 4). ~ **de pau** (coll.) blockhead. ~ **de ponte** 1. bridgehead (plate P 14). 2. (mil.) beachhead. ~ **de vento** (fam.) featherbrain, feather-brained. ~ **dura** thickhead, pigheaded, obstinate, stupid. ~ **de prego** nail-head (plate P 15). ~ **redonda** 1. bullet-head. 2. round head (of a screw) (plate P 4). ~ **magnética** magnetic head. ~ **sextavada** hexagonal head (of a screw) (plate P 4). **abaixar a** ~: a) to incline one's head. b) to give in, yield, submit. **acertar o prego na** ~ to hit the nail on the head. **andar com a** ~ **no ar** to be absent-minded. **andar de** ~ **erguida** 1. to look down upon others. 2. to go about proudly or boldly. **aprender de** ~ to learn by heart. **aquilo esquentou minha** ~ that made my blood boil. **assentar a** ~ to develop good sense, settle one's mind. **bater com a** ~ **na parede** to knock one's head against the wall. **cem** ~**s de gado** a hundred head of cattle. **coçar a** ~ to scratch one's head. **com a** ~ **para frente** head first. **da** ~ **aos pés** from head to foot, from top to toe. **dar com a** ~ **em** to knock one's head against. **de** ~ head. foremost. **de** ~ **chata** flat--headed. **de** ~ **para baixo** upside down. **de** ~ **redonda** round-headed. **dor de** ~ headache. **duro de** ~ stubborn, obstinate. **ele arrisca a sua** ~ he puts his life at stake. **ele não está com a** ~ **no lugar** he has not his wits about him. **ele não sabe onde andar com a** ~ he does not know which way to turn. **ele tem boa** ~ **para estudar** he has the brains for study. **ele vai levar na** ~ he will get it in the eye. **ficar quebrando a** ~ to busy one's brains. **fonte da** ~ (anat.) temple. **ganhar de** ~ to win by a head. **isto não quer entrar na minha** ~ I fail to understand that. **isto não tem pé nem** ~ there is neither rhyme nor reason in that. **levar na** ~ to suffer a financial loss, to be ruined, to get it in the neck. **manter a** ~ **levantada** to keep one's pecker up. **meter na** ~ 1. to learn by heart. 2. to take a fancy to. 3. to make s. o. believe, convince. **não cabe na** ~ **de ninguém** this is incomprehensible, it's absurd. **não é bicho de sete** ~**s** (fam.) it is not so difficult as it looks. **não encha a** ~ **dele!** don't put ideas into his head! **não levantar mais a** ~ not to be likely to recover, not to be able to retrieve one's loss. **não perca a** ~! keep your head! **não sair da** ~ not to get out of one's mind, to have always in mind. **não ter miolo na** ~ (pop.) to have no milk in the coco-nut. **parece um bicho de sete** ~**s** it looks like a poser. **o que a gente não tem na** ~, **tem de ter nos pés** a weak memory causes weary legs. **para salvar a sua** ~ to save his neck. **por** ~ per capita. **quebrar a** ~ to puzzle one's brain, to rack one's brains. **responder com a** ~ to answer with a nod. **sem** ~ headless, shallow-brained. **sem pés nem** ~ without rhyme or reason, neither head nor tail. **ser uma grande** ~ to have a good head on one's shoulders. **subir à** ~ to go to one's head. **ter** ~ to be intelligent, be naturally gifted. **uma** ~ **de couve** a head of cabbage. **você tem de tirar isto de sua** ~ you got to take that out of your head.

cabeça-azul s. m. (pl. **cabeças-azuis**), (Braz., ichth.) dorado, a dolphin of the genus Coryphaena.

cabeça-branca s. f. (pl. **cabeças-brancas**), (Braz., ornith.) a manakin (Pipra leucocilla).

cabeça-chata s. m. + f. (pl. **cabeças-chatas**), (Braz., depr.) native or inhabitant of the northern states of Brazil, flathead.

cabeçada s. f. 1. a bump with the head. 2. headstall, headgear of a harness. 3. blunder, folly, nonsense. 4. (ftb.) heading the ball. **dar uma** ~ 1. to commit a foolery. 2. (ftb.) to head a ball. 3. (com.) to be at the short end of a bargain.

cabeça-d'água s. f. (pl. **cabeças-d'água**), (Braz.) 1. torrent, impetuous current. 2. high water, flood.

cabeça-de-água s. f. (pl. **cabeças-de-água**), (pop.) hydrocephalus.

cabeça-de-boi s. f. (pl. **cabeças-de-boi**), (Braz., bot.) stanhopea (Stanhopea insignis).

cabeça-de-camarão s. m. + f. (pl. **cabeças-de-camarão**) blockhead.

cabeça-de-campo s. m. (pl. **cabeças-de-campo**), (N. Braz.) foreman of the cowboys, chief cowboy.

cabeça-de-casal s. m. (pl. **cabeças-de-casal**) the head (master) of a married couple.

cabeça-de-cavalo s. f. (pl. **cabeças-de-cavalo**), (N. Braz.) wooden water-pipe (used instead of a mill-race).

cabeça-de-coco s. m. + f. (pl. **cabeças-de-coco**) a feeble-minded or forgetful person.

cabeça-de-frade s. f. (pl. **cabeças-de-frade**), (Braz.) 1. dwarf water lily. 2. hedgehog cactus.

cabeça-de-negro s. m. (pl. **cabeças-de-negro**) 1. (bot.) an annonaceous shrub (Annona coriacea). 2. a firecracker with high explosion power.

cabeça-de-pedra s. f. (pl. **cabeças-de-pedra**), (Braz., ornith.) wood ibis.

cabeça-de-ponte s. f. (pl. **cabeças-de-ponte**) (mil.) bridgehead.

cabeça-de-porco s. f. (pl. **cabeças-de-porco**), (Braz., pop.) a slum, slum tenement, group of hovels or shacks.

cabeça-de-prego s. f. (pl. **cabeças-de-prego**), (Braz.) 1. a tadpole. 2. the larva of the anopheles (mosquito) in stagnant water. 3. pimple, pustule. 4. boil.

cabeça-de-urubu s. f. (pl. **cabeças-de-urubu**), (Braz.) a chocolate tree (Theobroma obovatum).

cabeça-de-vento s. m. + f. (pl. **cabeças-de-vento**) muddlehead.

cabeça-dura s. m. + f. (pl. **cabeças-duras**) blockhead, stupid fellow.

cabeça-inchada s. f. (N. Braz., pop.) 1. burning love, deep passion. 2. ardour, fervour. 3. jealousy. 4. lover's grief.

cabeçal s. m. (pl. -ais) 1. cotton pledget placed around a wound, compress. 2. headrest, pillow.

cabeçalho s. m. 1. pole or beam of a cart or carriage. 2. headrest, pillow. 3. head of a bed. 4. title page of any publication. 5. title (of a book). 6. head, heading (of a newspaper), date-line, header. 7. caption, billhead. 8. letterhead, heading (plate C 10). 9. subject-heading (on index or file cards).

cabeção s. m. (pl. -ões) 1. collar of a cape, coat or dress. 2. ornamental detachable dress front or neckpiece, tippet. 3. a scarf or scarflike garment worn by priests. 4. headstall, cavesson (plate C 12). 5. (Braz.) the upper, frequently bordered part of a woman's shirt, corset, cape. 6. (typogr.) vignette.

cabeçaria s. f. (archit.) roughhewn foundation stones.

cabeça-seca s. f. (pl. cabeças-secas) 1. (Braz., ornith.) a wood ibis. 2. m. (N. Braz., hist.): a) contemptuous designation for Negro slaves. b) soldier of a police force.

cabeceado s. m. (typogr.) headband.

cabeceador s. m. header, nodder, one who heads, nods or shakes his head. ‖ adj. heading, nodding, shaking.

cabecear v. 1. to beckon. 2. to shake the head, nod. 3. to doze. 4. to incline the head, lean to one side. 5. to deviate, change the course or direction. 6. (naut.) to swing. 7. (association ftb.) to head. 8. to gesture, make gestures with the head.

cabeceio s. m. 1. act of shaking the head. 2. headshake, nodding. 3. (association ftb.) heading the ball.

cabeceira (I) s. f. 1. cushion, pillow, bolster. 2. head of a bed (plate C 7). 3. headrest. 4. headband of a book (plate L 4). 5. upper end of a table. 6. high altar of a church. 7. the side opposite to the entrance (of a building). 8. (Braz.) spring or source of a river, headwater(s).

cabeceira (II) s. m. 1. (N. Braz.) chief cowboy who rides at the head of the drove, immediately behind the guide. 2. head, chief. 3. military chief or leader, head of a political faction.

cabeceiro s. m. (Braz.) butcher who cuts up the heads of slaughtered cattle (taking out the brain, tongue, etc.).

cabecel s. m. (pl. -éis) 1. principal leaseholder, partner or emphyteuta of a country estate. 2. vignette or heading at the top of a page.

cabecilha s. m. 1. head of a faction, political boss. 2. ringleader, chieftain. 3. caudillo.

cabecinha s. f. a stone specially prepared to serve as top lining of an irregular stone wall.

cabeço s. m. 1. the round top a mountain. 2. hill, hillock. 3. (naut.): a) head of the top-timber. b) mooring dolphin.

cabeçorra s. f. (pop.) a big head, pate.

cabeçorro s. m. hill, hillock, knoll.

cabeçote s. m. 1. headstock. 2. the adjustable sliding head of a lathe, spindle of a lathe. 3. (Braz.) bow of a yoke. 4. (Braz.) pommel of a saddle. 5. (Braz.) tadpole, polliwog.

~ de contra-pressão poppet of a grinder. ~ de máquina engine head. ~ divisor dividing head. ~ móvel, ~ corrediço (do torno) poppet-head, puppet, footstock (of a lathe).

cabeçuda s. f. (Braz.) 1. (zool.) an Amazonian turtle (Podecnemis dumeriliana). 2. (ent.) sauba ant.

cabeçudo s. m. 1. big-headed person. 2. pighead, obstinate or dullwitted person. 3. (Braz.) a freshwater fish (Pimelodus ornatus). ‖ adj. 1. big-headed. 2. headstrong, stubborn, obstinate. 3. wayward, contumacious. 4. self-willed.

cabedais s. m. pl. carpenters' rules used for checking plank surface finishing.

cabedal (I) s. m. (pl. -ais) 1. stock, funds, capital. 2. means, fortune, wealth. 3. property, money. 4. acquisition of intellectual or moral qualities. 5. expedient, resourcefulness. 6. esteem, account. 7. special leather for shoemaking. 8. -ais pl.: a) fixed assets. b) (carp.) level, ruler.

fazer ~ de to consider important.

cabedal (II) adj. m. + f. (pl. -ais) 1. principal, main. 2. important, momentous. 3. plentiful, abundant, copious.

cabedelo s. m. a small sandbank near the mouth of a river, down.

cabeio s. m. (Braz.) a violent whisking with the tail (horse).

cabeira s. f. (carp.) end mouldings on floor or ceiling panels.

cabeiro s. m. a maker of handles, hafts or knobs. ‖ adj. 1. last. 2. latest, hindmost. 3. final, ultimate.

dentes ~ wisdom teeth.

cabeladura s. f. 1. head of hair. 2. hair (with regard to its characteristic properties and natural growth).

cabelama s. f. 1. hairiness. 2. long hirsute hair.

cabelame s. m. 1. the root system of a plant. 2. (pop.) wig, peruke. 3. coiffure.

cabeleira s. f. 1. head of hair. 2. natural growth of long hair. 3. wig, peruke, toupee (plate P 8). 4. (astr.) nebula or tail of a comet. 5. horsehair, mane. 6. (bot.) fascicled growth of roots. 7. m.: a) a man with very long hair. b) an old-fashioned or conservative man. c) (Braz.) perverse individual. d) bandit, highway robber. 8. criminal.

ele serviu de pau de ~ he was used as a makeshift, he was the butt of the joke.

cebeleira-de-vênus s. f. (pl. cabeleiras-de-vênus) (min.) acicular, aureate inclusions in quartz.

cabeleireiro s. m. 1. hairdress, haircutter. 2. coiffeur, beautician. 3. wigmaker.

cabelo s. m. hair (plates C 18, P 8): 1. any growth of hair on the human body. 2. fell, fur. 3. a thread or string of hair. 4. hairspring (of a watch) (plate R 4). 5. down, flue.

~ anelado curled hair. ~ crespo crisp or frizzled hair. agarrar a ocasião pelos ~s to take the occasion by the forelock. arrancar-se os ~s to tear one's hair in anger. arrastar pelos ~s to drag along by sheer force, (fig.) to coerce, constrain to do s. th. arrumar os ~s to do the hair. ~ curto bob, crop. corte de ~ haircut. não lhe torceram um ~ sequer not a hair of his head was touched. pôr os ~ em pé to make one's hair stand on end. por um ~ by a hair's breadth. seus ~ eriçaram-se his hair stood on end. sua vida estava por um fio de ~ his life hung by a thread. ter bastante ~ to be well thatched. ter ~ no coração to be insensible, to be obdurate. de arrepiar os ~s horrifying, hair-raising.

cabelo-de-anjo s. m. (pl. cabelos-de-anjo) (Braz., cul.) pasta in the form of thin, solid threads, thinner than vermicelli.

cabelo-de-vênus s. m. (pl. cabelos-de-vênus), (Braz., bot.) maidenhair fern.

cabelouro s. m. tough band of tissue which runs from the nape (of cattle) to the articular extremities of the spine.

cabelo-vivo s. m. (pl. cabelos-vivos), (Braz., ent.) hairworm.

cabeluda s. f. (Braz.) tree of the family Myrtaceae.

cabeludo s. m. (Braz.) 1. (zool.) monk saki. 2. (hist.) nickname of the followers of one of the two principal political parties in Alagoas. ‖ adj. 1. hairy, long haired, hirsute. 2. complicated, intricate. 3. difficult. 4. obscene, immoral. 5. rough, rugged. 6. (bot.) comate.

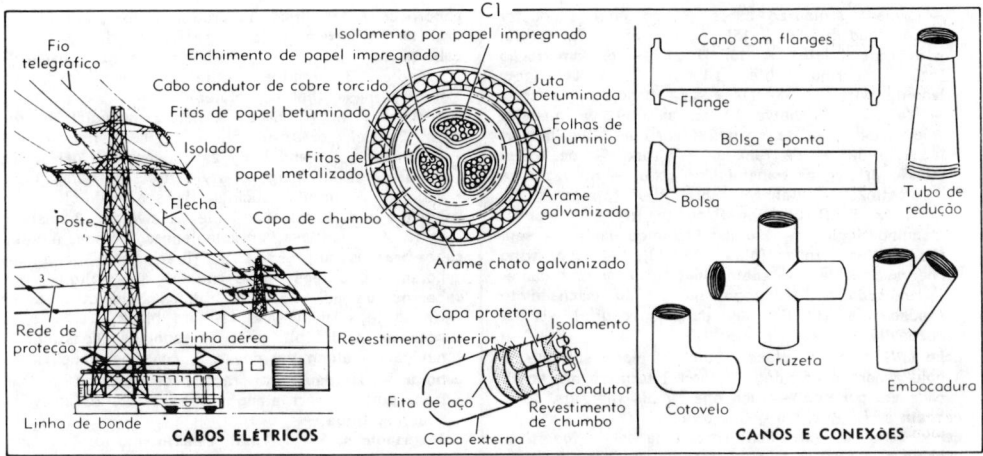

Cl

CABOS ELÉTRICOS

CANOS E CONEXÕES

caber v. 1. to be contained in. 2. to fit in or inside of. 3. to be containable in. 4. to be possible to be done, made or said. 5. to be proper, suitable or fit. 6. to be compatible with. 7. to fall to a person by partition or inheritance. 8. to be admissible. 9. to come or happen opportunely. 10. to be one's duty or one's given share of work. 11. to fall to one's lot. 12. to belong to, appertain. 13. (jur.) to accrue.
~ **com alguém** to be in favour of s. o., to be on good terms with s. o. **a propriedade coube a ele** the property fell to him. **dê-me o que me cabe** let me have my own. **isto não cabe em nossos dias** this is ill-timed nowadays. **isto cabe a** this falls to. **não ~ em si de contente** to be overjoyed, not to be able to contain o. s. for joy. **não ~ nas bainhas** to burst with pride. **não lhe cabe fazer tal coisa** he is not entitled to do such a thing, he can't do such thing. **não me cabe fazer crítica** it is not my place to find fault. **não pode ~ aqui tanta gente** there is not room enough for so many people. **no salão cabem 100 pessoas** the hall holds one hundred people. **os livros não cabem na prateleira** the books won't go on that stand.
cabide s. m. 1. rack, hatrack, hat-stand (plates B 3, M 14). 2. hanger, clothes hanger or coat-hanger (plate R 7). 3. peg (plate E 11). 4. (Braz.) jade, rosinante.
~ **de empregos** (Braz.) a person who holds many jobs. **colocar em ou sobre ~s** to rack.
cabidela s. f. 1. giblets. 2. (cul.) stewed giblets.
cabido (I) s. m. 1. chapter of a cathedral. 2. assembly of friars.
cabido (II) adj. 1. appropriate, proper. 2. fit, suitable. 3. deserved, merited. 4. well-liked. 5. opportune.
cabila s. m. + f. Kabyle, a Berber of Algeria or Tunisia. || adj. of, pertaining to or relative to the Kabyles.
cabilda s. f. 1. generic designation of several nomadic tribes who inhabit the coastal regions of North Africa. 2. gang, mob, band.
cabimento s. m. relevancy, pertinence. 2. acceptance, approval. 3. room, capacity. 4. opportunity, chance. 5. extent, content. 6. influence. 7. reason. 8. convenience. 9. interest(s). 10. favour. 11. credit. **isto não tem ~ algum** there is no rhyme nor reason in that. **sua reclamação não tem ~** there is no reason for his protest.

cabina s. f. 1. cabin (plates D 2, G 5, L 2). 2. berth. 3. box, booth. 4. (aeron.) cockpit (plate A 3).
~ **de banhista** cabina, bathing box, bathing hut, dressing cabin (plates B 3, P 17). ~ **de elevador** cage, car (elevator) (plate E 2). ~ **de popa** (naut.) after cabin. ~ **de pressão** pressure cabin. ~ **de sinaleiro** (railway) signal-box (plates E 12, V 4). ~ **de tombadilho** (naut.) roundhouse. ~ **telefônica** call-box, telephone booth (plate T 4).
cabinda s. m. + f. Cabinda, Bantu, native or inhabitant of the Cabinda territory (Africa). || adj. of, pertaining to or relative to the Cabindas.
cabine s. f. = cabina.
cabineiro s. m. 1. (railway) signalman. 2. (railway) waiter of a sleeping car, porter. 3. lift boy, elevator attendant.
cabisbaixo adj. 1. having the head lowered, with inclined head. 2. (fig.) downcast, depressed, crestfallen. 3. despondent, dejected. 4. ashamed, humiliated.
cabitu s. f. (Braz.) popular designation of leaf-cutting ants.
cabiú s. m. (Braz.) the thick juice of manioc tubers.
cabiúna s. f. 1. Brazilian rosewood, palisander. 2. m. (hist.) Negro illegally brought to Brazil after the abolition of slavery. || adj. m. + f. black, dark brown.
cabível adj. m. + f. (pl. -íveis) 1. founded on fact. 2. reasonable, sensible. 3. fitting, appropriate.
respondeu de maneira ~ he gave a fitting reply. **tomaram todas as medidas -íveis** they took all the necessary steps.
cablar v. to cable, transmit by submarine cable.
cabo (I) s. m. 1. (mil.) corporal. 2. commander, chief. 3. leader.
~ **de guerra** general, tug of war.
cabo (II) s. m. 1. terminal, end. 2. the extreme end of. 3. headland, promontory, cape.
Cabo da Boa Esperança (geogr.) the Cape of Good Hope. ~ **eleitoral** electioneerer. **de ~ a ~** from one end to the other, all over. **de ~ a rabo** from the beginning to the end, completely, thoroughly. **dobrar o ~** 1. to get over a difficulty. 2. to pass the age of fifty.
cabo (III) s. m. 1. handle, holder (plates B 7, 14, C 6, E 8, G 4, M 5, P 13). 2. haft, hilt, helve (plates A 1, E 4, P 1). 3. rope, cordage (plate G 5). 4. cable (plates E 2, P 14). 5. strand of a cable.

~ **armado** armoured cable. ~ **condutor** conductor cable, lead (plate B 15). ~ **de aço** steel cable, wire rope (plates A 10, D 2). ~ **de amarração** (naut.) mooring cable, gripes. ~ **de aterragem** landing wire. ~ **de ferramenta** handle of a tool. ~ **de machado** helve of an axe. ~ **de madeira** wood handle. ~ **de portaló** (naut.) entering ladder, ladder rope. ~ **de reboque** tow-rope. ~ **de transmissão** driving or transmission rope. ~ **de vassoura** broomstick. ~ **elétrico** cable, flex (plates B 15, C 1, M 5, R 8). ~**s fixos** (naut.) dead ropes, standing rigging. ~ **isolado** insulated cable. ~ **sem fim** endless rope (plate M 10). ~ **submarino** undersea cable. ~ **subterrâneo** underground cable. ~ **trançado** braided rope. **dar** ~ **ao machado** to expose o. s. (to ridicule, danger, rebuffs) without necessity.

cabo (IV) s. m. 1. place, room. 2. place suitable to hold a person or thing. 3. (arch.) turn, round, spell. **cada um por seu** ~ each one by his (her, its) turn.

caboatá s. f. (Braz.) a guara tree.

cabochão s. m. (pl. **-ões**) (Braz.) cabochon (gem).

cabocla s. f. (Braz.) 1. f. of **caboclo**. 2. (bot.) a zinnia (Zinnia multiflora).

caboclada s. f. (Braz.) 1. a group or reunion of **caboclos**. 2. action or trait typical of **caboclos**. 3. distrust, suspicion. 4. perfidy, treachery. 5. vindictiveness, revengefulness.

caboclinho s. m. (Braz.) 1. (ornith.) a seed-eater (Sporophyla bouvreuil), also called ~-**da-baía** and ~-**do- -norte**. 2. a popular dramatic dance. 3. dim. of **caboclo**.

caboclo s. m. (Braz.) 1. caboclo, civilized Brazilian Indian of pure blood. 2. a Brazilian half-breed (of white and Indian). 3. any copper-coloured mulatto with straight hair. 4. frontiersman, inlander, ranger. 5. an agricultural labourer, farm hand. 6. (fig.) a treacherous fellow. 7. name given by prospectors to any red or reddish-brown pebble (due to the presence of iron oxide). || adj. 1. copper-coloured, red-skinned. 2. of, pertaining to or relative to **caboclos**. 3. characteristic of a **caboclo**.

caboclo-d'água s. m. (pl. **caboclos-d'água**) (N. Braz., folkl.) fantastic creature said to turn over canoes at night and to haunt the inhabitants of the São Francisco river region.

caboclote s. m. (Braz.) a little **caboclo**.

caboclo-vermelho s. m. (pl. **caboclos-vermelhos**), (Braz., min.) popular name given by diamond prospectors to hematitic boulders and pebbles.

cabocó s. m. (Braz.) discharge canal through which the water runs after having driven a water-wheel.

cabo-de-esquadra s. m. (pl. **cabos-de-esquadra**) squad- -leader.

cabo-de-guerra s. m. (pl. **cabos-de-guerra**) high ranking army officer, general.

cabo-de-tropa s. m. (pl. **cabos-de-tropa**), (hist.) leader of a group of armed Brazilian explorers.

cabograma s. m. cable, cablegram, wire.

cabo-guia s. m. (pl. **cabos-guia**) 1. life line (used by firemen). 2. (naut.) thin cable tied to a tow cable in order to facilitate the approach to a buoy.

caboje s. m. (Braz.) a joint or section of sugar cane used for planting.

caborá s. m. (Braz., ornith.) a kind of owl (Atena brasiliensis).

caborje s. m. (Braz.) 1. witchcraft. 2. a charm or amulet worn around the neck. 3. a swamp fish.

caborjeiro s. m. sorcerer, enchanter, witch-doctor.

caborjudo adj. (Braz., pop.) invulnerable (due to witchcraft).

caboroca s. f. (N. Braz.) 1. act of clearing the ground for planting. (cacao). 2. newly cleared land.

caborocar v. (N. Braz.) to grub land for planting.

cabortar, cabortear v. to tell a falsehood, lie.

caborteirice s. f. 1. falsehood, lie. 2. rascality, swindle. 3. malice, spite. 4. unruliness, intractableness (horses, mules).

caborteiro s. m. (S. Braz.) 1. liar. 2. swindler, impostor. 3. tricky or artful fellow. 4. cheat, fraud. || adj. 1. deceptive, fraudulent. 2. obtained or performed by artifice. 3. sharp, crafty, artful. 4. lying, mendacious. 5. unruly, bucking (horses, mules).

cabortice s. f. 1. falsehood, lie. 2. swindle. 3. malice, spite. 4. unruliness, intractableness (horses, mules).

cabos-brancos adj. sg. + pl. (Braz.) said of a bay horse whose legs, mane and tail are white.

cabos-negros adj. sg. + pl. (Braz.) said of a horse whose legs, mane and tail are black.

cabotagem s. f. (pl. **-ens**) 1. cabotage, coasting. 2. navigation along the coast. 3. coasting trade.

cabotar v. 1. (naut.) to practice cabotage. 2. to sail from port to port along the coast. 3. to carry on coasting trade.

cabotinagem s. f. (pl. **-ens**), **cabotinismo** m. 1. action, life or behaviour of a wandering actor. 2. (fig.) cabotinage, charlatanry. 3. (fig.) dodge, trick.

cabotino s. m. 1. itinerant actor or performer. 2. bad actor, mediocre comedian. 3. cabotin. 4. (fig.) charlatan. || adj. charlatanic, pretentious.

caboto s. m. (N. Braz.) inlet or branch of the sea.

caboucador s. m. ditchdigger, digger, ditcher, trencher.

caboucar v. to dig, cut ditches or trenches.

cabouco s. m. 1. ditch, trench. 2. excavation made in order to make place for the substructure of a building. 3. pit, stonepit. 4. the space occupied by a water-wheel.

cabouqueiro s. m. ditchdigger, ditcher, trencher.

cabo-verde s. m. + f. (pl. **cabos-verdes**), (Braz.) 1. a half-breed of Negro and Indian. 2. m.: a) (ent.) a horsefly (Lepidoselaga lepidota). b) (bot.) a senna (Cassia speciosa). c) (min.) vulcanic rock consisting essentially of black diorite, Jewstone.

cabo-verdiano s. m. (pl. **cabo-verdianos**) native or inhabitant of the Cape Verde Islands. || adj. 1. of, pertaining to or relative to the archipelago of Cape Verde. 2. characteristic of the Cape Verde Islands.

cabra (I) s. f. 1. (zool.) she-goat, nanny-goat. 2. (pop.) a water spider. 3. (ichth.) goatfish. 4. (mech.) small winch or hoist. 5. (pop.) a woman of loose manners. 6. (fig.) a bad-tempered woman.

pé de ~ crowbar. **questão de lã de** ~ a matter of no importance.

cabra (II) s. m. (Braz.) 1. half-breed of Negro and mulatto. 2. fellow, individual. 3. farmer, farmhand, backwoodsman. 4. bodyguard. 5. hired killer.

~-**da-peste** (N. E. Braz.) a brave, corageous, intrepid individual. ~ **de sorte!** you lucky guy!

cabra-cega s. f. (pl. **cabras-cegas**) 1. blindman's buff. 2. (S. Braz.) popular designation of a dragonfly.

jogar a ~ to play blindman's buff; (fig.) to walk aimlessly around.

cabrada s. f. a flock of goats, many goats.

cabra-da-rede-rasgada s. m. (pl. **cabras-da-rede-rasgada**), (N. Braz.) impudent fellow, petulant or bold individual.

cabra-de-chifre s. m. (pl. **cabras-de-chifre**), (N. Braz.) bandit, outlaw.

cabralhada s. f. (N. Braz.) a gang of loafers or hoodlums.

cabra-macho s. m. (pl. **cabras-machos**) (Braz.) bully, rowdy, hector, ruffian, braggart, swashbuckler, daredevil.

cabramo s. m. a rope employed to tie the foot of an ox to its horn.

cabrão s. m. (pl. **-ões**) 1. buck, buck-goat, he-goat. 2. (pop.) a compliant cuckold. 3. squalling child, squaller.

~ montês (zool.) ibex.

cabrar v. (aeron.) to nose up.

cabra-sarado s. m. (pl. **cabras-sarados**), (Braz.) 1. sly or cunning fellow, slyboots. 2. sharper, swindler. 3. loafer, bum.

cabra-seco s. m. (pl. **cabras-secos**), (Braz.) 1. brute, bully, tough. 2. ruffian. 3. aggressive or tenacious Negro.

cabra-selvagem s. f. (pl. **cabras-selvagens**) bezoar-goat.

cabre s. m. = **calabre**.

cábrea s. f. hoist, gin, winch, crab.

cabreiro (I) s. m. 1. goatherd. 2. milkman. 3. (pop.) diligent or hard-working fellow. ‖ adj. 1. of, pertaining to or relative to the duties of a goatherd. 2. sly, cunning. 3. clever, sharp.

cabreiro (II) adj. said of cheese made from goat's milk.

cabrema s. f. a rope with a small wooden hook, used to fasten a load of sugar cane on the packsaddle.

cabrestante s. m. (naut.) capstan, winding-engine, winch, rundle (plate G 5).

cabrestão s. m. (pl. **-ões**) a reinforced halter.

cabresteador s. m. (Braz.) a maker or seller of halters. ‖ adj. of or relative to the production and sale of halters.

cabrestear v. (Braz.) 1. to follow docilely the halter rope. 2. to be led easily by the halter. 3. (fig.) to be docile, tame or tractable. 4. (fig.) to be obedient or submissive.

cabresteira s. f. (naut.) mooring bridle.

cabresteiro (I) s. m. manufacturer or seller of halters.

cabresteiro (II) adj. 1. following easily the halter rope. 2. tame, docile. 3. tractable. 4. submissive.

cabrestilho s. m. 1. a small halter. 2. (Braz.) leather strap or metal chain used to fasten the spurs on the boots.

cabresto s. m. 1. halter. 2. tame lead ox. 3. (naut.) bobstay. 4. (anat.) frenum.

trazer pelo ~ (fig.) to dominate, hold down.

cabrião s. m. (pl. **-ões**) importuner, teaser.

cabril (I) s. m. (pl. **-is**) stable for goats, goat pen.

cabril (II) adj. m. + f. (pl. **-is**) 1. rustic, agrestic. 2. rough, coarse. 3. rude, harsh. 4. steep, precipitous.

cabrilha s. f. 1. little goat, kid. 2. small gin or winch. 3. (naut.) capstan bar.

cabrim s. m. (pl. **-ins**) tanned goat hide.

cabrinete s. m. (Braz.) a man with a goatee beard.

cabrinha s. f. 1. little goat, female kid. 2. (ichth.) red gurnard, red crooner. 3. (N. Braz.) a variety of mango.

cabriola s. f. 1. leap of a goat. 2. caper, skip. 3. capriole, gambade. 4. somersault. 5. frisk, frolic, gambol.

cabriolar v. 1. to caper, cut capers. 2. to cavort, capriole. 3. to frisk, frolic, prance.

cabriolé s. m. 1. gig, dog-cart. 2. cabriolet, cab.

cabrita s. f. 1. a little goat. 2. a female kid. 3. catapult, ballista. 4. handle of a veneer-saw.

levar às ~s to carry pickaback.

cabritada s. f. (Braz.) a flock of kids.

cabritar, cabritear v. 1. to leap like a goat. 2. to skip, jump. 3. to caper, prance. 4. to frolic, frisk, romp.

cabriteiro s. m. 1. (ant.) a catapult maker. 2. goat keeper or breeder. 3. goat dealer.

cabritilha s. f. (Braz.) tanned goat hide.

cabritinho s. m. little kid, yearling goat.

cabritino adj. kidlike, kiddish, belonging to goats.

cabritismo s. m. (Braz.) 1. sensuality, voluptuousness. 2. lasciviousness, wantonness. 3. libidinousness.

cabrito s. m. 1. little buck, kid. 2. (Braz.) little child, youngster, kid. 3. mulatto, person of dark complexion.

~ montês roe. **carne de ~** kid flesh.

cabriúva s. f. (Braz.) 1. (bot.) cabreuva (Myrocarpus frondosus). 2. cabreuva balsam. 3. a drink made of ginger, sugar and brandy. 4. (cul.) an omelet flavoured with drops of brandy.

cabriúva-do-campo s. f. (pl. **cabriúvas-do-campo**) (Braz., bot.) cabreuva (Myrocarpus fastigiatus).

cabroada s. f. flock of billy-goats.

cabrobó s. m. (N. Braz.) 1. common or wretched fellow. 2. mobster. 3. good-for-nothing. 4. loafer, idler.

cabrocado s. m. (N. Braz.) cleared land, cleared field, backwoods plantation.

cabrocar v. (Braz.) to grub land for planting, cut the brushwood, clear.

cabrocha s. m. + f. (Braz.) 1. f. a very dark mulatto girl. 2. m. (also **cabroche**): a) a young dark-skinned mulatto, dark-skinned mulatto boy. b) any dark-skinned half-breed of Negro and mulatto.

cabrochão s. m. (pl. **-ões**), (Braz.) a stout or thickset mulatto.

cabroche s. m. (Braz.) = **cabrocha** 2. b.

cabroeira s. f., **cabroeiro** m. (Braz.) mob, gang of ruffians or bandits.

cabronaz s. m. big billy-goat.

cabrué s. m. (S. Braz., bot.) cabreuva.

cabrum adj. m. + f. (pl. **-uns**) caprine, of or belonging to goats.

gado ~ goats.

cabuchão s. m. (pl. **-ões**), (Braz.) any cone-shaped or coniform object.

cabucho s. m. 1. the coniform end of a sugar-loaf. 2. a cone-shaped lapidation (of a gem).

cabuçu s. m. (Braz., zool.) an armadillo of the genus Cabassous.

cabuim s. m. (pl. **-ins**) (Braz.) a shrub of the family Euphorbiaceae (Cicca inflata).

cábula s. m. 1. a lazy student, slacker. 2. truant, shirker. 3. f. truancy, absence from classes, class dodging. ‖ adj. m. + f. 1. idle, lazy. 2. sly, cunning. 3. truant.

cabulador s. m. truant, shirker, slacker.

cabular v. to play truant, cut classes, shirk obligations.

cabuletê s. m. (Braz.) 1. loafer, vagrant. 2. mobster. 3. common fellow, pauper. 4. good-for-nothing.

cabulice s. f. 1. truancy, act or habit of playing truant. 2. (fig.) idleness, laziness.

cabuloso adj. 1. unlucky, luckless, unfortunate. 2. irksome, wearisome. 3. unpropitious. 4. importune, importunate.

cabumbo-de-azeite s. m. (pl. **cabumbos-de-azeite**) (Braz.) a resin tree (Protium insigne).

cabundá s. m. (Braz., hist.) a thievish runaway slave.

cabungo s. m. (Braz.) 1. (hist.) a wooden box used as a portable privy or chamber pot. 2. untidy or dirty fellow. 3. a nobody, insignificant person.

cabungueiro s. m. (Braz., hist.) 1. servant who had to clean the portable privies. 2. dirty or despicable fellow. 3. fellow incapable to execute any but the lowest work.

cabúqui s. m. (theat.) kabuki.

caburé s. m. (Braz.) 1. a half-breed of Negro and Indian. 2. any dark-skinned **caboclo**. 3. a backwoodsman, ranger. 4. a glazed earthen vessel with a large body and a narrow neck. 5. a magic cup, vessel employed in sorcery. 6. a thickset or stout man. 7. a person who goes out only at night. 8. an ugly and sad-looking fellow. 9. (ornith.) a gnome owl (Glaucidium brasilianum).

caburé-de-orelha s. m. (pl. caburés-de-orelha), (Braz.) popular name of two owls of the family Bubonidae (Pisorhina crucifera, Pisorhina usta).

caburé-do-campo s. m. (pl. caburés-do-campo) a Brazilian burrowing owl (Speotyto cunicularia grallaria).

caca s. f. 1. feces, excrement(s). 2. turd, ordure, dung. 3. dirt, filth.

caça s. f. 1. act of hunting or chasing. 2. hunt, hunting, chasing. 3. game: the animals chased, quarry. 4. pursuit, persecution. 5. investigation, research. 6. sporting. 7. shooting, gunning. 8. huntsmanship. ~ à fortuna fortune-hunting. ~ à raposa fox-chase, fox-hunting. ~ de aves fowling. ~ de baleia whale--catching. ~ miúda small game. ~ de pena(s) feather, bird, feathered game. ~ de veados staghunt. cão de ~ tracker, sporting dog. ~ grossa big game, drag-hunt. ~ submarina underwater fishing. avião de ~ pursuit plane. dar ~ to follow after, run after, pursue. espantar a ~ to miss one's aim by precipitation. levantar a ~ to put up or raise the game, break cover. lugar de ~ hunting ground. percorrer em ~ to hunt. tempo defeso de ~ close time, close season. viver da ~ to live by chase.

caça-bombardeiro s. m. (pl. caças-bombardeiros) bomber-fighter.

cacaborrada s. f. (vulg.) 1. piece of stupidity, blunder. 2. foolishness. 3. botching, bungling. 4. nonsense.

cacada s. f. 1. a heap of potsherds. 2. potsherds, shards. 3. chipped old household goods.

caçada s. f. 1. hunting party. 2. hunt, chase. 3. safari. 4. the game killed at a hunting party; game, bag. 5. drive.

fiz uma boa ~ I made a good bag. não deite a ~ a perder don't give the game away.

caçadeira (I) s. f. 1. fowling piece, hunting gun. 2. hunting cape or coat.

caçadeira (II) s. f. (Braz.) any spider wasp.

caçadeiro adj. 1. proper or suitable for hunting. 2. fond of hunting.

arma -a fowling piece. rede -a hunting net.

caçado adj. 1. hunted, bagged. 2. chased. 3. pursued.

caçador s. m. 1. hunter, huntsman. 2. (mil.) gunner, sniper. 3. sportsman, woodsman. 4. chaser, courser. ~ de aves fowler, birdcatcher. ~ de espera deer--stalker. ~ de ratos rat-catcher. ~ de tartarugas turtler. ~ furtivo poacher.

caçadora s. f. huntress.

caçadores s. m. pl. (Braz.) tholes pegged on a wooden crossbar which is installed on raft logs astern, inclined outward and used for tying the sail sheet.

caça-dotes s. m. sg. + pl. dowry hunter, fortune hunter.

cacaieiro s. m. (Braz.) knapsack carrier. || adj. (Braz.) carrying a knapsack.

cacaio s. m. (Braz.) knapsack, satchel.

caçamba s. f. (Braz.) 1. bucket, pail. 2. well-bucket. 3. a shoelike stirrup. 4. dump-cart, tilting cart (drawn by one horse only). 5. a 5-gallon can (20 l) used for the transport of mortar or building cement (at the building sites). 6. a kind of yoke for small domestic animals (to prevent their passage through a fence). ~ de draga basket of a dredge. arear ~s (Braz.) 1. to loaf, lounge, lead an idle life. 2. to cajole, flatter.

caçambada s. f. a bucketful.

caçambar v. (Braz., student sl.) to denounce, inform against.

caçambeiro s. m. (Braz.) 1. flatterer, cajoler, wheedler. 2. carter, workman who handles the tipping carts (at earth moving operations). 3. a motorist's helper or assistant. || adj. flattering, cajoling, wheedling.

caça-minas s. m. sg. + pl (naut.) mine-sweeper.

caçanar s. m. a priest of the East Syrian Church.

caça-níquel s. m. (pl. caça-níqueis) a slot machine.

caçanje s. m. 1. a Portuguese dialect spoken by the creoles in Angola. 2. badly written or spoken Portuguese.

caçante adj. m. + f. 1. hunting. 2. (her.) prancing.

cação (I) s. m. (pl. -ões) (ichth.) shark, skate, dogfish.

cação (II) s. m. (Braz.) a drink or soup made of manioc flour, salt, pepper and water.

cação-anjo s. m. (pl. cações-anjo) angelfish, mongrel skate, puppyfish.

cação-da-areia s. m. (pl. cações-da-areia) sand shark.

cação-de-espinho s. m. (pl. cações-de-espinho) spiny dogfish.

cação-garoupa s. m. (pl. cações-garoupa) (Braz., ichth.) groupershark.

cação-martelo s. m. (pl. cações-martelo) hammerhead shark.

cação-prego s. m. (pl. cações-prego) spiny dogfish, piked dogfish.

caçapa s. f. (billiards) pocket.

caçapo (I) s. m. 1. young rabbit. 2. (fig.) a short and stout man.

caçapo (II) s. m. (Port., India) a butcher in a slaughterhouse.

caçapó s. f. (Braz.) popular designation of a sauba ant (Atta sextens).

caçar v. 1. to hunt, chase. 2. to pursue. 3. to get, catch, pick out. 4. (naut.) to haul in (sails), draw in (cables). 5. to follow, seek. 6. to smell, scent. 7. to make leeway. ~ à espreita to stalk. ~ aves to fowl, to go a birding. ~ caranguejos to crab. ~ coelhos to rabbit. ~ moscas (fam.) to busy o. s. with trifles, to get excited about nothing. ~ raposas to foxhunt. ele caçou com um falcão he flew a hawk. estar caçando to be hunting. sair para ~ to go out hunting.

cacará s. m. (Braz.) 1. disorderly or vulgar fellow. 2. mobster. 3. fool, simpleton. 4. scoundrel, rotter, rascal.

cacaracá s. m. (pop.) quite an insignificant matter.

cacarecos s. m. pl. chipped old household goods, old pieces of furniture.

cacarejador adj., cacarejante m. + f. 1. cackling. 2. chattering, tattling. 3. gossipy.

cacarejar v. 1. to cackle, cluck. 2. to chatter, prattle. 3. to boast, brag, swagger. 4. to giggle, chuckle.

cacarejo s. m. 1. cackling, clucking. 2. (fig.) silly chatter, prattle. 3. chuckle. 4. (fig.) loquacity.

caçareta s. f. drag-net, trawlnet, trammel.

cacaréus s. m. pl. 1. old household utensils. 2. old furniture. 3. lumber. 4. junk, trash. 5. raffle.

cacaria (I) s. f. 1. a heap of potsherds. 2. shards. 3. chipped, old household goods.

cacaria (II) s. f. (Braz.) 1. a gang of thieves and robbers. 2. thieves' lodging house or den.

caçaroba s. f. (Braz., ornith.) a pidgeon (Columba rufina).

caçarola s. f. casserole, soucepan, skillet (plate C 20).

caça-submarino s. m. (pl. caça-submarinos) (naut.) submarine chaser.

cacatua s. f. (ornith.) cockatoo.

cacau s. m. cacao-bean, cocoa, cacao.

gordura de ~ cocoa butter.

caçaú s. m. common name of two medicinal plants of the birthwort family (Aristolochia brasiliensis, Aristolochia cymbifera).

cacaual s. m. (pl. -als) cacao grove, cacao plantation.

cacau-do-mato s. m. (pl. cacaus-do-mato) (Braz., bot.) a small sterculiaceous tree (Theobroma sylvestris) which does not supply cacao.

cacau-do-peru s. m. (pl. cacaus-do-peru), (bot.) patashte.

cacaué s. m. (Braz.) a parrot (Aratinga solstitialis).

cacaueiro s. m. cacao tree, cocoa plant (Theobroma cacao).

cacauí s. m. a tree of the family Sterculiaceae (Theobroma speciosum).

cacauicultor s. m. (Braz.) cacao grower, cacao planter.

cacauicultura s. f. (Braz.) cacao plantation.

cacau-jacaré s. m. (pl. cacaus-jacaré) a tropical shrub of the family Sterculiaceae.

cacaulista s. m. (Braz.) cacao grower, cacao merchant.

cacaurana s. f. (Braz.) tree of the chocolate family (Theobroma microcarpum).

cacauzeiro s. m. cacao tree, cocoa plant.

caçava, caçave s. m. (Braz.) manioc flour, cassava starch.

cácea s. f. (naut.) deflection, leeway, drifting.

cacear v. (naut.) 1. to be deflected from the course (as by strong winds). 2. to drift. 3. to make leeway.

caceia (I) s. f. a system of extensive nets which are fastened to several fishing boats.

caceia (II) s. f. (naut.) deflection from the course, leeway, drifting.

cacerenga s. f. (Braz., pop.) an old worthless knife, handleless knife.

caceta (ê) (I) s. f. colander, strainer.

caceta (ê) (II) s. f. (Port., prov.) tablespoon, soupladle.

cacetada s. f. 1. a blow with a club. 2. beating, thrashing. 3. (Braz.) disagreeable or importunate matter. 4. importunity, bother.

cacetar v. 1. to beat with a club. 2. to beat, thrash, club. 3. to annoy, importunate, pester. 4. to bore.

cacete (ê) s. m. 1. club, mace. 2. cudgel, truncheon. 3. (fig.) annoying or tiresome person, bore, bother. 4. impertinence, insolence. ‖ adj. 1. importunate, tiresome. 2. obstrusive. 3. boresome.

é ~ mesmo it's a real nuisance.

caceteação s. f. (pl. -ões) 1. beating, thrashing (with a club). 2. (Braz.) disagreeable or annoying matter, nuisance. 3. importunation.

cacetear v. 1. to beat with a club, cudgel. 2. to beat, thrash. 3. to annoy, bother, pester. 4. to tease, rib.

caceteiro s. m. 1. clubman, soldier or watchman armed with a club. 2. rowdy, brawler. 3. annoying or tiresome fellow. 4. teaser, jeerer.

cacetinho s. m. 1. a small club. 2. (Braz.) a kind of biscuit.

cacha (I) s. f. 1. dissimulation. 2. trick, artifice, ruse. 3. mistake.

fazer ~ (cards) to raise the bet in spite of a bad hand.

cacha (II) s. f. (India) 1. a woolen cloth from which loincloths or sarongs are made. 2. cash: an Indian coin.

cacha (III) s. f. (Port., prov.) 1. the half of a sheet (cut diagonally). 2. the half of a fruit. 3. a half of anything.

cachaça s. f. 1. sugar-cane brandy, (white) rum. 2. (sl.) booze, hog-wash. 3. (sugar production) heavy foam which forms at the first boiling of the sugar--cane juice. 4. (fig.) passion, attachment. 5. inclination, strong feeling for.

um copo de ~ a glass of rum. um trago de ~ a swing of brandy.

cachação s. m. (pl. -ões) a blow on the nape of the neck.

cachaceira (I) s. f. a large nape.

cachaceira (II) s. f. crownpiece, poll piece of a bridle (harness) (plates A 12, C 12).

cachaceira (III) s. f. (Braz.) drunkenness.

cachaceiro (I) adj. haughty, proud, arrogant, overbearing.

cachaceiro (II) s. m. (Braz.) 1. fellow given to excessive drinking. 2. sot, tippler, swizzler. ‖ adj. given to excessive drinking.

cachaceiro (III) s. m. (Braz.) plant of the family Rutaceae (Hortia excelsa).

cachaço s. m. 1. the back of the neck, nape, crest (plates C 12, G 1). 2. (Braz.) a boar (selected for reproduction). 3. cervix.

cachaçudo adj. 1. large-necked. 2. proud, haughty. 3. arrogant, overbearing.

cachada s. f. a clearing of land by fire.

cachado adj. 1. ondulated. 2. in clusters. 3. wavy, curly.

cachalote s. m. (zool.) sperm whale, cachalot.

cachamorra s. f. club, mace, cudgel.

cachamorrada s. f. a blow with a club.

cachamorreiro s. m. clubman, club bearer, one who beats with a club.

cachão (I) s. m. (pl. -ões) 1. bubbling, gurgling. 2. gush, rush (of liquids). 3. boiling, seething. 4. bubble. 5. (Braz.) a large and high waterfall, cataract. 6. foam, spray.

cachão (II) s. m. (India) a strong head-wind which difficults the navigation between India and Sri Lanka.

cachaporra s. f. (vulg.) club, mace, cudgel.

cachaporrada s. f. a blow with a cudgel.

cachaporreiro s. m. (pop.) a person who uses a cudgel.

cachar (I) v. 1. to hide, conceal. 2. to cloak. 3. to close, stop up. 4. to set traps, lay a snare. 5. to betray, double-cross. 6. to mislead, mystify. 7. to act or proceed in an underhand way, do s. th. on the sly.

cachar (II) v. (Port. prov.) 1. to grub land. 2. to clear and break up the ground. 3. to bring land under cultivation.

cachar (III) v. 1. to bear fruits in form of bunches or clusters. 2. to cluster. 3. to develop spikes or ears (corn, rice). 4. to become ondulated (hair).

cacharolete s. m. a kind of cocktail, an alcoholic drink made by the mixture of several spirituous liquors.

cacharréu s. m. (N. Braz.) = cachalote.

cachê s. m. 1. salary of any performer of a theatrical group, or any movie actor. 2. payment made to a person who acts in a public performance.

cacheada s. f. (Braz.) a popular feast in celebration of Epiphany.

cacheado adj. (Braz.) 1. clustery, bunchy, in clusters. 2. curly, ondulated. 3. tressed, braided.

cachear (I) v. 1. to form clusters or tufts. 2. to cluster. 3. to ear, form ears. 4. to bear fruit in form of bunches. 5. (Braz.) to curl (hair).

cachear (II) v. 1. to work as a female custom-house inspector. 2. to search, frisk (woman suspects at a custom-house).

cachear (III) v. to copulate, cover (animals).

cachecol s. m. (pl. cachecóis) 1. neckerchief, neck--cloth. 2. scarf, muffler (plates R 6, 7). 3. wrap, comforter, tucker. 4. stole.

cacheira s. f. 1. a roughhewn cudgel or club. 2. a long pole. 3. a coarse woolen fabric.

cacheirada s. f. a blow with a cudgel or stick, drubbing.

cacheiro s. m. = cacheira. ‖ adj. 1. hiding, concealing (of an animal). 2. rolling itself up (said of the hedgehog). 3. (Port., prov.) sly, cunning.

cachenê s. m. comforter, muffler, scarf, neckerchief. ~ **comprido** tippet.

cacheta (ê) s. f. 1. (cards) cessation of bidding in spite of low cards (at black-jack). 2. a trumpet tree (Tabebuia cassinoides).

cachetar v. (Braz.) 1. to play around, cavort, romp. 2. to jest, banter, joke with. 3. to jeer, make fun of, mock at.

cachia s. f. the flower of the sweet acacia.

cachichola s. f. (N. Braz.) 1. a small, poor house. 2. cramped lodgings, a narrow room, close quarters.

cachimana s. f. 1. artifice, ruse, trick. 2. intrigue. 3. dodge.

cachimbada s. f. 1. a pipeful of tobacco. 2. the smoking of a pipe. 3. tobacco smoke (from a pipe). 4. a draw at the pipe. **uma** ~ a fill of tobacco.

cachimbador s. m. pipe smoker. ‖ adj. pipe-smoking.

cachimbar v. 1. to smoke a pipe, pipe. 2. (fig.) to deceive, delude, trick, double-cross. 3. to despise, disdain, slight. 4. (Braz.) to meditate, reflect, ponder.

cachimbo s. m. 1. tobacco-pipe, pipe (plate F 7). 2. hinge pin, socket. 3. candle socket, the hole of a candlestick. 4. (Braz.) common name of several plants of the family Gesneriaceae. ~ **bruyère** brier pipe. ~ **de barro** clay pipe. ~ **de raiz de urze** brierwood. **fumar** ~ to pipe. **limpador de** ~ pipe-cleaner. **raspador de** ~ pipe scraper. **tubo de** ~ pipe stem.

cachimbó s. m. (Braz., ornith.) a gray sparrow (Phleocryptes melanops).

cachimbo-de-jabuti s. m. (pl. **cachimbos-de-jabuti**) (Baz., bot.) an Amazonian tree (Erisma calcaratum) whose wood is used to make paper pulp.

cachimônia s. f. (pop.) 1. head. 2. shrewdness, cunningness. 3. brains, wit. 4. common sense. 5. a good memory.

cachinada s. f. 1. burst of laughter. 2. derision, scornful laughter. 3. mocking scoffing, jeering. 4. cachinnation.

cachinador s. m. mocker, jeerer, scoffer, taunter.

cachinar v. 1. to laugh in scorn, deride, sneer. 2. to break out into a fit of laughter. 3. to scoff, jeer, gibe. 4. to cachinnate.

cacho (I) s. m. 1. (bot.) racemose inflorescence, raceme. 2. cluster, bunch. 3. curl, ringlet (of hair). 4. (S. Braz.) horse-tail. **esta bananeira já deu** ~ (pop., fig.) he (she) has already done his (her) best, no further results may be expected (from him, her, it). **um** ~ **de uvas** a bunch of grapes (plate B 1).

cacho (II) s. m. (arch.) neck, nape of the neck.

cachoante adj. m. + f. bubbling, foaming.

cachoar v. 1. to form a waterfall or cataract. 2. to form foam on the surface of a liquid. 3. to bubble up, wallop. 4. to spurt, gush out. 5. (fig.) to stir up a tumult.

cachoeira s. f. 1. waterfall, overfall, chute. 2. cascade, linn, 3. cataract. 4. river rapids.

cachoeirista s. m. (Braz., Amazonas) river pilot, river guide, expert in shooting the rapids in a canoe.

cachoeiro s. m. (N. Braz.) waterfall, chute, cataract.

cachola s. f. (pop.) 1. the head. 2. pate, nut, noddle, costard. 3. shrewdness, cunningness. 4. brains, wit, common sense. 5. pork liver, hog's haslet.

cacholeta s. f. 1. a rap on the head (with the hand or with a stick). 2. reprimand, reproof, censure.

cachopa (I) s. f. (Port.) girl, lass, country maid.

cachopa (II) s. f. a tuft or bunch of flowers at the end of a bough.

cachopice s. f. 1. a youthful prank. 2. childishness, puerility. 3. a bunch of boys or young men. 4. boyishness.

cachopo (I) s. m. (Port.) boy, lad, young fellow.

cachopo (II) s. m. 1. shoal, shallow. 2. reef, cliff, shelf. 3. (fig.) hindrance, obstacle. 4. reverse of fortune, defeat.

cachorra s. f. 1. female puppy. 2. bitch, she-dog. 3. any young female of a species belonging to the family Canidae. 4. (ichth.) albacore. 5. (fig.) termagant, shrew. 6. strumpet, harlot, prostitute.

cachorrada s. f. 1. a pack of dogs. 2. (archit.) corbel(l)ing, corbel work, prop. 3. mob, rabble. 4. wickedness, mischievous or inisidious trick.

cachorrado adj. (archit.) corbel(l)ed (of a roof edge or balcony).

cachorreiro s. m. dog breeder, dog trainer.

cachorrice s. f. 1. wicked action or conduct. 2. dirty trick. 3. lowness, meanness. 4. indignity, outrage.

cachorrinho s. m. 1. puppy, whelp. 2. whiffet. 3. (ichth.) a kind of minnow.

cachorrinho-do-mato s. m. (pl. **cachorrinhos-do-mato**), (Braz., zool.) grison.

cachorrismo s. m. 1. insidious action or conduct. 2. dirty trick. 3. lowness, meanness, wickedness. 4. indignity, affront.

cachorro s. m. 1. little or young dog, pup, whelp. 2. the young of wild animals, cub. 3. (archit.) corbelling, corbel, prop. 4. (naval constr.) shore or support used in a shipyard. 5. dog: as expression of contempt. 6. scoundrel, wretch. 7. (Braz.) popular designation of a fiddlerfish. ~ **hidrófobo** mad dog. ~ **que late não morde** barking dogs do note bite. ~ **rosnador** growler. **chover de os** ~s **beberem água em pé** to rain cats and dogs, pour down. **eles vivem como gato e** ~ they live like cat and dog. **gostar de alguém como** ~ **gosta de couro** to dislike s. o. utterly. **lavar** ~s to labour in vain. **levar uma vida de** ~ to lead a dog's life. **manter um** ~ to keep a dog. **neste mato há** ~s! keep out, there are dogs watching! **quem não tem** ~ **caça com gato** half a penny is better than no one. **soltar os** ~ **em cima de** to give s. o. a severe scolding, give s. o. hell.

cachorro-d'água s. m. (pl. **cachorros-d'água**), (Braz., ent.) mole cricket.

cachorro-do-mato s. m. (pl. **cachorros-do-mato**), (zool.) bush dog.

cachorro-quente s. m. (pl. **cachorros-quentes**), (Braz., pop.) hot dog.

cachucha s. f. a lively, gracious Spanish dance, cachucha.

cachucho s. m. the pith of a quill.

cachudo s. m. (Port.) a variety of grapes. ‖ adj. having big clusters.

cacica s. f. (Braz.) chicken stewed with oil from the African oil palm (**dendê** oil), pumpkin pips and pepper.

cacical adj. m. + f. (pl. **-ais**) of, pertaining to or relative to a tribal chief.

cacicar v. to act as a tribal chief, rule as a tribal headman.

cacifar v. (Braz.) to collect the stakes at card games.

cacife s. m. (Braz.) 1. the amount of stakes bet by all gamblers at certain card games. 2. pool.

cacifeiro (I) s. m. canon of a diocese who acts as treasure of the chapter.

cacifeiro (II) s. m. the gambler who collects the stakes at certain card games.

cacifo, cacifro s. m. 1. chest, trunk. 2. box strongbox, safe. 3. drawer. 4. a dark room or recess. 5. (arch.) an ancient grain measure.

cacim s. m. (pl. **-ins**) a small vessel used by dyers.

cacimba s. f. 1. humid fog, heavy mist. 2. drizzle, fine rain. 3. (India) fog-bank. 4. small pool of stagnant water, puddle. 5. morning or night dew, dewfall. 6. water-hole, well.

cacimbado adj. (Braz.) 1. rich in water-holes or wells. 2. loamy, clayey, argillaceous; suitable for brick and tile manufacture. 3. soggy or waterlogged in some places.

cacimbão s. m. (pl. **-ões**) (Braz.) 1. big water-hole or well. 2. gully. 3. a deep gorge in the slope of a mountain.

cacimbar v. (Braz.) 1. to form a lot of water-holes. 2. to become waterlogged or swampy. 3. to envelop with fog, become foggy or misty.

cacimbeiro s. m. well digger, one who digs water-holes.

cacinheiro adj. (Braz.) following several tracks or scents (said of a hunting dog).

cacique s. m. (Braz.) 1. Indian tribal chief. 2. chieftain. 3. (fig.) political boss, big shot, bigwig. 4. elder. 5. cacique.

caciquismo s. m. 1. influence or power of a cacique. 2. rule of an Indian tribal chief. 3. (Braz.) caciquism, domination by petty political bosses. 4. arbitrary act.

cacite s. m. (Braz.) lye vat, leaching vat.

caco s. m. 1. potsherd, piece of broken earthenware. 2. shard, fragment. 3. chipped or worn out household utensil. 4. junk, lumber. 5. (fam.) head, noddle. 6. a sick or old person. 7. (Braz.) a very bad tooth. 8. toasted tobacco dust. 9. brickbat. 10. the headgear of a mount. 11. Brazilian saddle with a high pommel and cantle. 12. (Braz., theat.) funny extemporary remark. 13. ~s pl. rubbish, trash. ~ **de louça** crock. **ele tem um bom** ~ he has a good head (for studying). **fazer em** ~s, **reduzir a** ~s to break into pieces. **há um** ~ **de vidro aí no chão** there is a piece of broken glass on the floor. **sou um** ~ **velho** I am an old man.

caço s. m. 1. earthen frying pan. 2. casserole, saucepan. 3. ladle, spoon.

caçoada s. f. 1. act of jeering or jesting. 2. mockery, raillery, derision. 3. jest, joke. 4. banter. 5. ridicule. 6. persiflage. **fazer** ~**s de** to make fun of, make game of. **servir de** ~ **para todos** to be everybody's butt.

caçoador s. m. 1. joker, jester. 2. funster. 3. teaser. || adj. 1. mocking, jesting. 2. jeering. 3. teasing. 4. bantering.

cacoal s. m. (pl. **-ais**), (Braz.) cacao grove, cacao plantation.

caçoante s. m. + f. 1. mocker, jester. 2. teaser. || adj. mocking, jeering, teasing, bantering.

caçoar v. 1. to scoff, jeer, sneer. 2. to make fun of, poke fun at. 3. to mock, tease, kid. 4. to banter. 5. to deride. ~ **de** to make merry over. **todos caçoam dele** he is the laughingstock of everybody. **você está caçoando de mim** you are pulling my legs.

caco-de-telha s. m. (pl. **cacos-de-telha**) (Braz., min.) a flake of itabirite.

cacodilo s. m. (chem.) cacodyl, methyl arsenide.

caçoeira s. f. (Braz.) a special dragnet to catch sharks or for deep-sea fishery.

cacoeiro s. m. (bot.) cacao tree.

cacoépia s. f. cacoepy, bad or incorrect pronunciation.

cacoépico adj. cacoepistic.

cacoete s. m. cacoethes: 1. a bad habit. 2. addiction. 3. mania, itch. 4. grimace. 5. (med.) a bad tendency or disposition in a disease.

cacoeteiro s. m. one who has a tic. || adj. cacoethic.

cacofagia s. f. (med.) cacophagia: morbid desire of feeding on dirty or decayed matter.

cacófago adj. (med.) cacophagous.

cacófato, cacófaton s. m. a cacophonous word or expression.

cacofonia s. f. cacophony.

cacofoniar v. to cacophonize, make cacophonous.

cacofônico adj. cacophonic(al), cacophonous, ill-sounding.

cacofonista s. m. + f. cacophonist: person who introduces cacophony in his speech or musical compositions.

cacofonizar v. = **cacofoniar.**

cacofonofobia s. f. (med.) cacophonophobia, irrational aversion to cacophonous words or expressions.

cacografar v. to spell or write incorrectly.

cacografia s. f. cacography, bad or incorrect writing or spelling.

cacográfico adj. cacographic(al).

cacografismo s. m. (Braz.) cacographism: 1. habitual use of cacographies. 2. state of being cacographic. 3. cacography.

caçoila s. f. 1. earthen cooking pot 2. casserole. 3. censer, thurible, perfuming pan.

caçoilo s. m. (naut.) a small, cylindrical wooden device which is adapted to the stays.

caçoísta s. m. + f. joker, jester, teaser, moker. || adj. mocking, jesting, jeering, teasing, bantering.

caçoleta s. f. 1. (ant.) the fire-pan of a musket lock. 2. percussion cap. 3. cupel, test. 4. a small frying pan. 5. (Braz.) locket. **bater a** ~ (pop.) to kick the bucket, die.

cacologia s. f. cacology: 1. incorrect pronunciation. 2. bad diction.

cacológico adj. cacologic(al).

cacólogo s. m. person given to the use of cacologies.

cacongo s. m. (ichth.) a variety of African salmon.

cacopatia s. f. (med.) cacopathy: 1. malignant pain. 2. bad tendency or disposition in a disease.

cacopático adj. of or relative to cacopathy.

cacório adj. (Braz., vulg.) cunning, sly.

cacosmia s. f. (med.) the sense of bad odo(u)r, imaginary or resulting from a nasal lesion.

cacóstomo adj. (med.) affected with cacostomia.

cacotanásia s. f. (med.) death with pain and anguish.

caçote (I) s. m. (Braz.) popular designation of any small amphibian.

caçote (II) s. m. (Braz.) = **cabeçote.**

cacotecnia s. f. cacotechny, bad or mediocre art, lack of artistic sense.

cacotécnico adj. cacotechnic(al), of or relative to cacotechny.

cacotimia s. f. (med.) cacothymia, dejectedness.

cacotipia s. f. (typogr.) failure in graphic composition.

cacotrofia s. f. (med.) cacotrophy, malnutrition, alimentary deficiency.

caçoula s. f. 1. an earthen stewing pan 2. casserole. 3. censer, incense burner, perfuming pan.

cactácea s. f. 1. any plant of the family Cactaceae. 2. ~s pl. the Cactaceae, the cactus family.

cactáceo adj. (bot.) cactaceous.

cactiforme adj. m. + f. cactiform, cactoid, shaped like a cactus.

cacto s. m. 1. Cactus: a genus of plants of the family Cactaceae. 2. cactus: any plant of the cactus family.

cactóide adj. m. + f. cactoid, cactuslike.

caçuá s. m. (Braz.) 1. a large pannier, oblong hamper. 2. a kind of net with wide meshes.

caçuiroba s. f. (Braz.) a kind of pigeon (Columba rufina).

C 2

Espaldar

Moldura

Assento

Esteio   Pé

Cadeira de pãlhinha

Cadeira estofada

Mocho

Cadeira de jardim

Cadeira giratória

Espreguiçadeira

Assento de dobrar

Banquinho de lona dobradiça

Cadeira de criança

Cadeira de preguiça

Banquinho de piano

Cadeira de balanço

Poltrona de braços

Cadeira de braços

Poltrona de orelhas

Tripeça

Cadeira de rodas

Sofá

CADEIRAS E MÓVEIS ESTOFADOS

Divã

caçula, caçulê, caçulo s. m. (Braz.) the youngest child of a family, baby. ‖ adj. youngest (of several brothers and sisters).

caculo s. m. 1. excess, surplus. 2. superabundance.

caculucage s. m. (Braz., bot.) a marsh fleabane (Pluchea quitoco).

cacumbi s. m. (Braz.) a funnel-shaped wicker basket.

cacumbu (I) s. m. (Braz.) 1. a blunt and nearly worthless hoe or ax. 2. the period from Maundy Thursday noon until Good Friday noon.

cacumbu (II) s. m. (Braz.) a Negro dance.

cacunda s. f. (Braz.) 1. back, dorsum. 2. shoulders. 3. (fig.) protector, patron. 4. shelterer, harbourer. 5. conscience.

cacundê s. m. (Braz.) embroidered ribbon or chintz.

cacundeiro s. m. (Braz.) 1. porter, carrier. 2. pack animal that lags behind the troop. 3. common or vulgar fellow, hoodlum.

cacundo s. m. (Braz.) 1. back, shoulders. 2. hunch-back.

cacuri s. m. (N. Braz.) fish basket or pot, fish-garth made from wicker-work or nets.

cacutu s. m. (S. Braz.) bigwig, political boss.

cada adj. every, each.

a ~ momento every time. a ~ passo frequently, often. ~ dia every day. ~ dois ou três dias every two or three days. ~ qual com seu igual birds of a feather flock together. ~ qual de nós each of us. ~ qual fará o que melhor lhe parecer every one will do what he thinks best. ~ qual no seu ofício the cobbler must stick to his last. ~ qual sente o seu mal the wearer knows best where the shoe pinches. ~ um every one, each and all. ~ um

isoladamente every one. ~ um sabe as linhas com que cose every one knows what fits him best. ~ vez every time. ~ vez mais more and more. ~ vez melhor better and better. ~ vez que... whensoever... em ~ grupo in either group. está ficando ~ vez mais escuro it is becoming darker and darker. este menino faz ~ coisa that boy has a lot of bees in his bonnet. eu a espero a ~ momento I expect her every minute.

cadafalso s. m. 1. scaffolding, scaffold. 2. raised platform, dais. 3. stage. 4. gibbet, gallows.

cadarço s. m. 1. floss silk, flurt silk, cappadine. 2. ribbon or fabric made from the first silk spun by the silk worm. 3. tape, ribbon, ferret. 4. braid. ~ de sapatos shoestring.

cadarços s. m. pl. (typogr.) a set of ribbons used in printing presses that keep the paper adherent to the roll.

cadaste s. m. (naut.) 1. sternpost of a ship, post. 2. rudderpost, rudderstock.

cadastragem s. f. (pl. -ens) cadastration, organization of a cadastre.

cadastral adj. m. + f. (pl. -ais) cadastral.

cadastrar v. 1. to make a cadastre. 2. to register in a cadaster.

cadastro s. m. 1. cadastre, cadaster. 2. official register of real estate. 3. census. 4. a survey of population. 5. terrier. 6. dossier.

cadáver s. m. (pl. cadáveres) cadaver, corpse, dead body. 2. defunct, deceased. 3. mortal remain. 4. (fig.) ruin, complete destruction. 5. (Braz.) a person's creditor.

cadavérico adj. cadaveric, cadaverous, resembling a dead human body. ‖ **cadavericamente** adv. cadaverously.

cadaverização s. f. 1. act of suppressing any vital function (in an organ, limb, member of the body, etc.) 2. transformation into a cadaveric state.

cadaverizar v. to cadaverize: 1. suppress any vital function (of an organ, limb, member of the body, etc.) 2. reduce to a cadaveric form. 3. give the appearance of a cadaver to.

cadaveroso adj. 1. cadaverous, cadaveric. 2. resembling a cadaver.

cadê (Braz.) a popular expression meaning: what has become of?, what has happened to?, where is...?

cadeado s. m. padlock, portable lock, snap (plate F 1). **fechar a** ~ to padlock. **pôr um** ~ **na boca de alguém** to oblige s. o. to secrecy. **quebraram o** ~ **da mala** they broke the baglock open.

cadeia s. f. 1. chain, catena. 2. fetter(s), shackle(s). 3. jail, gaol, prison. 4. cage, coop. 5. (fig.) subjection, bondage. 6. sequel, train, series, succession (of things, acts, facts).

~ **de agrimensor** surveyor's chain, Gunter's chain. ~ **de engate** coupling chain. ~ **de entrave** stop--chain. ~ **de estações de rádio** hook-up of radio stations. ~ **de montanhas,** ~ **de montes** mountain--chain, mountain range, cordillera (plate M 11). **meter na** ~ to imprision, put in jail.

cadelão s. m. (pl. -ões), (Braz.) crosspieces which secure the siderails on the platform of an ox--cart.

cadeira s. f. 1. seat, chair (plates C 2, 20, D 4, R 5). 2. place. 3. stall. 4. a branch of science, subject of teaching. 5. coordinate discipline. 6. professorship. 7. ecclesiastical dignity. 8. seat of a diocese, diocesan center, see. 9. central or branch seat of a society (political, scientific, etc.). 10. ~s pl. hips.

~ **de armar** camp-chair. ~ **de balanço** rocking--chair, swing chair (plate C 2). ~ **de braços** arm-chair, easy chair (plates C 2, E 2). ~ **de dentista** dental chair (plate D 1). ~ **de palhinha** cane--chair (Plate C 2). ~ **de rodas** wheel chair, rolling chair, bath chair (Plate C 2). ~ **de vime** wicker -chair, basket chair. ~ **dobradiça** canvas chair, camp chair, folding-chair (plate C 2). ~ **elétrica** electric chair. ~ **estofada** upholstered chair (plate C 2). ~ **giratória** swivel chair, adjustable typing stool. ~ **presidencial** presidential chair. **falar de** ~ to speak with a perfect knowledge of a subject. **oferecer uma** ~ to motion a person to a chair. **o partido democrático ganhou oito** ~s **nas últimas eleições** the democratic party won eight seats at the last elections. **sentei-me entre duas** ~ I fell between two stools.

cadeirado (I) s. m. rows of chairs linked together and built into the wall of a choir, lecture hall, etc.

cadeirado (II) adj. large-hipped, having broad hips.

cadeiras s. f. pl. the hips.

cadeireiro s. m. 1. chairmaker, chair manufacturer. 2. (Braz., hist.) sedan-chair bearer.

cadeirinha s. f. 1. a little chair. 2. sedan-chair, portable chair. 3. pillion. 4. a seat formed by two persons who hold each other by the wrist, lady--chair.

cadeiruda adj. f. (Braz.) large-hipped (said of women).

cadeixo (I) s. m. 1. a piece of thread or string. 2. a curl of hair.

cadeixo (II) s. m. (Port., prov.) worthless old book.

cadela s. f. 1. female dog, bitch, she-dog. 2. (fam.) strumpet, prostitute.

cadelinha s. f. 1. dim. of. **cadela.** 2. a molusc (Donax trunculus).

cadena s. f. 1. a slip-knot or false knot which permits to remove without danger the halter rope from a steer's horns. 2. the pattern of dance figures in a fandango.

cadência s. f. 1. cadence, cadency. 2. (mus.) cadenza. 3. regularity of a movement, the rate of modulation. 4. rhytm. 5. talent. 6. disposition. 7. point of rest after a musical phrase. 8. trill. 9. (mus.) a sequence of chords ending a phrase.

a ~ **de um discurso** the fall of a discourse. ~ **de tiro** the rate of fire. ~ **do verso** the cadence of a verse. **não tem** ~ **para isto** his genius does not point this way.

cadenciado adj. 1. cadenced, regular, measured. 2. rhythmic(al). 3. harmonious.

cadenciar v. 1. to make cadenced. 2. to render rhythmical. 3. to cadence, accent. 4. to harmonize.

cadencioso adj. 1. cadenced, regular. 2. rhythmic(al). 3. harmonious.

cadente adj. m. + f. 1. cadenced, cadent. 2. falling. **estrela** ~ shooting star.

caderna s. f. (her.) a set of four similar pieces in an escutcheon.

cadernal s. m. (pl. -ais) (tech.) 1. pulley block. 2. double block, treble block. 3. rope block (plate G 5).

caderneta s. f. 1. notebook. 2. school register. 3. bank-book.

~ **bancária** bank-book. ~ **de caixa econômica** savings account book. ~ **de crediário** passbook. ~ **de passagens** circular ticket.

caderno s. m. 1. quire, loose sheet book. 2. memorandum book. 3. copy-book, exercise-book. 4. book.

~ **borrão** waste-book. ~ **de apontamentos** note-book, jotter. ~ **de esboços** sketch-book. ~ **de escrita** writing-book. ~ **de espiral** spiral-bound exercise-book.

cadete s. m. 1. cadet. 2. pupil of a superior military school.

~ **de aviação** flying cadet. **corpo de** ~s cadet corps. ~ **naval** naval cadet, midshipman.

cádi s. m. cadi, kadi: a judge or magistrate among the Mohammedans.

cadilho s. m. 1. a small cup for collecting the sap of rubber trees. 2. ~s pl.: a) the last threads of the warp. b) fringes. c) cares, worries, trouble.

cadimo adj. 1. dextrous, skilled. 2. cunning, sly. 3. artful, tricky, crafty. 4. common. 5. much frequented.

cadinhar v. to crucible, melt in a crucible.

cadinho s. m. crucible, melting pan or pot, melter. **aço de** ~ crucible steel. ~ **de recozer** annealing furnace. ~ **de refinar** fining-pot.

cadivo adj. 1. too ripe, overripe. 2. failing, decrepit. 3. (fig.) senile, decadent. 4. deciduous.

cadixe s. m. an Arab thoroughbred horse.

cádmio, cádmium s. m. (chem.) cadmium (symbol Cd).

cado s. m. (ant.) cadus, a kind of amphora, large vessel or jar.

cadorna s. f. (Braz., ornith.) a common quail (Nothura maculosa).

cadoz s. m. 1. burrow, hole. 2. (fig.) hiding-place, corner, nook. 3. garbage heap, dustbin. 4. (ichth.) gudgeon. 5. hovel, tumble-down shack. 6. (fig.) bottleneck.

caduca (I) s. f. ear-ornament worn by Indian dancing girls.

caduca (II) s. f. (anat.) decidua.

caducante adj. m. + f. 1. growing old. 2. decaying. 3. decadent.

caducar v. 1. to grow very old, age. 2. to weaken, enfeeble. 3. to become decrepit. 4. to decay, de-

C 3

Perdigueiro

Sabujo

Buldogue

Fox-pelo-duro

Buldogue-anão

Cão-d'água

Basset, baixote

Galgo

Collie

Dinamarquês

Pastor alemão

Grifom

Caça-raposa

Chinês

Mastim

"Labrador"

Dálmata

CÃES (Raças)

cline. 5. to dote. 6. (Braz.) to become feeble-minded or crazy (from old age). 7. to become extinct. 8. to lapse, forfeit.
o legado vai ~ the legacy will lapse.
caducário adj. 1. (jur.) subject to lapse or forfeit. 2. decayable. 3. of or relative to anything transitory or subject to aging.
caduceu s. m. 1. (Roman hist.) caduceus. 2. a staff with two serpents coiled around it (symbol of a physician).
caducidade s. f. (also **caduquez, caduquice**) 1. old age. 2. decadence, deterioration. 3. decrepitude, senility. 4. decay. 5. (jur.) caducity, forfeit, lapse. 6. obsoleteness. 7. deciduousness.
caducifólio adj. (bot.) caducous; deciduous.
caduco adj. 1. falling, ready to fall. 2. decrepit, senile. 3. caducous, fugacious. 4. age-worn. 5. decaying, decadent. 6. old and infirm, doting, bedridden. 7. transitory. 8. (jur.) subject to forfeit or lapse. 9. (bot.) deciduous. ‖ **-amente** adv. feebly, decadently, caducously.
esperanças -as vain hopes.
cães s. m., pl. of **cão** (plate C 3).
caetano s. m. (rel.) a monk of the Order of St. Cajetan.
caetê s. m. (Braz.) virgin forest.
cafajestada s. f. (also **cafajestice** f., **cafajestismo** m.) 1. action of common or vulgar people. 2. boorishness, churlishness. 3. mob, rabble.
cafajeste s. m. 1. boor, churl. 2. common, vulgar or despicable man. 3. rotter, scoundrel.
cafanga s. f. (Braz.) 1. squeamishness, touchiness. 2. simulated or false apology. 3. pretended refusal.
botar ~ **em alguém** to ascribe faults or defects to s. o.
cafangada s. f. (N. Braz.) fault, defect.
cafangar v. (Braz.) 1. to find fault- in, perceive a deficiency or defect. 2. to slander, malign. 3. to carp, nag. 4. to jeer, deride. 5. to threaten, menace. 6. to brag, boast.
cafangoso adj. full of faults or defects.
cafarnaú, cafarnaum s. m. (Braz.) 1. a depot for old things. 2. meeting place of rowdies or hoodlums.
café s. m. 1. coffee (fruit or tree). 2. a cup of coffee. 3. coffee-house.
~ **cantante** coffee-house with a music hall. ~ **com leite** white coffee. ~ **preto** black coffee. ~ **da manhã** breakfast. ~ **dançante** coffee-house with a dance hall. **cor de** ~ coffee-coloured. **é** ~ **pequenol** it's child-play! **grão de** ~ coffee bean, coffee berry. **jogo de** ~ coffee set. **não ganhar nem para o** ~ to earn very little. **o** ~ **está um pouco fraco** the coffee is rather weak. **serviço de** ~ coffee set. **sucedâneo do** ~ coffee substitute. **vamos tomar um** ~ let's have a coffee. **torrar** ~ to roast coffee.
café-caneca s. m. (pl. **cafés-caneca**), (Braz.) a second-class bar.
café-com-isca s. m. (pl. **cafés-com isca**), (Braz., pop.) coffee with a few drops of brandy, coffee served with delicacies.
café-com-leite adj. m. + f., sg. + pl. (Braz.) café-au--lait, light brown.
café-com-mistura s. m. (pl. **cafés-com-mistura**) (Braz.) coffee with delicatessen.
café-concerto s. m. (pl. **cafés-concerto**) coffee-house which offers musical entertainment.
café-do-mato s. m. (pl. **cafés-do-mato**), (Braz.) popular designation of several plants of the dogbane family (Tabernaemontana laeta, Cordia coffeoides, Cordia salicifolia, Trichilia laminensis).
cafedório s. m. (pop.) a weak watery coffee.
cafeeiral s. m. (pl. **-ais**) coffee plantation.

cafeeiro s. m. coffee tree, shrub, of the family Rubiaceae (Coffea arabica).
cafeicultor s. m. coffee grower, coffee planter.
cafeicultura s. f. coffee growing, coffee planting.
cafeína s. f. (chem.) caffeine.
cafelana s. f. a large coffee plantation.
cafelista s. m. + f. 1. coffee planter, coffee grower. 2. proprietor of a coffee plantation. 3. (Braz.) a person who is excessively fond of coffee.
cafelo s. m. mortar, building cement.
cafeocracia s. f. (Braz.) the rich and influential class of coffee growers, coffee barons.
caferana s. f. (Braz.) plant of the gentian family (Tachia guianensis).
cafetã s. m. caftan, kaftan.
cafetão s. m. (pl. **-ões**), (Braz., sl.) = **cáften**.
cafeteira s. f. 1. coffee-pot (plate V 2). 2. coffee percolator.
~ **com torneira** coffee urn.
cafeteiro s. m. (Braz.) proprietor of a coffee-house, barkeeper.
cafezal s. m. (pl. **-ais**) coffee plantation.
cafezeiro (I) s. m. (bot.) coffee tree, coffee.
cafezeiro (II) s. m. 1. coffee-grower, coffee planter. 2. worker or farmhand on a coffee plantation.
cafezinho s. m. (Braz.) 1. (ornith.) a jacana (Jacana spinosa jacana). 2. a small cup of coffee (usually served without milk). 3. common name of two plants (Maytenus alaternoides, Mouriria chamissoana).
cafezista s. m. + f. 1. coffee grower, coffee planter. 2. proprietor of a coffee plantation. 3. (Braz.) a person who is very fond of coffee.
cafifa s. m. + f. (Braz., pop.) 1. an unlucky gambler. 2. a person to whom a gambler attributes his bad luck. 3. a series of disappointments, setbacks or misfortunes. 4. importunity.
cafifar v. (Braz.) 1. to annoy or disturb a player. 2. to bring ill luck to. 3. to render unhappy.
cafife s. m. (Braz.) 1. persistent misfortune. 2. a series of disappointments. 3. constant lack of success. 4. uneasiness, indisposition. 5. dejectedness, dejection, depression. 6. lack of vitality.
cafifento s. m. (Braz.) an unlucky gambler. ‖ adj. bashful, peeved, diffident.
cafifice s. f., **cafifismo** m. 1. bad luck, misfortune. 2. indisposition. 3. uneasiness. 4. dejectedness.
cáfila s. f. 1. a large group of camels transporting goods. 2. caravan, cafila. 3. (fig.) band, gang, mob.
cafiote s. m. (N. Braz.) an old-fashioned trunk.
cafioto s. m. (Braz.) adherent of voodooism.
cafofa s. f. (Braz.) a dish made from roasted jerked meat and manioc flour.
cafofo s. m. (Braz.) marshy ground, the stagnant waters of which exhale foul smelling gases.
cafona s. m. + f. (Braz., sl.) one who tries the utmost to show off, but with remarkable bad taste. ‖ adj. showing off with bad taste.
cafonice s. f. (Braz., pop.) remarkable bad taste, show-off.
cafoto s. m. 1. (Braz.) latrine. 2. a narrow watercourse between rocks. 3. a narrow path between rocks.
cafraria s. f. 1. Kaffraria: region inhabited by Kaffirs (South Africa). 2. a group or assemblage of Kaffirs.
cafre s. m. + f. 1. Kaffrarian: native or inhabitant of Kaffraria. 2. (fig.) savage, barbarian. ‖ adj. Kaffrarian.
cafrice s. f. 1. action typical of Kaffirs. 2. (fig.) cruelty, barbarity.
cáften s. m. (pl. **caftens**) (f. **caftina**), (Braz., pop.) 1. fancy man, protector, bully. 2. panderer, procurer, pimp.

caftina s. f. (Braz.) panderess, procuress, bawd.

caftinagem s. f. (pl. **-ens)** panderage, act and practice of pandering, panderism.

caftinar v. to pander, procure for, act as a go-between.

caftinismo, caftismo s. m. (Braz.) 1. white slavery. 2. act or action of a procurer (procuress), panderage, panderism.

cafua s. f. 1. cavern, den, lair. 2. cavity, pit. 3. hide-out, hiding-place. 4. hovel, miserable hut. 5. dungeon, lock-up.

cafubá adj. (S. Braz.) pale yellow.

cafuca s. f. (Braz., pop.) charcoal pit.

cafuçu s. m. (N. Braz., pop.) devil, fiend.

cafuleta s. f. (N. Braz.) wooden trunk or chest with a leather cover (used on the jangadas for keeping food).

cafuleteiro s. m. (Braz.) 1. crew member of a whaler. 2. storekeeper.

cafumango s. m. 1. black cook (male), ship's cook. 2. vagabond, vagrant. 3. social outcast.

cafunar v. (children's play, Braz.) to drive a cashew-nut (like a marble).

cafundó, cafundoca, cafundório s. m. 1. = **cafua.** 2. a flat stretch of lowland between steep mountains. 3. a distant and secluded place (usually in the mountains and difficult to reach).

cafundó-do-judas s. m. (pl. **cafundós-do-judas)** (Braz.) the farthest corner of the world.

cafuné s. m. (Braz.) 1. a soft scratching or stroking on the head (to lull somebody into sleep). 2. scratching behind the ear (dogs, cats).

cafungar v. (Braz.) 1. to investigate in great detail. 2. to search thoroughly. 3. to scrutinize. 4. to ransack.

cafunje s. m. (Braz.) 1. pilferer, filcher, sneak-thief. 2. mischievous and sneaking street Arab.

cafurna s. f. 1. cavity, pit. 2. a deep and dark cavern. 3. hide-out.

cafus s. m. used in the adverbial locution: **pelos ~, ali pelos ~** at nightfall, in the dusk.

cafute s. m. (pop.) the devil.

cafuzo s. m. (also **cafuz** m. + f.) (Braz.) 1. the offspring of Negro and Indian. 2. a very dark-skinned, nearly black mulatto. 3. a plant of the sedge family (Cyprus lunciformis). ‖ adj. of or relative to the offspring of Negro and Indian.

caga (I) s. m. (vulg.) 1. a lovelorn or infatuated man. 2. an easily irritated fellow.

caga (II) s. f. (obs.) excrements.

cagaço s. m. (vulg.) fear, terror, fright.

cágado s. m. 1. (zool.) common name of several fresh-water and land turtles, a long-necked turtle. 2. (fig.) a slow or dull fellow, laggard.

caga-fogo s. m. (pl. **caga-fogos)** (Braz., pop.) 1. glowworm, firefly. 2. any firearm. 3. f. a black, slender bee of the family Apidae (Melipona tataira).

cagaiteira s. f. (Braz.) a tree of the myrtle family (Eugenia dysenterica).

caga-lume s. m. (pl. **caga-lumes),** (pop.) glowworm, firefly.

caganeira s. f. (vulg.) diarrhea, looseness of the bowels.

caganifância s. f. insignificant thing or matter.

cagar v. (vulg.) to defecate.

caga-regras s. m. + f., sg. + pl. (Braz.) smart aleck.

cagarolas s. m. sg. + pl. (vulg.) 1. weakling. 2. coward, dastard.

caga-sebinho s. m. (pl. **caga-sebinhos),** (Braz.) a bird of the family Tyrannidae (Phyllomias brevirostris), crested flycatcher.

caga-sebista s. m. (pl. **caga-sebistas)** proprietor of a second-hand bookshop, used books dealer.

caga-sebo s. m. (pl. **caga-sebos)** 1. a second-hand bookshop. 2. (ornith.) a crested flycatcher (Mysiophobus fasciatus).

cagatório s. m. (vulg.) latrine, privy.

cagosanga s. f. (Braz., bot.) ipecac (Cephaelis ipecacuanha).

cagotilho s. m. (Braz., pop.) an epizootic disease of mules.

caguincha, caguincho s. m. 1. coward, dastard. 2. weakling. 3. (cards) the two of clubs. ‖ **caguincha** adj. 1. weak, feeble. 2. cowardly, pusillanimous. 3. fearful. 4. anemic. 5. little, diminutive.

caguira s. f. (Braz.) 1. bad luck at gambling. 2. fear, dread, fright. 3. m. good-for-nothing, scamp.

caiabana s. f. (Braz.) a sort of cassava.

caiação s. f. (pl. **-ões)** whitewashing, whitewash, limewash.

caiadela s. f. the act of whitewashing.

caiado s. m. (Port., prov.) whitewash, limewash. ‖ adj. 1. covered with whitewash. 2. (fig.) whitened with rice powder or any other make-up.

caiador s. m. whitewasher.

caiadura s. f. 1. act or effect of whitewashing. 2. a coat of whitewash.

caiana (I) s. f. (Braz.) 1. a variety of sugar cane. 2. (pop.) rum.

caiana (II) s. m. (Braz.) a giant bat.

caiapiá s. m. (Braz.) the medicinal roots of several plants of the mulberry family.

caiapó (I) s. m. (Braz.) 1. a popular folk dance. 2. popular name of a kind of sauba ant (Atta sexdens).

caiapó (II) s. m. + f. Cayapo: native of an important tribe of Brazilian Indians. ‖ adj. of or relative to this tribe.

caiaque s. m. kayak (plate B 9).

caiar v. 1. to whitewash, limewash. 2. to white, whiten. 3. to disguise, conceal. 4. to overdo one's make-up. 5. to coat, paint.

caiarara s. m. (zool.) capuchin (Cebus gracilis).

caiaué s. m. (Braz.) a plant of the palm family (Elaeis melanococca).

caíba s. f. poor dry land, barren soil.

cãibra s. f. (med.) cramp, kink, crick, convulsion.
 ele foi atacado de ~ he was seized with a cramp.

caibral adj. m. + f. (pl. **-ais)** concerning, pertaining to or serving to fasten rafters.

caibramento s. m. the system of rafters of a roof, timberwork of a roof.

caibrar v. to rafter, provide with rafters.

caibro s. m. rafter(s), roof timber.

cãibro s. m. a pair of anything linked or grown together, esp. a pair of corncobs grown together on the same stalk.

caiçaca s. f. fer-de-lance, jararaca: one of the most common venomous vipers of Brazil.

caicaco s. m. (S. Braz.) a degraded or impoverished fellow, outcast.

caicai s. m. (Braz.) fishing-net.

caiçara s. f. 1. fence made of boughs or twigs. 2. a palisade around an Indian settlement. 3. a bundle of boughs put into the water in order to attract fish. 4. stable, corral. 5. the dead branches of felled trees. 6. a wooden enclosure or corral near the banks of a river where cattle is kept before shipment. 7. a rough fence around a piece of farmland (to ward off cattle). 8. a rude hunter's blind made of boughs and branches. 9. m.: a) vagabond, tramp. b) scoundrel. 10. m. + f. a brutish person of the backwoods.

caiçarada s. f. an assemblage of backwoods people.

caicau s. m. (Braz., bot.) black fig.

caiçuma s. f. a dish made from well-seasoned manioc juice thickened with manioc or potato flour.

caicurá s. f. (Braz.) bonfire.

caída s. f. 1. fall, falling. 2. (fig.) decay, decadence. 3. (Braz.) declivity, slope. 4. downcome, descent. 5. sag, sinking. 6. recession. 7. dump.

caideiro, caidiço adj. (Braz.) = caduco.

caído adj. 1. fallen. 2. decayed, decrepit. 3. sad, depressed, dejected. 4. indebted, in arrears. 5. overdue (payments). 6. overcome by (admiration, love, etc.), enamoured, in love with.

ele está caidinho por ela he is sopping on her.

caidor s. m. (Braz.) place where the cattle droves usually swim over a river. || adj. falling, tumbling, sinking.

caídos s. m. pl. 1. overdue and unpaid interest or income, arrears. 2. rests, pickings, scrapings. 3. passion, deep inclination. 4. flirtation, courtship.

caieira s. m. 1. lime-pit. 2. lime-kiln, lime-burner. 3. (Braz.) a furnace or kiln built from the raw bricks which are to be burned. 4. bonfire.

caieiro s. m. 1. whitewasher. 2. worker in a lime-kiln, lime-burner. 3. journeyman, mason's helper.

caiena (I) s. m. + f. one of the Cheyennes, a North American Indian tribe. || adj. of, pertaining to or relative to this tribe.

caiena (II) s. f. (Braz.) a sort of banana.

caiguá adj. (S. Braz.) mountainous, wild, sylvan.

caim (I) s. m. (pl. -ins) 1. Cain, fratricide. 2. (Port., prov.) scoundrel, rascal.

caim (II) s. m. (pl. -ins) yelp of a dog.

caimacão s. m. (pl. -ões) kaimakam, qaimaqam: a lieutenant or aide-de-camp of a grand vizier.

caimão s. m. (pl. -ões) (zool.) cayman, caiman.

caimbé s. m. (Braz., bot.) chaparro, sandpaper tree.

caimbezal s. m. (pl. -ais), (Braz., Amazonas) chaparro grove.

câimbra s. f. (med.) cramp, kink, crick, convulsion.

câimbro s. m. a pair of corncobs growing together on the same stalk.

caimento s. m. 1. act of falling, fall. 2. sinking, dropping. 3. decadence, decay. 4. prostration, despondency. 5. (fig.) dejectedness. 6. (Braz.) passion, deep inclination or love. 7. (naut.) sternway. 8. ~s pl. (Braz.) courtship, flirtation.

caimito s. m. (Braz., bot.) star apple.

cainca s. f. (Braz., bot.) Brazilian snakeroot.

cainça, cainçada, cainçalha s. f. (Braz.) 1. a pack of dogs. 2. barking, yelping.

cainhar (I) v. to yelp, bark (dogs).

cainhar (II) v. to be mean, act niggardly, grudge, give unwillingly.

cainheza s. f. 1. avarice, covetousness. 2. meanness, stinginess. 3. pettiness, paltriness.

cainho (I) adj. doggish, currish, like a dog, canine.

cainho (II) s. m. miser, avaricious fellow, skinflint. || adj. avaricious, niggardly, stingy, miserly.

caio s. m. 1. act or effect of whitewashing. 2. a coat of whitewash or white paint.

caiongo adj. 1. aging. 2. weak, feeble. 3. infirm.

caipira s. m. + f. (Braz.) 1. rustic, backwoodsman, back-settler. 2. yokel, hick, jake, clodhopper. 3. country bumpkin, hayseed. || adj. 1. of, pertaining to or relative to backwoods people. 2. rough, rude. 3. uncultured. 4. boorish.

deixe de bancar o ~ don't try to play the fool.

caipirada, caipiragem (pl. -ens), caipirice s. f., caipirismo m. 1. a crowd of backwoods people, an assemblage of back-settlers. 2. act typical of rustics. 3. awkward or uncultured behaviour. 4. foolishness, folly.

caipirinha s. f. (Braz.) a drink made of sliced or soaked lemon, sugar and ice cubes, mixed with white rum.

caipora s. m. + f. 1. goblin, imp. 2. person who brings bad luck. 3. unlucky fellow. 4. f. (Braz.) persistent misfortune. || adj. unfortunate, unlucky, luckless.

caiporice s. f. persistent misfortune.

caiporismo s. m. (Braz.) 1. persistent bad luck. 2. misfortune, run of ill luck. 3. adversity.

caíque s. m. 1. caique, fishing or coasting vessel. 2. kayak. .

cair v. 1. to fall: a) fall down. b) tumble, drop, succumb. c) set, sink, come down. d) decline, decay. e) be thrown to the ground. f) slope downwards. g) be overthrown. h) be mistaken. i) coincide, incur. j) be, become. k) fall for, yield to. l) hang downward, droop. m) happen by chance, befall, occur. n) sin, err. o) befall by inheritance. p) fall due, be payable. q) sag, sink down. r) (aeron.) crack-up. 2. to lessen, moderate. 3. to be dismissed or discharged. 4. to break down, collapse. 5. to go into, fit into. 6. to arrive unexpectedly. 7. to suit, match, harmonize with. 8. to surrender, capitulate. 9. to supervene, befall. 10. to fail to please (a play). 11. to look toward.

~ à ré (naut.) to fall astern. ~ ao mar to fall overboard. ~ como um pato to get it in the neck. ~ das mãos de alguém to fall out of one's hands. ~ das nuvens to be struck all of a heap. ~ de cama to be taken ill. ~ de joelhos to sink to one's knees. ~ de quatro to fall to the knees and hands. ~ do céu to happen unexpectedly. ~ em desuso to fall into disuse. ~ em esquecimento to fall into oblivion. ~ em má companhia to get into bad society. ~ em pecado to fall from grace. ~ em pedaços to tumble to pieces. ~ em prantos (pop.) to turn the tap on. ~ em si to recover one's senses. ~ em tal dia .to fall on (a certain day). ~ em tentação to yield to temptation. ~ em violência to lash out. ~ entre os selvagens to fall among savages. ~ fora 1. to fall out. 2. to be left out. ~ merto to drop dead. ~ na armadilha to go into the trap, (fig.) to swallow the bait. ~ na miséria to impoverish. ~ nas mãos de to fall into the hands of. ~ no desagrado de to run into displeasure. ~ no mato, ~ no mundo to fly, run away. ~ para trás to sink back, fall back. ~ sobre o inimigo to fall upon the enemy. ~ verticalmente to plummet. caíram em cima dele they set upon him. a criança caiu no sono the child dropped asleep. ao ~ da noite when night falls, at nightfall. caí ao comprido I fell with a run. caiu-lhe o coração aos pés his heart sank into his boots. caiu na esparrela he fell for it. deixar ~ 1. to drop, let fall. 2. to abandon. ela caiu de pé she fell on her legs. ele caiu em silêncio he subsided into silence. ele caiu na bebedeira he fell a prey to drink. ele caiu num erro he fell into an error. não ter onde ~ morto to be very poor. nessa eu não caio! you don't catch me! I don't go into the trap! no ano passado o Natal caiu num domingo Christmas fell on Sunday last year. o mal que de tua boca sai, em teu seio cai! chicken and curses come home to roost! o vestido cai bem the dress wears well. uma desgraça caiu sobre nós a misfortune has come over us.

cairara s. m. a kind of monkey. || adj. m. + f. very big, huge, gigantic.

cairel s. m. (pl. -éis) 1. border, edge. 2. rim, brink, margin. 3. guard, protection. 4. hem. 5. galloon, flounce, lace.

cairelado adj. laced, trimmed with galloons.

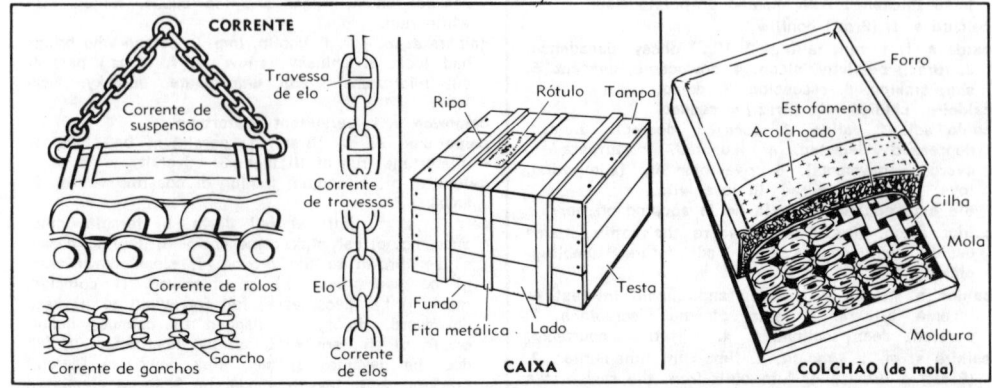

CORRENTE

Corrente de suspensão
Travessa de elo
Corrente de travessas
Corrente de rolos
Elo
Gancho
Corrente de ganchos
Corrente de elos

Ripa   Rótulo   Tampa
Testa
Lado
Fundo
Fita metálica

CAIXA

Forro
Estofamento
Acolchoado
Cilha
Mola
Moldura

COLCHÃO (de mola)

cairelar v. 1. to adorn with lace. 2. to lace, trim with galloons. 3. to hem, edge, border.

cairi s. m. (Braz.) a well-seasoned chicken stew.

cairota s. m. + f. native or inhabitant of Cairo (Egypt). || adj. of or relative to this city.

cairuçu s. m. (Braz.) name of several plants of the family Umbelliferae (genus: Hydrocotyle), Indian pennywort.

cais s. m., sg. + pl. 1. quay, wharf. 2. dock, pier. 3. mole. 4. goods platform, railway platform, side loading ramp (plate E 12). ~ **flutuante** floating pier.

cáiser s. m. Kaiser.

caité s. m. (Braz.) name of several plants of the family Marantaceae and of the canna family.

caititu s. m. (Braz.) 1. (zool.) peccary. 2., the wooden roller of a manioc grating machine.

caíva s. f. (Braz.) dry poor land, barren soil.

caixa s. f. 1. box (plate G 3, V 1). 2. case, chest (plate C 4). 3. kit, set. 4. casing (plates F 1, M 5). 5. coffer. 6. bin. 7. receptacle, container, vessel, tank (plate F 6). 8. frame. 9. road bed. 10. that part of a theater where the artists' dressing rooms are installed. 11. (typogr.) type case, letter-case. 12. purse, pouch. 13. treasury. 14. strongbox, safe. 15. treasurer, cashier, teller, receiver. 16. (com.) cash-book. 17. (com.) cashier's office or window. ~ **acústica** diaphragm. ~ **alta** (typogr.) upper case (for capital letters). ~ **baixa** (typogr.) lower case (for small and auxiliary types). ~ **beneficente** sick-club, relief society. ~ **cheia** a boxful. ~ **da direção** (mech.) steering box. ~ **de embreagem** (mot.) clutch housing (plate M 13). ~ **d'água,** reservoir, watertank (plate T 2). ~ **de bússola** (naut.) binnacle. ~ **de câmbio** 1. money changer, exchange broker. 2. (mech.) change gear. ~ **de charutos** cigar box. ~ **de chave** (electr.) switch box (plate M 5). ~ **de corte** miter box. ~ **de costura** sewing box. ~ **de cravelhas** (violin) peg box (plate V 5). ~ **de crédito** loan-office. ~ **de descarga** flushing cistern, flushing tank (plate R 4). ~ **de distribuição** (mech.) distribution box. ~ **de escape** (mech.) exhaust box. ~ **de esmolas** poor-box. ~ **de ferramentas** tool-box, tool kit (plate M 12). ~ **de folhas-de-flandres** tin case. ~ **de fósforos** matchbox. ~ **de fundição** molding box. ~ **de graxa** grease-box. ~ **de ligação** (electr.) junction box (plate E 3). ~ **de manivela** (mech.) crankcase. ~ **de munição** ammunition chest. ~ **de música** musical-box. ~ **de papelão** carton, cardboard-box, paper box (plate V 2). ~ **de pó-de-arroz** compact. ~ **de previdência**

provident fund. ~ **de relógio** watch-case (plate R 4). ~ **de tomada** (electr.) plug socket (plate E 3). ~ **econômica** savings bank, trust company. ~ **-forte** safe, strongbox. ~ **postal** postbox, letter-box (plate E 13). ~ **tipográfica** type case. **guardar a** ~ to keep book. **livro** ~ cashbook. **pagar na** ~ to pay at the desk. ~ **registradora** cash register. **tocar a** ~ (fig.) to beat the drum. **uma** ~ **de cerveja** a case of beer.

caixão s. m. (pl. **-ões**) 1. coffin. 2. great chest. 3. locker, trunk. 4. bin (plate E 11). 5. a bricklayer's hod. 6. (Braz.) river bottom. ~ **de bomba** (mech.) bomb chest. ~ **de defunto** coffin. ~ **-de-defunto** (ent.) a butterfly (Papilio thoas brasiliensis). ~ **flutuante** caisson.

caixa-pregos s. f. (Braz.) remote and isolated place, solitude.

caixaria (I) s. f. 1. a great quantity of chests or boxes. 2. (Braz., sugar mills) sugar deposit, stock of sugar.

caixaria (II) s. f. salesmanship, clerkship, profession of a salesman or saleswoman.

caixeirada s. f. (depr.) 1. the class of salesmen (collectively). 2. a group or assemblage of salesmen or saleswomen.

caixeiragem s. f. (pl. **-ens**), 1. the profession of salesmen. 2. salesmanship, clerkship. 3. shopman, shopwoman. 4. sales personnel of a store-house or magazine.

caixeiral adj. m. + f. (pl. **-ais**) of, pertaining to or relative to salespeople or salesmanship.

caixeirar v. (Braz.) 1. to belong to the sales personnel of a store-house. 2. to work as a (travelling) salesman or woman. 3. to act as cashier, keep the cash.

caixeiro s. m. 1. counter clerk, salesclerk. 2. shop-boy, errand-boy, porter, delivery-boy or man. 3. book-keeper, accountant. 4. cashier, treasurer. 5. box-maker, trunk manufacturer. 6. (Port.) drummer. ~ **de balcão** counter clerk. ~ **viajante** bagman, commercial traveller, travelling salesman.

caixeta s. f. 1. a little box. 2. pouch, little bag or case. 3. Brazilian cork tree.

caixeta-amarela s. f. (pl. **caixetas-amarelas**) (bot.) a tree of the genus Chrysophillum.

caixilharia s. f. moulding(s), framework.

caixilho s. m. 1. window-sash, casement (plate J 1). 2. framework. 3. (archit.) architrave. 4. frame, moulding. ~ **de porta** door-frame (plate A 13).

caixista s. m. + f. (typogr.) typesetter, hand compositor.

caixola s. f. little box, small case, casket.

caixotaria s. f. 1. a great quantity of packing boxes or cases. 2. box or trunk factory.

caixote s. m. 1. a crude chest or box. 2. packing-box, packing-case.
~ de lixo dustbin.

caixoteiro s. m. box maker, trunk or chest manufacturer.

caixotim s. m. (pl. -ins) (typogr.) each one of the square subdivisions of a type case, box.

cajá s. m. (bot.) hog-plum.

cajá-açu s. m. (pl. cajás-açus), (Braz.) a tree of the cashew family (Spondias macrocarpa).

cajadada s. f. a blow with a stick.
matar dois coelhos de uma ~ to kill two birds with one stone.

cajado s. m. 1. shepherd's stick, crook, crooked stick. 2. baculus, crozier. 3. cane, club.

cajá-manga s. m. (pl. cajás-manga), (Braz., bot.) Otaheite apple.

cajá-mirim s. m. (pl. cajás-mirins), (Braz., bot.) hog--plum.

cajarana s. f. (Braz., bot.) Otaheite apple, Malay apple.

cajazeira s. f. (Braz.), cajazeiro m. hog-plum tree.

cajetilha s. m. (S. Braz.) 1. city-bred boy. 2. city slicker. 3. poor but pretentious fellow.

cajila s. f. 1. good omen, happy presentiment. 2. bearer of glad tidings. 3. one who brings luck or causes happiness.

caju s. m. (bot.) cashew-nut, cashew, acajou.

cajuaçu s. m. (Braz.) a variety of cashew-trees (Anacardium giganteum).

cajuada s. f. (Braz.) 1. refreshing drink made from cashew-nut juice, water and sugar. 2. sweetmeat made from cashew-nuts. 3. (fig.) confusion, disorder.

cajual s. m. (pl. -ais) a grove of cashew-trees.

cajubi s. m. (ornith.) piping guan.

cajuçara s. f. (Braz.) popular name of two plants, one of the family Euphorbiaceae (Croton cajuçara), and the other of the family Malpighiaceae (Stygmaphyllon fulgens).

cajueiral s. m. (pl. -ais) a grove of cashew-trees.

cajueiro s. m. (also cajuzeiro) 1. cashew-tree. 2. cashew, acajou. 3. (pop.) extremely mean or avaricious fellow, miser.

cajueiro-do-campo s. m. (pl. cajueiros-do-campo) (Braz.) common designation of two subshrub species of the cashew family (Anacardium pumilum and A. nanum).

cajuí s. m. (Braz.) plant of the cashew family (Anacardium microcarpum).

cajuína s. f. cashew wine.

cajurana s. f. (Braz.) a simaba tree (Simaba guianensis).

cal (I) s. f. (pl. cales or cais) lime, whitewash.
~ apagada burned lime. ~ apagada no ar air slaked lime. ~ hidratada hydrated lime. ~ virgem, ~ viva quicklime. forno de ~ limekiln. leite de ~ limewater. pedra de ~ limestone.

cal s. m. feeder tube (of a waterwheel).

cala (I) s. f. 1. a recess in a shore, inlet. 2. creek. 3. plug, a piece cut out from a fruit to test its quality.

cala (II) s. f. (bot.) calla lily, arum lily.

cala (III) s. f. cordage made from the fiber of esparto grass.

cala (IV) s. f. 1. muteness. 2. silence, stillness.

cala (V) s. m. scoundrel, knave, crafty or deceitful fellow.

calaboca s. m. (Braz.) a short, thick club or cudgel.

calabouço s. m. 1. calaboose, dungeon. 2. prison, jail. 3. dog-house. 4. keep, donjon. 5. a shadowy, gloomy or somber place.

calabre s. m. (naut.) cord, rope, cable, hawser.

calabreada s. f. 1. act of confounding. 2. confusion, disorder. 3. mixture, blend. 4. deterioration. 5. perverting, corruption. 6. regulation. 7. alteration, change. 8. adulteration (of wine). 9. to deceive, cheat.

calabrear v. 1. to adulterate wine by false seasoning. 2. to season. 3. to mix up. 4. to change to worse. 5. to change, transform.

calabrês s. m. Calabrian: native or inhabitant (male) of Calabria (Italy). ‖ adj. Calabrian: of or pertaining to Calabria.

calabrote s. m. (naut.) 1. small and thin cable, cablet. 2. warp.

calabroteado adj. (naut.) cable-laid.

calabrotear v. (naut.) to twist three cables into one.

calabura s. f. (Braz.) calabur tree, silkwood.

calaçaria s. f. 1. laziness, slothfulness. 2. idleness. 3. vagrancy. 4. (S. Braz.) a gang of hoodlums or loafers.

calacear v. 1. to idle, loaf, loiter. 2. to lead a vagrant life, tramp about. 3. to live at other people's expense, sponge upon people, play the toady.

calaceirice s. f. 1. laziness, idleness. 2. vagrancy. 3. sponging, toadyism.

calaceiro s. m. 1. idler, lazibones. 2. loafer, lounger. 3. vagrant, bum. 4. sponger, toady.

calada s. f. 1. complete silence. 2. stillness, quietness. 3. hush. 4. cessation of any noise.
às ~s secretly, silently, tacitly. pela ~ da noite in the dead of the night, at an unearthly hour.

caladão s. m. a very silent person. ‖ adj. mum.

calado (I) s. m. load-displacement, load-draught (of a vessel), draught, sea-gauge.
o barco tem um ~ de dez pés the boat draws ten feet.

calado (II) s. m. (bot.) calla lily, arum lily.

calado (III) adj. (also p. p. of calar) 1. silent, quiet. 2. close, reserved. 3. secret, secretive. 4. close--tongued, mum. 5. taciturn, wordless. 6. sullen, dumb.
ele é um homem ~ he is a discreet man. eles ficaram ~s they kept silence. ele se mantém ~ he keeps mum.

caladura s. f. 1. silence, quietness. 2. reservedness. 3. taciturnity. 4. discretion. 5. muteness. 6. plug (of a fruit).

calafanje s. m. vulgar and despicable fellow.

calafate s. m. 1. calker, caulker. 2. (bot.) a barberry (Berberis ruscifolia). 3. (Braz.) a violent eastwind.

calafetação s. f. caulking.

calafetador s. m. 1. calker, caulker. 2. calking-iron.

calafetagem s. f. (pl. -ens), calafetamento m. (naut.) caulking, gasket.

calafetar v. 1. to calk, caulk. 2. to drive tarred oakum into the seams of a ship (to prevent leaking). 3. to stop up.

calafeto (ê) s. m. 1. (naut.) act or method of caulking. 2. joint, jointing.

calafriado adj. suffering from cold fits or shivers.

calafrio s. m. 1. fit of cold, shivering fit. 2. chill, shiver, shakes. 3. (med.) rigour.

calagem s. f. (pl. -ens), (agric.) liming of the soil.

calamar s. m. (Braz., ichth.) a squid, cuttlefish (Loligo brasiliensis).

calamidade s. f. 1. calamity. 2. calamitousness. 3. catastrophe, disaster. 4. affliction, woe, curse. 5. fatality. 6. misfortune, adversity. 7. scourge, plague. 8. disgrace.

calamídeo adj. calamiform.

calamífero adj. calamiferous.
calamiforme adj. m. + f. calamiform.
calamina s. f. (min.) calamine, hemimorphite, brass-ore.
calamistrado adj. curled, crimpy, frizzled (hair).
calamistrar v. to curl, crisp (hair).
calamistro s. m. curling or frizzling iron, curling tongs.
calamita s. f. 1. a kind of storax or resin tree. 2. (pal.) calamite. 3. (min.) calamine. 4. (arch.) magnetic needle.
calamite s. f. (pal.) calamite.
calamitoso adj. 1. calamitous. 2. catastrophic(al), disastrous. 3. wretched, unhappy, woeful. 4. tragic(al). 5. adverse.
cálamo s. m. 1. stalk, halm, blade of grass. 2. a reed pen, quill (for writing). 3. (poet.) flute. 4. (fig., poet.) stylus. 5. (bot.) calamus, sweet-flag, sweet-rush.
calamocada s. f. (vulg.) 1. a blow on the head. 2. (fig.) damage.
calamocar v. 1. to rap on the head. 2. to wound. 3. to vex.
calamofitáceas s. f. (pl. (paleobotany) Calamophytaceae.
calândar s. m. (pl. calândares) = calênder.
calandra (I) s. f. 1. (mech.) calender, rolling machine. 2. mangle, roll, hot-press. 3. (mech.) metal sheet bending machine.
calandra (II) s. f. 1. (ornith.) a skylark, calander. 2. (ent.) granary weevil (Calandra granaria). 3. (Braz.) a mockingbird (Mimus saturninus modulator).
calandrado adj. mangled, calendered.
calandragem s. f. (pl. -ens) act or method of calendering.
calandrar v. 1. to smooth in a calender, calender. 2. to mangle. 3. to roll, hot-press.
calandreiro s. m. calenderer, mangler, hot-press worker.
calandríni s. f. (Braz.) Egyptian grass, crowfoot grass.
calandrínia s. f. (bot.) a purslane (Calandrinia umbellata).
calandrista s. m. + f. (typogr.) calender stereotypist; (paper mill) calenderer.
calango, calangro s. m. (Braz.) 1. popular designation of several small lizards of the genus Anisolepis. 2. (pop.): a) biceps. b) little calf, newborn calf. c) soldier of the police force.
calão (I) s. m. 1. slang, jargon. 2. argot, patois. 3. cant.
calão (II) s. m. (pl. -ões) 1. a long rowing boat with bold bow used for tuna fishing. 2. (Braz.) yoke fitted to a person's shoulders for carrying pails and other loads. 3. short wooden sticks (which are fastened to both ends of a casting net). 4. a kind of trammel net.
calapídeos s. m. (pl. (zool.) Calappidae: a warm seas crab family.
calar (I) v. 1. not to speak, keep silent. 2. to silence. 3. to conceal, hide. 4. to dissemble, disguise. 5. to impose silence. 6. to lower, let down. 7. to pass over in silence. 8. ~-se to hold one's tongue, be silent, not to answer, stop to talk.
cala-te, que me pagarás! keep quiet, you'll pay for it. ~ a baioneta to fix the bayonet. ~ sua mágoa to conceal one's grief. cale a boca! hold your tongue, shut up!, shut your mouth! ela fê-lo ~ a boca she stopped his mouth. faça-o ~! shut him up! fazer ~ to strike dumb, command silence. quem cala consente silence gives consent.
calar (II) v. to plug, remove plugs from fruits (to test their quality).
~ o melão to cut a bit out of a melon.

calásia s. f. (path.) partial separation of the cornea from the sclera.
calátide s. f. (bot.) capitulum, anthodium.
calaveira s. m. 1. (Port., prov.) foolhardy or extravagant fellow. 2. (Braz.) scoundrel, swindler, cheat. 3. f. (Port., prov.) skull, death's head. ‖ adj. m. + f. foolhardy, rash, extravagant.
calaveirada s. f. 1. rascality, crookedness. 2. swindling, cheating. 3. vagabondage, vagrancy.
calaza s. f. 1. (bot., zool., biol.) chalaza. 2. (med.) chalazion.
calazar s. m. (path.) kala azar, visceral leishmaniasis.
calázio s. m. (med.) chalazion, sty, hordeolum.
calazógamo s. m. (bot.) chalazogam.
calca s. f. act of trampling, treading on or pressing down.
calça (I) s. f. = calças pl.
~ rancheira blue jeans, jeans (plate R 6).
calça (II) s. f. a leg band or mark for poultry.
calçada s. f. 1. pavement, (U. S. A.) sidewalk, sideway (plates C 8, R 8). 2. paved street, causeway. 3. steep street or path.
calcadeira s. f. stamper, rammer, tamp, tamper (plate F 7).
calçadeira s. f. shoe-horn.
calçado (I) s. m. 1. footwear (plate B 16). 2. shoe(s), boot(s).
calçado (II) adj. having spotted legs (cattle).
calçado (III) adj. 1. paved. 2. shod, footworn.
calcador s. m. 1. stamper, rammer, tamper. 2. clamp shoe of a sewing machine (which holds the cloth at sewing).
calcadouro s. m. 1. thrashing floor, floor of a barn. 2. mash-vat. 3. frequent ramming or tamping.
calcadura s. f., calcamento m. 1. act of stamping, ramming or pressing down. 2. treading, trampling. 3. (constr.) underpinning.
calça-fecho, calça-foice s. m. (Braz., pop.) vagabond, hoodlum.
calçamento s. m. 1. paving. 2. act or method of paving. 3. pavement. 4. paviour's work.
calcâneo s. m. (anat.) calcaneus, calcaneum, heel bone. ‖ adj. calcaneal.
calcanhar s. m. 1. heel (plate C 18). 2. the hinder part of any covering for the foot (sock, shoe, etc.). andar nos ~es de alguém to follow or run after a person. dar nos ~es to take to one's heels, run away. ele não lhe chega aos ~es he is not fit to hold a candle to him, he is no match for him. ter seu ~ de Aquiles to have one's Achilles' heel, have a weak or vulnerable spot. virar nos ~es to turn on one's heels.
calcanhar-de-judas s. m. (pl. calcanhares-de-judas) (Braz.) a distant and secluded place in the mountains.
calcante s. m. (Braz., sl.) 1. shoe(s), boot(s). 2. footwear. 3. foot, feet. ‖ adj. m. + f. (pop.) of, pertaining to or relative to feet and footwear.
calção s. m. (pl. -ões) 1. trousers. 2. trunks, shorts. 3. breeches.
~ de banho bathing trunks, slips (plates B 3, R 7). ~ de montaria riding breeches.
calção-de-couro s. m. (pl. calções-de-couro), (Braz., coll.) a dauntless and pertinaceous fellow.
calcar v. 1. to tread upon, step on. 2. to smash, crush. 3. to trample on (upon). 4. to squeeze, press. 5. to oppress. 6. to grind, crunch. 7. to trip up, knock down. 8. to treat with scorn, despise, spurn. 9. to place transparent paper on a drawing in order to retrace the outlines, copy a drawing by decalcomania. 10. to model, shape, mold.
calçar v. 1. to shoe, put on shoes. 2. to boot. 3. to put on (any footwear, stockings, socks, trousers,

pantaloons, gloves). 4. to supply with shoes. 5. to pave, cover with rock or stones. 6. to edge or point with steel, coat with steel. 7. (constr.) to underprop, underset, underpin. 8. (typogr.) to key (types). 9 to wedge, cleat. 10. to suit or fit well. ~ **um carro** to prop up a car. ~ **uma roda** to scotch a wheel. **estas luvas calçam bem** these gloves fit well.

calcário s. m. (min.) generic designation of calcareous rocks. ‖ adj. calcareous, limy, chalky. ~ **oolítico** (geol.) cornbrash. **pedra -a** limestone.

calças s. f. pl. 1. trousers, pants, pantaloons (plates R 6, 7). 2. (fam.) jeans, bags, breeches. 3. women's drawers, knickers. ~ **curtas** shorts. ~ **de couro** buckskins. ~ **esporte** trunks. ~ **de montaria** riding breeches. **estar metido em** ~ **pardas** to be at a pinch, be in a tight spot. **quem veste as** ~ **nesta casa é ela** she wears the breeches in this house. **um par de** ~ a pair of bags.

calcedônia s. f. (min.) chalcedony, calcedony, hornstone.

calcedônio adj. chalcedonic, chalcedonous.

calceiforme adj. m. + f. 1. shaped like a shoe. 2. (bot.) calceiform, calceolate.

calceiro s. m. trouser maker, tailor specialized in trousers.

calcemia s. f. (med.) calcemia, excess of calcium in the blood.

calceolária s. f. (bot.) slipperwort.

calcês s. m. (naut.) masthead.

calceta (ê) s. f. (ant.) 1. fetter or shackle for the feet. 2. hard labour, penal servitude. 3. galley slave, criminal condemned to forced labour.

calcetar v. to pave, lay or cover with stone, form a flooring of.

calcetaria s. f. process or method of paving, work of a paviour.

calceteiro (I) s. m. paver, paviour, flagger.

calceteiro (II) s. m. trouser maker, trouser manufacturer.

cálcico adj. calcic.

calcífero adj. (chem.) calciferous.

calcificação s. f. (pl. -ões) calcification, calcination.

calcificado adj. calcified.

calcificar v. 1. to calcify, calcinate. 2. ~-**se** to become calcified.

calciforme adj. m. + f. calciform.

calcífugo adj. calcifugous.

calcinação s. f. (pl. -ões) calcination, act or process of calcining.

calcinado adj. calcinated.

calcinar v. 1. to calcine, reduce to lime. 2. to oxidize by the action of heat. 3. to heat excessively. 4. to burn, cremate. 5. to burn to ashes. 6. to cauterize, sear. 7. (fig.) to inflame, excite, stimulate. 8. to burn, roast.

calcinatório adj. calcinatory, serving for calcination.

calcinável adj. m. + f. (pl. -áveis) calcinable.

calcinha s. f. pantie.

cálcio s. m. (chem.) calcium (symbol Ca).

calciose s. f. (path.) calcinosis.

calcioterapia s. f. (med.) calciotherapy.

calcita s. f. (min.) calcite, calespar.

calcitrapa s. f. (bot.) star thistle, caltrop.

calcitrar v. to recalcitrate.

calciúria, calciuria s. f. (med.) calcinuria, presence of calcium in the urine.

calço s. m. 1. wedge. 2. a piece of wood or a stone used to prop up an object. 3. chock. 4. scotch, skid. 5. cleat. 6. fid. 7. trig.

calcografar v. to engrave on copper or any other metal.

calcografia s. f. chalcography, art of engraving on copper, brass or any other metal.

calcográfico adj. chalcographic(al).

calcógrafo s. m. chalcographer, chalcographist.

calçolas s. f. pl. (N. Braz.) women's drawers, knickers.

calcopirita s. f. (min.) chalcopyrite, copper ore.

calcorreada s. f. (pop.) walk, hike, journey.

calcorrear v. 1. to walk, go on foot. 2. to walk a lot. 3. to travel a long way on foot.

calcosita s. f. (min.) chalcosite, copper glance.

calçudo adj. 1. having trousers or pants. 2. wearing trousers for the first time. 3. having the legs covered with feathers (certain birds).

calculação s. f. (pl. -ões) calculation, computation, reckoning.

calculado adj. 1. calculated, computed. 2. figured, estimated, rated. 3. deliberate. 4. scheming. ‖ -**amente** adv. calculatingly. **bem** ~ well-judged. **não** ~ unreckoned.

calculador s. m. 1. calculator, reckoner, computer. 2. scheming person. 3. accountant, counter. 4. calculating machine. ‖ adj. 1. computing, reckoning. 2. calculative, calculating.

calculante adj. m. + f. calculating, performing calculation(s).

calcular v. 1. to calculate, compute, reckon. 2. to count. 3. to evaluate, estimate. 4. to conjecture, guess, figure out. 5. to presume, surmise. 6. to foresee, anticipate. 7. to prepare. 8. to premeditate. 9. to account. 10. to reflect, consider, judge. ~ **a média** to average, strike an average. ~ **mentalmente** to reckon in one's head. ~ **o diferencial** (math.) to differentiate. ~ **o valor** to appraise. **ele calculou justo** he cut it fine. **ele não calcula o que é** he doesn't guess what it is. **ele sabe bem** ~ he is good at sums, he is quick at figures. **máquina para** ~ calculating machine. **sem** ~ **os esforços** not to mention the pains.

calculável adj. m. + f. (pl. -áveis) 1. computable, calculable. 2. countable. 3. estimable.

calculista s. m. + f. 1. calculator, reckoner, computer. 2. (com.) cost accountant. 3. calculist, mathematician, arithmetician. 4. calculating or scheming person. ‖ adj. calculating.

cálculo s. m. 1. calculation, computation, reckoning. 2. (math.) calculus. 3. counting, enumeration. 4. appraisal, valuation. 5. (med.) calculus, stone, concretion. 6. account. 7. forecast. 8. estimate, estimation. ~ **aproximado** rough estimate. ~ **biliar** (path.) calculus, gallstone. ~ **da posição do navio** (naut.) dead reckoning. ~ **das probabilidades** (math.) calculus of probabilities. ~ **das variações** (math.) calculus of variations. ~ **de perdas e danos** adjustment of average. ~ **de preço de custo** costing. ~ **do valor** appraisal. **enganei-me no** ~ **I** made a mistake in my calculation, I calculated erroneously. **eu calculo que vai dar certo** I reckon it will come off well. **fazer um** ~ **errado das coisas** to reckon without one's host. ~ **mental** mental arithmetic. ~ **por alto** rough calculation. **régua de** ~**s** slide rule, sliding-rule.

calculose s. f. (med.) morbid condition characterized by the presence of calculi in the organism, calculous concretion.

calda s. f. 1. solution of sugar in hot water. 2. syroup, sirup. 3. any medicated syrup, syrupy medicine. 4. preserves, fruit cooked with sugar. 5. incandescent iron. 6. ~**s** pl. hot springs. 7. ~**s** pl. residues of alcohol distillation. 8. weld, welding.

caldário adj. thermal; of, pertaining to or relative to hot springs.

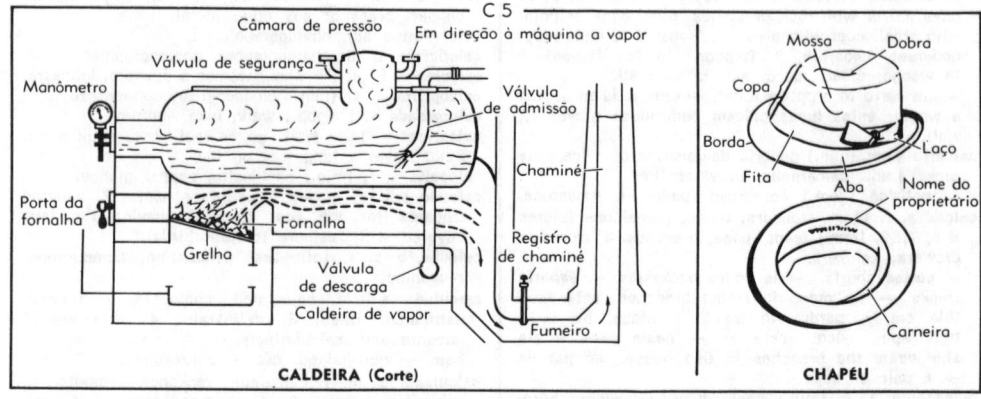

CALDEIRA (Corte)   CHAPÉU

caldeação s. f. (pl. **-ões**), **caldeamento** m. 1. act or process of making red-hot (metals). 2. welding, weld, forge welding. 3. tempering, annealing. 4. fusion. 5. mixture of races, crossbreed. 6. mixture. 7. amalgamation.

caldeado adj. red-hot, glowing, forge-welded.

caldear (I) v. 1. to make red-hot (iron or other metals). 2. to weld, forge-weld. 3. to temper, anneal. 4. to fuse, melt. 5. to unite by melting. 6. to interbreed, crossbreed. 7. to burn lime. 8. to amalgamate. 9. to blend, unite.

caldear (II) v. (S. Braz.) 1. to eat soup or broth. 2. to take preserved fruit or fruit juices.

caldeira s. f. 1. kettle, caldron. 2. boiler, seether (plate C 5). 3. hollow in the bottom of a lake (cistern, pool, well, etc.). 4. little ditch made around the trees to retain the rain-water (or manure). 5. little bay or inlet forming a natural harbour for small ships. 6. dock, quay for rowing boats or small ships. 7. furnace, firebox. ~ **cilíndrica** barrel boiler. ~ **de água benta** holy water vase. ~ **de cobre** copper (plate L 3). ~ **de pressão** pressure boiler, pressure cooker. ~ **a vapor** steam-boiler. ~ **tubular** tubular boiler.

caldeirada s. f. 1. a kettleful, quantity a kettle holds. 2. fish stew, chowder (especially when made by fishermen from fishes just caught).

caldeirão s. m. (pl. **-ões**) 1. large kettle, caldron, copper for boiling linen (plate C 6). 2. (mus.) rest, suspension. 3. (geol.) pothole in a riverbed. 4. hole in a roadbed. 5. dixie, water heater on a kitchen furnace. ~ **de lavar roupa** wash-boiler.

caldeiraria s. f. kettle or boiler factory.

caldeireiro s. m. 1. kettle maker, boilermaker. 2. coppersmith. 3. brazier, tinker. 4. (pop.) sign of coming rain. 5. (Braz.) worker in the boiler room of a sugar mill.

caldeireta s. f. mug, tankard.

caldeirinha s. f. 1. little kettle. 2. holy water vase. 3. (Braz.) a drinking cup which the wanderer wears on his belt. **estar entre a cruz e a** ~ to be between the devil and the deep sea, to be in a pinch.

caldeiro s. m. 1. cooking pot, casserole. 2. cooker, boiler. 3. bucket, pail (to draw water from a well). 4. rectangular evaporation vat in a saltern.

caldeu s. m. (hist.) Chaldean: native or inhabitant of Chaldea, Babylonian. ‖ adj. Chaldean, Chaldaic, Babylonian.

caldo s. m. 1. soup. 2. broth. 3. sauce. ~ **de cana** sugar-cane juice. ~ **de carne** bouillon, consommé, beef-tea. ~ **de carne com legumes** hotchpotch. ~ **de galinha** chicken broth. ~ **verde** a thick potato and cabbage soup. **entornaram o** ~ they made a mess of it. **muitos cozinheiros estragam o** ~ too many cooks spoil the broth. **o** ~ **está entornado** things look black. **remexer os** ~**s** to be overly concerned in a business. **você derramou o** ~**!** you have spoilt the whole show!

caldo-de-feijão s. m. (pl. **caldos-de-feijão**), (Braz., ornith.) talpacoti dove (Chamaepelia talpacoti).

caldoso adj. 1. soupy, brothy. 2. juicy. 3. succulent.

cale s. m. wooden gutter.

calear v. to limewash.

caleça s. f. (also **caleche**) 1. calash, light old-fashioned carriage. 2. fly. 3. barouche, victoria.

caleceiro s. m. coachman, carriage driver.

caledônio s. m. Caledonian: native or inhabitant of Caledonia (modern Scotland), Scotsman.

calefação s. f. (pl. **-ões**) 1. heating, warming. 2. calefaction. 3. act or method of heating.

calefaciente s. m. (med.) calefacient, a calefacient remedy. ‖ adj. m. + f. calefacient, calefactive, calefactory.

calefator s. m. calefactor, heater, radiator.

calefrio s. m. 1. fit of cold, shivering fit. 2. chill, shiver, shakes. 3. (med.) rigour.

caleidoscópio s. m. = **calidoscópio**.

caleira (I) s. f. 1. gutter, gutter pipe. 2. roofing tile.

caleira (II) s. f. prehistoric kitchen middens found on the Brazilian coast, sambaqui.

calejado adj. 1. callous, horny. 2. hardened, hardy. 3. (fig.) experienced, skilled. 4. practical, shrewd, sharp. **de mãos -as** hard-handed.

calejar v. 1. to make callous. 2. to harden, indurate. 3. to grow callous. 4. to become insensible.

calembur s. m. calembour, play on words, pun.

calemburar v. to make puns, indulge in quibbles or puns.

calemburgo s. m. play upon words, pun, quibble, paragram.

calemburista s. m. + f. punster.

calendar adj. m. + f. calendal, of or pertaining to the calends.

calendário s. m. 1. calendar, diary (plate E 2). 2. almanac. 3. chronological list or register (of documents, events). ~ **civil** calendar that considers the year as formed

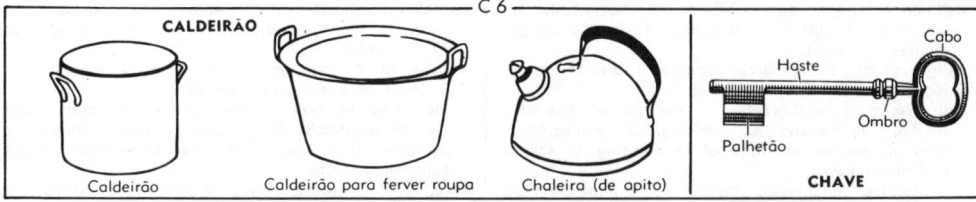

CALDEIRÃO — C 6

Caldeirão — Caldeirão para ferver roupa — Chaleira (de apito) — CHAVE

Cabo — Haste — Ombro — Palhetão — CHAVE

by determined number of days and months, in accordance with each country or people. ~ **gregoriano** Gregorian calendar. ~ **juliano** Julian calendar. ~ **lunar** calendar based on the revolutions of the moon.

calendarista s. m. + f. calendarian, calendar maker.

calendas s. f. pl. calends, kalends, the first day of the month in the ancient Roman calendar.

calênder s. m. (pl. **calênderes**) calender: mendicant dervish.

calêndula s. f. (bot.) calendula, marigold.

calentura s. f. (med.) calenture, thermic fever, heatstroke.

calepino s. m. 1. vocabulary, dictionary, lexicon. 2. (fam.) agenda, memorandum book. 3. notebook.

calete (ê) s. m. 1. gender, kind, sort. 2. quality, distinctive character. 3. category, class. 4. (Braz., fam.) complexion.

calha s. f. 1. gutter, gutter pipe. 2. channel, trough. 3. mill-race, mill-leat. 4. flume. 5. (archit.) drip. 6. chute. 7. tramway rails.

calhamaço s. m. (pop.) 1. a big, old book. 2. folio volume. 3. antiquated or old-fashioned book. 4. (vulg.) fat and ugly woman.

calhambeque s. m. 1. a small coasting vessel. 2. (fig.) an old carriage or chaise. 3. (pop.) rattletrap, jaloppy. 4. old trash.

calhambola, calhambora s. m. (Braz.) maroon, fugitive slave.

calhança s. f. (typogr.) anything which benefits the typesetter or linotypist concerning the composition.

calhandra s. f. (ornith.) calander, calandre, a large lark.

calhandra-de-crista s. f. (pl. **calhandras-de-crista**), (ornith.) crested titmouse.

calhandro s. m. 1. slop basin, slop bucket. 2. chamber-pot.

calhar v. 1. to fit well in, go into. 2. to come in time, be opportune. 3. to come about, come to pass. 4. to coincide with. 5. to be just right, suit, wear well.
velo-lhe a ~ it served his purpose.

calhau s. m. 1. fragment of a hard rock, flintstone. 2. pebble, pebblestone, stone. 3. (Braz., newspaper sl.) unimportant article held in reserve as a stop-gap matter. 4. boulder.

calhe s. f. 1. gutter, gutter pipe. 2. channel, trough, flume. 3. a narrow street, lane, walk.

calheta s. f. narrow inlet or bay, small creek.

calhorda s. m. vulgar or despicable fellow, low person, hoodlum.

cáli (I) s. m. (bot.) saltwort, barilla.

cáli (II) s. m. (chem.) alkali, potassium carbonate, potash.

caliandra s. f. common name of several ornamental plants of the genus Calliandra (family Mimosaceae).

calibração s. f. (pl. **-ões**) calibration.

calibrado adj. calibred, calibrated.

calibrador s. m. calibrator: 1. worker who calibrates. 2. gauge, caliber rule.

calibragem s. f. (pl. **-ens**) calibration, act of calibrating.

calibrar v. 1. to measure the calibre of, calibrate. 2. to gauge. 3. to standardize. 4. to give the correct calibre to. 5. to determine the bore of (a firearm).

calibre s. m. calibre, caliber: 1. the intern diameter of a firearm. 2. bore, gauge. 3. the diameter of a missile, size of a bullet. 4. dimension, measurement. 5. size. 6. capacity. 7. calibrator. 8. mark, sign (of graduations or measurements). 9. range (of firearms). 10. moulding iron (of a stuccoworker). ~ **de centragem** center-gauge. ~ **de perfuração** drill jig. ~ **de profundidade** depth gauge. **isto é uma mentira de grosso** ~ that's a monstrous lie, that's a whopper.

calibrina s. f. (Braz. sl.) any alcoholic beverage.

calibroso adj. (med.) relative to any duct (specially blood vessels) that shows expansion.

caliça s. f. pieces of dry mortar, debris, rubble.

cálice (I) s. m. 1. wine glass, liqueur-glass (plates C 14, R 5). 2. cup, chalice, calix, goblet (plate C 14). 3. (fig.) agonizing moment, anguish, ordeal, predicament.
beber o ~ **da amargura até as fezes** to drink the bowl of affliction to the dregs. ~ **de comunhão** (rel.) communion-cup.

cálice (II) s. m. 1. calyx of a flower, chalice. 2. (biol., bot.) envelope, integument.

cálice-de-vênus s. m. (pl. **cálices-de-vênus**), (bot.) angel's-trumpet.

calicerácea s. f. 1. plant of the Calyceraceae. 2. **Caliceráceas** pl. Calyceraceae: a small family of South American herbs.

caliciado adj. (bot.) caliced, chaliced.

calicida s. m. corn plaster, corn ring.

caliciforme adj. m. + f. cup-shaped, chaliced, caliciform.

calicinal adj. m. + f. (pl. **-ais**) calycinal, belonging to the calyx.

calicino adj. calycine.

calicose s. f. (med.) chalicosis: pulmonary affection caused by the inhalation of stone dust.

calicromo adj. having beautiful colours.

caliculado adj. (bot.) calyculate.

calículo s. m. calycle: 1. (bot.) epicalyx. 2. (zool.) calyculus.

cálido (I) adj. 1. hot, heated, very warm. 2. ardent, burning. 3. fiery, ablaze. 4. intense, impassioned.

cálido (II) adj. 1. shrewd, clever. 2. sagacious. 3. astute, smart.

calidoscópico adj. kaleidoscopic(al). || **calidoscopicamente** adv. kaleidoscopically.

calidoscópio s. m. kaleidoscope.

califa s. m. calif, caliph.

califado s. m. califate, caliphate, office or dignity of a kaliph.

califórnia s. f. (Braz.) 1. fortune, luck. 2. a source of riches, wealth. 3. (Port., prov.) a deep cavern.

californiano s. m. Californian: native or inhabitant of California. || adj. Californian.

califórnio s. m. (chem.) californium.

caligem s. f. (pl. **-ens**) 1. thick fog, heavy mist. 2. darkness, obscurity. 3. dimness. 4. (med.) caligo: dimness of sight.
caliginoso adj. 1. very dark, obscure. 2. dim. 3. misty, foggy. 4. tenebrous, appalling.
caligrafia s. f. calligraphy: 1. the art of beautiful writing. 2. handwriting, writing. 3. penmanship, hand. 4. manner and form of handwriting. 5. script. 6. (ironic) paw.
~ **forense** engrossing hand. ~ **vertical** vertical writing. **ele tem boa** ~ he writes a good hand. **uma** ~ **dura** a cramped hand.
caligráfico adj. calligraphic(al).
calígrafo s. m. 1. teacher of calligraphy. 2. calligrapher, calligraphist. 3. penman.
caligrama s. m. calligram.
calim s. m. (pl. **-ins**) (Braz., pop.) gipsy.
calinada s. f. 1. foolishness, folly. 2. blunder, nonsense.
calino (I) s. m. 1. blockhead, duffer. 2. blunderbuss, stupid fellow. || adj. silly, stupid, dumb.
calino (II) adj. (Port., prov.) hot, very warm, ardent.
calipal s. m. (pl. **-ais**) (pop.) eucalyptus grove.
calipígio adj. callipygian.
calipso s. m. calypso.
caliptra s. f. (bot.) a hooded corolla.
calista s. m. + f. chiropodist, pedicure.
calistenia s. f. calisthenics, callisthenics.
calisto (I) s. m. 1. unlucky fellow. 2. (fam.) person to whom a gambler attributes his bad luck.
calisto (II) s. m. little cup or chalice.
Calitricáceas s. f. pl. (bot.) Callitricaceae.
Calitriquídeos s. m. pl. (zool.) Callitrichidae, the true marmoset family.
cálix s. m. = **cálice**.
caliz s. m. (Braz.) wooden flume used in sugar mills for conveying water to the boiling vats.
calma s. f. 1. atmospheric heat, sultriness. 2. the hottest time of the day, noonday heat. 3. calm, lull. 4. serenity, composure. 5. tranquility, repose, reposedness, calmness. 6. equanimity, lenience, leniency. 7. sedateness, sobriety. 8. silence, peace. ~! keep your shirt on!, take it easy! **acabar na maior** ~ to finish at one's leisure. ~ **com isso!** hold your horses! **com** ~ at leisure. **com voz** ~ soft-voiced. **ela perdeu a** ~ she lost her temper. **ele recebeu o golpe com grande** ~ he bore the blow with great composure. **manter a** ~ to keep one's temper or countenance. **não ter nem** ~ **nem sossego** to be very restless. **o país está em** ~ the country is in peace and quietness.
calmante s. m. (med.) calmative, lenitive, sedative. || adj. m. + f. calmative, lenitive, mitigating, sedative, soothing.
calmar v. 1. to calm, quiet. 2. to tranquilize. 3. to appease. 4. to calm down. 5. to soothe, still.
calmaria s. f. 1. calm, lull. 2. becalmed sea. 3. sultriness, heat. 4. calmness, tranquility.
~ **equatorial** the doldrums.
calmeiro adj. (Braz.) navigable even in the slightest wind (said of a boat or ship).
calmo adj. 1. hot, warm. 2. sultry. 3. calm, still, quiet. 4. serene, undisturbed. 5. even-minded, even-tempered. 6. unimpassioned, lenient. 7. moderate. 8. unruffled, unmoved. 9. cool, serene. 10. stoical, dispassionate. 11. undisturbed, unembarrassed. 12. placid, silent. 13. windless. || **-amente** adv. calmly, evenly, peacefully, silently.
fique ~! keep calm!, keep your temper! **o mar está muito** ~ the sea is smooth.
calmoso adj. 1. calm, windless, still. 2. warm, hot, canicular.

calmuco s. m. Kalmuck, member of a nomad Tatar tribe (Mongolia). || adj. of, pertaining to or relative to this tribe.
calo s. m. 1. corn, callus. 2. callosity, callousness. 3. (fig.) hardness, indifference.
ele pisou no meu ~ he trod on my corn. **fazer** ~**s na paciência de alguém** to abuse someone's patience. **tirar (cortar) os** ~**s de alguém** to cut someone's corns.
calô s. m. thieves' cant, jargon of criminals and prostitutes.
calofilo adj. (bot.) having beautiful leaves.
caloji s. m. (N. Braz.) slum tenement.
calom s. m. (pl. **-ons**) a Brazilian gipsy.
calombento adj. 1. pustulate, covered with blisters. 2. covered with little knobs or earth mounds (said of a plot of land).
calombo s. m. (Braz.) 1. swelling, cyst. 2. pustule, blister. 3. mound, hillock, knoll. 4. ripples on the surface of water. 5. a race of zebu cattle.
calomelano s. m. (pharm.) calomel.
calóptero adj. (zool.) having beautiful wings.
calor s. m. 1. heat, warmth. 2. hotness, torridness. 3. sultriness, stuffiness. 4. animation, vivacity. 5. eagerness, fervour. 6. fire, fieriness. 7. (Braz.) courage, mettle.
~ **de fusão** smelting heat. ~ **específico** specific heat. ~ **humano** human warmth. ~ **febril** fever heat. ~ **radiante** radiant heat. **com** ~ fervently. **eu sinto** ~ I feel quite warm. **faz** ~ **hoje** it's warm to-day. **morrer de** ~ to swelter. **onda de** ~ heat-wave.
calorão s. m. excessive heat.
calorento adj. 1. hot, warm. 2. calorific. 3. (Braz.) sensitive to heat.
calorescência s. f. (phys.) calorescence.
caloria s. f. calorie, calory: unit of heat.
calórico s. m. caloric: the principle of heat. || adj. caloric.
calorífero s. m. heater, furnace, radiator. || adj. caloriferous, calorific, producing heat.
calorificação s. f. (pl. **-ões**) calorification.
calorífico s. m. heater, stove, radiator. || adj. caloric, calorific, producing heat. || **calorificamente** adv. calorifically.
capacidade -**a** heat capacity.
calorífugo adj. calorifugal, avoiding or dispelling heat.
calorígero adj. caloriferous, calorigenic, generating heat.
calorim s. m. (pl. **-ins**) a mollusc (Olivancillaria auricularia).
calorimetria s. f. (phys.) calorimetry.
calorimétrico adj. calorimetric(al).
calorímetro s. m. calorimeter, apparatus for measuring the specific heat.
calorização s. f. (chem.) calorization.
calor-nos-olhos s. m. (Braz., pop.) inflammation of the eyeball.
caloroso adj. 1. calm. 2. warm, hot. 3. sultry. 4. energetic, vigorous. 5. eager, ardent. 6. enthusiastic, effusive. || **-amente** adv. hotly, ardently, vigorously, effusively.
calose s. f. (bot.) callosity on certain cell walls.
calosidade s. f. 1. callosity, callousness. 2. hardened skin. 3. corn.
caloso adj. 1. having corns, affected with corns. 2. hardened, indurate. 3. corny. 4. horny, callous.
calota s. f. 1. cap, skullcap. 2. (geom., math.) spherical calotte. 3. hubcap (plate V 3). 4. (archit.) the superior part of a cupola.
~ **polar** polar icecap. ~ **craniana** brainpan.

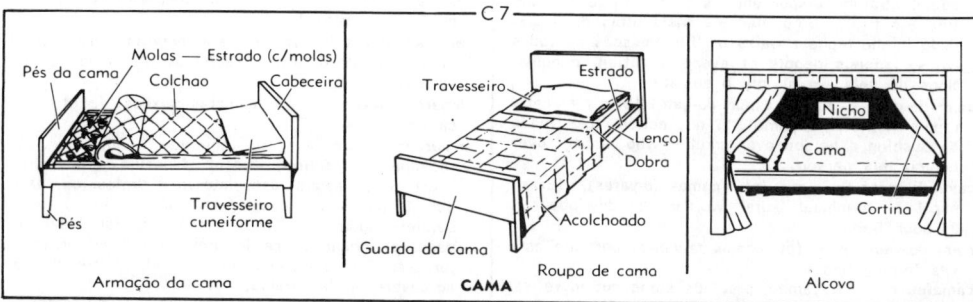

C 7

Pés da cama · Molas — Estrado (c/molas) · Colchao · Cabeceira · Travesseiro · Estrado · Lençol · Dobra · Travesseiro cuneiforme · Pés · Guarda da cama · Acolchoado · Roupa de cama · Nicho · Cama · Cortina

Armação da cama   **CAMA**   Álcova

calote s. m. 1. (fam.) unpaid debt or one contracted without intention to pay it back. 2. trick. 3. swindle, cheat.

calotear v. 1. not to pay a debt. 2. to contract debts without ability or intention to pay them back. 3. to swindle, cheat. 4. to bilk, welsh.

caloteiro s. m. 1. swindler, cheat. 2. sharper, welsher.

calotismo, caloteirismo s. m. 1. act or behaviour of a swindler. 2. crafty trick, swindle. 3. wile.

calourice s. f. 1. foolishness, folly. 2. piece of fun, jest. 3. inexperience, artlessness.

calouro s. m. 1. new pupil, new student. 2. freshman. 3. beginner, novice. 4. greenhorn. 5. a timid, bashful fellow. 6. fag.
~ **enfeitado** (fam.) student in the second year of a college or university course.

caluda interj. keep quiet!, quiet!, silence!

caluje s. m. (Braz., pop.) rude hut or shelter, cottage, thatched hut.

calumba s. f. (Braz., bot.) calumba, columba.

calumbá s. f. (Braz.) the juice of sugar cane (after its extraction).

calumbé s. m. (Braz.) oval trough or vessel used by gold and diamond washers.

calundu s. m. (Braz., pop.) 1. bad temper. 2. irascibility.

calunga s. f. (Braz.) 1. divinity of the Bantu cult. 2. fetish of the Bantu cult. 3. any small object. 4. plant of the family Simaroubaceae (Simaba ferruginea). 5. (zool.) a kind of dragonfly. 6. m.: a) a little doll. b) picture-book for little boys. c) a small rat. d) little fellow, short man. e) popular designation of a porgy. f) (pop.) Negro. g) a motorist's helper.

calungagem s. f. (pl. -ens) 1. grimace. 2. mimicry. 3. sentimental or amorous movement or look. 4. bad joke, mischievous trick. 5. ridiculous or despicable matter or thing. 6. vagrancy, vagabondage, idleness.

calungo s. m. (Braz., zool.) mouse.

calungueira s. f. (Braz.) fishing-boat.

calungueiro s. m. (Braz.) porgy fisher.

calúnia s. f. 1. act of slandering. 2. calumny, slander, calumniation. 3. defamation, detraction, vilification. 4. falsehood, imputation of evil. 5. libel. 6. scandal.

caluniado s. m. defamed person. ‖ adj. slandered, defamed.

caluniador s. m. 1. calumniator. 2. detractor, defamer. 3. disparager, maligner. 4. slanderer, vilifier. ‖ adj. calumniatory, slanderous, defamatory.

caluniar v. 1. to calumniate, slander. 2. to detract, defame. 3. to accuse falsely, belie, bespatter. 4. to scandalize, malign. 5. to backbite. 6. to asperse, traduce.

caluniável adj. m. + f. (pl. -áveis) subject or susceptible to calumny or slander.

calunioso adj. 1. calumnious, slanderous. 2. defamatory, detractive. 3. opprobrious, libelous. ‖ **-amente** adv. calumniously, slanderously, detractively, disparagingly.

calva s. f. 1. baldness, bald head, baldpate. 2. clearing in the woods. 3. (fig.) defect, fault, imperfection. 4. guilt, blame.
descobrir a ~ **de alguém** to expose someone's weakness or fault. **pôr a** ~ **à mostra** to show someone's weak points.

calvar v. to become bald.

calvário s. m. 1. Mount Calvary. 2. any elevation representing this place. 3. pedestal, base of a crucifix. 4. (ant.) ancient silver coin. 5. (fig.) toil, labour. 6. (fig.) suffering, martyrdom, torment.

calvejar v. to become bald.

calvície s. f. baldness.

calvinismo s. m. Calvinism, religious doctrine of Calvin.

calvinista s. m. + f. Calvinist, adherent of Calvinism. ‖ adj. Calvinistic(al), Calvinian.

calvinístico adj. Calvinistic(al), Calvinian.

calvo s. m. bald-headed person. ‖ adj. 1. bald, bald-headed. 2. hairless, bare. 3. without trees or any other vegetation. 4. evident, obvious (lie).

cama s. f. 1. bed (plates C 7, D 4). 2. sofa, couch. 3. resting place. 4. litter, strewing, bedding (plate E 11). 5. mattress. 6. stratum. 7. river-bed. 8. soft padding upon which fruits or fragile objects are laid. 9. (Braz.) usual resting place of cattle (in a pasture).
~ **beliche** double-decker bed. ~ **de campanha** camp-bed, tent bed. ~ **de casal** double bed. ~ **dobradiça** folding-bed, press-bed. **arejar a** ~ to air the bed. **armar uma** ~ to put up a bed. **arrumar uma** ~ to make a bed. **cair de** ~ to fall ill. **ele teve de recolher-se à** ~ he had to take to his bed. **ele ficou de** ~ **durante três anos** he lay on his back for three years. **estar de** ~ to be sick. **fazer a** ~ to make one's bed. **fazer a** ~ **a alguém** to accuse falsely or slander s. o., intrigue against s. o. **ficar na** ~ to remain in bed, stop in bed. **ir para a** ~ to go to bed, bed. **mudar a roupa de** ~ to sheet a bed. **prostrado na** ~ bedridden. **bed-fast. tirar da** ~ to drive s. o. out of his (her) bed.

camacã s. m. (Braz., bot.) bastard cedar, bay cedar.

camaçada s. f. 1. a beating, thrashing, spanking. 2. endemic venereal disease.

camacho s. m. cripple. ‖ adj. crippled.

camada s. f. 1. layer. 2. great quantity. 3. (geol.) stratum, seam, bed (plate F 7). 4. (fig.) class, category. 5. lay, tier. 6. coat, coating, couch (of paint).
as diversas ~**s sociais** the various strata of society.
~ **de concreto** surface concrete. ~ **social** class,

social stratum. **dispor em** ~s to put in layers. **em três** ~s triple-tiered. **nas** ~s **mais altas da sociedade** in the highest walks of life. **pessoas de todas as** ~s **sociais** people of every condition. **pneumáticos de seis** ~s six-ply pneumatics.

cama-de-gato s. f. (pl. **camas-de-gato**) (Braz.) 1. cat's cradle (children's game). 2. a practical joke made by pushing a person over another who is bent over behind this person.

cama-de-varas s. m. (pl. **camas-de-varas**), (Braz., pop.) 1. farmhand, rural worker. 2. day-labourer. 3. poor farmer.

cama-de-vento s. f. (pl. **camas-de-vento**) portable canvas folding bed.

camafeu s. m. 1. cameo, precious stone cut in relief. (plate J 2). 2. (pop.) very ugly woman. 3. (obs.) royal seal showing the ruler's bust. 4. baguette, baguet, intaglio.

camafonje s. m. (Braz.) 1. mischievous street Arab. 2. hoodlum, scoundrel. 3. base or vile person.

camaísma s. f. (Braz.) a tree from which the native Indians make arrows.

camal s. m. (pl. **-ais**), (hist.) camail: the neck and shoulder-guard of an armour.

camáldulas s. f. pl. large beads of a rosary.

camáldulo s. m. (rel.) Benedictine monk.

camaleão (I) s. m. (pl. **-ões**) 1. (zool.) chameleon. 2. (fig.) a fickle or inconstant person. 3. (fig.) hypocrite, pretender.

camaleão (II) s. m. (pl. **-ões**), (Braz., pop.) 1. the ridge between the ruts of a worn-out road. 2. knolls or earth mounds in a flat plot of land.

camaleônico adj. chamaleonic.

camalha s. f. woollen hood.

camalhão (I) s. m. (pl. **-ões**) 1. a piece of cultivated land lying between two furrows or trenches. 2. the ridge between the ruts of a worn-out dirt road.

camalhão (II) s. m. (pl. **-ões**), (ant.) a large camail.

camalho s. m. (ant.) camail.

camalote s. m. (S. Braz.) floating island of water-plants.

camândulas s. f. pl. the large beads of a rosary.

camapu s. m. (Braz.) 1. (bot.): a) cape gooseberry. b) strawberry-tomato. c) groundcherry. 2. (Amazonas) name of the water bubbles which are caused by the respiration of the arapaíma.

câmara s. f. 1. chamber, room. 2. bedroom. 3. camera. 4. audience room, stateroom. 5. town-council, municipal council. 6. town hall. 7. upper house and lower house of the parliament, House of Lords, House of Commons. 8. ecclesiastical court, consistory. 9. cabin (of a ship). 10. (anat.) aqueous chamber of the eye. 11. chamber of a gun. ~ **alta** the senate. ~ **baixa** the house of deputies. ~ **cinematográfica** motion picture camera. ~ **de ar** inner tube, air vessel (of a tire) (plate P 11). ~ **de carga** (mining) blasthole. ~ **de combustão** (mech.) combustion chamber. ~ **de compressão** airlock. ~ **de coração** (anat.) auricle, ventricle. ~ **de pressão** pressure chamber (plate C 5). ~ **de senado** senate. ~ **escura** 1. camera obscura. 2. darkroom. ~ **fotográfica** photographic camera. ~ **frigorífica** refrigerating chamber, cool chamber. ~ **letal** lethal chamber. ~ **municipal** municipal council. ~ **real** royal court, royal chamber, royal treasury. **filme em** ~ **lenta** slow motion picture. **moço de** ~ valet de chambre, groom of the bedchamber.

camará s. m. (bot.) red sage.

câmara-ardente s. f. (pl. **câmaras-ardentes**) mourning chamber (where the body of the deceased is laid out in state).

camará-branco s. m. (pl. **camarás-brancos**), (Braz., bot.) yerba sagrada.

camará-bravo s. m. (pl. **camarás-bravos**), (Braz., bot.) milkweed, blood flower, asclepias (Asclepias curassavica).

câmara-caixão s. f. (pl. **câmaras-caixões**) (phot.) box camera.

camarada s. m. + f. 1. comrade, companion. 2. roommate. 3. fellow student. 4. chum, crony, pal, sport. 5. colleague, associate in a profession, partner. 6. (N. Braz.) lover, paramour. 7. m.: a) (mil.) soldier, buddy. b) (navy) mate. c) farmhand. d) page, attendant. e) cattle drover. f) hired prospector. ‖ adj. 1. companionable. 2. kind, friendly. 3. agreeable. 4. favourable, advantageous. **ele é um** ~ **um tanto esquisito** he is rather a queer fellow. **faça um preço** ~! make a favourable (cheap) price! **vento** ~ agreeable or favourable wind.

camaradagem s. f. (pl. **-ens**) 1. comradeship, companionship. 2. good fellowship. 3. companionableness, companionability. 4. society. 5. solidarity, brotherhood.

câmara-de-ar s. f. (pl. **câmaras-de-ar**) inner tube (of a pneumatic).

camará-de-cheiro s. m. (pl. **camarás-de-cheiro**), (Braz.) plant of the laurel family (Acrondiclidium camará).

camará-de-espinho s. m. (pl. **camarás-de-espinho**) (Braz., bot.) spiny lantana.

camaradeiro adj. 1. chummy, sociable. 2. communicative. 3. friendly, amicable. 4. obliging.

camaradesco adj. 1. companionable. 2. kind, friendly, amicable. 3. agreeable. 4. favourable, advantageous.

camaradinha s. f. (bot.) a verbena (Verbena chamaedryfolia).

camarajuba s. f. (bot.) spiny lantana (Lantana aculeata).

camarambaia s. f. (bot.) a primrose willow (Jussiaea octonervia).

camaranchão s. m. = **caramanchão**.

camarão s. m. (pl. **-ões**) 1. (zool.) shrimp, prawn. 2. (ant.) an earthen vessel. 3. hook (for holding a lamp or chandelier).

camarão-de-água-doce s. m. (pl. **camarões-de-água-doce**) (ichth.) crayfish, crawfish.

camarão-rosa s. m. (pl. **camarões-rosas**) (Braz.) 1. common designation of shrimp species: a) Penaeus brasiliensis; b) Penaeus aztecus; c) Penaeus duorarum. 2. pink shrimp, pink prawn.

camararia s. f. office or duties of a chambermaid, groom, steward(ess) or chamberlain.

camarário s. m. ecclesiastical councillor. ‖ adj. of, pertaining to or relative to the council of an administrative court or tribunal.

camarata s. f. 1. dormitory, bed-chamber(s) in boarding-schools. 2. a group of beds in a dormitory.

camaratinga s. f. (bot.) yerba sagrada (Lantana brasiliensis).

camarazal s. m. (pl. **-ais**) a grove of red sage trees.

camarção s. m. (pl. **-ões**) 1. sandy soil. 2. tract of sandy land. 3. a thicket of small trees.

camarço s. m. 1. misfortune, calamity. 2. illness, sickness, disease. 3. (cards) capot. 4. bad luck. **dar** ~ to get all the tricks (at cards).

camareira s. f. 1. chambermaid. 2. lady-in-waiting, waiting maid, dresser. 3. tire woman.

camareiro (I) s. m. 1. chamberlain. 2. groom-in-waiting. 3. valet. 4. room servant (in a hotel), steward. 5. chamber-pot.

camareiro (II) s. m. shrimping net, bow-net.

camargo s. m. (S. Braz.) solution of coffee with sugar and fresh milk.

camarilha s. f. 1. camarilla. 2. clique, cabal. 3. group of favourites (surrounding royalty or high-standing personalities).

camarim s. m. (pl. -ins) 1. little room, cabinet. 2. dressing-room, tiring-room. 3. (rel.) space immediately over the tabernacle reserved for the exposition of the holy Host.

camarinha s. f. 1. room, bedroom. 2. hiding place, hide-out. 3. fruit of the crakeberry shrub, crowberry. 4. little round drops, droplets. 5. beads of sweat.

camarista s. m. 1. city councilman, alderman. 2. m. + f. Lord or Lady of the royal household, Lord chamberlain, Lady of the queen's bed-chamber.

camarlengo s. m. = camerlengo.

camarodontes s. m. pl. (zool.) Camarodonta, an order of echinoderm animals, including the sea urchin.

camaroeiro s. m. 1. shrimping net, bow-net. 2. shrimper. 3. black bow-net used as a storm flag or storm signal.

camarote s. m. 1. (theat.) box, box seat, loge (plates P 2, T 3). 2. cabin in a ship, berth.

camarote-do-torres s. m. (pl. camarotes-do-torres), (Braz., theat.) place in the highest gallery, the cheapest seats in the theater.

camaroteiro s. m. 1. boxkeeper. 2. box office clerk. 3. steward, cabinboy.

camartelada s. f. a blow with a stone-mason's hammer.

camartelo s. m. 1. a stone-mason's or bricklayer's hammer. 2. (fig.) destructive blow, demolition.

camarupi, camarupim (pl. -ins) s. m. (Braz., ichth.) tarpon.

camatanga s. f. (Braz.) a parrot (Amazona rhodocoryta).

camba (I) s. f. 1. felly, segment of the rim of a wheel. 2. curved beam of a plough. 3. small handmill. 4. bridle bar. 5. gore of a cape or skirt.

camba (II) s. f. 1. (Braz., ant.) girl slave employed as housemaid, nurse or companion. 2. m. + f. despicable Indian.

cambacã s. f. bastard cedar (Guazuma ulmifolia).

cambacica s. f. (ornith.) honey creeper.

cambada s. f. 1. a lot of things (birds, fishes, beads, etc.) strung on a thread. 2. a bunch of keys. 3. boodle, caboodle. 4. (fig.) gang, mob of thieves. 5. rabble, dregs of society.

cambadela s. f. 1. somersault. 2. heavy, headlong fall. 3. skip, trip.

cambado adj. 1. bent, twisted. 2. lopsided. 3. bandy-legged, bow-legged. 4. bootworn. 5. afflicted with chigoe fleas.

cambaí s. m. (bot.) shrub of the family Fabaceae (Sesbania marginata).

cambaiar v. to become twisted, lopsided or bowlegged.

cambaico s. m. native or inhabitant of Cambay (India). || adj. of, pertaining to or relative to this city.

cambaio adj. 1. bent, twisted. 2. disabled, hobbling. 3. bandy-legged, bow-legged. 4. weak-legged.

cambal s. m. (pl. -ais) guard plate around a millstone.

cambalacho s. m. 1. deceitful and fraudulent barter. 2. exchange, truck, barter. 3. permutation, interchange. 4. trick, swindle. 5. connivance, collusion.

cambaleante adj. m. + f. 1. reeling, staggering. 2. faltering. 3. groggy, dizzy. 4. tottering, tottery. || ~mente adv. reelingly, totteringly, wobblingly.

cambalear v. 1. to sway, reel. 2. to stagger, falter, totter. 3. to wobble. 4. to trip.

cambaleio s. m. 1. staggering, reeling. 2. stagger, totter.

cambalhota s. f. 1. caper, skip. 2. somersault, somerset. 3. capriole, gambade. 4. tumble, fall. 5. heavy fall, crashing down. 6. cart-wheel, flip-flap. 7. frisk, dido.
dar uma ~ 1. to suffer a heavy fall. 2. to turn a somersault. 3. to tumble head over heels.

cambalhotar v. 1. to tumble head over heels. 2. to suffer a heavy fall. 3. to turn somersaults, somerset. 4. to caper, capriole.

cambão s. m. (pl. -ões) 1. extension shaft or pole (used when a cart is drawn by two yokes of oxen). 2. yoke. 3. heavy piece of wood hung on the neck of roving cattle (used as a trammel). 4. a pair of oxen.

cambapé s. m. 1. trap, snare. 2. trick, ruse. 3. (wrestling) Cornish hug. 4. trip. 5. cheat, fraud.

cambar v. 1. to crook. 2. to twist, bend. 3. to become distorted or crooked. 4. to become bow-legged. 5. to change, turn around, turn from one side to the other. 6. to sway, reel, stagger. 7. to hobble. 8. to hang down. 9. to incline, bend. 10. to bring down, let down. 11. (obs.) to change, exchange. 12. (naut.) to change the course, veer.

cambará s. m. (Braz., bot.) red sage.

cambará-branco s. m (pl. cambarás-brancos), (bot.) yerba sagrada.

cambará-de-espinho s. m. (pl. cambarás-de-espinho), (bot.) red sage.

cambará-do-campo s. m. (pl. cambarás-do-campo) (Braz.) designation of two small trees: Moquinia gardneri and Vochysia sessilifolia.

cambará-roxo s. m. (pl. cambarás-roxos), (bot.) lilac lantana.

cambariçu s. m. (N. Braz.) 1. a kind of tom-tom used by Indians of the Amazonas region. 2. act of beating the tom-tom. 3. signalization by tom-tom.

cambau s. m. triangular wooden frame hung on the neck of goats, sheeps or other animals to prevent their passage through a fence.

cambembe s. m. (Braz., hist.) 1. a free farmhand who worked together with Negro slaves. 2. humble backwoods people. || adj. m. + f. 1. insignificant, unimportant. 2. clumsy, awkward. 3. bent, twisted. 4. lopsided. 5. bandy-legged.

cambeta (ê) s. m. + f. bandy-legged, footworn or weak-legged person. || adj. 1. bent, twisted. 2. weak-legged, hobbling. 3. bandy-legged, bow-legged.

cambetear v. 1. to sway, reel, stagger. 2. to hobble, limp.

cambeúva adj. m. + f. having inwards bent horns (cattle).

cambeva s. m. hammerhead shark.

cambiador s. m. 1. money-changer, banker. 2. exchanger.

cambial s. f. (pl. -ais) draft (drawn on a person in another city of the same country). || adj. m. + f. cambial, of or relative to the exchange of money or bills.

cambialidade s. f. exchangeability, characteristic of the bills of exchange.

cambiante s. m. 1. a changeable colour. 2. gradual differentiation of colour. 3. indistinct hue or colour. || adj. m. + f. 1. changing. 2. changeable, variable. 3. iridescent. 4. shot coloured. 5. indistinct (in hue or colour).

cambiar v. 1. to change (coins, money, drafts, bills). 2. to exchange. 3. to convert, interchange. 4. to barter, trade. 5. to permutate, permute. 6. to truck, traffic. 7. to change colours. 8. to make

changes (opinions, principles, system). 9. to undergo changes. 10. to move, remove.
~ a vela to trim a sail. **o vento está cambiando** the wind is shifting.
cambiário adj. relative to the juridical discipline of the bills of exchange.
cambiável adj. m. + f. exchangeable.
cambica s. f. (Braz.) a dish made from Barbados cheries, sugar and manioc flour.
cambindas s. f. pl. (Braz.) popular folk dance.
câmbio (I) s. m. 1. exchange of coins, banknotes, bills. 2. change, valuta. 3. barter, barter-trade. 4. conversion, interchange. 5. permutation, commutation. 6. banking business. 7. a banker's or money-changer's profits. 8. (mech.) switchgear, switching, change gear (plate M 13).
~ exterior foreign exchange. **~ manual** exchange made in cash where one of the currencies is foreign. **~ marítimo** loan contract warranted by a ship and her cargo. **~ negro** black market. **alavanca de ~** (mech.) gear lever, gear-shift lever, switch lever. **ao ~ do dia** at the current rate, at the rate of the day. **corretor de ~** bill broker. **garfo de ~** (mech.) striking fork. **letra de ~** paper, bill of exchange. **o ~ está muito alto** the rate of exchange is very high. **pelo ~ de** on the parity of. **preço de ~** rate of exchange. **tomar a ~** to take up money at interest. **venderemos com a taxa de ~ ao par** we shall sell at par.
câmbio (II) s. m. (bot.) cambium.
cambiroto s. m. (N. Braz.) headland, firm claybank projecting into the sea.
cambista s. m. + f. 1. cambist. 2. money-changer, banker. 3. exchange broker, bill broker. 4. ticket scalper, ticket jobber. 5. street peddler of lottery tickets.
cambitar v. to load an animal with a pack (of firewood, sugar-cane), put a load on the back of a pack animal.
cambiteira s. f. a small locomotive used to transport sugar-cane from the fields to the mill.
cambiteiro s. m. a driver of pack animals (especially on large-scale plantations).
cambito s. m. 1. a leg of pork. 2. thin leg. 3. hat-rack, coat-hanger. 4. a wooden double-hook used instead of a packsaddle. 5. a kind of reel used to wind strings of tobacco. 6. wooden stick used to tighten the straps of a packsaddle. 7. popular name of a dragonfly.
cambo (I) s. m. 1. long wooden pole used to pick fruit from trees or to beat them down. 2. extension pole or shaft (used when a cart is drawn by two yokes of oxen). 3. yoke. 4. a string of things (birds, fishes, beads).
cambo (II) adj. 1. crooked. 2. bent, twisted. 3. disabled. 4. hobbling. 5. bandy-legged, bow-legged.
camboa s. f. ·1. a shallow pond or lake near the seashore (where fishes are caught at low tide). 2. fish-garth.
camboatã s. m. (bot.) guara, guara tree (Cupania oblongifolia, Cupania racemosa).
~·bravo a shrub of the family Sapindaceae (Matayba guyanensis).
camboatá s. m. common name of several freshwater catfishes.
cambojano adj. Cambodian.
cambona s. f. 1. (naut.) veering, sudden change of the course. 2. (naut.) sudden shifting of sails, tacking. 3. backspin, reversal of rotation. 4. caper skip. 5. somersault.
cambondo s. m. 1. paramour. 2. lover, sweetheart. 3. friend. 4. young man, youth, lad.

cambota s. f. 1. (archit.) a semicircular framework used at the construction of archs and vaults; centering. 2. rim of a wheel. 3. (naut.) counter timber. 4. somersault. 5. m. + f. (S. Braz.) a bandy-legged or bow-legged person. || adj. m. + f. bow-legged, bandy-legged.
~s do navio (naut.) compass-timber. **voltar uma ~** (fam.) to turn a somersault.
cambraia s. f. 1. cambric: a fine closely woven linen or cotton fabric. 2. shalloon. 3. batting. || adj. m. + f. completely white (said of domestic animals).
~ transparente book-muslin.
cambraieta s. f. cambric of an inferior quality, lawn.
Câmbria s. f. (poet.) Cambria (modern Wales, England).
cambriano adj. Cambrian: 1. of or relative to Cambria, Welsh. 2. (geol.) of, pertaining to or designating the earliest division of the Paleozoic era.
câmbrico s. m. the Celtic (Keltic) language. || adj. Cambrian.
cambucá s. m. fruit of the **cambucazeiro**.
cambucarana s. f. (Braz.) a shrub of the family Myrtaceae (Eugenia cambucarana).
cambucazeiro s. m. a Brazilian myrtle tree (Myrcia plicato-costata).
cambuci s. m. 1. a tree of the myrtle family (Palvaea langsdorffii). 2. the fruit of this tree.
cambueiras s. f. pl. (Braz.) heavy spring rains (in September).
cambueiro s. m. 1. a violent south wind, souther, storm from the south. 2. heavy spring rains. 3. downpour, sudden shower, squall (before the beginning of the rainy season).
cambuí s. m. 1. (also **cambuizeiro**) tree of the myrtle family (Myrcia sphraerocarpa). 2. the fruit of this tree.
cambuizal s. m. (pl. -ais) a grove of **cambuí** trees.
cambulha s. f. 1. a bunch of keys. 2. a lot of little things.
cambulhada s. f. 1. a bunch of keys. 2. a string of things (birds, fishes, beads). 3. (fig.) intrigue. 4. confusion. 5. (fam.) hodgepodge, medley.
cambulho s. m. clay rings used by fishermen as sinkers.
cambuquira s. f. (S. Braz.) 1. pumpkin vine sprout. 2. roast beef served with a stew of pumpkin vine sprouts.
camburão s. m. Black Maria (police car).
cambuta s. m. 1. short, rachitic person. 2. bandy-legged person. || adj. 1. rachitic. 2. stunted, dwarfed. 3. crooked, twisted. 4. bandy-legged, bow-legged.
came s. f. (mech.) cam (on a wheel or shaft).
camelão s. m. 1. camlet: a fabric of camel's hair. 2. impermeable woollen fabric used for raincoats and capes. 3. impermeable cloth made from goat's hair.
~ ordinário common camlet.
cameleão s. m. (pl. **-ões**) 1. (zool.) chameleon, cameleon. 2. (fig.): a) a fickle or inconstant person. b) hypocrite, false pretender. 2. show-off.
cameleira s. f. camellia.
cameleiro s. m. camel driver, cameleer.
camélia s. f. (also **cameleira**) (bot.) camellia.
camelice s. f. 1. (pop.) foolishness, silliness. 2. stupidity. 3. blunder, nonsense. 4. brutality.
camélidas s. m. pl. (zool.) Camelidae, the camel family.
camelídeo s. m. any animal of the family Camelidae. || adj. of, pertaining to or relative to the Camelidae.
cameliforme adj. m. + f. resembling a camel, cameloid, cameline.
camelino adj. cameline.

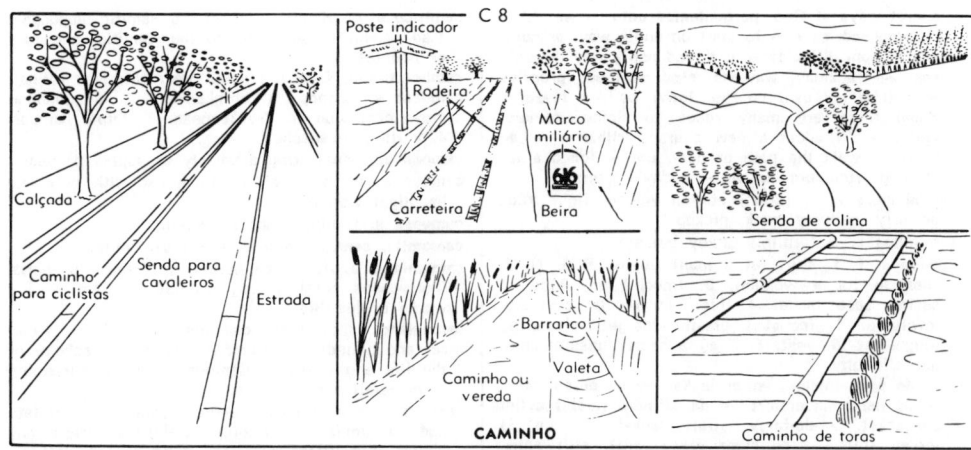

C 8

Poste indicador

Rodeira

Marco miliário

Carreteira

Beira

Calçada

Caminho para ciclistas

Senda para cavaleiros

Estrada

Senda de colina

Barranco

Caminho ou vereda

Valeta

CAMINHO

Caminho de toras

camelo s. m. 1. (zool.) camel, Bactrian camel. 2. (naut.) hawser. 3. ancient piece of ordnance. 4. (fig.) stupid fellow, blockhead, dunce.
lã de ~ mohair, camel's hair. **palha de ~** camel's hay.
camelô s. m. street peddler, hawker of cheap articles, pitcher.
camelório s. m. (fam.) big ass, big fool, dunce.
camenas s. f. pl. (poet.) the Muses.
câmera s. f. = **câmara.**
camerlengado s. m. 1. office, authority and functions of a camerlingo. 2. time during which a camerlingo exercises his authority.
camerlengo s. m. camerlingo, cardinal chancellor of the papal government in Rome.
cametau s. m. (Braz., ornith.) the horned screamer (Anhima cornuta).
camião s. m. (pl. **-ões**) = **caminhão** (II).
camilha s. f. 1. little bed, pallet. 2. sofa, couch. 3. easy chair.
camiliana s. f. collection of the works of the Portuguese author Camilo Castelo Branco.
camilista, camilianista s. m. + f., **camiliano** m. admirer or scholar of Camilo Castelo Branco's works.
camilano adj. of, pertaining to or relative to the works of Camilo Castelo Branco.
camina s. f. (Braz., Amazonas) a crude fish trap.
caminaú s. m. (Braz.) lake formed by the floodwaters of a river.
caminhada s. f. 1. walk, walking. 2. excursion, journey. 3. stroll, hike, jaunt, rove. 4. wayfaring. 5. a long walk, a long distance to be travelled all over. **~ inútil** fool's errand. **após uma ~ de três horas** after a three hours walk. **daqui até lá é uma boa ~** it is a good distance from here over there, it is a long way to that place.
caminhador s. m. 1. walker, hiker. 2. passer-by, pedestrian. 3. foot traveller, wayfarer. ‖ adj. walking.
caminhamento s. m. (topogr.) the exact distance between two places.
caminhante s. m. + f. 1. walker, hiker. 2. passer-by, pedestrian. 3. foot traveller, wayfarer. ‖ adj. walking, going, travelling.
caminhão (I) s. m. (pl. **-ões**) gum benzoin.
caminhão (II) s. m. (pl. **-ões**) lorry, truck, camion, autotruck, motor lorry (plate V 3).
~ basculante dumper-truck, dump-car, dump-cart.

caminhar v. 1. to walk, go on foot. 2. to hike, march. 3. to journey, travel. 4. to tramp. 5. to travel on foot. 6. to put in motion. 7. to camp, campaign. 8. to steer, sail, navigate. 9. to go or move towards, set out for. 10. to come or go after, proceed, follow.
~am muita terra they went a long way. **~am penosamente** they plodded along, they trudged along.
caminheiro s. m. 1. walker, hiker. 2. wayfarer, traveller. 3. messenger, express courier. 4. muleteer. 5. (ornith.) name of two pipits of the family Motacillidae (Anthus chii, Anthus natereri). ‖ adj. going, walking or moving easily and rapidly.
caminho s. m. 1. road, way, drive (plates A + C 8). 2. street. 3. path, pathway, walk. 4. highway. 5. route, course. 6. track, trail. 7. lane. 8. bypass, short cut, side trail. 9. direction. 10. (fig.) way, means, expedient. 11. passage, pass. 12. approach. 13. distance, long way travelled on foot. 14. (fig.) norm, rule, principle. 15. destination. 16. tendency. **~ batido** beaten track, trodden path. **~ de cabras** a steep, narrow footpath. **~ de carros** cart-way, carriageway. **~ de entrada** gateway. **~ de ferro** railway, railroad. **~ de gado** drift-way. **~ de toras** road paved with logs. (U.S.A.) corduroy road (plate C 8). **~ para ciclistas** cycle track (plate C 8). **~ para pedestres** footway. **~ público** highway. **~ reto** right or correct way. **~s cruzados** crossroads. **~ secreto** (fig.) by-way. **a ~** 1. on the way. 2. (naut.) under way, under weigh. **abrir ~** to pioneer, open the way, dig one's way, break a path. **a meio ~** halfway. **atravessar o ~** to cross the path. **cada qual tomou o seu ~** they each went their different ways. **~ da vida** walk of life. **cortar o ~** to take the shortest way (or cut). **ele atrapalhou meu ~** he put a spoke in my wheel. **ele está no meu ~** he is in my road. **eles erraram o ~** they lost their way. **ele tomou o ~ do mal** he fell on evil courses. **estar a ~** to be on the road. **estar no ~** to stand in the way. **fora do ~** afield, out of the way. **guarda de ~** highway guard; (railway) linekeeper. **indicar novos ~s** to take the lead. **ir fora do seu ~** to be out of one's way, (fig.) to go astray. **mostrar o ~** to show the right way (also fig.). **não é um ~ fácil** it's no royal road. **não sei que ~ hei de tomar** I don't know which way to turn. **~ no ~ errado** on the wrong tack. **no ~ para o sucesso** on the highroad to success. **o ~ pisado** the beaten track. **os ~s de Deus** the

secret ways of God. **perguntamos pelo** ~ we asked our way. **pôr-se a** ~ to start on one's way. **procurar seu** ~ **com dificuldade** to thread one's way through. **sem** ~ trackless, wayless. **sigo os meus próprios** ~ I take my own course. **todos os** ~**s levam a Roma** there are many roads to Rome. **tomarei outro** ~ I'll adopt a new course. **trilhar o** ~ **do dever** to walk the path of duty. **um** ~ **longo** a far or long fetch. **um dia de** ~ a day's journey.

caminhonete s. f. (Braz.) station wagon, light truck or lorry, delivery truck, pickup.

camiranga s. f. (ornith.) turkey buzzard.

camisa s. f. 1. shirt (of a man) (plates R 6, 7). 2. chemise (of a woman). 3. (mech.) any kind of casing, case, jacket. 4. (biol., bot.) outer covering, involucre. 5. (constr.) plaster, parget, plastering rough-cast. 6. vest. 7. (fig.) a nearly unsurmountable difficulty.
~ **de água** (mech.) water jacket. ~ **de ar** air case. ~ **de baixo** undershirt. ~ **de cilindro** (tech.) cylinder-jacket. ~**-de-força** strait jacket. ~ **de lã** jersey shirt. ~ **de rigor** dress shirt, stiff shirt. ~ **de vela** (naut.) bunt. ~ **do milho** hull of corn. ~ **engomada** evening shirt, boiled shirt. ~ **esporte** tunic shirt. ~ **negra** black shirt; (pol.) Blackshirt. **deixaram-no sem** ~ they just stripped him, they stripped him naked. **ele é capaz de lhe dar sua última** ~ he'd give you the shirt off his back. **em mangas de** ~ in shirt-sleeves. **não se meta em** ~ **de onze varas** don't put yourself into a mess. **não ter uma** ~ **para vestir** not to have a shirt to one's back. **pano de** ~ shirting. **peito de** ~ shirt-front. **punhos de** ~ shirt cuffs. **roubaram-no até a** ~ they bled him white. **tirar a** ~ **a alguém** to fleece s. o., to bring s. o. to ruin. **venderam até a** ~ they lost their whole property.

camisa-de-vênus s. f. (pl. **camisas-de-vênus**) condom: contraceptive or preventive sheath.

camisão s. m. (pl. **-ões**) 1. a long shirt. 2. a long, white linen vestment resembling an alb. 3. (Braz., pop.) peasant, yokel.

camisaria s. f. 1. shirt factory. 2. shirt shop, haberdashery.

camiseira (I) s. f. female shirtmaker.

camiseira (II) s. f. a closet for shirts, a chest of drawers (for shirts).

camiseiro (I) s. m. 1. a shirtmaker, shirt manufacturer. 2. proprietor, manager or salesman of a shirt shop, haberdasher.

camiseiro (II) s. m. a chest of drawers for keeping shirts.

camiseiro (III) adj. of, pertaining to or relative to shirts, their manufacture and sale.

camiseta s. f. 1. chemisette, sleeveless bodice worn by women. 2. undershirt, singlet. 3. vest (plate R 6).

camisinha s. f. 1. little shirt, children's shirt. 2. the upper, usually embroidered part of a woman's chemise. 3. chemisette. 4. petticoat.

camisola s. f. 1. night-shirt, night-dress (plate R 6). 2. night-gown, bed-gown. 3. camisole, corset cover. 4. vest, waistcoat. 5. smock, smock-frock.

camisola-de-força s. f. (pl. **camisolas-de-força**) strait jacket.

camisolão s. m. night-shirt.

camisote s. m. 1. a fine shirt with ruffles or embroideries. 2. (ant.) mail shirt of an armour.

camisu s. m. (N.E. Braz.) tee shirt.

camita s. m. + f. (bib.) Hamite, one of the descendants of Ham, Noah's second son. ‖ adj. Hamitic, pertaining to or relative to the Hamites.

camítico s. m. Hamitic: any of the Hamitic languages. ‖ adj. Hamitic, belonging to the Hamitic languages or peoples.

camocica s.m. (zool.) a small deer (Mazama rufina).

camoeca s. f. (pop.) 1. drunkenness. 2. somnolence, drowsiness due to drunkenness. 3. torpor, stupor. 4. a fit of headache.

camoês adj. desinating a variety of apples or pears.

camões s. m. sg. + pl. (pop.) a car with only one headlight working.

camoesa s. f. pippin apple, pippin.

camomila, camomilha s. f. (bot.) camomile.

camomiana s. f. 1. collection of Camões's works (Portuguese poet). 2. any treatise on Camões, his works or his life.

camoniano s. m. (also **camonista** m. + f.) 1. admirer and collector of Camões's works. 2. scholar of the life and works of Camões. ‖ adj. of, pertaining to or relative to Camões.

camorra s. f. 1. (hist.) a secret society of terrorists and criminals (at Naples, Italy). 2. (fig.) any clique of political terrorists, gang of criminals. 3. (S. Braz.) quarrel, strife. 4. (S. Braz.) provocation.

camote s. m. (S. Braz.) courtship. 2. love-making, love-affair. 3. flirtation. 4. lover, sweetheart.

camotim s. m. (pl. **-ins**) (Braz.) a pottery vessel used by Indians as a grave repository for their dead.

campa (I) s. f. 1. gravestone, tombstone. 2. grave, tomb.

campa (II) s. f. a little bell, handbell.

campação s. f. (pl. **-ões**) 1. camping. 2. camp, encampment. 3. gladness, joy. 4. vanity, conceit.

campador s. m. (Braz., pop.) night-walker, night-stroller who looks for amorous adventures.

campainha s. f. 1. small bell, handbell (plate B 11). 2. call-bell. 3. tinkler. 4. (archit.) bell-shaped architetonic ornament. 5. (bot.) bellflower, bluebell. 6. newsmonger, gossipper. 7. (anat.) uvula.
~ **da boca** (anat.) uvula, glottis. ~ **da porta** door-bell. ~ **de alarma** alarm bell, warning bell. ~ **da missa** saint's bell. ~ **elétrica** (tech.) electric bell (plate C 9). **a** ~ **está tocando** the bell rings. **atender a** ~ to answer the bell. **instalar uma** ~ to hang a bell.

campainhada s. f. 1. ringing of a bell. 2. pulling the bell-rope. 3. act of pushing the bell button.

campainha-dos-jardins s. f. (pl. **campainhas-dos-jardins**), (bot.) Canterbury bell, cuckooflower.

campainhar v. to ring the bell, pull the bell-rope, push the bell button.

campainha-vermelha s. f. (pl. **campainhas-vermelhas**), (bot.) Brazilian morning-glory.

campal s. m. (pl. **-ais**) (Braz.) a tract of open level country in the woods.‖ adj. m. + f. of, pertaining to or relative to the open field or country; rural.
batalha ~ a pitched battle. **missa** ~ celebration of Mass in the open air.

campana s. f. 1. bell, handbell. 2. (archit.) bell: the bell-shaped part of the capital of a column between the abacus and the neck moulding. 3. (mus.) the bell-shaped opening of horns, trumpets and similar instruments. 4. sleeve of a terra cotta pipe.

campanado adj. campaniform, bell-shaped.

campanário s. m. 1. campanile. 2. bell tower, belfry, steeple (plate A 4). 3. (fig.) parish, parishioners collectively. 4. (fig.) village.

campanha s. f. 1. open field country. 2. campaign, champaign. 3. wide plains, lowland. 4. camp, military camp, encampment. 5. (mil.) a series of coordinated military operations in open country, pitched battle. 6. (fig.) systematic operations in order to bring about some desired result.

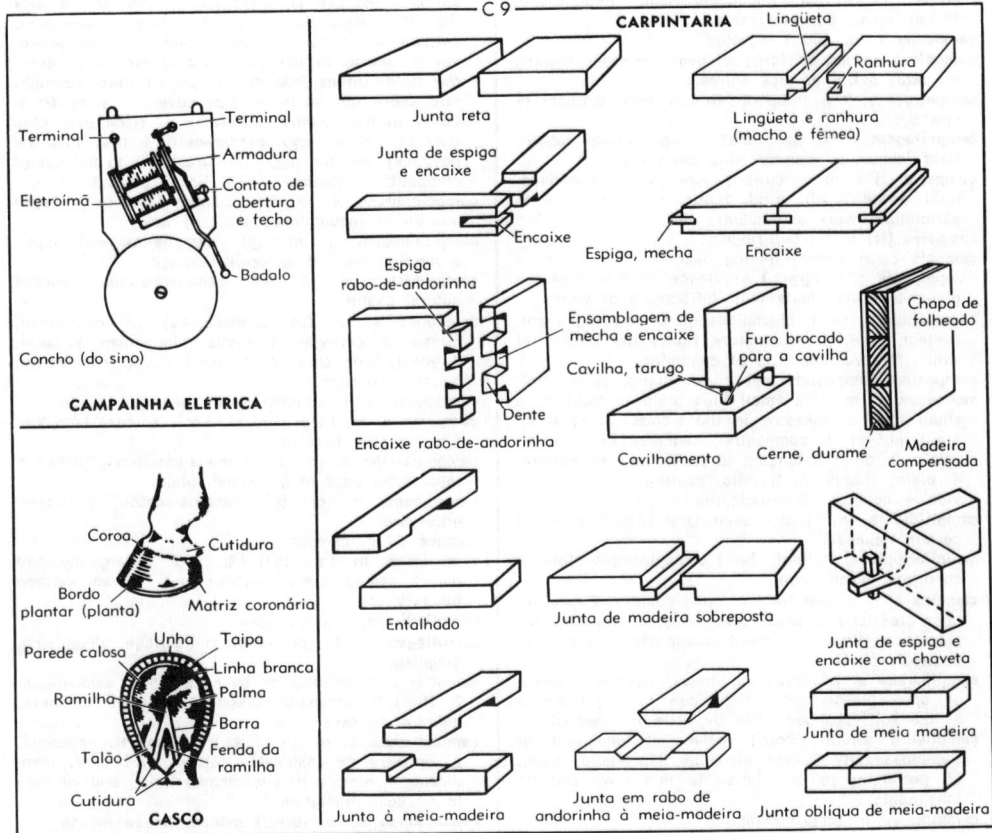

C 9

CAMPAINHA ELÉTRICA

Terminal, Armadura, Contato de abertura e fecho, Terminal, Badalo, Eletroímã, Concho (do sino)

CASCO

Coroa, Cutidura, Bordo plantar (planta), Matriz coronária, Parede calosa, Unha, Taipa, Linha branca, Ramilha, Palma, Barra, Talão, Fenda da ramilha, Cutidura

CARPINTARIA

Junta reta, Lingüeta, Ranhura, Lingüeta e ranhura (macho e fêmea), Junta de espiga e encaixe, Encaixe, Espiga, mecha, Encaixe, Espiga rabo-de-andorinha, Ensamblagem de mecha e encaixe, Furo brocado para a cavilha, Chapa de folheado, Cavilha, tarugo, Concho (do sino), Dente, Encaixe rabo-de-andorinha, Cavilhamento, Cerne, durame, Madeira compensada, Entalhado, Junta de madeira sobreposta, Junta de espiga e encaixe com chaveta, Junta de meia madeira, Junta à meia-madeira, Junta em rabo de andorinha à meia-madeira, Junta oblíqua de meia-madeira

~ **eleitoral** electoral campaign, campaign, electioneering. ~ **militar** (mil.) expedition. **abrir a** ~ to enter the field. **cama de** ~ field-bed. **cozinha de** ~ field kitchen. **entrar em** ~ to take the field. **meter-se em** ~ to begin the campaign, enter the field. **peça de** ~ (mil.) field gun, field-piece. **serviço de** ~ (mil.) field duty. **subsídio de** ~ (mil.) field-allowance.

campaniforme adj. m. + f. (bot.) campaniform.

campanil s. m. (pl. -is) bell metal.

campanólogo s. m. (mus.) carilloneur, one who plays on a carillon, campanaloger, campanologist.

campanudo adj. 1. bell-shaped. 2. campaniform, campanulate. 3. (fig.) pompous, ostentatious. 4. (fig.) bombastic, high-flown. 5. hyperbolic(al.) 6. inflated, bloated.

campânula s. f. 1. a bell-shaped glass, bell-glass, bell jar. 2. cloche. 3. campanula: any plant of the genus Campanula, bellflower. 4. (bot.) bell. 5. (electr.) petticoat insulator.

campanulácea s. f. 1. a plant of the family Campanulaceae. 2. ~s pl. Campanulaceae: a large family of herbs, shrubs and trees.

campanuláceo adj. (bot.) campanulaceous.

campanulado adj. 1. bell-shaped. 2. (bot.) campanulaceous. 3. campanulate, campaniform.

campanular (I) adj. 1. bell-shaped. 2. (bot.) campanulaceous. 3. campanulate, campaniform, campanular.

campanular (II) v. to tinkle or ring like bells.

campão s. m. (pl. -ões) (Braz.) a huge tract of open grassland or field.

campar v. 1. to camp. 2. to encamp, pitch a camp. 3. to sleep out of doors. 4. (Braz.) to stroll around at night looking for amorous adventures. 5. (fig.) to boast, brag, talk big. 6. to be remarkable, eminent or distinguished. 7. to shine, be brilliant. 8. to come out well. 9. to win a victory, be successful. 10. to take to flight.

campeã s. f. championess.

campeação s. f. (pl. -ões) (Braz.) act of riding all over the range looking for stray cattle or sick animals.

campeador s. m. 1. cowboy, hand on a cattle ranch. 2. one who is remarkable for his exploits, champion. ‖ adj. 1. rural, rustic. 2. of or relative to the duties of a cowboy. 3. remarkable, extraordinary.

campeão s. m. (pl. -ões) 1. (hist.) knight who fought in a tournament. 2. defender, paladin. 3. champion. champ. 4. ace. 5. protagonist. 6. ringer. 7. box champion. 8. fighter, combatant.

campear v. 1. to look for stray animals. 2. to look for, search for. 3. to fetch, bring in. 4. to display, show off. 5. to boast of (about). 6. to camp, encamp, pitch camp. 7. to live in the country. 8. to battle, fight, struggle against. 9. to win a victory, be victorious or triumphant. 10. to examine carefully. 11. to ride over the range looking into every corner. 12. to gain the upper hand, predominate. 13. to excel, be remarkable.

campeche s. m. (bot.) logwood.

campeio s. m. act of riding all over the range looking for stray cattle or sick animals.

campeirada s. f. a group of farmers, rural workers or cowboys.

campeiragem s. f. (pl. -ens) 1. agricultural labour, field labour. 2. country life, camp life.

campeiro (I) s. m. 1. cowboy, wrangler. 2. farmhand, rural worker. || adj. rural, rustic, of or relative to agricultural work and country life.

campeiro (II) s. m. bell-ringer.

campelo s. m. (Braz.) fishing gear.

campenomia s. f. (gram.) accidence: that part of the grammar which deals with inflections of words.

campeonato s. m. 1. championship. 2. sporting event, contest, bout. 3. eliminatory fights the winner of which receives the title of champion.

campesino, campesinho adj. rural, rustic, campestral.

campestre s. m. 1. a small high plain or field. 2. a small field or meadow in the woods. 3. clearing. || adj. m. + f. 1. campestral, campestrian. 2. rural, rustic. 3. of or belonging to fields and agriculture. 4. plain, simple. 5. bucolic, pastoral.
vida ~ country life, rustication.

campilídio s. m. (bot.) secondary fructification of certain lichens.

campilotropia s. f. (biol., bot.) campylotropic state or condition of an ovule.

campina s. f. 1. vast tract of open country. 2. prairie, open grassland. 3. plain, level land. 4. lea, meadow, natural pasture. 5. (zool.) Campine: a breed of domestic fowls.

campinarana s. f. (Braz., Amazonas) extensive space of open prairie-land which, due to improvement of the soil, changes little by little into woodland.

campineiro s. m. (Braz.) native or inhabitant of Campinas (city in the state of São Paulo). || adj. of, pertaining to or relative to this town and its inhabitants.

camping s. m. (Engl.) camping.

campino s. m. 1. farmer, rural worker, farmhand. 2. herdsman, herder. || adj. rural, rustic, campestral.

campir (arts) to outline the horizon in a drawing or painting.

campista s. m. cowboy in search of stray cattle or sick animals.

campo s. m. 1. field, corn land. 2. open country, prairie, meadow, grassland (plate A 4). 3. court, flat open place in front of the farmhouse. 4. village square. 5. camp, encampment. 6. arena, ring, 7. space, area. 8. opportunity, occasion. 9. (arts) background of a drawing or painting. 10. (her.) field: the whole surface of an escutcheon. 11. ground or prime colour of a cloth or painting. 12. territory, realm. 3. (sports) playing field, play-ground. 14. scope, range.
~ **de ação** field of activity, effective range. ~ **de aviação** air-field, flying field, aviation ground. ~ **de batalha** field, battlefield. ~ **de concentração** concentration camp. ~ **de desvio** deflecting field. ~ **de engorda** pasture for fattening cattle, winter pasture. ~ **de exercício** drilling camp. ~ **de futebol** football field, soccer field, (coll.) gridiron (plate F 9). ~ **de gelo** ice-field. ~ **de pouso** (aeron.) landing field. ~ **de radiação** radiation field. ~ **elétrico** electric field. ~ **gravitacional** gravitational field. ~ **magnético** magnetic field. ~ **para jogos** playing field, playfield. ~ **petrolífero** oil-field. **Campos Elísios** Elysian fields. ~ **visual** field of vision, field of view, verge. **abrir o** ~ to take the lead. **andar pelos** ~s to ramble through the fields.

as duas equipes entraram em ~ both teams took the field. **casa de** ~ country-house, country-seat. **cultivar o** ~ to till the ground. **em** ~ afield. **em** ~ **aberto** in the open. **entrar em** ~ to enter the field. **intensidade do** ~ (phys.) field strength. **isto cobre um vasto** ~ that covers a wide field. **no** ~ in the country, affield. **o** ~ **ficou para eles** they carried the day. **perderam o** ~ they lost the day, they lost the play. **pôr fora de** ~ to put out of competition. **queimar** ~ (S. Braz., pop.) to lie.

campo-dobrado s. m. (pl. **campos-dobrados**), (Braz.) uneven or mountainous tract of land.

campo-imagem s. m. (pl. **campos-imagem**) (opt.) projection area of an optical image.

campo-nativo s. m. (pl. **campos-nativos**), (Braz.) natural pasture.

camponês s. m. (pl. **camponeses**) 1. countryman, farmer. 2. cottager. 3. rustic, ploughman, peasant. 4. yokel, boor, churl. || adj. rural, rustic, campestral, bucolic, churlish.

camponesa s. f. countrywoman, peasant woman.

campônio s. m. (depr.) yokel, boor, country bumpkin. || adj. rustic, boorish.

campo-parelho s. m. (pl. **campos-parelhos**), (Braz.) a level open tract of grassland, plain.

campo-santo s. m. (pl. **campos-santos**) cemetery, graveyard.

campus s. m. campus.

camucim s. m. (pl. -ins) (Braz.) 1. a large-mouthed jar. 2. small black earthen pot. 3. an earthen funerary urn.

camuflado adj. camouflaged.

camuflagem s. f. (pl. -ens) camouflage, disguising, disguise.

camuflar v. 1. to disguise by camouflage, camouflage. 2. (fig.) to disemble, disguise. 3. (fig.) to mask, hide. 4. to fake.

camumbembe s. m. (N. Braz.) 1. vagrant, vagabond. 2. ordinary or despicable fellow. 3. beggar, mendicant. 4. simple backwoodsman living and working in a sugar plantation.

camundongo s. m. (Braz.) mouse, house mouse.

camunheca s. f. (Braz., pop.) drunken spree, binge.

camurça s. f. 1. (zool.) mountain goat, wild goat, chamois. 2. shammy, chamois leather. || adj. chamois-coloured.

camurçado adj. 1. chamois-coloured. 2. dressed or prepared like chamois leather.

camuri s. m. (Braz., Amazonas) small float used to support the bait line and to indicate the bite of a fish.

camurim s. m. (pl. -ins) (Braz., ichth.) robalo, snook.

camuripema s. m. (Braz., ichth.) a tarpon in its first stages of development.

camuripim (pl. **ins, camurupi, camurupim**) (pl. -ins) s. m. (Braz., ichth.) a tarpon.

cana s. f. 1. (bot.) cane, reed. 2. canna, any plant of the genus Canna. 3. sugar-cane. 4. haulm, stalk. 5. (anat.) an elongated cylindrical bone. 6. (Braz., sl.) prison, gaol, jail.
~ **da Índia, ~ de Bengala** fine Indian cane. ~ **de pescar** fishing-rod. ~ **de trigo** stalk of wheat. ~ **do leme** tiller (plate B 10). **chupar a** ~ (pop.) to howl with the dogs. **correr as** ~s to hurry away. **nó da** ~ knot or joint of a cane. **ter uma voz de** ~ **rachada** to chatter like a cracked kettle.

canabrás s. f. (bot.) cow-parsnip (Heraclium sphondylium).

canaca s. m. + f. Kanaka. a native Hawaiian.

canácea s. f. 1. any cannaceous plant. 2. **Canáceas** pl. Cannaceae: a small family of herbs (order Musales).

canáceo adj. (bot.) cannaceous.

canada (I) s. f. a blow with a cane.

canada (II) s. f. canada: ancient Portuguese liquid measure (2.622 l).

canada (III) s. f. 1. narrow trail, foot-path. 2. stakes driven into the river-bottom to indicate a ford. 3. ruts (of a road).

cana-de-açúcar s. f. (pl. canas-de-açúcar) sugar-cane (Saccharum officinarum).

cana-de-jacaré s. f. (pl. canas-de-jacaré), (bot.) a horsetail (Equisetum martii).

cana-de-macaco s. f. (pl. canas-de-macaco), common name of several plants of the ginger family (genus: Costus).

canadense s. m. + f. Canadian: native or inhabitant of Canada. ‖ adj. Canadian.

cana-de-são-paulo s. f. (pl. canas-de-são-paulo) (Braz. bot.) a palm tree (Chamaedorea lindeniana).

canadiano s. m. Canadian: native or inhabitant of Canada. ‖ adj. Canadian.

canado s. m. khanship: office, dignity and authority of a khan.

cana-do-brejo s. f. (pl. canas-do-brejo) (bot.) cardamom.

cana-do-reino s. f. (pl. canas-do-reino) (bot.) great reed, giant reed, reed-grass.

canafístula s. f. (bot.) 1. canafistula. 2. purging-cassia, cassia fistula. 3. pudding-pipe tree.

canafístula-verdadeira s. f. (pl. canafístulas-verdadeiras) drumstick tree.

canal (I) s. m. (pl. -ais) 1. canal. 2. waterway, watercourse, stream. 3. fosse, ditch, moat. 4. gutter. 5. channel, cut, groove. 6. conduit, duct, tube. 7. river-bed. 8. (anat.) meatus. 9. race, sluice. 10. river-branch, inlet of the sea. 11. (fig.) any intermediary element, medium, way, means. 12. (tech.) runway, fairway. 13. strait. 14. dike. 15. (radio, television) special wave-length of a radio or television transmitter. Canal da Mancha English Channel, (poet.) Silver Streak. ~ de alimentação (mech.) feeder. ~ de comunicação a communication channel. ~ de drenagem underdrain. ~ da uretra (anat.) urinary duct. ~ de televisão television channel. ~ de ventilação air flue, airway, cooling vent, (plate L 2). pelos canais competentes through official channels. ~ para gás de escape waste-gas flue. ~ subterrâneo underground channel.

canal (II) s. m. (pl. -ais) (Port., prov.) reed plot, cane plot.

canaleta s. f. gutter.

canalete s. m. 1. a small channel or canal. 2. groove. 3. furrow, rut. 4. race, leat.

canalha s. f. 1. rabble, mob. 2. dregs of society, scum; vulgar, low people. 3. m. + f. shameless fellow, rotter; wretch, miscreant; scoundrel, crook. ‖ adj. m. + f. 1. shameless, shameful. 2. disreputable, disgraceful. 3. infamous, vile, nefarious. 4. shifty, crooked.

canalhada, canalhice s. f., canalhismo m. 1. mean, base or vile action. 2. meanness, lowness, baseness. 3. rascality. 4. dirty trick, piece of roguery. 5. cheating, swindling.

canaliculado adj. (bot.) canaliculate, canaliculated.

canalículo s. m. 1. a small channel or canal. 2. groove. 3. furrow, rut. 4. (anat., bot.) canaliculus.

canaliforme adj. m. + f. canaliform, like a canal or groove.

canalização s. f. (pl. -ões) 1. canalization. 2. system of canals. 3. drainage system, sewerage, drains.

canalizador s. m. canal or sewerage constructor.

canalizar v. 1. to canalize, canal. 2. to construct a canal. 3. to sluice. 4. (also fig.) to provide with an outlet. 5. (fig.) to direct into channels.

canalizável adj. m. +f. (pl. -áveis) capable of being canalized.

canana s. f. a leathern cartridge box.

cananeu s. m. Cananaean: native or inhabitant of Canaan. ‖ adj. Canaanitic.

cananga s. f. a nutmeg tree (Myristica macrophylla).

canapé s. m. 1. settee. 2. couch, sofa. 3. canapé, appetizer.

canapu s. m. (Braz., bot.) a ground cherry.

canarana s. f. (Braz.) common name of several gramineous plants (of the genera Paspalum and Panicum).

canária s. f. (ornith.) female canary, hen-canary.

canaria s. f. large tubes, pipes or conduits collectively.

canarim s. m. + f. (pl. -ins) native or inhabitant of Goa (in former Portuguese India). ‖ adj. of, pertaining to or relative to Goa and its inhabitants.

canário (I) s. m. 1. (ornith.) canary, canary bird. 2. (fig.) a good singer. 3. native or inhabitant of the Canary islands (Span. possession). 4. (bot.) canary-bird flower. ‖ adj. of, pertaining to or relative to the Canary islands.

canário (II) s. m. a lively old French dance.

canário-da-terra s. m. (pl. canários-da-terra) common name of two birds of the family Fringillidae (Sicalis flaveola and Sicalis pelzelni).

canário-do-brejo s. m. (pl. canários-do-brejo) common name of several small birds of the family Dendrocolaptidae (esp. Synallaxis ruficapilla).

canário-do-campo s. m. (pl. canários-do-campo), (ornith.) a bird of the finch family.

canário-do-mato s. m. (pl. canários-do-mato) tanager: bird of the family Tanagridae (Piranga saira).

canas s. f. pl. leather straps or thongs (of a harness).

canastra s. f. 1. big basket made from thin and flexible strips of wood. 2. dorser, dosser, pannier. 3. wicker-basket. 4. (Braz., pop.) back, shoulders. 5. (Braz., pop.) hunchback. 6. (Braz., sl.) police raid. bater a ~ (Braz., sl.) to hit the bucket, die. pessoa com costas de ~ a person with good broad shoulders, kindhearted person.

canastrada s. f. 1. the load a large basket holds, a basketful. 2. a quantity of baskets, lots of baskets. 3. (collectively) the objects in a basket.

canastrão s. m. (pl. -ões) 1. a big hamper or wicker--basket. 2. old and outworn horse. 3. (Braz.) a cross-breed of pigs. 4. (theat. sl.) a bad actor, mediocre performer.

canastreiro s. m. 1. basketmaker, basket manufacturer. 2. basket vendor. 3. street vendor who carries his wares in a big basket. 4. special basket for the transport of fishes.

canastrel s. m. (pl. -éis) 1. small hamper or basket. 2. basket with a long handle. 3. a large hamper.

canastro s. m. 1. a splint basket with a broad rim. 2. (pop.) the human body, trunk.

cânave s. m. 1. hemp, hemp plant. 2. hempen rope.

canaveira s. f. hemp field, hemp plot, hemp plantation.

canavial s. m. (pl. -ais) place where reeds grow, reed plot.

canaz s. m. a big dog (also fig.)

cancã (I) s. m. cancan: a lively French dance and dance music.

cancã (II) s. m. (ornith.) masked duck.

cancaborrada s. f. 1. foolishness, foolery. 2. blunder. 3. botch, badly or clumsily executed work. 4. confusion, mess.

cancanista s. m. + f. cancan dancer. ‖ adj. of, pertaining to or relative to a cancan and its accompanying music.

cancão s. m. (pl. -ões) (ornith.) a jay.

canção s. m. (pl. -ões) 1. song. 2. singing. 3. chant. 4. chanson, folksong, ballad. 5. strain, tune, air. ~ **báquica** drinking-song. ~ **de amor** love-song. ~ **de Natal** noel, Christmas carol. ~ **fúnebre** epicedium, dirge, elegy. ~ **popular** folksong. ~ **sacra** hymn. **entoar uma** ~ to strike up a song.

câncaro s. m. (Braz.) one of the mountings of a door.

cancela s. f. 1. a grilled or grated door, wicket. 2. gate, farm gate. 3. barrier, railway gate.

cancelação s. f. (pl. -ões) cancellation.

cancelado adj. cancelled, abrogated, void.

canceladura s. f., **cancelamento** m. 1. act of cancelling. 2. cancellation. 3. abrogation, annulment, invalidation. 4. crossing or wiping out. 5. cassation, expunction. 6. withdrawal.

cancelar v. 1. to cancel. 2. to cross out, blot out, wipe out. 3. to annul, revoke, recall. 4. to invalidate, nullify. 5. to abolish. 6. to suppress, omit, delete. 7. to undo, unmake. 8. to abrogate. 9. to vitiate, vacate.

cancelário s. m. (ant.) cancellarius, chancellor, actual or honorary head of a university.

cancelável adj. m. + f. (pl. -áveis) 1. subject to cancellation. 2. abolishable, abrogable. 3. voidable.

cancelo (ê) s. m. small wicket or farm gate, rustic corral gate.

câncer s. m. (pl. **cânceres**) cancer: 1. (astr.): a) the fourth sign of the zodiac. b) Crab: zodiacal constellation. 2. (med.) malignant growth of tissue, canker, carcinoma, erosion.

cancerizar v. 1. to cancerate. 2. to canker. 3. to grow into a cancer, become cancerous. 4. (fig.) to rot, decay.

canceriforme adj. m. + f. (med.) cancriform, cancerous, cancroid.

cancerização s. f. (pl. -ões) cancerization, canceration.

cancerizar v. 1. to cancerate. 2. to canker. 3. to grow into a cancer, become cancerous.

cancerologia s. f. (med.) cancerology, oncology.

cancerológico adj. cancerologic(al), oncologic(al).

canceroso s. m. a person suffering from cancer. || adj. cancered, cancerous, cankered, affected with cancer.

cancha s. f. 1. race track. 2. football field, playing field, playground. 3. court, ground. 4. (brick-yard) place where raw bricks and tiles are deposited. 5. (Braz.) slaughterhouse.

canchal s. m. (pl. -ais) great quantity, abundance.

cancheado adj. dilacerated (said of the dry leaves of maté).

cancheador s. m. leaf cutting machine (for maté production).

canchear v. to dilacerate the dry leaves of the maté plant.

cancheiro adj. accustomed to races, race-broken (said of horses).

cancioneiro s. m. book or collection of songs, rhymes or poetry.

cancionista s. m. + f. composer of songs, ballad writer.

cançoneta s. f. 1. light and graceful little song. 2. lay, ditty. 3. canzonet, chansonnette.

cançonetista s. m. + f. 1. composer of songs. 2. ballad writer. 3. singer. 4. vocalist, balladier.

cancra s. f. (Braz.) sudden violent downpour.

cancrejo s. m. (ant.) crab.

cancro s. m. 1. (med.): a) generic designation of malignant tumours. b) cancer, canker, chancre. 2. canker of a plant. 3. dog, dog-bolt. 4. clamp,

holdfast, vice. 5. (fig.) deadly evil, inveterate vice. 6. (astr.) cancer. ~ **duro** (med.) hard chancre. ~ **mole** (med.) soft chancre.

cancróide adj. m. + f. cancriform, cancroid.

cancrose s. f. (bot.) citrus canker.

candado s. m. the part of a hoof which lies between the frog and the rim of the outer wall.

candango (I) s. m. nickname given to Portuguese settlers by African natives.

candango (II) s. m. (Braz.) 1. an evil individual. 2. a person with bad taste. 3. designation of the workers who participated in the construction of Brasília.

cande (I) s. m. (Port. India) a narrow pass, ravine, gorge.

cande (II) adj. crystallized, candied.

candeada, candeeirada s. f. a lampful of oil, the quantity of oil necessary to fill a lamp.

candeeiro s. m. 1. lamp, chandelier, candelabrum. 2. hanging lamp, sconce. 3. an oxcart driver. 4. street lamp.

candeia (I) s. f. 1. lamp, light. 2. candle. 3. common name of several shrubs of the genera Lychnophora, Piptocarpha, Vanillosmopsis and Vernonia. 4. ~**s** pl. Candlemas. **andar de** ~ **às avessas** to be on ill terms, be at variance. **bico de** ~ lamp burner.

candeia (II) s. m. + f. dandy or extremely elegant woman. || adj. elegant, beautiful.

candeio s. m. torch.

candela s. f. 1. lamp, light. 2. (opt.) candela, the unit of luminous intensity.

candelabro s. m. 1. chandelier, candelabrum. 2. hanging lamp, pendant lamp. 3. electrolier, gaselier, lighting fixture. 4. plant of the milkwort family (Polygala hygrophila). 5. girandole (fireworks).

Candelária s. f. 1. (rel.) Candlemas. 2. **candelária** (bot.) campion.

candelária-dos-jardins s. f. (pl. **candelárias-dos-jardins**) (bot.) rose-campion, mullein pink.

candeliça s. f. (naut.) small hoisting tackle, burton.

candelinha s. f. 1. a small candle. 2. (med.) catheter.

candembe s. m. (Braz.) fishing tackle.

candência s. f. candescence, white heat.

candente adj. m. + f. candescent, glowing, burning, ardent.

candial adj. m. + f. (pl. -ais) snow-white (said of a certain kind of wheat which yields a snow white flour).

candiar v. (Braz.) to guide a team of oxen or an oxcart.

cândida s. f. (N. Braz., pop.) white rum, sugar-cane brandy.

candidatar-se v. 1. to present o. s. as candidate. 2. to be a candidate for, put o. s. up as a candidate. 3. to make an application for (or to). 4. to stand for, throw in for. 5. to contend in rivalry, vie for.

candidato s. m. 1. candidate. 2. applicant. 3. contestant. 4. aspirant. **apresentar-se como** ~ to come forward as a candidate. **apresentar um** ~ to run a candidate. **ele é** ~ **à reeleição** he is up for reelection. **ser** ~ **para o parlamento** to stand for Parliament.

candidatura s. f. 1. candidateship, candidature. 2. claim, aspiration. 3. (fig.) solicitation, request.

candidez, candideza s. f. 1. whiteness, pureness. 2. (fig.) sincereness.

candidizar v. 1. to make white or pure. 2. to act sincerely.

cândido adj. 1. white, snow-white. 2. pure, innocent. 3. sincere, open, frank. 4. ingenuous, naive. 5.

candid, fair. 6. free. 7. simple. 8. truthful. ||
-amente adv. candidly, purely, sincerely, naively.
candil (I) s. m. (pl. **-is**) 1. lamp, light. 2. candle. 3.
phosphorescence of the water.
candil (II) s. m. (pl. **-is**), (Asia) 1. an ancient coin.
2. an ancient dry measure.
candil (III) adj. m. + f. (pl. **-is**) crystallized, candied.
candilar v. 1. to candy, coat with sugar. 2. to crystallize. 3. to conserve by boiling with sugar.
candimba s. m. (N. Braz.) 1. suffering. 2. distress,
anguish. 3. toil, labour. 4. hardship.
candimbá s. m. (N. Braz.) old household furniture,
trash.
candiota s. m. + f. Candiot, Candiote: native or inhab-
itant of Candia, Cretan. || adj. Candiot(e) Cretan:
of, pertaining to or relative to Candia or Crete.
candiru s. m. (ichth.) candiru (Vandelia cirrhosa).
candiru-branco s. m. (pl. **candirus-brancos** (Braz.,
ichht.) an Amazonian freshwater fish (Cetopsis
coecutiens).
candiubá s. f. (Braz., bot.) uva grass.
cando s. m. the part of a hoof which lies between
the frog and the rim of the outer wall.
candombe s. m. (Braz.) 1. shrimp net, bow-net. 2. a
lively Negro dance with foot-stamping and hand-
-clapping.
candombeiro s. m. (Braz.) 1. a **candombe** dancer. 2.
shrimp fisher.
candomblé s. m. (Braz.) 1. each one of the annual
voodooistic feasts. 2. rites of voodooism. 3. a
voodooistic ceremony or session. 4. any place where
voodoo rites are practised.
candonga (I) s. f. contraband of provisions and consumer goods (to avoid the payment of consumer
taxes).
candonga (II) s. f. 1. flattery, fawning. 2. dissimulation, shamming. 3. feigned friendliness or love. 4.
intrigue. 5. malicious gossip. 6. (Braz.): a) delight,
enchantment. b) passion, love. c) dearly beloved
person, darling.
vem cá, minha ~! come here, darling!
candongar (I) v. 1. to run contraband (of consumer
goods), smuggle.
candongar (II) v. 1. to flatter, fawn upon. 2. to
wheedle, cajole. 3. to feign friendliness or love. 4.
to intrigue, embroil. 5. to slander, gossip. 6. to
scheme, hatch plots.
candongueiro (I) s. m. 1. flatterer, adulator. 2.
wheedler, cajoler. 3. intriguer, intrigant. 4. troublemaker. 5. liar, impostor.
candongueiro (II) s. m. contrabandist.
candonguice s. f. 1. flattery, fawning. 2. dissimulation, shamming. 3. feigned friendliness or love. 4.
intrigue. 5. malicious gossip, slander.
candor s. m. (poet.) whiteness, pureness, innocence.
candoroso adj. (poet.) 1. white, snow-white. 2. pure.
3. innocent, guileless. 4. naive, simple.
candura (I) s. f. 1. whiteness, shining whiteness. 2.
pureness, purity. 3. innocence, guilelessness. 4.
maidenliness. 5. simplicity. 6. fairness, uprightness.
7. sincerity.
candura (II) s. f. dugout or canoe made from the
trunk of palm trees.
caneado adj. (N. Braz., pop.) drunk, tipsy, tight.
caneca s. f. mug, can, cup, tankard (plates C 14,
20, V 2).
escavadeira de ~s spoon dredge.
canecada s. f. the quantity a mug holds, a mugful.
caneco (I) s. m. a deep large mug, beer mug, a
deep tankard.
caneco (II) s. m. (Braz., pop.) the devil.
canéfora s. f. (archit.) canephorus: architectonic representation of a basket-bearing maid or woman.

caneiro s. m. 1. a narrow channel or canal. 2. river-
-crossing, ford. 3. the deepest part of the river-
-bed. 4. rocky creek, a narrow recess in a steep
and rocky shore. 5. fish-garth.
caneja s. f. (ichth.) dogfish, dog shark.
canejo adj. dog-like, canine.
canela (I) s. f. 1. the fragrant bark of the cinnamon
tree, cassia. 2. (bot.) cinnamon, canella. 3. (Braz.)
popular name of numerous plants of the laurel
family (esp. of the genera Nectandra and Ocotea).
água de ~ cinnamon water. **cor de ~** cinnamon
coloured, snuff coloured.
canela (II) s. f. 1. shinbone, shin (plate C 18). 2.
(anat.) tibia. 3. cannon, cannon-bone, shank (plates
C 12, G 1).
dar às ~s to bolt, run away. **ele tem ~s de maçarico** he has long and thin legs. **ensebar as ~s** to
take to flight. **esticar as ~s** (pop., sl.) to kick the
bucket, die.
canela (III) s. f. a weaver's quill or spindle.
caneláceas s. f. pl. (bot.) Canellaceae, the cinnamon
family.
canelada s. f. a blow on the shin-bone.
canela-de-ema s. f. (pl. **canelas-de-ema**), (bot.) tree-
-lily.
canela-de-velha s. f. (pl. **canelas-de-velha**), (bot.)
zinnia.
canelado adj. grooved, fluted.
caneladura s. f. 1. groove. 2. channeling, fluting. 3.
(bot.) striation.
canelagem s. f. (pl. **-ens**) 1. (Braz., pop.) jealousy.
2. fluting.
canelão (I) s. m. (pl. **-ões**) a heavy blow on the
shin-bone.
canelão (II) s. m. one of the stronger threads of a
spider web.
canelão (III) s. m. sugar-coated cinnamon comfit.
canela-preta s. f. (pl. **canelas-pretas**), (bot.) loblolly
whitewood.
canelar v. 1. to channel, flute. 2. to chamfer. 3. to
groove. 4. to thread a weaver's quill or spindle.
5. to carve grooves into.
canela-rajada s. f. (pl. **canelas-rajadas**) (Braz.) an 8
to 13 m high tree, of the family Lauraceae.
canela-seca s. f. (pl. **canelas-secas**), (bot.) shingle-
wood, whitewood.
canelas-ruivas s. f., sg. + pl. (zool.) a white-lipped
peccary (Pecari tajacu, Tayassu pecari).
caneleira (I) s. f. 1. canella, cinnamon, cinnamon-
-bark tree. 2. (ornith.) a chatterer (Hadretomus rufus).
caneleira (II) s. f. 1. female worker in a spinning
mill who threads the weaver's quills or spindles.
2. winding frame.
caneleira (III) s. f. (ant.) jamb of an armour. 2.
(ftb., sports) shin-guard, shin-pad.
caneleirinho s. m. (ornith.) a chatterer (Pachyrham-
phus polychropterus).
caneleiro (I) s. m. 1. canella, cinnamon, cinnamon-
-bark tree. 2. (ornith.) a chatterer.
caneleiro (II) s. m. (weav.) 1. spooler, winder, reeler.
2. spool, bobbin or spindle holder (of a winding
frame or spooling machine).
caneleiro (III) s. m. a careless and dangerous football player who kicks the opponents' shin-bones.
canelo (ê) s. m. 1. shin-bone. 2. an iron shoe for
oxen. 3. an old and worn horseshoe (that may
still be used).
caneludo s. m. (Braz., hist.) a contemptuous nickname
given to street vendors and itinerant pedlars. ||
adj. fluted, grooved, chamfered, striated.
canelura s. f. 1. fluting, flute. 2. groove, channel. 3.
(archit.) stria. 4. (mil.) cannelure, rifling (of a
gun). 5. (bot.) stria, striation, striature.

canescente adj. m. + f. (bot.) canescent.
caneta (I) s. f. 1. pen, penholder. 2. (med.) cautery--handle.
~ esferográfica ball-point pen.
caneta (II) s. m. (Braz., pop.) the evil one, the devil.
caneta-tinteiro s. f. (pl. canetas-tinteiro) (also caneta--fonte) fountain-pen, stylograph (plate C 11).
cânfora s. f. 1. camphor, gum camphor. 2. the tough gumlike resin extracted from several plants of the laurel family. 3. (bot.) camphor-laurel, camphor-tree.
canforado adj. camphorated, camphorate, containing camphor, treated with camphor.
canforar v. 1. to camphorate. 2. to mix with camphor. 3. to dissolve in camphor. 4. to impregnate or treat with camphor.
canforeira s. f., canforeiro m. (bot.) camphor-laurel, camphor-tree.
canga (I) s. f. 1. a yoke for oxen. 2. carrying poles. 3. (China) cangue: square wooden instrument of torture and punishment. 4. (fig.) oppression, repression, suppression, yoke.
canga (II) s. f. (Braz., min.) a kind of clayey iron ore.
cangá s. m. (N. Braz.) a kind of saddlebag.
cangaçais s. m. pl. (Braz., iron.) 1. poor people's furniture and possessions. 2. junk, trash. 3. worn--out or worthless things.
cangaceirada s. f. (N. Braz.) a gang of outlaws.
cangaceiro s. m. (N. Braz.) 1. bandit, brigand. 2. footpad, highway-robber. 3. outlaw.
cangaço s. m. 1. husks or skins of pressed fruits (esp. grapes). 2. (N. Braz.) the complete outfit of weapons a cangaceiro is used to wear. 3. poor people's furniture and belongings. 4. (also canga- ceirismo) the kind of life a highway-robber or cangaceiro leads. 5. the peduncle of a coconut palm.
cangalha s. f. 1. wooden frame of a packsaddle. 2. triangular wooden frame hung on the neck of small domestic animals (to prevent their passage through fences). 3. (prov.) cart drawn by one ox only. 4. shoulder yoke. 5. m. (N. Braz.) a bandy--legged fellow.
cangalhada s. f. 1. poor people's furniture and belongings. 2. junk, trash. 3. worn-out or worthless things.
cangalhão s. m. (pl. -ões) 1. wooden yoke, oxbow. 2. a man prematurely old.
cangalhas s. f. pl. 1. wooden framework of a packsad- dle. 2. (pop.) spectacles, eye-glasses. 3. supporting beam of a grain hopper (in a grain-mill).
cangalheiro s. m. 1. a driver of pack animals or draught oxen. 2. muleteer. 3. funeral undertaker. 4. a tree of the family Cunoniaceae (Belangera tomentosa).
cangalheta s. f. (Braz.) a rustic saddle.
cangalho (I) s. m. 1. a wooden yoke, oxbow. 2. old household furniture, trash. 3. worn-out or worthless things. 4. old, sick or useless person. 5. a small yoke for one draught animal only.
cangalho (II) s. m. dugout, Indian canoe.
cangambá s. m. (Braz., zool.) conepate, popular des- ignation of several kinds of skunks of the genus Conepatus.
cangancha s. f. (Braz.) 1. swindle, cheat. 2. trickery. 3. double-dealing, double-crossing.
cangancheiro s. m. (Braz.) swindler, cheat, double--crosser.
cangalo s. m. the naked stalk of a bunch of grapes.
cangar v. 1. to put the oxen into the yoke. 2. to subdue, suppress. 3. (fig.) to dominate, overcome, control. 4. (naut.) to become inclined, tilt. 5. to conquer, vanquish.

cangaraço s. m. (Braz.) 1. the rests of old things, worn out furniture. 2. the bones of an animal. 3. ruins, debris.
cangarilhada s. f. 1. deception, deceit. 2. swindle, trick.
cangatá s. m. (Braz.) 1. a string made from in- terwoven tufts of feathers. 2. popular designation of a marine catfish.
cangati s. m. a freshwater catfish.
cangoeira s. f. 1. a small Indian flute made from human bones. 2. an underfed suckling pig.
cangoncha s. f. (N. Braz.) a clumsily sculptured wooden image of a saint.
cangoncheiro s. m. (N. Braz.) carver of wooden images of saints, wood carver, wood statuary.
cangongo s. m. nickname given by backwoodsmen to the inhabitants of the sea shore.
cangorça s. f. (Port., prov.) 1. an old mare. 2. an ugly old woman.
cangosta s. f. 1. a long narrow street. 2. a narrow trail.
cangote s. m. (Braz., anat.) the occipital region.
cangotilho (I) s. m. (Braz., pop.) an epizootic disease of mules.
cangotilho (II) s. m. (Braz.) short trimming of a horse's mane.
cangotinho s. m. (Braz.) the most vulnerable region of a whale's body.
cangotudo adj. (Braz.) having a bulky occipital bone.
canguaí s. m. (Braz.) 1. backwoodsman. 2. peasant, farmhand. 3. boor, yokel, hayseed. 4. rustic.
canguara s. f. (Braz., pop.) white rum, sugar-cane brandy.
canguari s. m. (Braz., med.) popular designation of the ancylistomiasis (the hookworm disease).
canguçu s. m. (Braz., zool.) a jaguar (Felix onça).
cangueira s. f. (Braz.) a callosity on the neck of oxen and other draught animals caused by the constant friction of a yoke.
cangueiro adj. 1. bearing a yoke, capable of enduring a yoke. 2. (Braz.) lazy, indolent, sluggish. 3. slow, dawdling, loitering. 4. bent under a heavy load. 5. (fig.) oppressed, suppressed. 6. (fig.) obedient, submissive.
canguinhar v. 1. to be frail or puny. 2. to be weak. 3. to be irresolute, need a long time to come to a decision.
canguinhas s. m., sg. + pl. 1. a mean or narrow- -minded fellow. 2. weakling, feeble or frail man. 3. dejected or disheartened fellow, man lacking energy. 4. m. + f. an avaricious person, miser.
canguinho adj. avaricious, miserly, covetous.
cangulo s. m. (Braz.) 1. (ichth.) oldwife, triggerfish. 2. (fig.) a person whose teeth jut out.
cangurral s. m. (pl. -ais) (Braz.) the growth of brush- wood which is detrimental to the development of pastures.
canguru s. m. (Braz., ichth.) oldwife, triggerfish.
canguru s. m. (zool.) kangaroo.
filhote de ~ joey.
cangurupi s. m. (Braz., ichth.) a tarpon.
canha (I) s. f. (pop.) the left hand.
às ~s 1. left-handed. 2. clumsily, awkwardly. 3. done with the left hand. 4. contrary to the normal, contrarywise, inversely, reversely.
canha (II) s. f. (pop.) white rum, sugar-cane brandy.
canhada s. f. (S. Braz.) 1. a flat stretch of land lying between hills, lowland surrounded by knolls. 2. deep gorge, ravine. 3. deep gully excavated by running water.
canhadão s. m. (pl. -ões) (S. Braz.) deep valley, defile or gorge excavated by running water.

despenhar-se por um ~ abaixo (fig.) 1. to meet with failure, suffer a setback. 2. to act recklessly or overhasty.

canhamaço s. m. 1. a coarse hemp fabric. 2. sackcloth, packcloth. 3. hemp tow, canvas.

canhambola, canhambora s. m. (Braz., hist.) a fugitive slave.

canhameira s. f. a malvaceous plant (Althaea cannabina).

canhameiral s. m. (pl. -ais) hemp field, hemp plantation.

canhamiço adj. of, pertaining to or like hemp, hempen.

cânhamo s. m. 1. hemp, hemp plant. 2. hemp tow, packcloth, canvas. 3. hemp yarn. 4. common designation of several plants, the fibers of which are used in the textile industry.

cânhamo-brasileiro s. m. (pl. cânhamos-brasileiros), (Braz., bot.) brown Indian hemp, ambary, ambari.

cânhamo-de-manilha s. m. (pl. cânhamos-de-manilha) abaca, Manilla hemp plant (Musa textilis).

canhanha s. f. (ichth.) salema.

canhanho s. m. notebook, book for memoranda, register.

canhão s. m. (pl. -ões) 1. (mil.) cannon, gun, piece of ordnance. 2. gorge, defile, ravine. 3. canyon, cañon. 4. quill, stem or stalk of a quill (plate P 9). 5. top of boots, outward turned part of top-boots. 6. cuff on sleeves. 7. lapel, facings. 8. (Braz., pop.) an old and ugly woman. 9. -ões pl. (mil.) artillery.

~ antiaéreo anti-aircraft gun. ~ automático pom-pom. ~ de bota boot-tops. ~ de popa (naut.) stern-chaser. ~ de vestido facing of a dress. ~ eletrônico (electronics, TV) electron gun. ~ giratório swivel. alma do ~ the bore of a gun or cannon. bala de ~ cannon-ball, cannon-shot. culatra do ~ breech of a gun. dirigir um ~ contra to point a gun. o troar dos -ões the roar of guns.

canhão-azul s. m. (pl. canhões-azuis) (electronics, TV) in a kinescope, the electron gun that excites the blue component.

canhão-verde s. m. (pl. canhões-verdes) (electronics, TV) in a kinescope, the electron gun that excites the green component.

canhembora s. m. + f. (Braz., pop.) a fugitive Negro slave.

canhengue adj. m. + f. avaricious, miserly, covetous.

canhenho (I) s. m. 1. notebook, book for memoranda, register, diary. 2. (fig.) remembrance, memory.

canhenho (II) s. m. (Port., prov.) a left-handed person, left-hander. || adj. 1. left-handed. 2. done with the left hand. 3. clumsy, awkward. 4. inapt, unskilful.

canhestro adj. (pop.) 1. left-handed. 2. clumsy, awkward. 3. inapt, unskilful. 4. agrestic(al). 5. unwieldy, bulky. 6. wooden, woodenly. 7. ungainly. 8. timid, bashful.

canheta s. m. (Braz., pop.) the devil, the evil one.

canhim s. m. (pl. -ins) (Braz., pop.) the devil.

canho (I) adj. = canhoto.

canho (II) s. m. (pop.) ill-got profit(s), gains obtained by evil means.

canhonaço s. m. cannon-shot.

canhonada s. f. 1. cannonade, cannonry. 2. discharge of cannon(s), many cannon-shots fired at the same time, artillery fire. 3. roaring, booming (of or as of guns).

canhonar v. to provide with guns or cannons.

canhonear v. 1. to fire a cannon. 2. to bombard, shell, cannonade. 3. to attack, assail. 4. to reprehend, censure.

canhoneio s. m. cannonade, bombardment, shelling.

canhoneira s. f. 1. (fort.) embrasure, an opening in a wall or parapet through which cannons can be fired. 2. (naut.) gunboat.

canhoneiro adj. 1. cannoned, armed with cannons. 2. of, pertaining to or relative to artillery.

canhota s. f. (pop.) 1. the left hand. 2. a blow with the left hand.

canhota (ô) s. f. 1. a left-handed woman. 2. f. of canhoto.

canhoteiro s. m. left-hander.

canhoto s. m. (f. canhota) 1. left-hander, left-handed man. 2. the stub in or as in a checkbook, counterfoil. 3. (pop.) the devil, the evil one. 4. (mech.) a wooden or iron rod of a machine saw which transforms the rotative movement of the pulley into an oscillating one. || adj. 1. left-handed. 2. left. 3. done (better) with the left hand. 4. inapt, unskilful. 5. clumsy, awkward.

canibal s. m. + f. (pl. -ais) 1. cannibal, anthropophagite. 2. m. a brutal, cruel or ferocious man. || adj. cruel, barbarous, ferocious, inhuman.

canibalesco adj. 1. cannibal, cannibalic. 2. given to cannibalism. 3. (fig.) inhuman, ferocious, cruel.

canibalismo s. m. 1. cannibalism, man-eating. 2. anthropophagy. 3. ferocity of savages. 4. (fig.) brutality, cruelty. 5. act or fact of an animal devouring its own kind.

canibalização s. f. cannibalization.

canibalizar v. to cannibalize.

caniçada s. f. (also caniçalha) 1. trellis, latticework made from reeds or canes. 2. treillage, wattle. 3. a framework made for drying fish.

caniçal s. m. (pl. -ais) place where reeds grow, reedplot, canebrake, cane thicket.

canicho s. m. small dog, tiny dog, puppy.

canície, canícia s. f. 1. whiteness of hair. 2. gray hair, gray-hairedness. 3. (fig.) old age.

caniço s. m. 1. slender reed or cane. 2. a fishing fence made from reeds, weir. 3. fishing-rod, rod. 4. rush. 5. rushbroom. 6. (fig.) a lean or slender person.

de ~ reeden.

caniço-d'água s. m. (pl. caniços-d'água), (bot.) ditchreed, giant reed.

caniço-dos-brejos s. m. (pl. caniços-dos-brejos), (bot.) marsh reed.

canícula (I) s. f. (astr.) Syrius, dog-star. 2. the hottest period of the year, canicular days, dog-days. 3. sultriness.

canícula (II) s. f. 1. a small cane or reed. 2. (pop., vulg.) a slender shin-bone, very thin legs.

canicular (I) adj. m. + f. 1. of or pertaining to the canicular days. 2. hot, sultry. 3. canicular.

canicular (II) adj. m. + f. (astr.) of, pertaining to or relative to Syrius or Canicula.

canicultor s. m. breeder of dogs, dog-fancier.

canicultura s. f. breeding of dogs.

canicurá s. m. (Braz.) a civilized Indian, esp. one converted to Christianity.

canídeo s. m. (zool.) 1. animal of the family Canidae. 2. ~s pl. the Canidae: the family of dogs, wolves, jackals and foxes. || adj. canine: 1. of or pertaining to dogs or the family Canidae. 2. having the qualities of a dog.

canifraz s. m. extremely lean or scrawny man (like a hungry dog).

canil (I) s. m. (pl. -is) 1. dog-house, dog-hole. 2. kennel.

canil (II) s. m. (pl. -is) shin-bone of a horse.

canil (III) s. m. (pl. -is) 1. a wooden yoke. 2. old household furniture, trash. 3. worn-out or worthless things. 4. old, sick or useless person. 5. a small yoke for one draught-animal only.

caninana s. f. (Braz.) 1. (zool.) a harmless rat-snake (Spilotes pullatus). 2. a creeping plant of the family Polygalaceae (Securidaca lanceolata). 3. (fig.) an ill-natured, !rascible person.

canindé s. m. (Braz.) 1. (ornith.) blue-and-yellow macaw. 2. a long machete used in Ceará for clearing the underbrush.

caninha s. f. 1. diminutive form of **cana**. 2. (Braz., pop.) white rum, sugar-cane brandy.

caninha-verde s. f. (Port., Spain) a popular song and folk-dance in Minho.

canino s. m. (anat.) canine tooth, laniary tooth, fang. ‖ adj. 1. canine. 2. doglike, doggie. 3. of or relative to the eye-teeth.

ele tem uma fome -a he has a wolfish appetite.

canipreto adj. having black shanks (said of horses).

canista s. m. + f. (N. Braz.) habitual rum drinker.

canistrel s. m. = **canastrel**.

canitar s. m. (Braz.) Indian headdress made of feathers.

canivetaço s. m., **canivetada** f. (Braz.) lunge with a jackknife.

canivete s. m. 1. pocket-knife, penknife. 2. clasp-knife, jackknife. 3. knife. 4. a small fresh-water fish (Characidium sp.). 5. a coral tree (Erythrina reticulata). 6. (Braz., pop.) a small, weak and ugly horse.

vou fazê-lo, nem que chovam ~s I'll do it at any rate.

canivetear v. to cut or wound with a pocket-knife.

canja s. f. 1. chicken soup with rice, chicken broth. 2. (Braz., sl.) something very easy or agreeable to do, cinch.

~ com alho-porro cocky-leeky, cock-a-leekie. **é ~!** it's a lick! it's a pushover.

canjerê s. m. (Braz.) a group of persons (usually Negroes) meeting for the common practice of witchcraft or voodooism.

canjica s. f. (Braz.) 1. a dish made with grated green corn, sugar, coconut milk and cinnamon. 2. a soup made with crushed white maize, sugar, milk and cinnamon. 3. a kind of tobacco dust. 4. a kind of coarse clean river sand mixed with fine gravel. 5. cyst in the flesh of swine. 6. popular designation of several plants of the families Malpighiaceae, Rhamnaceae and Verbenaceae.

canjicada s. f. festive reunions on St. John's and St. Peter's feast-days at which usually **canjica** is served.

canjica-lustrosa s. f. (pl. **canjicas-lustrosas**) (Braz., min.) limonite found in coffee-brown pebbles.

canjiqueira s. f. (Braz.) corn grating machine, corn grater.

canjiquinha s. f. (Braz.) 1. name of the tapeworm larvae which are found in the flesh of swine. 2. a small tumefaction or swelling.

canjira s. m. (Braz.) male descendant.

canjirão s. m. (pl. **-ões**) 1. a wine jug with a wide mouth. 2. (fig.) a big and clumsy person or thing.

canjurupi, canjurupim s. m. (Braz., ichth.) tarpon.

cano s. m. 1. general designation of all kinds of tubes. 2. tube, pipe (plate C 1). 3. spout. 4. barrel, barrel of a gun. 5. conduit. 6. leg of a boot (plate B 16). 7. drain pipe, sewer. 8. water-main.

~ com flanges flanged pipe (plate C 1). **~ da chaminé** flue, chimney. **~ da coluna** shaft or shank of a pillar, chamfer. **~ de água** water conduit, water supply pipe (plate L 3). **~ de descarga** ejection pipe, flushing pipe (plate P 19). **~ de escapamento** (mot.) stack, silencer, suffler. **~ de escape** (mech.) escape pipe. **~ de esgoto** drain-pipe, waste-pipe, soil-pipe (plates E 3, P 19). **~ de órgão** organ-pipe. **~ isolador** (electr.) insulated conduit

(plate E 3). **~ para gás de escape** waste gas flue. **bota de ~ curto** halfboot. **entrar pelo ~** (pop.) to turn out badly in an event, go down the tubes. **espingarda de dois ~s** double-barrelled gun.

canoa s. f. 1. canoe. 2. boat, skiff, yawl. 3. dug-out, pitpan (plates B 8, 9). 4. a big bathtub. 5. frying-pan (shaped like a canoe). 6. fine decorative comb worn by women. 7. (Braz., gold-mining) an inclined flume for conveying water to the placer. 8. (N. Braz., sl.) a police raid.

ele tem o pé em duas ~s he has two strings to his bow. **não embarque em ~ furada** don't embark in a leaky boat; (fig.) don't embark in a risky enterprise.

canoeiro s. m. 1. canoeman, canoeist, wherryman. 2. manufacturer of canoes. 3. seller of canoes.

Cânon (I) s. m. (R. C. Church liturgy) Canon: the central and most important part of the mass.

cânon (II), **cânone** s. m. canon: 1. rule, precept. 2. decree, decision made by ecclesiastical authorities. 3. church law. 4. critical standard, criterion. 5. list, catalogue. 6. a catalogue of recognized saints. 7. book containing prescribed prayers. 8. table of contents, chart. 9. customary payment or right. 10. (mus.) a kind of continual fugue with repetition of the melodic theme. 11. (math.) general mathematical formula.

canonical adj. m. + f. (pl. **-ais**) canonic(al).

canonicato s. m. (eccl.) 1. dignity and authority of a canon or prebendary. 2. canonship, canonry.

canonicidade s. f. (eccl.) canonicalness.

canônico adj. 1. canonic(al). 2. canonistic(al). 3. (fig.) regular, methodical, orderly. ‖ **-amente** adv. canonically, canonistically, (fig.) regularly, methodically.

direito ~ canon law. **livros ~s da Sagrada Escritura** the canonical books of the Holy Scriptures. **horas -as** lauds, evensong, canonical hours.

canonisa s. f. (eccl.) canoness.

canonista s. m. (eccl.) canonist, teacher or scholar of canon law.

canonização s. f. (pl. **-ões**), (eccl., rel.) canonization, sanctification.

canonizado adj. canonized, sainted.

canonizador s. m. 1. (eccl.) canonizer: one who canonizes or declares a deceased person a saint. 2. (fig.) adulator, wheedler, flatterer. ‖ adj. 1. canonizing. 2. (fig.) flattering, wheedling.

canonizar v. 1. to canonize, declare saint. 2. to register in the book of saints. 3. (fig.) to flatter excessively, adulate, wheedle. 4. to sanctify, saint. 5. to consecrate, hallow. 6. to consider, ponder. 7. to declare.

canonizável adj. m. + f. (pl. **-áveis**) 1. capable of being canonized, worthy of canonization. 2. deserving canonization. 3. (fig.) meritorious, praiseworthy.

canopo s. m. 1. (hist.) canopic jar: a jar in which the Egyptians preserved the viscera of their deceased. 2. (astr.) Canopus: a first-magnitude star in the constellation Carina.

canoro adj. 1. canorous. 2. harmonious, melodious. 3. suave, sweet, pleasant (said of songs or voices). 4. singing, warbling. 5. well-sounding.

pássaro ~ singing bird, songbird.

canoura s. f. grain hopper, mill hopper.

cansacento adj. sick with fatigue, dead-tired, exhausted.

cansaço s. m. 1. fatigue, weariness. 2. tiredness. 3. weakness produced by illness or excessive exertion. 4. exhaustion. 5. lassitude. 6. jadedness, fag, frazzle.

ela estava acabada de ~ she was done up with fatigue. **ele caiu de ~** he dropped to the ground

for sheer exhaustion. **ele estava morto de** ~ he was tired to death.
cansado adj. 1. tired, fatigued. 2. weary, spent. 3. outworn, drawn, flagging. 4. weak, faint. 5. toilsome, wearisome. 6. jaded, exhausted. 7. fed up, squeamish. || **-amente** adv. tiredly, wearily, flaggingly, squeamishly.
agora estou ~ now I am weak and weary. ~ **deste mundo** world weary. ~ **de trabalhar** toil-worn. **estou** ~ **de ouvir sempre a mesma coisa** I am tired of hearing always the same thing. **estou** ~ **deste negócio** I am sick of that business, I am fed up with this business. **terra** -a worn-out or impoverished soil. **ter vista** -a (med.) to suffer from presbyopia.
cansanção s. m. (pl. **-ões**), (bot.) chichicaste.
cansanção-de-leite s. m. (pl. **cansanções-de-leite**), (Braz., bot.) spurge nettle, tread-softly.
cansão adj. (pl. **-ões**) easily tired or fatigued (said of horses).
cansar v. 1. to tire, fatigue. 2. to weary. 3. to cause fatigue, wear out or down. 4. to molest, annoy, trouble. 5. to flag, frazzle. 6. to irk, harass, pester. 7. to bore. 8. to grow tired, become fatigued. 9. to feel weariness or fatigue. 10. to cease, discontinue, leave off. 11. ~**-se:** a) to strive to do something, exert o. s., struggle for. b) to tire o. s. out. c) to become bored. d) to become annoyed.
~ **demais** to overfatigue. ~**-se em vão** to lose one's toil. **ela não cansou de desculpar-se** she exhausted herself in excuses. **ele cansou-se do negócio** he got fed up with the business. **este trabalho cansa muito** this work is very fatiguing. **isto é o que me cansa** that matter tires me out. **o esforço cansa-o** the effort wears on him. **você vai** ~**-se esperando por eles** you may whistle for them!
cansarina s. f. (bot.) a bougainvillea (Bougainvillea glabra).
cansativo adj. 1. tiring, fatiguing. 2. wearisome, toilsome. 3. boresome, tedious. 4. long-winded, ponderous. 5. heavy, rough. 6. stressful, killing. 7. slow. 8. trying. || **-amente** adv. wearisomely, tiresomely, wearily, irksomely, long-winded.
canseira s. f. 1. fatigue, weariness. 2. tiredness. 3. weakness, exhaustion. 4. lassitude. 5. hard work, toil, effort.
canseiroso adj. very tiresome, wearisome, toilsome.
cansim s. m. khamsin: a southerly wind, hot and dry, that occurs in Egypt during the high tide of the Nile.
canso s. m. 1. fatigue, weariness. 2. tiredness. 3. toil. || adj. (pop.) tired, fatigued, worn-out, weary.
cantã s. f. (bot.) plant of the arrowroot family.
cantábrio, cantábrico adj. Basque: of, pertaining to or relative to the Basques, their country and their language.
cântabro s. m. Basque: native or inhabitant of the Basque provinces in the western Pyrenees. || adj. Basque.
cantada s. f. 1. act of singing. 2. song, tune. 3. (Braz.,· pop.) seduction by flattering words and manners.
cantadeira s. f. 1. woman who is fond of singing or sings a lot. 2. songstress, woman singer. 3. (India) a hired girl singer. || adj. f. fond of singing (said with regard to women and girls).
cantadela s. f. (pop.) 1. act of singing. 2. ballad, popular song.
cantado adj. 1. sung, chanted, warbled. 2. expressed in a song. 3. celebrated or honoured with a song. **missa** -a high or grand mass.
cantador s. m. popular singer, street singer. || adj. singing, fond of singing, chanting.

canta-galo adj. (S. Braz.) bang-tailed (said of horsetails).
cantalupo s. m. 1. (bot.) cantaloupe, cantaloup. 2. muskmelon.
contante s. m. 1. good-for-nothing, vagabond. 2. loafer. 3. rascal, scoundrel. 4. swindler, crook. 5. commonplace fellow. || adj. m. + f. singing, cantative.
cantão s. m. (pl. **-ões**) 1. territorial division, district. 2. canton. 3. part of a province. 4. section of a highway or railroad. 5. (her.) each one of the four principal fields of an escutcheon.
dividiram a região em quatro -ões they cantoned the region in four sections.
cantar v. 1. to say or express one's feeling in songs. 2. to sing, chant. 3. to twitter, warble. 4. to celebrate or praise with a song. 5. to tune, flute. 6. to crow. 7. to vocalize. 8. to speak or perform pathetically. 9. (Braz.) to seduce by flattery. 10. to produce melodious rhythmical sounds. 11. to act as song leader.
~ **a missa** to sing a high mass. ~ **à primeira vista** to sing off. ~ **de ouvido** to sing by ear. ~ **em conjunto** to choir. ~ **errado** to sing out of tune. ~ **hinos** to hymn. ~ **uma modinha** to sing a tune. **cante para nós!** give us a song. ~ **vitória** to crow or cry victory. **disso eu sei** ~ **uma cantiga** I could tell a tale about that. **é fácil** ~ **isto** that's easy to sing. **ela canta baixo demais** she sings too flat. **ele canta seu próprio louvor** he blows his own trumpet. **ele cantou para nós** he gave us a tune. **quem canta no terreiro é o galo!** (pop.) I'm the boss of this show!
cântara s. f. a big-bellied water pitcher with a wide mouth.
cantareira s. f. 1. a shelf in the kitchen to set up pots, pans, jugs. 2. dish rack. 3. (Braz.) clavicle, collarbone.
cantarejar v. (pop.) to sing, hum, croon.
cantarejo s. m. singsong, humming, crooning.
cantaria s. f. 1. the art of stonecutting. 2. masonry. 3. ashlar.
cantaríase s. f. (med.) infestation by larvae of Coleoptera.
cantárida, cantáride s. f. blister beetle, Spanish fly.
cantarilho s. m. 1. (hist.) generic designation of ancient love songs and ditties sung by Portuguese troubadours. 2. (ichth.) pigfoot.
cântaro s. m. 1. a big-bellied water pitcher with one or two handles. 2. earthen pot, tin can, jar, jug. 3. urn. 4. (obs.) a measure of dry or liquid capacity varying from two to about 25 liters.
chove a ~**s** it's raining cats and dogs, it's pouring. **tantas vezes vai o** ~ **à fonte que por fim se quebra** the pitcher goes so often to the well that it is broken at last.
cantarola s. f. 1. singsong. 2. a song sung by many untrained voices. 3. song presented out of tune. 4. troll, catch, round. 5. song feast. 6. song presented in a low voice.
cantarolar v. 1. to sing with a low voice, hum. 2. to sing out of tune. 3. to warble, trill. 4. to troll, trollol.
cantata s. f. 1. cantata, choral composition. 2. narrative poem recited or chanted in a dramatic manner. 3. hymn. 4. musical composition for a single voice accompanied by one or more instruments. 5. (pop.) smooth talk, cunning double talk.
cantatriz s. f. 1. a talented professional songstress. 2. opera singer.
cantável adj. m. + f. (pl. **-áveis**) that can be sung, singable, cantabile.

cantear v. (typgr.) to round the corners (of paper or cardboard).

canteira s. f. stone pit, quarry.

canteiro (I) s. m. 1. stone-cutter, stone-mason. 2. sculptor. 3. flowerpot, flower box. 4. flower-bed, seed-bed or bed in a garden. 5. gantry. 6. plot, plat.
~ **de flores** flower-bed, parterre. ~ **para mudas** hotbed.

canteiro (II) s. m. trestle, horse, jack (for beer or wine barrels).

cânter s. m. (horse racing) canter, an easy gallop: the presentation gallop of a race-horse preceeding the actual race.

cântico s. m. 1. canticle, hymn. 2. chant. 3. symphonic poem.
~ **de Natal** Christmas carol. ~ **fúnebre** keen. ~ **sacro** sacred song. **O Cântico dos Cânticos** (bib.) The Song of Songs, Canticle of Canticles, Song of Solomon.

cantiga s. f. 1. poetry set to music. 2. symphonic poem. 3. ballad, ode. 4. quatrain, quartet. 5. air, tune. 6. cunning double talk, smooth talk.
cantar sempre a mesma ~ (pop.) to harp always upon the same string. ~ **amorosa** love-song. ~ **popular** descant.

cantil s. m. (pl. **-is**) 1. (carp.) rabbet plane, match plane. 2. water-bottle, canteen. 3. flask. 4. a stonecutter's or sculptor's smoothing chisel.

cantilena s. f. 1. ballad, ode. 2. ditty, quatrain, carol. 3. a tender love-song, lullaby or pastoral song. 4. symphonic poem. 5. (fam.) a boring, long drawn--out story. 6. warbling (of a bird).
voltar sempre à mesma ~ (fam.) to say the same thing over and again.

cantimplora s. m. = **catimplora**.

cantina s. f. 1. canteen. 2. mess, messroom. 3. tavern.

cantineira s. f. 1. a tavern-keeper's wife. 2. a female tavern-keeper, ale-wife.

cantineiro s. m. 1. tavern-keeper, proprietor of a canteen. 2. sutler. 3. a counterman who sells drinks in a bar or tavern.

cantinho s. m. 1. diminutive form of **canto** (I). 2. nook, corner. 3. retreat. 4. a little piece, fragment, slice (as of bread).

canto (I) s. m. 1. corner, edge (plate M 2). 2. angle. 3. nook. 4. arris. 5. brink, brow. 6. a lonely place, a remote, secluded spot. 7. canthus: each corner of the eye. 8. hedge.
~ **da boca** corner of the mouth. ~ **da rua** street corner. ~ **do olho** corner of the eye, canthus. **a criança foi colocada no** ~ **(de castigo)** the child was stood in the corner (for punishment). **meter-se em um** ~ to creep into a corner. **no** ~ **mais remoto** in the farthest corner. **pôr a um** ~ to put aside, neglect. **todos os** ~**s do mundo** every corner of the earth.

canto (II) s. m. 1. song, folk song, chant, lay. 2. singing 3. modulation of the human or animal voice. 4. music arranged or composed for the human voice. 5. lyrical poetry. 6. canto: chief division of a long poem.
~ **de galo** cockcrow, cockcrowing. ~ **do cisne** (fig.) the last work of a poet or composer: swan song. ~ **fúnebre** dirge, funeral song. ~ **gregoriano** Gregorian chant. ~ **orfeônico** community singing. ~ **popular** folk song. **aula de** ~ singing lesson. **professor de** ~ singing-master. **voz de** ~ singing--voice. **trazer alguém de** ~ **chorado** to bother or pester s. o.

canto (III) s. m. 1. a rough-hewn stone, corner-stone. 2. a stone block. 3. window or door frames made of stone.

cantochanista s. m. 1. chanter (esp. of Gregorian chants). 2. singer, songster. 3. cantor, chorister.

cantochão s. m. (pl. **-ões**) 1. chant, Gregorian chant. 2. (mus.) plain music. 3. church songs or hymns. 4. (fig.) often repeated and generally known theory or doctrine.

canto-de-sabiá s. m. (pl. **cantos-de-sabiá**), (Braz., med.) inflammatory and sometimes suppurative affection of the corners of the mouth.

cantoeira s. f. (archit., carp.) cramp-iron, angle-iron, cramp hook used to fix the corner-stones of a building.

cantonado adj. 1. cantoned, divided into sections or cantons. 2. (her.) having a charge in one or more corners of the escutcheon.

cantonal adj. m. + f. (pl. **-ais**) cantonal, of, pertaining to or relative to a canton.

cantoneira s. f. 1. a corner shelf or stand. 2. corner cupboard. 3. (tech.) angle plate, corner plate, angle bar, frame angle.
~ **de aço** angle steel. ~ **de abas iguais** equal angle-iron.

cantoneiro s. m. 1. section hand, section boss, man responsible for the maintenance of a railway or highway section. 2. street-sweeper.

cantonense s. m. + f. Cantonese. ‖ adj. m. + f. Cantonese.

cantor s. m. 1. singer, professional singer. 2. songster. 3. (radio) crooner. 4. chanter, chorister. 5. caroller. 6. warbler. 7. poet. 8. artist.
~ **ambulante** street singer. **ele é o melhor** ~ **negro** he is the best Negro minstrel. **um** ~ **excelente** a crack vocalist.

cantora s. f. songstress, opera singer, singer, chantress.

cantoria s. f. 1. choral singing. 2. troll, catch, round. 3 vocal music. 4. warbling. 5. the act or method of singing.

cantorina s. f. 1. songstress, singer. 2. (S. Braz.): a) symphonic poem. b) ode, ballad. c) ditty, carol. 3. singing festival.

cantorrafia s. f. (med.) canthoraphia.

cantotomia s. f. (surg.) the excision of one or both canthi of the eye.

canudinho s. m. 1. diminutive form of **canudo**. 2. drinking straw, straw.

canudo s. m. 1. long tube, pipe. 2. a piece of reed cut between two knots. 3. a starched pleat in a dress. 4. curls, ringlets (of hair). 5. (pop.) deceit, trick, swindle. 6. (Braz., bot.) ipomoea (Ipomoea fistulosa).
~ **de chupar** sipping straw, drinking straw, straw (plate R 5). ~ **de soprar** pea-shooter.

canudo-de-pito s. m. (pl. **canudos-de-pito**) (Braz.) 1. common name of several plants (some of which yield a medicinal oil used as a substitute for the chaulmoogra oil) of the family Flacourtiaceae. 2. (bot.) a senna (Cassia laevigata). 3. plant of the family Euphorbiaceae (Mabia augustiofolia).

cânula s. f. 1. (surg.) cannula: a metal, glass or hard rubber tube used with several surgical instruments. 2. pipe. 3. quill.

canutilho s. m. 1. gold, silver or brass purl (coiled). 2. a small tube. 3. small glass tube used as ornament on ladies' dresses.

canzá s. m. (Braz.) native musical instrument of African origin.

canzarrão s. m. (pl. **-ões**) augmentative form of **cão**: a very big dog.

canzil s. m. (pl. **-is**) 1. each one of the two wooden bows (of a yoke) which enclose the neck of a draught ox. 2. a wooden yoke, oxbow. 3. an identifying mark in the ear of cattle. 4. a dragonfly of the order Odonata (Libellula virgo).

canzoada s. f. 1. a great number of dogs. 2. a pack of dogs. 3. (fig.) a gang of hoodlums or scoundrels.

canzoal adj. m. + f. (pl. -ais) canine, doggish, doglike.

canzoeira s. f. 1. a great number of dogs. 2. a pack of dogs. 3. barking or yelping of dogs.

canzurral s. m. (Braz.) = **cangurral**.

cão (I) s. m. (pl. **cães**) (f. **cadela**) 1. dog: a carnivorous mammal of the family Canidae (Canis familiaris) (plate C 3). 2. hammer or cock of a gun. 3. name of two southern constellations: Canis Major, Canis Minor (the Greater Dog and the Lesser Dog). 4. (mil.) an ancient piece of ordnance. 5. a contemptible person.
~ **d'água** poodle (plate C 3). ~ **dálmata** Dalmatian (plate C 3). ~ **de busca** blood-hound, limer. ~ **de caça** hound, buckhound. ~ **de fila** mastiff dog, bulldog. ~ **de guarda** watchdog. ~ **de lareira** andiron (plate L 1). ~ **de pastor** shepherd's dog. ~ **de pedra** (archit.) corbel. ~ **de quinta** watchdog. ~ **de rua** cur, mutt, mongrel, street dog. ~ **dinamarquês** great Dane (plate C 3). ~ **fraldeiro** lap-dog. ~ **lebreiro** harrier. **Cão Maior** (astr.) Canis Major. **Cão Menor** (astr.) Canis Minor. ~ **pastor alemão** sheep-dog, Alsatian dog, Alsatian. ~ **perdigueiro** pointer. ~ **policial** police dog. ~ **que ladra não morde!** barking dogs seldom bite! **a** ~ **mordido os outros o mordem** give a dog a bad name and hang him. **andar a cair na boca dos cães** to come to grief, go to the dogs. **despertar o** ~ **que dorme** to look for trouble. **levaram uma vida de** ~ they led a dog's life. **quem bem quer ao Beltrão, bem quer ao seu** ~**!** love me, love my dog! **quem não tem** ~ **caça com gato** one makes the best of a bad job. **vivem como** ~ **e gato** they live like cat and dog.

cão (II) adj. (pl. **cãos**) (f. **cã**) 1. white-haired. 2. hoary. 3. white or gray with age.

caoba s. f. mahogany, plant of the mahogany family (Swietenia Mahagoni).

caoba-roxa s. f. (pl. **caobas-roxas**), red mahogany, forest mahogany.

caol s. m. liquid used for the cleaning of yellow metals.

caolho s. m. one-eyed or cross-eyed fellow. ‖ adj. one-eyed, cross-eyed, squint-eyed.

cão-marinho s. m. (pl. **cães-marinhos**) 1. (ichth.) nursehound. 2. sea-dog, seal.

cão-miúdo s. m. (pl. **cães-miúdos**), (Braz., pop.) the devil, the evil one.

caos s. m. 1. (theol.) confused, unorganized state of matter before the creation of the world. 2. chaos, utter confusion. 3. welter, tohu vabohu.

caótico adj. chaotic(al), completely confused.

cão-tinhoso s. m. (pl. **cães-tinhosos**), (pop.) the devil, the evil one.

caotização s. f. a turning things chaotic.

capa (I) s. f. 1. a sleeveless outdoor garment, cape. 2. coat, overcoat, wrap, mantle. 3. cover, covering (plate G 4). 4. (bullfight) banderole. 5. (naut.) main sail. 6. (fig.): a) shelter, protection. b) outward appearance, pretense, pretext. 7. envelop, envelopment. 8. (mining) the upper part of a mine gallery. 3. (tech.) cap, case.
~ **almofadada** a stuffed book cover. ~ **de asperges** cope, a priest's cope. ~ **de chuva** mackintosh, waterproof, raincoat (plate R 6). ~ **de inverno** winter coat (plate R 7). ~ **de livro** book cover, the binding of a book (plate L 4). ~ **de monge** cowl. ~ **de móveis** dust cloth. ~ **impermeável**

raincoat, waterproof, trench coat, burberry (plate (R 7). **pôr ou tirar a** ~ to put on or take off one's coat.

capa (II) s. f. (Braz.) castration of domestic animals.

capa-bode s. m. + f. (pl. **capa-bodes**) 1. backwoodsman, frontiersman, person of the backwoods. 2. inlander. 3. rustic.

capação s. f. (pl. -ões) 1. castration. 2. pruning of plants.

capacete s. m. 1. helmet, helm. 2. headpiece, casque, armet. 3. (bot.) galea. 4. head of an alembic. 5. the rotating roof of a windmill.
~ **de aço** steel helmet. ~ **de cortiça** sun-helmet. ~ **de gelo** ice bag. ~ **de proteção**, ~ **protetor** face-guard, crash helmet. **sem** ~ helmless.

capachismo s. m. 1. submissiveness, servility. 2. servile act. 3. lack of self-respect or dignity.

capacho s. m. 1. door-mat, mat (plates E 7, G 3). 2. rug. 3. mat used as a foot warmer. 4. base flatterer, servile adulator. 5. ~**s** pl. matting. **ele é apenas um** ~ he is nothing but a lickspittle.

capacidade s. f. 1. capacity, capability, capableness. 2. capaciousness, room, extent, scope. 3. content, volume. 4. size, measure. 5. ability, aptitude, aptness. 6. competence, competency. 7. skill, talent, bent. 8. integrity, honesty. 9. (jur.) legal qualification. 10. (electr.) capacitance. 11. gauge, calibre. 12. power, effect, load, effectiveness. 13. person of outstanding qualities. 14. command. 15. disposition. 16. faculty.
~ **aquisitiva** purchasing power. ~ **artística** artistry. ~ **calorífica** heat capacity. ~ **de absorção** capability of absorption. ~ **de carga de um navio** (naut.) burden, hold. ~ **de raciocínio** reasoning power. ~ **de refração** refractoriness. ~ **de resistência** resistance. ~ **de trabalho mecânico** performance. ~ **de um tanque** tankage. ~ **intelectual** apprehensiveness. ~ **produtiva** working power, or capacity. **conforme a minha** ~ according to my capacity. **de acordo com a sua** ~ according to his lights. **ele não tem** ~ **para isto** he has not the stuff for that. **ele tem a** ~ **de resistir a todos os ataques** he has the ability to resist crushing and shattering. **homem de grande** ~ a very able man. **medida de** ~ dry measure, measure of capacity. **isto ultrapassa nossas** ~**s** this is above our attainments.

capacitado adj. 1. capable, competent, able. 2. convinced.
ele está ~ **para cumprir a sua tarefa** he is equal to his task. **ele é um dos mais** ~**s** he is one of the first rate wits.

capacitância s. f. (electr.) capacitance.

capacitar v. 1. to capacitate, render capable. 2. to qualify. 3. to enable, make able. 4. to empower, authorize. 5. to convince, persuade. 6. to understand, comprehend. 7. ~**-se**: a) to be convinced. b) to persuade o. s.

capacitivo adj. (electr.) capacitive.

capacitor s. m. (electr.) capacitor, condensor.

capada (I) s. f. (hatmaking) a raw, preformed piece of felt.

capada (II) s. f. flock, herd, drove.

capada (III) s. f. a blow with a stick.

capadaria s. f. (Braz.) a lot of hogs or other animals set aside for fattening.

capadeira s. f. gelding knife.

capadeiro s. m. professional gelder or castrator.

capadete s. m. (S. Braz.) a castrated but not yet fattened young pig.

capadinho s. m. 1. (Braz., depr.) a small or insignificant school-book. 2. = **capadete**.

capado s. m. a castrated ram, goat or boar. ‖ adj. castrated.

capadoçada s. f. 1. an assemblage of rogues or scoundrels. 2. swindle, trickery, roguery.

capadoçagem s. f. (pl. **-ens**) knavish tricks, swindle, roguery.

capadoçal adj. m. + f. (pl. **-ais**) fraudulent, roguish, trickish.

capadócio (I) s. m. (also **capádoce** m. + f., hist.) Cappadocian: native or inhabitant of Cappadocia. ‖ adj. Cappadocian: of or pertaining to Cappadocia.

capadócio (II) s. m. 1. impostor, charlatan. 2. crook, sharper. 3. braggart, swaggerer, boaster. 4. bully, rowdy. ‖ adj. 1. fraudulent, roguish, trickish. 2. bragging, boasting.

capador s. m. 1. a professional gelder or castrator. 2. a shepherd's flute or pipe.

capadura s. f. gelding castration.

capa-homem s. m. (pl. **capa-homens**), (Braz.) savanna flower (Echites peltata).

capa-magna s. f. (pl. **capas-magnas**), (eccl.) a bishop's cope.

capanga s. m 1. a hired assassin, bully. 2. thug, ruffian, hoodlum. 3. (N. Braz.): a) the total value of the diamonds acquired by a purchasing agent. b) a lot of diamonds. 4. f. (Braz.) a money bag, a little pouch, purse.

capangada s. f. (Braz.) an assemblage of hired assassins or hoodlums.

capangagem s. f. (pl. **-ens**) 1. = **capangada**. 2. a brutal act, piece of roguery.

capangar v. (Braz.) 1. to buy diamonds from prospectors. 2. to peddle, hawk, sell from place to place.

capangueiro s. m. (N. Braz.) diamond purchaser (who buys directly from the prospectors).

capão (I) s. m. (pl. **-ões**) 1. capon, castrated male chicken. 2. gelding, castrated horse.

capão (II) s. m. copse, coppice, an isolated group of trees in the midst of an open plain.

capar v. 1‖ to castrate, deprive of generative power. 2. to emasculate. 3. to capon, caponize. 4. to geld, spay. 5. to prune, cut off the suckers of a plant, trim.

capara s. f. (Braz.) a large funnel-shaped leaf which is used as a cup.

caparidácea s. f. plant of the family Capparidaceae.

caparidáceas s. f. p. (bot.) Capparidaceae.

caparidáceo adj. (bot.) capparidaceous.

caparrosa s. f. 1. (chem.) popular designation of various sulphates. 2. (bot.): a) an evening primrose (Oenothera mollissima). b) a primrose willow (Jussievia caparosa).
~ **azul** (chem.) blue vitriol, chalcanthite. ~ **branca** (chem.) white vitriol, zinc sulphate. ~ **verde** (chem.) ferrous sulphate, green vitriol, copperas.

caparrosa-do-campo s. f. (pl. **caparrosas-do-campo**), plant of the family Nyctaginaceae (Neea theifera).

capataz s. m. 1. foreman, headman (plate A 7). 2. captain (of a gang of workmen). 3. taskmaster, master shifter. 4. warden, overseer. 5. keeper, guard.

capatazar, capatazear v. 1. to perform the duties of a foreman or headworkman. 2. to manage, direct, oversee.

capatazia s. f. 1. office, function and authority of a foreman. 2. group of workmen led by a foreman. 3. custom duty.

capa-verde s. m. (pl. **capas-verdes**), (Braz., pop.) the devil.

capaz adj. m. + f. (pl. **-es**) 1. capable, able. 2. apt, fit. 3. capacious. 4. good. 5. ample. 6. efficient. 7. obliging. 8. competent, skillful. 9. sufficient.

10. (jur.) capable of succeeding to an estate, heritable.
~ **de** capable of, able to.ˈ **ela é ~ de tudo** she has it in her. **ele é bem ~ de cometer tal tolice** he is equal to committing such a blunder. **ele é ~ de cometer toda e qualquer sujeira** he is up to any mean trick. **ele é ~ de tudo** he is game for anything. **nenhum remédio é ~ de salvá-lo** no remedies avail to save him. **você não é ~ de fazer isto?** are you unable to do this?

capcioso adj. 1. captious. 2. catchy, insidious. 3. cunning, sly. 4. fallacious. 5. crafty, tricky, deceitful. ‖ **-amente** adv. captiously, fallaciously.
argumento ~ sophistical argument. **ele é um indivíduo muito** ~ he is a faultfinding fellow. **o caráter** ~ **de sua argumentação** the captiousness of his reasoning.

capeado adj. hidden, disguised.

capeador s. m. 1. one who hides or covers up s. th. 2. deceiver, illuder. 3. bullfighter.

capeamento s. m. 1. coping of a wall. 2. the cover stone or crown stone of a wall or chimney-pot.

capear (I) v. 1. to cover with a cloak. 2. to hide, conceal. 3. to disguise, mask. 4. to face, coat (with stones, masonry). 5. to delude, deceive. 6. to call, summon. 7. to provoke, irritate (bulls with a banderole or red cape). 8. to make signs with a cape or cloak. 9. (naut.) to bring to, round to. 10. to by-pass a dangerous zone.

capear (II) v. to place copestones on the crown of the wall.

capeba s. m. 1. friend, comrade. 2. companion. 3. buddy, pal. 4. f. (Braz.) plant of the pepper family (Piper rohrii).

capeba-do-campo s. f. (pl. **capebas-do-campo**) (Braz.) a large herb of the family Piperaceae (Piper peltatum).

capeia s. f. copestone, copingstone.

capeirão s. m. (pl. **-ões**) a big cape or cloak.

capeiro s. m. 1. the bearer of a canopy or pluvial in a procession. 2. hat-rack, coat-hanger. 3. wardrobe, clothes closet. 4. keeper of a wardrobe, property master.

capela s. f. 1. chapel. 2. a small chapel in the country. 3. sanctuary, shrine. 4. a little church with one altar only. 5. side aisle of a church with its own altar. 6. a group of church musicians, band, choir. 7. eyelid. 8. bazaar, shop for fancy wares. 9. (tech.) dome of a furnace. 10. a glass-inclosed compartment used for chemical experiments. 11. pious bequest. 12. (Braz.) village, hamlet.
~ **de Nossa Senhora** Lady chapel. ~ **de olho** eyelid. ~ **real** royal chapel. **loja de** ~ millinery shop, toyshop. **mestre de** ~ chapel master, band leader.

capela (II) s. f. garland.

capelada (I) s. f. 1. holster cap. 2. leather strap on buskins.

capelada (II) s. f. a quantity of garlands.

capela-de-viúva s. f. (pl. **capelas-de-viúvas**), (bot.) purple wreath.

capela-mor s. f. (pl. **capelas-mores**) high altar, chancel.

capelânia s. f. office, dignity, authority and functions of a chaplain, chaplaincy, chaplainship.

capelão s. m. (pl. **-ões**) 1. chaplain, padre, priest. 2. (Braz.): a) old and cunning leader of a gang of monkeys. b) leader of a litany or prayer.

capelina s. f. 1. (arch.) head-piece of an armour, helmet. 2. headdress of women or children.

capelinha s. f. a small chapel.

casar na ~ **verde** (Braz., pop.) to get married in a police court, to have a shotgun wedding.

capelista s. m. + f. 1. proprietor or salesman (or saleswoman) of a millinery shop. 2. haberdasher. 3. draper. 4. (Braz.) inhabitant of a parish.

capelo s. m. 1. hood, cowl. 2. cap. 3. (arch.) headdress worn by widows and nuns. 4. doctor's cap. 5. cardinal's hat. 6. tester, canopy. 7. chimney-cap, chimney-pot, chimney-hood. ~ de cardeal red hat. ~ de viúva a widow's mourning veil. ~ giratório (archit.) turn-cap. ~ rotativo da chaminé chimney-jack.

capeludo adj. hooded, having a cowl: (of birds) crested, tufted.

capenga s. m. + f. 1. a cripple. 2. limping or hobbling person. || adj. lame, crippled, maimed, hobbling, limping.

capengante adj. m. + f. 1. lame. 2. crippled, maimed. 3. twisted, bent. 4. hobbling, limping.

capengar, capenguear v. to limp, hobble.

capepena s. f. (Braz.) 1. broken twigs and branches which help hunters to find their way back. 2. a rough trail formed by broken branches.

caperom s. m. (pl. -ons) (N. Braz.) pal, buddy, comrade, companion.

caperotada s. f. a stew made from the minced, roasted meat of fowl.

capeta s. m. (Braz., pop.) 1. the devil, the evil one. 2. a naughty or mischievous child.

capetagem s. f. (pl. -ens) (Braz., fam.) 1. mischievous act. 2. prank, lark. 3. devilish trick, deviltry. 4. sentimental or amorous expression or movement. 5. faces, grimaces.

capetão s. m. (pl. -ões) (Braz.) a long loaf of bread made from flour and mashed beans.

capete s. m. (N. Braz.) the devil.

capetinga s. f. (Braz.) blue-grass.

capetinha s. m. + f. a naughty or mischievous child.

capiangagem s. f. (pl. -ens) pilfering.

capiangar v. to steal cunningly, pilfer, filch.

capiango s. m. (Braz.) 1. pilferer, filcher. 2. scoundrel, crook. 3. sly thief, cunning robber.

capiau s. m. (f. capioa) backwoodsman, yokel, rustic.

capicongo s. m. derisive nickname of backwoods people.

capicua s. f. 1. (math.) a group of ciphers which give the same number, reading from either side (e. g. 787). 2. (game of dominoes) the domino which can be used to finish the game on either side.

capilar adj. m. + f. 1. capillary, capillaceous. 2. hairlike. 3. fine, very slender. 4. minute. artérias ~es capillary vessels. ação ~ cappillary action. tubo ou vaso ~ capillary, capillary tube.

capilária-do-canadá s. f. (pl. capilárias-do-canadá) (bot.) the maidenhair fern (Adiantum pedatum).

capilaridade s. f. capillarity.

capilé s. m. 1. a drink prepared with water, sugar and syrup. 2. capillaire: a syrup prepared from maidenhair juice.

capiliforme adj. m. + f. capilliform, hairlike.

capilossada s. f. (N. Braz.) a risky enterprise or adventure.

capim (I) s. m. (pl. -ins) 1. common name of several species of gramineous and ciperaceous plants. 2. grass, sedge. 3. hay. 4. (pop.) money, cash, salary. 5. herb, herbage.

capim (II) s. f. (pl. -ins) rough mortar of inferior quality made with sand and cement.

capim-amarelo s. m. (pl. capins-amarelos), (Braz., bot.) sword-grass, reed canary grass, gardener's garters.

capim-barba-de-bode s. m. (pl. capins-barba-de-bode), (Braz.) common name of two plants, one of the grass family (Sporobolus sprengelii), the other of the sedge family (Cyperus compressus).

capim-branco s. m. (pl. capins-brancos), (Braz.) feather grass.

capim-cabaiú s. m. (pl. capins-cabaiú), (Braz.) carpet grass, Louisiana grass.

capim-cabelo-de-negro s. m. (pl. capins-cabelo-de-negro), (Braz.) molasses grass.

capim-calandrínia s. m. (pl. capins-calandrínia), (Braz., bot.) Egyptian grass, crowfoot grass.

capim-camalote s. m. (pl. capins-camalote) buffalo grass. St. Augustine grass.

capim-catingueiro s. m. (pl. capins-catingueiros), (Braz.) molasses grass.

capim-cevadinha s. m. (pl. capins-cevadinha) 1. brome, brome grass. 2. awnless brome grass. 3. barren brome grass. 4. soft chess, goose corn.

capim-cheiroso s. m. (pl. capins-cheirosos) (Braz., bot.) a herb of the family Cyperaceae (Kyllinga odorata).

capim-chorão s. m. (pl. capins-chorões) weeping love grass.

capim-cidreira s. m. (pl. capins-cidreiras), lemon grass.

capim-cortesia s. m. (pl. capins-cortesia), black seed grass.

capim-da-cidade s. m. (pl. capins-da-cidade) 1. Bermuda grass. 2. dog's tooth, dog's tail grass. 3. crab grass.

capim-da-colônia s. m. (pl. capins-da-colônia) 1. shama millet. 2. guinea grass. 3. Pará grass.

capim-das-roças s. m. (pl. capins-das-roças), burgrass.

capim-de-bezerro s. m. (pl. capins-de-bezerro) 1. grass of tonga. 2. ridging grass.

capim-de-burro s. m. (pl. capins-de-burro) 1. Bermuda grass. 2. dog's tooth, dog's tail grass. 3. crab grass.

capim-de-cavalo s. m. (pl. capins-de-cavalo) 1. Pará grass. 2. guinea grass. 3. blue moss grass.

capim-de-cheiro s. m. (pl. capins-de-cheiro), (Braz.) 1. citronella grass. 2. lemon grass. 3. vetiver.

capim-de-hortas s. m. (pl. capins-de-hortas) crab grass.

capim-de-nossa-senhora s. m. (pl. capins-de-nossa-senhora), (bot.) Job's tears.

capim-de-pasto s. m. (pl. capins-de-pasto) Bahia grass.

capim-do-campo s. m. (pl. capins-do-campo) 1. smooth meadow grass. 2. June grass. 3. Kentucky bluegrass.

capim-doce s. m. (pl. capins-doces) 1. bulbous bluegrass. 2. sweet tussock.

capim-do-colorado s. m. (pl. capins-do-colorado) 1. Colorado grass. 2. Texas millet. 3. concho grass.

capim-do-pomar s. m. (pl. capins-do-pomar), (bot.) cocksfoot, orchard grass.

capim-do-prado s. m. (pl. capins-do-prado), (bot.) meadow fescue.

capim-dos-pampas s. m. (pl. capins-dos-pampas), (bot.) pampas grass.

capim-elefante s. m. (pl. capins-elefante), (bot.) elephant grass.

capim-gigante s. m. (pl. capins-gigantes), gama grass.

capim-gomoso s. m. (pl. capins-gomosos), (bot.) French weed.

capim-gordo s. m. (pl. capins-gordos) 1. West Indian sour grass. 2. Hilo grass. 3. molasses grass.

capim-gordura s. m. (pl. capins-gordura), molasses grass.

capim-limão s. m. (pl. capins-limão), lemon grass.

capim-lucas s. m. (pl. capins-lucas) blackseed grass.

capim-melado, capim-meloso s. m. (pl. capins-melados, capins-melosos) molasses grass.

capim-milhã s. m. (pl. capins-milhã) paspalum grass, crab grass.

capim-milhã-roxo s. m. (pl. capins-milhã-roxo), (bot.) browntop.

capim-mimoso s. m. (pl. capins-mimosos) 1. old witch grass. 2. lizardtail grass. 2. slender meadow grass. 4. feather grass.

capim-mimoso-do-agreste s. m. (pl. capins-mimosos--do-agreste), (Braz.) slender finger grass.

capim-mourão s. m. (pl. capins-mourão) blackseed grass.

capim-nó s. m. (pl. capins-nó) carpet grass, Louisiana grass.

capim-panasco s. m. (pl. capins-panasco), (bot.) bent, fiorin, creeping bent.

capim-pancuã s. m. (pl. capins-pancuã), (bot.) joint grass.

capim-paraturá s. m. (pl. capins-paraturá), (bot.) creek sedge.

capim-peba s. m. (pl. capins-peba) ridging grass.

capim-pé-de-galinha s. m. (pl. capins-pé-de-galinha), 1. barn grass, cockspur grass. 2. cocksfoot. 3. dog's tail grass, crab grass. 4. annual bluegrass, low spear grass. 5. shamalo grass, shama millet. 6. feather grass.

capim-peguento s. m. (pl. capins-peguentos) ginger grass.

capim-rabo-de-burro s. m. (pl. capins-rabo-de-burro), beard grass, little blue stem.

capim-relvão s. m. (pl. capins-relvão), (bot.) teff.

capim-salgado s. m. (pl. capins-salgados) 1. salt grass. 2. salt-marsh grass. 3. spart grass.

capim-sapé s. m. (pl. capins-sapé), (bot.) Brazilian satin tail.

capim-sempre-verde s. m. (pl. capins-sempre-verdes), wood meadow grass.

capim-verde s. m. (pl. capins-verdes) green foxtail--grass.

capim-vetiver s. m. (pl. capins-vetiver), (bot.) vetiver.

capina s. f. 1. act of cutting the grass of a meadow. 2. act of clearing a field from weeds. 3. weeding, hoeing, grubbing.

capinação s. f. (pl. -ões) weeding, hoeing or grubbing.

capinadeira s. f. 1. weeding machine. 2. cultivator.

capinado adj. cleared of weeds, weeded.

capinador s. m. weeder, hoer, mower.

capinal s. m. (pl. -ais) that part of a tract of land or farm which is covered with a dense growth of grass.

capinar v. 1. to clear a field from weeds. 2. to cut the grass of a meadow. 3. to weed, hoe. 4. (Braz., pop.) to defame, slander.

capincho s. m. (zool.) a male capybara or car-pincho.

capineira s. f. 1. that part of the farmland which is planted with grass. 2. meadow. 3. pasture, hay-field. 4. f. of capineiro.

capineiro s. m. (also capinheiro) 1. hoer, weeder. 2. grass mower. 3. mowing machine. 4. a freshwater fish (Anostomus knerii).

capinha s. f. 1. cape, dolman. 2. the red cape a bullfighter uses to irritate the bull. 3. m. bullfighter who carries a red cloak in order to irritate the bull, banderillero.

capinzal s. m. (pl. -ais) 1. land covered with a dense growth of grass. 2. pasture, hayfield.

capioa s. (f. of capiau) 1. backwoods woman. 2. wife of a backwoods farmer.

capiongo adj. (Braz.) 1. sad, mournful. 2. dejected, depressed. 3. glum, sullen, moody. 4. (pop.) suffering from an imperfection in one of the eyes.

capirocho s. m. (Braz., pop.) the devil.

capirote s. m. hood, old-fashioned cowl.

capiroto s. m. (Braz., pop.) the devil, demon, malignant spirit.

capiscar v. 1. to understand badly or insufficiently (a language, art or trade). 2. to begin to understand. 3. to grasp the sense of s. th. 4. to comprehend, understand.

capista s. m. + f. a book cover illustrator.

capitação s. f. (pl. -ões) 1. head tax, capitation. 2. poll-tax, poll. 3. tax or contribution levied on each member of a society or political group. 4. head--money.

capitado adj. capitate.

capital s. m. (pl. -ais) 1. capital. 2. available pecuniary resources. 3. funds, stock. 4. principal. 5. means, wealth. 6. capital stock of an industrial or business enterprise. 7. estate. 8. f.: a) capital, metropolis. b) capital letter. ‖ adj. m. + f. 1. capital. 2. essential, of special importance. 3. primal, primary. 4. vital, principal. 5. serious. 6 of or pertaining to the head. 7. (jur.) of, pertaining to or relative to capital punishment. 8. deadly, mortal, fatal. ∼ circulante floating capital. ∼ de comércio stock in trade. ∼ depositado em banco stock in bank. ∼ de um banco bank-stock. ∼ de risco risk capital. ∼ disponível capital at hand. ∼ em circulação floating stock, rolling capital. ∼ empatado dead capital, dormant capital. ∼ por ações capital stock. ∼ social joint stock. crime ∼ capital crime. de importância ∼ of vital importance. investir ∼ num negócio to put money in a business. ponto ∼ da questão pith of the question.

capital-ações s. m. pl. (com.) share capital.

capitalismo s. m. capitalism: 1. economic system in which the chief power lies in the hands of capitalists. 2. the ownership of capital.

capitalista s. m. + f. capitalist: 1. person who possesses capital. 2. person of large means. 3. partner of a business enterprise who supplies the necessary money, stockholder. ‖ adj. 1. of, pertaining to or relative to capitalism or capitalists. 2. capitalistic(al). 3. supplying working capital or funds (as partner of an enterprise).

capitalização s. f. (pl. -ões) capitalization: act of capitalizing or converting into capital.

capitalizar v. 1. to capitalize. 2. to convert into capital. 3. to estimate or compute the present value of a periodical income. 4. to accumulate, add to, increase. 5. to collect, amass money or wealth.

capitalizável adj. m. + f. (pl. -áveis) capitalizable, that can be capitalized, suitable for capitalization.

capital-obrigações s. m. pl. (com.) debenture capital.

capitanear v. 1. to command or act as a captain. 2. to lead, direct. 3. to command. 4. to govern.

capitania s. f. captainship: 1. condition, dignity or authority of a captain. 2. command, control. 3. (Braz., hist.) designation of the first administrative divisions of Brazil. 4. district or port under the command of a captain. 5. captaincy, leadership.

capitânia s. f. (navy, also capitaina) 1. admiralship, flagship. 2. admiral, naval commander in chief. ‖ adj. of, pertaining to or relative to a flagship or its commander.

capitão s. m. (pl. -ães) 1. captain. 2. commander of a company or troop; military commander. 3. leader, chief, headman. 4. officer of the army ranking below a major and above a lieutenant. 5. commander or master of a vessel, skipper. 6. formerly, the commander of local militias. 7. political boss, chieftain, hetman. 8. foreman of a group of workers. 9. (sports) leader of a team. 10. administrative officer, commander of territorial waters. ∼ de indústria industrial leader, tycoon.

capitão-aviador s. m. (pl. capitães-aviadores) air--force captain.

capitão-chico s. m. (pl. capitães-chicos) a crossbreed of Brazilian swine.

capitão-das-porcarias s. m. (pl. capitães-das-porcarias), a bird of the family Dendrocolaptidae (Lochmias nematura).

capitão-de-assaltos s. m. (pl. capitães-de-assaltos), (Baz., pop.) leader of a gang of ruffians who used to intimidate and enslave country-people.

capitão-de-cabotagem s. m. (pl. capitães-de-cabotagem) captain of a cabotage ship.

capitão-de-corveta s. m. (pl. capitães-de-corveta), (navy) captain of a corvette, lieutenant-commander.

capitão-de-fragata s. m. (pl. capitães-de-fragata), (navy) commander.

capitão-de-mar-e-guerra s. m. (pl. capitães-de-mar-e-guerra) 1. captain. 2. naval officer ranking immediately below a rear admiral.

capitão-de-saíra s. m. (pl. capitães-de-saíra), (Braz.) bird of the family Cotingidae (Attila rufus).

capitão-do-campo s. m. (pl. capitães-do-campo) 1. (Braz., hist.) pursuer and catcher of runaway slaves. 2. foreman of a group of Negro farmhands.

capitão-do-mato s. m. (pl. capitães-do-mato) 1. (Braz., hist.) pursuer and catcher of runaway slaves. 2. (ornith.): a) puffbird. b) (Notharchus swainsoni) a trogon (Trogon strigilatus). 3. (ent.) four-footed butterfly. 4. plant of the family Cucurbitaceae (Cayaponia cabocla).

capitão-mor s. m. (pl. capitães-mores) 1. commander of a militia. 2. commander of local police troops. 3. (Braz., hist.) governor of a capitania (province).

capitão-tenente s. m. (pl. capitães-tenentes) naval officer ranking immediately below a commander.

capitari s. m. (Braz.) 1. a male turtle. 2. plant of the family Bignoniaceae (Couralia taxophora).

capitato adj. capitate: 1. head-shaped, headlike in form. 2. (bot.) capitated, growing in a head. 3. having a head.

capitel s. m. (pl. -éis) 1. (archit.): a) capital: head of a column. b) chapiter, cushion capital. 2. (mil.) cap of the touch-hole of an old-fashioned cannon. 3. head of a skycrocket, warhead of a rocket. 4. (chem.) beaked cap of an alembic.

capitilúvio s. m. the act of washing only one's head.

capitolino adj. Capitoline, of or belonging to the Capitol.

capitólio s. m. 1. (Roman hist.) the Capitol: the temple of Jupiter at Rome. 2. (fig.) glory, triumph, splendour.

capitonídeos s. m. pl. (ornith.) Capitonidae, a family that comprises the barbets.

capitoso adj. 1. headstrong, obstinate, stubborn. 2. (bot.) capitate, capitated. 3. heady (said of strong wine).

capítula s. f. (rel.) a short passage or prayer from the breviary, capitulum, excerpt from the Scripture.

capitulação s. f. (pl. -ões) 1. capitulation. 2. act of capitulating. 3. surrender, rendition. 4. conditions of a surrender, conditions of an agreement between litigants. 5. (fig.) subjection, submission. 6. (fig.) cession, concession.

capitulada s. f. 1. accusation formulated in chapters or articles. 2. censure, reprimand, reproof.

capitulador s. m. 1. capitulator, one who surrenders or capitulates. 2. (arch.) accuser.

capitulante s. m. 1. member of a chapter. 2. capitulator. || adj. m. + f. 1. belonging to or having a voice in a chapter. 2. surrendering, capitulating.

capitular (I) s. m. full voting member of a chapter, capitular.

capitular (II) s. f. (typogr.) capital letters or characters at the beginning of a chapter. || adj. m. + f.

upper case, capital, of or pertaining to capital letters.

capitular (III) adj. m. + f. capitular, capitulary, of or pertaining to a chapter.

capitular (IV) v. 1. to capitulate, surrender on terms. 2. to agree on certain conditions. 3. to yield, relinquish. 4. to describe in chapters or articles. 5. to substantiate an accusation in paragraphs or chapters. 6. to separate in chapters. 7. to enumerate, number, specify. 8. to enunciate, articulate. 9. to classify. 10. to qualify. 11. to brand as, accuse. 12. to compromise, come to terms. 13. to read the divine service, officiate.

capitulares s. f. pl. (hist.) 1. royal decrees in medieval France. 2. civil or ecclesiastical ordinances.

capituleiro s. m. (R. C. Church) capitulary: book containing excerpts of the Bible read in the liturgy.

capituliforme adj. m. + f. (bot.) capituliform.

capítulo (I) s. m. 1. chapter, division of a book. 2. paragraph of a law. 3. section of a treatise, contract or agreement.

isto é um ~ à parte (coll.) that comes under another head, that is a horse of a different colour.

capítulo (II) s. m. chapter: 1. body of clergymen attached to a church. 2. meeting of the members of a religious order. 3. place where canons and other church dignitaries meet. 4. an organized branch of some society or fraternity.

capítulo (III) s. m. capitulum, flower-head of composite plants.

capivara s. f. (Braz.) 1. (zool.) capybara, capibara (Hydrochoerus capybara). 2. plant of the family Aristolochiaceae (Aristolochia birostris).

capixaba s. m. + f. (Braz.) 1. formerly a nickname of the inhabitants of Vitória (capital of Espírito Santo). 2. native or inhabitant of Espírito Santo. 3. m. small agricultural establishment, small farm or ranch. || adj. m. + f. of, pertaining to or relative to the Brazilian state of Espírito Santo or its capital Vitória.

capnófugo adj. capnofugal, smoke-preventing.

capnóide s. f. medicinal plant of the family Papaveraceae (Fumaris officinalis).

capnomancia s. f. capnomancy, divination by means of smoke.

capnomante s. m. + f. capnomancer, diviner by means of smoke.

capnomântico adj. capnomantic(al), of or relative to capnomancy.

capô s. m. (mot.) hood.

capoeira (I) s. f. 1. big chicken coop. 2. cage, mew. 3. place where capons are held for fattening. 4. (fort.): a) gabion. b) a deep defensive ditch with embrasures cut into it.

capoeira (II) s. f. (Braz.) 1. weeds and brushwood cut off and burned or otherwise destroyed. 2. new growth of herbs and shrubbery on cheared land. 3. copse, coppice. 4. knee timber, boscage, scrub, brushwood. 5. bird of the family Odontophoridae (Odontophorus capueira). 6. criminal technique of sudden, violent assault, characterized by agile movements of the body. 7. ruffian using the capoeira technique.

~ grossa brushwood country interspersed with big trees. ~ rala (N. Braz.) a tract of land cleared annually.

capoeiraçu s. f. (Braz.) dense woodland.

capoeirada (I) s. f. (Braz.) a group of capoeiristas.

capoeirada (II) s. f. a group of highwaymen or bandits.

capoeira-de-machado s. m. (pl. capoeiras-de-machado). (Braz., pop.) forest ready for cutting.

capoeira-de-pau-de-machado s. f. (pl. **capoeiras-de-pau-de-machado**), (Braz.) popular designation of a forest rich in hardwood trees.

capoeira-furada s. f. (pl. **capoeiras-furadas**), (Braz., pop.) clearings in dense virgin forests.

capoeiragem s. f. (pl. **-ens**) 1. fighting system of **capoeiras**. 2. behaviour or ways of life typical for **capoeiras**.

capoeirano s. m. (N. Braz.) backwoodsman.

capoeirão (I) s. m. (pl. **-ões**), (N. Braz.) 1. dense forest. 2. virgin forest.

capoeirão (II) s. m. (pl. **-ões**) broken old man. ‖ adj. sedate, calm, peaceful (said of old people).

capoeirar v. to practice **capoeira**.

capoeirinha s. f. (Braz.) open or sparse woodland.

capoeirista s. m. + f., **capoeira** m. a **capoeira** practitioner.

capoeiro (I) s. m. 1. chicken thief. 2. sneak thief, pilferer.

capoeiro (II) s. m. (Braz.) a kind of small deer without antlers. ‖ adj. of or pertaining to deforestable tracts of land.

capona s. f. a heavy cloak of a lady.

caponete s. m. (S. Braz.) a clump of a few trees in open country.

caponga s. f. (Braz.) 1. a small natural fresh-water lake in the sandy dunes of the seashore. 2. a ravine of wet sand usually covered with hygrophilous vegetation. 3. a fishline with a little ball instead of a hook which serves to attract the fish (they are readily caught with the hand).

caporal s. m. (pl. **-ais**) 1. squad leader, corporal. 2. a kind of coarse, minced tobacco.

capororoca s. f. (Braz.) 1. (ornith.) coscoroba. 2. common name of several plants of the family Myrsinaceae.

capota s. f. 1. cap, hood, lad's or children's headdress. 2. top or hood of a carriage or motorcar, capote (plate C 15). 3. canopy. ~ **conversível** folding-deck, convertible top (plate V 3). ~ **de caleche** calash. ~ **ou coberta de motor** motor cowling, engine cowling, cowl (plate A 3).

capotado adj. overturned, upturned, upset, capsized.

capotagem s. f. (pl. **-ens**) 1. capsize, capsizal. 2. act of capsizing. 3. upset, overturn.

capotar v. 1. to capsize. 2. to upset, overturn.

capote s. m. 1. a long and wide cape with a large collar or hood. 2. cloak, overcoat, mantle. 3. tabard, capot, throw-over. 4. a bullfighter's embroidered cape. 5. (fig.): a) disguise, mask. b) pretense, show, appearance. 6. (Braz.) tree of the family Sterculaceae (Sterculia speciosa). 7. (cards) capot. **dar um** ~ (cards) to win all the tricks, score a capot against. **levar** ~ (cards, fig.) to lose completely. **não é chuva para quem tem** ~ that's nothing for a man who has guts.

capoteira s. f. brief case, leather case for carrying documents.

capoteiro s. m. (Braz.) manufacturer or seller of motorcar bonnets, tops or cowling.

capotilha s. f. headcloth, kerchief worn by women.

capotilho s. m. small cloak or cape.

caprichar v. 1. to try to excel. 2. to perfect, elaborate carefully. 3. to take pride in doing a thing well. 4. to pride o. s. on (or upon). 5. to make it a point of honour or ambition.

capricho s. m. 1. caprice. 2. fancy, freak, whim. 3. freakishness, skittishness. 4. fitfulness, fickleness. 5. craze, rage. 6. notion, fad. 7. humour, humor. 8. (mus.) capriccio. 9. crotchet, perversity. 10. maggot, vagary. 11. hazard. 12. extravagance.

~ **da natureza** a freak of nature. **ele fez o serviço a** ~ he did his work to perfection. **homem de** ~ a whimsical fellow, capricious man.

caprichoso adj. 1. capricious. 2. fanciful, freakish, whimsical. 3. skittish. 4. fickle, fitful, faddish. 5. humoursome. 6. petulant, cantankerous. 7. vagarious. 8. temperamental. 9. arbitrary, difficult. 10. maggoty. 11. perverse. 12. obstinate, stubborn. 13. extravagant. 14. priding o. s. in doing everything well. 15. ambitious. ‖ **-amente** adv. capriciously, whimsically, freakishly, temperamentally. **o seu caráter** ~ his capriciousness. **pessoa -a** crotcheteer.

cáprico adj. (chem.) capric, of or pertaining to capric acid.

capricórnio s. m. 1. Capricorn: a) a southern zodiacal constellation. b) the tenth sign of the zodiac, sign of the winter solstice. 2. (ent.) capricorn beetle, goat chafer.

caprídeo adj. caprine: of, pertaining to or resembling a goat, caprid.

caprificação s. f. (pl. **-ões**) caprification: a treatment which furthers the maturing of figs.

caprificar v. to caprificate.

caprifigo s. m. (bot.) caprifig (Ficus carica sylvestris).

caprifoliácea s. f. 1. a caprifolium, any plant of the honeysuckle family. 2. a caprifoliaceous plant.

caprifoliáceo adj. (bot.) caprifoliaceous.

caprimulgídeos s. m. pl. (ornith.) Caprimulgidae: a nonpasserine bird family: goatsuckers, frogmouths, oilbirds.

caprimulgiformes s. m. pl. (ornith.) Caprimulgiformes, an order that comprises the goatsuckers.

caprino adj. caprine, caprinic, hircine, goatlike.

caprípede s. m. (poet.) capripede, satyr. ‖ adj. m. + f. capripede, having feet like a goat.

capro s. m. (poet.) he-goat, billy-goat.

capróico adj. (chem.) caproic, hexylic.

caprum adj. m. + f. (pl. **-uns**) caprine, caprinic, hircine.

capsela s. f. a small capsule, little pod.

cápsula s. f. 1. capsule: a) (bot.) a seed-vessel, pod, shuck, husk, case, boll. b) (chem.) a small shallow cup, tray, scorifer. c) cartridge case, fuse-cap. d) (med., pharm.) container of digestible material for remedies, cachet. e) (anat., biol., zool.) membraneous envelope of an organ. 2. small case or container (plate B 4).

capsulado adj. having a capsule, furnished with a capsule, enclosed in a capsule, capsuled.

capsular (I) adj. m. + f. capsular, pertaining to a capsule, resembling a capsule, capsulate, capsuliform.

capsular (II) v. to capsulate, enclose in a capsule.

capsulífero adj. capsuliferous.

capsuliforme adj. m. + f. capsuliform.

captação s. f. (pl. **-ões**) 1. captation, captivation. 2. impounding (of water). 3. act of captivating, inveigling.

captador s. m. captivator, inveigler, allurer.

captagem s. f. (pl. **-ens**) act of captivating or bringing in, collection, impounding (of water).

captante s. m. + f. 1. captivator. 2. inveigler, allurer. ‖ adj. m. + f. 1. captivating. 2. inveigling, alluring.

captar v. 1. to captivate. 2. to capture, catch. 3. to dominate, subdue. 4. to attract, fascinate, charm. 5. to ingratiate o. s. 6. to collect, impound (water), dam up. 7. (radio, T.V.) to pick up (a radio broadcast). ~ **a benevolência de** to curry favour. **~am a notícia** they picked up the news. **ela captou a amizade dele** she insinuated herself into his good graces.

captor s. m. capturer, captor.
captores s. m. pl. (Braz.) scientific term for aboriginal races who live as hunters or fruit collectors but do not know agriculture.
captura s. f. 1. act of capturing. 2. capture, seizure. 3. (mil.) taking. 4. arrest, detention. 5. prize. 6. caption. 7. catch, prey, booty.
capturador s. m. captor, capturer.
capturar v. 1. to capture. 2. to seize by force, take forcibly possession of. 3. (mil.) to conquer, occupy, take. 4. to corral (cattle, animals). 5. (hunt.) to catch, bag in. 6. to arrest, apprehend.
~am o tesouro they made prey of the treasure. o inimigo capturou a cidade the enemy carried the town.
capuaba s. m. (Braz.) 1. ground suitabe for clearing and agriculture. 2. newly cleared and planted field. 3. hut, hovel.
capuão s. m. = capão.
capuava s. m. (Braz.) 1. rustic b.ickwoodsman. 2. highwayman, robber. 3. a sparse forest made up of softwood or brushwood only.
capucha (I) s. f. a kind of hood, bonnet, cowl, capuchin.
capucha (II) s. f. 1. the religious order of the Capuchins. 2. a Capuchin convent.
à ~ unassumingly, modestly.
capuchana s. f. (naut.) hood or covering at the top of a companionway, hood or cover for a small boat.
capuchar v. 1. to outfit with a hood. 2. to cover with a hood. 3. (fig.) to disguise, cloak, veil.
capuchinha s. f. ornamental plant of the family Tropaeolaceae.
capuchinho s. m. 1. small hood or cowl. 2. (eccl.) Capuchin, Capuchin friar, monk of an austere branch of the Franciscan order. 3. (fig.) unpretentious modest man, man of austere character. ‖ adj. Capuchin: of, pertaining to or relative to this order.
capucho (I) s. m. (eccl.) a Capuchin friar or monk. ‖ adj. 1. (eccl.) of, pertaining to or relative to the Capuchin order. 2. penitent, repenting 3. austere, severe, strict. 4. solitary.
ele vive à -a he leads an austere life, he lives without ostentation.
capucho (II) s. m. (Braz.) 1. cotton boll, pod of a cotton plant. 2. the black seeds of a cotton plant (genus Gossypium).
capucho (III) s. m. (Port., prov.) a shock of rye.
capulho s. m. 1. (bot.) involucre of a flower, seed-vessel. 2. capsule, case. 3. cotton boll.
capurreiro s. m. (Braz., pop.) backwoodsman, rustic yokel.
capuz s. m. 1. hood. 2. cowl, cap. 3. bonnet.
capuz-de-fradinho s. m. (pl. capuzes-de-fradinho), (bot.) friar's cowl.
caqueado s. m. (N. E. Braz., vulg.) the sexual act.
caquear v. (Braz., theat. sl.) to improvise, introduce extempore remarks in the text.
caqueirada s. f. 1. a heap of potsherds or shards. 2. lots of broken, old or useless things, trash, junk. 3. a blow with a piece of broken earthenware. 4. act of throwing shards. 5. (Braz., sl.) a hard slap into the face.
caqueiro s. m. potsherd, shard, piece of broken earthenware.
caquemono s. m. kakemono: Japanese silk or paper painting.
caquera s. f. (Braz., bot.) Christmas bush.
caquético adj. (med.) cachectic, cachexic.
caquexia s. f. (med.) cachexy, cachexia, ill health, general weakness.

caqui s. m. (Braz.) kaki: the fruit of the Japanese persimmon tree.
cáqui s. m. khaki, khaki-coloured cotton cloth. ‖ adj. m. + f. khaki, khaki-coloured.
caquizeiro s. m. Japanese persimmon fruit and tree.
cara s. f. 1. face. 2. the front part of the head, visage. 3. countenance, appearance. 4. look, mien. 5. outward appearance, semblance. 6. (pop.) boldness, impudence.
~ a ~ face to face. ~ amarrada long face. ~ de gato pingado a drooping face. ~ de lua cheia pudding face. ~ de páscoa a smiling countenance. ~ de poucos amigos unpleasing face, unpleasant look, unfriendly countenance. ~ de quem comeu e não gostou a disappointed expression on the face. ~ de tacho a look of disapointment. ~ ou coroa heads or tails. à ~ descoberta bare-faced, frankly, openly. dar a alguém com a porta na ~ to shut the dor in a person's face. de ~ in front of. dizer na ~ de alguém to tell frankly or openly. ele pôs outra ~ he assumed a different expression. ele puxou uma ~ comprida he pulled a long face. está na ~ dele! that stands written on his brow! eu lho disse na ~ I gave it him straight. ficar com ~ de asno to be disappointed. livrar a ~ to come out well. meter a ~ 1. to penetrate, enter, appear daringly. 2. to attack. mostrar boa ou má ~ to show a kind or unfriendly face. não adianta puxar ~ feia it's no use frowning. não quero mais ver a ~ dele I do not want to see him again. não sabe onde tem a ~ he is a great simpleton. não ter ~ para not to have the guts to... nunca vi a ~ dele! I don't know him from Adam. pagar o olho da ~ to pay through the nose, pay an exorbitant price. quebrar a ~ to fail, misscarry. quem vê ~ não vê coração one can not judge from appearances. rir na ~ de alguém to laugh in a person's face. sem ~ faceless. só ~s conhecidas only familiar faces. ter duas ~s to have two faces, be false. torcer a ~ to be reluctant, show ill will. uma mão lava a outra, e ambas a ~! do a kindness, receive a kindness. virar a ~ to change one's mind, refuse s. th.
cará s. m. (Braz.) 1. common name of several plants of the family Dioscoreaceae; the yams. 2. a rustic ball. 3. common name of several fresh-water fishes (Mentricirrhus americanus).
Carabídeos s. m. pl. (ent.) Carabidae: a family of beetles.
carabina s. f. carabine, carbine, rifle.
carabinada s. f. a riffle-shot, discharge of a carabine.
carabineiro s. m. carabineer, rifleman.
caraca (I) s. f. an ancient Portuguese vessel of about 200 tons.
caraca (II) s. f. dried nasal mucus.
caraça s. f. 1. a paper mask, mask. 2. (fig.) a pudding face. 3. m. popular designation of a horse or ox with white spots on its muzzle.
caracará s. m. (ornith.) caracara (Milvago chimachima).
caracaraí s. m. (Braz., ornith.) chimango.
caracaxá s. m. (S. Braz.) children's rattle, rattle gourd.
Caracídeos s. m. pl. (ichth.) Characinidae, a family of freshwater fishes.
caraco s. m. 1. (Braz.) nickname given to the natives of Uruguay and Argentine. 2. (zool.) a kind of Chinese house-rat.
caracol s. m. (pl. -cóis) 1. caracol(e): a) (zool.) any land snail. b) a spiral shell. c) a spiral staircase. d) (bot.) a snailflower. 2. a curl of hair. 3. coil.

4. a spiral line, helix. 5. winding way. 6. a sharp half-turn on a horse.
casa de ~ snail shell. **escada em** ~ spiral staircase. **não vale dois caracóis** it is not worth a rush, he is not worth a flick of the finger. **pedra de** ~ snail stone.

caracolado adj. spiral-shaped, winding, curled.

caracolar, caracolear v. 1. to move in caracoles. 2. to caracol, wheel about. 3. to cavort, prance. 4. to spiral.

caracoleiro s. m. (bot.) snailflower (Phaseolus caracalla).

caractere s. m. (data processing) character.

caracteres s. m. pl. characters: 1. signs, marks. 2. written letters. 3. printing types, print, letters.

característica, caraterística s. f. 1. characteristic(s). 2. distinguishing mark, thing or quality which characterizes. 3. (math.) index or exponent of a logarithm. 4. (geom.) characteristic of a curve or graph. 5. property, quality.
ele tem as ~**s de um bibliômano** he shows the signs of a bookworm.

característico, caraterístico s. m. 1. characteristic(s). 2. typical trait, distinguishing mark. 3. character. 4. feature, signs, marks. 5. vestige. ‖ adj. 1. characteristic(al). 2. distinctive, distinguishing. 3. typic(al). 4. discriminating, discriminative. 5. peculiar, specific. 6. like, proper. 7. physiognomic(al). 8. symptomatic(al). 9. individual. 10. representative. ‖ **caracteristicamente** adv. characteristically, typically, symptomatically, specifically.

caracterização, caraterização s. f. (pl. **-ões**) 1. characterization. 2. act or process of characterizing. 3. artistic representation of a personality, impersonation. 4. making-up, make-up.

caracterizado, caraterizado adj. 1. characterized. 2. having a distinguishing mark or character. 3. (theat.) made-up.

caracterizador, caraterizador s. m. 1. characterizer. 2. (theat.) character actor, impersonator. ‖ adj. characterizing, impersonating.

caracterizante, caraterizante adj. m. + f. 1. characterizing. 2. suitable or appropriate for characterization.

caracterizar, caraterizar v. 1. to characterize. 2. to point out the specific qualities of. 3. to describe, delineate. 4. to distinguish, mark, stamp. 5. to individualize, particularize. 6. (theat.) to make up and dress (as an actor). 7. to feature, impersonate, personate, personalize. 2. ~-**s** to act in accordance with one's own character, manifest one's character.
isso o caracterizou como tolo that stamped him as a fool. **sua sinceridade caracteriza todos os seus atos** his sincerity gives colour to all he does.

caracterologia, caraterologia s. f. characterology: psychologic study of the different types of human character.

caracterológico, caraterológico adj. characterologic(al).

caracu s. m. (Braz.) 1. a crossbreed of Brazilian cattle. 2. bone marrow, medulla. ‖ adj. of, pertaining to or relative to **caracu** cattle.

cará-de-caboclo s. m. (pl. **carás-de-caboclo**), (Braz.) plant of the family Amaryllidaceae (Bomarea salsilloides).

cara-de-gato s. m. (pl. **caras-de-gato**), (Braz.) salt-water fish of the family Carangidae (Carangops amblyrhineus).

cara-de-mamão-macho s. m. (pl. **caras-de-mamão-macho**) (Braz., pop.) a long-faced individual.

cara-de-pau s. m. + f. (pl. **caras-de-pau**) (Braz., pop.) a straight-faced person. ‖ adj. straight-faced.

Caradriídeos s. m. pl. (ornith.) Charadriidae, a family of shore birds.

caradriiforme s. m. a bird belonging to the order Charadriiformes including rails, shore birds, plovers, crakes.

caradura s. m. + f. (Braz.) 1. (pop.) cynical or shameless fellow. 2. unconstrained or unceremonious person. 3. m. (Braz.): a) (fireworks) a kind of Bengal match. b) popular designation of a second-class tramway-car. c) the front bench of a tramway-car which faces the car.

caradurismo s. m. (Braz.) 1. cynism. 2. shamelessness, brazenness. 3. ease, unconstraint. 4. liveliness, briskness.

cara-fechada s. f. (pl. **caras-fechadas**), (Braz., pop.) a hard, unbroken sugar-loaf.

carafuz s. m. + f. (Braz.) mulatto, descendant of Indian and Negro. ‖ adj. mulatto (descending from Indian and Negro stock).

carafuzo s. m. male descendant of Indian and Negro. ‖ adj. descending from Indian and Negro.

caraguatá s. m. (Braz.) common name of several plants of the family Bromeliaceae, silk grass, caraguata.

caraguatal, caraguatazal s. m. (pl. **-ais**) a plot of caraguatas.

caraíba (I) s. m. + f. 1. Carib: Indian of the important Carib tribe. 2. important linguistic family of South American Indians. ‖ adj. Cariban, Caribal.

caraíba (II) s. m. (Braz.) 1. nickname given to Europeans by South American aborigines. 2. a supernatural being or thing.

caraíba (III) s. f. (Braz.) tree of the family Bignoniaceae (Tabebuia caraiba).

cara-inchada s. f. (pl. **caras-inchadas**), (Braz.) an epizootic disease of horses, mules, etc.

cará-inhame s. m. (pl. **carás-inhame**) (bot.) white yam.

caraipé s. m. (Braz.) name of various plants of the family Rosaceae, genus Licania.

carajá (I) s. m. (S. Braz.) 1. howling monkey of the genus Alouatta. 2. a variety of evergreen bamboo.

carajá (II) s. m. + f. (Braz.) Indian of the Carajá tribe. ‖ adj. of, pertaining to or relative to the Carajás.

carajé s. m. (Braz.) icing or frosting for cakes.

carajuru s. m. (N. Braz.) 1. plant of the family Bignoniaceae (Arrabidaea chica). 2. a red dyestuff extracted from this plant.

cara-lisa s. m. + f (pl. **caras-lisas**), (Braz., pop.) an impudent, cynical person.

caramanchão (pl. **-ões**), **caramanchel** (pl. **-éis**) s. m. 1. arbour, bower. 2. summer-house made of lattice-work. 3. pavillion. 4. alcove, pergola. 5. torch-light, signals given with torch-light.

caramba interj. exclamation expressing admiration or vexation: 1. dont't tell me!, by Jove! my!, blimey!, whew!, criminy!

carambina s. f. flake of ice or snow.

carambó adj. m. + f. having twisted horns (cattle).

carambola s. f. 1. the red ball at billiards. 2. carom, caramble (at billiards). 3. (fig.) cheat, fraud, deceit. 4. (bot.) carambola, Chinese gooseberry and its fruits.

carambolar v. 1. to caramble, carom (at billiards). 2. to deceive, cheat, trick. 3. to intrigue, plot, scheme. 4. to embroil, entangle. 5. to stir up trouble.

caramboleira s. f., **caramboleiro** m. carambola tree.

caramboleiro s. m. 1. swindler, cheater, impostor. 2. (fam.) liar. 3. intriguer, intrigant. 4. troublemaker.

carambolice s. f. swindle, trick, fraud. 2. intrigue, plot, scheme.

carambolim s. m. (pl. **-ins**) (cards) the simultaneous loss of three stakes at monte bank.

caramburu s. m. a refreshing drink made from Indian corn.

caramelado s. m. a caramel candy.

caramelo s. m. 1. frozen snow. 2. icicle, piece of ice. 3. molten and burnt sugar. 4. caramel, candy, blackjack. 5. (bot.) the balsam apple (Momordica charantia).

cara-metade s. f. (pl. **caras-metades**), (coll.) the better half, wife.

cará-mimoso s. m. (pl. **carás-mimosos**), (bot.) cush-cush.

caraminguás s. m. (pl. (Braz.) 1. trifles, baubles, odds and ends. 2. small change.

caraminhola s. f. 1. a crest of hair on the top of the head, forelock. 2. tuft of hair, long dishevelled hair. 3. intrigue, plot, scheme. 4. lie, falsehood.

caraminholas s. f. pl. 1. fantasies, inventions. 2. lies, petty falsehoods.

caramomom s. m. (pl. **-ons**) (Braz.) a bundle added to the usual burden of a pack animal.

caramujo 1. (zool.) any of various small marine univalve molluscs. 2. (bot.) a variety of cabbage. 3. the caking of salt in saltworks (due to the action of microorganisms). 4. (naut.) figurehead on the bow of a ship. 5. a very reticent person, a queer fellow.

caramunha s. f. 1. the wailing and whining of children. 2. lamentation, lament. 3. grimace, grin.

caramunhar v. 1. to wail, whine. 2. to lament, moan, bemoan. 3. to grieve. 4. to deplore, regret. 5. to pity.

caramunheiro adj. wailing, whining, lamenting.

caramuru s. m. (Braz.) 1. (ichth.): a) hamlet, spotted moray. b) lepidosiren. 2. (Braz., hist.): a) member of the monarchistic party headed by José Bonifácio. b) member of the conservative party (during the monarchic rule).

caramutanje s. m. (Braz., hist.) a Negro slave recently brought over from Africa, not yet adapted to the new environment. ‖ adj. of or relative to such a slave.

caraná s. f. a plant of the family Arecaceae (Mauritia carana) (in some places of Brazil also the wax palms or carnauba palms — Copernicia cerifera).

caraná-branca s. f. (pl. **caranás-brancas**), (bot.) white cedar.

caranaí s. f. (Braz., bot.) a palm tree (Mauritia limnophila).

carancho s. m. (ornith.) common caracara.

carandá s. f. (bot.) carnauba, wax-palm.

carandá-guaçu s. m. (pl. **carandás-guaçus**), (bot.) muriti palm, Brazilian wine palm.

carandazal s. m. (pl. **-ais**) a grove of carnauba palm trees.

Carangídeos s. m. pl. (ichth.) Carangidae, a family of percoid fishes inhabiting warm water seas.

carango s. m. 1. (vulg.) louse. 2. (mil. sl.) an infantryman. 3. (Braz.) itching caused by parasites.

carangonço s. m. (Braz.) popular name of a scorpion.

carangueja s. f. 1. (naut.) gaff (plate B 10). 2. (med.) cancer, sore.

carang007uejar v. 1. (pop.) to walk crabwise, sidle. 2. to dawdle, waste time, dally. 3. (fig.) to hesitate, vacillate.

caranguejeira s. f. (Braz., zool.) bird spider.

caranguejeiro s. m. 1. crab fisher, crabber. 2. (Braz.) humouristic nickname given to the citizen of Santos.

caranguejo s. m. 1. (zool.) crab: common name of various marine or land crustaceans of the order Decapoda. 2. **Caranguejo** (astr.) Crab: a zodiacal sign, Cancer. 3. (pop.) a lazy sluggish fellow.

andar para trás como o ~ to walk crablike, move backwards. ~ **de conchas** (zool.) hermit crab.

caranguejo-de-pedra s. m. (pl. **caranguejos-de-pedra**), (zool.) stone crab.

caranguejo-felpudo s. m. (pl. **caranguejos-felpudos**), (zool.) lady crab.

caranguejola s. f. 1. (pop.) any large crustacean resembling a crab. 2. a shaky wooden framework. 3. a rickety building. 4. a risky enterprise. 5. an unsteady or shaky pile of different things. 6. worn-out rattling vehicle.

caranha s. f. (Braz., ichth.) a marine fish of the family Lutjanidae.

caranha-do-mangue s. f. (pl. **caranhas-do-mangue**), (Braz., ichth.) gray snapper, mangrove snapper.

caranho s. m. (Braz., ichth.) common name of various species of lutjanid fishes.

caranho-vermelho s. m. (pl. **caranhos-vermelhos**), (ichth.) mutton snapper, muttonsfish.

carantonha s. f. 1. an ugly face. 2. a paper mask, mask. 3. grimace, scowl, frown.

carântulas s. f. pl. magic signs and symbols used by sorcerers.

carão (I) s. m. (pl. **-ões**) 1. a large and ugly face, pudding face. 2. the skin of the face. 3. (ornith.) courlan.

carão (II) s. m. (pl. **-ões**), (Braz., pop.) reprimand, censure.

caraolho s. m. (Braz., and Port. prov.) a cross-eyed person. ‖ adj. cross-eyed, strabismic(al).

carapaça s. f. (zool.) 1. carapace. 2. bony shield of an animal, cuirass, shell. 3. shard.

carapanã s. m. (Braz., Amazonas) a large mosquito of the family Culicidae (Culex fatigans).

carapanã-pinima s. m. (pl. **carapanãs-pinimas**), (Braz.) yellow fever mosquito.

carapanaúba s. m. (Braz.) 1. a tree of the family Apocinaceae (Aspidosperma nitidum). 2. paddlewood.

carapanta, carpanta s. f. (vulg.) 1. drinking bout, binge. 2. drunkenness. 3. reprimand, censure.

carapau s. m. 1. (ichth.) mackerel shad. 2. (fig.) a very lean person, bean pole.

carapeba s. f. (Braz.) fish of the family Gerridae (Diapterus rhombeus), a mojarra.

carapeba-listada s. f. (pl. **carapebas-listadas**), (Braz., ichth.) patao.

carapela s. f. 1. husk of Indian corn. 2. (med.) the dry crust of a sore, scab, eschar.

carapeta (ê) s. f. 1. whirligig, top. 2. knob of a lock, handle of a door. 3. an innocent lie, fib.

carapetal s. m. (pl. **-ais**) a kind of satchel or knapsack in which African Negroes use to carry their provisions.

carapetão s. m. (pl. **-ões**) 1. a big lie, whopper. 2. humbug, false rumour.

carapetar v. to tell wild stories, lie, tell a fib.

carapeteiro s. m. 1. liar, story-teller. 2. trickster. 3. impostor. 4. a kind of wild pear tree.

carapiá s. f. (Braz.) 1. a medicinal plant of the family Malvaceae (Sida macrodon). 2. a tropical herb of the family Moraceae (the mulberry family) (Dorstenia multiforme).

carapicu s. m. (Braz.) 1. common name of several fishes of the family Gerridae. 2. (ichth.) silver jenney, mojarra. 3. shrub of the family Malvaceae (the mallow family) (Urena sinuata).

carapina (I) s. m. (Braz., pop.) carpenter.

carapina (II) s. f. (Braz., chem.) carapine.

carapinha s. f. the crisp curled hair of Negroes.

carapinhada s. f. a deep-frozen fruit drink, esp. iced lemonade or orange-juice.

carapinheira s. f. a variety of pear tree which gives very juicy fruit.

carapinho adj. 1. crisp, coarse. 2. frizzled, curled.
carapinhudo adj. having crisp, curled hair, wool-pated.
carapitaia s. f. (Braz., bot.) Peruvian swamp lily.
carapitanga s. f. (Braz., ichth.) bastard snapper.
carapó s. m. (N. Braz., ichth.) carapo, electric eel.
carapobeba s. m. (Braz., zool.) a very venomous lizard.
carapuça s. f. 1. cap, skull cap. 2. hood, cowl. 3. any object resembling a fur cap. 4. (fig.) allusion, hint, insinuation. 5. (Braz.) caulker, caulking-iron. 6. (theat., sl.) part especially written to enhance the qualities of an actor.
   a ~ lhe assenta the cap fits you. **qual ~!** what a nonsense. **talhar ~s** to make allusions, hint.
carapuceiro s. m. capmaker.
carapulo s. m. cup of an acorn or similar fruits.
cara-quebrada s. f. (pl. **caras-quebradas**) a broken sugar-loaf.
carará s. m. American snakebird.
cara-suja s. m. (Braz.) (pl. **caras-sujas**) 1. (ornith.) tiriba. 2. (sl.) an unimportant person.
carataí s. m. (Braz.) a freshwater catfish of the family Doradidae (Doras weddellii).
caraté s. m. (path.) a dermatosis similar to vitiligo.
caratê s. m. (sports) karate.
caráter s. m. (pl. **caracteres**) 1. character. 2. stamp, mark, grain. 3. outline, form, feature. 4. (typogr.) character(s), letter(s). 5. badge, symbol. 6. colour, tone, note. 7. sort. 8. especiality, particularity. 9. nature. 10. type, structure, shape. 11. quality, vein, fiber. 12. abbreviated signs, abbreviation(s). 13. temperament, mettle. 14. force of will, strength of mind. 15. moral attitude, type of individuality. 16. artistic expression. 17. propriety. 18. peculiarity of character. 19. (N. Braz.) outward appearance, countenance, physiognomy.
   ~ adquirido acquired character. **~ agradável** pleasing ways. **~ agressivo** offensiveness. **~ alegre** jocularity. **~ autoritário** peremptoriness. **~ capcioso** captiousness. **~ caprichoso** whimsicality. **~ cerimonial** ceremoniousness. **~ clássico** classicality, classicalness. **~ conclusivo** conclusiveness. **~ comunicativo** communicativeness. **~ distintivo** characteristic trait. **~ duvidoso** fishiness. **~ efeminado** womanishness. **~es cuneiformes** cuneiform characters. **~ feminil** womanliness. **~ tipográfico** type. **ele agiu de acordo com seu ~** he acted in character. **ele mostrou seu verdadeiro ~** he came out in his true colours. **ele imprimiu seu ~ à sua época** he set his stamp upon his period. **ele não tem nenhum traço de falsidade em seu ~** he has not an atom of guile in his composition. **em ~ oficioso** of an informative or unofficial nature. **firmeza de ~** stability, stableness. **força de ~** strength of mind. **mostrar o seu verdadeiro ~** to unmask one's true character. **sem ~** unprincipled, boneless. **traços de ~ heróico** features cast in a heroic mould.
caratinga s. m. (Braz.) 1. (zool.) the white-headed saki (Hapales leucocephala). 2. (ichth.) a mojarra. 3. common name of various plants of the family Dioscoreaceae.
caratuã s. m. (Braz., Amazonas) the flesh of game animals dried or roasted by the hunters in the woods.
caraúba s. f. (Braz., bot.) fotui.
caraubal s. m. (pl. **-ais**), (Braz.) a grove or forest of fotui trees.
caraúna s. f. (Braz.) 1. (ichth.): a) rock hind. b) blue tang. 2. bird of the family Icteridae (Cassidix oryzivora).
caravana s. f. caravan: 1. a number of pilgrims, merchants or travelers who make their trip in one group. 2. a company of travelling people. 3. a group of tourists on a pleasure trip.
   ~ de carros wagon train, train of cars.
caravançará, caravançarai s. m. caravansary, caravanserai: (Orient) a kind of rest-house where caravans spend the night.
caravaneiro s. m. leader of a caravan, caravan guide.
caravela s. f. 1. (naut.) caravel(le), caravel, small sailing vessel. 2. an ancient silver coin. 3. (zool.) Portuguese man-of-war. 4. the stalk of a manioc plant.
caraveleiro s. m. sailor of a caravelle.
caraxixu s. m. (Braz., bot.) nightshade.
caraxué s. m. (Braz.) bird of the family Turdidae (Turdus fumigatus).
caraxué-da-capoeira s. m. (pl. **caraxués-da-capoeira**) (N. Braz., ornith.) a thrush (Turdus fumigatus).
carazal s. m. (Braz.) a plot where yams sprout.
carbamato s. m. (chem.) carbamate.
carbamida s. f. (chem.) carbamide, urea.
carbinol s. m. (pl. **-óis**), (chem.) carbinol, methanol.
carboidrato s. m. (chem.) carbohydrate.
carbólico adj. (chem.) carbolic, carbolated.
carbonado s. m. (min.) a black or carbon diamond, industrial diamond, carbonado. ‖ adj. (chem.) carbonized, containing carbon, treated with carbon, carbonaceous.
carbonante s. m. carburetant, carburant.
carbonar v. (chem.) to carbonate, carbonize, convert into a carbonate.
carbonário s. m. 1. (Italy) Carbonaro: member of a secret political society of anti-monarchistic tendencies. 2. member of any revolutionary secret society or group of terrorists.
carbonarismo s. m. Carbonarism: principles and fighting method adopted by Carbonari.
carbonatar v. (chem.) 1. to carbonate. 2. to saturate or impregnate with carbonic acid. 3. to transform into a carbonate.
carbonato s. m. (chem.) carbonate: generic designation of any salt or ester of carbonic acid.
   ~ de amônio (chem.) ammonium carbonate, salt of hartshorn. **~ de cálcio** (chem.) calcium carbonate. **~ de chumbo** (chem.) carbonate of lead, cerussite. **~ de cobre** (chem.) copper carbonate. **~ de magnésio** (chem.) magnesium carbonate. **~ de potássio** (chem.) potassium carbonate, potash. **~ de sódio** (chem.) sodium carbonate, barilla. **~ de zinco** (chem.) zinc carbonate.
carboneto (ê) s. m. (chem.) carbide, any binary compound of carbon, carburet.
   ~ de cálcio calcium carbide. **~ de cobre** copper carbide, malachite. **~ de silício** carborundum, carbon silicide. **~ de tungstênio** tungsten carbide.
carbônico adj. (chem.) carbonic.
carbonífero s. m. (geol.) 1. the Carboniferous period, Paleozoic period following the Devonian. 2. the system of rocks formed during this age. ‖ adj. 1. (geol.) of, pertaining to or relative to the Carboniferous period. 2. carboniferous, producing or containing coal, carbonaceous.
   formação -a (geol.) coal formation. **região -a** coal-district. **terreno ~** coal-field.
carbonial s. f. (chem.) carbonyl.
carbônio s. m. (also **carbono**) 1. (chem.) the chemical element carbon (symbol C). 2. (min.) a carbon diamond. 3. a carbon paper, carbon copy.
carbonização s. f. (pl. **-ões**) carbonization, act or process of carbonizing.
carbonizado adj. carbonized.
carbonizador s. m. 1. carbonizer, carbonizing agent. 2. appliance or retort for converting wood into charcoal.

carbonizar v. 1. (chem.) to carbonize. 2. to convert into carbon, coal, char. 3. to saturate or combine with carbon.

carbonizável adj. m. + f. (pl. -áveis) capable of being carbonized, subject to carbonization.

carbono s. m. (chem.) carbon.

carborundo s. m. (chem., tech.) carborundum: abrasive silicon carbide.

carboxila s. f. (chem.) carboxyl.

carbúnculo s. m. 1. (med.) carbuncle, boil. 2. (med., vet.) anthrax, blackleg. 3. (min.) ruby, cabochon.

carbunculoso adj. carbuncled, carbuncular.

carburação s. f. (pl. -ões) 1. carburetion, exposure to the action of carbon. 2. impregnation or saturation with gaseous carbon compounds. 3. process of carburet(t)ing, carburation.

carburado adj. carburet(t)ed.

carburador s. m. (tech.) carburet(t)or (plates M 12, 13).

bóia do ~ tickler. ~ de bóia float carburetor. ~ de pulverização ou vaporização spray carburetor. ~ invertido downdraft carburetor.

carburante s. m. (chem., tech.) carburetant.

carburar v. to carburize, carburet.

carbureto s. m. (chem.) carbide, carburet.

~ de cálcio (chem.) calcium carbide. ~ de boro (chem.) boron carbide. ~ de ferro (chem.) iron carbide.

carcaça s. f. 1. carcase, carcass. 2. skeleton. 3. framework. 4. old hull of a ship. 5. a ship without equipment. 6. frame of a woman's hat. 7. framework which supports the parts of a ship during its construction. 8. (mil.) fire shell, round carcass.

carcamano s. m. 1. boy, lad. 2. contemptuous nickname applied to Italian settlers in Brazil. 3. (N. Braz.) nickname applied to Syrians. 4. hawker, street peddler. 5. shoeshine boy, bootblack.

carcanel s. m. (pl. -éis) caulking-iron, caulker.

carcanha s. f. (Braz.) a marine fish of the family Hemulidae (Geniatremus luteus).

carcará s. m. = caracará.

carcás s. m. 1. (mil.) fire bomb, carcass. 2. quiver (arrow head).

cárcava s. f. (fort.) a defensive ditch surrounding a fortified place, moat, wide trench.

carcavar v. 1. to surround with a ditch or moat. 2. to make hollow. 3. to excavate, dig a trench or ditch. 4. to rip up. 5. to be torn up.

carcel s. m. (pl. -éis) 1. Carcel lamp, carcel. 2. hanging lamp.

carcela s. f. a strip of cloth with either buttons or buttonholes (sewn to uniform jackets).

carceragem s. f. (pl. -ens) 1. incarceration, act of putting into prison, imprisonment. 2. prison fee, jailer's fee.

carcerário adj. of, belonging to or relative to a jail.

cárcere s. m. 1. carcer, prison, jail. 2. an underground prison. 3. lock-up (in schools and universities). 4. (circus, theat.) room behind the arena where performers or animals wait for their appearance. 5. (fig.) obstacle.

carcereira s. f. jaileress, wardress.

carcereiro s. m. 1. governor or director of a prison. 2. jailer, gaoler. 3. warden, prison guard. 4. turnkey.

carcérula s. f. (bot.) cavity in certain indehiscent fruits.

carcharídeos s. m. pl. (ichth.) Carchariidae, a family of sand sharks.

carchear v. (Braz.) 1. to rob, plunder. 2. to despoil defenseless people or corpses. 3. to appropriate s. th. unlawfully.

carcheio s. m. (Braz.) robbery, looting, plundering.

carcinicultor s. m. a crab and other crustaceans breeder.

carcinicultura s. f. breeding of crabs and other crustaceans.

carcinóide s. m. (med.) not malignant carcinoid tumour. ‖ adj. m. + f. 1. (med.) carcinoid, resembling a carcinoma. 2. of, resembling or relative to crustaceans.

carcinologia s. f. carcinology: branch of zoology that studies crustaceans, crustaceology.

carcinológico adj. carcinological.

carcinologista s. m. + f., carcinólogo m. carcinologist, specialist in carcinology.

carcinólogo s. m. carcinologist.

carcinoma s. m. (med.) carcinoma, cancer of the epithelial tissue.

carcinomatoso adj. (med.) carcinomatous, cancerous.

carcinose s. f. (med.) carcinomatosis, simultaneous development of carcinomata in many parts of the body.

carcoma s. f. 1. woodworm. 2. putridity, rottenness. 3. worm-dust. 4. any damaging or destructive agent. 5. (fig.) the sting of conscience.

carcomer v. 1. to gnaw (wood). 2. to erode, corrode. 3. to make rotten, bring to ruin, destroy. 4. ~-se: a) to be affected with dry-rot. b) to be worm-eaten. c) (fig.) to grieve, fret, pine away.

carcomido adj. 1. worm-eaten, wormy. 2. rotten. 3. worn-out, consumed by use or time, wasted. 4. (fig.) utterly destroyed.

cárcova s. f. 1. (fort.) defensive ditch surrounding a fortified place. 2. (mil.) false door to a fortress (to deceive the enemy). 3. a covered way, covert.

carcunda s. m. + adj. = corcunda.

carda s. f. 1. (tech.) card, wool card. 2. (tech.) carding machine. 3. comb, flax-comb, comber. 4. separator, teasel. 5. hatchel, hackle. 6. a shoemaker's small tacks. 7. (hist.) a kind of hatchel used formerly as an instrument of torture. 8. clots of mud or filth in the pelt of domestic animals. 9. dirty spots on the skin (of persons).

cardação s. f. (pl. -ões) act of carding, carding, combing.

cardada s. f. quantity of wool combed at one time.

dar ao diabo a ~ (pop.) to lose one's courage, despair.

cardadeira s. f. 1. a female carder or hackler. 2. carding machine.

cardador s. m. 1. hackler, carder. 2. comber, wool comber. 3. corder, teaseler.

~ de feltro felt-carder. ~ de lã wool carder. ~ de linho flax-dresser.

cardadura s. f. 1. carding, act or process of preparing fibers for spinning. 2. combing, wool-combing. 3. a roll of carded wool, cotton or other fibres.

cardagem s. f. (pl. -ens) 1. carding, process or method of carding. 2. the art of carding or combing (fibers). 3. carding shop, carding mill.

cardal s. m. (pl. -ais) 1. a place where cardoons grow. 2. ground which produces nothing but thistles.

cardamomo s. m. (bot.) cardamom, cardamum.

cardão adj. (pl. -ões) thistle-coloured, bluish blue-red.

cardápio s. m. bill of fare, menu, carte (plate R 5).

cardar v. 1. to disentangle, unravel. 2. to card, comb (wool, flax). 3. to hatchel, teasel, rove. 4. (sl.) to strip s. o. artfully of money or property. 5. (sl.) to extort, steal, rob.

cardeal (I) s. m. (pl. -ais), cardinal, dignitary of the R. C. Church, prelate of the Sacred College in Rome.

cardeal (II) s. m. (pl. **-ais**) 1. common name of several birds in whose plumage predominates the red colour. 2. redbird, cardinal bird, cardinal.

cardeal (III) s. m. (pl. **-ais**) name of two ornamental plants of the family Labiateae: the cardinal flower and the scarlet salvia.

cardeal (IV) adj. m. + f. (pl. **-ais**) 1. cardinal, pre--eminent. 2. principal, chief, superior. 3. fundamental, basical.

pontos -ais cardinal points. **signos -ais** cardinal signs. **ventos -ais** cardinal winds. **virtudes -ais** cardinal virtues.

cardeal-amarelo s. m. (pl. **cardeais-amarelos**), (Braz., ornith.) the yellow cardinal (Gubernatrix cristata).

cardealina s. f. (bot.) cardinal flower, scarlet salvia.

cardeiro (I) s. m. card, comb or hackle maker.

cardeiro (II) s. m. plant of the family Bombacaceae, the silk-cotton tree (Catostemma micranthum).

cardenilho s. m. verdigris, green vitriol.

cárdeo, cárdeno adj. thistle-coloured, bluish blue-red.

cárdia s. f. (anat.) cardia: the cardiac end of the stomach.

cardíaco s. m. (med.) cardiac patient, person suffering from any heart disease. ‖ adj. cardiac(al): of, designating or relative to the heart or to the cardia.

cardial adj. m. + f. (pl. **-ais**) (med.) cardiac, cardial.

cardialgia s. f. (med.) cardialgy, pain in the region of the heart, heartburn.

cardiálgico adj. (med.) cardialgic.

cardiarticular adj. m. + f. of or relating to the heart and joints.

cárdice s. f. cameo showing a heart-shaped relief, gem carved in the form of a heart.

cardiço s. m. a small hatter's card.

Cardiídeos s. m. pl. (zool.) Cardiidae, the cockle family.

cardiectasia s. f. (med.) cardiectasia, partial or complete dilatation of the heart.

cardife adj. from Cardiff (referring to coal).

cardigã s. m. cardigan.

cardigueira s. f. (Braz., ornith.) a variety of wild dove (Zenaida auriculata virgata).

cardim adj. m. + f. (pl. **-ins**) having a white hide with some black spots. (cattle).

cardina s. f. 1. clots of mud or filth in the pelt of domestic animals. 2. dirty spots on the skin (of persons), grime, filth. 3. (pop.) drunkenness.

cardinal adj. m. + f. (pl. **-ais**) 1. cardinal, pre-eminent. 2. principal, chief, superior. 3. fundamental, basical. 4. of or belonging to hinges or movable joints.

número ~ cardinal number.

cardinala s. f. (bot.) = **cardealina**.

cardinalado, cardinalato s. m. cardinalate: office, dignity and scope of a cardinal; cardinal; cardinal's authority, cardinalship, purple.

cardinalício adj. of or pertaining to a cardinal.

chapéu ~ the scarlet hat. **dignidade -a** dignity of a cardinal.

cardinalista s. m. member of a cardinal's family or household.

cardiocele s. f. (med.) cardiocele, hernia or tumour of the heart.

cardiografia s. f. (med.) 1. cardiography: a) the part of anatomy which studies the heart. b) description of the heart. 2. cardiogram.

cardiográfico adj. (med.) cardiographic.

cardiógrafo s. m. (med.) cardiograph: instrument that registers the characteristic movements of the heart.

cardiograma s. m. (med.) cardiogram.

cardiologia s. f. (med.) cardiology: the science that treats of the heart, its function and diseases.

cardiológico adj. cardiological.

cardiologista s. m. + f., **cardiólogo** m. cardiologist.

cardiopalmia s. f. (med.) abnormal palpitations of the heart.

cardiopata s. m. + f. = **cardíaco**.

cardiopatia s. f. (med.) cardiopathy, any disease of the heart.

cardiopático adj. (med.) cardiopathic.

cardiopétalo adj. (bot.) having heart-shaped petals.

cardioplegia s. f. (med.) cardioplegy, cardioplegia, paralysis of the heart.

cardiosclerose s. f. (med.) cardiosclerosis.

cardiovascular adj. m. + f. cardiovascular.

cardite s. f. (med.) carditis, myocarditis, inflammation of the heart.

cardítico adj. (med.) carditic.

cardo s. m. 1. common name of several plants of the daisy family. 2. (bot.): a) shepherd's rod, shepherd's staff, teasel. b) cardoon, thistle. c) cockle-burr. 3. rope, string. ‖ adj. crisp, coarse.

semelhante ao ~ thistly, thistle-shaped.

cardo-bravo s. m. (pl. **cardos-bravos**), (bot.) sow--thistle.

cardo-corredor s. m. (pl. **cardos-corredor**), (bot.) fe-verweed.

cardo-de-isca s. m. (pl. **cardos-de-isca**), (bot.) globe thistle.

cardo-de-ouro s. m. (pl. **cardos-de-ouro**), (bot.) golden thistle, Spanish oyster plant.

cardo-de-santa-maria s. m. (pl. **cardos-de-santa-maria**), (bot.) milk-thistle.

cardo-melão s. m. (pl. **cardos-melão**) (Braz., bot.) a cactus (Echinocactus ottonis).

cardo-morto s. m. (pl. **cardos-mortos**), (bot.) groundsel, bird-seed.

cardo-negro s. m. (pl. **cardos-negros**), bot.) common thistle, bull thistle.

cardo-santo s. m. (pl. **cardos-santos**), (bot.) 1. blessed thistle. 2. Mexican poppy.

cardo-silvestre s. m. (pl. **cardos-silvestres**), (bot.) prickly artichoke.

carduça s. f. coarse carder, breaker card, a carding machine used to card or comb the raw fibers before further cleaning in the finisher card.

carduçador s. m. workman who operates a breaker card.

carduçar v. to card or comb raw fibers for the first time (before further cleaning and processing).

cardume s. m. 1. shoal of fish. 2. run, flock, cluster. 3. pod. 4. band, gang. 5. multitude, throng, crowd. 6. assemblage, gathering.

um ~ de arenques a shoal of herrings.

careação s. f. (pl. **-ões**) confrontation, act of bringing face to face, state of being confronted.

careador s. m. 1. allurer, enticer. 2. flatterer, cajoler. 3. admirer. 4. confronter. ‖ adj. 1. alluring, enticing. 2. flattering, cajoling. 3. face to face, confronting.

carear (I) v. 1. to attract, entice, allure. 2. to achieve, obtain. 3. to conduct, lead, convey. 4. to carry, transport.

carear (II) v. to bring face to face, confront. 2. to contrast, compare.

careca s. f. 1. baldness. 2. shedding of the hair, alopecia. 3. m. + f. a bald-headed person, baldpate, baldhead. 4. m. (Braz., pop.) the devil, the evil one. ‖ adj. m. + f. bald, bald-pated, bald-headed.

ele é completamente ~ he is as bald as a coot. **um pneu ~** a worn-out tyre.

carecedor s. m. a person in need, under privation, shortage, etc. ‖ adj. in need of.

carecente adj. m. + f. wanting, needy, deprived of, destitute.

carecer v. 1. not to have, not to possess. 2. to lack, need, want, necessitate. 3. to require. 4. to be in need of, be deficient in.
ele carece muito de educação he is rather uneducated.
carecido adj. lacking, wanting, destitute.
estou ~ de dinheiro I am hard up for money.
carecimento s. m. 1. want, need, lack. 2. privation, hardship. 3. poverty, necessity. 4. scarcity, scantiness.
careio s. m. 1. attraction, allurement, enticement. 2. ways or means employed in order to entice s. o. 3. confrontation.
careiro adj. 1. of, pertaining to or relative to a merchant or salesman who charges excessive prices. 2. dear, costly, expensive.
carena s. f. 1. keel, body of a vessel below the waterline. 2. (bot., zool.) carina, keel.
carenado adj. (bot., zool.) carinal.
carenal adj. m. + f. (bot.) 1. relative to **carena**. 2. carinal, said of a cochlear prefloration.
carenar v. 1. to careen, lay a ship on one side (in order to repair the hull). 2. to keel over.
carência s. f. 1. lack, wanting, want. 2. need, needfulness, necessity. 3. privation, penury. 4. failure. 5. dearth. 6. shortage.
carente adj. m. + f. destitute, wanting, shy.
carepa s. f. 1. dandruff, scurf. 2. squama. 3. the down of certain seed vessels. 4. husk. 5. knots or snags on the surface of rough-hewn boards.
carepento, careposo adj. 1. scaly. 2. downy, lanuginous (fruit).
carestia s. f. (also **careza**) 1. high prices. 2. accentuated rise of prices. 3. dearness, costliness. 4. dearth, scarcity. 5. need, necessity. 6. famine, hunger, starvation. 7. general destitution.
careta s. f. 1. grimace, faces. 2. mask. 3. scowl, mow. 4. antic.
fazer ~s to make grimaces, make or pull a face, mop and mow.
caretear v. to make faces or grimaces, grimace.
careteira s. f. (bot.) a balsam apple (Momordica charantia).
careteiro s. m. grimacer. ‖ adj. grimacing.
carfologia s. f. (med.) carphology, floccilation.
carfológico adj. (med.) carphologic(al).
carga s. f. load, burden. 2. freight, cargo, goods (plate E 12). 3. loading, lading (plate C 16). 4. bale. 5. shipment, freightage, draught. 6. a great quantity, great amount. 7. weight. 8. charge (of a gun). 9. oppression, hardship. 10. duty, task. 11. stress. 12. responsibility, obligation. 13. obstacle, hindrance. 14. accusation, charge. 15. attack, assault, onset. 16. simultaneous discharge of cannons or other firearms. 17. onus. 18. stowage, stowage capacity. 19. the accumulation of electricity in a battery. 20. (vet.) caustic plaster. 21. (tech.) charge of ore in a blast furnace. 22. (electr.) charging.
~ admissível working load. **~ alijada ao mar** (naut.) jetsam, jettison. **~ central** central load. **~ de compressão** compression load. **~ de detonante** firing-charge. **~ de ensaio** proof load. **~ de navio** ship-load; last of a ship. **~ de pólvora** powder charge. **~ de potência** power loading. **~ de profundidade** (navy) depth-charge, depth bomb. **~ de retorno** return cargo. **~ de roupa** a bundle of clothes. **~ de segurança** (mech.) working stress, working load. **~ elétrica** electric charge. **~ estática** (phys.) static load. **~ explosiva** bursting charge. **~ flutuante** floating cargo. **~ máxima** top load. **~ móvel** dynamic load. **~ onerosa** dead weight, dead load. **~ pesada** heavy load. (fig.) millstone. **~s**

da vida afflictions, tribulations. **~ viva** live load.
deitar ~ ao mar (coll.) to be seasick, vomit. **animal de ~** beast of burden. **caiu uma ~ d'água** it poured down. **enviaram a ~ a granel** they shipped the merchandise in bulk. **lançar a ~ a outro** (pop.) to put the load on other shoulders. **levar a ~** to have all the pains. **pôr ~ em** to pack. **por que ~ d'água!** (fam.) why on earth! **sem ~** freightless. **trabalhar sem ~** (tech.) to run idle. **trem de ~** (railways) freight train, luggage-train. **voltar à ~** to insist or return to the charge.
cargo s. m. 1. load, burden. 2. charge, duty, task. 3. office, employment. 4. dignity, authority. 5. public office. 6. responsibility, obligation. 7. expense, expenditure. 8. job, post, function, situation. 9. engagement, appointment. 10. quality, status, state. 11. capacity. 12. trust. 13. place. 14. bread. 15. character.
~ da consciência sense of responsibility. **~ de censor** censorship. **~ de confiança** position of trust. **~ de cônsul** consulship, consulate. **~ de coadjutor** (eccl.) curacy. **~ de escrevente ou escrivão** clerkship, clerkdom. **~ honorífico** honorary post. **a ~ de** under the responsibility of. **alto ~** high position, dignity. **dar a ~ a alguém** to intrust s. o. with. **demitir-se do seu ~** to resign one's position. **ele exerce um ~** he holds a position. **ele não está à altura de seu ~** 1. he is not up to his duties. 2. he is not equal to his duties. **exercer um ~ público** to be in office. **isto fica a seu ~** 1. that remains up to you. 2. you will remain in charge of this. **um ~ de confiança** a responsible position.
cargosear v. (Braz.) 1. to insist on, persist in. 2. to discuss, debate. 3. to boast, brag, talk big.
cargoso adj. (Braz.) 1. insistent, obstinate, stubborn. 2. impertinent, rude. 3. boasting, bragging.
cargueiro s. m. 1. (naut.) cargo boat, cargo vessel, freight ship, freighter (plate P 16). 2. muleteer, mule-driver. 3. guide of a pack-train. ‖ adj. 1. carrying a burden, burdened, freighted, loaded, laden. 2. (Braz.) showing poor horsemanship.
carguejar v. 1. to drive pack animals. 2. to transport by beasts of burden. 3. to ship in bales.
cariacu s. m. (Braz., zool.) a kind of fallow deer.
cariado adj. 1. (med., dent.) carious. 2. decayed.
Cariamídeos s. m. pl. (ornith.) Cariamidae, the crested cariama family.
cariar v. 1. to decay, rot. 2. (med., dent.) to become carious, grow carious. 3. to corrupt, pollute, spoil.
cariáster s. m. (biol.) a starlike grouping of chromosomes.
cariátide s. f. (archit.) caryatid, female figure supporting an entablature, beam or cornice.
cariba, caribe s. m. + f., adj. = **caraíba.**
caribé s. m. (Braz.) 1. a delicacy made from avocados. 2. a refreshing drink made with manioc flour. 3. porridge prepared from manioc or other kinds of flour.
cariboca s. m. + f. mestizo of European and Indian blood.
caricácea s. f. 1. a tree of the family Caricaceae. 2. **~s** pl. the Caricaceae: a family of tropical and subtropical trees, the papaya tree family.
caricáceo adj. (bot.) caricaceous.
caricato s. m. satirical actor, parodist, actor who plays a humouristic or satirical role in a drama. ‖ adj. 1. ridiculous. 2. funny, comical. 3. burlesque, grotesque. 4. caricatural.
caricatura s. f. 1. caricature. 2. humoristic or grotesque representation of persons or facts. 3. exaggeration. 4. travesty, parody. 5. funny impersonation. 6. a ridiculous person. 7. cartoon.
caricatural adj. m. + f. (pl. **-ais**) caricatural.

caricaturar v. 1. to caricature. 2. to draw a caricature of. 3. to mock or make ridiculous by burlesque.

caricaturesco adj. caricatural, grotesque, ludicrous, ridiculous.

caricaturista s. m. + f. caricaturist, cartoonist, distortionist.

carícia s. f. 1. caress, fondling. 2. expression of affection. 3. kind words, endearments. 4. gentleness, tenderness.

~s enganosas deceitful caresses.

cariciar v. 1. to caress, fondle. 2. to treat with kindness or affection. 3. to touch or stroke kindly, pet. 4. to cajole, flatter. 5. to cuddle.

cariciável adj. m. + f. (pl. **-áveis**) 1. caressing, fondling. 2. gentle, kind. 3. cuddlesome. 4. agreeable. 5. flattering.

caricioso adj. 1. caressing, fondling. 2. gentle, kind. 3. sweet, affectionate. 4. cuddlesome.

caridade s. f. 1. charity, charitableness. 2. virtue of loving God and fellow men for the sake of God. 3. kindliness, gentleness. 4. benevolence, benefaction. 5. almsgiving, generosity. 6. compassion, pity, mercy. 7. (rel.) virtue, grace of God. 8. (N. Braz.) a cake made with wheat flour, sugar, eggs.

a ~ começa em casa charity begins at home. **fazer ~ a um pobre** to bestow a charity upon a poor man. **irmã de ~** Sister of Charity. **por amor à ~** for pity's sake. **pretexto de ~** colour of charity. **um ato de ~** an act of mercy.

caridoso adj. 1. charitable. 2. gentle, kind. 3. benevolent. 4. almsgiving, eleemosynary. ‖ **-amente** adv. charitably.

cárie s. f. 1. (med.) caries, ulceration of bone. 2. (dent.) tooth decay. 3. (fig.) progressive destruction, ruin.

carijo s. m. (S. Braz.) a wooden framework for drying and toasting of Paraguay tea.

carijó (I) s. m. (Braz.) 1. mestizo of European and Indian blood. 2. a kind of liana. ‖ adj. m. + f. having black and white spotted feathers (said of a certain breed of chicken).

carijó (II) s. m. + f. (Braz.) former name of a large tribe of Indians, the Guaranis. ‖ of, belonging to or relative to this tribe.

caril s. m. (pl. **-is**) curry, curry sauce.

carimã s. f. (Braz.) 1. sun-dried cakes of grated and pressed manioc flour. 2. cake of manioc flour. 3. a dry and very fine manioc flour. 4. cattle with a pale-yellow hide. 5. a kind of cotton weevil.

carimbado adj. marked with a stamp, stamped, sealed.

carimbador s. m. stamper, rubber-stamper, mail canceller. ‖ adj. stamping, marking, cancelling, defacing.

carimbagem s. f. (pl. **-ens**) act or process of stamping.

carimbamba s. m. (Braz.) 1. (ichth.) popular designation of the cavalla after spawning. 2. quack, medicine man, witch doctor.

carimbar v. 1. to stamp, mark with a stamp. 2. to postmark, enstamp. 3. to seal. 4. to imprint. 5. (Braz.) to mark a fish with a cut in the gills or the tail (in order to know who bagged it).

carimbo s. m. 1. metal, wood or rubber stamp. 2. seal. 3. postage stamp. 4. signet. 5. dater (stamp). 6. imprint, impress.

~ datador dater, date stamp. **~ de borracha** rubber stamp. **~ oficial** hall-mark. **~ postal** postmark. **~ rolante** roller handstamp. **~ telegráfico** telegraph cancel. **almofada de ~** pad.

carimbó s. m. (N. Braz.) a hollow log drum.

carimboto s. m. (Braz., hist.) depreciatory nickname applied to legalist soldiers (1835).

carina s. f. 1. keel, body of a vessel below the waterline. 2. (bot., zool.) carina, keel.

carinegro adj. black-faced, sun-burnt.

carinha s. f. dim. form of **cara** face.

estar com a ~ n'água to be always content or merry. **uma ~ bonita** a pretty face.

carinho s. m. 1. kindness, gentleness. 2. caress, endearment, fondling. 3. affectionateness, lovingness. 4. love, affection. 5. care, caution, concern. **com ~** affectionately. **criado com amor e ~** brought up with loving care. **estudarei sua proposta com ~** I shall give your proposal my careful attention.

carinhoso adj. 1. kind, gentle. 2. full of love, affectionate. 3. caressing, fondling. 4. fond, loving, tender. ‖ **-amente** adv. 1. affectionately. 2. caressingly. 3. amorously.

com cuidado ~ with pious care. **ele é ~ com sua mãe** he is very devoted to his mother. **um olhar ~** a fond look.

cário, carió s. m. + f., adj. = **carijó** (II).

carioca s. m. + f. (Braz.) native or inhabitant of Rio de Janeiro. ‖ adj. 1. of, belonging to or relative to Rio de Janeiro or its inhabitants. 2. (pop.) designating strong coffee diluted with hot water. 3. of or pertaining to a certain cross-breed of Brazilian swine.

cariocaráceas s. f. pl. (bot.) Caryocaraceae, the souari tree family.

cariocinese s. f. (biol.) caryokinesis, mitosis.

cariocinético adj. (biol.) caryokinetic.

cariodiéres s. f. (biol.) division of the cellular nucleus.

cariofilácea s. f. 1. plant of the family Caryophyllaceae. 2. **~s** pl. the Caryophyllaceae: a family of tropical herbs.

cariofiláceo adj. (bot.) caryophyllaceous.

cariogameta s. m. (biol.) sexual nucleus.

cariogamia s. f. (biol.) karyogamy.

cariopse s. f. (bot.) caryopsis.

carioso adj. carious, cariated, rotten, decaying, putrid.

cariotina s. f. (biol.) = **cromatina.**

cariperana s. f. (Braz.) common name of several trees of the family Rosaceae (Parinarium barbatum, Hirtela tentaculata, Licania micrantha).

caripetirica s. f. (Braz.) a tree of the family Rosaceae (Licania sp.).

cariri s. m. (N. Braz.) 1. force, power. 2. effort.

carisma s. m. (theol.) charism, divine grace, the gift of divine mercy and forgiveness.

carismático adj. 1. charismatic. 2. epileptic.

caritativo adj. 1. charitable. 2. gentle, kind. 3. benevolent, beneficient. 4. merciful. 5. eleemosynary, almsgiving.

caritel s. m. (pl. **-éis**) the act of crying for help, screaming or shrieking in distress or horror.

caritó s. m. (N. Braz.) 1. hut, hovel. 2. wooden framework wherein crabs are kept for breeding and fattening. 3. a little niche made in the mudwall of their cottage where peasants keep small objects.

cariú, cariúa s. m. (pop.) nickname applied to white Brazilians by caboclos.

carixo s. m. (N. Braz., ornith.) a cowbird (Molothrus bonariensis).

cariz s. m. 1. face, visage. 2. countenance. 3. aspect, appearance. 4. (bot.) caraway. 5. caraway seed. 6. state or looks of the weather.

carlequim s. m. (pl. **-ins**) 1. instrument used to introduce the detonator into bombs, grenades, etc. 2. jack, lifting screw.

carlina (I) s. f. (bot.) carline thistle.

carlina (II) s. f. bridge stay, girder stay, bridge hoist.

carlindogue s. m. a kind of pug-dog.

carlinga s. f. 1. (naut.) keelson. 2. (naut.) mast step. 3. (aeron.) cockpit or cabin of an airplane.

Carlitos s. m. (pop.) Charlie Chaplin.

carma s. m. (philos.) karma.

carmanhola s. f. (hist.) carmagnole: a popular revolutionary song and dance (in the time of the French Revolution — 1793).

carme s. m. (poet.) song, poem, lyrical verses.

carmeador s. m. wool comber.

carmear v. 1. to disentangle, straighten out. 2. to comb wool or other fibers (before carding).

carmelita s. m. + f. Carmelite friar or nun, Carmelite, White Friar.

carmelitano s. m. Carmelite, White Friar. ‖ adj. of, belonging to or relative to the Carmelites.

carmelo s. m. Carmelite convent.

carmesim s. m. (pl. -ins) crimson. ‖ adj. m. + f. crimson, deep-red, bluish-red.

carmim s. m. (pl. -ins) 1. carmine, carmine lake. 2. (ent.) cochineal. 3. (ent.) apple blight, woolly apple aphid.

carminado adj. carmine, painted carmine red.

carminar v. to paint carmine red, carmine, apply carmine to.

carminativo s. m. (med.) carminative, carminative agent or remedy. ‖ adj. carminative.

carmíneo adj. carmine, carmine-coloured.

carmona s. f. cremone bolt.

carnaça s. f. 1. fleshy excrescence, carnosity. 2. a great quantity of meat.

carnação s. f. (pl. -ões) 1. artistic representation of the naked human body in its natural colour. 2. the colour of flesh.

carnada s. f. (S. Braz.) bait, lure.

carnadura s. f. 1. the fleshy parts of the body. 2. complexion, outward appearance. 3. countenance. 4. quality of meat. 5. brawn, muscles, musculature. 6. nature, disposition of the human body.

carnagem s. f. (pl. -ens) slaughter, carnage.

carnaíba s. f. (N. Braz.) vegetal tallow, carnauba wax.

carnaibal s. m. (pl. -ais) a grove of carnauba or wax palms.

carnal s. m. (pl. -ais) flesh time, time in which the eating of meat is allowed by the church. ‖ adj. m. + f. 1. fleshly, carnal. 2. consanguineous. 3. bodily, corporeal. 4. sensual. 5. lascivious, libidinous. ‖ ~mente adv. carnally.

carnalidade s. f. 1. carnality. 2. fleshiness. 3. sensuality. 4. lust, lasciviousness, fleshliness.

carnar v. to unite by kinship.

carnaúba s. f. (Braz.) 1. (bot., also carnaubeira) carnauba, wax palm. 2. carnauba wax.

carnaubal s. m. (pl. -ais) a grove of carnauba or wax palms.

carnaubeira s. f. (N. Braz.) = carnaúba.

carnaval s. m. (pl. -ais) 1. Shrovetide. 2. carnival: season of merrymaking, just before Lent.

festejar o ~ to hold carnival.

carnavalesco s. m. a merrymaker, carnivaller, reveller. ‖ adj. 1. of or relative to carnival. 2. funny, grotesque.

baile ~ carnival ball. corso ~ carnival parade. folias -as carnival frolics.

carnaz s. m. the inner side of the skin or leather.

carne (I) s. f. 1. flesh. 2. meat (plate A 2). 3. the fleshy, muscular part of the human body. 4. the pulp of fruits. 5. consanguinity, kinship. 6. carnal nature. 7. sensuality. 8. lasciviousness, concupiscence, lust.

~ assada roasted meat. ~ bem passada well done meat. ~ branca white meat. ~ congelada chilled meat. ~ de boi beef (plate A 2). ~ de canhão cannon-fodder. ~ de carneiro mutton. ~ de cavalo horse-flesh. ~ de cordeiro lamb. ~ de fumeiro smoked meat. ~ de minha ~ my child, my children. ~ de porco pork, pig (plate A 2). ~ de veado venison. ~ de vitela veal. ~ enlatada, ~ em conserva canned meat. ~ esponjosa (med.) proud flesh. ~ grelhada grill, broil. ~ magra lean, lean meat. ~ malpassada underdone meat. ~ salgada (de boi) bully, junk. ~ sem osso 1. meat without bones. 2. (fig.) lucrative and easy employment, profit without pain. ~ verde fresh meat. cor de ~ carnation. cortar até a ~ viva to cut to the quick. da cor de ~ flesh-coloured. ele é o diabo em ~ he is the very devil. em ~ e osso in the flesh, bodily, in person. estar por cima da ~ seca to be well-off. pão seco em casa é melhor do que ~ assada na casa alheia dry bread at home is better than roast meat abroad. ser de ~ e sangue to be a human being, have flesh and blood. ser ~ e unha to be hand and glove. sentir na ~ to feel it under one's own skin. sofrer na própria ~ to feel self-resentment.

carne (II) s. m. (Braz., sl.) 1. a rich loafer. 2. a stupid, common rich person. 3. a good-for-nothing.

carnê s. m. 1. notebook, address book. 2. booklet for instalment payments.

carneação s. f. (pl. -ões) (S. Braz.) act of slaughtering domestic or wild animals, slaughter.

carneador s. m. butcher in a slaughterhouse, slaughterer.

carnear v. 1. to butcher, slaughter (cattle). 2. to dress meat. 3. to make jerky, prepare meat for drying. 4. to kill, skin and quarter cattle.

carne-de-ceará s. f. (pl. carnes-de-ceará) jerked meat, jerky.

carne-de-sol s. f. (pl. carnes-de-sol) slightly salted, sun-dried meat.

carne-de-vaca s. f. (pl. carnes-de-vaca), Braz.) 1. plant of the family Proteaceae (Rhopala elegans). 2. deep-red or blood-coloured earth.

carne-de-vento, carne-do-ceará, carne-do-sertão, carne-do-sul s. f. different kinds of jerked meat.

carneeiro adj. (Braz., pop.) of, pertaining to or relative to slaughtering and meat packing.

carneira s. f. 1. cured sheepskin, sheep leather. 2. sheep, ewe. 3. sweatband of a hat (plate C 5).

carneirada s. f. 1. a flock of sheep. 2. the foamy crest of waves. 3. malarial fever. 4. (fig.) a group of defenseless or submissive people. 5. outbreak of endemic malaria.

carneireiro s. m. 1. sheep breeder. 2. shepherd.

carneiro (I) s. m. 1. sheep, ram, wether. 2. mutton. 3. (ent.) pea weevil. 4. battering ram. 5. foamy crest of a wave followed by others. 6. (astr.) Aries, the first sign of the zodiac. 7. (fig.) gentle, meek or kindhearted person.

~ castrado wether. ~ castiço, ~ de semente ram, tup. ~ de guia bellwether. ~ montês wild sheep. ~ silvestre bighorn. como um ~ rammish. criação de ~s sheep farm, sheep breeding. perna de ~ a leg of mutton.

carneiro (II) s. m. 1. charnel-house, place where the bones of the dead are kept, ossuary. 2. grave, tomb, sepulcre.

carneirum adj. m. + f. of or relative to sheeps.

cárneo adj. 1. flesh-coloured. 2. of flesh, carneous.

carne-quebrada s. f. (pl. carnes-quebradas) general weakness, general decline of physical forces.

carne-seca s. f. (pl. carnes-secas) jerked meat.

carniça s. f. 1. cattle for slaughtering. 2. prey, booty. 3. meat, quarry, edible flesh. 4. carnage, bloodshed.

massacre. 5. carrion, offal. 6. the butt of a joke. 7. (S. Braz.) leap-frog.

carniçal adj. m. + f. (pl. **-ais**) 1. carnivorous. 2. voracious, ravenous. 3. sanguinary, bloodthirsty. 4. (fig.) cruel.

carnicão s. m. (med.) the purulent and hard central core of a boil, a furuncle and of certain tumours.

carniçaria s. f. 1. carnage, bloodshed. 2. butchery, slaughter. 3. meat shop, butcher shop. 4. meat packing, the preparation of meat for sale.

carniceiro s. m. 1. butcher, slaughterer. 2. (Braz., sl.) a bungling surgeon. 3. ~s pl. (zool.) Carnivora: an order of carnivorous mammals. ‖ adj. carnivorous, feeding upon flesh. 2. (fig.) sanguinary, bloodthirsty.

carnícula s. f. a plant of the senna family (Caesalpinia bonducella).

carnificação s. f. (pl. **-ões**) (med.) carnification.

carnificar-se v. 1. to carnify. 2. to turn into flesh, become flesh. 3. to take on a fleshlike appearance or consistency.

carnífice s. m. executioner, hangman. ‖ adj. m. + f. sanguinary, bloodthirsty, cruel.

carnificina s. f. 1. carnage, bloodshed. 2. massacre. 3. mortality. 4. slaughter. 5. extermination, destruction, ruin.

carniforme adj. m. + f. carniform, resembling flesh.

carnijó s. m. + f. (N. Braz.) Indian of the Carnijó tribe. ‖ adj. of, belonging to or relative to this tribe.

carninga s. f. (Braz.) = **carlinga.**

carnita s. f. the bone of an ox-foot.

carnívoro s. m. (zool.) 1. carnivore: specimen of the Carnivora. 2. ~s pl. the Carnivora: an order of carnivorous mammals. ‖ adj. carnivorous, flesh--eating, feeding on flesh, creophagous.

carnosidade s. f. 1. (med.) abnormal fleshy excrescence. 2. carnosity, fleshiness.

carnoso adj. 1. full of flesh, covered with flesh. 2. meaty, carneous. 3. resembling flesh. 4. flesh--coloured. 5. (bot.) pulpous, pulpy, succulent. 6. (fam.) plump, corpulent.

carnudo adj. 1. full of flesh, well covered with flesh. 2. fleshy, meaty, carneous. 3. brawny, muscular. 4. fat, corpulent. 5. (Braz.) having a well developed body, neither too fat nor too lean (usually said with regard to animals). 6. pulpy, pulpous, succulent.

bem ~ (fam.) well-fed.

caro adj. 1. dear: a) highly valued or priced. b) costly, expensive. c) priced or esteemed higher than the real value. d) beloved, highly esteemed. e) kind, sweet. f) fond. 2. difficult, hard earned, requiring sacrifices or considerable expense. ‖ adv. 1. dearly. 2. costly, expensively. 3. under great efforts or costs, dear-bought.

aquela loja é demasiadamente -a that shop charges excessively high prices. **a vida aqui é muito -a** living is expensive here. **isto é muito** ~ that touches the pocket. **meu** ~ **senhor!** my man! my good man! **nada é demasiadamente** ~ **para ela** nothing is too dear to her. **o barato sai** ~**!** the cheapest comes dear in the long run!, the best is cheap!. **pagar** ~ to pay high. **tudo que nos é** ~ all that is dear to us. **vender** ~ **sua vida** to die hard.

caroá s. m. (Braz.) 1. (bot.) caroa. 2. the silky, resistant leaf fiber of this plant.

caroatal s. m. (pl. **-ais**) a grove of caroas.

caroável adj. m. + f. (pl. **-áveis**) 1. affectionate, kind, tender. 2. fond, loving. 3. pleasant, friendly. 4. propitious, opportune. 5. fertile, fruitful. 6. (Braz.) predisposed to, susceptible to.

caroazal s. m. (Braz.) = **caroatal.**

caroba s. f. (Braz.) common name of several plants of the family Bignoniaceae, genus Jacaranda.

caroba-branca s. f. (pl. **carobas-brancas**) (E. Braz.) a small tree of the family Bignoniaceae (Sparattosperma vernicosum).

caroba-brava s. f. (pl. **carobas-bravas**), (Braz.) tree of the family Araliaceae (Pentapanax angelicifolius).

carobinha s. f. (Braz.) common name of several plants of the family Bignoniaceae, which belong to the genera Jacaranda and Memora.

caroca s. f. (Braz., pop.) a noose or knot in the fishing-line.

caroçama s. f. (Braz.) 1. a lot of seed kernels or fruit pits. 2. many tumorous excrescences.

carocha s. f. 1. (ent.) stag beetle, ground beetle, dung beetle. 2. (hist.: Inquisition) a cap worn by condemned persons. 3. mask. 4. a dunce cap worn by naughty school children as punishment. 5. (Braz.) caulking can. 6. ~s pl.: a) witches. b) lies, false-hoods.

carochinha s. f. 1. dim. form of **carocha.** 2. puerility. **conto** or **história da** ~ nursery tale(s), old woman's tales, cock-and-bull story.

carocho (I) s. m. 1. small specimen of ground or dung beetles. 2. a salt-water fish (Scymnus lichia). 3. (pop.) the devil, the evil one.

carocho (II) adj. dark, dark brown.

caroço s. m. 1. stone in some kinds of fruits. 2. seed kernel, pip, pit. 3. (mech.) core-casting device or machine. 4. (med.) a turgid, hardened gland. 5. (med.) inflammatory swelling of a lymph. 6. (Braz., pop.) money, cash. 7. (Braz., fam.) a lump in the throat, momentary inhibition of speech. ~ **de algodão** cotton seed. ~ **de cereja** cherry-stone. ~ **de uva** grape-stone.

caroçudo adj. containing seed kernels.

carola (I) s. m. 1. man with a tonsurelike bald spot on the head. 2. m. + f. a very pious person, pietist, religionist, devotee. ‖ adj. sanctimonious, pietistic(al).

carola (II) s. f. an ancient round-dance and dance music.

carolice s. f. act of religious fanatism, pietism, devotion.

carolina s. f. (bot.) red sandalwood.

carolismo s. m. religious fanatism, sanctimoniousness, profound piety.

carolo s. m. 1. a blow on the head with a stick. 2. a rap on the fingers. 3. a spike of maize stripped of its grains. 4. badly ground maize kernels.

carombó adj. m. + f. having twisted horns (said of cattle).

carona s. f. 1. saddle blanket (of leather or raw hide). 2. a padded saddle-cloth. 3. (coll.) deadhead, dead beat.

dar ~ **a alguém** to give s. o. a lift. **dê-lhe uma** ~ give him a ride. **pedir uma** ~ to hitch a ride. **viajar de** ~ to travel on the thumb.

caronaço s. m. a blow with a saddle-cloth.

caronada s. f. a carronade, a short and light cannon with a large bore.

caronear v. (S. Braz.) 1. to tire out a horse. 2. (pop.) to deceive, delude. 3. to surpass, outstrip, pass by or over.

caroteno s. m. (chem.) carotene, carotin.

carotenóide s. m. (bot.) carotenoid.

carótico adj. (med.) carotic, stuporous.

carótida, carótide s. f. (anat.) carotid, each one of the two carotid arteries, external and internal carotid.

carotídeo adj. (anat.) carotid.

carpa (I) s. f. (ichth.) carp.

carpa (II) s. f. weeding, hoeing.

carpal adj. m. + f. (pl. **-ais**) carpal.

carpar v. to weed, hoe, clear a field from herbs.

carpear v. to rough-comb or disentangle raw wool (or other fibers).

carpelar adj. m. + f. (bot.) carpellary.

carpelo s. m. (bot.) carpel.

cárpeo adj. (bot.) relative to the fruit.

carpeta s. f. 1. the cloth which usually covers a card table. 2. game, play, gambling.

carpetear v. (S. Braz.) 1. to take part in hazard games. 2. to frequent gambling houses.

carpição s. f. (pl. **-ões**) hoeing, weeding.

carpideira s. f. 1. (arch.) a professional female mourner. 2. (agric.) a weeding machine.

carpido s. m. 1. wailing, lamentation. 2. (ornith.) moor-hen, coot. ‖ adj. 1. lamentable, deplorable. 2. mournful, doleful. 3. lugubrious.

carpidor s. m. weeder, hoer, mower. ‖ adj. weeding, hoeing.

carpidura s. f. 1. the act of hoeing or weeding. 2. lamentation, deploration. 3. wailing, weeping.

carpimento s. m. 1. action or process of hoeing, weeding. 2. lamentation, deploration. 3. mourning. 4. weeping, wailing.

carpina s. m. carpenter.

carpina s. m. pl. (S. Braz.) socks for men and children, short stockings worn by men.

carpintaria s. f. a carpenter's art, office and workshop, carpentry, house carpentry.

carpinteiro s. m. 1. carpenter, house-carpenter (plate A 7). 2. joiner, woodworker. 3. (obs.) cartwright, wheelwright, wheeler. 4. (theat.) stagehand. 5. (S. Braz.) a strong gale of wind blowing in from the ocean. 6. woodworm.

o ~ de Nazaré (bib.) Saint Joseph.

carpinteiro-da-praia s. m. (pl. **carpinteiros-da-praia**), (S. Braz.) a strong southeaster blowing in from the ocean.

carpintejar v. 1. to work as a carpenter. 2. to carpenter, work and square timber.

carpir v. 1. to gather, pick, pluck. 2. to weed, hoe, grub. 3. to tear one's hair (in despair or sorrow). 4. to mourn, lament. 5. to weep, wail. 6. (S. Braz.) to clear a piece of land and prepare it for cultivation.

carpo s. m. 1. (anat.) wrist. 2. pulse, pulsation. 3. (bot.) fruit.

osso do ~ (anat.) carpal bone.

carpófago s. m. fruit-eater. ‖ adj. carpophagous, feeding on fruit.

carpóforo s. m. (bot.) carpophore.

carpologia s. f. carpology: the study of fruits and seeds.

carpológico adj. (bot.) carpological.

carpomania s. f. (bot.) carpomania.

carpoptose s. f. (path.) paralysis of the extensors of the hands and fingers.

carpoteca s. f. (bot.) collection of preserved fruit, chiefly for scientific purpose.

carqueja s. f., **carque** m. 1. common name of several plants of the family Compositae (the daisy family). 2. (ornith.) a true coot (Fulica armillata).

carquilha s. f. 1. wrinkle. 2. pleat, fold, crease.

carrabouçal s. m. (pl. **-ais**) a steep slope or way.

carraca s. f. carrack: formerly a bulky freight ship.

carraça s. f. 1. a blood-sucking parasite, tick. 2. (zool.) nipper. 3. (fig.) importunate or troublesome person, clinger, hanger-on, toady.

carrada s. f. 1. regular load of a cart or carriage, carload, cart-load, waggon-load. 2. material transported by a cart at one time. 3. (fig.) a great quantity, lots.

às ~s: a) by cart-loads. b) in abundance, in plenty.

uma ~ de lenha a cart-load of firewood. **você tem ~s de razão** (pop.) you have lots of reasons, you are absolutely right.

carral adj. m. + f. (pl. **-ais**) of, pertaining to or relative to a car or carriage.

carranca s. f. 1. grave look or countenance. 2. an ugly face. 3. scowl, frown. 4. severe, forbidding expression of the face. 5. ill humour, depression. 6. bad manners. 7. (archit.) gargoyle. 2. bolt, hook or catch to fasten open shutters or windows 9. mask.

fazer ~s to frown.

carrança s. m. a person who is behind the times, old fogy.

carrancismo s. m. excessive conservativeness.

carrancudo adj. 1. scowling, frowning. 2. gruff, grim. 3. hard-faced, ugly-faced. 4. cantankerous, cranky. 5. surly, sullen. 6. in bad humour. 7. lowering. 8. dark, cloudy. 9. black-browed, grave.

carranquear v. 1. to scowl, frown. 2. to be sullen, gruff or cantankerous. 3. to be in ill humour. 4. to take up a threatening attitude. 5. to become crabbed or annoyed.

carrão s. m. (pl. **-ões**) 1. a large car, coach, omnibus. 2. a kind of cart or sled used by fishermen to drag their boat on the land.

carrapata s. f. a wound or sore which grows worse, obstinate sickness.

carrapatal s. m. (pl. **-ais**), (Braz.) 1. a meadow or pasture infested with ticks. 2. a grove or plantation of castor-oil plants.

carrapatar-se v. (S. Braz.) to cling with all one's force to (like a tick).

carrapatear v. 1. to clean an animal from ticks. 2. to make an animal immune to ticks.

carrapateira s. f. (bot.) ricinus, castor-oil plant, castor beans (Ricinus communis).

carrapateiro s. m. (ornith.) chimango.

carrapaticida s. m. a chemical agent used to destroy ticks.

carrapatinha s. f. a fern of the family Hymenophyllaceae (Trichomanes reptans).

carrapato s. m. 1. any of various arachnids of the order Acarida, tick, louse. 2. seeds of the castor--oil plant. 3. (zool.) carp louse. 4. (fig.) importunate or troublesome person, clinger, hanger-on, toady.

azeite de ~ ricinus or castor oil.

carrapato-das-galinhas s. m. (pl. **carrapatos-das-galinhas**), (Braz., ent.) chicken tick, adobe tick, Miana bug.

carrapato-de-boi s. m. (pl. **carrapatos-de-boi**), (ent.) cattle tick.

carrapato-de-cavalo s. m. (pl. **carrapatos-de-cavalo**) (Braz.) a star tick (Amblyomma cajannense).

carrapato-do-chão s. m. (pl. **carrapatos-do-chão**) (Braz.) a tick of the genus Ornithodorus.

carrapeta s. f. (bot.) bastard ironwood.

carrapicho s. m. 1. bun or knot of hair on the top or back of the head. 2. popular designation of the spiny seed kernels of various plants. 3. (bot.): a) bastard sensitive plant. b) burr, bur marigold. c) beggar's-lice, beggar-lice.

carrapicho-grande s. m. (pl. **carrapichos-grandes**). (bot.) common burdock.

carrapito s. m. 1. hornlet of a kid. 2. bun of hair.

carraria s. f. a lot of cars or carriages, waggon park.

carrascal s. m. (pl. **-ais**) brushwood, copsewood, thicket.

carrascão s. m. 1. a strong tinted wine. 2. wine of inferior quality mixed with brandy (to make it taste stronger). 3. (N. Braz.) brushwood, thicket. ‖ adj of or relative to a strong wine or one adulterated with brandy.

carrasco (I) s. m. 1. hangman, hanger. 2. executioner. 3. torturer. 4. (fig.) inhuman or cruel person.

carrasco (II) s. m. (also **carrasqueiro, carrasquenho**) 1. stony way, rocky road. 2. brushwood, copsewood. 3. sparse or dwarfed vegetation. 4. (bot.) a kind of holm-tree or holm-oak.

carrascoso, carrasquento adj. 1. full of brushwood. 2. covered with weeds or stunted vegetation.

carraspana s. f. (pop.) 1. binge, drunken spree, revelry. 2. censure, reproof, reprimand.

carreador, carreadouro s. m. 1. cart-road, carriageway. 2. path, lane, walk. 3. trail through woods or forests, foot-path.

carrear v. 1. to cart, carry. 2. to transport in a carriage or waggon. 3. to haul. 4. to drag along. 5. to drive cars. 6. to cause, occasion, give rise to.

carrega-bestas s. f. sg. + pl. a variety of grapes that grow in large bunches.

carregação s. f. (pl. **-ões**) 1. act of loading, loading. 2. cargo, load. 3. freight, shipment. 4. great quantity, lots. 5. disease, illness. 6. endemic eruption of venereal diseases. 7. agglomeration of threatening clouds, cloudiness.

~ **dos olhos** (med.) conjunctivitis.

carregadeira s. f. 1. (naut.) brail, clew-line. 2. a woman who bears loads on her head. 3. worker (sauba ant).

carregado adj. 1. cloudy, overcast. 2. threatening (weather). 3. loaded, charged. 4. oppressed. 5. full, replete, abundant. 6. gloomy, sullen. 7. dismal. 8. (Braz.) bad for the blood. 9. loaded (dice). 10. spawning. 11. suffering from venereal diseases. 12. indigestible.

~ **de anos** full of years. ~ **de vinho** (pop.) full of wine, drunk. ~ **de sono** sleepy. **cor -a** full or deep colour. **dados ~s** loaded or cogged dice. **ele está bem** ~ (fam.) he is half-seas-over, he is quite tipsy. **o ambiente está** ~ (fig.) there is a great wind up. **ser ~ pela água** to be washed away by the water.

carregador s. m. 1. loader, packer (plate C 16). 2. porter, carrier (plate E 13). 3. trucker, freighter. 4. bearer, baggage-man. 5. cartridge clip, charger. 6. stevedore. 7. conveyor.

~ **de baterias** charger.

carrega-madeira s. f. (pl. **carrega-madeiras**), (Braz.) bird of the family Furnariidae (Pachecellodomos rufifrons).

carregamento s. m. 1. the act of loading, lading, loading. 2. cargo, load. 3. oppression. 4. freight, shipment. 5. great amount. 6. weight, burden. 7. cargo. 8. charging. 9. waggonful, vanful. 10. (com.) consignment.

~ **de um navio** lastage.

carregão s. m. (pl. **-ões**) sudden jerk of a hooked fish.

carregar v. 1. to lay a load on, burden. 2. to load. 3. to lade, freight. 4. to bear, carry. 5. to weigh upon. 6. to bring to, transport to. 7. (naut.) to clew, furl (sails). 8. to make gloomy or sullen. 9. to place powder or a charge into a firearm. 10. to charge a battery, accumulate electricity in. 11. to attack impetuously, fall upon, make an assault. 12. to weigh down, encumber. 13. to become sad. 14. to impose heavy taxes or tributes. 15. to attribute, impute, ascribe to. 16. to overburden, overcharge. 17. to oppress. 18. to register. 19. to make severer or harder to bear. 20. to become darker. 21. to increase in intensity (wind, etc.). 22. to saddle, pack. 23. to convey. 24. to exaggerate. 25. ~-**se:** a) to shoulder (work, responsibility, etc.).

b) to undertake. c) to become cloudy. d) to become dejected, sad or sorrowful.

~ **ao inimigo** to charge or attack the enemy. ~ **armas de fogo** to charge firearms. ~ **as costas** to pack up. ~ **as sobrancelhas** to knit one's brows. ~ **as velas** to brail up, to down-haul or furl the sails. ~ **demasiado** (fam.) to drink too much, become tipsy. ~ **em procissão** to procession. ~ **em triunfo** to carry triumphantly. ~ **o estômago** to cram one's belly, overstuff one's belly. ~ **o povo** to overburden the people. ~-**se com alguma coisa** to take a load upon one's shoulders. **ele carregou sua espingarda** he loaded his rifle.

carrego (ê) s. m. 1. the act of carrying or loading. 2. a bale or any other kind of load put on the head or shoulders. 3. (pop.) qualms of conscience, compunction. 4. (Braz.) load of a cannon. 5. a bad case of venereal disease. 6. (N. Braz.) acute accent mark.

carregoso adj. 1. weighty, heavy. 2. burdensome, toilsome. 3. (fig.) annoying, vexatious. 4. grivous, injurious.

carreira (I) s. f. 1. cartway, carriageway. 2. trail. 3. route, track, course. 4. run, running. 5. profession, occupation. 6. slip, slipway. 7. race, racecourse, race ground. 8. current, river rapids. 9. row, line. 10. career, trade, vocation. 11. hair parting line. 12. mode of life. 13. scope or sphere of activity. 14. development and course of life. 15. ship lane. 16. way, road. 17. (Braz.) way formed by two rows of trees or shrubs on a plantation (coffee, Indian corn). 18. way, means. 19. behaviour.

~ **da vida humana** course of a man's life. **diplomata de** ~ a career diplomat. **às** ~**s** hastily, hurriedly, in full speed. **barco de** ~ liner. **ele iniciou sua** ~ he entered upon his career. **ele segue a** ~ **militar** he goes into the army. **encetar uma** ~ to enter upon a career. **estar na** ~ to follow a profession. **ir de** ~ to go with all speed. **parar no meio da** ~ to stop in full career. **seguir ou tomar a** ~ **militar** to take to the army. **viajaram no navio de** ~ they travelled in the packet-boat.

carreira (II) s. f. (bot.) a variety of Indian mangrove.

carreiramento s. m. (S. Braz.) a flat race, horse race without obstacles.

carreirismo s. m. careerism.

carreirista s. m. + f. horse racing fan.

carreiro s. m. 1. oxcart driver. 2. coachman, carman, carter. 3. a narrow way, foot-path. 4. bypath, sideway, short cut. 5. the space between two rows of planted trees. 6. path followed by roving ants. 7. hunting or wild animal's trail. || adj. of, pertaining to or relative to a cart or carriage and their drivers.

carrejar v. 1. to cart, carry, transport. 2. to haul. 3. to drag along. 4. to drive a car or cars.

carreta (ê) s. f. 1. cart, waggon. 2. gig. 3. cross--pieces and wheels of a common plough, wheel pair of other agricultural implements. 4. gun-carriage, caisson.

ir pelo caminho das ~**s** to follow the good old custom.

carretagem s. f. (pl. **-ens**) 1. cartage, act of carrying by cart or carriage. 2. the price paid for the transport of goods.

carretama s. f. (S. Braz.) a group of carts.

carretão s. m. (pl. **-ões**) 1. cart driver, carter, coachman. 2. (railway) a transfer table, traverse or transverse table. 3. a coffee shelling machine.

carretar v. 1. to cart, carry, transport. 2. to bring about.

carrete (ê) s. m. 1. spool, reel. 2. a small cart. 3. cogwheel, pinion, intermediary wheel of a gear.

carreteira s. f. cart road, carriage way (plate C 8).
carreteiro s. m. cart driver, carter, carman, coachman, carrier. ‖ adj. of or relative to freight barges or lighters.
carretel s. m. (pl. **-éis**) 1. spool, reel, bobbin (plates F 6, M 1, P 15). 2. small cart. 3. windlass, winch. 4. pulley. 5. (naut.) spinner of a long reel.
carreteleira s. f. (mech.) spool cutting machine.
carretilha s. f. 1. small roll or spool. 2. pastry cutter, pastry wheel (plate D 3). 3. pattern cutter (plate A 5). 4. a blacksmith's auger, wimble. 5. (N. Braz.) popular designation of a shooting star. 6. trolley, trolly.
~ **da vara para pescar** troll. ~ **de guia** guide pulley.
carreto (ê) s. m. 1. act of transporting by cart, carriage or waggon. 2. cartage, truckage, portage. 3. freight. 4. freight or carrying charges.
~ **de retorno** back carriage.
carriagem s. f. (pl. **-ens**) 1. a train of carts or carriages, waggon train. 2. cartage, transport by cart or carriage. 3. transport costs, price paid for carting.
carrião s. m. (pl. **-ões**) a double wheelbarrow.
carriça s. f. (ornith.) wren.
carriçada s. f. (Braz.) a number of boats, logs, barrels or the like fastened together for easier transport.
carriçal s. m. (pl. **-ais**) a plot where sedges or reed grass grows.
carricinha s. f. (ornith.) golden-crested kinglet.
carrieira s. f. popular name of an ant (Acromyrmex nigra).
carril s. m. (pl. **-is**) 1. tracks or ruts worn out by carts or carriages. 2. iron spike used to fasten a wheel on the axle. 3. (Port., prov.) carman, carter, coachman. 4. a narrow way. 5. rail, steel rail.
carrilhador,· carrilhanor s. m. carillonneur, chimer, carillon player.
carrilhão s. m. (pl. **-ões**) 1. carillon, set of bells. 2. musical clock.
carrinho s. m. 1. dim. form of **carro**. 2. small car or cart, cab, trolley, (U. S. A.) waggon (plate P 6). 3. a child's play car. 4. spool, reel. 5. wheelbarrow, push-cart. 6. iron shackles for the feet. 7. ~**s** pl. (pop.) the jaw-bones, maxillary bones.
~ **basculante** dump-waggon. ~ **de bagagem** luggage trolley (plate E 13). ~ **de bebê** baby buggy, perambulator, pram. ~ **de boneca** doll's pram, (U. S. A.) doll's carriage (plate P 6). ~ **de chá** tea waggon (plate R 5). ~ **de linhas** reel of cotton thread. ~ **de mão** wheelbarrow (plates A 7, E 11, P 6). ~ **de servir à mesa** dinner-wagon (plate M 14). ~ **de tombar** tilt-cart. ~ **elétrico** electric trolley (plate E 13). **empurrar o** ~ **de bebê** to wheel the pram.
carriola s. f. 1. cab, gig. 2. cariole, light one-horse carriage. 3. carryall. 4. (bot.) cornbind, corn bindweed.
carro s. m. 1. car, cart. 2. carriage, coach, hansom. 3. waggon, van. 4. lorry, truck. 5. automobile, motorcar. 6. railway carriage, coach (plate V 1). 7. (N. Braz.) spool, reel.
~ **aberto** tourer, touring car. ~ **alegórico** sightly decorated vehicle for festive parades, as in carnival. ~ **basculante** tiltcart. ~ **conversível** convertible (plate V 3)₁ ~ **de aluguel** hack, hackney. ~ **de assalto** armoured car, combat car. ~ **de bois** oxcart. ~ **de colheita** harvest waggon (plate C 16). ~ **de duas rodas** two-wheeler, gig. ~ **de entrega** delivery van, delivery waggon, supply waggon, speed waggon. ~ **de passeio** passenger car. ~ **de praça** taxicab. ~ **de presos** patrol waggon, Black Maria. ~ **de rádio-patrulha** cruiser, prowl car. ~ **de socorro** wrecker. ~ **direito** (railway) through car, through carriage. ~ **dormitório**
sleeping car. ~ **elétrico** electric tramway, street--car. ~ **fúnebre** catafalque, hearse. ~ **salão** (railway) saloon-car, chair car. ~ **tanque** tank--waggon, tank-car (plate E 2). **deixar passar** ~**s e carretas** to be absent-minded, not to be over-particular. **ir pelo caminho do** ~ (fam.) to follow the ruts, do as others do. **untar o** ~ (fam.) to grease someone's palm, bribe s. o. **pôr o** ~ **à frente dos bois** to put the cart before the oxen.
carroça s. f. 1. waggon, cart, transport van (plates C 16, S 1). 2. coach, waggon.
~ **de lixo** dust-cart. ~ **de vendedor ambulante** pushcart.
carroçada s. f. cart-load, waggon-load.
carroção s. m. (pl. **-ões**) 1. formerly a horse-drawn omnibus. 2. large van, truck, waggon. 2. the piece of double-six at dominoes. 4. (student sl.) a complicated mathematical problem. 5. prairie schooner.
carroçaria, carroceria s. f. the body of a motorcar, truck, van or waggon.
carroçável adj. m. + f. (pl. **-áveis**) carriageable.
carroceiro s. m. carter, cart-driver, coachman, waggoner, teamster.
carrocim s. m. (pl. **-ins**) little coach, small cart.
carrocinha s. f. a small dump-cart or tilt-cart.
carrossel s. m. (pl. **-éis**) merry-go-round, carrousel, whirligig, roundabout (plate P 6).
carruageiro s. m. carriage maker, manufacturer of cars and car-bodies.
carruagem (I) s. f. (pl. **-ens**) 1. carriage, coach. 2. car, cart. 3. four-wheeler, spring-carriage.
~ **a dois cavalos** carriage and pair. ~ **a quatro cavalos** carriage and four. ~ **de aluguel** hackney--carriage.
carruagem (II) s. f. (pl. **-ens**) (Braz., pop.) a great quantity of cars, waggon train.
carruajar v. 1. to drive in a car. 2. to cab.
carta s. f. 1. missive, letter. 2. epistle. 3. map, chart. 4. card, playing card. 5. charter, bill. 6. deed, instrument. 7. document. 8. degree, patent. 9. bill of fare. 10. diploma. 11. ~**s** pl. (cards) hand. 12. certificate.
~ **aberta** open letter. ~ **branca** blank paper, (fig.) free scope, full power. ~ **circular** circular letter. ~ **constitucional** constitution. ~ **de amor** love--letter, billet-doux. ~ **de apresentação** letter of introduction. ~ **de aviso** letter of advice. ~ **de crédito** letter of credit. ~ **devolvida** returned letter. ~ **de fiança** bond. ~ **de jogar** playing card, (fam.) devil's playthings. ~ **de nobreza** patent of nobility. ~ **de motorista** driver's licence. ~ **de recomendação** commendatory letter. ~ **expressa** express (letter). ~ **irrevogável** (com.) irrevocable letter. ~ **lembrete** follow-up letter. ~ **meteorológica** weather chart. ~ **patente** charter. ~ **registrada** registered letter (plate C 10). ~ **revogatória** writ of annulment. **acusamos o recebimento de sua estimada** ~ **de** we acknowledge receipt of your favour of... **baralhar as** ~**s** to shuffle the cards. **cortar as** ~**s** (cards) to cut the cards. **dar as** ~**s** 1. to deal the cards. 2. (fig.) to be one's own master. **deitar** ~**s** to tell fortunes. **jogar** ~**s** to play at cards. **jogar com as** ~**s na mesa** to put one's cards on the table, (fig.) act openly, be openhearted. **papel de** ~ note-paper. **pôr suas** ~**s na mesa** to show one's hand. **quem dá as** ~? whose deal is it? **ser** ~ **fora do baralho** to have no say. **ser** ~ **viva** to be lively, be on the spot. **ter** ~ **branca** to have a free hand, have full power. **ter as** ~**s na mão** to be master of the situation.
cartabuxa s. f. a wirebrush as used by printers and goldsmiths.

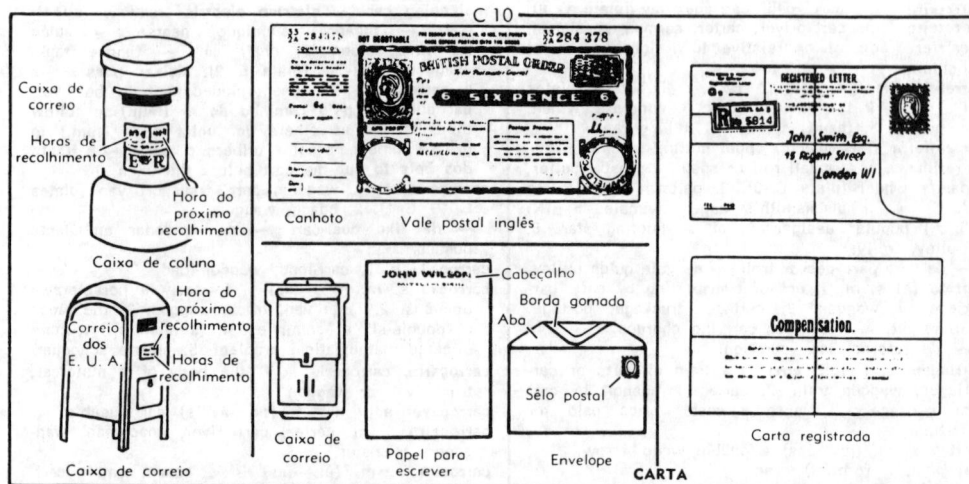

Caixa de correio
Horas de recolhimento
Hora do próximo recolhimento
Caixa de coluna
Hora do próximo recolhimento
Correio dos E. U. A.
Horas de recolhimento
Caixa de correio

C 10

Canhoto   Vale postal inglês

JOHN WILSON
Cabeçalho
Borda gomada
Aba
Sêlo postal

Caixa de correio   Papel para escrever   Envelope

REGISTERED LETTER
John Smith, Esq.
15 Regent Street
London W1

Compensation.

Carta registrada

CARTA

cartada s. f. 1. the playing or throwing of a card. 2. (fig.): a) blow, hit. b) attempt, effort. **jogar a última** ~ to play one's last card.

cartaginês s. m. (pl. -eses) (f. -esa, pl. esas) (hist.) Carthaginian: native or inhabitant of Carthage. ‖ adj. Carthaginian, Punic.

cartalogia s. f. a collection of maps.

cartamina s. f. (chem.) carthamin.

cartão s. m. (pl. -ões) 1. pasteboard, cardboard. 2. board, card. 3. cartoon. 4. visiting card. ~ **alcatroado** tarboard. ~ **couché** art cardboard. ~ **de amostras** show card. ~ **de colagem** = cartão. ~ **de estereotipia** flong, mat, matrix, stereotype paperboard. ~ **de felicitações para o Natal** Christmas card. ~ **de participação de casamento** wedding-card. ~ **de ponto** time-card, punching-card. ~ **-palha** strawboard. ~ **perfurado** (data processing) perforated card. ~**-postal** postal card, picture post card. ~ **prensado** pressboard. ~ **de visita** ticket, visiting card, calling card.

cartapácio s. m. 1. a large map. 2. a bulky old book. 3. manuscripts stitched together in form of a book, a mass of handwritten sheets. 4. a brief case for sundry documents.

cartas s. f. pl. a deck (of playing cards).

cartaz (I) s. m. 1. poster, placard. 2. bill, show bill. 3. billboard, advertisement board (plate E 13). 4. advertising. 5. display. 6. (fam.) popularity, fame. **afixar** ~**es** to placard. **ele não tem** ~ he is not much in favour. **é proibido colocar** ~**es!** stick no bills. **o filme mais novo do** ~ the newest film now showing.

cartaz (II) s. m. (hist.) a free trading charter granted by Portuguese administrators in the new colonies.

cartazeiro s. m. a poster gluer.

cartazista s. m. + f. posterist.

carteado s. m. (any) card game. ‖ adj. of card games.

carteamento, carteio s. m. 1. (cards) act of dealing cards. 2. calculation of ship's position. 3. (com.) exchange of correspondence.

cartear v. 1. to calculate a ship's position, plan its course. 2. to card, deal cards. 3. (com.) to entertain a correspondence with, correspond.

carteira s. f. 1. wallet, purse. 2. portfolio, letter-case. 3. notebook. 4. money-bag. 5. writing table, desk. 6. (com.) designation of the different departments of a bank.

batida de ~ (coll.) pickpocketing. **batedor de** ~**s** pickpocket, purse cutter. ~ **de bolso** wallet, billfold. ~ **de câmbio** (com.) exchange bureau. ~ **de compensação** clearinghouse. ~ **de habilitação de motorista** driving licence. ~ **escolar** desk, school desk. ~ **profissional** employment book. **uma** ~ **recheada** a well-filled purse. ~ **vazia** a light purse.

carteiro s. m. 1. postman, mailman, letter-carrier. 2. manufacturer of playing cards.

cartel s. m. (pl. -éis) 1. letter of challenge, summons to a duel. 2. provocation. 3. label, inscription. 4. trust, cartel. 5. (Port., prov.) high jinks, revelry, merry-making.

cartela s. f. tablet for inscriptions, memorial panel, commemorative or votive tablet.

cárter s. m. (mech.) crankcase.

cartesianismo s. m. Cartesianism, the philosophy of Descartes.

cartesiano adj. Cartesian, of or relative to Cartesianism and Descartes.

cartilagem s. f. (pl. -ens), (anat.) cartillage, gristle.

cartilaginoso adj. cartilaginous, gristly, cartilaginoid.

cartilha s. f. 1. primer, first reader. 2. speller, spelling book. **isto não está na** ~ that's not in the textbook, that is rather exceptional. **ler a** ~ **a alguém** to give s. o. a piece of one's mind, reprimand s. o. **ler pela mesma** ~ to follow the same system, do the same thing, to think in the same way. **não saber a** ~ to be an ignoramus.

cartismo s. m. (Engl. hist.) Chartism, the principles of a reformist and democratic group in the early 19th century.

cartista s. m. + f. Chartist, supporter of Chartism. ‖ adj. Chartist.

cartografia s. f. cartography, map-making, art of designing maps.

cartográfico adj. cartographic(al).

cartógrafo s. m. cartographer.

cartograma s. m. cartogram, plot chart.

cartola s. f. 1. tube, barrel. 2. top-hat, topper (plate R 7). 3. silk hat. 4. stove-pipe hat, shiner, crush-hat. 5. (Braz.) a sweetmeat made from fried banana strips, cheese and sugar.

cartolina s. f. light cardboard or pasteboard, board paper (plate L 4). ~ **para desenhos** Bristol-board.

cartomancia s. f. cartomancy, fortunetelling (by playing-cards).

cartomante s. m. + f. fortuneteller, cartomancer.

cartonado adj. in boards, (books) bound in boards.

cartonador s. m. bookbinder.

cartonagem s. f. (pl. -ens) 1. bookbinding. 2. manufacture of cardboard articles. 3. a cardboard covered book, paperback.

cartonar v. to board, bind books in pasteboard, wrap in cardboard.

cartonista s. m. + f. patternmaker (in cardboard) of tapestry.

cartorário s. m. 1. archivist, chartulary. 2. employee in a notary's office. 3. register (book) of deeds or donations.

cartório s. m. 1. registry, register office. 2. archives, records. 3. notary public's office, chartulary's office.

cartuchame s. m. provision or reserve stock of cartridges.

cartucheira s. f. 1. cartridge-box, cartouche. 2. bandoleer, bandolier, cartridge-belt. 3. pouch.

cartucho s. m. 1. cartridge, cartouche, shell. 2. a cartridge-shaped container (for money, gunpowder, etc.). 3. cornet, a cone-shaped piece of paper (used by retailers to enclose small wares). 4. socket. ~ carregado ball-cartridge. ~ com bala live cartridge. ~ de dinheiro a roll of coins (packed in paper). ~ de metralha case-shot. ~ de pólvora seca dummy cartridge. papel de ~ packing or wrapping paper. queimar os últimos ~s to resort to last measures. vinte ~s para cada homem twenty rounds of cartridges.

cártula s. f. scroll-shaped tablet (usually bearing an inscription) of a monument, cartouche.

cartulário s. m. 1. cartulary, chartulary. 2. archivist, keeper of records. 3. collection of deeds, charters or other documents.

cartusiano s. m. Carthusian monk. ‖ adj. Carthusian.

cartuxa s. f. 1. the Carthusian order. 2. a Carthusian monastery.

cartuxo s. m. Carthusian monk. ‖ adj. Carthusian.

caruá s. m. (S. Braz.) inflammatory swelling of the skin.

caruara s. f. (Braz.) 1. exhaustion, weakness. 2. evil eye. 3. an illness caused by another's evil eye. 4. rheumatic pain.

caruca s. f. (Braz., pop.) night, evening.

caruera s. f. (Braz.) clumps of grated manioc.

caruma s. f. pine leaf.

carumbá s. m. bucket.

carunchar v. to become worm-eaten or rotten.

carunchento adj. 1. worm-eaten, wormy. 2. rotten. 3. (fig.) very old. 4. downcast, prostrate, dejected.

caruncho s. m. 1. (ent.) woodworm, worm. 2. wormhole. 3. decay, deterioration. 4. dry rot. 5. (fig.) old age. 6. a breed of Brazilian swine.

caruncho-do-café s. m. (pl. carunchos-do-café) (Braz., ent.) coffee borer (Hypothenemus hampei).

carunchoso adj. 1. worm-eaten, wormy. 2. maggoty. 3. rotten. 4. (fig.) very old. 5. prostrate, dejected.

carúncula s. f. 1. (anat.) a fleshy excrescence. 2. caruncle: a fleshy excrescence on the wattles and comb of certain birds.

caruru s. m. (Braz.) 1. (bot.): a) green amaranth, redroot. b) rough amaranth, rough pigweed. 2. a dish prepared by stewing minced herbs with oil and spices.

caruru-amargoso s. m. (pl. carurus-amargosos), (Braz., bot.) pilewort, fireweed, burnweed.

caruru-azedo s. m. (pl. carurus-azedos), (Braz., bot.) roselle, Jamaica sorrel.

caruru-bravo s. m. (pl. carurus-bravos) (N. Braz.) a pokeweed (Phytolacca thyrsiflora).

cárus s. m. (med.) deep, deathlike coma, lethargy.

carusma s. f. sparkles and dust particles (which rise when blowing out a light or a fire).

carvalhal s. m. (pl. -ais) an oak grove, oak forest.

carvalheira s. f. 1. a thicket of young wild oak trees. 2. an oak grove, oak forest. 3. a young oak tree.

carvalheiro s. m. 1. an oak tree, esp. a young one. 2. oak club.

carvalhiça s. f. (bot.) kermes oak.

carvalhinha s. f. (bot.) water germander.

carvalho s. m. 1. (bot.) oak, oak tree. 2. oak wood. ~ novo oakling. de ~ oaken.

carvalho-branco s. m. (pl. carvalhos-brancos), (bot.) white oak.

carvalho-das-antilhas s. m. (pl. carvalhos-das-antilhas), (bot.) roble, American black oak.

carvalho-do-brasil s. m. (pl. carvalhos-do-brasil) any of several oaklike trees of the family Proteaceae (Rhopala brasiliensis).

carvão s. m. (pl. -ões) 1. coal, charcoal (plate M 10). 2. cinder. 3. fire-brand. 4. a piece of carbonized wood. 5. a charcoal drawing. 6. (sl.) a newspaper. 7. smut. 8. collective name of several parasitic fungi of the genera Puccinia, Tilletia and Ustilago. ~ animal char. ~ de arco carbon. ~ de fuligem swad. ~ de lenha, ~ vegetal charcoal, wood coal. ~ de pedra mineral or pit coal, stone-coal, forge coal (plate M 10). ~ em pó coal slack, coal-dust. abastecemo-nos de ~ we laid in coals. depósito de ~ coal depot. desenho a ~ charcoal, charcoal drawing. escova de ~ (electr.) carbon brush. jazida de ~ bed of coal. preto como ~ as black as a sloe. reduzir a ~ to carbonize, reduce to charcoal.

carvão-de-pedra s. m. (pl. carvões-de-pedra) pit-coal, mineral coal.

carvão-do-milho s. m. (pl. carvões-do-milho) corn smut.

carvoaria s. f. 1. coal-pit. 2. charcoal works, charcoal-burner's business. 3. charcoal kiln. 4. coal or charcoal dealer's shop.

carvoeira s. f. 1. coal-box. 2. coal-cellar, coal-bunker, bunker. 3. wife of charcoal burner or dealer. 4. female coal merchant.

carvoeiro s. m. 1. coalman, coal merchant, coal dealer. 2. coal-bunker, bunker. 3. collier. ‖ adj. coaly, charcoaly; of, pertaining to or relative to coal and its sale. carreta -a coal cart, coal waggon. navio ~ coaler.

carvoejar v. 1. to make charcoal. 2. to deal in charcoal.

carvoento adj. coallike, coally.

cãs s. f. pl. 1. white hair, whitish hair. 2. (fig.) old age.

casa s. f. 1. house (plates A 4, C 11, P 16). 2. building, edifice. 3. habitation, apartment. 4. abode, dwelling. 5. home. 6. lodging, room. 7. residence. 8. establishment. 9. household. 10. family. 11. household goods, furniture. 12. subdivisions of a box, drawer. 13. government office, section of a governmental office. 14. buttonhole. 15. square on a chess-board, draught-board, map or charter. 16. position of a figure within a number. 17. (Braz., bookbinding) the space between the spines of each group of sheets which make up a book. 18. roof, shelter. 19. tenement. 20. ~s pl. immovables. ~ bancária bank. Casa Branca the White House. ~ comercial emporium. ~ da cidade town house. ~ da comunidade common hall. ~ da moeda mint. ~ de bombas pump house. ~ das máquinas power-house. ~ de aldeia cottage (plate A 4). ~ de aluguel apartment-house, rented house. ~ de apar-

C 11

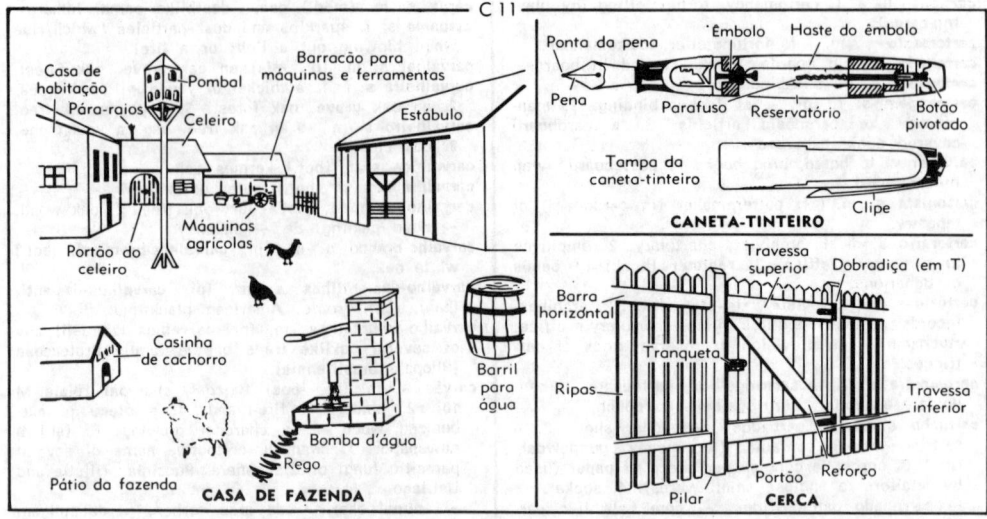

Casa de habitação · Pombal · Pára-raios · Celeiro · Barracão para máquinas e ferramentas · Estábulo · Portão do celeiro · Máquinas agrícolas · Casinha de cachorro · Barril para água · Bomba d'água · Rego · Pátio da fazenda · **CASA DE FAZENDA**

Ponta da pena · Pena · Parafuso · Émbolo · Haste do émbolo · Reservatório · Botão pivotado · Tampa da caneta-tinteiro · Clipe · **CANETA-TINTEIRO**

Barra horizontal · Travessa superior · Dobradiça (em T) · Tranqueta · Ripas · Travessa inferior · Pilar · Portão · Reforço · **CERCA**

tamento(s) a block of flats, apartmenthouse. ~ de campo country-house, cottage. ~ de comércio commercial house, commercial establishment. ~ de detenção house of detention. ~ de Deus church. ~ de fazenda farmhouse (plates A 4, C 11). ~ de jardim bower. ~ de jogo gambling house. ~ de madeira framehouse. ~ de má fama house of ill fame. ~ de negócios business house or firm. ~ de orates madhouse. ~ de pasto restaurant. ~ de penhores pawnhouse. ~ de saúde hospital. ~ de verão summerhouse, bower. ~ de vinho wineshop. ~ do leme (naut.) wheelhouse, pilothouse. ~ geminada duplex, duplex house. ~ noturna = boate. ~ popular popular house, built by institutions of social aid, for people of lower purchase power. ~ pública public house. ~ real royal palace, royal family. ~ roubada (fam., pop.) a badly furnished house. a ~ é sua! make yourself at home, feel at home! amanhã passarei em sua ~ I shall call on you tomorrow. andar de ~ em ~ to go from house to house. apartar a ~ to separate o. s. from family or friends. aqui não é a ~ da sogra! this is not liberty hall! arrombamento de ~ house-breaking. arrumar a ~ to tidy up the house. dentro de ~ within doors. ele está na ~ dos quarenta he is in his forties. ele está sendo esperado em ~ he is expected home. eles mantêm uma ~ grande they keep up a large establishment. em ~ home, indoors, at home. esta rodada fica por conta da ~ this is on the house. fazer como se estivesse em sua ~ to make o. s. at home. feito em ~ home-made, home-brewed. fica tudo em ~ (coll.) it remains between us. ficar em ~ to remain at home, keep the house. fora de ~ not at home. levarei você para ~ I'll see you home. não entre na minha ~! I don't cross my threshold! não sou cá de ~ (fam., pop.) I am a stranger here. não ter ~ nem lar to be homeless. Santa Casa de Misericórdia house of mercy (hospital). ser de ~ to be intimate, at home in. ter muita saudade de ~ to be longing for home. voltar a ~ to return home.

casabeque s. m. a light, short coat (for women).

casaca s. f. dress-coat, swallow-tailed coat, full dress.

cortar a ~ (fam.) to slander, defame, backbite. ele

vira a ~ facilmente he is the sport of every wind. ele virou a ~ he turned his coat.

casacão s. m. (pl. -ões) great-coat, top-coat.

casaco s. m. 1. coat, jacket (plate R 6). 2. overcoat, top-coat. 3. wrap, wrapper. 4. jacket (plate R 7).
~ de peles fur-coat, pelt (plate R 6). ~ de rigor tuxedo. ~ para uso caseiro house coat, smoking coat. sem ~ coatless.

casa-comum s. f. (pl. casas-comuns), (pop.) latrine, privy.

casacudo s. m. (Braz.) 1. a rich and important person. 2. rustic, farmer, backwoodsman.

casadeira s. f. girl or woman of marriageable age or willing to marry.

casadeiro adj. marriageable, desirous of marrying, nubile.

casadinhos s. m. pl. small round biscuits joined together with jam.

casado (I) s. m. 1. married man. 2. ~s pl. married people, a married couple. ‖ adj. 1. married, wedded. 2. (fig.) joined, united. 3. (fig.) settled. 4. very familiar with.

casado (II) s. m. (typogr.) imposition.

casadouro adj. 1. marriageable, nubile. 2. inclined or willing to marry. 3. seeking marriage. 4. of marriageable age.

casa-forte s. f. (pl. casas-fortes) safe deposit.

casa-grande s. f. (pl. casas-grandes) manor house, mansion.

casal s. m. (pl. -ais) village, hamlet. 2. farmhouse, farm. 3. a cluster of small farms. 4. a married couple, a couple. 5. a pair, male and female. 6. (weav.) creel. 7. (her.) baron and feme. 8. (fig.) married life.
um ~ de crianças a girl and a boy. um ~ de perdizes a brace of partridges. um ~ feliz a happy couple.

casalar v. to couple, pair, match.

casaleiro s. m. inhabitant of a hamlet or farmhouse. ‖ adj. of, belonging to or relative to a hamlet or farmhouse.

casalejo s. m. 1. little hamlet, little village. 2. hovel.

casamata s. f. (mil., fort.) casemate, bunker, pillbox.

casamatado adj. casemated, protected by casemates.

casamatar v. to build up a casemate.

casamentear v. 1. to induce s. o. to marry a certain person. 2. to act as matchmaker.

casamenteiro s. m. 1. a professional matchmaker. 2. matchmaker, love-monger. ‖ adj. match-making.

casamento s. m. 1. legal union of man and wife. 2. marriage, wedding. 3. wedlock, matrimony. 4. espousal. 5. (fig.) harmony. ~ **civil** civil marriage. ~ **clandestino** (pop.) hedge marriage. ~ **religioso** religious marriage ceremony. **ele a pediu em** ~ he asked her in marriage. **eles contraíram** ~ they contracted a marriage. **pedir em** ~ to ask the hand of. **unir-se em** ~ to marry, get married.

casa-mestra s. f. (pl. **casas-mestras**) the keel or bottom section of a ship.

casão s. m. (pl. **-ões**) 1. a very large house. 2. a rich house.

casaquinha s. a short jacket (for women) (plate R 6).

casar (I) v. 1. to marry, wed. 2. to get married. 3. to match, mate, espouse, husband, wive. 4. to unite, join, couple, pair. 5. to settle, establish o. s. **antes que cases, vê o que fazes!** look before you leap! ~ **dentro da família** to intermarry. ~ **mal** to mismate. ~ **novamente** to remarry. **ela casou-se** (pop.) she got off. **ele casou suas filhas** he got off his daughters. **eles casaram** they got married. **quem nasce bonita já nasce casada** beauty carries its face.

casar (II) v. (Port., prov.) to break, rend, fracture.

casarão s. m. (pl. **-ões**) a very large house or building.

casaria s. f., **casario** m. a row or group of houses.

casaveque s. m. a light, short coat (for women).

casca s. f. 1. bark, rind of trees. 2. husk, shuck. 3. peelings, peel, skin, shell. 4. (bot.) epicarp. 5. coat, jacket. 6. (fig.) outwardness, outward appearance. 7. sullenness, peevishness. 8. m. + f. miser, skinflint, close-fisted fellow. ‖ adj. m. + f. miserly, avaricious. ~ **de árvore** bark, rind, cortex. ~ **de caneleira** cinnamon. ~ **de carvalho** row tan. ~ **de ervilha ou vagem** hull. ~ **de laranja cristalizada** candied orange peels. ~ **de limão** lemon-peel. ~ **de ovo** egg-shell. ~ **de quina** Peruvian bark. ~ **de vidoeiro** birchbark. **com** ~ **e tudo** with stick and stone, completely. **dar à** ~ (Port., prov.) to die. **de** ~ **áspera, de** ~ **dura** hard-shelled, (fig.) uncouth, uneducated, rude. **ele se contenta com a** ~ (fig.) he reads the words but doesn't understand the meaning. **por** ~**s de alho** for trifles. **sair de sua** ~ to peep out of the shell, become lively. **sem** ~ shell-less. **ser uma** ~ **grossa** to be an uncouth fellow.

cascabulho s. m. 1. the skin of seeds or seed-grains (acorns, chestnuts). 2. a pile of husks or nutshells. 3. (Braz., fam.) crammer, student who crams for an examination.

casca-de-anta s. f. (pl. **cascas-de-anta**) winter's bark tree.

casca-doce s. f. (pl. **cascas-doces**) common name of three trees of the family Vochysiaceae (Vochysia oppugnata, V. rufa, V. ellyptica).

casca-grossa s. m. + f. (pl. **cascas-grossas**), (Braz., fam.) 1. a rude, coarse or uneducated person. 2. boor, yokel, backwoods person.

cascalhada (I) s. s. 1. gravel bed. 2. gravelly ground, pebbly soil. 3. alluvial deposit.

cascalhada (II) s. f. 1. burst of laughter, horselaugh. 2. (Braz.) violent blast of wind, storm. 3. (N. Braz.) a strong eastwind.

cascalhão s. m. (pl. **-ões**) 1. cobble gravel, boulder gravel. 2. (N. Braz.) banks of gravel rounded and smoothed by the action of rain water.

cascalhar v. to laugh, burst out laughing, chortle.

cascalheira s. f. 1. gravel bed. 2. gravelly ground, pebbly soil. 3. alluvial deposit. 4. the rattling sound produced by pouring gravel. 5. heavy or noisy breathing.

cascalhento adj. abounding with gravel, gravelly, pebbly.

cascalho s. m. 1. rock fragments, gravel. 2. pebbles. 3. crushed rock. 4. shingle, grit. 5. iron dross. 6. rubble, dirt. 7. ballasting, ballast. 8. (fam.) money, wealth, riches.

cascalhoso, cascalhudo adj. gravelly, pebbly, gritty, abounding with gravel.

cascalvo (I) adj. white-footed, white-hoofed (said of horses).

cascalvo (II) adj. albescent, whitish (said with regard to a certain strain of wheat).

cascão s. m. (pl. **-ões**) 1. thick bark, peel or shell. 2. hard crust. 3. a stratum of gravel or not yet hardened grit. 4. a crust of filth on someone's skin. 5. scale, dross. 6. scurf.

casca-preciosa s. f. (pl. **cascas-preciosas**) (S. Braz.) 1. sassafras (Sassafras albidum), a tree with an aromatic bark. 2. aniba, a large tree of the family Lauraceae (Aniba canelllla).

casca-preta s. f. (pl. **cascas-pretas**), (Braz., bot.) an ironweed.

cascar (I) v. 1. to beat, strike, hit. 2. to thrash, knock down. 3. to direct harsh or bitter words against. 4. to reply with bitterness. 5. to give s. o. a good thrashing. 6. to fib.

cascar (II) v. to peel, remove the skin (peel, hull, bark, etc.) of.

cáscara s. f. crude copper.

cáscara-sagrada s. f. (pl. **cáscaras-sagradas**), (pharm.) cascara sagrada, the dried bark of a buckthorn, chitten bark (used as a mild laxative).

cascaria s. f. 1. a lot of wine casks or kegs. 2. hoofs of animals collectively. 3. (Braz., pop.) good-for--nothing.

cascarilha s. f. (bot.) croton.

cascarrão (I) s. m. (pl. **-ões**) 1. trick skin, hull or shell (of fruits). 2. a large chip, large wood splinter. 3. anger, aversion, dislike.

cascarrão (II) s. m. (pl. **-ões**), (Braz.) stiff wind which blows from the ocean.

cascarria s. f. (S. Braz.) clots of dirt or filth in sheep's wool or in the pelt of other animals.

cascarrilha s. f. 1. (bot.) cascarilla. 2. the medicinal bark of several euphorbiaceous shrubs.

cascata s. f. 1. cascade. 2. waterfall. 3. (pop.) old wrinkled person. 3. (newspaper sl.) a worthless rhetoric.

cascateante adj. m. + f. cascading, falling in form of a waterfall.

cascatear v. to cascade, fall in form of a cascade.

cascateiro s. m. (Braz., sl.) 1. idle talker, lier. 2. boaster, swaggerer. ‖ adj. idling. 2. boasting.

cascavel s. m. (pl. **-éis**) 1. rattle, round bell. 2. bagatelle, trifle. 3. (fig.) foolishness. 4. f. (Braz.): a) (zool.) a rattlesnake, rattler (Crotalus terrificus). b) (fig.) a malignant, backbiting person. c) a kind of gate formed by several horizontal sliding poles.

cascavilhar v. to rummage, ransack, search by turning everything upside down.

casco s. m. 1. the skin covering the head, scalp. 2. skull, cranium. 3. cask, keg, barrel. 4. hide, skin. 5. hull, body of a ship. 6. hoof, ungula (plates C 9, 12). 7. shell. 8. (ant.) helmet, headpiece. 9. hood, cowl. 10. the wire-frame of a lady's hat. 11. (fig.) brain(s), wit, intelligence. 12. (Braz.) a small dugout canoe. 13. (Braz.) empty bottle.

~ de cavalo hoof (plates C 9, 12, G 1). ~ de casa (fam.) not yet furnished house. ~ de fortaleza fortress without garrison. ~ de marisco shell. ~ de navio hull, hulk or bottom of a ship. ~ de tartaruga turtleshell. ~ velho carcass, carcase. ~s valgos lady toed. ~s varos pigeon toed. ele é ligeiro dos ~s he is very heedless. ele tem um bom ~ (fam.) he has a good head. meter-se alguma coisa nos ~s to put s. th. into one's head, fancy s. th.

casco-de-burro s. m. (pl. cascos-de-burro) sandy river pothole, gravelly river bottom (with gold or diamond bearing sand).

casco-de-peba s. m. (pl. cascos-de-peba) 1. large straw-hat made from carnauba palm leaves. 2. hat made from plaited straw.

cascoso (I) adj. thick-shelled; having a thick peel, skin or husk.

cascoso (II) adj. 1. of, pertaining to or relative to hoofs. 2. having large hoofs or claws.

cascudinho s. m. (Braz., ichth.) a catfish of the family Loricariidae (Paraeioraphis duseni).

cascudo (I) s. m. (Braz.) 1. (ichth.) a catfish of the family Loricariidae (the body of which is covered with horny scales). 2. any horn-shelled beetle. ‖ adj. 1. having a thick bark, skin, peel or shell. 2. barky, husky. 3. shelly. 4. having thick hoofs or claws.

cascudo (II) s. m. a rap on the head with the fingers.

cascudo-comum s. m. (pl. cascudos-comuns) (Braz., ichth.) a catfish of the family Siluridae (Plecostomus plecostomus).

cascudo-espada s. m. (pl. cascudos-espada), (Braz.) collective name of horn-scaled catfishes (family Loricariidae, genus Loricaria).

cascudo-espinho s. m. (pl. cascudos-espinhos) (Braz., ichth.) a catfish of the family Loricariidae (Hemipsilichthys gobio).

caseação (I) s. f. (pl. -ões) act of making buttonholes.

caseação (II) s. f. (pl. -ões) 1. act of cheese-making, production of cheese. 2. transformation of milk into cheese, caseation.

caseadeira s. f. 1. woman who makes buttonholes. 2. buttonholer, buttonholing machine.

caseado s. m. 1. act or process of making buttonholes. 2. buttonhole stitch, blanket stitch.

caseador s. m. man who makes buttonholes by hand or machine.

casear v. 1. to sew buttonholes. 2. to furnish with buttonholes. 3. to work with buttonhole stitch.

casease s. f. (biochem.) casease.

casebre s. m. 1. little paltry cottage. 2. humble habitation. 3. hovel, hut, shack.

caseificação s. f. (pl. -ões) caseification, caseation.

caseificar v. 1. to casefy, caseate. 2. to make or become like cheese. 3. to transform into cheese.

caseiforme adj. m. + f. caseic, caseous, cheesy, like cheese.

caseína s. f. (biochem.) casein.

caseira s. f. 1. a farmer's wife. 2. peasant woman. 3. woman who takes care of a farm. 4. (N. Braz.) woman who does all the housework, housekeeper. 5. (pop.) concubine. 6. constipation. 7. hemorrhoids.

caseiro s. m. 1. tenant, lessee. 2. caretaker. 3. farm manager, farm administrator. 4. (fam.) family man. ‖ adj. 1. of or relative to house or home. 2. familiar, home-spun, home-made, domestic. 3. homely. 4. simple, modest.

ela é -a she has domestic tastes. mulher -a housewife. pão ~ home-baked bread. remédio ~ household medicine.

casela s. f. (bookbinding) the space between the raised bands.

caseoso adj. caseous, cheesy.

caserna s. f. (mil.) barracks, casern(e).

caserneiro s. m. (mil.) 1. casern commander. 2. soldier on duty (barracks). 3. inspector of barracks.

casimira s. f. 1. cashmere, cassimere, kerseymere. 2. fine woollen cloth of soft texture, broadcloth, suiting.

casinha s. f. 1. dim. form of casa. 2. small house, cottage.

~ de cachorro dog-house, dog-hutch, kennel (plate C 11).

casinhola, casinhota s. f., casinholo, casinhoto m. small and paltry house, poor cottage, hovel, hut, shack.

casita s. f. little house.

casleu s. m. Kislev: the third month of the Jewish calendar.

casmófito s. m. (ecol.) chasmophyte.

casmurral adj. m. + f. (pl. -ais) 1. obstinate, stubborn. 2. grumpy, sullen. 3. morose.

casmurrice s. f. 1. obstinacy, stubbornness. 2. sullenness, grumpiness. 3. moroseness.

casmurro s. m. a stubborn, dour or morose fellow. ‖ adj. 1. obstinate, stubborn. 2. grumpy, sullen. 3. dour. 4. morose. 5. sad, gloomy. 6. egocentric.

caso (I) s. m. 1. case. 2. event, occurrence. 3. chance, hap. 4. accident. 5. situation, condition. 6. fact, instance, circumstance. 7. matter. 8. difficulty, contingence, predicament. 9. esteem, high regard. 10. importance. 11. business. 12. (med.) an individual instance of illness or injury. 13. (med.) a patient under treatment. 14. (gram.) inflectional forms of nouns, pronouns and adjectives. 15. (Braz., pop.) a love affair. 16. (Braz.) story, tale.

~ de consciência a matter of conscience, scruples about an affair. ~ de honra affair of honour. ~ de necessidade exigence, exigency. ~ fortuito fortuity. ~ grave a serious affair, serious crime. ~ jurídico (law) suit. ~ particular private affair. dado o ~ in case, supposing that, admitting that, let us suppose it is so. de ~ pensado on purpose, deliberately. eis aqui como se passou o ~ it happened thus. em ~ de necessidade in case of need. em qualquer ~ at all events, at any rate, anyway. em todo (o) ~ upon all accounts, at all events, whatever happens, anyhow. em todo e qualquer ~ in any and every case. era um ~ imprevisto it was an unforeseen case. estar no ~ de to be able to (intervene), be fully informed of. é um ~ raríssimo it is a case in a million. eu não faço ~ de cartas I do not care about playing cards. eu tratarei do seu ~ I will fix you up. fazer muito ~ de to attribute great importance to. fazer pouco ~ de to treat off-handedly, treat without consideration, disregard. ir ao ~ to speak to the point. isto não faz ao ~ this has no bearing on the case, it is not to the purpose. na maioria dos ~s for the most part. não estou no ~ I am not mixed up in the case, I am not well informed about it. não faça ~ disto don't take any notice. não faça tanto ~ disto don't make much ado about it. não faço ~ dele I don't mind him. neste ~ thus, if so, in that case. ninguém faz ~ disto nobody cares a hoot about it. no ~ contrário in failure of which. no ~ de in the event of, if it should happen. no seu ~ in your instance. o ~ em pauta the matter in hand. o ~ é que... the fact is that... o ~ está perdido the matter is lost, it's all up. pelo mesmo ~ for the same cause or reason. tratar com pouco ~ to look down at. trata-se dum ~ reservado that's private business. um ~ perdido a lost case. é um ~ sério it is serious. vamos ao ~ let's come to

the point, let's get down to brass tacks. **vir ao ~** to be to the purpose, be suitable.
caso (II) conditional conj. if, supposing that, in case that.
~ ela vier if she should come. **~ que isso aconteça** in case that this should happen.
casório s. m. (pop.) marriage, wedding, betrothal.
caspa s. f. (med.) dandruff, scaly skin, scale, scurf.
caspento adj. dandruffy.
cáspite interj. indeed!, really!, whew!, by Jove!, by jingo!
casposo adj. dandruffy, scurfy, scabby, furfuraceous.
casqueira s. f. splinter or sliver of wood, strip of wood.
levado da ~ (S. Braz.) naughty, full of mischief (children).
casqueiro (I) s. m. 1. place where trees are decorticated (and made ready for sawing). 2. wood-cutter who strips trees from their bark. 3. (Braz.) a prehistoric shellmound. 4. (Braz.) a stiff southwind.
casqueiro (II) s. m. (S. Braz.) a farrier's helper, one who pares down horses' hoofs before shoeing.
casquejar v. 1. to grow a new skin, scar. 2. to heal up. 3. to form a new hoof.
casquento adj. 1. having a thick skin or shell. 2. hoofed. 3. horny.
casquete s. m. 1. hat, an old hat. 2. cap, skull-cap. 3. hood. 4. (mil.) forage-cap.
casquilha s. f. 1. a piece of bark, skin, peel or shell. 2. chip from a hoof.
casquilhada s. f. a lot of dandies.
casquilhar v. 1. to dress like a dandy. 2. to play the fop. 3. to act like a fop or dude.
casquilharia, casquilhice s. f. 1. dandyism, foppery. 2. exaggerated elegance, modish dress or trimming. 3. coxcombry.
casquilho s. m. 1. dandy. 2. fop, coxcomb. 3. fashion-monger. 4. dude. 5. (pop.) popinjay. 6. (mech.) metal sleeve. 7. (tech.) coupling-box. ‖ adj. 1. elegant, modish. 2. foppish, dandyish. 3. dudish, dapper, buckish.
casquinada s. f. 1. cackle, chortle. 2. horselaugh.
casquinar v. 1. to giggle. 2. to snicker, nicker. 3. to burst out into laughing. 4. to chuckle, titter.
casquinha s. f. 1. dim. form of **casca**. 2. a thin sheet of wood, veneer. 3. a sheet of valuable metal for inlaid work, metal plating. 4. m. (Braz., pop.): a) miser, niggardly fellow. b) mediocre teacher or school master.
tirar a sua ~ to have one's part in, make capital of, take advantage of.
casquinho adj. easily to be shod (said of certain horses).
cassa s. f. a transparent linen or cotton fabric, muslin.
~ arrendada lace muslin. **~ bordada de raminhos** spring muslin. **~ de riscas** striped muslin.
cassação s. f. (pl. **-ões**) 1. act of annulling or cancelling. 2. repeal, repealing. 3. annulling, abrogation, cassation.
cassaco s. m. 1. (zool.) any kind of opossum (of the genus Didelphis). 2. itinerant railway construction worker. 3. worker in a sugar-mill. 4. a baker's helper.
cassado s. m. (Braz., pol.) person with political rights annulled. ‖ adj. of or relating to such a person.
cassar v. 1. to annul, cancel. 2. to repeal, revoke. 3. to abrogate. 4. to make void. 5. to break (off or up, as relations), disrupt. 6. to quash.
cassete s. m. cassette.
cássia s. f. 1. Cassia: an important genus of herbs, shrubs and trees of the senna family. 2. (pharm.) cassia bark.

cássia-das-antilhas s. f. (pl. **cássias-das-antilhas**), (Braz., bot.) sensitive pea, partridge pea.
cássia-paulista s. f. (pl. **cássias-paulistas**), (Braz., bot.) ironwood.
cassineta s. f. cassinette, any fine fabric with a cotton warp and woollen or silk filling.
cassino s. m. 1. cassino, a game at cards for four players. 2. casino, building or club used for social gatherings, for dancing or gambling (plate P 17).
cassiopéia s. f. Cassiopeia, Cassiepeia: a northern constellation between Andromeda and Cepheus.
cassiterita s. f. (min.) cassiterite, tin-stone, tin ore.
casso adj. (obs.) cancelled, null, void.
cassoiro s. m. (naut.) trucks of the shrouds.
casta s. f. 1. caste. 2. race, lineage. 3. stock, breed, strain. 4. kind, sort, species. 5. family. 6. quality, nature.
da mesma ~ of the same stock or race, of the same sort. **de boa ~** of good stock. **fazer ~** to couple, pair. **sair à ~** to take after one's father. **vem-lhe de ~** it runs in his blood.
castanha s. f. 1. fruit of the chestnut tree, chestnut. 2. fruit of the common cashew. 3. a coiled knot of hair, topknot. 4. a horny excrescence on the head of a horse. 5. (vet.) chestnut, castor: callosities on the inner sides of a horse's legs (plate C 12). 6. **~s** pl. (naut.) cleats. 7. (radio) glass or porcelain insulators (for antennas) (plate A 10). 8. (mech.): a) spring clip. b) jaw of a lathe.
castanha-d'água s. f. (pl. **castanhas-d'água**), (bot.) water caltrop, water chestnut.
castanha-de-macaco s. f. (pl. **castanhas-de-macaco**), cannon-ball tree.
castanha-do-maranhão s. f. (pl. **castanhas-do-maranhão**) a silk-cotton tree.
castanha-do-pará s. f. (pl. **castanhas-do-pará**), (bot.) Brazil-nut.
castanhal s. m. (pl. **-ais**) a grove of chestnut trees, a chestnut plantation.
castanha-mineira s. f. (pl. **castanhas-mineiras**), (Braz.) a medicinal climbing plant of the family Cucurbitaceae (Anisosperma passiflora).
castanhedo s. m. a chestnut plantation.
castanheira s. f. 1. woman who sells roasted chestnuts. 2. (bot.) wild chestnut tree.
castanheiro s. m. 1. chestnut tree, chestnut. 2. (Braz.) gatherer of Brazil-nuts.
castanheiro-do-maranhão s. m. (pl. **castanheiros-do-maranhão**) provision tree.
castanheiro-do-pará s. m. (pl. **castanheiros-do-pará**), Brazil-nut tree.
castaneta s. f. 1. noise produced by snapping the fingers. 2. snappers, castanets. 3. (Braz., ornith.) a wading bird (Butorides striata).
castanho (I) s. m. 1. chestnut, chestnut tree. 2. chestnut wood.
castanho (II) s. m. chestnut brown, chestnut colour. ‖ adj. chestnut, nut-brown, maroon.
~ amarelado fawn, luteous. **~ avermelhado** puce.
castanholar v. to play castanets.
castanholas s. f. pl. castanets, bones.
castanita s. f. (min.) dark brown, chestnut-shaped rock or pebble.
castão s. m. (pl. **-ões**) head or knob of a walking stick.
casteado adj. (Braz.) cross-breed (said of cattle).
castear v. (Braz.) to breed, cross-breed, propagate (animals).
castelã s. f. chatelaine.
castelania s. f. castellanship, jurisdiction of a castellan.

castelão s. m. 1. castellan, lord of a castle. 2. feudal lord. 3. commander of a castle, governor of a province.

casteleiro s. m. lord of a castle, castellan. ‖ adj. of, pertaining to or relative to a castle or its castellan.

castelhanismo s. m. 1. idiomatic expression typical for the Spanish dialect spoken in Castile. 2. Castilian customs, mode and manner of living.

castelhano s. m. 1. Castilian: a) native or inhabitant of Castile (Spain). b) Spanish dialect spoken in Castile (now accepted as the official Spanish language). 2. (hist.) castellano: an old Spanish gold coin. 3. (S. Braz.) a native or inhabitant of Uruguay or Argentine. ‖ adj. 1. Castilian. 2. of, pertaining to or relative to Uruguay and Argentine or their inhabitants.

castelo s. m. 1. castle, manor-house. 2. fortress, fort. 3. stronghold, fortified place. 4. a lot of things in a heap. 5. (naut.) forecastle, poop deck. 6. (chess) castle, rook. 7. (N. Braz.) a home for bachelors. ~ **de água** water castle. **fazer** ~s **no ar** to build castles in the air. **seus planos ruíram como um** ~ **de cartas** his plans collapsed like a house of cards.

castiçal s. m. (pl. -ais) 1. candlestick, candle-holder. 2. branch light. 3. rush holder. 4. (Braz., bot.) paxiuba, stilt palm. ~ **de braço** sconce. **boca do** ~ socket of a candlestick.

castiçar v. 1. to make pure, purify. 2. to mate, copulate, cover (animals for breeding purposes).

casticismo s. m. 1. pureness, immaculateness. 2. vernacularness.

castiço adj. 1. pure, immaculate. 2. of good birth, of good stock. 3. genuine. 4. not degenerate. 5. of good quality, suitable for beginning a new strain or breed. 6. vernacular. **cavalo** ~ stallion kept for breeding purposes. **fidalgo** ~ a true nobleman. **português** ~ pure Portuguese.

castidade s. f. 1. chastity, chasteness. 2. purity. 3. continence, continency. 4. virtue, virtuousness. 5. honour. 6. correctness. ~ **conjugal** conjugal fidelity.

castificar v. 1. to make pure, purify. 2. to make chaste or virtuous. 3. to free from errors and faults. 4. to chasten.

castigado adj. 1. punished. 2. chastised. 3. corrected, amended. 4. (fig.) troubled, disturbed. 5. (fig.) mistreated. ~ **pelo mau tempo** weather-beaten.

castigador s. m. 1. castigator. 2. chastiser. 3. corrector. 4. punisher. 5. scourger. ‖ adj. chastising, punishing.

castigar v. 1. to castigate. 2. to punish. 3. to discipline, correct. 4. to chasten, chastise. 5. to scourge. 6. to flog, trounce. 7. to requite, repay, make return for. 8. to censure, reprimand. 9. ~-**se:** a) to do penance, feel sorry, regret. b) to punish o. s., give o. s. the rod. c) to subdue one's flesh. ~ **severamente** to strafe. ~ **um aluno** to discipline a pupil. **Deus me castigue!** strike me dead! **ele é castigado com...** he is cursed with...

castigável adj. m. + f. (pl. -áveis) punishable, castigatory, liable to punishment, that should be punished.

castigo s. m. 1. punishment, penalty. 2. castigation. 3. chastisement. 4. correction, emendation. 5. censure, reprimand. 6. mortification, self-discipline. 7. scourge, avengement. 8. pain. 9. requital, expiation, retribution. 10. wrath. **agüentar um** ~ to stand the gaff, stand the pain. ~ **disciplinar** discipline. ~ **do céu** (theol.) visitation. ~ **merecido** nemesis, condign punishment. **como** ~

for punishment. **o** ~ **vem!** retribution will come! **sem** ~ without punishment, unpunished, with impunity.

castilhismo s. m. (Braz.) the principles of a political party founded by Júlio de Castilhos.

castilhista (I) s. m. + f. admirer of the Portuguese poet Antônio Feliciano de Castilho (1800-1875).

castilhista (II) s. m. + f. (Braz.) follower of Júlio de Castilhos' political principles and party. ‖ adj. adherent to **castilhismo.**

castina s. f. 1. (min.) a calcareous stone used in iron foundries. 2. (met.) flux.

castinçal s. m. (pl. -ais) a grove of wild chestnut trees.

castinceira s. f., **castinceiro** m. wild chestnut tree.

casto adj. 1. chaste. 2. pure, clean. 3. virgin, virginal. 4. continent. 5. innocent, virtuous. 6. delicate. 7. unstained, undefiled. 8. honest. 9. unmingled, unmixed. 10. perfect. ‖ -**amente** adv. chastely, continently, virginally.

castor s. m. 1. (zool.) castor, beaver. 2. pelt or fur of a beaver. 3. (astr.) Castor: a bright star in the constellation Gemini.

castóreo s. m. (pharm.) castoreum.

castorina s. f. 1. (chem.) castorin. 2. a soft, brilliant woollen fabric.

castração s. f. (pl. -ões) 1. act of castrating. 2. castration, gelding. 3. emasculation.

castrado s. m. 1. castrate, eunuch. 2. castrated animal. ‖ adj. 1. castrated, gelded. 2. emasculate.

castrador s. m. castrator, gelder.

castrametação s. f. (pl. -ões) castrametation: art and technique of laying out a (permanent) camp, art of encamping.

castrametar v. 1. to plan a camp. 2. to lay out and build a camp. 3. to fortify an encampment.

castrar v. 1. to castrate, geld. 2. to spay, spade. 3. to destroy. 4. to emasculate. 5. to prune trees.

castrense adj. m. + f. castrensian, of or belonging to a camp.

castrismo s. m. (pol.) Castroism.

castrista s. m. + f. (pol.) Castroite. ‖ adj. Castroite.

castrolomancia s. f. divination by bottles or jars full of water.

castrorosa s. f. (Braz., tech.) machine used in hat-making.

casual adj. m. + f. (pl. -ais) 1. casual, happening or coming to pass by chance. 2. occasional, incidental. 3. accidental. 4. fortuitous, unforeseen, unpremeditated. 5. chance, chanceable. 6. odd. ‖ ~**mente** adv. casually, occasionally, fortuitously, haphazard, at random, by chance.

casualidade s. f. 1. casualty, casualness. 2. fortuity, fortuitousness. 3. circumstantialness, circumstantiality. 4. contingency. 5. accident, unfortunate occurrence, mishap. 6. hazard. 7. eventuality.

casuar s. m. (ornith.) cassowary.

casuariformes s. m. pl. (ornith.) Casuariiformes, an order of ratite birds (the cassowary and the emu).

casuarina s. f. (bot.) casuarina.

casuarinácea s. f. 1. casuarina, any casuarinaceous plant. 2. ~s pl. Casuarinaceae: a family of dicotyledonous trees and shrubs.

casuarináceo adj. (bot.) casuarinaceous.

casuísmo s. m. casuistry.

casuísta s. m. + f. casuist: one versed in casuistry, person skilled in deciding questions of conscience; one given to sophistical reasoning and interpretations.

casuística s. f. casuistry: 1. interpretation of cases of conscience. 2. sophistical reasoning.

casuístico adj. casuistic(al). ‖ **casuisticamente** adv. casuistically.

casula s. f. (eccl.) chasuble (plate P 5).

casulo s. m. 1. (bot.) boll, seed capsule. 2. (ent.) cocoon.

casuloso adj. (bot.) capsulate(d). 2. shaped like a capsule. 3. cocoon-shaped. 4. full of seed capsules.

cata s. f. 1. search. 2. investigation, examination. research. 3. quest. 4. (Braz.) the grading of the roasted coffee beans. 5. mine, pit. **à ~ de** in search of.

catabatismo s. m. a doctrine professed by members of an ancient Christian sect that refuted baptism as necessary for salvation.

catabatista s. m. + f. (rel.) catabaptist, person who opposes baptism. || adj. m. + f. catabaptistical.

catabi s. m. (N. Braz.) 1. a bump in the road, an uneven roadbed. 2. the jolting and jerking of vehicles which travel over rough ground.

catabiose s. f. (med.) catabiosis.

catabolismo s. m. (biol., med.) catabolism, destructive metabolism.

catacáustica s. f. (opt.) catacaustic, catacaustic curve.

catacego adj. (pop.) weak-sighted, near-sighted.

cataclase s. f. (geol.) cataclasis.

cataclísmico adj. cataclysmal, cataclysmic.

cataclismo s. m. 1. cataclysm. 2. flood, deluge, inundation. 3. violent geological transformations. 4. (fig.) catastrophe, disaster. 5. social or political upheaval. 6. ruin, debacle.

catacrese s. f. (rhet.) catachresis: misuse of terms.

catacumba s. f. 1. catacomb. 2. subterranean place for the burial of the dead. 3. vault, crypt.

catadeira s. f. (Braz.) female coffee gatherer.

catador s. m. (Braz.) coffee cleaning and grading machine. || adj. 1. searching. 2. scrutinizing. 3. cleaning, grading.

catádromo adj. (bot., zool.) catadromous.

catadupa s. f. waterfall, cataract.

catadupejar v. to fall like a waterfall.

catadura s. f. 1. outward appearance, countenance. 2. aspect, look. 3. temper, disposition. 4. humour, character. **ele é de má ~** he is an evil looking fellow. **estar de má ~** to be in bad humour. **olhar com má ~** to look furiously at.

catafalco s. m. catafalque, bier.

catáfase s. f. (philos.) affirmation, affirmative clause.

catafilo s. m. (bot.) cataphyll.

catáfora s. f. (med.) cataphora, lethargy, somnolency.

cataforese s. f. (biochem., med.) cataphoresis.

cataguá s. m. (Braz.) a tropical tree of the family Rutaceae.

catalânico adj. Catalan: 1. of or pertaining to Catalonia (Spain). 2. of or relative to the Catalan language.

catalão s. m. (pl. -ões) (f. **catalã**) Catalan: 1. native or inhabitant of Cataluña. 2. the Spanish dialect spoken in Cataluña, Valencia and vicinity.

cataléctico, catalético adj. (poet.) catalectic, wanting a syllable at the end of a verse.

catalecto s. m. catalecta, anthology of classic literature.

catalepsia s. f. (med.) 1. catalepsy. 2. cataplexy.

cataléptica s. f. (bot.) hingeflower.

cataléptico s. m. (med.) patient suffering from catalepsy. || adj. cataleptic.

catalisação s. f. (pl. -ões) (phys., chem.) catalysis, acceleration of a reaction produced by an agent (catalyst), activation.

catalisador s. m. 1. (phys., chem.) catalyser, catalyst. 2. (fig.) organizer, promoter (esp. political).

catalisar v. 1. (chem.) to catalize, accelerate a reaction. 2. to activate. 3. to promote, further.

catálise s. f. (phys., chem.) catalysis.

catalítico adj. (phys., chem.) catalytic. || **cataliticamente** adv. catalytically.

catalogação s. f. (pl. -ões) cataloguing: 1. act of organizing in form of a catalogue. 2. method or process of cataloguing.

catalogado adj. catalogued, registered in a catalogue.

catalogador s. m. cataloguer, cataloger, catalogist.

catalogar v. 1. to make a list of. 2. to put in order, arrange. 3. to inscribe in a catalogue, register. 4. to class, sort, classify. 5. to inventory, catalogue.

catalogizar v. to catalog.

catálogo s. m. 1. catalogue, catalog. 2. descriptive list. 3. register, roll. 4. detailed report.

catalografia s. f. the art and method of organizing a catalogue.

catalográfico adj. concerning the art of cataloguing.

catambá s. m. (N. Braz.) a popular ballet and dance.

catambuera s. f. (Braz.) popular designation of any stunted fruit. || adj. m. + f. stunted, atrophied (fruits).

catamenial adj. m. + f. (pl. -ais) (med.) catamenial.

catamênio s. m. (med.) catamenia, menses.

catamnésia s. f. (med.) a clinical follow-up.

catamorfismo s. m. (geol.) katamorphism, catamorphism.

catana s. f. 1. catan, a broad Japanese sword. 2. cutlass. 3. a scimitar, saber with a curved blade. 4. (pop.) popular name of several kinds of adventitious roots. 5. (bot.) spathe of a palm, spadix. || adj. (N. Braz.) having only one horn (said of cattle). **meter a ~ em alguém** to slander a person, to backbite. **ser ~** to have a serpent's tongue.

catanada s. f. 1. cut with a saber or sword. 2. smashing blow. 3. (fig.) severe censure or reprimand, violent rebuke.

catanduba, cantanduva s. f. 1. low-growing spiny herbs (indicating poor soil). 2. clayey, barren soil.

catanduval s. m. (pl. -ais), (S. Braz.) a grove of pine trees.

catanga s. f. (typogr.) part of the composition put aside for pertaining to several cases.

catangüera s. f. = **catambuera**.

catão s. m. (pl. -ões) (fig.) 1. an austere man. 2. person who feigns to be austere or virtuous.

catapereiro s. m. a wild pear tree.

cata-piolho s. m. (N. Braz., fam.) the index finger, forefinger.

cataplasma s. f. 1. (pharm.) cataplasm, poultice, plaster. 2. bit of a harness. 3. (fig.) a weak ailing person.

cataplasmado adj. 1. poulticed, covered with a cataplasm. 2. (fig.) weak, sickly, unhealthy, ailing.

cataplasmar v. **encataplasmar**.

catapléctico, cataplético adj. (physiol., med.) cataplectic.

cataplexia s. f. (med., physiol.) cataplexy, cataplexis.

catapora s. f. (usually **cataporas**), (Braz., med.) chicken pox, varicella.

catapulta s. f. catapult: 1. (hist.) ancient war engine used to throw stones and other missiles. 2. (aeron.) device for launching airplanes from the deck of a ship.

catar (I) v. 1. to seek, search for. 2. to strive after, try, attempt. 3. to discover, uncover. 4. to scrutinize, investigate carefully. 5. to delouse. 6. to gather, collect. 7. **~-se** to clean o. s. from vermin or parasites.

catar (II) v. 1. to respect, esteem, honour. 2. to keep away, guard. 3. to heed. 4. to treat respectfully. **~ respeito** 1. to command respect. 2. to treat with respect. 3. to deal respectfully with each other.

cataraca s. f. (Braz.) dried nasal mucus.

catarata s. f. cataract: 1. waterfall. 2. (med.) amaurosis, an opacity of the crystalline lens.
ele tem ~ nos olhos he is starblind. **operar a ~** (surg.) to couch a patient's cataract.
catarinense s. m. + f. native or inhabitant of Santa Catharina (state in S. Braz.). || adj. of, pertaining to or relative to this state and its inhabitants.
catarineta s. m. + f. (Braz.) a nickname applied to the natives of Santa Catarina (Brazil).
catarral s. f. (med.) acute bronchitis, catarrhal fever. || adj. m. + f. (pl. **-ais**) catarrhal, catarrhous. typical of a catarrh or common cold.
catarreira s. f. (fam.) nasal catarrh, running of the nose.
catarrento adj. 1. catarrhal, catarrhous. 2. highly susceptible to catarrhal fever and colds.
catarrinos s. m. pl. (zool.) Catharrina, a division of Old World monkeys.
catarro s. m. (med.) 1. catarrh, inflammation of mucous membranes. 2. common cold, cold. 3. nasal catarrh, running of the nose, defluxion.
catarroso adj. 1. catarrhal, catarrhous. 2. affected with a catarrh, suffering from a cold.
catarse s. f. catharsis: 1. purification, purifying. 2. (med.) purgation. 3. morale of a tragedy or dramatic play. 4. (psych.) abreaction.
catártico s. m. (med. + pharm.) cathartic, purgative, physic. || adj. cathartic(al), purgative.
Catartídeos s. m. pl. (ornith.) Cathartidae, the New World vulture family.
catartidiformes s. m. pl. (ornith.) Catharthidiformes.
catassol s. m. (pl. **-óis**) 1. a fine, brilliant woollen fabric. 2. iridescent colour, shot colour tinge, changeable luster (of a fabric).
catástase s. f. 1. general state of health. 2. constitution. 3. temperament. 4. the third part of a Greek drama, catastasis, height of action of a drama.
catástrofe s. f. catastrophe: 1. the tragic conclusion of a romance, drama or tragedy. 2. an unfortunate conclusion, final issue. 3. calamity, great misfortune. 4. drama.
catastrófico adj. catastrophic(al).
catatau s. m. 1. castigation, punishment. 2. rap, blow. 3. (Braz., fam.) discussion, controversy. 4. malicious gossip, slander. 5. an old sword. 6. scimitar.
catatermômetro s. m. instrument used for determining the degree of cold of a body or space.
catatonia s. f. (med.) catatonia, severe dementia praecox.
catatônico adj. (med.) catatonic.
catatraz interj. bang!, crash!, crack!
catatuá s. m. (Braz.) backwoodsman, yokel, rustic.
catau s. m. (naut.) sheepshank, sheepshank knot.
catauari s. m. (Braz.) a tropical shrub of the caper family (Crataeva Benthami).
cata-vento s. m. (pl. **cata-ventos**) 1. weather vane, vane, weathercock. 2. a fickle or capricious person. 3. (Braz.) popular designation of windmills which drive water pumps.
~ de papel pinwheel. **~ de penas** feather vane.
catazona s. f. (geol.) the deepest zone of metamorphism.
cateamento s. m. exploration of a mine, mining.
catear v. to mine, dig for ore or metal, pan for gold.
catecismo s. m. catechism: 1. religious instruction by questions and answers. 2. elementary manual or book which contains such instruction. 3. the act of catechizing. 4. (fig.) elementary indoctrination (regarding arts, politics, science).
catecol s. m. (chem.) catechin, catechol.

catecumenato s. m. (also **catecumenado**) catechumenate: 1. state or condition of a catechumen. 2. duration of the catechumenal status.
catecúmeno s. m. catechumen, neophyte.
cátedra s. f. cathedra: 1. a lecturer's chair, professor's chair. 2. apostolical see, pontifical chair.
catedral s. f. (pl. **-ais**) cathedral, minster, dome, head church of a diocese. || adj. m. + f. 1. cathedral. 2. principal, fundamental. 3. official, authoritative. || **~mente** adv. cathedrally, authoritatively.
catedrático s. m. 1. college or university professor. 2. administrative head of a faculty. 3. lecturer of a university. || adj. cathedratic, professorial.
ele é ~ de filologia he professes philology.
categorema s. m. (bot.) categorem, the quality of being taxonomically important.
categoremático adj. (log.) categorematic, self-significant.
categoria s. f. 1. category, class, order. 2. degree, rate. 3. series. 4. character, quality, nature, type. 5. hierarchy, rank. 6. rate, rating. 7. predicament. 8. (philos.) predicables.
~ gramatical part of a speech. **de alta ~** highly placed, first-rate. **terceira ~** third-rate.
categórico adj. 1. of or relative to a category, rank or class; categorial. 2. categorical, explicit. 3. absolute. 4. express, downright. 5. peremptory, positive. 6. decisive, decided. 7. adjuratory. || **categoricamente** adv. categorically, absolutely, peremptorily, definitely.
imperativo ~ (gram.) absolute imperative.
categorizado adj. 1. of good category or rank. 2. authoritative.
categorizar v. to class, classify, categorize.
categute s. m. catgut.
catenária s. f. (math.) catenary, catenary curve.
catenóide adj. m. + f. (geom.) catenoid.
catênula s. f. small chain.
catenulado adj. 1. chainlike. 2. (bot.) catenulate.
catequese s. f. 1. catechesis, catechetics: a) oral religious instruction. b) catechization, methodical introduction into the fundamental principles of Christian faith. 2. (fig.) indoctrination.
catequético adj. catechetical.
catequista s. m. + f. catechist, catechizer, catechiser. || adj. catechistic(al).
catequização s. f. (pl. **-ões**) 1. catechization, catechisation. 2. act of catechizing. 3. (fig.) indoctrination.
catequizador s. m. catechizer, catechiser, catechist. || adj. catechistic(al), catechizing.
catequizar v. 1. to catechize: a) give religious instruction. b) question systematically with regard to religious principles and faith. 2. to instruct, teach. 3. to convince, try to convince. 4. to entice, attract attention to. 5. to initiate, introduce. 6. to indoctrinate.
catérese s. f. weakness from medication.
cateretê s. m. (Braz.) a lively folk dance and accompanying dance songs (showing Tupian and African influence).
caterético adj. (med.) 1. slightly caustic. 2. debilitating.
caterina s. f. (Braz.) prostitute.
caterinete s. m. + f. = **catarineta**.
caterva s. f. 1. crowd, throng. 2. mob, gang. 3. a great number of animals, herd, flock. 4. (obs.) a great number of troops.
catervagem s. f. (pl. **-ens**), (Braz.) a considerable quantity or number, abundance.
catete s. m. (Braz., also **cateto**) 1. a variety of Indian corn. 2. a breed of pigs.
catetê s. m. Indian skilled in weaving, Indian weaver.
cateter s. m. (med., surg.) catheter, probe.

cateterismo s. m. (med.) catheterism, any surgical application of the catheter.

cateto s. m. 1. (geom.) cathetus. 2. (phys.) a beam of light reflected in perpendicular direction.

catetômetro s. m. cathetometer.

cati s. m. (Braz.) plant of the sedge family (Kyllinga triceps).

caticó s. m. (Braz.) = catatau.

catiguá s. f. (S. Braz.) a tree of the family Meliceae.

catilinária s. f. 1. (Roman hist.) each one of Cicero's three accusatory speeches (criticizing violently Catilina). 2. (fig.) violent accusation, eloquent critic.

catimbau, catimbaua s. m. (Braz.) 1. witchcraft, sorcery. 2. conjuration of evil spirits. 3. a small, old pipe. 4. a ridiculous man.

catimbauzeiro s. m. (also catimbozeiro) sorcerer.

catimbó s. m. (Braz.) 1. = catimbau. 2. backwoodsman, yokel.

catimbueira s. f. (Braz.) a stunted ear of Indian corn.

catimplora s. f. 1. a metalic water or wine cooler. 2. siphon. 3. oil-can with a long, narrow spout. 4. culvert, drainpipe. 5. sprinkler, watering can. 6. ice-cream freezer (operated by hand). 7. high hat, top hat.

catimpuera s. f. a fermented drink of cooked manioc flour, water and honey.

catinga (I) s. f. (Braz.) 1. a strong disagreeable smell. 2. offensive body odour. 3. fetid or foul smell. ter ~ de água (Braz., pop.) to be down on one's luck.

catinga (II) s. f. (Braz.) 1. a forest of dwarfed, knotty trees. 2. region of stunted vegetation. 3. a plant of the family Bignoniaceae (Tecoma catinga).

catinga (III) s. m. + f. 1. miser, niggard, mean and avaricious person. 2. f. avarice, greed, covetousness, meanness.

catinga-de-bode s. f. (pl. catingas-de-bode), (Braz., bot.) bastard hemp agrimony.

catinga-de-mulata s. f. (pl. catingas-de-mulata), (Braz., bot.) 1. tansy. 2. ivy geranium.

catinga-de-negro s. f. (pl. catingas-de-negro), (Braz., bot.) a giant spiderflower (Cleome gigantea).

catinga-de-tamanduá s. f. (pl. catingas-de-tamanduá), (Braz., bot.) a kind of mountain ebony (Bauhinia rufa).

catingal s. m. (pl. -ais) a large forest of dwarfed trees.

catingante adj. m. + f. rank, fetid or foul smelling.

catingar v. 1. to bicker, wrangle, haggle. 2. to be mean or avaricious, act niggardly. 3. to emit an offensive smell, stink.

catingoso adj. (also catinguento) 1. malodorous, ill--smelling. 2. foul, fetid or rank-smelling. 3. stinking.

catingudo adj. malodorous, foul-smelling, stinking.

catingueira s. f. (Braz.) 1. (bot.) croton. 2. vegetation typical for the northeastern dry areas.

catingueiro s. m. (Braz.) 1. native or inhabitant of the northeastern dry regions. 2. (zool.) a brocket (Mazama simplicicornis).

cátion, cationte s. m. (physical chem.) cation, kation.

catira s. f. (Braz.) a country dance.

catirumbava s. f. (ornith.) a passerine bird of the family Thraupidae.

catita (I) s. f. a small, triangular auxiliary sail.

catita (II) adj. m. + f. elegant, fine, adorned, decorated, trim.

catita (III) s. m. (Braz., zool.) house mouse.

catita (IV) s. f. (N. Braz., pop.) jail, prison.

catitice s. f., catitismo m. 1. elegance, neatness. 2. excessive elegance, dandyism, foppishness.

cativante adj. m. + f. 1. captivating, captivative. 2. charming, fascinating. 3. attractive. 4. seductive. 5. enthralling, bewitching. 6. catchy, catching. 7. arrestive. ‖ ~mente adv. captivatingly, attractively, winsome, winningly, prepossessingly.

um sorriso ~ an engaging smile.

cativar v. 1. to captivate. 2. to take prisoner, capture. 3. to hold captive. 4. to enfetter, enslave. 5. to charm, fascinate, enchant. 6. to bewitch, enthral(l). 7. ~-se: a) to become enraptured or fascinated. b) to lose one's (moral or physical) liberty. c) to surrender, submit o. s., yield. d) to feel obliged, bind o. s. to.

~ benevolências to curry favours. ela o cativou com seus modos despretensiosos she won him with her modesty. ele cativou minha simpatia he engaged my sympathy.

cativeiro s. m. 1. captivity. 2. bond, bondage. 3. slavery, servitude. 4. prison, jail. 5. thralldom, serfdom. 6. (fig.) preoccupation.

livrar do ~ to enfranchise. o ~ do vício the fetters of vice.

cativo s. m. 1. prisoner. 2. captive, slave. 3. (min.) anatase, titanium dioxide, octahedrite. ‖ adj. 1. captive, held in prison or bondage. 2. confined, constrained. 3. captivated, charmed, fascinating. 4. enamoured. 5. attractive, seductive, tempting. 6. (jur.): a) pawned, held under a mortgage. b) subject to obligations or pledges, liable to pay taxes, dutiable. ‖ -amente adv. captivatingly, attractively.

cativo-de-chumbo s. m. (pl. cativos-de-chumbo), (Braz., min.) anatase, titanium dioxide, octahedrite.

cativo-de-ferro s. m. (pl. cativos-de-ferro), (Braz., min.) octahedral iron ore.

catléia s. f. any Cattleya orchid.

catódico (I) adj. (phys.) cathodic(al), of, pertaining to or relative to a cathode.

catódico (II) adj. (phys.) of, pertaining to or relative to cathode rays.

catódio, cátodo s. m. (electr., phys.) cathode, kathode, the negative pole of an electrolytic cell.

cátodo fotossensível s. m. (electr., phys.) fotosensitive cathode.

catolicidade s. f. 1. Catholicity, faith and doctrines of the Catholic Church. 2. the Catholics and Catholic peoples collectively. 3. Catholicism. 4. the quality or fact of belonging to the Catholic Church.

catolicismo s. m. 1. Catholicism. 2. faith, principles and system of the Catholic Church. 3. universality of the Roman Catholic Church. 4. Roman Catholic people(s).

catolicização s. f. = catolização.

catolicizar v. = catolizar.

católico s. m. 1. a Catholic, one who embraces the Roman Catholic creed. 2. a Roman Catholic, a member of the Roman Catholic Church. ‖ adj. 1. Catholic, Catholical. 2. universal, general.

não estar muito ~ not to be perfect or sound.

catolização s. f. (pl. -ões) Catholization, act of Catholicizing.

catolizar v. to Catholicize.

catombo s. m. (N. Braz.) tumour, swelling, boil.

catoniano, catônico adj. (Roman hist.) Catonian: of, pertaining to or resembling Cato.

catonismo s. m. 1. Catonism, Catoism. 2. (fig.) austerity, harshness, severity. 3. quality or act characteristic of Cato.

catópode adj. m. + f. (ichth.) having ventral fins.

catoptromancia s. f. catoptromancy, divination by a mirror or crystal gazing.

catoptromante s. m. + f. catoptromancer.

catoptromântico adj. catoptromantic.

catorra s. f. (Braz., ornith.) monk parrot, monk parakeet.

catorze adj. (more used **quatorze**) fourteen.

catorzeno adj. (more used **quatorzeno**) the four-teenth.

catota s. f. (Braz., pop.) dried nasal secretion.

catrabucha s. f. 1. a fine wire brush, polishing brush. 2. (Braz.) any indeterminable object.

catraca s. f. 1. (tech.) ratchet, ratchet-brace (plate F 8). 2. ratchet, click of a watch (plate R 4). ~ **de avanço** feed-ratchet. ~ **de furar** ratchet-brace. ~ **de mudança** shift ratchet. ~ **motriz**, ~ **propulsora** driving ratchet.

catrafiar, catrafilar v. 1. to grasp, seize, lay hold of. 2. to arrest. 3. to imprison, incarcerate.

catraia s. f. 1. a small boat for one rower only. 2. sculler (plate B 9). 3. (Braz., vulg.) common prostitute, street-walker.

catraieiro s. m. boatman, rower of a sculler.

catrâmbias s. f. pl. somersault. ‖ interj. nuts! non-sense!

de ~ head over heels.

catrapoço s. m. (Braz.) any useless or worthless object.

catrapós, catrapus s. m. galloper, a fast running horse. ‖ interj. bang!, crash!, smash!, crack!

catre s. m. 1. truckle bed. 2. pallet, cot. 3. folding bed. 4. field-bed. 5. (Braz.) a kind of catamaran.

catrevage s. f. (Braz.) 1. unused construction material and implements. 2. a collection of objects (of any kind).

catrumano s. m. (Braz.) a backwoodsman, yokel, rustic.

catuaba s. f. (Braz.) 1. common name of two plants of the family Bignoniaceae (Anemopaegma glau-cum, Anemopaegma mirandum). 2. m. a strong or powerful man.

catuaba-do-mato s. f. (pl. **catuabas-do-mato**), (Braz., bot.) a holly (Ilex conocarpa).

catucação (pl. **-ões**), **catucada** s. f. nudging, jabbing, poking (with the finger or elbow).

catucaém s. m. (pl. **-ens**) = **carne-de-vaca**.

catucão s. m. (pl. **-ões**) violent jab or prod.

catucar v. 1. to nudge. 2. to jab, thrust, poke.

catueiro s. m. a heavy fishhook.

catulé s. m. 1. = **coco-da-quaresma**. 2. a palm tree.

cátulo s. m. little dog.

catumbi s. m. (Braz.) 1. a lively folk dance. 2. (gambling) a certain game of chance.

catunduva s. f. 1. low-growing, spiny herbs (indicating poor soil). 2. clayey, barren ground.

catupé s. m. (Braz.) an ancient folk dance.

catuqui, catuquim (pl. **-ins**) s. m. (Braz.) a gnat.

caturra s. m. + f. 1. stubborn, cantankerous person, faultfinding old fogey. 2. faddist. 3. castor-oil plant. 4. popular designation of two small parakeets. ‖ adj. cantankerous, crabby, faultfinding.

caturrada s. f. 1. obstinacy. 2. (naut.) the descending movement of the bow of a boat.

caturrar v. 1. to be obstinate, cantankerous or fault-finding. 2. to argue insistently. 3. to discuss insig-nificant matter. 4. (naut.) to plunge the bow of a vessel, make a vessel bow-heavy.

caturreira, caturrice s. f. 1. obstinacy, stubbornness. 2. fogyism, fogydom. 3. unfounded pertinacy. 4. act typical of a cantankerous, narrow-minded person.

caturrismo s. m. 1. act or saying typical of a narrow-minded, cantankerous or obstinate person. 2. fogyism, fogydom. 3. groundless dispute.

caturrita s. f. (ornith.) monk parrot, monk parakeet.

caturritar v. 1. to talk too much. 2. to chatter, babble. 3. to gossip.

catuta s. f. (Braz., pop.) sugar-cane brandy.

catuzado adj. (Braz.) worn-out, disabled, incapacitate, useless (said of old animals).

cauã s. f. (Braz.) bird of the family Falconidae (Herpethotheres cachinnans).

cauaba s. f. (Braz.) a drinking vessel.

cauaçu s. m. (bot.) a shrub: 1. of the family Marantaceae (Calathea lutea). 2. of the family Polygonaceae (Coccoloba latifolia). 3. of the family Rubiaceae (Exostemma australe).

caubi s. m. (Braz., Amazonas) green grassland or woodland.

caução s. f. (pl. **-ões**) 1. security. 2. guaranty, guarantee. 3. pledge, bond. 4. values deposited in a bank as a security or pledge. 5. bail. **prestar** ~ to give bail. **sob** ~ on bail. ~ **promissó-ria** promissory bond.

caucasiano, caucásico adj. Caucasian: of, pertaining to or relative to the Caucasus and its inhabitants. ‖ adj. Caucasian.

caucásio s. m. Caucasian: 1. native or inhabitant of the Caucasus. 2. member of the Caucasian race.

cauchal s. m. (pl.**-ais**) a grove or plantation of gum-trees. ‖ adj. m. + f. of, pertaining to or relative to gum-trees and their plantation.

caucheiro s. m. 1. a gatherer of wild rubber. 2. owner of a rubber or gum-tree plantation.

caucho s. m. 1. (bot.) a wild Braz. rubber tree (Castilloa ulei). 2. a wild Central American rubber tree (Castilloa elastica). 3. caoutchouc, gum-elastic.

cauchorana s. f. (Braz.) a tree of the family Moraceae (Perebea guinansis).

caucionado adj. bonded, pledged, pawned.

caucionante s. m. + f. 1. guarantor, warrantor. 2. bondsman, bailsman. 3. one who offers a guarantee. ‖ adj. serving as a security or bond.

caucionar v. 1. to give as security. 2. to bond, bail. 3. to guarantee, vouch for. 4. to pledge.

caucionário s. m. 1. guarantor, warrantor. 2. bonds-man, bailsman. ‖ adj. serving as a security or bond.

cauda s. f. 1. tail, prolongation of the rear-end of most of the animals. 2. horsetail. 3. tail feathers. 4. train of a gown (plate R 6). 5. (astr.) tail of a comet. 6. rear, rear-end (of marching troops, con-voy, wagon-train). 7. (mus.) the stem of a note. 8. stalk of certain fruits or flowers. 9. the body of a building stone. 10. trail. 11. (fig.) end, hind-part (plate M 7).

~ **de andorinha** dovetail. ~ **de avião** tail of an airplane. ~ **de cometa** tag, tail of a comet. ~ **de rato** rat's tail. ~ **de leque** fan tail. ~ **do dragão** the dragon's tail (also astr.). **enrolar a** ~ to sneak away with the tail between the legs; (fig.) to be afraid. **piano de** ~ grand piano.

cauda-le-leão s. f. (pl. **caudas-de-leão**), (bot.) mother-wort.

cauda-de-raposa s. f. (pl. **caudas-de-raposa**) 1. foxtail, fox-brush. 2. (bot.): a) love-lies-bleeding. b) flea-bane. c) beard-grass. d) meadow-foxtail. e) bit-terweed.

caudado adj. caudate(d).

caudados s. m. pl. (zool.) Caudata, an order of Amphibia.

caudal (I) s. m. (pl. **-ais**) 1. mighty river, stream. 2. current. 3. torrent. 4. waterfall. 5. volume of a river. ‖ adj. m. + f. 1. torrential. 2. capital. 3. great, large, voluminous. 4. (fig.) abundant.

caudal (II) adj. m. + f. (pl. **-ais**) (anat., zool.) caudal, posterior.

caudaloso adj. 1. torrential, carrying much water. 2. great, large. 3. voluminous. 4. mighty. 5. (fig.) abundant, copious. ‖ -amente adv. abundantly, copiously.

caudatário s. m. 1. train-bearer (to ecclesiastic dignitaries). 2. (fig.) servile or meanly submissive fellow.

caudato adj. caudate(d), tailed.

caudel s. m. (pl. -éis) = coudel.

caudelaria s. f. = coudelaria.

cáudex, cáudice s. m. (bot.) caudex.

caudiculado adj. (bot.) provided with caudicle.

caudículo s. m. (bot.) caudicle.

caudilhamento s. m. 1. act or fact of leading, commanding. 2. leadership in the hands of a military or political boss.

caudilhar v. 1. to lead, command. 2. to place under the command of a political or military leader.

caudilhismo s. m. 1. system and principles of autocratic leadership. 2. act typical of a caudillo. 3. (fig.) bossism, despotism.

caudilho s. m. 1. military leader, commander. 2. war chief. 3. caudillo, head of a party or political faction. 4. captain, general. 5. boss, chief, headman.

caudímano adj. (zool.) having a prehensile tail.

caudino (I) adj. made from one piece of timber.

caudino (II) s. m. (hist.) native or inhabitant of Caudio (Italy). ‖ adj. of, pertaining to or relative to this place.

cauíla adj. m. + f. avaricious, mean, parsimonious.

cauim s. m. (Braz.) a refreshing and intoxicating drink made from fermented manioc mixed with other fruits.

cauixi s. m. (Braz.) a black, caustic matter deposited on the river banks (the ashes of this material are mixed with clay and used by Indians for the production of earthenware).

caule s. m. (bot.) caulis, stalk, stem, shaft.
~ das gramíneas (bot.) culm.

cauleoso adj. (bot.) 1. caulescent, having a stem or stalk. 2. growing on a stem or stalk.

caulescência s. f. (bot.) caulescence, caulescency.

caulescente adj. m. + f. (bot.) caulescent, cauliferous.

caulícola s. m. + f. plant which lives on the stems of other plants. ‖ adj. caulicolous.

caulículo s. m. (bot.) caulicle, small or rudimentary stem.

caulídio s. m. (bot.) an organ similar to the stem in inferior plants.

caulificação s. f. (pl. -ões), (bot.) formation of a stalk or stem.

caulifloria s. f. (bot.) cauliflory.

caulifloro adj. (bot.) cauliflorous.

caulim s. m. kaolin(e), white clay, China clay, porcelain clay.

caulinar adj. m. + f. (bot.) cauline: relative to the stem.

caulinita s. f. (min.) kaolinite.

caulino (I) s. m. kaolin, porcelain clay.

caulino (II) adj. (bot.) cauline: 1. of or pertaining to a stalk or stem. 2. growing on a stem.

cauloma s. m. (bot.) caulome.

caúna s. f. (Braz.) common name of several plants of the genus Ilex, a holly.

cauré s. m. bird of the family Falconidae (Falco albigularis albigularis).

cauri (I), caurim, cauril s. m. 1. (zool.) cowrie, cowry, cowry shell, money shell. 2. (pop.) cheat, swindle, mean trick.

cauri (II) s. m. kauri resin.

caurinar v. 1. to deceive, dupe. 2. to swindle, cheat. 3. to play a mean trick.

caurineiro s. m. 1. swindler, cheat. 2. sponger. 3. rotter, hoodlum, scoundrel.

causa s. f. 1. cause. 2. ground, bottom. 3. causation. 4. motive, agent, reason. 5. root. 6. rise. 7. origin. 8. occasion. 9. (pol.) party, political faction. 10. concern, interest. 11. account. 12. justification. 13. (jur.) lawsuit, case, process, legal action.
~ concorrente concurrent fact. ~ final final cause. ~ motora fundamental motive. ~s secundárias adventitious causes. com conhecimento de ~ with special knowledge or experience. dar ~ a to give cause for. fazer ~ com to side with, make common cause with. ganhar uma ~ to win a lawsuit, recover a right. não se deve ser juiz em ~ própria no man should be a judge of his own cause. por ~ de by reason of, because of, on account of. por ~ de sua criança for the sake of her child. por ~ de quem? for whose sake? por ~ disto for that reason, on that account, thereupon, thereat. por minha ~ upon my account, for my sake, for my behalf. qual é a ~ da comoção? what is all this about? ser fiel à ~ to stick to one's colours. ser a ~ de to be instrumental in. uma ~ perdida a lost cause. uma ~ pública a public affair, a common cause.

causação s. f. (pl. -ões) causation, mutual relation between cause and effect, causality.

causador s. m. 1. cause, causer. 2. occasioner, originator. 3. raiser, doer. ‖ adj. causing, causative, productive.

causal s. f. (pl. -ais) 1. cause, causation. 2. motive, ground reason. 3. origin. ‖ adj. m. + f. causal, causative.
conjunção ~ (gram.) causative conjunction.

causalidade s. f. causality, causation, mutual relation between cause and effect.

causante adj. m. + f. causing, motivating.

causar v. 1. to cause, be the cause of. 2. to motivate, motive. 3. to occasion, effectuate, effect. 4. to engender, induce. 5. to originate, raise. 6. to produce, bring about, do, make. 7. to provoke. 8. to draw on. 9. to influence.
~ aversão a to be repulsive to. ~ colisão to cause a collision, dash. ~ dano to do harm to, damnify. ~ desespero to cause despair. ~ desgraça to disgrace. ~ dificuldades to stir up difficulties, ask for trouble. ~ dor to give pain, rankle. ~ irritação to irritate. ~ mágoa to grieve, cause grief. ~ ressentimento to cause resentment, rankle. ele causou grande impressão (theat.) he got across the footlights. ele causa boa impressão he impresses favourably, takes well. eles lhe causaram dificuldades they put difficulties in his way, put a spoke into his wheel. o acidente causou fortes reações the accident eventuated strong reactions. isto lhe causará bastante dor de cabeça that will cause him much trouble. tem causado muito bem it had worked much good.

causativo adj. 1. of, pertaining to or relative to a cause. 2. causative, causal, causing.
palavra ou frase -a (gram.) causative word or phrase.

causídico s. m. 1. lawyer, advocate. 2. barrister, inner barrister. 3. counsel for the defendant.

causo s. m. (pop.) 1. case. 2. tale, story, yarn.

causticação s. f. (pl. -ões) 1. act of cauterizing. 2. cauterization. 3. (fig.) trouble, bother, annoyance.

causticante adj. m. + f. 1. caustic(al). 2. cauterant. 3. burning, fiery. 4. pungent. 5. (fig.) wearisome, tedious.

causticar v. 1. to cauterize, sear with a cautery or caustic. 2. to burn, sear. 3. (fig.) to molest, annoy.

causticidade s. f. 1. causticity. 2. acridity, acridness. 3. (fig.) sharpness, mordacity, severity.

cáustico s. m. 1. caustic. 2. cautery. 3. caustic agent. ‖ adj. 1. caustic. 2. burning, corrosive. 3. biting, acrimonious, sharp. 4. (fig.) severe, bitter, vitriolic. ‖ **causticamente** adv. caustically, acrimoniously. **ele fez uma observação** -a he made a sarcastic remark.

caustobiólito s. m. (petrog.) sedimentary rock formed by residues of combustible organisms; charcoal, turf.

cautchu s. m. 1. latex. 2. caoutchouc, pure rubber.

cautela s. f. 1. caution, cautiousness. 2. guardedness, watchfulness. 3. vigilance. 4. care, carefulness, heedfulness. 5. prudence. 6. deliberation, deliberatedness. 7. pawn ticket. 8. voucher, ticket stub. 9. share of a lottery ticket. ~ **excessiva** overcaution, overcarefulness. à ~, por ~ as a preventive measure. com ~ cautiously, heedful.

cautelamento s. m. act or effect of cautioning or warning.

cautelar v. 1. to caution. 2. to warn, forewarn.

cauteleiro s. m. (Port.) a lottery ticket seller.

cauteloso adj. 1. cautious. 2. careful, heedful. 3. prudent. 4. watchful, vigilant. 5. reserved. 6. circumspect. 7. chary, shy, cagey. 8. wary. 9. calculative. 10. safe. ‖ **-amente** adv. 1. watchfully, vigilantly. 2. precautiously. 3. advertently. 4. foot by foot, prudently.

cautério s. m. 1. caustic. 2. cautery. 3. caustic agent, corrosive. 4. cauter, cauterizing iron. 5. (fig.) severe punishment.

cauterização s. f. (pl. **-ões**) cauterization, cautery.

cauterizar v. 1. to cauterize, sear with a cautery or a caustic. 2. to etch, sear, burn. 3. (fig.) to punish severely, reprove harshly. 4. to afflict. 5. to cure, heal. 6. to destroy completely. 7. to root out, extirpate.

cauto adj. 1. cautious. 2. careful, heedful. 3. prudent. 4. wary, shy. 5. circumspect. ‖ **-amente** adv. cautiously, guardedly, carefully.

cauxi s. m. (N. Braz.) spongy freshwater animals provided with spicules that cause irritation when in contact with human skin.

cava s. f. 1. act of digging. 2. furrow, trench, hole. 3. armhole of a coat. 4. cellar, basement. 5. butlery of a palace. ~ **da cunha** key-seat. ~ **de uma fortaleza** defensive trench around a fortress.

cavaca s. f. 1. a piece of firewood. 2. a splinter of wood. 3. a kind of biscuit, a hard, sweet cake.

cavação s. f. (pl. **-ões**) 1. act or effect of digging. 2. hole, pit. 3. (pop.) sharp practices. 4. (pop.) a source of easy income, easy position or business obtained as a favour.

cavacar v. = **cavar.**

cavaco (I) s. m. a chip or splinter of wood, wood-shaving.

cavaco (II) s. m. friendly conversation, chat. 2. attention, regard. 3. answer, reply. 4. gossip. 5. irritation, displeasure. **dar** ~ to take offense. **dar dois dedos de** ~ to chatter a little. **dar o** ~ **por** to be crazy about.

cavacué s m. (Braz., ornith.) the diademed parrot (Amazona diadema).

cavadeira s. f. a hoe.

cavadela s. f. 1. act of digging or hoeing. 2. a stroke with a hoe.

cavadiço adj. what is or may be digged out from the earth.

cavado s. m. hole, hollow, pit, furrow.

cavador s. m. 1. digger, hoer. 2. ploughman. 3. digging tool. 4. (Braz., pop.) one who tries to obtain an advantageous position or business even by unfair means. ‖ adj. diligent, industrious, hardworking.

cavadura s. f. 1. act of digging or hoeing. 2. a stroke with a hoe.

cavala s. f. (ichth.) a mackerel.

cavala-branca s. f. (pl. **cavalas-brancas**), (ichth.) cero, pintado (Scomberomus regalis).

cavalada s. f. 1. sheer folly, blunder, piece of stupidity. 2. brutal act, bestiality.

cavalagem s. f. (pl. **-ens**) 1. covering mares for breeding purposes. 2. stud fee. 3. trotting gait of a horse.

cavalão s. m. (pl. **-ões**) (f. **cavalona**) 1. a big horse. 2. a kind of mackerel. 3. (fig.) a well developed individual. 4. a mischievous, prankish lad. 5. a very tall person. 6. a physically well developed but not too bright and mannerly person.

cavalar (I) adj. m. + f. 1. equine: of, pertaining to or relative to horses. 2. of or belonging to a certain race of horses.

cavalar (II) v. = **cavaloar.**

cavalaria s. f. 1. a herd of horses. 2. a group of horsemen. 3. (mil.) military force which serves on horseback, cavalry. 4. horsemanship. 5. chivalry, gallantry, valour. ~ **ligeira** (mil.) light horse. ~ **pesada** (mil.) heavy cavalry. **meter-se em altas** ~**s** (fam.) to bite off more than one can chew.

cavalariano s. m. 1. (mil.) cavalryman, soldier belonging to the cavalry. 2. a horse dealer.

cavalariça s. f. 1. mews, a range of stables. 2. horse stable. 3. coach-house.

cavalariço s. m. 1. equerry, horseman. 2. hostler. 3. horse-boy, stable-boy, groom.

cavalear v. = **cavalgar.**

cavaleira s. f. horsewoman, equestrienne.

cavaleiro s. m. 1. horseman, rider, equestrian. 2. cavalryman, trooper. 3. nobleman, gentleman. 4. knight, chevalier. 5. cavalier. 6. paladin, banneret. 7. (fort.) raised defensive work of a bastion. 8. rider on the beam of a precision balance. ‖ adj. 1. of or pertaining to horsemen and horsemanship. 2. high, superior. 3. (fig.) noble. ~ **andante** paladin. ~ **armado** bachelor-at-arms. ~ **da Jarreteira** knight of the garter. **fazer de** ~ to affect dignity. **viver como** ~ to live in great style.

cavaleiroso adj. 1. chivalrous. 2. noble, gallant. 3. (fig.) generous. 4. gentlemanly. 5. famous.

cavalete s. m. 1. wooden horse, rack, stand, base (plates E 9, L 3, M 7). 2. trestle. 3. easel (plate P 12). 4. (hist.) instrument of torture. 5. (typogr.) rack. 6. bridge of string-instruments (plates G 2, P 10, V 5). 7. stays of a rack-wagon. 8. work bench. 9. corbel. ~ **de suspensão** drop hanger frame. ~ **secador** drying rack (plate F 6).

cavalgação s. f. (pl. **-ões**) (N. Braz., pop.) oestrus, rut.

cavalgada s. f. (also **cavalgata**) 1. cavalcade. 2. meeting of horsemen and women. 3. rodeo. 4. procession or parade of horsemen.

cavalgadura s. f. 1. mount. 2. saddle animal, beast. 3. (fig.) boor, a coarse stupid fellow.

cavalgamento s. m. (poet.) enjambment.

cavalgante s. m. + f. horseman, horsewoman. ‖ adj. riding.

cavalgar v. 1. to ride on horseback, mount a horse. 2. to bestride, bestraddle. 3. to jockey. 4. to pass by (on a horse). 5. (fig.) to override. 6. to spring or leap over. 7. to sit astraddle.

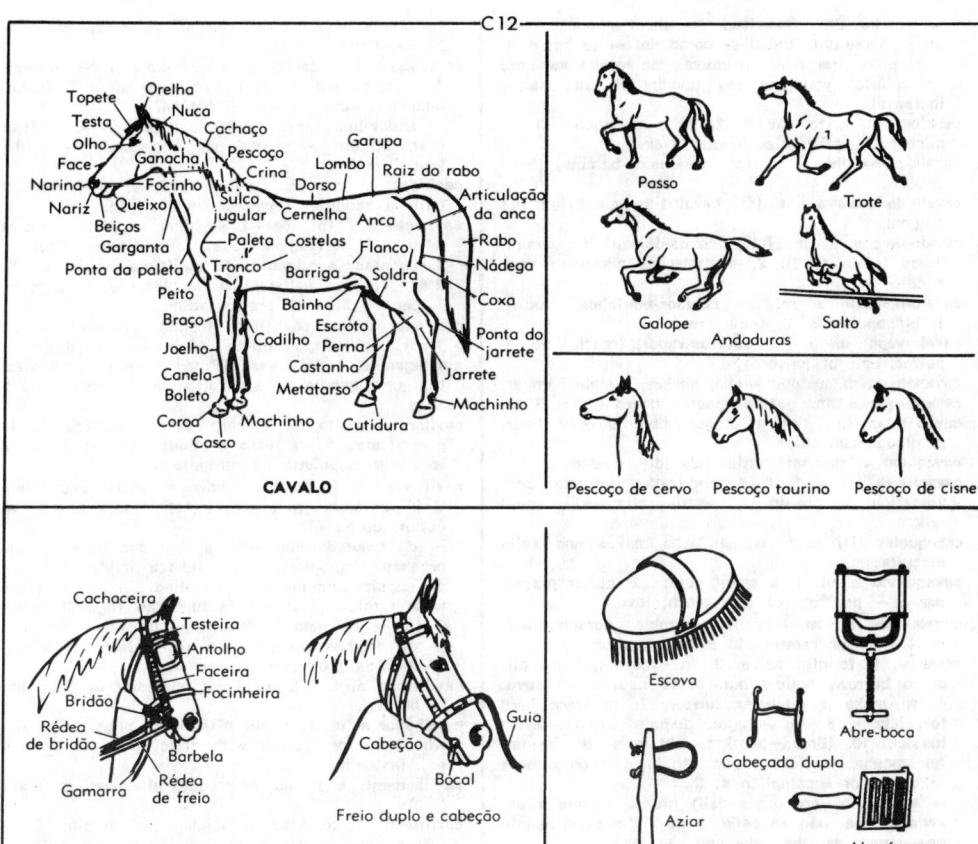

C 12

CAVALO

Passo

Trote

Galope — Salto

Andaduras

Pescoço de cervo — Pescoço taurino — Pescoço de cisne

Escova

Abre-boca

Cabeçada dupla

Aziar

Almofaça

Tratamento de cavalos

Cachaceira
Testeira
Antolho
Faceira
Focinheira
Bridão
Rédea
de bridão
Barbela
Gamarra
Rédea
de freio

Cabeção
Guia
Bocal

Freio duplo e cabeção

Topete, Orelha, Testa, Nuca, Olho, Cachaço, Face, Ganacha, Pescoço, Garupa, Narina, Focinho, Crina, Lombo, Raiz do rabo, Nariz, Queixo, Dorso, Sulco jugular, Cernelha, Anca, Articulação da anca, Beiços, Paleta, Costelas, Flanco, Rabo, Garganta, Tronco, Barriga, Soldra, Nádega, Ponta da paleta, Peito, Bainha, Coxa, Braço, Escroto, Codilho, Perna, Ponta do jarrete, Joelho, Castanha, Canela, Metatarso, Jarrete, Boleto, Machinho, Coroa, Machinho, Cutidura, Casco

---

cavalhada s. f. 1. a herd of horses. 2. horses, donkeys, mules collectively. 3. popular amusement or sport. 4. a popular contest, tournament. 5. cavalcade.

cavalheiresco adj. 1. chivalrous, chivalric. 2. noble, gallant. 3. knightly, gentlemanly. 4. distinguished.

cavalheirismo s. m. 1. chivalrousness, chivalry. 2. noble or generous act. 3. knightliness. 4. gallantry.

cavalheiro s. m. 1. gentleman, cavalier. 2. nobleman. 3. don, squire. 4. well-bred and well-educated man. ‖ adj. 1. noble, distinguished. 2. gentlemanly. 3. chivalrous.
indigno de um ~ ungentlemanlike.

cavalheiroso adj. 1. chivalrous, chivalric. 2. noble, gallant.

cavalice s. f. (Braz.) 1. = **cavalada**. 2. exaggerated lickerishness.

cavalicoque s. m. (pop.) a small worn-out horse, jade.

cavalinha s. f. 1. dim. form of **cavala**. 2. (ichth.) a small mackerel. 3. (bot.): a) horsetail. b) bottle brush.

cavalinho s. m. 1. dim. form of **cavalo**. 2. cockhorse, rockinghorse. 3. (S. Braz.) tanned horsehide.

cavalinho-d'água s. m. (pl. **cavalinhos-d'água**) (bot.) water milfoil.

cavalinho-de-judeu s. m. (pl. **cavalinhos-de-judeu**) (ent.) a dragonfly.

cavalinho-do-mar s. m. (pl. **cavalinhos-do-mar**) (ichth.) sea-horse.

cavalo s. m. 1. (zool.) horse (plate C 12). 2. (hort.) rootstock for grafting. 3. trestle. 4. (med., pop.) venereal chancre. 5. (chess, cards) knight (plate X). 6. cavalryman. 7. (fort.) cavalier. 8. sawing horse, rack.
~ alazão sorrel. **~ branco** white horse. **~ de aluguel** hack, hackney, job-horse. **~ de balanço** rocking horse. **~ de batalha** 1. war horse, steed, charger. 2. hobby-horse, favorite topic. 3. encumbrance, difficulty. **~ de carga** packhorse. **~ de cavalaria** troop-horse. **~ de corridas** race-horse. **~ de meia jornada** old outworn horse. **~ de montaria** mount. **~ de tiro** cart-horse, draught-horse, dray-horse. **~ dianteiro** forehold, leader. **~ empinador** prancer. **~ estradeiro** padnag, pad. **~ puro-sangue** blood-horse. **~s ao freio** (tech.) brake horse-power. **~ trotador** trotter. **~ velho** hack, jade. **~ veloz** courser, pelter. **a ~** on horseback, astraddle. **a ~!** (mil. command) to horse! **a ~ dado não se olham os dentes** never look a gift-horse into the mouth. **andar no ~ dos frades** (pop.) to go on foot. **corrida de ~s** horses-racing. **estar a ~** to be on horseback. **fazer ~ de batalha** to insist upon an argument, make a mountain out of a molehill. **montar a ~** to ride on horseback.

no ~ de São Francisco on shank's mare. **rabo de** ~ horse-tail. **trabalhar como um** ~ to horse it. **você pode tirar o** ~ **da chuva, não haverá aumento de salário!** you can say goodby to that salary increase!.

cavaloar v. 1. to cavort. 2. to skip, amble. 3. to misbehave, play mischievous tricks.

cavalo-de-batalha s. m. (pl. **cavalos-de-batalha**) (bot.) bebeeru.

cavalo-de-judeu s. m. (pl. **cavalos-de-judeu**) (ent.) a dragonfly.

cavalo-de-pau s. m. (pl. **cavalos-de-pau**) 1. (gymn.) horse (plate G 3). 2. a turnabout maneuver with a car.

cavalo-marinho s. m. (pl. **cavalos-marinhos**) (zool.): 1. hippopotamus. 2. sea-horse.

cavalo-vapor s. m. (pl. **cavalos-vapor**) (mech.) horse-power, unit of power.

cavanejo s. m. a deep wicker basket, a main hamper.

cavanhaque s. m. goatee, goatee beard (plate B 6).

cavão s. m. (pl. **-ões**) 1. digger, ditchdigger. 2. hoer. 3. ploughman, tiller.

cavaquear v. to chat, tattle, talk idly, gossip.

cavaqueira (I) s. f. 1. a long-lasting intimate conversation. 2. gossip. 3. prattle, chat, idle small talk.

cavaqueira (II) s. f. woman who makes and sells biscuits.

cavaquinho s. m. 1. a small guitar. 2. guitar player. **dar o** ~ **por** to like very much, love.

cavaquista s. m. + f. an irritable person. || adj. m. + f. of or relating to such a person.

cavar v. 1. to dig, delve. 2. to excavate, hole, pit. 3. to burrow, hollow out. 4. to hoe. 5. to cave. 6. to make a ditch or furrow. 7. to work hard for, labour. 8. to wrangle, dispute angrily. 9. to fossick. 10. (Braz., pop.) to obtain s. th. by unfair means. 11. (Braz., pop.) to have much trouble to obtain or accomplish s. th. ~ **a vida** to earn one's daily bread. ~ **com a enxada** to hoe. **não se pode** ~ **na vinha e no bacelo** one cannot eat the cake and have it.

cavatina s. f. (mus.) cavatina, a simple aria.

cavedal s. m. (pl. **-ais**) a gunsmith's tool.

caveira s. f. 1. skull, death's-head. 2. (fig.) death. 3. (pop.) a lean face, leanness. ~ **de burro** (pop.) bad luck. **fazer a** ~ **de alguém** (pop.) to lay a snare for a person.

caveira-de-pau s. m. (pl. **caveiras-de-pau**) (Braz., naut. sl.) an officer on duty.

caveiroso adj. 1. like a skull, resembling a skull. 2. very lean, haggard.

caverna s. f. 1. cave, cavern. 2. grotto, den, delve. 3. undercroft. 4. crypt, vault. 5. ~**s** pl. (naut.) the ribs of a ship (plate B 10). 6. (med.) oedema of the lungs.

cavernal adj. m. + f. (pl. **-ais**) cavernal, cavernous.

cavername s. m. 1. the ribs of a ship, boat timbers. 2. (fam.) skeleton, bones of a skeleton.

cavernícola s. m. + f. cavernicole. || adj. m. + f. cavernicolous.

cavernite s. f. (med.) inflammation of the cavernous bodies.

cavernosidade s. f. cavernous character or quality.

cavernoso adj. 1. cavernous. 2. full of caverns or caves. 3. resembling a cavern or cavity. 4. hollow. 5. hollow-sounding. 6. (anat.) of or pertaining to the cavernous bodies. || **-amente** adv. cavernously.

caveto s. m. (archit.) cavetto, throat, channel, flute.

cavi s. f. (bot.) root of the oca.

caviar s. m. caviar.

cavicórneo s. m. (zool.) 1. ruminant belonging to the Cavicornia. 2. ~**s** pl. the Cavicornia: a group of ruminants whose horns are hollow. || adj. cavicorn, having hollow horns.

cavidade s. f. 1. cavity. 2. hole, hollow. 3. hollowness. 4. cave, cavern. 5. depression, excavation. 6. (anat.) chamber, bursa, sinus. 7. lacuna. ~ **abdominal** (anat.) abdominal cavity. ~ **linfática** (nat.) cistern. ~ **natural** pan, depression. ~ **ocular** (anat.) orbit.

cavídeos s. m. pl. (zool.) Caviidae, a family of tailless rodents: capybara, guinea pig.

cavilação s. f. (pl. **-ões**) 1. sophism, sophistical act or saying. 2. stratagem, ruse. 3. cavilation, trickery. 4. cunning, astuteness. 5. malicious irony. 6. (N. Braz.) feigned satisfaction or pleasure, simulation. 7. captiousness. 8. prevarication.

cavilador s. m. cavil(l)er, sophist, deceiver, cheat. || adj. cavil(l)ing, captious, sophistical, deceptive.

cavilagem s. f. (pl. **-ens**), (Braz.) 1. feigned satisfaction or pleasure. 2. simulation. 3. cunning, astuteness.

cavilar v. 1. to cavil, carp. 2. to pettyfog. 3. to prevaricate. 4. to raise captious objections. 5. to fool with sophistic interpretations.

cavilha s. f. 1. dowel, wooden or metal peg (plate C 9). 2. spike, pin, plug (plate C 15). 3. bolt. 4. cotter, cotter pin. ~ **da amurada** bolt with a ring and hook. ~ **de organéu** ring-bolts. ~ **de cabeça** fender bolt. ~ **de engate** coupling iron, coupling pin. ~ **de escatelar** forelock bolt. ~ **de fundação** rag-bolt (plate P 4). ~ **de gato** hook-bolt. ~ **de olhal** eye-bolt. ~ **de orelhas** wing nut. ~ **de rebitar** clinch-bolt. ~ **roscada** grub screw.

cavilhação s. f. (pl. **-ões**) act or result of fastening or bolting.

cavilhador s. m. 1. maker of bolts or pegs. 2. person who joins or fastens with bolts, pegs or keys. || adj. fastening.

cavilhamento s. m. act or process of dowelling (plate C 9).

cavilhar v. 1. to drive in wooden or iron pins. 2. to fasten, join, attach. 3. to dowel, peg, pin, bolt.

caviloso adj. 1. cavilling, captious. 2. fraudulent, deceptive, deceitful. 3. disputative. 4. tricky. 5. (N. Braz.): a) feigning satisfaction or pleasure. b) cunning, artful. || **-amente** adv. captiously, deceptively, cunningly.

cavirão s. m. (naut.) 1. a long wooden or iron piece to fasten an equipment to a strap. 2. a shutter, iron lock pin.

cavirrostro adj. (zool.) cavirostrate, having a hollow beak.

cavitação s. f. (pl. **-ões**) cavitation.

caviúna s. f. (Braz.) = **cabiúna.**

cavo adj. 1. concave, hollow. 2. deep, profound. 3. void. 4. cavernous. 5. hollow-sounding. **veia** -a (anat.) vena cava.

cavodá s. m. (Braz.) the hole which remains in the walls of a newly built house after the removal of the scaffold.

cavorteiro s. m. + adj. = **caborteiro.**

cavoucador s. m. digger, ditchdigger, delver, grubber.

cavoucar v. 1. to dig, delve. 2. to break up the earth, grub. 3. to hollow out, excavate. 4. (fig.) to work hard.

cavouco s. m. 1. ditch, trench. 2. excavation. 3. cave, hollow. 4. stone pit, quarry.

cavouqueiro s. m. 1. digger, delver. 2. ditchdigger. 3. quarryman, quarrier. 4. (fig.): a) bungler. b) liar.

cavu s. m. (Braz., pop.) cape, cloak.

cavucador s. m. (Braz., pop.) a persevering worker, dogged labourer.

cavucar v. (Braz., pop.) 1. to work doggedly and persistently. 2. to work hard for one's daily bread.

caxa s. f. 1. (India) a small coin. 2. (sl.) cashbox, safe.

caxambu s. m. (Braz.) a coarse, lively Negro dance.

caxango s. m. (Braz.) ox or cattle to be slaughtered.

caxarela, caxarelo, caxaréu s. m. (Braz.) a full-grown, male whale.

caxeta s. f. (Braz., bot.) a bignoniaceous tree (Tabebuia cassinoides).

caxexa adj. m. + f. (Braz.) dwarfed, weak, wasted, rickety, rachitic (said of human beings and animals.)

caxias s. m. + f., sg. + pl. martinet. || adj. m. + f., sg. + pl. martinetish.

caxicaém s. m. (Braz., bot.) a snow bell.

caxiense s. m. + f. (Braz.) native or inhabitant of Caxias (towns in Maranhão and in Rio Grande do Sul). || adj. of, pertaining to or relative to these towns and their inhabitants.

caxinduba s. f. (Braz.) plant of the family Euphorbiaceae (Hippomane spinosa).

caxinga s. f. (Braz.) = **catinga** (I).

caxingar v. (Braz., pop.) to limp, hobble.

caxingó adj. m. + f. (Braz., pop.) lame, hobbling, limping, crippled.

caxinguelê s. m. (Braz., zool.) popular designation of several rodents of the squirrel family.

caxinguento adj. 1. malodorous, ill-smelling. 2. foul, fetid, rank. 3. stinking.

caxinxa s. m. + f. gap-toothed person; person with one or more front teeth missing.

caxirengue, caxirenguengue s. m. (Braz., also **caxerenga, caxerenguengue, caxeringuengue**) 1. useless old knife. 2. old knife without a handle.

caxiri, caxirim (pl. **-ins**) s. m. 1. a sweetmeat made with manioc flour. 2. casiri beer.

caxixe (I) s. m. (Braz.) 1. a kind of squirrel. 2. astuteness, shrewdness. 3. sharp dealing.

caxixe (II) s. m. (Braz., bot.) chayote.

caxixeiro s. m. (N. Braz.) 1. a person who makes speculative negotiations with chocolate-producing landed properties. 2. a person who practices fraudulent deals.

caxixi s. f. white rum of inferior quality. || adj. common, ordinary, of inferior quality (white rum).

caxumba s. f. (Braz., med.) mumps, parotitis.

cazumbi s. m. (Braz.) zombi, deity of the voodoo cults.

cear v. to sup, take supper, eat one's supper.

ceará s. f. (Braz.) salted and dried beef, jerked beef.

cearense s. m. + f. native or inhabitant of the state of Ceará (Braz.). || adj. of, pertaining to or relative to this state and its inhabitants.

ceata s. f. a sumptuous supper, lavish repast, banquet.

cebídeo s. m. 1. monkey of the family Cebidae. 2. **~s** pl. Cebidae: a family of New World monkeys. || adj. cebid, cebine.

cebo s. m. scientific designation of any monkey of the family Cebidae, genus Cebus.

cebola s. f. 1. (bot.) onion (Allium cepa). 2. the edible bulb of this plant. 3. (bot.) any bulbous root. 4. (fig., pop.) an old clumsy silver watch, turnip. 5. (fam.) a weak, exhausted or indolent person. **chorar pelas ~s do Egito** to pine for the flesh-pots of Egypt.

cebola-branca s. f. (pl. **cebolas-brancas**), (bot.) shallot, scallion.

cebola-cecém s. f. (pl. **cebolas-cecém**), (bot.) belladonna lily.

cebolada s. f. onion stew or any other dish made mainly with onions, onion souce.

cebola-de-cheiro s. f. (pl. **cebolas-de-cheiro**), (bot.) Welsh onion.

cebolal s. m. (pl. **-ais**) onion field, onion plantation.

cebolão s. m. (pl. **-ões**), (pop.) an old clumsy silver watch, turnip.

cebolinha s. f. (bot.) 1. any small onion. 2. Welsh onion.

cebolinha-capim s. f. (pl. **cebolinhas-capím**), (bot.) chive, chive garlic.

cebolinho s. m. (bot.) 1. onion seed. 2. young onion shoot. 3. cive, chive, chive garlic.

cebolinho-branco s. m. (pl. **cebolinhos-brancos**), (bot.) daffodil garlic.

cebolinho-cheiroso s. m. (pl. **cebolinhos-cheirosos**), (bot.) fragrant, false garlic.

cebolório interj. exclamation expressing contempt or dissatisfaction: hooey!, nonsense!, fie!

ceca s. f. only used in the proverbial locution: **andar de ~ em meca, correr ~ e meca** to go from pillar to post.

cecal adj. m. + f. (pl. **-ais**), (anat.) caecal.

ceceadura s. f. lisping, lisp.

cecear v. 1. to lisp. 2. to speak or pronounce in a faltering manner. 3. to talk in an affected manner.

ceceio s. m. act of lisping, lisp.

cecém s. f. (pl. **-éns**) poetical name of the madonna lily.

ceceoso adj. lisping.

cecídio s. m. (bot.) cecidium.

cecília s. f. (zool.) a wormlike, burrowing amphibian of the genus Caecilia, family Caecilidae.

cecilídeos s. m. pl. (zool.) Caecilidae: a family of wormlike amphibians.

ceco s. m. (anat.) caecum.

cecografia s. f. a system of printing for the blind, invented by the French Louis Braille.

cécum s. m. (anat.) caecum: the first part of the large intestine.

cê-dê-efe s. m. + f. (pl. **cê-dê-efes**) (Braz., student sl.) swotter.

cedência s. f. 1. cession. 2. transfer. 3. yielding, giving up.

cedente s. m. + f. 1. cessionary. 2. transferor, transferee. 3. assignee, grantee. 4. one who yields or gives up. || adj. transfering, assigning, yielding.

ceder v. 1. to cede, assign, transfer. 2. to give way, yield. 3. to back away, submit. 4. to founder, falter. 5. to waver, stagger. 6. to abandon, desist, relent. 7. to surrender, fall. 8. to sign away, hand over. 9. to comply, remit. 10. to collapse, break, snap. 11. to forego, quitclaim, waive. 12. to subordinate o. s. 13. to renounce. 14. to knuckle under. 15. to concede. 16. to grant.

~ à razão to yield to reason. **~ ao segurado** to condescend with the insured. **~ com dificuldade** to yield with great reluctance. **~ de seu direito** to give up one's right. **~ direitos** (jur.) to assign, remise. **eles ~am facilmente** they gave way without resistance. **não ~** to stand out, stick in, wait it out. **não ~ a palma a ninguém** to be second to none. **os muros ~am** the walls caved in.

cediço adj. 1. corrupt, rotten. 2. stagnant. 3. stale, musty. 4. (of news or information) very old, grown uninteresting, generally known.

cedido adj. granted, relinquished, transferred.

cedilha s. f. (gram.) cedilla: mark ( ) placed under the letter C.

cedilhado adj. market with a cedilla.

cedilhar v. to mark with a cedilla.

cedimento s. m. 1. act of yielding or transferring. 2. cession. 3. transfer. 4. yelding, giving up.

cedinho adv. 1. very early, at daybreak. 2. very soon in the morning. 3. (fam.) soon.

cedível adj. m. + f. (pl. -íveis) 1. transferable. 2. that may be assigned or handed over. 3. alienable, yieldable.

cedo adv. 1. early, betimes. 2. soon, in a short time. 3. untimely, prematurely. 4. promptly, quickly. 5. forehanded, timely, timeous. ~ demais too early. ~ ou tarde sooner or later. bem ~ na vida at an early age. chegar suficientemente ~ to be in good time. de manhã ~ early in the morning. de manhã ~ até a noite from early morning till evening. demasiado ~ oversoon, untimely. ele chegou ~ he arrived early. fez-se desde ~ uma tentativa an early attempt was made. mais ~ ou mais tarde sooner or later, in the long run. muito ~ very early, too soon. tão ~! so early!

cedrão s. m. (pl. -ões) a big, old cedar-tree.

cedrinho s. m. a type of cedar used for quicksets.

cedro s. m. (bot.) 1. cedar, cedar-tree. 2. cedrela. 3. common juniper. 4. common larch. 5. the wood of a cedar-tree.

cedro-do-líbano s. m. (bot.) (pl. cedros-do-líbano) cedar of Lebanon (Cedrus libani).

cedro-japonês s. m. (pl. cedros-japoneses), (bot.) Japan cedar, Japanese cryptomeria.

cedro-português s. m. (pl. cedros-portugueses), (bot.) cedar of Goa.

cedrorana s. f. (bot.) American muskwood.

cedro-vermelho s. m. (pl. cedros-vermelhos), (bot.) red cedar.

cédula s. f. 1. note, short letter. 2. various kinds of written documents. 3. ticket. 4. bond, share. 5. banknote, bill, currency note. 6. voting paper, ballot (paper). 7. promissory note, I O U. 8. schedule. ~ de banco banknote, bill. ~ de testamento codicil. ~ eleitoral vote. ~ hipotecária mortgage bill.

cefalalgia s. f. (med.) cephalalgia, headache.

cefalálgico adj. (med.) cephalalgic.

cefaléia s. f. (med.) chronic headache, sick headache.

cefálico adj. cephalic, of or pertaining to the head, cerebral.

cefalídio s. m. (biol.) cephalodium.

cefalite s. f. (med.) cephalitis, inflammation of the brain.

cefalóide adj. m. + f. cephaloid.

cefalômetro s. m. (med.) cephalometer.

cefalópode s. m. (zool.) cephalopod, cephalopodan. || adj. cephalopodan.

cefalotácea s. f. (bot.) 1. Australian pitcher plant (Cephalotus follicularis). 2. Cephalotaceae: a family of tropical plants.

cefaloteca s. f. (zool.) cephalotheca.

cefalotomia s. f. (med., surg.) cephalotomy.

cefalotórax s. m. (zool., anat.) cephalothorax.

cefeu s. m. (astr.) Cepheus.

cega s. f. a blind woman.

cegamento s. m. 1. blindness. 2. deprivation of sight, blinding. 3. (fig.) blind ignorance or fanatism.

cegante adj. m. + f. 1. blinding, depriving of sight. 2. (fig.) dazzling. 3. (fig.) obfuscating, rendering obscure.

cega-olho s. m. (pl. cega-olhos) plant of the family Aesculeaceae (Asclepias campestris, A. mellodora, A. umbellata).

cegar v. 1. to blind, strike blind. 2. to deprive of sight. 3. to dazzle, daze. 4. (fig.) to fascinate, charm. 5. to render deranged, make s. o. lose his (her) head. 6. to pervert, corrupt. 7. to deceive, delude, dupe. 8. (fig.) to cloud, darken. 9. to efface, eclipse. 10. to make blunt. 11. to lose one's sight, become blind. 12. to mislead, let in the dark. 13.

to be mistaken. 14. ~-se: a) to deceive o. s. b) to become hallucinated, become deranged. isto é tão claro que cega os olhos that is so plain that it strikes you at first sight.

cega-rega s. f. (pl. cega-regas) 1. a cicada, cricket. 2. an instrument which imitates the shrill cry of a cicada. 3. (fig.) prattler, chatterer, chatterbox.

cegas word only used in the adverbial locution: às cegas blindly, heedless, overhastily, rashly. fazer as coisas às ~ to go blindly to work.

cego s. m. blind man. || adj. 1. blind. 2. eyeless, sightless. 3. blinded, dazzled, fascinated. 4. (fig.) unreasoning, unquestioning. 5. out of one's mind, hallucinated. 6. ignorant. 7. inconsiderate. 8. (of a knife) blunt, dull. 9. dark, rayless, black. 10. obliterated, effaced. 11. (of a knot) difficult to be opened. 12. (of pipes, ditches, etc.) choked. 13. rash. || -amente adv. blindly, unreasoningly, rashly. ~ de nascença blind born. ~ de uma vista blink--eyed, blind of one eye. ~ para com o mundo oblivious to the world. a faca é -a the knife is blunt. amor ~ blind love. andar ~ em to act blindly. completamente ~ stone-blind. comprar algo -amente to buy a pig in a poke. entre ~s quem tem um olho é rei among the blind the one-eyed is king. fazer as coisas -amente to go blindly to work. intestino ~ (anat.) the blind gut. nó ~ a very hard or intricate knot, a knot difficult to be untied. pancada de ~ (fig.) a desparate blow. ser ~ para com... to be blind to...

cegonha s. f. 1. (ornith.) stork. 2. (Braz., ornith.) manguari. 3. sweep, water-raising device consisting of a long pole moved on a fulcrum, used to raise and lower a bucket. 4. the iron fork to which the bell-rope is fastened.

cegude s. f. (bot.) poison hemlock.

cegueira, ceguidade, s. f. 1. blindness, want of sight, cecity, sightlessness. 2. infatuation, passion. 3. fanatism. 4. darkness. 5. fatuity. 6 ignorance, stupidity. 7. inconsiderateness, thoughtlessness.

ceguinha s. f. (Braz.) a vasp from the Iguape region.

ceguinho s. m. (Braz.) catfish of the family Siluridae (Typhlobagrus kronei). || adj. somewhat blind.

ceia s. f. 1. supper, evening meal. 2. (pop.) picture representing the Lord's supper. a ~ do Senhor, a Santa Ceia (rel.): 1. the Lord's Supper, the Lord's Table. 2. Eucharist, sacrament.

ceifa s. f. 1. the act of reaping or harvesting. 2. harvest, crop. 3. harvest time. 4. math, reaping. 5. shearing. 6. massacre, slaughter, carnage. 7. mortality. 8 considerable or excessive wear and tear.

ceifar v. 1. to harvest, crop. 2. to cut, mow. 3. to shear. 4. to reap. 5. (fig.) to cause the death of, kill. 6. (fig.) to destroy.

ceifeira s. f. 1. harvest-woman. 2. reaper, reaping machine.

ceifeiro s. m. (also ceifadeiro, ceifador) 1. reaper, harvest-man (plate C 16). 2. cutter, mower, scytheman. 3. reaping machine, scythe. || adj. of or pertaining to harvest, harvesting, reaping.

ceita s. f. (hist.) an exempt tax formerly paid to the Spanish kings.

ceitil s. m. (pl. -is) 1. ancient Portuguese coin, Portuguese farthing. 2. farthing, penny. 3. (fig.) insignificant matter, trifle, small sum of money. não vale um ~ it isn't worth a fillip.

cela s. f. 1. cell. 2. very small room or dormitory. 3. alcove. 4. prison cell, ward, pen. 5. compartment of a honeycomb.

celacanto s. m. (ichth.) coelacanth.

celação s. f. (pl. -ões) celation, concealment.

celada s. f. (hist.) helmet, iron head-piece.

celagem s. f. (pl. **-ens**) 1. the colour of the sky at sunrise and sunset. 2. aurora, sunset glow. 3. the looks of the weather.

celamim s. m. (pl. **-ins**) 1. celemin: an ancient dry and liquid measure. 2. peck: the fourth part of a bushel.

celastráceas s. f. (bot.) Celastraceae.

celebração s. f. (pl. **-ões**) 1. act of celebrating. 2. celebration, commemoration. 3. solemnization, solemnity.

celebrado adj. 1. celebrated. 2. renowned, famous. 3. praised, commended, glorified.

celebrador s. m. celebrator.

celebrante s. m. (rel.) celebrant, officiating priest. ‖ adj. m. + f. celebrant, celebrative.

celebrar v. 1. to celebrate, perform a solemn ceremony. 2. to commemorate, call to remembrance. 3. to officiate. 4. to entertain, carol, jolly. 5. to laud, fame. 6. to inaugurate. 7. to honour publicly. 8. (ironic.) to exaggerate greatly the capacity and achievements of.

~ **matrimônio** to celebrate one's wedding, give a wedding party. ~ **um concílio** to hold a council. ~ **um contrato** to make a bargain with, come to an agreement. **ele celebra a missa** he says mass.

celebrável adj. m. + f. (pl. **-áveis**) praiseworthy.

célebre adj. m. + f. 1. celebrated. 2. famed, famous. 3. distinguished, renowned, noted. 4. eminent. 5. epochal. 6. (fam.) extravagant. 7. (fam.) odd, strange. 8. (fam.) original. ‖ **celebremente** adv. celebratedly, famously.

~ **pelo mundo afora** far-famed. **tornar** ~ to immortalize. **tornar-se** ~ to get a name, arrive.

celebreira s. f. (fam.) 1. extravagance. 2. folly, wildness. 3. fad, craze, obsession. 4. oddness, queerness.

celebridade s. f. 1. celebrity. 2. fame, renown. 3. famousness, illustriousness, notedness. 4. famous person or thing.

celebrização s. f. (pl. **-ões**) process of making or becoming famous.

celebrizar v. 1. to render famous, fame. 2. ~-**se** to become famous, get fame.

celeireiro s. m. watchman or administrator of a storehouse, deposit or barn; cellarer.

celeiro s. m. 1. cellar. 2. granary. 3. corn-floor, loft, corn-loft. 4. barrack, depository, barn (plates A 4, C 11). 5. (fig.) provision.

celelmintos s. m. pl. (zool.) Coelhelminthes, metazoan invertebrate animals, comprising the Annelida and Chaetognatha.

celenterado s. m. (zool.) coelenterate. ‖ adj. coelenterate.

celêntero s. m. (zool.) coelenteron.

celerado s. m. criminal, malefactor, felon, perverted fellow. ‖ adj. criminal, perverted, corrupt, vicious.

célere adj. m. + f. 1. swift, quick. 2. rapid. 3. light fleet.

celeridade s. f. 1. celerity. 2. rapidity, rapidness. 3. swiftness, quickness. 4. velocity. 5. haste. 6. agility.

celerígrado adj. (zool.) said of an animal that moves about or runs swiftly.

celerímetro s. m. 1. speed counter, tachometer. 2. distance meter.

celerípede adj. m. + f. (poet.) swift-footed, nimble--footed.

celescópio s. m. (astr.) an assembly of four telescopes, each one equipped with a television camera, installed in a satellite.

celeste s. f. (mus.) celesta: pianolike instrument of the carillon type. ‖ adj. m. + f. (also **celestial**) 1. celeste, celestial: a) of or pertaining to the sky.

b) heavenly, ethereal. c) supernal, divine, paradisiac(al). d) firmamental. 2. (fig.) perfect. 3. (fig.) splendid, delicious.

as forças ~**s** the powers above. **vosso Pai Celeste** your Father in Heaven.

celestial adj. m. + f. (pl. **-ais**) 1. celestial, celeste. 2. firmamental. 3. unearthly. ‖ ~**mente** adv. celestially, divinely, heavenly.

celestina s. f. (bot.) an ageratum.

celestino (I) s. m. (rel.) Celestine: monk of an austere group of Benedictines.

celestino (II) adj. (poet.) celestial blue, sky-blue.

celestita s. f. (min.) celestite, celestine.

celeuma s. m. 1. the shouts of seamen or workmen who join their forces in common work. 2. noise, clamour. 3. the cries of boatsmen. 4. racket, uproar, din. 5. alarm, tumult.

celga s. f. (bot.) beet.

celha s. f. 1. fish-basket, fish-tub. 2. ~**s** pl. eyelashes. 3. (biol., bot., zool.) cilia.

celheado adj. (biol., bot., zool.) ciliate.

celíaco adj. (anat., med.) coeliac, celiac, abdominal.

celibatário s. m. celibate, bachelor. ‖ adj. unmarried, single, celibate, celibatarian.

celibatarismo s. m. 1. the principle of celibacy. 2. single life. 3. condition of a celibatarian.

celibato s. m. 1. state or condition of being unmarried. 2. celibacy. 3. bachelorship, singleness, bachelorhood.

célico adj. (poet.) celeste, celestial, heavenly.

celícola s. m. + f. inhabitant of heaven.

celidônia s. f. (bot.) celandine.

celífluo adj. emanating or flowing from heaven.

celígena adj. m. + f. heaven-born, sky-born.

celioscopia s. f. (med.) coelioscopy.

celipotente adj. m. + f. ruling the heavens.

celofane s. m. cellophane.

celoma s. m. (anat.) coelom, celom, celoma.

celomado s. m. (anat., zool.) 1. coelomate, coelomate animal. 2. specimen of the Coelomata. ‖ adj. coelomate.

celsitude s. f. celsitude, exaltation, sublimation.

celso adj. 1. high. 2. noble. 3. excellent. 4. sublime.

celta s. 1. m. + f. Celt, Kelt; individual belonging to a Celtic-speaking people or to the Celtic race. 2. m. Celtic, Keltic: the Celtic idiom, a Celtic language. ‖ adj. m. + f. Celtic, Keltic.

celtibero s. m. (hist.) Celtiberian: native or inhabitant of Celtiberia. ‖ adj. Celtiberian.

céltico s. m. 1. Celt, Kelt. 2. the Celtic language. ‖ adj. Celtic.

célula s. f. 1. dim. form of **cela**. 2. (biol., bot., anat., zool.) the structural and fundamental unit of an organism. 3. (biol.) the body of a cell, mass of protoplasm containing a nucleous. 4. (anat.) a small cavity. 5. (aeron.) the complete wing structure of an airplane. 6. cell, cellule, corpuscule. 7. (bot.) embryo.

~ **fotelétrica** electric eye, photo-electric cell.

célula-ovo s. f. (pl. **células-ovos**) egg cell.

celular adj. m. + f. cellular, consisting of cells or cavities.

estrutura ~ (bot.) cellular tissue, parenchyma, pulp. **prisão** ~ isolated imprisonment. **tecido** ~ (anat.) cellular membrane.

celulífero adj. culluliferous, containing many cells, cellulous.

celuliforme adj. m + f. celluliform, celliform, cell--shaped.

celulite s. f. (med.) cellulitis, inflammation of the cellular tissue.

celulóide s. m. (chem.) celluloid.

celulose s. f. (chem.) cellulose.

celulósico adj. (chem.) cellulosic.
celulosidade s. f. cellulosity.
celuloso adj. cellulous, cellular.
celulótico adj. cellulosic.
cem (I) s. m. one hundred. ‖ adj. num. hundred.
~ **vezes** a hundred times. ~ **vezes mais** hundred-fold. **ele vale por** ~ he is a host in himself.
cem (II) s. m. (India) formerly a linear measure of about 400 meters.
cêmbalo s. m. (mus.) cymbal(s).
cem-dobrar v. 1. to centuplicate, increase a hundredfold. 2. to yield a hundredfold more.
cem-dobro s. m. 1. twice one hundred. 2. centuplicate. 3. a hundredfold. ‖ adv. (fig.) in quantities, abundantly.
cementação s. f. (pl. -ões), (met.) cementation, case-hardening.
~ **superficial** face hardening.
cementado adj. (met.) cemented, case-hardened.
aço ~ (met.) blister steel.
cementar v. to cement, case-harden (iron, steel).
cemento s. m. cement: 1. (constr.) basic material used in the production of concrete and mortar. 2. (met.) a powder used in the cementation of ferrous metals. 3. (anat.) cementum.
cem-folhas s. f. sg. + pl. (bot.) cabbage rose.
cemiterial adj. m. + f. (pl. -ais) cemeterial, of, pertaining to or relative to a cemetery.
cemitério s. m. 1. cemetery, necropolis. 2. churchyard, graveyard (plate A 4). 3. charnel. 4. burying ground, burying place, God's acre.
porta do ~ lych gate.
cempasso s. m. (Braz.) formerly a measure of one hundred paces square.
cena s. f. f. scene, subdivision of an act (during which there is no change of place). 2. stage, stage setting. 3. part of a play, drama or any other theatrical spectacle. 4. picture, sequence of pictures. 5. stage decoration. 6. the place of any occurrence or action. 7. scenery. 8. dramatic event. 9. emotional explosion, violent discussion, exhibition of strong feelings. 10. landscape, panorama. 11. dramatic art.
~ **cômica** the comedy. ~ **lírica** the opera. **a** ~ **começa com um diálogo** the scene opens with a conversation. **a** ~ **passa-se em Verona** the scene lies in Verona. **direção de** ~ stage-management. **diretor de** ~ stage director. **eles entraram em** ~ they entered the stage. **ele se retira da** ~ 1. he goes off stage. 2. (fig.) he retires from active service. **não faça** ~**s!** now, do not make scenes!, don't make a row! **pôr em** ~ to put or bring to the stage. **ser posto em** ~ to be staged.
cenáculo s. m. 1. dining-room, mess hall, refectory. 2. the room where Christ's last supper took place. 3. (fig.) companionship, familiarity, intimacy. 4. group of persons bound together by common ideals or aims.
cenário (I) s. m. 1. scenery (plate P 2). 2. stage setting, theater decoration. 3. set, flat scene. 4. (cin.) scenario. 5. picturesque view, landscape, view. 6. background of an event, where something occurs.
o ~ **do crime** the wheres and hows of the crime.
cenário (II) (also **cenatório**) adj. of, pertaining to or relative to the supper.
cenarista s. m. + f. scenarist: 1. writer of scenarios for movies. 2. person who adapts a romance or play to motion picture representation.
cendal s. m. (pl. -ais) a fine, ash-gray veil.
cendrado adj. ash-gray, gray-coloured.
cenestesia s. f. (psych.) coenesthesis, awareness of physical existence, vital sense.

cenho s. m. 1. (vet.) disease of the bulbs of a hoof. 2. severe or awe inspiring countenance. 3. frown, scowl.
cenhoso adj. cross, surly, cantankerous, grim.
cênico adj. 1. scenic(al). 2. of or pertaining to a scenery or a stage setting. 3. theatrical.
superintendente ~ stage-manager.
cenismo s. m. (rhet.) 1. the excessive use of foreign idiomatic expressions in a book or discourse. 2. uncorrect speech or elocution.
ceno s. m. (obs.) mudhole, slough.
cenóbio s. m. cenoby, convent, monastery.
cenobiose s. f. (biol.) group of individuals of same species but without common substratum.
cenobismo s. m. cenobitis, cenobitic life, monastic life.
cenobita s. m. + f. cenobite, monk or nun living in a religious community.
cenobítico adj. cenobitic(al).
cenobitismo s. m. cenobitism: system, principles and practice of cenobitic life.
cenografia s. f. scenography: 1. art of painting stage decorations, or stage settings. 2. art of perspective representation of objects or landscapes. 3. (collectively) the objects thus represented.
cenográfico adj. scenographic(al), drawn or painted in perspective.
cenógrafo s. m. scenographer, scenographis, scene-painter.
cenolestídeos s. m. pl. (zool.) mammals of the family Caenolestidae (opossum rat).
cenologia (I) s. f. a medical council.
cenologia (II) s. f. (phys.) that part of physics that treats of vacuum and empty spaces.
cenológico adj. of, pertaining to or relative to: 1. a medical council. 2. the study of rarefied atmosphere, vacuum or empty spaces.
cenoplastia s, f. (theat.) = **cenografia**.
cenosidade s. f. 1. filth, dirt, grime. 2. obscenity, lewdness. 3. slough, puddle, mudhole.
cenoso adj. 1. dirty, filthy, unclean. 2. lewd, obscene. 3. muddy, miry. 4. base, vile, sordid.
cenotáfio s. m. cenotaph, empty tomb or monument.
cenotécnica s. f. (theat.) the technique in stage setting.
cenotécnico s. m. (theat.) stage setting technician. ‖ adj. of or relating to stage setting.
cenoura s. f. (bot.) carrot, wild carrot.
cenozóico adj. (geol.) Cenozoic.
cenrada s. f. a solution of lye.
cenreira s. f. (pop.) 1. stubbornness, obstinacy. 2. fight, brawl. 3. quarrel, squabble, dispute. 4. aversion, antipathy.
censatário, censionário, censitário s. m. 1. rent payer, renter, feudatory. 2. a census or taxpayer. ‖ adj. 1. liable to pay quit-rent. 2. of, pertaining to or relative to a census.
censo s. m. 1. census, registration of the number, condition, and the property of the citizens. 2. cense, rank. 3. yearly rent, quit-rent. 4. computation of inhabitants. 5. charge, tribute. 6. annual revenue.
~ **demográfico** demographic census. ~ **perpétuo** perpetual rent. ~ **reservativo** (jur.) a long lease, emphyteusis. ~ **vitalício** annuity for life. **dar a** ~ to let out a farm for a yearly rent. **pagar o** ~ **comum** (fam.) to die. **sem** ~ clear from all debts. **tomar um** ~ to take a census.
censor s. m. 1. censor. 2. (hist.) census taker, tax collector. 3. person appointed to examine all plays, books, movies, in order to avoid the publication of objectionable matter. 4. critic, censurer. 5. con-

troller, reviewer. 6. licenser. 7. (Braz.) school supervisor, disciplinarian.

censório adj. censorial, censorian.

censual adj. m. + f. (pl. **-ais**) censual, censorial, censorian.

censualista s. m. tax or rent receiver.

censuário s. m. taxpayer, rent payer, tenant.

censura s. f. 1. office, dignity and authority of a censor. 2. critical examination and control of literary works, works of art, newspapers, etc. 3. (R. C. Church) index. 4. censorship. 5. censure, reproach, reprehension, rebuke. 6. criticism, comment. 7. faultfinding, condemnation. 8. exprobration, expostulation. 9. correction. 10. admonition, admonishment. 11. sermon.

censurado adj. censured, reproved, condemned.

ele foi severamente ~ he was reproached severely.

censurador s. m. 1. censor, censurer. 2. faultfinder. 3. critic. 4. reviewer, reviser. 5. upbraider. 6. carper. || adj. 1. censorious, censuring. 2. captious, faultfinding. 3. carping, critical.

censurar v. 1. to censure, control, examine carefully. 2. to subject to censure. 3. to find fault with, reprimand, reproach, reprehend. 4. to criticize, censor. 5. to complain. 6. to condemn, impeach. 7. to inculpate. 8. to correct. 9. to admonish. 10. to carp. 11. to comment. 12. to expostulate. 13. (R. C. Church) to put on the index.

~ **abertamente** to criminate. ~ **a alguém pelos erros cometidos** to upbraid s. o. for the faults he has committed. ~ **publicamente** to decry. ~ **severamente** to berate. ~ **vivamente** to deprecate. **censuram-no por isto** they twitted him with it. **não o censure por causa disto** don't blame him for it, don't throw that in his teeth.

censurável adj. m. + f. (pl. **-áveis**) 1. censurable, subject to censure. 2. reprehensible, blameworthy, blameful. 3. objectionable, reprovable. 4. criticizable. 5. culpable, rebukable. || **censuravelmente** adv. censurably, objectionably, blameworthy.

centafolho s. m. tripe, mesentery, part of the stomach of a ruminant that contains innumerous folds.

centão s. m. (pl. **-ões**) 1. a torn old cloak. 2. a cover for engines made of a coarse cotton cloth. 3. cento: a poetic composition made up of different verses from different poets. 4. (Braz., pop.) one hundred cruzeiros.

centáurea s. f. (bot.) centaury, knapweed.

centáurea-menor s. f. (pl. **centáureas-menores**), (bot.) lesser centaury.

centauro s. m. (myth.) centaur. 2. (astr.) Centaurus, Centaur: a constellation between Cruz and Hydra.

centavo s. m. 1. centavo: a coin representing a hundredth part of a cruzeiro (or peso, sucre, etc.). 2. penny, pence. 3. hundreth part.

ele não tem um ~ **no bolso** he hasn't got a cent in his pocket. **ele os pagou até o último** ~ (fam.) he paid them scot and lot. **não vale um** ~ it is not worth a rush.

centeal s. m. (pl. **-ais**) rye field.

centeio s. m. (bot.) rye (Secale cereale).

centeio-espigado s. m. (pl. **centeios-espigados**), (bot., plant path.) ergot of rye.

centelha s. f. 1. spark, scintilla. 2. sparkle, flash. 3. flicker. 4. (fig.) brain wave, flash of inspiration.

~ **da vida** the spark of life. ~ **intelectual** coruscation of wit. **a última** ~ **de esperança** the last flicker of hope. **ignição por** ~s spark ignition. **não há nisto nenhuma** ~ **de verdade** there is not a trace of truth in it.

centelhador s. m. (tech.) spark discharger, spark plug.

centelhar v. to scintillate, sparkle.

centena s. f. 1. a hundred, position of hundreds in a number. 2. a group of one hundred.

às ~s by the hundred. ~s **de vezes** hundreds of times. ~s **e mais** ~s hundreds upon hundreds.

centenário s. m. 1. centenarian, a hundred years old person. 2. centennial, one hundredth anniversary, centennial commemoration. 3. (hist.) centurion. || adj. centennial, centuple, centenary, centuplicate, hundredfold.

centenoso adj. rye-producing, ryelike, of or relative to rye.

centesimal adj. m. + f. (pl. **-ais**) centesimal: of or relative to a hundredth part of, hundredth.

centésimo s. m. 1. centesimal, a hundredth. 2. centesimo: a coin representing a hundredth part of a lira (or peso). || adj. centesimal, hundredth.

centiare s. m. 1. a square measure equivalent to one square meter. 2. a hundredth part of an are.

centifólio adj. centifolious, having hundred leaves.

centigrado s. m. (math.) one hundredth of a grad.

centígrado adj. centigrade.

centigrama s. m. centigram, centigramme: one hundredth part of a gram.

centil s. m. (statistics) centile, percentile.

centilitro s. m. centiliter, centilitre: a liquid measure equal to one hundredth of a liter.

centímano adj. having one hundred hands.

centímetro s. m. centimeter, centimetre.

cêntimo s. m. centime: a coin representing the hundredth part of a franc (or gourde - of Haiti).

centípede adj. m. + f. centipede, having one hundred feet.

centipoise s. m. (phys.) centipoise.

cento s. m. 1. a hundred. 2. a group of one hundred. 3. the number hundred. || adj. hundred.

alguns ~s several hundred. **cinco por** ~ five in the hundred. **encaixotado aos** ~s boxed by hundreds. **por** ~ percent, per cent. **um** ~ **de ovos** one hundred eggs.

centóculo adj. having one hundred eyes.

centopeia s. f. 1. (zool.) the centipede. 2. (fig.) a horrible woman.

central s. f. (pl. **-ais**) 1. central, telephone exchange. 2. headquarters, central office. || adj. m. + f. 1. central. 2. centric(al). 3. placed in the centre or amidst. 4. midland. 5. pivotal. 6. (fig.) principal. || ~**mente** adv. centrically, centrally.

~ **da polícia** police headquarters. ~ **do correio** chief or central post office. ~ **elétrica** power station. **banco** ~ bank of issue. **forças** **-ais** central forces. **ponto** ~ nucleus. **terra** ~ inland country.

centralidade s. f. centralness, centricity.

centralismo s. m. centralism, centralization.

centralista s. m. + f. centralist. || adj. centralist, centralistic(al).

centralização s. f. (pl. **-ões**) centralization.

centralizado adj. centralized.

centralizar v. 1. to centralize, bring to a central point. 2. to unite in one central point. 3. (fig.) to concentrate power in one hand or central agency.

centrar v. 1. to center, centre. 2. to place or fix in a center. 3. to form a center. 4. to concentrate (in one point). 5. to middle. 6. to true.

centrífuga s. f. centrifuge, machine for centrifuging, hydro-extractor, separator (plate A 11).

centrifugação s. f. (pl. **-ões**) centrifugation.

centrifugador s. m. centrifuge, centrifuging machine.

centrifugar v. 1. to centrifuge. 2. to spin in a centrifuge. 3. to remove from the center. 4. to hydro-extract.

centrífugo adj. centrifugal, receding from the center. || **centrifugamente** adv. centrifugally.

força -a centrifugal force or power, tangential force.
centrípeto adj. centripetal, directed toward the center. ‖ **centripetamente** adv. centripetally.
centro s. m. 1. center, centre. 2. the middle point of a circle. 3. focal point. 4. nucleus. 5. principal aim or end of an action. 6. pivot. 7. centrum, core. 8. commercial or financial center. 9. (theat.) actor playing the role of a middle-aged person. 10. (fig.) bowels, bosom, heart. 11. bull's eye. 12. casino, club, center of social reunions. 13. (Braz.) the inner region of a seringal (rubber plantation).
~ **alto** (theatre) the back center of a scene. ~ **comercial** emporium. ~ **da roda** hub of wheel. ~ **de atração** cynosure. ~ **de escudo** (her.) fesse-point. ~ **de gravidade** center of gravity. ~ **de massa** center of mass, of inertia. ~ **de percussão** percussion center. ~ **de rotação** pivotal point, centre of motion. ~ **do alvo** bull's eye. ~ **óptico** optical center. ~ **telefônico** telephon exchange. **deslocação do** ~ **de gravidade** eccentricity of the centre of gravity. **no** ~ **da cidade** in the center of the town.
centroavante s. m. (pl. **centroavantes**), (ftb.) centre-forward (plate F 9).
centrodonte adj. m. + f. (zool.) having sharp-pointed teeth.
centromédio s. m. (ftb.) center-half, position of player in the game of soccer (plate F 9).
centro-oeste s. m. (Braz. geogr.) Middle West.
centropino s. m. (typogr.) center-pin.
centrosfera s. f. (geogr.) astrosphere.
centrossomo s. m. (biol.) centrosome.
centunviral adj. m. + f. (pl. **-ais**), (Roman hist.) centumviral.
centunvirato s. m. (also **centunvirado**) (Roman hist.) centumvirate: office, dignity and authority of a centumvir.
centúnviro s. m. (Roman hist.) centumvir.
centuplicado adj. centuplicate, hundredfold.
centuplicar v. 1. centuple, multiply by one hundred. 2. to increase a hundredfold. 3. (fig.) to increase the volume of, increase considerably.
cêntuplo s. m. centuplicate, the result of a multiplication by one hundred. ‖ adj. centuple, centuplicate.
centúria s. f. 1. a hundred. 2. a group of one hundred objects of the same kind. 3. (Roman hist.) one of the political divisions of the Roman people. 4. (Roman hist.) century: a subdivision of the Roman legion, consisting of 100 soldiers. 5. centennial, one hundredth anniversary. 6. centenary, century. 7. (lit.) historical narration subdivided into periods of one hundred years.
centurial adj. m. + f. (pl. **-ais**) 1. centurial. 2. of, pertaining or relative to a centurion.
centurião s. m. (pl. **-ões**) (Roman hist.) centurion.
cenuro s. m. (zool.) coenurus.
cepa s. f. 1. (bot.) cepa, onion. 2. grapevine, vinestock. 3. stub, stump (plate A 14). 4. rootage. 5. strain. 6. (fig.) pith, mettle. 7. (fig.) ancestry, stock. **não passar de** ~ **torta** (fam.) to make no progress. **sair da** ~ **torta** (pop.) to get ahead, rise. **um homem de boa** ~ a man of the true kidney.
cepáceo adj. (bot.) cepacious, onionlike.
cepilhar v. to smooth down, plane.
cepilho s. m. 1. smoothing plane, block plane. 2. dead-smooth polishing file. 3. pommel of a saddle.
cepo s. m. 1. stock or stump of a tree. 2. log, block of timber (plate L 1). 3. clump. 4. chopping block (plate A 2). 5. a snare for birds, small trap. 6. wooden block for an anvil. 7. (Braz.) a wooden brake shoe (plate C 15). 8. stock of a plane. 9. (fig.) a clumsy or indolent person.

~ **de âncora** the stock of an anchor (plate A 6). ~ **do freio** brake block, brake shoe (plate C 15).
cepticismo, ceticismo s. m. scepticism, skepticism: 1. philosophical doctrine which considers doubt as the correct mental attitude with regard to the evidence of thought. 2. a sceptical principle or system.
céptico, cético s. m. 1. a sceptic, a philosophic doubter. 2. agnostic. ‖ adj. sceptic(al), doubting, agnostic(al), cynical.
cepudo adj. of, pertaining to or resembling a stump of a tree.
cequim s. m. (pl. **-ins**) an ancient Italian gold coin.
cera (ê) s. f. 1. wax, beeswax. 2. any vegetable product that resembles beeswax. 3. candle, wax-candle, wax-torch. 4. (fig.) a soft or tender-hearted person. 5. (fig.) unprincipled, weak or wavering person. 6. (fig.) work badly done. 7. (ornith.) cere. 8. (physiol.) cerumen.
~ **amarela** virgin wax. ~ **branca** bleached wax. ~ **de abelha** beeswax. ~ **de carnaúba** Brazil wax. ~ **de parafina** paraffin wax. **de** ~ waxen. ~ **para assoalho** rubbing wax, floor wax. ~ **virgem** beeswax. **cor de** ~ wax-coloured. **ele é feito de** ~ he is an unprincipled man. **ele faz** ~ he works slowly on purpose. **feito de** ~ waxy, waxen. **mole como** ~ as soft as putty. **não gaste** ~ **com ruim defunto** (fig.) don't waste good deeds on a bad fellow; don't flog a dead horse. **vela de** ~ wax-candle.
ceráceo adj. waxen, ceraceous, waxy.
cerambicídeos s. m. pl. (ent.) Cerambycidae, the long-horned beetle family.
cerâmica s. f. 1. ceramics: the art of making earthenware. 2. any article formed of baked clay, pottery, earthenware.
cerâmico adj. ceramic.
ceramista s. m. + f. ceramist, ceramic artist, manufacturer of ceramics. ‖ adj. ceramic.
céramo s. m. a vase made of burnt clay.
ceramografia s. f. ceramography.
cerar v. 1. to wax. 2. to cover or fill with wax. 3. to seal with wax, seal.
cerasina (I) s. f. (min.) ozocerite.
cerasina (II) s. f. 1. (pharm.) cerasein. 2. (chem.) cerasin. 3. formerly a refreshing drink made of cherries.
ceratite s. f. (med.) keratitis: inflammation of the cornea.
cerato s. m. unguent, ointment (using wax as principal ingredient).
ceratocone s. m. (med.) keratoconus: conical protrusion of the cornea.
ceratodonitídeos s. m. pl. (ichth.) Ceratodontidae.
ceratoplastia s. f. (surg.) keratoplasty: surgical restoration of the cornea.
ceratosas s. f. pl. (zool.) poriferan: spongy animals of the order Keratosa.
ceratose s. f. (med.) keratosis.
ceráunia s. f. 1. thunderbolt. 2. (archeol.) keraunion, thunderstone.
cérbero s. m. 1. (myth.) Cerberus, three-headed dog, hellhound. 2. (fig.) vigilant and brutal guardian.
cerca (ê) (I) s. f. 1. fence, railing (plates A 4, C 11, E 11, P 6). 2. wall. 3. paling. 4. close, enclosure. 5. stockade. 6. hedge, haw, quickset. 7. a piece of land closed by a wall.
~ **de arame** wire fence. ~ **de madeira** a palisade. ~ **de parque** park paling. ~ **viva** quickset. **separar por** ~ to hedge off.
cerca (ê) (II) adv. 1. near, close by. 2. approximate, circa. 3. about, around.
~ **de** approximately, about. ~ **de quatrocentas crianças** about four hundred children. ~ **de vinte** some twenty.

cercada s. f. fishgarth, fishpound, fishtrap.
cercado s. m. 1. enclosure, yard. 2. park. 3. pound. 4. (Braz.) ward, lair. 5. field protected by a fence or hedge, fenced-in land. ‖ adj. enclosed, walled or hedged in. **~ de terras** land-locked. **~ para bois** bull pen. **~ para gado** ward. **~ pelo gelo** ice-bound.
cercadura s. f. 1. any kind of border, trimming or adornment. 2. rim, edge. 3. hem, fringe. 4. embroidery.
cercal s. m. (pl. **-ais**) a grove of oak trees.
cercania s. f. (usually used in pl.) 1. neighbourhood. 2. outskirts. 3. environs, surroundings. 4. adjacency.
cercante s. m. + f. 1. besieger, blocker. 2. surrounding element or medium. ‖ adj. surrounding.
cercão s. m. (pl. **-ões**) 1. neighbourhood, environs. 2. neighbour. 3. kin, kinsfolk. ‖ adj. near, near-by, neighbouring, proximate.
cercar v. 1. to surround with a fence, hedge or wall. 2. to enclose, close in. 3. to barrier in, cordon, corral. 4. to hedge up, rail. 5. to coop. 6. to encircle, encompass, circumfuse. 7. to constrict, restrict, coerce. 8. (fig.) to persecute, harrass. 9. to surround, round, encircle. 10. to hem in. 11. (mil.) to lay siege to, besiege, beleaguer. 12. **~-se** to approach slowly, draw near, surround o. s with. **~ com dique** to bank or dike in. **~ com arame** to wire in. **~ com paliçadas ou estacadas** to palisade, picket. **~ o inimigo** to envelop the enemy. **~-se de amigos** to associate with friends, surround o. s. with friends.
cercária s. f. cercaria, larval form of the trematodes.
cerce adv. 1. close, closely, close to. 2. even with, even with the root. 3. short.
cércea s. f. 1. template. 2. gauge. 3. a kind of scaffold at railway stations that indicates the maximum loading height of freight cars. 4. curve-templet.
cerceador s. m. one who clips or cuts round.
cerceadura s. f. clipping, cutting short, act of trimming.
cerceamento s. m. art or method of clipping.
cercear v. 1. to cut or clip around. 2. to retrench. 3. to cut short. 4. to lessen, diminish. 5. to cut near the root. 6. to unmake, dissolve. 7. to restrict. 8. to depreciate. 9. to destroy.
cerceio s. m. art or method of cutting short.
cérceo adj. cut short, cut near the roots. ‖ adv. close-clipped, closely cut.
cercilhado adj. tonsured, close-shaven.
cercilhar v. to shave the head of, tonsure.
cercilho s. m. tonsure.
cerco (ê) s. m. 1. the act of encircling. 2. encirclement, envelopment. 3. circle, circuit. 4. siege, beleaguerment. 5. enclosure. 6. fishgarth, fishpound. 7. (hunt.) battue. 8. a kind of fishing-net. 9. halo around the moon or some stars. **apertar o ~** to close the siege. **levantar o ~** to raise the siege. **pôr ~ a** to lay siege to. **sustentar o ~** to continue the siege.
cercopídeos s. m. pl. (ent.) Cercopidae.
cerda s. f. bristle (plate E 8).
cerdear v. to shear (an animal).
cerdo s. m. hog, boar.
cerdoso adj. 1. bristly. 2. covered with bristles. 3. wiry, coarse like bristles.
cereal s. m. (pl. **-ais**) 1. cereal. 2. corn, edible grain, breadstuff. 3. cornfield, corn land. ‖ adj. m. + f. cereal.
cerealífero adj. 1. of, pertaining to or relative to cereals. 2. grain producing.
cerealista s. m. + f. cerealist: cereal dealer. ‖ adj. m. + f. of or relating to the cereal trade.

cerebelar adj. m. + f. (anat.) cerebellar.
cerebelo s. m. (anat.) cerebellum, parencephalon.
cerebeloso adj. (anat.) cerebellar.
cerebídeos s. m. pl. (ornith.) passeriform birds of the family Cerebidae.
cerebração s. f. (pl. **-ões**) 1. cerebration. 2. intellectual power. 3. mental activity, thought.
cerebral adj. m. + f. (pl. **-ais**) cerebral.
cerebrastenia s. f. (med.) cerebral asthenia, brain-fag.
cerebrino adj. 1. cerebral. 2. fanciful, phantastic. 3. extraordinary, uncommon.
cérebro s. m. 1. (anat.) brain, cerebrum. 2. (fig.) intelligence, intellectual capacity.
cérebro-espinhal, cerebrospinal adj. m. + f. (pl. **-ais**) cerebrospinal.
cerefólio, cerefolho s. m. (bot.) chervil.
cereja s. f. 1. the fruit of the cherry tree, cherry. 2. any fruit resembling a cherry. 3. (Braz.) a ripe, red coffee berry. ‖ adj. cherry-red, cherry-coloured.
cereja-de-purga s. f. (pl. **cerejas-de-purga**), (bot.) creeping cucumber.
cereja-dos-passarinhos s. f. (pl. **cerejas-dos-passarinhos**), (bot.) 1. gean. 2. hedge berry. 3. mazard, merry. 4. bird cherry.
cerejal s. m. (pl. **-ais**), cherry orchard, cherry plantation.
cerejeira s. f. 1. cherry tree, cherry. 2. cherry wood.
cerejeira-das-antilhas s. f. (pl. **cerejeiras-das-antilhas**), (bot.) Barbados cherry.
cerejeira-do-pará s. f. (pl. **cerejeiras-do-pará**), (bot.) Barbados cherry.
céreo adj. 1. waxen, waxy. 2. pale, wax-coloured.
Ceres s. f. 1. (myth.) Ceres. 2. (fig.) vegetation, field.
ceriantários s. m. pl. (zool.) Cerianthария.
cerianto s. m. (zool.) cerianthid.
cérica s. f. an unguent made of wax and oil (applied to cracked lips or skin).
cerieira s. f. a plant that produces vegetable wax.
cerieiro s. m. wax-worker, wax-chandler, candle-maker.
cerífero adj. wax producing, ceriferous.
cerificação s. f. (bot.) a process in which the epidermic cells of the leaves and stems form a waxen revestment.
cerimônia s. f. 1. ceremony. 2. solemnization, solemnity. 3. rite. 4. form, civility, urbanity. 5. function, exercise. 6. etiquette. 7. excessive politeness. 8. (fig.) shyness, timidity, bashfulness. 9. **~s** pl. rites or legal ceremonies, ceremonial rules. 10. book of ceremonies. **~ de casamento** espousals. **~ de formatura** commencement. **~ do batismo** baptismal service. **de ~** formally, solemnly. **ele não faz muitas ~s** he is not to be trifled with. **não faça ~** 1. please, make yourself at home. 2. don't stand on ceremony. 3. don't be silly. 4. don't be bashful! **sem ~s** unconventional, without formalities. **traje de ~** evening dress, dress suit. **visita de ~** a formal call.
cerimonial s. m. (pl. **-ais**) 1. system of ceremonies, rules of worship, rites. 2. ceremonial, ritual. 3. etiquette. 4. book containing ceremonial rules. 5. book of etiquette. ‖ adj. m. + f. ceremonial, ritual.
cerimoniar v. 1. to assist at ceremonies. 2. to act ceremoniously, act as master of ceremonies. 3. to treat with formality.
cerimoniário s. m. (rel.) cerimoniarius.
cerimoniático adj. 1. ceremonious, formal. 2. standing upon ceremonies. 3. fussy. ‖ **cerimoniaticamente** adv. ceremoniously.

cerimonioso adj. 1. ceremonious, ceremonial. 2. formal, solemn. 3. precise, exacting. 4. stiff. || -amente adv. ceremoniously, ceremonially.

cério s. m. (chem.) cerium (symbol Ce).

cerita s. f. (min.) cerite.

cernambi s. m. (Braz.) 1. an eatable mollusc (Mesoderma mactroides). 2. rubber of inferior quality.

cernar v. 1. to cut to the core. 2. to extract the core or pith of. 3. (fig.) to uncover the underlying reason, discern.

cerne s. m. 1. (bot.) duramen. 2. pith, core (plate C 9). 3. heartwood. 4. (fig.) an old but still vigorous person.

cerneira s. f. 1. the hard, tough, woody core of a tree. 2. boards cut from this wood.

cerneiro adj. of, pertaining to or relative to the hardwood core of a tree.

cernelha s. f. withers (of animals) (plate C 12).

cernideira s. f. a wooden piece on which the wheat sieve rests.

cernir v. 1. to sift, screen, separate the wheat from the chaff. 2. to walk or dance with a swaying motion.

ceró s. m. (Braz., pop.) a waxy secretion, cerumen, earwax.

ceroferário s. m. ceropheary, candle-bearer or torch-bearer in a procession, acolyte, altar-boy.

ceróide adj. m. + f. waxlike.

cerol s. m. (pl. -óis) wax, shoemaker's wax.

ceroma s. f. cere of birds.

ceromancia s. f. ceromancy: divination by melted wax and wax figures.

ceromante s. m. + f. ceromancer.

ceromântico adj. of, pertaining to or relative to ceromancy.

cerome s. m. a long cloak for a woman.

ceromel s. m. (pl. -éis) a salve or unguent made of wax and honey.

ceroplastia, ceroplástica s. f. ceroplastics, the art of modeling in wax.

ceroto s. m. 1. cerate, salve or unguent made of wax and other medicinal ingredients. 2. filth, dirt.

ceroulas s. f. pl. drawers, pants.

~ **curtas** trunk-drawers.

cerqueiro adj. fencing or hedging in, surrounding, envolving.

rede -a sweep-net, drag-net.

cerração s. f. (pl. -ões) 1. fog, fogginess. 2. mist, haze. 3. darkness, gloom. 4. cloudiness. 5. vapour. 6. (fig.) hoarseness, shortness of breath, suffocation.

~ **do tempo** cloudy or gloomy weather.

cerradal s. m. (pl. -ais) (N. Braz.) a natural pasture closed in by hedgelike shrubs and trees.

cerradão s. m. (pl. -ões) an extensive tract of barren land.

cerrado s. m. 1. fence, hedge. 2. a fenced-in tract of land. 3. open pasture with patches of stunted vegetation. || adj. 1. compact, close. 2. dense, thick. 3. joined, united. 4. tight. 5. heavy (of colours). 6. threatening (of weather). 7. hard to understand. 8. foggy. || -amente adv. tightly, densely, thickly.

cerradouro s. m. drawstring(s) (to close pouches and sacks with).

cerradura s. f. (†) a fence, a wall.

cerra-fila s. m. (pl. **cerra-filas**) 1. (mil.) the last soldier in a file, file closer. 2. (navy) the last ship of a convoy.

cerramento s. m. the act of closing or tightening.

cerrar v. 1. to close, shut. 2. to join, unite. 3. to tighten. 4. to enclose, fence in. 5. to finish, conclude. 6. to silence. 7. to cover up, conceal, hide. 8. to come close together, crowd together. 9. to reach full age, be full grown (said of horses). 10.

to grow dark or threatening (weather). 11. ~-se: a) to shut up. b) not to yield, to persist, persevere. c) to stop speaking or writing.

~ **a boca** to stop to talk, to silence. ~**am fileiras** they closed the ranks. ~**am-se todas as portas** (fam., fig.) there was no way out. ~ **o punho** to double or clench the fist. **ele cerrou os dentes** he set his teeth. **ele cerrou os olhos para** he closed his eyes to.

cerrilha s. f. the white rim of worn-down incisors (of old horses, mules).

cerrito s. m. 1. knoll, hillock. 2. high rocky place.

cerro (ê) (I) s. m. 1. small hill, hillock, knoll. 2. softly rising ground. 3. crag, cliff.

cerro (ê) (II) s. m. (Port., prov.) a small rest of liquid in a glass or cup.

certa s. f. 1. certainty, certitude. 2. sureness, surety. 3. veracity.

na ~! (Braz., pop.) beyond doubt, doubtless, certainly.

certame s. m. (also **certâmen**, pl. **certamens, certâmenes**) 1. fight, combat. 2. discussion, argument. 3. controversy, dispute. 4. literary contest. 5. scientific, industrial or sportive competition.

certão adj. (pl. -ões) (f. **certã**) (ant.) certain, sure, correct.

certar v. 1. to fight, combat. 2. to argue, plead. 3. to discuss, debate. 4. to endeavour, strain hard for. 5. to fail, go bankrupt.

certeiro adj. 1. well-aimed. 2. (fig.) adequate, convenient. 3. well-managed, well-directed, well-advised. 4. right, correct, accurate.

com um tiro ~ with a well-aimed shot. **tiro** ~ toucher.

certeza s. f. 1. certainty, certitude. 2. positiveness, definiteness. 3. conviction. 4. exact knowledge. 5. confidence, assurance, sureness. 6. safeness, security. 7. unfailingness, indubitableness. 8. stability. ~ **absoluta** dead certainty, (sl.) dead cert. **com** ~ unerringly. **com toda** ~ as sure as can be, as sure as eggs. **sabia disso com toda** ~ I knew that for certain. **tenho** ~ **de que** I feel sure that. **tenho absoluta** ~ I am quite sure of it, I know for certain. **você tem** ~? are you sure of it?

certidão s. f. (pl. -ões) 1. certificate. 2. attestation, testimonial. 3. acknowledgement. 4. voucher.

~ **de alfândega** debenture. ~ **de casamento** marriage licence. ~ **de sentença** judgement.

certificação s. f. (pl. -ões) act of certifying, certification.

certificado s. m. 1. certification, certificate. 2. testimonial. 3. attestation, attest. 4. voucher, warrant, docket. || adj. certified, certificated.

~ **consular** consular certificate. ~ **de reservista** military service certificate. ~ **de transferência** deed of settlement.

certificador s. m., **certificante** m. + f. certifier. || adj. certifying.

certificar v. 1. to certify, certificate. 2. to attest. 3. to acknowledge, confirm. 4. to authenticate. 5. to make known, make sure, affirm. 6. to convince. 7. to warrant. 8. to docket. 9. to seal. 10. ~-se to convince o. s., have the assurance.

certificamo-nos da sua ajuda we made sure of her help.

certificativo adj. certificatory, certificable.

certo s. m. 1. certainty. 2. the right or correct thing. 3. the metal value of a coin. || adj. 1. certain. 2. true, truthful, veracious. 3. exact, accurate, right, precise. 4. evident. 5. sure, assured. 6. unfailing, unquestionable. 7. correct, perfect. 8. authentical. 9. confident. 10. positive. 11. absolute. 12. suitable. 13. some, a certain one. || interj. that's so!, so!, that's right, all right!. ‖ **certamente** adv. 1. certainly. 2. exactly, indeed. 3. undoubtedly, unquestionably. 4. positively, surely. **∼ como a morte** (fam.) as sure as death and taxes. **∼ de** informed of, convinced of. **∼ dia fiquei aborrecido** one day I got disgusted. **absolutamente ∼** absolutely certain, cock-sure, (sl.) on the peg. **andar ∼ (relógio)** to go true (watch). **ao ∼** with certainty, exactly. **até ∼ ponto** to some extent, in a sense. **devagar mas ∼** slowly but surely. **é ∼ demais** it is only too true. **está o sr. ∼ do que diz?** are you sure of what you say? **está ∼, eu vou!** all right, I shall go! **eu tenho por ∼ que iremos** I take it for granted that we go. **isso é o ∼** that's the right thing, (coll.) that's the dandy, (sl.) that's just the ticket. **isto é mais que ∼** that's cock-sure, you can kiss the book on that. **não se sabe ao ∼** it is not exactly known. **nunca deixe o ∼ pelo duvidoso** never quit certainty for hope. **o ∼ é que eu não sabia disso** the truth is that I did not know anything about it. **o fato é ∼** the fact is certain. **pode estar ∼ de que** you may be sure of it. **pode-se estar ∼ de que ele virá** he is safe to come. **tomar por ∼** to believe, assume. **uma -a decepção** somewhat of a disappointment. **um ∼ homem** a certain man. **um homem ∼** a reliable man. **você pode ficar ∼ de que** you may rest assured that.

cerúleo, cérulo adj. cerulean, ceruleous, sky-coloured, azure.

cerume, cerúmen (pl. **cerumens, cerúmenes**) s. m. (med.) cerumen, earwax, wax.

ceruminoso adj. ceruminous.

cerusita s. f. (min.) cerusite, cerussite, native lead carbonate.

cerva s. f. (zool.) doe, female of deer.

cerval (I) adj. m. + f. (pl. **-ais**) of, pertaining to or relative to a deer.

cerval (II) s. m. (pl. **-ais**), (zool.) serval.

cervantesco adj. of, pertaining to or relative to the Spanish poet Miguel de Cervantes Saavedra and/or his works.

cervantista s. m. + f. Cervantist, an admirer of Cervantes.

cervato s. m. (zool.) a young deer.

cerveja s. f. beer, ale.
∼ amarga bitter. **∼ escura** bock (beer). **∼ escura e forte** stout. **∼ forte** double ale, entire. **∼ fraca** swipes, small beer. **∼ fresca do barril** draught beer. **de ∼** beery. **ele gosta de beber uma ∼** he is fond of a bottle of beer. **vamos tomar um copo de ∼!** let's have a glass of beer!

cervejada s. f. 1. (fam.) a glass of beer. 2. a group of friends drinking beer, party of beer tipplers.

cerveja-de-barbante s. f. (pl. **cervejas-de-barbante**), (N. Braz., pop.) a kind of root beer made by Indians.

cervejar v. to drink beer.

cervejaria s. f. 1. beershop, ale-house, beerhouse. 2. brewing house, brewery.

cervejeiro s. m. brewer.

cervical adj. m. + f. (pl. **-ais**), (anat.) cervical.

cervicartrose s. f. (path.) arthrosis envolving one or more cervical articulations.

cervicite s. f. (med.) cervicitis.

cervicórneo adj. (zool.) cervicorn.

cervídeo s. m. (zool.) ruminant mammal of the family Cervidae. ‖ adj. cervine, cervoid.

cervino adj. cervine.

cerviz s. f. (anat.) cervix, neck, nape. **dobrar a ∼** to eat humble pie, humble o. s. **ele é de dura ∼** he is obstinate, he is incorrigible.

cervo s. m. (zool.) deer.

cerzideira s. f. 1. woman who darns clothes. 2. woman fine-drawer.

cerzido s. m. 1. darned fabric. 2. a darning. 3. a clothes' mending made with very small stitches. ‖ adj. darned.

cerzidor s. m. darner, fine-drawer. ‖ adj. darning, fine-drawing.

cerzidura s. f. darning, fine-drawing.

cerzimento s. m. act or method of darning, darning, fine-drawing.

cerzir v. 1. to darn, patch, fine-draw. 2. to knit up. 3. to join, unite. 4. to compose, compound. 5. to form, shape. 6. to insert, intercalate.

cesáreo adj. (Rom. hist.) Caesarian: of, pertaining to or relative to Caesar.

cesariana s. f. (med., surg.) Caesarian, Caesarian operation, abdominal delivery.‖ ‖adj. Caesarian.

cesariano adj. of or relative to Caesarism, Caesarian.

cesarismo s. m. Caesarism: 1. absolute or autocratic government. 2. despotism, despotic government. 3. imperialism.

cesarista s. m. + f. Caesarist: supporter or defender of absolutism. ‖ adj. Caesaristic(al).

césio s. m. (chem.) caesium, cesium.

céspede s. m. a piece of sod, turf.

cespitoso adj. 1. covered with turf, turfy, turfed. 2. (bot.) cespitose, growing in clusters.

cessação s. f. (pl. **-ões**) cessation, ceasing. 2. interruption, discontinuance. 3. suspension. 4. break. 6. intermission. 6. (jur.) surcease.
∼ das hostilidades suspension of hostilities.

cessamento s. m. = **cessação.**

cessante adj. m. + f. cessant, inactive, intermissive.

cessão s. f. (pl. **-ões**) 1. act of ceding or yielding. 2. cession. 3. demise, release, transfer. 4. alienation. 5. disposal. 6. desistance.
∼ de bens surrender of effects. **∼ de calor** (tech.) delivery of heat. **∼ de um direito** (jur.) remise. **∼ testamentária** (jur.) demise.

cessar v. 1. to cease. 2. to come to an end, stop. 3. to make an end of, discontinue, break off. 4. to interrupt. 5. to desist. 6. to leave off, let up. 7. to drop, pass off. 8. to surcease.
∼ de falar to stop talking. (sl.) dry up. **∼ o fogo** (mil.) to stop firing. **∼ por algum tempo** to intermit. **cessou de ventar** it fell calm. **não cessa de chover** it continues raining. **sem ∼** continually, incessantly, without intermission.

cessibilidade s. f. assignability, transferability.

cessionário s. m. cessionary, assignee, releasee.

cessível adj. m. + f. (pl. **-íveis**) assignable, transferable.

cesta s. f. basket, coop.
∼ de roupa usada clothes basket. **∼ de madeira para jardineiros** trug. **∼ de tiras de madeira** chip-basket. **∼ de vime** wicker-basket.

cestada s. f. basketful.

cestão s. m. (pl. **-ões**) 1. large basket. 2. (fort.) gabion. 3. large river raft.

cesteiro s. m. basketmaker.

cesto (I) s. m. (ant.) a heavy leather whip.

cesto (II) s. m. (ant.) 1. belt, waistband. 2. (zool.) Venus' girdle.

cesto (ê) (III) s. m. basket, back-basket, scuttle (plate B 11).
∼ da gávea (naut.) crow's nest, bird's nest. **∼ de pão** bread-basket (plates M 1, 8). **∼ de vime** hamper, pannier, crib. **∼ para papéis** litter basket, waste basket (plates P 6, R 8). **∼ para peixes** creel, fishing basket (plate P 9).

cestodários s. m. pl. (zool.) metazoan animals of the subclass Cestodaria.

cestóide s. m. (zool.) cestoid. ‖ adj. m. + f. cestoid.

cestro s. m. (bot.) cestrum, night jasmine.
cesura s. f. 1. act of cutting, incision. 2. scar of a wound. 3. (mus., poet.) caesura, break.
cesurar v. 1. to cut, make an incision. 2. (mus., poet.) to pause, break, intercalate a caesura.
cetáceo s. m. (zool.) cetacean, whale. ‖ adj. cetacean, cetaceous.
cetim s. m. (pl. **-ins**) satin.
cetina s. f. spermaceti.
cetíneo adj. satiny, satin, silky, satin-finished.
cetineta s. f. satinette, sateen.
cetinoso adj. satin, satiny, smooth, silky.
cetona s. f. (chem.) ketone.
cetose s. f. (med.) ketosis.
cetra s. f. (hist.) a leather-covered shield or buckler.
cetrária s. f. (bot.) iceland moss.
cetraria s. f. falconry.
cetras s. f. pl. 1. sign manual, abbreviated signature. 2. flourishes on old manuscripts. 3. sign, mark. 4. signature.
cetrino adj. (poet.) red.
cetro s. m. 1. scepter, sceptre. 2. (fig.) royal dignity and authority. 3. mace, staff, baton. 4. wand.
depor o ~ to abdicate, resign. **empunhar o ~** to wield the sceptre, rule.
céu s. m. 1. sky, heaven. 2. firmament. 3. above, sphere, air. 4, canopy. 5. (rel.) paradise. 6. atmosphere. 7. (fig.) God. 8. providence.
~ da boca (anat.) roof of the mouth, palate. **céus!** for heaven's sake!, my word! good heavens! **alto como o ~** sky-high. **aquilo é um ~ aberto** that is heaven on earth. **cair do ~** (fig.) to fall from the sky, appear unexpectedly. **ganhar o ~** to win the paradise by kind deeds. **isto brada aos ~s** it cries to heaven. **elogiaram-no até aos ~s** they praised him to the skies. **no sétimo ~** in paradise. **pôr a boca no ~** to talk about things one doesn't understand. **revolver ~ e terra** to move heaven and earth. **um ~ aberto** (fig.) 1. a great adventure. 2. paradise on earth. 3. an unclouded sky. **um ~ encoberto** a troubled sky. **tomar o ~ com as mãos** to cry for the moon. **~ claro** (meteor.) clear sky.
ceva s. f. 1. act or method of fattening animals. 2. special mast feed, hogwash. 3. bait, lure, grain or other feed laid out to attract game. 4. place where such bait is laid out, decoy.
cevada s. f. barley.
cevadal s. m. (pl. **-ais**) barley field.
cevadeira s. f. 1. nose-bag, feed bag. 2. (naut.) spritsail.
cevadeiro s. m. 1. fattening pen. 2. decoy, place where a bait is laid out. 3. stable master. 4. falconer.
cevadiço adj. easy to fatten.
cevadilha s. f. (bot.) sabadilla, cevadilla, sneeze-wort.
cevadinha s. f. 1. pearl barley. 2. (bot.) rescue grass.
cevado s. m. 1. a fattened hog. 2. fatling, fat animal. 3. a very fat man. ‖ adj. fattened, fat.
cevador s. m. 1. feeder, fattener, one who fattens animals for slaughter. 2. (S. Braz.) one who prepares and serves maté to his friends.
cevadouro s. m. 1. fattening pen or coop. 2. pasture. 3. decoy.
cevadura s. f. 1. mast-feed, special feed for fattening. 2. pasture. 3. remains of animals which have been used as bait or lure. 4. carnage, slaughter.
cevagem s. f. = **ceva**.
cevão s. m. (pl. **-ões**) a fattened hog.
cevar v. 1. to make fat, fatten. 2. to bait, chum (fish). 3. to feed, nourish. 4. to satiate, satisfy. 5. to enrich. 6. to stimulate, foment, encourage. 7. to prepare manioc flour. 8. to place ground

maté into the drinking vessel before pouring boiling water over it. 9. to regale, feast, entertain sumptuously. 10. to become satiated. 11. to become rich.
~ com grão to feed with corn. **~ o desejo** to gratify one's desire. **eles ~m a sua ira** they took revenge. **eles ~am a vista na paisagem** they feasted their eyes with the landscape.
cevatício adj. good for fattening, fattening, nourishing.
ceveiro s. m. adequate place to lay out bait or to chum fish.
cevo (ê) s. m. 1. fattening, mast. 2. bait, lure. 3. feed, food. 4. (fig.) enticement, charm. 5. chum.
chá s. m. 1. (bot.) tea bush, tea-plant. 2. the dry leaves of this shrub. 3. tea, aromatic beverage prepared from tea-leaves and the leaves of several other medicinal plants. 4. tea-party. 5. (coll.) an ingrained habit, addiction.
~ dançante informal tea-time dancing party. **~ das cinco horas** afternoon tea, five o'clock tea. **~ de camomila** camomile tea. **~ elegante** pink tea. **~ preto** black-tea. **~ verde** green tea. **aparelho de ~** tea-service, tea-things, tea-set. **bandeja de ~** tea-tray. **carrinho para servir ~** tea wagon. **colher de ~** teaspoon. **eu gosto de ~ sem açúcar** I like tea without sugar. **folha de ~** tea-leaf. **lata para ~** tea-caddy. **hora do ~** teatime. **o que há para o ~?** what is there for tea? **provador de ~** tea taster. **salão de ~** tea room. **ter tomado ~ em pequeno** to be properly educated. **tomar ~ de cadeira** 1. to be a wallflower at a dancing party. 2. to be kept waiting for an interview. **tomar ~ de sumiço** to be long absent from a place one is costumarily present. **tomar ~ de pouco caso** to care little, give but little importance to. **uma chávena para ~** a tea-cup. **venha tomar ~ conosco** come to tea with us.
chã s. f. 1. a level tract of land. 2. plain, plateau. 3. a round of beef.
chabu s. m. (Braz.) the explosion of a fire cracker.
chabuco s. m. whip, scourge.
chaça s. f. 1. the spot where the ball stops or bounces twice, in the **péla** game. 2. moral shock. 3. argument, fight.
o cavalo fez ~ the horse reared up.
chacal s. m. (pl. **-ais**), (zool.) jackal.
chaçar v. to have advantage over, surpass s. o.
chácara s. f. 1. country house on the outskirts of a town. 2. country seat, rural residence. 3. a small farm.
chacareiro s. m. 1. proprietor of a country house or small farm near the town. 2. administrator of a rural residence. 3. truck farmer.
chacarola s. f. a small **chácara**.
chacim s. m. (pl.-ins) hog, pig.
chacina s. f. 1. act of slaughtering. 2. slaughter. 3. massacre. 4. minced pork. 5. minced, salted and smoked meat.
chacinado adj. 1. slaughtered. 2. (fig.) lean, meagre.
chacinador s. m. 1. meat packer, meat salter. 2. slaughterer. 3. massacrer, killer.
chacinar v. 1. to slaughter. 2. to mince, salt, smoke or pack meat. 3. to massacre, kill. 4. to scrutinize.
chaço (I) s. m. 1. a cooper's tool. 2. iron tire. 3. driver. 4. holder, holdfast, clamp.
chaço (II) s. m. (Port., prov.) bargain.
chaço (III) s. m. (Port., prov.) darned heel of a stocking.
chacoalhar v. 1. to shake violently. 2. to agitate, stir up.
chacona s. f. (mus.) chaconne: 1. an old, slow Spanish dance. 2. the accompanying dance music. 3. a

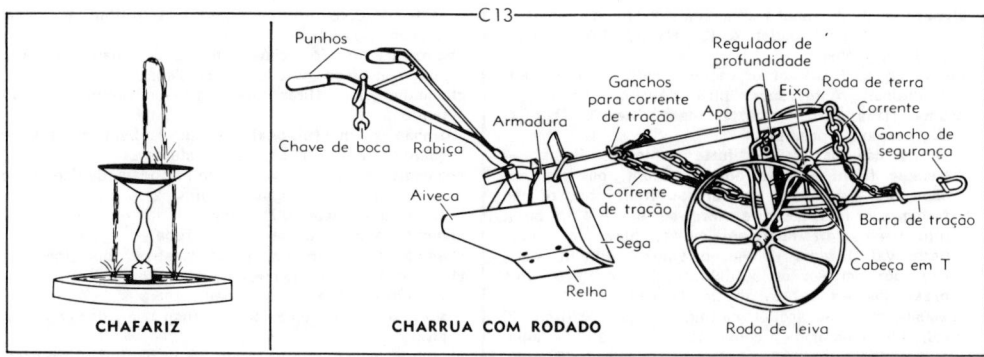

────C13────

CHAFARIZ | **CHARRUA COM RODADO**

Punhos / Chave de boca / Rabiça / Aiveca / Armadura / Ganchos para corrente de tração / Regulador de profundidade / Eixo / Apo / Roda de terra / Corrente / Gancho de segurança / Corrente de tração / Sega / Relha / Barra de tração / Cabeça em T / Roda de leiva

composition written in a moderate three-quarter measure.

chacota s. f. 1. banter, derision. 2. mockery. 3. joke. 4. revelry, spree. 5. an old popular song. 6. a satirical song.
fazer ~ de alguém to scoff at a person.

chacoteação s. f. (pl. **-ões**) joke, jest, mockery.

chacoteador s. m. jester, joker, merry maker, reveller, mocker.

chacotear v. 1. to joke, jest. 2. to mock, poke fun at. 3. to scoff at, ridicule. 4. to revel, go on a spree.

chacrinha s. f. (Braz., fam.) an informal and intimate group meeting.

chá-da-índia s. m. (pl. **chás-da-índia**) (Braz.) tree or bush of the tea family.

chá-de-casca-de-vaca s. m. (pl. **chás-de-casca-de-vaca**), (S. Braz., pop.) a good, sound thrashing with a rawhide whip.

chá-de-cozinha s. m. (pl. **chás-de-cozinha**) (Braz.) tea-party programmed by young ladies with presents for a bride-to-be.

chafalhão (I) s. m. (pl. **-ões**) a big, old, rusty sword.

chafalhão (II) (pl. **-ões**) adj. prankish, frolicsome.

chafalho s. m. an old, useless sword.

chafarica s. f. 1. a Freemasonic lodge. 2. ordinary eating place. 3. common tavern, pub. 4. small grocery store.

chafariz s. m. fountain, spout, waterworks (plate C 13).

chafurda s. f. 1. pig stable, pigsty. 2. bog, mudhole. 3. dirty house. 4. dirt, filth. 5. wallow.

chafurdar v. 1. to roll in the mire. 2. to wallow, welter, mire. 3. to splash, bespatter. 4. to flounder. 5. to become filthy. 6. (fig.) to become perverted, become depraved.

chafurdeiro s. m. 1. pigsty. 2. bog, mire. 3. wallower. 4. one who becomes depraved or degrades himself.

chafurdice s. f. 1. wallow, act of wallowing. 2. mean or common action.

chaga s. f. 1. an oppen wound, sore. 2. ulcer, fester. 3. a cut in the bark of a tree. 4. (fig.) affliction, tribulation, grievous distress. 5. misfortune, calamity. 6. **~s** pl. (bot.): a) common nasturtium (Tropaeolum majus). b) tall nasturtium, Indian cress, lark's heel. 7. the flower of nasturtium.
com o corpo todo em ~s with sores all over the body. **pelas ~s de Cristo!** for heaven's sake! for the love of God. **mal de Chagas** (med.) barber bug fever, Chagas' disease.

chagado adj. 1. covered with sores, wounded, ulcerated. 2. (fig.) afflicted, tormented.

chagar v. 1. to ulcerate. 2. to affect with sores. 3. to wound, injure. 4. to molest, trouble, annoy. 5. to torment, afflict. 6. to become ulcerated.

chagásico s. m. a person with Chagas' disease. ‖ adj. relative to the Chagas' disease.

chagoma s. m. (pathol.) chagoma, a swelling from the sting of the barber bug.

chagrém s. m. (pl. **-éns**) shagreen.

chagueira s. f. (bot.) common nasturtium, tall nasturtium, Indian cress, lark's heel.

chaguento adj. full of sores, ulcerated.

chaguer s. m. a leather vessel used as water cooler.

chaira s. f. a piece of steel used for sharpening knives.

chairar v. 1. to whet, sharpen, hone (knives). 2. to crop the mane of a horse.

chairel s. m. (pl. **-éis**) saddlecloth.

chalaça s. f. 1. a funny saying, bon mot. 2. witty remark. 3. mockery. 4. derision, ridicule. 5. banter. 6. scoff, jeer. 7. joke, jest.

chalaçar, chalacear v. 1. to joke, jest. 2. to gibe, jeer. 3. to poke fun at, make sport of. 4. to banter. 5. to kid, tease.

chalaceador s. m. jester, joker, teaser, jeerer. ‖ adj. jesting.

chalaceiro s. m. jester, joker, jeerer.

chalana s. f. (Braz.) a flat-bottomed boat.

chalavagão s. m. (pl. **-ões**) a large vessel with two banks of oars.

chalé s. m. chalet, log cabin, lodge, cottage.

chaleira, s. f. 1. tea-kettle, tea-urn (plates C 6, 20). 2. kettle. 3. (naut.) platform on the bow of a whaling boat. 4. m. + f. (pop.) flatterer, wheedler, fawner. ‖ adj. m. + f. flattering, wheedling.
~ com torneira tea-urn.

chaleiramento s. m. act of flattering, fawning; adulation.

chaleirar v. to flatter, wheedle, fawn.

chaleirismo s. m. adulation, flattery.

chaleirista s. m. + f. flatterer, wheedler, cajoler. ‖ adj. flattering, cajoling.

chalo s. m. cot, rustic bedstead.

chalrar, charear v. 1. to prattle, talk happily, chatter. 2. to chirp, twitter. 3. to babble.

chalreada s. f. 1. the murmur of many voices. 2. chatter, prattle. 3. gabbling, babbling. 4. chirping, twittering.

chalreador s. m. 1. babbler. 2. chatterer, chatterbox. 3. endless talker. ‖ adj. babbling, prattling, chirping.

chalreio s. m. 1. the hum of voices. 2. chatter, prattle. 3. chirping, warble, twittering.

chalrote s. m. the bark of a pine-tree.

chalupa s. f. 1. (naut.) long-boat. 2. (naut.) shallop, sloop. 3. (naut.) tender. 4. (cards) the three highest cards at omber.

chama (I) s. f. 1. act of calling, call. 2. jure, bait. 3. birdcall. 4. m. decoy bird, decoy, call-bird.

chama (II) s. f. 1. flame. 2. blaze, fire. 3. light. 4. (fig.) ardour, passion.
~ **de gás** gas-jet. ~ **forte** explosive flame. ~ **trêmula** flare. **em** ~**s** ablaze, alight, on fire. **escapar às** ~**s e cair nas brasas** (fam.) out of the frying pan into the fire. **fazer-se em** ~**s** to burst into flames. **irromper em** ~**s** to burst in flame. **perto vai o fumo da** ~ no smoke without some fire. **pôr em** ~**s** to set ablaze, set on fire. **uma presa das** ~**s** a prey to the flames.

chamada s. f. 1. act of calling. 2. call, calling. 3. roll-call, muster. 4. convocation. 5. call or summons of the bell. 6. (typogr.) catchword. 7. note. 8. (pop.) censure, reprimand.
~ **de nota** the letter, number or sign used to refer from the text to the foot-note. ~ **interurbana** long-distance call. ~ **telefônica** telephone call. **fazer a** ~ to call the roll(s).

chamado s. m. 1. call, act of calling. 2. convocation. ‖ adj. called, summoned.

chamador s. m. 1. caller, summoner. 2. proclaimer, crier, town-crier. 3. (Braz.) leader of a drove of cattle, oxman, oxen driver.

chamalote s. m. 1. camlet, camel's hair cloth. 2. wave, wavy lines, water-lines.

chama-maré s. m. (pl. **chama-marés**), (zool.) fiddler crab.

chamamento s. m. 1. act of calling. 2. convocation. 3. call, calling.

chamar v. 1. to call, shout s. o.'s name. 2. to hallo, hail. 3. to summon. 4. to invoke, evoke. 5. to convoke, call together, call for. 6. to wake up. 7. to attract. 8. to demand, require. 9. to entitle, call o. s. 10. to choose, select. 11. to invite. 12. to name, term, denominate. 13. to ring, toll. 14. to christen. 15. to beckon, call with a movement of the hand or any other signal. 16. (Braz.) to lead a drove of cattle. 17. ~**-se**: a) to be called or named. b) to allege, pretend. c) to appeal to. 18. to allure, entice. 19. to exclaim.
~ **à ordem** to call to order. ~ **às armas** to beat to arms. ~ **a atenção a** to advert, draw the attention to. ~**am-no já por duas vezes** you have been called twice. ~**am por mim** they called for me. ~**am por socorro** they shouted for help. ~ **com a mão** to beckon, waft. **chamarei de novo (pelo telefone)** I shall call again. ~ **para exame** to call in question. ~ **um navio à fala** to hail a ship. **como o senhor chama isso?** what do you call that? **ele chama a atenção** he stands out like a sore thumb. **ele chamou-a de casa** he called to her from the house. **ele chamou a si a responsabilidade** he shouldered the responsibility. **ele foi chamado à ordem** he was called on the carpet. **ele foi chamado por telegrama** he was wired for. **ele me chamou** he cried to me. **ele se chama** he answers to the name of. **muitos são os chamados mas poucos os escolhidos** many are called but few are chosen. **não possuo nada que possa** ~ **meu** I have nothing to call my own. **permito-me chamar-lhe a atenção para** may I call your attention to. **tive de chamá-lo à razão** I had to bring him to his senses.

chamarisco s. m. 1. lure, bait, decoy. 2. enticement, attraction.

chama-rita s. f. = **chimarrita**.

chamariz s. m. 1. anything calling the attention to. 2. advertisement. 3. attraction. 4. bait, lure. 5.

bird-call. 6. call-bird, decoy. 7. bird-lime. 8. stool-pigeon.

chá-mate s. m. (pl. **chás-mate**) (Braz.) maté, aromatic beverage used chiefly in S. America.

chamativo adj. (Braz.) calling or claiming for attention.

chambão s. m. (pl.-ões) 1. leg. 2. beef of inferior quality. ‖ adj. coarse, rude, clumsy.

chambaril s. m. 1. a curved wooden device used for hanging up slaughtered pigs. 2. a stingy person. 3. an ugly, worn-out woman.

chamboado adj. coarse, rough, rude.

chamboíce s. f. rudeness, coarseness, clumsiness.

chambre s. m. 1. housecoat, morning coat. 2. dressing gown, robe. 3. negligee.
abrir o ~ or **abrir do** ~ (pop.) to decamp, run away.

chambrié s. m. a long whip used by horse trainers.

chamego s. m. 1. sexual excitement. 2. flirtation, love-making. 3. uneasiness, unrest, anxiety. 4. hastiness, fidgetiness. 5. intimate friendship. 6. infatuation. 7. intimacy.

chameguento adj. infatuated, flirtaceous, intimate, fidgety.

chamejamento s. m. act of flaming.

chamejante adj. m. + f. flaming, flamy. 2. ablaze, fiery. 3. flashing, flamboyant.

chamejar v. 1. to flame. 2. to blaze, flare. 3. to flicker. 4. to glitter, sparkle. 5. to flash, fulgurate. 6. (fig.) to be enraptured. 7. (fig.) to grow angry, flare up.

chamelote s. m.= **chamalote**.

chamiça s. f. 1. (bot.) a variety of wild rush, matweed. 2. a string or rope made of matweed fibers.

chamiceiro s. m. maker or vendor of matweed articles.

chamiço s. m. kindling, small brushwood, small sticks or twigs.

chaminé s. f. 1. chimney (plate C 5). 2. chimney flue, stove-pipe. 3. funnel. 4. chimney stalk, smoke stack (plate A 4). 5. hole of a candlestick. 6. (geol.) the orifice of a volcano.
cão da ~ andiron. ~ **de ventilação** vent pipe (plate B 3). **limpador de** ~ chimney-sweeper. **quadro da** ~ chimney-piece.

chá-mineiro s. m. (pl. **chás-mineiros**), (bot.) a burhead.

chamorro s. m. contemptuous nickname formerly given by Spaniards to Portuguese. ‖ adj. shorn, shaved.

champanha, champanhe s. m. champaign, champagne.

champignon s. m. (bot.) champignon.

champil s. m. (pl. **-is**) that part of a snare or trap whereupon the bait is laid out.

champirrear v. to make clumsily, botch.

champunha s. m. handstand, handspring.

champurrião s. m. (pl. **-ões**) binge, drunken spree.

chamurro s. m. castrated yearling.

chamusca s. f. act of singeing, slight burn.

chamuscado adj. slightly burned, singed.

chamuscador s. m. singer: one who or that which singes. ‖ adj. singeing.

chamuscadura s. f. act of singeing, slight burn.

chamuscar v. 1. to singe, burn slightly. 2. to sear, scorch. 3. to toast. 4. to char.

chamusco s. m. 1. the smell of something that has been singed, burnt smell. 2. singe, slight burn. 3. elevated plain. 4. encounter, skirmish.
cheirar a ~ 1. to smell of burning. 2. (fig.) to have the smell of danger.

chanana s. f. (bot.) yellow alder.

chanca s. f. (pop.) 1. a long foot. 2. brogue (plate B 16). 3. a slender and long leg (of a man).

chança s. f. 1. jest, joke. 2. wisecrack. 3. scoffing, scoff. 4. vanity, self-conceit. 5. stand-offishness, arrogance.

chancarina, chancarona s. f. (ichth.) sea bream.

chance s. f. (Fr.) 1. chance. 2. opportunity, vantage, venture.

a melhor ~ the main chance. ~ desfavorável em apostas long odds. ~ igual an even chance. nenhuma ~ not an earthly hap. vamos dar-lhe uma ~ we'll give you a chance.

chancear v. 1. to scoff, gibe. 2. to persecute with sarcastic saying. 3. to talk mockingly.

chanceiro s. m. scoffer, jester, mocker.

chancela s. f. 1. seal, official seal. 2. abbreviated signature, autograph initials. 3. act of signing. 4. flourish added to a signature.

chancelar v. 1. to seal. 2. to stamp. 3. to sign, put one's signature to. 4. (fig.) to approve.

chancelaria s. f. 1. office, dignity and authority of a chancellor. 2. chancellorship. 3. chancellery, chancery court.

chanceler s. m. chancellor.

chanchada s. f. (theat.) a worthless play.

chaneco s. m. plain, barren prairie land.

chanfalho s. m. 1. a rusty old sword. 2. a musical instrument which is out of tune. 3. a worn-out tool.

chanfana s. f. 1. (pop.) a liver stew. 2. pimple, blister. 3. a badly cooked dish. 4. = chanfalho.

chanfaneiro s. m. proprietor of a cheap cookshop. tavern keeper.

chanfrado adj. beveled, bezeled, cant, featheredged, notched.

chanfrador s. m. chamfer(ing) plane, chaser.

chanfradura s. f. 1. the result of chamfering. 2. bevel, bezel, chamfer (plate A 7). 3. chase, cant.

chanfrar v. 1. to chamfer. 2. to groove, flute. 3. to cant, bevel. 4. to notch, dent, nick.

chanfreta s. f. mockery, jest, banter.

chanfro s. m. 1. chamfer, bevel. 2. notch. 3. featheredge. 4. rabbet.

changa s. f. 1. transport by handcart. 2. profit. 3. tip.

boa ~ good business.

changador s. m. porter, carter, deliveryman.

changar, changuear v. to work as a porter or deliveryman.

changueiro s. m. a mediocre race-horse.

changui s. m. respite.

não dar ~ ao inimigo to give no respite to the enemy.

chanqueta s. f. a kind of moccasin.

chanta s. f. a twig or branch used for planting, cutting.

chantadura s. f. the plantation of cuttings.

chantagem (I) s. f. (pl. -ens) blackmail, extortion, (jur.) chantage.

fazer ~ to blackmail.

chantagem (II) s. f. (pl. -ens) act or process of planting cuttings.

chantagista s. m. + f. blackmailer, extortionist, highflyer. ‖ adj. blackmailing.

chantão s. m. (pl. -ões) plant cutting, shoot.

chantar v. 1. to drive (a stake) into the ground. 2. to plant cuttings or shoots. 3. to become fixed.

chantel s. m. (pl. -éis) cantlet of a barrel or vat.

chanto s. m. (obs.) lament, wailing, mourning.

chantoeira s. f. a field replanted with cuttings.

chantrado s. m. office and dignity of a precentor.

chantre s. m. precentor, chanter, cantor, choir leader.

chantria s. f. office and dignity of a precentor.

chanura s. f. plain, prairie.

chão s. m. (pl. chãos) 1. level ground, ground. 2. earth. 3. a small area of ground, plot. 4. floor. 5.

background of a painting. ‖ adj. (pl. chãos) (f. chã) 1. level, flat. 2. plain. 3. even. 4. smooth. 5. quiet, peaceful. 6. frank, free. 7. simple, sincere. 8. vulgar, humble.

deitar no ~ to throw upon the ground. medir o ~ to fall on the ground. riscar o ~ (pop.) to run away.

chão-parado s. m. (pl. chãos-parados) (Braz., pop.) a large area of level ground, plain, lowland, prairie.

chapa s. f. 1. metal sheet, plate, sheet-metal. 2. lamina. 3. engraved plate, gravure. 4. cliché. 5. pane, foil. 6. tag, tablet. 7. licence plate (of a motor vehicle (plate M 12). 8. phonograph record. 9. (pol.) list of candidates of a political group. 10. common-place phrase in a discourse, trite phrase or expression. 11. cymbal: a musical instrument (made of two metal half globes).

~ de aço steel plate. ~ de aquecimento elétrico hot plate (plate C 20). ~ de automóvel (also placa de licença) index-number, license plate (plate V 3). ~ de blindagem, ~ de couraça armour plate. ~ de corte (typogr.) card cutter, ~ de empregado badge. ~ de ferro sheet iron. ~ de ferro corrugada carrugated iron. ~ de ferro estanhada tin plate. ~ de fogão hearthplate, hot plate (plate F 3). ~ de diapositivo (phot.) glass diapositive (plate E 5). ~ de testa face plate (plate F 1). ~ de vidro glass plate. ~ eleitoral a list of candidates for election. ~ fotográfica plate. ~ fria (mot.) a fake license plate. ~ furada perforated sheet. ~ para caldeiras boiler plate. ~ para estampas stamping sheet. ~ seca dry-plate. ~ universal (de torno) face-plate (of a lathe). homem de ~ a well-deserving man. não mudar a ~ to harp always on the same string.

chapa-branca s. m. (pl. chapas-brancas) (Braz.) Public Service vehicle with license plates.

chapada s. f. 1. a clearing in the woods. 2. plateau, tableland. 3. blow, stroke. 4. a squirt of any liquid. 5. (Braz.) a clear, level space or walk on the top of a mountain.

chapadão s. m. (pl. -ões) 1. a large area of level land. 2. several clearings in a forest. 3. ridge, brow of a hill. 4. plain, prairie.

chapadeiro s. m. (Braz.) 1. yokel, backwoodsman. 2. name of a crossbreed of cattle.

chapado adj. (pop.) 1. accomplished, perfect. 2. complete.

ele é um burro ~ he is a perfect fool. homem ~ honest man, sensible fellow.

chapar v. 1. to plate, adorn or cover with plates. 2. to fix with plates. 3. to coin, mint. 4. to give the form of a plate to. 5. to mark with a badge or plate. 6. to tell to one's face, be outspoken. 7. to fall flat on the ground.

chaparia s. f. 1. a lot of sheet-metal or plates. 2. metal ornaments, trimmings of sheet-metal.

chaparral s. m. (pl. -ais) chaparral, thicket of dwarf oaks.

chaparreiro, chaparro s. m. 1. a young oak tree that does not yet bear acorns. 2. a stunted tree.

chapatesta s. f. striking plate of a lock.

chá-paulista s. m. (pl. chás-paulistas) tea dance, dance tea.

chape s. m. 1. a blow on the surface of the water. 2. a splashing noise, splash. ‖ interj. splash!, plash!, clap! slap!.

chapeado s. m. veneering. ‖ adj. adorned with small pieces of sheet-metal, plated.

chapear v. 1. to cover or adorn with plates. 2. to fix with plates. 3. to trim, adorn with iron work. 4. to plate, inlay. 5. to plaster a wall. 6. to veneer.

chape-chape s. m. (pl. chape-chapes) (Braz.) 1. hard, barren soil. 2. an arid tract of land.

chapeirada s. f. a hatful, a kettleful.

chapeirão s. m. (pl. -ões) 1. a hat with a broad brim. 2. hat, hood. 3. a reef or ridge of sand lying near the surface of the water.

chapelada s. f. a hatful, capful.

chapelão s. m. (pl. -ões) a big or broad-brimmed hat.

chapelaria s. f. 1. hatmaker's or hatter's shop, hattery. 2. hat store. 3. millinery, millinery shop.

chapeleira s. f. 1. a hatter's wife. 2. hat box.

chapeleiro s. m. hatter, hatmaker.

chapeleta s. 1. a little hat, a children's or woman's hat. 2. (mech.) valve flap, bonnet of a valve (plate E 10). 3. a ricochet. 4. rosy spot(s) in the face, red cheeks.

chapelina s. f. (N. Braz.) a type of hat used by women from the inland.

chapetão adj. (pl. -ões) stupid, indolent.

chapetonada s. f. foolishness, blunder, nonsense.

chapéu s. m. 1. hat (plate C 5). 2. dregs of wine. 3. an umbraculiform mushroom. 4. (naut.) spindle-head of a capstan. 5. the captain's share of the freight charges. 6. (fig.) dignity, authority. **alfinete de** ~ hatpin. ~ **cardinalício** cardinal's hat, red hat. ~ **coco** Derby, bowler, billycock (plate R 7). ~ **com aba virada para cima** cock-up. ~ **de aba larga** broadbrim. ~ **de capitão** a contracted remuneration paid to a merchant marine captain for bringing his ship safely ashore. ~ **de feltro** felt hat, hamburg (plate R 7). ~ **de palha** brimmer, straw-hat. ~ **panamá** panama. **de** ~ **na mão** with one's hat off, humbly. **fita de** ~ hatband. **isto é de se tirar o** ~ that's to take one's hat off, that feat commands respect. **pôr o** ~ to put on one's hat. **sem** ~ hatless, bareheaded. **tirar o** ~ **a alguém** to raise hat to, bow down. **tirei o** ~ **diante de** l uncovered myself to, l uncovered myself. **vir com o** ~ **na mão** to come hat in hand.

chapéu-armado s. m. (pl. **chapéus-armados**), (Braz., ichth.) a hammerhead shark.

chapéu-coco s. m. (pl. **chapéus-cocos**) derby hat.

chapéu-de-chuva s. m. (pl. **chapéus-de-chuva**) umbrella.

chapéu-de-cobra .s m. (pl. **chapéus-de-cobra**), (bot.) chanterelle.

chapéu-de-couro s. m. (pl. **chapéus-de-couro**), (bot.) a burhead.

chapéu-de-ferro s. m. (pl. **chapéus-de-ferro**), (min.) native iron oxid, gossan, iron hat.

chapéu-de-frade s. m. (pl. **chapéus-de-frade**) 1. a triangle-shaped diamond of very low value. 2. a small diamond crystal. 3. a bush of the family Bignoniaceae (Zeyheria montana).

chapéu-de-napoleão s. m. (pl. **chapéus-de-napoleão**), (bot.) yellow oleander, trumpet flower.

chapéu-de-sol s. m. (pl. **chapéus-de-sol**) 1. sunshade, umbrella. 2. (fig.) protection, defence. 3. (bot.) Malabar almond.

chapéu-velho s. m. (pl. **chapéus-velhos**), (pop.) reheated, stale coffee.

chapeuzinho s. m. 1. dim. form of **chapéu**. 2. circumflex accent.

chapim s. m. (pl. -ins) 1. a kind of lady's slippers. 2 a high-soled half-boot. 3. skate. 4. steel-plates forming a connecting passageway between railway cars. 5. (fig.) basis, base plate, pedestal (of a column). 6. base plate of an iron column. 7. an elegant shoe of a lady. 8. (ornith.): a) titmouse, tomtit. b) coalmouse. c) nun. d) bluebonnet, blue-cap.

chapineiro s. m. a manufacturer or vendor of slippers.

chapinhar v. 1. to plash, splash. 2. to paddle, dabble. 3. to beat water with hands or feet. 4. to slap water with the hand. 5. to wade in water.

chapista s. m. + f. (typogr.) platemaker.

chapo adj. 1. common, low, ordinary. 2. vulgar. 3. obstrusive. 4. conspicuous, showy.

chapota s. f. act of pruning.

chapotar, chapodar v. 1. to prune (plants). 2. to cut off.

chapriz s. f. a lady's slipper or half-boot.

chapuz s. m. 1. a piece of wood fixed in the wall (to hold nails). 2. wooden peg, dowel. 3. cleat. 4. (mech.): a) bearing, pillow-block. b) rail cradle. 5. wooden wedge. **de** ~ with the head downwards.

chapuzar v. 1. to throw s. o. into the water head foremost. 2. to take a header. 3. to place with the head downwards. 4. to crouch, squat.

chara s. f. (Orient) habit, manner of living, custom.

charada s. f. 1. charades. 2. riddle, conundrum. 3. (fig.) problem. 4. phrase or conversation of unintelligible meaning. 5. (Braz., pop.) allusion, hint, sarcastic remark. ~ **casal** a riddle having two part solutions that end with the letters a and o. ~ **invertida** a riddle having two part solutions, one being the inverse of the other. ~ **novíssima** a riddle with two or more part solutions that when put together give the final solution. ~ **tônica** a riddle with two key solutions having the same letter composition but with different pronunciation.

charadismo s. m. 1. special fondness for charades and their solution. 2. elaboration of charades.

charadista s. m. + f. charadist: one who composes or likes to solve charades. || adj. charadistic(al).

charamba s. f. (Azores) a popular folk dance.

charamela s. f. (mus.) shawn, a kind of oboe.

charameleiro s. m. (mus.) a shawn player.

charanga s. f. 1. a small music band. 2. brass band, band. 3. (mus.) flourish.

charangueiro s. m. player of a brass band, bugler.

charão s. m. (pl. -ões) 1. lac-varnish, Chinese lacquer. 2. any object painted with Chinese lacquer. 3. (bot.) sumac, sumach (Rhus succedanea). 4. japan lac.

charco s. m. 1. dirty, stagnant water. 2. bog, mire, slough. 3. pool, moor. 4. quag, marsh, everglade. **isto é chapejar no** ~ that's labour in vain.

charcoso adj. stagnant, marshy, swampy.

charcutaria charcuteria s. f. 1. delicatessen shop, sausage shop. 2. meat chop. 3. sausage factory.

charcuteiro s. m. sausage maker or dealer, pork-butcher.

charivari s. m. confusion, disorder, tumult.

charla s. f. empty talk, prattle.

charlador s. m. endless talker, prattler, chatterbox. || adj. prattling, garrulous.

charlar v. 1. to chatter, talk thoughtlessly. 2. to prattle, jabber, prate. 3. to gossip.

charlata s. m. (fam.) charlatan, false pretender, quack.

charlatanaria s. f. 1. behaviour and mannerisms of a charlatan. 2. charlatanism, charlatanry. 3. quackery. 4. cheating, fraud, imposture.

charlatanear v. 1. to behave or act like a charlatan. 2. to double talk, illude. 3. to cheat, dupe, mountebank.

charlatanesco adj. charlatanic(al), charlatanistic, charlatanish, quackish, false, illuding. || -**amente** adv. charlatanically.

charlatanice s. f., charlatanismo m. 1. charlatanism, charlatanry. 2. charlatanish act. 3. mountebankery. 4. imposture.

cahrlatão s. m. (pl. -ões) (f. -ona) 1. charlatan. 2. quack, quacksalver, medicaster. 3. mountebank, impostor. 4. boaster, braggart. 5. pettifogger. 6. faker, swindler, cheat.

charlateira s. f. (mil.) a kind of epaulettes.

charlote s. m. a kind of handwoven and embroidered shoe for ladies.

charme s. m. charm.

charminho s. m. used in the locution fazer ~ to act with pretense charm.

charmoso adj. (Braz., fam.) charming.

charneca s. f. 1. large area of barren land. 2. heath, fell. 3. (bot.) Guinea pepper, redpepper.

charneira s. f. 1. joint. 2. hinge, folding-joint (plate M 3). 3. sphincter muscle of a shellfish or clam. 4. short strap to which a shoe-buckle is sewn.

charola s. f. 1. a bier to carry images or statues in procession. 2. niche in a churchwall for the statues of saints. 3. semi-circular passageway in a church.
levar em ~ to carry on one's shoulders (in order to demonstrate high regard or esteem).

charpa s. f. scarf, sash.

charque s. m. salted and dried meat, jerked beef, junk.

charqueação s. f. (pl. -ões) act or process of jerking (beef).

charqueada s. f. place or farm where jerked beef is made.
fazer ~ (pop.) to defeat utterly an opponent (at play, contest, sports).

charqueador s. m. manufacturer of jerked beef.

charquear v. to salt and dry meat, jerk.

charque-de-vento s. m. (pl. charques-de-vento), (Braz.) jerked beef made from thin, slightly salted, wind--dried slices of meat.

charqueio s. m. act or process of jerking (beef).

charqueiro s. m. 1. dirty, stagnant water. 2. bog, mire, slough. 3. quag, marsh, swamp.

charrasca s. f. (ornith.) brak-cap.

charravascal s. m. (pl. -ais) a nearly impenetrable thicket.

charrete s. f. a light two-wheeled cart, drawn by a horse.

charro adj. 1. rustic. 2. coarse. 3. ill-bred, awkward.

charrua s. f. 1. plough, moldboard, plough (plate C 13). 2. draining plough. 3. (fig.) agriculture. 4. (ant.) a large freight vessel. 5. a plant of the daisy family (Eupatorium macrophyllum).
puxar pela ~ to work very hard.

charruada s. f. a plowed field.

charruar v. to break up the soil with a plough: to plough, till the land.

charutaria s. f. cigar shop, tobacco shop.

charutear v. to smoke a cigar.

charuteira s. f. cigar case.

charuteiro s. m. 1. cigar maker, cigar manufacturer. 2. proprietor or salesman of a cigar shop.

charuto s. m. 1. cigar, cheroot, stogy (plate F 7). 2. a cigar-shaped cake. 3. a fermented drink of honey and wine.

chasco (I) s. m. 1. witty saying or remark. 2. mockery, derision. 3. flout, fleer.

chasco (II) s. m. act of pulling suddenly the reins in.

chasco (III) s. m. (ornith.) whinchat.

chasque s. m. 1. messenger, courier, dispatch-rider. 2. deliveryman. 3. private messenger.

chasqueador s. m. mocker, scoffer, teaser, banterer. || adj. scoffing, mocking, bantering, teasing.

chasquear v. 1. to joke, jest. 2. to banter. 3. to poke fun at. 4. to scoff, jeer. 5. to fool.

chasqueiro adj. tossing (said of a certain disagreeable gait of horses).

chasquento adj. 1. jolly, funny. 2. nice, beautiful. 3. interesting. 4. well-dressed, well-groomed.

chassi s. m. (mech., tech.) chassis, frame, body (plates B 15, V 3).

chata (I) s. f. (naut.) flatboat, lighter, barge (plate P 16).

chata (II) s. f. (hist.) funeral repast.

chatada s. f. 1. a disagreeable answer or remark. 2. a gruff allusion. 3. reprimand, censure.

chateação s. f. (pl. -ões) 1. act of annoying or bothering. 2. importunity, molestation. 3. bother.

chatear v. 1. to annoy, importune. 2. to bother, molest. 3. to plague, pester. 4. to crouch, squat.

chateza, chatice s. f. 1. flatness. 2. lowness, meanness. 3. (fig.) shallowness, platitude. 4. coarseness, rudeness.

chatim s. m. (pl. -ins) 1. a crooked dealer. 2. swindler, crook.

chatinar v. 1. to deal without consideration or crookedly. 2. to deceive, swindle, cheat. 3. to traffic. 4. to buy, purchase. 5. to bribe, suborn.

chato s. m. (zool.) crablouse. || adj. 1. smooth. 2. even, flat, plain (plate L 3). 3. (pop.) importunate, troublesome, annoying. 4. obtrusive. 5. (fig.) vulgar, low, creeping. 6. dull, dusty, trite, shallow.
ele tem um nariz ~ he is flat-nosed. que trabalho ~ what a dull and boring job. pé ~ flat foot.

chatobriã s. m. a thick loin steak.

chauã s. m. (Braz.) a parrot of the genus Amazona (A. rhodocorytha).

chauvinismo s. m. chauvinism, exaggerated patriotism; jingoism.

chauvinista s. m. + f. chauvinist. || adj. chauvinistic(al.)

chavão s. m. (pl. -ões) a large key. 2. cakemould. 3. model, pattern. 4. formule. 5. (coll.) cliché, platitude. 6. (fam.) authoritative personality or book.

chavaria s. f. a lot of keys, collection of keys.

chavascada s. f. 1. blow, stroke. 2. lashing with a whip, whipping.

chavascado adj. coarse, rough, rude, clumsy.

chavascal s. m. (pl. -ais) 1. a dirty place or room. 2. pigsty. 3. barren soil. 4. a nearly impenetrable thicket. 5. bushland, heath.

chavascar v. 1. to bungle, botch. 2. to make in a crude or imperfect manner. 3. to tinker.

chavasco adj. rough. coarse, crude, bungled, imperfect.

chavasqueiro s. m. = chavascal. || adj. 1. uncouth, uncivil, impolite. 2. rough, coarse.

chavasquice s. f. 1. rudeness, impoliteness. 2. coarseness, crudeness. 3. imperfect or clumsy work, botch, bungle.

chave s. f. 1. key (plates C 6, F 1). 2. wrench, spanner. 3. any tool for opening, tightening, closing, mounting or dismounting. 4. lever of brass instruments or keyboard instruments. 5. watch or clock key. 6. (mus.) stop, stopping. 7. (mus.) keynote. 8. electric switch (plates B 15, E 3, M 5). 9 (mil.) strategic position, key-position. 10. clue, solution, explication. 11. symbol of authority. 12. (archit.) keystone, closer (plates A 7, 12). 13. (mus., typogr.) brace. 14 (poet.) climax or envoy of a poem. 15. peg, dowel. 16. the palm of the hand. 17. width of the sole of the foot. 18. (typogr.) bracket. 19. control. 20. key of a cypher. 21. the crucial point of a problem. 22. (zool.) a mollusc of the family Cipraedidae (Ciprea exanthema).
~ combinada de boca fixa e boca fechada (tech.) combination open-end and box-end wrench. ~ comutadora (electr.) change-over switch. ~ da abó-

bada (archit.) arch-stone, keystone. ~ de alavanca (electr.) tumbler switch. ~ de boca coach-wrench, screw-key, open-ended spanner (plate C 13). ~ de boca fechada box-end wrench, double-ended nut spanner (plate P 4). ~ de botão button-switch (plate M 5). ~ de cachimbo, ~ de caixa socket wrench, socket spanner, box wrench, box spanner (plate P 4). ~ de comando control lever, controller. ~ de escrita secreta cypher-code, cypher-key. ~ de fenda screw-driver, turn-screw (plates F 1, M 4, P 4). ~ de ignição spark lever, ignition key. ~ de inversão (tech.) double-throw switch. ~ de parafuso screw key, wrench, spanner (plate F 1). ~ de partida starter. ~ de pulso (wrestling) wristlock. ~ de roda wheel bolt wrench. ~ de trinco latch-key. ~ de tubos pipe wrench. ~ eletrônica electronic switch. ~ em trilhos rail switch. ~ faca (railway) knife switch. ~ falsa skeleton key, double key. ~ geral (electr.) house main switch (plate E 3). ~ inglesa screw wrench, adjustable wrench, monkey wrench, king-dick (plate P 4). ~ mestra passkey, passepartout, master-key. agulha de ~ (railway) points. debaixo de ~ under lock and key. fechar a sete ~s to put under lock and key. fechar com ~ de ouro to bring to a good end. isto é a ~ do mistério this is the key of the mystery. sem ~ keyless. sinal de ~ (railway) switch signal. ter a ~ na mão to be the master of, have the power of the keys. um molho de ~s a bunch of keys.

chavear v. to lock with a key.

chaveira s. f. (vet.) measles of domestic animals, scab.

craveirão s. m. (pl. -ões) 1. a large key. 2. (her.) chevron.

chaveirento adj. (vet.) suffering from measles (animals).

chaveiro (I) s. m. 1. key keeper. 2. doorman. 3. key rack. 4. jailkeeper, jailer. 5. butler, steward. 6. key maker, locksmith.

chaveiro (II) s. m. a pair of wheels on the same axle-tree.

chaveiroso adj. (vet.) suffering from measles, scabby.

chavelha s. f. 1. peg, pin. 2. dowel, plug. 3. beam of a plough or carriage.

chavelhão s. m. (pl. -ões) 1. iron pole-pin. 2. iron axle-pin of a plough.

chavelho s. m. 1. horn. 2. feeler (of an insect). 3. tentacle.

chávena s. f. tea-cup, cup.

chaveta (ê) s. f. 1. axle-pin, pin, peg. 2. lichpin. 3. key, slot key. 4. cotter. 5. forelock. 6. chock. 7. hinge pin. 8. (typogr.) bracket, brace.
~ chata (tech.) flat key. ~ dobrada (tech.) cotter pin.

chavetar v. 1. to fasten or secure with a cotter. 2. to introduce a pin into.

chaviano s. m. native or inhabitant of Chaves (town and health resort in Portugal). ‖ adj. 1. of or relative to the town of Chaves. 2. designative of a certain kind of black pudding.

chavo s. m. 1. farthing. 2. any small coin. 3. little value.

chazeiro (I) s. m. the sideboards of a cart or wagon.

chazeiro (II) s. m. tea lover, tea friend. ‖ adj. tea loving, fond of tea.

ché (I) s. f. (mus.) a Chinese lyre.

ché, chê interj. dont't tell me!, hooey, nonsense! como vai, chê! hello, how are you!

checador s. m. checker, verifier.

checar v. (Braz.) to write out a cheque.

cheda s. f. the sideboards of a cart or wagon.

chefão s. m. (pl. -ões) 1. political leader, boss. 2. top manager, top dog. 3. (hum.) panjandrum, big shot.

chefatura s. f. chieftaincy, chieftainship, headquarters.

chefe s. m. + f. 1. chief, principal. 2. leader, commander, commandress. 3. manager, director, boss. 4. headman, head, master. 5. captain, conductor. 6. authority. 7. (pop.) a chummy form of address to strangers (whose name is unknown). 8. provost. 9. standard bearer. 10. ~s pl. betters. 11. top-dog, big shot.
~ de divisão a division commander. ~ de escritório head clerk. ~ de estrada de ferro station-master. ~ de família the head of the family, householder. ~ de seção (com.) department head. ~ de serviço works manager. ~ de trem conductor. ~ de tribo chief, chieftain, cacique, elder. ~ de um pelotão (mil.) section leader. ~ supremo overlord, paramount.

chefete s. m. (depr.) straw boss.

chefia s. f. 1. leadership, managership. 2. chieftaincy, chieftainship. 3. office or authority of a manager. 4. leadership, command.

chefiar v. 1. to direct, manage. 2. to govern. 3. to be boss, chief, manager or master. 4. to head, command, lead.

chega (I) s. m. + f. (Port. usually f.), (fam.) censure, reprimand, rebuke, upbraiding.

chega (II) s. f. (ant., jur.) citation, letter of citation (to recover a debt).

chega (III) interj. that's enough!, stop that!, enough!.

chegada s. f. 1. act of coming or approaching. 2. arrival. 3. (sports) home, homestretch. 4. approximation, approach. 5. coming, incoming, landing. 6. advent, forthcoming.
linha de ~ home stretch. marco da ~ winning post, betting post.

chegadeira s. f. a blacksmith's coal shovel, fire-tongs.

chegadela s. f. 1. approximation, approach. 2. sudden arrival. 3. censure, reprimand, rebuke. 4. flogging, thrashing.

chegadiço s. m. (ant.) 1. a foreigner, person who comes from abroad. 2. intrusive or meddlesome person. ‖ adj. 1. adventitious, foreign. 2. meddlesome, intrusive.

chegadinha s. f. a medicinal plant of the mint family (Aeolanthus suavis).

chegado adj. (also p. p. of chegar) 1. near, close, intimate. 2. proximate, not distant. 3. propense. 4. allied. 5. arrived, landed. 6. prone to, fond of. eles são muito chegados a brincadeiras they are very fond of jests.

chegador s. m. 1. comer, new-comer, foreigner. 2. stoker, fireman. 3. rent or tax collector. ‖ adj. (S. Braz., pop.) bold, courageous, aggressive.

chega-e-vira s. f., sg. + pl. (ornith.) widow duck.

chegamento s. m. 1. act or process of coming. 2. arrival, landing, coming. 3. approaching. 4. (obs., jur.) letter of citation, citation.

chegança s. f. 1. (ant.) = chegamento. 2. (hist.) formerly an erotic dance. 3. (Braz.) popular Christmas festivities and merrymaking, public folk plays with historical background. 4. ~s pl. carols and popular songs offered to neighbours and friends by merrymakers (at Christmas and Epiphany).

cheganço s. m. 1. (pop.) censure, reprimand, rebuke. 2. (billiards) a backspin stroke with the cue.

chegar v. 1. to come, arrive. 2. to reach a certain place. 3. to begin, start. 4. to move toward, approach, approximate. 5. to border. 6. to be enough, suffice. 7. to attain. 8. to come close to, bring or transport near to. 9. to match, be equal to. 10. to conclude. 11. to fetch. 12. to enter. 13. to amount to. 14. ~-se: a) to approach, draw nearer. b) to adjust o. s. to. c) to resign o. s. to. ~ a casa to reach home. ~ a entender to get the hang of, begin to understand. ~ a fazer fortuna to come into property. ~am às vias de fato they came to blows. ~ à meta final to get home. ~ ao fim to draw to its close. ~ ao ponto de afirmar to go so far as to say. ~ a uma conclusão to reach a conclusion. ~ a um acordo to come to terms. ~ a um fim to terminate. ~ a um impasse to come to a stand. ~ a um ponto morto to come to a deadlock. ~ à vista to come into sight. ~ inesperadamente to drop in. ~ tarde to be late. chega para hoje! let's call it a day. chegamos a falar sobre isto we got to talking about it. cheguemos ao assunto! let's get on to business. como você chegou a saber isto? how came you to know this? ela chegou a crê-lo she came to believe it. ela chegou finalmente she has turned up at last. ele chegou a professor he rose to be professor. ele não me chega aos calcanhares he is no match for me. eles ~am a ser amigos they got to be friends. isto chega em boa hora that comes in useful. isto chega para uma semana that will last me a week. isto não chega that will not do, that will not be sufficient. não chega a ser satisfatório it is short of satisfactory. aonde você quer ~? where do you aim at? os conservadores chegam ao poder the conservatives come in. o trem deve ~ às oito horas the train is due at eight o'clock. o verão chegou summer is in. uma desgraça nunca chega só it never rains but pours.

cheia s. f. 1. inundation, flood. 2. overflowing, flow. 3. freshet. 4. full of the moon. 5. abundance.

cheio s. m. the dried leaves of marijuana. ‖ adj. 1. full, filled up (plate Q). 2. replete, crammed. 3. ample, big. 4. massive, dense. 5. pregnant. 6. crowded, packed. 7. round, rotund. 8. stout, fat, full bodied. 9. copious, plentiful, abundant. 10. not interrupted (line). 11. generous, rich. 12. (sl.) drunk. 13. busy, overburdened (with work). 14. happy. 15. well-fed, saturate. 16. large, broad. ~ até a borda brimmed, top-full. ~ de água watery. ~ de ar inflated. ~ de arbustos bushy. ~ de caprichos whimsical. ~ de ervas daninhas weedy. ~ de fé em que... possessed with the faith that... ~ de flores blooming, blossomy. ~ de idéias full of ideas, planful. ~ de luz suffused with light. ~ demais overfull. ~ de restolhos stubby. ~ de si inflated. ~ de terror terror--stricken. ~ de vida lively, full of beans. a lua cheia the full moon. a lua está cheia the moon is at the full. a rua está cheia de gente the street is crowded with people. a rua está cheia de poeira the street is thick with dust. completamente ~ chock-full, choke-full. de rosto ~ full--faced. ela está cheia de si she fancies herself. ele está ~ de serviço his work is cut out for him. ele me atingiu em ~ na vista he hit me full in the eye. estar ~ até a borda to be full to the brim. estar ~ (sl.) to be fed up to the teeth. o livro está ~ de erros the book is full of mistakes. quando o coração está ~, transborda a boca out of the abundance of the heart the mouth speaketh. ser ~ de to abound with (in). uma cesta cheia de maçãs a basket full with apples.

cheira-cheira s. m. (Braz., sl.) a meddlesome or inquisitive person.

cheiradeira s. f. snuff-box.

cheirador s. m. 1. smeller. 2. professional smeller, perfume smeller. 3. (fig.) a prying or inquisitive person.

cheirante adj. m. + f. 1. smelly. 2. fragrant, odoriferous.

cheirar v. 1. to smell, sniff. 2. to snuff, snuffle. 3. to scent. 4. to search into, investigate. 5. to nose out, detect. 6. to suspect. 7. (fig.) to guess, conjecture. 8. to perfume, make fragrant. 9. to pry, snoop. 10. to give pleasure, try to please. ~ de to flavour of. ~ o perigo to smell a rat. ~ uma flor to smell a flower. ele o cheirou he sniffed at it. está cheirando agradavelmente a it is fragrant with. este negócio não cheira bem that business is somewhat fishy. este quarto cheira mal this room is fetid. não posso nem ~ aquilo I can't even stand the sight of it.

cheiro s. m. 1. smell. 2. scent, odour. 3. perfume, frangrance, aroma. 4. clue, trace, vestige. 5. fame. 6. ~s pl.: a) perfumes, aromatic essences. b) herbs, spices. 8. suspicion. 9. whiff. 10. stench. ~ desagradável reek. ~ de peixe fishiness. ervilha de ~ (bot.) sweet-pea. frasco de ~ smelling bottle. mau ~ fetidness, stink, rammishness, stench. sem ~ inodorous.

cheiros s. m. pl. 1. aromatic essences. 2. green spices.

cheiroso adj. 1. smelly. 2. fragrant, odoriferous. 3. savoury. 4. flavourous, scented, redolent.

cheiro-verde s. m. (pl. cheiros-verdes) (Braz.) = cheiros 2.

chela s. m. (India) chela, Buddhist novice.

chelpa s. f. (sl.) money.

chepe-chepe s. m. (pl. chepe-chepes) swampy or soggy ground.

cheque s. m. cheque, bank cheque (U. S. A. = check). ~ ao portador (com.) bearer-cheque. ~ cruzado crossed cheque. ~ de compensação transfer ticket. ~ de viagem traveller's cheque. ~ em branco blank cheque. ~ sem fundo (com. sl.) stumer.

cheque-ouro s. m. (pl. cheques-ouro) (Braz.) a especial cheque that is also payable in overdraft up to a fixed amount.

chercônia s. f. (India) circassian, an Indian silk and cotton fabric.

cherimólia s. f. (bot.) cherimoya.

cherna s. f., cherne, chernote m. (ichth.) black grouper, black jewfish.

cherne-vermelho s. m. (pl. chernes-vermelhos), (ichth.) red snapper.

cheta s. f. (sl.) 1. small copper coin. 2. farthing.

cheviote s. m. cheviot, English cotton or wool fabric.

chiada s. f. 1. act of hissing or squeaking. 2. chirping. 3. creak, squeak. 4. hiss. 5. shrill disagreeable sound.

chiadeira s. f. 1. squeaking, creaking, screaking, fizzle. 2. clamour, din, uproar. 3. impertinent question or complaint.

chiado s. m. shrill sound, squeaking, screaking. ‖ adj. 1. sly, cunning. 2. malicious. 3. squeaky.

chiar v. 1. to creak, squeak. 2. to shriek, make a shrill noise. 3. to hiss, siss, sizzle, fizzle. 4. to screech. 5. to peep, chirp.

chiata s. f. 1. jest, joke. 2. quip. 3. prank.

chiatar v. to play jokes, jest, banter.

chiba (I) s. f. young goat, kid.

chiba (II) s. f. (Port., prov.) boasting, bragging.

chiba (III) s. f. blister on a hand (not accustomed to hard work).

chibamba s. m. (Braz., folklore) imp, hobgoblin.

chibanca s. f. root breaker, root cutter, root mattock.

cribança s. f. 1. haughtiness. 2. boasting, bragging.

chibantaria s. f. boast, act of bragging, vaingloriousness.

chibante s. m. 1. braggart, boaster. 2. (ornith.) a cotingilid bird (Tijuca atra). ‖ adj. m. + f. 1. bragging, boasting, vainglorious. 2. foppish.

chibantear v. to brag, boast, swagger.

chibantesco adj. bragging, boastful, vainglorious.

chibantice s. f., **chibantismo** m. 1. haughtiness. 2. boastful act or saying.

chibar v. to brag, boast, swagger.

chibarrada s. f. a small flock of goats.

chibarreiro s. m. goatherd

chibarro (I) s. m. a young, castrated he-goat.

chibarro (II) s. m. (zool.) vinegar eel.

chibata s. f. rush, stick, rod, cane.

chibatada s. f. a blow with a cane.

chibatão s. m. (N. Braz.) a large tree of the family Anacardiaceae (Astronium fraxinifolium).

chibatar, chibatear v. to cane, whip, punish with a cane, flog.

chibateiro s. m. vulgar, low, common.

chibato s. m. kid (he-goat from six to twelve months old).

chibé s. m. a refreshing drink of manioc flour, water and sugar.

chibo s. m. young buck not yet one year old.

chica s. f. 1. a Negro dance. 2. a strong alcoholic drink flavoured with herbs. 3. a cigarette butt.

chicana s. f. 1. chicane, chicanery. 2. intrigue, stratagem. 3. subterfuge. 4. sophistic reasoning, pettifoggery.

chicanar, chicanear v. to chicane, use chicanery, quibble over, pettifog.

chicaneiro s. m. chicaner, pettifogger, trickster, sharper. ‖ adj. tricky, pettifogging, deceitful.

chicanice s. f. chicane, chicanery, pettifoggery.

chicanista s. m. + f. chicaner, pettifogger. ‖ adj. pettifogging.

chicante adj. m. + f. well-dressed, elegant.

chicarola s. f. (bot.) prickly lettuce.

chicha s. f. 1. meat. 2. tidbit. 3. (students' sl.) interlinear translation. 4. note, annotation. 5. chicha: a fermented liquor made from maize, nuts, honey and other ingredients.

chícharo s. m. (bot.) chick-pea, chickling.

chicharro s. m. (ichth.) a saurel.

chicharro-pintado s. m. (pl. **chicharros-pintados**) (ichth.) round scad, cigarfish (Decapterus punctatus).

chichelo s. m. old and outworn house slipper.

chichiar v. to squeak, creak.

chichisbéu s. m. cicisbeo, an importunate suitor.

chicle s. m. 1. plant of the dogbane family (Zschokkea latescens). 2. chewing gum, chicle.

chiclete s. m. chewing gum.

chico s. m. 1. **Chico**: a nickname for Francisco. 2. petname applied to domestic monkeys. 3. a suckling pig, young pig. 4. (Braz., pop.) menses.

chico-da-ronda s. f. (pl. **chicos-da-ronda**) a kind of fandango.

chicolerê s. m. (pl. **chicolerês**), (ornith.) puffbird.

chico-preto s. m. (pl. **chicos-pretos**), (ornith.) a grackle.

chicória s. f. (bot.) endive, chicory.

chicotada s. f., **chicotaço** m. a stroke with a whip, lashing, whip-lash, flogging, cut, flick.

chicotar, chicotear v. to whip, lash, flog, spank, scourge.

chicote s. m. 1. whip, horsewhip, lash (plate R 7). 2. (naut.) end of a rope or cable. 3. pigtail, tress.
~ **de couro cru** rawhide whip.

chicote-queimado s. m. (pl. **chicotes-queimados**) (Braz.) a juvenile sport played with a catcher.

chicuta s. f. (pop.) baby, little child.

chidova s. m. (ichth.) a caribe (Serrasalmus undulatus).

chifarote s. m. a short, straight sword.

chifra s. f. an iron scraper, smoothing iron (for leatherdressing, book-binding).

chifrada s. f., **chifraço** m. a thrust with the horns.

chifradeira s. f. a leather strap bound on the horns by which two oxen are joined for working together.

chifrar (I) v. to scrape, rasp, make smooth (raw hides, leather).

chifrar (II) v. to attack with horns, gore with horns, horn.

chifre s. m. horns of an animal, horn (plates C 17, G 1).
~ **de bigorna** beak, horn (plate B 12). ~ **de carneiro** ram's horn. **cabo de** ~ handle of horn. **ele é do** ~ **furado** (pop.) he is a daring fellow.

chifre-de-boi s. m. (pl. **chifres-de-boi**), (Braz., min.) fibrolite.

chifre-de-cabra s. m. (pl. **chifres-de-cabra**), (Braz., pop.) 1. a stingy person, miser. 2. worthless fellow, good-for-nothing.

chifre-de-veado s. m. (pl. **chifres-de-veado**), (bot.) unicorn plant, devil's-claw.

chifre-furado s. m. (pl. **chifres-furados**), (pop.) an entirely trustworthy or reliable matter or affair.

chifrudo s. m. (pop.) cuckold. ‖ adj. having big horns.

chila (I) s. f. (bot.) Malabar gourd.

chila (II) s. f. plain English cotton fabric, chintz.

chilenas s. f. pl. (Braz., pop.) very long spurs.

chileno s. m. 1. Chilean: native or inhabitant of Chile. 2. (S. Braz.) a crossbreed of cattle. ‖ adj. Chilean.

chilido s. m. peep, chirp, a peeping sound.

chilindrão s. m. a sort of a card game.

chilique s. m. (pop.) 1. faint, swoon. 2. fit, seizure. 3. nervous breakdown. 4. (med.) syncope.

chilrada, chilreada s. f. 1. chirping, twittering. 2. chatter.

chilrão s. m. (pl. **-ões**) shrimp net.

chilrar, chilrear v. 1. to chirp, twitter, chirrup. 2. to warble. 3. to chatter, babble. 4. (fig.) to sing.

chilreador s. m. 1. chirping or warbling bird. 2. (fig.) chatterbox, blabbermouth, prattler. ‖ adj. (also **chilreiro**) chirping, warbling, (fig.) prattling.

chilreante adj. m. + f. chirping, warbling.

chilreio, chilro s. m. 1. act of chirping, chirp. 2. warbling, twitter. 3. peep, cheep.

chilro adj. 1. unseasoned. 2. stale, flat, insipid. 3. insignificant, unimportant. 4. worthless.

chim s. m. (pl. **chins**), (sl.) Chinese. ‖ adj. Chinese.

chimango s. m. (ornith.) chimango.

chimarrão s. m. 1. maté, tea, coffee or any other hot beverage served without sugar. 2. roving wild cattle. 3. stray dog. ‖ adj. 1. unsweetened (hot beverage). 2. straying and growing wild (domestic animals).

chimarrear v. (S. Braz.) to drink hot, unsugared maté.

chimarrita s. f. (S. Braz.) 1. a popular dance. 2. the accompanying music and songs.

chimarronear v. (S. Braz.) to drink hot, unsugared maté.

chimbear v. to loaf, bum around, loiter.

chimpanzé s. m. (zool.) chimpanzee.

chimpar v. 1. to deal a blow, slap, strike. 2. ~-**se** to sit down, rest, settle o. s.

china (I) s. m. + f. Chinese: native or inhabitant of China.

china (II) s. f. (Braz.) 1. Indian woman or girl, squaw. 2. a dark-skinned countrywoman of mixed race. 3. (pop.) a kept woman.

chinarada s. f. a lot or group of native country women.

C 14

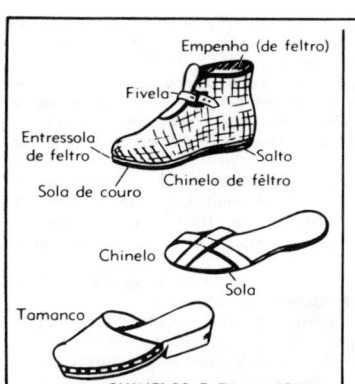

CHINELOS E TAMANCO

COPOS

chincada (I) s. f. 1. act of proving or tasting. 2. enjoyment, use. 3. staggering, lurch.

chincada (II) s. f. 1. indirect rebuke. 2. a coarse allusion.

chincar (I) v. 1. to prove, taste. 2. to enjoy, use up. 3. to make stagger, lurch.

chincar (II) v. 1. to rebuke in a roundabout manner. 2. to make a pointed remark, make a coarse allusion.

chincha s. f. 1. a fishing boat. 2. a small trawling net.

chinchar v. 1. to form in a cheese press. 2. to dry on a rack.

chinchila s. f. 1. (zool.) chinchilla. 2. a misshapen man. 3. name of a certain rabbit breed.

chinchorro s. m. 1. a kind of fishing vessel. 2. trawling net. 3. (fig.) slow, indolent fellow, sluggard. 4. a slow car, boat, animal or person.

chincoã s. m. common name of several birds of the cuckoo family.

chinear v. to lead a profligate life, live in the company of prostitutes.

chineiro s. m. fancy man, bully. ‖ adj. dissolute.

chinela s. f. house slipper.

chinelada s. f. a blow with a slipper.

chineleiro s. m. 1. manufacturer of slippers. 2. a low, common fellow.

chinelo s. m. 1. slipper (plates C. 14, R 6). 2. an old shoe (esp. a shoe run down at the heels). 3. scuff. ~ de feltro carpet-slipper, felt shoe (plate C 14). botar no ~, pôr no ~ (fig.) to surpass a person in s. th.

chinês s. m. (pl. -eses), (f.-esa, pl. -esas) Chinese: 1. native or inhabitant of China. 2. the Chinese language. ‖ adj. Chinese. templo ~ joss-house.

chinesice s. f. 1. Chinese behaviour or mannerisms. 2. gewgaws, trinket. 3. trifle, bagatelle. 4. any object made with great skill and special patience.

chinfrão s. m. (pl. -ões) an ancient Portuguese coin (about the value of 14 reis).

chinfreiro adj. (Braz., sl.) which is up-to-date in fashion.

chinfrim s. m. (pl. -ins) 1. racket, row. 2. clamour, din. 3. disorder, confusion. ‖ adj. m. + f. 1. insignificant, trifling. 2. vulgar, low, paltry.

chinfrinada, chinfrineira, chinfrinice s. f. 1. racket, row. 2. clamour, din, uproar. 3. ridiculous thing or matter.

chinfrinar v. 1. to make a racket, clamour. 2. to cause a tumult or disorder. 3. (sl.) to poke fun

at, deride, ridicule. 4. to provoke. 5. to agitate, disturb. 6. to exasperate.

chinguiço s. m. cloth pad placed under a pole or any other object carried on the shoulders.

chininha s. f. (Braz.) a half-bred country girl.

chino s. m. Chinese. ‖ adj. Chinese.

chinó s. m. 1. chignon. 2. wig, peruke, periwig.

chinoca s. f. (Braz.) half-bred country girl.

chinocão s. m. a beautiful caboclo girl.

chinquilho s. m. (pop.) game of quoits.

chio s. m. 1. squeak, squeaking sound. 2. squeal, shriek. 3. shrill wild cry of certain animals. 4. fuse or powder line of a firecracker.

chioba s. m. muttonfish.

chipa s. f. (Braz.) a kind of doughnut made from cornmeal, milk and grated cheese.

chique (I) s. m. insignificant thing, trifling matter. nem ~ nem mique (fam.) nothing at all.

chique (II) adj. m. + f. 1. elegant, well-dressed. 2. beautiful, handsome. 3. smart, chic. 4. cheesy.

chiqueira s. f. (ornith.) terutero, teruteru.

chiqueirá, chiqueirador s. m. horse whip with a short handle.

chiqueirar v. to separate the calves from their mother cows.

chiqueireiro adj. used to sleep in the pen (said of animals).

chiqueiro s. m. 1. pigsty, piggery, pigpen (plate E 11). 2. pen, enclosure. 3. a dirty house. 4. the second basket of a fishgarth (from where the fishes cannot escape any more). 5. a weir, fishgarth. 6. small corral, barnyard. 7. (min.) low dike or dam made around placers.

chiquismo s. m. elegance, stylishness, smartness.

chiquito s. m. baby shoe, children's shoes.

chirca s. f. (Braz., bot.) crabweed.

chircal s. m. (pl. -ais) a plot infested with crabweed.

chirinola s. f. (pop.) 1. confusion, perplexity. 2. uncomprehensible or complicated matter. 3. rigmarole. 4. trick. 5. trap, snare, pitfall.

chiripa s. f. any accidental stroke of luck.

chiripear v. to win by an accidental stroke of luck.

chiripento s. m. (gambling) a lucky chap, player favoured by a fluke. ‖ adj. lucky at gambling.

chirivia s. f. (S. Braz., bot.) parsnip (Pastinaca sativa).

chirriante adj. m. + f. 1. shrill. 2. shrieking. 3. resembling the cry of an owl.

chirriar v. 1. to make a shrill noise, shriek. 2. to hoot (as an owl).

chiru s. m. (f. **chirua**), (Braz.) 1. a South American Indian. 2. caboclo, mestizo. 3. backwoodsman, rustic. || adj. of or relative to a caboclo, rural, rustic.

chispa s. f. 1. spark. 2. a sudden flash of light, sudden glare. 3. (fig.) talent, high mental ability, superior intelligence. 4. (fig.) genius. 5. flake.

chispada s. f. 1. a sudden headlong scamper, a wild running away. 2. a rapid race. 3. rush, stampede.

chispante adj. m. + f. sparkling, fiery.

chispar, chispear v. 1. to sparkle, spark, scintillate. 2. to grow angry, flare up. 3. to scamper headlong away, rush along, spank, whisk.

chispe s. m. 1. the inferior part of the foot. 2. pig's foot, pettitoes.

chiste s. m. 1. jocoseness, jocosity. 2. joke, jest. 3. wit, witty remark. 4. pleasantry. 5. facetiae. 6. quip, wisecrack. 7. prank.

chistoso adj. 1. witty, funny, jocular. 2. facetious, jocose. 3. pleasant. 4. amusing, droll, waggish. 5. clever, ingenious. || **-amente** adv. wittily, facetiously, clever.

chita (I) s. f. (zool.) cheetah.

chita (II) s. f. 1. plain common cotton cloth. 2. calico, chintz. 3. common name of several orchids of the family Oncidium. || adj. white and reddish-brown speckled (cattle).

chitado adj. white and reddish-brown speckled (cattle).

chitão (I) interj. (also **chitom**) keep quiet!, shut up!, silence!, hush!

chitão (II) s. m. printed cotton, chintz.

chitaria s. f. cotton weaving mill, cotton weaving.

choca (I) s. f. 1. stick, mallet (used by boys in a bowling game). 2. bowl, ball.

choca (II) s. f. 1. a big bell. 2. a cowbell. 3. bell cow, leading cow of a herd.

choca (III) s. f. (fam.) smutch or stain on a skirt.

choca (IV) s. f. (ornith.) ant shrike.

choça s. f. hut, hovel, shack, cabin.

~ **de barro** clay hut. ~ **de palha** straw shack.

chocadeira s. f. 1. a broody hen. 2. brooder, hatcher. ~ **elétrica** incubator.

chocagem s. f. (pl. **-ens**) act or process of hatching eggs.

chocalhada s. f. 1. act of jingling, clanging. 2. a lot of little bells. 3. rattling, jingling, tinkling. 4. laughter.

chocalhado adj. 1. agitated, shaken. 2. rattled. 3. stirred up.

chocalhar v. 1. to shake, stir up. 2. to tinkle, produce or emit a series of short clinking notes. 3. to brattle, rattle. 4. to chime, play on musical bells. 5. (mus.) to accompany on chimes. 6. to break out in laughter, guffaw. 7. to let out secrets, blab.

chocalheiro s. m. 1. blabber, blab, telltale. 2. an indiscreet fellow, gossip. 3. busybody, inquisitive or meddlesome person. || adj. 1. babbling, chattering. 2. tinkling, jingling. 3. rattling. 4. inquisitive, meddlesome. 5. indiscreet, gossipy.

chocalhice s. f. 1. indiscretion, gossip. 2. babbling, prattling. 3. inquisitiveness, meddlesomeness.

chocalho s. m. 1. cattle bell, bell. 2. rattle, clapper. 3. gossip, newsmonger, chatterbox. 4. (bot.) yellow lupine. 5. (bot.) rattlebox.

chocante adj. m. + f. shocking, frightful, scandalous.

chocão s. m. (ornith.) an ant shrike (Hypoedaleus guttatus).

chocar (I) v. 1. to collide, strike against, knock against. 2. to run or bump into. 3. to crash into. 4. to dash against, clash. 5. to offend, pique. 6. to hurt, wound. 7. to shock, scandalize. 8. to

startle, stun. 9. to discord, conflict. 10. ~-**se** to become shocked. 11. ~-**se com** to stumble at, fall out with s. o. abruptly.

ele ficou chocado com o comportamento dela he was shocked at (or by) her behaviour. **fiquei seriamente chocado** I got the shock of my life. **o navio chocou-se contra um rochedo** the ship run upon a rock.

chocar (II) v. 1. to hatch, brood. 2. to incubate. 3. to set, sit on. 4. to premeditate, plan, scheme. 5. to intimidate, frighten. 6. (fam., fig.) to think a long time about a matter. 7. to spoil, rot, grow rotten.

chocarrear v. 1. to jest, joke. 2. to poke fun at. 3. to jeer, scoff. 4. to droll.

chocarreiro s. m. jester, joker, scoffer. || adj. droll, jocose, waggish, foolish, scurrilous.

chocarrice s. f. 1. a coarse jest. 2. jeering, scoffing. 3. drollery, buffoonery. 4. waggishness, waggery. 5. fooling.

chocar v. to be or become tasteless, empty or insignificant.

chochice s. f. 1. insipidity, staleness. 2. emptiness. 3. uselessness, futileness. 4. foolishness. 5. rottenness. 6. insignificance. 7. weakness, giddiness.

chochinha s. m. + f. 1. a small, thin and weak person. 2. a fool, a numskull. 3. m. John Doe.

chocho (ô) (I) s. m. smack, loud kiss.

chocho (ô) (II) adj. 1. juiceless, sapless. 2. thoughtless, foolish. 3. without kernel, coreless. 4. dry. 5. rotten. 6. (fig.) empty, hollow. 7. futile, useless. 8. insignificant, worthless. 9. weak, feeble.

choco (ô) (I) s. m. (ichth.) cuttlefish, cuttle.

choco (ô) (II) s. m. 1. brooding, hatching. 2. incubation. 3. period of incubation. 4. sitting or lying upon.

estar de ~, **estar no** ~ (fam.) to be abed.

choco (ô) (III) adj. 1. being hatched. 2. broody. 3. not fresh. 4. tasteless, insipid. 5. addled, spoiled, rotten. 6. vapid, dull. 7. witless, ungraceful. 8. stagnant.

água choca stagnant water. **galinha choca** broody hen.

chocolataria s. f. 1. chocolate factory. 2. chocolate shop.

chocolate s. m. 1. chocolate, cacao. 2. chocolate served as a beverage. 3. the colour of chocolate.

chocolateira s. f. 1. chocolate pot, chocolate kettle. 2. metallic vessel for boiling water. 3. (Braz., sl.) face, head.

chocolateiro s. m. 1. chocolate maker, chocolate manufacturer. 2. chocolate dealer. 3. cacao planter or dealer.

chocorreta s. f. gulp or swallow of wine.

chofer s. m. chauffeur, motorist, driver.

~ **de caminhão** trucker, truckman. ~ **de ônibus** busman, bus driver. ~ **de praça** cab-driver, taxi-man.

chofrada s. f. 1. a sudden blow or shot. 2. random shot, chance-shot.

chofrar v. 1. to give a sudden blow to. 2. to strike unexpectedly. 3. to wound or hurt all of a sudden. 4. to annoy, pester, disappoint. 5. to go to meet, meet halfway. 6. to shoot or throw at random.

chofre (ô) s. m. 1. a sudden blow or stroke. 2. a random shot, chance shot. 3. (billiards) a stroke with the cue.

de ~ suddenly, unexpectedly, unawares.

chofreiro s. m. one who acts all of a sudden; rash or overhasty person, chance or random shooter. || adj. rash, abrupt, overhasty.

choldra s. f. (pop.) 1. a worthless thing. 2. trifle, bauble. 3. riffraff, common people, mob. 4. promiscuous collection of people, crowd. 5. medley, hodgepodge.

choldraboldra s. f. 1. a worthless thing, trifle. 2. confusion, disorder. 3. mob, crowd. 4. medley.

chopa s. f. (typogr.) the metal point of a footstick.

chopada s. f. draught (U. S. A. draft) beer session or party.

chope s. m. 1. draught beer, fresh beer from the barrel. 2. a tropical tree of the family Lecythidaceae (Gustavia longifolia).

chope-duplo s. m. (pl. **chopes-duplos**) a double-sized mug of beer.

choque s. m. 1. collision. 2. crash, clash. 3. impact, concussion. 4. encounter, combat, skirmish, fight. 5. (med.) shock. 6. jolt, jostle. 7. bump. 8. startle. 9. electric shock. 10. conflict. 11. (fig.) dispute, opposition. 12. (fig.) commotion, agitation. ~ **traumático** a traumatic shock. **a perda do emprego foi um grande ~ para ele** the loss of his position was a great shock to him. **à prova de ~** shock-proof. **ele tem de agüentar o ~** he has to bear the brunt of. **entrei em ~ com ele** I came into collision with him. **prova de ~** shock test. **tratamento de ~** (med.) shock therapy. **tropas de ~** (mil.) shock troops.

choqueiro s. m. hen nest, hen house, brooding coop.

choquento (I) adj. 1. hatching, brooding. 2. broody. 3. rotten. 4. weak, feeble. 5. indisposed, out of sorts.

choquento (II) adj. muddled, sullied, dirty, mud--splashed.

choradeira s. f. 1. weeping, wailing. 2. whimpering, whining, crying. 3. a professional mourner (woman), hired weeper. 4. lamentation. 5. (fam.) a tearful request or complaint, jeremiad.

choradinho s. m. (mus.) a slow, mournful folksong and dance.

chorado s. m. (Braz., mus.) plaintive tune, a slow mournful folksong and dance. || adj. 1. mournful, sad. 2. bemoaned, regretted. 3. (mus.) blue, melancholic (tune).

chora-lua s. m. (pl. **chora-luas**), (Braz., ornith.) a goatsucker.

choramingador, choramigador s. m. whimperer, whiner, sniveler. || adj. whimpering, crying, whining.

choramingar, choramigar v. 1. to whimper, whine. 2. to cry, weep. 3. to wail, moan. 4. to bleat. 5. to snivel. 6. to make a tearful request or complaint.

choramingas, choramigas s. m. + f., sg. + pl. whimperer, whiner, sniveler.

choramingueiro, choramigueiro s. m. whimperer, whiner, crybaby. || adj. whimpering, whining, puling.

chorão (I) s. m. (pl. **-ões**) (f. **-ona**) 1. whimperer, whiner. 2. crybaby. 3. sniveler. || adj. whimpering, whining, crying, puling.

chorão (II) s. m. (pl. **-ões**) 1. (bot.) weeping willow, drooping willow. 2. (bot.) beefwood, swamp oak. 3. (ichth.) a freshwater catfish (Trachycoristes galeatus). 4. (ornith.) a large parrot (Amazona pretrei).

chorão-salgueiro s. m. (pl. **chorões-salgueiro**), (bot.) weeping willow (Salix babylonica).

chorar v. 1. to weep, cry. 2. to mourn, bemoan, bewail. 3. to regret, lament. 4. to shed tears. 5. to repent, be sorry for. 6. to snivel, snuffle, sob. 7. to complain tearfully. 8. to exaggerate one's misfortune. ~ **por** to bewail, whine for. ~ **sobre** to bemoan, beweep. **acabar de ~** to leave off mourning. **a criança chorou até pegar no sono** the child cried itself to sleep. **as crianças choram por pão** the children want for bread. **ela chorou bastante** she had a good weep. **ela chorou em vez de rir** she cried instead of laughing. **ela chorou lágrimas**

amargas she wept bitter tears. **ela chorou muito** she cried her eyes out. **ele chorou como uma criança** he wept like a child. **ele riu até ~** he laughed himself to tears. **não adianta ~** crying will not help, it's too late for crying. **quem não chora não mama** you must cry to be helped.

choraria s. f. 1. act of weeping. 2. endless crying or weeping. 3. weeping fit (by one or several persons together).

choro (ô) s. m. 1. act of weeping or crying. 2. sobbing. 3. weep, whine. 4. wail, whimpering. 5. tearfulness. 6. mourning, sorrowing. 7. (mus.) popular musical recital executed by a small orchestra. 8. (mus.) the tunes played at such a recital. ~ **convulsivo** paroxysm of crying. **romper em ~** to burst into tears.

chorolambre s. m. a small catfish (Rhamdia vittata).

chorona s. f. 1. f. of **chorão** (I). 2. big spurs used by horse tamers. || adj. f. tearful, crying, whimpering.

chororó s. m. small waterfall, cascade.

choroso adj. 1. weeping, weepy. 2. tearful, wailful. 3. whimpering, whining, wailing. 4. sobbing, sniveling. 5. in tears. 6. pitiful, touching. || **-amente** adv. weepingly, shedding tears, pityingly, tearfully. **com os olhos ~s** with tears in his (her) eyes. **todo ~** melting in tears.

chorrar v. to gush out, spurt, spout out, spring forth.

chorrilho s. m. 1. series, sequence. 2. a group of very similar persons or things. 3. a rapid, uninterrupted succession of events. 4. rush of words, spate.

chorro (ô) s. m. 1. spouting, gushing out, spurting. 2. rush, impetuous forward movement. 3. spate.

chorudo adj. (pop.) 1. fat, fatty, greasy. 2. succulent, juicy. 3. profitable, lucrative.

chorume s. m. 1. lard, animal fat. 2. grease. 3. (fig.) abundance, opulency. 4. fortune, wealth.

chorumela s. f. thing of little value, trifle, bauble.

chorumento adj. 1. succulent, juicy. 2. wealthy, rich.

choupa s. f. metal point of a spear or goad.

choupal s. m. (pl. **-ais**) a grove of poplar-trees.

choupana s. f. 1. cottage, cabin. 2. hut, hovel. 3. thatched hut, grass shack. 4. cot-house, cot, shanty.

choupaneiro s. m. hut dweller, cottager.

choupo s. m. (bot.) poplar.

choupo-branco s. m. (pl. **choupos-brancos**), (bot.) white poplar, silver poplar, abele.

choupo-preto s. m. (pl. **choupos-pretos**), (bot.) black poplar.

chourém s. m. (pl. **-éns**) a sickly person.

chouriça s. f. 1. = **chouriço**. 2. (student sl.) interlinear translation of a foreign language text.

chouriçada s. f. 1. a great quantity of sausages, a string of sausages. 2. smoking chamber. 3. a blow with a sandbag.

chouriceiro s. m. sausage maker, sausage dealer.

chouriço s. m. 1. sausage, smoked sausage. 2. blood pudding. 3. a long sausagelike bag filled with sand or sawdust (placed against the slit at the foot of a window or door it impedes draughts). 4. a coiled knot of hair (used as a pad in order to increase the height of the hairdo). ~ **de fígado** white pudding.

choutador, choutão adj. (pl. **-es, -ões**) hard-trotting, high-stepping (horse).

choutar, choutear v. to jog along, trot hard (horse).

chouteiro adj. hard-trotting, high-stepping.

chouto s. m. jog, hard trot, jolting gait of a horse.

chovediço adj. 1. rainy, showery. 2. of or pertaining to rain, pluvial. 3. threatening rain.

chovedouro s. m. weather-side, the side from where usually the rain comes.

chove-não-molha s. m., sg. + pl. 1. any affair which does neither go ahead nor fall back. 2. a blasé personality.

chover v. 1. to rain, pour down. 2. (fig.) to fall down. 3. to fall or appear in great quantities. 4. to spill, shed, spatter. 5. to let fall. 6. to storm.

chove muito it's raining hard. ~ **a cântaros** to pour down, rain cats and dogs, rain pitchforks. **~am cartas** the letters came thick and fast. ~ **no molhado** to spend one's time in useless effort, carry coals to Newcastle. ~ **pedras** to hail. **ameaça** ~ it looks like rain. **é ~ no molhado** it is utterly useless. **está num chove e não molha** it is uncertain. **os presentes ~am no meu aniversário** gifts snowed in on my birthday. **quer chova, quer faça sol** rain or shine.

chovido adj. wet or moistened by rain.

chuá s. m. (Braz.) a kind of basket for fruits (made of cipó).

chuça s. f. 1. spear. 2. harpoon. 3. goad. 4. (fam.) lancet.

chuca-chuca s. m. (pl. **chuca-chucas**) a curl made on a lock of hair on the top of a baby's head.

chuçada s. f. blow with a spear or harpoon.

chuçar v. 1. to throw a spear or harpoon. 2. to stab with a lance. 3. to wound with a pike or spear. **ir ~-se a si mesmo** to cause one's own ruin.

chuceiro s. m. lancer, soldier armed with a lance.

chucha s. f. 1. act of suckling. 2. breast, mother's milk. 3. nutriment, nurture, food. 4. titty-bag, sucking bag.

chuchadeira s. f. 1. = **chucha**. 2. (fam.) an unexpected gain or profit, profitable business. 3. mockery.

chuchado adj. 1. sucked. 2. very thin, lean, skinny.

chuchar v. 1. to suck, suckle. 2. to receive s. th. **ficar chuchando no dedo** (pop.) to be disappointed, be frustrated.

chucho s. m. ((Braz.) 1. chill(s), shivering. 2. recurrent fever, ague.

chuchu s. m. 1. (bot.) chayote (Sechium edule). 2. the fruit of this plant. 3. (Braz.) a nickname applied to persons born in Petropolis (State of Rio de Janeiro). 4. (pop.) a sociable fellow. **é caro pra ~** (coll.) it is awfully expensive. **ele tem dinheiro pra ~** he has heaps of money.

chuchurreado adj. (of kisses) smacking, noisy and long drawn out.

chuchurrear v. 1. to sip, drink slowly little by little. 2. to eat or drink with sucking noises. 3. to gurgle.

chuço s. m. spear, dart, goad.

chucrute s. m. sauerkraut.

chué adj. m. + f. 1. insignificant, unimportant, trifling. 2. ordinary, common. 3. mean, evil. 4. poor, paltry. 5. poorly dressed, shabby. 6. (dress) of poor quality.

chufa (I) s. f. 1. mockery, derision. 2. jest, coarse joke. 3. an offensive remark, scoff, quirk. 4. banter. 5. a spicy story or remark.

chufa (II) s. f. 1. a sweetmeat made from the sugared roots of the chufa sedge. 2. a refreshing drink made from the sweet sedge. 3. (bot.) chufa.

chufar v. 1. to poke fun at, mock. 2. to sneer at, scoff. 3. to tell coarse jokes. 4. to treat with ridicule.

chufista s. m. + f. witty fellow, punster, jokist, buffoon. ‖ adj. witty, funny, scoffing, ridiculous.

chula (I) s. f. 1. a popular dance, country dance. 2. the accompanying dance music. 3. vulgar ballad, street song.

chula (II) s. f. (Braz., bot.) mistletoe cactus.

chularia s. f. 1. jocosity, joke, jest. 2. waggery, drollery. 3. a coarse or indecent remark. 4. indecency, vulgarity.

chulé s. m. (vulg.) 1. filth accumulated between unwashed toes. 2. the rank smell of perspiring feet.

chuleado s. m. (Braz.) whipstitch.

chulear v. to stitch, whipstitch.

chuleio s. m. 1. act or result of stitching. 2. stitch, whipstich.

chuleiro s. m. 1. one who plays popular dance tunes. 2. a dancer.

chulepento s. m. a filthy fellow. ‖ adj. filthy, dirty, unclean.

chulice s. f. 1. a coarse or indecent remark. 2. a spicy story. 3. vulgarity, commonness. 4. crude expression.

chulipa (I) s. f. (pop.) a railroad sleeper, crosstie.

chulipa (II) s. f. (pop.) a kick in the pants.

chulismo s. m. coarse, dirty or indecent remark.

chulista s. m. + f. 1. = **chuleiro**. 2. person who tells smutty or indecent stories. 3. nasty, indecent fellow.

chulo adj. 1. coarse, crude. 2. common, vulgar. 3. jesting, joking, funny. 4. smutty, indecent.

chumaçar v. 1. to pad, stuff. 2. to quilt.

chumaceira s. f. 1. a kind of wooden bearing (for the axle-tree of a carriage). 2. a leather strap used to fix the oar in the thole pin. 3. pillow block, plummer block.

chumacete s. m. 1. a small cushion. 2. pad, padding, wad.

chumaço s. m. 1. padding, stuffing. 2. pad, wad. 3. compress. 4. pillow. 5. wooden pillow block, plummer block.

chumbada s. f. 1. a load of shot, buckshot. 2. the wounds caused by the shot pellets. 3. sinker, plumb, weight of lead attached to fishing lines or nets (plate P 9).

chumbado adj. 1. soldered with lead. 2. plugged up or filled out with lead, leaded. 3. wounded (by shot or buckshot). 4. (coll.) tipsy, drunk. 5. (fam.) deeply in love. 6. infected with a contagious disease. 7. sober, weighty. 8. grave, serious. **ele estava ~** (fig.) he was drunk.

chumbador s. m. 1. anchor bolt, jag bolt. 2. workman who anchors bolts with lead or concrete. 3. person who seals with lead.

chumbagem s. f. (pl. **-ens**) 1. act or result of plumbing. 2. anchoring in lead or concrete. 3. act or process of tailing in.

chumbalé s. m. (Braz.) a children's nightgown.

chumbar v. 1. to fasten, fix or plug up with lead, lead. 2. to solder or weld with lead. 3. to wound with shot or buckshot. 4. to tail in, anchor a bolt. 5. to seal with lead. 6. to weigh down with sinkers. 7. (fig.) to fix, fasten firmly. 8. (coll.) to get drunk. 9. to unite, join. 10. to give a leaden or dull gray colour to.

chumbeado adj. (Braz., fig.) drunk.

chumbear v. to wound with buckshot.

chúmbeas s. f. pl. (naut.) a piece of timber used to strengthen a mast or yardarm.

chumbeira s. f. 1. a casting net with sinkers. 2. the sinkers of a net or fishing line. 3. a circular fishing net. 4. a leather container for shot or buckshot.

chumbeiro s. m. 1. a leather container for shot. 2. shot, pellet of lead. 3. (Braz. hist.) contemptuous nickname applied to Portuguese citizens at the time of the independence movement.

chumbinho s. m. 1. (Braz.) nickname applied to Portuguese settlers in Minas Gerais. 2. (fireworks) torpedo. 3. small shot. 4. printing type.

chumbo s. m. 1. lead (chemical symbol Pb). 2. shot, lead pellet. 3. leaden sinker of fishing lines or nets. 4. (fig.) circumspection. 5. any very heavy object. 6. (fam.) intelligence, wit, common sense. ~ de caçar shot. ~ grosso para caça de pêlo buckshot. ~ miúdo small shot, bird shot. ~ para tipografia type-metal. andar com pés de ~ to walk along very heavily and slowly. cor de ~ dove-coloured. fundição de ~ lead-works. minério de ~ lead ore.

chumear v. (naut.) to strengthen with fishes (masts, yards).

chúmeas s. f. pl. (naut.) fishes, fishlike wooden pieces used to strengthen masts or yards.

chumeco s. m. shoemaker, cobbler.

chupa s. f. 1. tree of the family Lecythidaceae (Gustavia speciosa). 2. a peeled orange.

chupa-caldo s. m. (pl. chupa-caldos) 1. pander, procurer, pimp. 2. base flatterer, lickspittle.

chupada s. f. 1. act of sucking. 2. suck, sucking. 3. suction. 4. (Braz., pop.) scold, tongue-lash.

chupadela s. f. suck, sucking, suction.

chupa-dente s. m. (pl. chupa-dentes), (ornith.) ant pipit.

chupado adj. (fam., pop.) very lean, skinny, meager, sucked.

chupador s. m. 1. sucker, one who sucks. 2. proboscis of insects. ‖ adj. sucking.

chupador-de-anta s. m. (pl. chupadores-de-anta), (N. Braz.) an outcrop of native salt, salt lick (frequented by tapirs and other wild animals).

chupadouro s. m. 1. sucking port. 2. sucking tube. 3. pacifier (rubber nipple). 4. constant sucking.

chupadura s. f. 1. act of sucking. 2. suck, sucking. 3. suction.

chupa-flor s. m. (pl. chupa-flores), a hummingbird.

chupa-galhetas s. m., sg. + pl. (Braz.) acolyte, altar boy.

chupa-mel s. m. (pl. chupa-meles, chupa-méis) 1. (bot.) honeysuckle. 2. (ornith.) hummingbird.

chupamento s. m. suck, sucking, suction.

chupança s. f. (Braz., ent.) barber bug.

chupão s. m. (pl. -ões) 1. loud kiss, smack. 2. (f. chupona) sucker, one who sucks. ‖ adj. sucking.

chupa-ovo s. m. (pl. chupa-ovos) 1. common name of two snakes of the genus Spilotes. 2. (ornith.) an ant shrike, ant bird.

chupar v. 1. to suck. 2. to absorb, soak in. 3. to imbibe. 4. (fig.) to profit, gain. 5. to eat, consume. 6. to obtain, get. 7. to achieve, succeed in. 8. (Braz., sl.) to tipple, indulge in hard drinks. ~ o dedo to suck one's thumb. ~ o sangue de alguém (fig.) to suck the blood of s. o.

chuparino s. m. 1. sucker, one who sucks. 2. proboscis of an insect.

chupa-rolha s. m. (pl. chupa-rolhas) drunkard, tippler.

chupa-sangue s. m. (pl. chupa-sangues) 1. (fig.) parasite, bloodsucker. 2. leech, human leech. 3. (ftb.) a lazy or negligent player.

chupeta s. f. 1. sucking tube. 2. sucking bag, titty bag. 3. sucker. 4. (fam.) soother, pacifier. 5. sipping straw. 6. teat. 7. rubber nipple. de ~ delectable, first class. isto é de ~ that's a choice morsel.

chupim s. m. (pl. -ins) 1. man who lets his wife support him. 2. (ornith.) the shiny cowbird. 3. (fig.) sucker.

chupim-do-brejo s. m. (pl. chupins-do-brejo), (ornith.) maize-eater.

chupista s. m. + f. 1. tippler, drunkard. 2. parasite, sponge.

chupita s. f. (Braz., ichth.) a kind of caribe.

chupitar v. 1. to tipple, indulge in hard drinks. 2. to obtain, get. 3. to achieve, succeed in.

churdo s. m. 1. villain. 2. nasty, disagreeable person. ‖ adj. raw, coarse, dirty (said of wool).

churma s. f. 1. the whole crew of a ship. 2. (ant.) the galley-slaves. 3. crowd, throng.

churrascada s. f. 1. barbecue, joint roasted on the spit. 2. assemblage of friends invited to a barbecue.

churrascaria s. f. rotisserie, restaurant specialized in roast meat.

churrasco s. m. barbecue, roasted meat, meat roasted on the spit.

churrasqueada s. f. 1. act of preparing meat for a barbecue. 2. eating and savouring a barbecue.

churrasquear v. 1. to prepare meat for barbecuing. 2. to barbecue, eat roasted meat. 3. to have a sligth repast.

churrasqueira s. f. (Braz.) barbecue (framework).

churrasqueiro s. m. (Braz.) person specialized in barbecue roasting.

churrasquinho s. m. (Braz.) chopped barbecue on a small spit.

churrião s. m. (pl. -ões) a heavy cart.

churro adj. raw, coarse, dirty.

chus adv. not at all, in no wise. não dizer ~ nem bus not to utter one single word, not to retort.

chusma s. f. 1. crew, the whole crew of a ship. 2. (ant.) the slaves of a galley collectivelly. 3. great quantity, a lot, a heap of things. 4. crowd, throng.

chusmado adj. provided with a crew.

chusmar v. to man a ship.

chuta interj. quiet!, shut up!

chutador s. m. (ftb.) kicker, a good soccer player.

chutar v. (ftb.) to kick the ball, boot the ball.

chute s. m. (ftb.) a kick, act of kicking the ball. 2. a kick, a blow with the foot.

chuteira s. f. football boots, football shoes.

chuva s. f. 1. rain, shower. 2. downpour. 3. (fig.) any matter coming forth freely and abundantly. 4. (fig.) great quantity, lots, heaps. 5. (Braz., sl.) drunkenness. 6. s. m. (Braz.) drunkard, tippler. ~ artificial artificial rain. ~ de estrelas meteor shower. ~ de pedra hail. ~ fina drizzle. ~ forte heavy rainfall, rainstorm. ~ miúda a mizzling rain. ~ torrencial torrents of rain. banho de ~ a shower bath. com ~ ou bom tempo in rain or fine weather. ele está na ~ (pop.) he is tipsy. estava ameaçando ~ there was a threat of rain. quanta ~! fine weather for ducks! sem ~ rainless. tempo de ~ rainy weather, rainy season. tomamos ~ we had a wetting.

chuva-criadeira s. f. (pl. chuvas-criadeiras) a steady, lasting drizzle which soaks the soil thoroughly.

chuvada s. f. 1. abundant rain, downpour. 2. rainy weather.

chuva-de-caju s. f. (pl. chuvas-de-caju), (N. Braz.) the first heavy rains (September, October) which further the ripening of the cashew nuts (also called chuva-dos-cajueiros).

chuva-de-ouro s. m. (pl. chuvas-de-ouro), (Braz., bot.) popular name of: 1. the drumstick tree. 2. an orchid (Oncidium flexuosum).

chuva-de-rama, chuva-de-santa-luzia s. f. (Braz.) equinoctial rains.

chuvão s. m. (pl. -ões), chuvarada f. downpour, uninterrupted rain, flood, drencher, soaking rainfall.

chuvirinho s. m. (Braz., ftb.) a kind of pass.

chuveiro s. m. 1. heavy but short rainfall. 2. (fig.) any matter coming forth freely and in rapid succession. 3. a shower-bath nozzle (plate B 3). 4. the shower-bath compartment of a bathroom. 5. the nozzle of a sprinkler. 6. lasting and abundant winter rain.

chuvinha s. f. 1. drizzle, mizzle. 2. scud.

chuviscar v. to drizzle, mizzle, dribble, sprinkle.

chuvisco s. m. 1. fine drizzling rain, mizzle, drizzle, dribble, a sprinkling of rain. 2. scud.

chuvisqueiro s. m. drizzle, mizzle.

chuvoso adj. 1. pluvious, pluviose. 2. rainy, drizzly, showery. 3. moist, wet, watery.

tempo ~ rainy weather. **um dia** ~ a rainy day.

cianamida s. f. (chem.) cyanamide, cyanamid.

cianato s. m. (chem.) cyanate.

cianetação s. f. (chem.) the cyanide process.

cianeto s. m. (chem.) cyanide, prussiate.

~ **de cobre** copper cyanide. ~ **de ferro** ferrocyanide. ~ **de ouro** gold cyanide. ~ **de potássio** potassium cyanide.

ciânico adj. (chem.) cyanic.

cianicórneo adj. (zool.) having blue or blueish antlers or feelers.

cianídrico adj. (chem.) hydrocyanic.

ácido ~ hydrocyanic or prussic acid.

cianípede adj. m. + f. (zool.) having blue feet or paws.

cianirrostro adj. (zool.) having a blue or blueish beak.

cianita s. f. (min.) cyanite, disthene.

ciano s. m. a greenish-blue colour. || adj. greenish--blue.

cianocarpo adj. (bot.) cyanocarpous, having blueish seed kernels.

cianocéfalo adj. (zool.) cyanocephalous.

cianogênico ad. (chem.) cyanogenic.

cianômetro s. m. cyanometer: instrument to measure the intensity of blueness (of a dye, sky).

cianóptero adj. (zool.) having blueish wings or fins.

cianosar v. to look sickly, appear as if affected with cyanosis.

cianose s. f. 1. (min.) cyanose, chalanthite, blue-stone. 2. (med.) cyanosis, cyanopathy.

cianótico adj. (med.) cyanotic.

cianotipia s. f. (phot.) cyanotype.

cianureto s. m. (chem.) cyanide.

cianúria s. f. (med.) the elimination of blue-coloured urine.

cianúrico adj. (chem.) cyanuric.

ácido ~ cyanuric acid.

ciar (I) to row backwards.

ciar (II) v. 1. to be jealous of. 2. to be envious of.

ciateáceas s. f. pl. Cyatheaceae: a family of tropical ferns.

ciateáceo adj. (bot.) cyatheaceous.

ciática s. f. (med.) sciatica, neuralgia of the sciatic nerve.

ciático s. m. (anat.) sciatic nerve. || adj. sciatic, ischiatic.

ciatiforme adj. m. + f. cyathiform, shaped like a cup.

cíato s. m. (hist.) cyathus: 1. a long-handled ladle for filling cups with wine. 2. a liquid measure of about 45 ml. (=0.079 pint).

cia-voga s. f. (naut.) a rotative movement of a boat produced by the rowers, who row forward on one side of the boat and backward on the other.

cibalho s. m. food for wild birds.

cibernética s. f. cybernetics.

cibo s. m. food (esp. for birds).

cibório s. m. (R. C. Church) ciborium, pyx.

cica s. f. acridity, harshness, astringency (as caused by tasting unripe fruit).

cicadáceas s. f. pl. Cycadaceae: a family of tropical gymnospermous plants.

cicadáceo adj. (bot.) cycadaceous.

cicadídeos s. m. pl. (ent.) Cicadidae: the cicada family.

cicatricial adj. m. + f. (pl. -ais) (med.) cicatricial.

cicatrícula s. f. 1. (med.) a small cicatrix, small scar, seam (of a wound). 2. (embriol.) cicatricle, tread, small disc of protoplasm on the egg-yolk. 3. (bot.) the hilum of a seed.

cicatriz s. f. 1. (med.) cicatrix, cicatrice, scar, seam. 2. (fig.) stigma, any psychical mark caused by offense or disgrace. 3. (bot.) a permanent mark on the stem after the fall of a leaf or branch. 4. (fig.) stain, blemish.

cicatrização s. f. (pl. -ões) cicatrization.

cicatrizado adj. 1. scarred, scarry, cicatrized, cicatrizate. 2. (fig.) rescued, saved, cured, healed.

cicatrizante adj. m. + f. cicatrizant, furthering the process of healing.

cicatrizar v. 1. (med.) to cicatrize, scar, heal, skin over. 2. (fig.) to make forget or forget a dolorous experience. 3. ~-se to become closed (a wound).

cicatrizável adj. m. + f. (pl. -áveis) cicatrisive, capable of being healed.

cicerado adj. (typogr.) marked, measured and graded in picas (12 points).

ciceragem s. f. (typogr.) 1. measuring in picas. 2. number of picas.

cícero s. m. (typogr.) 1. pica, a certain size of type (12 points). 2. quad.

cicerone s. m. cicerone, tourist guide.

ciceroniano adj. 1. (hist.) Ciceronian, of, pertaining to or relative to Cicero. 2. (fig.) eloquent, sublime, winged.

ciciar v. 1. to lisp. 2. to whisper, murmur.

cicindelídeos s. m. pl. (ent.) Cicindelidae, the tiger beetle family.

cicio s. m. 1. a lisp, lisping. 2. whisper, murmur. 3. a rustle, sough.

cicioso adj. lisping, murmuring, rustling.

cíclame, ciclâmen s. m. (bot.) cyclamen.

ciclantáceas s. f. pl. Cyclanthaceae: a small family of tropical plants.

ciclantáceo adj. (bot.) cyclanthaceous.

ciclarídeos s. m. pl. (ornith.) Cyclarhidae: a family of passerine birds.

cíclico s. m. (Greek hist.) a cyclic poet. || adj. cyclic(al): 1. of, relative to or being a part of a cycle. 2. (med.) recurrent at definite periods. 3. (chem.) regular (sequence of reactions). 4. (mus.) recurring (said of the fundamental motive of a sonata).

ciclism s. m. (sport) cyclism, art and practice of riding a bicycle.

ciclista s. m. + f. cyclist, bicyclist.

ciclo s. m. cycle: 1. a series of regularly recurrent phenomena. 2. the space of time necessary to complete the cycle of a phenomenon. 3. a series of legends connected with some mythical subject. 4. (bot.) the section between two leaves on the same stem. 5. a long period. 6. (sociol.) the cyclic repetion of cultural or social conditions. 7. (mus.) a song cycle. 8. circle, round.

~ **básico** the preparatory course preceeding the professionalizing courses. ~ **cultural** a grouping of elements that present the same characteristics of culture. ~ **menstrual** the menstrual cycle (menses).

cicloidal adj. m. + f. (pl. -ais) cycloidal, belonging to a cycloid.

ciclóide s. f. 1. (geom.) cycloid, cycloid curve. 2. m. (med.) cyclothymic condition of a patient. || adj. m. + f. (med.) cyclothymic(al).

ciclometria s. f. cyclometry.

ciclométrico adj. cyclometric(al).

ciclone s. m. cyclone, hurricane, twister (U.S.A.).

ciclônico adj. cyclonic(al), typhonic(al).
ciclope s. m. 1. (greek myth.) Cyclops, Cyclopes. 2. (zool.) Cyclops: a genus of minute freshwater crustaceans.
ciclópeo, ciclópico adj. 1. (myth.) Cyclopean. 2. cyclopean. 3. (fig.) one-eyed, gigantic. 4. (archit.) pertaining to a massive type of architecture, consisting of irregular huge blocks of stones.
ciclorama s. f. cyclorama.
ciclostomados s. m. pl. (ichth.) Cyclostomata.
ciclóstomo s. m. cyclostome: a fish of the class Cyclostomata. ‖ adj. cyclostomate.
ciclotimia s. f. (med., psych.) cyclothymia.
ciclotímico adj. (med., psych.) cyclothimic(al), cycloid.
ciclótomo s. m. (surg.) cyclotome.
ciclotron, ciclotrônio s. m. (phys.) cyclotron.
ciconídeas s. f. pl. (ornith.) the Ciconiidae, the stork family.
ciconiforme s. m. 1. a storklike bird. 2. a wading-bird of the order Ciconiformes. ‖ adj. m. + f. ciconiform.
cicuta s .f. (bot.) 1. water hemlock, cowbane. 2. poison hemlock, spotted parsley. 3. hemlock dropwort. 4. water fennel, horsebane. 5. cicuta.
cidadã s. f. (f. of cidadão) citizeness.
cidadania s. f. 1. citizenship, citizenhood. 2. status of rights of a citizen. 3. franchise. 4. freedom of a city.
cidadão s. m. (pl. -ãos) 1. citizen, denizen. 2. commoner, townsman, freeman. 3. inhabitant. 4. townee, burgher. 5. pl. people, citizenry, townsfolk.
cidade s. f. 1. city, town. 2. capital. 3. borough, burg(h). 4. the inhabitants of a city collectively. 5. (Braz.) a big underground nest of the sauba ants.
~ aberta open city. ~ alta uptown: the elevated part of a city in contraposition to the lower part. ~ baixa the lower part of a city in contraposition to the uptown.
Cidade Eterna Eternal City, Rome. ~ jardim garden city. ~ natal home town. ~ pequena townlet. Cidade Santa Holy City, Jerusalém. ~ soberana city-state. andei pela ~ durante três horas I walked the streets for three hours. em direção à ~ townward. ir ao centro da ~ to go downtown.
cidadela s. f. 1. citadel, fortress. 2. tower, stronghold. 3. (Braz., ftb.) goal.
cidade-satélite s. f. (pl. cidades-satélites) (Braz.) satellite town.
cidra s. f. 1. (bot.) Persian apple, citron (Citrus medica). 2. the fruit of this tree. 3. crystallized citron rind. 4. citron cider.
cidrada s. f. a sweetmeat made of crystallized citron rind.
cidral s. m. (pl. -ais) citron garden, citron plantation.
cidrão s. m. (pl. -ões) 1. (bot.): a) a lemon-scented verbena. b) white brush. 2. a sweetmeat of jelly made from citron peels or juice.
cidreira s. f. (bot.) citron, cedrat (Citrus cedra).
ciecié s. m. (zool.) a genus of small fiddler crabs.
cieiro s. m. (med.) 1. roughness of the skin. 2. dermatitis of the lips, cracked lips.
ciência s. f. 1. science. 2. knowledge, wisdom, learning. 3. art. 4. skill, vocation.
~ aplicada applied science, technique. ~ eletrônica electronics. ~ farmacêutica pharmaceutics, pharmacy. ~ física physical science. ~s humanas humanities. ~ naturais natural science, natural philosophy. ~s sociais social ciences. ~ técnica technical science. as ~s exatas the exact sciences. ele tem ~ dos acontecimentos he is well aware of the facts.

ciente adj. m. + f. 1. aware, knowing, cognizant. 2. sensible, conscious. 3. wise. ‖ ~mente adv. knowingly, wittingly, on purpose, intentional.
~ da culpa guilty. ele está ~ disso he is cognizant of it. estou ~ disso I am aware of it, I am conscious of it.
cientificar v. 1. to inform, advise. 2. to make known, placard. 3. to take cognizance of, notice. 4. (fam.) to let into. 5. to warn.
científico adj. scientific, sciential, well versed in science, according to science. ‖ cientificamente adv. scientifically, scientially, in a scientific manner.
cientismo s. m. (phil.) scientism: doctrine maintaining the exclusive importance of science research for the advancement of learning.
cientista s. m. + f. scientist, man of science, savant.
cifa (I) s. f. moulding sand used by goldsmiths.
cifa (II) s. f. 1. fish-oil. 2. the painting of a ship's hull with fish-oil.
cifé s. m. (Braz., pop.) the devil, the evil one.
cifela s. f. (bot.) Cyphella: a genus of cup-shaped fungi.
cifoftalmos s. m. pl. (zool.) invertebrate, arthropod animals without eyes or with marginal eyes.
cifose s. f. (med.) kyphosis.
cifótico adj. (med.) kyphotic(al), hunchbacked.
cifozoário s. m. (zool.) an acaleph(e).
cifra s. f. 1. cipher, cypher. 2. naught, nought, zero. 3. figure. 4. code. 5. (com.) sum, total amount. 6. monogram. 7. (mus.) key of a chord.
cifrado adj. written in code.
cifrão s. m. (pl. -ões) symbol used to indicate the currency (dollar $, cruzeiro Cr$, pound sterling L).
cifrar v. 1. to cipher, cypher. 2. to write in code, code. 3. to resume, sum up, epitomize. 4. to include, comprise. 5. ~-se to be reduced to, be included in.
cigalho s. m. a small portion, crumb, morsel.
cigana s. f. 1. (f. of cigano) gypsy woman. 2. (ornith.) stinkbird, hoatzin. 3. (ornith.) screamer. 4. (ent.) Argentine ant. 5. ~s pl. a kind of large ear-rings.
ciganada, ciganaria s. f. 1. a band or gang of gypsies. 2. behaviour or mannerism of gypsies. 3. gypsy life. 4. underhand tricks, cheating.
ciganear v. 1. to wander aimlessly around. 2. to lead a gypsy life. 3. to live like a Bohemian.
ciganice s. f. 1. behaviour or act typical of a gypsy. 2. underhand trick, trickery. 3. cheating, fraud. 4. sly flattery. 5. importunate begging, mendicancy.
cigano s. m. 1. gypsy. 2. horse-dealer. 3. (fig.) cunning fellow. 4. vagrant, vagabond. 5. hawker, street peddler. 6. Bohemian. 7. sharper, trickster. ‖ adj. sly, cunning, deceitful, errant, Bohemian.
casa de ~ disorderly house.
cigarra s. f. (ent.) cicada, harvest fly, locust, balm cricket.
cigarrar v. to smoke cigarettes.
cigarraria s. f. cigarette and tobacco shop.
cigarreira s. f. 1. woman who works in a cigarette factory. 2. cigar case, cigarette etui.
cigarreiro s. m. 1. cigar or cigarette maker. 2. workman of a cigarette factory. 3. a kind of tobacco.
cigarrilha s. f. 1. cigarillo, small cheap cigar (plate F 7). 2. whiff.
cigarrinha s. f. 1. cigarillo. 2. (ent.) hopper, frog hopper.
cigarrista s. m. + f. a cigarrete smoker.
cigarro s. m. cigarette (plate F 7).
cigude s. m. (pop.) = cicuta.
cilada s. f. 1. ambush, ambuscade. 2. snare, trap, entrapment. 3. treachery, treason. 4. pitfal. 5. trick, trickery, crafty wile.
~s da memória tricks of memory. armar uma ~

to lay a snare, waylay. **ele caiu na** ~ he was caught in the trap. **ele caiu na própria** ~ he was hoisted with his own petard. **ele lhe armou uma** ~ he laid wait for him.

cilha s. f. 1. cinch, girth, back-band, belly-band (plate S 2). 2. webbing (plate C 4).

cilhado adj. striped (resembling a belly-band).

cilhão s. m. (pl. -ões) 1. a large girth, surcingle, harness saddle (plate A 12). 2. a saddle-backed horse. ‖ adj. saddle-backed.

cilhar v. to girth, cinch, draw the back-band tightly.

ciliado s. m. (zool.) a ciliate. ‖ adj. (bot., zool.) ciliate(d) (plate F 5).

ciliar adj. 1. (anat.) ciliary, belonging to the eyelashes. 2. bordering rivers, ponds and lakes (said of certain plants).

ciliciar v. 1. to wear sackcloth. 2. to practise self--mortification. 3. (fig.) to be penitent.

cilício s. m. 1. cilice, hairshirt, sackcloth (worn as a penance). 2. (fig.) voluntary sacrifice. 3. (fig.) torment.

ciliforme adj. m. + f. ciliform.

cilígero adj. having or producing cilia.

cilindrada s. f. (tech., mech.) piston displacement.

cilindragem s. f. (pl. -ens) act or process of rolling or calendering.

cilindrar v. to cylinder, subject to the pressure of a heavy roll, press, level with a roller.

cilindreiro s. m. (typogr.) inker (worker).

cilindricidade s. f. quality of being cylindrical, cylindricity.

cilíndrico adj. cylindric(al), having the form or properties of a cylinder. ‖ **cilindricamente** adv. cylindrically.

cilindrifloro adj. (bot.) cylindriflorous, having cylindrical flowers.

cilindriforme adj. m. + f. cylindriform.

cilindrista s. m. + f. (typogr.) the operator of a cylinder press.

cilindro s. m. 1. cylinder. 2. roll, roller. 3. any body of cylindrical form. 4. barrel of a pump. 5. (tech.) motor block, cylinder of a motor (plate M 13). ~ **da roda do leme** (naut.) barrel of the steering wheel. ~ **das fechaduras** drum of a lock. ~ **de comando** controlling cylinder. ~ **de freio** brake-drum. ~ **de margeação** (typogr.) the cylinder in front of the **cilindro de retiração**. ~ **de retiração** (typogr.) second-impression cylinder. ~ **de tinta** (typogr.) printing roller, ductor roller ~ **de realejo** barrel (of an organ). ~ **de tear** cloth beam. ~ **holandês** breaker (paper mill).

cilindróide adj. m. + f. cylindroid, cylindric(al).

cílio s. m. 1. eyelash, lash. 2. (bot., zool.) cilium, cilia.

ciliófoto s. m. (zool.) infusorian of the class of Ciliophora.

cilíolo s. m. (bot.) a minute cilium.

cima s. f. 1. the highest part of. 2. top, summit. 3. apex. 4. (fig.) accomplishment, achievement. **de** ~ from above, atop. **de** ~ **para baixo** from top to bottom. **de quinze anos para** ~ from fifteen years upward. **em** ~ over, on, above, up, high up (plate Q). **em** ~ **de** on top of, moreover. **em** ~**, na página dez** at the top of page ten. **está embaixo ou em** ~? are you downstairs or upstairs? **ficar de** ~ to get the better of. **lá em** ~ up there. **para** ~ up, upwards. **para** ~ **e para baixo** up and down. **passar por** ~ to surmount. **por** ~ on, above, over (plate P 18). **por** ~ **de** on top of.

cimácio s. m. (archit.) cymatium, ogee, talon.

cimalha s. f. 1. summit, top. 2. (archit.) cymatium, cyma, entablature, entablement.

cimba s. f. a flat-boat, skiff.

cimbalária s. f. (bot.) ivywort, Kenilworth ivy.

címbalo s. m. 1. (mus.) cymbal: a) ancient string instrument. b) a pair of brass half globes. 2. psaltery.

cimbiforme adj. m. + f. cymbiform, boat-shaped.

cimbrar v. 1. to fold, plait. 2. to curve, bend.

cimbre s. m. (archit.) 1. wooden framework for the construction of an arch. 2. centering, centre (of an arch). 3. falsework, frame.

címbrico adj. (hist.) Cimbric, Cimbrian.

cimbro s. m. (hist.) Cimbrian, member of the Cimbrian people. ‖ adj. of, pertaining to or relative to this people.

cimeira (I) s. f. 1. crest of a helmet. 2. top, summit, apex.

cimeira (II) s. f. (bot.) cyme.

cimeiro adj. 1. situated on the top. 2. high, elevated. 3. crested. 4. uppermost.

cimélio s. m. cimelia: a rare and very valuable object, heirloom, treasure.

cimentação s. f. (pl. -ões) 1. act of cementing, cementation. 2. foundation, 3. consolidation.

cimentar v. 1. to cement, unite by means of cement. 2. to lay a foundation, found. 3. to consolidate, strengthen. 4. (fig.) to unite firmly.

cimento s. m. 1. cement (plates A 7, E 10). 2. concrete. 3. (geol.) the basic groundmass in which the different components of clastic rocks are embedded. 4. (fig.) foundation, basis. 5. (fig.) uniting element, bond of union. ~ **armado** reinforced concrete. ~ **hidráulico** hydraulic cement.

cimério adj. 1. lugubrious, doleful, gloomy. 2. infernal.

cimicídeos s. m. pl. (ent.) Cimicidae, the bedbugs family.

cimicífuga s. f. (bot.) 1. bugbane. 2. black cohosh, black snakeroot.

cimitarra s. f. scimitar, falchion.

cimo s. m. 1. top of a mountain. 2. summit, apex. 3. crest. 4. acme. 5. crown. 6. zenith.

cimoso adj. (bot.) cymose.

cimótrico adj. cymotrichous: of a person with wavy or curly hair.

cinabre, cinábrio s. m. 1. (min.) cinnabar. 2. red lead, vermilion (colour).

cinabrino adj. 1. cinnabar-coloured, vermilion. 2. made with cinnabar.

cinabrita s. f. (min.) cinnabar.

cinâmico adj. cinnamonic(al), cinnamon-coloured.

cinamomo s. m. (bot.) chinaberry tree, pride of China, pride of India, cinnamon.

cínara s. f. (bot.) cynara, artichoke.

cinastráceas s. f. pl. (bot.) a family of herbaceous and floriferous plants from tropical Africa.

cinca s. f. 1. (bowling) the loss of five points. 2. (fig.) mistake, error, bungle, blunder.

cincada s. f. mistake, error, blunder, bungle.

cincar (I) v. 1. to make a mistake, blunder, flounder. 2. (bowling) to lose five points. 3. to misunderstand.

cincar (II) v. (Port., prov.) 1. to spill, pour out. 2. to drain.

cinceiro s. m. (Braz.) a thick fog.

cincerro s. m. bell hung about the neck of the leading pack animal.

cincha s. f. cinc, saddle belt, saddle girth.

cinchador s. m. leather or iron ring used to fasten the loose end of a belt.

cinchão s. m. (pl. -ões) broad ornamental saddle girth.

cinchar v. to cinch, girth tightly.

cincho s. m. cheese-press, cheesevat.

cinchona s. f. 1. (bot.) Cinchona: a large genus of trees of the madder family. 2. (pharm) cinchona.
cinchonina s. f. (chem.) cinchonine.
cincídeo s. m. (zool.) skink: a lizard of the family Scincidae.
cínclise s. f. (med.) nervous twitching of the eyelid.
cinco s. m. five, the number five. || adj. five.
~ por cento five percent, a shilling in the pound. ir a ~ e ~ to go five by five.
cinco-folhas s. f. sg. + pl. (bot.) cinquefoil.
cindir v. to cut, split, separate.
cine s. m. abbr. form of cinema: motion picture theater.
cineasta s. m. + f. cinematographer.
cineclube s. m. a movie-club.
cinegética' s. f. art and practice of hunting with dogs, the art of hunting, huntsmanship.
cinegético adj. cynegetic.
cinegrafista s. m. cameraman.
cinema s. m. 1. cinema, movies, pictures. 2. picture-house, movie theatre, motion picture theater.
ir ao ~ to go to the movies. ~ falado talkie, a sound motion picture. ~ mudo a soundless motion picture.
cinemascópio s. m. cinemascope.
cinemateca s. f. = filmoteca.
cinemática s. f. (phys.) kinematics.
cinemático adj. cinematic(al) kinematic(al).
cinematografar v. to take motion pictures.
cinematografia s. f. cinematography.
cinematográfico adj. cinematographic(al). || cinematograficamente adv. cinematographically.
cinematógrafo s. m. 1. motion-picture projector, cinematograph, kinematograph. 2. motion-picture theater.
cinemeiro s. m. an assiduous movie-goer. || adj. regular movie-goer.
cineração s. f. cineration, incineration, cremation.
cineral s. m. (pl. -ais) ash-heap.
cinerama s. m. Cinerama: trade-mark of a motion-picture process.
cinerar v. to reduce to ashes, incinerate, cremate.
cinerária s. f. (bot.) 1. cineraria. 2. dusty miller. 3. blue daisy.
cinerário s. m. cinerarium, cinerary-urn, funeral urn. || adj. of, pertaining to or containing ashes, cinerary.
cinérea s. f. a very resistent variety of American grapes.
cinéreo adj. cinereous, ashen, ash-coloured.
cineriforme adj. m. + f. cinereal, cinereous, ash-like.
cinerradiografia s. f. (med.) an X-ray of an organ in motion.
cinestesia s. f. kinesthesis.
cinética s. f. (phys.) kinematics, kinetics, dynamics.
cinético adj. (phys.) kinetic.
cingalês s. m. (pl. -eses) (f. -esa, pl. -esas) Cingalese: native or inhabitant of Ceylon (Sri Lanka). || adj. Cingalese.
cingel (pl. -éis) s. m., cingelada f. a yoke of oxen.
cingeleiro s. m. person who owns, hires or guides a yoke of oxen.
cingideira s. f. each one of the middle claws of a bird of prey.
cingidouro s. m. 1. belt, girdle, sash. 2. buckle, clasp.
cingir v. 1. to gird, put on a belt. 2. to belt, begird, enclasp. 3. to unite, join. 4. to surround, encompass. 5. to repress, constrain, restrain. 6. to entwine, entwist. 7. to tie, bind, bandage. 8. to skirt along. 9. to embrace. 10. to crown. 11. to embellish, adorn. 12. ~-se: a) to draw near, approximate. b) to keep close to, stick to, cling to. c) to restrain o. s. 13. to zone.

ele cingiu-a com os braços he folded his arms round her. ele cingiu a espada he put on his sword.
cíngulo s. m. cingulum: girdle of a priest's alb.
cínico s. m. 1. cynic. 2. (hist., philos.) one of the Cynics. || adj. 1. cynic(al). 2. impudent, shameless. 3. (hist., philos.) of, pertaining to or relative to the Cynics.
cinipídeos s. m. pl. (ent.) Cynipidae (gall wasps).
cinira s. f. (hist.) an ancient lyre-shaped string instrument.
cinismo s. m. 1. cynicism. 2. impudence, shamelessness. 3. (hist.) doctrine of the Cynics.
cinocéfalo s. m. (zool.) a cynocephalous ape, flying lemur.
cinófilo adj. cynophilous.
cinofobia s. f. cynophobia: fear of dogs.
cinologia s. f. cynology: the study of dogs and their behaviour.
cinoglossa s. f. (bot.) dog's-tongue, hound's tongue.
cinografia s. f. cynography, a treatise on dogs.
cinográfico adj. cynographic(al).
cinórrodo s. m. the fruit of the dogrose, cynorrhodon.
cinosura s. f. (astr.) Cynosure: the constellation Ursa Minor.
cinosuro s. m. (bot.) dog's-tail. || adj. resembling a dog's-tail.
cinquena s. f. 1. (R. C. Church) a five day's devotion. 2. a period of five days.
cinqüenta s. m. 1. fifty, the number fifty. 2. f. (Braz.) formerly a square measure (about 12,000 m²). || adj. fifty.
cinqüentão s. m. (pl. -ões) (f. cinqüentona) (pop.) a man in his fifties. || adj. fiftyish.
cinqüentenário s. m. the fiftieth anniversary.
cinta s. f. 1. girdle, sash. 2. waistband, belt (plate R 7). 3. (archit.) cincture, truss. 4. (naut.) wale. 5. ribbon, tie. 6. zone. 7. wrapper, postal wrapper (of newspaper, books).
~ antimagnética a device installed on the ship's hull as a protection against mine explosions. ~ couraçada a set of armour plates mounted and placed on a battleship's waterline. ~ grossa (naut.) main-wale. apertar a ~ (also fig.) to tighten the belt.
cinta-calça s. f. (pl. cintas-calças) panty girdle.
cintado (I) s. m. (naut.) the strakes and wales of a ship.
cintado (II) adj. belted, girded.
cinta-liga s. f. (pl. cintas-ligas) garter belt.
cintar v. 1. to put on a belt. 2. to belt, band. 3. to bind. 4. to rap (newspapers, books, etc.). 5. (archit.) to form a cincture or fillet.
cinteiro s. m. 1. belt maker or dealer. 2. bellyband. 3. belt, sash. 4. hatband.
cintel s. m. (pl. -éis) 1. trammel, beam compass. 2. gin race, track of a horse turning a gin. 3. region, zone. 4. enclosed piece of land.
cintilação s. f. (pl. -ões) 1. scintillation. 2. sparkling, sparkle. 3. twinkle, twinkling. 4. blink. 5. dazzling brightness, glare, splendour.
cintilante adj. m. + f. 1. scintillant. 2. sparkling, flaring. 3. blinking, twinkling. 4. flashy. 5. dazzling, coruscant.
cintilar v. 1. to scintillate. 2. to sparkle, flare. 3. to twinkle, blink. 4. to flash, glare. 5. to fulgurate, coruscate. 6. to irradiate, radiate.
cintilho s .m. 1. dim. form of cinto. 2. small girdle, sash or belt. 3. a richly ornamented belt or one studded with precious stones.
cintilograma s. m. (med.) scintigram.
cinto s. m. 1. leather strap, belting, belt (plate R 6). 2. waistband, girdle, sash. 3. (anat., zool.) cingu-

lum. 4. cincture. 5. zone, region. 6. fenced-in land, enclosed tract of land.

~ **frio** (poet.) the cold zone. ~ **de segurança** safety belt. ~ **salva-vidas** life-belt. **apertar o** ~ (fig.) to reduce expenses, to cut down on the budget.

cinto-de-couro s. m. (pl. **cintos-de-couro**) a broad rawhide belt used as a heavy shakle for criminals.

cintura s. f. 1. waist, waistline (plate C 18). 2. waistband, sash, belt. 3. middle (of the body), stomach. 4. bodice (of a dress).

~ **de calça** waistband. ~ **de vespa** wasp waist. ~ **escapular** pectoral arch, pectoral girdle. ~ **pélvica** (anat.) pelvic arch, pelvic girdle.

cinturado adj. 1. belted, girt, girded. 2. well tightened at the waistline.

cinturão s. m. (pl. **-ões**) 1. broad sash or waistband. 2. leather belt. 3. shoulder-strap, cartridge belt. 4. moneybelt. 5. waistline. 6. cincture.

~ **da espada** sword-belt. ~ **verde** greenbelt (surrounding a city).

cinza s. f. 1. ash(es), ember, cinder. 2. ~**s** pl. mortal remains, dust. 3. (fig.) annihilation, destruction. 4. bereavement, mourning, grief. 5. humiliation. || adj. m. + f. 1. ashen, cindery. 2. ash-coloured, gray. 3. dove-coloured. 4. coesious. 5. pepper-and--salt coloured.

~ **vulcânica** volcanic ash. **botar** ~ **nos olhos de** to shield, cut off from observation. **coberto de** ~ ashy. **cor de** ~ ash gray. **embaixo da** ~ **há brasa** (proverb) under the dead ashes still smothers a fire, still waters run deep. **quarta-feira de** ~**s** Ash Wednesday. **recipiente de** ~ ash can. **reduzir a** ~**s** to turn to dust and ashes.

cinzar v. 1. to make ash-coloured, give an ashen hue to. 2. to deceive, cheat, fool. 3. to inveigle. 4. ~**-se** to become ash-coloured, turn ashen.

cinzeiro s. m. 1. ash-heap. 2. ash-tray (plates F 7, R 5). 3. ash-pit of a furnace. 4. a very fine drizzling rain. 5. ash-pan, ash-bin (plate F 3). 6. (Braz.) workman who cleans the ash-pit of a furnace. 7. tree of the genus Vochysia (Qualea multiflora).

cinzel s. m. (pl. **-éis**) 1. chisel, sculptor's chisel, boasting-chisel (plates F 2, M 6). 2. graver, burin. 3. scooper.

cinzelado adj. chiselled, engraved, carved.

cinzelador s. m. 1. chisel(l)er. 2. sculptor. 3. carver. 4. engraver. || adj. (chisel(l)ing, engraving, carving.

cinzeladura s. f. engraving, engraved work, sculpture.

cinzelamento s. m. act or process of carving or engraving.

cinzelar v. 1. to chisel, chip, hew. 2. to engrave, chase. 3. to carve, shape by cutting. 4. (fig.) to perfect, refine, work delicately.

cinzento s. m. gray, gray colour, ash gray. || adj. 1. cinereous, gray, grey, ashen, grizzly. 2. boasting, boastful (talk).

cio s. m. rut, heat, oestrus; (of fishes) spawning.

cioba s. f. 1. (ichth.) dog snapper. 2. m. (fig.) pedantic adulator.

ciografia s. f. 1. (archit.) skiagraphy, vertical section (of a building, machine), sectional drawing. 2. (astr.) skiagraphy.

ciográfico adj. (archit., astr.) skiagraphic(al).

ciógrafo s. m. skiagrapher.

cióptico, ciótico adj. scioptic(al).

cioso adj. 1. jealous, envious. 2. careful, cautious, mindful. 3. passionate, ardorous. || **-amente** adv. jealously.

ciotomia s. f. (surg.) uvulectomy.

ciperáceas s. f. pl. (bot.) Cyperaceae, the sedge family.

ciperáceo adj. (bot.) cyperaceous.

cipo s. m. 1. (hist.) cippus, post, pillar. 2. a column without capital. 3. gravestone. 4. (her.) genealogical tree.

cipó s. m. cipo, liana, liane.

cipoaba s. m. a tropical shrub of the family Combretaceae (Combretum leprosum).

cipoada s. f. 1. a blow with a cipo. 2. whipping, lashing. 3. (fig.) difficulty.

cipoal s. m. (pl. **-ais**) 1. a place where lianas grow in abundance. 2. (fig.) an intricate matter or affair. 3. complication, difficulty.

cipoar v. to flog with a piece of cipo.

cipó-cabeludo s. m. (pl. **cipós-cabeludos**), (bot.) a climbing vine of the thistle family (Micania hirsutissima).

cipó-caboclo s. m. (pl. **cipós-caboclos**), (bot.) a dilleniad.

cipó-café s. m. (pl. **cipós-café**), (bot.) moonflower.

cipó-cravo s. m. (pl. **cipós-cravo**) a medicinal plant of the family Bignoniaceae (Tynnanthus fascinaculus, Tynnanthus elegans).

cipó-cruz s. m. (pl. **cipós-cruz**), (bot.) 1. carajura. 2. virgin's-bower. 3. dilleniaceous hemp.

cipó-d'alho s. m. (pl. **cipós-d'alho**), (bot.) garlic shrub.

cipó-de-são-joão s. m. (pl. **cipós-de-são-joão**), (bot.) 1. flame vine. 2. orange creeper.

cipó-do-reino s. m. (pl. **cipós-do-reino**), (bot.) virgin's--bower.

cipoíra s. m. a plant of the family Annonaceae (Guatteria scandens).

cipolino s. m. cipolin, a light-coloured Roman marble.

cipó-mole s. m. (pl. **cipós-moles**), (bot.) cockspur.

cipó-seco s. m. (pl. **cipós-secos**) (ent.) walking stick: an insect of the family Phasmidae.

cipó-suma s. m. (pl. **cipós-suma**), a medicinal plant of the family Violaceae (Anchietea salutaris).

cipotaia s. m. a medicinal plant of the family Capparidaceae (Capparis urens).

cipó-vermelho s. m. (pl. **cipós-vermelhos**), (bot.) red creeper.

ciprestal s. m. (pl. **-ais**) a grove of cypress trees.

cipreste s. m. 1. bot.): a) cypress, cypress tree. b) ginger pine, white cedar. c) incense cedar. d) arbor-vitae. e) Chinese arbor-vitae. f) red cedar, canoe cedar. g) akeki, Japanese arbor-vitae. 2. (fig.) death, mourning, sadness.

cipreste-calvo s. m. (pl. **ciprestes-calvos**), (bot.) bald cypress.

cipreste-chorão s. m. (pl. **ciprestes-chorões**), (bot.) white fir.

cipreste-do-brejo s. m. (pl. **ciprestes-do-brejo**), (bot.) pond cypress.

cipreste-do-japão s. m. (pl. **ciprestes-do-japão**), (bot.) sawara cypress.

ciprínidas s. f. pl. Cyprinidae: an important family of fresh-water fishes including carps, barbels.

ciprinídeo, ciprinóide s. m. (ichth.) cyprinid, a cyprinoid fish. || adj. (**ciprinóide** m. + f.) cyprinid, cyprinoid.

ciprino s. m. + adj. = **cíprio**.

ciprinocultor s. m. a breeder of carps.

ciprinocultura s. f. carp breeding.

cíprio s. m., **cipriota** m. + f. Cypriot(e), native or inhabitant of Cyprus. || adj. Cyprian, Cypriot(e).

cipselídeo s. m. 1. a cypseline bird. 2. Cypselidae: a family of birds, the swifts. || adj. cypseline.

ciranda s. f. 1. a coarse sifting screen (for sand, grain). 2. van, winnow, riddle. 3. fanner, fanning machine. 4. a popular dance and dance music.

cirandagem s. f. (pl. **-ens**) 1. act of screening or winnowing. 2. the quantity screened at one time. 3. chaff.

cirandar v. to screen, winnow, riddle.

cirandinha s. f. a popular dance, dance music and accompanying songs.

circassiano s. m. Circassian: 1. native or inhabitant of Circassia. 2. individual of a group of Caucasian tribes. 3. the language of the Circassian tribes. ‖ adj. Circassian.

circatejano adj. habiting the banks of the river Tagus (Spain, Port.).

circéia s. f. (bot.) enchanter's nightshade, wild mandrake.

circense adj. m. + f. circensian, circensial: of or relative to a circus.

circenses s. m. pl. 1. circus performances. 2. (hist.) Circensian games.

circinado adj. (bot.) circinate, circinal, gyrate.

circinal adj. m. + f. (pl. **-ais**), (bot.) gyrate, circinal.

circo s. m. 1. circus, amphitheater. 2. circular enclosure, ring. 3. canvas. 4. (geol.) cirque. 5. cheese-press circle. 6. (Braz.) roundup.

~ **de cavalinhos** circus. **ser de** ~ 1. to have extraordinary skill. 2. to be able to solve complicated problems. 3. to have remarkable willingness to act when confronted with problems.

circuição s. f. (pl. **-ões**) 1. circuity, act of going in a circle. 2. a circular movement. 3. circuit.

circuitar v. 1. to circuit, walk in a circle. 2. to encompass, encircle. 3. to gyrate, circulate.

circuito s. m. 1. circumference, circle. 2. circuit. 3. short walk, round. 4. an enclosed tract of land, space within a circle. 5. succession of recurrent phenomena. 6. (electr.) the complete path of an electric current. 7. the act of moving or passing around. 8. ambit, scope. 9. zone. 10. cycle. 11. circuital tour.

~ **aberto** (electr.) open or broken circuit. ~ **de palavras** 1. circumlocution. 2. redundancy. ~ **de viagem** circular tour. ~ **direto** direct circuit. ~ **elétrico** live wire, electric circuit. ~ **em paralelo** (electr.) parallel circuit. ~ **fechado** (electr.) closed circuit. ~ **impresso** (electronics) printed circuit. ~ **sintonizado** (radio) tuned circuit. **curto-**~ (electr.) short circuit. **fazer um** ~ to make a tour.

circulação s. f. (pl. **-ões**) 1. act of circulating, circulation. 2. rotation, gyration. 3. course, route. 4. orbit. 5. transit, passage, traffic. 6. flow. 7. currency.

~ **da corrente** flow of current. ~ **do sangue** the circulation of the blood. ~ **fiduciária** currency duly issued in paper money. ~ **forçada** forced circulation. ~ **monetária** metal currency, gold or silver currency. **em** ~ out, afloat. **pôr em** ~ to emit, issue, give currency to.

circulador s. m. 1. a circulation apparatus. 2. an electronic circulator. ‖ adj. circulating.

circulante adj. m. + f. circulating, circulatory, current, floating, circling, abroad.

capital ~ (com.) floating capital. **lubrificação** ~ (tech.) flood lubrication.

circular (I) s. f. circular, circular letter, bill. ‖ adj. m. + f. 1. circular. 2. round, ring-shaped. 3. cyclic(al), cycloid. 4. rotund. 5. circulatory. 6. cochleate(d). 7. orbiculate, orbicular. 8. of, pertaining to or relative to a circular letter. ‖ ~**mente** adv. circular, circlewise, around, roundly.

ele faz um vôo ~ he flies a circuit.

circular (II) v. 1. to circulate. 2. to move in a circle. 3. to surround, encompass. 4. to garnish, trim round about. 5. to circle, pass through, traverse. 6. to gyrate, rotate. 7. to spread, diffuse. 8. to put into circulation. 9. to renew (air). 10. to be accepted as legal currency (money, banknotes). 11. to flow, float.

circulatório adj. circulative, circulatory, gyratory.

círculo s. m. 1. circle (plate A 9). 2. belt, strip. 3. ring, circumference, arc. 4. gyration, rotation. 5. round, rondure. 6. zone, area, region. 7. circumscription, district. 8. cycle. 9. circle of friends, society, guild, clique.

~ **de ação** range. ~ **de amigos** set of friends. ~ **de eleitores** constituency. ~ **de fogo** the strip formed by active and extinct volcanoes along the Pacific coast. ~ **de latitude** (geogr.) parallel of latitude. ~ **divisor** (geom.) pitch line. ~ **equinocial** (geogr.) equinoctial circle. ~ **familiar** family, home circle. ~ **máximo** (geom.) great circle. ~ **polar** polar circle. ~ **social** social circle. ~ **vicioso** 1. vicious circle. 2. (logic) sophistic argument which is based on hypothetical reasoning. **você argumenta dentro de um** ~ **vicioso** you argue in a circle.

circum-adjacente adj. m. + f. (pl. **circum-adjacentes**) circumjacent.

circum-ambiente adj. m. + f. (pl. **circum-ambientes**) circumambient.

circumpolar adj. m. + f. circumpolar.

circumurado adj. completely walled in, surrounded by walls.

circunavegação s. f. (pl. **-ões**) circumnavigation.

circunavegador s. m. circumnavigator.

circunavegar v. 1. to circumnavigate, sail round (the earth, a continent, island). 2. to double (a cape).

circuncidar v. to circumcise.

circuncisão s. f. (pl. **-ões**) circumcision.

circunciso s. m. a circumcised man. ‖ adj. circumcised.

circundamento s. m. 1. act of encompassing. 2. circumambience, circumambiency. 3. compassing, surrounding.

circundante adj. m. + f. circumambient, environmental, surrounding.

circundar v. 1. to circle, encompass. 2. to surround, round. 3. to enclose, belt, cincture. 4. to embrace. 5. to circuit.

circundução s. f. (pl. **-ões**) circumduction, circumvolution, rotation.

circundutar v. 1. (jur.) to circumduct. 2. to rotate, circumvolve.

circunduto adj. (jur.) that has to be repeated in view of a preceding annulment.

circunferência s. f. 1. circumference. 2. circle. 3. periphery, perimeter. 4. circuit, compass.

~ **primitiva** pitch chain. **em** ~ in extent, around. **dentro de cinco milhas de** ~ five miles about. **uma árvore com três pés de** ~ a tree three feet about.

circunferencial adj. m. + f. (pl. **-ais**) circumferential, encircling.

circunferente adj. m. + f. circumferential, encircling, surrounding.

circunflexão s. f. (pl. **-ões**) circumflexion, circuity, act of bending round, curvature.

circunflexo adj. circumflex, bent, round, curved.

acento ~ (gram.) circumflex, circumflex accent.

circunfluência s. f. circumfluence.

circunfluente adj .m. + f. circumfluent, circumfluous.

circunfluir v. to flow around.

circunfundir v. 1. to circumfuse. 2. to spread or diffuse round. 3. to envelop or bathe by pouring around. 4. to spread about. 5. to shed.

circunfuso adj. (poet.) circumfluous, surrounded.

circungirar v. 1. to circumgyrate. 2. to circle. 3. to glance over, peruse. 4. to go or pass around (a center).

circunjacente adj. m. + f. circumjacent, surrounding, circumambient, neighbouring.

circunjazer v. 1. to surround, encompass. 2. to envelop completely. 3. to border on, neighbour.

circunlocução s. f. (pl. **-ões**), **circunlóquio** m. 1. circumlocution. 2. redundancy, verbosity. 3. circumvolution. 4. periphrasis. 5. (hum.) circumbendibus. 6. ambages.

circunscrever v. 1. to circumscribe. 2. to draw a line around, encircle. 3. to bound, limit. 4. to determine, define. 5. to comprehend, include. 6. to restrict, confine. 7. to concentrate on.

circunscrição s. f. circumscription: 1. act of circumscribing. 2. outline, periphery. 3. boundary, limitation. 4. district, borough. 5. margin, verge.

circunscritivo adj. circumscriptive, limitative, peripheral.

circunscrito adj. circumscribed, circumscript, limitary.

circunsessão s. f. (teol.) the unity of three hypostases in the mystery of Trinity.

circunsoante adj. m. + f. circumsonant, sounding on all sides, sounding round about.

circunspeção, circunspecção s. f. (pl. **-ões**) 1. circumspection, circumspectness. 2. careful attention, caution. 3. considerateness, carefulness. 4. prudence. 5. meditation. 6. discretion, discreetness. 7. reserve.

circunspeto, circunspecto adj. 1. circumspect, circumspective. 2. cautious, prudent. 3. heedful, wary. 4. discreet, reserved. 5. deliberate. || **-amente** adv. circumspectly, cautiously.

circunstância s. f. 1. circumstance. 2. state, condition. 3. concurrent fact, detail. 4. particularity. 5. position, situation. 6. incident. 7. motive. 8. (Braz.) importance. 9. occasion, opportunity. 10. ~s pl. surroundings.
em boas ou más ~s well or badly off. **em iguais** ~s under equal circumstances. **nessas** ~s under these conditions.

circunstanciado adj. 1. circumstanced, circumstantial. 2. detailed. 3. incidental. || **-amente** adv. circumstantially, in detail, minutely, incidentally.

circunstancial adj. m. + f. (pl. **-ais**) circumstantial, (gram.) attributive, relating to.

circunstanciar v. 1. to circumstantiate. 2. to tell or describe in detail. 3. to particularize. 4. to bring forward important details (in proof of).

circunstante s. m. + f. 1. bystander, onlooker. 2. spectator. 3. ~s pl. an audience. || adj. circumstant, circumjacent, surrounding, ambient.

circunstar v. 1. to be present, be at hand. 2. to surround, envelop. 3. to be visible or near.

circunvagante adj. m. + f. circumvagrant, wandering or roving about.

circunvagar v. 1. to wander or rove about. 2. to move in a circle. 3. to let rotate, gyrate. 4. to look searchingly about. 5. to digress. 6. to circumviate.

circúnvago adj. 1. wandering about. 2. roving. 3. surrounding. 4. ambient. 5. aimless.

circunvalação s. f. (pl. **-ões**) 1. circumvallation. 2. (mil.) fieldworks, ramparts, enceinte. 3. protective stockade, wall or trench around a village.

circunvalado adj. circumvallate, surrounded with a protective rampart or trench.

circunvalar v. 1. to circumvallate. 2. to surround with a rampart, wall or trench. 3. to enclose. 4. to fortify, defend. 5. to ditch.

circunver v. to look around, see on all sides.

circunvizinhança s. f. 1. suburb. 2. adjacency, environs. 3. vicinity. 4. neighbourhood, neighbours.

circunvizinhar v. 1. to circumviate, surround. 2. to be in the neighbourhood of. 3. to be in the suburbs of.

circunvizinho adj. 1. circumambient, circumjacent. 2. neighbouring. 3. confining. 4. limiting, bounding. 5. surrounding.

circunvoar v. to circumaviate, fly around.

circunvolução s. f. (pl. **-ões**) 1. circumvolution, rotation. 2. tortuous or sinuous winding around, convolution.

circunvolver v. 1. to circumvolve. 2. to turn round, revolve, rotate. 3. to ensphere. 4. to envelop.

cirenaico s. m. Cyrenaic: native or inhabitant of Cyrenaica (Lybia). || adj. Cyrenaic, Cyrenian.

cireneu s. m. (f. **cirenéia**) Cyrenian: native or inhabitant of Cyrene (Lybia). || adj. Cyrenian.

cirial s. m. (pl. **-ais**) large candlestick of a church, chandelier.

cirieiro s. m. wax chandler, candle manufacturer or dealer.

ciriláceas s. f. pl. (bot.) Cyrillaceae: a family of shrubs and trees of the order Sapindales.

cirílica s. f. Cyrillic: the Cyrillic alphabet, Slavic alphabet.

cirílico adj. Cyrillic, of or designating the old Slavic alphabet.

círio s. m. 1. a large wax candle, taper. 2. a procession in which lighted candles are born to a place of veneration. 3. pilgrimage. 4. (bot.) Cereus: a genus of tropical American cacti.

círio-de-nossa-senhora s. m. (pl. **círios-de-nossa-senhora**), (bot.) a yucca (Yucca gloriosa).

círio-do-norte s. m. (pl. **círios-do-norte**), (bot.) evening primrose (Oenothera biennis).

ciriologia s. f. (hist.) curiology, curiologics, pictorial writings (i. e. hieroglyphs which represent pictures instead of symbols).

ciriológico adj. (hist.) curiologic(al).

cirrífero adj. cirriferous.

cirrípede s. m. + f. (zool.) 1. cirriped. 2. Cirripedia: a class of marine Crustaceae.

cirro s. m. 1. (bot.) cirrus, tendril. 2. slender, flexible appendages (arms of barnacles, barbels of fishes, tufts of hair on the legs of insects). 3. (meteor.) cirrus cloud, spindrift cloud (plate N 2). 4. (med.) stertorious breathing, death rattles. 5. (med.) cancer of the fibrous tissue.

cirro-cúmulo s. m. (pl. **cirros-cúmulos**) (meteor.) cirro--cumulus (plate N 2).

cirro-estrato s. m. (pl. **cirros-estratos**) (meteor.) cirro--stratus (plate N 2).

cirrose s. f. (med.) cirrhosis, sclerosis.
~ **alcoólica** (med., pop.) whisky-liver.

cirrosidade s. f. (med.) cirrhotic condition or state, scirrhosity, cancerous tumour.

cirroso adj. 1. (med.) scirrhous, scirrhoid, cirrhotic. 2. (meteor.) cirrous, like cirrus clouds. 3. (bot., zool.) cirrose, cirriferous, cirriform.

cirrótico adj. (med.) cirrhotic, scirrhoid, scirrhous.

cirurgia s. f. (med.) surgery.
~ **estética** aesthetic surgery. ~ **plástica** plastic surgery, plastics, anaplasty. ~ **protética** prosthetics.

cirurgião s. m. (pl. **-ões**) (f. **cirurgiã**) (med.) surgeon.

cirurgião-dentista s. m. (pl. **cirurgiões-dentistas**) (f. **cirurgiã-dentista**) surgeon-dentist, dental surgeon.

cirúrgico adj. surgical.
tratamento ~ surgical treatment.

cisalha s. f. 1. shear. 2. ~s pl. sheet metal parings, metal shavings, scissel(s).

cisalhamento s. m. (act of) shearing, shear.

cisalpino adj. cisalpine, pertaining or situated on this side of the Alps (usually the south side).

cisandino adj. cisandine, on the hither side of the Andes.

cisão s. f. (pl. **-ões**) 1. act of separating or splitting. 2. scission, split. 3. divergence, disagreement. 4. dissension, contentious division. 5. discord. 6. secession.

cisatlântico adj. cisatlantic.

cisbordo s. m. (naut.) starboard.

ciscada s. f. heap of coal-dust or coal sweepings.
ciscador s. m. iron rake. ‖ adj. scraping or raking together.
ciscalhada, ciscalhagem s. f. 1. a heap of sweepings. 2. scourings. 3. plant refuse, detritus of Algae.
ciscalho s. m. 1. rubbish, refuse. 2. sweepings, scourings.
ciscar (I) v. 1. to clean up trash. 2. to weed a field. 3. to sweep, rake up. 4. to instigate, incite, sick on (dogs). 5. to scratch the earth (chicken).
ciscar (II) v. (Port., prov.) to hide.
cisco s. m. 1. trash, rubbish, refuse. 2. dust. 3. dead branches, wood chips, kindling. 4. sweepings, scourings. 5. soot, smut. 6. speck of dust, mote.
cisdanubiano adj. cisdanubian.
cisirão s. m. (pl. **-ões**), (bot.) vetchling.
cisjurano adj. cisjurane, on this (usually the western) side of the Jura Mountains.
cisma (I) s. m. 1. (rel.) schism. 2. rent, split. 3. division, separation. 4. dissidence, disagreement.
cisma (II) s. f. 1. act of musing or pondering. 2. daydreaming, reverie. 3. preoccupation, worry. 4. suspicion, doubt. 5. caprice, craze. 6. superstitious fear.
   tirar a ~ de alguém (pop.) to humble or reduce o. s.
cismado adj. 1. suspicious, distrustful. 2. worried. 3. wary, cautious, forewarned.
cismar v. 1. to ponder, meditate. 2. to daydream. 3. to be worried, worry over. 4. to think hard, ratiocinate. 5. to distrust, have doubts. 6. to brood over. 7. to dwell upon, get an idea into one's head. 8. to become convinced of.
   ela cismou estar doente she fancied herself to be ill.
cismarento adj. 1. worried, preoccupied. 2. meditative, pondering. 3. apprehensive, anxious, fearful.
cismático (I) s. m. schismatic, heretic, separatist. ‖ adj. schismatic(al), heretical. ‖ **cismaticamente** adv. schismatically, heretically.
cismático (II) adj. 1. worried, preoccupied. 2. pondering, meditative. 3. dreaming. 4. apprehensive, fearful. ‖ **cismaticamente** adv. worriedly, meditatively, dreamingly.
cismativo adj. 1. worried, preoccupied. 2. pondering, meditative. 3. distrustful, suspicious. 4. fearful.
cisne s. m. 1. (ornith.) swan, cob. 2. (astr.) Cygnus, Swan: a northern constellation. 3. (fig.) a famous poet, orator or musician.
   ~ novo cygnet. **canto de ~** swan-song. **com colo de ~** swan-necked (said of horses).
cisne-de-pescoço-preto s. m. (pl. **cisnes-de-pescoço-preto**) (Braz.) = **pato-arminho**.
cispadano adj. cispadane, situated on this side of the river Po (Italy).
cisplatino adj. cisplatine, situated on this side of the Rio de la Plata (Argentine).
cisqueiro s. m. 1. rubbish heap, heap of trash. 2. garbage collector.
cisrenano adj. cisrhenane, situated on this side of the river Rhine (Germany).
cissiparidade s. f. (biol.) schizogenesis.
cissíparo adj. (biol.) fissiparous, schizogenous.
cisso s. m. (bot.) Cissus: a genus of tropical vines.
cissóide s. f. (math., geom.) cissoid. ‖ adj. m. + f. cissoidal.
cissura s. f. 1. (anat.) fissure, sulcus. 2. crack, cleft, split. 3. incision, cut. 4. (fig.) break of peace or friendship.
cista s. f. cist, kist.
cistáceas s. f. pl. Cistaceae: a family of woody herbs, the rockrose family.
cistáceo adj. (bot.) cistaceous.
cistalgia s. f. (med.) cystalgia, pain in the bladder.

cistálgico adj. (med.) cystalgic.
cisterciense adj. m. + f. (rel.) Cistercian.
cisterna s. f. 1. cistern, water-tank. 2. well, water-hole.
cisticerco s. m. (ent.) bladder worm, cysticercus.
cisticercose s. f. (med.) cysticercosis.
cístico adj. (med.) cystic.
cistina s. f. (biochem.) cystine.
cistite s. f. (med.) cystitis, inflammation of the bladder.
cisto s. m. (bot., med., zool.) cyst.
cistocarpo s. m. (bot.) cystocarp.
cistocele s. f. (med.) cystocele, hernia of the bladder.
cistóide adj. m. + f. (med.) cystoid, bladderlike.
   formação ~ (med.) a cystoid formation.
cistólito s. m. (med.) cystolith, urinary calculus.
cistometria s. f. (med.) cystometry: a method for measuring the pressure within the urinary bladder.
cistopielite s. f. (med.) cystopyelitis, inflammation of the bladder and the pelvis of the kidneys.
cistoplegia s. f. (med.) cystoplegy, paralysation of the bladder.
cistoplégico adj. (med.) cystoplegic(al).
cistoscopia s. f. (med.) cystoscopy: endoscopic examination of the bladder.
cistotomia s. f. (med., surg.) cystotomy.
cistótomo s. m. (surg.) cystotome.
cita (I) s. f. citation, quotation.
cita (II) s. m. + f. (hist.) Scythian: one of an ancient nomadic people of Iranian origin. ‖ adj. Scythian.
citação s. f. (pl. **-ões**) 1. citation, quotation. 2. official summons, arraignment. 3. (jur.) subpoena. 4. excerpt. 5. (jur.) monition.
   ~ comum commonplace quotation. **terminar uma ~** to unquote.
citadino s. m. city dweller, citizen, cit, townsman. ‖ adj. city-bred, citizen, civic, urban.
   ele é um ~ he is a man about town.
citado adj. 1. summoned, arraigned, subpoenaed. 2. said. 3. quoted, cited. 4. mentioned.
   não ~ unquoted.
citador s. m. 1. summoner. 2. one who quotes. ‖ adj. summoning.
citar v. 1. to cite, quote. 2. to summon, subpoena. 3. to name, mention. 4. to notice. 5. to convene. 6. to adduce. 7. to make reference to.
   ~ na íntegra to quote in full. **~ como exemplo** to demonstrate by an instance. **cite-me os nomes** give me the names.
citara s. f. (mus.) cither, cithara, zither(n).
citaredo s. m. person who accompanies his songs on a cither (zither).
citarista s. m. + f. citharist, zitherist.
citatório adj. citatory.
citável adj. m. + f. (pl. **-áveis**) citable, quotable, mentionable, adduceable, adducible.
   não ~ unquotable.
citerior adj. m. + f. hither, situated on this (the nearer) side, belonging to this side.
cítico adj. Scythian, of or pertaining to the Scythians.
citígrado adj. walking rapidly, swift-footed.
citíneas s. f. pl. Cytinaceae: a family of tropical and subtropical plants (order Aristolochiales).
citíneo adj. (bot.) cytinaceous.
citiso s. m. (bot.) cytisus (Cytisus racemosus).
citissa s. f. a Scythian woman.
citoblasto s. m. (biol.) cytoblast.
citocinese s. f. (biol.) cytokinesis.
citoclástico adj. (biol.) cytoclastic.
citodiagnóstico s. m. (med.) cytodiagnosis: the examination of cells found in organic secretion.

cítola (I) s. f. millclapper, clack of a mill.
cítola (II) s. f. (mus.) cithara, cither, zither.
citólise s. f. (physiol.) cytolysis.
citologia s. f. (biol.) cytology.
citológico adj. (biol.) cytological.
citologista s. m. + f., citólogo s. m. cytologist.
citoplasma s. m. (biol.) cytoplasm.
citoplasmático, citoplásmico adj. (biol.) cytoplasmic.
citoplasto s. m. (biol.) cytoplast.
citostático adj. (biol.) cytostatic: that which inhibits the growing of cells.
citotaxia s. f. (physiol.) cytotaxis.
citráceo adj. citrine, relative to or resembling a citron.
citral s. m. (pl. -ais), (chem.) citral.
citrato s. m. (chem.) citrate.
cítreo adj. citrus, citrine.
cítrico adj. 1. (bot.) citrus, citrine, citrean. 2. (chem.) citric(al).
    ácido ~ citric acid, lemon acid.
citrina s. f. 1. lemon essence. 2. (min.) citrine, a yellow variety of quartz.
citrino adj. citrinous, pale-yellow, citrine.
citronela s. f. (bot.) citronella, citronella grass, common balm mint, horse balm, lemon-verbena.
ciumada, ciumagem (pl. -ens) s. f. 1. deep-rooted jealousy or envy. 2. sudden outburst of jealousy.
ciumar v. to be jealous or envious of, envy.
ciumaria s. f. 1. a deep-rooted jealousy or envy. 2. a sudden outburst of jealousy, fit of jealousy.
ciúme s. m. 1. jealousy. 2. emulation, ambitious rivalry. 3. envy. 4. (bot.) mudar.
    dar ~s a alguém to make s. o. jealous. ele está louco de ~ he is mad with jealousy. ter ~s de alguém to be jealous of s. o.
ciumeira s. f. (pop.) exaggerated jealousy or envy.
ciumento s. m. a jealous person. || adj. jealous, envious.
    ela é -a she is jealous, looks yellow. ele a observou de modo ~ he looked at her jealously.
ciurídeo s. m. 1. a sciurine animal, sciurine. 2. ~s pl. the Sciuridae: the squirrel family. || adj. sciurid, sciurine.
cível s. m. (pl. cíveis) the jurisdiction of civil courts. || adj. m. + f. (jur.) of, pertaining to or relative to civil law, civil. || civelmente adv. civilly.
cívico adj. 1. civic, civil. 2. of or pertaining to a city. 3. relative to citizenship. 4. patriotic(al). || civicamente adv. civically.
    isto é um dever ~ this is a civic duty.
civil s. m. (pl. -is) 1. civilian, (non-military) citizen. 2. gownsman. || adj. m. + f. 1. civil, urbane. 2. polite, courteous. 3. well-bred. 4. friendly, sociable. 5. civilian. 6. of or pertaining to civil law. || ~mente adv. civilly, courteously, sociably.
    casamento ~ civil marriage. causa ~ (jur.) civil cause, civil suit. direito ~ (jur.) civil law. engenheiro ~ civil engineer. guerra ~ civil war, intestine war. posse ~ (jur.) legal possession. tribunal ~ civil court.
civilidade s. f. 1. civility. 2. urbaneness, urbanity. 3. politeness, courtesy. 4. good breeding. 5. niceness, refinedness. 6. good manners.
civilismo s. m. civilism: 1. government by civilians. 2. political party which defends government by civilians.
civilista s. m. + f. 1. civilian, civilist. 2. scholar of civil law. 3. defender of civilism. || adj. civilist, civilian, defending or upholding civil government.
civilização s. f. (pl. -ões) civilization: 1. act of civilizing. 2. culture. 3. state of human development and social progress. 4. refinement, enlightenment.

civilizado adj. 1. civilized. 2. cultured, cultivated. 3. civil, courteous, polite, urbane. 4. well educated, well-bred. 5. refined.
civilizador s. m. civilizer. || adj. civilizing.
civilizar v. 1. to civilize, bring civilization to. 2. to reclaim from (a barbarous state). 3. to instruct, teach, educate. 4. to make urbane or polite. 5. to cultivate. 6. to become civilized.
civilizável adj. m. + f. (pl. -áveis) civilizable.
civismo s. m. 1. civism, principles of good citizenship. 2. patriotism. 3. devotion to public interests and welfare.
cizânia s. f. 1. (bot.) tare, cockle, darnel. 2. (fig.) discord, disharmony. 3. strife, quarrel, brawl.
    semear ~ to foment discord.
cizirão s. m. (pl. -ões) (bot.) 1. tufted vetch, cow vetch. 2. everlasting pea.
clã s. m. 1. clan. 2. tribe, family. 3. a group of families of common extraction. 4. party, society. 5. clique.
cladanto adj. (bot.) cladanthous.
cladóceros s. m. pl. (zool.) Cladocera: an order of branchiopod crustaceans (the water fleas).
cladódio s. m. (bot.) cladode, cladophyll.
clamador s. m. 1. crier, town-crier. 2. clamourer. || adj. crying, clamouring, clamant.
clamante adj. m. + f. clamant, crying out, clamourous, loud.
clamar v. 1. to cry, shout. 2. to clamour, vociferate. 3. to protest or complain loudly. 4. to implore, beseech, supplicate. 5. to plead, beg. 6. to claim.
    ~ aos céus to cry aloud to heaven. ~ em vão to bark at the moon. ~ por justiça to clamour for justice. ~ por socorro to call out for help. ~ vingança to cry out for vengeance.
clâmide s. f. (Greek hist.) chlamys: a short mantle fastened with a clasp in front or at the shoulder.
clamidósporo s. m. (mycology) chlamydospore.
clamor s. m. 1. clamour. 2. great outcry, vociferation. 3. loud call, exclamation. 4. row, racket. 5. complaint. 6. lamentation. 7. alarm. 8. rumour.
clamoroso adj. 1. clamourous. 2. shouting, crying out loudly. 3. vociferous, vociferant. 4. noisy, loud. 5. clamant. 6. complaining, plaintive. || -amente adv. clamourously, vociferously, plaintively.
    é uma injustiça -a it's a crying wrong.
clandestinidade s. f. clandestineness, secrecy, underhandedness.
clandestino s. m. person who acts illegally or clandestinely, esp. a stowaway or illegal passenger. || adj. 1. clandestine. 2. illegal, illicit. 3. underhand. 4. covert, secret. 5. furtive, stealthy. || -amente adv. clandestinely, surreptitiously, underhandedly.
    casamento ~ clandestine marriage, hedge-marriage. fizeram ligação -a no fio telefônico they tapped the telephone wire. temos um passageiro ~ a bordo we have a deadhead on board.
clangor s. m. blare of a trumpet, clang, clangour, peal, rattle.
clangorar, clangorejar v. 1. to blare, clangour, clang, jar. 2. to proclaim, make publicly known, announce.
clangoroso adj. clangorous, plangent. || -amente adv. clangorously.
claque (I) s. f. claqueur(s), a group of paid applauders.
claque (II) s. f. collapsible opera hat, crush-hat, folding hat.
claquista s. m. + f. claqueur, claquer.
clara (I) s. f. 1. the white of an egg. 2. (anat.) sclera. 3. clearing in the woods.
clara (II) s. f. (naut.) helm hole, rudder-hole.
clarabóia s. f. 1. skylight. 2. top-lantern, top-light. 3. louver. 4. fanlight, eye. 5. peep-hole.

clarão (I) s. m. (pl. -ões) 1. glaring radiance, clearness of the sky. 2. brightness, brilliancy. 3. intense light. 4. (fig.) intellectual brightness. 5. (Braz.) clearing in the woods.
clarão (II) s. m. (mus.) clarion (organ stop).
clareação s. f. (pl. -ões) act or process of making clear or lighter, clarification.
clarear v. 1. to clear, clarify. 2. to brighten, illuminate, illume. 3. to enlighten. 4. to make scarce or rare. 5. to enkindle, spark. 6. to dawn. 7. to become light. 8. to be or become dotted with clearings (a forest). 9. (fig.) to become comprehensible or intelligible.
o tempo está clareando the weather is getting brighter.
clareira s. f. clearing in the woods, glade, opening, break (plate F 4).
clarejar v. = clarear.
clarete s. m. claret, a red wine, any red Bordeaux wine. ‖ adj. claret-coloured, dark red.
clareza s. f. 1. clearness, clarity. 2. intelligibility, explicitness. 3. purity, fineness. 4. distinctness. 5. plainness, simplicity. 6. perspicuity. 7. obviousness, evidence. 8. lucidity, lucidness. 9. deed, document containing the terms of a contract.
~ de estilo pureness of style. com ~ distinctly, perspicuously. falar com ~ to speak plainly. falta de ~ obscureness.
claridade s. f. 1. clarity, clearness. 2. brightness, brilliancy. 3. light, shine. 4. blankness. 5. day, sunshine. 6. evidence, plainness. 7. lucidity.
clarificação s. f. (pl. -ões) clarification, act of clarifying.
clarificador s. m. clarifier. ‖ adj. clarifying.
clarificar v. 1. to clarify, make clear. 2. to purify, fine. 3. to explain, elucidate. 4. to purge, cleanse. 5. to purify, refine. 6. to become pure or clear. 7. to repent, regret.
clarificativo adj. clarificative, tending to clarify.
clarim s. m. (pl. -ins) 1. trumpet, clarion, bugle. 2. bugler, trumpeter, clarioner.
clarinada s. f. flourish of horns, fanfare.
clarinar v. to clarion, blow the clarion.
clarineta s. f. (also clarineto, clarinete m.) (mus.) 1. clarinet. 2. clarinet(t)ist, clarinet player.
clarinetista s. m. + f. clarinet(t)ist, clarinet player.
clarissa, clarista s. f. Clarist, nun of the order of St. Clare. ‖ adj. Clarist.
clarividência s. f. 1. clear-sightedness. 2. clairvoyance. 3. perception, sagacity. 4. divination.
clarividente adj. m. + f. 1. clear-sighted. 2. clairvoyant. 3. prudent, cautious. 4. scrutinizing, examining. 5. wise, clever, discerning.
claro s. m. 1. clear space, blank space. 2. a clearing in the wood. 3. the illuminated part of an object. 4. clarity, clearness. 5. brilliancy, brightness. ‖ adj. 1. clear. 2. luminous, bright, brilliant. 3. shining, lucid, light. 4. transparent, evident. 4. limpid, cloudless, unclouded. 6. apparent, evident. 7. clean, pure. 8. express, explicit. 9. frank, open. 10. visible. 11. blond, light-coloured, fair. 12. undeniable, unmistakable. 13. certain. 14. whity, whitish. 15. legible, intelligible. 16. clear-sighted, sharp, penetrative. 17. sunny. 18. unequivocal. 19. distinct. 20. noted, eminent, illustrious. ‖ -amente adv. 1. clearly, clear. 2. brightly, lucidly. 3. cloudlessly. 4. visibly. 5. expressly, explicitly. 6. evident(ly). 7. distinctly. 8. apparently. 9. illustriously.
às claras in the face of the day, in the open, evidently. claro!, está ~! sure!, of course!, it goes without saying! é -amente visível it leaps to the eye. é ~, está ~ it is quite clear. ele deixou esta parte em ~ he omitted that part, he did not

mention that part. ele falou em voz alta e -a he spoke loud and clear. falei -amente com ele I spoke in the vernacular to him. isto é ~ como água that's as plain as a pikestaff; it stares one in the face. passamos a noite em ~ we sat up all night. uma noite em ~ a sleepless night. ~ de entrada the space left blank on the beginning of a paragraph.
claro-escuro s. m. (pl. claros-escuros) 1. the transition from bright light to darkness. 2. chiaroscuro. 3. the contrast of light and shadow and its artistic representation.
claro-escurista s. m. + f. (pl. claro-escuristas) chiaroscurist.
classe s. f. 1. class. 2. category, group. 3. division. 4. school, schoolroom. 5. lecture. 6. kind, caste, sort, variety. 7. group of pupils of about the same age and intellectual standing. 8. (sociology) a social group, social stratum. 9. rank, place. 10. order. 11. type. 12. form, school bench. 13. degree.
~ de alunos class, pupils of a class. ~ média middle class. ~s trabalhadoras working classes. a ~ baixa low life. a ~ dos advogados the legal faculty. a ~ dos proprietários proprietary. a ~ médica the faculty. de alta ~, de primeira ~ first-class, first-rate, a number one, excellent. de ~ classy. é autor de primeira ~ he is a first-rate author. toda a ~ dos negociantes the whole tribe of tradesmen. vida das ~s abastadas high life.
classicismo s. m. classicism: 1. classical system or principles. 2. classic style or phrase. 3. classical literature.
clássico s. m. a classic author, classic(s). ‖ adj. 1. classic(al). 2. of or belonging to a school, schoolroom or course, academic(al). 3. of or relative to Greek or Latin literature. 4. ancient, old, antique. 5. inveterate, deep-rooted. 6. model, serving as an example. ‖ classicamente adv. classically.
autor ~ standard author. educação -a classical scholarship. ele estuda filologia -a he is a student of the classics.
classificação s. f. (pl. -ões) 1. classification, act of classifying. 2. arrangement, assortment. 3. grouping, sorting. 4. qualification. 5. distribution, division (in classes). 6. rating. 7. graduation.
classificado adj. classified, assorted, ranked, systematic(al).
classificador s. m. 1. classifier, assorter, one who groups or arranges. 2. document file, file. ‖ adj. classifying, assorting, classificatory.
~ de algodão cotton sampler. ~ de lã woolsorter, wool stapler.
classificar v. 1. to classify, class. 2. to assort, arrange in groups or ranks. 3. to label, catalogue. 4. to qualify, graduate, grade. 5. to order, rank. 6. to rate. 7. to distribute. 8. to codify.
eles ~am os livros de novo they resorted the books.
classificável adj. m. + f. (pl. -áveis) classifiable, classable.
classismo s. m. = classicismo.
classista s. m. + f. 1. representative or member of a class. 2. one who upholds the system of social classes (as distinguished from the masses). ‖ adj. divided into social classes or ranks, classified.
clástico adj. (geol.) clastic, fragmentary.
rochedos ~s (geol.) clastic rocks.
claudicação s. f. (pl. -ões) 1. claudication. 2. limping. 3. lameness. 4. (fig.) error, mistake, omission. 5. (fig.) imperfection.
claudicante adj. m. + f. 1. claudicant. 2. limping, lame. 3. halting, wavering. 4. (fig.) wrong, imperfect.

claudicar v. 1. to claudicate. 2. to walk lamely. 3. to be lame. 4. (fig.) to halt, waver. 5. to commit a fault. 6. to hobble. 7. to do s. th. imperfectly. 8. to err, go wrong.

claustral s. m. (pl. -ais) the inner patio of a cloister. ‖ adj. m. + f. claustral, cloistral.

claustro s. m. 1. monastery, cloister, convent. 2. inner courtyard of a cloister, patio. 3. (fig.) monastic life. 4. congregation of professors of a university.

claustrofobia s. f. (med.) claustrophobia.

claustrófobo s. m. (med.) person suffering from claustrophobia.

cláusula s. f. 1. clause. 2. condition, stipulation of a contract. 3. passage, proviso. 4. article. 5. precept, rule. 6. rider, additional clause. 7. (mus.) cadence. 8. ~s pl. terms.
~ adicional codicil, rider. ~ condicional (gram.) conditional. ~ de contrato covenant. ~ de ressalva (com., jur.) saving clause.

clausular (I) adj. m. + f. clausular: of, pertaining to or consisting of clauses, clausal.

clausular (II) v. 1. to insert clauses in. 2. to make one's terms, lay down conditions. 3. to divide in clauses or sections. 4. to limit, restrict. 5. to establish clauses.

clausura s. f. 1. clausure. 2. enclosure. 3. claustral confinement. 4. seclusion, retirement. 5. monastic life.

clausurado adj. cloistered, secluded.

clausurar v. 1. to cloister, confine in a cloister. 2. to seclude, immure. 3. (fig.) to lead a secluded life. 4. ~-se to become a monk; take veil.

clava s. f. 1. club, mace, bludgeon. 2. (mus.) clef. ~ dos indígenas waddy, battle-club.

clave s. f. 1. (mus.) clef (plate N 1). 2. axle pin, cotter pin.
~ de fa bass clef (plate N 1). ~ de sol treble clef (plate N 1).

clavecinista s. m. + f. (mus.) clavecinist, clavecin player.

clavecino s. m. (mus.) clavecin, harpsichord.

clavicilindro s. m. (mus.) clavicylinder.

clavicímbalo s. m. (mus.) clavicymbal, clavichord, harpsichord.

clavicítara s. f. (mus.) clavicytherium.

clavicórdio s. m. (mus.) clavichord.

clavicórneo adj. (ent.) clavicorn, having club-shaped feelers.

clavícula s. f. (anat.) clavicle, collar-bone.

claviculado adj. (zool.) claviculate.

clavicular adj. m. + f. clavicular.

claviculário s. m. turnkey, key keeper.

clavifoliado adj. (bot.) clavifoliate, having club-shaped leaves.

claviforme adj. m. + f. claviform, clavate, club--shaped, clubbed.

clavígero adj. (poet.) clavigerous.

clavija s. f. peg, pin, plug, coupling pin.

clavina s. f. carbine, light rifle.

clavinaço s. m. 1. heavy rifle. 2. rifle-shot.

clavineiro s. m. carabineer, gunsmith.

clavinotaço s. m. shot from a light rifle.

clavinote s. m. carbine, light rifle.

clavinoteiro s. m. 1. bandit or soldier armed with a light rifle. 2. criminal, thug.

claviórgão s. m. (pl. claviórgãos), (mus.) claviorgan.

clematite s. f. (bot.) 1. vine bower. 2. clematis, traveller's joy, virgin's bower.

clemência s. f. 1. clemency. 2. indulgence. 3. lenity, mercifulness, forgivingness. 4. kindness, mildness. 5. mercy. 6. amenity, affability.
a ~ do tempo the mildness of weather, temperate-ness.

clemenciar v. to treat with clemency.

clemente adj. m. + f. 1. clement. 2. indulgent. 3. merciful, lenient. 4. forgiving. 5. kind, mild, com-passionate. ‖ ~mente adv. clemently, forgivingly, compassionately.

clenáceas s. f. pl. (bot.) a plant family of the order Malvales (from Madagascar).

clepsidra s. f. water-clock, clepsydra.

cleptofobia s. f. kleptophobia.

cleptomania s. f. (med., psych.) cleptomania, klepto-mania.

cleptomaníaco, cleptômano s. m. (med., psych.) clep-tomaniac, kleptomaniac.

clerestório s. m. (archit.) clerestory, central or prin-cipal part of a church.

clerezia s. f. 1. the clergy (collectively or as a class). 2. priesthood.

clerical adj. m. + f. (pl. -ais) 1. cleric(al). 2. priestly, parsonic(al). 3. ecclesiastic(al). ‖ ~mente adv. cler-ically, priestly, ecclesiastically.

clericalismo s. m. 1. clericalism, sacerdotage. 2. (pol.) clerical party. 3. clerical principles and practices.

clericalista s. m. + f. clericalist.

clericalizar v. to clericalize.

clericato s. m. clerkship, office, dignity and authority of a clergyman, clericate, clericality.

clérigo s. m. 1. cleric, clergyman. 2. churchman, minister. 3. clerk. 4. parson, priest. 5. ecclesiastic.
tornar-se ~ to go into the church.

clero s. m. 1. the clergy (as a class). 2. priesthood. 3. the body of clergymen of a church, chapter of a church.

clerodendro s. m. (bot.) clerodendron.

cleromancia s. f. cleromancy, divination by means of casting dice.

cleromante s. m. + f. cleromancer.

cleromântico adj. cleromantic(al).

cletráceas s. f. pl. Clethraceae: a small family of plants (order Ericales).

cletráceo adj. (bot.) clethraceous.

clianto s. m. (bot.) glory pea.

clichagem s. f. (typogr.) = estereotipagem.

clichê s. m. 1. (typogr.) cliché, stereotype plate. 2. (typogr.) block, electrotype, electroplate. 3. (phot.) negative. 4. (fig.) commonplace, trite phrase or ex-pression.
~ a meio-tom = autotipia. ~ a traço a line-drawn photogravure. segundo ~ second edition of a daily, containing the latest news.

clicheria s. f. 1. cliché manufacture. 2. workshop in which clichés are made.

clicherista s. m. + f. a cliché maker.

cliente s. m. + f. 1. client. 2. dependent, protected person. 3. customer, patron. 4. patient. 5. protegee. ~ externo (med.) outpatient. sem ~s clientless, briefless.

clientela s. f. 1. clientage, body of clients, clientele. 2. customers, patronage. 3. (pol., jur.) constituency. 4. (med.) those who habitually consult with a doctor.
ter boa ~ to have numerous customers.

clima s. m. 1. the average conditions of the weather in a certain place. 2. climate, clime. 3. climatic region. 4. zone, sphere. 5. predominant weather. 6. country. 7. medium, environment, ambient. 8. field of action. 9. latitude(s).
~ subtropical subtropical climate.

clímace s. m. (obs.) climax, culmination.

climatérico adj. 1. (med.) climateric(al). 2. a critical point or period of life. 3. (physiol.) of or referring to the menopause. 4. (fig.) critical, dangerous.

climatério s. m. (med.) climacterium, climacteric, menopause.

climático adj. climatic(al), climatal. ‖ **climaticamente** adv. climatically.
climatização s. f. climatization.
climatizar v. to climatize, acclimate.
climatologia s. f. climatology.
climatológico adj. climatologic(al), climatic(al).
clímax s. m. 1. climax. 2. the highest point, culmination. 3. apex. 4. crown. 5. (rhet.) gradation. **no** ~ at the full.
clina s. f. horsehair, mane, tail, crine.
clinândrio s. m. (bot.) clinandrium, androclinium.
clinanto s. m. (bot.) clinanthium.
clínica s. f. (med.) 1. hospital, clinic, medical establishment. 2. a doctor's patients collectively. 3. practice of medicine.
exercer ~ to practise medicine. **médico de** ~ **geral** general practitioner.
clinicar v. to practise medicine.
clínico s. m. doctor, physician, general practitioner, clinician. ‖ adj. clinical.
ensino ~ practical medical instruction.
clinocloro s. m. (min.) clinochlore, ripidolite.
clinomania s. f. (path.) a morbid and exaggerated staying in bed.
clinômetro s. m. clinometer, instrument for measuring the inclination of slopes.
clinométrico adj. clinometric(al).
clínquer s. m. clinker.
clinudo adj. 1. having a long mane. 2. hairy, shaggy.
clipe s. m. clip (plate C 11).
clipeado adj. clypeate.
clipeiforme adj. m. + f. clypeiform, scutiform.
clípeo s. m. 1. (zool.) clypeus. 2. (poet.) shield, clipeus.
clíper s. m. (naut.) clipper, clipper ship.
clique s. m. clique, set, coterie. ‖ interj. click!: light sharp noise, clicking noise.
clister s. m. (med., also **clisma**) clyster, enema.
clitelo s. m. (zool.) clitellum.
clitoridiano adj. clitoridean.
clitóris s. m. sg. + pl. (anat.) clitoris.
clivagem s. f. (pl. **-ens**), (cryst.) cleavage.
clivar v. to cleave (in accordance with the structure of a crystal).
clívia s. f. (bot.) Kaffir lily.
clivo s. m. 1. sideway, steep street. 2. hill, hillock, knoll. 3. slope, hillside, acclivity.
clivoso adj. 1. steep. 2. acclivitous, declivitous. 3. hilly.
cloaca s. f. 1. sewer, sink. 2. cesspit, cesspool. 3. latrine. 4. filthy, bad-smelling place. 5. (fig.) moral corruption. 6. (zool.) cloaca.
cloacal adj. m. + f. (pl. **-ais**) cloacal.
cloacino adj. 1. of or pertaining to a sewer or sewer system. 2. of or relative to a latrine. 3. (fig.) indecent.
cloacite s. f. (vet.) cloacitis, inflammation of the cloaca.
cloasma s. m. (med.) chloasma, liver spots.
cloasonado adj. cloisonné.
clone s. m. (biol., bot.) clone.
clônico adj. (med.) clonic.
clopemania s. f. (med., psych.) cleptomania.
cloração s. f. (pl. **-ões**) chlorination.
clorado adj. (chem.) chlorinated.
cloral s. m. (pl. **-ais**), (chem.) chloral. chloral hydrate.
cloranfenicol s. m. (chem.) chloramphenicol.
clorantáceas s. f. pl. (bot.) Chloranthaceae: a family of tropical herbs (order Piperales).
clorantia s. f. (bot.) chloranthy.
cloranto adj. having green flowers.
clorar v. to chlorinate, treat with chlorine.

clorato s. m. (chem.) chlorate.
~ **de bário** barium chlorate. ~ **de cálcio** calcium chlorate. ~ **de potássio** potassium chlorate.
clorela s. f. (bot.) Chlorella: a genus of green algae.
cloremia s. f. (med.) chloremia, chlorosis.
clorênquima s. m. (bot.) chlorenchyma: a vegetable tissue provided with chlorophyl.
cloretemia s. f. (med.) morbid state caused by the presence of chlorine in the blood.
cloreto s. m. (chem.) chloride.
~ **áurico** aurous chloride, gold chloride. ~ **de alumínio** aluminum chloride. ~ **de cal** lime chloride. ~ **de cálcio** calcium chloride. ~ **de cobre** cupric chloride. ~ **de enxofre** sulphur monochloride. ~ **de estanho** stannic chloride. ~ **de sódio** sodium chloride. ~ **mercuroso** mercurous chloride. ~ **platínico** platinic chloride.
clórico adj. (chem.) chloric.
clorídrico adj. (chem.) hydrochloric, chloridic, muriatic. **ácido** ~ hydrochloric acid.
clorita s. f. (min.) chlorite.
clorito s. m. (chem.) chlorite.
clorítico adj. (chem.) chloritic.
cloritóide s. m. (min.) chloritoid.
cloritoso adj. (chem.) chloritic.
cloro s. m. (chem.) chlorine.
clorocisto s. m. (bot.) a series of cells containing chlorophyl which are found in certain moss.
clorofana s. f. (min.) chlorophane.
clorofânio s. m. (physiol.) chlorophane.
clorofenol s. m. (chem.) chlorophenol.
cloroficeas s. f. pl. (bot.) Chlorophyceae: a class of light green algae.
clorofila s. f. (bot.) chlorophyll.
clorofilado adj. chlorophyllaceous, consisting of or containing chlorophyll.
clorofilase s. f. (biochem.) chlorophyllase.
cloroformado adj. treated with chloroform.
clorofórmico adj. chloroformic.
clorofórmio s. m. (chem., med.) chloroform.
cloroformização s. f. (pl. **-ões**) chloroformization.
cloroformizar v. to chloroform, chloroformize.
cloroleucito s. m. (biol., bot.) chloroleucite, chloroplast.
clorometria s. f. (chem.) chlorometry.
clorométrico adj. (chem.) chlorometric.
clorômetro s. m. (chem.) chlorometer.
cloromicetina s. f. (pharm.) chloromycetin.
cloropicrina s. f. (chem.) chloropicrin, chlorpicrin.
cloroplastídio, cloroplasto s. m. (biol.) chloroplast, chloroplastid.
clorose s. f. 1. (med.) chlorosis, green-sickness. 2. (bot.) chlorosis, etiolation.
cloroso adj. (chem.) chlorous.
clorótico adj. chlorotic: 1. (med.) affected by chlorosis. 2. (bot.) destitute of chlorophyll.
clube s. m. 1. club. 2. club-house. 3. sorority. 4. association, society. 5. assembly, gathering. 6. guild.
clubista s. m. + f. clubber, club-member.
clunâmbulo s. m. cripple; stunted or deformed person, who moves about on his buttocks.
cluniacense s. m. Cluniac monk. ‖ adj. Cluniac.
clupeio s. m. (ichth.) common designation of the clupeid fish (sardines, herrings).
clupeídeos s. m. pl. (ichth.) Clupeideae: sardines, herrings.
clúpeo s. m. (ichth.) clupeoid, clupeoid fish.
cnêmide, cnêmida s. f. (hist.) protective armour for the shinbone.
cnidário s. m. (zool.) cnidarian, coelenterate.
cnidoblasto s. m. (zool.) cnidoblast.
cnidose s. f. (med.) urticaria.
cnute s. m. knout.

coa agglutination of the words **com** and **a** = with the.

côa s. f. straining, filtration.

coabitação s. f. (pl. -ões) cohabitation, companionate marriage, dwelling together.

coabitador s. m. cohabitant. ‖ adj. cohabiting.

coabitante s. m. + f. cohabitant, cohabiter.

coabitar v. 1. to cohabit, dwell together. 2. to live together. 3. to bed, live as husband and wife.

coação (I) s. f. (pl. -ões) straining, filtration.

coação (II) s. f. (pl. -ões) 1. coaction. 2. compulsion. 3. constraint. 4. enforcement.

coacervar v. 1. to accumulate, coacervate. 2. to pile up, heap up. 3. to collect, bring together (crowd).

co-acusado s. m. (jur.) codefendant.

coada s. f. 1. a solution of lye. 2. filtered water (used for the preparation of lye). 3. strained vegetables.

coadjutor s. m. 1. (R. C. Church) coadjutor, assistant of a parish priest or bishop. 2. assistant, helper. 3. accomplice.

coadjutora s. f. coadjutress, coadjutrix.

coadjutoria s. f. coadjutorship.

coadjuvação s. f. (pl. -ões) coadjuvancy, co-operation.

coadjuvante adj. m. + f. coadjuvant, co-operating.

coadjuvar v. 1. to coadjuvate. 2. to help, assist, aid. 3. to work for a common cause, co-operate.

co-administração s. f. (pl. **co-administrações**) co--administration.

co-administrador s. m. (pl. **co-administradores**) co-administrator.

co-administrar v. to co-administer.

coado adj. filtered, strained.

coador s. m. 1. percolator. 2. filter, strainer. 3. sieve. 4. colander (plate C 20). 5. perforated cup or cloth bag of a coffee percolator.

coadquirente s. m. + f. co-acquirer, partner of a joint acquisition. ‖ adj. acquiring jointly.

coadquirir v. to acquire jointly, acquire together with another person.

coadunação s. f. (pl. -ões) 1. coadunation, act of uniting dissimilar substances in one mass. 2. union, congregation. 3. joinder. 4. combination. 5. incorporation.

coadunado adj. coadunate, united, incorporated, adapted.

coadunar v. 1. to coadunate, unite into one. 2. to join, incorporate. 3. to combine. 4. ~-se: a) to adjust o. s. to. b) to resign o. s. to. c) to agree with.

coadunável adj. m. + f. (pl. -áveis) capable of being united.

coadura s. f. 1. act of straining, filtration. 2. the passage of liquid through a filter or percolator. 3. the filtered liquid.

coagente adj. m. + f. coercive, coactive.

coagido adj. constrained, strained, forced, unspontaneous.

coagir v. 1. to coerce. 2. to constrain, restrain. 3. to force. 4. to oblige, compel. 5. to drive on, throng upon. 6. to bulldoze.

coagmentação s. f. (pl. -ões) 1. act of joining. 2. moulding. 3. kneading. 4. cementing.

coagmentar v. 1. to mould, mold. 2. to join, put together. 3. to knead, amass. 4. to cement.

coagmento s. m. act of joining or putting together.

coagulação s. f. (pl. -ões) 1. coagulation. 2. the jellylike substance formed by coagulation.

coagulado adj. coagulated, curdy, grumous.

coagulador s. m. 1. abomasum. 2. rennet. 3. coagulator. ‖ adj. coagulative, coagulatory.

coagulante s. m. coagulant, coagulant agent. ‖ adj. m. + f. coagulative, coagulatory, coagulating.

coagular v. 1. to coagulate. 2. to curdle, clot. 3. to clabber. 4. to congeal. 5. to cause or produce the coagulation of. 6. to become solid, thicken, set.

coagulável adj. m. + f. (pl. -áveis) coagulable.

coágulo s. m. 1. the coagulated part or particle of a liquid, coagulum, clot. 2. coagulase, coagulant. 3. coagulation. 4. the result of a coagulative process. 5. rennet.

coajerucu s. m. tree of the family Annonaceae, the custard-apple family (Xylopia fructescens).

coala s. m. (zool.) koala.

coalescência s. f. 1. adhesion. 2. coalescence, coalition. 3. combination. 4. agglutination.

coalescente adj. m. + f. coalescent, cohering, growing together.

coalescer v. 1. to coalesce. 2. to adhere. 3. to unite by growth, grow together. 4. to combine. 5. to agglutinate.

coalhada s. f. curdled milk, clabber.

~ **e soro de leite** curds and whey.

coalhado adj. 1. curdled, curdy. 2. jellied. 3. sour. 4. solidified. 5. full of.

coalhadura s. f. 1. process or result of curdling. 2. curdled substance. 3. coagulation.

coalha-leite s. f. (pl. **coalhas-leite**), (bot.) cardoon.

coalhar v. 1. to curdle, curd. 2. to turn, clabber. 3. to clod, set. 4. to coagulate. 5. ~-se to thicken, become coagulated.

coalheira (I) s. f. 1. rennet. 2. (zool.) abomasum.

coalheira (II) s. f. (Port., prov.) collar, hame.

coalho s. m. 1. coagulum. 2. rennet. 3. (zool.) abomasum. 4. curd(s). 5. coagulator. 6. (bot.) cardoon. 7. clot.

coalizão s. f. (pl. -ões) (also **coalização**) coalition, alliance, union.

coalizar-se v. 1. to coalesce with, coalize. 2. to unite, confederate.

coaltar s. m. coal tar, pitch.

co-aluno s. m. (pl. **co-alunos**) a schoolmate.

cóano s. m. (anat.) choana.

coanócito s. m. (zool.) choanocyte.

co-apóstolo s. m. (pl. **co-apóstolos**) co-apostle.

coaptação s. f. (pl. -ões), (med., surg.) coaptation.

coar v. 1. to filter, strain. 2. to percolate. 3. to distill. 4. to cast, found, pour the molten metal into the mould. 5. to infiltrate. 6. to drip, drop. 7. to penetrate little by little. 8. to pass along furtively. 9. to enter in, penetrate.

Coaraci s. m. sun-god of the Tupi tribes.

coarctação, coartação s. f. (pl. -ões) 1. restriction in size. 2. coarctation. 3. restriction, limitation. 4. (med.) the narrowing of a canal or orifice. 5. squeeze.

coarctada, coartada s. f. (jur.) 1. justification, excuse. 2. vigorous reply, refutation. 3. coarctation.

coarctado, coartado adj. coarctate, restrained, restricted.

coarctar, coartar v. to coarct, restrain, restrict, confine.

co-arrendamento s. m. (pl. **co-arrendamentos**) co--leasing.

co-arrendar v. to co-lease.

coativo adj. coactive, coercive.

coato, coacto adj. obliged, forced, coerced.

co-autor s. m. (pl. **co-autores**) 1. co-author, collaborator. 2. (jur.) complice, accomplice, associate.

co-autoria s. f. (pl. **co-autorias**) co-authorship.

co-avalista s. m. + f. (pl. **co-avalistas**) co-guarantor.

coaxação (pl. -ões), **coaxada** s. f. croaking (of a frog).

coaxante adj. m. + f. croaky.

coaxar v. to croak.

coaxi s. m. (N. Braz.) soft mud that remains on the fields after an inundation.

coaxo s. m. croak, croaking.

cobaia s. f. (zool.) guinea-pig, cavy.
ela fê-lo sua ~ she made him her cat's paw.

cobáltico adj. (min.) cobaltic.

cobaltífero adj. (min.) cobaltiferous.

cobalto s. m. (chem., min.) cobalt (chemical symbol Co).

cobaltoso adj. (chem.) cobaltous.

cobarde s. m. + f. 1. coward, faint-heart. 2. poltroon. 3. treacherous or perfidious fellow. ‖ adj. 1. timid, fearful. 2. cowardly, craven. 3. treacherous, tricky, perfidious.
mostrar-se ~ to show the white feather.

cobardia, cobardice s. f. 1. timidity, faint-heartedness. 2. pusillanimity. 3. cowardice. 4. treachery, perfidious act.

coberta s. f. 1. cover, cap (plate L 2). 2. covering, coverture, coverlet, coverlid. 3. blanket, bedspread, spread. 4. hood (plate L 1). 5. case, casing, casement. 6. roof, material used to cover a building. 7. shelter. 8. envelope, sheath, wrapper. 9. (naut.) deck. 10. clothing. 11. course or sequence of dishes at a meal.
~ **de cama** quilt. ~ **de lona** tilt. ~ **de penas** featherbed. ~ **de proa** (naut.) foredeck. **baralhar as** ~s to get into a conflict. **navio de três** ~s (naut.) three-decker. **pôr-se à** ~ to put o. s. on the safe side, protect o. s. **segunda** ~ **de um navio** (naut.) tonnage-deck. **sem** ~ bare.

coberto s. m. 1. shed, shelter. 2. veranda, porch. ‖ adj. + p. p. 1. covered. 2. hooded. 3. protected, sheltered. 4. coated. 5. hidden. 6. lidded. 7. clothed, clad, dressed. 8. outbid (at an auction). 9. obscure, dark.
a mesa estava -a de moscas the table was thick with flies. ~ **com bolhas** beady. ~ **com nuvens** cloudy, cloud-capped. ~ **de árvores** woody, bosky. ~ **de cinza** cindery. ~ **de folhagem** bowery. ~ **de grama** grass-grown, green, grassy, turf-clad. ~ **de lágrimas** suffused with tears. ~ **de mato** wooded. ~ **de nós** knobby. ~ **de palha** straw-thatched. ~ **de pústulas** blotched, blotchy. ~ **de vime** wattled. **barco** ~ a decked boat. **estar** ~ to be covered by sufficient security.

cobertor s. m. 1. blanket. 2. coverlet, quilt. 3. counterpane, bedspread. 4. hangings, wall drapery. 5. wrapper.
~ **pespontado de cama** comforter. ~ **elétrico** electric blanket. ~ **para viagem** steamer rug.

cobertura s. f. 1. cover, covering (plates F 7, T 5). 2. envelope, wrapper. 3. headdress. 4. overlay, facing. 5. case, casing. 6. roof (plates A 11, V 1). 7. roofing, roof covering (plate T 5). 8. coat, cape. 9. canopy. 10. escort, bodyguard.
~ **acolchoada** duvet. ~ **de fundos** provision of funds. ~ **superior** (de navio) (naut.) saloon deck. **a** ~ **da casa** the roofing of the house (plate T 5).

cobiça s. f. 1. avarice, avariciousness. 2. envy, enviousness. 3. violent desire or longing. 4. greediness, avidity. 5. eagerness. 6. acquisitiveness. 7. covetousness.

cobiçante adj. m. + f. covetous, greedy.

cobiçar v. 1. to covet, lust after. 2. to desire, long for. 3. to envy. 4. to desire ambitiously or covetously.
ele está cobiçando com os olhos he looks longingly at.

cobiçável adj. m. + f. (pl. **-áveis**) enviable, covetable.

cobiçoso adj. 1. covetous, greedy. 2. avaricious. 3. desirous, longing for. 4. ambitious. ‖ **-amente** adv. covetously, avariciously.

cobol s. f. (data processing) Cobol (abbr. of co(mmon) b(usiness) o(riented) l(anguage)).

cobra s. f. 1. (zool.) snake, serpent, adder. 2. any object resembling a snake. 3. (fig.) a sneaking, treacherous person, wicked tongue.
dizer ~s **e lagartos de alguém** to defame another person, speak ill of s. o. **ele comeu** ~ he is very ill-humoured. **ele ficou** ~ he grew very angry. **encantador de** ~s snake-charmer. **picada de** ~ snake bite. **matar a** ~ **e mostrar o pau** to make a statement and further prove it. **ruim como a** ~ wily, crafty or cunning as a snake. **saber mais que as** ~s to be more cunning than snakes.

cobra-cega s. f. (pl. **cobras-cegas**), (zool.) slow-worm, blind-worm, any limbless lizard.

cobra-coral s. f. (pl. **cobras-coral**), (zool.) coral-snake.

cobra-d'água s. f. (pl. **cobras-d'água**), (zool.) 1. grass-snake, ringed snake. 2. water-snake. 3. water moccasin.

cobra-de-asa s. f. (pl. **cobras-de-asa**), (ent.) lantern fly.

cobra-de-cabelo s. f. (pl. **cobras-de-cabelo**), (zool.) hair-worm.

cobra-de-duas-cabeças s. f. (pl. **cobras-de-duas-cabeças**) (Braz.) slow-worm, blind-worm.

cobra-de-veado s. f. (pl. **cobras-de-veado**), (Braz., zool.) boa constrictor.

cobra-de-vidro s. f. (pl. **cobras-de-vidro**), (zool.) glass snake, slow-worm, blind-worm.

cobrado adj. gathered, collected.

cobra-do-ar s. f. (pl. **cobras-do-ar**), (ent.) lantern fly.

cobra-do-banhado s. f. (pl. **cobras-do-banhado**), (zool.) pantherine snake.

cobra-do-mar s. f. (pl. **cobras-do-mar**), (ichth.) 1. sea-serpent, sea-snake. 2. snake eel.

cobrador s. m. 1. bill collector, collector. 2. receiver. 3. tax-exacter, tax-gatherer.
~ **importuno** dun, dunner.

cobrança s. f. 1. act or result of collecting. 2. collection, encashment. 3. exaction (of taxes).

cobra-papagaio s. f. (pl. **cobras-papagaio**), (zool.) a pit viper (Bothrops bilineata).

cobrar v. 1. to receive, take back (debts). 2. to get in. 3. to collect, encash. 4. to recover, reacquire, regain. 5. to charge. 6. to exact. 7. to recover strength, restore o. s. 8. (whale fishing) to take in the harpoon rope. 9. (ftb.) to kick (as a penalty).
~ **aluguel** to collect rent. ~ **em excesso** to rack, supercharge. ~ **forças** to recover one's strength. ~ **impostos** to gather taxes, levy taxes. ~ **pedágio** to take toll of. ~ **preço inferior ao usual** to undercharge. ~ **uma dívida** to charge a debt. **ele não cobrou ânimo** he did not yet take a heart. **eles cobram preços absurdos** they charge awfully high prices.

cobra-topete s. f. (pl. **cobras-topete**), (zool.) a pit viper (Bothrops jararacussu).

cobrável adj. m. + f. (pl. **-áveis**) chargeable, collectable.

cobre s. m. 1. copper (chemical symbol Cu). 2. any copper coin. 3. (fig.) money.
~ **amarelo** brass. ~ **bruto** coarse copper. ~ **fundido** cast copper. **cair com os** ~s, **espichar os** ~s, **passar os** ~s to pay. **lâminas de** ~ copper plates, copper sheating. **liga de** ~ **e zinco** tombac, tomback. **semelhante ao** ~ coppery. **torrar nos** ~s (Braz., pop.) to sell at any price.

cobreamento s. m. copper-facing.

cobrear v. 1. to cover or sheath with copper. 2. to copper, coat with copper. 3. to treat with copper.

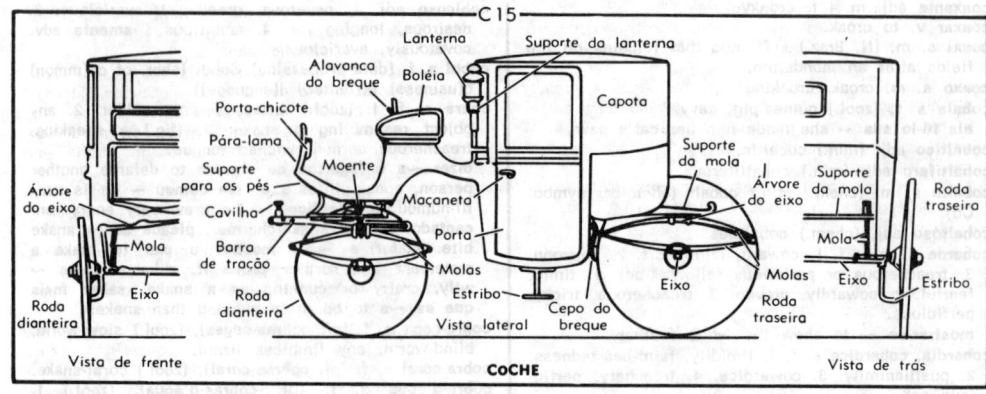

C 15

Vista de frente

Vista lateral

COCHE

Vista de trás

cobreira s. f. (pop.) sugar cane brandy.

cobreiro s. m. (Braz., med., pop.) shingles (an inflammation of the skin), herpes zoster.

cobrejar v. to serpentine, twist, wind, meander.

cobrelo s. m. 1. (zool.) any small snake. 2. (med., pop.) herpes zoster, shingles.

cobre-nuca s. m. (pl. cobre-nucas) neck-cloth.

cobre-peito s. m. (pl. cobre-peitos) a kind of leather apron used by farmers and esp. cowboys.

cobricama s. f. coverlet, counterpane, bedspread.

cobrição s. f. (pl. -ões) copulation (of horses, cattle, dogs).

cobrimento s. m. 1. act of covering. 2. coverage, covering. 3. coating, facing. 4. roofing.

cobrinha s. f. 1. a small snake. 2. any long snakelike creature. 3. a long line of people.

cobrir v. 1. to cover, place or spread s. th. over. 2. to hide, conceal. 3. to cloak, hood. 4. to sheathe, shield. 5. to curtain. 6. to shroud, enshroud, enfold. 7. to mantle, case. 8. to coat, line, face. 9. to protect, defend. 10. to envelop, wrap. 11. to overlay, overspread. 12. to spread, strew, scatter. 13. to disguise, dissimulate. 14. to clothe. 15. to outdo, surpass. 16. to stop up, plug. 17. to copulate with (domestic animals). 18. to overcast, obscure, encloud. 19. to travel over a certain distance, cover a distance, run through. 20. to put on the hat (or cap, hood). 21. to pay, compensate. 22. to roof a building. 23. ~-se: a) to take shelter, cover o. s. b) to become cloudy (sky). c) (com.) to obtain sufficient security for one's risks. d) to become sad or worried.

~ com abóbada to vault. ~ com açúcar to cover with crystallized sugar, to glaze, ice. ~ com grama to turf, grass. ~ com imundície to befoul. ~ com neve to cover with snow. ~ com nuvens to becloud. ~ com tábuas to clapboard, board. ~ com tinta to overpaint. ~ com véu to veil. ~ de cera to coat with wax. ~ de neve to oversnow. ~ de pano to drape. ~ de pedregulho to gravel. ~ de vegetação to overgrow. ~ grande distância to pass over a great distance. ~ habitualmente um percurso to ply a course. ~ por completo to overcover. ~ um lance (em leilão) to overbid, outbid (at an auction). ~-se de folhas to burst into leaf, to leaf. ~-se de suor to be all in perspiration. cobrimos a distância de três milhas we covered a distance of three miles. cobriram suas cabeças they covered their heads. cubra-se! put on your hat! ela cobriu bem a criança she tucked the child well up. ele cobriu a criança de beijos he stifled (or smothered) the

child with kisses. esta quantia cobrirá toda a despesa this sum will pay everything. o preço não cobre as despesas the price does not cover the cost.

cobro (ô) (I) s. m. 1. end, termination, ending close. 2. collection, encashment. 3. fee.

cobro (ô) (II) s. m. 1. any small snake. 2. (med., pop.) herpes zoster, shingles. 3. (naut.) one coil of the anchor rope.

cobu s. m. a biscuit made of cornmeal baked in banana leaves.

coca (I) s. f. watching, spying, act of spying out.
estar à ~ to be on the watch or lookout, lurk for.

coca (II) s. f. 1. (bot.) coca (Erythroxylon coca). 2. the dried leaves of this plant. 3. (pharm.) any alkaloid extracted from this plant.
dar ~ (pop.) to fascinate.

coca (III) s. f. kink (of a rope or cable).

coca (IV) s. f. (bot.) any one of the hollow cells of a pericarp.

coca (V) s. f. (hist., naut.) a kind of pinnace.

coca (V) s. f. (Port., prov.) pumpkin, gourd.

coca (ô) (I) s. f. 1. head scarf. 2. hood, cowl. 3. bogeyman, hobgoblin, bugbear.

coca (ô) (II) s. f. (Port., prov.) scratch.

coça s. f. (pop.) 1. act of scratching. 2. a volley of blows, a sound thrashing.

cocada s. f. 1. a sweetmeat made of coconuts and sugar. 2. (pop.) a blow on the head. 3. messenger or person who serves as a go-between for lovers. 4. pander, procurer.

coçado adj. threadbare, shiny, shabby.

coçadura s. f. act or consequence of scratching.

cocaína s. f. (pharm.) cocain(e), dope (sl.)

cocainismo s. m. (med.) cocainism.

cocainização s. f. (pl. -ões) cocainization.

cocainizar v. to cocainize, treat or anaesthetize with cocaine.

cocainomania s. f. (med.) cocainomania.

cocainômano s. m. (med.) cocainomaniac, drug addict, drug fiend.

cocal s. m. (pl. -ais) a grove of coconut palms or related species.

cocanha s. f. a climbing pole (frequently covered with tallow) on the top of which hang prizes or surprise packages.

cocão s. m. (pl. -ões) the rustic wooden bearing(s) of an oxcart.

cocar (I) s. m. 1. the plume of a helmet. 2. cockade, rosette. 3. knot, topknot. 4. crest.

cocar (II) v. to be on the lookout, lurk for.

coçar v. 1. to scratch. 2. to itch. 3. to rub. 4. to tickle. 5. (pop.) to give a sound thrashing. 6. to meet with difficulties. 7. (fig.) to excite, irritate. 8. ~-se to scratch o. s.

ele já tem com que se ~ he has already enough difficulties to overcome. **não ter tempo para se ~** to have not even a moment to waste.

cócaras s. f. pl. squatting.

cocarda s. f. cockade.

cocção s. f. (pl. **-ões**) 1. the act of cooking. 2. cooking, boiling. 3. concoction. 4. digestion of food.

coccídio s. m. (zool.) 1. scale insect. 2. ~s pl. Coccidae: a family of homopterous insects. ‖ adj. coccid.

coccídia s. f. (zool.) 1. coccidian. 2. ~s pl. Coccidia: an order of protozoans.

coccígeo, coccigiano adj. (anat.) coccygeal.

coccinelídeo s. m. (ent.) any insect of the genus Coccinella.

coccíneo adj. scarlet, garnet-red.

cóccix s. m. (anat.) coccyx.

cócegas s. f. pl. 1. tickle, tickling. 2. titillation. 3. itching. 4. (fig.) desire, sensual appetite. 5. (fig.) impatience, restlessness.

fazer ~ a alguém to tickle a person. **ter ~ na língua** to have a mind to speak.

coceguento adj. ticklish.

coceira s. f. itching, itch.

causar ~ to tickle.

cocha s. f. 1. (naut.) each strand of a rope or cable. 2. act of twisting several strands into a rope. 3. zeal, diligence. 4. recommendation. 5. (Braz.) courage, bravery, spirit. 6. dexterity, skill.

~ de cabo (naut.) kink in a rope. **dar ~s num cabo** (naut.) to lay a cable. **perder a ~** to lose heart, become discouraged.

cocha (ô) s. f. wooden trough.

cochada s. f. a coachful.

cochado adj. 1. (naut.) close-hauled. 2. (fig.) tight, close. 3. thick, dense.

cochar v. 1. (naut.) to lay a rope or cable. 2. to tighten, compress, constrict. 3. to recommend.

coche (ô) (I) s. m. coach, carriage (plate C 15).

coche (ô) (II) s. m. hod, wooden tray for mortar.

cocheira s. f. coach-house, box, cart-house.

cocheiro s. m. 1. coachman, cab-driver, driver, coachee. 2. the Greater Bear: a northern constellation.

cochichada s. f. 1. a crushed or cocked hat. 2. a blow on the hat of an opponent.

cochichador s. m. whisperer, one who murmurs. ‖ adj. whispering.

cochichar v. 1. to whisper, murmur. 2. to mutter. 3. to buzz. 4. to speak in a low voice.

cochicho (I) s. m. act of whispering, whisper, buzz, muttering.

cochicho (II) s. m. 1. (ornith.) skylark, field-lark. 2. a children's plaything which imitates the call of a lark. 3. a very small hut or room. 4. an old hat. 5. (Braz., ornith.) a bird of the family Dendrocolaptidae, the tree creeper (Anumbius anumbi).

cochicholo, cochichó s. m. a very small hut or room, hovel, dog-hole.

cochila s. f. (Braz.) a treeless mountain range.

cochilar v. 1. to nod off, doze away. 2. to nap, doze, snooze, drowse. 3. (fig.) to become careless or negligent. 4. (fig.) to err, make a mistake.

cochilo s. m. 1. act of dozing. 2. nap, doze, drowse. 3. (fig.) carelessness, negligence. 4. (fig.) mistake, error, oversight, slip.

cochinada s. f. 1. a herd of small pigs. 2. dirt, filth. 3. (fig.) an indecorous act, indecency.

cochinar v. 1. to grunt (as a pig). 2. to make a clamour, shout, outcry.

Cochinchina s. f. Cochin-China.

cochinchino s. m. (also **cochinchinense** m. + f., **cochinchinês** m. pl. **-eses**; f. **-esa**) 1. Cochin-Chinese: native or inhabitant of Cochin-China. 2. the language spoken in this country. ‖ adj. of, pertaining to or relative to Cochin-China, its inhabitants and language.

cochinês s. m. (pl. **-eses**) (f. **-esa**) native or inhabitant of Cochin or Madras (India). ‖ adj. of or relative to this state and its people.

cochinilha s. f. 1. (ent.) cochineal insect. 2. cochineal, a scarlet dyestuff extracted from these insects.

cochino s. m. 1. hog, pig. 2. a filthy person. 3. grumbler, grouchy fellow. ‖ adj. dirty, filthy.

cocho (ô) (I) s. m. (pl. **cochos**) 1. hod, trug (plate A 7). 2. trough (plate E 11). 3. coconut. 4. bearing housing of a whetstone.

comer no mesmo ~ to place o. s. on the same level with.

cocho (ô) (II) s. m. (pl. **cochos**) (Port., prov.) pig.

cochonilha s. f. = **cochinilha**.

cochonilha-verde s. f. (pl. **cochonilhas-verdes**) (Braz.) a green scale louse (Coccus viridis).

cociente s. m. quotient.

cóclea s. f. 1. (anat.) cochlea. 2. caracole, spiral stair. 3. Archimedean screw.

cocleado adj., **coclear** adj. m. + f. 1. cochlear, cochleate(d). 2. spirally, helical. 3. twisted, winding. 4. in form of a screw.

cocleária s. f. (bot.) cochlearia, scurvy-grass.

cocleariforme adj. m. + f. (bot.) cochleariform: spoon-shaped (plate F 5).

coclearídeos s. m. pl. (ornith.) Cochlearidae: a family of wading birds (boat-billed heron).

cocleiforme adj. m. + f. cochleate(d), cochleiform.

coclospermáceas s. f. pl. Cochlospermaceae: a family of tropical shrubs or trees (order Hypericales).

coclospermáceo adj. (bot.) cochlospermaceous.

coco (I) s. m. (bact.) coccus, bacteria.

coco (II) s. m. koku: a Japanese dry measure equivalent to about 180 litres.

coco (ô) (I) s. m. 1. common name of numerous palm trees, coconut tree or palm. 2. the fruit of these palms, coconut. 3. a drinking vessel made of a coconut shell. 4. cup. 5. dipper, ladle. 6. (pop.) head, skull. 7. (pop.) lots of money.

leite de ~ coconut milk. **óleo de ~** coconut oil.

coco (ô) (II) s. m. act of watching or spying.

coco (ô) (III) s. m. (N. Braz.) a popular dance and dance music.

cocó s. m. topknot, feminine hairdo consisting of a coiled knot of hair on the top of the head.

cocô s. m. excrement.

coco-amargoso s. m. (pl. **cocos-amargosos**) the fruit of a palm tree (Syagrus oleracea).

coco-da-baía s. m. (pl. **cocos-da-baía**), (bot.) common coconut palm.

coco-das-ilhas s. m. (pl. **cocos-das-ilhas**), (bot.) sea coconut.

coco-de-catarro s. m. (pl. **cocos-de-catarro**), mucaja palm tree, macaw-tree.

coco-de-colher s. m. (pl. **cocos-de-colher**) a green coconut the pulp of which may be eaten with a spoon.

coco-de-purga s. m. (pl. **cocos-de-purga**), (bot.) andá.

coco-de-quaresma s. m. (pl. **cocos-de-quaresma**), (bot.) a coconut palm (Cocos pycrophylla).

coco-de-vassoura s. m. (pl. **cocos-de-vassoura**), (bot.) spiny clubpalm.

coco-do-mar s. m. (pl. **cocos-do-mar**), (bot.) sea coconut.

coco-indaiá s. m. (pl. **cocos-indaiás**) (Braz.) = anajá.
coco-macaúba s. m. (pl. **cocos-macaúbas**) (Braz.) = coco-de-catarro.
cócoras s. f. (pl. squatting.
estar de ~ to squat, sit upon the hams or heels.
cocoré s. m. row, fracas, brawl.
cocoricar v. to crow.
cocório adj. 1. tricky, deceitful. 2. fraudulent. 3. feigned, simulated. 4. false.
cocoroca s. f. (ichth.) the yellow grunt.
cocorocó, cocorocô s. m. (also **cocoricó, cocoricô**) a cock's crow, crowing.
cocorote s. m. a blow on the head with the knuckles.
cocote s. f. cocotte, strumpet, prostitute.
cocre s. m. 1. boat-hook, grapnel. 2. grappling-iron. 3. a rap on the head with the knuckles.
co-credor s. m. (pl. **co-credores**) (com.) cocreditor, joint creditor.
cocular v. to heap up, fill up.
coculina s. f. (Braz.) cocculin: a poison extracted from the juice and berries of the anamirta vine (Anamirta cocculus).
coculo s. m. overmeasure, overfilling, overflow, excess.
cocoruta s. f., **cocoruto** m. 1. top, summit, apex. 2. the crown of the head (plates C 18, P 8). 3. vertex, zenith. 4. knoll, hillock. 5. the hump of zebu cattle.
coda s. f. (mus.) coda.
codagem s. f. (pl. **-ens**), (bot.) Indian pennywort.
codamina s. f. (chem.) codamine.
códão s. m. 1. frozen soil, ground frost. 2. icicle. 3. freezing, frost, rime.
côdea s. f. 1. hull, husk. 2. crust, incrustation. 3. scab. 4. crust of bread. 5. a speck on clothes.
cobrir de ~ to crust. cobrir-se de ~ to become covered with a scab.
codeína s. f. (chem., pharm.) codeine.
co-delinqüência s. f. (pl. **co-delinqüências**) codelinquency.
co-delinqüente adj. m. + f. (pl. **co-delinqüentes**) codelinquent.
codessal s. m. (pl. **-ais**), **codesseira** f. a place where laburnum shrubs grow.
codesso s. m. (bot.) laburnum.
codesso-bastardo s. m. (pl. **codessos-bastardos**), (bot.) bean trefoil, laburnum.
codeúdo adj. covered with a heavy crust, crusty.
co-devedor s. m. (pl. **co-devedores**) codebtor.
códex, códice s. m. 1. ancient manuscript, manuscript book. 2. codex, code. 3. works of classical authors.
co-dialeto s. m. dialect which developed under the influence of a foreign language.
codicilar adj. m. + f. codicillary.
codicilo s. m. codicil, appendix (of a will), rider.
codificação s. f. (pl. **-ões**) codification.
codificador s. m. codifier.
codificar v. 1. to code, codify. 2. to reduce to a code, systematize. 3. to unite in a book or code. 4. to collect, compile. 5. to classify.
código s. m. 1. code, systematic collection of laws. 2. a collection of rules or basic principles. 3. (com.) telegraph code. 4. code, codex. 5. key (of a code).
~ civil (jur.) statute book (England). ~ de honra code of honour. ~ morse Morse code. ~ penal (jur.) penal code. escrito em ~ written in code, coded.
codilhar v. 1. to deceive, cheat. 2. (gambling) to break the bank. 3. to thwart, frustrate.
codilheira s. f. (vet.) a tumour on the elbow.
codilho (I) s. m. 1. (cards) codille (at omber). 2. (fig.) deceit.

codilho (II) s. m. slight saliency on a horse's elbow (plate C 12).
co-diretor s. m. (pl. **co-diretores**) co-director.
codo s. m. = **códão**.
co-doador s. m. (pl. **co-doadores**) co-donor.
co-donatário s. m. (pl. **co-donatários**) co-donee.
codório s. m. a sip of wine or brandy.
codorna s. f. a bird of the family Tinamidae, the tinamou (Nothura maculosa).
codorna-buraqueira s. f. (pl. **codornas-buraqueiras**), (ornith.) the burrowing tinamou (Taoniscus nanos).
codorna-mineira s. f. (pl. **codornas-mineiras**), (ornith.) a tinamou (Nothura minor).
codorniz s. f. (ornith.) quail.
codornizão s. m. (pl. **-ões**) (ornith.) landrail, corn-crake, crake (Crex pratensis).
codorno s. m. 1. nap, snooze, doze. 2. siesta.
codorno (ô) s. m. a variety of giant pear.
co-educação s. f. (pl. **co-educações**) coeducation.
co-educacional adj. m. + f. (pl. **co-educacionais**) coeducational. ‖ ~mente adv. coeducationally.
co-educar v. to coeducate, educate together.
co-educativo adj. coeducative, coeducational.
coeficiente s. m. 1. coefficient, joint agent. 2. (math.) factor. 3. (phys.) rate, ratio.
~ binomial binomial coefficient. ~ de resistência drag coefficient. ~ de amplificação amplification coefficient. ~ de atrito coefficient of friction. ~ de dilatação coefficient of expansion. ~ de elasticidade elastic modulus. ~ de escoamento exponent of discharge. ~ de saturação saturation factor. ~ de natalidade birth-rate. ~ de velocidade coefficient of velocity.
coéforos s. m. pl. (Greek hist.) Choephorae.
coelha s. f. doe rabbit.
coelheira (I) s. f. rabbit-warren, rabbitry, hutch, rabbit-hutch.
coelheira (II) s. f. collar-harness, collar, hame, neck strap, neckband (plate A 12).
coelheiro s. m. rabbit-hunter.
coelho s. m. (zool.) rabbit, jack rabbit, coney, buck coney.
aí há dente de ~ (pop.) this seems to be fishy. cova de ~ rabbit burrow. deste mato não sai ~ there is nothing to be gained here. levantar um ~ (hunt.) to start up a rabbit. matar dois ~s com uma só cajadada (fig.) to kill two birds with one stone. pele de ~ coney skin.
coelho-do-mato s. m. (pl. **coelhos-do-mato**) (zool.) a small rabbitlike rodent (Sylvilagus minensis).
coelho-no-prato s. m. (pl. **coelhos-no-prato**) a climbing plant of the senna family (Periandra coccinea).
coempção s. f. (pl. **-ões**), (jur.) 1. coemption. 2. joint purchase. 3. reciprocal purchase, exchange.
coentrada s. f. coriander sauce.
coentrilho s. m. (bot.) prickly ash (Xanthoxylum hyemale).
coentro s. m. (bot.) coriander (Coriandrum sativum).
coentro-bravo s. m. (pl. **coentros-bravos**) (bot., also **coentro-da-colônia, coentro-de-caboclo**) fitweed.
coenzima s. f. (biochem.) coenzyme.
coerana s. f. (bot.) willow-leaved jasmine.
coerção s. f. (pl. **-ões**) 1. act of restraining. 2. coercion, repression. 3. coaction. 4. force. 5. compulsion.
coercibilidade s. f. coercibility, coercibleness, coerciveness.
coercitividade s. f. compulsiveness, compulsoriness.
coercitivo adj. coercitive, coactive.
coercível adj. m. + f. (pl. **-íveis**) coercible.
coercivo adj. coercive, compulsory, exerting coercion. ‖ ~amente adv. coercively.

coerência s. f. 1. quality or state of being coherent. 2. coherence, coherency. 3. cohesion, consistency. 4. logical sequence of thought. 5. logic, congruity, congruence. 5. harmony.
~ **dum discurso** congruency of the different parts of a discourse.

coerente adj. m. + f. 1. coherent. 2. sticking together, consistent, cohesive. 3. consequent, logical. 4. consonant. 5. congruous. 6. sequacious. 7. agreeable. ‖ ~**mente** adv. coherently, agreeably, conformably.

coerir v. 1. to cohere, stick together. 2. to adhere. 3. to agree, fit. 4. to be congruous or logical.

coesão s. f. (pl. -ões) act of cohering. 2. cohesion, coherence. 3. mutual molecular attraction. 4. continuity. 5. tenacity. 6. harmony, concord. 7. intimate relationship.
~ **tribal** clanship. **força de** ~ power of cohesion.

coesivo adj. cohesive. ‖ -amente adv. cohesively.

coeso adj. 1. united, joined, combined. 2. associated. 3. coherent. 4. harmonious.

coesor s. m. (phys.) coherer: an instrument that detects electromagnetic waves.

coessência s. f. coessentialness, coessentiality, common essence.

coessencial adj. m. + f. (pl. -ais) coessential, having the same essence or substance as another one. ‖ ~**mente** adv. coessentially.

coestaduano adj. of or pertaining to the same state.

coestender v. to coextend, extend over the same space, extend simultaneously.

coetâneo s. m. contemporary. ‖ adj. coetaneous, living at the same period, contemporary.

coeternidade s. f. coeternity.

coeterno adj. coeternal, jointly, eternal. ‖ -amente adv. coenternally.

coevo s. m. coeval, contemporary, one of the same age or period. ‖ adj. coeval, coetaneous, contemporary.

coexistência s. f. coexistence, simultaneous existence.

coexistente adj. m. + f. coexistent.

coexistir v. to coexist, exist together, exist at the same time.

cofator s. m. (math.) cofactor.

co-fiador s. m. co-surety, joint warrantor.

cofiar v. to smooth down, stroke with the hand (over the hair or beard).

cofo (I) s. m. (ant.) slipper, pantofle.

cofo (II) s. m. an oblong wicker-basket with a narrow mouth in which fishermen carry their catch.

cofose s. f. (med.) cophosis, deafness.

cofre s. m. 1. strongbox, box. 2. chest, trunk. 3. money-box, safe. 4. (mil.) rear limber (of a gun carriage). 5. (mot.) hood (plate V 3).
arrombador de ~**s** safeblower. ~ **de carga** container. ~ **de segredo** combination safe.

cogitabundo adj. meditative, pensive, wrapt up in thought.

cogitação s. f. (pl. -ões) 1. cogitation. 2. reflection, meditation. 3. thought. 4. pensiveness.
isto é fora de ~ this is out of question.

cogitar v. 1. to cogitate. 2. to think over, meditate, ponder. 3. to recollect. 4. to consider, reflect, take into consideration. 5. to pay atention to. 6. to imagine.
ele cogitou de... he toyed with the idea...

cogitativo adj. cogitative, meditative, pensive. ‖ -amente adv. cogitatively, pensively.

cognação s. f. cognation, blood relationship by the mother's side, cognateness.

cognado s. m. cognate, blood relative. ‖ adj. cognate, related on the mother's side.
língua -a cognate language.

cognático adj. cognatic, relative to cognation.

cognato s. m. cognate, blood relative. ‖ adj. 1. cognate, related on the mother's side. 2. (gram.) having the same root, of the same derivation, conjugate. 3. paronymic.

cognição s. f. (pl. -ões) cognition. 2. faculty of knowing, knowledge. 3. perception. 4. understanding.

cognitivo adj. cognitative, meditative, cognitional, cognitive.

cógnito adj. known, cognized.

cognome s. m. 1. cognomen. 2. surname, nickname. 3. epithet. 4. byname. 5. alias.

cognominação s. f. (pl. -ões) cognomination.

cognominadas s. f. pl. (gram.) words with a common root.

cognominar v. 1. to cognominate. 2. to surname, dub.

cognoscibilidade s. f. cognoscibility.

cognoscitivo adj. cognoscitive. ‖ -amente adv. cognoscitively.

cognoscível adj. m. + f. (pl. -íveis) cognizable, capable of being known, recognizable.

cogote s. m. (pop.) nape of the head, scruff.
ele pegou o cachorro pelo ~ he took the dog by the scruff.

cogotilho s. m. a short trim of a horse's mane.

cogotudo adj. having a well developed scruff, strong-naped.

cogula s. f. 1. a monk's cowl or hood. 2. chasuble.

cogular v. to heap up (a grain measure), fill to capacity.

cogulhado adj. (archit.) adorned with rosettes.

cogulho s. m. (archit.) rosette.

cogulo s. m. 1. overmeasure. 2. overfilling, overflowing. 3. excess, surplus.

cogumelo s. m. (bot.) 1. mushroom. 2. fungal, fungus. 3. toadstool.

cogumelo-do-mar s. m. (pl. **cogumelos-do-mar**), (zool.) sea kidney (Renilla reniformis).

co-herdar v. to inherit jointly.

co-herdeira s. f. coheiress.

co-herdeiro s. m. coheir, coheritor, joint heir, parcener.

coibição s. f. (pl. -ões) 1. act of restraining. 2. cohibition. 3. restraint, check. 4. limitation.

coibir v. 1. to cohibit. 2. to repress, restrain. 3. to hamper, hinder. 4. to limit, restrict. 5. ~**-se**: a) to contain o. s. b) to control o. s. c) to deprive o. s. of. d) to abstain from.

coibitivo adj. cohibitive.

coice s. m. 1. rear, rear guard. 2. the rear end of anything. 3. backward kick. 4. recoil of a fire-arm. 5. fling. 6. jointer of a plough. 7. heel. 8. sash of a door. 9. (pop.) clothes moth. 10. (fig.) brutality. 11. ingratitude.
dar ~ **(cavalo)** to savage, lash out (horse). **dar a alguém o** ~ to give a person the sack. **ele lhe deu um** ~ he returned evil for good.

coicear v. to kick, lash out.

coiceira s. f. 1. jamb post of a door. 2. sash of a door.

coiceiro s. m. kicker, kicking horse. ‖ adj. kicking.

coifa s. f. 1. a fine hair-net used by women. 2. coif. 3. (anat.) caul. 4. kerchief. 5. (bot.) root cap. 6. (mil.) primer cap. 7. bell-shaped gas flue (of chemical laboratories).

coima s. f. 1. fine, penalty. 2. indemnification, compensation. 3. damages.

coimar v. to impose a fine or penalty, fine.

coimável adj. m. + f. (pl. **-áveis**) subject to fine or penalty; liable, responsible.

coimbrão s. m. (pl **-ões**) (f. **coimbrã**) Coimbran: native or inhabitant of Coimbra (Port.). ‖ adj. of, pertaining to or relative to Coimbra and its inhabitants.

coimeiro (I) s. m. collector of fines or penalties.

coimeiro (II) adj. 1. subject to a fine or penalty. 2. liable, responsible. 3. forbidden, prohibited (to trespass).

coincidência s. f. 1. coincidence. 2. concurrence, concurrency. 3. happening together. 4. juxtaposition. 5. simultaneousness of events.

é pura ~ it is pure chance. **encontrei-o por** ~ I happened across him. **por** ~ **também vou lá** as it happens I am going there too.

coincidente adj. m. + f. coincident(al). ‖ ~**mente** adv. coincidentally, coincidently.

coincidir v. 1. to coincide (with). 2. to occur at the same time, concur. 3. to agree, correspond exactly to. 4. to contemporize. 5. to combine.

coincidível adj. m. + f. (pl. **-íveis**) capable of coinciding.

co-interessado s. m. (pl. **co-interessados**) a co-concerned person. ‖ adj. co-concerned.

colo s. m. (pop.) 1. hiding place, lurking place. 2. hide-out for criminals. 3. asylum, sanctuary.

coló s. m. 1. a ridiculous lover or admirer. 2. a silly boy. 3. (ichth.) batfish, butterfly fish. ‖ adj. silly, ridiculous, foolishly infatuated.

colote s. m. (zool.) coyote, prairie wolf.

coirana s. f. (bot.) poisonberry.

coirana-branca s. f. (pl. **coiranas-brancas**) a medicinal plant of the nightshade family (Cestrum laevigatum).

coirela s. f. 1. a long and narrow tract of land. 2. an ancient square measure equivalent to about 5,788 sq. yd.

coirmão s. m. (pl. **coirmãos**) (f. **coirmã**) first cousin.

coisa s. f. 1. thing, object. 2. matter, substance. 3. affair, event. 4. fact, act. 5. business. 6. article. 7. kind, sort. 8. mystery. 9. ~**s** pl. goods, means, possessions.

~ **antiquada** back number, old-fashioned thing. ~ **apimentada** (pop.) hot stuff. ~ **de duas horas** about two hours (ago). ~ **de riso** ridiculous thing. ~ **desanimadora** a disheartening thing, wet blanket. ~ **desconhecida** nondescript matter or affair. ~ **de ver** a thing worth seeing. ~ **fácil** an easy thing, (U.S.A., sl.) cinch. ~ **lógica** an understood thing. ~**s costumeiras** customary things. ~ **secundária** non-essential matter. ~**s diversas** sundries, sundry matter. ~ **sem valor** trash, trumpery, hog-wash. **aí é que está a** ~ that's the point of the question. **alguma** ~ somewhat, something. **as** ~**s como são** things as they are. **as nossas** ~**s** our affairs. **como as** ~**s andam** as things go. **como vão as** ~**s com você?** how goes the world with you? **defender uma** ~ **justa** to stand for a just cause. **é a mesma** ~ there is no difference, it is the same thing. **ele conhece as** ~**s como são** he knows a thing or two. **ele não leva as** ~**s a sério** he does not take things seriously. **ele vê** ~**s** he sees snakes. **este sistema tem as suas** ~ **boas** there is something good in that system. **eu estou pronto para qualquer** ~ I'm game for anything. **falar é uma** ~, **fazer é outra** talking is easy, doing is hard; it takes money to buy whisky. **foi pouca** ~ it was not much. **há qualquer** ~? is anything wrong? **isto é outra** ~ that's quite different. **não conte com** ~**s que não possui** don't count your chickens before they are hatched. **não é lá grande** ~ it's not worth a while. **não pude esperar a** ~ **terminar** I couldn't stick it out. **não**

se importe com ~ **alheia!** go about your own business! **nunca vi tal** ~! never have I seen such a sight! **ponhamos estas** ~**s à parte** let those things alone. **que** ~! what a job! **saber uma** ~ **na ponta da língua** to have something at one's finger's end. **são** ~**s que acontecem** that just happens. **suspeitar de alguma** ~ to smell a rat. **tomar as** ~**s como são** to take things as one finds them. **uma** ~ **lógica** a matter of course. **você faria uma** ~ **dessas?!** would you do such a thing? would you be such a fool?!

coisada s. f. a lot or pile of heterogeneous things.

coisa-feia s. f. (pl. **coisas-feias**) 1. exorcism, conjuration. 2. romping, shindy, clamour.

coisa-má s. m. (Braz., pop.) the devil.

coisar v. (sl.) 1. to ponder, meditate. 2. to think s. th. over. 3. to imagine, form an opinion. 4. to take care of.

coisificar v. to reduce human and related values to mere material value.

coisinha s. f. 1. dim. form of **coisa**. 2. trifle, bauble. 3. toy, plaything.

coita (I) s. f. 1. pain, ache. 2. suffering, affliction. 3. misfortune, adversity, trouble.

coita (II) s. f. 1. a big kitchen knife. 2. a machete.

coitado s. m. poor or miserable fellow, wretch, underdog. ‖ adj. poor, miserable, wretched, pitiful. ‖ interj. poor soul!, poor fellow!, poor thing!

~ **de mim!**, poor me! **um pobre** ~ a poor stick.

coitar (I) v. to fence a field.

coitar (II) v. 1. to cause pain. 2. to afflict, torment. 3. to worry, trouble. 4. to make unhappy, bring misfortune to.

coité s. f. a drinking vessel made from a gourd.

coiteiro s. m. 1. gamekeeper, game warden. 2. one who shelters and protects criminals.

coito (I) s. m. 1. coitus, coition. 2. copulation, coupling.

coito (II) s. m. hideout, shelter for criminals or vagabonds.

coito (III) s. m. fenced-in land, enclosure, warren.

coivara s. f. (Braz.) a heap of half-burned brushwood gathered for final burning.

coivarar v. to gather and heap up half-burned firewood for final burning.

cola (I) s. f. 1. glue (plate M 4). 2. paste, adhesive. 3. (Braz., student sl.) the act of copying or cheating in an exam. 4. size. 5. sizing.

~ **de amido** starch. ~ **de peixe** isinglass. ~ **forte** joiner's glue.

cola (II) s. f. (bot.) cola, kola.

cola (III) s. f. 1. track, trace. 2. (S. Braz.) tail.

colaboração s. f. (pl. **-ões**) 1. collaboration, co-operation. 2. common work. 3. help, assistance. 4. contribution. 5. concurrence, concurrency.

colaborador s. m. 1. collaborator. 2. co-worker, helpmate. 3. co-author. 4. contributor (of a newspaper). 5. fellow worker. ‖ adj. collaborative, concurrent.

colaborar v. 1. to collaborate. 2. to co-operate, work together, act jointly. 3. to contribute.

colaborativo adj. collaborative.

colação s. f. (pl. **-ões**) 1. collation, act of bestowing a dignity, title or benefit. 2. a light repast. 3. comparison. 4. conference.

~ **de grau** graduation. **ele está se preparando para a** ~ **de grau** he is reading for his honour. **trazer à** ~ to quote.

colacia s. f. 1. relationship or affinity of foster-brothers and foster-sisters. 2. intimacy, familiarity.

colacionar v. 1. to confer, bestow on (or upon). 2. to compare, confront. 3. to collate. 4. to check, control.

colaço s. m. foster-brother. ‖ adj. intimate, familiar.

colada s. f. mountain pass, col.
coladeira s. f. (typogr.) gluer, gluing machine.
colado adj. agglutinate.
colador s. m. 1. collator. 2. gluer, paster.
colagem s. f. (pl. -ens) 1. gluing, pasting. 2. purification of wine.
colágeno s. m. (biol.) collagen.
colagenose s. f. (pathol.) collagenosis, collagen disease.
colagogo s. m. (med., pharm.) cholagogue, cholagogic agent. ‖ adj. cholagogue, cholagogic.
colangiectasia s. f. (med.) expansion of the biliary ducts.
colangite s. f. (pathol.) inflammation of the colon vessels.
colante adj. close-fitting (dress).
colapsar v. to cause collapse.
colapso s. m. 1. collapse. 2. break-down, burst up, break-up. 3. (med.) shock, fit. 4. crash, drop. 5. failure.
   sofrer um ~ mental to suffer a mental crack-up.
colar (I) s. m. 1. necklace; string, band or chain worn round the neck. 2. collar, shirt collar. 3. (tech.) fast collar, collar, neck (plate P 4). 4. (naut.) hoop.
   ~ de pérolas string of pearls, chaplet.
colar (II) v. 1. to bestow a benefice on. 2. to install in office, confer a title or privilege. 3. to receive an academic or professional degree, graduate.
colar (III) v. 1. to glue, unite or fasten with glue. 2. to conglutinate, agglutinate. 3. to stick on, stick together. 4. to attach, bill (advice, warning, communication). 5. (student sl.) to cheat or crib at examinations. 6. to clarify (wine). 7. to adhere, hold together. 8. ~-se: a) to lean against. b) to join o. s. to. c) to combine with (for a common purpose).
colarejo s. m. native or inhabitant of Colares (Portugal). ‖ adj. of or relative to this town and its inhabitants.
colarinho s. m. 1. collar of a dress, shirt collar, collar (plate R 7). 2. collaret, neckband. 3. (archit.) a small necking near the top of a column. 2. the white foam on a glass of beer. 5. neck.
   ~ de bico wing collar. ~ de senhoras collaret(te). ~ duro stick-up collar, stand-up collar. ~ mole soft collar. ~ pendente rabat. ~ virado turn--down collar (plate R 7). mudar o ~ 1. to have a drink. 2. to change shirts. 3. to change the collar of a shirt.
colatório s. m. one upon whom a degree, privilege or benefice is bestowed.
colateral adj. m. + f. (pl. -ais) collateral, subordinate. ‖ -mente adv. collaterally.
colaterabilidade s. f. collaterality.
colativo adj. collative.
colbaque s. m. busby.
colcha s. f. 1. blanket, bedspread. 2. coverlet, coverlid. 3. counterpane. 4. quilt.
   ~ de penas feather-bed. ~ de retalhos patchwork quilt.
colchão s. m. (pl. -ões) mattress (plate C 7).
   ~ de molas spring-mattress (plate C 4).
colchão-de-noiva s. m. (pl. colchões-de-noiva) roly--poly (pastry).
colcheia s. f. (mus.) quaver, eighth note (plate N 1).
colcheiro s. m. quilt maker.
colcheta (ê) s. f. ear, eye (of a hook and eye fastener) (plate G 2).
colchetar v. 1. to close or fasten with a hook and eye fastener, clasp. 2. to provide with a hook and eye fastener.

colchete (ê) s. m. 1. hook, clasp (plate B 16). 2. hook and eye (plate G 2). 3. meat hook. 4. (typogr., mus.) bracket, brace, crotchet. 5. fastening. 6. agraffe.
   ~ de gancho hook and eye fastener. ~ de pressão snap fastener.
colchoaria s. f. mattress factory, mattress shop.
colchoeiro s. m. matress maker, quilter, mattress dealer.
coldre s. m. holster, saddle-case.
coleado adj. sinuous, winding, flexible.
coleante adj. m. + f. winding, wriggly, eely.
colear (I) v. 1. to meander. 2. to glide, crawl, slither. 3. to wriggle, wiggle. 4. to squirm.
colear (II) v. to throw cattle by twisting the animal's tail.
coleção s. f. (pl. -ões) 1. collection. 2. compilation, assortment. 3. gathering, accumulation, aggregation. 4. set, stock. 5. kit. 6. crop.
   ~ completa de obras (de um autor) the complete works (of an author), corpus. ~ de amostras sampler: a collection of samples. ~ de quadros picture gallery. ~ de selos stamp collection.
colecionação s. f. (pl. -ões) act of collecting, gathering.
colecionado adj. collected, compiled.
colecionador s. m. 1. collector. 2 compiler. 3. gatherer.
   ~ de livros bookhunter. ~ de selos stamp collector, philatelist.
colecionar v. 1. to collect. 2. to gather, accumulate, aggregate. 3. to compile. 4. to collate.
colecionista s. m. + f. = colecionador.
coleciste, colecisto s. m. (anat.) cholecyst, gall bladder.
colecistectomia s. f. (surg.) cholecistectomy, removal of the gall bladder.
colecistite s. f. (med.) cholecystitis.
colecistotomia s. f. (surg.) cholecystotomy, the surgical opening of the gall bladder.
colédoco s. m. (anat.) the choledoch duct, common bile duct.
colega s. m. + f. 1. colleague. 2. co-partner, associate. 3. co-worker in the same profession or office. 4. schoolmate, class-fellow, condisciple. 5. friend, pal. 6. comrade, companion, mate, fellow. 7. chum, crony.
   ~ de farra boon companion.
colegatário s. m. co-legatee.
colegiada s. f. 1. chapter of a church. 2. a collegiate church. 3. the student body (of a school).
colegiado adj. collegiate.
colegial s. m. + f. (pl. -ais) student of a college. ‖ adj. collegial, collegiate.
   ~ interno colleger.
colegiatura s. f. fellowship.
colégio s. m. 1. college. 2. public school, high school. 3. body of persons of equal standing, profession or authority. 4. an electoral college. 5. guild, society, chapter of a church or convent.
   Sacro Colégio (R. C. Church) the Sacred College of Cardinals.
coleguismo s. m. 1. collegiality, colleagueship. 2. companionship, fellowship. 3. esprit de corps, camaraderie.
coleira (I) s. f. collar (for animals), dog-collar, horse collar.
coleira (II) s. f. common name of two canarylike finches of the family Fringillidae (Sporophila caerulescens, Sporophila lineola).
coleira (III) s. m. (N. Braz.) 1. (ent.) a kind of tick. 2. (pop.) crook, rascal. 3. bad debtor.
coleirado adj. 1. wearing a collar. 2. having collar-like spots on the neck (animals).

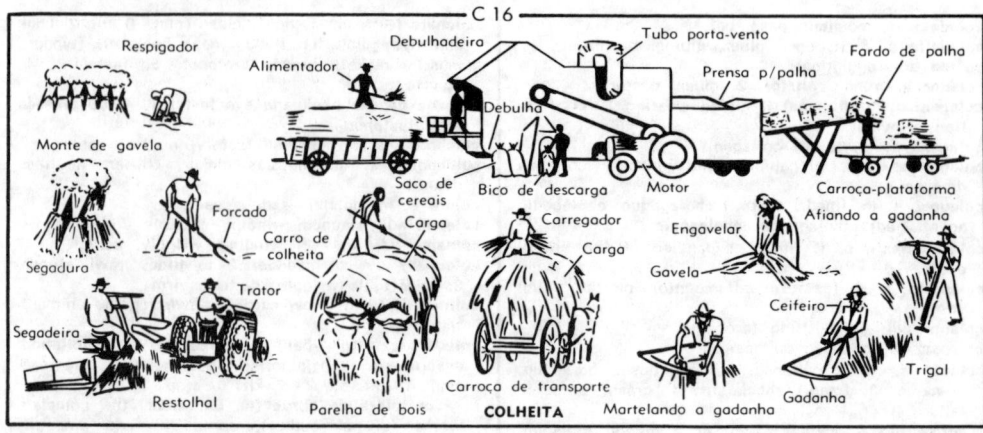

Respigador · Debulhadeira · Tubo porta-vento · Fardo de palha · Alimentador · Prensa p/palha · Debulha · Monte de gavela · Saco de cereais · Bico de descarga · Motor · Carroça-plataforma · Forcado · Carga · Carregador · Engavelar · Afiando a gadanha · Carro de colheita · Carga · Gavela · Segadura · Trator · Ceifeiro · Segadeira · Restolhal · Parelha de bois · COLHEITA · Carroça de transporte · Martelando a gadanha · Gadanha · Trigal

C 16

coleira-do-brejo s. f. (pl. coleiras-do-brejo) common name of two birds of the family Fringillidae (Sporophila pileata, Sporophila ochrascens).

coleirinha s. m. (ornith.) = coleira (II).

coleiro s. m. (ornith.) collared seedeater.

colelitíase s. f. (med.) cholelithiasis, gallstones.

colélito s. m. (med.) biliary calculus, gallstone.

colemia s. f. (med.) cholemia.

colendo adj. respectable, venerable.

colênquima s. m. (bot.) chollenchyma.

coleóptero s. m. (ent.) 1. coleopter, coleopteran. 2. ~s pl. the Coleoptera: an order of insects. ‖ adj. coleopterous.

cólera (I) s. f. 1. passion, fervour. 2. anger, irritation. 3. choler, bile. 4. wrath, rage, ire. 5. angriness. 6. indignation, resentment.

estar em ~ to be very angry, be in passion.

cólera (II) s. f. (also cólera-morbo) (med.) cholera; cholera morbus.

colerado adj. furious, angry.

colerético adj. (med.) increasing the bilious secretion, furthering the bilious secretion.

colérico (I) adj. 1. choleric, irascible. 2. furious, ireful. 3. passionate, hot-headed, fiery. 4. atrabilious. 5. irate, wrathful. ‖ colericamente adv. irately, wrathfully, passionately.

colérico (II) s. m. person attacked by cholera morbus. ‖ adj. (med.) choleric.

colesterina s. f. (biochem.) cholesterine, cholesterol.

colesterol s. m. (biochem.) cholesterine, cholesterol.

coleta s. f. 1. collection, church collection. 2. gathering, collecting (of alms). 3. levy. 4. amount paid as contribution or tax. 5. collect, a short prayer said before the Epistle.

a ~ para domingo de páscoa the collect for Easter Sunday. fazer uma ~ to raise a collection, to pass the hat. fizemos uma ~ em seu benefício we clubbeb together for you, we collected money for you.

coleta (ê) s. f. a bullfighter's pigtail.

coletado s. m. a tax payer. ‖ adj. collected.

coletânea s. f. collectanea.

coletâneo adj. excerptive, excerpted, selected, compiled.

coletar v. 1. to collect, gather. 2. to impose a tax or tribute. 3. to assess, levy. 4. to rate.

coletável adj. m. + f. (pl. -áveis) collectable, collectible.

colete (ê) s. m. 1. waistcoat, vest (plate R 7). 2. corset, halter. 3. jumper.

~ ortopédico orthopedic corset. ~ salva-vidas life jacket, air-jacket.

colete-curto s. m. (pl. coletes-curtos), (N. Braz.) pander, procurer.

coleteiro s. m. waistcoat or corset maker.

coletício adj. (hist.) called to the arms (without order or selection).

coletividade s. f. 1. collectivity. 2. society, social community. 3. set, group, team.

coletivismo s. m. collectivism.

coletivista s. m. + f. collectivist, socialist. ‖ adj. collectivist(ic).

coletivizar v. to communize, socialize.

coletivo s. m. 1. (Braz.) tramway-car, omnibus. 2. (gram.) collective noun. ‖ adj. 1. collective. 2. common, general. 3. aggregative. 4. social. 5. socialistic, collectivistic. ‖ -amente adv. collectively, aggregatively.

coleto (I) s. m. (bot.) connecting point of root and stem of a plant.

coleto (II) collected, compiled, gathered.

coletor s. m. 1. collector. 2. gatherer. 3. tax collector. 4. (electr.) collector, shoe. ‖ adj. collecting.

~ de graxa (tech.) grease-trap. ~ de óleo (tech.) oil sump, engine sump (plate M 13).

coletoria s. f. tax collector's office.

colgado adj. 1. hanging. 2. adorned with draperies.

colgadura s. f. hangings, draperies.

colgar v. 1. to hang draperies. 2. to adorn with draperies. 3. to hang, suspend. 4. to hang (by the neck).

colha s. f. (N. Braz.) the harvest of latex.

colhedeira s. f. 1. harvester, reaper. 2. stick used by painters to scrape together their ground colours.

colhedor s. m. 1. gatherer, collector. 2. ~es pl. (naut.) lanyards. ‖ adj. gathering, collecting.

colheita s. f. 1. harvest (plate C 16). 2. crop, math. 3. picking, ingathering. 4. harvest time. 5. hoard. 6. (fig.) profit, gain.

ação de graças pela ~ harvest thanksgiving. ~ de hortaliças green-crop. ~ do feno hay harvest. má ~ failure of crops. mês de ~ harvest month. segunda ~ no mesmo ano aftermath, aftercrop. uma rica ~ a rich harvest.

colheitadeira s. f. (S. Braz.) harvester: a harvesting machine.

colheiteiro s. m. harvestman, labourer in harvest.

colher s. f. 1. spoon (plates D 3, M 8, T 1). 2. a spoonful. 3. any spoonlike object. 4. ladle.

~ de chá tea-spoon, caddy spoon (plate M 8). ~ de pedreiro float, trowel. ~ de sobremesa dessert--spoon (plate M 1). ~ de sopa tablespoon (plate

M 1). **isto é de** ~ (pop.) that's a cinch, that's very easy.

colher (ê) v. 1. to harvest. 2. to pick (off), pluck. 3. to reap, crop, gather. 4. to cut (flowers). 5. to surprise. 6. to obtain, get, achieve. 7. to learn. 8. to perceive. 9. to receive in payment or as a reward. 10. to conclude, deduce. 11. to be conclusive. 12. to infer.
~ **água em cesto** to lose one's time, work in vain. ~ **as velas** (naut.) to down-haul, furl the sails. ~ **os frutos do próprio trabalho** to reap the fruits of one's labour. **a chuva nos colheu na metade do caminho** the rain caught us half-ways. **cada um colhe o que semeia** such seeds he sows, such harvest shall he find. **colhi informações** I gathered information. **quem semeia vento, colhe tempestade** he who sows winds will gather tempests.

colhera s. f. 1. harness for a team of horses or a yoke of oxen. 2. (fig.) two persons who are always seen together.

colherada s. f. spoonful, ladleful.
às ~**s** by spoonfuls, by ladlefuls.

colherão s. m. 1. a big spoon. 2. ladle, pot ladle, scoop (plate C 20). 3. drainer.

colhereira s. f. (ornith.) shoveller.

colhereiro s. m. 1. spoon manufacturer or dealer. 2. (ornith.) spoonbill, shoveller duck.

colherete s. m. the strike of the ball on any person watching the game.

colheril (pl. **-is**), **colherim** (pl. **-ins**) s. m. a stucco--worker's trowel.

colhimento s. m. gathering, picking (fruit).

colibri s. m. (ornith.) colibri, hummingbird.

cólica s. f. 1. (med.) colic, pain or cramp in the abdomen. 2. belly-ache, throe. 3. ~**s** pl.: a) gripes. b) (fig.) difficulties, predicament.
~ **saturnina** (med.) painter's colic. ~**s uterinas** (med.) after-pains.

cólico (I) adj. colic: of or pertaining to the colon, colicky.

cólico (II) adj. cholic, of, pertaining to or of the nature of bile.

colidir v. 1. to collide. 2. to knock against, shock, dash. 3. to crash. 4. to bump into. 5. to clash. 6. to conflict, be in conflict, be in opposition. 7. to contradict one another. 8. to interfere.
~ **com** 1. to knock against. 2. (naut.) to run foul of.

coligação s. f. (pl. **-ões**) 1. colligation. 2. alliance, coalition, union. 3. confederation. 4. assimilation. 5. scheme, plot. 6. (logics) the accumulation of isolated facts in order to deduce from them a general principle.
~ **de nações** axis (of nations).

coligado adj. confederate, allied.

coligar v. 1. to colligate. 2. to approximate. 3. to unite, join, connect. 4. (logics) to unite by colligation. 5. ~**-se** to band together, league, confederate.

coligativo adj. colligative, colligate, tending to colligate.

coligido adj. collected, united (in a collection), deduced.

coligir v. 1. to gather, collect. 2. to unite in a collection. 3. to compile. 4. to infer, conclude, deduce. 5. to codify.

coligível adj. m. + f. (pl. **-íveis**) collectable, colligible.

colim s. m. (pl. **-ins**), (ornith.) bobwhite.

colimação s. f. (pl. **-ões**), (phys.) collimation, collineation.

colimador s. m. (phys.) collimator.

colimar v. 1. (phys.) collimate, render parallel. 2. to aim at. 3. to have in view.

colimbiformes s. f. pl. Colymbiformes: an order of birds including the grebe family.

colimbo s. m. (ornith.) 1. Colymbus: a genus of birds. 2. ember-goose, western grebe.

colina (I) s. f. 1. knoll, hill. 2. small mountain. mount. 3. siope, mountainside. 4. mound. 5. fell.

colina (II) s. f. (biochem.) choline.

colinear adj. m. + f. collinear. ‖ ~**mente** adv. collinearly.

colinoso adj. hilly, abounding in hills.

coliquação s. f. (pl. **-ões**) (med.) colliquation.

coliquar v. to colliquate, melt, liquefy.

coliquativo adj. colliquative, causing colliquation, dissolvent.

colírio s. m. (med.) collyrium, eye drops.

colisão s. f. (pl. **-ões**) 1. collision. 2. crash, shock, clash. 3. impact, smashing. 4. bump. 5. fight. 6. conflict. 7. difficulty. 8. opposition. 9. (phon.) a sequence of sibilants in a word which creates a harsh, disagreeable sound. 10. interference.

coliseu s. m. 1. (Roman hist.) Colosseum. 2. coliseum, amphitheater, stadium.

colite s. f. (med.) colitis.

colitigante s. m. + f. (jur.) joint plaintiff.

colmado s m. straw hut, thatch hut.

colmagem s. f. (pl. **-ens**) thatching.

colmar (I) to thatch, cover with palm leaves or straw.

colmar (II) 1. to elevate. 2. to sublimate, exalt. 3. to conclude, complete.

colmatagem s. f. (pl. **-ens**) (agric.) act or process of changing the course of rivers rich in sediments, so that they inundate marshy lowlands (filling them up little by little).

colmeal s. m. (pl. **-eais**) apiary, a group of beehives.

colmeeiro s. m. apiarist, beekeeper, hiver.

colmeia s. f. 1. beehive, hive. 2. skep, bee stock (plate A 11). 3. apiary. 4. a swarm of bees. 6. an overfurnished house. 7. (naut.) the hull of a ship not yet outfitted with a bridge.

colmilho s. m. canine, canine tooth, tusk, fang.

colmilhoso adj. hav'ng fangs, tusked.

colmilhudo adj. 1. having long fangs. 2. tusked. 3. (of horses) having well developed canine teeth, old, outworn. 4. (fig.) of old (persons).

colmo (ô) s. m. 1. stem, stalk. 2. straw. 3. culm. 4. thatch, thatching.

colo (I) s. m. 1. neck. 2. lap. 3. any neck-shaped object (plate A 6). 4. bosom, breast.
cavalo com ~ **de cisne** a swannecked horse. **ter um menino no** ~ to have a boy on one's lap. **trazer ao** ~: 1. to hold in one's arms. 2. (fig.) to protect s. o., do everything for s. o.

colo (II) s. m. (anat.) colon.

colobacilo s. m. (bact.) colon bacillus.

colóbio s. m. colobium, dalmatic.

coloboma s. f. (med.) coloboma.

colocação s. f. (pl. **-ões**) 1. act of placing, placement. 2. collocation. 3. emplacement, setting. 4. situation. 5. job, place. 6. appointment. 7. installation. 8. rank, order.
~ **metódica** methodical arrangement. **ele obteve** ~ **para as finais** (sports) he placed himself for the finals.

colocado adj. placed, situated, appointed.

colocar v. 1. to place, put in place. 2. to dispose, arrange. 3. to employ, make use of. 4. to install, place in office, collocate. 5. to lodge, set. 6. to plant. 7. to coordinate. 8. to situate, station. 9. ~**-se** to place o. s., get a job. 10. to provide employment for others. 11. to bestow.
~ **acima de...** to put over... ~ **entre parênteses** to put in brackets. ~ **mal** to misplace. ~

um **pedido** to place an order. **~-se entre** to interpose. **ele colocou o livro na prateleira** he placed the book on the shelf. **ele colocou tudo atrás** (also fig.) he set everything behind. **ele colocou-se diante dela** he squared up to her. **ele colocou-se em situação difícil** he placed himself in an awkward position. **ele colocou-se muito bem** he obtained a good position. **eles ~am todas as velas** (naut.) they crowded the sails. **foi colocada uma coroa no dente** the tooth was crowned. **foi de propósito que ele colocou o livro aqui** he placed the book here deliberately. **se você se coloca em meu lugar** if you think yourself in my place.

colocíntida, colocíntide s. f. (bot., pharm.) colocynth, bitter cucumber, bitter apple.

colocutor s. m. collocutor, colloquist, interlocutor.

colódio s. m. (chem.) collodion, collodium.

colofão, cólofon s. m. colophon, inscription or emblem placed on the title page or at the end of a book.

colofônia s. f. colophony, rosin.

cologaritmo s. m. (math.) cologarithm.

coloidal adj. m. + f. (pl. -ais) colloid(al).

colóide s. m. (phys., chem.) colloid. ‖ adj. m. + f. colloid(al).

colombiano (I), **colombino** s. m. Colombian: native or inhabitant of Colombia. ‖ adj. Colombian.

colombiano (II) adj. Columbian: of, pertaining to or relative to Christopher Columbus.

colômbio s. m. (chem.) columbium, niobium (chemical symbol Cb).

colombina s. f. (teath.) Columbine.

colombita s. f. (chem.) columbite.

colombofilia s. f. the art of raising carrier pigeons.

colombófilo s. m. pigeon breeder.

colomi s. m. boy, lad, servant.

cólon s. m. (anat.) colon.

colondro s. m. (bot.) bottle gourd.

colonia s. f. (Port.) a kind of labour contract closed between a tenant-farmer and a landlord.

colônia s. f. 1. colony, possession. 2. territory. 3. a group of immigrants in a foreign country. 4. protectorate. 5. settlement, community. **~ de férias** summer camp. **~ de povoamento** settlement: an early-stage colony. **formar uma ~** to colonize. **~ agrícola** 1. a field colony of farmers. 2. a prison camp.

colonial s. m. + f. (pl. -ais) 1. colonial, citizen or inhabitant of a colony. 2. one well versed in colonial affairs. 3. colonist. ‖ adj. colonial, of, pertaining to or forming a colony. ‖ **~mente** adv. colonially. **~ brasileiro** (archit.) Brazilian colonial style.

colonialismo s. m. colonialism.

colônico adj. of or pertaining to colonists and colonies, colonial.

colonista s. m. + f. colonist.

colonização s. f. (pl. -ões) 1. colonization. 2. act of settling. 3. settlement. 4. plantation.

colonizado adj. colonized, settled.

colonizador s. m. colonizer, colonist.

colonizar v. 1. to colonize, establish a colony in. 2. to settle, plant (with inhabitants). 3. to work as a farm-hand or tenant-farmer.

colonizável adj. m. + f. (pl. -áveis) colonizable.

colono s. m. 1. colonist, member or inhabitant of a colony. 2. settler, planter. 3. farm-hand, tenant--farmer.

colopatia s. f. (med.) colonopathy.

coloquial adj. m. + f. (pl. -iais) colloquial. **linguagem ~** common parlance.

colóquio s. m. colloquy, conversation, debate, discussion.

color s. f. (obs.) 1. colour. 2. m. adornment, ornament. **sob ~ de** under the pretext of, under the disguise of.

coloração s. f. (pl. -ões) 1. act of colouring. 2. colouration. 3. tinction, tinct. 4. hue.

colorado adj. reddish, red.

colorante adj. m. + f. colouring, tinctorial.

colorar v. 1. to colour, paint with colours. 2. to make bright or lively with gay colours. 3. to embellish, adorn. 4. to perfect, make excellent.

coloratura s. f. (mus.) coloratura.

colorau s. m. paprika, paprica.

colorear v. 1. to colour, paint with colours. 2. to show a red hue. 3. to disguise, conceal. 4. to allege, use s. th. as a pretext.

colorido s. m. 1. colour, colouring. 2. combination of colours (in works of art, nature). 3. variegation. 4. tincture, tinge, hue. 5. (rig.) brilliancy, bright vivid colouring, colourfulness. ‖ adj. 1. coloured, tinted, hued. 2. bright-coloured. 3. colourful. **~ local** local colour. **~ vivo** warmness (of colours). **filme ~** Technicolor. **vidro ~** stained glass. **dar ~ demasiadamente forte:** 1. to overpaint. 2. (fig.) to exaggerate the description of a scene.

colorífico adj. colourific, producing or communicating colour.

colorimetria s. f. colorimetry.

colorimétrico adj. colorimetric(al).

colorímetro s. m. colorimeter, tintometer.

colorir v. 1. to colour, paint, bepaint. 2. to blend colours, dye, tinge, stain. 3. to variegate. 4. to touch up. 5. to adorn or brighten with colours. 6. to describe vividly. 1. (fig.) to cover up, excuse. 8. (fig.) to disguise, conceal. 9. to become coloured.

colorismo s. m. system and principles of artistic painting or (fig.) brilliant writing.

colorista s. m + f. 1. colourist, colourer, brilliant painter. 2. (fig.) a brilliant imaginative writer.

colorização s. f. (pl. -ões) 1. colouration. 2. hue, brilliance (of colours). 3. change of colours.

colossal adj. m.+f. (pl. -ais) 1. colossal. 2. enormous, huge. 3. gigantic, gigantesque. 4. very extensive. ‖ **~mente** adv. colossally, enormously.

colosso s. m. 1. colossus. 2. a gigantic statue. 3. (fig.): a) big person. b) any object of gigantic dimensions. c) power. d) powerful person. 4. (Braz.) an advantageous, favourable or delightful matter or affair. 5. (pop.) a great quantity, lots of (persons or things). **ele é um ~** (pop.) he is a great guy. **ele é um ~ de pés de barro** (fam.) he is a colossus with feet of clay. **ele é um ~ em tênis** he is a whale at tennis.

colostro s. m. (med.) colostrum.

colotomia s. f. (surg.) colotomy.

colpite s. f. (med.) colpitis.

colpo s. m. (bot.) germinal furrow (in pollen grains).

colquicina s. f. (chem.) colchicine.

cólquico s. m. (bot.) meadow saffron, autumn crocus.

coltar s. m. 1. coal tar. 2. escape gas (from hearths, furnaces). 3. pitch.

colubreado adj. shaped like a serpent, serpentiform.

colubrear, colubrejar v. to crawl like a snake, meander.

colubrídeos s. m. pl. (zool.) Colubridae: a large family of snakes.

colubrina s. f. 1. culverin. 2. (bot.) devil's turnip, common bryony. 3. creese, Malayan dagger.

colubrino adj. colubrine, snakelike, serpentine.

columbário s. m. (Roman hist.) columbarium.

columbicultor s. m. pigeon breeder.

columbicultura s. f. pigeon breeding.

columbídeos s. m. pl. (zool.) Columbidae: the dove and pigeon family.

columbiformes s. m. pl. (ornith.) Columbiformes: an order of birds including pigeons, doves, grouse and related specimens.

columbiano s. m. Columbian: native or inhabitant of Colombia. ‖ adj. Colombian.

columbino (I) adj. 1. columbine, of or pertaining to doves. 2. dovelike. 3. dove-coloured. 4. (fig.) innocent, pure.

columbino (II) adj. Colombian, of or relative to Colombia.

columbofilia s. f. the art of raising carrier pigeons.

columbófilo s. m. a breeder of carrier pigeons.

columela s. f. columella: 1. (bot.) carpophore. 2. (anat.) a columnlike bone. 3. (zool.) the central axis of a univalve shell.

coluna s. f. 1. column, supporting pillar. 2. any cylindrical, columnlike object. 3. post. 4. upright section (of a newspaper, periodical, book). 5. (mil.) a military column. 6. a row. 7. a vertical column of figures. 8. shaft, axle-tree. 9. support. 10. (bot.) gynostemium.

~ **cerrada** (mil.) closed column. ~ **composta** (archit.) compound pillar. ~ **de fumaça** column of smoke, plume. ~ **de haver** (com.) credit side (of an account). ~ **de notícias fúnebres** agony column (of a newspaper). ~ **espinal** spinal column (plate C 18). ~ **móvel** flying column. ~ **por um** single file. ~ **vertebral** vertebral column, backbone (plate P 7). **em** ~ **de dois** in double file. **entre** ~**s** intercolumnar.

colunar (I) s. f. ancient Paraguayan silver coin. ‖ adj. m. + f. columnar, columnal, columnate, columned.

colunar (II) v. 1. to give the form of a column to. 2. to arrange in columns.

colunário adj. showing or representing columns.

colunata s. f. 1. a range of columns. 2. portico, arcade, peristyle, colonnade.

colunelo s. m. 1. a small column or pillar. 2. mark, boundary mark. 3. small columns of a balustrade.

coluneta s. f. a small slender column, colonette.

colunista s. m. + f. columnist, the author of a regular newspaper column.

coluro s. m. (astr., geogr.) colure.

colusão s. f. (pl. -ões) collusion, deceit, fraud.

colutório s. m. (med.) collutory.

colza s. f. (bot.) 1. rape, colza. 2. rapeseed.

óleo de ~ rape-oil. **torta de** ~ rape-cake.

com prep. 1. with. 2. among. 3. in, at.

~ **aquiescência** assentingly. ~ **estas palavras** with these words. ~ **facilidade** easily. ~ **isto** with this, herewith, hereby. ~ **o cabelo ondulado** curly-haired. ~ **o rosto pálido** pale-faced. ~ **prudência** prudently. ~ **reservas** subject to reservation. ~ **seu auxílio** through your help. ~ **sol** in sunshine. ~ **tempo ruim** in bad weather. ~ **todos os seus sofrimentos ela não é infeliz** with all her pains she is not unhappy. ~ **tudo isto, eu irei!** in spite of all that I shall go. ~ **uma risada** with a laugh. **confundi-o** ~ **meu amigo** I mistook him for my friend. **ele adoeceu** ~ **gripe** he fell ill with influenza. **ele está** ~ **inveja dela** he envies her. **ele está** ~ **menos de dez anos de idade** he is under ten years old. **ela teve de lidar** ~ **ele** she had dealings with him. **eu estou** ~ **ele** I agree with him. **eu estou** ~ **medo** I am afraid. **isto é lá** ~ **ele** that's up to him. **nisto não concordo** ~ **você** in that you differ with me. **vim** ~ **ele** I came with him.

coma (I) s. f. 1. a head of hair. 2. mane. 3. horsehair. 4. plume, ornamental tuft of feathers.

coma (II) s. m. + f. (med.) coma, torpor.

coma (III) s. f. coma: 1. (astr.) a comet's head. 2. (bot.) a tuft of hair, bracts or branches.

coma (IV) s. f. 1. (mus.) pause, rest, interval. 2. comma. 3. ~**s** pl. quotation marks.

comado adj. 1. comate, hairy, comose. 2. frondose, leafy.

comadre s. f. 1. godmother (in relation to the godchild's parents). 2. (pop.) midwife. 3. a bedpan.

comadresco adj. godmotherly, of or relative to a godmother.

comadrice s. f. 1. gossip, intrigue, chitchat. 2. machination, scheme.

comandância s. f. commandership.

comandante s. m. 1. commander, commandant. 2. chief, chieftain. 3. leader, head. 4. officer. 5. (naut.) captain. ‖ adj. m. + f. commanding.

~ **do porto** port commander, port admiral. ~ **de uma esquadra da armada** admiral. ~ **supremo** commander-in-chief.

comandar v. 1. to command. 2. to have the command over. 3. to direct, order. 4. to captain. 5. to control, govern. 6. to dominate. 7. to overlook.

comandita s. f. (com.) 1. shareholder in a limited society. 2. silent partner. 3. limited partnership.

comanditar v. (com.) 1. to supply funds as a silent partner. 2. to manage the funds of a company with limited liability.

comanditário s. m. (com.) 1. financier of a limited company. 2. silent partner, sleeping partner. ‖ adj. sleeping, silent (said of the capitalist partner in a limited society).

comando s. m. 1. act of commanding. 2. command, order. 3. mandate, authority. 4. power, control. 5. commandership, leadership. 6. direction. 7. commando. 8. (tech.) control (plate D 1).

~ **à distância** (mech.) remote control, distant control. ~ **a pedal** (mech.) foot control. ~ **supremo** the supreme command, chief command. **assumir o** ~ to take the lead. **alavanca de** ~ (aeron.) steering rod. **sob** ~ by command. **voz de** ~ word of command.

comarca s. f. 1. (Braz.) judiciary district of a state, judicature. 2. district, county. 3. region. 4. limits, frontier, boundaries.

comarcão adj. (pl. **comarcãos**) (f. **comarcã**) 1. of or pertaining to a judiciary district. 2. bordering upon, adjacent.

comatoso adj. (med.) comatose.

comba s. f. a narrow valley between high mountains, glen.

combacilo s. m. (bact.) comma bacillus.

combalido adj. 1. indisposed. 2. weak, frail, enfeebled. 3. dejected, downcast.

combalir v. 1. to weaken, enfeeble. 2. to despond, become discouraged. 3. to upset, discompose, shock. 4. to become foul or rotten. 5. ~-**se** to grow weak.

combate s. m. 1. combat, fight, battle. 2. (mil.) action, engagement. 3. brush, fray, encounter. 4. conflict. 5. warfare.

~ **aéreo** air fighting. ~ **em retirada** running fight. **dar** ~ **ao inimigo** to fight the enemy. **entrar em** ~ to come into action. **fora de** ~ down and out. **interromper o** ~ to break off an action. **o soldado morreu em** ~ the soldier died in action. **pôr fora de** ~ to put out of action.

combatente s. m. + f. 1. fighter, combatant. 2. warrior. 3. (ornith.) ruff. ‖ adj. fighting, combatant.

combater v. 1. to combat, fight, battle. 2. to strive against, struggle with. 3. to contend, contest. 4. to antagonize, oppose. 5. to conflict. 6. to be in disagreement. 7. to attack, assault.

~ **as suas paixões** to master one's passions. ~ **corpo a corpo** to fight at close quarters. **a maneira** de ~ the way of fighting. **ele combateu estas coisas com bastante efeito** he waged an effective war on these things.

combatível adj. m. + f. (pl. -íveis) combatable, contestable.

combatividade s. f. 1. combativity, combativeness. 2. pugnacity.

combativo adj. 1. combative. 2. disposed to fight, pugnacious. 3. militant. || **-amente** adv. combatively, pugnaciously.
a força -a diminuiu the fighting fitness diminished. **ele é ~** he shows fight.

combinação s. f. (pl. -ões) 1. combination: a) act or result of combining. b) adjustment, arrangement. c) aggregation. d) agreement, understanding. e) (chem.) formation of a chemical compound, the compound thus formed. f) underskirt, slip (plate R 6). g) (math.) grouping of certain numbers or quantities in every possible manner. h) union, association. i) coalition. j) fusion. 2. conjunction, conjugation.
~ fraudulenta collusiveness. **~ linear** (math.) a linear combination. **conforme ~** by agreement. **ela comprou uma ~ de seda** she bought a silk combination. **em ~ com** in conjunction with. **segundo ~ particular** by private contract.

combinada s. f. (agric.) combine, threshing machine.

combinado s. m. 1. (sport) a scratch team. 2. (chem.) compound. 3. agreement. || adj. 1. combined, agreed. 2. consolidate(d). 3. adjusted, arranged. 4. united, allied. 5. collusive.
~! agreed!, all right!, put it there! **como ~ as** agreed upon. **está ~?** is that a bargain? **está tudo ~** (pop.) it's all cut and dried, it's agreed upon.

combinador s. m. combiner. || adj. combining.

combinar v. 1. to combine. 2. to group, rank, place in a certain order. 3. to join together, unite, connect. 4. to arrange, assort. 5. to make a pact, stipulate. 6. to agree, correspond. 7. to mix, mingle, blend. 8. to synthesize. 9. to consider, reflect, ponder. 10. to match. 11. **~-se** to concur with, agree to. 12. (chem.) to form a chemical compound. 13. to consolidate. 14. to compose. 15. to coincide, conjugate.
~ bem to blend well. **eles combinam muito bem** they suit each other well, they are a good match. **eles ~am um bom negócio** they came to terms about a good bargain. **estas cores não combinam uma com outra** these colours are out of harmony with each other, (sl.) swear at each other. **isto combina bem com meu vestido** this is a good match for my dress. **~ um preço** to agree on a price.

combinativo adj. combinative.

combinatório adj. combinatory, combinative.

combinável adj. m. + f. (pl. -áveis) combinable, compoundable.

combóia s. f. (Braz.) a big wicker basket used for the transport of sugar-cane to the mills.

comboiar v. 1. to guide. 2. to convoy, escort. 3. to waft. 4. to guard, protect. 5. to accompany.

comboieiro s. m. escort, escort ship.

comboio s. m. 1. convoy. 2. wagon train accompanied by an armed escort. 3. vessels of a convoy. 4. transport of wounded soldiers or prisoners. 5. the locomotive and carriages which make up a railway train.

combona s. f. a small ditch or channel near the sea-shore (used as a fish-trap), fish-garth.

comborça s. f. concubine who lives with a married man.

comborçaria s. f. concubinage.

comborço s. m. man who lives in concubinage with a married woman.

combretáceas s. f. pl. Combretaceae: a family of tropical and subtropical shrubs or trees.

combretáceo adj. (bot.) combretaceous.

combro s. m. knoll, hill, hillock.

comburente s. m. + f. fuel. || adj. causing combustion, burning, inflaming.

comburir v. to burn, consume with fire.

combustão s. f. (pl. -ões) 1. combustion. 2. act of burning. 3. ignition, inflammation. 4. moral conflagration. 5. tumult, hubbub, agitation. 6. revolution, civil war.
gás de ~ stack gas. **motor de ~ interna** internal-combustion engine. **resíduos de ~** residue of combustion. **~ espontânea** spontaneous combustion.

combustar v. to burn, consume with fire.

combustibilidade s. f. combustibility, inflammability.

combustível s. m. (pl. -íveis) 1. combustible, fuel. 2. firewood, coal. 3. gasoline, gas. || adj. m. + f. 1. combustible. 2. combustive, burnable. 3. ignitable, piceous.
~ atômico nuclear fuel. **~ nuclear = combustível atômico.**

combustivo adj. combustive, combustible.

combusto adj. burning; burnt.

combustor s. m. (Braz.) street lamp.

come-aranha s. m. (pl. **come-aranhas**) popular designation of any spider-wasp (of the genus Pepsis).

começado adj. inchoate, just begun.

começador s. m. beginner. || adj. beginning.

começante adj. m. + f. beginning, initiating, incipient.

começar v. 1. to begin, commence. 2. to start. 3. to introduce, enter on. 4. to originate. 5. to take rise. 6. to launch. 7. to initiate, inchoate.
~ a escrever to set pen to paper. **~ a trabalhar** to set to work. **~ com novos planos** to start on new plans. **~am um negócio arriscado** they embarked upon a dangerous enterprise. **~ novamente com** to start anew, start over again. **~ uma briga** to pick up a quarrel. **~ uma conversa** to fall into conversation. **~ uma vida nova** to enter upon a new life. **~ um negócio** to start in business. **começou a cair neve** it came on to snow. **começou a chover** it came on to rain. **começou um forte temporal** a heavy storm set in. **ele começou a estudar direito** he took up law. **ele começou a fazê-lo** he sat down to do it. **ele começou a rezar** he fell to praying. **ele começou a trabalhar por conta própria** he set up for himself. **ele começou do nada** he started from the scratch. **eles ~am a ler** they took up reading. **eu vou ~** I'll make the beginning. **o fogo começou na cozinha** the fire originated in the kitchen. **o navio começou a fazer água** the ship sprang a leak. **quando começa?** when does it come off?

começo (ê) s. m. (pl. **começos**) 1. commencement, beginning. 2. inception, birth, infancy. 3. start; outset. 4. opening, onset. 5. (fig.) bud. 6. inchoateness, incipience. 7. origin. 8. pl. test(s), experiment(s).
desde o ~ from the foundation. **do ~ ao fim** from first to last, from title page to colophon, from alpha to omega. **isto ainda está no ~** it is still in its infancy. **isto é apenas o ~** this is only the beginning, is the thin end of the wedge. **no ~ da noite** early in the evening. **no ~ de sua carreira** at the outset of his career. **no ~ deste ano** on the threshold of this year. **no ~ tudo ia bem** at first all ran smoothly. **para o ~ está bom** quite good for the beginning. **tivemos um bom ~** we had a good start. **todo o ~ é difícil** nothing so hard as the beginning. **um novo ~** a new departure.

comedeira s. f. graft, exploitation.

comedela s. f. 1. alimony. 2. aliments, food, victuals. 3. (fig.) illicit profit.

comedia s. f. (Braz.) 1. pasture, grazing. 2. feeding grounds. 3. place where wild animals feed on fallen fruits.

comédia s. f. 1. (theat.) comedy, sketch, farce. 2. (fig.) a ridiculous fact or matter. 3. (fig.) dissimulation. ~ de costumes (theat.) comedy of manners. ~ musical (theat.) musical comedy.

comédia-de-arte s. f. (pl. comédias-de-arte) (theat.) commedia dell'arte.

comediante s. m. + f. comedian, comedienne, comic actor or actress.

comediar v. to transform into a comedy, write a farce or comedy.

comedido adj. 1. moderate, modest. 2. unpretentious. 3. prudent, cautious. 4. philosophic(al). 5. discreet.

comedimento s. m. 1. moderation. 2. modesty. 3. unpretentiousness. 4. prudence. 5. discretion.

comediografia s. f. the art of writing or staging a comedy.

comediógrafo s. m. comedist: author of comedies.

comedir v. 1. to moderate. 2. to contain, restrain. 3. to make respectful. 4. to regulate conveniently. 5. to impose the fulfilment of a duty. 6. ~-se: a) to behave modestly. b) to comply with. c) to restrain o. s.

comedista s. m. + f. author of a comedy.

comedor s. m. 1. eater. 2. a great eater, glutton. 3. wastrel, spendthrift. 4. parasite, sponger. ‖ adj. eating, feeding.

homem farto não é ~ enough is as good as a feast.

comedoria s. f., comedorias pl. 1. alimony. 2. aliments, victuals, food.

comedouro s. m. 1. feeding place (of wild animals). 2. feedbin, feedbag, food-trough, feedbox. 3. feed-drawer of a bird-cage. ‖ adj. good to eat.

comelináceas s. f. pl. Commelinaceae: a family of herbs.

comelináceo adj. (bot.) commelinaceous.

come-longe s. m. + f., sg. + pl. 1. geophagist, eater of earth or clay. 2. a pallid person.

comemoração s. f. (pl. -ões) 1. commemoration. 2. celebration. 3. memorialization.

comemorador s. m. commemorator, celebrator. ‖ adj. commemorating.

comemorar v. 1. to commemorate. 2. to remember, memorialize. 3. to celebrate. 4. to solemnize.

comemorativo adj. 1. commemorative, commemoratory. 2. memorial, recordative. 3. votive. ‖ -amente adv. commemoratively.

medalha -a votive medal. placa -a votive tablet.

comemorável adj. m. + f. (pl. -áveis) commemorable.

comenda s. f. 1. (eccl.) commendam, ecclesiastical benefice. 2. (hist.) commandery, knighthood. 3. badge, insignia (of a commander). 4. distinction.

comendador s. m. (f. comendadeira) a commendatary, commander (of a religious or military order).

comendadoria s. f. 1. office, dignity or authority of a commendatary. 2. commendam, ecclesiastical benefice. 3. income from and fruition of a benefice.

comendataria s. f. commendam.

comendatário s. m. a commendatary, beneficiary of a commendam. ‖ adj. commendatory.

comendatício adj. commendable, laudatory, laudable.

comendativo adj. recommendatory, commendable, laudatory.

comendatório adj. commendatory.

comenos s. m. 1. moment, instant. 2. occasion, opportunity.

neste ~ at that moment, in the meanwhile, at that opportunity.

comensal s. m. + f. (pl. -ais) 1. commensal, one who eats at the same table, messmate. 2. regular guest at a restaurant, boarder.

comensalidade s. f. commensality.

comensalismo s. m. commensalism.

comensurabilidade s. f. commensurability, commensurableness, commensurateness.

comensurado adj. commensurate.

comensurar v. 1. to reduce to a common measure. 2. to commensurate, proportion. 3. to compare.

comensurável adj. m. + f. (pl. -áveis) commensurable, commensurate. ‖ comensuravelmente adv. commensurably, commensurately.

comentação s. f. (pl. -ões) 1. commentation. 2. commentary.

comentado adj. commented, discussed.

comentador s. m. commentator, expounder, expositor.

comentar v. 1. to coment, commentate. 2. to explain, expound. 3. to annotate. 4. to observe. 5. to interpret.

~ de passagem to remark parenthetically.

comentário s. m. 1. comment, commentary. 2. note, annotation. 3. critical analysis, careful consideration (of facts). 4. explication, interpretation. 5. malicious critique. 6. remark.

~ formal dictum. não faça ~! don't make comments! sem ~ without remark.

comentarista s. m. + f. 1. commentator, annotator. 2. author of a commentary. 3. columnist, paragrapher. 4. interpreter.

comentício adj. 1. notable, remarkable. 2. fictitious.

comento s. m. 1. comment, commentary. 2. interpretation.

comer s. m. 1. act of eating. 2. eating, meal. 3. food. ‖ v. 1. to eat, consume. 2. to devour, swallow, gulp down. 3. to chew, mastigate. 4. to spend (for food), waste. 5. to corrode. 6. to feed. 7. to believe easily, be gullible. 8. to deceive, delude, dupe. 9. to cheat, defraud. 10. to take a man (at chess or checkers). 11. ~-se: a) to be consumed with, pine away. b) to become upset, fret. c) to be consumed with anger. 12. to i¹tch.

~ as palavras to mumble. ~ avidamente to devour, wolf down. ~ à vontade to eat one's fill. ~ bem to take one's teeth to, keep a good table. ~ como um lobo to eat like a wolf. ~ demais to overeat, overfeed, stuff, stodge. ~ e calar to eat one's fill and keep quiet. ~ em pensão to board. ~ fora de casa to eat out. ~ gato por lebre (fig.) to take an owl for an ivy-bush. ~ regaladamente to feast, feed high. ~-se de inveja to be eaten with envy. ~-se uns aos outros to eat up one another. dar de ~ to feed. ela não come muito she is not a great eater, she is a poor eater. ele come-lhe os olhos da cara he eats him out of house and home. ele come muito bem he plays a good knife and fork. ele está comendo gambá errado! (fam.) he's got hold of the wrong end of the stick. ele faz hoje para ~ amanhã he lives from hand to mouth. isto é do seu ~ that is to his liking. não é possível ~ aquilo that is just uneatable. não ter que ~ to have nothing to eat. gostamos de ~ bem we are fond of good eating. nós comemos em cinco we are five at a mess. um guloso vive para ~, um sábio come para viver a glutton lives to eat, a wise man eats to live.

comercial adj. m. + f. (pl. -ais) commercial, mercantile, staple, trading. ‖ ~mente adv. commercially.

casa ~ emporium. direito ~ commercial law. junta ~ trade board. movimento ~ trade. nome ~ trade name. valor ~ economic value.

comercialismo s. m. commercialism, commercial practice, spirit and method.
comercialista s. m. + f. commercialist, person well versed in commercial law. ‖ adj. commercialistic(al).
comercialização s. f. (pl. -ões) commercialization.
comercializar v. to commercialize, render commercial.
comerciante s. m. + f. 1. merchant, trader, tradesman. 2. businessman. 3. tradeswoman, businesswoman. 4. trafficker. ‖ adj. trading, commercial.
~ **por atacado** wholesale trader. ~ **rico** merchant prince. **ele é** ~ he is in trade.
comerciar v. 1. to trade, deal. 2. to carry on commerce. 3. to traffic. 4. to barter. 5. to do business, commerce.
comerciário s. m. commercial employee.
comerciável adj. m. + f. (pl. -áveis) marketable, negotiable, sellable, commercial.
comercinho s. m. (Braz.) small market town.
comércio s. m. 1. commerce, trade. 2. trading, business, dealing. 3. truck, barter. 4. traffic. 5. the class of merchants. 6. mercantile affairs. 7. illicit sexual intercourse.
~ **a varejo** retail trade. ~ **clandestino** clandestine trade. ~ **de bufarinheiro** peddling. ~ **de cabotagem** coasting trade. ~ **de cereais** corn trade. ~ **de importação** import and export trade. ~ **de livros** book trade. ~ **de troca** barter. ~ **exterior** foreign trade. ~ **intermediário** intermediate trade, commission business. ~ **interno** home trade. ~ **nacional** domestic trade. ~ **por atacado** wholesale trade. ~ **vantajoso** bargain. ~ **varejista** retail trade. **câmara do** ~, **ministério do** ~ Board of Trade. **o** ~ **está paralisado** there is a trade depression. **de fechar o** ~ gorgeous, splendid, lavishing, sensational, extraordinary (said of a woman). **tratado de** ~ commercial treaty.
comes s. m. pl. comestibles, food.
~ **e bebes** (pop.) eating and drinking, food and drink.
comestibilidade s. f. comestibility, edibility, edibleness.
comestível s. m. + f. (pl. -íveis) comestible(s), edible(s), food, eatable(s), eats, viand. ‖ adj. comestible, eatable, esculent.
cometa s. m. 1. (astr.) comet. 2. travelling salesman.
cauda de ~ tail of a comet.
cometário adj. of, pertaining to or relative to a comet.
cometedor s. m. committer or perpetrator of a crime. ‖ adj. committing, perpetrating.
cometer v. 1. to commit, practise, perform. 2. to perpetrate. 3. to make, undertake. 4. to entrust with, charge. 5. to affront, insult. 6. to attack, assault. 7. to propose.
~ **falta** to trespass, err. ~ **faltas no jogo de futebol** to make foul. ~ **perjúrio** to perjure. ~ **uma jornada** to set out upon a journey. ~ **um erro** to blunder, make a mistake. ~ **um pecado** to commit a sin. **ele cometeu um lapso** he made a slip. **ter cometido um crime** to be guilty of a crime.
cometida s. f. attack, assault.
cometimento s. m. 1. act of committing, committal, commitment. 2. comission, undertaking. 3. fault, crime. 4. enterprise, bold action. 5. attack.
cometomancia s. f. cometomancy, divination based on the observation of comets.
cometomante s. m. + f. cometomancer.
comezaina s. f. (pop.) 1. a rich repast, tuck-in. 2. binge, reverly, merrymaking.
comezinho adj. 1. good to eat, appetizing, palatable. 2. (fig.) easy to be understood. 3. plain, simple. 4. homemade.

comicha adj. m. + f. importune, meddlesome.
comichão s. f. (pl. -ões) 1. itching, pruritus, prickle. 2. (med.) formication. 3. ardent desire, longing. **senti** ~ **na mão** it pricked my hand. **ter** ~ **na língua** to have a mind to speak.
comichar v. 1. to itch, creep. 2. to formicate.
comichoso adj. 1. itchy, creepy. 2. ticklish. 3. hard to please. 4. longing, desiring, having an itch for.
comicial adj. m. + f. (pl. -ais) of or relative to a meeting, rally or assembly, comitial.
comicidade s. f. 1. comicality, comicalness. 2. comic, ridiculousness. 3. ludicrousness.
comício s. m. 1. meeting, rally. 2. assembly. 3. demonstration. 4. (hist.) comitia.
cômico s. m. comedian, comic actor, comic. ‖ adj. 1. comic(al), funny. 2. jocular, burlesque. 3. droll, farcical. 4. humourous. ‖ **-amente** adv. 1. comically. 2. jocularly, farcically. 3. ludicrously.
comida s. f. 1. food, aliment. 2. eating, fare, meal. 3. feed, feeding. 4. grub, chow. 5. cuisine. 6. ~**s** pl. illicit dealings or business relations.
~ **caseira** household fare. ~ **de cachorro** food fit for a dog. ~ **e bebida** food and drink, meat and drink. ~ **para porcos** pigwash. ~ **pesada** stodge. ~ **simples** plain diet. **a** ~ **aqui é boa** you fare well here. **dar** ~ **a alguém** to give a person something to eat.
comido adj. 1. eaten, consumed. 2. corroded. 3. chewed, ingested, swallowed. 4. betrayed, deceived.
comigo pron. with me, in my society, as for me, as to myself, upon my account.
dizendo ~ saying to myself. **eu levo tudo** ~ I carry everything with me. **isso não é** ~ that is not my business. **isto é** ~ it falls to my lot, that is my affair. **não agiram bem para** ~ they did not treat me well. **para** ~ towards me.
comigo-ninguém-pode s. m. (Braz.), popular name of the **aningapara**, an ornamental araceous plant (Dieffenbacchia picta) with a deadly poisonous juice.
comilança, comilância s. f. (pop.) 1. act or habit of eating too much. 2. (fig.) rascality, thievery, swindle.
comilão s. m. (pl. -ões) (f. **comilona**) 1. a heavy eater, greedy feeder. 2. glutton, stodger, guttler. ‖ adj. edacious, aluttonous, greedy.
cominação s. f. (pl. -ões) 1. commination. 2. threat, act of threatening. 3. punishment. 4. menace.
cominador s. m. one who threatens, threatener. ‖ adj. comminatory, threatening, menacing.
cominar v. 1. to comminate. 2. to threaten, menace. 3. to threaten with punishment. 4. to impose a penalty, prescribe a punishment.
cominativo, cominatório adj. comminatory, threatening.
cominho s. m. (bot.) cumin, cummin.
não vale um ~ it is not worth a straw.
cominho-armênio s. m. (pl. **cominhos-armênios**), (bot.) caraway-seeds.
cominho-bastardo s. m. (pl. **cominhos-bastardos**), (bot.) wild cumin.
cominuir v. 1. to comminute. 2. to reduce to small particles. 3. to break into fragments, shatter, crumble.
cominutivo adj. crumbled, shattered, comminute.
cominuto adj. comminute.
comiseração s. f. (pl. -ões) 1. commiseration. 2. compassion, pity.
comiserador s. m. commiserator. ‖ adj. commiserating, merciful.
comiserar v. 1. to commiserate. 2. to move to pity. 3. to feel pity or compassion. 4. to condole with, grieve with.

comiserativo adj. commiserative, compassionate.
comissão s. f. (pl. -ões) 1. commission. 2. act of committing or performing. 3. act of entrusting or giving in charge. 4. executive body, group of persons united to perform a task or duty. 5. committee. 6. retribution, recompense, gratification. 7. percentage paid (to a commission agent). 8. brokerage, factorage. 9. (hist.) letters of marque. 10. provisional position, office or duty. 11. (mil.) warrant of authority or command.
dar ~ to commissionate, give a commission. **vender por** ~ to sell for a third party.
comissária s. f. stewardess.
comissária de bordo s. f. airline stewardess.
comissariado s. m. 1. office, authority or duty of a commissary. 2. commissariat. 3. commissaryship, commissionership.
comissariaria s. f. commissaryship.
comissário s. m. 1. commissary, commissioner. 2. commissar. 3. police officer, sheriff. 4. deputy, delegate. 5. judge. 6. agent. 7. steward, purser.
~ **da marinha mercante** (naut.) paymaster, purser. ~ **da polícia** police commissioner, justice of peace. ~ **de bordo** purser, supercargo. ~ **volante** (com.) travel(l)ing salesman.
comissionado s. m. commissioned officer or civil authority, deputy, delegate. ‖ adj. commissioned, commissionary.
comissionar v. 1. to commission, commissionate. 2. to give authority to, empower. 3. to confide in, rely on. 4. to entrust, charge with.
comisso s. m. fine, forfeit, penalty imposed for non--fulfilment of a contract.
comissório adj. obligatory.
comissura s. f. 1. commissure. 2. joint, seam. 3. suture. 4. cleft, crack, fissure.
comissural adj. m. + f. (pl. -ais) commissural.
comitê s. m. 1. committee. 2. group of persons united to perform a duty. 3. group of persons appointed to represent associates (in a common cause). 4. commission.
ele pertence ao ~ he is on the committee. **em** ~ in private, privately.
comitente s. m. + f. 1. committer. 2. employer. 3. consigner. 4. constituent. ‖ adj. committing, constituent.
comitiva s. f. 1. train, retinue of attendants. 2. company, suit. 3. cortège. 4. following, tail, equipage.
comível adj. m. + f. (pl. -íveis) eatable, edible.
como adv. 1. how, by what means, in what manner. 2. wherein. 3. to what degree. 4. for what reason. 5. to what effect. ‖ conj. as, when, while, because, why. ‖ interj. what!, why!
~ **aconteceu isso?** how did it happen?, how comes? ~ **assim?** how that?, why so? ~ **as coisas estão atualmente!** as affairs stand! ~ **disse?** I beg your pardon? ~ **é isso?** what does that mean? ~ **está?** how are you? how is it? ~ **quem diz que isto não é nada** that's like giving to understand that it is nothing. ~ **quer que seja** whatever it may be. ~ **quiser** as you like it. ~ **se** as if, as though. ~ **segue** as follows. ~ **também** as well as. ~ **vai?** how do you do?, how are you? ~ **você está!** what a sight you are! **a sua posição** ~ **banqueiro** his position as a banker. **deixe-me dizer-lhe** ~ **amigo** let me tell you as a friend. **diga-me,** ~ **é que isto se chama?** tell me, what do you call it? **diligente** ~ **uma abelha** busy as a bee. **duro** ~ **pedra** stonehard. **ele** ~ **ela** he as well as she. **faça** ~ **quiser** do as you wish. **livros clássicos** ~ **dramas de Racine** classical books as the plays of Racine. **nada** ~ **este avião em velocidade** nothing can touch this

plane for speed. **não** ~ **professor, mas** ~ **amigo** not as a master, but as a friend. **parecia** ~ **se eles lutassem de fato** it looked as if they were really fighting. **pesado** ~ **chumbo** heavy as lead. **seja** ~ for however it may be. **temos de aceitá-lo tal** ~ **está** we must accept it as it is. **velho** ~ **é, devia sabê-lo melhor!** old as he is he should know it better.
comoção s. f. (pl. -ões) 1. commotion. 2. agitation, disturbance. 3. ferment, fermentation, effervescence. 4. revolt, riot. 5. eruption. 6. disorder, perturbation. 7. sensation, emotion. 8. squall, flurry.
cômoda s. f. commode, chest of drawers, bureau.
comodante s. m. accommodation lender, one who lends as a favour.
comodatário s. m. (jur.) commodatary, receiver of a commodation or commodatum.
comodato s. m. (com., jur.) commodation, commodatum.
comodidade s. f. 1. comfortableness, cosiness. 2. commodiousness, ease. 3. convenience, opportunity. 4. leisureliness. 5. comfort. 6. suitableness, handiness. 7. well-being.
com todas as ~**s** with all conveniences.
comodismo s. m. 1. selfishness. 2. self-indulgence.
comodista s. m. + f. a selfish or self-indulgent person, egotist. ‖ adj. selfish, self-indulgent.
ele é muito ~ he is an easy-going fellow.
cômodo s. m. 1. room, accommodation. 2. comfort, ease. 3. comfortableness. 4. shelter. 5. hospitality. ‖ adj. 1. commodious. 2. useful. 3. suitable, fit, handy. 4. favourable. 5. comfortable, easy. ‖ -amente adv. comfortably, commodiously, easily, leisurely.
~ **mobiliado para alugar** a furnished room to let. **em -as prestações** in easy instalments. **homem** ~ an easy-tempered man, an indulgent fellow. **preço** ~ **a** reasonable price. **ter para viver -amente** to have a fair livelihood.
comodoro s. m. 1. (naut.) commodore, commander of a fleet. 2. senior captain of a line of ships. 3. president of a naval club. 4. honorific title.
comoração s. f. (pl. -ões) a dwelling upon a certain subject (discourse).
cômoro s. m. 1. hillock, knoll, monticle, mound. 2. ledge. 3. flower-bed, flower-box.
comoso adj. 1. hairy, downy, comose. 2. (med.) comatose.
comovedor adj., **comovente** adj. m. + f. 1. moving, touching. 2. soul-stirring. 3. impressive. 4. dramatic, poignant. 5. vibrant, piteous. ‖ **comovedoramente** adv. touchingly, movingly.
comover v. 1. to move, affect. 2. to agitate, stir up. 3. to upset. 4. to impress. 5. to arouse, stimulate. 6. to commove, move to compassion. 7. ~-**se** to become moved, to be touched with pity, take to the heart. **o sofrimento dos pobres me comoveu** the sufferings of the poor have come home to me. **um aspecto assim me comove bastante** I am deeply touched by such a sight.
comovido adj. 1. shaken, upset. 2. moved, touched. 3. struck. 4. deeply impressed by. 5. impassioned, impassionate. ‖ -amente adv. feeling, impassionately.
ele ficou ~ it has come home to him. **ele ficou** ~ **de pesar** he was smitten with grief. **ele ficou profundamente** ~ he was touched to the quick.
compacidade s. f. compactness, denseness, closeness.
compacto adj. 1. compact. 2. close, massy, massive. 3. dense, close-grained. 4. thick. 5. solid, consolidate. 6. numerous. 7. crowded. 8. compressed. 9. tight. ‖ -amente adv. compactly, tightly, massively, solidly.

compadecedor adj. compassionate, pitiful, merciful.
compadecer v. 1. to pity, compassionate, regret. 2. to deplore, commiserate. 3. to condole, sympathize. 4. to endure, bear. 5. to resign o. s. to. 6. to feel pity for.
compadecido adj. compassionate, pitiful, ruthful, sympathetic. ‖ **-amente** adv. compassionately, sympathetically, pitifully.
compadecimento s. m. 1. compassion. 2. commiseration. 3. sympathy. 4. condolence, mercy, pity.
compadrado s. m. 1. compaternity. 2. sponsorship, godfathership. 3. (fig.) intimacy, familiarity. ‖ adj. related (by godfathership).
compadrar v. 1. to be or become godfather. 2. to enter into an intimate relationship with. 3. to maintain (as godfather) an intimate relationship with the child's actual parents.
compadre s. m. 1. godfather (in relation to the godchild's parents). 2. father (in his relationship with his child's godfather). 3. companion, friend, crony.
compadrear v. to become godfather.
compadresco adj. of or concerning the relationship between a godfather and the child's parents.
compadrice s. f., **compadrio** m. 1. compaternity, spiritual relationship between a godfather and the child's parents. 2. intimity, familiarity. 3. exaggerated or unjustified protection, sponsorship, favouritism.
compadrismo s. m. political partiality or favouritism.
compaginação s. f. (pl. **-ões**) compagination.
compaginado adj. (bot.) said of plant parts with their surfaces joined together.
compaginador s. m. (typogr.) = **paginador**.
compaginar (I) v. to compaginate, unite firmly, join, hold together.
compaginar (II) v. to paginate.
compaixão s. f. (pl. **-ões**) 1. compassion. 2. commiseration. pity. 3. sympathy. 4. mercy, condolence.
companha s. f. 1. a ship's crew. 2. a fishermen's guild. 3. (obs.): a) company. b) companion.
companheira s. f. 1. a female companion. 2. woman (in relation to the man with whom she lives). 3. chaperon(e). 4. (pop.) wife. 5. female partner, mate.
companheirão s. m. (pl. **-ões**) (f. **companheirona**) a trustworthy, loyal friend, unfailing comrade.
companheirismo s. m. companionship, comradeship.
companheiro s. m. 1. companion, friend, fellow. 2. consort, colleague. 3. pal, crony, buddy, mate. 4. associate, partner. 5. (pop.) husband, spouse. ‖ adj. accompanying, companionate, matched.
~ **de armas** fellow soldier. ~ **de classe** classmate, schoolmate. ~ **de folguedos** playmate. ~ **de infortúnio** fellow sufferer. ~ **de mesa** commensal. ~ **de quarto** roommate, chamber-fellow, chum. ~ **de sofrimento** fellow sufferer. ~ **de trabalho** fellow worker, work companion, colleague, chum. ~ **de viagem** travelling companion, fellow passenger, fellow traveller. **bom** ~ good companion, boon companion. **eles são** ~**s íntimos** (fam.) they are hand in glove with each other.
companhia s. f. company: 1. society. 2. act of accompanying. 3. state of being a companion. 4. person or thing associated with others. 5. any assemblage of persons. 6. companionship, partnership. 7. firm, corporation, business concern. 8. train, retinue, entourage. 9. social intercourse. 10. (mil.) subdivision of a battalion under the command of a captain. 11. the officers and crew of a ship. 12. band. 13. body of actors of a theatre.
Companhia de Jesus Society of Jesus. ~ **de seguros** insurance company, underwriters. ~ **de transportes rápidos** express company. ~ **fiduciária** trust

company. ~ **filiada,** ~ **subsidiária** subsidiary company. **ele tem má** ~ he keeps bad company. **em** ~ in company, accompanied by, along, together. **evito sua** ~ I avoid his society. **fazer** ~ **a alguém** to keep s. o. company. **gosto de** ~ I am fond of company. **ir de** ~ to go together with. **regra de** ~ rule of fellowship.
cômpar adj. m. + f. 1. equal, exactly the same. 2. (mus.) accompanying. 3. similar, like. 4. analogous. 5. on a par with, even.
comparabilidade s. f. comparableness, comparability.
comparação s. f. (pl. **-ões**) 1. act or result of comparing. 2. comparison, confrontation. 3. similitude, parallel.
acima de qualquer ~, **sem** ~ beyond comparison. ~ **injuriosa** disparagement. **em** ~ **com** in comparison with, when compared with, in respect of. **fazer -ões** to draw comparisons, draw parallels. **graus de** ~ degrees of comparison. **isto não é nada em** ~ **com aquilo** this is nothing to that. **não há sombra de** ~! it's not in the least to be compared with, (sl.) not a patch on it!
comparado adj. comparate, comparative, confronted, similar.
comparador s. m. 1. comparer, confronter. 2. (phys.) comparator. ‖ adj. comparing, confronting, comparative.
comparar v. 1. to compare. 2. to regard discriminatingly. 3. to confront, liken, parallel. 4. to collate, check. 5. to measure. 6. to confer, contrast. 7. to equal, equalize, equate, even. 8. ~-**se**: a) to put o. s. on a level with. b) to be or pretend to be equal to. c) to enter into competition with, rival with.
comparamo-nos a... we put ourselves on a parallel with. **não se pode compará-lo ao seu irmão** he does not sustain a comparison with his brother. **não se pode compará-los** they are not to be compared. **ninguém se pode** ~ **a ele** he stands second to none.
comparatista s. m. + f. student or scholar of comparative literature.
comparativo s. m. (gram.) comparative degree. ‖ adj. comparative, comparable, relative.
comparável adj. m. + f. (pl. **-áveis**) comparable, similar, matchable.
é ~ **com** it sustains comparison with. **não é** ~ **com** it is not to be compared with; (fam.) it is not in the same street with.
comparecência s. f. 1. attendance. 2. (jur.) appearance (in court).
comparecente adj. m. + f. 1. attending, present. 2. (jur.) appearing (in court upon summons).
comparecer v. 1. to attend to, be present with. 2. (jur.) to appear in court. 3. to report, show up.
~ **de acordo com a intimação** (jur.) to save one's bail. ~ **em pessoa** to appear in person.
comparecimento s. m. 1. attendance, presence. 2. (jur.) appearance (in court upon summons). 3. (fam.) call.
comparoquiano s. m. fellow parishioner.
comparsa s. m. + f. 1. (theat.) figurant, walking gentleman, dummy, supernumerary. 2. (theat.) figurante, walking lady. 3. (com.) a person of little or no account in business dealings. 4. (pop.) accomplice.
comparsaria s. f. (theat.) a group of figurants.
comparte s. m. + f. companion, partner, participator. ‖ adj. participant, participating, sharing.
compartilhar v. 1. to participate, partake. 2. to take part in, have a share in. 3. to apportion, share.
compartilhei da sua tristeza I shared your grief.

compartimento s. m. 1. compartment. 2. room, chamber. 3. division, subdivision (of a house, railway carriage, drawer, etc.) (plate V 1). 4. cubicle, box.
compartir v. 1. to divide, separate. 2. to distribute. 3. to participate, share.
compáscuo s. m. common pasture, public grazing ground.
compassado adj. 1. measured. 2. regulated, regular. 3. rhythmic(al). 4. slow, moderate. 5. paced, cadenced. ‖ -amente adv. measuredly, rhythmically, regularly.
compassageiro s. m. fellow passenger.
compassar v. 1. to measure with a compass. 2. to cadence, pace. 3. to calculate. 4. (mus.) to beat time. 5. to slow down, make moderate (time). 6. to regulate, order. 7. to space. 8. to proportion.
compassível adj. m. + f. (pl. -íveis) merciful, pitiful.
compassividade s. f. compassionateness.
compassivo adj. 1. compassionate, commiserative. 2. merciful, feeling, pitiful. 3. kind-hearted, mild. 4. sympathetic. 5. sentimental. ‖ -amente adv. compassionately, relentingly, commiseratively.
compasso s. m. 1. compasses, instrument for describing circles (plates D 2, F 2). 2. (mus.) measure, tact, beat. 3. pace, time. 4. regular movement. 5. rhythm. 6. rule, precept. 7. (astr.) Compass, Circinus: a southern constellation. 8. distance. 9. interval.
~ de calibre calyper. ~ de mola bow-compasses (plate D 2). ~ de pontas direitas straight compasses. ~ de pontas fixas divider (plate D 2). ~ de vara trammel. ao ~ de in proportion of. dançamos ao ~ da música we dance to the rhythm of the music. fazer tudo ao ~ (fam.) to do everything by rule and compass. fora do ~ (mus.) out of time. manter o ~ to keep time. tirar alguém do seu ~ to disconcert s. o.
compaternidade s. f. compaternity, co-paternity.
compatibilidade s. f. 1. compatibility, compatibleness. 2. consistency, consilience. 3. associability.
compatível adj. m. + f. (pl. -íveis) compatible, conformable, consistent, harmonious. ‖ compativelmente adv. compatibly.
compatrício s. m. fellow citizen. ‖ adj. compatriotic.
compatriota s. m. + f. 1. compatriot, fellow countryman. 2. fellow countrywoman. ‖ adj. compatriotic.
compatriotismo s. m. compatriotism, kinship.
compelação s. f. (pl. -ões) 1. (jur.) arraignment, hearing. 2. accusation, charge. 3. interrogatory, judicial examination.
compelativo adj. compellative, compelling.
compelir v. 1. to compel, oblige. 2. to coerce, force. 3. to constrain. 4. to drive, impel. 5. to press.
compelível adj. m. + f. (pl. -íveis) compellable.
compendiador s. m. abridger, epitomizer, epitomist. ‖ adj. summarizing.
compendiar v. to summarize, epitomize, synthesize.
compêndio s. m. 1. compendium. 2. abstract, summary. 3. text-book, schoolbook, workbook. 4. manual.
compendioso adj. compendious, abridged, summarized.
compenetração s. f. (pl. -ões) compenetration, conviction.
compenetrado adj. deeply convinced.
compenetrar v. 1. to compenetrate, pervade. 2. to convince. 3. to enroot. 4. ~-se: a) to convince o. s., make sure of. b) to master s. th. completely. ele compenetrou-se disso he woke to it.
compensação s. f. (pl. -ões) 1. compensation. 2. recompense, remuneration. 3. indemnity, reparation. 4. counterbalance, counterpoise. 5. allowance. 6.

amends, correction. 7. (com.) balance. 8. satisfaction.
compensado s. m. veneer.
compensador s. m. 1. compensator. 2. (tech.) equalizer. ‖ adj. compensational, compensative, compensatory.
compensar v. 1. to compensate. 2. to recompense. 3. to make amends for, reimburse, repay. 4. to indemnify. 5. to counterbalance, even. 6. (tech.) to equalize. 7. (com.) to balance, clear. 8. ~-se to be compensated.
~ a perda a alguém to make good a loss to s. o. o crime não compensa crime does not pay.
compensativo adj. 1. compensative, compensatory, compensational. 2. recompensive. 3. (com.) profitable.
compensatório adj. compensatory.
compensável adj. m. + f. (pl. -áveis) compensable.
comperto adj. uncovered, discovered, evident, clear.
competência s. f. 1. competence, competency. 2. ability, capacity. 3. aptitude, adeptness. 4. faculty. 5. efficiency. 6. jurisdiction, sphere of influence. 7. fight, conflict. 8. competition, concurrence. 9. rivalry.
isto é de sua ~ this is within his scope. isto é fora da minha ~ that is out of my sphere. por falta de ~ for lack of ability.
competente adj. m. + f. 1. competent. 2. capable, able, apt. 3. sufficient. 4. cognizant. 5. proper, lawful. 6. due. 7. authoritative. 8. efficient. 9. qualified, fit. ‖ ~mente adv. 1. competently. 2. capably, aptly, ably. 3. authoritatively. 4. suitably. 5. properly.
ele não é ~ para... he is not competent to be... juiz ~ a competent judge.
competição s. f. (pl. -ões) 1. competition. 2. competitiveness. 3. contest, tournament. 4. rivalry. 5. match, race.
-ões de atletismo athletic events.
competidor s. m. 1. competitor. 2. contestant, contender. 3. rival. 4. emulator. 5. concurrent. ‖ adj. competing, competitive, rival, emulous.
superar todos os ~es to hold the field.
competidora s. f. competitress.
competir v. 1. to compete. 2. (com.) to be or stand in competition. 3. to contest, contend. 4. to rival. 5. to match. 6. to dispute, vie with, emulate. 7. to belong to (lawfull). 8. to behoove, be incumbent to. 9. to belong to the sphere of influence of.
apto para ~ able to compete. compete ao senhor fazer a proposta it is for you to propose. compete a ele it is due to him. esta pintura compete favoravelmente com aquela this painting is gaining on that one. isso compete a ela it falls to her. não lhe compete decidir he is not entitled to decide.
compilação s. f. (pl. -ões) 1. compilation. 2. collection. 3. digest.
compilador s. m. compiler, collector. ‖ adj. compiling.
compilar v. 1. to compile. 2. to collect. 3. to unite, put together, compose.
compilatório adj. compilatory.
compita s. f. 1. competition, concurrence. 2. rivalry. 3. strife.
à ~ in rivalry, in a spirit of competition.
cômpito (I) s. m. crossroads.
cômbito (II) s. m. (Port., prov.) measure, gauge.
complacência s. f. 1. complacence, complacency, complaisance. 2. compliance, yieldingness. 3. facility. 4. softness. 5. indulgence, deference. 6. accomodativeness. 7. conformity.
complacente adj. m. + f. 1. compliant, complaisant. 2. yielding, acquiescent. 3. sympathetic, pleasing, obliging. 4. indulgent, kind. 5. obsequious. 6. tracta-

ble, ductile. ‖ ~mente adv. yieldingly, sympathetically, complacently.

complanar v. 1. to level, make even, grade. 2. to be extended on a plane surface.

compleição s. f. (pl. -ões) 1. complexion. 2. physique, build, frame. 3. disposition, frame of mind. 4. temperament.

ele tem uma ~ forte he has a strong constitution.

compleicional adj. m. + f. (pl. -ais) complexional.

compleiçoado adj. complexioned.

complementação s. f. (pl. -ões) 1. completion. 2. conclusion.

complementador s. m. completer. ‖ adj. completing.

complementar (I) adj. m. + f. 1. complemental, complementary, completing. 2. supplementary. 3. appendaged. 4. new.

complementar (II) v. 1. to complement. 2. to complete, finish, conclude.

complementário adj. complementary.

complemento s. m. complement: 1. anything that makes complete or perfect. 2. (gram.) a word by which a predication is made complete. 3. (math.) complemental angle.

completação s. f. (pl. -ões) act of completing, completion.

completador s. m. completer, fulfiller. ‖ adj. completing.

completamento s. m. 1. act or process of completing, completion. 2. finish. 3. conclusion.

completar v. 1. to complete, complement. 2. to accomplish, fulfill. 3. to finish, conclude. 4. to cap, crown. 5. to perfect. 6. to integrate.

~ o estoque to replenish the stock. ~am as suas fileiras they brought their number to full. ela completou 18 anos agora she has just turned eighteen. eles ~am a refeição com sorvete they topped off the meal with icecream.

completas s. f. pl. (eccl.) complin.

completeza s. f. (math.) completeness.

completível adj. m. + f. (pl. -íveis) capable of being completed or included.

completivo (I) s. m. complement, supplement. ‖ adj. completive, completory.

completivo (II) adj. embodying, inclusive, comprehensive.

completo s. m. 1. a complete or finished thing or task. 2. the whole. 3. appurtenance. ‖ adj. 1. complete. 2. entire. 3. finished, concluded, done. 4. fulfilled. 5. whole, integral. 6. full. 7. perfect. ‖ -amente adv. completely, perfectly, fully, through and through.

-amente bêbado dead-drunk. -amente cheio brimful. -amente errado quite wrong. -amente estragado rotten to the core. -amente molhado soaked to the skin, sopping wet. -amente surdo stone-deaf. deixamo-lo em -a desordem we turned upside down. disparate ~ pure nonsense. eu sou -amente estranho aqui I am an utter stranger here. isto é coisa -amente diferente that is quite another thing. por ~ entirely, out and out. uma educação -a an all-round education. um tolo ~ an absolute fool. você ficou -amente maluco you have gone completely mad.

completório s. m. 1. (eccl.) complin. 2. end, finish, termination.

complexão s. f. (pl. -ões) 1. complexity. 2. concatenation of things or matter. 3. a whole. 4. assemblage. 5. union.

complexidade s. f. 1. complexity. 2. complicatedness, complicity. 3. intricacy, complication. 4. involution.

complexo s. m. 1. complex, conjunction of several elements or parts. 2. concatenation of things or matter. 3. (chem.) compound. 4. (psych.) a psychological complex. 5. composite. 6. synthesis. ‖ adj. 1. complex. 2. complicated, intricate. 3. synthetic(al). ‖ -amente adv. complexly.

~ de inferioridade (psych.) inferiority complex. ~ de superioridade (psych.) exaltation.

complicação s. f. (pl. -ões) 1. complication. 2. difficulty. 3. entanglement. 4. complicacy, complicatedness. 5. intricacy.

com muitas -ões with much trouble. ele meteu-se em -ões he got into trouble.

complicado adj. complicated, intricate, tricky, complex. ‖ -amente adv. complicatedly, intricately.

coisa -a a complicated matter or affair. um problema ~ an intricate problem.

complicador s. m. one who complicates. ‖ adj. complicating, complicative.

complicar v. 1. to complicate, render difficult or complex. 2. to embarrass. 3. to confuse. 4. to entangle, involve. 5. to become complicated.

complô s. m. (Fr.) complot, plot, conspiracy.

componedor s. m. (typogr.) 1. composing stick. 2. typesetter.

componenda s. f. (eccl.) agreement as to the payment of papal perquisites.

componente s. m. + f. component part, constituent part, ingredient. ‖ adj. component, constituent.

componista s. m. + f. (mus.) composer, writer of music.

componível adj. m. + f. (pl. -íveis) composable.

compor v. 1. to compose: a) enter into composition. b) arrange, put together. c) (typogr.) set up (type). d) write music. e) write or produce (as a literary or musical work). f) constitute, create, produce. g) compound. 2. to invent. 3. to repair, set in order. 4. to adorn, embellish. 5. to tranquilize, soothe. 6. ~-se: a) to set (o.s.) up as, constitute as. b) to conform (o.s.) to. 7. to reconcile, harmonize.

a obra compõe-se de... the work consists of... ~-se com seus inimigos to become reconciled with one's enemies. ~ a dois (typogr.) to set up types line by line. ~ limpo (typogr.) to typeset with practically no mistakes. ~ um poema to compose a poem.

comporta (I) s. f. canal lock, sluice, flood-gate.

comporta (II) s. f. (hist.) an ancient popular dance and dance tune.

comportação s. f. (pl. -ões) 1. behaviour. 2. conduct, demeanour. 3. bearing, carriage. 4. good manners.

comportamento s. m. 1. manner, conduct. 2. behaviour. 3. (sociol.) individual reaction caused by a definite social environment.

comportar v. 1. to be proportionate to. 2. to admit. 3. to bear, suffer. 4. to be able to hold or contain. 5. ~-se to behave, comport o. s.

a sala comportava cem pessoas the room could seat one hundred persons. o ônibus comporta cinqüenta passageiros the bus carries fifty passengers. o preço comporta todas as despesas the price is inclusive expenses.

comportável adj. m. + f. (pl. -áveis) tolerable, sufferable.

composição s. f. (pl. -ões) 1. composition: a) the art of composing. b) essay, writing. c) literary or musical work. d) mixture, compound. e) (typogr.) typesetting, composed type (plate T 6). f) disposition, arrangement. 2. constitution. 3. construction. 4. framing, setting. 5. harmonization of litigant parties. 6. (Braz.) the railway carriages which make up a train. 7. agreement, settlement.

~ **a frio** (typogr.) cold-type composition, photocomposition. ~ **humorística** humoresque. ~ **manual** (typogr.) hand composition. ~ **musical** opus, concerto. ~ **pequena** (mus.) bagatelle. ~ **simples** straight matter. ~ **centrada** (typogr.) centered composition. ~ **recorrida** (typogr.) straight matter. **prova de** ~ (typogr.) specimen of type, proof.

compósita adj. (archit.) Composite.

compositivo adj. compositive.

compositor s. m. 1. compositor. 2. (mus.) composer, maestro. 3. (typogr.) typesetter, typographer.
~ **de jazz** jazzer. ~ **de pastorais** pastoralist.

compostas s. f. pl. Compositae: an important family of herbs, shrubs and trees; the daisy family.

composto s. m. 1. composition, mixture. 2. compound. 3. composite. 4. amalgam. ‖ adj. 1. composed of, consisting of. 2. compound. 3. composite. 4. articulate. 5. modest, sober. 6. self-possessed, discreet, reserved.

compostura s. f. 1. composition, composing. 2. repair. 3. composure. 4. composedness. 5. countenance. 6. structure. 7. modesty, decency. 8. reservedness, soberness 9. falsity, imposture.
ele manteve a ~ he kept his countenance.

compota s. f. compote, fruit preserve, preserve.
um vidro de ~ a glass of jam.

compoteira s. f. compote, compotier, a glass or cup in which compote is served.

compra s. f. 1. act or result of purchasing. 2. purchase, buy. 3. acquisition. 4. buying, shopping. 5. object bought. 6. (cards) a drawing of a certain number of cards.
~ **a crédito** purchase on credit. ~ **de ocasião** bargain. ~ **e venda** purchase and sale (contract). ~ **muito barata** dead bargain. **por** ~ by purchase. **registro de** ~s purchase book. **sobrepujar nas** ~s to outbuy.

compradiço adj. easily bought, easily bribed, purchasable.

comprador s. m. 1. purchaser, purchasing agent. 2. (jur.) bargainee. 3. buyer, shopper, customer. 4. vendee.

compradora s. f. female buyer, shopper or customer.

comprar v. 1. to purchase, buy. 2. to acquire. 3. (cards) to draw a certain number of cards from the pack. 4. (fig.) to bribe, corrupt.
~ **a crédito** to buy on credit, buy on trust. ~ **a dinheiro** to buy cash down. ~ **por atacado** to purchase at wholesale. ~ **muito caro** to overbuy. ~ **a preço inferior do usual** to underbuy. ~ **desvantajosamente** to buy to disadvantage. ~ **gato por lebre** to buy a pig in a poke. ~ **passagens** to book. ~ **por uma bagatela** to pick up for a song. **ele comprou muito bem** he got good value for his money. **o dinheiro não compra felicidade** money cannot buy happiness.

comprável adj. m. + f. (pl. -**áveis**) 1. buyable, purchasable. 2. capable of being bribed, corruptible. 3. marketable, negotiable.

comprazedor s. m. 1. an obliging, obsequious person. 2. complier. ‖ adj. obliging, obsequious, deferential.

comprazer v. 1. to please, humour. 2. to comply with. 3. to gladden. 4. to assent, give in. 5. ~-**se** to have a great pleasure in, rejoice, be pleased with.

comprazimento s. m. 1. pleasing. 2. pleasure. 3. complaisance, affability. 4. compliance.

compreender v. 1. to comprehend, comprise, include. 2. to contain, hold. 3. to consist of, embrace, constitute. 4. to perceive, grasp, understand. 5. to sense, pick up, catch. 6. to conceive, apprehend. 7. to compass. 8. ~-**se** to be included in, be contained in.

compreenda o que quero dizer! now understand me! **compreende isto?** can you make sense of this? **compreende-me?** do you follow me? ~ **mal** to misunderstand. **compreendi que ele disse...** I understood him to say... **compreendo perfeitamente que** I am not unapprehensive that... **agora estou compreendendo** now I see light, now I have it. **ele é um tanto vagaroso em** ~ he is rather slow of apprehension. **eu não compreendi bem o que você disse** I did not quite catch what you said. **eu não o posso** ~ I cannot make him out. **eu o compreendi mal** I mistook your meaning. **como é que se deve** ~ **uma coisa dessas?** what construction is to be put upon such a thing? **isto se compreende por si** that goes without saying. **não compreendo isto!** I cannot make it out!, (coll.) that beats me! **não o compreendi bem** I didn't get you straight. **não compreendo a sua intenção** his purpose escapes me. **não posso compreender como chegou a isto** I cannot conceive how it came to that. **um fato que não se compreende facilmente** a fact not easily apprehended. **você compreende o que ele quer dizer?** do you see what he is driving at? **você me compreende?** do you understand me?, (sl.) do you get me?

compreendido adj. 1. included, comprised. 2. understood.

compreensão s. f. (pl. -**ões**) 1. comprehension, comprehensiveness. 2. apprehension, understanding. 3. (logics) connotation. 4. conception, grasp, knowing. 5. insight. 6. sense. 7. brain. 8. open-mindedness.
além da ~ over one's head, over one's light. **cada qual age de acordo com a sua** ~ everyone acts according to his lights. **ele não tem** ~ **para estas coisas** he cannot see the point of such things.

compreensibilidade s. f. comprehensibility, conceivableness.

compreensiva s. f. perception, understanding.

compreensível adj. m. + f. (pl. -**íveis**) comprehensible, intelligible, perceivable, understandable. ‖ **compreensivelmente** adv. comprehensibly, understandably, pellucidly.
fazer-se ~ to make o. s. understood. **tornar** ~ to clear, make plain. **um homem** ~ a man of understanding.

compreensivo adj. comprehensive, appreciative, wise, open-minded.
ele mostrou-se pouco ~ he showed but little understanding.

compressa s. f. compress, dressing, wet-dressing, bandage.

compressão s. f. (pl. -**ões**) 1. compression. 2. compressure, pressure. 3. constriction. 4. squeeze. 5. tension.

compressibilidade s. f. compressibility.

compressicaule adj. m. + f. (bot.) having a flat stem or stalk.

compressível adj. m. + f. (pl. -**íveis**) compressible.

compressivo adj. 1. compressive, tending to compress. 2. repressive.

compressor s. m. (all senses) compressor. ‖ adj. compressive.
~ **de ar** air compressor. ~ **de pistão** piston supercharger. **rolo** ~ roller, steam roller.

compressório adj. compressive.

compridez s. f. length.

comprido s. m. length. ‖ adj. 1. long, lengthy (plate Q). 2. elongated.
ao ~ longitudinally, lengthwise. **ele tem a língua muito -a** he is a gossipmonger.

comprimente adj. m. + f. compressive, compressing, repressing.

comprimento s. m. 1. length. 2. longitudinal dimension, extent. 3. distance. 4. size. ~ **de onda** (radio) wave-length.

comprimido s. m. tablet, pill. ‖ adj. compressed, tight, crowded.

comprimir v. 1. to compress, press together. 2. to reduce in size, squeeze down, condense. 3. to compact. 4. to repress, constrain, check. 5. ~-**se** to become reduced (in size), shrink.

comprimível adj. m. + f. (pl. -**íveis**) compressible.

comprobação s. f. (pl. -**ões**) proof, evidence, corroboration.

comprobante s. m. 1. confirmation. 2. receipt, voucher. 3. corroboration, substantiation. ‖ adj. m. + f. proving, confirming, corroborative.

comprobativo, comprobatório adj. corroborative, probative, evidential.

cópia -a voucher copy.

comprometedor adj. 1. compromising. 2. exposing.

comprometer v. 1. to compromise. 2. to promise, pledge. 3. to engage, bind. 4. to involve, implicate. 5. to endanger, jeopardize. 6. to expose, bring into question or doubt. 7. ~-**se:** a) to expose o. s. to doubt or suspicion. b) to bond o. s. (to do s. th.). c) to undertake s. th. d) to accept responsibility for.

as suas palavras comprometem-no his own words bind him. **ele comprometeu-se a** 1. he pledged himself to. 2. he gave himself away. **eles ~am a boa reputação da moça** they jeopardized the girl's good reputation.

comprometido adj. engaged, implicated, under obligation.

comprometimento s. m. compromising, exposure.

compromissário s. m. arbitrator. ‖ adj. obliged, bound by compromise.

compromissivo adj. compromissary, committable.

compromisso s. m. 1. compromise. 2. liability, obligation. 3. promise, pledge. 4. engagement. 5. settlement by arbitration, agreement. 6. debt, commitment. 7. appointment. 8. political covenant. 9. (jur.) entailed writ or deed.

assumir um ~ to undertake a responsibility. **chegar a um ~** to make a compromise. **eu honro meus ~s** I meet my engagements. **sem ~** without engagement. **tenho o ~ de não falar** my lips are sealed. **ter um ~** to have an obligation. **você tem um ~ a satisfazer** you have an engagement (liability) to meet.

compromissório adj. compromissary, compromissorial.

compromitente s. m. + f. 1. compromiser, one who compromises or subjects himself to the terms of an arbitral decision. 2. (jur.) party of a contract. ‖ adj. compromising, promising, compromissary.

comprovação s. f. (pl. -**ões**) 1. proof, evidence. 2. corroboration, substantiation. 3. confirmation. 4. verification. 5. adduction. 6. authentication. 7. receipt, voucher.

comprovador s. m. authenticator, verifier, corroborator. ‖ adj. confirming.

comprovante s. m. 1. receipt, voucher. 2. proof, evidence. ‖ adj. m. + f. confirming, proving, probative, corroborative.

comprovar v. 1. to prove, accumulate evidence. 2. to confirm. 3. to aver, justify, verify. 4. to corroborate.

~ com documentos to support by voucher. **ele é um malandro comprovado** he is an out and out rascal.

comprovativo adj. corroborative, confirmatory, conclusive.

comprovável adj. m. + f. (pl. -**áveis**) averrable.

compsotlipídeos s. m. pl. (ornith.) Compsothlypidae, the wood warbler family.

compulsação s. f. (pl. -**ões**) 1. examination (books, documents). 2. scrutiny, close inspection.

compulsador s. m. examiner, (jur.) compeller. ‖ adj. scrutinizing, examining.

compulsão s. f. (pl. -**ões**) 1. compulsion, constraint. 2. coercion, duress. 3. necessitation.

compulsar v. 1. to examine carefully (books, documents). 2. to scrutinize, scan. 3. to thumb, leaf through (the pages of a book). 4. to consult, study. 5. (obs.) to compel, oblige.

compulsivo adj. compulsive, compelling, coercive.

compulsória s. f. (jur.) mandate from a superior court or officer to an inferior instance.

compulsório adj. compulsive, compulsory, obligatory, forced. ‖ **compulsoriamente** adv. compulsively, compulsorily.

ajuste ~ compulsory settlement.

compunção s. f., **compungimento** m. 1. compunction, sense of guilt. 2. remorse, regret. 3. penitence. 4. contrition, repentance.

compungir v. 1. to move, touch. 2. to cause remorse, move to compunction. 3. to feel remorse, regret, repent.

compungitivo adj. compunctious, remorseful, contrite.

computação s. f. (pl. -**ões**) 1. computation. 2. calculation, reckoning. 3. representation.

computador s. m. computer, estimator, calculator.

computar v. 1. to compute. 2. to calculate, reckon. 3. to count, enumerate. 4. to estimate.

computável adj. m. + f. (pl. -**áveis**) computable, calculable, enumerative.

computista s. m. + f. 1. computist. 2. computor.

cômputo s. m. 1. computation. 2. calculation, reckoning. 3. estimate. 4. account. 5. appreciation.

comtiano s. m. (philos.) Comtist. ‖ adj. Comtian.

comtismo s. m. (philos.) Comtism, Positivism.

comtista s. m. + f. (philos.) Comtist, Positivist. ‖ adj. Comtian, Positivist(ic).

comua s. f. latrine, privy.

comum s. m. (pl. -**uns**) 1. the common people, commonality. 2. vulgarity, commonness. 3. the usual, the commonplace. ‖ adj. m. + f. 1. common. 2. usual, regular, unexceptional, normal. 3. habitual, customary. 4. vulgar, coarse, base. 5. trivial, commonplace. 6. simple. 7. cheap, mediocre. 8. widespread. 9. public, collective. ‖ **~ente** adv. commonly, usually, currently, vulgarly, familiarly, unexceptionally.

~ acordo joint consent. **~ a todos** common to all. **adágio ~** a common saying. **de ~ acordo** unanimously. **em ~** in common. **fora do ~** out of the common, uncommon, unfamiliar, exceptional. **preço ~** common rate. **o mínimo múltiplo ~** (math.) the least common multiple. **senso ~** common sense. **um aspecto muito ~** a very familiar sight. **viver em ~** to live in common.

comum-de-dois adj. (pl. **comuns-de-dois**), (gram.) having the same form for both genders.

comuna s. f. 1. commune. 2. community. 3. administrative district.

comunal s. m. + f. (pl. -**ais**) inhabitant of a commune. ‖ adj. communal. ‖ **~mente** adv. communally.

comuneiro s. m. inhabitant of a commune.

comungado adj. having received the Lord's Supper, communicant.

comungante s. m. + f. communicant. ‖ adj. communicant.

comungar v. 1. (rel.) to communicate, commune: a) administer the communion to. b) receive the Lord's Supper, partake of the Holy Communion. c) share in common, participate in. 2. to be a member of a parish, sect, faction or political group.

comungatório s. m. Communion altar, place where the Eucharist is administered. ‖ adj. communional, communionable.

comunhão s. f. 1. (rel.) Communion, Lord's Supper, Eucharist. 2. act of administering or receiving the Lord's Supper. 3. a sharing, participation. 4. fellowship. 5. community.
~ **de bens** community of goods. ~ **mútua** intercommunion.

comunial adj. m. + f. (pl. -ais) communional.

comunicabilidade s. f. communicability, communicativeness.

comunicação s. f. (pl. -ões) 1. communication. 2. message, information, correspondence. 3. transmission, conveyance. 4. connection, passage. 5. fellowship.
~ **de massa** mass communication. ~ **ferroviária** train service. **estou em** ~ **com** I am in communication with.

comunicado s. m. communication, communiqué, official report.

comunicador s. m. 1. communicant. 2. communicator. ‖ adj. communicating.

comunicante s. m. + f. communicant. ‖ adj. communicant, communicating.

comunicar v. 1. to communicate. 2. to impart, tell. 3. to notify, announce. 4. to report, write. 5. to correspond with. 6. to spread, diffuse. 7. to reveal. 8. to have dealings with. 9. to converse, speak with, keep company. 10. to participate, share in. 11. to connect, unite. 12. to transmit, convey.
~**-se mutuamente** to intercommunicate. **comunicamos a transferência por telegrama** we communicated the transfer by cable. **ele comunicou-se com a sua firma** he got in touch with his company. **ele comunicou-se com seu amigo** he contacted his friend.

comunicativo adj. 1. communicative. 2. approachable, sociable. 3. communicable. 4. expansive. ‖ -amente adv. communicatively.

comunicável adj. m. + f. (pl. -áveis) 1. communicable. 2. communicative, free-speaking. 3. expansive.

comunidade s. f. 1. community. 2. commonalty. 3. commonness, joint property. 4. society. 5. religious or civil association. 6. parish. 7. commune, township, district. 8. (sociol.) a close-knit social group, tribe.

comunismo s. m. communism, Bolshevism.

comunista s. m. + f. Communist, Bolshevik, Bolshevist. ‖ adj. communistic(al).

comunitário adj. (sociology) of, pertaining to or relative to a tribe or any other close-knit primitive group of people.

comutabilidade s. f. commutability.

comutação s. f. (pl. -ões) 1. commutation. 2. alteration, mutation. 3. substitution. 4. (electr.) reversal of the flow of current, change-over. 5. (jur.) attenuation of a penalty. 6. (gram.) metathesis.

comutador s. m. 1. one who commutates or attenuates. 2. (electr.): a) commutator. b) cutout. ‖ adj. commutative.

comutar v. 1. to commutate. 2. to commute. 3. to change, permute, exchange. 4. to substitute. 5. to attenuate.
a sentença de morte foi comutada para prisão perpétua the death sentence was commuted to penal servitude for life.

comutatividade s. f. (math.) commutativity.

comutativo adj. commutative. ‖ -amente adv. commutatively.

comutável adj. m. + f. (pl. -áveis) commutable.

conabi s. m. a medicinal plant of the family Euphorbiaceae (Phyllanthus conami)..

conação s. f. (pl. -ões), (psych.) conation.

conairu s. m. a freshwater fish (Pimelodela insignus).

conaráceas s. f. Connaraceae: a family of dicotyledonous plants.

conaráceo adj. (bot.) connaraceous.

conato adj. connate: 1. conascent (plate F 5). 2. innate, connatural.

conatural adj. m. + f. (pl. -ais) 1. congenital. 2. connatural, natural. 3. appropriate, proper.

conca s. f. 1. (anat.) concha of the ear. 2. quoit. 3. a small bowl or porringer.

concameração s. f. (pl. -ões), (archit.) concameration, vaulting.

concani, concanim (pl. -ins) s. m. + f. 1. native or inhabitant of Goa, Goanese. 2. the language spoken in Goa (India). ‖ adj. Goanese.

concassor s. m. (Braz.) a rustic coffee-processing machine.

concatenação s. f. (pl. -ões), **concatenamento** m. 1. concatenation, catenation. 2. connection, linking. 3. dependence.

concatenar v. 1. to concatenate, catenate. 2. to enchain, form a chain. 3. to link together, join. 4. to tie, bind. 5. to correlate, connect with.

concausa s. f. concause, joint cause, concomitant cause.

concausal adj. m. + f. (pl. -ais) concausal, concomitant.

concavar v. to render concave, hollow out.

concavidade s. f. 1. concaveness, concavity. 2. hollow, hollowness. 3. cavity. 4. (geol.) fold.

concavifoliado adj. (bot.) having concavous leaves.

côncavo s. m. concavity, concaveness. ‖ adj. 1. concavous. 2. hollow. 3. incavate.

côncavo-convexo adj. (pl. côncavo-convexos) concavo-convex.

conceber v. to conceive: 1. become pregnant, generate, procreate. 2. think out, ideate. 3. meditate, ponder. 4. understand. 5. picture, imagine. 6. frame. 7. perceive. 8. realize.
pode-se ~ **uma coisa destas!** can you think of such a thing! **um plano bem concebido** a well conceived plan.

concebimento s. m. 1. conceipt. 2. conception. 3. conceivability.

concebível adj. m. + f. (pl. -íveis) conceivable, cogitable, possible, imaginable.

concedente s. m. + f. concessor. ‖ adj. concessive.

conceder v. 1. to concede, grant. 2. to confer, impart. 3. to permit, allow, propitiate. 4. to yield, cede. 5. to agree with. 6. to award. 7. to assent, consent. 8. to dispense.
~ **a palavra a alguém** to allow a person to speak. ~ **facilidades** to grant facilities. ~ **uma patente** to file a patent. ~ **um desconto** to grant a discount. ~ **uma entrevista** to grant a person an interview. ~ **licença** to furlough. **ele concedeu em fazê-lo** he agreed to do it. **ele lhe concede um prazo para pagamento** he allows him time for payment. **seu pai lhe concede 200 libras por ano** his father allows him 200 pounds a year.

concedido adj. permitted, granted, conceded, admitted.

concedível adj. m. + f. (pl. -íveis) permissible, allowable, conferrable, grantable.

conceição (I) s. f. (pl. -ões), (rel.) the dogma of the Immaculate Conception.
Conceição Imaculada de Nossa Senhora (rel.) the Immaculate Conception of Our Lady.

conceição (II) s. f. (pl. -ões), an ancient Portuguese gold coin.

conceito s. m. 1. idea, thought. 2. notion, conception, concept, conceit. 3. immagination. 4. opinion. 5. reputation. 6. maxim. 7. fame, credit. 8. moral or meaning of a story. 9. project, intention.
explicar bem os seus ~s to explain clearly one's intentions. **formar um ~ de alguém** to form a definite opinion about s. o. **fazer mau ~ de uma pessoa** to think badly of a person. **gozar de bom ~** to enjoy a good reputation.
conceituado adj. esteemed, respected, worthy.
bem ~ well-thought-of, highly esteemed, reputable. **mal ~** ill-reputed.
conceituar v. 1. to form an opinion about, judge. 2. to rank, classify. 3. to appraise, evaluate. 4. to brand as, repute as. 5. to esteem, regard.
conceituoso adj. 1. witty, spirited. 2. ingenious, clever. 3. sententious.
concelebrar v. to concelebrate (a liturgic ceremony).
concelhio adj. (also **concelheiro**) municipal, public.
concelho s. m. 1. administrative subdivision of a district. 2. circumscription. 3. municipality, council.
concento s. m. 1. consonance, accordance, concent. 2. harmony.
concentração s. f. (pl. **-ões**) concentration: 1. act or result of concentrating. 2. convergence to one point. 3. increase of strength or density (of a solution).
concentrado s. m. 1. concentrate. 2. concentration. 3. essence. ‖ adj. 1. concentrated. 2. centralized. 3. limited. 4. tight, close. 5. intent, absorbed, deeply in thought. 6. hidden. 7. latent. 8. conglobate.
concentrador s. m. concentrator. ‖ adj. concentrative.
concentrar v. to concentrate: 1. centralize, unite in one central point. 2. increase the strength or density of. 3. consolidate, compact. 4. intensify. 5. condense, inspissate. 6. focus. 7. **~-se** to fix one's attention on, meditate deeply, ponder.
concentrativo adj. concentrative.
concentricidade s. f. concentricity.
concêntrico adj. (geom.) concentric(al).
concepção s. f. (pl. **-ões**) 1. conception, concept. 2. generation. 3. notion. 4. ideation. 5. conceiving, imagining. 6. faculty of perception. 7. comprehension.
conceptáculo s. m. 1. receptacle. 2. (bot.) conceptacle.
conceptibilidade s. f. conceivability.
conceptível adj. m. + f. (pl. **-íveis**) conceivable, comprehensible.
conceptivo adj. conceptive, conceptional.
conceptual adj. m. + f. (pl. **-ais**) conceptual.
conceptualismo s. m. (phil.) conceptualism.
conceptualista s. m. + f. (phil.) conceptualist. ‖ adj. conceptualistic.
concernência s. f. 1. relationship, relation, affinity. 2. concern, concernment.
concernente adj. m. + f. 1. relative to, with regard or respect to. 2. concerning, regarding. 3. pertinent. 4. apropos.
concernir v. 1. to concern. 2. to relate or belong to, regard. 3. to appertain, pertain, impart. 4. to interest. 5. to touch, respect. 6. to apply to.
concertado adj. 1. soft, mild. 2. serene, tranquil. 3. favourable. 4. affected. 5. perfect. 6. modest. 7. put in order. 8. prudent, reserved.
concertador s. m. conciliator, arbitrator, mediator. ‖ adj. conciliatory.
concertamento s. m. act or process of conciliating, arrangement.
concertante s. m. (mus.) concertante. ‖ adj. m. + f. 1. litigant. 2. fighting, struggling. 3. (mus.) concertante.
concertar v. 1. to put in order. 2. to adjust, regulate. 3. to arrange or dispose in the best possible manner. 4. to adorn, decorate. 5. to concert. 6. to harmonize, reconcile. 7. to compose. 8. to settle, agree. 9. to deliberate. 10. to assent to agreements, enter into combinations or adjustments. 11. **~-se:** a) to be reconciled with. b) to agree to.
~ um relógio to repair or regulate a watch.
concertina s. f. (mus.) concertina.
concertista s. m. + f. concertist, concert performer.
concerto (ê) s. m. 1. (mus.) concert, concerto, musical entertainment. 2. consonance, harmony. 3. disposition, order.
~ ao ar livre promenade concert. **de ~** in conformity, unanimously. **fazer alguma coisa de ~** to do s. th. by general consent.
concessão s. f. (pl. **-ões**) 1. act of conceding. 2. concession, grant, permission. 3. assent, compliance. 4. conferment, bestowal. 5. privilege, award. 6. cession. 7. compromise. 8. acquiescence.
não fazer -ões not to give in. **você recebeu a ~?** have you got the lease?
concessionário s. m. concessionaire, grantee, leaser of a concession. ‖ adj. concessionary.
concessível adj. m. + f. (pl. **-íveis**) concessible, grantable.
concessivo adj. concessive, concessional.
concessor s. m. concessor, grantor, licenser.
concessório adj. concessory, concessive, permissive.
concha s. f. 1. shell. 2. any object resembling a shell (plates C 9, T 4). 3. scale of a balance. 4. the concave part of the key of wind instruments. 5. the auricle of the ear. 6. ladle, soup ladle (plates C 20, M 1). 7. scoop (plate P 1).
~ de báscula (tech.) tipping hopper. **~ de berbigão** cockle-shell. **~ de marisco** clam-shell. **cal de ~** shell-lime. **sair da ~** (fam.) to gain courage.
conchada s. f. scoopful, ladleful.
conchado adj. shell-shaped.
conchar v. to adorn or face with shells.
concharia s. f. lots of shells, a heap of shells.
conchavado s. m. 1. participant in a collusion. 2. farm-hand, workman. 3. partner of an agreement. ‖ adj. collusive.
conchavar v. 1. to compound, combine. 2. to adjust. 3. to join, unite. 4. to contract (the services of). 5. **~-se** to plot, connive. 6. to enter the service of, hire o. s. out.
conchavo s. m. 1. plot, conspiracy. 2. collusion. 3. protection. 4. domestic service.
concheado adj. shell-shaped, shell-like.
conchear v. to adorn or face with shells.
conchegado adj. 1. near, close. 2. in contact with. 3. sheltered. 4. comfortable. 5. comforted, strengthened. 6. (Braz.) thickset, stocky.
conchegar v. 1. to bring nearer, approach. 2. to make comfortable. 3. to bring into contact. 4. **~-se:** a) to snuggle up, nestle. b) to join, put together. c) to make o. s. comfortable. d) to wrap o. s. up, take shelter. e) to adhere to.
conchegativo adj. comfortable, providing comfort and shelter.
conchego s. m. 1. comfort, ease. 2. coziness. 3. protection, assistance. 4. shelter. 5. protector, shelterer.
concheira s. f. (Braz., hist.) prehistoric shell mound.
conchelo s. m. (bot.) 1. hipwort. 2. navelwort.
conchífero adj. conchiferous, rich in shells.
concho (I) adj. 1. self-confident. 2. vain, conceited.
concho (II) s. m. (Port., prov.) a rustic pail or bucket.
conchóide s. f. (geom.) conchoid.
conchoso adj. shelly, full of shells.
conchudo adj. 1. shelly, rich in shells. 2. shell-shaped. 3. (pop.) self-confident. 4. (pop.) vain.
concidadão s. m. (pl. **concidadãos**) (f. **concidadã**) fellow citizen.

conciliábulo s. m. 1. (eccl.) conciliabulum. 2. reunion, assembly. 3. secret meeting. 4. conspiracy, collusion.

conciliação s. f. (pl. -ões) 1. conciliation. 2. reconciliation, appeasement. 3. settlement of a dispute, arrangement. 4. compromise. 5. adjustment, accommodation. 6. agreement.

conciliador s. m. conciliator, harmonizer, appeaser, reconciler. ‖ adj. conciliating, conciliative, friendly.

conciliante adj. m. + f. conciliative, appeasing.

conciliar (I) adj. m. + f. conciliar.

conciliar (II) v. 1. to conciliate, reconcile. 2. to harmonize, attemper. 3. to adjust, arrange. 4. to unite. 5. to appease. 6. to render accordant. 7. to attract, win over. 8. to placate. 9. to be in agreement with. 10. to accommodate. 11. to obtain, get, achieve.

~ **opiniões diferentes** to reconcile different opinions. **não consegui** ~ **o sono** I was not able to fall asleep. **temos de** ~ **os nossos interesses** we have to harmonize our interests.

conciliário adj. conciliar.

conciliativo adj. conciliative.

conciliatório adj. conciliatory, placatory, pacificatory, propiciatory.

conciliável adj. m. + f. (pl. -áveis) concillable, compatible, appeasable, adjustable, propitiable.

concílio s. m. 1. (eccl.) council. 2. assembly of ecclesiastics. 3. reunion of an administrative body. 4. ~s pl. resolution(s), deliberation(s).

concional adj. m. + f. (pl. -ais) concional, concionary.

concionar v. 1. to speak in public, concionate. 2. to preach.

concionário adj. concionary, concional.

concisão s. f. (pl. -ões) 1. briefness, brevity. 2. conciseness. 3. curtness, terseness. 4. laconism. 5. precision, exactness. 6. concinnity (of style).

conciso adj. 1. concise, told in a few words. 2. terse, curt, short, brief. 3. laconic(al). 4. precise, exact. 5. sententious. 6. concinnate. ‖ -amente adv. concisely.

estilo ~ close style.

concitação s. f. (pl. -ões) concitation, agitation, instigation, incitement, trouble.

concitador s. m. instigator, inciter. ‖ adj. exciting, inciting.

concitar v. 1. to stir up, incite, rouse. 2. to instigate, provoke. 3. to touch, move. 4. to preach.

concitativo adj. concitative, exciting, inciting, rousing.

conclamação s. f. (pl. -ões) conclamation.

conclamar v. 1. to shout, yell. 2. clamour, roar. 3. to cry out simultaneously with others, scream. 4. to vociferate. 5. to acclaim, elect (by acclamation).

conclave s. m. conclave: 1. (eccl.) reunion, assembly. 2. private or secret meeting.

conclavista s. m. + f. conclavist: 1. (eccl.) a cardinal in conclave. 2. participant in a secret or private meeting.

concludente adj. m. + f. 1. concluding, conclusive. 2. cogent. 3. convincing, demonstrative. 4. finishing. 5. decisive.

concluído adj. concluded, finished, done, complete.

concluidor s. m. concluder, finisher, closer. ‖ adj. finishing, concluding, terminative.

concluimento s. m. conclusion, termination.

concluinte s. m. + f. student who is about to complete the prescribed course, pre-graduate student. ‖ adj. (obs.) concluding, conclusive, finishing.

concluir v. 1. to conclude, bring to an end, finish. 2. to end, terminate. 3. to decide, resolve, determine. 4. to complete, achieve. 5. to imply, infer.

6. to reason, elicit. 7. to apply the finishing touches to (treaty, contract). 8. to be conclusive. 9. to perfect. 10. to settle. 11. to argue.

concluindo, o orador disse... concluding, the speaker said... ~ **um acordo** to come to an agreement. ~ **um negócio** to strike a bargain. ~ **um trabalho** to finish a work. **conclui-se que...** it follows that... **pelo que dizem, concluímos ser a verdade** judging from what they say, we believe it is true.

conclusão s. f. (pl. -ões) conclusion: 1. close, closing. 2. termination, end. 3. illation, inference. 4. consequence, upshot. 5. decision, determination. 6. thesis. 7. deduction. 8. corollary. 9. implication. 10. completion. 11. finish. 12. (jur.) verdict or final judgement on legal proceedings.

chegar à ~ **(duma tarefa)** to come to the end (of a task). **chego à** ~ **de que...** I come to the conclusion that... **ele chegou a uma** ~ **errada** he arrived at a wrong conclusion, got the wrong sow by the ears. **em** ~, **a verdade é esta** in conclusion, this is the truth. **tirar uma** ~ to deduce an inference, draw a conclusion. **vir à** ~ to come to the conclusion.

conclusionista s. m. + f. university graduate who defends a thesis.

conclusivo adj. 1. conclusive. 2. illative. 3. final, definitive. 4. decisive. ‖ -amente adv. conclusively.

concluso adj. concluded (legal proceedings).

concocção s. f. (med.) concoction: preliminary digestion of food in the stomach.

concoctivo adj. (med.) concoctive.

concoidal adj. m. + f. (pl. -ais) conchoidal.

concóide s. f. (geom.) conchoid. ‖ adj. m. + f. conchoidal.

concologia s. f. (zool.) conchology.

concomitância s. f. 1. concomitance, concomitancy. 2. concurrence. 3. concomitant thing or fact. 4. accompaniment.

concomitante adj. m. + f. 1. concomitant. 2. coincident, concurrent. 3. collateral. 4. accessory. ‖ ~mente adv. concomitantly.

concomitar v. to concomitate, accompany.

concordado adj. concordal, concordant.

concordância s. f. 1. concordance. 2. agreement, conformity. 3. consonance, congruity. 4. (gram.) concord. 5. harmony, harmoniousness. 6. reconciliation. 7. coincidence. 8. (geol.) parallel stratification of deposits. 9. (mus.) accord. 10. correspondence, rapport. 11. sympathy. 12. adhesion. 13. abidance.

concordante adj. m. + f. 1. concordant. 2. agreeing, conformable. 3. correspondent. 4. concurrent, coincident. 5. (mus.) harmonious. 6. sympathetic.

concordar v. 1. to concord. 2. to agree, assent. 3. to reconcile, acquiesce. 4. to correspond, concur. 5. to harmonize. 6. to be in accordance with. 7. to coincide. 8. to accord. 9. to settle, arrange. 10. to adhere to. 11. to sympathize. 12. to accept. 13. to comply (with). 14. (gram.) to be in grammatical concord.

~ **com** to sympathize with, say yes to, sustain the same opinion. ~ **com as condições** to yield to conditions. ~ **com as palavras de alguém** to agree with a person's words. **concordo com a sua opinião** I give in to your opinion. **concordo com você** I agree with you, I concur with you. **ela sempre concorda com ele** she always chimes in with him. **ele concordou com meus desejos** he was compliant with my wishes. **eles** ~**am muito bem** they got along very well. **eles** ~**am unanimemente** they agreed with one accord. **não posso** ~ **consigo nisto** I can't go to that length with you. **nisto concordo com você** there I join with you. **você concorda comigo?** do you agree with me?, (coll.)

do you go with me? **você concorda com isso?** do you agree to that?

concordata s. f. 1. (eccl.) concordat. 2. agreement, covenant, contract. 3. (com.) forced agreement.

concordatário s. m. (com.) businessman who has entered into a composition with his creditors. ‖ adj. concordatory.

concordável adj. m. + f. (pl. **-áveis**) reconcilable, concordable.

concorde adj. m. + f. concordant, of the same opinion, pursuant, conformable, unisonous.

concórdia s. f. 1. concordance. 2. harmony, harmoniousness. 3. peace. 4. agreement. 5. concord. 6. union, unity. 7. oneness. 8. atonement.

concorrência s. f. 1. concourse, flocking together. 2. affluence. 3. competition, emulation. 4. competitiveness. 5. rivalry. 6. crowd, throng. 7. (jur.) legal claim.

~ **desleal** unfair competition. ~ **pública** submission. **fora de** ~ unmarketable.

concorrente s. m. + f. 1. competitor. 2. contestant, rival. 3. (sports) entrant. 4. adversary. ‖ adj. 1. competitive, concurrent. 2. ~**s** pl. (geom.) intersecting.

~ **desleal** unfair competitor, dumper.

concorrer v. 1. to compete with. 2. to rival, contest. 3. to concur, act jointly, cooperate. 4. to contribute. 5. to meet, come together.

~**am à vaga** they applied for the vacancy. ~ **para** to try for. **não** ~**am para o êxito** they had no share in the success.

concorrido adj. crowded, numerous (in the sense of attendance).

concreção s. f. (pl. **-ões**) 1. concretion, solidification of concreted matter. 2. accretion. 3. (geol.) concretions, sinter. 4. calcification.

concrecionado adj. concretionary.

concrecionar v. to concrete, solidify, harden.

concrescência s. f. concrescence, adhesion.

concrescibilidade s. f. quality of being concrescible.

concrescível adj. m. + f. (pl. **-íveis**) concrescible, concretionary.

concretar v. to fill moulds with concrete.

concretismo s. m. (paint., lit.) concretism.

concretista s. m. + f. (paint., lit.) concretist: adept of concretism. ‖ adj. m. + f. concretist.

concretização s. f. (pl. **-ões**) substantiation, realization, concretion.

concretizar v. to render concrete, substantiate, materialize.

concreto s. m. 1. concretion. 2. concreteness. 3. (phil.) the concrete, positive fact. (archit.) concrete (plate A 7). ‖ adj. 1. concrete. 2. positive, factual. 3. real, material. ‖ **-amente** adv. concretely.

~ **armado** (constr.) steel concrete, reinforced concrete, iron concrete. **chegar a resultados** ~**s na discussão** to touch ground in the discussion. **o que há de** ~ **a respeito?** what is concrete about that?

concriação s. f. (pl. **-ões**) 1. concreation: creation of two things at the same time. 2. collaboration.

concriar v. to concreate, create together.

concubina s. f. concubine, mistress.

concubinagem s. f. concubinage.

concubinário s. m. concubinary. ‖ adj. concubinary.

concubinar-se v. to co-habit.

concubinato s. m. concubinage.

concúbito s. m. concubitus, coitus, copulation.

conculcado adj. downtrodden.

conculcador s. m. oppressor, vilifier.

conculcar v. 1. to conculcate, trample down. 2. to oppress. 3. to slight, vilify.

concunhada s. f. wife of the husband's brother.

concunhado s. m. husband of the wife's sister. ‖ adj. of or concerning this relationship.

concupiscência s. f. 1. concupiscence. 2. lust, lustfulness. 3. appetence. 4. cupidity.

concupiscente adj. m. + f. 1. concupiscent. 2. lustful.

concupiscível adj. m. + f. (pl. **-íveis**) concupiscible.

concurso s. m. 1. concurrence. 2. affluence, confluence. 3. concourse. 4. contest, contestation. 5. competition, rivalry. 6. throng, crowd. 7. cooperation. 8. resort. 9. examination, test.

abrir um ~ to set a competition, open a competition. ~ **de prêmios** prize competition. **ele tomou parte num** ~ he entered a competition. **por** ~ by competition.

concussão s. f. (pl. **-ões**) 1. concussion. 2. violent shock, impact. 3. peculation, public graft.

concussionário s. m. grafter, peculator. ‖ adj. concussional, concussive, peculating.

concutir v. to shake, tremble, concuss.

condado s. m. 1. dignity or authority of a count. 2. earldom. 3. county, shire.

condal adj. m. + f. (pl. **-ais**) of or belonging to a count.

condão s. m. (pl. **-ões**) 1. special virtue, magic power. 2. privilege, prerogative. 3. talent, mental power, ability.

vara de ~ the magic wand.

conde s. m. 1. (hist.) military commander of a district. 2. count, earl. 3. knave at cards.

condecoração s. f. (pl. **-ões**) 1. act of decorating. 2. decoration, badge of honour. 3. citation.

condecorado s. m. decorated man. ‖ adj. decorated.

condecorar v. 1. to decorate. 2. to adorn, embellish. 3. to distinguish, honour. 4. to award a decoration to.

ele foi condecorado com uma medalha he was distinguished with a medal.

condenação s. f. (pl. **-ões**) 1. act of condemning. 2. condemnation. 3. conviction. 4. censure, disapprobation. 5. penalty, fine. 6. doom. 7. judgement. ~ **a degredo** deportation. ~ **à morte** capital sentence. ~ **eterna** perdition.

condenado s. m. 1. convict. 2. felon, criminal, culprit. 3. (pop.) malefactor, wicked fellow. ‖ adj. condemned, damned, reprobate, fated, doomed.

~ **à morte** under sentence of death.

condenador s. m. condemner, reprover. ‖ adj. condemning, condemnatory, reproving, reproachful.

condenar v. 1. to condemn. 2. to sentence, pronounce judgement. 3. to declare guilty. 4. to censure, reprobate. 5. to disapprove. 6. to denounce. 7. to doom. 8. ~**-se** to denounce o. s., plead guilty.

~ **a atitude de alguém** to reprove a person's attitude. **estar condenado** to stand condemned. **é uma doutrina condenada** it is a rejected doctrine. **suas próprias palavras o condenam** his own words condemn him.

condenatório adj. condemnatory, damnatory, convictional, blameful.

condenável adj. m. + f. (pl. **-áveis**) condemnable, damnable, reproachful.

condensabilidade s. f. condensability, condensibility.

condensação s. f. (pl. **-ões**) 1. condensation. 2. compression. 3. digest.

condensador s. m. condenser, capacitor, condensator. ‖ adj. condensing.

condensante adj. m. + f. condensing.

condensar v. 1. to condense, condensate. 2. to compress, compact. 3. to concentrate. 4. to abridge, abbreviate. 5. to epitomize.

condensativo adj. condensative.

condensável adj. m. + f. (pl. **-áveis**) condensable, condensible.

condescendência s. f. 1. condescendence, condescension. 2. tolerance, compliance. 3. acquiescence. 4. patronage. 5. concession. 6. conformity. 7. accommodation.

condescendente adj. m. + f. condescending, compliant, acquiescent, willing. ‖ ~mente adv. condescendingly, willingly, patronizingly.

ela é ~ conosco she stoops to us.

condescender v. 1. to condescend, deign. 2. to stoop to. 3. to comply (with), acquiesce. 4. to yield, submit.

condessa (ê) (I) s. f. countess.

condessa (ê) (II) s. f. a small delicately shaped basket with cover.

condessar v. to guard, keep, retain.

condestável s. m. (pl. -áveis) (hist.) 1. supreme commander of the army. 2. high judicial officer, Lord High Constable.

condição s. f. (pl. -ões) 1. condition. 2. circumstance, state, situation. 3. quality, nature. 4. character. 5. social position, rank. 6. clause, stipulation, proviso. 7. high social standing, distinction. 8. plight, predicament. 9. size, form. 10. postulate. 11. -ões pl. terms.

~ de mulher womanhood. ~ social social standing, walk. ~ prévia prerequisite. -ões de fornecimento delivery terms. -ões de serviço working conditions. -ões iguais para todos fair field and no favour. a máquina não está em -ões the machine is out of conditions. diante das -ões atuais under present circumstances. ele o estipulou como ~ he made it a condition. em -ões fáceis on easy terms. em boa ~ in good fettle, in good fig. em boas -ões físicas in good form. estamos em -ões de fornecer os livros we are in position to supply the books. nestas -ões under these circumstances. pessoa de ~ a person of rank. pessoas de humildes -ões plain people. sob a ~ de... with the proviso that, on condition that...

condicente adj. m. + f. suitable, fit, agreeable.

condicionado adj. subject, conditioned.

condicionador s. m. conditioner. ‖ adj. that conditions (a person or thing).

condicional s. m. (pl. -ais) 1. conditional. 2. conditionality. 3. (gram.) the conditional mood, conditional word or clause. ‖ adj. m. + f. 1. conditional, depending upon. 2. (psych.) conditioned. ‖ ~mente adv. conditionally.

condicionalidade s. f. conditionality.

condicionamento s. m. conditioning.

condicionante s. f. restriction, imposition. ‖ adj. m. + f. imposing, depending on a condition.

condicionar v. 1. to subject to a condition, stipulate. 2. to condition. 3. to put in proper condition. 4. to render conditional. 5. to regulate.

condignidade s. f. 1. condignity. 2. worthiness, merit. 3. suitableness. 4. agreeableness.

condigno adj. 1. condign. 2. proportional to worth or merit. 3. suitable, agreeable.

condiliano adj. (anat.) condylar.

côndilo s. m. (anat.) condyle.

condilóide adj. m. + f. (anat.) condyloid.

condilomar s. m. (anat., med.) condyloma.

condimentação s. f. (pl. -ões) seasoning (of food).

condimentado adj. spicy.

condimentar v. 1. to season (food), spice. 2. to flavour. 3. to relish, zest. 4. to farce.

um prato bem condimentado a well seasoned dish.

condimentício adj. condimental.

condimento s. m. 1. seasoning, condiment. 2. dung, manure. 3. spice. 4. flavouring. 5. relish, zest.

condimentoso adj. condimental, condimentary.

condir v. 1. to season. 2. to condite. 3. (pharm.) to prepare remedies, make up a prescription.

condiscípulo s. m. condisciple, fellow student, classmate.

condizente adj. m. + f. 1. suitable, agreeable. 2. worthy. 3. proper, adequate. 4. harmonious.

condizer v. 1. to suit, fit well. 2. to agree, match. 3. to be in the right proportion to. 4. to correspond to 5. to be harmonious. 6. to answer.

condoer v. 1. to arouse pity in. 2. to move to compassion. 3. ~-se to be sorry for, sympathize with, condole.

condoído adj. pitiful, commiserative.

condoimento s. m. compassion. pity, commiseration.

condolência s. f. 1. condolence, condolement. 2. sympathetic sorrow, pity, compassion. 3. sympathy.

condolente adj. m. + f. condolent, condolatory, condoling.

condomínio s. m. joint ownership, joint-tenancy, condominium.

condômino s. m. joint owner.

condor s. m. (ornith.) condor.

condoreirismo s. m. (Braz.) high-flown literary style.

condoreiro adj. (Braz.) exalted, high-flown (said of a school of Brazilian writers).

condralgia s. f. (pathol.) chondralgia: a pain in a cartilage.

condrina s. f. (biochem.) chondrin.

condroblasto s. m. (med.) chondroblast, a cell of cartilaginous tissue.

condróide adj. m. + f. (med.) chondroid.

condroma s. m. (med.) chondroma.

condrictes s. m. (pl. (ichth.) Chondrichthyes: a class of cartilaginous fishes (sharks).

condrósteos s. m. pl. (ichth.) Chondrostei: an order of Teleostomi (sturgeons, paddlefishes).

condrotomia s. f. (med., surg.) chondrotomy.

condução s. f. (pl. -ões) 1. act or result of conducting. 2. conduction. 3. conveyance, transport. 4. driving. 5. (pop.) vehicle, carriage.

há falta de ~ there is a shortage of public vehicles. não há ~ para lá there is no conveyance to that place.

conducente adj. m. + f. conducive, conducible, leading.

conduplicação s. f. (pl. -ões) 1. doubling, duplication. 2. (bot.) conduplication.

conduplicado adj. (bot.) complicate, conduplicate.

condurango s. m. a medicinal plant of the family Asclepiadaceae (Marsdenia cundurango).

conduru s. m. (bot.) a jacaranda.

conduru-de-sangue s m. (pl. condurus-de-sangue), (bot.) satiné.

conduta s. f. 1. conduct. 2. behaviour, deportment. 3. levy. 4. conveying of people, conveyance. 5. morals, manners. 6. proceeding, procedure. 7. way, course. 8. demeanour. 9. management.

contra as regras da boa ~ against etiquette. boa ~ propriety of conduct. mudar de ~ to change the line of conduct.

codutância s. f. (electr.) conductance.

condutar v. (pop.) 1. to eat bread (together with some other food). 2. to save, economize.

condutibilidade s. f. (phys.) conductibility, conductivity.

~ de calor (phys.) heat conductance.

condutível adj. m. + f. (pl. -íveis) conductible.

condutividade s. f. conduction, conductance.

condutivo adj. conductive, conducent.

conduto s. m. 1. duct. 2. pipe, tube, conduit. 3. (anat.) channel. 4. (pop.) anything eaten with bread

~ **auditivo** (anat.) auditory canal, auditory meatus (plate C 17).
condutor s. m. 1. conductor: a) leader, guide. b) (phys.) body capable of transmitting electricity, heat, etc. c) conduit. d) gutter, leader. e) fare collector in a tramway or omnibus. 2. (electr.) wire. 3. driver. ‖ adj. conductive, conducting, leading, guiding.
~ **de água** conduit, race, channel. ~ **de carro** waggoner. ~ **de gado** drover. ~ **de pára-raios** lightning-conductor. ~ **sem corrente** (electr.) dead wire. ~ **sob tensão** (electr.) live wire. **eles colocaram um** ~ they fitted a circuit.
condutora s. f. conductress.
conduzir v. 1. to conduct: a) lead, guide. b) direct, usher. c) transmit. d) manage. e) (mus.) direct. 2. convey, carry, transport. 3. to drive. 4. to accompany. 5. to lead to. 6. to tend to (as a result). 7. to bring about, effect. 8. ~-**se** to behave, conduct o. s.
~ **a espada** to wield the sword. ~ **ao altar** to lead to the altar. ~ **perante o juiz** to carry before the magistrate. ~-**se mal** to misconduct. ~ **uma pessoa pela mão** to lead a person by the hand. **a porta conduz à cozinha** the door gives entrance to the kitchen. **ele não se conduziu como devia** he did not conduct himself as he should.
cone s. m. (geom.) cone.
conectivo adj. = **conetivo.**
conector s. m. connector.
cônega s. f. (rel.) canoness.
cônego s. m. (rel.) canon of a chapter, capitular, prebendary.
conetivo, conectivo s. m. 1. (bot.) connective. 2. (gram.) a connective word or clause. 3. (anat.) connective tissue. ‖ adj. connective, conjunctive, connectional, connectible.
conexão s. f. (pl. -**ões**) 1. connection. 2. link. 3. junction. 3. relation, relationship. 5. union. 6. (mech.) sleeve, socket. 7. dependence. 8. analogy. 9. coherence. 10. continuity. 11. liaison. 12. (tech.) coupling.
~ **em estrela** (electr.) star connection. ~ **em triângulo** (electr.) delta connection.
conexidade s. f. 1. connexity. 2. connection. 3. connectivity.
conexivo adj. connective, conjunctive.
conexo adj. 1. connected. 2. linked, joined. 3. dependent. 4. coherent, logical.
conezia s. f. 1. canonry, canonship. 2. (fig.) sinecure.
confabulação s. f. (pl.-**ões**) confabulation.
confabular v. to confabulate, chat, converse, talk familiarly to.
confecção s. f. (pl. -**ões**) 1. making, confection. 2. finish, finishing, conclusion. 3. ready-made articles.
confeccionador s. m. 1. manufacturer of ready-made articles. 2. producer, maker. ‖ adj. confectionary.
confeccionar v. 1. to make, prepare. 2. to fabricate, manufacture. 3. to confection. 4. to finish. 5. to compose. 6. to execute, realize. 7. to organize.
confederação s. f. 1. (pl. -**ões**) confederation, confederacy. 2. league, alliance.
confederado s. m. 1. confederate, ally. 2. leaguer. ‖ adj. associate, confederate, federative, united, allied.
confederar v. 1. to confederate, federate. 2. to unite, league. 3. to ally. 4. to associate. 5. ~-**se** to enter into a league.
confederativo adj. confederative.
confeição s. f. (pl. -**ões**) confection, composition, manufacture.

confeiçoar v. 1. to put up a prescription. 2. to confection. 3. to prepare or make sweetmeats, cookies, cakes.
confeitada s. f. (Port., prov.) Easter cake (given as a present).
confeitadeira s. f. = **confeiteira.**
confeitado adj. candied.
confeitar v. 1. to confect, confection. 2. to cover with sugar, candy. 3. to preserve. 4. to dissimulate, disguise.
confeitaria s. f. candy shop, confectionary, sweetshop.
confeiteira s. f. 1. a confectioner's wife. 2. a woman who makes and/or sells sweetmeats. 3. plate for sweetmeats.
confeiteiro s. m. confectioner.
confeito s. m. sweetmeat, comfit, cake, sweet, candy, confection.
conferência s. f. 1. conference. 2. parley, palaver. 3. council, convention. 4. consultation. 5. lecture, address. 6. speech, talk. 7. interview.
fazer uma ~ to read a paper.
conferenciador s. m. public speaker, lecturer.
conferencial adj. m. + f. (pl. -**ais**) conferential.
conferenciar v. 1. to confer, hold a conference. 2. to interview. 3. to talk, parley. 4. to consult. 5. to discuss.
conferencista s. m. + f. public speaker, lecturer.
conferente s. m. + f. 1. lecturer. 2. conferee. 3. proof-reader. 4. checking clerk. ‖ adj. conferential.
conferir v. 1. to confer. 2. to compare, confront. 3. to check, control. 4. to verify. 5. to give, bestow, grant. 6. to award. 7. to speak, talk, lecture. 8. to discuss business dealings. 9. to accord, allow. 10. to accredit. 11. to be in conformity with, agree. 12 to collate.
~ **amplos poderes** to confer full powers. ~ **um direito** to confer a right. **foi-lhe conferido o poder** power was delegated to him.
confertifloro adj. (bot.) with conferted flowers.
confessado s. m. confessionaire, confessant, confessionalist, confessionist. ‖ adj. confessed, declared, avowed.
confessar v. 1. to confess. 2. to declare, assert openly. 3. to reveal, disclose. 4. to acknowledge, admit, avow. 5. (also ~-**se**) to tell one's sins to a priest (to obtain absolution). 6. to hear confessions (priest). 7. to recognize one's faults. 2. to squeal, come across.
~ **tudo** to confess all, (sl.) come clean. **confesso que fiquei muito surpreso** I must admit that I was very much surprised. **ele confessou tudo** he made a clean breast of it. **ele se confessou o causador do erro** he avowed himself the perpetrator of the blunder. **ele teve de confessá-lo** he had to admit it. **ele vai** ~-**se** he goes to confession.
confessional adj. m. + f. (pl. -**ais**) confessional, denominational: of, pertaining to or of the nature of a confession.
confessionário s. m. (eccl.) 1. confessional, place where a priest sits to hear confessions. 2. penitential tribunal.
confesso s. m. 1. lay brother. 2. confessant, confessionalist. ‖ adj. confessed, confessional.
confesso (ê) s. m. 1. confession. 2. (ant.) any kind of confession.
confessor s. m. confessor: 1. a priest who hears confessions. 2. one who professes Christianity. 3. martyr.
confessório adj. confessionary.
confete s. m. 1. confetti. 2. (pop.) praise, compliments.

confiado adj. 1. confident. 2. familiar. 3. cocksure. 4. fiducial. 5. (pop.) impertinent. ‖ **-amente** adv. 1. confidentially, undoubtingly. 2. fiducially.
ele é muito ~ he is rather bold.
confiança s. f. 1. confidence. 2. trust, 3. assurance, assuredness. 4. reliance, reliability, affiance. 5. hope, hopefulness. 6. familiarity. 7. courage. 8. boldness. 9. dependability. 10. impertinence. 11. friendship, intimacy.
~ **em si mesmo** self-reliance, self-assurance. ~ **excessiva** overconfidence, overcredulity. **abuso de** ~ breach of trust. **cargo de** ~ position of trust. **com** ~ trustingly. **de** ~ confidential, fiduciary, trustable, reliable, **de pouca** ~ unsure, doubtful, unreliable. **de toda** ~ as good as gold. **ele é digno de** ~ he is to be depended upon, he can be relied on. **ele tem muita** ~ **em seu amigo** he swears by his friend. **em** ~ in trust, trustfully. **faltou-lhe** ~ **em si mesmo** he lacked confidence. **indigno de** ~ untrustworthy. **não tenho nenhuma** ~ **nele** I do not trust him round the corner. **não se pode ter** ~ **nele** there is no trust to be placed in him, there is no reckoning on him. **o homem é de** ~? is the man safe? **temos** ~ **em Deus** our trust is in God. **ter** ~ **em** to place reliance on. **você deve ter** ~ **nele** you must trust yourself to him.
confiante adj. m. + f. 1. confident. 2. sure, assured. 3. trustful, undoubting. 4. secure. ‖ ~**mente** adv. confidently, assuredly, reliably, hopefully.
~ **em si mesmo** self-reliant. ~ **em sua força** confident of his own strength. **ele procedeu** ~**mente** he advanced with confidence.
confiar v. 1. to confide, trust. 2. to believe in. 3. to hope. 4. to rely on, count with. 5. to communicate, transmit. 6. to entrust, deliver upon trust. 7. to accredit. 8. to disembosom, impart (secret to).
~ **à guarda de** to deposit with, put in the charge of. ~ **alguma coisa a alguém** to trust s. o. with s. th. ~ **demais em** to overtrust. ~ **no conselho de um amigo** to lean on a friend's advice. ~ **uma coisa a alguém** to entrust a thing to a person. **confio em** I put faith in. **confio em você** I put great trust in you. **confio inteiramente nele** I quite depend on him. **confio-lhe o rapaz** I place the boy with you. **confio nas suas palavras** I give credit to his report. **confio nele** I trust him. **ele me confiou sua filha** he gave his daughter into my charge. **não se pode** ~**-lhe uma soma tão grande** he cannot be trusted with so large a sum. **pode** ~ **nele** you may confide in him. **você pode** ~ **no que ele diz** you may rely upon his words.
confidência s. f. 1. confidence. 2. confidentiality, confidentialness. 3. trust. 4. confidential communication, secret. 5. whisper. 6. intimacy.
confidencial adj. m. + f. (pl. **-ais**) confidential, classified, private. ‖ ~**mente** adv. confidentially, privately.
caráter ~ privateness. **ela falou** ~**mente comigo** she made confidences to me about, she spoke under the rose. **estritamente** ~ in strict confidence. **informação** ~ inside information.
confidenciar v. to entrust a secret, disclose, reveal (secrets).
confidencioso adj. confidential.
confidente s. m. + f. confidant, confidante, trusted friend, inside man. ‖ adj. confident, trustworthy.
fazer alguém seu ~ to admit s. o. into one's confidence.
configuração s. f. (pl. **-ões**) 1. configuration, conformation. 2. form, shape, aspect. 3. figure, figuration. 4. face. 5. constitution. 6. (psych.) physiognomy.

configurar v. 1. to configure. 2. to shape according to a model. 3. to figure, form. 4. to hew out.
configurativo adj. configurative.
confim s. m. 1. confine. 2. limit, abutment. 3. barrier. 4. **-ins** pl. boundaries, frontier. 5. extremity. 6. ambit. ‖ adj. m. + f. bordering, limiting. **nos -ins do mundo** at the farthest corner of the world.
confinante adj. m. + f. bordering upon, neighbouring, limitary.
confinar v. 1. to circumscribe. 2. to demarcate. 3. to limit. 4. to have a common border. 5. to confine, constrain, restrict. 6. to neighbour. 7. to bound, border.
confinidade s. f. 1. confinement. 2. confinity. 3. contiguity.
confioso adj. full of self-confidence.
confirmação s. f. (pl. **-ões**) 1. (eccl.) Confirmation. 2. confirmation, affirmation. 3. ratification, homologation. 4. sanction. 5. acknowledgement. 6. corroboration.
confirmador s. m. confirmer. ‖ adj. confirming, corroborant.
confirmado s. m. confirmee. ‖ adj. confirmed.
confirmante adj. m. + f. confirming, ratifying.
confirmar v. 1. to confirm, affirm. 2. to approve, sustain. 3. to validate, corroborate. 4. to homologate. 5. to sanction. 6. (eccl.) to administer the rite of Confirmation to. 7. to support, fortify. 8. to hold good or true. 9. ~**-se** to receive Confirmation.
a exceção confirma a regra the exception confirms the rule. **a sentença foi confirmada** the verdict was sanctioned. **as notícias** ~**am-se** the news proved to be true.
confirmativo adj. confirmative, corroborative, ratifying.
confirmatório adj. confirmatory, affirmative, corroboratory.
confiscação s. f. (pl. **-ões**) 1. confiscation. 2. sequestration. 3. requisition. 4. seizure.
confiscado adj. confiscate.
confiscador s. m. confiscator. ‖ adj. confiscatory.
confiscar v. 1. to confiscate. 2. to sequestrate. 3. to requisition. 4. to seize, embargo.
confiscável adj. m. + f. (pl. **-áveis**) confiscable, forfeitable.
confisco s. m. confiscation, forfeiture, requisition.
confissão s. f. (pl. **-ões**) confession: 1. (rel.) act of confessing before a priest. 2. (rel.) the prayer said before confession. 3. admission. 4. acknowledgement. 5. declaration. 6. profession.
ir à ~ (rel.) to go to confession. **ouvir a** ~ (rel.) to hear a confession.
confitente s. m. + f. confessor, confessant. ‖ adj. confessing.
conflagração s. f. (pl. **-ões**) 1. fire, combustion. 2. conflagration.
~ **mundial** world war.
conflagrar v. t. conflagrate.
conflitante adj. m. + f. conflicting.
conflitar v. to conflict.
conflito s. m. conflict: 1. heated discussion. 2. discord, disagreement. 3. encounter, skirmish. 4. war, battle.
ele entrou em ~ **com** he came into conflict with.
confluência s. f. 1. confluence: a) meeting, junction. b) place of junction of two or more rivers. 2. (med.) skin eruption.
confluente s. m. confluent, tributary, confluent stream. ‖ adj. m. + f. confluent.
confluir v. 1. to flow together. 2. to flow into one another. 3. to join, meet.
confocal adj. m. + f. (math.) confocal.

conformação s. f. (pl. -ões) 1. configuration, conformation. 2. frame, shape. 3. constitution. 4. resignation.
~ **anormal** abnormal conformation. ~ **defeituosa** malformation.
conformado adj. resigned, patient.
conformador s. m. conformator. || adj. conformating.
conformar v. 1. to form, shape. 2. to adapt, suit, accommodate. 3. to configurate. 4. to reconcile. 5. to tolerate. 6. to make similar. 7. to conform. 8. to agree with. 9. ~-se: a) to adjust o. s. to. b) to resign, submit o. s. c) to stand pat. d) to comply with. ~-se com a sua sorte to resign o. s. to one's fate, (dial.) to dree one's weird; (pop.) to take one's medicine. ~-se com os tempos to yield to the times. **ele tem de se** ~ **com os fatos** he must face the facts. **ele se conformará com a perda** he will get over the loss.
conformativo adj. conformative.
conforme adj. m. + f. 1. conform, conformable. 2. accordant, accordable. 3. correspondent, corresponding. 4. congruous. 5. pursuant. 6. resigned, uncomplaining, patient. 7. harmonious. 8. identical. || **conforme,** ~**mente** adv. conformably, accordingly, agreeably, correspondingly. || conj. as, according to, how, as per.
conforme! it depends! ~ **a natureza** true to nature. ~ **fatura anexa** as per enclosed invoice. ~ **pedido** as requested. **Deus dá o frio** ~ **o cobertor** Our Lord tempers the wind to the shorn lamb. **isto não está** ~ it does not agree, it is not in accordance.
conformidade s. f. 1. conformity. 2. conformance, accordance. 3. agreement. 4. consentaneity, consonance. 5. conformation, submission. 6. compliance. 7. convenience, suitableness. 8. harmony. 9. (geol.) concordance.
em ~ **com o seu desejo** in compliance with your request. **não há** ~ **entre os dois** there is no harmony between the two of them.
conformismo s. m. acquiescence on principle.
conformista s. m. + f. conformist, conformer. || adj. conformistical.
confortabilidade s. f. comfortableness.
confortado adj. comforted, strengthened, sheltered, protected.
confortador s. m. comforter, consoler. || adj. comforting, consoling.
confortante adj. m. + f. comforting, consoling, strengthening.
confortar v. 1. to comfort. 2. to console, soothe, solace. 3. to stimulate, animate.
ele confortou-se com... he solaced himself with...
confortativo s. m. (pharm.) a tonic medicine. || adj. comforting.
confortável adj. m. + f. (pl. -áveis) comfortable, at ease, commodious.
conforto (ô) s. m. 1. comfort, comfortableness. 2. well-being. 3. solace, consolation. 4. ease, coziness. 5. relief.
a filha era o seu único ~ her daughter was her sole comfort. **procurar o próprio** ~ to seek one's own convenience. **sem** ~ uneasy, comfortless. **ser amigo do** ~ to be fond of comfort. **uma casa com todo o** ~ a house with every convenience.
confrade s. m. 1. member of a fraternity. 2. confrere, fellow. 3. colleague, comrade.
confragoso adj. rugged, confragose, uneven, rough.
confrangedor adj. distressing, tormenting, heart-breaking.
confranger v. 1. to torment, distress. 2. to oppress. 3. to torture, afflict. 4. to anguish.
confrangido adj. tormented, distressed, oppressed, tortured.

confrangimento s. m. 1. affliction, anguish. 2. oppression.
confraria s. f. 1. brotherhood, fraternity. 2. confraternity. 3. friary, fraternal order.
ser da mesma ~ (pop.) to sihg the same song.
confraternar v. to fraternize with, enter a brotherhood.
confraternidade s. f. confraternity, brotherhood.
confraternização s. f. (pl. -ões) confraternization.
confraternizar v. 1. to fraternize with. 2. to live in a brotherly manner. 3. to forgather, consort socially.
confrontação s. f. (pl. -ões) 1. confrontation. 2. -ões pl. outlines of a building.
confrontador s. m. confronter.
confrontante adj. m. + f. confronting.
confrontar v. 1. to confront, bring face to face. 2. to compare. 3. to collate. 4. to be opposite. 5. to parallel.
~ **as testemunhas com o acusado** to confront the witnesses with the defendant.
confronte adj. m. + f. fronting, facing, opposite. || prep. in front of, before.
confronto s. m. confrontation, comparison, parallel.
confuciano adj. Confucian, of or relating to the Chinese philosopher Confucius.
confucionismo s. m. (phil.) Confucianism.
confucionista s. m. + f. Confucian, Confucianist, follower of Confucius or Confucianism. || adj. Confucianist.
confugir v. 1. to run away, make one's escape with other persons. 2. to resort to, have recourse to.
confundas s. f. pl. (pop.) the depths of hell.
confundido adj. 1. confused, perplexed. 2. frightened. 3. embarrassed. 4. ashamed. 5. concerned.
confundir v. 1. to confound, confuse. 2. to mix together, disarray. 3. to bewilder, perplex. 4. to mistake. 5. to humble, abash, make ashamed. 6. to baffle, amaze, dumbfound. 7. to disconcert, discomfit. 8. to entangle, enmesh. 9. to amalgamate, blend. 10. to distract, fog. 11. ~-se to be puzzled or perplexed, become mixed up, be confounded.
confundível adj. m. + f (pl. -íveis) confusable.
confusão s. f. (pl. -ões) 1. confusion, confusedness. 2. uproar, clamour, tumult, hubbub. 3. perplexity, perplexedness. 4. pandemonium. 5. throng, disorganized crowd. 6. entanglement. 7. shame. 8. bewilderment. 9. disorder, chaos. 10. disturbance, discomfiture, disarray. 11. medley, complication, welter.
em completa ~ upside down, topsy-turvy. ~ **uma** ~ **dos diabos** an up-and-down disorder.
confuso adj. 1. confused. 2. disorderly, disarranged. 3. medley, upside-down. 4. obscure. 5. perplexed, confounded. 6. promiscuous. 7. undistinct. || -**amente** adv. equivocally, chaotically, confoundedly.
ela estava -a she was in a maze. **eles ficaram** ~s they were put to confusion. **está muito** ~ it is all gone haywire. **eu estou muito** ~ I am off the hinges, I am in a fog. **minha cabeça está -a** my head is in a whirl. **situação -a** troubled waters.
confutação s. f. (pl. -ões) confutation, refutation.
confutador s. m. confuter.
confutar v. 1. to confute, refute. 2. to disprove. 3. to impugn, oppose. 4. to expose one's own faults or mistakes.
confutável adj. m. + f. (pl. -áveis) confutable.
conga (I) s. f. (N. Braz.) multure, miller's fee.
conga (II) s. f. conga: a lively dance and dance music.
congada s. f., **congado** m. (Braz.) a pantomimic folk dance of African origin.
congelação s. f. (pl. -ões) 1. congelation, congealment. 2. frozenness, freezing.

congelado s. m. 1. any frozen material. 2. (com.) frozen credit, frozen asset. ‖ adj. frozen, icy.

congelador s. m. freezer, freezing compartment of an icebox. ‖ adj. freezing, congealing.

congelamento s. m. 1. freezing: a method for preserving food. 2. (econ.) freeze (of prices, wages, etc.).

congelar v. 1. to freeze, congeal. 2. to chill. 3. to ice. 4. ~-se: a) to become frozen. b) (fig.) to become embarrassed.

congelativo adj. congelative.

congelável adj. m. + f. (pl. -áveis) congealable, congelable.

congeminação s. f. (pl. -ões) double and simultaneous formation.

congeminar v. 1. to meditate, ponder. 2. to muse. 3. to think.

congênere s. m. congener, congenerousness. ‖ adj. m. + f. congenerous, congeneric(al).

congeneridade s. f. congeneracy, congenerousness.

congenial adj. m. + f. (pl. -ais) congenial, sympathetic, congenital, native.

congenialidade s. f. congeniality.

congênito adj. 1. congenital, inborn, connate. 2. (fig.) appropriate.

congérie s. f. congeries, aggregation, heap, mass.

congestão s. f. (pl. -ões), (med.) congestion.

~ **cerebral** (med.) apoplexy.

congestionado adj. 1. congested. 2. apoplectic. 3. jammed, crowded.

congestionamento s. m. 1. congestion. 2. traffic jam.

congestionar v. 1. to congest, produce congestion in. 2. to become congested. 3. to become flushed with anger.

congestionável adj. m. + f. (pl. -áveis) subject to congestion.

congestivo adj. congestive.

congesto adj. congested.

conglobação s. f. (pl. -ões) conglobation, accumulation.

conglobado adj. conglobate.

conglobar v. 1. to conglobate. 2. to give the form of a ball to. 3. to amass, accumulate. 4. to concentrate. 5. to summarize, make an abstract of.

conglomeração s. f. (pl. -ões) conglomeration, agglomerate, compages.

conglomerado s. m. 1. conglomerate. 2. (geol.) conglomerate, pudding stone. ‖ adj. conglomerate.

conglomerar v. 1. to conglomerate. 2. to collect into a round mass. 3. to heap up, amass, accumulate. 4. to join (o. s.) to.

conglutinação s. f. (pl. -ões) conglutination.

conglutinante adj. m. + f. conglutinant.

conglutinar v. 1. to conglutinate. 2. to adhere, stick together. 3. to be or remain conglutinate.

conglutinoso adj. glutinous, sticky, viscous.

congo (I) s. m. 1. Congolese, native or inhabitant of the Congo region (Africa). 2. (Braz.) = congada.

congo (II) adj. designating a certain variety of tea.

congonha s. f. designation of several plants similar to holly (families: Aquifoliaceae, Ochnaceae, Solanaceae).

congonha-brava s. f. (pl. **congonhas-bravas**) (Braz.) a celastraceous plant (Maytenus communis).

congonha-do-campo s. f. (pl. **congonhas-do-campo**) (Braz.) an ochnaceous plant (Luxenburgia polyandra).

congonheiro s. m. a tree of the family Vochysiaceae (Vochysia oppugnata).

congorsa s. f. (bot.) periwinkle.

congosta s. f. a long and small street, narrow lane.

congote s. m. nape, scruff.

congoxa (ô) s. f. 1. anguish, agony. 2. affliction. 3. trouble.

congraçador s. m. conciliator, pacifier. ‖ adj. conciliatory.

congraçar v. 1. to reconcile. 2. to harmonize. 3. to atone for. 4. to ingratiate (o. s.).

congratulação s. f. (pl. -ões) congratulation, felicitation.

congratulador s. m. congratulator.

congratulante adj. m. + f. congratulant.

congratular v. 1. to felicitate, congratulate. 2. to compliment. 3. to praise, applaud. 4. ~-se to congratulate o. s.

~-**am-lhe a vitória** they congratulated him on his victory.

congratulatório adj. congratulatory.

congregação s. f. (pl. -ões) 1. congregation. 2. reunion, assembly. 3. fraternity, sisterhood. 4. friary, fraternal order. 5. flock, parish.

congregado s. m. member of a congregation, congregant.

congregante s. m. + f. member of a congregation, congregant. ‖ adj. congregational, congregating.

congregar v. 1. to congregate. 2. to assemble, bring together. 3. to convene, forgather, meet, unite. 4. to coexist.

congressional adj. m. + f. (pl. -ais) congressional.

congressista s. m. + f. member of the Congress, Congressman. ‖ adj. congressional.

congresso s. m. 1. Congress. 2. congress. 3. conference. 4. session, reunion, assembly.

Congresso Eucarístico Eucharistic Congress.

congro s. m. (ichth.) conger eel, conger.

côngrua s. f. ecclesiastical revenue, allowance.

congruência s. f. 1. congruence, congruency. 2. congruity, congruousness. 3. coherence. 4. consistency. 5. propriety, appropriateness. 6. convenience.

congruente adj. m. + f. congruent, congruous, consonant. ‖ ~**mente** adv. congruently, congruously.

congruidade s. f. congruousness, congruity, congruence.

congruísmo s. m. (theol.) congruism.

congruísta s. m. + f. congruist. ‖ adj. congruistic(al).

côngruo adj. suitable, adequate. 2. congruous. 3. apt, fit, competent. 4. said with precision.

conguês s. m. (pl. -eses) (f. -esa; pl. -esas) Congolese, native or inhabitant of the Congo region (Africa). ‖ adj. Congolese.

conha s. f. gnarl, a knot in the wood of a tree.

conhaque s. m. cognac, brandy.

conhecedor s. m. 1. connoisseur. 2. expert, specialist. 3. good judge. ‖ adj. knowing, expert.

conhecença s. f. knowledge.

conhecer v. 1. to know, have a notion of. 2. to perceive, understand. 3. to be acquainted with. 4. to be familiar with. 5. to be well versed in, have experience in. 6. to be informed about. 7. to judge, appraise, evaluate. 8. to recognize, be aware of. 9. to feel, know intimately. 10. to be thankful. 11 to be convinced of. 12. to know intimately, have carnal knowledge of. 13. ~-se to know o. s.

~ **de nome** to know by name. ~ **de vista** to know by sight. ~ **os meios** to know one's way about. ~ **pessoalmente** to know personally. **dar-se a** ~ to make o. s. known. **quem não te conhece que te compre** only those who don't know you will fall for you.

conhecido s. m. acquaintance. ‖ adj. 1. known, well known. 2. notorious. 3. public. 4. famous, illustrious. 5. proverbial. 6. familiar, conversant. 7. out.

bem ~ well known. **ela o faz para tornar-se -a** she does it to advertise herself. **é largamente** ~ it is common knowledge. **eu não sou** ~ **aqui** I am a stranger here. **nós somos** ~**s** we are acquainted.

pouco ~ unfamiliar. **repetir o já** ~ to go over the old ground again. **ser** ~ **pelo nome de Zé** to go under the name of Joe. **suas obras mais -as** his best-known works. **tornar-se** ~ to take air, leak out, transpire.

conhecimento s. m. 1. knowledge, know, knowing. 2. cognizance, awareness. 3. intelligence. 4. acquaintance, familiarity. 5. information. 6. understanding. 7. self-consciousness. 8. experience, learning. 9. conscience, cognition. 10. bill of lading, waybill, forwarding note. 11. **~s** pl. acquirements, attainment.

adquirir ~s consideráveis to acquire a large range of knowledge. **chegar ao ~ de** to come under one's notice. **chegou ao ~ de seu pai** it came to his father's ears. **com seu ~ e consentimento** with his privity and consent. **é de ~ geral** it is common ground, it is all about. **ele falou com ~ de causa** he spoke with knowledge of the subject. **ele não tomou ~ de** he took no note of. **ele tem ótimos ~s de grego** he is an excellent Greek scholar. **levar ao seu ~** to bring to his notice. **meu ~ deste fato** my acquaintance with this fact. **não tomar ~ de** to overlook, take no notice of. **sem o meu ~** unknown to me. **tentar travar ~s** to approach s. o. **um ~ superficial** a superficial knowledge. **~ aéreo** airway bill. **~ de depósito** 1. a receipt for warehousing goods. 2. a bonded bill of store issued with the warrant. **~ de carga** bill of lading.

conhecível adj. m. + f. (pl. **-íveis**) knowable, cognizable.

conicidade s. f. conicity, conicalness, angle of taper.

cônico adj. conical, conic, cone-shaped, tapering (plate A 14). ‖ **-amente** adv. conically.

figura -a (geom.) cone.

conídio s. m. (biol.) conidium.

conífera s. f. 1. conifer: tree or shrub of the order Pinales (pine family). 2. **Coníferas** pl. Coniferae.

conifloro adj. (bot.) coniflorous, having cone-shaped flowers.

coniforme adj. m. + f. coniform, conic(al), conoid.

coniina s. f. (chem.) coniine.

conimbricense, conimbrigense s. m. + f. native or inhabitant of Coimbra (Port.). ‖ adj. of, pertaining to or relative to Coimbra and its inhabitants.

conirrostro s. m. Conirostres, group of birds with a conical bill. ‖ adj. conirostral.

conivalve adj. m. + f. (zool.) having a conical shell.

conivência s. f. 1. connivance, connivancy, collusion. 2. (jur.) guilty consent to wrongdoing. **estão de ~** they are hand in glove.

conivente adj. m. + f. conniving, connivent, accessory.

conjetura s. f. 1. conjecture, supposition. 2. guess. 3. presumption, surmise. 4. hypothesis.

conjeturador s. m. conjecturer, guesser. ‖ adj. conjecturing.

conjetural adj. m. + f. (pl. **-ais**) conjectural, depending on conjecture, involving conjecture.

conjeturar v. 1. to conjecture. 2. to presume, surmise. 3. to suppose, presuppose. 4. to guess. 5. to suspect.

conjeturável adj. m. + f. (pl. **-áveis**) conjecturable.

conjugação s. f. (pl.-**ões**) conjugation: 1. act of conjugating. 2. conjunction, assemblage, union. 3. (gram.) the inflectional forms of a verb. 4. (bot.) reproduction by fusion of two gametes.

conjugado adj. conjugate.

conjugal adj. m. + f. (pl. **-ais**) conjugal, matrimonial, connubial, married. ‖ **~mente** adv. conjugally.

conjugar v. to conjugate: 1. (gram.) inflect a verb. 2. join simultaneously, unite. 3. (bot., biol.) fuse by conjugation. 4. coordinate (efforts).

conjugativo adj. conjugative.

conjugável adj. m. + f. (pl. **-áveis**) conjugable.

cônjuge s. m. + f. 1. consort, spouse. 2. mate. 3. partner. 4. **~s** pl. married couple.

conjunção s. f. (pl. **-ões**) conjuction: 1. union, association. 2. conjuncture, opportunity. 3. connexion. 4. the passing of two or more celestial bodies, transit. 5. (gram.) connective word or clause. **~ concessiva** (gram.) concessive conjunction. **~ coordenativa** (gram.) coordinating conjunction. **~ correlativa** (gram.) correlative conjunction. **~ subordinativa** (gram.) subordinate conjunction.

conjuncional adj. m. + f. (pl. **-ais**) conjunctional.

conjunta s. f. one of the thongs used to fasten the yoke to the horns of an ox.

conjuntar v. 1. to conjoin, join. 2. to unite. 3. to combine.

conjuntiva s. f. (anat.) conjunctiva.

conjuntivite s. f. (med.) conjunctivitis, inflammation of the conjunctiva.

conjuntivo s. m. (gram.) conjunctive (mood). ‖ adj. conjunctive, additive, connective. ‖ **-amente** adv. conjunctively, connectively.

conjunto s. m. 1. a complex whole, entirety. 2. set, kit. 3. suite, complete apartment. 4. (ftb.) team. 5. ensemble: a) troupe. b) (tail.) costume (plate R 6). 6. assemblage. ‖ adj. 1. conjunct, conjoint. 2. united. 3. concurrent. 4. combined. 5. adjacent. 6. near, proximate, close by. ‖ **-amente** adv. conjunctly, concurrently, jointly.

em ~ concerted, together, on the whole, in the lump. **lutar em ~** to fight together. **tudo em ~** all together. **trabalho em ~** joint work, team-work. **vamos fazê-lo -amente** let's do it among us. **~ crítico** (nuclear physics) critical sustaining of a chain reaction. **~ residencial** a group of houses.

conjuntura s. f. 1. conjuncture. 2. sequence of events or circumstances. 3. difficulty, complication. 4. event, a happening. 5. affair. 6. opportunity. 7. predicament.

conjuração s. f. (pl. **-ões**) (also **conjura**) 1. conjuration, conspiracy. 2. complot, conspiration. 3. plot.

conjurado s. m. 1. complotter, conspirator. 2. = **conjurador**.

conjurador s. m. conjurer, conjuror.

conjurante adj. m. + f. conjuring.

conjurar v. 1. to conjure. 2. to exorcise. 3. to ward off, avoid a danger. 4. to implore, beseech, entreat. 5. to conspire, plot, scheme. 6. to invoke. 7. to incite. 8. to swear together. 9. to take part in a complot. 10. to rise or revolt against.

conjuratório adj. concerning a conspiration.

conjuro s. m. 1. conjuration. 2. incantation, magic, sorcery. 3. exorcism. 4. words used in exorcising.

conluiado adj. collusive, done in collusion.

conluir v. 1. to collude. 2. to scheme, plot. 3. to conspire, connive. 4. to dupe, cheat (with the help of others). 5. to confederate. 6. to enter into collusion with, act in concert.

conluio s. m. 1. collusion, collusiveness. 2. machination, plot, artful scheme. 3. frame-up. 4. covin, cabal. 5. confederacy. 6. conspiration.

conocarpo adj. (bot.) conocarpous.

conócito s. m. (bot.) the epidermic cell of the plants of the family Cyperaceae.

conoidal adj. m. + f. (pl. **-ais**) conoid, conoidal, coniform.

conóide s. m. (geom.) conoid. ‖ adj. m + f. conoid(al), cone-shaped.

conosco pron. with us, to us, for us, together with us, to ourselves, addressed or directed to us.

conotação s. f. (pl. **-ões**) 1. connotation. 2. denotation. 3. inference, implication. 4. signification.

conotativo adj. connotative. ‖ -amente adv. connotatively.

conquanto conj. although, though, inasmuch as, notwithstanding.

conquiliologia s. f. (zool.) conchology.

conquiliológico adj. (zool.) conchologic(al).

conquiliologista s. m. + f. conchologist.

conquista s. f. 1. conquest, conquering. 2. victory. 3. the conquered thing, that which is conquered. 4. effort. 5. acquisiton.
ele fez uma ~ he made a great capture. não é lá grande ~ it is no catch.

conquistado adj. conquered, won, dominated, defeated.

conquistador s. m. 1. conqueror, conquistador. 2. victor. 3. (fig.) lady-killer, wolf.

conquistar v. 1. to conquer. 2. to overcome, subdue, defeat. 3. to acquire, take. 4. to win a victory. 5. to attract (sympathy, love). 6. to win one's heart or affection. 7. (fig.) to achieve.
ele conquistou a estima de todos he won the respect of all. ele conquistou todos he carried all before him. ele nos havia conquistado para o seu partido he won us over to his side. isto a conquistará that will serve to win her over.

conquistável adj. m. + f. (pl. -áveis) conquerable, vincible.

consabido adj. whatever many people know about.

consagração s. f. (pl. -ões) 1. consecration. 2. dedication. 3. devotion. 4. sacring, anointing.

consagrado adj. consecrate(d), holy, sanctified, devoted, sainted.

consagrador s. m. consecrator. ‖ adj. consecratory.

consagrante s. m. + f. consecrator, officiant. ‖ adj. consecrating, consecratory.

consagrar v. 1. to consecrate, render sacred. 2. to dedicate to the worship of God. 3. to sanctify, bless. 4. to anoint. 5. to devote. 6. to ordain. 7. to authorize, sanction. 8. to elect, acclaim. 9. ~-se to devote o. s.

consangüíneo s. m. a blood relation. ‖ adj. consanguine, consanguineous.

consangüinidade s. f. 1. consanguinity. 2. relationship by blood (on the father's side), kinship. 3. (fam.) blood, flesh. 4. (pal.) relationship existing between different rocks of the same petrographic region.

consciência (I) s. f. 1. conscience. 2. consciousness. 3. perception, awareness. 4. conscientiousness. 5. scruple, compunction. 6. rectitude, uprightness. 7. fairness, justice. 8. sense of duty.
apelar à ~ de alguém to appeal to a person's conscience. com uma ~ tranqüila with a safe conscience. de sã ~ with a good conscience. ela perdeu a ~ she lost consciousness. falta de ~ unscrupulousness. há uma coisa que me pesa na ~ I have s. th. on my conscience. meter a mão na ~ to listen to one's conscience. o limiar da ~ the threshold of consciousness. por descargo de ~ for the sake of conscience. questão de ~ matter of conscience. sem ~ unconscionable, unprincipled. ter ~ to be scrupulous. ter a ~ larga not to be overscrupulous. um homem com vários crimes na ~ a man with several crimes on his conscience. ~ coletiva a joint conscience. ~ moral a moral conscience.

consciência (II) s. f. breast-plate of a breast-drill.

conscienciosa adj. 1. conscientious. 2. conscionable. 3. scrupulous, exact. 4. faithful, religious. ‖ -amente adv. conscientiously, scrupulously.

consciente adj. m. + f. 1. conscious. 2. aware, sensible. 3. knowing. 4. conscientious. ‖ ~mente adv. consciously.

conscientização s. f. 1. the act of acquiring knowledge about. 2. the act of having an idea about.

conscientizar v. 1. to acquire knowledge about. 2. to have an idea about.

cônscio adj. 1. conscious. 2. cognizant, aware. 3. sensible. 4. knowing. 5. (fam.) wise.

conscrição s. f. (pl.-ões) conscription, draft.

conscrito s. m. conscript, recrute. ‖ adj. conscript, recruited.

consecratório adj. consecratory.

consecução s. f. (pl. -ões) consecution, obtainment. 2. success, achievement. 3. procuration, procurement. 4. fruition.
de difícil ~ difficult to achieve.

consecutivo adj. consecutive, successive, sequent(ial). ‖ -amente adv. consecutively, sequentially.
imagem -a (psych.) after-image. três vezes -as three times over. três dias ~s three days on end.

conseguidor s. m. achiever, accomplisher. ‖ adj. accomplishing.

conseguimento s. m. 1. consecution. 2. achievement, attainment.

conseguinte adj. m. + f. 1. consecutive, sequential. 2. consequent, following, subsequent.
por ~ then, therefore, ergo. por ~ eu não vou consequently I will not go.

conseguir v. 1. to obtain, achieve, get. 2. to succeed in. 3. to happen as consequence or result. 4. to provide, purchase. 5. to manage. 6. to contrive.
consegui ajudar meu amigo I succeeded in helping my friend. consegui a ligação telefônica I got the telephone connection, (fam.) I got through to him. ~am resolver o problema they brought it about to solve the problem. ele conseguiu escapar he contrived to escape. ele conseguiu perder todo o dinheiro he contrived to lose all his money. ele conseguiu seus objetivos com astúcia he attained his end by art. ele conseguiu terminar esta obra it was given him to complete this work. não consegui ser atendido por ele I could not gain his ear. você consegue arranjar-se sem ela? can you make shift without her?

conseguível adj. m. + f. (pl. -íveis) obtainable.

conselhar v. (obs.) to counsel, advise.

conselheiral adj. m. + f. (pl. -ais), conselheirático, conselheiresco 1. of, pertaining to or typical of a counselor. 2. serious, grave, ponderous.

conselheirismo s. m. 1. behaviour of a counselor. 2. seriousness.

conselheiro s. m. 1. counselor, counsel. 2. member of a council. 3. adviser. 4. council-man, alderman. ‖ adj. counseling, advising.
~ de legação counsellor of legation. ele foi nomeado ~ real he has taken silk.

conselho s. m. 1. counsel. 2. council, synod. 3. court, board. 4. advice, recommendation. 5. warning, admonition, exhortation. 6. opinion. 7. prudence.
a ~ de by the advice of. a ~ médico on medical advice. a ~ de um amigo at a friend's suggestion. câmara do ~ council-chamber. ~ privado privy council. ~ de guerra court-martial. ~ de ministros cabinet council. ele pediu meu ~ he asked counsel of me. ele seguiu meu ~ he followed my advice, took my tip. ouça meus ~s be guided by me. ouvir ~ to listen to reason. um bom ~ a piece of advice.

consenciente adj. m. + f. consentient, consenting.

consensial adj. m. + f. (pl. -ais) consensual.

consenso s. m. 1. consensus. 2. consent, consentment. 3. agreement, accord. 4. harmony.

~ **das gentes** the proof of the existence of God through the consensus of belief of all peoples.
consensual adj. m. + f. (pl. **-ais**) consensual.
consensualidade s. f. consension, character or quality of being consensual.
consentâneo adj. consentaneous, adequate, suitable, proper.
consentimento s. m. 1. consent, consentment. 2. approbation, approval. 3. permission. 4. acquiescence, agreeableness. 5. acceptance, agreement. 6. adhesion. 7. compliance. 8. tolerance. 9. assent, admission.
com o ~ **de todos** by common consent. **obtido o seu** ~, **saí** having obtained his consent, I left. **obtive o seu** ~ I got his will. **sem o meu** ~ **e aprovação** without my knowledge and consent.
consentir v. 1. to consent. 2. to concede, grant. 3. to tolerate. 4. to make possible. 5. to authorize, permit. 6. to yield, acquiesce. 7. to agree, admit. 8. to approve. 9. to comply with.
ele resolveu ~ **na adoção deste plano** he decided to acquiesce in the adoption of this plan. **quem cala consente** silence gives consent.
conseqüência s. f. 1. consequence. 2. product, result. 3. sequence, sequel. 4. conclusion, deduction. 5. pursuance. 6. outcome, issue. 7. aftermath, fruit. 8. importance, import. 9. inference.
arco com as ~s I take the consequences. **a crise teve o desemprego como** ~ the crisis resulted in unemployment. **as** ~s **não se farão esperar** you will hear of it. **como** ~ **natural disso** as a corollary to this. **em** ~ **de** in pursuance of, therefore, as a result of. **pensar nas** ~s to count the cost. **ser a** ~ **de** to be consequential on. **tem alguma coisa como** ~ it brings s. th. in its train.
conseqüente adj. m. + f. 1. consequent, consequential. 2. resultant, attendant, following. ‖ ~**mente** adv. consequently.
consertador s. m. repairer, repairman, mender.
consertar v. 1. to repair. 2. to mend, patch up, fix. 3. to adjust. 4. to darn. 5. to refit. 6. to service.
conserto (ê) s. m. repair, restoration, fixing, refitting.
em ~ under repair. **não há cura nem** ~ there is neither help nor hope. **necessitando de** ~ in need of repair. **sem** ~ beyond repair.
conserva s. f. conserve, preserve, comfit.
abridor de latas de ~s tin-opener, (U.S.A.) can opener. **carne de** ~ canned meat. ~s **alimentícias** canned food. **fábrica de** ~s factory of canned goods. **navegar de** ~ to navigate a ship accompanied by another ship.
conservação s. f. (pl. **-ões**) 1. conservation. 2. conservancy. 3. maintenance, upkeep.
a ~ **das estradas** the preservation of the roads. **a** ~ **dos costumes** the retention of the customs. **em bom estado de** ~ in good order, shape or repair. **o instinto de** ~ the instinct of self-preservation.
conservador s. m. 1. conservator, conserver, preserver. 2. curator. 3. conservative (in politics), Tory, member of the conservative party. ‖ adj. conservative, conservatory.
conservadorismo s. m. conservativeness.
conservante adj. m. + f. conservant, conserving, preserving.
conservantismo s. m. 1. conservatism. 2. traditionalism.
conservantista s. m. + f. 1. conservative. 2. traditionalist. ‖ adj. conservative, traditionalistic.
conservar v. 1. to conserve, preserve from destruction. 2. to maintain, sustain. 3. to keep, guard. 4. to save, reserve. 5. to keep in mind, remember. 6. to retain. 7. to remain, stay, last.

a casa não está bem conservada the house is in bad repair. ~**am-se em silêncio** they kept silent. ~ **carne** to cure meat. ~ **em bom estado** to maintain in good conditions. ~ **em salmoura** to pickle--cure. **bem conservado** well-preserved, well-kept. ~ **um emprego** to keep a job. **ela se conserva jovem** she wears well.
conservativo adj. conservative, conservatory, preservative.
conservatório s. m. conservatory. ‖ adj. conservatory.
conservável adj. m. + f. (pl. **-áveis**) conservable, preservable.
conserveiro s. m. 1. manufacturer of canned goods, canner. 2. conserver, preserver. 3. confectioner. 4. dealer in canned goods.
consideração s. f. (pl. **-ões**) 1. act of considering. 2. consideration. 3. appreciation, respect, regard. 4. considerateness, regardfulness. 5. importance. 6. reflection, meditation, ponderation. 7. cogitation, speculation. 8. **-ões** pl. reasons, motives.
em ~ **a** by token of, out of consideration for. **eu a tenho em** ~ I care for her. **falta de** ~ want of consideration, inconsiderateness. **não o tomo em** ~ I leave it out of account. **sem** ~ unscrupulous, unmindful, irrespective. **sem** ~ **à minha saúde** unmindful of my health. **...subscrevemo-nos com toda estima e** ~ (in commercial letters) we remain cordially yours... **temos de tomar em** ~ **que** we must take into consideration that. **ter** ~ **por** to be tender of. **ter alguém em grande** ~ to make a great deal of, hold s. o. in high respect. **tomar em** ~ to take into account, make allowance for.
considerado adj. considerate, considered, deliberate, respected, prudent, thoughtful. ‖ **-amente** adv. considerately.
considerando s. m. motive, reason, fundamental considerations.
considerar v. 1. to consider: a) take into consideration. b) ponder, meditate. c) examine carefully, observe. d) esteem, appreciate highly, respect. e) judge, estimate. f) think, cogitate, reflect, speculate. 2. to believe, suppose.
considerando todos os fatos all things considered. **considerando que a paz está em perigo** whereas peace is in danger. **considero-o meu amigo** I consider him my friend. **ele foi considerado um gênio** he was counted a genius. **ele o considera como mérito seu** he takes credit for it. **ele pode** ~-**se feliz** he may consider himself lucky. **eu o considero uma honra** I esteem it an honour. **não** ~ to ignore. **não se considere um sábio!** be not wise in your own conceits! **precisamos** ~ **seus sentimentos** we must consult his feelings.
considerável adj. m. + f. (pl. **-áveis**) 1. considerable. 2. notable, important. 3. remarkable, eminent. 4. ponderable. 5. fair. 6. respectable. 7. enormous. ‖ **consideravelmente** adv. considerably.
consignação s. f. (pl. **-ões**) consignation, consignment, deposit, trust.
~ **bancária** bank-transfer. **em** ~ on sale or return. ~ **em pagamento** a deposit under judicial sanction to cover a claimed debt. ~ **em folha** a monthly deduction from the payroll of government personnel.
consignador s. m. consigner, consignor. ‖ adj. consigning.
consignante s. m. + f. consigner, consignor. ‖ adj. consigning.
consignar v. 1. to consign. 2. to seal, sign. 3. to send, address to, ship to. 4. to deposit, entrust, commit. 5. to register, record, bill. 6. to devote, assign.
consignatário s. m. consignee, consignatary, receiver, trustee.

consignativo adj. of, concerning or relative to the value (money, funds, estate) consigned to the contractor of a perpetual or temporary annuity.
consignável adj. m. + f. (pl. -áveis) consignable.
consigo pron. with him (her, it), with himself (herself, itself, themselves).
ela não tinha dinheiro ~ she had no money about her. eles disseram ~ mesmos que... they said to themselves that... isto não é ~ that is none of your business.
consiliário s. m. = conselheiro.
consistência s. f. 1. consistence, consistency. 2. denseness. 3. (fig.) stability, stableness. 4. firmness. 5. substance. 6. body.
consistente adj. m. + f. consistent, solid, dense, thick, tough.
consistir v. 1. to consist in (or of). 2. to rest in. 3. to be constituted or composed of. 4. to comprise.
o plano consiste na criação de novas bases the plan consists in forming new bases.
consistorial adj. m. + f. (pl. -ais) consistorial.
consistório s. m. 1. (eccl.) consistory. 2. council, convention.
consoada s. f. 1. light supper (as on a fast day). 2. Christmas gift box. 3. Christmas supper. 4. Christmas gift.
consoante (I) s. f. consonant. ‖ adj. m. + f. consonant(al), consonous.
consoante (II) s. m. rhyme. ‖ adj. m. + f. rhyming.
consoante (III) prep. conformable, consonant with, according to.
consoar v. 1. to take a light supper. 2. to be consonant. 3. to rhyme, form a rhyme.
consociação s. f. (pl. -ões) consociation, association.
consociar v. 1. to consociate. 2. to unite, join. 3. to associate.
consociável adj. m. + f. (pl. -áveis) consociable.
consócio s. m. consociate, associate, partner, colleague.
consogra s. f. mother in relation to her child's mother-in-law.
consogro s. m. father in relation to his child's father-in-law.
consola s. f. 1. (archit.) console, bracket. 2. console table.
consolação s. f. (pl. -ões) 1. consolation. 2. relief, easement. 3. comfort. 4. cheer.
consolado adj. consoled, comforted, mitigated, content.
consolador s. m. 1. consoler, comforter. 2. rubber nipple, pacifier. ‖ adj. comforting, mitigating, consolatory, consoling. ‖ -amente adv. consolingly, consolatorily.
consolante adj. m. + f. comforting, consolatory, consoling.
consolar v. 1. to console. 2. to comfort, solace. 3. to ease. 4. to mitigate, relieve. 5. to encourage, cheer (up). 6. ~-se: a) to be comforted. b) to console o. s.
~ alguém to speak to a person's heart. ele não se consola he is inconsolable. ele teve de ~-se com o segundo lugar he had to put up with the second place.
consolativo adj. consolatory, consoling, comforting.
consolatório adj. consolatory.
consolável adj. m. + f. (pl. -áveis) consolable.
consolda s. f. (bot.) comfrey.
consolda-do-cáucaso s. f. (pl. consoldas-do-cáucaso), (bot.) rough comfrey.
consolda-grande s. f. (pl. consoldas-grandes), (bot.) great consound.
consolda-real s. f. (pl. consoldas-reais), (bot.) rocket larkspur.

consólida s. f. (bot.) comfrey, consound.
consolidação s. f. (pl. -ões) 1. consolidation. 2. solidification. 3. (com.) merger of two or more corporations. 4. combination. 5. strengthening, stiffening.
consolidado s. m. (com.) consolidated stock. ‖ adj. consolidated.
consolidador s. m. consolidator. ‖ adj. consolidating.
consolidar v. 1. to consolidate. 2. to solidify, become hard. 3. to fund (debts). 4. to heal over, close up (wound). 5. to be or become stable. 6. to ratify (laws).
consolidativo adj. consolidative.
consolo s. m. 1. (archit.) console, bracket, truss. 2. corbel. 3. console table.
consolo (ô) s. m. consolation, solace, comfort.
consomê s. m. (cul.) consommé.
consonância s. f. 1. consonance, consonancy. 2. accord. 3. harmony. 4. rhyme. 5. (fig.) agreement, concord.
consonantal adj. m. + f. (pl. -ais) consonant(al).
consonante adj. m. + f. consonant, consonous.
consonantismo s. m. (gram.) consonantism.
consonantização s. f. (pl. -ões), (phon.) transformation of a semivowel into a consonant, shifting of sounds.
consonantizar v. (phon.) to transform a semivowel into a consonant.
consonar v. 1. to produce a consonance. 2. to harmonize.
cônsono adj. consonous, consonant(al).
consorciar v. 1. to associate. 2. to consort, unite by marriage. 3. to join, unite. 4. to marry.
consórcio s. m. 1. consortium. 2. partnership, fellowship. 3. association, society. 4. marriage. 5. (com.) trust.
consorte s. m. + f. 1. spouse, husband or wife. 2. partner, associate. 3. mate, companion. 4. consort.
conspecto, conspeto s. m. conspectus, presence, sight.
conspicuidade s. f. conspicuity, conspicuousness.
conspícuo adj. 1. conspicuous. 2. notable, eminent, prominent. 3. illustrious, famous. 4. respectable. ‖ conspicuamente adv. conspicuously.
conspiração s. f. (pl. -ões) 1. conspiration. 2. plotting, plot. 3. collusion, covin. 4. machination. 5. frame-up.
conspirador s. m. 1. conspirator, complotter. 2. machinator, schemer. ‖ adj. conspiring, conspiratorial.
conspiradora s. f. conspiratress.
conspirar v. 1. to conspire, complot. 2. to collude, connive. 3. to machinate, scheme, intrigue.
conspirata s. f. conspiration, conspiracy.
conspirativo adj. conspiring, conspirative, conspiratorial.
conspiratório adj. conspiratorial, collusive.
conspurcação s. f. (pl. -ões) 1. conspurcation, defilement. 2. moral corruption. 3. debasement, depravation.
conspurcar v. 1. to conspurcate, defile. 2. to corrupt, affect with corruption. 3. to debase, pervert.
conspurcável adj. m. + f. (pl. -áveis) corruptible, pervertible.
consta s. m. rumour, report (taken for granted).
constância s. f. 1. constancy. 2. fidelity, faithfulness. 3. faith. 4. fortitude. 5. firmness, steadiness. 6. stability. 7. perseverance. 8. uniformity. 9. courage, resolution.
constante s. f. (logics, math., phys.) constant. ‖ adj. m. + f. 1. constant. 2. unremitting, persistent. 3. invariable, unchangeable. 4. faithful, true. 5. stable, steadfast. 6. continuous, ceaseless. 7. courageous, resolute. ‖ ~mente adv. constantly, unremittingly, ceaselessly, ever.
ele é muito ~ he is rather regular. o vento é ~

the wind sits fair. ~ **de desintegração** (nuclear physics) disintegration, decay constant. ~ **de integração** (math.) constant of integration. ~ **radioativa = constante de desintegração.**
constantinopolitano s. m. Constantinopolitan: native or inhabitant of Constantinople. ‖ adj. Constantinopolitan.
constar v. 1. to consist of. 2. to be known, be evident. 3. to be taken for true or granted. 4. to be reported.
conforme consta as the story has it. **consta ainda que...** added to this is that... **consta que** it is reported, it is said. **consta que ele fugiu** the truth is that he run away.
constatar v. 1. to evidence, establish positively. 2. to discover, find out. 3. to verify, certify. 4. to prove. 5. to testify.
constelação s. f. (pl. -ões) constellation.
constelado adj. constellate(d), star-spangled, star-shaped.
constelar v. to constellate.
consternação s. f. (pl. -ões) 1. consternation. 2. desolation, despair. 3. fright, dread. 4. alarm, panic. 5. abashment.
consternado adj. dejected, depressed, disconsolate, aghast, consternated.
consternador adj. consternating, alarming, frightful.
consternar v. to fill with consternation, dismay, confound.
constipação s. f. (med.) 1. constipation, costiveness. 2. common cold. 3. astriction.
eu peguei uma ~ I have caught a cold.
constipado adj. 1. constipated, costive. 2. suffering from a cold.
constipar v. 1. to constipate, cause a constipation. 2. to catch a cold.
constitucional s. m. (pl. -ais) constitutionalist. ‖ adj. m. + f. constitutional: 1. (pol.) of, pertaining to or based on a constitution. 2. inherent in the body or in the natural disposition. ‖ ~**mente** adv. constitutionally.
constitucionalidade s. f. constitutionality.
constitucionalismo s. m. constitutionalism.
constitucionalista s. m. + f. constitutionalist. ‖ adj. constitutionalistic(al).
constitucionalizar v. to constitutionalize.
constituição s. f. (pl. -ões) constitution: 1. formation, act of establishing. 2. organization. 3. nature, physical disposition. 4. temperament, character. 5. fundamental law of state, magna charta. 6. texture. 7. statutes of a corporation, by-laws. 8. ordination.
a ~ **do mundo** the creation of the world.
constituinte s. m. + f. 1. constituent, representative. 2. voter. 3. member of a constituent assembly. 4. component. 5. principal. ‖ adj. constituent, component, forming an elementary part of, having the power of constituting.
constituir v. 1. to constitute. 2. to form, put together, establish, compose. 3. to appoint or elect to an office. 4. ~**-se:** a) to consist of. b) to constitute o. s. (as). c) to arrogate to o. s. the right to...
constitutivo adj. constitutive, elemental, determinative.
constrangedor adj. constraining, compelling.
constranger v. 1. to constrain. 2. to urge, impel. 3. to oblige. 4. to coerce, force. 5. to restrain, astrict. 6. to bind, enfetter, chain.
constrangido adj. 1. constrained. 2. restrained, compelled. 3. uneasy, stiff, uncomfortable. 4. self-conscious. 5. bound, forced. 6. distressed.
constrangimento s. m. 1. constraint, compulsion. 2. force, coercion. 3. embarrassment. 4. duress. 5. manacle, fetter.

constrição s. f. (pl. -ões) constriction, contraction.
constringente adj. m. + f. constringent.
constringir v. 1. to constringe, constrict. 2. to press. 3. to contract. 4. ~**-se** to become narrower or tighter.
constritivo adj. constrictive.
constrito adj. 1. narrow, compressed. 2. constrained.
constritor s. m. 1. (anat.) constrictor. 2. (zool.) boa constrictor. ‖ adj. constricting, constrictive, constringent.
construção s. f. (pl. -ões) 1. art, process or result of constructing. 2. construction, building, edification. 3. structure. 4. assembly. 5. fabrication. 6. organism. 7. (gram.) syntax (of a clause).
~ **aeronáutica** aircraft construction. ~ **civil** civil architecture. ~ **de frases** (gram.) structure of sentences. ~ **de madeira** timberwork. ~ **gramatical** syntax. ~ **naval** shipbuilding, naval architecture. **a casa está em** ~ the house is in course of construction. **casa de** ~ **sólida** a well-built house. **escritório de -ões** surveyor's office. **madeira para** ~ structural timber.
construir v. 1. to construct. 2. to erect, build. 3. to form, frame. 4. to compose, assemble. 5. (gram.) to construe, combine grammatically. 6. to organize. 7. to found.
~ **castelos no ar** to build castles in the air.
construtivismo s. m. constructivism, constructionism, any constructive activity in art, literature, politics or society.
construtivo adj. constructive, organic, implicit, imaginative. ‖ **-amente** adv. constructively, imaginatively.
construtor s. m. constructor, builder, architect, erector.
~ **de carros** wheelwright. ~ **de casas** housebuilder. ~ **de máquinas** engine builder. ~ **de navios** shipbuilder.
construtura s. f. manner or method of constructing.
consubstanciação s. f. (pl. -ões), (theol.) consubstantiation, impanation.
consubstancial adj. m. + f. (pl. -ais) consubstantial.
consubstancialidade s. f. (theol.) consubstantiality.
consubstanciar v. 1. to consubstantiate. 2. to consolidate, make firm. 3. (theol.) to impanate. 4. to unite, join intimately.
consueto adj. usual, customary.
consuetudinário adj. consuetudinary, customary, common.
direito ~ (jur.) common law.
cônsul s. m. (f. **consulesa,** pl. **cônsules**) consul: 1. (Roman hist.) supreme magistrate in ancient Rome. 2. (hist.) chief magistrate during the French revolution. 3. representative of a nation in a foreign country.
consulado s. m. 1. consulate. 2. consulship. 3. dignity, office or authority of a consul.
consulagem s. f. (pl. -ens) consulage.
consular adj. m. + f. consular.
consulente s. m. + f. 1. consultant, consulter. 2. consultant, consultee. ‖ adj. consulting, consultatory.
consulesa s. f. 1. a woman consul. 2. a consul's wife.
consulta s. f. 1. consultation. 2. council, conference. 3. counsel. 4. deliberation.
uma obra de ~ a book of reference.
consultador s. m. consultant. ‖ adj. consulting, consultative.
consultante s. m. + f. consultant. ‖ adj. consulting, consultative, consultatory.
consultar v. 1. to consult. 2. to ask for advice or counsel. 3. to deliberate. 4. to confer with. 5. to seek information. 6. to sound out, probe. 7. to examine. 8. to meditate, ponder. 9. to offer advice or counsel.

~ **o travesseiro** (fam.) to consult one's pillow, sleep s. th. over. ~ **um médico** to take medical advice. **consultei de novo o relógio** I looked again on my watch. **tenho de** ~ **um médico** I must see a doctor. **tenho de** ~ **um livro** I must consult a book.

consultivo adj. consultive, consultory, consultable, prudential, advisory, deliberative. || **-amente** adv. consultively.

consultor s. m. consultant, consultee, counsel(l)or, examiner.

consultório s .m. 1. consultation room. 2. doctor's office, surgery.

ela trabalha num ~ **médico** she is receptionist to a doctor.

consumação (I) s. f. (pl. **-ões**) 1. consummation. 2. accomplishment, achievement. 3. completion.

consumação (II) s. f. (pl. **-ões**) 1. cover charge. 2. food and drinks consumed at one time in a restaurant.

consumado adj. 1. consummate. 2. accomplished, well-versed. 3. thorough-going, competent. 4. perfect. 5. distinguished.

fato ~ **fait accompli. patife** ~ accomplished scoundrel. **um cavalheiro** ~ a perfect gentleman.

consumador s. m. consummator. || adj. consummative.

consumar v. 1. to terminate, finish. 2. to consummate, complete. 3. to fulfil. 4. to bring to perfection.

consumido adj. consumed, wasted.

consumidor s. m. consumer. || adj. consuming, wasting, afflicting.

consumir v. 1. to consume. 2. to eat up, devour. 3. to spend, waste. 4. to use, wear. 5. to destroy. 6. to squander. 7. to wear out, exhaust. 8. to vex, distress, trouble. 9. to absorb. 10. to mortify. 11. to decay. 12. **~-se** to be consumed, waste away, pine away.

as preocupações ~am-no his troubles have told on him. **ele se consome de inveja** he is consumed with envy.

consumível adj. m. + f. (pl. **-íveis**) consumable.

consumo s. m. 1. consumption. 2. act of consuming. 3. use, wear. 4. waste. 5. absorption. 6. (com.) sale of goods. 7. (com.) expenditure, disbursement.

consumpção, consunção s. f. (pl. **-ões**) (med.) consumption, phthisis.

consumptibilidade, consuntibilidade s. f. quality of being consumptible.

consumptível, consuntível adj. m. + f. (pl. **-íveis**) consumptible.

consumptivo, consuntivo adj. consumptive.

consumpto, consunto adj. consumed, spent, wasted, worn out.

consútil adj. m. + f. (pl. **-úteis**) having a seam.

conta s. f. 1. act or result of counting. 2. account. 3. count, numeration, reckoning, calculation. 4. bead (of a rosary). 5. sum, total. 6. bill, note, report. 7. statement (of account). 8. repute, esteem. 9. responsibility. 10. justification. 11. expenditure, disbursement.

~ **a pagar** an account payable. ~ **a receber** active debt. ~ **atrasada** overdue bill. ~ **bancária** bank account. ~ **corrente** current account, account, drawing account. ~ **de caixa** cash-account. ~ **de capital** stock account. **abrir uma** ~ to open an account. **acertar as ~s** (com.) to adjust accounts. **à** ~ **(de)** on account (of). **afinal de ~s** after all. **à minha** ~ on my own account. **as ~s do rosário espalharam-se no chão** the beads from the rosary scattered all over the floor. **bobagens sem** ~ (fam.) endless nonsense. **dar** ~ **do recado** to be up to the thing. **ele ficou por** ~ (pop.) he got awfully angry. **ele não pôde dar** ~ **do dinheiro que lhe foi confiado** he could not account for the money he

had received in trust. **este é o estado em que se encontram as nossas ~s** the account stands thus between us. **eu não faço** ~ **disso** I really don't mind. **eu tomo isto à minha** ~ I take it upon myself, I will answer for it. **incluir na** ~ to count in. **isto é de sua ~!** that's your own concern! **isto me saiu bem em** ~ I bought it rather cheap. **isto não é de sua** ~ that's no concern of yours, it is none of your business. **lançar ao débito de sua** ~ (com.) to place it to his account. **lançar a uma nova** ~ to carry to a new account. **levar em** ~ to take into account. **liquidar uma** ~ to settle an account. **não é de minha** ~ I have no concern with (it). **não sei onde eu pus a** ~ **da luz** I wonder where I put that light bill. **no fim das ~s** when all is said and done. **o mato está tomando** ~ **do jardim** the garden runs to loss. **perdi a** ~ I lost count. **ponha na** ~ put it down to my score, (U. S. A., coll.) put it on the cuff. **por** ~ **(de)** on account (of). **por** ~ **própria** for my own account, for one's own hand, at his (her) own charge. **por minha** ~ at my cost. **prestar ~s** to account for. **tenho uma** ~ **a acertar com ele** I have a crow to pluck with him. **ter em grande** ~ to esteem s. o. highly. **tomarei** ~ **da menina** I shall take charge of the girl. **vamos prestar ~s uma vez por ano** whe shall render accounts once yearly. **você pode pôr isto na minha** ~ you can put that down to my score.

contábil adj. m. + f. (pl. **-ábeis**) of, pertaining to or relative to the art of bookkeeping.

contabilidade s. f. 1. accountancy, accountantship. 2. computation, calculation. 3. counting-house, counting room, accounting department.

contabilista s. m. + f. accountant.

contabilização s. f. booking, accounting.

contabilizar v. to book, register.

contado adj. 1. counted, recounted. 2. calculated, computed. 3. related, reported, told.

de ~ ready money, cash. **não** ~ 1. untold, not reported. 2. uncounted, unnumbered. **são favas -as** (pop.) that's very obvious.

contador s. m. 1. bookkeeper, accountant. 2. auditor. 3. counter, computer, reckoner. 4. teller, head clerk, paymaster. 5. meter, instrument for measuring and recording the consumption (gas, electricity, water). 6. storyteller, taleteller, fabulist. 7. chest of many small drawers. 8. pendant of a rosary.

perito-~ certified accountant.

contadoria s. f. accounting department.

conta-fios s. m., sg. + pl. thread counter.

contagem s. f. (pl. **-ens**) 1. count, counting. 2. reckoning. 3. telling. 4. score.

~ **do original** (typogr.) calculation of the composition required, based on the original text. ~ **regressiva** countdown.

contagiante adj. m. + f. contagious, infectious.

contagião s. f. (pl. **-ões**), (obs.) contagion.

contagiar v. 1. to infect, contaminate. 2. to corrupt, defile. 3. to pervert.

contágio s. m. 1. infection, contagion. 2. pollution, corruption.

contagiosidade s. f. contagiousness, infectiveness.

contagioso adj. infectious, contagious, infective, zymotic.

conta-gotas s. m., sg. + pl. dropper, filler.

contaminação s. f. (pl. **-ões**) 1. contamination, infection. 2. pollution. 3. contagion. 4. the interplay of two plots in a Latin comedy (according to the ancient Greek style).

contaminado adj. contaminated, affected, polluted, vitiated.

fui ~ I caught an infection.

contaminador s. m. contaminator, vitiator, corrupter. ‖ adj. contaminative, infective, infectious.

contaminar v. 1. to contaminate, infect. 2. to corrupt. 3. to defile. 4. to affect. 5. to taint, attaint.

contaminável adj. m. + f. (pl. -áveis) contaminable.

contanto que conj. as long as, as, provided that, if, on condition that.

conta-passos s. m., sg. + pl. pedometer.

conta-quilômetros s. m. sg. + pl. speedometer.

contar v. 1. to count. 2. to calculate, reckon. 3. to recount. 4. to number, numerate. 5. to compute. 6. to score. 7. to tell, narrate, relate, report. 8. to confide in, depend on. 9. to include, enclose. 10. to expect, hope for. 11. to respect, esteem. 12. ~-se to consider o. s. ~ com to reckon with, figure on. ~ como segredo to confide. ~ mal to miscount. ~ minuciosamente to describe, tell in details, retail. ~ prosa to boast. ~ uma história to pitch a yarn, spin a yarn, tell a tale. ~ vantagem to talk big, blow, come the heavy, pull the long bow. contamos com o seu auxílio we reckon upon your help. conta-se it is reported. conte-me o segredo! tell me the secret! a ~ de from... on. ela sabe ~ até dez she can count up to ten. ele não é contado entre os melhores he does not rank among the best. não conte com ele! don't trust him for that! não conte histórias do not tell fibs. não conte mais com isto you cannot any more reckon on that, (U. S. A., coll.) you can put that on the ice. quem te contou isto? who told you that? sem ~ os velhos without counting the old ones. vá ~ isso a outro! tell that to the marines! você não pode ~ com ele you can't count on him. você pode ~ comigo you can reckon on me.

contas-correntes s. m., sg. + pl. (com.) current account book.

contatar v. to contact.

contato, contacto s. m. 1. contact. 2. touch, touching. 3. influence. 4. proximity. 5. social or business connection(s). 6. (geol.) surface of contact formed by two different strata of rocks. 7. (electr.) contact (plate M 5). ~ de abertura e fecho (electr.) make and break contact (plate C 9). ~ de agência (advertising) a dealer contact, a go-between. ~ de partida starting contact, starter. ~ de veículos a contact of media. cópia de ~ (phot.) contact print. ele estabelece ~ com he makes contact with. ele rompeu o ~ he broke contact. em ~ com in contact with. entrar em ~ com to get in touch with. entrar em ~ direto to come to close quarters. não quero qualquer ~ com ele I won't touch him with a barge pole. por simples ~ at a touch. sem ~ com out of touch with.

contável adj. m. + f. (pl. -áveis) countable, tellable.

conteira s. f. 1. chape of a scabbard. 2. cascabel of an ancient cannon. 3. trail of a cannon.

conteirar v. to traverse, move crosswise.

conteiro s. m. bead manufacturer or dealer.

contemplação s. f. (pl. -ões) 1. contemplation. 2. meditation, pondering. 3. thought. 4. observation. 5. (fig.) consideration, deference. 6. (fig.) care, kindness. estar perdido em -ões to be lost in contemplation. sem ~ regardless.

contemplador s. m. contemplater. ‖ adj. contemplating.

contemplante adj. m. + f. contemplative, contemplant.

contemplar v. 1. to contemplate. 2. to regard, observe, gaze upon. 3. to meditate, ponder. 4. to admire. 5. to eye with love or devotion. 6. to appreciate. 7. ~-se to contemplate o. s. (self--complacently in a mirror).

contemplativa s. f. 1. faculty of thought. 2. contemplativeness.

contemplatividade s. f. contemplativeness.

contemplativo adj. contemplative, pensive, speculative. ‖ adj. -amente adv. contemplatively.

contemporaneidade s. f. contemporaneousness, contemporariness.

contemporâneo s. m. contemporanian, contemporary, coeval. ‖ adj. contemporaneous, contemporary, coetaneous, coeval. ‖ -amente adv. contemporaneously, coevally.

contemporização s. f. (pl. -ões) temporization, cunctation.

contemporizador s. m. temporizer, cunctator. ‖ adj. temporizing.

contemporizar v. 1. to temporize. 2. to conform (o. s.) to circumstances. 3. to acquiesce, comply with. 4. to give time to, grant a respite to.

contemptível adj. m. + f. (pl. -íveis) contemptible, base, vile, disdainful. ‖ contemptivelmente adv. contemptibly.

contempto s. m. contempt, disdain, scorn, contemptuousness.

contemptor s. m. spurner, despiser, detractor. ‖ adj. contemptuous.

contenção (I) s. f. (pl. -ões) 1. contention. 2. quarrel, dispute. 3. effort. 4. fight. 5. debate, controversy.

contenção (II) s. f. (pl. -ões) restraint, self-restraint.

contencioso s. m. governmental office for litigious matter. ‖ adj. 1. litigious, contentious. 2. doubtful. 3. controversial, disputatious. 4. contestable.

contenda s. f. 1. contention. 2. quarrel, dispute. 3. strife, row, wrangle. 4. fight, battle. 5. dissension. 6. plea.

contendedor s. m. contestant, contender, protagonist.

contender v. 1. to contend. 2. to fight, struggle. 3. to altercate, debate, dispute. 4. to strive for. 5. to challenge. 6. to compete, rival.

contendor s. m. contestant, contender, rival.

contensão s. f. (pl. -ões) 1. endeavour, effort. 2. contention.

contentadiço adj. easily satisfied, moderate.

contentamento s. m. 1. contentment, contentedness. 2. satisfaction. 3. complacence. 4. joy, cheerfulness, exhilaration.

contentar v. 1. to content, satisfy. 2. to suffice. 3. to give pleasure, please. 4. to be or become satisfied. 5. to reconcile. ~-se com a sua sorte to acquiesce in one's fate. ele não se contenta com um simples "não" he won't take "no" for an answer. tenho de ~-me com pouco I must be contented with little.

contentável adj. m. + f. (pl. -áveis) contentable.

contente adj. m. + f. 1. content, contented. 2. cheerful, joyful, hilarious. 3. satisfied. 4. comfortable. 5. happy, glad, pleased. ‖ ~mente adv. contentedly. a notícia me deixou ~ the news made me happy. ele estava muito ~ he was as gay as a cricket. estou ~ de que você gosta disto I am glad you like this.

contento (I) s. m. contentment, joy, satisfaction. a ~ 1. to one's heart's content. 2. satisfactory.

contento (II) s. m. content(s).

conter v. 1. to contain. 2. to enclose, hold within. 3. to comprise, comprehend. 4. to restrain, refrain. 5. to hold back. 6. to repress, check. 7. to moderate. 8. to implicate, imply. 9. to possess. 10. ~-se to refrain from, moderate o. s., curb one's passion. 11. to involve, embrace.

ele se conteve he contained himself, he ruled himself. **estas moedas contêm muito ouro** these coins carry a lot of gold.
contérmino s. m. boundary, limit, conterminousness. ‖ adj. conterminal, conterminous, adjoining.
conterrâneo s. m. fellow citizen, fellow countryman. ‖ adj. belonging to the same country.
contestabilidade s. f. contestability.
contestação s. f. (pl. **-ões**) 1. contestation. 2. plea, defense. 3. answer. 4. disputation, debate. 5. contradiction. 6. disproof. 7. impugnment, impeachment. 8. conformity of testimonies (made by different witnesses).
contestado adj. refuted, contradicted, replied, proved by witnesses.
contestador s. m. contester, impeacher, refuter. ‖ adj. refuting.
contestante s. m. + f. contestant, contester, refuter. ‖ adj. refuting, disputant, adversary.
contestar v. 1. to contest, refute. 2. to bear witness. 3. to agree upon, confirm. 4. to plead, argue. 5. to impugn, impeach. 6. to contradict. 7. to object, oppose o. s. 8. to defy, disprove. 9. to reply.
contestável adj. m. + f. (pl. **-áveis**) 1. contestable. 2. disputable, debatable. 3. litigable, impeachable. 4. exceptionable. 5. challengeable. ‖ **contestavelmente** adv. contestably.
conteste adj. m. + f. corroborative, concurring, confirmatory, confirming the evidence (of another witness).
conteúdo s. m. 1. content(s). 2. matter contained. 3. tenor, gist, purport. 4. subject, matter. ‖ adj. included.
o ~ **da conversa** the meaning of the conversation. o ~ **do romance** the tenor of the novel. o ~ **em álcool** the alcoholic strength.
contexto s. m. 1. context. 2. body of a document. 3. contexture. 4. composition. 5. argument.
contextura s. f. 1. contexture, structure. 2. context.
contido adj. 1. contained. 2. included, enclosed. 3. repressed, pent-up. 4. curbed. 5. moderate.
com ódio ~ with pent rage.
contigo pron. with you, in your company.
contigüidade s. f. 1. contiguousness, contiguity. 2. nearness, proximity. 3. adjacency.
contíguo adj. 1. contiguous. 2. conterminal, conterminous. 3. near, close, proximate. 4. next. 5. neighbouring, adjoining. 6. coadjacent. ‖ **contiguamente** adv. contiguously.
continência s. f. 1. continence. 2. chastity. 3. abstinence. 4. moderation. 5. (mil.) honours, salute. 6. capacity.
continental adj. m. + f. (pl. **-ais**) continental.
continente (I) s. m. 1. (geogr.) continent. 2. (geogr.) mainland. 3. content, container. ‖ adj. m. + f. 1. continental. 2. containing, including.
continente (II) adj. m. + f. chaste, moderate, continent, abstinent.
contingência s. f. 1. contingence, contingency. 2. eventuality, possibility. 3. uncertainty. 4. (phil.) fortuitousness of life. 5. accident.
contingenciamento s. m. (econ., com.) curtailment.
contingente s. m. 1. contingent. 2. quota, proportional share. 3. (mil.) effectives. ‖ adj. m. + f. 1. contingent. 2. doubtful, uncertain. 3. dependent. 4. eventual.
continuação s. f. (pl. **-ões**) 1. continuation, continuance, continuity. 2. sequel, prosecution, sequence. 3. proceeding, procedure. 4. prolongation. 5. train.
continuado adj. continued, continual, prolonged. ‖ **-amente** adv. continuedly, pauselessly, all along.
continuador s. m. continuator, prosecutor. ‖ adj. continuing.

continuar v. 1. to continue. 2. to go on, proceed. 3. to persevere, hold on, pursue. 4. to remain, stay. 5. to prolong, extend. 6. to last. 7. to endure. 8. to prosecute, progress. 9. to resume.
~ **a ser** to continue to be. ~ **ininterruptamente** to follow on, pass on. **a lei continua em vigor** the law remains in force. **a menina continuou com o berreiro** the girl kept on howling. **ele continua em forma** he is still in form, he is still going. **ele continuou falando** he went on talking. **estas planícies continuam até o mar** these plains reach over to the sea. **eu continuo cansado** I am still tired. **eu continuo sem dinheiro** I have no money yet. **o mundo continua** the world goes on. **você não pode** ~ **desta maneira** you can't go on the way you've been.
continuativo adj. continuative.
continuidade s. f. 1. continuity, continuance. 2. permanence, duration.
contínuo s. m. servant, attendant. ‖ adj. 1. continued, continuous, continual. 2. ongoing, successive. 3. incessant, perpetual, constant. 4. unremitting, unabated, pauseless. 5. persistent. 6. enduring. ‖ **continuamente** adv. continuously, forever, unremittingly. **febre -a** (med.) continual fever. **fogo** ~ (mil.) rapid-fire. **provocações -as** constant provocations.
contista s. m. + f. author of stories, story-teller.
conto (I) s. m. 1. narrative, story, tale. 2. fable, yarn. 3. account. 4. invention, tall story. 5. fraud. 6. intrigue.
~ **de aventuras** adventure story. ~ **infantil** fairy tale. ~ **policial** detective story. ~ **popular** folk tale. **livro de** ~s story-book.
conto (II) s. m. 1. number. 2. thousand Cruzeiros (formerly Milréis).
conto (III) s. m. the butt of a lance.
contoada s. f. a blow with the butt of a lance.
conto-do-vigário s. m. (pl. **contos-do-vigário**) (Braz.) confidence trick, swindle.
o **maior** ~ **do século** it was the century's worst swindle.
contorção s. f. (pl. **-ões**) 1. contortion. 2. distortion, twisting.
contorcer v. 1. to contort. 2. to distort, twist. 3. to squirm, writhe. 4. to screw. 5. to strain.
~ **o rosto** to screw one's face up, twitch one's face. **ele se contorceu de dores** he was convulsed with pain. **seu rosto se contorceu de dor** his face worked with pain.
contorcionista, contorcista s. m. + f. contortionist, distortionist.
contornar, contornear v. 1. to contour. 2. to profile. 3. to turn round, wind round. 4. profile. 5. to round. 6. to bypass.
contornável adj. m. + f. possible of being bypassed.
contorneado adj. contorniate.
contorno s. m. 1. contour, configuration. 2. form, shape, outline. 3. profile. 4. circuit, periphery.
contra s. m. 1. objection. 2. opposition. 3. obstacle. 4. reply, refutation, rebuttal. ‖ adv. contra, contrariwise, adversely, dissentingly. ‖ prep. against, counter to, contrary to, versus, athwart.
bater ~ to hit against. ~ **a lei** against the law, lawlessly. ~ **os bons costumes** against morals. ~ **pagamento à vista** for cash down. **fê-lo** ~ **sua vontade** he was slow to do it. **ela lhe deu o** ~ she gave him the brush-off (or the mitten). **eu dei o** ~ I opposed myself to it. **isto fala** ~ **ele** that is against him. **lutar** ~ to fight against. **os prós e** ~s the pros and cons. **sou** ~ **a guerra** I am against war.
contra-abertura s. f. (pl. **contra-aberturas**) counter-opening, counter-fissure.

contra-alísio s. m. (pl. **contra-alísios**) (meteor.) antitrades.

contra-almirante s. m. (pl. **contra-almirantes**) rear-admiral.

contra-amura s. f. (pl. **contra-amuras**), (naut.) tack, tackle.

contra-atacar v. to counter-attack.

contra-ataque s. m. (pl. **contra-ataques**) counter-attack.

contrabaixista s. m. + f. (mus.) contrabass player or singer.

contrabaixo s. m. (mus.) contrabass, double-bass, violone.

contrabalançado adj. equilibrative, counterbalanced, compensated.

contrabalançar v. 1. to counterbalance, counterpoise. 2. to counteract, neutralize. 3. to compensate, equilibrate. 4. to counterweigh. 5. to countervail.

contrabalanço s. m. 1. counterweight. 2. compensation.

contrabandear v. to smuggle, contraband, run goods.

contrabandista s. m. + f. 1. contrabandist, smuggler. 2. runner. 3. bootlegger, moonshiner. 4. peddler, hawker.

contrabando s. m. 1. illegal commerce, prohibited traffic. 2. smuggled goods. 3. smuggling, running (illegal goods), contraband. 4. wrong or unlawful behaviour. 5. (fig.) dubious affair. 6. low people, populace.
de ~ 1. illicitly, illegally. 2. contraband, smuggled. (sl.) bootleg. **mercadoria de** ~ prohibited goods.

contrabater v. to repel, counter-attack, counter-fire.

contrabateria s. f. counterbattery.

contrabordo s. m. (naut.) used in the locution **a ~ de** alongside of.

contrabracear v. (naut.) to counter-brace.

contrabraço s. m. (naut.) counter-brace.

contracadaste s. m. (naut.) inner post.

contracaixa s. f. (typogr.) the right side of the upper type case.

contracambiar v. 1. to counterchange. 2. to pay badly, short-change. 3. to exchange, swap. 4. to repay badly a good turn, be ungrateful.

contracâmbio s. m. 1. counterchange. 2. re-exchange. 3. act of short-changing.

contracanto s. m. (mus.) a word or phrase sung in response to the principal theme.

contração s. f. (pl. **-ões**) 1. contraction. 2. (anat.) retraction or shrinking of organs. 3. shrinking. 4. (med.) convulsion. 5. (gram.) coalescence of two or more vowels. 6. constringency.

contracapa s. f. (typogr.) inside cover (of a book).

contracédula s. f. counter-deed, annulment, defeasance.

contracena s. f. (theat.) background action on the open scene.

contracenar v. (theat.) to express or represent by pantomime.

contracepção s. f. contraception.

contraceptivo s. m. contraceptive. ‖ adj. contraceptive.

contracheque s. m. (com.) a paycheck voucher.

contrachoque s. m. countershock.

contracifra s. f. key to a code or cipher.

contracobra s. f. shrub of the family Verbenaceae (Aegiphila salutaris).

contracolagem s. f. (typogr.) the act of glueing the end paper to the colour flyleaf.

contracolar v. (typogr.) to glue the end paper to the colour flyleaf.

contracorrente s. f. countercurrent, backset, eddy.

contracosta s. f. the opposite shore or coastline.

contracunhar v. to coin again, recoin.

contracunho s. m. counterpunch.

contradança s. f. square dance, contra-dance, quadrille.

contradançar v. to execute a square dance.

contradição s. f. (pl. **-ões**) 1. contradiction. 2. contradictoriness. 3. incoherence, incoherency, variance. 4. disclaiming, denial, disavowal. 5. opposition.
ela caiu em -ões she became entangled in contradictions. **espírito de** ~ spirit of contradiction. **sem** ~ unquestionable, incontestable.

contradita s. f. (jur.) objection, refutation, impugnation.

contraditado adj. contested, impugned.

contraditar v. 1. to contradict. 2. to oppose. 3. to refute, disprove. 4. to contest, deny. 5. to impugn.

contraditável adj. m. + f. (pl. **-áveis**) contradictable.

contradito adj. contradicted, refuted, denied.

contraditor s. m. contradicter, denier, gainsayer, impugner. ‖ adj. 1. contradictory, contradictive, contradictious. 2. discordant, conflicting. 3. incoherent.

contraditório adj. 1. contradictory, contradictive, contradictious. 2. discordant, conflicting. 3. incoherent. 4. gainsaying. 5. inconsecutive, inconsistent. ‖ **contraditoriamente** adv. contradictorily, contradictively.

contradizer v. 1. to contradict. 2. to contest, refute. 3. to gainsay, speak against. 4. to deny, disaffirm. 5. to oppose. 6. to impugn. 7. **~-se** to contradict o. s., eat one's words.
ele contradisse minha declaração he contradicted my statement. **estas afirmativas se contradizem** these statements contradict each other.

contra-emboscada s. f. (pl. **contra-emboscadas**) counterambush.

contraente s. m. + f. contrahent, contracting party. ‖ adj. contracting, contrahent.

contra-erva s. f. (pl. **contra-ervas**), (bot.) contrayerva.

contra-escarpa s. f. (pl. **contra-escarpas**), (fort.) counterscarp.

contra-escota s. f. (pl. **contra-escotas**), (naut.) preventer.

contra-escritura s. f. (pl. **contra-escrituras**) counter-deed, defeasance.

contra-espionagem s. f. (pl. **contra-espionagens**) counterintelligence, counter-espionage.

contra-estais s. f. pl. (naut.) preventer.

contra-estímulo s. m. (pl. **contra-estímulos**) counter-incentive.

contrafação s. f. (pl. **-ões**) 1. counterfeit, fake, forgery. 2. imitation.

contrafaixa s. f. (her.) counterfess.

contrafaixado adj. (her.) counterfessed.

contrafator s. m. counterfeiter, faker, forger.

contrafazedor s. m. 1. counterfeiter, forger. 2. imitator.

contrafazer v. 1. to counterfeit, fake. 2. to imitate. 3. to falsify. 4. to disguise, conceal. 5. to restrain, curb.

contrafé s. f. authenticated copy of a deed or summons.

contrafecho s. m. (archit.) the voussoirs adjacent to the keystone.

contrafeição s. f. (pl. **-ões**) 1. counterfeit, fake, forgery. 2. imitation.

contrafeito (I) s. m. eaves board.

contrafeito (II) s. m. forgery, counterfeit. ‖ adj. 1. counterfeit, false. 2. constrained, coerced.

contrafilé s. m. (Braz.) sirloin.

contrafileira s. f. 1. a row behind another one. 2. counterguard. 3. (archit.) strut (of a roof).

contrafixa s. f. (archit.) strut (of a roof).

contrafixo s. m. (mech.) cap of a bearing.

contrafloreado adj. (her.) counterflory.

contraforma s. f. (typogr.) in colour printing, the second and following forms.

contraforte s. m. 1. counter: a stiffener of leather around the heel of a shoe upper. 2. (fort.) counterfort. 3. (constr.) buttress. 4. foothill or mountain which runs parallel or crosswise to a mountain range.

contrafrechal s. m. (pl. -ais), (constr.) pole plate (of a roof).

contrafuga s. f. (mus.) counterfugue.

contrafundo adj. downwards.

contrage s. f. spoke of the great wheel in a sugar-mill.

contragolpe s. m. 1. counterblow. 2. counterplot. 3. (sports) backstroke, ripost(e), backhand.

contragosto s. m. dislike, aversion, antipathy.

contraguarda s. f. (fort.) counterguard.

contraído adj. contracted, tight, shrunken, narrow.

contra-indicação s. f. (pl. contra-indicações), (med.) counterindication.

contra-indicar v. (med.) to counterindicate, contraindicate.

contra-informação s. f. (pl. contra-informações) counterintelligence.

contrair v. to contract: 1. tighten, constrict, constringe, compress. 2. reduce. 3. shorten. 4. make narrower. 5. make a contract. 6. acquire, catch. 7. stipulate. 8. ~-se shrink, shrivel.
~ matrimônio to espouse, wed. eles ~am núpcias they got married. nós contraímos dívidas we ran into debts.

contraível adj. m. + f. (pl. -íveis) contractible, contractile.

contralto s. m. (mus.) contralto.

contraluz s. f. counter-light.

contramalha s. f. double mesh.

contramalhar v. to double mesh.

contramandado s. m. counterorder, countermand.

contramandar v. to countermand.

contramangas s. f. pl. oversleeves.

contramão s. f. (Braz.) the opposite direction of a one-way street.

contramarca s. f. 1. countermark. 2. theater ticket stub.

contramarcar v. to countermark.

contramarcha s. f. countermarch.

contramarchar v. to countermarch.

contramaré s. f. neaptide.

contramargem s. f. (pl. -ens) a tract of marginal land.

contramedida s. f. counteraction.

contramestra s. f. forewoman.

contramestre s. m. 1. foreman. 2. foremanship. 3. (naut.) boatswain. 4. overseer, overlooker.

contramezena s. f. (naut.) mizzenmast.

contramina s. f. 1. countermine. 2. counterplot.

contraminar v. to countermine, counterplot, frustrate.

contraminuta s. f. (jur.) the written reasons presented by a claimee in response to a claimant.

contramoldagem s. f. (pl. -ens) countermoulding.

contramoldar v. to countermould.

contramolde s. m. countermould.

contramovimento s. m. countermovement.

contramurar v. to countermure, (fig.) defend.

contramuro s. m. countermure.

contranatural adj. m. + f. (pl. -ais) counternatural.

contranaturalidade s. f. unnaturalness.

contranitência s. f. (phys.) resistance.

contranitente adj. m. + f. resisting, resistant, repulsive.

contranivelar v. (surv.) to cross-level.

contra-ofensiva s. f. (pl. contra-ofensivas) (mil.) counter-offensive.

contra-oferta s. f. (pl. contra-ofertas) counterproposal.

contra-oitava s. f. (pl. contra-oitavas), (mus.) contraoctave.

contra-ordem s. f. (pl. contra-ordens) counterorder, countermand.

contra-ordenar v. to countermand, give contrary orders, revoke.

contrapala s. f. (her.) counterpale.

contraparente s. m. + f. 1. a distant relation. 2. kinship by marriage.

contraparentesco s. m. 1. distant relationship. 2. quality or state of being related by marriage.

contraparte s. f. (mus.) counterpart.

contrapartida s. f. a book entry made in compensation of an entry on another account.

contrapassantes adj. m. + f. pl. (her.) counterpassant.

contrapasso s. m. 1. counterstep, short dance-step. 2. (mil.) change of step.

contrapé s. m. 1. (cards) partner who plays before the forehand. 2. support, prop.

contrapeçonha s. f. (pop.) counterpoison, antidote.

contrapelo s. m. position or movement against the grain.
a ~ against the grain, the wrong way.

contrapesar v. 1. to counterpoise. 2. to counterbalance. 3. to compensate. 4. to compare, examine, consider.

contrapeso (ê) s. m. 1. (pl. contrapesos) counterweight. 2. counterpoise, equipoise. 3. counterbalance (plate D 1). 4. balance weight. 5. (fig.) compensation amends.
alavanca de ~ balance level.

contrapilastra s. f. (archit.) counterpillar, buttress, counterpilaster.

contrapino s. m. cotter pin, cotter key, forelock (plate P 4).

contrapontado adj. (her.) counterpointed.

contraponteador s. m. (pop.) habitual objector.

contrapontear v. 1. (mus.) to compose in counterpoint. 2. (pop.) to disappoint, annoy. 3. (pop.) to contradict.

contrapontista s. m. + f. (mus.) contrapuntist, polyphonist.

contrapontístico adj. (mus.) contrapuntal, polyphonic.

contraponto s. m. (mus.) counterpoint, polyphony, art of composing polyphonic music.

contrapor v. 1. to put against, oppose. 2. to put in front of. 3. to compare, collate. 4. to expose, show simultaneously (two or more objects). 5. to refute. 6. to interpose. 7. ~-se to oppose o. s. to.

contraporca s. f. lock-nut, check-nut (plate P 4).

contraposição s. f. (pl. -ões) 1. contraposition. 2. (fig.) opposition, resistance. 3. antithesis. 4. contrast. 5. reluctance.

contraposto adj. opposed, opposite, contrary.

contraprestação s. f. (jur.) reciprocal fulfilment of obligations in a bilateral contract.

contraproducente adj. m. + f. producing the opposite result, self-defeating, miscarrying.

contrapropaganda s. f. counterpropaganda.

contrapropor v. to make a counterproposal.

contraproposta s. f. counterproposal.

contraprotesto s. m. counterprotest.

contraprova s. f. 1. (jur.) impugnation. 2. (jur.) counterevidence, alibi. 3. (typogr.) second proof, counter-proof. 4. (logics) elenchus.

contraprovar v. 1. to counterprove. 2. to produce counterevidence. 3. (jur.) to upset an indictment.

contrapunção s. m. (typogr.) counterpunch.

contrapunho s. m. (naut.) tack tackle.

contraquarteado adj. (her.) counterquartered.

contraquartel s. m. (pl. -éis), (her.) counterquarter.
contraquilha s. f. (naut.) false keel.
contra-rapantes adj. m. + f. pl. (her.) counterrampant.
contra-regra s. m. (pl. contra-regras), (theat.) stage manager, prompter.
contra-reparo s. m. (pl. contra-reparos), (fort.) counter-approaches.
contra-réplica s. f. (pl. contra-réplicas), (jur.) rejoinder.
contra-retábulo s. m. (pl. contra-retábulos) altar-piece.
contra-revolução s. f. (pl. contra-revoluções) counter-revolution.
contrariado adj. vexed, annoyed, upset.
contrariador s. m. contradictor, opposer, gainsayer. ‖ adj. contradicting.
contrariante adj. m. + f. contrariant, opposing, antagonistic.
contrariar v. 1. to counter, counteract. 2. to oppose, contest. 3. to refute. 4. to antagonize. 5. to contradict. 6. to thwart. 7. to disappoint, vex. 8. to frustrate. 9. to hinder, embarrass. 10. to transgress.
contrariável adj. m. + f. (pl. -áveis) contradictable, disputable.
contrariedade s. f. 1. opposition, resistance. 2. contrariety, contrariness. 3. difficulty, setback. 4. anger, annoyance. 5. worry, vexation, anxiety. 6. (jur.) rejoinder.
contrário s. m. opponent, adversary, enemy, rival. ‖ adj. 1. contrary, contrariant. 2. opposite, opposed. 3. adverse, antagonistic. 4. inverse. 5. unfavourable. 6. negative. 7. unconformable. 8. discrepant. 9. repugnant. ‖ contrariamente adv. oppositely, adversely, unfavourably, repugnantly, negatively.
absolutamente ~ dead against. ao ~ on the contrary, to the contrary, unlike, the other way about. caso ~ otherwise. do ~ if not, else, otherwise. eu sou decididamente ~ I am full against. foi ~ aos meus planos it ran counter to my plans. foi o ~ it was the reverse. isto é ~ a tudo que tenho acreditado that is in contrast to all I have believed. justamente o ~ just the opposite. muito ao ~ much the reverse. pelo ~ on the contrary. vento ~ counterblast.
contra-rotura, contra-ruptura s. f. (pl. contra-roturas, contra-rupturas) (surg.) contrarupture, double rupture. ‖ adj. preventing or healing ruptures.
contra-selar v. to counterseal.
contra-selo s. m. (pl. contra-selos) counterseal.
contra-senha s. f. (pl. contra-senhas) 1. watchword, password. 2. counter-ticket, stub. 3. countersign, signal.
contra-senso s. m. (pl. contra-sensos) 1. nonsense, absurdity. 2. incongruity.
contra-significação s. f. (pl. contra-significações) opposite meaning, countersignification.
contra-sinal s. m. (pl. contra-sinais) 1. watchword, password. 2. countersign, signal. 3. dissimulation, disguise.
contra-soca s. f. (pl. contra-socas), (Braz.) the fourth cutting of sugar cane.
contrastado adj. contrasted.
contrastante adj. m. + f. contrasting, contradistinctive.
contrastar v. 1. to contrast, form a contrast. 2. to fight against. 3. to oppose, withstand. 4. to defy, affront. 5. to counteract. 6. to appraise, evaluate. 7. to assay.
contrastaria s. f. an assayer's office.
contrastável adj. m. + f. (pl. -áveis) contrastable.
contraste s. m. 1. contrast. 2. opposition. 3. assay. 4. assayer. 5. set-off, difference. 6. clash, dispute, quarrel. 7. nuance, delicate gradations of light or hues.

ele e seu pai formam um grande ~ he is a great contrast to his father. que ~ com a vida em Londres! what a far cry from life in London!
contrasteação s. f. (pl. -ões) act of contrasting, contrastment.
contrasteador s. m. assayer, appraiser.
contrastear v. to evaluate, appraise, assay.
contrata s. f. 1. act of contracting temporary services. 2. (pop.) contract, agreement. 3. engagement.
contratação s. f. (pl. -ões) 1. act of contracting. 2. contract, agreement. 3. traffic, trade, dealing.
contratado adj. agreed upon.
contratador s. m. contractor. ‖ adj. contracting.
contratante s. m. + f. contractor, covenanter, contracting party. ‖ adj. m + f. contracting.
contratar v. 1. to contract, enter into mutual obligations. 2. to stipulate, agree upon. 3. to engage, hire. 4. to acquire by contract. 5. to deal, trade. 6. to bargain. 7. to charter. 8. to undertake. 9. ~-se to take employment for wages, give one's services for hire.
eu estou contratado para I am under engagement to. o direito de ~ e despedir the right to hire and dismiss, (sl.) to hire and fire.
contratável adj. m. + f. (pl. -áveis) contractable, negotiable.
contratelar v. to provide old paintings with a protective linen reinforcement.
contratempo (I) s. m. 1. mischance, mishap. 2. accident. 3. backset, check. 4. disappointment, annoyance. 5. obstacle, hindrance.
contratempo (II) s. m. 1. (mus.) contretemps, syncopation. 2. ancient dance step.
contrátil, contráctil adj. m. + f. (pl. -eis) contractile, contractible.
contratilidade, contractilidade s. f. contractibility, contractility.
contratista s. m. (Braz.) sharecropper of a cacao plantation.
contrativo, contractivo adj. contractive.
contrato s. m. 1. contract. 2. covenant, agreement. 3. deed. 4. bargain. 5. engagement. 6. settlement. 7. commerce, traffic.
~ de casamento marriage contract, marriage settlement, covenant of marriage, betrothal. ~ de sociedade social contract, deed of partnership. ~ de trabalho labour agreement. ~ formal formal contract. ~ selado contract under seal. fechar um ~ to make a contract. firmei um ~ de trabalho com ele I contracted with him for work. fiz um ~ I made a contract.
contratorpedeiro s. m. torpedo-boat destroyer.
~-escolta an escort torpedo-boat destroyer. ~-líder a larger torpedo-boat destroyer with quarters for a fleet commander and his general staff.
contratrilho s. m. (railway) guardrail (plate V 4).
contratual adj. m. + f. (pl. -ais) contractual, pactional.
contratualismo s. m. philosophical doctrine which considers the State as a contract existing between the sovereign and the people.
contratura s. f. act or result of contracting.
contravalação s. f. (pl. -ões), (fort.) contravallation.
contravalar v. (fort.) to erect contravallations.
contravapor s. m. 1. countersteam. 2. (pop.) immediate reaction.
contraveirado adj. (her.) countervairy.
contraveiro s. m. (her.) countervair.
contravenção s. f. (pl. -ões) 1. contravention. 2. infraction. 3. transgression, trespass. 4. violation, breach (of contract).
contraveneno s. m. counterpoison, antidote.

contraveniente s. m. + f. contravener, transgressor, offender, forfeiter. ‖ adj. contravening.
contravento s. m. 1. wind screen. 2. windbreak. 3. window shutter. 4. (naut.) a strong headwind, contrary wind.
contraventor s. m. contravener, transgressor, offender, forfeitor. ‖ adj. contravening, transgressing, forfeiting.
contraversão s. f. (pl. -ões) contraversion, inversion.
contraverter v. 1. to invert. 2. to return to the opposite side. 3. to misinterpret. 4. to put in confusion.
contravigia s. f. (Braz.) a small raft used by fishermen.
contravir v. 1. to reply, answer. 2. to retort. 3. to transgress, contravene. 4. to violate a law, rule or regulation. 5. to infringe, commit a breach of.
contravolta s. f. turn, twist, counterturn.
contrectação s. f. (pl. -ões), (jur.) expropriation.
contribuição s. f. (pl. -ões) 1. contribution. 2. quota, share. 3. assessment. 4. tribute, tax. 5. donation, offering. 6. subscription. 7. rate. 8. (gambling) ante.
contribuidor s. m. contributor. ‖ adj. contributory.
contribuinte s. m. + f. 1. contributor. 2. taxpayer, ratepayer. ‖ adj. contributory, tributary, contributive.
contribuir v. 1. to contribute. 2. to pay taxes. 3. to donate, give. 4. to add to, cooperate. 5. to concur, bear a part. 6. to pay contributions. 7. to furnish. **ele contribui para o sucesso** he is accessory to the success. **eles ~am para o seu êxito** they put him in way of success. **isso contribuiu muito para convencer-me** this went far to convince me. **isto ~á muito para melhorar a situação** this will go a long way to improve the situation.
contributário s. m. contributor, taxpayer, contributory. ‖ adj. contributory, tributary.
contributivo adj. contributive, subscriptive, contributory.
contrição s. f. (pl. -ões) 1. contrition, contriteness. 2. sorrow. 3. repentance, remorse.
contristação s. f. (pl. -ões) sadness, sorrow, affliction.
contristador s. m. griever, afflicter. ‖ adj. grievous. afflicting, afflictive.
contristar v. 1. to make very sad, grieve. 2. to afflict, distress. 3. **~-se** to feel sorry.
contrito adj. 1. contrite. 2. sorrowful, sorry. 3. compunctious. 4. remorseful, penitent. ‖ **-amente** adv. contritely.
contro interj. (naut.) forwards!, onwards!
controlado adj. 1. dispassionate, self-possessed. 2. sober-minded. 3. managed, supervised. 4. ruled, dominated. 5. curbed, checked. **ele é muito ~** he has great command over himself.
controlador s. m. supervisor, controller. ‖ adj. controlling.
controlar v. to control: 1. supervise, manage, boss. 2. dominate, hold in leash, bridle, master. 3. curb, check. 4. guide. 5. rein, rule. **~ alguém** to keep tab on s. o. **ele controlou suas paixões** he contained his passion.
controlável adj. m. + f. (pl. -áveis) controllable, manageable.
controle (ô) s. m. 1. control, controlment. 2. regulation. 3. direction, management. 4. domination, rule, command, upper hand. 5. arrestment, check. 6. reserve, restraint. 7. (mech.) any mechanical controlling device. **alavanca de ~** switching handle. **~ de ar do carburador** choke-control. **~ sobre si mesmo** self-discipline. **de difícil ~** unwieldy. **estar sob o ~ de uma pessoa** to be under a person's thumb. **perder**

o ~ to lose self-control, see red. **sem ~** undisciplined. **ter o ~ do dinheiro** to bear the bag.
controlista s. m. + f. (Braz., naut.) an intermediate between ship and agent.
controvérsia s. f. 1. controversy. 2. contest, contestation. 3. dispute, debate. 4. difference. 5. argumentation.
controversial adj. m. + f. (pl. -ais) controversial, argumentative, eristic(al).
controversista s. m. + f. controvertist, controversialist, disputer, polemist.
controverso adj. controversial, contentious, litigious.
controverter v. 1. to controvert, invert. 2. to dispute, debate, discuss. 3. to misinterpret. 4. to deny, contradict. 5. to impugn, object to.
controvertível adj. m. + f. (pl. -íveis) controvertible, controversial, disputable, arguable.
contubernal s. m. + f. (pl. -ais) commensal, contubernal. ‖ adj. contubernal, commensal, living together.
contubernar-se v. to cohabit, live with, dwell together as husband and wife.
contubérnio s. m. 1. contubernium. 2. cohabitation, concubinage. 3. familiarity, close companionship. 4. tent.
contudo conj. however, yet, although, nevertheless.
contumácia s. f. 1. contumacy, contumaciousness. 2. obstinacy, stubbornness. 3. disobedience. 4. (jur.) contempt of court.
contumaz s. m. + f. contumacious person. ‖ adj. contumacious.
contumélia s. f. 1. contumely, contumeliousness. 2. insult, outrage. 3. reproach.
contumelioso adj. contumelious, outrageous, shameful, contemptuous.
contundente adj. m. + f. contusing, bruising.
contundir v. 1. to contuse, bruise, injure. 2. to squash, squeeze. 3. to grind, crush.
conturbação s. f. (pl. -ões) 1. agitation. 2. disturbance. 3. riot, tumult. 4. trouble. 5. act of disturbing.
conturbador s. m. trouble rouser, disturber. ‖ adj. disorderly, turbulent, disturbing.
conturbar v. 1. to disturb, perturb. 2. to excite, stir up. 3. to alter, change. 4. to confound, perplex. 5. **~-se** to become vexed or troubled.
conturbativo adj. irritating, alarming, disturbing.
contusão s. f. (pl. -ões) 1. contusion, bruise. 2. (fig.) impression. 3. notch, dent, indentation. 4. resentment, hurt feelings.
contuso adj. contused, bruised.
conubial adj. m. + f. (pl. -ais) connubial, nuptial.
conúbio s. m. marriage, wedding, matrimony.
conurbação s. f. conurbation.
convalária s. f. (bot.) lily of the valley.
convale adj. m. + f. of or designating a white lily.
convalescença s. f. convalescence, recovery from disease. **entrar em ~** to be convalescent.
convalescente s. m. + f. convalescent. ‖ adj. convalescent.
convalescer v. 1. to convalesce, recover. 2. to regain health or forces. 3. to fortify, strengthen.
convalidar v. 1. to validate. 2. to re-establish the validity of.
convecção s. f. (pl. -ões), (phys.) convection.
convelir v. 1. to displace, remove. 2. to subvert, upset. 3. to overturn, overthrow. 4. to destroy. 5. to convulse.
convenção s. f. (pl. -ões) 1. convention(s). 2. covenant, agreement. 3. compact, pact. 4. formality. **~ social** social convention. **~ teatral** theatrical convention.
convencedor adj. convincing.

convencer v. 1. to convince. 2. to persuade. 3. to overcome, subdue. 4. to prove guilty. 5. to make s. o. acknowledge his (her) guilt. 6. to argue. **convencemo-nos de que...** we persuaded ourselves that. **convenci-o da necessidade** I impressed the necessity on him. **convenci-o do seu erro** I convicted him of his error. **ela me convenceu** she carried conviction to me. **ele convenceu-me da sua honestidade** he convinced me of his honesty. **ele convenceu a corte** he satisfied the court. **ele convenceu-o** he persuaded him, talked him round. **ele não se deixa ~** he won't be dissuaded, talked out of it. **procurar ~ uma pessoa** to argue with a person.

convencido adj. 1. convinced. 2. satisfied, assured. 3. sure of o. s. 4. (pop.) conceited, vain. 5. smart-alecky, stand-offish.
ele é muito ~ de si mesmo he is full of conceit, (coll.) he thinks no small beer of himself. **ele está ~ de que** he has a notion that. **estou ~ da sinceridade dele** I am assured of his good faith. **estou ~ de que** I feel confident that. **pode ficar ~ disto** you may rest assured of that.

convencimento s. m. 1. act or result of convincing. 2. argument, persuasion. 3. satisfaction. 4. self-importance.

convencionado adj. stipulated, agreed upon, covenanted.

convencional s. m. + f. (pl. **-ais**) conventional, conventionalist. ‖ adj. 1. conventional. 2. stipulated, contractual. 3. usual, customary. 4. formal. 5. academic(al).

convencionalidade s. f. conventionality.

convencionalismo s. m. conventionalism.

convencionalista s. m. + f. 1. conventional, conventionalist. 2. (phil.) formalist. ‖ adj. conventional.

convencionar v. 1. to stipulate, arrange definitely. 2. to contract. 3. to agree upon. 4. to arbitrate.

convencível adj. m. + f. (pl. **-íveis**) convincible.

conveniência s. f. 1. convenience. 2. appropriateness. suitability, seasonableness. 3. fittingness, becomingness. 4. advantage, profit. 5. expedience. 6. advisability. 7. **~s** pl. social rules. 8. favourableness.
não vejo nenhuma ~ nisto I do not see any advantage therein. **por ~** for convenience. **por ~ própria** in one's own benefit.

conveniente adj. m. + f. 1. convenient. 2. suitable, fitting. 3. befitting, seemingly, becoming. 4. useful, advantageous. 5. decent, proper. 6. favourable. 7. right.
acho ~ ir I think it fit to go. **é ~ fazê-lo** it is fit to do it. **é muito ~ para mim** it is a great convenience to me. **não é ~** it is not fit. **o livro mais ~ é este** this is the most suitable book. **se for ~ para você** if you can make it convenient.

convênio s. m. 1. convention. 2. covenant, accord. 3. concordat. 4. international pact.

conventicular adj. m. + f. 1. conventicular. 2. clandestine.

conventículo s. m. 1. conventicle. 2. secret meeting. 3. collusion, connivance. 4. conspiracy.

conventilho s. m. (pop.) brothel.

convento s. m. convent, cloister, monastery.
~ de freiras nunnery.

conventual s. m. + f. (pl. **-ais**) conventual, inmate of a convent. ‖ adj. conventual.

conventualidade s. f. permanent residence in a convent.

convergência s. f. convergence.

convergente adj. m. + f. convergent, converging.

convergir v. to converge, tend to one point, approach one center.

conversa (I) s. f. 1. conversation. 2. talk, talking. 3. speech, discourse. 4. consultation, collocution. 5. comment. 6. small talk, gabble, chatter. 7. understanding, adjustment of differences.
~ fiada idle talk, drivel, clitter-clatter, poppycock. **~ inútil** talky talk. **~ mole** fiddle-faddle, claptrap. **dois dedos de ~** a bit of small talk. **fazer ~ fiada** to talk idly. **ele teve uma ~ particular com ela** he had a private talk with her, he was closeted with her. **é o assunto da ~ da cidade** it's the talk of the town. **muita ~ a respeito de nada** much ado about nothing.

conversa (II) s. f. a lay sister in a nunnery.

conversação s. f. (pl. **-ões**) 1. conversation. 2. colloquy, converse, palaver. 3. interview. 4. discourse. 5. (fig.) companionship, familiarity.

conversadeira s. f. a double chair or bench (the seats of which face each other), a kind of love seat.

conversado s. m. sweetheart, lover.

conversador s. m. converser, conversationalist, proser. ‖ adj. conversational, chatty, gabby.

conversa-fiada s. m. + f. (pl. **conversas-fiadas**) person who has no intention to make good his (her) promises; boaster.

conversante adj. m. + f. talking, conversable, conversant, disposed to converse, conversational.

conversão s. f. (pl. **-ões**) 1. conversion, commutation. 2. (sociology) converse, convertite. 3. change, alteration. 4. (mech.) reduction. 5. transformation.

conversar v. 1. to converse, chat, talk. 2. to discourse. 3. to visit (with), be familiar (with). 4. to consult (with). 5. to confabulate. 6. to live or reside with.
eu preciso ~ com você I must have a word with you. **vamos ~ mais tarde a respeito** we shall discuss that later. **vou ~ com o travesseiro** I shall take counsel of my pillow.

conversável adj. m. + f. (pl. **-áveis**) conversable, sociable, easy.

conversibilidade s. f. conversibility.

conversível adj. m. + f. (pl. **-íveis**) convertible, reducible, exchangeable, reciprocal.

conversivo adj. conversive.

converso (I) s. m. 1. conversation. 2. colloquy, converse. 3. parlour, visiting room.

converso (II) s. m. 1. convert. 2. lay brother who lives or works in a convent. ‖ adj. converted.

conversor s. m. (electr., met.) converter.

convertedor s. m. converter. ‖ adj. converting.

converter v. 1. to convert, proselyte. 2. to transform, transubstantiate. 3. to invert. 4. to reduce. 5. to change. 6. **~-se**: a) to be or become converted. b) (pop.) to turn round.
~ ao cristianismo to Christianize. **~ em** to turn into. **~ em capital** to capitalize. **ele converteu-se ao cristianismo** he turned Christian.

convertibilidade s. f. convertibility.

convertido s. m. convert, proselyte. ‖ adj. converted, regenerate.

convertimento s. m. conversion.

convertível adj. m. + f. (pl. **-íveis**) convertible.

convés s. m. (naut.) deck (of a ship), ship-board.
~ corrido flush-deck. **~ da ré** after-deck. **sob o ~** under hatches. **~ superior** hurricane-deck.

convescote s. m. picnic.

convexidade s. f. 1. convexity, convexness. 2. (tech.) camber.

convexirrostro adj. (ornith.) convexorostrate.

convexo adj. convex, curved, rounded.

convexo-côncavo adj. convex-concave.

convicção s. f. (pl. **-ões**) 1. conviction. 2. certitude, certainty. 3. confidence, belief. 4. persuasion. 5. assurance.

~ **plena** positiveness. **eles têm as mesmas -ões** they are like-minded. **poder de** ~ cogency.
convício s. m. insult, affront, outrage.
convicioso adj. offensive, outrageous.
convicto s. m. convicted criminal, convict. ‖ adj. 1. convinced, assured, persuaded. 2. convicted, sentenced.
convidado s. m. guest, visitor, one who received an invitation. ‖ adj. invited.
ele foi meu ~ he was a guest at my house.
convidador s. m. inviter, host.
convidar v. 1. to invite. 2. to ask, bid. 3. to attract, tempt. 4. to summon. 5. to treat. 6. ~-**se:** a) to offer o. s., make a proffer. b) to consider o. s. invited.
convidei-o para o almoço I asked him to lunch. **convide-o para subir** ask him upstairs. **ele convidou-me para ir à sua casa** he asked me to his house. **mandar** ~ **uma pessoa** to send for a person.
convidativo adj. inviting, invitory. ‖ -**amente** adv. invitingly.
convincente adj. m. + f. 1. convincing. 2. strong, potent, powerful. 3. cogent, conclusive. 4. forcible, evincible, evincive. 5. weighty. 6. valid. ‖ ~**mente** adv. convincingly.
teoria ~ tenable theory. **uma conclusão** ~ a suasive conclusion.
convindo adj. convenient, suitable, acceptable.
convinhável adj. m. + f. (pl. -**áveis**) convenient, suitable.
convir v. 1. to agree to, be suitable. 2. to beho(o)ve, beseem, befit. 3. to correspond. 4. to go well together. 5. to coincide. 6. to fit, do. 7. to comport. 8. to be convenient, useful or proper.
agora não me convém mais now it does not suit me any more, now the shoe is on the other foot. **convém notar** it is worthy of notice. **ele sabe o que lhe convém** he knows what suits him best. **ele trabalha quando lhe convém** he works when he feels like it. **farei o que me convier** I shall do as I choose. **isto não convém** that will not do. ...**qualquer tempo que lhe convier!** ...any time that suits your convenience.
convite s. m. 1. invitation. 2. call, convocation. 3. engagement. 4. donation, gift. 5. banquet.
aceitei o ~ I accepted the invitation. **eu tenho um** ~ **para segunda-feira** I am engaged on Monday.
conviva s. m. + f. commensal, feaster, banqueter, guest.
convival adj. m. + f. (pl. -**ais**) convival, convivial, festive.
convivência s. m. 1. act or result of living in society. 2. company, companionship. 3. acquaintanceship. 4. familiarity, intimacy. 5. sociability.
convivente s. m. + f. 1. sociable person. 2. friend, companion. ‖ adj. affable, sociable, convivial, familiar.
conviver v. 1. to live together, cohabit. 2. to be familiar or intimate with. 3. to be sociable.
convívio s. m. 1. banquet. 2. society. 3. conviviality. 4. social contact. 5. familiarity, intimacy.
convizinhança s. f. neighbourhood.
convizinhar v. 1. to be or live in the neighbourhood. 2. to be similar, resemble. 3. to approach, come nearer.
convizinho s. m. neighbour. ‖ adj. 1. neighbouring, bordering. 2. near. 3. (fig.) similar, like.
convocação s. f. (pl. -**ões**) 1. convocation. 2. invitation. 3. convening, meeting. 4. summons. 5. call-(ing).
~ **às armas** call to arms. ~ **para o serviço militar** induction order. **lugar de** ~ induction station.

convocado s. m. (mil.) draftee. ‖ adj. 1. (mil.) drafted. 2. summoned.
convocador s. m. convoker, convocator. ‖ adj. convocative.
convocar v. to convoke, call together, summon.
~ **uma assembléia** to call together an assembly.
convocatório adj. convoking, convocative, convocational.
convolação s. f. (pl. -**ões**) (jur.) change of civil status.
convolar v. 1. to change the civil status. 2. (fig.) to change one's mind (or feelings, convictions).
convolução s. f. (pl. -**ões**) convolution.
convoluto adj. convolute(d). ‖ -**amente** adv. convolutely.
convolvuláceas s. f. pl. Convolvulaceae: a family of vines, shrubs and trees (the morning-glory family).
convolvuláceo adj. convolvulaceous.
convólvulo s. m. (bot.) convolvulus.
convosco pron. with you.
convulsão s. f. (pl. -**ões**) 1. convulsion, convulsive fit. 2. cataclism. 3. tumult, commotion.
ela foi atacada de -ões she was seized with convulsions.
convulsar v. to convulse. 2. to agitate, disturb. 3. to suffer from convulsions.
convulsibilidade s. f. (med.) convulsiveness.
convulsionar v. 1. to convulse. 2. to agitate, disturb. 3. to revolutionize, revolt. 4. to be caught by convulsions.
convulsionário s. m. (med.) convulsionary, convulsionist. ‖ adj. convulsionary, convulsive.
convulsivo adj. 1. convulsive. 2. spasmodic(al), jerky. 3. effervescent. ‖ -**amente** adv. convulsively.
convulso adj. convulsive, tremulous, shaky.
coobação s. f. (pl. -**ões**) cohobation.
coobar v. to cohobate.
coobrigação s. f. co-obligation.
coocupar v. to co-occupy.
cooficiar v. to co-officiate.
coonestação s. f. (pl. -**ões**) whitewashing, rehabilitation.
coonestador adj. rehabilitating.
coonestar v. to whitewash, rehabilitate.
cooperação s. f. (pl. -**ões**) co-operation, coaction, concurrency.
espírito de ~ team-spirit. **falta de** ~ non-co-operation.
cooperador s. m. co-operator. ‖ adj. co-operating, concurrent.
cooperante adj. m. + f. co-operative.
cooperar v. 1. to co-operate, work together. 2. to collaborate, coact, concur.
cooperativa s. f. co-operative, co-operative society.
cooperativismo s. m. co-operativism.
cooperativista s. m. + f. co-operativist, defender or supporter of co-operativism. ‖ adj. co-operativistic(al).
cooperativo adj. co-operative.
cooptação s. f. (pl. -**ões**) co-optation.
cooptar v. to co-opt, co-optate.
coordenação s. f. (pl. -**ões**) co-ordination, co-ordinateness.
coordenadas s. f. pl. (math.) co-ordinates.
~**s cartesianas** Cartesian co-ordinates. ~**s parabólicas** parabolic co-ordinates.
coordenado adj. 1. co-ordinative, co-ordinate. 2. collateral. 3. concurrent.
coordenador s. m. co-ordinator. ‖ adj. co-ordinating.
coordenar v. 1. to co-ordinate. 2. to put in a certain order or rank, classify. 3. to organize. 4. to arrange, order.

coordenativo adj. co-ordinative.

coorte s. f. cohort.

copa (I) s. f. 1. pressing vat. 2. top or crown of a tree (plate A 14). 3. crown of hat.

copa (II) s. f. pantry, butler's pantry.

copa (III) s. f. 1. chalice, cup, goblet. 2. ~s pl. (cards) hearts (place P 6).

copaço s. m. a large glassful.

copa-cozinha s. f. (pl. **copas-cozinhas**) a kitchen and pantry.

copada (I) s. f. 1. a glassful. 2. (archit.) torus.

copada (II) s. f. 1. big crown of a tree. 2. a tree with a big crown.

copado adj. 1. tuffy, bushy. 2. convex. 3. puffed up. 4. leafy, leaved.

copagem s. f. (pl. -ens) foliage.

copaíba s. f. 1. copaiba tree (Copaifera officinalis). 2. (pharm.) copaiba, copaiba balsam.

copaibal s. m. (pl. -ais) a grove of copaiba trees.

copaibarana s. f. a wallaba tree (Eperua purpurea).

copaíba-vermelha s. f. (pl. **copaíbas-vermelhas**), a copal tree (Copaifera langsdorfii).

copaibeiro s. m. copaiba oil extractor.

copaié s. m. (bot.) etaballi.

copal s. m. copal, copal resin.

copar v. 1. to prune the crown of a tree or brush. 2. to embower. 3. to trim the hair around the top of the head. 4. to give a convex form to.

coparrão s. m. (pl. -ões) a large glassful.

co-participação s. f. (pl. -ões) copartnership, collective participation, communion.

co-participante s. m. + f. copartaker, copartner.

co-participar v. to share, take part jointly.

copázio s. m. 1. a large glass, rummer (plate C 14). 2. large glassful.

cope s. m. (Braz.) the central part of a fishing net.

copé s. m. (Braz) a wooden straw-covered shack, a large Indian hut that houses more than one family.

copeira s. f. 1. pantry. 2. cupboard, side-board. 3. waitress.

copeiragem s. f. (Braz.) 1. the work performed by a butler or waitress, butlership. 2. a group of butlers or waitresses.

copeirar v. to work as butler (or waitress).

copeiro s. m. butler, waiter.

copejada s. f. central part of a fishing net; the fishes caught in it.

copejador s. m. harpooner (of fish).

copejadura s. f. act of harpooning, fishing with a harpoon.

copejar v. to harpoon, catch or kill with a harpoon.

copel s. m. (pl. **copéis**) the fine-meshed bag of a dragnet.

copela s. f. (met.) cupel.

copelação s. f. (pl. -ões), (met.) cupellation.

copelar v. (met.) to cupel, refine by means of a cupel furnace.

copépodes s. m. pl. (zool.) the Copepoda: a large subclass of crustaceans.

copeque s. m. kopeck, a minor Russian coin.

cópia s. f. 1. copy. 2. reproduction. 3. transcript, replication. 4. repetition. 5. imitation. 6. estreat, true duplicate or extract. 7. similitude, semblance. 8. abundance, copiousness.
~ **em papel carbônio** carbon copy. ~ **fotográfica** print. ~ **fotomecânica** photoprint. ~ **heliográfica** cyanotype. ~ **xerográfica** xerographic print. **ela fez uma** ~ **a limpo** she made a fair copy. **ele tirou negativas**.
uma ~ he took a copy from it. **fazer uma** ~ to replicate. **produzir uma** ~ to print.

copiá s. m. (Braz.) veranda, porch.

copiadeira s. f. (phot.) printer: a machine for copying

copiador s. m. 1. copier, copyist. 2. transcriber. 3. copy-book, letter-book. 4. (phot.) printer (plate F 6). 5. tracer.

copiadora s. f. 1. female copyist. 2. copying or duplicating machine.

copião (s. m. (cin.) a soundless copy of a film.

copiar (I) v. 1. to copy, reproduce. 2. to transcribe, duplicate. 3. to imitate. 4. to plagiarize. 5. to transfer. 6. to trace, pattern. 7. (phot.) to print.

copiar (II) s. m. (also **copiara** f.) veranda, porch.

copilação s. f. (pl. -ões) compilation.

co-piloto s. m. copilot.

copiografar v. to reproduce on a duplicating machine, copy.

copiógrafo s. m. duplicating machine, copying press.

copiosidade s. f. 1. copiousness. 2. abundance, plenty.

copioso adj. 1. copious, plenty, plentiful. 2. abundant, opulent. 3. ample, large. 4. rich, wealthy. 5. voluminous. 6. flush, full. 7. bounteous, profuse. ‖ -**amente** adv. copiously, plentifully, abundantly.

copirraite s. m. (jur.) copyright.

copista s. m. + f. 1. copier, copyist. 2. transcriber, amanuensis. 3. plagiarist. 4. (pop.) hard drinker, tippler.

copla s. f. couplet, stanza, strophe, distich.

copo s. m. 1. cup (plates G 2, V 2). 2. glass, drinking glass, goblet, tumbler (plates C 14, M 1, P 12, R 5). 3. glassful. 4. any object resembling a cup. ~ **de óleo** oil-cup. ~ **para cerveja** beer glass, (U. S. A.) schooner (plate C 14). ~ **para vinho** wineglass (plate C 14). ~ **a mais** he has had a glass too much. **tempestade num** ~ **d'água** storm in a tea-cup.

copo-d'água s. m. (pl. **copos-d'água**), (Braz.) a slight repast offered to friends.

copo-de-caçador s. m. (pl. **copos-de-caçador**), (bot.) pitcher plant.

copo-de-leite s. m. (pl. **copos-de-leite**), (bot.) 1. calla lily, arum lily. 2. water arum, wild calla. 3. trumpet lily.

copofone s. m. musical glasses.

copos s. m. pl. 1. metal adornments on both sides of the bridle bit. 2. basket-hilt of a sword.

copra s. f. copra, dried coconut meat.

copraol s. m. copra oil, coconut oil.

co-produção s. f. (pl. **co-produções**) co-production.

co-produtor s. m. (pl. **co-produtores**) co-producer.

co-produtos s. m. pl. (econ., com.) co-products.

co-produzir v. to co-produce.

coprofagia s. f. (med., zool.) coprophagy.

coprófago adj. coprophagous.

coprolalia s. f. (med. psych.) coprolalia.

coprólito s. m. (pal.) coprolite.

coprologia s. f. (med.) coprology.

coprológico adj. (med.) coprologic(al).

co-proprietário s. m. co-proprietor, co-owner, joint--owner, part owner.

copta s. m. + f. 1. Copt, a member of the old Egyptian race. 2. Coptic (language). 3. member of the Coptic church. ‖ adj. Coptic.

cóptico adj. Coptic.

copuda s. m. rosacean plant (Licania parinarioides).

copudo adj. having a large crown (tree).

cópula s. f. 1. coition, coitus. 2. copulation, coupling. 3. (gram.) copula, predicative connecting word. 4. (logics) word which connects the subject and predicate of a proposition. 5. (mus.) coupler of an organ.

copulação s. f. (pl. -ões) copulation, copula.

copulador adj. copulative, copulating.

copular v. 1. to copulate. 2. to unite in sexual intercourse. 3. to have sexual contact with. 4. to join, unite. 5. to couple, join in pairs.

copulativo adj. copular, copulative, copulatory. ‖ -amente adv. copulatively.
coque (I) s. m. 1. a rap on the head. 2. a knot of hair on the top of the head. 3. a male cook.
coque (II) s. m. coke. ~ em pó coke dust. ~ metalúrgico foundry coke.
coqueiral s. m. (pl. -ais) a grove of coco trees, coconut palm plantation.
coqueiro (I) s. m. 1. popular designation of all nut-bearing palm trees. 2. (bot.) coconut palm.
coqueiro (II) s. m. (pop.) swindler, cheater, adventurer.
coqueiro-cabeçudo s. m. (pl. coqueiros-cabeçudos), (bot.) cauldron palm.
coqueiro-catulé s. m. (pl. coqueiros-catulé), (bot.) a wild palm (Syagrus comosa).
coqueiro-da-baía s. m. (pl. coqueiros-da-baía) (bot.) coconut palm, coconut tree, coco (Cocos nucifera).
coqueiro-macho s. m. (pl. coqueiros-machos), (bot.) tree fern.
coqueiro-tucum s. m. (pl. coqueiros-tucum), (bot.) tucum palm.
coqueluche s. f. 1. (med.) whooping cough. 2. (pop.) craze, fad.
coquetaria s. f. coquetry.
coquete s. f. coquette, flirtatious girl. ‖ adj. f. coquet, coquettish, flirtatious, kittenish.
coquetear v. to flirt, coquet.
coquetel s. m. (pl. coquetéis) cocktail.
coqueteleira s. f. cocktail shaker.
coquetice s. f. coquettishness, flirtatiousness.
coquetismo s. m. coquetry, coquettishness.
coquilho s. m. 1. (bot.) a canna (Canna glauca). 2. the meat or kernels of palm nuts from which oil is extracted.
coquinha s. f. a plant of the family Melastomaceae.
coquinho s. m. 1. a small cocoanut. 2. (bot.) pindo palm.
coquinho-babá s. m. (pl. coquinhos-babá) a palm tree of the family Arecaceae (Desmoncus setosus).
cor s. m. 1. (obs.) heart. 2. will, wish, desire. 3. inclination.
de ~ by heart. saber de ~ to know by heart.
cor s. f. colour. 2. hue, tint. 3. paint, dye. 4. ruddiness, healthy complexion. 5. general character. 6. colours, flag, ensign. 7. tone. 8. political colour, political party. 9. quality. 10. pretext, pretense, excuse. 11. semblance, appearance. 12. rouge.
~ de aço steel-blue. ~ de laranja orange. ~ de vinho wine-coloured. ~es básicas fundamental colours. ~es berrantes glaring colours. ~ firme fast dye, fast colour. ~ mista composite colour, secondary colour. ~ vermelho-clara claret. de ~ firme unfading. de ~ fixa of a fast colour. ele mudou de ~ he changed colours. ficar sem ~ to turn pale. não saber de que ~ é not to have the slightest notion of a thing. perder a ~ to fade away. sem ~ tintless. ter boa ~ to have much colour. uma ~ discreta a quiet colour. uma ~ viva a lively colour. um homem de ~ a coloured man. variação de ~es play of colours. ~ pastel 1. a pale colour. 2. pastel colour.
cora s. f. bleaching of white clothes.
coração (I) s. m. (pl. -ões) 1. (anat.) heart. 2. (fig.) courage, mettle. 3. (fig.) feeling(s), sentiment. 4. kindness, generosity. 5. bosom, breast. 6. (railway) frog (plate V 4). 7. center, core. 8. love, affection. 9. popular designation of several plants.
abrir o ~ a alguém to open one's heart to s. o., make a clean breast of. aquilo me dilacerou o ~ that broke my heart. caiu-lhe o ~ aos pés his heart went down to his heels. com o ~ sangrando with a bleeding heart. com todo o meu ~ with all my heart. conquistar o ~ de to win the heart of. de bom ~ sweet-tempered. de todo o ~ with all my heart and soul, willingly. ele sofre do ~ he has a heart trouble. ele tem um ~ de pedra he hás a heart of flint. fazer das tripas ~ to pluck up courage. fazer o ~ saltar de alegria to make the heart leap with joy. isto transpassa-me o ~ it cuts me to the heart. meter no ~ to take to one's heart. mãos frias, ~ quente a cold hand, a warm heart. o que os olhos não vêem o ~ não sente what the eye does not see the heart does not grieve over. música que fala ao ~ a touching tune (or music). não se pode ver até o ~ you cannot search the heart. no ~ inwardly. no ~ da cidade in the heart of the town. no fundo do seu ~ deep in his heart. no ~ do inverno in the depth of winter. não ter ~ to be heartless. sem ~ heartless, bloodless. ser um ~ aberto to be an open-hearted person. tenha ~! have a heart! ter o ~ na boca to wear one's heart on one's sleeve. ter um ~ alegre to be lighthearted. ter um ~ de ouro to have a heart of gold.
coração (II) s. f. (pl. -ões) 1. act or result of dyeing. 2. blushing.
coração (III) s. m. (Braz.) 1. a big room. 2. veranda.
coração-da-índia s. m. (pl. corações-da-índia), (bot.) 1. balloon vine. 2. heart pea, heart seed.
coração-de-boi s. m. (pl. corações-de-boi), (bot.) custard apple (Annona reticulata).
coração-de-estudante s. m. (pl. corações-de-estudante), popular designation of several plants of the family Bignoniaceae.
coração-de-maria s. m. (pl. corações-de-maria), (bot.) bleeding heart.
coração-de-negro s. m. (pl. corações-de-negro), (bot.) 1. lebbek. 2. chatterbox tree. 3. siris.
coração-de-rainha s. m. (pl. corações-de-rainha), (bot.) cherimoya.
coração-magoado s. m. (pl. corações-magoados), (bot.) a bloodleaf (Iresine herbstii).
coraçãozinho s. m. 1. little heart. 2. (pop.) chick-abiddy.
coraciiformes s. m. pl. (ornith.) Coraciiformes: an order of birds to which belong the kingfishers.
coracoidal adj. m. + f. (pl. -ais) coracoidal.
coracóide s. m. (anat.) the coracoid bone. ‖ adj. m. + f. coracoid.
coracóideo adj. coracoid(al).
coraçonada s. f. 1. instinctive sentiment or impulse. 2. hunch, intuitive impression.
co-radical adj. m. + f. (pl. -ais), (phil.) co-radicate, having the same radical.
corado adj. 1. red-faced, ruddy, rosy. 2. fresh, florid. 3. full-blooded. 4. ablush, ashamed. 5. bashful, modest. ‖ -amente adv. ruddily, rosily, ablush.
coradouro s. m. bleaching ground, bleaching yard, bleachery.
coragem s. f. 1. courage, daring, fearlessness. 2. valour, valiantness, gut, pluk. 3. boldness, undauntedness, bravery, nerve. 4. fortitude, spirit, enterprise. 5. heart, great-heartedness. 6. moral courage, assurance. ‖ interj. have courage!, pluck up!, never say die!
criar ~ to take courage. é preciso muita ~ it takes grit. ele perdeu a ~ his nerve failed him. eles não têm ~ their hearts fail them. ele tinha a ~ de responder pelas suas opiniões he had the courage of his opinions. não perca a ~! don't be discouraged!, keep a stiff underlip! não perder a ~ to keep one's pecker up. sem ~ tame.
corajoso adj. 1. courageous, daring. 2. valiant, valorous, doutless 3. bold, brave, plucky. 4. gallant,

spirited. 5. fortitudinous. 6. enterprising. || **-amente** adv. courageously, dauntlessly, bravely, boldly.

corajudo adj. courageous.

coral (I) s. m. (pl. **-ais**) 1. (zool.) coral. 2. calcareous substance secreted by marine polyps, a piece of coral. 3. coral red. 4. coral red caruncles of certain birds.

coral (II) s. f. (pl. **-ais**) 1. coral plant. 2. mountain rose. 3. scarlet plume.

coral (III) s. f. (pl. **-ais**) coral snake.

coral (IV) s. m. (pl. **-ais**), (Braz.) a porridge made from grated green corn, coconut milk, sugar and cinnamon.

coral (V) s. m. (pl. **-ais**) (mus.) choral(e), chorus. || adj. m. + f. choral, choric.

coraleira s. f. 1. a coral fishing boat. 2. coral tree, coral wood.

coraleiro s. m. 1. coral fisher, coral diver. 2. coral fishing boat. 3. a parrot (Amazona vinacea). || adj. coral-fishing.

coraliários s. m. pl. (zool.) Coralligena: a group of Anthozoa, consisting of the corals and their allies.

coralina (I) s. f. coraline.

coralina (II) s. f. (min.) carnelian.

coralíneo adj. coralline, coralloid.

coralino adj. coral red.

coral-verdadeira s. f. (pl. **corais-verdadeiras**), a coral snake (family Elapidae).

coramastro s. m. (Braz., naut.) quartermaster.

coramina s. f. Coramine: trademark of a heart stimulant.

corandel s. m. (pl. **corandéis**), (typogr.) small text columns which surround a picture.

corante s. m. colour, dye, pigment, colouring. || adj. m. + f. colouring, dyeing, colorific.

corar v. 1. to colour. 2. to dye, paint. 3. to bleach, expose to the sun, whiten. 4. to disguise, conceal. 5. to attenuate. 6. to blush, redden. 7. **~-se** to be or become ashamed.

corbelha s. f. a small basket for sweets, fruits or flowers.

corça s. f. (zool.) doe, hind.

corcel s. m. (pl. **corcéis**) charger, courser (horse).

corcha s. f. 1. bark of a tree. 2. cork, corkwood. 3. a wooden muzzle cover (of a cannon).

corcho s. m. a vase or vessel made of cork-bark.

corço s. m. (zool.) roebuck, roe deer.

corcoroca s. f. (Braz., ichth.) grunt: common designation of teleost fishes, esp. the yellow grunt (Haemulon sciurus).

corcoroca-boca-de-fogo s. f. (pl. **corcorocas-bocas-de-fogo**), (ichth.) white grunt.

corcoroca-mulata s. f. (pl. **corcorocas-mulatas**), (ichth.) common grunt.

corcova (I) s. f. 1. hump, hunch. 2. hunchback, humpback. 3. crookedness.

corcova (II) s. f. 1. bucking of a horse, a horse's curvet. 2. leap.

corcovado s. m. a bird of the family Odontophoridae (Odontophorus guianensis). || adj. humpy, humped, hunchbacked, knobbed.

corcovadura s. f. 1. act or result of curving. 2. hunchback, humpback. 3. leap, jump.

corcovar v. 1. to curve, bend, crook. 2. to curvet, buck, leap (horses). 3. to hump, hunch. 4. to give the form of an arch. 5. **~-se** to become curved or arched.

corcovear v. to curvet, buck, caper, jib.

corcovo (ô) s. m. (pl. **corcovos**) curvet, capriole, caper (of a horse).

corcunda s. m. + f. 1. humpback, hunchback, crookback. 2. f. hump, hunch. || adj. humped, humpbacked.

corda s. f. 1. cord, rope, line (plates A 2, 7, E 6, G 3, P 2, 6, T 2). 2. leash, thong, sinew, tendon. 4. twine. 5. cable. 6. (naut.) lashing. 7. (mus.) fiddlestring, string (plates B 4, G 2, H, P 10). 8. spring of a watch or clock. 9. halter, tether. 10. (math., geom.) chord. 11. (anat.) vocal chord.
~ de arco bowstring, chord, string. **~ de fibra de coco** coir rope. **~ de rebocador** tow-line, tow-rope. **~ de sino** bell-rope. **dançar na ~ bamba** (pop.) to be in a nice mess. **dar ~ ao relógio** to wind up the watch. **dar ~ em excesso** to overwind. **deram ~ nele** they played on him, they made him talk. **estar com a ~ no pescoço** to be frightfully hard-pressed. **instrumentos de ~** string instruments. **não toque nessa ~** don't touch upon that string. **quarteto de ~s** string quartet. **sem ~** unwound. **sua ~ sensível** his sore spot. **subir muito à ~** to carry matters a peg too high. **tambor de ~** snare drum. **roer a ~** 1. to be absent in an engagement. 2. to break up a deal or contract.

corda-d'água s. f. (pl. **cordas-d'água**) a heavy rainfall.

cordados s. m. pl. (zool.) Chordata: a subkingdom of animals which have a notochord.

corda-dorsal s. f. (pl. **cordas-dorsais**), (anat., zool.) chorda dorsalis.

cordal adj. m. + f. (pl. **-ais**) chordal.

cordame s. m. 1. rope(s). 2. cordage. 3. (naut.) tackling, rigging, ropery.

cordão s. m. (pl. **-ões**) 1. string, thread. 2. twist, fillet. 3. rank(s). 4. lace, lacing, girdle. 5. cordon. 6. strap. 7. a group of carnival revellers. 8. cable made up of several strands of fine copper wire, cord.
~ de bolsa purse string(s). **~ de campainha** bell-pull, bell-rope. **~ de isolamento** cordon. **~ de sapato** shoe-lace, shoestring, latchet (plate B 16). **~ umbilical** umbilical cord, navel string. **entrar no ~** to join in.

cordão-de-frade s. m. (pl. **cordões-de-frade**), (bot.) lion's-ear.

cordão-de-freira s. m. (pl. **cordões-de-freira**), (bot.) fringed heath.

cordas s. f. pl. the strings (in an orchestra).

cordato adj. prudent, wise, sensible.

cordeação s. f. (pl. **-ões**) 1. act of measuring with a cord. 2. alignment of buildings, laying out of streets.

cordeador s. m. town surveyor, municipal clerk who supervises the alignment of buildings and constructions.

cordeamento s. m. act of supervising the alignment of buildings and the layout of streets.

cordear v. 1. to measure with a cord. 2. to align, line up. 3. to lay out streets. 4. to supervise the alignment of buildings.

cordeira s. f. 1. lamb, ewe lamb. 2. a lambskin.

cordeiragem s. f. (pl. **-ens**) a flock of lambs.

cordeirinho s. m. a little lamb, lambkin.

cordeiro s. m. 1. lamb. 2. (fig.) a gentle, sweet-tempered person. 3. (fig.) an innocent being.
~ pascoal paschoal lamb, passover. **ele é um lobo em pele de ~** he is a wolf in sheep's clothing.

cordel s. m. (pl. **-éis**) twine, fine string. 2. thread. 3. bobbin. 4. cord.
apertar os -éis to oblige a person to do s. th. against his will. **~ de chicote** whipcord, whiplash. **literatura de ~** cheap literature. **puxar os -éis** to pull strings.

cordeona s. f. (mus.) concertina.

cor-de-rosa s. m. damask, rose. || adj. m. + f., sg. + pl. pink, roseate, rose-coloured, damask, rosy.
ver tudo ~ to see everything through rose-coloured spectacles, to see only the bright side of everything.

cordíaca s. f. a heart disease of horses.
cordial (I) s. m. (pl. **-ais**) cordial, invigorating or stimulating drink.
cordial (II) adj. m. + f. (pl. **-ais**) 1. cordial. 2. sincere, heartfelt. 3. kind, amiable. 4. warm, friendly, amicable. 5. genial, open. 6. affectionate. ‖ ~**mente** adv. cordially, kindly, genially, whole-heartedly. **cordiais felicitações!** I wish you joy!
cordialidade s. f. 1. cordiality, cordialness. 2. warm-hertedness, heartiness. 3. sincerity. 4. affection. 5. friendliness, amicability. 6. kindness.
cordierita s. f. (min.) iolite.
cordifoliado adj. (bot.) cordifolious, having heart-shaped leaves.
cordiforme adj. m. + f. cordiform, heart-shaped (plate F 5).
cordilha s. f. designation of a tuna fish in its first stages of life.
cordilheira s. f. 1. cordillera, mountain range. 2. range, ridge. 3. chain or system of mountains.
cordoada s. f. 1. a blow with a rope. 2. ropery, rigging of a ship. 3. (pop.) a torrential rain.
cordoalha s. f. 1. cordage, ropery. 2. a ship's tackle, rigging, gear.
cordoaria s. f. rope factory, ropewalk, ropery.
córdoba s. m. cordoba: the monetary unit of Nicaragua.
cordoeiro s. m. rope manufacturer, ropemaker, rope dealer.
cordovaneiro s. m. a manufacturer of or dealer in Cordovan leather.
cordovão s. m. (pl. **-ões**) Cordovan leather, cordwain, cordovan.
cordoveias s. f. pl. popular designation of the jugular veins.
cordovês s. m. Cordovan, native or inhabitant of Cordoba (Spain). ‖ adj. Cordovan.
cordura s. f. 1. prudence, wisdom. 2. good sense. 3. discretion. 4. seriousness.
coreano s. m. Korean: 1. native or inhabitant of Korea (East Asia). 2. the Korean language. ‖ adj. Korean.
corê-corê s. m. (pl. **corê-corês**), (pop.) prattler, endless talker. ‖ adj. garrulous, talkative.
co-redator s. m. (pl. **co-redatores**) co-editor.
co-regência s. f. (pl. **co-regências**) co-regency.
co-regente s. m. + f. (pl. **co-regentes**) co-regent.
coregia s. f. co-regence, co-regency.
corego s. m. co-regent, dancing master.
coregrafia s. f. choreography, choregraphy: 1. the art of dancing. 2. the art of composing dances and ballets.
coregráfico adj. choreographic(al).
coréia s. f. (med.) chorea, St. Vitus' dance.
coreideos s. m. pl. (ent.) Coreidae: the true bug family.
coreiro adj. (med.) choreic, choreatic.
coreografia s. f. choreography, choregraphy.
coreográfico adj. choreographic(al).
coreógrafo s. m. (also **corégrafo**) choreographer.
coreotripanose s. f. (med.) Chagas' disease.
corera s. f. = **crueira.**
co-responsabilidade s. f. (pl. **co-responsabilidades**) co-responsability.
co-responsável adj. m. + f. (pl. **co-responsáveis**) co-responsible, jointly responsible.
coreto s. m. bandstand.
coreu s. m. (Greek poet.) choreus, trochee.
co-réu s. m. (pl. **co-réus**) co-defendant.
corenta s. m. pop. form of **quarenta** forty.
coriáceo adj. 1. coriaceous, leathery, leatherlike. 2. tough.
coriambo s. m. (Greek poet.) choriamb, choriambus.

coriandro s. m. (bot.) coriander.
coriária s. f. 1. Coriaria: a small genus of shrubs. 2. sumach (Coriaria myrtifolia). 3. tanning substance extracted from this plant.
coriariáceas s. f. pl. Coriariaceae: a family of shrubs.
coriariáceo adj. (bot.) coriariaceous.
cariarina s. f. (biochem.) coriin.
coriavo s. m. (ornith.) a nighthawk (Nyctidromus albicolis).
coribântico adj. (Greek myth.) Corybantian, Corybantic.
coribanto s. m. (Greek myth.) Corybant.
corículo s. m. leather strap, thong.
corifeu s. m. 1. (Greek hist.) coryphaeus, co-regent. 2. leader of a religious sect or school of thought. 3. head of a political party.
corimbífero adj. (bot.) corymbiferous.
corimbo s. m. corymb: a panicle in which all the flowers rise to the same level.
corimbó-da-mata s. m. (pl. **corimbós-da-mata**) a climbing plant of the family Bignoniaceae (Tanaecium nocturnum).
corimboso adj. (bot.) corymbous, corymbose, corymbiate.
corincho s. m. boasting, swaggering, braggartism. **quebrar o** ~ to outstrip or ridicule a braggart.
corindiba, corindiúba s. f. (bot.) a hackberry (Celtis brasiliensis).
coríndon, corindo s. m. (min.) corundum.
coringa s. f. 1. a small triangular sail. 2. m. cabin boy, cabin attendant. 3. (fig.) weak and ugly fellow.
coríntio s. m. Corinthian: native or inhabitant of Corinth (Greece). ‖ adj. Corinthian.
corinto s. m. a variety of currants.
córion, cório s. m. 1. (anat.) chorium, a membrane which envelops the fetus of mammals. 2. (anat.) corium, derma of the skin, cutis vera.
corisa s. f. 1. a boatbug. 2. Corixa: a genus of aquatic carnivorous insects.
coriscação s. f. (pl. **-ões**) coruscation, a sudden flash of light, sparkling, gleaming.
coriscada s. f. a lot of scintillating sparks, flashes of lightning.
coriscado adj. struck by lightning, seared.
coriscante adj. m. + f. coruscant, flashing, glittering.
coriscar v. 1. to coruscate, glitter, gleam in flashes. 2. to scintillate, sparkle. 3. to strike (lightning). 4. to hurl, throw.
corisco s. m. 1. electric spark, lightning, sheet-lightning. 3. coruscation, glittering, sparkling. 4. flashing. 5. (pop.) unexpected visitor or guest.
corista s. m. + f. 1. chorist(er). 2. choirman, choirboy. 3. singer. 4. chorus girl.
corixa s. f. (also **corixe**) outlet of ponds, lakes or marshes.
corixão s. m. (pl. **-ões**) large outlet of a lake or marsh.
corixo s. m. 1. = **chupim.** 2. = **corixa.**
coriza s. f. (med.) coryza, nasal catarrh, cold in the head.
corja s. f. 1. rabble, mob. 2. multitude, throng. 3. dregs of society, scum. 4. (obs.) twenty.
cornaca s. m. elephant guide, elephant driver, mahout.
cornáceas s. f. pl. Cornaceae: a family of trees, shrubs and herbs (dogwood family).
cornáceo adj. (bot.) cornaceous.
cornaço s. m. a horn-thrust.
cornada s. f. a piercing with horns os tusks.
cornadura s. f. the horns of animals, horns, antlers.
cornal s. m. (pl. **-ais**) (also **corneira** f.) a leather strap with which the horns are bound to the yoke.

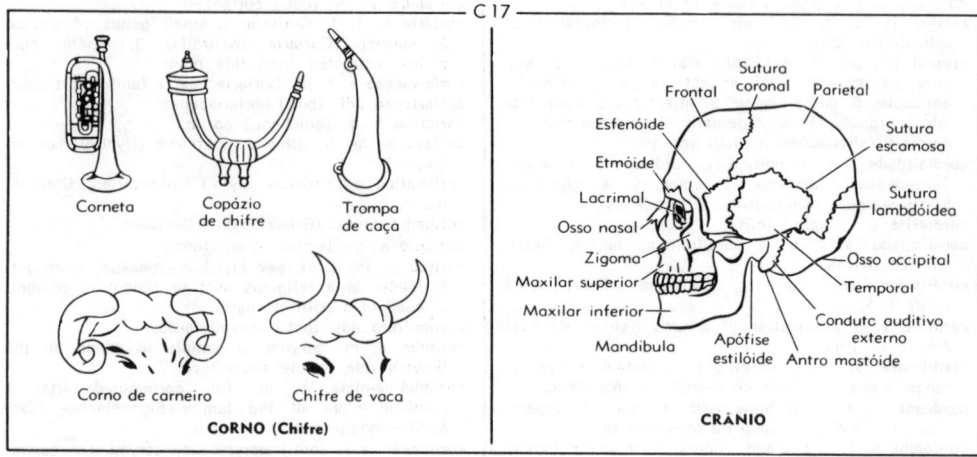

CORNO (Chifre)

CRÂNIO

cornalina s. f. (min.) cornelian.
cornamusa s. f. a bagpipe, pipe.
cornante adj. m. + f. horny, cornigerous, cornific.
cornar v. to gore, pierce of wound with horns.
corne s. m. (mus.) trumpet, horn.
~ inglês (mus.) English horn, oboe.
córnea (I) s. f. (anat.) cornea: the outer cover of the eye (plate O).
córnea (II) s. f. a family of dicotyledonous plants.
corneador adj. prone to attack with the horns (said of bulls).
corneal adj. m. + f. (pl. -ais) corneal.
cornear v. 1. to attack or gore with the horns; to horn. 2. to butt. 3. to wound (with the horns). 4. (pop.) to be unfaithful (wife or husband).
corneliano adj. of, pertaining to or relative to the French poet Corneille or his works.
córneo adj. 1. (anat.) corneal: of or pertaining to the cornea. 2. horny, hornish, keratoid. 3. corneous.
córner s. m. 1. each of the four corners of a soccer field. 2. the corner penalty in a soccer game.
corneta s. f. 1. (mus.) bugle: a) trumpet, bugle-horn (plate C 17). b) hunting horn. 2. auto horn. 3. organ-stop. 4. m. trumpeter, bugler. ‖ adj. meddlesome.
~ acústica ear-trumpet, speaking trumpet.
cornetada s. f. bugle-call, trumpet-blast.
corneteiro s. m. horner, hornblower, trumpeter, bugler.
cornetim s. m. (pl. -ins) 1. (mus.) cornet, small trumpet with three piston stops. 2. cornet(t)ist.
corneto s. m. (anat.) turbinal bones.
cornicabra s. f. 1. (bot.) a capsicum (Capsicum annuum). 2. (bot.) bush pepper, chili (Capsicum frutescens). 3. a tract of wasteland, heath.
cornicabra-dos-algarvios s. f. (pl. cornicabras-dos-algarvios), (bot.) sea grape.
cornichão s. m. (pl. -ões) (bot.) 1. ground-honeysuckle. 2. bird's-eye, lesser bird's-foot trefoil.
cornicho s. m. 1. a small horn. 2. cornicle. 3. feeler, antenna. 4. a horn-shaped vessel.
córnico s. m. Cornish, a Celtic dialect spoken in Cornwall (England). ‖ adj. Cornish.
cornicurto adj. shorthorned.
cornífero adj. cornific, cornigerous, horn-shaped.
corniforme adj. m. + f. corniform, horn-shaped, cornute(d).
cornígero adj. cornigerous.

cornija s. f. (archit.) 1. cornice. 2. corona, cordon. 3. moulding, label.
~ da lareira mantelpiece, chimney-piece (plate L 1).
cornilargo adj. broad-horned, large-horned.
cornilongo adj. long-horned.
cornimboque s. m. a snuff or tobacco box made from the point of a horn.
cornípede adj. m. + f. horn-footed.
corniso s. m. cornel, cornelian cherry, dogberry tree.
cornisolo s. m. dogberry, fruit of the dogberry tree.
corno (ô) s. m. (pl. cornos) 1. horn: a) pl. head defenses of ruminants, antlers (plate C 17). b) feeler, antenna. c) any hornlike object. 2. (fam.) cuckold.
lançar os cornos ao sol (fig.) to grow bold. não vale um ~ it is not worth a pin. pegar o touro pelos cornos to take the bull by the horns. pôr alguém nos cornos da lua to praise a person up to the skies. quebrar os cornos a alguém (fig.) to humble s. o. roer um ~ to have neither bite nor sup. ver-se nos cornos do touro to be in great danger.
cornos-do-diabo s. m., sg. + pl. unicorn-plant, devil's--claw.
cornucópia s. f. cornucopia: 1. (myth.) the horn of plenty, horn of Amalthea. 2. a vessel shaped like a horn.
cornuda s. f. (ichth.) hammerhead.
cornudo adj. cornute, horned.
cornúpeto adj. that attacks with the horns.
cornuto adj. having horns, cornific, horn-shaped, cornigerous, cornute(d), horny.
raciocínio ~ a difficult or perplexing problem, a dilemma.
coro (ô) s. m. (pl. coros) 1. choir. 2. chorus. 3. a group of singers. 4. a musical composition intended to be sung by a number of voices.
em ~ (mus.) concerted, simultaneously, unanimously. fazer ~ to agree with.
coró s. m. (zool.) maggot.
coroa s. f. 1. crown: a) sovereign's headdress, diadem. b) wreath, garland, fillet. c) regal power and authority, sovereignty. d) anything crown--shaped (plate S 3). e) topmost part of the skull. f) top part of a tooth. g) (dent.) artificial crown of a tooth. h) the top part of a diamond or any other gem. i) monetary unit in several countries (Krona, Krone, Crown). j) top of a tree. k) tuft of

hair or feathers on the head of certain animals.
l) (bot.) corona. 2. (astr.) corona. 3. (fig.) acme,
perfection. 4. winder (of a watch) (plate R 4).
~ **circular** (geom.) annulus. ~ **dentada** (tech.)
face wheel. ~ **do casco do cavalo** (Zool.) coronet
(plates C 9, 12). ~ **de clérigo** tonsure. ~ **de dente**
(dent.) coronal. ~ **de espinhos** 1. Christ's crown
of thorns. 2. (fig.) affliction, torment. ~ **de louros**
laurel wreath. ~ **de mastro** pendant, pendent. ~
imperial imperial crown. ~ **mural** coping. **cara ou**
~**?** heads or tails? **pequena** ~ coronet. **suceder à** ~
to succeed to the crown. **uma** ~ **de flores** a wreath
of flowers.
coroá s. m. 1. (bot.) caroa (Neoglaziovia variegata).
2. caroa fibers (used for rope-making).
coroação s. f. (pl. **-ões**) 1. act of crowning. 2. crowning, coronation. 3. antlers. 4. (Braz.) formation of a
small earth wall around the trunk of a coffee tree.
a ~ **do seu trabalho** the completion of his work,
the crowning of his work.
coroa-da-terra s. f. (pl. **coroas-da-terra**) (bot.) ground
lily.
coroa-de-cristo s. f. (pl. **coroas-de-cristo**), (bot.) 1.
milk hedge. 2. Jew's-thorn. 3. Christ's-thorn.
coroa-de-moçambique s. f. (pl. **coroas-de-moçambique**),
(bot.) blood lily, Cape tulip.
coroa-de-viúva s. f. (pl. **coroas-de-viúva**), (bot.) a
petrea (Petrea subserrata).
coroado (l) adj. 1. crowned, coroneted. 2. crested. 3.
blushing. 4. royal, regal.
cabeças -as crowned heads. ~ **de louros** laureate.
coroado (II) s. m. a kind of sparrow (Aremon taci-
turnus).
coroa-imperial s. f. (pl. **coroas-imperiais**) 1. (bot.)
crown-imperial (Fritillaria imperialis). 2. (zool.) a
volute (Voluta imperialis).
coroamento s. m. 1. coronation, ceremony of investing a sovereign with a royal crown. 2. (archit.)
crowning, coping of a building. 3. finish, completion.
coroanha s. f. common name of two plants of the
family Leguminosae (Dioclea erecta, Dioclea violacea).
coroar v. 1. to crown, invest with royalty, enthrone.
2. to decorate with a crown. 3. to acclaim, elect.
4. to top, cap. 5. (dent.) to put an artificial crown
on a tooth. 6. to finish, complete. 7. to reward,
recompense. 8. to perfect. 9. (Braz.) to form a
small earth wall around the trunk of a coffee tree.
10. ~**-se** to surround o. s. with. 11. to enwreathe.
12. to crest.
~ **com louros** to laureate. ~ **um rei** to king. **ele**
foi coroado rei he was crowned king. **o fim coroa**
a obra all's well that ends well.
coroa-real s. f. (pl. **coroas-reais**), (bot.) yellow sweet-
clover.
corobicho adj. strong, resistant (said of horses).
coroboca s. f. 1. an isolated place in the backwoods.
2. dwelling place in the backwoods, faraway abode.
coroca (l) s. f. an ugly old woman, hag. ‖ adj. m. + f.
old, decrepit, failing, doting.
coroca (II) s. f. (Braz.) a knot or kink in the fishing-
-line.
coroça s. f. 1. a straw cape used by fishermen and
peasants. 2. straw hut. 3. (jur.) abusive formalism
in legal proceedings.
coró-coró s. m. (pl. **coró-corós**), (ornith.) an ibis
(Phimosus infuscatus nudifrons).
corocotéu s. m. (ornith.) a cotingid (Ampelion cuculatus).
corocoxó s. m. (ornith.) common name of two cotingids
(Ampelion cuculatus Swains, Ampelion melanoce-
phalus).

corografia s. f. chorography.
corográfico adj. chorographic(al). ‖ **corograficamente**
adv. chorographically.
corógrafo s. m. chorographer.
coróia s. f. a knot or kink in the fishing-line.
coróide s. f. (anat.) choroid.
coroidéia s. f. (anat.) choroid.
coroidite s. f. (med.) choroiditis.
coroinha s. f. 1. dim. form of **coroa**, small crown. 2.
m. a choir-boy, altar-boy, server.
corola s. f. (bot.) corolla.
coroláceo adj. corollaceous.
corolado adj. (bot.) corollate(d).
corolário s. m. 1. corollary. 2. consequence, deduction. 3. additional proof. 4. inference.
corolífero adj. (bot.) corolliferous.
coroliforme adj. m. + f. (bot.) corolliform.
corolítico adj. (archit.) corollitic(al), foliated (said with
regard to the shaft of a column).
corologia s. f. chorology.
corólula s. f. (bot.) corollet, a small corolla.
corona s. f. (bot., electr.) corona.
coronadas s. f. pl. (zool.) Coronatae: an order of
Scyphomedusae (deep-sea jellyfishishes).
coronal s. m. (pl. **-ais**) (anat.) 1. frontal bone. 2.
corona, upper part of a tooth or of the skull. ‖
adj. m. + f. coronal, of or pertaining to a crown
or corona, coronary.
coronária s. f. (anat.) coronary artery.
coronário adj. 1. (anat.) coronary. 2. of or pertaining
to a crown. 3. crown-shaped.
corondel s. m. (typogr.) = **corandel**.
corondó s. m. (zool.) a small freshwater snail of the
genus Planorbis.
coronel (l) s. m. (pl. **-éis**) 1. colonel, commander of a
regiment. 2. (aeron.) group captain. 3. (pop.) the
butt of a party, one who has to pay the expenses.
coronel (II) s. m. (pl. **-éis**), (her.) a crown on the top
of an escutcheon.
coronelato s. m. colonelcy, office, rank and authority
of a colonel.
coronelício adj. 1. (depr.) of, pertaining to or relative
to a colonel. 2. showy, ostentatious, pretentious.
coronha s. f. 1. butt of a rifle, gun-stock, stock,
butt. 2. (bot.) sweet acacia.
coronhada s. f. a blow with the butt of a rifle or
gun.
coronheiro (l) s. m. rifle butt manufacturer.
coronheiro (II) s. m. (Port., prov.) porter, carrier.
corônide s. f. 1. cornice. 2. top, summit. 3. crown,
crownwork.
coroniforme adj. m. + f. crown-shaped.
coronilha s. f. 1. (bot.) coronilla, coronillo, axseed.
2. (pop.) a strong, courageous fellow, tough, ruffian.
coronilha-dos-jardins s. f. (pl. **coronilhas-dos-jardins**),
(bot.) scorpion senna.
coronóide adj. m. + f., **coronóideo** adj. resembling
the beak of a crow.
cororô s. m. scorched rice which sticks to the walls
of the pan.
cororoá s. m. a rope or sling made of red leather.
corote s. m. a small cask, water keg.
corotéu s. m. (ornith.) a cotingid (Ampellio cuculatus).
corozil s. m. a kind of thatch.
corozo s. m. 1. (bot.) corozo palm, ivory palm. 2.
corozo nut. 3. corozo fiber.
corpanzil s. m. (pl. **-is**) a big body. 2. stoutness,
tallness; stature. 3. a stout person.
corpeada s. f. rapid movement with the body, wheeling
round, feint.
corpete s. m. 1. bodice, corselet. 2. camisole. 3.
corsage.

C 18

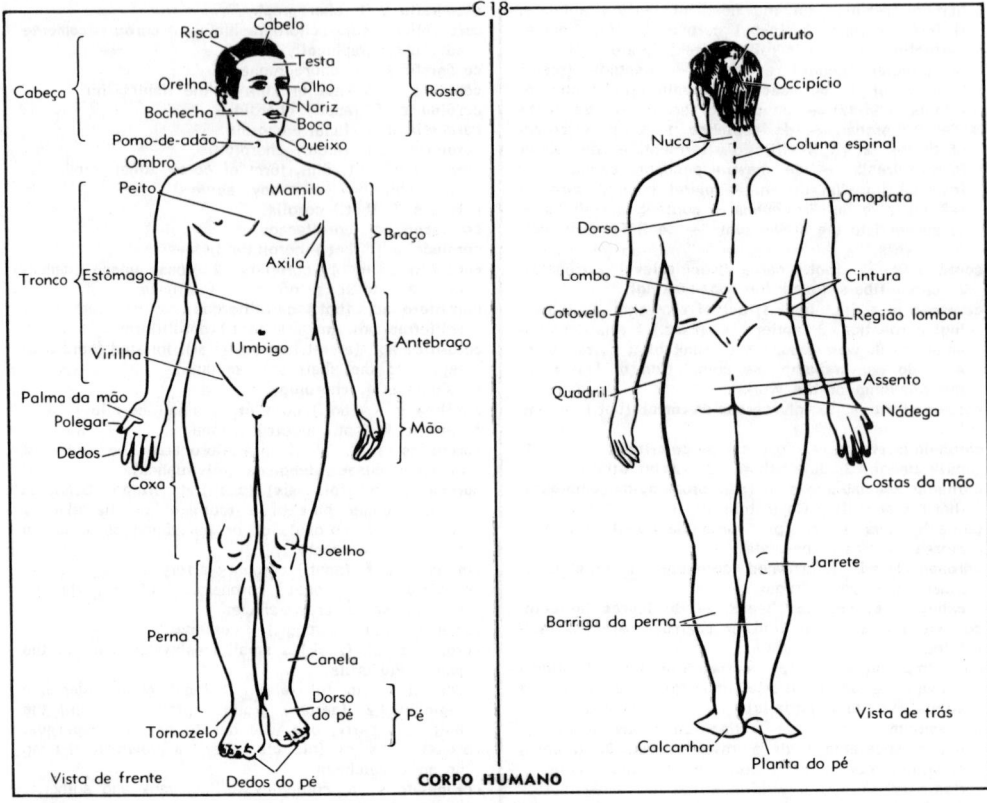

Vista de frente   Dedos do pé   **CORPO HUMANO**

Labels (Vista de frente): Risca, Cabelo, Testa, Orelha, Olho, Nariz, Boca, Queixo, Cabeça, Bochecha, Pomo-de-adão, Ombro, Rosto, Peito, Mamilo, Braço, Axila, Tronco, Estômago, Virilha, Umbigo, Antebraço, Palma da mão, Polegar, Dedos, Mão, Coxa, Joelho, Perna, Canela, Dorso do pé, Pé, Tornozelo

Labels (Vista de trás): Cocuruto, Occipício, Nuca, Coluna espinal, Omoplata, Dorso, Lombo, Cintura, Cotovelo, Região lombar, Quadril, Assento, Nádega, Costas da mão, Jarrete, Barriga da perna, Vista de trás, Calcanhar, Planta do pé

corpinho s. m. 1. dim. form of **corpo,** small body. 2. = **corpete.**

corpo s. m. 1. body: a) structure of man or animal. b) limited portion of matter. c) corpus, mass, bulk. d) main part (plates L 4, R 3). e) figure, frame. f) (mus.) resonance base (plates G 2, H). g) thickness. h) barrel, trunk. i) consistence. j) crowd, throng. k) collection. l) (mil.) regiment, brigade. m) basis, base (plate P 4). n) matter, material. o) society, company. p) context, contexture. q) (geom.) a solid figure. 2. (archit.) the main structure of a building. 3. shape, form. 4. importance. 5. (typogr.) point. ~ **celeste** heavenly body, star. ~ **de bailado** ballet, corps de ballet. ~ **de bombeiros** fire brigade. ~ **de cadetes** cadet corps. ~ **de delito** corpus delicti, proof or evidence. **Corpo de Deus** (rel.) Corpus Christi. ~ **de parafusos** shank of a screw (plate P 4). ~ **de prego** stem of a nail (plate P 15). ~ **de tropas** body of troops. ~ **de vestido** waist (of a dress). ~ **diplomático** diplomatic corps. ~ **docente** teaching staff, faculty. ~ **do exército** army corps. ~ **humano** human body (plate C 18). **atacar o serviço com** ~ **e alma** to throw o. s. with heart and soul into one's work. **ele se empenha com** ~ **e alma no seu trabalho** he puts his heart in his work. **ele tem um** ~ **estranho na vista** he has a foreign body in his eye. **lutar** ~ **a** ~ to fight hand to hand. **na hora do aperto ele tira o** ~ **fora** if it comes to a pinch he slips the collar. **ele tem realmente o diabo no** ~ he is a sheer devil. **um** ~ **bem feito** a well-knit frame. **vinho de** ~ full--bodied wine. **fazer** ~ **mole** to dawdle away, loiter.

corpo-a-corpo s. m. a close fight, (sport) clinch.

corpo-lúteo s. m. (pl. **corpos-lúteos**) corpus luteum.

corporação s. f. (pl. **-ões**) 1. corporation. 2. association, guild. 3. fraternity.

corporal (I) adj. m. + f. (pl. **-ais**) corporal, corporeal, material.

corporal (II) s. m. (pl. **-ais**), (eccl.) Communion cloth, corporal.

corporal (III) s. m. (pl. **-ais**), (archit.) the part of the nave which lies between the main door and the transept.

corporalidade s. f. 1. corporality, corporeality. 2. corporeity, corporealness. 3. fleshliness. 4. material existence.

corporalizar v. 1. to give a corporeal form to, embody. 2. to assume corporeity. 3. to materialize, corporealize.

corporativismo s. m. (sociology). 1. government based principally on the productive classes as represented by corporations. 2. collectivism. 3. communism.

corporativista s. m. + f. sympathizer or defender of corporative government, collectivist. ‖ adj. of, pertaining to or relative to a corporative government, collectivistic(al).

corporativo adj. corporative, collective.

corporatura s. f. 1. the external form of a body. 2. form, shape. 3. stature, physique.

corporeidade s. f. corporeity, corporality.

corpóreo adj. 1. corporal, corporeal. 2. bodily, bodied. 3. external, outward. 4. fleshly. 5. material. 6. physical.

corporificação s. f. (pl. **-ões**) 1. corporification. 2. incorporation, incarnation. 3. embodiment.
corporificar v. 1. to corporify, assume a corporeal form. 2. to embody. 3. to externalize. 4. to materialize. 5. **~-se** to be or become corporified. 6. to incorporate.
corpo-seco s. m. (pl. **corpos-secos**) (Braz.) 1. skeleton. 2. sylvan spirit, goblin (appearing in the form of a skeleton).
corpudo adj. (pop.) 1. corpulent, stout. 2. courageous, valiant. 3. tall, big.
corpulência s. f. 1. corpulence, corpulency. 2. stoutness, fatness. 3. fleshiness, fullness. 4. portliness.
corpulento adj. 1. corpulent. 2. stout, fat. 3. fleshy, chunky, gross, burly. 4. big-bodied, big, portly.
corpuscular adj. m. + f. corpuscular.
corpúsculo s. m. 1. corpuscule, corpuscle. 2. molecule, atom. 3. mite, mote.
corra s. f. 1. a rope made from esparto fibers. 2. leather strap, thong. 3. a strip of wood, batten.
corrão adj. (pl. **-ões**) swift-footed.
corrasão s. f. (geol.) corrasion.
correada s. f. a blow with a leather strap.
correagem s. f. (pl. **-ens**), **correame** m. leather belts and straps (esp. of a uniform), harness, belting.
correão s. m. (pl. **-ões**) a long, broad or heavy leather strap.
correaria s. f. leather goods factory, saddlery.
corre-campo s. f. (pl. **corre-campos**) (zool.) a colubrid snake. (Dryophylax pallidus).
correção s. f. (pl. **-ões**) 1. correction. 2. correctness. 3. rectitude, rightness. 4. rectification, amendment. 5. emendation. 6. revisal. 7. expurgation. 8. reformatory, workhouse, penitentiary. 9. pressing-down, chastisement.
~ da deriva drift-correction. **~ de Bessel** (stat.) Bessel's adjustment. **~ monetária** monetary correction. **~ tipográfica** correction, emendation. **casa de ~** reform school.
correcional s. m. (pl. **-ais**) jurisdiction of a correctional court. ‖ adj. m. + f. 1. correctional, of or pertaining to correction. 2. reformatory. 3. of or relative to a correctional court.
instituto ~ house of correction.
correcionalidade s. f. a nature of infringements subject to correctional jurisdiction.
corre-corre s. m. 1. (bot.) a convolvulaceous plant (Evolvulus alsinoides). 2. headlong flight. 3. rout, stampede.
corredeira s. f. 1. chute, river rapids. 2. (pop.) diarrhea.
corredela s. f. 1. running, run. 2. hurrying.
corrediça s. f. 1. slide, slider. 2. sash-window. 3. race, strong current of water, chute. 4. coulisse. 5. blind. 6. sliding curtain. 7. groove, slot.
corrediço, corredio adj. 1. sliding, gliding. 2. slipping easily. 3. running. 4. smooth, even. 5. unencumbered, free, easy.
amarra -a slip-rope. **assento ~** sliding seat. **biombo ~** sliding panel. **janela -a** sash-window. **roda ~ dentada -a** sliding gear. **peso ~** sliding weight.
corredor s. m. 1. runner, racer. 2. corridor, gangway. 3. passage, aisle, gallery. 4. narrow mouth of a river. 5. narrow way, passageway in a garden. ‖ adj. running, racing.
corredora s. f. (fort.) portcullis.
corredoura s. f. the inferior stone in a set of millstones.
corredouro s. m. 1. track, race track. 2. continued running.
corredura s. f. 1. running, hurrying. 2. race. 3. the rest of a liquid which remains in the measuring vessel.

correeiro s. m. beltmaker, saddler.
corregedor s. m. (jur.) corregidor.
corregedoria s. f. office, dignity and authority of a corregidor.
correger (I) v. (ant.) 1. to correct, rectify. 2. to amend, emend. 3. to repair, reform, mend.
correger (II) v. (pop.) 1. to survey, inspect. 2. to examine carefully. 3. to search. 4. to run through.
corregimento s. m. 1. correction. 2. fine, penalty. 3. ornament, decoration. 4. household furnishings or decorations.
córrego s. m. 1. streamlet, stream. 2. brooklet, runlet. 3. a narrow road in the mountains or running between walls. 4. ravine, gully. 5. small tributary stream.
córrego-seco s. m. (pl. **córregos-secos**) a deep ravine worn out by temporary rainfalls.
corregozinho s. m. rillet, very small watercourse.
correia s. f. 1. leather strap, thong (plate M 3). 2. belt, belting. 3. leash, dog lead.
~ articulada chain-belt. **~ de fibras têxteis** fabric belt. **~ de transmissão** driving band, driving belt (plate M 1). **~ de transporte** conveyor belt. **~ em V** V-belt. **~ suspensa** overhead conveyor.
correição s. f. (pl. **-ões**) 1. correction. 2. a corregidor's visit. 3. popular designation of any variety of army ants. 4. a swarm of ants or other insects.
correio s. m. 1. messenger, courier. 2. mailman. 3. mail, post. 4. post office, postal service. 5. prediction. 6. letters, correspondence.
~ aéreo air mail. **~ pneumático** pneumatic dispatch, pneumatic post. **caixa de ~** mailbox. **com o ~ de hoje** by to-day's post. **ir ao ~** to go to the post. **leve estas cartas ao ~** take these letters to the post. **pela volta do ~** by return of mail. **por ~ expresso** by dispatch. **por ~ separado** under separate cover.
correlação s. f. (pl. **-ões**) correlation, correlativity.
correlacional v. to correlate, establish a relationship, connect systematically.
correlatar v. to put in relation with each other, be in correlation, be reciprocal, correlate.
correlatividade s. f. correlativity.
correlativo adj. correlative, correlate, reciprocal, correspondent. ‖ **-amente** adv. correlatively, reciprocally.
correligionário s. m. coreligionist. ‖ adj. coreligionary.
correligionarismo s. m. principles of coreligionary solidarity, community of interests.
correntada s. f. river rapids, chute.
correntão adj. (pl. **-ões**) (f. **-ona**) 1. unencumbered, unconstrained. 2. free, easy. 3. loquacious. 4. affable, amiable.
corrente (I) s. f. 1. chain, metal chain, tie (plates B 4, 11, C 4, 13, E 11, J 3, P 19, V 3). 2. cable, rope, hawser. 3. fetters, shackle.
~ articulada sprocket chain. **~ calibrada** pitch chain. **~ de elos** open link chain (plate C 4). **~ de entrave** stop chain. **~ de ganchos** hook link chain, band chain (plate C 4). **~ de rolos** roller chain (plate C 4). **~ de segurança** guard chain. **~ de suspensão** (chain) sling, sling chain (plate C 4). **~ de tração** draught-chain (plate C 13). **~ de travessas (de estais)** stud-link chain (plate C 4). **~ motriz** drive chain. **~ pequena** chainlet. **~ sem-fim** caterpillar. **roda para ~** sprocket wheel.
corrente (II) s. f. 1. current. 2. stream, watercourse. 3. torrent. 4. flux, flow. 5. circulation. 6. tide. 7. (fig.) tendency. ‖ adj. m. + f. 1. current. 2. running, fluent. 3. floating, afloat. 4. common, usual. 5. known, public. 6. easy. 7. prevailing, prevalent. 8. circulating. 9. smooth. 10. ruling. 11. passable.

‖ ~**mente** adv. currently, fluently, readily, easily, commonly, generally.
~ **alternada** (electr.) alternating current. ~ **contínua** (electr.) continuous current, direct current. ~ **de carga** (electr.) charging current. ~ **de indução** induced current. ~ **dielétrica** displacement current. ~ **do alimentador** (electr.) feeder current. **água** ~ running water. **a opinião** ~ **é...** the current opinion is... **contra a** ~ upstream. **em dinheiro** ~ in current money. **estar ao** ~ to be well informed of. **nadar contra a** ~ to swim against the tide. **pôr alguém ao** ~ to inform s. o. of s. th., put a person up to the ropes. **preço** ~ the market price. **uma** ~ **de ar** a draught.
corrente (III) s. m. the current month.
no dia 5 do ~ on the 5th instant.
correnteza s. f. 1. current. 2. stream, watercourse. 3. flow, drift. 4. row, rank, range (as of houses). 5. chute, river rapid. 6. (fig.) briskness, liveliness. 7. (fig.) ease.
~ **de ar** draughtiness. **ele nada contra a** ~ he goes against the stream.
correntino s. m. native or inhabitant of Corrientes (an Argentine province). ‖ adj. of or relative to this province and its inhabitants.
correntio adj. 1. swift, swift-footed, rapid. 2. common, usual. 3. current. 4. generally accepted.
correntista s. m. + f. clerk in charge of the current accounts.
correntoso adj. fast-flowing, swift.
correr v. 1. to run, run after. 2. to travel. 3. to go rapidly, hurry. 4. to chase, hunt, pursue. 5. to be exposed or subject to. 6. to subject o. s. to. 7. to pass along, range over. 8. to go about. 9. to peruse, consult. 10. to refer to for information (to a book, dictionary, etc.). 11. to flee, fly, bolt. 12. to ladder (stockings). 13. to slip away, elapse (time). 14. to spread, make known (a notice, news). 15. to pass from hand to hand, circulate. 16. to flow, pour. 17. to ooze, leak. 18. to fuse, melt. 19. to extend, go on, proceed. 20. to gush, surge. 21. to move quickly towards. 22. to compete with. 23. to run through. 24. to expel, drive out. 25. to take to one's heels.
corra! shake a leg! **corremos a cidade inteira à procura do livro** we ran through the whole town in search of the book. **corre o boato que...** there is a rumor that... ~ **às armas** to fly to arms. ~ **atrás de alguém** to run after a person. ~ **em auxílio de alguém** to run to a person's aid. ~ **o risco** to run the risk, risk. ~ **perigo** to expose o. s. to danger. **correu muito sangue** much blood has been shed. **apenas corri os olhos pela carta** I just glanced over the letter. **deixa o barco** ~! let the thing slide! **ela correu para seu quarto** she ran to her room. **ele correu de medo** he showed a clean pair of heels. **ele correu para salvar a sua vida** he ran for his life. **ele deixa as coisas** ~em he lets things slide. **ele partiu correndo** he sped his way. **ele saiu corrido daqui** he was chased out here. **isto corre por sua conta** that goes to your account. **ninguém corre parelha com ele** no man is equal to him. **no** ~ **dos séculos** down the centuries. **o processo correu em ausência do réu** the law-suit went by default. **sair correndo precipitadamente** to rush headlong away. **tudo lhe corre muito bem** he is very successfull, he's in clover.
correria s. f. 1. running, scurry, rushing around. 2. foray, incursion, inroad.
correspondência s. f. 1. correspondence, exchange of communications. 2. letters, art of letter-writing. 3. conformity, congruity. 4. respondence. 5. agreement, harmony. 6. coincidence. 7. uniformity.

~ **atrasada** overdue correspondence. ~ **comercial** commercial correspondence. **em** ~ **com** in accordance with.
correspondente s. m. + f. correspondent. 2. newspaper correspondent. 3. representative. ‖ adj. 1. correspondent, corresponding. 2. suitable, agreeable. 3. congruent. 4. concordant, accordable. 5. identic(al). 6. pursuant. 7. respective. ‖ ~**mente** adv. correspondingly, respectively, accordantly.
corresponder v. 1. to correspond. 2. to retribute, repay, reciprocate. 3. to answer, reply. 4. to satisfy. 5. to agree with, conform to. 6. to coincide. 7. to suit. 8. to be equal (to). 9. to be in communication with.
~ **às exigências** to meet the requirements, (coll.) to come up to the mark. **a qualidade não corresponde ao preço** the quality falls short with the price. **ele não corresponde à tarefa** he is not up to his job. **ele não correspondeu às minhas expectativas** he did not come up to my expectations. **isto corresponde!** that's according! **isto corresponde à sua descrição** this answers to your description. **isto não corresponde ao ideal** this falls short of the ideal. **não posso** ~ **ao seu pedido** I cannot comply with your request. **o prato corresponde ao seu gosto** the dish suits his taste. **seu amor não é correspondido** his (her) love is not returned.
corretagem s. f. (pl. **-ens**) 1. brokerage, factorage. 2. jobbing. 3. fee, commission.
~ **de penhores** pawnbroking.
corretar v. 1. to work as a broker. 2. to traffic, negotiate.
corretismo s. m. correctitude, correctness, irreprehensible conduct.
corretivo s. m. 1. corrective; corrective agent. 2. penalty, punishment. 3. remedy. ‖ adj. 1. corrective. 2. amendatory. 3. tending to rectify. ‖ -**amente** adv. correctively.
correto adj. 1. correct. 2. irreprehensible, perfect. 3. true, free from error, accurate, exact. 4. upright, aboveboard, right. 5. proper. 6. sound. 7. okay, all right. 8. dignified. 9. elegant. ‖ -**amente** adv. correctly, uprightly, properly, righteously.
ele não agiu de modo ~ he did not act as he should. **um homem** ~ an upright man.
corretor (I) s. m. 1. corrector. 2. corrector of the press, reader, reviser. 3. disciplinarian.
corretor (II) s. m. 1. broker, commission agent. 2. agent. 3. jobber.
~ **de ações** share-broker. ~ **de câmbio** discount broker, exchange broker, bill-broker. ~ **de fundos** stock broker. ~ **de imóveis** realtor, house-agent. ~ **marítimo** ship-broker. ~ **de seguros** insurance broker.
corretoria s. f. office, dignity or authority of a corregidor.
corretório s. m. registration of penalties. ‖ adj. corrective.
corrião s. m. (pl. **-ões**) a broad leather belt with a buckle.
corrição s. m. (pl. **-ões**), (hunt.) the starting of game with the help of dogs, the pursuit of running game with dogs.
corricar (I) v. 1. to walk slowly. 2. to run with short steps. 3. to walk up and down, go from one side to the other. 4. to perambulate. 5. to loaf around.
corricar (II) v. to fish by drawing the bait on a long line behind a moving boat.
corricas s. f. pl. wrinkles.
corrico s. m. troll-fishing.
corrida s. f. 1. run, the act of running. 2. scurrying, scurry, rushing around, scamper, skedaddle. 3. way, distance. 4. track, course, race-course. 5. run-

ning, coursing. 6. race, racing. 7. horse race. 8. (met.) the pouring of metal. 9. bullfight. 10. run on a bank or banks (to withdraw funds or deposits). 11. (mech.) the strokes of a piston. 12. trip in a taxi. ~ **armamentista** arms race, armamental race. ~ **breve** dash. ~ **de cavalos** horse race, flat race. ~ **de cavalos com obstáculos** steeplechase, hurdle race. ~ **de galgos** dog race. ~ **de revezamento** relay race. ~ **final** (sports) final heat, last event, decider. ~ **de olhos** once-over, glance-over. ~ **de touros** bullfight. ~ **de treino** (sports) hollow race. ~ **de trote** trotting, trotting match. ~ **empatada** dead heat. **de** ~ hastily, in a hurry. **ele disputou a** ~ he ran the race. **ganhar a** ~ to make the running. **nas** ~**s de cavalo** on the turf. **pista de** ~ speedway.
corrido (I) adj. 1. drawn (lottery ticket). 2. drained off. 3. expelled, ousted. 4. confused, confounded, vexed. 5. ashamed, abashed. 6. degraded. 7. worn, wasted.
corrido (II) s. m. pebble gravel.
corrigenda s. f. 1. corrigendum. 2. a list of errors to be corrected. 3. errata.
corrigibilidade s. f. corrigibility.
corrigir v. 1. to correct, rectify. 2. to amend, emendate. 3. to set right, bring in order. 4. to reform, right. 5. to regenerate, revive. 6. to revise. 7. to improve, better, ameliorate. 8. to censure, reprimand. 9. to punish, castigate. 10. to discipline. 11. to repress. 12. to reclaim, retrieve. 13. to remedy. 14. ~**-se:** a) to change one's ways or life, turn over a new leaf. b) to chastise o. s. c) to grow better, correct o. s.
~ **o rumo** (naut.) to correct the course, make up for deviation. ~ **provas** to correct proof, proofread. **ele corrigiu-se** he mended his ways. **isto é uma edição corrigida** this is a revised edition. **você precisa** ~ **o seu modo de viver** you must improve your standards.
corrigível adj. m. + f. (pl. **-íveis**) 1. corrigible, correctable. 2. reclaimable. 3. reformable. 4. emendable, mendable. 5. revisable. ‖ **corrigivelmente** adv. corrigibly, reformably, revisably.
corrilheiro s. m. 1. promoter of secret or closed meetings. 2. frequenter of such reunions. 3. intriguer, schemer. 4. tough, ruffian.
corrilho s. m. 1. conciliabulum. 2. clandestine meeting (esp. of partisans or conspirators). 3. conventicle.
corrimaca s. f. (Braz.) 1. a great quantity, lots. 2. a boatload, batch.
corrimaça s. f. 1. hoots and jeers. 2. uproar, hubbub. 3. riot. 4. persecution with railing or offending remarks. 5. run, chase.
corrimão s. m. (pl. **-ões**) 1. stair rail. 2. handrail, guardrail (plates A 8, E 7). 3. balustrade, banister.
corrimboque s. m. = **cornimboque**.
corrimento s. m. 1. act of flowing. 2. (path.) flow(ing) of humours, rheum. 3. hooting, hoot and cry. 4. noisy pursuit. 5. vexation.
corriola s. f. 1. a kind of game in which a folded ribbon is used. 2. hooting, hoot and cry. 3. noisy pursuit. 4. (fam.) cheat, trick.
cair na ~ to fall into the snare. **fazer alguém cair na** ~ to trick or cheat s. o.
corriqueirice s. f. triviality, commonplaceness, vulgarity.
corriqueirismo s. m. (Braz.) affectedness, presumptuousness.
corriqueiro s. m. (N. Braz.) small kerosene lamp. ‖ adj. 1. current. 2. trivial, commonplace, trite. 3. vulgar. 4. (Braz.) affected, presumptuous. 5. (Braz.) unquiet, turbulent. 6. (Port. prov.) tale-bearing.
corrixo s. m. (Braz., ornith.) cowbird (Molothrus bonariensis), also known as **chupim.**

corro s. m. (arch.) 1. circus. 2. arena, ring. 3. assembly. 4. circle, society, club. 5. gang, band. 6. multitude, throng.
corró s. m. (N. Braz.) small fishes in irrigation ponds.
corroboração s. f. (pl. **-ões**) 1. corroboration, confirmation. 2. strengthening.
corroborante adj. m. + f. 1. corroborant. 2. strengthening.
corroborar v. 1. to corroborate, confirm. 2. to strengthen. 3. to valiate. 4. ~**-se** to gain strength; to be confirmed.
corroborativo adj. corroborative, corroboratory.
corroer v. 1. to corrode, erode. 2. to gnaw at, eat away. 3. to waste away. 4. to destroy slowly. 5. to deprave. 6. ~**-se:** a) to be consumed or wasted away. b) to become corrupt. c) to wear out. d) to become vitiated.
corroído adj. 1. corroded, eroded. 2. worm-eaten. 3. worn away, time-worn. 4. vitiated.
corrompedor s. m. corruptor. ‖ adj. corrupting.
corromper v. 1. to corrupt: a) taint, spoil, adulterate, desfigure, mar. b) deprave, pervert, debauch, seduce. c) brible. 2. ~**-se:** a) to putrify, rot, deteriorate. b) to become adulterated. c) to degenerate, become perverted.
corrompido adj. corrupted, corrupt.
corrompimento s. m. = **corrução.**
corrosão s. f. (pl. **-ões**) corrosion, erosion.
~ **eólica** (geol.) deflation, wind erosion (of rocks). ~ **magmática** (petrog.) resorption borders of phenocrysts.
corrosibilidade s. f. corrosibility, corrosibleness.
corrosível adj. m.+f. (pl. **-íveis**) corrosible, corrodible.
corrosividade s. f. corrosiveness.
corrosivo s. m. corrosive. ‖ adj. corrosive.
líquido ~ corrosive liquor. **sublimado** ~ corrosive sublimate.
corrubiana, corrupiana s. f. (Braz.) cold fog accompanied by a southeast wind, in some mountaineous regions of Minas Gerais.
corrução, corrupção s. f. (pl. **-ões**) 1. (also **corrompimento** m.) corruption: a) spoiling, tainting, putrefaction, deterioration, rottenness. b) adulteration, alteration, perversion. c) perversity, depravation, debauchment. d) bribery. e) seduction. 2. = **maculo.**
corruchiar v. (Braz.) to sing continuously in a low tone (canaries and other songbirds).
corrugação s. f. (pl. **-ões**) corrugation: act or effect of corrugation.
corrugado adj. corrugated, wrinkled.
chapa -a corrugated (sheet) iron.
corrugar v. to corrugate, wrinkle.
corruíra s. f. (Braz.) common name of several birds of the wren family (Troglodytes musculus, etc.).
corruiraçu s. f. (Braz., ornith.) a wren (Thryothorus longirostris longirostris).
corruíra-do-brejo s. f. (pl. **corruíras-do-brejo**) = **curutié.**
corrume s. m. slide groove, slide slot.
corrupiana s. f. = **corrubiana.**
corrupião s. m. (Braz.) 1. = **sofrê.** 2. bird of the family Pipridae (Chiromachaesis gutturosus).
corrupiar v. (Braz.) 1. to whirl round, spin round, twirl. 2. to cause to go around.
corrupiê, corrupié s. m. (Braz.) croupier: superintendent of a gambling table.
corrupio s. m. 1. name of several children's games. 2. (fam.) incessant movement, overbusiness, bustle, fuss. 3. whirlwind. 4. toy windmill. 5. (Braz.) sea urchin.
corrupixel s. m. (pl. **-éis**) (N. Braz.) small bag at the end of a pole for plucking fruits.
corrutela, corruptela s. f. 1. corruption. 2. wrong manner of speaking or writing a word. 3. alteration.

4. abuse. 5. agent of corruption. 6. (Braz.) small camping ground of diamond miners at the entrance of the diamond fields.

corrutibilidade, corruptibilidade s. f. corruptibility.

corrutível, corruptível adj. m. + f. (pl. **-íveis**) corruptible: 1. perishable. 2. venal, bribable. 3. seducible.

corrutivo, corruptivo adj. corruptive, venal.

corruto, corrupto adj. 1. corrupt: a) dissolute, lewd. b) depraved, demoralised. c) decomposed, putrid. d) venal, bribable. 2. vitiated, incorrect (language).

corrutor, corruptor s. m. 1. corrupter, briber. 2. vitiator of language. ‖ adj. corrupting, corruptive.

corsário s. m. corsair, privateer: 1. privateering vessel. 2. one engaged in privateering, pirate.

corsear v. to privateer.

corselete s. m. (also **cossolete, cossoleto**) 1. corselet. 2. bodice.

córsico s. m. (also **corso**) Corsican: native or inhabitant of Corsica. ‖ adj. Corsican: relating to Corsica or its inhabitants.

corso (I) s. m. 1. privateering cruise, privateering. 2. piracy. 3. pillage. 4. corso: procession of carriages or automobiles.

corso (II) s. m. school of sardines.

corso (III) s. m. Corsican. ‖ adj. 1. Corsican. 2. (N. Braz.) living in shallow water (fishes).

corta s. f. 1. cutting: action of the verb to cut. 2. pruning.

corta-água s. f. (pl. **corta-águas**) (Braz. ornith.) black skimmer (Rhinchops nigra cineracens).

corta-asma s. f. (pl. **corta-asmas**) (Braz.) medicinal plant of the family Rubiaceae (Psychotria involucrata).

corta-bainha s. f. (pl. **corta-bainhas**) (N. Braz.) = **cachaça** white rum.

corta-brocha s. m. (pl. **corta-brochas**) (N. Braz., pop.) heated discussion, altercation, strife.

corta-charutos s. m. sg. + pl. cigar cutter (plate F 7).

corta-chefe s. f. (pl. **corta-chefes**) (carp.) drawknife, drawing knife, drawshave (plate F 2).

cortadeira s. f. 1. pastry cutter, jagging iron. 2. (Braz.) agricultural instrument for breaking up the soil. 3. (Braz., also **saúva**) sauba ant.

cortado s. m. 1. (S. Braz.) quarter part of the boliviano, a silver coin formerly in circulation in Rio Grande do Sul. 2. (Braz.) incessant movement, overbusines, bustle, fuss. 3. pinch, strait, tight spot. 4. persecution. 5. continuous petty domestic persecution. ‖ adj. 1. cut, severed. 2. interrupted during the dry season (rivers).
andar num ~ to be very busy, be in a pinch. **trazer alguém num** ~ to persecute incessantly.

cortador s. m. 1. cutter: a) cutting tool or machine (plates A 2, B 12). b) meat cutter, butcher. c) (tail) cutter. d) wood-cutter. 2. (N. Braz.) flirter, ladykiller. ‖ adj. 1. cutting. 2. (N. Braz.) flirtatious.
~ **de grama** lawn-mower.

cortador-chanfrador s. m. (pl. **cortadores-chanfradores**) (typogr.) cutter and creaser, cutting and creasing press.

cortadouro, cortadoiro s. m. (Port., prov.) pass between mountains.

cortadura s. f. (also **cortadela**) 1. cut, incision, gash. 2. draining ditch. 3. gap between mountains.

corta-frio s. m. (pl. **corta-frios**) cold chisel, cold set.

cortagem s. f. 1. cutting. 2. meat cutting.

corta-jaca s. f. (pl. **corta-jacas**) 1. (Braz.) a kind of tap-dancing. 2. (N. Braz. sl.) flatterer, lick-spittle.

corta-mão s. m. (pl. **corta-mãos**) (carp.) square.

corta-mar s. m. (pl. **corta-mares**) 1. breakwater. 2. angular prolongation of bridge pillars to strengthen the structure. 3. (Braz.) = **bico-rasteiro**.

cortamento s. m. 1. cut, cutting. 2. cutting-off, amputation, mutilation. 3. crossing, interception.

cortante adj. m. + f. 1. cutting: a) that cuts. b) keen, sharp-edged. 2. keen, biting, nipping (cold).

corta-palha s. m. (pl. **corta-palhas**) fixed saw for chopping straw.

corta-papel s. m. (pl. **corta-papéis**) paper cutter.

cortar v. 1. to cut: a) make a cut; incise, gash, sever, cut or hew down, fell; cut through, in two; cut up, chop, slice; cut out, carve, saw off; mow; cut off; amputate. b) wound with a sharp instrument. c) cut to measure. d) divide a pack of cards. e) pierce. f) trim, clip, prune. g) suppress. h) be sharp or sharp-edged. i) cross, intersect. j) intercept. k) bar, block (way). l) shorten, diminish. m) interrupt, cut one short. n) end, finish, make an end. o) shut off (water), turn off (steam). p) suspend (deliveries). 2. to afflict. 3. to obstruct, encumber. 4. to adulterate, doctor (wine). 5. (S. Braz.) to separate cattle from the herd. 6. (N. Braz.) to dry up in summer (river). 7. to plough (the sea). 8. (N. Braz.) to court, make love. 9. ~-se: a) to wound o. s. with a cutting instrument. b) (S. Braz.) to separate o. s. from, part from. c) (S. Braz.) to interrupt the course (river).
~ **a cabeça** to decapitate, behead. ~ **a febre** to make cease the fever. ~ **a grama** to mow the lawn. ~ **a palavra a alguém** to cut a person short. ~ **a retirada ao inimigo** to cut off the enemy's retreat. ~ **as asas** (also fig.) to clip the wings. ~ **as ondas, o mar** to plough the waves, the sea. ~ **as unhas** to pare, cut, clip the nails. ~ **à esquerda** to take the turning to the left. ~ **com os dentes** to bite off. ~ **direito** to act correctly. ~ **em pedaços** to cut up, mince. ~ **largo** 1. to spend largely. 2. to be large-minded, not to attach importance to trifles. ~ **lenha** to cut, cleave wood. ~ **na casaca de alguém** to slander, backbite, speak ill of s. o. ~ **nas despesas** to curtail, reduce one's expenses. ~ **o cabelo** to have one's hair cut. ~ **o coração** to break the heart. ~ **o dedo** to cut one's finger. ~ **o mal pela raiz** to pull up the evil by the roots. ~ **o naipe** to cut (at cards). ~ **o vestido** to cut out the dress. ~ **os ares** to fly. ~ **relações com** to break with (a person). ~ **um caminho** to block a road. ~ **uma carta (um trunfo)** to trump a card.

corta-vento s. m. (pl. **corta-ventos**) (Braz.) 1. windmill. 2. (ornith.) Paraguayan snipe (Capella paraguaiae).

corte (I) s. m. 1. cut: a) act of cutting, blow, stroke with a cutting instrument. b) incision, slab, gash, stab. c) cutting edge of a knife, etc. d) cutting, cut-off piece. e) notch, indentation, slit. f) cutting, passage, excavation, trench. g) supression (of a passage); the passage supressed. h) shortening (of an article). 2. (archit.) section, profile, plan. 3. felling of trees. 4. slaughter(ing) of cattle. 5. interruption. 6. (archit.) each of the faces of the intrados of an arch. 7. (typogr.) nick (plate T 6). 8. piece of cloth sufficient for a garment. 9. cut, make, pattern of a dress or coat. 10. cutting at cards. 11. (typogr.) edge (of a book) (plate L 4).
~ **da abertura** (typogr.) fore edge. ~ **da cabeça** (typogr.) head edge. ~ **da espada** edge of a sword. ~ **de cabelo** haircut (plate P 8). ~ **de vestido** a piece of cloth for a dress. ~ **do pé,** ~ **inferior** (typogr.) tail of the book. ~ **transversal** transverse section, cross section. **aquele vestido tem mau** ~ that dress is badly cut. **curso de** ~ **e costura** course of dress-making. **gado de** ~ cattle for slaughter. **sem** ~ blunt (plate Q).

corte (II) s. f. 1. stable, sty, pen, corral, fold. 2. butchery, slaughterhouse, shamble.

corte (ô) s. f. 1. court: a) a sovereign's residence, household, retinue, residential city. b) the sovereign and his government. 2. courtship, love-making. 3. ~ muxirão. 4. ~s pl.: a) parliament, (house of) parliament. b) (hist.) assembly pf the three estates of the Portuguese kingdom, viz. clergy, nobility and commonalty. c) the representative chambers in Portugal and Spain.
fazer a ~ a alguém 1. to pay one's court to s. o., to court s. o. 2. to pay one's courtship to a lady, (fam.) to flirt with a girl, woo.
corteiro s. m. (N. Braz.) railway excavation contractor.
cortejador s. m. 1. an overcourteous person, flatterer. 2. a wooer, suitor (of a lady). ‖ adj. overcourteous.
cortejar v. 1. to treat courteously. 2. to greet, salute. 3. compliment, flatter. 4. to court, pay one's court to. 5. to woo, make love to, flirt with.
cortejo s. m. 1. courteous treatment. 2. homage, complimentation. 3. courtship, wooing. 4. solemn greeting, salutation. 5. suite, retinue, train. 6. procession. 7. (fig.) acessory.
~ fúnebre funeral procession.
corteleiro s. m. (Braz.) tame ox which always returns to the corral.
cortelha s. f., cortelho m. stable, corral, pigsty.
cortês adj. m. + f. (pl. -eses) courteous, polite, civil, affable, urbane.
cortesã s. f. 1. lady of the court. 2. coụrtesan: luxurious fancy woman, elegant prostitute.
cortesania s. f. 1. a courtier's manners. 2. courteous manners.
cortesanice s. f. 1. affected politeness. 2. simulated urbanity. 3. a courtier's intrigue.
cortesão s. m. (pl. cortesãos, cortesões) (f. cortesã) 1. courtier: a) person in attendance at a sovereign's court. b) person with courtly manners. 2. adulater. ‖ adj. courtly: relative to a princely court.
cortesia s. f. 1. a courtier's manners. 2. courtesy, courteousness, politeness, civility, urbanity, affableness, delicacy, gentleness. 3. salutation, bow, curtsy.
fazer uma ~ to bow to, (mil.) to salute. fazer ~ com o chapéu dos outros to be generous at another's expense.
córtex, córtice s. m. cortex: 1. (bot.) bark of a tree. 2. (anat.) outer, barklike layer of several organs. 3. superficial layer of the brain.
cortiça s. f. 1. cork: bark of the cork-tree. 2. bark. 3. crust. 4. = córtex. 5. ~s pl.: a) floats (of a fishing-net). b) swimmers' life-belt.
cortiçada s. f. 1. great quantity of cork. 2. a number of beehives.
cortical adj. m. + f. (pl. -ais) (bot. + anat.) cortical: relating to the cortex.
corticeira s. f. 1. storage place for cork. 2. (also flor-de-coral, mulungu) cockscomb coral bean (Erythrina crista-galli).
corticeiro s. m. 1. cork gatherer (from the trees). 2. cork worker. 3. cork dealer. ‖ adj. relating to cork or its industry.
corticento adj. barky: resembling bark, of the nature of bark.
cortíceo adj. (made) of bark or cork.
corticícola adj. m. + f. living in the bark of trees.
corticífero adj. corticiferous; producing bark.
corticiforme adj. m. + f. corticiform: resembling bark.
cortiço s. m. 1. hive, beehive, skep. 2. (Braz.): a) slum tenement-house. b) (also cabeça-de-porco f.) a group of slum-dwellings around a common courtyard.
corticoso adj. thick-barked.

cortil s. m. (pl. -is) small cut.
cortilha s. m. jagging iron, pastry-cutter.
cortina s. f. 1. curtain: a) hanging screen of a window, (plates D 4, V 1). b) (fort.) rampart connecting two bastions. 2. low wall along a roadside over a precipice. 3. (Braz., theat.) drop-scene, act-drop in a revue.
~ da cama bed curtain. ~ da janela a window curtain (plates C 7, 20). ~ de bambu (pol.) bamboo curtain. ~ de cena scene curtain (plate P 2). ~ de ferro (de segurança) (theat.) 1. safety curtain (plate P 2). 2. (pol.) iron curtain. ~ de fogo curtain fire. ~ de fumaça smoke screen. correr a ~ 1. to draw the curtain. 2. to show, make patent, let talk the facts. por detrás da ~ (also fig.) behind the curtain.
cortinado s. m. (a set of) curtains, hangings or bed-hangings.
cortinar v. to curtain: 1. provide with curtains. 2. veil, screen, mask as with curtains.
cortineiro s. m. 1. a curtain maker. 2. the stage-curtain operator.
coruchéu s. m. 1. (archit.) spire, pinnacle of a steeple, turret. 2. mitre of pasteboard, used formerly by disciplinants.
coruja s. f. 1. owl, owlet, screech-owl. 2. (fig.) hag, witch: old and ugly woman. 3. (ent.) butterfly of the family Brassolidae (Caligo 'eurilochus).
coruja-de-igreja s. f. (pl. corujas-de-igreja) (Braz., also suindara) barn owl.
coruja-do-campo s. f. (pl. corujas-do-campo) (Braz., also corujinha-buraqueira pl. corujinhas-buraqueiras) burrowing owl.
coruja-do-mato s. f. (pl. corujas-do-mato) (Braz.) wood owl.
corujão s. m. (pl. -ões) 1. a large owl (Pulsatrix perspicillata). 2. (N. Braz.) a variety of paper kite.
corujeira s. f. hamlet in a rocky place.
corujeiro adj. (S. Braz.) 1. good. 2. of excellent appearance. 3. good-looking.
corujinha s. f. (Braz., ent.) noctuid, owlet, moth.
corumbaense s. m. + f. native or inhabitant of Corumbá. ‖ adj. of Corumbá.
corumbamba s. m. (Braz.) intricate event.
corumbás s. m. pl. (Braz., also used in the singular) forgotten, despised or distant places.
coruscação s. f. (pl. -ões) coruscation: 1. act of coruscating. 2. flash, sudden fulgor.
coruscante adj. m. + f. coruscant, fulgurant, sparkling.
coruscar v. to coruscate: 1. fulgurate, gleam, glitter, sparkle, flash. 2. to dart, send forth.
seus olhos coruscavam chispas de ódio his eyes flashed with anger.
coruta s. f., coruto m. 1. pinnacle, summit, top. 2. (bot.) maize tassel, panicled top of some plants.
corvacho s. m. small raven.
corvéia s. f. (hist.) 1. corvee: unpaid labour for a feudal lord. 2. forced labour for the government.
corvejamento s. m. 1. act of croaking or cawing. 2. tedious repetition of a subject, rumination of an idea.
corvejar v. 1. to caw, croak. 2. to tell over and over, to weary repeating the same thing. 3. to ruminate, muse upon.
corveta s. f. 1. (naut.) corvette. 2. (Braz.): a) zigzag. b) winding, sinuosity. c) roundabout way, circumlocution, evasion. d) curvet (horse).
corvetear v. (Braz.) 1. to zigzag. 2. to wind, form a sinuous line. 3. to use a roundabout or evasive procedure or language. 4. to curvet (horse).
corvídeo s. m. a specimen of the Corvidae, to which belong the ravens and crows. ‖ adj. ravenlike, crow-like.

corvina s. f. corvina: a sort of seafish with black fins.

corvino adj. corvine: relating to the ravens or crows.

corvo s. m. 1. raven, crow. 2. (archit.) modillion. 3. (astr.) the constellation Corvus.

corvo-marinho s. m. (pl. **corvos-marinhos**) (also **biguá**) cormorant, sea raven.

cós s. m. sg. + pl. (pl. also **coses**) waistband of a garment, especially trousers.

cosca(s) s. f. (pl.) (Braz. + Port. prov.) (also **cócegas**) tickle.

coscorão s. m. (pl. **-ões**) 1. omelet, pancake, fritter. 2. (med.) eschar. 3. (S. Braz.) bumpkin, clodhopper.

coscoro s. m. 1. crust. 2. callosity. 3. stiff and crumpled state of cloth after being washed and dried. 4. wrinkling of the skin.

coscos s. m. pl. 1. small coin, change. 2. savings.

coscós s. m. (S. Braz.) iron rosette on a bridle which makes a noise when the horse moves the tongue.

coscosear v. (S. Braz.) to move the **coscós**, producing the characteristic noise.

coscuvilhar v. 1. to intrigue, gossip. 2. (N. Braz.) to ransack, rummage.

coscuvilheiro s. m. intriguer, gossiper. ‖ adj. intriguing, gossiping, gossipy.

coscuvilhice s. f. intrigue, gossip.

co-secante s. f. (pl. **co-secantes**) (math.) cosecant. ‖ adj. being a cosecant.

cosedor s. m. stitcher (bookbindery).

cosedura s. f. sewing.

co-seguro s. m. (pl. **co-seguros**) co-insurance.

co-seno s. m. (pl. **co-senos**) (math.) cosine.

coser v. 1. to sew, stitch, stitch up. 2. to unite, join, attach. 3. to lean against. 4. to stab with a knife. 5. **~-se:** a) to cling to. b) to arrange, settle. c) to lean against, to go together.

~-se com a terra 1. to lie flat upon the ground. 2. to coast along, keep to the shore.

cosicador s. m. 1. (Braz.) mender (of clothes, etc.), hand sewer (of slight things). 2. (fig.) person who unites incoherent things.

cosicar v. (Braz.) 1. to mend, patch (by sewing). 2. to hand-sew (slight things).

co-signatário s. m. (pl. **co-signatários**) co-signer.

cosmético s. m. cosmetic: external application for conserving or improving the beauty of the skin. ‖ adj. cosmetic: beautifying the skin.

cósmico s. m. celestial globe. ‖ adj. 1. cosmic(al): pertaining to the universe. 2. designating the star that rises and sets with the sun.

poeiras -as cosmic dust. **radiação -a** cosmic radiation.

cosmo s. m. cosmos: the universe, cosmic system.

cosmogonia s. f. cosmogony: hypothetical system of the formation of the universe.

cosmogônico adj. cosmogonic(al): relating to cosmogony.

cosmogonista s. m. + f. cosmogonist: person who occupies himself with cosmogony.

cosmografia s. f. cosmography: description of the universe.

cosmográfico adj. cosmographic(al): relating to cosmography.

cosmógrafo s. m. cosmographer.

cosmolábio s. m. cosmolabe: ancient instrument for taking the altitude of the stars.

cosmologia s. f. cosmology: science of the law that rules the physical world.

cosmológico adj. cosmological: relating to cosmology.

cosmólogo s. m. cosmologist.

cosmometria s. f. cosmometry: science of the measurement of cosmical distances.

cosmométrico adj. relating to cosmometry.

cosmonauta s. m. (astron.) cosmonaut, astronaut.

cosmonáutica s. f. astronautics.

cosmonave s. f. spaceship.

cosmonomia s. f. cosmonomy: the cosmic laws.

cosmonômico adj. relating to cosmonomy.

cosmopolita s. m. + f. cosmopolite, cosmopolitan: citizen of the world. ‖ adj. cosmopolitan: 1. at home in any part of the world. 2. (bot.) spread in several parts of the world, widespread.

cosmopolitismo s. m. cosmopolitism, cosmopolitanism: character or manner of life of a cosmopolitan.

cosmorama s. m. 1. cosmorama: a series of amplified views of several countries and facts. 2. peep-show apparatus for viewing a cosmorama. 3. cosmorama peep-show.

cosmos s. m. 1. = **cosmo**. 2. cosmos: ornamental plant (Cosmos caudatus).

cosmovisão s. f. world view.

cosmurgia s. f. creation of the world.

cospe-cospe s. m. (pl. **cospe-cospes**) (N. Braz., pop.) very small fish.

cosquento, cosquilhento, cosquilhoso, cosquilhudo adj. (S. Braz.) ticklish: 1. sensible to tickling. 2. (fig.) oversensitive, susceptible, touchy.

cossa s. f. (pop. for **acossa**) 1. harassment, pursuit. 2. fatigue, toil.

cossaco s. m. (ethn.) Cossack.

cosseira s. f. (naut.) 1. port sill of a gunport. 2. **~s** pl. spirketing.

cosso, cusso s. m. (Braz.) a medicinal tree of the family Rosaceae (Ilagenia abyssinica).

cossolete, cossoleto s. m. = **corselete**.

cossouro, cossoiro s. m. 1. (naut.) truck of a mast. 2. rowel (of a spur).

costa s. f. 1. coast, sea-shore (plate C 19). 2. declivity, slope of a hill. 3. back, backside. 4. **~s** pl.: a) (anat.) costa, loin. b) absence. c) reverse, opposite. d) bank of a river, brook; border of a lake, swamp, region, forest, plane, etc.

~ arriba or **acima** upwards, with difficulty. **~ da faca** back of a knife. **~ rochosa** rocky coast (plate C 19). **~s da cadeira** back of the chair. **~s da mão** the back of the hand (plate C 18). **~s do navio** ribs, side-timber of a ship. **~s com ~s** back to back. **às ~s** on the back, on the shoulders. **cair de ~s** to fall on one's back, backwards. **cair de ~s e quebrar o nariz** to have incredible bad luck. **dar à ~** 1. to run ashore, aground. 2. (fig.) to suffer an ill success. **dar as ~s** to take to one's heels, flee. **de ~s** on the back, backwards. **desejar ver pelas ~s** to desire a person's absence. **falar pelas ~s** to backbite, speak ill of s. o. behind his back. **ir ~ abaixo** (fig.) to decay, decline. **levar alguém às ~s** to carry s. o. on one's back. **pelas ~s** 1. from behind, from the back. 2. (fig.) behind one's back, perfidiously, in an underhand way. **pôr às ~s** to take on one's shoulders, load o. s. with. **ter às ~s** (fig.) to be encumbered or saddled with; to have to provide for. **ter as ~s quentes** or **largas** to rely on someone's patronage, be well backed or patronized. **virar as ~s a alguém** to turn one's back upon s. o.; to forsake s. o. **voltar as ~s** 1. to flee. 2. to turn one's back on s. o., show discontent or contempt.

costa-abaixo s. m. (pl. **costas-abaixo**) (Braz.) declivity, downward slope of a hill-side or mountain-side.

costa-acima s. f. (pl. **costas-acima**) acclivity, upward slope of a hill-side or a mountain-side.

costado s. m. 1. (anat.) back. 2. barrel (plate G 1). 3. side, flank, ship's side, broadside (plate B 8).

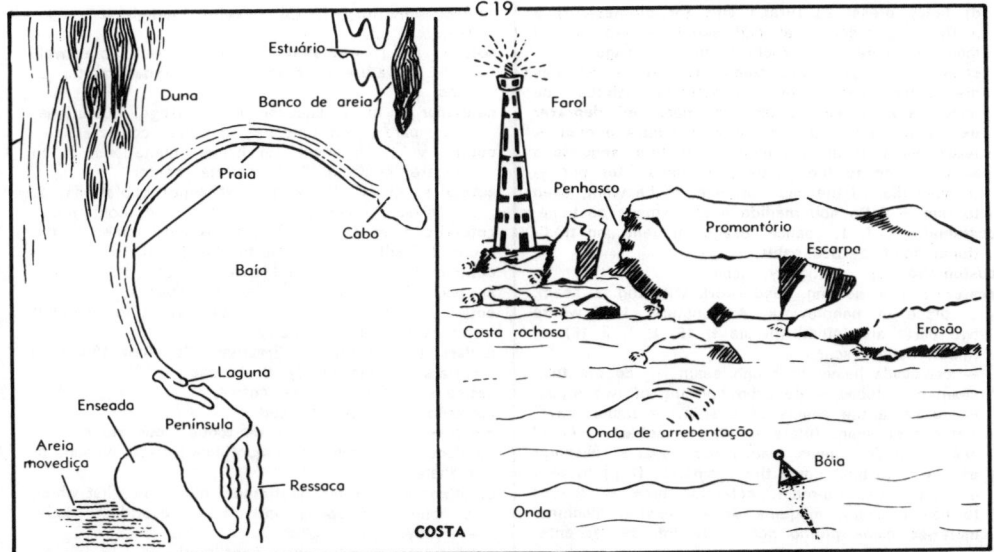

C 19

Estuário

Duna

Banco de areia

Praia

Cabo

Baía

Laguna

Enseada

Areia movediça

Península

Ressaca

Farol

Penhasco

Promontório

Escarpa

Costa rochosa

Erosão

Onda de arrebentação

Bóia

Onda

COSTA

4. (geneal.) each of the four grandparents of a person. 5. (fig.): a) responsibility. b) conscience. ~ **de fuselagem** (aeron.) fuselage side. **dos quatro ~s** (fig.) dyed-in-the-wool. **medir o ~** to give a hiding, thrash. **os ~s do navio** the planks which cover a ship's sides. **os quatro ~s** the four grandparents.

costal s. m. (pl. **-ais**) 1. burden, load which one can carry on one's back at a time. 2. threads to tie a skein to prevent it from getting entangled. 3. (Braz.) part of a carrying yoke. 4. (Port.) load of 60 kg. ‖ adj. m. + f. costal.

costalgia s. f. (med.) costalgia: violent pain in the costal region.

costálgico adj. relating to costalgia.

costaneira (I) s. f. 1. paper of inferior quality which protects the sides of the reams. 2. coarse ordinary paper. 3. slab, flitch: outside board of a sawed tree trunk. 4. (Braz. + Port. prov.) (com.) wastebook, day-book.

costaneira (II) s. m. (N. Braz.) cowboy who rides at the side of the herd.

costaneiro s. m. back, loin. ‖ adj. 1. outside, slab. 2. (fig.) cheap.

papel ~ outside paper (of a ream).

costão s. m. (pl. **-ões**) (Braz.) wild coast without inlets.

costarriquenho s. m. Costa Rican: native or inhabitant of Costa Rica. ‖ adj. Costa Rican: of Costa Rica.

costeado adj. (S. Braz.) put in a pasture or a corral to be tamed.

costeagem s. f. (pl. **-ens**) 1. (naut.) coasting. 2. rounding. 3. act of following closely, pursuit. 4. (Braz.) herding (of cattle). 5. (S. Braz.) punishment in requital. 6. approach in a vessel. 7. act of belting, girding.

costear v. 1. to coast, sail along, follow the shore. 2. to round, go around, go along. 3. to follow closely, pursue. 4. (Braz.) to herd, round-up cattle at determinate times to accustom it to certain places of the ranch. (5. Braz.) to punish, make s. o. suffer in requital, causing him envy, etc.

~ uma ilha to sail around an island.

costeio s. m. (Braz., also **costeagem**) temporary pasturage of cattle.

dar um ~ em alguém to deal energically with s. o., to reprehend s. o.

costeira s. f. (arch.) coast, sea-shore. 2. (Braz.) steep mountain range at the sea-shore.

costeiras s. f. pl. (naut.) partners of the mast.

costeiro adj. 1. coastal. 2. (naut.) coasting: a) that sails along the coast. b) that sails from port to port along the same coast.

costela s. f. 1. (anat.) rib (plate C 12). 2. (naut.) rib (of a vessel). 3. a sort of snare (for birds). 4. (bot.) midrib (of a leaf). 5. (Braz., fam.) wife: one's better half.

~ de reforço stiffening rib. **~ de reforço da asa** (aeron.) rib of a wing. **podem-se-lhe contar as ~s** he is so lean that one might count his ribs.

costela-de-vaca s. f. (pl. **costelas-de-vaca**) = **catabi**.

costelar v. (N. Braz.) to fold at the centre (leaves of tobacco) so that ribs come to lie upon ribs.

costeleta s. f. 1. (pork, mutton) chop; (veal) cutlet. 2. (Braz.) sideburns.

costilhar s. m. (S. Braz.) 1. costal region of beeves. 2. rib cut of beef for a roast. 3. roasted rib cut of beef.

costilhas s. f. pl. (mus.) the sides of the resonance box of a string instrument (plates G 2, V 5).

costumado s. m. that which is wonted, accustomed, habitual. ‖ adj. wonted, accustomed, inured, customary, habitual, usual.

costumar v. 1. to be accustomed, inured, used or wont to. 2. to be in the habit of; to use to. 3. **~-se:** a) to get accustomed, habituated or used to. b) to contract the habit of. c) to become familiar(ized) with a foreign surrounding.

~ fazer to use to do. **como se costuma dizer** as one usually says, as the saying goes.

costumário adj. customary, accustomed, habitual.

costumbrismo s. m. (lit.) realistic description of folk life (in Spanish romantic literature).

costume s. m. 1. custom: a) habit, usage, use, way, practice, inurement. b) (jur.) prescriptive law, common law, prescription right. 2. customary behavior. 3. particularity. 4. menstruation. 5. costume: a) fashion (style of dress). b) adequate or characteristic garment. c) attire of an actor or actress.

d) fancy dress. e) (Braz.) suit (of clothes). f) a feminine garment (coat and skirt). 6. **~s** pl.: a) manners, morals. b) (sociol.) custom, usage. **como de** ~ as usual. **como era seu** ~ as was his custom. **de** ~, **do** ~ customary, habitual. **de bons** ~s well-bread, behaved or mannered. **depravar os** ~s to corrupt the manners. **é contra o meu** ~ **fazer isso** it is not my habit to do this. **segundo o** ~ according to the custom, as usual. **ter por** ~ to have (be in) the habit of, use, to be wont, used to. **um** ~ **feito sob medida** a tailor-made costume.

costumeira s. f. 1. usance, usage, ancient and traditional habit. 2. bad habit.

costumeiro adj. customary, usual.

costura s. f. 1. sewing, needlework stitching. 2. seam. 3. piece of needlework. 4. juncture: line where two parts are joined (plates B 16, L 3, P 16). 5. (med.) suture, scar.
~ **carregada** heavy or rough seam. ~ **de um tubo** seam of a tube. ~ **de cabo** splicing of two ropes. ~ **do navio** the seams of a ship. ~ **impermeável** water-proof seam (plate B 16). ~ **soldada** welded seam. ~**s do convés** (naut.) deck seams. **assentar as** ~**s** 1. to beat down the seams. 2. (fig.) to beat on the back, rib-roast. **calafetar uma** ~ (naut.) to pay a seam. **máquina de** ~ sewing machine. **meter-se como piolho por** ~ to intrude: 1. enter without being invited. 2. to force o. s. upon others.

costuradeira s. f. (Braz.) stitcher, machine for sewing brochures.

costurador s. m. (typogr.) 1. thread sewing machine. 2. sewer: thread sewing machine operator.

costuragem s. f. (pl. **-ens**) (Braz.) stitching (of brochures).

costurar v. 1. to sew, do needlework. 2. (S. Braz.) to stab.

costureira s. f. seamstress, sewing woman, needlewoman, dressmaker.

costureiro s. m. 1. seamster, ladies' tailor. 2. (anat. also **sartório**) sartorius: muscle of the thigh. ‖ adj. (anat.) sartorial: of or pertaining to the sartorius.

cota (I) s. f. (also ~ **de malha**) coat of mail, hauberk.

cota (II) s. f. 1. quota, share, portion, part. 2. instalment. 3. note, notation. 4. marginal note. 5. contribution. 6. (jur.) reference letter or number on records. 7. elevation (above a determinate point).

cota (III) s. f. back of a cutting instrument.
~ **de faca** back of a knife. ~ **parte** share. ~ **social** (com.) brought in capital, partner's share.

cotação s. f. (pl. **-ões**) 1. quotation (of prices of goods, stocks). 2. list of quotations. 3. notation. 4. a marking with reference letters or numbers. 5. assessment. 6. taxation, valuation, estimation. 7. classification. 8. (fig.) prestige, credit, good repute.
~ **do câmbio** quotation of exchange. ~ **do preço** quotation of price. ~ **efetuada** rate of exchange. **ter fraca** ~ 1. to have a low rate of exchange. 2. (fig.) not to be much esteemed.

cotado adj. well-reputed, esteemed.

cotador s. m. one who puts marginal notes.

cotamento s. m. (jur.) marking of records.

co-tangente s. f. (pl. **co-tangentes**) (math.) cotangent.

cotanilho s. m. 1. dim. of **cotão** (I) 2. (bot.) tomentum, pubescence, down.

cotanilhoso adj. (bot.) tomentose, tomentous, pubescent, downy.

cotão (I) s. m. (pl. **-ões**) 1. rubbed off nap of cloth. 2. down on some fruits. 3. fluff under furnitures.

cotão (II) s. m. augm. of **cota**: coat of mail.

cotar v. 1. to mark with reference letters or numbers. 2. to tax: fix the tax or cost of. 3. to indicate the level of. 4. to valuate, estimate. 5. to classify.

cotável adj. m. + f. (pl. **-áveis**) marketable, negotiable.

cote s. m. 1. whetstone, hone. 2. (naut.) blackwall hitch, curvature of a mast. 3. everyday matter or thing.

cotejador s. m. 1. checker of (exchange) quotations. 2. comparer, confronter. 3. collator, conferrer.

cotejar v. 1. to check (exchange) quotations. 2. to compare, confront. 3. to collate, confer.

cotejo s. m. 1. check of (exchange) quotations. 2. comparison, confrontation. 3. collation, conferment.

coteleiro s. m. (N. Braz.) tame ox accustomed to the corral. ‖ adj. accustomed to the corral.

cotia s. f. (naut.) ancient Oriental vessel.

cotiado adj. 1. daily used. 2. threadbare.

cotiar v. 1. to whet (on a whetstone). 2. to wear out (by use). 3. to use daily.

cotiara s. f. (Braz.) a Brazilian pit viper (Bothrops cotiara) of the family Crotalidae.

cotica s. f. (her.) cotise, cotice.

coticado adj. (her.) cotised.

cotícula s. f. (also **pedra de toque**) touchstone.

cotidade s. f. (com. also **quotidade**) fixed amount of a share.

cotidiano s. m. (also **quotidiano**) quotidian: that which is done or happens daily. ‖ adj. quotidian, daily, everyday.

cotil s. m. (Braz.) a very light cloth.

cotilédone s. m. cotyledon: 1. (bot.): a) seed-leaf. b) plant of the family Crassulaceae (Cotyledon secunda). 2. (anat.) any of the subdivisions of the uterine surface of the placenta.

cotiledôneo adj. cotyledonous: possessing cotyledons.

cotilhão s. m. (pl. **-ões**) cotillion (dance).

cótilo s. m. (anat.) cotylo: socket of a joint, articular cavity.

cotilóforo adj. cotyledonous, having articular cavities.

cotilóide adj. m. + f., **cotilóideo** (anat.) shaped like an articular cavity.
cavidade ~**a** cotyloid cavity, acetabulum.

cotim s. m. drill, tick, ticking, duck.

cotinga s. f. (Braz., ornith.) cotinga, waxwing, chatterer.

cotio (I) s. m. daily use.
a ~ daily, every day. **de** ~ everyday.

cotio (II) adj. said of a genus of chick-pea.

cotista s. m. + f. (com.) a shareholder of a limited company, (U. S. A.) of a corporation.

cotização s. f. (pl. **-ões**) 1. assessment, taxation, allotment, rating. 2. quota, share.

cotizar v. (also **quotizar**) 1. to assess, tax, allot, rate. 2. ~**se** to participate, share, contribute.

cotizável adj. m. + f. (pl. **-áveis**) (also **quotizável**) assessable, taxable, ratable.

coto (ô) s. m. 1. stump: a) of a candle, torch, etc. b) of an amputated arm or leg. 2. part of a bird's wing from which grow the feathers. 3. feather-edged file, slitting file. 4. **cotos** pl. knuckles.

cotó (I) s. m. (Braz.) person with a mutilated arm or leg. ‖ adj. 1. having a mutilated arm or leg. 2. bob-tailed.

cotó (II) s. m. 1. (obs.) large knife, cutlass. 2. (Braz.) small ordinary knife. 3. small thing. 4. stump.

cotoco s. m. (Braz., also **coto**) stump of an amputated arm or leg.

cotonaria s. f. (also **algodoaria**) cotton factory, cotton mill.

cotonária, cotoneira s. f. any plant with cottony leaves.

cotonete s. m. a small wooden or plastic stick with cotton tufts on both ends, used for hygienic purpose.

cotonicultor s. m. (Braz.) a cotton farmer.

cotonicultura s. f. (Braz.) cotton culture.

cotonifício s. m. (Braz.) cotton mill.

cotovelada s. f., cotovelão (pl. -ões) m. nudge, dig, blow with the elbow.

abrir caminho a ~s to elbow one's way (through a crowd).

cotovelar v. (also acotovelar) to elbow.

cotoveleira s. f. an elbow pad (in some sports).

cotovelo (ê) s. m. (pl. cotovelos) elbow: 1. (anat.) articulation between forearm and upperarm (plates C 18, G 1). 2. outer curve formed by this articulation. 3. bend of a road or river. 4. (tech.) elbow bend, knee (plates C 1, E 3, 10). 5. any elbow--shaped angle, bend or corner.

dobrado em ~ bent 90 degrees. dor de ~ jealousy.

falar pelos cotovelos to talk nineteen to the dozen.

apoiar-se sobre os cotovelos to lean on one's elbows.

cotovia s. f. (ornith.) lark, sky-lark.

~ de poupa crested lark.

cotréia s. f. (N. Braz.) white rum of inferior quality.

cotriba s. m. (Braz., sl.) would-be ruffian, bully; braggart, braggadocio.

cotruco s. m. 1. (Braz.) itinerant vender of cloths and haberdashery. 2. (N. Braz.) dagger.

coturnado adj. cothurned: 1. wearing the cothurnus. 2. shaped like a cothurnus.

coturno s. m. 1. (ant.) cothurnus: buskin worn by Greek and Roman tragedians. 2. sock, half-stocking.

de alto ~ of high position.

couçoeira s. f. (Braz.) timber to be cut up and finished.

coudel s. m. (pl. -éis) (also caudel) manager of a stud-farm.

coudelaria s. f. (also caudelaria) stud, stud-farm.

coura s. f. (also coira) 1. ancient buff-coat for warriors. 2. cuirass.

couraça s. f. (also coiraça) 1. cuirass, breastplate. 2. armour of a warship. 3. (fig.) callousness to slander or bad luck.

couraçado s. m. (also coiraçado) 1. ironclad, battleship. 2. fish resembling the armoured catfish (Hemipsilichthys gobis). || adj. 1. armoured, ironclad, armour-plated, cuirassed. 2. iron-sheathed, iron--coated.

couraçar v. (also coiraçar) 1. to armour: a) cover or protect with a cuirass. b) sheathe with iron-plating. 2. ~-se: a) to put on a cuirass. b) to protect o. s. c) to become indifferent or insensible.

couraceiro s. m. (also coiraceiro) cuirassier: soldier that wears a cuirass.

courama s. f. (also coirama) 1. great quantity of raw hides. 2. (N. Braz.) leather apparel of cattle herders.

courão s. m. (also coirão) 1. augm. of couro. 2. (vulg.) old prostitute. 3. hag.

coureador s. m. (also coireador) (S. Braz.) skinner of perished cattle.

courear v. (also coirear) (S. Braz.) to skin cattle (perished of plage, starvation or accident).

coureiro s. m. (also coireiro) dealer in leather.

courinho s. m. (also coirinho) (N. Braz.) goatskin.

couro s. m. (also coiro) 1. leather. 2. hide. 3. (fig.) skin. 4. hag. 5. old despicable prostitute. 6. (Braz. ftb.) ball, pigskin. 7. ~s pl. (N. Braz.) leather clothing of the inlander.

~ cabeludo scalp. ~ cru rawhide, untanned hide. ~ curtido tanned hide. ~ de bezerro calf, calfskin. ~ de boi ox-hide. ~ de jacaré crocodile leather. ~ de porco pigskin. ~ fresco, ~ verde green hide.

comer o ~ a (or de alguém) (N. Braz.) to give s. o. a hiding. dar no ~ (Braz., fig.) to hit the mark, make a good hit. dar o ~ às varas (fig.) to kick the bucket. fazer ~ duro to resist.

couro-n'água s. m. (pl. couros-n'água) (Braz., pop.) rowdy, bully.

coutada s. f. (also coitada) (hunt.) game preserve, game reserve, covert.

coutar v. (also coitar) 1. to prohibit hunting in a determinate place. 2. to enclose, fence.

couteiro s. m. (also coiteiro) game keeper.

couto (also coito, valhacouto) s. m. 1. asylum, sanctuary, refuge. 2. shelter, covert.

couval s. m. (pl. -ais) cabbage field, cabbage plantation.

couve s. f. cabbage, cole, kale.

~ repolhuda cabbage. ~ lombarda white cabbage. ~ marroquina, ~ vermelha red cabbage. ~-de--bruxelas Brussels sprouts. ~ galega green kale.

couve-brócolos s. f. (pl. couves-brócolos) broccoli.

couve-flor s. f. (pl. couves-flores) cauliflower.

couve-nabo s. f. (pl. couves-nabos) Swedish turnip.

couve-rábano s. f. (pl. couves-rábanos) turnip cabbage.

couvetinga s. f. (Braz.) two shrubs belonging to the nightshades (Solanum auriculatum and Solanum subumbellatum).

cova s. f. 1. hole, hollow, cavity, depression, cavern, pit. 2. excavation. 3. alveolus. 4. grave. 5. (Braz.) small elevated manioc bed, generally for one plant only.

não caber na ~ de um dente not to be enough to fill the hollow of a tooth. estar com os pés na ~ to have one foot in the grave; be on the brink of the grave.

covacho s. m. dim. of cova.

covada s. f. (N. Braz.) a hole, where a tortoise lays her eggs.

cova-de-touro s. f. (pl. covas-de-touro) (S. Braz.) depression made by bulls with their feet and horns and sometimes much deepened by rain.

côvado s. m. ell.

covagem s. f. (pl. -ens) 1. grave-making. 2. a grave--digger's fee.

coval s. m. (pl. covais) 1. burial-ground, burial-place. 2. price of a burial-place.

covanca s. f. (S. Braz.) circular valley with one entrance only; extremity of a valley.

covão s. m. 1. large hole, cavity. 2. (N. Braz.) deep pool in a river.

côvão s. m. wicker fish-trap of the bow-net type for catching fishes in rivers.

covarde s. m. + f. (also cobarde) coward, poltroon, dastard. || adj. 1. coward, cowardly, dastard. 2. vile, base, mean, treacherous.

covardia s. f. (also cobardia) 1. cowardliness, cowardice. 2. treacherousness.

covas-de-mandioca s. f. pl. (N. Braz.) small clouds announcing a tempest.

covato s. m. 1. grave-digging. 2. burying-ground.

covear v. (Braz.) to dig holes for coffee seedlings.

coveiro s. m. grave-digger.

coveta s. f. (N. E. Braz.) hole for sugar-cane cuttings.

covil s. m. (pl. -is) 1. den: a) lair of a wild beast. b) lurking-place of robbers. 2. hovel. 3. burrow.

~ de ladrões den of thieves. ~ de raposa fox-earth.

covileiro adj. said of a ground-game tracker.

covilhete s. m. shallow soucer for cakes or sweetmeats.

covinha s. f. 1. dim. of cova. 2. dimple.

covo s. m. (Braz.) 1. fish-trap made of matting. 2. (sl.) watch of inferior quality.

covo (ô) s. m. wicker fish-trap of the bow-net type. || adj. 1. concave. 2. deep, hollow.

covoá s. m. low hills on the central plateau of Brazil.

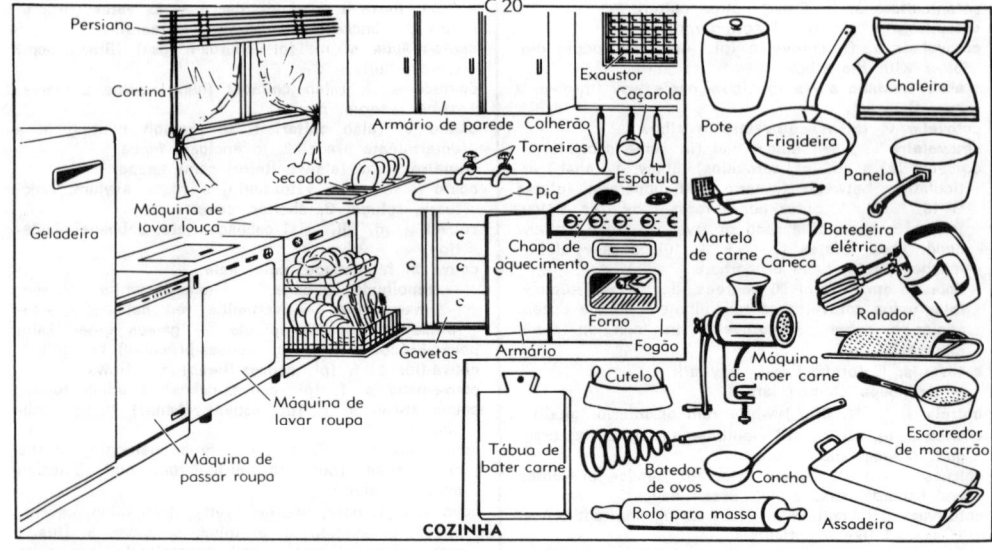

COZINHA

covoada s. f. 1. range of holes, hollows, cavities. 2. (N. Braz.) slope or ondulation of a mountain range, more or less covered with vegetation. 3. (Braz.) swampy depression.

covoão s. m. (N. Braz.) deep and narrow low-land.

covoca s. f. (Braz.) subsided ground, forming a depression or cave at the foot of a hill or mountain.

coxa s. f. thigh (plates C 12, 18).

coxa-de-frango s. f. (pl. coxas-de-frango) plant of the family Oleaceae (Linociera mandiocana).

coval adj. m. + f. (pl. -ais) belonging to the thigh. osso ~ thigh-bone.

coxalgia s. f. (med.) 1. coxalgia: hip ache. 2. hip disease: tuberculosis of the hip-joint.

coxálgico adj. relating to coxalgia or the hip disease

coxartria s. f. (path.) an inflammatory illness of the hip-bone.

coxé adj. m. + f. (N. Braz.) 1. having one leg shorter than the other. 2. lame of one leg.

coxeadura s. f. limping, hobble, lameness.

coxear v. 1. to limp, halt, hobble, be or become lame. 2. (fig.) to halt, be defective, err, commit a fault, falter.

ele coxeia um pouco he has a slight limp.

coxeira s. f. 1. lameness (of an animal). 2. an elastic sleeve for distentions of the thigh muscles.

coxêndico adj. (anat.) said of the hip-bones which, together with the sacrum, form the pelvis.

coxia s. f. 1. central walk, aisle, gangway (plate V 1). 2. (naut.) coursey, gangway plank. 3. (aeron.) catwalk. 4. a horse's box, stall. 5. folding-seat. 6. (N. Braz.): a) stack of bricks and several other objects piled in an orderly manner. b) hillock breaking the uniformity of plains.

correr a ~ 1. to idle, lounge, lead the life of a vagabond. 2. to roam, rove, ramble about.

coxilha s. f. (S. Braz.) 1. hilly grassland. 2. grassy hill used for pasturage.

coxilhão s. m. (S. Braz.) extensive hilly grassland.

coxim s. m. (pl. -ins) 1. cushion, pad (plate A 5). 2. padded backless bench. 3. seat of a saddle (plate S 2). 4. leather cushion to cut leather on. 5. (archit.) abutment, impost. 6. rail-chair (plate V 4). 7. (electr.) cushion rubber.

coximpim s. m. (pl. -ins) (Braz., also arre-burrinho) see-saw.

coxinilho, coxonilho s. m. (Braz.) black, woollen saddle-cloth.

coxo s. m. 1. lame or limping person, hobbler. 2. (N. Braz., pop.) the devil. ‖ adj. 1. lame, limping, halting. 2. missing a leg (chair, table). 3. (fig.) incomplete.

ser (estar) ~ to be lame.

coxote s. m. (form.) cuisse, cuish: plate-armour for the thighs.

cozedura s. f. 1. cookery, cooking, boiling, baking. 2. food or quantity of food cooked at a time. 3. solid part of the broth.

cozer v. 1. to cook, boil, bake. 2. to digest.
~ a carne to boil the meat. ~ o pão (no forno) to bake the bread. ~ tijolos to burn (or bake) bricks. ~ a bebedeira to sleep off one's intoxication, to sleep o. s. sober.

cozido s. m. Portuguese dish consisting of boiled beef, vegetables, eggs, potatoes, etc. ‖ adj. cooked, boiled, baked.

cozimento s. m. 1. cooking, boiling, baking. 2. digestion. 3. decoction. 4. infusion.

cozinha s. f. 1. kitchen, cuisine (plate C 20). 2. cuisine, cookery: a) art of cooking. b) preparation of dishes.

cozinhado s. m. cooked food, dish.

cozinhador s. m. 1. male cook. 2. an autoclave, a digestor.

cozinhar v. 1. to cook, boil. 2. to stew, simmer. 3. to do the cooking.

cozinheira s. f. (female) cook (plate R 5).

cozinheiro s. m. (male) cook (plate R 5).

craca s. f. 1. goose barnacle. 2. (Braz.) acorn barnacle, rock barnacle. 3. flute of a column. 4. stria.

crachá s. m. identitication card.

cracoviana s. f. cracovienne: dance of Polish origin.

cracoviano s. m. Cracowian: native or inhabitant of Cracow. ‖ adj. Cracowian: of Cracow.

craguatá s. f. (Braz.) = caraguatá.

craniano adj. (anat.) cranian, cranial; cranic, belonging to the cranium.

craniectomia s. f. craniectomy: surgical operation on the skull.

crânio s. m. 1. cranium, skull, brainpan (plate C 17). 2. death's head. 3. (Braz., sl.) a clever head.

craniografia s. f. craniography: scientific description of the cranium.

craniográfico adj. relating to craniography.

craniolar adj. m. + f. skull-shaped.

craniolária s. f. shell representing a skull.

craniologia s. f. craniology: study of crania.

craniológico adj. craniological: relating to craniology. || **craniologicamente** adv. craniologically.

craniologista, craniólogo s. m. + f. craniologist: person versed in or practising craniology.

craniomancia s. f. phrenology.

craniomante s. m. + f. phrenologist.

craniometria s. f. craniometry: measuring of the skull.

craniométrico adj. craniometric(al): relating to craniometry. || **craniometricamente** adv. craniometrically.

craniômetro s. m. craniometer: instrument for measuring skulls.

cranioscopia s. f. cranioscopy: art of determining the mental and moral faculties by examination of the skull.

cranioscópico adj. cranioscopical: relating to cranioscopy.

cranioscópio s. m. instrument for examining the skull.

craniotomia s. f. (surg.) craniotomy.

crápula s. f. 1. crapulence, intemperance. 2. debauchery, dissoluteness. 3. debauchee; scamp.

crapuloso adj, 1. crapulous, crapulent. 2. debauched, licentious.

craque (I) interj. (onomatopoeic) crack! crash! bang!

craque (II) s. m. (Braz.) excellent race-horse or footballer.

craquelê s. m. crackle: the crack on chinaware enamel.

crás s. m. croak (of a raven). || adv. (obs.) tomorrow.

crase s. f. crasis: 1. (gram.): a) contraction of two vowels into one. b) contraction of **aa** into **à**. c) the accent indicating a crasis. 2. (med.) mixture, equilibrium of the constituents of blood or other organic liquids. 3. temper. 4. constitution.

crasear v. to put an accent on a vowel to indicate a crasis.

craspedota adj. (zool.) craspedote, craspedotal: relating to the veiled medusae.

crassicaude adj. m. + f. (zool.) thick-tailed.

crassicaule adj. m. + f. (bot.) thick-stalked, thick--stemmed.

crassicolo adj. thick-necked.

crassicórneo adj. (zool.) having thick horns or antennae.

crassidade, crassidão (pl. -ões) s. f. (also **crassície**) crassness, crassitude; thickness, grossness, coarseness; density; enormity, completeness.

crassifoliado adj. (bot.) thick-leaved.

crassilíngüe s. m. saurian, reptile. || adj. m. + f. crassilingual, thick-tongued.

crassinérveo adj. (bot.) thick-ribbed.

crassipene adj. m. + f. (zool.) dense-feathered, strong--winged.

crassirrostro adj. (zool.) thick-billed.

crasso adj. crass; thick, gross, coarse; dense; great, big, complete. || **-amente** adv. crassly.
ignorância -a crass ignorance.

crassulácea s. f. (bot.) specimen of the Crassulaceae, a family of succulent dicotyledonous herbs.

crassuláceo adj. (bot.) crassulaceous: relating to the family Crassulaceae.

crástino adj. (poet.) 1. of tomorrow. 2. matutinal.

cratera s. f. 1. crater: a) (geol.) mouth of a volcano (plate M 11); funnel-shaped cavity. b) hole in the earth caused by a bomb, shellburst, etc. c) ancient Roman cup. 2. (fig.) calamity, origin of misfortunes.
~ adventícia craterlet, lateral crater (plate M 11).

cratera-lago s. f. (pl. **crateras-lago**) (geol.) crater lake.

crateriforme adj. m. + f. crateriform.

crauá s. m. (Braz.) = **caroá, cruá.**

crauaçu, crauatá s. m. (Braz.) = **caraguatá.**

crauça, graucá s. m. (Braz. zool.) sprite crab.

crauçanga s. f. (N. Braz.) a red ant.

craúna s. f. (Braz.) = **araúna.**

cravação (pl. -ões), **cravadura** s. f. 1. nailing, riveting. 2. ornament of studwork. 3. setting of gems. 4. relief of type on the opposite side of a printed paper.

cravador s. m. 1. nailer, riveter, studder, gem setter. 2. awl, punch.

cravagem s. f. (also **fungão, morrão, centeio-espigado** m.) ergot, spur.

cravar v. 1. to drive, thrust in (as a nail). 2. to set (gems). 3. to fix, fasten (with nails, rivets). 4. **~-se:** a) to penetrate. b) to take root.
~ os olhos em to stare at.

craveira s. f. 1. standard for measuring the height of men. 2. size stick, rule. 3. nail hole (in a horseshoe). 4. heading tool, heading machine.
não chegar à ~ 1. not to have the necessary height. 2. (fig.) not to be suffent or apt.

craveiro s. m. 1. pink, carnation, gillyflower (plant). 2. flowerpot to hold carnations. 3. (N. Braz.) pyrotechnic piece which imitates a carnation. 4. musical instrument resembling a guitar. 5. (form.) key-keeper; turnkey. 6. person who makes horseshoe nails, nailsmith. || adj. according to or measured by the Port. standard.
palmo ~ one span (Port. standard = 12 inches).
braça ~ a fathom of 10 spans (Port. standard).

cravejador s. m. 1. gem setter. 2. nailer (one who nails). 3. inserter, interposer. 4. nailsmith, horseshoe nailer.

cravejamento s. m. 1. gem-setting. 2. nailing, studding. 3. intercalation, interposition.

cravejar v. 1. to set gems. 2. to stud with nails. 3. to intercalate, interpose.

cravelha s. f. 1. tuning peg or pin (in stringed instruments) (plates B 4, G 2, P 10, V 5) = **cravelho.**
apertar as -s to tighten the reins.

cravelhame s. m. peg box (of a string instrument) (plate G 2).

cravelho s. m. crude wooden latch of a door or gate.

cravete s. m. buckle tongue.

cravija s. f. pole-bolt of a coach.

cravina s. f. 1. (bot.) China pink. 2. (Braz.) = **carabina.**

cravina-dos-poetas s. f. (pl. **cravinas-dos-poetas**) (bot.) sweet William, sweet John.

cravinho s. m. 1. small carnation. 2. clove (spice). 3. tack, small nail.

cravinoso adj. caryophyllaceous: having a flower like the pink.

cravista s. m. + f. 1. harpsichordist. 2. horseshoe nailer.

cravo s. m. 1. horseshoe nail (plate P 15). 2. shoe tack (plate P 15). 3. crucifixion nail, spike. 4. (med.) comedo, blackhead. 5. (vet.) callous tumour on the hoof of a horse. 6. (mus.) harpsichord. 7. (bot.) carnation, pink.
dar no ~ to hit the nail on the head. **uma no ~ outra na ferradura** to hit and miss alternately.

cravoária s. f., **cravo-da-índia** m. (pl. **cravos-da-índia**), **cravo-de-cabecinha** m. (pl. **cravos-de-cabecinha**) clove (tree).

cravo-da-roça s. m. (pl. **cravos-da-roça**) (Braz. also .cravorana, **ambrósia-americana** f.) two ragweeds (Ambrosia psilostachia and A. artemisifolia).
cravo-de-amor s. m. (pl. **cravos-de-amor**) (also **gipsófila** f.) (bot.) baby's-breath.
cravo-de-bouba s. m. (pl. **cravos-de-bouba**) (med.) verrucous efflorescence of the framboesia.
cravo-de-defunto s. m. (pl. **cravos-de-defunto**) common name of the marigolds of the genus Tagetes.
cravo-do-maranhão s. m. (pl. **cravos-do-maranhão**) (Braz.) clove cinnamon.
cré (I) s. m. limestone.
cré (II) s. m. used only in the locution: **lé com lé, ~ com ~** birds of a feather flock together.
crebro adj. frequent, oft-recurring, repeated.
creca s. m. 1. (Braz., pop.) bald-head. 2. (S. Braz.) baldness.
creche s. f. day nursery for poor children.
credência s. f. (church) credence-table, prothesis.
credenciais s. f. pl. credentials: 1. that which entitles to credit or confidence. 2. credential letter of a diplomat.
credencial adj. m. + f. (pl. **-ais**) credential, accrediting.
cartas -ais credential letters.
credenciário s. m. (church) person in charge of a credence-table.
crediário s. m. (S. Braz., also **facilitário, auxiliário**) instalment system.
crediarista s. m. + f. (S. Braz.) person who buys on the instalment plan.
credibilidade s. f. credibility.
creditar v. 1. to credit (a sum to a person). 2. to guarantee, warrant.
creditício adj. relating to public credit.
crédito s. m. credit: 1. trust, trustworthiness. 2. good reputation, repute, prestige, esteem, regard, merit, honour. 3. reliance .in a person's solvency. 4. authority, power, influence. 5. faith, belief. 6. trust, commercial credit. 7. outstanding debt, claim. 8. facility in receiving a loan. 9. entry on the credit side of an account.
~ aberto credit opened. **~ a longo (curto) prazo** long (short) credit. **~ em mercadorias** credit on goods. **~ ilimitado** blank credit. **abri um ~ com ele** I had a credit opened with him. **carta de ~** letter of credit. **comprar a ~** to buy on credit. **dar ~ a alguém** 1. to give credit to s. o. 2. to believe s. o. **levar a ~ de** to carry to the credit of. **merecer ~** to deserve credit.
creditório adj. relating to credit.
credo s. m. 1. (church) a) Credo; Creed, credo, creed. b) symbol of the apostles. c) profession of faith. d) time necessary to pray the Credo. 2. rule, line of conduct. 3. (pol.) party programme. ‖ interj. (also **credo-em-cruz**) goodness alive! good gracious! **num ~** in a trice. **com o ~ na boca** in great peril; with great fear.
credor s. m. 1. creditor. 2. person deserving credit, worthy of or entitled to credit, consideration, etc.
credulidade s. f. credulity, credulousness, gullibility, simple-mindedness.
crédulo s. m. credulous, simple-minded person, gull. ‖ adj. credulous, gullible, simple-minded.
creiom s. m. (pl. **-ons**) crayon: 1. the pencil. 2. the drawing.
crejuá s. m. (Braz.) = **corocotéu**.
cremação s. f. cremation: disposal of a corpse by burning it; incineration.
cremado adj. 1. creme-coloured. 2. cremated, incinerated.
cremador s. m. cremator: person who cremates, incinerates or destroys. ‖ adj. crematory.

cremalheira s. f. 1. pot-hook and chain, pot-hanger, trammel. 2. rack rail. 3. rack, rack bar.
~ circular rack wheel. **~ e pinhão** rack and pinion.
engrenagem de ~ rack gear.
estrada (de ferro) de ~ rack railway, rack road.
cremar v. to cremate (corpses), incinerate.
crematório s. m. crematorium, crematory: place where corpses are cremated. ‖ adj. crematory: employed in or relating to cremation.
creme s. m. 1. cream: a) greasy part of milk. b) custard. c) a whitish-yellow colour. 2. a dense liqueur. ‖ adj. cream-coloured.
~ chantilly whipped cream.
cremona s. f. 1. Cremona (violin). 2. (Braz.) cremone bolt.
cremor s. m. cremor: thick decoction (of a plant).
~ de tártaro cream of tartar.
crena (I) s. f. (dim. **crenazinha, crênula**) 1. (tech.) space between the cogs of a wheel. 2. (bot.) crenature.
crena (II) s. f. (obs.) = **querena**.
crenado adj. (bot. + zool.) crenate, crenated (plate F 5).
crenar v. (N. Braz.) = **carenar**.
crença s. f. 1. belief, faith, creed. 2. opinion, conviction, persuasion.
crendeirice s. f. 1. credulity, credulousness, gullibility, simple-mindedness. 2. superstition, absurd belief.
crendeiro s. m. 1. credulous or superstitious person, gull. 2. simpleton. ‖ adj. superstitious, credulous, gullible.
crendice s. f. superstition, absurd belief.
crenirrostro adj. (ornith.) dentirostral.
crenoterapia s. f. (med.) mineral water therapy.
crente s. m. + f. (rel.) 1. believer. 2. (N. Braz.) Protestant. ‖ adj. believing.
crênula s. f. dim. of **crena** (I).
crenulado adj. (bot.) crenulate(d).
creofagia s. f. creophagy: habit of flesh-eating.
creófago s. m. creophagist: flesh-eater, carnivore. ‖ adj. creophagous, carnivorous, flesh-eating.
creolina s. f. Creolin, creolin (desinfectant).
creosotagem s. f. (pl. **-ens**) impregnation with creosote.
creosotar v. to creosote: impregnate with creosote.
creosoto (ô) s. m. creosote: preserve of organic substances, extracted from wood tar.
crepe s. m. 1. crape: a) gauzy fabric. b) mourning band, mourning crape. 2. crepe: crapy fabric. 3. (Braz.) creperubber.
~ da China crepe de Chine: raw silk crape.
crépido adj. (poet.) crisped, curled, frizzled.
crepitação s. f. (pl. **-ões**) crepitation, crackle.
crepitante adj. m. + f. crepitant, crackling.
crepitar v. to crepitate, crackle.
crepom s. m. crépon: coarse crepe of silk and wool.
papel ~ crepe paper.
crepuscular adj. m. + f. (also **crepusculino** m.) crepuscular.
crepusculário s. m. crepuscular insect (appearing or flying about at twilight).
crepúsculo s. m. 1. crepuscle, crepusculum, twilight, dusk. 2. (fig.) decadence, decline, close sunset.
~ dos deuses Ragnarok, Twilight of the Gods. **~ da manhã, ~ matutino** dawn, daybreak. **~ da vida** evening (decline, close) of life. **~ vespertino** evening twilight.
crer v. 1. to believe: a) hold to be true, give credit to. b) have confidence in, trust in. c) think, judge, be of opinion. d) presume, suppose. e) have faith. 2. **~-se (de)** to trust s. o.
~ a olhos fechados to believe blindly. **~ piamente** to believe a thing piously. **creio em Deus** I believe

In God. **creio em você** I have confidence in you. **creio que sim** I think so. **ver e** ~ first see and then believe. **ver para** ~ seeing is believing.

crescença s. f. 1. growth: a) act of growing. b) increase, augmentation. c) development, thriving. 2. overplus, surplus, excess.

crescendo s. m. 1. (mus.) crescendo. 2. progression. 3. gradation.

crescente s. m. 1. crescent: a) increasing moon, half--moon (first quarter). b) crescent-shaped object. c) Turkish flag. 2. period during which the moon increases, from new moon to full moon. 3. (Arabian archit.) arch, greater than a semicircle. 4. crescent-shaped bun or roll (in hairdressing). 5. f. flood of a river; tide, highwater. || adj. m. + f. 1. crescent, increasing, growing. 2. (gram.) said of the diphtong in which the semivowel sounds before the vowel.
quarto ~ (**da lua**) the first quarter (of the moon).
ditongo ~ improper diphtong.

crescer v. 1. to grow: a) increase in height, bulk. b) multiply, increase in number or quantity. c) augment, enlarge, expand, wax. d) swell, rise, become tumid. e) shoot, sprout, spring up; strike root. f) develop, grow up. 2. to improve, meliorate, thrive, progress. 3. to superabound. 4. to make grow.
~ **para alguém** to rise against s. o., face s. o. in a defying manner. **a criança cresce** the child grows up. **a dívida pública cresce** the public debt increases. **a massa cresce** the dough rises. **a·planta cresce** the plant grows. **deixar** ~ **a barba** to grow a beard. **o rio cresce na época das chuvas** the river swells in the rainy season.

crescidos s. m. pl. 1. added meshes (in knitting). 2. leavings, leftovers. || **crescido** adj. (dim. **crescidinho**) 1. grown, grown up, adult. 2. augmented, increased, enlarged. 3. developed. 4. swollen.

crescimento s. m. 1. growth, increase, augmentation, enlargement, development, progress. 2. ~**s** pl. (pop.) intermittent, intermittent fever.

créscimo s. m. 1. excess, surplus. 2. residues, remnants, remainders.

cresol s. m. (chem.) cresol: mixture of three isomeric phenols extracted from tar.

crespar v. to curl, crisp, frizz, frizzle, ripple.

crespidão s. f. (pl. **-ões**) 1. crispness, curliness, frizziness. 2. roughness, ruggedness, cragginess.

crespina s. f. 1. (zool.) reticulum: second stomach of ruminants. 2. (obs.) coif to keep the hair in place.

crespir v. 1. = **encrespar**. 2. to undulate, wave. 3. to besprinkle with paint so as to imitate stone.

crespo (ê) s. m. (pl. **crespos**) 1. wrinkles. 2. plater. || adj. 1. rough, rugged, craggy. 2. wrinkled. 3. bristling. 4. (hair) crisped, curly, curled, frizzled. 5. (sea) agitated, rough. 6. perilous. 7. menacing, threatening.

cresta s. f. (also **crestamento** m.) 1. toasting, singeing, scorching, parching. 2. tanning (of the skin, by exposure to the sun). 3. the cutting of the honeycombs. 4. (fig.) sack, pillage. 5. (fig.) defalcation, embezzlement. 6. extortion. 7. reduction of quantity.

crestadeira s. f. 1. instrument for cutting the honeycombs. 2. (cul.) browning iron.

crestadura s. f. scorch, singe, sunburn.

crestamento s. m. 1 = **cresta**. 2. sunburning.

crestar v. 1. to singe, scorch, parch, toast. 2. to tan, brown. 3. to cut the honeycombs from the beehive. 4. (fig.) to sack, pillage. 5. (fig.) to defalcate: a) embezzle. b) reduce the quantity of.
a carestia crestou-lhe os meios de subsistência the dearth defalcated his means of subsistence. **a**

geada crestou as árvores de café the frost nipped the coffee trees, the coffee trees were frostbitten.

cresto (ê) s. m. kid castrated when eight days old.

crestomatia s. f. 1. chrestomathy: selection of choice passages from good authors. 2. anthology.

creta s. f. 1. creta, chalk. 2. (bot.) sea fennel.

cretáceo s. m. (geol.) Cretaceous (period or system).

cretense s. m. + f. Cretan: native or inhabitant of Crete. || adj. Cretan: of Crete.

cretinice s. f. cretinism, imbecility.

cretinismo s. m. cretinism: morbid condition owing to absence or insuff**e**ncy of the thyroid gland.

cretinização s. f. 1. progressive brutification. 2. condition of a cretin.

cretinizar v. 1. to cretinize. 2. to idiotize, brutalize.

cretino s. m. cretin, idiot, imbecile.

cretinoso adj. cretinous: relating or peculiar to a cretin.

cretone s. m. cretonne (a cotton fabric).

cria s. f. 1. suckling (animal), young, breed, brood, litter, calf, foal, kid. 2. stable-bred cattle; cattle. 3. (Braz.) poor person brought up in other people's home.
gado de ~ young cattle.

criação s. f. (pl. **-ões**) 1. creation: a) act or effect of creating. b) all the created beings, universe. c) invention. d) institution, foundation, establishment. 2. breeding, rearing, raising. 3. suckling, nursing, upbringing, nurture. 4. education, breeding. 5. breed, brood, the young. 6. generation, propagation of species, origination, production. 7. cattle; poultry. 8. (N. Braz.) small cattle (caprine and ovine). 9. (S. Braz., constr.) filling consisting of gravel and mortar.
~ **de gado** breeding of cattle. ~ **miúda** small cattle and poultry. **a última** ~ **da moda** the newest fashion; dernier cri.

criacionismo s. m. (lit.) creationism.

criada s. f. woman-servant, maid-servant, maid.
~ **grave**, ~ **de quarto** chamber-maid, waiting-maid, waiting-woman.

criadagem s. f. (pl. **-ens**) the (class of) household servants.

criadeira s. f. 1. wet-nurse. 2. brooder (for newly hatched chicken). 3. incubator (for babies). 4. (Braz.) cow for breeding. 5. = **chuva-criadeira** prolonged drizzle. || adj. 1. well nursing. 2. fecund, fertile.
a chuva miúda é mais ~ **do que um aguaceiro** a prolonged drizzle is more fecund than a heavy shower.

criado s. m. servant, man-servant, domestic. || adj. 1. created. 2. bred, reared, brought up, raised, educated. 3. nursed, suckled.
~ **de mesa** waiter. ~ **particular** valet. **bem** ~ 1. well-bred, well-educated. 2. well-nursed, well-nourished.

criado-mudo s. m. (pl. **criados-mudos**) (Braz., also **bidê**) bedside table, night table.

criador s. m. 1. creator, maker; the Creator, God. 2. cattle breeder. 3. (Braz.) owner of a cattle farm. || adj. 1. creative. 2. breeding, raising. 3. fecund, fertile, fruitful. 4. nourishing.

criadouro s. m. (hort., also **criadoiro**) 1. nursery. 2. creche. || adj. capable of thriving.

criança s. f. child, infant, baby.

criançada s. f. 1. children collectively, bunch of children. 2. childish act or behaviour.

criancice s. f. childishness, puerility, childish action, remark or ways.

criançola s. m. childish, silly youth.

criar v. 1. to create: a) generate, produce, originate, bring forth, cause. b) invent. c) institute, establish, found. 2. to nurse, suckle, nourish, feed. 3. to

breed: a) promote procreation, raise. b) rear up, bring up, nurture. c) educate, instruct. 4. to grow, cultivate, put on (fat). 5. to acquire, get, obtain. 6. ~-se: a) to grow, arise, come forth. b) to develop, grow up. c) to form o. s., cultivate one's mind.
~ **afeição a alguém** to take a liking to s. o. ~ **ao peito** to suckle. ~ **bolor** to grow mouldy. ~ **carne** to put on weight. ~ **coragem** to take courage, heart; sum up pluck. ~ **dificuldades** to raise difficulties; to raise objections to a thing. ~ **forças** to acquire strength. ~ **gado** to raise cattle. ~ **juízo** to develop good sense. ~ **raízes** to strike or take root.
criativo adj. creative.
criatório s. m. (Braz.) 1. cattle. 2. cattle farm.
criatura s. f. 1. creation: effect of creating. 2. creature: a) each of the created beings. b) man, individual, person. c) person servilely attached to another by gratitude.
cribriforme adj. m. + f. cribriform: sievelike.
criciúma s. f. (Braz.) name of several bamboo grasses, genera Arundinaria, Chusquea and Olyra.
cricóide adj. m. + f. (anat.) cricoid: designating the annular cartilage at the bottom of the larynx.
cartilagem ~ cricoid cartilage.
cricóstomo adj. round-mouthed.
cricri, cricrido s. m. (Braz.) a cricket's stridulation.
cricrilar v. to stridulate, chirp as a cricket.
cricrió s. m. (Braz.) bird of the family Cotingideae (Lathria cinerea).
crila s. m. (Braz.) (also **menino**) boy, kid.
crilada s. f. (Braz.) group of boys.
crime s. m. crime, misdeed, felony, offence, delinquency, trespass, outrage, murder.
~ **capital** capital crime. ~ **contra a natureza** crime against nature. ~ **de Estado** treason against the State. ~ **de lesa-majestade** lese-majesty, high--treason. ~ **de lesa-pátria** treason against one's country. ~ **de lesa-razão** crime against reason. ~ **político** political crime. ~ **privativo** an imaginary fellony.
criminação s. f. (pl. -ões) crimination, incrimination, accusation.
criminador s. m. criminator, incriminator, accuser.
criminal s. m. (pl. -ais) 1. criminal case. 2. criminal jurisdiction, criminal court. ‖ adj. m. + f. criminal: relating to crime.
criminalidade s. f. 1. criminality, guiltiness, culpability. 2. crime (collectively). 3. history of crimes.
criminalista s. m. + f. 1. criminalist. 2. (Braz., pop.) severe juror who always tends to condemn the accused.
criminar v. 1. to criminate, incriminate, consider as a criminal. 2. ~-se to incriminate o. s.
criminável adj. m. + f. (pl. -áveis) liable to be criminated, culpable, accusable.
criminologia s. f. criminology: science of crime and penal law.
criminológico adj. criminologic: relating to criminology.
criminologista s. m. + f. criminologist: person versed in criminology.
criminoso s. m. criminal, felon, offender, delinquent, trespasser, murderer. ‖ adj. criminal.
crimodinia s. f. (med.) crymodynia: rheumatic pain.
crimófilo adj. that endures well the cold climate.
crina s. f. (also **clina**) crine, horse-hair; hair of the mane and the tail of some animals (plate C 12).
~ **vegetal** fibres of agaves and some other plants used in upholstery.
crinal s. m. (pl. -ais) = **crineira**. ‖ adj. m. + f. crinal: of or relating to horse-hair and its equivalents.

crindiúva s. f. tree of the family Ulmaceae (Trema micrantha).
crineira s. f. 1. mane (of a horse). 2. lion's mane. 3. plume, crest of a helmet.
crinicórneo adj. (bot.) having crinose antennae.
crinífero adj. criniferous: having a crine.
criniforme adj. m. + f. capillary: resembling a hair.
crinipreto adj. black-maned and black-tailed.
crinito adj. crinite, comate; maned.
crino s. m. a kind of daffodil.
crinóide s. m. (zool.) crinoid: echinoderm with featherlike arms.
crinolina s. f. crinoline: 1. fabric made of horse-hair. 2. stiff cloth for lining the fringes of gowns. 3. hoop-pettycoat, hoop-skirt.
crinudo adj. (Braz.) thick-maned.
criocirurgia s. f. cryosurgery.
criolita s. f. (min.) cryolite: a sodium-aluminum fluoride.
crioula s. f. 1. tree of the family Melastomaceae (Mousiria guianensis). 2. fem. of **crioulo**.
crioulada s. f. bunch of creoles.
criouléu s. m. (Braz.) public creole dance.
crioulinho s. m. (dim. of **crioulo**) little creole. ‖ adj. of or relating to a little creole.
Crioulinho do Pastoureio (S. Braz.) = **Negrinho do Pastoreio** a folkloristic phantom of the pampas.
crioulismo s. m. (lit.) creolism: Spanish American nativistic tendency in literature.
crioulo s. m. (Braz.) 1. creole: a) originally a home--born slave, now any Negro. b) any native of Rio Grande do Sul. 2. cigarette made of twist with a maize leaf cover. ‖ adj. 1. creole.: a) pertaining to the natives of a region. b) Negro, black-skinned. c) in colonial times said of the white born in America or other transoceanic colonies. d) designative of the dialect spoken by creoles. e) designative of the Portuguese dialect spoken in Cabo Verde and of other Portuguese African dialects. 2. said of the common fowl without race nor type.
cripta s. f. crypt: 1. vault, catacomb, cavern. 2. (anat.): a) follicle. b) small gland in mucous membranes.
criptandro adj. said of the vegetals without apparent masculine organs.
críptico adj. cryptic, cryptical: pertaining to a crypt.
criptocarpo adj. (bot.) cryptocarpic, cryptocarpous.
criptocristalina adj. f. cryptocrystalline: said of a crystalline texture so fine that its components are undistinguishable.
criptogamia s. f. 1. cryptogamy: state or character of a plant with hidden sexual organs. 2. Cryptogamia: order of plants comprising all those with hidden sexual organs or, generically, which produce no flowers or seeds.
criptogâmica s. f. (bot.) a specimen of the Cryptogamias.
criptogâmico adj. (bot.) cryptogamic: relating to cryptogamy.
criptógamo s. m. cryptogam: cryptogamic plant. ‖ adj. cryptogamic.
criptografia s. f. cryptography: art of writing in secret characters or in ciphers.
criptográfico adj. cryptographic: relating to cryptography.
criptograma s. m. cryptogram: a writing in secret characters or ciphers.
criptologia s. f. 1. cryptology: secret language; cryptography. 2. occult science, occultism.
criptológico adj. relating to criptology.
criptoméria s. f. 1. (biol.) cryptomere: factor not apparent but demonstrable by crossing. 2. cryptomeria: genus of plants of the family Pinaceae.

criptorquia, criptorquidia s. f. (med. + vet.) cryptor-chidism, cryptorchism.
criquete s. m. cricket (the game).
cris (I) s. m. creese, kris: Malayan dagger.
cris (II) s. m. (astr., obs., also criso) eclipse. ‖ adj. 1. (obs.) eclipsed. 2. m. + f.: a) grayish, greyish. b) obscure, dark. c) gray, grey.
crisálida, crisálide s. f. 1. (zool.) chrysalis, pupa, cocoon. 2. latent thing.
crisântemo s. m. (Braz., also monsenhor) chrysan-themum.
crise (I) s. f. crisis: 1. turning point: a) (med.) decisive change in a disease. b) decisive moment. 2. (fig.) juncture. 3. difficult political situation of the government. 4. economic depression.
~ de nervos nervous fit. ~ econômica economic crisis. ~ social crisis: transition between two cultural standards.
crise (II) s. f. ancient kind of cloth.
criselefantino adj. chryselephantine: of gold and ivory.
crisma s. m. + f. (eccles.) chrism: 1. consecrated oil. 2. anointment. 3. confirmation.
crismar v. 1. (eccles.) to chrism.: a) confirm. b) anoint. 2. to surname, nick-name. 3. ~-se: a) to receive the confirmation. b) to be called, surnamed or nick-named. c) to have or adopt a surname; call o. s.
criso s. m. (also cris) eclipse.
crisoberilo s. m. (min.) chrysoberyl: glucinium alumi-nate.
crisofilo adj. (bot.) chrysophyll: golden-leaved.
crisófitas s. f. pl. (bot.) Chrysophita: a group of algae with light coloured pigments.
crisografia s. f. chrysography.
crisol s. m. (pl. -óis) crucible: 1. a melting pot. 2. severe test, trial.
crisolita s. f. (min.) chrysolite, olivine, peridot.
crisólita s. f. a golden-yellow gem.
crisomelídeos s. m. pl. (ent.) Chrysomelidae: a large family of beetles.
crisopídeos s. m. pl. (ent.) Chrysopidae: the lacewing family.
crisópraso s. m. (min.) chrysoprase: light-green variety of chalcedony.
crisóstomo adj. golden-mouthed: eloquent.
crispação, crispatura s. f. crispamento m. crispation. crispature, contraction.
~ dos nervos contraction of the nerves.
crispar v. 1. = encrespar. 2. to crimp, crinkle, wrin-kle, crisp, curl. 3. to contract, shrink. 4. ~-se to contract spasmodically.
crispim s. m. (pl. -ins) (N. Braz., also saci) a folkloric one-legged Negro phantom.
crista s. f. 1. crest: a) cockscomb. b) plume of a helmet. c) tuft of feathers. d) ridge, chine (plate M 11). e) peak, top, pinnacle. 2. name of several plants.
abaixar a ~ a alguém to take s. o. down a peg or two. levantar a ~ to grow arrogant.
crista-de-galo s. f. (pl. cristas-de-galo) (Braz.) com-mon name of some plants of the genus Amaran-thus and Celosia, the cockscomb.
crista-de-mutum s. f. (pl. cristas-de-mutum) (Braz., bot.) a mucuna (Mucuna huberi): climber of the family Leguminosae.
crista-de-peru s. f. (pl. cristas-de-peru) name of sever-al ornamental plants of the genus Acalypha, as the chenille (A. hispida, also called rabo-de-macaco m., A. illustrata, A. marginata and A. wilkesiana).
cristado adj. crested, that has a crest.
cristal s. m. (pl. -ais). 1. (min.) crystal. 2. crystal glass. 3. glass of superior quality. 4. -ais pl. crystalware: glassware of superior quality.

~ de rocha rock crystal, quartz. ~ lapidado cut crystal, cut glass.
cristaleira s. f. crystal closet, china-closet.
cristaleiro s. m. (Braz.) 1. crystal prospector, explorer. 2. gatherer of gold sand or of diamonds.
cristalífero adj. crystalliferous, crystalligerous: con-taining crystals.
cristalinidade s. f. 1. crystallinity: state or quality of being crystalline. 2. (petrog.) characteristic of rocks composed of crystals or fragments of crystals.
cristalino s. m. crystalline lens (of the eye) (plate O). ‖ adj. crystalline: 1. relating to crystal. 2. having a structure like a crystal. 3. limpid, flawless like crystal.
água -a limpid water.
cristalização s. f. crystallization: act or effect of crystallizing.
cristalizador s. m. (Braz.) crystallizer: 1. crystallizing tank in a sugarmill. 2. low, cylindrical crystallizing vessel.
cristalizar v. 1. to crystallize. 2. ~-se: a) to crystal-lize; congeal in crystals. b) (fig.) to assume a fixed and definite form.
cristalizável adj. m. + f. (pl. -áveis) crystallizable.
cristalografia s. f. crystallography: science of crystals and crystallization.
cristalográfico adj. crystallographic: relating to crys-tallography.
cristalógrafo s. m. crystallographer.
cristalóide s. m. 1. chorioid coat or membrane (of the eye). 2. (chem.) crystalloid: crystallizable substance which diffuses through membranes of dialyzators. 3. (petrog.) minute body without geo-metrical contour, which polarizes light. ‖ adj. m. + f. crystalloid: resembling a crystal.
cristandade s. f. Christendom, Christianity.
cristão s. m. (pl. cristãos) (fem. cristã) Christian: 1. adherent of Christianity. 2. (Braz.) human being, person. ‖ adj. Christian. ‖ -âmente. adv. Christian-like, like a Christian, Christianly, charitably.
cristear v. (S. Braz.) to take in a fool.
cristel s. m. (pl. -éis) (pop.) clyster, enema.
cristianismo s. m. Christianism: Christian religion.
cristianização s. f. Christianization: act of Christian-izing, conversion to Christianity.
cristianizador s. m. Christianizer: person who Chris-tianizes. ‖ adj. Christianizing.
cristianizar v. 1. to Christianize: a) render Christian; convert to Christianity. b) include in the dis-cipline or practice of Christianism. 2. ~-se to become a Christian.
Cristo s. m. 1. Cristo: Christ, Jesus, the Saviour. 2. crucifix. 3. (Braz., sl.) sufferer. 4. (Braz.) victim of mistakes, tricks or ill-treats.
bancar o ~, ser o ~ to be made the goat.
cristologia s. f. Christology.
critério s. m. 1. criterion, standard, rule. 2. judgement, discernment, discretion.
deixar a ~ de alguém to leave to a person's discre-tion. homem de ~ a judicious man.
criteriologia s. f. criteriology: that part of logic which deals with the criterions of truth.
criterioso adj. discerning; sensible, judicious, clear--sighted.
crítica s. f. 1. critique, criticism: a) the art of judging works of art, literature or science. - b) written account of such works, review, recension. c) discus-sion of historical facts. d) censure, fault-finding, disparagement. 2. minute appreciation. 3. discern-ment.
fazer a ~ de to review, comment upon.
criticador s. m. critic, fault-finder, carper, disparager.
criticalidade s. f. (nuclear engineering) criticality.

criticar v. 1. to criticise, critique, review, judge. 2. censure, disparage, carp, find fault with. 3. evaluate, appraise the qualities of.

criticastro, critiqueiro s. m. (depr.) criticaster: bad critic, criticule, petty critic.

criticável adj. m. + f. (pl. **-áveis**) criticizable: open to or deserving criticism.

criticismo s. m. criticism: 1. critical reasoning. 2. critical philosophy (founded by Kant).

criticista s. m. + f. adherent of critical philosophy. ‖ adj. relating to critical philosophy or its adherents.

crítico s. m. 1. critic, reviewer, recensor. 2. censurer, fault-finder, carper. ‖ adj. critical: 1. relating to critique, censorious. 2. relating to a crisis: serious, crucial, dangerous.

critiqueiro s. m. criticaster, carper.

critiquice s. f. (depr.) criticasterism, criticastry.

crivação s. f. (pl. **-ões**) 1. sifting, screening, riddling. 2. act or fact of perforating.

crivado adj. 1. riddled; perforated or pierced in many places. 2. studded, covered. 3. speckled, spotted, flecked.
~ **de balas** riddled with shot. ~ **de feridas** covered with wounds.

crivar v. 1. to stud, cover. 2. to riddle: a) sift, sieve, screen. b) perforate. 3. ~-**se** to become riddled or pierced.

crível adj. m. + f. (pl. **críveis**) (abs. synt. superl. **credibilíssimo**) credible, believable, worthy of belief.

crivo s. m. 1. sieve, screen, riddle. 2. colander, strainer. 3. rose (of a watering can), spraying rose, rosehead. 4. grate (of a sinkhole). 5. any object full of holes. 6. (Braz.): a) fire-grate of the furnace of a sugar mill. b) the bars of such a fire-grate. 7. skimmer. 8. peep-hole, spy-hole (or window).

cró s. m. card game in which wins the partner who first puts together a complete suit of cards.

croata s. m. + f. Croatian, Croat: native or inhabitant of Croatia. ‖ (also **croácio**) adj. Croatian.

croatá s. m. (Braz.) name of several Bromeliaceae of the genera Atananas, Dickia, Nidularia, Quesnelia and Vrisia.

croca (I) s. f. a mother without love for her children.

croca (II) s. f. plough-staff.

croça s. f. crosier (of a bishop).

crocal s. m. (pl. **-ais**) cherry- or saffron-coloured precious stone.

cróceo adj. saffron(-coloured).

crochê s. m. crochet, crochet work.

crocidismo s. m. (med.) floccillation: involuntary agitation of a sick person's hands, which seem to pick fuzzes from the bedclothes.

crocitante adj. m. + f. croaking, cawing.

crocitar v. to croak, caw (raven, crow), make a croaking sound.

crocito s. m. croak (of a raven, crow and other such birds).

crocodiliano s. m. crocodilian: specimen of the Crocodilia.

crocodilo s. m. (zool.) crocodile.

crocoíta s. f. (min.) crocoite: lead chromate.

crocoroca s. f. (Braz.) name of several species of fishes of the genera Haemulon and Orthopristis.

crocoroca-jurumim s. f. (pl. **crocorocas-jurumim**) (Braz.) pigfish (Orthopristis ruber).

croinha s. m. (Braz.) 1. (also **coroinha**) altar boy. 2. sacristan; choir boy.

cromado adj. 1. chromated, chromatized. 2. chrome-plated, chromium-plated.

cromar v. 1. to chromate, chromatize. 2. to plate with chromium.

cromática s. f. chromatics, chromatology: science of colours.

cromático adj. chromatic: 1. (phys.) relating to colours. 2. (mus.) composed of a series of semitones.

cromatina s. f. (biol., also **nucleína**) chromatin: substance contained in the cell nuclei.

cromatismo s. m. 1. (phys.) chromatism: dispersion of light. 2. recomposition of light which has traversed diaphanous bodies.

cromato s. m. (chem.) chromate: any salt containing the bivalent anion CrO_4.
~ **de chumbo** lead chromate, chrome yellow. ~ **de potássio** potassium chromate. ~ **de zinco** chromate of zinc, zink yellow.

cromatóforo s. m. (zool.) chromatophore: pigmented cells (of animals which change colour).

crômel s. m. (chem.) a metallic alloy composed of 90% nickel and 10% chromium.

crômico adj. 1. chromatic: relating to colours. 2. (chem.) chromic: pertaining to or derived from chromium.

cromidrose s. f. (med.) chromidrosis.

cromista s. m. + f. (typogr.) colour etcher.

cromo s. m. 1. (chem.) chromium. 2. chromolithograph, chromolith, chromo: coloured lithograph.

cromolitografia s. f. chromolithography.

cromolitográfico adj. cromolithographic, cromolithic: relating to chromolithography.

cromoplastofonia s. f. an artistic composition characterized by using simultaneously colours, visual forms and sound.

cromossomo s. m. (biol.) chromosome: one of the chromatin fragments of the cell nucleous, previous to the mitotic division of the cell.

cromotipia s. f. (typogr.) any colour printing process.

crônica s. f. chronicle: 1. chronological record of historical events, annals. 2. narrative, account, record. 3. news-section in a newspaper. 4. scientific or literary column in a newspaper.
~ **policial** police-news section.

cronicão, crônicon s. m. voluminous medieval chronicle.

cronicidade s. f. (med.) chronicity.

crônico adj. chronic, chronical: 1. of long duration. 2. (fig.) inveterate.
doença -a chronic disease.

croniqueiro s. m. (fam.) news writer, news editor in charge of local news.

cronista s. m. + f. cronicler, annalist, columnist, historian.

cronografia, cronologia s. f. chronography, chronology: 1. treatise on the divisions of time. 2. treatise on historical dates, chronological table.

cronográfico adj. chronographic: relating to chronography.

cronógrafo s. m. chronograph: instrument for measuring or recording time.

cronograma s. m. chronogram: 1. an enigmatic date, formed by Roman numeral letters contained in an inscription or phrase. 2. a step-by-step schedule for the execution of a job.

cronologia s. f. 1. = **cronografia**. 2. chronology: science of the division of time and the proper sequence of dates of events.

cronológico adj. chronologic(al): 1. relating to chronology. 2. according to the order of time or occurrence.
ordem -a chronological order.

cronologista s. m. + f. chronologist: person versed in chronology.

cronometragem s. f. timekeeping.

cronometrar v. to timekeep.

cronometria s. f. chronometry.

cronômetro s. m. chronometer: 1. instrument for measuring time, timekeeper (plate R 4). 2. precision watch.

cronônimo s. m. 1. name of historical epochs. 2. designation of divers names indicating epochs: June, Hegira, Middle Ages, etc.

cronoscópio s. m. chronoscope: a chronometer.

croque s. m. 1. boat-hook. 2. (Braz. + Port. prov.; also cocre) light blow on the head with the knuckles or also with a stick or cane.

croquete s. m. (cul.) croquette: ball of minced meat.

croqui s. m. croquis: sketch of a design or painting.

cróssima s. f. (Braz.) triangular piece of a railroad switch.

crosta s. f. 1. crust, rind. 2. (med.) eschar, scab. ~ da Terra crust of the earth; lithosphere.

crotalídeo s. m. specimen of the family Crotalidae, snakes typified by the genus Crotalus. || adj. crotalic, crotaline.

crótalo s. m. 1. Crotalus: the genus of the rattlesnakes. 2. (ant.) crotalum: a kind of castanet.

crotalóide adj. m. + f. crotaloid, crotaline: resembling a rattlesnake.

cróton s. m. (also crotão) croton: a genus of medicinal plants.

cru adj. (f. crua) 1. raw: a) uncooked. b) not prepared or dressed, unprocessed. 2. crude, rough, coarse. 3. cruel, hard, barbarous. 4. afflictive. 5. blunt, plain, unvarnished, unadorned. 6. shocking, rude (language). 7. crude, immature, ill-considered. 8. unbleached.
algodão ~ unbleached cotton, raw cotton. couro ~ rawhide, green skin. desastre ~ afflictive disaster. seda ~a raw silk. verdade nua e ~a unvarnished truth.

cruá s. f. (also melão-caboclo m.) (Braz., bot.) cassabanana, musk cucumber (Sicana odorifera).

crubixá s. m. black coral found at several points of the Brazilian coast.

cruciação s. f. (pl. -ões) mortification, torture, torment, martyrization.

cruciador s. m. mortifier, tormentor, torturer, excruciator. || adj. (also cruciante m. + f., cruciário) mortifying, torturing, tormenting, excruciating, heart-rending.

crucial adj. m. + f. (pl. -ais) crucial: 1. cruciate, cruciform, cross-shaped. 2. decisive, critical.

cruciana s. f. (Braz.) a kind of bamboo.

cruciante adj. m. + f. crucial.

cruciar v. to mortify, afflict, torture, torment, martyrize.

crucífera s. f. (bot.) crucifer: specimen of the Cruciferae or Brassicaceae, the cabbage family.

cruciferário s. m. cross-bearer (at processions).

crucífero, crucígero adj. cruciferous: 1. bearing a cross. 2. having a cross-shaped flower; relating to the Cruciferae.

crucificação, crucifixão (pl. -ões) s. f., crucificamento m. crucifixion.

crucificado s. m. the Crucified, the Crucifixed, Christ. || adj. crucifixed; nailed to the cross.

crucificador s. m. crucifier.

crucificar, crucifixar v. to crucify: 1. nail to the cross. 2. torture, excruciate, mortify.

crucifixo s. m. crucifix (plate M 11). || adj. crucified.

cruciforme adj. m. + f. cruciform: cruciate, cross-shaped.

crucígero adj. crucigerous: bearing a cross; marked with a cross.

crucirrostro adj. (ornith.) curvirostral (said of the beak of the crossbill).

crudívoro adj. living on uncooked food.

crueira s. f. 1. (Braz., also corera, cruera, curuera) residue of manioc-flour which at the fabrication does not pass through the sieve. 2. (N. Braz.) dry tumour on the head of Gallinaceae. 3. (N. Braz., also cuiuíra, cuinhira, cunhira) a 15-minute flux and equal reflux at the beginning of the flood tide, in some rivers.

cruel adj. m. + f. (pl. -éis) (abs. synt. superl. cruelíssimo and crudelíssimo) cruel, fierce, inhuman, barbarous; ferocious; tyrant; hard, severe, dolorous, grievous, insensible, unmerciful, merciless, sanguinary, bloodthirsty. || ~mente adv. cruelly, fiercely, unmercifully.

crueldade s. f. cruelty, inhumanity, ferocity; cruel action.

cruentação s. f. (pl. -ões) act of making cruel, bloody.

cruentar v. to bloody, ensanguine; make bloody, stain with blood.

cruento adj. bloody: 1. containing blood. 2. ensanguined, bloodstained. 3. cruel, bloodthirsty, ferocious.

crueza s. f. 1. rawness, crudity; state of being uncooked. 2. cruelty, rudeness, brutality. 3. ill digestion.

crúmen s. m. (pl. crumens, crúmenes) (also crume) crumen: suborbital gland of certain ruminants.

cruor s. m. 1. (poet.) the blood which is shed. 2. cruor, gore, crassamentum: coagulum of blood. 3. hemachrome: colouring matter of the blood.

crupe s. m. (med., also garrotilho) croup.

crupiê s. m. croupier: gambling table attendant.

crural adj. m. + f. (pl. -ais) (anat.) crural: of or relating to the thigh.

crusta s. f. (also crosta) crust.

crustáceo s. m. (zool.) crustacean: specimen of the Crustacea. || adj. crustaceous: 1. covered with a crustlike shell or scab. 2. crustacean: relating to the Crustacea.

cruviana s. f. (N. Braz.) 1. very cold wind. 2. drizzle. 3. terral: fresh morning breeze.

cruz s. f. 1. cross: a) ancient instrument of torture. b) Christianism. c) Christian symbol of redemption. d) affliction, trouble, tribulation. e) symbol of some military or religious orders. f) sign of the cross. 2. Passion of Christ. 3. (Braz.) name of several plants of the genus Jussiaea. 4. ~es pl.: a) loins, small of the back. b) reverse of a coin, showing a cross. c) withers of a horse. || cruzes! interj. indicating horror or shockedness: good heavens!
~ da âncora, crown, cross of an anchor (plate A 6). ~ de Lorena Lorraine cross. ~ de Malta Maltese cross. ~ de Santo André St. Andrew's cross. ~ gamada swastika. ~ grega Greek cross. ~ latina Latin cross. ~ vermelha, ~ de Genebra red cross, Geneva cross. ~es ou cunhos cross or pile, head or tail. assinar de ~ 1. to sign by a criss-cross. 2. (fig.) to sign without reading; have no opinion, be transigent. em ~ crosswise. entre a ~ e a caldeirinha in a dilemma, in a critical situation. fazer ~ na boca 1. to have nothing to eat. 2. (fig.) to be too late in the field. fazer o sinal da ~ to cross o. s., sign o. s. with the cross, make the sign of the cross. levar a ~ ao calvário to accomplish a difficult task. todos têm a sua ~ every one has his affliction or tribulation.

cruza s. f. (S. Braz.) 1. cross(-breeding). 2. cross (-breed), hybrid. 3. cross-ploughing.

cruza-bico s. m. (pl. cruza-bicos) (ornith.) crossbill, crossbeak.

cruzada (I) s. f. cruzade: 1. medieval military expedition against infidels or heretics. 2. any campaign against some evil.

cruzada (II) s. f. (S. Braz.) 1. crossway, crossroad(s): intersection of two or more roads. 2. = cruzamento.

cruzadista s. m. + f. crossworder: one who solves crossword puzzles.

cruzado s. m. 1. crusader. 2. ancient Portuguese gold coin. 3. coin of the value of 40 centavos. ‖ adj. crossed, crosswise, intersected.
cheque ~ crossed cheque. fogo ~ (mil.) cross fire. mar ~ cross-sea. palavras -as crossword puzzle. primos ~s first cousins.

cruzador s. m. 1. crosser: one who or that which crosses. 2. (navy) cruiser.

cruzamento s. m. crossing: 1. act or fact of crossing. 2. effect of that action. 3. intersection, street crossing (plate R 8). 4. cross-breeding. 5. crossing over.

cruzar v. 1. to cross: a) put crosswise. b) traverse, pass over. c) pass through in various directions. d) cross-breed, intercross, interbreed. e) cruise (the sea). 2. ~ -se: a) to intercross, cross each other, intersect each other. b) to meet passing in opposite directions. c) to cross o. s., make the sign of the cross.
~ as mãos to resign o. s. to patience. ~ os braços to cross (or fold) one's arms; (fig.) to rest on one's oars, stay idle. ~-se com alguém to cross s. o. (meet him and pass by). eles cruzaram-se na rua they crossed in the street.

cruzeira s. f. (S. Braz., also urutu) urutu: a pit viper (Bothrops alternata).

cruzeiro s. m. 1. large cross of stone, erected in churchyards, squares, cemeteries. 2. (archit.) transept: transversal part of a church, between the nave and the main altar. 3. (naut.) sea route, maritime route. 4. (naut.) cruiser. 5. cruise. 6. Cruzeiro (astr. also Cruzeiro do Sul) Southern Cross. 7. Brazilian monetary unit. 8. Brazilian military medal. 9. (Braz.) ~ urutu. 10. plant of the family Rubiaceae (Declieuxia chiococcoides). ‖ adj. crossed: that has a cross or is marked with a cross.

cruzeta s. f. 1. a little cross. 2. surveyor's square. 3. (N. Braz.) coat hanger. 4. (tech): a) crosshead. b) double tee junction, four-way union (plate C 1).

cruzetado adj. that has the form of a little cross.

crúzio s. m. member of the congregation of Santa Cruz de Coimbra. ‖ adj. said of that congregation.

cruzo s. m. (S. Braz.) crossroad: 1. road that crosses another. 2. crossing: place where two roads cross.

ctenóforo s. m. (zool.) ctenophore: specimen of the Ctenophora.

cu s. m. (vulg.) arse; bum, buttocks, butt.

cuada s. f. (vulg.) 1. a bump with the buttocks. 2. seat of a pair of trousers or drawers.

cuandu s. m. (also ouriço-cacheiro) (Braz.) 1. coendou: prehensile-tailed porcupine. 2. young carnauba (palm).

cuatá s. m. (Braz.) a spider monkey (Ateles paniscus).

cuba (I) s. f. 1. tub, vat, cask, press tub, press vat. 2. shaft (of a blast-furnace) (plate A 6). 3. Cuban (tobacco).

cuba (II) s. m. (N. Braz.) 1. (also cuebas, mancueba) big shot: influential personality; sage; artful fellow. 2. sorcerer, wizard.

cubagem s. f. (pl. -ens) 1. cubature: calculation of the cubic contents. 2. (math.) a raising to the third power. 3. cubage, volume: cubic contents of a solid or enclosed space.

cubano s. m. Cuban: native or inhabitant of Cuba. ‖ adj. Cuban: of Cuba.

cubar v. (also cubicar) to cube: 1. calculate the cubic contents of a solid or enclosed space. 2. raise to the third power.

cubata s. f. 1. Negroes' hut. 2. former slave-house on Brazilian farms. 3. habitation, abode.

cubatão s. m. (Braz.) foothill.

cubatura s. f. (geom.) cubature: reduction of any solid to a cube of equivalent volume.

cubé s. m. (Braz., also cubiú) small fish of the Amazon.

cubeba s. f. cubeb pepper: 1. the shrub. 2. its fruit.

cúbico adj. cubic, cubical.
metro ~ cubic meter. raiz -a (math.) cube root. sistema ~ (min.) isometric system.

cubicular adj. m. + f. cubicular: relating to a cubicle or cubiculum.

cubículo s. m. 1. cubiculum, cubicle: a) small room, small compartment, cubby-hole. b) (obs.) bedchamber, partitioned sleeping place. 2. a monk's or nun's cell. 3. (Braz.) jail, prison.

cúbio s. m. (Braz.) a nightshade (Solanum sessiliflorum).

cubismo s. m. (paint.) cubism.

cubista s. m. + f. cubist: artist who paints according to cubism. ‖ adj. cubist: said of an adherent of cubism.

cubital adj. m. + f. (pl. -ais) (anat.) cubital: of or pertaining to the cubitus.

cúbito s. m. 1. = côvado. 2. (anat.) cubitus: bone of the forearm.

cubiú s. m. (Braz.) = cubé.

cubo s. m. 1. cube: a) (geom.) regular hexahedron. b) (math.) third power, cubic number, cubic quantity. 2. hub, nave (of a wheel). 3. bucket of a water wheel. 4. overshot water channel (of a water-mill).
~ de um número the third power of a number.

cubóide s. m. (anat.) cuboid: short tarsal bone. ‖ adj. m. + f. cuboid, cuboidal: aproximately cube-shaped.

cubomancia s. f. cubomancy: divination by means of dice.

cuca s. f. 1. (Braz.): a) bogery, bugbear, hobgoblin. b) (N.) hag, ugly woman. c) also (cuque) cake prepared with eggs, flour, butter and yeast. d) (N.) luxury. e) cook. f) m. = mestre-cuca cook, male cook, man cook. 2. (Port., prov.) dark pebble gravel for underlaying stonework and masonry. 3. (Braz., pop.) head. ‖ cuca! interj. (Port. prov.) out you go!, get out! be off!

cucar v. 1. (also cucular) to cuckoo, cry cuckoo. 2. (also cocar) to be on the lookout, lie in wait. 3. (Port. prov., fam.) to go away, retire, withdraw.

cucharra s. f. (S. Braz.) horn spoon, wooden spoon used in the country.

cuchê adj. coated (paper).
papel ~ art paper.

cuco s. m. 1. (ornith.) cuckoo. 2. cuckoo-clock. 3. (bot., also campainha-amarela) cuckoo-flower. 4. (obs., Port. prov.) cuckold: husband of an unfaithful wife. ‖ adj. cuckold: said of a cuckold.

cucular (I) adj. m. + f. cuculliform: hood-shaped.

cucular (II) v. 1. (also cucar) to cuckoo, cry cuckoo. 2. (N. Braz., pop.) = cogular, acogular.

cuculiforme s. m +f. a specimen of the Cuculiformes, an order of birds typified by the cuckoo.

cuculo s. m. 1. hood, cap. 2. (N. Braz., pop., also cogulo) overmeasure, excess.

cucura s. f. (Braz., also matapi) plant of the family Moraceae (Pourouma cecropiaefolia).

cucúrbito s. f. cucurbit: 1. (chem.) part of an alambic. 2. plant of the genus Cucurbita.

cucurbitácea s. f. (bot.) a specimen of the Cucurbitaceae, family typified by the cucurbit.

cucurbitáceo adj. (bot.) cucurbitaceous: relating to the family Cucurbitaceae; relating to or resembling a gourd.

cucurbitino adj. (bot.) cucurbitine: resembling a gourd or gourd-seed.

cucuricar, cucuritar v. to crow (cock).

cu-de-boi s. m. (pl. **cus-de-boi**) (Braz., pop.) rot, row, disorder, melee.

cu-de-ferro s. m. (pl. **cus-de-ferro**) (school sl.) student who never shirks a lesson.

cudelume s. m. (Braz., pop., also **pirilampo**) firefly.

cuebas s. m. (Braz., also **cuba**) big shot, influential person.

cuecas s. f. pl. short drawers, shorts (plate R 7).

cueiro s. m. swaddling-clothes, swathe, diaper, baby's napkin, clouts.

deixar os ~s to leave childhood. **desde os ~s** from the cradle. **ele ainda cheira a ~s** his number is still wet, he is as green as grass.

cuera s. f. (S. Braz., also **unheira, tubuna**) saddle gall.

cuerudo adj. (S. Braz.) saddle-galled.

cuí s. m. 1. (Braz.) refuse tobacco dust. 2. (N. Braz.) fine sifted flour.

cuia s. f. 1. (Braz., also **cuitê, cuité**) bottle gourd. 2. (S. Braz.) maté gourd: drinking vessel made of a gourd and from which maté tea is drunk with a silver tube. 3. (sl.) head. 4. prostitute. 5. (N. Braz.) dry measure holding 0.43 liter; the contents of such a measure.

juntar as ~s (Braz., pop.) to change one's residence.

cuiabana s. f. (Braz.) a carpenter ant (Prepolepis fulva).

cuiabano s. m. (Braz.) 1. native or inhabitant of Cuiabá, State capital of Mato Grosso. 2. native or inhabitant of Mato Grosso. ‖ adj. of Cuiabá.

cuiada s. f. (Braz.) gourdful of maté tea.

cuia-de-macaco s. f. (pl. **cuias-de-macaco**) (Braz.) plant of the family Lecideaceae (Couropita lentula).

cuia-do-brejo s. f. (pl. **cuias-do-brejo**) (Braz.) plant of the family Styracaceae (Styra camporum).

cuiambuca, cumbuca s. f. (Braz.) gourd bottle.

cuiame s. m. (Braz.) great number of bottle gourds or vessels made thereof.

cuiapeua s. f. (N. Braz.) flat gourd used in ceramics for polishing manufactured ware.

cuiapitinga s. f. (N. Braz.) black, lustrous gourd vessel.

cuiara s. m. (Braz.) 1. sharp gambler. 2. rogue, knave. 3. crafty or shrewd fellow. ‖ adj. 1. sharp. 2. roguish. 3. crafty, shrewd.

cuiarana s. f. (Braz.) tree of the family Combretaceae (Buchenavia grandis).

cuíca s. f. 1. (Braz., zool., also **goiacuíca**) the mouse opossum and some other marsupials of the family Didelphyidae. 2. a drumlike instrument open at one end and having a stick attached to the center of the drum-skin which, when rubbed, produces a grunting noise.

quebrar a ~ a alguém to take s. o. down a peg.

cuíca-d'água s. f. (pl. **cuícas-d'água**) (Braz., zool.) yapok (Chironectes minimus), an aquatic opossum of South America.

cuidado s. m. care: 1. precaution, caution, watchfulness, heed. 2. diligence, attention, solicitude. 3. uneasiness, anxiety, concern. 4. trouble, worry, grief, sorrow. 5. object of care. ‖ adj. considered, cared for. ‖ **cuidado!** interj. take care!, look out! **~ com o degrau!** watch out for the step. **~ com os batedores de carteiras!** beware of pickpockets! **~! não caias!** take care you don't fall. **~! não virar!** attention! don't tilt. **ao ~ de** (abbr. a/c) in care of, care of (abbr. c/o). **com ~** careful, heedful. **deixar ao ~ de** to leave to the care of. **deixe isto ao meu ~** let that be my care. **estar**

com ~ to be uneasy. **isto dá-me ~** this makes me uneasy. **não lhe dê isso ~** never mind that, don't trouble yourself about that. **por, ter, tomar ~** to look to, to take care of. **ter ~** to take care, mind. **tomar ~** to take heed.

cuidador s. m. (f. **cuidadeira**) carer: one who cares; caretaker.

cuidadoso, cuidoso adj. careful: 1. cautious, heedful, mindful. 2. attentive, solicitous. 3. diligent, zelous. 4. painstaking, conscientious, scrupulous, particular. ‖ **-amente** adv. carefully.

cuidar v. 1. to care. 2. to cogitate, consider. 3. to imagine, suppose, think, believe, presume. 4. to take care of, look after, take charge of. 5. to care for, attend to. 6. to pay attention to, feel interested. 7. **~-se**: a) to believe o. s. to be s. th. b) to take care of o. s.

~ em to consider, think of. **não ~ do seu alinho** to neglect one's dress. **quem cuidaria de tal** who could imagine that.

cuidaru s. m. (Braz., also **tamarana**) flat, edged Indian club, about one yard long.

cuieira s. f. (Braz., also **cabaceiro**) calabash tree.

cuietê, cuieté s. m. (Braz.) bottle gourd, gourd.

cuim s. m. (pl. **-ins**) 1. (Braz., also **ouriço-cacheiro**) coendou. 2. squeal of a suffering hog. 3. (Braz.) rice chaff.

cuinchar, cuinhar v. to squeal (hog).

cuinhira s. f. (N. Braz., also **crueira**) manioc-flour residue.

cuintau s. m. (Braz., also **anhuma**) horned screamer.

cuipuna s. f. (Braz.) tree of the family Myrtaceae (Myrcia tingens).

cuíra adj. m. + f. (N. Braz.) turbulent, restless, fidgety, squirmish, frolicsome (child or horse).

cuité s. m. + f. (Braz., also **coité**) bottle gourd, gourd.

cuitelão s. m. (Braz., ornith.) a three-toed jacamar.

cuitelo s. m. (Braz., pop., also **beija-flor**) humming-bird.

cuitezeira s. f. (Braz., also **cabaceira**) calabash tree.

cuiú-cuiú s. m. (pl. **cuiú-culús**) (Braz.) 1. a crested parrot (Pionopsitta pileata). 2. a river catfish (Ovidorus niger).

cuiuíra s. f. (N. Braz, also **crueira**) manioc flour residue.

cujara s. m. (Braz.) a rice rat (Oryzomis leucogaster).

cujo s. m. (Braz., fam., also **dito-cujo**) 1. the said person, such a one, individual. 2. the devil. ‖ rel. pron. whose, of whom, of which.

em ~ testemunho falei in witness whereof I spoke. **o homem ~ livro perdi** the man whose book I lost. **Pedro, de -a casa eu venho** Peter, from whose house I come.

cujuba s. f. (N. Braz.) small gourd (vessel). ‖ interj. something like "heave ho!" used by lumbermen to pull all at the same time.

cujubi, cajubim s. m. (Braz., ornith.) piping guan.

culape s. m. (Braz.) 1. startle, shock. 2. large piece (of bread, meat).

culatra s. f. 1. breech: a) part of a firearm at the rear of the bore; breech piece of a cannon. b) (sl.) buttocks. 2. (S. Braz.) remnant of a lot of cattle. 3. rear of a herd of cattle.

~ de um ímã yoke of a magnet. **sair o tiro pela ~** 1. to backfire. 2. (fig.): a) to be contrary to expectation (result). b) to prejudice the author (the act).

culatrear v. (S. Braz.) 1. to herd: follow at the rear of a herd, driving it. 2. (fig.) to follow up, pursue.

cule s. m. coolie, cooly: Chinese labourer.

culicídeos s. m. pl. (ent.) Culicidae: the mosquito family.

culinária s. f. cookery, culinary art.

culinário adj. culinary: relating to the kitchen or cooking.
arte -a culinary art.
culminação s. f. (astr.) culmination, transit.
culminância s. f. apex, apogee, zenith, summit, acme.
culminante adj. m. + f. culminant.
momento ~ acme, decisive moment. **ponto** ~ culminating point, acme, apex, climax.
culminar v. 1. to culminate: reach the summit or perfection. 2. to terminate brilliantly.
a comemoração culminou em uma apoteose patriótica the commemoration culminated in a patriotic apotheosis.
culote s. m. + f. (Braz.) riding breeches.
culpa s. f. 1. (jur.) culpa, delict, offence, delinquency, crime. 2. sin. 3. fault, blame, guilt, cause of an evil.
a ~ é minha it is my fault. **a ~ não é nossa** it is not our own fault. **dar a ~ de alguma coisa a alguém, deitar, lançar a ~ de alguma coisa sobre alguém** to lay the blame for a thing on s. o. **de quem é a ~** whose fault is it? **é por sua ~** it is his fault, he is to blame. **lançar a ~ a outrem** to throw the blame on another, to lay it at another person's door. **ter a ~ de** to be the cause of, to be to blame for. **ter ~ em** to be implicated in a fault. **ter ~s no cartório** to have a guilty conscience.
culpabilidade s. f. culpability, guilt.
culpado s. m. culprit, criminal, the guilty person. ‖ adj. culpable, guilty, criminal, blameworthy.
quem é ~ disso? who is to blame for this? **quem é o ~** who is the criminal?
culpar v. 1. to inculpate, accuse, incriminate, charge. 2. to blame, censure. 3. ~-se: a) to become guilty. b) to confess o. s. guilty; incriminate o. s.
culpável adj. m. + f. (pl. -áveis) 1. culpable, guilty. 2. censurable, blamable.
culposo adj. (jur.) culpose; guilty.
culteranismo s. m. (lit.) cultism, Gongorism: style imitative of that of the Spanish poet Góngora.
culteranista s. m. + f. cultist, Gongorist: adherent of cultism. ‖ adj. gongoristic.
cultismo s. m. 1. culturization, civilization. 2. culteranism, cultism.
cultista s. m. + f. cultist: adherent of cultism. ‖ adj. gongoristic: relating to cultism (Gongorism).
cultivação s. f. cultivation, culture: act of cultivating.
cultivador s. m. 1. cultivator: a) one who cultivates s. th. b) agricultural implement to break up the soil (plate E 4). 2. tiller, farmer, husbandman, grower.
cultivar v. 1. to cultivate: a) till, manure. b) apply o. s. to. c) promote, favour. d) grow (plants). e) develop. f) maintain, keep up. 2. ~-se to acquire culture, knowledge.
~ amizades to cultivate friendships. **~ as artes** to cultivate the arts. **~ flores** to cultivate, grow flowers. **~ um talento** to cultivate, develop a talent. **~ a terra** to cultivate, till the ground.
cultivável adj. m. + f. (pl. -áveis) cultivable, cultivatable, that can be cultivated.
cultivo s. m. cultivation; culture; tillage.
~ do feijão culture of beans.
culto s. m. cult: worship, adoration, veneration. ‖ adj. cultivated, enlightened, cultured, learned, educated, civilized; refined; elegant (style).
~ divino divine service, worship. **liberdade de ~** freedom of worship, religious freedom.
cultor s. m. 1. = **cultivador**. 2. (fig.) follower, adherent; worshiper. 3. person engaged in a determinate study.

cultrifoliado adj. m. + f. (bot.) having cultriform leaves.
cultriforme adj. m. + f. cultriform, cultrate: shaped like the blade of a knife.
cultrirrostro s. m. a specimen of the Cultirostres, a family of cultirostral wading-birds. ‖ adj. (zool.) cultirostral, having a long, pointed bill shaped like the blade of a knife.
cultual adj. m. + f. (pl. -ais) cultual: relating to a cult.
cultuar v. to worship, adore, make an object of worship of.
cultura s. f. culture: 1. cultivation, tillage, growing, rearing, breeding. 2. promotion of arts or sciences. 3. intellectual development, learning, education. 4. civilization. 5. refinement.
~ dos campos agriculture, farming. **~ geral** general knowledge. **homem de grande ~** a man of wide culture. **sem ~** unlettered, ignorant.
cultural adj. m. + f. (pl. -ais) cultural, relating to culture.
cumachama s. m. + f. (N. Braz., pop.) so-and-so, what's-his-name, what's-her-name.
cumaí s. m. (Braz.) couma, cow tree, sorva.
cumandatiá s. f. (Braz.) lablab: hyacinth bean.
cumari, cumarim s. m. (Braz.) 1. (also **cumbari, cumbarim**) a palm (Astrocaryum vulgare). 2. chili, goat pepper: a solanaceous shrub which yields the Cayenne pepper.
cumaru, cumbaru, cumburu s. m. (Braz.) coumarou: tonka-bean tree.
cumarurana s. f. (Braz.) two trees of the genus Coumcrouna or Dipteryx.
cumati s. m. (Braz.) tree of the family Myrtaceae (Myrcia atramentifera).
cumã-uaçu s. f. (Braz.) tree of the dogbane family (Couma macrocarpa).
cumba s. m. (Braz., sl.) strong dexterous man; bully; provoker. ‖ adj. strong, dexterous; provoking.
cumbaca s. f. (Braz., also **anujá**) a freshwater catfish.
cumbé s. m. (Braz.) any soft-bodied wormlike animal as leeches or slugs.
cumbuca s. f. (Braz.) 1. = **cuiambuca**. 2. raffle, lottery. 3. (sl.) gambling house.
cume s. m. 1. summit, peak, montaintop, hilltop (plate M 11). 2. (fig.) climax, apogee.
cumeada s. f. (also **encumeada**) 1. mountain ridge or crest. 2. = **cumeeira**.
cumeeira s. f. 1. root ridge, ridge beam or pole (plate T 5). 2. mountain ridge (plate M 11).
cúmplice s. m. + f. accomplice: 1. accessory to a crime. 2. co-operator, partner in an action, supporter.
cumpliciar(-se) v. to implicate o. s. in an offence.
cumplicidade s. f. complicity.
cumpridor s. m. 1. accomplisher, executer, fulfiller (of a promise, duty, etc.). 2. executor (of a will). ‖ adj. executant, performing; trustworthy, reliable.
cumprimentar v. 1. to salute, greet, bow to, hail, welcome. 2. to compliment, pay one's compliments to, congratulate, gratulate.
cumprimenteiro adj. overcourteous, exceedingly complimentary.
cumprimento s. m. 1. accomplishment, execution, fulfilment, performance. 2. compliment, salutation, salute, greeting, bow, hail, welcome. 3. congratulation, gratulation, felicitation. 4. ~s pl. compliments, respects, regards; short visit or call; letter of congratulation.
~s rasgados exaggerated compliments. **apresentar seus ~s a** to pay one's respects to.
cumprir v. 1. to accomplish, execute, fulfil, keep, perform, carry out, make good, meet, satisfy, serve. 2. to be necessary, convenient, profitable. 3. to

complete. 4. to behoove, be incumbent, upon o. s. 5. ~-se to come true.

~ a palavra to keep one's word. ~ a sua promessa to fulfil one's promise. ~ (com) a ordem to execute an order. ~ (com) os seus deveres to perform one's duties. cumpre fazer face aos fatos it is necessary to face the facts. ele cumpriu sete anos de prisão he served a seven years' term of prison.

cumulação s. f. (pl. -ões) (also acumulação) cumulation, accumulation.

cumular v. (also acumular) to cumulate, accumulate.

cumulativo adj. 1. cumulative: formed by, or being part of a cumulation.

cúmulo s. m. 1. cumulus, accumulation, heap. 2. acme, apex, summit, top. 3. addition. 4. ~s pl. (meteor.) cumulus (plate N 2).

chegar ao ~ da imprudência to carry things to the last extreme of imprudence. é o ~! that's the limit! para ~ da desgraça to crown it all. por ~ to make matters worse.

cúmulo-nimbos s. m. pl. cumulo-nimbus (plate N 2).

cuna s. f. 1. (poet.) cunabula, cradle. 2. (fig.) origin.

cunabi, cunambi s. m. (Braz.) poisonous plant of the family Compositae (Ichthyothera cunabi).

cunauaru s. m. (N. Braz.) 1. a toad, believed by the natives to be of good augury. 2. fragrant resin secreted by that toad.

cunca s. f. (Braz.) 1. succulent tubercles on the roots of the hog plum, with which cattlemen and hunters quench their thirst, for want of water. 2. m. a card game.

cundurango s. m. (Braz.) several plants of the family Compositae, genus Mikania.

cunduru s. m. (Braz.) tree of the family Urticaceae.

cuneano adj. cuneiform: wedge-shaped.

cuneifoliado adj. (bot.) cuneate, cuneated: having wedge-shaped leaves.

cuneiforme s. m. cuneiform: 1. ~s pl. cuneiform characters, arrowhead characters, wedge-characters. 2. (anat.) cuneiform bones. ǁ adj. m. + f. cuneiform, arrowheaded, wedge-shaped.

cuneirrostro adj. (ornith.) wedge-billed.

cunha s. f. 1. wedge, (typogr.) quoin (plates M 6, V 4). 2. (fig.) influential interceder, protector. 3. intercession, recommendation, protection of an influential person. 4. suplementary word to round off a word or period.

~ da plaina wedge of a plane (plate P 13). ~ esférica (math.) spherical wedge. à ~ replete, cram-full, crowded, closely packed, jammed.

cunhã s. f. (N. Braz.) woman (Tupi-Guarani).

cunhada s. f. sister-in-law.

cunhadia s. f., cunhadio m. relationship of brothers-in-law and sisters-in-law.

cunhado s. m. 1. brother-in-law. 2. (N. Braz.) manner of addressing between halfbreeds, meaning "fellow", "friend", "Mister", etc. ǁ adj. 1. coined: a) minted, stamped, embossed. b) invented. 2. enhanced, exalted.

cunhador s. m. coiner, minter, coin stamper.

cunhagem s. f. (pl. -ens) coinage, mintage, stamping.

cunhal s. m. (pl. -ais) external angle formed by two walls; corner.

cunhantã, cunhatã, cunhantaim s. f. (N. Braz.) 1. girl (Tupi-Guarani). 2. babe, infant.

cunhar v. 1. to coin: a) mint, stamp, emboss. b) invent. 2. (fig.) to enhance, exalt.

~ uma palavra to coin a word.

cunharapixaba adj. (N. Braz.) 1. fond of women. 2. effeminate, whomanish, sissy.

cunhete s. m. wooden ammunition-box.

cunho s. m. 1. coiner's die, matrix; stamp. 2. stamped mark, stamp, seal. 3. side of a coin bearing arms.

4. mark, character, characteristic. 5. (Port. prov.) large rock in a river.

cunicultor s. m. rabbit breeder.

cunicultura s. f. rabbit breeding.

cuntatório, cunctatório adj. cunctatory: dilatory, sluggish, temporising.

cupaí s. m. (Braz., bot.) pitch apple (Clusia rosea).

cupão s. m. = cupom.

cupê s. m. 1. four-wheeled closed carriage with two seats. 2. also such an automobile.

cupé s. m. (N. Braz.) depreciative surname given to the Portuguese in colonial times.

cupidez s. f. 1. cupidity, concupiscence, greed, avidity. 2. ambition.

cupidíneo adj. relating to Cupid or love.

cupidinoso adj. cupidinous, desirous, amorous.

cupido s. m. 1. Cupid: personification of love. 2. love. 3. ridiculous, conceited beau, coxcomb. 4. (N. Braz., also capivara) capybara.

cúpido adj. 1. covetous, avid, greedy. 2. overambitious.

cupim s. m. (Braz.) 1. termite: white ant. 2. termitary. 3. (N. Braz.) the hair of Negroes. 4. occiput, hind head, nape. 5. hump of steers and zebus.

cupincha s. m. + f. buddy, pal.

cupineira s. f. (Braz.) a bee living in abandoned termitaries.

cupinudo adj. (S. Braz.) 1. big-humped (steer). 2. (fig.) bull-necked: big and headstrong, bullish. 3. braggart, swaggering.

cupinzama s. f. (S. Braz.) 1. agglomeration of termites. 2. great quantity of termitaries.

cupinzeiro s. m. (Braz., also cupineiro) 1. termitary. 2. decaying tree inhabited by termites.

cupira s. f. (Braz.) 1. = boca-de-barro. 2. several species of bees that inhabit termitaries.

cupom s. m. (pl. -ns) (also cupão) coupon: 1. dividend-warrant. 2. voting-paper for a public competition or part of an advertisement (which is to be used as an order form or the like) to be cut from newspapers, magazines, etc.

cupressiforme adj. m. + f. resembling a cypress.

cúprico adj. (chem.) cupric: of copper, containing copper (bivalent copper compound).

cuprífero adj. cupriferous: copper-bearing.

cúprino adj. cupric, cuprous: relating to copper.

cupripene adj. m. + f. (zool.) having copper-coloured wings or elytrons.

cuprirrosto adj. (zool.) having a copper-coloured bill.

cuprita s. f. (min.) cuprite: red copper ore.

cuproso adj. (chem.) cuprous.

cupu s. m. (N. Braz.) 1. fruit resembling a cacao bean. 2. sweetmeat and refreshing beverage made of that fruit.

cupuaçu s. m. (Braz.) 1. a plant of the cacao tree family (Theobroma grandiflorum). 2. its fruit.

cúpula s. f. 1. (archit.): a) cupula, dome. b) vault. 2. anything shaped like a cupula (plate S 3). 3. (bot.) cupule. 4. [tech., also forno de ~) cupula (furnace).

cupulado adj. cupolate: having a cupula.

cupulíferas s. f. (pl. (bot.) Cupuliferae: catkin-bearing trees and shrubs (oaks, chestnuts, beeches, birches, etc.).

cupuliforme adj. m. + f. cupuliform: shaped like a cupula, cup-shaped.

cuque s. m. (Braz., also cuca) cake prepared with eggs, flour, butter and yeast.

cuqueiro adj. (Braz.) fond of luxury.

cura (I) s. f. 1. cure: a) healing, sanation, recovery. b) treatment of a disease, medication. c) restoration to health. d) spiritual charge, care of souls. e) curing by heat, drying. f) seasoning, hardening. 2.

amendment (of moral defects or manners). 3. bleaching. 4. (Braz.) seasoning, preparation.
ter ~ to be curable; to be remediable.
cura (II) s. m. (eccl.) 1. curate, rector, parish priest, parson. 2. curate's assistant.
~ **de almas** minister, priest.
curabi s. m. (N. Braz.) small poisoned arrow used by the savages.
curabilidade s. f. curability, curableness.
curaca s. m. (N. Braz., also **cacique**) cacique, Indian chief.
curaçau s. m. curaçao: liqueur prepared with the peel of bitter oranges.
curadá s. m. (N. Braz.) large tapioca cake with minced chestnuts as an ingredient.
curado adj. 1. cured: a) healed, restored, recovered. b) seasoned, hardened (cheese). c) sun-dried, dried by heat. 2. (Braz.) invulnerable, proof against snake poison, knife stabs and bullets by sorcery.
~ **no fumo** smoked.
curador s. m. 1. curator, guardian, tutor, trustee. 2. (Braz.) sorcerer or quack who pretends to heal snake bites or make that a person is avoided by snakes.
~ **de ausentes** official of the prosecuting counsel before the district judges of orphans and absent persons. ~ **de massas falidas** official of the prosecuting counsel before the district judges in civil and criminal cases. ~ **de menores** official of the prosecuting counsel before the district judges of minors and juvenile delinquents. ~ **de resíduos** official of the prosecuting counsel before the district judge of purveyance and residues.
curadoria, curatela s. f. curatory, curatorship, tutelage, guardianship, trusteeship.
curanchim s. m. (S. Braz.) 1. (also **uropígio**) the tail bone of a bird. 2. (fam.) the coccyx of man.
curandeirismo s. m. (Braz.) quackery, witch-doctory, charlatanism.
curandeiro s. m. quack, quackster, quacksalver, witch--doctor, charlatan.
curandice s. f. quackery: quack medical treatment.
curar v. 1. to cure: a) heal, remedy. b) treat, medicate, dress. c) restore to health. d) recover (from disease). e) practise medicine. f) preserve by drying (meat, fruits). g) season, harden (cheese, wood). h) (Braz.) prepare, improve (by smoking, salting etc.) 2. to amend (a person of his faults). 3. to bleach. 4. ~-**se**: a) to medicate o. s., to recover, restore one's health. b) to mend one's ways.
~ **carne no fumeiro** to smoke meat. ~ **de** to deal with, treat. ~ **um enfermo** to cure a sick man. ~ **uma ferida** to dress a wound.
curare s. m. (Braz.: also **ervadura, ervagem, ticuna, uirari, voorara**) curare, curara: arrow poison used by S. American Indians.
curarização s. f. (Braz.) curarization: act or effect of poisoning with curare.
curarizante adj. m. + f. (Braz.) that curarizes.
curarizar v. (Braz.) to poison with curare.
curatá s. f. (bot.) a sea-grape (Coccoloba cordifolia).
curatela s. f. (also **curadoria**) curatel.
curatelado s. m. (Braz.) ward: person under curatory, wardship, guardianship, tutelage.
curativo s. m. 1. curative, remedy. 2. treatment, medication. 3. dressing, plaster. ‖ adj. curative, curatory.
receber ~ **de** to be treated of. ~ **dum ferimento** dressing, bandaging of a wound.
curato s. m. 1. curacy, rectorate: office of a curate or rector. 2. curatage, rectory: residence of a curate or rector. 3. parish, rectory, parsonage.

curau s. m. (Braz.) 1. a parrot (Amazonia aestiva). 2. countryman, rustic. 3. (N. Braz.) migrant from the drought-stricken arid regions of the Northeast. 4. (N. Braz.) dish made of salted meat brayed together with manioc flour. 5. (also **coral**) pap made of green maize and milk. ‖ adj. foolish; green, inexperienced.
curauá s. m. (N. Braz.) 1. white hair of horses. 2. plant of the pineapple family with spineless leaves yielding textile fibres.
curável adj. m. + f. (pl. **-áveis**) curable, remediable, amendable.
curcúligo s. m. ornamental plant of the family Amaryllidacea (Curculigo orchioides).
curculionídeo s. m. curculionid, curcullio: a snout beetle or weevil. ‖ adj. curculionid: 1. relating to the Curculionidae, the family of snout beetles or weevils. 2. relating to or resembling weevils.
curcurana s. f. (N. Braz.) marsh, swamp.
curdo s. m. Kurd: native or inhabitant of Kurdistan. ‖ adj. Kurdish: of Kurdistan.
curema s. m. (N. Braz.) 1. (also **valentão**) rowdy. 2. big shot, bigwig.
curera s. f. (N. Braz.) squeezed out manioc pulp, improper for making flour.
cureta (ê) s. f. (surg.) curette: scraping instrument.
curetagem s. f. (pl. **-ens**) (surg.) curettage, curettement: scraping by means of a curette.
curetar v. (surg.) to curette: scrape with a curette.
cúria s. f. 1. curia: a) Curia (Romana): the Papal Court. b) ancient subdivision of Roman tribes. c) ancient Roman Senate. d) ancient Roman senate house. 2. episcopal tribunal.
curial s. m. + f. (pl. **-ais**) curial: 1. official of the Papal Court. 2. member of an ancient Roman curia. ‖ adj. 1. curial: pertaining to a curia. 2. (fig.) proper, convenient.
curiangada s. f. (S. Braz.) a flock of goatsuckers.
curiango, curiangu s. m. (Braz., ornith.) goatsucker (family Caprimulgidae).
curiantã s. m. (Braz. ornith. also **guriatã**) tanagra.
curião s. m. (pl. **-ões**) chief of a Roman curia.
curiboca s. m. (N. Braz., also **cariboca**) Amerindian half-breed.
curica s. f. (N. Braz.) small paper kite without a frame.
curiaca, curucaca s. f. (Braz., ornith.) two ibises (Theristicus caudatus and Plegadis guarauna).
curieterapia s. f. (med.) curietherapy: radiumtherapy.
curimã s. m. (Braz., ichth.) striped mullet.
curimatá, curimataú s. m. (also **catinga**) North Brazilian cattle region.
curimbatá s. m. (Braz.) common designation of freshwater fishes of the family Characidae, genus Prochilodus.
curimbó s. m. (Braz., also **tabaque**) 1. tree of the Amazon region. 2. drum used by Negroes and Indians, made of a hollow tree trunk, open at one end beaten with the hands.
curinga s. m. (Braz., also **dunga**) (cards) joker; wild card.
curingão s. m. big joker (the wild card at the canasta game).
curió s. m. (Braz., also **avinhado, bico-de-furo**) a rice finch (Oryzoborus angolensis).
curiosidade s. f. curiosity: 1. inquisitiveness, eagerness for seeing, knowing, detecting; indiscretion. 2. rarity, oddity, object of interest. 3. fancy for rare or original things.
aguardar com ~ to be anxiously awaiting a thing. **estar com** ~ **de** to be curious to know.
curioso s. m. 1. curious, inquisitive individual. 2. looker-on, bystander. 3. (Braz.) jack-of-all-trades,

dilettante. 4. practician; professional without a diploma. 5. quack, empiric. ‖ adj. curious: 1. inquisitive, attentive, studious. 2. prying, indiscreet. 3. odd, strange, singular, queer. 4. interesting. 5. diligent. ‖ -amente adv. curiously.
estar ~ por to be anxious to know if.
curista s. m. + f. (Braz.) visitor of a health-resort or a spa.
curitibano s. m. (Braz.) Curitiban: native or inhabitant of Curitiba, capital of Paraná. ‖ adj. Curitiban: of Curitiba.
curiúva s. f. Brazilian pine-tree (Araucaria brasiliana).
curral s. m. (pl. -ais) 1. corral, stable, farmyard, pen, sheepfold. 2. (also cocuri) a fish-trap.
curralada s. f. (S. Braz.) a series of corrals.
curralagem s. f. (pl. -ens) stallage: rent formerly paid for stabling cattle in a municipal corral.
curraleira s. f. (Braz.) 1. euphorbiaceous shrub of the genus Croton (C. antisyphilliticus). 2. a country dance. 3. a bovine race.
curraleiro adj. 1. corralled, stabled. 2. said of a certain bovine race.
gado ~ cattle kept in a corral or stable.
currículo s. m. 1. curriculum, course. 2. (Braz.) part of a literary course. 3. path, run.
curriqueiro s. m. (Braz.) an ovenbird (Geositta cunicularia cunicalaria).
curro s. m. 1. bull corral appertaining to a bull ring. 2. (Braz., form.) slave quarters. 3. (Port. prov.) stallion.
currupira s. m. (Braz.) = curupira.
cursar v. 1. to course: a) follow a course of studies: attend, frequent a university. b) run through or over, cross. 2. to travel, cruise, navegate, voyage. 3. (med.) to evacuate, defecate. 4. to range, carry, reach.
cursilhista s. m. + f. the participant of a cursilho.
cursilho s. m. a spiritual retreat movement for religious orientation.
cursinho s. m. a preparatory course for the university admission test.
cursista s. m. + f. frequenter of a course, student.
cursivo s. m. cursine: 1. cursive character or script. 2. (typogr.) italics; italic type. ‖ adj. 1. italic: relating to italic type. 2. running, flowing, fluent (writing).
curso s. m. 1. course: a) run, running, career, race. b) motion. c) direction. d) progress, sequence. e) course of studies, term; the subject matter of one term. f) circulation, currency, vogue. 2. (tech.) stroke, travel, throw, lift: extent of motion. 3. (astr.) revolution, orbit. 4. route, path, way, track. 5. (med.) alvine evacuation, stool. 6. (Braz.): a) a bovine disease. b) (also piracema) shoal of fishes; spawning time.
o ~ dos astros the revolution of the stars. ~ do corpo evacuation; stool. ~ de êmbolo piston stroke. ~ de filosofia the study of philosophy. ~ de válvula lift of valve. ~ primário primary grade, elementary school. ~ secundário secondary grades. ~ superior university study, college study. ~ vestibular pre-university course, pre-college course. dar livre ~ a alguma coisa to let a thing take its natural course. em ~ 1. in operation, in progress. 2. in circulation. 3. running, current, present. fazer o ~ de medicina to study medicine. o ano em ~ the present year. ter ~ 1. to be in circulation. 2. to be quoted. 3. (fig.) to be in use, current. ter um ~ to have studied.
cursor s. m. 1. slave footman, who followed his master's carriage. 2. a papal messenger. 3. (tech.) cursor, slider, slide (plate R 3). ‖ adj. sliding or running along s. th.

~ de balança sliding weight or poise.
curta s. f. shortness, lightness, only used in: à ~ in short-clothes: lightly, cooly dressed.
andar à ~ to wear short clothes.
curtamão s. m. (pl. curtamãos) (Braz.) large square of a mason.
curta-metragem s. f. (pl. curtas-metragens) (cin.) a short motion picture.
curtarém s. m. (India) headdress of female dancers.
curteza s. f. 1. shortness; scantiness, scarcity. 2. timidity, timidness, shyness. 3. ignorancy, deficiency of intellect: thick-headedness.
~ dos meios shortness of means.
curtição s. f. 1. tanning, tannage. 2. (Braz., sl.) ecstasy from drugs. 3. (Braz., sl.) the act of finding pleasure and joy in; the act of delighting in.
vamos à ~ na praia let us delight in the beach.
curtido adj. 1. tanned. 2. hardened, inured, tough.
curtidor s. m. tanner. ‖ adj. of or referring to tanning.
curtimenta s. f. 1. fermentation of must together with the husks. 2. tanning of hides.
curtimento s. m. (also curtidura) 1. tanning, tannage. 2. hardening, inuring. 3. steeping of flax. 4. pickling.
curtir v. 1. to tan hides. 2. to steep flax or hemp. 3. to pickle olives. 4. to harden, inure, toughen. 5. to suffer, sustain, endure, undergo. 6. (Braz., sl.) to enjoy, take pleasure or delight in.
~ um agradável bate-papo to take pleasure in an agreeable chat.
curto adj. 1. short, brief (plate Q). 2. scant, scarce. 3. (fig.) obtuse, dull, thickheaded. 4. timid, shy. ~ de entendimento slow-witted, obtuse, thickheaded. ~ de meios short of means. ~ de palavras brief in words, sparing of words, laconic. ~ de vista short-sighted. ser ~ de espírito, ter o espírito ~ to be narrow-minded.
curto-circuito s. m. (pl. curtos-circuitos) (electr.) short circuit.
curtume s. m. 1. tanning, tannage: act or process of tanning. 2. tannery: tanning establishment. 3. substance used for tanning, tanning extract.
curuá s. m. (Braz.) several palm trees of the genus Attalea.
curuatá s. m. (N. Braz.) perianth of certain palm trees.
curuatá-açu s. m. (pl. curuatás-açus) (N. Braz., bot.) agave.
curuba s. f. (Braz.) 1. itch, mange. 2. itch-mite.
curubento s. m. itchy person; mangy animal. ‖ adj. itchy, mangy.
curubixá, grumixá s. m. (Braz.) larvae of some insects, living in cocoons on the bottom of water.
curuca s. f. (Braz.) agitation of fishes which come to the surface at the spawning time.
curuiri s. m. (Braz., also pitombeira-da-baía) tree of the family Myrtaceae (Eugenia luschnathiana).
curul s. f. (Roman, hist.) curule chair. ‖ adj. curule: relating to certain Roman magistrates.
curumatá, curumatã s. f. curumatão m. (Braz.) several species of fishes of the Amazon and São Francisco rivers.
curumba s. m. (N. Braz.) 1. (depr.) ragged hiker or rider travelling on the roads. 2. migrant worker from the back country. 3. back country man, rustic. 4. f. old woman.
curumbatá s. m. (Braz., also curimbatá, curimatá) freshwater fish of the genus Prochilodus.
curumi, curumim s. m. (N. Braz., var. corumim, colomi, colomim) 1. boy, urchin, youth, youngster. stripling. 2. servant. 3. fishing rod.
curuminzada s. f. (N. Braz.) bunch of boys.

curungo (Braz.) adj. (also **coroca**) decrepit, doting.

curuperê s. m. (N. Braz.) intermittent brook or affluent of a main river-branch.

curupiá s. f. (Braz.) a hackberry (Celtis glycicarpa).

curupira, currupira s. m. (Braz.) folkloric sylvan phantom with backwards pointing feet.

curupitã s. m. (Braz.) tree of the family Euphorbiaceae (Sapium curupita).

curupuruí s. m. (Braz., ornith.) a wren (Troglodytes musculus).

curuquerê s. m. (Braz.) cotton worm.

cururu s. m. (Braz.) 1. a terrestrial toad. 2. a gopherlike rodent (Ctenomys brasiliensis). 3. round dance with a singing competition.

cururuá s. m. (Braz.) a myomorph rodent (Loncheres nigrispinea).

curutié s. m. (Braz., ornith., also **canário-do-brejo, corruíra-do-brejo, turucué** and **tururié**) a tree creeper (Synallaxis ruficapilla).

curva s. f. 1. curve: a) (geom.) a curved line. b) bend, turn, crook, bow. c) arch, arc. d) (math.) graph of co-ordinates. 2. ~s pl. ribs of a ship. ~ **acentuada** sharp curve, quick curve. ~ **da perna** bend, hollow of the knee, ham. ~ **de estrada** bend of the road. ~ **de nível** (math.) contour curve. ~ **de probabilidade** (stat.) probability curve. ~ **em U** (mot.) U-turn. ~ **fechada** hairpin bend, sharp curve (plate E 14). ~ **plana** plane curve. ~s **anaclásticas** (geol.) anaclastic curves. ~s **exponenciais** (math.) exponential curves.

curvaça s. f. (vet.) jarde, jardon.

curvado adj. 1. curved, arched, bent, crooked. 2. bowed down, bent, stooping (with age). 3. resigned, downcast, subdued.

curvador s. m. (typogr.) a device used for bending the lead into curved forms.

curval adj. m. + f. (pl. -ais) relating to the bend of the knee.

curvar v. 1. to curve, incurvate, bend, arch, crook, inflect, bow, stoop, bend over. 2. to warp, sag. 3. (fig.) to humble, oppress, subdue. 4. ~-se: a) to bend, form a curve. b) to bow, incline, curtsy, prostrate. c) to resign, submit, humiliate, abase o. s. d) to decline, decay, fail. ~ **o arco** to bend, draw the (long) bow. ~ **a cabeça** to hang one's head. ~ **os joelhos** to bend the knees. ~-**se aos pés de alguém** to prostrate before s. o. **ele curvou-se ao peso dos anos** he curved under the weight of years.

curvatura s. f. curvature, bend, incurvation, sag, flection (plate V 5).

curvejão s. m. (pl. -ões) (vet., also **curvilhão**) hock, hough.

curveta s. f. 1. small curve. 2. bend of a road. 3. curvet (of a horse).

curvetear v. to curvet: 1. make a curvet: bound. 2. cause to curvet.

curvicórneo adj. (zool.) having curved horns.

curvifloro adj. (bot.) having curved corollas.

curvígrafo s. m. curvograph, arcograph: instrument for drawing arcs.

curvilhão s. m. = **curvejão.**

curvilíneo adj. 1. curvineal, curvilinear: a) consisting of curves. b) following a curved line. 2. curviform, curvous.

curvípede adj. m. + f. crooked-legged.

curvirrostro adj. (zool.) curvirostral, crook-billed.

curvo adj. curved, bent, crooked, arched (plate Q).

cuscada s. f. (S. Braz.) 1. pack of small curs (dogs). 2. small curs, collectivelly. 3. (fig.) fry; mob, rabble.

cusco s. m. (S. Braz.) 1. small cur (mongrel dog). 2. small person of no consequence.

cuscuz s. m., sg. + pl. (Braz.) couscous: dish of North African origin, made of steamed rice or maize flour.

cuscuzeira s. f. (Braz.) couscous kettle.

cuscuzeiro s. m. (Braz.) 1. round peak rising from a plateau. 2. couscous-mould of sheet-metal or clay.

cuscuz-paulista s. m. (pl. **cuscuz-paulistas**) (Braz.) couscous made of maize flour and fish.

cuspada, cusparada s. f. (Braz.) 1. profuse spitting. 2. = **cuspidela, cuspidura.**

cuspe s. m. pop. var. of **cuspo.**

cuspidal s. m. (pl. -ais) (stat., also **moda**) mode.

cuspidado adj. cuspidate, cuspidated: terminating in a cusp or point.

cúspide s. f. 1. cuspis, cusp, point, peak, sharp end. 2. Neptune's trident. 3. a bee's or scorpion's sting. 4. (bot.) sharp, long terminal point of some leaves.

cuspideira s. f. cuspidor, spittoon.

cuspidiforme adj. m. + f. cuspate, cuspidal: cusp--shaped, pointed, peaked.

cuspidor s. m. 1. spitter. 2. cuspidor, spittoon. ‖ adj. spitting.

cuspidura s. f. (also **cuspidela**) 1. spitting. 2. great quantity of spittle.

cuspinhada s. f. large quantity of spittle.

cuspinhador s. m. person who spits or salivates continually. ‖ adj. spitting frequently, salivating.

cuspinhar v. (also **cuspilhar**) to spit often, to salivate.

cuspir v. 1. to spit, spit out, expectorate. 2. to eject, reject, cast off, toss. 3. to fling insults at; affront, defame, slander. 4. to hurl into the face. ~ **calúnias** to calumniate. ~ **uma injúria à face de alguém** to hurl an insult at someone's face. ~ **sangue** to spit blood. **o cavalo cuspiu-o ao chão** the horse threw him off.

cuspo s. m. (var. **cuspe**) spit, spittle, saliva.

custa s. f. 1. cost, expense, expenditure, outlay, charge, price paid. 2. pain, toil, labour. 3. ~s pl. (jur.) costs of a lawsuit, law costs. **a quanto montam as** ~s what do the costs amount to? **viver à** ~ **de outrem** to live at another's cost.

custar v. 1. to cost: a) be obtainable at the price of, at the cost of or by dint of. b) cause the expenditure of, be worth. 2. to be difficult or painful. 3. (Braz.) to have difficulty, be slow, be long. ~ **caro** to be dear. ~ **a crer** to be difficult or hard to believe. ~ **os olhos da cara** to cost a fortune. **custa-me dizer-lhe isso** it pains me to (have to) tell him that. **custe o que custar** cost what it may! whatever it may cost! **custou-lhe caro a brincadeira** he had to pay dearly for the joke. **custa-lhe compreender** he is slow to understand. **custa à gente acreditar isso** one is reluctant to believe that. **não custa (nada) experimentar** it's worth while to try. **quanto lhe custou o seu chapéu?** how much did your hat cost? what did you pay for your hat? **sua imprudência custou-lhes a vida** their imprudence cost them their lives.

custeamento, custeio s. m. 1. defrayal. 2. expenditure, expense, outlay, disbursement, costs. 3. estimate of costs.

custear v. 1. to defray, bear the expense. 2. to finance, provide capital for. 3. to estimate the costs of. ~ **uma expedição** to defray the expenses of an expedition.

custo s. m. 1. cost, expense, price. 2. worth. 3. (fig.) difficulty, trouble, pain. 4. (Braz.) delay, slowness, retardment. **o** ~ **da vida** the cost of living. ~, **seguro e frete** cost, insurance and freight (abbr. C.I.F.). ~s **de produção** production costs. **a** ~ with difficulty. **a** ~ **de** by means of, by dint of. **a muito** ~ with great difficulty, hardly, barely. **a todo o** ~ at all cost, by all means. **preço de** ~ cost price; prime cost. ~ **fixo** fixed cost. ~ **variável** variable cost.

custódia s. f. custody: 1. custodia, keeping, safekeeping, charge, guardianship, protection. 2. ward, prison, place of custody. 3. detention, imprisionment. 4. (R. C. Church) custodial, monstrance. ~ **protetora** protective custody.

custodiar v. 1. to keep in custody. 2. to safekeep, guard, protect.

custódio s. m. custodian, guardian. ‖ adj. custodial: that guards, protects.

custoso adj. 1. expensive, costly. 2. difficult, painful, troublesome. 3. (Braz.) slow, lingering.

cutâneo adj. cutaneous: of or relating to the skin.

cutela s. f. 1. a butcher's cleaver, chopper. 2. pruning-knife.

cutelaria s. f. cutlery: 1. art or shop of a cutler. 2. a cutler's ware.

cuteleiro s. m. cutler.

cutelo s. m. 1. chopping knife, mincing knife (plate C 20). 2. pruning-knife. 3. hunting knife, hanger, cutlass. 4. (poet.) sword. 5. ~**s** pl. studding sails, stay sails.

cúter s. m. (pl. **cúteres**) (naut.) cutter (plate B 8).

cutia s. f. 1. (Braz., also **aguti**) (zool.) agouti: a rodent of the family Caviidae (Dasyprocta aguti). 2. tree of the family Rutaceae (Policarpus, sp.).

cutícola adj. living on the skin.

cutícula s. f. 1. (bot.) cuticle. 2. scarf-skin epidermis. 3. pellicle.

cuticular adj. m. + f. cuticular, epidermal.

cutículo s. m. (zool.) cuticle: scarf-skin, pellicle, membrane.

cuticuloso adj. like a cuticle or small membrane.

cutidura s. f. (zool.) cutidure, coronary cushion.

cutilada s. f. stroke with a cutlass, sabre; sword, cut, stab with a knife.

cutilão s. m. (pl. **-ões**) (augm. of **cutelo**) large chopping knife.

cutilar v. (Braz.) to wound with a cutlass or the like.

cutiliquê s. m. (var. **quotiliquê**) nonentity: person or matter without importance. **de** ~ of little importance, of no consequence. **razões de** ~ futile reasons. **questões de** ~ trifling questions.

cutipaca s. m. (Braz., also **cavaleiro**) a prawn.

cutipuruí s. m. (Braz.) = **corruíra**.

cutirreação s. f. (med., vet.) cutireaction.

cútis s. f. sg. + pl. 1. (anat.) cutis, derma, corium. 2. skin. 3. complexion: hue of the skin.

cutisação s. f. (med.) cutization.

cutiú-preto s. m. (pl. **cutiús-pretos**) (also **gavião pega-macaco**) a hawk-eagle.

cutuba adj. m. + f. (N. Braz.) 1. important. 2. strong. 3. courageous, valiant. 4. learned. 5. very intelligent, clever. 6. good. 7. beautiful.

cutuca s. f. (Braz.) small saddle with two high saddle-bows for breaking in horses.

cutucação, cutucada s. f. (Braz., pop., var. **catucação, catucada**) a jogging, nudging, poking (as to arouse attention).

cutucão s. m. (pl. **-ões**) (Braz., pop.) 1. jab, vigorous nudge to arouse attention. 2. sword-cut, stab with a knife.

cutucar v. (Braz., var. **catucar**) to jog, nudge, poke (as to arouse attention).

cutucurim s. m. (also **gavião-real**) the South American harpy eagle.

cuvilheira s. f. (also **coscuvilheira**) gossiping, talebearing, intriguing hussy. ‖ adj. gossiping, talebearing, intriguing.

cuvu s. m. (Braz., also **juquiá**) a kind of bow net for fishing in shallow or muddy places.

cuxá s. m. (Blaz.) sauce made of vinegar, ginger and other seasonings.

cuxiú s. m. (Braz.) several species of apes of the genus Chiroptes.

czar s. m. (f. **czarina**) czar, tsar: title of the former emperors of Russia.

czarda s. f. (also **xarda**) czardas: a Hungarian dance.

czaréviche s. m. 1. czarevitch, tsarevitch: son of a czar. 2. cesarevitch, tsesarevitch: formerly, title of the eldest son of a czar, the heir to the Russian throne.

czarevna s. f. czarevna, tsarevna: 1. daughter of a czar. 2. wife of a czarevitch. 3. title of a heiress to the Russian throne.

czarina s. f. czarina, tsarina: title of an empress of Russia.

czarismo s. m. czarism, tsarism: autocratic political system prevailing in Russia under the czar.

czarista s. m. + f. czarist, tsarist: adherent of czarism. ‖ adj. czaristic, tsaristic.

D

D, d s. m. 1. the fourth letter of the Portuguese alphabet. 2. abbr. of: a) **Digno** estimable, worthy, noble. b) **Dom** (honorific title). c) **Dona** miss, mistress. 3. (com.) **deve** debit.

da contr. of the prep. **de** with the feminine article **a** of, from.

eu o vi ~ janela I saw him from the window.

dábliu s. m. name of the letter W.

dacolá (Port.) contr. of the prep. **de** and the adv. **acolá** from there, from yonder.

dácron s. m. (trademark) 1. dacron, a synthetic fiber; 2. a fabric made of Dacron fiber.

dactílico, datílico adj. dactylic.

dactilino, datilino adj. digitiform, digitate, digitated, dactyloid: finger-shaped.

dáctilo, dátilo s. m. dactyl: metrical foot. ‖ adj. dactylic.

dactilografado, datilografado adj. typewritten, typed.

dactilografar, datilografar v. to typewrite.

dactilografia, datilografia s. f. typewriting.

dactilógrafo, datilógrafo s. m. typist.

dactilologia s. f. dactylology, dactylography.

dactilomancia s. f. dactyliomancy.

dactiloscopia, datiloscopia s. f. dactyloscopy, classification of fingerprints.

dactiloscópico, datiloscópico adj. dactyloscopic.

dactiloscrito, datiloscrito s. m. typewritten sheet.

dada s. f. give, giving, bestowing.

~ de cartas card dealing.

dadeira s. f. 1. a woman subject to attacks. 2. whore. ‖ adj. (Braz.) of or relating to a woman subject to attacks.

dádiva s. f. gift, present, donation.

dadivar v. to gift, present, bestow.

dadivoso adj. liberal, bountiful, generous.

dado (I) s. m. 1. die: a) small cube for gaming. b) (mech.) link block. c) (archit.) dado: pedestal of a column. 2. datum, figure. 3. basis, fundamental principle. 4. (Braz.) beam of stone. 5. nature, character (of things only). ‖ adj. 1. allowed, permitted, licit. 2. given, gratis, free. 3. addicted to, inclined to, fond of. 4. affable, communicative, amiable, good-natured. 5. dated.

dado (II) conj. in view of, considering that.

dadas as peculiaridades in view of the peculiarities. **~ que** provided that, though.

dador s. m. giver, donor, donator.

dafnifiláceas s. f. pl. (bot.) Daphniphyllaceae.

daguerreotipar v. to daguerreotype.

daguerreotipia s. f. daguerreotype, daguerreotypy.

daguerreótipo s. m. daguerreotype.

daí contr. of the prep. **de** with the adv. **aí.** 1. thence, from there. 2. (fig.) for that reason, that for, therefore.

~ em diante thenceforth, thenceforward, thereafter. **e ~?** and what then? what of this? (of that? of it?)

daiquiri s. m. daiquiri, a cocktail made of rum, lime or lemon juice and sugar.

dala (I) s. f. spout, dale (plate B 14).

dala (II) s. f. path between mountains.

dalcerídios s. m. pl. (zool.) family of insects, order of the Lepidoptera.

dali contr. of the prep. **de** and the adv. **ali.** 1. thence, therefrom, from there. 2. (fig.) therefore, for this. **os visitantes chegaram daqui e ~** the visitors came from here and there.

dália s. f. (bot.) dahlia.

dálmata, dalmatense s. m. + f. Dalmatian; native or inhabitant of Dalmatia. ‖ adj. Dalmatian.

dalmática s. f. (eccl.) dalmatic (plate P 5).

dálton s. m. (chem.) name sometimes used for the atomic mass unit.

daltônico s. m. daltonian, daltonist. ‖ adj. daltonic.

daltonismo s. m. daltonism, colour-blindness.

dama s. f. 1. lady, maid. 2. actress. 3. female partner (at a ball). 4. queen (at chess and cards). 5. king (at draughts). 6. **~s** pl. draughts, (E. U. A.) checkers.

~ de companhia lady in waiting. **~ de copas** (cards) queen of hearts (plate B 5). **a primeira ~ do país** the first lady of the country. **fazer ~** to make a king at checkers or a queen at chess.

dama-do-lago s. f. (pl. **damas-do-lago**) (Braz., bot.) water hyacinth.

dama-entre-verdes s. f. (pl. **damas-entre-verdes**) fennelflower, love-in-a-mist.

damaísmo s. m. 1. a group of ladies. 2. ladies collectively. 3. lady's manners.

damas s. f. pl. checkers.

damasceno s. m. Damascene: a native of Damascus. ‖ adj. Damascene.

damasco s. m. 1. (bot.) damson, damson plum. 2. damask.

damasqueiro s. m. damson (tree).

damasquilho, damasquim s. m. any damasklike fabric.

damasquinagem s. f. (pl. **-ens**) damascening.

damasquinar v. to damascene, ornament metal with wavy patterns.

damasquino adj. damascene: 1. relating to damascening. 2. Damascene: of or relating to Damascus.

damejar v. to please, court, make love to, woo.

damice s. f. prudery, affection.

danação s. f. (pl. **-ões**) 1. damagement, impairment. 2. rage, anger, fury. 3. hydrophobia, rabies.

danado adj. 1. damned, condemned. 2. damaged, impaired. 3. ruined, decayed. 4. furious, angry. 5. (Braz.) smart, keen, clever. 6. valiant, courageous. 7. bad, wicked. 8. torturing, distressing. 9. impious, ungodly. 10. hydrophobic, rabid, mad.

danaida, danaide s. f. (mach.) danaide.

danaídeos s. m. pl. (ent.) Danaidae.

danar v. 1. to harm, hurt, injure, damage. 2. to irritate, provoke, annoy, make angry. 3. to prejudice, ruin. 4. to infect with rabies. 5. **~-se:** a) to become angry, exasperate o. s. b) to become rabid.

dança s. f. 1. dance. 2. dancing, ball. 3. (fig.) work, attributions, business.

~ de roda round dance. **~ de São Guido ou de São Vito** St. Vitus's dance, chorea. **~ folclórica** folk dance. **~ rodada** skirt dance. **ele se meteu na ~** (fig.) he was involved into the business. **entrar na ~** to join the dance. **estar na ~** to be in the dance. **iniciar a ~** to lead the dance.

dançadeira s. f. dancer, dancing-girl, ballerina.

dançador s. m. dancer. ‖ adj. dancing.

dançante adj. m. + f. dancing.

chá ~ an afternoon dancing party at which tea is served, afternoons's dancing party.

dançar v. 1. to dance. 2. (coll.) to shake a leg. 3. to bob, turn around.

~ conforme a música to adapt o. s. to a situation. **~ conforme tocam** to dance to the tune of.

dançarina s. f. dancer, dancing-girl, ballerina.

dançarino s. m. dancer, ballet dancer.

dandá s. m. (Braz., bot.) 1. chufa. 2. nutgrass, coco grass.

dandão s. m. (pl. -ões) (Braz.) nightmare.

dândi s. m. dandy, fop, coxcomb.

dandismo s. m. dandyism.

danificação s. f. (pl. -ões) damnification, impairing, damaging.

danificador s. m. injurer. ‖ adj. damaging, injuring, imparing.

danificar v. to damage, harm, injure, hurt, impair.

danífico, daninho adj. damaging, detrimental, prejudicial, harmful.

ervas daninhas weeds.

dano s. m. 1. damage, harm, injury. 2. prejudice. 3. loss. 4. disadvantage.

o temporal causou muito ~ the storm caused much harm.

danoso adj. damaging, prejudicial, hurtful, noxious.

danou-se (interj.) (Braz.) expression denoting surprise, fright, admiration or enthusiasm.

dantes adv. formerly, heretofore, hitherto.

dantesco adj. 1. awful, horrible. 2. Dantean, Dantesque.

danubiano, danubino adj. Danubian.

daquele contr. of the prep. **de** and the dem. pron. **aquele** from that, of that.

ela não é -as mulheres que she is not that kind of women who.

daqueles (fem. **daquelas**) (fam.) adj. sg. + pl. uncommon, unspeakable.

daquém contr. of the prep. **de** and the adv. **aquém** from there.

daqui contr. of the prep. **de** and the adv. **aqui** from here, within.

~ **a oito dias** within a week. ~ **a pouco** in a little while, shortly. ~ **a quatro semanas será Páscoa** Easter is four weeks off. ~ **a quinze dias** today fortnight. ~ **em diante** from now on, henceforth, henceforward.

daquilo contr. of the prep. **de** and the pron. dem. **aquilo** from that, of that.

dar v. 1. to give, offer, bestow, present. 2. to beat, thrash. 3. to administer. 4. to hand over, deliver. 5. to dedicate to, spend for. 6. to grant, concede. 7. to confer, bestow. 8. to allow, permit. 9. to attribute. 10. to produce, yield, bring forth. 11. to notice, inform, publish. 12. to amount to, result in. 13. to lead to. 14. to take to. 15. to come across, find. 16. to suffice, be enough or adequate. 17. to be sufficient. 18. ~-se: a) to happen, come to be, occur. b) to feel o. s. c) to agree, live in harmony.

~ **a César o que é de César** to give the devil his due. ~ **a mão à palmatória** to admit of being wrong. ~ **a saber** to make known, to state. ~ **as boas-vindas a** to welcome, extend a welcome to. ~ **às de Vila Diogo** to take to one's heels. ~ **baixa** (mil.) to quit the service, (U. S. A. dial.) take felt. ~ **cartas** to deal cards. ~ **cabo de** to kill. ~ **com** to meet, run across. ~ **com a língua nos dentes** to blab, tattle. ~ **de si.** 1. to yield: a) give way (a structure). b) comply, consent. 2. to result in, bring about. ~ **em alguém** to thrash s. o. ~ **em nada** to fail. ~ **margens a dúvidas** to admit of a doubt. ~ **murro em ponta de faca** to commit o. s. to a difficult and dangerous task. ~ **na vista** to strike the eye. ~ **o fora** to take to one's heels. ~ **pancadas** to lay blows. ~ **parte de doente** to feign illness. ~ **passagem** to step aside, make way for. ~ **se bem com** to get on well with, be on good terms with. ~-**se conta de** to awaken to, realize. ~-**se pressa** to make haste. ~-**se por vencido** to give in, yield. ~ **tento de** to see, notice.

~ **um passeio** to take a walk, take the air. ~ **uma pancada** to deal, fetch a blow. ~ **uma volta** to take a stroll. ~ **voltas** 1. to walk around. 2. to bestir o. s. to some purpose. **dê-lhe o dedo, tomará o braço** give him an inch, he'll take an ell. **dê-lhe os meus cumprimentos** give him my best respects, (fam.) give him my love. **dê o foral** go (get) along with you! **dei-lhe uma ensaboadela por causa de** I told him off for. **dei-lhe uma gorjeta** I gave (fam. tipped) him a gratuity. **dê-me um cigarro!** give me a cigarette. **demos uma festa** we threw a party. **deram parte à polícia** they informed the police. **deu-me na cabeça escrever** I took it into my head to write. **dou fé** I certify. **ele deu-me a entender** he gave me to understand. **ele dá a impressão de estar envergonhado** he has an air of being ashamed of himself. **ele sempre dá a impressão de sentir-se desassossegado** he always has an appearance of being ill at ease. **ela deu à luz uma filha** she gave birth to a daughter. **ele deu-me a mão** he gave me his hand. **ele deu sua palavra** he gave his word. **não darei o braço a torcer** I will not yield. **ele deu uma cambalhota** he cut a caper. **isto não dará certo** this won't work, that cock won't fight. **ela não sabe onde dar com a cabeça** she does not know which way to turn. **o navio deu contra o recife** the ship struck the reef. **foi dado de lambugem** it was thrown into the bargain. **ele deu estalos com a língua** he clicked his tongue. **a menina deu gritos** the girl cried out. **isto dá uma idéia** it conveys an idea. **eles não deram ouvidos à mulher** they did not give ear to the woman. **a janela dá para o mar** the window looks on the sea, the window faces the sea. **eles lhe deram os parabéns** they congratulated him. **o caminhão deu passagem ao carro** the truck gave room to the car. **não se** ~ **por achado** to feign ignorance. **o crime deu que falar** the crime was much talked about. **isto lhe dá muito trabalho** it costs him much trouble. **eles lhe deram uma lição** they taught him better. **ela lhe deu uma tábua** she gave him a denial (rebuff, the mitten). **ele foi dar um passeio** he went for a walk. **ele se dá bem com seus professores** he succeeds with his teachers. **isto dá** it's enough. **nós nos damos muito bem** we get along very well together. **pouco se lhe dava** little he recked. **quantos anos lhe dá?** how old do you take him? **o relógio deu cinco horas** the clock struck five. **será que dá?** will it suffice? **vamos** ~ **um fim nisso** let's put an end to it.

dardada s. f. throw of the javelin.

dardejamento s. m. throw of or transfixion with a javelin or dart.

dardejante adj. m. + f. darting.

dardejar v. (also **dardar**) 1. to throw the javelin or the dart. 2. to hurt or pierce (with a dart). 3. to shoot out or emit suddenly. 4. to twinkle, sparkle.

dardo s. m. 1. dart. 2. small spear. 3. (fig.) anything that pierces our wounds like a dart. 4. sting (of certain insects). 5. sarcasm, irony. 6. tongue of a snake.

dares s. m. pl. (as **dares e tomares**) quarrel, controversy, dispute.

darico s. m. daric: golden coin of ancient Persia.

darma s. m. (philos.) in Indian philosophies and religions: dharma.

daroês s. m. = **dervixe.**

darsonvalização s. f. therapeutic application of d'Arsonval currents.

dartrial s. m. (pl. -ais) (bot.) ringworm bush.

dartro s. m. (med.) dartre, tetter.

dartroso adj. dartrous.

darwiniano s. m. = **darwinista**. || adj. Darwinist, Darwinistic.

darwinismo s. m. Darwinism.

darwinista s. m. + f. Darwinist, Darwinite, Darwinian. || adj. Darwinist, Darwinistic.

das contr. of the prep. **de** and the art. pl. **as** from the, of the.

dasiatídeos s. m. pl. (zool.) Dasyatidae.

dasimetria s. f. dasymetry.

dasímetro s. m. (phys.) dasymeter.

dasipodídeo s. m. any animal of the family Dasypodidae. || adj. dasypodoid.

dasiproctídeos s. m. pl. (zool.) Dasyproctidae.

data s. f. 1. date. 2. dose, small amount. 3. large quantity. 4. (Braz.) mine of gold or precious stones. 5. (Braz.) piece of land (about 22 × 44 m).
de longa ~ of old, from former times. ~ **de vencimento**, due date, maturity date.

datar v. 1. to date. 2. to star, reckon from, count from. 3. to persist, exist, last.
a carta está datada do dia 12 the letter is dated from the 12th. **a casa data do século 13** the house goes back to the 13th century (dates from the...).

dataria s. f. (eccl.) dataria, datary.

datil s. m. (pl. **-is**) date: fruit of the date palm.

datileira s. f. (bot.) date palm.

dativo s. m. (gram.) dative (case). || adj. appointed by a magistrate and not by a law.

datolita s. f. datolite.

D.D.T. s. m. (chem.) DDT.

de prep. 1. of. 2. from (plate P 18). 3. by. 4. to. 5. with. 6. on. 7. in.
~ **boa fé** in good faith. ~ **boa mente** willingly. ~ **cima** from above. ~ **dia a dia** from day to day. ~ **mau humor** in bad humour. ~ **onde é você?** where are you from? ~ **preto** in black. ~ **segunda a sexta-feira inclusive** Monday through Friday. ~ **trás da árvore** from behind the tree. ~ **uniforme**, ~ **farda** in uniform. **a fim** ~ **que** in order that. **cego** ~ **um olho** blind on one eye. **deixar** ~ **castigo** (school) to keep in. **do lado** ~ **lá da cerca** on the thither side of the fence. **dormir** ~ **cansaço** to fall asleep through exhaustion. **seis pés** ~ **comprimento** six feet in length.

deado s. m. deanship, deanery.

dealbação s. f. bleach, bleaching, blanching, whitening.

dealbar, dealvar v. 1. to bleach, blanch, whiten. 2. to purify.

deambulação s. f. (pl. **-ões**) 1. digression. 2. walk, deambulation, stroll, ramble.

deambular v. to walk abroad, stroll, ramble.

deambulatório s. m. deambulatory. || adj. 1. walking, strolling, rambling. 2. variable. 3. errant.

deão s. m. (pl. **deãos, deães, deões**) dean.

dearticulação s. f. (pl. **-ões**) clear articulation or pronunciation.

dearticular v. to articulate clearly.

debaixo adv. 1. under, beneath, below. 2. inferior. 3. decadently.

debalde adv. in vain, to no purpose.
foi ~ it was for nothing.

debandada s. f. flight, escape, disbandment.

debandar v. 1. to put to flight, scatter. 2. to flee, disperse. 3. (mil.) to fall out.

debate s. m. 1. debate, discussion. 2. contention, contest (of arguments).
a questão está em ~ the matter lies at issue. **encerrar o** ~ to apply the closure.

debater v. 1. to discuss, dispute. 2. to contend, debate. 3. to contest, argue. 4. ~-**se**: a) to fight, struggle, attempt to free o. s. b) to flutter (birds).

debatidiço adj. fluttering.

debatidura s. f. fluttering, ruffle.

debelação s. f. (pl. **-ões**) 1. control, restraint, check. 2. cure, healing. 3. subduing, subjection.

debelador s. m. 1. subduer, vanquisher, conqueror. 2. healer. || adj. (also **debelatório**) 1. subduing, conquering. 2. healing, curing.

debelar v. 1. to subject, subdue, overcome. 2. to conquer, defeat, vanquish. 3. to cure, heal. 4. to repress, restrain.
a febre foi debelada the fever was overcome.

debenturagem s. f. (pl. **-ens**) (Braz.) issuance of debentures.

debenturar v. (Braz.) to issue debentures.

debênture s. f. (Braz.) debenture.

debenturista s. m. + f. (Braz.) holder of debentures.

debicação s. f. nibbling, pecking.

debicar v. 1. to try, test. 2. to nibble, eat dainties. 3. to taunt, jeer at, gibe. 4. to peck.

débil adj. m. + f. (pl. **débeis**) 1. weak. 2. vacillating, irresolute, fainthearted. 3. feeble, frail, infirm. 4. soft, delicate. 5. insignificant. 6. dim, indistinct, faint. || **debilmente** adv. weakly, feebly.

debilidade s. f. 1. debility, weakness. 2. fragility. 3. feebleness, frailty. 4. softness.

debilitação s. f. (pl. **-ões**) debilitation, weakening.

debilitante adj. m. + f. weakening, debilitating.

debilitar v. 1. to weaken, debilitate. 2. to prejudice, disable, harm.

debilitável adj. m. + f. (pl. **-áveis**) liable to being weakened.

debilóide s. m. + f. somewhat feeble-minded individual. || adj. m. + f. feeble-minded.

debique s. m. taut, gibe, sarcasm, sneer.

debitar v. to bill, enter as a debt, debit, charge.
~ **em conta** to charge to the account.

débito s. m. debt, obligation, debit.
~ **escriturado** claim as per accounts. **ao** ~ **de** to the debit of. **levamos a quantia de Cr$ 1.000,00 ao seu** ~ we charged Cr$ 1.000,00 to your account.

deblaterar v. 1. to claim violently, demand. 2. to shout.

debochado adj. 1. lewd, licentious, indecent, obscene. 2. (Braz.) scoffing, mocking.

debochador s. m. (Braz.) debaucher, scoffer. || adj. 1. sarcastic. 2. jeering, mocking, taunting.

debochar v. 1. to debauch, corrupt, pervert. 2. (Braz.) to jeer, mock, scoff.

debochativo adj. (Braz.) taunting, scoffing, jeering, sarcastic.

deboche s. m. 1. debauch, debauchery. 2. mockery, jeer.

deborcar v. to turn downwards, turn upside down.

debrear v. to throw out of gear, disengage.

debruadeira s. f. (Braz.) hemming machine.

debruado adj. 1. with a hem, doubled and sewn. 2. (Braz.) with white stripes (horse).

debruar v. 1. to hem, border and sew. 2. (fig.) to adorn, trim.

debruçar v. 1. to stoop, bend forward, lean over. 2. to incline, curve. 3. ~-**se** to bend o. s., stoop.

debrum s. m. hem, edging, border, binding (plate P 15).

debulha s. f. thrashing, stripping, peeling, husking (plate C 16).

debulhador s. m. 1. thrasher, thresher, husker. 2. thrashing machine. || adj. thrashing, threshing.

debulhadora s. f. thrashing (threshing) machine, thrashing mill (plate C 16).

debulhar v. 1. to thrash, thresh. 2. to peel, husk. ~-**se em lágrimas** to dissolve in tears, melt into tears.

debulho s. m. chaff.

debutante s. f. debutante.
   ela foi ~ o ano passado she came out last year.
debutar v. to appear for the first time in public.
debute s. m. debut, first appearance in public.
debuxador s. m. sketcher, drawer, depicter. ‖ adj. sketching, drawing.
debuxante adj. m. + f. sketching, drawing.
debuxar v. 1. to sketch, draw, depict. 2. to outline. 3. (fig.) to plan. 4. to manifest, express. 5. ~-se to be reflected.
debuxo s. m. sketch, outline, design, rough drawing, project, scheme.
década s. f. decade.
decadáctilo, decadátilo adj. having ten fingers.
decadência s. f. decadence, decline, decay.
   ele está em ~ (fig.) his star has set.
decadente adj. m. + f. decadent, decaying, deteriorating.
decadismo s. m. decadence: the literary movement of the decadents.
decadista s. m. + f. decadent. ‖ adj. decadent.
decaedro s. m. (geom.) decahedron. ‖ adj. decahedral.
decagonal adj. m. + f. (pl. -ais) (geom.) decagonal.
decágono s. m. (geom.) decagon.
decagrama s. m. decagramme, decagram.
decaída s. f. 1. decay, decline, fall. 2. whore, strumpet.
decaído s. m. a person or thing decayed. ‖ adj. decayed, declined, ruined, rotten; (fig.) far gone, at low ebb.
decaimento s. m. decay, decline, fall.
decair v. 1. to decay, decline, fall away. 2. to lose position, fall. 3. to diminish, abate, moderate.
   ele decaiu muito he has come down in the world, he has sunk very low. **ele está decaindo rapidamente** he is sinking fast. **o interesse do rapaz decaiu** the boy's interest lapsed.
decalcar v. 1. to trace, reproduce by copying or by decalcomania. 2. to copy, imitate.
decalcomania s. f. decalcomania.
decalitro s. m. decalitre.
decálogo s. m. decalogue, decalog: the Ten Commandments.
decalque s. m. (also **decalco**) 1. tracing, copying. 2. decalcomania. 3. copy. 4. plagiarism, plagiary.
decâmetro s. m. decameter, decametre.
decampamento s. m. decampment.
decampar v. 1. to decamp, break camp. 2. to run away, (pop.) give leg-bail, light out.
decanado s. m. deanship, deanery, decanate.
decandria s. f. (bot.) decandria.
decandro adj. (bot.) decandrian, decandrous.
decangular adj. m. + f. = **decagonal**.
decania s. f. 1. deanship. 2. deaconry: corporation presided over by a dean. 3. group of ten persons.
decano s. m. dean, elder, senior (of a corporation).
decantação s. f. (pl. -ões) decantation, separation by decanting, pouring off.
decantador s. m. decanter: vessel used for decanting.
decantar (I) v. to decant, pour off.
decantar (II) v. to praise, celebrate in song.
decapagem s. f. (pl. -ens) scouring or pickling (met.).
decapar v. to scoure, pickle (met.).
decapê s. m. a wood treatment process with plaster.
decapitação s. f. (pl. -ões) decapitation, beheading.
decapitar v. to decapitate, behead.
decápode s. m. (zool.) decapod, decapodan. ‖ adj. m. + f. decapod, decapodal, decapodous.
decassílabo s. m. decasyllable. ‖ adj. decasyllabic.
decastere, decastéreo s. m. decastere, dekastere.
decatlo s. m. decathlon.
decatron s. m. (electr.) decatron, a gas valve with 10 cathodes.

deceinar v. to wash (yarn), remove the ash of the bleaching bath.
decenal adj. m. + f. (pl. -ais) decennial.
decenário s. m. decennial, tenth anniversary. ‖ adj. decennary.
decência s. f. decency, propriety, decorum.
decendial adj. m. + f. (pl. -ais) lasting ten days.
decêndio s. m. period of ten days.
decênio s. m. decennium.
decenovenal adj. m. + f. (pl. -ais) lasting nineteen years.
decente adj. m. + f. 1. decent, proper, decorous. 2. honest, fair. 3. convenient. 4. suitable, adequate, befitting. 5. clean, tidy.
decenvirado, decenvirato s. m. decemvirate.
decênviro s. m. decemvir.
decepador adj. cutting off, amputating, severing.
decepamento s. m. cutting off, amputation, severance.
decepar v. 1. to cut off, amputate, sever, maim. 2. to interrupt, break off. 3. to mutilate. 4. to stop, restrain, check. 5. to intercept. 6. to deprive of life, kill. 7. to truncate.
decepção s. f. (pl. -ões) 1. disappointment, disillusion(ment). 2. deception, deceit. 3. fraud.
decepcionar v. 1. to disappoint, surprise. 2. to deceive.
decerto adv. certainly, surely.
decesso s. m. decease, death.
decidido adj. 1. resolute, decided. 2. courageous, bold. 3. determined, unwavering. 4. firm, unflinching. ‖ **-amente** adv. 1. resolutely. 2. courageously. 3. steadily.
   estar quase ~ a to have some thought of. **estou ~ a ir** I am resolved to go. **-amente a favor** flatly in favour of.
decidir v. 1. to decide. 2. to resolve. 3. to determine. 4. to settle, sentence. 5. to convince, persuade. 6. to choose, be in favour of. 7. to reach a decision. 8. ~-se to make up one's mind.
   ~ pelas armas to fight out. **decidi morar na cidade** I settled on living in town. **~ a favor de** (jur.) to find for. **isto decide o assunto** that clinches matters. **tenho uma questão para ~ com você!** I have a bone to pick with you.
decíduo adj. deciduous, caducous.
decifração s. f. (pl. -ões) ʹdecipherment, deciphering.
decifrador s. m. decipherer. ‖ adj. deciphering.
decifrar v. 1. to decipher. 2. to interpret. 3. to guess.
   você será capaz de ~ este mapa? can you make any sense out of this map?
decifrável adj. m. + f. (pl. -áveis) decipherable.
decigrama s. m. decigram, decigramme.
decil s. m. (pl. -is) decile, decil.
decilitro s. m. decilitre, deciliter.
décima s. f. 1. decimal, decimal fraction. 2. tithe (one tenth of the income). 3. tax, tribute, duty. 4. (poet.) stanza of ten verses.
decimal s. f. (pl. -ais) decimal (fraction). ‖ adj. m. + f. decimal.
decimável adj. m. + f. (pl. -áveis) 1. tithable. 2. taxable.
decímetro s. m. decimetre, decimeter.
décimo s. m. tenth, tenth part. ‖ adj. tenth.
decisão s. f. (pl. -ões) 1. decision. 2. resolution, determination. 3. judgment, verdict. 4. firmness, steadfastness. 5. courage.
   chegar a uma ~ to come to a resolution. **forçar uma ~** to force an issue. **por ~ do Senado** by grace of the Senate. **tomar uma ~** to take a decision.
decisivo adj. 1. decisive, conclusive. 2. resolutive. 3. clear, evident, obvious. 4. positive, final, ultimate. ‖ **-amente** adv. decisively, evidently, positively.

isto foi ~ this was decisive, turned the balance.
resposta -a final answer.
decisório adj. (jur.) having the power to decide.
decistere, decistéreo s. m. decistere.
declamação s. f. (pl. -ões) s. f. 1. declamation. 2. empty talk. 3. rhetorical speech.
declamador s. m. declaimer. ‖ adj. declaiming.
declamar v. 1. to declaim. 2. to recite. 3. to proclaim. 4. to speak in rhetorical style, harangue. 5. to inveigh.
~ versos ao desafio to cap verses.
declamatório adj. declamatory.
declaração s. f. (pl. -ões) 1. declaration, assertion. 2. statement. 3. document. 4. announcement. 5. declaration of love.
~ de falência declaration of insolvency. ~ de guerra declaration of war. ~ de valor statement of value. ~ juramentada, ~ sob juramento sworn affidavit, sworn statement. fazer uma ~ to make a declaration.
declarado adj. 1. manifest, proved, obvious, apparent, evident, clear. 2. asserted, declared. 3. confessed, sworn, avowed. ‖ -amente adv. declaredly, openly. inimigo ~ sworn enemy.
declarador s. m. declarer. ‖ adj. declaring.
declarante s. m. + f. declarant. ‖ adj. declaring.
declarar v. 1. to declare, assert, state. 2. to pronounce, announce. 3. to manifest, state. 4. to confess, admit of. 5. to explain, explicate. 6. to publish, disclose. 7. to proclaim. 8. to appoint. 9. to elect. 10. to adjudge. 11. ~-se a) to break out (disease, fire, etc.). b) to pronounce o. s. c) to manifest o. s. or itself.
~ alguém culpado (jur.) to adjudge s. o. guilty. ~ guerra to declare war. ~ inocente to clear from blame. ~ o jogo to call one's hand. ~-se quite com to cry quits. ~ sob juramento to swear under an oath. declaro-o isento de responsabilidade I acquit him of responsibility. ele declarou-se a favor de he declared himself for. ele declarou-se à senhora he proposed to the lady. ele declarou-se satisfeito he professed himself contented. tem algo a ~? (at customs) have you anything to declare?
declarativo adj. declarative.
declaratório adj. declaratory.
declinação s. f. (pl. -ões) 1. declination. 2. decline, deterioration, decay. 3. (astr.) declination: angular difference or distance. 4. (gram.) declension.
declinador s. m. declinometer, declinator.
declinante adj. m. + f. 1. declining. 2. falling, decaying.
declinar v. 1. to reject, refuse. 2. to bend downwards. 3. to declare, reveal. 4. to inflect. 5. to deviate from. 6. to lean, incline. 7. to decline, sink, fall, decrease, decay. 8. to approach the close. 9. to lower, diminish. 10. ~-se to tend to, be inclined towards.
está declinando it is on the wane. suas forças declinam rapidamente he is failing fast.
declinativo adj. (gram.) declensional.
declinatória s. f. (jur.) declinatory plea, (Scot.) declinature.
declinatório adj. declinatory, declinational.
declinável adj. m. + f. (pl. -áveis) declinable.
declínio s. m. 1. decline, inclination. 2. decay, decadence.
declinoso adj. declivous, declivitous, sloping downward.
declivar v. 1. to decline, slope down, incline. 2. to render declivous.
declive s. m., declividade f. (also declívio) descending slope, declivity. ‖ adj. declivous, declivitous.
~ de manobra (railway) hump (plate E 12).

declivoso adj. declivous, declivitous, sloping down.
decoada s. f. 1. lye. 2. extraction of ash with water.
decoar v. to put into lye.
decocção s. f. (pl. -ões) 1. decoction. 2. boiling.
decocto s. m. 1. product of decoction. 2. decoction.
decolagem s. f. (pl. -ens) (aeron.) take-off.
pista de ~ landing strip.
decolar v. (aeron.) to take off.
decomponente adj. m. + f. decomposing.
decomponível adj. m. + f. (pl. -íveis) decomposable.
decompor v. 1. to decompose, decompound. 2. to separate. 3. to alter, modify. 4. to analyse. 5. to study. 6. to spoil, rot, decay, putrefy.
decomposição s. f. (pl. -ões) 1. decomposition. 2. analysis. 3. separation. 4. disorganization, disintegration.
~ de forças resolution of forces.
decoração s. f. (pl. -ões) 1. decoration. 2. ornamentation, adornment. 3. scenery, décor.
~ de vitrina window-dressing (plate V 5).
decorador (I) s. m. person who learns by heart. ‖ adj. learning or knowing by heart.
decorador (II) s. m. decorator.
decorar (I) v. 1. to learn by heart. 2. to know by heart. 3. to remember, retain, keep in mind.
decorar (II) v. 1. to decorate. 2. to adorn, ornament, embellish. 3. to honour. 4. to bestow a decoration upon.
eles decoraram a sala com azevinho they dressed the room with holly.
decorativo adj. decorative, ornamental.
decoreba s. f. (Braz., sl.) 1. habit of learning school tests, etc. by heart, without understanding. 2. m. + f. an individual having such a habit.
decoro (ô) s. m. 1. decorum, propriety. 2. decency. 3. honour, honor. 4. honest character. 5. propriety of words or style.
as normas do ~ the proprieties.
decoroso adj. 1. decorous, proper, becoming. 2. deserving, worthy. 3. decent. 4. honourable.
decorrente adj. m. + f. 1. current, passing, elapsing. 2. deriving, resulting from, due to. 3. (bot.) decurrent.
decorrer v. 1. to elapse, pass away. 2. to happen, occur. 3. to derive, originate from.
no ~ do tempo in course of time.
decorrido adj. passed, elapsed.
decorticação s. f. (pl. -ões) decortication.
decorticar v. to decorticate.
decotado adj. low-necked, décolleté.
decotar v. 1. to cut off (the neck of a dress), make low-necked. 2. to top, trim, prune. 3. to pare, clip.
decote s. m. 1. low neck (of a dress). 2. topping, pruning, trimming.
decremento s. m. decrease, diminution, decrement.
decrepitação s. f. (pl. -ões) decrepitation.
decrépito adj. 1. decrepit. 2. old, infirm, feeble. 3. declining. 4. weak. 5. worn out. 6. decayed.
decrepitude s. f. (also decrepidez) 1. decrepitude, feebleness. 2. infirmity, old age.
decrescente adj. m. + f. decrescent, decreasing, waning.
decrescer v. 1. to diminish, decrease, grow less. 2. to wane, subside, decline.
decrescimento, decréscimo s. m. decrease, diminution, lessening.
decretação s. f. (pl. -ões) decreement, decreeing.
decretado adj. (Braz.) intentionally, deliberately, on purpose.
decretal s. f. (pl. -ais) decretal.
decretar v. 1. to decree, proclaim. 2. to determine, ordain. 3. to destine.
~ a falência de alguém to adjudge s. o. bankrupt.

decreto s. m. 1. decree, edict. 2. designation. **nem por** ~ (fig.) never, on no account.
decreto-lei s. m. (pl. **decretos-leis**) decree-law.
decretório adj. 1. decretory, decisive. 2. deciding. 3. (med.) critical.
decriptar v. to decrypt.
decrua s. f. first tillage or cultivation.
decruagem s. f. (pl. **-ens**) 1. = **decrua**. 2. washing of raw silk.
decruar v. 1. to till, cultivate. 2. to wash raw silk.
decúbito s. m. decubitus, decumbency, decumbent position, lying down.
decumbente adj. m. + f. decumbent, reclining.
decuplar, decuplicar v. to decuple, increase tenfold.
décuplo s. m. decuple, tenfold number. ‖ adj. decuple, tenfold.
decúria s. f. decury, decuria.
decuriado s. m. decurionate.
decurião s. m. (pl. **-ões**) decurion.
decursivo adj. = **decorrente**.
decurso s. m. 1. continuation, succession. 2. duration, continuance. 3. passing, going by. 4. going, moving, running. ‖ adj. past, gone by. **no** ~ **do ano** during the year.
dedada s. f. 1. pinch, bit. 2. fingerprint.
dedal s. m. (pl. **-ais**) 1. thimble (plate A 5, P 15). 2. bit, small quantity. 3. (Braz., bot., also **dedaleira**) digitalis, foxglove.
dedáleo adj. dedalous, daedalian, intricate, skillful, ingenious.
dédalo s. m. 1. labyrinth. 2. confusion, mess.
dedecorar v. to dishonour, dishonor.
dedeira s. f. 1. fingerstall, thumbstall. 2. a small device used to pluck the strings of musical instruments.
dedetizar v. to spray with insecticide, to debug.
dedicação s. f. (pl. **-ões**) 1. devotion, affection, fondness. 2. dedication. 3. faithfulness. 4. consecration. 5. self-abandonment. ~ **simulada** lip-homage, lip-worship.
dedicado adj. 1. dedicated, devoted. 2. consecrated. 3. zealous. **ser** ~ **a** to be attached to.
dedicador s. m. dedicator. ‖ adj. dedicatory, devotional.
dedicar v. 1. to dedicate, devote, hallow. 2. to consecrate. 3. to vote. 4. to offer. 5. to apply. 6. to intend, destine. 7. ~-**se** to devote o. s. ~-**se aos estudos** to take to study. ~-**se de corpo e alma a** to put one's back into. **ele se dedica ao seu trabalho** he sticks to his work. **estamo-nos dedicando à leitura** we are taken with reading.
dedicatória s. f. dedication.
dedignação s. f. (pl. **-ões**) 1. disdain. 2. condescension.
dedignar-se v. 1. to disdain. 2. to deign, condescend.
dedilhação s. f. (pl. **-ões**), **dedilhado**, **dedilhamento** m. fingering.
dedilhar v. 1. to finger, to play with the fingers. 2. to mark (a piece of music), to indicate which fingers should be used.
dedo s. m. 1. finger (plate C 18). 2. finger of a glove (plate L 3). 3. the width of a finger. 4. (fig.) skill. ~ **anular** ring finger. ~ **de Deus** divine providence, God's hand. ~ **do pé** toe (plate C 18). ~ **indicador** forefinger, index finger. ~ **médio** middle finger. ~ **mínimo**, ~ **mindinho** little finger. ~ **polegar** thumb. **ela está a dois** ~s **da morte** she is close to death. **eles deram dois** ~s **de prosa** they talked a little. **fiquei cheio de** ~s I got completely mixed up. **lamber os** ~s to lick one's fingers. **nem um** ~ **faz mão, nem uma andorinha verão** one swallow does not make a summer. **ponta do** ~ finger-

-tip. **saber nas pontas dos** ~s to have at one's finger-tips. **ter** ~ to have skill.
dedo-duro s. m. + f. (pl. **dedos-duros**) delator, informer, stool pigeon, stoolie.
dedução s. f. (pl. **-ões**) 1. deduction, subtraction. 2. abatement, allowance. 3. reasoning, conclusion, inference.
deducional adj. m. + f. (pl. **-ais**) made through deduction.
dedutivo adj. deductive, inferential.
deduzir v. 1. to deduce. 2. to draw or trace from facts. 3. to reduce. 4. to deduct, subtract. 5. to infer. 6. to draw as a conclusion. **isto se deduz de** it is implied from.
defasagem s. f. (pl. **-ens**) (electr.) phase displacement.
defasar v. (electr.) to dephase.
defecação s. f. (pl. **-ões**) 1. defecation. 2. purification, refining.
defecado adj. 1. defecated. 2. purified, refined. 3. lean, meager.
defecador s. m. defecator: an apparatus to remove albuminoid matter from cane juice. ‖ adj. defecating.
defecar v. 1. to defecate. 2. to purify, clarify. 3. ~-**se** to cast off impurities, to become pure.
defecatório adj. 1. defecating. 2. purifying.
defecção s. f. (pl. **-ões**) 1. defection, desertion. 2. apostasy.
defectibilidade s. f. defectibility.
defectível adj. m. + f. (pl. **-íveis**) defectible.
defectivo adj. defective, imperfect, faulty.
defedação s. f. (pl. **-ões**) mark, stain on the skin.
defeito s. m. 1. defect. 2. fault, imperfection, deficiency. 3. deformity. 4. blemish, stain. 5. addiction, vice. 6. flaw, blister. **localizador de** ~s faults-man. **todos têm seus** ~s everybody has his shortcomings.
defeituoso adj. defective, faulty, imperfect, incomplete.
defendente s. m. + f. defender. ‖ adj. defensive.
defender v. 1. to defend, protect. 2. to help, aid, support. 3. to prohibit, forbid. 4. to hinder, hamper, embarrass. 5. (Braz.) to get, obtain (by more or less crooked ways). 6. to guard shield, shelter. 7. to resist, withstand, defy. 8. (Braz.) ~-**se**: a) to earn one's living (through smartness). b) to uphold, excuse, sustain. ~ **algo** to defend s. th.; stand by a thing. ~ **uma causa** to be the counsel in a case. **ela defendeu sua opinião** she stood up for her opinion. **ele defendeu-se** (coll.) he saved his bacon. **ele me defendeu** he defended me, was at my back. **ele o defende** he defends him, (coll.) sticks up for him. **ele se defende com biscates** (Braz.) he earns his living with odd jobs. **ele se defende de qualquer modo** he gets around somehow. **eles defenderam-me** they defended me, (fig.) they took up the cudgels for me.
defendimento s. m. (rare) defense.
defendível adj. m. + f. (pl. **-íveis**) defendable, defensible.
defenestração s. f. (pl. **-ões**) defenestration.
defensa s. f. 1. = **defesa**. 2. ~s pl. (naut.) fender.
defensável, defensível adj. m. + f. (pl. **-áveis, -íveis**) defendable, defensible. ‖ **defensavelmente** adv. defendably.
defensiva s. f. defensive, position of defence. **estar na** ~ to be on the defensive.
defensivo s. m. protection, preservative, safeguard. ‖ adj. defensive, protective.
defensor s. m. 1. defender, protector. 2. (jur.) defensor. ‖ adj. defensive, protective.
defensório adj. defensive.

deferência s. f. deference, respect, regard.
deferente adj. m. + f. deferent, deferential, respectful. ‖ ~mente adv. deferentially, respectfully.
deferido adj. granted, conferred, conceded.
deferimento s. m. grant, concession.
adiar o ~ de um pedido to postpone the granting of a request. pede ~ asks for granting.
deferir v. 1. to grant, concede. 2. to confer, bestow.
deferível adj. m. + f. (pl. -íveis) grantable.
defesa (I) s. f. 1. defence, defense. 2. justification, vindication. 3. (jur.) defender. 4. guard, protection. 5. tusk. 6. (zool.) either of the two horns, antlers. 7. prohibition. 8. (Braz.) profit cunningly obtained. em ~ de in advocacy of. em ~ de suas teorias in support of his theories. em ~ própria in self--defence.
defesa (II) s. m. (ftb.) backfield (plate F 9).
defeso s. m. = defesso. ‖ adj. prohibited, forbidden.
defesso s. m. (hunt.) fence season, close(d) season. ‖ adj. tired, weary.
deficiência s. f. 1. deficiency. 2. lack, want, need. 3. insufficiency, shortage. 4. imperfection.
deficiente adj. m. + f. 1. deficient, defective, imperfect, faulty. 2. insufficient, wanting. ‖ ~mente adv. deficiently, imperfectly.
déficit s. m. deficit, shortage.
deficitário adj. deficient, giving deficit, affording loss.
definhado adj. 1. meager, thin. 2. weak, debilitated, feeble.
definhamento s. m. 1. emaciation. 2. weakening. 3. decay.
definhar v. 1. to make thin or meager. 2. to debilitate, weaken. 3. to waste o. s. 4. to emaciate, languish, dwindle. 5. to dry out, decay. 6. to wither. 7. ~-se to waste away, to peak and pine. ele está definhando com uma doença he is being wasted by a disease.
definibilidade s. f. definability.
definição s. f. (pl. -ões) 1. definition, definement. 2. explanation. 3. decision.
definido s. m. a defined matter or subject. ‖ adj. 1. defined, definite. 2. determined, explicit, unequivocal. 3. definitive, positive.
artigo ~ definite article. bem ~ sharp-cut.
definidor s. m. 1. definer. 2. (eccl.) definitor: high officer of certain religious orders. ‖ adj. defining.
definir v. 1. to define. 2. to determine, fix, decide. 3. to describe precisely.
definitivo adj. 1. definitive. 2. conclusive, final. 3. decisive. ‖ -amente adv. definitively, conclusively. eles compraram -amente they bought firm. minhas intenções são -as my intentions are fixed. oferta -a firm bid, firm offer. uma resposta -a a definite answer.
definitório s. m. (eccl.) 1. council of definitors. 2. meeting place of the definitors.
definível adj. m. + f. (pl. -íveis) definable.
deflação s. f. (pl. -ões) (finance, phys., geogr.) deflation.
deflacionista s. m. + f. deflationist. ‖ adj. deflationary.
deflagração s. f. (pl. -ões) 1. deflagration. 2. outburst (of war).
deflagrar v. 1. to deflagrate. 2. to burn, explode. 3. to inflame, excite, kindle.
deflectir v. to deflect.
deflegmação s. f. (pl. -ões) (chem.) fractionation, fractional distillation.
deflegmar v. (chem.) to fractionate, to subject to fractional distillation.
defletor s. m. (mech.) deflector, cooling baffle.
deflexão s. f. (pl. -ões) deflection, deflexion.
deflexo adj. curved or bent down.
defloração s. f. (pl. -ões) defloration.

deflorador s. m. deflowerer.
defloramento s. m. defloration.
deflorar v. 1. to deflorate. 2. to deflower, violate, ravish. 3. to compile the best passages of a literary work.
defluência s. f. = influência.
defluente adj. m. + f. defluent, flowing down.
defluir v. 1. to flow down. 2. to emanate from, issue (a liquid), flow out.
deflúvio s. m. 1. defluent. 2. emanation (of liquids).
defluxão s. f. 1. = deflúvio. 2. (med.) defluxion.
defluxo s. m. common cold, nasal discharge, catarrh.
deforete s. m. (N. Braz.) 1. rest, interruption during work. 2. joke of bad taste.
deformação s. f. (pl. -ões) 1. deformation, disfigurement, disfiguration. 2. deformity.
deformador s. m. deformer. ‖ adj. deforming.
deformar v. 1. to deform, disfigure, misshape. 2. to warp. 3. to become deformed, to lose the shape.
deformatório adj. deforming, disfiguring.
deforme adj. m. + f. 1. deformed. 2. disfigured, misshapen. 3. ugly, unsightly.
deformidade s. f. 1. deformity, disfigurement, malformation. 2. bodily defect.
defraudação s. f. (pl. -ões) defraudation, cheating.
defraudador s. m. defrauder, cheater. ‖ adj. defrauding, cheating.
defraudar v. 1. to defraud, cheat. 2. to deprive of.
defrontação s. f. (pl. -ões) confrontation.
defrontante adj. m. + f. confronting, facing, opposing.
defrontar v. 1. to confront, stand facing. 2. to face, meet, encounter. 3. to place before. 4. to be opposite to, to front upon.
defronte adv. face to face, opposite to, in front of. ~ de in face of.
defumação s. f. (pl. -ões) 1. smoking, curing (of meat or fish). 2. (Braz.) curing of latex.
defumado adj. smoke-dried, cured.
carne -a smoked meat.
defumador s. m. 1. smoker: one who cures or smokes. 2. vessel for fumigating. 3. (Braz.) room for the curing of latex. ‖ adj. smoking, curing.
defumadouro s. m. 1. substance used for smoking or curing. 2. smokehouse. 3. receptacle for curing or smoking.
defumadura s. f. 1. smoking, curing. 2. perfuming.
defumar v. 1. to smoke-dry, to cure with smoke. 2. ~-se to perfume o. s.
defunção s. f. (pl. -ões) death, obit, decease.
defunto s. m. deceased, dead person. ‖ adj. dead, extinct, deceased.
degas s. m., sg. + pl. (Braz.) myself (manner to refer to oneself always preceded by the article o).
degelar v. 1. to deice, defrost, thaw. 2. to heat, warm, animate.
degelo (ê) s. m. thawing, thaw: the act of defrosting. o ~ começou the thaw has set in.
degeneração s. f. (pl. -ões) 1. degeneration, degeneracy, debasement. 2. degradation.
degenerado s. m. a degenerate person. ‖ adj. 1. degenerate, degraded, sunk. 2. corrupt, depraved, perverted.
degenerar v. 1. to degenerate. 2. to fall off, deteriorate. 3. to decline. 4. to become corrupt.
degenerativo adj. degenerative.
degenerescência s. f. 1. degeneration. 2. disposition to degenerate.
degenerescente adj. m. + f. degenerating.
deglutição s. f. (pl. -ões) deglutition, swallowing.
deglutinação s. f. (gram.) a form of aphaeresis by which the initial phonemes a or o of a word are separated.
deglutir v. to swallow.

degola, degolação (pl. ~s, -ões), **degoladura** s. f. 1. decollation, decapitation, beheading. 2. (fig.) mass failure at an examination.

degolador s. m. 1. cutthroat. 2. fuller, fullering tool.

degolar v. to decollate, behead, decapitate.

degradação s. f. (pl. -ões), **degradamento** m. 1. degradation, deposition, demotion. 2. degeneration, decay. 3. (fig.) abasement, debasement. 4. (geol.) degradation: a wearing down by erosion.

degradador s. m. degrader: one who degrades. ‖ adj. degrading, debasing.

degradante adj. m. + f. degrading, debasing.

degradar v. 1. to degrade. 2. to debase, lower. 3. = **degredar**.

ele degradou-se he abased himself.

degranar v. to thresh, thrash, separate the grain.

degrau s. m. 1. stair, stairstep, step (plate E 7). 2. rung, tread (of a ladder) (plate E 6). 3. (fig.) degree or grade of progress.

espelho de ~ step. **piso do** ~ tread (plate E 7).

degredado s. m. deportee, exilé. ‖ adj. banished, expatried.

degredar v. to exile, banish, expatriate, deport.

degredo s. m. 1. exile, banishment, expatriation, deportation. 2. place of exile.

degressivo adj. decreasing, decrescent.

degringolada s. f. 1. a rolling down, fall. 2. decay, decadence.

degringolar v. 1. to roll down, fall. 2. to come down, decay.

degustação s. f. (pl. -ões) degustation, tasting.

degustar v. to degust, taste.

déia s. f. (poet.) goddess.

deicida s. m. + f. deicide. ‖ adj. deicidal.

deicídio s. m. deicide.

deícola s. m. + f. deist.

deidade s. f. 1. deity, divinity. 2. goddess. 3. (fig.) a woman of great beauty.

deificação s. f. (pl. -ões) deification.

deificador s. m. deifier.

deificar v. to deify, to make godlike.

deífico adj. 1. deific. 2. godlike, divine.

deiforme adj. m. + f. 1. deiform. 2. godlike.

deiscência s. f. (bot.) dehiscence.

deiscente adj. m. + f. (bot.) dehiscent.

deísmo s. m. deism.

deísta s. m. + f. deist.

deita s. f. the act of lying down, going to bed.

deitado adj. 1. lying, stretched out. 2. in bed.

deitar v. 1. to lie, lay (down), put down horizontally. 2. to let fall. 3. to exhale, emit. 4. to produce, create, put forth. 5. to put to bed. 6. to incline, 7. to pour. 8. to spill, shed (liquid); to let out. 9. to cast down. 10. ~-**se**: a) to lie down. b) to go to bed. c) to throw a. s. into. d) to fall upon, attack.

~ **abaixo** to pull down, demolish, destroy. ~ **a fugir** to take to one's heels. ~ **água no mar** to carry coals to Newcastle. ~ **âncora** to cast anchor. ~ **a perder** to spoil, impair, ruin. ~ **fora** to throw away. ~ **raízes** to take root. ~ **sortes** to cast lots. ~-**se na cama** to go to bed. **deitei-o no chão** I threw him down. **deite o leite numa xícara!** pour the milk into a cup! **as flores estão deitando brotos** the flowers are blossoming. **deite isto fora!** throw that away! **deitamos duas galinhas** we set two hens. **ele deitou-lhe as mãos ao pescoço** he seized him by the neck. **ele deitou sangue pela boca** he bled through the mouth. **ele deitou-se aos inimigos** he fell upon the enemies. **o barco foi deitado ao mar** the ship was launched. **o senhor deita-se muito tarde** you go to bed very late.

deixa, deixação (pl. -ões) s. f. 1. letting. 2. legacy. 3. (theat.) catchword, cue word.

deixar v. 1. to leave, quit. 2. to abandon, forsake. 3. to release, let go. 4. to leave alone. 5. to overlook, not to mention. 6. to allow, permit. 7. to postpone, put off. 8. to yield, bring as a result. 9. to interrupt, suspend. 10. to give up, renounce. 11. to omit, leave out. 12. to let, cause to. 13. to institute, appoint to. 14. to avoid. 15. to bequeath, leave by will. 16. to leave, desist from, abstain from. 17. to stop, discontinue. 18. to cease to be. 19. to let lie. 20. to neglect.

~ **alguém com a pulga atrás da orelha** to put a bug (or flea) in some one's ear. ~ **cair** 1. to drop, let fall. 2. to let down. ~ **de fumar** to give up smoking, to stop smoking. ~ **entrar** to let in, to admit. ~ **escapar** to let slip. ~ **escapar uma oportunidade** to miss an opportunity. ~ **impune** to let unpunished, let off. ~ **muito a desejar** to be quite unsatisfactory. ~ **para trás** to leave behind. ~ **partir** to let go. ~ **saber** to let know, let into. ~ **sair** to let out. ~ **só** to leave, let alone. ~ **um emprego** to quit a job. **deixe de conversa!** (coll.) cut the cackle! **deixe disso!** come out of that! give it a miss! **deixe isto a critério dele!** leave that to him! **deixe-me em paz, deixe-me só!** leave me alone! **deixe-me ver** let me see. **deixe-o fazer** let him have his run. **deixo-o a seu critério** I put it to you. **ela deixou cair o prato** she dropped the dish. **ela me deixa nervoso** she is a strain on my nerves, she gets on my nerves. **ele deixou crescer a barba** he grew a beard. **ele deixou-me em situação difícil** he got me into difficulties. **ele deixou-me na mão** he let me down, failed me, left me holding the bag. **ele deixou todos para trás** he left everybody behind. **ele nunca deixou de vir** he never failed to come. **ele o deixou à mercê de seu destino** he abandoned him to his fate. **não deixe de fazê-lo!** be sure and do it! **não posso deixar de fazê-lo** I cannot but do it. **não posso** ~ **de mostrar a aversão que sinto por ele** I cannot restrain from showing the aversion I feel towards him. **não posso deixar de observar** I cannot forbear observing. **não se deixe dominar pelas suas paixões!** don't let your passions overcome you! **não se deixe levar** (coll.) don't go in on it. **o negócio deixou muito lucro** the business yielded a large profit. **vamos** ~ **como está, para ver como fica** let's wait and see.

dêixis s. f. (ling.) the ability of language to designate something by showing, not by conceptualizing it.

dejarretar v. to hamstring, to disable by cutting the hamstrings.

dejeção s. f. (pl. -ões) 1. dejection, defecation. 2. (geol.) substances expelled by volcanoes.

dejejua s. f., **dejejuadouro** m. = **desjejua**.

dejejuar v. = **desjejuar**.

dejetar v. to defecate.

dejeto s. m. 1. dejection, evacuation, defecation. 2. excrements, feces.

dejetório s. m. (Braz.) privy, latrine.

dejua, dejuação s. f. (pl. ~s, -ões) = **desjejua**.

dejungir v. = **desjungir**.

dejúrio s. m. oath, solemn swearing.

dela contr. of the prep. **de** and the pronoun **ela** her, hers, of her, from her.

delação s. f. (pl. -ões) delation, denouncement, accusation.

delamber-se v. 1. to lick the body (animals). 2. to rejoice, delight, cheer. 3. to affect.

delambido s. m. dandy, fop. ‖ adj. foppish, dapper, spruce.

delatar v. 1. to delate, to inform against. 2. to denounce, accuse. 3. to reveal.
delatável adj. m. + f. (pl. -áveis) revealable, what can or should be denounced.
delator s. m. delator, informer.
delatório adj. denouncing, revealing.
dele contr. of the prep. **de** and the pronoun **ele** his, of his, from his, of him.
a culpa foi ~s the fault was theirs. **viram a casa diante ~s** they saw the house before them.
delegação s. f. (pl. -ões) 1. delegation: a) investing with authority. b) a body of delegates. 2. commissionership. 3. office of a commissioner.
delegacia s. f. 1. delegateship, commissionership. 2. police station.
delegado s. m. 1. delegate, representative, deputy. 2. commissioner. 3. police officer.
delegante s. m. + f. one who delegates. || adj. delegating, assigning, appointing.
delegar v. 1. to delegate, depute, authorize. 2. to assign, appoint. 3. to transmit (by delegation). 4. to entrust, charge, commit.
~ poderes a to delegate authority to.
delegatório adj. delegating, appointing.
deleitação s. f. (pl. -ões), **deleitamento** m. delight, pleasure, enjoyment, diversion.
deleitante adj. m. + f. delectable, delightful, pleasing.
deleitar v. 1. to delight, please, gratify, enchant. 2. **~-se** to be delighted, take delight in, be pleased.
deleitei os olhos com I fed my eyes on.
deleitável adj. m. + f. (pl. -áveis) delighting, pleasing.
deleite s. m. delight, pleasure, delectation, enjoyment.
deleitoso adj. delightful, charming.
deletério adj. deleterious, injurious, noxious, pernicious.
deletrear v. 1. to spell. 2. to read with difficulty.
delével adj. m. + f. (pl. -éveis) delible, erasable.
délfico adj. Delphic, Delphian.
delfim (I) s. m. (pl. -ins) 1. (ichth.) dolphin. 2. (astr.) Delphinus.
delfim (II) s. m. (pl. -ins) (chess) bishop.
delfim (III) s. m. dauphin.
delfinídeos s. m. pl. (zool.) Delphinidae.
delgadeza s. f. slenderness, slimness, thinness.
delgado s. m. a thin part. || adj. 1. thin, lean, slender (plate Q). 2. meagre, lank.
delibação s. f. (pl. -ões) tasting, sipping.
delibar v. 1. to prove, taste, sip. 2. to touch with the lips.
deliberação s. f. (pl. -ões) 1. deliberation, consideration. 2. resolution, decision.
deliberado adj. deliberate, intentional, studied, premeditated. || **-amente** adv. deliberately, of set purpose, intentionally.
deliberante s. m. + f. one who deliberates. || adj. m. + f. deliberative, deliberating.
deliberar v. 1. to deliberate, ponder, reflect upon. 2. to premeditate. 3. to determine, resolve. 4. to discuss, debate, argue. 5. to decide (o. s.).
deliberativo adj. deliberative.
Conselho Deliberativo deliberative body.
delicadeza s. f. 1. delicacy. 2. politeness, courtesy. 3. weakness, fragility, frailty. 4. fineness, slightness. 5. subtlety, sensitiviy. 6. dainty, luxury. 7. susceptibility.
delicado adj. 1. delicate. 2. courteous, polite. 3. feeble, weak. 4. fragile, frail. 5. slender, slight. 6. elegant. 7. tender, soft. 8. fine, smooth. 9. subtle. 10. sensitive. 11. critical. 12. refined, exquisite. || **-amente** adv. courteously, politely.

delícia s. f. 1. delicacy, dainty. 2. delight, pleasure.
isto é uma ~ this is delicious.
deliciar v. 1. to delight, please greatly, gratify, charm. 2. to be pleased, have pleasure in, enjoy.
ela se deliciou com uma xícara de café she indulged in a cup of coffee.
delicioso adj. 1. delicious, delightful, dainty. 2. perfect. || **-amente** adv. deliciously, delightfully.
deligação s. f. (pl. -ões) 1. deligation, bandaging. 2. ligature, bandage.
delimitação s. f. (pl. -ões) delimitation.
delimitador s. m. delimiter. || adj. limiting, delimitative.
delimitar v. 1. to delimitate, delimit, bound, demarcate. 2. to restric, circumscribe.
delineador s. m. delineator, sketcher. || adj. 1. limiting. 2. outlining, tracing, sketching.
delineamento s. m. (also **delineação** f.). 1. delineation. 2. sketch, drawing, outlining, plan.
delinear v. 1. to delineate, sketch out, outline. 2. to trace, draw, portray, picture. 3. to describe, represent. 4. to plan, devise, contrive. 5. to delimit, demarcate.
delineativo adj. delineatory, delineative.
delinqüência s. f. 1. delinquency. 2. fault, guilt, misdemeanor.
delinqüente s. m. + f. delinquent, transgressor. || adj. delinquent.
~ primário first offender.
delinqüir v. to commit or perpetrate a crime.
deliqüescência s. f. deliquescence.
deliqüescente adj. m. + f. deliquescent.
delíquio s. m. 1. deliquescence. 2. (med.) fainting, swooning.
delir v. 1. to undo, efface, erase, blot out. 2. to dissolve, melt, liquefy.
delirado adj. delirious, frantic, mad, crazy, deranged.
delirante adj. m. + f. 1. delirious, insane, lightheaded. 2. frantic, excited, raving. || **~mente** adv. 1. deliriously, lightheadedly. 2. frantically.
delirar v. 1. to be delirious, talk nonsense, rave, wander in mind. 2. to be madly in love. 3. to be very happy.
delírio s. m. 1. delirium, derangement, insanity. 2. excitement, enthusiasm. 3. ecstasy.
delitescência s. f. (med.) delitescence.
delito s. m. delict, fault, crime.
em flagrante ~ in the very act.
delituoso adj. wrong, criminal, punishable.
delivramento s. m. (med.) delivering of the afterbirth.
delonga s. f. delay, postponement, procrastination.
sem ~s without any delay.
delongador s. m. delayer, postponer. || adj. delaying, postponing.
delongar v. 1. to delay, tarry, loiter. 2. to postpone, put off, procrastinate. 3. to detain, retard.
delta s. m. delta: 1. the fourth letter of the Greek alphabet. 2. alluvial deposit at the mouth of a river.
deltacismo s. m. articulation vice exchanging the d for the t.
delta-mais s. m. (nucl. phys.) baryon in the fundamental state having a mass equal to 1,330 units of atomic mass, a spin of 3/2, positive parity and positive charge one or two times that of the proton.
delta-menos s. m. (nucl. phys.) baryon in the fundamental state having a mass equal to 1,330 units of atomic mass, a spin of 3/2, positive parity and a negative charge equal to that of the electron.
delta-zero s. m. (pl. **deltas-zero**) (nucl. phys.) baryon in the fundamental state having a mass equal to 1,330 units of the atomic mass, a spin of 3/2, positive parity and electric charge zero.

deltocarpo adj. (bot.) having delta-shaped fruits.
deltóide s. m. (anat., math.) deltoid. ‖ adj. m. + f. (also **deltóideo**) deltoid(al), delta-shaped.
deltoidiano adj. (anat.) deltoid: pertaining to a deltoid muscle.
deludir v. 1. to delude, deceive, evade, shun. 2. to infringe, trespass, violate.
delusão s. f. (pl. -ões) 1. delusion, deceiving, misleading. 2. (med.) delirium.
deluso adj. deluding, deceiving.
delusório adj. 1. delusory, delusive, deceptive. 2. illusory, illusive.
deluzir-se v. to fade, grow dim, turn pale.
demagogia s. f. demagogy, demagogism.
demagógico adj. demagogic(al).
demagogo s. m. demagogue, demagog.
demais (I) adj. too much, excessive, overmuch. ‖ adv. excessively, more than enough.
   amadurecer ~ to overripen. **aquecer** ~ to overheat. **arriscar-se** ~ to risk too much. **beber** ~ to overdrink, to drink too much. **bom** ~ **para ser verdade** too good a thing to be true. **cansar** ~ to overfatigue, overwork. **cedo** ~ too soon. **cheio** ~ overfull. **comer** ~ to overeat. **confiar** ~ to overtrust. **difícil** ~ **para você** too difficult for you. **dormir** ~ to oversleep. **encher** ~ to overfill. **esperto** ~ overcunning. **estudar** ~ to overstudy. **excitar** ~ to overexcite. **expor** ~ to overexpose. **expor** ~ **à ação do tempo** to overweather. **expor** ~ **uma chapa fotográfica** to overtime a photographic exposure. **falar** ~ to overspeak, to talk too much. **fermentar** ~ to overleaven. **ferver** ~ to overboil. **ficar** ~ to overstay. **isso é** ~ that's to much, that beats the Dutch. **levar longe** ~ to overcarry, to go too far. **longe** ~ too far off. **não será** ~? isn't it too much? **o que é** ~ **faz mal** enough is as good as a feast. **ser zeloso** ~ to be overzealous, overburn. **tarde** ~ too late, overlate. **um pouco** ~ (coll.) a bit thick.
demais (II) adv. besides, moreover.
demais (III) adj. + pron. pl. the others, the rest.
demanda s. f. 1. lawsuit, prosecution. 2. contest, dispute. 3. discussion. 4. (poet.) combat, fight, warfare.
   em ~ in search of. **estar em** ~ to be at law. **ganhar a** ~ to gain one's cause.
demandador s. m. plaintiff, demandant, demander.
demandante adj. m. + f. suing, demanding.
demandar v. 1. to seek, search for. 2. to require, call for. 3. to demand, request, entreat, beseech. 4. to sue at law, prosecute. 5. to question, dispute. 6. to claim.
demandista s. m. + f. 1. plaintiff, demandant. 2. person who likes to sue at law.
demão s. f. (pl. -ãos) 1. coat, coating (of paint, etc.). 2. help, assistance.
   dar uma ~ **de tinta** to apply a coat of paint. **última** ~ **(de tinta)** paint finish.
demarcação s. f. (pl. -ões) 1. demarcation. 2. boundary, limit.
   linha de ~ line of demarcation.
demarcador s. m. demarcator. ‖ adj. demarcating, delimiting.
demarcar v. 1. to demarcate, delimit, line off. 2. to define, fix, mark. 3. to separate. 4. to stake out.
demarcativo adj. 1. serving to demarcate. 2. denotative.
demarcável adj. m. + f. (pl. -áveis) 1. capable of being demarcated. 2. definable, determinable.
demasia s. f. 1. surplus, overplus. 2. excess. 3. remainder. 4. superfluity, superanbundance. 5. intemperance, immoderateness. 6. abuse.

comprar em ~ to overbuy. **descuidado em** ~ overcareless. **saciar em** ~ to overcloy. **eles comeram em** ~ they ate too much.
demasiado adj. 1. excessive, overmuch, too much. 2. superfluous, superabundant. 3. intemperate, immoderate. 4. exaggerated. 5. abusive. ‖ **-amente** adv. excessively, overmuch, too.
   esta mesada é -a para um estudante tão jovem that allowance is too large for so young a student. **o** ~ **rigor do professor amargurou o aluno** the excessive rigour of the teacher embittered the pupil. **-amente ativo** overactive. **-amente curioso** overcurious. **estou -amente cansado!** I am too tired!
demasiar-se v. to exaggerate, overact, go too far.
demência, dementação s. f. (pl. ~s, -ões) 1. (med.) dementia. 2. (pop.) insanity, madness, craziness.
   ~ **precoce** (med.) dementia praecox, schizophrenia.
dementar v. 1. to madden, craze, drive to madness. 2. to become mad.
demente s. m. + f. (also **dementado**) 1. (med.) demented person. 2. (pop.) madman, madling, lunatic. ‖ adj. 1. (med.) demented. 2. (pop.) insane, mad, crazy, lunatic.
demerara s. m. (Braz.) demerara crystals (raw cane-sugar).
demérito s. m. demerit, want of merit, fault. ‖ adj. (also **demeritório**) demeritorious.
demissão s. f. (pl. -ões) 1. demission, dismissal. 2. resignation, abdication.
   solicitei minha ~ I sent in my resignation.
demissionário adj. (also **demitente** m. + f.) resigning.
demissível adj. m. + f. (pl. -íveis) dismissible, dismissible.
demitido adj. dismissed.
   ele foi ~ he got the pay-off, he was dismissed.
demitir v. 1. to dismiss, discharge, fire. 2. to give leave of departure. 3. to disband. 4. to remove from (office). 5. to renounce, give up. 6. to resign, quit.
demiúrgico adj. demiurgic(al), demiurgeous.
demiurgo s. m. demiurge.
demo s. m. 1. demon, devil. 2. turbulent or cunning person.
democracia s. f. democracy.
democrata s. m. + f. democrat. ‖ adj. democratic(al).
democrático adj. democratic, democratical. ‖ **democraticamente** adv. democratically.
democratização s. f. (pl. -ões) democratization.
democratizado adj. democratized.
democratizar v. to democratize.
demofilia s. f. love or sympathy for the people.
demografia s. f. demography.
demográfico adj. demographic(al).
demógrafo s. m. demographer, demographist.
demolhar v. to steep, soak (in water).
demolição s. f. (pl. -ões) 1. demolition, demolishment. 2. destruction.
demolidor s. m. 1. demolisher. 2. destroyer. ‖ adj. demolishing, destroying.
demolir v. 1. to demolish, pull down, peck down. 2. to raze. 3. to ruin, destroy.
demolitório adj. fit for demolition.
demologia s. f. 1. demology. 2. folklore.
demonete s. m. deviling, devilkin, imp.
demonetização s. f. (pl. -ões) demonetization.
demonetizar v. to demonetize.
demoníaco adj. demoniac(al), demonic, devilish.
demonico s. m. deviling, devilkin.
demônio s. m. 1. demon, devil. 2. evil spirit. 3. wicked person. 4. reckless or dashing person.
   com mil ~s! the deuce! **como um** ~ like a devil, like the deuce.

demonismo s. m. demonism.

demonista s. m. + f. demonist. ‖ adj. believing in demons.

demonólatra s. m. + f. demonolater, demon worshipper.

demonolatria s. f. demonolatry.

demonolátrico adj. demonolatrous.

demonologia s. f. (also demonografia) demonology, demonography.

demonológico adj. (also demonográfico) demonologic(al).

demonólogo s. m. (also demonógrafo) demonologer, demonologist, demonographer.

demonomancia s. f. (also demonopatia) divination through the influence of demons.

demonomania s. f. (med.) demonomania.

demonomaníaco s. m. (also demonopata, demonópata) person suffering from demonomania. ‖ adj. suffering from demonomania.

demonomante s. m. + f. a person practising divination through the influence of demons.

demonstrabilidade s. f. demonstrability, demonstrableness.

demonstração s. f. (pl. -ões) 1. demonstration. 2. proof, evidence. 3. manifestation, exhibition, display. 4. exposition.

~ de lucros statement of earnings.

demonstrador s. m. demonstrator. ‖ adj. demonstrative, demonstratory.

demonstrante adj. m. + f. 1. demonstrative, demonstratory. 2. demonstrational.

demonstrar v. to demonstrate: 1. prove by reasoning. 2. explain by examples, etc. 3. give evidence of, evince, show. 4. manifest, display. 5. make a demonstration. 6. show publicly (a merchandise). ela demonstrou ser boa filha she proved herself a good daughter. ele demonstrou muita perseverança he showed great steadfastness.

demonstrativo adj. 1. demonstrative, evincing. 2. illustrative.

adjetivo ~ demonstrative adjective. pronome ~ demonstrative pronoun.

demonstrável adj. m. + f. (pl. -áveis) demonstrable.

demopsicologia s. f. 1. study of the psychology of a people. 2. folklore.

demopsicológico adj. concerned with or pertaining to the study of a people's psychology.

demora s. f. 1. delay, retardation, lateness. 2. procrastination, deterring, postponement. 3. lingering. 4. stay, abode (temporary).

venha sem ~! come at once!

demorado adj. 1. long, lasting, slow. 2. late, dilatory, lengthy.

um processo muito ~ a very slow procedure.

demorar v. 1. to retard, keep back, detain. 2. to be located, be situated. 3. to stay, dwell, live, abide, sojourn. 4. to stop off. 5. to delay, defer, put off. 6. to stop for a longer or shorter period. 7. to linger, loiter, tarry. 8. to take time. 9. (also ~-se) to be late, be long.

a operação demorou muito the operation took a long time. demorei-me muito no Rio de Janeiro I stayed a long time in Rio de Janeiro. o mensageiro demorou-se muito the messenger was late; he kept us waiting a long time.

demostênico adj. Demosthenic, Demosthenean, Demosthenian.

demostração s. f. (pl. -ões) demonstration, ·display.

demostrador s. m. demonstrator.

demostrar v. 1. to demonstrate, explain, illustrate. 2. to evince, show, reveal.

demótico adj. demotic.

demover v. 1. to dissuade, divert, deter, discourage. 2. to move, change the position of. 3. ~-se to move from one place to another.

demudado adj. 1. changed, altered. 2. disfigured. 3. upset, disturbed.

demudar v. 1. to change, alter. 2. to upset, perturb, disturb. 3. ~-se to change one's character or disposition.

demulcente s. m. (med.) demulcent. ‖ adj. m. + f. demulcent, softening, mollifying, soothing.

denário (I) adj. denary.

denário (II) s. m. denarius.

dendê s. m. (Braz., bot.) 1. (also dendezeiro) African oil palm (Elaeis guineensis). 2. its fruit.

dendo s. m. (bot.) Lagos ebony, billetwood, Calabar ebony (Diospyros dendo).

dendraxônio s. m. (anat.) neuron in which the cylinder at leaving the cell is divided in terminal filaments.

dendria s. f. (min.) dendrite.

dendrite s. f. (geol.) 1. a fossil tree. 2. (anat.) dendrite.

dendrito s. m. (geol.) dendrite.

dendrobata, dendróbata adj. m. + f. dendrophilous, living on trees.

dendróbio s. m. (bot.) dendrobium.

dendrocélios s. m. pl. (zool.) Dendrocoela.

dendrocolaptídeos s. m. pl. (zool.) Dendrocolaptidae.

dendrófobo s. m. one who injures trees. ‖ adj. injuring trees.

dendróide adj. m. + f. (also dendróideo) dendroid(al), arborescent.

dendrólatra s. m. + f. tree worshiper. ‖ adj. practising tree worship.

dendrolatria s. f. tree worship, tree cult.

dendrolite s. m. dendrite: a fossil tree.

dendrologia s. f. dendrology.

dendrológico adj. dendrologic(al), dendrologous.

dendrômetro s. m. dendrometer.

dendroquirotos s. m. pl. (zool.) Dendrochirota.

denegação s. f. (pl. -ões) 1. denial, refusal to grant, rejection (of a request). 2. contradiction, negation, contestation.

denegar v. 1. to deny, refuse. 2. to gainsay, contradict, refute. 3. to disown, abjure, disawow. 4. to hinder, impede, prevent.

denegrido adj. denigrated, blackened, tawny.

denegridor s. m. 1. denigrator. 2. defamer, slanderer. ‖ adj. (also denegrativo) 1. denigrating. 2. defamatory, slanderous.

denegrir v. (also denegrecer) 1. to denigrate, blacken. 2. to sully, stain, defile. 3. to defame, slander, calumniate.

~ com fumo to besmoke.

dengoso adj. (also dengueiro) 1. affected, finical, dainty. 2. vain, conceited. 3. effeminate, womanly. 4. whining. ‖ -amente adv. affectedly.

dengue (I) s. m. (also dengo) 1. primness, prudery. 2. coquetry, vanity. 3. affectation, finicalness. 4. whine, whining. ‖ adj. 1. affected, finical. 2. effeminate, womanly. 3. vain, conceited.

dengue (II) s. f. (med.) dengue, breakbone fever, dandy.

denguice s. f. 1. affectation, prudery. 2. coquetry. 3. womanly pride.

denigração s. f. (pl. -ões) 1. denigration. 2. defamation, detraction, calumny.

denodado adj. 1. bold, daring, courageous, dauntless. 2. impetuous, headlong, eager.

denodar v. to untwine, disentangle, untie, unwind.

denodo (ô) s. m. 1. boldness, bravery, courage. 2. impetuousness, eagerness.

denominação s. f. (pl. -ões) denomination: 1. denominating, naming. 2. designation, name. 3. a sect.

denominado adj. (Port.) so-called.
denominador s. m. denominator. ‖ adj. denominative. ~ **comum** (math.) common denominator.
denominar v. 1. to denominate, name, call, entitle, designate. 2. ~-**se** to be called, be named.
denominativo adj. denominative. ‖ -**mente** adv. denominatively.
denominável adj. m. + f. (pl. -**áveis**) denominable.
denotação s. f. (pl. -**ões**) 1. denotation, denotement. 2. sign, token.
denotador s. m. someone who or that which denotes. ‖ adj. denotative.
denotar v. 1. to show, indicate, point out, connote. 2. to signify, mean, symbolize.
densidade, densidão s. f. (pl. ~s, -**ões**) 1. density, thickness, compactness, closeness. 2. (stat.) density of population.
~ **dinâmica** (sociol.) dynamic density. ~ **do vapor** vapour density. ~ **de corrente,** ~ **elétrica** electric density, current density. ~ **magnética** magnetic density, flux density. ~ **volumétrica** volumetric density.
densifoliado adj. (bot.) densifoliate, set close together (of leaves).
densimetria s. f. densimetry.
densimétrico adj. densimetric.
densímetro s. m. densimeter.
denso adj. dense: 1. thick, compact. 2. close, tight. 3. (fig.) dark. ‖ -**amente** adv. densely.
tornar ~ to condense.
dentada s. f. 1. bite, biting. 2. wound made by biting. 3. morsel. 4. biting remark.
dentado adj. 1. toothed. 2. (bot.) dentate. 3. serrate, serrulate(d), cogged, indented.
roda -a cogwheel, toothed wheel.
dentadura s. f. 1. denture, set of teeth. 2. (mech.) rim of a gear wheel.
~ **frontal** (mech.) face cog.
dental (I) s. f. (pl. -**ais**) (phon.) dental consonant. ‖ adj. m. + f. dental, odontic.
dental (II) s. m. (pl. -**ais**) point of the ploughshare.
dentão s. m. (pl. -**ões**) 1. large tooth. 2. (ichth.) dentex.
dentar v. 1. to bite, snap. 2. to indent, engrail, notch.
dentária s. f. (bot.) dentaria, toothwort, coralwort, pepperwort.
dentário adj. dental.
dente s. m. 1. tooth. 2. fang, tusk. 3. (mech.) cog, gear tooth. 4. jag. 5. prong, tine (of a fork, etc.) (plate A 1).
~ **abalado** loose tooth. ~ **bicúspide** bicuspid, premolar tooth. ~ **de alho** clove of garlic. ~ **de coelho** (fig.) trick, scheme, cheat. ~ **canino** canine tooth, eyetooth, cuspid, cuspidate tooth, dog-tooth. ~ **de cremalheira** rack tooth. ~ **de engrenagem** gear tooth, cog, dent. ~ **de forcado ou de garfo** prong, tine. ~ **de leite** milk tooth. ~ **de serra** saw tooth (plates F 2, S 2). ~ **do siso** wisdom tooth. ~ **incisivo** incisor. ~ **molar** molar, cheek tooth, grinder. ~ **por** ~ a tooth for a tooth, tit for tat. ~ **pré-molar** premolar tooth, bicuspid. ~ **saliente** bucktooth. **armado até os** ~s armed to the teeth. **arrancar um** ~ to have a tooth pulled. **arreganhar os** ~s to bare the teeth. **dar com a língua nos** ~s to blab, to spill the beans. **obturar um** ~ to fill a tooth, to have a tooth filled. **ela defendeu-se com unhas e** ~s she fought tooth and nail. **ela sofreu de dor de** ~s she had the toothache. **ele mente com quantos** ~s **tem na boca** he lies in his throat. **ele mostrou os** ~s he showed his teeth, offered opposition. **escovar os** ~ to

clean one's teeth. **extração de** ~s teeth drawing. **nasceu-lhe o primeiro** ~ he cut his first tooth.
denteação s. f. (pl. -**ões**) 1. dentition. 2. indentation, denting.
denteado adj. 1. indented, jagged, notched, serrate(d). 2. (philately) perforated. 3. (bot., zool.) dentate (plate F 5).
dentear v. to indent, notch, engrail, jag.
dentebrum s. m. (bot.) male fern.
dente-de-leão s. m. (pl. **dentes-de-leão**) (bot.) dandelion.
dente-de-ovo s. m. (pl. **dentes-de-ovo**) (Braz.) egg tooth.
dentel s. m. (pl. -**éis**) (carp.) notch.
dentelária s. f. (bot.) toothwort, leadwort.
dente-seco s. m. (pl. **dentes-secos**) braggart, bully. ‖ adj. bragging.
dentição s. f. (pl. -**ões**) dentition, teething.
denticulado adj. denticulate(d), indented.
denticular v. to indent, notch, jag, tooth. ‖ adj. m.+f. denticular, denticulate, indented.
dentículo s. m. 1. dentice, a small tooth. 2. (archit.) dentil. 3. (Bot.) dentate leaf margin.
dentificação s. f. (pl. -**ões**) dentification.
dentiforme adj. m. + f. dentiform, tooth-shaped.
dentifrício s. m. dentifrice, tooth paste, tooth powder.
dentígero adj. dentigerous.
dentilha s. f. (ichth.) cuckoo wrasse.
dentilhão s. m. (pl. -**ões**) 1. large tooth. 2. (archit.) dentil.
dentina s. f. dentine, dentin, ivory.
dentirrostro adj. (zool.) dentirostral, dentirostrate.
dentista s. m. + f. (coll.) dentist, dental surgeon (plate D 1).
dentola s. f. 1. (coll.) large tooth. 2. bucktooth.
dentolas s. m. + f. person having large, ugly teeth.
dentre prep. 1. among(st), in the midst of. 2. from among.
dentro adv. inside, within, indoors.
~ **de alguns minutos** within a few minutes. ~ **de casa** indoors. ~ **de cinco milhas de circunferência** five miles about. ~ **de quinze dias** within a fortnight. ~ **de sua capacidade** within the compass of his powers. ~ **de um ano** in the course of a year. ~ **do espírito da lei** within the meaning of the law. ~ **em breve nos encontraremos** we shall meet soon. **a árvore estava oca por** ~ the tree was hollow inside. **aqui** ~ in here. **de** ~ from within. **lá** ~ in there. **para** ~ inwards, into. **pôr uma mão** ~ **da outra** to join hand to hand. **já para** ~! in with you!
dentuça s. f. buckteeth.
dentuço s. m. person having large teeth or buckteeth. ‖ adj. 1. big-toothed. 2. buck-toothed.
dentudo s. m. 1. person having large teeth. 2. (ichth.) tope. ‖ adj. big-toothed, large-toothed.
denudação s. f. (pl. -**ões**) denudation, divestment.
denudar v. 1. to denude, denudate, divest, lay bare. 2. ~-**se** to undress, unclothe, take off one's clothes.
denúncia, denunciação s. f. (pl. ~s, -**ões**) 1. denunciation: a) denouncement, accusation, delation. b) formal denouncing of a treaty. 2. exposure, exposition, revelation. 3. complaint. 4. (law) indictment.
denunciado s. m. defendant.
denunciador s. m., **denunciante** m. + f. denouncer, denunciator, delator, accuser, informer. ‖ adj. denouncing, denunciatory.
denunciar v. 1. to denounce, denunciate, accuse, inform against. 2. to betray, spill, split, squeal. 3. to reveal, expose, divulge, proclaim. 4. to give notice of termination (of a treaty, etc.) 5. (law) to indict. 6. to nominate, appoint. 7. to repute, deem, consider. 8. to come to light. 9. ~-**se** to reveal o. s. or itself.

Ð 1

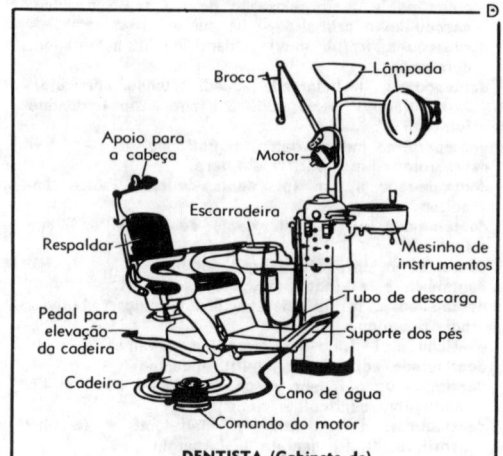

DENTISTA (Gabinete de)

Broca — Lâmpada
Apoio para a cabeça — Motor
Escarradeira
Respaldar
Mesinha de instrumentos
Tubo de descarga
Pedal para elevação da cadeira
Suporte dos pés
Cadeira
Cano de água
Comando do motor

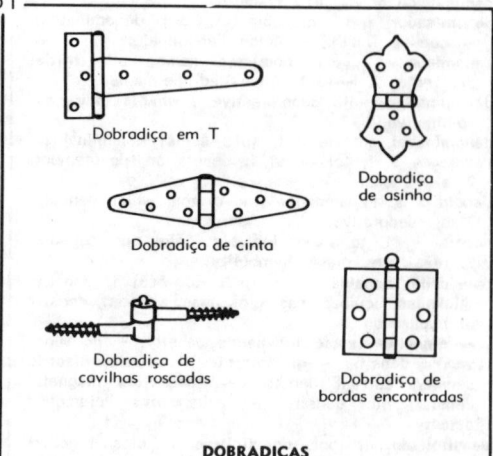

DOBRADIÇAS

Dobradiça em T
Dobradiça de asinha
Dobradiça de cinta
Dobradiça de cavilhas roscadas
Dobradiça de bordas encontradas

~ **alguém** to inform against s. o. **denunciamos o tratado** we denounced the treaty. **não me denuncie!** don't inform on me! **o cheiro denunciou sua presença** the smell denounced his presence.
denunciativo adj. denunciative.
denunciatório adj. denunciatory.
denunciável adj. m. + f. (pl. **-áveis**) denounceable.
deontologia s. f. deontology.
deontológico adj. deontological.
deparador s. m. finder, discoverer. ‖ adj. finding, discovering.
deparar v. 1. to cause to appear suddenly. 2. to find, fall in with, come upon. 3. to appear, present itself, turn up. 4. to offer, give. 5. to afford, provide, furnish. 6. to encounter, stumble upon, come across.
~ **com** to come across.
departamental adj. m. + f. (pl. **-ais**) departmental.
departamento s. m. department: 1. a territorial division. 2. a division or branch of governmental administration. 3. a division of a business concern.
~ **dos Correios e Telégrafos** Post Office Department. ~ **Técnico** Engineering Department.
departimento s. m. departure, separation, partition.
departir v. 1. to divide, distribute, apportion, impart. 2. to separate, sunder, sever. 3. to detail, particularize, report minutely. 4. to talk, converse. 5. to depart, quit, leave. 6. to turn aside from, deviate from.
depauperador adj. (also **depauperante**) 1. depauperating, impoverishing, pauperizing. 2. enfeebling, debilitating, weakening.
depauperamento s. m. (also **depauperação**) 1. depauperation, impoverishment. 2. enervation, weakening.
depauperar v. 1. to depauperate, impoverish, pauperize. 2. to enfeeble, enervate, weaken, deplete.
depenado adj. 1. plucked, deplumed. 2. (coll.) penniless, flat broke.
depenador s. m. 1. plucker. 2. one who deprives another of money by cunning.
depenar v. 1. to pluck, deplume, pick. 2. (fig.) to fleece, skin, strip of money. 3. ~-**se** to molt, moult.
dependência s. f. 1. dependence, subjection. 2. pendency. 3. subordination. 4. dependency. 5. accessories, appurtenances. 6. (Braz.) annex, outbuilding, outhouse. 7. (Braz.) room, apartment, chamber. 8. contingency.

dependente s. m. + f. dependent. ‖ adj. m. + f. 1. dependent, subject. 2. be conditioned on, be based on. 3. to be pending.
~ **escolar** (school) a repeat, a repeater.
depender v. 1. to depend on, be continent on. 2. to be conditioned on, be based on. 3. to be pending, hang in suspense. 4. to depend on or upon, trust, rely. 5. to be subject to. 6. to be subordinate to. 7. to be dependent on or upon.
depende de sua aprovação it is subject to your approval. ~ **de alguém** to depend on s. o., lie on or upon s. o. ~ **de si mesmo** to be thrown upon o. s. **ela não depende de ninguém** she is independent. **ele dependeu de sua própria habilidade** he was thrown back upon his own ability. **estamos dependendo do tempo** we are tied to time. **isso depende das circunstâncias** that depends upon circumstances. **depende inteiramente de você** it all depends upon you.
dependura s. f. hanging, hangings; that which is hung.
estar na ~ to be in a bad plight.
dependurado s. m. (Braz.) naked mountain flank. ‖ adj. 1. suspended, hanging, dangling. 2. (Braz.) dulled, saddened (eyes).
dependurar v. = **pendurar**.
depenicar v. 1. to pull at, pluck at (esp. with the mouth or with the fingers). 2. to preen. 3. to nibble at.
deperecer v. to fade away, decline, droop, pine away.
deperecimento s. m. drooping, languishment.
depilação s. f. (pl. **-ões**) depilation.
depilar v. to depilate, divert of hair.
depilatório s. m. depilatory. ‖ adj. depilatory.
depleção s. f. (pl. **-ões**) (med.) depletion.
depletivo adj. depletive, depletory.
deploração s. f. (pl. **-ões**) deploration, lamentation, wail.
deplorador s. m. deplorer.
deplorar v. 1. to deplore, lament, bewail, bemoan. 2. to rue, regret.
deplorativo adj. 1. deploring, lamenting. 2. pitiful, lamentable.
deploratório adj. deploring, lamenting.
deplorável adj. m. + f. (pl. **-áveis**) 1. deplorable, lamentable. 2. detestable, abominable. 3. pitiable, pitiful. ‖ **deploravelmente** adv. deplorably, detestably.

ele se encontrava em estado ~ he was in a deplorable plight.

deplumar v. = **depenar.**

depoente s. m. + f. deponent, affiant. ‖ adj. (gram.) deponent.

depoimento s. m. 1. deposition, affidavit, testimony. 2. declaration, statement.

prestar ~ to bear testimony.

depois adv. 1. after, afterward(s), later on, subsequently, then. 2. besides, moreover. ~ **de** behind, following. ~ **de amanhã** the day after tomorrow. ~ **de anoitecer** after dark. ~ **disso** thereafter. ~ **e não antes** then and not till then. ~ **que** after, subsequent to. **seis meses** ~ six months later.

depolarização s. f. (pl. **-ões**) (phys.) depolarization.

depolarizar v. (phys.) fo depolarize.

depopular v. = **despovoar.**

depor v. 1. to put down, lay down, set aside. 2. to depose, divest or deprive of office, discharge, dethrone. 3. to put aside. 4. to testify, witness, depone, bear witness. 5. to abdicate, renounce, resign. 6. to lay down (arms), surrender. 7. to entrust, commit to. 8. to deposit. 9. to give evidence of. ~ **contra o acusado** to testify against the defendant.

deportação s. f. (pl. **-ões**) deportation, banishment, expatriation.

deportado s. m. deportee, transport. ‖ adj. deported, banished, exiled.

deportar v. to deport, transport, banish, exile, expatriate.

deposição s. f. (pl. **-ões**) deposition: 1. putting down, laying aside. 2. displacement, deposal, dismissal. 3. testimony, evidence, statement.

depositador s. m. depositor.

depositante s. m. + f. 1. depositor. 2. consignor, consigner. ‖ adj. depositing.

depositar v. 1. to deposit, commit to for custody, entrust, lodge with for safekeeping. 2. to lay down, set down. 3. to trust, rely upon. 4. to bin. 5. ~**-se** to settle, be precipitated, sink to the bottom. ~ **em banco** to bank. **ele depositou confiança nela** he placed confidence in her. **ele depositou seu dinheiro** he took his money to the bank.

depositário s. m. 1. depositary, depository. 2. trustee. 3. (fig.) confidant.

depósito s. m. deposit: 1. act of depositing, deposition. 2. that which is deposited, esp. money lodged with a bank. 3. pledge, security. 4. depot, depository, store, storehouse, warehouse, storage yard, reservoir, tank (plate A 7). 5. matter precipitated from a solution; sediment, fur, dregs. 6. (geol., mining) natural occurrence of mineral material. ~ **aluvial** (geol.) warp. ~ **de armas e munições** armoury, arsenal. ~ **de bagagem** baggage room, luggage room, left luggage deposit (plate E 13). ~ **de carvão** coal depot, coal dump (plate E 12). ~ **de móveis** pantechnicon. **ele deixou um** ~ **de 5.000 cruzeiros** he left a deposit of 5,000 cruzeiros. **em** ~ on hand, in stock.

depravação s. f. (pl. **-ões**) depravation, depravity, corruption, perversion, degeneracy.

depravado adj. depraved, corrupt, wicked, vicious, degenerate. ‖ **-amente** adv. depravedly.

depravador s. m. depraver, corrupter, defiler. ‖ adj. depraving, corrupting.

depravar v. 1. to deprave, corrupt, pervert, vitiate. 2. to forge, falsify, counterfeit. 3. ~**-se** to degenerate, become depraved.

deprecação s. f. (pl. **-ões**) plea, prayer, entreaty, request.

deprecada s. f. (jur.) requisition.

deprecado adj. (jur.) designative of a judge to whom a requisition has been made.

deprecante s. m. + f. deprecator, petitioner. ‖ adj. deprecating, entreating.

deprecar v. 1. to supplicate, beseech, entreat. 2. to invoke.

deprecativo, deprecatório adj. beseeching, supplicating, entreating.

depreciação s. f. (pl. **-ões**) 1. depreciation. 2. (fig.) disparagement, detraction.

depreciador s. m. depreciator, disparager, decrier. ‖ adj. depreciating, depreciant, depreciative.

depreciar v. to depreciate: 1. lessen in price or estimated value, lower the worth of. 2. disparage, undervalue, belittle.

depreciativo adj. depreciative, depreciatory. ‖ **-amente** adv. depreciatively.

depreciável adj. m. + f. (pl. **-áveis**) depreciable.

depredação s. f. (pl. **-ões**) depredation, brigandage, pillage, plunder.

depredar v. to depredate, despoil, lay waste, prey upon, plunder.

depredatório adj. depredatory, plundering, predatory, pillaging.

depreender v. to infer, gather, deduce, conclude.

depressa adv. 1. fast, quickly, swiftly, readily, speedily. 2. hurriedly, hastily. ~**!** hurry up, make haste!

depressão s. f. (pl. **-ões**) depression: 1. act of depressing, lowering, sinking. 2. hollow, cavity, pit. 3. stagnation or reduction in business, stringency. 4. (fig.) dejection, despondency, low-spiritedness, doldrums, the dumps, the blues.

depressivo adj. depressive, depressing. ‖ **-amente** adv. depressively.

depresso adj. depressed: 1. dejected, low-spirited, dispirited. 2. lowered, sunk. 3. (bot.) vertically flattened.

depressor s. m. depressor. ‖ adj. depressive, depressing.

deprimente adj. m. + f. 1. depressive, depressing. 2. debasing, degrading. ‖ ~**mente** adv. depressively.

deprimido adj. depressed, dejected, dispirited, downcast, low-spirited.

deprimir v. to depress: 1. lower, press down. 2. enfeeble, weaken, enervate. 3. disparage, depreciate, debase. 4. deject, sadden, dispirit.

depuração s. f. (pl. **-ões**) depuration, purification, expurgation.

depurador s. m. depurator, purifier. ‖ adj. (also **depurante** m. + f.) depurant, purifying.

depurar v. 1. to depurate, purify, cleanse. 2. to purify o. s., cleanse o. s.

depurativo m. depurative. ‖ adj. depurative, purifying, cleansing.

deputação s. f. (pl. **-ões**) deputation: 1. act of deputing or appointing. 2. delegation.

deputado s. m. deputy: 1. representative, delegate, commissioner. 2. a member of the House of Deputies, congressman, assemblyman, burgess.

deputar v. 1. to depute, delegate, commission. 2. to assign, destinate, consign.

deque s. m. deck.

dequitação (pl. **-ões**), **dequitadura** s. f. (med.) = **delivramento.**

dequitar-se v. (med.) to expel the afterbirth.

deriva s. f. 1. (naut.) drift, leeway. 2. (mil.) deflection. 3. (aeron.) drift angle.
andar à ~ to drift, float along.

derivação s. f. (pl. **-ões**) 1. derivation. 2. deviation, shift, drift. 3. (fig.) origin, source. 4. (mech.) tap (ping), branch. 5. (electr.) shunt.

derivada s. f. (math.) derivative.
derivado s. m. 1. (gram., mus.) derivative. 2. by-product. ‖ adj. derivative, secondary. **produto** ~ by-product.
derivante adj. m. + f. derivational.
derivar v. 1. to derive: a) turn the course of, deflect, cause to deviate. b) form from, create from. c) trace the origin or derivation of. d) deduce, gather, infer. 2. to originate from, arise from, issue, descend. 3. to run, flow. 4. to elapse, pass away, slip away (time). 5. to be carried away. 6. to spread, become dispersed. 7. (electr.) to branch off. 8. (naut.) to drift.
derivativo s. m. 1. (med.) derivative, revulsive. 2. (Braz.) diversion: an occupation, amusement or hobby intended to turn the mind away from sad thoughts, fixed ideas, etc. ‖ adj. (also **derivatório**) derivative, derivational. ‖ **-amente** adv. derivatively.
derivável adj. m. + f. (pl. **-áveis**) derivable.
derma s. m. (also **derme** anat., zool.) derma, dermis, cutis vera.
dermanissídeos s. m. pl. (zool.) Dermanyssidae.
dermatite s. f. (also **dermite**) (med.) dermatitis.
dermatogênio s. m. (bot.) dermatogen.
dermatóide adj. m. + f. dermatoid.
dermatologia s. f. dermatology.
dermatológico adj. dermatological.
dermatologista s. m. + f. dermatologist.
dermatose s. f. (med.) dermatosis.
dérmico adj. dermic.
dermóide adj. m. + f. dermoid, dermatoid.
dermópteros s. m. pl. (zool.) Dermoptera.
derrabado adj. bobtail(ed), docked.
derrabar v. 1. to bobtail, dock. 2. to cut the flap of a garment.
derradeiras s. f. pl. (Braz.) afterbirth.
derradeiro adj. 1. last, hindmost. 2. final, conclusive, ultimate. ‖ **-amente** adv. lastly.
derrama (I) s. f. lopping, pruning (of branches).
derrama (II) s. f. local tax assessed according to the income of each taxpayer.
derrama (III) s. f. (Braz.) = **derrame** (3).
derramador s. m. spiller, spreader. ‖ adj. spilling, spreading.
derramamento s. m. 1. lopping, pruning. 2. strewing, sprinkling. 3. shedding, effusion, diffusion. 4. spillage. 5. emanation, emission, discharge. 6. distribution, apportionment. 7. yielding, furnishing. 8. spreading, diffusion. 9. dissemination, propagation. 10. emanation, issuance. 11. dispersion, scattering. 12. hydrophobia, rabies.
derramar v. 1. to lop, prune. 2. to strew, sprinkle. 3. to shed, pour out, emit, effuse, diffuse. 4. to spill. 5. to exhale, give forth, discharge, emanate. 6. to distribute, deal out. 7. to issue, spread, diffuse. 8. to disseminate, propagate. 9. to cause to flow or fall from a cut or wound. 10. to disperse, drive asunder, scatter. 11. ~-se to become hydrophobic.
~ **lágrimas** to shed tears. ~ **sangue** to shed blood.
derrame s. m. 1. = **derramamento**. 2. (med.) liquid or gaseous accumulation inside a natural or accidental cavity. 3. (Braz.) long ridge of a hill.
derrancar (I) v. 1. to spoil, mar, deteriorate, turn rancid. 2. to corrupt, pervert, deprave. 3. to become deteriorated, to grow rancid. 4. to become perverted or depraved. 5. ~-se to become hydrophobic.
derrancar (II) v. (Braz.) to flee, run away.
derranco s. m. 1. spoilage, spoiling, deterioration. 2. corruption, perversion, depravation.
derrapagem s. f. (pl. **-ens**) (Braz.) skidding, sideslip.
derrapar v. (Braz.) to skid, sideslip.

derreado adj. bowed down, worn out, jaded.
derreamento s. m. exhaustion, prostration.
derrear v. 1. to bend down, stoop. 2. to wear out, exhaust. 3. to jade, sag. 4. to beat, thrash, drub. 5. to discredit, defame.
derredor adv. around, about.
derregar v. to dig drainage ditches.
derrelito adj. derelict, abandoned.
derrengado adj. 1. sway-backed. 2. (Braz.) affected, pretentious.
derrengar v. 1. to beat up. 2. to mince, behave in an affected manner. 3. to move the body with affected twists.
derrengue, derrengo s. m. (Braz.) affected twisting of the body.
derretedura s. f. melting, liquefaction.
derreter v. 1. to melt, liquefy, fuse, dissolve. 2. to soften, mollify, mellow. 3. to vex, torment, harass. 4. to waste, lavish, squander. 5. to melt away, break up, disappear. 6. to thaw. 7. to become softhearted, become tender.
derretido adj. 1. melted, molten, drawn (butter). 2. deeply in love.
derretimento s. m. 1. melting, liquefaction, fusion. 2. (fig.) affectation. 3. (fig.) tenderheartedness.
derribada s. f. (Braz.) = **derrubada**.
derribadinha s. f. (Braz.) clearing of a small tract of land with an axe or scythe.
derribamento s. m. 1. knocking down. 2. demolition, felling. 3. destruction, annihilation. 4. prostration. 5. overthrow, dismissal, discharge.
derribar v. 1. to throw down, knock down, strike down. 2. to pull down, demolish, fell. 3. to destroy, annihilate. 4. to enfeeble, enervate, prostrate. 5. to overthrow, to cause to fall or resign. 6. to discharge, dismiss, deprive of office. 7. ~-se to throw o. s. on the ground.
derriça s. f. 1. act of untangling, untwining. 2. derision, scoffing. 3. quarrel, row. 4. (pop.) flirtation. 5. (Braz.) stripping of coffee berries from the branches.
derriçador s. m. philanderer. ‖ adj. philandering.
derriçar v. 1. to untangle, disentangle, untwine. 2. to tug at, pull at (with the teeth), to tear. 3. to scoff at, banter, chaff. 4. to quarrel, wrangle. 5. (pop.) to flirt, philander, woo. 6. (Braz.) to strip coffee berries from the branches.
derriço s. m. 1. flirtation, dalliance, courtship. 2. sweetheart. 3. banter, scoff, mockery.
derrisão s. f. (pl. **-ões**) derision, scorn, mockery.
derriscar v. 1. to efface, blot out, cancel. 2. to exclude, eliminate.
derrisório adj. derisory, derisive. ‖ **derrisoriamente** adv. derisorily.
derrocada s. f. destruction, demolition, overthrow, ruin, debacle.
derrocado adj. demolished, overthrown, ruined.
derrocador s. m. demolisher, destroyer. ‖ adj. destructive, demolishing.
derrocar v. 1. to demolish, destroy, raze, ruin. 2. to overthrow, overturn. 3. to humble, abase, subdue. 4. to fall in, cave in.
derrogação s. f. (pl. **-ões**) (also **derrogamento** m.) derogation.
derrogador s. m. derogator, detractor.
derrogante adj. m. + f. derogative (to or of).
derrogar v. 1. to derogate, annul in part, repeal partly. 2. to produce essential alterations to. 3. to contain directions contrary to.
derrogatório adj. derogatory.
derrota (I) s. f. 1. defeat, rout, overthrow, discomfiture, foil. 2. barbarous thinning out (of trees). 3. ruin. 4. (Braz.) thing of little worth or bad quality.

derrota (II) s. f. 1. (naut.) course, route. 2. (astr.) orbit. 3. path, way. 4. voyage, journey.

derrotado adj. 1. defeated, routed, beaten. 2. (Braz.) downcast, dispirited, despondent. 3. (naut.) off course.

derrotador s. m. defeater. ‖ adj. defeating.

derrotar (I) v. 1. to defeat, rout, vanquish, foil, discomfit, overthrow. 2. to beat, outdo. 3. to exhaust, wear out, tire out.

derrotar (II) v. 1. (naut.) to be driven off course. 2. (naut.) to follow a given course. 3. to lose one's way.

derrotismo s. m. defeatism.

derrotista s. m. + f. defeatist. ‖ adj. defeatist.

derruba, derrubada s. f. (Braz., also **derrube** m.) 1. felling of trees (to clear the land for plantations). 2. wholesale dismissal of public servants when a new party or administration takes over.

derrubado adj. 1. demolished, felled, overthrown. 2. ruined.

derrubamento s. m. 1. overthrowal, overturning. 2. falling down, sinking to the ground (of animals). 3. exhaustion. prostration. 4. discharge from office.

derrubar v. 1. to throw down, throw to the ground; knock down. 2. to overthrow, overturn. 3. to demolish, pull down; overthrow. 4. to cut down (trees). 5. to shoot down (plane). 6. to dismiss, discharge (from a position).

derruído adj. thrown down; knocked down; destroyed.

derruimento s. m. 1. collapse. 2. foundering. 3. destruction. 4. throwing down, overthrow. 5. annulment.

derruir v. 1. to collapse. 2. to founder; sink in. 3. to destroy, knock down. 4. to annul.

dervixe, dervis s. m. (also **daroês**) dervis(e), derwish; fakir.

dês prep. = desde.

desabado s. m. slope, declivity, hillside, acclivity. ‖ adj. pulled down, turned down (the brim of a hat). **chapéu ~** slouch hat (a hat with a flexible brim).

desabafado adj. 1. uncovered, unsheltered. 2. unreserved, unrestricted, frank. 3. tranquil, calm, quiet. ‖ **-amente** adv. frankly, tranquilly.

desabafar v. 1. to uncover, expose to the air. 2. to open, reveal, disclose. 3. to breathe freely. 4. to free, rid, disencumber, clear. 5. to vent, give vent to. 6. to relieve from. 7. **~-se:** a) to uncover o. s. b) to open or disclose one's heart to.
~(-se) com um amigo to discover one's heart to a friend. **~ a sua cólera** to breathe out one's anger. **~-se da roupa** to pull the heavy clothes off and dress light ones. **ela se desabafou** she poured out her heart.

desabafo s. m. (also **desabafamento**) 1. ease, relief, alleviation, disencumbering. 2. expansiveness, opening of one's heart.

desabalado adj. (pop.) 1. enormous, immense, vast, huge, unmeasurable. 2. precipitate, overhasty, hurried, rash, abrupt, headlong. ‖ **-amente** adv. enormously; precipitately.

desabalroamento s. m. separation of two ships that have collided.

desabalroar v. to separate two ships that have collided.

desabamento s. m. 1. pulling down (the brim of a hat), turning down. 2. crumbling, falling, tumbling. 3. collapse.

desabar v. 1. to pull down, turn down (the brim of a hat). 2. to crumble, fall down, tumble. 3. **~-se** to prostrate; collapse.

desabe s. m. crumbling, tumbling, falling down; crumbled part of a wall or building.

desabelhar v. to disband, disperse, put to flight (as a swarm of bees).

desabilidade s. f. lack of ability or competence; unskillfulness, incapacity.

desabilitar v. to incapacitate, disable, render unfit; disqualify.

desabitado adj. uninhabited, unoccupied, empty; deserted, waste, secluded; solitary.

desabitar v. 1. to quit, abandon (a house). 2. to depopulate, deprive of inhabitants, dispeople.

desábito s. m. want of habit or practice.

desabituação s. f. (pl. **-ões**) break of a habit, disaccustoming, dishabituating, disuse.

desabituar v. 1. to dishabituate, disaccustom, break off a habit, free from a habit; wean. 2. **~-se** to give up, leave off.
~ de to cure of a habit. **~-se de fumar** to wean from smoking.

desabocar v. (Braz.) to talk nonsense, go wrong.

desaboçar v. (naut.) to take off the stoppers.

desabonado adj. 1. without sponsor or bondsman, discredited, disreputed, ill-reputed. 2. penniless, destitute.

desabonador s. m. depreciator, person who destroys the credit of; scaremonger. ‖ adj. discrediting, bringing into discredit, disgracing.

desabonar v. 1. to discredit, disbelieve, destroy the credit, bring into discredit. 2. **~-se** to lose one's credit, reputation, good name or prestige.

desabonatório adj. discreditable, disgraceful, disreputable.

desabono s. m. discredit, disrepute; prejudice, disesteem, harm, damage.
falar em ~ de alguém to speak ill of s. o.

desabordar v. to detach a grappled ship; disengage, separate a ship from another, ungrapple.

desabotinado adj. (S. Braz.) insane, delirious; crack-brained, senseless, reasonless, crazy.

desabotoadura s. f., **desabotoamento** m. unbuttoning.
~ das flores the blowing of flowers.

desabotoar v. 1. to unbutton, lose the buttons (of). 2. (bot.) to open, spread, blow (as flowers). 3. **~-se** to open one's heart, loosen one's tongue.
~ o vestido to unbutton the dress.

desabraçar v. 1. to unclasp, release from an embrace. 2. **~-se** to disengage from one's arms.

desabrido adj. 1. rude, insolent, disrespectful, haughty. 2. harsh, severe, rigorous, untractable, unfriendly. 3. violent, sharp, rugged.
um homem ~ an ill-tempered man. **inverno ~** sharp winter. **linguagem -a** unrestrained language. **maneiras -as** rough manners. **uma resposta -a** a sharp answer.

desabrigado adj. 1. unsheltered, unprotected, uncovered. 2. exposed, open. 3. abandoned, forsaken. 4. harsh. ‖ **-amente** adv. openly.

desabrigar v. 1. to uncover, unshelter, strip of. 2. to abandon, give up, cast off. 3. **~-se** to leave the shelter, expose o. s. to wind and air.

desabrigo s. m. 1. want of a shelter or roof. 2. lack of protection, forlornness; distress; defenselessness.

desabrimento s. m. 1. rudeness, insipidity, sharpness, bitterness, harshness, roughness. 2. severity of weather.
~ das palavras bitterness of words. **falar com ~** to inveigh bitterly against, utter severe denunciations.

desabrir v. 1. to abandon, desist, leave off, give up. 2. **~-se** to become irritable; fall out or be disgusted with s. o.

desabrochado adj. 1. unclasped, loose, disconnected. detached, not fastened; open; free. 2. blooming, sprouting.

desabrochamento s. m. (also **desabrocho**) unclasping, loosening; blooming, opening (as a flower); sprouting.

desabrochar v. 1. to unclasp, loosen, free, unbutton, unfasten. 2. to blow, bloom, open (flower); sprout. 3. ~-se to free o. s., get loose.

desabrolhar v. to bloom, blossom, flower, unfold; burgeon, sprout.

desabusado adj. 1. unprejudiced; impartial. 2. impudent, bold-faced, impertinent, intrepid. 3. improper, incorrect, inaccurate.

desabusar v. 1. to disabuse, undeceive, set right. 2. to disillusion, disenchant. 3. ~-se: a) to be undeceived. b) to lose one's illusions.

desabuso s. m. 1. disabusing, undeceiving. 2. disillusionment, disenchantment.

desaçaimar, desaçamar v. to unmuzzle, remove the muzzle.

desacampar v. to break or strike camp.

desacanhado adj. 1. bold, daring, audacious. 2. self-assured, self-reliant, complacent. || **-amente** adv. boldly.

desacanhar v. 1. to embolden, encourage. 2. ~-se to cast off timidity, lose shyness; behave with ease.

desacasalar v. to separate (animals which have been joined for breeding).

desacatamento s. m. disrespect, disregard, discourtesy; incivility; insolence; profanation.

desacatar v. 1. to disrespect, disregard, slight, neglect. 2. to affront, insult. 3. to profane, desecrate. 4. to vex, annoy, trouble. 5. (Braz., sl.) to gape at or comment with disrespect (e. g. a woman).

desacato s. m. 1. disrespect, disregard, discourtesy. 2. profanation, desecration. 3. (Braz., sl.): a) gaping at discourteously; gazing at with disrespect (especially at a woman). b) showy, elegant woman.

desacaudilhado adj. without a chief, in disorder, abandoned.

desacautelado adj. 1. careless, heedless, negligent, incautious. 2. improvident, inconsiderate, thriftless. || **-amente** adv. carelessly.

desacautelar v. 1. to be careless. 2. ~-se: a) to want providence or prudence. b) to be heedless or incautious. c) to be off one's guard.

desacavalar v. to separate, remove (superposed things).

desaceitar v. to decline, reject, refuse.

desaceleração s. f. (pl. **-ões**) deceleration.

desacelerar v. to decelerate, decrease speed, retard.

desacentuar v. to take the accents away; simplify.

desacerbar v. 1. to take the bitterness, soften. 2. to temper, mitigate.

desacertado adj. 1. imprudent, unwise, unconsiderate, injudicious. 2. mistaken, wrong. || **-amente** adv. imprudently, astray.

desacertar v. 1. to bungle, botch. 2. to mistake, miss, err. 3. to take wrong measures, act imprudently. 4. ~-se to fail, miscarry; be disappointed.
~ **o passo** to break step.

desacerto (ê) s. m. mistake, error, fault, oversight, blunder; nonsense.

desachegar v. 1. to separate, divide, part, disunite, disapproach. 2. ~-se to go away, retire; part or withdraw from.

desacidificação s. f. (pl. **-ões**) desacidification.

desacidificar v. to desacidify, neutralize or destroy the acidity.

desaclimação s. f. (pl. **-ões**) fact of unacclimatizing.

desaclimar, desaclimatar v. to unacclimatize.

desacobardar v. (also **desacovardar**) 1. to embolden, encourage. 2. to animate, hearten, inspire. 3. ~-se to grow bold, become courageous.

desacochar v. (Braz.) to come down a peg or two, eat humble pie; be at one's wits end.

desacoimar v. 1. to discharge of a fine. 2. to rehabilitate, re-establish, restore, reinstate.

desacoitado adj. shelterless; defenceless, unprotected.

desacoitar v. (also **desacoutar**) 1. to rouse, drive up, frighten up (game). 2. to dislodge.

desacolchetar v. 1. to unhook, unfasten a hook. 2. to unbutton, unclasp, unloose.

desacolher v. 1. to receive unfriendly. 2. to refuse hospitality.

desacolherar v. to unpen (animals).

desacolhimento s. m. unfriendly reception; a turning away from the door.

desacomodado adj. displaced, dislodged; disturbed, disarranged, disordered.

desacomodar v. 1. to displace, dislodge. 2. to discommode, disorder, disturb, disarrange. 3. to dismiss. 4. ~-se to lose one's employment.

desacompanhado adj. unaccompanied, alone, lonely, solitary; isolated, single.

desacompanhar v. 1. to abandon, leave alone, forsake. 2. not to agree with, not to suit.

desaconchegar v. to discomfort, disturb the comfort.

desaconselhado adj. 1. inconsiderate. 2. ill-advised. 3. dissuaded.

desaconselhar v. to dissuade, exhort against, advise to the contrary, persuade not to do s. th.

desaconselhável adj. m. + f. (pl. **-áveis**) inadvisable, inexpedient.

desacorçoar v. = **descoroçoar**.

desacordado adj. unconscious, not aware, senseless.

desacordante adj. m. + f. differing, in disagreement.

desacordar v. 1. to disaccord, disagree, dissent, differ. 2. to disunite, set a variance; untune; discompose, disarrange. 3. to lose one's sense, become unconscious; forget. 4. to contradict, quarrel.

desacorde adj. m. + f. 1. discordant, disagreeing. 2. dissonant, inharmonious.

desacordo (ô) s. m. 1. disagreement, disaccord, discord, dissension, divergency, difference, disharmony. 2. disunion, contrariety, variance; conflict, quarrel. 3. loss of consciousness, swoon, faint.
estar em ~ to be at variance.

desacoroçoado adj., **desacoroçoar** v. = **descoroçoado, descoroçoar**.

desacorrentamento s. m. unchaining, unleashing, unfettering, loosening.

desacorrentar v. to unchain; unleash, unfetter, untie; free, unfasten, loosen.

desacostumado adj. unaccustomed, unusual, disused, uncommon, not habitual; strange. || **-amente** adv. unusually.

desacostumar v. 1. to disaccustom, wean, disuse, dishabituate. 2. ~-se to break o. s. of a habit, get out of a habit, doff, leave off.
~ **uma criança dos maus hábitos** to break a child of his tricks. ~-se **de fumar** to leave off smoking.

desacreditado adj. discredited, disreputable, disesteemed; notorious.

desacreditador s. m. disgracer, slanderer, defamer. || adj. discrediting, disgracing, slanderous.

desacreditar v. 1. to discredit, disparage, slander, defame, derogate, disgrace, decry. 2. ~-se to lose one's credit, reputation, prestige.
~ **alguém** to bring s. o. in discredit.

desacumular v. to unplie, unstack.

desacunhar v. (naut.) to unwedge, take off the wedges.

desadmoestar v. = **desaconselhar**.

desadoração s. f. (pl. **-ões**) detestation, abhorrence, hate; antipathy, distaste, repugnancy.

desadorado adj. (Braz.) indisposed; annoyed; upset, impertinent, impish.

desadorador s. m. person who detests, hates, distates. || adj. detesting, hating, hateful.

desadorar (I) v. 1. to detest, hate, dislike, despise. 2. to cease worship, disapprove. ~ **com impaciência** to be impatient. **fazer** ~ to anger.

desadorar (II) v. (N. Braz.) 1. to suffer pain. 2. to importune, annoy, incommode. 3. ~-**se** to become indignant, get angry.

desadormecer v. 1. to awake, wake up, rouse from sleep. 2. to reanimate, vivify. 3. to quicken (limbs).

desadornado adj. unadorned, unornamented, uncoloured, disgarnished; simple, single.

desadornar v. to disadorn, disgarnish, strip the ornaments, disembellish.

desadorno (ô) s. m. 1. want of ornaments, grace or elegance; simplicity. 2. untidiness, unkemptness.

desadoro (ô) s. m. (Braz.) 1. suffering, great pain. 2. annoyance, vexation. 3. insolence. 4. large quantity.

desadunado adj. (bot.) distinct, separate, disconnected.

desadvertido adj. inadvertent, unaware, thoughtless; bird-witted. || -**amente** adv. inadvertently.

desafabilidade s. f. want of affability; arrogance, haughtiness, pride.

desafaimar v. 1. to appease hunger, feed the hungry; satiate, saturate. 2. (fig.) to satisfy.

desafamar v. to defame, discredit, disgrace, slander.

desafastar v. to remove, weep away, dismiss.

desafável adj. m. + f. (pl. -**áveis**) uncourteous, rough, impolite, rude. || **desafavelmente** adv. uncourteously.

desafazer v. 1. to disaccustom, dishabituate, wean. 2. ~-**se** to break o. s. of a habit.

desafear v. to take away the ugliness; embellish.

desafeição s. f. (pl. -**ões**) disaffection, dislike, aversion, antipathy.

desafeiçoado adj. disaffected, estranged, disloyal; inimical, unfriendly, contrary, adverse. || -**amente** adv. disaffectedly.

desafeiçoar (I) v. 1. to disfigure, deform, disfeature. 2. ~-**se** to change colour, turn pale, pallid.

desafeiçoar (II) v. 1. to disaffect, dislike, detest, distaste, estrange. 2. ~-**se** to become disaffected; lose one's affection.

desafeitar v. = **desenfeitar**.

desafeito adj. unaccustomed, uncommon, unusual, not habitual, strange.

desaferrar v. 1. to unhook, loosen from a hook. 2. to loosen, unfasten, untie, free. 3. to dissuade, exhort against, advise to the contrary. 4. (naut.) to weigh anchor. 5. ~-**se** to free o. s. of, get rid of, let go.

desaferrolhar v. 1. to unbolt, unlock, unbar; open. 2. to set free, release. 3. ~-**se** to get loose, come untied, unlocked or free.
~ **grilhões** to unshackle.

desafervorar v. to cool the fervour, moderate the force.

desafetação s. f. (pl. -**ões**) unaffectedness, frankness, naturalness, simplicity; sincerity.

desafetado adj. unaffected, simple, frank, natural, sincere, genuine. || -**amente** adv. unaffectedly.

desafeto s. m. 1. disaffection, alienation, disloyalty. 2. (Braz.) adversary, opponent, enemy, foe, rival. || adj. disaffected, disloyal.

desafiado adj. 1. blunt, edgeless, dull. 2. challenged, provoked, incited.

desafiador s. m., **desafiante** m. + f. challenger; provoker, defier, darer. || adj. defiant, challenging, defying, provoking, inciting.

desafiar v. 1. to challenge, defy, provoke, dare, beard, brave, tempt. 2. to invite (to a match or game). 3. to incite. 4. to blunt, dull.

~ **para um duelo** to challenge or summon to a duel. ~ **para um jogo** to invite to a game.

desafinação s. f. (pl. -**ões**) (also **desafinamento** m.) (mus.) discord, disharmony, dissonance.

desafinado adj. dissonant, inharmonious, out of tune, jarring, tuneless; faise. || -**amente** adv. dissonantly. **o piano está** ~ the piano is out of tune.

desafinar v. 1. to untune, discord, sing or play out of tune. 2. ~-**se** to get out of tune; get angry.

desafio s. m. 1. challenge, defiance, provocation, defy; contest, competition. 2. (Braz.) a musical competition between two popular singers.
aceitar um ~ to pick up the gauntlet, take up the glove. **cartel de** ~ cartel, challenge to a duel, letter of defiance. **entrar em** ~ **com a morte** to defy death.

desafivelar v. to unbuckle, detach the buckle, unclasp, unfasten.

desafixar v. to unfix, detach, loosen, unfasten.

desafogado adj. 1. relieved, easy, free from cares. 2. frank, free. 3. open, clear, unencumbered, ample, spacious. || -**amente** adv. freely, easily.

desafogar v. 1. to disencumber, relieve, ease. 2. to vent, wreak. 3. to unbosom, disclose, disburden. 4. ~-**se** to relieve o. s., set o. s. at ease, make o. s. comfortable; make a clean breast of.
~ **a sua cólera** to give vent to one's anger. ~ **o coração** to ease, unburden one's heart. ~ **com alguém o seu sentimento** to communicate one's trouble to another, unbosom o. s. ~-**se em lágrimas** to relieve one's distress by weeping.

desafogo (ô) s. m. 1. ease, relief, disencumbering, vent. 2. respite, relaxation, diversion, recreation. 3. abundance, wealth. 4. space.
viver com ~ to live at ease.

desafoguear v. 1. to cool, refresh. 2. soften.

desaforado adj. 1. insolent, impertinent. 2. rude, abusive, shameless, saucy, impudent. || -**amente** adv. insolently.

desaforama s. f. (S. Braz.) a lot of insults or dirty words.

desaforar v. 1. to exempt from ground-rent, free from rent payment. 2. to deprive of a privilege, encroach on one's rights, disfranchise. 3. to renounce a right or privilege. 4. ~-**se** to become insolent, impudent or abusive.

desaforo (ô) s. m. 1. insolence, impudence, impertinence. 2. insult, injury, affront, effrontery, sauciness, outrage. 3. shamelessness, abusiveness, brazenness. **que** ~! what a cheek!

desafortunado adj. luckless, unlucky, unhappy, unfortunate, sad, wretched. || -**amente** adv. unhappily.

desafreguesar v. 1. to take away the customers, make a shop lose its customers. 2. ~-**se** to cease to be a customer, discontinue to patronize.

desafronta s. f. 1. revenge, retaliation, requital. 2. redress, amends.

desafrontado adj. 1. revenged, retaliated. 2. redressed, repaid. 3. eased, free.

desafrontador s. m. revenger, redresser. || adj. revengeful, retaliatory, vindictive.

desafrontar v. 1. to revenge, avenge, retaliate, vindicate. 2. to requite, repay. 3. to free, ease, relieve. 4. ~-**se** to take vengeance.

desagaloar v. to take away the gold braid; degrade.

desagarrar v. 1. to detach, unfix, unloosen. 2. to extirpate, eradicate. 3. to relax.

desagasalhado adj. 1. unsheltered, unhoused, roofless, homeless. 2. uncovered; dressed lightly or insufficiently.

desagasalhar v. 1. to unshelter, unhouse, deprive of shelter or home. 2. to uncover, dress insufficiently.

3. ~-se: a) to take off the warmer clothes. b) to quit one's lodgement.

desagasalho s. m. 1. want of lodgement, house or home. 2. bad reception, lack of welcome. 3. want of clothes; light or inadequate clothing.

desagastamento s. m. freedom from passions, calmness, tranquility, appeasement.

desagastar v. 1. to appease, calm, pacify, quiet, soothe. 2. ~-se to grow calm, cool down; cheer up.

deságio s. m. (econ.) loss of the agio.

desaglomerar v. to unpile, unstack; separate, part (what was agglomerated).

desagradado adj. discontent, disgusted, displeased, dissatisfied, disliked.

desagradar v. 1. to discontent, disgust, displease, dissatisfy, dislike. 2. ~-se to become disgusted with.

a coisa que mais me desagrada the thing I dislike most. **isso me desagrada** I don't like that.

desagradável adj. m. + f. (pl. **-áveis**) 1. disagreeable, unpleasant, displeasing; awkward, bad, abominable, unpalatable. 2. nasty, troublesome. 3. rash, rough. 4. joyless; offensive. || **desagradavelmente** adv. disagreeably.

dizer coisas -áveis to say rude things. **tempo ~** bad weather.

desagradecer v. to fail to thank, be ungrateful.

desagradecido adj. ungrateful, thankless, unthankful. || **-amente** adv. ungratefully.

desagradecimento s. m. ingratitude, unthankfulness, thanklessness.

desagrado s. m. unpleasantness, distaste, displeasure, dislike, discontent; disfavour, disapproval, antipathy, disagreeableness.

cair no ~ to lose a person's favour, be disgraced, be in someone's black books.

desagravador s. m. revenger, redresser, amender. || adj. revengeful, redressing, vindictive, amendatory.

desagravar v. 1. to right, redress, give satisfaction, amend. 2. to avenge, revenge, vindicate. 3. to soften, soothe, ease, allay. 4. to reverse a sentence of a court. 5. ~-se to avenge o. s., take vengeance.

desagravo s. m. 1. revenge, retaliation, requital, redress; amends, satisfaction, reparation. 2. sentence by which the judgement of an inferior court is reversed.

desagregação s. f. (pl. **-ões**) disaggregation, dissolution, dissociation, disintegration; separation, disuniting.

desagregante adj. m. + f. disaggregating, dissolving, disintegrating.

desagregar v. 1. to disaggregate, dissolve, disintegrate; shatter; disincorporate, disunite, separate, dispense. 2. ~-se to crumble, decompose.

desagregável adj. m. + f. (pl. **-áveis**) disintegrable, separable.

desagrilhoar v. to unbolt, unlock, unbar; set free.

desaguadouro s. m. (also **desaguadoiro**) ditch, drain, gutter, outlet.

desaguamento s. m. draining, drainage; effluence.

desaguar v. 1. to drain, dry. 2. (also ~-se) to disembogue, flow into, disgorge, discharge. 3. (Braz.) to urinate.

~ uma mina to bail out the water from a mine.

desaguaxado adj. (S. Braz.) trained, exercised (a horse which was put at rest for a long time).

desaguaxar v. (S. Braz.) to train, exercise (horse).

desaguisado s. m. dispute, disagreement, quarrel, conflict, wrangle, squabble.

desainado adj. thinning, emaciated, skinny.

desairar v. 1. to render inelegant, disfigure, uglify, deprive of grace. 2. ~-se to become graceless, ugly or inelegant.

desaire s. m. 1. inelegance, want of grace or distinction. 2. gaucherie, awkwardness, impoliteness. 3. blemish, stain. 4. unseemliness, impropriety.

desairoso adj. 1. inelegant, graceless, ungraceful. 2. awkward, unhandsome, unbecoming. 3. embarrassing, inconvenient, dowdy, improper. || **-amente** adv. inelegantly.

desajeitado adj. 1. unskillful, awkward, clumsy. 2. maladroit, gauche, fumbling, left-handed, uncouth, thumby, dowdy. 3. stupid, rough, coarse, boorish. || **-amente** adv. unskillfully.

desajeitamento s. m. unskillfulness, awkwardness, clumsiness, dowdiness, floppiness, gaucherie, maladroitness.

desajeitar v. to disfigure, disarrange, deform, turn awkward.

desajoujar v. 1. to unyoke, unleash, unharness. 2. to loosen, unfasten, untie, set free.

desajudado adj. unhelped, unaided, unassisted; helpless, poor.

desajudar v. to refuse help, fail to aid, disoblige; hinder or forbear assistance.

desajuizado s. m. harum-scarum. || adj. witless, unwise, injudicious, thoughtless, senseless, foolish. || **-amente** adv. injudiciously.

desajuizar v. to deprive of one's wits, render foolish; fluster.

desajuntar v. 1. to disjoin, disunite. 2. to detach, disconnect, separate, uncouple.

desajustamento s. m. 1. disagreement. 2. inadaptation, unsuitableness.

desajustar v. 1. to disagree, break an agreement, disadjust. 2. to disarrange, disturb. 3. to disunite, separate, disconnect, discompose.

desajuste s. m. disagreement, breaking of a contract or an agreement.

desalagar v. 1. to drain, dry. 2. (naut.) to set afloat. 3. to free of, disentangle.

desalastrar v. 1. to diminish the ballast, unburden. 2. to unballast, take the ballast off.

desalbardar v. to take off the packsaddle, unsaddle.

desalegre adj. m. + f. joyless, melancholic, sad; unhappy, wretched. || **~mente** adv. melancholically.

desaleitar v. to wean.

desalentado adj. discouraged, depressed, dejected, downhearted, forsaken, dispirited, exanimate, weary, fatigued. || **-amente** adv. without courage.

desalentador s. m. discourager. || adj. discouraging, dejecting, depressing.

desalentar v. 1. to dishearten, discourage, depress; deter. 2. ~-se to lose courage, be discouraged.

desalento s. m. 1. discouragement, disheartenment, faintness, timorousness, dispiritedness. 2. dejection, seediness, prostration, dismay; despondency.

desalforjar v. to take s. th. off the saddlebag, unpack; empty.

desalgemar v. to lose from shackles, unshackle, unfetter; set free.

desalhear v. 1. to alienate, estrange. 2. to dissipate, waste, distract.

desaliar v. to disallay, disunite, disjoin, separate from union or alliance.

desalijar v. 1. to jettison, unburden, unload. 2. to spill, empty, vacate. 3. to ease, alleviate, lighten.

desalinhado adj. 1. out of line, disorderly. 2. careless, sluttish, sloppy, dowdy, frumpish, disheveled, sloven, slipshod, untidy, unkempt. || **-amente** adv. carelessly.

desalinhar v. 1. to put out of line; dishevel, disorder, disarray, disarrange, derange, deviate, discompose; strip of ornaments. 2. ~-se to get out of order, become deranged.

desalinhavar v. to take away the basting stitches.

desalinho s. m. 1. disorder, disarray, dishevelment, frumpiness, frowziness, untidiness. 2. negligence, carelessness, unkemptness. 3. trouble, affiction.

desalistar v. 1. to remove, eliminate from a list. 2. to disenroll, muster out (recruit).

desaliviar v. to alleviate, ease, lighten.

desalmado adj. soulless, inhuman, perverse, wicked, cruel, merciless. ‖ **-amente** adv. inhumanly.

desalmamento s. m. inhumanity, cruelty, perversity, wickedness, mercilessness, meanness.

desalojamento s. m. dislodgement, removal, departure, displacement.

desalojar v. 1. to dislodge, unhouse, drive out. 2. to break camp. 3. to give up one's post. 4. to remove, quit one's house.

desalterar v. 1. to still, calm, appease. 2. to quench (thirst). 3. ~**-se** to relent, grow tranquil.

desalumiado adj. 1. unenlightened, dark, gloomy. 2. ignorant. ‖ **-amente** adv. darkly; ignorantly.

desamabilidade s. f. discourtesy, unamiability, unfriendliness, uncivility, impoliteness.

desamagoar-se v. (Braz.) to relieve from grief or sorrow, console o. s.

desamalgamar v. to deamalgamate, separate or part (what has been amalgamated); disconnect, discompose, part.

desamamentar v. (also **desmamar**) to wean.

desamanhar v. to put in disorder, disarrange, neglect.

desamar v. 1. to love no more, cease to love. 2. to hate, detest, abhor.

desamam-se they dislike each other.

desamarrar v. 1. to untie, unfasten, loosen, detach, unbind, unlace. 2. (naut.) to unlash; unmoor; unbend; weigh anchor. 3. (aeron.) to take off. 4. ~**-se** to get loose.

desamarrotar v. to unwrinkle, smoothe, uncrumple.

desamassar v. 1. to unknead (dough). 2. to smooth, unwrinkle.

desamável adj. m. + f. (pl. **-áveis**) unkind, unfriendly, unamiable, unlovable, ungracious, tactless, indelicate. ‖ **desamavelmente** adv. unkindly.

desambição s. f. (pl. **-ões**) unambitiousness, want of ambition; modesty, unselfishness, disinterestedness.

desambicioso adj. 1. unambitious, indifferent, disinterested. 2. modest. ‖ **-amente** adv. unambitiously.

desambientado adj. strange, unadapted to a new environment.

desambientar v. 1. to take away from the environment or habitat, displace. 2. ~**-se** to leave one's habitual surroundings.

desamigar v. to cease to be friends, dissolve friendship.

desamigo adj. unfriendly, fallen out (with), hostile, inimical.

desamizade s. f. want of friendship, unfriendliness.

desamoador s. m. (Braz.) a carpenter's or calker's tool for extracting pegs or nails.

desamodorrar v. to awake, stir up; quicken, excite, stimulate, enliven.

desamoedação s. f. (pl. **-ões**) demonetization, depreciation of money.

desamoedar v. to demonetize: depreciate money, take its character as money.

desamolgar v. to smooth out (what has been bruised or battered).

desamontoar v. to unpile, unstack.

desamor s. m. 1. want of love, lovelessness, disaffection, aversion, antipathy, dislike, hatred. 2. cruelty, inhumanity, atrocity, barbarity.

desamorado adj. loveless, unkindly, unfriendly.

desamorável adj. m. + f. (pl. **-áveis**), **desamoroso** unloving, disagreeable, unkindly, harsh.

desamortalhar v. to take off the shroud, unshroud.

desamortização s. f. (pl. **-ões**) exemption from- entail.

desamortizar v. to disentail, free from entail.

desamortizável adj. m. + f (pl. **-áveis**) disentailable.

desamotinar v. 1. to suppress a rebellion, mutiny or revolt, appease a resistance. 2. ~**-se** to return to obedience.

desamparado adj. abandoned, unhelped, unaided, forlorn, forsaken; desolate, solitary, deserted, destitute. ‖ **-amente** adv. forsakenly.

desamparar v. 1. to abandon, quit, leave, forsake, desert. 2. to deprive of help or protection, neglect. 3. ~**-se** to go astray, lose one's way.

desamparo s. m. abandonment, lurch, destitution, dereliction, forsaking; helplessnes, friendlessness, defencelessness.

deixar tudo ao ~ to leave all at random, leave everything in confusion. **estar no maior** ~ to be forsaken by everybody. **viver ao** ~ to live forsaken.

desamuar v. to make merry again; cease to be sulky.

desancador s. m. thrasher; bully, ruffian.

desancamento s. m. thrashing, beating.

desancar v. 1. to thrash, beat soundly, pommel. 2. to maltreat, mishandle, outrage. 3. to triumph in debating.

desancorar v. to disanchor, weigh anchor.

desanda s. f. (also **descompostura**) 1. reprimand, scolding. 2. insult. 3. beating, thrashing.

desandar v. 1. to turn or draw back. 2. to unscrew, undo. 3. to retrocede; worsen. 4. to deteriorate.

~ **a correr** to break into a run. ~ **numa risada** to burst into laughter. **quanto anda tanto desanda** he does nothing but to do and undo.

desando s. m. 1. turning or drawing back. 2. decline, worsening. 3. spoiling.

desanelar v. to unroll, uncurl.

desanexação s. f. (pl. **-ões**) disconnection, disjunction, disunion, dissolution.

desanexar v. to disconnect, dissolve, disunite, disannex.

desanexo adj. disannexed, detached, separated, divided.

desanichar v. 1. to take out of a niche. 2. to dislodge, unhouse, unshelter.

desanimação s. f. (pl. **-ões**) discouragement, dejection, depression, disheartenment; spiritlessness, despondency; dismay.

desanimado adj. discouraged, dispirited, downhearted, exanimate, hopeless, depressed, dejected, broken-down, crestfallen, desponding. ‖ **-amente** adv. downheartedly.

estar ~ to be discouraged, have the blues.

desanimar v. 1. to discourage, dishearten, depress, deject, dispirit, despond. 2. to deter from; discountenance. 3. ~**-se** to dispair, be discouraged.

~ **alguém** to put s. o. out of countenance, discourage a person. ~ **uma iniciativa** to throw cold water on an enterprise.

desânimo s. m. discouragement, disheartenment, dispiritedness, doldrums, despondency; dejection, depression, dismay, prostration, faintness of heart, hopelessness.

desaninhar v. 1. to take out of the nest, unnestle. 2. (fig.) to dislodge, unhouse, drive out. 3. to trace out, track.

desanojar v. 1. to leave off mourning. 2. to condole. 3. to cheer, comfort. 4. ~**-se** to cheer up, get merry.

desanojo (ô) s. m. reanimation.

desanuviar v. 1. to uncloud, disperse clouds, clear up. 2. ~**-se** to grow calm or tranquil.

desapadrinhar v. 1. to disapprove, disallow. 2. to deny one's further protection.

desapagar v. 1. to wipe out, extinguish. 2. to erase, blot out, efface, obliterate.

desapaixonado adj. dispassionate, unmotional, unimpassioned, passionless, unbiased; impartial, cold-livered, unconcerned. ‖ **-amente** adv. dispassionately, impartially.

desapaixonar v. 1. to calm, appease, quiet, ease, free from passion. 2. ~-se to calm down, moderate one's passion.

desaparafusagem s. f. unscrewing, screwing off.

desaparafusar v. 1. to unscrew, screw off. 2. ~-se to get loose (screw).

desaparecer v. 1. to disappear, vanish, go out of sight. 2. (fig.) to die; go away, leave. ~ **deste mundo** to pass away; die. **o dinheiro desapareceu** the money disappeared. **ele desapareceu da cidade** he disappeared from town.

desaparecido s. m. missing person. ‖ adj. absent, disappeared, vanished, missing.

desaparecimento s. m. disappearance, vanishing, evanishment; fading; loss.

desaparelhado adj. unequipped.

desaparelhar v. 1. to dismantle. 2. to unharness (a horse). 3. (naut.) to strip, unrig, dismast. 4. to take away, disgarnish. 5. to uncouple, unleash. 6. (fig.) to die.

desaparição s. f. (pl. **-ões**) disappearance, vanishing.

desapartar v. to part, separate, break off.

desapavorar v. to relieve from fear or fright.

desapear v. 1. to alight, dismount. 2. to disembark, descend. 3. to unhorse. 4. to help to dismount, take down from or as from a horse.

desapegado adj. 1. unattached, detached, disaffected; indifferent. 2. independent, free. ‖ **-amente** adv. indifferently, without attachment.

desapegar v. = **despegar**.

desapego (ê) s. m. (also **desapegamento**) 1. indifference. 2. disaffection, want of love. 3. disinterestedness, unconcern.

desaperceber v. 1. to deprive of provisions or munitions; unfurnish, leave unprovided. 2. ~-se to fail to provide, be careless, neglect.

desapercebido adj. 1. unprovided, unprepared, destitute, unfurnished, unequipped; deprived of. 2. incautious, careless, negligent; unguarded. ‖ **-amente** adv. unprovidedly.
estar ~ **de tudo** to be deprived of everything. **tomar alguém** ~ to catch one napping, surprise a person.

desapercebimento s. m. improvidence, destitution, unpreparedness, want of foresight.

desaperrar v. to uncock (gun).

desapertar v. 1. to loosen. 2. to unlace, unbrace, unfasten, untie. 3. to unscrew. 4. to enlarge, widen, broaden. 5. to unbutton. 6. to alleviate, lighten, ease. 7. ~-se: a) to become unfastened, get loose. b) (Braz.) to slink away.

desaperto (ê) s. m. 1. unfastening. 2. ease, relief. 3. (sl.) loophole.

desapiedado adj. pitiless, unpitying, unmerciful, ruthless, remorseless, unfeeling, uncompassionate, heartless, harsh, cruel, inhuman. ‖ **-amente** adv. unmercifully, ruthlessly.

desapiedar v. 1. to make pitiless or inhuman; harden the heart. 2. ~-se to grow merciless.

desaplaudir v. to disapprove, reject; not to applaud.

desaplauso s. m. want of applause or acclamation; disapprobation, reproval, rejection.

desaplicação s. f. (pl. **-ões**) 1. want of application, inapplication, negligence. 2. withdrawal (as of investments).

desaplicar v. 1. to hinder from application, cease applying, distract, neglect. 2. to withdraw, take off.

desaplumar v. = **desaprumar**.

desapoderado adj. 1. deprived, dispossessed, destitute. 2. (fig.) impetuous, furious; immense, mighty. ‖ **-amente** adv. impetuously.

desapoderar v. 1. to dispossess, take the power, deprive. 2. ~-se to abstain from power or possessions; to deprive o. s. of.

desapoiar v. 1. to deprive of assistance, not to give one's support, disapprove. 2. to unprop, take away the props.

desapoio s. m. want of assistance, helplessness, destitution, forlornness.

desapolvilhar v. to comb out the powder (of or as of one's hair); dust off.

desapontado adj. disappointed, frustrated, thwarted, disgruntled. ‖ **-amente** adv. disappointedly.

desapontamento s. m. (also **desaponto**) disappointment, frustration, baffling, letdown.

desapontar (I) v. to aim badly, miss one's aiming.

desapontar (II) v. to disappoint, frustrate, baffle, thwart; disgruntle.

desapoquentar v. to appease, calm, tranquilize, encourage, animate.

desaportuguesar v. to deprive of its peculiar Portuguese aspect.

desaposentar v. 1. to deprive of lodgings, unhouse. 2. to stir up.

desapossar v. 1. to dispossess, deprive, divest, oust, expropriate; usurp, despoil. 2. ~-se to renounce a possession, abstain from power.

desaprazer v. to displease, cause displeasure; annoy, disgust, discontent.

desaprazível adj. m. + f. (pl. **-íveis**) unpleasant, disagreeable. ‖ **desaprazivelmente** adv. unpleasantly.

desapreciar v. to disparage, depreciate, undervalue, underrate, belittle.

desapreço s. m. depreciation, disparagement, disregard, slight, lack of esteem or appreciation.

desaprender v. to unlearn, forget; fall out.

desapresilhar v. to unfasten, untie, loosen; unbuckle, unclasp.

desapressar v. 1. to slacken down, slow down. 2. ~-se to free o. s. from, get rid of.

desaprimorado adj. clumsy, rude, sloven; impolite, uncivil. ‖ **-amente** adv. clumsily.

desapropositado adj. 1. unsuitable, unseasonable. 2. absurd; irrelevant, preposterous, improper, out of question. ‖ **-amente** adv. absurdly; preposterously.

desapropósito s. m. absurdity, nonsense, foolery; impropriety.

desapropriação s. f. (pl. **-ões**) dispossession, ouster, divestiture, expropriation.

desapropriar v. 1. to dispossess, deprive, expropriate, divest, oust. 2. ~-se to deprive o. s., of, renounce to.

desaprovação s. f. (pl. **-ões**) disapprobation, disapproval; criticism, censure; disallowance, dispraise, disfavour, disclaiming, reproval.

desaprovador s. m. disapprover, blamer. ‖ adj. disapproving, disclaiming, disliking.

desaprovar v. 1. to disapprove, disallow, disclaim, disfavour, dislike, dispraise, disprize, disavow, disacknowledge. 2. to censure, damn, condemn, criticise.

desaprovativo adj. disapprobative, disapprobatory.

desaproveitado adj. 1. not used to advantage, vain, useless, fruitless. 2. waste, abandoned. 3. squandered. 4. uneconomical, prodigal. ‖ **-amente** adv. vainly.

desaproveitamento s. m. 1. inapplication, want of progress. 2. waste, prodigality, squandering.

desaproveitar v. 1. not to profit; misuse. 2. to waste, squander away, consume.

desaprumar v. 1. to put out of plumb. 2. (fig.) to put out of the mark. 3. ~-se: a) to get out of plumb, be inclined. b) (fig.) to get out of the mark.

desaprumo s. m. want of perpendicularity, divergence from the vertical line, lack of plumbness.

desapurado adj. clumsy, sloven, negligent, careless. ‖ **-amente** adv. clumsily.

desapuro s. m. clumsiness, slovenliness, carelessness; inelegance.

desaquartelar v. to dislodge, unhouse, deprive of lodgement or quarters.

desaquinhoar v. 1. to deprive s. o. of his share, cheat s. o. out of his part or portion. 2. ~-se to give up one's share, desist of one's portion.

desar s. m. 1. inelegance, want of grace or distinction. 2. blemish, stain. 3. misfortune, unhappiness, ill luck.

desaranhar v. 1. to take away cobwebs. 2. (fig.) to enlighten, explain, clarify, clear up.

desarar v. 1. to fall off, get loose (hoofs of horses, mules). 2. (fig.) to disarrange, upset, disorder.

desarborizar v. to take away the trees, deprive of trees; cut down trees, deforest.

desarcar v. to remove the hoops, unhoop.

desarear v. to clean from sand, take off the sand.

desarmado adj. 1. unarmed, unprotected. 2. not assembled, knocked down.

desarmamento s. m. 1. disarming, disarmament, reduction of troops. 2. unmanning of a ship, unrigging.

desarmar v. 1. to disarm, unarm, deprive of arms. 2. (naut.) to unrig, dismantle, unship; unman a ship. 3. to dismount, disjoint, disassemble, knock down. 4. to disband troops. 5. to frustrate, disappoint, deceive. 6. ~-se to relent, strip. ~ **uma espingarda** to uncock a gun. ~ **um navio** to unman a ship.

desarmonia s. f. 1. disharmony, dissonance. 2. discordance, disaccord, variance.

desarmônico adj. inharmonous, discordant; harsh. ‖ **-amente** adv. inharmoniously.

desarmonizador s. m. person who destroys harmony, brawler. ‖ adj. destroying harmony, disharmonizing, causing disharmony, setting at variance.

desarmonizar v. to disharmonize, destroy harmony, create disharmony, set at variance.

desaromar, desaromatizar v. to deprive of its aroma, turn tasteless or insipid.

desarraigamento s. m. uprooting, eradication, extirpation; destruction.

desarraigar v. (also **desarreigar**) 1. to unroot, uproot, pluck, eradicate, extirpate. 2. to expulse, banish, eliminate, have done with. 3. ~-se to be extinguished or rooted out, die out.

desarrancar v. to pull out violently, snatch, wrench, root up.

desarranchar v. (mil.) to separate or exclude from the mess.

desarranjado adj. out of shape; not working properly.

desarranjador s. m. person who causes disorder or confusion. ‖ adj. disarranging, disordering, putting out of order.

desarranjar v. 1. to disarrange, discompose, displace, disorder, dislocate. 2. to ruffle, upset, confound, trouble, disturb, derange, unsettle. 3. ~-se: a) to get out of order. b) to disagree, break out with s. o.

desarranjo s. m. 1. disarrangement, disorder, derangement, distemper, disconcertment; breakdown. 2. setback, mishap, reverse, annoyance; variance. 3. (fig.) diarrhea.

desarrazoado adj. 1. unreasonable, unreasoning, senseless, thoughtless, nonsensical. 2. unjust, wrong, absurd. ‖ **-amente** adv. unreasonably.

desarrazoar v. to talk nonsense, act without common sense.

desarrear v. 1. to unharness, take off the harness; unsaddle. 2. to ungear.

desarredondar v. to cause to lose its round shape, change the round form.

desarregaçar v. to untuck, roll down (as tucked sleeves).

desarrimar v. 1. to take away the support. 2. to abandon, forsake. 3. to unprop.

desarrimo s. m. lack of support; forlornness, abandonment, destitution; distress.

desarriscar v. 1. to strike out, erase. 2. ~-se to free o. s. from one's Easter duty.

desarrochar v. to loosen, unlace, relax.

desarrolhar (I) v. to uncork, unplug, unstop; open, draw the cork.

desarrolhar (II) v. (S. Braz.) to scatter (cattle).

desarroupado adj. unclothed, uncovered, naked, nude. ‖ **-amente** adv. nakedly.

desarruar v. to disregard street planning.

desarrufar v. 1. to reconcile; cease to pout or be sulky. 2. ~-se to cheer up again.

desarrufo s. m. reconciliation; return to good humour.

desarrugamento s. m. unwrinkling.

desarrugar v. = **desenrugar**.

desarrumação s. f. (pl. -ões) disarray, disorder, derange, untidiness, jumble; confusion, disturbance, trouble.

desarrumar v. 1. to disarrange, put out of place, displace, dislocate. 2. to disorder, derange, disturb, put in confusion.

desarticulação s. f. (pl. -ões) disarticulation, dislocation, disjointedness, luxation.

desarticular v. 1. to disarticulate, dislocate, disjoint, luxate. 2. to disconnect, break up (the connexion).

desartificioso adj. 1. uningenious, unskillful. 2. (fig.) unaffected, simple, modest.

desarvorado adj. 1. dismasted. 2. dismantled, unequipped, unprovided with. 3. disorientated, aimless, purposeless. 4. (Braz.) lost, bewildered. ‖ **-amente** adv. aimlessly.

desarvoramento s. m. dismasting, dismantling.

desarvorar v. 1. to dismantle, unequip. 2. (naut.) to dismast; lose the masts; be unmasted. 3. (fig.) to run away, break away, bolt.

desasa s. f. (Braz.) molt, moult (of birds).

desasado adj. 1. drooping (wings). 2. bowed down, knocked down.

desasar v. 1. to clip the wings. 2. (fig.) to break the back. 3. to belabour; beat soundly, drub.

desasir v. 1. to loose, release, set free. 2. ~-se to get loose, get rid of.

desasnar v. 1. to open a person's eyes, enlighten. 2. to disillusion. 3. to instruct.

desassanhar v. 1. to calm, appease the anger, placate. 2. ~-se to grow calm, quiet down.

desassazonado adj. unseasonable, untimely; ill-timed, unripe; inopportune. ‖ **-amente** adv. unseasonably.

desasseado adj. unclean, untidy, dirty, filthy, soiled; impure. ‖ **-amente** adv. uncleanly.

desassear v. to make unclean; pollute, soil, defile.

desasseio s. m. 1. uncleanliness, dirtiness. 2. untidiness. 3. defilement.

desasselvajar v. to civilize, polish, improve the manners; reclaim from barbarism.

desassemelhar v. to render unlike or dissimilar.

desassenhorear v. to deprive of possession, dispossess.

desassestar v. to disarrange, put out of focus or aim.

desassimilação s. f. (pl. -ões) disassimiliation, catabolism.

desassimilar v. to unassimilate; convert.

desassisado s. m. fool. ‖ adj. injudicious, inconsiderate, senseless; foolish, silly, crazy. ‖ **-amente** adv. injudiciously.

desassisar v. 1. to deprive of good sense, make crazy, stun. 2. to get crazy, lose one's good sense.

desassociar v. to dissociate, disassociate, separate, disunite, disconnect.

desassombrado adj. 1. not shady, unshaded, sunny, exposed to the sun. 2. fearless, bold. 3. frank, open. ‖ **-amente** adv. boldly.

desassombrar v. 1. to expose to the sun, brighten. 2. to embolden, encourage. 3. to free from care or trouble; to calm, tranquillize, appease. 4. ~-**se** to recover one's cold blood or self-possession, become fearless.

desassombro s. m. 1. frankness; firmness, resolution. 2. fearlessness, boldness, intrepidity. 3. calm, tranquility, quiet. 4. self-possession.

desassossegado adj. unquiet, disturbed, restless, worried, uneasy, feverish, hectic. ‖ **-amente** adv. unquietly.

desassossegar v. 1. to disquiet, perturb, disturb, trouble, vex. 2. ~-**se** to become worried.

desassossego (ê) s. m. 1. unquietness, disquietude, uneasiness, unrest, restlessness, peacelessness, disturbance, perturbance. 2. feverishness.

desassustar v. 1. to take away fear, reassure. 2. ~-**se** to lose fear, recover from fear.

desastrado adj. 1. disastrous. 2. awkward, clumsy, maladroit, fumbling. 3. unhappy, unfortunate, unlucky. ‖ **-amente** adv. disastrously.

desastre s. m. disaster: 1. calamity, misfortune, unhappiness. 2. accident. 3. loss, damage.
ter um ~ to come to grief, meet with an accident.

desastroso adj. disastrous, calamitous, sinister, black; unhappy, unlucky, unfortunate. ‖ **-amente** adv. disastrously.

desatabafar v. 1. to ease, lighten. 2. to make a clean breast of, unbosom, disclose one's heart. 3. to breathe freely.

desatacar v. 1. to unlace, untie, loosen. 2. to unbutton. 3. to unload (a gun). 4. to spill, pour out.

desatado adj. 1. unfastened, untied, loose. 2. unbuttoned. 3. unbuckled, unclasped. 4. open, free. ‖ **-amente** adv. openly, loosely.
discurso ~ a discourse that has neither rhyme nor reason. **homem** ~ awkward fellow.

desatadura s. f., **desatamento** m. loosening, unlacing, unfastening; dissolving.

desatar v. 1. to unfasten, untie, unbind, unlace, unlash; unbrace, unbuckle, unclasp; loosen. 2. to release, disengage. 3. to begin, start. 4. ~-**se** to get untied, unfastened or loose.
~ **a chorar** to burst into tears. ~ **às gargalhadas** to burst into a laughter. ~ **a língua** to speak freely.

desatarraxar v. to unscrew, unbolt, screw off.

desatascar v. 1. to take out of the mire, pull or draw out of a mudhole. 2. to clear (a pipe), open (a sewer).

desataviado adj. unadorned, ungarnished, untrimmed; simple. ‖ **-amente** adv. unadornedly.

desataviar v. to take away adornments, strip or divest of ornaments.

desatavio s. m. lack of ornaments or decorations, simplicity; disarray, untidiness.

desate s. m. outcome, upshot, denouement, end.

desatemorizar v. 1. to free from fear, embolden, encourage. 2. to reassure; restore confidence.

desatenção s. f. (pl. **-ões**) 1. inattention, absence of mind, carelessness, heedlessness, regardlessness, disregard, negligence, distraction, woolgathering. 2. want of respect, impoliteness, incivility; lack of consideration.

desatencioso adj. 1. inattentive, disregardful, disobliging, unmindful. 2. unkind, impolite, uncourteous, uncivil. ‖ **-amente** adv. inattentively.

desatender v. 1. to be inattentive, disregard, neglect, give no attention. 2. to disrespect, dispise, disdain, refuse.

desatendível adj. m. + f. (pl. **-íveis**) negligible, that is not worth attention.

desatentar v. 1. to take no notice of. 2. to neglect, forget about, be careless.

desatento adj. inadvertent, heedless, careless, negligent, distracted, thoughtless, regardless, forgetful, unmindful. ‖ **-amente** adv. heedlessly.

desaterrar v. 1. to raze (a hill). 2. to remove earth, level ground. 3. to excavate, hollow out (ground).

desaterro (ê) s. m. 1. level(l)ing of ground. 2. level(l)ed ground.

desatestar v. to disembarrass, disentangle, clear.

desatilado adj. dull, stupid, foolish, silly; rude, awkward. ‖ **-amente** adv. stupidly.

desatinado adj. 1. foolish, silly, wrong-headed. 2. hot-headed. 3. crazy, giddy, mad. ‖ **-amente** adv. madly.

desatinar v. 1. to render crazy, make a person lose his sense, madden. 2. to talk nonsense or misbehave. 3. ~-**se** to be mad, be out of one's wits.

desatino s. m. madness, wrong-headedness, folly, extravagancy, nonsense.

desativação s. f. (nucl. eng.) decommissioning.

desatolado adj. (N. Braz., pop.) self-assured, self-reliant, forward. ‖ **-amente** adv. forwardly.

desatolar (I) v. to take out of the mud, pull or draw out of the mire.

desatolar (II) v. (N. Braz., pop.) to lose shyness, acquire self-assurance, embolden.

desatordoar v. 1. to make a person recover his senses. 2. to help a person to recover and be his own self again.

desatracação s. f. (pl. **-ões**) 1. (naut.) unmooring, putting off. 2. getting clear.

desatracar v. 1. (naut.) to unmoor, put off. 2. to get clear. 3. ~-**se** to weigh anchor.

desatravancar v. to disencumber, take away obstructions, remove any hindrance.
~ **a linha** to clear the line (as of a railway).

desatravessar v. 1. to take away (what is lying across), clear the way, disembarrass. 2. ~-**se** to give way, make place.

desatrelar v. 1. to unleash, unharness, unhitch, outspan, unyoke. 2. to release, set free.

desautoração s. f. (pl. **-ões**) degradation, degrading, deprivation of rank or position.

desautorado adj. degraded, deprived of rank or position, discredited.

desautorar v. 1. to degrade, deprive of rank or position. 2. to take the authority, depose, discredit. 3. ~-**se**: a) to lose authority. b) (fig.) to rebel against the authorities.

desautoridade s. f. (obs.) want of authority; unworthiness, indignity.

desautorização s. f. (pl. **-ões**) degradation, loss of authority, discredit.

desautorizar v. 1. to deprive of authority, discredit, disauthorize, lessen the authority or power. 2. to deny, forbid.

desavagar v. to unshoe a horse.

desavença s. f. dissension, disagreement, discord, difference, disaffection, disunion, estrangement; falling out, quarrel, debate, strife.
em ~ at variance, at loggerheads.

desaverbar v. to efface, strike out, cancel.

desavergonhado s. m. shameless person. ‖ adj. shameless, impudent, brazen-faced, insolent, unblushing, waggish, saucy, unabashed, unashamed. ‖ **-amente** adv. shamelessly.

desavergonhar v. 1. to induce to impudence or insolence. 2. ~-**se** to lose all shame, grow shameless, become impudent.

desavexar v. to remove the cause of vexation.

desavezar v. 1. to break of a custom or habit; to wean, dishabituate, disaccustom. 2. ~-**se** to leave off a custom.

desaviar v. to obstruct, frustrate.

desavindo adj. disagreeing, on bad terms with, at variance.

desavir v. 1. to disagree, discord, set at variance, estrange, dissent, differ. 2. ~-**se** to fall out with, quarrel, dispute.

desavisado adj. ill-advised, not informed, ignorant; imprudent. ‖ **-amente** adv. imprudently, unaware.

desavisar v. 1. to countermand, revoke an order. 2. to render imprudent. 3. ~-**se** not to pay attention, not to perceive.

desaviso s. m. 1. countermand, contrary order. 2. want of advice, disinvitation. 3. imprudence, indiscretion; folly, levity, frivolity.

desavistar v. to lose sight of, fail to see.

desavolumar v. to lessen the volume of, diminish, reduce.

desazado adj. 1. ungainly, awkward, gauche. 2. foolish. 3. careless, negligent. 4. fumbling. ‖ **-amente** adv. awkwardly.

desazo s. m. awkwardness, ineptness, clumsiness, unskillfulness; unseasonableness, inconvenience.

desbabar v. to clean of slime or slobber.

desbagoar v. to pick grapes (from a bunch).

desbagulhar v. to pick out the seeds of fruits, as of grapes.

desbalizar v. to take away the seamarks or landmarks.

desbancar v. 1. to take away the benches. 2. to break the bank (as in gambling). 3. to surpass, excel, supplant, beat, outclass.
~ **alguém na disputa** to run one down in a dispute.

desbandeirar v. 1. to take away the flag. 2. to deprive the corn plants of their panicles.

desbaratador s. m. dilapidator, waster, destroyer, consumer, spendthrift. ‖ adj. wasting, consuming, dissipating.

desbaratamento s. m. (also **desbarate, desbarato**) 1. wasting, consuming, squandering. 2. defeat, rout. 3. havoc.

desbaratar v. 1. to waste, squander, scatter, consume, spend. 2. to disarray, turn away. 3. to disorder. 4. to demolish, destroy. 5. to beat, overcome. 6. to rout, defeat. 7. ~-**se** to go broke; run to ruin.

desbarbado adj. beardless, without beard; shaved.

desbarbar v. 1. to shave. 2. to cut off, trim, clip.

desbarrancado s. m. (Braz.) 1. precipice, cliff, declivity. 2. gully, gutter.

desbarrancamento s. m. landslide, landslip.

desbarrancar v. (Braz.) 1. to remove earth, excavate, hollow out (ground). 2. to fill up gullies or ravines with earth. 3. to slip or slide (masses of earth).

desbarrar (I) v. to unbolt, unbar; open.

desbarrar (II) v. to take away the clay or mud; clean from clay.

desbarretar v. 1. to deprive s. o. of his cap. 2. ~-**se** to cap, take off one's cap or hat in order to greet.

desbarrigado adj. 1. having a thin belly, thin-bellied, meagre. 2. famished (animal).

desbastador s. m. 1. (carp.) jack plane (plate P 13). 2. rough-hewer. 3. lopper. ‖ adj. 1. rough-hewing. 2. pruning, lopping (trees).

desbastamento s. m. 1. rough-hewing. 2. pruning, lopping (trees).

desbastar v. 1. to pare, rough-hew, cut off, thin out, straighten. 2. to chop, lop, prune. 3. to fashion, polish, form.
~ **um pedaço de madeira** to rough-hew a piece of timber. ~ **os ramos das plantas** to thin the plants.

desbastardar v. to legitimate (bastards).

desbaste s. m. 1. rough-hewing, paring. 2. pruning, lopping. 3. (N. Braz.) lopping of cotton plants.

desbatizar v. 1. to cause to lose the grace of baptism, excommunicate. 2. to take another name. 3. to lose or change the baptismal name.

desbeiçar v. to break or chip (as the edge of a cup or a plate).

desbloquear v. to raise the blockade, cease to blockade.

desbloqueio s. m. raising of the blockade.

desbocado adj. 1. unrestrained, foul-mouthed. 2. shocking, indecent; lewd, wanton. 3. hard-mouthed (horse). ‖ **-amente** adv. unrestrainedly; shockingly.

desbocamento s. m. unreservedness, impudence, sauciness, impertinence; loose talk.

desbocar v. 1. to cause a horse to be hard-mouthed. 2. to empty, pour out, spill. 3. ~-**se** to talk rashly or imprudently.

desbolado adj. cock-brained, crack-brained, mad, foolish, insane. ‖ **-amente** adv. madly.

desbolinar v. 1. (naut.) to straighten a sail that had been hauled. 2. to undo, remove or avoid kinks (of a cable).

desborcar v. to turn over.

desborcinar v. to chip, break off an edge.

desbordante adj. m. + f. overflowing, brimful.

desbordar v. to overflow, flow over the brim, flow out; overspread.

desboroar v. to reduce to dust, pulverize.

desborrar v. to clear of lees or dregs.

desbotado adj. discoloured, washed-out, faded, dingy, lack-lustre. ‖ **-amente** adv. discolouredly.

desbotadura s. f., **desbotamento** m. discolourment; tarnishing.

desbotar v. 1. to discolour, deface the colour; weather. 2. ~-**se** to fade, tarnish, be discoloured.

desbote s. m. discolouring, fading.

desbragado s. m. shameless person. ‖ adj. immoderate, coarse, shameless, indecorous, impudent, shocking, indecent. ‖ **-amente** adv. shamelessly.

desbragamento s. m. impudence, shamelessness, rudeness, want of good behaviour.

desbragar v. 1. to unchain (galley-slaves). 2. (fig.) to cause dissolution, set free, let loose.

desbravador s. m. 1. tamer (animals). 2. grubber (land). ‖ adj. 1. taming (animals). 2. grubbing, cultivating (land).

desbravar v. 1. to tame, domesticate (animals). 2. to break, cultivate (land), grub up; pioneer. 3. ~-**se** to grow calm or quiet.

desbravejado adj. (S. Braz.) cleared of thicket (ground).

desbravejar v. (S. Braz.) to clear of thicket, grub land (for planting).

desbriado s. m. person without pride or self-respect. ‖ adj. undignified, infamous, shameless. ‖ **-amente** adv. infamously.

desbriar v. 1. to deprive of dignity, humble s. o. 2. ~-**se** to lose one's pride or self-respect.

desbridar v. to take off the bridle, unbridle.

desbrio s. m. (also **desbriamento**) want of dignity or pride, shamelessness, infamousness.

desbrioso adj. undignified, infamous, shameless. ‖ **-amente** adv. infamously.

desbulhar v. to thrash (corn), peel, shell, husk.

desbundar v. (Braz.) 1. to lose self-control because of drugs. 2. to lose one's temper.

descabaçar v. (Braz.) to take the virginity.

descabeçado adj. (Braz.) headless, brainless, rattle-brained, crazy, insane. ‖ **-amente** adv. headlessly.

descabeçar v. 1. to behead, take the head off, decapitate. 2. (S. Braz.) to clean of roots or stumps (land). 3. to fall (the tide).

descabelado adj. 1. hairless, bald-headed. 2. (fig.) offensive, violent. ‖ **-amente** adv. bald-headedly.

descabelar v. 1. to unhair, pull out someone's hair. 2. **~-se** to tear one's hair, dishevel one's hair.

descaber v. not to suit, be improper, not to pertain to.

descabido adj. improper, unbecoming, inopportune, not suitable. ‖ **-amente** adv. improperly.

descachaçar v. (Braz.) to clean, scum (ebullient cane juice).

descadeirado adj. (Braz.) luxated, disjointed; hip-shot.

descadeirar v. 1. to disjoint, luxate; break one's back. 2. to beat, whip. 3. **~-se** to move (excessively) the hips especially in dancing.

descaída s. f. 1. chicken pluck (of fricassee). 2. (pop.) slip, oversight, fault. 3. inattention, negligence, carelessness.

descaído adj. fallen, inclined, sloping; tumbled, fallen down, turned over.

descaimento s. m. 1. falling (down), crash. 2. decay, decadence, declension, decline. 3. feebleness, weakness, faintness, wanness. 4. discouragement, debility, depression, dejection.

descair v. 1. to drop, decay, decline, sink, fall. 2. to worsen, weaken, droop. 3. (naut.) to drop astern, drift off. 4. to deviate, come away, drive from the right course.

~ da sua esperança to lose one's expectation, be disappointed. **~ da sua grandeza** to fall from one's greatness.

descalabro s. m. 1. breakdown, ruin. 2. damage, loss. 3. rout, defeat. 4. trouble, calamity, misfortune.

descalçadeira s. f. 1. bootjack. 2. (fig.): a) reprimand, scolding. b) abuse, insult.

descalçadela s. f. (pop.) dressing down, reprimand, reproof, reprehension.

descalçador s. m. bootjack. ‖ adj. pulling off (shoes, stockings, etc.).

descalçar v. 1. to take or slip off (shoes, stockings, gloves), unboot. 2. to take off wedges or chocks. 3. to take away (paving stones). 4. to deprive of recourse, fail to help. 5. **~-se** to pull off one's shoes.

~ a bota to get out of a scrape.

descalço adj. 1. unshod, shoeless, bare-footed. 2. (fig.) unprepared, improvided, destitute. 3. unpaved.

descalhoar v. to take away the stones, clear a ground of stones.

descalicino adj. (bot.) having no calyx.

flor -a acalycinous flower.

descalvado adj. (also **escalvado**) bald, hairless; bare, naked. ‖ **-amente** adv. baldly.

descalvar v. (also **escalvar**) to bare, render bald.

o calor descalva os montes cerrados de neve heat bares the snowy crown of mountains.

descamação s. f. (pl. **-ões**) 1. desquamation, scaling off. 2. (geol.) exfoliation.

descamar v. to scale off.

descambação s. f. (pl. **-ões**) slide, fall.

descambada s. f. (Braz.) 1. slip, oversight, fault. 2. (S.) slope, declivity.

descambado s. m. (Braz.) slope, declivity.

descambar v. 1. to slide, swerve, topple, tumble. 2. (fig.) to talk imprudently. 3. (S. Braz.) to descend, incline. 4. to degenerate into.

descaminhar v. (also **desencaminhar**) 1. to mislead, misguide, lead astray, go astray. 2. to pervert, corrupt.

descaminho s. m. 1. embezzlement, purloining, ill use, ill conduct. 2. mistake, error.

descamisa, descamisada s. f. husking of the grains of corn.

descamisado s. m. ragamuffin, ragged fellow. ‖ adj. shirtless; wretched, very poor.

descamisar v. 1. to take or pull off the shirt. 2. to husk the grains of corn, unhusk.

descampado s. m. desert, open field, plain, wold; moor. ‖ adj. unsheltered, uninhabitated.

em ~ in the open field, in the open air. **a casa está construída num ~** the house is built on the open field.

descampar v. 1. to decamp, run away; break camp; disappear. 2. (naut.) to put to sea.

descangotado adj. (Braz.) 1. mopish. 2. weakened, enfeebled; depressed, dejected. ‖ **-amente** adv. mopishly.

descangotar v. (Braz.) to weaken, impair; enfeeble, knock down.

descanhotar v. (Braz.) 1. to disjoint, dismember, disarticulate. 2. (S.) to walk with ease.

descanjicar v. (Braz., pop.) to beat violently, tear to pieces; shatter.

descansadeiro s. m. resting-place.

descansado adj. quiet, easy, undisturbed, untroubled, calm, tranquil, sedate, restful; slow, tardy. ‖ **-amente** adv. easily.

esteja ~! be easy! don't worry!. **terra -a** fallow ground. **vida -a** quiet or idle life. **viver ~** to live at one's ease. **você pode ficar ~!** don't worry about!

descansar v. 1. to rest: a) repose, give rest, put at rest. b) relax, be at ease. c) pause. d) slumber, sleep. e) lie upon, be supported, lean against, recline. 2. to help, relieve. 3. to place, set, put, lay (in or on). 4. to rely on. 5. **~-se** to rest from, take a rest.

~ armas to trail arms. **~ no cemitério** to rest in the churchyard. **~ um pouco** to take a short rest. **~ as terras** to lie fallow. **descansamos aqui!** let us rest here! **descanse em paz!** rest in peace! **sem ~** without intermission, incessantly, continually.

descanso s. m. 1. rest, resting, restfulness, repose, refreshment, recess, relaxation, recumbence. 2. quietness, calm, tranquility, ease, comfort. 3. prop, support, lap, brace. 4. (mil.) catch, halt, stay. 5. sleep, slumber; eternal rest.

~ para livros book-rest (plate B 2). **~ de turco** (naut.) supporter of the cathead. **dar ~** to give some rest; relax. **em ~** at rest, quietly, sedately. **lugar de ~** resting place. **sem ~** without interruption, without letup. **tomar ~** to respire, breathe.

descantar v. 1. to descant, sing, serenade. 2. to talk ill of s. o., criticise, censure, reprehend, blame. 3. = **descantear**.

descante s. m. 1. descant. 2. popular song, ballad. 3. a small guitar.

descantear v. to remove the edges of stones.

descanto s. m. part song; part singing.

descapacitar-se v. to change one's mind.

descaracterizar, descaraterizar v. 1. to deprive of the characteristics. 2. **~-se** to become commonplace.

descarado s. m. shameless person. ‖ adj. shameless, saucy, impudent, insolent, brazen-faced, unabashed, barefaced, unblushing, rude, bold; cheeky. ‖ **-amente** adv. shamelessly.

descaramento s. m. (also **descaro**) shamelessness, impudence, barefacedness, sauciness, insolence; cheek, affrontery.

ele teve o ~ de dizer he had the cheek to say.

descarapuçar v. to take off the cap, uncover.
descarar v. 1. to make s. o. bold or impudent. 2. ~-se to grow impudent, become shameless.
descarbonizar v. to decarbonize, decarburize.
descarboxilar v. (chem.) to decarboxylate.
descarga s. f. 1. discharge: a) unlading, unloading. b) volley, flight. c) firing, gunfire. d) exhaust, issue; flush. 2. (med.) evacuation, excretion. ~ atmosférica atmospheric discharge. ~s de artilharia discharge of guns, volley. ~ da culpa excuse, clearing. cais para ~ discharging berth. cano de ~ eduction pipe, discharge pipe. dar uma ~ to fire a round. dar uma ~ inteira (naut.) to give a broadside. licença de ~ discharging permit. proceder a ~ to discharge.
descargo s. m. 1. unloading, unlading, discharge. 2. acquittal. 3. ease, release, relief. 4. excuse, clearing. por ~ da minha consciência for the acquittal of my conscience; in conscience, for conscience's sake.
descaridade s. f. want of charitableness, uncharitableness.
descaridoso adj. uncharitable; harsh, censorious.
descarinhoso adj. unkind, unloving; harsh, intractable. ‖ -amente adv. unkindly.
descarnado adj. lean, meagre, gaunt, lanky, thin, not fleshy; fleshless. ‖ -amente adv. meagrely.
descarnadura s. f. taking off of the flesh, clearing from flesh.
descarnar v. 1. to pick the flesh off, cut the meat from the bones. 2. to scrape hides. 3. to make lean, thin or lank. 4. to waste away. 5. ~-se to grow lean or thin. ~ a terra to wash away the ground (waves, tides).
descaro s. m. = descaramento.
descaroável adj. m. + f. (pl. -áveis) unkind, uncharitable; pitiless, unmerciful. ‖ descaroavelmente adv. unkindly.
descaroçador s. m. coring, stoning or seed removing machine. ‖ adj. seed removing. ~ de algodão cotton gin.
descaroçamento s. m. coring, stoning, removing seeds.
descaroçar v. 1. to clean of grains, kernels or seeds (as cotton.) 2. to seed, stone, pit. 3. (pop.) to tell in detail, tell one's beads.
descarrar v. 1. to take down from the cart. 2. to unload.
descarregador s. m. 1. unloader, porter; docker. 2. (tech.) discharger. ‖ adj. discharging, unloading.
descarregadouro s. m. (also descarregadoiro) place of discharge, loading-place; wharf, dock.
descarregamento s. m. discharge, unloading, unlading, disembarkment.
descarregar v. 1. to discharge: a) unload, unburden, unlade, disembark. b) dump. c) fire off, shoot off (a gun). d) volley. e) relieve, exonerate, exculpate, acquit. 2. to vent, give vent to, wreak. 3. to ease, lighten, alleviate. 4. to strike (a blow). 5. to disembogue, empty. 6. ~-se to relieve o. s., get rid, grow calm. ~ a bateria to discharge the battery, run the battery down. ~ do carro ou da carreta to uncart. ~ a consciência to clear one's conscience. ~ a culpa sobre alguém to put the blame on another. ~ um golpe to strike a blow. ~ sua ira sobre alguém to glut one's revenge upon s. o. ~ um navio to clear a ship. ~ os seus negócios sobre alguém to charge another with one's business. ~ vapor to blow off, let off (steam). ~ um vagão to unload a railroad freight car.
descarreirar v. to lead astray, mislead, misdirect; put on a wrong way.

descarreto (ê) s. m. place of a river where vessels must be either unloaded or lightened on account of navigational difficulties.
descarrilamento, descarrilhamento s. m. derailment, running off the rails.
descarrilar, descarrilhar v. 1. to derail, jump or get off the rails; run off the track. 2. (fig.) to make a slip, behave uncorrectly; become lost, run to ruin. o trem descarrilhou the train jumped the rails.
descartar v. 1. to discard, reject, throw aside; dismiss. 2. ~-se de to get rid of, put off, leave alone.
descarte s. m. 1. discard: a) discardment, discarding. b) the card or cards thrown out (at cardplaying). 2. (fig.) excuse, subterfuge; evasion.
descasalar v. = desacasalar.
descasamento s. m. 1. divorce, divorcement, dissolution of marriage. 2. separation.
descasar v. 1. to divorce, dissolve marriage, unmarry. 2. to separate, unmatch, disunite.
descascação s. f. (pl. -ões) (also descasca, descascadura f., descascamento m.) peeling, barking, shelling, husking.
descascadela s. f. reprehension, reproof, reprimand, rebuke.
descascadinha s. f. (S. Braz.) very fair woman.
descascador s. m. 1. husker, peeler, barker, decorticator. 2. pulping mill, hulling or peeling machine. ‖ adj. husking, peeling, barking.
descascar (I) v. 1. to peel, shell; rind, bark, husk, hull, decorticate; skin, scale. 2. (Braz.) to reprimand, reproof, censure, condemn, scold, chide, admonish, rebuke; talk ill of s. o. 3. (S. Braz.) to unsheathe (as a knife). 4. to hide, take the hide from.
descascar (II) v. to lose the hoof.
descaso s. m. negligence, inattention; disregard, indifference, carelessness, heedlessness.
descaspar v. to clean from dandruff.
descasque s. m. = descascação.
descativar v. to free from slavery, release from captivity, set free.
descaudado adj. (also descaudato) tailless, without a tail; stalkless, stemless.
descaudar v. to deprive of the tail; crop the tail (of a horse).
descaulino adj. (bot.) acaulous, acaulose, acauline, stemless.
descautela s. f. lack of caution; carelessness, negligence, indifference.
descavalgamento s. m. dismounting (as from a horse).
descavalgar(-se) v. to dismount: descend, alight or get off (from or as from a horse). ~ a artilharia to dismount the cannons.
descavar v. (also escavar) to excavate, dig out, hollow out.
descaveirado adj. (also escaveirado) emaciated, lean, thinny.
descaxelado adj. = desqueixelado.
descelular v. to destroy the cells, decompose.
descendência s. f. 1. descent, family, lineage, pedigree, generation. 2. issue, offspring. de baixa ~ lowborn. de ~ ilustre highborn. sem ~ without issue.
descendente s. m. + f. 1. descendant. 2. ~s pl. descendants, progeny, offspring, posterity. ‖ adj. m. + f. descending, descendent; proceeding.
descender v. 1. to descend, proceed, come from, be derived from, draw one's origin from. 2. ~-se to arise from.
descendimento s. m. (also descida f.) descension.
descensão s. f. (pl. -ões), descenso m. descent, descension, fall; lowering, lessening.

descensional adj. m. + f. (pl. **-ais**) descensional. **diferença** ~ (astr.) descensional difference.

descente s. f. descent. ‖ adj. m. + f. descending. ~ **da maré** reflux, the ebbing of the tide.

descentralização s. f. (pl. **-ões**) decentralization; separation.

descentralizador s. m. person who decentralizes. ‖ adj. decentralizing.

descentralizar v. to decentralize; separate.

descentralizável adj. m. + f. (pl. **-áveis**) that may be decentralized or separated.

descer v. 1. to descend: a) go down, come down, dismount, light, alight, step down. b) proceed, be derived (from). 2. to get off, get out, disembark. 3. to down, bring down, put down, take down, get down. 4. to sink, fall, drop; relapse. 5. to throw down, swoop. 6. to lower, lessen, diminish. 7. to humble, stoop, abase. 8. ~**-se** to debase, demean o. s. ~ **na consideração de alguém** to sink in someone's estimation, lose prestige. ~ **a cortina** to drop the curtain. ~ **a escada** to go downstairs. ~ **a ladeira** to coast. ~ **um monte** to descend a hill. ~ **a miudezas** to enter into particulars. ~ **do ônibus** to debus. **sem** ~ **em pormenores** without going into details. ~ **um rio** to sail down (a river). **desça!** down! below! **desça as malas!** get down the trunks! **os preços estão descendo** prices are falling.

descercar v. 1. to pull down a fence, to unfence. 2. to raise a siege.

descerco (ê) s. m. raising of a siege.

descerebração s. f. (pl. **-ões**) decerebration.

descerebrado s. m. 1. person deprived of brain. 2. idiot, imbecile, cretin. ‖ adj. 1. (surg.) decerebrated, deprived of brain. 2. idiotic, silly, absurd.

descerebrar v. 1. (surg.) to decerebrate, deprive of brain. 2. to render idiotic.

descerimônia s. f. informality, familiarity.

descerimonioso adj. unceremonious, informal, unconstrained, free, familiar. ‖ **-amente** adv. familiarly.

descerrar v. 1. to unseal, open, break open. 2. to discover, disclose.

deschancelar v. to break the seal, unseal.

deschapelar-se v. to take off one's hat; bare one's head.

descida s. f. 1. descent, descending, going or coming down; fall, drop. 2. decay. 3. declivity, slope, hillside. 4. lowering, lessening, diminution. ~ **de antena** fair-lead. ~ **da maré** ebb of the tide.

descimbramento s. m. (archit.) removing of the centres (vault, arch).

descimbrar v. to take away the centres (of an arch or vault after it is built).

descimentar v. to take the cement away from; demolish; ruin.

descimento s. m. 1. descent, descending. 2. (Braz., hist.) transportation of captured Indians as slaves to the coast.

descingir v. 1. to ungird; unbuckle, unclasp. 2. to loosen, unfasten. 3. to stretch, widen.

desclaridade s. f. want of light, lack of clearness.

desclassificação s. f. (pl. **-ões**) disqualification; disability, incapacity. ~ **de navio** withdrawal of the classification of a ship.

desclassificado s. m. disqualified person, outcast. ‖ adj. disqualified; unclassified; outcast, unworthy.

desclassificar v. 1. to disqualify, disable, unfit; unplace. 2. to lower, discredit, degrade, dishonour, disgrace.

descoagulação s. f. (pl. **-ões**), **descoagulamento** m. decoagulation, liquefaction, melting, dissolution.

descoagular v. to decoagulate, melt, dissolve, liquify.

descoalhar v. 1. to melt, liquify, fuse, dissolve. 2. ~**-se** to thaw.

descoberta s. f. 1. discovery, invention, finding, disclosure. 2. discovered land. 3. detection, espial. **às** ~**s** publicly, without concealment.

descoberto s. m. (Braz.) place where a gold mine has been found. ‖ adj. 1. discovered. 2. (also mil. + com.) uncovered, bare, bare-headed, naked, nude. 3. exposed, open. 4. divulged, disclosed, spread abroad. ‖ **-amente** adv. openly. **em** ~ without shelter, exposed to wind and weather. **homem** ~ openhearted person. **a peito** ~ openly, frankly.

descobridor s. m. discoverer, explorer, finder; detector. ‖ adj. discovering, exploring; detecting.

descobrimento s. m. 1. discovery, discovering; disclosure. 2. invention. 3. detection, espial. **o** ~ **do Brasil** the discovery of Brazil. ~ **do peito** opening or disclosing of one's heart.

descobrir v. 1. to discover, uncover, lay bare, lay open, disclose, expose, make visible, show; open. 2. to exhibit, betray, manifest. 3. to make known, impart, declare, tell, reveal. 4. to find, bring light to; detect, espy, perceive, see. 5. to unfurnish, disgarnish, deprive, strip. 6. to clear up (weather). 7. ~**-se** to cap, take one's cap off; unmask o. s. ~ **a cara** to show the face, unmask. ~ **uma conspiração** to discover a plot. ~ **a alguém seu coração** to unbosom o. s. to another. ~ **o fio** to be threadbare. ~ **uma mina de ouro** to discover a gold mine. ~ **o Santíssimo** to expose the Sacrament. ~ **uma terra** to discover a new country. ~ **a verdade** to catch the truth. **ele descobriu a América** (fig.) it dawned upon him. **isto há de** ~**-se algum dia** time will bring it to light.

descocado adj. bold, saucy, impudent, insolent; cheeky. ‖ **-amente** adv. boldly.

descocar-se v. to grow impudent or bold.

descochar v. (also **desacochar**) to disentangle, unravel.

descoco (ô) s. m. insolence, impudence, sauciness; audacity.

descodear v. to cut off or nip the crust of bread.

descoimar v. to dispense from a penalty, release of a fine.

descoivarar v. (Braz.) to clear a ground of half-burned tree trunks.

descolagem s. f. (pl. **-ens**) 1. unglueing. 2. (aeron.) taking off.

descolar v. 1. to unglue, unpaste. 2. to detach. 3. to take off, rise (airplane). **o livro descolou** the book has come apart.

descoloração s. f. (pl. **-ões**) discolouration, decolourization.

descolorar, descolorir v. 1. to discolour, decolourate; tain; fade. 2. ~**-se** to change the colour, grow pale.

descomedido adj. 1. immoderate, unreserved, exorbitant. 2. riotous, ungovernable, free, unbridled. 3. precipitate, rash, rude. ‖ **-amente** adv. immoderately.

descomedimento s. m. 1. immoderacy, exorbitancy; excess, extravagance. 2. uncivility, impoliteness, want of good manners, rudeness.

descomedir-se v. to behave immoderately, be rash or impolite.

descometer v. to exempt from an obligation, release of a charge or duty.

descomodidade s. f., **descômodo** m. incommodity, inconvenience, trouble; discomfort, want of comfort.

descomover v. to appease, calm, quiet.

descompadrar v. 1. to set at variance, disaffect, estrange; disunite. 2. ~**-se** to fall out (with s. o.).

descompaixão s. f. (pl. **-ões**) lack of compassion; hard-heartedness; indifference, disaffection.

descompassado adj. out of measure, immense, excessive; disorderly. ‖ **-amente** adv. immensely.

descompassar v. 1. (mus.) to put or get out of time. 2. to exaggerate, overstate. 3. ~-**se** to behave without moderation.

descompasso s. m. 1. (mus.) unsteadiness in keeping time. 2. immoderation, exaggeration; disorder, confusion, commotion; irregularity.

descomponenda s. f. insulting words; chiding.

descompor v. 1. to discompose, disarrange, derange, unsettle, disconcert, jumble, disorder. 2. to disturb, confuse, disorder, trouble, vex, irritate, agitate, ruffle. 3. to affront, insult. 4. to upset, set at variance, discord. 5. to displace. 6. ~-**se** to get upset; be irritated.

descomposição s. f. (pl. **-ões**) discomposure; disorder; trouble; perplexity; vexation, anger.

descomposto adj. 1. disordered; confused; perplexed. 2. immodest, exigent, demanding. ‖ **-amente** adv. out of order, immodestly.

descompostura s. f. 1. discomposure, disorder, agitation, disturbance, perturbation. 2. chiding, admonition; reprimand, censure. 3. immodesty, indecency, sauciness. 4. injury; insult, affront, abuse.

descomprazente adj. m. + f. displeasing, unpleasing, uncompliant, disobliging.

descomprazer v. to displace, be unpleasing to; disoblige, dissatisfy, not to comply with.

descompressão s. f. (pl. **-ões**) lack of compression, low pressure.

descomunal adj. m. + f. (pl. **-ais**) (also **escomunal**) 1. uncommon, rare, infrequent. 2. extraordinary, remarkable, strange, formidable. 3. excessive, huge, colossal, enormous, gigantic. ‖ **~mente** adv. uncommonly.

descomungar v. to annul the excommunication.

descomunhão s. f. (pl. **-ões**) annulment of an excommunication.

desconceito s. m. discredit, disrepute, disesteem; dishonour.

desconceituado adj. discredited, ill-famed, defamed, disesteemed.

desconceituar v. 1. to discredit, disrepute, bring into disgrace. 2. to slander, calumniate.

desconcentrar v. to deconcentrate; deviate from the center; decentralize.

desconcertado adj. 1. disorderly, disarranged, broken. 2. disconcerted, upset, confused, disturbed. ‖ **-amente** adv. out of order, confusedly.

desconcertador s. m. disturber, agitator. ‖ adj. disconcerting, disturbing, discomposing.

desconcertante adj. m. + f. 1. disconcerting, disarranging; upsetting, disturbing, baffling, perplexing.

desconcertar v. 1. to disconcert, disarrange, disorder, derange. 2. to discompose, trouble, confound, confuse, upset, baffle, puzzle, embarrass, perplex. 3. ~-**se** to become upset, get confused; be perplexed, bewildered, puzzled or confounded.

~ **alguém** to put someone's nose out of joint. ~ **um relógio** to put a watch out of order. ~-**se na vida** to take to bad courses. **esta notícia o desconcertou** he was put out by this news.

desconcerto (ê) s. m. 1. disorder, disarrangement. 2. confusion, trouble, perturbation, disturbance. 3. disharmony, disunion, discord.

desconchavar v. 1. to disjoint, disconnect, disunite, uncouple. 2. to differ, dissent, fall out (with), set at variance. 3. ~-**se** to be deranged, talk idly, act foolishly.

desconchavo s. m. 1. disorder; derangement. 2. nonsense, misconduct, foolishness.

desconchegar v. 1. to separate, disunite. 2. to unshelter.

desconciliar v. to disunite, set at variance; alienate.

desconcordância s. f. 1. variance, discordance, disagreement, difference, discord; opposition. 2. error of grammar.

desconcordante adj. m. + f. (also **desconcorde**) 1. discordant, dissonant, dissenting, different. 2. opposite, contradictory, contrary. 3. inharmonious, harsh. ‖ **~mente** adv. discordantly.

desconcordar v. 1. to discord, set at variance, vary, dissent, disagree, jarr. 2. ~-**se** to be discordant or dissonant.

desconcórdia s. f. disharmony, discord, disunity, variance, opposition; dissonance.

descondensar v. 1. to diminish the density of, dilute, rarefy. 2. ~-**se** to rarefy, grow less dense.

desconexão s. f. (pl. **-ões**) disconnection, disunion, interruption; separation.

desconexo adj. 1. disconnect(ed), unconnected, separate. 2. incoherent, abrupt (style), rambling. 3. fragmentary, scrappy. ‖ **-amente** adv. separately; incoherently.

desconfiado adj. 1. distrustful, mistrustful, suspicious, defiant; jealous. 2. shy, diffident. ‖ **-amente** adv. suspiciously; diffidently.

desconfiança s. f. 1. suspicion, suspiciousness, distrust, mistrust, dubiousness; jealousness; unbelief. 2. shyness, diffidence.

entrar em ~ to begin to mistrust.

desconfiante adj. m. + f. distrustful, mistrusting, suspicious; jealous. ‖ **~mente** adv. distrustfully.

desconfiar v. 1. to distrust, mistrust, suspect, doubt, not to rely on; despair. 2. to discourage, dispirit, deject.

~ **com alguém** to fall out with one. ~ **de si** to fall in despair.

desconfiômetro s. m. (Braz.) the capacity to perceive, suspect, sense something.

desconformar v. 1. to set at variance, dissent, trouble. 2. to disagree, differ.

desconforme adj. m. + f. 1. at variance, contrary, opposed, disagreeing, different. 2. uncommon, unusual; huge. 3. disproportional, unequal. ‖ **~mente** adv. contrarily; uncommonly.

desconformidade s. f. disconformity, discordance; disproportion, inequality; dissidence, difference; disharmony, contrariety (of opinion).

desconfortar v. 1. to discomfort, discourage, dishearten, dispirit, distress. 2. to afflict, trouble.

desconforto (ô) s. m. uncomfortableness, discomfort, comfortlessness; disconsolateness, discouragement, dejection, dispiritedness.

descongelação s. f. (pl. **-ões**) 1. breaking of the ice (of a river). 2. defrosting.

descongelar v. to thaw, defrost, melt.

descongestionante s. m. (med.) laxative. ‖ adj. m. + f. depleting; purgative.

descongestionar v. 1. to relieve of congestion, deplete. 2. ~-**se** to free of, clear.

desconhecedor s. m. ignorant. ‖ adj. 1. ignorant, disowning. 2. thankless, ungrateful. ‖ **~amente** adv. ignorantly; ungratefully.

desconhecer v. 1. to ignore, not to know. 2. to disown, dissemble. 3. to be ignorant of, estrange. 4. to be ungrateful. 5. ~-**se** (fig.) not to recognize o. s.

~-**se com alguém** to treat a person like a stranger.

desconhecido s. m. anonym, stranger, an unknown person. ‖ adj. 1. unknown, anonymous, nameless, unnoted, unheard of, unrecorded. 2. strange, obscure, unascertained. 3. thankless, ungrateful.

a bela -a the fair uknnown. ilustre ~ an obscure individual. o soldado ~ the unknown soldier.

desconhecimento s. m. 1. ignorance, want of knowledge, non-acquaintance, unfamiliarity; obscurity. 2. disowning. 3. ungratefulness, thanklessness.

desconhecível adj. m. + f. (pl. -íveis) that cannot be known, unknowable.

desconjunção s. f. (pl. -ões), desconjuntamento m. (also desconjuntura) disjointedness, disarticulation, luxation, dislocation; separation, disunion.

desconjuntar v. 1. to disjoint, dislocate, disarticulate, luxate. 2. to separate, disunite. 3. ~-se to be disunited, come asunder.

desconjunto adj. 1. disjoint(ed), out of joint, dislocated, disarticulated, luxated. 2. separate(d), divided, disunited. 3. discordant, contrary, opposite. ‖ -amente adv. separately.

desconjurar v. 1. to exorcise, conjure. 2. to insult, offend.

desconsagração s. f. (pl. -ões) profanation, blasphemy, desecration; irreverence.

desconsagrar v. to profane, blaspheme, desecrate; revile.

desconsciência s. f. unconscientiousness, want of conscience, unscrupulousness.

desconsentimento s. m. refusal, denial, disagreement.

desconsentir v. to disconsent, disagree, dissent; refuse, deny.

desconsideração s. f. (pl. -ões) disrespect, disregard, disesteem, slight, inconsiderateness; impoliteness, imprudence.

desconsiderar v. 1. to disrespect, disregard, disesteem, not to consider, pay no attention, discredit. 2. to lose one's reputation.

desconsolação s. f. (pl. -ões) disconsolateness, desolation; affliction, uncomfortableness, distress, sadness; misfortune.

desconsolado adj. 1. disconsolate, comfortless, desolate, sad, afflicted, sorry; cheerless, forlorn, forsaken. 2. displeasing, insipid, dull. ‖ -amente adv. desolately, sadly.

ele está muito ~ he is down, in poor spirits.

desconsolador adj. desolating, afflictive, grievous.

desconsolar v. 1. to discomfort, sadden, afflict, discourage, dispirit, dishearten. 2. ~-se to become sad, be afflicted, to grieve.

desconsolativo adj. displeasing, sad, grievous, desolating. ‖ -amente adv. sadly, grievously.

deconsolável adj. m. + f. (pl. -áveis) inconsolable. ‖ desconsolavelmente adv. inconsolably.

desconsolo (ô) s. m. disconsolateness, affliction, sadness, trouble, distress, discomfort.

descontar v. 1. to discount (promissory note, bill of exchange). 2. to abate, rebate, allow, deduct, reckon off, diminish, lessen. 3. to leave out, disregard.

~ uma letra de câmbio to discount an exchange bill.

descontário, descontatário s. m. the legitimate holder of a discounted title.

descontentadiço adj. discontented, hard to please, peevish, sulky.

descontentamento s. m. (also descontento) discontentment, displeasure, dissatisfaction, disgust; fret, trouble, sorrow.

descontentar v. 1. to discontent, displease, dissatisfy, disoblige, disgust. 2. to disgruntle, disaffect. 3. ~-se: a) to be displeased, disgusted. b) to grow sad, be tired.

descontente s. m. + f. grumbler, repiner; malcontent. ‖ adj. discontent, unsatisfied, ill-pleased, malcontent, disgruntled, disaffected; snuffy. ‖ ~mente adv. discontently.

estar ~ to repine. viver ~ de sua vida to live a discontented life.

descontinência s. f. incontinence; unchastity.

descontinuação s. f. (pl. -ões) discontinuance, discontinuation, intermission, interruption, cessation.

descontinuar v. 1. to discontinue, leave off, cease, stop. 2. to suspend, interrupt, intermit, break off (for a time). 3. ~-se to be discontinued, suspended.

descontinuidade s. f. discontinuance, discontinuity, discontinuousness.

descontínuo adj. discontinuous, incoherent, intermittent, disconnected. ‖ descontinuamente adv. discontinuously.

desconto s. m. 1. discount(ing). 2. abatement, deduction, reduction, allowance, rebate; compensation. 3. (Braz.) loss in weight due to the transportation (of cattle).

~ sobre o frete allowance on weight. ~ pelo pagamento à vista cash discount. ~ para revenda trade discount. sem ~ without rebate, straight.

descontratar v. to annul or cancel a contract.

descontrolado adj. uncontrolled; unruled, unbridled, unrestrained, reinless, ungoverned; upset.

descontrolar v. not to control, abandon, give away. neglect.

desconvencer v. to dissuade, advise against.

desconveniência s. f. 1. inconvenience. 2. disadvantage. 3. prejudice.

desconveniente adj. m. + f. inconvenient, not suitable, disadvantageous. ‖ ~mente adv. inconveniently.

desconversação s. f. (pl. -ões) unsociableness; impoliteness.

desconversar v. 1. to break off a conversation. 2. to change the subject of a discourse. 3. to dissimulate, dissemble.

desconversável adj. m. + f. (pl. -áveis) 1. unsociable. 2. rough, harsh, coarse, rude. 3. solitary, lonely. ‖ ~mente adv. unsociably.

desconverter v. to cause a converted person to relapse.

desconvidar v. to disinvite, recall an invitation.

desconvir v. to disagree, discord, not to suit, be inconvenient.

descoordenar v. to disarrange what had been coordinated.

descor s. f. lack of colour, colourlessness.

descorado adj. 1. discoloured, colourless. 2. pale, palid, wan, bloodless. 3. rusty, weathering, faded.

descoramento s. m. want of colour, colourlessness, paleness, wanness, bleaching, discolourment.

descorante s. m. decolourizer, bleacher, decolourant. ‖ adj. m. + f. discolouring, decolourizing, bleaching.

descorar (I) v. 1. to discolour, decolourize, bleach, weather, fade. 2. ~-se to grow pale, fade away, pale.

descorar (II) v. to forget, not to remember.

descorçoar v. = descorçoar.

descordo (ô) s. m. a sort of troubadour's ballad.

descornar v. 1. to break the horns (animal). 2. to poll.

descoroar v. to discrown, uncrown, deprive of a crown, dethrone.

descoroçoado adj. (also descorçoado) discouraged, disheartened, dejected, drooping, despondent, dispirited, downcast. ‖ -amente adv. discouragedly.

descoroçoar v. (also descorçoar) to discourage, dishearten, deject, dispirit, depress, discountenance, dismay.

descorolado adj. (bot.) apetalous, without petals.

descorrelacionar v. to break a correlation.

descortejar v. to be discourteous, disrespect, disregard.

descortês adj. m. + f. (pl. descorteses) discourteous, unkind, uncivil, ungracious, ill-mannered, misbehaved, impolite, disobliging, rude, unfriendly, ungentle. ‖ ~mente adv. discourteously, unkindly.

descortesia s. f. discourteousness, discourtesy, unkindness, incivility, ungraciousness, impoliteness, rudeness, unfriendliness, ungentleness, ill manners, unmannerliness, rudeness, coarseness, grossness, disrespect, disregard.

descortiçamento s. m. decortication, barking, stripping off (bark).

descortiçar v. 1. to decorticate, bark, strip off the bark. 2. to peel, pare.

descorticar v. to shell, husk, peel, pare.

descortinar v. 1. to pull the curtain, disclose, lay open, expose to view, show. 2. to reveal, make known, bring to light, discover, find out. 3. (Braz.): a) to penetrate (into the jungle). b) to clear, stub (woods).

descortinável adj. m. + f. (pl. -áveis) noticeable, visible.

descortino s. m. (Braz.) 1. discovering, seeing from afar. 2. (fig.) sagacity, intelligence, perspicacity.

descosedura s. f. ripping, unsewing, unstitching.

descoser v. 1. to rip, unsew, unstitch, pick out stitches. 2. to separate, disunite. 3. ~-se to tear, rip, rend apart, be unsewed, unstitched.
~ a amizade to break gradually with a friendship. ~ a vida a alguém to find fault with, censure. ~ as orelhas a alguém (fig.) to reprimand s. o.

descosido adj. 1. unstitched, unsewed. 2. loose, incoherent, disconnected.

descostumar v. = **desacostumar**.

descostume s. m. disuse, disusage, cessation of practice or exercise, desuetude.

descotoar v. to take away the cotton (down), clean of fluff.

descravar v. 1. to pull out nails, unnail. 2. to turn away the eyes, shut one's eyes.

descravejar v. 1. to take away the nails of a horseshoe. 2. to take a jewel or stone out of its setting.

descravizar v. to disenthral, (set) free from slavery; emancipate.

descrédito s. m. discredit, disgrace, disesteem, disparagement, defame, dishonour, disrepute; scandal.

descremação s. f. (pl. -ões) skimming the cream from the milk.

descremar v. to skim, separate the cream from the milk.

descrença s. f. incredulity, want of faith, faithlessness, disbelief, ungodliness; doubt.

descrente s. m. + f. unbeliever, infidel. ‖ adj. incredulous, unbelieving, infidel. ‖ ~mente adv. incredulously.

descrer v. 1. to disbelieve, refuse to believe, deny the truth. 2. to discredit, fail to give credit to. ~ a fé to renounce one's faith.

descrever v. 1. to describe, make a description of, relate, narrate, portray, explain. 2. to draw, trace, outline, delineate.
~ um círculo to trace or draw a circle. ~ uma gravura to describe a picture.

descrição s. f. (pl. -ões). 1. description, report, narration, depiction, portrayal, definement; picture. 2. delineation, marking out. 3. enumeration, specification.
~ completa full description. ~ de um festa description of a festival. ~ de uma paisagem portrayal of a landscape.

descrido s. m. disbeliever, unbeliever, infidel, atheist. ‖ adj. unbelieving, sceptic, ungodly, trustless, faithless, unfaithful.

descriminar v. to justify, absolve (from crime), exculpate, acquit.

descristianização s. f. (pl. -ões) dechristianization.

descristianizar v. to dechristianize, turn away from Christianity, to paganize.

descritível adj. m. + f. (pl. -íveis) describable, that can be described.

descritivo s. m. description. ‖ adj. descriptive; graphic(al). ‖ -amente adv. descriptively; by description.

descritor s. m. describer, person who describes or depicts; reporter. ‖ adj. describing, depicting; reporting.

descruzar v. to uncross, change from a cross-wise position.
~ as pernas to uncross one's legs.

descuidado s. m. 1. want of application, negligence, forgetfulness, carelessness, heedlessness; inadvertence. 2. neglecter, forgetter, incautious person. ‖ adj. 1. incautious, careless, heedless, regardless, reckless. 2. mindless, brainless, forgetful, thoughtless. 2. inattentive. 3. negligent, disregardful, unguarded, slack, flighty, supine. 4. untidy, slovenly. 5. lazy, indolent, idle. ‖ -amente adv. incautiously, absentmindedly.
apanhar uma pessoa -a to take s. o. napping.

descuidar v. 1. to treat carelessly, neglect, slight, disregard. 2. to forget, oversee, overlook. 3. ~-se: a) to become careless. b) to forget o. s.
~-se de fazer a lição to fail to make one's (school) task. ~-se de seus deveres to neglect one's duties. ele descuida de sua roupa he is careless of his clothes.

descuidista s. m. + f. (Braz., sl.) a thief who takes advantage of his victim's weak point.

descuido s. m. 1. incautiousness, carelessness, unguardedness, disregard, negligence, heedlessness. 2. lapse, default, oversight, overslip. 3. inadvertence, inadvertency, unwariness.
num momento de ~ in an unguarded moment.

descuidoso adj. unheeding, careless, thoughtless, unobservant, casual, unguarded, negligent. ‖ -amente adv. carelessly, anyway.

desculpa s. f. 1. excuse, pardon, apology. 2. exculpation, exoneration, absolution, defence, extenuation. 3. evasion, subterfuge, pretext.
não há ~ alguma there is no excuse whatsoever. peço-lhe ~s I beg your pardon. pedir ~s to ask for a person's pardon.

desculpador s. m. excuser, defender. ‖ adj. apologetic, excusing, forgiving.

desculpar v. 1. to excuse, pardon, apologize, forgive, exculpate. 2. to acquit, justify, exonerate, extenuate, condone. 3. ~-se to excuse o. s., beg pardon; eat humble pie.
~-se com a ignorância to plead ignorance. ~-se por chegar atrasado to excuse o. s. for coming late. desculpe! sorry! desculpe-me! I beg your pardon. desculpe o meu atraso will you, please, excuse me for being late. ele desculpou-se dizendo he apologized by saying. não tente ~-se! don't back out! queira ~ o incômodo excuse my intrusion.

desculpável adj. m. + f. (pl. -áveis) excusable, pardonable.

descultivar v. to fail to cultivate, lay fallow; abandon.

desculto s. m. 1. want of worship, disaffection. 2. disrespect.

descumprir v. to disobey, disregard; not to comply with.

descuramento s. m. neglect, negligence, carelessness; dereliction, laxity.

descurar v. to neglect, be careless, disregard; omit, slight, forget; relinquish, abandon, forsake.

descuriosidade s. f. lack of curiosity, incuriousness, incuriosity, indifference.

descurioso adj. incurious, indifferent; lazy. ‖ **-amente** adv. incuriously.

descurvar v. to unmake a curve, unbend, make straight, straighten.

desdar v. 1. to unlace, unbind; untie, unfasten. 2. to retake, regain. 3. ∼**-se:** a) to be undone, unlaced. b) get loose.

desde prep. since, from; after.
∼ **agora,** ∼ **o presente** henceforth, from thence, from that time on. ∼ **aquele tempo** thence, from thenceforward. ∼ **aquele tempo em diante** thenceforth, thenceforward. ∼ **aqui** from this place on. ∼ **o berço** from the cradle. ∼ **cedo** early. ∼ **a criação do mundo** since the creation of the world. ∼ **criança** from or since childhood. ∼ **então** thenceforth, thenceforward, ever since, from that time. ∼ **já,** ∼ **logo** at once, immediately, directly. ∼ **ontem** since yesterday. ∼ **quando?** since when, how long ago? ∼ **que** since, as soon as, inasmuch as, provided, now. ∼ **que é assim, não há nada mais que fazer** since that is so, there is nothing more to be done. ∼ **que nasci** since I was born. ∼ **sempre** since always.

desdém s. m. 1. disdain, disdainfulness, depreciation, contempt, abomination, despite, scorn. 2. haughtiness, pride, arrogance, presumption.

desdenhador s. m. person who disdains, scorner, despiser. ‖ adj. disdaining, despising, scorning.

desdenhar v. to disdain, scorn, despise, condemn, spurn; disregard, disesteem, depreciate.

desdenhativo adj. disdainful, scornful, contemptuous.

desdenhável adj. m. +f. (pl. **-áveis**) contemptible, despicable, worthless, mean. ‖ **desdenhavelmente** adv. despicably.

desdenhoso adj. disdainful, scornful, contemptuous, fleering, supercilious, demure, depreciating. ‖ **-amente** adv. disdainfully.

desdentado s. m. (zool.) edentate: one of an order of mammals without teeth. ‖ adj. edentate, without teeth; fangless.
animal ∼ an edentate animal.

desdentar v. 1. to break or draw the teeth, make toothless. 2. ∼**-se** to lose the teeth.

desdita s. f. 1. misfortune, unluckiness, infelicity. wretchedness. 2. disaster, mischange. 3. misery. poverty.

desditoso adj. (also, but less common **desditado, desdito**) unfortunate, fortuneless, unhappy, wretched, unlucky; miserable. ‖ **-mente** adv. unfortunately, miserably.

desdizer v. 1. to unsay, deny, contradict, recant, gainsay. 2. to differ, oppose, discord. 3. ∼**-se** to retract, disavow.

desdobramento s. m. 1. unrolling, unfolding. 2. development, evolution.

desdobrar v. 1. to unfold, unroll; display. 2. (fig.) to disintegrate, separate into fractions. 3. to develop, expand, extend. 4. (mil.) to deploy. 5. ∼**-se** to be unfold or displayed.
desdobramos nossos esforços para terminar em tempo we doubled our efforts to finish in time.

desdobrável adj. m. + f. (pl. **-áveis**) that can be unfolded.

desdobre s. m. (Braz.) 1. unfolding; displaying. 2. development, evolution.

desdobro (ô) s. m. cutting of logs into planks.

desdormido adj. (Braz.) fatigued, worn out.

desdourar v. (also **desdoirar**). 1. to ungild, deprive of gilding, darken, tarnish. 2. to obscure, stain one's glory or reputation. 3. to discredit, dishonour. 4. ∼**-se:** a) to become dull. b) to fade, decay, lose its gilding.

desdouro s. m. (also **desdoiro**) 1. tarnish, blemish, stain. blot. 2. dishonour, discredit.

deseclipsar v. 1. to discover, bring to light, uncover. 2. to uncloud, shine again, reappear (after an eclipse). 3. to restore one's reputation. 4. ∼**-se** to be enlightened.

desedificação s. f. (pl. **-ões**) bad example, demoralization; scandal.

desedificar v. to give a bad example, demoralize, scandalize.

deseducação s. f. (pl. **-ões**) want of education, poor education.

deseducado adj. uneducated, ill-mannered, uncivil, impolite.

deseducar v. to neglect the education of, not to educate.

deseixar v. 1. to take away the axle, deprive of the axle. 2. to remove from the axle.

desejador s. m. wisher, desirer. ‖ adj. wishing, desiring, wanting, eager.

desejar v. 1. to wish, want, will, desire, covet. 2. to hanker after, crave, long for. 3. to envy.
∼ **com ânsia alguma coisa** to pant after a thing. ∼ **ardentemente** to suspire, rave, ambition. ∼ **ver alguém pelas costas** to want to see someone's back. **desejo boas melhoras** I trust you will soon be better. **desejamos muito um carro** we wish we had a car. **como** ∼**!** as you please! **deixa muito a** ∼ it is far from being what one might wish. **não** ∼ **mal a ninguém** to wish nobody ill. **que deseja?** what do you want?

desejável adj. m. + f. (pl. **-áveis**) desirable, eligible; covetable. ‖ **desejavelmente** adv. desirably.

desejo s. m. desire, want, wish, will; wishfulness, mind. 2. longing, hankering, urge, passion. 3. (fig.) appetite, hunger, thirst.
à medida de seus ∼**s** according to your wishes. **com nossos melhores** ∼**s** with our best wishes. **seus** ∼**s, para nós, são ordens** your wishes are commands to us.

desejoso adj. desirous, solicitous, anxious, eager; wishful, yearning, willing. ‖ **-amente** adv. desirously.

deselegância s. f. want of elegance, inelegance, ungainliness.

deselegante adj. m. + f. inelegant, ungraceful, ungainly, unhandsome; frumpish, dowdy, slouchy. ‖ ∼**mente** adv. inelegantly.

desemaçar v. to open a bundle (of documents, deeds, notes), unbundle, unpack.

desemadeirar v. to take away the planking or boarding.

desemalar v. to unpack (a trunk or box).

desemalhar v. to take out of the meshes of a net.

desemaranhar v. 1. to unravel, disembarrass, disentangle. 2. to unknit, untwine, unweave, unthread. 3. to unsnarl. 4. (fig.) to unriddle, solve.

desembaciar v. to clean (as a window from mist), render untarnished.

desembainhar v. 1. to unseam, unsew, rip up. 2. to draw, unsheathe, uncover (as a sword).
∼ **a língua cortadora** to lampoon, satirize.

desembalagem s. f. (pl. **-ens**) unpacking.

desembalar v. 1. to unpack, unbale, open a bale, uncase, unwrap. 2. to separate the bullet from the cartridge.

desembandeirar v. 1. to strike the flag. 2. to remove a flag or flags.

desembaraçado adj. 1. unembarrassed, disengaged, unencumbered, unhindered, unimpeded, unrestrained. 2. free, easy, clear(ed), ready, prompt, quick, agile. ‖ **-amente** adv. freely, easily.
um estilo ∼ an unlaboured style. **uma moça -a** an unaffected girl.

desembaraçar v. 1. to disembarass, disencumber, disentangle, disengage, disembroil. 2. to free, clear, rid. 3. to unknit, untwine, unwind, outwind. 4. to unravel, extricate. 5. to unriddle. 6. ~-se to free o. s., get rid of.
~-se de alguém to get rid of s. o. ~-se de todos os cuidados to rid o. s. of all cares. ~-se de um negócio trabalhoso to disentangle o. s. from a tedious business.

desembaraçável adj. m. + f. (pl. -áveis) extricable.

desembaraço s. m. 1. disembarrassment, disengagement, unrestraint, unreserve, familiarity. 2. readiness, ease, easiness, facility, agility. 3. vivacity, quickness, liveliness, promptness, briskness. 4. courage, self-reliance, self-assurance.

desembaralhar v. to disintricate, extricate, disentangle, unravel, set in order, clear.

desembarcação s. f. (pl. -ões) disembarkment, landing.

desembarcadouro s. m. (also **desembarcadoiro**) 1. landing-place, wharf, quay (plate P 16). 2. ~s pl. wharfage.
~flutuante landing-stage.

desembarcar v. 1. to disembark, debark, land, set on shore. 2. to unship, discharge, unlade, unload. ~ mercadorias to unship or unload goods. ~ passageiros to land passengers. ao ~ at one's landing.

desembargador s. m. chief judge, judge at the High Court, judge at the Court of Appeals.

desembargar v. 1. to remove an embargo. 2. to set free, set at liberty. 3. to dispatch, expedite, forward.

desembargo s. m. 1. raising of an embargo. 2. clearing, dispatching, expedition. 3. (jur.) replevin.

desembarque s. m. disembarkation, debarkation, landing.
~ de mercadorias discharging of merchandises. ~ de passageiros landing of passengers. **despacho de** ~ order of disembarkation.

desembarrancar v. to take out of the mire, draw out of mud.

desembarrigado adj. (S. Braz.) thin-bellied, meagre.-

desembarrigar v. (S. Braz.) to emaciate, grow thin or lean.

desembarrilar v. 1. to take or pour out of a barrel, empty. 2. (fig.) to tell a person the plain truth.

desembaular v. to take out of a trunk or chest.

desembebedar v. 1. to make sober, sober up. 2. to recover from drunkenness, grow sober.

desembestada s. f. a furious runaway (horse), galloping run.

desembestado adj. unbridled, unruled, ungoverned, unrestraint, unmanageable; furious. ‖ -amente adv. unmanageably.

desembestamento s. m. furiosity; loss of control.

desembestar v. 1. to shoot, let fly an arrow. 2. to run furiously, run away (horse). 3. to fly into a passion.

desembezerrar v. to regain one's good humour, cease to be sulky.

desembirrar v. 1. to calm, appease, make reasonable, bring to reason. 2. ~-se to come to reason.

desembocadura s. f. 1. discharge (of a river). 2. mouth (of a river), issue.

desembocar v. 1. to discharge, disembogue, disgorge, fall or flow into (river). 2. to run into (street), lead, emerge.
esta travessa vai ~ **no mercado** this lane leads into the market-place.

desembolsar v. to disburse, spend, lay out, make payments, expend, come down with money.

desembolso (ô) s. m. disbursement; outlay, payment, expenditure.

desemborcar v. to replace to its proper position (a fallen object).

desemborrachar v. (pop.) to make sober, sober up.

desemborrascar v. 1. to clear up (weather), brighten. 2. to appease, quiet, calm.

desemboscar v. 1. to drive out from an ambuscade; dislodge, turn out, displace. 2. ~-se to rush out from an ambuscade.

desembotar v. 1. to make sharp, sharpen. 2. to make nimble.

desembraçar v. to take from the arm, let loose.

desembramar v. (Braz.) to disentangle, unsnarl; unriddle.

desembravecer v. 1. to tame, make tame, domesticate. 2. ~-se: a) to become tame or appeased. b) to grow gentle.

desembrear v. 1. to clean from tar. 2. (mot.) to declutch, ungear.

desembrenhar v. 1. to force to leave the sheltering bushes. 2. to expel from the brambles; startle. 3. ~-se (fig.) to get rid of; extricate.

desembriagar v. 1. to make sober. 2. ~-se to sober up.

desembridar v. to take away the bridle, unbridle.

desembrulhado adj. 1. unpacked. 2. (fig.) disentangled, cleared up.

desembrulhar v. 1. to unpack, unroll, unfold, unravel, unwrap, open. 2. to disentangle, disembroil, disintricate. 3. to set in order, clear up, explain.

desembrulho s. m. 1. disentangling, unravelling, unfolding. 2. clearing up, explanation.

desembruscar v. to uncloud, clear up.

desembrutecer v. 1. to polish, refine. 2. to civilize, teach, educate. 3. to humanize, domesticate, tame.

desembruxar v. to free from sorcery, disenchant.

desembuçar v. 1. to unmuffle, unveil, uncover. 2. to disclose, reveal, manifest. 3. ~-se to reveal o. s., show one's colours.

desembuchar v. 1. to disgorge, throw out, pour out. 2. to unstop. 3. to reveal (secrets), blab out; speak frankly, say openly, unbosom.
desembuche! (pop.) weigh in! spit it out!

desemburrar v. 1. to polish, refine, civilize, educate. 2. ~-se: a) to become reasonable. b) to improve o. s.

desembutir v. to unmortise, loosen the mortises or joints.

desemedar v. to take away the hay from a heap or a rick.

desemoinhar v. to sift, separate the chaff.

desemoldurar v. to take out of a frame, unframe, take apart.

desempacar v. (Braz.) to cease balking (horse).

desempachar v. 1. to deobstruct, disencumber. 2. ~-se to get rid of, free o. s. of.

desempacho s. m. riddance, clearing from incumbrance; unblocking; extrication.

desempacotamento s. m. unpacking, unwrapping.

desempacotar v. 1. to take out of a package. 2. to unpack, unwrap.

desempalhar v. 1. to remove from the straw, take out from the straw. 2. to take away the straw.

desempalmar v. to release, loose (what had been concealed in the hand).

desempambado adj. (N. Braz.) free, easy, frank. ‖ -amente adv. easily, freely.

desempanado adj. 1. untarnished; cleared up, enlightened. 2. (Braz.) frank, sincere, open, ingenious.

desempanar v. 1. to unvail. 2. (fig.) to enlighten, brighten, clear up, explain. 3. to wipe clean (glass, mirror).

desempapelar v. to take away the paper, unpack. unfold, unwrap; remove the wall-paper.

desempar v. to take away the props or pales from the vines.

desemparceirar v. to separate partners.

desemparedar v. to destroy the immurement.

desemparelhar v. to unmatch, unyoke, separate (a pair).

desempastar v. to unpaste, dissolve.

desempastelar v. (typogr.) to straighten out pi, distribute pied matter (types or other printing material that had been disarranged or mixed up).

desempatador s. m. arbitrator, umpire; referee, judge.

desempatar v. 1. to decide, resolve. 2. to give the casting vote, clear a difficulty. 3. ~-se to make up one's mind, arrive at a decision, be decided.

desempate s. m. 1. decision; resolution. 2. clearing up of a difficulty, settling of a matter.
partida de ~ play-off game. ponto de ~ vantage. voto de ~ casting vote.

desempavesar v. 1. to take away the pavese (large shield). 2. (fig.) to stop being arrogant.

desempeçar, desempecer v. 1. to free from incumbrance, disentangle, disencumber, remove hindrances, extricate. 2. ~-se to get rid of, free o. s. from.

desempecilhar v. 1. to remove hindrances, disentangle, disencumber. 2. ~-se to free o. s. from, get rid of.

desempeço (ê) s. m. riddance, disencumbrance, clearing from difficulties.

desempedernir v. 1. to soften, mollify. 2. to assuage, mitigate, palliate.

desempedrar v. 1. to clear of stones. 2. to unpave. 3. to soften, mollify.

desempegar v. to take out of an abyss, river or lake.

desempenadeira s. f. (constr.) float, mortar board, trowel (plate A 7).

desempenado adj. 1. straight, unwarped. 2. (Braz.): a) strong, robust, powerful. b) gallant, chivalrous.

desempenar v. 1. to straighten, unwarp. 2. ~-se to straighten up, become straight again.

desempenhar v. 1. to take out or redeem of a pawn. 2. to fulfill, acquit, discharge, perform (promise). 3. to execute, practise, attend; act, represent, officiate. 4. to effect, pay off (one's debts). 5. ~-se to acquit o. s. of.
~ bem o seu papel to act one's part well. ~ a outrem das suas dívidas to rid s. o. of his debts, pay the debts for him. ~ a palavra, ~ a promessa to perform one's promise, fulfill one's promise, keep one's word. ~ o papel do chefe to play the role of the boss, to boss. ~ um papel secundário to play the second fiddle.

desempenho s. m. 1. redemption of a pledge. 2. acquittal, discharge, fulfillment. 3. performance; practice. 4. execution, acting.
~ das obrigações acquittal of one's obligations. o ~ de suas funções the pursuance of his vocation.

desempeno s. m. 1. straightening, unwarping. 2. uprightness; gracefulness, dignified appearance: deftness, versatility. 3. a carpenter's level or ruler.

desemperramento s. m. (also desemperro) yielding.

desemperrar v. 1. to break stubbornness or obstinacy, render compliant. 2. to loosen; appease, mitigate. 3. to yield. 4. ~-se to become compliant.

desempestar v. to disinfect, cleanse from infection, purify.

desempilhar v. to unpile, unstack; derange, disarrange, put in disorder or confusion.

desemplastrar v. to remove the (medicinal) plaster.

desemplumar v. to deplume, pluck out the plumes or feathers.

desempoado adj. affable, frank, sincere; modest. ‖ -amente adv. affably, frankly.

desempoar v. 1. to dust, clean from dust or shake off the dust. 2. (fig.) to show sincerity, become affable.

desempobrecer v. 1. to free from poverty, render rich. 2. to become rich, recover from poverty.

desempoçar v. 1. to draw out of a well (water). 2. to dry or remove ponds or pools.

desempoladeira s. f. (also trolha) a mason's trowel, mortar board.

desempolar v. 1. to remove bubbles or blisters. 2. to level, flatten, smooth (plaster).

desempoleirar v. 1. to unroost. 2. (fig.) to expulse from a high position or place; to reduce, lower.

desempolgadura s. f. release (as of claws).

desempolgar v. to loosen, release, let go, set free, quit, stray.

desempossar v. to dispossess, deprive, divest, oust, expropriate, abridge.

desempregado s. m. 1. an unemployed. 2. ~s pl. the unemployed. ‖ adj. unemployed, unengaged, unoccupied, unplaced, out of job, out of work, breadless, workless.

desempregar v. 1. to remove s. o. from office, service or employment, dismiss. 2. ~-se to lose one's job or employment.

desemprego (ê) s. m. unemployment, want of employment.
seguro de ~ unemployment benefit, employment insurance.

desemprenhar v. 1. to lie in, bring forth. 2. (fig.) to communicate a secret; blab out.

desemproar v. to humble, lower, take s. o. down a peg or two.

desempunhar v. to unhand, take the hands from; release, let go.

desemudecer v. 1. to break silence, cease to be silent. 2. to regain speech.

desenamorar v. 1. to cause s. o. to renounce his love. 2. to cease to be in love with.

desenastrar v. to unbind, unfasten, untie.

desencabar v. to unhaft, release or loose the handle of.

desencabeçar v. 1. to dissuade, advise against. 2. (Braz.) to lead astray.

desencabrestar v. 1. to unyoke, unhalter. 2. (fig.) to render ungovernable. 3. ~-se to give o. s. over to passions, run riot.

desencabritar v. (Braz.) to fly in great haste, to decamp.

desencabular v. to win (horse) a race after finishing always as second or third.

desencadear v. 1. to unleash, unchain, unfetter, unloose, unlink. 2. to break out, burst forth (storm). 3. ~-se to break or get loose.
desencadeou-se uma grande tempestade a violent storm broke out.

desencadernação s. f. (pl. -ões) unbinding of books.

desencadernado adj. 1. unbound (as books). 2. (fig.) disconnected, loose.

desencadernar v. 1. to unbind (books). 2. (fig.) to disjoint, disconnect, separate.

desencalporar v. (Braz.) to cease to be unhappy or unlucky, return to happiness; recover from bad luck.

desencaixadura s. f., **desencaixamento** m. (also desencaixe) dislocation, disarticulation, disjointedness; separation, disunion.

desencaixar v. 1. to dislocate, disjoint, disarticulate, put out of joint. 2. to disunite, separate, dismount. 3. ~-se to be disunited, get asunder.

desencaixilhar v. to take out of the frame, unframe.

desencaixotamento s. m. unpacking, unboxing.

desencaixotar v. to unpack, unbox, uncase; take out of a box or case.

desencalacração s. f. (pl. -ões) riddance of difficulties or debts.

desencalacrar v. 1. to free of difficulties or debts. 2. to get free of debts.

desencalhar v. 1. to put afloat. 2. to set going. 3. to remove impediments, to disencumber.

desencalhe, desencalho s. m. a getting afloat, bringing off (a stranded vessel); removal of a hindrance.

desencalmar v. 1. to cool, refresh. 2. (fig.) to moderate, appease, tranquilize, calm. 3. ~-se to refresh o. s.

desencaminhado adj. out of the right way, astray, lost, devious, misguided; perverted. ‖ -amente adv. deviously.

desencaminhador s. m. 1. misleader. 2. seducer, corruptor. ‖ adj. 1. misleading. 2. seducing, corrupting.

desencaminhar v. 1. to misguide, misdirect, mislead, lead astray; seduce. 2. to embezzle, misemploy, deviate, misappropriate. 3. ~-se to go astray, take a bad course; disappear.

desencamisar v. = descamisar.

desencampar v. to give back s. th., return s. th. to its proprietor (that had been expropriated).

desencanar v. to deviate from a channel or pipe; go astray.

desencanastrar v. 1. to take out of a basket. 2. to unplait, untwist.

desencantação s. f. (pl. -ões) (also **desencantamento**) disenchantment, disillusion, disillusionment, break of spell.

desencantador s. m. disenchanter. ‖ adj. disenchanting, discharming.

desencantar v. 1. to disenchant, decharm, disillusion. 2. to discover, find what had been lost.

desencanto s. m. 1. disenchantment, disillusion. 2. freeing of witchcraft.

desencantoar v. to withdraw from retirement; raise from the dust.

desencapar v. t deprive of the cover; uncover.

desencapelar v. 1. to grow calm (sea). 2. (naut.) to unrig the mast. 3. to appease, calm, quiet.

desencapotar v. 1. to take off one's cloak, uncloak. 2. (fig.) to manifest, discover, reveal. 3. ~-se to discover o. s., reveal o. s.

desencaprichar v. 1. to cure a person from a whim. 2. to cease to be capricious or whimsical.

desencaracolar v. to unroll, uncurl, spread out.

desencarapelar v. to uncurl; straighten.

desencarapinhar v. to uncurl, straighten out, unkink.

desencarcerar v. to discharge (a prisoner), set free, release from a prison, disincarcerate, liberate, disimprison, set free from confinement.

desencardimento s. m. cleaning, cleansing, expurgation.

desencardir v. 1. to clean, cleanse, wash, bleach, whiten. 2. to purify, purge, expurgate.

desencarecer v. 1. to reduce or lower a price, abate; grow cheaper. 2. to depreciate, disesteem, undervalue, belittle.

desencargo s. m. fulfilment of one's duty, disengagement, release.

por ~ de consciência for the sake of one's conscience.

desencarnar v. to leave the body (as the soul).

desencarquilhar v. to remove the wrinkles, unwrinkle; smooth.

desencarrancar v. 1. to cheer (up). 2. to make cheerful again, cease to be sulky.

desencarregar v. 1. to discharge, disburden, unburden. 2. to exempt, free, acquit, rid. 3. to dismiss, remove from a position or employment. 4. ~-se to clear o. s., get rid.

~ a consciência to discharge one's conscience. **~ uma pessoa de todos os trabalhos** to rid a person of all troubles. **~-se de uma culpa, pondo-a em alguém** to cast the fault upon another.

desencarreirar v. to lead astray, mislead, misguide, misdirect; put on a wrong way.

desencarretar v. to dismount (a gun).

desencarrilar, desencarrilhar v. = descarrilar, descarrilhar.

desencartar v. to dismiss, remove or oust from an employment.

desencasar v. 1. to unhouse, dislodge; displace. 2. to remove from its socket or groove.

desencascar (I) v. to take out of a cask.

desencascar (II) v. to clean, cleanse, wash, bleach, whiten.

desencasquetar v. to dissuade, advise against, deter.

desencastelar v. 1. to drive out of a castle, beat out of a fortress; expel. 2. to throw down a pile or heap, unpile, unstack.

desencastoar v. to take out a stone of a ring, unset (a stone), remove a stone from its setting.

desencatarroar v. 1. to cure s. o. from a catarrh. 2. ~-se to recover from a catarrh.

desencavar v. (Braz.) 1. to dig up, dig out; ferret. 2. to find out, discover.

desencavernar v. to drive out from a lair or cavern.

desencavilhar v. to unpeg, unpin; unfasten, untie.

desencepar v. (also **desencarretar**) to dismount a cannon.

desencerar v. to take the wax off, dewax.

desencerramento s. m. 1. release, setting at liberty. 2. disclosing, opening; manifestation.

desencerrar v. 1. to release, set at liberty, set free. 2. to disclose, expose to, show, manifest; unfold, let out. 3. ~-se to be set at liberty; free o. s.

desencharcar v. to drain, dry.

desencher v. 1. to empty, pour out, spill. 2. to discharge, deflate.

desencilhar v. 1. to take off the saddle-girth. 2. (Braz.) to unsaddle, unharness.

desenclaustrar v. to make leave a cloister or monastery, to uncloister.

desenclavinhar v. to unclench, unclinch, open, force open.

desencobrir v. to uncover, lay bare, lay open, disclose, expose, make visible, show, open, manifest.

desencoifar v. to take off the coif or kerchief.

desencoivarar v. (Braz.) = descoivarar.

desencolar v. to plane off the edges of a board.

desencolerizar v. 1. to appease, calm; pacify, moderate. 2. ~-se to grow calm.

desencolher v. 1. to extend, stretch out. 2. to unshrink. 3. ~-se to grow bold, lose one's shyness.

desencomendar v. 1. to countermand, contradict, cancel former orders. 2. ~-se to refuse to fulfill another's orders.

desenconchar v. 1. to take out of the shell (as pearls). 2. to set free, release. 3. ~-se to come out of a hiding-place or a prison.

desencontrar v. 1. to fail to meet one another, cause to go different ways. 2. ~-se to disagree, dissent, be of a contrary opinion, diverge.

eles andaram desencontrados they were going different ways.

desencontro s. m. 1. failure in meeting. 2. divergency, disagreement, difference.

desencorajado adj. discouraged; weak-hearted, downcast, dejected, depressed.

desencorajar v. to discourage, depress, deject, dishearten, dispirit.

desencordoar v. to unstring, take off the strings (as of an instrument or tennis racket).

desencorpar v. to make meagre or lean; reduce the volume.

desencorporar v. 1. to disincorporate, detach from a corporation. 2. to separate, loosen. 3. ~-se to withdraw from a corporation.

desencorrear v. to uncord, untie, unfasten (animals).

desencortiçar v. to unwrinkle, smooth, polish.

desencoscorar v. 1. to smooth the wrinkles, unwrinkle. 2. to uncurl. 3. to remove the scab or crust.

desencostar v. 1. to deprive of a support; straighten. 2. ~-se to straighten up, not to lean upon or against.

desencovador adj. 1. digging up, ferreting out. 2. discovering, finding out.

desencovar v. 1. to dig out, dig up, ferret out, drive out of a hiding-place. 2. to discover, find out, bring to light.

desencovilhar v. 1. to drive out from a lair or den. 2. to give up a hiding-place.

desencravar v. to pull out (nails), unnail, unpin, unfix.

desencravilhar v. 1. to untie, loosen, make loose. 2. (fig.) to get s. o. out of difficulties, relieve s. o. of troubles.

desencrencar v. (Braz.) to settle a hitch or a problem, to smoothen things.

desencrespar v. 1. to uncurl. 2. ~-se to grow calm (sea).

desencruzar v. = **descruzar**.

desencurralar v. 1. to drive out of a pen, unpen; let out of the stable. 2. to set at liberty, disengage.

desencurvar v. 1. to make straight, straighten. eliminate any bends. 2. ~-se to grow straight.

desendemoninhar v. 1. to drive out the demon, exorcise the devil. 2. (fig.) to appease, calm, moderate.

desendeusar v. to divest of divinity, deprive of divine attributes, undeify, ungod.

desendividar v. 1. to acquit a person from an obligation or debts. 2. ~-se to get out of debt, pay one's debts.

desenegrecer v. to make white, whiten, bleach; clear.

desenervação s. f. (pl. -ões) toning up, invigoration.

desenervar v. to tone up, strengthen, invigorate.

desenevoar v. 1. to disperse the fog, clear of fog; uncloud. 2. to clear up, enlighten, brighten, illuminate. 3. to make glad, gladden, cheer.

desenfadadiço adj. pleasant, delightful, amusing, entertaining, sportful, diverting.

desenfadamento s. m. 1. diversion, amusement; recreation, entertainment. 1. rest, relaxation, repose.

desenfadar v. 1. to relax, repose, rest; refresh. 2. to divert, amuse, entertain, please, cheer up, recreate. 3. ~-se to divert o. s., have a good time.

desenfado s. m. 1. rest, relaxation, repose. 2. amusement, recreation, pleasure, sport. 3. ease, calmness, tranquility, quietness, composedness.

desenfaixar v. 1. to unswathe, unswaddle; unwind; unbind, unroll. 2. ~-se to become unswathed.

desenfardamento s. m. (also **desenfardo**) unpacking, opening a pack or bale.

desenfardar v. to open a pack or bale, unpack.

desenfarpelar(-se) v. to undress, take one's clothes off.

desenfastiadiço adj. (also **desenfastioso**). 1. appetizing, delicious, dainty. 2. pretty, smart, graceful, witty.

desenfastiar v. 1. to stimulate, whet the appetite, provoke appetite. 2. to amuse, entertain, divert, please, recreate, make merry. 3. ~-se to amuse o. s., take pleasure in.

desenfeitar v. 1. to take away the ornaments or attire, disembellish, disfigure. 2. ~-se: a) to take off ornaments, remove make-up. b) to undress.

desenfeitiçar v. 1, to disenchant, unbewitch, free of sorcery or witchcraft. 2. (fig.) to deliver from a passion.

desenfeixar v. to untie a bundle, unbundle, open (as a sheaf).

desenfermar v. to recover, convalesce.

desenferrujado adj. rustless, free of rust.

desenferrujar v. 1. to remove the rust; polish, make glossy .2. (fig.): a) to cheer up. b) to bring into form or fettle.

~ **a língua** to prate, chatter, blab.

desenfezar v. 1. to improve growth or health; strengthen. 2. to calm. 3. to cheer. 4. ~-se: a) to become healthy. b) to grow, invigorate.

desenfiar v. 1. to unstring, unthread; untie; loose, relax. 2. ~-se to withdraw.

~ **a agulha** to unthread the needle. ~ **um instrumento** to unstring or untune an instrument. ~ **pérolas** to unstring pearls.

desenfileirar v. to take out of the line or rank.

desenflorar v. 1. to deflower, deprive of flowers. 2. ~-se to lose the flowers.

desenforjar v. to take from the forge.

desenformar v. to take out of a mould.

desenfornar v. to draw out of the oven or kiln.

desenfrascar v. to pour out, spill out of a flask or bottle.

desenfreado adj. 1. unruled, unbridled, ungoverned, uncurbed, unrestrained, uncontrolled. 2. reinless, riotous, wild, checkless; free. ‖ **-amente** adv. wildly, riotously.

desenfreamento s. m. (also **desenfreio**) unruliness, immoderation, excess; turbulence, intemperance, outrage.

desenfrear v. 1. to unbridle, let loose, set free. 2. ~-se: a) to throw off the bridle. b) (fig.) to grow unruly, give rein to one's passions, lose self-control. c) to fly into a passion.

desenfrenar v. (S. Braz.) to unbridle.

desenfronhar v. 1. to take the pillow-case from the pillow. 2. to show, make known, disclose.

desenfueirar v. to remove the stakes of a cart.

desenfunar-se v. 1. to cease from swelling, unswell. 2. (fig.) to resign o. s., become modest.

desenfurecer v. 1. to appease one's anger or passion, to placate. 2. ~-se to grow calm, quiet down.

desenfurnar v. to take out of a cave.

desenfuscar v. to clear up, brighten.

desengaçadeira s. f. grape picker, instrument for stripping the grapes from the bunch.

desengaçar v. 1. to strip the grapes from the bunch. 2. (pop.) to devour, eat up swiftly.

desengaiolar v. 1. to set free from a cage, uncage, release. 2. (fig.) to release from prison. 3. ~-se to get out of prison.

desengajado adj. residing outside and not within the military quarters.

desengajar v. to dismiss (from an employment), disengage, release.

desengalfinhar v. to separate two fighting persons.

desenganado adj. 1. undeceived. 2. disillusioned.

~ **dos médicos** given over or up by the physicians. ~ **do mundo** disgusted with the world.

desenganador s. m. undeceiver, person who disillusions. ‖ adj. undeceiving, disillusioning.

desenganar v. 1. to undeceive, disillusion, open a person's eyes. 2. (med.) to give up a case. 3. (S. Braz.) to break in a horse. 4. ~-se to undeceive o. s., see clearly, see one's mistake, come to reason. ~-se de alguma coisa to be undeceived about something. ~-se com alguém to be plain with s. o.

desenganchar v. to unhook, unclasp, unhitch; unfasten, untie.

desengano s. m. 1. disillusion, undeceiving. 2. ~s pl. bitter experiences.

desengarrafar v. to pour out of the bottle.

— D 2 —

Compasso de pontas fixas

Compasso de mola

Porta tira-linhas

Estojo de pontas e lápis

Compasso articulado

Ponta   Tira-linhas

DESENHO GEOMÉTRICO (instrumentos)

Cabo de aço para guincho e comando

Garras e caçamba

Pau-de-carga

Braço do guindaste

Cabina

Lagartas do trator

DRAGA E ESCAVADORA

desengasgar v. 1. to clear the throat. 2. (fig.) to disentangle, disembarrass.

desengastar v. to take a stone out of a ring, unset a stone, take a precious stone out of its setting.

desengatar v. to uncouple, unlimber, unset, disconnect, uncramp, unlink; (tech.) disengage.

desengatilhar v. 1. to pull the trigger; uncock, fire. 2. (fig.) to inspire; unchain; have as a consequence.

desengavetar v. 1. to take out of a drawer. 2. to retrieve, resume something that had been put aside or forgotten.

desengenhoso adj. simple-minded, unskilful, awkward, clumsy, unhandy. ‖ -**amente** adv. unskilfully.

desenglobar v. to set apart from the whole.

desengodar v. to make less interesting or attractive; disillusion.

desengolfar v. 1. to take or come out of a gulf 2. (fig.) to rescue s. o. from danger or mistake.

desengomar v. to dissolve the gum, unstarch.

desengonçado adj. 1. disjoint, unhinged, out of joint. 2. tottering, loose, gangling, floppy. ‖ -**amente** adv. floppily.

desengonçar v. 1. to disjoint, unhinge, put out of joint. 2. to disunite, loosen. 3. to totter. 4. ~-**se** to be put out of joint, fall apart.

desengonço s. m. unhinging, putting out of joint; distortion; floppiness.

desengordar v. 1. to lose fatness, grow thin or lean, waste away. 2. to emaciate, cause meagerness.

desengordurar v. to take away the fat, degrease, clean from spots of grease.

desengraçado s. m. an ungainly boresome person. ‖ adj. 1. unpleasant, inelegant, ungraceful, unhandsome, awkward. 2. insipid, vapid, flat, banal, dull. 3. stupid, dense, crass. ‖ -**amente** adv. undhandsomely, awkwardly.

desengraçar v. 1. to deprive of grace. 2. (pop.) to dislike, disrelish.

desengrandecer v. to lessen, lower, decrease, disparage, belittle, minimize; undervalue, underestimate, underrate.

desengranzar v. (also **desengrazar**) to unstring beads.

desengravescer v. 1. to make less grave or serious, diminish, lessen the importance. 2. to facilitate, relieve, mitigate, alleviate, ease.

desengraxar v. 1. to unoil, degrease; render unpolished. 2. (pop.) to undye.

desengrenar v. to put out of gear, ungear, uncouple; disengage.

desengrenhar v. = **desgrenhar**.

desengrimpar-se v. to come down from the high horse.

desengrinaldar v. 1. to take away the garland or wreath, to unwreathe. 2. ~-**se** to be unwreathed.

desengrossar v. 1. to thin, make thinner, less thick. 2. to attenuate. 3. to reduce, shrink (as a swelling).

desengrumar v. to clean from the grume or clot, dissolve grumes or clumps.

desenguaranchar v. (Braz.) to clean a piece of land either for planting or building.

desenguiçar v. 1. to free from a spell. 2. to disentangle, free, set going.

desengulhar v. to free from nausea; relieve of melancholy; amuse, entertain.

desenhador s. m. designer, drawer, drafter, draftsman, draughtsman.

desenhar v. 1. to design, draw, outline, sketch, delineate, draft, trace. 2. to picture, represent by picture, create, figure. 3. to project, plan, scheme. 4. ~-**se** to take form, take shape, appear.

desenhista s. m. + f. tracer, drawer, sketcher, draftsman, draughtsman, designer.

desenho s. m. 1. design, sketch, drawing, draft, outline, draught, delineation (plate D 2). 2. picture, figure, layout, representation; pattern, device, motif. 3. purpose, project, enterprise, intention, plan.
~ **animado** trick picture. ~ **a carvão** charcoal drawing. ~ **em escala** drawing to scale. ~ **a mão livre** freehand sketching. ~ **de máquinas** machine drawing. ~ **em pastel** crayon, pastel. **estojo de** ~ drawing set. **livro de** ~**s** drawing book. **professor de** ~ art master.

desenjoar v. 1. to free from nausea, relieve of melancholy, make merry, amuse, entertain. 2. ~-**se** to amuse o. s., overcome melancholy.

desenjoativo s. m. aperitif, appetizer. ‖ adj. appetizing, tasty, delicious.

desenlaçamento s. m. unlacing; disentangling.

desenlaçar v. 1. to unthread, unlace, unknot, undo, untie; loose. 2. (fig.) to disentangle; settle, resolve, decide, determine. 3. ~-**se** to detach o. s., get loose; come off; get away.

desenlace s. m. conclusion, outcome, end, ending, denouement, issue, upshot; finish, epilogue.

desenlambuzar v. (pop.) to clean, cleanse, tidy up.

desenlamear v. 1. to clean of mud or mire, rub off the dirt, brush (off). 2. ~-**se** to get clean.

desenlapar v. 1. to drive out of a den or hiding-place (animal). 2. ~-**se** to give up a hiding-place, come out of a lair.

desenleado adj. 1. expeditious, efficient, quick, ready, prompt. 2. frank, open-hearted, outspoken. ‖ -**amente** adv. efficiently; frankly.

desenlear v. 1. to untie, loosen, unsnarl, unravel. 2. to disentangle, disembarrass, disencumber, release; liberate, relieve from difficulties. 3. ~-se to get free from difficulties.

desenleio s. m. loosening, unravelling, disentanglement, disembarrassment.

desenlevar v. to disenchant, disillusion, free from a spell.

desenliçar v. ·1. to unweave, untwine. 2. to disentangle, disencumber, unravel. 3. ~-se to get free, get loose.

desenlodar v. = desenlamear.

desenlouquecer v. 1. to cure of madness. 2. ~-se to recover from insanity, listen to reason.

desenlutar v. 1. to console, comfort. 2. ~-se to come out of mourning; cheer up.

desenobrecer v. (also **desnobrecer**) 1. to deprive of nobility; degrade, disenoble, debase, vilify. 2. ~-se: a) to lose one's title of nobility. b) to degrade o. s.

desenodoar v. to clean from spots or stains.

desenojar v. to free from nausea, to cheer, comfort.

desenovelar v. (also **desnovelar**) 1. to unwind, unroll, wind off; unthread. 2. (fig.) to find or follow the thread of (a narrative, plot). 3. ~-se to unroll itself, uncoil.

desenquadrar v. to take out of the frame, unframe.

desenraivecer v. 1. to appease, calm, quiet. 2. ~-se to grow calm, cool one's anger.

desenraizar v. = desarraigar.

desenramar (I) v. to divest of twigs or branches.

desenramar (II) v. to take (the typographic composition) out of the printer's chase.

desenrascar v. 1. to disentangle, disencumber, remove difficulties. 2. ~-se to free o. s. of difficulties, rid o. s. of.

desenredador s. m. one who disentangles, extricates.

desenredar v. 1. to untwine, unknot, unsnarl. 2. to disentangle, extricate, unravel, untangle, disembarrass, disengage. 3. to explain, explicate, show, elucidate, clear up. 4. ~-se to disentangle o. s., get rid of a trouble.
~ um mistério to solve a mystery.

desenredo (ô) s. m. 1. disentanglement, extrication, denouement, unravelling. 2. explanation, solution, clearing up, explication.

desenregelar v. 1. to unfreeze, thaw, melt. 2. to warm, heat.

desenriçar v. to uncurl, unroll, ·smooth, polish.

desenrijar v. to soften, weaken, make tender.

desenriquecer v. 1. to deprive of wealth, make poor, impoverish. 2. ~-se to become poor, lose riches.

desenristar v. to take the lance from its rest.

desenrodilhar v. 1. to unroll, uncoil, spread out. 2. ~-se to unroll, uncoil itself.

desenrolamento s. m. 1. unrolling, uncurling. 2. development, evolution, course of events.

desenrolar v. 1. to unroll, uncoil, uncurl, unwind, untwine. 2. ~-se: a) to develop, progress, take its way or course. b) to uncoil, unfold itself.
~ muitos textos to allege many texts, word by word. a tragédia desenrolou-se do seguinte modo the tragedy came to be the following way.

desenroscar v. 1. to untwine, untwist. 2. to unscrew. 3. ~-se to become disentangled.

desenroupar v. to deprive of clothes, undress, disrobe.

desenrubescer v. 1. to destroy the red colour; decolour, fade. 2. ~-se to lose the red colour, grow pale; pass out, faint, swoon.

desenrugar v. to take away the wrinkles, unwrinkle, make smooth.
~ o rosto to smooth one's brow.

desensaboar v. to remove the soap from, clean of soap, rinse (washed clothes).

desensaburrar v. to clean from ballast or sand.

desensacar v. to take out of a sack, unsack.

desensangüentar v. to wipe off the blood, clean from blood.

desensarado s. m. (Braz.) person who did not recover from a serious illness.

desensarilhar v. to unpile, unstack (arms).

desensebar v. to scour, clean of grease or fat (spots).

desensinar v. to unteach: 1. to consign to oblivion. 2. to cause to forget.

desensino s. m. unteaching, want of instruction, ignorance; oblivion.

desensoberbecer v. 1. to break one's pride, humble, humiliate; abash. 2. ~-se to lose one's pride, become humble or modest.

desensombrar v. 1. to clear up, brighten, lighten. 2. to uncloud. 3. to gladden, make glad.

desensopar v. to dry (up).

desensurdecer v. 1. to cure from deafness. 2. ~-se to lose deafness.

desentabuar v. to take away the planks (of the floor or ceiling).

desentaipar v. 1. to take away the framework. 2. to unpen, liberate, relieve, free. 3. to redress, avenge.

desentalar v. 1. to take away the laths or splints. 2. to deliver from trouble or difficulties, disentangle. 3. ~-se to get free from troubles or difficulties.

desentaramelar v. to loosen one's tongue, chatter, patter, prate, gabble, gibber, jabber.

desentarraxar v. to unscrew, unfasten.

desentediar v. 1. to free of nausea. 2. to amuse, entertain, recreate, divert; enliven.

desentender v. 1. to misunderstand, misconceive, misapprehend. 2. to pretend ignorance, feign misunderstanding. 3. ~-se to come to grips.

desentendido s. m. ignorant. ‖ adj. ignorant; misunderstood, mistaken. ‖ -amente adv. misunderstandingly, under the pretext of ignorance.
dar-se por ~ to feign ignorance, to do as if one did not understand.

desentendimento s. m. 1. misunderstanding, misapprehension, ignorance. 2. unpleasantness, disagreement, dissension.

desentenebrecer v. 1. to uncloud, clear up, brighten, lighten. 2. to illuminate, enlighten.

desenternecer v. 1. to disaffect, cause the loss of love or tenderness. 2. ~-se to become unloving.

desenterrado adj. exhumed, disentombed; (fig.) unearthed, discovered.

desenterrador s. m. 1. person who exhumes dead bodies. 2. (fig.) person who discloses or uncovers. ‖ adj. 1. exhuming, digging out. 2. discovering, disclosing.

desenterramento s. m. 1. exhumation, disinterment, unburying. 2. (fig.) discovering, revelation.

desenterrar v. 1. to unbury, disinter, exhume, excavate, dig up, unearth. 2. (fig.) to discover, bring to light, find out; investigate.

desenterroar v. to hack or break up clods (of soil).

desentesar v. 1. to unstiffen, loosen. 2. ~-se to grow loose; to slacken.

desentesourar v. 1. to take out of a treasury. 2. (fig.) to find out, communicate or publish (important facts).

desentibiar v. to encourage, embolden, animate.

desentoação s. f. (pl. -ões) singing out of tune, dissonance.

desentoado adj. out of tune, dissonant, discordant, inharmonious. ‖ -amente adv. dissonantly.

desentoar v. 1. to untune, discord, sing or play out of tune, jar. 2. (fig.) to speak boldly, talk unreasonably.

desentocar v. to unkennel, unearth, ferret out, drive out of a hiding-place.

desentolher v. to unbenumb, relieve from numbness, free of torpidity or stiffness.

desentonar v. to humble, humiliate.

desentorpecer v. 1. to free of torpidity or numbness. 2. (fig.) to reanimate, revive, quicken, wake up, enliven. 3. ~-se to cheer up, be unbenumbed, recover strength.

desentortar v. to unbend, make straight, straighten.

desentrançar v. (also **destrançar**) to unplait (hair), unbraid, untwine.

desentranhar v. 1. to unbowel, eviscerate, disembowel. 2. (fig.) to examine, sift, search. 3. to tear out of one's innermost. 4. ~-se: a) to kill o. s. by harakiri. b) to sacrifice o. s., do all one can for another person. c) to make a clean breast of, disclose one's feelings.

desentravar v. = **destravar**.

desentrelinhar v. (typogr.) to delete interlines.

desentrincheirar v. to drive out of the trenches, dislodge.

desentristecer v. 1. to drive away grief, banish sadness, make merry. 2. ~-se to gladden, cheer up, become merry again.

desentronizar v. to dethrone, disenthrone, uncrown, unking, depose.

desentropilhar v. (S. Braz.) to mix animals of different colours in one group.

desentrouxar v. to unpack, open a truss, bundle or fardel; to untruss.

desentulhador s. m. person who clears or removes rubbish. ‖ adj. clearing from rubbish, removing debris.

desentulhar v. to clear from rubbish, remove debris. ~ **um poço** to cleanse a well.

desentulho s. m. 1. clearing from rubbish. 2. rubbish, debris.

desentupido adj. unstopped, open.

desentupimento s. m. unstopping, opening; clearing.

desentupir v. 1. to unstop, cleanse, open, clear. 2. to free from obstructions, remove impediments. 3. (fig.) to blurt out, blab out, divulge.

desenturmado adj. in racing, the horse rated below the average.

desenturvar v. to uncloud, clear up.

desenvasar v. 1. to take out of the mud. 2. to cleanse from mud. 3. (naut.): a) to launch. b) to set afloat again.

desenvasilhar v. to take out or pour out of a vessel or cask.

desenvencilhar v. (also **desenvincilhar**) 1. to disentangle, disengage, loosen; untie, unfasten. 2. ~-se to become disengaged, get rid of.

desenvenenar v. 1. to unpoisen, free of poison. 2. to administer an antidote.

desenvergar v. 1. to unbend (the sails from their yards). 2. (pop.) to undress, disrobe.

desenvernizar v. to remove the varnish, unpolish; dull, sully.

desenviesar v. to take away the bias (of cloth).

desenviolar v. to hallow again, reconsecrate (as a church after a crime).

desenviscar v. to take away the lime, unglue.

desenvolto adj. 1. nimble, agile, brisk, light, spry, quick. 2. licentious, dissolute, wanton, indecent, bold, impudent. 3. dishonest, unscrupulous. ‖ **-amente** adv. nimbly; licentiously.

desenvoltura s. f. 1. nimbleness, agility. 2. boldness, insolence. 3. licentiousness, impudence, indecency.

desenvolvente adj. m. + f. developmental, developing; evolutionary.

desenvolver v. 1. to develop: a) unwrap, unroll, unfold, expand. b) disclose, explain, explicate, show, display, elucidate. clear. c) advance, progress, form, build. 2. ~-se to grow, ripen, mature, unfold, expand. ~ **uma idéia** to unfold an idea. ~ **um problema** (math.) to develop a problem. ~ **o serviço** to develop one's work.

desenvolvido adj. developed, grown, advanced, ahead, forward; instructed; ripe, mature.

desenvolvimento s. m. (also **desenvolução**) development: 1. building up, improvement, upgrowth, growth, progress, evolution. 2. explication, display, explanation, disclosure, unfolding. 3. systematic unfolding of a musical theme. ~ **de uma obra** the development of a work. ~ **de uma planta** the development of a plant. **em** ~ in progress.

desenvolvível adj. m. + f. (pl. **-íveis**) developable, improvable.

desenxabidez s. f. (also **desenxabimento**) insipidity, flatness, vapidity, unsavouriness, tastelessness, want of grace.

desenxabido adj. (also **desenxavido**) insipid, flat, banal, spiritless, unsavoury, vapid, tasteless; sottish, silly, foolish, absurd. ‖ **-amente** adv. insipidly, absurdly.

desenxabir v. to render unsavoury.

desenxamear v. to destroy or disperse a swarm.

desenxarciar v. to unrig, strip off the tackle.

desenxoframento s. m. desulphurization.

desenxofrar v. 1. to desulphurize, clean of sulphur, extract the sulphur. 2. (fig.) to apease, calm, quiet. 3. ~-se to grow calm, recover one's good humour.

desenxovalhado adj. 1. clean, neat, tidy, spotless. 2. well-dressed, elegant. ‖ **-amente** adv. cleanly, tidily.

desenxovalhar v. 1. to clean, cleanse, wash. 2. to unwrinkle, smooth. 3. to redress, revenge.

desenxovalho s. m. 1. cleanness, neatness, tidiness. 2. redress, reparation.

desenxovar v. to take out of a dungeon, liberate, set free.

desequilibrado adj. 1. unbalanced, unequaled, unsteady, deranged. 2. (fig.) crazy, top-heavy, insane.

desequilibrar v. 1. to unbalance, throw out of balance, derange, upset. 2. ~-se to be unbalanced, lose one's balance. ~ **a conta** to unbalance an account. ~ **os nervos** to shatter one's nerves.

desequilíbrio s. m. unbalance, distemper, disequilibrium, derangement; unstability, unsteadiness.

deserção s. f. (pl. **-ões**) desertion, defection, dereliction, abandonment, running from the colours.

deserdação s. f. (pl. **-ões**) disinheritance, disinheriting.

deserdado adj. 1. disinherited, deprived of heritage. 2. ungifted, unskillful, untalented.

deserdar v. 1. to disinherit, deprive of heritage, prevent s. o. from the right to inherit, exheredate. 2. ~-se to abstain from (an inheritance).

desertar v. 1. to unpeople, turn into a desert, lay waste. 2. to desert, abandon (forsake, overrun, renegade). 3. to leave, depart, quit, fly.

desértico adj. like a desert.

deserto s. m. 1. desert, wilderness, waste, bad lands. 2. desolation, solitude, isolation. ‖ adj. desert, uninhabited, wild, waste, unfrequented, solitary, forsaken. ‖ **-amente** adv. desertedly. **pregar no** ~ to cry out in the desert; to preach to deaf ears.

desertor s. m. deserter, runaway, fugitive, runagate, absconder, transfuge, renegade, turn-coat, flincher.

desescalada s. f. deescalation.
desesperação s. f. (pl. -ões) 1. despair, hopelessness, desperation, forlornness, despondency. 2. anger, rage, indignation, fury, ire.
desesperado adj. 1. hopeless, desperate, despondent, unpromising. 2. precipitant, rash, resolute, mad, furious. || -**amente** adv. desperately.
desesperador adj. despairing, hopeless.
desesperança s. f. despair, desperation, hopelessness.
desesperançar v. 1. to put one out of hopes, dash hopes; discourage, dishearten, depress. 2. ~-**se** to lose hope.
desesperante adj. m. + f. despairing, hopeless, desponding.
desesperar v. 1. to give no hopes, drive to despair; tease, tantalize, worry, torment. 2. to despair, despond, be cast down. 3. ~-**se**: a) to rave, anger, become impatient. b) to lose all hope.
desespero (ê) s. m. 1. despair, hopelessness, desperation, forlornness, despondency. 2. rage, anger, fury, irritation.
dar o ~ (Braz.) to get angry, lose one's temper. **em** ~ in despair. **no auge do** ~ in the deepest despair. **ele faz um jogo de** ~ he is playing a losing game.
desespero-dos-pintores s. m. (pl. **desesperos-dos-pintores**) (bot.) London pride, none-so-pretty.
desestagnar v. to cause stagnant waters to flow again or away.
desesteirar v. to take away the mats of a room; (fig.) discover, bring to light.
desestima, desestimação s. f. (pl. -ões) disesteem, disregard, disgrace, disfavour, despite, scorn, bad repute, contempt.
desestimador s. m. depreciator, columniator, slanderer. || adj. disesteeming, disregarding, disparaging.
desestimar v. 1. to disesteem, disrespect, disregard, despise, disgrace, disfavour. 2. to undervalue, depreciate, disparage. 3. ~-**se** to suffer from an inferiority complex.
desestorvar v. to remove obstacles or difficulties, disencumber, disimpede.
desestorvo (ô) s. m. removal of obstacles.
desevangelizar v. to unevangelize; annul the effects of a certain doctrine.
desexcomungar v. to withdraw an excommunication, disexcommunicate, absolve from excommunication.
desexcomunhão s. f. (pl. -ões) withdrawing of an excommunication, absolution from excommunication.
desfabricar v. 1. to unmake, undo. 2. to raze, destroy. 3. to disarrange, put out of order, upset.
desfabular v. to recant a fable or fiction, tell the truth.
desfaçado adj. barefaced, impudent, insolent, shameless. || -**amente** adv. impudently.
desfaçamento s. m. (also **desfaçatez**) impudence, shamelessness, barefacedness, effrontery, sauciness, insolence.
desfaçar-se v. to grow impudent, speak brazenly, become shameless.
desfaçatez s. f. shamelessness, cheek, impudence.
desfadiga s. f. rest, repose, ease, sleep.
desfadigar v. 1. to rest, restore, refresh; alleviate, relieve, assuage. 2. ~-**se** to repose, take a rest.
desfalcar v. 1. to defalcate, peculate, misappropriate, embezzle. 2. to diminish, lessen, lower. 3. to steal, rob, rifle, plunder.
desfalecente adj. m. + f. weakening, fainting, enfeebling, decaying, swooning; frail.
desfalecer v. 1. to faint, swoon, decay, waste away, grow weak and feeble, droop, vanish. 2. to collapse, die. 3. to forsake, depress, deject.

~ **no cumprimento da promessa** to fail to fulfil one's promise. ~ **na paga** not to pay, fail to pay. **não** ~ **em prudência** to be prudent.
desfalecido adj. faint(ed), drooping, exanimate, amort.
desfalecimento s. m. faintness, weakness, feebleness, breakdown; drooping, languishment, faint; exhaustion.
desfalque s. m. 1. defalcation, peculation, embezzlement, graft. 2. diminution, keeping back, stealing.
desfanatizar v. to free from fanaticism.
desfarelar v. (also **esfarelar**) to crumble, disintegrate, reduce to sawdust.
desfastio s. m. 1. appetite, desire of eating. 2. cheerfulness; entertainment, pastime.
desfavor s. m. 1. disfavour, disgrace, disesteem, disrepute, disregard, dislike. 2. contempt, disdain, scorn, repugnance, aversion, antipathy.
desfavorável adj. m. + f. (pl. -**áveis**) 1. unfavourable, disadvantageous, bad, unpropitious; unlucky. 2. unfriendly, inimical, adverse, contrary; uncomplimentary. || **desfavoravelmente** adv. unfavourably, adversely.
desfavorecer v. 1. to disfavour, discountenance; reject, repulse; disapprove, not to accept, not to support or back. 2. to hurt, prejudice, thwart.
desfavorecido adj. 1. unprotected, not supported. 2. disgraced. 3. not endowed with, ill-favoured.
~ **da natureza** not endowed with gifts of nature.
desfazedor s. m. undoer; destroyer. || adj. undoing, unmaking, destroying, breaking.
desfazer v. 1. to undo, unmake. 2. to demolish, break, destroy, ruin, pull down. 3. to deprive of, strip of, rid of, free of. 4. to unknit; rip up, take asunder. 5. to annul, cancel. 6. to abolish, annihilate, extinguish. 7. to depreciate, find fault with, undervalue, underrate. 8. to defeat, rout, beat. 9. to dissolve, dilute. 10. to disperse. 11. to disjoint, dismount. 12. ~-**se**: a) to get rid of, ease o. s. b) to disappear, be dispersed, melt. c) to be unripped, unsewed or disunited. d) to grow weak or thin.
~ **agravos** to redress grievances. ~ **um contrato** to break or violate a contract. ~ **um engano, erro** to clear up a mistake. ~ **um nó** to untie a knot. ~ **o noivado** to break up an engagement. ~ **os pacotes** to open the parcels. ~ **um tecido** to unweave, unknit, unrip. ~ **a venda** to annul a sale. ~-**se em bocados** to go to pieces. ~-**se uma coisa entre as mãos** to melt like butter before the sun. ~-**se dos criados** to dismiss the servants. ~-**se em desculpas** to ask a thousand pardons, offer many excuses. ~-**se como fumo** to vanish into smoke, come to nothing. ~-**se de um hábito** to get rid of a habit. ~-**se em lágrimas** to melt into tears. ~-**se de um ofício** to divest o. s. of an office. ~-**se em pó** to crumble into dust. **ela o desfez por completo** she picked him to pieces. **fazer e** ~ to do and undo. **a manteiga se desfez** the butter melted.
desfazimento s. m. undoing, annulling, abolishment, annihilation.
desfear v. to disfigure, make ugly, deface.
desfechar v. 1. to fire, shoot off, discharge (a gun). 2. to open, unlock, unfasten. 3. to break a seal. 4. to break or burst out (as a tempest). 5. to finish, end, conclude, result. 6. ~-**se** to go off (as the cock of a gun).
desfecho s. m. issue, outcome, conclusion, solution, result, effect, upshot, sequel, consequence.
desfeita (I) s. f. 1. affront, insult, outrage, ill usage. 2. (mil.) defeat, overthrow.
desfeita (II) s. f. (pop., also **desfeito**) a sort of purée prepared of codfish, chick-peas and onion.

desfeiteador s. m. offender, insulter; flouter.

desfeitear v. 1. to insult, abuse, affront, offend, outrage. 2. to flout, abase, slight, ignore, disregard.

desfeito adj. 1. undone. 2. disfigured, defaced. 3. violent, furious, dreadful, fierce. 4. dissolved, diluted, melted. 5. excessive, out of measure, enormous. || **-amente** adv. violently, excessively.
fugida -a a hasty or rapid escape or flight. **tempestade** -a a furious storm.

desferir v. 1. to brandish (as a sword). 2. to strike the strings of an instrument; emit sounds. 3. to fling, throw. 4. (naut.) to loosen (sails), unfurl. 5. to set sail, put to sea.

desferrar v. 1. to unshoe a horse. 2. to unfetter, unchain. 3. (naut.) to unfurl, loosen, heave out the sails. 4. **~-se** to lose or cast the horseshoe.

desferrolhar v. to unbolt, withdraw a latch; open.

desfervoroso adj. impassive, phlegmatic, dispassionate, nonchalant. || **-amente** adv. impassively.

desfiado s. m. 1. unweaving. 2. **~s** pl. stringy fringes. || adj. untwisted, unspun, unwoven; shredded.

desfiadura s. f. unweaving, untwisting, unthreading, unravelling.

desfiar v. 1. to unweave, untwist, unknit, unthread, unravel, unknot, fray. 2. to separate, divide, parcel out; examine or analyse minutely. 3. to enumerate, tell one's beads. 4. **~-se** to be reduced to threads, become frayed.

desfibrador s. m. 1. shredder. 2. shredding machine, doffer.

desfibramento s. m. shredding, removal of the fibres.

desfibrante adj. m. + f. shredding.

desfibrar v. 1. to remove the fibres, shred, defiber. 2. to analyse, split hairs; relate in details, scrutinize.

desfibrinar v. (chem.) to take away the fibrine, defibrinate.

desfiguração s. f. (pl. **-ões**) disfigurement, defacement, deformation; transformation; haggardness.

desfigurado adj. 1. disfigured, deformed, defeatured. 2. altered, modified. 3. haggard, worn.

desfigurador s. m. deformer, one who disfigures. || adj. disfiguring, deforming, defeaturing.

desfigurar v. 1. to disfigure, disfeature, defeature, deface, deform, disproportion. 2. to mar, blemish. 3. to disguise, feign, dissemble. 4. to alter, vary, change, transform. 5. **~-se** to be disfigured, put out of form.

desfigurável adj. m. + f. (pl. **-áveis**) defaceable.

desfilada s. f. file, marching, parade.
à ~ at full speed. **correr à ~** to run away hastily. **marchar à ~** to file off, parade.

disfiladeiro s. m. defile, narrow, ravine, col, gorge, hollow, kloof, dingle; pass, couloir.

desfilar v. to file, defile, march off in line or by files; parade.
~ em procissão to procession.

desfile s. m. 1. march, filing off, parade, review. 2. pageant, display, spectacle. 3. procession.

desfilhar v. 1. (bot.) to deprive of buds, disbud, nip or prune off the buttons. 2. to take away the children. 3. to separate a swarm of bees. 4. to unpeople, depopulate, dispeople, deprive of inhabitants. 5. **~-se** to be unpeopled.

desfitar v. to turn away the eyes, cease staring.

desfivelar v. to unbuckle, unclasp; unfasten, untie.

desfloração s. f. (pl. **-ões**) (also **desfloramento**) 1. defloration, deflowering. 2. ravishment, rape.

desflorador s. m. 1. deflowerer. 2. ravisher. || adj. 1. deflowering. 2. ravisKing.

desflorar v. 1. to deflorate, take away the flowers. 2. to deflower, deflour, despoil of beauty, damage,

vitiate. 3. to ravish, violate, rape. 4. (S. Braz.) to maltreat, mishandle (a horse).

desflorescer v. 1. to cease flowering, shed the blossoms; to fade, wither. 2. **~-se** to lose blossoms, be out of blossom.

desflorescimento s. m. fall or loss of the blossoms or flowers.

desflorestador s. m. (Braz.) deforester.

desflorestamento s. m. (Braz.) deforestation.

desflorestar v. to deforest, cut down the forests of a tract of land, clearing of timber.

desflorido adj. without flowers, bloomless.

desflorir v. 1. to cease flowering; fade, wither. 2. **~-se** to grow withered; decay.

desfolha, desfolhação s. f. (pl. **-ões**) 1. fall of the leaves; defoliation. 2. season of the falling of the leaves; fall.

desfolhada s. f. husking of maize or corn.

desfolhador s. m. person who takes away the leaves. || adj. divesting of leaves.

desfolhamento s. m. removal of the leaves; defoliation.

desfolhar v. 1. to take away the leaves or petals, defoliate, exfoliate. 2. to husk (maize or corn). 3. (N. Braz.) to unsheathe, draw a dagger or knife. 4. **~-se** to shed the leaves.
~ a vinha to lop the leafy branches of a vine.

desfolho (ô) s. m. defoliation, the work of pulling or tearing off the leaves.

desforçado adj. avenged, redressed, revenged.

desforçador s. m. avenger of wrongs.

desforçar v. 1. to avenge, revenge, redress, pay back, vindicate. 2. **~-se** to avenge o. s.

desforço (ô) s. m. vengeance, revenge, satisfaction, retaliation, acquittal.

desformar v. = **deformar**.

desforra s. f. (also **desforro**) revenge, retaliation, satisfaction, retribution, avengement.
em ~ in return, in requital. **tirar uma ~** to get even, take revenge.

desforrar (I) v. to take out the lining, unline.

desforrar (II) v. 1. to avenge, revenge, requite, compensate, repay. 2. to win one's money back (at gambling). 3. **~-se** to get even, be revenged of.

desfortalecer v. to disarm, dismantle, weaken.

desfortuna s. f. misfortune, mischance, ill luck; disaster, calamity, catastrophe.

desfradar v. 1. to disfriar, unfrock, expulse from a religious order. 2. **~-se** (rel.) to forsake one's order, become worldly.

desfraldar v. 1. to spread, furl. 2. **~-se** to fly (as a flag), unfurl (sails).

desfrangir, desfranjar v. 1. to take away the fringes. 2. to unwrinkle, smooth.

desfranzir v. 1. to undo the gathers or plaits. 2. to unwrinkle, smooth.

desfrechar v. 1. to let fly, shoot (arrows). 2. to throw, pitch, cast.

desfreqüentado adj. unfrequented, solitary, deserted, forsaken.

desfruir v. to enjoy, take advantage, have use of, usufruct.

desfruta s. f. (N. Braz.) harvest of coconuts.

desfrutador s. m. 1. usufructuary, enjoyer. 2. parasite. 3. jester. || adj. enjoing, having use of.

desfrutar v. 1. to gather the fruit of. 2. to usufruct, hold in usufruct. 3. to relish, delight, like. 4. to jeer, gibe, jest, make fun of, mock. 5. to sponge on.
~ alguém to take advantage of another's friendship, to sponge a person. **~ dinheiro** to waste money.

420 desfrutável — desidrogenar

desfrutável adj. m. + f. (pl. -áveis) 1. that may be usufructed or enjoyed. 2. (Braz.) tending to ridicule.

desfrute, desfruto s. m. 1. usufruct, enjoyment, right to use. 2. mockery, derision, scorn. 3. (Braz.) scandal, indignation.

desfundar v. to stave a cask, deprive of the bottom (tube or pipe).

desgabar v. to blame, discommend, find fault with; undervalue, underrate, belittle, depreciate.

desgabo s. m. disregard, contempt, depreciation, disparagement.

desgadelhado adj., **desgadelhar** v. = **desguedelhado, desguedelhar.**

desgalante adj. m. + f. uncourteous, uncivil, impolite. ‖ ~mente adv. uncourteously.

desgalgar v. to hurtle down, throw headlong; precipitate, cast down.

desgalhar v. to cut or tear off the branches, lop a tree.

desgarrada s. f. extempore popular song.

desgarrado adj. strawy, disorderly, lost; licentious, dissolute, libertine, lewd. ‖ -amente adv. disorderly, dissolutely, shamelessly.

flecha -a stray arrow. **ovelha** -a a lost sheep.

desgarrão s. m. (pl. -ões) violent push. ‖ adj. misleading.

desgarrar v. 1. to lead astray, mislead, misguide. 2. to miss one's way, be led into error. 3. (naut.) to fall off the course. 4. ~-se to break out, take to bad courses; straggle.

desgarre, desgarro s. m. 1. straying, going out of the way. 2. impudence, sauciness, boldness, effrontery. 3. elegance. 4. courage, bravery.

desgarronar v. (S. Braz.) to hamstring (animal).

desgastar v. 1. to consume, absorb, abrade, wear down, waste, destroy. 2. (pop.) to digest. 3. ~-se: a) to wear o. s. out. b) to be worn down.

desgaste, desgasto s. m. wearing, consuming, wastage, wear and tear; abrasion, erosion.

~ **das rochas** weathering. ~ **por atrito** detrition.

desgelar v. = **degelar.**

desgorjado adj. barenecked.

desgornir v. (naut.) to unreeve a rope.

desgostar v. 1. to disrelish, disgust, displease, dislike, distaste, loathe, irritate, vex, annoy. 2. to offend, pain; disgruntle, grieve. 3. ~-se to be displeased, grow weary.

desgosto (ô) s. m. 1. disgust; displeasure, annoyance, vexation. 2. shock; offence; trouble, grief, sorrow. 3. distastefulness.

a ~ with regret; in spite of. **imensos** ~s a sea of troubles. **sofrer** ~s to meet troubles.

desgostoso adj. 1. displeased, dissatisfied, discontent. 2. regretful, disgustful, annoying. 3. sorrowful, grieved. 4. tasteless, unsavoury. ‖ -amente adv. sorrowly; unsavourily.

desgovernação s. f. (pl. -ões) misgovernment, misgovernance, mismanagement, uncontrollableness.

desgovernado adj. 1. ungoverned, misgoverned, disordered, unruled, uncontrolled, undirected. 2. afloat, adrift. 3. masterless, guideless, rudderless. 4. mindless, careless. ‖ -amente adv. without control, disorderly.

desgovernar v. 1. to misgovern, mismanage, upset, overthrow. 2. ~-se: a) to become uncontrolled. b) to drift at the mercy of the waves. c) to lose self-control, behave ill, lead a disorderly life.

desgoverno (ê) s. m. misgovernment, mismanagement, misrule; misbehaviour, misconduct, excess, disorderly life.

desgraça s. f. (also **desgraceira**) 1. misfortune, ill luck, unluckiness, misadventure. 2. disaster, catastrophe, ruination, fatality. 3. trouble, grievousness, calam-

ity, downfall, affliction. 4. disgrace. 5. gracelessness.

cair em ~ to be out of favour. **a causa da nossa** ~ the rock on which we foundered. **ele é a** ~ **da família** he is the curse of his family. **nunca uma** ~ **vem só** misfortunes seldom come alone, one misfortune comes on the back of another. **para maior** ~ **sua** to complete his misfortune. **por** ~ unfortunately. **prevalecer-se da** ~ **alheia** to take advantage of another's misfortune. **ser perseguido pela** ~ to have ill luck, be unhappy.

desgraçado s. m. 1. poor fellow. 2. (sl.) wretch; rascal, scoundrel, devil. ‖ adj. unhappy, unlucky, unfortunate, miserable; disastrous, ill-fated, wretched. ‖ -amente adv. unhappily, unfortunately.

~ **de mim** poor me!

desgraçar v. 1. to render unhappy or unlucky, to ruin s. o., bring misfortune to. 2. (sl.) to violate, ravish. 3. ~-se to become unhappy, ruin o. s.

desgraceira s. f. (Braz.) continuous misfortunes.

desgracioso adj. 1. ungraceful, untoward, awkward, clumsy, ungainly, unlovely. 2. inelegant, uncouth. ‖ -amente adv. awkwardly, inelegantly.

desgranido adj. (S. Braz., sl.) wretched, miserable.

desgravidar v. to interrupt the pregnancy of; give birth to.

desgraxamento s. m. degreasing.

desgraxar v. to degrease, remove the grease from.

desgrenhado adj. 1. dishevelled, shaggy, unkempt, tousled, disorderly. 2. (fig.) topsy-turvy, untidy. ‖ -amente adv. shaggily.

desgrenhamento s. m. dishevelling, dishevelment.

desgrenhar v. to dishevel, tousle; rumple.

desgrilhoar v. to unfetter, unchain, unshackle.

desgrinaldar v. to remove the wreathes, unwreathe.

desgrudar v. 1. to deglutinate, unglue, come off. 2. ~-se to become unglued.

desgrumar v. to break (clumps) in particles, grind.

desguampar v. (S. Braz.) to deprive of horns, dehorn.

desguardar v. 1. not to guard. 2. to neglect, be careless.

desguaritar v. (Braz.) 1. to stray, get lost. 2. to seclude o. s.

desguarnecer v. 1. to disgarnish, divest, strip, disfurnish. 2. (mil.) to unman; deprive of munition. 3. ~-se to divest, deprive o. s.

~ **a espada** to take off the hilt of a sword. ~ **as mulas ou cavalos** to unharness, remove the harness from mules or horses.

desguarnecido adj. 1. disgarnished, disfurnished. 2. unprotected. 3. (mil.) disarmed, unprovided of munition; unmanned.

desguedelhado adj. (also **desgadelhado**) dishevelled, tousy, unkempt, disarranged, disorderly.

desguedelhar v. (also **desgadelhar**) to dishevel, disarrange, tousle, rumple, put in disorder (as the hair).

desguiar v. (Braz., sl.) to walk out on.

desiderativo adj. desiderative.

desiderato s. m. desideratum; aim, purpose, goal.

desídia s. f. laziness, remissness, slothfulness, idleness; inertness, indolence, sluggishness; negligence.

desidioso adj. lazy, remiss, idle, slothful; negligent, indolent, sluggish. ‖ -amente adv. idly, indolently.

desidratação s. f. (pl. -ões) anhydration, dehydration; removal of water.

desidratar v. to anhydrate, dehydrate; remove water from, free of water.

desidremia s. f. (med.) reduction of the water content in blood.

desidrogenação s. f. (pl. -ões) dehydrogenization, removal of hydrogen.

desidrogenar v. to dehydrogenate, dehydrogenize, remove hydrogen from, free of hydrogen.

designação s. f. (pl. **-ões**) 1. designation, denomination, indication, denotation, title, appelative. 2. assignment, appointment, relegation.

designador s. m. indicator. ‖ adj. designating, denominating, indicating.

designar v. 1. to designate, appoint, mark, point out, denote, denominate. 2. to determinate, destine, project, term. 3. to indicate, call, name, express, signify, characterize. 4. to nominate, elect, assign. ~ **para deputado** to deputize. ~ **uma hora** to set a time.

designatário s. m. (com.) (Braz.) the bank designated to receive the amount of a crossed check.

designativo adj. indicative, distinctive, characteristic.

desígnio s. m. design, intention, purpose, aim; resolution, project, plan.

desigual adj. m. + f. (pl. **-ais**) 1. unequal, unlike, different, irregular, disparate, disproportional. 2. uneven, rough, rugged. 3. variable, inconstant, changeable. ‖ ~**mente** adv. unequally, unevenly.

desigualar v. 1. to unequalize, make uneven, unequal. 2. to mismatch, disorder, discompose. 3. ~**-se** to grow different, be unequal.

desigualdade s. f. 1. inequality, unlikeness, disparity, disproportion, dissimilarity, difference. 2. unevenness, roughness, raggedness. 3. variableness, inconstancy, changeableness.
~ **do solo** unevenness of the ground. ~ **do tempo** changeableness of the weather.

desiludido s. m. person without illusions. ‖ adj. disillusioned, disenchanted, undeceived; realistic.

desiludir v. 1. to disillusion, free of illusions, disenchant, undeceive. 2. to lose illusions. 3. ~**-se** to be disillusioned, despair of.

desilusão s. f. (pl. **-ões**) 1. disillusion, disenchantment, common-sense. 2. disappointment, deception.

desilusivo adj. disillusive.

desimaginar v. 1. to forget about, wipe out of the memory. 2. to dissuade. 3. ~**-se** to forget, fail to remember.

desimpedido adj. 1. unimpeded, unhindered, unfettered, unrestrained, unstopped, unobstructed, free, clear. 2. clean, afloat. ‖ **-amente** adv. unrestrainedly; clearly.

desimpedimento s. m. 1. disengagement, disencumbrance, riddance. 2. facilitation, easeness.

desimpedir v. 1. to disencumber, disengage, disembarrass. 2. to clear up, unstop. 3. to facilitate, ease.

desimplicar v. to disentangle, disengage; simplify.

desimprensar v. to take out of the press.

desimpressionar v. 1. to blot out an impression. 2. ~**-se** to be untouched, not impressed at all.

desinçar v. 1. to extirpate, root out, destroy. 2. to disentangle.

desinchar v. 1. to reduce a swelling. 2. to bring down one's pride; to humble. 3. ~**-se:** a) to unswell. b) to humiliate o. s., eat humble pie.

desinclinação s. f. (pl. **-ões**) disinclination, unwillingness, disaffection, dislike.

desinclinar v. 1. to straighten up, put in a perpendicular position. 2. to disincline, dislike, disaffect, make unwilling.

desincompatibilizar v. to free of incompatibility, cease to be incompatible.

desincorporação s. f. (pl. **-ões**) disincorporation: 1. privation of the rights of a corporation. 2. detachment of a body, disembodiment.

desincorporar v. 1. to disincorporate, disembody. 2. ~**-se** to separate or detach o. s. of a corporation or society.

desincumbir-se v. to acquit o. s. of, execute, carry out. ~ **de sua tarefa** to hoe one's row.

desindividualizar v. 1. to deprive of individualism, generalize. 2. to lose individualism.

desinência s. f. 1. extremity, end, termination. 2. (gram.) ending, inflection.

desinfamar v. to clear of a mark of infamy, rehabilitate, re-establish one's reputation.

desinfe(c)ção s. f. (pl. **-ões**) disinfection, decontamination, deodorization; asepsis.

desinfe(c)cionar v. (also **desinficionar**) to disinfect, purify, deodorize.

desinfelicidade s. f. (pop.) unhappiness, unluckiness, misfortune.

desinfeliz adj. m. + f. (pop.) unhappy, unlucky, unfortunate.

desinfernar v. to calm, quiet, appease.

desinfestar v. to disinfest.

desinfetador s. m. disinfector, deodorizer. ‖ adj. disinfecting, deodorizing.

desinfetante s. m. + f. disinfectant, deodorant. ‖ adj. disinfecting, antiseptic.

desinfetar v. 1. to disinfect, antisepticize, deodorize, decontaminate. 2. to cleanse, purify. 3. (Braz., sl.) to disappear, make o. s. scarce.

desinfetório s. m. (Braz.) disinfecting station.

desinflamação s. f. (pl. **-ões**) reduction of an inflammation, assuagement.

desinflamar v. to cure an inflammation; to unswell.

desinfluir v. to cease influencing; discourage, depress, deject.

desingurgitar v. to free from an engorgement, disgorge.

desinjuriar v. to revenge, avenge, vindicate, redress.

desinquietação s. f. (pl. **-ões**) 1. disquiet, disquietude, disturbance; alarm. 2. a misleading.

desinquietador s. m. disquieter, intruder, marplot. ‖ adj. disquieting; turbulent; alarming.

desinquietar v. to disquiet, disturb, alarm, vex, trouble, annoy, worry, make anxious.

desinquieto adj. disquiet, turbulent, disturbing; troubled; impatient, restless.

desintegração s. f. (pl. **-ões**) disintegration, disassociation, decomposition, dissolution, fission.
~ **espontânea,** ~ **natural** natural desintegration. ~ **ramificada** multiple desintegration.

desintegrado adj. 1. disintegrated. 2. (geol.) detrited.

desintegrar v. 1. to disintegrate, decompose, degrade, dissolve, split, weather. 2. ~**-se** to dissolve, crumble away, break off in pieces, split.

desinteirar v. (Braz.) to disunite, separate, divide.

desinteiriçar-se v. to cease to be rigid.

desinteligência s. f. misunderstanding, alienation, variance; rupture, friction, dissension, difference, discord.

desintencional adj. m. + f. (pl. **-ais**) unintentional, casual, accidental, fortuitous. ‖ ~**mente** adv. unintentionally.

desinteressado adj. disinterested, detached, unselfish, nonchalant, impartial, ambitionless. ‖ **-amente** adv. impartially, unselfishly.

desinteressante adj. m. + f. uninteresting, insignificant, dry-as-dust.

desinteressar v. 1. to divest of interest, disinterest. 2. to indemnify. 3. not to matter, to neglect. 4. ~**-se** to lose interest.

desinteresse (ê) s. m. 1. disinterest, indifference, nonchalance, aloofness. 2. unselfishness, self-denial, abnegation; detachment.

desinteresseiro adj. disinterested, unbiased, impartial, unselfish.

desinternar v. to take out of an internment, take away from a boarding-school, cease to be a resident pupil or an inpatient.

desintimidar v. to rid of shyness or timidity; encourage, animate, quicken.

desintoxicar v. to free of poison, unpoison.

desintri(n)car v. to disentangle, disembarrass, disencumber; make clear, clear up; simplify.

desintumescer v. 1. to reduce a swelling. 2. ~-se to become less swollen, unswell.

desinvernar v. 1. to leave the winter quarters (as soldiers). 2. to cease, come to an end (winter).

desinvestir v. 1. to deprive of a right or authority. 2. to dismiss, deprive of an employment, discharge.

desipotecar v. (Braz.) to call in or pay off a mortgage.

desiriado adj. achromatic; colourless.

desirmanado adj. odd, unmatched, asunder. ‖ **-amente** adv. separately, without its match.

desirmanar v. 1. to unmatch, divide a pair. 2. ~-se not to behave like a brother, fall out with (a brother).

desirmão adj. (pl. ~s) 1. odd, unmatched. 2. unequal, unlike, different.

desiscar v. to eat away the bait (as a fish).

desistência s. f. 1. desistance, cessation, stopping. 2. giving up. 3. discontinuance; nonsuit.

~**da herança** forsaking of an inheritance.

desistente adj. m. + f. desisting, renouncing, forsaking.

desistir v. 1. to desist, cease, discontinue, stop. 2. to renounce, recede, forsake, abdicate, wave; forbear, relinquish. 3. to quit, leave; desert, depart.

~ **de fazer** to desist from doing. ~ **de fumar** to give up smoking. ~ **de uma herança** to forsake an inheritance. ~ **de uma intenção** to give up a purpose. ~ **de um negócio** to go out of a business. ~ **de uma pretensão** to give up a claim.

desistivo adj. purgative.

desjarretar v. to hamstring, lame by cutting the hamstring.

desjeito s. m. awkwardness, clumsiness, unskilfulness.

desjeitoso adj. unskilful, clumsy, awkward; gauche, maladroit. ‖ **-amente** adv. unskilfully.

desjejua s. f. (also **desjejum**) breaking of one's fast; first breakfast.

desjejuar v. to break one's fast.

desjuizar v. = desajuizar.

desjungir v. to unyoke; unteam, unharness.

deslabiado adj. (Braz.) without lips, lipless.

deslaçamento s. m. unlacing; disentangling.

deslaçar v. 1. to unlace, untie, unfasten, loose, set free. 2. ~-se to detach o. s., get loose, break out.

deslacrar v. to break the seal, unseal.

desladrilhar v. to remove the bricks or tiles; to unpave.

deslajear v. to take away the flagstones.

deslambido adj. (Braz.) 1. affected, prudish, conceited, excentric. 2. cynical, shameless, impudent, saucy.

deslanar v. to shear sheep.

deslanchar v. to get moving, to go ahead, progress, proceed.

deslapar v. to take out of a den, hunt up, dig up.

deslassar v. to make slack, loosen.

deslastrador s. m. ballast remover, ballast unloader.

deslastrar, deslastrear v. to take out the ballast, unballast.

deslastre s. m. (naut.) unballasting, unloading of ballast.

deslavado adj. 1. discoloured, faded, pale. 2. insipid. 3. (fig.) shameless, impudent, saucy, bare-faced. ‖ **-amente** adv. palely; shamelessly.

cara -a brazen face.

deslavamento s. m. 1. discolouring, bleaching, weakness of colour, paleness. 2. (fig.) shamelessness, impudence, insipidity.

deslavar v. 1. to discolour, bleach, fade. 2. to turn insipid. 3. (fig.) to render shameless.

deslavrar v. to give the soil the second tilth, plough for the second time.

desleal adj. m. + f. (pl. **-ais**) (also **deslealdoso**) disloyal, false, dishonest, disaffected, perfidious, unfair, raw, treacherous, trustless, faithless, untrue. ‖ ~**mente** adv. disloyally, falsely, unfairly.

deslealdade s. f. disloyalty, falseness, disaffection, dishonesty, infidelity, treachery, unfairness, betrayal, perfidity.

deslealdar v. 1. to betray, deceive. 2. to treat disloyally, be unfair.

deslegitimar v. to take the legitimacy from.

desleitar v. 1. to draw the milk (from a cow). 2. to wean.

desleixado s. m. neglecter, careless person. ‖ adj. careless, neglectful, negligent, untidy, unkempt, disordered, sloven, slouchy, remiss, derelict. ‖ **-amente** adv. carelessly, neglectfully.

desleixamento s. m. (also **desleixação** f.) neglect, carelessness, laxness, slackness, remissness, indifference.

desleixar v. 1. to neglect, disregard, ignore, omit, slight. 2. ~-se to be negligent, become careless.

desleixo s. m. negligence, remissness, carelessness, laxness, indifference, nonchalance, disregard; slatternliness, floppiness, untidiness.

deslembrado adj. forgetful, oblivious, thoughtless.

deslembrança s. f. lack of memory, forgetfulness, heedlessness, inattention.

deslembrar v. 1. to forget, omit, slight. 2. ~-se to forget o. s.

deslembrativo adj. forgettable.

deslendear v. to clean of nits.

desligado adj. 1. (tech.) off, out, turned off. 2. disconnected, disjoint; unattached, untied, loose. 3. indifferent, disinterested.

desligadura s. f., **desligamento** m. disconnection, disunion, separation, unfastening, untying; detachment.

desligar v. (also **desliar**) 1. to untie, unfasten, undo, uncouple, unlink, unloose. 2. to separate, disunite, disjoint, disconnect, detach. 3. to stop, switch off or out; declutch. 4. ~-se to get loose, detach o. s. ~ **a máquina** to stop the engine. ~ **o rádio** to turn off the radio.

desligável adj. m. + f. (pl. **-áveis**) detachable.

deslindação s. f. (pl. **-ões**) (also **deslindamento, deslinde**) clearing up, disentanglement; explanation, explication.

deslindador s. m. person who unravels, disintricates, clears.

deslindar v. 1. to extricate, unravel, unfold; clear up, disentangle. 2. to explain, explicate. 3. to investigate, examine. 4. to bound, fix the bounds, survey (ground).

deslinguado adj. 1. tongueless. 2. (fig.) loose-tongued, backbiting, slanderous.

deslinguar v. 1. to pull out or cut the tongue. 2. (fig.) to talk loosely, have an ill tongue.

deslisura s. f. lack of smoothness; harshness, roughness, unevenness.

deslizadeiro s. m. 1. slide (plate P 6). 2. slope.

deslizador s. m. (Braz.) 1. skid. 2. small boat used on the rivers of Mato Grosso. ‖ adj. sliding, slipping.

deslizamento s. m. sliding, slipping, gliding.

deslizar v. 1. to glide, slide, skid. 2. to slip, overlook. 3. ~-se to pass lightly over.

deslize s. m. 1. slip, sliding, gliding, skidding. 2. fault, error, lapse. 3. stumble, misstep, false step.

deslocação s. f. (pl. **-ões**) 1. dislocation, luxation. 2. dislodgment, displacement, transposition; motion.

deslocado adj. 1. dislocated, out of joint. 2. displaced, out; strange.

deslocador adj. dislocated, disjointing; displacing.

deslocamento s. m. displacement, shifting.

deslocar v. 1. to dislocate, disjoint, put out of joint, luxate. 2. to displace, move, transport, transfer, shift. 3. ~-**se** to be put out of joint; shift one's place.

deslocável adj. m. + f. (pl. **-áveis**) displaceable.

deslodar v. to cleanse of dirt or mud, wash away.

deslograr v. not to obtain, be unsuccessful.

deslombar v. 1. to break the back, thrash, beat. 2. (fig.) to defeat, overcome.

desloucar v. to harrow (the soil).

deslouvar v. to disparage, depreciate, belittle, undervalue, underrate; blame, find fault with.

deslouvor s. m. blame, reproach.

deslumbrado s. m. (Braz., sl.) too easily enthusiastic individual. ‖ adj. fascinated, enchanted, dazzled.

deslumbrador s. m. dazzler, fascinator. ‖ adj. dazzling, fascinating; seducing.

deslumbramento s. m. dazzling (of the sun); fascination, captivation, hallucination; blindness, folly.

deslumbrante adj. m. + f. (also **deslumbrativo**) dazzling, blinding; flaring, fulgent; seducing. ‖ ~**mente** adv. flaringly.

deslumbrar v. 1. to dazzle, overpower with light, blind. 2. to fascinate, seduce, tempt, beguile. 3. ~-**se** to be fascinated, seduced or enchanted.

deslustrador s. m. tarnisher. ‖ adj. tarnishable, tarnishing, taking away the lustre; dulling.

deslustrar v. 1. to take away the lustre, tarnish, dull. 2. to sully, stain (reputation), dishonour, blemish. 3. ~-**se** to defile o. s.

deslustre, deslustro s. m. 1. tarnish, dulling; dimness. 2. blemish, stain, note of infamy.

deslustroso adj. 1. tarnished, lackluster, dull, dim. 2. disgraceful, shameful; dishonourable.

desluzido adj. 1. lustreless; obscure, dull, dim. 2. scanty (of weight or measure).

desluzimento s. m. 1. lack of gloss or lustre. 2. dishonour, blemish, spot, stain, reproach.

desluzir v. 1. to deprive of lustre or brilliance, dim, tarnish, dull, obscure, darken. 2. to stain one's reputation, dishonour, discredit. 3. ~-**se** to become obscure, grow dark.

desmagnetização s. f. (pl. **-ões**) demagnetization; demesmerization.

desmagnetizar v. 1. to demagnetize. 2. ~-**se** to lose the magnetic power.

desmaiado adj. 1. faint, exanimate, unconscious, pallid. 2. dull, dim; imperceptible.

desmaiar v. 1. to swoon, faint, turn faint, collapse. 2. to discolour, fade, turn pale. 3. to discourage, despond. 4. ~-**se** to lose courage, be disheartened.

desmaio s. m. 1. swoon, collapse, faint, fainting, fit. 2. discouragement, feebleness, paleness.

desmalhar v. to undo the meshes of.

desmalicioso adj. without malicious intention; good-natured, benignant.

desmama, desmamação (pl. **-ões**) s. f. weaning.

desmamar v. to wean, ablactate.

~ **uma criança** to wean a child.

desmanar v. 1. to separate from the herd. 2. ~-**se** to stray from the herd.

desmancha s. f. (Braz.) preparation of manioc meal.

desmanchadão s. m. (pl. **-ões**) 1. careless or ungainly person; sloven. 2. loose or reckless fellow, rake.

‖ adj. 1. negligent, disorderly, slipshod. 2. loose, reckless. 3. unhandsome, clumsy, awkward.

desmanchadiço adj. breakable, derangeable.

desmancha-prazeres s. m. + f., sg. + pl. spoil-sport, kill-joy, damper; wet blanket.

desmanchar v. 1. to undo, unmake, take to pieces, break up. 2. to disarrange, put out of joint; ruffle, confuse, disorder, derange. 3. ~-**se** to become deranged, be put out of joint, be disordered; to misbehave, lead a disorderly life.

~ **a casa** to disarrange the house. ~ **o noivado** to break up an engagement. ~ **a panelinha** to unmask a clique. ~-**se em desculpas** to overdo o. s. in excuses. ~ **um vestido** to rip up a garment.

desmancha-sambas s. m., sg. + pl. (N. Braz.) rowdy, ruffian, hooligan, hoodlum.

desmancho s. m. 1. undoing, taking to pieces. 2. spoiling. 3. disorder, confusion. 4. miscarriage, abortion. 5. (Braz.) ugly business.

desmandar v. 1. to countermand, give contrary orders, repeal an order. 2. to deprive of the command. 3. to disobey, baffle, disregard. 4. ~-**se** to go beyond the orders, go too far; swerve from duty.

desmandibular v. to gape (mouth).

desmando s. m. 1. disobedience, insubordination. 2. disorder, irregularity, excess; outrage.

desmanear v. (S. Braz.) to unshackle, unfetter (an animal).

desmangolado adj. (N. Braz., pop.) misshapen, ill-formed.

desmanivado adj. (N. Braz., pop.) bewildered, touched, groggy.

desmanivar v. (N. Braz.) 1. to crop or prune manioc shrubs. 2. to settle a business. 3. to overcome a trouble. 4. to dissipate, squander.

desmantelado adj. 1. dismantled, demolished; run-down. 2. unrigged, unmasted. 3. abandoned. 4. unequipped, unprovided.

desmantelamento s. m. (also **desmantelo**) dismantling dismantlement, unrigging.

desmantelar v. 1. to dismantle, demolish, throw down (walls or works), ruin. 2. (naut.) to unrig, unmast. 3. to abandon, forsake. 4. to clear out (gang). 5. ~-**se** to fall in, tumble down.

desmarcado adj. enormous, colossal, huge, out of measure; excessive, immoderate. ‖ **-amente** adv. enormously.

desmarcar v. 1. to take away or efface the marks or signs. 2. to remove the boundary-stones. 3. to render excessive. 4. ~-**se** to become excessive, enormous.

desmarcializar v. to give an unmartial appearance.

desmarear v. 1. to clean of stains. 2. ~-**se** to be ill steered, be out of control (as a ship).

desmascarar v. 1. to unmask, remove the mask. 2. to expose, reveal, disclose, bring to light. 3. ~-**se** to take off one's mask, discover o. s. (to one's friend).

~ **as mentiras de alguém** to expose a person for a liar.

desmastrar v. (naut., also **desmastrear**) 1. to take away the masts, unmast. 2. ~-**se** to lose the masts.

desmastreamento s. m. removal or loss of the masts.

desmatamento s. m. (Braz.) deforestation, clearing of timber.

desmatar v. (Braz.) to deforest, clear of timber.

desmaterialização s. f. (pl. **-ões**) dematerialization, immateriality.

desmaterializar v. to dematerialize, immaterialize, turn immaterial.

desmazelado s. m. slipshod fellow, sloven. ‖ adj. negligent, careless, slack, lax, indolent; slut, slovenly, reckless, slipshod. ‖ **-amente** adv. negligently.

desmazelar-se v. to neglect one's affairs, be careless, become slovenly.

desmazelo (ê) s. m. 1. negligence, carelessness, disarray, untidiness, frowziness, indolence. 2. (Braz.) safety pin.

desmazorrar v. (Braz.) to cheer up.

desmedido adj. excessive, immoderate, immense, colossal, enormous, out of measure, huge. ‖ **-amente** adv. immensely, excessively.

desmedir-se v. = descomedir-se.

desmedra s. f. (Braz.) retardation, check (of progress).

desmedrado adj. 1. checked, restrained, hindered. 2. diminished, impaired. 3. stunted.

desmedramento s. m. 1. checking. 2. stunting, withholding. 3. diminution, loss.

desmedrança s. f. lack of growth or development.

desmedrar v. 1. to check. 2. to stunt, go backward, decay. 3. ~-se to grow lean; be stunted.

desmedro s. m. decay, diminution.

desmedroso adj. fearless, courageous, daring, audacious. ‖ **-amente** adv. courageously.

desmedular v. to take out the marrow.

desmelancolizar v. to free of melancholy, cheer up, gladden.

desmelhorar v. 1. to make worse, impair. 2. ~-se to grow worse.

desmelindrar v. to redress, revenge, avenge; give satisfaction.

desmembração s. f. (pl. -ões) 1. dismembering, dividing, detaching, abruption. 2. (fig.) partition, division.

desmembrado adj. (fig.) destitute, cast down, dejected.

desmembramento s. m. dismemberment, detachment, abruption.

desmembrar v. 1. to dismember, dislimb, disjoint. 2. to separate, disunite, divide. 3. ~-se to be dismembered, separated into portions.

desmemória s. f. forgetfulness, obliviousness; negligence, disregard.

desmemoriado s. m. person who lost his memory (as by a disaster). ‖ adj. forgetful, negligent; deprived of memory.

desmemoriar v. 1. to cause loss of memory. 2. to cause to fall in oblivion. 3. to lose one's memory. 4. ~-se to forget.

desmentido s. m. dementi, disavowel, denial, recantation, disaffirmation; contradiction. ‖ adj. contradicted, denied.

desmentidor s. m. disavower.

desmentidura s. f. (N. Braz.) luxation, dislocation of a bone; wrench, sprain.

desmentir v. 1. to belie, give the lie, contradict. 2. to deny, gainsay, negate. 3. to disprove, disclaim, disavow, controvert. 4. (N. Braz.) to luxate, dislocate, put out of joint. 5. ~-se to contradict o. s.

desmerecedor s. m. unworthy person. ‖ adj. unworthy, ill-merited, undeserving.

desmerecer v. 1. to demerit, not to deserve, undeserve. 2. to deprive of merit, depreciate, discredit. 3. to fade, discolour. 4. ~-se to lose one's merit, be unworthy.

~ **para com alguém** to demerit in another's eyes. **ele a desmerece** he is unworthy of her. **não ~ de alguém** not to be inferior to one in merit.

desmerecido adj. 1. unworthy, unmerited, undeserved. 2. faded, colourless. 3. (Braz., pop.) anemic, feeble, weak. ‖ **-amente** adv. unworthily.

desmerecimento s. m. 1. demerit, unworthiness, undeservedness. 2. depreciation, discredit.

desmesura s. f. discourtesy, incivility, impoliteness, rudeness, unkindness, ungentleness.

desmesurado adj. immeasurable, excessive, huge, enormous, colossal, immense. ‖ **-amente** adv. excessively.

desmesurar v. 1. to exaggerate, pass the limits. 2. ~-se to commit excesses; dissipate.

desmesurável adj. m. + f. (pl. -áveis) immeasurable.

desmidiácea s. f. (bot.) desmid (a group of freshwater algae).

desmilitarização s. f. (pl. -ões) demilitarization, demobilization, disarmament.

desmilitarizar v. to demilitarize, demobilize, disarm.

desmineralizar v. (Braz.) to immineralize.

desmiolado s. m. rattlehead, rattlepate. ‖ adj. crack-brained, brainless, shallow-brained, rattle-pated.

desmiolar v. 1. to pull out the brains. 2. to take out the insides of bread. 3. (fig.) to make someone lose his sense, render crazy, madden.

desmiudar v. to break into small pieces, crumble; detail, particularize.

desmobilar, desmobilhar, desmobiliar v. to deprive of furniture, unfurnish, disgarnish.

desmobilização s. f. (pl. -ões) demobilization, disarmament.

desmobilizar v. to demobilize, disarm; disband.

desmobilizável adj. m. + f. (pl. -áveis) that can be demobilized.

desmochar v. to take away the horns; mutilate.

desmoderar v. 1. to act without moderation, lose moderation. 2. ~-se to grow immoderate.

desmodulação s. f. (electr.) demodulation.

desmoita s. f. clearing or stubbing (soil).

desmoitar v. 1. to clear, stub the soil (in order to cultivate it). 2. (fig.) to instruct, educate, bring culture or civilization to.

desmomiário s. m. (ent.) a species of phosphoric insects.

desmonetização s. f. (pl. -ões) demonetization.

desmonetizar v. to demonetize.

desmonopolizar v. to free of a monopoly, destroy the monopoly, demonopolize.

desmontada s. f. dismounting, getting off (a horse).

desmontado adj. 1. dismounted, unhorsed. 2. dismantled, disassembled, apart.

desmontar v. 1. to unhorse, throw from the saddle, beat from a horse. 2. to dismantle, disjoint, disassemble, take to pieces. 3. to pull down, lower, level (a hill), raze. 4. (S. Braz.) to humble, brownbeat (an adversary). 5. ~-se to get off, alight (from).

~ **uma máquina** to dismount an engine. ~ **um navio** to unship.

desmontável adj. m. + f. (pl. -áveis) dismountable, removable.

desmonte s. m. 1. dismounting, taking to pieces, disassembly. 2. levelling (of hills). 3. the earth thus removed. 4. extraction of minerals.

desmoralização s. f. (pl. -ões) demoralization, disparagement, corruption.

desmoralizador s. m. demoralizer. ‖ adj. demoralizing, deleterious.

desmoralizar v. 1. to demoralize, corrupt, undermine the morals, pervert, deprave. 2. to deprive of energy, dishearten, discourage. 3. to disorganize, bring into disorder, confuse (mentally). 4. ~-se to become perverted or depraved.

desmoronadiço adj. shaky, tottering, ready to fall, in decay.

desmoronamento s. m. collapse, tumbling, falling in, crumbling, ruin.

~ **de montanha** mountain creep. ~ **de túnel** cave-in of a tunnel.

desmoronar v. 1. to pull down, demolish, ruin, undermine, destroy, cave. 2. ~-se to collapse, fall to pieces; moulder away.
~ **uma mina** to underlay a mine. **os muros desmoronaram** the walls gave way.

desmorrer v. to recover from dangerous illness; return to life.

desmortificar v. (Braz.) to cease mortifying, alleviate, lighten.

desmotivado adj. unfounded, groundless, not motivated, unjustifiable.

desmunhecar v. (Braz.) 1. to cut off a limb (esp. the hand). 2. (fig.) to take away a part (of a whole), disunite.

desmurar v. to destroy the walls, raze, demolish.

desnacionalização s. f. (pl. -ões) denationalization.

desnacionalizar v. 1. to denationalize, denaturalize, expatriate, deprive of citizenship. 2. to lose citizenship.

desnalgado adj. dry, meager, thin.

desnalgar-se v. to waddle, move the hips excessively (at dancing).

desnarigado adj. noseless or having a small nose.

desnarigar v. to cutt off the nose.

desnasalação s. f. elimination of nasal sounds.

desnasalar v. to rid of nasal sounds.

desnastrar v. to take away the tapes, ribbons or plints.

desnatação s. f. (pl. -ões) skimming, creaming (milk).

desnatadeira s. f. milk skimmer, cream-separator, centrifuge.

desnatar v. 1. to take away the cream (of milk), skim. 2. (fig.) to take away the best of a thing.

desnaturação s. f. (pl. -ões) denaturation, making unnatural.

desnaturado s. m. monster. ‖ adj. unnatural, disnatured, monstrous, cruel.
álcool ~ denatured alcohol. **pai** ~ monstrous father.

desnatural adj. m. + f. (pl. -ais) unnatural, contrary to the laws of nature; inhuman; odd; artificial.

desnaturalização s. f. (pl. -ões) denaturalization, expatriation; banishment.

desnaturalizar v. 1. to disnaturalize, disnature, deprive of the rights of a citizen. 2. to change the citizenship, renounce to the rights of a citizen. 3. ~-se to quit one's native country.

desnaturante adj. m. + f. denaturing, changing the nature (of s. th.).
~ **nuclear** nuclear denaturant.

desnaturar v. 1. to denature, change the nature, pervert. 2. to render inhuman, cruel or unnatural. 3. ~-se to become unnatural or cruel.

desnecessário adj. unnecessary, useless, needless, superfluous. ‖ -amente adv. uselessly, unnecessarily.

desnecessidade s. f. unnecessariness, needlessness, uselessness, superfluousness, inutility.

desnegociar v. to cancel an order, undo a business, call off a transaction.

desnervar v. to enervate, deprive of strength, weaken.

desnevada s. f. melting of snow thawing.

desnevar v. to melt, thaw (snow).

desniquelagem s. f. (pl. -ens) loss of nickel.

desniquelar v. to deprive of nickel.

desnível s. m. (pl. -íveis) unevenness, difference in level.

desnivelamento s. m. unlevelling, making uneven.

desnivelar v. to unlevel, make uneven.

desnobre adj. m. + f. ignoble, vile, base, mean.

desnobrecer v. to disenoble, vilify, deprive of nobility, degrade.

desnodoar v. to clean of spots.

desnodoso adj. knotless, unknotted, without snags.

desnoivar v. 1. to break off an engagement. 2. (fig.) to deprive of.

desnorteado adj. 1. bewildered, lost, perplexed, confused. 2. distempered, thoughtless, disorientated. 3. dizzy, giddy, crazy, foolish.

desnorteador adj. m., **desnorteante** m. + f. baffling, confusing, bewildering.

desnortear v. 1. to turn from the north, throw off course. 2. to misguide, mislead, lead astray, turn aside. 3. to bewilder, confuse, perturb. 4. ~-se to be lost or bewildered.

desnotar v. to take away a note (from).

desnovelar v. to unwind (a skein).

desnuar v. to denude, undress, unclothe; lay bare.

desnublado adj. cloudless; diaphanous, pellucid, transparent.

desnublar v. 1. to uncloud, clear up. 2. ~-se to become clear.

desnucar v. 1. to break or hurt the nape. 2. (S. Braz.) to kill (cattle) with a stab into the nape.

desnudamento s. m. denudation, undressing, unclothing.

desnudar v. 1. to denudate, undress, unclothe, strip of. 2. to bare, lay bare. 3. ~-se to undress o. s.

desnudez s. f. nudity, nakedness, want of covering.

desnudo adj. naked, denuded, undressed, uncovered, unclothed; bare.

desnutrição s. f. (pl. -ões) want of nutrition, malnutrition, underfeeding; emaciation, growing thin.

desnutrir v. to nourish poorly, unfeed.

desobedecer v. 1. to disobey, transgress; be disobedient, violate (a command). 2. disregard.

desobediência s. f. disobedience, insubordination, rebellion, recalcitration, waywardness, indiscipline; naughtiness; contempt.

desobediente adj. m. + f. disobedient, contumacious, naughty, wayward; insubordinate, rebellious; unruly, ungovernable. ‖ ~mente adv. disobediently.

desobriga, desobrigação (pl. -ões) s. f. dispensation, exemption, release, acquittance, disengagement, discharge.

desobrigado adj. unpledged, unobligated, disengaged, exempt, free.

desobrigar v. 1. to exempt, release, dispense. 2. to free, acquit, loose, unbind. 3. to disengage, disembarass. 4. ~-se to disengage o.s., meet one's engagements.
~-se **dos filhos** to neglect the duty of a father.
~-se **da sua promessa** to fulfill one's promise.

desobrigatório adj. unobligatory.

desobscurecer v. to illuminate, clarify, enlighten; clear up.

desobstrução s. f. (pl. -ões) removal of a hindrance, deoppilation, clearance.

desobstruir v. 1. to remove obstructions, unstop, disencumber, deobstruct, deoppilate. 2. to free, open, unbar, clear.

desobstrutivo adj. deobstruent, deoppilative, deoppilatory.

desocupação s. f. (pl. -ões) 1. inoccupation, leisure, vacancy. 2. unemployment.

desocupado s. m. unemployed person. ‖ adj. 1. unemployed, disengaged, unoccupied. 2. idle, leisurely. 3. free, vacant, open. 4. untenanted. 5. void, empty. ‖ -amente adv. vacantly, at leisure, without employment.

desocupar v. 1. to vacate, disoccupy. 2. to empty. 3. to evacuate. 4. to cease to employ s. o., dismiss. 5. ~-se to retire from a business, be unoccupied.

desodorizante s. m. deodorant. ‖ adj. m. + f. deodorant, disinfecting.

desodorizar v to deodorize, make scentless, disinfect.

desoficialização s. f. (pl. -ões) making unofficial or informal.
desoficializar v. to make unofficial or informal.
desofuscar v. 1. to uncloud, clear up; enlighten, illuminate. 2. ~-se to clear up, become clear.
desolação s. f. (pl. -ões) 1. desolation, destruction, ravage, ruin, devastation. 2. desolateness, afflictedness, forlornness, wretchedness, loneliness, sadness, misery.
desolado adj. 1. desolate, forlorn, lonely, waste, bereaved; ruined. 2. miserable, wretched, bleak, afflicted, inconsolable. ‖ -amente adv. desolately.
desolador s. m. desolator, destroyer. ‖ adj. desolating, distressing, destroying, afflicting, grievous.
desolar v. 1. to lay waste, desolate, depopulate, ruin, destroy. 2. to distress, afflict, sadden, torment, worry, annoy, depress. 3. ~-se to become deserted.
desolha s. f. removal of the buds of plants.
desolhar v. 1. to take away the buds of plants, disbud. 2. (Braz.) to unbewitch, free of an evil eye.
desoneração s. f. (pl. -ões) disinvesting of a charge, exoneration, dispensation.
desonerar (I) v. to exonerate, dispense.
desonerar (II) v. (pop.) to degenerate.
desonestar v. = desonrar.
desonestidade s. f. 1. dishonesty, crookedness, knavery, fraud, corruption, foul play. 2. immorality, immodesty, obscenity, indecency.
desonesto s. m. dishonest person, scoundrel, knave. ‖ adj. 1. dishonest, crooked, corrupt, foul, unfair, false, rotten, deceitful, unscrupulous, nasty. 2. immodest, dishonourable, indecent, immoral, obscene, lewd. ‖ -amente adv. dishonestly.
por meios ~s on the cross.
desonra s. f. 1. dishonour, disgrace, discredit, disrepute, defame. 2. baseness, vileness, dishonesty, shame.
desonradez s. f. infamy, dishonesty, dishonourableness.
desonrado adj. dishonoured, disgraced, fallen, soiled, ruined.
desonrador s. m. disgracer, dishonourer, disparager, violator. ‖ adj. dishonourable, shameful, disgracing.
desonrante adj. m. + f. dishonourable, disgracing, disreputable.
desonrar v. 1. to dishonour, discredit, disgrace, disrepute, defame. 2. to ravish, violate, deflower, ruin, wrong. 3. to sully, spot, defile, foul. 4. ~-se to disgrace o. s., bring shame upon o. s.
desonroso adj. dishonourable, discreditable, unworthy, shameful, disgraceful. ‖ -amente adv. dishonourably.
desopilação s. f. (pl. -ões) 1. deoppilation. 2. (med.) purgation.
desopilante adj. m. + f. (also **desopilativo**) 1. relieving, stimulating. 2. (med.) purgative.
desopilar v. 1. to deoppilate, deobstruct. 2. (med.) to purge, cleanse. 3. to cheer up, enliven.
desoportuno adj. inopportune, inconvenient, unseasonable.
desopressão s. f. (pl. -ões) freeness from oppression, relief, ease, lightening.
desopressor s. m. liberator. ‖ adj. easing, liberating.
desoprimir v. (also **desopressar**) 1. to free from oppression, liberate, ease, lighten. 2. ~-se to get rid of oppressions.
desoras adv. lately, inopportunely, unseasonably.
a ~ untimely, out of hours, at an unseasonable hour.
desorbitar v. to throw out of the orbit.
desordeiro s. m. rampager, ruffian, rowdy, rioter, hooligan. ‖ adj. turbulent, rowdy, rough, riotous, ruffianly, raffish, unruly. ‖ -amente adv. turbulently.

desordem s. f. (pl. -ens) 1. disorder, confusion, disturbance, jumble, tumble, disarrangement, disarray, rout, trouble, derangement. 2. untidiness, litter, muddle, shindy. 3. riot, tumult, turmoil, upset, uproar, affray, row, commotion, brawl, quarrel. 4. illness, disease, discomposure.
em ~ topsy-turvy, upside down, pell-mell, in a muddle. **estar em ~** to lie about. **lançar em ~** to pell-mell, kick up a shindy. **pôr em ~** to unsettle, upset, tousle. **promover ~** to rampage, stir up a storm. **provocar -ens** to riot.
desordenado adj. 1. disordered, untidy, turbid, deranged, confused. 2. troublesome, tumultuary, upset. 3. unruly, loose, disordinate.
desordenador s. m. disturber, mischief-maker, rowdy, rioter, disorderly fellow. ‖ adj. disturbing, disordering, disarranging, ruffling.
desordenar v. 1. to disorder, disarrange, derange, disarray, put out of order, ruffle, confuse. 2. to discompose, disease, distemper. 3. to displace, dislocate. 4. to disturb, upset, stir up. 5. ~-se to be disordered, lead a disorderly life, commit excesses.
desorelhado adj. earless.
desorelhamento s. m. cutting off the ears.
desorelhar v. to cut off the ears.
desorganização s. f. (pl. -ões) disorganization, disorder, chaos, disarrangement.
desorganizador s. m. disorganizer. ‖ adj. confusing, planless, wild-cat.
desorganizar v. 1. to disorganize, disorder, disarrange, subvert, muddle, disturb, confuse, unsettle. 2. to dissolve an organization.
desorientação s. f. (pl. -ões) disorientation, bewilderment, perplexity, confusion; nonsense, foolishness.
desorientado adj. 1. disorientated, perplexed, bewildered, confused. 2. lost, adrift, rudderless. ‖ -amente adv. confusedly, at random.
desorientador s. m. disorientator. ‖ adj. perplexing, bewildering, leading astray.
desorientar v. 1. to put out of the away or rout. 2. to lead astray; bewilder, perplex, confuse, throw into confusion. 3. ~-se to lose one's way.
desornado adj. 1. unadorned, plain; unornamented.
desornar v. to divest of ornaments, disembellish, disgarnish.
desossado adj. boned, separated from the flesh.
desossar v. to bone, separate the bone from the flesh.
desova s. f., **desovamento** m. spawning of fishes, laying (of eggs).
desovar v. 1. to spawn, lay eggs (as fishes). 2. to unload a great part of a cargo (of a ship). 3. (Braz., fig.) to reveal.
desoxidação s. f. (pl. -ões) deoxidation.
desoxidante adj. m. + f. deoxidizing.
desoxidar v. to deoxidize.
desoxigenação s. f. (pl. -ões) deoxygenation.
desoxigenante adj. m. + f. deoxygenating.
desoxigenar v. to deoxygenate.
despachadão s. m. (pl. -ões) (Braz.) rough-and-ready person. ‖ adj. rough, forward, pert.
despachado adj. 1. settled, resolved. 2. posted, dispatched. 3. expedite, quick of dispatch, speedy, swift, ready. 4. frank, sincere. 5. valient, intrepid, courageous. ‖ -amente adv. quickly, readily.
despachador s. m. man of quick dispatch, dispatcher. ‖ adj. dispatching, forwarding, expediting.
despachante s. m. + f. dispatcher, forwarder, forwarding agent, customhouse clerk, forwarding merchant. ‖ adj. forwarding, dispatching, expediting.
despachar v. 1. to forward, dispatch, despatch, send, expedite. 2. to clear, discharge, put on the way. 3. to clear (goods at the customhouse). 4. (Braz.)

to dismiss, dispense, deprive of employment. 5. to kill, put s. o. out of the way. 6. to hasten, speed. 7. ~-se to conclude one's affairs, make haste, hurry.

~ bagagem to book one's luggage. ~ a correspondência to post the correspondence. ~ documentos to clear documents, put documents on their way. ~ uma encomenda to express a parcel. ~ um navio to clear a ship. despache-se com isso! make haste!

despacho s. m. 1. despatch, dispatch, forwarding, shipping, posting, expedition. 2. decision, resolution, determination, sentence, ruling, rescript. 3. clearance (as of goods at the customhouse). 4. speed, haste, diligence. 5. execution, conclusion. 6. enactment, writ, order. 7. execution (of a deed). 8. grant, allowance. 9. (Braz.) witchcraft, sorcery. ~ ministerial official communication relating to public affairs. ~ de um navio clearance of a ship. ~ do porto anchorage, groundage. ~ telegráfico wire, telegram. dar-se ~ to make haste.

despadrar v. 1. to deprive of ecclesiastic dignity, unfrock. 2. ~-se to cease to be a priest.

despalatalizar v. (phon., also despalatizar) to unpalatize.

despaletar, despaletear v. (S. Braz.) to disjoint the shoulder blade (of an animal).

despalha s. f. (Braz.) removal of the straw from sugar cane.

despalhar v. to take away the straw.

despalmar v. to pare a horse's hoof.

despalmilhado adj. without an inner sole.

despalmilhar v. to take out the inner sole.

despampanar v. to lop the leafy branches of a vine.

despapar v. to lift or hold up the head too much (a horse).

desparafusar v. 1. to unscrew, screw off. 2. (N. Braz.) to get annoyed, become irritated.

desparamentar v. to deprive of vestments, take off the vestments.

despargir v. (also espargir, desparzir) to spread, disperse, pour out, shed, scatter; strew.

desparramar-se v. to spread out; sprawl.

desparrar v. to lop the leafy branches of a vine.

despartir v. 1. to separate, divide. 2. to part, break off.

despassar v. to pass over or beyond.

despatriota s. m. + f. unpatriotic person. ‖ adj. unpatriotic.

despatriótico adj. unpatriotic.

despautério s. m. nonsense, folly, foolishness, senselessness, absurdity, stupidity.

despavorido adj. fearless, intrepid, courageous. ‖ -amente adv. fearlessly.

despavorir v. to frighten, terrify, make afraid, scare.

despear (I) v. 1. to unshackle, unfetter, unlock (a horse). 2. ~-se to get loose, be unfettered.

despear (II) v. 1. to tire the feet. 2. to wear out the hoofs.

despedaçador s. m. (also fig.) person who shatters, tears to pieces. ‖ adj. tearing to pieces.

despedaçamento s. m. tearing to pieces, laceration, smashing, breaking.

despedaçar v. 1. to tear into pieces, smash, shatter, hackle, break, pull to pieces; crash, destroy, disintegrate. 2. to rend, rip, lacerate. 3. ~-se to break, be torn.

despedida s. f. 1. farewell, adieu, valediction, leave-taking, parting, departure. 2. discharge, dismissal; separation. 3. (fig.) end, conclusion.

carta de ~ farewell letter. discurso de ~ valedictory address. jantar de ~ farewell dinner. visita de ~ farewell visit. ir à despedida to send off.

despedimento s. m. 1. taking leave of. 2. shooting, letting fly, discharge. 3. dismissal.

despedir v. 1. to discharge, dismiss, 2. to turn away, disband, discard. 3. to fire, shoot, let off. 4. to send, forward. 5. to cease, end, conclude. 6. ~-se to take leave, part, say farewell.

~ alguém to sack s. o., give s. o. the sack. ~ a alma to give up one's ghost. ~ um criado to turn off, dismiss a servant. ~ as mágoas to banish melancholy. ~-se de alguém to send s. o. off. ~-se à francesa to take a French leave. ~-se da sociedade to withdraw from a company. estar a ~-se to be at death's door, be dying.

despegado adj. 1. unattached, unglued, unstuck. 2. hard, cross, unkind, disaffected, disinterested, unmoved, indifferent. 3. free, independent. ‖ -amente adv. loosely, without affection, independently.

orelhas -as protruding ears (donkey's ears).

despegar v. 1. to unglue, detach, separate, unstick, unfix. 2. to set at variance; make indifferent. 3. ~-se to become disaffected; get loose, come off.

despego (ê) s. m. (also desapego) 1. unattachment, detachment. 2. disaffection, unconcern, disinterestedness, indifference.

despeitado (I) s. m. hurt, angry or indisposed person. ‖ adj. 1. slighted, hurt, offended; averse. 2. annoyed, angry. 3. indisposed. ‖ -amente adv. despitefully.

despeitado (II) adj. small-chested, hollow-chested.

despeitador s. m. slighter, despiser, hurter, offender.

despeitar v. 1. to despite, treat with contempt, despise. 2. to annoy, vex, fret, offend, spite. 3. ~-se to grow angry, be offended.

despeito s. m. spite, disgust, despite, resentment, grudge; anger, rage, fury, contempt; languor, feintness, dejection.

a ~ de in spite of, despite, notwithstanding.

despeitorar v. 1. to uncover the breast, cut low (as a dress). 2. ~-se (fig.) to open one's heart.

despeitoso adj. despiteful, peevish, malicious, spleenful. ‖ -amente adv. despitefully.

despejado adj. 1. unhoused, unoccupied, vacant, emptied. 2. impudent, shameless, licentious, indecent, obscene. ‖ -amente adv. shamelessly; vacantly.

despejamento s. m. 1. spilling. 2. removal, emptying, quitting, vacating. 3. impudence, shamelessness, licentiousness.

despejar (I) v. 1. to spill, pour or throw out, empty, effuse, decant. 2. to remove, evacuate, unhouse, vacate, oust. 3. to dispossess, evict, quit. 4. ~-se to get rid of, free o. s.

despejar (II) v. 1. to rid of timidity or shyness. 2. ~-se to free o. s. of shyness.

despejo (I) s. m. 1. pouring out, spilling, emptying. 2. evacuation, eviction, removing, clearing a place. 3. closet, lumber-room, limbo. 4. litter, garbage, slop, rubbish.

despejo (II) s. m. impudence, lack of shame, boldness, licentiousness.

despela s. f. skinning, flaying; hulling, peeling.

despelar v. 1. to skin, flay. 2. to peel, shell; rind, bark, husk, hull, decorticate.

despenar (I) v. 1. to deplume, deprive of feathers. 2. to relieve of cares, free of troubles, console. 3. ~-se to get rid of troubles.

despenar (II) v. 1. to deprive of feathers, deplume. 2. (Braz., pop.) to strip the leaves and runners from a plant.

despencar v. (Braz.) 1. to take (bananas or grapes) from the bunch. 2. to fall down disastrously from a high place.

despendedor s. m. disburser, squanderer, spendthrift, defrayer.

despender v. 1. to spend, expend, disburse. 2. to outlay, lay out, apply. 3. to squander, dissipate, waste.

~ **tempo** to kill the time, consume the time.

despendurar v. to take down something that was hanging, unhook, take off the hook, unhang.

despenhadeiro s. m. precipice, crag, declivity, cliff, slope.

despenhamento s. m. (also **despenho**) precipitation, precipitous fall, fall from a high place, downfall.

despenhar v. 1. to precipitate, hurl, cast down; fall headlong. 2. (aeron.) to crash. 3. to disgrace, disfavour. 4. ~-se: a) to hurl o. s. b) to run headlong into danger.

despenhoso adj. precipitous, craggy, steep. ‖ -amente adv. precipitously.

despenque s. m. (S. Braz.) galloping run (of a horse).

despensa s. f. buttery, pantry, larder, spence, store--room.

despenseiro s. m. steward, layer-out, pantryman, butler, cellarist, provider; cup-bearer.

despenteado adj. unkempt, disheveled, rough, slovenly.

despentear v. to tousle, ruffle, dishevel.

desperceber v. not to observe or perceive, disregard, pay no attention, fail to see.

despercebido adj. unperceived, unobserved, unheeded, unheard, unmarked, unseen, unnoticed, unnoted, unfelt.

passar ~ to escape one's notice.

despercebimento s. m. inattention.

desperdiçado s. m. waster, prodigal, spendthrift. ‖ adj. wasted, lost.

desperdiçador s. m. waster, prodigal, lavisher. ‖ adj. wasting.

desperdiçar v. to waste, throw away, fiddle, squander, lavish, misspend, scatter, dissipate, cast away, fritter away.

~ **sua fortuna** to chuck away one's fortune. ~ **as palavras** to spend one's breath in vain. ~ **o tempo** to dilly-dally, doze away, potter away one's time, trifle time away.

desperdício s. m. wastefulness, waste, wastage, thriftlessness, dissipation, lavishness, prodigality, squandering, loss.

desperfilamento s. m. getting out of line.

desperfilar v. 1. to disorder, disarrange the alignment. 2. to get out of line.

despersonalização s. f. (pl. -ões) depersonalization, loss of personality.

despersonalizar v. 1. to depersonalize, disindividualize, deprive of personality or individuality. 2. ~-se: a) to change one's character. b) to act contrary to one's personality.

despersuadir v. 1. to dissuade, advise to the contrary, divert from. 2. ~-se to be undeceived.

despersuasão s. f. (pl. -ões) dissuasion, diversion from a purpose, dehortation.

despertado adj. awake, roused from sleep.

despertador s. m. alarm-clock, alarm-bell (plate R 4). ‖ adj. awakening, rousing.

despertar s. m. awakening. ‖ v. 1. to awake, rouse from sleep, wake, stir up. 2. to excite, revive, stimulate, put in motion.

~ **a quem dorme** to wake sorrow when it is asleep. ~ **interesse** to arouse interest. ~ **do sonho** to arouse from one's dream.

desperto adj. awake, roused from sleep.

despesa s. f. 1. disbursement, expense, outgo, outlay. 2. charge, cost, payment.

~**s adicionais** additional charges. ~**s alfandegárias** (customs) duties. ~**s bancárias** bank fees. ~**s de carreto** portage. ~**s a deduzir** charges to be

deducted. ~**s de desembarque** discharging expenses. ~**s de embarque** shipping charges. ~**s de exploração** working expenses. ~**s gerais** overhead charges. ~**s imprevistas** unforeseen expenses. ~**s de instalação** outfit charges. ~**s a liquidar** outstanding expenses. ~**s miúdas**, ~**s pequenas** petty charges, idle expenses. ~**s de porte** postage. ~**s postais** postage. ~**s de representação** representation fees. ~**s suplementares** extra costs. ~**s de transporte** carriage. ~**s de viagem** travelling expenses. **cobri as minhas** ~**s** I found my costs. **deduzidas as** ~**s** clear of all charges. **livro de** ~**s** book of charges. **não olhar as** ~**s** not to spare money. **ter grandes** ~**s** to suffer in one's pocket.

despescar v. (N. Braz.) 1. to catch fishes with a net. 2. (fig.) to steal another's objects of value.

despetalado adj. (bot.) apetalous.

despicador s. m. revenger.

despicar v. 1. to revenge, avenge, vindicate, take revenge. 2. ~-se to return like for like, be revenged, retaliate an injury.

despicativo adj. taking revenge; depreciating.

despiciendo adj. despicable; worthless.

despiciente adj. m. + f. despising, disdaining.

despido adj. 1. uncovered, undressed, unclothed, naked, nude, denudate; bare. 2. exempt, free.

despiedade s. f. unmercifulness, inhumanity, cruelty, pitilessness, barbarism.

despiedado adj. unmerciful, inhuman, cruel, pitiless, ruthless, barbarous, fierce. ‖ -amente adv. unmercifully.

despiedar v. = **desapiedar**.

despiedoso adj. inhuman, unmerciful, pitiless, cruel, fierce.

despigmentação s. f. (pl. -ões) lack of pigmentation.

despilchar v. (S. Braz.) to despoil of; to steal.

despimento s. m. divestment, divestiture, undressing, unclothing.

despinçar v. to take away with a pincette.

despinicar v. (Braz., pop.) 1. to fray out, separate into threads. 2. to separate the foliage of peanuts.

despintar v. 1. to blot out, efface (a painting). 2. to disfigure, falsify, misrepresent. 3. to vilify, debase, undervalue. 4. ~-se to be disfigured.

despique s. m. 1. satisfaction, avenge, revenge, spite. 2. (N. Braz.) vengeance.

despir v. 1. to undress, unclothe, disrobe, strip, throw off. 2. to divest. 3. to disarray, dismantle. 4. to lay bare, bare, uncover. 5. ~-se: a) to pull off one's clothes, undress o. s. b) to be divested of. ~ **alguém** to leave one as naked as the hand.

despistar v. to foil, throw off the scent; mislead, misguide, lead astray.

desplantar v. to displant, transplant, remove a plant to a new place.

desplante s. m. 1. an oblique position in fencing. 2. (fig.) sauciness, boldness; cheek, impudence, insolence.

desplumar v. to deprive of feathers, strip of the feathers, deplume, unfeather.

despoético adj. unpoetic(al), prosaic.

despoetizar v. to render unpoetical, make prosaic, disenchant, disillusion.

despojador s. m. plunderer, spoliator, spoiler, stripper. ‖ adj. bereaving, plundering, spoiling.

despojamento s. m. 1. robbing, plundering; despoilment, divestment, bereavement. 2. dispossession, divestiture, deposal.

despojar v. to deprive, divest, dispossess, strip, spoil, rob, bereave. 2. to depose, disthrone, discrown; disestablish, disinherit, expropriate. 3. ~-se: a) to divest o. s. of. b) to renounce to.

despojo (ô) s. m. 1. booty. 2. plunder, robbing, spoiling, despoliation. 3. ~s pl. leavings, leftovers.
~s **do mar** jetsam. ~s **mortais** mortal remains.
despolarizante adj. m. + f. depolarizing.
despolidez s. f. 1. want of politeness, impoliteness, incivility, rudeness. 2. want of polish.
despolir v. to take away the polish; to tarnish, dull.
despolpador s. m. engine for hulling coffee.
despolpar v. 1. to hull coffee grains. 2. to pulp.
despoluir v. to unpollute, fight pollution.
desponderar v. not to consider, disregard, disesteem, pay no attention.
desponsório s. m. = **desposório**.
despontado adj. 1. edgeless, without point; trimmed. 2. numbed, torpid.
despontante adj. m. + f. blunting, taking away the point.
despontar v. 1. to blunt, take away the point. 2. to unfold, rise, appear, come to view. 3. (bot.) to blow, bud, sprout. 4. to break (the day). 5. to come to mind. 6. ~-se to become blunt.
~o **cabelo** to trim the hair. ~a **maré** to begin to ebb. **ao** ~ **do dia** at the break of day.
desponte s. m. (Braz.) lopping of the tops of corn stalks.
despontuar v. to remove the punctuation.
despopularizar v. 1. to make unpopular. 2. ~-se to become unpopular.
desporte s. m. (also **desporto**) 1. sport; play, game. 2. recreation, amusement, diversion.
desportilhar v. to break or thrust open a door or gate.
desportista s. m. + f. athlete, sportsman; sportswoman. ‖ adj. sportive.
desportivo adj. athletic, sportive, sporting; relating to sport.
desposado s. m. bridegroom. ‖ adj. 1. engaged, betrothed. 2. married.
desposar v. 1. to affiance, betroth. 2. to marry, wed. 3. ~-se to get married.
ele desposou-a he married her.
desposório s. m. (also **desponsório**) betrothal, wedding, marriage.
despossar v. = **desapossar**.
despossuir v. to deprive of a possession, dispossess; lose the possession of.
déspota s. m. + f. despot, tyrant, oppressor.
despótico adj. despotic(al), autocratic(al), absolute in power, oppressive, tyrannic(al), imperious. ‖ **despoticamente** adv. despotically.
despotismo s. m. 1. despotism, absolutism, dictatorship, tyranny, autocracy, oppression. 2. (Braz.): a) multitude. b) hidden place (in the woods).
despotizar v. to despotize, govern despotically, tyrannize.
despovoação s. f. (pl. -ões) (also **despovoamento**) depopulation, expulsion of inhabitants; solitude, seclusion; lonely place.
despovoado s. m. desert place. ‖ adj. unpeopled, desert, uninhabited, depopulated, empty; wild, desolate.
despovoar v. 1. to depopulate, dispeople, unpeople, desolate, lay waste. 2. (fig.) to deprive of adornments. 3. ~-se to grow into desert, become depopulated.
despratear v. to take or scrape the silver off.
desprazer s. m. (also **desprazimento**) displeasure, disgust, distaste, dissatisfaction, discontent; vexation, grief. ‖ v. to displease, disgust, dissatisfy, distaste, discontent; vex.
desprazível adj. m. + f. (pl. -íveis) unpleasant, unpleasing, ungracious, disagreeable. ‖ **desprazivelmente** adv. unpleasantly.

desprecatado adj. improvident, neglecting, careless, heedless. ‖ **-amente** adv. improvidently.
desprecatar-se v. to act imprudently, neglect, be forgetful.
desprecaver(-se) v. to be heedless, careless or incautious.
despregado adj. 1. unfurled, displayed. 2. loose, untied, unfastened, unnailed, unpinned. 3. impertinent, impudent, insolent.
despregadura s. f. 1. unplaiting, undoing the plaits. 2. unnailing.
despregar (I) v. 1. to unhook, unnail, unpin, unplait; unfasten, untie. 2. ~-se to become unnailed, get loose.
despregar (II) v. 1. to unfurl, spread (out). 2. to unwrinkle, smooth out.
~**as velas** to spread the sails.
despreguiçar(-se) v. to strech (out); to idle, lounge.
despremiar v. not to reward or recompense.
desprendado adj awkward, untalented, unskilful, unaccomplished. ‖ **-amente** adv. awkwardly.
desprender v. 1. to loosen, unfasten, untie, unhook, unfix, unlink, unhitch, untruss. 2. to disengage, extricate, disembarrass. 3. to take away, detach. 4. to release (as from a prison). 5. ~-se to get loose, become disengaged.
desprendido adj. 1. unfastened, loose, untied. 2. disinterested, indifferent.
desprendimento s. m. 1. unfastening, loosening, unfixing. 2. detachment, disinterest, indifference. 3. altruism, unselfishness, self-denial. 4. independence, liberty, freedom.
despreocupação s. f. (pl. -ões) freedom of prejudice or care; easiness, carefreeness, insouciance.
despreocupado adj. insouciant, light, easy, carefree. ‖ **-amente** adv. at ease.
despreocupar v. to free from care or prejudice; to rid, ease, relieve of worry.
despreparo s. m. 1. want of preparation, unpreparedness. 2. disarrangement, disorganization, disorder, confusion.
despresilhar v. to unfetter, unshackle.
desprestigiar v. 1. to lessen prestige; depreciate, discredit, disrespect, disrepute. 2. to lose one's reputation or prestige.
desprestígio s. m. want of prestige; disreputation, discredit, disrespect, disgrace; loss of authority or reputation.
despretensão s. f. (pl. -ões) unambitiousness, unpretentiousness; modesty.
despretensioso adj. unpretentious, unambitious, unpresuming, unassuming; unostentatious; simple, modest, humble; austere. ‖ **-amente** adv. unpretentiously.
desprevenção s. f. (pl. -ões) want of foresight, improvidence, carelessness, heedlessness, incautiousness.
desprevenido adj. 1. unprovided, unready, unprepared, unwary, unaware. 2. (pop.) pennyless.
apanhar ~ to take one napping.
desprevenir v. 1. not to provide, fail to prepare, neglect. 2. ~-se to be heedless.
desprezador s. m. despiser, scorner, contemner. ‖ adj. scornful, contemptuous, despising, disdainful.
desprezar v. 1. to despise, scorn, contemn, slight, disdain, scout, look down upon. 2. to spurn, repudiate, reject, defy. 3. to disesteem, disregard, misprize, abominate, detest. 4. to throw away, undervalue, underrate. 5. ~-se: a) to feel ashamed. b) to degrade or debase o. s.
~ **uma lei** to disregard a law.
desprezativo adj. contemptuous, disdainful; depreciative.

desprezilho s. m. disdain, contempt, scorn; disregard, despite.

desprezível adj. m. + f. (pl. -íveis) 1. despicable, contemptible, pitiable, scurvy, beggarly. 2. vile, mean, sordid, worthless, base, abject, ignoble, dirty, paltry. 3. miserable, poor, low, little. 4. negligible, inappreciable. ‖ **desprezivelmente** adv. despicably.

desprezivo adj. 1. = desprezativo. 2. depreciative.

desprezo (ê) s. m. 1. contempt, contemptuousness, disdain, disdainfulness, scorn, despicableness, slightness. 2. disregard, disesteem, defiance. 3. neglect, carelessness, heedlessness.

dar-se ao ~ to disgrace o. s.

desprimor s. m. want of delicacy or elegance, unfairness, impoliteness, ungentleness, incivility.

desprimorar v. 1. to take away the lustre; to blemish, stain, tarnish; dishonour. 2. ~-se to disgrace o. s., lower o. s.

desprimoroso adj. 1. impolite, ungentle, unkind, unfriendly, discourteous. 2. dishonourable, mean, base, vile. ‖ -amente adv. impolitely.

desprivança s. f. disgrace, disfavour, exclusion.

desprivar v. 1. to disgrace, put out of favour, reject, slight. 2. to lose a person's favour.

desprivilegiar v. to deprive of privilege; generalize.

desprofanar v. to purify what had been profaned.

despronúncia s. f. rejection of an indictment, acquittal.

despronunciar v. to reject an indictment, cancel an accusation; acquit, absolve.

despropério s. m. (C. Braz.) offense, affront, insult.

desproporção s. f. (pl. -ões) disproportion, inequality, inadequacy, want of symmetry, disparity.

desproporcionado adj. disproportionate, unsymmetric(al), unequal, inadequate; unshapely, oversize. ‖ -amente adv. disproportionately.

desproporcionar v. 1. to disproportion, mismatch. 2. ~-se to become unproportional.

despropositado adj. purposeless, unmeaning; nonsensical, absurd, unreasonable; foolish, impertinent. ‖ -mente adv. nonsensically.

despropositar v. 1. to act unreasonably, talk at random, extravagate, dote. 2. to be impertinent, be out of the way.

despropósito s. m. 1. preposterousness, extravagance; absurdity, nonsense; impertinence. 2. (Barz.) abundance; multitude; plenty.

desproteção s. f. (pl. -ões) want of protection, defencelessness, helplessness.

desproteger v. 1. to fail to protect, deprive of shelter, unshelter. 2. to forsake, abandon, fail to help.

desprotegido adj. 1. unprotected, guardless, defenceless, unsheltered. 2. exposed, open; naked.

desproveito s. m. disadvantage, prejudice, waste, detriment.

desprover v. to deprive of, unfurnish, digarnish.

desprovido adj. unprovided, unfurnished, destitute, unaccommodated, wanting.

desprovimento s. m. want of provision or necessaries, destitution, resourcelessness.

despudor s. m. shamelessness, insolence, impudence, immodesty.

despudorado s. m. shameless fellow. ‖ adj. impudent, insolent, shameless, licentious, impertinent. ‖ -amente adv. impudently.

despundonor s. m. want of dignity, irreverence, disrespect.

despundonoroso adj. undignified, irreverent, unchivalrous.

desquadrar v. not to tally with.

desqualificação s. f. (pl. -ões) disqualification, elimination.

desqualificado s. m. disqualified person. ‖ adj. disqualified, eliminated; worthless; dinhonourable.

desqualificar v. 1. to disqualify, eliminate (as in a game). 2. to incapacitate, unfit. 3. ~-se to become disqualified.

desqualificativo adj. disqualifying, eliminating.

desquartar v. (Braz.) 1. to suffer (animal) from disarticulation in one of the haunches. 2. to lose (animal) fatness in the haunches.

desqueixado adj. jawless.

desqueixar v. to tear the jaws from, break the jaws.

desqueixelado adj. (Braz.) open-mouthed, agape; surprised, amazed, astonished.

desquerer v. to love no more, dislike, disaffect, disgust, disregard, distaste.

desquerido adj. unloved, disliked, disaffected.

desquiciar v. to put out of joint, unhinge.

desquietar v. to disquiet, worry, trouble, perturb, disturb, annoy.

desquitação s. f. (pl. -ões) divorce, separation, disunion.

desquitar v. 1. to divorce, separate, disunite. 2. ~-se to be divorced.

desquite s. m. divorce, dissolution of marriage, separation, disunion.

~ **amigável** an amicable dissolution of marriage.

desrabar v. = derrabar.

desraigar, desraizar v. = desarraigar, desenraizar.

desramar v. to disbranch, lop or prune a tree.

desratização s. f. (pl. -ões) extirpation of mice or rats.

desratizar v. to exterminate mice.

desrazão s. f. (pl. -ões) unreason, lack of reason, unreasonableness, nonsense, absurdity.

desrazoável adj. m. + f. (pl. -áveis) unreasonable, foolish, nonsensical.

desregrado s. m. disorderly, dissolute or intemperate person. ‖ adj. disorderly, unruly, loose, unrestrained, dissolute; intemperate, extravagant. ‖ -amente adv. disorderly, dissolutely.

desregramento s. m. 1. disorder, iregularity, unruliness, unsteadiness. 2. dissipation. 3. immoderation, excess. 4. immorality, wantonness, licentiousness.

desregrar v. 1. to disorder, put out of order, distemper. 2. to misconduct. 3. to dissipate. 4. ~-se to lead a loose life.

desrelvar v. to cut the grass.

desremediado adj. remediless; unlucky, needy, poor, miserable, wretched.

desremediar v. to make worse, aggravate, cause difficulties.

desrespeitador s. m. disrespectful person. ‖ adj. disrespectful.

desrespeitar v. to disrespect, disesteem, disregard; affront; worry, annoy.

desrespeito s. m. disrespect, contempt, affront, defiance; impoliteness, incivility.

desrespeitoso adj. disrespectful, regardless, flippant. ‖ -amente adv. disrespectfully.

desresponsabilizar v. 1. to free of responsibility. 2. ~-se not to take responsibility, decline responsibility.

desresvestir-se v. to divest, take off the vestments (a priest after celebrating the mass).

desriçar v. to uncurl, unroll.

desrolhar v. to uncork, unstop; open (a bottle).

desrugar v. = desenrugar.

dessaber v. 1. to show ignorance. 2. to forget. 3. ~-se to be ignorant.

dessabor s. m. want of taste or flavour, distaste, insipidity, usavouriness.

dessaborar v. to render unsavoury, insipid or tasteless.

dessaborido, dessaboroso adj. unsavoury, insipid; tasteless, distasteful.

dessaburrar v. = **desensaburrar.**

dessagrar v. to desecrate; profane.

dessalgado adj. without salt, unsalted; insipid, unsavoury.

dessalgar v. 1. to deprive of salt, desalt. 2. to render unsavoury, make insipid. 3. to render ungracious.

dessamoucar v. to clean from the crust, remove the scab.

dessangrar v. 1. to exsanguinate, draw blood from. 2. to bleed. 3. (fig.) to drain a person's purse. 4. ~-se to bleed to death.

dessaudar v. not to salute or greet.

desaudoso adj. unlamented, not deplored.

dessazonado adj. 1. unseasoned, not well seasoned. 2. unripe.

dessazonar v. to deprive of seasoning, unseason.

desse (ê) contr. of **de** and **esse** from that, of that. ~ **lado** thither. ~ **tempo** from that time.

dessecação s. f. (pl. **-ões**) **dessecamento** m. desiccation, making dry, depriving of moisture; drying; drainage.

dessecante adj. m. + f. desiccative, desiccant, drying.

dessecar v. to desiccate, exsiccate, dry, dry up, drain.

dessecativo s. m. (med.) desiccant. ‖ adj. desiccant, desiccative.

dessedentar v. 1. to quench or slack the thirst of. 2. ~-se to quench one's thirst.

dessegredo (ê) s. m. lack of secrecy.

desseguir v. to fail to accompany, not to follow.

dessegurar v. to make insecure, expose to danger, deprive of safety.

desseivar v. to remove the sap from.

desselar (I) v. to remove the saddle, unsaddle.

desselar (II) v. to unseal, break the seal.

dessemelhança s. f. dissimilarity, dissimilitude, diverseness, diversity, disparateness, disparity, unlikeness, difference.

dessemelhante adj. m. + f. dissimilar, disparate, diverse, distinct, different, unlike. ‖ ~**mente** adv. differently, distinctly.

dessemelhar v. 1. to make dissimilar or unlike. 2. ~-se to become dissimilar or unlike, differ from.

dessepultar v. to take out of a grave, exhume, disinter.

dessepulto adj. unburied.

desserviçal adj. m. + f. (pl. **-ais**) unserviceable, useless; disobliging.

desserviço s. m. disservice, ill turn.

desservido adj. hurtful, unhelpful, badly served.

desservir v. to disserve, serve baddly, misserve, hurt.

dessexuado adj. 1. unsexed. 2. (fig.) without sexual appetites.

dessexuar, dessexualizar v. to unsex, deprive of sexual characters.

dessimetria s. f. want of symmetry, dissymmetry, asymmetry.

dessimétrico adj. dissymmetric(al), asymmetric(al).

dessimpatizar v. not to sympathize; to have an antipathy against, dislike, disaffect.

dessitiar v. to liberate of a siege; unfence, set free.

dessociável adj. m. + f. (pl. **-áveis**) unsociable, reserved.

dessocorrer v. to fail to help or support; to give up, abandon, forsake.

dessolar v. to deprive of soles (shoes).

dessoldar v. to unsolder, separate, disunite, dissolve.

dessolhar v. to pull out the floor.

dessorado adj. 1. converted into a serum. 2. feeble, languishing.

dessorar v. 1. to make serous. 2. to weaken. 3. ~-se to become serous.

dessossegar v. = **desassossegar.**

dessoterrar v. = **desenterrar.**

dessuar v. to cease sweating; clean of sweat.

dessubjugar v. to liberate from subjection or submission.

dessubstanciar v. to take away the substance or essence.

dessuetude s. f. desuetude, obsoleteness, disuse.

dessujar v. to clean of dirt, cleanse, sweep.

dessujeito adj. not subdued, independent, free.

dessulfurar v. to desulphurate, free from sulphur, desulphurize.

dessultório adj. desultory, not persistent.

dessumir v. 1. to summarize, condense. 2. to deduct, conclude.

dessurdo adj. not deaf; open-eared.

destabocado adj. (Braz., also **destalado**) 1. eccentric, wild. 2. nuts. 3. daring. 4. insolent. 5. talkative. 6. prankish.

destabocar(-se) v. (Braz.) to behave boisterously or inconveniently, play the fool, talk idly.

destacamento s. m. detachment (of an army).

destacar v. 1. to detach, put a body of troops on their way. 2. to exceed, overtop, surpass, go beyond. 3. to make salient, make stand out, put in relief. 4. (mus.) to staccato, accent, accentuate, contrast. 5. (Braz.) to expulse, oust, kill. 6. ~-se to be detached; be separated (from); be outstanding, to distinguish o. s.

destalingar v. (naut.) to unbend. ~ **a amarra** to unbend the cable.

destampado adj. 1. lidless, bare, uncovered, open. 2. inopportune, preposterous.

destampar v. 1. to take off the lid; to tap, open. 2. to dote, lose one's wits, play the fool.

destampatório s. m. (Braz.) 1. dispute, discussion, quarrel. 2. scolding, a dressing down.

destapamento s. m. uncovering, disclosure.

destapar v. 1. to uncover, open. 2. to uncork, unstop. ~ **uma garrafa** to uncork or crack a bottle.

destaque s. m. prominence, eminence, distinction, notability, superiority.

dar um ~ em (Braz.) to give s. o. to understand he is undesired. **família de ~** an illustrious family.

deste (ê) contr. of **de** and **este** of this, from this.

destecedura s. f. unweaving, unravelling.

destecer v. 1. to unweave, unravel, unwrap, separate the threads of texture. 2. (fig.) to untwine.

destelar v. to fall down (fruits from a tree because of ripeness or blown down by the wind).

destelhar v. to take away the tiles, untile, unroof.

destemer v. 1. to have no fear, be fearless, be unafraid. 2. not to care or mind.

destemidez s. f. fearlessness, intrepidity, boldness.

destemido adj. fearless, dreadless, dauntless; daring, bold, valiant, intrepid, impavid, brave. ‖ **-amente** adv. boldy, intrepidly.

destemor s. m. fearlessness, daringness, dauntlessness, boldness, intrepidity.

destempero s. f. 1. dissension, disorder, distemper. 2. untempering (of steel).

destemperado adj. 1. disordered, dissolute. 2. distempered, unreserved, violent. 3. (mus.) out of tune, disonant. 4. immoderate, excessive, exorbitant. 5. crazy, insane, mad, cracked. ‖ **-amente** adv. immoderately.

barriga -a diarrhoea, flux. **clima ~** raw climate.

destemperança s. f. intemperance, want of moderation; excess.

destemperar v. 1. to dilute, make thin, attenuate, weaken. 2. to soften, untemper, anneal (steel or other metals). 3. (mus.) to put out of tune, make

dissonant. 4. to derange, upset, disturb (as the stomach). 5. to distemper, spoil the temper. 6. ~-se: a) to be put out of tuhe. b) to be softened (steel). c) to commit excesses. d) to become immoderate.
~ com alguém to fall out with one. ~ o vinho com água to treat wine with water, dilute wine.
destempero (ê) s. m. 1. intemperature, distemper, disorder, excess. 2. impertinence, folly, dotage. 3. transport, passion. 4. (pop.) diarrhoea, gastro-intestinal disturbance.
desteridade s. f. (also destreza) adroitness, skill, expertness, handiness.
desterneirar v. (S. Braz.) to take away the calves from the cows.
desterrado s. m. outcast, exile. ‖ adj. banished, exiled, expatriated, outcast.
desterrador s. m. banisher. ‖ adj. driving out, expelling.
desterrar v. 1. to drive out, expel, dispel. 2. to exile, expatriate, banish, deport. 3. ~-se to leave one's country, emigrate.
desterro (ê) s. m. 1. deportation, expatriation, banishment, relegation. 2. exile. 3. wilderness, desert.
desterroar v. to break clods; drag, harrow.
destetadeira s. f. (S. Braz.) small board put on a lamb's muzzle to prevent it from sucking.
destetar v. to wean, accustom to live without the mother's milk.
destilação s. f. (pl. -ões) 1. distillation. 2. distillery. ~ com decomposição, ~ destrutiva destructive distillation. ~ seca dry distillation.
destilador s. m. 1. still, retort. 2. distiller.
destilar v. 1. to distil, extract, evaporate and condense again. 2. to drip, pour out in drops, trickle. 3. (fig.) to instill, insinuate, introduce.
destilaria s. f. distillery, boilery.
destilatório adj. distillatory.
destimidez s. f. boldness, intrepidity, courage.
destímido adj. bold, intrepid, brave, daring. ‖ destimidamente adv. boldly.
destinação s. f. (pl. -ões) destination, fate, fatality, fortune.
destinador s. m. determiner, designator. ‖ adj. determining, designative, destinating, appointing.
destinar v. 1. to destine, fate, doom, consecrate. 2. to purpose, mean, reserve, consign, allot. 3. to apply, appropriate, appoint, determine. 4. ~-se: a) to devote or dedicate o. s. to. b) to be meant for. c) to be destined or addressed to.
destinatário s. m. addressee, receiver, consignee. sem ~ unmailable, unclaimed.
destingir v. 1. (also ~-se) to discolour, bleach; to lose colour, fade. 2. to remove the colour.
destino (I) s. m. 1. destiny, lot, fate, fatality, future, fortune, karma, kismet, predestination, doom. 2. destination, appointment, designation, designment. 3. purpose, intention, aim, end.
destino (II) s. m. (Braz., pop.) folly, madness, craziness.
destinto adj. discoloured, colourless, faded.
destitulção s. f. (pl. -ões) 1. dismissal, deposing. 2. deprivation, need, want, destitution. 3. abandonment, forsaking.
destituído adj. 1. dismissed, deposed, deprived of an office or employment. 2. wanting, destitute, needy. 3. unprovided; void, devoid, unaccommodated, bare.
destituir v. 1. to depose, demit, dismiss, displace, fire (position, employment). 2. to deprive, take away, divest of. 3. ~-se: a) to abstain (from), renounce. b) to be destitute or devoid of.

destoante adj. m. + f. dissonant, discordant, untunely, inharmonious. ‖ ~mente adv. dissonantly.
destoar v. 1. to sound untunely, to discord. 2. to jar, clash. 3. to differ, disaccord, diverge.
destocador s. m. machine for grubbing up the stubs of trees.
destocamento s. m. clearing of the soil from stubs or trunks.
destocar (I) v. 1. to clear from stubs or trunks. 2. to make arable.
destocar (II) v. to disconnect, separate, unmatch, uncouple.
destocar (III) v. (Braz.) to take out, startle or rout animals from their hiding-place.
destoldar v. 1. to take away the awning or tilt. 2. to clarify, bring to light. 3. to purify, cleanse. 4. ~-se to uncloud, clear up.
destom s. m. disharmony, discord, dissonance, divergence, disagreement.
destopetear v. 1. to deprive of the foretop. 2. (S. Braz.) to cut a horse's foretop.
destorar v. to separate the twigs from the trunk.
destorcedor s. m. (Braz.) 1. sugar-cane press used in cheap bars. 2. person who does not keep his word.
destorcer v. 1. to untwist, unwrap, untwine. 2. to redress, reform. 3. to disentangle, unravel, disembarrass. 4. to deflect from due course. 5. to deviate (from a subject). 6. ~-se to exert o. s., do one's utmost.
destorcido adj. lively, gay; skilful; valiant, bold.
destorpecer v. = desentorpecer.
destorroamento s. m. harrowing, breaking of clods.
destorroar v. = desterroar.
destoucar v. 1. to take off the bonnet. 2. to dishevel, tousle the hair. 3. (fig.) to disembellish.
destra s. f. the right hand.
destramar v. 1. to unweave, unravel, unwrap a woof. 2. to discover a plot.
destrambelhado adj. giddy, foolish, silly, crazy.
destrambelhar v. to behave crazily, play the fool.
destrambelho s. m. disorder, disarray, confusion; absurdity, folly, nonsense.
destrancar v. to unlock, unbar, unbolt.
destrançar v. = desentrançar.
destranque s. m. (Braz.) quarrel, brawl, squabble.
destratar v. to affront, abuse (with ill language), insult, outrage, offend.
destravancar v. = desatravancar.
destravar v. to unlock, unfetter, unshackle; stop braking.
destrelar v. = desatrelar.
destrepar v. to come down, clamber down, descend.
destreza s. f. 1. dexterity, ability, skill, skilfulness, handiness, deftness, knack. 2. expertness, aptitude, ingenuity, cleverness, adroitness, cunning. 3. facility, finesse, art, artfulness. 4. craft, feat, slight. 5. readiness, quickness, industry.
destribar-se v. to lose one's stirrups, become unpropped or unsupported.
destrimanismo s. m. righthandedness.
destrímano adj. righthanded.
destrinça s. f. disentangling; specification, detail, particularization; individualization.
destrinçador s. m. disentangler. ‖ adj. disentangling, unravelling, extricating.
destrincar v. to snap with the fingers.
destrinçar v. 1. to disentangle, unravel, extricate, clear. 2. to specify, particularize, expound minutely, detail; individualize.
destrinçável adj. m. + f. (pl. -áveis) specifiable.
destrinchar v. (Braz.) to resolve; explain; clear up, untangle.
destripar v. to gut, paunch, eviscerate.

destripular v. (naut.) to unman, unrig (a ship).

destristecer v. 1. to free of melancholy, make merry, cheer (up.) 2. to cease to be sorrowful, get merry.

destro adj. 1. dexterous, habile, skillful, handy, deft, facile, fine-fingered, agile, artful. 2. expert, apt, ingenious, clever, adroit, cunning; sagacious, intelligent. ‖ **-amente** adv. skilfully, dexterously, adroitly, expertly.

destroca s. f. a changing back to the original form or situation.

destroçador s. m. destroyer, wrecker, overthrower. ‖ adj. wrecking, destroying, ruining, disarraying.

destrocar v. to change again, change back to the original form or state.

destroçar v. 1. to break or cut into pieces, raze, ruin, devastate, wreck, destroy. 2. to defeat, foil, overthrow. 3. to disperse, disband.

destroço (ô) s. m. 1. discomfiture, havock; destruction, devastation. 2. ~s pl. wreckage, rack, ruins. ~s **de fortuna** remains of one's fortune. ~ **de um navio** the remains of a ship (destroyed by storm or rocks). **que** ~ what a wreck!

destronamento s. m. dethronement; deposition, lowering of position; let down; abdication.

destronar v. 1. to dethrone, disenthrone, decrown, unthrone; abdicate. 2. to lower in position, reduce, let down.

destroncado adj. out of joint; dismembered; mutilated; decapitated.

destroncar v. 1. to truncate, lop, cut down the trunk of a tree. 2. to dismember, mutilate, maim; decapitate. 3. to put out of joint, sprain.

destronização s. f. (pl. **-ões**) dethronement; deposition.

destronizar v. to dethrone, unthrone, disenthrone, decrown, depose.

destruição s. f. (pl. **-ões**) 1. destruction, devastation, demolition, rack and ruin, ruination, ravage, havoc, overthrowal, wrack. 2. dissolution, annihilation, extermination, extinction, end.

destruído adj. demolished, broken; extinguished.

destruidor s. m. (also **destrutor**) destructor, destroyer, demolisher, impairer. ‖ adj. destructive, demolishing, ruinous.

destruir v. 1. to destroy, demolish, pull or throw down, crush, raze, smash, ruinate, blast, waste, wreck. 3. devastate, overthrow, subvert, shatter, ruin. 3. to unmake, undo. 4. to extinguish, extirpate, efface, end; kill. 5. ~-se to kill o. s., come to ruin. ~ **uma fortaleza** to raze a fortress. ~ **totalmente** to raze to the ground.

destrunfar (I) v. to unmake the headdress.

destrunfar (II) v. to oblige to play trump, draw the trumps (at cards).

destrutibilidade s. f. destructibility, destructibleness.

destrutível adj. m. + f. (pl. **-íveis**) destructible.

destrutivo adj. destructive, ruinous, hurtful.

desultrajar v. 1. to redress, revenge. 2. ~-se to revenge o. s.

desumanar v. (also **desumanizar**) to render inhuman, make cruel.

desumanidade s. f. inhumanity, cruelty, barbarism.

desumano adj. inhuman(e), brutal, cruel, barbarous, fierce, savage, pitiless, ruthless. ‖ -amente adv. inhumanly.

desunhar v. 1. to pluck off the nails, tear out the nails. 2. to tire, fatigue. 3. (Braz.) to put o. s. to work, make efforts. 4. (Braz., sl.) to bolt, escape, run away.

desunião s. f. (pl. **-ões**) 1. disunion, disjunction, separation. 2. dissension, misunderstanding, discord, variance. 3. breach, quarrel, brawl, wrangle.

desunificar v. to disunify.

desunir v. 1. to disunite, disjoint, separate, divide, disengage, dismatch, discouple. 2. to set at variance, alienate. 3. to dispute, quarrel. 4. ~-se to separate o. s., become detached.

desurdir v. to unwrap a woof, unweave, unravel.

desusado adj. unused, uncommon, unfrequent, unaccustomed; obsolete.

desusar v. 1. to disuse, disaccustom, use no more. 2. to omit, not to employ. 3. ~-se to grow out of use.

desuso s. m. disuse, desuetude, want of practice, discontinuance. **cair em** ~ to fall out of use or grow out of fashion.

desvaecer v. to dispel, disappear, dispense.

desvaidade s. f. modesty, absence of vanity or presumptuousness.

desvairado adj. wild, frenetic, hallucinated; crack-brained, crazy; confused, bewildered. ‖ -amente adv. crazily.

desvairador s. m. cause of bewilderment or crazyness. ‖ adj. hallucinating, distracting, confusing, bewildering.

desvairamento s. m. hallucination, distraction; strangeness; misbehaviour; bewilderment.

desvairança s. f. 1. hallucination; madness. 2. contrariety, discrepance, variance, dissention.

desvairar v. 1. to hallucinate, unhinge, make crazy; infatuate, crack; bewilder. 2. to vary, disagree, dissent. 3. ~-se to lose one's head, behave crazily.

desvairo s. m. (obs.) discrepance, discord, disagreement, dissention, variance.

desvalente adj. m. + f. out of favour; valueless.

desvaler v. 1. to be out of favour, lose value. 2. not to help; to abandon, neglect.

desvalia s. f. (also **desvalimento** m.) 1. disgrace, disfavour, destitution, dereliction. 2. depreciation, diminution or lessening of value.

desvaliar v. 1. to depreciate, undervalue, underrate, belittle. 2. to discredit, disfavour, disgrace. 3. to lose value or merit.

desvalidar v. to invalidate, render infirm.

desvalido s. m. wretched person. ‖ helpless, friendless, abandoned, forsaken; disfavoured, unlucky.

desvalijar v. to rob a person's portmanteau or bags; to strip; steal.

desvalioso adj. depreciated, undervalued; disfavoured, disgraced; worthless.

desvalor s. m. worthlessness, trashiness; depreciation, diminution of value; discredit, disfavour, disgrace.

desvalorização s. f. (pl. **-ões**) depreciation, devaluation; demonetization; disesteem, discredit.

desvalorizador s. m. depreciator. ‖ adj. depreciating, underrating, devaluating.

desvalorizar v. 1. to devaluate, depreciate, depress. 2. to undervalue, underrate, belittle; disesteem.

desvalvulado adj. (bot.) valveless.

desvanecedor adj. 1. frustrating. 2. extinguishing. 3. causing to disappear. 4. causing pride.

desvanecer v. 1. to disperse, dispel, make disappear, dissolve, dissipate, vanish, evanesce, delate. 2. to frustrate, fail; disappoint, deceive. 3. to puff s. o. up with pride. 4. ~-se: a) to vanish, pass away, disappear. b) to grow proud. ~ **a cabeça** to make giddy, cause confusion. ~ **as esperanças** to cut off from expectations, frustrate one's hopes. ~ **todas as dúvidas** to dispel all doubts. ~-se **de** to pride o. s. of, be blown or puffed up with.

desvanecido adj. 1. dispelled, dissipated, vanished. 2. proud, elate, arrogant, haughty. 3. (N. Braz.) excessive, exaggerated, immoderate. ‖ -amente adv. proudly.

desvanecimento s. m. 1. fading, disappearance, evanescence. 2. giddiness, dizziness. 3. pride, arrogance, vanity, presumption; complacency.
desvanecível adj. m. + f. (pl. **-íveis**) evanescent, disappearing.
desvantagem s. f. (pl. **-ens**) disadvantage, prejudice, handicap, drawback, inconvenience, unprofitableness; inferiority, detriment.
a única ~ **é** the pity of it is.
desvantajoso adj. disadvantageous, prejudicial, inexpedient, inconvenient, unprofitable, unfavourable. ‖ **-amente** adv. disadvantageously.
desvão s. m. (pl. **desvãos**) garret, corner, attic; hiding-place, hide-out.
desvariado adj. 1. foolish, heedless, doting, delirious. 2. different, unlike.
desvariar v. 1. to vary, be inconstant or unsteady. 2. to rave, rage, be delirious, extravagate, dote.
desvario s. m. 1. loss of wits, derangement. 2. franticness, delirium, raving. 3. dotage, absurdity, folly. 4. extravagance, caprice.
desvelado (I) adj. watchful, careful, cautious, zealous, solicitous. ‖ **-amente** adv. carefully.
desvelado (II) adj. unveiled, disclosed, uncovered.
desvelar (I) v. 1. to watch, care for, attend, guard. 2. to keep or remain awake. 3. ~**-se** to be careful or diligent.
desvelar (II) v. 1. to remove the veil of, unveil, uncover, disclose. 2. ~**-se** to disclose o. s.
desvelejar v. (naut.) 1. to furl the sails, shorten sails. 2. to take a contrary course.
desvelo (ê) s. m. attention, carefulness, zeal, watchfulness; diligence; devotion.
desvencilhar v. = **desenvencilhar.**
desvendar v. 1. to take the blindfold from the eyes. 2. (fig.): a) to unmask, unveil, uncover, reveal, disclose. b) to disentangle, unriddle.
~ **um mistério** to solve a mystery. ~ **um tesouro** to discover a treasure.
desveneração s. f. (pl. **-ões**) want of veneration, irreverence, disrespect, disesteem.
desvenerar v. to disrespect, disesteem, disregard, slight.
desvenosa adj. (bot.) said of the leaves without venation.
desventoso adj. calm, tranquil, not windy or gusty.
desventrar v. to slit the belly, take out the entrails; to gut, disembowel.
desventura s. f. misadventure, misfortune, unhappiness, unfortunateness, unluckiness, unsuccessfulness; ill fortune, bad luck; calamity.
desventurado s. m. wretch, miserable creature. ‖ adj. unhappy, unlucky, unfortunate, unsuccessful, distressful, infelicitous, miserable. ‖ **-amente** adv. unfortunately.
desventurar v. to make unhappy, render infelicitous.
desventuroso adj. unhappy, unlucky, unfortunate, infelicitous.
desverde adj. withered, faded.
desverdecer v. to lose the green colour, wither, fade.
desvergonha s. f. want of shame, shamelessness, impudence, insolence, sauciness, impertinence; licentiousness.
desvergonhamento s. m. loss of shame, shamelessness.
desvergonhar v. = **desavergonhar.**
desvestir v. 1. to divest, strip, undress, unclothe, make naked, denude. 2. ~**-se** to undress o. s.
desvezado adj. unaccustomed, unfamiliar, unusual, uncommon.
desviado adj. put out of the way, astray, afield, distant, apart, devious; erring.
desviar v. 1. to put out of the way, remove, turn aside, deflect, ward off, diverge, digress. 2. to

deviate, switch, swerve, decline, shunt, sheer, sidetrack. 3. to dissuade, divert, baffle. 4. to misappropriate, misapply, embezzle. 5. ~**-se** to miss one's way, wander, go astray, err, straggle.
~ **alguém do caminho** to put a person out of his road. ~ **alguém do estudo** to divert s. o. from his study. ~ **alguém do perigo** to keep s. o. from danger. ~ **alguém da sua resolução** to dissuade s. o. from his resolution. ~ **a âncora** (naut.) to bear off the anchor. ~ **dinheiro** to purloin or embezzle money. ~ **um golpe** to shun or parry a blow. ~ **o pensamento** to withdraw the mind. ~ **a suspeita** to divert suspicion. ~**-se do assunto** to digress from the main subject. ~**-se de um costume** to depart from a custom. ~**-se da sua obrigação** to deviate from one's duty. ~**-se de um perigo** to shun a danger. ~**-se da verdade** to deviate from the truth. ~**-se da virtude** to forsake virtue.
desvirtuar-se v. to lose the glaze, become dull.
desvigar v. to deprive of framework, take away the beams.
desvigiar v. to cease to watch, render unguarded, unguard.
desvigorar, desvigorizar v. 1. to deprive of strength, weaken, impair. 2. ~**-se** to lose vigour, grow weak, wilt.
desvincar v. to unwrinkle, smooth.
desvincilhar v. = **desenvencilhar.**
desvinculação s. f. (pl. **-ões**) disentail, act of disentailing.
desvincular v. 1. to disentail, free from entail. 2. to free from connection, divest. 3. ~**-se** to become disentailed; become separated.
desvio s. m. 1. deviation, declination. 2. deflection, diversion. 3. detour, bypass, pathway. 4. switch, side-track, shunt, swerve. 5. dissuasion. 6. embezzlement, defalcation, turning away, misapplication, misemployment. 7. subterfuge, shift, escape, evasion. 8. misguidance, aberration, aberrance. 9. error, lapse.
~ **da agulha magnética** deflection of the compass needle. ~ **do assunto** digression of the subject. ~ **de dinheiro** embezzlement of money. **no** ~ (coll.) unoccupied, jobless, unemployed.
desvio-padrão s. m. (pl. **desvios-padrão**) (stat.) standard deviation.
desvirar v. to turn back to the normal position.
desvirgar, desvirginar, desvirginizar v. to deflower, violate, ravish, deprive of virginity.
desvirgular v. not to insert commas.
desvirilizar v. to unman, divest of virility, emasculate.
desvirtuação s. f. (pl. **-ões**) depreciation, disrepute.
desvirtuar v. to depreciate, disparage, warp, pervert, wrench; wrest, misrepresent.
desvirtude s. f. want of virtue; vice.
desvirtuoso adj. virtueless, unvirtuous, vicious.
desviscerado adj. disembowelled.
desvitalizar v. to deprive of vitality, devitalize.
desviver v. to cease to live, to die.
desvizinhar v. to be no more one's neighbour.
deszelar v. to unguard, neglect, cease to take care of.
detalhado adj. detailed, circumstantial. ‖ **-amente** adv. particularly, fully, from point to point, minutely, at length.
detalhar v. to detail, give full account, specify, particularize.
detalhe s. m. detail, circumstance, particularity.
~**s biográficos** biographical dates. ~**s técnicos** technicalities. **dar todos os** ~**s necessários** to give full details. **entrar em** ~**s** to go (enter) into par-

ticulars. **para maiores** ~s **dirija-se a** for further details apply to.

detective s. m. (also **detetive**) 1. detective; (sl.) gumshoe. 2. (fig.) beagle, bloodhound.

detector s. m. (phys.) detector.

detença s. f. delay, retardation, detainment, demurrage; stay.

detenção s. f. (pl. **-ões**) detention, imprisonment, confinement, constraint, arrest; apprehension.

detento s. m. (Braz.) prisoner.

detentor s. m. 1. detainer, withholder. 2. holder, trustee. 3. proprietor.

~ **de um prêmio** prizeman.

deter v. 1. to detain, withhold, retain, keep back, hinder, check. 2. to stop, retard, stay. 3. to hold in custody, keep in arrest. 4. ~**-se:** a) to linger, delay. b) to be detained.

~ **alguém com palavras** to keep s. o. at bay. ~ **o pranto** to forbear crying. ~**-se com detalhes** to dwell on details.

detergente s. m. (med.) detergent. ‖ adj. m. + f. detergent, cleansing, purging, abstergent.

detergir v. (med.) to deterge, absterge, cleanse.

deterioração s. f. (pl. **-ões**) 1. deterioration, decay, rot. 2. waste, dilapidation. 3. derogation.

deteriorante adj. m. + f. deteriorative, tending to deteriorate.

deteriorar v. 1. to deteriorate: a) make worse, impair, spoil. b) rot, putrify. c) decay, degenerate, retrograde. 2. ~**-se** to grow worse; become rotten.

deteriorável adj. m. + f. (pl. **-áveis**) deteriorative; decayable.

determinação s. f. (pl. **-ões**) 1. determination, resolution, decision. 2. order, instruction. 3. resoluteness, firmness. 4. courage, boldness.

falar com ~ to speak with a conscious air. **força de** ~ strength of purpose.

determinado adj. 1. determinate, definitive, decisive; bound, fixed, certain, concrete. 2. bold, resolute, courageous. ‖ **-amente** adv. determinately.

determinador s.m. determinator, person who determines. ‖ adj. determinating.

determinante s. f. (math.) determinant. ‖ adj. m. + f. determinative; decisive, definitive.

determinar v. 1. to determine, order, command, enjoin. 2. to stipulate, establish. 3. to settle, decide, ascertain, regulate, resolve. 4. to limit, bound, mark, fix. 5. ~**-se** to be determined, make up one's mind.

determinativo adj. determinative, conclusive.

determinável adj. m. + f. (pl. **-áveis**) determinable, definable.

determinismo s. m. determinism.

determinista s. m. + f. determinist, follower of determinism. ‖ adj. deterministic, relating to determinism, necessitarian.

detersão s. f. (pl. **-ões**) (med.) detersion, cleansing.

detersivo, detersório adj. detersive, cleansing, detergent.

detestação s. f. (pl. **-ões**) detestation, abhorrence, horror; detestability.

detestar v. to detest, abhor, abominate, loathe, execrate, hate, dislike greatly.

detestável adj. m. + f. (pl. **-áveis**) (also **detestando**) 1. detestable, odious, abominable, abhorrent, execrable, hateful. 2. vile, mean, damnable. ‖ **detestavelmente** adv. detestably.

detido s. m. person in preventive arrest or protective custody. ‖ adj. detained, retarded, delayed; stopped, hindered.

detonação s. f. (pl. **-ões**) detonation, explosion, sudden report, fulmination, blast.

detonante adj. m. + f. detonating.

detonar v. 1. to detonate, explode, fulminate. 2. (by extension) to fire (a gun). discharge.

detorar v. to lop or prune (trees).

detração s. f. (pl. **-ões**) detraction, derogation, disparagement; slander, calumny, defamation.

detrair v. to detract, derogate; slander, calumniate, backbite, defame, libel.

detrás adv. after, behind, back.

por ~ behind one's back, in the absence of.

detratar v. 1. (Braz.) to detract, derogate, depreciate. 2. to insult, affront, contempt.

detrativo adj. detractive, derogative.

detrator s. m. detractor, maligner, blackmouth, slanderer, backbiter. ‖ adj. detracting, slandering, defaming.

detrição s. f. detrition.

detrimento s. m. detriment, damage, hurt, loss, disadvantage, prejudice.

detrítico adj. dreggy; detrital.

detrito s. m. detritus, remains, debris, dreg.

detruncar v. to truncate; mutilate (as a text).

detumescência s. f. (med.) assuagement of a swelling, detumescence.

deturbação s. f. (pl. **-ões**) perturbation, agitation, trouble, disorder, confusion.

deturbar v. to perturb, disturb, disquiet, agitate, trouble.

deturpação s. f. (pl. **-ões**) 1. disfigurement, falsification, alteration. 2. perversion, pervertedness. 3. debasement, defilement, corruption.

deturpador s. m. 1. distorter, mutilator. 2. (fig.) corrupter.

deturpar v. 1. to disfigure, deform, distort; stretch; falsify, warp, wrench, wrest, misrepresent. 2. to corrupt, defile.

déu s. m. used in the expression: **de déu em déu** from house to house.

Deus s. m. 1. God, the Supreme Being, Creator of the Universe. 2. Lord, Providence, Spirit, The Everlasting. 3. deity, a god, divinity.

~ **castiga quem merece** the mills of God grind slowly yet they grind exceedingly small. ~ **te guarde!** God bless you! ~ **nos livre!** God forbid! ~ **lhe pague** God reward you! ~ **permita** God grant. ~ **o sabe!** God knows! ~ **me é testemunha** God is my witness. ~ **Todo-Poderoso** All Mighty God. **a** ~ **nada é impossível** there is nothing impossible to God. **com o auxílio de** ~ under God. **entregar-se nas mãos de** ~ to commit o. s. to Providence. **estar bem com** ~ **e o diabo** to make the best of both worlds. **graças a** ~ thanks God, thanks be to God! **o homem propõe e** ~ **dispõe** man proposes, but God disposes. **meu** ~ Good Lord! My Lord! Begad! **não queira** ~ God forbid! **não serve a** ~**, nem ao diabo** it is good for nothing. **em nome de** ~ in the name of God. **pelo amor de** ~! for God's sake! **por** ~ egad! **se** ~ **quiser** God willing. **sem** ~ godless. **vá com** ~ God speed you, God be with you!

deusa s. f. goddess, deity, divinity. 2. (fig.) adored woman.

deus-dará s. m. used in the expression: **ao deus-dará** at random, haphazardly.

deus-nos-acuda s. m. (used always with the article **um**) hubbub, tumult, chaos, jumble; uproar, riot.

deutério s. m. (chem.) deuterium.

deuterogamia s. f. deuterogamy, second marriage after the death of the first husband (or wife).

deuterógamo s. m. deuterogamist.

deuterologia s. f. (hist.) speech of the defender (at an Athenian law court).

dêuteron s. m. (nucl. phys.) deuteron.

Deuteronômio s. m. Deuteronomy, the fifth book of the Pentateuch.

deuteropatia s. f. (med.) deuteropathy, a secondary affection.

deuteroprisma s. m. deuteroprism.

deuterose s. f. 1. repetition or reproduction of something. 2. tradition.

deutocloreto s. m. (chem.) deutochloride.

deutoplasma s. m. (biol.) deutoplasm, the food substance in the yolk of an egg or ovum.

devação s. f. (pl. -ões) (obs.) = **devoção**.

devagar adv. slowly, at leisure, softly. || interj. steady! easy! hold your horses!

~ **se vai ao longe** fair and softly goes far.

devaneador s. m. castle-builder, daydreamer, dreamer. || adj. dreaming, doting.

devanear v. to dote, daydream; meditate, ponder, muse; extravagate.

devaneio s. m. dream, daydream, cloudland, reverie, illusion; chimera, fancy; brown study.

devassa s. f. 1. hearing of witnesses; judicial inquiry. 2. (by extension) inquest, inquiry, information.

devassado adj. obvious to the sight, exposed to view.

devassador s. m. 1. divulger. 2. corrupter. || adj. opening, exposing to view.

devassamento s. m. 1. hearing of witnesses. 2. indiscretion; licentiousness.

devassante adj. m. + f. inquiring, examining, making inquiries.

devassar (I) v. 1. to trespass, encroach, entrench, invade, enter, penetrate. 2. to divulge, disclose, make public. 3. to inquire, fathom, examine, interrogate, question. 4. ~-se to become public, be divulged, spread.

devassar (II) v. 1. to render lax or loose. 2. to become licentious, take a lewd course of life.

devassidão s. f. (pl. -ões) licentiousness, looseness of manners, dissoluteness, wantonness, debauchery, libertinism, lewdness; prostitution.

devasso s. m. debauchee, libertine, profligate person, reveller. || adj. debauched, dissolute, profligate, licentious, libertine, lewd, wanton, immoral, rakish.

devastação s. f. (pl. -ões) devastation, waste, havoc, desolation, ravage, foraging, depredation; destruction.

devastador s. m. waster, spoiler, ravager, devastator; desolator; plunderer. || adj. devastating, wasting, wasteful, depredatory, ravaging, desolating, destroying, destructing.

devastar v. to devastate, lay waste, havoc, rage, destruct, destroy, desolate, forage.

deve s. m. debit (in bookkeeping).

~ **e haver** debit and credit.

devedor s. m. debtor. || adj. in debt, owing.

deventre s. m. entrails, intestines, bowels (of animals).

dever s. m. obligation, duty, task; business, job, burden, charge; part. || v. 1. to need, have (to do), be obliged. 2. to owe, be indebted, be in debt. 3. ~-se to apply o.s., dedicate o. s.

~ **favores a alguém** to be under an obligation to s. o. ~ **ao terço e ao quarto** to be in everybody's debt. **deve-se fazer isso** this should be done. **deve-se obedecer às leis** we ought to obey the law. **deve-se respeito aos pais** we have to respect our parents. **deve seguir pela direita** you must keep to the right. **deve ser meio-dia** it must be twelve-o'clock. **devia fazê-lo melhor** you ought to do it better. **devia ter feito isso** you should have done that. **devia ser louco** only if you were a fool. **ele deve a fortuna aos seus pais** he owes his fortune to his parents. **ele deve vir hoje** he is to come to-day. **eu devo ir** I must go, I have to

go. **isso não deve admirar** it is not astonishing. **que devemos fazer?** what shall we do?

deveras adv. indeed, downrightly, in earnest, truly, really, certainly, in fact.

eu estou ~ **aborrecido** I am truly fed up.

deveres s. m. duties, obligations.

~ **domésticos** domestic duties. ~ **sacerdotais** pastoral duties.

devesa s. f. a row of trees delimiting a ground.

deviação s. f. (pl. -ões) deviation, alteration of the course.

devido adj. due, just, owing. || -amente adv. duly, orderly, properly.

~ **a** due to, on account of, through. ~ **aos custos altos** due to the high costs. **com todo o respeito** ~ with all due respect. **o trem chegou no tempo** ~ the train arrived in due course.

dévio adj. 1. missing. 2. strayed. 3. impassable, intransitable.

devir s. m. (also **devenir**) a series of transformations. || v. to become, turn out.

devitrificação s. f. (pl. -ões) devitrification.

devitrificar v. to devitrify, deprive of the vitreous qualities.

devoção s. f. (pl. -ões) devotion: 1. adoration, cult, religious fervour, godliness, religion. 2. dedication, attachment, adherence. 3. fidelity, constancy. 4. affection, devotedness. 5. attention.

devocionário s. m. prayer-book.

devolução s. f. (pl. -ões) devolution, restitution, restoration, reddition, return; redelivery; reversion; refund.

devolutivo adj. (also **devolutório**) devolutive, reversional, returnable.

devoluto adj. 1. devolved, returned, escheated. 2. vacant, empty, uninhabited, unoccupied.

devolver v. 1. to devolve, return, remise, redeliver, render, restore, recede, give back; refund. 2. (S. Braz., pop.) to vomit, spew. 3. ~-se to develop (itself).

devoniano s. m. (geol.) Devonian. || adj. Devonian.

devoração s. f. (pl. -ões) devouring.

devorador s. m. devourer. || adj. devouring, wolfish, ravenous, voracious, edacious, avid.

chamas ~as devouring flames.

devorante adj. m. + f. devouring, ravenous, greedy.

devorar v. 1. to devour, ingurgitate, wolf, eat up greedily, lick up, gulp, engorge, englut. 2. to consume, absorb, destroy, squander.

~ **sua fortuna** to squander away one's fortune. ~ **seu lanche** to devour one's breakfast. ~ **os livros** to devour books, read eagerly, pore day and night over books. ~ **a presa** to devour the prey (animal).

devorismo s. m. 1. wasting of money. 2. embezzlement of public funds.

devorista s. m. + f. squanderer, waster (of money). || adj. squandering, wasteful.

devotação s. f. (pl. -ões) devotement; devotion.

devotado adj. 1. devoted, pious, religious. 2. attached, affectionate, dedicated.

devotamento s. m. devotement, dedication, fidelity, allegiance.

devotar v. 1. to devote, dedicate. 2. to consecrate. 3. to adhere, affect. 4. ~-se to dedicate o. s. to, give o. s. to.

devoto s. m. devotee, ascetic votarist, cultist, church-goer. || adj. devoted, religious, pious, heavenly-minded.

dextrina s. f. (chem.) dextrin, starch-gum.

dextrogiro adj. dextral, dextrorotary, dextro-gyrate; clockwise.

dextrose s. f. (chem.) dextrose, dextroglucose.

dez s. m. ten, the number ten. ‖ num. ten.
~ **por um** ten to one. ~ **vezes** ten times. **aos** ~ by tens. **nove em** ~ nine out of ten.

dezembro s. m. December, last month of the year.

dezena s. f. 1. ten; a set of ten. 2. ten days. 3. half a score.

dezeno adj. tenth.

dezenove s. m. (also **dezanove**) nineteen. ‖ num. nineteen.

dezesseis s. m. (also **dezasseis**) sixteen. ‖ num. sixteen.

dezessete s. m. (also **dezassete**) seventeen. ‖ num. seventeen.

dezoito s. m. eighteen. ‖ num. eighteen.

dezoito-grande s. m. (pl. **dezoitos-grandes**) (N. Braz.) a special fishing instrument.

dezoito-pequeno s. m. (pl. **dezoitos-pequenos**) (N. Braz.) a kind of fishing tool.

dez-réis s. m. ancient Portuguese coin, corresponding to the present **centavo**.
~ **de mel coado** lowest amount, trifle, bagatelle.

dia s. m. day, daylight, daytime.
~ **a** ~ daily, day by day. ~ **de abstinência**, ~ **de jejum** fast day, fish day. ~ **de ano-bom** New Year's Day. ~ **de anos** birthday. ~ **de azar** black Monday. ~ **dos bobos** (1st. of April) All Fool's Day. ~ **de carne** meat day. ~ **de casamento** wedding-day. ~ **claro** clear day or weather. ~ **do Espírito Santo** Whit-Sunday. ~ **feriado** holiday. ~ **de finados** All Souls' Day. ~ **de folga** playday. ~ **de gala** collar-day. **o** ~ **de hoje** to-day. ~ **do Juízo** doomsday, dies irae. ~ **letivo** school day. ~ **de Natal** Christmas Day. ~ **de pagamento** pay-off, pay-day. ~ **de Páscoa** Easter day. ~ **pesado** gloomy, dull weather. ~ **de Reis** Epiphany, twelfth-day. ~ **santo** holiday, Sunday. ~ **de semana** weekday. ~ **do Senhor** Sunday, sabbath. ~ **de todos os santos** All Saints' (day). ~ **de trabalho**, ~ **útil** weekday. ~ **de verão** summer day. **algum** ~ someday. **ao declinar do** ~ at night-fall. **ao romper do** ~ at daybreak. **até outro** ~! so long! **bom** ~! **bons** ~s! good morning! **cada** ~ day by day. **de** ~ in the daytime, by day. **deixar para outro** ~ to postpone, leave for another day. **de** ~ **em** ~ from day to day. **de** ~ **e de noite** by day and night. **de três em três** ~s every third day. **dum** ~ **para outro** overnight, suddenly. **é** ~ **claro** it is broad daylight. **em** ~ up--to-date. **em nossos** ~s in our days. **fazer do** ~ **noite** to turn day into night. **há** ~s some days ago, some time ago. **hoje em** ~ nowadays. **jornada de um** ~ a day's journey. **mais** ~ **menos** ~ sooner or later. **marcar um** ~ to set a day. **meio** ~ midday, noon. **não há** ~ **sem tarde** the longest day must have an end. **não se vão os** ~s **debalde** time leaves its traces. **neste** ~ this day, today. **o** ~ **todo** all the day long. **o pão de cada** ~ the daily bread. **outro** ~ recently. **pôr em** ~ to update. **na semana dos nove** ~s when two Sundays come together; never. **que** ~ **é hoje?** what day is it? **seu** ~ one's happy day (birthday or name-day). **ter os** ~s **contados** to have one's days numbered. **um** ~ **é da caça, outro do caçador** every dog has his day. **um** ~ **destes** one of these days. **um** ~ **sim um** ~ **não** every other day. **um homem de** ~s an aged man. **viver aos** ~s to live from hand to mouth.

diá s. m. (Braz., pop.) devil.

diaba s. f. (also **diáboa, diabra**) demoness, she-devil; fury; shrew.

diabada s. f. (Braz.) a lot of devils or wrong fellows.

diábase s. f., **diabásio** m. (min.) diabase, diorite.

diabelha s. f. bock's horn, dog's tooth (medicinal plant).
~ **do reino** plantago lusitanica.

diabetes, diabete s. m. + f. (med.) diabetes.

diabético adj. (med.) diabetic, relating to diabetes.

diabetologia s. f. branch of medicine dealing with diabetes.

diabetólogo s. m. (med.) specialist in diabetes.

diabinho s. m. 1. litle devil, imp, devilkin; little hussy. 2. (N. Braz.) a species of firecracker used on midsummer day.

diabo s. m. (also **diacho**) devil, evil spirit, demon, Satan, dickens, Beelzebub, Old Nick, Belial, bogy, fiend.
~ **coxo** the devil upon crutches. ~ **pregador** person who speaks like a saint and acts like a knave. ~s **me levem!** I will be blowed, if... **aí é que está o** ~! there lies the difficulty! **anda o** ~ **soltol** the hell is broken loose. **cair nas mãos do** ~ to fall into the devil's clutches. **bom** ~ a good-natured fellow. **dar-se a todos os** ~s to fret and fume. **fazer o** ~ **a quatro** to play the devil. **nem sempre o** ~ **está atrás da porta** every flow will have its ebb. **há muitos** ~s **que se parecem uns com os outros** there are more Jacks than one. **oh** ~! **hoity-toity!** **o** ~ **não é tão feio como o pintam!** he (it) is not so bad as he (it) seems to be; the devil is not so black as he is painted. **o** ~ **o dá e o** ~ **o leva** what is got over the devil's back is spent under his belly. **pintar o** ~ to raise the devil. **pobre** ~! poor devil, poor wretch! **por arte do** ~ by devilish tricks. **que** ~! what the devil! **que** ~ **aconteceu?** what the deuce has happened? **que** ~ **quer você?** what the devil do you want? **sorte do** ~ devil's luck. **valha-te o** ~! the devil take you.

diabólico adj. 1. devilish, hellish, diabolical, impish, infernal, satanic(al), deuced, fiendish, demoniacal. 2. very wicked. 3. intricate, obscure, abstruse. ‖ **diabolicamente** adv. diabolically, devilishy; intricately.

diabolismo s. m. 1. (Braz.) meanness, brutality, cruelty. 2. diabolism.

diabolô s. m. diabolo, devil on two sticks (a toy).

diabo-marinho s. m. (pl. **diabos-marinhos**) devil-fish, frog-fish, toad-fish, angler.

diabrete s. m. 1. little devil. 2. mischievous child. 3. a certain game at cards.

diabrose s. f. (med.) erosion, corrosion of the bones.

diabrótico adj. (med.) diabrotic.

diabrura s. f. 1. diablerie, deviltry, devilishness, develish trick. 2. mischief of a child.

diacáustico s. m. diacaustic, a double-convex lens.

diacidrão s. m. candy of citron peel.

diacódio s. m. (pharm.) diacodium, a sirup of white poppies.

diaconal adj. m. + f. (pl. **-ais**) diaconal, pertaining to a deacon.

diaconato s. m. (also **diaconado**) diaconate: office or dignity of a deacon, deaconship, deaconry.

diaconia s. f. deaconship, deaconry.

diaconisa s. f. deaconess.

diácono s. m. deacon.

diácope s. f. diacope: 1. (gram.) tmesis. 2. (surg.) a longitudinal fracture.

diacrítico adj. diacritic(al): 1. (gram.) said of a mark, point or sign serving to distinguish or separate. 2. (med.) diagnostic(al).

diactínico adj. (phys.) diactinic, capable of transmitting the chemical rays of light.

diactinismo s. m. (phys.) diactinism.

diacústica s. f. diacoustics, the science of refracted sounds.

díade, díada s. f. dyad, pair, couple, group of two.

diadelfia s. f. diadelph: plant with stamens united into two bundles.

diadelfo adj. (bot.) diadelphian, diadelphious.

diadema s. m. 1. diadem, crown, tiara. 2. (fig.) supreme power, sovereignty.

diademado adj. having a diadem on the head, crowned.

diademar v. to diadem, adorn with a diadem; crown.

diadema-real s. f. (pl. **diademas-reais**) plant of the family Amaryllidaceae.

diafa s. f. bounty, bonus (payable at the end of the task).

diafaneidade s. f. diaphaneity, power of transmitting light, diaphanousness, pellucidity, transparency.

diáfano adj. 1. diaphanic, diaphanous, transparent, translucent, clear, pellucid. 2. (fig.) lean, meagre.

diafanômetro s. m. diaphanometer, an instrument for testing the transparency of the air.

diafilme s. m. (Braz.) a positive slide (film).

diáfora s. f. (gram.) repetition of a word in the same phrase, however, with different signification.

diaforese s. f. (med.) diaphoresis, (artificial) perspiration.

diaforético adj. diaphoretic, increasing perspiration, sudorific.

diafragma s. m. diaphragm: 1. partition, separation. 2. (anat.) midriff, the musculomembranous partition between the thoracic and abdominal cavity. 3. (opt.) aperture. 4. a vibrating disk (telephone, phonograph).

diafragmático adj. diaphragmal, diaphragmatic; separating, partitioning.

diagnose s. f. 1. (med.) diagnosis, scientific discrimination of disease. 2. (biol.) distinctive description of an animal or plant. 3. analysis.

diagnosticador s. m. diagnostician, expert in diagosis.

diagnosticar v. to diagnose, diagnosticate.

diagnosticável adj. m. + f. (pl. **-áveis**) that can be diagnosed.

diagnóstico s. m. diagnosis: 1. determination based on symptoms. 2. the symptoms of a diagnose. 3. summary of characteristics. 4. discrimination, definition. ‖ adj. diagnostic: specifying diagnostically, indicative of the nature of.

diagonal s. f. (pl. **-ais**) diagonal line or direction. ‖ adj. m. + f. diagonal, oblique, bias, transverse, cater-cornered. ‖ ~**mente** adv. diagonally.

diágrafo s. m. diagraph, a drawing instrument (scale and protractor).

diagrama s. m. diagram, scheme, sketch, graph, figure.

diagramático adj. diagrammatic, schematic.

dial s. m. (pl. **-ais**) dial. ‖ adj. m. + f. quotidian; daily.

diale s. m. (N. Braz., pop.) = **diabo**.

dialetal adj. m. + f. (pl. **-ais**) dialectal, dialectic.

dialética s. f. dialectic, dialectics, disputation, critical examination of an opinion, logical reasoning.

dialético s. m. dialectician, logician; a good reasoner. ‖ adj. dialectic.

dialeto s. m. dialect, idiom of a locality, manner of speaking, accent; vernacular.

dialetologia s. f. dialectology, branch of philology which examines the dialects.

dialetológico adj. dialectological, of or relating to dialectology.

dialetólogo s. m. dialectologist, dialectologer.

dialho s. m. (pop.) = **diabo**.

dialiocarpelar adj. (bot.) dialycarpous, apocarpous: bearing fruit with separate carpels.

dialiopétalo adj. (bot.) dialypetalous, polypetalous.

dialiossépalo adj. (bot.) dialysepalous, polysepalous, having a calix of separate sepals.

dialiostêmone adj. (bot.) dialystaminous.

dialipetalantáceas s. f. pl. (bot.) Dialypetalanthaceae.

dialisador s. m. (chem.) dialyser.

dialisar v. (chem.) to dialyse, separate by dialysis.

diálise s. f. (chem.) dialysis: process of separating crystalloyd substance from the colloid.

dialogado adj. put in the form of dialogue, dialogued.

dialogador s. m. dialoguer, dialogist.

dialogal adj. m. + f. (pl. **-ais**) (also **dialógico**) dialogic(al), dialogistic.

dialogar v. 1. to dialogue, put in the form of a dialogue, write dialogues. 2. to take part in a dialogue, converse, talk.

dialogia s. f. = **diáfora**.

dialogismo s. m. dialogism: 1. art of writing dialogues. 2. (rhet.) expression of ideas in the form of a dialogue.

dialogista s. m. dialogist: 1. a writer of dialogues. 2. a good reasoner.

dialogístico adj. dialogistic(al), having the form of a dialogue, consisting in a dialogue. ‖ **dialogisticamente** adv. in the form of a dialogue.

diálogo s. m. dialogue: 1. conversation between two persons. 2. (by extension) conversation between more persons, colloquy, interlocution. 3. a literary work in the form of a dialogue.
os ~s de Platão the dialogues of Plato. pôr em ~ to dialogize.

diamagnético adj. (phys.) diamagnetic, exhibiting diamagnetism.

diamagnetismo s. m. diamagnetism, the branch of physics treating of the phenomena of diamagnetic bodies.

diamantário s. m. (Central Braz.) diamond trader, diamond dealer.

diamante s. m. (also but obs. **diamão**). 1. diamond, adamant, brilliant. 2. (N. Braz.) a sort of chisel. ~ **abrasivo** abrasive diamond. ~ **bruto** rough diamond. ~ **negro** black diamond, carbon diamond. ~ **de vidraceiro** glacier's diamond. **ponta de** ~ diamond point. **bodas de** ~ diamond wedding.

diamante-rosa s. m. (pl. **diamantes-rosa**) rose diamond, rose cut.

diamantífero adj. diamantiferous: yielding or bearing diamonds, producing diamonds. **distrito** ~ diamantiferous district, diamond-field.

diamantino adj. diamantine, adamantine, diamond, resembling a diamond, hard as a diamond.

diamantista s. m. + f. diamond cutter, diamond dealer.

diamantizar v. 1. to diamondize, polish as a diamond. 2. to esteem highly, value.

diamantóide s. m. diamantoid.

diamba s. f. (bot.) marijuana (the dried leaves and flowers are smoked as a narcotic).

diambarana s. f. medicinal plant of the gentian family.

diametral adj. m. + f. (pl. **-ais**) diametric(al), diametral. ‖ ~**mente** adv. diametrically.

diâmetro s. m. diameter (plate A 9). ~ **externo** (tech.) external diameter. ~ **interno** (tech.) bore, size. ~ **de rotação** axis of rotation.

Diana s. f. 1. (mythol.) Diana, the goddess of hunting. 2. (poet.) the moon.

diandria s. f. attribute of diandrous plants.

diândria s. f. Diandria: an order of plants with perfect flowers, having only two stamens.

diandro adj. (bot.) diandrous, diandrian, having two stamens.

diangas, dianho s. m. = **diabo**.

diante adv. before, in front.
~ **de** in front of. ~ **de Deus e todo o mundo** in the face of God and the world. ~ **do perigo** in the presence of danger. **daqui em** ~ hereafter, henceforth, from now on, from this time on. **em** ~ upward, up, on, forward. **ir por** ~ to go on, continue. **para** ~ ahead, along, onward, forward. **quem ao** ~ **não olha, atrás torna** he who does not look ahead finds himself behind. **do século décimo em** ~ from the tenth century upwards. **tocar para** ~ to go ahead.

dianteira s. f. 1. fore-part, foreside, front. 2. lead. 3. vanguard. 4. pre-eminence, priority.
~ **do exército** the van of an army. **dar a** ~ **a alguém** to let a person take the lead. **na** ~ ahead, leading. **tomar a** ~ to overrun, pass, outpace.

dianteiro s. m. front line player. ‖ adj. fore, foremost, headmost, front, first, leading.

diapalmo s. m. (pharm.) diapalma, plaster or salve prepared of palm leaves.

diapasão s. m. (pl. -ões) 1. (mus.) diapason: a) the entire compass of a voice or instrument. b) (obs.) octave. c) pitch, tune. d) concert pitch, tuning-fork. 2. (fig.) standard, state of equality. 3. (Braz., sl.) blade (as of a dagger or foil).

diapedese s. f. (med.) diapedesis.

diapensiácea s. f. (bot.) a species of the genus Diapensiaceae, a small order of dicotylodons.

diapensiáceo adj. (bot.) relating to the genus Diapensiaceae.

diaporese s. f. (rhet.) a figure by which the speaker manifests doubt or irresolution.

diapositivo s. m. (Braz.) diapositive, slide, transparency.

diaquilão s. m. (pharm.) diachylon, diachylum, lead plaster.

diária s. f. 1. daily wages or income. 2. daily expenses or rate (as of a board or hotel).

diário s. m. 1. diary, daybook, daily record. 2. journal, daily newspaper, magazine. 3. (fam.) daily expenses. 4. a bookkeeper's journal. ‖ adj. daily, diurnal, quotidian, everyday.
~ **de bordo** log-book. ~ **de tempo** diary of the weather. ~ **de viagem** a traveler's diary.

diarismo s. m. daily journalism, daily press.

diarista (I) s. m. + f. editor of a daily newspaper, journalist, reviewer; diarist.

diarista (II) s. m. (Braz.) day-labourer, day-worker.

diarito s. m. greenstone.

diarquia s. f. 1. state ruled (at the same time) by two kings. 2. diarchy.

diarréia s. f. (med.) diarrhea, diarrhoea, intestinal catarrh; looseness.

diarréico s. m. person suffering from diarrhea. ‖ adj. diarrheal, diarrhoeal, catarrhal (referring to the intestines), lax.

diartrose s. f. (anat.) diarthrosis, articulation of bones in any direction.

dia-santo s. m. (pl. **dias-santos**) (Braz., pop. Port., prov.) hole in the stocking.

diascopia s. f. projection of slides or transparencies.

diascórdio s. m. (pharm.) diascordium; a stomachic remedy prepared from scordium or water germander.

diaspídeos s. m. pl. (ent.) family of insects, order homoptera, a pest for fruit trees.

diáspora s. f. diaspora.

diaspório s. m. diaspore, orthorombic mineral, hydrate of aluminium.

diassintomia s. f. (biol.) change of genes among analogous chromosomes.

diástase s. f. 1. (chem.) diastase: a substance existing in barley, wheat and oats after germination.

2. (anat.) diastasis: dislocation, luxation. 3. (mil.) division.

diastema s. m. (zool., anat.) diastema: an interval between two contiguous teeth.

diastilo s. m. (archit.) diastyle: mode of arrangement of columns, in which the intercolumnation measures three diameters.

diástole s. f. 1. (anat.) diastole, dilatation or expansion of the heart or other blood vessels. 2. extension of a syllable by which the stress of a syllable is transferred to the next one.

diastólico adj. diastolic, relating to diastole.

diastrofia s. f. (anat.) dislocation of nerves or muscles; luxation, sprain of bones.

diatermanismo s. m. diathermanism.

diatérmano adj. diathermous, diathermanous, diathermic.

diatermia s. f. (med.) diathermy, application of high-frequency currents to heat the tissues.

diatérmico adj. (med.) diathermic.

diátese s. f. (med.) diathesis, constitutional predisposition, particular disposition or habit.

diatético adj. (also **diatésico**) diathetic, constitutional.

diatomáceas s. f. pl. (bot.) Diatomaceae.

diatônico adj. (mus.) diatonic, said of the tones of the standard scales without chromatic alteration.

diatribe s. f. diatribe, bitter and violent criticism, strain of invective, philippic.

diaulo (I) s. m. ancient Greek instrument consisting of two flutes.

diaulo (II) s. m. ancient Greek measure.

dibrânquio s. m. (zool.) mollusc with two gills.

dica s. f. (Braz.) a tip, helpful advice.

dicacidade s. f. dicacity, pertness, satiricalness, waggery, banter; sauciness, causticity.

dição, dicção s. f. (pl. -ões) diction, style expression, way of speaking or writing, use of words, phraseology; parlance.

dicapetaláceas s. f. pl. (bot.) Dichapetalaceae.

dicar v. 1. to dedicate, consecrate, devote. 2. to pay respect and homage. 3. to sacrifice.

dicarpelar adj. m. + f. (bot.) dicarpellary, composed of two carpels.

dicásio s. m. (bot.) dichasium, a cyme with two axes.

dicataléctico, dicatalético adj. dicatalectic.

dicaz adj. m. + f. satirical, sarcastic, jeering, bantering.

dicéfalo adj. dicephalous, two-headed, bicapitate.

dichote s. m. scoff, jest, sneer, jeer; scorn, disdain.

dicíclico adj. (bot.) dicyclic, having two verticils.

dicionário s. m. dictionary, wordbook, lexicon, vocabulary, glossary.
~ **de algibeira**, ~ **de bolso** pocket dictionary. ~ **ambulante** (fig.) walking dictionary. ~ **latim-português** Latin-Portuguese dictionary. ~ **poliglota** polyglot dictionary. ~ **técnico** technical dictionary. **compilar um** ~ to compile a dictionary. **manejar bem um** ~ to handle a dictionary well. **ele nunca se serve do** ~ he never uses a dictionary. **procure a palavra no** ~! look up the word in the dictionary!

dicionarista s. m. + f. lexicographer, author of a dictionary, dictionarian, compiler of a dictionary.

dicionarizar v. (also **dicionariar**) 1. to include in a dictionary. 2. to compile or organize a dictionary.

diclamídeo adj. (bot.) having two whorls.

diclidanteráceas s. f. pl. (bot.) family of trees, order Ebenales, comprising only a few Brazilian species of two genera.

diclínea adj. (bot.) diclinous: having the stamens and pistils on separate flowers.

diclinismo s. m. (bot.) diclinism.

dicogamia s. f. (bot.) dichogamy, maturity of stamens and pistils at different times in order to prevent self-fertilization (of hermaphrodite flowers).

dicógamo adj. (bot.) dichogamous, characterized by dichogamy.

diconroque s. m. (Braz.) tree of the family Moraceae.

dicotiledôneo adj. (bot.) dicotyledonous, having two cotyledons.

dicotilídeo s. m. (bot.) dicotyledon.

dicotomia s. f. dichotomy: 1. (astr.) that phase of the moon in which it shows only half its disk. 2. (bot.) a mode of branching by constant forking.

dicotômico adj. dichotomous: pertaining to or consisting of a pair; divided into two.

dicromático, dicrômico adj. dichromatic, having or producing two colours.

dicrotismo s. m. (med.) the state of being dichrotic (pulse).

dícroto adj. dicrotic, double-beating, having a double or resounding pulse.

dictiólde adj. m. + f. reticulate.

dictite s. f. (med.) inflammation of the retina.

didáctilo, didátilo adj. (zool.) didactyl, didactyle, didactylous, two-fingered, two-toed.

didactologia, didatologia s. f. didactics, the art or science of teaching, pedagogy, pedagogics.

didactológico, didatológico adj. didactic, pedagogic(al), instructive, doctrinal, expository.

didascálico adj. 1. didactic, preceptive, instructive. 2. didascalic, didascalar.

didática s. f. didactics, pedagogics, art of teaching.

didático adj. didactic, instructive, pedagogical, preceptive, expository.

    livro ~ schoolbook, textbook. **método** ~ method of teaching. **poema** ~ didactic poem.

didelfídeos s. m. pl. (zool.) Didelphidae.

didi-da-porteira s. f. (pl. **didis-da-porteira**) (Braz.) a medicinal plant of the spiderwort family.

dídimo (I) s. m. (chem.) didymium.

dídimo (II) adj. (bot.) didymous, twofold, twin, growing double, bigeminate, bijugous.

didínamo adj. (bot.) didynamic, didynamian, didynamous, having four stamens in two unequal pairs.

didoniano s. m. a kind of printing type. || adj. relating to this type.

diecia s. f. Diocecia: class of plants which have male flowers on one individual and female on another.

diédrico adj. dihedral.

    ângulo ~ dihedral angle.

diedro s. m. (math.) dihedron, a figure with two sides or surfaces. || adj. dihedral.

dielétrico s. m. dielectric: non-conducting material. || adj. dielectric, non-conducting, insulating.

diérese s. f. (gram.) diaeresis, dieresis: 1. separate pronunciation of two vowels (diphtong). 2. the sign for this separation.

dierético adj. dieretic, diaeretic; corrosive, escharotic.

diesar v. (mus.) to raise a semitone in pitch.

diese s. f. (mus.) diesis, semitone, sharp.

dieta (I) s. f. diet: 1. (med.) regimen, course of food according to medical rules. 2. allowance of provision, supply of food.

    fazer ~ to diet o. s. **o doutor pôs o doente em** ~ **rigorosa** the doctor put the patient on a strict diet. **devo pôr-me em** ~? must I diet myself?

dieta (II) s. f. diet, assembly, a meeting of dignitaries or delegates.

dietética s. f. dietetics, branch of medicine relating to the diet.

dietético adj. (med.) dietary, dietetic(al). || **dieteticamente** adv. dietetically.

dietista s. m. + f. dietitian, dietician.

difamação s. f. (pl. -ões) defamation, aspersion, libel, columny, reproach, backbiting, detraction, vilification, slander; scandal.

difamador s. m. defamer, detractor, slanderer. || adj. defamatory, detractive, slanderous, defaming, calumniatory, scandalous. || ~**amente** adv. slanderously.

difamante adj. m. + f. defaming, abusive, slanderous, detractory, calumnious.

difamar v. 1. to defame, vilify, calumniate, malign, blemish, traduce, asperse, slander, libel; discredit, decry, disparage. 2. ~**-se** to lose one's credit, prestige or reputation.

difamatório adj. defamatory, calumnious, libel(l)ous, slanderous. || **difamatoriamente** adv. slanderously, libel(l)ously.

    libelo ~ defamatory libel, lampoon. **ele fez um libelo** ~ **contra o governo** he wrote a lampoon against the government.

difásico adj. (electr.) diphase, diphasic.

difenilo s. m. (chem.) diphenyl, biphenyl.

diferença s. f. 1. difference, dissimilarity, inequality, unlikeness, disparity. 2. deviation, variety. 3. distinction, contrast. 4. divergence, diversity. 5. variance, discord, disagreement. 6. result of a subtraction. 7. ~**s** pl.: a) dispute, quarrel, dissension, debate. b) odds.

    ~ **mínima** a small difference, shade. ~ **potencial** (electr.) potential difference, voltage. ~ **de preço** difference in price. ~ **de temperatura** difference in temperature. **com pouca** ~ with a small difference, about, near. **ele pagou a** ~ he paid the difference. **fazer** ~ to difference, distinguish, be different; make a difference. **faz pouca** ~ it matters little. **há muita** ~ there wants a great deal. **não faz** ~ it does not matter. **eu parto a** ~ **ao meio** I split the difference. **sem** ~ without difference. **uma** ~ **notável ou enorme** a marked difference.

diferençar v. 1. to difference, differentiate. 2. to distinguish, discriminate, discern, note the difference. 3. ~**-se:** a) to vary, differ, be distinguished from. b) to grow unlike, become different.

diferençável adj. m. + f. (pl. -áveis) differentiable, distinguishable.

diferenciação s. f. (pl. -ões) differentiation: 1. discrimination of varieties. 2. (math.) operation of finding the differential.

diferencial s. f. (pl. -ais) 1. (math.) differential, infinitesimal difference between two values of a variable quantity. 2. m. (mech.) differential gear (plate V 3). || adj. m. + f. differential, discriminating, distinguishing; special.

    cálculo ~ differential calculus, analysis of infinitesimals. **quantidade** ~ differential quantity or capacity. **quociente** ~ differential quotient, derivative or coefficient.

diferenciar v. 1. to difference, discriminate, differentiate. 2. (math.) to calculate the differential of. 3. ~**-se** to differ, contrast.

diferente adj. m. + f. 1. different, unlike, dissimilar, unequal. 2. distinct, particular. 3. other, another, else. 4. divergent. 5. ~**s** pl. several, diverse, sundry, various. || ~**mente** adv. differently.

    ~ **um do outro** unlike each other. **agir de modo** ~ **dos outros** to act unlike others. **agora o caso é** ~ it is quite another story now. **ele é de opinião** ~ he differs in opinion. **é uma coisa completamente** ~ it is quite another matter. **isto é muito** ~ that is quite different. **muitas coisas** ~**s** a lot of different things.

diferimento s. m. deferment, postponement, putting off, delay.

diferir v. 1. to defer, postpone, delay, put off, retard, prolong; adjourn, protract. 2. to differ: a) disagree, dissent, conflict. b) be unlike or dissimilar; vary.
difícil adj. m. + f. (pl. -ceis) 1. difficult, hard, uneasy, arduous, painful, toilsome, laborious. 2. intricate, complicated, involved, knotty, obscure, entangled. 3. onerous, burdensome. 4. perilous, wearisome. ‖ dificilmente adv. hardly, difficultly, probably not.
~ de contentar hard to please. circunstâncias -eis strained circumstances. empreitada ~ a tough job. ele está colocado numa situação ~ he is in a awkward position, he is in a hole. uma obrigação ~ a tall order. um problema ~ a tough problem. ser de ~ compreensão to be slow in the uptake. venda ~ slow sale.
dificílimo adj. (abs. superl. of difícil) very difficult.
dificuldade s. f. 1. difficulty, hardness, laboriousness, arduousness. 2. complication, trouble, annoyance, embarrassment, intricacy. 3. obstacle, impediment, obstruction, hindrance. 4. distress, dilemma, quandry, predicament. 5. exigency; pinch, strait.
~s financeiras (financial) embarrassment. achar-se em grandes ~s to labour under great difficulties. aplanar ~s to smooth over difficulties. buscar ~s onde não há to stumble upon plain ground. causa ~s it makes heavy weather. criar ~s to raise objections. desembaraçar-se de ~ to get out of a scrape. estar livre de ~s (pop.) to be out of the wood. eu compreendo muito bem a sua ~ I quite understand your difficulty. fica em pé a ~ (fig.) the difficulty is not removed, the question is not yet decided. fugir de uma ~ to evade a difficulty. ganhar sem ~ to win hands down. meter-se em ~s to get into troubles. respirar com ~ to gasp for breath. ter uma montanha de ~s na sua frente to be up against a brick wall. ter ~ em compreender to have difficulty in understanding. ter grandes ~s to be in deep water. vencer uma ~ to master a difficulty, turn the corner.
dificultação s. f. (pl. -ões) difficultating, making difficult.
dificultar v. 1. to difficultate, render difficult, raise difficulties or objections; to hamper, encumber, embarras, handicap. 2. ~-se to grow difficult, become painful.
dificultoso adj. difficult, hard, laborious, troublesome. ‖ -amente adv. difficultly.
difidência s. f. diffidence: 1. distrust, mistrust, suspicion, want of confidence. 2. want of self-confidence, shyness, timidity, modesty, hesitation.
difidente adj. m. + f. diffident: 1. distrustful, mistrustful, suspicious. 2. shy, bashful, timid, reserved, modest.
difilobotrídeos s. m. pl. (zool.) Diphyllobothriidae.
difilídeos s. m. pl. (zool.) Diphyllidae.
difiodonte adj. m. + f. (zool.) diphyodont: having two sets of teeth.
difluente adj. m. + f. diffluent, fluid, readily dissolving, melting.
difluir v. 1. to spread as a liquid; flow away, pour. 2. ~-se to become liquid, liquefy.
diforme adj. m. + f. difform, irregular in form, anomalous, deformed.
difração s. f. (phys.) diffraction, spreading of light.
difratar v. to diffract; deflect.
difrativo adj. diffractive, causing diffraction or relating to diffraction.
difringente adj. m. + f. diffractive.
difteria s. f. (med.) diphteria, diphteritis.
diftérico adj. (med.) diphtheritic, diphterial.

difundido adj. 1. spread, scattered. 2. divulged; diffused, widespread. 3. broadcast.
muito ~ world-widely.
difundir v. 1. to diffuse, pour out. 2. to spread, scatter, disseminate. 3. to publish, divulge, propagate. 4. to broadcast; send. 5. ~-se to be scattered, spread or divulged.
difusão s. f. (pl. -ões) 1. diffusion, scattering, dissemination. 2. interfusion, infiltration. 3. diffusiveness, prolixity. 4. divulgation, propagation, spread, transmission. 5. broadcasting.
~ do estilo diffusion of style. ~ da luz diffusion of light. estação de rádio ~ broadcasting station.
difusível adj. m. + f. (pl. -íveis) diffusible, diffusive.
difusivo adj. diffusive.
difuso adj. diffuse, diffused, spread; dispersed, scattered; prolix. ‖ -amente adv. diffusively.
difusora s. f. broadcasting or television station.
dígamo adj. (bot.) digamous, androgynous.
digástrico adj. (anat.) digastric.
digêneos s. m. pl. (zool.) Digenea.
digerido adj. (also digesto) digested, transformed by digestion.
digerir v. 1. to digest, undergo digestion, assimilate. 2. to tolerate, bear patiently, brook, put up with, endure, suffer. 3. to study, ponder, meditate, work upon.
digerível adj. m. + f. (pl. -íveis) (also digestível) digestible, capable of being digested.
digestão s. f. (pl. -ões) digestion, concoction.
boa ~ good digestion. homem de má ~ (fig.) raw, untractable person. negócio de má ~ difficult business.
digestibilidade s. f. digestibility, digestibleness.
digestir v. (S. Braz.) to tolerate, put up with, endure.
digestivo adj. digestive: 1. relating to digestion. 2. promoting digestion.
aparelho ~ (anat.) digestive system. distúrbio ~ indigestion. tubo ~ (anat.) alimentary canal.
digesto s. m. collection of Roman laws prepared by order of the emperor Justinian; Digest, Pandects.
digestor s. m. digester, digestor (apparatus). ‖ adj. digestive.
digestório adj. digesting, digestive.
digitação s. f. (pl. -ões) digitation: 1. (mus.) finger exercise. 2. digitiform arrangement of parts. 3. state of being digitate.
digitado adj. digitate, digitiform, fingerlike, arranged like a set of fingers.
digital (I) s. f. (pl. -ais) (bot.) digitalis, foxglove.
digital (II) adj. m. + f. digital, digitate.
impressão ~ finger-print.
digitalina s. f. (med., chem.) digitalin, digitaline, a substance obtained from the foxglove leaves.
digitifoliado adj. (bot.) digitate.
digitiforme adj. m. + f. digitiform, digitate, fingerlike.
digitígrado adj. (zool.) digitigrade, walking on the toes.
dígito s. m. 1. (astr.) digit: the twelfth part of the diameter of the sun or moon. 2. (poet.) finger. ‖ adj. (math.) digital.
digitonina s. f. (chem.) digitonin.
digitoxina s. f. (chem.) digitoxin, a poisonous substance obtained from the foxglove.
digladiação s. f. (pl. -ões) 1. digladiation, a combat with swords. 2. (by extension) a dispute, quarrel.
digladiador s. m. gladiator, swordsman, fencer, fighter. ‖ adj. gladiatorial.
digladiar(-se) v. to digladiate, fence, quarrel, fight for life or death.
diglifo s. m. (archit.) diglyph.
dignação s. f. (pl. -ões) 1. condescension, complaisance. 2. mercy, grace, benefit.

dignar-se v. to condescend, deign, be pleased, vouchsafe.

não se dignou dar-me uma resposta he vouchsafed me no answer, he did not deign to give me an answer. **o presidente dignou-se conceder uma audiência** the president deigned to grant an audience. **dignidade** s. f. 1. dignity, nobleness, honourableness, elevation of mind, lordliness, worthiness; gracefulness. 2. (fig.) importance, rank, title. 3. honour, merit, excellence, eminence. 4. (obs.) dignitary. **abaixo da sua** ~ beneath his dignity, infra dignitatem. **prezar-se da sua** ~ to insist upon one's dignity.

dignificação s. f. (pl. -ões) dignification, elevation, exaltation, promotion; ennoblement.

dignificador adj. dignified, exalted, honoured, invested with dignity.

dignificar v. 1. to dignify, raise to dignity, honour, ennoble, exalt, promote, elevate; render illustrous. 2. ~-se to ennoble o. s.

dignitário s. m. dignitary.

~ **eclesiástico** canon, dean, bishop.

digno adj. 1. worthy, condign, deserving, estimable. 2. honourable, respectable, regardable. || -amente adv. deservingly, worthily.

~ **de confiança** trustworthy. ~ **de louvor** worthy of praise. **ele é** ~ **de admiração** he is deserving of admiration. **ele não é** ~ **dela** he is not worthy of her. **um livro** ~ **de ser lido** a book worth reading. **nada** ~ **de menção** nothing to speak of.

dígono adj. (math.) digonous, having two angles.

dígrafo, digrama s. m. (Braz., gram.) digraph, two letters representing one sound (as "th" in father, "ea" in weather).

digressão s. f. (pl. -ões) (also **digresso** m.) 1. digression, deviation. 2. excursion, walk, outing. 3. subterfuge, evasion.

digressionar v. to digress, turn aside, deviate.

digressivo adj. digressive, digressional, departing from the main subject.

diguice s. f. (Braz.) nonsense, absurdity.

dilação s. f. (pl. -ões) deferment, postponement, putting off, delay, retardation, protraction, adjournment.

dilaceração s. f. (pl. -ões) dilaceration, laceration, tearing asunder.

dilacerador s. m. tearer. || adj. lacerating, dilacerating.

dilacerante adj. m. + f. lacerating, pungent; cruel.

dilacerar v. 1. to dilacerate, lacerate, tear, rend asunder. 2. to distress. 3. to defame, slander. 4. ~-se to hurt o. s.

dilacera-me o coração it breaks my heart.

dilapidação s. f. (pl. -ões) 1. dilapidation, waste, embezzlement, squandering. 2. robbery.

dilapidador s. m. dilapidator, waster; spendthrift.

dilapidar v. 1. to dilapidate: a) ruin, decay, deteriorate. b) waste, squander, spend inconsiderately. 2. to embezzle, defraud.

dilatabilidade s. f. dilatability, elasticity.

dilatação s. f. (pl. -ões) 1. dilation, expansion, extension; enlargement, widening; stretching. 2. prorogation, delay, prolongation.

dilatado adj. dilated: 1. expanded, extensive, diffused. 2. stretched, enlarged, distended. 3. delayed, deferred, put off. || -amente adv. amply, largely.

dilatador s. m. dilator; delayer. || adj. dilating.

dilatante adj. m. + f. dilatant, dilating.

dilatar v. 1. to dilate: a) enlarge, widen; stretch, expand, swell. b) spread abroad, diffuse, distend, extend. c) delay, put off, postpone, defer. 2. ~-se to grow wide, expand.

dilatável adj. m. + f. (pl. -áveis) dilatable, elastic, expansible, distensible.

dilatório adj. dilatory, slow, tardy, moratory, long.

dileção s. f. (pl. -ões) dilection, preference, affection, esteem; love.

dilema s. m. dilemma, problem, difficult choice, predicament, quandary.

dilemático adj. dilemmatic.

dileniáceas s. f. pl. (bot.) Dilleniaceae.

diletante s. m. + f. dilettante, an admirer of fine arts; amateur; dabbler. || adj. dilettante, unprofessional.

diletantismo s. m. dilletantism, amateurism.

dileto adj. dear, beloved, preferred, favourite.

diligência s. f. diligence: 1. assiduity, industry, application, laboriousness, activity. 2. care, attention, heed, caution, circumspection, vigilance. 3. judicial execution (security for debt). 4. stage-coach, post-coach.

fazer as suas ~s to do one's utmost. **pôr** ~ **no trabalho** to work with caution. **oficial de** ~ bailiff, sheriff.

diligenciador s. m. diligent person. || adj. diligent, industrious, assiduous.

diligenciar v. 1. to endeavour, make efforts, ply, do one's best. 2. ~-se to exert o. s.

diligente adj. m. + f. diligent: 1. assiduous, industrious, active, laborious, busy, painstaking, sedulous, persevering. 2. careful, cautious, attentive. 3. expeditious, quick, swift. || ~-mente adv. diligently.

dilobulado adj. having two lobes, bilobular.

dilogia s. f. = **diáfora**.

dilucidação s. f. (pl. -ões), **dilucidamento** m. dilucidation, making clear, explanation, explication, illustration, interpretation.

dilucidar v. to elucidate, make clear, explicate, explain, unfold, illustrate.

dilúcido adj. lucid, clear, light, bright.

dilucular adj. m. + f. dawning.

dilúculo s. m. dawn, dawning, day-break.

diluente adj. m. + f. diluent, diluting.

diluição s. f. (pl. -ões) (also **diluimento** m.) dilution, diluteness, thinness; attenuation.

diluído adj. dilute, thin, waterish, attenuated; weak, poor, paltry.

diluir v. 1. to dilute, render more liquid, make thin, attenuate, thin. 2. ~-se to become thinner or more liquid; dissolve.

diluto adj. 1. dilute. 2. (S. Braz.) said of wine or any other drink mixed with water.

diluvial adj. m. + f. (pl. -ais) diluvial, diluvian.

diluviano adj. 1. diluvian, relating to a deluge. 2. (fig.) torrential, overflowing.

diluvião s. m. (pl. -ões) (geol.) diluvium, ground with diluvial deposits.

diluviar v. to rain abundantly, flood.

dilúvio s. m. 1. Deluge. 2. flood, inundation, overflowing, cataract. 3. heavy rainfall, shower, torrent. 4. (fig.) abundance, large quantity.

~ **de cartas** a deluge of letters. ~ **de palavras** flood of words.

dimanação s. f. (pl. -ões) issuing, coming from, emanation, derivation, flowing.

dimanante adj. m. + f. issuing, proceeding; rising.

dimanar v. 1. to flow, emanate, stream, come or proceed from, issue. 2. to derive, result. 3. to originate, start (from.)

dimensão s. f. (pl. -ões) 1. dimension, extension. 2. size, measure, volume, magnitude. 3. -ões pl. proportions.

dimensível adj. m. + f. (pl. -íveis) dimensional, measurable.

dimensório adj. dimensional.

dímero adj. (biol.) dimerous, dipartite.

dimetilbenzeno s. m. (chem.) dimethylbenzene, zylene.

dímetro s. m. (pros.) dimeter, verse of four feet or two dipodies.

dimiários s. m. pl. (zool.) Dimyarin.

dimidiação s. f. (pl. -ões) dimidiation, division into two equal parts, halving.

dimidiar v. to dimidiate, divide into two equal parts or halves; to halve.

dimidiato adj. dimidiate, halved, divided into two equal parts.

diminuendo s. m. (math.) minuend. ‖ adv. (mus.) diminuendo, indication to lessen the volume of sound.

diminuente adj. m. + f. diminishing, subtracting, lessening.

diminuição s. f. (pl. -ões) 1. diminution, decrease, reduction, abridgement, abatement, impairment, depletion. 2. (math.) subtraction.

diminuidor s. m. 1. (math.) subtrahend. 2. diminisher. ‖ adj. diminishing, diminutive.

diminuir v. 1. to diminish, reduce, lessen, impair, decrease, abate. 2. to shorten, curtail, contract, shrink. 3. to take away, subtract. 4. to weaken, soften, slacken. 5. to slow down. 6. to moderate, temper, mitigate. 7. to thin down, taper. 8. to rarefy. 9. ~-se: a) to deprive o. s. of. b) to grow less; grow weak. ~ o crédito de alguém to reduce someone's credit. ~ a velocidade to decelerate, slow down. ~ o volume (radio) to fade out. a produção está diminuindo the wind abates. seu trabalho prova que a sua energia não diminuiu your works shows that your energy is unabated.

diminutivo s. m. diminutive, a word that lessens the original word from which it is derived. ‖ adj. (gram.) diminutive.

diminuto adj. diminutive, minute, small, little, tiny, microscopic; narrow; contracted.

dimissórias s. f. pl. (eccl.) dimissorials, dimissory leters (authorizing the bearer to be ordained).

dimorfia s. f., **dimorfismo** m. dimorphism: crystallization in two distinct forms.

dimorfo adj. dimorphic, dimorphous, existing in two distinct forms.

dimorfoteca s. f. (bot.) cape marigold.

dina s. m. (phys.) dyne, unity of force or power.

Dinamarca s. f. Denmark.

dinamarquês s. m. (pl. -eses) (f. -esa, pl. -esas) 1. Dane, inhabitant of Denmark. 2. Danish (language). ‖ adj. Danish, of or relating to Denmark. **cão** ~ Danish dog, Dalmatian dog.

dinâmetro s. m. dynameter, instrument for measuring the magnifying power of telescopes.

dinâmica s. f. dynamics, the science which treats of the motion of bodies.

dinâmico adj. 1. (phys.) dynamic(al), relating to dynamics. 2. energetic, vigorous, strenuous. **amortecedor** ~ dynamic damper. **freio** ~ dynamic brake.

dinamismo s. m. dynamism: 1. (philos.) doctrine which all substance involves forces. 2. push, rush; verve; energy. **o ~ da vida moderna** the rush of modern life.

dinamista s. m. + f. dynamist, follower of dynamism. ‖ adj. m. + f. dynamistic, relating to dynamism.

dinamitar v. to dynamite, destroy with dynamite.

dinamite s. f. dynamite, blasting powder, explosive.

dinamiteiro s. m. dynamiter, a terrorist who employes dynamite.

dinamitista s. m. + f. 1. manufacturer of dynamite. 2. dynamiter, blaster. ‖ adj. dynamiting.

dinamização s. f. (pl. -ões) dynamization.

dinamizar v. to dynamize, increase the power of a medicament.

dínamo s. m. (electr.) dynamo, generator (plate B 11). ~ **compensador** balancer, buffer dynamo. ~ **de reforço** booster. **acionamento do** ~ dynamo drive. **coletor de** ~ commutator.

dinamoelétrico adj. dynamo electric.

dinamogenia s. f. dynamogenesis.

dinamogênico adj. dynamogenic.

dinamometria s. f. (also **dinamiometria**) dynamometry, measurement of working forces or power.

dinamométrico adj. (also **dinamiométrico**) dynamometrical.

dinamômetro s. m. (also **dinamiômetro**) dynamometer, apparatus for measuring working forces or power. ~ **registrador** dynamograph.

dinasta s. m. + f. dynast, feudal lord, member of a dynasty.

dinastia s. f. dynasty, a series of sovereigns of the same family.

dinástico adj. dynastic(al). ‖ **dinasticamente** adv. dynastically.

dindinha s. f. (N. Braz., fam., also **dinda**) godmother or grandmother.

dindinho s. m. (N. Braz., fam.) godfather or grandfather.

dingo s. m. dingo, the Australian dog.

dinheirada, dinheirama s. f. (also **dinheiral, dinheirão** m.) a lot of money, great quantity of money.

dinheirento adj. rich, well off, wealthy.

dinheirinho s. m. a little money.

dinheiro s. m. money, any sort of coin; currency; cash; capital. ~ **amoedado** coinage. ~ **em barda,** ~ **a rodo** plenty of money, money to be raked in, money to burn. ~ **é a causa de muitos males** money is the root of many evils. ~ **é um bom companheiro, mas mau conselheiro** money is a god servant but a bad master. ~ **em caixa** cash in hand. **o** ~ **chegou numa ocasião muito oportuna** the money came at a most fortunate time. ~ **efetivo** real money. ~ **emprestado,** ~ **gastado** money lent, money spent. ~ **falso** flash-money. ~ **ganha** ~ money makes money. **o** ~ **faz girar o mundo** money makes the world go round. ~ **à mão** balance in hand, hard cash. ~ **miúdo** small change. ~ **não compra felicidade** money cannot buy happiness. ~ **é a mola real** money makes the mare go. ~ **não nasce na algibeira** money does not grow on trees. ~ **sempre faz falta** money is always needed. ~ **à vista** ready cash. **o** ~ **voa, tem asas** money takes to itself wings. **abonado de** ~ flushed of money. **ajuntar** ~ to hoard money. **algibeiras abarrotadas de** ~ pockets filled with money. **arranjar** ~ to raise money. **arriscar** ~ to risk money. **atormentar alguém com constantes pedidos de** ~ to torment s. o. with constant demands for money. **bolsa para** ~ moneybag. **caixa para** ~ cashbox. **com pouco** ~ short of money. **compra a** ~, **compra à vista** cash transaction. **comprar a** ~ to buy for cash. **contribuir com** ~ **para obras de caridade** to contribute to charity. **custar muito** ~ to cost a lot of money. **empregar** ~ **em fundos** to invest money. **empreste-me o** ~ **que puder** lend me what money you can. **estar bem de** ~ to be flush of money. **estar embaraçado com falta de** ~ to be pushed for money. **estar sem** ~ to be without money, be penniless, be in Queer Street. **estragar** ~ to play ducks and drakes with the money. **falta de** ~ impecuniosity, pennilessness. **fugir com o** ~ to make off with the money. **ganhar** ~ to make money. **ganhar** ~ **honestamente** to turn a honest penny. **ganhar** ~ **rapidamente** to coin money. **gastar** ~ **à bessa** to spend money like water. **gastar o** ~ **num instante** to make the money fly. **gas-**

taram muito ~ they spent much treasure. **guardar** ~ to put money by. **hei de receber** ~ **amanhã** I am to receive money tomorrow. **homem cheio de** ~ a moneyed man. **manejar o** ~ to hold the purse strings. **levantar o** ~ **do banco** to take out money from a bank. **nadar em** ~ to be rolling in money. **não é uma questão de** ~ money is no object. **não gastes mais** ~ **do que tens** cut your coat according to your cloth. **não há** ~ money is tight. **não jogue fora seu** ~! do not play ducks with your money! **não tenho o** ~ **necessário** I have not the wherewithal. **negócios de** ~ money matters. **nem por** ~ **algum!** not for the life of me! **o obstáculo é não termos** ~ **suficiente** the snag is we have not money enough. **perder** ~ **em apostas** (pop.) to spill money. **perder** ~ **em negócios** to lose money over a deal. **pôr** ~ **a juros** to put out money. **prêmio em** ~ cash prize. **prepara-te para gastares** ~! be prepared to put your hand in your pocket! **sacar** ~ **sobre navio e carga** to borrow on bottomry, on the ship's security. **sem** ~ without money, broke, impecunious, penniless, stone-broke. **sem** ~, **sem casa e sem amigos** without money, home or friends. **soma importante de** ~ a good round sum. **tempo é** ~ time is money. **ter grande necessidade de** ~ to be hard up (for money). **todo o meu** ~ **está empatado** all my capital is tied up.

dinheiroso, dinheirudo adj. rich, wealthy, well-to-do, moneyed.

dinodo s. m. (electron.) dynode.

dinossauro s. m. dinosaur, an extinct reptile of gigantic size.

dinotério s. m. dinothere, an extinct proboscidean quadruped related to the elephants and mammoths.

dintel s. m. (pl. **-éis**) (archit.) lintel, a beam over a door or window.

dinumerar v. to enumerate.

diocesano s. m. diocesan, a bishop of a diocese. ‖ adj. diocesan, pertaining to a diocese.

diocese s. f. diocese: 1. (obs.) district, province. 2. a district and its population under the care of a bishop, episcopacy.

diodo s. m. (electron.) diode.

diogo s. m. (Braz., and Port. prov.) = **diabo.**

dióica adj. (bot.) dioecious, unisexual.

dionéia s. f. (bot.) Dionaea, Venu's fly-trap.

dionisíaco adj. Dionysian, relating to Dionysius, god of wine.

dioptásio s. m. (min.) dioptase, emerald copper ore; silicate of copper, crystallized in sixsided prisms.

dioptria s. f. 1. dioptric. 2. diopter: unit of refractic power of a lens.

dióptrica s. f. dioptrics, the part of optics treating of the refraction of light.

diorama s. m. diorama.

diorâmico adj. dioramic, relating to a diorama.

diorito s. m. (min.) diorite, greenstone.

dioscoreácea s. f. (bot.) one of the Dioscoreaceae, Chinese or Japan yam.

diósmea s. f. a genus of heathlike rutaceous plants.

dioso adj. aged, old, elderly.

dipétalo adj. (bot.) dipetalous, having two petals.

diplegia s. f. (med.) diplegia.

diplococo s. m. (biol.) diplococcus.

diploe s. f. (anat., also **díploa**) diploe, the medullary substance between the plates of the cranial bones.

diploglossados s. m. pl. (zool.) Diploglossata.

diplóide s. m. robe formerly used among the orientals. ‖ adj. m. + f. (biol.) diploid.

diploma s. m. 1. diploma, document, charter, patent. 2. degress, certificate.

~ **universitário** university degree.

diplomação s. f. (pl. **-ões**) (Braz.) the granting of a certificate or diploma.

diplomacia s. f. 1. diplomacy. 2. tact; adroitness, skill. 3. diplomatic body, all ministers at a foreign court.

falta de ~ bad policy.

diplomaciar v. 1. to diplomatize, practise diplomacy. 2. to use diplomatic art or skill; to handle with tact.

diplomado adj. certificated, licensed; graduate.

enfermeira -a trained nurse. **engenheiro** ~ certified engineer. **oficial** ~ commissioned officer.

diplomar v. 1. to grant a certificate or diploma. 2. ~-se to graduate, receive a diploma.

diplomata s. m. + f. 1. diplomat, ambassador, diplomatist, attaché, member of a diplomatic body. 2. (fig.) person skilled in diplomacy, tactful person.

diplomática s. f. diplomatics, paleograph, science of deciphering diplomas.

diplomático s. m. diplomatist. ‖ adj. 1. diplomatic(al). 2. tactful, adroit, skillful. 3. discrete, corteous, well-mannered.

corpo ~ the diplomatic body, the body of foreign ambassadors, ministers and attachés accredited to a court or government. **serviço** ~ diplomatic service.

diplomatista s. m. diplomatist.

diplopia s. f. (med.) diplopia, diplopy: disorder of sight in which a single object appears double.

diplóide s. m. one of the Diplopoda or Chilognatha, a millepede, milliped.

diplostêmone adj. m. + f. (bot.) diplostemonous: having twice as many stamens as petals.

dipneusta s. m. (ichth.) dipnoi.

dipode adj. m. + f. biped, walking on two feet.

dipsacáceo adj. (bot.) dipsacaceous.

diprosopia s. f. (pat.) diprosapus.

dipsético adj. dipsetic, producing thirst.

dipsomania s. f. (med.) dipsomania: irresistible craving for alcoholic drinks; alcoholism.

dipsomaníaco s. m. dipsomaniac: heavy drinker. ‖ adj. dipsomaniac.

diptérico adj. (ornith., ent.) dipteral, dipterous, two-winged.

díptero s. m. dipteron: a class of insects having two wings. ‖ adj. dipteran, dipterous.

díptico s. m. diptych: a two-leaved tablet with waxed inner surfaces used by Greeks and Romans for writing.

dique s. m. 1. dike: a) dam, dyke, embankment. b) (geol.) a fissure in a rock filled with lava. c) (fig.) stopping, obstacle, barrier, defence. 2. flood-gate. 3. pond, pool. 4. dry basin, dock.

~ **seco** dry dock. **romper os** ~**s** to break or open the dikes. **talude de um** ~ slope of an embankment.

direção s. f. (pl. **-ões**) direction: 1. course, route, run (plate V 4). 2. management, administration, government, superintendence, presidency, control. 3. order, instruction, regulation. 4. guidance, tendency, lead. 5. destination, end, object. 6. pointing, aiming. 7. address.

~ **da corrente** set of the current. ~ **da marcha** direction of running. ~ **norte** northerliness, northward. ~ **técnica** technical direction. ~ **do tiro** firing control. ~ **do vento** eye of the wind. ~ **de vôo** direction of flight. **assumir a** ~ to take the lead. **barra de** ~ steering gear connecting rod. **caixa de** ~ steering box. **eixo de direção** steering axle. **em** ~ a toward. **em** ~ **da casa** homeward. **engrenagem de** ~ steering gear. **indicador de** ~ direction indicator, trafficator. **mostrar a** ~ to show the way. **seguir -ões opostas** to go in opposite

directions. **sempre na mesma** ~ all in one direction, straight on. **volante de** ~ steering wheel.
direita s. f. 1. right side, right hand. 2. the conservative party. 3. protection, favour.
à ~ on the right. **à** ~ **da mesa** at the right side of the table. **à sua** ~ at his (her, your) right hand. **às** ~**s** as it should be, honest, upright. **conservar-se à** ~, **seguir pela** ~ to keep the right. **homem às** ~**s** upright man. **perfilar pela** ~ to dress by the right. **rotação à** ~ clockwise rotation. **virar à** ~ to turn to the right.
direiteiro s. m. (S. Braz.) bachelor of law.
direiteza s. f. 1. righteousness, honesty, uprightness. 2. straightness. 3. direction.
direitinho adj. diminutive of **direito**. ‖ adv. (Braz., pop.) exactly, just as, just like.
andar ~ to go straight (also fig.). **o menino é** ~ **o pai** the boy is just like the father.
direitista s. m. + f. (Braz.) rightist, a member o the rights (in politics). ‖ adj. rightist, pertaining to the rightists.
direito s. m. 1. right. 2. law; jurisprudence. 3. justice, equity. 4. rectitude, righteousness, honesty, fairness. 5. prerogative, privilege. 6. claim, interest, patent. 7. authority, power. 8. right side, right hand. 9. fee, duty, tax. 10. (Braz., box) right-hander. ‖ adj. 1. right, right-hand. 2. straight. 3. even, level, flat. 4. honest, loyal, righteous, correct, true. 5. fit, suitable. 6. erect, upright. 7. equitable, just. 8. sincere, frank. 9. dextral. 10. direct. ‖ -**amente** adv. rightly, directly.
~**s aduaneiros**, ~**s alfandegários** custom duties, tariff. ~**s de ancoragem** anchorage, groundage, harbour dues. ~**s de armazenagem** storage fees. ~ **de cais** wharfage. ~**s autorais** copyright. ~ **canônico** canon law. ~ **civil** civil law. ~ **comercial** commercial law. ~ **como um fuso** as straight as a die. ~ **consuetudinário** right founded upon custom, unwritten law. ~ **eclesiástico** ecclesistical law. ~**s de entrada** entrance fees. ~**s específicos** fixed duties. ~**s de exportação** export duties. ~ **das gentes** right of nations. ~ **hereditário** right of succession. ~ **inalienável** an inalienable right. ~ **internacional** international law. ~ **marítimo** marine law, shipping law. ~ **natural** the law of nature. ~ **de passagem** right of way. ~**s portuários** keelage. ~ **de propriedade** ownership. ~ **de primogenitura** birthright. ~ **de trânsito** transit duty. **os** ~**s do indivíduo devem ser protegidos** the rights of the individual must be protected. **abolir um** ~ to abolish a duty. **adquirir um** ~ to acquire a right. **ambos os sócios têm o** ~ **de assinar** both partners are entitled to sign. **ande** ~, **velho amigo!** go straight, old chap! **a torto e a** ~ (fig.) at random. **dar** ~ to invest, entitle. **doutor em** ~ doctor of laws. **edição com** ~**s reservados** copyright edition. **está** ~ it's all right. **estudar** ~ to keep terms, read law, read for the Bar. **faculdade de** ~ faculty of law. **fazer valer seus** ~**s** to assert one's rights, put in a claim. **foi** ~ **à porta** he went straight up to the door. **fora os** ~**s** besides duties. **isento de** ~**s, livre de** ~**s** duty-free. **perda de** ~**s** forfeiture. **por** ~, **baseado na lei** in the eyes of the law. **renunciar aos seus** ~**s** to give up one's rights. **reservados todos os** ~**s** all rights reserved. **seguir sempre** ~ to follow one's nose. **sujeito a** ~**s** liable to duties. **ter o** ~ **de** to be entitled to, have the authority. **ela tem** ~ **ao meu amparo** she has a claim to my care.
direitura s. f. 1. straightness, rightness, directness. 2. (fig.) righteousness, honesty, uprightness, integrity.
em ~ straight on, directly.

diretiva s. f. (geom.) diretrix: a fixed line (straight or not) required for the description of a curve.
diretivo adj. directive: 1. directing. 2. pointing, indicating, prescribing. 3. managerial.
direto s. m. (Braz., box) right-hander. ‖ adj. 1. direct, straight, undeviating. 2. immediate, instantaneous. 3. clear, evident, explicit. 4. straightforward, ingenious, open, sincere. 5. plain, express, positive. 6. (gram.) deictic. ‖ -**amente** adv. directly.
carro ~ through car. **comboio** ~ through train. **ele comprou um bilhete** ~ he booked through. **contribuições** -**as** direct taxes. **discurso** ~ direct speech. **iluminação** -**a** direct lighting. **notícias** -**as** direct news. **passagem** -**a** through passage. **pergunta** -**a** direct question. **serviço** ~ through service. **trânsito** ~ through traffic. **o trem é** ~ the train goes through. **vôo** ~ nonstop flight. **a pedra caiu-lhe diretamente na cabeça** the stone hit him fair in the head.
diretor s. m. 1. director, head, headmaster, manager, superintendent, disposer; entrepreneur. 2. conductor. 3. mentor, guide, rector. 4. administrator, provost, warden. ‖ adj. ruling, guiding, managing.
~ **de cena** stage director. ~ **da escola** schoolmaster, rector. ~ **geral da casa de moeda** mintmaster. ~ **gerente** managing director. ~ **técnico** engineering manager, technical director.
diretora s. f. directrix, directress, headmistress, manageress; conductress; governess.
diretorado s. m. directorate: 1. the office of a director, directorship. 2. the body of directors.
diretoria s. f. 1. direction, administration, management. 2. board of directors, directory body. 3. directorship, director's office.
diretorial adj. m. + f. (pl. -**ais**) directorial: 1. referring to a director. 2. invested with direction.
diretório s. m. directory: 1. directorate, a board of directors. 2. a book containing rules or laws. 3. the body of five executive directors in France during the revolutionary epoch. ‖ adj. directive, guiding or directing.
diretriz s. f. 1. (geom.) directrix. 2. route, line of direction. 3. governess, conductress, directress. ‖ adj. (f. of **diretor**) directive, guiding or directing.
dirigente s. m. + f. director, leader, controller, manager. ‖ adj. head, directing, leading.
*~ **de coro** chorister. ~ **de orquestra** orchestra leader. **classes** ~**s** ruling classes.
dirigido adj. directed, ruled, managed; pointed, aimed. ~ **a** pointed towards. ~ **para frente** onward. **bem** ~ well-directed.
dirigio s. m. (also **diamba** f.) (bot.) marijuana, hemp.
dirigir v. 1. to direct: a) govern, rule, command; superintend, head, boss, preside. b) regulate, control. c) manage, dispose, manipulate, administer. d) order, prescribe, instruct. e) tend, point toward, aim. f) (mus.) act as a director or conductor. g) superscribe, address; dedicate 2. to conduct, guide, lead, drive, steer, pilot. 3. ~-**se** a) to address o. s. to, apply to. b) to be directed.
~ **um aeroplano** to fly an aeroplane. ~ **a atenção para alguém** to direct one's attention to a person. ~ **uma carta** to write a letter. ~ **um hotel** to run a hotel. ~ **mal** to misdirect. ~ **um negócio** to run a business. ~ **para** to turn toward, apply to, make for. ~ **os passos para** to turn the steps toward. ~-**se para casa** to make one's way home. ~ **petições a** to address petitions to. **dirigiram-se a nós** they turned to us. **ele não dirige uma palavra amável a ninguém** he has not a word to throw at a dog. **ele dirige os negócios da família** he manages the affairs of the family. **este discurso dirige-se a vós somente** this speech regards

none but you. **queira** ~-**se ao Sr.** ... please, apply to Mr.... **quem está dirigindo o negócio?** who is managing the business?, who is bossing the show?

dirigível s. m. (pl. **-íveis**) dirigible airship, zeppelin. ‖ adj. m. + f. controllable, dirigible, steerable.

dirijo s. m. (Braz., bot.) marijuana, hemp.

dirimente adj. m. + f. 1. diriment, nullifying, rendering null and void. 2. (law) extenuating, attenuating. **impedimento** ~ an absolute impediment that invalidates a marriage.

dirimir v. 1. to nullify, cancel, annul. 2. to obstruct, prevent. 3. to extinguish, dissolve, put an end to. 4. to determine, decide, settle.

diro adj. dire, awful, fearful, terrific; cruel, inhuman.

diruir v. = **derruir.**

dirupção s. f. (pl. **-ões**) disruption; ruin.

diruptivo adj. disruptive.

disartria s. f. defective articulation (sounds, speech).

disbasia s. f. (med.) locomotive difficulties.

discagem s. f. (Braz.) dialing (teleph.).

discar v. (Braz., teleph.) to dial.

discente s. m. pupil, student, disciple. ‖ adj. m. + f. learning.

disceptação s. f. (pl. **-ões**) disceptation, controversy, disputation, dissension.

discernente adj. m. + f. discerning, distinguishing, discriminating.

discernimento s. m. discernment, discernance, discrimination, judgement, criterion; perception.

discernir v. to discern: 1. distinguish, discriminate. 2. separate. 3. perceive, note, descry, discover, see.

discernível adj. m. + f. (pl. **-íveis**) discernible, distinguishable.

disciforme adj. m. + f. disciform, having the form of a disk; discoidal.

disciplina s. f. 1. discipline: a) order, training, system of regulations or rules. b) education, instruction; branch of instruction. c) correction, chastisement, punishment. 2. ~**s** pl. scourge.
~ **militar** military discipline, drill. **manter** ~ to preserve discipline, subordinate.

disciplinado adj. disciplined, correct, orderly.

disciplinador s. m. disciplinarian, discipliner, tutor; scourger, whipper. ‖ adj. disciplinarian, chastening.

disciplinante s. m. flagellant, a person who scourges himself. ‖ adj. m. + f. disciplinant.

disciplinar (I) v. 1. to discipline, train, educate, instruct, drill. 2. to correct. 3. to chastise, punish, scourge, whip. 4. ~-**se** to scourge o. s., discipline o. s.

disciplinar (II) adj. m. + f. disciplinal, disciplinary.

disciplinas-de-freira s. f. pl. (bot.) love-lies-bleeding.

disciplinável adj. m. + f. (pl. **-áveis**) disciplinable.

discipulado s. m. 1. pupils of a school, number of scholars. 2. discipleship, apprenticeship. 3. period of apprenticeship.

discípulo s. m. 1. disciple, follower (of a doctrine or religion), adherent. 2. scholar, student, pupil.

disco s. m. 1. disk, disc, roundel. 2. discus, quoit. 3. paten. 4. record (gramophone). 5. dial (plates M 3, T 4). 6. distance-signal (railway). 7. (bot.) disk.
~ **de frenagem** brake wheel. ~ **da lua** disk of the moon. ~ **para polir** rag-wheel. ~ **voador** flying saucer. **mudar o** ~ (pop.) to change the tune.

discóbolo s. m. discobolus, discus thrower.

discografia s. f. discography.

discóide adj. m. + f. discoid(al), discous, having the form of a disk.

díscolo s. m. rowdy, rough, rioter. ‖ adj. unsociable, unruly, obstinate, unconversable, sullen, pettish.

discomedusas s. f. pl. (zool.) Discomedusae.

discordância s. f. 1. discordance, discordancy, disharmony, disagreement, divergence, variance, opposition, disaccord. 2. conflict, clash.
~ **de camadas** (geol.) unconformity.

discordante s. m. + f. person who disagrees, opponent. ‖ adj. discordant, disagreeing, opposite, contrary; inharmonious, dissonant. ‖ ~**mente** adv. discordantly.

discordar v. 1. to disaccord, dissent, disagree, vary, differ, take issue. 2. to disharmonize, untune, be out of tune. 3. to be incompatible with.

discorde adj. 1. discorded, at variance, disagreeing, clashing, incompatible, incongruous. 2. dissonant, jarring, out of tune, harsh.

discórdia s. f. 1. discord, disharmony, incongruity; dissension, difference. 2. variance, debate, strife, quarrel, contention.
o pomo da ~ the bone of contention. **lançar o pomo da** ~ to sow the seeds of discord, sow division.

discorrer v. 1. to run or flow over, run to and fro, travel through or along. 2. to discourse, converse, expatiate. 3. to reason, argue; discuss, talk over. 4. to narrate, tell, relate. 5. to meditate, consider, think out.
~ **os meios** to think about an expedient. ~ **a respeito de** to discourse about. ~ **por várias terras** to travel through different countries.

discorrimento s. m. reasoning, discernment, discrimination.

discoteca s. f. record cabinet, record collection.

discrepância s. f. discrepancy, difference, disagreement, contrariety, incongruity, divergence.

discrepante adj. m. + f. discrepant, disagreeing, at variance, contrary; jarring, contradictory, opposed.

discrepar v. 1. to disagree, discord, differ, vary, contradict, dissent. 2. ~-**se** to be contradictory.

discreteador s. m. a fine tattler; person who speaks discreetly. ‖ adj. speaking discreetly.

discretear v. 1. to discourse (upon), converse, hold forth in speech. 2. to speak discreetly; chat.

discretivo adj. discretive, disjunctive, distinct, separate.

discreto adj. 1. discreet, tactful, wise, unobtrusive, cautious, prudent, circumspect. 2. discrete, distinct. 3. reserved. ‖ **-amente** adv. discreetly.
pintura -a distinct make-up. **quantidade -a** small quantity.

discrição s. f. (pl. **-ões**) 1. discretion, tactfulness, reserve, distance, modesty. 2. discreetness, prudence, caution, sagacity, circumspection, carefulness, wariness.
à ~ at one's own pleasure, at will, at one's discretion. **correr à** ~ **dos mares** to be committed to the waves (a ship). **entregar-se à** ~ to surrender at discretion, yield without terms.

discricional adj. m. + f. (pl. **-ais**) (Braz.) discretional, discretionary.

discricionário adj. discretional, discretionary; unconditional; optional, arbitrary; capricious, inconstant.

discrime, discrimen s. m. 1. difference, diversity. 2. discernment. 3. risk, danger. 4. fight.

discriminação s. f. (pl. **-ões**) discrimination, distinction; separation, selection.

discriminador s. m. discriminator. ‖ adj. discriminatory, discriminating, distinguishing.

discriminar v. 1. to discriminate, distinguish, differentiate, make a difference between. 2. to select, separate, discern; divide, part.

discriminável adj. m. + f. (pl. **-áveis**) discriminable; distinguishable.

discursador s. m. speaker, orator, haranger, discourser; narrator. ‖ adj. discoursing; narrative.

discursar v. to discourse: 1. make a speach, deliver an address, hold forth, expatiate, orate; preach. 2. reason, argue. 3. narrate, tell, talk or speak about, converse.

discurseira s. f. (Braz.) a lot of speeches; verbosity, verboseness; talkativeness.

discursista s. m. + f. discourser, speaker, haranger.‖ adj. discoursing, speaking.

discursivo adj. discursive; communicative; thoughtful.

discurso s. m. discourse, speech, oration, sermon; lecture, dissertation, address.
~ **de despedida** valedictory. ~ **de estréia** maiden speech. ~ **preparado** ready-made speech, set speech. **fazer um** ~ to make a speech, deliver an address.

discursório s. m. (Braz.) 1. a lot of speeches, speechification. 2. wordiness, verbosity.

discussão, discutição s. f. (pl. **-ões**) 1. discussion, debate, disquisition, disputation. 2. contestation, altercation, wrangle, quarrel, controversy, strife. 3. argumentation.
sem ~ out of question, without question. **ter uma** ~ to have a discussion.

discutidor s. m. discusser, arguer, disputant, debater, wrangler. ‖ adj. disputant, discussing, debating.

discutir v. 1. to discuss, argue, reason, agitate, dispute, debate. 2. to consider, examine, thrash, treat. 3. to wrangle, controvert, quarrel.
~ **calorosamente** to argufy. ~ **com** to pick a bone with. ~ **sobre ninharias** to dispute about trifles. ~ **a opinião de alguém** to join issue with s. o. ~ **sobre política** to talk politics. **não discuta!** don't argue! **você discutiu com ele?** had you words with him?

discutível adj. m. + f. (pl. **-íveis**) discussable, disputable, arguable, controvertible, debatable; problematic, doubtful; moot.

disemia s. f. (med.) dyshemia.

disenteria s. f. (med.) dysentery, looseness.
~ **amebiana** amoebic dysentery. ~ **bacilar** bacillary dysentery.

disentérico s. m. (med.) dysenteric, person who suffers from dysentery. ‖ adj. dysenteric, relating to or suffering from dysentery.

diserto adj. 1. speaking fluently, eloquent. 2. well--spoken, clear, selected.

disestesia s. f. (med.) dysesthesia: derangement of a sense, esp. of the sense of touch.

disfagia s. f. (med.) dysphagy.

disfarçado adj. 1. disguised, dissembled, masked, veiled, cloaked. 2. simulated, insincere, false, feigned. ‖ **-amente** adv. disguisedly.

disfarçador s. m. disguiser, disfigurer; masker, mummer. ‖ adj. disguising, dissembling.

disfarçar v. to disguise: 1. cover, mask, veil, dissemble, cloak. 2. simulate, shift, feign. 3. ~**-se** to disguise o. s.
~ **a bandeira** to hoist a false flag.

disfarce s. m. disguise(ment), mask, veil, mummery, cloak; dissimulation, deception, pretence.
agir sob ~ to sail under false colours.

disfasia s. f. (med.) dysphasia, loss of the power of language.

disferir v. to enlarge, aggrandize, widen, dilate.

disfonia s. f. (med.) dysphonia.

disforia s. f. (med.) dysphoria, indisposition, dissatisfaction.

disformar v. to deform, disfigure, deface, distort.

disforme adj. m. + f. 1. deformed, disfigured, defaced. 2. enormous, huge, colossal, monstrous. 3. ugly, misshapen, hideous, miscreated. ‖ ~**mente** adv. in a disfigured manner; enormously.

disformidade s. f. 1. deformity, disfigurement. 2. ugliness, malformation. 3. hugeness, monstrousness, exorbitance, enormity.

disga, disgra s. f. (Braz., sl.) penury, poverty, lack of money, pennilessness.

disgenesia s. f. (biol.) dysgenesis, barrenness.

disgenético adj. (biol.) dysgenetic.

disidria s. f. (med.) dyshidrosis.

disjunção s. f. (pl. **-ões**) 1. separation, disjunction, disconnection. 2. (gram.) suppression of conjunctions. 3. (log.) a disjunctive proposition.

disjungir v. 1. to unyoke. 2. to disconnect, disjoin. 3. to separate, keep apart, divide, disunite.

disjuntivo adj. (also gram.) disjunctive, separating, dividing, distinguishing.
particula -a disjunctive particle.

disjunto adj. disjoined, disjunct, disconnected, separated, distinct.

disjuntor s. m. (electr.) circuit breaker.

dislalia s. f. (med.) dyslalia, difficulty in the articulation of words.

dislate s. m. extravagance, nonsense, folly, silliness, absurdity.

dislexia s. f. (med.) dyslexia, difficulty to read and understand writing.

dislogia s. f. (med.) dyslogia.

dislógico adj. (med.) dyslogic(al).

dismnésia, dismnesia s. f. (med.) enfeeblement of the memory.

disopia s. f. (med.) dysopia, enfeeblement of the strength of vision.

disorexia s. f. (med.) dysorexy, want of appetite.

disosmia s. f. (med.) dysosmia, derangement of the sense of smelling.

dispar adj. m. + f. unequal, unlike, dissimilar, disparate.

disparada s. f. (Braz.) stampede or escape of animals.

disparado adj. bold, fearless, brave, courageous, intrepid, daring; undaunted.

disparador s. m. 1. trigger, hair-trigger. 2. (phot.) shutter release (plate M 3).
~ **automático** (phot.) self-timer (plate F 6).

disparador (II) adj. 1. obstinate, hard-mouthed (horse). 2. fainthearted, fearful; coward, craven.

disparar v. 1. to discharge, fire off, shoot. 2. to let fly, to cast or throw violently. 3. to affront. 4. to start (race). 5. ~**-se** to go off (fire-arm).
~ **uma arma** to let off a gun. ~ **uma bandeira** to display a flag, unfold the flag. ~ **injúria contra alguém** to affront s. o. **o navio disparou uma salva** the ship thundered a salute.

disparatado adj. foolish, silly, heedless, senseless, nonsensical, ridiculous, absurd. ‖ **-amente** adv. absurdly, sillily.

disparatar v. 1. to play the fool, talk foolishly, dote, rave. 2. to blunder, commit faults.

disparate s. m. folly, foolishness, absurdity, nonsense, stupidity; silly action, blunder, indiscretion, thrash.
dizer ~**s** to talk nonsense. **grande** ~ perfect nonsense. **que** ~! what a thrash!

disparidade s. f. 1. disparity, dissimilitude, disproportion, difference; unlikeness, inequality. 2. nonsense, foolishness.

disparo s. m. discharge, shooting, shot; detonation.

dispartir v. 1. to disperse, divide, distribute; scatter. 2. ~**-se** to be separated or dispersed.

dispêndio s. m. 1. (great) expense, expenditure, disbursement. 2. consumption. 3. waste, prodigality. 4. disadvantage, prejudice, damage, loss.

dispendioso adj. expensive, costly, dear. ‖ **-amente** adv. expensively.

dispensa s. f. 1. dispensation, dispense, exemption. 2. leave, license. 3. dismissal.

dispensabilidade s. f. dispensability.
dispensação s. f. (pl. **-ões**) dispensation, exemption, remission.
dispensador s. m. 1. dispenser, dispensator. 2. distributer.
dispensar v. to dispense: 1. grant dispensation, exempt, excuse, release, free from an obligation. 2. leave, not to need or want, forego, do without. 3. distribute, deal out, give forth. 4. administer. 5. bestow. 6. **~-se** to avoid, feel free. **~ alguma coisa** to spare s. th. **~atenção** to show kindness (careful consideration). **~ honras** to confer honours on. **~ os serviços de alguém** to dispense with a person's services, excuse from work. **fui dispensado de comparecer** I was excused from attendance.
dispensário s. m. dispensary, a place where medical advice is given and medicines are furnished free (to the poor).
dispensatário s. m. person who grants dispensation.
dispensativo adj. dispensative, dispensable; granting dispensations, dispensatory.
dispensatório s. m. dispensatory: 1. laboratory, dispensary. 2. pharmacopeia.
dispensável adj. m. + f. (pl. **-áveis**) dispensable, excusable; unessential.
dispepsia s. f. (med.) dyspepsy, dyspepsia, indigestion, bad digestion.
dispéptico s. m. person afflicted with bad digestion. || adj. dyspeptic(al).
disperder v. to ruin, destroy, waste.
dispermático, dispermo adj. (bot.) dispermatous, dispermous: containing only two seeds.
dispersador s. m. disperser. || adj. dispersive, diffusive.
dispersão s. f. (pl. **-ões**) dispersion: 1. act of dispersing, scattering; diffusion. 2. disbandment, breakup. 3. (opt.) separation of the different coloured rays in refraction.
dispersar v. 1. to disperse: a) diffuse, spread, scatter; dissipate. b) break up, disband, put to flight, dispart. 2. **~-se** to become diffused or spread. **~ uma multidão** to scatter a crowd. **os rebeldes foram dispersados** the rebels were put to flight.
dispersivo adj. dispersive; diffusive; scattering.
disperso adj. 1. dispersed, scattered. 2. disbanded, fugitive. 3. diffused, spread, sparse. || **-amente** adv. sparsely.
displástico adj. (med.) dysplastic, abnormal, anomalous.
displicência s. f. 1. disgust, displeasure, annoyance; sorrow, discomfort, uneasiness, ill humour. 2. (Braz.) carelessness, negligence, indifference, unconcern; slovenliness.
displicente s. m. + f. (Braz.) disorderly person. || adj. 1. unpleasant, disagreeable. 2. ill-humoured, uneasy. 3. (Braz.) disorderly, negligent, careless, indifferent.
dispnéia s. f. (med.) dyspneia, dyspnoea, laboured respiration.
dispnéico adj. (med.) dyspneal, dyspnoeal, dyspneic, dyspnoeic.
disponente s. m. + f. disponer, a person who transfers property to another one. || adj. disponent, disposing.
disponibilidade s. f. 1. disposability, availability, availableness. 2. assessibility. 3. reserve, disposable force (of an army).
disponível adj. m. + f. (pl. **-íveis**) disposable, available, ready for use. || **disponivelmente** adv. availably. **estoque ~** floating supply. **fundos -veis** ready money. **tempo ~** time at one's disposal. **não ter dinheiro ~** to have no spare cash.

dispor s. m. disposal, disposition. || v. 1. to dispose, regulate, order, adjust, fit. 2. to place, put, lay out. 3. to rank, group, range. 4. to arrange, organize. 5. to prepare, predispose, make dispositions. 6. to alienate, bestow; make over, part with. 7. to resolve, determine, decide, settle. 8. **~-se** to prepare o. s., make o. s. ready. **~ árvores** to plant trees (in a particular order). **~ em camadas** to arrange in layers, stratify. **~ em capítulos** to chapter. **~ em classe** to class, classify. **~ as suas coisas** to settle one's affairs. **~ de** to dispose of. **~ de fundos** to dispose of funds or resources. **~ em gradação** to gradate. **~ de si** to dispose of o. s., be disengaged. **~-se para o que der e vier** to be ready for anything that may happen. **ao seu inteiro ~** at your disposal, at your service. **não ~ de tempo** to be pushed for time. **os alunos dispunham-se em fila, por ordem crescente de altura** the pupils ranged in a row from the shortest to the tallest. **o homem põe, Deus dispõe** man proposes, God disposes. **pode ~ de mim** you can count on my help. **você dispõe de um momento para mim?** can you spare me a moment?
disposição s. f. (pl. **-ões**) disposition: 1. disposal, arrangement, classification, grouping, order. 2. guidance, control. 3. clause of a contract. 4. aptitude, inclination, tendency, bent, mind. 5. temper, mood, nature, spirit. 6. state of health, bodily well-being. 7. predisposition. 8. readiness, willingness. 9. formation, structure. 10. provision, forethought. **~ animada** flow of spirits. **~ em camadas** arrangements in layers. **~ do céu, ~ divina** the divine providence, the divine disposal. **~ do temperamento** attitude of mind. **~ testamentária** last will. **achar-se em ~** to be in good condition, be ready. **à sua ~** at your disposal, at your service. **com boa ~** good tempered, in great form. **estar à ~** to be available. **não estou com ~ para brincar** I am not in the vein for joking. **render-se à ~ do vencedor** to surrender at discretion. **tomar -ões** to make arrangements.
dispositivo s. m. 1. gadget, device, appliance, contrivance, contraption. 2. apparatus, mechanism. || adj. dispositive, disposing, regulating. **~ de avanço** feed attachment. **~ de comando** control mechanism. **~ de ligação** connector.
disposto s. m. determination, rule, precept. || adj. 1. disposed, ordered. 2. prepared, ready, willing, eager. 3. inclined, bent. 4. arranged, settled. 5. laid out. 6. (Braz.) animated, vivacious; laborious, courageous, daring. **estar alegre e bem ~** to be full of beans, feel quite o. s., be at one's best. **estar mal ~** to be not quite the thing, be indisposed. **não estou ~ para cantar** I do not feel inclined to sing. **eu me sinto bem ~** I feel fresh.
disprósio s. m. (chem.) dysprosium, a magnetic element.
disputa s. f. dispute: 1. discussion, controversy, debate, altercation. 2. wrangling, contention, contestation, jangle, strife, quarrel, jar. 3. wrestle, row. 4. plea, moot. 5. difference, disagreement. 6. contest, match. **em ~** at strife. **entrar na ~** to enter the lists. **estar em ~** to be in dispute, be under discussion. **fora de ~** beyond dispute, indisputable. **pôr em ~** to put in question, dispute about. **sobre o gosto não há ~** there is no accounting for tastes.
disputador s. m. disputer, debate, wrangler, contender, quarreller, squabbler. || adj. disputant, disputatious, contentious, controversial.
disputante adj. m. + f. disputant.

disputar v. 1. to dispute, debate, discuss, argue. 2. to squab, quarrel, bicker, wrangle, brawl, contest, fight. 3. to controvert, disagree, altercate. 4. to contend, rival; challenge.
~ **alguma coisa com alguém** to vie with s. o for s. th. ~ **a coroa** to contend for the crown. ~ **regatas** to run rowing or sailing races. **cerca de quarenta barcos disputarão a taça "Comodoro"** about forty boats are going to enter for the "Comodore" cup.
disputativo adj. disputative, disputatious, argumentative.
disputável adj. m. + f. (pl. **-áveis**) disputable, controversial, questionable, uncertain.
disquisição s. f. (pl. **-ões**) disquisition, search, investigation, inquiry.
dissabor s. m. (also **dessabor**) 1. unsavouriness, insipidity. 2. (fig.) disgust, displeasure, contrariety, annoyance.
causar ~es a alguém to put a person to inconvenience.
dissaborear v. 1. to make unsavoury or insipid. 2. to discontent, dissatisfy, displease.
dissaborido, dissaboroso adj. (also **dessaborido, dessaboroso**) 1. unsavoury, insipid, tasteless. 2. (fig.) annoying, disgusting, saddening.
dissecação s. f. (pl. **-ões**) (also **dissecção**) 1. dissection, anatomization. 2. (fig.) rigorous examination.
dissecar v. 1. to dissect, anatomize. 2. to analyze, examine part by part or point by point.
dissector s. m. 1. dissector, anatomist. 2. dissecting knife.
disseminação s. f. (pl. **-ões**) 1. dissemination, propagation, diffusion, spreading, scattering. 2. sowing.
disseminador s. m. disseminator, diffuser. || adj. 1. disseminating, diffusing, scattering. 2. sowing.
disseminar v. to disseminate, scatter, sow, spread, diffuse, propagate.
dissenção s. f. (pl. **-ões**) (also **dissídio** m.) dissension, discord, disunion, variance, difference, divergence; dispute.
dissentâneo adj. dissentaneous, disagreeing, contrary, inconsistent.
dissentimento s. m. dissentience, dissent, dissension, disagreement, difference, variance, controversy.
dissentir v. 1. to dissent, differ, disagree. 2. ~**-se** to fall out (with).
dissépalo adj. (bot.) disepalous, having two sepals.
dissepimento s. m. (anat., bot.) septum, partition.
dissertação s. f. (pl. **-ões**) dissertation: 1. a written essay or treatise. 2. a set of formal discourses.
dissertador s. m. dissertator: 1. person who discourses formally; long-winded speaker. 2. person who writes an essay or treatise.
dissertar v. to dissertate: 1. write dissertations. 2. talk, debate, discuss, examine, argue, discourse.
dissidência s. f. dissidence. disagreement, dissent, difference or division of opinions.
dissidente s. m. + f. dissident; opponent. || adj. dissident, at variance; dissenting, not conforming, in disagreement.
dissidiar v. to render dissident, dissent, disagree, differ; divide, separate.
dissilábico adj. (gram.) dissyllabic, consisting of two syllables only.
dissilabo s. m. (gram.) dissyllable, a word consisting of two syllables. || adj. dissyllabic.
dissimetria s. f. dissymmetry, want of symmetry.
dissimétrico adj. dissymmetric(al), unsymmetric(al).
dissímil adj. h. + f. (pl. **-ímeis**) dissimilar, unlike, different.
dissimilação s. f. (pl. **-ões**) dissimilation, the change of one sound for another.

dissimilar (I) adj. m. + f. dissimilar, unlike, different.
dissimilar (II) v. to dissimilate, make unlike, cause to differ.
dissimilitude s. f. dissimilitude, want of resemblance, unlikeness, difference.
dissimulação s. f. (pl. **-ões**) dissimulation, hypocrisy, disguise, deceit, falseness, comouflage, palliation, feigning veil.
dissimulado s. m. dissimulator, dissembler. || adj. dissimulative, dissembling, feigned, furtive, hyprocritical, veiled.
dissimulador s. m. disguiser, dissimulator, dissembler, feigner. || adj. dissimulative, dissembling, feigning.
dissimular v. 1. to dissimulate, dissemble, conceal, cloak, disguise. 2. to feign, deceive, pretend.
~ **ignorância** to feign o. s. ignorant. ~ **com os maus** to connive with the wicked. ~ **uma ofensa** to dissemble an affront.
dissipação s. f. (pl. **-ões**) dissipation: 1. dispersion, scattering. 2. waste, destruction. 3. expenditure, prodigality, squandering; extravagance; debauchery.
dissipado adj. dissipated, wasted, consumed, squandered, destroyed; unsettled, dissolute. || **-amente** adv. with dissipation.
dissipador s. m. prodigal, lavisher, unthrift, dissipator, devourer, waster. || adj. squandering, wasting, dissipating.
dissipar v. 1. to dissipate, dispel, scatter, disperse. 2. to consume, waste, spend, misspend, squander, fritter away. 3. to enervate, weaken, enfeeble. 4. to dissolve, melt away, evaporate, evanish, disappear. 5. ~**-se** to be dispersed, disappear.
~ **as dúvidas** to remove the doubts. ~ **uma fortuna** to dissipate a fortune, waste a fortune. ~ **os humores** to dispel the humours.
dissipável adj. m. + f. (pl. **-áveis**) dissipative, dispersive.
disso contr. of the prep. **de** and pron. **isso** of that, thereof, about that, therefrom. || adv. hence.
acerca ~ with regard to that. **além** ~ thereto, besides, furthermore. **apesar** ~ even so. **nada** ~ nothing of the sort, nothing of the kind.
dissociabilidade s. f. dissociability, want of sociability.
dissociação s. f. (pl. **-ões**) dissociation, separation, disunion.
dissocial adj. m. + f. (pl. **-ais**) dissocial, unfriendly, contracted, selfish, unsocial. || ~**mente** adv. dissocially.
dissociar v. 1. to dissociate, make unsocial, separate, disunite, disconnect. 2. (chem.) to decompose. 3. ~**-se** to become desunited or decomposed.
dissociável adj. m. + f. (pl. **-áveis**) dissociable, not sociable, incongruous, not reconcilable.
dissolubilidade s. f. dissolubility, disolvability, solubility, dissolubleness.
dissolução s. f. (pl. **-ões**) (also **dissolvência**) dissolution: 1. breakup, separation, disunion. 2. (chem.) deliquation, liquefaction, solution, decomposition, disintegration. 3. dissoluteness, lewdness, licentiousness, depravation. 4. dismissal of an assembly.
~ **do parlamento** dissolution of Parliament. ~ **do sangue** dissolution of the blood.
dissolutivo adj. dissolutive, dissolving, dissoluble.
dissoluto adj. 1. dissolute, loose, relaxed, enfeebled. 2. vicious, wanton. 3. lewd, wicked, debauched, licentious. || **-amente** adv. dissolutely.
vida -a dissolute life.
dissolúvel adj. m. + f. (pl. **-áveis**) dissoluble, dissolvable.
dissolvente s. m. dissolvent, solvent; disintegrating; resolvente. || adj. m. + f. dissolvent.
dissolver v. 1. to dissolve: a) liquefy, melt, fuse, thaw. b) disunite, break up, separate; put an end

to; annul. c) consume, vanish, destroy. 2. to corrupt. 3. ~-se to be dissolved; become fluid.

dissolvido adj. liquified, melted, dissolved; broken up, separated, disunited.

dissonância s. f. 1. (mus.) dissonance, discord. 2. (fig.) disagreement, incongruity, disproportion, impropriety. 3. variance, clash, jarring, jangle. **fazer** ~ to be contrary to, clash with.

dissonante adj. m. + f. (also **dissonoro, díssono**) dissonant: 1. discordant, harsh, inharmonious, tuneless. 2. disagreeing, incongruous. ‖ ~-**mente** adv. dissonantly. **acorde** ~ dissonant accord. **intervalo** ~ dissonant interval.

dissonar v. 1. (mus.) to be dissonant. 2. to disagree, be contrary, clash with.

dissuadir v. 1. to dissuade, advise or exhort against, deter, divert from; turn. 2. to discourage, bring or call off. 3. ~-se to change one's mind. ~ **alguém da sua intenção** to dissuade s. o. from his purpose. **ele não se deixou** ~ there was no holding him.

dissuasão s. f. (pl. -ões) dissuasion, dehortation, advice against something, diversion (from).

dissuasivo adj. (also **dissuasório**) dissuasive, tending to dissuade, dissuasory, dehortatory.

dissuasor s. m. dissuader, dehorter. ‖ adj. dissuading, dissuasive.

distal adj. m. + f. (anat.) distal, terminal, peripheral.

distância s. f. distance: 1. farness, remoteness, extension. 2. space. 3. (mus.) interval, difference between two tones. 4. reserve of manners, coldness. ~ **entre dois eixos** wheel-base (plate E 1). ~ **focal** (opt.) focal length, focal distance. ~ **de planeamento** (aeron.) gliding distance. ~ **percorrida** length of route. ~ **entre rodas** gauge. ~ **de tiro** gunshot. **a** ~ aloof, aside. **à** ~ **de um braço** at arm's length. **a grande** ~ **daqui** a long way off, afar, far-off. **a pouca** ~ at a short distance, near. **a que** ~? how far? **cobrir uma** ~ to cover a distance. **conservar à** ~ to keep s. o. at a distance. **guardar** ~s to avoid familiarity. **o som repercutiu-se de uma grande** ~ the sound reverberated from a great distance. **tomar a** ~ **de alguém** to get the start of s. o. **uma longa** ~ a long way off.

distanciado adj. distant: 1. reserved, not cordial. 2. apart, asunder. ‖ -**amente** adv. distantly.

distanciar v. 1. to distance: a) place at a distance, situate remotely, space. b) get in advance of, outdo, excel, outstrip. 2. ~-se to withdraw, keep away from.

distanciômetro s. m. range finder.

distante adj. m. + f. distant: 1. far, far-off, far-away, remote. 2. reserved, cool, not cordial; shy, haughty, frigid. ‖ ~-**mente** adv. distantly, far-away. ~ **de** remote from. **cidade** ~ far-away town. **mais** ~ farther, ulterior. **o mais** ~ farthest, farthermost.

distar v. 1. to be distant. 2. (fig.) to differ, vary, be unlike, dissimilar.

disteleologia s. f. dysteleology.

distender v. 1. to distend, dilate, expand, swell out, enlarge, stretch or spread (on all directions). 2. ~-se to become distended, swell.

distendido adj. distended, dilated, wide; bagged, blown.

distênio s. m. disthene, cyanite: a mineral of unequal hardness.

distensão s. f. (pl. -ões) distension: 1. distending, dilatation, stretching, tension. 2. extension, expansion. 3. sprain, wrench, wrest. **sofri uma** ~ **do pé** I gave my foot a wrench.

distenso adj. 1. distended, dilated; wide. 2. sprained, wrenched.

distensor s. m. distender, expander. ‖ adj. distending, distensive.

dístico s. m. 1. (pros.) distich, a group of two lines or verses, couplet. 2. inscription, label. ‖ adj. (bot.) distich, distichous, having two rows or ranks, two-ranked.

distinção s. f. (pl. -ões) distinction: 1. discrimination, discernment, difference. 2. division, separation. 3. distinctness, good breeding, urbanity, discreetness; elegance. 4. rank, name, title, dignity. 5. superiority, respectability. 6. eminence, prominence, ennoblement, honour, mark of honour, renown. 7. first-class honours (exam). **homem de grande** ~ a man of note. **pessoas de** ~ people of quality. **sem** ~ unexceptional. **sem** ~ **de sexo ou idade** without distinction of sex or age.

distinguidor s. m. distinctor, one who distinguishes or makes distinctions, distinguisher.

distinguir v. 1. to distinguish; distinct, differentiate, discern, discriminate. 2. to remark, note, mark, descry, single, know, perceive. 3. to honour, make famous or eminent. 4. to separate, differ, divide. 5. ~-se: a) to take the first-class honours (examination). b) to distinguish o. s., signalize o. s., stand out, win one's spurs. ~ **o bem do mal** to discern good from evil, distinguish between right and wrong. ~-se **na sua profissão** to distinguish o. s. in the profession. **não** ~ **o branco do preto** to be an ignoramus. **você não é capaz de** ~ **um do outro** you cannot tell them apart, you cannot know one from another. **você sabe** ~ **as duas coisas?** do you know which is which?

distinguível adj. m. + f. (pl. -íveis) distinguishable, discernible.

distintivo s. m. distinctive, decoration, emblem, attribute, badge, symbol. ‖ adj. distinctive, characteristic; discerning.

distinto adj. 1. distinct: a) distinctive, distinguished, separate, different, diverse. b) special, individual. c) clear, determinate, explicit, well-marked, unmistakable, indubitable, positive. d) famous, eminent, remarkable, grand, conspicuous, illustrous; high-bred. 2. fine, elegant. **um artista** ~ an artist of rank. **um homem** ~ a man of distinction, gentleman, nobleman. **uma moça -a** smart girl. **uma senhora -a** a fine lady, a lady of quality. **ter um porte** ~ to have a distinguished bearing, have refined manners.

distiquíase s. f. (med.) distichiasis: malformation consisting of a double row of eyelashes.

disto contr. of the prep. **de** and the pron. **isto** of this, of it, at it, hereof, herefrom. **muito antes** ~ long before this. **por meio** ~ by this.

distomatose s. f. (med.) distomiasis, disease caused by trematoid worms or flukes.

dístomo adj. (zool.) distomatous, two-mouthed.

distonia s. f. dystonia.

distorção s. f. (pl. -ões) (phot.) distortion, deviation from the regular shape; deformation, malformation.

distração s. f. (pl. -ões) (also **distraimento** m.) distraction: 1. absence of mind, inattention, mindlessness, brown study. 2. amusement, diversion, recreation, relaxation, pastime. **a leitura é uma boa** ~ reading is a good diversion. **ser sujeito a** -ões to be prone to inattention.

distraído s. m. absent-minded person. ‖ adj. 1. distracted, inattentive, absent-minded, forgetful, thoughtless. 2. amused, entertained. **ele anda muito** ~ he is being rather absent-minded.

distrair v. 1. t distract, draw away (the attention from an object). 2. to embezzle. 3. to amuse, entertain. 4. ~-se: a) to commit a mistake. b) to amuse o. s., enjoy o. s.

distratar v. to cancel, make void an agreement, annul a contract, break a pact, revoke.

distrativo adj. distractive, distractious, entertaining.

distrato s. m. (also **distrate**) rescission, dissolution of an agreement, cancelling, annulling.

distribuição s. f. (pl. **-ões**) 1. distribution, dividing, parcelling, sharing; division. 2. arrangement, regulation; classification. 3. delivery (of letters). 4. allotment, allocation, partitionment. 5. distribution of types into their boxes (after printing) . ~ **de alimentos** distribution of food. ~ **de bilhetes** issue of tickets. ~ **da carga** the trim of the hold. ~ **da energia elétrica** distribution of electricity. ~ **de livros** book circulation. ~ **de papéis** (theat.) cast. ~ **postal** delivery of letters. ~ **de massa falida** bankrupt's division. **estação de** ~ switching station. **quadro de** ~ (electr.) switchboard. **tubo de** ~ distributing tube or pipe.

distribuidor s. m. 1. distributer, allocator, allotter. 2. disposer, circulator. 3. letter carrier, postman. ‖ adj. distributing, dividing.

distribuir v. 1. to distribute: a) divide, deal out, allot, allocate, apportion; proportionate. b) separate and put in order, arrange, classify, dispose. c) spread, scatter, disperse. d) deliver, hand out. 2. ~-se to be distributed. ~ **dividendo** to strike a dividend. ~ **a ração** to ration, feed. ~ **socos a esmo** to lay about one.

distributivo adj. distributive, distributional, expressing division or separation. **justiça** -a distributive justice. **partícula** -a distributive particle.

distrição s. f. (pl. **-ões**) affliction, anxiety, trouble.

distrital adj. m. + f. (pl. **-ais**) belonging to a district.

distrito s. m. 1. district, circuit, quarter. 2. territory, region, section, zone. ~ **eleitoral** precinct, borough. ~ **mineiro** mining district. **sede do** ~ county town.

distrofia s. f. (med.) dystrophy, nutritional perturbation.

disturbar v. to disturb: 1. stir, trouble, agitate, molest, perturb. 2. interrupt, hinder, incommode, derange. 3. discompose, disquiet, disorder, upset.

distúrbio s. m. 1. disturb, disturbance, perturbation, trouble. 2. misunderstanding, dissension, division, discord, distemper. 3. noise, commotion, row. 4. tumult, uproar, riot. ~ **mental** mental disorder. **provocar** ~ to cause disturbance, to riot.

disúria, disuria s. f. (med.) dysuria, difficulty in discharging urine.

disúrico s. m. person suffering from dysuria. ‖ adj. relative to dysuria (dysury).

dita (I) s. f. fortune, happiness, good luck, chance, felicity.

dita (II) s. f. (Braz., pop.) jail, prison.

ditado s. m. 1. dictation. 2. proverb, saying, sentence, adage.

ditador s. m. dictator, despot, tyrant, absolute sovereign, oppressor.

ditadura s. f. 1. dictatorship. 2. despotism, absolutism, tyranny.

ditame s. m. dictate, rule, principle, precept, maxim; admonition, injunction. **obedecer aos** ~**s do coração** to follow the dictates of the heart. **seguir os** ~**s da razão** to follow the dictates of reason.

ditar v. 1. to dictate (for another to write down). 2. to impose, command, prescribe, decree, require. 3. to suggest, inspire, teach, show. **o chefe ditou uma carta à secretária** the boss dictated a letter to the clerk. **o aluno escreveu o**

trecho ditado pelo professor the pupil wrote the passage at the teacher's dictation.

ditatorial adj. m. + f. (pl. **-ais**) (also **ditatório**) dictatorial, absolute, unlimited; dogmatic, authoritative, imperious, magisterial. ‖ ~**mente** adv. dictatorially.

ditério s. m. 1. jest, witticism, scoff, quirk. 2. (S. Braz., pop.) meddling, tittle-tattle.

ditinho s. m. intrigue; meddling, tittle-tattle; insinuation, hint.

ditirâmbico adj. dithyrambic, bacchanalian; lyrical.

ditirambo s. m. dithyramb, dithyrambus: 1. a form of Greek lyrical composition. 2. (ant.) a song in honour of Dionysus.

dito s. m. 1. ditto, the same, the aforesaid thing. 2. dictum, aphorism, maxim, axiom, sentence. ‖ adj. said, surnamed, stated; aforesaid. ~! done! ~ **chistoso** conceit, wisecrack. ~ **e feito** no sooner said than done, suiting the action to the words. **como foi** ~ as stated. **dar o** ~ **por não** ~ to retract o. s. **dizer** ~ (N. Braz.) to use obscene words or expressions. **fi-lo cumprir o que havia** ~ I took him at his word.

dito-cujo s. m. Braz., pop.) Mr. So-and-So.

ditografia s. f. dittography.

ditologia s. f. dittology, a twofold reading or interpretation.

ditongação s. f. (pl. **-ões**) diphthongization, diphthongation, formation of a diphthong.

ditongal adj. m. + f. (pl. **-ais**) diphthongal: 1. belonging to a diphthong. 2. consisting of two vowels pronounced in one syllable.

ditongar v. to diphthongize, form a diphthong.

ditongo s. m. diphthong, union of two vowels pronounced in one syllable. ~ **crescente** rising diphthong. ~ **decrescente** falling diphthong.

dítono s. m. (mus.) ditone, interval of two tones.

ditoso adj. happy, lucky, felicitous, fortunate, prosperous. ‖ -**amente** adv. happily.

ditríglifo s. m. (archit.) ditriglyph.

diurese s. f. (med.) diuresis.

diurético s. m. (med.) diuretic, a medicine that excites the discharge of urine. ‖ adj. (med.) diuretic.

diurnal s. m. diurnal, a Roman Catholic book of prayers containing the little hours. ‖ adj. m. + f (pl. **-ais**) diurnal, daily, happening every day.

diurno adj. diurn(e), diurnal, daily, of the day.

diuturnidade s. f. diuturnity, length of time, long space of time.

diuturno adj. diuturnal, lasting, being of a long continuance.

diva s. f. diva, a prima donna, distinguished female singer.

divã s. m. 1. divan, a kind of couch (plates C 2, D 4). 2. (hist.) council of state esp. in Turkey.

divagação s. f. (pl. **-ões**) 1. divagation, deviation, digression. 2. (fig.) departure from the main subject. 3. wandering.

divagador s. ím. 1. rambler. 2. vagabond. 3. dreamer, daydreamer. ‖ adj. 1. rambling, wandering, deviating, roving. 2. dreaming.

divagante adj. m. + f. wandering, rambling, far afield; aimless, uncertain; discoursive.

divagar v. 1. to divagate, wander, deviate, digress, rove, ramble. 2. to depart from the main subject. 3. to daydream.

divaricado adj. divaricate(d), diverged (from), branched off.

divergência s. f. divergence, divergency: 1. deviation, divarication. 2. contrariety, variance, oppositeness, discrepancy. 3. difference, dissension, misunderstanding, disagreement. ~ **de opinião** difference of opinion, disagreement.

divergente adj. m. + f. divergent: 1. devious, divaricate, diverging. 2. variant, opposite, discrepant. 3. different, varicoloured. 4. disagreeing. **lente** ~ diverging lens.

divergir v. to diverge: 1. deviate, divaricate. 2. to discord, disagree, dissent. 3. to differ. ~ **de opinião** to differ in opinion.

diversão s. f. (pl. **-ões**) diversion: 1. deviation, a turning aside or diverting from. 2. distraction, entertainment, amusement, pastime, relaxation, recreation, jollification. **parque de** ~ amusement park.

diversicolor adj. m. + f. diversicoloured, having different colours; variegated.

diversidade s. f. diversity, diverseness, dissimilarity, unlikeness, difference, distinction, variousness; variegation, diversification.

diversificação s. f. (pl. **-ões**) diversification, variation, change, alteration.

diversificado adj. diversified. **indústria** -a diversified industry. **paisagem** -a diversified landscape.

diversificante adj. m. + f. diversifying, varying.

diversificar v. 1. to diversify, vary, modify, variegate. 2. ~**-se** to differ.

diversificável adj. m. + f. (pl. **-áveis**) diversifiable, variable.

diversifloro adj. (bot.) diversiflorous, bearing flowers of two or more kinds.

diversiforme adj. m. + f. diversiform, of various forms, different.

diversionismo s. m. (pol.) a maneuver used to divert the attention.

diversivo adj. diversive; revulsive.

diverso adj. 1. divers(e), different, various, multiform, manifold, unlike, else, variegated. 2. ~**s** pl. several, sundry, divers; a number of. ~**s dias** a number of days, a few days. **-as vezes** several times. **carga -a** mixed cargo. **é coisa muito -a** that is quite different. **o assunto pode ser visto de -as maneiras** the subject may be viewed in different ways.

diversório s. m. diversion. ‖ adj. diversive, diversory.

divertículo s. m. (anat.) diverticulum, coecum, cul--de-sac.

divertido adj. 1. deviated, drawn to another course. 2. amusing, entertaining, pleasing, diverting. 3. comical, droll, funny. 4. merry, gay, exhilarant, jolly, jocund, enjoyable. 5. festive, sportive. 6. distracted, inattentive, absent-minded. ‖ **-amente** adv. merrily, in an amusing manner. **é muito** ~ it is great fun, it is as good as play. **quanto mais, mais** ~ the more the merrier. **que** ~**!** what fun!

divertimento s. m. 1. diversion, amusement, pastime, entertainment. 2. merry-making, enjoyment. 3. play, game, festival; sport, fun. 4. distraction, inattention, absence of mind, heedlessness. **bom** ~**!** I have a good time! **organizar um** ~ to organize an entertainment. **que** ~ what capital sport!

divertir v. 1. to divert: a) draw away, turn aside. b) change the direction, aim or destination. c) distract, digress. d) entertain, amuse, jolly, recreate. 2. ~**-se** to divert o. s., take one's pleasure, make merry, have fun. ~**-se à custa alheia** to be amused at people's expense, be witty at another's expense. ~**-se imensamente** to be hugely amused, have a royal time. ~**-se muito com a história** to be greatly tickled by the story. **diverti-me muito no baile** I had much fun at the dancing party. **ele divertiu-se bastante** he had his fling. **deixe-o** ~**-se à vontade** let him have his full swing of pleasure. **não é fácil di-**

verti-lo he is not easy to amuse. **gosto de ver gente nova** ~**-se** I like to see young people enjoying themselves.

divícia s. f. wealth, richness.

dívida s. f. 1. debt, money or thing one is owing; arrears, arrearage, debit. 2. indebtedness, liability, obligation, duty, due. ~**s ativas** book debts, outstandings. ~ **consolidada** funded dept. ~ **externa** external debt. ~ **flutuante** floating debt. ~ **de gratidão** debt of gratitude. ~ **hipotecária** martgage debt. ~ **de honra** debt of honour. ~ **de jogo** play debt. ~ **pública** public debt, national debt. **carregado de** ~**s** deeply in debt. **cobrar** ~**s** to collect debts. **confessar uma** ~ to acknowledge a trespass. **contrair** ~**s** to contract debts, run into debts. **em** ~ in debt. **estar crivado de** ~**s** to be deep in debts. **fazer** ~**s** to get into debt, incur debts. **isento de** ~, **sem** ~ clear of debts, free of debts. **não ter** ~**s** to pay one's way. **obrigar alguém a pagar a** ~ to impel s. o. to pay his debt. **pagar uma** ~ to honour a debt, clear the debt, answer one's debt. **pagou a** ~ **com o trabalho** he worked off his debt. **perdoai-nos as nossas** ~**s!** forgive us our debts! **satisfazer uma** ~ to meet a debt. **ter** ~**s** to owe.

dividendo s. m. dividend: 1. (math.) a number or quantity which is to be divided. 2. share, portion, bonus, quote. ‖ adj. dividing, distributing, separating.

dividido adj. 1. divided, separated, disunited, parted. 2. distributed, cleft, split. ~ **em compartimentos** chambered. ~ **ao meio** dimidiate. ~ **em quatro partes** quartered.

dividor s. m. divider, diviser, distributer.

dividir v. 1. to divide: a) part, share, average, allot, apportion. b) distribute, parcel out, deal out. c) separate, disjoin, disunite, break, sunder, sever, dissever, dismember, cleave; divorce. d) cut, slice, section, intersection; split. 2. ~**-se** to become separated, be disunited; fall out (with). ~ **em compartimentos** to compart. ~ **em distritos** to district, canton. ~ **em partes iguais** to go shares. ~ **em duas partes** to halve; bisect, bifurcate. ~ **em parágrafos** to paragraph, chapter. ~ **em parcelas** to parcel, branch. ~ **o tempo entre o trabalho e a distração** to divide one's time between work and play. ~ **entre três irmãos** to divide between three brothers. ~ **em triângulos** to triangulate.

dividivi s. m. divi-divi, a tree, whose pods are used for inkmaking.

divíduo adj. dividual, divisible.

divinação s. f. (pl. **-ões**) divination, clairvoyance; perception, discernment; intuition.

divinal adj. m. + f. (pl. **-ais**) = **divino**.

divinatório adj. divinatory, divining.

divindade s. f. 1. divineness, divinity, sanctity, heavenliness. 2. Divinity; God, the Supreme Being, deity.

divinização s. f. (pl. **-ões**) divinization, divinizing, deification, apotheosis.

divinizador s. m. person who divinizes. ‖ adj. divinizing, deifying.

divinizante adj. m. + f, divinizing, deifying.

divinizar v. 1. to divinize, deify, render divine, regard as divine. 2. to idolize, adore, worship. 3. ~**-se** to become divine.

divino s. m. (Braz.) the Holy Ghost. ‖ adj. (also **divinal**) divine: 1. holy, deific, supernal, heavenly, celestial, godlike. 2. excellent, extraordinary, supreme, admirable. 3. supernatural. ‖ **-amente** adv. divinely. **O Divino Espírito Santo** the Holy Ghost. **assistência** -a divine assistance. **culto** ~ divine service, religion. **direito** ~ divine right. **serviço** ~ the public worship of God.

divisa s. f. 1. device, slogan, motto, catchword, posy. 2. emblem, symbol, badge. 3. boundary, ambit, cincture, verge, frontier. 4. (mil.) stripe. 5. (Braz.) brand mark (cattle). 6. ~s pl. exchange value.

divisão s. f. (pl. **-ões**) 1. division: a) section, segment, septum. b) separation, distribution, partition. c) discord, disunion, variance, difference. d) classification, category. 2. dividing line, demarcation. 3. compartment, repartition. 4. district, department. 5. portion, share, parcel. 6. (gram.) hyphen. ~ **por fatores** (math.) division by factors. ~ **harmônica** (math.) harmonic division of a line. ~ **de sílabas** division of syllables, end-of-line break. ~ **do trabalho** division of labour. **assumir o comando de uma** ~ to take the head of a division. **general de** ~ general of division, major general.

divisar v. 1. to espy, see, descry, discern, perceive. 2. delimit(ate), fix the boundaries, bound.

divisibilidade s. f. divisibility, divisibleness, partibility.

divisional adj. m. + f. (pl. **-ais**) divisional, divisionary. || ~**mente** adv. divisionally.

divisionário adj. divisionary, divisional.

moeda -a divisional coin.

divisível adj. m. + f. (pl. **-íveis**) divisible, dividable, partible.

o número 6 ~ **por três** the number is divisible by three.

diviso adj. divided, parted, separated, distributed; disunited.

divisor s. m. 1. (arith.) divisor, a number by which another one is divided. 2. divider. || adj. dividing, divisive.

~ **comum** common divisor. ~ **de tensão** (radio) potentiometer. **máximo** ~ **comum** greatest common divisor.

divisória s. f. 1. separating line, demarcation. 2. partition, screen, division; shed.

~ **de água** watershed.

divisório s. m. (typogr.) text-holder, copy-holder. || adj. divisory, divisive, dividing, parting; distributing, separating.

caixa de válvula -a slide valve case. **linha** -a parting line. **parede** -a partition wall.

divo s. m. 1. divinized person. 2. God. || adj. divine, godlike, saint, heavenly.

divorciar v. 1. to divorce, dissolve the marriage contract. 2. (fig.) to separate, disunite, set at variance, force asunder. 3. ~**se** to get divorced, become separated.

divórcio s. m. 1. divorce, dissolution of marriage. 2. (fig.) separation, disunion, disjunction, repudiation.

requerer ~ to sue for divorce.

divorcista s. m. + f. person pleading for divorce. || adj. favouring divorce; pleading for divorce.

divulgação s. f. (pl. **-ões**) divulgation, propagation, publishing, diffusion, disclosure.

divulgador s. m. divulger, publisher, propagandist. || adj. divulging, publishing, making public; disclosing.

divulgar v. 1. to divulge, make public, publish, scatter abroad. 2. to jet out, disclose, betray, impart, communicate. 3. ~**se** to become known, be published.

~ **um segredo** to spill the beans. **a notícia foi divulgada pelo jornal** the news was published in the paper.

divulsão s. f. (pl. **-ões**) divulsion, rending asunder; violent separation.

dixe s. m. 1. jewel, ornament. 2. trinket, watch charm.

dizedor s. m. 1. teller, jester. 2. talker, chatterer. || adj. talking, chattering, telling.

dizer s. m. saying, what is said, words, sentence. || v. 1. to say, speak, tell, talk. 2. to utter, express. 3. to declare, affirm, assert. 4. to relate, narrate, report, recount, describe, recite. 5. to indicate, demonstrate, denote. 6. ~**se** to call o. s., give o. s. out as.

~ **adeus** to take one's leave, bid farewell, say good-bye. ~ **bem de alguém** to speak well of s. o., praise him. ~ **cobras e lagartos** to have no good word to say of s.o. ~ **com seus botões** to say to o. s. ~ **mal de alguém** to speak ill of s. o., slander. ~ **missa** to say mass, celebrate mass. ~ **uma coisa e fazer outra** to say one thing and do another. ~ **respeito a** to concern. **andar dizendo** to spread abroad. **bem dito! well spoken! como ia dizendo** as I was about to say. **come se costuma** ~ as the saying goes. **dar o dito por não dito** to call off the deal. **diga-me** I ask you. **digam o que disserem** they may say what they please. **digamos vinte** let's say twenty. **digo que não** I say it is not. **digo que sim!** I say it is. **dito e feito** no sooner said than done. **dize-me com quem andas e dir-te-ei quem és** a man is known by the company he keeps. **diz-se** it says, they say, it is whispered. **é o que ele diz** so he says. **é isto o que eu queria** ~ I should just say so. **ele disse o que tinha a** ~ he said his say. **ela lhe disse em voz baixa que viesse** she whispered him to come. **isso não quer** ~ **nada** that signifies nothing. **isto não se deve** ~ this is not to be repeated. **isto quer** ~ that is to say. **lamento** ~ I am sorry to say. **mais fácil** ~ **que fazer** easier said than done. **não diga a ninguém** keep it to yourself. **não** ~ **sim nem não** to give an evasive answer. **não me diga** you don't say so. **não posso deixar de** ~ I can't help saying. **não ter que** ~ to have nothing to say or to answer. **no que diz respeito** as regards. **ouvi** ~ I was told. **para assim** ~, **por modo de** ~ as it were. **para** ~ **a verdade** to tell the truth. **para** ~ **tudo em uma palavra** to wind up all in one word. **para melhor** ~ let us speak more correctly. **por assim** ~ so to say. **quem diz A, também diz B** in for a penny, in for a pound. **quer que lhe diga o que estou pensando?** shall I tell you what I think? **somente queria** ~ all I wanted to say was.

dize-tu-direi-eu s. m., sg. + pl hot discussion, endless altercation.

dízima s. f. tithe, contribution of a tenth.

~ **periódica** circulating decimal, circulating fraction. **cobrar a** ~ to tithe. **sujeito à** ~ tithable.

dizimação s. f. (pl. **-ões**) 1. decimation. 2. restriction, reduction.

dizimador s. m. decimator. || adj. 1. decimating. 2. tithing.

dizimar v. to decimate: 1. tithe, take the tenth part of. 2. pick out every tenth soldier for capital punishment. 3. (fig.) defalcate, deduct, diminish.

dizimeiro s. m. tithe collector, tithingman, tither.

dízimo s. m. tithe, a tenth, tenth part.

dizível adj. m. + f. (pl. **-íveis**) that can be said, easy to be said, utterable.

diz-que, diz-que-diz, diz-que-diz-que s. m., sg. + pl. (Braz.) rumour, report.

djalmaíta s. f. (min.) djalmaite.

djim s. m. jinnee, a spirit or demon in Arabian mythology.

do contr. of the prep. **de** and the art. **o** of the, from the.

~ **bom e** ~ **melhor** of the best. ~ **começo ao fim** from end to end. **a casa** ~ **pai** the house of the father. **mais ~ que bom!** more than good, excellent.

dó (I) s. m. (mus.) do, C.

dó (II) s. m. 1. pity, compassion; empathy, condolence, mourning. 2. mercy, clemency; charity.
fazer dó to arouse pity. **ter ~ de alguém** to pity s. o., have compassion, take pity on s. o.

doação s. f. (pl. **-ões**) donation, gift, present, grant, endowment; granting, bestowing, benefaction.
~ por morte donatio mortis causa, bequest. **~ de terras pelo governo** land grant.

doado adj. donated, given as a gift.

doador s. m. donor, donator, giver, endower; benefactor.
~ de sangue blood donor.

doar v. to donate, give, present as a gift, endow; contribute, bestow.
~ seus bens to make over one's goods by deed or gift.

dobadeira s. f. woman that winds skeins or bottoms, female yarn winder.

dobadoura s. f. (also **dobadoira**) 1. reel, spindle, windle, winding frame. 2. (pop.) hurry, rush, flurry. **andar numa ~** to be always stirring. **fazer andar alguém numa ~** to cause trouble to s. o.

dobagem s. f. (pl. **-ens**) 1. reeling, windling (yarn). 2. reeling room (in a spinning mill).

dobar v. to reel: 1. wind, spool. 2. (fig.) turn round, whirl, stagger.

doble s. m. (S. Braz.) double. ‖ adj. m. + f. 1. double, coupled, twofold. 2. two-faced, deceitful.

doblete s. m. doublet, a false stone, counterfeit gem.

doblez s. f. hypocrisy, disingenuousness, falsety, deceit, duplicity.

dobra (I) s. f. plait, fold, plication, pucker (plate C 5)
~ em folha de livro dog's-ear.

dobra (II) s. f. doubloon; ancient Portuguese gold coin.

dobração s. f. (pl. **-ões**) (Braz.) driving in (cattle).

dobrada (I) s. f. 1. tripe, intestines of an ox. 2. tripe ragout.

dobrada (II) s. f. (S. Braz.) 1. descent (from the top of a hill). 2. ondulation or unevenness in a ground.

dobradeira s. f. folding stick, an instrument that bookbinders use to fold the sheets of a book; folding machine.

dobradiça s. f. 1. hinge, joint (of a door, window, etc.) (plates A 1, C 11, D 1, J 1, P 10). 2. (theat.) tip-up seat. 3. (N. Braz.) a certain dancing step. **~ de asinha** flap hinge (plate D 1). **eixo da ~** axle of a hinge.

dobradiço adj. folding, collapsible, flexible, supple, pliable; bending easily.

dobradinha s. f. (Braz.) tripe stew or ragout.

dobrado s. m. (Braz.) 1. (mil.) marching music. 2. hilly ground. ‖ adj. 1. folded, doubled, plicate; double, bent. 2. (Braz.) strong, vigorous, robust.

dobrador s. m. doubler, folder, furler, lapper, winder.

dobradura s. f. fold, folding, plication; duplication, doubling.

dobramento s. m. 1. folding, curvature, plication, flexure. 2. (geol.) fold.

dobrão s. m. (pl. **-ões**) doubloon: 1. ancient Portuguese gold coin. 2. a gold of Spain and the Spanish-American states. 3. (N. Braz.) copper coin.

dobrar v. 1. to double: a) make double, increase, enlarge, extend. b) fold, fold up, plait, ply, plicate. c) turn, round, curve, bow, bend. d) duplicate, repeat. 2. **~-se:** a) to become double, be the double of. b) (fig.) to humble o. s. c) to change one's mind.
~ um cabo to turn a cape. **~ uma carta** to fold a letter. **~ a esquina** to turn the corner. **~ a**

finados to toll the funeral knell. **~ a ganância** to get twice as much. **~ o joelho** to bend the knees, humble o. s. **~ a parada** to double the stake (gambling). **~-se ao partido de alguém** to take someone's part. **~ o passo** to mend one's pace, quicken one's step. **~ o sino** to ring, toll a bell. **~ a voz** to trill, quaver, stake. **ao ~ do século** at the century's turn. **dobrando a esquina** past the corner. **tenho de ~ minha roupa** I must lay my clothes flat.

dobrável adj. m. + f. (pl. **-áveis**) folding, pliable, bending, flexible.

dobre (I) s. m. knell, death-bell, ding-dong, passing-bell.

dobre (II) adj. m. + f. double, double-dealing; double-minded, double-faced, deceitful.

dobrez s. f. doubleness, duplicity; double-dealing, falsehood.

dobro (ô) s. m. double, doubleness, duplication.
pagar em ~ to give double the price. **a soma em ~** twice the sum. **ele tem o ~ da força** he has twice the strength.

doca (I) s. f. dock, basin, quay.
~ de abrigo wet dock. **~ flutuante** floating dock. **~ seca** graving dock, dry dock. **direitos de ~** dock rent, dockage. **entrar em ~** to be docked. **estaleiro de ~** dockyard. **inspetor da ~** dock-master. **piloto de ~** dock pilot.

doca (II) adj. m. + f. (Braz.) one-eyed.

doçaria s. f. 1. large quantity of sweetmeats. 2. a confectioner's shop, sweets shop.

doce s. m. sweetmeat, sweets, comfit, confection; bonbon, cooky, sweety. ‖ adj. m. + f. 1. sweet, sugared, honeyed, candied. 2. soft, mild, lenient; gentle. 3. agreeable, pleasant, comfortable, easy. 4. harmonious, melodious. 5. ductile, supple, pliable. ‖ **~mente** adv. sweetly.
~ (de casca de) cidra citron peel. **~ de frutas** tutti-frutti. **~ em calda** compote. **de falas ~s** honey-tongued. **é ~** it tastes sweet. **metal ~** flowing metal. **palavras ~s** flattering speech, courteous language, sugared words. **peixe de água ~** fresh-water fish.

doce-de-pimenta s. m. (pl. **doces-de-pimenta**) (Braz.) cake prepared of manioc, sugar and black pepper.

doceira s. f. 1. f. of **doceiro**. 2. any ant living on sugar or sweets.

doceiro s. m. confectioner, seller of sweetmeats.

docência s. f. teaching, instruction.

docente s. m. teacher, professor, instructor, lecturer, prelecter; academician. ‖ adj. m. + f. teaching, instructing, lecturing.
corpo ~ professoriate, teaching staff, teaching body.

docente-livre s. m. + f. (pl. **docentes-livres**) full professor.

dócil adj. m. + f. (pl. **-eis**) 1. docile, teachable, amenable, guidable, manageable, tractable, corrigible. 2. pliant, ductile, tame, supple, sweet-tempered, facile, submissive. ‖ **docilmente** adv. with docility.

docilidade s. f. docility, teachableness, tractableness, suppleness, towardness, pliancy, flexibleness, tameness.

docilizar v. 1. to make docile, tame, soften. 2. **~-se** to be docile, submit o. s.

docimasia s. f. (chem.) docimacy, docimasy, art of assaying (metals), docimastic assay.

docimástico adj. (chem.) docimastic, assaying.

docoglossos s. m. pl. (zool.) Docoglossa.

doctilóquio s. m. eloquence, elocution, oratory.

doctíloquo adj. (also **doctiloqüente**) eloquent, voluble, fluent, expressing.

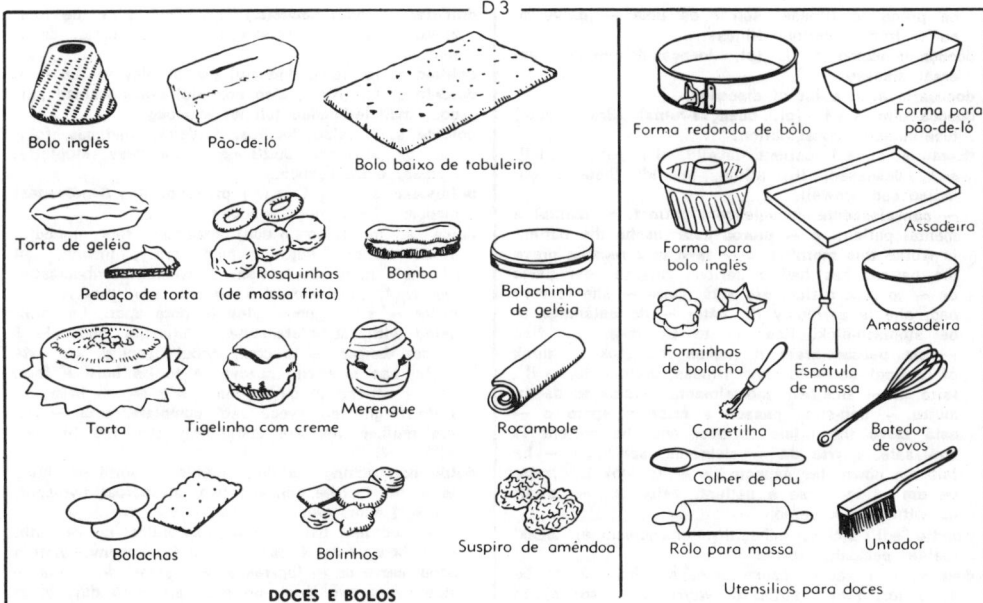

— D 3 —

Bolo inglês

Pão-de-ló

Bolo baixo de tabuleiro

Torta de geléia

Pedaço de torta

Rosquinhas (de massa frita)

Bomba

Bolachinha de geléia

Torta

Tigelinha com creme

Merengue

Rocambole

Bolachas

Bolinhos

Suspiro de amêndoa

Forma redonda de bôlo

Forma para pão-de-ló

Assadeira

Forma para bolo inglês

Forminhas de bolacha

Amassadeira

Espátula de massa

Carretilha

Batedor de ovos

Colher de pau

Rôlo para massa

Untador

DOCES E BOLOS

Utensilios para doces

documentação s. f. (pl. **-ões**) 1. documentation, documents. 2. argumentation.

documentado adj. documentary, proved by or based on documents.

documental adj. m. + f. (pl. **-ais**) documental, documentary, derived from documents.

documentar v. 1. to document, prove, bring evidence. 2. to provide with documents, furnish with proofs. 3. ~-**se** to prove one's identity.

documentário s. m. set of documents, dossier. ‖ adj. documentary.
    filme ~ documentary film.

documentativo adj. documental, documentary.

documentável adj. m. + f. (pl. **-áveis**) provable, demonstrable.

documento s. m. 1. document, muniment, deed, writ, act; paper, record, voucher; bill. 2. ~**s** pl. dossier. ~ **de carga** bill of lading. ~ **de embarque** shipping document. ~ **falso** pseudograph. ~ **histórico** historical document. ~ **legal** act and deed. **autenticar um** ~, **legalizar um** ~ to legalize a document. **contestar a validade de um** ~ to contest the validity of a document. **entregar os** ~**s** to deliver the documents. **juntar os** ~**s** to attach documents. **pagamento contra** ~**s** cash on delivery. **registro de** ~**s** registration of documents. **tamanho não é** ~ men are not to be measured by inches. **verificar um** ~ to check a bill.

doçura s. f. 1. sweetness, sugariness, honey. 2. softness, gentleness, mildness, smoothness, meekness. 3. delight, pleasure, comfort.
    falar com ~ to speak courteously.

dodecaédrico adj. (geom.) dodecahedral: having the form of a solid of twelve faces.

dodecaedro s. m. (geom.) dodecahedron: solid having twelve faces.

dodecágino adj. (bot.) dodecagynous, dodecagynal, having twelve styles or pistils.

dodecafonismo s. m. (mús.) dodecaphonism.

dodecagonal adj. m. + f. (pl. **-ais**) dodecagonal: having twelve sides and twelve angles.

dodecágono s. m. dodecagon: a polygon having twelve sides and twelve angles.

dodecandria s. f. dodecandria: a class of plants having twelve stamens.

dodecandro adj. (bot.) dodecandrian, dodecandrous.

dodecapétalo adj. (bot.) dodecapetalous, having twelve petals.

dodecassílabo s. m. dodecasyllable, a word of twelve syllables. ‖ adj. dodecasyllabic, having twelve syllables.

dodói s. m. (Braz., pop.) woe, pain. ‖ adj. sick, ill.

doença s. f. disease, illness, sickness, affection, ailment, malady, complaint; distemper, infirmity, indisposition.
    ~ **de Basedow** Basedow's disease. ~ **contagiosa** contagious disease, contagion. ~ **estacionária** stationary disease. ~ **do fígado** hepatic disease. ~ **da garganta** disease of the throat. ~ **hereditária** hereditary disease. ~ **incurável** incurable disease. ~ **latente** latent disease. ~ **mortal** fatal illness. ~ **dos olhos** eye disease. ~ **orgânica** organic disease. ~ **de pele** skin disease. ~ **profissional** occupational disease. ~ **rebelde** a protracted illness. ~ **renal** renal disease. ~ **de São Vito** chorea. ~ **do sono** sleeping sickness. ~ **simulada** feigned disease. ~ **tropical** tropical disease. **a** ~ **inutilizou-o para o trabalho** illness incapacitated him for work. **a** ~ **progrediu rapidamente** the disease made rapid progress. **alegar** ~ to allege illness. **apanhar uma** ~ to catch a disease. **as apoquentações e a** ~ **envelhecem-nos** worry and illness age a man. **combater uma** ~ to fight a disease. **convalescer de uma** ~ **grave** to convalesce from a serious illness. **curar uma** ~ to cure a disease. **especialista em** ~**s mentais** mental specialist. **foco de** ~ focus of disease. **licença por** ~ sick-leave. **livrar-se de uma** ~ to turn the corner in an illness. **a pobreza é preferível à** ~ poverty is preferable to ill health. **propagação de** ~**s** spread or propagation of disease. **recair gravemente de uma** ~ to have a serious relapse in an illness. **ser afeito a** ~**s** to

be prone to illness. **sofrer de uma ~ grave** to suffer from a serious illness.

doença-do-mundo s. f. (pl. **doenças-do-mundo**) venereal disease.

doençaria s. f. a lot of diseases.

doença-ruim s. f. (pl. **doenças-ruins**) (Braz., pop.) tuberculosis, consumption.

doente s. m. + f. patient, invalid, sick person. ‖ adj. sick, deseased, ill, ailing, invalid; distempered, indisposed, unwell.
~ **convalescente** convalescent patient. ~ **mental** a mental patient. **o ~ piorou esta manhã** the patient is worse this morning. **o ~ teve uma recaída grave** the patient has had a serious relapse. **dar parte de ~** to report sick. **ela está muito ~** she is very bad, she is seriously ill. **estar ~ do estômago** to be stomach-sick. **ficar ~** to be taken ill. **fico ~ em pensar nisto** it makes me sick to think of it. **fingir-se ~** to sham illness, pretend to be ill. **leito de ~** sick-bed. **mortalmente ~** sick to death. **muito ~** dog-sick. **passou a crise e agora o ~ está salvo** the crisis is over and the patient is now safe. **quarto de ~** sickroom. **sentiu-se ~** he felt run down. **ter aspecto de ~** to look ill. **tratar de um ~** to nurse a patient. **velar um ~** to sit up with a sick person.

doentio adj. sickly, unhealthy, unwholesome; weak, feeble, peakish, morbid.

doer v. 1. to ache, cause pain, ail, hurt. 2. to be sorry for, feel distressed, worry. 3. **~-se:** a) to pity, take pity. b) to complain.
~ **a alguém os dentes** to have the tooth-ache. **dói-me tudo** I am aching all over. ~ **o cabelo a alguém** to smell a rat, distrust s. th. **dói muito?** does it ache much? **faz-me ~ o coração** it wrings my heart.

doestador s. m. injurer, affronter. ‖ adj. injuring, infamous, opprobrious, offensive.

doestar v. to injure, insult, affront, offend, reproach, blame, revile.

doesto s. m. injury, affront, offence, insult, blame; vituperation.

dogal adj. m. + f. (pl. **-ais**) pertaining to a doge.

doge s. m. doge, the title of the chief magistrate of the former republics of Venice and Genoa.

dogma s. m. dogma, principle, maxim, tenet; doctrine.

dogmático adj. dogmatic(al), pragmatic, pronunciative, doctrinal, positive, dictatorial. ‖ **dogmaticamente** adv. dogmatically.
tom ~ dogmatical tone, peremptoriness.

dogmatismo s. m. dogmatism, pragmatism; authoritative assertion of opinion.

dogmatista s. m. + f. dogmatist. ‖ adj. dogmatic; authoritative, positive; arrogant.

dogmatizador s. m., **dogmatizante** m. + f. dogmatizer, dogmatist; arrogant asserter, authoritative teacher. ‖ adj. dogmatizing.

dogmatizar v. to dogmatize: 1. make dogmatic assertions, assert; set down as a dogma. 2. treat dogmatically, speak authoritatively; assert with arrogance.

dogre s. m. Dutch dogger, dogger boat.

dogue s. m. pug(dog).

doida s. f. (also **douda**) (vet.) a disease of sheep. ‖ adj. f. of **doido**.

doidaria s. f. (also **doudaria**) 1. a lot of insane persons. 2. madness, silliness, foolishness, nonsense, crazyness.

doidarrão s. m. (pl. **-ões**) (also **doudarrão**) fool, idiot, blockhead, madman. ‖ adj. mad, foolish, insane, extravagant.

doidejante adj. m. + f. (also **doudejante**) playing the fool, acting crazily.

doidejar v. (also **doudejar**) 1. to fool, play the fool. 2. to romp, play boisterously. 3. to trifle, dally, jest.

doidejo s. m. (also **doudejo**) act of playing the fool.

doidelo s. m. (Braz., also **doudelo**) crack-brained person, muddle-headed fellow, windbag.

doidice s. f. (also **doudice, doideira**) madness, foolishness, silliness, sottishness, craziness; stupidity, excess, extravagance.

doidivanas s. m. + f., sg. + pl. (pop. also **doudivanas**) madcap, fool, mug, windbag.

doido s. m. (also **doudo**) madman, fool, muddle-head person. ‖ adj. 1. mad, crazy, insane, out of one's mind. 2. foolish. 3. wanton, enthusiastic, merry. 4. impassioned. ‖ **-amente** adv. madly.
andar ~ em alguma coisa to dote upon, be infatuated with. **completamente ~** starring mad. **ele é ~ por dançar** he is crazy about dancing. **ele está ~** he has a worm. **nascer ~** to be born a fool. **ser ~ varrido** to be as mad as a March hare, be a downright fool. **você está completamente ~ por sua mulher** you are completely wrapped in your wife.

doído adj. aching, painful; troubled, aggrieved, hurt.

dois s. m. 1. (the number) two. 2. (cards) two-spot, deuce. ‖ num. two.
a ~ two and two, in twos, by pairs. **os ~** both. **~ é bom, três é demais** two's company, three's none. **carro de ~ lugares** a two-seater. **de ~ em ~ dias** every two days, on each alternate day. **jogar com pau de ~ bicos** to hunt with the hounds and run with the hare. **espada de ~ gumes** two-edged sword. **espingarda de ~ canos** double-barrelled gun. **jantar de ~ pratos** two course dinner. **não cabem ~ galos num poleiro** there is no room for more than one at the top. **não cabem ~ proveitos no mesmo saco** you cannot eat your cake and have it. **qualquer dos ~** one or other of the two. **tão certo como ~ e ~ são quatro** as sure as eggs are eggs. **um homem prevenido vale por ~** forewarned is forearmed.

dois-amigos, dois-irmãos s. m., sg. + pl. slipper plant, bird cactus.

dois-de-paus s. m. (Braz.) a person of no importance, a nobody.

dólar s. m. (pl. **dólares**) dollar; (sl.) buck.

dolência s. f. melancholy, dejection, depression; sorrow, dolour, distress, grieve; lamentation.

dolente adj. m. + f. sorrowful, painful, doleful, lamentable; plaintive, grieved.

dolerite s. m. (min.) dolerite, a basaltic greenstone.

dolero adj. (N. Braz., pop.) beautiful, handsome, elegant.

dolicocefalia s. f. dolichoephalism, dolichocephaly.

dolicocéfalo adj. dolichocephalous, long-headed.
raça -a dolichocephalous race.

dolicópode adj. m. + f. (zool.) dolichopodous, having long feet.

doliolídeos s. m. pl. (zool.) Doliolidae.

dólmã s. m. jacket of the uniform of a hussar.

dólmen s. m. (pl. **dolmens**) dolmen, cromlech: a structure consisting of one large unhown stone, resting on two others.

dolo (I) s. m. 1. fraud, deceit, cheating, swindling, duplicity, trickery. 2. stratagem; craftiness.
~ **de guerra** stratagem of war. **por ~** fraudulently.

dolo (II) s. m. a kind of dagger used formerly in Spain.

dolomia, dolomita s. f. (min.) dolomite, a rock consisting of carbonate of calcium and magnesium.

dolorido adj. 1. dolorific(al), dolorous, painful, aching, sore. 2. sorrowful; bad, bitter. ‖ **-amente** adv. painfully.

dolorífico adj. dolorific(al).

doloroso adj. 1. dolorous, aching, sore. 2. cruel, bitter; doleful. 3. grievous, distressing, harrowing, poignant. ‖ -amente adv. painfully, grievously.
é um caso ~ it is a painful case. ele nunca se esqueceu daquele ~ incidente he has never forgotten that painful incident. uma história -a a tale of woe.

doloso adj. fraudulent, deceitful, knavish, crafty, crooked. ‖ -amente adv. fraudulently.

dom s. m. (pl. dons) 1. gift, present, donation. 2. readiness, talent, qualification, ability, dowry, endowment, accomplishment. 3. Dom Don, Dom, a honorific title.
~ de falar bem, ~ da palavra gift of speech or eloquence. ~ de profecia gift of divination. ~ da natureza a natural gift. Dom Pedro, primeiro imperador do Brasil Dom Pedro, first emperor of Brazil. Dom Bosco, fundador da ordem salesiana Dom Bosco, founder of the order of the Salesians.

doma s. f. taming, breaking (of a horse).

domação s. f. (pl. -ões) break-in.

domado adj. 1. tamed, broken, domesticated. 2. submissive.

domador s. m. 1. tamer, horse-breaker. 2. subduer; vanquisher. ‖ adj. 1. taming. 2. vanquishing.

domar v. 1. to tame, domesticate, break in (horses). 2. to vanquish, overcome, subdue. 3. to check, control. 4. ~-se to control o. s., refrain o. s.

domável adj. m. + f. (pl. -áveis) tamable, that can be tamed; domesticable.

dom-bernardo s. m. (Braz.) plant of the family Rubiaceae.

domesticação s. f. (pl. -ões) domestication, break-in, taming.

domesticado adj. broken, tamed, domesticated.

domesticador s. m. tamer, breaker, subduer. ‖ adj. taming, breaking, domesticating.

domesticar v. 1. to domesticate, tame, break in. 2. (fig.) to civilize. 3. ~-se: a) to be tamed. b) to become civilized.

domesticável adj. m. + f. (pl. -áveis) domesticable, reclaimable, tamable.

domesticidade s. f. domestication; domesticity, homeliness, familiarity.

doméstico s. m. domestic, servant. ‖ adj. domestic: 1. familiar, private. 2. internal, not foreign. 3. tame, broken. 4. home-made, household.
água para gastos ~s water for domestic use. acessórios de instalações -as accessories for domestic fittings. assuntos ~s household affairs. empregada -a domestic servant. fazer serviço ~ to keep house. orçamento ~ family budget.

domiciliar v. 1. to domiciliate, domicile, establish in a place, settle down. 2. ~-se to settle o. s. in a place, fix one's abode. ‖ adj. m. + f. = domiciliário.

domiciliário adj. domiciliary, relating to a domicile.

domicílio s. m. domicile, dwelling, abode, residence, house, home, habitation.
~ legal legal domicile. entrega a ~ home delivery.

dominação s. f. (pl. -ões) 1. domination, dominance, dominancy, command, rule, control, authority, sovereignty. 2. -ões pl. dominations, an order of angels.

dominado adj. dominated, governed.
~ pela mulher wife-ridden. ~ pelo medo terror-stricken.

dominador s. m. dominator, ruler, subduer, vanquisher. ‖ adj. dominating, dominative, ruling, overbearing, magisterial.

dominância s. f. (Braz.) domination, dominance.

dominante s. f. 1. dominant: a) the reciting tone in the scale. b) the fifth tone in the scale. 2. m. + f. dominator, ruler. ‖ adj. m. + f. dominant, governing, predominant, commanding, overmastering, overbearing, ascendant, authoritative, dictatorial. ‖ ~mente adv. dominantly.
o princípio ~ the governing principle. uma vista ~ a commanding view.

dominar v. 1. to dominate: a) rule, be lord, command, reign. b) control, govern, sway. c) predominate, prevail. d) overbear, overcome, triumph, vanquish, conquer. 2. ~-se to control o. s., refrain o. s.
~ as dificuldades to master the difficulties. ~ sobre to have the rule over. dominamos a situação the matter is well in hand. ele domina he sways the sceptre. o castelo domina a cidade the castle overlooks the town.

dominável adj. m. + f. (pl. -áveis) vanquishable, restrainable, controllable.

dominga s. f. sunday, especially of advent, lent.

domingo s. m. Sunday, Lord's day.
~ após a Páscoa, Pascoela Low Sunday. ~ de Espírito Santo Whitsunday. ~ de Lázaro Passion Sunday. ~ da Páscoa Easter Sunday. ~ de Ramos Palm Sunday. ~ de Rosas Rose Sunday. aos ~s on Sundays. no ~ on Sunday.

domingueiro adj. of or pertaining to the Sunday.
roupa -a best Sunday clothes, Sunday best.

dominguinha s. f. (Braz.) plant of the nightshade family.

dominial adj. m. + f. (pl. -ais) dominial, relating to domains.

dominical adj. m. + f. (pl. -ais) dominical, relating to Sunday or the Lord's Day.
escola ~ Sunday school. oração ~ the Lord's prayer.

dominicano s. m. Dominican: 1. an order of mendicant friars, founded by Domingo de Guzmán. 2. native or inhabitant of the Dominican Republic. ‖ adj. Dominican: 1. relating to the order of Dominicans. 2. relating to the Dominican Republic.

dominico s. m. Dominican monk or friar.

domínio s. m. dominion: 1. rule, sovereignty, lordship, authority. 2. power, domination, territory, domain, region, estate. 3. patrimony, crownlands. 4. field of action.
~ de si próprio self-command, self-control. ~ público public property. ~s ultramarinos overseas dominions. ~ vinculado fee tail. estar sob o ~ de to be under the lash of. exercer ~ sobre alguém to exercise an influence upon a person. ele perdeu o ~ sobre si he lost his balance. ter o ~ pleno de to hold in fee. todo o ~ da história the whole field of history.

dominó s. m. domino: 1. a masquerade dress. 2. the game.
jogar ~s to play at dominos.

dom-joão s. m. (pl. dom-jões) don-juan.

domo s. m. 1. dome, cathedral, church. 2. cupola.

dona s. f. 1. donna, lady, mistress. 2. proprietress, proprietrix. 3. a common title of respect prefixed to the Christian name of a woman. 4. (Braz.) woman, wife, spouse.
~-de-casa housewife, mistress of the house.

dona-branca s. f. (pl. donas-brancas) (Braz.) 1. fire-water, white rum. 2. frost.

donacídeos s. m. pl. (zool.) Donacidae.

donaire s. m. 1. grace, gracefulness, debonairness, elegance; comeliness. 2. good behaviour; amenity. 3. witticism.

donairear v. to speak or behave gracefully or elegantly; to have fine manners.

donairoso adj. debonair, graceful, pleasant, agreeable, gentle; facetious. ‖ -amente adv. debonairly.

donataria s. f. (Braz., hist.) jurisdiction of a province.
donatário s. m. 1. donee: a) person to whom a donation is made. b) (Braz., hist.) lord of a province. 2. proprietary. 3. appointee.
donativo s. m. (also but less used **donadio**) 1. gift, present, donation. 2. alms, dole. 3. contribution.
pede-se o favor de conceder um ~ your alms are requested.
donato s. m. lay brother.
donde contr. of prep. **de** and the adv. **onde** where, from where, whence, wherefrom.
~ se faz fogo, sai fumo no smoke without fire. **~ você vem?** where do you come from?
doninha s. f. 1. diminutive of **dona**. 2. (zool.) weasel, ferret. 3. (ichth.) dolphin, sea lamprey.
~ fedorenta (zool.) polecat.
dono s. m. 1. master. 2. keeper, holder. 3. owner, proprietor. 4. lord, landlord.
mudar de ~ to change hands. **~ da casa** 1. landlord. 2. head of the house. **~ de loja** storekeeper. **sem ~** unowned, unpossessed.
dono-de-serra s. m. (pl. **donos-de-serra**) (N. Braz.) owner of a diamond field.
donoso adj. 1. pleasant, pretty, agreeable, gracious, charming. 2. witty. 3. gentle, polite.
donzel s. m. (pl. **-éis**) esquire, shield-bearer, a young nobleman. ‖ adj. soft, docile, manageable.
donzela s. f. maid, maiden, damsel; virgin.
donzela-de-candeeiro s. f. (pl. **donzelas-de-candeeiro**) table or bench on which a night-light is placed.
donzelaria s. f. a train of damsels.
donzelice s. f. maidenhood, maidhood; virginity.
donzelinha s. f. 1. dim. of **donzela**. 2. dragon-fly.
donzelo s. m. virgin man, chaste man.
donzelona s. f. (pop.) old maid or spinster.
dopado adj. doped (horse).
dopar v. to dope (race horse).
doqueiro s. m. docker, a dock worker.
dor (I) s. f. 1. ache, pain, ail, suffering. 2. sorrow, grief, dolour, trouble, worry. 3. affliction. 4. misery, passion.
~ aguda severe pain. **~ de cabeça** headache. **~ de cotovelo, ~ de canela** (Braz., sl.) jealousy. **lombar** backache. **a ~ de dentes inchou-o** the toothache caused one side of his face to swell (up). **aliviar sua ~** to ease one's pain. **como suporta ele a ~?** how does he stand the pain? **com pena e ~** painfully, grievously. **em ~es do parto** in the throes. **esmagado pela ~** overwhelmed by grief. **estar com ~ de garganta** to have a sore throat. **gemer com ~** to groan with pain. **grito de ~** a scream of pain. **sofrer uma ~** to suffer pain. **suas feições contorciam-se com ~** his features twisted with pain. **trespassado pela ~** pierced with sorrow.
dor (II) s. m. a prayer of the Parsees.
dor-de-cotovelo s. f. (pl. **dores-de-cotovelo**) (Braz.) jealousy, resentment or suffering caused by love.
dor-d'olhos s. f. (pl. **dores-d'olhos**) (Braz., pop.) any disease of the eyes.
dórico s. m. the Doric dialect. ‖ adj. Dorian, Doric.
ordem -a Doric order.
dorido adj. 1. aching, painful. 2. sad, depressed, dejected. 3. sorry, afflicted, grieved. 4. compassionate. ‖ **-amente** adv. painfully.
dorilíneos s. m. pl. (zool.) Dorylinae.
dórios s. m. pl. Dorians, natives or inhabitants of Doris in ancient Greece.
dorme-dorme s. m. (pl. **dorme-dormes, dormes-dormes**) (S. Braz.) sleepy person, sleepyhead.
dorme-maria s. f. (pl. **dorme-marias**) (Braz., bot., also **dormideira**) 1. drowsiness, dormancy. 2. (bot.) opium poppy.

dormência s. f. (Braz.) dormancy, quiescence, torpidity.
dormente s. m. 1. railway sleeper (plates E 13, V 4). 2. (archit.) beam, girder. 3. (naut.) clamp of the deck beams. ‖ adj. m. + f. 1. dormant, sleeping. 2. benumbed, stiff, torpid. 3. quiescent, inactive. 4. (N. Braz.) insensible, cold-blooded; indifferent.
dormião s. m. (pl. **-ões**) (Braz., ornith.) puffbird.
dormida s. f. 1. lodging for the night. 2. sleep; time of sleep. 3. sleeping place of animals.
dormideira s. f. 1. somnolence. 2. (bot.) opium poppy.
dormido adj. stale (bread).
tive uma noite bem -a I had a good night rest.
dormidor s. m. 1. sleeper. 2. sleephead. ‖ adj. fond of sleeping; drowsy; dull.
dorminhar v. (N. Braz.) 1. = **dormitar, dormir**. 2. to be disinterested, pay no attention to.
dorminhoco s. m. 1. lie-a-bed, sleepyhead. 2. (ornith.) black-crowned night heron. ‖ adj. given to sleep much; sleepy, drowsy, somnolent, slumberous.
dormir s. m. sleep, slumber. ‖ v. 1. to sleep, slumber, fall asleep. 2. to repose, lie, rest. 3. to be quiet, calm. 4. to neglect, lie dormant (matter). 5. to be dead.
~ ao relento to sleep in the open air. **~ com os olhos abertos** to sleep like a hare. **~ como uma pedra** to sleep like a log. **~ em pé** to sleep standing, not to be able to keep one's eyes open. **~ fora de casa** to sleep out, lie out, lie abroad. **~ no chão nu** to lie upon the ground, sleep on the bare earth. **~ o sono do justo, ~ tranqüilamente** to sleep the sleep of the just. **~ o caso** to sleep on the matter, take council with one's pillow. **~ sobre os louros** to rest on one's laurels. **~ a sesta, tirar uma soneca** to take a nap. **~ um bom sono** to have a very good sleep. **cria fama e deita-te a ~** rest on your laurels. **estar com vontade de ~** to feel quite drowsy, feel sleepy. **fingir que dorme** to feign to be asleep. **não ~** (fig.) to be very alert or active. **não fazer nada senão comer e ~** to do nothing but eat and sleep. **passei uma hora dormindo** I slumbered away an hour. **vá ~** go to roost!
dormitar v. to slumber, doze, nod, sleep lightly, drowse, nap.
dormitivo adj. dormitive, somniferous, causing sleep.
dormitoreiro s. m. (S. Braz.) valet, porter of a sleeping-car.
dormitório s. m. 1. dormitory, bedroom, bedchamber (plate D 4). 2. the whole furniture for a bedroom (plate D 4). 3. sleeping place of animals, especially of birds.
carro ~ sleeping car (railway).
dorna s. f. vintage tub, vat.
tempo de ~ vintage time.
dornacho s. m. a small vintage tub.
dorneira s. f. mill hopper, millstone.
dorônico s. m. (bot.) leopard's bane.
dorsal adj. m. + f. (pl. **-ais**) dorsal, pertaining to the back, posterior.
dores -ais pains in the back. **espinha ~** spine.
dorsífero adj. dorsiferous, dorsiparous.
dorsifixo adj. dorsifixed, attached dorsally.
dorsiventral adj. m. + f. (pl. **-ais**) (bot.) dorsiventral, bifacial.
dorso s. m. 1. (anat.) back, dorsum. 2. reverse.
~ do pé instep (plate C 18). **~ do cavalo** horseback (plate C 12).
dosagem s. f. (pl. **-ens**) (also **doseamento**) dosage, dosing, proportion; mixture.
dosar v. (also **dosear**) to dose, portion, administer in doses, give doses to.
~ insuficientemente to underdose.

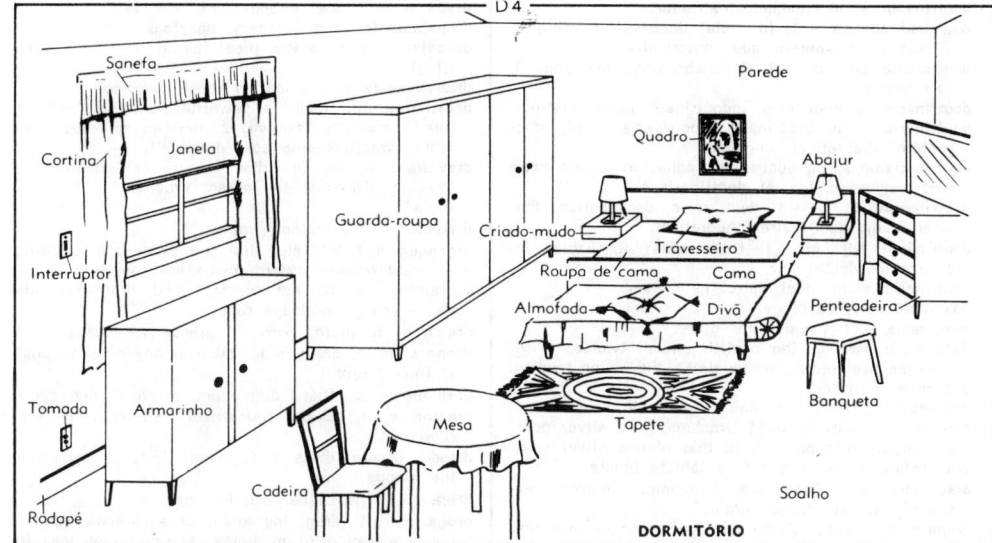

Sanefa · Parede · Cortina · Janela · Quadro · Abajur · Guarda-roupa · Criado-mudo · Travesseiro · Interruptor · Roupa de cama · Cama · Almofada · Divã · Penteadeira · Tomada · Armarinho · Mesa · Tapete · Banqueta · Cadeira · Soalho · Rodapé

DORMITÓRIO

dose s. f. dose, quantity, proportion.
a ~ produziu efeito instantâneo the dose produced an instantaneous effect. **dar ~ insuficiente** to underdose. **exagerar na ~** to overdose.
dosificar v. 1. to divide into doses. 2. to reduce to doses.
dosimetria s. f. dosimetry, dosology, the science of apportioning medicines in doses.
dosimétrico adj. dosimetric.
dosímetro s. m. dosimeter, drop meter.
dossel s. m. (pl. **-éis**) dossal, dossel, canopy, tester. **cobrir com ~** to canopy.
dossiê s. m. dossier, minutes of a case.
dotação s. f. (pl. **-ões**) 1. dotation, endowment, foundation. 2. patrimony (church). 3. appanage.
dotado adj. endowed with, gifted, portioned; talented.
dotador s. m. person who endows, endower.
dotal adj. m. + f. (pl. **-ais**), **dotalício** m. dotal, pertaining to a dower or dowry.
dotar v. 1. to dot, endow, dower. 2. to give a dowry, present.
~ uma igreja to endow a church. **dotado de excelentes qualidades** endowed with excellent qualities.
dote s. m. 1. dot, dotal gift, dowry, fortune, marriage portion. 2. dower, talent, natural gift, mental quality.
douração s. m. (pl. **-ões**) 1. gilding. 2. gold lettering.
dourada s. f. (Braz., ichth.) (also **doirada**) dory, gilthead.
douradão s. m. (pl. **-ões**) (also **doiradão**) a kind of card game.
douradinha s. f. (also **doiradinha**) 1. (bot.): a) bitter blain. b) golden shrub. c) lady-fern, wall-fern. d) polypody, adder's foot. 2. a kind of card game. 3. the queen of diamonds in this game. 4. (ornith.) golden plover. 5. (sl.) a gold coin.
dourado s. m. (also **doirado**) (ichth.) dorado, dolphin. ‖ adj. golden, gilt, gilded.
cavaleiros de espora -a the knights of the golden spur. **escaravelho ~** rose-chafer. **espigas -as** (poet.) the golden ears of corn. **idade -a** the golden age. **parcialmente ~** parcel-gilt. **prata -a** gilded silver, silver gilt.
dourador s. m. (also **doirador**) gilder.

douradura s. f. (also **doiradura**) 1. gold leaf. 2. gold laid on a surface. 3. gilt object. 4. gilding, the art of gilding.
douramento s. m. (also **doiramento**) gilding.
dourar v. (also **doirar**) 1. to gild, gild over, cover with a thin gold layer. 2. to embellish, adorn, brighten.
~ a pílula to gild a pill.
douto adj. learned, erudite; well-informed, well-instructed. ‖ **-amente** adv. learnedly.
doutor s. m. 1. doctor, holder of the highest degree of a faculty or university. 2. lawyer. 3. physician. 4. learned man, well-instructed person.
~ da Igreja Doctor of the Church. **~ em Lei** Doctor of Law. **~ in honoris causa** doctor honoris causa. **capelo de ~** Doctor's cap. **grau de ~** degree of doctor.
doutora (ô) s. f. 1. lady doctor, doctoress. 2. (fam.) bluestocking.
doutoraço s. m. 1. augm. of **doutor**. 2. (fig.) ridiculous wiseacre.
doutorado s. m. doctorate, doctorship, the degree of doctor.
doutoral adj. m. + f. (pl. **-ais**) doctoral, relating to the degree or profession of a doctor.
doutoramento s. m. graduation.
doutorando s. m. candidate for a doctor's degree, inceptor.
doutorar v. 1. to doctorate, graduate, give the degree of a doctor. 2. **~-se** to graduate, receive a doctor's degree.
doutorice s. f. airs of a know-it-all.
doutrina s. f. doctrine: 1. principle or body of principles relating to religion, science or politics; formula, dogma, maxim, precept, tenet. 2. instruction, teaching, course of discipline.
~ cristã Christian doctrine. **~ falsa** unsound doctrine. **~ de Monroe** Monroe doctrine. **aceitação de uma ~** acceptance of a doctrine. **fazer ~ às crianças** to instruct children in the Christian faith. **propagar ~s** to propagate doctrines.
doutrinação s. f. (pl. **-ões**) (also **doutrinamento**) catechesis, indoctrination; instruction, teaching.
doutrinado adj. learned, instructed.

doutrinador s. m. teacher, instructor.
doutrinal adj. m. + f. (pl. **-ais**) doctrinal, relating to a doctrine. ‖ **~mente** adv. doctrinally.
doutrinante adj. m. + f. 1. instructing, teaching. 2. catechetical.
doutrinar v. to doctrinize, indoctrinate, teach, instruct.
doutrinário s. m. doctrinaire, doctrinarian. ‖ adj. doctrinaire, theoretical, doctrinal.
doutrinarismo s. m. doctrinism, adhesion to one-sided theories; principles of doctrinarians.
doutrinarista s. m. + f. doctrinaire, doctrinarian, theorist. ‖ adj. doctrinaire, theoretical.
doutrinável adj. m. + f. (pl. **-áveis**) teachable, instructable, docile.
doutrineiro s. m. doctrinaire, catechiser.
doxologia s. f. doxology.
doxomania s. f. passion for glory.
doze s. m. twelve; the twelfth. ‖ num. twelve.
~ vezes twelvefold, twelve times. **dia ~** the twelfth.
dozena s. f. dozen.
dracena s. f. (bot.) Dracaena, a genus of the Lilaceae.
dracma s. f. (Greek hist.) Drachma: 1. a silver coin. 2. weight corresponding to that of one silver coin.
dracocéfalo s. m. a genus of labiate plants.
draconiano adj. Draconian, Draconic, rigorous, extremely severe, harsh, cruel.
draga s. f. 1. drag, dredge, dredger, dredging machine (plate D 2). 2. excavator. 3. dumb barge.
~ a nora chain dredger. **~ seca** steam navy. **barco de ~** drag boat.
dragado adj. dredged.
dragador s. m. dredger: 1. person who works with a dredge. 2. vessel used in dredging. 3. dredging machine.
dragagem s. f. (pl. **-ens**) dredging.
dragão s. m. (pl. **-ões**) dragon: 1. a fabulous animal. 2. (zool.) a lizard of the genus Draco, flying dragon. 3. (ornith.) dragoon, a kind of carrier pigeon. 4. a violent person, spiteful woman. 5. (astr.) **Dragão**: the northern constellation Draco. 6. (mil.) dragoon, dragooner.
~ alado wyvern, flying dragon. **~ infernal** Devil, Satan.
dragão-fedorento s. m. (pl. **dragões-fedorentos**) (Braz., bot.) a species of monstera.
dragar v. to drag, dredge, remove sand or mud from the bottom of a river or canal.
dragoeiro s. m. dragon tree.
dragomano s. m. dragoman, interpreter.
dragona s. f. shoulder strap, epaulet(te).
dragonete s. m. (her.) dragon's head.
dragontéia s. f. (bot., also **serpentária**) serpentine stone.
dragontino adj. of a dragon.
draino s. m. = **dreno**.
drama s. m. drama: 1. (theat.) a play, tragedy. 2. dramatic literature. 3. catastrophe, terrible event.
dramalhão s. m. (pl. **-ões**) melodrama.
dramaticidade s. f. (Braz.) dramatic nature, dramatization.
dramático adj. dramatic, represented by action; tragic(al).
autor ~ playwright. **poesia -a** dramatic poetry.
dramatização s. f. (pl. **--es**) dramatization, dramatizing, dramatic construction, dramatic representation.
dramatizar v. to dramatize: 1. make a drama of, put in a dramatic form. 2. express dramatically.
dramatologia s. f. (also **dramaturgia**) dramaturgy: 1. dramatic art. 2. theatrical representation.
dramatológico adj. dramaturgic, theatrical, stagy.
dramaturgo s. m. (also **dramatista** m. + f.) dramaturge, dramaturgist, playwright, author of a dramatic composition, dramatist.

drapê s. m. drape, arrangement in folds.
drapejamento s. m. drapery, hangings.
drapejar v. 1. to drape, pleat (cloth). 2. to fly, wave (flag).
drapetomania s. f. a loafing about, vagrancy.
drástico s. m. (med.) a powerful purgative. ‖ adj. 1. (med.) strongly laxative. 2. drastic, powerful, violent. ‖ **drasticamente** adv. drastically.
dravidiano s. m. Dravidian, native or inhabitant of Dravida, (Dravira) an ancient province of Southern India.
drenador s. m. drainer, ditcher.
drenagem s. f. (pl. **-ens**) drainage, process of draining. **~ subterrânea** underdrainage. **~ superficial** top draining. **~ de um terreno** land drainage. **tubo de ~** (surg.) drainage tube.
drenar v. to drain, draw off gradually, exhaust.
dreno s. m. 1. drain (pipe, ditch or any other means). 2. (med.) tent.
drepânio s. m. (bot.) drepanium, sickle-shaped cyme.
dresina s. f. (Braz.) four-wheel self-propelled railroad car.
dríade, dríada, drias s. f. dryad, deity or nymph of the woods.
driça s. f. (naut.) halyard, halliard.
droga s. f. 1. drug, ingredient or substance used in the preparation of medicine. 2. thing that lost its value, thrash, junk. 3. unsalable commodity. 4. m. (Braz., pop.) devil.
isto é uma ~ this is not worth a pin, it is a drug.
drogaria s. f. 1. drugstore, pharmacy, chemist's shop. 2. trash, rubbish, junk.
drogomano s. m. (also **dragomano**) dragoman, interpreter.
droguete s. m. drugget, linsey-woolsey.
~ lavrado figured duroy. **~ liso** plain duroy.
droguista s. m. + f. druggist, chemist, apothecary.
dromedário s. m. (zool.) dromedary, Arabian camel, bred and used especially for riding.
dromomania s. f. (path.) dromomania.
drope s. m. drop (candy).
drósera s. f. drosera: an order of polypetalous insectivorous herbs.
droseráceas s. f. pl. (bot.) Droseraceae.
drosometria s. f. drosometry.
drosômetro s. m. drosometer.
druida s. m. druid, priest among the ancient Celts of Gaul, Britain and Ireland.
druidesa s. f. druidess.
druídico adj. druidic(al), of or pertaining to the druids.
druidismo s. m. druidism, the religion of the druids.
drupa s. f. drupe, a stone-fruit (as a cherry, apricot, peach).
drupáceo adj. drupaceous, relating to or resembling a drupe.
drupéola s. f. a little drupe, drupelet, drupel, drupeole.
drupeolado adj. drupaceous, relating to drupel or drupelet.
drusa s. f. (min.) druse, aeode, a rock cavity covered with minute crystals.
drusiforme adj. m. + f. (min.) drusy, covered with minute crystals.
dual s. m. (gram.) dual, the number relating to two, the dula number. ‖ adj. m. + f. dual, double, twofold, binary, dualistic.
dualidade s. f. duality, twoness, twofold division, twofold character.
dualismo s. m. dualism, division into two, doctrine of two eternal principles (one good and the other evil).

dualista s. m. + f. dualist, an adherent of the dualistic doctrine, opponent of monism. ‖ adj. dualistic, pertaining to dualism.

dualístico adj. dualistic.

dualizador s. m. dualist.

duas s. f. two (f. form of **dois**). ‖ num. two, twain. **~ partes iguais** two equal parts. **~ vezes** twice. **~ vezes por ano** twice a year, half-yearly. **chave de ~ bocas** double-ended spanner. **com ~ pedras na mão** ready to start a fight. **de ~ em ~ horas** bihourly. **de ~ uma** one of two things. **em ~ colunas** in double columns. **impressão em ~ cores** two-colour printing. **pano de ~ faces** reversible cloth. **parecidos como ~ gotas d'água** as like as two peas. **pense ~ vezes antes de fazer isto** think twice before you do that. **pessoa de ~ caras** double-faced person.

dubá s. m. (Braz., pop.) devil.

dubiedade s. f. dubiety, doubtfulness, dubiousness, uncertainty; fishiness.

dúbio adj. dubious, doubting, hesitant, uncertain, vague, ambiguous; suspicious, skeptical. ‖ **dubiamente** adv. dubiously.

dubitação s. f. (pl. **-ões**) dubitation, doubt, hesitation, skepticism.

dubitativo adj. dubitative, doubting. ‖ **-amente** adv. dubitatively.

dubitável adj. m. + f. (pl. **-áveis**) dubitable, doubful, uncertain, skeptic, questionable.

dublagem s. f. (cin.) doubling.

duboisina s. f. duboisine: alkaloid obtained from the Duboisia shrub.

ducado (I) s. m. dukedom: 1. the jurisdiction or territory of a duke. 2. the rank of a duke.

ducado (II) s. m. ducat, a gold coin of varying form and value, formerly used in various countries.

ducal adj. m. + f. (pl. **-ais**) ducal, pertaining to a duke.

ducatão s. m. (pl. **-ões**) ducatoon, ancient Portuguese coin.

ducentésimo s. m. a two-hundredth. ‖ num. two-hundredth.

ducha s. f. 1. douche: a) a jet of water or vapor applied for medicinal purposes. b) an instrument for administering such a jet. 2. shower-bath. 3. (fig.) wet blanket; reprehension. 4. **~s** pl. bathhouse.

banho de ~ shower-bath.

duchal adj. m. + f. (pl. **-ais**) relating to douche.

duchar v. 1. to douche. 2. to take a shower-bath.

duchista s. m. + f. person who administers douches.

ducina s. f. cyma, molding with a wavelike profile.

dúctil adj. m. + f. (pl. **-eis**) ductile: 1. flexible, pliable, supple, soft, malleable. 2. tractable, complying.

ductilidade s. f. ductility: 1. tractility, ductileness, flexibility, malleability, distensibility. 2. compliance.

ducto s. m. (anat.) duct.

~ lacrimal tear-duct.

duelar (I) adj. m. + f. duel(l)ing, referring to a duel.

duelar (II) v. to duel: 1. to engage in a duel, fight a duel. 2. to overcome in a duel.

duelista s. m. + f. duel(l)er, duel(l)ist.

duelístico adj. duel(l)ing.

duelo s. m. duel, duello, encounter, single combat.

duende s. m. 1. dwarf, kobold, elf, imp, puck. 2. spirit, sprite, pixy, hobgoblin, boglin, spook, bogey.

duenha s. f. duenna, governess, chaperon of young girls in Spain.

duerno s. m. two sheets of printed paper laid one in the other.

duetista s. m. + f. duetist, duet singer.

dueto s. m. duet, duetto: 1. musical composition either for two voices or for two instruments. 2. (pop.) conversation between two persons.

dugão s. m. (pl. **-ões**), **dugongo** (zool.) dugong.

duidade s. f. twoness.

dulcamara s. f. (bot.) dulcamara, bitter-sweet, felonwort, woody nightshade.

dúlcido adj. sweet, soft.

dulcificação s. f. (pl. **-ões**) dulcification, sweetening.

dulcificado adj. 1. dulcified, sweetened, sweetish. 2. (fig.) calm, appeased.

dulcificante adj. m. + f. dulcifying, sweetening.

dulcificar v. to dulcify: 1. sweeten, render more agreeable to the taste. 2. (fig.) to alleviate, soften, mollify. 3. **~-se** to be appeased.

dulcífico adj. 1. dulcifying. 2. sweet.

dulcífluo adj. dulcifluous, flowing sweetly.

dulcíloquo adj. sweet-spoken.

dulcinéia s. f. Dulcinea, ladylove of Don Quixote; (pop.) sweetheart.

dulcíssono adj. sweet-sounding, melodious, harmonious.

dulçor s. m. 1. sweetness. 2. caress(es).

dulçoroso adj. 1. sweet, sugary. 2. gentle, mild, soft.

dulia s. f. (theol.) dulia: worship paid to saints and angels.

dum contraction of the prep. **de** and the art. **um** of a, from a, of one, from one.

os resultados ~ erro the consequences of a mistake.

duma contr. of the prep. **de** and the art. **uma** of a, from a, of one, from one.

~ vez at one stroke. **recuperei-me ~ doença** I recovered from a sickness.

duna s. f. dune, a hill of loose sand, heaped up by the wind, sand dune, sand hill; down (plate C 19).

dundu s. m. (Braz.) fresh-water catfish.

dundum s. f. dumdum bullet.

dunga s. m. (Braz.) 1. chief, boss; bully. 2. (cards) joker.

dunguinha s. m. (Braz.) childish fellow; insignificant person.

dunito s. m. (geol.) dunite.

dunquerque s. m. bracket, shelf.

duo s. m. duo, duet, duetto.

duodecimal adj. m. + f. (pl. **-ais**) duodecimal, reckoning by twelves.

duodécimo s. m. the twelfth. ‖ num. twelfth.

duodécuplo s. m. quantity or amount twelve times as large as another. ‖ num. duodecuple.

duodenal adj. m. + f. (pl. **-ais**) duodenal, relating to the duodenum.

úlcera ~ duodenal ulcer.

duodenário adj. duodenary, in sets of twelve.

escala -a duodenary scale.

duodenite s. f. (med.) duodenitis, inflammation of the duodenum.

duodeno s. m. (anat.) duodenum: the first portion of the small intestine, twelve-inch intestine.

dupla s. f. couple; two persons appearing or acting together.

dúplex, dúplice adj. duplex, double, twofold.

duplicação s. f. (pl. **-ões**) 1. duplication, doubling, duplicating. 2. repeating.

duplicado s. m. duplicate, copy, transcript. ‖ adj. duplicate, double, twofold.

duplicador s. m. 1. duplicator. 2. duplicating machine, machine for reproducing copies.

duplicante adj. m. + f. duplicating.

duplicar v. 1. to double, duplicate. 2. to copy. 3. to repeat. 4. **~-se** to become twice as much; be repeated.

duplicata s. f. 1. duplicate, counterpart, double, copy. 2. promissory note, bill.
duplicativo adj. duplicative, duplicating, doubling.
duplicatura s. f. duplicature, doubling, duplication.
duplicável adj. m. + f. (pl. **-áveis**) duplicable.
dúplice adj. m. + f. double, duplex, duplicated, twofold.
duplicidade s. f. 1. duplicity, doubleness. 2. double--dealing, deception.
duplo s. m. the double. ‖ num. double, duplex, twofold, twice as much, dual, duplicate. ‖ **-amente** adv. doubly.
~ **efeito** double acting. **adaptador** ~ double-nipple. **espoleta de** ~ **efeito** time and percussion fuse. **fundo** ~ double bottom. **manivela -a** double crank. **pneumonia -a** double pneumonia. **via -a** double line (railway).
duque (I) s. m. duke.
grão-~ grand duke.
duque (II) s. m. 1. (cards) deuce, two. 2. (N. Braz.) suit of clothes (of two pieces).
duquesa s. f. 1. duchess, wife of a duke, woman holding the sovereignty of a duchy. 2. a sort of cotton fabric.
dura s. f. duration, durability.
coisa de muita ~ resistant, lasting thing. **sol de pouca** ~ a flash in the pan.
durabilidade s. f. 1. durability, durableness, duration. 2. lastingness, enduringness, wear.
duração s. f. 1. duration, run, continuance, length of time, term. 2. endurance, lastingness.
~ **de um contrato** duration of a contract. **de curta** ~ of short duration.
duradouro adj. (also **duradoiro**) 1. lasting. 2. durable, enduring. ‖ **-amente** adv. durably; lastingly.
dural s. m. abb. of **duralumínio** Duralumin.
dura-máter s. f. (anat.) dura mater, the outermost membrane of the brain and the spinal cord.
durame, durâmen s. m. (pl. **duramens, durâmenes**) duramen, core: the central wood or heartwood of a tree.
durante prep. during, while, in the time of, in the course of, for, by.
~ **a noite** during the night. ~ **a próxima semana** over the next week. ~ **a vida** in life, as long as one lives. ~ **minha estada** during my stay. ~ **algum tempo** for some time. ~ **horas** for hours. ~ **muitos séculos** for ages. ~ **o seu sono** in his sleep. ~ **o vôo** on the flight. ~ **todo o ano** throughout the year. **ele afogou-se** ~ **o banho** he drowned while bathing. **esperam-se revelações espantosas** ~ **o julgamento** amazing revelations are expected during the trial. **fui seu hóspede** ~ **três semanas** I was his guest for three weeks. **perdi-o de vista** ~ **muitos anos** I have lost sight of him for many years.
durão s. m. (pl. **-ões**) (Braz., pop.) bully, ruffian.
duraque s. m. a sort of serge formerly used for shoemaking.
durar v. 1. to last, continue, remain, abide. 2. to be resistent, endure. 3. to wear well. 4. to live, stay.
~ **mais tempo que** to outwear. **isto durará muito** that will go far. **isto durará por muito tempo** it will go a long way. **como te curas, duras!** as one makes his bed, so one must lie in it! **não pode** ~ **para sempre** it cannot last for ever. **quanto tempo vai** ~**?** how long will it last?
durasnal s. m. (pl. **-ais**) (S. Braz.) uncared peach tree plantation.
durasno s. m. peach.
durável adj. m. + f. (pl. **-áveis**) durable, lasting, stable. ‖ **duravelmente** adv. durably.

durázio adj. 1. hard-shelled, hard, hard-grained. 2. (fig.) oldish, elderly.
mulher -a middle-aged woman.
dureza s. f. 1. hardness, quality or state of being hard. 2. consistency, compactness, solidity. 3. stiffness, toughness. 4. severity, insensibility, unkindliness. 5. harshness, rudeness, sharpness. 6. strength, firmness.
~ **de coração** hardheartedness. ~ **de estilo** roughness of style. **ele trata o homem com** ~ he is harp upon the man.
durião s. m. (pl. **-ões**) durian (tree).
durina s. f. (Braz.) a horse disease.
durindana s. f. 1. Roland's sword. 2. (by extension) any sword, dagger.
duro (I) s. m. Spanish silver coin.
duro (II) s. m. (N. Braz.) hard sandy bottom of a river. ‖ adj. 1. hard. 2. firm, solid, consistent, compact, dense. 3. strong, vigorous. 4. difficult, painful. 5. rude, rough. 6. cruel, inclement, hardhearted. 7. severe, unkind, insensible, unfeeling. ‖ **-mente** adv. hardly.
~ **como um calhau** as hard as flint. ~ **de boca** hard-mouthed (horse). ~ **de ouvido** hard of hearing, dunny. **água mole em pedra -a tanto bate até que fura!** constant dripping wears away the stone! **de casca -a** hard-shelled. **ele tem queixo** ~ he is as obstinate as a mule. **ferro** ~ chill casting. **homem** ~ **dos fechos** a man that is not easily persuaded. **pele -a** tough skin. **pez muito** ~ stone--pitch. **uma vida -a** a hard life. **um osso** ~ **de roer** a hard nut to crack. **tratamento** ~ unkind treatment.
duro-a-fogo s. m. 1. (N. Braz.) tobacco of inferior quality. 2. (fig.): a) tricky person, scalawag, crook. b) pachyderm.
duunvirado s. m. (also **duunvirato**) duumvirate, the union of two men in the same government or office.
duunviral adj. m. + f. (pl. **-ais**) duumviral, pertaining to a duumvirate.
duúnviro s. m. (Roman hist.) duumvir, one of the two persons of a joint government or public function.
dúvida s. f. 1. doubt. 2. dubiety, dubiousness. 3. incertainty, incertitude, quandary. 4. discredit, distrust, disbelief, suspicion. 5. scrouple, hesitation, irresolution, indecision.
é fora de ~ **que...** there is no question but... **ela sem** ~ **cumprirá sua promessa** she is sure to fulfill her promise. **estar em** ~ to hang, halt, be hazy about. **eu o creio sem** ~ I should rather think so. **fora de** ~ beyond doubt, without question, certainly. **não o deixei em** ~ **sobre minhas intenções** I left him in no doubt as to my intentions. **não há** ~ **alguma** there is no doubt about it, there is not the slightest doubt. **não tenha** ~ don't kid yourself. **pôr em** ~ to arraign, impeach. **qualquer** ~ **que tenha** whatever doubt you may have. **sem** ~ **alguma** undoubtedly. **sem** ~ I am sure of it, out of question. **surge uma** ~ a doubt arises. **tenho minhas** ~**s a respeito** I call it in question.
duvidador s. m. doubter, sceptic, person who doubts.
duvidança s. f. (obs.) doubt, incertitude.
duvidar v. to doubt: 1. to be uncertain. 2. disbelieve, discredit. 3. question. 4. suspect, distrust. 5. waver, hesitate.
duvida-se it is not certain. **duvido da sua competência para tal cargo** I doubt his competence for such a post. **duvido de sua coragem** I suspect his (her, your) courage. **duvido disso** I doubt it. **duvido que ele venha** I doubt that he will come. **não duvido** I dare say.

duvidoso adj. 1. dubious, doubtful, uncertain, questionable. 2. undecided, problematic, unsettled. 3. suspicious, ambiguous. ‖ **-amente** adv. doubtfully, dubiously.

caráter ~ a doubtful character. **deixar o certo pelo** ~ to grasp at the shadow and lose the substance. **freguês** ~ doubtful customer. **parece** ~ it looks a bit fishy. **procedência -a** doubtful origin. **promessa -a** doubtful promise, **uma coisa bastante -a** too doubtful a matter.

duzentos s. m. two hundred. ‖ num. two hundred. **de** ~ **anos** bicentennial.

dúzia s. f. 1. dozen (twelve). 2. (fig.) a lot (of things). ~ **de frade** baker's dozen, devil's dozen, printer's dozen (thirteen). **às** ~**s** by the dozen, by dozens. **cinqüenta cruzeiros a** ~ fifty cruzeiros a dozen. **falta uma** ~ there is a dozen short. **meia** ~ half a dozen. **por** ~ by the dozen.

dzeta s. m. zeta, the sixth letter of the Greek alphabet.

E

E, e s. m. 1. the fifth letter of the Portuguese alphabet. 2. (mus., obs.) mi. 3. abbr. for **Este**, east. ‖ conj. and.

~ **comercial** (&) ampersand. ~ **isto** ~ **aquilo** this and that. **bonito** ~ **quente (tempo)** nice and warm (weather).

ebâneo adj. ebony, ebon, like ebony, black.

ebanista s. m. + f. 1. ebonist, worker in ebony. 2. cabinet-maker, joiner. 3. wood carver.

ebanizar v. to ebonize: 1. stain in imitation of ebony, make ebonylike. 2. to stain black, tinge with the colour of ebony.

ébano s. m. ebony: 1. the tree (also ebon(y) tree). 2. the wood. 3. anything resembling ebony in colour, grain or texture.

ebenácea s. f. shrub or tree of the ebony family.

ebenáceo adj. (bot.) referring to the Ebenaceae.

ébia s. f. (Braz.) 1. foolishness, folly, stupidity. 2. mistake, error, blunder.

cair na ~ to blunder.

ebionitas s. m. pl. (eccl., hist.) ebionite: member of a gnostic sect.

ebó s. m. (also **ebô**) (Braz.) 1. sacrifice or oblation used in macumba. 2. a kind of food made of corn and "dendê" oil, to which sometimes a kind of toasted bean is added.

ebonite s. f. vulcanite, ebonite, hard rubber.

eborário s. m. ivory turner, ivory worker.

ebóreo adj. (poet. also **ebúrneo**) 1. eburnean, ivory. 2. eburneous. 3. ivory-coloured.

ebracteado adj. without bracts.

ebriático adj. (also **ebriativo**) intoxicating, intoxicant, intoxicative.

ebriedade, ebriez s. f. drunkenness, inebriation, intoxication, ebriety.

ebrifestivo adj. (also **ebrifestante** m. + f.) 1. tipsy, tight. 2. frolicsome, wanton, very jolly (under alcoholic influence).

ébrio (also **bêbedo, bêbado;** sl. **pau-d'água**) s. m. drunkard, toper, tippler. ‖ adj. drunk(en), intoxicated, inebriated.

todos se mostraram -s de alegria they all were drunken with joy.

ebrioso adj. 1. given to drink, dipsomaniacal, habitually intoxicated. 2. tipsy, drunk.

ebulição s. f. (pl. **-ões**) ebullition, ebullience: 1. effervescency, boiling. 2. (fig.) agitation, excitement. **temperatura de** ~ boiling heat. ~ **de sangue** boiling up of the blood.

ebuliente adj. ebullient, boiling.

ebuliômetro, ebulioscópio s. m. ebulliometer, ebullioscope.

ebulioscopia s. f. ebullioscopy: the determination of boiling-points.

ebulir v. to boil: 1. reach the boiling-point, effervesce. 2. be agitated.

ébulo s. m. (bot.) dwarf elder, Danewort.

eburnação s. f. (pl. **-ões**) (path.) eburnation: morbid change in bone, by which it becomes hard and dense, like ivory.

ebúrneo adj. 1. eburnean: of or like ivory. 2. ivory-coloured. 3. smooth like ivory.

ecar v. to communicate something aloud.

écbase s. f. (rhet.) digression in a discourse.

ecdise s. f. (biol.) ecdysis: shedding of an outer integument (insects, crustaceans), a molting.

ecdótica s. f. textual criticism.

ecfonema s. m. ecphonesis, rhetorical exclamation, sudden utterance expressive of strong feelings.

écfora s. f. (archit.) ecphora: the projection of any molding before the face of the molding next below it.

ecfrático adj. deobstructive, aperient.

echarpe s. f. scarf.

eclampsia s. f. (med.) eclampsia.

eclâmptico adj. (med.) eclamptic.

eclegma s. m. eclegma: a medicine of syrupy consistency.

eclesial adj. of or relating to the Church.

eclesiástico s. m. ecclesiastic: priest, clergyman, churchman. ‖ adj. ecclesiastic(al), clerical; canonical. ‖ **eclesiasticamente** adv. ecclesiastically.

eclético s. m. eclectic, philosopher. ‖ adj. eclectic.

ecletismo s. m. 1. eclecticism. 2. eclectic sect or doctrine.

eclipsar v. to eclipse: 1. (astr.) hide by intervention. 2. overshadow, surpass, outshine, outdo. 3. cover up. 4. obscure, obfuscate, darken. 5. ~-**se** hide, disappear (a heavenly body).

fazer ~ to cause to disappear. **Miguel Ângelo eclipsou todos os pintores** Michelangelo overshadowed all painters. **sua formosura parecia** ~ **a das outras** her beauty appeared to obscure that of the others.

eclipse s. m. 1. eclipse: a) (astr.) an interception of a heavenly body by the interposition of another heavenly body. b) (fig.) overshadowing, any state of obscuration. 2. (fig): a) occultation, disappearance. b) intellectual or moral obscuration.

~ **total** total eclipse. ~ **parcial** partial eclipse. ~ **do sol** eclipse of the sun. ~ **da lua** eclipse of the moon.

eclíptica s. f. (astr.) ecliptic, apparent orbit of the sun.

eclíptico adj. ecliptic(al): of or pertaining to eclipses or to the ecliptic.

eclodir v. to come to light, arise, appear.

écloga s. f. eclogue, a pastoral poem, bucolic.

eclosão s. f. (pl. **-ões**) 1. (zool.) eclosion: (hatching, emergence). 2. appearance. 3. development.

eclusa s. f. 1. canal lock, lockage. 2. floodgate. 3. dam.

eco s. m. 1. echo: a) reflection of sound, resonance. b) repetition, resound. c) person who repeats or imitates another. d) (mus.) soft repetition of a phrase. e) (Gr. myth.) Echo: a nymph. 2. reflection, repercussion. 3. (N. Braz.) a cry.

as sugestões dele não encontraram ~ his suggestions did not meet with response. **fazer-se** ~ **de** to repeat submissively what another says.

ecoar v. 1. to echo: a) reflect the sound of. b) resound, repeat. c) reverberate. d) emit an echo. 2. (fig.) become famous.

ecofonia s. f. (med.) a sound similar to an echo after a vocal sound in thoracic auscultation.

ecolalia s. f. (med.) echolalia: the senseless repetition of words.

ecologia s. f. (biol., sociol.) (o)ecology, bionomics: the study of the relations between organisms and their environment.

ecológico adj. (biol.) (o)ecologic(al), bionomic(al).

ecometria s. f. echometry: measurement of sounds and resonance.

ecômetro s. m. echometer.

economato s. m. stewardship: office or functions of a steward.

econometria s. f. econometrics.

economia s. f. 1. economy: a) husbandry. b) organization, regulation, method, system. c) private or public administration as management, government. d) thrift, frugality, frugalness, parsimony. 2. ~s pl. savings, economies; scrapings. ~ **dirigida** planned economy. ~ **doméstica** domestic economy. ~ **livre** private enterprise. ~ **política** economics, political economy. **ele faz** ~**s** he puts by. **ele tem algumas** ~**s** he has some money put by. **fazer** ~**s** to make savings, economize.

econômico adj. 1. economic(al): a) of, referring to or belonging to economy. b) thrifty, frugal. 2. saving. 3. unexpensive, cheap. || **-amente** adv. 1. economically. 2. savingly. 3. unexpensively. **ano** ~ financial year. **caixa -a** Savings Bank. **ciências -as** economics. **ele é econômico** he is economical. **funcionamento** ~ economical operation.

economista s. m. + f. economist.

economizar v. 1. to economize: a) husband, administer or manage economically. b) be frugal or economical. c) avoid waste. d) use or spend sparingly. 2. to accumulate, amass, hoard. 3. to economize, save. 4. to lay up. **ele economiza alguma coisa para o seu futuro** he keeps something for a rainy day. **ele economizou muito dinheiro** he saved a lot of money. **quem economiza em tempo, tem quando precisa** waste not want not.

ecônomo s. m. 1. burser, steward, manager; pantryman. 2. housekeeper.

ecosfera s. f. (geophys.) region in the atmosphere where no living beings exist.

ecossondador s. m. (naut.) echo sounder.

éctase s. f. (pros.) ectasis: lengthening of a short syllable.

ectasia s. f. (med.) ectasia: dilatation of a hollow organ or of a canal.

éctima s. m. ecthyma: a cutaneous eruption.

éctipo s. m. ectype, reproduction. 2. coin mould, die.

ectipografia s. f. ectypography: method of etching in relief.

ectlipse s. f. (gram.) ecthlipsis: elision or suppression of a final m.

ectocarpácea s. f. (bot.) alga of the family Ectocarpaceae.

ectoderma s. m. (zool.) ectoderm.

ectoparasito s. m. (zool.) ectoparasite: external parasite.

ectoplasma s. m. ectoplasm: 1. (spiritualism) emanation from a spiritualistic medium while in a trance. 2. (zool.) outer portion of the cytoplasm in the cell of a protozoan.

ectozoário s. m. ectozoon, external parasite.

ectrópio, ectrópion s. m. (med.) ectropion, ectropium: morbid eversion of the eyelids.

ecúleo s. m. 1. (hist.) rack: torturing instrument. 2. (fig.) torment, scourge, calamity.

ecumênico adj. (o)ecumenic(al): 1. general, universal. 2. belonging to the entire Christian Church. **concílio** ~ ecumenical or general council.

ecumenismo s. m. (rel.) ecumenism.

eczema s. m. 1. (med.) eczema. 2. (pop.) tetter.

eczematoso adj. eczematous: 1. afflicted with eczema. 2. having the nature of eczema.

edacidade s. f. edacity, voracity.

edáfico adj. edaphic.

edafologia s. f. edaphology, pedology: science of soils.

edaz adj. m. + f. edacious, voracious, ravenous, devouring, eating much.

edelvais s. m. (bot.) ~~edelweiss~~ (~~Leontopodium~~ alpinum).

edema s. m. (med.) ~~oedema, edema:~~ abnormal accumulation of serous fluid in the tissues of the body. ~ **maligno** carbuncle.

edemaciar v. to produce edemas.

edemático adj. (med.) edemic, (o)edematous: relating to (o)edema.

edematoso adj. (med.) (o)edematous: affected with (o)edema.

Éden s. m. Eden, paradise.

edênico adj. Edenic: of or pertaining to Eden, paradisiac(al).

edentado s. m. (zool.) edentate: 1. one of the Edentata. 2. toothless creature.

edeologia s. f. (med.) edeology, aedeoology: science of the organs of generation.

edeológico adj. (med.) edeologic: of or referring to edeology.

edeoscopia s. f. (med.) edeoscopy.

edição s. f. (pl. -ões) edition: 1. impression, publication (of a book, etc.). 2. total number of copies of a book, magazine, newspaper, etc. published together. ~ **abreviada** abridged edition. ~ **de bolso** pocket edition. ~ **matinal** morning edition. ~ **príncipe** first edition of a book. ~ **revista** revised edition. **a** ~ **esgotou-se** the edition is sold out. **a última** ~ the latest edition. **este livro teve quatro -ões** this book has gone through four editions.

edícula s. f. 1. little house. 2. niche. 3. oratory, little chapel.

edificação s. f. (pl. -ões) 1. erection, construction, edifying, building. 2. (fig.) edification, improvement, good example. 3. an edifice, a building. **dar** ~ to set good examples, to edify.

edificador s. m. 1. builder, constructor. 2. edifier. || adj. 1. edifying. 2. constructive.

edificante adj. m. + f. 1. edifying: a) building, constructing. b) constructive, setting a good example, instructive, moralizing. 2. (depr.) scandalous. **exemplo** ~ shining example.

edificar v. 1. to edify: a) construct, build, erect. b) found, institute. c) set good examples. d) instruct, enlighten. 2. ~**-se** to receive edifying impressions. **ele edificou na areia** he built on sand.

edificativo adj. edifying: 1. building, constructing. 2. instructing, instructive, uplifting, exemplary.

edifício s. m. 1. edifice, building, structure, construction. 2. house. ~ **sólido** substantial building. **alçado de um** ~ elevation of a building. **acesso ao** ~ access to the building. **fachada de um** ~ façade of a building.

edil s. m. (pl. **edis**) 1. (hist.) aedile, edile: Roman magistrate. 2. councilman, alderman.

edilidade s. f. 1. (hist.) aedility, edility. 2. edileship: the office of an edile or councilman. 3. town council.

editação s. f. (pl. -ões) edital, edition, publication.

edital s. m. (pl. -ais) 1. authenticated copy of an edict, proclamation. 2. poster, bill, placard. || adj. m. + f. edictal: relating to or announced by an edict. **citação** ~ (law) edictal citation, summons.

editar v. to edit, publish (a book, magazine, etc.).

editimo s. m. (Roman hist.) a temple guard.

édito s. m. 1. edict, proclamation. 2. ordinance, decree. 3. court order.

edito s. m. a decree, edict or the rule or law proclaimed.

editor s. m. publisher, editor. || adj. publishing.

editora (ô) s. f. publishing house or company.

editoração s. f. (pl. -ões) editorial business, publishing, publication.

editorar v. = editar.

editorial s. m. (pl. -ais) 1. editorial, leading article. 2. f. publishing house or company. ‖ adj. m. + f. editorial: of or pertaining to publishing.

editorialista s. m. + f. editorialist.

edredão s. m. (pl. -ões) eiderdown: 1. the down of the eider duck. 2. down quilt.

educabilidade s. f. educability.

educação s. f. (pl. -ões) 1. education: a) instruction, teaching. b) breeding, rearing. c) knowledge, culture, acquirements. d) training, discipline, upbringing. e) improvement, development. 2. civility, courtesy, good manners.

~ **física** physical education. ~ **superior** higher education. **a boa** ~ **nada custa** civility costs nothing. **boa** ~ good upbringing, good manners. **falta de** ~ ill breeding. **sem** ~ ill-bred, uncivil, uneducated.

educacional adj. m. + f. (pl. -ais) educational: of or pertaining to education.

educado adj. 1. educated, trained. 2. well-bred, polite, courteous, urbane, well-mannered.

bem ~ true-bred. **ela é bem -a** she is polite, she has good manners.

educador s. m. educator: 1. teacher, tutor. 2. master, preceptor. 3. instructor, trainer. ‖ adj. educating; educative, educatory.

educandário s. m. school, educational establishment.

educando s. m. pupil, scholar, student.

edução s. f. (pl. -ões) eduction, elicitation, deduction.

educar v. 1. to educate, bring up, rear. 2. to teach, instruct, school. 3. to train, discipline. 4. to breed. 5. to cultivate, civilize. 6. to develop morally and mentally by instruction. 7. to domesticate. 8. ~-se to acquire learning, study.

ela educou o ouvido she trained the ear. **ela educou seus filhos** she brought up her children.

educativo adj. educative, educatory.

educável adj. m. + f. (pl. -áveis) educable, teachable.

edulcorar v. 1. to edulcorate: a) sweeten, make sweet. b) purify, free from acids, salts, etc. 2. to soften, assuage.

édulo adj. eatable, edible, esculent.

eduzir v. to educe: 1. extract, bring out. 2. draw out, take out of. 3. deduce, infer.

efe s. m. name of the letter **f**.

efebo s. m. (hist.) ephebe, ephebus.

efeito s. m. effect: 1. result, consequence, outcome. 2. realization, execution, fulfilment, accomplishment. 3. intention, purpose, end, aim. 4. application. 5. efficacy. 6. validity, legality, force. 7. impression. 8. ~s pl. effects, goods, possessions.

~ **da temperatura** effect of temperature. ~ **de válvula** valve action. ~ **teatral** stage effect. **com** ~ in effect, in fact, as a matter of fact. **espere o** ~ wait for the effect, leave it to do its work. **faz (causa)** ~ it makes an effect, it operates. **levar a** ~ to effectuate. **não produzir** ~ to take no effect. **o** ~ **do radium** the action of radium. **para** ~s **bancários** for bank purposes. **para este** ~ therefore, for this purpose. **para todos os** ~s to all intents and purposes. **sem** ~ without effect. **ter** ~ **sobre** to act (up)on.

efeituar v. (usually **efetuar**) 1. to effectuate: a) realize. b) accomplish, achieve. c) bring to pass. 2. ~-se to take place, occur.

efélide s. f. (med.) ephelis, freckle.

efemérida s. f. (ent.) ephemerid, May fly.

efemérides s. f. pl. ephemeris (pl. ephemerides): 1. (astr.) astronomical almanac. 2. diary. 3. chronological register of past events. 4. an almanac, a calendar.

efemerina s. f. (bot.) dayflower (genus Tradescantia).

efêmero adj. ephemeral: 1. short-lived, lasting only one day. 2. transitory, passing, fleeting. 3. (bot.) fugacious. 4. faddy.

prazeres ~s ephemeral pleasures.

efeminação s. f. (pl. -ões) (also **afeminação**) effeminacy, womanishness.

efeminado adj. (also **afeminado**) 1. effeminate: a) womanish, womanlike (said of men). b) unmanly. c) delicate, softish. 2. weak. 3. timid. ‖ -amente adv. effeminately, like a woman.

efeminar v. (also **afeminar**) 1. to effeminate: a) womanize, make or become womanish (men). b) emasculate, weaken. c) unman. 2. to sensualize, enervate, soften.

eferente adj. m. + f. efferent: 1. conveying outward or away. 2. (physiol.) said of efferent nerves or vessels.

efervescência s. f. effervescence: 1. bubbling, ebullition. 2. ebullience, boiling. 3. (fig.) commotion; excitement; agitation.

efervescente adj. m. + f. effervescent: 1. bubbling, effervescing. 2. (fig.) irascible, irritable; agitable.

efervescer v. to effervesce: 1. bubble up. 2. be in the state of ebullition. 3. (fig.) be excited or boisterous.

efes-e-erres s. m. pl. minuteness, smallest details.

efésio s. m. Ephesian: a native or inhabitant of Ephesus. ‖ adj. Ephesian: of or relating to Ephesus.

efetivação s. f. act or result of effecting: act or effect of engaging an employee or civil servant for a permanent position.

efetivar v. to effect: 1. execute, accomplish. 2. realize, produce as a result.

efetível adj. m. + f. (pl. -íveis) effectible, realizable.

efetividade s. f. 1. effectiveness. 2. activity.

efetivo s. m. effective: 1. (mil.) ready or fit for active service. 2. that which effects or actually exists. 3. strength: number of troops, persons, or animals. ‖ adj. effective: 1. efficient, efficacious, effectual. 2. active. 3. real, actual, positive. ‖ -amente adv. 1. effectively, matter-of-factly. 2. really.

funcionário ~ employee officially in charge or position. **homem** ~ **nas promessas** a punctual man (a man of his words). **amor** ~ active charity or love. **prova** -a satisfactory proof, a convincing argument.

efetuação s. f. (pl. -ões) effectuation: 1. act of effectuating. 2. accomplishment, realization, fulfilment. 3. execution, performance.

efetuar v. 1. to effectuate: a) bring to pass, effect. b) accomplish, realize, fulfil, achieve. 2. to execute, perform, make. 3. to complete, conclude. 4. to cause. 5. ~-se to take place, occur.

efetuou o pagamento he made the payment.

eficácia s. f. 1. efficacy, efficiency, effectiveness. 2. force, power.

eficaz adj. m. + f. 1. efficacious, efficient, effective. 2. productive. 3. forceful, powerful. ‖ -mente adv. 1. efficaciously, efficiently. 2. productively.

remédio ~ efficient medicine.

eficiência s. f. 1. efficiency, efficience, efficacy. 2. effectiveness, reality. 3. activity, vigour, power. 4. capacity, smartness.

eficiente adj. m. + f. 1. efficient, efficacious. 2. capable, competent. 3. vigorous, energetic, powerful. 4. operative.

efigiar v. 1. to form or represent a person's image. 2. to execute in effigy. 3. to paint the effigy of.

efígie s. f. effigy, image: a figure representing a person.

efipídeos s. m. pl. (ichth.) Ephippidae: the spadefish family.

eflorescência s. f. efflorescence, efflorescency: 1. (bot.) the act (or time) of flowering. 2. (med.) skin eruption, rash.

eflorescente adj. m. + f. efflorescent, efflorescing.

eflorescer v. to effloresce: blossom, bloom, come into flower.

efluência s. f. effluence: 1. emanation. 2. outflow, flowing out, efflux. 3. effusion, pouring out.

efluente adj. m. + f. effluent, flowing out, emanating.

eflúvio s. m. 1. effluvium: a) invisible exhalation. b) emanation. 2. (poet.) aroma, fragrance, perfume. ~ elétrico electrical effluvium.

efluvioso adj. effluvious: emitting an effluvium.

efluxão s. f. (pl. -ões) abortion in the beginning of pregnancy.

efluxo s. m. efflux.

efó s. m. (Braz.) typical Bahia dish made of green vegetables, dried shrimp, "dendê"-palm oil, pepper, etc.

efúgio s. m. 1. subterfuge, evasion, tergiversation. 2. (fig.) loophole, pretext.

efundir v. 1. to effuse: shed, spill; outpour. 2. to breath, exhale. 3. ~-se to spread, scatter about. ~ lágrimas to shed tears.

efusão s. f. (pl. -ões) 1. effusion: shedding, outpouring. 2. fervour of friendship. ~ do coração opening or disclosing of one's heart. ~ de sangue bloodshed. com ~ tenderly.

efusiômetro s. m. (phys.) effusiometer.

efusivo adj. 1. effusive, effluent, flowing out. 2. expressive. 3. copious, profuse. 4. ardent, fervent. ‖ -amente adv. effusively. rocha -a volcanic rock. ~s agradecimentos profuse thanks.

efuso adj. effuse: poured out, spilled, spilt, shed.

Egéria s. f. 1. (Rom., myth.) Egeria: a nymph. 2. (fig.) inspiration, inspiring woman.

égide s. f. (a)egis: 1. shield or defensive armour. 2. (fig.) shelter, protection, support, defense.

egípcio, egipcíaco, egipciano s. m. Egyptian: native or inhabitant of Egypt. ‖ adj. Egyptian.

egiptologia s. f. Egyptology: the science of Egyptian antiquities.

egiptológico adj. Egyptologic(al).

egiptólogo s. m. Egyptologist: person versed in Egyptology.

eglanduloso adj. (bot.) without glands.

égloga s. f. (also écloga) eclogue.

ego s. m. (psych.) ego: the "I"; self.

egocêntrico adj. egocentric, self-centered.

egofonia s. f. (med.) egophony: a form of vocal resonance heard in auscultation.

egofônico adj. (med.) egophonic.

egoísmo s. m. egoism, selfishness, self-interest.

egoísta s. m. + f. 1. egoist. 2. self-seeking person. ‖ adj. 1. egoistic(al), selfish. 2. self-seeking.

egoístico adj. egoistic(al), selfish, self-centered.

ególatra s. m. + f. (Braz.) self-worshipper.

egolatria s. f. (Braz.) self-worship.

egotismo s. m. egotism: 1. an excessive self-esteem. 2. self-conceit, selfishness.

egotista s. m. + f. egotist. ‖ adj. egotistic(al).

egrégio adj. 1. prominent, eminent, distinguished, noted, illustrious (lineage). 2. admirable, great, remarkable.

egressão s. f. egress(ion): going out.

egresso s. m. 1. egress: a) exit. b) departure. 2. monk who has quitted a convent; person who has withdrawn from a community. ‖ adj. egressed.

egreta s. f. egret: an egret's plume, also called aigrette.

égrio s. m. plant of the mustard family (Nasturtium pumilum).

égua s. f. 1. (zool.) mare. 2. (N. Braz., sl.) prostitute, harlot. ~ madrinha (Braz.) 1. leading mare, bell mare. 2. (fig.) person fond of giving advice. lavar a ~ (Braz., ftb.) to win easily.

eguada s. f. (S. Braz.) a herd of mares.

eguariço s. m. 1. breeder of horses. 2. (h)ostler. ‖ adj. of or referring to mares or mules.

eh, êh interj. 1. (to call attention to s. th. or make animals go) hey!, look out!, go on!; stop! wo!, whoa! 2. (Braz., interj. of surprise, astonishment) whoop!, oh!

eia! interj. come on! cheer up!

eiconal s. f. (opt.) function used in optical geometry to calculate the trajectory of a light beam through a lens or a system.

ei-la, ei-lo contr. of eis + la, eis + lo, there he (she, it) is; here he (she, it) is. ei-lo que chega! (or aí vem ele!) here he comes! ei-los aqui! here they are!

eigenvalor s. m. (math.) eigenvalue.

einstêinio s. m. (chem.) einsteinium.

eira s. f. 1. threshing floor, barn floor. 2. cane store in sugar mills. 3. salt deposit near a sea saltern. sem ~ nem beira in poverty, in distress, down and out.

eirada s. f. quantity of wheat or corn placed on the barn floor for one threshing.

eirado s. m. open or roof terrace. ‖ adj. (Braz., coll.) said of a pig about to be fattened.

eirante s. m. farmhand.

eis adv. (also aqui está) here is, this is, here are, these are, here it is. ~ os meus livros here are my books. ~-me aqui here am I. ~! você não viu? there! didn't you see that? ~ a questão that's the question. ~ o motivo that's why.

eito s. m. 1. sequence, row, succession. 2. (Braz.) clearing of a plantation by gangs working with hoes. 3. (Braz., hist.) plantation or field where Negro slaves worked. a ~ uninterruptedly, continually, without intermission.

eiva s. f. 1. flaw, crack, fissure. 2. rottten spot of a fruit. 3. (fig.) blemish, blot.

eivar v. 1. to contaminate, infect. 2. to stain. 3. to vitiate. 4. ~-se: a) to become weak or sickly. b) to get cracked, get flaws (glass). c) to become rotten (fruit). d) to be contaminated. eivou-se a maçã the apple became rotten. eivou-se o vidro the glass is cracked.

eixo s. m. 1. (tech.): a) axle, axle-tree, axle-shaft, axis, pivot (plates B 4, C 13, 15). b) spindle, shaft, arbor, (horology) staff (plates E 2, T 6). 2. (geom., astr.) axis, center line (plate E 1). 3. (fig.) main point, pivotal question. ~ acionador driving-shaft. ~ cardan cardan shaft. ~ da dobradiça axle of a hinge. eixo da hélice propeller shaft. ~ da roda axle-tree, pin. ~ das abscissas (geom.) axis of abscissae (plate E 1). ~ das ordenadas (geom.) axis of ordinates (plate E 1). ~ de acionamento driving-shaft (plate F 8). ~ de comando (tech.) camshaft (plate E 2). ~ de direção steering axle. ~ de incidência axis of incidence. ~ de manivela crankshaft (plate E 2). ~ de pinhão (tech.) pinion shaft. ~ de rotação axis of rotation (plate E 1). ~ de simetria axis of symmetry. ~ dianteiro front axle. ~ fixo

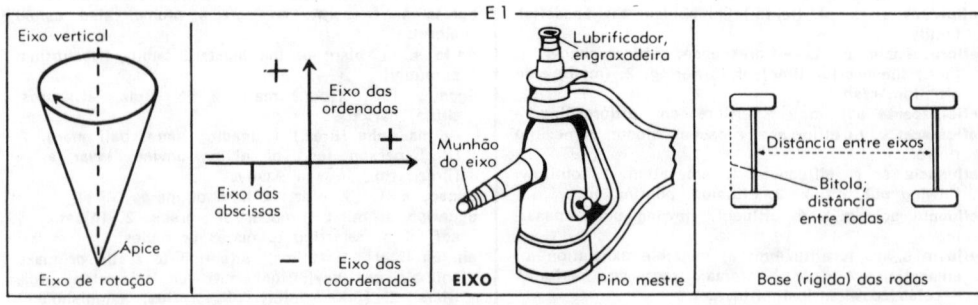

Eixo vertical — Eixo de rotação — Ápice — Eixo das ordenadas — Eixo das abscissas — Eixo das coordenadas — **EIXO** — Lubrificador, engraxadeira — Munhão do eixo — Pino mestre — Distância entre eixos — Bitola; distância entre rodas — Base (rígida) das rodas — E 1

stationary shaft. ~ intermediário (mech.) intermediate shaft, coupling shaft. ~ do motor driving--shaft. ~ móvel jointed cross shaft or axle. ~ oscilante (mech.) floating axle, spring axle. ~ óptico (or visual) optic axis. ~ transversal lateral axis, transverse axis. ~ traseiro rear axle. ~s das coordenadas co-ordinate axes (plate E 1). andar fora dos ~s (fig.) to be out of order, lead a disorderly life. carga de ~ axial load. cavilha do ~ axle-pin. com dois ~s biaxially. entrar nos ~s (fig.) to straighten, become straight. espaço entre ~s wheel base. está fora dos ~s it is off the hinges. girar sobre um ~ to turn on a pivot. pôr nos ~s to put in order, regulate. a terra gira em volta do seu próprio eixo the earth rotates about its own axis. tirar uma coisa dos seus ~s to put s. th. out of joint, throw s. th. into desorder.

eixo-badeixo s. m. (Braz.) (game) leapfrog.

eixu s. m. (Braz.) a small wasp (Nectarina lecheguana).

ejaculação s. f. (pl. -ões) 1. ejaculation, exclamation. 2. discharge, spur. 3. jet, gush. 4. spilling, pouring.

ejaculador s. m. ejaculator. ‖ adj. ejaculatory, ejaculating.

ejacular v. 1. to ejaculate, eject, discharge. 2. to exclaim or utter vehemently.

ejaculatório adj. ejaculatory; exclamatory.

ejeção s. f. (pl. -ões) 1. ejection, expulsion. 2. (med.) dejection.

ejetar v. to eject, to expell.

ejeto, ejetamento s. m. (geol.) ejecta, ejectamenta: matter issued from a volcano.

ejetor s. m. (tech.) ejector; jet pump.

el archaic form of the masculine definite article o. ~-rei the king.

ela pron. f. 1. she, it. 2. her. 3. ~s pl. they.
~ gosta muito de você she loves you very much. ~s por ~s tit for tat. ~s não sabem they don't know. aí é que são ~s now, there is (begins) the difficulty, (fam.) there is the rub.

elaboração s. f. (pl. -ões) 1. elaboration: the act of elaborating. 2. working up; preparation, improvement. 3. (physiol.) digestion.
~ de um projeto the working up of a project.

elaborar v. 1. to elaborate, work out in detail. 2. to organize. 3. to prepare. 4. (physiol.) to digest. 5. ~-se: to develop.
por fim, decidiu-se ~ um relatório finally it was decided to work out a report. a seiva elabora-se nas folhas the sap develops in the leaves.

elação s. f. (pl. -ões) elation: 1. haughtiness, pride, arrogance. 2. sublimity, exultation.

élan s. m. (Fr.) élan.

elafiano adj. elaphine.

elaiúria s. f. (path.) morbid change in the urine indicated by its oleaginous aspect.

elanguescente adj. m. + f. languid; faint; sickly.

elanguescer v. to languish: 1. debilitate, enfeeble, become feeble. 2. droop, pine. 3. lose strength or animation.
os olhos da viscondessa elanguesciam the eyes of the viscountess became wistful.

elasmobrânquio s. m. (ichth.) elasmobranch: a fishlike vertebrate of the class Elasmobranquii.

elastecer v. (Braz.) to dilate, enlarge, expand; make elastic.

elastério s. m. 1. elastic force, elasticity. 2. (fig.) energy; reaction.

elasticidade s. f. 1. elasticity, resilience, springiness. 2. flexibility. 3. reaction. 4. energy. 5. (fig.) unscrupulousness.
ter ~ de consciência not to be overscrupulous. falta de ~ inelasticity.

elástico s. m. elastic cord or string, an elastic (band) (plate R 7). ‖ adj. elastic: 1. resilient, pliant, supple (limbs). 2. flexible. 3. distensible.
força -a elasticity, elastic force. fita -a elastic. mesa -a telescope table, sliding-table, pull-out table. não ~ inelastic.

elastômero s. m. (chem.) elastomer.

élate s. m. a genus of palm trees (resembling the date-palm).

elaterídeo s. m. (ent.) elaterid.

elaterina s. f. (chem.) elaterin(e).

elatério s. m. 1. (pharm.) elaterium. 2. (bot.) wild cucumber. 3. (bot.) elater.

elaterite s. f. (min.) elaterite: an elastic mineral resin.

elaterômetro s. m. elaterometer.

elatina s. f. (bot.) waterwort.

elator s. m. elator, elate: one who or that which elates. ‖ adj. lifting up, elevating.

Eldorado s. m. El Dorado: 1. imaginary land of gold in South America. 2. (fig.) ideal land of plenty, Tom Tiddler's ground.

ele s. m. name of the letter L.

ele (ê) pron. m. 1. he; it; him. 2. ~s pl. they.
~ próprio he himself. ~s foram ao cinema they went to the movies. é ~ that's he.

eleatismo s. m. (philos.) eleaticism.

elé(c)trio s. m. = eléctron.

ele(c)tro s. m. 1. yellow amber. 2. (min.) electrum: alloy of gold and silver.

ele(c)trocardiografia s. f. electrocardiography.

ele(c)trocardiográfico adj. electrocardiographic.

ele(c)trocardiógrafo s. m. (med.) electrocardiograph.

ele(c)trocardiograma s. m. (med.) electrocardiogram.

ele(c)trochoque s. m. electroshock.

ele(c)trodinâmica s. f. (phys.) electrodynamics.

ele(c)trodinâmico adj. (phys.) electrodynamic.

ele(c)tródio s. m. (electr.) electrode.

elé(c)trodo s. m. (electr.) electrode.
~ massa ground electrode.

ele(c)troforese s. f. (phys.) electrophoresis.

ele(c)tróforo s. m. (phys.) electrophore, electrophorus.

E 2

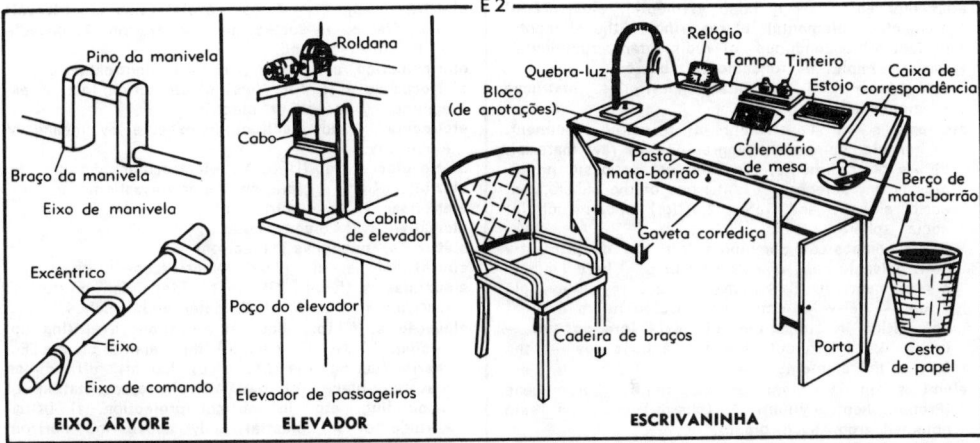

| EIXO, ÁRVORE | ELEVADOR | ESCRIVANINHA |

ele(c)trogalvânico adj. (electr.) electrogalvanic.
ele(c)trogalvanismo s. m. (electr.) electrogalvanism.
ele(c)trogêneo adj. (electr.) electrogenous.
ele(c)trografia s. f. electrography.
ele(c)troímã s. m. electromagnet (plate C 9).
~ **de levantamento** lifting magnet. ~ **de suspensão** crane magnet.
ele(c)trólito s. m. (chem., phys.) electrolyte.
ele(c)tromagnético adj. electromagnetic(al).
ele(c)tromagnetismo s. m. electromagnetism.
elé(c)tron s. m. (chem., phys.) electron.
ele(c)trônica s. f. electronics.
ele(c)trônico adj. electronic(al).
descarga ~a electronic discharge.
ele(c)troquímica s. f. electrochemistry.
ele(c)troscopia s. f. electric charge detection and measuring.
ele(c)troscópio s. m. electroscope.
ele(c)trostática s. f. electrostatics.
ele(c)trostático adj. electrostatic(al).
ele(c)trotécnico s. m. electrotechnician. ‖ adj. electrotechnic(al).
ele(c)troterapia s. f. (med.) electrotherapy, electrotherapeutics.
ele(c)trotipia s. f. electrotypy.
elefanta s. f. she-elephant.
elefante s. m. (zool.) elephant.
~-**do-mar**, ~-**marinho** elephant seal. **tromba de** ~ elephant's trunk.
elefantíase s. f. (med.) elephantiasis.
elefantíase-dos-árabes s. f. (pl. **elefantíases-dos-árabes**) (med.) filariasis.
elefantíase-dos-gregos s. f. (pl. **elefantíases-dos-gregos**) (med.) leprosy.
elefântico, elefantino adj. 1. elephantine: pertaining to or resembling an elephant. 2. elephantiac: affected with elephantiasis.
elefantófago adj. of or relating to one who feeds on elephant meat.
elefantóide adj. m. + f. elephantoid: having the form of an elephant.
elegância s. f. 1. elegance, grace(fulness), smartness. 2. delicacy, genteelness, refinement. 3. handsomeness. 4. fashionableness. 5. politeness, gallantry (of speech, manners, etc.). 6. stylishness, modishness.
~ **do estilo** elegance of style. **com** ~ elegantly. **perder a** ~ to become corpulent. **o supra-sumo das** ~**s** the height of elegance. **tem um ar de** ~ it looks quite smart.

elegante s. m. + f. elegant or smart person. ‖ adj. 1. elegant, fine, smart, graceful. 2. handsome, neat. 3. fashionable. 4. polished, cultivated, refined, genteel, polite. 5. well-dressed, spruce, trim. 6. well-proportioned. 7. stylish. ‖ ~**mente** adv. 1. elegantly, gracefully. 2. genteelly. 3. stylishly.
a sociedade ~ the fashionable society. **um casamento** ~ a smart wedding. **um vestido** ~ a very stylish dress.
elegendo s. m. person who is to be elected.
eleger v. to elect: 1. choose by vote. 2. give preference to, prefer. 3. select, pick.
eles elegeram o seu representante they elected their delegate. **ele foi eleito presidente** he was elected president.
elegia s. f. elegy: a plaintive poem.
elegíaco adj. elegiac(al), plaintive.
elegíada s. f. elegiac poem.
elegibilidade s. f. eligibility, eligibleness.
elegível adj. m. + f. (pl. -**íveis**) eligible, fit to be elected, subject to election.
eleição s. f. (pl. -**ões**) 1. election. 2. choice, choosing, selection. 3. preference. 4. option, will; mind, pleasure.
~ **prévia** pre-election. **foi proclamada uma** ~ **geral** a general election was called. **obter o maior número de votos numa** ~ to head a poll. **as próximas eleições** the coming election.
eleídrico adj. said of a painting made with oil and water.
eleito s. m. elect, the chosen. ‖ adj. elect(ed), selected, chosen.
os ~**s do Senhor** the Lord's elect, the elect. **o** ~ **da fortuna** the darling of fortune. **presidente** ~ the president elect.
eleitor s. m. elector: 1. person who elects; voter, constituent. 2. a prince who had the right to take part in the election of the Emperor in ancient Germany.
~**es do império** the electors of the empire.
eleitora s. f. elect(o)ress.
eleitorado s. m. electorate: 1. body of electors. 2. the right to elect. 3. (German hist.) the territory of an elector.
eleitoral adj. m. + f. (pl. -**ais**) 1. electoral, elective. 2. (German hist.) of or referring to an elector.
assembléia ~ electoral assembly. **caderno** ~ pollbook, electoral register. **influência** ~ influence of the electorate. **urna** ~ ballot-box.

elementar adj. m. + f. (also **elemental, elementário**) elementary, elemental: a) referring to the elements. b) (chem.) uncombined. c) rudimentary, rudimental, initial, simple. d) fundamental, basic. **conhecimento** ~ elementary knowledge. **instrução** ~ elementary instruction.

elemento s. m. 1. element: a) principle, rudiment. b) particle, component, ingredient. c) raw material. d) ~**s** pl. rudiments, the simplest or basic principles of any science. e) (ant.) one of the substances: earth, air, fire and water. 2. (fig.) ambient; circle; social sphere.
~ **de composição** combining form. ~ **de pilha** dry cell, galvanic cell. **aí estou no meu** ~ here I am in my element, (U. S. A.) that's right my alley. **ele é um** ~ **de valor em nosso círculo** he is a great acquisition in our circle. **ele está fora do seu** ~ he is like a fish out of water. **a fúria dos** ~**s** the fury of the elements.

elemi s. m. 1. plant of the family Burceraceae (Protium heptaphyllum). 2. (pharm.) elemi: a resin obtained from such plants.

elena s. f. Saint Elmo's fire.

elenco s. m. 1. (theat., Braz.) cast (set of actors). 2. list, catalogue, index.
o ~ **da peça é bom** (theat.) the play is well cast.

eleoceróleo s. m. plaster made with wax and oil.

eleóleo s. m. medicament containing an oily excipient.

eleolita s. f. (min.) eleolite.

eletividade s. f. (also **electividade**) electivity, selectivity.

eletivo adj. (also **electivo**) elective: 1. referring to election. 2. designated, named by election. 3. selecting, choosing.
reino ~ an elective kingdom.

eletrão s. m. (Port.) electron.

eletricidade s. f. (also **eletricismo**) electricity (plate E 3).
~ **magnética** magneto-electricity. **carregado de** ~ electrically charged, electricity-laden. **descarregar** ~ to discharge electricity.

eletricista s. m. + f. electrician.

elétrico s. m. electric: tram(car), tramway, streetcar. ‖ adj. electric(al): 1. of or pertaining to electricity. 2. containing or producing electricity. ‖ **eletricamente** adv. electrically.
abastecimento de energia -a supply of electrical energy. **acendedor** ~ electric lighter. **acionado por um motor** ~ driven by an electric motor. **almofada** -a electric cushion. **cabo** ~ electric cable. **carro** ~ tramcar. **central** -a power station. **choque** ~ electric shock. **circuito** ~ electric circuit. **cortar a corrente** -a to break the electric(al) current. **eu vou de** ~ I go by tram. **ferro** ~ electric iron. **lâmpada** -a electric lamp or bulb. **medidor** ~ electricity meter, supply meter. **rede** -a electrical supply system. **trem** ~ electric train. **usina** -a electricity works. **ventoinha** -a electric fan.

eletrificação s. f. (pl. -ões) electrification, electrifying.

eletrificar v. to electrify.

eletrino adj. amber: 1. of or referring to amber. 2. made of amber.

eletrização s. f. (pl. -ões) electrization.

eletrizador s. m. electrizer, electrifier. ‖ adj. electrifying.

eletrizante adj. m. + f. electrifying.

eletrizar v. to electrify, electrize: 1. charge with electricity. 2. give an electric shock to. 3. (fig.) thrill, excite. 4. (fig.) delight s. o., fill s. o. with enthusiasm. 5. ~**-se** (fig.) become enthusiastic or excited.

eletrizável adj. m. + f. (pl. -áveis) (also **electrizável**) electrifiable: 1. subject to electrization. 2. capable of being electrified.

eletrocinético adj. (phys., chem.) electrokinetic.

eletrocussão s. f. (pl. -ões) electrocution: act of executing by means of electricity.

eletrocutar v. to electrocute: execute by means of electricity.

eletrocutor s. m. (U. S. A.) electrocuter.

eletrolisação s. f. (pl. -ões) electrolyzation.

eletrolisar v. to electrolyse.

eletrólise s. f. electrolysis.

elétron s. m. (phys.) electron.

eletroscópio s. m. (phys.) electroscope.

eleusínias s. f. pl. (Gr. hist.) Eleusinian mysteries: festivals in honour of Demeter and Bacchus.

elevação s. f. (pl. -ões) 1. elevation: a) lifting up, raising. b) (R. C. Church) the raising of the Eucharist during the Mass. c) height, hill. d) an elevated place. c) geometrical representation of a building, etc. in vertical projection. f) (astr.) altitude of a celestial body above the horizon. 2. ascension. 3. (up)rising. 4. preferment, promotion, advancement. 5. increase, augmentation. 6. distinction, dignity. 7. culture, refinement.
~ **da Hóstia** Elevation of the Host. ~ **da temperatura** rise in temperature. ~ **de estilo** sublimity of style. ~ **do espírito a Deus** elevation of the mind to God. ~ **do nível da água** raising of the water level. **pequena** ~ **de terra** a swell, a hill.

elevado s. m. elevated expressway, viaduct, overpass. ‖ adj. 1. elevated: a) lifted up, raised, lofty, high. b) noble, sublime. c) rapt, ravished. 2. (mus.) forte, full-toned. 3. promoted.
acharam o preço ~ they found the price too high. **estilo** ~ elevated style. **renda** -a high rent. **temperatura** -a high temperature. **tensão arterial** -a high blood pressure. **ele foi** ~ **à categoria de** he was promoted to...

elevador s. m. elevator, lift (plate E 2). ‖ adj. elevating, elevatory.
~ **contínuo** continuous chain passenger lift. ~ **de cargas, de serviço** goods lift, luggage hoist (plate E 13). ~ **de cozinha** dumb-waiter. ~ **de nora** bucket elevator. ~ **de passageiros** passenger elevator, passenger lift (plate E 2). **poço de** ~ elevator shaft.

elevar v. 1. to elevate: a) raise, lift (up). b) hoist. c) exalt, ennoble, aggrandize, praise. d) promote, advance. e) put in high spirits. 2. to augment, increase (price). 3. to heighten, enlarge. 4. to erect (wall), raise (a building). 5. ~**-se:** a) to be lofty, ascend. b) to rise. c) to enrapture. d) to amount, run up to. e) to tower.
~ **à terceira potência** (math.) to raise to the third power. ~ **a voz** to speak louder. ~ **o pensamento a Deus** to lift up one's thoughts to God. **as despesas elevam-se a Cr$ 500,00** the expenses amount to Cr$ 500,00. **as enormes montanhas elevam-se acima das nuvens** the enormous mountains tower above the clouds. **elevou-se no ar** it rose into the air. **ele foi elevado a presidente** he was made a chairman. **o missionário elevou-se à santidade** the missionary lifted himself into sainthood. **os preços estão se elevando rapidamente** the prices are shooting up.

elevatória s. f. (Braz.) pumping station in water supply or sewage systems.

elevatório adj. 1. elevatory: raising or tending to raise. 2. referring to elevation.

elfo s. m. (myth.) elf (pl. elves): a sprite.

eliciar v. to elicit: 1. expel, draw out. 2. throw s. o. out.

~ **maus espíritos de** to exorcize evil spirits from. **a associação eliciou diversos elementos** the association expelled various elements.
elidir v. to elide: 1. cut off. 2. omit (in pronunciation), make an elision. 3. suppress, eliminate.
eliminação s. f. (pl. **-ões**) elimination: 1. removal expulsion. 2. exclusion, banishment.
eliminar v. 1. to eliminate: a) remove, banish, expulse. b) blot out, put or turn out, cut out. c) get rid of, leave out. 2. (fig.) to extirpate, kill.
eliminatório adj. eliminatory, eliminating.
provas -as 1. eliminating tests. 2. (sport) trial match, (U. S. A.) elimination tournament.
eliminável adj. m. + f. (pl. **-áveis**) eliminable.
elipse s. f. 1. (gram.) ellipsis: omission of a word or words necessary to complete a sentence. 2. (geom.) ellipse: an oval figure.
~ **paraláctica** (astr.) parallactic orbit.
elipsógrafo s. m. ellipsograph: an elliptic trammel.
elipsoidal adj. m. + f. (pl. **-ais**) ellipsoidal: having the form of an ellipsoid.
elipsóide s. m. (geom.) ellipsoid: a solid figure of which every plane section is an ellipse. ‖ adj. m + f. ellipsoidal.
elíptico, elítico adj. alliptic(al) (plate F 5). ‖ **elipticamente** adv. elliptically.
elisão s. f. (pl. **-ões**) 1. (gram.) elision: elimination of a vowel at the end of one word when the next word begins with a vowel (e. g. **dum = de um**). 2. suppression, elimination.
eliseu s. m. (myth.) Elysium, Elysian fields.
Elísio s. m. Elysium: 1. the abode of the blessed after death. 2. paradise. 3. bliss, blessedness. ‖ adj. Elysian: 1. of or relative to Elysium. 2. blissful, delightful.
Campos ~s Elysian fields.
elite s. f. elite: 1. the choicest part. 2. the cream or flower of a group or society. 3. influential people, leading circles.
a ~ da sociedade the cream of society. **regimento da ~** crack regiment.
elitrite s. f. vaginitis: inflammation of the vagina.
élitro s. m. (zool.) elytrum, elytron: wing cover of certain insects.
elitrocele s. f. (med.) elytrocele: vaginal hernia.
elitroplastia s. f. (surg.) elytroplasty: an operation to restore a part of the vagina.
elitrorragia s. f. (path.) vaginal hemorrhage.
elixir s. m. elixir: 1. (pharm.) a sweetened alcoholic medicine. 2. (alchemy: a) panacea. b) philosopher's stone. 3. (fig.) delicious beverage.
~ **paregórico** paregoric.
elmo s. m. 1. (mil.) helmet. 2. (med.) dandruff on the head of babies. 3. burgonet; casque.
~ **de ponta** spiked helmet.
elo s. m. 1. link (of a chain) (plate C 4). 2. (bot.) tendril. 3. (fig.) connexion, connecting link.
elocução s. f. (pl. **-ões**) elocution: 1. manner of speaking, utterance, diction. 2. style (speaking and writing).
eloendro s. m. (bot.) oleander (Nerium oleander).
elogiar v. 1. to eulogize: a) speak or write of praisingly. b) praise, extol, commend, laud, panegyrize. 2. to exalt.
~ **alguém altamente** to bestow great praise upon s. o. ~ **um ator em jornal** to write up an actor. **ele a elogia** he praises her highly. **ele o elogiou sobejamente** he praised him to the sky.
elogiável adj. m. + f. (pl. **-áveis**) laudable; praiseworthy.
elogio s. m. eulogy: 1. a spoken or written laudation. 2. a praise, extol(l)ment. 3. commendation. 4. panegyric, encomium.

digno de ~s praiseworthily. **ele lhe fez um grande ~** he commended him highly. **fazer um ~ a alguém** to extol s. o.
elogioso adj. 1. eulogistic(al), eulogious, laudatory. 2. panegyrical, flattering, complimentary. ‖ **-amente** adv. flatteringly, eulogistically, laudatorily.
ela fala dele em termos ~s she speaks highly of him. **falou acerca dele com palavras -as** he spoke about him in the most flattering terms.
elongação s. f. (pl. **-ões**) elongation: 1. (astr.) angular distance of a planet from the sun. 2. distance of an oscillatory point from its original position. 3. (med.) luxation of a joint.
eloqüência s. f. eloquence: 1. fluency of speech. 2. oratory. 3. elocution. 4. (fig.) persuasiveness.
cores da ~ rhetorical colours.
eloqüente adj. m. + f. 1. eloquent: a) fluent, ready in speaking, silver-tongued. b) persuasive, convincing. 2. (fig.) expressive. ‖ **~mente** adv. eloquently.
ele é ~ he has a fluent (ready) speech.
elóquio s. m. 1. speech, oration; discourse. 2. talk, conversation.
elucidação s. f. (pl. **-ões**) 1. elucidation, clearing up, explanation. 2. exposition, commentary.
elucidar v. 1. to elucidate: a) explain, make clear, make plain. b) comment. c) illuminate. 2. **~-se** to be enlightened.
elucidário s. m. 1. glossary: any explanatory vocabulary. 2. commentary.
elucidativo adj. elucidative, explanatory, elucidating.
elucubração s. f. (pl. **-ões**) lucubration: 1. night work (study). 2. close meditation. 3. (fig.) composition of too elaborate a character.
eludir v. to elude: 1. avoid or escape by dextery. 2. evade.
~ **uma lei** to evade a law. ~ **o regulamento** to get round the regulations.
eluir v. (chem.) to elute.
eluvião s. f. (geol.) eluvium.
elzevir s. m. Elzevir: 1. book printed by one of the Elzevir family. 2. a style of printing type.
elzeviriano adj. Elzevirian.
em prep. in, into, up, at, on, upon, during, within, by, to.
~ **alto grau** to a high degree. ~ **atenção a** in consideration of. ~ **boa hora** at a good time, opportunely. ~ **boas mãos** in good hands. ~ **breve** soon. ~ **casa** at home. ~ **caso afirmativo** in the affirmative case. ~ **cena** on the stage. ~ **cheio** fully, smack on. ~ **cima** 1. above. 2. upstairs. ~ **cinco dias** in five days. ~ **compensação** on the other hand. ~ **conseqüência disso** by reason of that. ~ **conta (barato)** at a cheap rate. ~ **demasia** in excess. ~ **direção a** toward. ~ **excesso** excessively. **enfim** finally. ~ **forma** in form. ~ **frente de** in front of. ~ **geral** generally. ~ **guerra** at war. ~ **honra de Deus** in honour of God. ~ **liberdade** at liberty. ~ **lugar de:** 1. in place of. 2. instead of. ~ **mãos** 1. at one's possession. 2. (com.) care of. ~ **movimento** in motion. ~ **nossos dias** nowadays. ~ **particular** privately. ~ **ponto** exactly (in time). ~ **quantidade** in abundance. ~ **seguida** afterwards. ~ **silêncio** silently. ~ **situação difícil** in straightened circumstances. ~ **sonho** in a dream. ~ **sua passagem** during his passage. ~ **suma** in a word. ~ **tempo** in time. ~ **vão** in vain, idly. ~ **verdade** in truth. ~ **virtude de** by virtue of. ~ **sinal de** as a proof that, in token of. ~ **proveito de seu irmão** to his brother's advantage or benefit. **de ano ~ ano** year by year. **baseado ~ fatos** based on facts. **cair ~ sorte** to fall to one's share, come in one's way. **dormir**

~ **terra** to sleep on the bare earth. **ele vai ~ busca de** he goes in search of. **ir à igreja ~ jejum** to go to church without breakfast.

ema s. f. 1. (ornith.) rhea: Brazilian ostrich. 2. (N. Braz.) drunkenness.

montado na ~ (N. Braz., sl.) drunk.

emaçar v. 1. to bundle. 2. to wrap up.

emaciação s. f. (pl. **-ões**) (med.) emaciation.

emaciar v. to emaciate: 1. cause excessive meagerness. 2. weaken, debilitate. 3. get thin.

emadeiramento s. m. timberwork, wooden framework of a building.

emadeirar v. 1. to timber, make the timberwork. 2. to cover with planks. 3. to make the wooden framework (of a house).

emadeixar v. to arrange in or put into skeins or roves (wool).

emagotar v. to heap up, make heaps.

emagrecer v. (also **emagrentar**) 1. to emaciate: a) (also **~-se**) grow lean or thin. b) get thin, lose flesh. 2. to diminish in importance or value.

você está emagrecendo you are getting thin.

emagrecido adj. emaciate.

emagrecimento s. m. 1. emaciation, thinning. 2. weakness.

emalar v. 1. to put in a trunk, bag or suitcase. 2. to pack up.

emalhar v. 1. to cover with a (chain-)mail. 2. to entangle, net. 3. to hold together by means of a net.

emalhetamento s. m. mortising, morticing, joinery, fastening by tenon and mortise.

emalhetar v. 1. to mortise: tenon, join (by tenon and mortise). 2. to dovetail.

emanação s. f. (pl. **-ões**) emanation: 1. efflux, effluvium, a flowing or issuing from. 2. provenience, evaporation, exhalation, (ir)radiation, effluence.

-ões das fossas sewer-gas.

emanacionismo s. m. (theol.) the theories of creation by emanation of God.

emanante adj. m. + f. emanative, emanating.

emanar v. 1. to emanate: a) arise, spring, flow out, issue forth. b) proceed or come from. c) originate in, stem from. 2. to exhale.

emanatismo s. m. (philos.) emanatism, emanationism.

emancipação s. f. (pl. **-ões**) emancipation: 1. freeing, setting free. 2. liberation, abolition (slavery).

emancipar v. 1. to emancipate: a) set at liberty, set free. b) release from (parental control). 2. **~-se** to emancipate o. s.: a) free o. s. from another's jurisdiction. b) take too much liberty. c) grow licentious. d) liberate.

emanquecer v. to lame, become or grow lame, become crippled.

a queda emanqueceu-o the fall lamed him. **o cavalo emanqueceu** the horse grew lame.

emaranhada s. f. (Braz., coll.) something tangled, a confusion.

uma ~ dos diabos (Braz., coll.) a hell of a mess.

emaranhamento s. m. 1. entanglement, complication, intricacy. 2. confusion, tangle.

emaranhar v. 1. to embarrass, puzzle. 2. to tangle, snare. 3. to entangle, complicate, implicate, make intricate. 4. **~-se**: a) to entangle o. s., become entangled. b) to get involved or mixed in. c) (fam.) to get mixed up with. d) to let o. s. in for (difficulties).

emarar-se v. to put out to sea.

emarelecer v. to yellow: 1. grow (or turn) yellow. 2. make yellow. 3. become yellow.

emartilhar v. (Braz.) to unlock, cock (one's gun).

emascarar v. to mask, disguise.

emasculação s. f. (pl. **-ões**) 1. emasculation. 2. gelding, castration.

emascular v. 1. to emasculate: a) deprive of virility, castrate, geld. b) unman. 2. **~-se**: a) to lose virility or vigour. b) to become weak, weaken.

emassar v. to convert into a mass or paste.

emassilhar v. to putty, apply putty to (window panes).

emastrar, emastrear v. to mast (a ship).

embaçadela s. f. 1. cheat, trickery, deceit, fraud, swindle. 2. embarrassment.

embaçado adj. 1. dimmed, dull, lusterless. 2. obfuscated. 3. cheated, deceived.

embaçador s. m. person who or that which dims, duller, tarnisher. ‖ adj. dimming, causing dullness (on window panes).

embaçar v. 1. to dim, dull (as window panes with mist). 2. to obfuscate. 3. to trick, hoodwink, deceive. 4. to perplex, confuse, stun, embarrass. 5. to tarnish. 6. **~-se** to deceive o. s., fool o. s.

embacelar v. to plant (vines).

embaciar v. 1. to dim, make dull, tarnish, be obscured. 2. **~-se** a) to become dimmed. b) to grow dull.

o brilho do ouro ia embaciando the lustre of the gold slowly tarnished.

embaidor s. m. 1. swindler, cheat, coaxer, deceiver. 2. circumventor. 3. seducer. ‖ adj. 1. cheating, deceitful. 2. seductive.

embaimento s. m. 1. deceit, cheat, deception. 2. fascination, seduction.

embainhar v. 1. to sheathe (sword). 2. to hem: a) make a hem in. b) edge, border.

ela embainhou uma saia she hemmed a skirt. **ele embainhou a sua espada** he sheathed his sword.

embair v. 1. to coax, delude, deceive by fair words. 2. to wheedle, allure.

embaixada s. f. embassy: 1. the function or mission of an ambassador. 2. the official residence of an ambassador. 3. (fig.) private message, mission, legation.

ele mandou uma ~ he sent an embassy. **ele foi fazer uma ~** he went upon an embassy.

embaixador s. m. ambassador; emissary.

o governo retirou o ~ de sua missão the government recalled the ambassador.

embaixadora s. f. 1. ambassadress: a female ambassador. 2. mediatress.

embaixatriz s. f. ambassadress, ambassador's wife.

embaixo adv. 1. below, beneath, under(neath). 2. downstairs.

cá ~ herebelow. **lá ~** down there.

embala s. f. 1. slave house. 2. hut of an African tribal chief.

embalada adj. (Braz.) said of a loaded gun.

embaladeira s. f. a woman who rocks a child.

embalado adj. 1. (Braz.) loaded (gun). 2. (Port.) well off, wealthy.

embalador s. m. 1. rocker: person who rocks the cradle. 2. packer, wrapper. ‖ adj. 1. lulling. 2. delusive, deceptive.

embalagem s. f. (pl. **-ens**) 1. packing up. 2. package, packaging. 3. wrapping.

~ original original package. **caixa de ~** packing-case. **secção de -ens** packery.

embalançar v. 1. to balance, swing. 2. to oscillate.

embalar (I) v. 1. to rock (a child) to sleep; cradle. 2. to cajole or lull s. o. into. 3. to soothe. 4. to coax s. o.

~ uma esperança to hold out hopes for, to cherish.

embalar (II) v. to wrap up, pack (up); bale.

embalar (III) v. (Braz.) to load (a gun).

embalde adv. = **debalde.**

embalete s. m. pump handle.

embalo s. m. lulling, rocking.

embalsamador s. m. embalmer: person who embalms. || adj. embalming.

embalsamamento s. m., embalsamação f. embalmment: act or process of embalming.

embalsamar v. 1. to embalm, anoint (bodies) with balm for preservation. 2. to make fragrant, perfume.

embalsamento s. m. 1. vatting. 2. embarkation on a raft.

embalsar v. 1. to put into a vat. 2. to go aboard a raft.

embamata s. f. (Braz.) thick sauce.

embambecer v. 1. to loosen, slacken. 2. (Braz.) to make loose or slack.

embananamento s. m. (Braz., sl.) embarrassment, confusion.

embananar-se v. (Braz., sl.) to get embarrassed, become confused.

embandar v. 1. to sew on, provide with stripes. 2. to adorn with bands. 3. to join a swarm, or a flight (of birds).

embandeirado adj. 1. adorned with flags. 2. (fig.) dressed up (person).

embandeiramento s. m. decoration with flags.

embandeirar v. 1. to flag, adorn with flags. 2. (Braz., fig.) to celebrate; praise. 3. to flatter. 4. ~-se (fig.) to dress o. s. up.

~ em arco to dress or decorate in a semicircle.

embaraçado adj. 1. embarrassed, ill at ease, perplexed, puzzled. 2. disconcerted, nonplussed. 3. tangled. 4. confused. || -amente adv. 1. embarrassingly. 2. perplexedly, with difficulty. 3. confusedly

ela está -a she is embarrassed, she is at a loss. ele está ~ he is ill at ease. iniciativa -a pela falta de interesse initiative hampered by indifference.

embaraçador s. m. embarrassing person. || adj. 1. embarrassing. 2. difficult, worrying, troublesome.

embaraçar v. 1. to embarrass, hinder, hamper. 2. to obstruct. 3. to block up, bar, barricade (way). 4. to encumber (with). 5. to discompose, disconcert. 6. to abash, derange. 7. to puzzle (a question). 8. to nonplus, disturb. 9. to complicate, mix up. 10. to perplex. 11. ~-se to get entangled, get embarrassed, get o. s. into a scrape.

ela embaraçou-se com ele she was at variance with him, she fell out with him. ele embaraçou-se num negócio he got entangled in a business. ela me embaraça o caminho she obstructs (or stops up) my way. isso não embaraça that's no obstacle.

embaraço s. m. 1. embarrassment: a) impediment, encumbrance, hindrance, obstacle. b) perplexity. c) intricacy, entanglement, confusion. d) obstruction, difficulty (esp. in business). e) disconcertment. f) involvement (as by debt or unfavourable circumstances). 2. (med.) gastric disorder.

ele evita os ~s he steers clear of scrapes. fiquei livre de ~s I got out of troubles.

embaraçoso adj. embarrassing: 1. causing embarrassment. 2. troublesome. 3. perplexing; puzzling. 4. annoying, cumbersome.

ele está numa situação -a he finds himself in an embarrassing situation.

embarafustar v. (Braz.) 1. to burst (into a room), come bursting in. 2. to penetrate, enter into.

embaralhar v. 1. to shuffle (cards). 2. to mix (up), jumble, clutter (up). 3. to confuse, disconcert. 4. to entangle, complicate. 5. ~-se to become confused.

embarbar v. 1. to rabbet, join, incase. 2. to fit into, set in.

embarbascar v. 1. to intoxicate (fish) by certain weeds. 2. to be stunned, embarrassed or perplexed. 3. to get stuck in the mud.

embarbecer v. to grow a beard.

embarbelar v. 1. to hold, cling fast to a bull's dewlap. 2. ~-se (Braz., coll.) to be in a fix.

embarcação s. f. (pl. -ões) 1. embarkation: act of putting or going on board a vessel or boat. 2. vessel, ship, craft; boat.

~ de recreio pleasure-boat. ~ de remos row(ing)-boat. ~ fluvial river boat.

embarcadiço s. m. 1. seafaring person. 2. seafarer, mariner, sailor.

embarcadouro s. m. (also embarcadoiro) 1. landing-place; landing-stage. 2. quay, wharf, jetty. 3. (railway) platform.

embarcamento s. m. = embarque.

embarcar v. 1. to embark, take a ship. 2. to put on board, load. 3. to go on board. 4. to board (train, ship, plane, etc.) 5. to depart, leave (for). 6. (Braz., pop.) to die. 7. (Braz., sl.) to fall into a snare.

~! all aboard! ~ num navio to go aboard a ship. ele embarcou para o Rio 1. he took the train to Rio. 2. he embarked for Rio (in a steamer).

embargado adj. 1. seized, stopped, paralyzed, held up. 2. under an embargo.

ele é ~ na fala he has an impediment in his speech.

embargador s. m. 1. person who lays an embargo (on a ship). 2. caveator. || adj. 1. hindering, embarrassing. 2. troublesome.

embargar v. 1. to embargo, lay an embargo (up)on. 2. to detain, seize, confiscate. 3. to hinder, impede, embarrass. 4. (law) to attach.

~ um navio to embargo a ship. isto não embarga this does not hinder.

embargável adj. m. + f. (pl. -áveis) 1. liable to embargo. 2. seizable; confiscable.

embargo s. m. 1. embargo, seizure, arrest. 2. impediment, hindrance, encumbrance. 3. (jur.): a) caveat, exception at law; appeal. b) attachment.

~ de bens estrangeiros foreign attachment. sem ~ nevertheless, notwithstanding.

embarque s. m. 1. embarkment, embarkation: act of embarking, shipping. 2. place of embarkation.

~ de mercadorias shipment of goods. ~ de passageiros embarkation of passengers. pronto para o ~ ready for shipping.

embarramento s. m. (Braz.) filling of clay in walls of a mud cottage.

embarrancar v. 1. to cause to fall down a slope or into a gully (ravine). 2. to embarrass, thwart. 3. to run against a slope. 4. ~-se: a) to be embarrassed. b) to get stuck in mud.

embarrar (I) v. (also embarrear) 1. to daub with clay. 2. to fill out with clay (wall of a mud cottage).

embarrar (II) v. 1. to run against, strike upon. 2. to touch slightly, graze.

embarrear v. to daub or coat with clay.

embarreirar v. to surround with barriers.

embarrelar v. 1. to put in lye. 2. to apply lye to something.

embarricar v. 1. to barrel: put or pack in a barrel. 2. to barricade, stow up. 3. ~-se to defend o. s. by means of barricades.

embarrigar v. 1. to grow big-bellied (fat). 2. to become pregnant, be with young.

embarrilagem s. f. (pl. -ens) act of barrelling, filling into a barrel.

embarrilar v. 1. to barrel: fill into a barrel. 2. (pop.) a) to annoy. b) to cheat.

embasamento s. m. (archit., constr.) 1. basement. 2. base. 3. foundation.

embasar v. 1. to base, found (on, upon). 2. ~-se to be based upon.

embasbacar v. 1. to gape (in wonder). 2. to be stupefied, be taken aback, be dumbfounded. 3. to stupefy, amaze. 4. ~-se to be amazed.

embastar v. to quilt, baste (a mattress).

embastecer, embastir v. 1. to thicken, condense, inspissate. 2. to make dense.

embate s. m. 1. collision, clash, impact, shock. 2. knock, dash (against). 3. (fig.) resistance, opposition. 4. assault, onset. 5. ~s (fig.) reverses of fate.

embater v. 1. to knock, clash, dash against. 2. (fig.) to offer resistance. 3. ~-se (com) to bump against, colide with.

as ondas embatem nos rochedos the waves beat against the rocks. **tantas idéias que se embatem** so many contradictory ideas.

embatocar v. to bung up, plug with a bung.

embatucar v. 1. to silence, stop a person's mouth. 2. to dumbfound. 3. to become speechless, be dumbfounded. 4. to hold one's tongue, shut up.

embatumar v. (Braz.) 1. to fill up, overfill, cram. 2. to accumulate.

embaucador s. m. 1. deceiver, decoyer, duper. 2. coaxer, wheedler, cajoler. ‖ adj. 1. deceiving. 2. coaxing.

embaucar v. 1. to hoax, beguile, deceive, cheat, decoy, dupe. 2. to coax, wheedle.

embaular v. 1. to put into a trunk. 2. to store away.

embeaxió s. m. (N. Braz.) a kind of bamboo flute.

embebecer v. = **embevecer**.

embebedar v. 1. to intoxicate, make drunk, fuddle, inebriate. 2. to make drowsy. 3. to infatuate, befool. 4. ~-se: a) to get drunk. b) (fig.) to be intoxicated with, go out of one's head, become hallucinated.

embeber v. 1. to imbibe, soak up, absorb; steep, drench. 2. to infiltrate. 3. to plunge (a dagger in), thrust (a sword through). 4. ~-se: a) to be imbibed or soaked in, become absorbed. b) (fig.) to be wrapt up in, be enraptured with.

~ em si uma doutrina to imbibe a doctrine. **ela embebeu as lágrimas num lenço** she dried her tears in her handkerchief. **ele embebeu-se na leitura dos escritores modernos** he got absorbed in (reading) modern authors. **a esponja embebeu todo o líquido** the sponge soaked in all the liquid. **o pão embebeu-se no caldo** the bread soaked in the broth.

embeberar v. 1. to water, lead to water (animals), give to drink. 2. to soak, imbibe.

embibição s. f. (pl. -ões) imbibition, absorption, soaking.

embeiçado adj. 1. in love with, smitten with; enchanted. 2. infatuated with.

João está ~ por Maria John is dotingly in love with Mary.

embeiçamento s. m. (Braz.) amorous infatuation.

embeiçar v. 1. to infatuate. 2. to twist a person round one's finger. 3. to enchant, bewitch. 4. ~-se to fall in love.

embelecar v. 1. to coax, wheedle, beguile, dupe, decoy. 2. ~-se to let o. s. be deceived by, let o. s. be taken in.

não nos podemos ~ com esses truques we cannot let ourselves be deceived by these tricks.

embelecer v. 1. to embellish, beautify. 2. to adorn, decorate.

embeleco (ê) s. m. 1. deceit, hoax, trick, imposture, humbug. 2. coaxing, wheedling. 3. lure, bait. 4. (Braz.) obstacle, impediment.

embelezador adj. embellishing; adorning; decorative.

embelezamento s. m. 1. embellishment, beautification. 2. adornment.

embelezar v. 1. to embellish, beautify. 2. to decorate, adorn, ornament. 3. to charm, enrapture. 4. ~-se: a) to embellish o. s. b) (fig.) to be enchanted.

embernar v. to infest with the larvae of botflies.

embespinhar-se v. 1. to become irritated; to get one's bristles up. 2. to take a huff.

embestar v. 1. to make stupid, besot, brutalize. 2. (Braz.): a) to be obstinate, be stubborn. b) to persist.

embetara s. f. (ornith.) ant shrike.

embetesgar v. 1. to corral, bring to a deadlock. 2. ~-se to reach a deadlock, become corralled.

embevecer v. 1. to strike with amazement, stupefy. 2. to charm, captivate. 3. ~-se to be enraptured.

embevecido adj. rapt, stupefied, wrapt up in admiration.

embevecimento s. m. 1. stupefaction, astonishment. 2. ravishment, rapture, extasy.

embezerrado adj. (pop.) frowning, sulky, moody.

embezerrar(-se) v. 1. to frown, sulk. 2. to become sullen. 3. to be stubborn. 4. to become obstinate.

embiara s. f. (N. Braz.) prey; booty.

embicado adj. beak-shaped, rostriform.

embicador s. m. stumbler, a stumbling horse. ‖ adj. stumbling.

embicadura s. f. (naut.) entry, entering into a port.

embicar v. 1. to shape like a beak. 2. to trip, stumble, slip. 3. to be confused or embarrassed. 4. to slide into a blunder. 5. to touch. 6. (N. Braz.) to drink, sip. 7. (naut.) to enter a port. 8. ~-se to direct one's way towards, head towards.

~ o chapéu to cock one's hat.

embigada s. f. (pop. form for **umbigada**) 1. push with the navel or the paunch. 2. the umbilical region.

embigo s. m. (pop. form for **umbigo**) navel.

embilocar v. 1. to rush through. 2. to put in, introduce.

embiocar v. 1. to cover and hide the face (woman). 2. to muffle, cover. 3. ~-se to disguise o. s., muffle o. s.

embira s. f. (Braz., also **embiratanha**) embira: any of several bast fibers derived from trees of the family Thymelaeaceae used for making nets, ropes, etc. **ele está na ~** he is in pecuniary difficulties. **eles ficam na ~** they are in great straits for money. **lamber ~** to live in extreme poverty, starve. **meter (passar) nas ~s** to tie up, arrest s. o.

embira-da-mata-branca s. f. (pl. **embiras-da-mata--branca**) (bot.) screw tree.

embirar v. (N. Braz.) to tie, bind, fasten (with embira).

embiricica s. f. (N. Braz.) 1. string, file, rank. 2. act of arranging or ordering in ranks or files.

embirra, embirração, embirrância s. f. 1. obstinacy, stubbornness, wilfulness. 2. aversion, antipathy. 3. tiff.

embirrar v. 1. to be obstinate or stubborn, persist obstinately. 2. to dislike, feel antipathy or aversion for. 3. to sulk.

~ com alguém to take a dislike to. **ele embirra com qualquer coisa** he is nettled at everything.

embirrento, embirrativo adj. 1. stubborn, obstinate. 2. pettish, sullen. 3. annoying.

emblema s. m. 1. emblem, badge; ensign. 2. allegory; symbol.

emblemar v. 1. to emblematize, emblemize. 2. to symbolize. 3. to be the emblem of.

emblemático adj. 1. emblematic(al). 2. significative; symbolical. ‖ **emblematicamente** adv. emblematically.

emboaba, emboava s. m. + f. nickname applied by the Brazilians to Portuguese or other foreigners who came into the hinterland in quest of gold and precious stones.

emboca s. m. (N. Braz.) gate crasher, party crasher.

emboçador s. m. mason who puts on the first layer of plaster; hence plasterer or, by extension, mason.

embocadura s. f. 1. mouthpiece of a musical instrument (as a trumpet or flute). 2. nozzle. 3. bit of a bridle. 4. mouth or passage (as of a river); estuary. 5. (fig.) tendency, propensity, inclination. 6. branch (plumbing) (plate C 1).

emboçamento s. m. act of plastering the ridge tiles onto a roof.

embocar v. 1. to set a wind instrument to one's mouth. 2. to put the mouthpiece on an instrument (trumpet, flute, etc.). 3. to put to one's mouth. 4. to empty (glass, bottle). 5. to bit a horse. 6. to fall or flow into (river). 7. to run into (street). 8. (Braz., pop.): a) to shoot into the hole (marbles). b) to hole (golf).

emboçar v. 1. to plaster (walls, etc.). 2. to roughcast a wall. 3. to plaster the ridge tiles onto a roof.

emboço (ô) s. m. (pl. **emboços**) first layer of plaster, roughcast.

embodegar v. 1. to make dirty, soil. 2. to begrime, befoul. 3. to stain, besmear, smirch.

embodocar-se v. (S. Braz.) 1. to curve or bend to take the shape of a slingshot fork. 2. to harden the loin (horse) preparing to caper.

embófia s. f. 1. presumption, conceit, haughtiness. 2. emposture, sham.

embolação s. f. (pl. **-ões**) act of padding the horns of a bull.

embolada s. f. 1. (N. Braz.) a sort of music. 2. (tech.) piston stroke.

embolar v. 1. to pad the horns of bulls to prevent them from hurting people. 2. to shape into a ball.

embolia s. f. (med.) embolism: the stopping up of a vein or artery.

embolismo s. m. embolism: intercalation of days in a year for the adjustment of the calendar.

êmbolo s. m. 1. (mech.) piston (plates B 14, C 11). 2. (med.) embolus: any body that forms an obstruction in a blood vessel.

bomba de ~ piston pump. haste do ~ piston rod.

embolorado, embolorecido adj. (also **abolorecido**) mouldy, musty.

embolorar, embolorecer v. (also **abolorecer**) to become mouldy or musty.

embolsar v. 1. to pocket, pouch, purse, put into a pocket, purse or pouch. 2. to pay, reimburse, refund.

embolso (ô) s. m. (pl. **embolsos**) 1. pocketing up, act of pouching. 2. getting in, receipt of payment. 3. reimbursement, (re)payment.

embonar v. to refit or sheathe the hull of a ship.

embondeiro s. m. (bot.) baobab, monkey bread.

embondo s. m. trouble, embarrassment.

embonecar v. 1. to adorn, doll up. 2. to dress like a doll. 3. ~-se to adorn o. s., dress o. s. up. 4. (agric.) to ear.

embonecrar v. (Braz.) = **embonecar** 4.

embora adv. (obs.) auspiciously, in a good time; even so. ‖ conj. (al)though, albeit, however, in despite of. ‖ vá ~! interj. begone!, go away!, be off! ~ fosse tarde, decidimos partir though it was late, we decided to set out. ele mandou-me ~ he sent me away. ir ~ to go away, leave, depart. muito ~ seja assim although it really is so. queira desculpar-me, mas tenho de ir-me ~ if you will kindly excuse me, I'm afraid I must be going now. tenho de ir-me ~ I must be off.

emboras s. m. pl. congratulations, compliments.

emborcação s. f. (pl. **-ões**) 1. act of turning upside down. 2. emptying (drinking up). 3. fall. 4. (med.) embrocation.

emborcar v. (S. Braz., also **emborquilhar**) 1. to turn mouth downwards, upside down (glass, vessel). 2. to empty to the last drop, drain off. 3. to pour out, empty. 4. to fall, tumble.

emborco s. m. = **embarcação.**

embornal s. m. (pl. **-ais**) 1. foddersack, nose-bag, feed bag. 2. **-ais** pl. (naut.) scupper holes.

embornalar v. 1. to put into the foddersack. 2. (fig.) to economize, spare, save.

emborque s. m. 1. act of keeling a ship. 2. emptying (of a glass, bottle, etc.).

emborrachar v. 1. to intoxicate, make drunk. 2. ~-se to get drunk.

emborralhar v. 1. to cover with ashes or burning coals. 2. to begrime with ashes. 3. ~-se to wallow in ashes (like a cat).

emborrascar v. 1. to darken. 2. to overcloud, grow dark or stormy. 3. to agitate. 4. to lash up (the sea).

emboscada s. f. 1. ambush, ambuscade: a) act of lying in wait to surprise or attack an enemy. b) hiding place. 2. snare, trap. 3. (fig.) treason. ficar de ~ to lie in ambuscade.

emboscar v. (also ~-se) to ambush: 1. hide in order to attack unexpectedly. 2. ambuscade, attack from an ambush. 3. lie in wait for.

embostar, embostear v. to besmear with dung.

embostelar v. 1. to cover with blisters or pimples. 2. to pustulate. 3. to dirty, begrime.

embotadeira s. f. tops: kneepieces of boots.

embotador adj. blunting: that which dulls the edge of.

embotadura s. f. **embotamento** m. blunting, bluntness, dullness, obtuseness, want of edge.

embotar v. 1. to blunt: dull the edge of. 2. to benumb, make insensible. 3. to grow feeble, weaken, enervate. 4. ~-se: a) to be blunted, grow dull. b) to grow weak, lose force.
~ os dentes to set the teeth on edge.

embotelhar v. to bottle, put in bottles.

embotijar v. 1. to put in a jug or jugs. 2. (naut.) to reinforce cards or ropes.

embraçadeira s. f. = **braçadeira.**

embraçar v. 1. to hold with the arm. 2. to give one's arm to, support. 3. to carry under the arm.

embrace s. m. curtain hook.

embragueira s. f. recess in the shaft of oxcarts.

embramar v. to enrage, grow furious.

embrancar v. 1. to whiten, make or become white. 2. to grow white.

embrandecer v. 1. to soften, slacken, relax. 2. to calm, soothe, still, relent. 3. to move, stir.

embranquecer v. 1. to whiten, bleach, make white. 2. ~-se: a) to grow white. b) to turn gray (hair). ~ de velho to get white hair.

embravear, embravecer v. 1. to enrage, infuriate. 2. to make fierce or furious. 3. ~-se: a) to rage, get mad, wild or angry; become irritated. b) to grow rough (sea).

embravecido adj. 1. furious, angry. 2. fierce. 3. rough, stormy (sea). mar ~ rough sea.

embravecimento s. m. 1. anger, rage, enragement, fury. 2. fierceness. 3. roughness (of the sea).

embreadura s. f. act of pitching, tarring.

embreagem s. f. (pl. **-ens**) (tech.) 1. coupling, clutch (plate M 13). 2. connection.
~ acionadora drive clutch. ~ de dentes claw clutch. ~ de discos disk clutch. ~ de manga

clutch coupling. ~ **presa** jammed clutch. **eixo da** ~ clutch shaft. **pedal de** ~ clutch pedal.

embrear (I) v. to pitch, tar, cover with pitch or tar.

embrear (II) v. (tech.) to let the clutch in, throw into gear, couple, connect.

embrechado s. m. 1. shell-work. 2. decorative masonry of little stones, pebbles or shells, for grottos or wells. 3. (fam.) annoying person. 4. (fig.) impediment.

embrechar v. 1. to adorn with shells, pebbles or stones. 2. to interfere, meddle.

embrenhar v. 1. to hide in the thicket of a wood. 2. to penetrate into the woods. 3. ~**-se** to hide o. s. in the woods.

embretada s. f. (S. Braz.) fix, difficulty, mess.

ele meteu-se numa ~ (S. Braz.) he got into a fix.

embriagado adj. 1. drunk(en), tipsy, intoxicated, inebriated. 2. (fig.) enchanted, (en)raptured, rapt.

completamente ~ drunk and incapable. **ele ainda não estava** ~ he was not drunk yet, (coll.) he walked the chalk. **ele chegou a casa** ~ he came home drunk, (sl.) he came home with a skinful. **ele está** ~ he is drunk. **ele estava bastante** ~ he was the worse for drink.

embriagador adj., **embriagante** m. + f. 1. intoxicating, intoxicant. 2. (fig.) exciting, entrancing, inebriating. **perfume** ~ inebriating perfume.

embriagar v. 1. to make drunk, intoxicate, alcoholize, inebriate. 2. (fig.) to enchant, charm; amaze. 3. (fig.) to ravish, infatuate, enrapture, besot. 4. ~**-se**: a) to drink to excess, get drunk. b) (fig.) to be enraptured, become enchanted.

embriaguez s. f. 1. drunkenness, intoxication, inebriety, tipsiness. 2. (fig.) ecstasy, rapture, enthusiasm.

embrião s. m. (pl. **-ões**) 1. (zool.) embryo, germ. 2. (bot.) plantule, plantlet. 3. (anat.) foetus (until the third month of development). 4. (fig.) beginning, origin; anything yet unfinished.

embridar v. 1. to bridle, put a bridle on. 2. to pace with the head lifted up, lift the head elegantly (horse). 3. (fig.) to be proud or arrogant.

embrincar v. 1. to adorn, trim. 2. to embellish, beautify.

embriocardia s. f. (med.) embryocardia: heart-beat resembling that of a fetus.

embriogenia s. f. (med.) embryogeny: formation or origin of the embryo.

embriologia s. f. (biol.) embryology: science of the development of the embryo.

embriológico adj. embryologic(al): of or pertaining to embryology.

embriologista s. m. + f. embryologist: an expert in embryology.

embrionário adj. (med.) embryonic, embryolike.

embrionífero adj. (med.) embryoniferous: containing an embryo.

embrioniforme adj. m. + f. embryoniform: resembling an embryo.

embriopatia s. f. (path.) embryopathy.

embriotomia s. f. (surg.) embryotomy: cutting up of a fetus to facilitate delivery.

embriótomo s. m. (surg.) embryotome: cutting instrument used in embryotomy.

embriulco s. m. (surg.) embryulcus: a sort of blunt hook to remove the dead fetus from the uterus.

embrocação s. f. (pl. **-ões**) (med.) embrocation: 1. application of a liquid medicament. 2. a liquid medicine for external use.

embroma s. m. (also **embromação** f., pl. **-ões**) (Braz.) 1. cheating, deceiving, humbug, fake. 2. mockery. 3. delaying, a putting off (business). 4.

false promise. 5. boasting, boastful talk. 6. derision, mockery.

embromador s. m. (also **embromeiro**) (Braz.) swindler, cheat, deceiver; cunning fellow, talker.

embromar v. (Braz.) 1. to swindle, cheat, defraud, deceive. 2. to make false promise. 3. to make fun of, scoff, mock. 4. to boast, brag. 5. to delay, put off (business). 6. to move or walk slowly. 7. to jest, joke.

embruacar v. (Braz.) to put in a **bruaca**.

embrulhada s. f. 1. confusion, disorder, complication. 2. entanglement, imbroglio; mix-up, imbroilment. 3. muddle, mess. 4. embarrassment, difficulty, fix, knotty problem, hot water. 5. (fig.) quarrel, intrigue.

fiz uma ~ I made a mess of it. **meti-me numa** ~ **dos diabos** I got in a hell of a mess.

embrulhado adj. 1. wrapped up. 2. entangled, confused, muddled, involved. 3. (fig.) deluded, deceived. **tenho o estômago** ~ (fig.) I am in a kecking mood. **ele foi** ~ he was cheated, taken in.

embrulhador s. m. 1. wrapper. 2. (fig.): a) entangler, muddler. b) cheat. || adj. 1. confusing, embroiling. 2. baffling.

embrulhamento s. m. 1. packing or wrapping up, package. 2. = **embrulhada.**

embrulhar v. 1. to wrap up, pack up. 2. to double, fold, bundle. 3. to confuse, complicate, intricate, entangle, embarrass. 4. to perplex, confound. 5. to nauseate. 6. (Braz.) to deceive, cheat. 7. ~**-se**: a) to stammer, hesitate, hem and haw. b) to wrap o. s. up (in a coat). c) to become overcast, get cloudy (weather).

embrulhei-me todo (falando) I stammered, I got embarrassed. **ele embrulhou-me** (Braz.) he got over me. **embrulhe-o em papel de seda** wrap it in tissue paper. **ele embrulhou-se no discurso** he lost the thread of the speech. **ele embrulhou-se no seu capote** he wrapped himself in his cloak. **você está me embrulhando!** you are trying to diddle me! **isto me embrulhou o estômago** it turned my stomach.

embrulho s. m. 1. bundle, parcel, packet, package. 2. intrigue, plot. 3. confusion, entanglement. 4. (Braz.) swindle, trick.

atar um ~ to tie up a parcel. **estou num** ~**!** I'm in a mess! **fazer um** ~ to wrap a parcel. **fui no** ~ (sl.) I was tricked. **papel de** ~ brown paper, wrapping paper.

embruscar(-se) v. 1. to darken, grow cloudy. 2. to be overcast (sky). 3. (fig.) to be sad or afflicted. 4. to become annoyed.

embrutecer v. (also **embrutar**) 1. to brutalize, bestialize. 2. to become brutish or coarse. 3. to stupidify, besot, make stupid. 4. ~**-se** to become brutish, grow stupid.

embrutecimento s. m. 1. brutalization. 2. stupefying. 3. coarsening.

embruxar v. to bewitch, affect by sorcery or magic.

embuá s. m. (Braz., zool.) myriapod, centiped.

embuçadela s. f. (S. Braz.) act of putting a halter on a horse.

embuçado adj. 1. wrapped up, muffled up. 2. feigned, disguised; cloaked. || **-amente** adv. dissemblingly.

embuçalador s. m. (S. Braz.) 1. person who puts a halter on a horse. 2. (fig.) scoundrel, rogue.

embuçalar v. 1. to put a halter on a horse. 2. (fig.) to deceive, cheat.

embuçar v. 1. to cloak, veil. 2. to disguise, dissemble. 3. ~**-se**: a) to muffle or wrap o. s. up (in a cloak). b) to disguise o. s.

~ **a parede** to roughcast a wall. **embucei-me na capa** I wrapt myself in my cloak.

embuchado adj. 1. glutted, gorged, full-fed, replete. 2. reserved, uncommunicative. 3. mischievous, brooding.

embuchar (I) v. 1. to stuff one's craw (or belly), to glut. 2. to satiate. 3. to shut up, keep silent, stop one's gab. 4. to be or become shy. 5. (Braz.) to pout, sulk.

embuchar (II) v. (tech.) to bush, fit with a bushing.

embuço s. m. 1. wrap, muffler, veil. 2. disguise, dissimulation.

embudar v. 1. to dope (fishes, throwing poisonous plants into the water). 2. (fig.) to sulk, pout.

embude s. m. 1. fish poison. 2. (bot.) poison hemlock. 3. a kind of funnel.

embuizar v. (obs.) to bend, curve.

emburacar(-se) v. (N. Braz.) 1. to hole, get or haste into a hole. 2. to disappear, vanish. 3. to lose money.

emburrado s. m. (Braz.) place covered with rounded stones. ‖ adj. 1. sulky, moody, out of humour. 2. annoyed, angry. 3. bored, irksome.

hoje ele está ~ he is out of humour today.

emburramento s. m. the state of being moody, out of humour.

emburrar v. 1. to become brutish. 2. to sulk, pout, grouch. 3. to become sullen.

emburricar v. 1. to bewitch, seduce, fascinate. 2. to deceive, cheat.

embuste s. m. (also **embustice** f.) 1. a sly lie, falsehood. 2. ruse, stratagem, clever trick, artifice. 3. fraud, deceit, cheat, imposture, hoax. 4. flimflam.

embustear v. 1. to cheat, hoax, trick, deceive. 2. to tell lies, pretend, sham.

embusteiro s. m. liar, deceiver, impostor, cheater, swindler, trickster. ‖ adj. 1. lying, cheating. 2. deceptive, fraudulent, tricky.

embutideira s. f. a device to make buttons in relief.

embutido s. m. inlaid work, intarsia, mosaic. ‖ adj. 1. inlaid, inserted. 2. forced in. 3. (archit.) built-in.

armário ~ built-in closet.

embutidura s. f. inlaid work, intarsia.

embutir v. 1. to inlay, encrustate, imbed, incrust. 2. to make intarsia work. 3. to joggle.

embuziar v. 1. to soil, besmear, make dirty. 2. ~-se: a) to get annoyed or disgusted. b) to enrage, become furious.

embuzinado adj. sounding like a horn.

embuzinar v. 1. to resound like a horn. 2. to soil, make dirty.

eme s. m. name of the letter **M**.

emedar v. to rick, heap up in ricks; stack, pile (grain, hay, etc.).

emelar v. 1. to sweeten, add honey to. 2. to cover with honey. 3. (fig.) to make pleasant or gratifying. 4. to become covered or besmeared with honey.

emelia s. f. emmeleia.

emenagogo s. m. (med.) emmenagogue: any medicine that stimulates the menstrual flow. ‖ adj. emmenagogic, promoting menstruation.

emenda s. f. 1. correction: a) emendation, rectification. b) amendment, regeneration. c) reformation. 2. a proofreader's corrections. 3. piece joined on, joining. 4. seam. 5. (fig.) repair; patch; patched place or spot.

~ **em alça** (naut.) eye splice. **é pior a** ~ **do que o soneto** the remedy is worse than the disease. **não tem** ~ it is beyond amendment, it is past praying for. **sem** ~ seamless.

emendar v. 1. to correct, remove faults or errors from, amend, emend. 2. to ameliorate, improve, get better. 3. to repair, mend; patch. 4. to modify,

charge. 5. ~-se: a) to repent, reform. b) to regenerate o. s. c) to mend one's ways.

~ **cabos** (naut.) to splice ropes. ~ **a vida** to mend one's ways. **nunca é tarde para nos emendarmos** it is never too late to begin a new life.

emendável adj. m. + f. (pl. **-áveis**) amendable, emendable, improvable, reparable.

ementa s. f. 1. roll, list. 2. memorandum book. 3. annotation. 4. summary. 5. reminiscence, commemoration.

ementar v. 1. to point out. 2. to make a note. 3. to recall, call to mind.

ementário s. m. memorandum book, record, register.

emergência s. f. 1. emergency: a) incident. b) dangerous or crucial moment, crisis. c) necessity, exigency. 2. emergence: a) act of emerging. b) rising, emersion, appearance. c) (bot.) outgrowth.

chamada de ~ emergency call. **em caso de** ~ in case of emergency. **freio de** ~ emergency brake. **porta de** ~ emergency door. **pronto para todas as** ~**s** ready for all emergencies. **saída de** ~ emergency exit.

emergente adj. m. + f. 1. emergent, emerging. 2. resultant.

emergir v. to emerge: 1. rise out from or as from a fluid. 2. appear, become manifest. 3. come into view.

emérito adj. 1. emeritus, honourably retired. 2. eminent, illustrious. 3. wise, sage.

êmero s. m. scorpion senna: a yellow-flowered shrub (Coronilla emerus).

emersão s. f. (pl. **-ões**) emersion: 1. emergence. 2. reappearance of a celestial body after an eclipse.

emerso adj. emersed, emerged, emergent; buoyant, afloat.

emeticidade s. f. (med.) emetic quality or effect.

emético s. m. (med.) emetic: agent which causes vomiting. ‖ adj. emetic(al), vomitory.

emetina s. f. (chem.) emetine: alkaloid found in ipecacuanha.

emetizar v. to mix with an emetic (as medicine).

emetrope adj. (anat.) emmetropic (eye).

emigração s. f. (pl. **-ões**) 1. emigration: a) act of emigrating. b) emigrants collectively. 2. migration (of animals).

emigrado s. m., **emigrante** m. + f. emigrant; migrator. ‖ adj. emigrant.

emigrar v. 1. to emigrate: leave one's own country or region to settle in another. 2. to migrate, move from one place to settle (temporarily) in another (animals).

eminência s. f. 1. eminence, height. 2. hill, elevated ground. 3. excellence, superiority. 4. elevation, moral exaltation. 5. Eminency, Eminence (a cardinal's title).

Vossa Eminência Your Eminency.

eminente adj. m. + f. 1. eminent, prominent. 2. high, elevated. 3. supreme, excellent. 4. famous, illustrious. ‖ ~**mente** adv. 1. eminently. 2. highly. 3. in the highest degree.

ele foi um estadista ~ he was an eminent statesman. **ele tornou-se** ~ he became eminent, he came to the top.

Eminentíssimo adj. absolute sup. of **eminente** most eminent (an archbishop's or cardinal's title).

emir s. m. emir, emeer (title of dignity among Mohammedan peoples).

emirado s. m. emirate: 1. office or rank of an emir. 2. a country ruled by an emir.

emissão s. f. (pl. **-ões**) 1. emission: a) act of emitting. b) publication. c) act of putting into circulation, issuing, emanation. 2. ejection, discharge. 3. radio broadcast.

~ **atmosférica** airglow. ~ **de notas de banco** issue of bank-notes. ~ **de papel-moeda** issue of paper-currency.

emissário s. m. 1. emissary, agent. 2. messenger. 3. spy, secret agent. 4. drainage channel. ‖ adj. emissary.

emissivo adj. 1. emissive, issuable. 2. that emits.

emissor s. m. 1. sender, emitter. 2. transmitter. 3. issuing agent or element. ‖ adj. emissory, issuing, emissive.

banco ~ issuing bank.

emissora s. f. broadcasting station.

Emissora Nacional National Broadcasting Station.

emitir v. 1. to emit, issue. 2. to expel, eject, discharge. 3. to put into circulation; publish. 4. to broadcast. 5. to utter (an opinion). 6. to produce, bring forth, give out. 7. ~-se to be emitted or issued.

~ **notas de banco** to issue bank-notes. ~ **som** to emit sound. ~ **uma opinião** to utter an opinion. **ela emitiu a sua opinião** she gave her opinion.

emoção s. f. (pl. -ões) emotion, thrill, excitement, commotion.

emocionado adj. emotioned, thrilled; affected, touched. **ficar** ~ **com a interpretação de uma peça** to be thrilled by the play.

emocional adj. m. + f. (pl. -ais) emotional. ‖ ~mente adv. emotionally.

emocionante adj. m. + f. 1. emotive, causing emotion. 2. exciting, thrilling. 3. impressive.

um espetáculo ~ an impressive sight.

emocionar v. 1. to thrill, cause emotion. 2. to move, touch, affect. 3. to impress. 4. ~-se to feel emotion, be impressed.

emoldar v. 1. to mold, shape, form. 2. = **emoldurar**.

emoldurar v. to frame: 1. set in a frame. 2. case. 3. surround, frame with.

emoliente s. m. + f. (med.) emollient: a softening or soothing external application. ‖ adj. m. + f. emollient, softening, soothing.

emolir v. (med.) to mollify, soften, soothe, mitigate.

emolumento s. m. 1. emolument: a) salary, fee. b) gain, profit. c) advantage. 2. ~s pl. eventual returns, profits, perquisites.

~s **consulares** consular fees. ~s **judiciais** judicial fees.

emonar-se v. (pop.) 1. to become sullen, to pout. 2. to become ruffled or irritated. 3. to be sulky.

emordaçar v. (usually **amordaçar**) to gag, muzzle.

emortecer v. less used form of **amortecer**.

emostar v. 1. to ripen, sweeten (grapes). 2. to put into must.

emotividade s. f. emotivity, emotionality, emotiveness.

emotivo adj. emotive, emotional. ‖ -**amente** adv. emotively.

emouquecer v. to deafen, make or become deaf.

empa s. f. tying, staking or propping up (vines).

empacador s. m. 1. (Braz.) a balky horse or beast. 2. (S. Braz.) stutterer.

empacar v. (Braz.) 1. to balk: stop short and refuse to go (horse or beast). 2. = **empacotar**.

empacavirar v. (N. Braz.) to wrap up twisted tobacco in **pacavira** (Heliconia pendula) leaves for preservation purposes.

empachado adj. 1. surfeited, crammed with food. 2. encumbered, overloaded, overfilled, overfull. 3. big-bellied.

empachamento s. m. 1. surfeit, repletion. 2. overloading. 3. obstacle, obstruction, hindrance.

~ **do estômago** overloading of the stomach.

empachar v. 1. to overfeed, overload, cram the stomach, cloy. 2. to encumber, overburden. 3. to hin-

der, obstruct, clog. 4. ~-se: a) to be crammed with food. b) to be overfreighted (as a ship).

empache s. f. (N. Braz.) peevishness, impertinence.

empacho s. m. 1. surfeit, repletion, cramming. 2. overloading, encumbrance. 3. obstacle, obstruction, hindrance, clog.

empachoso adj. 1. embarrassing, troublesome, cloggy. 2. (fig.) timid, bashful.

empaçocar v. (Braz.) 1. to crumple, wrinkle. 2. to eat one's fill of **paçoca** (Brazilian dish of fried meat ground with manioc flour). 3. to tangle, ensnare. 4. (fig.) to cram, glut.

empacotador s. m. 1. packer, wrapper. 2. binder; baler. ‖ adj. packing, wrapping.

empacotadora s. f. (also **empacotadeira**) baler: baling machine.

empacotamento s. m. 1. package, wrappage: act or process of packing. 2. binding, baling.

empacotar v. 1. to pack or wrap up. 2. to package. 3. to bale, form into a bundle. 4. to incase, box.

empada s. f. 1. patty: pastry made with meat, shrimp, fish or the like. 2. (fam.) meddlesome person.

empadroar v. 1. to register (tax-payers). 2. ~-se: a) to be registered. b) to inscribe or enrol o. s.

empáfia s. f. 1. haughtiness. 2. pride, arrogance, conceit, self-esteem. 3. presumption. 4. m. conceited person.

empaiolar v. to keep in a locker or silo.

empalação s. f. (hist.) impalement: punishment by empaling.

empalamado, empalemado adj. 1. covered with plasters. 2. full of sores or ulcers. 3. sick, weak, ill. 4. ulcerated. 5. pale.

empalamar-se v. (S. Braz.) to grow sick.

empalar v. 1. to impale: pierce with sharp stakes. 2. (fig.) to torture.

empaletar v. (naut.) to place packs, goods on pallets.

empalhação s. f. (pl. -ões) (also **empalhamento** m.) 1. packing in straw. 2. stuffing or covering with straw. 3. (fig.) delaying, retardation, procrastination. 4. (fam.) subterfuge, evasion.

empalhador s. m. 1. person who covers, packs or stuffs with straw. 2. cane-worker. ‖ adj. (S. Braz.) lazy, idle, truant.

~ **de cadeira** chair-bottomer.

empalhar v. 1. to pack in straw (fruits, etc.). 2. to stuff with straw (animals). 3. to cover with straw (glasses, bottles). 4. to cane (as chairs); put straw seats in chairs. 5. (fig.) to put off, delay; defer, procrastinate.

empalheirar v. 1. to gather hay or straw into the barn. 2. to put a straw bottom in chairs; to cane.

empalidecer v. (also **empalecer**) 1. to pale: make or turn pale. 2. to blanch. 3. (fig.) to fade.

empalmação s. f. (pl. -ões) 1. palming, sleight of hand. 2. pilfering, snatching, (U. S. A.) swiping, sly theft.

empalmador s. m. 1. palmer, prestidigitator. 2. pilferer, thief, swindler.

empalmar v. 1. to palm: hide in the hand (as in sleight of hand tricks); grasp. 2. to pilfer, filch, snatch.

~ **o dinheiro a alguém** to rob one.

empambado adj. (N. Braz.) 1. pale, bloodless. 2. anemic.

empampanar v. to become covered with shoots (a vine).

empanada s. f. 1. big pie of meat or shrimps. 2. window-frame covered with paper or linen (instead of glass).

empanado s. m. (N. Braz.) person who wears cashmere or cotton suits (and no leather garments). ‖

adj. 1. wrapped up in or covered with cloth. 2. lusterless. 3. dull, dim.

empanamento s. m. 1. wrappage in or covering with cloth. 2. tarnishing, dulling. 3. dimness, dullness.

empanar v. 1. to cover (with cloth), wrap up. 2. to darken, obscure. 3. to dim, dull. 4. to tarnish, sully, stain. 5. to cloak, hide, conceal. 6. ~-se to grow dull or tarnished.

empancar v. 1. to latch, secure with a wooden lever. 2. to sustain, refrain. 3. to dam up. 4. to clog, hold back, hinder.

empandeirar v. 1. to swell (sails), be puffed up. 2. to cause to rise or increase. 3. to squander, waste. 4. to deceive, cheat. 5. to get rid of.

empandilhar v. 1. to swindle, cheat (at cards). 2. (fam.) to steal dexterously. 3. ~-se to join in a plot in order to cheat (esp. at cards).

empaneirar v. to put into a pannier.

empangar v. (S. Braz.) to be inert, be inactive; feel cold or down.

empanque s. m. stuffing, packing, gasket.

caixa de ~ packing box.

empantanar v. 1. to make swampy. 2. to put or throw into the dirt or mire. 3. ~-se: a) to sink into the mud, stick in the mire. b) to grow swampy or marshy (fields, etc.).

empantufar-se v. 1. to put on one's slippers. 2. (fig.) to flaunt, strut, boast; fill o. s. with pride.

empanturrar v. 1. to stuff, glut, cram, gorge (with food). 2. ~-se: a) to fill one's belly, eat one's fill, cram o. s. b) to grow proud, become haughty or arrogant.

empanzinador s. m. 1. glutton, greedy eater, gorger. 2. swindler, cheat.

empanzinamento s. m. glut, surfeit, stuffing, cramming.

empanzinar v. 1. to surfeit, stuff, glut, gorge, cram. 2. to shock, surprise disagreeably. 3. to humbug, deceive, cheat. 4. ~-se to fill one's belly, eat one's fill.

empapar v. 1. to cover with a paste or poultice. 2. to make soft as pap. 3. to drench, soak, sop. 4. to imbibe, steep. 5. to immerge. 6. (bullfighting) to wave the muleta (red flag) before the bull's eyes (to arrest the animal's attention). 7. ~-se to be or become wet through, get soaked; be drenched. 8. (Braz.): a) to eat a cropful, stuff the craw (goose, duck, etc.). b) (fig.) to pocket, get, obtain.

empapelador s. m. 1. packer: person who makes up paper parcels or bundles. 2. paperer, paper hanger.

empapelar v. 1. to wrap in paper, pack up in parcels. 2. to paper (wall). 3. to keep or store away very carefully.

empapelo s. m. the wrapping of tobacco in paper (in factories).

empapuçado adj. 1. pouchy, puffed up, swollen. 2. stuffed, satiated.

olhos ~s swollen eyes, puffy eyes.

empapuçar v. 1. to fold, crease, plait. 2. to bloat, puff up. 3. ~-se to become bloated or swollen.

empaquetamento s. m. (S. Braz.) act of dressing o. s. up or of adorning o. s.

empaquetar-se v. (S. Braz.) to trim or tuck o. s. up, make o. s. fine.

empar v. to stake, prop (vines).

~ **a vinha** to prop a vine.

emparceirar v. 1. to unite, join. 2. to match up, couple, pair, fit together. 3. to link. 4. ~-se to associate with, unite in company with.

empardar v. (S. Braz.) to pair, arrange in a pair.

empardecer v. 1. to darken. 2. to make grey or brown. 3. ~-se to become grey, dark or brown.

emparedado adj. walled in, enclosed in walls, shut in or up.

emparedar v. 1. to wall in, cloister, shut up between walls. 2. ~-se to immure o. s.

emparelhado adj. 1. paired, coupled. 2. abreast; in pairs. 3. yoked, matched.

emparelhamento s. m. 1. pairing, matching, coupling. 2. equalizing.

emparelhar v. 1. to pair, couple. 2. to unite, join, link. 3. to yoke. 4. to make equal or alike. 5. to match, mate. 6. to assort, classify. 7. to fit, suit, make suitable. 8. to resemble, be like or similar. 9. to compare with, parallel, rival. 10. to level, make even. 11. to stand on a par. 12. to team up. 13. ~-se to be or become equal, matched or coupled.

emparrar v. 1. to leaf, grow leaves (vines). 2. to be covered with leaves (vines).

emparreirar v. to trellis; stake up vines.

emparvamento s. m. (S. Braz.) piling up of sheaves of grain.

emparvar(-se), emparvoecer(-se) v. 1. to make or become silly or stupid. 2. (S. Braz.) to make up into ricks or shocks (sheaves of grain).

emparvecer v. = emparvar, emparvoecer.

empasma s. m. empasm: perfumed powder used to remove any disagreeable body odour.

empastado adj. 1. impasted. 2. plastered down (as wet hair).

empastamento s. m. (also **empaste**) impastation: 1. pasting up. 2. plastering. 3. (painting) act of applying impasto to.

empastar v. to impast: 1. paste, plaster. 2. turn into paste. 3. (painting) apply impasto to. 4. to apply paint in great quantities. 5. (bookbinding) to case in.

empastatriz s. f. (tech.) mixing and kneading machine.

empastelamento s. m. devastation, ravage of the installations of a newspaper (usually for political reasons).

empastelar v. 1. (typogr.) to pie (types). 2. to destroy the installations of a newspaper. 3. to become disarranged, out of order (form, letter-board or setting-rule).

empata s. m. 1. (sl.) spoil-sport, mar-feast, disturber, intruder. 2. (Port.) embargo, confiscation.

empatado adj. 1. drawn (game). 2. invested (money). 3. put off, delayed, suspended.

capital ~ engaged capital. **o jogo terminou** ~ the game ended in a draw.

empatar v. 1. (gambling, sports, etc.) to be or end drawn. 2. to tie up, bind money in business. 3. (chess) to stalemate. 4. to stop, hinder, intercept. 5. to embarrass, disturb. 6. to tie, be or become equal. 7. to make equal, equalize (votes).

empatei capital em I tied up money in. ~ **tempo com alguma coisa** to dwell on something. **eu não quero** ~ **o seu tempo** I will not detain you, I will not keep you long. **os quadros de futebol empataram** the two teams played a drawn game.

empate s. m. 1. act or effect of being or becoming equal; equality. 2. (gambling, sports, etc.) draw, dead heat, tie. 3. (chess) stalemate (plate X). 4. irresolution, indecision. 5. unprofitable investment of capital. 6. obstacle, hindrance.

houve ~ **na eleição** there was a parity of votes.

empavesar v. 1. to flag, put on flags, adorn (ships) with a number of flags, pendants, etc. 2. ~-se: a) to grow proud, become vain. b) to smarten, spruce.

empavonar v. 1. to make proud. 2. to fill with pride. 3. ~-se: a) to become vain. b) to strut, flaunt.

c) to fill o. s. with pride. d) (fig.) to talk big, give o. s. great airs.

empeçar v. 1. to oppose, hinder, obstruct. 2. to entangle, embarrass; tangle. 3. to stumble against, meet with difficulties. 4. ~-se to be or become confused or embarrassed. 5. (Braz.) to begin, start.

empecer v. 1. to damage, hurt, harm. 2. to oppose, hinder, hamper. 3. to stop, impede. 4. to be embarrassed or confused. 5. to find obstacles, meet with difficulties.

empecilho s. m. impediment, difficulty, obstruction, check, snag, obstacle, hindrance, rub, trouble; drawback.

ele é um ~ he is a snag.

empecimento s. m. 1. (act or fact of) hindering. 2. obstacle, hindrance, cumbrance. 3. damage, harm.

empecível adj. m. + f. (pl. -íveis) (also **empecivo**) 1. hurtful. 2. obstructive.

empeço (ê) s. m. (pl. **empeços**) 1. obstacle, impediment, snag, obstruction. 2. (S. Braz.) beginning.

empeçonhar, empeçonhentar v. 1. to poison. 2. (fig.) to pervert, deprave; corrupt. 3. ~-se to take poison.

empedernido adj. petrified: 1. stony, hardened. 2. (fig.) unfeeling, insensible, heartless, obdurate. ‖ -amente adv. insensibly, obdurately.

empedernir v. (also **empedernecer**) to petrify: 1. to convert into stone. 2. (fig.): a) to become cruel. b) to harden, indurate (heart). c) to make insensible, obdurate. d) ~-se to be or become unfeeling, callous or cruel.

empedrado s. m. ground paved with stones or covered with gravel; stone pavement. ‖ adj. 1. covered with gravel, paved with stones. 2. hardened.

empedrador s. m. paver; person who lays cobblestones.

empedradura s. f. 1. = **empedramento**. 2. windgall: soft tumour on the fetlock joint of horses.

empedramento s. m. act or process of paving; gravelling.

empedrar v. 1. to pave, cover with a layer of gravel or stones. 2. (also ~-se) to petrify: a) become stony, convert into stone. b) harden, become motionless like stone.

empedrouçado adj. (Braz.) stony, full of stones.

empegar v. 1. to engulf, swallow up. 2. to throw into a pit, abyss, or whirlpool.

empeireirado adj. (N. Braz.) 1. rickety, affected with rickets. 2. rachitic.

empeireirar v. 1. to stop the growth of. 2. to atrophy. 3. to become rickety.

empeiticação s. f. (pl. -ões) (N. Braz.) obstination, obstinacy, stubbornness.

empeiticar v. (N. Braz.) to be obstinate or stubborn, to behave or act obstinately.

empelamar v. to put skins into a tan pit.

empelicar v. 1. to prepare kid leather or other fine skins. 2. to cover with kid leather.

empelo (ê) s. m. 1. lump of bread dough ready for the oven. 2. boiled vegetables pressed through a sieve (to be used as vegetable purée).

empelota s. f. small bottle, vial, ampulla, glass phial.

empena s. f. 1. gable, gable-end of a house (plate T 5). 2. warping of a board. 3. roof rafter, hip rafter, entablature of a roof. 4. a wood piece from the roof beam to the ridge beam. 5. the upper part of a wall in the shape of an isosceles triangle.

empenachar v. 1. to adorn with plumes or feathers. 2. (fig.) to make or become lively or elegant.

empenado adj. 1. feathered. 2. warped (wood, board).

empenagem s .f. (pl. -ens) (aeron.) empennage: tail unit.

empenamento s. m. warping, warpage, bending (wood, board).

empenar v. 1. to feather: a) (also ~-se) cover or become covered with feathers or plumes; fledge. b) fit or adorn with feathers. 2. to warp, bend (board).

o sol empenou a tábua the sun has warped the board.

empencado adj. (N. Braz.) clustered (like a bunch of bananas).

empendoar v. (Braz.) 1. to unclasp, bloom (as of the tassel of Indian corn). 2. to decorate with standards or banners.

empenha s. f. 1. the upper leather, uppers (of boots or shoes) (plates B 16, C 14). 2. patch, botch (on a shoe).

empenhado adj. 1. indebt(ed). 2. pledged, engaged, mortgaged. 3. pawned, put in pawn. 4. interested, concerned in.

estou muito ~ em fazer bem o serviço I am highly interested in doing well my work. **ele está ~ até os olhos** (fam.) he is hopelessly in debt. **eles estão ~s numa guerra total contra o crime** they are engaged in an all out war against crime.

empenhar v. 1. to pawn, mortgage, hypothecate. 2. to induce, attract. 3. to oblige, compel, impel. 4. to employ, apply. 5. to engage. 6. ~-se: a) to run into debts, indebt. b) to lay o. s. under an obligation. c) to take interest in, make every effort. d) to strive, bend, exert o. s. e) to insist, persevere.

~-se por alguém to put in for one. **ela empenhou-se muito** she engaged herself too far. **ele empenhou sua palavra** he pledged his faith (word). **eu me empenho** I exert myself.

empenho s. m. (also **empenhamento**) 1. act of pawning or mortgaging. 2. pledge, pawn. 3. engagement, promise. 4. obligation, liability. 5. protection, protector. 6. interest, diligence. 7. debt. 8. ardent desire, assiduity. 9. earnest striving. 10. allocation of funds for budget items.

com ~ earnestly, vehemently. **dar-se com todo o ~ a** to devote o. s. entirely to. **ele pôs grande ~ em conseguir o intento** he strained every nerve to obtain his end.

empenhoramento s. m. pawning, mortgaing, pledging.

empenhorar v. 1. to put in pawn, give as security. 2. to mortgage. 3. to pledge. 4. = **empenhar**.

empeno s. m. 1. warping, warpage, bending. 2. (fig.) obstacle, difficulty. 3. (pop.) mistake.

empepinar v. (sl.) 1. to embarrass, confuse. 2. ~-se to become confused, embarrassed.

emperiquitar-se v. (Braz.) to adorn o. s. in excess, overdress.

emperlar v. 1. to adorn with pearls. 2. to shape like pearls. 3. ~-se to adorn o. s. with pearls.

empernar v. to cross one's feet.

emperrado adj. 1. hard to open (as a lock). 2. jammed. 3. (fig.) obstinate, stiff, stubborn.

emperramento s. m. (also **emperro**) 1. act of jamming. 2. sticking fast. 3. obstinacy, stubbornness.

emperrar v. 1. to stick fast, jam, get jammed. 2. to harden, make hard. 3. to indurate (heart). 4. to stiffen. 5. to make angry. 6. to be stubborn, to sulk. 7. ~-se to make or become obstinate.

empertigado adj. 1. stiff, upright, erect. 2. supercilious, proud, haughty. 3. hard. 4. prim. 5. perky.

empertigar v. 1. to erect, raise. 2. to stiffen. 3. to straighten. 4. to bridle up. 5. to make proud. 6. ~-se to be or become proud or haughty.

~ o pescoço to hold up one's head.

empesgadura s. f. 1. coat of pitch. 2. pitching, covering with pitch.

empesgar v. to pitch: smear, cover, stain or treat with pitch.

empestar v. 1. to infect with plague, become pestiferous. 2. to contaminate. 3. (fig.) to corrupt, demoralize; deprave. 4. (fig.) to turn unpleasant through the contamination of the environment by noxious or harmful elements. 5. to become infected by a pest, become pestilent.

empetecar v. to adorn or to dress o. s. in an exaggerate and inaesthetic manner, overdress.

empetrácea s. f. plant of the family Empetraceae.

empetráceo adj. (bot.) empetraceous.

empezar v. 1. to pitch, cover with pitch. 2. to fumigate with pitch.

empezinhar v. 1. to pitch: cover or besmear with pitch. 2. to soil with pitch.

empicotar v. 1. to put on the top or summit. 2. to pillory, expose to scorn or ridicule.

empiema s. m. (med.) empyema.

empiemático adj. (med.) empyematic, empyemic.

empilchar v. (S. Braz.) 1. to cover with jewels or ornaments. 2. ~-se to cover o. s. with jewels or ornaments. 3. to get much money.

empilhamento s. m. heaping or piling up.

empilhar v. 1. to heap or pile up, stack. 2. to accumulate, amass.

empilhadeira de feno haystacking machine (plate S 1).

empinado adj. 1. straight, upright. 2. steep, precipitous, craggy. 3. rearing, prancing (horse). 4. elevated, raised up. 5. bombastic (style). 6. (fig.) exalted, sublime; proud, haughty.

empinar v. 1. to raise or lift up. 2. to put straight. 3. to tope, drink hard. 4. ~-se: a) to prance, rear up (horse). b) to stand on tiptoe. c) to tower above. d) (fig.) to grow proud, become arrogant or conceited, to give o. s. airs.

~ um papagaio to fly a kite. ele empina um copo he drinks a whole glass, he empties a glass. empinam-se as ondas the waves run mountain-high. o cavalo empinou-se the horse reared up. ~ as orelhas (cavalo) to prick up, erect the ears (horse).

empino s. m. 1. act or effect or standing or lifting up. 2. raising, lifting. 3. prancing, rearing (of a horse). 4. (fig.) haughtiness, pride, arrogance.

empiônfalo s. m. (path.) abscess in the navel.

empiorar v. (more usually piorar) 1. to worsen, make or become worse. 2. to aggravate. 3. ~-se to grow or become worse.

empiose s. f. (path.) formation of an empyema.

empipocar v. (Braz.) 1. to crackle, pop; burst. 2. to break out in pustules or bubbles.

empíreo s. m. empyrean: 1. the highest heaven. 2. the abode of God and angels. ‖ adj. empyreal, celestial, heavenly; divine, supernal.

empireuma s. m. empyreuma: disagreeable odor of burnt organic matter.

empírico s. m. empiric, quack, empiricist. ‖ adj. empiric(al), experimental. ‖ empiricamente adv. empirically, experimentally; by rote.

empirismo s. m. empiricism: 1. empirical method, individual experience. 2. quackery, charlatanry. 3. metaphysical theory that all ideas are derived from experience.

empirrear v. (N. Braz.) to brood, sit on eggs, incubate, hatch.

empirreio s. m. (Braz.) hatching, brooding.

emplacamento s. m. (Braz.) act or method of supplying with a plate (licence plate, number plate, etc.) or plaque.

emplacar v. (Braz.) to supply with a plate or plaque.

emplasmado adj. 1. covered with plasters. 2. full of sores, badly wounded. 3. sickly, given to aches and pains.

emplasmar v. to cover with plasters.

emplastação (pl. -ões), emplastagem (pl. -ens) s. f., emplastamento m. plastering, application of a plaster.

emplastrar v. (also emplastar) to plaster: 1. apply a plaster. 2. cover with a plaster.

emplástrico adj. useful or used as a plaster. medicamentos ~s (pharm.) emplastics.

emplastro s. m. (also emplasto) 1. (pharm.) plaster. 2. (fig.) patch(work). 3. (pop.) ailing, sick or troublesome person.

emplumação s. f. (pl. -ões) 1. feathering, getting a plumage. 2. decoration with feathers.

emplumado adj. feathered, plumed, adorned with feathers.

emplumar v. 1. to feather, fledge, cover or adorn with feathers. 2. ~-se: a) to become feathered. b) to adorn o. s.

empoado adj. covered with dust, powdered, dusty.

empoar v. to cover with dust; to dust, powder.

empobrecer v. 1. to make poor, impoverish, pauperize. 2. to exhaust, weaken, wear out. 3. to deplete (soil). 4. ~-se to grow poor, become impoverished.

empobrecimento s. m. 1. impoverishment: a reducing to indigence. 2. exhaustion. 3. depletion (of soil).

empoçado adj. 1. put in a well or puddle. 2. converted into a puddle.

empoçar v. 1. to put into a well or puddle. 2. to form a puddle or pool. 3. ~-se: to stick or sink in a mire.

empocilgar v. 1. to put in a pigsty. 2. to corral, shut in a pen.

empoeirar v. 1. to dust: a) cover with dust. b) make dusty. 2. (fig.) to obscure. 3. ~-se: to be dusty, become covered with dust.

empofe s. m. (N. Braz.) pride, arrogance, conceit.

empola (ô) s. f. (also ampola) 1. (air)bubble. 2. blister, pustule, vesicle. 3. ampoule, ampul(e). 4. knoll, mound. 5. (obs.) oasis.

empoláceo adj. (also empolar m. + f.) ampullaceous, bladderlike, shaped like an ampule.

empolado adj. 1. swollen: a) protruded. b) puffed up, proud; bombastic. 2. blistered. 3. rough (sea). ‖ -amente adv. 1. in a swollen manner. 2. (fig.) bombastically.

estilo ~ highflown style. mar ~ swelling sea, rough sea.

empolamento s. m. 1. act or effect of blistering. 2. a dry paint bubble. 3. volume increase in earthfill or excavation materials.

empolar v. 1. to blister, raise blisters on. 2. to swell, roughen, run high (sea). 3. ~-se to be or become proud, puffed up, haughty or arrogant.

empolear v. (India) 1. to pollute, profane, debase. 2. ~-se to become polluted, unclean.

empoleirar(-se) v. 1. to roost: perch or sit on a roost (birds). 2. (fig.): a) to raise to a dignity, rise in position. b) to grow proud, haughty or arrogant.

empolgadeira s. f. the notch or hole on each extremity of a crossbow.

empolgadura s. f. 1. grasping, handgrip, seizure. 2. ~s pl. notches or holes at each extremity of a crossbow.

empolgante adj. m. + f. 1. grasping, gripping. 2. exciting, thrilling, striking, overpowering.

empolgar v. 1. to grasp, grip, seize, grab, catch, lay hold of, clutch; take forcibly. 2. to thrill, excite, arrest, engross, absorb, grip (attention, interest). ~ alguém to overwhelm s. o., carry s. o. off his feet.

empolhar v. to brood, incubate, hatch, sit on eggs.

empolmar v. to inspissate, reduce to paste.

empombação s. f. (pl. **-ões**) (Braz.) 1. the refilling of a typesetting machine with lead slugs. 2. (fig.): a) persecution. b) anger.

empombar v. (Braz.) to anger, enrage.

empopar v. (N. Braz.) to have (a boat) more load--draught astern than at the forepart.

emporcalhar v. 1. to dirty, soil, mess up. 2. ∼-**se:** a) to drabble, dirt o. s. b) to degrade, debase or demean o. s.

empório s. m. 1. emporium: a) place of trade, market. b) trade center. 2. warehouse. 3. (Braz.) a grocer's store or shop.

empossado adj. vested, installed in office.

empossar v. 1. to give possession to or put in possession of. 2. ∼-**se:** a) to take possession of, appropriate. b) to assume office, install in office.

emposse s. f. 1. act of taking possession of. 2. seizure, occupation.

emposta s. f. 1. impost: the uppermost part of a column on which the end of an arch rests. 2. hindrance, obstacle.

empostação s. f. (pl. **-ões**) a pitching of the voice.

empostar v. 1. to pitch the voice properly. 2. (Port.) to bundle, arrange in bundles; to faggot.

emprazador s. m. 1. summoner, assigner. 2. beater, person who beats up game. ‖ adj. summoning, citing.

emprazamento s. m. 1. emphyteusis, cop/hold. 2. summons or warning to appear before the judge on an appointed day. 3. appointed date.

emprazar v. 1. to summon to appear, order to come, cite (at a given date). 2. to appoint, set a term, fix a date. 3. to convoke. 4. to challenge. 5. to let by emphyteusis. 6. to agree upon a meeting.

empreendedor s. m. 1. contractor, enterpriser, entrepreneur. 2. undertaker. ‖ adj. 1. pushing, active, bold. 2. enterprising. 3. adventurous. 4. courageous, daring.

ela tem um espírito ∼ she has a speculative spirit.

empreender v. 1. to undertake, attempt, take upon o. s., start, begin. 2. to enterprise, venture. 3. to have a go at, try, endeavour. 4. to outline, delineate, plan.

∼ **alguma coisa** to undertake s. th., lay hands on a thing. **empreenderei esta tarefa arriscada** I shall venture on (dial.: have a shot at this) risky business. **empreendi um negócio** I undertook a business. **ela empreendeu a obra com entusiasmo** she threw herself into her work.

empreendimento s. m. 1. undertaking, enterprise. 2. (ad)venture; attempt; speculation. 3. business; work; job.

∼ **arriscado** risky undertaking. ∼ **extravagante** fanciful venture.

empregada s. f. (Braz., also ∼ **doméstica**) maid, servant-girl, domestic servant.

empregado s. m. 1. employee. 2. functionary, office-holder. 3. clerk; servant. ‖ adj. 1. employed, occupied, busy. 2. applied.

∼ **bancário** bank clerk. ∼ **público** civil servant. **bem** ∼ (fam.) well-done, well-spent. **mal** ∼ ill--spent. **ela está -a como secretária** she is engaged as a secretary. **ele está** ∼ **em** he is employed in.

empregador s. m. 1. employer: person engaging or keeping others in service. 2. owner; boss, master.

empregar v. 1. to employ: a) make use of, utilize. b) give a job, engage, set to work. c) exert, apply, devote. 2. to invest, spend (money). 3. ∼-**se:** a) to employ o. s., get a job. b) to hold a public or private position, be in office.

∼ **bem** to make good use of. ∼ **a força** to use violence. ∼ **mal** to misuse. ∼ **o tempo no estudo** to devote time in studying. ∼ **todos os meios** to

have resort to all means. **empreguei bem o dinheiro** I placed the money on good security. **ele empregou seu dinheiro** he invested his money. **ele empregou-se nas minas** he found work in the mines.

emprego (ê) s. m. (pl. **empregos**) 1. employment: a) use, application, utilization, function, office post, position. b) charge. c) job, work, business, occupation. 2. public appointment.

∼ **fácil** soft job. **abandonar o** ∼ to leave one's job, quit. **agência de empregos** employment bureau. **ele está sem** ∼ he is out of employment. **sem** ∼ **de força** without resort to force. **solicitar um** ∼ to apply for a job.

empreguiçar v. to make or become lazy.

empreguismo s. m. (Braz.) tendency to give public office position abundantly and easily for political reasons.

empreguista s. m. + f. (Braz.) adherent or defender of **empreguismo**. ‖ adj. m. + f. of or relating to **empreguismo**.

empreita s. f. 1. stripe of esparto or matgrass used for making mats, creels, baskets, etc. 2. anything made of esparto. 3. = **empreitada**.

empreitada s. f. contract job, taskwork, piecework. **de** ∼ by the job, by contract. **trabalho por** ∼ work done by contract.

empreiteira s. f. (Braz.) a firm that contracts to be responsible for the performance of a construction job; building contracting firm working on a contract basis.

empreitar v. to job: take over on a contract basis.

empreiteiro s. m. 1. contractor, undertaker, entrepreneur. 2. jobber, person who works by the job, pieceworker.

emprenhar v. to impregnate, make pregnant, fecundate, beget.

empresa (ê) s. f. 1. enterprise, undertaking. 2. business. 3. company, firm. 4. intention, design, purpose.

∼ **árdua** hard task. ∼ **de navegação** shipping interest. ∼ **funerária** undertaking concern, mortuary.

empresar v. 1. to stop, dam up. 2. (theat.) to act as impresario.

empresariado s. m. the entrepreneurial class.

empresarial adj. m. + f. of or relating to enterprises, entrepreneurial.

empresário s. m. 1. undertaker, entrepreneur, contractor. 2. (theat.) impresario. ‖ adj. of or pertaining to an undertaking.

emprestado adj. 1. lent, loaned. 2. borrowed. **tomar ou pedir** ∼ to borrow.

emprestador s. m. loaner, lender.

emprestar v. 1. to lend, loan (**a** to). 2. to borrow (**de** from). 3. to communicate. 4. ∼-**se** to help one another.

empreste-me um lápis! lend me a pencil! **emprestei o livro a ela** I lent her the book. **emprestei a caneta dela** I borrowed her pen(holder).

empréstimo s. m. 1. a loan, lending. 2. borrowing. ∼ **hipotecário** a mortgage loan. **levantar um** ∼ to raise a loan.

emprisionar v. (usually **aprisionar**) to imprison.

emproado adj. 1. (naut.) sailing towards, headed for. 2. (fig.) proud, haughty, pretentious, arrogant.

emproar v. 1. (naut.) to steer right forward, head for. 2. ∼-**se** (fig.) to be or become proud, haughty or arrogant.

emprostótono s. m. (med.) emprosthotonos: convulsive contraction of the body.

empubescer(-se) v. 1. to reach puberty or manhood. 2. to become covered with hair or down.

empulhar v. 1. to jeer, jest, rally, banter. 2. to trick, cheat, make a fool of.

empunhadura s. f. hilt: the handle and guard of a sword or dagger; haft.
empunhar v. 1. to grasp, grip, gripe, lay hold of (by the handle, as a sword). 2. to hold up.
ele empunhou a espada he laid hold of the sword.
empurra s. f. act of pushing.
jogo de ~ passing the buck.
empurrão s. m. (pl. **-ões**) push, shove, jostle, thrust, poke.
aos -ões shovingly, violently, forcibly. **dei-lhe um ~** I gave him a shove. **ele abriu caminho aos -ões por entre a multidão** he shouldered his way through the crowd.
empurrar v. 1. to push, thrust (aside, away). 2. to press, force. 3. to shove, jostle, poke. 4. to drive. **~ para diante** to shove on. **~ alguém para fora** to push s. o. out. **~ para o lado** to shove aside. **empurraram-no para fora** they shouldered him out. **empurraram a tarefa para ele** they thrust the task upon him. **empurrei para frente** I thrust forward. **empurrei-lhe um serviço** I forced a task upon him. **não empurrei** don't push! **ser empurrado de cá para lá** to be tossed from post to pillar.
empurro s. m. (Braz.) the act of pushing.
empuxador s. m. pusher: person who thrusts forward or pushes away.
empuxão s. m. (pl. **-ões**) rough push, thrust, shove.
empuxar v. 1. to push, thrust, shove. 2. to shake. 3. to pull. 4. (fig.) to persuade, stir up.
empuxo s. m. 1. act of pushing. 2. thrust (also phys. and archit.).
~ da hélice (aeron.) propeller thrust.
emudecer v. 1. to silence, still. 2. to make quiet 3. **~-se:** a) to become silent, remain speechless. b) to be struck dumb, grow mute.
emulação s. f. (pl. **-ões**) emulation: 1. desire or ambition to equal or excel. 2. rivalry, competition, envy.
emular v. to emulate: 1. strive to equal or excel. 2. (also **~-se**) vie or compete with, rival. 3. imitate.
emulgente adj. m. + f. emulgent: said of the renal arteries or vessels.
êmulo s. m. emulator; rival; imitator, follower. ‖ adj. emulous; rivalling.
emulsão s. f. (pl. **-ões**) (chem., pharm., phot.) emulsion.
emulsina s. f. (chem.) emulsin: a caseous substance found in certain almonds.
emulsionar v. (also **emulsificar**) to emulsionize, emulsify: make an emulsion of, form into an emulsion.
emulsivo adj. emulsive: producing oil when pressed (as emulsive seeds).
emunctório s. m. (anat.) emunctory, excretory duct.
emundação s. f. (pl. **-ões**) purification, cleaning.
emundar v. to purify, clean, cleanse.
emurchecer v. to wither, wilt: 1. become or cause to become limp or dry (as flowers). 2. lose freshness, droop, fade.
enação s. f. (pl. **-ões**) (bot.) enation: a superficial outgrowth.
enágua s. f. underskirt, petticoat.
enálage s. f. (gram.) enallage: change of words.
enaltecer v. (also **enaltar**) 1. to exalt, aggrandize, ennoble. 2. to praise, laud.
enaltecimento s. m. exaltation, aggrandizement.
enamorado adj. enamo(u)red, infatuated, in love.
estou loucamente ~ I am madly in love.
enamorar v. 1. to enamo(u)r, inspire with love. 2. to enchant, charm, fascinate. 3. **~-se:** a) to become enamo(u)red. b) to fall in love (**de** with).

João enamorou-se de Maria John fell in love with Mary.
enantema s. m. (med.) enanthema: an eruption upon a mucous surface.
enântico adj. oenanthic, enanthic: relating to the fragrance of a wine.
enantiomorfo adj. enantiomorphous: similar but superposable.
enantiopatia s. f. (med.) enantiopathy, allopathy.
enantiopático adj. enantiopathic, allopathic.
enanto s. m. (bot.) oenanthe, a kind of dropwort.
enapupés s. m. (Braz., ornith.) a variety of tinamou.
enarmonia s. f. (mus.) enharmonic chord or note.
enarmônico adj. (mus.) enharmonic.
enartrodial adj. m. + f. (pl. **-ais**) enarthrodial: of or referring to a ball and socket joint.
enartrose s. f. (anat.) enarthrosis: ball and socket joint, the insertion of one bone into another to form a joint.
enastrar v. to adorn (the hair) with ribbons.
enatar v. to cream, cover with cream.
enateirar v. to cover with mud.
encabadouro s. m. (also **encabadoiro**) the eye of any tool in which the handle is inserted (as an axe, hammer, etc.) (plates A 1, P 1).
encabar v. (also **encabeirar**) to helve, haft, supply with a handle (an axe, hammer, etc.).
encabeçar v. 1. to head, lead, direct. 2. to inculcate, persuade. 3. to begin, start. 4. to title, entitle, give a title to. 5. **~-se:** a) to put into one's head. b) (fig.) to be convinced.
ele encabeçou a greve he was the strike leader.
encabeira s. f. (carp.) header.
encabelado adj. covered with hair.
encabeladura s. f. 1. act of covering with hair. 2. head of hair.
encabelar v. 1. to grow hair. 2. to (re-)cover with hair.
encabelizar v. to cover with hair.
encabrestadura s. f. excoriation or sore caused by a halter (horse).
encabrestamento s. m. haltering: act of putting a halter on.
encabrestar v. to halter: 1. put a halter on (a horse). 2. attach as with a halter.
encabritar-se v. 1. to rear up, prance (as a goat). 2. to climb (as a boy).
encabruado adj. willful, stubborn, bullheaded.
encabulação s. f. (pl. **-ões**) (Braz.) 1. embarrassment, abashment. 2. vexation. 3. constraint.
encabulado adj. (Braz.) 1. bashful. 2. constrained, restrained. 3. timid, shy. 4. vexed.
encabular v. 1. to abash. 2. to constrain, restrain. 3. to ashame. 4. to bring bad luck to. 5. **~-se** to become thoughtful about, to worry.
encachaçar-se v. 1. to get drunk with sugar-cane brandy. 2. to take a liking to s. o., have a passion for s. o.
encachar-se v. to cover the body with a loin-cloth (Indians).
encacho s. m. (also **tanga**) loin-cloth.
encachoeiramento s. m. (Braz.) 1. formation of a waterfall. 2. waterfall, cascade.
encachoeirar v. to transform into a waterfall or cataract, take the shape of a waterfall.
encacholar v. (Braz.) to hammer a thing into a person's head.
encadeado adj. 1. chained (up), linked. 2. coherent, connected. 3. joined in a series, concatenate.
encadeamento s. m. (also **encadeação** f.; pl. **-ões**) 1. chaining, linkage, enchainment. 2. concatenation. 3. series. 4. union, junction, connexion. 5. (post.) enjambement.

encadear v. 1. to enchain, fetter. 2. to concatenate, join in a series. 3. to link, connect, joint, unite. 4. (fig.) to captivate. 5. ~-se to form a chain.

encadeirar v. 1. to put or set on a chair. 2. to enthrone: a) seat on a throne. b) install (as a bishop).

encadernação s. f. (pl. -ões) 1. bookbinding. 2. binding, cover (of a book). 3. (fig.) apparel.
~ de luxo de luxe binding. ~ em couro leather binding. ~ em pano cloth binding. oficina de ~ bookbindery.

encadernado adj. bound, provided with a cover (book). bem ~ (fam.) well-dressed. o livro ainda não foi ~ the book is still in sheets.

encadernador s. m. bookbinder: person who binds books.
agulha de ~ bookbinder's needle.

encadernar v. 1. to bind (books). 2. (fig.) to put on new clothes.

encafifar v. (Braz.) 1. to abash: a) make ashamed. b) turn shy. 2. to dislike; displease. 3. to become bored or annoyed.

encafuar, encafurnar v. 1. to shut up in a cave or den. 2. ~-se to hide o. s.

encaibramento s. m. timberwork (or its erection) of a roof.

encaibrar v. 1. to erect the timberwork of a roof. 2. to provide or support with rafters.

encaleirar v. (Braz.) to form a lime-kiln.

encalpirar-se v. (Braz., more usually acaipirar-se) to become a rustic, acquire boorish habits.

encalporar v. (Braz.) 1. to render unhappy. 2. to bring or cause bad luck to. 3. ~-se: a) to become unlucky. b) to become hoodoo.

encaixamento s. m. 1. grating, boxing, incasement, packing. 2. fitting or setting (into a rabbet, groove or mortise). 3. insertion.

encaixar v. 1. to box: put into or enclose in a box; incase, case. 2. to mortise: fit into a mortise (as a tenon). 3. to set or fit into a groove. 4. (carp.) to rabbet, dovetail. 5. to inlay, incase. 6. to introduce, insert. 7. (fig.) to come in handy, suit the purpose. 8. to penetrate, intrude.
~ alguma coisa na cabeça to put or take a thing into one's head. isto encaixou direitinho it fitted perfectly. os tubos foram encaixados um no outro the pipes were fitted into each other.

encaixe s. m. (also encaixo) 1. mortise, dovetail, groove, rabbet; notch, recess (plate C 9). 2. setting or fitting in. 3. encasement.
abrir ~ to cut notches, to dovetail.

encaixilhar v. 1. to frame: surround with or put into a frame. 2. to sash: furnish with a sash (as windows).

encaixotador s. m. packer: person who packs (goods) in boxes or cases.

encaixotamento s. m. act of packing (goods) in boxes, incasement.

encaixotar v. to box, pack (goods) in boxes; incase.

encalacração (pl. -ões), **encalacradela** s. f. 1. act of putting or state of being in trouble, in a bad mess. 2. risky enterprise.

encalacrar v. 1. to put s. o. in trouble; let s. o. down. 2. ~-se: a) to run into debt. b) to run risks.

encalamechar v. (N. E. Braz.) to put in, insert.

encalamento s. m. (naut.) wooden reinforcing crosspiece of a boat.

encalamistrar v. to frizzle, curl (hair).

encalcadeira s. f. calking tool.

encalcar v. to calk; tighten.

encalçar v. 1. to be at one's heels, pursue. 2. to follow closely.

encalço s. m. 1. pursuit, chase. 2. footprint, track, trail.
a polícia anda-lhe ao ~ the police is on his tracks. em seu ~ in the wake of her (him, them). fomos ao ~ dele we pursued him.

encaldeiração s. f. (pl. -ões) (agric.) act of digging a water-hole around trees.

encaldeirar v. (agric.) to dig water-holes around trees.

encalecer v. to callus, grow a corn, become horny.

encaleirar v. to cause to flow through a gutter.

encalhação s. f. (pl. -ões), **encalhamento** m. = encalhe.

encalhado adj. aground, stranded.
~ no seco high and dry. o navio está ~ the ship is aground.

encalhar v. 1. to run aground or ashore (ship). 2. to strike on a sand-bank. 3. to stagnate, stick fast, come to a stand, stop. 4. (fig.) to become embarrassed or entangled.

encalhe s. m. (also encalhação f., pl. -ões; encalhamento m.) 1. stranding: running aground (ship). 2. hindrance, obstacle, obstruction, check; burden. 3. deadlock. 4. unsold merchandise (esp. books, newspapers and magazines).

encalho s. m. 1. sand-bank, place where a ship runs aground. 2. that part of the horseshoe on which the hoof rests.

encaliçar v. to cover with pieces of dry mortar or debris.

encalir v. 1. to braise or roast meat slightly in order to preserve it. 2. to parboil, brown.

encalistar v. (fam.) to bring or cause bad luck to.

encalistamento s. m. (Braz.) abashment: act of making or getting ashamed.

encalistrar v. (Braz.) 1. to abash: a) put to shame. b) confuse, embarrass, trouble. 2. to sulk. 3. to be obstinate.

encalmadiço adj. that is easily stifled with heat.

encalmamento s. m. act of heating.

encalmar v. 1. to heat, warm, stifle with heat. 2. to make angry, provoke, excite, inflame. 3. to feel hot. 4. ~-se to grow calm, calm down.

encalombar v. (Braz.) to develop swellings, as a result of blows or bites.

encalvecer v. to grow bald (the head).

encamar v. 1. to place or put in layers. 2. to take to or be confined to one's bed. 3. to fall sick abed.

encamarotar v. to put in a ship cabin.

encambar v. to string together (fish, onions, etc.).

encambitar v. (Braz.) 1. to proceed with the tail lifted up (horse). 2. to pursue.

encamboar v. (Braz.) to leash, couple, string together (horse).

encambulhada s. f. a bunch of things of the same kind.

encambulhar v. 1. to string together. 2. to unite, join. 3. to tie. 4. ~-se to become (en)tangled.

encame s. m. a lair of a boar or some other wild animals.

encaminhador s. m. 1. guide, conductor. 2. person who puts another on his way, or who makes something follow its proper course. || adj. guiding, directing.

encaminhamento s. m. direction, guiding, leading.

encaminhar v. 1. to conduct, lead, guide, direct, show the way, orient. 2. to put on the way. 3. to help onward. 4. to advise, counsel, recommend. 5. to set on foot. 6. ~-se to go to or towards, take one's way, turn to, set out for.
encaminhei-o em tempo I put it on its way in time.

encamisada s. f. 1. (hist.) camisado, camisade: a surprise attack at night by soldiers wearing shirts

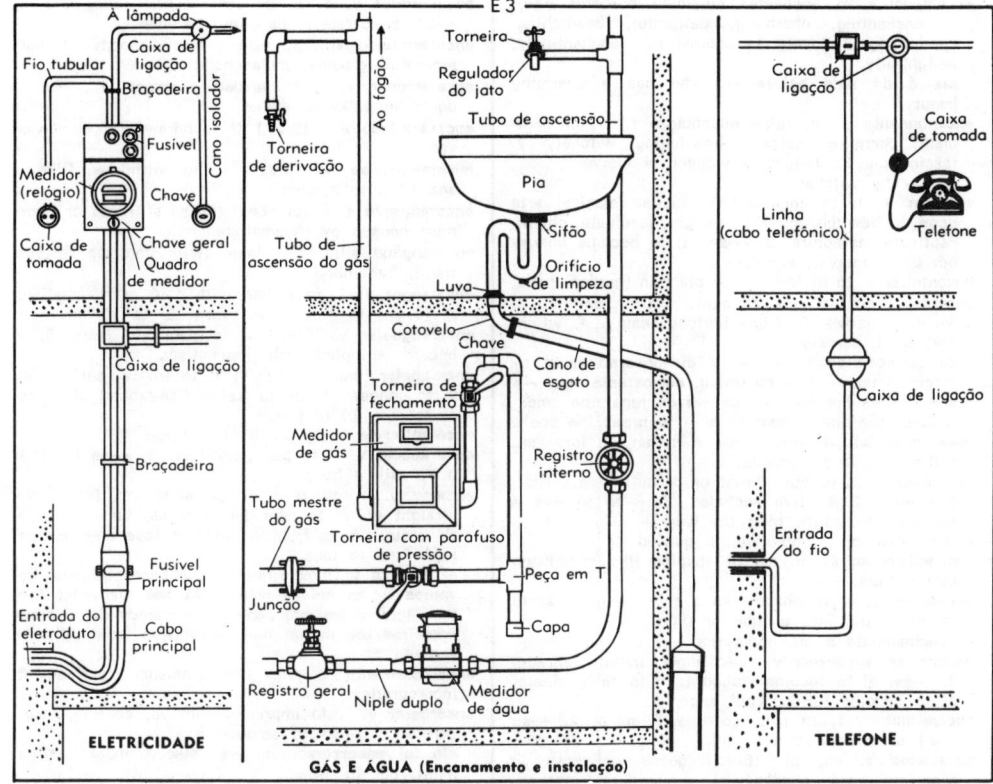

E 3

ELETRICIDADE

GÁS E ÁGUA (Encanamento e instalação)

TELEFONE

over their armour. 2. entanglement, confusion. 3. a sort of masquerade.

encamisar v. (Braz.) to cover (a kiln, charcoal pile, etc.) with straw and mud in order to keep in the heat.

encampação s. f. (pl. -ões) 1. cancellation of a lease contract; rescission. 2. expropriation: a taking from a private owner for public use (real estate, company).

encampador s. m. 1. person who rescinds or cancels a lease contract, agreement, etc. 2. expropriator.

encampar v. 1. to rescind a lease contract, cancel an agreement on lease. 2. to annul, cancel, revoke (by legal means). 3. to expropriate: take over for public use (properties, companies, utilities, etc.)

ençampar v. (Braz., coll.) to deceive, cheat.

encamurçar v. 1. to cover with chamois leather (the hammers of a piano). 2. to warp (wood).

encanação s. f. (pl. -ões) 1. act of providing with pipes; piping (of a house). 2. = **encanamento**.

encanado adj. 1. (more usually **canalizado**) canalized, piped. 2. set in (a splint in a broken bone).
ar ~ current of air.

encanador s. m. plumber: person who makes a business of plumbing; pipe fitter, drainer.

encanamento s. m. plumbing, piping: 1. installation of all the pipes of a building (for water, gas, sewage) canalization. 2. the pipe system of a building (plate E 3). 3. ~s pl. drainage (pipes) of a house (plate E 10).

encanar v. 1. to channel: a) conduct or convey (water, etc.) through a channel. b) flute a column.

2. to lay pipes. 3. to convey in pipes. 4. (surg.) to set (a fracture). 5. (Braz., sl.) to imprison.

encanastrado s. m. network like basketry or wickerwork.

encanastrar v. 1. to put in a large basket. 2. to braid, plait. 3. (theatre, sl.) to cause s. o. to be a ham actor. 4. a) to lose (an actor) incentive or interest; b) ~-se to become a ham actor.

encancerar v. (med.) to cancerate: 1. develop into a cancer. 2. ~-se to become cancerous or malignant.

encandear v. 1. to dazzle (eye). 2. to daze (fish). 3. (fig.) to hallucinate, fascinate, charm. 4. ~-se: to be dazzled.

encandilar v. to candy. 2. ~-se to crystallize as sugar candy.

encanecer v. 1. to grow white or whitish. 2. to grow grey-headed. 3. to turn grey or hoary (hair). 4. (fig.) to grow old.

encanelar v. 1. to wind up, spool. 2. to wind on a reel.

encanfinfar v. (Braz.) = **encafifar**.

encangalhar v. 1. to yoke, join, tie together. 2. (Braz.) to saddle a pack animal with panniers. 3. ~-se to be or become involved in or with.

encangar v. to yoke: put the yoke on oxen.

encaniçar v. to surround with trellis or latticework.

encanoar v. to wrap, curl (a board).

encantado adj. 1. enchanted, enraptured, charmed, delighted; bewitched. 2. overjoyed.
ela deixou-me ~ she has cast a spell over me. estou ~ com I am delighted with. estar ~ por to be attached to.

encantador s. m. enchanter, magician, sorcerer. ‖ adj. 1. enchanting, charming, delightful, bewitching, captivating. 2. lovely. ‖ ~amente adv. enchantingly, delightfully.
ela é de uma beleza ~a she has a charming beauty.
encantamento s. m. (also **encantação** f.) 1. enchantment: charming, sorcery, bewitching, witchery. 2. fascination. 3. delight, a wonder, a marvel.
por ~ by witchery.
encantar v. 1. to enchant: a) practise magical arts upon. b) bewitch, spell. c) delight, fascinate, charm, captivate, enrapture. 2. ~-se: a) to become charmed. b) to marvel, wonder.
encanteirar v. to divide into or plant in (garden) beds.
encanto s. m. 1. enchantment, charm, delight. 2. wonder, marvel. 3. (fig.) perfect beauty. 4. witchery, spell, sorcery.
desapareceu como por ~ it disappeared as if by magic. **é um** ~ it is charming. **ela ostenta seus** ~s she flashes her charms. **os** ~s **do lugar** the amenities of the place. **quebrar o** ~ to break the spell.
encantoado adj. 1. thrust into a corner. 2. forsaken, solitary; retired, secluded.
encantoar v. 1. to put, thrust or drive into a corner, to corner. 2. to live secluded. 3. ~-se to live a solitary life, retire from the world.
encanudado adj. 1. tubelike. 2. quilled.
encanudamento s. m. act of shaping like or putting into a tube.
encanudar v. 1. to shape like a tube or pipe. 2. to thrust or put into a tube or pipe.
encanzinamento s. m. obduration.
encanzinar, encanzoar v. 1. to anger, irritate, enrage. 2. ~-se: a) to become stubborn. b) to be obstinate. c) to become furious, get angry.
encapachar v. 1. to mat, cover with mats. 2. ~-se (fig.) to demean o. s.
encapados s. m. pl. (Braz.) goods delivered in sackcloth. ‖ adj. **encapado** 1. covered. 2. cloaked. 3. wrapped up.
encapar v. 1. to put a cover on (book). 2. to cloak. 3. to wrap up.
encapelado adj. rough, swollen, turbulent, choppy (sea).
encapeladura s. f. shrouds and other riggings at the mast-head.
encapelar v. 1. to roughen, swell, rise (sea). 2. ~-se to become rough (sea). 3. to bequeath a property to the building of a chapel.
encapetado adj. (Braz.) 1. devilish, mischievous. 2. playful. 3. truant.
encapetar-se v. (Braz.) 1. to become mischievous. 2. to play pranks. 3. to romp about.
encapoeirar v. to pen up, put into a pen or cage; to coop.
encapotado s. m. person wearing an overcoat, cape or cloak. ‖ adj. 1. covered with a cape or cloak. 2. (fig.) disguised, concealed.
encapotar v. 1. to cover with a cape or cloak. 2. to cloak, muffle. 3. to disguise, conceal. 4. (also ~-se) to grow cloudy, dark, or overcast.
encaprichar-se v. 1. to get an idea into one's head. 2. to become obstinate or stubborn about something. 3. to act capriciously.
encapsulação s. f. (med.) encapsulation.
encapsular v. to encapsulate.
encapuzar v. 1. to hood, cover with a hood. 2. ~-se to cover o. s. with a hood.
encaração s. f. (pl. -ões) (Braz.) 1. staring or glaring (at) 2. meddlesomeness. 3. (sl.) free ticket.
encaracolar v. 1. to spiral. 2. to twist and turn, twine (as spirals). 3. ~-se to curl, crisp.

encaramelar v. 1. to congeal, curdle, coagulate. 2. ~-se. to caramel: turn into caramel.
encaramonado adj. 1. sullen, surly, moody. 2. sad, mournful, gloomy, melancholic.
encaramonar v. 1. to sadden, overcast. 2. ~-se to pout: be sulky or sullen.
encaramujado adj. (Braz.) 1. withdrawn. 2. somewhat sad.
encaramujar-se v. (Braz.) 1. to withdraw (like a snail). 2. to sadden.
encarangação s. f. (pl. -ões) (Braz.) stiffness or lameness caused by rheumatism.
encarangado adj. stiff, lame (with cold or rheumatism); benumbed.
encaranguejar v. 1. to stiffen with cold or rheumatism. 2. (Braz.) to shrink: withdraw. 3. to sicken.
encaranguejar v. (Braz.) 1. to paralyse, lame. 2. to become crippled with rheumatism.
encarapelar, encarapinhar v. 1. to frizzle, curl, crisp. 2. to congeal, begin to freeze (ice-cream). 3. ~-se: a) to curl. b) to freeze.
encarapitar-se v. to climb on the top.
encarapuçar v. 1. to put a hood on. 2. ~-se to cover o. s. with a hood.
encarar v. 1. to look or stare at; to face, look straight at. 2. to consider, analyse, view (a question, etc.). 3. to front. 4. ~-se to face one another, look face to face.
~ **alguém** to look straight in a person's face. **devemos** ~ **as coisas como elas são** we must face the facts. **o assunto pode ser encarado de diversas maneiras** the matter may be viewed from different angles.
encarceramento s. m. imprisonment, confinement, incarceration.
encarcerar v. 1. to imprison, shut up, confine, incarcerate. 2. ~-se to seclude o. s.
ele foi encarcerado he was placed under confinement, put in jail.
encardido adj. 1. soiled, dirty, grimy, nasty, unclean. 2. threatening, scowling. 3. shady (business).
encardir v. 1. to soil, dirty, grime. 2. to wash badly.
encardumar v. (Braz.) to shoal, form into a shoal (fish).
encarecedor s. m. 1. person who forces prices up. 2. exaggerator. 3. enhancer. ‖ adj. 1. raising the price of. 2. exaggerating.
encarecer v. 1. to raise the prices. 2. to grow dear. 3. to exalt. 4. to exaggerate; amplify; enhance. 5. to endear.
encarecimento s. m. 1. raising (of prices). 2. enhancement. 3. interest. 4. exaggeration.
encaretado adj. masked, disguised.
encaretar-se v. to mask, disguise o. s.
encargar v. 1. to charge. 2. to load up. 3. (Braz.) to fill (up).
encargo s. m. 1. incumbency, responsibility, duty. 2. charge, mission, office. 3. tax. 4. order.
tenho muitos ~s I have many duties.
encarna s. f. mortise, groove, notch.
encarnação s. f. (pl. -ões) 1. incarnation: a) embodiment. b) Incarnation: the assumption of human nature by Jesus Christ. c) personification. 2. the use of flesh-colour in painting.
~ **do Verbo Divino** Incarnation of the Word.
encarnado s. m. flesh-colour; red, scarlet. ‖ adj. incarnate: 1. invested with flesh. 2. personified. 3. flesh-coloured; red, scarlet.
encarnar v. 1. to incarnate: a) embody. b) personify. 2. to apply flesh-colour in painting. 3. to give a flesh-colour to (images). 4. to put on flesh. 5. ~-se (theat.) to live a part.

encarne s. m. 1. act of incarnating. 2. painting in flesh-colour.

encarneirar-se v. 1. to foam, become choppy, roughen (sea). 2. to become covered with cloudlets (sky).

encarniçado adj. 1. bloodthirsty, sanguinary, bloody. 2. furious, fierce, cruel. 3. irritated.
luta -a bloody battle. **olhos ~s** bloodshot eyes.

encarniçamento s. m. 1. ferocity, cruelty, fierceness. 2. fury, rage. 3. taking of the prey (wild animals).

encarniçar v. 1. to flesh (a hound). 2. to instigate, incite; sick on (dogs). 3. **~-se:** a) to become enraged. b) to be or become fierce (fight). c) to take the prey (wild animals).

encaroçada s. f. (S. Braz.) lumpy red soil.

encaroçado adj. lumpy, full of lumps.

encaroçar v. 1. to become lumpy. 2. to break out in pustules. 3. to falter (during a speech).

encarochar v. 1. to bewitch, hex. 2. (hist.) to put a painted cap like a mitre on the head of one condemned by the Inquisition.

encarpo s. m. (archit.) encarpus: a sculptured ornament in imitation of a festoon of fruits, leaves, flowers, etc.

encarquilhado adj. 1. wrinkled, crumpled, rugose. 2. parched, wilted.

encarquilhar v. 1. to wrinkle, furrow, crumple, make rugose. 2. **~-se** to become wrinkled.

encarrancar(-se) v. 1. to frown, scowl. 2. to be or become sullen. 3. to grow overcast or cloudy.

encarrapichar-se v. (Braz.) to become full of beggar's--lice (one's clothes, the fur of an animal).

encarrapitar-se v. (also **encarapitar-se**) to climb on the top.

encarrar v. to put into the car.

encarrascar-se v. to get drunk with bad wine.

encarraspanar-se v. to get drunk.

encarregado s. m. 1. person in charge. 2. commissioner; manager. ‖ adj. charged, entrusted with, in charge.
~ da seção department head.

encarregar v. 1. to charge, commit, intrust. 2. to put in charge of. 3. **~-se:** a) to take upon o. s. b) to take charge of, take care of. c) to undertake to. **ele encarregou-se do assunto** he took the task upon himself, saddled himself with the task. **eu me encarrego dele** I'll tackle him, fix him. **encarregue-se disso** take this in hand, take it of my hands. **eu me encarregarei disso** I will see to it.

encarrego (ê) s. m. act of charging or entrusting.

encarreirar v. 1. to direct, guide. 2. to put on the right way. 3. **~-se** to direct one's steps to; take or follow one's way.

encarretar v. to mount (up), limber (gun).

encarrilhamento s. m. placing (a railroad car or engine) on the rails.

encarrilhar v. (also **encarrilar**) 1. to put on the rails (car, engine, etc.). 2. to direct, orient. 3. to put on the right way. 4. (fig.) to follow the right way.

encartação s. f. (pl. -ões) **encartamento** m. 1. investment, appointment (office, etc.). 2. = **encarte.**

encartar v. 1. to invest with an office. 2. (obs.) to banish.

encarte s. m. (cards) 1. winning of a trick, overtrumping. 2. registration (of a diploma, commission, letter patent, etc.).

encartuchar v. 1. to put in a paper-bag. 2. to make cartridges. 3. to load cartridges.

encarvoar v. 1. to soil with coal. 2. **~-se:** a) to soil or blacken o. s. with coal. b) to coal: convert into coal.

encarvoejar v. 1. = **encarvoar.** 2. to darken, denigrate, obscure.

encasacar-se v. 1. to put on a coat. 2. to dress up.

encasamento s. m. notch, cut, groove.

encasar v. 1. to fit or set in. 2. to mortise; incase; engage. 3. **~-se** to harmonize with.

encascar v. 1. to barrel, put in a cask. 2. to plaster: cover walls with plaster. 3. to form a crust (soil). 4. to grow bark (trees).

encasmurrar v. to make or become sad, obstinate or stubborn.

encasquetar v. 1. to persuade, make believe. 2. to cover with or as with a cap; to hat. 3. **~-se:** a) to get something into one's head; be obsessed (as by a fixed idea). b) to put on one's cap.

encasquilhar v. 1. to put a metal coating on. 2. to dress like a coxcomb or dandy.

encastelado adj. 1. castellated, castled, fortified. 2. superposed. 3. (vet.) hoofbound.

encastelamento s. m. 1. castellation, building of or fortifying with castles. 2. piling up, heaping up (clouds).

encastelar v. 1. to castle: a) place in a castle. b) fortify with castles. 2. to pile up, heap up (clouds). 3. **~-se:** a) to resort to a castle. b) (fig.) to get strong, strengthen o. s.

encastoar v. 1. to enchase, set (precious stones). 2. to mount (canes, sticks, etc.).

encasular v. 1. to form into a cocoon. 2. (fig.) to shut in.

encataplasmar v. 1. to cover with a cataplasm. 2. to become sick, fall ill.

encatarrar-se, encatarroar-se v. to catch a catarrh or a cold.

encatrinar-se v. (pop.) to get drunk.

encauchar v. to rubberize: impermeabilize (a cloth or a bag) with a preparation of rubber.

encausta s. m. (also **encaustes** sg. + pl.) a painter in encaustic.

encáustica s. f. 1. encaustic: art, method or practice of encaustic painting. 2. floor or furniture wax.

encausticar v. to apply encaustic to.

encáustico adj. encaustic: of or referring to encaustic painting.

encavacado adj. 1. moody, sullen. 2. angry, annoyed.

encavacar v. 1. to pout, sulk. 2. to be angry. 3. to become embarrassed.

encavalar v. 1. to fix or put on or upon as a tab. 2. = **encavalgar.**

encavalgadura s. f. (usually **cavalgadura**) mount (horse, etc.).

encavalgar v. (usually **cavalgar**) to ride on horseback, mount a horse.

encavar v. 1. to put in a cavity. 2. to dig, excavate.

encavernar v. 1. to cavern: shut up or place in a cavern or den. 2. **~-se** (fig.) to hide o. s.

encavilhar v. to peg: 1. to drive a peg into. 2. to fasten with a peg.

encavo s. m. 1. rabbet, mortise, groove. 2. incavation.

encefalograma s. m. (med.) encephalogram.

encefalalgia s. f. (med.) encephalalgia: pain within the head.

encefálico adj. (anat.) encephalic: pertaining to the encephalon.

encefalite s. f. (med.) encephalitis: inflammation of the brain.

encéfalo s. m. (anat.) encephalon, brain.

encefalocele s. f. (med.) encephalocele: hernia of the brain.

encefalóide adj. m. + f. encephaloid: resembling the brain.

encefalólito s. m. (med.) encephalolith: a brain calculus.

encefalologia s. f. encephalology: the science of the brain.

encefaloma s. m. (path.) tumour or hernia in the encephalon.

enceguecer v. to become blind.

encegueirado adj. (Braz., coll.) passionate, smitten, wrapped up, nuts.

encelar v. 1. to shut up in a cell. 2. to cloister.

enceleirar v. 1. to store up (grain). 2. to warehouse. 3. to amass.

encelialgia s. f. (med.) enc(o)elialgia: pain in the intestines.

encelite s. f. (med.) encelitis: inflammation of the intestines.

encenação s. f. (pl. -ões) 1. staging: putting a play on the stage, mise en scène. 2. (fig., sl.) feigning, simulation.

encenar v. 1. to stage: mount, arrange for, or exhibit on the stage (a play). 2. to show, exhibit, display. ~ **uma peça** to get up a play.

encendrar v. 1. to clean with ash. 2. to purify; refine.

encentrar v. (also **concentrar**) to concentrate.

enceradeira s. f. (Braz.) floor polisher (machine).

encerado s. m. oilcloth, waxed cloth; tarpaulin. ‖ adj. 1. waxed. 2. wax-coloured.

encerador s. m. (Braz.) floor waxer.

enceradura s. f., **enceramento** m. waxing: coating or treating with wax.

encerar v. 1. to wax: coat or treat with wax. 2. to give the colour of wax to. 3. to mix with wax. ~ **o soalho** to wax or polish the floor.

encerebração s. f. (pl. -ões) 1. intellectual development. 2. way of thinking.

encerebrar v. 1. to fix in one's memory. 2. to learn by heart.

enceroular v. to give the shape of drawers to. 2. to wear as drawers.

encerra s. f. (Braz.) an enclosure for holding cattle.

encerrador s. m. closer, ender. ‖ adj. closing, final.

encerramento s. m. 1. closing. 2. termination, finishing, end. 3. conclusion. 4. enclosure. 5. confinement.

encerrar v. 1. to enclose, encompass. 2. to contain, hold. 3. to comprehend, include, comprise. 4. to conclude, close, finish, terminate, bring to an end. 5. to keep, lock up, confine. 6. ~-se: a) to shut o. s. up, seclude o. s. b) to become a recluse. ~ **a sessão** to close the meeting. ~ **uma conta** to close an account. **ele encerrou o assunto** he put an end to the matter.

encerro (ê) s. m. 1. end, finish, close, conclusion. 2. shutting up. 3. retirement, secluded place.

encestamento s. m. (Braz.) 1. act of putting in baskets. 2. (basketball) throw-in.

encestar v. 1. to basket: put in baskets. 2. (basketball) to score, throw in, put the ball in the basket.

encetamento s. m. (also **encetadura** f.) 1. beginning, start. 2. the first cut or slice.

encetar v. 1. to begin, start, enter upon. 2. to broach. 3. to cut or make the first cut. 4. to try, experiment. 5. to take a part of (a thing). 6. ~-se to do (a thing) for the first time. ~ **um assunto** to broach a subject. ~ **uma carreira** to enter upon a career.

enchacotar v. to kiln-dry vessels which are to be glazed.

enchafurdar v. 1. to wallow, welter in the mud. 2. to flounder. 3. ~-se to sink in a mire; to bog.

enchamboado adj. (Braz.) 1. ungainly, cumbersome. 2. ragged, badly dressed.

enchapelar-se v. 1. to cover o. s. with a hat. 2. to put on (a woman) a hat, to go to a feast or ceremony.

encharcadiço adj. swampy, muddy, slimy.

encharcado adj. 1. swampy, marshy. 2. flooded, soppy. 3. waterlogged. 4. sopping wet, soaked to the skin.

estou ~ **até aos ossos** I am wet to the skin. **ele estava** ~ he was soaking wet, he ran with rain. **roupas -as** wet clothes.

encharcar v. 1. to form into a puddle. 2. to flood, inundate, deluge. 3. to soak, wet, drench. 4. ~-se: a) to get thoroughly wet. b) to get into a mire (also fig.).

encharolar v. to niche, put in a niche.

enchavetar v. to key, fix with a key or pin.

encheção s. f. act or effect of boring; annoyance, weariness.

enchedeira s. f. filler, a little funnel (to fill sausages).

enche-mão s. f. used in the adj. locution **de enche-mão** (also **de mão cheia**) best, excellent, perfect.

enchente s. f. 1. inundation: a) flood, deluge, overflow. b) superabundance. c) crowd, great number of people. 2. high water. 3. torrent. 4. (theat.) a full house. ~ **da lua** full of the moon. ~ **da maré** flood-tide. **a** ~ **está em declínio** the flood abates.

encher v. 1. to fill: a) make full. b) satisfy, satiate, saturate, glut. 2. to abound. 3. to stuff, load, charge. 4. to crowd. 5. ~-se: a) to become full. b) to surfeit, satiate o. s. ~ **a paciência** to bore, tire, annoy. ~ **alguém de medo** to strike s. o. with fear. ~ **a mochila** to feather one's nest. ~ **as medidas** to exhaust another's patience. ~ **até a borda** to brim. ~ **completamente** to fill up. ~ **demais** to overfill. ~ **um tanque** to fill up a tank; (U. S. A., mot.) to gas up. ~ **um pneumático** to pump up a tire. **de grão em grão a galinha enche o papo** little drops of water make the ocean, little strokes fell great oaks. **ele encheu a pança** (fam.) he crammed his guts. **ele encheu-se de orgulho** he swelled with pride. **ele encheu um copo de vinho** he filled a glass with wine. **enchi-me de ânimo** I cheered up. **não encha a cabeça dele** don't put ideas into his head. **palavras não enchem barriga** (fig.) a hungry belly has no ears. **a sua voz encheu o aposento** his voice filled the room.

enchido s. m. 1. padding, stuffing; wadding. 2. sausage. ‖ adj. full, filled up.

enchimento s. m. 1. filling up. 2. stuffing; wadding. 3. inflation (tire). 4. forcemeat.

enchiqueirador s. m. (Braz.) person who pens (animals).

enchiqueirar v. (Braz.) 1. to pen (animals). 2. to be caught (fishes) in a fish-garth.

enchocalhação s. f. (pl. -ões) act of putting a bell around the neck (of cattle).

enchocalhar v. to bell, put a bell around the neck (of cattle).

enchoçar v. 1. to put in a hut. 2. to corral. 3. ~-se. a) to take shelter in a hut. b) to hide o. s.

enchombrar v. (Braz.) to remain slightly wet (wash).

enchouriçado adj. (also **enchoiriçado**) 1. haughty, arrogant. 2. cylindrical, round like a sausage.

enchouriçar v. (also **enchoiriçar**) 1. to give the form of a sausage to. 2. ~-se: a) to bristle up, become roily. b) to be puffed up.

enchova s. f. (ichth.) 1. anchovy. 2. bluefish, tailor.

enchova-preta s. f. (pl. **enchovas-pretas**) (ichth.) escolar, oilfish (Ruvettus pretiosus).

enchumaçar v. to pad, stuff, wad.

enciclia s. f. circle formed on the surface of water by something dropped therein.

encíclica s. f. encyclic(al): a circular letter from the Pope to the bishops all over the world.

encíclico adj. 1. encyclic(al): said of circular letters from the Pope. 2. circular.

enciclopédia s. f. encyclop(a)edia: 1. a work or book giving information on all branches of knowledge. 2. a summary of knowledge or a branch of knowledge.

enciclopédico adj. encyclop(a)edic: of or pertaining to an encyclop(a)edia or to general knowledge.

enciclopedismo s. m. Encyclop(a)edism, encyclop(a)edism.

enciclopedista s. m. + f. encyclop(a)edist: compiler of an encyclop(a)edia.

encilhada s. f. (S. Braz.) act of girthing and mounting (colt, horse).

este potro tem três ~s this colt has been mounted thrice.

encilhadela s. f. (S. Braz.) 1. act of girthing and mounting (colt, horse). 2. additional maté to the one still in use, to render it stronger.

encilhador s. m. (S. Braz.) person who girths or saddles an animal.

encilhamento s. m. (Braz.) 1. act of girthing and mounting. 2. a period of wild speculation in the early days of the republic.

encilhar v. 1. to girth; saddle (animals). 2. (S. Braz.) to add maté tea leaves to the brew.

encimado adj. 1. placed above, on the top; high up. 2. (fig.) crowned.

encimar v. 1. to top, place above or on the top, put high up. 2. (fig.) to crown. 3. to surmount. 4. to raise (up), elevate.

cumes encimados com neve mountain peaks crowned with snow.

encinchar v. to press (cheese).

encintar v. 1. to belt: a) gird. b) surround, encircle. 2. to furnish with girdles, belts, bands.

encinzar v. 1. to cover with ashes. 2. to dirty or soil with ashes.

encistamento s. m. = **enquistamento.**

encistar v. = **enquistar.**

enciumar-se v. to be or become jealous.

enclaustramento s. m. 1. act of cloistering. 2. closure; seclusion; cloister.

enclaustrar v. 1. to cloister: a) seclude. b) confine in a cloister. 2. ~-se: a) to retire as in a convent. b) to become a recluse.

enclausura s. f. (also **clausura**) closure.

enclausurar v. 1. to cloister. 2. to confine in an enclosure. 3. to refrain from society. 4. ~-se: a) to shut o. s. up in or as in a convent. b) to lead a secluded life, retire.

enclavinhar v. to clasp, interlock, entwine (fingers).

enclenque adj. m. + f. (S. Braz.) 1. indisposed. 2. sickly, ailing. 3. (fig.) weak; coward.

ênclise s. f. (gram.) enclisis: pronunciation as an enclitic.

enclítica s. f. (gram.) enclitic: a word connected with a preceding one so that it loses its independent accent.

enclítico adj. (gram.) enclitic.

encloacar v. to put in a sewer or sink.

encoadura s. f. provisional water reservoir, pond, for fishes that are still alive.

encobardar v. (also **encovardar**) 1. to intimidate, frighten. 2. ~-se: to lose courage, get scared, become a coward.

encoberta s. f. 1. shelter, hiding-place. 2. cubbyhole. 3. pretext, excuse, subterfuge, dissimulation. 4. (fig.) cunning; snare.

às ~s surreptitiously, furtively.

encobertar v. (usually **acobertar**) 1. to cover. 2. to conceal, hide; disguise, dissimulate. 3. ~-se to cover o. s.

encoberto adj. 1. covered: a) hidden, occult. b) secret, covert. c) concealed, disguised, dissimulated. 2. unknown. 3. clandestine. 4. cloudy, overcast (sky).

a ilha está -a de nevoeiro the isle is wrapped in mist. **o céu está ~ hoje** the sky is overcast today.

encobridor s. m. 1. dissimulator, dissembler. 2. concealer. 3. fence (receiver of stolen goods). || adj. covering, concealing, dissimulative.

encobrimento s. m. 1. covering, hiding, concealing, concealment. 2. dissimulation. 3. receiving of stolen goods.

encobrir v. 1. to cover. 2. to hide, occult, conceal. 3. to disguise, dissimulate, dissemble. 4. to keep secret. 5. ~-se: a) to hide or disguise o. s. b) to become cloudy, be overcast (sky).

encobriremos isto we shall throw a veil over that.

encocurutar v. (Braz.) to put (s. th.) on the top or highest part of anything.

encodeamento s. m. 1. crusting. 2. crust (of bread). 3. husk.

encodear v. 1. to crust. 2. ~-se to form into a crust.

o pão começa a ~ the bread begins to crust.

encofar v. to store in a basket.

encofrar v. to coffer: place in a coffer.

encoifar v. (obs.) to cap the touchhole of a cannon.

encoimar v. (also **acoimar**) 1. to punish, fine; reproach, censure 2. ~-se to reprove o. s., recognize one's fault or guilt.

encolar v. 1. to gum. 2. to glue, cover or draw over with glue; stick. 3. to hold (a child) in one's arms; to pamper, coddle (a child).

encoleirar v. to put a collar on (an animal).

encolerizar v. 1. to make angry, enrage, infuriate, irritate, exasperate. 2. ~-se to get angry, fly into a passion.

ela encolerizou-se she fell into a passion (or rage). **ele encolerizou-se contra mim** he flared out against me.

encolha s. f. (also **encolhimento** m.) contraction, shrinkage.

meter-se nas ~s to be quiet; shut up; draw in one's horns.

encolher v. 1. to shrink, contract, draw up. 2. to make narrower, cramp. 3. to restrain, restrict, hold back. 4. to shrug (shoulder). 5. to flinch, recoil, wince. 6. ~-se: a) to be shy, timid, disheartened. b) to humble o. s. c) to cringe, crouch, cower.

~ na lavagem to run up in the wash (clothes). **ele encolheu os ombros** he shrugged his shoulders, he gave a shrug. **esta fazenda não encolhe com a lavagem** this cloth does not shrink in the wash.

encolhido s. m. a timid, shy or bashful person. || adj. 1. shrunken, contracted. 2. timid, shy, bashful. **ele está ~ de frio** he is hunched up with cold.

encolhimento s. m. 1. shrinking, shrinkage, contraction. 2. diminution, diminishing.

encólpio s. m. encolpion: small reliquary.

encolpismo s. m. (med.) medication through the vagina.

encomenda s. f. 1. order (for goods). 2. thing ordered. 3. indent. 4. task, incumbency. 5. commission, charge. 6. (Braz., sl.) sorcery, witchcraft.

~ postal parcel post. **eu mandei uma ~** I sent an order. **feito de ~** made to order. **trabalho de ~** ordered work.

encomendação s. f. (pl. -ões) 1. order(ing). 2. recommendation. 3. (eccl.) commendation.

encomendado adj. 1. ordered, made to order. 2. recommended.

encomendar v. 1. to order, ask for. 2. to charge, command, recommend. 3. to indent. 4. to commit, entrust. 5. ~-se: to present one's compliments.

encomendei alguma coisa dele I indented upon him for something. **encomendei o livro** I called for the book. **ele encomendou sua alma a Deus** he commended his soul to God.

encomendeiro s. m. 1. person whose job was to collect orders and to do the (collective) purchasing for others (as in the country). 2. person who takes or executes orders (for goods).

encomiar v. 1. to praise, laud, extol. 2. to eulogize.

encomiasta s. m. + f. 1. encomiast, eulogist. 2. panegyrist. ‖ adj. 1. encomiastic. 2. panegyrical.

encomiástico adj. 1. encomiastic(al), eulogistic. 2. laudatory ‖ **encomiasticamente** adv. eulogistically.

encômio s. m. encomium: 1. a formal expression of praise. 2. eulogy.

encomoroçar v. 1. to put on the top (of or as of a hill). 2. to heap or pile up.

encompridar v. (Braz.) 1. to lengthen, make longer. 2. to prolong. 3. to piece on (to).

enconcar v. 1. to bend, curve. 2. ∼-se: a) to become concave. b) to warp.

enconchar v. 1. to shell: a) enclose in a shell. b) cover with shells. 2. ∼-se: to withdraw (as into a shell).

encondar v. to give the title of count to, make s. o. a count.

encondroma s. m. (med.) enchondroma: a cartilaginous tumour.

encontradiço adj. 1. frequently met with. 2. easily encountered, easily found.

encontrado adj. 1. joined, close. 2. contrary, opposite.

encontrão s. m. (pl. **-ões**) (also **encontrada, encontroada** f.) 1. collision, impact, shock. 2. push, shove, jostle.

encontrar v. 1. to meet (with), encounter. 2. to find, find out, discover. 3. to come across, stumble upon. 4. to come face to face with. 5. to fall in with. 6. ∼-se: a) to be (in a certain place or disposition), feel o. s., find o. s. b) to collide (with). c) to come across. d) to meet up with.
∼ **alguém por acaso** to run across s. o., to drop upon. ∼ **dificuldades inesperadas** to run into a snag. ∼ **um amigo** to come across a friend. **encontramos dificuldades** we met with difficulties. **encontramo-nos freqüentemente** we met frequently, were much thrown together. **encontraram-se** they came together. **encontrei-a chorando** I found her in tears. **encontrei-me por acaso com meu amigo** I ran up against my friend. **encontrei-o na rua** I met him in the street. **eu sempre encontro obstáculos** I always meet with obstacles. **isto encontra-se à venda** this is on sale. **onde você o encontrou?** where did you come across him? **por acaso encontrei um velho amigo** it happened I came across an old friend. **a primeira pessoa que encontrei** the first person I came across. **saí para o ∼** I went to meet you.

encontro s. m. 1. meeting, encounter. 2. shock, impact, collision, crash. 3. find. 4. fight, contest. 5. a casual engagement; rencounter. 6. a chance meeting. 7. conjuncture. 8. (zool.) elbow of a bird's wing. 9. ∼**s** pl.: a) abutments of an arch (plate A 12). b) (fam.) shoulders.
∼ **marcado** a set engagement. **de ∼ a** a) opposed to, contrary to. b) against. **ele foi ao ∼ dela** he went to meet her. **ele marcou ∼ comigo** he made an appointment with me. **marcar um ∼** to make an appointment, (coll.) make (or have) a date. **o carro foi de ∼ à árvore** the car ran into a tree.

encontroar v. to thrust one's way (through a crowd); to elbow, jostle one's way.

encopar v. 1. to branch out, develop a crown (tree). 2. to top, prune. 3. to swell.

encoquinar, encoquinhar v. to hide, conceal.

encorajamento s. m. encouragement: 1. act of encouraging. 2. incitement, stimulation.

encorajar v. to encourage: 1. give courage to, inspire with courage. 2. stimulate, incite. 3. animate, hearten, cheer up. 4. help.

encorcundar v. (also **acorcundar-se**) 1. to make s. o. humped, hunchbacked. 2. ∼-se to become hunchbacked, humped.

encórdio s. m. (med.) bubo.

encordoamento s. m. 1. act of stringing (a musical instrument). 2. (Braz.) all the strings of an instrument.

encordoar v. 1. to string (musical instruments). 2. to cord: furnish with cords. 3. (fig.): a) to mistrust. b) to be sullen. 4. to form an Indian file.
∼ **uma guitarra** to string a guitar.

encornar v. (Braz., sl.) to sleep.

encoronhado adj. (vet.) hurt or sick (hoof).

encoronhar v. to assemble the butt to the barrel (firearm).

encorpado adj. 1. corpulent, full-bodied. 2. thick; dense. 3. resistent, solid, firm. 4. close-woven (cloth).

encorpadura s. f. thickness; density.

encorpar v. 1. to thicken: a) make or become thicker. b) make or become more dense. 2. to increase the body or consistence of. 3. to grow; grow fat; fatten. 4. to swell, enlarge.

encorreadura s. f. leather belts and straps.

encorreamento s. m. binding or fastening with leather straps.

encorrear v. 1. to bind or fasten with leather straps. 2. ∼-se: a) to become leathery. b) to grow wrinkly.

encorriar v. to tame only partially.

encorrilhar v. 1. (also ∼-se) to involve in a conventicle. 2. (also **encorrugir**) to wrinkle; become wrinkly, corrugate. 3. to wither.

encortelhar v. to stable, put into a stable.

encortiçar v. 1. to put bees in a beehive. 2. to cover with cork. 3. to make rough (like cork). 4. ∼-se to form bark.

encortinar v. to curtain: provide with curtains.

encorujar-se v. (Braz.) 1. to be sad, be in the dumps. 2. to seclude o. s. from human society.

encoscorar v. 1. to wrinkle, crinkle, shrink. 2. to shrivel. 3. to harden, crust.

encóspias s. f. pl. boot trees, shoe trees.
meter-se nas ∼ to be quiet, shut up, draw in one's horns.

encosta s. f. (also **vertente**) 1. hillside, rising of a hill (plate M 11). 2. ascent, slope, declivity, acclivity (plate M 11).

encostadela s. f. (pop.) tap, a touch for a favour or money.

encostado s. m. sponger, parasite, dependent. ‖ adj. 1. close, nearby. 2. leaning on, propped, supported, recumbent. 3. set aside (as old things). 4. (Braz.) indolent; lazy.
∼ **à parede** flat against the wall.

encostador s. m. person used to taps or touches for money; borrower.

encostalar v. to bundle, pack up.

encostamento s. m. act or fact of leaning against or upon.

encostão s. m. (pl. **-ões**) (f. **-ona**) (Braz., coll.) lazy or indolent person. ‖ adj. lazy; indolent.

encostar v. 1. to lean (against), prop. 2. to place against. 3. to ask for money. 4. ∼-se: a) to lean back, recline, rest. b) to lie down. c) to seek protection, shelter, support.

~ **a cabeça** (**em, contra**) to rest one's head (on, upon). ~ **alguém à parede** (fig.) to drive s. o. to the wall. ~ **ao meio-fio** to pull up at the curb, pull over. ~**se nos cotovelos** to rest upon one's elbows. ~**se a uma árvore** to lean against a tree. **encostamo-lo à parede** (fig.) we pinned him to the wall. **encoste a porta, por favor!** please, close the door!; please, leave the door ajar! **não encoste o guarda-chuva na mesa!** don't stand the umbrella against the table!

encoste s. m. 1. act of pairing or mating (animals). 2. ~**s** pl.: a) abutments, counterforts, struts. b) support; protection.

encostelar v. to match.

encosto (ô) s. m. 1. prop, stay, strut, support. 2. back (of a chair, etc.) (plates B 2, V 1). 3. (fig.) protection. 4. grassland enclosed by woods and marshes, with only one entryway.

sem ~ backless.

encouchar v. 1. to curve, bend. 2. to humble. 3. to depress, lower. 4. to crouch, squat down.

encouraçado s. m. (also **encoiraçado**, usually **couraçado**) battleship. ‖ adj. 1. cuirassed. 2. armoured, ironclad.

encouraçar v. (also **encoiraçar, couraçar**) 1. to provide with a cuirass. 2. to protect (ships) with armour plates. 3. ~**se** to put on a mail.

encourado s. m. (also **encoirado**) person dressed in leather. ‖ adj. dressed in, or covered with leather.

encourar v. (also **encoirar**) 1. to cover or line with leather. 2. (Braz.): a) to tan. b) to beat, thrash, flog. 3. ~**se** to cicatrize: form a scar, heal.

encovar v. 1. to inter, bury. 2. to hide. 3. to cause to become hollow or fallen in (as the eyes). 4. to pick up a person. 5. ~**se**: a) to retire, seclude, withdraw. b) to burrow (as an animal).

encovardar v. (also **encobardar**) to become a coward.

encovilar v. to shut up in a den.

encrassar v. to become crass.

encrava, encravação (pl. **-ões**) s. f. 1. = **encravamento**. 2. (fig.) deceit, fraud; lie.

encravado adj. 1. nailed; driven in (with a nail). 2. inlaid, imbedded. 3. set (as gems). 4. stuck.

unha -a ingrowing nail.

encravadouro s. m. (also **encravadoiro**) hole or place where something is stuck or fixed in.

encravadura s. f. 1. horseshoe nails. 2. (vet.) wound caused by a horseshoe nail.

encravamento s. m. 1. nailing, fastening with nails. 2. a sticking or fixing in; inlaying. 3. that which is fixed in or inlaid.

encravar v. 1. to nail: drive in or fasten with nails. 2. to inlay, imbed. 3. to set (gems). 4. to deceive. 5. (vet.) to prick, wound with horseshoe nails. 6. (mil.) to spike (guns). 7. ~**se**: a) to become fixed or imbedded in. b) to stick (as in mire). c) to get involved in difficulties.

~**no lodo** to stick in the mud.

encrave s. m. = **encravo**.

encravelhação s. f. (pl. **-ões**) 1. embarrassment, difficult situation, difficulty; fix, corner, rub. 2. act of providing a musical instrument with pegs.

encravelhar, encravilhar v. 1. to embarrass. 2. to put s. o. in a difficult situation, to corner a person. 3. to peg: provide a musical instrument with pegs. 4. ~**se**: a) to engage o. s. b) to run into debt.

encravo s. m. (vet., also **encrave**) wound occasioned by the prick of a horseshoe nail.

encrenca s. f. (Braz., sl.) 1. obstacle, difficulty, trouble; complication. 2. intrigue; disorder, row.

armar ~ to kick up a dust (or row). **uma** ~ **dos diabos** a devil of a row. **não procure** ~**s** don't ask for trouble. **você vai expor-se a grandes** ~**s**

por causa dele you will lay open yourself to much trouble for his sake, you will get in hot water for him.

encrencar v. (Braz., sl.) 1. to embarrass, confuse, embroil (a situation). 2. to complicate. 3. to stall, break down (esp. car). 4. ~**se** to become complicated.

o carro encrencou na subida the car stalled on the upgrade. **o caso está muito encrencado** the case is deeply entangled, it is a regular muddle.

encrenqueiro s. m. 1. troublemaker. 2. person who creates difficulties or complications. ‖ adj. bothersome, creating difficulties, quarrelsome.

encrespação s. f. (pl. **-ões**) 1. curling, frizzling. 2. rippling (of the sea).

encrespado adj. 1. (also **crespo**): a) crisp, curled; fuzzy, frizzled (hair). b) rippled, choppy (sea). 2. (fig.) irritated; furious; angry.

encrespador s. m. curling the hair. ‖ adj. curling, frizzling.

encrespadura s. f., **encrespamento** m. 1. curling, frizzling. 2. rippling, popple (of the sea).

encrespar v. 1. to curl, frizzle, crisp (hair). 2. to bristle, ridge. 3. to ripple. 4. ~**se**: a) to bristle up, stand on end, (hair, quills). b) to roughen, become white-capped, choppy; c) get angry, fly into a passion.

~ **o cabelo** to curl the hair. **ele encrespou-se com seu amigo** he fell out with his friend.

encrisar v. (N. Braz.) to darken, get cloudy.

encristar-se v. 1. to raise up the crest (bird). 2. (fig.): a) to become proud or haughty. b) to toss the head.

encrostar v. to crust: form or gather into a crust.

encruamento s. m. 1. toughness; hardness, rawness. 2. indigestion. 3. cruelty.

encruar v. 1. to harden, toughen, make or become tough or hard. 2. to cause indigestion. 3. to brutalize, make or become cruel. 4. to retrogress. 5. ~**se**: a) to become cruel. b) to become aggravated.

encrudelecer(-se) v. (also **encruelecer-se**) 1. to grow cruel, become brutalized. 2. to enrage.

encruecer v. 1. = **encruar**. 2. to become fierce, cruel or bloody.

encruentar v. to become furious or bloody (as a battle).

encruzamento s. m. 1. crossing (act, fact or place). 2. intersection.

encruzar v. (also **encruzilhar**) 1. to cross: a) transverse, intersect. b) place crosswise. 2. ~**se** to sit crosslegged.

~ **os braços** to fold one's arms.

encruzilhada s. f. (also **encruzada**) cross-road, crossway, carfax, place where roads cross.

na ~ **dos caminhos** at the parting of the ways. **numa** ~ at a cross-road.

encubação s. f. (pl. **-ões**) act of putting (wine) in vats.

encubar v. to put (liquids) in vats, tuns or pipes.

encurar v. (Braz., sl.) to become troubled, or worried over.

encueirar v. to swaddle.

encumeada s. f. summit, ridge.

encumear v. to place or put on the top.

encurralamento s. m. act of corralling, poundage.

encurralar v. to corral: 1. shut up in a corral (cattle); pound, pen up. 2. confine, shut up. 3. corner, drive into 'a corner. 4. ~**se** to take refuge, take shelter.

encurtador s. m. person who or thing that shortens. ‖ adj. shortening.

encurtamento s. m. shortening (act or fact), diminution, curtailment; abridging.

encurtar v. to shorten: 1. curtail, cut short. 2. diminish, reduce. 3. abbreviate, abridge. 4. limit, restrict, contract.
~ **o caminho** to cut across (way).
encurvação (pl. **-ões**), **encurvadura** s. f., **encurvamento** m. 1. incurvation, act of curving or bending. 2. curvature, arching, bowing.
encurvar v. 1. to incurvate, curve, bend, arch, bow. 2. (fig.) to humble, humiliate. 3. ~-**se**: a) to bend. b) to bow, stoop. c) to be humble, submit.
~-**se debaixo do peso** to sink under a burden.
endecha s. f. dirge, threnody: an ode or song of lamentation.
endechador s. m. (obs.) threnodist, author of a dirge.
endechar v. (obs.) to sing dirges or threnodies.
endefluxar-se v. to catch a cold.
endemia s. f. (med.) endemic disease: a disease confined to a given locality.
endemicidade s. f. endemicity, endemism.
endêmico adj. endemic(al): 1. referring to endemic diseases. 2. peculiar to a certain country or people.
|| **-amente** adv. endemically.
endemoninhado adj. 1. demoniac, demonian: possessed by a demon or evil spirit, devilish. 2. mischievous (child).
endemoninhar v. 1. to demonize: control by a demon. 2. to enrage, infuriate.
endentação s. f. (pl. **-ões**) entanglement (gear teeth).
endentar v. to mesh, tooth: be or become interlocked or entangled (gear teeth).
endentecer v. to teethe: cut one's teeth.
endereçamento s. m. address, direction.
endereçar v. 1. to address: a) superscribe or direct to (letter, words, etc.). b) aim at any object. 2. ~-**se**, to address o. s. to, betake o. s. to, make for, go or move towards.
~ **uma carta a alguém** to address a letter to s. o. **máquina de** ~ mailer: an addressing machine.
endereço (ê) s. m. (pl. **endereços**) address: name, place and residence of a person.
~ **desconhecido** unknown address. ~ **telegráfico** telegraphic address. **ao** ~ **de** to the consignation of. **ponha o** ~ **nesta carta** address this letter.
endérmico adj. (med.) endermic.
endeusado adj. deified, divinized.
endeusamento s. m. 1. deification, divinization. 2. apotheosis. 3. (fig.) pride, haughtiness.
endeusar v. 1. to deify, divinize. 2. (fig.): a) to ecstasy. b) to grow vain or haughty.
endez s. m. (also **indez**) nest-egg.
endiabrado adj. 1. devilish, devilishly bad. 2. mischievous, impish, naughty (child). 3. furious, mad. 4. demoniac.
um fulano ~ a devilish fellow.
endiabrar v. 1. to demonize. 2. to become devilish or furious.
endinheirado adj. moneyed, rich, wealthy, opulent.
endireita s. m. 1. bonesetter: person who sets broken bones. 2. (pop.) charlatan.
endireitar v. 1. to straighten: a) set to right. b) make straight. c) reform. 2. to make better, improve, ameliorate. 3. to guide. 4. to rectify. 5. ~-**se**: to straighten: a) become straight. b) stand upright. c) mend one's ways.
isto vai endireitar-se outra vez this will straighten again, this will dry straight." **quem nasce torto, tarde ou nunca se endireita** what is bred in the bone will come out in the flesh.
endívia s. f. (bot.) endive, scarole (Chichorium endivia).
endividado adj. in debt, indebted.
estou ~ I am in debt.

endividar v. 1. to indebt, make one run into debt. 2. to lay under obligation. 3. ~-**se**: a) to run into debt. b) to bind o. s.
endoado adj. draped in mourning, mournful, sad.
endobiose s. f. (biol.) life within a host as parasite.
endobiótico adj. (biol.) endobiotic: living within the tissues of the host.
endocárdio s. m. (med.) endocardium: the endothelial membrane lining the cavities of the heart.
endocardite s. f. (med.) endocarditis: inflammation of the endocardium.
endocárpio s. m. (bot.) endocarp: the inner layer of a pericarp.
endocéfalo adj. (biol.) endocephalous.
endocraniano adj. (anat.) endocranial: within the cranium.
endocrínico, endócrino adj. (med.) endocrinous: of or pertaining to a gland producing internal secretion.
endocrinologia s. f. (med.) endocrinology: the study of internal secretion.
endocrinopatia s. f. (med.) endocrinopathy: any disease due to disorder of internal secretion.
endoderma s. m. (biol.) endoderm, entoderm: the innermost of the three primary germ layers of the embryo.
endoenças s. f. pl. (R. C. Church) rites of Maundy Thursday.
endogamia s. f. endogamy: the custom of marriage within the group, class, caste or tribe.
endógamo adj. endogamous: of or pertaining to endogamy.
endógeno adj. (also **endógene**) endogenous: growing or proceeding from within.
endoidecer v. (also **endoudecer, endoidar, endoudar**) to madden: 1. make mad or crazy. 2. become insane, go crazy.
endoidecimento s. m. (also **endoudecimento**) act of going mad or crazy.
endolinfa s. f. (anat.) endolymph: the serous fluid that fills the membranous labyrinth of the ear.
endométrio s. m. (med.) endometrium: the mucous membrane that lines the uterus.
endometrite s. f. (med.) endometritis: inflammation of the endometrium.
endomingado adj. (fam.) 1. in Sunday clothes. 2. elegant; fashionable.
endomingar-se v. 1. to put on Sunday clothes. 2. to dress well or fashionably.
endomorfismo s. m. (geol.) endomorphism: the changes produced in igneous rocks by the action upon them of underlying and intrusive magmatic material.
endoplasma s. m. (biol.) endoplasm.
endorsar v. (typogr.) (also **alombar**) to line up the back of a book.
endoscopia s. f. endoscopy.
endoscópio s. m. (med.) endoscope: instrument for the examination of any cavity of the body.
endosmômetro s. m. endosmometer: instrument for determining the rate and extent of endosmosis.
endosmose s. f. (phys.) endosmos, endosmosis: a movement in liquids of different densities, separated by a membranous or porous septum.
endosmótico adj. endosmotic: of or pertaining to endosmosis.
endosperma, endospermo s. m. (bot.) endosperm: the albumen of a seed.
endospérmico adj. endospermic: containing endosperm (applied to seeds and embryos).
endósporo s. m. (bot.) endospore: a spore formed within a cell.
endossado s. m. (also **endossatário**) endorsee: a person to whom a note or bill is endorsed. || adj. endorsed.

endossamento s. m. endorsement (as of a bill).

endossante s. m. + f. (also endossador m.) endorser: person who endorses (a bill, check, etc.). ‖ adj. endorsing.

~ anterior previous endorser. ~ posterior later endorser.

endossar v. 1. to endorse: a) write one's name on the back of (a bill, check, draft, etc.). b) give sanction to. 2. (fig.) to defend, protect, back, uphold.

~ um cheque to back a check.

endosso (ô), endosse s. m. endorsement (as of a bill, check, note, etc.).

~-caução endorsement "value as security". ~ sem responsabilidade endorsement free from liability.

endoteca s. f. (bot.) endothecium.

endotélio s. m. (anat.) endothelium: a membrane that lines blood vessels, lymphatic tubes and cavities.

endotelioma s. m. (med.) endothelioma: a tumour developed from the endothelial linings.

endotérmico adj. endothermic: relating to absorption of heat.

endovenoso adj. (also intravenoso) intravenous: into or within a vein.

injeção -a intravenous injection.

endrão s. m. (pl. -ões) (bot.) wild dill.

endro s. m. (bot.) dill.

endrômina s. f. artifice, stratagem; imposture.

enduração s. f. (pl. -ões) induration: 1. act of indurating. 2. (also- med.) obduracy; hardening of the heart.

endurado adj. indurate: 1. hard(ened). 2. contumacious, obdurate, obstinate.

endurecer v. (also endurar, endurentar) to harden: 1. (also ~-se) make or become hard or solid. 2. toughen, strengthen. 3. (also ~-se) make or become insensible or cruel. 4. ~-se: a) become hard--hearted. b) inure o. s. (to labour, fatigue, etc.). ~-se no vício to become inured in vice. o gesso endureceu the plaster has fastened.

endurecimento s. m. 1. act of hardening. 2. an indurated part, callosity, tumour.

eneágino adj. (bot.) enneagynous: having nine pistils or styles.

eneagonal adj. m. + f. (pl. -ais) enneagonal: having nine angles.

eneágono s. m. (geom.) enneagon: a polygon with nine angles.

eneandro adj. (bot.) enneandrous: having nine stamens.

eneassépalo adj. (bot.) enneasepalous: having nine sepals.

eneassílabo s. m. enneasyllabic word or verse.

enegrecer v. 1. to blacken; darken. 2. to begrime; denigrate. 3. (fig.) to defame; tarnish. 4. ~-se to grow dark or black.

enegrecido adj. blackish; smoke-stained.

enegrecimento s. m. 1. blackening; darkening. 2. (fig.) defamation, slander.

enema s. m. (med.) enema: a clyster, injection into the rectum.

êneo adj. bronze, brazen.

enequim s. m. (pl. -ins) (Braz., ichth.) man-eater: a large shark (Carcharodon carcharias).

energia s. f. energy: 1. power, strength. 2. force, vigour, soul, zip, heartiness, activity, peppiness, sinew. 3. firmness. 4. courage. 5. power to produce motion.

~ atômica atomic energy. ~ cinética kinetic energy. ~ elétrica electrical energy. ~ hidráulica water power. ~ mecânica mechanical energy. ~ nuclear nuclear energy. ~ química chemical energy. ~ térmica heat energy. ~ vital vital energy. central de ~ hidráulica water power station. com ~ with a

will, energetically. consumo de ~ power consumption. ele age com ~ he acts energetically. ele trabalha com ~ he works with a will. produção de ~ power generation. sem ~ fecklessly. trabalhe com ~! work earnestly, (U. S. A., sl.) put some pep into your work!

enérgico adj. energetic: 1. powerful, strenuous. 2. vigorous, active, forceful. 3. strong-willed. ‖ energicamente adv. energetically, vigorously; forcibly. agir energicamente to act energetically. apoiar energicamente to give strong support to. ela é uma garota -a e de ação she is an energetic and active girl. falei energicamente com ele I spoke sternly to him. insistir energicamente em to press hard for. protestei energicamente I protested strongly.

enérgide s. f. (bot.) energid, protoplast.

energúmero s. m. 1. energumen: a) demoniac person; person possessed by a devil. b) a fanatical enthusiast. 2. (fig.) muddler.

enervação s. f. (pl. -ões) (also enervamento m.) 1. enervation: a) act of enervating or state of being enervated. b) debility, weakness. 2. nervation.

enervante adj. m. + f. (also enervador) enervating; weakening.

enervar v. to enervate: 1. unnerve: deprive of nerve, energy or vigour; weaken, debilitate. 2. render effeminate. 3. provide with nerves. 4. ~-se: lose strength, grow weak.

enerve adj. m. + f. enervate: 1. weakened. 2. rendered effeminate or feeble.

enesgar v. to have the form of a gore.

enevoado adj. 1. foggy, misty. 2. overcast, covered with clouds, cloudy.

enevoar v. 1. to fog, haze, mist, cover with mist or fog. 2. to cloud, darken, obscure. 3. (fig.) to sadden. 4. ~-se: a) to become overcast, grow cloudy. b) to become foggy.

enfadadiço adj. 1. easily tired. 2. irascible, touchy. 3. peevish, petulant.

enfadar v. 1. to tire, irk. 2. to bore, annoy, disturb, vex. 3. to put out of humour, worry. 4. to peeve, rile. 5. ~-se: a) to become tired, bored, annoyed or riled. b) to worry o. s.

enfado s. m. (also enfadamento) 1. unpleasantness, tediousness, boredom, displeasure. 2. uneasiness, indisposition. 3. annoyance; nuisance, weariness.

encher-se de ~ to become bored.

enfadonho, enfadoso adj. 1. tiresome, irksome, boring, tedious, wearisome. 2. annoying, troublesome. ‖ -amente adv. wearisomely; annoyingly.

conversa -a prosy talk. tarefa -a troublesome task.

enfaixar v. to swathe: bind, swaddle, bandage.

~ o nenê to dress the baby.

enfanicar-se v. (fam.) to faint, swoon.

enfaramento s. m. 1. loathing, disgust; aversion. 2. weariness. 3. nausea, surfeit.

enfarar v. 1. to loathe, disgust. 2. to nauseate, surfeit, turn one's stomach, sicken.

enfardadeira s. f. baler: hay baling machine.

enfardador s. m. 1. baler, binder, packer. 2. bundler. ‖ adj. that packs up.

enfardamento s. m. 1. baling, packing up. 2. bundling.

enfardar v. 1. to bale, bind, pack up. 2. to bundle: make into a bundle.

enfardelar v. to put up into a bundle.

enfarelar v. to mix or cover with bran.

enfarinhadela s. f. 1. sprinkling or covering with flour or meal. 2. smattering, superficial knowledge.

enfarinhar v. 1. to flour: sprinkle or cover with flour or meal. 2. to powder. 3. to make white (with flour). 4. to get a smattering or superficial knowledge of. 5. ~-se to cover o. s. with flour.

enfaro s. m. 1. loathing, disgust, aversion. 2. nausea, surfeit, repugnance.

enfaroso adj. (Braz.) 1. loathed; fed up. 2. annoyed, bored.

enfarpelado adj. dressed up in new or Sunday clothes.

enfarpelar-se v. to dress up in new or Sunday clothes.

enfarrapar v. 1. to cover with rags. 2. to dress in rags, tatters.

enfarruscar v. 1. to soot: cover with soot. 2. to soil or blacken (as with coal). 3. (Braz.) (also ~-se) to become sullen; get angry. 4. ~-se to become covered or soiled with soot.

enfartação s. f. (pl. -ões) = enfarte.

enfartado adj. 1. glutted, sated, satisfied. 2. replete, full.

enfartar v. 1. (med.) to cause an infarct to. 2. to glut, satiate, fill, stuff. 3. to cram. 4. to obstruct, congest.

enfarte s. m. (also **enfartamento**) 1. glutting; repletion; stuffing. 2. cramming. 3. (med., pathol.) = **infarto**.

ênfase s. f. 1. emphasis: a) a stress laid upon some word or words (in speaking or reading). b) expressiveness. 2. ostentation, pomp.
dar ~ to emphasize. **sem** ~ unexpressive.

enfastiadiço adj. 1. easily tired or bored. 2. wearisome. 3. tedious.

enfastiamento s. m. 1. boredom, tiring. 2. weariness. 3. tediousness.

enfastiar v. 1. to tire, irk, weary. 2. to bore, annoy, vex. 3. to pall: make tasteless. 4. ~-se: to become bored, tired or annoyed.

enfastioso adj. (also **enfastiante** m. + f.) 1. loathsome, disgusting. 2. tedious, irksome.

enfático adj. 1. emphatic(al): having emphasis or stress. 2. with a flourish. 3. pompous. || **enfaticamente** adv. emphatically; pompously.

enfatiotar-se v. (Braz.) to dress up, spruce o. s. up.

enfatismo s. m. quality of being emphatic.

enfatizar v. to emphasize.

enfatuação s. f. (pl. -ões), **enfatuamento** m. 1. act of making vain. 2. conceit, presumption. 3. fatuousness.

enfatuar v. 1. to make vain or conceited. 2. to make fatuous. 3. ~-se to be or become vain; pride o. s.

enfear v. (usually **afear**) to uglify.

enfebrecer v. to fever: throw into or affect with fever.

enfeirar v. to buy and sell at a fair.

enfeitado adj. adorned, trimmed, embellished, spruce.
a mesa estava -a com flores the table was gay with flowers.

enfeitador s. m. adorner; decorator. || adj. adorning, embellishing; beautifying.

enfeitar v. 1. to adorn, decorate, ornament, trim, embellish, beautify, prank. 2. to flourish. 3. ~-se: a) to make o. s. beautiful. b) to spruce up, dress o. s. up.
ela enfeitou-se com jóias she adorned herself with jewels. **ela não enfeita os seus vestidos** she does not trim her dresses. **ele enfeitou o discurso** he flourished his speech. **enfeitei a sala com quadros** I decorated the room with pictures. **gobelinos enfeitavam as paredes** gobelins pranked the walls.

enfeite s. m. 1. ornament, decoration, trimming, embellishment, adornment. 2. ~s pl. fripperies.

enfeitiçado adj. enchanted, charmed, bewitched, spellbound, fascinated.

enfeitiçamento s. m. (be)witchery, charming, fascination.

enfeitiçar v. 1. to bewitch, charm, fascinate; hex. 2. to enchant, seduce. 3. ~-se to be charmed or fascinated.
ela enfeitiçou-me she cast a spell on me.

enfeixamento s. m. act of bundling up.

enfeixar v. 1. to fagot, tie together (as sticks). 2. to bundle up.

enfeltrar v. to felt: 1. convert into felt. 2. overlay with felt.

enfelujar v. to soot, soil with soot.

enfenecer v. (usually **fenecer**) 1. to finish, end. 2. to die.

enfermagem s. f. (pl. -ens) (sick-)nursing: care of the sick.

enfermar v. 1. to sicken: make or become sick. 2. to weaken.

enfermaria s. f. 1. infirmary: place for treatment of the sick. 2. sickroom, hospital ward.

enfermeira s. f. nurse: woman trained to wait upon the sick.

enfermeiro s. m. 1. male nurse. 2. hospital orderly.

enfermiço adj. sickly, unhealthy, infirm.

enfermidade s. f. infirmity: 1. disease, sickness, ailment, illness, complaint. 2. weakness.

enfermo (ê) s. m. (pl. **enfermos**) patient, a sick person; patient; sufferer. || adj. 1. sick, diseaded, infirm, ill. 2. weak, feeble.

enferrujado adj. rusty: covered or affected with rust.

enferrujar v. to rust: 1. affect or become affected with rust. 2. (fam.) deteriorate through disuse. 3. ~-se become rusty.

enfesta s. f. summit, peak, acme.

enfestação s. f. (Braz.) act of folding lengthwise (a piece of cloth).

enfestado adj. 1. folded lengthwise (a piece of cloth). 2. reinforced. 3. (obs.) turned upside; lifted up.

enfestador s. m. (Braz.) person who cheats in a game.

enfestar v. 1. to fold lengthwise (a piece of cloth). 2. to increase (as an account). 3. (Braz.): a) to cheat in a game. b) to exaggerate. c) to tire, weary; bore.

enfesto (ê) adj. steep, sheer, sloping.

enfestoar v. (also **afestoar**) to festoon, decorate with festoons.

enfeudação s. f. (pl. -ões) enfeoffment: act of giving the fee of an estate.

enfeudar v. 1. to enfeoff: sell or give and convey lands in fee. 2. to submit, subject.

enfezado adj. 1. rachitic, rickety, stunted, dwarfish. 2. (fig.): a) annoyed, exasperated. b) irksome, bored; peevish.

enfezamento s. m. 1. rachitis, rickets, stuntedness. 2. (fig.): a) annoyance, irritation. b) boredom; peevishness.

enfezar v. 1. to stunt, dwarf. 2. to check the natural development of. 3. (fig.): a) to annoy, irritate. b) to tire, bore; rile. 4. ~-se: a) to wither, droop, decay. b) to become riled or irritated.
não o enfeze! don't get his back up!

enfiada s. f. 1. file, range, string. 2. series (of happenings, words, etc.). 3. number of things ranged in line.

enfiador s. m. (N. Braz.) shoe-string.

enfiadura s. f. 1. needleful. 2. threading. 3. eye of a needle.

enfiamento s. m. (also **enfiação** f.) 1. stringing, threading (of needles, beads, etc.). 2. scare, fright.

enfiar v. 1. to thread (as a needle). 2. to string (pearls, beads, etc.). 3. to range into files. 4. to slip on (dresses, shoes, etc.). 5. to run through, pierce (as with a sword). 6. ~-se to enter in, penetrate.
~ **em** to insert in. ~ **no bolso** to tuck away into the pocket. ~ **pérolas** to string pearls. **a galinha enfiou a cabeça debaixo da asa** the hen tucked her head under her wing. **enfiei-me numa rua escura** I plunged into a dark street.

enfileiramento s. m. alinement, alignment: ranging in a line or file.

enfileirar v. 1. to range in a file or line. 2. to align, set in a row, form a line; rank. 3. ~-se: a) to get into line. b) to align o. s.

enfim adv. at last, finally, after all, ultimately.
até que ~ ele chegou! he finally came after all!

enfincar v. (Braz., pop. usually **fincar**) to stick, drive, plant into.

enfisema s. m. (med.) emphysema: a swelling or inflation due to the presence of air in the interstices of the connective tissues.

enfisemático, enfisematoso adj. emphysematous: of the nature of or affected with emphysema.

enfistular v. 1. to fistulize, make fistulous. 2. (also ~-se): a) to become fistulous. b) to become ulcerated.

enfitar v. 1. to trim with ribbons. 2. to fix the eyes on, stare at.

enfiteuse s. f. (jur.) emphyteusis: long or inheritable lease of lands or tenements.

enfiteuta s. m. + f. emphyteuta: a tenant by emphyteusis.

enfiteuticar v. to grant by emphyteusis.

enfitêutico adj. emphyteutic: pertaining to emphyteusis.

enfivelamento s. m. buckling: act of providing or fastening with buckles.

enfivelar v. to buckle: provide or fasten with a buckle.

enfixar v. (Braz.) 1. to put hinges on (doors, windows). 2. to connect rails with fishplates.

enflanelar v. to flannel: cover or wrap with flannel.

enflorar, enflorear v. to flower: 1. (also ~-se) blossom, bloom, effloresce, produce flowers. 2. cause to blossom. 3. decorate with flowers. 4. adorn, embellish.

enflorescer v. = **florescer**.

enflorestado adj. forested.

enfobiar v. to anger, irritate, enrage.

enfocação s. f. (pl. **-ões**) focalization: act of focalizing.

enfocar v. to focus, focalize: adjust, bring or come to a focus.

enfogar v. to burn, put on fire.

enfolhamento s. m. act of forming into leaves.

enfolhar v. 1. to form into a leaf or leaves. 2. to grow leaves. 3. to cover with leaves.

enfolipar v. to form bulges or folds (in a badly-fitting dress).

enfoque s. m. way of focussing a question.

enforcado s. m. hanged person: 1. one who hanged himself. 2. one who was executed on the gallows. ‖ adj. 1. hanged. 2. (Braz.) pressed for money.

enforcamento s. m. hanging: 1. the act of one who hangs himself (by the neck). 2. execution on the gallows.

enforcar v. 1. to hang: execute on the gallows. 2. to squander. 3. to sell at a loss, to dump. 4. ~-se a) to hang o. s. (by the neck). b) to marry.
ele merece ser enforcado por seu crime he deserves to be hanged for his crime. **morrer enforcado** to die by hanging. **que me enforquem se...** I'll be hanged if...

enforjar v. to put into the forge.

enformar v. 1. to put in a mould. 2. to shape. 3. to develop. 4. to increase the body or consistency of. ~ **o sapato** to put the shoe on the last. ~ **o chapéu** to block the hat.

enfornar v. 1. to put into the oven (as bread). 2. to eat too much.

enfortir v. to full (cloth).

enfragar v. to lead to a cliff, a steep rock (a mine, a road).

enfranque s. m. 1. the shank of a shoe. 2. the part of a coat covering the waist.

enfraquecer v. (also **enfraquentar**) 1. to weaken, debilitate, enfeeble. 2. to lose courage. 3. ~-se to grow weak or feeble.

enfraquecido adj. weak, feeble, debilitated.

enfraquecimento s. m. weakness, feebleness, debility.

enfrascar v. 1. to bottle, put into a flask or bottle. 2. ~-se: a) to be or become impregnated. b) to get drunk. c) to entangle o. s.

enfreamento s. m. braking, curbing.

enfrear v. 1. to curb, bride, restrain. 2. to brake, apply the brakes. 3. to break in, tame. 4. ~-se: a) to control o. s. b) to curb one's desires.

enfrechadura s. f., **enfrechate** m. (naut.) ratline; ship ladder.

enfrenar v. to bridle, curb.

enfrenesiar v. 1. to frenzy, make frantic. 2. to grow impatient.

enfrentar v. 1. to face, front, meet. 2. to come face to face with, confront. 3. to stand up to. 4. to brave. 5. to defy.
~ **algo com coragem** to face s. th. courageously, face up to s. th. ~ **resolutamente** to look in the face. ~ **a situação** to face the situation, (coll.) take the bull by the horns. **você conhece as dificuldades a ~?** do you know what you are about?

enfrestar v. 1. to provide openings, slits, gaps in. 2. to separate by slits.

enfriar v. to cool, make cool.

enfronhado adj. 1. in a pillowcase. 2. well versed in a subject, skilled, expert. 3. learned, instructed.

enfronhar v. 1. to put the pillow into the pillowcase. 2. to put or slip on (one's clothes). 3. to teach a person a subject. 4. ~-se: a) to acquire learning. b) to become versed in (a subject).
enfronhei-a no assunto I taught her the subject. ~-**se num assunto** to make o. s. acquainted with a subject.

enfrouxecer v. (also **enfroixecer**) 1. to loosen, slacken. 2. to debilitate, weaken.

enfrutecer v. to frutify, bear fruit.

enfueirada s. f. a full cart-load.

enfueirar v. 1. to provide a cart with stakes. 2. to load the cart up to the stakes.

enfulijar v. to soot, soil with soot.

enfumaçar, enfumar, enfumarar v. to smoke: fill or cover with smoke.

enfunação s. f. (pl. **-ões**) presumption, arrogance, vainglory.

enfunar v. 1. to belly: swell out or fill (as a sail). 2. (fig.) to puff up with pride. 3. ~-se: a) to become bellied (sails). b) to become proud. c) to become sullen; be irritated, get angry.

enfunilamento s. m. act of pouring liquids through a funnel.

enfunilar v. 1. to shape like a funnel. 2. to pour liquids through a funnel.

enfurecer v. (also **enfuriar**) 1. to infuriate, enrage, make furious. 2. to be furious. 3. ~-se: a) to become furious; lose one's temper. b) to swell, become rough (as the sea).
~ **alguém** to put a person in rage.

enfurecido adj. (also **enfuriado**) 1. furious, enraged, infuriated, angry. 2. rough (as the sea).

enfurnar v. 1. to shut or hide in or as in a cave or grotto. 2. (naut.) to step (masts).

enfusar v. (Braz.) to go or run aground.

enfusca s. f. (N. Braz.) hiding-place.

enfuscar v. to obfuscate, darken, blacken.

enfusta s. f. (N. Braz.) oblique prop.

enfustar v. (Port.) to come in or out hastily.

engabelação s. f. (pl. -ões) (Braz.; also **engabelo**) deceit, act of deceiving (with fair words).

engabelador s. m. (Braz.) deceiver, cheat. ‖ adj. deceiving, cheating.

engabelar v. (Braz., also **engambelar**) 1. to deceive, dupe (with fair words), lead a person up the garden path. 2. to cheat, coax, decoy.

engaçar v. to break the clots of earth in a field (with a rake).

engaço s. m. 1. the stalk of a bunch of grapes. 2. husk (of fruits). 3. rake.

engadanhar-se v. 1. to have one's hands stiffened with cold. 2. to become embarrassed. 3. to be perplexed or nonplussed.

engadelhar v. to dishevel, disorder (the hair).

engafecer v. 1. to cause dog mange or leprosy. 2. to become a leper.

engaiar v. (naut.) to wind a rope or marline around a fixed cable to make its surface smooth.

engaifonar v. (also **gaifonar**) to make faces or grimaces.

engaio s. m. (naut.) rope to worm a cable.

engaiolar v. 1. to cage: a) shut up in or as in a cage (birds, etc.). b) (fig.) imprison. 2. ~-se: to withdraw, isolate o. s., seclude o. s.

engajado s. m. person who is engaged for work. ‖ adj. engaged (for work).

engajador s. m. engager, emigration agent, shipping--master, crimp.

engajamento s. m. 1. engagement, employment. 2. enlistment, enrollment.

engajar v. 1. to engage: hire, employ. 2. ~-se: a) to engage o. s., take an employment. b) to enlist o. s.

engalanado adj. 1. adorned, trimmed. 2. elegant, chic. **ele estava** ~ he was figged out.

engalanar v. (also **agalanar**) 1. to adorn, decorate, ornament (with ribbons or lace). 2. to embellish, beautify. 3. ~-se to put on gala dress.

engalar v. 1. to erect or set up the neck (horse). 2. ~-se to become proud or haughty.

engalfinhar-se v. 1. to wrestle, grapple (with another person). 2. to get entangled.

engalgar v. to show (the hare) to the greyhounds.

engalhardetar v. to deck with pennants or flags (as a ship).

engalinhar v. to bring or cause bad luck to.

engalispar-se v. to ruffle or bristle like a cockalorum (with anger).

engambelar v. (Braz.) 1. to deceive with false hopes, to cheat. 2. to entertain, to rock.

engambitar v. (Braz.) to traverse or step across (trench, ditch).

enganadiço adj. that deceives easily, leads to a mistake.

enganado adj. 1. wrong, mistaken. 2. deceived, deluded. 3. betrayed; sold.
estar redondamente ~ to be quite beside the mark. **fui** ~ I was led into error. **você está** ~ you are under a mistake, you are in error.

enganador s. m. deceiver, cheater, swindler. ‖ adj. 1. deceiving, deceptive, delusive. 2. false, illusory.

enganar v. 1. to deceive, mislead, delude. 2. to cheat, trick, coax, wheedle. 3. to seduce, entice, decoy, beguile. 4. to conceal. 5. to lead into error. 6. to give a wrong impression. 7. ~-se: a) to make a mistake. b) to be mistaken.
~ **alguém** to impose upon s. o. ~ **as horas** to beguile the time. ~ **o estômago** to stay the stomach. **as aparências enganam** appearances are deceptive. **deixar-se** ~ **por alguém** to be the dupe of s. o. **ele o está enganando** he puts a cheat upon you. **ele enganou-me** he juggled with me. **ele quer me** ~

he wants to take me in. **ele engana-se em** he is thrown out in. **enganei-me** I made a mistake.

engana-tico s. m. (pl. **engana-ticos**) (Braz.) a variety of cowbird (genus Molothrus).

engana-tolo s. f. (pl. **engana-tolos**) (Braz.) a butterfly of the family Nymphalidae.

engana-vista s. m. (pl. **engana-vistas**) trompe l'oeil.

enganchar v. 1. to hook: hold, fasten, catch with a hook. 2. ~-se: a) to hook into. b) to be caught as by a hook.

engangorrado adj. captured in a snare or trap (animal).

enganjento adj. 1. foolish, silly. 2. presumptuous, vain, self-conceited.

engano s. m. 1. mistake, error, fault. 2. delusion, swindle, deception. 3. fraud, trick, hoax. 4. deceit, cheating, swindle.

enganoso adj. 1. deceiving. 2. deceitful, illusory. 3. fallacious, false. 4. simulated, make-believe, insidious. ‖ **-amente** adv. deceivingly.

engarapar v. (N. Braz.) 1. to give **garapa** (beverage made of the juice of sugar-cane) to. 2. to deceive, cheat s. o.

engar v. 1. to get used to (game). 2. to wrangle, pick a quarrel. 3. to recalcitrate, wince.

engaravitado adj. stiff with cold.

engaravitar-se v. to grow stiff with cold.

engargantar v. 1. to swallow. 2. to indent.

engarrafadeira s. f. (Braz.) bottling machine.

engarrafado adj. 1. bottled, in bottles. 2. (fig.) blocked up.
vinho ~ bottled wine.

engarrafador s. m. bottler: person who bottles.

engarrafamento s. m. (also **engarrafagem** f.) 1. bottling: act or process of putting into bottles. 2. (fig.) obstruction.
~ **de trânsito** traffic jam.

engarrafar v. to bottle: put into a bottle or bottles.

engarupar-se v. to ride on a crupper.

engasgalhar-se v. 1. to be choked. 2. to swallow the wrong way. 3. (fig.) to grapple.

engasgamento s. m. 1. act of choking. 2. suffocation. 3. (fig.) embarrassment.

engasgar v. 1. to choke, obstruct the windpipe. 2. ~-se: a) to be choked. b) to suffocate. c) to have something sticking in the throat. d) to swallow the wrong way. 3. (fig.) to be embarrassed, confound o. s., break down in one's speech.

engasgo s. m. (also **engasgue**) 1. act of choking. 2. obstacle that hinders the respiration. 3. (fig.) embarrassment, confusion.

engastador s. m. setter: person who sets gems.

engastalhar v. 1. to clamp. 2. to clasp, join or bind with clasps.

engastar v. 1. to set (gems). 2. to inlay, incase. 3. to intercalate.
~ **um brilhante** to mount a diamond.

engaste s. m. setting or mounting (of gems).

engatar v. 1. to clamp: bind or join with or as with a clamp. 2. to leash. 3. to hook. 4. to couple (railway carriages). 5. to hitch up (horses).

engate s. m. 1. clamp, hook; cramp. 2. coupling gear. 3. coupling (railway carriage) (plate V 1).
~ **articulado** toggle-joint. **barra de** ~ coupling bar.

engatilhar v. 1. to cock (as a firearm, gun). 2. (fig.) to prepare.

engatinhar v. 1. to creep, crawl on all fours (as children). 2. to be a beginner.

engavelar v. to sheaf: bind or tie up the corn in sheaves (plate C 16).

engavetamento s. m. 1. act of putting into a drawer. 2. (fig.) postponement. 3. telescoping (of railway carriages in a collision).

engavetar v. 1. to put into a drawer. 2. (fig.) to postpone, put off. 3. to telescope: be forced into one another (railway carriages in a collision).

engazopador s. m. cheater, imposter, lier. ‖ adj. untruthful, mendacious, false.

engazopar v. (also **engazupar**) 1. to deceive, delude. 2. to tell a lie. 3. to cheat, trick. 4. to imprison.

engelhado adj. 1. wrinkled, withered, shriveled. 2. (fig.) entangled.

engelhar v. 1. to wrinkle, shrivel, wilt. 2. ~-**se**: a) to become wrinkled or dry. b) to corrugate.

engendrar v. 1. to engender: a) produce, create, originate, cause. b) generate, beget. c) invent, contrive, make up, engineer. 2. to imagine, devise. 3. to hatch (a plot).

engenhador s. m. inventor: person who invents, contrives or schemes. ‖ adj. 1. ingenious, inventive. 2. inventing.

engenhar v. 1. to engineer: scheme, conceive, machinate, plan; hatch. 2. to form ideas. 3. to invent, contrive. 4. to devise, imagine. 5. ~-**se** to be endeavouring, apply one's mind.
engenhei uma máquina I invented a machine.

engenharia s. f. 1. engineering: the science of engineers. 2. engineers collectively. 3. (mil.) engineer corps.
~ **civil** civil engineering. ~ **elétrica** electrical engineering. ~ **hidráulica** hydraulic engineering. ~ **mecânica** mechanical engineering. ~ **militar** military engineering.

engenheirando s. m. senior student of or person about to graduate in engineering.

engenheiro s. m. 1. engineer: person versed in or practicing any branch of engineering. 2. (Braz.) an owner of a sugar-mill.
~ **chefe** chief engineer. ~ **civil** civil engineer. ~ **eletricista** electrical engineer. ~ **mecânico** mechanical engineer. **corpo de** ~**s** (mil.) corps of engineers, engineer corps. ~-**residente** resident engineer.

engenheiro-agrônomo s. m. (pl. **engenheiros-agrônomos**) agronomist.

engenho s. m. 1. inventive power, ingeniousness, inventiveness, wit. 2. skill, dexterity, ability. 3. talent, faculty, aptitude. 4. engine; machine. 5. mill.
~ **de açúcar** sugar-mill. ~ **de guerra** petard; missile. ~ **de serra** sawmill.

engenhoca s. f. 1. gadget: any simple mechanical device or contrivance. 2. artifice, stratagem. 3. (Braz.) small sugar-mill which produces mostly sugar-cane brandy.

engenhosidade s. f. (Braz.) quality of being ingenious, inventive or clever, cleverness.

engenhoso adj. 1. ingenious, witty, inventive. 2. artful. 3. talented, clever, adroit, resourceful. ‖ -**amente** adv. 1. ingeniously, wittily. 2. artfully.
um homem ~ a man full of devices.

engessador s. m. plasterer: 1. stuccoworker. 2. person who applies plaster casts to fractured arms or legs. ‖ adj. 1. coating with plaster. 2. applying a plaster cast.

engessar v. to plaster: 1. (archit.) coat with plaster. 2. (surg.) apply a plaster cast to a fractured arm or leg.

englobar v. 1. to conglobate: gather or form into a globe. 2. to embody. 3. to unite. 4. to conglomerate.

englobular v. to transform into a globule.

engodado adj. 1. allured, enticed, persuaded (with flattery or false promises). 2. deceived, deluded.

engodamento s. m. 1. allurement, enticement, fascination. 2. act of baiting.

engodar v. 1. to allure, lure, entice, persuade (with flattery or false promises). 2. to bait. 3. to wheedle, decoy, cajole.

engodativo adj. alluring, enticing, fit to allure.

engodilhar v. 1. to form lumps or knots. 2. to embarrass, confuse.

engodo s. m. 1. allure(ment), enticement, decoy. 2. bait (esp. to catch fish). 3. artful flattery, coaxing.

engoiado adj. meager, lean; rickety, rachitic.

engoiar-se v. 1. to shrink up. 2. to become rickety or rachitic.

engole-vento s. m. (pl. **engole-ventos**) = **curiango**.

engolfar v. 1. to engulf: swallow up in or as in a gulf. 2. ~-**se**: a) to enter deeply, penetrate. b) to become absorbed. c) to plunge or be plunged (em in).

engolição s. f. (pl. -**ões**) the act of swallowing, absorption.

engolideiras s. f. pl. (sl.) gullet, throat, gorge.

engolipar v. (sl.) to swallow.

engolir v. 1. to swallow, take into the stomach. 2. to devour, gulp down, englut. 3. to absorb, drink in or suck up. 4. (fig.) to believe.
~ **a pílula** (pop.) to swallow the pill. ~ **em seco** to bite one's tongue. **ela não engole uma injúria** she doesn't swallow an affront. **ele engole suas palavras** he slurs his words. **ele engoliu a ofensa** he sat down under the insult. **ele engoliu a poção de um (só) trago** he swallowed the potion in one gulp. **ele engole sem mastigar** he swallows without chewing. **fazer alguém** ~ **alguma coisa** (fig.) to thrust s. th. down some one's throat. **isto não se pode** ~ (fig.) it is a hard thing to bear.

engomadaria s. f. establishment where clothes are ironed.

engomadeira s. f. 1. ironer: woman who irons clothes. 2. ironing machine: a machine for hot-pressing clothes.

engomadela s. f. light starching, touch ironing.

engomadura, engomagem (pl. -**ens**) s. f. starching and ironing of clothes with a flatiron.

engomar v. 1. to starch and iron clothes with a flatiron. 2. to launder.
~ **colarinho** to starch collars. **ferro de** ~ flatiron, smoothing-iron.

engonçar v. to hinge: 1. provide with hinges. 2. attach with hinges.

engonço s. m. hinge, movable joint.
boneco de ~ puppet, marionette.

engorda s. f. 1. fattening (of animals for sale). 2. feed for such a purpose.

engordar v. 1. to fatten. 2. to grow fat. 3. (fig.) to grow rich. 4. to nourish, feed.
ela tem tendência para ~ she has a tendency to corpulence.

engorduramento s. m. act of greasing.

engordurar v. 1. to grease: smear with grease. 2. to stain (especially clothes) with grease.

engorovinhado adj. wizened, wrinkled.

engoteirado adj. leaky, full of holes or rotten spots (roof).

engra s. f. corner; angle.

engraçado s. m. funny or witty person. ‖ adj. 1. graceful; having grace. 2. funny, comic, amusing; jocose. 3. witty, clever, spirited. 4. merry, jolly.
ele é muito ~ he is full of fun. **esta anedota é -a** this anecdote is funny. **que** ~! what fun! how funny.

engraçamento s. m. 1. gallantry, politeness. 2. confidence, intimacy.

engraçar v. 1. to grace, make gracious. 2. to heighten the splendour. 3. (Braz., also ~-**se**) to take a liking to, to fall for. 4. ~-se to ingratiate o. s. (with). ~ com alguém: a) to take a liking to s. o. b) to win some one's good graces.

engradado s. m. (Braz.) crate: a framework of slats used to pack articles; packing box.

engradamento s. m. railing; grating.

engradar v. 1. to rail, grate: a) shut in with railing or grating. b) fit with, put in or surround with a grate. 2. (mil.) to put together the gun-carriage.

engradecer v. to make o. s. agreeable.

engraecer v. to seed: run into seed.

engrambelar v. = engabelar.

engrampador s. m. deceiver, cheater, swindler.

engrampar v. to deceive, cheat, trick.

engramponar-se v. to grow proud or haughty.

engrandecer v. 1. to enlarge; augment. 2. to aggrandize. 3. to increase, raise (in power, rank, riches, wealth). 4. ~-se: a) to become greater. b) to exalt o. s.; make o. s. proud.

engrandecimento s. m. 1. enlargement, increase, rise. 2. aggrandizement. 3. exaltation, elevation.

engranzagem s. f., engranzamento m. 1. act of stringing (beads, pearls). 2. (mach.) meshing (gears).

engranzar v. (also engrazar) 1. to string (beads, pearls) on a gold or silver wire. 2. to hook. 3. to gear, mesh.

engravatar-se, engravatizar-se v. to put on a tie.

engravescer v. 1. to make worse. 2. ~-se: a) to take a bad turn, worsen (situation). b) to aggravate (an evil).

engravidar v. to render pregnant.

ela engravidou she is in the family way.

engravitar-se v. 1. to straighten o. s. up, stand up straight. 2. to react. 3. to recalcitrate.

engraxadeira s. f. (tech.) lubricator, grease cup (plate E 1).

engraxadela s. f. shine, shining (of shoes).

engraxador s. m. 1. = engraxate. 2. (fig.) toady, lick-spittle.

engraxamento s. m. 1. act of shining (shoes). 2. smearing (with grease).

engraxar v. 1. to shine (shoes). 2. to smear (with grease).

~ as botas a alguém to cringe before s. o.

engraxataria s. f. (Braz.) place where shoes are shined.

engraxate s. m. (also engraxador) shoeshiner, bootblack, shoeblack.

engrelar v. to stand upright.

engrerfagem s. f. (pl. -ens) 1. gear, gearings, works; cogwheel. 2. (fig.) organization.

~ acionadora drive gear, main gear. ~ anular ring gear. ~ cilíndrica spur gear. ~ cônica bevel gear. ~ da coroa crown wheel. ~ da direção steering gear. ~ de avanço feed gear. ~ de câmbio switch gear. ~ de controle control gear. ~ de reversão reversing gear. ~ de rosca worm gearing. ~ diferencial differential gearing. ~ dupla double gear. ~ helicoidal screw gear. ~ intermediária transmission gear. ~ interna internal gear. ~ motriz drive gear. ~ planetária planetary gear, sun-and-planet gear. ~ redutora back gear. ~ sincronizada synchro-mesh gear. roda de ~ gear wheel.

engrenar v. 1. to gear, mesh. 2. to put in gear. 3. to tooth.

engrenhar v. (obs.) to put the hair in order.

engrifar v. 1. to show the claws (animals ready to attack). 2. to seize control of. 3. to hold on, catch.

engrilar v. 1. to set upright, prick (ears). 2. ~-se: to become angry or upset.

engriguilhado adj. (S. E. Braz., sl.) entangled, complicated, embarrassed.

engrimanço s. m. 1. affectation (in speaking or doing anything). 2. unintelligible manner of speaking. 3. artifice, ruse.

engrimpar-se, engrimpinar-se, engrimponar-se v. 1. to climb, clamber to the top. 2. to grow proud.

engrinaldar v. 1. to engarland: adorn with garlands, to wreathe, festoon. 2. to adorn, embellish. 3. ~-se to bedeck, trim o. s.

engrolar v. 1. to parboil. 2. to bungle. 3. to pronounce badly, sputter. 4. ~-se to be half raw.

engrossador s. m. (Braz., sl.) flatterer, coaxer, fawner.

engrossamento s. m. 1. thickening, swelling, enlarging; augmentation, increase. 2. (archit.) entasis. 3. (Braz., sl.) adulation, coaxing, flattery.

engrossante s. m. (N. Braz.) a sort of sloppy food for babies.

engrossar v. 1. to enlarge, swell, thicken. 2. to augment, increase. 3. to fertilize. 4. to enrich. 5. (Braz., sl.) to flatter, coax, adulate. 6. ~-se: a) to grow rich or mighty. b) to become thick or thicker. c) to inspissate. d) to become deeper (the voice). 7. to treat s. o. coarsely. 8. to show o. s. impolite, rude.

a puberdade engrossa a voz the age of puberty makes the voice stronger.

engrouvinhado adj. 1. thin and tall, lanky, thin as a lath (person). 2. dishevelled (hair).

engrujado adj., engrujar-se v. = engurujado, engurujar-se.

engrunação s. f. (N. E. Braz.) underground section of a river.

engrunhido adj. 1. lazy, idle, sluggish, indolent. 2. benumbed. 3. stiff (with cold).

engrunhir v. 1. to benumb. 2. to become lazy, idle. 3. to stiffen (with cold).

engrupir v. (Braz., sl.) to deceive, cheat.

enguaxumado adj. (Braz.) covered with guaxuma (Caesar weed).

enguia s. f. (ichth.) eel.

~ elétrica electric eel.

enguiçador s. m. 1. person who has bad luck, ill-starred fellow. 2. a bearer of ill luck. || adj. bearing or causing bad luck.

enguiçar v. 1. to stunt. 2. to bewitch, bring bad luck. 3. to stall, break down (esp. a car). 4. to get out of order. 5. (Braz., pop.) to mismanage, embroil.

o motor enguiçou na subida the motor stalled on an acclivity. meu carro enguiçou my car broke down.

enguiço s. m. (also enguiçamento) 1. impediment, difficulty, rub, hitch, snag. 2. breakdown (mot.) 3. mishap, bad luck. 4. ill omen. 5. evil eye.

há um ~ there is a hitch somewhere, there is no go in it.

enguirlandar v. (usually engrinaldar) to engarland, adorn with garlands.

engulhado adj. nauseated, affected with nausea.

engulhar v. 1. to nauseate, make squeamish. 2. to be affected with nausea.

engulho s. m. 1. nausea, qualm. 2. (fig.): a) desire. b) temptation.

engulhoso adj. (also engulhento) nauseous, causing nausea, qualmish.

engulosinar v. 1. to make sweet-toothed, use to sweets. 2. to whet the appetite. 3. ~-se to become fond of or used to sweetmeats.

engunhar v. to wither (fruit).

engurujar-se v. (also engrujar-se) 1. to stiffen (with cold). 2. to dishevel (feathers, hair). 3. to muffle o. s. up. 4. to retire, become shy.

enho s. m. fawn, young deer.

enícola adj. m. + f. (com.) dealing in wine.

enigma s. m. enigma: 1. riddle. 2. anything puzzling or inexplicable. 3. (fig.) mystery. 4. problem. 5. enigmatic person.

enigmar v. to enigmatize: 1. make enigmatic. 2. express enigmatically.

enigmático adj. enigmatic(al): 1. puzzling, perplexing. 2. mysterious. 3. obscure. ‖ enigmaticamente adv. enigmatically.

carta -a rebus: a riddle made up of enigmatical representations of words by figures.

enigmatista, enigmista s. m. + f. enigmatist: 1. a person who makes or deciphers enigmas or riddles. 2. person who talks in enigmas.

enjambrar v. 1. to warp, twist. 2. ~-se to become bashful, timid or confuse.

enjangar v. to raft: form into a raft, give the form of a raft.

enjaular v. to (en)jail: 1. cage, put into a cage. 2. put in jail, imprison, confine.

enjeitado s. m. foundling: baby abandoned by its unknown parents. ‖ adj. 1. rejected. 2. abandoned.

enjeitador s. m. person who exposes, abandons a child. ‖ adj. rejecting, abandoning (child).

enjeitamento s. m. 1. rejection, casting off, repudiation. 2. abandonment, forsaking. 3. exposing (a child).

enjeitar v. 1. to despise, reject, expose (a child), repudiate. 2. to abandon, forsake.

enjerido adj. 1. wrinkled, shriveled. 2. shrunk, stiff (with cold).

enjerir-se v. to shrink, stiffen (with cold).

enjerizar-se v. (Braz.) 1. to make or become angry. 2. to show an aversion or antipathy towards.

enjica s. f. (N. Braz., pop.) 1. annoyance; boredom. 2. ill will.

enjicar v. (N. Braz., pop.) 1. to annoy, bore. 2. to pick on (someone).

enjoadiço adj. squeamish, easily nauseated, qualmish.

enjoado adj. 1. nauseated, seasick, afflicted with nausea. 2. nauseating, disgusting. 3. insupportable, intolerable, unsufferable. 4. (Braz.): a) out of humour, in a bad temper. b) antipathetic.

ele é muito ~ he is very squeamish. ele ficou ~ com esta azáfama toda he was disgusted with all that fuss. é para ficar ~ it's sickening. estou ~ I am seasick. que homem ~! what a bore!

enjoar v. 1. to nauseate: a) cause nausea or repugnance. b) feel nausea or repugnance for. c) make (sea)sick. d) sicken, turn one's stomach. 2. to bore, annoy, irk. 3. to pall. 4. ~-se to become tired of.

enjoativo adj. 1. nauseating, nauseous. 2. repugnant, nasty, loathsome.

este bolo é ~ this cake is disagreeably sweet.

enjôo s. m. (also enjoamento) 1. nausea: a) queasy feeling. b) seasickness. c) repugnance, loathing. 2. (fig.) boredom.

~ de vôo airsickness.

enjugamento s. m. the act of yoking oxen.

enjugar v. to yoke oxen.

enlabiar v. to persuade with fine words.

enlabirintar v. 1. to convert into a labyrinth. 2. to confuse, disarrange.

enlaçado adj. 1. tied, fastened. 2. laced. 3. linked. 4. spliced. 5. embraced.

enlaçador s. m. 1. person who entangles, ties, etc. 2. lassoer: person who catches (animals) with a lasso.

enlaçadura s. f. 1. enlacing, enlacement. 2. lacing. 3. chinband of a helmet.

enlaçar v. 1. to interlace, entwine. 2. to tie, bind, fasten. 3. to unite, link, join. 4. to marry. 5. to entangle, ensnare. 6. to splice. 7. ~-se: a) to join with. b) to be bound. c) to become entangled.

enlace s. m. (also enlaçamento) 1. enlacement, interlacing. 2. union, concatenation. 3. marriage. 4. splice.

~ matrimonial bonds of matrimony, marriage.

enladeirado adj. inclined, declivous, sloping down.

enladeirar v. to incline, become declivous or steep.

enlaivar v. 1. to stain, spot, tarnish, dirty, soil. 2. ~-se: a) to soil, dirty o. s. b) to maculate o. s.

enlambuzar v. (usually lambuzar) 1. to dirty, soil, stain. 2. to (be)smear. 3. ~-se to eat without table manners: smear one's face or soil one's clothes with food.

enlameado adj. 1. muddied, muddy, covered or soiled with mud. 2. spotted, stained. 3. vilipended, slandered.

enlameadura s. f. 1. dirtying, soiling. 2. slandering.

enlamear v. 1. to dirty, puddle, spatter, soil with mud. 2. to cover with mud. 3. to foul. 4. to stain, spot. 5. (fig.) to slander, defame, depreciate. 6. ~-se: a) to get dirty, soiled with mud. b) to degrade o. s.

enlaminar v. to line or cover with metal plates.

enlanguescer(-se) v. to languish: 1. become languid. 2. become weak, droop. 3. lose energy. 4. pine away.

enlanzar v. (Braz., fam.) to dress warmly in woolly clothes.

enlapado adj. 1. shut up into a den or cave. 2. hidden, concealed.

enlapar v. 1. to shut up in a den or cave. 2. to hide. 3. ~-se to hide o. s.

enlatado adj. 1. canned, put in a can. 2. trelliced (as vines).

enlatamento s. m. canning, tinning: act of putting (fruits, meat) into a can or tin.

enlatar v. 1. to tin, can: put (fruits, meat) into a can or tin. 2. to trellis (vines).

enleado adj. 1. interlaced, interwoven. 2. (en)tangled, enmeshed. 3. (fig.): a) perplexed, perturbed. b) irresolute, undecided. c) confused.

enlear v. 1. to tie, fasten, attach, bind. 2. to (en)tangle, ensnare. 3. to involve, implicate. 4. to confuse, embarrass. 5. ~-se: a) to become entangled. b) to be perplexed. c) to flounder.

ele enleou-se num negócio perigoso he entangled himself in a dangerous business.

enleio s. m. (also enleamento) 1. tie, bond, interlacing. 2. entanglement. 3. confusion, perplexity, embarrassment. 4. doubt.

~s de amor affairs with ladies.

enleitado adj. well-laid (stones, bricks).

enleivamento s. m. levelling of ground, operation of moving, filling in and levelling with earth.

enleivar v. to move earth in order to level the ground.

enlerdar v. to make slow, lazy, heavy, stupid, dull.

enlevação s. f. (pl. -ões), enlevamento m. 1. rapture, ecstasy. 2. enchantment. 3. delight. 4. trance. 5. wonder, marvel.

enlevado adj. 1. (en)rapt, enraptured. 2. enchanted. 3. ecstatic(al). 4. fascinated.

enlevar v. 1. to enrapture, enchant, bewitch. 2. to entrance. 3. to delight, charm, fascinate. 4. to captivate. 5. ~-se a) to be delighted, filled with joy. b) to become enraptured, charmed. c) to be astonished. d) to fall into an ecstasy. e) to marvel, wonder.

enlevo s. m. 1. enchantment, charm. 2. rapture, ecstasy; delight, overjoy. 3. trance. 4. marvel.

enliçador s. m. 1. weaver. 2. (fig.) deceiver, cheater.

enliçar v. 1. to weave. 2. (weaving) to put in the woof the threads that cross the warp. 3. (fig.):

a) to entangle. b) to deceive, cheat. 4. ~-se: to become embarrassed.

enliço s. m. 1. bad warp. 2. (fig.) deceit, cheat, fraud.

enlocar v. to shut up or hide in a den or cave.

enlodaçar v. to transform into a mudhole.

enlodado adj. 1. muddy, miry. 2. sullied.

enlodar v. 1. to muddy, sully, begrime. 2. to spatter with mud. 3. to make or become dirty. 4. to contaminate, infect.

enlojamento s. m. warehousing, storing.

enlojar v. to warehouse: store or put in a warehouse.

enlouquecer v. 1. to madden, craze: make or become crazy. 2. to lose one's reason, become insane. 3. to lose one's head. 4. to hallucinate.
~ **de amor** to be infatuated. **não me faça** ~**!** I don't drive me out of my wits!

enlouquecimento s. m. madness, act or fact of maddening.

enlourado adj. 1. crowned or decked with laurels. 2. (fig.) victorious; successful.

enlourar v. (also **enloirar**) 1. to crown or deck with laurels. 2. (also **alourar**) to dye one's hair to make it blond.

enlourecer v. 1. to make or become blond (hair). 2. to turn yellow.

enlousamento s. m. (also **enloisamento**) act of covering with slates or flagstones.

enlousar v. (also **enloisar**) to slate: cover with slates or flagstones.

enluarado adj. moonlit: lighted or illuminated by the moon.
noite -a moonligt night.

enludrar v. to make or become dirty.

enlurar v. 1. to shut up in a cave or den. 2. to bury, hide (as in a den).

enlutado adj. 1. clad or draped in mourning. 2. afflicted, mournful. 3. darkish.

enlutar v. 1. to put on mourning, to clothe or drape in mourning. 2. to mourn: a) feel or show sorrow for. b) grieve. c) lament. 3. ~-se: a) to go into mourning. b) to be consternated.
a perda do filho enlutou os pais the loss of their son threw the parents into mourning.

enluvado adj. gloved.

enobrecedor s. m. ennobler; cause of ennoblement. ‖ adj. ennobling.

enobrecer v. 1. to ennoble: a) make noble, confer a title of nobility. b) dignify, exalt. c) glorify, make famous. 2. to enrich. 3. to embellish. 4. ~-se to become greater, richer.

enobrecimento s. m. 1. ennoblement: a) raising to nobility. b) exaltation, dignity. 2. celebrity; renown, fame.

enodar v. to knot: 1. tie or twine together in a knot 2. entangle in knots.

enodo adj. (bot.) knotless, destitute of knots.

enodoar v. 1. to spot, soil, stain. 2. (fig.) to defame, dishonour; tarnish (reputation), slander. 3. ~-se to disgrace o. s.

enofilia s. f. oenophily: fondness of wine.

enófilo s. m. oenophilist: a lover of wine. ‖ adj. wine-loving.

enofobia s. f. oenophoby: aversion to wine.

enófobo s. m. oenophobist: person who has an aversion for wine. ‖ adj. having horror of wine.

enoftalmia s. f. (med.) enophthalmus: retraction of the bulb of the eye.

enoitecer v. (also **enoitar**; usually **anoitecer**) 1. to grow night. 2. to darken, make or grow dark. 3. to sadden, grieve.

enojadiço adj. 1. squeamish, easily nauseated. 2. choleric, irascible.

enojado adj. 1. nauseated, squeamish; fed up. 2. disgusted. 3. irksome, boresome.

enojar v. 1. to nauseate: a) cause nausea or repugnance. b) make (sea)sick. 2. to tire, bore, irk. 3. ~-se: a) to feel nausea for. b) to turn one's stomach. c) to become tired or bored.

enojo (ô) s. m. (pl. **enojos**) (also **enojamento, nojo**) 1. nausea; seasickness. 2. disgust, loathing. 3. annoyance, boredom, tediousness. 4. mourning.

enol s. m. (chem.) enol.

enólico adj. enolic: of or pertaining to an enol compound.

enolina s. f. (chem.) oenolin: the red colouring matter of wine.

enologia s. f. oenology: the study of wines.

enológico adj. oenological: of or pertaining to oenology.

enologista s. m. + f., **enólogo** m. oenologist: person versed in oenology.

enomancia s. f. oenomancy: divination by the colour or other peculiarities of wine.

enomania s. f. a morbid and uncontrollable craving for wine.

enomel s. m. (pl. **-éis**) oenomel: a beverage consisting of wine and honey.

enômetro s. m. oenometer: an alcoholometer for testing wines.

enora s. f. (naut.) partner, mast hole.

enorme adj. m. + f. enormous: 1. extremely large. 2. huge, outsize. 3. vast. 4. gigantic, prodigious, colossal, big. ‖ ~**mente** adv. enormously; vastly; prodigiously.

enormidade s. f. enormity, enormousness: 1. hugeness. 2. extraordinary greatness or largeness. 3. vastness (in size). 4. that which surpasses endurable limits. 5. atrociousness, atrocity.

enosteose s. f. (med.) enostosis: a bony growth developed within the cavity of a bone or on the internal surface of the bone cortex.

enouriçar v. (also **enoiriçar**; usually **ouriçar**) to bristle.

enoveladeira s. f. yarn windle, yarn spooler: a winding machine for filling spools or bobbins.

enovelado adj. 1. wound: formed into a hank or ball. 2. rolled. 3. entangled, snarled.

enovelar v. (also **anovelar**) 1. to wind or gather into a hank or ball (thread). 2. to reel. 3. to coil, curl. 4. to become confused. 5. ~-se to curl; roll up.

enquadramento s. m. 1. framing. 2. fitting. 3. (mil.) bracket.

enquadrar v. 1. to frame: put into a frame. 2. to fit (in). 3. ~-se to square, conform, accommodate with.
isto se enquadra no meu plano it fits in my plan.

enquadrilhamento s. m. (Braz.) 1. rounding up (animals). 2. act of gathering (people).

enquadrilhar v. (Braz.) 1. to round up (animals). 2. ~-se to gather, assemble, crowd (people).

enquanto conj. 1. while, whilst. 2. as long as. 3. during the time that. 4. whereas.
~ **eu escrevia ela foi embora** while I was writing she went away. ~ **eu viver** as long as I live. ~ **há vida, há esperança** while there's life, there's hope. **meu chapéu é cor de cinza enquanto o seu é preto** my hat is grey while yours is black. **por** ~ for the time being. **por** ~ **ainda não** not yet, not so far.

enquartar v. to quarter; cut into quarters.

enque s. m. (naut.) preventer stay.

enqueijar v. to curdle, turn into cheese (milk).

enquete s. f. (fr.) survey, search.

enquilhar v. (naut.) to provide with a keel.

enquistado adj. 1. encysted: inclosed in a cyst. 2 circumscribed.

enquistamento s. m. encystment: an enclosure in a cyst.

enquistar(-se) v. to encyst: 1. enclose in a cyst. 2. be or become encysted.

enquitar v. to obstruct, impede, oppose.

enquizilado adj. marked by repugnance, antipathy, aversion, misunderstanding.

enquizilar v. = **quizilar.**

enrabar v. (S. Braz.) 1. to follow on the heels of, pursue closely. 2. to follow insistently. 3. to tie to the tail of another beast or to the rear part of another vehicle.

enrabichado adj. 1. pig-tailed. 2. (fig.) infatuated; in love, enamoured.

enrabichar v. 1. to give the form of a pigtail. 2. to tie with a ribbon. 3. (fig.): a) to put in a tight corner. b) ~-se to be infatuated with, fall in love with.

enradicado adj. deep-rooted, inveterate.

enraiar v. to spoke: fit or provide (a wheel) with spokes.

enraivar, enraivecer v. 1. to enrage, irritate, infuriate, anger, make angry. 2. ~-se to become angry, irritated, furious.

enraivecido adj. enraged, choleric, angry, irate, infuriated.

enraizado adj. 1. rooted; deep-rooted. 2. (fig.) fixed, inveterate, radicated.

enraizar v. to root: 1. take or strike root. 2. (fig.) establish o. s.

enramada s. f. branches, leafage.

enramado adj. branched, ramate, full of boughs.

enramalhar v. to adorn with branches or boughs.

enramalhetar v. (also **enramilhetar**) 1. to form into bunches or nosegays. 2. to adorn with nosegays.

enramamento s. m. 1. covering or adorning with branches or boughs. 2. interlacing. 3. joining.

enramar v. 1. to cover or adorn with boughs or branches. 2. to interlace, interweave. 3. to bunch, form into a nosegay. 4. to join, unite.

enrançar v. 1. to make rancid. 2. ~-se to become rancid or musty.

enranchar v. 1. (Braz.) to lodge. 2. (also ~-se) to form a group, join in a group (persons).

enrarecer v. 1. to rarefy: a) diminish the denseness. b) ~-se become rarefied. 2. to make scarce.

enrascada s. f. (Braz.) 1. difficulty, embarrassment. 2. tight spot, rub, hitch, dangerous situation.

estar numa bela ~ to be in a pretty mess. **meti-me numa** ~ I got into a scrape.

enrascadela, enrascadura s. f. 1. act of fishing with a net. 2. entanglement, embroilment. 3. embarrassment, difficulties, straits, fix, dilemma. 4. scrape, predicament.

enrascar v. 1. to catch in a net (fish). 2. to snarl, tangle. 3. to deceive, delude. 4. to catch in a trap, ensnare. 5. to complicate. 6. ~-se: a) to become embarrassed, entangled or complicated. b) to get into trouble.

enredadeira s. f. 1. a female talebearer, intriguer. 2. (Braz., bot.) a creeper of the family Convolvulaceae (Polygonum convolvulus).

enredadela s. f. 1. entanglement, embroilment. 2. intrigue, plot.

enredado adj. 1. netlike. 2. tangled; foul. 3. complicated, involved, entangled. 4. jeopardized.

enredador s. m. (f. ~a, enredadeira) 1. talebearer, plotter, intriguer. 2. mischief-maker. ‖ adj. 1. talebearing. 2. mischief-making.

enredar v. 1. to net, catch in a net (as fish). 2. to snarl, embroil, tangle. 3. to embarrass, entangle, complicate. 4. to hatch plots; lie, contrive. 5. to bind, tie. 6. to set at variance. 7. ~-se to become entangled, embarrassed or complicated.

enredear v. 1. to form into a net. 2. to interweave, intertwine, interlace.

enredeiro s. m. (Braz.) 1. talebearer, intriguer, plotter. 2. mischief-maker. ‖ adj. 1. talebearing. 2. mischief-making.

enrediça s. f. common name of climbing and sarmentose plants.

enrediço adj. used to hatch plots; intriguing.

enredo (ê) s. m. (also **enredamento**) 1. plot of a drama, story. 2. intrigue. 3. tittle-tattle, meddling. 4. intricate lie. 5. embarrassment, entanglement. 6. confusion. 7. act of netting.

o ~ da novela the plot of the novel. **qual é o ~ do filme?** what is the picture about?

enredoso adj. 1. entangled, full of snares. 2. confused. 3. complicated, involved.

enredouçar v. (also **enredoiçar**) to swing.

enregelado adj. frozen, congelated; frost-bitten.

enregelamento s. m. freezing, congelation; frost-bite.

enregelar v. 1. to freeze, chill, congeal; frost-bite. 2. (fig.) to discourage, depress; throw a wet blanket on. 3. ~-se: a) to be frozen. b) to catch a cold. c) to lose heart.

enrelhar v. (Braz.) to tie up (young cattle) with a rope.

enrenquear v. to range, align, set in a row.

enresinar v. 1. to resin: cover, treat or rub with resin. 2. (also ~-se) to resinify: a) change into resin. b) make or become resinous.

enresmar v. = **resmar.**

enrestado adj. (S. Braz., coll.) satiate, fed-up.

enrestar-se v. to become fed-up, satiate.

enricar v. = **enriquecer.**

enriçar v. 1. to curl, frizzle, crisp (the hair). 2. to entangle.

enrijar(-se), enrijecer(-se) v. 1. to rigidify: make or become rigid. 2. to harden, make hard; stiffen. 3. (fig.) to fortify, strengthen.

enrilhar v. 1. = **enrijar.** 2. to become leathery. 3. (med.) to cause constipation in.

enrinconar v. (S. Braz.) to lead (cattle) to the pasture in a secluded place.

enripamento s. m. (Braz.) act of covering or lining with laths (as a roof).

enripar v. (Braz.) to lath: cover or line with laths (as a roof).

enriquecer v. (also **enricar**) 1. to enrich: a) make rich or riches. b) embellish, adorn. c) improve the quality. 2. to increase, augment, enlarge. 3. ~-se to grow rich.

enriquecimento s. m. enrichment.

enristar v. 1. to couch or set (a lance), tilt (with a lance). 2. to invest.

enrizar v. (inaut.) to reef, take in a reef.

enrobustecer v. 1. to make robust. 2. to strengthen, vitalize. 3. to grow strong.

enrocado adj. 1. rocky: full of or abounding in rocks. 2. craggy: abounding in crags.

enrocamento s. m. a sea-wall of large rocks.

enrocar v. 1. to tie or fix flax or tow to a distaff. 2. (obs.) to adorn (a dress) with ornamental slits. 3. (naut.) to clamp, strengthen a mast with clamps. 4. (chess) (usually **rocar**) to castle.

enrodelar v. to shield: protect with a buckler.

enrola-cabelo s. m. (pl. **enrola-cabelos**) = **torce-cabelos.**

enrodilhar v. 1. to wind around. 2. to twist, twine. 3. to entangle. 4. to snarl, tangle. 5. ~-se to curl, form into curls.

enrolada s. f. (N. Braz.) a road in the Hevea rubber tree area without any certain direction.

enroladouro s. m. (also **enroladoiro**) the core of a clew of thread.

enrolamento s. m. 1. rolling up. 2. (electr.) winding. 3. coiling, twisting.
~ **a tambor** (tech.) drum winding. ~ **do primário (de transformador) de alta tensão** (tech.) high--voltage primary winding. ~ **em série** (tech.) series winding. ~ **indutor,** ~ **de campo** (tech.) field-winding. ~ **secundário** (tech.) secondary winding.

enrolar (I) v. 1. to roll, roll up. 2. to wind (around), coil, twist. 3. to curl. 4. (fig.) to wrap up, involve, enfold. 5. (Braz.) to reel, wind on a reel. 6. ~-se: a) to roll, furl. b) to wind, coil up. c) to swell, roughen (waves). d) to revolve. 7. (Braz., sl.) to confuse, complicate. 8. (Braz., sl.) to cheat.
a cobra enrolou-se the snake coiled up.

enrolar (II) v. (Port.) to fondle (children).

enroscado adj. 1. threadlike; spiraled. 2. rolled, coiled. 3. twined, twisted. 4. entangled, tangled.

enroscadura s. f., **enroscamento** m. 1. screw thread; spiral. 2. winding up.

enroscar v. 1. to twine, twist. 2. to thread (as a screw). 3. to wind around; roll up; coil. 4. ~-se: a) to spiral: move in a spiral. b) to entangle, tangle: get twisted up and caught.

enroupado adj. 1. clothed; dressed. 2. (fam.) provided with a good wardrobe.

enroupar v. 1. to clothe: a) put garments on. b) cover with clothes, dress. 2. ~-se to provide o. s. with clothes.

enrouquecer v. 1. to hoarsen: make hoarse (the voice). 2. (also ~-se) to become hoarse.

enrouquecimento s. m. (also **rouquidão** f.) hoarseness.

enroxar-se v. to become purple.

enrubescer(-se) v. to redden: 1. make or become red. 2. blush, flush: make or become red because of shame, confusion or excitement.

enrubescido adj. erubescent: 1. reddish. 2. blushing.

enrubescimento s. m. erubescence, erubescency: 1. blushing. 2. redness of the skin.

enruçar-se v. to become brownish (hair).

enrudecer v. 1. to make or become rude, cruel, stupid. 2. to brutalize: make or become brutal.

enrufar-se v. 1. to become ruffled, irritated. 2. to get angry with.

enrugado adj. 1. wrinkled, furrowed, shrunken. 2. crisp. 3. wizened, shrivelled.
de rosto ~ wizen-faced.

enrugamento s. m. wrinkling, shrivelling; rugosity.

enrugar v. 1. to wrinkle, crinkle, crease. 2. to shrivel, dry up. 3. to corrugate. 4. to pucker.
as preocupações enrugaram o seu semblante his face was lined with care.

enrustir v. (Braz., sl.) 1. to deceive accomplices in the partition of stolen goods. 2. to hide, conceal. (s. th. stolen).

ensaboadela s. f. (also **ensaboadura**) 1. soaping, washing with soap. 2. reprehension, rebuke, reprimand.
eu terei que lhe dar uma ~ (fig.) I must comb his hair for him. **dei-lhe uma** ~ (fig.) I told him where to get off.

ensaboado s. m. wash, washing of linen. ‖ adj. 1. soapy, lathery. 2. clean.

ensaboadura s. f. 1. soaping, washing in soap. 2. wash, quantity of linen washed. 3. (fig.) reprehension, reprimand, rebuke.

ensaboar v. 1. to soap, wash with soap. 2. (fam.) to rebuke, reprehend, reprove. 3. ~-se to rub o. s. with soap, wash o. s.

ensaburrar v. (also **saburrar**) 1. to ballast a ship. 2. (vet.) to cause the formation of saburra.

ensacador s. m. 1. sacker: person who sacks or bags. 2. (Braz.) exporter of green coffee.

ensacamento s. m. (also **ensaca** f.) act of filling into a sack or bag.

ensacar v. 1. to bag, sack: fill into a bag or sack. (flour, rice). 2. (fig.) to keep, store away. 3. to make sausages.

ensaiador s. m. 1. assayer. 2. trier; tester. 3. (theat.) rehearser.

ensaiar v. 1. to assay: a) analyze. b) try, test, examine. 2. to essay, attempt. 3. to train, drill, instruct. 4. to exercise, practise. 5. (theat.) to rehearse. 6. (also ~-se) to make or get ready, prepare o. s.
atores ensaiam a peça the actors rehearse the play.

ensaibrar v. to cover with gravel.

ensaio s. m. 1. assay: a) an analysis. b) trial, test, examination, experience, proof. 2. essay, attempt. 3. training. 4. exercise, practice. 5. (theat.) rehearsal. 6. endeavour.
~ **de dureza** hardness test. ~ **de forjamento** forge test. ~ **de laboratório** laboratory test. ~ **de perfuração** drill test. ~ **de rendimento** efficiency test. ~ **geral (com vestimenta)** (theat.) dress rehearsal. **aparelho de** ~ tester. **a título de** ~ by way of trial. **balão de** ~ trial balloon. **carga de** ~ proof load. **ele fez o** ~ **de suas forças** he tried his strength or his abilities. **resultado de** ~ test result. **tubo de** ~ test tube.

ensaísta s. m. + f. essayist: a writer of essays.

ensalada s. f. 1. salad. 2. (obs.) a sort of poetry including words of different languages.

ensalmador s. m. (also **ensalmeiro**) witch-doctor, medicine man, quack.

ensalmar v. to pretend to cure by witchery or the like.

ensalmo s. m. 1. pretended way of curing by blessings. 2. witchcraft, sorcery.

ensalmourar v. (also **ensalmoirar**) to brine: 1. treat with brine. 2. steep in or saturate with brine.

ensamambaiado adj. ferny, covered with ferns.

ensamarrar v. (obs.) to dress o. s. in sheepskin garments.

ensambenitar v. = **sambenitar.**

ensamblador s. m. 1. joiner, carpenter. 2. wood carver.

ensambladura, ensamblagem (pl. **-ens**) s. f. **ensamblamento** m. (carp.) 1. joinery. 2. dovetailed joint, rabbet, scarf.
~ **de mecha e encaixe** mortise and tenon joint (plate C 9).

ensamblar v. (carp.) 1. to join or fit together (wood) by means of rabbets, dovetails, etc. 2. to inlay, imbed. 3. to scarf. 4. to carve (wood). 5. to mortise.

ensancha s. f. 1. a wide hem. 2. width, breadth. 3. leftover, surplus. 4. liberty, freedom. 5. ~s pl. opportunity, chance.

ensanchar v. 1. to enlarge, extend, widen, broaden. 2. to amplify, augment.

ensandalar v. to anoint or aromatize with sandalwood oil.

ensandecer v. 1. to make or become mad, insane or crazy. 2. to become a fool.

ensanefar v. to adorn with valances.

ensangüentado adj. blooded, bloody, imbrued with blood, bloodstained.
cenas -as red scenes, bloody scenes.

ensangüentar v. (also **ensanguinhar**) 1. to bloody: stain with blood, imbrue with blood. 2. (fig.) to stain, spot, blemish. 3. ~-se: a) to stain o. s. with blood. b) to become bloodstained.

ensapezado adj. (Braz.) covered with **sapé** (sape grass vegetation).

ensaque s. m. act of sacking or bagging (cereals, flour).

ensarilhar v. 1. to reel (thread, yarn). 2. to embroil, entangle. 3. to stack (arms). 4. to walk up and down.

ensarnecer v. to become infected with itch or scab; become itchy or mangy.

ensartar v. to string (beads).

enseada s. f. 1. cove, inlet, small bay, creek, lagoon (plate C 19). 2. (Braz.) an area between two **igarapés** or at the bend of a river.

ensebado adj. 1. greasy: smeared or soiled with grease. 2. covered with grease. 3. (fig.) soiled, dirty.

ensebar v. 1. to grease: smear or soil with grease. 2. to cover with grease. 3. (fig.) to stain, soil. 4. (Port.) to hedge: fence in with a hedge.

ensecadeira s. f. cofferdam: a watertight enclosure used in laying foundations below the water.

ensecar v. 1. to drain, dry up. 2. to beach a boat. 3. to empty, exhaust. 4. to run aground. 5. (obs.): a) to follow, pursue. b) to investigate.

enseio s. m. depression, opening or passage between two mountains.

enseirar v. to put into a wicker basket.

ensejar v. 1. to wait for a chance or a good opportunity. 2. to try. 3. (also ~-se) to present itself (an opportunity).

ensejo s. m. opportunity, occasion; chance.

aproveito o ~ para lhe apresentar felicitações | avail myself of the opportunity to congratulate you.

ensemble s. f. (Fr.) ensemble (suit).

ensementar v. (Braz.) to sow, scatter seed.

ensenhorear-se v. (usually **assenhorear-se**) 1. to take possession of. 2. to lay hold of.

ensífero adj. ensiferous: bearing or carrying a sword.

ensiforme adj. m. + f. (bot., zool.) ensiform: sword--shaped.

ensilado adj. (Braz.) stored, ensiled (cereals, fodder).

ensilagem s. f. (pl. **-ens**) ensilage: the storage of fodder or cereals in a silo (plate S 1).

ensilar v. to ensile, silo: put or store (fodder, grains, etc.) in a silo.

ensimesmar-se v. 1. to be lost in thought, be self--absorbed. 2. to concentrate, fix one's attention.

ensinadela s. f. 1. scolding, punishment. 2. rebuke, admonition.

ensinamento s. m. (also **ensinação** f., pl. **-ões**) 1. teaching, training, instruction. 2. education. 3. doctrine. 4. lesson.

ensinar v. 1. to teach, instruct. 2. to train, drill, coach (as animals). 3. to educate. 4. to (in)doctrinate. 5. to castigate, punish. 6. to explain, show, disclose. 7. ~-se to learn by o. s.

ela ensinou o menino a andar she taught the boy how to go. ele ensinou-me o caminho he showed me the way. este professor ensina muito bem this teacher is most efficient. eu lhe ensino como fazer isto | teach you (or him) how to do this. você não pode ensiná-lo a comportar-se? can't you teach him manners? ensinei meu cão | trained my dog.

ensino s. m. 1. teaching, instruction. 2. education. 3. training, drilling. 4. indoctrination.

~ elementar elementary education. estabelecimento de ~ any school. livro de ~ text book. método de ~ methods of teaching.

ensirrostro adj. (ornith.) having an ensiform beak.

ensoado adj. 1. flacid, drooping, flabby, wilted. 2. weakened on account of heat. 3. tasteless, insipid.

ensoamento s. m. 1. wilting. 2. etiolation. 3. insolation, sunstroke.

ensoar v. 1. to wilt, droop. 2. to etiolate. 3. to be affected with a sunstroke. 4. (Port., obs.) to intone.

ensoberbecer v. 1. to make proud, haughty, exalted. 2. ~-se: a) to grow proud or haughty. b) to pride o. s. on, take pride in.

ensobradar v. (usually **assobradar**) to build a house of two or more storeys.

ensofregar v. 1. to make greedy or voracious. 2. to incite, instigate. 3. to sick on (dogs).

ensolarado adj. sun-drenched, sunny.

ensolarar v. to expose to the sun.

ensolvar v. (obs.) to prevent the firing of a cannon by wetting the powder.

ensombrar, ensombrear v. 1. to shade, shadow: a) make dark, obscure. b) make sad or gloomy. 2. ~-se to grow dark or gloomy.

ensombro s. m. 1. shading. 2. awning. 3. shelter, refuge, protection.

ensopado s. m. stew, ragout, fricassee. ‖ adj. soaked to the skin, sopping wet, dripping wet.

~ de carne a stew of meat. fiquei ~ até aos ossos | was wet to the skin.

ensopar v. 1. to sop in. 2. to soak, drench, steep. 3. to stew, make into a stew. 4. to wet, moisten. 5. ~-se: a) to get soaked or sopping wet. b) to be drenched.

ensornar v. (S. E. Braz.) 1. to be slow in accomplishing an order. 2. to delay, put off. 3. to loiter.

ensumagrar v. to sumach: treat or prepare (leather) with sumach.

ensurdecedor adj. deafening, stunning with noise.

ensurdecência s. f. deafness: inability to hear.

ensurdecer v. 1. to deafen: a) make deaf. b) stun with noise. c) deaden (sound). 2. (fig.) to turn a deaf ear to. 3. to grow deaf.

ensurdecimento s. m. 1. act of deafening. 2. deafness.

ensurroar-se v. (S. Braz.) to become fed-up, eat one's fill.

entablamento s. m. (archit.) entablature: that part of a wall which rests horizontally upon the columns and consists of the architrave, frieze and cornice.

entabocar v. (Braz.) 1. to put between splints. 2. to press, squeeze.

entabuamento s. m. 1. act of boarding up. 2. planking. 3. board floor.

entabuar v. 1. to board, cover or line with boards; to plank. 2. to floor. 3. ~-se to become as stiff or hard as a board.

~ o costado do navio to plank a ship.

entabular v. 1. = **entabuar**. 2. to prepare, arrange, dispose. 3. (fig.) to enter upon, set on foot, begin, open, start (conversation or business).

~ conversa to engage in a conversation. ~ negociações to start negotiations.

entaipado s. m. enclosure, fence. ‖ adj. 1. surrounded with a wall of lath-and-plaster or mud. 2. immured.

entaipar v. 1. to surround with a wall of lath-and--plaster or with a mud wall. 2. to immure, fence in. 3. to enclose, shut up; cloister.

entalação (pl. **-ões**), **entalada, entaladela** s. f. 1. (med.) a placing between splints. 2. tight corner, predicament, embarrassment, difficulty, scrape, strait. 3. compromising, discrediting.

entalado adj. 1. pressed, pinched. 2. put between splints. 3. in a difficult situation.

estar ~ to be in a tight corner.

entalar v. 1. to splint, put between splints. 2. to put s. o. into an embarrassment, in an awkward situation or in a tight spot. 3. ~-se to get stuck in a fix, get into trouble, be bunkered.

entalecer v. to grow in a stalk.
entaleigar v. 1. to bag, put into bags, sack. 2. to satiate, stuff. 3. ~-se to eat one's fill.
entalha s. f. incision, cut, notch, jag, groove, carve (in wood).
entalhador s. m. 1. wood carver, cutter. 2. engraver. 3. ripping chisel.
entalhadura s. f., **entalhamento** m. 1. wood carving. 2. carved work. 3. notch. 4. mortise.
entalhar v. 1. to carve (in wood). 2. to engrave (plate Q). 3. to intaglio: carve or execute in intaglio. 4. to sculpture (in wood). 5. to mortise, rabbet, notch (plate C 9). 6. to cut.
entalhe s. m. 1. incision, notch, cut, jag. 2. = **entalho**.
entalho s. m. 1. wood carving. 2. a sculpture in wood. 3. intaglio; carved work (plate J 2). 4. rabbet, mortise; notch, slot.
entaliscar v. 1. to put, press or force in (as in an opening or slot). 2. (Braz.) to join with splines. 3. ~-se to find o. s. caught in or as in a crevice.
entalpia s. f. (phys.) enthalpy.
entancar v. (Braz.) to dam up (water).
entanguecer v. 1. to stiffen (with cold). 2. to shrink up.
entanguido adj. (also **entanguitado**) 1. benumbed, stiff (with cold). 2. (fig.) rachitic, stunted, wizened.
entanguir-se v. 1. to stiffen (with cold). 2. to become stunted.
entanto adv. in the meantime, meanwhile.
no ~ nevertheless, notwithstanding, however, still, yet.
então adv. 1. then, at that time. 2. on that occasion. 3. in that case. 4. after that. 5. so. ‖ interj. well? so what?! now then!
~ **eu não falei?** well then, did I not say it? ~ **por que você não diz?** then why don't you say so? ~ **você quer dizer que...** then you mean to say that... **até** ~ till then, up to that time. **bem,** ~ **ele devia ter recusado** well, then he should have refused. **desde** ~ since that time, ever since. **e** ~? what then?, what about it? **o** ~ **rei** the then king. **se isto é assim,** ~ if that is so, then. **somente** ~ not till then.
entapizar v. 1. to carpet. 2. to cloth again. 3. to adorn, decorate.
entaramelar v. 1. to tongue-tie. 2. ~-se: a) to stutter, falter. b) to get entangled, become embarrassed.
entardecer s. m. late afternoon, nightfall, setting of the sun. ‖ v. 1. to grow dark, grow night. 2. to grow late.
entarraxar v. to screw or rivet together.
ente s. m. a being: 1. that which exists (object, thing, substance). 2. life, existence. 3. a person, living creature.
~ **de Deus** (N. Braz., pop.) a person. ~s **queridos** dear ones, loved ones.
enteada s. f. stepdaughter.
enteado s. m. stepson.
entear v. 1. to weave. 2. to interweave, interlace. 3. to twine together.
entecar v. (S. Braz.) 1. to be absolutely motionless. 2. to become sick.
entediar, entejar v. 1. to bore, tire: make weary. 2. ~-se to become bored or weary, to have about enough of a thing.
entejo s. m. 1. weariness, boredom. 2. aversion, repugnance.
entelar v. 1. to reinforce (stamps, maps) by placing on fine cloth. 2. to put wire screens on doors and windows to keep out mosquitoes.
enteléquia s. f. (philos.) entelechy: a realization or actuality as opposed to a potentiality.

entendedor s. m. 1. comprehensive or quick-witted person. 2. connoisseur, expert; critical judge.
a bom ~ **meia palavra basta** a word to the wise is enough.
entender s. m. 1. understanding. 2. opinion, judgement, statement. ‖ v. 1. to understand: a) get the meaning of. b) comprehend, apprehend, perceive. c) know. d) be informed, hear. e) have a knowledge of. 2. to conceive, imagine, mean. 3. to judge, suppose. 4. to believe, think. 5. to contend, dispute. 6. ~-se: a) to understand each other, agree. b) to be in agreement with. c) to concern o. s. with.
~ **do assunto** to be well acquainted with a matter. ~ **mal** to misunderstand. **agora entendi** now I understand, now I got it. **assim como eu entendo** as I understand it. **como geralmente se entende** according to the general opinion. **dar a** ~ to insinuate, give a hint of, give to understand. **deram-me a** ~ I was given to understand. **disso eu não entendo nada** I understand nothing about it. **ela entende de negócio** she is an expert in business. **ele deu a** ~ **que estava muito contrariado** he indicated that he was very displeased. **ele entende de cavalos** he has a good eye for horses. **ele entende de música** he understands music. **ele me deu a** ~ he has as good as told me. **eles lá se entendem.** they play booty. **eles não se entendem** they are at cross-purposes. **estamos falando sem nos entendermos** we are talking at cross-purposes. **eu cá me entendo** I understand my own business. **faça como** ~ have it your own way. **faço-me** ~ I explain my thoughts. **não consigo** ~ I fail to see, understand. **não consegui** ~ **as suas intenções** I could not catch his drift. **não conseguimos** ~-**nos com eles** we could not make ourselves understood. **não posso** ~! I can't make it out! **no meu** ~, **isto está errado** according to my opinion, this is wrong, to the best of my knowledge, this is wrong. **nós nos entendemos** we understand each other. **pelo que eu posso** ~ as far as I can see. **que entende você por isso?** what do you mean by that? **vou me** ~ **com ele** I shall get that straight with him.
entendido s. m. expert, knower. ‖ adj. 1. understood. 2. learned, skilled, erudite. 3. known. 4. knowing. 5. wise. 6. agreed.
está ~! that is understood! **não me tenho na conta de** ~ I don't profess to be an expert. **ser** ~ **em um assunto** to know a subject, be happy of s. th. **bem** ~ to be sure, doubtlessly, of course.
entendimento s. m. 1. understanding: a) act of understanding. b) comprehension. c) apprehension, perception, discernment. d) intelligence. e) knowledge. 2. talent, capacity. 3. judgement. 4. agreement, accord.
chegar a um ~ to come to an agreement. **estar em bons** ~s **com alguém** to stand fair with a person.
entenebrecer(-se) v. to darken: make or become dark or darker; obscure.
entenrecer v. 1. to soften: make soft. 2. to tender: make or become tender.
enteomania s. f. theomania: religious mania in which the patient believes to be inspired by God.
enteralgia s. f. (med.) enteralgia: neuralgia of the intestines.
entérico adj. enteric, intestinal: belonging to the intestines.
enterite s. f. (med.) enteritis: inflammation of the intestines.
enternecedor adj. moving, touching, pathetic(al), impressive. ‖ ~**amente** adv. movingly, pathetically.

enternecer v. 1. to move to compassion, touch, affect. 2. ~-se: a) to be moved, touched. b) to condole, pity; feel sorry.

enternecimento s. m. 1. compassion, pity, commiseration. 2. tenderness.

enterocele s. f. (path.) enterocele: any hernia of the intestine.

enterocistocele s. f. (path.) enterocystocele: hernia of the bladder and intestine.

enteróclise s. f. (med.) enteroclysis: injection of a medicinal liquid into the intestine, an enema.

enterodelo adj. (zool.) enterodelous: having an intestine as an infusorian.

enterodinia s. f. (med.) enterodynia: pains in the intestine.

enterogastrite s. f. (path.) gastro-enteritis: inflammation of the stomach and the intestines.

enterografia s. f. enterography: the anatomical description of the intestines.

enterográfico adj. of or pertaining to enterography.

enterólito s. m. enterolith, enterolite: an intestinal concretion or calculus.

enterologia s. f. enterology.

enterológico adj. of or pertaining to enterology.

enteroquinase s. f. (med.) enterokinase: enzyme of the intestinal juice.

enterose s. f. (med.) generic term for any intestinal disease.

enterotomia s. f. (surg.) enterotomy: dissection of the intestine.

enterótomo s. m. (surg.) enterotome: an instrument for slitting the intestine.

enterozoário s. m. enterozoon: an animal parasite inhabiting or infesting the intestines (as an intestinal worm).

enterramento s. m. 1. burial: act of burying. 2. a funeral, interment, inhumation.

enterrar v. 1. to bury: a) put (a dead body) into the earth, inter. b) (fig.) cover up, hide, secrete. 2. to lead s. o. into ruin. 3. to ram; plunge, thrust (dagger). 4. ~-se: a) to ruin o. s. b) to get involved in difficulties. c) to bury o. s. in solitude. **ele enterrou-se numa cadeira de braços** he sank down into an armchair.

enterreirar v. to form into a yard, court, courtyard, backyard (cutting away the herbs).

enterro (ê) s. m. (pl. **enterros**) burial: a) interment, entombment. b) act of burying.

entesar v. 1. to stretch, harden, toughen, stiffen. 2. ~-se: a) to become stiff, taut, tight. b) to resist obstinately.
~ **um arco** to string a bow.

entesourador s. m. (also **entesoirador**) hoarder, person who lays up a treasure.

entesourar v. (also **entesoirar**) 1. to (en)treasure, hoard; lay up (money, jewels). 2. to enshrine. 3. (fig.) to accumulate; heap up.

entestar v. 1. to border upon, confine, limit. 2. to confront, compare. 3. to face, be opposite (as buildings). 4. (Port.) to put a lid (cover) on a pot.

enteu adj. (f. **entéia**) entheate: 1. divinely inspired. 2. filled with holy enthusiasm.

entibiamento s. m. lukewarmness, half-heartedness, want of ardour.

entibiar v. (also **entibecer**) 1. to cool down, make lukewarm. 2. ~-se: a) to grow lukewarm, cool, indifferent. b) to weaken, grow lame.

entica s. f. (Braz.) provocation, provoking.

enticador adj. m., **enticante** m. + f. (Braz.) provoking, irritating, vexatious.

enticar v. 1. to provoke, pick up a quarrel, exasperate, vex. 2. to be at variance with.

entidade s. f. 1. entity: a) a being. b) essence; existence. c) the essential nature of a thing. d) anything that has real existence. 2. corporation, society, body (collective group). 3. importance. ~ **divina** the divine essence. ~ **oficial** official personage.

entijolar v. to line with bricks.

entijucado adj. morassic, muddied, sullied.

entijucar v. to spatter with mud or morass.

entimema s. m. (log.) enthymeme.

entintar v. (typogr.) to ink up (forms, rollers).

entisicar v. 1. to cause to suffer phthisis. 2. to result in consumption. 3. to emaciate. 4. (fig.) to importune. 5. ~-se: a) to become consumptive or weak, waste away. b) to be phthisical.

entivação s. f. lining with planks, planking.

entivar v. to line with planks, to plank.

entoação s. f. (pl. **-ões**) intonation: 1. act of intonating or intoning. 2. modulation or inflection of the voice. 3. tone.

entoador s. m. intoner: 1. (mus.) person who intones. 2. (fig.) a singer. ‖ adj. intoning.

entoar v. 1. to intone: a) indicate the tone or tune. b) vocalize. c) utter a tone. d) sing, chant. e) tune. 2. to begin (a song). 3. (Braz.) to please, delight.
isto não me entoa that does not please me at all.

entocar-se v. (Braz.) 1. to burrow, hide in a cave or hole. 2. to hide or shut o. s. up, seclude, retire.

entófito s. m. entophyte: a parasite growing within a plant.

entojado adj. 1. nauseated, disgusted. 2. (Braz., pop.) proud, self-conceited, puffed up.

entojar v. 1. to loathe, nauseate, disgust. 2. to cause repugnance to, abhor. 3. to bore. 4. (Braz.) to feel nausea (a pregnant woman).

entojo (ô) s. m. (pl. **entojos**) nausea; odd, fanciful wishes peculiar to the period of pregnancy.

entogástrio s. m. (ent.) a part of the abdomen of insects.

entômico adj. entomic(al): relating to insects.

entomofilia s. f. (bot.) entomophily: pollination by the agency of insects.

entomógeno adj. (bot.) entomogenous (fungi).

entomologia s. f. entomology: that part of zoology which treats of insects.

entomológico adj. entomologic(al): of or pertaining to entomology.

entomologista s. m. + f., **entomólogo** m. entomologist: person versed or engaged in the study of entomology.

entomostráceo s. m. any crustacean of the subclass Entomostraca.

entonação s. f. (pl. **-ões**) (also **entoação**) intonation.

entonar v. 1. to raise the head proudly or haughtily. 2. ~-se: a) to be puffed up with pride. b) to put on airs.

entono s. m. 1. pride, haughtiness. 2. arrogance, superciliousness. 3. imposture.

entontecedor adj. 1. dizzying, giddying. 2. stunning, bewildering, stupefying.

entontecer v. 1. to make or become giddy or dizzy. 2. to inebriate. 3. to stun, bewilder. 4. to hallucinate, madden. 5. to lose one's head or reason.

entontecimento s. m. 1. giddiness, dizziness. 2. inebriation. 3. bewilderment, stupefaction.

entornado adj. 1. shed, spilled, upset, overturned. 2. scattered. 3. (fig.) lost.

entornadura s. f. 1. spilling, shedding, pouring out. 2. scattering.

entornar v. 1. to spill, pour (on, in, out), shed. 2. to upset, overturn, cant over. 3. to prodigalize, squander. 4. (also ~-se): a) to scatter, spread.

b) to flow off. c) to diffuse. d) to fail, come to nothing. 5. (fig.) to take over to drinking.
~ o caldo (fig.) to aggravate one's situation by lack of tact and prudence; to upset the applecart.
entorpecente s. m. any narcotic. ‖ adj. m. + f. 1. narcotic. 2. (be)numbing.
entorpecer v. 1. to torpify: a) make torpid. b) benumb, numb. 2. to paralyse. 3. to weaken. 4. **~-se:** a) to grow torpid or benumbed. b) to grow dull or inactive.
entorpecido adj. 1. torpid, benumbed, numb. 2. dull.
entorpecimento s. m. 1. torpor: a) torpid condition, numbness. b) sluggish inactivity. c) dullness, apathy, lethargy. 2. paralysis. 3. laziness.
entorroar v. to form into clods or clots (earth).
entorse s. f. sprain: a violent straining or wrenching of a joint or muscle.
entortadura s. f. 1. crooking; bending. 2. twisting, torsion. 3. wrench.
entortar v. 1. to crook, curve, bend, bow, twist. 2. to warp. 3. (fig.) to lead astray, mislead. 4. **~-se:** a) to become crooked. b) to get drunk. c) (fig.) to go astray. d) to ruin o. s.
~ os olhos to squint, look asquint.
entótico adj. entotic.
entouçar v. (also **entoiçar**) 1. to grow up to a thicket. 2. to thicken. 3. (fig.) to grow strong.
entozoário s. m. entozoon: an internal parasite.
entrada s. f. 1. entrance: a) act of entering. b) entry, ingress. c) opening, inlet, gate, portal, passage (plates A 11, E 3, P 16, V 5). d) access, admission, admittance. e) beginning, initiation, introduction. 2. (game) entrance-money. 3. ticket, card of admission (as a theater ticket). 4. (Braz., com.) first instalment. 5. (com.) receipts, income, cash. 6. (theat.) scene. 7. (mil.) raid.
~ franca, ~ gratuita free access, free admission. **~ proibida** no entrance. **à ~ da avenida** at the beginning of the avenue. **bilhete de ~** admission ticket. **dar ~** 1. (also com.) to enter. 2. to lead to (way, door). **dar ~ a um requerimento** to give in a petition. **é proibida a ~** no admittance. **meia ~** half-price (ticket). **na ~ do verão** at the beginning of summer.
entrado adj. 1. entered, come in. 2. elderly, advanced in years. 3. (fig.) drunken. 4. free, used to take liberties.
entra-e-sai s. m., sg. + pl. (Braz.) a continuous coming and going.
entrajar v. 1. to clothe. 2. to dress.
entraje s. m. 1. act of clothing. 2. suit, dress, clothing.
entralhar v. 1. to net: a) make network. b) ensnare. 2. to embroil, entangle. 3. to catch. 4. **~-se:** to be entangled, get caught.
entrançado s. m. = **entrelaçamento**. ‖ adj. 1. twisted, braided, plaited. 2. interlaced, interwoven.
entrançadura s. f., **entrançamento** m. 1. braiding, plaiting. 2. interlacing.
entrançar v. 1. to twist, braid, plait. 2. to interlace, interweave. 3. (fig.) to loaf.
~ o cabelo to braid the hair.
entranha s. f. 1. a viscera. 2. **~s** pl.: a) entrails, bowels. b) womb. c) (fig.) character, temper. d) (coll.) profundity; insides; core.
entranhar v. 1. to pierce, penetrate. 2. to pierce to the bottom of the heart. 3. **~-se:** a) to dive: enter deeply into anything. b) (fig.) to apply, devote o. s. to.
~-se na floresta to penetrate deeply into the forest. **~-se no estudo** to be lost in study.
entranhável adj. m. + f. (pl. **-áveis**) 1. hearty, sincere. 2. deep, piercing, penetrating, profound.

entranqueirar v. 1. to intrench: a) surround with a trench. b) fortify, barricade. 2. **~-se** to defend, fortify o. s. (as by means of intrenchments).
entrante adj. m. + f. 1. beginning. 2. entering. 3. ready to enter or begin.
ano ~ beginning year.
entrapar v. 1. to cover with or wrap in clouts or rags. 2. to bandage. 3. **~-se** to cover o. s. with rags.
entrar v. 1. to enter: a) come or go in (or into). b) get into. c) penetrate into, pierce. d) go inside of. e) join, enlist, become a member. f) begin, initiate, start. g) get involved. 2. to arrive. 3. to flow or run into. 4. to partake, participate. 5. (Braz.) to delight, please.
~ bem (fig.) 1. to have a good start. 2. (Braz., sl.) to fall a cropper. **~ com ímpeto** to burst into. **~ com o pé direito** (fig.) to have a good start. **~ de roldão** to rush in. **~ em contato com** to get in touch with. **~ em detalhes** to hold forth, to enter into details. **~ em forma** (mil.) to fall in line. **~ em greve** to come out, go on strike. **~ em jogo** to come into play. **~ em negociações** to enter into negotiations. **~ em vigor** to take effect. **~ e sair** to go in and out. **~ na casa** to go into the house. **~ na moda** to come into vogue. **~ no exército** to join the army. **~ no assunto** to come to the point. **~ num acordo** to enter into an arrangement. **~ pelo cano** (pop.) to go down the tubes. **~ por um ouvido e sair pelo outro** to go in an ear and out the other. **~ sorrateiramente** to steal in(to). **a doença entrou numa fase perigosa** the illness settled into a state of danger. **deixar ~** to admit. **deixe ~ a luz** let in light. **ela entrou de tropel** she came bursting in. **ele entrou com o pé direito** he made a good start. **ele entrou em ação** he got in play. **ele entrou no comércio** he went into business. **ele entrou no exército** he joined the army. **ele não há de ~ na minha casa** he shall not set foot in my house. **entramos em choque** we joined battle. **entre!** come in! **entrei em cena** I entered the scene. **entrei em convalescença** I became convalescent. **entrei em conversa com ele** I entered upon a conversation with him. **entrei na sala de aula** I went into the classroom. **entrei na universidade** I entered the university. **faça o favor de ~** please, come in. **hoje, entro em função** today, I enter into function. **isto entra na classe B** this falls under class B. **isto não me entra** it doesn't please me; I do not understand that. **mande-o ~!** show him in! **não posso ~ em detalhes** I can't enter into details. **o navio entrou no porto** the ship put into the port. **por favor, deixe-me ~** please, let me in. **Romeu, entra em cena** enter, Romeo. **você entra no jogo?** do you join in the game? **vou ~ na faca amanhã** (coll.) I am going to be operated tomorrow.
entravar v. 1. to impede, hinder. 2. to trammel, hamper, fetter. 3. to clog, obstruct, block. 4. to lock (as a wheel).
entrave s. m. 1. fetter, shackle, clog. 2. device to lock a wheel. 3. (fig.) impediment, obstacle, hindrance.
corrente de ~s stop-chain.
entre prep. 1. between (plate P 18). 2. among, amongst. 3. during the interval. 4. amid.
~ a cruz e a espada between the devil and the deep blue sea. **~ nós** among ourselves. **~ os gregos antigos** among the old Greeks. **~ outras coisas** among other things. **ele disse isso ~ aplausos** he said this amid cheers. **isto foi dividido ~ nós** it was divided among us.
entreaberta s. f. act of opening partially.

entreaberto adj. half-open, not entirely opened, ajar. **a janela está -a** the window is ajar.
entreabrir v. 1. to open partially. 2. to set ajar (a door). 3. to open carefully or quietly. 4. ~-se: a) to bloom, blossom. b) to uncloud.
entreato s. m. (theat.) interact, entr'acte: 1. interval between two acts of a play. 2. a short performance between two acts.
entrebater-se v. 1. to fight (as with swords). 2. to wrangle.
entrebranco adj. whitish, whitened.
entrecambado adj. tangled; involved.
entrecana s. f. (archit.) arris: fillet between flutes.
entrecasca s. f. (bot.) liber: 1. inner bark. 2. bast tissue, phloem.
entrecasco s. m. 1. the upper part of a hoop. 2. = **entrecasca**.
entrecena s. f. (theat.) interscene: interval between two scenes.
entrecerrar v. to shut or close partially (door, eyes).
entrechar v. 1. to plot: make a plot of a play. 2. to intrigue.
entrecho s. m. 1. plot of a play. 2. intrigue.
entrechocar-se v. 1. to collide with. 2. to fight. 3. (fig.) to be contradictory.
entrechoque s. m. collision, crashing, clash.
entrecoberta s. f. (naut.) between-decks.
entreconhecer v. 1. to know vaguely, imperfectly, not to know well. 2. ~-se to know one another.
entrecoro s. m. chancel: space between the altar and the choir.
entrecorrer v. 1. to run between. 2. to happen, occur between two other occurrences.
entrecortar v. 1. to intersect, cut. 2. to interrupt. 3. ~-se to cross each other.
entrecorte s. m. intersecting, point of intersection.
entrecosto s. m. ribs of an animal (plate G 1).
entrecozer v. to parboil.
entrecruzamento s. m. act of crossing.
entrecruzar-se v. to cross; intersect (reciprocally).
entrededo s. m. interdigital region.
entredilacerar-se v. to lacerate each other.
entredizer v. 1. to soliloquize: talk or say to o. s. 2. ~-se to say to one another.
entredormido adj. drowsy, half-asleep.
entrefala s. f. = **entrevista**.
entrefalar v. (Braz.) = **entredizer**.
entrefechado adj. half-closed.
entrefechar v. to close slightly.
entrefino adj. neither thick nor thin.
entrefolha (ô) s. f. interleaf: insert (either blank or printed).
entrefolhar v. to interleave: insert blank or printed leaves in a book.
entrefolho (ô) s. m. hiding-place, cubbyhole.
entreforro s. m. 1. buckram. 2. ceiling.
entrega s. f. 1. delivery. 2. surrender. 3. treachery, treason. 4. cession.
~ **a domicílio** home delivery. ~ **imediata** prompt delivery. ~ **urgente** express delivery. **contra** ~ on delivery. **nota de** ~ bill of delivery. **prazo de** ~ time of delivery.
entregador s. m. 1. deliverer: person who delivers or makes deliveries (goods, parcels). 2. traitor, perfidious person. 3. (also ~ **de jornais**) deliverer of newspapers.
entregar v. 1. to deliver. 2. to hand over, remit. 3. to restore, return, give back. 4. to confide in. 5. to betray. 6. to cede. 7. ~-se: a) to apply or devote o. s. to. b) to abandon o. s. c) to surrender, give o. s. up.
~ **a alma a Deus** to die. ~ **a rapadura** (fig.) to throw in the sponge. ~-**se ao desespero** to yield

to despair. **o carteiro entregou-me uma carta** the postman handed me over a letter. **ela entrega-se toda ao trabalho** she applies herself earnestly to work. **ele entregou-se ao jogo** he took to gambling. **ele entregou-se ao vício da bebida** he took to drinking. **ele entregou-se à tristeza** he gave himself up to melancholy. **entrego-o em suas mãos** I place it in your hands. **não se entregue ao desespero** don't abandon yourself to despair.
entregue adj. m. + f. 1. delivered, handed over. 2. addicted. 3. devoted to, attached, busy. 4. (Braz., fig.) exhausted.
ele foi ~ **a um júri para ser julgado** he was committed for trial. **estou** ~**!** I am down and out.
entrelaçado s. m. 1. = **entrelaçamento**. 2. any interlaced or interwoven thing. ‖ adj. interlaced, interlinked, interwoven.
arcos ~**s** (archit.) interlacing arches.
entrelaçamento s. m. (also **entrelace, entrelaço**) interlacement: 1. act of interlacing. 2. state of being interlaced.
entrelaçar(-se) v. to interlace: 1. interweave, intertwine. 2. unite as by lacing. 3. mix, blend.
entrelembrar-se v. to remember vaguely, have a faint memory of.
entrelinha s. f. 1. interlineation: a) insertion of matter between the lines of writing or print. b) the matter thus inserted. 2. space between two lines. 3. (printing) lead: a thin strip of metal for widening the space between lines. 4. (fig.) comment. 5. ~**s** pl. (fig.) implied sense, meaning; deduction, conclusion.
entrelinhar v. 1. to interline, interlineate: write, print or mark between the lines. 2. (typogr.) to lead: insert leads between lines. 3. (fig.) to comment.
entrelopo s. m. 1. (Braz., hist.) interloper, contrabandist, smuggler. 2. adventurer, soldier of fortune.
entreluzir v. 1. to shine through. 2. to begin to shine. 3. to glimmer: a) shine faintly. b) twinkle. c) ~-se appear faintly or dimly.
entremaduro adj. half-ripe.
entremanhã s. f. daybreak, dawn.
entrematar-se v. to kill each other.
entremear v. 1. to intermix, intermingle. 2. to interpose, put between. 3. to intersperse, interlard. 4. ~-se to be intermingled.
ele entremeou suas palavras de gemidos he punctuated his words with groans.
entremeio s. m. 1. interval (of space or time). 2. an intermediate space. 3. insertion (embroidery, needlework, lace).
nos ~**s** in the meantime, meanwhile.
entrementes adv. meantime, meanwhile: 1. in the intervening time, in the interim. 2. during that time. 3. at the same time.
entremesa s. f. time of a meal (the time it is taken or the time necessary to have it).
entremeter v .1. to interpose: put or place between. 2. ~-se: a) to intermeddle. b) to interfere, intervene. c) to intrude o. s. d) to poke one's nose in other people's business.
entremetimento s. m. 1. interposition, interposal. 2. intervention, interference. 3. meddling.
entremez s. m. 1. interlude, intermezzo: entertainment between two acts. 2. a farce.
entremezada s. f. 1. farce, ridiculousness, ridiculous action. 2. farcicality.
entremezista s. m. + f. an author or actor of intermezzos or farces.
entremisturar v. 1. to intermix, mingle. 2. to confuse.
entremodilhão s. m. (pl. -ões) (archit.) intermodillion: the space between two modillions.

entremontano adj. intermontane: situated between mountains.

entremostrar v. 1. to show but indistinctly. 2. ~-se to appear faintly.

entrenó s. m. (bot.) internode: space between two nodes or leaf knots.

entrenublar-se v. 1. to become lightly clouded. 2. to appear between clouds.

entreolhar-se v. to look at one another, to exchange looks.

entreouvir v. to hear but indistinctly.

entrepano s. m. divider, partition board between shelves.

entreparar v. to stop for a moment.

entrepausa s. f. intermission: 1. a pause. 2. a temporary cessation.

entreperna s. f. 1. crotch (also **entrepernas**). 2. meat from cattle appropriate for barbecue or roast. 3. roast or barbecue from such meat.

entrepilastras s. m., sg. + pl. (archit.) interpilaster: the interval between pilasters.

entrepor v. (usually **interpor**) 1. to interpose, place between. 2. ~-se: a) to interfere, intervene. b) to be placed between. c) to be an obstacle.

entreposto s. m. (also **entrepósito**) entrepôt: 1. a warehouse. 2. emporium. 3. mart, center to which goods are sent for redistribution.

entrepresa s. f. enterprise, undertaking.

entrequerer-se v. to like, love one another.

entrescolher v. to choose superficially.

entresilhar v. 1. to emaciate. 2. to weaken.

entressachar v. 1. to intermix, intermingle. 2. to interweave, interlace. 3. to intersperse. 4. to put between. 5. ~-se to intermeddle, meddle in.

entressafra s. f. period between two harvests of a product.

entresseio s. m. 1. sinuosity. 2. hollow, cavity.

entressemear v. 1. to sow between. 2. to intersperse: scatter, place here and there among other things. 3. to spatter, splash.

entressola s. f. insole: the inner sole (plates B 16, C 14) of a shoe.

entressolhar v. to provide (a house) with an entresol.

entressolho (ô) s. m. (pl. **entressolhos**) entresol, mezzanine: an intermediate story.

entressonhar v. 1. to imagine vaguely, dreamily. 2. to muse, daydream.

entretalhadura s. f. 1. bas-relief, low relief. 2. ornate carving.

entretalhar v. 1. to carve, sculpture in bas-relief. 2. to cut, fashion (as paper or cloth).

entretalho s. m. 1. cut clothwork, cut paperwork. 2. bas-relief.

entretanto (I) adv. meantime, meanwhile, in the meantime, in the meanwhile. ‖ conj. nevertheless, however, notwithstanding.

eu esperava, ~, que você lhe tivesse dito I hoped you had told him, though.

entretanto (II) s. m. the meantime, interim, intervening time.

entretecedor s. m. person who interweaves, intertwists or intertwines. ‖ adj. interweaving.

entretecer v. 1. to interweave, intertwist, intertwine. 2. to interlace. 3. to intermix, intermingle. 4. to intercalate, insert between.

entretecimento s. m. (also **entretecedura** f.) 1. interweaving, intertwinement. 2. interlacing. 3. insertion.

entretela s. f. 1. buckram: a linen or cotton fabric stiffened with gum (used for garments or binding books). 2. interlining of a garment.

entretelar v. 1. to buckram: stiffen with or as with buckram. 2. to interline: insert a lining (garment).

entretempo s. m. meantime, interim, intermediate time.

nesse ~ in the meantime, meanwhile.

entretenimento s. m. (also pop. **entretém; entretimento**) 1. entertainment, diversion, pastime, amusement, recreation. 2. delaying.

entreter v. 1. to entertain, divert, amuse, recreate. 2. to delay, postpone, detain, retard. 3. to distract, draw the attention from. 4. ~-se: a) to amuse o. s. b) to have a good time. c) to concern o. s. with, occupy o. s. d) to linger.

ele se entretém com a leitura he amuses himself with reading.

entretinho s. m. food for birds.

entretom s. m. nuance, gradation between two colours.

entretrópico adj. intertropical: situated between the tropics.

entreturbado adj. slightly perturbed.

entreturbar v. to disturb slightly, discomfort.

entrevação s. f. (pl. -ões) (also **entrevecimento** m.) 1. maiming, paralysing. 2. lameness.

entrevado s. m. maimed person, paralytic, cripple. ‖ adj. maimed, paralytic, crippled, lamed.

entrevar, entrevecer v. 1. to paralyse: a) affect with paralysis, cripple. b) ~-se be affected with or become a paralytic. 2. to darken: a) make dark, obscure, render gloomy. b) ~-se become dark or obscure; grow clouded.

entrever v. 1. to see indistinctly. 2. to catch a glimpse or sight of. 3. to have a presentiment; foresee. 4. ~-se to have an interview with.

entreverar v. (S. Braz.) to mix, confuse, blend.

entrevero (ê) s. m. (S. Braz.) 1. mixture, disorder, confusion. 2. melee of troops (at a combat); dog-fight, mix-up.

entrevia s. f. distance between two railway lines (between up way and down way).

entrevinda s. f. a sudden or unexpected arrival.

entrevisão s. f. (pl. -ões) indistinct sight.

entrevista s. f. interview: 1. meeting. 2. formal meeting for a conference. 3. a meeting between a reporter and a person from whom information is sought for publication. 4. the published report thereof; appointment.

conceder uma ~ to grant an interview.

entrevistador s. m. (Braz.) interviewer: person who interviews (a reporter).

entrevistar v. to interview: have an interview with (especially to obtain information for publication).

entrezar v. 1. to interweave, intermingle. 2. to interlace.

entrincheirado adj. entrenched: fortified or defended with or as with trenches.

entrincheiramento s. m. entrenchment: 1. act of entrenching. 2. trench, parapet.

entrincheirar v. 1. to entrench: fortify, defend or protect with or as with trenches. 2. ~-se: a) to fortify o. s. b) (fig.) to establish o. s.

entristecedor adj. saddening: that makes sad.

entristecer v. to sadden: 1. make sad. 2. afflict, grieve. 3. ~-se be saddened; feel sorry; become sad.

sua morte entristeceu a festa his death cast a cloud over the festival.

entristecimento s. m. 1. act of saddening. 2. sadness, sorrow.

entrita s. f. panada: pap made of crumbs of bread soaked in water or milk.

entroncado adj. 1. broad-shouldered. 2. strong, corpulent. 3. well-set.

entroncamento s. m. 1. crossing point. 2. junction (as of a railway). ~ ferroviário railway junction.
entroncar v. 1. to make a junction. 2. to strengthen, make robust. 3. to join, connect.
entronchado adj. thick-stalked.
entronchar v. to grow a thick stalk.
entronização s. f. (pl. -ões) enthronement, enthronization; act of enthroning or enthronizing.
entronizar v. (also entronar) 1. to enthrone, enthronize: a) place on a throne. b) raise to the seat of royalty. c) (fig.) exalt, aggrandize. d) ~-se mount the throne; dominate. 2. ~-se to put a sacred image on an altar or a picture of a saint on the wall.
entronquecer v. to grow or form into a trunk.
entropia s. f. (phys.) entropy.
entropicar v. (N. Braz., usually tropeçar) to stumble.
entropigaitar v. (Braz., pop.) 1. to confuse, embarrass. 2. to bewilder. 3. ~-se: a) to be or become confused or embarrassed. b) to fall silent.
entropilhar v. to join into groups, to troop (animals).
entrópio(n) s. m. (med.) entropion: the inversion of the edge of the eyelid.
entrosa s. f., entrós m. 1. cog-wheel, gear, toothed wheel. 2. the space between the teeth of a cog--wheel.
entrosagem s. f. (pl. -ens) 1. gearing or meshing of gears. 2. (fig.) interplay.
entrosar v. 1. to gear, mesh (the teeth of two gears). 2. to fit or set (one part into another). 3. ~-se to be adapted or suited to.
entrouxar v. (also entroixar) to bundle: 1. make up into a bundle (as clothes). 2. wrap up, pack up.
entrouxo s. m. (Braz.; also entroixo) padding, stuffing.
entroviscada s. f. poisoning and catching of fishes by means of spurge flax.
entroviscar v. 1. to catch fish by poisoning them with spurge flax. 2. to cloud. 3. ~-se to become cloudy or overcast.
entrudada s. f. revelry, carnival frolics.
entrudar v. 1. to celebrate carnival. 2. to make merry during the carnival. 3. to mock, jest.
entrudesco adj. of or referring to carnival.
entrudo s. m. (usually carnaval) carnival: 1. the season immediately preceding Lent. 2. the festivity of this season. 3. revelry.
entrupicar v. 1. (Braz., pop., also tropeçar) to stumble. 2. to fall.
entuchamento s. m. (Braz.) swallowing, gulping down.
entuchar v. (Braz.) 1. to swallow up. 2. to gulp down. 3. to hold one's tongue.
entufado adj. 1. swollen, puffed up. 2. proud, haughty. 3. arrogant. 4. (Braz.) chafed, angry.
entufar v. 1. to swell. 2. to be proud, haughty or arrogant. 3. ~-se (Braz.): a) to become sullen. b) to get angry.
entujucado adj. (Braz., also entijucado) morassic, muddied, sullied.
entujucar v. (Braz., also entijucar) to spatter with mud or morass.
entulhar(-se) v. 1. to fill up with rubbish. 2. to choke, block up. 3. to obstruct. 4. to heap up, hoard. 5. to put into a granary.
entulho s. m. 1. rubbish, waste or refuse material. 2. fragments of dry mortar or plaster. 3. ruins, debris. 4. encumbrance.
entuna s. f. (S. Braz.) the act of hunting or wandering through mountain regions.
entunicado adj. (bot.) tunicate: having a series of concentric layers (as a bulb).

entupido adj. 1. obstructed. 2. stopped or blocked up, clogged. 3. (fig.) dumbfounded.
entupigaitação s. f. (pl. -ões) (Braz., pop.) 1. embarrassment, perplexity, confusion, fluster. 2. speechlessness.
entupigaitar v. (Braz., pop.). 1. to disturb, perturb, muddle. 2. to embarrass. 3. ~-se: a) to become confused. b) to hold one's tongue, fall silent.
entupimento s. m. 1. choking or stopping up, clogging. 2. obstruction.
entupir v. 1. to block, stop or choke up, clog. 2. to obstruct. 3. to grow mute; hold one's tongue. 4. ~-se: to become obstructed, jammed.
enturvação s. f. (pl. -ões) 1. clouding. 2. perturbation, disturbance. 3. sadness. 4. uneasiness.
enturvado adj. 1. muddy. 2. troubled. 3. turbid, disturbed.
enturvar v. 1. to make turbid. 2. to muddy. 3. to cloud. 4. to muddle. 5. (fig.) to sadden; perturb. 6. ~-se: a) to become turbid or obscure. b) to get angry.
enturviscar-se v. to overcast, overcloud, darken (sky).
entusiasmado adj. 1. ravished, enraptured. 2. full of enthusiasm; elated. 3. (Braz.) exalted, proud, haughty.
ela está -a com a sua carreira she is enthusiastic about her work. ele está ~ com isso he is strong for it. ele ficou ~ he was thrown into rapture.
entusiasmar v. 1. to ravish, enrapture. 2. to fill with enthusiasm. 3. to animate, give life to. 4. ~-se: a) to become enraptured. b) to be enthusiastic.
entusiasmo s. m. 1. enthusiasm: a) zeal, eager interest, eagerness. b) excitement. c) ecstasy. d) fervour, ardour; passion, devotion. 2. rapture, ravishment. 3. admiration.
a assistência delirou de ~ quando o violinista apareceu the audience went wild with excitement when the violinist appeared.
entusiasta s. m. + f. enthusiast: 1. zealot. 2. devotee. 3. person prone to entusiasm. || adj. having enthusiasm; given to enthusiasm.
entusiástico adj. 1. enthusiastic(al): a) zealous, eager. b) devoted. c) inspired by enthusiasm. 2. vibrant. 3. rapturous. || entusiasticamente adv. enthusiastically, with great enthusiasm; vibrantly.
entuviada s. f. fighting, riot, tumult.
enublar v. to overcast: 1. cloud, overspread with clouds (the sky). 2. darken. 3. ~-se become cloudy or dark.
enucleação s. f. (pl. -ões) enucleation: act of enucleating.
enuclear v. to enucleate: 1. remove (as a kernel, tumour, etc.) from its cover. 2. (fig.) lay open, explain, elucidate.
enumeração s. f. (pl. -ões) 1. enumeration: a) act of enumerating. b) numeration, numbering. c) recapitulation. 2. computation, reckoning. 3. specification; description.
enumerador s. m. 1. enumerator: person who enumerates. 2. specificator. || adj. enumerative.
enumerar v. 1. to enumerate: a) count. b) mention in details. c) number. d) recount. e) recapitulate. 2. to specify.
enumerável adj. m. + f. (pl. -áveis) enumerable: 1. capable of being enumerated. 2. numerable. 3. (math.) said of a collection or ensemble that can be put into one-to-one correspondence with integer numbers.
enunciação s. f. (pl. -ões) enunciation: 1. act of enunciating. 2. manner of utterance, pronunciation. 3. proposition. 4. expression. 5. positive statement.

enunciado s. m. enunciation; proposition; statement. ‖ adj. declared, stated, uttered.

enunciar v. to enunciate: 1. state, utter. 2. express. 3. declare. 4. propound. 5. ~-se to exhibit or express o. s.

enunciativo adj. enunciative, enunciatory.

enurese, enuresia s. f. (med.) enuresis: incontinence of the urine.

enuviar v. to overcast: 1. cloud, overspread with clouds (the sky). 2. darken.

envaidar v. (also **envaidecer**) 1. to make proud or vain; puff up with pride. 2. to fill with vanity. 3. ~-se to become proud, vain, haughty.

envaidecedor adj. that which makes proud or vain.

envalar v. to entrench: 1. ditch. 2. fortify with entrenchments.

envarar v. to wattle: make a fence, wall or the like of rods or stakes interwoven with twigs or branches.

envaretado adj. (S. Braz.) disappointed, abashed.

envaretar v. (S. Braz.) to disappoint, baffle, disconcert.

envasamento s. m. (also **envasadura** f.) 1. = **envasilhamento**. 2. act of planting (flowers) in pots. 3. (archit.) base of a column or pillar.

envasar v. 1. = **envasilhar**. 2. to plant (as flowers) in pots. 3. to give the form of a pot.

envasilhamento s. m. act or effect of bottling, casking, tunning, barrelling.

envasilhar v. 1. to put into vessels. 2. to bottle, cask, tun, barrel.

envelhacar(-se) v. to be or become a rascal.

envelhecer v. (also **envelhentar**) 1. to age: a) grow old. b) take on characteristics of age. c) make old (in years, appearance). d) cause to grow old. 2. to fall into disuse, become obsolete.

envelhecimento s. m. act or effect of aging.

envelopar v. to envelope, put in an envelope.

envelope s. m. 1. envelope: a cover for a letter or the like (plate C 10). 2. (Braz.) boiler jacket. ~ **selado** stamped envelope.

envencilhado adj. 1. tangled, snarled. 2. complicated, involved, entangled.

envencilhar v. 1. to bind, tie, fasten. 2. to tangle, snarl. ‖ ~-se to become (en)tangled.

envenenado adj. poisoned, poisonous: 1. full of or containing poison. 2. malignant, highly pernicious.

envenenamento s. m. poisoning, intoxication.

envenenar v. 1. to poison: a) put poison in. b) give poison to. c) kill with poison. d) (fig.) ruin, corrupt, affect perniciously. 2. to taint, infect, contaminate. 3. to intoxicate. 4. ~-se to take poison.

enventanar v. to throw a ball into the pocket (at billiards).

enverdecer, enverdejar v. 1. to green: a) make green. b) ~-se grow green or become covered with greens. 2. (fig.): a) to rejuvenate. b) to recover one's strength.

enveredar v. 1. to direct one's steps (to or toward a given place). 2. to make one's way (to or toward). 3. to go toward. 4. to guide, lead.

envergadura s. f. 1. (naut.) breadth of the sails from one stop of the yard cleats to the other. 2. spread of a bird's wing. 3. (aeron.) span. 4. capacity, extent. ~ **das asas** (aeron.) wingspan.

envergamento s. m. 1. tying or fastening of the sails. 2. curvity, crookedness.

envergar v. 1. (naut.) to tie or fasten the sails to the yards. 2. to bend, curve, crook. 3. to wear, put on. 4. ~-se to bow, bend over.

envergando uma camisa verde wearing a green shirt.

envergonhado adj. ashamed, bashful. **ele devia ficar** ~ he ought to be ashamed. **ele ficou muito** ~ **com isto** he felt much shame at it. **ele sentiu-se** ~ he felt ashamed.

envergonhar v. 1. to shame: a) cause to feel shame. b) make ashamed. c) (fig.) disgrace, dishonour. 2. to humble. 3. ~-se: a) to be ashamed, bashful or shy. b) to blush. **envergonharam-no em público** they put him to shame publicly. **ela o envergonhou** she put him out of countenance.

envergues s. m. pl. (naut.) ropes with which a sail is fastened to the yard.

envermelhar, envermelhecer v. (usually **avermelhar**) 1. to make red. 2. ~-se to blush, turn red.

envernizado adj. 1. varnished. 2. polished. 3. (pop.) drunk. **couro** ~ patent leather.

envernizador s. m. varnisher: person who lays varnish on; a lacquerer.

envernizar v. 1. to varnish: lay varnish on. 2. to polish. 3. (pop.) to get drunk.

enverrugado adj. 1. wrinkled. 2. warty, full of warts. 3. crumpled.

enverrugar v. 1. to wrinkle, rumple. 2. to fill with warts. 3. ~-se: a) to be or become covered with warts. b) to be wrinkled.

envesgar v. 1. to squint. 2. to look asquint.

envessado adj. 1. turned inside out (a piece of garment). 2. (fig.) inverted.

envessar v. (also **envesar**) 1. to turn the inside out (the wrong side of a cloth). 2. to invert the order of things.

envesso (ê) s. m. (usually **avesso**) 1. the other side. 2. the wrong side. 3. reverse.

enviado s. m. 1. envoy, messenger. 2. person in charge. ‖ adj. sent, dispatched.

enviar v. 1. to send, emit, dispatch. 2. to depute 3. to remit. **enviei-lhe uma carta** I sent him a letter.

envidar v. 1. to vie or make a wager or bet (at cards). 2. to invite. 3. to exert, endeavour. 4. ~-se to strive, exert o. s.

envide s. m. act of betting or making a wager (at cards).

envidilha s. f. = **bacelo**.

envidilhar v. to wind around a shoot of vine.

envidraçado adj. glazed: 1. provided with glass (as a window). 2. glassy, vitreous (as the eyes).

envidraçamento s. m. glazing: act of furnishing or fitting with glass.

envidraçar v. 1. to glaze: a) furnish or fit with glass (as a window). b) cover with glass (as a picture). c) become glazed or glassy. 2. ~-se to grow dull or dim.

enviés s. m. (pl. **envieses**) (usually **viés**) bias binding (as in sewing).

enviesado adj. 1. set on the bias; oblique, diagonal, slant(ing). 2. cut on the bias.

enviesar v. 1. to set on the bias. 2. to cut on the bias or obliquely. 3. to slant, slope. 4. ~-se to be or become oblique.

envigamento s. m. beamwork.

envilecer v. 1. to vilify: a) degrade, debase, abase. b) make vile. c) defame. 2. to tarnish, dull. 3. ~-se: a) to debase o. s., become vile. b) to lose value.

envilecimento s. m. 1. abasement; degradation; disgrace. 2. undervaluing, undervaluation.

envinagrado adj. vinegary: 1. mixed with vinegar. 2. like vinegar.

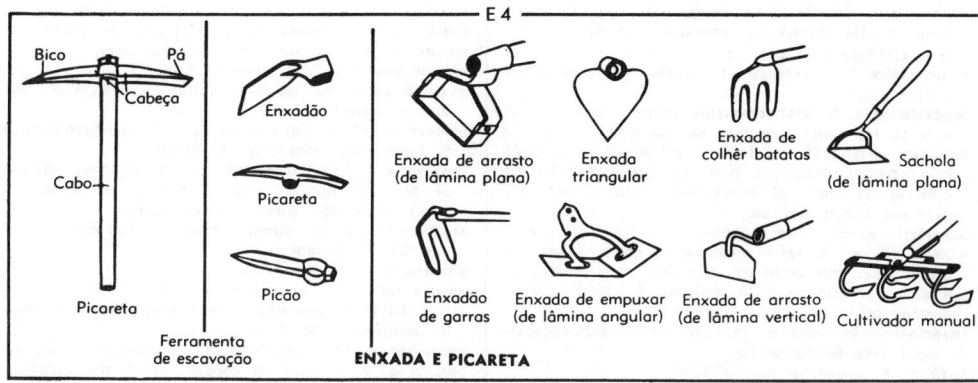

E 4

Bico — Pá — Cabeça — Cabo — Picareta — Picareta — Enxadão — Picareta — Picão — Ferramenta de escavação

Enxada de arrasto (de lâmina plana) — Enxada triangular — Enxada de colhêr batatas — Sachola (de lâmina plana)

Enxadão de garras — Enxada de empuxar (de lâmina angular) — Enxada de arrasto (de lâmina vertical) — Cultivador manual

ENXADA E PICARETA

envinagrar v. 1. to vinegar: a) add vinegar to. b) mix with vinegar. 2. to render sour. 3. to cause ill-humour. 4. ~-se: a) to turn sour. b) to become irritated.

envincilhar v. = **envencilhar**.

envio s. m. 1. sending, forwarding, remittance, dispatch. 2. shipment, consignment.

enviperado adj. furious like a viper.

enviperar v. 1. to make furious, to irritate. 2. ~-se: a) to grow furious like a viper. b) to become irritated.

envira s. f. = **embira**.

enviscar v. 1. to lime, smear with lime. 2. to catch with birdlime. 3. (fig.) to lure. 4. ~-se: a) to be caught with birdlime. b) (fig.) to fall into a lure.

enviuvar v. to widow: 1. deprive a woman of her husband or a man of his wife. 2. become a widow or widower. 3. (fig.) deprive of.

enviveirar v. 1. to keep in a fishpond. 2. to plant in seedbeds.

envolta s. f. confusion, uproar, noise.

de ~ 1. confusedly. 2. promiscuously. 3. simultaneously.

envolta (ô) s. f. (Port.) bandage, ligature.

envolto adj. 1. wrapped (up). 2. embarrassed. 3. mixed, mingled.

~ **em silêncio** wrapped in silence. **a casa estava toda -a em chamas** the house was alight with flames.

envoltório s. m. wrapper, cover, covering, packing-sheet.

envoltura s. f. 1. wrapping up, envelopment. 2. a baby's blanket.

envolvedor s. m. 1. wrapper, cover. 2. intriguer. ‖ adj. involving, covering.

envolvente adj. m. + f. involving: 1. complicating, entangling. 2. wrapping, enveloping.

envolver v. 1. to involve: a) wrap up, cover, envelop. b) include (in). c) comprehend, contain, hold. d) entangle, complicate. e) implicate in, imply. 2. to hide, conceal. 3. to surround, enclose. 4. to captivate. 5. to trouble. 6. to cause to be turbid. 7. ~-se: a) to be involved in anything. b) to wrap o. s. up (as in a coat). c) to take part in. d) to grow dark, become overcast (sky).

ela envolveu o filho em seus braços she wound he arms round her child.

envolvido adj. 1. wrapt up. 2. ˙involved in. 3. embarrassed.

~ **em crimes** steeped in crime. **ele está ~ nisto** he is in it. **estar ~** to be entangled in.

envolvimento s. m. envolvement: act of involving or the state of being involved.

enxabidez s. f. 1. insipidity, tastelessness. 2. (fig.) spiritlessness.

enxabido adj. (usually **desenxabido**) 1. insipid, tasteless. 2. (fig.) spiritless, unamusing; ungraceful.

enxacoco s. m. a person who speaks badly a foreign language.

enxada s. f. 1. hoe, spade (plates E 4, J 2). 2. (fig.) job, profession. 3. (Braz., ichth.) spadefish (Chaetodipterus faber).

enxadada s. f. stroke with a hoe.

enxadão s. m. (pl. -ões) 1. (also **alvião**) mattock (plate E 4). 2. a big hoe.

enxadeiro s. m. (Braz.) hoer.

enxadrez s. m. (obs. form of **xadrez**) chess.

enxadrezado adj. checkered: marked with squares like a checker-board.

enxadrezar v. (also **enxequetar**) to checker: mark like a checker-board with squares of alternating colours.

enxadrismo s. m. chess playing.

enxadrista s. m. + f. chess player.

enxaguadura s. f. rinsing, washing.

enxaguar v. to rinse, wash lightly (as clothes, dishes).

enxaimel s. m. (pl. -éis) (Braz.) pillar of a mud hut.

enxalmar v. to cover with **enxalmo**.

enxalmo s. m. 1. a blanket placed on a packsaddle to level its seat. 2. worthless person.

enxama s. f. oarlock; rowlock.

enxambrado adj. humid, damp.

enxambrar v. to dry partially (as linen that is to be ironed).

enxame s. m. 1. a swarm of bees. 2. (fig.) multitude, crowd.

enxamear, enxaimear (Braz.) v. 1. to swarm (like bees). 2. to hive, put into a hive. 3. to people. 4. to teem, pullulate. 5. to set the pillars of a mud hut. 6. ~-se to crowd together.

enxaqueca s. f. megrim, migraine, hemicrania: a severe headache usually on one side only.

enxara s. f. dense thicket, woods.

enxárcia s. f. shrouds of a ship.

enxaropar v. 1. to give a syrup (as a remedy). 2. ~-se: a) to take syrup. b) to drink very much; get drunk.

enxequetar v. (her.) = **enxadrezar**.

enxerçar v. to salt and dry meat.

enxerga (ê) s. f. 1. straw bed; simple and very poor bed. 2. pallet.

enxergão s. m. (pl. -ões) 1. a sort of straw mattress. 2. steel mattress. 3. saddle blanket.

enxergar v. 1. to discover, discern, descry. 2. to see. 3. to catch a glimpse or sight of. 4. to foresee. 5. (pop.) to be an expert in.

enxerir v. 1. (obs.): a) to insert, put in. b) to intercede. 2. (N. Braz.) to interfere; put one's nose into someone's affairs.

enxertadeira s. f. grafting knife, budding knife (plate J 2).

enxertadura s. f. (also **enxertia**) grafting: insertion of a scion from one tree into another one.

enxertar v. to graft: 1. bud, insert a scion or graft into another plant. 2. treat by the operation of grafting. 3. (fig.): a) insert into or incorporate in. b) ~-se introduce o. s.

enxertário s. m. (naut.) parrel.

enxerto (ê) s. m. (also **enxertia** f.) graft: 1. act of grafting. 2. the point of insertion of a scion. 3. a shoot or bud used in grafting. 4. (surg.) transplanted piece of skin or bone.

enxerto-de-passarinho s. m. (pl. **enxertos-de-passarinho**) = **erva-de-passarinho**.

enxó s. f. adz(e): a cutting tool.

enxoada s. f. a tumour on the hoof of a horse.

enxofradeira s. f. sulphurator: instrument used in sulphurizing.

enxofrado adj. 1. sulphurated; powdered with sulphur. 2. (pop.) vexed, annoyed.

enxofrar v. 1. to sulphurize, sulphurate, sulfurate: treat, combine or impregnate with sulphur, the fumes of burning sulfur, or the like. 2. ~-se (fig.) to get angry or cross.

enxofre (ô) s. m. (chem.) brimstone, sulphur. ~ em barras thick sulphur. mina de ~ sulphur pit. pau de ~ brimstone roll.

enxofreira s. f. a volcano from which sulfuric gases emane.

enxofrento adj. containing brimstone, sulphureous.

enxofria s. f. 1. sulphurizing. 2. pulverization of sea water resulting from the breaking of waves.

enxota-cães s. m., sg. + pl. (fam.) doorkeeper of a church who keeps out dogs.

enxota-diabos s. m., sg. + pl. (pop.) laic exorcist.

enxotadura s. f., **enxotamento** m. expelling, expulsion, driving away.

enxota-moscas s. m., sg. + pl. fly-flap.

enxotar v. 1. to scare, fright or drive away. 2. to expel, throw out. 3. to banish. ~ moscas to drive away flies.

enxoval s. m. (pl. **-ais**) 1. trousseau: a bride's outfit of clothes, linen, etc. 2. layette: set of clothes, bedding, for a newborn baby. 3. (fig.) simpleton.

enxovalhamento s. m. (also **enxovalho**) 1. dirtiness. 2. untidiness, slovenliness.

enxovalhar v. 1. to dirty, soil, stain. 2. to spot, tarnish. 3. to wrinkle, crumple. 4. (fig.) to affront, insult. 5. (Braz.) to overflow (esp. the deck of a ship). 6. ~-se: a) to become dirty or nasty. b) to stain one's reputation.

enxovar v. (obs.) to dungeon: 1. confine in a dungeon. 2. imprison.

enxovedo s. m. (fam.) simpleton, imbecile, fool.

enxovia s. f. (also **enxova**) dungeon: a dark underground cell to keep prisoners in.

enxu s. m. 1. a social wasp (Nectarina lecheguana). 2. its nest.

enxugador s. m. 1. drier, wiper: device or machine that removes water as by heat or air. 2. (fam.) towel.

enxugadouro s. m. (also **enxugadoiró**) place for drying.

enxugar v. 1. to dry: a) make dry; wipe. b) cause to evaporate. c) ~-se become dry, lose moisture. 2. to imbebe. 3. (fig.) to empty; drink. ~ as lágrimas to wipe off one's tears. ~ uma garrafa to empty a bottle. ela enxugou as mãos she dried her hands.

enxugo s. m. 1. drying. 2. = enxugadouro.

enxuí s. m. (Braz.) a wasp (Polybia sedula).

enxúndia s. f. axunge: fat esp. of pigs or geese.

enxundiar v. to fatten, make fat (animals).

enxundioso adj. fatty, greasy; oily.

enxurdar-se v. to wallow, welter or grovel in the dirt as swine.

enxurdeiro s. m. (also **enxurreira** f., **enxurreiro** m.) 1. mire, mud, quagmire. 2. pigsty.

enxurrada s. f. (also **enxurro** m.) 1. a heavy shower of rain. 2. torrent, rushing stream of water. 3. (fig.) abundance, plenty, great quantity.

enxurrar v. 1. to stream, flow in torrents. 2. to overflow, inundate.

enxurro s. m. = **enxurrada**.

enxuto adj. 1. dry: a) not wet. b) of little or no rain (time or season). 2. sheltered from the rain. 3. neither fat nor thin.

enzampar v. 1. to overfeed. 2. to swindle, trick.

enzima s. f. (chem.) enzym(e): any of the unorganized ferments as diastase.

enzímico adj. enzymotic: pertaining to the unorganized chemical ferments.

eoceno s. m. Eocene.

eólico adj. Aeolian, Aeolic: of or pertaining to Aeolia in ancient Greece.

eolina s. f. a small ancient organ.

eólio (I) s. m. Aeolian: one of the Greek peoples who founded ancient Aeolia. ‖ adj. Aeolian: of or pertaining to Aeolia.

eólio (II) adj. eolian: pertaining to or caused by the winds.

éolo s. m. a strong wind.

eosina s. f. (chem.) oesin(e): a reddish colouring matter.

eosinofilia s. f. (med.) eosinophilia: accumulation of an unusual number of eosinophil cells in the blood.

eosinófilo adj. (med.) eosinophile: readily stainable with eosin.

epacridácea s. f. any plant of the family Epacridaceae.

epacridáceo adj. (bot.) of or pertaining to the family Epacridaceae.

epacta s. f. epact: the excess of the solar year above the lunar year.

epactal adj. m. + f. (pl. **-ais**) (anat.) epactal.

epagoge s. f. (philos.) epagoge, induction.

epagógico adj. (philos.) epagogic: pertaining to induction.

epanadiplose s. f. (rhet.) epanadiplosis: use of a word at the beginning as well as at the end of a sentence.

epanáfora s. f. (rhet.) epanaphora: repetition of a word at the beginning of two or more successive clauses.

epanalepse s. f. (rhet.) epanalepsis: repetition of the same word.

epanástrofe s. f. (rhet.) epanastrophe: repetition of a word which ends a sentence at the beginning of the next sentence.

epânodo s. m. (rhet.) epanodos: a figure in which the second member of a sentence is an inversion of the first.

epanortose s. f. (rhet.) epanorthosis: immediate revocation of a word in order to correct it.

eparquia s. f. eparchy: a district corresponding to a Roman province under the jurisdiction of an eparch.

epêndima s. m. (anat.) ependyma: the lining membrane of the ventricles of the brain and of the central canal of the spinal cord.

epêntese s. f. (gram.) epenthesis: insertion of a letter within a word, chiefly to facilitate pronunciation.

epentético adj. epenthetic: referring to an epenthesis.

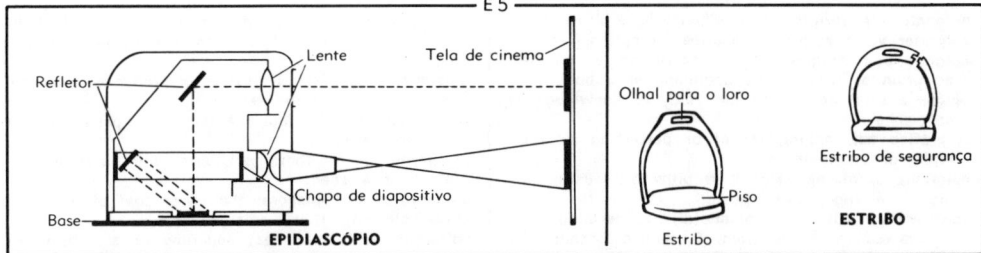

E 5

EPIDIASCÓPIO

ESTRIBO

epiblema s. m. (bot.) epiblema: the epidermis of a growing root.
epicanto s. m. (med.) epicanthus: a fold of skin concealing the inner canthus of the eye.
epicárpico adj. of or referring to the epicarp.
epicárpio s. m. (bot.) epicarp: the outer skin of a fruit.
epicédio s. m. epicedium: a funeral song or dirge.
epiceno adj. (gram.) epicene: said of a noun that has only one form of gender for both sexes of animals.
epicentro s. m. epicenter: the point on the earth's surface vertically above the focus of an earthquake.
epiciclo s. m. (astr.) epicycle: a small circle whose center moves on the periphery of a larger circle.
epicicloidal adj. m. + f. (pl. -ais) epicycloidal: having the form of an epicycloid.
epiciclóide s. f. (geom.) epicycloid: a curve formed by the motion of a point on the circumference of a circle which rolls upon the convex side of a fixed circle.
epiclese s. f. (rel.) epiklesis, epiclesis.
epiclino adj. (bot.) epiclinal: situated on the receptacle of a flower.
épico s. m. an epic poet. ‖ adj. epic(al): pertaining to or constituting an epos or heroic poem.
epicondiliano adj. epicondylian: pertaining to an epicondyle.
epicôndilo s. m. (anat.) epicondyle.
epicraniano, epicrânico adj. epicranial: pertaining to the epicranium.
epicrânio s. m. (anat.) epicranium: 1. covering of the cranium. 2. (ent.) the upper surface of an insect's head.
epícrise s. f. (med.) epicrisis: a critical analysis or discussion of a case of disease after its termination.
epicrítico adj. epicritic: relating to an epicrisis.
epicureu s. m. Epicurean: 1. a follower of Epicurus. 2. a sensualist. ‖ adj. Epicurean: of or pertaining to Epicureanism.
epicurismo s. m. Epicureanism: the doctrine of Epicurus that pleasure is the chief good in life.
epidemia s. f. epidemic: wide-spread disease in a certain region.
epidemiar v. to transmit an epidemic disease to; infect.
epidemicidade s. f. epidemicity: the quality or fact of being epidemic.
epidêmico adj. epidemic(al): of the character of an epidemic.
epidemiologia s. f. epidemiology: treatise on or the science of epidemics.
epidemiológico adj. epidemiological: pertaining to epidemiology.
epidemiologista s. m. + f., **epidemiólogo** m. epidemiologist: a specialist in epidemic diseases.

epidendro s. m. Epidendrum: a genus of orchids growing on trees.
epiderme s. f. (anat.) epidermis: the cuticle or outer skin; scarf-skin.
epidérmico adj. epidermic(al): of or relating to the epidermis.
epidiascópio s. m. epidiascope: a device for projecting the images of opaque or transparent objects (plate E 5).
epidíctico, epidítico adj. (rhet.) epidictic, demonstrative.
epididimite s. f. (med.) epididymitis: inflammation of the epididymis.
epidídimo s. m. (anat.) epididymis: an oblong body attached to the upper part of the testicle.
epifania s. f. Epiphany: a feast observed on January 6 to commemorate the manifestation of Christ to the Magi.
epifauna s. f. (biol.) epifauna; the sea floor fauna.
epifenômeno s. m. epiphenomenon: a phenomenon which is secondary to one or more other phenomena.
epifilo adj. (bot.) epiphyllous: growing upon a leaf.
epífise s. f. (anat.) epiphysis: 1. a process of separate ossification. 2. the pineal gland.
epífito s. m. epiphyte: a plant growing non-parasitically upon another.
epiflora s. f. (biol.) the sea floor flora.
epifonema s. m. (rhet.) epiphonema: an exclamatory sentence or striking reflection which concludes a passage.
epífora s. f. (med.) epiphora: an overflow of tears down the cheek mainly due to an obstruction of the lachrymal passages.
epífrase s. f. (rhet.) addition to a phrase which seemed complete, in order to develop secondary ideas.
epigastralgia s. f. (med.) epigastralgia: pain in the epigastrium.
epigástrico adj. epigastric: pertaining to the epigastrium.
epigástrio s. m. (anat.) epigastrium: the epigastric region, the upper portion of the abdomen.
epigenesia s. f. epigenesis: generation by successive formations.
epigenesista s. m. + f. epigenesist: one who supports the theory of epigenesis. ‖ adj. epigenetic.
epigenético adj. epigenetic: pertaining to epigenesis.
epigeu adj. (bot.) epigeous: 1. growing on or out of the earth. 2. borne above ground in germination (as the cotyledons of beans).
epígino adj. (bot.) epigynous: growing upon the top of the ovary.
epiglote s. f. (anat.) epiglottis: the lidlike structure which covers the entrance to the larynx.
epiglótico adj. epiglottic: pertaining to the epiglottis.
epiglotite s. f. (med.) epiglottitis: inflammation of the epiglottis.

epígnato adj. (ornith.) epignathous: hook-billed.

epigrafar v. to epigraph: inscribe an epigraph on.

epígrafe s. f. epigraph: 1. an inscription. 2. a superscription or title at the beginning of a book.

epigrafia s. f. epigraphy: the study or knowledge of epigraphs.

epigráfico adj. epigraphic: of or pertaining to epigraphy or on epigraph.

epigrama s. m. epigram: 1. a pithy or caustic saying. 2. a short, pithy poem.

epigramático adj. epigrammatic(al): 1. pertaining to, or marked by an epigram. 2. satirical, caustic. ‖ **epigramaticamente** adv. epigrammatically.

epigramatista s. m. + f. epigrammatist: person who composes epigrams.

epigramatizar v. to epigrammatize: 1. represent or express by epigrams. 2. write epigrammatically.

epilação s. f. (pl. -ões) depilation: the removal of hair by the roots.

epilatório s. m. depilatory: an agent which effects the destruction of hairs. ‖ adj. depilatory: having the power to remove hair.

epilepsia s. f. (med.) epilepsy: a chronic nervous affection.

epiléptico, epilético s. m. epileptic: person affected with epilepsy. ‖ adj. epileptic: pertaining to or affected with epilepsy.

epilogação s. f. (pl. -ões) 1. act of epilogizing. 2. recapitulation, summing up.

epilogador s. m. epilogist: person who epilogizes.

epilogar v. to epilogize: 1. write or pronounce an epilogue. 2. recapitulate, summarize, sum up.

epílogo s. m. 1. epilog(ue): a) the conclusion or closing part of a discourse or oration. b) recapitulation, summary. 2. (theat.) after-piece.

epimítio s. m. epimyth: a moral as of a fable.

epinastia s. f. (bot.) epinasty: a curvation due to a more active development of one side (as of a leaf).

epinefrina s. f. = **adrenalina.**

epinício s. m. epinicion: 1. a song of triumph. 2. a poem to celebrate a victory.

epiódia s. f. (ancient Gr.) funeral march.

epipétalo adj. (bot.) epipetalous: said of the stamens inserted in the corolla.

epiplocele s. f. (surg.) hernia of the epiploon.

epiploíte s. f. (med.) epiploitis: inflammation of the epiploon.

epíploo(n) s. m. (anat.) epiploon: the great omentum.

epipterado adj. (bot.) epipterous: having a wing on the summit (seeds).

epiquirema s. m. (logic) epichirema: a syllogism having the truth of one or both of its premises confirmed by a proposition annexed.

epirota s. m. + f. Epirot(e): native or inhabitant of Epirus. ‖ adj. (also **epirótico**) Epirotic: of or pertaining to Epirus or the Epirotes.

episcênio s. m. (ancient Gr. theat.) upper floor of the scene.

episcopado s. m. 1. episcopate: the office or dignity of a bishop. 2. episcopacy: a) the government of a church by bishops. b) the body of bishops collectively.

episcopal adj. m. + f. (pl. -ais) episcopal: of or pertaining to a bishop.

episodiar v. to adorn with episodes.

episódico adj. episodic(al): pertaining to or of the character of an episode.

episódio s. m. episode: 1. an incident or story in a literary work separable from the main subject but arising from it. 2. (mus.) an intermediate section of a composition. 3. a happening in real life or in a story.

epispádias s. f. pl. (med.) epispadias: a defect in which the urethra opens on the dorsum of the penis.

epispástico adj. (med.) epispastic: producing a blister when applied to the skin.

epispermático adj. (bot.) epispermic: pertaining to the episperm.

epispermo s. m. (bot.) episperm: the outer integument of a seed.

epísporo s. m. epispore: the outer coat of a spore.

epissépalo adj. (bot.) episepalous.

epistação s. f. (pl. -ões) pounding of something in a mortar.

epistar v. to pound in a mortar.

epístase s. f. (med.) epistasis: a pellicle on the surface of urine.

epistasia s. f. (biol.) epistasy.

epistaxe s. f. (med.) epistaxis: nosebleed, hemorrhage from the nose.

epistemologia s. f. epistemology: the science of the methods and validity of knowledge.

epistílio s. m. (archit.) epistyle: the lower member of the entablature.

epístola s. f. 1. epistle: a written message, a letter. 2. Epistle: a letter of an apostle in the New Testament. 3. (eccl.) the side of an altar from which the Epistle is read.

~**s de São Paulo** the Epistles of St. Paul.

epistolar (I) adj. m. + f. epistolary: pertaining to epistles or letters.

epistolar (II) v. to epistolize: write epistles or letters.

epistolário s. m. epistolary: a book containing the epistles of a liturgy.

epistolografia s. f. epistolography: art or practice of writing letters.

epistolográfico adj. epistolographic.

epistológrafo s. m. (also **epistoleiro**) epistolographist: a writer of letters.

epístrofe s. f. (rhet.) epistrophe: a repetition in which successive sentences end with the same word.

epitáfio s. m. epitaph: 1. an inscription on a tomb or monument in memory of the dead. 2. a brief test written as if for inscription on a tomb.

epitafista s. m. + f. epitaphist: a writer of epitaphs.

epitalâmico adj. epithalamic: relating to an epithalamium.

epitalâmio s. m. epithalamium: a nuptial poem or song.

epítase s. f. epitasis: the main action of a play.

epitélio s. m. (med.) epithelium: the covering of skin and mucous membranes.

epitelioma s. m. (med.) epithelioma: an epithelial cancer.

epítese s. f. (gram., also **paragoge**) paragoge: addition of a sound or syllable at the end of a word.

epitetar v. to epithet: 1. entitle. 2. describe by epithets.

epitético adj. epithetic(al): pertaining to or characterized by an epithet.

epíteto s. m. epithet: 1. additional descriptive word or phrase. 2. a nickname, cognomen.

epitomar v. to epitomize: 1. reduce to an epitome. 2. reduce, condense, summarize.

epítome s. m. epitome: 1. summary, abridgement. 2. a compendium. 3. synopsis.

epítrope s. f. (rhet.) epitrope: a figure by which one allows or concedes esp. ironically.

epíxilo adj. (bot.) epixylous: growing upon wood (as many fungi).

epizeuxe, epizêuxis s. f. (rhet.) epizeuxis: immediate repetition of a word.

epizoário s. m. (zool.) epizoon: an external animal parasite. ‖ adj. epizoan, epizoic: living on the surface or in the skin of animals.

epizootia s. f. epizootic: a disease common to or affecting many animals at the same time.

época s. f. 1. epoch, era, period, age. 2. season, time, tide. 3. cycle. 4. (geol.) a division of geological time.

~ **de inverno** wintertide, wintertime. ~ **de Natal** Christmastide, Yuletide. ~ **morta** dead season. **em nossa** ~ in our age. **em qualquer** ~ in season or out of season, always. **fora de** ~ unseasonable.

epódico adj. epodic: pertaining to or containing an epode.

epodo s. m. epode: the third stanza of a Greek ode.

epônimo s. m. eponymist: person after whom a country or people is named. ‖ adj. eponymic.

epopéia s. f. 1. epopee, epopoeia, epic poem. 2. (fig.) epic histories or actions.

epopéico adj. epic: 1. pertaining to an heroic poem. 2. heroic, grand.

epsomita s. f. (min.) epsomite, Epson salt.

épulas s. f. pl. appetizing food.

epúlida, epúlide s. f. (med.) epulis: a small tumour of the gums.

epulótico adj. favouring cicatrization.

equabilidade s. f. equability, equableness.

equação s. f. (pl. -ões) (math.) equation.

~ **biquadrada** (math.) biquadratic equation. ~ **exponencial** (math.) exponential equation. ~ **linear** (math.) linear equation, equation of the first degree.

equador s. m. equator:˙ the imaginary great circle of the earth, at right angles to the earth's axis and equidistant from the poles.

~ **magnético** magnetic equator, aclinic line.

equânime adj. m. + f. equanimous, even-minded.

equanimidade s. f. equanimity: 1. evenness of mind or temper. 2. calmness, firmness, composure, self--control.

equatorial (I) adj. m. + f. (pl. -ais) equatorial: of or pertaining to the equator.

equatorial (II) s. m. equatorial: an instrument to determine the ascension and declination of a heavenly body.

equatoriano s. m. Ecuadorian: native or inhabitant of Ecuador. ‖ adj. Ecuadorian: of or pertaining to Ecuador.

equável adj. m. + f. (pl. -áveis) equable, steady; equal, uniform.

eqüestre adj. m. + f. equestrian: pertaining to or relating to horses or horsemanship.

estátua ~ equestrian statue.

eqüevo adj. coeval, of the same age, equaeval, coetaneous, contemporary.

eqüiângulo adj. equiangled, equiangular: having equal angles.

eqüidade, equidade s. f. equity: 1. fairness, impartiality. 2. equal justice. 3. rightness. 4. equality.

eqüídeo s. m. a horse or related animal. ‖ adj. equine: of, pertaining to or like a horse.

eqüidiferente adj. m. + f. equidifferent: having equal differences.

eqüidistância s. f. equidistance, equal distance.

eqüidistante adj. m. + f. equidistant, equally distant.

eqüidistar v. to be equidistant.

équidna s. f. (zool.) echidna: the typical genus of the family Echidnidae.

equidnina s. f. echidnine: serpent poison.

eqüilateral adj. m. + f. (pl. -ais), **eqüilátero** equilateral: having all the sides equal.

triângulo eqüilátero equilateral triangle.

equilibração s. f. (pl. -ões) equilibration, equipoise.

equilibrador adj. m., **equilibrante** m. + f. equilibratory: tending or serving to equilibrate or balance.

equilibrar v. 1. to equilibrate: a) balance equally. b) keep in equipoise. c) counterpoise, counterbalance. 2. to compensate. 3. ~-se to maintain o. s. in equilibrium; make the ends meet.

bem equilibrado well poised. **estar equilibrado** to be well-balanced, tremble in the balance. **ele sabe** ~ **o barco** (fig.) he makes both ends meet.

equilíbrio s. m. 1. equilibrium, balance, poise, equipoise. 2. equilibration.

~ **de forças** balance of power. ~ **instável** unstable equilibrium. **ele perdeu o** ~ he lost his balance. **pistão de** ~ balance piston.

equilibrista s. m. + f. equilibrist: ropewalker, acrobat.

equimosar-se v. to become ecchymosed.

equimose s. f. (med.) ecchymosis: discoloration of the skin caused by the extravasation of blood.

equimótico adj. ecchymotic: pertaining to or of the nature of an ecchymosis.

eqüimultíplice adj. m. + f. **eqüimúltiplo** m. (math.) equimultiple.

equino s. m. (archit.) echinus, quarter-round.

eqüino adj. equine: of, pertaining to or resembling a horse.

equinocial adj. m. + f. (pl. -ais) equinoctial: of or referring to the equinox.

equinócio s. m. equinox: point at which the sun crosses the celestial equator, when the days and nights are equal.

equinococo s. m. (zool.) echinococcus: a genus of tapeworms.

equinodermo s. m. echinoderm: one of the Echinodermata.

equinoftalmia s. f. (med.) echinophthalmia: inflammation of the eyelids marked by projection of the lashes.

equinóide s. m. (zool.) echinoid: one of the Echinoidea.

equinospermo adj. (bot.) having rough downy seeds.

equipagem s. f. (pl. -ens) 1. equipage: a) accoutrements. b) baggage, equipment. c) outfit. d) furniture. e) retinue. 2. the crew of a ship.

equipamento s. m. equipment: 1. act of equipping, of fitting out. 2. gear, outfit, tackle (plate P 9). 3. accoutrements. 4. kit.

equipar v. to equip: 1. furnish or fit out with all the necessary supplies. 2. outfit. 3. man. 4. ~-se be equipped with.

~ **um navio** to equip a ship.

equiparação s. f. (pl. -ões) equalization, levelling, matching, making equal.

equiparar v. 1. to equal(ize), match, compare. 2. to put up to the level of, make equal. 4. to parallel.

equiparável adj. m. + f. (pl. -áveis 1. comparable. 2. that can be equalized.

equipe s. f. 1. team: (sport) a number of players of the same side. 2. a group of persons engaged in joint work.

~ **de futebol** football team. ~ **de salvamento** search-party; rescue-party. **trabalho de** ~ teamwork.

eqüípede adj. m. + f. equipedal, equal-footed.

eqüipendência s. f. equipendency, equiponderance.

eqüipendente adj. m. + f. equipendent: 1. of equal value. 2. equal in weight.

equipo s. m. (tech., radio) a set of circuits.

eqüipolência s. f. equipollence: 1. equality of power or force. 2. (math.) equality of length with parallelism of direction.

eqüipolente adj. m. + f. equipollent: 1. having equal power or force, equivalent. 2. having the same meaning. 3. (math.) equal.

eqüponderância s. f. equiponderance, equality of weight, equipoise.

eqüponderante adj. m. + f. equiponderant: 1. equal in weight. 2. evenly balanced.

eqüponderar v. to equiponderate: 1. equipoise. 2. counterbalance. 3. ~-se be equal in weight.

eqüissetácea s. f. an equisetaceous plant.

eqüissetáceo adj. (bot.) equisetaceous: of or pertaining to the Equisetaceae.

eqüisseto s. m. Equisetum: a genus of plants constituting the order Equisetaceae.

eqüissonância s. f. (mus.) equisonance: consonance as that which exists between octaves.

eqüissonante adj. m. + f. equisonant: marked by equisonance.

equitação s. f. (pl. -ões) equitation, horsemanship: art of riding on horseback.

equitador s. m. a rider, equestrian, horseman.

eqüitativo adj. equitable, just, reasonable, fair-minded. ‖ -amente adv. equitably.

equivalência, eqüivalência s. f. equivalence, equal value.

equivalente, eqüivalente s. m. equivalent: something equal in value, power or effect. ‖ adj. m. + f. equivalent, of equal value, force, power or weight. ‖ ~mente adv. equivalently, in an equivalent manner.

equivaler, eqüivaler v. to equivale: be equal or equivalent to, be on a par with.

eqüivalve adj. m. + f. equivalve: having equal valves.

equivocação s. f. (pl. -ões) error, mistake (in meaning).

equivocado adj. mistaken, in error.

equivocar(-se) v. 1. to mistake, make a mistake (as in speaking). 2. to take one thing for another. **estar equivocado** to be wrong.

equívoco s. m. 1. mistake, error. 2. a word of double meaning. 3. ambiguity, equivocation. 4. ambiguous interpretation. ‖ adj. 1. equivocal, of doubtful signification. 2. dubious, ambiguous. 3. double meaning.

aconteceu por ~ it happened by mistake. **resultar num** ~ to give rise to a misunderstanding. **surgiu um** ~ a misunderstanding arose.

equóreo adj. (poet.) equorean: belonging to the sea.

era s. f. 1. era: a) epoch, a period of time. b) date, age or time marked by a remarkable event. 2. (Braz.) age, time of life.

~ **cristã** Christian era.

erado adj. (of animals) full grown, fully developed; good to be slaughtered.

erário s. m. exchequer: 1. the treasury (of a state), fisc. 2. finance. 3. public purse.

erásmico adj. Erasmian: pertaining to the famous Dutch theologian Erasmus.

erbina s. f. (chem.) erbia: the oxid of the metal erbium.

Érebo s. m. (myth.) Erebus: the infernal region.

ereção s. f. (pl. -ões) erection: 1. act of erecting or state of being erect. 2. raising. 3. institution, foundation.

eremita s. m. + f. hermit, eremite, anchorite.

eremita-bernardo s. m. hermit crab: a crustacean of the genus Pagurus.

eremitério s. m. habitation of hermits, hermitage.

eremítico adj. hermitic(al), eremitic(al): referring to hermits.

éreo adj. (poet.) made of copper or brass.

erepsina s. f. (med.) erepsin.

erétil adj. m. + f. (pl. **eréteis**) (also **eréctil** pl. **erécteis**) erectile.

eretilidade s. f. (also **erectilidade**) erectility: quality of being erectile.

eretismo s. m. (med.) erethism: excitement or stimulation of any organ or tissue (esp. of the organs of generation).

ereto adj. (also **erecto**) 1. erected, raised (up), founded. 2. erect, upright, straight, plumb (plate Q). 3. lifted (up).

eretor s. m. (f. **eretriz**) (also **erector**) erector, erecter: person who or thing that arises or erects.

ereutofobia s. f. (med.) fear of blushing.

erg s. m. (phys.) erg: the unit of work in the centimeter-gram-second system.

ergastenia s. f. (path.) asthenia (from excess of work).

ergástulo s. m. dungeon, prison; house of correction.

ergofobia s. f. ergophobia: aversion to work.

ergógrafo s. m. ergograph: instrument for registering work done in muscular exertion.

ergologia s. f. ergology.

ergotina s. f. ergotine: an amorphous alkaloid of ergot.

ergotismo s. m. ergotism: 1. a logical inference. 2. chronic poisoning from excessive use of ergot.

erguer v. 1. to raise, lift (up). 2. to elevate, rear. 3. to build, erect. 4. to found. 5. to increase (strength of voice). 6. to set upright. 7. ~-se: a) to rise. b) to get or stand up. c) to rear (horse). ~ **os olhos** to raise the eyes. ~ **um brinde** to propose a toast, to give a rouse.

erica s. f. (bot.) a kind of heath.

ericácea s. f. an ericaceous plant.

ericáceo adj. (bot.) ericaceous: of or pertaining to the heath family.

eriçado adj. 1. hispid, bristly, brushy; patchy. 2. frizzled, rough. 3. spiked. 4. prickly, thorny.

eriçar(-se) v. 1. to bristle (up). 2. to ruffle. 3. to make hair stand on end.

Erídano s. m. Eridanus: a southern constellation.

erigir v. 1. to erect, raise, set up, lift up. 2. to build, edify. 3. to found. 4. to elevate, rear.

erináceo adj. (zool.) erinaceous: resembling a hedgehog.

erinacídeo s. m. erinaceid: an animal of the family Erinaceidae. ‖ adj. of or pertaining to the Erinaceidae.

erisipela s. f. (med.) erysipelas: an acute inflammatory disease of the skin.

erisipelar v. to be affected with erysipelas.

erisipeloso adj. (med.) erysipelatous: 1. of the nature of erysipelas. 2. affected with erysipelas.

erística s. f. (logic) eristic: the art of disputation.

eritema s. m. (med.) erythema: a superficial redness of some portions of the skin.

eritemático adj. erythematic, erythematous: of, pertaining to or of the nature of erythema.

eritrocarpo adj. (bot.) erythrocarpous: red-fruited.

eritrócero adj. (zool.) having red antennae.

eritrodermo adj. (zool.) red-skinned.

eritrófilo adj. (bot.) red-leaved.

eritróide adj. m. + f. erytroid: red-coloured.

eritrópode adj. m. + f. (zool.) red-rooted.

eritropsia s. f. (med.) erythropia: condition in which all objects appear reddish.

eritróptero adj. (zool.) red-winged.

eritróstomo adj. (zool.) red-mouthed.

eritróxilo adj. (bot.) of red wood.

ermamento s. m. 1. depopulation. 2. devastation.

ermar v. 1. to devastate. 2. to lay waste, desolate, depopulate. 3. to live in solitude, live a retired life. 4. ~-se to become depopulated.

ermida s. f. 1. out of the way chapel (as a hermitage). 2. a small church.

ermita s. m. (also eremita) hermit.

ermitágio s. m. (also eremitério) hermitage.

ermitão s. m. (pl. -ãos, -ães, -ões) (f. ermitã, ermitoa). 1. (also eremita) hermit. 2. the hermit in charge of the chapel of a hermitage.

ermitério s. m. (also eremitério) hermitage.

ermitoa s. f. hermitess: 1. a woman who retired for devotion. 2. a woman who takes care of a hermitage.

ermo (ê) s. m. hermitage, wilderness, desert, solitary place. || adj. solitary, retired, secluded, desert.

erodir v. to erode.

erosão s. f. erosion, act of eroding, corrosion (plate C 19).

erosivo adj. m. (also erodente m. + f.) erosive, corrosive.

erótico adj. erotic(al): 1. belonging to love, amorous. 2. sensual. 3. lubric, lascivious.

erotismo s. m. 1. eroticism, a passion of love. 2. lubricity.

erotofobia s. f. (med.) aversion to sexual intercourse.

erotomania s. f. erotomania: 1. mental alienation caused by sexual love. 2. love-sickness.

erotomaníaco, erotômano s. m. erotomaniac: person suffering from or afflicted with erotomania.

erpe adj. (Braz., coll.) boasting, self-praising.

errabundo adj. vagrant, erring, errant.

errada s. f. (Braz.) 1. crossroads. 2. error, mistake.

erradicação s. f. (pl. -ões) eradication: 1. act of plucking up by the roots. 2. extirpation.

erradicante adj. m. + f. eradicative: tending to eradicate or extirpate.

erradicar v. to eradicate: 1. pull up by the roots. 2. extirpate. 3. cure radically.

erradicativo adj. eradicative: 1. tending to eradicate. 2. that which cures radically. || -amente adv. radically.

erradio adj. 1. errant, vagrant, wandering. 2. confused, lost.

errado adj. 1. mistaken, erroneous. 2. wrong. 3. false, incorrect. 4. faulty. || -amente adv. mistakenly, erroneously.

andar ~ to err, go astray. ele começou do lado ~ he has begun at the wrong end, he has got hold of the wrong end of the stick. ele está ~ he is wrong, he is mistaken. ele lhe deu informação -a he told him wrong. eles lhe podem provar que você está ~ they can prove you are wrong. ligação -a 1. (tech.) faulty control. 2. (teleph.) wrong number. meu relógio está ~ my watch is wrong. uma coisa -a a wrong thing. você topou com a pessoa -a you hit upon the wrong person.

errar v. 1. to miss, mistake, make a mistake, be mistaken. 2. to take one thing for another. 3. to fail. 4. to ramble, wander, roam, err, go astray. 5. to sin, trespass, offend.

~ o alvo 1. (shooting) to miss the mark, miss one's aim. 2. to deviate from the purpose. ~ o caminho to lose one's way. ela errou a vocação she mistook her vocation. errei com meu palpite I guessed wrong.

errata s. f. 1. erratum: typographical error, misprint. 2. errata: the list of the errata of a book.

errático adj. erratic: 1. wandering. 2. (astr.) moving, not fixed. 3. (med.) changeable, appearing at indeterminate intervals (as some intermittent fevers). 4. (geol.) said of a block which has been conveyed from its original site, probably by ice.

erriçar v. = eriçar.

errino adj. (med.) errhine: 1. affecting the nose. 2. designated to be snuffed. 3. sternutative: occasioning sneezing and increased discharge from the nose.

erro (ê) s. m. 1. error, fault, mistake. 2. false judgement. 3. blunder, oversight, slip; miss. 4. incorrectness. 5. trespass, sin; wrong.

~ é ~ a miss is a good as a mile. ~ de cálculo (medição, leitura) error in calculation (measurement, reading). ~ de composição (typogr.) a wrong letter. ~ de montagem faulty mounting. ~ ortográfico scribal error. admito meu ~ I stand corrected. ele cometeu um ~ crasso he made a blunder, a bad mistake. foi um ~ dele it was wrong of him. pegamo-lo num ~ we caught him tripping.

errôneo adj. 1. erroneous, false, mistaken. 2. untrue. || -amente adv. erroneously, falsely.

erronia s. f. a deep-rooted error.

erubescer v. (also enrubescer) to make red, redden.

eructação s. f. (pl. -ões) eructation, belching, a belch.

erudição s. f. (pl. -ões) erudition: extensive reading, knowledge, scholarship.

erudito s. m. erudite: a learned person. || adj. erudite: well-read, learned, skilful. || -amente adv. eruditely, with erudition.

falar -amente to talk fine.

eruginoso adj. (a)eruginous, rusty.

erupção s. f. (pl. -ões) eruption: 1. a bursting forth. 2. (med.) breaking out, rash, eruption of the skin. 3. outbreak.

~ vulcânica vulcanic eruption.

eruptivo adj. eruptive: 1. (med.) causing eruption. 2. of or referring to eruption.

febre -a an eruptive fever.

erva s. f. 1. herb. 2. grass; grassland, meadow. 3. (Braz.) venomous plant. 4. herbage. 5. (Braz., sl.) money. 6. ~s pl. greens, herbs, vegetables.

erva-abelha s. f. (pl. ervas-abelhas) (bot.) bee-orchis.

erva-agulheira s. f. (pl. ervas-agulheiras) (bot.) shepherd's needle, needle-weed.

erva-andorinha s. f. (pl. ervas-andorinhas) (Braz.) name common to three plants of the genus Euphorbia (Euphorbia brasiliensis, Euphorbia pilulifera and Euphorbia coecorum).

erva-aranha s. f. (pl. ervas-aranhas) (bot.) spider orchis.

erva-babosa s. f. (pl. ervas-babosas) (bot.) barbados aloe.

erva-benta s. f. (pl. ervas-bentas) (bot.) avens, herb bennet.

erva-besteira s. f. (pl. ervas-besteiras) (bot.) the fetid or black hellebore.

erva-bicha s. f. (pl. ervas-bichas) plant of the natural order Aristolochiaceae (Aristolochia longa).

erva-botão s. f. (pl. ervas-botões) (bot.) dyeweed (Eclipta alba).

ervaçal s. m. (pl. -ais) pasture, grassland.

erva-castelhana s. f. (pl. ervas-castelhanas) rye-grass.

erva-chumbo s. f. (pl. ervas-chumbo) (bot.) white mangrove (Avicennia alveolata).

erva-cidreira s. f. (pl. ervas-cidreiras) (bot.) 1. balm-mint (Melissa officinalis). 2. lemon-scented verbena (Lippia geminata).

erva-coalheira s. f. (pl. ervas-coalheiras) (bot.) yellow galium, lady's bedstraw.

erva-colégio s. f. (pl. ervas-colégios) (bot.) woolly elephant's-foot, devil's-grandmother.

erva-de-bicho s. f. (pl. ervas-de-bicho) (bot.) water smartweed (Polygonum acre).

erva-de-cobra s. f. (pl. ervas-de-cobra) = caacambuí.

erva-de-passarinho s. f. (pl. ervas-de-passarinho) (bot.) mistletoe.

erva-de-santa-lúcia s. f. (pl. ervas-de-santa-lúcia) (bot.) plant of the family Commelinaceae (Commelina sulcata).

erva-de-santa-maria s. f. (pl. **ervas-de-santa-maria**) (bot.) wormseed (Chenopodium ambrosioides).

erva-de-santo-estêvão s. f. (pl. **ervas-de-santo-estêvão**) (bot.) enchanter's nightshade, wild mandrake.

erva-de-são-joão s. f. (pl. **ervas-de-são-joão**) (bot.) St. John's wort.

ervado adj. 1. envenomed, poisoned (by herbs). 2. grassy. 3. (fig.) moneyed.

erva-doce s. f. (pl. **ervas-doces**) (bot.) anise (Pimpinella anisum).

erva-dos-gatos s. f. (pl. **ervas-dos-gatos**) (bot.) = **gatária.**

ervagem s. f. (pl. **-ens**) 1. herbage: plenty of herbs, greens, vegetables. 2. pasture.

erva-gigante s. f. (pl. **ervas-gigantes**) (bot.) acanthus, brank-ursine.

erval s. m. (pl. **-ais**) (Braz.) maté plantation, place abounding in maté.

erva-mate s. f. (pl. **ervas-mates**) (Braz., bot.) maté, Paraguay-tea (Ilex paraguaiensis).

erva-moura s. f. (pl. **ervas-mouras**) (also **erva-moira**) (bot.) nightshade, banewort (Solanum nigrum).

ervanaria s. f. (Braz.) herb shop.

ervanário s. m. (also **herbanário**) 1. herb shop, a herbalist's shop. 2. herb dealer, herbalist.

ervançal s. m. (pl. **-ais**) chick-pea plantation.

ervanço s. m. chick-pea: 1. a leguminous plant (Cicer arietinum). 2. its seeds.

ervar v. to envenom, poison by rubbing with venomous herbs.

ervatário s. m. (Braz.) herbman, gatherer and seller of medicinal plants.

ervateiro s. m. (Braz.) person who cultivates maté or dealer in maté.

ervecer v. to grass, become covered with grass.

ervicida s. m. (also **herbicida**) herbicide.

ervilha s. f. pea: 1. a leguminous plant (Pisum sativum). 2. its edible seeds. 3. pea-pod.

ervilhaca s. f. (bot.) tare, vetch (Vicia sativa).

ervilha-de-cheiro s. f. (pl. **ervilhas-de-cheiro**) sweet-pea (Lathyrus adoratus).

ervilhal s. m. (pl. **-ais**) pea plantation.

ervoeira s. f. (pop.) prostitute.

ervoso adj. grassy, herbous, full of herbs.

esbaforido adj. 1. hasty. 2. panting, puffing, gasping, breathless. 3. tired.

esbaforir-se v. 1. to pant, puff, breathe hard. 2. to put o. s. out of breath. 3. to grow weary.

esbagaçar v. 1. to tear to or break into pieces. 2. to smash, shatter.

esbagachar v. to denude the breasts.

esbaganhar v. to clean, pull flax.

esbagoar v. 1. to pick (as grapes out of a bunch). 2. **~-se** to drop from the bunch (as overripe grapes).

esbagulhar v. to take out the seeds, grains, kernels.

esbambear v. = **bambear.**

esbamboar-se v. to swing, see-saw; shake the hips.

esbandalhado adj. 1. disbanded, dispersed, runaway, strayed. 2. destroyed, shattered. 3. tattered, torn, ragged.

esbandalhar v. 1. to break to pieces, destroy. 2. to tatter, tear. 3. **~-se** to disband, disperse, run away, stray (as cattle).

esbandeirar v. 1. to cut the panicle (of corn plants). 2. **~-se** to throw o. s., make a rush for, pitch into, go for.

esbandulhar v. to slit up the belly (of s. o.).

esbanjador s. m. lavisher, squanderer, dissipator; profuse man, prodigal, spendthrift. ‖ adj. prodigal, lavish, squandering.

esbanjamento s. m. dissipation, waste, squandering; profusion.

esbanjar v. to dissipate, misspend, waste, lavish, squander, overspend.

~ o dinheiro to trifle away the money, throw one's money to the dogs.

esbaralhar v. (obs.) to shuffle cards.

esbarbar v. to burr; remove burrs from a sharp edge.

esbarbotar v. to burl (cloth).

esbarrada s. f. 1. a slight shock. 2. (Braz.) an abrupt stop or halt (horse).

esbarrancar v. (Braz.) = **desbarrancar.**

esbarrão s. m. (pl. **-ões**) 1. shock, collision, clash, dashing together. 2. trip. 3. shove, jostle.

esbarrar v. 1. to dash; collide with (com, contra). 2. to run against, stumble. 3. to beat slightly against. 4. **~-se** to elbow, jostle one another.

esbarrigar v. 1. to bring forth young (animals). 2. to slit up the belly of.

esbarro s. m. (S. Braz.) shove, jostle.

esbarrocamento s. m. 1. collapse (as of a wall). 2. landslide; washout.

esbarrocar v. 1. to demolish. 2. to tumble down. 3. to form into a gully.

esbarrondadeiro s. m. precipice; gully; cliff.

esbarrondar v. 1. to destroy, demolish, tumble down. 2. to throw down. 3. to attack, invest, inveigh. 4. **~-se:** a) to precipitate o. s. upon, fall away. b) to fall to ruin.

esbater v. 1. to cause to stand out in relief (a figure). 2. to temper paint, shade off, adumbrate. 3. (also **~-se**) to dilute (colours).

esbatimento s. m. a putting in relief (figures).

esbeatado adj. unravelled, separated into threads.

esbeatar v. to ravel, frazzle.

esbeiçar v. 1. to break off the edges, to chip (cup, plate). 2. to hang over, stick out. 3. **~-se** to confine, touch.

esbeltar v. 1. to make slender, give an elegant shape to. 2. **~-se:** a) to carry o. s. elegantly. b) to make a show of (o. s.).

esbeltez(a) s. f. slenderness, elegance, gracefulness, gracility.

esbelto adj. 1. slender, tall and thin, svelte, slim. 2. elegant, graceful, gracious.

conservar-se ~ to keep one's figure. **garota -a** a slender girl.

esbilhotar v. (Braz., pop.) to chatter; gossip; intrigue.

esbirrar v. (naut.) to prop.

esbirro s. m. 1. bailiff, constable. 2. prop: a) (naut.) support used in careening. b) wooden support used during the operation of underpinning a wall.

esboçar v. to sketch: 1. make the first draught. 2. roughdraw, outline, delineate. 3. present in rough draft or outline without details. 4. plan. **ele esboçou seu plano** he plotted out his plan.

esboço (ô) s. m. (pl. **esboços**) 1. sketch, outline, rough draught, first plan; project. 2. (fig.) summary, synopsis.

esbodegação s. f. (pl. **-ões**) (Braz.) 1. spoiling. 2. squandering. 3. exhaustion.

esbodegado adj. (S. Braz.) 1. panting, breathless. 2. tired, worn out. 3. spoiled. 4. dissipated squandered.

esbodegar v. (Braz.) 1. (pop.) to spoil, mar, destroy; waste, squander. 2. **~-se:** a) to become negligent. b) to put o. s. out of breath, pant. c) to be tired, fagged, worn out.

esbofado adj. breathless, panting, out of breath.

esbofar v. 1. to tire out, fatigue, fag. 2. **~-se:** a) to put o. s. out of breath. b) to gasp, puff, pant.

esbofetear v. to slap, strike with a slap in the face box a person's ears.

esbombardear v. to bombard.

esborcelar, esborcinar v. to remove the edges of.

esbordar v. to overflow, spill or run over.
esbordoar v. to cudgel, beat with a cudgel or stick.
esbórnia s. f. (Braz.) orgy, wild revel, a drunken carouse.
esborniador s. m. (Braz.) person given to orgies.
esborniar v. (Braz.) to live in orgies.
esboroamento s. m. (also **esborôo**) 1. a reducing to pieces, powdering. 2. collapse (as of a wall); ruin, decay.
esboroar, esbroar v. 1. to powder, reduce to powder or dust. 2. to destroy, demolish, tumble down.
esborrachado adj. burst, crushed, squashed; smashed.
esborrachar v. 1. to burst, crush, squash. 2. to pulp by a fall. 3. to flatten. 4. (fig.) to strike with a slap in the face. 5. ~-se to fall sprawling.
esborralhada s. f. 1. scattering, dispersing. 2. demolition.
esborralhadouro s. m. oven broom.
esborralhar v. 1. to put out, extinguish, or scatter embers. 2. to demolish, destroy. 3. to disperse, scatter. 4. ~-se to crumble or moulder away.
esborrar v. 1. to overflow, spill over, run over. 2. to skim; cleanse of dregs.
esborratadela s. f. 1. act of blotting. 2. an ink blot.
esborratar v. (also **esborretar**) to blot out, stain, spot (with ink).
esborregar v. to level (skins).
esborrifar v. (also **borrifar**) to sprinkle, spray.
esborrifo s. m. sprinkling, spraying.
esborro (ô) s. m. act of frothing over, overflowing.
esbouçar v. to cultivate the soil for grapevine plantation.
esbrabejado adj. (N. Braz., pop.) tamed, domesticated.
esbracejar v. to move, agitate one's arms, gesticulate.
esbraguilhado adj. unzipped, unbuttonned, open (fly of trousers).
esbranquiçado adj. 1. whitish, pale, inclined to white. 2. discoloured, faded.
esbraseado adj. 1. fiery, burning, inflamed. 2. flame-coloured, red-hot.
esbrasear v. 1. to set abraze. 2. to heat, burn. 3. to redden, make red-hot. 4. to inflame, excite. 5. ~-se to become inflamed.
esbravecer v. 1. to become furious, infuriate, enrage. 2. to rage.
esbravejar v. (also **esbravear**) 1. = **esbravecer**. 2. to roar, shout, cry out. 3. to rage violently, to fret and fume.
esbregue s. m. (Braz., pop.) 1. reprehension, reprimand, reproof. 2. noise, disturbance.
esbugalhado adj. staring, bulging, pop-eyed.
olhos ~s prominent eyes, goggle-eyes.
esbugalhar v. to pop out (eyes); stare, gaze, gape.
esbulhado adj. plundered, despoiled, robbed.
esbulhador s. m. plunderer, robber; usurper. ‖ adj. plundering; usurping.
esbulhar v. to despoil: 1. rob, plunder. 2. strip (of possessions), expropriate. 3. deprive, divest. 4. usurp.
esbulho s. m. 1. despoliation, plundering. 2. expropriation, dispossession.
esburacado adj. (also **esburaquento**) 1. bored, perfurated. 2. full of holes. 3. broken; tattered, torn, ragged.
esburacar v. 1. to make a hole or many holes, fill with holes. 2. to bore, perforate. 3. ~-se to become full of holes (as a street).
esburaquento adj. = **esburacado.**
esburgar v. (also **esbrugar**) 1. to peel, shell. 2. to skin, take off the skin. 3. to pick bones.
esburnir v. to give but unwillingly.
esbuxar v. (obs.) to dismember, disjoint.

escabecear v. to beckon, nod.
escabeche s. m. 1. souse, marinade, pickle used for fish or meat. 2. disguise.
escabela s. f. removal of the fur from the skin before tanning.
escabelar v. 1. to dishevel, tousle, spread the hair disorderly. 2. to pull out the hair (by the roots). 3. ~-se to tear one's hair.
escabelo (ê) s. m. footstool (plate B 2).
escabichar v. to investigate patiently, sound.
escabiosa s. f. scabious: plant of the family Scabiosa. ~ dos jardins musk scabious.
escabiose s. f. (med.) scabies, itch: a skin disease produced by the itch mite Sarcoptes scabiei.
escabioso adj. (med.) scabious, itchy.
escabreação s. f. anger, fury, rage.
escabreado adj. (Braz.) 1. suspicious, skittish, timorous. 2. repentant, sorry. 3. wise.
escabrear v. 1. to irritate, tease, exasperate. 2. ~-se: a) to be angry. b) to distrust, suspect. c) to become skittish. d) (Braz.) to repent.
escabrosidade s. f. 1. roughness, harshness, scabrousness, asperity; craggedness, rockiness, abundance of prominent rocks. 2. difficulty.
escabroso adj. 1. rough, rugged, uneven, scabrous, craggy, rutted (plate Q). 2. difficult, hard, harsh. 3. unseemly.
escabujar v. to struggle (with feet and hands).
escabulhar v. 1. to peel, shell, pod, take off the hull or husk of. 2. to expurgate.
escabulho s. m. husk, hull, peel (inclosing the seeds).
escacar v. to shatter, reduce to pieces or fragments; to smash.
escachar v. 1. to cleave, part asunder. 2. to break up into pieces. 3. to slit, rent, split. 4. to spread apart, straddle. 5. (fig.): a) to squelch, reduce to silence. b) to ridicule.
escachoar v. 1. to bubble with foam (as in a waterfall). 2. to form into a waterfall.
escacholar v. to break a person's skull.
escada s. f. 1. staircase, stairs (plate E 7). 2. flight of steps. 3. ladder (plates A 7, 8, B 3, E 6). 4. (fig.) means to attain one's aim. 5. ~s pl. = **escadaria.**
~ de corda rope ladder (plate E 6). ~ de emergência escape ladder. ~ de escotilha companion-ladder. ~ de ganchos hook ladder (plate E 6). ~ de mão ladder (plate E 6). ~ de pintor painter's trestle. ~ de serviço backstairs. ~ dobradiça step-ladder (plates A 8, E 6). ~ caracol winding staircase, winding stair (plate E 7). ~ rolante moving staircase. ~ secreta private staircase. alcatifar a ~ to carpet the stairs. ele caiu pela ~ abaixo he fell downstairs. desci as ~s I went downstairs. eles subiram as ~s they went upstairs, they climbed the stairs.
escadaria s. f. (also **escadório** m.) 1. a flight of stairs. 2. a wide and fine stair (at the entrance of a church or theatre).
escádea s. f. a part of a bunch of grapes broken off.
escadear v. to make or build in the way of stairs or a ladder.
escadeirar v. 1. to knock down, beat, drub. 2. to disjoint the hip, break one's back. 3. to disembowel, cut to pieces (cattle).
escadelecer v. (pop.) to slumber, doze, nod.
escadote s. m. step-ladder, platform ladder (plate E 6).
escafandrista s. m. + f. diver (wearing a diving-dress).
escafandro s. m. diving-dress: waterproof clothing and breathing-helmet for divers working at the bottom of the sea.

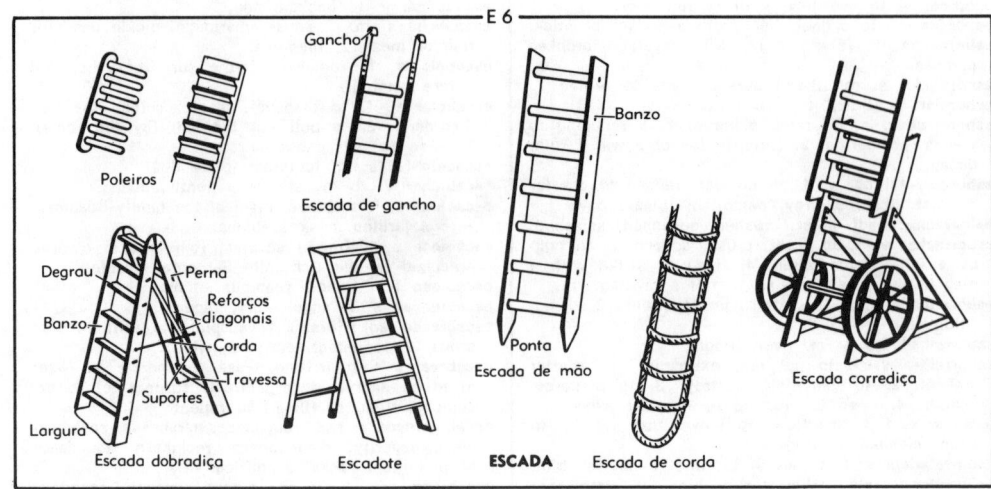

— E 6 —

Gancho

Banzo

Poleiros

Escada de gancho

Degrau — Perna

Reforços diagonais

Banzo — Corda

Travessa

Suportes

Largura

Ponta

Escada de mão

Escada corrediça

Escada dobradiça   Escadote   **ESCADA**   Escada de corda

---

escafeder-se v. (pop.) 1. to run away, take to one's heels. 2. to steal away, make o. s. scarce.

escafóide s. m. (anat.) scaphoid bone. ‖ adj. m. + f. scaphoid, boat-shaped.

escaiola s. f. scagliola.

escala s. f. 1. scale: a) a series of degrees; ladder. b) a series of marks made along a line to be used in measuring (plates B 4, M 2, 7, 9, R 3). c) proportional size of a plan, map or model. d) (mus.) a series of ascending and descending tones. 2. sea-port. 3. (aeron.) intermediate landing. ~ **cromática** chromatic scale. ~ **diatônica** diatonic scale. **desenhar em** ~ to draw to scale. **importar em larga** ~ to import to a large extent. **em grande** ~ on a large scale. **porto de** ~ port of call.

escalada s. f. (also **escalamento** m.) 1. scaling, climbing, storming with ladders. 2. (mil.) escalade.

escalador s. m. 1. scaler: person scaling or storming with ladders. 2. (mil.) escalader.

escalafobético adj. (Braz., sl.) 1. clumsy. 2. ramshackle. 3. ridiculous.

escalafrio s. m. shivering, fits of cold, chill.

escalão s. m. (pl. **-ões**) 1. step, stair. 2. (mil.) echelon: the arrangement of troops as in a series of steps.

escalar v. 1. to scale: a) storm, take by storm. b) climb by or as by a ladder. c) escalade, mount or enter by means of a ladder. d) clean and disembowel fish. 2. (fig.) to devastate. 3. to designate (persons) for a specific purpose.

escalavradura s. f., **escalavramento** m. 1. scratch or abrasion, bruise, slight wound. 2. ruin.

escalavrar v. 1. to graze or scratch the skin, bruise. 2. to make a slight wound.

escalda s. f. 1. act of scalding, burning. 2. a very sharp sauce.

escaldadela s. f. 1. = **escaldadura**. 2. lesson, costly experience. 3. reproof, scolding.

escaldadiço adj. 1. easy to be scalded. 2. (fig.) easy to be impressed or influenced.

escaldado adj. 1. scalded, burned. 2. (fig.) warned, made wise by experience.

gato ~ **da água fria tem medo** (fig.) a burnt child dreads the fire; a scalded cat dreads cold water.

escaldador s. m. scalder. ‖ adj. scalding.

escaldadura s. f., **escaldão** m. (pl. ~s, -ões) scalding, burning. 2. a slight wound. 3. a reprehension, reprimand.

escalda-pés s. m., sg. + pl. quite a hot footbath.

escaldar v. 1. to scald, burn, parch. 2. to inflame, heat. 3. (fig.) to rebuke, reprimand. 4. ~-**se**: a) to scald o. s. b) to take a warning, grow wise by experience.

escalda-rabo s. m. (pl. **escalda-rabos**) (sl.) rebuke, reprimand, reprehension.

escaldo (I) s. m. (Braz.) premature ripening of wheat.

escaldo (II) s. m. scald, skald: an ancient Scandinavian poet.

escaleira s. f. 1. staircase; ladder. 2. step (of a staircase).

escaleno adj. scalene: 1. of or pertaining to the scalene muscle. 2. (triangle) having three unequal sides. 3. (of a cone, etc.) having the axis inclined to the base.

escalenoedro s. m. scalenohedron: a hemihedral form of the hexagonal system in which the faces are scalene triangles.

escaler s. m. 1. sloop, ship, boat, gig (plate B 8). 2. cutter.

escaletas s. f. pl. (mil., naut., obs.) square cuts in the cheeks of the carriage of a piece of ordenance forming degrees.

escalete, escaleto s. m. a very thin person.

escalfador s. m. a vessel used to heat water in and keep it warm for kitchen purposes.

escalfar v. 1. to heat water (for kitchen purposes). 2. to rinse or pass through hot water (as dishes). 3. (Port.) to exhaust, overtire. ~ **ovos** to poach eggs.

escalfeta s. f. a kind of warming-pan for the feet.

escaliçar v. (also **descaliçar**) to remove pieces of dry mortar or debris.

escalinata s. f. flight of stairs.

escalonamento s. m. (aeron.) stagger, projection of the edge of an upper wing beyond that below it (plate A 3).

escalonar v. 1. to give the form of a stair to. 2. (mil.) to echelon.

escalpação s. f. (pl. **-ões**), **escalpamento** m. act of tearing or cutting the scalp (skin of the skull) from.

escalpar v. to scalp: tear the scalp (skin of the head) from.

E 7

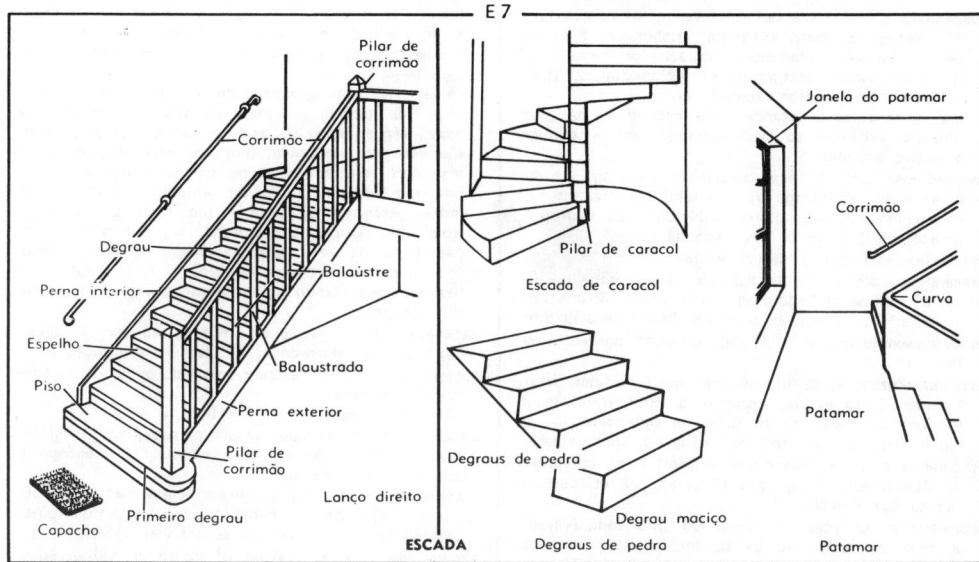

Pilar de corrimão
Corrimão
Degrau
Perna interior
Balaústre
Espelho
Balaustrada
Piso
Perna exterior
Pilar de corrimão
Primeiro degrau
Capacho
Lanço direito
ESCADA

Pilar de caracol
Escada de caracol
Degraus de pedra
Degrau maciço
Degraus de pedra

Janela do patamar
Corrimão
Curva
Patamar
Patamar

escalpelar, escalpelizar v. 1. (surg.) to open or dissect with a scalpel. 2. to analyse carefully.

escalpelo (ê) s. m. scalpel: a dissecting knife.

escalpo s. m. scalp: the skin and hair of the skull cut from a person's head.

escalrachar v. to clear of dog's grass.

escalracho s. m. (bot.) dog's grass, couch-grass.

escalrichado adj. insipid, unsalted; tasteless, savourless.

escalvação s. f. (pl. -ões) a becoming bare or bald.

escalvado adj. 1. bare: without any kind of vegetation. 2. bald: without hair.

escalvar v. 1. to make bald. 2. to bare: make barren or sterile.

escama s. f. (zool., bot., med.) scale (of or as of a fish) (plate P 7).

escamação s. f. (pl. -ões) 1. scaling (of fishes, plants, etc.). 2. anger, aversion.

escamadeira s. f. woman who scales fish.

escamado adj. scaled: having the scales removed. 2. angry, irritated, annoyed.

escamadura s. f. scaling (as of fishes).

escamar v. 1. to scale: remove the scales of (fish). 2. (fig.): a) to get angry. b) to run away.

escambador s. m. changer; exchanger.

escambar v. to change; exchange.

escambichar v. (Braz.) 1. to knock down, beat. 2. to disjoint the hip; break one's back.

escambo s. m. change; barter, trade.

escambroeiro s. m. (bot.) buckthorn (Rhamnus catharticus).

escameado adj. scaly: covered with or abounding in scales.

escamel s. m. (pl. -éis) frame or bench of a sword-cutler or furbisher.

escamiforme adj. m. + f. scalelike, scaly.

escamisar v. to remove the shirt of.

escamônea s. f. scammony: 1. a climbing plant (Convolvulus ammonea). 2. a resin extracted from this plant.

escamoso adj. (also **escamento, escamífero, escamígero**) 1. scaly: a) covered with scales. b) provided with scales. 2. squamous.

escamotar v. (also **escamotear**) 1. to pilfer, filch. 2. to perform sleight of hand tricks; to conjure. 3. to palm. 4. (aeron.) to retract. 5. ~-se to make away, make o. s. scarce.

escamoteação s. f. (pl. -ões) 1. pilfering, swiping. 2. prestidigitation, sleight of hand, legerdemain. 3. palming.

escampado s. m. desert, open field. ‖ adj. (also **escampo**) 1. unsheltered. 2. unpeopled, uninhabited. 3. open; desert (field). 4. settled, clear (weather).

escampar v. 1. to stop raining. 2. to settle (weather); to clear (the sky). 3. to escape, run away.

escâmula s. f. a little scale.

escamurrengar v. (S. Braz.) to become sad or taciturn.

escanado adj. adult, full-grown.

escanção s. m. (pl. -ões) cupbearer: person who serves wine (esp. in royal or noble households).

escançar v. (also **escancear**) 1. to serve or pour out wine. 2. to come to happen by good luck.

escâncara s. f. estate of being patent, open, public, manifest.

às ~s openly, in public.

escancarado adj. 1. wide-open (door). 2. patent, public, manifest.

escancarar v. 1. to set (a door) wide open. 2. to open; show. 3. ~-se: a) to open widely. b) to become public, manifest.

escancelar v. (Braz.) to open widely (the mouth, eyes), gape; stare.

escanchar v. 1. to spread open, widen. 2. to halve. 3. ~-se to spread one's legs, stride, straddle.

escandalizador s. m. scandalizer, scandal-monger: person who scandalizes or spreads defamatory reports concerning the character of others. ‖ adj. scandalous, defamatory, scandalizing.

escandalizar v. 1. to scandalize: offend, give offence to, defame, slander, shock. 2. to behave ill. 3. to make a scandal. 4. ~-se: a) to take offence. b) to be scandalized or offended at.

eles ficaram escandalizados com o seu procedimento they were scandalized at his (her, your) conduct.

escândalo s. m. 1. scandal: a) offence. b) opprobrium. c) shame, reproach, disgrace, dishonour. d) slander, columny; defamatory speech or report. e) (jur.) defamatory statement. f) indignation. 2. (fig.) agitation, perturbation, tumult, noise.
dar ~ to raise a scandal. **ele causou** ~ he gave offence. **evitar** ~ to avoid scandal. **um** ~ **público** a public scandal.

escandaloso adj. 1. scandalous: a) causing scandal or offense; shocking. b) shameful, disgraceful. c) defamatory. 2. pernicious, injurious. 3. improper, indecorous. || **-amente** adv. scandalously.

escândea s. f. (bot.) durum wheat.

escandescência s. f. 1. incandescence, glowing. 2. act of making or becoming incandescent. 3. passion. 4. irritation, violent anger. 5. (S. Braz.) constipation.

escandescente adj. m. + f. incandescent, aglow, glowing.

escandescer v. 1. to incandesce, make red-hot, heat, inflame. 2. to excite, provoke. 3. to irritate, make furious. 4. ~-se: a) to grow incandescent. b) to catch fire. c) to become inflamed, enthusiastic.

escandinavo s. m. Scandinavian: native or inhabitant of Scandinavia. || adj. Scandinavian: of or pertaining to Scandinavia.

escandir v. to scan: 1. mark off into feet (verse). 2. read or recite so as to indicate the metrical structure.

escanelado adj. 1. having long and slim legs. 2. thin, lean (person).

escangalhado adj. 1. out of order; broken, severed. 2. spoiled. 3. done for.

escangalhar v. 1. to break, break to pieces. 2. to disarrange, put out of order. 3. to spoil, ruin, destroy. 4. to dislocate, put out of joint. 5. ~-se: a) to become undone. b) to be disjointed.
~-se de tanto rir to die with laughing. o telefone está escangalhado the phone is out of order.

escangalho s. m. 1. retaining wall: a massive wall built to support and hold back the earth of an embankment. 2. (Braz.) confusion, disorder; tumult.

escanganhadeira s. f. a sort of screen to strip the grapes from the bunch.

escanganhar v. to strip the grapes from the bunch.

escangotar v. to seize a person by the scruff of his neck.

escanhoar(-se) v. to shave very close.

escanifrado adj. very thin or lean, meager, skinny.

escanifrar v. to cause to become thin or lean.

escaninho s. m. 1. a small partition or division within a drawer or chest; secret drawer; pigeon-hole. 2. hidden corner; lurking-hole. 3. a small footstool.

escano s. m. a footstool.

escansão s. f. (pl. -ões) scansion: act of scanning.

escanteio s. m. (ftb.) corner.

escantilhado adj. (carp.) bevel.

escantilhão s. m. (pl. -ões) gauge; pattern; standard.
de ~ falling, tumbling.

escantilhar v. (carp.) to bevel.

escanzelado adj. meager, very thin; lean.

escanzurrado adj. (S. Braz.) tired, worn-out, fatigued.

escanzurrar(-se) v. (S. Braz.) to become tired, be fatigued, worn-out.

escapada, escapadela s. f. 1. escape, evasion, flight. 2. escapade, a freak, prank.

escapadiço adj. 1. prone to run away. 2. fugitive, runaway.

escapamento s. m. 1. (mot.) exhaust. 2. escapement; escape: act of escaping.

escapar v. 1. to escape, get free, get out, run away. 2. to flee, bolt. 3. to avoid, slip (danger). 4. to fall. 5. to omit. 6. to forget. 7. to let fall or drop. 8. to survive, be saved, rescued. 9. ~-se: a) to run away. b) to escape from, free from. c) to free o. s.
deixei ~ **uma oportunidade** I let an opportunity slip. **ela deixou** ~ **uma palavra** she dropped a word. **ele escapou de boa** he had a narrow escape. **ele escapou por pouco (por um triz)** he just saved his skin. **ele me escapou** he gave me the slip. **isto me escapou** it is an omission of myself. o **ladrão escapou da polícia** the thief broke loose from the police. **escapou-me da memória** it escaped my memory. **nada lhe escapa** nothing escapes him. **nem sequer um escapou** not a single one has escaped. **tenho de** ~ **deste perigo** I must fly this danger.

escaparate s. m. 1. glass bell, glass jar. 2. glass cupboard. 3. show-case. 4. (fam.) subterfuge.

escapatória s. f. 1. excuse, pretext, evasion. 2. subterfuge, escape.
não tem ~ there is no loophole.

escape s. m. 1. escape: a) act of escaping. b) flight, evasion. c) leakage (gas, water). 2. = escapo. || adj. m. + f. = escapo.
corrente de ~ leakage current. **curva de** ~ exhaust curve. **tubo de** ~ exhaust pipe, eduction pipe. **válvula de** ~ escape valve, exhaust valve.

escapelada s. f. a husking of maize or Indian corn.

escapelar v. 1. to strip the husks from maize or Indian corn. 2. to strip of (leaves).

escapismo s. m. escapism.

escapo s. m. 1. escapement (of a clock, watch or typewriter). 2. escape. || adj. safe, sure, free.

escápole adj. m. + f. exempt, free from (obligations).

escapula s. f. = escapadela.

escápula s. f. 1. a hook. 2. support, stay. 3. scapula, blade-bone.

escapulal (pl. -ais), **escapular** (pl. ~es) adj. m. + f. scapular, of or pertaining to the shoulders or the shoulder-blade.

escapulário s. m. scapular: 1. (R. C. Church) a long narrow strip of cloth hanging from the shoulders, worn by certain religious orders. 2. two small pieces of cloth worn over the shoulder by Roman Catholics as a mark of religious devotion.

escapulida s. f. flight, escape, runaway.

escapulir(-se) v. 1. to slip out of the hand. 2. to steal away. 3. to slip or run away. 4. to escape, disappear.

escaquear v. to divide into squares like a chessboard.

escaqueirar v. to break into pieces, shatter.

escaques s. m. pl. 1. squares of a chessboard. 2. (her.) a division into squares of alternate colours.

escara s. f. (med.) scab of an ulcer or sore.

escarabeu s. m. beetle.

escarabídeo s. m. a scarab, beetle. || adj. of or pertaining to the Scarabaeidae.

escarabocho s. m. scrawl, an awkward writing or drawing.

escarafunchar v. 1. to scratch, pick, rake, scrape. 2. to inquire about, poke one's nose into, hunt up. 3. to investigate, examine; smell out, ferret out; rummage.

escarambar-se v. to overdry and open into cracks (earth).

escaramuça s. f. (also **escaramuceada** f., **escaramuceio** m.) 1. skirmish: a petty fight. 2. contest, debate, dispute, quarrel. 3. disorder. 4. threat, menace.

escaramuçador s. m. skirmisher, bickerer. || adj. bickering.

escaramuçar v. 1. to skirmish, bicker, fight. 2. to frighten away.

escarapela s. f. a fray or brawl in which the contenders cuff and scratch one another.

escarapelar v. 1. to scratch, cuff. 2. ~-se: a) to scratch one another. b) to fight and fall pulling a person's ears.

escaravelhar v. to move like a beetle.

escaravelho s. m. (ent.) beetle, scarab, tumblebug. ~ aquático aquatic beetle. ~ bosteiro black-beetle. ~ dos estercos dung-beetle.

escarça s. f. a wound in a horse's hoof.

escarçar v. 1. to take wax or honeycombs from a beehive. 2. to fray (cloth).

escarcavelar v. (pop.) 1. to break open. 2. to disjoint, disarrange.

escarcear v. 1. to make a great fuss (about nothing). 2. to storm, rage.

escarcela s. f. 1. a large leather purse (as a birding pouch). 2. tasses: the armour from the waist to the thighs.

escarcéu s. m. 1. a huge wave, billow. 2. (fig.): a) clamour, ado, uproar, tumult, riot. b) exaggeration, excess.

fazer grandes ~s to make great fuss about nothing.

escarcha s. f. 1. hoar-frost, rime. 2. a sort of gold or silver embroidery; tinsel. 3. rough or rugged thing.

escarchado adj. covered with hoar-frost.

escarchar v. 1. to make rough; to crisp. 2. to frost, cover with hoar-frost or rime.

escarço s. m. act of taking wax or honeycombs from a beehive.

escardado s. m. a frayed horn (from bumping against hard obstacles).

escardear v. 1. to clear of thistles, to weed, hoe. 2. to clean. 3. to graze (excoriate in passing). 4. to scatter (shot).

escardilhar v. to weed, hoe.

escardilho s. m. weedhook, hoe.

escarduçador s. m. wool carder, wool comber. ‖ adj. wool-carding, wool-combing.

escarduçar v. to card or comb wool.

escareador s. m. 1. reamer: an instrument or tool used in reaming. 2. countersink bit (plate M 4).

escarear v. 1. to ream: widen or enlarge a hole. 2. to countersink.

escarificação s. f. (pl. -ões) scarification: act of scarifying.

escarificador s. m. 1. (surg.) scarificator: instrument for making simultaneously several superficial incisions. 2. (agric.) scarifier; implement for stirring the soil.

escarificar v. to scarify: 1. (surg.) scratch or make superficial incisions in. 2. (agric.) to stir (soil).

escarioso adj. scarious: 1. (bot.) membranous and dry (as bracts). 2. (zool.) scaly; scurfy.

escarlate s. m. (also **escarlata** f.) scarlet: 1. a brilliant red colour. 2. scarlet dye. 3. cloth of scarlet colour. ‖ adj. scarlet, bright red.

escarlatim s. m. (pl. -ins) a sort of scarlet cloth of inferior quality.

escarlatina s. f. (med.) scarlatina, scarlet fever.

escarmentado adj. 1. warned, punished. 2. made wise by costly experience. 3. disillusioned.

escarmentar v. 1. to reprehend, reprove, punish severely. 2. (also ~-se) to make or become wise by experience, to get one's object-lesson.

escarmento s. m. 1. warning taken by punishment or experience. 2. reprimand, rebuke, punishment. 3. a warning example, object-lesson. 4. disillusionment.

escarna, escarnação (pl. -ões) s. f. 1. a picking of the flesh from the bones. 2. lancing of gums by a dentist.

escarnador s. m. 1. fleam, lancet. 2. instrument used by dentists to lance gums.

escarnar v. 1. (surg.) to separate the flesh from the bones. 2. (dent.) to lance gums. 3. to scrape hides before tanning. 4. (fig.) to investigate, examine.

escarnecedor s. m. jester, mocker, derider, flouter, scoffer. ‖ adj. jeering, mocking, derisive, flouting.

escarnecer v. 1. to mock, laugh at, deride, jeer, scoff, gibe, ridicule, make fun of. 2. to illude, cheat.

escarnecido adj. (also **escarnido**) 1. mocked, offended. 2. illuded, taken in.

escarnecível adj. m. + f. (pl. -íveis) 1. execrable. 2. ridiculous.

escarnicação s. f. (pl. -ões) act or fact of ridiculing.

escarnicar v. to crack jokes, make fun of, play the joker.

escarnificação s. f. (pl. -ões) laceration, martyrization, torture.

escarnificar v. to lacerate the flesh, to torture, martyr.

escarninho adj. sneering, fleering, flouting.

escárnio s. m. (also **escarnecimento**) 1. mockery, derision, scoffing, scorn, contempt, laugh. 2. joke, raillery.

ele foi o alvo do seu ~ he was their scorn. **de ~** scornfully.

escarnir v. = **escarnecer**.

escaro s. m. scar, parrot fish. ‖ adj. (Port.) ill-tempered, intractable, rude.

escarola s. f. endive: a variety of chicory (Cichorium endivia) much cultived for use in salads.

escarolado adj. 1. said of the corn removed from its cob. 2. clear, trimmed up. 3. (pop.) shameless, impudent; malicious.

escarolador s. m. shelling machine (for corn).

escarolar v. 1. to clear the corn (removing it from its cob). 2. to grow bald. 3. to clear, clean. 4. ~-se to take off one's hat.

escarótico s. m. (med.) escharotic, caustic. ‖ adj. escharotic, caustic.

escarpa s. f. 1. scarp, escarpment, slope, acclivity (plates C 19, M 11). 2. talus.

escarpado adj. sloped, steep, sheer.

escarpadura s. f. **escarpamento** m. slope, talus, cliff, escarpment.

escarpar v. to slope, scarp, cut steep down.

escarpelar v. 1. to strip a plant of leaves. 2. to shuck (corn). 3. to scratch with the nails.

escarpes s. m. pl. (hist.) iron shoes (as instruments of torture).

escarpetear v. (S. Braz.) = **escrapetear**.

escarpim s. m. (pl. -ins) a shoe with a very thin sole; pump (plates B 16, R 6).

escarradeira s. f. spitton, cuspidor (plate D 1).

escarrado adj. 1. spit; expectorated. 2. (fig.) similar, like.

escarrador s. m. 1. spitter. 2. spittoon.

escarradura s. f. 1. spitting. 2. spittle, ejected saliva.

escarranchado adj. astraddle, astride.

escarranchar(-se) v. 1. to open, spread the legs (as sitting on a·horse). 2. to sit astraddle.

escarrapachar(-se) v. 1. to straddle the legs. 2. (fig.) to fall flat on the ground, fall sprawling.

escarrapiçar, escarrapichar v. 1. to untangle, explain, unriddle. 2. to comb.

escarrar v. to spit (out), expectorate. ~ **sangue** to spit blood.

escarro s. m. 1. spittle, saliva, spawl, mucus. 2. (pop.) despicable person.

escarva s. f. (carp.) scarf: a joint by which the ends of two pieces of timber are united so as to form a continuous piece.

escarvador s. m. instrument for scarfing. ‖ adj. scarfing.

escarvar v. 1. (carp.) to scarf. 2. to scrape or rake up the ground. 3. to corrode. 4. to paw, beat with the forefoot (horse).

escarvoar v. to sketch, crayon, draw with crayon.

escascar v. to peel, pare; shell.

escasquear v. 1. to clean (up), tidy (up). 2. (also ~-se) to wash (o. s.). 3. (fig.) to play the dandy.

escassear v. 1. to give (something) niggardly; to scrimb, pinch. 2. to be scanty of. 3. to make or become scarce. 4. to fail, grow less, wane. 5. to diminish, slacken, abate, cease.

escassez s. f. scarcity, scarceness: 1. state or condition of being scarce. 2. dearth, want, lack; famine. 3. sparingness, parsimony, niggardliness. 4. scantiness. 5. need, privation.

escassilho s. m. a little piece.

escasso adj. scarce: 1. sparing, niggardly, stingy. 2. scant(y), not abundant. 3. insufficient, deficient. 4. rare, uncommon, infrequent. ‖ -amente adv. scarcely, sparingly, scantily.

meios ~ narrow means. meu tempo é muito ~ I have many claims on my time. uma colheita -a a thin crop.

escatel s. m. (pl. escatéis) hole for a forelock; keyway; mortise slot.

escatelar v. to forelock, secure by a forelock; to slot; mortise.

escatima s. f. (obs.) 1. fault, defect. 2. lack, shortage. 3. fraud, deceit.

escatimar v. 1. to give (something) niggardly. 2. to defraud, cheat. 3. to viciate, taint. 4. to ill-treat.

escatófago adj. scatophagous: feeding on excrements, as a dung-fly.

escatófilo adj. coprophylous.

escatologia s. f. 1. scatology: the science or study of fossil excrement. 2. (theol.) eschatology: the study of the end of the world and man's condition or state after death.

escatológico adj. 1. of or pertaining to scatology. 2. (theol.) eschatologic(al): of or pertaining to eschatology.

escavação s. f. (N. Braz., also escavacação) (pl. -ões) 1. excavation: a) act of excavating. b) digging up. c) digging out (esp. for archaelogical research). d) cutting (as for a road, railway or canal). 2. (fig.) investigation.

escavacar v. 1. to break into pieces, shatter. 2. to ruin, destroy, demolish. 3. = escavar.

escavador s. m. 1. excavator: one who or that which excavates. 2. (fig.) investigator. ‖ adj. excavatory.

escavadora, escavadeira s. f. excavator, digging machine, digger, grab (plate D 2).

escavar v. 1. to excavate: a) hollow, scoop. b) dig away or out (esp. for archaeological research). c) cut (as for a road, railway). 2. (fig.) to investigate.

escaveirado adj. 1. cadaverous: a) like a cadaver. b) pale and ghastly. c) thin, lean. 2. emaciated.

escaveirar v. 1. to make very lean or thin. 2. to become like a skeleton.

escindir v. 1. to rescind, cancel. 2. to cut, separate; tear. 3. to divert, turn aside.

escirpo s. m. (bot.) club-rush.

esclarecer v. 1. to clear, enlighten, brighten, give light to. 2. to clarify, illumine, elucidate, explain. 3. to make famous. 4. to render illustrious. 5. to dawn, grow light. 6. ~-se to instruct o. s., be informed.

~ **alguma coisa** to shed light upon something. **esclarecemos o caso** we cleared up the matter, got it right. **isto esclarece tudo** that accounts for everything.

esclarecido adj. 1. clear; cleared up. 2. apparent, evident. 3. illustrious, renowned, enlightened.

esclarecimento s. m. 1. clearing up, explanation, elucidation. 2. light, clearness, brightness; enlightenment. 3. renown, reputation.

ele sempre pede ~s he always asks for explanations. para o ~ de in exemplification of. prestei ~ I gave information.

esclareia s. f. clary: a labiate plant (Salvia sclarea).

esclavina s. f. a sort of mantle worn by pilgrims.

esclavônio s. m. (also esclavão, pl. -ões) Slavonian: native or inhabitant of Slavonia. ‖ adj. Slavonian; of or pertaining to Slavonia.

escleral adj. m. + f. (pl. -ais) 1. sclerous, hard, firm, indurated. 2. fibrous.

esclerênquima s. m. sclerenchyma: the tissue forming the hard parts of plants.

esclerodermia s. f. (med.) sclerodermia: a chronic induration of the skin.

escleroma s. m. (med.) scleroma: hardening of cellular tissue.

esclerosar v. (med.) to indurate, form a sclerosis.

esclerose s. f. (med.) sclerosis: hardening or induration of a tissue.

esclerótica s. f. (anat.) sclerotic: the white membrane forming the outer coat of the eye (plate O).

esclusa s. f. lock: an enclosure in a canal for raising and lowering vessels by introduction of water; canal lock.

escoadouro s. m. (also escoadoiro) canal, sewer, gutter, sink, drain (plate L 3).

escoadura s. f. 1. drain pipe, outlet. 2. = escoamento. 3. lees, dregs (of casks).

escoamento s. m. 1. flowing off, drainage, flowage. 2. discharge, outlet.

~ **das águas da enchente** the flowoff of the inundation. ~ **de aparas** (tech.) flow of chips. ~ **do material** (tech.) flowing of the material.

escoar(-se) v. 1. to flow off, drain, empty. 2. to decant. 3. to filter, filtrate. 4. to guide away, slip away. 5. to leak, trickle. 6. to make a passage for water. 7. to fade away; run away. 8. (com.) to market.

escocês s. m. Scotch(man): native or inhabitant of Scotland. ‖ adj. Scotch, Scottish: of or pertaining to Scotland or its inhabitants.

escocesa s. f. 1. Scotchwoman. 2. a Scottish dance.

escócia s. f. (archit.) scotia: a concave molding in the base of a column.

escoda s. f. bushhammer, patent hammer, patent ax: hammer used for dressing stones (plate M 6).

escodar v. 1. to smooth or polish stones. 2. to prepare or dress skins.

escodear v. 1. to cut away the crust of bread. 2. (fig.) to peel.

escoicear v. (also escoucear, encoicinhar) 1. to kick (horse). 2. (fig.): a) to affront, insult, injure. b) to maltreat, mistreat.

escoimar v. 1. to free from a fine. 2. to purify, free from impurities. 3. ~-se to avoid, escape, get away.

escol s. m. (pl. -óis) elite, the choice, prime, pick, plower, cream, the best part (of a group or society).

escola s. f. 1. school. 2. schoolhouse (plate A 4). 3. method of teaching. 4. (fig.) experience; example. 5. education.

~ **de comércio** commercial school. ~ **de dança** dancing-school. ~ **de equitação** riding-school. ~ **de**

esgrima fencing school. ~ **de mineralogia** school of mines. ~ **dominical** Sunday school. ~ **elementar** elementary school. ~ **naval** naval college. ~ **noturna** night-school. ~ **preparatória** preparatory school. ~ **pré-primária** preschool. ~ **primária** elementary school. ~ **secundária** high school. ~ **superior de medicina veterinária** veterinary college. ~ **técnica** technical school. **colega de** ~ schoolfellow. **festa de** ~ school-treat. **ir à** ~ to go to school. **jornal de** ~ school magazine. **mensalidade de** ~ school fee. **navio-**~ training-ship. **tempo de** ~ school days.

escolado adj. 1. smart, cunning. 2. tested, trained. 3. wise. **ele é muito** ~ he is very artful, (coll.) he is a deep one.

escolar s. m. + f. scholar, student, schoolboy, schoolgirl. ‖ adj. scholastic: of or pertaining to school. **idade** ~ school age. **livro** ~ school-book. **material** ~ educational material.

escolaridade s. f. education, school apprenticeship.

escolarização s. f. act or effect of schooling.

escolarizar v. to submit to education in a school.

escolástica s. f., **escolasticismo** m. scholasticism: the Aristotelean teaching of medieval schools.

escolástico s. m. scholastic: 1. a student or studious person, a scholar. 2. schoolman. ‖ adj. scholastic: 1. of or pertaining to schools or scholars. 2. pertaining to or characteristic by scholasticism. ‖ **escolasticamente** adv. scholastically.

escólex, escolece s. m. (zool.) scolex.

escolha s. f. (also **escolhimento** m.) 1. choice, election, selection, option. 2. prime, elite, flower. 3. preference. 4. (Braz.) a cereal of inferior quality. **deixo à sua** ~ I let you make your choice. **na** ~ **de um livro** in the choice of a book.

escolher v. 1. to choose, make a choice of, pick out, select. 2. to elect. ~ **a dedo** to pick and choose. ~ **entre** to choose between. **de dois males, escolha o menor** of two evils, choose the lesser. **ela escolheu cuidadosamente o seu caminho por entre as poças d'água** she picked her way through the puddles. **ele não escolhe suas palavras!** he does not mince matters, he is not very mealy-mouthed. **ele escolheu outra profissão** he made choice of another profession. **eles escolheram-no seu chefe** they elected him their chief, boss. **escolhi a ocasião propícia** I chose the proper time. **escolhi-o como amigo** I chose him as my friend. **a mulher que escolhi** the woman of my choice. **quem pede não escolhe** beggars cannot be choosers.

escolhido s. m. person or thing chosen, the elect, faithful. ‖ adj. chosen, elected, choice; first-rate.

escolho s. m. 1. rock, cliff, shelf, reef. 2. (fig.) obstacle; danger.

escoliar v. to make scholia; write commentaries.

escoliasta s. m. + f. (also **escoliador** m.) scholiast: 1. person who makes scholia. 2. a commentator.

escólio s. m. scholium: 1. a commentary, annotation, remark. 2. explanatory comment or remark on Greek and Latin authors by an early grammarian.

escolmar v. to unthatch.

escolopendra s. f. (ent.) scolopendra, streaked centiped.

escolta s. f. (mil.) guard, convoy, escort.

escoltar v. to escort, convoy; conduct, accompany.

escombrídeo s. m. a scombroid fish. ‖ adj. (ichth.) scombroid: of or pertaining to the Scombroidea.

escombro s. m. 1. rubbish, rubble. 2. ~**s** pl. debris, ruins.

escomunal adj. m. + f. (pl. **-ais**) 1. uncommon. 2. immeasurable, prodigious.

escondedor s. m. 1. hider: person who hides or conceals. 2. receiver of stolen goods.

escondedura s. f. hiding, concealment.

esconde-esconde s. m. hide-and-seek: a children's game.

esconder v. 1. to hide: a) put, keep or retain out of sight. b) occult, conceal, secret, veil. c) cover up. d) keep secret. e) disguise, dissimulate, dissemble. 2. ~**-se:** a) to steal away from. b) to hide or disguise o. s. c) to skulk, abscond. **ela escondeu-se atrás da árvore** she hid behind the tree. **ele se esconde** he hides himself, keeps himself close. **escondi a minha mágoa** I concealed my grief, pocketed my sorrow. **jogo de** ~ hide-and-seek, hide and coop. **nós escondemo-lo dele** we hid it from him.

esconderijo s. m. (also **escondedouro, escondedoiro**) hiding-place, hiding corner, lurking-place, lurking-hole, coverture.

escondidas s. f. pl. 1. (also **jogos das escondidas**) hide-and-seek: a children's game. 2. word used in the adverbial locution: **às escondidas** secretly, covertly, in secret, furtively, clandestinely. **sair às** ~ to steal away.

escondido s. m. (Braz., also **grunado, itararé, sumidouro**) sinkhole. ‖ adj. hidden, concealed, occult, secret. **a casa está -a** the house is out of sight, tucked away. **ele vive** ~ he is living in concealment, he is in a cloud.

escondimento s. m. hiding, concealment.

esconjurar v. 1. to exorcize, adjure by some holy name, lay evil spirits. 2. to conjure, supplicate, entreat. 3. ~**-se** to complain.

esconjurativo adj. having the power to exorcize.

esconjuro s. m. (also **esconjuração** f.; pl. **-ões**) 1. exorcism. 2. conjuration.

esconsas s. f. pl. used only in the adverbial phrase **às** ~ secretly, clandestinely.

esconso s. m. 1. hiding-place. 2. angle, corner; nook. ‖ adj. inclined, slanting, sloping. **abóbada -a** half-barrel vault.

escopa s. f. (Braz.) a sort of card game.

escopeta s. f. (formerly) a short rifle or carbine.

escopetear v. (obs.) to shoot with a rifle.

escopeteiro s. m. (obs.) rifleman, soldier armed with a carbine. ‖ adj. (N. Braz.): 1. good at shooting (soldier). 2. able, adroit, dexterous.

escopo s. m. 1. mark, target. 2. aim, end, design, goal, purpose.

escopro s. m. chisel: an edged tool for cutting wood, iron or stone (plates E 9, F 2, M 6).

escora s. f. 1. prop, stay, shore, brace (plate A 8). 2. (fig.) support, aid, help, protection.

escoramento s. m. staying, timbering, propping.

escorar v. 1. to prop, stay, brace, support, uphold, sustain, underpin. 2. to make firm. 3. to resist. 4. (Braz.): a) to ambush. b) to meet face to face. 5. ~**-se:** a) to seek shelter. b) to lean upon. c) to base o. s. on, rely upon. ~ **um navio** to prop a ship.

escorbútico adj. (med.) scorbutic: 1. pertaining to or of the nature of scurvy. 2. suffering from scurvy.

escorbuto s. m. (med.) scurvy: a disease due to deficiency of vitamin C.

escorçar v. (paint.) to shorten, foreshorten, represent foreshortened.

escorchado adj. 1. flayed, excoriated. 2. peeled. 3. dispoiled, robbed.

escorchador s. m. 1. flayer. 2. person who peels or barks. ‖ adj. 1. flaying; robbing. 2. that which peels.

escorchar v. 1. to flay, skin, excoriate. 2. to bark, peel, strip. 3. to scratch. 4. to wound, injure.

5. to despoil, fleece, rob. 6. to scorch (beehive). ~ o povo to overtax the people.

escorcioneira s. f. (bot.) 1. viper's-grass. 2. Scorzonera: a genus of composite plants.

escorço (ô) s. m. 1. (paint.) foreshortening: the representation of a figure in such a manner as to convey to the mind the impression of its just lenght. 2. summary.

escordar v. 1. to awake, rouse from sleep. 2. (also ~-se) to remember.

escórdio s. m. (bot.) scordium, water germander (Teucrium scordium).

escore s. m. score: record of points made in a game. o ~ foi de 2 a 1 a nosso favor the score was 2 to 1 in our favour.

escória s. f. 1. scoria, dross, slag, recrement of metal. 2. dregs. 3. scum, refuse. 4. (fig.) mob, rabble. ~ social the dregs of society.

escoriação s. f. (pl. -ões) 1. excoriation, scratch or abrasion of the skin. 2. a light wound.

escoriar v. 1. to excoriate, strip off the skin, to flay. 2. ~-se to scratch, hurt o. s. 3. to purify, cleanse; remove the scoria from.

escorificar v. to scorify; purify, cleanse.

escorificatório s. m. scorifier (metals). ‖ adj. scorifying, purifying.

escorjar v. 1. to distort, contort. 2. to twist. 3. to constrain, restrain. 4. ~-se to writhe (in pain).

escornado adj. 1. punched or gored with a horn. 2. driven out or away; expulsed. 3. (Braz., sl.) dog-tired.

escornar, escornear, escornichar v. 1. (also ~-se) to wound, punch or gore with the horns. 2. (fig.) to ill-treat, treat with contempt. 3. to debase, vilify. 4. to drive out or away.

escoroar v. to uncrown, dethrone.

escorpião s. m. (pl. -ões) (ent.) scorpion: a venomous arachnid of the order Scorpionida. ~-d'água a predaceous water bug (family Belostomatidae).

Escorpião s. m. Scorpio, Scorpion: 1. (astr.) a zodiacal constellation. 2. the eighth sign of the zodiac.

escorpióide adj. m. + f. scorpioid: resembling the tail of a scorpion.

escorpionídeo s. m. (ent.) one of the order Scorpionida. ‖ adj. scorpioid: belonging to the Scorpionida.

escorraçar v. 1. to put to flight, drive away, banish, expulse. 2. (Braz.) to reject, refuse.

escorralhas s. f. pl., **escorralho** m. 1. remains of liquids (as wine) in a vessel; dregs. 2. residue. 3. (fig.) mob, the masses.

escorregadela s. f. (also **escorregadura** f., **escorregamento, escorregão, escorrego** m.) 1. slipping, sliding. 2. a slip, false step. 3. fault, error, mistake.

escorregadiço, escorregadio adj. m. (also **escorregável** m. + f.; pl. -áveis) 1. slipping, that slips easily. 2. slippery, lubricous.

escorregador adj. 1. slipping, sliding, slippery. 2. untruthful, lying, mendacious.

escorregadouro s. m. slippery place.

escorregar v. 1. to slide, slip, skid, glide, miss one's step (or footing). 2. (fig.) to err, fall into error, commit a sin. 3. (Braz.) to exaggerate; lie. 4. to incur.

escorreito adj. sound, healthy; sane, able-bodied.

escorrência s. f. 1. quality of that which streams or runs like water; fluency. 2. ease in trickling. 3. that which flows or streams.

escorrer v. 1. to let flow off, empty. 2. to drain. 3. to drop, trickle, drip, dribble. 4. to run or flow out, to stream.

ele escorria em suor he ran with sweat, he was dripping with sweat.

escorrido adj. drained, emptied; exhausted.

escorrimento s. m. 1. flowing, running out. 2. dropping or dripping out, oozing. 3. (Braz.) process of separation of butter from milk.

escorropichadela s. f. 1. draining. 2. drinking up to the last drop.

escorropicha-galhetas s. m., sg. + pl. (pop.) sacristan, sexton.

escorropichar v. 1. to drain; empty, not to leave a drop. 2. to drink up to the last drop.

escorva s. f. 1. (obs.) fire-pan of a gun. 2. primer of a firearm.

escorvar v. 1. to prime a gun. 2. (fig.) prepare, make ready.

escota s. f. (naut.) sheet: a rope that controls the angle at which a sail is set in relation to the wind. ~ do traquete (naut.) foresheet. punho de ~ (naut.) clew of a sheet.

escote s. m. share, contribution, quota, part.

escoteirismo s. m. (also **escotismo**; (Port.) **escutismo**) an organization founded by Lord Baden-Powell for training and disciplining Boy Scouts.

escoteiro s. m. 1. person who travels without baggage. 2. a Boy Scout; a scout. ‖ adj. 1. traveling without baggage. 2. (Braz., obs.) alone; unrestrained.

escotilha s. f. (naut.) hatchway. ~ de proa forehatchway. ~ de popa afterhatchway, stern hatchway (plate L 2).

escotilhão s. m. (pl. -ões) (naut.) scuttle, small hatchway.

escotoma s. m. (med.) scotoma: a dark spot in the visual field.

escova (ô) s. f. 1. brush (plates C 12, E 8). 2. (fig.) a bore. 3. (electr.) brush (of a generator). ~ de aço, ~ de arame wire brush (plates E 8, P 12). ~ de cabelo hairbrush. ~ de calçados shoe-brush. ~ de chapéu hatbrush ~ de dentes toothbrush. ~ de mesa crumb-brush. ~ de roupa clothesbrush.

escova-botas s. m. + f., sg. + pl. servile flatterer, bootlicker.

escovadeira s. f. a coarse brush.

escovadela s. f. (also **escova, escovação**) 1. brushing. 2. (fig.) punishment, castigation; reprehension, rebuke.

escovador s. m. 1. brusher person who brushes. 2. a machine for cleaning wheat. ‖ adj. brushing.

escovão s. m. 1. big brush. 2. floor polisher: a heavy, long-handled brush.

escovar v. 1. to brush. 2. (fig.) to reprehend; give a scolding to. escove o meu chapéu brush my hat. eu escovo meu cabelo I brush my hair. escovo os dentes todos os dias I brush my teeth every day.

escoveiro s. m. 1. a dealer in brushes. 2. box or the like to keep brushes in.

escovém s. m. (pl. -éns) (naut.) hawse(-hole).

escovilha s. f. 1. act of cleaning or purifying gold or silver. 2. a goldsmith's sweepings.

escovilhão s. m. (pl. -ões) (mil.) sponge: a kind of mop for cleaning a cannonbore after a discharge.

escovilhar v. to clear gold or silver.

escovinha s. f. 1. a little brush. 2. (Braz., fam.) toothbrush. 3. (bot.) bluebottle, cornflower. cabelo à ~ a la brosse, crew-cut (hair) (plate P 8).

escrachado adj. (Braz., sl.) 1. booked in a police register. 2. clear, open, obvious. 3. wicked, depraved (person). 4. slovenly (dress, person).

escrachar v. (Braz., sl.) 1. to photograph and book s. o. in a police register. 2. to unmask s. o.,

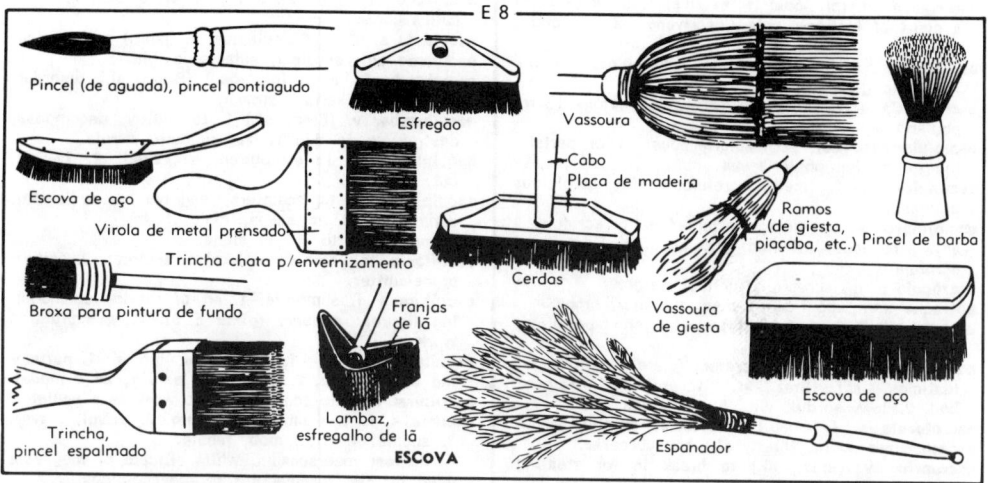

E 8

Pincel (de aguada), pincel pontiagudo

Esfregão

Vassoura

Escova de aço

Virola de metal prensado

Cabo
Placa de madeira

Ramos
(de giesta,
piaçaba, etc.) Pincel de barba

Trincha chata p/envernizamento

Cerdas

Broxa para pintura de fundo

Franjas
de lã

Vassoura
de giesta

Trincha,
pincel espalmado

Lambaz,
esfregalho de lã

Escova de aço

Espanador

ESCOVA

exposing his hidden intentions. 3. to shatter, ridicule s. o.

escrachetar v. to break, destroy, demolish.

escrapetear v. 1. to curvet, prance, run away (horse). 2. to stamp one's foot (with rage).

escravaria s. f. a great number of slaves.

escravatura s. f. 1. slave-trade. 2. slavery.

escravidão s. f. (pl. **-ões**) slavery: 1. the condition of a slave. 2. bondage, servitude. 3. the practice of keeping human beings in a state of servitude; enslavement.

escravismo s. m. proslaver system, proslavery.

escravista s. m. + f. proslaver: a proslavery advocate. ‖ adj. 1. slavish: of, pertaining to or characteristic of slaves. 2. proslavery, favouring slavery.

escravizar v. to enslave: 1. make a slave of. 2. reduce to slavery. 3. (fig.) **~-se** be enslaved.

escravo s. m. slave, bond-servant, serf. ‖ adj. 1. slave; slavish, bond. 2. captive. 3. (fig.) enamoured, infatuated.
-a branca white slave. **~ do trabalho** drudge(r). **~ negro** black ivory, Negro slave. **ela é -a de sua casa** she is a prisoner to her house. **hoje trabalhei como um ~** today I worked like a slave. **mercado de ~s** slave-trade. **nascido como ~** slave-born. **traficante de ~s** slave-trader.

escravocrata s. m. + f. slavocrat, proslaver: a proslavery advocate. ‖ adj. proslavery, favouring slavery.

escrete s. m. (ftb.) scratch team.

escrevedor s. m. 1. writer: person who writes. 2. = **escrevinhador**.

escrevedura s. f. (fam.) writing.

escrevente s. m. + f. clerk, copyist, scribe, notary; an official or public writer.

escrever v. 1. to write. 2. to write or send a letter to. 3. **~-se** to sign up, enlist s. o.
~ a lápis to pencil, write with a pencil. **~ a limpo** to copy out. **~ depressa** to write off. **~ mal** to miswrite. **~ para um jornal** to write for a newspaper, contribute to a newspaper. **~ por extenso** to write out, write down in full. **como se escreve isto?** how do you spell this? **ela escreve claramente** she writes plain. **ela lhe escreveu uma carta** she wrote a letter to him. **ele escreve seu nome com "e"** he spells his name with an "e". **ele escreve perguntando se...** he writes to ask if...

escreverei pedindo o livro I shall write for the book. **máquina de ~** typewriter. **não saber ~ corretamente** not to spell correctly. **você sabe ~ à máquina?** can you typewrite?

escrevinhador s. m. (also **escrevinhadeiro**) scrawler, scribbler, petty author, writer of no reputation.

escrevinhadura s. f. act of writing badly; scribbling.

escrevinhar v. to scrawl, scribble, write badly.

escriba s. m. scribe: 1. (hist.) a teacher of the Jewish law. 2. a writer, penman. 3. a copyist. 4. (pop.) scribbler, petty author.

escrínio s. m. 1. chest, safe. 2. a small closet. 3. writing-desk.

escrita s. f. 1. writing. 2. handwriting: the style of writing. 3. book-keeping, accounting.
~ comum long-hand: **erro de ~** error in writing, slip of the pen.

escritinho adv. (Braz., fam.) exactly like, just like.

escrito s. m. 1. a writing; a work. 2. literary composition. ‖ adj. written; described.
~ à máquina typewritten. **acusação -a** bill of indictment. **contrato por ~** contract in writing. **decifrei uma carta mal -a** I deciphered a badly written letter. **ele o fez por ~** he put it in writing. **ele responde por ~** he writes back. **narração por ~** write-up. **por ~** by letter. **prova -a** written test.

escritor s. m. writer, author, literary man.

escritório s. m. office, counting-house, scriptorium; bureau.
~ central head office. **~ da obra** (constr.) site office (plate A 7).

escritura s. f. 1. deed, legal document, writ. 2. conveyance, transfer of ownership. 3. contract. 4. writing.
passar a ~ de uma casa to write up the document of conveyance of a house. **a Sagrada Escritura** the Holy Writ; the Bible.

escrituração s. f. (pl. **-ões**) 1. book-keeping, entry, accounting. 2. contract.

escriturar v. 1. to enter into a book, keep books, keep account. 2. to make a deed.

escriturário s. m. 1. clerk of a counting-house; book-keeper. 2. scribe, clerk.

escrivania s. f. the business of a clerk or notary; clerkdom.

escrivaninha s. f. desk, writing-desk, writing-table (plate E 2).

escrivão s. m. (pl. -ões) (f. **escrivã**) 1. clerk (esp. in a court of justice); notary, scrivener. 2. secretary, copyist.

escrófula s. f. (med.) scrofula: tuberculosis of the lymphatic glands.

escrofulária s. f. (bot.) figwort, water betony (Scrophularia aquatica).

escrofuláceo adj. scrophulariaceous: of or pertaining to the Scrophulariaceae.

escrofulose s. f. (med.) scrofulosis: the scrofulous diathesis.

escrofuloso s. m. person affected with scrofula. ‖ adj. scrofulous: affected with or of the nature of scrofula.

escrópulo s. m. scruple: a unit of weight.

escroque s. m. confidence man, swindler, crook.

escrotal adj. m. + f. (pl. -ais) scrotal: of or pertaining to the scrotum.

escroto s. m. 1. (anat.) scrotum (plate C 12). 2. ~s testicles. ‖ adj. (Braz., sl.): 1. ordinary, mediocre, bad. 2. low, sordid, vile. 3. ill-formed.

escrotocele s. f. (med.) scrotocele, scrotal hernia.

escrunchante s. m. (Braz., sl.) housebreaker.

escrunchar v. (Braz., sl.) to break in for stealing.

escruncho s. m. (Braz., sl.) housebreaking.

escrupulear, escrupulizar v. to scruple: 1. have scruples (about). 2. hesitate about doing a thing. 3. be reluctant.

escrúpulo s. m. 1. scruple: a) uneasiness of conscience. b) hesitation in doubt as to the properness of an action. 2. susceptibility. 3. remorse. 4. zeal. **ele não tem ~s** he has no scruples, (fam.) he sticks at nothing.

escrupulosidade s. f. scrupulousness: scrupulous character or disposition.

escrupuloso adj. scrupulous: 1. having scruples. 2. hesitant. 3. precise, rigorous, punctilious, meticulous, careful. ‖ **-amente** adv. scrupulously. **com cuidado ~** with scrupulous care. **estar excessivamente ~** to be excessively scrupulous, to strain at a gnat.

escrutador s. m. scrutator: 1. person who scrutinizes. 2. a close examiner or inquirer. ‖ adj. scrutinizing, examining closely.

escrutar v. to scrutinize, investigate, examine, inquire, search.

escrutinador s. m. scrutineer: person who scrutinizes; examiner of votes.

escrutinar v. to scrutinize: 1. examine, search, inquire. 2. collect and count the votes.

escrutínio s. m. 1. scrutiny. a) close examination. b) (R. C. Church) one of the three methods used for electing a pope. 2. balloting. 3. ballot-box. 4. counting of votes. **votação por ~** secret ballot.

escudar v. 1. to shield, protect with a shield. 2. to defend, protect, guard. 3. ~-se: a) to cover o. s. with or as with a shield. b) to base o. s. on or upon.

escudeirar v. to squire.

escudeiro s. m. 1. shield-bearer, squire. 2. upper servant, valet.

escudela s. f. a wooden porringer.

escudelar v. 1. to serve (a meal) in wooden porringers. 2. to put in wooden porringers.

escudete s. m. 1. a small scutcheon. 2. scutcheon of a lock.

escudo s. m. 1. shield, buckler. 2. (her.) scutcheon, arms. 3. a Portuguese coin. 4. (fig.) shelter, protection, defence. **~ de armas** coat of arms.

esculachar v. (Braz.) 1. to beat, blow. 2. (fig.) to shatter, destroy; ridicule.

esculacho s. m. (Braz., sl.) 1. blow, stroke. 2. = **esculhambação**.

esculápio s. m. 1. Aesculapius. 2. (poet.) a physician.

esculento adj. esculent, eatable, edible.

esculhambação s. f. (pl. -ões) (Braz., sl.) disorder, confusion, disarray, anarchy.

esculhambar v. (Braz., sl.) 1. to shatter, decompose, destroy. 2. to demoralize, ridicule, deride.

esculpido adj. 1. sculptured, engraved. 2. carved; cut, polished.

esculpir v. 1. to sculpture, engrave. 2. to chisel, carve, cut. 3. to shape, mold, form. **~ em pedra** to cut in stone.

escultor s. m. (also **esculpidor**) 1. sculptor. 2. carver; stone-cuttter.

escultura s. f. sculpture: 1. art of carving or modeling figures; statuary (plate E 9). 2. a sculptured work.

escultural adj. m. + f. (pl. -ais) sculptural: 1. pertaining to sculpture. 2. (sculpture) serving as a model.

esculturar v. 1. to sculpture. 2. to work as a sculptor.

escuma s. f. 1. scum, froth, foam. 2. drivel, slaver. 3. spume. 4. (fig.) mob, rabble. **~ do mar** meerschaum: white silicate of magnesia used for the manufacture of tobacco-pipes.

escumadeira s. f. skimmer; skimming ladle.

escumador s. m. 1. one who or that which foams. 2. skimmer, scummer. ‖ adj. 1. frothy, foaming. 2. skimming, scumming.

escumalha s. f. (sl.) mob, rabble, scum of society.

escumante adj. m. + f. scumming, foaming.

escumar v. 1. to skim, scum. 2. to slabber, drivel, slaver. 3. to foam, froth. 4. to boil, bubble.

escumilha s. f. 1. birdshot, small shot to kill birds. 2. gauze. 3. (bot.) crape myrtle, (U. S. A.) crepe myrtle (Lagerstroemia indica).

escumilhar v. to embroider on gauzelike material.

escumoso adj. frothy, foamy.

escuna s. f. schooner: a two-masted vessel with fore--and-aft rigging (plate B 10).

escurão s. m. (pl. -ões) nightfall.

escuras s. f. pl. word used in the adverbial locution: **às ~** 1. in the dark, blindly. 2. occultly. **andar às ~** to be in the dark (about anything). **apalpar às ~** to grope in the dark.

escurecedor s. m. one who darkens, darkener. ‖ adj. darkening, making dark.

escurecer v. (also **escurentar**) 1. to darken, obscure, cloud, make dark. 2. to obfuscate, eclipse, overshadow. 3. to make turbid. 4. to perturb, disturb. 5. to grow night. 6. ~-se: a) to grow dark. b) to become dull, dimmed, tarnished. **está escurecendo** it is growing dark, night is coming on.

escurecimento s. m. darkening.

escurejar v. 1. to appear dark. 2. to grow dark.

escuriço adj. (Braz.) dark in colour.

escuridade s. f. 1. darkness, obscurity. 2. (fig.) difficulty; mystery.

escuridão s. f. (pl. -ões) (also **escureza**) 1. darkness, obscurity; blackness. 2. (fig.) blindness, ignorance.

escuro s. m. 1. darkness, obscurity. 2. (fig.) night. ‖ adj. 1. dark, obscure, lightless, dim. 2. cloudy, overcast; swarthy. 3. somber, shady, shadowy. 4. tenebrous. 5. sad, melancholic. 6. mysterious, intricate. **azul-~ (castanho-~, verde-~, vermelho-~)** dark-blue (-brown, -green, -red). **câmara -a** camera obscura, darkroom. **cor -a** dark colour. **dia ~** cloudy day. **ficar no ~** to remain in darkness. **no ~, todos os gatos são pardos** (fig.) in the dark all cats are grey. **um pulo no ~** a leap in the dark.

E 9

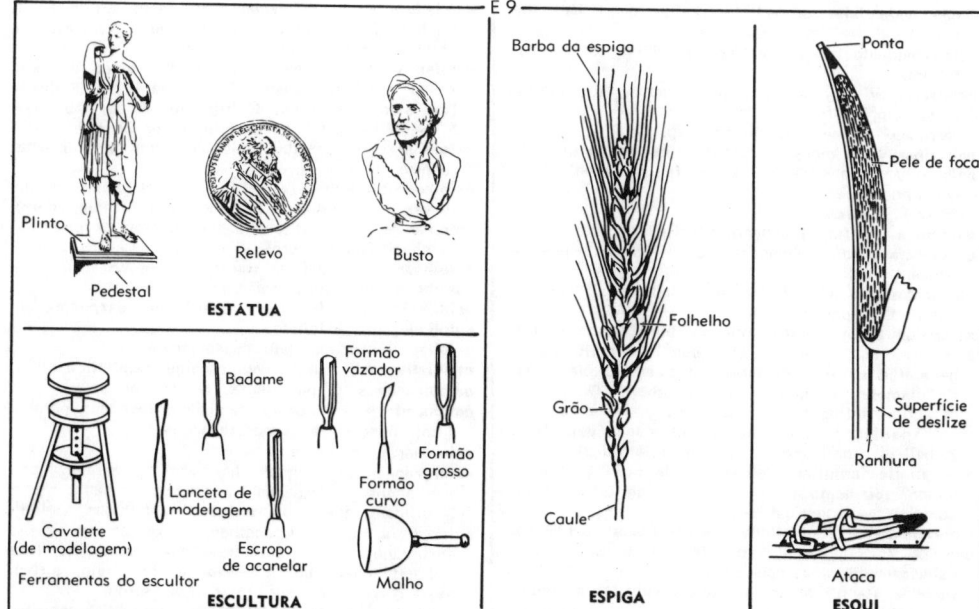

Plinto / Pedestal / Relevo / Busto / **ESTÁTUA**

Cavalete (de modelagem) / Badame / Lanceta de modelagem / Escropo de acanelar / Formão vazador / Formão curvo / Formão grosso / Malho / Ferramentas do escultor / **ESCULTURA**

Barba da espiga / Folhelho / Grão / Caule / **ESPIGA**

Ponta / Pele de foca / Superfície de deslize / Ranhura / Ataca / **ESQUI**

escusa, escusação (pl. **-ões**) s. f. 1. excuse; apology. 2. dispensation, exemption, discharge.
ele apresentou a sua ~ he advanced an excuse.
escusado adj. 1. useless, needless. 2. superfluous. 3. unnecessary.
é ~ **it is useless.**
escusar v. 1. to excuse, pardon, forgive. 2. to justify, vindicate. 3. to exempt, release. 4. to dispense. 5. to avoid. 6. not to want. 7. ~-**se**: a) to forgive o. s. b) to excuse o. s. from, apologize for. c) to refuse to.
escusatório adj. excusatory, making or containing excuse.
escusável adj. m. + f. (pl. **-áveis**) 1. excusable, pardonable. 2. useless. 3. dispensable.
escuso adj. 1. exempt, excused. 2. useless, unnecessary. 3. secret, hidden, recondite.
escuta s. f. 1. listening, hearkening. 2. (obs.) listener, hearkener.
aparelho de ~ sound locator. **serviço de** ~ interception service.
escutador s. m. listener, hearkener.
escutar v. 1. to hearken, give ear to. 2. to listen. 3. to hear. 4. (fig.) to spy. 5. to auscultate.
escute! listen to me!, I say! **escute-me!** lend me an ear!
escutiforme adj. m. + f. scutiform, shield-shaped.
esdruxular v. to write dactylic verses, versify in dactyls.
esdruxularia s. f. 1. singularity, extravagance. 2. oddness.
esdruxulizar v. 1. to give a singular or extravagant appearance to. 2. to become odd. 3. to write dactylic verses, versify in dactyls.
esdrúxulo s. m. dactyl, dactylic verse. ‖ adj. 1. (gram.) proparoxytone. 2. dactylic (verse). 3. (fig.) odd, strange, extravagant.
esfacelado adj. 1. shattered, broken up, in pieces. 2. ruined; destroyed, spoiled. 3. mangled, lacerated. 4. (med.) sphacelated.

esfacelar v. 1. (med.) to sphacelate. 2. to break up. 3. to spoil, ruin, destroy. 4. ~-**se**: a) to corrupt. b) to ruin o. s. c) to dissolve.
esfácelo s. m. (med.) sphacelus, necrosis, gangrene.
esfacelo (ê) s. m. 1. destruction, ruin. 2. corruption. 3. laceration.
esfachear v. (Braz.) to break up, destroy.
esfaimado s. m. famished, starving, ravenous person. ‖ adj. ravenous, starving, famished, hungry.
esfaimar v. to famish, starve.
esfalfado adj. overtired, exhausted, worn-out.
esfalfamento s. m. 1. fatigue, weariness. 2. annoyance.
esfalfar v. 1. to fatigue, tire, exhaust, weary, fag. 2. ~-**se**: a) to tire o. s. b) to get tired, grow weary. c) to overwork.
~ **a montaria** to ride to death.
esfanicado adj. 1. shattered, broken up. 2. thin, slender, slim.
esfanicar v. to cut or break to pieces.
esfaqueado adj. knifed, stabbed.
esfaquear v. 1. to stab, pierce or wound with a knife. 2. to cut (into pieces) with a knife.
esfarelado adj. 1. reduced to bran. 2. crumbled.
esfarelar v. 1. to reduce to bran. 2. to bolt, sift (meal). 3. ~-**se**: a) to crumble (into dust). b) to be reduced to bran.
o bolo esfarelou-se the cake was reduced to crumbs.
esfarinhado adj. 1. crumbled. 2. reduced to flour.
esfarinhar v. 1. to crumble. 2. to reduce to flour; to mill.
esfarpado adj. 1. torn; tattered, ragged. 2. unravelled. 3. splintered.
esfarpar v. 1. to tear; to shred, tear into shreds. 2. to unravel. 3. to splinter.
esfarrapadeira s. f. shredder, shredding machine.
esfarrapado s. m. ragamuffin, tatterdemalion. ‖ adj. torn, rent, tattered, ragged, dressed in tatters, shabby.
desculpa -a lame excuse, professed excuse. **o roto**

não pode falar do ~! the kettle can't call the pot black!

esfarrapamento s. m. act of reducing to shreds, tatters.

esfarrapar v. 1. to rend, tear, reduce to tatters. 2. to ruin, destroy.

esfarripado adj. wispy, sparse (esp. hair).

esfarripar v. to make or dispose like scarce hair.

esfatiar v. 1. to slice, cut slices (as of bread). 2. to cut into pieces.

esfazer v. = **desfazer.**

esfênio s. m. (min.) sphene, titanite.

esfenocéfalo adj. sphenocephalous: having a wedge--shaped head.

esfenoidal adj. m. + f. (pl. -ais) sphenoidal: pertaining to the sphenoid bone.

esfenóide s. m. (anat.) sphenoid bone (plate C 17).

esfera s. f. 1. sphere: a) (geom.) a solid figure generated by the revolution of a semicircle about its diameter. b) globe, ball. c) orb. d) (fig.) field of action, influence; position; scope, range; authority; knowledge. 2. an ancient Portuguese gold coin. 3. ball of a ball and socket joint (plate J 3).

~ **armilar** armillary sphere. ~ **de ação** sphere of action. **rolamento de ~s** ball bearing (plate R 2). **setor de ~** spherical sector.

esfericidade s. f. sphericity, sphericalness, roundness.

esférico adj. spherical, orbicular, globular, round. ‖ **esfericamente** adv. spherically.

fresa -a (tech.) spherical cutter. **válvula -a** (tech.) ball valve.

esferoidal adj. m. + f. (pl. -ais) spheroidal: of, pertaining to or having the form of a spheroid.

esferóide s. m. (geom.) spheroid: a body almost but not perfectly spherical.

esferômetro s. m. spherometer: instrument for measuring the radii of spheres.

esférula s. f. 1. spherule: a little sphere or spherical body. 2. a drop.

esfervilhação s. f. (pl. -ões) act of swarming.

esfervilhar v. to swarm; seethe; agitate, stir.

esfiapar, esfiar v. (also **esfiampar**) to ravel, fray out, unthread, shred (into threads).

esfigmógrafo s. m. sphygmograph: instrument for recording the movements of the pulse.

esfigmômetro s. m. sphygmometer: instrument for measuring the strength of the pulse beat.

esfíncter, esfincter s. m. (anat.) sphincter: a ringlike muscle which closes a natural orifice.

esfinge s. f. 1. sphinx: a fabulous Egyptian monster having a human face and the body of a lion. 2. (ent.) hawk-moth. 3. (fig.) taciturn, reserved, enigmatic person.

esfíngico adj. 1. of or pertaining to a sphinx. 2. enigmatic(al), mysterious.

esfingídeo s. m. a moth of the family Sphingidae. ‖ adj. of or pertaining to the family Sphingidae.

esflorar v. 1. to deflorate, strip of flowers. 2. to deflower, ravish. 3. to touch the surface of anything.

esfoguear-se v. (Braz.) 1. to blush, redden. 2. to hasten, hurry. 3. to become impatient.

esfogueteado s. m. foolhardy person; simpleton. ‖ adj. foolhardy, rattlebrained; foolish.

esfoguetear v. 1. to let off fireworks (as a celebration). 2. to censure, rebuke, reprehend. 3. to drive away.

esfoladela s. f. 1. = **esfoladura.** 2. (fig.): a) fraud, swindle. b) illicit gain, graft. c) (Braz.) a touch (for a gift or money).

esfolador s. m. 1. flayer. 2. scratcher, scraper. ‖ adj. flaying; scratching.

esfoladura s. f., **esfolamento** m. (also **esfola** f.) 1. flaying. 2. a scratch, light wound, excoriation, abrasion of the skin. 3. a scrape.

esfolar v. 1. to flay, strip off the skin; to skin. 2. to scratch; scrape. 3. to graze, rub, abrade (the skin); excoriate. 4. (fig.) to fleece, rob, flay. 5. ~-**se** to suffer an excoriation or scratch.

esfolegar v. to breathe, draw or catch one's breath; respire.

esfolhada, esfolhadela s. f. 1. a stripping of the leaves from a plant. 2. shucking (of Indian corn).

esfolhar v. 1. to strip the leaves from a plant. 2. to shuck (Indian corn).

esfolhear v. to leaf, to run through a book.

esfolhoso adj. (bot.) leafless.

esfoliação s. f. (pl. -ões) exfoliation, desquamation.

esfoliado adj. exfoliated.

esfoliar v. to exfoliate, desquamate.

esfoliativo adj. exfoliative: causing exfoliation.

esfomeação s. f. hungriness, ravenousness.

esfomeado s. m. hungry, famished, ravenous person. ‖ adj. hungry, famished, ravenous.

esfomear v. to famish, starve.

esforçado s. m. diligent, hard-working person. ‖ adj. 1. valiant, courageous. 2. strong, robust, stout. 3. diligent, assiduous, active. 4. impetuous, violent.

esforçar v. 1. to strengthen, make strong. 2. to encourage, incite, stimulate, activate. 3. to take a heart, cheer up. 4. ~-**se:** a) to strain, strive, exert o. s., endeavour. b) to grow strong.

~-**se inutilmente** to labour in vain, beat the air. ~-**se para** to take pains for. **ele esforçou-se à toa** he had his labour for his pain. **ele esforçou-se para conseguir um emprego** he tried hard for a job. **esforçamo-nos em fazê-lo** we endeavoured to do it. **esforçamo-nos para obter o dinheiro** we made a push for the money. **você precisa ~-se mais** you must try harder. **você precisa ~ sua memória** you must tax your memory.

esforço (ô) s. m. (pl. **esforços**) 1. effort, endeavour. 2. struggle, attempt. 3. exertion. 4. courage, valour. 5. strength, vigour, energy. 6. sense of honour. 7. vitality, animation. 8. care, zeal.

esforços mútuos mutual efforts. **com o máximo ~** with the utmost effort, for all one is worth. **ela não poupa esforços** she spares no pains, she is unsparing in her efforts. **ele fez grandes esforços para esclarecer esta questão** he went to great pains to clarify this matter. **ele não suporta o ~** he can't stand the strain. **empregar todos os seus esforços** to do one's level best. **fazer um grande ~** to be at great pains. **poupem os esforços** spare your pains. **todos os nossos esforços foram baldados** all our efforts were in vain. **trabalhar com todo ~** to work to the utmost of one's power, work tooth and nail. **este trabalho é um ~ penoso** this work is a heavy burden. **você não deve afrouxar os seus esforços** you must not relax in your efforts.

esfragística s. f. sphragistics, sigillography.

esfraldar v. (Braz.) to unfurl (flags or sails).

esfrançar v. to cut off the dry branches of a tree, to lop.

esfrangalhar v. to reduce to tatters, rend, tear to pieces; tatter.

esfrega s. f. 1. (also **esfregação**, pl. -ões) wiping, rubbing, friction, scrubbing. 2. (fig.) reprimand, scolding; punishment. 3. (fam.) beating, thrashing. **ele levou uma ~** he took a severe beating.

esfregação (pl. -ões), **esfregadela** s. f. (also **esfregadura**) a rubbing or scrubbing; friction.

esfregalho s. m. rubbing clout, rubbing brush, mop (plate E 8).

esfregão s. m. (pl. **-ões**) 1. rubbing clout, rubbing cloth, rubber, scrubber. 2. dish-clout, mop. 3. rubbing brush, scrubbing-brush (plate E 8).

esfregar v. 1. to rub, scour, scrub, scrape. 2. to fray, chafe. 3. to clean. 4. to wash (as with a rubbing brush); mop up. 5. ~-**se**: a) to rub or massage o. s. b) to scratch o. s.
ele esfregou-o he wiped it, gave it a wipe. **enquanto o diabo esfrega um olho** in a trice, in an instant. ~-**se contra alguma coisa** to scrape against something.

esfria s. m. + f. (Braz., newspaper sl.) one who conceals a piece of news from a reporter.

esfriadouro s. m. (also **esfriadoiro**) cooler, cooling vessel.

esfriamento s. m. cooling; refrigeration.

esfriar v. 1. to cool, make cool, chill. 2. to refresh, refrigerate; freeze. 3. to despond, lose heart. 4. ~-**se**: a) to grow cold. b) to lose heart or enthusiasm. ~ **o entusiasmo** to cool one's enthusiasm. **ponha-o fora da janela para** ~ put it outside the window to get cool. **o tempo esfriou** the weather has turned cooler.

esfria-verruma s. m. (pl. **esfria-verrumas**) (N. Braz.) 1. person who hangs on or sticks to another. 2. adulator, fawner, base flatterer. 3. attendant.

esfrolar v. = **esfolar**.

esfulinhar v. to remove cobwebs and soot from the corners of a room.

esfumação s. f. (pl. **-ões**) 1. drawing with crayon. 2. shading, padding (picture).

esfumaçar v. 1. to fill (a place) with smoke. 2. to overshadow with smoke.

esfumado s. m. charcoal drawing.

esfumador s. m. (paint.) stump.

esfumar v. 1. to shade or rub down (a drawing) with a stump. 2. to draw with crayon. 3. to smoke; blacken with smoke. 4. ~-**se**: a) to dissolve in smoke. b) to fade away, disappear (like smoke).

esfumarar v. to cover with smoke.

esfumear v. to fume, smoke, emit smoke.

esfuminho s. m. (drawing) stump: an implement used to rub down crayon drawings.

esfuracar v. 1. to fill with holes. 2. to perforate, bore.

esfuziada s. f. firing, gunfire; shooting affray, volley.

esfuziante adj. m. + f. 1. whistling, hissing. 2. whizzing. 3. sibilant.

esfuziar v. 1. to whistle, hiss (wind). 2. to whiz through the air (volley).

esfuzilar v. 1. to scintillate, sparkle, glitter. 2. to flash (as lightning).

esgaçar v. = **esgarçar**.

esgadanhar v. 1. to scratch with a claw. 2. to pull out hair or feathers. 3. ~-**se**: to hurt o. s.; suffer a scratch (with a claw).

esgadelhar v. to dishevel, tousle, rumple (hair).

esgaivar v. to excavate, dig, hollow.

esgaivotado adj. 1. resembling a gull. 2. thin, lean, lank.

esgalamido adj. (N. Braz., pop.) gluttonish, greedy.

esgaldripado adj. long but with few fruits (bunch of grapes).

esgaldripar v. to become **esgaldripado**.

esgalgado adj. 1. thin as a starving dog, lanky, skinny. 2. needy, indigent.

esgalgar v. to emaciate, grow thin.

esgalha s. f. 1. branching, ramification. 2. pruning (of trees). 3. a branch.

esgalhado adj. 1. full of shoots or branches; branched. 2. pruned (tree).

esgalhar v. 1. to cut off branches, trim, prune, lop. 2. to ramify.

esgalho s. m. 1. branch, shoot, spring. 2. antler (of a deer). 3. the remaining knotty part of a branch that has been cut off. 4. ramification.

esgalopado adj. gluttonish, greedy.

esgana s. f. 1. = **esganação**. 2. chin-cough, hooping--cough.

esganação s. f. (pl. **-ões**) (also **esganadura**) 1. strangulation. 2. desire, avidity, eagerness, impatience. 3. greediness.

esganado s. m. gluton; greedy or famished person. ‖ adj. 1. famished, starving. 2. gluttonish, greedy. 3. eager, desirous. 4. (fig.) mean, niggardly.

esganar v. 1. to strangle, stifle, suffocate. 2. ~-**se**: a) to hang o. s., strangle o. s. b) to envy, covet; to be eaten up with envy.

esganiçar v. 1. to howl (as dogs). 2. to sing in a loud yelling way. 3. to screech, scream, yell, shriek.

esgar s. m. 1. grimace, wry face. 2. ~**es** pl. mouths.

esgarabulhão s. m. (pl. **-ões**) hopping or skipping top.

esgarabulhar v. to hop or skip (a top).

esgaratujar v. to scrawl, scribble.

esgaravatador s. m. 1. toothpick. 2. ear-pick. 3. (forge) poker. ‖ adj. 1. raking, scraping, scratching. 2. picking (teeth, ears, etc.). 3. searching, investigating, prying (into).

esgaravatana s. f. (also **esgarapatana**) 1. (obs.) megaphone. 2. (Braz.) blowgun used by Indians.

esgaravatar, esgaravatear v. 1. to rake, scrape. 2. to pick the teeth or ears. 3. to scratch. 4. (fig.) to search, investigate, inquire, ask about.

esgaravatil s. m. (pl. **-is**) a joiner's tool for making mortises.

esgarçar v. 1. to tear, slit, rend, shred (cloth). 2. to fray out, separate into threads. 3. to wound. 4. ~-**se** to fade away; to wear out.

esgardunhar v. to scratch; to tear with or as with claws.

esgargalar v. to cut low (neckline of a dress); discover the neck or breast.

esgargalhar-se v. to laugh out or aloud, have a hearty laugh.

esgarrão adj. (pl. **-ões**) (naut.) contrary (winds).

esgarrar v. 1. to lead astray. 2. to drive out of the course, scatter (ships). 3. ~-**se**: a) to stray from the course. b) to become scattered (ships). c) to withdraw from, separate o. s. from.

esgatanhar v. 1. to claw, scratch (as a cat). 2. to pull out hair or feathers.

esgazeado adj. 1. pale, wan, blanched. 2. brilliant, staring (eyes).

esgazear v. 1. to stare into the space, into vacancy. 2. to be pale or faded.

esgoelar v. 1. (also ~-**se**) to cry or call out, bawl, yell, cry very much. 2. to strangle, stifle, choke.

esgorjar v. 1. to uncover the neck or breast. 2. to desire very earnestly; crave for, be eager about.

esgotado adj. 1. drained, emptied, exhausted. 2. wasted. 3. broken-down. 4. finished. 5. out of print. 6. dog-tired.
a edição está -a the edition is out of print. **ele está muito** ~ he is tired out. **estar com os recursos** ~**s** to be at the end of one's tether. **estou** ~ I am run-down. **um homem** ~ a tired man.

esgotadouro s. m. (also **esgotadoiro**) drain pipe.

esgotadura s. f. exhausting, exhaustion, draining, emptying.

esgotamento s. m. 1. = **esgotadura**. 2. depauperation. 3. prostration, weakness, debility. 4. fatigue. ~ **nervoso** nervous breakdown.

esgotante adj. m. + f. debilitating, exhausting.

esgotar v. 1. to drain to the last drop. 2. to exhaust, dry, empty, deplete. 3. ~-**se**: a) to exhaust o. s.,

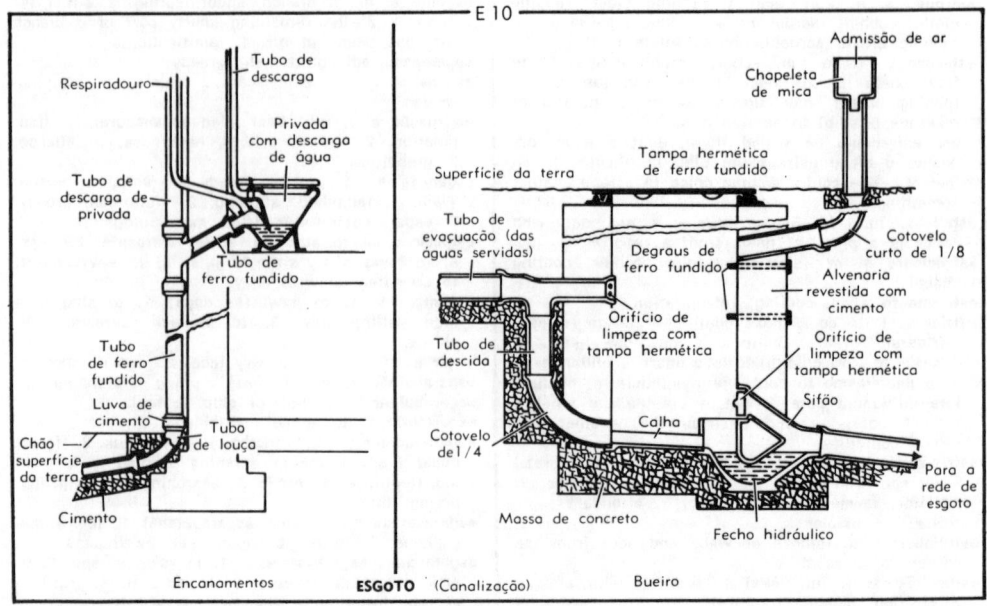

E 10

Encanamentos — **ESGOTO** (Canalização) — Bueiro

become exhausted. b) to dry up. c) to tire, fatigue, spend o. s. d) to debilitate. e) to be sold out, go out of print.
a edição esgotou-se em um mês the edition was sold out in a month. **o escritor simplesmente esgotou as (próprias) idéias** the writer simply ran out of ideas. **esgotei-lhe a paciência** I exhausted his patience, got up his back. **eu esgotei todos os recursos** I am at the end of my resources.
esgotável adj. m. + f. (pl. **-áveis**) 1. drainable. 2. exhaustible.
esgote s. m. = **esgotadura, esgotamento.**
esgoto (ô) s. m. drain(age), sewer(age) (plate E 10). **cano de ~** discharging pipe. **rede de ~** sewerage system.
esgrafiar v. to paint in sgrafitto.
esgrafito s. m. sgrafitto: scribbling scratched, painted or otherwise marked on a wall, tablet, column, or other surface.
esgravatar, esgravatear v. = **esgaravatar.**
esgrima s. f. (also **esgrimidura**) fencing (art or act). **mestre de ~** fencing master.
esgrimidor s. m. = **esgrimista.** ‖ adj. fencing.
esgrimir v. 1. to shake, brandish, wave. 2. to fence, tilt. 3. (fig.) to wrangle, quarrel; dispute, argue.
esgrimista s. m. + f. fencer: person who fences or practises the art of fencing with a sword or foil.
esgrouviado, esgrouvinhado adj. 1. tall and thin; like a crane. 2. disheveled.
esguardar v. 1. to respect, consider. 2. to look at. 3. **~-se** to be wary, be on one's guard.
esguedelhado adj. disheveled, uncombed, unkempt (hair).
esguedelhar v. to dishevel, tousle, rumple, ruffle; spread the hair disorderly.
esgueirar v. 1. to steal artfully. 2. **~-se:** to steal away, sneak out; make o. s. scarce.
esguelha s. f. 1. obliquity. 2. bias, slant. 3. diagonal. **andar de ~** to sidle. **de ~** obliquely, aslant, sideways.

esguelhar v. 1. to place obliquely or sideways. 2. to lay across, set awry. 3. to cut on the bias.
esguião s. m. fine linen or cotton fabric.
esguichadela s. f. squirt, a jet (of liquid), water--spout.
esguichar v. 1. to spirt (up), spurt. 2. to squirt, syringe, jet. 3. to spout out, gush, spring.
esguicho s. m. 1. squirt (instrument). 2. jet, water--spout, gush. 3. clyster-pipe.
esguio adj. long and thin, lanky; tall and thin.
esguncho s. m. (naut.) skeet: a shovel used to water the sides of a ship or to throw water on the deck.
esgurido adj. (Braz., pop.) famished, starved.
esipra s. f. (N. Braz., pop.) erysipelas.
eslabão s. m. (vet.) spavin: tumour on the inside of a horse's leg.
esladroar v. to sucker: cut off the useless suckers of a tree.
eslagartar v. to clear or rid trees of caterpillars.
eslávico adj. Slavic: of or pertaining to the Slavs, their country or language.
eslavo s. m. Slav, Slavonian. ‖ adj. Slav, Slavonian, Slavic.
eslinga s. f. (naut.) sling for hoisting heavy things.
eslingar v. (naut.) to sling, hoist with a sling.
eslovaco s. m. Slovak: a member of a Slavic race (central Czechoslovakia). ‖ adj. Slovak.
esloveno s. m. Slovene: one of a southern Slavic group (Yugoslavia). ‖ adj. Slovene.
esmadrigado adj. strayed, runaway (cattle).
esmadrigar v. to stray, lead astray (from the herd).
esmaecer(-se) v. 1. to discolour, fade. 2. to turn pale, faint. 3. to grow weak, feeble. 4. to discourage.
esmaecimento s. m. 1. fainting, swoon. 2. weakness.
esmagador s. m. (Braz.) crusher of a sugar-mill. ‖ adj. smashing, crushing.
ele obteve ~a vitória he had a crushing victory. **uma resposta ~a** a crushing retort.
esmagadura s. f., **esmagamento** m. (also **esmagação**) 1. compressing, squeezing. 2. crushing, squashing. 3. bruise, contusion

esmagar v. 1. to compress, squeeze, press. 2. to crush, smash, bruise, squash. 3. to break. 4. to trample on or upon. 5. to triturate; jam. 6. to macerate, steep. 7. to tyranize; enslave, destroy utterly. 8. (fig.) to present an irrefutable argument. 9. ~-se to be crushed.

esmaiar v. to faint, swoon; turn pale.

esmaleitado adj. having the tertian fever.

esmalhar v. to cut the mails (of an armour).

esmaltador s. m. enameller, enamellist.

esmaltagem s. f. (pl. -ens) act or method of enamelling.

esmaltar v. 1. to enamel. 2. (fig.): a) to adorn, embellish, decorate. b) to brighten; polish.

esmalte s. m. 1. enamel. 2. enamel of the teeth. 3. enamel work. 4. (fig.): a) splendour. b) brightness. c) ornament, adornment. 5. (her.) colours. ~ de unhas nail polish.

esmalhada adj. f. with sagging breasts (woman).

esmaniado adj. senseless, crack-brained, maniacal.

esmaniar v. to be whimsical; act crazily; be madly fond of.

esmar v. 1. to estimate. 2. to appraise, evaluate, value. 3. to conjecture, guess.

esmarelido adj. somewhat yellow, yellowish.

esmarrido adj. 1. dry; arid, parched. 2. downhearted, discouraged.

esmechada s. f. a blow on the head.

esmechar v. 1. to wound on the head with a stick or stone. 2. to be burning hot (sun).

esmega s. m. (med.) smegma: a secretion found under the prepuce and around the labia minora.

esmerado adj. 1. performed with care. 2. accurate, neat, spruce. 3. fine, elegant, trim. 4. perfect, accomplished, finished.
acabamento ~ perfect finish. serviço ~ irreproachable service.

esmeralda s. f. 1. (min.) emerald. 2. (ornith.) a variety of the bird of paradise.
verde-~ chrome green (colour). ~-do-brasil (min.) green tourmaline.

esmeraldear v. 1. to give a green colour to. 2. to green, make green.

esmeraldino adj. smaragdine, emerald, green.

esmerar v. 1. to perform with care. 2. to perfect, bring to perfection. 3. to polish. 4. to accomplish; finish. 5. ~-se: a) to exert o. s.; to make as good as possible, do one's best. b) to work with care.

esmeril s. m. (pl. -is) 1. emery. 2. emery-wheel, corundum-wheel. 3. (N. Braz.) unskilful chauffeur; spoiler of cars.
lixa de ~ emery-paper. pedra de ~ emery-stone.

esmerilador s. m. polisher: person who rubs or polishes with an emery.

esmerilar v. (also **esmerilhar**) 1. to rub or polish with emery. 2. (fig.): a) to search, investigate. b) to perfect.

esmerilhão s. m. (pl. -ões) 1. (ornith.) merlin. 2. an ancient musket.

esmero (ê) s. m. 1. care, diligence, carefulness. 2. perfection. 3. accuracy. 4. correctness. 5. cleanliness.
ela veste-se com ~ she dresses up.

esmigalhador s. m. crusher. || adj. crushing, crumbling.

esmigalhadura s. f. trituration, a crumbling or breaking into small pieces, fragmentation.

esmigalhar v. 1. to crumb(le), break into fragments, to triturate. 2. to shatter. 3. ~-se to fall into small pieces.

esmiolado adj. 1. foolish, silly, rattle-brained. 2. brainless.

esmiolar v. 1. to take out the inside, to crumb (bread). 2. (fig.) to make crazy, madden.

esmirrar-se v. 1. to dry up, parch. 2. to grow lean, decay; wilt. 3. (fig.) to escape, fade away, sneak away.

esmiuçado adj. 1. broken or divided into small pieces. 2. minute, detailed; precise.

esmiuçador s. m. 1. pounder (person). 2. person who goes to the bottom of things, who stands upon niceties, who explains minutely. || adj. 1. fragmentizing, crushing. 2. scrutinizing. 3. explaining minutely.

esmiuçar, esmiudar v. 1. to crumble, pound, fragmentize. 2. to examine, scrutinize, make a strict inquiry into. 3. to explain minutely or in details. 4. to stand upon niceties.

esmo (ê) s. m. 1. conjecture, guess. 2. rough calculation, estimate, estimation.
a ~ by the sight; rashly, at random. atirar a ~ to shoot at random.

esmocar v. to beat, sock, buffet, thrash, spank, cudgel.

esmochar v. to cut off the horns, poll (cattle).

esmoer v. 1. to munch. 2. to digest. 3. to ruminate, chew the cud.

esmola s. f. 1. alms, charity, almsdeed. 2. benefit, favour. 3. (coll.) beating.
ele pediu uma ~ he asked an alms. passar a pedir ~s to take to begging. pedir ~s to ask for alms, beg, panhandle.

esmolador s. m. 1. almsgiver. 2. beggar, mendicant. || adj. giving alms.

esmolambado adj. (Braz.) torn, tattered, ragged, in tatters.

esmolambador s. m. (Braz.) 1. tatterdemalion. 2. debaser || adj. 1. ragged, shabby. 2. scoffing, debasing.

esmolambar v. (Braz.) 1. to debase, degrade. 2. to mock, ridicule. 3. to be all tattered and torn.

esmolar v. 1. to give alms; bestow charity upon. 2. to beg, ask for alms. 3. to live by begging.

esmolaria s. f. almoner's office or dignity, almonry.

esmoleira s. f. a beggar's pouch, purse or sack.

esmoleiro s. m. 1. beggar, indigent, pauper. 2. a mendicant friar who goes about to beg for his monastery. || adj. mendicant (said of a friar).

esmolento adj. almsgiving, charitable.

esmoler s. m. 1. almoner. 2. (Braz., pop.) beggar, mendicant. || adj. charitable; almsgiving.

esmoncar v. 1. to wipe the nose. 2. ~-se to blow one's nose.

esmondar v. 1. to weed; peel, husk. 2. to emend, correct.

esmordaçar, esmordicar v. 1. to bite (into), snap. 2. to tear with the teeth.

esmorecer v. 1. to dismay, discourage, depress. 2. to lose one's courage or enthusiasm. 3. to lose heart. 4. to faint away; swoon. 5. to become loose or slack. 6. to grow weak, feeble. 7. to go out (fire or light).

esmorecido adj. 1. discouraged, dejected; down. 2. disheartened, downhearted. 3. weak. || -amente adv. downheartedly.

esmorecimento s. m. 1. discouragement, despondency, disheartening. 2. dejection, depression. 3. faintness.

esmorraçar, esmorrar v. to snuff the candle.

esmoucar v. 1. to damage, breaking the edges. 2. to beat.

esmurrar v. (also **esmurraçar, esmurre(n)gar** 1. to cuff, box, sock, pummel. 2. to mistreat; beat.

és-não-és s. m. somewhat, a little, a speck.
por um ~ almost, nearly, within an ace of.

esnobe s. m. + f. snob. || adj. snobbish, snobby.

esnobismo s. m. snobbism, snobbery, snobbishness.

esnocar v. 1. to snapp off the branches, to prune. 2. to cut away, amputate.

esnoga s. f. synagogue.

esoderma s. m. (ent.) esorderm.

esofagiano, esofágico adj. esophageal: of or pertaining to the esophagus.

esofagismo s. m. (med.) esophagism(us): spasm of the esophagus.

esofagite s. f. (med.) esophagitis: inflammation of the esophagus.

esôfago s. m. (anat.) esophagus, gullet: the canal extending from the pharynx to the stomach.

esofagotomia s. f. (surg.) esophagotomy: the opening of the esophagus by an incision.

esópico adj. Aesopian: pertaining to Aesop.

esotérico adj. esoteric (doctrine).

esoterismo s. m. esoterism, esotericism: esoteric doctrine or principles.

espaçado adj. 1. spaced, set at intervals, divided into spaces. 2. slow, sluggish.

espaçamento s. m. 1. spacing. 2. postponement.

espaçar, espacear v. 1. to space: a) set at intervals. b) divide into spaces. 2. to delay, retard, slow down. 3. to adjourn. 4. to enlarge, extend.

espacejamento s. m. (typogr.) spacing (plate L 4).

espacejar v. 1. (typogr.) to space: arrange the spaces and intervals in or between (words, lines or letters). 2. = **espaçar.**

espacial adj. m. + f. (pl. **-ais**) spatial: a) of or pertaining to the space. b) existing in the space. **foguete** ~ space-rocket.

espácio s. m. (Braz.) a wide-horned animal. ‖ adj. wide horned.

espaço s. m. 1. space: a) unlimited room; the ether. b) room, area, place. c) length of time, duration, while. d) interval. e) (mus.) an interval between the lines of a staff (plate N 1). f) (typogr.) blank types used to separate words. g) distance. 2. delay, retardation.
~ **acanhado** narrow space. ~ **amplo para todos** ample room for everyone. ~ **para livros** accommodation for books. **barra de** ~ (typewriter) space-bar (plate M 2). **a** ~**s** from time to time, now and then. **de** ~ slowly, leisurely. **não há** ~ **neste ônibus** there is no room in this bus. **no** ~ **de uma semana** within the space of a week. **pelo** ~ **de...** for a period of... **a terra gira no** ~ **the earth** moves through the space.

espaçoso adj. 1. spacious: a) wide, extended; extensive. b) roomy, large. c) ample, broad. 2. slow, unhurried. ‖ **-amente** adv. spaciously, widely; slowly.

espada s. f. 1. sword. 2. ~**s** pl. (cards) spades (plate B 5). 3. m. (bullfight) matador: the person appointed to kill the bull.
~ **de fogo** (fig.) fiery sword. ~ **de vingança** avenging sword. **à ponta de** ~ at the point of the sword. **à prova de** ~ swordproof. **bainha de** ~ sheath, scabbard (sword). **com o lado largo da** ~ with the flat of the sword. **desembainhar a** ~ to draw one's sword. **entre a cruz e a** ~ between the devil and the deep blue sea; between wind and weather. **golpe de** ~ stroke with the sword, sword-cut. **lâmina de** ~ sword-blade. **medir a** ~ **com alguém, lutar à** ~ **com alguém** to fight a duel with s. o. **luta de** ~ fight with swords. **passar à** ~ to kill with the sword. ~**s são trunfos** spades are trump.

espadachim s. m. (pl. **-ins**) 1. swordsman. 2. duelist. 3. bully, bravo, swaggerer.

espadachinar v. 1. to be a swordsman. 2. to act or behave like a swordsman or a duelist.

espadada s. f. sword-cut, stroke with a sword.

espadagão s. m. (pl. **-ões**) a large and old sword.

espadana s. f. 1. (bot.) flag, Spanish iris. 2. flame, blaze. 3. jet, shoot, spout (as of water). 4. the tail of a comet. 5. fin (of a fish).

espadanal s. m. (pl. **-ais**) place where flags grow.

espadanar v. to gush, spout, spring; to bubble, pour forth.

espadâneo adj. (bot.) ensiform (leaves).

espadão s. m. (pl. **-ões**) 1. augmentative of **espada.** 2. a broad and heavy sword.

espadar v. = **espadelar.**

espadarte s. m. (ichth.) swordfish, sawfish (Xiphias gladius).

espadas s. f. pl. (cards) spades.
rei de ~ king of spades.

espadaúdo adj. 1. broad-shouldered. 2. full-bodied, stout, corpulent.

espadeira s. f. (bot.) wallaba (Eperua falcata).

espadeirada s. f. cut or stroke with a sword.

espadeirão s. m. (pl. **-ões**) a long and narrow sword.

espadeirar v. to cut, wound or strike with a sword.

espadeiro s. m. sword maker, sword cutler; blade-smith; swordsman.

espadela s. f. 1. brake, scutcher, swingle: a wooden instrument for beating flax or hemp. 2. a large oar used as a helm.

espadeladeira s. f. woman who beats or scutches flax or hemp.

espadelagem s. f. (pl. **-ens**) scutching, swingling of flax or hemp.

espadelar v. to beat, swingle, to scutch hemp or flax.

espadice s. f. (bot.) spadix.

espadilha s. f. 1. (cards) spadille: the ace of spades. 2. (ichth.) sprat. 3. (fig.) chief, boss.

espadim s. m. (pl. **-ins**) a small sword; rapier.

espadista s. m. + f. (Braz.) swordsman; duelist.

espadongado adj. (Braz.) = **espandongado.**

espádua s. f. (anat.) shoulder: the junction of the arm and trunk; scapula, shoulder blade.

espaduar v. to put the shoulder out of joint.

espagíria s. f. alchemy.

espaguete s. m. (It.) (cul.) spaghetti.

espairecer(-se) v. to amuse, entertain, recreate, distract, divert (also o. s.).

espairecimento s. m. amusement, entertainment, recreation.

espalda s. f. 1. shoulder, shoulder blade. 2. = **espaldar.**

espaldão s. m. (pl. **-ões**) (fort.) epaulment.

espaldar s. m. back rest, back of a chair (plates C 2, D 1, V 1).

espaldear v. (naut.) 1. to drive back. 2. to repel, repulse.

espaldeira s. f. 1. cover for the back of a chair, antimacassar. 2. espalier.

espaldeirada s. f. = **espadeirada.**

espaldeirar v. = **espadeirar.**

espaleira s. f. (gym.) wall bars (plate P 6).

espalha s. m. 1. gabbler, prater, very talkative person. 2. = **espalha-brasas.**

espalha-brasas s. m., sg. + pl. (Braz., fam.) 1. hothead, hotspur. 2. rowdy, blatant, noisy person.

espalhada s. f. 1. spreading, dispersing, scattering. 2. noise, bluster, confusion.

espalhadeira s. f. (agric., also **espalhadoura, espalhadoira**) pitchfork, hayfork.

espalhado s. m. noise; confusion. ‖ adj. 1. scattered, dispersed, spread. 2. divulgated, diffused.
~ **aos quatro ventos** scattered to the wind. **coisas -as pelo chão** things lying about. **estar** ~ to lie about.

espalhador s. m. disperser, dispeller: one who or that which disperses, scatters; divulger. ‖ adj. 1. dispersing, scatterring. 2. divulging.

espalhafatar v. 1. to fuss: make much bother about small matters. 2. to make a noise.

espalhafato s. m. 1. fuss, much bother about small matters. 2. noise, disorder, confusion; uproar.

espalhafatoso adj. 1. fussy. 2. noisy, blatant. 3. ostentatious, flaunting. 4. tawdry, garish. ‖ -amente adv. 1. fussily. 2. noisily.

rir -amente to scream with laughter.

espalhagar v. to separate the straw from the wheat or the grain from the chaff.

espalhamento s. m. spreading: 1. dissemination, scattering, dispersion. 2. diffusion, divulgation.

espalhar v. 1. to spread. 2. to scatter about, strew, disperse, dispel. 3. to divulge, reveal, make known. 4. to broadcast. 5. to disseminate. 6. ~-se: a) to disband, scatter, disperse. b) to become known. c) to spread easily (plants). d) to get abroad. e) to stretch.

~ **um boato** to spread a rumour, go about saying. **o boato espalhou-se rapidamente** the rumour spread like wildfire. **ela espalha tristeza à sua volta** she difuses sadness around her. **ele o espalhou** he sounded it abroad. **não deve espalhá-lo aos quatro ventos** you don't have to shout it from the housetops.

espalmado adj. 1. flat, even, plane. 2. palmate(d). 3. laminate(d).

espalmar v. 1. to flatten, make flat, spread. 2. to smooth. 3. to enlarge, distend, stretch out. 4. (naut.) to clean and tar. 5. ~-se to become flat.

espalto s. m. (min.) spalt: a white scaly mineral used as a flux for metals.

espamparar v. (also **escancarar**) to open wide (as a door).

espanador s. m. feather broom, feather duster, duster, dust-cloth (plate E 8).

espanar v. 1. to dust, clean from dust, wipe off the dust. 2. to strip (screw thread).

espancador s. m. 1. drubber, agressor, attacker. 2. bully, scuffer, brawler. 3. quarrelsome person.

espancamento s. m. spanking, beating, drubbing.

espancar v. 1. to beat, thrash, cudgel, drub. 2. to spank, strike with the open hand (esp. on the buttocks). 3. to frighten away. 4. to disperse.

espanquei-o I dusted his jacket.

espandongado adj. (Braz.) 1. careless, slipshod, slovenly, sloppy, frowsy, slouchy, slack, lax. 2. shabby; tattered, down at the heels.

espandongamento s. m. (Braz.) 1. untidiness, unkemptness, inelegance; slovenliness, carelessness, laxity. 2. disorder, disarray.

espandongar v. (Braz.) 1. to disorder, disarrange. 2. to injure. 3. to blemish, damage. 4. to shatter.

espanéfico adj. (pop.) 1. conceited, vain. 2. priggish. 3. foppish, dandyish.

espanejar v. 1. (also **espanar**) to dust. 2. ~-se to flap the wings and shake off the dust (birds).

espanhol s. m. (pl. **-óis**) 1. Spaniard: native or inhabitant of Spain. 2. Spanish: the language of Spain. ‖ adj. Spanish: of or pertaining to Spain, its people or their language.

espanhola s. f. (pop.) the influenza of 1918.

espanholada s. f. 1. exaggeration; a figure of speech expressing much more than the truth. 2. swaggering, bragging. 3. a group of Spaniards.

espanta-boiada s. m. (pl. **espanta-boiadas**) (Braz., ornith.) terutero (Belonepterus chilenis).

espantadão s. m. simpleton; an easily astonished person. ‖ adj. foolish.

espantadiço adj. fearful, timid, timorous, skittish; easily frightened.

cavalo ~ a skittish horse.

espantado adj. 1. afraid, frightened. 2. surprised, amazed, astonished.

ela olhou-me com os olhos ~s she gazed at me with wondering eyes.

espantador s. m. one who or that which frightens or astonishes; frightener. ‖ adj. frightening, startling.

espantalho s. m. scarecrow: 1. a man of straw set in a field to frighten birds away from crops. 2. shabby or ugly person; guy.

este vestido me transforma em ~ this dress makes a sight of me.

espanta-lobos s. m., sg. + pl. 1. (pop.) chatterbox, talkative person. 2. (bot.) bladder senna.

espantar v. 1. to frighten, terrify, alarm, scare. 2. to put to flight; drive away. 3. to surprise, astonish, amaze; startle. 4. to marvel (at). 5. ~-se: a) to be startled, marvelled or astonished. b) to be surprised. c) to become frightened, get scared.

ele espantou o gato he frightened away the cat.

espanto s. m. 1. fright, terror. 2. scare, fear. 3. amazement, astonishment. 4. admiration, surprise. 5. marvel, wonder.

causar ~ to cause astonishment. **ele olhou com ~ e admiração para o rosto dela** he stared with astonishment and admiration at her face. **para grande ~ meu** to my great surprise.

espantoso adj. (also **espantável**; pl. **-áveis**) 1. dreadful, frightful, fearful. 2. terrible, horrible. 3. amazing, astonishing, marvellous, wonderful, admirable. 4. extraordinary, uncommon.

com velocidade -a at a terrific velocity. **esperam-se revelações -as** amazing revelations are expected.

espapaçado adj. soft, pappy.

espapaçar v. 1. to make pappy, soft or insipid. 2. ~-se to become pappy, soft or insipid.

espapar v. (also **despapar**) to lift or hold up the head too much (horse).

esparadrapo s. m. adhesive tape.

esparavão s. m. (pl. **-ões**) spavin: a disease in horses affecting the hock joint.

esparavel s. m. (pl. **-éis**) 1. a sort of fishing-net. 2. tester of a bed. 3. fringe (as of a curtain). 4. a mason's float, hand float, panel trowel (plate A 7).

esparavonado adj. spavined (horse).

espargimento s. m. 1. spreading, diffusion. 2. scattering. 3. pouring out, shedding. 4. sprinkling.

espargir v. 1. to scatter about, spread. 2. to spill, shed (liquids). 3. to diffuse. 4. to strew. 5. to sprinkle, spray.

espargo s. m. (bot.) asparagus (Asparagus officinalis).

esparguta s. f. (bot.) spurry, spurrey (Spergula arvensis).

esparóide s. m. a sparoid fish.

esparolação s. f. (Braz.) 1. levity, frivolity. 2. rapture, ecstasy. 3. carelessness; thoughtlessness.

esparolado s. m. (Braz.) 1. frivolous or thoughtless person. 2. lier. 3. boaster, braggart. ‖ adj. 1. frivolous; thoughtless. 2. talkative, garrulous. 3. untruthful.

esparralhar v. 1. to spread about. 2. = **derramar**.

esparramado adj. (Braz.) 1. scattered, dispersed, spread. 2. hotheaded. 3. intemperate, extravagant. 4. disorderly. 5. unkempt, untidy.

esparramar v. 1. to scatter about, spread, strew; disperse. 2. ~-se to disband, disperse.

esparrame, esparramo s. m. 1. scattering, spreading. 2. rout, stampede, dispersion. 3. ostentation; exaggeration. 4. noisy quarrel, brawl, row.

esparrar-se v. (Braz.) 1. to come a cropper. 2. to be mistaken. 3. to talk rubbish.

esparregado s. m. a dish of herbs boiled and seasoned with vinegar, oil and salt.

esparregar v. to boil and season herbs.

esparrela s. f. 1. springe, noose, snare. 2. trap, pitfall. 3. fraud, trick, hoax.

cair na ~ to fall into the snare.

esparrinhar v. 1. to sprinkle about; to splash about. 2. to spill, pour out.

esparro s. m. (Braz., sl.) 1. stall: a pickpocket's helper who diverts attention while the theft is committed. 2. noise, humming, buzzing.

esparsa s. f. a sort of poetry having verses of six syllables.

esparso adj. 1. scattered, dispersed, spread, sparse. 2. diffuse. 3. separate. 4. overturned.

espartal s. m. (pl. **-ais**) place where esparto grows.

espartano s. m. Spartan: native or inhabitant of Sparta. ‖ adj. 1. Spartan: of or pertaining to Sparta. 2. (fig.) austere, severe, rigorous, strict.

espartaria s. f. 1. esparto articles (as baskets, ropes, mats). 2. place where such articles are made or sold.

esparteína s. f. (chem.) spartein(e).

esparteiro s. m. person who makes or sells articles of esparto.

espartenhas s. f. pl. sandals made of esparto.

espartilhado adj. 1. fitted with a corset. 2. (fig.) elegant, graceful.

espartilhar(-se) v. to corset.

espartilheiro s. m. person who makes corsets or stays.

espartilho s. m. stays, bodice, corset.

espartir v. to separate, disunite, part; break off.

esparto s. m. (bot.) esparto: a kind of coarse grass (Stipa tenacissima) used for making ropes, baskets, mats.

esparzeta s. f. (bot.) sainfoin (Onobrichy sativa).

esparzir v. = **espargir.**

espasmar v. 1. to cause spasms, cramp. 2. ~-se to be affected or seized with a cramp; to suffer a spasm.

espasmo s. m. 1. (med.) spasm: excessive muscular contraction; cramp, convulsion. 2. (fig.) ecstasy, delight, rapture.

espasmódico adj. spasmodic, convulsive.

espasmofilia s. f. (med.) spasmophilia, a spasmophilic diathesis.

espástico adj. (med.) spastic, spasmodic.

espata s. f. 1. (bot.) spathe: a large bract enveloping the spadix. 2. spatha: a double-edged broadsword.

espatáceo adj. (bot.) spathaceous, spathal: enclosed in a spathe.

espatela s. f. tongue depressor: a wooden spatula used to depress the tongue in order to examine the throat.

espático adj. (min.) spathic: of or relating to spar.

espatifado adj. broken into pieces; shattered.

espatifar v. 1. to shatter, smash. 2. to break into or tear to pieces. 3. (fig.) to dissipate, squander.

o avião espatifou-se contra o solo the plane crashed. **ele espatifou-se no chão** he fell flat on the ground.

espato s. m. (min.) spar: name for various lustrous minerals.

~ **calcário** calc(arious)-spar.

espatódea s. f. tree of the family Bignoniaceae (Spathodea campanulata).

espato-pesado s. m. (pl. **espatos-pesados**) (min.) barite.

espátula s. f. 1. spatula, spattle; slice (plates C 20, D 3, P 12). 2. trowel. 3. (ichth.) paddlefish. 4. paper knife.

~ **de pintor** palette knife.

espatulado adj. (bot.) spatular, spatulate, shaped like a spatula.

espatuleta s. f. a small spatula.

espaventar v. 1. to frighten. 2. to astonish, amaze. 3. (fig.) to puff up, make arrogant or haughty. 4. ~-se to be frightened or alarmed; to get scared.

espavento s. m. 1. terror, fright, scare, alarm. 2. astonishment. 3. (fig.) pomp, ostentation, display.

espaventoso adj. 1. frightful, dreadful. 2. frightening. 3. astonishing. 4. pompous, showy, ostentatious. 5. self-important.

espavorido adj. frightened, terrified, appalled, terror-stricken, afraid.

espavorir, espavorizar v. (also **espavorecer**) 1. to frighten, scare; terrify, appall. 2. ~-se to become frightened, scared, appalled, horror-stricken.

especar v. 1. to prop, stay, support, sustain. 2. to protect. 3. to stop short. 4. ~-se to rest on or against, be supported by.

espeçar v. to make longer.

especial s. m. (pl. **-ais**) private courier or messenger. ‖ adj. m. + f. 1. especial, special, particular, peculiar, individual, singular. 2. reserved, extra (as a train). 3. excellent, very good. ‖ ~**mente** adv. especially; principally.

oferta ~ (com.) special bargain. **ônibus** ~ special bus.

especialidade s. f. speciality, particularity, peculiarity, specialty, special branch.

especialista s. m. + f. specialist, expert.

~ **de doenças do coração** heart specialist.

especialização s. f. (pl. **-ões**) specialization, specialty.

especializado adj. specialized.

operário ~ skilled workman. **ramo** ~ especial line.

especializar v. 1. to specialize, differentiate, particularize. 2. to distinguish. 3. ~-se: a) to distinguish o. s. b) to train o. s. for a special branch.

especiaria s. f. (also **espécia**) spices (in general), spicery.

espécie s. f. 1. species, sort, kind, variety. 2. class, genus, group, order. 3. spice. 4. nature, gender, quality, character. 5. specie, metal money. 6. (jur.) particular case.

~**s sacramentais, as santas** ~**s** (R. C. Church) sacramental species, the sacramental elements. **de toda a** ~ of all sorts. **ela é uma** ~ **de arrumadeira** she is something like a maid. **pagar em** ~ to pay in goods (not in money). **uma** ~ **de:** 1. a species, sort, kind or variety of. 2. something like. **valor em** ~ value in cash.

especieiro s. m. person who sells spices.

especificação s. f. (pl. **-ões**) specification, act of specifying; particularization.

especificado adj. 1. specified. 2. detailed, minute, complete. 3. particularized.

especificador s. m. specifier. ‖ adj. specifying.

especificar v. to specify, mention or name precisely, indicate, stipulate; particularize, individualize.

especificativo adj. specificative: tending or serving to specify.

específico s. m. specific remedy: a medicine that cures a particular disease. ‖ adj. specific, peculiar, particular, special, concrete, explicit. ‖ **especificamente** adv. specifically.

calor ~ specific heat. **caráter** ~ specific character. **peso** ~ specific gravity.

especilho s. m. (surg.) probe.

espécime(n) s. m. (pl. **-ens, -ímenes**) specimen, example, sample, instance, model.

especiosidade s. f. speciousness: 1. plausible or fair appearance. 2. beauty.

especioso adj. specious: 1. plausible, fair. 2. beautiful. 3. seducible. ‖ **-amente** adv. speciously.

espectador s. m. spectator, looker-on, onlooker, observer, witness, bystander, beholder.
ela causou admiração a todos os ~es she was the admiration of all beholders. **filas cerradas de ~es** serried rows of spectators.
espectadora s. f. spectatress.
espectável adj. m. + f. (pl. -áveis) remarkable.
espectral, espetral adj. m. + f. (pl. -ais) spectral: 1. of or pertaining to a specter, ghostlike, ghostly. 2. concerning the solar spectrum.
espectro, espetro s. m. 1. specter, ghost, spirit, apparition, phantom. 2. (phys.) spectrum: an image produced by the decomposition of rays of light by means of a prism. 3. (fig.) skeleton, very thin person.
~ solar solar spectrum.
espectrologia, espetrologia s. f. (phys.) spectrology: the science of spectral analysis.
espectrológico, espetrológico adj. spectrological: of or pertaining to spectrology.
espectrometria, espetrometria s. f. (phys.) spectrometry.
espectrômetro, espetrômetro s. m. spectrometer: instrument for measuring the angular deviation of a ray of light passing through a prism.
espectroscopia, espetroscopia s. f. (phys.) spectroscopy, spectrum analysis.
espectroscópico, espetroscópico adj. (phys.) spectroscopic.
espectroscópio, espetroscópio s. m. (phys.) spectroscope: instrument for forming and analysing the spectra of rays emitted by bodies.
especula s. m. + f. (Braz., pop.) busybody, meddler, snooper.
especulação s. f. (pl. -ões) speculation: 1. act of speculating. 2. inspection, examination. 3. (com.) speculative business transaction or investment.
~ de bolsa stock-jobbing. **preço de ~** speculative price.
especulador s. m. speculator: 1. observer, onlooker. 2. person who practises speculation; speculating merchant. || adj. speculative.
~ de terras land-jobber.
especular (I) v. to speculate: 1. observe, consider, view. 2. inspect, examine, investigate. 3. theorize. 4. meditate, conjecture, contemplate upon. 5. invest money; make purchases or investments on the chance of profit. 6. traffic, carry on business.
especular (II) adj. m. + f. 1. specular: of or pertaining to a mirror. 2. diaphanous, transparent, pelucid.
especulária s. f. (opt.) catoptries: the science of reflected light.
especulativo adj. speculative: 1. pertaining or given to speculation. 2. contemplative. 3. theorical, not practical. || **-amente** adv. speculatively.
espéculo s. m. (surg.) speculum.
espedaçar v. (also **despedaçar**) to break into or tear to pieces; to shatter, smash, hackle; crash.
espedregar v. to take away the stones (from a field).
espeleologia s. f. speleology: the scientific study of caves.
espeleológico adj. speleological: of or pertaining to speleology.
espeleologista s. m. + f., **espeleólogo** m. speleologist: person who practises speleology.
espelhado adj. smooth as a mirror, clear, bright, polished, burnished, shining.
espelhamento s. m. (also **espelhação**) 1. act of giving a high polish to. 2. reflection (as of a mirror).
espelhar v. 1. to polish, bright, make smooth as a mirror. 2. to mirror, reflect in or as in a mirror. 3. **~-se:** a) to look at o. s. in a mirror. b) to reflect.

espelharia s. f. mirror factory or shop.
espelheiro s. m. person who makes or sells mirrors.
espelhento adj. polished, clear, mirrorlike.
espelhim s. m. a white lustrous plaster.
espelho s. m. 1. mirror, looking-glass (plates B 3, M 14, P 19). 2. (fig.) model, example. 3. (also ~ de fechadura) escutcheon of a lock. 4. riser (of a step). 5. (tech.) face. 6. (electr.) switch plate. 7. (mus.) sound-hole (as of a guitar) (plates G 2, V 5). 8. (typogr.) type area (plate L 4).
~ plano-côncavo plano-concave mirror (plate M 9).
~ de toucador dressing glass. **~ retrovisor** (plate V 4) rear-vision mirror, driving mirror.
espelho-de-vênus s. m. (pl. **espelhos-de-vênus**) (bot.) 1. cardinal-flower. 2. musk plant. 3. Venus's looking-glass.
espelina s. f. (Braz.) a plant of the family Cucurbitaceae (Cayoponia espelina).
espeloteado s. m. (Braz.) 1. person without discernment. 2. hotheaded, muddleheaded, foolish fellow. || adj. 1. undiscerned; careless. 2. hotheaded. 3. rattlebrained; foolish. 4. muddleheaded. 5. unquiet, turbulent.
espeloteamento s. m. (Braz., also **espeloteio**) 1. emptyheadedness, giddiness, foolishness. 2. wildness.
espelotear v. (Braz.) to act or behave senselessly, rashly.
espelta s. m. spelt: a kind of wheat (Triticum spelta).
espelunca s. f. 1. cavern, den, hole. 2. miserable room or house. 3. den of vice; gambling hell.
espenda s. f. skirt of a saddle.
espenejar v. (also **espanejar**) 1. to dust. 2. **~-se:** a) to shake off the dust (clothes). b) to rig o. s. up.
espenicar v. 1. to pluck, pick, pull (feathers). 2. **~-se:** to preen: a) trim (feathers) with the beak (birds). b) trim, rig o. s. up.
espenifre s. m. ancient card game where the two of clubs was the highest card.
espeque s. m. 1. prop, stay, brace, support. 2. (fig.) aid, protection. 3. handspoke.
espera s. f. 1. expectation, expecting, waiting for. 2. a wait. 3. pause, respite. 4. delay. 5. hope. 6. (hunt.) station, stand. 7. ambush. 8. (Braz.) toolpost of a lathe. 9. (N. Braz.) place of waiting. || **~!** interj. wait!
ele estava à sua ~ he was waiting for you (him or her). **sala de ~** waiting room.
esperado adj. 1. expected, hoped (for), wished. 2. probable, likely. 3. foreseen; prospective.
não ~ unexpected; unhoped for.
esperadouro s. m. (also **esperadoiro**) 1. watchtower. 2. place of waiting.
espera-marido s. m. (pl. **espera-maridos**) (Braz.) a sweet made with burned sugar and eggs.
esperança s. f. hope: 1. an expectant desire. 2. expectation. 3. the object of hope. 4. (R. C. Church) one of the theological virtues.
acalentado pela ~ rocked in hopes. **aquém das minhas ~s** beyond my expectations. **dar ~s a** to hold out hopes to. **eles estão sem nenhuma ~** they have no hope whatever. **mas nesta vez não há ~** but this time there is not a chance. **na ~ de** in the hope of. **não há ~s** there is no room for hope. **não há mais ~** it is past hope. **não ter mais ~** to be out of hope. **sem ~** void of hope.
esperançado adj. hopeful.
esperançar v. 1. to give hopes. 2. to make one hope. 3. **~-se:** a) to have hope. b) to place one's confidence in.
esperançoso adj. hopeful, full of hope, expectant. || **-amente** adv. hopefully.
jovem ~ young hopeful.

esperantista s. m. + f. Esperantist. ‖ adj. Esperantist, Esperantic.

esperanto s. m. Esperanto: an international auxiliary language.

esperar v. 1. to hope for. 2. to wait (for), expect, await. 3. to look for, watch. 4. to suppose, presume. 5. to conjecture. 6. to count on, rely, trust in. 7. to have hope. 8. to ambush.
~ **em fila** to wait in line. ~ **em pé pacientemente** to kick one's heels. ~ **por** to wait for. ~ **por sapato de defunto** to hope against hope. **algo que não esperávamos** something we have not calculated upon. **apanhei-o sem ele** ~ I caught him unawares, (sl.) on the hop. **assim o espero** I hope so. **ela espera com ansiedade** she waits anxiously. **ela está esperando (bebê)** she is expecting, she is in the family way. **ele esperou em vão por seu dinheiro** he failed to get his money, (coll.) he whistled for his money. **ele esperou sua oportunidade** he bided his time. **eles tiveram que** ~ **muito no portão** they had a long wait at the gate. **era de se** ~ it was seen to come. **era uma resposta que não tinha esperado** it was an answer I had not expected. **esperamos que nada lhe tenha acontecido** let us hope nothing has happened to him. **espera-se que você trabalhe o dia inteiro** you are supposed to work all day. **espere o resultado** wait for it. **espere pelo momento oportuno** watch your time. **espere um momento!** wait a moment! **espero encontrá-la no restaurante** I expect to meet her in the restaurant. **espero o melhor** I hope for the best. **espero que ela venha** I expect (that) she will come. **espero que você seja capaz de fazê-lo** you shall be able to do it, I trust. **espero um bom resultado** I anticipate a good result. **fazer alguém** ~ **to keep s. o. waiting. ficaram esperando** they were kept waiting, (coll.) they cooled their heels. **fizemo-lo** ~ we kept him waiting. **não pude** ~ **a coisa terminar** I couldn't stay to the end of it. **quando a gente menos espera é que acontece** the unexpected always happens. **sabemos o que temos de** ~ we know what we are up to. **o tempo e a maré não esperam por ninguém** time and tide wait for no man.

esperável adj. m. + f. (pl. **-áveis**) probable; that may be expected or hoped for.

esperdiçador s. m. lavisher, prodigal, squanderer, dissipator, spendthrift. ‖ adj. lavishing, prodigal.

esperdiçar v. to lavish, squander, dissipate, waste, misspend, spend prodigally.
~ **o tempo** to squander away one's time.

esperdício s. m. lavishness, prodigality, waste, foolish expenses, squandering.

esperma s. m. (biol.) sperm, semen, testicular secretion.

espermacete s. m. spermaceti: a white fatty substance found in the head of the sperm whale or cachalot.

espermático adj. spermatic, pertaining to the semen.

espermatizar v. 1. to spermatize. 2. to fecundate.

espermatocele s. f. (med.) spermatocele: a cyst of the epididymus or testicles containing spermatozoa.

espermatófito s. m. (bot.) spermatophyte.

espermatologia s. f. spermatology: the scientific study of sperm.

espermatológico adj. spermatological: referring to spermatology.

espermatorréia s. f. (med.) spermatorrhea: involuntary discharge of semen.

espermatose s. f. (physiol.) spermatogenesis: the process of formation of spermatozoa.

espermatozóide s. m. 1. (biol.) spermatozoon: a mature male germ cell. 2. spermatozoid: the male germ cell of plants.

espernear v. 1. to kick about, shake one's legs. 2. to jump, leap or fidget about.

espernegar v. 1. = **espernear.** 2. to straddle, sprawl; spread the legs.

espertador s. m. 1. waker, wakener. 2. one who or that which animates, stimulates or encourages. ‖ adj. 1. awakening, arousing. 2. animating, heartening, inciting.

espertalhão s. m. (pl. **-ões**) (f. **-ona**) 1. slicker, sly or tricky person. 2. a bad and dishonest person, villain, rascal.

espertar v. 1. to awake, rouse from sleep. 2. to stimulate, incite, stir up, animate. 3. to revive, give new life to. 4. to call. 5. ~-**se**: a) to awaken, arouse. b) to take a heart.

esperteza s. f. 1. briskness, quickness, sprightliness, liveliness, smartness, sharpness. 2. vivacity, vivaciousness. 3. astuteness, cunning(ness).

espertina s. f. (also **insônia**) insomnia, sleeplessness.

espertinar v. 1. to cause insomnia. 2. to suffer from insomnia.

esperto adj. 1. sprightly, brisk, lively, alive, quick. 2. agile, spry. 3. vivacious. 4. active, smart, alert, nimble. 5. intelligent, bright, acute. 6. sharp, ready-witted. 7. astute, cunning, sly. 8. clever, tricky, trickish. 9. energetic, vigorous. 10. warm (water). ‖ **-amente** adv. 1. quickly; actively. 2. astutely. 3. trickily.
ela é -a she is quick-witted, (sl.) she was born with her eyes open. **ele é demasiado** ~ he knows too much for me. **ficar** ~ to learn wit. **garoto** ~ sharp boy.

espescoçar v. 1. to bare the root of a vine. 2. ~-**se** to stretch one's neck.

espessar v. 1. to thicken, make thick. 2. to condense, condensate. 3. ~-**se** to grow thick or thicker.

espessidão s. f. (pl. **-ões**) 1. thickness. 2. darkness, obscurity. 3. denseness, density.

espesso (ê) adj. (pl. **espessos**). 1. thick. 2. dense, consistent. 3. opaque, obscure. 4. shady (tree).

espessura s. f. 1. thickness. 2. denseness, density. 3. (fig.) woods, forest, thick wood.

espetacular adj. m. + f. (Braz.) spectacular; splendid, grand, excellent; magnificent. ‖ ~**mente** adv. spectacularly.
uma coisa ~ a splendid affair.

espetáculo s. m. 1. spectacle: a) a sight, thing to look at. b) a public show or display; a play. 2. view, scene. 3. perspective. 4. scandal.
o ~ **começa às 8 horas** the performance begins at eight o'clock. **que** ~! what a show! **sala de** ~**s** playhouse auditorium. **um** ~ **comovente** a moving spectacle. **um** ~ **que alegra a vista** a sight to rejoice one's eyes. **um triste** ~ a sorry sight.

espetaculosidade s. f. 1. spectacularity. 2. ostentation, display, pomp. 3. din, uproar, noisy show, fanfare.

espetaculoso adj. 1. spectacular. 2. pompous, showy, ostentatious.

espetada s. f. 1. a blow, thrust with or as with a spit. 2. a jab, sticking.

espetadela s. f. 1. = **espetada.** 2. difficulties. 3. (fig.) fraud, swindle.

espetado adj. 1. stiff, straight as a pin. 2. on a spit, sticked. 3. (fig.) erect, upright.

espetanço s. m. (Braz., sl.) = **espetadela** 2 and 3.

espetão s. m. (pl. **-ões**) 1. hooked iron for drawing crucibles out of the fire. 2. a big spit.

espetar v. 1. to spit, put on the spit; broach, impale. 2. to pierce, prick. 3. to thrust, drive, stick, stab, run (in). 4. to poke (as with a stick). 5. to cheat, deceive, take in. 6. ~-**se**: a) to get hurt. b) to get stuck.

ela se espetou com um alfinete she pricked herself with a pin.

espeto (ê) s. m. (pl. **espetos**) 1. spit (as for roasting meat). 2. a sharp-pointed stick. 3. broach. 4. (fig.) tall and thin person. 5. (Braz., sl.): a) a difficult thing, a rub. b) trick, deception. c) annoyance, nuisance.

ela é magra como um ~ she is a thin as a lath. **isto é um** ~! (coll.) that's a fix, tough situation!

espevitadeira s. f. (a pair of) snuffers.

espevitado adj. 1. snuffed (wick as of a candle). 2. (fig.): a) brisk, lively. b) insolent, flippant, petulant. c) talkative, garrulous. d) pretentious, affected.

espevitar v. 1. to snuff: cut or pinch off the burned wick. 2. to make pretentious or affected. 3. to incite, stimulate. 4. ~-**se**: a) to speak in a chosen or affected manner. b) to become irritated, get angry.

espezinhado adj. scorned, despised, humbled, oppressed, vexed.

espezinhador s. m. one who scorns, oppresses or ill--treats another. ǁ adj. 1. ill-treating. 2. humiliating.

espezinhar v. 1. to trample on. 2. to ill-treat, oppress, vex. 3. to humiliate, depress.

espia s. m. + f. 1. spy, watcher; informer. 2. sentinel, sentry; lookout. 3. m. (Braz.) fisher in charge of spotting the shoal which is to be caught with the net. 4. f. (naut.) tow-rope, drag-rope, warp; guy wire.

espiada s. f. (Braz.) look, glance, squint, ogle.

espia-maré s. m. (pl. **espia-marés**) (Braz.) 1. (zool.) ghost crab. 2. tide-gauge.

espiantador s. m. (Braz., sl.) shoplifter (who runs away after stealing).

espiantar v. (Braz.) to run away (after shoplifting).

espião s. m. (pl. **-ões**) (f. **espiã**) spy, intelligencer, secret agent, undercover man.

espiar v. 1. to spy, watch, observe, dog. 2. to pry into. 3. to wait for an opportunity. 4. (Braz.) to look at, observe. 5. (naut.) to warp.

~ **alguém** to spy upon s. o.

espicaçado adj. 1. pecked by birds (as a fruit). 2. striked. 3. (fig.) tortured, tormented. 4. hurt. 5. aggrieved. 6. incited, goaded.

espicaçar v. 1. to peck (as a bird). 2. to strike, hit (with a pointed instrument). 3. to needle. 4. to prick, sting. 5. to pierce. 6. to stimulate, incite, instigate. 7. to afflict, grieve. 8. to torture, torment.

espicha s. f. 1. a string of fish. 2. (naut.) sprit. 3. (Braz.) fiasco, failure in a public performance.

vela de ~ (naut.) spritsail, sprit lug.

espichar v. 1. to string by the gills (fish). 2. to broach, tap a cask. 3. to stretch, extend. 4. to prolong. 5. to enlarge. 6. (pop.) to die, kick the bucket. 7. ~-**se**: a) to stretch o. s. out. b) to be mistaken. c) to prove a fiasco; to fail.

espiche s. m. 1. = **espicho**. 2. (fam.) allocution, speech.

espicho s. m. 1. spigot, faucet, tap, plug (plate B 4). 2. perforator, punch. 3. (fig.) a very thin and tall person. 4. (Braz.): a) nervousness at an examination. b) fiasco, failure.

espiciforme adj. m. + f. (bot. also **espiculado**) spiciform: having the form of a spike.

espícula s. f. spicule, spikelet.

espicular v. 1. to give the form of a spike to. 2. to spiculate, taper, point.

espículo s. m. 1. spicule. 2. sting, spike, prick. 3. point.

espiga s. f. 1. ear of corn, spike (plate E 9). 2. (carp.) tenon, dowel, pin (plate C 9). 3. hangnail:

flaw at the root of the nails. 4. the star Spica 5. (fig.): a) disappointment, deception. b) annoyance, nuisance. c) contrariety. d) prejudice; fraud, swindle.

~ **de encaixe** (carp.) mortise tenon (plate C 9). ~ **de ferramenta** tang (plate S 3). ~ **de madeira** (carp.) tenon. ~ **de milho** corn-cob. ~ **de trigo** wheatear. **junta de** ~ **e encaixe** tenon joint. **sem** ~ earless.

espiga-d'água s. f. (pl. **espigas-d'água**) (bot.) pondweed.

espigado adj. 1. spicate, eared, bearing spikes. 2. (fig.): a) developed, grown up. b) tall, slender.

espigaitado adj. (Braz.) 1. excited. 2. intoxicated.

espigame s. m. (agric.) a heap of ears.

espigão s. m. (pl. **-ões**) 1. a great ear or spike. 2. ridge, ridge-pole. 3. hip of a roof, hip rafter. (plate T 5). 4. top of a wall. 5. (archit.) buttress. 6. ridge of a mountain. 7. iron spike. 8. sharp point of any tool. 9. spur. 10. sting.

espigar v. 1. to ear, form ears. 2. to seed. 3. to grow up, develop. 4. to cheat, deceive. 5. (Port.) to investigate (a person). 6. ~-**se** to suffer damage.

espigo s. m. 1. sharp end, point (of iron or wood). 2. sprout of vegetables.

espigoso adj. spiky: 1. eared, spiciform. 2. having spikes; covered with spikes.

espigueiro s. m. granary, corn-loft, corn crib.

espigueta s. f. spicule, spikelet, small spike or ear.

espigueto s. m. the high or shrill sound of a flute.

espiguilha s. f. a sort of narrow lace.

espiguilhar v. to adorn with narrow laces.

espinafração s. f. (pl. **-ões**) (Braz.) 1. act of ridiculing. 2. a scolding, reproach.

espinafrar v. (Braz.) 1. to ridicule, deride, laugh at. 2. to reprove or admonish severely.

espinafre s. m. (bot.) spinach (Spinacia oleracea).

espinafre-da-guiana s. m. (pl. **espinafres-da-guiana**) inkweed, ink plant (Phytolacca octandra).

espinal adj. m. + f. (pl. **-ais**) (also **espinhal**) spinal: 1. of or pertaining to the spine or spinal column. 2. resembling a spine.

espinça s. f. napping (of cloth).

espinçar v. to nap, burl (cloth).

espinel s. m. (pl. **-éis**) = **espinhel.**

espinélio s. m. (min.) spinel.

espíneo, espinhoso adj. prickly, thorny, spiny, having thorns or spines.

espinescente adj. m. + f. (bot.) 1. spinescent, spinose, spinous, full of spines or thorns. 2. spiniform, spinelike, having the form of a spine or thorn.

espinescido adj. ending in a point or thorn.

espineta s. f. spinet: an ancient musical instrument.

espingarda s. f. (hand)gun, rifle, shot-gun, musket. ~ **a ar comprimido** air gun, air rifle. ~ **de dois canos** double-barreled gun. **cano de** ~ barrel. **cão da** ~ cock (of a gun). **desarmar uma** ~ to uncock a gun.

espingardada s. f. musket-shot, gunshot.

espingardão s. m. (pl. **-ões**) musketoon.

espingardaria s. f. 1. musketeers. 2. plenty of muskets or handguns. 3. fusillade, volley.

espingardear v. to shoot, put to death by shooting (with a musket or rifle).

espingardeira s. f. loophole for muskets or musketoons.

espingardeiro s. m. 1. gunsmith, gunmaker. 2. (obs.) musketeer.

espingolado adj. (Braz.) tall, lean and clumsy (person).

espinha s. f. 1. (anat.) spine, backbone, spinal column. 2. fishbone (plate P 7). 3. pimple, whelk, wheal. 4. (fig.) obstacle, difficulty, trouble.

~ de fundidor wimble, drill. ~ dorsal dorsal column, backbone. curvatura da ~ curvature of the spine. ponto de ~ feather whalebone stitch. estar na ~ to be very lean, weak or poor.

espinhaço s. m. 1. backbone, spine, chine. 2. mountain chain. 3. crest, ridge of a mountain (plate M 11). 4. dorsum. 5. back.

espinhal s. m. (pl. -ais) (also espinheiral) brier patch, place where briers grow, thorn. || adj. m. + f. spinal: of or pertaining to the spine or spinal column. medula ~ (anat.) spinal marrow.

espinhar(-se) v. 1. to prick (like or with a thorn). 2. (fig.): a) to nettle, sting, irritate. b) to offend, pique, hurt. c) to be offended, take offence.

espinheiro s. m. (bot.) 1. brier, bramble, Christ's--thorn. 2. bastard ironwood, wild lime.

espinheiro-bravo s. m. (pl. espinheiros-bravos) (bot.) common designation for several shrubs of the family Leguminosae.

espinheiro-da-virgínia s. m. (pl. espinheiros-da-virgínia) (bot.) honey-locust (Gleditschia triacanthos).

espinheiro-de-cristo s. m. (pl. espinheiros-de-cristo) (bot.) Christ's-thorn paliurus.

espinheiro-preto s. m. (pl. espinheiros-pretos) (bot.) black haw.

espinhel s. m. (pl. -éis) (Braz.) paternoster line.

espinhela s. f. the tip or extremity of the sternum.

espinhento adj. thorny, prickly.

espinho s. m. 1. thorn, prickle. 2. a small sharp point; sting. 3. quill of a porcupine. 4. spine. 5. (fig.) difficulty, hindrance, tough problem, rub; affliction, uneasiness. cheio de ~s full of thorns, thorny. não há rosa sem ~s no rose without a thorn, no joy without annoy.

espinho-de-agulha s. m. (pl. espinhos-de-agulha) (bot.) sheep bur, Paraguay bur.

espinho-de-carneiro s. m. (pl. espinhos-de-carneiro) (bot.) 1. cockspur. 2. cocklebur. 3. spiny clot-bur.

espinho-de-cerca s. m. (pl. espinhos-de-cerca) (bot.) Mysore thorn (Caesalpina sepiaria).

espinho-de-cristo s. m. (pl. espinhos-de-cristo) (bot.) 1. Christ's-thorn. 2. coronilla.

espinho-de-judeu s. m. (pl. espinhos-de-judeu) (bot.) jew's-thorn.

espinhoso adj. 1. thorny, prickly. 2. spiny. 3. (fig.) spinous, difficult, arduous; disagreeable. ponto ~ knotty point.

espinicar-se v. to dress o. s. with great care and nicety; to rig o. s. up.

espiniforme adj. m. + f. spiniform: having the form of a spine or thorn.

espinilho s. m. (Braz., bot.) coronilla, coronillo (Gleditschia amorphoides).

espinoteado adj. (Braz.) frivolous, flippant; rattle-brained; inconsiderate, thoughtless.

espinotear v. 1. to curvet, buck, leap. 2. to leap or bound about. 3. to become angry, to rave.

espiolhar v. 1. to louse, delouse, clean from lice. 2. (fig.) to investigate or examine minutely, to sift.

espionagem s. f. (pl. -ens) 1. spying, espionage, intelligence service. 2. a body of spies.

espionar v. 1. to spy (out). 2. to observe, watch (in secret). 3. to work as a spy.

espipar v. 1. to spring forth; gush, spout. 2. to burst.

espipocar v. = empipocar.

espique s. m. stem or trunk of a palm tree.

espiqueado adj. having a stem like a palm tree.

espira s. f. spire: 1. a spiral, a coil. 2. spiral line, a single turn of a spiral. 3. thread of a screw.

espiráculo s. m. spiracle, air-hole, vent-hole.

espiral s. f. (pl. -ais) 1. spiral: a spiral curve, formation, spring or the like (as the thread of a screw). 2. hair-spring (of a watch). || adj. spiral, coiled, helical.

elevar-se em linha ~ to spiral up. linha ~ spiral line, spiral gear. uma ~ de fumaça a wreath of smoke.

espiralado adj. spiralled: having the form of a spiral.

espiralar v. to spiral: 1. make spiral. 2. form into a spiral. 3. ~-se to move spirally.

espirante adj. m. + f. 1. breathing. 2. living, alive.

espirar v. 1. to breathe. 2. to exhale, emit, pour out. 3. to live, be alive.

espirema s. m. (biol.) spireme: the chromatin of a cell nucleus when in the form of a thread.

espírilo s. m. (med.) spirillum: a spiral-structured microbe.

espirilose s. f. (med.) spirillosis.

espírita s. m. + f. (also espiritista) spiritualist, spiritist: person who believes in spiritualism or communication with departed spirits. || adj. spiritualistic: of or pertaining to spiritualism or communication with departed spirits.

espiritar v. 1. to bring under the control of the devil. 2. to cause to be mischievous or naughty. 3. to inspire, infuse. 4. to insinuate. 5. to incite, provoke, instigate.

espiriteira s. f. (Braz.) etna: a heating apparatus.

espiritismo s. m. spiritualism: a system of professed communication with departed spirits esp. through mediums.

espírito s. m. 1. spirit: a) soul, immaterial part of man; mind. b) a supernatural being (as an angel). c) a ghost, phantasm, apparition, spectre. d) an elf, fairy, sprite. e) vigour of mind or intellect. f) vivacity, energy, ardour. g) enthusiasm, animation, life. h) temper, disposition. i) person, personality. j) mood, humour, wit. k) distilled alcohol. l) pure alcohol. 2. imagination. 3. tendency.

~ de camaradagem team spirit. ~ de contradição, ~ de porco spirit of contradiction. ~ de vingança vindictive spirit. ~ forte freethinker, unbeliever. ~ maligno devil, demon. ~ plácido placid mind. ~ prático practical mind. ~s animais (vitais) animal (vital) spirits. Espírito Santo Holy Ghost, Holy Spirit. abatimento de ~ depression of mind. abstração de ~ absence of mind. ausente do corpo, presente em ~ absent in body, present in spirit. batidas dos ~s spirit-rapping. bem-aventurados os pobres de ~ blessed are the poor in spirit. cultivar o ~ to cultivate the mind. homem de ~ a man of genius. jogar com ~ esportivo to play fair. pessoa de ~ person of wit. presença de ~ presence of mind, readiness of mind. sossegar o ~ to set one's heart at rest. sossego de ~ peace of mind. um ~ ativo an active mind.

espírito-santense s. m. + f. (pl. espírito-santenses) (Braz.) native or inhabitant of the state of Espírito Santo. || adj. of or pertaining to this state.

espiritual adj. m. + f. (pl. -ais) spiritual, immaterial, incorporeal, bodiless; mental, intellectual; mystic(al); devout, religious; ecclesiastic(al). padre ~ father-confessor.

espiritualidade s. f. spirituality, immateriality; religiousness, sanctity.

espiritualismo s. m. (philos.) spiritualism: the doctrine of the existence of spirit as distinct from matter.

espiritualista s. m. + f. spiritualist: person who accepts philosophical spiritualism. || adj. spiritualistic.

espiritualização s. f. (pl. -ões) spiritualization: act of spiritualizing or the state of being spiritualized.

espiritualizar v. to spiritualize: 1. make spiritual. 2. refine the intellect. 3. animate, inspirit. 4. revive. 5. distil, extract spirit from. 6. ~-se: a) recover one's spirits. b) become spiritualized.

espirituoso adj. 1. spirituous, alcoholic. 2. witty, spirited, clever. ‖ -amente adv. 1. spirituously. 2. wittily.

espirógrafo s. m. spirograph.

espiróide adj. m. + f. spiroid(al): like a screw or spiral.

espirômetro s. m. spirometer: an instrument that measures the capacity of the lungs.

espiroqueta, espiroqueto s. m. spirochete: a microbe of the order Spirochaetales.

espirra-canivetes s. m. + f., sg. + pl. hot-headed, hot-brained, irritable person. ‖ adj. hot-headed.

espirradeira s. f. (bot.) oleander (Nerium oleander).

espirrar v. 1. to sneeze. 2. to crackle. 3. to crepitate. 4. to expel, eject. 5. to squirt, spur, gush (out). 6. to burst out. 7. to be irritated.
fazer alguém ~ de um lugar (fig.) to make one run away in a hurry.

espirro s. m. sneeze, sneezing.
dar um ~ to sneeze.

esplanada s. f. esplanade: 1. a level space as for public walks. 2. the open space between the citadel and the houses of a town.

esplâncnico adj. (anat.) splanchnic: pertaining to the viscera.

esplancnografia s. f. splanchnography: the descriptive anatomy of the viscera.

esplancnográfico adj. splanchnographical.

esplancnologia s. f. (anat.) splanchnology: the study of viscera.

esplancnológico adj. splanchnological: of or pertaining to splanchnology.

esplancnotomia s. f. (anat.) splanchnotomy: the dissection of the viscera.

esplenalgia s. f. (med.) splenalgia: neuralgic pain in the spleen.

esplenálgico adj. splenalgic: 1. relating to splenalgia. 2. affected with splenalgia.

esplendecência s. f. resplendence: brilliant luster, splendour.

esplendente adj. m. + f. resplendent, splendid, shining with brilliant luster.

esplender v. (also **esplendecer, esplendorar**) to resplend, shine, be resplendent.

esplendidez s. f. 1. splendidness. 2. splendour. 3. magnificence.

esplêndido adj. splendid: 1. brilliant, shining. 2. magnificent, sumptuous, grand. 3. admirable, wonderful, beautiful. 4. excellent, very fine. ‖ **esplendidamente** adv. splendidly.

esplendor s. m. splendour: 1. great brightness, brilliant luster, brilliance, refulgence. 2. magnificence, pomp, glory. 3. sumptuousness.
ela está no ~ da sua beleza she is in the flush of her beauty.

esplendoroso adj. splendorous, bright; magnificent; sumptuous.

esplenectomia s. f. (surg.) splenectomy: extirpation of the spleen.

esplenético s. m. splenetic: person affected with a splenetic disorder. ‖ adj. splenetic: affected with splenic disorder.

esplênico adj. (anat.) splenic: pertaining to the spleen.

esplenificação s. f. (pl. -ões) (path.) splenization: intumescence of the lungs or the liver.

esplênio s. m. (anat.) splenius (muscle).

esplenite s. f. (med.) splenitis: inflammation of the spleen.

esplenocele s. f. (med.) splenocele: hernia of the spleen.

esplenografia s. f. splenography: a description of the spleen.

esplenográfico adj. splenographical.

esplenóide adj. m. + f. splenoid: resembling the spleen.

esplenologia s. f. (med.) splenology: the study of the spleen.

esplenológico adj. splenological.

esplenomegalia s. f. (med.) splenomegaly: enlargement of the spleen.

esplenopatia s. f. (med.) splenopathy: any disease of the spleen.

esplenopático adj. of or pertaining to splenopathy.

esplenotomia s. f. (anat.) splenotomy: dissection of the spleen.

esplim s. m. spleen, ill humour, low spirits.

espoar v. 1. to sift again. 2. to dust, sweep away the dust from.

espojadouro s. m. (also **espojadoiro, espojeiro**) place where beasts wallow or tumble about.

espojar(-se) (also **espolinhar-se**) v. to wallow: roll or tumble in the dust (beasts).

espoldra s. f. the second pruning of vine.

espoldrar v. to prune (vine).

espoleta (ê) s. f. 1. fuse, cap of a gun: 2. detonator. 3. m. + f. (Braz.): a) pander, procurer. b) intriguer. c) talebearer. d) henchman. e) (fam.) mischievous child.

espoletear v. (Braz.) to become dizzy.

espoliação s. f. (pl. -ões) spoliation, spoliating, plunder, robbery; dispossession, usurpation.

espoliador s. m. spoliator, spoiler, plunderer. ‖ adj. spoliating, plundering.

espoliar v. 1. to spoil, spoliate, rob, despoil, plunder. 2. to deprive of possessions or rights. 3. to usurp.

espoliativo adj. 1. spoliatory, causing spoliation. 2. (med.) spoliative.

espolim s. m. a small shuttle for interweaving designs in upholstery material.

espolinar v. to interweave with the **espolim**.

espólio s. m. 1. (jur.) assets, estate; property or goods of a deceased person. 2. spoil, booty, plundering. 3. remains.

espondaico adj. spondaic(al).

espondeu s. m. (ancient pros.) spondee.

espondílico adj. spondylous: pertaining to a vertebra.

espondilite s. f. (med.) spondylitis: inflammation of the vertebrae.

espôndilo s. m. (anat.) spondyl(e), a vertebra.

espongiário s. m. (zool.) spongean: a member of the Spongiae; a sponge.

esponja s. f. 1. sponge: a) a marine animal. b) its soft elastic framework used for soaking up water as in bathing. c) any spongelike substance. 2. parasite, sponger, dead beat. 3. (fig.) drunkard, boozer, soak. 4. (Braz., bot.) an acacia (Acacia Farnesiana).
banho de ~ sponge bath. **ele o apagou com a ~** he sponged it out. **passar a ~ em** (or **sobre**) (fig.) to forgive, forget.

esponjar v. to sponge: 1. wipe out with a sponge. 2. (up) absorb.

esponjeira s. f. 1. sponge basket, sponge holder. 2. (Braz., bot.) sweet acacia.

esponjosidade s. f. sponginess; softness; porosity.

esponjoso adj. spongeous, spongy.

esponsais s. m. pl. (also **esponsálias** f. pl.) 1. espousals, betrothment, marriage contract or promise. 2. celebration of the espousals.

esponsal adj. m. + f. (pl. -ais), **esponsalício** m. spousal, nuptial, bridal.

espontaneidade s. f. spontaneity, spontaneousness, voluntariness, free will.

espontâneo adj. spontaneous: 1. voluntary, free. 2. growing naturally. 3. unstudied. ‖ **-amente** adv. spontaneously, voluntarily.

espontar v. to clip, cut, shear (hair); prune, lop (tree).

espora s. f. 1. spur: a) instrument on a horseman's heel to goad the horse (plate R 7). b) the spine on a cock's leg. c) (fig.) anything which goads; incitement, incentive, stimulus. 2. (bot.) larkspur. ‖ adj. m. + f. (Braz.) 1. poor, inferior. 2. ragged. **chamar nas ~s** 1. to spur. 2. (fig.) to reprove, reprimand. **ele meteu as ~s no cavalo** he set spurs to his horse.

esporada s. f. 1. prick with a spur. 2. (fig.) incentive, stimulus. 3. (fam.) reprehension, reproof, reprimand.

esporadicidade s. f. sporadicalness.

esporádico adj. sporadic(al), separate, scattered; occurring singly. ‖ **esporadicamente** adv. sporadically. **doença -a** sporadic disease.

esporângio s. m. (bot.) sporangium: a spore case.

esporão s. m. (pl. **-ões**) 1. spur: a) a stiff, sharp spine on the legs of certain birds (esp. the spine on a cock's leg). b) (archit., fort.) counterfort, reinforcing buttress of masonry. c) (bot.) a spur-like appendage of a corolla. 2. (naut.) the beak of a ship, ram.

esporão-de-galo s. m. (pl. **esporões-de-galo**) (bot.) cockspur (Pisonia aculeata).

esporar, esporear v. to spur: 1. clap spurs to the horse; prick with spurs. 2. spur on, incite.

esporeira s. f. (bot.) larkspur.

esporífero, esporígeno adj. (bot., zool.) sporiferous.

esporim s. m. (pl. **-ins**) a small spur without a rowel.

espório s. m. (bot., biol., zool.) spore.

esporogônio s. m. (bot.) sporogonium.

esporro (ô) s. m. (Braz., sl.) 1. quarrel, row, brawl. 2. a fit of rage. 3. reprimand, reproof, severe rebuke.

esporta s. f. frail, drum, rush basket.

esporte s. m. sports: 1. form of amusement or play. 2. athletic or outdoor game.
~ aquático watercraft. **~s de inverno** winter sports. **blusão de ~** swing-away jacket. **capa ~** sports coat. **ele pratica ~** he goes in for sport. **equipamento para ~** sports kit.

esportismo s. m. sportsmanship; sport, the practice of sports.

esportista s. m. + f. 1. sportsman. 2. sportswoman. ‖ adj. sporting; referring to sport.
ele é um ~ moderno e competente he is the last word as sportsman. **seja ~!** (fig.) be a sport!

esportiva s. f. fair-mindedness, state of being good-tempered, sportsmanship.
loteria ~ soccer lottery, in which bets are made relating to the winner teams in thirteen soccer games.

esportivo adj. sporting: of or pertaining to sports. **notícias -as** sporting news.

espórtula s. f. alms, tip, fees, gratuity, dole.

esportular v. 1. to give alms, tips or gratuities. 2. **~-se** to be generous.

esporulação s. f. (pl. **-ões**) (bot.) sporulation: formation of spores.

espórulo s. m. (bot.) sporule: a small spore.

esposa (ô) s. f. 1. wife, consort, spouse. 2. bride, fiancée.
ela tem sido boa ~ (para ele) she has been a good wife (to him). **sua ~** his (your) wife. **os meus cumprimentos para a sua ~!** remember me to your wife!

esposar v. 1. to marry; get married. 2. to betroth, espouse. 3. (fig.) to prop, support, shelter.

esposo (ô) s. m. 1. husband, spouse, consort. 2. bridegroom.

esposório s. m. 1. espousals, act or ceremony of marriage. 2. wedding party.

espostejado adj. shredded, slashed; cut into pieces.

espostejar v. 1. to cut in slices or pieces; to shred. 2. to tear apart.

espote s. m. (Engl., radio, TV) 1. spot announcement. 2. time scheduled for a spot announcement.

espraiado s. m. 1. seashore (at low tide). 2. (Braz.) broadening or expansion of a river bed. ‖ adj. 1. cast on the shore (sea). 2. (fig.) scattered, spread.

espraiamento s. m. 1. ebbing of the sea. 2. stretch along the shore or banks from which the water subsided. 3. scattering, spreading. 4. prolixity.

espraiar v. 1. to cast on the shore or strand (sea). 2. to drive ashore. 3. to extend, stretch, spread abroad. 4. to scatter. 5. **~-se**: a) to overflow, run over the banks (river or sea). b) to speak at length upon.

espreguiçadeira s. f., **espreguiçador** m. couch (plate C 2), bed for taking the siesta, chaise longue, lounge.

espreguiçamento s. m. stretching (of arms and legs, after sleep).

espreguiçar v. 1. to rouse one (from sleep). 2. **~-se**: a) to stretch o. s. and yawn (after sleep). b) to sprawl, lounge.

espreita s. f. (also **espreitadela**) 1. peep, sly close look, pry. 2. watch, vigil. 3. spying, espionage. 4. lookout. 5. ambush.
ele está de ~ he is on the watch.

espreitadeira s. f. a peephole, eyehole. ‖ adj. f. curious, prying (woman).

espreitador s. m., **espreitante** m. + f. 1. prier, observer, peeper. 2. watcher. 3. spy. 4. waylayer. ‖ adj. 1. prying, peeping. 2. spying.

espreitar v. 1. to peep, pry, observe attentively. 2. to watch. 3. to spy: look slyly, closely or curiously. 4. to ambush. 5. **~-se** to take care of o. s.
~ pelo buraco da fechadura to spy through the keyhole.

espremedor s. m. squeezer, smasher. ‖ adj. squeezing, pressing.
~ de batatas 1. potato masher. 2. ricer: a kitchen utensil to press potates with. **~ de limão** lemon-squeezer.

espremedura s. f. 1. pressing or squeezing out. 2. oppression.

espremer v. 1. to press, squeeze out, compress. 2. to express; crush. 3. to contract, constrict. 4. to worry. 5. to oppress. 6. **~-se**: a) to strain. b) to press, crowd (together). 7. to find out thoroughly, omit nothing. 8. to interrogate insistently. 9. to try to expel.

espritar-se v. (N. Braz., pop.) to become furious, lose one's temper.

espulgar v. to flea, clear or rid of fleas.

espuma s. f. 1. scum, froth, foam, spume; lather, suds. **~ de sabão** soap-suds, lather (plate B 7).

espumadeira s. f. skimmer, skimming spoon.

espuma-do-mar s. f. (pl. **espumas-do-mar**) meerschaum, sepiolite.

espumante adj. m. + f. foaming, frothy, foamy, bubbly. 2. sparkling. 3. (fig.) excited, angry, furious.
vinho ~ sparkling wine.

espumar v. 1. to skim, scum. 2. to slabber, drivel. 3. to foam, froth. 4. to bubble.

espumarada s. f. a lot of foam.

espumejar v. 1. to foam, froth (with anger). 2. to get angry.
ele espumejou (de raiva) he foamed with rage.

espúmeo, espumífero adj. covered with foam; frothy.
espumosidade s. f. foaminess, frothiness.
espumoso adj. (also espumento, espumígero) 1. frothy, full of scum, foamy, spumous, spumy, scummy. 2. sparkling. ‖ -amente adv. foamily.
espurcícia s. f. 1. filth, dirt, impurity. 2. turpitude, vileness.
espurco adj. 1. filthy, foul, dirty. 2. sordid, vile.
espuriedade s. f. spuriousness: 1. illegitimacy, bastardy. 2. spuriousness, falseness.
espúrio adj. spurious: 1. illegitimate, bastard, adulterine. 2. (fig.) false, not genuine, counterfeit, adulterated.
esputação s. f. (pl. -ões) 1. act of spitting. 2. (med.) an excessive flow of saliva.
esputar v. to spit (out), eject saliva; to drivel.
esputo s. m. sputum, saliva, spittle.
esquadra s. f. squadron: 1. (naut.) a part or unit of a naval fleet; naval fleet. 2. (mil.) squad (infantry). 3. a military formation of airplanes. coluna de ~ (naut.) squadron column. testa de ~ (naut.) lead of fleet.
esquadrado adj. squared, put at right angles.
esquadrão s. m. (pl. -ões) 1. squadron: a main division of a cavalry regiment. 2. (fig.) crowd, multitude.
esquadrar v. (also esquadriar) 1. to square, put at right angles. 2. to form into squadrons (troops).
esquadrejamento s. m. squaring (of timber).
esquadrejar v. to cut or saw square.
esquadria s. f. 1. square: instrument for determining or making right angles. 2. a right angle. 3. building block of stone. 4. (constr.) generic designation for sashes, frames, doors and the like.
esquadrilha s. f. 1. flotilla: a fleet of small vessels. 2. (aeron.) squadron: formation of two or more flights.
esquadrilhado adj. 1. bowed down; worn out. 2. hipshot. 3. hipped.
esquadrilhar v. to dislocate the hips of.
esquadrinhador s. m. 1. investigator, searcher, researcher. 2. observer. ‖ adj. investigating, searching.
esquadrinhadura s. f., esquadrinhamento m. investigation, examining, inquiry, research, careful inquiry.
esquadrinhar v. 1. to investigate, search, examine, scan, scrutinize, inquire into, ferret out, sift. 2. to watch, observe.
~ o horizonte (com binóculos) to scan the horizon.
esquadro s. m. square: an L- or T-shaped instrument for laying out and testing right angles (plate F 1). ~ para desenho set-square (plate A 5). ~ de encosto try square (plates F 2. M 4). em ~ at right angles. no ~ on the square.
esqualidez s. f. squalidness, squalidity, sordidness, squalor.
esquálido adj. squalid, sordid, filthy, foul, nasty; extremely dirty. ‖ esqualidamente adv. squalidly.
esqualo s. m. a shark, dogfish.
esquarroso adj. squarrous, squarrose, jagged.
esquartejado adj. quartered, cut into quarters.
esquartejamento s. m. quartering.
esquartejar v. 1. to quarter, cut into quarters. 2. to cut into slices or pieces. 3. to shred. 4. to lacerate, tear to pieces.
esquartelar v. (her.) to quarter, divide into four.
esquecer v. 1. to forget, disremember; neglect. 2. to omit, leave out. 3. (fig.) to pardon. 4. ~-se: a) to forget o. s. b) to be forgotten or forgetful. c) to fall into oblivion. d) to be absent-minded. ~ as suas obrigações to forget one's duties. ~ o passado to wipe off the slate; to let bygones be bygones. ~ uma ofensa to forget an injury; to pardon. esqueci-me completamente disso I never

thought of it. esqueci o nome I forgot the name. não o esqueça! have it in mind! não se esqueça de aparecer remember to come. vamos ~ isso let's pass the sponge over it.
esquecidiço adj. forgetful, unmindful.
esquecido s. m. forgetter: a forgetful person. ‖ adj. 1. forgotten. 2. forgetful, unmindful. 3. oblivious. 4. (pop.) paralytic. 5. (Braz.) said of the cocks without spurs. ‖ -amente adv. forgetfully, obliviously.
~ de sua presença oblivious of his presence. ele é ~ he is forgetful. ele foi ~ he has grown out of memory. sentir-se ~ to think o. s. neglected, (sl.) feel out of it.
esquecimento s. m. 1. forgetfulness, oblivion. 2. omission. 3. negligence, carelessness.
esquelético adj. skeleton: 1. skeletal: of, pertaining to or resembling a skeleton. 2. (fig.) very lean, thin (person).
esqueleto s. m. skeleton: 1. (anat., zool.) the bones of a body, carcass. 2. framework, frame; timberwork. 3. (fig.): a) outline, rough sketch. b) a very thin person or animal.
esquema s. m. 1. scheme, project, plan; model, design, diagram. 2. summary; synoptic chart.
esquemático adj. schematic: of, pertaining to or in conformity with a scheme or plan. ‖ esquematicamente adv. schematically.
esquematismo s. m. schematism.
esquematizar v. to schematize: form a scheme; to arrange according to a scheme.
esquentação s. f. (pl. -ões) 1. heating, overheating. 2. (fig.) quarrel, brawl, heated discussion.
esquentada s. f. the hour of greatest heat during a day.
esquentado adj. 1. heated, warmed, warmish. 2. (fig.) hot-tempered, irritated, exasperated.
esquentador s. m. heater; warming-pan; bed-pan.
esquentamento s. m. 1. = esquentação. 2. (pop.) gonorrhoea.
esquenta-mulher s. m. (pl. esquenta-mulheres) (N. E. Braz.) a quartet (two fifes, a snare drum and a bass drum) for dancing and processional purposes.
esquenta-por-dentro s. m., sg. + pl. (Braz., pop.) = cachaça.
esquentar v. 1. to heat, warm, overheat, make warm. 2. (fig.) to inflame, incense, animate; provoke. 3. ~-se: a) to grow warm. b) to overheat o. s. c) to grow angry, become irritated, lose one's temper. o motor esquentou the motor ran hot.
esquerda s. f. 1. the left side or hand. 2. (pol.) the opposition.
~ volver! (mil.) left turn! à ~ to the left. as ~s (pol.) the left wing.
esquerdismo s. m. 1. leftism: radicalism. 2. the leftists collectively.
esquerdista s. m. + f. (pol.) leftist, left winger. ‖ adj. leftist, left wing.
esquerdo adj. 1. left. 2. left-handed. 3. crooked, oblique. 4. clumsy, awkward.
do lado ~ 1. leftwards, on the left. 2. from the left. ele levantou-se da cama com o pé ~ he got out of bed the wrong side. mão -a left hand. pé ~ left foot.
esquete s. m. (Engl.) sketch, a short theatrical, radio or television act, pochade.
esqui s. m. ski (snow-shoe) (plate E 9).
~ aquático aquaplaning.
esquiação s. f. skiing.
esquiar v. to ski.
bastão de ~ ski-stick. botas de ~ ski boots.
esquiça s. f. peg, spigot.
esquifar v. to make coffins or tombs.

esquife s. m. 1. coffin, casket; bier. 2. skiff: a small boat propelled by oars (plate B 9).

esquila s. f. (S. Braz., pop.) shearing.

esquilar v. (S. Braz., pop.) to shear.

esquilo s. m. (zool.) squirrel.

esquimó s. m. + f. Eskimo: a member of a race inhabiting Greenland and the adjacent parts of North America. ‖ adj. Eskimo: of or pertaining to the Eskimos.

esquina s. f. corner: 1. street corner. 2. angle. **ele dobrou (virou) a** ~ he came round the corner; he turned the corner. **na** ~ at the corner. **na próxima** ~ at the next corner.

esquinar v. 1. to corner: furnish with corners. 2. to cut in angles. 3. to facet (gems). 4. ~-se to get drunk.

esquinência s. f. (med.) amygdalitis: inflammation of a tonsil.

esquipação s. f. (pl. -ões) 1. fitting out, equipment or equipage of a ship. 2. act of equipping a ship. 3. suit, garments, dress.

esquipado s. m. (Braz.) amble: the pace like that of an ambling horse. ‖ adj. 1. equipped, fitted, rigged (ship). 2. (fig.) embellished, adorned, dressed.

esquipamento s. m. equipment, fitting out or manning of a ship.

esquipar v. 1. to fit out, equip, rig out, man (a ship). 2. (Braz.) to amble: a) move (horse) by lifting the two feet on one side alternately with the two feet on the other. b) move like an ambling horse. 3. ~-se (fig.) to adorn, dress, rig o. s. up.

esquipático adj. 1. odd, queer, singular. 2. fanciful, fantastic. 3. extravagant.

esquírola s. f. 1. splint or splinter of a bone. 2. a hard thin plate.

esquisitão s. m. (pl. -ões) (f. -ona) queer fellow; eccentric person. ‖ adj. peculiar, queer, odd.

esquisitice s. f. extravagance, eccentricity, oddity, queerness, strangeness.

esquisito s. m. (Braz.) 1. a desert place. 2. a narrow track. ‖ adj. 1. singular, rare, exquisite. 2. strange, curious. 3. odd, queer, peculiar. 4. eccentric(al). 5. fanciful, funny, freak(ish). ‖ -amente adv. oddly, queerly; eccentrically; freakishly. **bastante** ~ curiously enough. **ele é um homem** ~ he is a queer fellow, (coll.) a queer fish. **modos** ~s particular ways. **um sujeito** ~ a comical customer, (U. S. A., sl.) comical cuss.

esquisto s. m. schist (rock).

esquiva s. f. 1. shunning, avoidance. 2. ducking (as of a blow).

esquivança, esquivez, esquiveza s. f. 1. disdain, contempt, unkindliness, scorn. 2. refusal, rejection. 3. repugnance, aversion.

esquivar v. 1. to shun, avoid, dodge. 2. to duck, parry (a blow). 3. to scorn, despise, treat with disdain. 4. to stray, digress. 5. to draw back, withdraw from. 6. ~-se: a) to retreat, avoid, escape, keep away from. b) to steal away from. c) to avoid doing something. ~-se a uma responsabilidade avoid a liability.

esquivo(so) adj. 1. disdainful, supercilious, scornful. 2. untractable, rude, crude, sullen, stubborn. 3. rare, singular, exceptional. 4. difficult or hard to find or to get at.

esquizofrenia s. f. (med.) schizophrenia, dementia praecox.

esquizofrênico s. m. schizophrenic: person affected with schizophrenia. ‖ adj. schizophrenic: pertaining to or affected with schizophrenia.

esquizóide s. m. + f. schizoid: person of schizoid personality. ‖ adj. schizoid.

esquizotímico adj. (med.) schizothymic, schizoid: characterized by schizoidism.

essa (l) s. f. catafalque: 1. a stand or frame to support the coffin in which a dead person lies; cenotaph, bier. 2. (R. C. Church) a coffin-shaped structure at requiem masses.

essa (II) demonstrative pron. f. of **esse:** 1. that. 2. ~s pl. those. ~ é boa! that's a good one! ~ é a moça que eu tinha visto that is the girl I had seen. ~s são as garotas those are the girls. **ainda mais** ~! how now!, and now this! **ora** ~! well now!

esse s. m. 1. ess: the name of the letter S. 2. something S-shaped (as a double hairpin). **andar aos** ~s to reel (an intoxicated person).

esse (ê) demonstrative pron. 1. that, that one. 2. ~s pl. those. ~ é o homem that is the man. ~s são os homens those are the men. **durante** ~s três dias during those three days. **prefiro** ~ **livro** I prefer that book. **que grito foi** ~? what is that cry? **quem é** ~? who is that?

essedário s. m. a Roman gladiator who fought standing on a chariot.

éssedo s. m. essed(a): a two-wheel war chariot used by ancient Britons and Gauls.

essência s. f. 1. essence: a) substance, nature. b) existence, life, being. c) essentiality. d) extract, solution obtained by distillation. e) essential oil. f) perfume, scent. 2. species (of trees).

essencial s. m. (pl. -ais) the essential, main or principal point. ‖ adj. m. + f. essential: 1. substantial, natural, constitutive. 2. principal, main, absolutely necessary, indispensable. 3. fundamental, pivotal. ‖ ~mente adv. essentially, substantially. **a parte** ~ **disto** the sum and substance of it. **o** ~ **da questão** the heart of the matter.

essencialidade s. f. essenciality, essentialness.

essênio s. m. (hist.) Essene: a member of a brotherhood or cenobite order among the Jews.

és-sueste s. m. east-southeast.

esta adj. + demonstrative pron. f. of **este:** 1. this. 2. the latter. 3. ~s pl. these. ~ **mulher** this woman. ~ **noite** last night. **com** ~ **me vou!** enough!, that's enough! **por** ~ **vez** (for) this time.

estabanado adj. 1. overhasty, headlong. 2. unquiet, uneasy. 3. rattlebrained, crackbrained, crazy. 4. careless, clumsy, awkward, devil-may-care.

estabelecedor s. m. person who establishes; founder. ‖ adj. establishing.

estabelecer v. 1. to establish: a) settle, fix, set up. b) institute, found, make, create. c) ordain, determine, appoint. d) make firm, stable or sure. 2. ~-se: a) to settle or establish o. s. b) to become fixed. c) to base o. s. on. ~-se **solidamente** to establish o. s. firmly, (coll.) get a footing. **o governo estabeleceu uma nova lei** the government laid down a new rule. **o clube estabeleceu um novo comitê** the club set up a new committee.

estabelecido adj. established: 1. having an establishment. 2. fixed, put down, prescribed. 3. settled. 4. determinate, ordained, ordered. **antes da expiração do prazo** ~ previous to the expiration of the fixed time.

estabelecimento s. m. establishment: 1. act of establishing. 2. an organization, institution, foundation, settlement. 3. a business organization; shop; a store. 4. a house. 5. an institute. ~ **de ensino** a school. ~ **público** public building or institution.

E 11

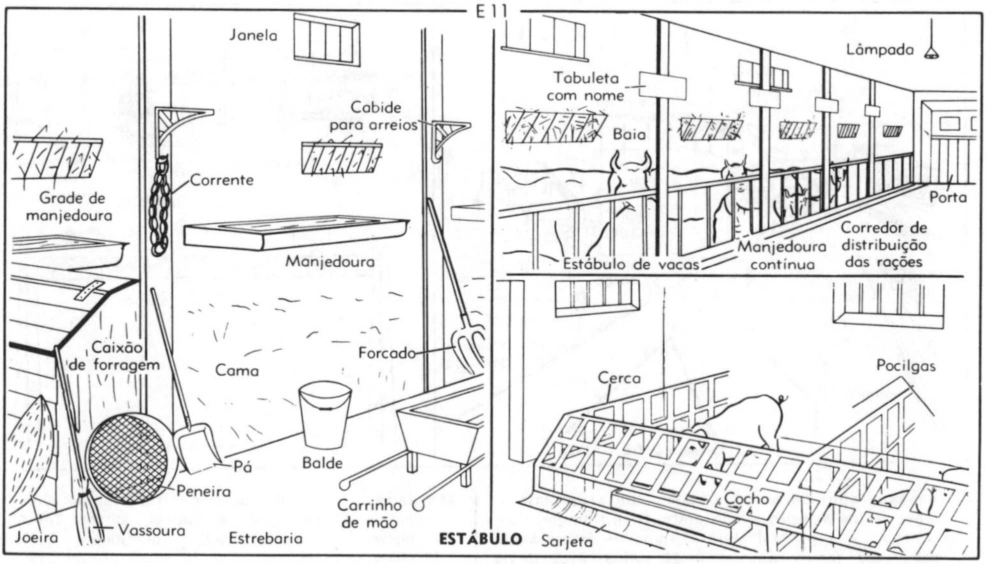

ESTÁBULO

estabilidade s. f. stability, stableness, steadiness, firmness; security, safety.
~ **dinâmica** dynamic stability.
estabilização s. f. (pl. **-ões**) (Braz.) stabilization: act of rendering or of becoming stable, fixed.
estabilizador s. m. (aeron.) stabilizer, tail-fin (plate A 3).
estabilizar v. 1. to stabilize: fix, fixate, settle. 2. **~-se** to become stabilized, fixed or settled.
estabulação s. f. (pl. **-ões**) stabling: a putting and raising animals in a stable.
estabular v. to stable: put, keep or raise (cattle) in a stable. ‖ adj. m. + f. of or pertaining to a stable.
estábulo s. m. stable: a building where cattle are kept and fed (plates A 4, C 11, E 11).
estaca s. f. 1. stake, pale, pole, post, picket. 2. pile; palisade. 3. slip, tree prop. 4. peg (plate T 2). **fixar com ~s** to stake in. **marcar com ~s** to peg out.
estacada s. f. 1. stockade. 2. paling, pale-work; palisade. 3. picket fence. 4. corral, barnyard.
estação s. f. (pl. **-ões**) 1. station: a) stand(ing), place where a person or thing stands. b) stand; short stay. c) police post. d) railway station (plates E 12, 13). e) stop, stopping place, bus stop. f) (R. C. Church) any of a series of 14 pictures representing successive scenes of Christ's passion. 2. a season of the year. 3. season, term, time. 4. opportunity, occasion. 5. (Braz.) telephone center. ~ **climatérica** climatic resort. ~ **de águas** watering resort. ~ **de monta** stud farm. ~ **de rádio** broadcasting station. ~ **de televisão** telestation. ~ **de veraneio** summer resort. ~ **meteorológica** weather station. ~ **radiotelegráfica** wireless station. ~ **telefônica** telephone exchange. **até à** ~ up to the station. **chefe de** ~ (railway) station-master. **em plena** ~ at the height of the season.
estaca-prancha s. f. (pl. **estacas-pranchas**) sheet pile.
estacar v. 1. to stake: fasten, support or protect with a stake or stakes. 2. to stop short, stay, halt. 3. to support, protect, shield. 4. to be still, motionless, perplexed, confused or undecided.
estacaria s. f. 1. stockade. 2. pale-work, piling. 3. a great number of pales or piles.
estacional adj. m. + f. (pl. **-ais**) 1. stational: of or pertaining to a station. 2. stationary. 3. seasonal.
estacionamento s. m. 1. parking. 2. state of being stationary.
~ **proibido** parking prohibited. **ponto de** ~ parking place.
estacionar v. 1. to stop in a place; to station. 2. to settle. 3. to be stationary; come to a standstill, remain stationed. 4. to park (automobiles).
estacionário s. m. person in charge of a weather station. ‖ adj. 1. stationary, motionless, still. 2. stagnant, dull.
estada s. f. 1. abode, residence. 2. sojourn, stay, stop.
estadão s. m. (pl. **-ões**) pomp, luxury, magnificence, display.
estadear v. 1. to boast, brag, flaunt. 2. to exhibit. display, show off. 3. **~-se:** a) to pride o. s., boast of. b) to become proud or haughty.
estadia s. f. 1. lay days: the days allowed by the charter party for loading or unloading a vessel. 2. permanence; stay, sojourn. 3. delay.
estádia s. f. (geom.) stadia: an instrument for measuring distances.
estádio s. m. stadium: 1. a structure with rows of seats around a large open space for athletic games. 2. a Greek measure of length. 3. stage, period; epoch; season.
estadismo s. m. statism: belief in a state government.
estadista s. m. + f. statesman, stateswoman, politician.
estadística s. f. politics, statesmanship, science of government.
estadístico adj. concerning the science of government; political.
estado s. m. state: 1. condition, constitution, circumstance. 2. situation, position, rank, station, status. 3. dignity, pomp, magnificence. 4. show, ostentation. 5. government, administration. 6. (also **Estado**) state, State: a) part of a federal republic. b) nation, country.
~ **civil** civil status. ~ **de casado** married status. ~ **de graça** state of grace. ~ **de inocência** state of innocence. ~ **de inércia** (state of) inertia. ~

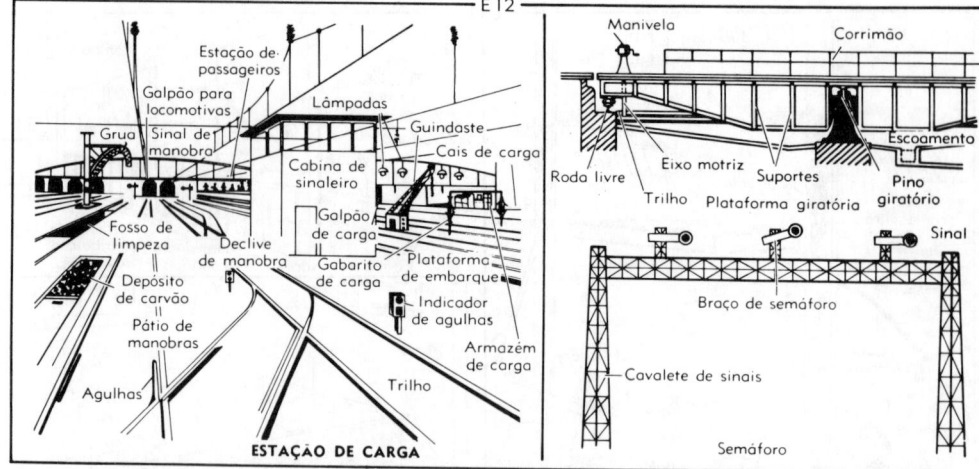

E 12

ESTAÇÃO DE CARGA

desesperador desesperate state. ~ **de sítio** state of siege. ~ **de solteiro** single state, (fam.) single blessedness. ~ **espiritual** state of mind. ~ **interessante** pregnancy, family way. ~ **legal** status. **à custa do** ~ at government expense. **conselho de** ~ State Council. **em bom** ~ in good repair, in good heart, sound, well. **em** ~ **deplorável** in a deplorable plight. **em** ~ **lamentável** in a miserable condition. **em** ~ **natural** in a state of nature. **em mau** ~ out of repair. **homem de** ~ statesman. **manter em bom** ~ **de conservação** to keep in thorough repair. **mudar de** ~ to change one's civil status. **o navio não está em** ~ **de navegar** the ship is not in navigable condition. **negócio de** ~ state affair. **num triste** ~ in a sorry plight. **receita do** ~ public revenue. **servidores do** ~ civil servants. **seus nervos estão em** ~ **alarmante** his nerves are in a shocking state. **tomar** ~ to get married. **~-tampão** (pol.) buffer state.

estado-maior s. m. (pl. **estados-maiores**) 1. general staff. 2. captain-general.
oficial do ~ staff officer.

estadual adj. m. + f. (pl. **-ais**) (Braz.) state: of or pertaining to the State.
controle ~ state control.

estadulho s. m. cart stake.

estadunidense s. m. + f. North American: native or inhabitant of the U. S. A. ‖ adj. American: of or pertaining to the U. S. A.

estafa s. f., **estafamento** m. 1. hard work, tiring work, irksome task. 2. fatigue.

estafado adj. weary, fatigued, tired.

estafante adj. m. + f. 1. fatiguing, wearying, tiring. 2. toilsome.

estafar v. 1. to tire, weary, fatigue; jade. 2. to irk, bore, importune. 3. to overlabour. 4. **~-se:** a) to get tired, tire o. s. out. b) to grow weary. c) to be tedious.

estafermo s. m. 1. a good-for-nothing. 2. simpleton, dullard, nincompoop. 3. scarecrow.

estafeta s. m. 1. courier, estafette, an express, a messenger. 2. postman. 3. (Braz.) deliverer of telegrams.

estafilococo s. m. (bact.) staphylococcus.

estafiloma s. m. (path.) staphyloma: protrusion of the cornea resulting from inflammation.

estagiar v. to serve as apprentice, receive training.

estagiário s. m. probationer, trainee: person on probation or trial (esp. a student, student teacher, a nurse in training). ‖ adj. probationary: serving for trial.

estágio s. m. 1. probation: period of probation. 2. apprenticeship: period of training.

estagnação s. f. 1. stagnation, stagnancy: a) condition of being stagnant. b) cessation of flow (as stagnation of blood). c) (fig.) inertia, inertness. 2. stoppage, interruption.

estagnado adj. stagnant: 1. motionless, without current. 2. inert, inactive, sluggish.
água -a stagnant water, backwater.

estagnar(-se) v. 1. to stagnate: a) cease to run or flow. b) be motionless; not to circulate. c) become inert, sluggish or dull. 2. to remain stationary.

estagnícola adj. m. + f. stagnicolous: living in stagnant waters.

estai s. m. (naut.) stay: a rope that supports a mast. ~ **da bujarrona** jibstay. ~ **do traquete** forestay.

estala s. f. stall (also **estábulo**) 1. stable. 2. a (usually canopied) seat for a clergyman in a (large) church.

estalactífero adj. stalactific: containing stalactites.

estalactite s. f. (min.) stalactite: a deposit of carbonate of lime; dripstone.

estalactítico adj. stalactitic: having the form of stalactites.

estalada s. f. 1. crack: sound as of a thing suddenly broken. 2. noise, sound. 3. mutiny, riot, tumult.

estalador adj. cracking, popping.

estalagem s. f. (pl. **-ens**) 1. inn, lodge, hostel(ry). 2. auberge. 3. a group of poor houses built around a common courtyard.

estalagmite s. f. (min.) stalagmite: carbonate of lime deposited on the floor of a cavern.

estalajadeiro s. m. innkeeper, host, landlord.

estalão s. m. (pl. **-ões**) standard; measuring stick, gauge.

estalar (v. also **estalejar**) 1. to crack, split, break into pieces. 2. to crackle, crepitate, pop. 3. to burst, explode. 4. to snap (as with a whip).
~ **a paciência** (fam.) to lose patience. ~ **um chicote** to snap a whip, crack a whip. **ele estalou os dedos** he cracked his fingers.

estalecido adj. (Braz., pop.) asthmatic.

estaleiro s. m. shipyard, dockyard: a yard where ships are built or repaired (plate P 16).

estalia s. f. (also **estadia**) lay days (of ships).

─ E13 ─

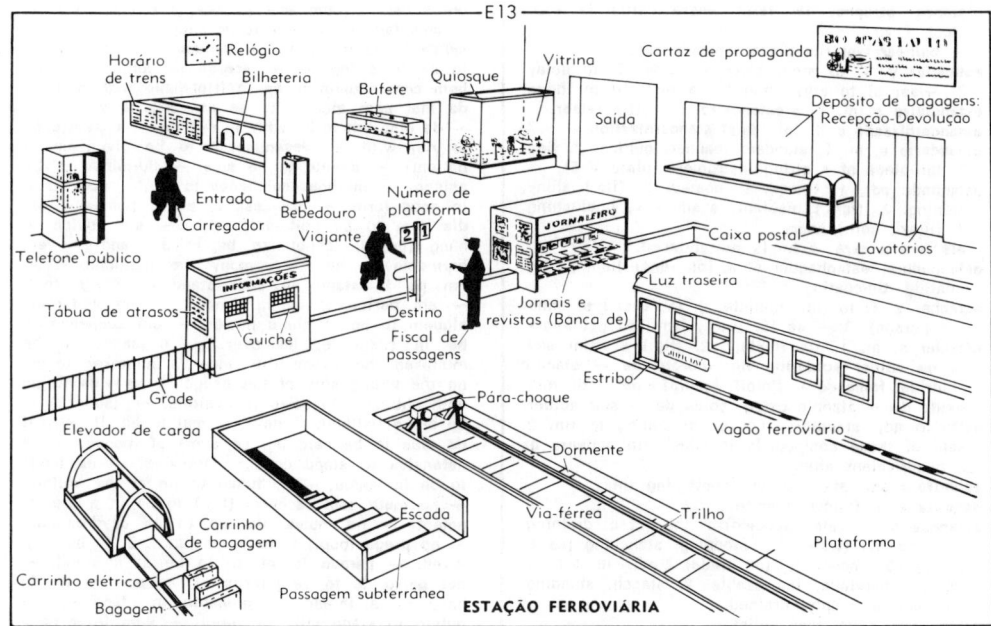

ESTAÇÃO FERROVIÁRIA

estalicar v. (pop.) 1. to emaciate, grow thin. 2. to crack the fingers.

estalicídio s. m. (Braz., obs., pop.) coryza.

estalidar v. to make a clapping or cracking noise (with the tongue).

estalido s. m. 1. clapping, cracking, smacking, snapping. 2. cracking noise.

estalo s. m. 1. crack: a) sharp noise. b) a sound made by things suddenly broken. 2. cracking, crackling, burst. 3. (Braz.) torpedo: a small firework which explodes when thrown against a hard object.

estambrar v. to twist wool.

estambre s. m. worsted, woollen thread.

estame s. m. 1. a woollen or silk yarn. 2. stamen: the male or fertilizing organ of flowering plants.

estamenha s. f. estamene, estamin, woollen cloth, bolting-cloth.

estamináceo adj. (bot.) stamineous: referring to stamens.

estaminado adj. 1. reduced to a thread (wool). 2. (bot.) staminate (flower): producing stamens but no pistils.

estaminal adj. m. + f. (pl. **-ais**) (bot.) staminal: pertaining to a stamen or stamens.

estaminífero adj. (bot.) staminiferous: bearing or having stamens.

estaminódio s. m. (bot.) staminodium: a sterile or abortive stamen.

estaminoso adj. (bot.) stamineous: having a salient stamen.

estampa s. f. 1. impression, print (of a picture). 2. a printed image, picture or figure. 3. gravure. 4. cast. 5. model, pattern, stencil (plate P 12). 6. vestige, trace, step. 7. (fig.) beautiful thing. ~ **de forja** swage-block. **dar à** ~ to put in print, publish, bring out.

estampado s. m. printed cloth. ‖ adj. 1. printed, impressed, stamped. 2. published. **papel** ~ embossed paper. **tecido de algodão** ~ printed cotton.

estampador s. m. person who prints or stamps. ‖ adj. printing, stamping.

estampagem s. f. (pl. **-ens**) stamping: 1. printing. 2. (met.) swaging; die forging, cutting out.

estampar v. 1. to print, impress, imprint, stamp, press. 2. to engrave (on copper). 3. (tech.) to swage. 4. (fig.) to infix, inculcate. 5. to design, draw, picture, paint. 6. to make patent, show, make a show of. 7. ~**-se**: a) to be impressed, printed, stamped or engraved. b) to become infixed.

estamparia s. f. 1. printworks, printery. 2. print shop. 3. (met.) factory for stamping articles.

estampeiro s. m. 1. stamper. 2. print-seller.

estampido s. m. 1. clap, crack, report (as of a gun). 2. explosion, detonation, burst, blast. 3. roar, great noise.

estampilha s. f. 1. small stamp. 2. (Braz.) revenue stamp. 3. postage stamp.

estampilhado adj. provided with revenue stamps (documents) or a postage stamp (letter).

estampilhar v. to affix revenue stamps (document) or postage stamps (letter).
~ **uma carta** to stamp a letter.

estanato s. m. (chem.) stannate: a salt of stannic acid.

estancamento s. m. stopping, stanching (as of blood).

estancar v. 1. to stanch, stop, hinder from running or flowing (as blood). 2. to drain, dry up, exhaust. 3. to stop, check. 4. to stagnate. 5. to put an end to. 6. to monopolize. 7. ~**-se**: a) to halt, come to a standstill. b) to stanch, stop, cease running. c) to become exhausted. d) to end, finish.

estanca-rios s. m., sg. + pl. water-engine.

estanceiro s. m. 1. owner of a timber-yard. 2. rancher.

estância s. f. (also **estança**) 1. stay, abode, home, residence, dwelling(-place). 2. ranch(o), estate, country seat. 3. stand. 4. enclosed place. 5. pause, temporary stop. 6. resting place; resort. 7. anchorage (place). 8. station. 9. watering place. 10. timber-yard. 11. coal or wood yard. 12. (poet.)

stanza, strophe. 13. farm where cattle is kept; stock farm.

~ **balnear** watering-place, seaside resort.

estanciar v. 1. to stop, sojourn, abide. 2. to delay. 3. ~-se: a) to stay, stop for a rest. b) to lodge.

estancieiro s. m. 1. = **estanceiro**. 2. cattle raiser.

estandardização s. f. (pl. **-ões**) standardization.

estandarte s. m. 1. standard, banner, guidon. 2. flag. 3. tail-piece of a string instrument (plate V 5).

estanhado adj. 1. tinned, tin-coated. 2. (fig.) shiny, shining. 3. (fam.) insolent, shameless, unblushing. 4. (Braz., coll.) angry.

ele tem a cara -a he is brazen-faced.

estanhadura, estanhagem s. f. (pl. **-ens**) tinning, tin--plating, tin-coating.

estanhar v. 1. to tin, tin-plate. 2. (S. Braz.) to shoot (a person). 3. ~-se (S. Braz., fam.) to get angry.

estanho s. m. 1. tin (metal). 2. (fig.) a calm sea. ~ **de soldar** soldering tin. **cloreto de** ~ stannic chloride. **folha de** ~ tinfoil. **fundipão de** ~ tinwork. **óxido de** ~ stannic oxide. **solda de** ~ soft solder.

estânico adj. stannic: 1. of or pertaining to tin. 2. said of those compounds in which tin appears as a quadrivalent atom.

estanífero adj. stanniferous: containing tin.

estanita s. f. (min.) stannite.

estanque s. m. (also **estanco**) 1. the act of draining, pumping out (water). 2. stopping, stanching (as of blood). 3. monopoly (of trade). ‖ adj. m. + f. 1. tight, impervious, impassable. 2. stanch, standing, stagnant. 3. empty, drained.

estanqueiro s. m. monopolist.

estante s. f. 1. bookstand, bookshelf, bookcase, bookrack (plates A 13, M 14). 2. lectern, reading--desk (plate T 4). 3. stand. 4. canterbury, music--stand (plates M 14, P 10).

~ **de regente** rostrum (plate P 2). ~ **para flores** flower-stand (plate M 14).

estapafúrdio adj. 1. heedless, hare-brained. 2. extravagant, irregular, strange. 3. odd, queer, freakish, peculiar. 4. eccentric.

estape s. m. (Braz.) a plant of the family Bignoneaceae (Jacaranda intermedia).

estapear v. (Braz.) to mistreat by slapping someone's face.

estaqueação s. f. (pl. **-ões**) (also **estaqueamento** m.) 1. act of staking, propping up with stakes. 2. (also **estaquelo** m.) act of stretching (hides) in order to dry.

estaqueadouro s. m. (also **estaqueadoiro**) place for stretching and drying hides.

estaquear v. 1. to prop up (stakes); to stake. 2. to make firm. 3. to fence in (with stakes). 4. (S. Braz.) to stretch (hides) in order to dry. 5. (N. Braz.) to tear up; to reduce to pieces or slices.

estaqueira s. f. (Braz., coll.) hatrack; coat-hanger.

estáquida-do-japão s. f. (pl. **estáquidas-do-japão**) (bot.) japanese artichoke, chorogi, knotroot (Stachys affinis).

estar s. m. act or state of being. ‖ v. to be: 1. (also ~-se) find o. s. (in a given place or condition). 2. stand, keep o. s., remain, stay, lie. 3. exist; be present, attend.

~ **à capa** (naut.) to lie to. ~ **afeiçoado por alguma coisa** to be attached to s. th., to hang upon s. th. ~ **à mão** to be at one's hand. ~ **a ponto de** to be on the verge of. ~ **às portas da morte** to be at death's door. ~ **atrapalhado** to be quite puzzled. ~ **boquiaberto** to stare open-mouthed. ~ **certo** to be sure of a thing, feel certain. ~ **cheio de** (fig. sl.) to be fed up with. ~ **com alguém** 1. to be with s. o. 2. (sl.) to agree with s. o. ~ **com a pulga atrás da orelha** (fig.) to have a flea in

one's ear. ~ **com azar** to have a run of ill luck. ~ **com falta de víveres** to go short of food. ~ **com saúde** to be in health. ~ **confuso** to be perplexed, to be in a fog. ~ **de acordo** to conform. ~ **de bem com alguém** to be in friendship with s. o. ~ **de mal com alguém** to be at variance with s. o. ~ **de olho em** to be with an eye on. ~ **desenfreado** to run wild. ~ **desenganado** to be given up (a patient). ~ **doente** to be sick. ~ **dormindo** to be asleep. ~ **em boas condições** to be in good state, in good form. ~ **em casa** to be at home. ~ **em dia com** to be up-to-date with. ~ **em dúvida** to hang (be) in doubt; to be at a stand. ~ **em harmonia** to be in harmony, be harmonious. ~ **em pé** to stand on end; stand on one's foot. ~ **em perigo** to be in danger. ~ **em poder de alguém** to be in one's power. ~ **em suspenso** to be in suspense, lie over. ~ **enganado** to be mistaken, be wrong, lie under a mistake; to be on the wrong side of the hedge. ~ **grávida** to go with child. ~ **indeciso** to hesitate. ~ **liso** (sl.) to be broke (without money). ~ **mal** to be ill. ~ **mal de vida** to be hard up, be short of money. ~ **na defensiva** to stand on the defensive. ~ **na moda** to be in vogue. ~ **no fundo** to lie at the bottom. ~ **no mato sem cachorro** (fig.) to be in a predicament. ~ **no mundo da lua** to be daydreaming. ~ **no prego** (pop.) 1. to be in pawn. 2. to be dog--tired. ~ **parado (perplexo)** to be at a stand. ~ **por baixo de** to be inferior to. ~ **por um fio** to hang by a thread. ~ **presente** to stand by. ~ **quieto** to stand still, be quiet. ~ **sem fazer nada** to do nothing. ~ **sujo com** to lose confidence in or from (after deceit or disappointment). ~ **sozinho** to stand alone. ~ **visível** to stick out, be evident. **ainda está em tempo** it is in time yet. ~ **pronto (teso, sem dinheiro)** to be moneyless, (sl.) broke. **como estamos?** how do we stand? **como está você?** how do you do?, how goes the time with you? **deixe ~ isso!** let that alone! **ela está ausente** she stays away. **ele está com esta idéia na cabeça** he got the idea into his head. ~ **numa boa** (sl.) to feel well, be well-off. **ela está em más circunstâncias** she is in reduced circumstances. **ele está louco por ela** he is dead nuts on her. **ele está fingindo** he is dissembling, puts it on. **ele está nas últimas** he is about to die. **ele esteve lá por acaso** he happened to be there. **está a meu cargo** it is incumbent on me, it lies on me. **está bem!** all right! O. K. **está bom!** it is good! **está chovendo** it rains. **esta casa está para cair** this house is ready to fall in. **está combinado!** that's understood! **está em discussão** it is under discussion. **estamos muito bem onde estamos** we are quite all right where we are. **está para acontecer alguma coisa** s. th. is about to happen, there is something in the air. **está para chover** it is going to rain. **está pela hora da morte** (sl.) it is exorbitant in price. **eu estava sem capa, e fiquei ensopado** I didn't have my raincoat on, and I got soaked. **estou a cavalo** I am on horseback. **estou ansioso por** I am anxious for. **estou ardendo de calor** I'm simply roasting. ~ **frito** (sl.) to be in a fix, in a sad plight. **estou com pressa** I am in a hurry. **estou indo bem** I am doing well. **estou lendo** I am reading. **estou na fé que...** I believe that... **estou nas mesmas circunstâncias** I am in the same situation, I am in the same boat. **estou para casar-me** I am going to be married. **estou para comprar um cavalo** I am about buying a horse. **estou para ir** I am going, I am ready to go. **não deves sair sem agasalho porque estás constipado** you should not go out with so little on because you have got a cold. **no pé em que as coisas estão...** as things stand... **quando ele ʔstava à morte** when he came to die. **quem está ʔí?** who goes there? **sala de** ~ living room. **tenho de** ~ **no escritório às dez horas** I am due at the office at ten o'clock. **a vida está para você** life lies before you. **você está arruinado** you are ruined, broken, (fam.) you go to pot.

estardalhaçar, estardalhar v. (Braz.) to make a noisy show or confusion.

estardalhaço s. m. 1. noise, din, bustle. 2. roar, rattle. 3. noisy display, showing-off or confusion. 4. (fig.) ostentation, boasting.

ele fez muito ~ he made a great stir, splash (sl.).

estarrecer v. 1. to frighten, strike with fear, terrorize, terrify. 2. to appall, dismay. 3. to startle. 4. ~-se: a) to become frightened. b) to become appalled or dismayed.

estase s. f. (path.) stasis: stagnation of the blood or humours.

estasiofobia s. f. (path.) stasiphobia: morbid dread of standing erect.

estatal adj. m. + f. (pl. -ais) of or referring to the state.

estatelado adj. 1. immovable, motionless, still. 2. stretched out.

estatelamento s. m. a knocking down; stunning.

estatelar v. 1. to throw or knock down. 2. to be stretched out on the ground. 3. to be or become stunned, dizzy. 4. ~-se to fall flat down.

~-se no solo to fall down full length, measure one's length.

estática s. f. 1. (phys.) statics: that branch of mechanics which treats of relations between forces in equilibrium. 2. (electr.) atmospherics, radio static.

estático adj. static: 1. standing still, at rest. 2. of or pertaining to atmospheric electricity that interferes with radio reception. 3. (electr.) pertaining to forces in equilibrium. || **estaticamente** adv. statically.

carga -a static load.

estatística s. f. statistics.

estatístico s. m. statistician: person versed in statistics. || adj. statistic(al): of or pertaining to statistics.

levantamento ~ statistic investigation.

estatização s. f. nationalization: act or effect of nationalizing.

estatizar v. 1. to nationalize. 2. to bring (a private enterprise) under the ownership of the government. 3. to appropriate (natural resources, certain economic activities) for the exclusive exploitation by the State.

estátua s. f. 1. statue (plate E 9). 2. (fig.) person without energy, humdrum.

~ **eqüestre** equestrian statue. ~ **pedestre** pedestrian statue.

estatuar v. to statue, make a statue of.

estatuaria s. f. statuary: 1. collection of statues. 2. statues collectivelly.

estatuária s. f. statuary sculpture: the art of making statues.

estatuário s. m. statuary sculptor: person who makes statues. || adj. statuary: of or pertaining to a statue or statuary.

estatueta s. f. statuette: a small statue.

estatuir v. to decree, establish, determine, enact, ordain.

estatura s. f. stature, natural height of a living being, tallness, size.

de ~ **média** middle-sized.

estatutário adj. (also **estatucional** m. + f.) statutory: according or relating to statutes.

estatuto s. m. statute, decree, rule, law, ordinance. ~ **adicional** bylaw.

estaurolita s. f. (min.) staurolite.

estavanado adj. = **estabanado**.

estável adj. m. + f. (pl. -áveis) 1. stable, firm, solid, fixed. 2. durable, lasting, enduring. 3. steady, permanent.

temperatura ~ steady temperature.

estazador s. m. person who overtires an animal. || adj. fatiguing, wearing.

estazamento s. m. overfatiguing (an animal).

estazar v. to overtire, overfatigue (an animal).

este s. m. 1. east. 2. east wind.

este (ê) demonstrative pron. 1. this. 2. the latter. 3. ~s pl. these, these ones.

~ **aqui** this one. ~ **é meu amigo** this is my friend. ~ **livro** this book. ~ **lugar** this place. **quem são** ~s? who are these?

estear v. 1. to stay, shore, prop, support. 2. to protect, shield. 3. to lean upon; base, rest.

estearato s. m. (chem.) stearate: a salt of stearic acid.

esteárico adj. (chem.) stearic: obtained from stearin.

estearina s. f. stearin: glyceride formed by the combination of stearic acid and glycerin.

vela de ~ stearin candle.

stearinaria s. f. factory of stearin products.

esteatita s. f. (min.) steatite, soapstone: an impure massive variety of talc.

esteatoma s. m. (path.) steatoma: a sebaceous cyst.

esteatomático adj. steatomatous: of the nature of a steatoma.

esteatopigia s. f. (med.) steatopygia, steatopygy: excessive fatness of the buttocks.

esteatorréia s. f. (path.) steatorrhoea, steatorrhea.

esteatose s. f. (path.) steatosis: fatty degeneration.

estefanote s. m. (bot.) stephanotis, waxflower (Stephanotis floribunda).

estégano adj. (ornith.) steganopod: having all four toes webbed.

esteganografia s. f. steganography: the art of writing in ciphers or secret characters.

esteganográfico adj. steganographical: relating to steganography.

esteganógrafo s. m. steganographist: person skilled in steganography.

esteio s. m. 1. shore, prop, stay, support, brace (plates C 2, M 2, T 6). 2. strut. 3. rod, staff. 4. (fig.) help, protection, aid, assistance.

ele é o ~ **de sua família** he is the support of his family.

esteira s. f. 1. mat (plate P 17): a piece of coarse fabric made of woven grass, straw or hemp. 2. (naut.) wake of a ship. 3. course, direction. 4. vestige, track. 5. norm.

esteirado adj. matted: covered with a mat or mats.

esteirão s. m. (pl. -ões) a coarse large mat.

esteirar v. 1. to mat, cover with or as with a mat. 2. (naut.) to sail, follow a course.

esteireiro s. m. mat maker or seller.

esteiro s. m. 1. creek, inlet of the sea, arm of a river. 2. estuary.

estela s. f. 1. stele: a pillar or upright slab, mostly with inscriptions and sculptured. 2. monolith.

estelante adj. m. + f. 1. shining, scintillating as the stars. 2. starry, star-studded.

estelar adj. m. + f. stellar: of or pertaining to stars.

estelífero adj. stelliferous: full of stars; starry, starred.

estelionatário s. m. (jur.) person guilty of stellionate.

estelionato s. m. (jur.) stellionate: a fraud, esp. a sale of the same property to different persons.

estelo s. m. stele: the central cylinder in the stems and roots of vascular plants.

estema s. m. 1. crown, garland or wreath of flowers. 2. stemma: a) a family tree or pedigree. b) (zool.) the simple eye of an invertebrate.

estêncil s. m. (pl. **-eis**) stencil: a paraffin-coated sheet to reproduce written or typewritten matter.

estendedouro s. m. (also **estendedoiro, estendal**) drying place or ground, drying loft.

estender v. 1. to extend, stretch out. 2. to enlarge, expand, widen, amplify. 3. to dilate, prolong, lenghten, draw out, procrastinate. 4. to prostrate, overthrow 5. to spread, propagate, divulge, diffuse, disseminate, scatter. 6. to reach or arrive at. 7. **~-se**: a) to extend, stretch, dilate, expand, widen, be enlarged. b) to be stretched out, extended, dilated, expanded. **~ a mão** 1. to put out one's hand. 2. (fig.): a) to offer peace. b) to offer help. **~ a roupa** to hang out the washing or linen. **~ mãos amigas** to lend a willing hand. **~ os braços** to stretch one's arms. **~-se ao comprido na areia** to stretch o. s. at full length on the sands. **~-se de um século a outro** to lap over from one century to another. **~-se sobre** to enlarge upon. **as montanhas estendem-se para o oeste** the run of the mountains is to the west. **um grande futuro estende-se diante dele** a great future opens up to him.

estenderete s. m. 1. a sort of card game. 2. fiasco, failure, flop; sorry figure. 3. bad example. 4. place to spread washing to dry.

estendível adj. m. + f. (pl. **-íveis**) extendible, extensible.

estenia s. f. (med.) sthenia: strenght and activity.

estenocardia s. f. (med.) stenocardia, angina pectoris.

estenocefalia s. f. stenocephalia, stenocephaly: excessive narrowness of the nead.

estenocéfalo adj. stenocephalous: narrow-headed.

estenodactilografia, estenodatilografia s. f. shorthand and typewriting.

estenodactilógrafo, estenodatilógrafo s. m. shorthand typist: stenographer and typist.

estenografar v. to write shorthand.

estenografia s. f. stenography, shorthand.

estenográfico adj. stenographic(al): of or pertaining to stenography.

estenógrafo s. m. stenographer, shorthand writer.

estenosar v. (med.) to cause stenosis in.

estenose s. f. (med.) stenosis: narrowing or stricture of a duct or canal.

estentor s. m. stentor: person with a powerful voice.

estentóreo, estentórico adj. stentorian (voice).

estepe s. f. steppe: vast stretches of level land (as in Asiatic Russia).

éster s. m. (pl. **ésteres**) (chem.) ester.

estercado adj. fertilized, manured.

estercar v. 1. to manure, dung, fertilize (soil). 2. to defecate.

esterco (ê) s. m. 1. dung, manure. 2. excrement. 3. garbage. 4. dirt.

estercoral adj. m. + f. (pl. **-ais**) stercoral, stercoraceous: pertaining to or resembling dung or excrement.

estercorário adj. stercoraceous: living in or feeding on dung.

estercoreiro s. m. (ent.) dorbeetle, dung-beetle.

estercúlia s. f. Sterculia: a genus of plants of the order Sterculiaceae.

esterculiácea s. f. a sterculiaceous plant.

esterculiáceo adj. sterculiaceous: of or pertaining to the Sterculiaceae (chocolate family).

estéreo s. m. (also **estere**) stere, a cubic meter.

estereocromia s. f. stereochromy.

estereografia s. f. stereography: the art of delineating solid forms on a plane.

estereográfico adj. stereographic(al): of or pertaining to stereography.

estereologia s. f. the study of the solid parts of animal bodies.

estereoma s. m. (bot.) stereome.

estereometria s. f. stereometry: 1. the art of measuring volumes. 2. solid geometry.

estereométrico adj. stereometric(al): pertaining to stereometry.

estereômetro s. m. stereometer: an instrument for measuring the volume of solid bodies.

estereoscopia s. f. stereoscopy: the use or construction of stereoscopes.

estereoscópico adj. stereoscopic(al): of, pertaining to or resembling a stereoscope.

estereoscópio s. m. stereoscope: an instrument to give a three-dimensional lifelike appearance to pictures.

estereostática s. f. (phys.) stereostatics: the statics of solids.

estereotipagem s. f. (pl. **-ens**) 1. stereotypography: act of printing from stereotype. 2. stereotyping: act or process of making stereotypes.

estereotipar v. to stereotype: 1. make a stereotype of; cast a stereotype plate from. 2. print from stereotypes. 3. give a fixed or settled form to.

estereotipia s. f. stereotypy: the art or business of making stereotype plates.

estereótipo s. m. stereotype: a printing plate cast from a mould.

estereotomia s. f. stereotomy: the cutting of solids into figures by certain sections.

estereotômico adj. stereotomic: of or pertaining to stereotomy.

esterigma s. m. (bot.) sterigma, a stalk or support.

estéril adj. m. + f. (pl. **estéreis**) sterile: 1. barren, unfruitful, unproductive, infertile, unprolific. 2. infecund. 3. sterilized, free from living germs. **mulher ~** infecund woman. **terra ~** barren soil.

esterilidade s. f. 1. sterility, unfruitfulness, barrenness, infertility, infecundity. 2. scarcity.

esterilização s. f. (pl. **-ões**) 1. sterilization: the act or process of making sterile, esp. the process of freeing from living germs. 2. destruction, devastation.

esterilizado adj. sterilized, free from living germs.

esterilizador s. m. sterilizer: 1. person who sterilizes. 2. an apparatus for rendering substances free from living germs (as by means of heat). ‖ adj. sterilizing.

esterilizante adj. m. + f. sterilizing.

esterilizar v. (also **esterilecer**) 1. to sterilize: a) make sterile or barren. b) deprive of fecundity. c) free from living germs (as by heating or boiling). 2. (fig.) to make useless. 3. **~-se** to become sterile.

esterlino s. m. pound sterling. ‖ adj. sterling: of or pertaining to the pound sterling. **uma libra -a** one pound sterling.

esternal adj. m. + f. (pl. **-ais**) (anat.) sternal: pertaining to the sternum.

esternalgia s. f. (med.) sternalgia: angina pectoris.

estérnebra s. f. (anat.) sternebra: any of the segments of the sternum.

esternebral adj. m. + f. (anat.) sternebral: pertaining to the sternebra.

esterno s. m. (anat.) sternum, breast-bone.

esternoclidomastóideo s. m. (anat.) sternocleidomastoid muscle. ‖ adj. sternocleidomastoid.

esternutação s. f. (pl. **-ões**) sternutation, sneezing, a sneeze.

esternutatório s. m. sternutatory: an agent that causes sneezing. ‖ adj. sternutatory: causing sneezes.

esterqueira s. f., **esterqueiro, esterquilínio** m. 1. dunghill, laystall. 2. any place full of ordure. 3. (fig.) dirty place.

esterrecer v. = **estarrecer.**

esterroada s. f. 1. act of breaking up clods (as with a harrow). 2. (fig.) noise, din.

esterroador s. m. tool or implement to break clods.

esterroar v. 1. to harrow, break the clods. 2. to remove earth.

estertor s. m. (pl. **estertores**) (med.) stertor: stertorous breathing; death-rattle.

estertorante adj. m. + f. 1. stertorous. 2. dying, moribund.

estertorar v. to agonize.

estertoroso adj. stertorous; rattling.

estese, estesia s. f. esthesia, esthesis, perception, feeling, sensibility.

esteta s. m. + f. (a)esthete: person versed in (a)esthetics.

estética s. f. (a)esthetics: 1. the study or science of the beautiful. 2. the theory or philosophy of the fine arts.

esteticismo s. m. aestheticism.

esteticista s. m. + f. 1. (philos.) aesthetician, aestheticist. 2. (Braz.) beautician, cosmetologist: an expert in beauty (make-up, hairdressing, etc.).

estetizar v. to study or consider s. th. under the aesthetic point of view.

estético adj. (a)esthetic: pertaining to the science of (a)esthetics. ‖ **esteticamente** adv. (a)esthetically.

estetoscópio s. m. stethoscope: instrument used in auscultation.

esteva (ê) s. f. 1. (bot.) rock-rose (Cistus ladeniferus). 2. plough handle, plow handle.

esteval s. m. (pl. **-ais**) place where rock-roses grow.

estiado adj. dry (weather).

estiagem s. f. (pl. **-ens**) (also **estiada**) drought: 1. dryness, aridity. 2. dry weather. 3. want of rain.

estiar v. 1. to stop raining, rain no more, to settle. 2. to dry up. 3. (fig.) to slacken, relax, flag.

estibiado adj. stibiated: impregnated with antimony.

estíbio s. m. stibium, antimony.

estibordo s. m. starboard, right side of a ship.

estica s. f. (fig.) 1. leanness. 2. thin person. 3. (N. Braz.) elegance.

ele está na ~ 1. (N. Braz.) he is dressed very well. 2. (S. Braz.) to be poverty-stricken.

esticado adj. 1. stretched. 2. (fig.) well dressed.

esticador s. m. 1. stretcher. 2. (tech.) tensioner (Plate M 1). 3. that stretches.

~ **de corrente da bicicleta** chain tensioner (plate B 11). **molete** ~ tension roller.

esticar v. 1. to stretch out, extend, tighten. 2. to lengthen, draw out, pull. 3. to prolong, dilate. 4. **~-se** to stretch out.

~ **as canelas** (sl.) to die.

estígio adj. (myth.) Stygian.

estigma s. m. stigma: 1. mark, spot. 2. cicatrix, scar. 3. a mark of infamy, blemish, macula. 4. blotch, stain. 5. brand. 6. (bot.) the part of the pistil which receives the pollen. 7. (ent.) a spiracle of an insect.

estigmatizar v. (also **estigmar**) 1. to stigmatize: mark with a stigma or brand. 2. (fig.) to censure, blame.

estilar v. 1. to distill. 2. to drip, drop, let fall in drops. 3. to squeeze. 4. **~-se** to pine or waste away; to decay.

estilete s. m. 1. (surg.) probe, sound. 2. stiletto. 3. (bot.) style.

estiletear v. (Braz.) to stab with a stiletto.

estilha s. f. (also **estila**) 1. chip, wood **splinter.** 2. fragment, scrap.

estilhaçar v. (also **estilhar**) 1. to break into small pieces. 2. to shatter, splinter, shiver, burst.

estilhaço s. m. splinter, fragment, chip.

à prova de ~**s** splinter-proof.

estilicídio s. m. dripping (like drops falling from the eaves).

estilingue s. m. (Braz.) slingshot: a forked stick with two elastic bands attached to it, for shooting with small stones.

estilismo s. m. excessive care in speech or language; pedantism.

estilista s. m. + f. stylist: 1. a writer having or cultivating a good style. 2. a writer having individual style. ‖ adj. stylistic(al).

estilística s. f. stylistic(s): 1. art of forming a good style in writing. 2. a treatise on style.

estilizar v. to stylize: 1. draw according to a style. 2. conform to a style.

estilo s. m. style: 1. a pointed instrument used by the ancients for writing on wax-covered tablets. 2. fashion. 3. distinctive mode of presentation, construction or execution in any fine art. 4. way of writing or speaking; characteristic made · of expression. 5. manner, method, way. 6. (fig.) usage, custom.

~ **elevado** lofty style. ~ **forçado** forced style. ~ **gótico** Gothic style. **seu** ~ **de corrida não é bom** his form in running is bad. **seu** ~ **de escrever é formidável** he wields a formidable pen.

estilofaríngeo adj. (anat.) stylopharyngeal (muscle).

estiloglosso s. m. (anat.) styloglossus: a muscle arising from the styloid process and inserted into the tongue.

estilógrafo s. m. (usually **caneta-tinteiro)** fountain pen.

estilóide adj. m. + f. styloid.

estilometria s. f. art of measuring columns.

estilômetro s. m. stylometer: an instrument for measuring columns.

estima s. f. (also **estimação**, pl. **-ões**) 1. esteem, respect, regard. 2. affection, fondness. 3. consideration, attention. 4. appraisal, valuation, account.

ela o trata com ~ she makes much of him. **ele conquistou a** ~ **de todos** he has won the respect of all. **este cachorro é de estimação this is a pet dog. objeto de estimação** prized possession. **temo-lo em alta** ~ we hold him in high regard.

estimar v. 1. to esteem: a) hold in high estimation. b) regard with respect. c) prize. d) consider, reckon. 2. to estimate: a) appreciate, value, set a value on. b) appraise, rate, size up. 3. to like, admire. 4. to be glad, rejoice. 5. **~-se: a)** to esteem o. s., count o. s. for, know one's worth. b) to like one another. c) to be esteemed, beloved. **ele a estima muito** he likes her much. **estimo muito vê-lo com saúde** I am very glad to see you in good health.

estimativa s. f. 1. estimation, valuation, apprizement. 2. calculation, reckoning, computation. 3. judgement. 4. consideration, attention.

estimativo adj. estimative, esteeming.

valor ~ sentimental value, rough guess value.

estimável adj. m. + f. (pl. **-áveis**) 1. estimable, worthy of esteem or regard; valuable. 2. respectable. 3. appraisable.

ele é um rapaz ~ he is an amiable fellow.

estimulação s. f. (pl. **-ões**) stimulation, excitement, incitation, encouragement.

estimulador s. m. stimulator: person or thing that stimulates. ‖ adj. stimulating, stimulative.

estimulante s. m. + f. stimulant, stimulus. ‖ adj. stimulant, stimulative; incitant, excitant, exciting; provocative.

estimular v. 1. to stimulate: a) incite, instigate, excite, arouse, spur on, rouse, stir up. b) animate, revive, encourage, activate. 2. to irritate, provoke, vex. 3. ~-se: to be resentful, brisk o. s. up, be offended.

estímulo s. m. 1. stimulus, incentive, impulse, encouragement. 2. prick, goad. 3. excitant, stimulant.

estingar v. (naut.) to brail or clue up a sail.

estingue s. m. (naut.) clue-garnet, clue-line.

estinha s. f. the second crop of honey of a hive.

estinhar v. 1. to gather the second crop of honey from a hive. 2. (Port.) = **estiar**.

estio s. m. summer. ‖ adj. = **estival**.

no rigor do ~ in the height of summer.

estiolamento s. m. 1. etiolation. 2. emaciation. 3. weakness.

estiolar(-se) v. to etiolate: 1. (bot.) blanch, become blanched due to privation of light. 2. become pale, look unhealthy. 3. grow weak.

estipe s. m. stipe: trunk of a palm tree.

estipela s. f. (bot.) stipel: a secondary stipule at the base of leaflets.

estipendiar v. to stipend: 1. pay (a salary). 2. hire for wages. 3. provide with a stipend.

estipendiário adj. stipendiary: receiving wages or a salary.

estipêndio s. m. stipend, wages, salary, pay, allowance.

estipitado adj. stipitate: having stipes.

estípite s. m. 1. stipe, stalk, stem. 2. (fig.) origin, stock.

estíptico, estítico adj. styptic, bitter, astringent.

estípula s. f. (bot.) stipulate: one of a pair of lateral appendages at the base of the peciole of many leaves (plate F 5).

estipulação s. f. (pl. -ões) stipulation: 1. adjustment, settlement, agreement. 2. condition, clause (as of a contract).

estipulado adj. 1. stipulated, adjusted, agreed, combined; conventional. 2. (bot.) stipulate: having stipules.

data de entrega -a stipulated date for delivery. **está ~ por lei** it is provided by law.

estipulador s. m., **estipulante** m. + f. stipulator: person who stipulates. ‖ adj. stipulating.

estipular (I) v. to stipulate, contract, settle terms, agree upon, covenant, condition.

estipular (II) adj. m. + f. (bot.) stipular: of or belonging to stipules.

estipuloso adj. (bot.) stipulate: having stipules.

estiracácea s. f. styracaceous plant.

estiracáceo adj. styracaceous: of or pertaining to the Styracaceae.

estirada s. f. 1. long or tiring walk. 2. great distance. **de uma** ~ without interruption, in one go.

estirado adj. 1. extended, stretched out; flat. 2. extensive, large, wide. 3. prolix, diffuse, long-winded. 4. drawn.

estirador s. m. drawing-board.

estirão s. m. (pl. -ões) 1. tiring walk, long way. 2. (N. Braz.) a straight stretch of river.

estirar v. (also **estiraçar**). 1. to extend, stretch, lengthen. 2. to distend, strain. 3. to draw, pull, drag. 4. to throw down. 5. to exceed. 6. to range, set in a row. ~-se: a) to stretch. o. s. (out). b) to grow long. c) to humble, humiliate o. s.

~-se no chão to stretch or be stretched out on the ground.

estirpe s. f. stirps: 1. stock, race, origin, lineage, source. 2. family tree. 3. pedigree, ancestry, genealogy.

estiva s. f. 1. trimming of a ship, stowage. 2. grate, (wooden) grating. 3. bilge or ballast of a ship. 4. ship's hold. 5. cross beams of a wooden bridge. 6. (S. Braz.) coarse wooden bridge.

estivação (I) s. f. (pl. -ões) trimming of a ship, stowage.

estivação (II) s. f. (bot.) aestivation, prefloration.

estivado s. m. (N. Braz.) a sort of wooden bridge. ‖ adj. (Braz.) 1. stowed, trimmed, loaded (ship). 2. full.

estivador s. m. 1. stower, stevedore: one who loads or unloads ships. 2. (Braz.) grocer; provision merchant. ‖ adj. stowing.

estivagem s. f. (pl. -ens) stevedoring, stowing, loading and unloading of a ship.

estival adj. m. + f. (pl. -ais) (also **estio, estivo** m.) (a)estival: of or belonging to the summer; summery.

estivar v. 1. (naut.) to stow, load and unload ships. 2. to weight. 3. to summer, pass the summer.

esto s. m. 1. great heat, hotness. 2. ardour, passion, fervour. 3. flood, inundation. 4. high tide. 5. the roar of waves.

estocada s. f. 1. thrust, lunge, jab. 2. a stab with a dagger. 3. (fig.) disagreeable surprise.

estocar v. 1. to hit s. o. with a rapier. 2. to stock, build up a stock of.

estofa (ô) s. f. 1. stuff: woven material; woollen fabric. 2. (fig.) kind, sort, ilk; condition.

estofado adj. 1. upholstered: furnished (chairs) with stuffing, cushions, coverings. 2. quilted.

móveis ~s upholstered furnitures.

estofador s. m. 1. upholsterer: person who furnishes or adorns (as chairs) with stuffing, cushions, coverings. 2. person who sells upholstery (furniture or interior fittings).

estofar v. 1. to upholster, stuff, cover, bolster. 2. to wad, pad, quilt.

estofo (ô) (I) s. m. (pl. **estofos**) 1. stuff: woven material. 2. padding, wadding, stuffing (of cotton, feathers, straw). 3. interlining. 4. pl. upholstery.

estofo (ô) (II) adj. (pl. **estofos**) 1. calm, smooth, not tiding (sea). 2. stagnant (water).

estoicidade s. f. 1. stoicalness: quality of being stoical. 2. firmness. 3. austerity. 4. resignation.

estoicismo s. m. 1. stoicism, stoic philosophy or way of living. 2. austerity. 3. rigour, rigidness.

estóico s. m. stoic (person). ‖ adj. 1. Stoic(al): of or pertaining to the Stoics. 2. stoic: a) insensible, unconcerned, impassive. b) severe, austere, rigid.

estojar v. to put into a box, case or kit.

estojo (ô) s. m. (pl. **estojos**) case, box, etui, container, kit, set (plates D 2, F 6, P 12).

~ de barba shaving set. **~ de costura** workbag, sewing kit. **~ de desenho** drawing set. **~ de pintura** colour-box. **~ de tintas** paint-box. **~ para escrever** writing-case. **~ para pó-de-arroz** vanity case.

estol s. m. (pl. -óis) (aeron.) 1. loss of velocity. 2. stunt flying.

estola s. f. (eccl.) stole (plate P 5).

estolho s. m. (bot.) stolon.

estolhoso adj. (bot.) stoloniferous: producing or bearing stolons.

estólido adj. 1. rattlebrained. 2. foolish, stupid, dull, stolid. ‖ **estolidamente** adv. foolishly, stolidly.

estoma s. m. (bot.; also **estomato**) stoma.

estomacal adj. m. + f. (pl. -ais) (also **estomáquico** m.) stomachic(al), stomachal: 1. good for the stomach. 2. of or pertaining to the stomach.

estomagar v. 1. to vex, annoy. 2. to make angry. 3. to scandalize, offend. 4. ~-se: a) to become angry. b) to be scandalized or offended. c) to resent.

estômago s. m. 1. (anat.) stomach (plate C 18). 2. (fig.): a) disposition, animation, courage, resolution. b) appetite. c) patience.
   boca do ~ pit of the stomach. dor de ~ stomach--ache. forrar o ~ to eat less than usually. isto me vira o ~ that goes against my stomach. lavagem do ~ gastric lavage.

estomático adj. stomatic: said of medicines for diseases of the mouth.

estomatite s. f. (path.) stomatitis: inflammation of the interior of the mouth.

estomatópode s. m. (zool.) stomatopod: a member of the Stomatopoda. || adj. m. + f. stomatopod: having some of the legs near the mouth (as a mantis shrimp).

estomatoscópio s. m. (med.) stomatoscope: an instrument for keeping the mouth open.

estomentar v. to scutch, hatchel (hemp, flax).

estonado adj. peeled, decorticated, skinned.

estonar v. to bark, peel, skin, decorticate.

estoniano s. m. Estonian: native or inhabitant of Estonia. || adj. Estonian.

estonteado adj. 1. giddy, dizzy. 2. stunned, puzzled. 3. muddle-headed.

estonteamento s. m. 1. act of stunning. 2. perturbation, disturbance.

estonteante adj. m. + f., estonteador m. 1. stunning. 2. perturbing, confusing, disturbing. 3. dazzling. 4. dizzying.

estontear v. 1. to stun, puzzle; perplex, astonish. 2. to dazzle. 3. to make dizzy. 4. to perturb, disturb. 5. to fuddle. 6. ~-se: to become perturbed or confused.

estopa (ô) s. f. 1. tow, hards, hurds; oakum. 2. waste of cotton.

estopada s. f. 1. a lot of tow. 2. tow for a plaster. 3. (fig.): a) tiresome or tedious thing; nuisance. b) irksome talk. c) blunder, piece of stupidity.
   que ~! what a nuisance! what a howler!

estopador adj. m., estopante m. + f. 1. importunate, troublesome. 2. tedious, boring.

estopar (I) adj. said of a sort of nail with a broad head (like scupper-nails).

estopar (II) v. 1. to fill with tow or oakum. 2. to calk with tow. 3. (fam.) to tire, irk, bore.

estopento adj. fibrous, like tow.

estopetar v. to dishevel, tousle; muss (hair).

estopim s. m. (pl. -ins) quickmatch, fuse, lunt.
   ~ à prova d'água sump fuse.

estopinha s. f. very fine flax.

estoque (I) s. m. rapier, tuck.

estoque (II) s. m. 1. stock (of goods). 2. (fig.) reserve, supply.
   levantamento do ~ stock-taking. manter em ~ to keep in stock. ter em ~ to have in stock.

estoquear v. to thrust, hurt with a rapier.

estoquésia s. f. (bot.) stokes' aster (Stokesia cyanea).

estoquista s. m. + f. stockman: person in charge of the stock of an establishment.

estoraque s. m. storax: 1. the resin. 2. the tree.

estorcegão s. m. (pl. -ões) 1. twisting. 2. a pinch.

estorcegar v. 1. = estorcer. 2. to pinch, nip. 3. to bruise, crush, hurt.

estorcer v. 1. to twist, contort; squirm, strain. 2. to agitate. 3. to change direction. 4. ~-se to writhe (as in pain).

estorço s. m. forced or affected attitude.

estore s. m. 1. spring blind, roller blind. 2. window shade.

estória s. f. story, tale.

estornar v. 1. (com.) to cancel: debit or credit an account for what it had been mistakenly credited or debited. 2. (naut.) to rescind an insurance contract.

estorninho s. m. (Braz., ornith.) a starling.

estorno (ô) s. m. 1. (com.) act or fact of cancellation: debiting or crediting an account for what it had been mistakenly credited or debited. 2. (naut.) rescission (insurance).

estorrador s. m. (agric.) harrow, harrower.

estorricado adj. 1. dry, arid. 2. toasted, parched.

estorricar v. 1. to dry (up). 2. to toast, parch, overroast.

estorroar v. to harrow.

estortegar v. 1. to writhe. 2. to dislocate, luxate. 3. to twist.

estorva s. f. 1. hindrance, impediment. 2. embarrassment. 3. the seams of a ship.

estorvador s. m. hinderer; (fig.) drag, spoke. || adj. hindering, obstructive.

estorvar v. 1. to hinder, embarrass, obstruct, impede. 2. to importune, disturb, perturb.

estorvilho s. m. a little hindrance or impediment.

estorvo (ô) s. m. (pl. estorvos) (also estorvamento) 1. hindrance, impediment, embarrassment, obstruction, obstacle. 2. difficulty. 3. opposition.

estou-fraca s. f., sg. + pl. (a pop. name for galinha--d'angola) the guinea-fowl.

estourada s. f. (also estoirada) 1. great noise of explosions or detonations. 2. brawling, scolding. 3. dogfight, brawl, row.

estourado s. m. boisterous, turbulent person. || adj. (also estoirado) 1. burst. 2. (fig.) crack-brained, turbulent, rattlebrained; boisterous, unrestrained.

estourar v. (also estoirar) 1. to cause to burst. 2. to burst (with great noise); explode. 3. to split, crack, clatter; break up, shatter. 4. to blow out. 5. to stampede (cattle). 6. (fig.) to enrage, lose one's temper; scold, rail, bawl.
   de volta para casa um pneu estourou on my driving home a tire blew out. a garrafa estourou the bottle burst asunder, pop went the bottle. por pouco ele estoura (fig.) he is about to fly into a passion of rage, (coll.) he'll take off any minute now. quase estourei de riso I almost burst with laughter.

estoura-vergas s. m., sg. + pl. (also estoira-vergas) hothead, hotspur.

estouraz adj. m. + f. 1. that explodes (with great noise). 2. noisy.

estouro s. m. (also estoiro) 1. burst, bursting. 2. noise of bursting objects. 3. crack, clap, peal, detonation, report, explosion. 4. (Braz.) a rebuke, severe admonition.
   ~ da boiada the stampede of cattle.

estouvado adj. 1. hotheaded, lightheaded. 2. rash, rattlebrained. 3. foolhardy. 4. unreflecting, heedless.

estouvamento s. m. 1. rashness, inconsiderateness, heedlessness, recklessness. 2. carelessness.

estovaína s. f. (pharm.) stovaine: a compound used as a local anesthetic.

estrabada s. f. dung.

estrabão s. m. (pl. -ões) cross-eyed person. || adj. cross-eyed.

estrabar v. to void, defecate, dung.

estrábico s. m. cross-eyed person. || adj. 1. cross--eyed, squinting, strabismic. 2. of or pertaining to strabism.

estrabismo s. m. squinting, strabismus.

estrabo s. m. dung, excrement of animals.

estrabômetro s. m. strabometer: instrument for measuring strabismus.

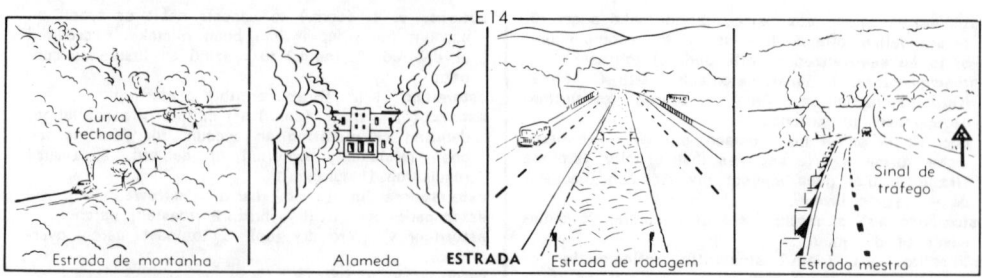

E 14

Curva fechada

Estrada de montanha | Alameda **ESTRADA** Estrada de rodagem | Sinal de tráfego Estrada mestra

estrabotomia s. f. (surg.) strabotomy: the cutting of an ocular tendon in order to cure strabismus.

estrabulega s. m. (S. Braz.) 1. a mad, insane or hotheaded person. 2. prodigal, squanderer. 3. naughty, mischievous person.

estrabuleguice s. f. (S. Braz.) 1. madness, foolishness. 2. disorder, confusion. 3. noisy merry-making, spree.

estraçalhar, estracinhar, estraçoar v. 1. to cut, tear, rend to pieces. 2. to shred, slash. 3. to smash, shatter.

estrada s. f. 1. road, highway, main road, public road (plates C 8, E 14). 2. (fig.): a) way, means. b) rule, method, course.
~ **de duas vias** two-way road. ~ **de ferro** railway, railroad. ~ **de rodagem** arterial road, highway, (U. S. A.) super highway (plate E 14). ~ **de uma só via** one-way road. ~ **real,** ~ **mestra,** ~ **principal** main road, (U. S. A.) highway (plates A 4, E 14). ~ **secundária** by-road, lane (plate A 4). **consertar uma** ~ to mend a road. **conservação das** ~**s** preservation of roads. **eles abriram uma** ~ they opened a road. **ladrão de** ~**s** highwayman. **a linha férrea atravessa a** ~ **neste ponto** the railway line crosses the road at this point. **plano e construção das** ~**s** highway planning and building. **uma curva na** ~ a curve in the road.

estradar (I) v. 1. to open or build a road. 2. to go towards, take one's way to. 3. to follow a road.

estradar (II) v. to provide with a floor or platform.

estradeiro adj. (Braz.) 1. usually away from home, always on the road. 2. scoundrelly, crooked; deceitful, rascal.

estradiota s. f. a style of riding with stretched legs and steadied in the stirrups.

estradioto s. m. (obs.) highwayman.

estradivário s. m. a Stradivarius violin.

estrado (I) s. m. 1. estrade: a slightly raised platform. 2. mattress frame, bedframe (plate C 7). 3. footstool. 4. broad bench.
~ **com molas (da cama)** steel mattress (plate C 7).

estrado (II) adj. strewn.

estradona s. f. (N. Braz.; also **estradão** m.) a very broad road.

estrafegar v. 1. to shatter, smash. 2. to tear to pieces.

estrafego (ê) s. m. (Braz.) 1. act of shattering. 2. laceration.

estraga-albardas s. m., sg. + pl. hothead, hotspur, spendthrift.

estragado adj. 1. damnified, rotten, deteriorated, damaged. 2. corrupt(ed). 3. spoiled, dissipated. 4. (fig.) syphilitic.
meu sapato está muito ~ my shoe is much worn.

estragador s. m. 1. spendthrift, squanderer. 2. waster, lavisher. 3. corrupter. ‖ adj. destructive, spoiling.

estragão s. m. (pl. **-ões**) (bot.) tarragon (Artemisia dracunculus).

estraga-prazeres s. m., sg. + pl. spoil-sport, kill-joy, wet blanket.

estragar v. 1. to destroy, ruin, spoil, damage. 2. to hurt, injure. 3. to waste. 4. to corrupt, deprave 5. to deteriorate. 6. to rot, decay. 7. to vitiate. 8. ~**-se**: a) to ruin o. s. b) to become depraved, spoiled or damaged. c) to grow corrupt. d) to deteriorate.
ele estragou-me os planos he undid my plans, (sl.) cooked my goose. **ele me estragou o dia** he put me out of conceit with the day.

estrago s. m. 1. damage, prejudice, harm. 2. hurt, injury. 3. ruin, destruction. 4. spoilage, havoc. 5. waste, squandering, dissipation. 6. deterioration. 7. corruption, depravity.
causar grandes ~**s ao inimigo** to do great execution upon the enemy.

estralada s. f. 1. noise, clamour. 2. snapping sound, crackling. 3. disorder, confusion, conflict. 4. a brawl.

estralar, estralejar v. to crack, crackle, burst.

estralheira s. f. (naut.) foretackle; becket.

estrambótico adj. (also **estrambólico**) 1. extravagant, irregular. 2. odd, queer, freakish. 3. ridiculous.
ela tem um nome estrambólico she has an odd name.

estramônio s. m. (bot.) stramonium, thorn-apple (Datura stramonium).

estramontado adj. 1. bewildered; confused. 2. very irritated, furious.

estrangeirada s. f. (depr.) a lot of foreigners; foreigners collectively.

estrangeirado adj. 1. adopting foreign customs. 2. imitating foreigners.

estrangeirice s. f. 1. foreignism, imitation of foreign usages. 2. fondness for foreign things. 3. foreign ways.

estrangeirismo s. m. 1. = estrangeirice. 2. the usage of foreign words or expressions.

estrangeiro s. m. 1. foreigner, stranger. 2. foreign countries. ‖ adj. 1. foreign, outlandish, alien. 2. exotic.
carta do ~ foreign letter. **comércio** ~ foreign trade. **crédito** ~ foreign credit. **ele é** ~ **na sua pátria** he is a stranger in his own country; he is stranger to its customs. **ele mora no** ~ he resides abroad. **no** ~ abroad, under a foreign sky. **tanto** ~ **como nacional** both foreign and domestic. **valores** ~**s** foreign assets. **viver no** ~ to live abroad.

estrangulação s. f. (pl. **-ões**) 1. strangulation, suffocation. 2. choke, choking, throttling. 3. constriction.

estrangulador s. m. 1. strangler. 2. choker, throttle. ‖ adj. strangling, choking.

estrangulamento s. m. strangulation, suffocation.

estrangular v. 1. to strangle, suffocate. 2. (med.) to strangulate. 3. to choke, throttle. 4. to restrain.

check. 5. ~-se: a) to strangle o. s. b) to be suffocated or choked.

estrangúria, estranguria s. f. (med.) stranguria, strangury: slow and painful discharge of urine.

estranhado adj. 1. timid, shy, bashful. 2. strange.

estranhamento s. m. 1. the act or fact of finding s. th. strange or curious. 2. unfamiliarity. 3. surprise. 4. blame, reprehension.

estranhão s. m. (pl. -ões) (f. -ona) (fam.) a shy person. ‖ adj. shy, coy, timid, bashful.

estranhar v. 1. to find queer, odd or strange. 2. to wonder, admire. 3. to be surprised. 4. not to be used to, not to get accustomed to. 5. to feel uneasiness in the presence of unknown persons. 6. to consider reprehensible, blamable. 7. ~-se to estrange o. s., to shun, avoid, desert, forsake. **estou estranhando o seu modo de proceder** I am surprised at your conduct. **o menino estranha as pessoas desconhecidas** the child feels ill at ease with strangers.

estranhável adj. m. + f. (pl. -áveis) 1. strange; causing strangeness. 2. censurable, blamable.

estranheza s. f. 1. strangeness, queerness, oddity. 2. astonishment, wonder, amazement. 3. surprise. 4. shyness, timidity; unfamiliarity.

estranho s. m. stranger, foreigner. ‖ adj. 1. foreign, strange, outlandish, alien. 2. extraneous. 3. wonderful. 4. odd, queer, freakish. 5. exotic, singular. 6. unaccustomed. 7. unknown, unfamiliar. **é ~!** it is strange! **por ~ que pareça ele escreveu isso** oddly enough he wrote that. **quão ~** how odd. **um tipo ~ de moça** a strange sort of girl.

estranja s. f. 1. foreign countries. 2. m. + f. foreigner, stranger.

estransilhar-se v. (S. Braz.) to tire out (horse).

estrapada s. f. strappado: a former military punishment.

estrapilho s. m. (S. Braz.) (usually **maltrapilho**) tatterdemalion. ‖ adj. ragged, in tatters.

estrapilhar v. (S. Braz.) to reduce to tatters, rags (dress).

estratagema s. m. stratagem: 1. ruse, artifice, trick. 2. artfulness, astuteness; cunning.

estratégia s. f. 1. strategics, strategy: the art of war, generalship; military science. 2. stratagem, artifice, trick.

estratégico s. m. strategist. ‖ adj. 1. strategic(al): of or pertaining to strategy. 2. cunning, artful, astute, tricky.

estrategista s. m. + f. strategist: person skilled in the art of war.

estratificação s. f. (pl. -ões) stratification.

estratificar v. to stratify: 1. form into a layer. 2. lay or arrange in strata.

estratiforme adj. m. + f. stratiform: resembling strata.

estratigrafia s. f. stratigraphy: that branch of geology which treats of the arrangement and succession of strata.

estrato s. m. 1. (geol.) stratum, bed, layer. 2. stratus: a continuous horizontal sheet of clouds.

estrato-cirro s. m. (meteor.) (pl. estratos-cirros) cirrostratus.

estratocracia s. f. stratocracy: military government or despotism.

estrato-cúmulo s. m. (pl. estratos-cúmulos) cumulostratus, stratocumulus (plate N 2): cumulus clouds with a stratified appearance.

estratografia s. f. stratography: description of armies and their equipments.

estratográfico adj. stratographic(al): pertaining to stratography.

estrato-nimbo s. m. (pl. estratos-nimbos) (meteor.) nimbostratus.

estratosfera s. f. stratosphere.

estravar v. to void, defecate, dung.

estreante s. m. + f. 1. debutant(e). 2. beginner, novice. ‖ adj. inicial, beginning; that appears for the first time.

estrear v. 1. to handsel: a) use for the first time. b) be the first to use. 2. to inaugurate; iniciate; begin. 3. ~-se: a) to do a thing for the first time. b) to make one's debut. **~ um vestido** to handsel a dress.

estrebaria s. f. horse stable.

estrebuchamento s. m. struggle, violent or convulsive motion of the arms and legs.

estrebuchar(-se) v. 1. to struggle with feet and hands. 2. to move convulsively; sprawl, kick. 3. to flounder, toss.

estréia s. f. 1. handsel, the first sale. 2. the first use of anything. 3. (theat.) première: the first performance of a play; first night. 4. beginning, debut, first appearance.

estreitamento s. m. narrowing, straitening, shortening, tightening.

estreitar v. 1. to narrow, straiten. 2. to make narrower. 3. to grip, crimp. 4. to diminish, shorten, reduce. 5. to confine, limit, restrict. 6. to press, clasp. 7. to tighten. 8. to constrict. 9. ~-se: a) to grow narrower. b) to restrict o. s. **~ nos braços** to clasp in one's arms. **~ os laços de amizade** to become close friends.

estreiteza s. f. 1. narrowness, straitness. 2. shortness. 3. tightness. 4. closeness, intimacy. 5. pettiness, stinginess. 6. indigence, penury. **~ de visão** narrow-mindedness.

estreito s. m. a strait. ‖ adj. 1. narrow, strait (plates F 5, Q). 2. close. 3. thin. 4. sparing, scanty. 5. narrow-minded. ‖ -amente adv. narrowly. **~ de Gibraltar** the straits of Gibraltar. **de bitola -a** narrow gauge (railway).

estreitura s. f. 1. = estreiteza. 2. = estreitamento.

estrela (ê) s. f. star: 1. any heavenly body appearing as a luminous point. 2. anything which resembles a star. 3. fate, fortune, destiny; guide. 4. person of brilliant qualities. 5. leading actress, film star (leading actor = **astro**). **~ cadente** shooting star, falling star. **~ da manhã, ~ da tarde, ~ do pastor, ~ matutina** morning star. **ler nas ~** to horoscope, foretell the future by the observation of stars. **levantar-se com as ~** to get up very early. **as ~ cintilam** the stars scintillate. **o filme apresenta uma nova ~** the picture is starring a new actress. **sua ~ é ascendente** (fig.) his star is in the ascendant. **ver ~s ao meio-dia** (fig.) to be stunned.

estrela-d'alva s. f. (pl. estrelas-d'alva) morning star, day star; evening star.

estreladeira s. f. pan for poached eggs.

estrela-de-jerusalém s. f. (pl. estrelas-de-jerusalém) (bot.) snow-in-harvest, snow-in-summer (Cerastium tomentosum).

estrela-de-rabo s. f. (pl. estrelas-de-rabo) (Braz., pop.) comet.

estrelado adj. 1. starry, starred, studded or covered with stars. 2. fried (eggs). **noite de céu ~** starlit night. **ovos ~s** fried eggs.

estrela-do-mar s. f. (pl. estrelas-do-mar) (Braz., zool.) starfish; five-finger.

estrelar v. 1. to star: a) set, spangle or adorn with stars. b) (theat., cin.) play as a star. 2. to fry (eggs). 3. to shine, scintillate. 4. to adorn, ornament. 5. ~-se: to become covered with stars.

estrelário adj. starlike, shaped like a star.

estrelato s. m. stardom.

estreleiro adj. lifting the head too much (horse).

estrelejar v .to become covered with stars (sky).
estrelinha s. f. 1. starlet, little star. 2. asterisk. 3. a star-shaped paste for the soup. 4. sparkler: a firework of brilliant sparks.
estrelo (ê) adj. (N. Braz.) blazed (ox).
estrém s. m. (pl. -éns) (naut.) anchor-cable.
estrema s. f. landmark: boundary line.
estremadela s. f. (pop.) 1. demarcation. 2. separation.
estremado adj. 1. delimited, demarcated. 2. divided, confined.
estremadura s. f. frontier, limit, bound, border.
estremar(-se) v. 1. to bound, demarcate, fix the bounds of (land); delimitate. 2. to border. 3. to separate, divide, distinguish. 4. to choose, select.
estreme adj. m. + f. pure, unmixed, genuine; sheer.
estremeção s. m. (pl. -ões) shaking, shuddering, tremor; start.
estremecer v. 1. to tremble, shake. 2. to excite, affect, shock; frighten, start. 3. to agitate, vibrate. 4. to love very much. 5. ~-se: a) to tremble, quake, shake. b) to shudder. c) to become frightened.
~ **com todo o corpo** to tremble all over. **a mera idéia fê-lo** ~ the very idea gave him a start.
estremecido adj. 1. shocked, startled, scared. 2. loved very much.
estremecimento s. m. 1. shudder(ing), trembling. 2. fright, start, shock. 3. vibration, concussion. 4. extreme love.
estremunhar(-se) v. 1. to awake with a start, to startle from sleep. 2. to become confused, bewildered.
estrênuo adj. valiant, strenuous, bold, brave; active, diligent.
estrepada s. f. wound caused by a sharp point or caltrop.
estrepar v. 1. to provide with sharp points or caltrops. 2. ~-se: a) to be wounded by a caltrop, thorn or sharp point. b) (Braz.) to come off badly, fail.
ele estrepou-se com isto he came off badly, got his teeth into it.
estrepe s. m. 1. pointed stake. 2. caltrop. 3. thorn. 4. (Braz., sl.) an ugly and lean woman.
estrepeiro s. m. thorn tree, hawthorn.
estrepitante adj. m. + f. 1. noisy, loud, clamorous. 2. showy, ostentatious.
estrepitar v. 1. to make a great noise. 2. to crash, crack, thunder, peal.
estrépito s. m. 1. great noise. 2. clap, crack, crash, peal, thunder. 3. rattle, racket. 4. confusion, tumult, uproar. 5. pomp, display, ostentation.
estrepitoso adj. noisy, clamorous, thundering, roaring. ‖ -**amente** adv. noisily.
estreptococo s. m. (bact.) streptococus.
estreptomicina s. f. (pharm.) streptomycin.
estresir v. (drawing) to pounce.
estressar v. (med.) to stress.
estresse s. m. (med.) stress.
estressor s. m. (med.) stress agent.
estria (I) s. f. 1. furrow, groove, channel. 2. (archit.) stria: a fillet between the flutes of columns. 3. rifling (gun).
estria (II) s. f. vampire, bloodsucker.
estriamento s. m. 1. striation. 2. rifling (gun).
estriar v. 1. to chamfer, flute, channel, groove. 2. to rifle (gun). 3. to striate, form in striae.
vidro estriado corrugated glass.
estribado adj. 1. supported in stirrups. 2. propped, firm. 3. (fig.) based, well-founded.
estribar v. 1. to put one's feet in the stirrups. 2. to prop, support. 3. to base. 4. ~-se: a) to steady o. s. on horseback resting one's feet firmly on the

stirrups. b) to lean or rest upon. c) to base o. s. on.
estribeira s. f. 1. step, foot-board (of a coach). 2. stirrup.
perder as ~**s** to lose one's temper, (sl.) fly off the handle.
estribeiro s. m. stableman, equerry, master of the horses.
estribilhar v. (Braz.) to repeat a verse (as a refrain).
estribilho s. m. 1. a verse often repeated, refrain, ritornello, chorus, burden. 2. (fig.) pet phrase or expression.
estribo s. m. 1. stirrup (plates B 14, E 5, S 2). 2. step or foot-board of a coach (plate C 15). 3. (mot.) running-board (plate V 3). 4. (anat.) stirrup bone, stapes. 5. any stirrup-shaped piece (plates F 1, M 9). (fig.) prop, support.
correia do ~ stirrup-leather. **ter o pé em dois** ~**s** to have two strings to one's bow, to be Jack on both sides.
estricnina s. f. (chem.) strychnine: a poisonous alkaloid.
estridência s. f. stridence, stridency.
estridente adj. m. + f. (also **estrídulo, estriduloso** m.) 1. strident, shrill, whistling; creaking, harsh, grating. 2. noisy. 3. penetrating.
estridor s. m. 1. stridor: a) shrill or whistling sound; creak. b) harsh, creaking noise. 2. roar, rattle, din.
estridulação s. f. (pl. -ões) stridulation, a grating sound.
estridulante adj. m. + f. 1. = **estridente**. 2. stridulant, stridulous (insects).
estridular v. to stridulate: 1. make a stridulous noise. 2. grate, scrape, creak. 3. shrill, chirr.
estriga s. f. strike of flax; handful of combed flax fit for spinning.
~ **de cabelos** a braid of hair.
estrigado adj. as thin or fine as hatcheled flax.
estrigar v. 1. to card, comb (flax). 2. to put it on the distaff.
estrige s. f. vampire, horn-owl.
estrigídeo s. m. a bird of the family Strigidae. ‖ adj. of or pertaining to the Strigidae.
estrilador adj. (Braz., sl.) given to shouting, yelling.
estrilar v. (Braz., sl.) 1. to protest noisily. 2. to rail (against). 3. to shout, bawl. 4. to enfuriate, enrage.
estrilo s. m. (Braz., pop.) 1. loud protest. 2. rail. 3. fury, anger, fit of rage. 4. shout, bawl, squawk.
estrincar v. to crack, snap one's finger joints.
estrinchar v. 1. to play. 2. to leap, jump, romp.
estringir v. to tighten, bind closely.
estripação s. f. (pl. -ões) 1. unboweling, disembowelment, evisceration. 2. extirpation.
estripar v. 1. to unbowel, disembowel, unrip, eviscerate. 2. to extirpate.
estripulento adj. (Braz., sl.) 1. mischievous, naughty. 2. rowdy.
estripulia s. f. (Braz., fam.) 1. mischief, naughtiness. 2. confusion, tumult, racket, din. 3. lark, prank. 4. disorder.
não faça ~**s** don't play the giddy goat.
estrito adj. strict: 1. rigorous, severe, rigid. 2. exact, accurate, precise. ‖ -**amente** adv. strictly.
estritura s. f. stricture; compression; binding.
estro s. m. 1. oestrum, oestrus: a) a gadfly. b) violent impulse, passion. c) sensual desire. 2. inspiration, poetic rage.
estróbilo s. m. (bot.) strobile, cone.
estroço s. m. 1. wreckage, devastation. 2. swarm of bees that moved to another hive.
estrofanto s. m. plant of the family Apocynaceae (Strophantus gratus).
estrofe s. f. strophe, stanza; verse.

estrófico adj. strophic: of or pertaining to strophes or stanzas.

estrófulo s. m. (med.) strophulus: an eruption peculiar to infants.

estróina s. m. + f. 1. wastrel, spendthrift. 2. harum-scarum. 3. hot-head. 4. cutup, playboy. ‖ adj. 1. extravagant, irregular. 2. hare-brained, waggish, rattle-brained. 3. dissipated, wild, wanton.

estroinar v. to be used to or fond of extravagances; lead a playboy's life.

estroinice s. f. 1. extravagance, folly. 2. light-mindedness.

estroma s. m. stroma: 1. (bot.) in fungi, a variously shaped more or less continuous layer of cellular tissue. 2. (anat.) the framework of tissue or an organ or cell.

estrompa adj. m. + f. (N. Braz., pop.) 1. clumsy, awkward, unskilful. 2. desagreeable, unpleasant. 3. coarse, rough, uncouth, rude.

estrompado adj. 1. worn-out; damaged. 2. (S. Braz.) stupid; brash, rash, foolhardy.

estrompar v. 1. to ruin. 2. to fatigue, tire out. 3. to wear out. 4. (N. Braz., pop.) to perturb, disturb.

estrompido s. m. 1. noise, din, racket. 2. crack, explosion.

estronca s. f. prop, stay, strut.

estroncamento s. m. 1. dismembering. 2. truncating. 3. sprain.

estroncar v. 1. to truncate. 2. to mutilate, maim. 3. to dismember. 4. to sprain (as an ankle).

estroncianita s. f. (min.) strontianite.

estrôncio s. m. (chem.) strontium.

estrondeante adj. m. + f. rumbling, thundering, roaring.

estrondear v. (also **estrondar**) 1. to roar, thunder, rumble, resound, boom. 2. to make a great noise. 3. to shout. 4. to be notorious. 5. to cause sensation.

estrondo s. m. 1. noise, buzz, din, cracking, boom, thundering, roaring, rumble. 2. racket, rattle. 3. report, detonation, explosion, blast. 4. noisy fanfare. 5. rumour, report. 6. reputation, renown.
~ **de trovão** thunder-clap.

estrondoso adj. 1. noisy, tumultuous, strepitous. 2. loud, clamorous. 3. resounding. 4. famous, renowned. 5. pompous, ostentatious; sumptuous. ‖ **-amente** adv. 1. with much noise. 2. stately; sumptuously.
aplausos ~**s** thunderous applause.

estropalho s. m. 1. dish-clout, washing clout, dishrag, mop. 2. rag.

estropeada s. f. 1. tramping of feet. 2. hubbub, uproar; tumultuous crowd.

estropear v. 1. to make a great noise. 2. to trample. 3. to knock violently against a door.

estropiar v. 1. to maim, mutilate, mangle, cripple. 2. to deform, disfigure. 3. to overfatigue. 4. to garble (a text). 5. to mispronounce. 6. to misread. 7. ~**-se** to maim o. s.

estropício s. m. 1. hurt, damage. 2. evil deed, wrong.

estropo s. m. 1. strap. 2. (railway) eccentric strap. 3. (naut.) grummet.

estrosca s. f. (Braz., sl.) embarrassment, difficulty.

estrotejar v. to trot; ride (a horse) at a trot.

estrouxar v. (S. Braz.) to take away all honeycombs from a beehive.

estrovenga s. f. (Braz.) 1. gear, gearing. 2. any complicated mechanical apparatus.

estrovo s. m. fishing line.

estrugido s. m. roar, rattle, racket, bluster.

estrugidor adj. roaring, blustering, rumbling.

estrugimento s. m. 1. roaring, booming, thundering. 2. deafening, stunning.

estrugir v. 1. to roar, thunder, boom, rumble. 2. to stun (with noise), din, deafen. 3. to vibrate, burst forth.

estruir v. 1. = **destruir**. 2. (N. Braz., pop.) to fritter away.

estruma s. f. (path.) struma: 1. scrofula. 2. goiter.

estrumação s. f. (pl. **-ões**) manuring.

estrumada s. f. a pile of manure, dung-heap.

estrumar v. to fertilize, manure, dung.

estrume s. m. manure, dung, fertilizer.

estrumeira s. f. dunghill, dung-heap, manure pile.

estrumoso adj. (path.) strumous, scrofulous: of, pertaining to or affected with struma.

estrupada s. f. 1. puff of wind. 2. assault, attack. 3. skirmish.

estrupício s. m. (Braz., pop.) 1. mutiny, riot, revolt, tumult. 2. conflict, struggle. 3. a great quantity. 4. an indefinite thing. 5. (fig.) blunder, a piece of stupidity.

estrupidante adj. m. + f. 1. noisy, roaring, rumbling. 2. thunderous.

estrupidar v. 1. to rumble, roar, boom, bluster. 2. to tramp, trample.

estrupido s. m. 1. rumble, roar, boom, great noise. 2. tumult. 3. tramping, trampling. 4. clatter of hoofs.

estrutura s. f. 1. structure; framing, frame(work). 2. the disposure of parts of a discourse or poem; composition.
~ **colunar** (geol.) columnar structure. ~ **cristalina** crystalline system. ~ **social** social structure. ~ **zonada**, ~ **zonar** zonal structure. **esta** ~ **política está em conformidade com a nossa tradição** this political framework is in keeping with our historical tradition. **peso de** ~ (aeron.) structural weight.

estruturação s. f. structuration.

estrutural adj. m. + f. (pl. **-ais**) structural: of or pertaining to a structure; constructional; constructive.

estruturar v. to structure.

estuação s. f. (pl. **-ões**) 1. fervour, fervency. 2. the burning of a fever. 3. great heat. 4. seasickness, nausea.

estuante adj. m. + f. 1. burning, hot, ardent. 2. febrile, feverish.

estuar v. 1. to be very hot; (fig.) burn. 2. to boil, bubble.

estuário s. m. estuary: the mouth of a river in which the tide meets the current (plate C 19).

estucador s. m. plasterer, stuccoer: person who works in stucco.

estucar v. to stucco, coat with stucco, plaster.

estucha s. f. wedge, peg.

estuchar v. to hammer or wedge in.

estudado adj. 1. studied: a) instructed, versed, learned. b) examined, analyzed; elaborate. 2. (fig.) affected; ingenious.
é um assunto para ser ~ it is a matter for consideration.

estudantaço s. m. (fam., also **estudantão**) a great student; studious person.

estudantada s. f. 1. a great number of students. 2. prank of students.

estudante s. m. + f. student, scholar.

estudantina s. f. 1. multitude of students. 2. song of students.

estudar v. to study: 1. apply o. s. to study; be a student. 2. learn. 3. inquire into, investigate. 4. meditate, reflect, consider. 5. observe. 6. ~**-se** to analyze, examine o. s.
~ **até altas horas** to study far into the night, burn the midnight oil. ~ **com aplicação** to study hard, fag at. ~ **Direito** to study for law, read for the

bar. ~ o papel to get up the part. **ando estudando** I am studying. **ele estuda muito** he is a hard student. **ele estudou Arquitetura** he was trained to architecture. **estar estudando francês** to work at French. **estudei a fundo esta questão** I entered deeply into this question. **estudei bem o assunto** I thought it out.

estúdio s. m. (Braz.) studio: 1. working room as of a painter, photographer; atelier. 2. place where motion pictures are made. 3. place from where radio programmes are broadcast.

estudiosidade s. f. studiousness; diligence in study.

estudioso adj. studious: 1. given to study or learning; bookish. 2. diligent, careful.

estudo s. m. 1. study: a) act of studying. b) application, learning, effort to learn. c) tractate, treatise. d) examination. e) particular branch of learning. f) sketch for a picture, story, work; plan. g) (mus.) an étude. 2. dissimulation. **atrasado nos ~s** backward in one's studies. **bolsa de ~s** a scholarship. **comissão de ~s** research staff. **curso de ~s** curriculum. **ele se dedica aos ~s** he devotes himself to study. **os seus ~s abrangem muitas matérias** his studies embrace many subjects.

estufa s. f. 1. stove. 2. hot-house, greenhouse. 3. sterilizer. 4. (fig.) very hot place. **planta de ~** hot-house plant.

estufadeira s. f. stew-pan.

estufado s. m. stewed meat. ‖ adj. 1. put or placed in a hot-house. 2. stewed (meat).

estufagem s. f. (pl. -ens) stewing (of meat).

estufar v. 1. to stew (meat). 2. to heat. 3. to put into a hot-house.

estufilha s. f. dungeon: a close and stuffy prison.

estufim s. m. (pl. -ins) garden-frame, bell-glass (for plants).

estugar v. to accelerate, quicken one's step, hurry along.

estultícia s. f. folly, foolishness, silliness, stupidity.

estultificação s. f. (pl. -ões) stultification.

estultificar v. 1. to stultify: a) make or become foolish or stupid. b) regard as a fool. 2. to go insane. 3. to brutalize.

estultilóquio s. m. stultiloquy: foolish talk.

estulto adj. 1. foolish, silly, stupid, dull. 2. ignorant. ‖ -amente adv. foolishly.

estumar v. (Braz.) to instigate, incite, sick on (dogs).

estuoso adj. 1. seething, boiling, very hot. 2. turbulent, raging (sea).

estupefação s. f. 1. (med.) stupefaction, benumbing, stupor, suspension of sensibility. 2. (fig.) perplexity, wonder, astonishment, amazement.

estupefaciente adj. m. + f., **estupefativo** stupefacient, facient, narcotic, stupefying.

estupefato adj. 1. stupefied. 2. (fig.) astonished, amazed.

estupefazer, estupeficar v. 1. to stupefy: a) make stupid or senseless. b) deprive of sensibility. 2. to amaze, astonish, stun, perplex, flabbergast.

estupendo adj. 1. stupendous, amazing, astonishing, wonderful, startling, admirable. 2. extraordinary, uncommon. ‖ -amente adv. stupendously.

estupidarrão s. m. (pl. -ões) (f. -ona) a very stupid person. ‖ adj. very stupid.

estupidez s. f. 1. stupidity, foolishness, dullness, heaviness of mind. 2. blunder, piece of stupidity. 3. (Braz.) coarseness, rudeness; discourtesy. **~ crassa** crass stupidity.

estupidificar v. 1. to dumbfound. 2. to brutalize. 3. **~-se** to become brutish.

estúpido s. m. 1. brute. 2. dunce, blockhead, half--wit, dullard, stupid person. ‖ adj. 1. stupid, dull,

blockish, heavy, doltish, idiotic(al), silly, obtuse. 2. senseless, spiritless, witless. 3. coarse, rude, rough, brutish, brute, ill-mannered. ‖ **estupidamente** adv. 1. in a stupid manner; doltishly. 2. brutally, coarsely. **não seja ~!** don't be a fool. **ele é muito ~** he is very ignorant.

estupor s. m. (pl. **estupores**) 1. stupor: a) suspension or great diminution of sensibility; torpidity of feeling, trance. b) dullness of perception. 2. (fig.) an evil or ugly person.

estuporado adj. 1. stuporous: marked by stupor. 2. spoiled; damaged. 3. ugly. 4. evil, bad.

estuporar v. 1. to cause stupor. 2. to astonish, startle. 3. **~-se**: a) to become spoiled or damaged. b) (also fig.) to become rotten.

estuprador s. m. ravisher, deflowerer, violator. ‖ adj. debauching, ravishing.

estuprar v. to rape, debauch, ravish, deflower.

estupro s. m. stuprum, indecent assault, violation of chastity by force.

estuque s. m. stucco: 1. plaster of Paris, fine plaster. 2. a work made of stucco. 3. (Braz.) stuccoed ceiling.

estúrdia s. f. 1. frolic, prank, wanton trick. 2. extravagance.

esturdiar v. 1. to frolic, play tricks. 2. to commit extravagances.

estúrdio adj. 1. frolicsome, waggish, hare-brained. 2. dissipated. 3. frivolous, fickle. 4. extravagant. 5. odd, queer; strange.

esturjão s. m. (pl. -ões) sturgeon: a large anadromous fish which yields caviar.

esturrado adj. 1. parched, scorched. 2. ardent, hot, burning. 3. hot-tempered, irritated. 4. intransigent. 5. radical.

esturrar v. 1. to parch, scorch; toast, brown. 2. **~-se**: a) to overdry (meat.) b) to become toasted. c) to become irritated.

esturricar v. = **estorricar**.

esturrinho s. m. a variety of snuff.

esturro s. m. 1. roasting (esp. of coffee beans). 2. = **esturrinho**. 3. the roar of an ounce (Felis uncia).

esturvinhado adj. stunned, dazed.

ésula s. f. (bot.) leafy spurge (genus Tithymalus).

esurino adj. (med.) that stimulates the appetite.

esvaecer v. (also **esvanecer**) 1. to make disappear. 2. to evanesce, vanish. 3. to extinguish, dissolve. 4. to dissipate, disperse, dispel. 5. to make vain. 6. to faint, decay. 7. **~-se**: a) to disappear, vanish. b) to decay, weaken. c) to become discouraged, depressed.

esvaecido adj. 1. undone. 2. dissipated. 3. weak, discouraged, enfeebled. 4. proud, vainglorious.

esvaecimento s. m. 1. pride, vanity. 2. evanescence. 3. giddiness, fainting. 4. weakness, enfeeblement. 5. discouragement.

esvair v. 1. to disperse, dissipate. 2. to evaporate. 3. **~-se**: a) to evanesce, vanish, disappear gradually. b) to faint, swoon. c) to become exhausted. **~-se em sangue** to bleed to death.

esvão s. m. (pl. **esvãos**) garret.

esvaziamento s. m. 1. emptying. 2. exhaustion; evacuation. 3. deflation (as of a balloon).

esvaziar v. 1. (also **esvazar**) to empty, exhaust; evacuate. 2. to bleed. 3. to deflate (as a tire). 4. **~-se** to become exhausted, empty or devoid of. **ele esvaziou uma garrafa** he drank a bottle, (fam.) crushed a bottle.

esventar v. (mil.) to burn powder in a cannon in order to dry it out.

esverdeado adj. greeny, greenish.

esverdear v. 1. to make or paint green or greenish, give a green colour to. 2. to become green.

esverdinhado adj. greenish, light green, somewhat green.

esverdinhar v. to make or become green or light green.

esvidar, esvidigar v. to remove the vine branches that have been cut off.

esviscerado adj. 1. eviscerated, disemboweled. 2. (fig.) insensible, hard; cruel.

esviscerar v. 1. to eviscerate, disembowel. 2. (fig.) to become cruel or insensible.

esvoaçar v. to flutter, flit, flicker, fly.

eles esvoaçaram para cá e para lá they flitted about.

esvurmar v. 1. to squeeze pus (out of a sore). 2. (fig.) to lay open.

eta s. m. eta: the seventh letter of the Greek alphabet.

eta (ê) interj. (also **eta-mundo, eta-pau**) wow!, hot diggity!

etal s. m. (chem.) ethal: cetyl alcohol.

etapa s. f. 1. (mil.): a) the daily allowance for soldiers, a day's ration. b) stopping place. 2. stage.

etário adj. of or relating to the age.

éter s. m. ether: 1. (chem.) a volatile and inflammable fluid. 2. the upper air; higher regions of the sky. 3. (phys.) a fluid supposed to be the medium of transmission of light and heat.

etéreo adj. 1. ethereal, ethereous. 2. (fig.) heavenly, celestial; aerial; sublime. ǁ **etereamente** adv. ethereally.

eterificação s. f. (pl. -ões) etherification, etherizing.

eterificar v. to etherify: make or convert into ether.

eterismo s. m. (med.) etherism: the effects produced by the administration of ether as an anaesthetic.

eterização s. f. (pl. -ões) etherizing.

eterizar v. 1. to etherize: a) to convert into ether. b) subject to the influence of ether. 2. ~-se: to dissolve; evaporate.

eternidade s. f. eternity: 1. eternal duration. 2. future life; sempiternity. 3. immortality, deathlessness.

esperei uma ~ I have been waiting ages. para ~s! (fig.) for worlds! uma ~ (muito tempo) (coll.) a long while, a week of Sundays.

eternizar v. 1. to eternalize, eternize: a) make eternal, everlasting or endless. b) perpetuate. c) make famous, immortalize. 2. ~-se: to immortalize o. s.

Eterno s. m. the Eternal, the Everlasting, God.

eterno adj. (also **eternal**) 1. eternal: a) without beginning or end. b) everlasting, endless, imperishable, perpetual. 2. immortal, deathless. 3. unalterable, unchanging. ǁ **-amente** adv. 1. eternally, everlastingly. 2. ever, forever, evermore. 3. immortally.

Roma, a cidade ~ the Eternal City (Rome).

etésios s. m. etesian (winds).

ética s. f. ethics: the moral science or philosophy.

ético adj. ethic(al), moral: relating to morals or principles of morality. ǁ **eticamente** adv. ethically.

etileno s. m. (chem.) ethylene.

etílico adj. (chem.) ethylic.

etilo s. m. (chem.) ethyl.

étimo s. m. etymon: 1. the original element of a word. 2. the root or primitive.

etimologia s. f. etymology: 1. the study of the origin and history of words. 2. the derivation of a word from its original.

etimológico adj. etymologic(al): of or pertaining to etymology. ǁ **etimologicamente** adv. etymologically.

etimologismo s. m. etymologization.

etimologista s. m. + f. (also **etimólogo** m.) etymologist: person versed in etymology.

etimologizar v. to etymologize: 1. study etymology. 2. suggest or provide etymologies for words.

etiologia s. f. (a)etiology: 1. the philosophy of causation. 2. (med.) the science of the causes of disease.

etíope s. m. + f. Ethiopian: native or inhabitant of Ethiopia. ǁ adj. m. + f. Ethiopian: of or pertaining to Ethiopia.

etiópico adj. Ethiopic: of or pertaining to Ethiopia.

etiqueta (ê) s. f. etiquette: 1. the conventional rules of behaviour in polite society. 2. the ceremonial of the court. 3. label, ticket, tag. 4. formality.

etiquetagem s. f. (pl. -ens) labelling.

etiquetar v. to label, ticket, tag.

etmoidal adj. m. + f. (pl. -ais) (also **etmóide** m.) ethmoidal: pertaining to the ethmoid.

etmóide s. m. (anat.) ethmoid bone (plate C 17).

etnia s. f. ethnos, ethnic group.

etnicismo s. m. ethnicism, heathenism, paganism, idolatry.

étnico s. m. ethnic: a heathen, a gentile, a pagan. ǁ adj. ethnic(al): relating to race or people.

etnogenia s. f. ethnogeny: the science of the origin of human races.

etnografia s. f. ethnography: the scientific description and classification of the races and nations of mankind.

etnográfico adj. ethnographic(al): pertaining to ethnography.

etnógrafo s. m. ethnographer.

etnologia s. f. ethnology: the study of human races, their character, history, customs and institutions.

etnológico adj. ethnologic(al): relating to ethnology.

etnologista s. m. + f., **etnólogo** m. ethnologist: 1. person skilled in ethnology. 2. a student of ethnology.

etocracia s. f. government founded on morality.

etogenia s. f. the science of the moral characteristics of man.

etografia s. f. (philos.) ethography: a description of moral characteristics of man.

etográfico adj. referring to ethography.

etologia s. f. ethology: the science of ethics.

etológico adj. ethologic(al): pertaining to ethology.

etopéia s. f. ethopoeia.

etrusco s. m. Etruscan, Etrurian: native or inhabitant of Etruria. ǁ adj. Etruscan, Etrurian: of or pertaining to Etruria.

eu s. m. (metaphysics) I: the ego; the self-conscious subject; self. ǁ pron. I.

~ mesmo myself. ~, por exemplo take me, for example. como ~ like me, as I. sou ~ it is I, it is me.

eucaliptal s. m. (pl. -ais) place abounding in eucalyptus.

eucalipto s. m. eucalypt: tree of the genus Eucalyptus (E. globulus).

eucaliptol s. m. eucalyptol: an oil obtained from the Eucalyptus globulus.

Eucaristia s. f. Eucharist: the sacrament of the Lord's Supper, the communion; the elements, bread and wine, given in this sacrament.

eucarístico adj. Eucharistic(al): relating to the Eucharist.

comunhão -a the Lord's Supper.

eucológio s. m. euchology: ritual book of the Greek Church.

eucólogo s. m. the liturgy of the Greek Church.

eucrasia s. f. (med.) eucrasia.

eucrásico adj. relating to eucrasia.

eudemonismo s. m. eud(a)emonism: the doctrine of happiness.

eudiometria s. f. eudiometry.

eudiômetro s. m. eudiometer: an instrument for ascertaining the purity of the air or the quantity of oxigen it contains.

eufemia s. f. prayer.

eufêmico adj. euphemistic(al): referring to euphemism.

eufemismo s. m. euphemism: the use of a pleasing term for one that is harsh or offensive.

eufonia s. f. euphony: 1. an agreeable sound. 2. a pleasing pronunciation.

eufônico adj. euphonic(al), agreeable, pleasing, melodious. ‖ **-amente** adv. euphonically.

êufono, eufono s. m. euphonium: a musical instrument. ‖ adj. euphonious, well-sounding.

euforbiácea s. f. an euphorbiaceous plant.

euforbiáceo adj. euphorbiaceous: of or pertaining to the Euphorbiaceae.

euforia s. f. euphoria: a sense of well-being.

eufórico adj. euphoric.

eufuísmo s. m. euphuism: an affected literary style.

eufuísta s. m. + f. euphuist: person who writes euphuistically.

eufuístico adj. euphuistic (style).

euge s. m. an exclamation of applause. ‖ interj. euge!, well done! good!

eugenia s. f. eugenics: the science of generative or procreative development.

eugênia s. f. Eugenia: a genus of myrtaceous shrubs and trees.

eugênico adj. eugenic: of or pertaining to the improvement of the (human) offspring.

euipnia s. f. normal sleep.

eumatia s. f. facility of learning.

eulalia s. f. good manners of speaking, good diction.

eulália s. f. a plant of the grass family (Miscanthus sinensis).

eunuco s. m. eunuch: a castrated man (esp. an attendant in a harem).

eupatia s. f. eupathy, resignation, patience.

eupatório s. m. Eupatorium: a genus of the natural order Compositae.

eupepsia s. f. (med.) eupepsia, eupepsy, good digestion.

euplástico adj. (med.) euplastic.

eupnéia s. f. eupnea, eupnoea, easy or normal respiration.

euquinina s. f. (chem.) quinine ethyl carbonate.

euricéfalo adj. eurycelphalic, eurycephalous, having a wide head.

eurícero adj. (zool.) eurycerous: having broad horns.

eurígnato adj. eurygnathic: having a wide jaw.

euripo s. m. euripus: strait or narrow sea where the flow of the tide in both directions is violent.

eurístomo adj. eurystomatous: having a wide mouth.

euro s. m. Eurus: the southeast wind.

europeização s. f. (pl. **-ões**) Europeanization: process of making or becoming European.

europeizar v. to Europeanize: 1. make or cause to become European. 2. assimilate to Europeans in any respect.

europeu s. m. (f. **européia**) European: a native or inhabitant of Europe. ‖ adj. European: of or pertaining to Europe.

eurritmia s. f. eurythmy: 1. elegance of proportion. 2. (med.) regularity of pulse.

eutanásia, eutanasia s. f. euthanasia: 1. an easy or painless death. 2. the putting to death of a person suffering from an incurable disease.

eutaxia s. f. eutaxy.

euterpe s. f. Euterpe: 1. (Gr. myth.) the Muse of music. 2. a genus of South American palms.

eutimia s. f. euthymia, tranquility.

eutocia s. f. eutocia: safe, easy or natural parturition or childbirth.

eutócico adj. of or pertaining to eutocia.

eutrapelia s. f. pleasant jesting.

eutrofia s. f. eutrophia: a healthy state of nutrition.

evacuação s. f. (pl. **-ões**) 1. evacuation. 2. excretion, discharge, defecation.

evacuar v. 1. to evacuate: a) empty, void, clear. b) withdraw from (troops). 2. to excrete, defecate. 3. ~-se to leave.

evacuativo, evacuatório adj. evacuative, evacuant.

evadir v. 1. to avoid, shun, escape. 2. to delude, deceive, evade, elude (by artifice). 3. ~-se: a) to steal away, make one's escape. b) to disappear, abscond, run away.

evagação s. f. (pl. **-ões**) 1. distraction. 2. divagation.

evanescente adj. m. + f. evanescent, vanishing. ‖ ~mente adv. evanescently.

evangelho s. m. Gospel, Evangel.

pregar o ~ to preach the Gospel.

evangeliário s. m. evangelistary: a book containing passages from the Gospels to be read at the divine service.

evangélico adj. evangelic(al): 1. relating to the Gospels or to the doctrine of Christ. 2. Protestant, relating to Protestantism.

evangelismo s. m. evangelism: adherence to and insistence upon evangelical doctrines.

evangelista s. m. 1. Evangelist: a) one of the writers of the four Evangels or Gospels. b) m. + f. a preacher of the Gospel. 2. m. + f. a Protestant.

evangelização s. f. (pl. **-ões**) evangelization.

evangelizador s. m. evangelist, preacher. ‖ adj. (also **evangelizante** m. + f.) evangelizing.

evangelizar v. to evangelize: preach the Gospel to.

evaporação s. f. (pl. **-ões**) evaporation, exhalation.

evaporadeira s. f. (Braz.) evaporator (of a sugar mill).

evaporado adj. 1. evaporated. 2. (fig.) ratte-brained.

evaporar v. (also **evaporizar**) 1. to evaporate: a) convert into vapour, vaporize. b) exhale. c) dissipate. d) consume; waste, destroy. 2. ~-se: a) to evaporate, be exhaled, pass off in vapour. b) to vanish, dissipate, fume away, disappear.

evaporativo adj. evaporative, that causes evaporation.

evaporatório s. m. 1. exhaust hole for vapours. 2. evaporator: an apparatus used to facilitate evaporation. ‖ adj. evaporative.

evaporável adj. m. + f. (pl. **-áveis**) evaporable.

evaporômetro s. m. evaporometer, evaporimeter, atmometer: an instrument for ascertaining the rate of evaporating power of the air.

evasão s. f. (pl. **-ões**) 1. escape, flight, elopement. 2. (fig.) evasion, shift, subterfuge.

evasiva s. f. evasion, subterfuge, elusion, dodgery.

evasivo adj. evasive, artfully, illusory.

resposta -a evasive answer.

evecção s. f. (pl. **-ões**) (astr.) evection.

evencer v. (jur.) to despoil, strip (of possessions).

evento s. m. event, occurrence, happening.

eventração s. f. (med.) eventration: 1. ventral hernia. 2. protrusion of the bowels.

eventrar v. to eviscerate, cause eventration.

eventual adj. m. + f. (pl. **-ais**) eventual, fortuitous, occasional, contingent, casual. ‖ ~mente adv. eventually, occasionally.

gastos -ais incidental expenses.

eventualidade s. f. eventuality, event, contingency, casualty, chance, fortuity.

preocupar-se com ~s to worry about perhapses.

eversão s. f. (pl. **-ões**) eversion, destruction, ruin, overthrow.

eversivo adj. 1. subversive. 2. destructive.

everter v. to overthrow, subvert; destroy.

evicção s. f. (pl. **-ões**) (jur.) eviction: the recovery of a thing by law.

evictor s. m. evictor.

evidência s. f. evidence, evidentness, clearness, unequivocalness, obviousness.
~ **esmagadora** damning evidence. ~ **interna** internal evidence. **em** ~ up, forward.

evidenciar v. 1. to evidence: a) make evident or clear. b) show clearly. 2. **~-se** to become evident, clear.
ele evidenciou energia nisso he displayed energy in it, came it strong. **evidenciou-se que tinham conhecimento** they proved to know.

evidente adj. m. + f. evident, clear, plain, manifest, obvious, patent, unequivocal. ‖ **~mente** adv. evidently, clearly, obviously.
é ~ it is evident, lies on the surface. **isto é** ~ that is understood.

evisceração s. f. (pl. **-ões**) evisceration, disembowelment, removal of the viscera.

eviscerar v. to eviscerate: remove the viscera from; to disembowel.

evitação s. f. (pl. **-ões**) 1. avoiding, avoidance; a shunning. 2. pretext, evasion.

evitar v. 1. to avoid, shun, spare, escape, dodge; keep clear of. 2. to impede, hinder, prevent. 3. to forestall, forerun. 4. **~-se**: a) to deprive. b) to refuse, avoid (to do a thing).
a fim de ~ **mal-entendidos** in order to avoid misunderstandings. **ele evita o seu próximo** he flees his fellowman. **ele não pôde** ~ **sua ruína financeira** he could not avoid his financial ruin, didn't keep his head above water. **ele procurava ~-me** he sought to avoid me, sought to shy of me. **não pode ser evitado** it can't be helped. **para** ~ **acidentes** for fear of accidents. **por que você me evita?** why do you draw away from me?

evitável adj. m. + f. (pl. **-áveis**) avoidable, that can be avoided.

eviternidade s. f. eviternity.

eviterno adj. eviternal, eternal.

evo s. m. (poet.) eternity, infinite duration.

evocação s. f. (pl. **-ões**) evocation: 1. calling forth; raising up (spirits). 2. reminiscence, recollection. 3. (jur.) the removal of a suit from an inferior to a superior tribunal.

evocar v. to evocate, evoke: 1. call or summon forth or out, invoke. 2. remember, remind. 3. conjure, raise up (spirits).
~ **os espíritos** to conjure up spirits.

evocativo, evocatório adj. evocative.

evocável adj. m. + f. (pl. **-áveis**) evocable.

evoé interj. evoe!

evolar-se v. 1. to evaporate; dissolve. 2. to disappear. 3. to soar, fly away.

evolução s. f. (pl. **-ões**) evolution: 1. gradual development. 2. movement of ships or soldiers, maneuver. 3. theory that all living things developed from a few simple forms of life.

evolucionar v. to evolutionize, evolve, unfold, develop, improve.

evolucionário adj. evolutionary, developmental.

evolucionismo s. m. evolutionism: the metaphysical or the biological doctrine of evolution or development.

evolucionista s. m. + f. evolutionist. ‖ adj. evolutionist: of or pertaining to the doctrine of evolution.

evoluir v. 1. to develop, unfold, evolve, progress. 2. to perform evolution. 3. to become developed.

evoluta s. f. (geom.) evolute: a curve which by its evolution forms another curve.

evolutivo, evolucional adj. evolutive, evolutionary.

evolvente s. f. (geom.) evolvent: a curve considered as correlative to its evolute.

evolver(-se) v. = **evolucionar, evoluir.**

evonimina s. f. euonymin: a bitter substance obtained from the euonymus.

evônimo s. m. (bot.) spindle tree.

evulsão s. f. (pl. **-ões**) evulsion: act of plucking or pulling out by force; forcible extraction.

evulsivo adj. evulsive.

ex- pref., forming words as:
ex-combatente ex-serviceman. **ex-libris** ex-libris, book-plate.

exabundância s. f. superabundance.

exabundante adj. m. + f. superabundant.

exação s. f. (pl. **-ões**) 1. exaction. 2. exigency, demand. 3. exactness, accuracy.

exacerbação s. f. (pl. **-ões**) exacerbation: 1. act of exacerbating; irritation, exasperation. 2. (med.) aggravation of a disease.

exacerbar v. 1. to exacerbate, embitter, aggravate, exasperate, irritate; provoke. 2. **~-se**: to get worse, become aggravated.

exageração s. f. (pl. **-ões**) exaggeration, amplification, excessiveness, overstatement.

exagerado s. m. exaggerator: one who exaggerates. ‖ adj. exaggerating; exaggerated, excessive. ‖ **-amente** adv. exaggeratedly.
ela é -a she is an exaggerator, all her geese are swans. **ele tem uma idéia -a de sua própria importância** he is self-conceited, (U. S. A., coll.) he has a swelled head.

exagerador s. m. exaggerator: one who exaggerates. ‖ adj. exaggerating.

exagerar v. 1. to exaggerate, amplify, magnify, overstate, enhance; to come it strong. 2. **~-se** to use exaggerations in speech or writing.
~ **a modéstia** to carry modesty to an extreme. ~ **bastante** (coll.) to lay it on (thick). **ela exagera a sua prestimosidade** she carries her eagerness to excess. **não se exagere tanto** don't overact, (coll.) draw it mild.

exagero (ê) s. m. exaggeration, amplification, excessiveness, overstatement.
falaram sem ~ they spoke within compass.

exagitado adj. agitated (violently).

exagitar v. 1. to shake or agitate violently. 2. **~-se** to get angry; become irritated.

exalação s. f. (pl. **-ões**) 1. exhalation: a) act or process of exhaling. b) evaporation; vapour. c) emanation, effluvium. 2. perfume, odour. 3. rapid, meteoric light.

exalante adj. m. + f. exhaling, evaporating, exhalant.

exalar v. 1. to exhale, emit; emanate. 2. to evaporate. 3. to breathe out. 4. to expand, manifest. 5. to vent, give vent. 6. (fig.) to die. 7. **~-se**: a) to evaporate, vapour. b) to be exhaled.

exaltação s. f. (pl. **-ões**) (also **exalçamento** m.) exaltation: 1. elevation to power or dignity. 2. state of dignity. 3. mental elevation, deliriousness, excitement; enthusiasm.
~ **da Santa Cruz** (R. C. Church) exaltation of the Holy Cross.

exaltado s. m. person who gets exalted easily. ‖ adj. 1. eccentric, exalted, extravagant. 2. overexcited, fanatical. 3. ardent, hot-tempered. 4. easily irritable.
ele está ~ **e furioso** he frets and fumes. **esta criança é -a** this child is hotheaded.

exaltar v. (also **exalçar**) 1. to exalt: a) magnify, glorify, praise, extol. b) ennoble, dignify, aggran-

dize, elevate. c) excite. 2. ~-se: a) to extol o. s., to boast, pride, to become vain. b) to grow hot, get angry, become irritated, exasperate.
ela foi se exaltando she was becoming irritated. **não se exalte!** keep your temper!, don't ruffle your feathers! don't make a fuss!
exalviçado adj. whitish, somewhat white.
exame s. m. examination: 1. interrogatory, questioning. 2. test of knowledge. 3. inquiry, investigation, search, scrutiny, survey.
~ **de admissão** entrance examination. ~ **de aptidão** University entrance examination. ~ **de consciência** examination of one's conscience. ~ **de sangue** blood count. ~ **médico** medical examination. ~ **oral** oral examination. **ele foi aprovado num** ~ he passed an examination. **ele foi reprovado num** ~ he failed in an examination. **ele submeteu-se a um** ~ he went in for examination. **farei um** ~ **detalhado disto** I'll make a check-up of it. **fui bem no** ~ I did well in the examination. **livre** ~ free inquiry. **o pequeno atrapalhou-se no** ~ the child muddled his examination. **prestar um** ~ (university) to take a class.
examinador s. m. examiner, examinator. ‖ adj. examining.
banca ~**a** board of examination.
examinando s. m. examinee.
examinar v. 1. to examine: a) search, inquire into, interrogate. b) scrutinize, investigate, study, consider, canvass; discuss. c) test, try, analyze; prove. 2. ~-se to examine one's conscience.
ela examinou a situação com serenidade she took a calm survey of the situation. **ela examinou os livros criticamente** she viewed the books with a critical eye. **ele examinou o caso de mais perto** he took a nearer view of the affair. **eu examinei os cadernos dos meus alunos** I looked over my pupils' copybooks. **examinando melhor** on nearer view. **examinaremos isto** we'll see into this. **examinei uma conta** I looked through an account.
examinável adj. m. + f. (pl. -áveis) examinable.
exangue adj. m. + f. 1. bloodless, without blood. 2. (fig.) feeble, faint, languid, week, debilitated.
exania s. f. (med.) exania: prolapse of the rectum.
exanimação s. f. (pl. -ões) exanimation: 1. apparent death. 2. unconsciousness. 3. coma; faintness.
exânime adj. m. + f. exanimate, inanimate, lifeless.
exantema s. m. (med.) exanthem(a): any eruptive disease.
exantemático, exantematoso adj. exanthematous: pertaining to, characterized by or of the nature of an exanthem.
tifo ~ typhous fever, typhus exanthemicus.
exarar v. 1. to engrave, cut, carve. 2. to imprint. 3. (fig.) to write down, register.
exarcado s. m. exarchate: the dignity of an exarch.
exarticulação s. f. (pl. -ões) dislocation, disarticulation.
exarticular v. = **desarticular.**
exasperação s. f. (pl. -ões) (also **exaspero** m.) exasperation: 1. act of exasperating; irritation. 2. exacerbation; indignation, embitterment.
exasperador s. m. exasperater. ‖ adj. exasperating, vexatious.
exasperar v. 1. to exasperate: a) provoke, enrage, irritate, anger, vex. b) exacerbate, aggravate. c) drive to dispair. 2. ~-se: a) to become exasperated. b) to grow furious. c) to grow worse.
~ **alguém** to exasperate s. o., drive s. o. mad. **ele exasperou-se** he flew into a rage, jumped out of his skin.

exatidão s. f. (pl. -ões) exactness: 1. accuracy, precision. 2. punctuality, punctualness. 3. certainty. 4. carefulness; perfection.
~ **das medidas** accuracy to size. ~ **do trabalho** accuracy of work.
exato adj. exact: 1. accurate, precise. 2. punctual. 3. correct, right, certain; strict. 4. careful; perfect. 5. true, faithful. ‖ **-amente** adv. 1. exactly. 2. just. **-amente assim!** that's just it! **-amente duas horas** just two hours. **-amente o contrário** quite the contrary. **-amente o que eu estava procurando** exactly what I was looking for. **à hora -a** at the right time. **cálculo** ~ accurate calculation. **é -amente o contrário** it is all the other way about. **é -amente o que preciso** it is exactly what I want, it suits me to a T. **é isso -amente o que lhe convém** that will just suit him. **fiz -amente o contrário** I did just the reverse. **isto é -amente o motivo por que...** that is the very reason why... **no sentido** ~ in the strict sense. **são -amente três horas** it is just three o'clock.
exator s. m. 1. collector, tax-gatherer. 2. exacter.
exaurir v. (also **exaustar**) 1. to exhaust: a) draw out, drain, empty. b) expend, waste. c) tire very much, fag, weary out. 2. to deplete. 3. to pauperize, impoverish. 4. ~-se to become exhausted, depleted, or tired out.
~ **as suas forças** to exhaust one's strength.
exaurível adj. m. + f. (pl. -íveis) exhaustible.
exaustão s. f. (pl. -ões) exhausting, exhaustion.
exaustivo adj. exhaustive, exhausting, wearisome. ‖ **-amente** adv. exhaustively.
exausto adj. exhausted, drained, emptied, drawn out; dog-tired, worn-out.
estou completamente ~ I am thoroughly drained, quite knocked up. **estou** ~ **depois de ter estudado tanto** I am tired out after so much study.
exaustor s. m. exhaust(er), suction fan, ventilator (plate C 20).
exautoração s. f. (pl. -ões) exauctoration, degradation.
exautorar v. to exauctorate, degrade, deprive of position or dignity.
excarcerar v. to set free (as from a prison).
exceção s. f. (pl. -ões) exception, excepting; prerogative, privilege.
a ~ **comprova a regra** the exception proves the rule. **à** ~ **de** except. **com** ~ **de, exceto** with the exception of, excepting. **não há regra sem** ~ there is no rule without exception. **no meu caso ela fez uma** ~ she made an exception of me. **por** ~ by way of exception. **sem** ~ without exception. **todos, com** ~ **de você** all except you. **todos, sem** ~ all without exception. **uma** ~ **da regra** an exception to the rule.
excedente s. m. excess, surplus, overplus, remainder. ‖ adj. m. + f. exceeding, excessive; spare.
receitas ~**s** surplus receipts.
exceder v. 1. to exceed: a) pass or go beyond, transcend. b) go too far, overstep. c) surpass, be superior to; excel, outdo, outstrip. 2. to transgress, trespass. 3. ~-se: a) to exceed o. s. b) to go too far. c) to become furious or enraged.
~ **no peso** to outpoise, overweigh. ~ **os limites** (fig.) to overstep the limits. ~-se **em algo** to carry a thing too far. **ele excedeu-se** he went too far, he strained a point. **eu excedi o crédito do banco** I overdrew the banking account. **você já se excedeu** you went beyond the limit.
excedível adj. m. + f. (pl. -íveis) surpassable: capable of being exceeded.
Excelência s. f. Excellence, Excellency.
Vossa ~ Your Excellency.

excelência s. f. excellence, excellency, primacy, supremacy.
por ~ par excellence.
excelente adj. m. + f. excellent, eminent, worthy, fine, admirable, choice, of superior quality; exquisite. **~! fine!, splendid! aprendo inglês com um ~ professor** I am learning English with an excellent teacher. **isto parece ~** this sounds just perfect. **uma coisa ~** an excellent thing, (sl.) a thundering good thing. **um ~ contador de histórias** a great story teller. **um nadador ~** an expert at swimming. **variedade de pratos ~s** a variety of excellent dishes.
excelentíssimo adj. (absolute, sup. of **excelente**) most excellent.
Exmo. Senhor (in letters) Dear Sir. **Exma. Senhora** (in letters) Dear Madam.
exceler, excelir v. to excel, surpass, exceed, be superior to, outdo.
excelsitude s. f. sublimity, loftiness, eminence; highness.
excelso adj. 1. high, lofty, eminent, exalted, sublime, excellent. 2. superior.
excentricidade s. f. 1. eccentricity, deviation from a center. 2. (fig.): a) originality. b) extravagance, vagary. c) oddity.
excêntrico s. m. 1. (tech.) eccentric. 2. (fig.) queer person. ‖ adj. 1. eccentric(al), not located or situated in the center, away from the center or axis. 2. (fig.) peculiar, extravagant, odd, queer. ‖ **-amente** adv. eccentrically.
colar ~ (tech.) eccentric strap. **eixo ~** (tech.) eccentric shaft.
excepcional, excecional adj. m. + f. (pl. **-ais**) exceptional: 1. forming an exception. 2. irregular, unusual, uncommon, unnatural, peculiar, anomalous. ‖ **~mente** adv. exceptionally; once in a way.
excepcionar, excecionar v. to except: 1. make an exception. 2. (jur.) object, make an objection.
exceptiva, exceptiva s. f. an exceptive condition, a clause.
exceptivo, excetivo adj. exceptive, that makes or contains an exception.
excerto s. m. excerpt, extract, choice.
excessivo adj. excessive, exceeding, immoderate, beyond measure, undue, exaggerate, exorbitant. ‖ **-amente** adv. excessively, exceedingly; too.
-amente generoso generous to a fault. **cuidado ~** overcare. **trabalho ~** overwork.
excesso s. m. 1. excess: a) immoredation, exorbitance. b) superabundance. c) surplus, overplus, over-measure; superfluity. d) intemperance, luxury, debauch. 2. redundance. 3. abuse, outrage.
~ de bagagem excess luggage. **~ de bondade** excess of kindness. **~ de população** congestion of population. **a casa tem móveis em ~** the house superabounds with furniture. **cometer ~s** to run riot. **nós trabalhamos em ~** we work too hard, work ourselves to a shadow. **todo ~ é prejudicial** too much of a thing is good for nothing.
exceto prep. except(ing), save, unless, excluding, with the exception of.
~ minha filha saving my daughter. **todos, ~ meu amigo** all, save my friend.
excetuar v. 1. to except, exclude, bar out. 2. to free, save, exempt, let off. 3. **~-se:** a) to be excluded. b) to make an exception.
excetuam-se os presentes the present company excepted.
excídio s. m. (poet.) ruin, devastation, destruction, desolation.
excipiente s. m. (pharm.) excipient: the basis of a compound medicine.

excisão s. m. (pl. **-ões**) (surg.) 1. excision. 2. amputation.
excisar v. to excise, remove surgically.
excitabilidade s. f. excitability, excitablenes; nervousness, irritability.
excitação s. f. (pl. **-ões**) (also **excitamento** m.) exitation: 1. excitement, stimulation. 2. agitation; commotion. 3. irritation. 4. instigation.
~ luminosa (phys.) quantity of light. **~ nervosa** nervous excitement.
excitador s. m. (also **excitante** m. + f., **excitativo** m.) 1. inciter, instigator. 2. dynamo or battery necessary to operate a motor or another dynamo. ‖ adj. excitant, exciting, inciting.
excitar v. 1. to excite: a) stimulate, incite, arouse, instigate, animate, stir up. b) encourage. c) thrill. d) provoke, irritate; make angry. 2. **~-se:** a) to take heart. b) to become enraged, furious or irritated; to fly off the handle.
excitável adj. m. + f. (pl. **-áveis**) excitable.
exclamação s. f. (pl. **-ões**) exclamation: 1. act of exclaiming. 2. outcry; ejaculation. 3. (also **ponto de ~**) exclamation mark, exclamation point (!).
exclamador s. m. exclaimer. ‖ adj. exclamatory.
exclamar v. exclaim, cry out, say loudly.
exclamativo, exclamatório adj. exclamative, exclamatory.
excluir v. 1. to exclude, preclude, seclude or debar from, shut out. 2. to eliminate. 3. to abandon, forsake. 4. to refuse, reject. 5. to emit, neglect. 6. **~-se:** a) to deprive o. s. of, abstain from. b) to eliminate o. s.
circunstância excludente (jur.) excluding circumstance.
exclusão s. f. (pl. **-ões**) (also **exclusiva**) exclusion: 1. act of excluding. 2. debarring, seclusion. 3. elimination. 4. exception.
exclusive adv. (Latin) exclusively.
exclusividade s. f. exclusiveness.
exclusivismo s. m. exclusivism, exclusionism: exclusive principles or practice.
exclusivista s. m. + f. exclusivist. ‖ adj. inclined to exclusivism.
exclusivo adj. 1. exclusive. 2. restricted, limited. 3. private, particular. ‖ **-amente** adv. exclusively.
excluso adj. excluded.
excogitação s. f. (pl. **-ões**) excogitation, contrivance, cogitation.
excogitar v. to excogitate, think out, contrive, imagine, invent.
excogitável adj. m. + f. (pl. **-áveis**) excogitable.
excomungado s. m. excommunicate: excommunicated person. ‖ adj. excommunicated.
ele foi ~ he was laid under a ban.
excomungar v. to excommunicate, anathematize, ban.
excomunhão s. f. (pl. **-ões**) excommunication: the formal exclusion of a person from a religious communion and religious privileges; ban.
excreção s. f. (pl. **-ões**) excretion: 1. act of excreting. 2. the substance excreted.
excrementício adj. (also **excrementoso**) excrementitious: 1. pertaining to excrement. 2. of the nature of excrement.
excremento s. m. excrement, fecal matter, feces.
excrescência s. f. 1. excrescence, excrescency. 2. wart, tubercle, outgrowth. 3. superfluity.
excrescente adj. m. + f. 1. excrescent. 2. superfluous.
excrescer v. 1. to swell, tumefy, form an excrescence. 2. to outgrow, grow too much.
excretado adj. excreted.
excretar v. 1. to excrete. 2. to expel, secrete, discharge. 3. to evacuate.

excreto s. m. (also **excreta**) excreta: useless matter eliminated from the living baby (as urine or sweat). ‖ adj. excreted.

excretor, excretório adj. excretory, excretive.

excruciante adj. m. + f. excruciating, tormenting, extremely painful.

excruciar v. 1. to excruciate, torture, torment, martyrize. 2. ~-se to fret, grieve.

exculpar v. to excuse, exculpate.

excursão s. f. (pl. -ões) (also **excurso** m.) excursion: 1. journey, trip, ramble, tour, jaunt. 2. sally, raid. 3. (fig.) digression, deviation.

bilhete de ~ excursion ticket.

excursionista s. m. + f. excursionist, tourist, tripper.

excussão s. f. (pl. -ões) (jur.) excussion, a seizing by law.

excutir v. (jur.) to attach, distrain.

execração s. f. (pl. -ões) execration, curse, imprecation; detestation, abhorrence.

execrar v. to execrate, curse, imprecate; abhor, abominate, detest, hate.

execratório adj. execrative, execratory, containing an execration.

execrável adj. m. + f. (pl. -áveis) (also **execrando** m.) execrable, abominable, detestable, cursed, odious. ‖ **execravelmente** adv. execrably.

execução s. f. execution: 1. act of executing. 2. accomplishment. 3. style or mode of performance (as in mus.). 4. infliction of capital punishment. 5. effective action, effectuation.

acelerar a ~ to press the execution. **auto de** ~ writ of execution. **ele acelerou a** ~ **dos trabalhos** he pushed on the work. **isto é de difícil** ~ this is of difficult execution. **isto foi posto em** ~ this was carried out. ~ **sumária** summary execution.

executado s. m. person who has been executed. ‖ adj. executed: 1. put to death. 2. performed, accomplished.

a ser ~ **imediatamente** (com.) to receive immediate attention. **o assassino foi** ~ the murderer was put to death.

executante s. m. + f. 1. (jur.) executor. 2. (mus.) executant, performer. ‖ adj. executing.

executar v. 1. to execute: a) perform, realize, effectuate, carry out, accomplish, put in practice. b) distrain (goods). c) (jur.) put one to death. d) play, perform (as a piece of music). 2. ~-se to occur, take place.

~ **uma operação** to perform an operation. ~ **um pedido** to fill an order. **descuidar-se de** ~ **uma ordem** to fail to execute an order. **ele executou-o** he carried it into effect.

executável adj. m. + f. (pl. -áveis) executable: capable of being executed or carried out.

executivo s. m. executive: 1. a person with administrative authority (as in an enterprise). 2. the executive branch of a government. ‖ adj. 1. executive: concerned with or pertaining to executing, performing or carrying into effect. 2. resolute, courageous; brisk; active. ‖ **-amente** adv. executively. **ônibus** ~ a special bus intended primarily for higher income passengers.

executor s. m. 1. executor, executer: one who executes. 2. executioner: a) person who carries into effect a death sentence. b) hangman, headsman. ‖ adj. executive.

executório adj. executory, executive.

êxedra s. f. exedra: a portico in a Grecian palaestra used for disputations.

exegese s. f. exegesis: exposition or interpretation of a literary product or passage (more particularly the exposition or interpretation of the Holy Scriptures).

exegeta s. m. + f. exegete, exegetist: person skilled in exegesis.

exegética s. f. (theol.) exegetics, exegetical theology.

exegético adj. exegetic(al), of or pertaining to exegesis.

exemplar (I) s. m. example, exemplar, model, pattern, specimen, copy, sample. ‖ adj. exemplary. ~ **de exposição** display specimen. ~ **de publicidade** press copy. ~ **de serviço** copy in use. ~ **grátis** specimen copy. ~**es vendidos** sold copies.

exemplar (II) v. 1. to make an example of. 2. to punish exemplarily.

exemplaridade s. f. exemplariness: the state or quality of being exemplary.

exemplário s. m. collection of examples.

exemplificação s. f. (pl. -ões) exemplification: act of exemplifying.

exemplificar v. to exemplify: show or illustrate by example.

exemplificativo adj. exemplifying.

exemplo s. m. example, model; instance, procedent; pattern.

castigar para servir de ~ **aos outros** to make an example of. **dar bom** ~ to set a good example. **outro** ~ **de seu desleixo** another version of your carelessness. **para citar um** ~ by way of example. **por** ~ for instance, for example. **quando ela saiu, os outros seguiram o seu** ~ when she went out, the others followed suit. **seguir o** ~ **de alguém** to follow someone's example. **servir de** ~ to serve as example. **tomar como** ~ to take pattern by. **tomar** ~ **de alguém** to take an example by someone. **um** ~ **para** an instance of.

exenteração s. f. (pl. -ões) exenteration, disemboweling, evisceration.

exeqüente s. m. (jur.) suitor for attachment. ‖ adj. m. + f. sueing for attachment.

exequial adj. m. + f. (pl. -ais) exequial, funereal.

exéquias s. f. pl. exequies, funeral rites, obsequies.

exeqüibilidade s. f. feasibility, workability.

exeqüível adj. m. + f. (pl. -íveis) feasible, performable, executable.

exercer v. 1. to exercise: a) practise, put in practice. b) carry out or put in action. c) perform the function or duties of; pursue. 2. to exert. ~ **um cargo** to hold an office. ~ **clínica** to practise medicine. ~ **pressão sobre** to put pressure on. ~ **uma profissão** to follow a profession. **ela exerce a medicina** she professes medicine. **ele exerce a advocacia** he practises law. **exerceram pressão sobre ele** they put pressure on him, (sl.) put the screw on him.

exercício s. m. 1. exercise, practice, exercitation. 2. work, labour, service, task, lesson. 3. training. 4. use, custom. 5. (mil.) drill; manoeuvres. 6. holding of a position or job.

~ **de ginástica** bodily exercise. ~ **militar** military exercise. ~**s espirituais** spiritual exercises; exercises of devotion. **campo de** ~**s** parade ground. **faço diariamente alguns** ~**s de ginástica** I take some exercises every day. **fazer** ~ to take exercise.

exercitação s. f. (pl. -ões) exercitation, exercise, practice, use.

exercitador s. m. exerciser: person who exercises, trains, drills. ‖ adj. exercising.

exercitante s. m. + f. person who attends to spiritual exercises. ‖ adj. exercising.

exercitar v. 1. to exercise, practise. 2. to dress, drill, train, instruct. 3. ~-se to exercise o. s., practise or train o. s. in.

~ **a memória** to exercise one's memory. **eu exer-**

cito minha mente estudando línguas I exercise my mind by studying languages.
exército s. m. army: 1. troops. 2. a multitude, host. 3. an organized body.
exerdação s. f. (pl. -ões) exheredation, disinheritance.
exerdar v. to exheredate, disinherit.
exérese s. f. exeresis: a surgical excision.
exergo s. m. exergue (of a coin).
exfetação s. f. (med.) exfetation, extrauterine pregnancy.
exfoliado adj. (bot.) subdivided in laminae (bark of trees).
exibição s. f. (pl. -ões) exhibition: 1. act of exhibiting or display(ing) (as for inspection). 2. a showing; exposition. 3. ostentation.
~ **aviatória** air display. ~ **industrial** Industrial exhibition. **dois meses de** ~ (theat.) a run of two months.
exibicionismo s. m. exhibitionism.
exibicionista s. m. + f. exhibitionist: person given to exhibitionism. ‖ adj. exhibitionistic.
exibir v. 1. to exhibit: a) show, display. b) expose. c) unfold, reveal, manifest. d) present, offer. e) flaunt, boast, show off. 2. ~-se to pride; show o. s. **o bilhete deve ser exibido quando for exigido** the ticket must be produced on demand. **ela exibiu seu vestido novo** she made a show of her new dress.
exibitório adj. exhibitive, exhibitory.
exicial adj. m. + f. (pl. -ais) pernicious, ruinous, fatal.
exício s. m. ruin, destruction, perdition, doom.
exido s. m. common open ground, public land.
exigência s. f. 1. exigence, exigency, requisiteness, exaction, demand. 2. necessity, need. 3. insistent request. 4. requirement.
corresponder às ~s to meet with the requirements. **ela não corresponde às** ~s she is not up to the standard. **este trabalho satisfez as suas** ~s this work fulfilled your (his) requirements.
exigente adj. m. + f. 1. exigent, exacting, urgent, demanding. 2. impertinent, difficult, fussy. 3. pretentious.
uma tarefa ~ an exacting task.
exigir v. 1. to claim, exact, demand, require, urge. 2. to impose (as an obligation).
~ **demais** to ask too much. **ele exigiu um quarto para si só...** he stipulated for a room of his own. **este crime exige castigo** this crime calls for punishment. **este serviço exige cuidado especial** this work asks for great care. **exijo uma explicação** I demand an explanation. **isto não se pode** ~ **de ninguém** it is too much to ask of anyone. **quando as circunstâncias o exigirem** as occasion may require.
exigível adj. m. + f. (pl. -íveis) demandable, exigible, requirable.
exigüidade s. f. exiguity, smallness, slenderness, scantiness.
exíguo adj. exiguous, small, slender, scanty.
exilado s. m. exile, a banished person, deportee. ‖ adj. banished, exiled.
exilar v. 1. to exile, banish, expatriate; deport. 2. ~-se to separate o. s. from one's country.
exílio s. m. exile, expulsion from one's country, banishment, expatriation.
exímio adj. eminent, conspicuous, excellent, extraordinary, distinguished.
eximir v. 1. to exempt, free, deliver, dispense, release. 2. exonerate from (of) obligation. 3. ~-se to refuse to, escape, shy away from, shun.
~-**se de uma responsabilidade** to shun a responsibility.

exinanição s. f. (pl. -ões) exinanition: 1. evacuation, exhaustion, prostration. 2. weakening.
exinanir v. 1. to exinanite: a) make empty, drain, exhaust. b) weaken. c) belittle. 2. to destroy, annihilate. 3. ~-se: to become exhausted or debilitated.
existência s. f. 1. existence, existency: a) being, life. b) reality, truth. 2. (Port.) stock of goods.
mínimo para a ~ minimum of subsistence.
existencial adj. m. + f. (pl. -ais) existential: of or pertaining to existence.
existencialismo s. m. (philos.) existentialism.
existencialista s. m. + f. existentialist.
existente s. m. + f. existent, being. ‖ adj. 1. existent, existing, living; subsistent. 2. at hand, on hand.
existir v. 1. to exist, be, live, be alive. 2. to subsist. 3. to endure, last. 4. to be at or on hand.
êxito s. m. effect, result, outcome, success, triumph, issue.
consegui bom ~ I had good success. **ela teve muito** ~ **na vida** she had much success in her life, she carried the world before her. **ele assegura o** ~ he ensures the success. **ele tem muito** ~ he is a big success. **ele teve bom** ~ he turned out well. **eu contribuo para o bom** ~ I contribute to the success.
Êxodo s. m. Exodus: the second book of the Old Testament.
êxodo s. m. exodus: departure, migration.
exoftalmia s. f. (med.) exophtalmos, exophtalmus: protrusion of the eyeball.
exoftálmico adj. exophtalmic: pertaining to or affected with exophtalmus.
exogamia s. f. exogamy: prohibition to marry a woman of the own tribe.
exógamo adj. exogamous: of or pertaining to exogamy.
exógeno adj. exogenous.
exometria s. f. (surg.) uterine dislocation.
exomologese s. f. exomologesis: public confession.
exoneração s. f. (pl. -ões) exoneration, dismissal, discharge.
exonerar v. 1. to exonerate: a) discharge, dismiss (as from a job). b) exempt, free, release. 2. ~-se to exonerate o. s., resign (from).
exonirose s. f. (med.) nocturnal emission (of semen), wet dream.
exorar v. 1. to entreat earnestly for; to implore, supplicate, beseech, entreat. 2. to invoke.
exorável adj. m. + f. (pl. -áveis) exorable, compassionate, susceptible of being moved, inclined to pity.
exorbitância s. f. 1. exorbitance, exorbitancy, extravagance, excessiveness. 2. excessive price.
exorbitante adj. m. + f. exorbitant, excessive, extravagant, unreasonable, inordinate. ‖ ~**mente** adv. exorbitantly, excessively.
preços ~s fancy prices.
exorbitar v. 1. to exorbitate: a) go beyond the usual orbit. b) deviate from the track. 2. to exceed. 3. to go beyond the limits. 4. to go too far.
exorcismar v. (also **exorcizar**) to exorcise, conjure, adjure, drive away (spirits).
exorcismo s. m. exorcism: expulsion of evil spirits by conjuration.
exorcista s. m. + f. exorcist: 1. exorciser, person who exorcises evil spirits. 2. m. (R. C. Church) a member of the third minor order.
exordial adj. m. + f. (pl. -ais) exordial: 1. pertaining to an exordium. 2. introductory, initial.
exordiar v. 1. to make an exordium or preface. 2. to begin (as a speech).

exórdio s. m. exordium: 1. preface, introduction. 2. prologue. 3. the introductory part of a discourse. 4. (fig.) beginning, origin.

exornação s. f. (pl. -ões) 1. ornamentation, decoration. 2. embellishment.

exornar v. 1. to adorn, ornament. 2. to embellish.

exornativo adj. that adorns or embellishes.

exortação s. f. (pl. -ões) exhortation, admonition, act of exhorting.

exortador s. m. exhorter: person who exhorts.

exortar v. 1. to exhort: a) admonish, advise, warn, counsel. b) incite, stimulate, encourage, animate. c) appeal to. 2. to persuade, induce.

exortativo, exortatório adj. exhortative, hortative, hortatory, containing exhortation.

exortatória s. f. exhortative speech or address.

exosmose s. f. (phys.) exosmosis.

exosmótico adj. exosmotic: of or pertaining to exosmosis.

exósporo s. m. (bot.) exospore: the outer coat of a spore.

exóstoma s. m. (bot.) exostome.

exostose s. f. exostosis: 1. (path.) a morbid growth on the surface of a bone. 2. the formation of woody excrescences upon the stems of plants.

exotérico adj. exoteric(al): of or pertaining to exoterics.

exoterismo s. m. (phil.) the exoteric doctrine.

exotérmico adj. exothermic, exothermous.

exótico adj. 1. exotic(al), foreign, not native. 2. odd, strange, queer. 3. extravagant. 4. clumsy, awkward. ‖ **exoticamente** adv. exotically.

exotismo s. m. exoticism: the state of being exotic.

expandir v. 1. to expand: a) spread or stretch out, unfold. b) extend, open, enlarge, widen, broaden. c) amplify, augment, dilate. 2. ~-se: a) to expand, become dilated, distended or enlarged. b) to be expansive. c) to express o. s. freely. d) to develop, grow.

expansão s. f. (pl. -ões) 1. expansion: a) act of expanding. b) enlargement, dilatation, spreading. 2. expansiveness. 3. free expression of one's feelings. 4. frankness, sincerity.
a vasta ~ **do mar** the vast expanse of the sea. **ele deu** ~ **a seus sentimentos** he gave free scope to his feelings.

expansibilidade s. f. expansibility: 1. quality of being expansible. 2. capacity of extension in surface or bulk (as the expansibility of air).

expansionismo s. m. expansionism.

expansionista s. m. + f. expansionist.

expansível adj. m. + f. (pl. -íveis) expansible, expansive.

expansivo adj. 1. expansive. 2. (fig.): a) enthusiastic. b) frank, free, sincere. ‖ **-amente:** 1. expansively. 2. enthusiastically. 3. sincerely.

expatriação s. f. (pl. -ões) 1. expatriation, banishment, exile. 2. (e)migration.

expatriado s. m. an exile (person). ‖ adj. exiled, banished.

expatriar v. 1. to expatriate, exile, banish, deport. 2. ~-se: a) to quit one's own country. b) to go into exile.

expectador, expetador s. m. expectator, expectant: 1. one who waits or awaits. 2. person who has expectations.

expectante, expetante adj. m. + f. expectant, expecting.

expectativa, expetativa s. f. (also **expectação, expetação;** pl. -ões) expectation: 1. hopes. 2. anticipation, expectance, expectancy, reliance, presumption.
a peça não corresponde às minhas ~s the play falls short of my expectations. **as** ~s **são boas** expectations are good, (coll.) the goose hangs high. **contra toda** ~ contrary to all expectation, against all expectation. **mantenha-o na** ~ keep him in suspense. **na** ~ **da sua chegada** in expectation of your arrival, against your arrival. **na** ~ **de suas ordens** (letters) trusting to receive your orders. **na** ~ **de uma breve resposta** expecting an early reply. **segundo todas as** ~s according to all expectations, humanly speaking.

expectável, expetável adj. m. + f. (pl. -áveis) 1. expectable, that may be expected. 2. probable.

expectoração, expetoração s. f. (pl. -ões) expectoration: 1. act of expectorating. 2. the matter expectorated.

expectorante, expetorante s. m. (pharm.) expectorant: a medicine that promotes or facilitates expectoration. ‖ adj. m. + f. expectorant: promoting or facilitating expectoration.

expectorar, expetorar v. to expectorate.

expedição s. f. (pl. -ões) expedition: 1. despatch(ing) (as of goods). 2. haste, speed, activity, promptness. 3. excursion, journey, trip, raid. 4. military expedition.

expedicionário s. m. person who takes part in an expedition. ‖ adj. expeditionary: of or pertaining to an expedition.

expedicioneiro s. m. (Vatican) officer who dispatches breves, bulls.

expedidor s. m. dispatcher, forwarder, shipper, forwarding-agent. ‖ adj. dispatching, forwarding.

expediência s. f. 1. activity, speed, expeditiousness. 2. facility, readiness.

expediente s. m. 1. business or office hours. 2. the work of an office or governmental bureau. 3. expedient, means, resource. ‖ adj. m. + f. 1. expeditious, quick, hasty, speedy; active. 2. dispatching.
ele vive de ~s he lives on his wits. **tenho de inventar um** ~ I must think of a way out, of a loophole.

expedir v. 1. to dispatch, forward, express, ship (goods). 2. to remit, send, deliver. 3. to promulgate, publish. 4. to hasten, expedite. 5. to expel, eject. 6. ~-se: a) to disentangle o. s. b) to make haste.
expedi as malas (do correio) I made up the mails.

expedito adj. (also **expeditivo**) 1. expeditious: a) quick, swift, hasty, speedy. b) active, diligent. 2. disengaged, freed.

expedrar v. to clear a piece of land from stones.

expelir v. 1. to expel, force or throw out, eject. 2. to expectorate, spit out. 3. to reject.

expender v. 1. to weigh, ponder, consider, examine. 2. to make plain, expound. 3. to spend, lay out (money).

expensão s. f. (pl. -ões) ponderation, an expounding or expending.

expensas s. f. pl. expenses.
a ~ **de** at the expenses of.

experiência s. f. 1. experience. 2. practice, knowledge (as of life). 3. experiment, proof, trial, test. 4. tentative.
~ **do mundo** worldly wisdom. **a título de** ~ by way of trial. **em** ~ on probation. **eu sei por** ~ I know it by experience. **pela própria** ~ by my own experience. **um homem de** ~ a man of experience.

experiente s. m. + f. expert: an experienced or skilful person. ‖ adj. experienced, skilful, skilled, expert.

experimentação s. f. (pl. -ões) (also **experimenta)** experimentation, experiment, trial, test, tryout.

experimentado adj. experienced, tried, tested; able, apt, skilled.
marinheiro ~ old sea-dog. **um professor** ~ a teacher of tried experience. **um soldado** ~ a seasoned soldier. **um velho** ~ an old hand.
experimental adj. m. + f. (pl. **-ais**) experimental: pertaining to or derived from experiments.
experimentar v. 1. to experiment, experimentalize, try, test, prove, examine. 2. to attempt, essay. 3. to practise. 4. to taste. 5. to feel; suffer, undergo, experience. 6. ~-**se**: a) to make a trial. b) to be tried, proved, experienced.
~ **alguma coisa** to give something a trial. ~ **fazer alguma coisa** to try one's hand at something. ~ **um pouco** to take a taste of. **ele experimentou** he tried his hand at it. **experimentamos este jogo** we tried at this play. **experimente a sua sorte!** try your luck. **experimente outra vez!** try a second time! **preciso** ~ **este carro antes de dizer que ele é bom** I want to try out this car before saying it is good.
experimentável adj. m. + f. (pl. **-áveis**) capable of being tried or examined.
experimento s. m. 1. experiment, trial, test, proof. 2. experimentation, experience.
experto s. m. an expert. || adj. 1. skilful, expert. 2. experienced.
expiação s. f. (pl. **-ões**) expiation, atonement, reparation.
expiar v. to expiate: 1. atone for. 2. give satisfaction or offer reparations for, pay for a crime or sin. 3. propitiate.
~ **uma falta** to atone for a fault. ~ **um crime** to serve time.
expiatório adj. expiatory.
bode ~ scapegoat.
expiável adj. m. + f. (pl. **-áveis**) expiable.
expilação s. f. (pl. **-ões**) (jur.) expilation.
expilar v. (jur.) to expilate.
expiração s. f. (pl. **-ões**) expiration: 1. breathing out, exhalation. 2. cessation, conclusion, termination, end (as of a term).
expirante adj. m. + f. expiring, dying, moribund.
expirar v. to expire: 1. exhale, breathe out. 2. die, emit one's last breath. 3. end, conclude, terminate, finish. 4. come to an end.
o prazo expirou the time is up.
expiratório adj. expiratory.
explanação s. f. (pl. **-ões**) explanation, explication, interpretation, elucidation.
explanador s. m. explainer, interpreter, expositor. || adj. explaining, elucidative.
explanar v. to explain, explicate, expound, interpret, elucidate, illustrate, make plain.
explanatório, explanativo adj. explanatory.
expletivo s. m. (also **expletiva**) (gram.) expletive. || adj. expletive.
explicação s. f. (pl. **-ões**) 1. explication, explanation, elucidation. 2. solution, definition. 3. commentary. 4. interpretation. 5. pl. repetitional lessons.
~ **de símbolos** explanation of symbols. **dar uma** ~ **de alguma coisa** to give an explanation of something. **reclamar** ~ to call to account.
explicador s. m. 1. explainer, interpreter, expositor, elucidator. 2. coach: a tutor who assists students in examinations.
explicar v. 1. to explicate, explain, expound, illustrate, interpret, elucidate, make clear. 2. to account for. 3. to teach, coach. 4. ~-**se** to explain or express o. s.
como se explica isso? how do you account for that. **expliquei-me com ele** I came to an explanation with him, I had it out with him. **que isto**

fique explicado de uma vez para sempre let this be made clear once for all.
explicativo adj. explicative, explicatory, elucidative, explanatory.
explicável adj. m. + f. (pl. **-áveis**) explainable, explicable, accountable.
explícito adj. explicit, plain, clear, express, categorical, positive. || **explicitamente** adv. explicitly.
explodir v. 1. to explode, blow up, detonate, burst. 2. to roar out, vociferate.
fazer ~ **uma mina** to spring a mine.
exploração s. f. (pl. **-ões**) 1. exploration, close search, strict or careful examination; investigation, inquiry. 2. exploitation, exploitage. 3. robbery. 4. (TV, radio) scanning.
explorador s. m. 1. explorer, researcher. 2. exploiter, sweater. || adj. 1. exploring. 2. explorative, exploiting.
explorar v. 1. to explore, search, inquire into. 2. to exploit, fleece, soak, plunder, strip.
~ **alguém** to exploit s. o., play fast and loose with a person.
exploratório s. m. (surg.) sound, catheter. || adj. 1. exploratory, exploring. 2. exploiting.
explorável adj. m. + f. (pl. **-áveis**) 1. that can be explored. 2. exploitable.
explosão s. f. (pl. **-ões**) explosion: 1. blowing up, blast, burst; detonation. 2. (fig.) a sudden manifestation, outburst.
explosível adj. m. + f. (pl. **-íveis**) explosible.
explosivo s. m. explosive: an explosive agent or substance (as dynamite, gunpowder). || adj. explosive.
pólvora -a explosive powder. **projetil** ~ explosive projectile.
explotar v. to exploit.
expluir v. = **explodir.**
expoente s. m. exponent: 1. (math.) number expressing the degree of the power to which another number is raised. 2. one who expounds or explains. 3. (fig.) great man in his field.
expolição s. f. (pl. **-ões**) (rhet.) expolition.
exponencial adj. m. + f. (pl. **-ais**) (math.) exponential.
função ~ exponential function.
expor v. 1. to expose, lay out, exhibit, show, display. 2. to offer for sale. 3. to explain, expound, make clear, lay open, disclose. 4. to declare. 5. to narrate, relate, report, tell. 6. to risk, endanger, hazard. 7. to abandon (as a child). 8. ~-**se**: a) to expose o. s. to danger. b) to show o. s.
~ **à mostra** to hang out. ~ **à venda** to expose for sale. ~-**se ao perigo** to expose o. s. to a danger, incur a risk, put one's fingers in the fire. ~-**se ao ridículo** to hold o. s. up to ridicule, make an ass of o. s. **ela expôs o caso** she stated the case.
exportação s. f. (pl. **-ões**) exportation, export.
artigos de ~ exports. **comércio de** ~ export trade.
exportador s. m. exporter. || adj. exporting.
casa ~**a** exporting firm.
exportar v. to export: carry or send (goods) to foreign countries.
exposição s. f. (pl. **-ões**) exposition: 1. act of exposing. 2. (phot.) an exposure. 3. a public exhibition or show, display. 4. explanation, interpretation, account, statement.
~ **de gado** cattle-show. ~ **de quadros** picture gallery. **sala de** ~ show-room.
expositivo adj. expositive, expository.
expositor s. m. expositor, explainer, interpreter: one who or that which (as a book) expounds.
exposto s. m. a foundling, exposed child. || adj. 1. exposed. 2. bare. 3. patent, open, evident.
~ **ao público** on public exhibition. **está** ~ it is on show. **pede-se o favor de não tocar nos objetos**

~s visitors are requested not to touch the exhibits. **pelas razões -as** for the reasons shown.
expostulação s. f. (pl. **-ões**) expostulation, dissuasion, remonstrance.
expressão s. f. (pl. **-ões**) 1. expression: a) act of expressing (squeezing out). b) utterance, saying; a word, phrase, term, sentence; way of expressing one's thought. c) (mus.) effective execution; expressiveness. d) a combination of algebrical symbols. 2. countenance, look.
desculpe a ~, mas... forgive the word, but... **-ões vulgares** everyday expressions, vulgar expressions. **rosto de ~ angélica** an angelic expression of countenance.
expressar v. (also **exprimir**) to express.
ele expressou os nossos sentimentos he gave voice to our feelings. **ele o expressou muito bem** he put it well.
expressionismo s. m. (art) expressionism.
expressionista s. m. + f. expressionist. ‖ adj. expressionist(ic).
expressividade s. f. expressiveness: the quality of being expressive.
expressivo adj. expressive, significant, significative; meaning. ‖ **-amente** adv. expressively.
expresso s. m. 1. courier, special messenger. 2. express train. ‖ adj. express: clearly made known, explicit, plain, clear.
carta -a special delivery letter. **uma ordem -a** an express command.
exprimir v. 1. to express: a) utter, describe, phrase, speak, say. b) represent, signify. c) manifest, reveal. 2. **~-se** to express o. s., give expression to one's feelings.
~ os seus pensamentos to frame one's thoughts into words. **ele exprimiu sua satisfação** he expressed his satisfaction at. **exprimimos nossos agradecimentos** we tendered our thanks.
exprimível adj. m. + f. (pl. **-íveis**) expressible, significant, significative, utterable.
exprobração, exprobação s. f. (pl. **-ões**) exprobration, reproach, blame, rebuke, reprimand.
exprobrador, exprobador s. m. reproacher, blamer, upbraider. ‖ adj. (also **exprobrante** m. +f.) reproachful, upbraiding.
exprobrar, exprobar v. to exprobrate, upbraid, reproach, blame, censure.
exprobratório adj. reproachful, rebuking, upbraiding.
expromissor s. m. (jur.) expromissor.
expropriação s. f. (pl. **-ões**) expropriation; dispossession.
expropriador s. m. expropriator, dispossessor. ‖ adj. expropriating.
expropriar v. to expropriate, take from, dispossess (esp. for public use).
expugnação s. f. (pl. **-ões**) expugnation: conquest, overcoming or taking by assault.
expugnar v. to overcome, conquer, take by assault.
expugnável adj. m. + f. (pl. **-áveis**) expugnable, conquerable.
expulsão s. f. (pl. **-ões**) 1. expulsion, driving away. 2. exclusion, dismissal. 3. banishment. 4. (med.) expelling, ejection, excretion.
expulsar v. 1. to expel, drive away, turn out. 2. to dismiss, cast forth. 3. to banish. 4. (med.) to eject. **~ da corte** to banish from the court. **~ da escola** to expel from school.
expulsivo adj. expulsive: serving to expel.
expulso adj. expelled, turned out, driven away.
ele foi ~ da escola he was expelled from school.
expulsor s. m. (f. **expultriz**) 1. one who expels or turns out. 2. (typogr.) type-pusher. ‖ adj. turning out, expelling.

expunção s. f. (pl. **-ões**) expunction: act of expunging or erasing.
expungir v. to expunge, blot out, erase, delete.
expurgação s. f. (pl. **-ões**) (also **expurgo** m.) 1. expurgation. 2. purification; cleansing.
expurgado adj. cleansed, purged.
expurgador s. m. expurgator. ‖ adj. expurgating.
expurgar v. 1. to purge, expurgate, cleanse. 2. to purify, clear.
~ um livro to expurgate a book. **expurgamos os estábulos** we smoked the stables out.
expurgatório s. m. (R. C. Church) expurgatory index: the list of books anathematized by the pope. ‖ adj. expurgatory.
exsicação s. f. (pl. **-ões**) exsiccation; desiccation, dryness; dehydration.
exsicante adj. m. + f. (also med.) exsiccant, drying.
exsicar v. to exsiccate, desiccate, dry up.
exsicata s. f. exsiccatae: dried specimens of plants.
exsicativo adj. exsiccative: having the power of drying (as a medicine).
exsolver v. to dissolve; resolve; pay.
exspuição s. f. act of spitting.
exsucção, exsução s. f. (pl. **-ões**) exsuction, act of sucking, suction.
exsudação s. f. (pl. **-ões**) exudation, sweating out.
exsudar v. (also **exsuar**) to exude, ooze, discharge through the pores (sweat).
exsurgir v. to arise, issue.
êxtase s. m. ecstasy: a) rapture, excessive delight, trance, transport. b) (med.) a morbid state of the nervous system.
absorto em ~ wrapped up in an ecstasy.
extasiado adj. 1. ecstasied, ecstatic, rapt, enraptured, ravished. 2. aghast.
extasiar v. 1. to ecstasy, ravish, enrapture, transport, entrance. 2. **~-se**: a) to fall into an ecstasy. b) to be enchanted, delighted. c) to become enraptured.
extático adj. 1. ecstatic(al), ecstasied, ravished, raptured, enchanted. 2. raving, frenzied. ‖ **extaticamente** adv. ecstatically.
extemporaneidade f. extemporaneousness: the quality of being extemporaneous.
extemporâneo adj. extemporaneous, extemporary. ‖ **-amente** adv. extemporaneously.
extensão s. f. (pl. **-ões**) 1. extension, stretching. 2. enlargement, expansion, amplification; prolongation. 3. extent, range, space, length. 4. duration. 5. generalization. 6. a short telephone extension.
a vasta ~ do céu the vast extent of sky. **em toda ~** at full length. **em toda ~ da palavra** in the full meaning of the word. **mesa de ~** sliding-table.
extensibilidade s. f. extensibility, extensibleness: the quality of being extensible.
extensível adj. m. + f. (pl. **-íveis**) extensible, extendible.
extensivo adj. 1. extensive, extensible, extendible. 2. expansive. ‖ **-amente** adv. extensively.
extenso adj. 1. extensive, ample, large, vast. 2. spread, stretched. 3. prolonged, diffuse, prolix, detailed. 4. wide, broad. ‖ **-amente** adv. extensively, fully; wide.
é favor escrever por ~ please, write in full. **por ~** at full length.
extensor s. m. 1. (anat.) extensor (muscle.) 2. extender. ‖ adj. serving to extend.
extenuação s. f. (pl. **-ões**) 1. extenuating, lessening, falling away, enfeeblement. 2. debility, feebleness, weakness.
extenuado adj. 1. exhausted, worn out. 2. tired out. 3. enfeebled, weakened.

extenuador adj. **extenuante** m. + f. (also **extenuativo** m.) exhaustive, weakening, debilitating.
extenuar v. 1. to exhaust. 2. to debilitate, weaken, enfeeble, prostrate. 3. ~-**se** to lose strength; grow weak or feeble.
exterior s. m. 1. the exterior, external, outside. 2. the foreign countries. ‖ adj. m. + f. exterior, external, outer, outward, outside. ‖ ~**mente** adv. externally. **do** ~ from abroad. **Ministro do Exterior** Minister of the Exterior. **obras** ~**es** outer works. **o mundo** ~ the external world. **no** ~ abroad, in foreign parts. **relações** ~**es** foreign affairs.
exterioridade s. f. 1. appearance, outside. 2. externality, outwardness, exteriority.
exteriorização s. f. (pl. -**ões**) 1. externalization. 2. expression, utterance.
exteriorizar v. 1. to utter, express. 2. to manifest. 3. ~-**se** to manifest, show itself.
exterminação s. f. (pl. -**ões**) extermination: act of exterminating.
exterminador s. m. exterminator, extirpator. ‖ adj. exterminatory.
exterminar v. to exterminate: 1. drive away, expel, banish. 2. destroy, annihilate, uproot, extinguish, extirpate. 3. to kill.
extermínio s. m. extermination, extirpation, destruction, desolation, ruin, extinction.
externar, exteriorizar v. 1. to utter, express. 2. to manifest, declare.
externato s. m. day-school.
externo adj. external, exterior, outward, outside, outer. ‖ -**amente** adv. externally.
aluno ~ extern, a day-scholar. **para uso** ~ (pharm.) for external application.
exterritorialidade s. f. exterritoriality.
extinção s. f. (pl. -**ões**) extinction, extinguishment, destruction; abolition.
extinguir v. 1. to extinguish: a) put out, quench, stifle. b) destroy, put an end to. c) abolish, annul, suppress. 2. ~-**se**: a) to be extinguished, go out. b) to become extinct. c) to die.
o título extinguiu-se the title lapsed.
extinguível adj. m. + f. (pl. -**íveis**) extinguishable, that may be extinguished.
extinto s. m. a dead person. ‖ adj. 1. extinct, extinguished, put out. 2. dead, defunct.
vulcão ~ extinct volcano.
extintor s. m. 1. extinguisher (plate F 7). 2. (also ~ **de incêndio**) fire-extinguisher. ‖ adj. extinguishing.
extirpação s. f. (pl. -**ões**) extirpation: 1. act of extirpating. 2. destruction. 3. eradication. 4. excision.
extirpador s. m. extirpator: one who or that which extirpates or roots out. ‖ adj. extirpating.
extirpar v. to extirpate: 1. pull out by the roots; root out, eradicate, uproot. 2. destroy totally. 3. (surg.) make an incision.
é difícil ~ **preconceitos** it is difficult to root out prejudices.
extorquir v. to extort: 1. wrest or wring from (by force), obtain by violence. 2. exact. 3. rob, steal.
extorsão s. f. (pl. -**ões**) (also **extorso** m.) 1. extortion, exaction, concussion. 2. blackmail. 3. usurpation.
extorsionário s. m. extortioner: person who practises extortion. ‖ adj. (also **extorsivo**) extortionary: practising extortion.
extra s. m. + f. extra: an extra paper or person. ‖ adj. 1. extra, additional, supplementary. 2. extraordinary. 3. extrafine.
edição ~ special edition. **hora** ~ overhour. **trabalho** ~ surplus work.
extração s. f. (pl. -**ões**) 1. extraction: a) act of extracting or pulling out. b) that which is ex-

tracted. 2. sale, market, vent. 3. (math.) process of extracting a root. 4. mining. 5. drawing (lottery). 6. derivation, lineage, origin.
extraconjugal adj. extramatrimonial, extramarital.
extracontinental adj. extracontinental.
extradição s. f. (pl. -**ões**) extradition: the surrender of fugitive criminals.
extraditar v. to extradite, surrender, deliver (a fugitive criminal).
extradorso s. m. (archit.) extrados: the upper or convex surface of an arch or of a vault (plate A 12).
extrafino adj. extrafine, superfine.
extrafoliáceo, extrafólio adj. (bot.) extrafoliaceous.
extragenital adj. extragenital.
extra-humano adj. (pl. **extra-humanos**) superhuman.
extrair v. 1. to extract: a) draw out, withdraw, pull out. b) (math.) calculate or find (as the root of a number). 2. to make an extract of. 3. to pick, pluck.
~ **o suco das uvas** to express the juice of grapes. ~ **um dente** to pull a tooth.
extraível adj. m. + f. (pl. -**íveis**) extractable.
extrajudicial adj. m. + f. (pl. -**ais**) extrajudicial: out of the regular course of legal procedure.
extrajurídico adj. illegal, unlawful.
extralegal adj. m. + f. (pl. -**ais**) extralegal, illegal.
extramural adj. m. + f. (pl. -**ais**) extramural: outside of the walls.
extranatural adj. m. + f. (pl. -**ais**) supernatural.
extranumeral s. m. + f. (pl. -**ais**), **extranumerário** m. extra worker. ‖ adj. supernumerary.
extraordinário adj. m. 1. anything unusual or uncommon. 2. extra expenses or work. ‖ adj. extraordinary: 1. unusual, extra, uncommon, not ordinary, rare. 2. remarkable, exceptional, phenomenal. 3. astonishing. ‖ **extraordinariamente** adv. extraordinarily.
aquele é um caso ~ that is an uncommon case. **caso** ~ extraordinary case. **eles trabalham horas -as, eles fazem** ~ they work overtime. **isto não é nada de** ~ that is all in the day's work. **uma memória -a** a portent of memory. **um rapaz** ~ a jolly good fellow.
extrapassar v. to exceed, surpass, overstep.
extrapolar v. to extrapolate.
extrapor v. to put out, away.
extraprograma s. m. part of a performance not on the programme. ‖ adj. m. + f., sg. + pl. not on the programme.
extra-regulamentar adj. m. + f. (pl. **extra-regulamentares**) irregular.
extratar v. 1. to extract. 2. to summarize, make an abstract of.
extraterreno adj. extraterrestrial: outside of the earth.
extraterritorial adj. m. + f. (pl. -**ais**) extraterritorial.
extrativo adj. extractive, extracting.
extrato s. m. extract: 1. that which is extracted or drawn out. 2. abridgement, summary, compendium, exerpt, quotation, citation. 3. a copy. 4. an essence (as of tincture or perfume).
~ **de conta** extract or statement of account. ~ **de rosas** extract of roses.
extrator s. m. extractor: one who or that which extracts (plate M 5). ‖ adj. extracting.
extratorácico adj. extrathoracic: on the outside of the thorax.
extra-uterino adj. (pl. **extra-uterinos**) extrauterine: outside of the uterus.
gravidez -a extrauterine pregnancy.
extravagância s. f. 1. extravagance, extravagancy: a) wildness, absurdity, folly. b) excess, exorbitance. c) dissipation. d) extravagant action or thing. 2. oddity, oddness, queerness. 3. ~**s** excesses (as of drink).

ele **arruinou-se com suas** ~s he was ruined by his own extravagance.

extravaganciar v. 1. to live extravagantly. 2. to waste, dissipate (as money). 3. to lead a wild life.

extravagante s. m. + f. 1. dissipator, squanderer, spendthrift, waster. 2. playboy, giddy-head, madcap. 3. loafer, vagrant. ‖ adj. 1. extravagant, wild. 2. odd, strange, singular. 3. exorbitant; prodigal; excessive. 4. fantastic.

as suas idéias são ~s your ideas are extravagant. **não seja tão** ~! don't be so extravagant.

extravagar v. to extravagate: 1. pass the limits. 2. wander about, divagate.

extravasamento s. m. 1. extravasation. 2. overflow(ing).

extravasar v. 1. to extravasate: force out or let out of the proper vessels (e. g. blood). 2. to pour over. 3. ~-se to overflow.

extraviado adj. 1. astray, lost, amiss. 2. depraved, corrupt, perverted. 3. bashful, embarrassed.

carta -a miscarried letter. **objetos** ~s lost property.

extraviar v. 1. to lead astray, put out of the way, 2. to misdirect, mislead. 3. to embezzle. 4. to seduce, pervert, corrupt. 5. ~-se to be or to become lost.

a carta extraviou-se the letter has been lost.

extravio s. m. misleading, misguiding, deviation. 2. miscarriage. 3. loss; misplacement. 4. embezzlement, purloining. 5. corruption.

extrema-direita s. m. (pl. **extremas-direitas**) (ftb.) outside-right.

extremado adj. 1. extraordinary. 2. distinct, distinguished, eminent.

extrema-esquerda s. m. (pl. **extremas-esquerdas**) (ftb.) outside-left.

extremar v. 1. to mark out. 2. to exalt, elevate, sublimate. 3. ~-se to distinguish o. s.

extrema-unção s. f. (pl. **extremas-unções, extrema-unções**) (rel.) extreme unction.

extremidade s. f. 1. extremity: a) the utmost point or side. b) edge, border, margin, tip. c) end. 2. misery, distress, acute need.

na ~ **oposta** at the other extreme.

extremismo s. m. extremism, ultraism.

extremista s. m. + f. extremist.

extremo s. m. 1. extreme: a) extremity, end. b) utmost point or limit. c) highest degree. d) (math.) either of the first and last terms of a proportion. 2. (fig.) the last resource. ~s pl. excessive fondness. ‖ adj. 1. extreme: a) last, final. b) utmost, greatest. c) farthest, most distant. d) highest. e) extravagant, excessive. 2. perfect. ‖ -amente adv. extremely.

-a miséria deep poverty. **até os limites** ~s to its utmost limits. **cair no** ~ **oposto, ir aos** ~s to fly to the opposite extreme. **de** ~ **a** ~ from out to out. **ela vive em -a miséria** she lives in abject poverty. **ele é -amente humorístico** he is the per-

fection of wit. **ele irá ao** ~ he will go to the limit. **levar uma coisa ao** ~ to carry a thing too far.

Extremo-Oriente s. m. Far East.

extremos s. m. pl. 1. extreme kindness, lovingness. 2. (fig.) last resort. 3. excess, exaggeration.

extremosa s. f. (bot.) crape myrtle. 2. queen's--flower.

extremoso adj. 1. extreme, excessive. 2. excessively fond, affectionate. 3. kind. 4. devote, tender, attached. 5. most perfect.

extrínseco adj. extrinsic(al), external, exterior.

extrofia s. f. (path.) extrophia.

extrorso adj. (bot.) extrorse, turned outward (anther).

extrusão s. f. (pl. **-ões**) extrusion, expulsion.

exu s. m. (Braz.) 1. (in voodoo rites) an evil spirit. 2. (pop.) the devil.

virar ~ to enter into trance (voodoo rites).

exuberância s. f. exuberance, exuberancy, superabundance, plenty, profusion.

exuberante adj. m. + f. exuberant: 1. superabundant, plenteous, copious, profuse, rich. 2. luxuriant, rank, lush. 3. effusive, full of life.

exuberar v. to exuberate: 1. abound, superabound. 2. be in exuberance, exist in great abundance; teem with.

exúbere adj. m. + f. weaned.

êxul adj. m. + f. (pl. **êxules**) = **êxule**.

exular v. to quit one's own country; expatriate o. s., emigrate.

exulceração s. f. (pl. **-ões**) exulceration: 1. formation of ulcers. 2. (fig.) fretting, affliction.

exulcerante adj. m. + f. exulcerating.

exulcerar v. to exulcerate: 1. produce an ulcer; ulcerate. 2. (fig.) corrode, fret; afflict. 3. ~-se to become ulcerous.

exulcerativo adj. exulcerative.

êxule adj. m. + f. exiled, banished.

exultação s. f. (pl. **-ões**) exultation, joy, rapturous delight, jubilation; triumph.

exultante adj. m. + f. exultant, exulting, jubilant, radiant; triumphant.

exultar v. to exult, rejoice, jubilate, radiate; triumph.

exumação s. f. (pl. **-ões**) exhumation, disinterment.

exumar v. to exhume, disinter, dig out of the ground (a corpse).

exutório s. m. (med.) fontanel(le): an issue for the discharge of humours from the body.

exúvia s. f. exuviae: cast-off skins, shells or other coverings of animals.

exuviabilidade s. f. exuviability: capability of exuviating.

exuviável adj. m. + f. (pl. **-áveis**) exuviable: capable of being cast or thrown off.

exúvio s. m. (bot.) remains on the upper parts of fruits left by the chalice or corolla.

ex-voto s. m. (pl. **ex-votos**) ex-voto: an object offered to a divinity for a favour received.

F

F, f s. m. the sixth letter of the Portuguese alphabet. || adj. m. + f. sixth.
com todos os ff e rr with the greatest exactness.
F. 1. abbr. of: a) **Fulano** Mr. So-and-so, Mr. what's--his-name. b) Fahrenheit, thermometer and system. 2. (chem.) symbol of fluorine.
f (mus.) abbr. of **forte** (**ff fortíssimo**).
fá s. m. (mus.) fa: the fourth note of the diatonic scale.
fã s. m. + f. devotee, admirer, fan (abbr. of fanatic).
fabagela s. f. (bot. also: **falso-alcaparreiro** m.) bean--caper.
fabela s. f. little fable or tale.
fabiana (I) s. f. (bot.) fabiana, false heather.
fabiana (II) s. f. (Braz., pop.) wound, sore, ulcer.
fabordão s. m. (pl. -**ões**) 1. (ant. mus.) faburden: 1. hymn in counterpoint. 2. (fig.) insipidity.
fábrica s. f. 1. factory, workshop. 2. mill, plant, work(s), manufactory, industry. 3. personnel, workmen, operatives, hands. 4. construction of a building. 5. ingenious device. 6. (eccl.) prebend, benefice. 7. workmanship, skill. 8. m. (Braz.) farm hand, help.
~ **de açúcar** (**engenho**) sugar refinery. ~ **de arames** (**trefilaria**) wireworks. ~ **de armas** (**armaria**) arms factory (armo(u)ry). ~ **de automóveis** automobile plant. ~ **de cerâmica** earthenware factory. ~ **de conservas** cannery. ~ **de fiação** spinning mill. ~ **de folhas de cobre** copper mill. ~ **de igreja** funds of a church. ~ **de lacticínios** dairy. ~ **de louça** pottery. ~ **de obras de bronze** brass works. ~ **de papel** paper mill. ~ **de seda** silk factory. ~ **de produtos químicos** chemical works. ~ **têxtil** (**tecelagem**) textile factory. **de boa** ~ well-made or well-worked. **preço de** ~ cost price.
fabricação s. f. (pl. -**ões**) 1. manufacture, fabrication. 2. making, make, production. 3. work.
~ **de cabos** cable manufacture. ~ **de cerveja** beer brewing. ~ **de ferramentas** tool making. ~ **de moldes** pattern making. ~ **em massa,** ~ **em grande escala** mass production. ~ **em série** 1. series manufacture. 2. gang work.
fabricado adj. made, built.
~ **sob encomenda** custom-made.
fabricador s. m. 1. constructor, builder, maker. 2. workman, operative. 3. (fig.) rumourmonger. || adj. manufacturing.
~ **de enredos** intriguer. ~ **de mentiras** coiner of lies. **todo homem é** ~ **de sua fortuna** every man is the maker of his own fortune.
fabricante s. m. + f. 1. manufacturer, maker, producer, fabricant. 2. industrialist. 3. organizer, inventor.
~ **de cerveja** brewer. ~ **de conservas** conserver. ~ **de ferramentas** tool maker. ~ **de lacticínios** dairyman. ~ **de papel** paper maker. ~ **de velas** tallow chandler.
fabricar v. 1. to produce, manufacture, make. 2. to form, frame, mill, prepare, make ready, fit out. 3. to edify, construct. 4. to coin, mint. 5. to cultivate, till. 6. to repair, reconstruct. 7. to invent, contrive, devise. 8. to forge, fabricate. 9. to maintain a factory. 10. to put to work, let work.
~ **moeda** to coin money. ~ **a sua ruína** to cause one's own misfortune. **ele fabricou esta história** he concocted this story.
fabricável adj. m. + f. (pl. -**áveis**) producible, capable of being manufactured.

fabrico s. m. 1. production: a) act or process of producing, preparation, fabrication. b) the product, work, workmanship. 2. tillage, cultivation, husbandry. 3. (naut.) ship repair, refitting.
fabril adj. m. + f. (pl. -**is**) 1. industrial: of, pertaining to or relative to a factory. 2. mechanical, operative. 3. productive, originative.
indústria ~ heavy industry, (U. S. A.) big business. **união** ~ manufacturing combine.
fabriqueiro s. m. (also **fabricário**) church-warden.
fabro s. m. (poet.) artisan, craftsman.
fábula s. f. fable: 1. fictitious narrative. 2. legend, myth. 3. story made up to teach a lesson. 4. plot of a literary composition (epic or dramatic). 5. untruth, lie, fabrication, falsehood, invention.
~**s de Esopo** Aesop's fables. **ganhou uma** ~ **na transação** he made a packet (killing) on the deal.
fabulação s. f. (pl. -**ões**) 1. fabled (fictious) story. 2. lie, fantastic report. 3. romance, fiction, tale. 4. moral of a fable.
fabulador s. m. 1. fabler, fabulist. 2. liar. || adj. 1. fabling. 2. lying.
fabular v. (also **fabulizar**) to fable; fabulize: 1. write fables. 2. invent, contrive or concoct stories. 3. feign, simulate, fib, lie. 4. talk idly. || adj. m. + f. 1. fabulous, fictitious. 2. of or relative to fables.
fabulário s. m. collection of fables, fable book.
fabulista s. m. + f. 1. fabulist, fabler, legendist, 2. liar.
fabuloso adj. 1. fabulous: a) fictitious, imaginary, feigned, invented, legendary. b) fabled, like a fable. c) mythologic, mythic(al). d) incredible, not believable. e) admirable, astonishing. f) great, magnificent. 2. obscure. || **-amente** adv. fabulously.
faca (I) s. f. 1. knife (plates M 1, 8, T 1). 2. cutting blade or tool in a machine.
~ **de cozinha** kitchen knife. ~ **de curtidor** grainer. ~ **de dois gumes** (also fig.) two-edged knife. ~ **de mato** machete, hunting knife. ~ **de mesa** table knife. ~ **de trinchar** carver, carving knife. ~ **para cortar queijo** cheesecutter. ~ **para enxertar** budding knife. ~ **para peixe** fish carver. **amolador de** ~**s** knife grinder. **ele está uma** ~ (sports, sl.) he is well trained. **à ponta de** ~ brutally. **pôr a** ~ **em** to stab. **entrar na** ~ (sl.) to be operated, to undergo an operation. **lâmina de** ~ knife blade. **meter a** ~ **aos peitos** to put a knife to a person's throat. **ter a** (or **estar com**) ~ **e o queijo na mão** to have all the trumps in hand. **uma** ~ **afiada** a sharp knife.
faca (II) s. f. saddle horse, ambler, pacer, palfrey.
facada s. f. 1. stab, thrust with a knife. 2. painful surprise, shock. 3. (Braz., sl.) act of touching a person for a loan or gift of money.
dar uma ~ **em** to try to borrow money from, to tap, (sl.) to touch a p. for. **levei uma** ~ I was touched for money. **matar às** ~**s** to stab, pierce (kill).
facadista s. m. + f. (Braz., sl.) habitual borrower.
facalhão (pl. -**ões**), **facalhaz** s. m. big knife.
façalvo adj. blazy, marked with a white blaze on the forehead (horse).
façanha s. f. 1. achievement, exploit, feat, prowess, performance, adventure, stunt. 2. evil deed, perversity.
uma vida de ~**s** a life of adventure.
façanheiro s. m. braggart, boaster. || adj. boastful, braggart.

façanhoso, façanhudo adj. 1. courageous, brave, valiant. 2. heroic(al). 3. admirable, memorable.

facão s. m. (pl. **-ões**) 1. large, heavy knife, machete, scythe. 2. saber, sabre.
~ **de caça** bowie knife.

fac(c)ção s. f. (pl. **-ões**) 1. feat, military exploit. 2. cabal, clique, set. 3. faction, part, wing, political party or group, sect. 4. partiality, bias, favouritism.

fac(c)ionar v. 1. to split in factions, divide. 2. to revolt, rebel.

fac(c)ionário s. m. factionary, factionist, partisan, party follower. ‖ adj. factionary.

fac(c)ionismo s. m. factiousness.

fac(c)iosidade s. f., **fac(c)iosismo** m. 1. partiality, bias, factiousness, cliquishness, cliquism. 2. factious spirit, party feeling.

fac(c)ioso adj. 1. partial, factious, biassed, partisan, cliquish. 2. seditious, rebellious. ‖ **-amente** adv. 1. factiously, clannishly. 2. seditiously.

face s. f. 1. face: a) countenance, visage (plate C 12). b) look, expression, aspect. c) appearance, semblance. d) surface, superficies (plate B 12). e) head (coin). f) side, right side, forepart, (arch.) front, façade. g) (Braz., archit.) any side of a building. h) (geom.) any of the limiting surfaces of a solid. 2. cheek, jowl.
~ **do martelo** face of a hammer (plate M 5). ~ **externa** outface. ~ **a** ~ face to face, opposite. ~ **posterior** back. ~**s muito magras** lantern jaws. **à** ~ **do mundo** in the face of the whole world (or the public). **a** ~ **da Terra** the face of the earth. **de** ~**s coradas** pippin-faced. **de** ~ **pálida** pale-visaged, pale-cheeked. **em** ~ **de** or **na** ~ **de** in the face (or presence) of. **este negócio tem duas** ~**s** there are two sides to this business. **fazer** ~ **a** to oppose, resist, meet. **fazer** ~ **às despesas** to meet expenses.

facear v. 1. to square: a) make rectangular. b) smooth, level. 2. to be in front of or in the presence of. 3. to face: a) be opposite to. b) meet. **ferramenta de** ~ facing tool.

facécia s. f. 1. facetiousness, buffoonery, drollery, waggishness, friskiness. 2. witticism, witty remark.

facecioso adj. facetious, merry, jocose.

faceira (I) s. f. 1. ox chaps or chops. 2. (fam.) jowl, double chin, fat cheeks. 3. cheekpiece (of a horse's head harness) (plate A 12, C 9).

faceira (II) s. m. 1. dandy, fop. 2. f. an affected or conceited woman.

faceiraço adj. (Braz.) very coquettish, foppish, coxcombical, swell(ish).

faceirar v. 1. to beautify, decorate, adorn. 2. to array, dress up, display elegance, show off, parade.

faceirice s. f. 1. ostentation, display, pomp. 2. foppishness, coquetry, coquettishness. 3. arrogance. 4. ridiculous aspect or sight.

faceiro adj. 1. coquettish, dressed up, foppish, swell(ish), coxcombical. 2. elegant, graceful, fashionable. 3. foplike, dandyish. 4. cheerful, gay. 5. contented, satisfied. 6. swan-necked (horse). ‖ **-amente** adv. coquettishly, etc.

faceta (ê) s. f. facet: any of the polished surfaces of precious stones. 2. any of the features of a person or thing. 3. pane.

facetar v. 1. to facet, cut facets on. 2. to polish. 3. (fig.) to improve, perfect.

facetear v. 1. to joke, jest, play a trick. 2. to frolic, make merry. 3. = **facetar**.

faceto (ê) adj. (pl. **facetos**) 1. gay, cheerful. ‖ 2. merry, witty, jocose, waggish, droll. 3. facetious. ‖ **-amente** adv. facetiously, gaily.

fachada s. f. 1. face of a building, front, façade. 2. (coll.) face, countenance. 3. frontispiece, title page. 4. window dressing.

fachear v. (N. Braz.) 1. to fish or work at torchlight. 2. to splinter, split, break.

facheiro s. m. 1. torch-bearer, linkboy, linkman. 2. torch support, torch-holder. 3. (hist.) hatchetman.

facho s. m. 1. torch, torchlight, flambeau. 2. lighthouse, beacon. 3. lantern, signal light, search or spotlight.
~ **de luz** beam of light. **sair ao** ~ to take a walk.

fachudaço, fachudo adj. (S. Braz.) handsome, nice, beautiful.

facial adj. m. + f. (pl. **-ais**) facial. ‖ ~**mente** adv. facially.
ângulo ~ facial or visual angle. **nevralgia** ~ face-ache.

fácies s. m. pl. (geol.) face, facies.

fácil adj. m. + f. (pl. **fáceis**) 1. easy, simple, effortless. 2. fluent, flowing. 3. fast, ready. 4. common, natural. 5. clear, comprehensible, intelligible. 6. compliant, indulgent. 7. tractable, docile. 8. sincere, frank. 9. gentle, soft, mild, smooth. 10. naïve, naive, ingenuous. 11. accessible, attainable. 12. (Braz., coll.) easy of morals (woman). 13. fickle, unsteady. 14. precipitated. ‖ **facilmente** adv. easily, simply, naturally, sincerely, frankly, readily, etc.
~ **de fazer** easy to do. **é** ~ **de obter** it is easy to get. **ele tem um estilo** ~ he has an easy style. **lugar de trabalho** ~ soft spot. **mais** ~ **falar do que realizar** easier said than done. **é facílimo** it is dead easy. **facilmente acessível** easy of access. **isto suja facilmente** it shows dirt. **vai facilmente** it goes swimmingly. **ser facilmente vendável** to command a ready sale.

facilidade s. f. 1. facility, ease, easiness, simplicity. 2. promptness, readiness. 3. clearness, comprehensibility. 4. agility, cleverness, skill, aptitude. 5. compliance, indulgence. 6. heedlessness, frivolity. 7. directness, forwardness, offhandedness. 8. handiness. 9. favour. 10. flowingness. 11. ~**s** pl.: a) condescension. b) recklessness in attaining one's ends.
~ **de manobra** handiness. ~ **de trabalho** workableness. ~ **em falar** readiness of speech. **com** ~ easily, with a wet finger. **com** ~**s** (payment) by instalments. **ele aprende com** ~ he has great facility in learning.

facilitação s. f. (pl. **-ões**) facilitation.

facilitador s. m. facilitator. ‖ adj. facilitative.

facilitar v. 1. to facilitate, make easy, free from difficulty, favour, smooth. 2. to be ready or willing. 3. to become easy. 4. to exercise o. s., acquire skill. 5. (Braz.) to risk, expose o. s. to danger. 6. ~**-se** to consent (to do).

facilitário s. m. (Braz., pop.) instalment sales plan.

facínora s. m. criminal, villain, malefactor, gangster.

facinoroso adj. facinorous, criminal, wicked, perverted.

facistol s. m. (pl. **-tóis**) 1. a chorister's desk in a church, choir, psalter shelf. 2. faldstool, bishop's seat in the chancel.

facocele s. f. (med.) phacocele: hernia of the eye lens.

facóide adj. m. + f. phacoid, lens-shaped, lenticular.

façoila s. f. (sl.) jowl, plump cheek.

facólito s. m. (min.) phacolite.

facômetro s. m. phacometer: instrument for measuring the refracting power of lenses.

facosclerose s. f. (med.) phacosclerosis.

facote s. m. (surg.) bone scraper.

fac-similado adj. m. (pl. **fac-similados**) (Braz., also **fac-similar** m. + f., pl. **fac-similares**) facsimile.

fac-similar v. to facsimile, facsimilize, be or make an exact copy of.

fac-símile s. m. (pl. **fac-símiles**) facsimile, exact copy, duplicate, replica, counterpart.

fa(c)tício adj. factitious, artificial, unnatural. ‖ **facticiamente** adv. factitiously.
fa(c)tível adj. m. + f. (pl. **-íveis**) feasible, practicable, possible, doable, contrivable.
factótum s. m. (pl. **-ns**) 1. factotum. 2. confidant. 3. (joc.) busybody, jack of all trades.
façudo adj. broad-faced, chub-cheeked.
fácula s. f. (astr.) facula, flaming sunspot.
faculdade s. f. 1. faculty: a) capacity, power, ability, reach. b) natural aptitude, talent. c) moral authority, intellectual capability. d) right, legal power. e) authorization, permission, licence, license. f) any of the departments of learning at a university. g) teaching body in any of these departments. h) establishment of higher education, college. 2. opportunity, chance. 3. **~s** pl. resources.
~ de concentração concentrativeness. **~ de lembrar** power of recollection. **~ de medicina** the Faculty (of Medicine). **~ de perceber** conception. **~s mentais** lights, wits. **as quatro ~s** the four faculties. **ele pediu a ~ de sair a qualquer hora** he asked for leave to withdraw at any time. **estar em plena posse de suas ~s mentais** to be in one's right or perfect mind.
facultar v. 1. to grant, permit, facilitate, empower, authorize. 2. to · place at a person's command. 3. to afford facilities, render service. 4. to offer, propose.
facultativo s. m. physician, (fam.) doctor. ‖ adj. facultative, nonobligatory, optional. ‖ **-amente** adv. optionally.
facultoso adj. opulent, rich, wealthy.
facúndia, facundidade s. f. eloquence, fluency of speech.
facundo adj. eloquent, facund.
fada s. f. 1. fairy, fay, faerie, sprite. 2. (fig.) charming woman.
fadado adj. 1. predestinate, predestined. 2. fated, doomed, weird, devoted.
bem ~ happy, fortunate. **ele está ~ a uma decepção** he will inevitably be disappointed.
fadar v. 1. to predestine, foreordain, foredoom, fate, preordain. 2. foretell, presage, augur. 3. to endow with (talent, fortune, etc.). 4. to favour.
fadário s. m. 1. fate, destiny. 2. misfortune, fatality. 3. hard life or lot, tribulation, vicissitudes.
fadejar v. 1. to submit or live up to one's fate. 2. to play or sing a **fado** or the like.
fadiga s. f. 1. fatigue, tiredness, lassitude, weariness. 2. work, labour, drudgery, toil. 3. hardship, difficulty.
~ ocular eyestrain.
fadiga-corrosão s. f. (pl. **fadigas-corrosão**) corrosion fatigue.
fadigar v. to fatigue, fag-out, weary, exhaust, make or become tired.
fadigoso adj. (also **fatigante** m. + f.) 1. troublesome, wearisome. 2. tiring, fatiguing. 3. painful, hardy.
fading, fádingue s. m. (radio) fading.
fadista s. 1. m. + f. player or singer of Portuguese folk songs. 2. m. rowdy, vagrant. 3. f. prostitute.
fadistagem s. f. (pl. **-ens**) 1. fado singers or players. 2. their ways and manners.
fado s. m. 1. destiny, fate, lot, future; (fig.) cup, die. 2. predestination, foredoom. 3. fortune. 4. fatality. 5. Portuguese folk song, dance and music. 6. last hour, death.
faéton, faetonte s. m. phaeton: light four-wheeled open carriage.
faetontídeos s. m. pl. (ornith.) Phaetontidae, pelican-like sea birds.
fagedênico adj. (med.) phagedenic(al).
fagedenismo s. m. (med.) phaged(a)ena.

fagícola adj. m. + f. (bot.) that grows on beeches.
fagócito s. m. phagocyte.
fagocitose s. f. phagocytosis.
fagópiro s. m. (bot.) buckwheat.
fagote s. m. (mus.) bassoon.
fagotista s. m. + f. (mus.) bassoonist.
fagueiro adj. 1. tender, fond, lovely, gracious. 2. affectionate, loving, sweet. 3. soft. 4. flattering.
fagulha s. f. 1. spark, flash(ing), flake. 2. (coll.) busybody, meddler.
fagulhar v. 1. to emit sparks, spark. 2. to scintillate, sparkle. 3. (fig.) to meddle with.
fagulhento adj. 1. emitting sparks, flashing. 2. sparkling. 3. (fig.) turbulent, restless.
faia (I) s. f. 1. beech-tree. 2. beechwood (timber).
~ branca (bot.) white poplar. **~ preta** (bot.) asp. **de ~** beechen, aspen.
faia (II) s. f. (typogr.) lead.
faia (III) s. m. = **fadista**.
faial s. m. (pl. **-ais**) beechwood (forest).
faiança s. f. faience: glazed earthenware.
~ italiana maiolica, majolica.
faiar v. 1. (typogr.) to lead: insert leads between lines. 2. (sl.) to steal, pilfer.
faille s. f. (Fr.) faille (silk fabric).
faim s. m. 1. small sword. 2. lance head, spear head.
faina s. f. 1. working, routine work on a ship. 2. labour, toil, work, drudgery, plod, trouble. 3. haste, stir, fuss. 4. fatigue.
faisão s. m. (pl. **-ões**) (ornith.) pheasant.
viveiro de -ões pheasantry.
faísca s. f. 1. spark, flashing, gleam, flake, fire. 2. flash of lightning, thunderbolt. 3. lump of gold, nugget. ‖ (Braz.) adj. m. + f. 1. brilliant, flashy, sparkling. 2. valiant, daring, brave.
~ de ignição striker. **brecha de ~** (radio) spark gap.
faiscação s. f. (pl. **-ões**) sparkling: 1. scintillating. 2. flying of sparks.
faiscador, faisqueiro s. m. prospector, gold washer, gold-digger.
faiscante adj. m. + f. sparkling, scintillating, flashy, fiery.
faiscar v. 1. to spark, produce or emit sparks. 2. to sparkle, flash, coruscate, scintillate, twinkle. 3. to dazzle, daze, fascinate. 4. to prospect for gold or diamonds, to pan.
faisqueira s. f. 1. gold lode, gold mine, gold streak. 2. (Braz.) broken rock or gravel abandoned by gold-diggers.
faixa s. f. 1. band, strip, stripe, streak, bar (plate P 7). 2. waistband, sash, stole. 3. belt, ribbon, fillet, collar. 4. bandage, swathe, binding, binder. 5. zone, area. 6. (archit.) fascia. 7. (astr.) fascia, planet rings or bands. 8. strip of land. 9. (her.) fesse. 10. (anat., zool.) cingulum.
~ com gravação de som (film) sound track (plate F 3). **~ de crepe para luto** crape. **~ de freqüência** (radio) channel, frequency band. **~ de onda** wave band. **~ de rodagem** roadway. **~ de segurança** (traffic regulation) area for pedestrians. **~ de transmissão** communication band.
faixar v. to swathe; to bind or tie up.
fajuto, farjuto adj. (Braz., sl.) of poor quality, shoddy (textile), fake.
fala s. f. 1. speech, talk, conversation. 2. discourse, allocution. 3. words. 4. voice. its timbre or character. 5. style of speech. 6. say.
~ do trono royal speech. **~ ininteligível** babble. **boas ~s!** glad to hear it! **defeito na ~** speech impediment. **ele perdeu a ~** he lost his tongue. **fazer perder a ~** to strike one dumb. **fazer uma**

~ to make a speech. **negar a** ~ to protest tacitly, refuse to talk. **perder a** ~ to lose one's speech. **sem** ~ tongueless. **vir à** ~ (naut.) to come within hail.

falaça s. f. stake to which offenders were shackled, in order to be whipped.

falação s. f. (pl. **-ões**) (Braz., pop.) verbiage, discourse, idle talk.

deitar ~ to discourse.

falácia s. f. 1. fallacy: a) misconception. b) deceit, fraud. c) sophism, sophistry. d) illusion. e) fallaciousness. 2. din of voices, clamour. 3. talkativeness.

falacioso adj. fallacious: 1. deceitful, deceptive. 2. misleading. 3. erroneous.

falaço s. m. (Braz., pop.) rumour.

falacrocoracídeos s. m. pl. (ornith.) Phalacrocoracidae, pelicanlike, hook-billed diving birds.

falacrose s. f. (med.) phalacrosis: baldness.

falada s. f. 1. rumour, report. 2. din of voices, clamour. 3. talk, prattle.

faladeira s. f. gossip, chatterbox, tattler (woman).

falado adj. 1. notable, famous. 2. known. 3. talked over, settled. 4. (Braz., pop.) loose, frivolous (woman).

bem ~, ~ **com propriedade** well-spoken. **foi muito** ~ it was very much commented.

falador s. m. 1. talker, speaker, prattler, chatterbox, (sl.) windjammer, telltale, windbag, rattler. 2. indiscreet fellow. ‖ adj. talkative, indiscreet, slandering, long-tongued, telltale, gabby, communicative.

falange s. f. 1. phalanx: a) (hist.) battle formation of the Greek infantry. b) (anat. also phalange) digital bones of the hand or foot. c) (fig.) multitude, crowd. 2. body of soldiers.

falangeal adj. m. + f. (pl. **-ais**) (anat.) phalangeal.

falangeta s. f. (anat.) terminal phalanx.

falângico adj. phalangeal.

falanginha s. f. (anat.) middle phalanx.

falansteriano s. m. phalansterian, member of a phalanstery.

falanstério s. m. phalanstery.

falante adj. m. + f. 1. that speaks, speaking. 2. eloquent, expressive.

falar v. 1. to speak, say, tell, communicate, talk. 2. to converse, discuss, discourse. 3. to combine, adjust. 4. to explain, teach, make understand. 5. to exhort, preach. 6. to enunciate, pronounce. 7. to utter. 8. to express, be expressive. 9. to be on speaking terms, be good friends with. 10. to address. 11. to flash. 12. to ramble, yarn.

~ **a um auditório** to address an audience. ~ **alto** to talk up. ~ **a um surdo** to preach to deaf ears. ~ **autoritariamente** to lay down the law. ~ **com** to talk to. ~ **com alguém** to speak to someone. ~ **com franqueza** to outspeak. ~ **de papo** to talk big. ~ **do ofício** to talk shop. ~ **é fácil** talk is cheap. ~ **francamente** not to mince matters or words. ~ **mais alto que** to outspeak. ~ **no ar** to talk idly, whithout purpose. ~ **pelos cotovelos** to talk nineteen to the dozen. ~ **por enigmas** to speak riddles. ~ **por entre os dentes** to mutter. ~ **por** ~ to talk at random, babble. ~ **por quantas juntas tem** to talk blue streak. ~ **sem rodeios** to speak to the point. ~ **sobre** to talk of, to tell about. ~ **só** to soliloquize. ~**am com juízo** they talked sense. **a coisa fala por si** the thing tells its own tale. **aqui fala Brown!** (teleph.) this is Brown, Brown (is) speaking (here). **aqui se fala inglês** English spoken here. **aqui quem fala sou eu!** I have the say here! **conheço-o pelo** ~ I know him by his speech. **deixe-o** ~ let him have his say. **deu o que** ~ it was widely commented. **ela falou-lhe**

em palavras doces she spoke him fair. **ele fala por dois** he talks his head off. **ele falou a meu favor** he spoke up for me. **ele falou sem chegar ao assunto** he talked round it. **ele falou sobre isto durante meia hora** he went on about it for half an hour. **ele falou sobre o mesmo assunto** he spoke on the same subject. **ele mesmo pode** ~ he can speak for himself. **eu estou falando sério** I mean it, I mean business. **falando nisso** talking of it. **falando seriamente** joking apart. **fala-se muito nisso** it is much talked of. **fale!** speak out!, (sl.) spit it out. **fale logo!** say away! **fale mais alto!** speak up! **fale o que está pensando** speak your mind. **falei com ela de um modo amável** I gave her fair words. **ficar falando sozinho** to get no answer. **foi impossível conseguir** ~ **uma só palavra** it was impossible to get a word in edgeways. **gostaria de falar-lhe** I should like to speak to you. **isto fala a seu favor** that speaks well for him. **isto fala contra você** that tells against you. **isto fala por si mesmo** that speaks for itself. **isso fala por livros** that speaks volumes. **modo de** ~ manner of speech. **não falemos mais nisso** forget it, will you. **não falo mais com ele** I am no more on speaking terms with him. **não o deixaram** ~ they talked him down. **posso** ~ **com o Sr. Silva?** can I see Mr. Silva? **sem** ~ **das despesas** not to speak of expenses, let alone the costs. **sem** ~ **de** apart from, except for, without counting. **só ela falou** she did all the talking. **você fala de barriga cheia!** you can talk!

falárica s. f. fire lance.

falaropídeos s. m. pl. (ornith.) Phalaropes, small aquatic birds.

falastrão s. m. (pl. **-ões**) (f. **falastrona**) speaker, talker, chatterbox. ‖ adj. talkative, long-tongued.

falatório, falario s. m. (Braz., also **falaraz**) 1. din of voices 2. whisper(ing). 3. chit-chat, gossip, cackle, yap, jabber. 4. slander. 5. locutory.

deram motivo a ~ they set the tongues wagging.

fala-verdade s. m. (pl. **fala-verdades**) (Braz., pop.) knife, pistol or any arm of self-defense.

falaz adj. m. + f. 1. fallacious, misleading. 2. sly, shrewd. 3. deceitful, deceptive, fraudulent. 4. vain, futile. 5. illusory, phantastic. ‖ ~**mente** adv. fallaciously.

falbalá s. m. furbelow, flounce.

falca s. f. 1. square piece of timber. 2. (naut.) washboard.

falcaça s. f. (naut.) whip.

falcaçar v. (naut.) to whip, whip a rope.

falcado adj. falcate(d), falciform, sickle-shaped.

falcão s. m. (pl. **-ões**) falcon: 1. (ornith.) hawk, harrier. 2. (hist.) a light piece of artillery.

falcato adj. 1. armed with a sickle or scythe. 2. falcated, falciform, sickle-shaped.

falcatrua s. f. 1. imposture, fraud. 2. deceit, trick, hoax.

falcatruar v. to cheat, trick, sharp, hoax.

falcífero adj. (poet.) armed with or bearing a sickle, falcated.

falcifoliado adj. (bot.) falcifoliate.

falciforme adj. m. + f. falciform, falcate.

falcípede adj. m. + f. (poet.) club-footed, clump-footed.

falcoada s. f. 1. flock of falcons. 2. (hist., mil.) falcon shot.

falcoado adj. pursued by a hawk.

falcoar v. to hawk, hunt with a falcon.

falcoaria s. f. 1. falconry, hawking: a) art of training falcons. b) hunting with falcons. 2. breeding place of falcons.

falcoeira s. f. (ornith.) herring gull.

falcoeiro s. m. falconer, hawker: breeder and trainer of hunting hawks.

falconete s. m. falconet: 1. (hist.) small piece of ordnance. 2. (ornith.) saker, any of some small Asiatic falcons.

falconídeo s. m. any bird of the family Falconidae. ‖ adj. falconine.

falconiformes s. m. pl. (ornith.) Falconiformes, the order of falconlike birds of prey.

falda s. f. 1. skirt, train, lower part of a shirt. 2. base of a hill, foot of a mountain.

faldistório s. m. faldstool: a bishop's seat within the chancel.

falecer v. 1. to decease, die, expire, pass away, leave. 2. to dwindle, waste away. 3. to become scarce, fall short. 4. to be short of, stand in need, want. 5. to fail, miss, omit. 6. to be inadequate. **ele faleceu** he is no more, he died. **faleço de** I am short of, I lack.

falecido s. m. dead, deceased. ‖ adj. 1. dead, deceased, late, departed. 2. lacking, wanting, short of. 3. defective.
~ **de recursos** wanting resources. **orações por intenção de um** ~ last offices. **meu** ~ **pai** my late father.

falecimento s. m. 1. death, departure, dying, pass, decease, disappearance. 2. failure, imperfection. 3. scarcity, shortness. 4. incapacity, inability. 5. want, need, privation.

falena s. f. moth.

falência s. f. 1. insolvency, bankruptcy, collapse, crash, ruin, smash(up), blowup. 2. failure, fault, mistake, omission. 3. scarceness, scarcity.
~ **de um banco** collapse of a bank. **ele requereu** ~ he filed a petition in bankruptcy. ~ **fraudulenta** fraudulent bankruptcy. **abrir** ~, **ir à** ~ to go bankrupt, (U. S. A., sl.) to (go) bust, smash. **levar à** ~ to bankrupt, (U. S. A., sl.) to bust, smash. **pedido de** ~ bankruptcy notice.

falerno s. m. 1. Falernian wine. 2. (fig.) any good wine.

falésia s. f. cliff, mountainous coast.

falha s. f. 1. crack, fissure, rent. 2. defect(iveness), flaw, imperfection, rub, fault. 3. error, mistake, slip, failure, miss, break. 4. omission, lacuna, gap. 5. blame. 6. mania, craze, obsession. 7. (geol.) fault, stepfault. 8. fragment, splinter. 9. blister, blowhole.
formar ~ (geol.) to fault. **sem** ~ without fail.

falhadão s. m. (pl. **-ões**) (Braz.) void in a coffee plantation where several plants have died.

falhado s. m. failure (person). ‖ adj. 1. flawy, imperfect, defective. 2. wrong, mistaken. 3. cracked, fractured, split. 4. (Braz.) barren (domestic animals). 5. failed.

falhar v. 1. to fail: a) be wanting. b) not to succeed. c) come out badly. d) not to do or occur. e) lack. f) lose strength, (sl.) peter out. g) go bankrupt. h) fade or die away. i) err, be mistaken, miss, lapse, balk. j) (aeron.) conk out. 2. to split, crack, cleave. 3. to splinter, sliver. 4. to be underweight or undersized. 5. to miscarry. 6. to misfire. 7. (Braz.) to be barren, sterile (domestic animals). 8. (Braz.) to postpone or discontinue a trip (due to accidents, etc.). 9. (cards) to pass.
~ **ao compromisso** to break one's word. **a tentativa falhou completamente** the experiment fell flat, flopped. **os seus planos** ~**am** his plans came to nothing, fell through, failed. **sua vista falhou** her (his) sight failed.

falho adj. 1. defective, imperfect, bad, deficient, flawy, lame. 2. wanting, underweight. 3. effectless,

unsuccessful, fruitless. 4. (cards) short-suited. 5. (Braz.) sterile, barren (domestic animals).
de modo ~ lamely.

falhudo adj. (Braz.) imperfect, flawy, defective, wanting.

falibilidade s. f. fallibility, fallibleness, unreliableness.

falicismo s. m. phallicism, worship of the phallus.

fálico adj. phalic(al).

falido s. m. bankrupt. ‖ adj. 1. failed. 2. faulty, imperfect. 3. barren, fruitless. 4. empty or hollow (nut). 5. bankrupt, ruined, insolvent; (sl.) stony, on the rocks, broke.
~ **em esperanças** bankrupt in hopes. ~ **que não obteve concordata** uncertificated bankrupt. **declarar alguém** ~ to adjudge someone a bankrupt. **dar-se por** ~ to file a petition in bankruptcy. **massa falida** a bankrupt's or insolvent's estate or assets.

falimento s. m. failing, failure: 1. omission, mistake. 2. scarcity. 3. unsuccessfulness. 4. death, decease.

falir v. to fail: 1. break, be unable to pay, stop payment, go bankrupt, become insolvent, (sl.) bust, crash, crack. 2. lack, be destitute. 3. be unsuccessful. 4. become scarce, wane. 5. ruin.
a empresa faliu the enterprise failed, went bankrupt.

falite s. f. (med.) phallitis.

falível adj. m. + f. (pl. **-íveis**) fallible, unreliable, liable to err, faulty. ‖ **falivelmente** adv. fallibly.

falo s. m. phallus.

falqueador s. m. person who roughhews or squares timber.

falque(j)ar v. 1. to ax, square, chip or roughhew wood. 2. to wedge up, fasten with wedges.

falquejo s. m. roughhewing, squaring of timber, chipping of wood.

falqueta s. f. jump shot (at billiards).

falripas s. f. pl. thin and scarce hair (on the head).

falsa s. f. (mus.) 1. dissonance, discord, disharmony. 2. false note or tune.

falsa-acácia s. f. (pl. **falsas-acácias**) locust tree, red locust.

falsa-braga s. f. (pl. **falsas-bragas**) 1. bastion, outer bulwark. 2. barbican. 3. counterbreastwork.

falsa-camomila s. f. (pl. **falsas-camomilas**) field camomile.

falsa-ervilha s. f. (pl. **falsas-ervilhas**) bush vetch.

falsa-posição s. f. (arith.) false position.
regra de ~ the rule of the false position.

falsa-quina s. f. (pl. **falsas-quinas**) (bot.) copalche.

falsar v. 1. to falsify, adulterate, counterfeit. 2. to deceive, cheat. 3. to shortweight, shortmeasure. 4. to frustrate, thwart. 5. to break, split, crack. 6. to tell lies, lie. 7. to begin to split, break or go to ruin. 8. to begin to fall in or to slide.
~ **o pé** to take a false step.

falsa-rédea s. f. (pl. **falsas-rédeas**) double cavesson.

falsário s. m. 1. forger, falsifier, counterfeiter. 2. swindler. 3. perjurer, false witness. 4. person who breaks his word.
~ **de moedas** coiner, money forger.

falsa-verônica s. f. (pl. **falsas-verônicas**) (bot.) bastard speedwell.

falseamento s. m. 1. falsification, adulteration. 2. counterfeiting, forgery. 3. frustration, uselessness. 4. discord, disharmony. 5. ill success, failure. 6. adversity. 7. betrayal, treachery. 8. misrepresentation.

falsear v. 1. to falsify, adulterate. 2. to counterfeit, forge, distort. 3. to deceive, cheat, betray. 4. to frustrate, make useless. 5. to bring or sing out of tune, to untune. 6. to tell lies, lie. 7. to fail. 8. to err.

falseta s. f. (Braz., sl.) misrepresentation, deceit, hoax, bluff.

falsete s. m. falsetto: 1. the voice. 2. the singer.

falsetear v. to speak or sing falsetto.

falsidade s. f. 1. falseness, falsehood, mendacity, untruth(fulness), lie. 2. hypocrisy, hollowness. 3. deceit, cheat, fraud, imposture. 4. slander, defamation, calumny. 5. double-dealing, spuriousness, foulness. 6. wrongness, erroneousness. 7. unfaithfulness.
~ **me causa nojo** untruthfulness makes me sick, is my abhorrence.

falsídico adj. 1. lying, false, deceitful, mendacious. 2. distorted.

falsificação s. f. (pl. -ões) 1. falsification, counterfeit, fake(ment), pinchbeck, bogus. 2. adulteration. 3. forgery.

falsificado adj. 1. falsified, counterfeit, fake, false. 2. adulterate. 3. imitated. ‖ -**amente** adv. adulterately. **não** ~ straight, unsophisticated.

falsificador s. m. forger, falsifier, counterfeiter, adulterator, fake(r), tamperer, fabricator, false coiner. ‖ adj. falsifying.

falsificar v. 1. to falsify, counterfeit, forge, fake. 2. to adulterate, sophisticate. 3. to imitate, copy, plagiarize. 4. to feign.
~ **bebidas** to hocus drinks. ~ **moedas** to forge coins. ~ **vinho** to doctor wine. **a carta foi falsificada** the letter has been tampered with.

falsificável adj. m. + f. (pl. -**áveis**) falsifiable, adulterable.

falsinérveo adj. (bot.) pseudo-nervated.

falso adj. 1. false, untrue. 2. fraudulent, spurious, crooked, artificial, fictitious. 3. sham, simulate, adulterated, fake, feigned, bogus, pinchbeck, mock. 4. disloyal, unfaithful, treacherous, double-dealing, double-faced. 5. unfounded, baseless. 6. wrong, erroneous, inaccurate, faulty. 7. falsified, counterfeit, forged, sophisticated, make-believe, shoddy, distortional. 8. perfidious, deceitful, snaky, insincere, slippery, lying, snide. ‖ -**amente** adv. falsely, unfaithfully, etc.
alarma ~ false alarm. **chave** -**a** skeleton-key. **em** ~ in vain. **fundo** ~ double or false bottom. **juramento** ~ perjury. **moeda** -**a** false coin. **não há nada de mais** ~ there is nothing more untrue. **passo em** ~ a false step. **presságio** ~ false boding. **sentença** -**a** false verdict.

falso-alcaparreiro s. m. (pl. **falsos-alcaparreiros**) (bot.) bean caper.

falso-pinho s. m. (pl. **falsos-pinhos**) (bot.) Norway spruce.

falso-plátano s. m. (pl. **falsos-plátanos**) (bot.) sycamore.

falta s. f. 1. lack, want, need, destitution, scantiness. 2. absence. 3. privation, necessity. 4. shortage, deficiency, shortcoming, scarceness. 5. defect, flaw. 6. fault, mistake, error, slip, stumble, balk. 7. omission. 8. failing, failure. 9. sin, guilt. 10. blame. 11. default. 12. ullage. 13. (ftb.) charge, foul.
~ **de água** water famine. ~ **de civismo** incivism. ~ **de comparecimento** (aulas) (school) cut. ~ **de compreensão** incomprehension. ~ **de cumprimento do dever** dereliction. ~ **de desenvolvimento** stuntedness, non-development. ~ **de educação** rudeness, bad form. ~ **de entrega** non-delivery. ~ **de graça** gracelessness. ~ **de importação** non-importation. ~ **de jeito** gaucherie, cumbersomeness. ~ **de juízo** injudiciousness, witlessness. ~ **de lisura** unfairness. ~ **de motivo** groundlessness, causelessness. ~ **de pagamento** default, non-payment. ~ **de sorte** haplessness, bad luck. **acusar alguém de alguma** ~ to charge somebody with a fault. **com** ~ **de ar**

shortwinded. **cometer uma** ~ to commit a fault. **dar três** ~**s** to be absent or to be missing three times. **deixe uma notícia sem** ~**l** be sure you leave a message! **ele tem** ~ **de ar** he is short of breath. **eles falharam por** ~ **de dinheiro** they failed for want of money. **em** ~ lacking, out of stock. **estamos com** ~ **de farinha** we are short of flour. **estar em** ~ **com alguém** to feel guilty, to have a bad conscience with respect to s. o. **estar em** ~ **de uma carta** to be owing a letter. **ficar em** ~ to neglect one's duty. **isto não me faz** ~ I can make shift without it. **por** ~ **de provas** for want or in default of evidence. **sem** ~**l** 1. without fail, unfailingly. 2. blameless. **sentimos muito a** ~ **dele** we miss him very much. **sofrer** ~ **de** to starve for. **ter** ~ **de** to be deficient in. **uma** ~ **gritante** a howler. **uma** ~ **há muito sentida** a longfelt want.

faltar v. 1. to miss. 2. not to be existent. 3. to be absent, to be missing. 4. to be or run short of, lack. 5. to be wanting, deficient. 6. to be necessary, feel the scarcity or necessity of. 7. not to do, leave undone, not to fulfil, omit, neglect. 8. not to aid. 9. to fail, lose strength. 10. to die, decease. 11. to forfeit.
~ **à aula** to be missing (absent). ~ **à palavra** to break one's word, to go back on one's word, to back out of one's promise. ~ **à verdade** not to tell the truth. ~ **aos seus compromissos** not to keep one's engagements. ~ **às aulas para vadiar** to play truant. (U. S. A.) to cut (lessons). **era só o que faltava!** it wanted only that! **falta água** water fails, water is lacking. **falta-lhe coragem** he lacks courage. **falta-lhes instrução** they want knowledge. **falta-lhes pão** they go short of bread. **faltam cinco minutos para doze horas** it is five minutes to twelve. **faltam diversos livros** there are several books missing. **faltam-me palavras** words fail me. **não falta quem diga** there are some that say. **não faltava mais nada!** that's the limit!, that would just finish it up! **não lhes deixe** ~ **nada** let them want for nothing. **pouco lhe faltou para ser atropelado** he was very near being run over.

falto adj. 1. needy, necessitous, needful. 2. lacking, deficient, devoid, destitute. 3. effectless, failing. 4. minus.

faltoso s. m. delinquent. ‖ adj. 1. faulty, blamable, delinquent. 2. peccant. 3. truant.

falua s. f. (sailing) barge.

falucho s. m., **faluca** f. felucca: fast Mediterranean vessel.

falueiro s. m. master of a felucca, bargee. ‖ adj. of or relative to a felucca.

falupa s. f. (Braz.) a silkworm cocoon.

fálus s. m., sg. + pl. phallus.

fama s. f. 1. fame, renown, glory, honour. 2. report, rumour. 3. reputation, standing, prestige, name, repute, (sl.) kudos. 4. credit. 5. celebrity: famous person. 6. authority.
ele alcançou ~ **mundial** he gained a world-wide reputation. **dar** ~ to bring into fashion. **ganhar** ~ **com** to gain honour by. **gozar de má** ~ to be ill--famed, to be under a cloud. **grande** ~ famousness. **de má** ~ of bad repute, ill-famed. **ter fama** to flourish. **ela tem** ~ **de** she is famed for. **ele tem** ~ **de ser consciencioso** he has a character for conscientiousness.

famanado adj. m., **famanaz** m. + f. very famous, renowned, celebrated.

famelga s. m. + f. starveling, starver, lean person.

famelguita s. f. lean or undernourished child.

famélico adj. 1. hungry, famishing, starving. 2. greedy, ravenous.

famigerado, famígero adj. famous, renowned, celebrated.

família s. f. 1. family: a) father, mother and children; people in one house under one head; folks. b) household, house, home. c) tribe, clan, kin, kinsfolk, kindred, race, flesh. d) lineage. e) a group of related plants or animals forming a category. 2. (gram.) words with the same root. **carregar-se de** ~ to have a large family. **chefe de** ~ head of the family. **de boa** ~ wellborn. **jazigo de** ~ family vault. **nome de** ~ surname, family name. **pessoa de** ~ relation, relative. **questões de** ~ family affairs. **seio da** ~ family circle. **a Sagrada Família** the Holy Family. **segredo (escândalo) de** ~ the skeleton in the cupboard.

familial adj. m. + f. (pl. **-ais**) familial.

familiar s. m. 1. relative, kinsman, kinswoman, familiar. 2. member of a household. 3. servant. 4. fellow member of a religious order. 5. (hist.) bailiff of the Inquisition. ‖ adj. m. + f. 1. familiar, familial. 2. domestic, home(like). 3. vulgar, common, popular, colloquial. 4. well-known, intimate, close, near. 5. habitual. ‖ ~**mente** adv. familiarly, in a family way, freely, colloquially, etc. **círculo** ~ home circle. **estilo** ~ easy style. **expressão** ~ colloquialism. **não** ~ unconversant. **palavra** ~ household word. **trato** ~ familiarity.

familiaridade s. f. 1. familiarity, intimacy. 2. frankness. 3. confidence, reliance. 4. accustomedness. **agir com** ~ **indevida** to take liberties. **muita** ~ **é causa de menosprezo** too much familiarity breeds contempt.

familiarização s. f. (pl. **-ões**) domestication, familiarization.

familiarizado adj. well-acquainted, familiar with, conversant. **não** ~ unconversant.

familiarizar v. 1. to familiarize, make or become familiar. 2. to habituate, accustom. 3. to vulgarize. 4. to get acquainted with. 5. to domesticate. 6. to forgather. 7. ~**-se (com)** to make o. s. conversant or acquainted with, grow familiar with. **ele familiarizou-se com seu trabalho** he got the swing of his work. **ele não está familiarizado com este trabalho** he is strange to this work.

faminto adj. 1. hungry, starving, famishing, peckish, starveling. 2. craving, greedy, voracious. 3. eager, covetous. **estou** ~ I am starved (out). **de modo** ~ hungrily.

famoso adj. famous: 1. famed, renowned, celebrated, noted. 2. notable, remarkable, distinguished, eminent. 3. excellent, great, extraordinary. ‖ **-amente** adv. famously, etc.

famulagem s. f. (pl. **-ens**) servants or attendants collectively, retinue, suite.

famular v. 1. to act as a famulus. 2. ~**-se** to help each other.

famulatício adj. famulary, serving, attending.

famulato s. m. service and duties of a famulus.

famulatório adj. famulary.

famulento adj. 1. hungry, starving. 2. greedy, voracious.

fâmulo s. m. famulus: servant, attendant, assistant, follower.

fanal s. m. (pl. **-ais**) 1. fanal, beacon, a ship's light. 2. (fig.) guide. 3. (fig.) north, polestar. 4. torch, lighthouse.

fanar v. 1. to cut short, pare, curtail, trim, crop. 2. to wither, fade.

fanático s. m. 1. fanatic. 2. enthusiast, fan. 3. zealot, bigot. 4. fiend, energumen. ‖ adj. 1. fanatic(al). 2. very enthusiastic. 3. bigoted. 4. phrenetic, rabid.

‖ **fanaticamente** adv. fanatically, phrenetically, enthusiastically, rabidly, bigotedly. ~ **de futebol** football fiend. ~ **por cinema** film fan.

fanatismo s. m. 1. fanaticism. 2. excessive enthusiasm or zeal. 3. bigotry, zealotry. 4. passion, fervour.

fanatizador s. m. person who fanaticizes. ‖ adj. fanaticizing, fanatical.

fanatizar v. 1. to fanaticize: cause to become a fanatic. 2. to inspire enthusiasm or zeal. 3. ~**-se** to become a fanatic. 4. (fig.) to Jacobinize.

fanca s. f. (Braz.) drapery: cloth, fabric, linen, etc. for sale.

fancaria s. f. cloth trade, drapery. **obra de** ~ botchery.

fanchona s. f. (pop.) a lesbian.

fanchone s. m. truck: four-wheeled little wagon (used in shops, stores, factories).

fandangaçu s. m. (Braz.) popular noisy carnival ball.

fandango s. m. 1. fandango: a lively Spanish dance. 2. (Braz.): a) popular dance. b) revelry, amusement, frolic, merrymaking. c) noise, clamour, brawl.

fandanguear v. 1. to dance a fandango. 2. (Braz.) to take part in sprees, revelries.

fandangueiro s. m., **fandanguista** m. + f. fandango dancer or fan. ‖ adj. of, pertaining to or related to the fandango and its music.

faneca s. f. 1. (ichth.) bib, pout. 2. empty nut. 3. (pop.) piece or morsel of bread. ‖ adj. m. + f. 1. lean, meagre, scant. 2. dry. **ele veio ao pintar da** ~ (pop.) he came just in the nick of time, at the right moment.

faneco (I) s. m. 1. piece, slice, or morsel of bread. 2. piece, morsel. 3. (Port.) bread. **pintar o** ~ to amuse o. s. greatly, frolic, carry out practical jokes.

faneco (II) adj. 1. curtailed, cropped, trimmed. 2. empty (nut). 3. withered, faded.

fânega s. f. (also **fanga**) fanega.

fanerocarpo adj. phanerocarpous: with visible seeds or fruits.

faneróforo adj. (anat.) phanerophorous.

fanerogâmico adj. (bot.) phanerogamic, phanerogamous.

fanerógamo s. m. (bot.) phanerogam.

fanerozônios s. m. pl. (ichth.) Phanerozonia, an order of starfishes.

fanfa s. m. (pop.) boaster, braggart.

fanfã s. m. plant of the mallow (Malvaceae) family; (Hibiscus bifurcatus).

fanfarra s. f. 1. flourish of trumpets. 2. fanfare. 3. brass band.

fanfarrão s. m. (pl. **-ões**) 1. boaster, braggart, four-flusher, scaramouch, talker, windbag, blatherskite, blusterer. 2. pretender. 3. bully, rowdy, roisterer. ‖ adj. 1. boastful, bragging, gassy, windy. 2. roistering.

fanfarrear v. 1. to boast, brag, talk big, swagger. 2. to bully, browbeat, roister. 3. to show off.

fanfarrice s. f. (also **fanfarada, fanfarria, fanfarronada, fanfarronice**) 1. swagger(ing), boasting, brag(ging), blow, fanfaronade, rant, vaunt, gasconade, jactation, blatancy, windiness. 2. ostentation, pretension. 3. foppery, bluff.

fanfarronar v. (also **fanfarrear**) to fanfaronade, vapour, swash, ruffle.

fanfreluche s. f. cheap trinket, imitation jewel.

fanga s. f. fanega: measure for grain (**4 alqueires** about 1½ bushel). ~ **de terra** field requiring one fanega of seed grain.

fanhosear v. to snuffle: speak through the nose, have a nasal twang.

fanhoso adj. snuffling, nasal. ‖ **-amente** adv. snuffingly.

fanicar v. to chase after small business.
fanico s. m. 1. fragment, bit, morsel. 2. casual profit, small gain.
partir em ~s to go to pieces.
faniqueiro s. m. small trader, peddler, hawker.
faniquito s. m. (fam.) nervous fit, fainting fit.
fanisco s. m. lean and short person.
fanqueiro s. m. clothier, linen draper.
fantascópio s. m. phantascope.
fantasia s. f. 1. fantasy: a) imagination, fancy, unreality, moonshine, fancyfulness, imagery. b) caprice, extravagancy, whim. c) (mus.) fantasia. d) illusion, delusion, utopia. e) concept, mental image. f) vision. g) (art.) nonrepresentational painting, fancy painting or drawing. 2. (typogr.) fancy type. 3. (Braz.) fancy dress.
artigos de ~ fancy goods, doodads. **ela tem uma** ~ **bonita** she has a nice fancy dress. **ele deixa levar-se pela** ~ he lets himself carry away by his fancy.
fantasiador s. m. fantast, dreamer, visionary. ‖ adj. fantastic(al), imaginary.
fantasiar v. 1. to fantasy, fancy, imagine. 2. to indulge in dreams, be given to reveries. 3. (mus.) to play or sing fantasias. 4. ~-se to wear a fancy dress.
fantasioso adj. 1. fantastic(al), fanciful. 2. imaginary, visionary.
fantasista s. m. + f. 1. fantast, dreamer. 2. imaginative, creative person. ‖ adj. fantastic(al).
fantasma s. m. 1. phantasm: a) phantom. b) apparition, ghost, specter, haunt, spook, spirit. c) delusion, vision, imagination, fancy. 2. lean and weak person.
exorcismar um ~ to lay a ghost. **navio** ~ phantom ship.
fantasmagoria s. f. 1. phantasmagoria. 2. phantasm, phantom. 3. delusion.
fantasmagórico adj. phantasmagoric, phantasmagorial, spooky, wraithlike.
fantasmático adj. apparitional.
fantástico s. m. fantasticality, imagination, creation of the mind, reverie. ‖ adj. 1. fantastic, vagarious, imaginary, unreal. 2. quaint, queer, fancy. 3. incredible, made up, false. 4. capricious, freakish, fanciful. 5. weird, phantasmal. 6. chimeric, air-built. 7. baroque, grotesque, bizarre, arabesque, extravagant. 8. wild, tremendous. ‖ **fantasticamente** adv. fantastically, whimsically, capriciously, etc.
fantastiquice s. f. 1. fantasticality. 2. extravagance, eccentricity, oddness. 3. boasting, bragging. 4. flightiness.
fantil adj. m. + f. (pl. -is) thoroughbred (horse).
fantochada s. f. 1. puppetry. 2. puppet show. 3. puppets. 4. (fig.) blunder, ridiculousness.
fantoche s. m. puppet: 1. marionette, small doll. 2. (fig.) pawn, dummy, tool.
governo ~ puppet government.
faquear v. 1. (also **esfaquear**) to stab, knife. 2. (Braz., sl.) to ask for money, borrow.
faqueiro s. m. 1. case for knives, forks and spoons. 2. knife box. 3. knifesmith.
faquinha s. f. 1. diminutive of **faca**: little knife. 2. m. (Braz.) worker who cuts whale meat into smaller pieces.
faquir s. m. fakir, fakeer.
faquirismo s. m. fakirism.
faquista s. m. + f. cutthroat, murderer, ruffian.
farad s. m. farad: unit of electrical capacity.
farádico adj. faradic.
faradismo s. m., **faradização** f. (pl. -ões) (med.) faradism, faradization.
faradizar v. (med.) to faradize.

farândola s. f. 1. farandole: lively dance, of Provençal origin. 2. (also **farandolagem**, pl. -ens): a) rag, tatter. b) gang of vagrants, rags.
farandolar v. to dance the farandole.
faraó s. m. 1. (hist.) Pharaoh. 2. (cards) faro.
faraônico adj. Pharaonic.
farar v. to seek, search, (after, for), (in order to steal).
farauta s. m. old ewe.
faraute s. m. 1. interpreter. 2. guide. 3. (fig.) meddler.
farcino s. m. (vet.) 1. cattle or bovine farcy. 2. tropical actinomycosis.
farda s. f. 1. uniform, regimentals, military dress. 2. livery, garb, service dress.
despir a ~ to retire from military service. **enlamear a** ~ to disgrace the colours. **tecido para** ~s **militares** army cloth.
fardado adj. uniformed, in uniform.
fardagem s. f. (pl. -ens) (also **fardelagem**) 1. baggage, luggage, cargo. 2. a lot of packages or bundles. 3. clothing. 4. rags.
fardalhão s. m. (pl. -ões) showy uniform.
fardamenta s. f., **fardamento** m. (Braz.) uniform: 1. full military dress. 2. distinctive garb, dress or livery (club, school, servants).
fardão s. m. (pl. -ões) (Braz.) 1. pompous uniform. 2. full vestments of the members of the Academy of Letters.
fardar v. 1. to uniform, equip with a uniform. 2. to put on a uniform.
fardel s. m. (pl. -éis) 1. luncheon package, food parcel. 2. knapsack, bundle, truss. 3. haversack. 4. provisions. 5. prog.
fardeta s. f. (mil.) undress, fatigue dress.
fardete s. m. small bale, little bundle, package.
fardo s. m. 1. bale, bunch, bundle, truss, pack, package (plate C 16). 2. load, burden (also fig.), infliction. 3. charge, freight.
~ **de algodão** cotton bale. ~ **de lã** wool-pack. ~s **volumosos** bulky packages. **fazer um** ~ to bale or package. **o** ~ **dos anos** the burden of the years.
fardola s. m. (Braz., pop.) pedant, meddler.
farejar v. 1. to scent: a) smell out. b) trace, track down, wind, follow the scent (game). c) suspect, follow a clue. 2. to sniff, snuffle (after, for), search or find out, discover.
ele farejou algo he got wind of something.
farejo s. m. 1. scent(ing), smell(ing). 2. (fig.) inkling, clue, suspicion.
faráceo adj. 1. branny, like bran. 2. farinaceous, furfuraceous.
farelada s. f. 1. portion of bran. 2. swill of bran and water, bran mash.
farelagem s. f. (pl. -ens) 1. quantity of bran. 2. insignificancy, trifle.
farelento adj. branny: full of (or rich in) bran, mealy.
farelhão s. m. (pl. -ões) 1. little promontory or cape. 2. reef, cliff.
farelice s. f. (also **fanfarrice**) 1. swaggering, boasting, bragging. 2. ostentation, pretension. 3. foppery, bluff.
farelo s. m. 1. bran, pollard. 2. wood meal, wood flour. 3. insignificancy, bagatelle, trifle.
poupar o ~ **e estragar a farinha** penny-wise and pound-foolish.
farelório s. m. 1. trifle, odds and ends, trash. 2. twaddle, prattle, idle talk.
fáretra s. f. quiver.
farfalha s. f. 1. rustle, murmur, sough. 2. parings, filings, limature. 3. (fig.) trifles, baubles.
farfalhada s. f. (also **farfalharia, farfalheira**) 1. rustle, murmur, sough. 2. twaddle, idle talk, prattle. 3. boasting, bragging, ostentation. 4. loquacity.

farfalhador s. m. (also farfalhão, f. farfalhona) boaster, braggart, chatterer.
farfalhante adj. m. + f. 1. boastful, bragging, ostentatious. 2. rustling, murmuring.
farfalhar v. 1. to boast, brag, show off. 2. to speak at random, fudge, talk idly, prattle. 3. to rustle.
farfalheiro adj. 1. showy, ostentatious. 2. talkative, noisy.
farfalhento adj. 1. boastful, braggart, ostentatious. 2. talkative, verbose.
farfalhice, farfância s. f. 1. swaggering, boasting. 2. pompous ostentation.
farfalho s. m. 1. boast(ing), brag(ging). 2. rustle. 3. prattle, idle talk.
farfalhoso, farfalhudo adj. 1. showy, ostentatious. 2. gaudy, flashy. 3. bombastic, ranting. 4. conceited, vainglorious.
farfante s. m. + f. (also fanfarrão m.) 1. boaster, braggart. 2. impostor, pretender. 3. bully, rowdy.
fárfara s. f. (bot.) coltsfoot.
farfúgio s. m. leopard plant.
farináceo adj. farinaceous: yielding flour, mealy, farinose.
farinar v. to reduce to flour, triturate.
faringe s. f. (anat.) pharynx.
faríngeo adj. pharyng(e)al.
faringógnatos s. m. pl. (ichth.) Pharyngognathi: a division of teleost fishes.
faringite s. f. (med.) pharyngitis.
faringologia s. f. (anat.) pharyngology.
farinha s. f. 1. flour. 2. meal. 3. farina. 4. breadstuff. ~ de arroz rice flour. ~ de aveia oatmeal. ~ de centeio rye flour. ~ de cevada barley meal. ~ de linhaça linseed meal. ~ de madeira wood meal. ~ de mandioca cassava, manioc flour. ~ de milho maize flour, (U. S. A.) Indian meal. ~ de ossos bone meal, bone dust. ~ de trigo wheat flour. ~ grosseira grout. ~ integral whole meal. ~ láctea dried milk. ainda tem muita ~ que comer that will be many a long day to come. como ~ abundantly, much. não fazem boa ~ they cannot agree. ser ~ do mesmo saco birds of a feather flock together. tirar ~ com alguém (Braz.) to provoke a quarrel, demand satisfaction. vender ~ (Braz.) to walk with one's shirt-tails showing.
farinhada s. f. (Braz.) manufacture of manioc flour.
farinha-d'água s. f. (pl. farinhas-d'água) (N. Braz.) flour made of fermented manioc.
farinha-do-reino s. f. (pl. farinhas-do-reino) wheat flour.
farinha-queimada s. f. Brazilian folk dance.
farinha-seca s. f. (pl. farinhas-secas) popular designation of several tropical shrubs and trees of the families Leguminosae, Sapindaceae and Ochnaceae.
farinheira s. f. 1. woman who sells meal or flour. 2. (Braz.) flour pan, mealpot.
farinheiro s. m. flour dealer, meal merchant. ‖ adj. farinaceous, floury, mealy, starchy.
farinhento, farinhoso adj. farinaceous, mealy, floury, farinose.
farinhudo adj. (usually with respect to the pulp or meat of certain fruits) farinaceous, mealy, floury.
farisaico adj. Pharisaic(al): 1. of or pertaining to the Pharisees. 2. (fig.) hypocritical, self-righteous.
farisaísmo s. m. 1. Pharisaism: the doctrines and ceremonies of the Pharisees. 2. pharisaism: pharisaicalness, hyprocrisy.
fariscar v. = farejar.
farisco s. m. = farejo.
fariseu s. m. 1. (hist.) Pharisee: member of a Jewish sect. 2. (fig.) pharisee: hypocrite.
farmacêutico s. m. pharmaceutist, pharmacist, apothecary, druggist, chemist. ‖ adj. pharmaceutic(al).

farmácia s. f. pharmacy: 1. pharmaceutics, art and practice of preparing and storing drugs. 2. drugstore, apothecary's or chemist's shop. relativo a ~ pharmic.
farmacodinâmica s. f. pharmacodynamics.
farmacognosia s. f. pharmacognosy.
farmacografia s. f. pharmacography.
farmacográfico adj. pharmacographic.
farmacolando s. m. student who takes a pharmacist's degree.
farmacolita s. f. (min.) pharmacolite.
farmacologia s. f. pharmacology.
farmacológico adj. pharmacologic(al).
farmacologista s. m. + f. pharmacologist.
farmacopéia s. f. pharmacopoeia: 1. book of pharmacological standards. 2. collection of basic medicinal prescriptions. 3. dispensary. 4. materia medica. 5. stock of basic drugs.
farmacopola s. m. (joc.) pillmonger, charlatan, quack.
farmacotecnia s. f. pharmacotechnics, pharmacotechnique.
farmacotécnico adj. pharmacotechnic(al).
farnel s. m. (pl. -éis) = fardel.
farnesia s. f. (obs. form of frenesia) frenzy, rage, raving, madness.
farnesim s. m. (pop.) frenzy, rage.
faro s. m. 1. scent: a) odour. b) sense of smell(ing), (fig.) nose. 2. sagacity, flair. 3. (fig.) trail, wind, clue, vestige, sign. 4. (naut.) beacon, lighthouse, pharos. ele tem um ~ para isso he has a snout or nose for it. a matilha seguiu pelo ~ the pack followed the scent. tomar o ~ de alguma coisa to smell a rat, to get an inkling.
farofa s. f. 1. manioc flour toasted in butter or olive oil (sometimes mixed with meat or eggs). 2. boast, swagger, pretension. 3. trifle, trash. 4. powdered sugar. 5. (Braz.) chitchat, empty talk.
farofada s. f. = fanfarrice.
farofeiro s. m. (Braz.) 1. boaster, braggart. 2. pretender. 3. bully, rowdy. ‖ adj. boastful, bragging.
farofento adj. (Braz.) boastful, vainglorious, ostentatious.
farófia s. f. 1. meringue, cream puff. 2. trifle, worthless matter. 3. boast, bragging, ostentation.
farol s. m. (pl. -óis) 1. lighthouse, beacon, pharos, seamark, warning light (plates C 19, P 16). 2. searchlight. 3. (mot.) headlight (plates B 15, M 12, V 3). 4. lantern (plate L 2). 5. (fig.): a) light, luminary. b) guide, direction. c) (Braz.) show, ostentation, brag(ging), buncombe, frothiness, claptrap. 6. individual paid in order to make bids at auctions. 7. a ring with an exceedingly big brilliant. ~ auxiliar (mot.) spotlight (plate V 3). ~ de bombordo port light. ~ de estibordo starboard light. ~ de sinais signal lantern. ~ flutuante lightship. ~ pisca-pisca, ~ intermitente blinker, flashing beacon. ~ verde green light. ~ vermelho stop light. abaixar os faróis (mot.) to dim the headlights, to switch on the dim lights.
farolagem s. f. (Braz.) = fanfarrice.
faroleiro (I) s. m. lighthouse keeper.
faroleiro (II) s. m. (Braz., sl.) braggart, boaster, bladder, squirt, prancer, claptrap.
farolete s. m. (Braz.) 1. pocket lamp. 2. (mot.): a) rear light, taillight. b) small light on mudguard. c) spot lamp.
farolice s. f. prattle, idle talk.
farolim s. m. (pl. -ins) small lighthouse, beacon.
farpa s. f. 1. fluke: barbed head of an arrow, lance, harpoon, etc. (plate A 2). 2. beard, barb, hook.

3. banderilla (bullfighting). 4. tear, rent (in cloth). 5. splinter (of wood).
~ **do anzol** barb of a fishing hook.
farpado adj. barbed, pronged, bearded.
arame ~ barbed wire.
farpante adj. m. + f. 1. stinging, stingy. 2. splintering, tearing. 3. dilacerating.
farpão s. m. (pl. **-ões**) 1. harpoon. 2. pike, javelin. 3. (barbed) hook, barb, prong. 4. (fig.) painful blow, shock. 5. aggression. 6. (Port.) rent, tear.
farpar v. 1. to barb, form into barbs. 2. to tear into pieces, rend. 3. = **farpear**.
o vento farpou as velas the wind tore the sails asunder.
farpear v. 1. to wound with a fluke. 2. to stick banderillas into a bull's neck.
farpela s. f. 1. (coll.) clothes, (sl.) togs. 2. hook (of a crochet needle).
farra s. f. 1. (ichth.) lavaret, whitefish. 2. (Braz.) carousal, binge, spree, bust, bum, bender.
fazer uma ~ to go on a spree. **fizemos uma** ~ we were on the spree.
farracho s. m. (Braz.) a kind of cudgel (to stun or kill fishes).
farrafaiado s. m. (Braz.) a natural thinning out of the trees in a forest.
farragem s. f. (pl. **-ens**) meddley, hodgepodge, trash, lumber, farrago.
farrambamba s. f. (Braz.) 1. boast, bragging. 2. vanity, conceit. 3. stir, fuss, bustle. 4. ostentation, show.
farrancho s. m. (pop.) 1. group of pilgrims. 2. picnickers.
farrapada s. f. 1. heap of rags or tatters. 2. (Braz., hist.) party of the **farrapos**, republicans of Rio Grande do Sul, in 1835.
farrapagem s. f. (pl. **-ens**) (also **farraparia**) a heap or lot of rags.
farrapão s. m. (pl. **-ões**) (f. **farrapona**) 1. tatterdemalion, ragamuffin. 2. rag, tatter, trash.
farrapeira s. f. ragpicker (woman), female rag dealer.
farrapeiro s. m. rag dealer, ragseller.
farrapo s. m. 1. rag, shred, clout, junk, frazzle. 2. rags, tatter; worn-out, tattered clothing; dud. 3. shabby fellow, scamp, ragamuffin. 4. waste, remnants, refuse, rubbish. 5. (Braz., hist.) member of the republican party of Rio Grande do Sul (1835).
farrear v. to go on a spree (or on the loose, racket); (U. S. A.) to go on the bat.
fárreo s. m. wheat cake. ‖ adj. wheaten.
farricoco s. m. (Port.) 1. pallbearer. 2. hooded lay brother who accompanies a penitentiary procession.
farripas s. f. pl. thin and scarce hair (on the head).
farrista s. m. + f. carouser, reveller, gadabout, one who often goes on a spree.
farro s. m. 1. wheat cake. 2. barley water.
farroma s. m. braggart, boaster, swaggerer.
farromba s. f. (sl.) swagger(ing), brag(ging).
farrombeiro s. m. (Braz., also **farromeiro**) braggart, boaster. ‖ adj. boastful, talking big, vainglorious.
farromear v. 1. to boast, brag, vaunt. 2. to show off.
farronca s. m. + f. bravado, ostentation, boasting.
farroupa, farroupilha s. m. + f. 1. ragamuffin, tatterdemalion. 2. scamp, rascal, wretch.
farroupo s. m. farrow, young pig.
farruma s. f. = **fanfarrice**.
farrusca s. f. 1. mask, disguise. 2. old, rusty sword. 3. dark stain, blot, smut.
farrusco adj. 1. dirty, smutty, sooty. 2. dark, black.
farsa s. f. 1. farce, burlesque, burletta, satirical composition or play. 2. buffoonery, joke, jest, drollery, lark.

farsada s. f. 1. farce. 2. farcicality, buffoonery, drollery, foolery, mockery, ridiculous action.
farsalhão s. m. (pl. **-ões**) elaborate but worthless farce.
farsante s. m. + f. 1. buffoon, farcist, trickster. 2. impostor.
farsantear v. 1. to play farces or tricks, play the buffoon. 2. to joke, jest.
farsilhão s. m. (pl. **-ões**) tongue of a buckle.
farsista s. m. + f. 1. buffon, farcist. 2. clown, jack-pudding, (hist.) pickle-herring. 3. trickster, impostor. ‖ adj. farcical, ludicrous.
farsola s. m. + f. 1. buffoon, clown. 2. boaster, braggart.
farsolar v. 1. to joke, jest. 2. to boast, brag, vaunt.
farsolice s. f. 1. boast(ing), brag(ging). 2. joke, jest.
fartação s. f. (pl. **-ões**) 1. satiation, satiety. 2. ful(l)ness. 3. overfeeding, repletion.
tomar uma ~ to fill one's belly.
fartadela s. f. (pop.) 1. satiety, satiation. 2. repletion, bellyful, excessive eating or drinking.
fartar v. 1. to satiate, saturate, (over-)cloy, glut, fill the belly, satisfy one's hunger or thirst. 2. to sate, surfeit, cram, stuff. 3. to cause troubles, annoy. 4. to tire, wear out. 5. ~-**se** to become annoyed, sick of or weary. 6. to heap up. 7. to be sufficient, abound.
comer até ~-**se** to eat one's fill. **eles** ~**am sua vingança** they took revenge. **suas brincadeiras absurdas fartam a gente** his silly jokes are annoying to everybody.
fartável adj. m. + f. (pl. **-áveis**) 1. satiable. 2. satisfying. 3. enough, abounding.
farte, farto s. m. (also **fartalejo**) almond cake.
farto adj. 1. satiated, full, fed, quenched (thirst). 2. satisfied. 3. sated (with), crammed, glutted. 4. well-fed, fat. 5. abundant, bounteous, plenty, plenteous, plentiful, replete, opulent. 6. tired, weary, disgusted, sick (of). 7. extensive. 8. liberal, generous. ‖ -**amente** adv. fully, richly, etc.
~ **de** fed up with. **estou** ~ **disto** I have had enough of it. **já estou** ~ **de esperar** I am sick of waiting. **ele levou uma vida -a em dificuldades** he led a life full of difficulties.
fartum s. m. rancid smell, stench.
fartura s. f. 1. abundance, wealth, profusion, plenty. 2. fullness, repletion, surfeit, satiation. 3. affluence, shower.
fas s. m. right, just or righteous action.
por ~ **e por nefas** right or wrong, in any case, by hook or by crook.
fascal s. m. (pl. **-ais**) rick, pile of sheaves of corn.
fasces s. m. pl. (Roman hist.) fasces.
fasciação s. f. (pl. **-ões**) (bot.) fasciation.
fasciado adj. fasciated.
fasciculado adj. fasciculate(d), fascicular.
fascicular adj. m. + f. fascicular.
fascículo s. m. fascicle: 1. fascicule. 2. small bundle, cluster. 3. (bot.) glomerule. 4. fasciculus: division of a book issued in sections.
aparecer em ~**s** to be issued in sections (book).
fascinação s. f. (pl. **-ões**) 1. fascination, captivation, •charm(ingness). 2. dazzle, enchantment, spell. 3. allure(ment), alluringness. 4. witching, witchcraft, witchery.
fascinado adj. fascinated, spellbound, entranced, captive, enamoured.
fascinador s. m. 1. charmer, enchanter. 2. fascinating person, fascinator, captivator. ‖ adj. 1. fascinating. 2. charming, bewitching. ‖ ~**amente** adv. fascinatingly, etc.
fascinante adj. m. + f. 1. charming, enchanting. 2. fascinating, prepossessing, captivating, catching. 3.

bewitching, entrancing. 4. alluring, lovely. ‖ ~mente adv. fascinatingly, charmingly.

orador ~ spellbinder.

fascinar v. to fascinate: 1. captivate, attract. 2. allure, entice. 3. enchant, becharm, (be)witch, ensorcel, bedevil. 4. grip, catch. 5. ensnare.

ele fascinou os ouvintes he held the audience. **ele estava fascinado pela beleza da paisagem** he was spellbound by the beauty of the landscape. **este problema fascinou-me** this problem caught my fancy.

fascínio s. m. 1. fascination, charm. 2. enchantment, spell. 3. evil eye.

estão sob seu ~ they are under his spell.

fascíola s. f. (zool.) fluke worm, fasciola.

fasciolária s.- f. (zool.) fasciolaria: a genus of large marine snails.

fasciolídeos s. m. pl. (zool.) Fasciolidae, a family of platyhelminthic worms.

fascismo s. m. Fascism, fascism.

fascista s. m. + f. Fascist, fascist, Black Shirt. ‖ adj. Fascist, fascist(ic).

fase s. f. phase, phasis: 1. (also astr.) a) state of change or development. b) aspect. c) period. 2. side, angle or aspect of a question, situation, etc. 3. (biol., chem., phys.) definite stage in the development of cells, matter, motion, etc. 4. (med.) stadium.

~ **adiantada** (electr.) leading phase. ~ **neutra** (electr.) neutral leg. ~ **retardada** (electr.) lagging phase. **de ou relativo à** ~ phasic. **divisor de** ~ (electr.) phase splitter. **entrar na última** ~ to enter upon the last phase. **na** ~ **de crescimento** in the course of growing. **transformador de** ~s (electr.) phase transformer.

faseolar adj. m. + f. bean-shaped.

faseolina s. f. (biochem.) phaseolin.

fasianídeos s. m. pl. (ornith.) Phasianidae, the pheasant family.

fasímetro s. m. (electr.) phasemeter, power factor indicator.

fasmóide s. m. insect of the family Phasmatidae.

fasquia s. f. 1. lath, narrow strip of wood, batten. 2. wood splinter.

fasquiar v. 1. to lath, board. 2. to saw into narrow strips of wood. 3. to lattice.

fastidioso adj. 1. tedious, wearisome, troublesome, tiresome. 2. fastidious, meticulous, critical. ‖ -amente adv. 1. fastidiously, tediously, wearifully. 2. disdainfully, disgustingly. 3. fulsomely.

fastigiado adj. (bot.) fastigiate(d).

fastígio s. m. 1. apex, summit, top. 2. high position, eminence. 3. fastigiate form of a tree. 4. (Roman hist.) acroterium. 5. (archit.) frontal.

fastigioso adj. fastigious.

fastio s. m. 1. lack of appetite, fulsomeness. 2. disgust, distaste, disrelish. 3. aversion, dislike, loathing. 4. fastidiousness.

fasto s. m. 1. pomp, show, ostentation. 2. pride, vanity. ‖ adj. prosperous, happy, lucky.

fastos s. m. pl. 1. (Roman hist.) fasti. 2. (fig.) annals, chronicles.

fast(u)oso s. m. fastidious person, indulger in luxury. ‖ adj. 1. pompous, showy, proud. 2. arrogant.

fataça s. f. (ichth.) striped mullet.

fatacaz s. m. large piece or slice (bread, cheese, etc.).

fatagear v. to rummage for, poke into, turn inside out (suits of clothes, pockets, etc.).

fatal adj. m. + f. (pl. -ais) fatal: 1. destructive, ruinous, pernicious, baleful. 2. deadly, mortal. 3. portentous, ominous. 4. fateful. 5. inevitable. 6.

harmful. ‖ ~mente adv. fatally, destructively, ruinously.

ele lhe deu o golpe ~ he gave him the fatal blow. **sua vida tomou o seu curso** ~ his life took its inevitable course. **ela sofreu um acidente** ~ she suffered a deadly accident. **a hora** ~ the dying hour.

fatalidade s. f. fatality: 1. destiny, fate. 2. misfortune, disaster. 3. inevitableness. 4. fatefulness.

por ~ **viajou neste trem** unfortunately he travelled in this train.

fatalismo s. m. fatalism: doctrine of the predetermination and inevitableness of fate.

fatalista s. m. + f. fatalist, predestinatarian. ‖ adj. fatalistic(al).

de modo ~ fatalistically.

fateiro (I) s. m. tripeman, tripe dealer.

fateiro (II) adj. 1. of or relative to clothes. 2. fit for keeping clothes.

fateixa s. f. 1. grapnel: a) small anchor. b) grappling iron or grappling hook. c) drag hook, grab. 2. (Braz.) stone used as an anchor. 3. meat-hook.

~ **de rocegar** drag.

fateixar v. to grapple: seize with a grapnel, drag.

fatejar v. 1. = **fateixar.** 2. (Braz.) to tidy up, repair, or patch clothes.

fateusim s. f. (civil law) emphyteusis. ‖ adj. emphyteutic.

fatia s. f. 1. slice, chop, chip, piece. 2. cantle, section.

~ **de carne** steak, cutlet. ~ **grossa** hunch. ~ **pequena** collop. ~ **torrada** toast. **uma** ~ **de pão com manteiga** a piece of bread and butter.

fatia-de-parida, fatia-dourada s. f. (pl. **fatias-de-parida, fatias-douradas**) (also **rabanada**) fritter: slice of roll, soaked in milk and fried in eggs beaten up with sugar.

fatiar v. to slice, cut in rashers.

fatídico adj. fatidic(al), fateful, weird, prophetic(al), ominous, portentous, fatal. ‖ **fatidicamente** adv. fatidically, prophetically, weirdly, ominously, portentously, fatefully.

fatigado adj. worn-out, weary, run-down, tired.

muito ~ tired to death, quite done up.

fatigador s. m. tiresome or dull person, bore. ‖ adj. tiring, boring, fatiguing.

fatigamento s. m. 1. fatigue, weariness. 2. exhaustion, lassitude.

fatigante adj. m. + f. (also **fatigoso** m.) 1. fatiguing, wearisome, tiresome, wearing, tiring. 2. exhausting, hard, arduous. 3. tedious. 4. dreary. ‖ ~mente adv. fatiguingly, tediously, etc.

fatigar v. 1. to fatigue, wear out, exhaust, tire, tucker, flog. 2. to importune, pester, moider. 3. ~-se to tire out, weary, loath, moil, overdo, jade.

~ **a montaria** to override a horse. ~ **os animais** to overdrive the animals.

fatiloqüente adj. m. + f., **fatíloquo** m. (poet.) fatidic(al), prophetic(al), portentous.

fatímida s. m. + f. Fatimid, Fatimite: descendant of Mohammed's daughter Fatima. ‖ adj. Fatimid, Fatimite: 1. descended from Fatima. 2. of or pertaining to the period of the Fatimid dynasty.

fatiota s. f. (pop.) 1. dress, clothes, (fam.) duds. 2. old rags.

levantar a ~ to pack up one's traps.

fato (I) s. m. 1. suit of clothes, dress. 2. clothes, garments, vestment.

fato (II) s. m. 1. flock of sheep, drove of cattle. 2. entrails (of animals).

fato (III) s. m. fact: 1. factum, thing, deed, doing. 2. event, occurrence. 3. actuality, reality, truth.

de ~ as a matter of fact, in fact. **esteve lá de** ~? were you there indeed? **baseado em** ~s founded on facts. **o** ~ **da minha presença** the fact that I was present, the fact of my being present. **os** ~s **por ele alegados são duvidosos** his facts are doubtful. **ele está ao** ~ 1. he is aware of or informed of. 2. he is sure or certain of. **é um** ~ **consumado** it is a consummate fact. **ir às vias de** ~ to come to grips.

fator s. m. factor: 1. agent, managing clerk, foreman. 2. (math.) multiplicand, multiplier, measure. 3. component part, element. 4. (phys.) coefficient. ~ **comum** (math.) common divisor. ~ **constante** constant. ~ **de desvio** deflecting factor. ~ **Rh** (med.) Rh factor.

fatorar v. (math.) to factor.

fatorial s. m. (pl. **-ais**) (math.) factorial. **análise** ~ factor analysis.

fatual adj. m. + f. (pl. **-ais**) factual, actual.

fatuidade s. f. fatuity, fatuousness, dullness, foolishness, silliness, finicalness, puppyism.

fátuo adj. 1. fatuous, foolish, stupid, silly. 2. arrogant, conceited. 3. vain, vainglorious. 4. futile, ineffectual. 5. finical. 6. foppish, dandy(ish), puppyish. 7. dull. ‖ **fatuamente** adv. 1. fatuously, foolishly. 2. conceitedly, vainly.

fatura s. f. 1. invoice, bill, bill of parcels, voucher. 2. (also **feitura**): a) making, manufacture. b) workmanship. **conforme** ~ as invoiced, as per invoice. **fazer uma** ~ to (make out an) invoice.

faturar v. 1. (Braz.) to invoice, bill. 2. (Braz.) to include (merchandise) in an invoice. 3. (Braz., pop.) to derive (monetary) advantage from.

faturista s. m. + f. (Braz.) invoice clerk.

faucal adj. m. + f. (pl. **-ais**) faucal.

fauce s. f. 1. (anat.) fauces. 2. throat, gullet. 3. (bot.) inner perianth.

faúla s. f. = **fagulha.**

faular v. to emit or form sparks, scintillate.

faúlha s. f. 1. spark, sparkle, flash. 2. fine dust of flour. 3. bustler, busybody. 4. ~s pl. trifles, baubles.

faulhento adj. 1. emitting sparks, scintillating, sparkling. 2. raising dust (flour).

fauna s. f. fauna: animals and animal life of a region.

fauniano adj. faunal: 1. relating to a fauna. 2. of or pertaining to a fauna. **região -a** faunal region.

faunístico adj. faunal, faunistic(al), of or relative to a fauna.

fauno s. m. (myth.) faunus, faun.

fáunula s. f. (pal., zool.) faunule.

fausti(a)no adj. Faustian, of or pertaining to Faust or Faustus.

fausto s. m. luxury, ostentation, pomp, pageant(ry). ‖ adj. lucky, fortunate, auspicious.

faust(u)oso adj. pompous, magnificent, luxurious.

fautor s. m. (f. **fautriz**) fautor: 1. favourer, protector. 2. promoter, supporter, well-wisher. 3. patron. 4. framer, performer, realizer. ‖ adj. promotive, favouring, supporting. ~ **de guerra** warmonger, war agitator.

fautoria s. f. fautorship, abetment, favouring, promotion, aid.

fautorizar v. to favour, help, support, back, uphold.

fava s. f. 1. (bot.) broad bean. 2. its seeds. 3. swelling on the roof of the mouth (horse, cattle). **casca de** ~ pod of a bean. **vá às** ~s! go to hell (blazes), get you gone! **vá plantar** ~s! leave me alone! I'll see you further first! **são** ~s **contadas**

that's quite sure, I'm cocksure of it, there is no doubt about it. **ele paga as** ~s he is the scapegoat (or whipping boy).

fava-café, fava-coceira s. f. (pl. **favas-café, favas-coceiras**) (bot.) cowhage.

fava-da-índia s. f. (pl. **favas-da-índia**) (also **fava-de-cheiro**, pl. **favas-de-cheiro**, bot.) tanka bean.

fava-de-calabar s. f. (pl. **favas-de-calabar**) (bot.) Calabar bean.

fava-de-malaca s. f. (pl. **favas-de-malaca**) (bot.) Malacca bean, marking nut.

favado adj. (Braz.) unsuccessful.

faval s. m. (pl. **-ais**) field of broad beans, beanfield.

favar v. (Braz.) to fail, miscarry, meet with ill success.

favaria s. f. 1. = **faval.** 2. a lot of beans. 3. a lot of honeycombs.

favária s. f. (bot.) orpine.

faveira s. f. 1. bean plant. 2. popular designation of several plants of the family Leguminosae. 3. (bot.) holly, honey locust.

faveiro s. m. popular name of a few trees of the family Mimosaceae.

favela s. f. (Braz.) slum: quarter of primitive houses, usually on hills.

faveolado adj. faveolate, alveolate, honeycombed.

faviforme adj. m. + f. shaped like a honeycomb.

favila s. f. ashes, embers.

favo s. m. 1. honeycomb. 2. any similar object. 3. confection, sweet. 4. (med.) favus. ~ **de mel** honeycomb (plate A 11).

favonear v. 1. to favour, protect. 2. to back, uphold. 3. to authorize.

favônio s. m. zephyr, gentle breeze. ‖ adj. favonian.

favor s. m. favour: 1. regard, esteem. 2. interest, credit. 3. protection, assistance, support, help. 4. benefit, privilege, benefaction. 5. partiality, favouritism. 6. permission, authorization, consent. 7. sympathy, charm. 8. attention, courtesy, kindness, grace, boon, obligation, complaisance. 9. letter, card, communication. 10. pleasure. 11. behalf. 12. turn, accommodation. 13. blessing. **a** ~ **de** pro, for, in behalf of, on account of, to the credit of. **a** ~ **da correnteza** with the stream. **diga-me, por** ~ pray, tell me. **fale em** ~ **dele** put in a good word for him. **com o** ~ **da noite** favoured by night. **faça-me o** ~ do me the kindness. **posso pedir-lhe um** ~? may I ask a favour of you? **faça o** ~ **de ajudar-me** be kind enough to help me. **faça o** ~ **de informar-me** do me the favour of letting me know. **faça o** ~ **de sentar-se!** please, be seated! **fazer um** ~ to do a favour. **negar um** ~ to refuse a favour. **intercedi em seu** ~ I pleaded in his favour. **esperamos o** ~ **de uma breve resposta** we await the favour of an early reply. **recebi seu** ~ **de 10 do corrente** I have received your favour of the 10th inst. **saldo a seu** ~ balance in your favour. **ser a** ~ **de** to be in favour of. **tem muito a** ~ **disto** there is much to be said for it. **é um** ~ **retirar-se** I will thank you to go. **um** ~ **merece outro** one good turn deserves another.

favorável adj. m. + f. (pl. **-áveis**) favourable: 1. favouring, well-inclined, toward(ly), friendly. 2. advantageous, propitious. 3. helpful, benefic, suitable, opportune. 4. lucky, happy, fortunate. 5. prosperous. 6. accommodating. 7. (naut.) fair, free. ‖ **favoravelmente** adv. favourably, kindly, propitiously, etc. **o vento está** ~ the wind sits fair. **a sorte lhe é** ~ fortune smiles upon him. **ter opinião demasiadamente** ~ **sobre** to take too bright a view of. **trazer um negócio** ~ to bring grist to the mill. **em con-**

dições favoráveis on easy terms. **disposição** ~ propitiousness. **muito** ~ optimal.

favorecedor s. m. 1. favourer, fautor, protector, friend, furtherer, fosterer. 2. promoter, supporter, helper, sider. ‖ adj. favouring, promoting, beneficial.

favorecer v. to favour: 1. promote, help, aid, assist, further. 2. back, support, protect, sustain, encourage, side, foster, patronize. 3. point out the merits of, enhance. 4. collaborate, cooperate, corroborate. 5. speed, forward. 6. praise, exalt, endear, hold up. 7. oblige, do a favour. 8. advantage, benefit. 9. prosper. 10. flatter, honour. 11. friend, befriend. 12. **~-se** avail o. s. of, take advantage of, make use of, profit by.
ele tenta ~ **o seu irmão** he tries to play into his brother's hand. **eles favorecem os planos** they promote the plans. **o retrato a favorece** the portrait flatters her.

favorecido adj. 1. favoured, protected, supported. 2. (portrait) flattering. 3. fortunate.
~ **pela sorte** fortune-favoured. ~ **pela noite** favoured by night.

favorecimento s. m. aiding and abetting.
~ **de partidários políticos** spoil system.

favorita s. f. favourite, darling, pet, minion.

favoritismo s. m. favouritism, nepotism, preference.
~ **político** spoil system.

favorito s. m. favourite: 1. predilect person or thing. 2. fondling, pet. 3. protegé, minion. 4. (racing) probable winner. ‖ adj. favourite, beloved, preferred, pet, fond, great.

favoso adj. 1. alveolar, alveolate. 2. (med., vet.) seized with favus, scabious.

faxina (I) s. f. 1. (engin., mil.) fascine. 2. fag(g)ot, bundle of brushwood. 3. wood measure (about 60 kg). 4. (mil.) fatigue duty. 5. (Braz.) damage, defalcation. 6. (Braz.) pasture (with tall trees).
estar de ~ to be on fatigue.

faxina (II) s. m. (Braz.) soldier on fatigue duty.

faxinal s. m. (pl. **-ais**) (Braz.) field penetrating into the virgin forest.

faxinar v. 1. to bundle into fascines or faggots. 2. to provide or strengthen with fascines.

faxina-vermelha s. f. (pl. **faxinas-vermelhas**) akeake: sapindaceous tree (Dodonaea viscosa).

faxineiro s. m. (mil.) soldier on fatigue duty.

faz-de-conta s. m., sg. + pl. 1. fantasy, imagination. 2. (Braz., fam.) cuckold. ‖ adj. cuckoldly.

fazedor s. m. 1. factor, executer. 2. maker, doer.

fazedouro adj. that may or should be done.

fazenda s. f. 1. farm, (U. S. A.) ranch (plate A 4). 2. estate, property, homestead, holding. 3. farm building. 4. cultivated land. 5. public finances, treasury. 6. cloth, stuff, textile material. 7. goods, wares, merchandise. 8. (fig.) quality.
~ **de café** coffee plantation. **~s de lã** wool, wool(l)en cloth. ~ **pastoril** cattle farm. ~ **real** the king's revenue, exchequer. ~ **senhorial** barton. **boa ~ depressa se vende** please the eye and pick the purse. **conselho da** ~ the exchequer or treasury court. **ministério da** ~ treasury department. **ministro da** ~ minister of finance.

fazendão s. m. (Braz., sl.) stout woman.

fazendário adj. financial, fiscal, economic(al).

fazendeiro s. m. 1. farmer: a) cattleman. b) husbandman. c) planter, agriculturist, granger. 2. (Braz.) great landholder. 3. (bot.) French weed.
círculos de ~s the landed interest.

fazendista s. m. + f. finance expert.

fazendola, fazendinha s. f. small farm.

fazer v. 1. to do, make, create. 2. to form, fashion, mo(u)ld. 3. to construct, build, erect. 4. to manufacture, produce, fabricate. 5. to compose, assemble. 6. to write. 7. to realize, execute, perform. 8. to arrange, prepare. 9. to cook, bake. 10. to represent, act a part or role. 11. to regard, consider. 12. to say, pronounce, express. 13. to cause to exist or appear. 14. to reach, attain, get. 15. to pretend, simulate, seem. 16. to formulate, conceive, frame in one's mind. 17. to convert, change into. 18. to inspire, incite, stir up. 19. to adjust, fit, adapt. 20. to compute, calculate. 21. to give, bestow. 22. to attribute, ascribe. 23. to elevate, advance. 24. to convert into. 25. to interest, concern. 26. **~-se:** a) to establish o. s. b) to transform o. s. into. c) to dedicate o. s. to.
~ **adição** to add up. ~ **água** (naut.) to (spring a) leak. ~ **uma asneira** to blunder. ~ **baldeação** to change (trains). ~ **a barba no barbeiro** to get a shave at the barber's. ~ **um bolo** to make a cake. ~ **caça à raposa** to give chase to the fox. ~ **alguém cair** to give one a fall. ~ **a cama** to make the bed. ~ **uma caminhada** to go a way. ~ **caso** to esteem, value. ~ **cavalo de batalha de** to harp upon. ~ **centro** to centre, center. ~ **cera,** ~ **hora** to stall, dillydally, kill the time. ~ **a chamada** to call the roll. ~ **cócegas** to kittle. ~ **companhia a** to keep s. o. company. ~ **compressas quentes** to stupe. ~ **concorrência** to compete with. ~ **corar** to put to blush. ~ **a corte a** to dangle, woo. ~ **depressa** to make haste. ~ **o seu dever** to do one's duty. ~ **dieta** to diet. ~ **diferença ou distinção entre** to differentiate, discern between. ~ **um discurso** to make a speech. ~ **dormir** to put to sleep. ~ **economias** to retrench, economize. ~ **efeito** to operate. ~ **envergonhar** to put to shame. ~ **exame de consciência** to take stock of one's own conscience. ~ **uma expedição** to go on an expedition. ~ **extraordinário** to overwork. ~ **face ao inimigo** to face the enemy. ~ **um favor** to do a favour, do a kindness. ~ **festa(s) a alguém** to celebrate, welcome heartily. ~ **fiasco** to flunk. ~ **folia** to revel. ~ **força** to get up steam. ~ **gato e sapato de** to play horse with. ~ **gazeta às aulas** to play truant. ~ **greve** to (go on) strike. ~ **uma herança** to come in for an inheritance. ~ **justiça** to do justice. ~ **um laço** to tie in a bow. ~ **lugar** to make room. ~ **mal** to do harm, to hurt, wrong. ~ **maus negócios** to do badly. ~ **um negócio** to do a business. ~ **o papel de** to personate. ~ **novamente** to do again. ~ **parte de** to compose, constitute. ~ **um passeio** to have a walk. ~ **uma pausa** to rest. ~ **em pedaços** to pick to pieces, cut to pieces. ~ **uma pergunta** to make a question. ~ **planos** to lay plans. ~ **o mais possível** to do all one's ability. ~ **pouco de** to disparage, bob. ~ **às pressas** to patch, clap. ~ **progresso** to make headway. ~ **uma prova** to have a try. ~ **questão da sua dignidade** to stand on one's dignity. ~ **com que** 1. to do (act) as if. 2. to manage to, to succeed in. ~ **um requerimento** to file an application. ~ **saber** to let know, denounce. ~ **sensação** to cause sensation. ~ **sumir** to spirit away. ~ **de tolo** to make a fool of. ~ **um trabalho** to do a job. ~ **transfusão de sangue** to transfuse. ~ **um tratamento** to undergo a (medical) treatment. ~ **trocadilhos** to play on (or upon) words. ~ **uma viagem** to go on a journey. ~ **uma visita** to pay a visit. ~ **a vontade de alguém** to comply with someone's desire. ~ **zombaria de alguém** to mock a person. **~-se ao largo** to clear the land. **~-se ao mar** (naut.) to put to sea. **~-se passar por** to pretend to be. **~-se de rogado** (fig.) to hang back (hesitate). **~-se tarde** to grow late. **façam abrir as janelas** let the windows be opened. **ontem eu fiz vinte e cinco anos** I became 25 years

old yesterday. **não façais mais assim!** don't do it any more! **ele fez seu balanço** he cast his accounts. **eu faria bem em...** I had as well... **acho que você fez muito bem em** dizê-lo I think you did the right thing in saying that. **faz calor** it is warm. **fizemo-lo compreender à viva força** we pounded it into him. **faço-lhe concessão de tanto** I give you so much. **ela fez de conta que não me viu** she pretended or affected she didn't see me. **ele fez de conta que não a conhecia** he affected not to know her. **fiz de conta que não vi** I winked at it. **ele fez uma dama** (draughts) he crowned a man. **fez bom efeito** it told well. **o remédio não fez efeito** the medicine did not act. **faça-o entrar** have him in. **não se fazia de escritor famoso** he did not present himself as a famous writer. **ele faz um exame** he sits for an examination. **é este o homem que faz falta!** that is the man for me! **o que mais nos faz falta são bons técnicos** what we need most are good technicians. **você fez falta ontem na festa** we missed you at the party last night. **faz frio** it is cold. **ele fez o pião girar** he sent the top spinning. **estou fazendo horas até ir ao dentista** I am killing time before going to the dentist. **ele fez-me uma injustiça** he put me in the wrong. **ela fê-lo jurar** she put him on his oath. **fizeram a testemunha jurar** they tendered an oath to the witness. **a comida fez mal ao meu estômago** the food has upset me. **isto não faz mal** that won't hurt, it does not matter. **frutas verdes me fazem mal** unripe fruit does not agree with me. **você fez muito mal em dizer isso** you should never have said that. **não faz mal** never mind. **ela está fazendo sua maquilagem** she puts her make-up on. **isto não me faz nada** that does not concern me. **eles fazem negócio** they carry on business. **ele faz o papel de vilão** he figures as the villain. **ele fez um triste papel** he cut a sorry figure. **façamo-lo de pé!** let us walk it. **faça-o sem pensar muito!** do not think twice about doing that! **fizemos o que quisemos** we did pretty much as we liked. **faça como quiser** do as you like, have it your own way, take it or leave it. **você me faz rir** you amuse me, make me laugh. **fizeram o serviço juntos** they joined in the work. **fi-lo subir** I had him up. **ela me fez uma surpresa** she sprang a surprise on me. **faz tempo que não o vejo** I have not seen him for a long time. **faça uma tentativa** have a go at it! **ela fê-lo trabalhar** she put him to work. **a enfermeira fez as vezes do médico** the nurse acted as the doctor's substitute. **logo irei ~-lhe uma visita** I shall come and see you soon. **faça como se estivesse em casa** make yourself at home. **faça-o como deve ser** do it the proper way. **não faça aos outros o que não queres que te façam** do as you would be done by. **que faremos hoje?** what is the programme for today? **não faria isto se eu fosse você** I should not do that if I were you. **o hábito faz o monge** the dress proclaims the man. **isto não se faz** it is not seemly. **quanto tempo faz que você o viu?** how long is it since you saw him? **tanto faz!** that's all the same to me! **para mim tanto faz se ele vem ou não** I do not care whether he comes or not. **mandei fazê-lo** I got it done. **provavelmente vou fazê-lo** I am apt (or likely) to do it. **você mesmo é capaz de fazê-lo?** can you do it yourself? **você tem de fazê-lo** you have got do to it. **uma coisa é dizer, outra é ~** sooner said than done. **não há nada mais a ~** there is nothing you could do about it. **sem ter o que ~** to be at a loose end. **não sei o que ~** I am at my wit's end, I don't know which way to turn. **que hei de ~?** what am I to do? **do dizer ao ~ há muita coisa a ver** there's many a slip twixt the cup and the lip. **ele fez das tripas coração** he plucked up courage, he took heart. **o navio fez-se ao mar** the ship put out on the sea. **fi-lo eu mesmo** I did it myself.

fazível adj. m. + f. (pl. **-íveis**) feasible, practicable.

faz-tudo s. m., sg. + pl. handy man, factotum, jack-of-all-trades.

fé s. f. 1. faith, creed. 2. religion, persuasion, profession. 3. belief, trust, credit, conviction. 4. loyalty, fidelity, faithfulness. 5. confidence, reliance, dependence, dependability, fiance. 6. (rel.) the first of the three theological virtues (faith, hope, charity). 7. statement, assertion. 8. (fig.) divinity. 9. (law) notorial evidence, testimony.

~ cega, ~ de carvoeiro blind or implicit faith. **~ dos padrinhos** wavering faith. **dar ~ a** to give faith to. **de boa ~** in good faith, bona fide. **de ~ católica** of Catholic persuasion. **de má ~** in bad faith. **usar de má ~** to act perfidiously. **em ~ de que** in testimony whereof, in verification of which. **em ~ disto** in witness whereof. **estar na ~ de** to believe, suppose. **estou nesta ~** this is my opinion. **excesso de boa ~** overcredulity. **falta de ~** infidelity. **homem de boa ~** trustful man. **homem digno de ~** trustworthy man. **à minha ~** upon my honour. **pela minha ~** by my truth. **quebrar a ~** to break a contract of promise. **sem ~** unfaithful. **ter ~ em** to have faith in, put trust in a person.

fealdade s. f. 1. ugliness, deformity, unseemliness, ungracefulness; (U.S.A.) homeliness (face). 2. blemish. 3. indignity.

fearrão s. m. (pl. **-ões**) (f. **fearrona**) ugly person. || adj. ugly, (U.S.A.) homely.

febeu adj. Phoebean, of or relative to Phoebus, god of the sun and poetry.

febra s. f. 1. boneless and fatless meat, fibre. 2. (fig.) strength, power, energy.

febrão s. m. (pl. **-ões**) violent fever.

febre (I) s. f. 1. fever, temperature, pyrexia. 2. (fig.) excitement, agitation.

~ aftosa foot-and-mouth disease. **~ amarela** yellow fever, black vomit. **~ intermitente** intermittent fever. **~ ligeira** febricula. **~ palustre** malaria, paludal fever. **~ puerperal** milk fever. **~ recorrente** relapsing fever. **~ reumática** rheumatic fever. **~ tifóide** camp fever, gastric fever, typhoid. **atacado pela ~** ague-struck. **sem ~** feverless.

febre (II) s. m. underweight of a coin. || adj. underweight, wanting in legal weight (coin).

febre-de-caroço s. f. (pl. **febres-de-caroço**) (Braz., pop.) bubonic plague.

febrento s. m. person inclined to fever fits. || adj. feverish, excited.

febricitante adj. m. + f. 1. feverish, fever-sick, feverous, fevered. 2. exalted, excited.

febricitar v. to fever, be feverish.

febrícula s. f. slight fever, febricula.

febriculoso adj. feverish, feverous.

febrífugo s. m. febrifuge, antifebrile, antipyretic. || adj. febrifugal, febrifuge, antifebrile.

febril adj. m. + f. (pl. **-ris**) 1. febril, feverous, feverish, fevered, hectic, aguish, pyretic. 2. agitated, raving. || **~mente** adv. feverishly, aguishly.

febrilizar v. to become feverish.

febriologia s. f. (med.) treatise on fevers, pyretography.

febriológico adj. (med.) pyretologic.

fecal adj. m. + f. (pl. **-ais**) f(a)ecal, excremental, excrementitious.

matéria ~ excremental matter.

fecalóide adj. m. + f. fecaloid.

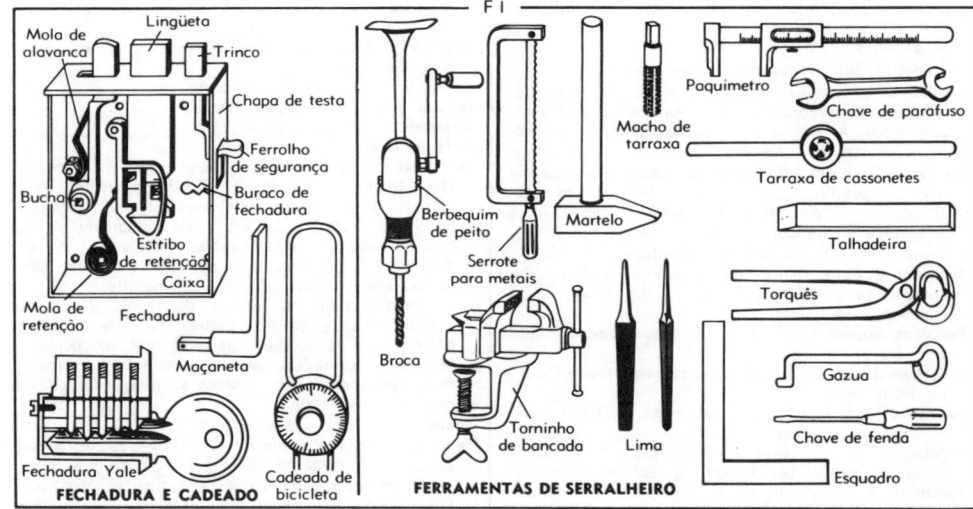

F I

Mola de alavanca — Lingüeta — Trinco — Chapa de testa — Ferrolho de segurança — Bucha — Buraco de fechadura — Estribo de retenção — Caixa — Mola de retenção — Fechadura — Maçaneta — Fechadura Yale — Cadeado de bicicleta

FECHADURA E CADEADO

Berbequim de peito — Serrote para metais — Broca — Martelo — Torninho de bancada — Lima — Paquímetro — Macho de tarraxa — Chave de parafuso — Tarraxa de cassonetes — Talhadeira — Torquês — Gazua — Chave de fenda — Esquadro

FERRAMENTAS DE SERRALHEIRO

fecha s. m. (Braz.) clamour, noise, disorder.
fecha-bodegas s. m., sg. + pl. (Braz., pop.) rowdy, brawler.
fechação s. f. (N. Braz.) roundup of cattle.
fechado s. m. (N. Braz.) dense thicket or wood. ‖ adj. 1. close(d), shut, enclosed, shut in, locked, unopened (plate Q). 2. secluded, hidden. 3. narrow, confined. 4. reserved, close-mouthed, stand-offish, self-contained. 5. strict, rigorous. 6. close-fisted, niggardly, tight. 7. (zool.) bisulcate. 8. bushy.
~ **com grade ou cerca de vime** watled. **circuito** ~ closed circuit. **ele é um homem** ~ he is a reticent man. **não** ~ unclosed. **noite -a** dark night. **à porta -a** in private. **ter alguma coisa -a na mão** (fig.) to have something at one's command.
fechadura s. f. lock (plates F 1, P 10).
~ **de mola** snap-lock. ~ **de segredo** puzzle-lock. ~ **de segurança** chubb-lock, safety-lock.
fecha-fecha s. m. (Braz.) hasty closing of shops at the outbreak of riots, street fights, etc.
fechamento s. m. 1. shutting or locking up. 2. closure, closing. 3. stopping, fastening. 4. (archit.) keystone, arch stone.
fechar v. 1. to close: a) shut, shut up. b) unite, join, link. c) close with a key, lock up. d) latch, bar (up), bolt. e) stop, stopper, plug up, bung. f) enclose, barrier in, hurdle, encompass, (em)bar, surround. g) finish, conclude, terminate. h) limit, restrict. i) cicatrize, heal. j) fill. k) agree, come to terms. l) collapse. m) box. n) fasten. o) seal. 2. to impede, hamper, obstruct. 3. (N. Braz.) to round up cattle in a corral. 4. ~-se: a) to close o. s. up or in. b) (mil.) to close ranks. c) to be reserved. d) to be tightfisted.
~ **com barro** to clay. ~ **a boca a alguém** to stop somebody's mouth, to silence s. o. ~ **nos braços** to inarm. ~ **uma carta** to seal a letter. ~ **com cerca** to fence off (or out). ~ **à chave** to lock (up), to key. ~ **as contas** to close an account. ~ **num curral** to corral. ~ **com o ferrolho** to bolt. ~ **com grade** to bar up. ~ **a mão** to clench one's fist. ~ **o negócio** to close or strike a bargain. ~ **o olho** to die. ~ **os olhos** 1. to shut the eyes. 2. (fig.) not to take notice of a thing. ~ **os ouvidos a** to refuse to listen to. ~ **a porta na cara de alguém** to slam the door in a person's face. ~ **no redil**

to cot. ~ **com solda** to solder up. ~ **a torneira** to turn off. ~ **com a tranca** to bar. ~ **violentamente** to fling to, clash, bang, slam. **ele fechou a cara para mim** he frowned at me. **ele fechou a porta** he clicked the door to. **ele fechou a porta atrás dela** he closed the door upon her. **ele fechou as mãos (para rezar)** he clasped his hands. **ele fechou um olho** he closed his eyes to it, he blinked a thing. **ele fechou-se em copas** he was reticent. **a fábrica foi fechada** the factory was shut. **isso se fecha com um botão** it fastens with a button. **a janela foi fechada** the window was shut down. **a janela não fecha** the window will not fasten. **as lojas ~am suas portas** the shops closed down. **feche bem os olhos** shut your eyes fast.
fecharia s. f. gunlock, breech mechanism.
fecho s. m. 1. bolt, latch, bar. 2. any device to shut or lock. 3. clasp, hasp. 4. fastening, fastener, clip (plates J 1, 3). 5. (archit.) closer, keystone (plate A 12). 6. conclusion, termination, closure. 7. seal. 8. ~**s** pl.: a) gunlock. b) clasp.
~ **da abóbada** arch stone of a vault. ~ **de correr** zipper, sliding fastener. ~ **de segredo** combination lock. ~ **hidráulico** water seal (plate E 10). **homem duro dos** ~**s** a hard-hearted man.
fecial s. m. (pl. -ais) (Roman hist.) pater patratus: member of the priestly board of fetiales.
fécio s. m. (N. Braz.) stench.
fécula s. f. 1. fecula, starch, farina. 2. lees, sediment. ~ **de batatas** potato flour.
fecularia s. f. (Braz.) starch factory.
feculência s. f. 1. feculence, feculency. 2. sediment, dregs.
feculento adj. (also **feculoso**) 1. feculent, fecal. 2. foul, turpid. 3. starchy.
feculóideo adj. starchy, amylaceous.
fecundação s. f. (pl. -ões) 1. (biol.) fecundation, fertilization, impregnation, insemination. 2. (bot.) fructification.
fecundado adj. impregnate(d).
fecundador s. m. fructifier, fecundator. ‖ adj. fructifying, fecundating.
fecundante adj. m. + f. fecundative, fecundatory, fructifying.
fecundar v. 1. (biol.) to fecundate, inseminate, impregnate, fertilize. 2. (bot.) to fructify. 3. (fig.)

to fertilize, develop, evolve, enrich. 4. (ichth.) to milt. 5. to tup (sheep).
~ **as artes** to foster the arts.
fecundativo adj. fecundative, fecundatory.
fecundidade, fecundez, fecúndia s. f. 1. fecundity, fertility. 2. pregnancy. 3. abundance, profusion, prolificacy. 4. fruitfulness, copiousness. 5. productivity. 6. creative power.
fecundo adj. 1. fecund, fertile. 2. conceptive, procreative. 3. prolific, productive, fruitful. 4. copious, abundant. 5. pregnant. 6. inventive, creative. ‖ **-amente** adv. copiously, fruitfully, etc.
fedegosa s. f. (bot.) stinking goosefoot.
fedegoso s. m. 1. (bot.) seaside heliotrope. 2. popular designation of several plants of the family Leguminosae. ‖ adj. fetid, stinking.
fedegoso-do-pará s. m. (pl. **fedegosos-do-pará**) (bot.) wild clary.
fedegoso-grande s. m. (pl. **fedegosos-grandes**) (Braz.) ringworm bush.
fedelhice s. f. 1. filthiness, dirtiness. 2. nasty habit or trick.
fedelho s. m. 1. (fam.) bantling, brat. 2. stripling, ninny. 3. cheeky boy or girl, greenhorn.
fedentina s. f. stench, stink, fetidness, malodorousness.
feder v. 1. to stink, reek, smell badly. 2. (fig.) to cause troubles, bore.
esta carne fede this meat stinks. **quem muito pede, muito fede** who asks too much is troublesome.
federação s. f. (pl. **-ões**) 1. federation, federacy, union, alliance. 2. confederation.
federado s. m. federal(ist). ‖ adj. federate.
federal s. m. (pl. **-ais**) (hist.) Federal: supporter or soldier of the government of the United States in the Civil War. ‖ adj. m. + f. federal, allied, confederated.
federalismo s. m. federalism.
federalista s. m. + f. federal(ist). ‖ adj. federalist(ic).
federar, federalizar v. 1. to federate, federalize. 2. to confederate, ally.
federativo adj. federative, federal.
fedor adj. m. stench, stink, fetidness, bad smell, malodorousness, frowziness, fetor.
fedorentina s. f. = **fedentina**.
fedorento adj. (also **fedido**) fetid, stinking, malodorous, rotten, rammy. ‖ **-amente** adv. fetidly, malodorously.
pedra -a stinkstone.
feérico adj. fairylike, marvellous, prodigious.
feianchão s. m. (pl. **-ões**) (f. **feianchona**) very ugly person. ‖ adj. ugly, hideous, horrid.
feição s. f. (pl. **-ões**) 1. feature: a) form, figure, shape. b) make, style, kind. c) (also **-ões** pl.) physiognomical expression, physiognomy, countenance. d) lineament. 2. aspect, appearance, look. 3. manner, behaviour. 4. humour. 5. character, trait. 6. touch. 7. fashion.
de -ões acentuadas with marked features. **de -ões duras** hard-featured. **-ões regulares** clean-cut features. **homem de boa** ~ a jovial or kindhearted man. **pôr em** ~ (mil.) to put in ranks. **suas -ões fazem lembrar o seu pai** his traits remind us of his father. **falar à** ~ **de alguém** to chime in with s. o., to fawn on s. o.
feijão s. m. (pl. **-ões**) (bot.) bean, frijol.
isto é ~ **com carne-seca** that's quite a trivial affair.
feijão-bravo s. m. (pl. **feijões-bravos**) Mexican rosary plant.
feijão-cru s. m. (pl. **feijões-crus**) rain tree.
feijão-manteiga s. m. (pl. **feijões-manteiga**) wax bean, butter bean.

feijão-soja s. m. (pl. **feijões-soja**) soy bean, soya bean.
feijoada s. f. dish of beans cooked with dried meat, pork, sausages, etc.
feijoal s. m. (pl. **-ais**) field of beans.
feijoca s. f. large French beans.
feijoeiro s. m. bean, bean plant.
feila s. f. fine flour dust.
feio s. m. 1. awkward or improper situation. 2. repulsive, immoral attitude. 3. (fig.) bad figure. ‖ adj. 1. ugly, ill-favoured, unsightly, uncomely, haggish. (U. S. A.) homely. 2. deformed, disproportionate, hard-featured. 3. disagreeable, unpleasing. 4. indecorous, base, low. 5. unbearable. ‖ **-amente** adv. uglily, unbecomingly, basely, shamefully.
~ **como o diabo** as ugly as the devil. ~ **como o pecado** as ugly as sin. **patinho** ~ ugly duckling. **como é** ~ **aquilo** how naughty that is! **quem o feio ama, bonito lhe parece** never was a mistress foul. **nem tudo é tão** ~ **como se pinta** every cloud has its silver lining.
feioso adj. plain, unsightly.
feira s. f. 1. fair. 2. market. 3. (fig.) clamour, noise, shouting. 4. (Braz.) bargain sale, rummage sale.
~ **de amostras** sample fair. ~ **industrial** industries' fair. ~ **do livro** bookseller's fair. ~ **de roupas velhas** rag fair. ~ **livre** free market. **dia de** ~ market day.
feirante s. m. + f. marketer, merchant, huckster or stallkeeper in a fair.
feirar v. to buy or sell at a fair.
feita s. f. 1. act, action. 2. occasion, juncture, opportunity.
desta ~ this time, at this occasion, now.
feital s. m. (Braz., pl. **-ais**) exhausted soil.
feitar v. (Braz.) to make, do.
feitiar v. 1. to form, shape. 2. to adapt, fit.
feitiçaria s. f. 1. witchcraft, witchery, sorcery, black art, bedevilment. 2. charm, enchantment, fascination, incantation.
feiticeira s. f. 1. witch, sorceress, wise woman. 2. ugly old woman, hag. 3. charming woman, enchantress. 4. (Bras. ent.) black bee.
feiticeiro s. m. 1. sorcerer, wizard, wise man, charmer, enchanter, witch doctor, medicine man. 2. magician, conjurer. 3. interesting or attractive person. ‖ adj. charming, attractive, fascinating, fairylike.
feiticismo s. m. fetishism, fetichism.
feiticista s. m. + f. fetishist, fetichist.
feitiço (I) s. m. 1. witchcraft, sorcery, black magic. 2. magic, occult power. 3. amulet, talisman. 4. charm, fascination. 5. spell, incantation, hex, enchantment.
virar o ~ **contra o feiticeiro** to turn the tables, (on, upon s. o.). **fazer** ~**s** to practise magic.
feitiço (II) adj. artificial, fictitious, feigned.
feitio s. m. 1. workmanship, make, fabric. 2. feature, form, shape, fashion, pattern. 3. style, cut. 4. (con)figuration. 5. temper, frame of mind. 6. character. 7. work of art. 8. cost of or charge for making something.
isto não é de seu ~ that's quite unlike him (her). **do** ~ **de** like, after the manner of. **perder o tempo e o** ~ to lose both cost and pains.
feito ' (I) s. m. 1. fact, deed. 2. act, action. 3. undertaking, enterprise. 4. feat, achievement, attainment. 5. exploit, accomplishment. 6. lawsuit, legal procedure. 7. ~**s** pl. legal acts.
um ~ **imortal** an immortal deed. **um** ~ **brilhante** a stroke of genius. **todo o seu** ~ **é ganhar dinheiro** all his thoughts are bent on money. **de** ~ in fact as a (matter of) fact.

feito (II) adj. 1. made, done, built, wrought, fashioned. 2. accomplished, finished. 3. accustomed, used, inured to. 4. adult, grown-up. 5. ripe, mature. 6. established, settled, constituted. 7. trained, drilled. 8. ready, prepared. ‖ conj. (Braz.) like. ~! agreed!, all right!, that's a bargain! ~ é! it is done! ~ a mão handmade. ~ de propósito intentionally done, done on purpose. ~ sob encomenda custom-made. ~ sob medida tailor-made, made to measure. bem ~ 1. well-done. 2. it serves you (him, her, etc.) right. dito e ~ no sooner said than done. ele é um homem ~ he is grown-up, an adult. estar ~ com alguém to combine in a plot with s. o. isto até que está muito bem ~ that's very well done considering. já ~ ready-made. nada ~! no soap! que é ~ dele? what has become of him? o que está ~, está ~ what cannot be cured must be endured, it is no use crying over spilt milk. um terno bem ~ a well-tailored suit. o homem espumava ~ cachorro doido the man foamed (with rage) like a mad dog.

feitor s. m. 1. administrator, factor. 2. manager, foreman, overman. 3. farm bailiff. 4. maker, manufacturer. 5. author, creator. ‖ adj. factorial.

feitorar, feitoriar, feitorizar v. 1. to administrate, manage. 2. to superintend. 3. to manufacture, make (wine). 4. to usufruct.

feitoria s. f. 1. factorship, position of a factor or steward. 2. administration, management. 3. commercial establishment, factory. 4. (Braz., hist.) trading post. 5. wine making. 6. (hist.) farm, farm building. 7. (Braz.) camp, clearing, encampment. 8. a fisherman's hut. 9. place where fish are salted.

feitoriar v. to factor.

feitura s. f. 1. act, or mode of making. 2. work, structure. 3. production. 4. (tail.) make, style, fashion.

~ de um poço well-sinking.

feiúme s. m. (Braz.) 1. ugliness, unbecomingness. 2. ugly or repulsive object.

feiúra s. f. (Braz., fam.) 1. ugliness, (U. S. A.) homeliness. 2. wickedness, turpitude. 3. indignity, outrage. 4. ill-favouredness.

feixas-fradinho s. m. (pl. **feixas-fradinhos**) Cape pigeon.

feixe s. m. 1. sheaf, bundle, faggot. 2. handful. 3. bob, bunch. 4. beam, shaft (light). 5. (opt.) pencil. **formado em** ~ bobbed. ~ de gravetos bavin. ele é um ~ de nervos he is a bundle of nerves.

feixinho s. m. fascicle, fascicule.

fel s. m. (pl. **féis**) 1. gall, bile. 2. (fig.) bad temper, anger, hate. 3. rancour, grudge, bitterness.

não há mel sem ~ no rose without thorns. pouco ~ faz amargo muito mel a drop of bitterness often mars a happy spell.

fela s. f. (sl.) face, mug.

felá s. m. (f. **felaína**) fellah, Arabian peasant.

fel-da-terra s. m. (pl. **féis-da-terra**) designation of various plants of the family Balanophoraceae.

feldspático adj. (min.) feldspathic.

feldspato s. m. (min.) feldspar.

féleo adj. bilious, biliary.

felga s. f. clod (of earth).

felgudo adj. cloddy, lumpy.

felícia s. f. familiar form of **felicidade**.

felicidade s. f. 1. happiness, bliss, felicity. 2. luckiness, good luck, fortunateness, good fortune. 3. satisfaction, contentment. 4. success. 5. welfare, weal, well-being. 6. paradise.

por ~ by good luck. por nossa ~ fortunately for us. a eterna ~ salvation. a ~ suprema blissfulness, beatitude. desejo-lhe ~s I wish you good luck, I hope you will be very happy. muitas ~s! good luck to you! with all good wishes for...

felicíssimo adj. (abs. sup. of **feliz**) overhappy.

felicitação s. f. (pl. **-ões**) felicitation, congratulation, good wishes.

apresento minhas **-ões** por... I offer you my congratulations on... carta de **-ões** letter of congratulation(s). **-ões cordiais!** (aniversary compliments) many happy returns of the day!

felicitar v. 1. to felicitate: a) make happy, bring happiness to. b) congratulate, compliment, wish luck. 2. ~-se to congratulate o. s. with.

felicito-me por I hug myself on.

felídeos s. m. pl. (zool.) Felidae: the cat family.

felídeo s. m. (zool.) felid, feline, of the cat family. ‖ adj. feline.

felino s. m. (zool.) felid, animal of the cat family. ‖ adj. 1. feline, felid. 2. catlike, cattish. 3. (fig.) sly, stealthy, treacherous. ‖ **felinamente** adv. felinely.

feliz adj. m. + f. (pl. ~es) 1. lucky, in luck, happy. 2. felicitous, boon, fain, sunny. 3. fortunate, blessed, blissful. 4. prosperous, palmy, successful. 5. opportune, timely. 6. satisfied, content. 7. carefree. ‖ ~mente adv. happily, fortunately, luckily. ter-se por ~ to consider o. s. happy. dou-me por ~ I congratulate myself on, I count myself happy. sou muito ~ I am very fortunate, happy. momentos ~s snatches of happiness. um ~ acaso a hap. ele é muito ~ he swims in joy. ele é ~ por ter filhos bons he is fortunate in his children. ~mente! as good luck would have it! by good fortune!

felizão (pl. **-ões**) (f. **felizona**), **felizardo** s. m. lucky fellow, (coll.) lucky dog or chap, person favoured by fortune.

felô s. m. (Braz.) sugar plum.

feloderma s. m. (bot.) phelloderm.

felogênico adj. (bot.) phellogenetic, phellogenic.

felogênio, felógeno s. m. (bot.) phellogen.

felonia s. f. 1. felony, crime. 2. perfidy, treachery. 3. cruelty. 4. meanness.

feloplástica s. f. phelloplastics: art of sculpturing or carving in cork.

felpa (ê) s. f. 1. nap of cloth, shag, fuzz. 2. flue, down, fluffy feathers. 3. pelt, fur, pile. 4. pubescence, velvety coat of some plants or fruits. 5. scurf. 6. (Braz., pop.) character, principle.

toalha de ~ Turkish (or bath, rough) towel. ele é um homem de boa ~ he is a man of firm character.

felpar v. to fuzz, raise a nap on, make shaggy or fluffy.

felpazinha (ê) s. f. flue, fluff.

felpo (ê) s. m. (pl. **felpos**) = **felpa**. ‖ adj. = **felpudo**.

felpudo adj. (also **felpado**) 1. hairy, shaggy. 2. fluffy, downy. 3. nappy, pily, fuzzy, piled, plushy. 4. fleecy, cottony.

felsítico adj. (min.) felsitic.

felsito s. m. (min.) felsite.

feltradeira s. f. 1. felting machine. 2. female felt worker.

feltrador s. m. feltmaker, felt worker.

feltragem s. f. felting, feltmaking, fabrication of felt.

feltrar v. to felt: 1. make into felt. 2. cover with felt. 3. stuff with felt.

feltro (ê) s. m. 1. felt, shag. 2. fibrous asbestos. ~ asfaltado felt roofing, asphaltic felt. ~ de amianto asbestos felt. chapéu de ~ felt hat. sapatos de ~ felt-shoes.

felugem s. f. (pl. **-ens**) (also **fuligem**) soot.

fêmea s. f. 1. female. 2. a) female animal. b) hen. c) jenny. d) dam. 3. pistillate plant. 4. (naut.) brace of the rudder, gudgeon. 5. eye of a hook. 6. nut of a screw. 7. undertile (plate T 5).

~ **do leme**, ~ **de governo** (Braz., naut.) rudder brace, rudder gudgeon. ~ **do lobo** bitch-wolf, she- -wolf. ~ **do pardal** hen-sparrow.

femeaço s. m. 1. womenfolk, womankind, women of a town. 2. loose women, prostitutes.

femeal adj. m. + f. (pl. **-ais**) womanish.

femeeiro s. m. 1. lady killer. 2. group of prostitutes. || adj. given to amorous affairs.

fementido adj. 1. perjured, forsworn. 2. false, faith- less. 3. treacherous, perfidious. 4. fraudulent.

fêmeo adj. female, relating to the female.

jacaré ~ (zool.) female caiman.

feminela s. f. (artillery) cylindric hole in the head- piece of a ramrod.

feminidade s. f. feminity, womanliness, feminality.

feminifloro adj. (bot.) pistillate: having a pistil but no stamens.

feminil adj. m. + f. (pl. **-is**) (also **feminal** m. + f., **femíneo** m.) 1. female, feminine. 2. womanish, womanlike, womanly. 3. petticoat. 4. effeminate. || ~**mente** adv. womanishly.

feminilidade s. f. feminineness, feminality, femininity, womanishness.

feminino adj. female, feminine, womanly, womanish, womanlike, petticoat.

equipe -a women's team. **sexo** ~ female; feminine sex. **gênero** ~ feminine gender. **sufrágio** ~ woman suffrage. **trabalho** ~ female labour.

feminismo s. m. feminism.

feminista s. m. + f. feminist. || adj. feminist, femi- nistic.

feminizar v. to feminize, make effeminate.

femoral adj. m. + f. (pl. **-ais**) (anat.) femoral, crural.

artéria ~ femoral artery.

fêmur s. m. (anat.) femur, thighbone.

fenação s. f. (pl. **-ões**) haymaking, hay harvest.

fenacetina s. f. (pharm.) phenacetin.

fenar v. (Braz.) to grow alfalfa, clover, grass, etc. for hay.

fenato s. m. (chem.) phenate, phenoxide.

fenda s. f. 1. crack, chink. 2. fissure, chap, cleft (plate C 9). 3. gap, crevice. 4. rent, slot, slit, notch, hack. 5. rift, burst, break, breach, fracture. 6. (geol.) shake, split, chasm.

cheio de ~**s** cracky. ~ **de geleira** crevasse.

fendedor s. m. splitter. || adj. splitting, cracking

fendeleira s. f. iron wedge, splitter [plate M 6].

fendente s. m. a cutting blow. || adj. m. + f. splitting, cleaving.

fender v. 1. to cleave, spring, flaw, split, cut. 2. to separate by cutting, disrupt, open, divide. 3. to crack, chap, chink, fissure, slit. 4. to chop, rift. 5. to rip (up), tear open. 6. ~**-se** to break or cleave asunder. 7. (fig.) to move, affect, touch. 8. to cross, plough (seas).

fendido adj. 1. cleft, split, cloven. 2. fissured, cracked, rimous. 3. choppy. 4. creviced. 5. (zool.) bisulcate, cloven-hoofed.

fendidura s. f. cleavage.

fendimento s. m. 1. act or process of cleaving. 2. rent, crack, fissure, fission, disruption, fracture.

fendível adj. m. + f. (pl. **-íveis**) fissile.

fenecer v. 1. to end, finish, terminate, expire. 2. to die out, become extinct. 3. to die, decease. 4. to fade, wither.

fenecimento s. m. 1. end, conclusion. 2. death. 3. dying out. 4. fading, withering.

feneco s. m. (zool.) fennec.

feneiro s. m. hayloft.

fenestrado adj. fenestrate(d).

fenestragem s. f. (archit.) fenestration.

fenestral s. m. (pl. **-ais**) vent, air hole. || adj. m. + f. fenestral.

fenetidina s. f. (chem.) phenetidin(e).

fenetol s. m. (chem.) phenetol(e).

fenfém s. m. (pl. **-éns**) (Braz.) imp, goblin, puck.

feniano s. m. Fenian: member of the Irish Republican Brotherhood. || adj. Fenian.

fenicado adj. carbolic, carbolated.

fenício s. m. Phoenician. || adj. Phoenician.

fênico adj. (chem.) phenic, carbolic, carbolated.

ácido ~ carbolic acid.

fenicopteriformes s. m. pl. (ornith.) Phoenicopteri- formes, the order to which belongs the flamingo.

feníigeno adj. that produces hay, haylike.

fenigma s. m. (med., ant.) phoenigm, redness of the skin (caused by illness or an application).

fenilacético adj. (chem.) phenylacetic.

fenilo s. m. (chem.) phenyl.

fênix s. f. phoenix, phenix: 1. (myth.) legendary, immortal bird. 2. (fig.) person of high excellence, paragon. 3. Phoenix: (astr.) southern constellation.

feno s. m. hay.

espalhar o ~ to ted. **preparador de** ~ haymaker. **febre do** ~ hay-fever. **colheita de** ~ hay harvest or crop. **meda de** ~ haymow, haystack. ~ **serôdio** aftergrass, aftermath, eddish.

fenobarbital s. m. + f. (pl. **-ais**) (pharm.) phenobarbital.

fenocópia s. f. (biol.) phaenocopy: mutation obtained experimentally that shows the characteristics of the natural strain.

fenocristal s. m. (pl. **-ais**) (petrog.) phenocryst.

feno-de-cheiro s. m. (pl. **fenos-de-cheiro**) sweet vernal grass.

feno-grego s. m. (pl. **fenos-gregos**) (bot.) fenugreek.

fenol s. m. (pl. **-óis**) (chem.) phenol, carbolic acid.

fenolftaleína s. f. (chem.) phenolphtalein.

papel de ~ litmus paper.

fenólico adj. (chem.) phenolic.

fenolizar v. (chem., pharm.) to phenolize.

fenologia s. f. phenology.

fenológico adj. phenological.

fenologista s. m. + f. phenologist.

fenomenal adj. m. + f. (pl. **-ais**) 1. phenomenal: a) of the nature of a phenomenon. b) extraordinary, remarkable, unusual. 2. frightful, enormous. 3. admirable, wonderful. || ~**mente** adv. phenomenally.

fenomenalidade s. f. phenomenality, remarkability.

fenomenismo s. m. (phil.) phenomenalism.

fenômeno s. m. phenomenon: 1. any observable action, appearance, change or fact, symptom. 2. rare or unusual event, exceptional or abnormal occurrence, thing or person. 3. person of outstand- ing talents or capacity.

~ **aperiódico** aperiodic phenomenon. ~ **físico ou químico** physical or chemical phenomenon.

fenomenologia s. f. phenomenology.

fenomenológico adj. phenomenologic(al).

fenotípico adj. (biol.) phenotypic(al).

fenótipo s. m. (biol.) phenotype.

feofíceas s. f. pl. (bot.) Phaeophyceae, a large class of brown algae.

fera s. f. 1. wild animal or beast, beast of prey. 2. (fig.) brutal person. 3. (astr.) a constellation of the Southern Hemisphere.

feracidade s. f. feracity, fertility, fruitfulness.

feral adj. m. + f. (pl. **-ais**) 1. funereal, mournful. 2. lugubrious, ominous. 3. fatal, deadly. 4. cruel, sanguinary, feral.

feramina s. f. (min.) pyrite.

feraz adj. m. + f. (pl. ~**es**) feracious, fertile, produc- tive, prolific.

férculo s. m. bier, baldachin, canopy (in pagan rites).

fere-folha s. m. + f. (pl. **fere-folhas**) busybody, med- dlesome person, intriguer.

fere-lume s. m. (pl. **fere-lumes**) glowworm.

féretro s. m. 1. grave, tomb. 2. coffin, hearse, bier, feretory.

fereza s. f. 1. ferocity, cruelty, ferociousness. 2. wildness, fierceness.

féria s. f. 1. weekday, working day. 2. salary. 3. weekly pay, wages. 4. rest, repose, recreation. 5. proceeds, sales receipts, returns. 6. ~s pl. holidays, vacations.

dia de ~ payday. ele está de ~s he is on holiday. ele passou as ~s na praia he spent his holiday at the seaside. eles passaram uns dias em ~s they spent a few days on leave of absence.

feriado s. m. holiday, feast day, red-letter day, vacation. ‖ adj. like a holiday, festive.
~ bancário bank holiday. ~ nacional national red--letter day.

ferial adj. m. + f. (pl. -ais) ferial: 1. referring to a holiday or vacations. 2. referring to week days.

feriar v. 1. to rest from labour, repose. 2. to be in vacation, spend vacations. 3. to concede rest days or vacations. 4. to be idle.

feriável adj. m. + f. (pl. -áveis) ferial.

ferida s. f. 1. wound, sore, trauma, hurt. 2. cut, flesh-wound, slash. 3. ulcer, boil. 4. (fig.) injury, offense, damage. 5. affront, insult. 6. pain, grievance, affliction. 7. (Port.) mill-race. 8. entrance (to a beehive).

uma ~ aberta an open sore. ~ mortal mortal wound. ~ por mordida tooth wound, bite. renovar a ~ to reopen old sores. deixar cicatrizar a ~ (fig.) to bury in oblivion a painful occurrence. tocar na ~ (fig.) to touch a sore spot.

feridade s. f. ferocity, fierceness.

feridagem s. f. simultaneous outcropping of many sores.

feridento adj. full of sores, covered with wounds.

ferido s. m. wounded person. ‖ adj. 1. wounded, hurt. 2. sore. 3. smitten, stricken, cut. 4. grieved, offended.
~ de raio thunderstruck. ~ por garras ou unhas clawed. ela tem um dedo ~ she has a hurt finger. ele está ligeiramente ~ he is slightly wounded. ele foi ~ gravemente he received severe injuries. estar mortalmente ~ to be wounded to death. a sua mão foi ferida pela faca his hand was hit by the knife.

feridor s. m. (pl. ~es) wounder, hurter, harmer. ‖ adj. wounding, hurting.

ferimento s. m. 1. wound, trauma, sore, injury. 2. hack. 3. act or effect of wounding.
sem ~ unscarred. sofrer ~ to bleed. ~ interno internal injury. receber muitos ~s to be badly wounded.

ferino adj. 1. ferine, feral. 2. cruel, brutal. 3. ferocious, savage. 4. inhuman, atrocious.

ferir v. 1. to wound, injure, bruise. 2. to beat, strike, smite, hit, bayonet. 3. to pain, damage or harm. 4. to hurt, cut, sting. 5. to afflict, annoy, vex, harrow, attack. 6. to split. 7. to touch, impress, shock. 8. to offend, wrong, scarify, ding. 9. to punish. 10. to wage (battle). 11. ~-se: a) to wound or hurt o. s. b) to become angry or offended about s. th.
~ o alvo to hit the mark. ~ a batalha to engage in battle. ~ com os cornos to horn. ~ com os dentes to tusk, bite. ~ ligeiramente to raze. ~ até a medula to cut to the quick. ~ num ponto sensível to touch on the raw. ~ o ponto to hit the nail on the head. ~ sensivelmente to rasp. ~ a unhas to claw, crab. ~ a vista to strike the sight, to dazzle. ele feriu a sua honra he wounded her honour. ele feriu os dedos he cut his fingers. ele feriu-me com palavras he snapped at me.

ele o feriu na perna he wounded him in his leg. isto fere os seus sentimentos it hurts his feelings. sua grosseria me feriu o coração his unkindness cut me to the heart. a notícia feriu-lhe o coração the news stabbed him to the heart.

fermata s. f. (mus.) fermata, pause.

fermentação s. f. (pl. -ões) 1. fermentation, leavening, working, heat. 2. (fig.) agitation, unrest.
em ~ (fig.) in a ferment.

fermentáceo adj. fermentable, fermentative, fermenting, barmy.

fermentante adj. m. + f. fermentative, fermenting, yeasty.

fermentar v. to ferment: 1. leaven, yeast, cause or undergo fermentation. 2. excite, agitate, arouse, stir up. 3. get excited, become agitated.
~ a massa to leaven the dough. ~ demais to overleaven.

fermentativo adj. fermentative.

fermentável adj. m. + f. (pl. -áveis) fermentable.

fermentescente adj. m. + f. fermentescible, fermentative.

fermentescibilidade s. f. fermentability, fermentativeness.

fermentescível adj. m. + f. (pl. -íveis) fermentescible, fermentitious.

fermento s. m. ferment: 1. leaven(ing), yeast. 2. unrest, agitation, excitement. 3. cause, fomentation.
~ de discórdia cause of discord. sem ~ unleavened. ~ em pó yeast powder or baking powder. ~ solúvel enzyme. a ociosidade é o ~ de vícios idleness is the root of all evil.

fermentoso adj. fermentative, fermentatory, zymotic.

férmion s. m. (phys.) fermion.

fero s. m. 1. threat, menace. 2. ~s pl. bragging, boast. ‖ adj. 1. ferocious, savage, ferine. 2. wild, uncultivated. 3. furious, fierce, violent, cruel. 4. indomitable, unyielding. 5. rustic, rural, coarse. 6. strong, sturdy. 7. severe, harsh. 8. sound, vigorous.

ferocidade, ferócia s. f. 1. ferocity, ferociousness, fierceness. 2. wildness, savageness, savagery, fellness, wolfishness. 3. brutality, cruelty, atrocity.

feroz adj. m. + f. 1. ferocious, fierce. 2. wild, savage, wolfish, tigerish, feral, fell, truculent. 3. indomitable. 4. furious, violent, sanguinary. 5. wicked, depraved. 6. threatening, menacing. 7. arrogant, haughty. ‖ ~mente adv. ferociously, fiercely, felly, wildly, furiously, menacingly, haughtily.

ferra s. f. 1. shovel, fire-shovel. 2. branding iron. 3. (Braz.) time of cattle branding.

ferrã s. f. green fodder (mostly barley).

ferrabrás s. m., sg. + pl. 1. braggart, boaster, swash-buckler. 2. rowdy, rough, bully. ‖ adj. 1. boasting, boastful. 2. rough.
ele é um ~ he is a pugnacious fellow.

ferraça s. f. hearth ring.

ferrado (I) s. m. 1. act of covering or protecting with iron. 2. shoeing of horses. ‖ adj. 1. shod, bound, plated or tipped with iron. 2. marked (with a branding iron). 3. shod (horses). 4. (fig.) stubborn, obstinate.
é um navio ~ it is an ironbound ship. sapato ~ spiked shoe.

ferrado (II) s. m. 1. first faeces of babies. 2. milk-pail.

ferrador s. m. blacksmith, farrier, shoeing smith.
oficina de ~, ofício de ~ farriery.

ferradura s. f. horseshoe, shoe.
~ para calçados calk.

ferradurinha s. f. (bot.) horseshoe vetch.

ferrageiro s. m. ironmonger, hardware dealer.

F 2

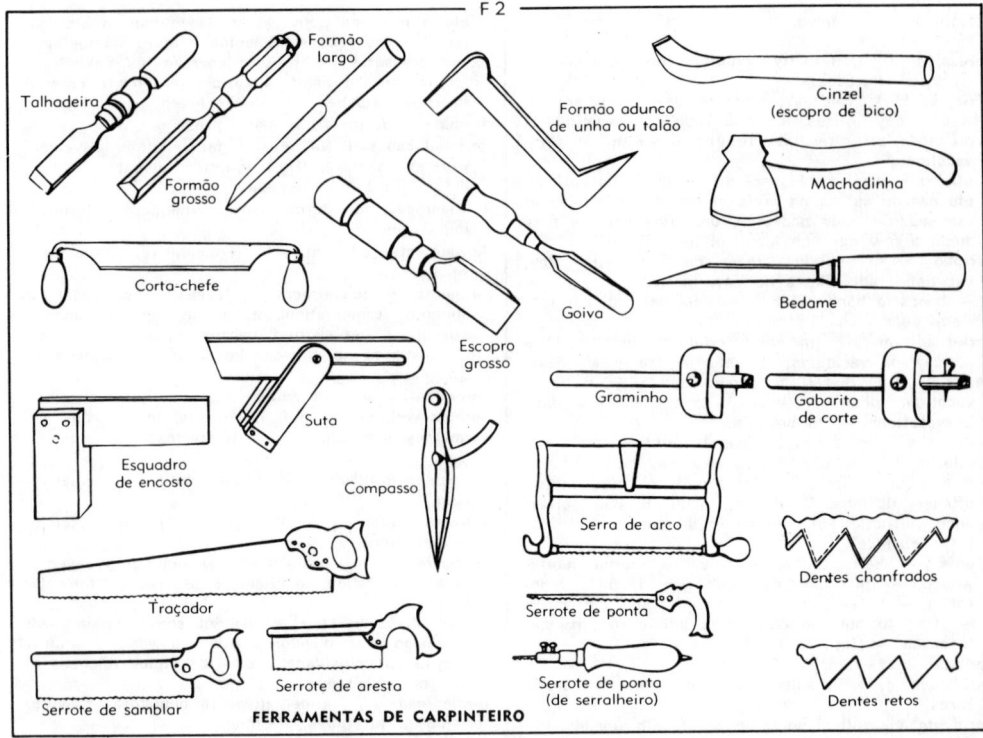

Talhadeira
Formão largo
Formão grosso
Formão adunco de unha ou talão
Cinzel (escopro de bico)
Machadinha
Corta-chefe
Goiva
Bedame
Escopro grosso
Suta
Graminho
Gabarito de corte
Esquadro de encosto
Compasso
Serra de arco
Dentes chanfrados
Traçador
Serrote de ponta
Serrote de ponta (de serralheiro)
Serrote de aresta
Serrote de samblar
Dentes retos

FERRAMENTAS DE CARPINTEIRO

ferragem s. f. (pl. **-ens**) 1. hardware, ironware. 2. iron fittings or trimmings (plate D 1). 3. cutlery. 4. iron tools or utensils. 5. horseshoes.
~ **de esquadria** angle hinge. **loja de -ens** hardware shop.
ferragista s. m. + f. (Braz.) hardware dealer, ironmonger.
ferragoulo s. m. (ant.) felt cloak with hood.
ferrajaria s. f. iron mill, ironwork.
ferral adj. m. + f. (pl. **-ais**) iron-coloured.
ferramenta s. f. tool(s), instrument(s), implement(s), utensil(s), findings, iron (plates E 4, 9, F 1, 2, J 2, M 4, 6).
~ **de acabamento** finishing tool. ~**s de carpinteiro e marceneiro** tools for joiners and cabinetmakers. ~ **de corte** cutter, cutting tool. ~ **de facear** facing tool. ~**s de ferrador** shoeing tools. **caixa de ferramentas** tool box. **estojo para** ~ tool bag. **trabalhar com** ~, **usar** ~ to tool.
ferramenteiro s. m. toolmaker.
ferrão s. m. (pl. **-ões**) sting, prickle, ferret, dart, piercer.
sem ~ stingless.
ferrar v. 1. to iron, provide or cover with iron. 2. to fit or garnish with iron parts. 3. to shoe, horseshoe. 4. to calk, furnish with calks. 5. to brand or mark with a hot iron. 6. to nail, strike, hammer. 7. to grapple, grasp. 8. to force, penetrate violently, pierce. 9. to devote or dedicate o. s. seriously to. 10. to drop the anchor. 11. (naut.) to reef, furl.
~ **com alguém**, ~ **com alguma coisa** to cling, to stick fast to. ~ **o cavalo** to shoe the horse. ~ **o pano** (naut.) to reef. ~ **o porto, a barra** (naut.) to cast anchor. **ele está ferrado no sono** he is sound asleep. **ele ferrou no trabalho** he put hand to work, he was hot on his work.

ferraria s. f. 1. ironworks, iron mill or forge. 2. hardware shop, workshop, smith, smithery. 3. blacksmiths' quarters. 4. ironware, hardware.
ferrária s. f. Ferraria: a genus of dwarf plants of the family Iridaceae.
ferrato s. m. (chem.) ferrate, salt of ferric acid.
ferreiro s. m. 1. smith, hammersmith, blacksmith, farrier, forger, forgeman. 2. ironmonger, hardware dealer. 3. (ornith.) a) swift. b) bellbird, campanero. 4. (zool.) a tree toad (Hyla faber). ‖ adj. rat-coloured.
tenaz de ~ smith's tongs. **trabalho de** ~ blackwork.
ferrejar v. to cut green fodder for horses and cattle.
ferrejo s. m. green (barley) fodder.
ferrenho adj. 1. ironlike, ferruginous. 2. iron-grey, iron-coloured. 3. hard as iron. 4. intransigent, uncompromising. 5. despotic, tyrannical. 6. tenacious, persevering.
férreo adj. 1. ferrous, ferruginous. 2. iron. 3. (chem.) ferric. 4. hard, strong. 5. intransigent, uncompromising, inflexible. 6. hard, rigorous, unrelenting. 7. cruel, merciless.
água férrea chalybeate. **linha -a** railway track, railroad. **rede férrea** railway network. **extensão de linha férrea** trackage.
ferreta (ê) s. f. 1. sting, prickle. 2. iron point, tip.
ferret(e)ar v. 1. to brand, mark with a branding iron. 2. to afflict, torment, pain. 3. to blemish, taint, stigmatize. 4. to reproach, censure.
ferrete (ê) s. m. 1. branding iron. 2. mark of infamy or disgrace. 3. stigma, brand. 4. blemish, stain.
ferretoada s. f. 1. sting, prick. 2. witty retort, sarcastic criticism. 3. gibe, scoff.
ferretoar v. 1. to sting, prick, goad. 2. to tease, gibe. 3. to reprimand, blame.
férrico adj. (chem.) ferric, ferrous.

ferrífero adj. ferriferous.

ferrificação s. f. (pl. -ões) formation of iron.

ferrinhos s. m. pl. (mus.) triangle.

ferro s. m. 1. iron (symbol Fe). 2. cutting blade, knife, sword, dagger, iron head of a lance or arrow. 3. tool, implement, instrument (plate T 5). 4. flat--iron. 5. (Port., pop.) worry, trouble, anger. 6. ~s pl.: a) chains, fetters. b) (fig.) jail, prison, captivity. c) anchor. d) tongs. 7. any piece of iron. 8. (fig.) hardness, strength. 9. (tail.) flat (or smoothing) iron, goose (pl. gooses). ~ de calafate reeming iron. ~ de engomar iron, smoothing iron, pressing iron (plate A 5). ~ de plaina plane iron, cutting iron, bit (plate P 13). ~ em barras bar iron. ~ em folhas sheet-iron. ~ em lingotes pig iron. ~ em T T iron, T bar. ~ U channel iron. ~ forjado forged or wrought iron. ~ fundido cast iron. ~ gusa cast iron. ~ laminado rolled iron (bars). ~ maleável malleable iron. ~ redondo round bar iron. ~ velho swap iron. a ~ e a fogo by any means. a ~ quente malhar de repente strike the iron whilst it is hot. cobrir com ~ to iron. coração de ~ heart of steel. devastar com ~ e fogo to devastate with fire and sword. estar sobre ~s (naut.) to ride at anchor. lançar ~s to cast anchor. levantar ~s to weigh anchor. limalha de ~ iron filings. malhar em ~ frio to labour in vain, to preach to the winds. meter em ~s to put in shackles. passar a ~ o vestido to iron the dress. pau-~ ironwood. peça de ~ fundido iron casting. quem com ~ fere com ~ será ferido who slayeth with the sword shall perish with the sword. ele tem saúde de ~ he has an iron constitution. ele é ~ velho he is on the shelf.

ferroada s. f. sting, prick, goad, jab, bite.

ferroar v. 1. to sting, prickle, goad, bite. 2. to tease, gibe. 3. to reprimand, blame.

ferrolhar v. 1. to bolt, latch. 2. (fig.) to imprison.

ferrolho (ô) s. m. (pl. ferrolhos) bolt, push bolt, door bolt, latch, snap, closing clasp, fastening, stop (plates A 13, F 1).

ferromoça s. f. (Braz.) passenger train stewardess.

ferropear v. to put in irons, fetter, shackle.

ferropéia s. f. shackles, fetters.

ferroso adj. ferrous, ferruginous, ferriferous.

ferro-velho s. m. (pl. ferros-velhos) junk-dealer, fripperer.

ferrovia s. f. railway, railroad.

ferroviário s. m. railway man, railroader, railway employee. || adj. railroad: of, pertaining to or relative to railways. comunicação -a train service.

ferrugem s. f. (pl. -ens) 1. rust, rustiness. 2. (chem.) ferric oxyde. 3. (bot.) rust fungus, smut, blight, brand, ergot, blast. 4. (fig.) ignorance, dullness. 5. (fig.) stagnation, idleness, negligence. ~ do trigo dust-brand, wheat rust. mancha de ~ iron-mould. ele tirou ~ da língua he let loose his tongue. eles criaram ~ they grew rusty.

ferrugento adj. 1. rusty, blighted. 2. antiquated, old--fashioned. 3. tasteless, of bad taste. ela é uma agulha -a she is an intriguing person.

ferrugíneo adj. 1. dark, dusky. 2. sooty, black. 3. rust-coloured, ferrugineous, rubiginous.

ferruginosidade s. f. ferrousness, ferruginosity.

ferruginoso adj. 1. ferrous, ferruginous. 2. chalybeate.

ferruncho s. m. 1. spite, grudge. 2. jealousy.

fértil adj. m. + f. (pl. -eis) 1. fertile, fruitful, fructuous, fecund. 2. abundant, plentiful, rich, generous. 3. productive. 4. fat, rank. 5. luxuriant. || **fertilmente** adv. fertilely, fruitfully, abundantly, productively, prolifically, richly.

fertilidade s. f. 1. fertility, fruitfulness, prolificacy. 2. (fig.) fecundity, pregnancy. 3. (fig.) abundance, copiousness, opulency, richness. 4. fatness, rankness. 5. luxuriance.

fertilização s. f. (pl. -ões) fertilization, fecundation, fructification.

fertilizador s. m. fertilizer. || adj. fertilizing, fecundating.

fertilizante s. m. fertilizer, manure. || adj. m. + f. fertilizing.

fertilizar v. 1. to fertilize, fecundate, impregnate. 2. to fructify, make productive or fruitful. 3. to manure, fatten. 4. to prolificate, enrich.

fertilizável adj. m. + f. (pl. -áveis) fertilizable.

fertilizina s. f. (biol.) cytoplasm.

férula s. f. 1. (bot.) ferula. 2. ferule, palmer.

fervedouro s. m. 1. bubbling, gushing, boiling up. 2. (fig.) agitation, excitement.

fervença, fervência s. f. 1. boiling, bubbling. 2. effervescence, ebullition. 3. fervour, ardour, zeal. 4. vivacity. 5. liveliness.

ferventar v. to parboil.

fervente adj. m. + f. 1. seething, boiling, ebullient. 2. fervent, ardent. 3. tempestuous, violent. 4. eager, zealous. 5. piping hot.

ferver v. 1. to boil, cook, seethe. 2. to be agitated, stirred up. 3. to bubble up, foam, steam. 4. to heap or pile up. 5. to appear in great numbers, swarm. 6. to become very hot, be boiling or scalding hot. 7. to glow, blaze. 8. to excite, rouse up. 9. to be keen on. 10. to be eager or restless. ~ demais to overboil. ~ em água fria to draw out, protract (as a debate). ~ em pouca água to get excited about nothing. ~ em ira to boil with rage. fervem as águas de peixes the water swarms with fishes. o leite está fervendo the milk boils over. o mar está fervendo the sea is agitated. pouco ~ (or quente) (egg) soft-boiled.

fervescente adj. m. + f. 1. seething, boiling. 2. fervent, hot. 3. tempestuous, violent. 4. eager, full of zeal. 5. fervescent.

férvido adj. 1. hot, burning. 2. (fig.) fiery, ardent, eager. 3. fervid, fervent.

fervilha s. m. lively, very active or vivacious person.

fervilhar v. 1. to boil frequently. 2. to simmer. 3. to get excited or irritated frequently. 4. to swarm with, throng together, teem. 5. to effervesce, bubble, foam. 6. to be very active or vivacious.

fervo s. m. (Braz.) row, conflict, tumult.

fervor s. m. 1. boiling, seething. 2. ebullition, bubbling up. 3. warmth, heat, warmness, hotness. 4. fervency, fervour, ardour, fire, fieriness. 5. devotion, devoutness, dedication (to a cause), mettle(someness). 6. enthusiasm, zeal, unction. 7. vivacity, liveliness. 8. yearning, eager desire. 9. earnestness, seriousness. 10. activity, industriousness. 11. (med.) rhonchus. o ~ da mocidade the fire of youth. ~ do sangue (pop.) eczema.

fervoroso adj. 1. fervorous, fervent. 2. fervid. 3. devoted, zealous, unctuous. 4. eager, keen. 5. ardent, vehement. 6. forward. 7. vivacious, lively. || -amente adv. fervently, fervidly, zealously, ardently, unctuously, vivaciously, vehemently.

fervura s. f. 1. ebullition, ebullience, a bubbling up, boil(ing), simmer. 2. effervescence, fervency. 3. (fig.) agitation, commotion. levantar ~ to bubble up, to rise in bubbles. dar uma ~ to let boil or bubble up, bring to a simmer. deitar água na ~ to throw oil upon troubled waters, to curb, repress.

fescenino adj. 1. Fescennine: a) of Fescennia, town in Italy. b) scurrilous, obscene. 2. burlesque.

festa s. f. 1. feast(ing), festival, entertainment, merry-making, party, treat. 2. holiday, day of rest, off day. 3. celebration, commemoration. 4. pilgrimage, popular festival. 5. (fam.) drudgery, toil. 6. ~s pl. caresses, fondling. ~ **comemorativa** jubilee. ~ **de bodas** wedding feast. ~ **de carregação** (N. Braz.) feast without music. ~ **de colheita** harvest-festival, thanksgiving. ~ **de confraternização** bean-feast, (students) end-of-term party. ~ **de guarda** (rel.) strict holiday. ~ **de Reis** Twelfthtide. ~ **do Natal** Christmas festival. ~ **escolar** school treat; gaudy; speech-day. ~s **(i)móveis** (im)movable feasts. ~ **social** reunion. **Boas festas!** a merry Christmas and happy New Year! **dar as boas** ~s to wish a happy Christmas, send the compliments of the season. **foi dada uma** ~ **em sua honra** a party was given for her. **dias de** ~ feast days. **ela gostou da** ~ **musical** she liked the musical entertainment. **ele não está para** ~s (fam.) he is out of humour. **fazer a** ~ **e soltar os foguetes** to applaud one's own feasts. **fazer a uma criança** to fondle a child. **dias de** ~ **gala** or red-letter days. **hoje ele está de** ~ today he is in high spirits. **sair no melhor da** ~ to disappoint, to leave a feast at its height. **vestido de** ~ holiday dress. **furar uma** ~ to crash a feast.

festança s. f. 1. festivity, solemnity. 2. banquet. 3. rich feast, revel(ry), carousal. 4. merrymaking, jollification. 5. (sl.) racket, blowout, do.

festão (I) s. m. (pl. -ões) festoon, garland, wreath of flowers.

festão (II) s. m. (pl. -ões) (Braz.) big feast, merry or very noisy entertainment.

festar v. 1. to celebrate. 2. to dance. 3. to revel, carouse.

festarola s. f. 1. feast, festivity. 2. amusement, entertainment.

festeiro s. m. 1. host, entertainer, (fig.) amphitryon. 2. merrymaker, reveller. 3. patron, sponsor. ‖ adj. 1. festive. 2. revelling, carousing. 3. endearing, fondling. 4. patronizing.

festejador s. m. feaster, entertainer, host. ‖ adj. 1. festive, revelling. 2. merry, gay, cheerful.

festejar v. 1. to feast, entertain, fête. 2. to celebrate, commemorate, hold. 3. to junket, regale. 4. to revel, racket. 5. to applaud, praise. 6. to caress, fondle. 7. to salute, welcome. ~ **consigo** to laugh into one's sleeve. ~ **por lisonja** to fawn upon, to wag the tail at. **eles** ~am **bastante** they made a night of it.

festejo s. m. 1. feast, festivity, fête. 2. entertainment, frolic. 3. celebration. 4. kind reception. 5. caress, endearment. 6. flirtation.

festim s. m. (pl. -ins) 1. feasting, private feast, party, festive family gathering. 2. repast, regale, banquet. 3. entertainment, treat, jollification. 4. revel. **passar a vida em** -ins to feast away one's life.

festival s. m. (pl. -ais) 1. festival, fête. 2. time of feasting or celebration, feast-day. 3. public procession. ‖ adj. m. + f. 1. festival, festive, feastful. 2. gay, merry, convivial.

festividade s. f. 1. feast, festiveness, festivity. 2. religious feast, church festival. 3. rejoicing, jollity, jolliness. 4. solemnity, celebration, function. **programa das** ~s table of events.

festivo adj. festive, feastful, festal, merry, joyful, cheerful, pleasureful, gay. ‖ -**amente** adv. festively, merrily, joyfully, cheerfully, gaily, convivially.

festo s. m. (Braz.) 1. feast, festivity. 2. ball, dancing party. 3. spree, carousal. 4. entertainment, amusement. ‖ adj. = **festivo**.

festo (ê) s. m. 1. width, breadth of cloth. 2. the middle fold in a bale of cloth. **cortar o pano pelo** ~ to cut the cloth along the middle. **subir a** ~ to go straight uphill.

festonadas s. f. pl. architectural ornaments, tracery work.

festo(n)ar v. to festoon, garland.

festuca s. f. (bot.) 1. tall fescue. 2. sheep's fescue.

fetação s. f. (pl. -ões) f(o)etation.

fetal (I) s. m. (pl. -ais) fernery, fern plot, ferny ground.

fetal (II) adj. m. + f. (pl. -ais) 1. f(o)etal. 2. of, pertaining to or relative to ferns.

fetiche s. m. 1. fetish, fetich, charm. 2. (fig.) person or object of special devotion, idol.

fetíchico adj. fetishistic, fetichistic.

fetichismo s. m. 1. fetishism, fetichism. 2. (fig.) partiality, bias. 3. (fig.) servility, submissiveness.

fetichista s. m. + f. fetishist, fetichist. ‖ adj. fetichist(ic).

feticida s. m. + f. person who provokes a f(o)eticide.

feticídio s. m. f(o)eticide.

fetidez s. f. stench, stinking, fetidness.

fétido s. m. stench, fetidness, fetor. ‖ adj. 1. fetid, stinking, rank, malodorous, putrid, frowzy, rotten, feculent. 2. (fig.) hircine. ‖ **fetidamente** adv. fetidly, stinkingly, rottenly, etc.

feto s. m. 1. (anat.) f(o)etus, embryo, germ. 2. (bot.) fern, frond.

feto-macho s. m. (pl. **fetos-machos**) male fern.

feudal adj. m. + f. (pl. -ais) feudal(istic), liege. ‖ ~**mente** adv. feudally. **direito** ~ feudal law. **regime** ~ feudal system. **senhor** ~ feudal lord, liege, (jur.) feoffor, feoffer.

feudalidade s. f. feudality.

feudalismo s. m. feudalism, feudal system.

feudalista s. m. + f. feudalist. ‖ adj. feudalistic.

feudatário s. m. feudatory, liegeman, feudal tenant, vassal. ‖ adj. feudatory, beneficiary.

feudo s. m. 1. feud, fief, feod, feudal tenure, feudality. 2. fee, feudal benefice. 3. vassalage.

fevereiro s. m. 1. February. 2. (Braz., ornith.) puffbird. **o dia 29 de** ~ leap-day.

fevra, fêvera s. f. 1. filament, fibre. 2. thread. 3. tissue, brawn.

fez (ê) s. m. fez: Turkish cap, tarboosh.

fezes s. f. pl. (sg. **fez** now rare) 1. lees, dregs. 2. sediments. 3. refuse. 4. dross, slag, scoria. 5. f(a)eces, excrements, excreta, feculence, rejections. 6. (fig.) mob, scum.

fezinha s. f. (Braz., pop.) modest or timid bet.

fiã s. f. 1. (arch.) measure of capacity. 2. = **fiada**.

fiação s. f. (pl. -ões) 1. spinning. 2. spinning mill, spinnery.

fiacre s. m. fiacre, hackney coach.

fiada s. f. 1. layer of bricks, tier of stones. 2. line, row, file, swath.

fiadeiro s. m. (f. **fiadeira**) spinner.

fiadilho s. m. floss silk, silk waste, unreelable silk fibers.

fiado s. m. 1. yarn, filament, fibre, thread. ‖ adj. 1. spun, thrown twisted (into a thread). 2. trusting, trustful, confiding. ‖ adv. on credit, trust or tick. ~ **de algodão** cotton-yarn. ~ **em** dependent on. **conversa** -a small or idle talk. **dar** ~ to lend. **vender ou comprar** ~ to tick, sell or buy on credit.

fiador s. m. 1. guarantor, warrantor, truster, sponsor, guarantee. 2. guaranty, bond(sman), bail, security, surety. 3. rifle prop or rifle rest. 4. rein, strap of a bridle. 5. sword knot. 6. (naut.) mooring bridle. ~ **de seda** (spin.) thrower. **ser** ~ to stand security.

fiadoria s. f. security, bail.

fiadura s. f. 1. spinning. 2. security, bail.

fiambre s. m. 1. cured cold meat, cold ham. 2. (S. Braz.) foodstuff for a trip.
fiança s. f. 1. security, bail, caution, surety, guaranty. 2. pledge, warrant(y). 3. deposit, gage, amount of security or bail. 4. responsibility, sponsion. 5. (S. Braz.) favourite or very reliable horse. **dar** ~, **prestar** ~ to go bail for, give security, stand surety. **em** ~ on trust.
fiançar v. to bail.
fiandeira s. f. 1. spinster, female spinner, woman working at a spinning machine. 2. (tech.) spinning jenny. 3. (zool.) spinneret, spinning wart, arachnidean mammila.
fiandeiro s. m. spinner, worker at a spinning jenny.
fiango s. m. (Braz.) hammock.
fiapo s. m. 1. fine thread. 2. (Braz., pop.) glance, quick look.
fiar (I) v. 1. to spin, twist into threads. 2. to pull through dies, draw into wires. 3. (weaving) to warp, weave, form threads into a web, throw (silk). 4. to cut lengthwise (wooden boards, battens).
fiar (II) v. 1. to stand bail, guarantee, warrant, give security. 2. to rely, trust, confide in. 3. to sell on credit. 4. to hope for, expect. 5. to submit to arbitration. 6. to hand over on good faith, give on trust. 7. ~-se to rely, bank, or depend on or upon.
fiasco s. m. 1. fiasco, failure. 2. (sl.) fizzle, frost, flop, flunk. 3. ridiculous, shameful or vexatious mistake, blunder. 4. poor figure, sorry customer. **fazer** ~ to go completely amiss.
fiável adj. m. + f. (pl. -áveis) 1. spinnable. 2. bailable, warrantable.
fibra s. f. 1. fibre, filament, thread, strand. 2. (fig.) nerve, strength, energy, toughness, wiriness. 3. (bot.) string. 4. chip. ~ **de ráfia** raffia bass. ~ **têxtil** textile fibre. ~ **vegetal** harl(e). **de** ~ **curta** short-grained. **ele é um homem de** ~ he is a man of firm character. **sem** ~ fibreless.
fibrazinha s. f. fibril.
fibriforme adj. m. + f. fibriform.
fibrilação s. f. fibrillation.
fibrilar adj. m. + f. fibrillar(y), fibrillose.
fibril(h)a s. f. 1. fibril. 2. (bot.) root hair.
fibrílifero adj. fibrilliferous.
fibriloso adj. fibrillose.
fibrina s. f. (biochem.) fibrin, vegetable fibrin.
fibrino adj. fibrillate, fibrillar.
fibrofermento s. m. (biochem.) thrombin, fibrin ferment.
fibrinogênio s. m. (biochem.) fibrinogen.
fibrinoso adj. fibrinous, fibrinogenous.
fibroblasto s. m. (anat.) fibroblast.
fibrocartilagem s. f. (pl. -ens) (anat.) fibrocartilage.
fibrocartilagíneo, fibrocartilaginoso adj. (anat.) fibrocartilaginous.
fibrocelular adj. m. + f. fibrocellular.
fibrogranular adj. m. + f. fibrogranular.
fibróide adj. m. + f. fibroid.
fibrolita s. f. (min.) fibrolite.
fibroma s. m. (med.) fibroma, fibrous tumor.
fibrose s. f. (med.) fibrosis.
fibrosidade s. f. fibrousness.
fibroso adj. fibrose, fibrous, fibriform, fibred, wiry, thready, filamentous.
fíbula s. f. fibula: 1. buckle, clasp, brooch. 2. (anat., zool.) perone: the outer and smaller of the two bones of the leg.
ficáceo adj. 1. of, pertaining to or relative to fig trees. 2. figlike, shaped like a fig.
ficada s. f. 1. (act of) staying, remaining. 2. abiding place, sojourn.

ficar v. 1. to remain, stay, tarry. 2. to abide, rest, sojourn. 3. to stop in one place. 4. to be situated or located, lie. 5. to be known or noted. 6. to continue, last, endure. 7. to be left over or out. 8. to lag behind. 9. to adjust, agree on. 10. to fit, suit, become. 11. to be postponed, be put off. 12. to acquire, get. 13. to agree, combine. 14. to promise. 15. to subsist. 16. to grow, become. 17. to assure, guarantee, stand bail. 18. to keep, retain. 19. to become fixed in someone's memory, impress. 20. to die, decease. 21. to serve as pledge. 22. to spend the night, get a night's shelter. 23. to keep up, retain (custom, etc.). 24. to come to a person as inheritance. 25. to maintain the same quality. 26. ~-se: a) to stay, abide. b) to stop short. c) to keep to o. s.
~ **à âncora** to lie at anchor. ~ **afastado** to stay away. ~ **ajoelhado** to remain on one's knees. ~ **ativo** to stir. ~ **à toa** to (lie) idle, loll, stand or hang about, quiddle, trifle. ~ **atrás** to lag, draggle, stay behind. ~ **ausente** to stay away. ~ **à vontade** 1. to unbend o. s. 2. (U. S. A.) to stay put. ~ **bem ou mal** to be appropriate or unappropriate. ~ **bravo** to grow angry. ~ **bronzeado** (face) to tan. ~ **colado** to stick on. ~ **com o serviço** to hold down a job. ~ **conhecido** (news) to transpire. ~ **convencido** to be persuaded, convinced. ~ **debaixo** to succumb, be overcome. ~ **de boca aberta** to stand gaping. ~ **de cama** to lie up. ~ **de emboscada** to lie in wait. ~ **de fora** to be left out. ~ **de lado** to hold aloof, stand off (person). ~ **de joelhos** to kneel. ~ **demais** to overstay. ~ **em casa** to stay in, stay home, stick indoors. ~ **em volta de alguém** to dangle about a person. ~ **ensopado** to become soaking wet. ~ **fora de uso** to grow out of use. ~ **fora** to stay out. ~ **forte** to grow strong. ~ **frio** to cool. ~ **grudado** to stick on. ~ **inteirado** to be informed. ~ **em pé** 1. to stand. 2. to be in force (law). 3. to stick up (hair). ~ **indeciso, irresoluto** to vacillate. ~ **junto** to stick or stay together. ~ **louco** to run mad. ~ **molhado** to get wet. ~ **no tinteiro** (pop.) to be left out. ~ **pálido** to blanch, turn pale. ~ **para o chá** to stay for tea. ~ **parado** to be at (come to) a standstill, to stand. ~ **para trás** to stay behind. ~ **por aí** to stick around. ~ **por alguma coisa** to warrant for s. th. ~ **por herdeiro** to be left out. ~ **quieto** to be quiet, hold one's peace. ~ **riscado** to become streaked. ~ **sabendo** to hear. ~ **sem dinheiro** to run out of cash. ~ **senhor de si** to have self-control. ~ **tonto** to turn giddy. **a roupa fica bem** the suit wears well. **isto não fica bem a um homem de sua posição** this does not become a man of your position. **não te fica bem** it miscomes you. **este chapéu lhe fica bem** this hat suits you. **ele ficou com medo** he was afraid, (fam.) got the wind up. **ela ficou com o melhor** she had the best of it. **pode** ~ **com o troco** keep the change. **ele ficará com você?** will he stay with you? **ficamos de partir no dia seguinte** we agreed to set out the next day. **ficamos devendo na loja** we are indebted at the store. **fiquei doente** I was taken ill. **ela ficou doente** she took to her bed. **a boneca ficou em pedaços** the doll has gone to pieces. **fiquei estupefato** it fairly took my breath. **ele ficou fora de si** he was taken out of himself. **ele ficou impune** he went unpunished. **pois fiquei logrado!** I have been had! **fiquei mais tempo do que ele** I sat him out. **ela ficou mais moderada** she came down a peg or two. **eles ficaram noivos** they became engaged. **ficaram para esperar meu marido** they stopped for my husband. **ficaram para tomar chá!** they stopped for tea. **fico res-**

ponsável por isso I'll answer for it. o papagaio ficou preso numa árvore the kite lodged in a tree. fique sabendo que... let it be a warning to you (that)... fiquei mais satisfeito em sair I was only too glad to leave. ele ficou sentido he took it to heart. ela ficou séria she straightened her face. não fique triste don't be sad, don't fret. ele ficou zangado he cut up rough. ficarei se V. S. o desejar I shall stay if you wish me to do so. não me fica mais que dizer I have nothing else to say. se ainda fica alguma esperança if there be still any hope left. eu tinha ficado dias sem comer I had not tasted food for days. afinal, em que ficamos? after all what shall we agree upon? não ficou nada there was nothing left.

ficária s. f. (bot.) lesser celandine, pilewort.

ficção s. f. (pl. -ões) 1. (lit.) fiction, romance, fable, legend. 2. invention, creation of the mind, fabrication, nonentity, figment. 3. falsehood, untruth, forgery, simulation.

ficcionista s. m. + f. (lit.) fictionist, storyteller.

ficela s. f. (Braz.) a deceitful trick (card games).

ficha s. f. 1. counter, fish (at cards), chip, check, mark. 2. filing card, index card. 3. entrance form, record. 4. slip, ticket. ~ de consolação consolation prize. ~ de identidade tag. ~ de trabalho timecard, time sheet.

fichado adj. on file (esp. card index).

fichar v. 1. to annotate, note down, mark. 2. to register, record, card, file, enter in a file. 3. to catalogue, make a list of.

fichário s. m. 1. card index, card registry. 2. file, filing cabinet (plate M 14).

ficheiro s. m. 1. money changer in a gambling house. 2. card registry.

fichu s. m. fichu: triangular kerchief for women.

ficiforme adj. m. + f. shaped like a fig.

ficitídeos s. m. pl. (ent.) Phycitidae: an order of moths and butterflies.

ficocianina s. f. (bot.) phycocyanin.

ficóide adj. m. + f. (bot.) algal, phyceous.

ficoíte s. m. fossilized fig tree.

ficologia s. f. phycology, algology.

ficológico adj. phycologic(al).

ficologista s. m. + f. phycologist.

ficomicetos s. m. pl. (micol.) Phycomycetes: a class of fungi.

fictício adj. 1. fictitious, imaginary. 2. fabled, fabulous, fairy, romantic. 3. feigned, assumed, unreal. 4. not genuine, false, counterfeit, artificial, make-believe. 5. paper, straw. || **ficticiamente** adv. fictitiously, etc. **personagem ~ da novela** fictitious character of the novel. **ela deu um nome ~** she gave an assumed name.

ficto adj. 1. fictive, fictitious. 2. imaginary, feigned. 3. supposed, assumed. 4. counterfeit, sham. 5. unreal, illusory.

fidalga s. f. gentlewoman, noblewoman, lady, peeress.

fidalgal adj. m. + f. (pl. -ais) noble, noble-minded, magnanimous.

fidalgaria s. f. 1. nobility, peerage. 2. nobleness.

fidalgo s. m. 1. nobleman, noble, lord, peer, knight, armiger. 2. person of rank, (U. S. A., coll.) tycoon, aristocrat. || adj. 1. noble. 2. noble-minded, magnanimous. || **-amente** adv. nobly, magnanimously, loftily.

fidalgoso adj. squirely.

fidalgote s. m. lordling, squireling, insignificant nobleman.

fidalgueiro s. m. courtier, carpet-knight, person who tries to mingle with the nobility. || adj. (also **fidalguesco**) 1. courtly, courtierly. 2. noble, genteel.

fidalguia s. f. 1. nobility, the nobles, knighthood. 2. nobleness, knightliness. 3. magnanimity, generosity. 4. gracefulness, elegance.

fidalguice s. f. haughtiness, arrogance, ostentation.

fidalguinho-dos-jardins s. m. (pl. **fidalguinhos-dos--jardins**) cornflower, corn-bluebottle, ragged sailor.

fidedignidade s. f. trustworthiness, reliability, credit.

fidedigno adj. 1. trustworthy, worthy of confidence, reliable, credible, dependable. 2. authentical. **novidades -as** authentic news.

fideicomissário s. m. (law) fideicomissary, beneficiary of a fideicomissum, trustee. || adj. fideicommissary.

fideicomisso s. m. (law) fideicommissum, family trust, entail(ment). ~ **parcialmente anulado** (jur.) base fee.

fideicomissório adj. fideicomissary.

fideísmo s. m. (philos., rel.) fideism.

fideísta s. m. + f. (philos., rel.) fideist.

fidejussória s. f. (law) fidejussion, contract of guaranty.

fidejussório adj. (law) fidejussionary, fidejussory.

fidelidade s. f. 1. fidelity, faithfulness, fealty. 2. loyalty, abidance. 3. veracity, honesty, truth. 4. exactness, accuracy. 5. integrity, probity, trustiness, trustworthiness. 6. piety. 7. constancy.

fidéus s. m. pl. vermicelli.

fido adj. (poet.) faithful, true, loyal, devoted.

fidúcia s. f. 1. confidence, trust. 2. self-reliance, self-confidence. 3. (pop.) boldness, courage. 4. (law) fiducia.

fiducial adj. m. + f. (pl. -ais) fiducial, fiduciary, founded on trust.

fiduciário s. m. fiduciary, trustee, fideicommissor, fideicommissioner. || adj. fiducial, fiduciary. **emprego ~ de capital** investment of trust money. **circulação -a** paper currency.

fieira s. f. 1. (tech.) drawplate, drawing frame, die for wire drawing. 2. file, row, alignment. 3. vein of mineral rock. 4. practical experience, trial. 5. (Braz.) fishing-line. 6. children's whiplash (to spin a top). ~ **de pérolas** beads. **dar pela ~** to give but very little. **passar pela ~** to stand a severe trial. **pela ~ da justiça** strictly according to the law. **puxar a ~** to be the first, to push forward.

fiel s. m. (pl. **fiéis**) 1. a treasurer's assistant, cashier. 2. tongue, cock, pointer or hand of a balance or weighing-machine. 3. pl. (rel.) the faithful, true believers, followers, churchgoers. 4. regular. || adj. m. + f. 1. faithful, true, trusty. 2. loyal, devoted, leal. 3. sincere, honest. 4. trustworthy, reliable, sure. 5. punctual, exact, accurate, unfailing. || ~**mente** adv. faithfully, loyally, sincerely, surely, reliably. **ficar ~ a** to abide by, adhere. **fique ~ aos seus juramentos** adhere to your vows. ~ **à sua promessa** true to his promise. **manter-se ~ a** to stick by. **você me será ~?** will you be true to me? **ele é o ~ da balança** he will decide the question.

fieldade s. f. = **fidelidade**.

fífia s. f. shrill sound, discordance.

fifó s. m. (S. E. Braz.) a small kerosene lamp with wick but no chimney.

figa s. f. 1. (bot.) fico, fig. 2. fig: gesture of contempt made by placing the thumb between two of the closed fingers. 3. charm, talisman. 4. amulet, mascot. 5. (fig.) mockery, contempt. **dar uma ~ a alguém** not to care, send to hell. **fazer ~** to show contempt. **embrulhão de uma ~!** (pop.) you dirty swindler! **não vale uma ~!** it isn't worth a penny!

figadal adj. m. + f. (pl. -ais) 1. hepatic: of or pertaining to the liver. 2. intimate, confidential.

3. profound, thorough. 4. intense, intensive. ‖ ~mente adv. intimately, confidentially.
ódio ~ mortal hatred.

figadeira s. f. 1. (vet.) disease of the liver. 2. (pop.) liver complaint, inflammation of the liver.

fígado s. m. 1. (anat.) liver. 2. (fig.): a) courage, tenacity. b) character, moral firmness.
~ **de alcoólatra** whisky liver. **ele tem maus** ~s he is a vindictive man. **ela tem** ~ she has courage. **óleo de** ~ **de bacalhau** codliver oil.

fígaro s. m. (pop.) figaro, barber.

figle s. m. ophicleide: musical wind instrument, having usually eleven keys.

figo s. m. fig.
isto não vale um ~ this is not worth a fig, not worth a rush.

figueira s. f. (bot.) fig, fig tree.
plantar uma ~ to come a cropper.

figueira-maldita s. f. (pl. **figueiras-malditas**) balsam fig, chigoe poison, pitch apple.

figueiral s. m. (pl. **-ais**) fig grove, fig plantation.

figueiredo s. m. 1. fig grove, fig plantation. 2. (sl.) liver.

figueirinha-hera s. f. (pl. **figueirinhas-hera**) creeping fig.

figulina s. f. (obs.) figuline, piece of pottery, earthenware.

figulino adj. 1. figuline, made of clay. 2. suitable for pottery. 3. (fig.) soft, bland.

figura s. f. 1. figure: a) appearance. b) figuration, aspect, conformation, shape, frame, outward form. c) social importance, eminence. d) person, personality, individuality. e) drawing, design. f) construction plan, layout, diagram. g) performer, actor, player, character. h) countenance, looks. i) image, effigy, picture. j) symbol. k) rhetoric figure, metaphor. 2. chessman, piece. 3. honour, card face, court-card.
~ **de cera** waxwork. ~ **de um escudo** armorial bearings. ~ **de retórica** figure of speech. **ele é apenas uma** ~ **de proa** he is nothing but a figure head. **depois daquela minha conversa com ele o caso mudou de** ~ after that conversation with him the case looked quite different. **em** ~ in attitude, in posture. **fazer** ~ to cut a figure, cut a dash. **fazer boa** ~ to cut a good figure. **ele faz triste** ~ he cuts a sorry figure. **estar em boa** ~ to be in a fair way. **mudar de** ~ to put a new face on things, become different.

figuração s. f. (pl. **-ões**) 1. figuration. 2. act or process of shaping something. 3. form, shape, outline, contour. 4. configuration of stars and its interpretation.

figurado adj. 1. figurative, figured, allegoric. 2. tropologic(al), metaphorical. 3. imitative, representative.

figural adj. m. + f. (pl. **-ais**) figural, figurate.

figuralidade s. f. 1. (phys.) shape. 2. figurability.

figurante s. m. + f. 1. (theat.) figurant(e), super (numerary), (fam.) dummy. 2. (theat.) each of the actors and figurants appearing on the stage.

figurão s. m. (pl. **-ões**) (f. **figurona**) 1. person of consequence, eminent personality. 2. (sl.) toff, panjandrum, bigwig. 3. ostentation, display.
fazer um ~ to make o. s. conspicuous.

figurar v. 1. to figure, portray. 2. to outline, trace, draw, figure. 3. to shape, form. 4. to represent, symbolize. 5. to feign. 6. to suppose. 7. to be renowned, be well-thought of. 8. to act on the stage, play, perform. 9. to participate, partake. 10. to resemble, have the appearance of. 11. ~-se to fancy, imagine.
~ **de** to pose as, appear as. ~ **em** to belong to.

~ **em primeiro lugar** to rank first. **ele figurava 30 anos** he looked about 30 years of age.

figurarias s. f. pl. grimaces, gests to entertain children.

figurativa s. f. (gram.) ending, termination (of declinable words).

figurativo adj. 1. figurative, representative, symbolic(al). 2. tropological. ‖ **-amente** adv. 1. figuratively, symbolically. 2. tropologically.

figurável adj. m. + f. (pl. **-áveis**) figurable, capable of being expressed figuratively.

figurilha s. m. + f. little or unsightly person, shrimp.

figurinha s. f. figurine.

figurino s. m. 1. model, fashion plate, pattern (for cutting a dress). 2. ~s pl. pattern book, fashion jornal or magazine. 3. dandy, fop. 4. (fig.) example, standard.

figurismo s. m. (phil., rel., theol.) figurism.

figurista s. m. + f. (phil., rel., theol.) figurist. ‖ adj. (paint.) specialized in portraying the human figure.

figuro s. m. 1. eccentric (fellow). 2. dubious character.

fila s. f. 1. file, line. 2. row, rank. 3. tier. 4. queue. 5. train.
~ **da frente** front row. ~ **indiana** single file. **em** ~ in file. **formar** ~ to queue up, rank, tier. **pôr em** ~ to set in a row.

filaça s. f. filasse, yarn, lint, harl, charpie.
~ **de cânhamo** harl of hemp.

filactério s. m. phylactery, amulet.

filadelfo s. m. Philadelphian. ‖ adj. Philadelphian.

filamentar adj. m. + f. filamentar(y).

filamento s. m. 1. filament (plate L 1). 2. fibre, thin thread, string. 3. mineral fibre.
circuito de ~ filament circuit. ~ **de quartzo** quartz fibre. **sem** ~ filamentless, fibreless.

filamentoso adj. filamentose, filamentous, filamentary, thready, filose.

filandras s. f. pl. 1. long, thin threads. 2. gossamer. 3. filamentous seaweed. 4. filanders: bird disease caused by worms.

filandroso adj. fibrous, fibrose.

filante s. m. + f. (Braz., sl.) cadger; (U. S. A., sl.) deadhead. ‖ adj. cadging.

filanto s. m. (bot.) 1. snowbush. 2. Phylantus: a large genus of tropical plants.

filantropia s. f. philanthropy, love for mankind, good will.
praticar a ~ to philanthropize.

filantrópico adj. philanthropic(al), benevolent. ‖ **filantropicamente** adv. philanthropically.
tornar ~ to philanthropize.

filantropismo s. m. philanthropism.

filantropo s. m. philanthropist, humanitarian. ‖ adj. philanthropist.

filão s. m. (pl. **-ões**) 1. (min.) lode, vein, seam, streak. 2. (Braz.) loaf of (wheaten) bread (plate P 3). 3. (fig.) source.

filar v. 1. to fasten, tie. 2. to seize with the teeth, grip, clutch. 3. to pounce upon, claw. 4. to grasp, take hold of. 5. to catch, capture. 6. to steer in the wind, tack. 7. to incite, instigate. 8. to obtain as a gift. 9. (Braz.) to ask as a favour, beg, scrounge, cadge, bum, prog. 10. (gambling) to appreciate one's cards with gusto. 11. to crib, copy.

filargíria s. f. avarice.

filária s. f. (zool.) filaria, guinea worm.

filaríase, filariose s. f. (med.) filariasis.

filarídeos s. m. pl. (zool.) Filariidae, a family of nematode worms.

filarmônica s. f. Philharmonic: philharmonic society, concert or orchestra.

filarmônico adj. philharmonic: fond of music.

filástica s. f. 1. tow, strand of rope. 2. oakum.

filatelia s. f. philately.

filatélico adj. philatelic(al), philatelist.

filatelista s. m. + f. philatelist, stamp collector.

filatório s. m. spinning machine, jenny. ‖ adj. of, pertaining to or related to spinning.

filáucia s. f. 1. egoism, egotism. 2. vanity, conceit.

filaucioso adj. 1. egoistic, egotistic. 2. vain, conceited.

filé s. m. 1. fil(l)et: piece of lean meat, flat slice of fish, (U. S. A.) undercut, tenderloin. 2. broiled or cooked steak. 3. filet or net lace. **eu queria um ~ com batatas** I would like a steak with potatoes.

fileira s. f. 1. row, rank, tier, range. 2. file, line, string, rope. 3. wing, ala. 4. course. 5. train. 6. **~s** pl. military life or active service. **~ de tijolos** stretching course. **cerrar as ~s** to close the ranks. **em ~s** in tiers. **paletó de uma ~ de botões** a single-breasted coat. **uma ~ de soldados** a column.

filelenismo s. m. Philhellenism.

filerete s. m. 1. jointer, joiner's plane. 2. (naut.) netting.

filetar v. 1. to hem or border. 2. to adorn with fillets or listels. 3. to groove. 4. to cut a thread, to thread a screw.

filete (ê) s. m. 1. thread, thin thread. 2. beading. 3. (archit.) fillet, moulding, listel, string-course, reglet, quadra. 4. (bot.) filament. 5. (anat.): a) fine band of fibers. b) nervule. 6. (mech.) rim, border. 7. thin slice of meat or fish. 8. (tech.) turn of a thread, thread of a screw, worm (plate P 4). 9. (typogr.) rule. **~ duplo** double thread. **~ externo** male screw.

filha s. f. daughter. **~ adotiva** foster daughter. **~ de madrasta ou padrasto** stepsister. **as ~s de Eva** the fair sex. **a ambição é ~ do orgulho** ambition is the daughter of pride.

filhação s. f. (pl. -ões) 1. filiation, descent. 2. parentage. 3. dependency.

filhada s. f. 1. grasping, seizure.

filha-de-senhor-de-engenho s. f. (pl. **filhas-de-senhor--de-engenho**) (Braz., sl.) sugar-cane brandy.

filhar v. 1. to affiliate, adopt. 2. (bot.) to sprout, shoot up, bud. 3. to grasp, seize, take hold by force. 4. to appropriate barren land.

filharada s. f. large family, great number of children.

filharar v. (bot.) to bud, sprout.

filheiro adj. 1. prolific, fruitful, fecund. 2. fond of one's own children.

filhento adj. prolific, fecund, fruitful.

filhinho s. m. little son, chikabiddy, sonny. **ele é ~ de papai** he was born with a silver spoon in his mouth.

filho s. m. 1. son. 2. descendant, offspring, fruit. 3. (zool.) younglet, young animal, nestling, (dog) pup. 4. (bot.) sprout, shoot. 5. native, national. 6. **~s** pl. children. 7. (fig.) product, effect. ‖ adj. proceeding, resulting. **~ adotivo** adopted son, fosterling. **~ de criação** foster child. **~ das ervas** foundling. **~ de leite** child in relation to its wet nurse. **~ da sua mãe** son who takes after his mother. **~ do mar** able seaman. **~ de São Paulo** native of São Paulo. **~ ilegítimo** bastard. **~ mais moço** cadet. **~ natural** natural child. **~ primogênito** first-born son. **~ pródigo** (bib.) prodigal (son). **Filho do Homem** Son of Man (Jesus). **cada um é ~ de suas obras** his good deeds commend the man. **ele é ~ de peixe** he is a chip of the old block. **ele é também ~ de Deus** he has the same rights. **fazer de um ~ e de outro, enteado** to act unjustly or unfairly. **im-**

próprio de um ~ unfilial. **os ~s da candinha** (Braz. pop.) the common people, the man in the street, the wicked tongues. **sem ~** sonless. **todos somos ~s de Adão** we are all poor sinners.

filhó, filhós s. m. + f. (pl. **filhoses**) tortilla, pancake, wafer, fritter.

filho-família(s) s. m. (pl. **filhos-família(s)**) son who lives on his rich parents' expenses.

filhotão s. m. (pl. -ões) half-grown animal or plant.

filhote s. m. 1. native, descendant. 2. younglet, nestling. 3. litter, brood, fry. 4. **~s** (pl.) young. 5. protégé, beneficiary, favourite. **~ de águia** eaglet. **~ de aves de rapina** aerie, aery, eyrie. **~ de cachorro** pup(py), whelp. **~ de leão** baby lion. **~ de urso, leão, lobo, raposa** cub.

filhotismo s. m. (Braz.) 1. favouritism, patronage. 2. political protectionism.

filiação s. f. (pl. -ões) 1. descent, extraction. 2. filiation. 3. affiliation, adoption. 4. dependency, subordination. 5. admission, admittance, enrolment.

filial s. f. (pl. -ais) 1. branch, branch office or establishment, suboffice. 2. chain store. ‖ adj. m. + f. filial, (biol.) daughter. ‖ **~mente** adv. filially. **~ de banco** branch bank. **obediência ~** filial obedience.

filiar v. 1. to adopt, affiliate. 2. to branch out, spring off. 3. to admit, enroll, incorporate. 4. to procriate. 5. to proceed from, originate. 6. **~-se** to enter, join (a group or party). **companhia filiada** subsidiary company. **eles não se filiam a nenhum partido** they affiliate with no party. **pessoa ou organização filiada** affiliate.

filicida s. m. + f. filicide: parent who kills a son or daughter.

filicídio s. m. filicide: act of killing a son or daughter.

filicífero adj. (bot.) filiferous.

filicíneo adj. (bot.) filical, filicinean.

filicíneas s. f. pl. (bot.) Filicales.

filicite s. m. (pal.) filicite, fossil fern.

filicórneo adj. (zool.) having hornlike antenna(e).

filidráceas s. f. pl. (bot.) Philydraceae, a family of flowering herbs.

filífero adj. (bot.) filiferous.

filifolha (ô) s. f. (bot.) fern.

filiforme adj. m. + f. 1. (bot., zool.) filiform, thready, threadlike. 2. (med.) weak (pulse).

filigrana s. f. 1. filigree, filigrane, filigree work. 2. (typogr.) watermark.

filigranado adj. filigree.

filigranar v. 1. to filigree, adorn with or work in filigree. 2. (fig.) to do delicate, artistic work.

filigraneiro s. m., **filigranista** m. + f. filigree worker.

filipêndula s. f. (bot.) dropwort.

filípica s. f. (hist.) Philippic. 2. (fig.) philippic: acrimonious oration, invective.

filipina s. f. philippina, philopena: 1. sharing of a nut, that has two kernels, between two persons, each one trying to obtain a forfeit. 2. the forfeit. ‖ adj. of, pertaining to or relative to this game.

filipino s. m. Filipino (f. **filipina**): native or inhabitant of the Philippine Islands. ‖ adj. Filipino, Philippine.

filipluma s. f. filoplume: feather with a slender quill.

filipsita s. f. (min.) phillipsite.

filirostro adj. (zool.) filirostrate.

filisteu s. m. (f. **filistéia**) 1. (bib.) Philistine. 2. (fig.) a narrow-minded fellow, pedant, fog(e)y. 3. (school sl.) townee. ‖ adj. Philistine.

filmagem s. f. (pl. -ens) (cin.) 1. filming, putting on the screen, motion picture shot, shoot. 2. film version. **~ de ângulo** angle shot.

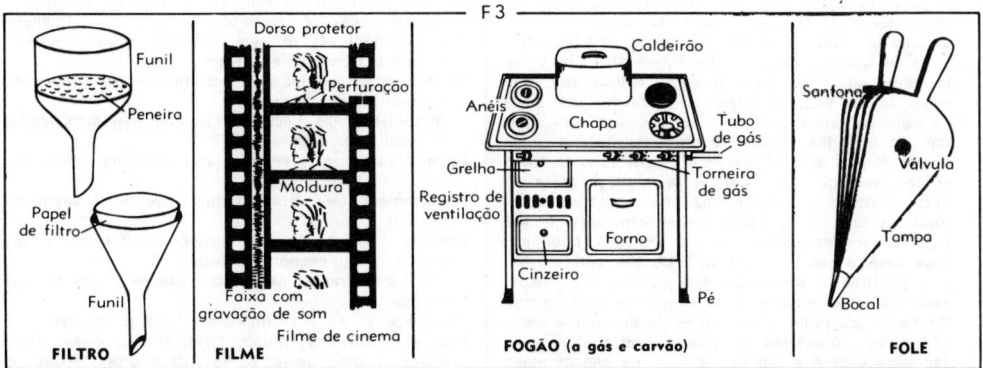

F 3

FILTRO — Funil, Peneira, Papel de filtro, Funil
FILME — Dorso protetor, Perfuração, Moldura, Faixa com gravação de som, Filme de cinema
FOGÃO (a gás e carvão) — Caldeirão, Anéis, Chapa, Tubo de gás, Grelha, Torneira de gás, Registro de ventilação, Forno, Cinzeiro, Pé
FOLE — Sanfona, Válvula, Tampa, Bocal

filmar v. to film, screen, cinematize, shoot, picture, reel.

que pode ser filmado filmable.

filme s. m. film: 1. movie, motion picture. 2. pellicle, thin layer, haze. 3. film strip (plate F 3). ~ **cinematográfico** motion picture. ~ **de desenho** trick film. ~ **de longa-metragem** feature. ~ **exibido por televisão** telefilm. ~ **em rolo** roll film, film cartridge (plate F 6). ~ **sonoro** sound film. **rodar um** ~ to take a film.

fílmico adj. filmic. ‖ **filmicamente** adv. filmically.

filmoteca s. f. 1. collection of films or motion pictures. 2. its keeping place.

filo s. m. (biol.) phylum: one of the primary divisions of the animal or vegetable kingdom.

filó s. m. tulle, bride, bobbinet.

filobrânquios s. m. pl. (zool.) Phylobranchiae: an order of bivalve molluscs.

filocínico s. m. cynophile, dog lover. ‖ adj. cynophilic.

filocládio s. m. (bot.) phylloclade.

filodendro s. m. (bot.) philodendron.

filodérmico adj. philodermic.

filódio s. m. (bot.) phyllode, phyllodium.

filófago s. m. (zool.) 1. animal that feeds on leaves, leaf eater. 2. Phyllophaga: a large genus of beetles. ‖ adj. feeding on leaves, phyllophagous.

filogenético adj. (bot.) phyllogenetic.

filogenia s. f. (biol.) phylogeny, phylogenesis.

filogênico adj. (biol.) phylogenetic(al).

filoginia s. f. philogyny, fondness for women.

filoginio, filógino s. m. 1. philogynist, admirer or lover of women. 2. lady's man, amorous fool. ‖ adj. philogynous, fond of women.

filóide adj. m. + f. (bot.) phylloid: leaflike.

filologia s. f. philology: 1. humanities, study of literature. 2. linguistic science.

ele estuda ~ **clássica** he is a student of the classics.

filológico adj. philologic(al).

filologista s. m. + f. philologer, philologist, student of languages.

filólogo s. m. philologer, philologist, philologian grammarian.

~ **de línguas antigas** classic.

filomatia s. f. philomathy, love of learning.

filomático adj. philomathic(al).

filomela s. f. 1. (myth.) Philomela. 2. (poet.) nightingale.

filonar adj. m. + f. veinous, veiny, streaked.

filoneísmo s. m. philoneism.

filosela s. f. filature, filoselle.

filosofal adj. m. + f. (pl. **-ais**) philosophic(al).

pedra ~ philosopher's (philosophers') stone.

filosofante s. m. + f. 1. philosopher. 2. (depr.) philosophaster. ‖ adj. 1. philosophic(al). 2. (depr.) philosophastering.

filosofar v. 1. to philosophize, interpret philosophically. 2. to reason; argue, ponder. 3. to debate, discuss, draw subtle conclusions. 4. to dabble in philosophy, feign eruditeness.

filosofastro s. m. philosophaster, philosophist.

filosofia s. f. philosophy: 1. love of wisdom and search for it. 2. study of laws, causes and principles of the universe. 3. system of moral principles, ethics. 4. rational explanation and theory of any branch of learning. 5. (fig.) calmness, fortitude, serenity, composure.

filosófico adj. philosophic(al). ‖ **filosoficamente** adv. philosophically.

filosofismo s. m. philosophism, sophistry, false philosophy.

filósofo s. m. 1. philosopher. 2. quiet thinker, calm reasoner. 3. queer fellow.

filostomídeos s. m. pl. (zool.) Phylostomidae, a large family of leaf-nosed bats.

filotaxia s. f. (bot.) phyllotaxy, phyllotaxis.

filotecnia s. f. philotechnique.

filotécnico adj. philotechnic(al).

filoxera s. f. (zool.) phylloxera, vine fretter, vine louse.

filtração s. f. (pl. **-ões**) (also **filtramento** m., **filtragem** f.) filtration: act or process of filtering; percolation.

filtrado s. m. filtrate.

filtrador s. m. filter(er). ‖ adj. filtering.

material ~ filtering material.

filtragem s. f. (pl. **-ens**) filtration.

filtrante adj. m. + f. filtering.

filtrar v. 1. to filter, filtrate. 2. to strain, percolate, ooze through, permeate. 3. (fig.) to instil, inspire (confidence, courage). 4. ~**-se** to ingratiate o. s., worm into.

filtrável adj. m. + f. (pl. **-áveis**) filtrable.

filtreiro s. m. filter, strainer, colander, percolator.

filtro s. m. 1. filter, strainer, percolator (plate F 3). 2. filtering material (bag, cloth, porous mass, paper, etc.). 3. philter, philtre.

~ **amoroso** love potion. ~ **amatório** philter. ~ **de algodão** bag filter. ~ **de ar** air filter (plate M 13). **papel** ~ filtering paper.

filustria s. f. (Braz.) 1. feat, prowess, exploit. 2. boast, bragging.

fim s. m. (pl. **fins**) 1. end, conclusion, termination. 2. terminal, expiration, ending. 3. closure, close, closing. 4. aim, intention, design, destination, finality, motive. 5. extremity, tail, tail end. 6.

stop. 7. finish. 8. tag, last. 9. come-off, outgoing. 10. winding-up. 11. (fig.) wane. 12. death.
a ~ de in order to, by way of, to the end that, for. **a ~ de que** so that, to the intent that, in order to. **levar ao ~** to carry through. **chegar ao ~** to come to an end, to draw to a close. **até o ~** through. **fiel até o ~** faithful to the last. **eles lutaram até o ~** they fought to the finish. **até o ~ do mundo** to the end of the world. **em fins de maio** at the end of May. **dar ~ a alguma coisa** to finish, accomplish something. **do começo ao ~** from one end to the other. **no ~** terminally, in the end. **no ~ das contas, no ~ de tudo** after all. **você será o meu ~** you will be the end of me. **o ~ justifica os meios** the end justifies the means. **para que ~?** to what end? **o ~ está se aproximando** the sands are running out. **no ~ do dia** at the close of the day. **pomos um ~ nisto** we put a stop to it. **não sabe qual é o começo e o ~** he cannot make head or tail of it. **a partida está no ~** the game is up. **por ~** at last. **ter ~** to be at an end. **~ de semana** weekend. **para o ~ da semana** towards the end of the week. **com o ~ de** in order to.
fima s. f. (med.) phyma.
fimatose s. f. (med.) phymatiasis, phymatiosis, tuberculosis.
fímbria s. f. 1. fringe, border of a gown. 2. (anat., bot.) fimbria.
fimbriado adj. fimbriate(d).
fim-d'águas s. m. (pl. **fins-d'águas**) (N. Braz.) refluence of high water (approaching normal water-level).
fim-de-século adj. m. + f., sg. + pl. 1. of the turn of the century. 2. modern, up-to-date. 3. refined.
fimícola adj. m. + f. (biol.) fimicolous.
fimose s. f. (med.) phimosis.
finado s. m. deceased, departed, dead. ‖ adj. dead, defunct, deceased.
Finados All Souls' Day.
final s. m. (pl. **-ais**) 1. conclusion, finish, end, last. 2. final, upshot. 3. terminus, terminal. 4. tail, tag. 5. result, outcome, come-off. 6. (mus.) finale. ‖ adj. m. + f. final: 1. last. 2. terminal, terminative, ultimate. 3. decisive, conclusive, definite, definitive, peremptory. 4. concluding, finishing. 5. closing, eventual. ‖ **~mente** adv. at last, lastly, finally, conclusively, ultimately, at length, eventually.
aguardar o resultado ~ to watch the final result or event. **causa ~** final cause. **cláusula ~** final clause. **o dia ~, o juízo ~** day of judgement, doomsday. **linha ~** tag line. **no ~ das contas** In the long run, in the upshot. **objetivo ~** final aim. **parte ~** tail end. **sessão ~** (jur.) final hearing. **tomar parte no ~** to be in at the finish. **ele escreveu ~mente** he wrote at last. **~mente ela tem razão** finally she is right.
finalidade s. f. 1. ultimate object, purpose, finality. 2. end, design, intention, effect. 3. motive, sake. 4. use, function.
qual foi a ~ disto? what was it intended for? **com esta ~** for this purpose. **com que ~?** for what purpose? **com a ~** to the effect. **ausência de ~** aimlessness.
finalismo s. m. finalism (teleological doctrine).
finalista s. m. + f. finalist: 1. believer in finalism. 2. contestant in the final round of a competition. ‖ adj. finalist, teleological.
finalização s. f. (pl. **-ões**) conclusion, termination, end, finish, finishing.
finalizado adj. finished, accomplished.
finalizar v. 1. to finish, terminate, conclude, accomplish. 2. to put an end to, bring to a conclusion.
finamento s. m. death, decease, end.

finanças s. f. pl. finance(s): 1. fund(s), capital. 2. the science of monetary affairs. 3. financial management. 4. revenue, income, public revenue. 5. public treasury, exchequer.
financeiro s. m. financier, capitalist. ‖ adj. financial. ‖ **-amente** adv. financially.
dificuldades -as pecuniary trouble. **em dificuldades -as** (coll.) hard-up.
financial adj. m. + f. (pl. **-ais**) financial, monetary, fiscal.
financiamento s. m. financing, capital investment, floating.
financiar v. 1. to finance, provide capital for, supply money. 2. to support, maintain.
ela lhe financiou os estudos she put him through college.
financista s. m. + f. financier, banker, capitalist.
finar v. 1. to end, finish, terminate. 2. **~-se:** a) to waste or pine away. b) to wither away, decay. c) to grow lean, lose flesh. d) to die.
finca s. f. prop, support, stay.
fincão s. m. (pl. **fincões**) (ent.) barbeiro, barber bug.
finca-pé s. m. (pl. **finca-pés**) 1. foothold, foot support. 2. (fig.) stubbornness, pertinacity, obstinacy.
fazer ~ to put one's foot down, persist in.
fincar v. 1. to thrust in, nail in, drive in, ram down (piles), dig, stick, plunge. 2. **~-se:** a) to stand still, stop, remain fixed on the spot. b) to persevere, persist, to be pertinacious.
finco s. m. (ant.) 1. deed. 2. contract, obligation.
fincudo s. m. (Braz., ent.) barbeiro, barber bug.
findar v. 1. to finish, conclude. 2. to complete, accomplish, fulfil. 3. to terminate, come to an end. 4. to put an end to. 5. to die, perish.
findável adj. m. + f. (pl. **-áveis**) finishable.
findo adj. finished, over, past, out.
finês s. m. (pl. **-eses**) (f. **-esa**) 1. Finn: native of Finland. 2. Finnish: language spoken in Finland and some adjacent regions. ‖ adj. 1. Finnic. 2. Finnish.
fineza s. f. 1. slimness, slenderness, thinness. 2. perfection, elegance, gracefulness. 3. delicacy, attentiveness, gentleness. 4. purity, fineness. 5. favour, kindness, helpfulness. 6. courtesy, politeness. 7. finesse, refinement, subtleness. 8. **~s** pl. compliments, attentions.
~ das cores brightness of colours. **com ~** friendly, obligingly. **dever uma ~** to be under an obligation. **fazer uma ~** to do a kindness. **faça-me a ~** be so kind. **feito com ~** delicately done.
fingido adj. 1. feigned, fictitious, assumed, sham, artificial, fabled, forced, fake, disguised. 2. insincere, false, hypocrite, hypocritical, feline, cattish, double-faced, double-hearted. ‖ **-amente** adv. simulatively, artificially, feigningly, feignedly, falsely, deceivingly, felinely.
lágrimas -as false tears. **dedicação -a** spurious devotion. **não ~** unfeigned. **ser ~** to cant.
fingidor s. m. dissembler, feigner, simulator.
fingimento s. m. 1. simulation, hypocrisy, dissimulation, feigning, feignedness. 2. deceit, deception, fraud. 3. camouflage, disguise(ment). 4. pretense, affectation. 5. cant.
fingir v. 1. to (dis)simulate, feign, make believe, sham, play-act, fake, assume. 2. to pretend, affect. 3. to fancy, imagine. 4. to invent, fable. 5. to imitate, copy, counterfeit. 6. camouflage, disguise.
~ não conhecer alguém to cut s. o. **~-se doente** to feign sickness. **fingiu ir-se** he made a feint of going. **ele fingiu inocência** he had a face of innocence. **eles ~am a sua identidade** they sailed under false colours. **ela fingiu-se ingênua** she feigned ingenuousness.

finidade s. f. (philos.) finiteness, finite, finitude.
fininha s. f. (Braz., pop., med.) consumption.
fininho s. m. (N. Braz., pop.) a leaf of Indian hemp.
finítimo adj. 1. bordering upon. 2. adjacent, contiguous. 3. neighbouring.
finito s. m. 1. finite (also philos.). 2. (gram.) indicative mood. 3. (math.) a definite number. ‖ adj. 1. limited, bounded. 2. transitory, temporary. 3. finite, terminable. 4. contingent. 5. (math.) terminate. ‖ **-amente** adv. finitely.
finlandês s. m. (pl. **-eses**) (f. **-esa**) (also **fino**) 1. Finn, Finlander. 2. Finnish (language). ‖ adj. Finnic, Finnish.
fino s. m. a fine, slender, delicate or elegant thing or matter. ‖ adj. 1. thin, slim, slender (plate Q). 2. filmy, tenuous, wispy, aerial, subtile. 3. graceful, elegant, pretty, tasteful, nice. 4. delicate, gentle. 5. pure, fine. 6. excellent, superior, refined, exquisite, choice. 7. polite, courteous, well-bred, noble, gallant. 8. sharp, shrewd, cunning, subtle, wizen, keen, wise. 9. kind, affectionate. 10. perfect, accomplished. 11. sharp, pointed. 12. (mus.) classical. 13. light (fabric). 14. (fig.) thready. 15. (joc.) proper. ‖ **-amente** adv. 1. finely, delicately. 2. handsomely. 3. politely. 4. affectionately, fondly. 5. thinly, etc.
~ como uma cobra sly as a snake. **~ como um sarrafo** lathy. **ela é muito -a** she is very shrewd. **um tanto ~** thinnish. **beber do ~** to be well informed about political secrets or important transactions, etc. **à -a força** by mere force. **pedras -as** precious stones.
finório s. m. cunning fellow, artful dodger; (sl.) file. ‖ adj. 1. sly, cunning. 2. sharp, keen, perspicacious. 3. foxy.
fins-d'água s. m. pl. (N. Braz.) the end of the rainy season.
finta s. f. 1. additional tax, tribute, contribution. 2. feint, dodge. 3. spar, jink.
fintador s. m. swindler, cheat, sharper. ‖ adj. deceitful, fraudulent.
fintar v. 1. to tax, impose tribute. 2. to contribute. 3. (Braz., pop.) to swindle, cheat. 4. (sport) to feint, trick, jink.
finura s. f. 1. thinness, slimness, exility. 2. subtleness, slyness, cunning, wit. 3. courtesy, politeness. 4. sharpness. 5. malice, mischievousness. 6. niceness. 7. fineness. 8. daintiness, delicacy. 9. finesse.
fio s. m. 1. thread, twine, yarn. 2. file, row, line. 3. wire. 4. trickle. 5. connection, link. 6. string. 7. cutting edge. 8. (bot.) filament, fibre. 9. **~s** pl. means, methods. 10. cutting pattern (drawn on wooden boards or timber).
~ condutor conducting wire. **~s cruzados** cross wires. **~ de água** dribble. **~ de algodão** cotton yarn. **~ de cabelo** one hair. **~ de campainha** bell-wire. **~ de descida de antena** (radio) lead-in. **~ de enfardar** pack thread. **~ de lã** wool fibre. wool yarn. **~ de linha** sewing-thread. **~ de navalha** razor's edge. **~ de ouro** spun gold. **~ de prata** silver wire. **~ de prumo** plumb line. **~ de retícula** cross hair. **~ de retrós** sewing-silk, twine. **~s de teia de aranha** (flutuantes no ar) air threads, gossamer. **~ de tripa** gut. **~ de vela** (naut.) twine. **~ elétrico** wire (plates A 6, C 1, E 3, L 1). **~ flexível** (electr.) flex (wire) (plate T 4). **~ grosso (de lã)** thrum. **~ neutro** (electr.) neutral wire. **~ sem corrente** (electr.) dead wire. **~ torcido** twist. **~ trançado** braided wire. **cinco anos a ~** five years running. **por horas a ~** hours and hours. **achar o ~ da meada** to find the clue of the problem. **o ~ arrebentou** the thread

is broken. **correr em ~** to trickle. **cortar o ~** to break off, discontinue. **dar um ~ à língua** to slander. **de ~ a pavio** from the beginning to the end. **de dois ~s** bifilar. **de três ~s** three-ply. **embotar os ~s** to take off the edge. **o ~ da espada** the edge of the sword. **meu paletó está no ~** my jacket is threadbare. **ficar no ~** to become shabby. **em forma de ~** threadlike. **minha vida estava por um ~** my life hung by a thin thread. **ir pelo ~ da gente** to go after the multitude. **levar tudo a ~ de espada** to destroy (or smash) everything radically. **retomar o ~ do discurso** to resume a discourse. **perder o ~ da meada** to lose o. s., to hum and haw. **ela perdeu o ~ da sua história** she lost the thread of her tale. **por um ~ (de cabelo)** (fig.) within a hair's breadth, by a fraction of an inch, to a fit. **estava por um ~ de cabelo** it was touch and go. **foi por um ~ que** it was a matter of touch-and-go. **reatar o ~ da conversa** to resume (or take up) the thread. **sem ~** without cutting edge, edgeless. **~ da vida** the thread of life, fatal thread.
fiofó s. m. (Braz., sl.) behind, posterior, anus.
fiorde s. m. fiord, fjord.
fiorita s. f. (min.) fiorite.
fioritura s. f. 1. (mus.) fioritura. 2. (fig.) melodic, oratorical or artistic ornaments.
fiota, fiote adj. (N. Braz., pop.) dandy, swell, fop.
fio-terra s. m. (radio) ground wire, earth wire.
fique s. f. (bot.) portulaca (family Portulaceae).
firma s. f. 1. firm: a) trade or business name. b) commercial or industrial establishment; concern, house, business. 2. signature. 3. seal, subscription. 4. support, foothold.
uma ~ muito acreditada a firm of good reputation. **assinar pela ~** to sign for the firm. **bandeira de uma ~** house flag. **a ~ extinta** the late firm. **nome de ~** trade name. **sua prezada ~** (com. correspondence) your esteemed firm. **~ reconhecida** authenticated signature.
firmã s. m. (Orient) firman: mandate issued by a rule or royal decree.
firmação s. f. (pl. **-ões**) 1. signing, signature. 2. authentication. 3. fastening.
firmador s. m. signer, subscriber, authenticator.
firmal s. m. (pl. **-ais**) 1. brooch. 2. reliquary. 3. seal, signet. 4. **-ais** pl. small hooks or clasps.
firmamento s. m. 1. firmament, sky, heaven, azure. 2. support, prop. 3. foundation.
firmar v. 1. to firm, make or become fast, fix, fixate, secure, set. 2. to settle, establish definitely, steady, stabilize, consolidate. 3. to confirm, sanction. 4. to contract, pact, conclude, bind. 5. to sign, ratify, subscribe, undersign, underwrite, seal. 6. to authenticate, agree to, authorize. 7. to support, back. 8. **~-se:** a) to rely on, lean upon. b) to convince o. s. c) to take firm hold, hold on. d) to base upon. e) to fasten, steady.
eles se ~am em they held firm to. **ele firmou um seguro sobre** he effected an insurance on. **ela firmou de próprio punho** she signed by her own hand. **~ com grampo ou sargento** to clamp. **um contrato** to sign an agreement.
firme (I) s. m. (Braz., Amazonas) plot of land above the high-water level.
firme (II) adj. m. + f. 1. firm, fixed, set. 2. strong, durable. 3. robust, stout. 4. compact, solid. 5. stable, immovable, static(al). 6. unswerving, steadfast, determined, tenacious, decided, sturdy, uncompromising. 7. unfailing, secure, sure. 8. constant, resolute. 9. rigid, stern. 10. contumacious, unruly. 11. definite, unequivocal. 12. with fixed prices or terms. 13. well-founded, settled. 14. definite. 15.

(of colours) genuine, unfading, fast-dyed, fadeless, fast. ‖ ~mente adv. firmly, fast, unswervingly, resolutely, steadfastly, sternly, strongly, solidly, etc. conservar-se ~ to keep steady. o tempo está ~ the weather is settled. de cor ~ dyed in the grain. estar ~ to stand fast. estar ~ em to persist in. manter-se ~ to keep one's ground. memória ~ tenacious memory. tomar uma resolução ~ to fix upon a resolution. ela está ~mente decidida she is hard-set. que não é ~ (colour) unserviceable. não ~ unsound.

firmeza s. f. 1. firmness, fortitude, fixedness. 2. stability, immobility. 3. solidity, steadiness. 4. durability. 5. constancy, steadfastness, tenaciousness. 6. strength, vigour, sturdiness. 7. resolution, determination, resolvedness, decidedness. 8. backbone, energy, hardness. 9. character. **sem** ~ unsteadily, unstable, (fig.) invertebrate. ~ **de vontade** firmness of purpose. **ele mostrou** ~ **de ânimo** he showed valour. **devido à** ~ **de seu braço** due to his arm's strength. **ela falou com** ~ she spoke with determination. **dar** ~ to brace.

firmeza-dos-homens s. f. (pl. **firmezas-dos-homens**) (bot.) cotton rose, Confederate rose.

firmisternos s. m. pl. (zool.) Firmisternia, a division of the amphibian order Linguata.

firo s. m. (Braz.) game similar to checkers.

fisalita s. f. (min.) physalite.

fiscal s. m. (pl. -**ais**) 1. custom inspector, surveyor of taxes, revenue officer. 2. controller, inspector, check (plate E 13). 3. supervisor. 4. fiscal. ‖ adj. m. + f. fiscal, supervisory; assessorial, of, pertaining to or relative to the public treasury or revenue. ~ **de obras** inspector of works.

fiscalização s. f. (pl. -**ões**) 1. fiscalization, control. 2. supervision, inspection. 3. surveillance, inspectorate. ~ **do tráfego** traffic control. **comissão de** ~ visiting committee.

fiscalizar v. 1. to fiscalize, subject to fiscal control. 2. to act as a fiscal or revenue officer. 3. to observe, examine. 4. to control, check, inspect, supervise. 5. to investigate, inquire.

fiscela s. f. muzzle (cover for an animal's mouth, made of straps).

fisco s. m. 1. public revenue, public treasury, the Exchequer. 2. (Roman hist.) fiscus. 3. revenue office, board of assessment.

fiseterídeos s. m. pl. (zool.) Physeteridae, the sperm whale family.

fisga s. f. 1. harpoon, fish-spear, eel-spear, gig, gaff, grains. 2. chink, split, fissure.

fisgada s. f. 1. stabbing. 2. sharp pain, pang.

fisgador s. m. harpooner. ‖ adj. harpooning.

fisgar v. 1. to hook, gaff. 2. to catch. 3. to perceive or understand readily.

fisgo s. m. (Braz.) barbed hook, barb, hook of an angle or harpoon.

física s. f. 1. physics. 2. natural science.

fisicismo s. m. physicism, materialism.

fisicista s. m. + f. physicist. ‖ adj. versed in physics.

físico s. m. 1. constitution, build, physique. 2. physicist. 3. configuration, external aspect. 4. (ant.) physician, doctor of medicine. ‖ adj. 1. physical. 2. bodily, corporeal, personal. 3. natural, material. 4. external. ‖ **fisicamente** adv. 1. physically. 2. animally. **condição** -**a** physical condition. **cultura** -**a** physical culture. **as propriedades** -**as** the physical properties. **treinamento** ~ physical training, physical exercise, gymnastics.

físico-química s. f. physicochemistry.

físico-químico adj. physicochemical.

fisiocracia s. f. physiocracy: physiocratic doctrine or system.

fisiocrata s. m. + f. physiocrat.

fisiocrático adj. physiocratic(al).

fisiogenia s. f. physiogeny.

fisiognomonia s. f. physiognomy: character study from outward appearance and facial features.

fisiognomônico adj. physiognomic(al).

fisiognomonista s. m. + f. physiognomist.

fisiografia s. f. physiography, physical geography.

fisiográfico adj. physiographic(al).

fisiógrafo s. m. physiographer.

fisiologia s. f. 1. physiology, bionomy. 2. treatise on physiology. ~ **de plantas** physiology of plants.

fisiológico adj. physiologic(al), bionomical. ‖ **fisiologicamente** adv. physiologically.

fisiologista s. m. + f., **fisiólogo** m. physiologist, physiologue.

fisionomia s. f. 1. physio(g)nomy, face, semblance, countenance. 2. facial features, characteristic expression. 3. air, countenance, look, aspect. 4. brow.

fisionômico adj. physiognomic(al).

fisionomista s. m. + f. 1. physiognomist. 2. person who has a retentive memory for faces.

fisiopatia s. f. (med.) physiopathology.

fisiopático adj. physiopathological.

fisioterapêutico, fisioterápico adj. (med.) physiotherapeutic(al).

fisocele s. f. (med.) physocele.

fisoclistos s. m. pl. (ichth.) Physoclisti, an order of teleost fishes.

fisóide adj. m. + f. bladdery.

fisometria s. f. (med.) physometra.

fissão s. f. 1. division, splitting, cleavage. 2. (nucl. phys.) nuclear fission, splitting of the atom with release of energy.

fissifloro adj. (bot.) fissiflorous.

fissil adj. m. + f. (pl. -**eis**) fissile.

fissiparidade s. f. (biol.) fissiparism, (reproduction by) fission.

fissíparo adj. (biol.) fissiparous.

fissípede adj. m. + f. (zool.) fissiped(al), fissipedate, fissipedial, cloven-footed, cloven-hoofed.

fissipene adj. m. + f. (ornith.) fissipennate.

fissirrostro s. m. specimen of the Fissirostres: birds with cleft beaks. ‖ adj. fissirostral, fissirostrate.

fissura s. f. 1. chink, split, crack, rime, cleft, cranny. 2. (anat.) fissure, sulcus. 3. (path.) lesion.

fissuração s. f. (pl. -**ões**) fissuration, act of cleaving or splitting, state of being fissured.

fístula s. f. 1. (med.) fistula, sinus, syrinx. 2. (poet.) flute, reed pipe. 3. (fig.) repulsive character.

fistular (I) adj. m. + f. (also **fistulado, fistuloso** m.) 1. fistulated. 2. fistulous. 3. fistular, fistuliform. 4. tubular.

fistular (II) v. to fistulate.

fistulivalve adj. tubular (shell, conche).

fistuloso adj. fistulous, fistular.

fita s. f. 1. ribbon, band, braid, streamer, fillet, ferret, snood. 2. edging. 3. bind(er), string. 4. tape, clamp. 5. (anat.) taenia. 6. strip, zone, belt. 7. riband, ribbon of an order, cordon. 8. (Braz.): a) movie, film, picture, flick. b) show, make-believe. c) deception, lie, falsehood. d) love-making, courtship. 9. act of staring, stare, glare. ~ **azul** (naut.) blue ribbon. ~ **de aço ou de ferro** hoop-iron. ~**s do avental** apron strings. ~ **de chapéu** hatband (plate C 5). ~ **de máquina de escrever** typewriter ribbon. ~ **isolante** insulation tape, friction tape, rubber tape. ~ **métrica** tape line, tape measure (plates A 5, M 7). **fazer** ~ to playact,

dissemble. **queimar a** ~ to spoil or mar the pleasure. **gravação de som em** ~ tape recording.
fitáceo adj. 1. ribbonlike, ribbon-shaped, taenioid. 2. (bot.) taeniform (leaves).
fita-de-moça s. f. (pl. **fitas-de-moça**) centipede plant.
fita-do-mar s. f. (pl. **fitas-do-mar**) eel-grass.
fitar v. 1. to turn upon s. o. or s. th. (attention, thought, etc.). 2. to stare, gaze, fix the glance upon, to eye, envisage. 3. to prick the ears (dogs, cats, etc.). 4. to gaze at each other.
~ **alguém desconfiadamente** to look askance at s. o. **o cachorro fitou as orelhas** the dog cocked his ears. **ele fitou-me com os olhos** he stared at me. **deixe de me** ~ **boquiaberto** don't gape at me.
fitaria s. f. lot of ribbons, ribbandry.
fiteiro (I) s. m. 1. ribbonmaker, ribbon manufacturer. 2. (Braz.): a) bouncer, braggart, humbug. b) lover, flirter. c) doggie. ‖ adj. (Braz.) 1. untruthful, bragging, bouncing. 2. flirting.
fiteiro (II) s. m. (Braz.) show-case, show-window.
fitilho s. m. 1. narrow ribbon, tape. 2. flat packthread, paper string.
fitina s. f. (biochem.) phytin.
fitinha s. f. 1. little ribbon. 2. (fam.) decoration.
fito s. m. 1. aim, target, mark. 2. purpose, intent, design, end, plan. ‖ adj. 1. fixed, staring, firm, immovable. 2. pricked up, upright.
a ~ fixedly, staringly. **com o** ~ **de** with a view to. **pôr o** ~ **em** to aim at.
fitocrenáceas s. f. pl. (bot.) a small family of plants of the order Sapindales.
fitófago s. m. (zool.) phytophagan: specimen of the Phytophaga. ‖ adj. phytophagous, herbivorous.
fitogêneo adj. phytogenic, phytogenous.
fitogenia s. f. phytogeny, phytogenetics.
fitógrafo s. m. phytographer.
fitóide adj. m. + f. phytoid, vegetal.
fitolacáceas s. f. pl. (bot.) Phytolaccaceae.
fitólito s. m. phytolite, phytolith, fossilized plant.
fitologia s. f. phytology, botany, phytography.
fitológico adj. phytologic(al).
fitólogo s. m. phytologist, botanist.
fitônia s. f. ornamental plant of the acanthus family.
fitonomia s. f. phytonomy, plant physiology.
fitopatologia s. f. phytopathology.
fitopatológico adj. phytopathologic(al).
fitoquímica s. f. phytochemistry.
fitossociologia s. f. phytosociology, vegetal sociology.
fitotecnia s. f. 1. phytotechny. 2. phytotaxonomy. 3. economic botany.
fitotécnico adj. phytotechnical.
fitotomia s. f. phytotomy.
fitozoário s. m. (zool.) phytozoon, specimen of the Phytozoa or Phytozoaria, zoophyte.
fiúza s. f. hope, trust, faith.
fiúzo s. m. (ichth.) smooth dogfish.
fivela s. f. buckle, clasp, loop (plates C 14, R 7).
fivelão s. m. (pl. **-ões**) large buckle.
fiveleta s. f. 1. little buckle. 2. old dance.
fixa s. f. 1. a surveyor's staff. 2. joint pin, joint frame (of a door hinge). 3. plug. 4. (railway) fishplate.
~ **e tomada** (Port.) plug and socket. ~ **de comutador** (Port.) plug switch.
fixação s. f. (pl. **-ões**) 1. fixing, fastening. 2. settling, settlement. 3. determination. 4. fixation, fixture. 5. (chem.) solidification.
fixado adj. fixed, set, stated.
fixador s. m. 1. fixer, fixator. 2. clamp, locking device. 3. (chem.) fixative. 4. fixature. 5. (phot.) fixing bath. ‖ adj. fixative.
~ **de maiúsculas** (typewriter) shift lock (plate M 2).

fixar v. 1. to fix: a) fasten, (make) firm, affix, truss, steady, tie. b) attach. c) stick on. d) (naut.) ship. e) lodge. f) settle, establish, set, define, fixate. g) (chem.) render solid (a volatile compound). h) (phot.) fix a negative or positive. 2. to remember, retain in the memory. 3. to determine. 4. to appoint, assign. 5. to stare at.
~ **com agulha** to bestick. ~ **cartazes** to fix posters on, to bill. ~ **uma data** to date, schedule. ~ **os olhos sobre** to look attentively upon. ~ **o pensamento em** to concentrate upon. ~ **o preço** to appraise, rate. ~ **rações** to ration. ~ **seguramente** to make fast. ~ **taxas** to asses (taxes). **ele fixou-me com os olhos** he glared at me. **ela fixou sua residência em Campinas** she made her abode at Campinas.
fixativo s. m. fixature, fixative. ‖ adj. fixative.
fixe adj. (Braz., coll.) fixed, steady, settled, immovable.
fixidade, fixidez s. f. 1. fixidity, fastness, fixity. fixture. 2. permanence, settled state. 3. constancy.
fixo s. m. fixture, permanent appendage. ‖ adj. 1. fixed, firm. 2. stable, steadfast. 3. steady, constant, durable. 4. settled, established, set, vested. 5. stationary. 6. stereotyped. 7. certain, sure. 8. determined, decided, determinate. 9. appointed, definitely, termed (payment, price, etc.). 10. fast, unfadable, fadeless. ‖ **-amente** adv. fixedly, fast, attentively, earnestly, carefully.
estrelas -as fixed stars. **idéia -a** fixed idea. **renda -a** sure income. **uma soma -a** a stationary sum. **não** ~ unsteady.
flabelação s. f. (pl. **-ões**) flabellation, fanning.
flabelado adj. m., **flabelar** m. + f. flabellate, fan-shaped, flabelliform.
flabelar v. 1. to fan. 2. to move to and fro like a fan, agitate.
flabelífero adj. flabelliferous.
flabelifoliado adj. (bot.) flabellifoliate.
flabeliforme adj. m. + f. (bot.) flabelliform.
flabelípede adj. m. + f. (zool.) flabellipede.
flabelo s. m. 1. fan. 2. (eccl.) flabellum, rhipidion. 3. (bot.) paspalum.
flacidez s. f. 1. flaccidity, flaccidness. 2. slackness, flabbiness, lack of tension.
flácido adj. 1. flaccid, flabby, limp. 2. languid, flagging. 3. soft, slack. 4. adipous, fatty. 5. weak, feeble. 6. relaxed. 7. pulpy. ‖ **flacidamente** adv. flaccidly, flabbily, etc.
flaco adj. (Braz.) weak, feeble, meagre, lean.
flacurtiáceas s. f. pl. (bot.) Flacourtiaceae, a small family of tropical shrubs and trees.
flagelação s. f. (pl. **-ões**) 1. flagellation, flogging, whipping. 2. scourge, affliction.
flagelado s. m. (zool.) flagellate, flagellate protozoan or alga. ‖ adj. 1. (biol.) flagellate. 2. tortured, afflicted, tormented.
flagelador s. m. flagellator, flagellant, scourger. ‖ adj. flagellant.
flagelante adj. m. + f. flagellant.
flagelar v. 1. to flagellate, whip, flog. 2. to punish. 3. to torture, scourge. 4. to afflict, harass. 5. ~**-se** to chastise o. s.
flagelífero adj. flagelliferous.
flageliforme adj. m. + f. flagelliform, shaped like a whip or flagellum, flagellate.
flagelo s. m. 1. scourge, whip. 2. punishment, chastise. 3. calamity, plague. 4. torment, affliction. 5. (biol.) flagellum.
flagiciar v. 1. to defame, slander. 2. to disgrace, shame.
flagício s. m. 1. infamy. 2. crime. 3. ignominy.

flagicioso adj. flagitious: 1. shamefully criminal. 2. heinous, wicked. 3. villainous, corrupt.

flagra s. m. (Braz.) the condition of flagrancy.
ser apanhado no ~ (Braz., pop.) to be caught red-handed, in the very act.

flagrância s. f. flagrantness, flagrancy: the very moment of a flagrant act.

flagrante s. m. 1. the very act. 2. instant, moment. 3. opportunity, chance. 4. (phot.) snapshot. ‖ adj. m. + f. 1. flagrant. 2. ardent, flaming. 3. pressing, urgent. 4. rank, notorious. 5. gross, crying. 6. incontestable, evident. ‖ ~**mente** adv. flagrantly.
em ~ in the very deed, in the act, red-handed. **autuar alguém em** ~ (jur.) to take proceedings against s. o. based on an eyewitness report (within a definite time after the crime). **pegar em** ~ to take by surprise. **ele foi pego (preso) em** ~ he was caught flagrante delicto, in the very act. **lavrar o** ~ (jur.) to take down the eyewitness report concerning a crime. **uma violação** ~ **dos tratados** a flagrant violation of the treaties.

flagrar v. 1. to burn, glow. 2. to inflame.

flajolé s. m. (mus.) flageolet, little flute.

flama s. f. 1. flame, blaze. 2. ardour, eagerness. 3. enthusiasm, fervour, passion.

flamância s. f. 1. flame, blaze. 2. glow. 3. brightness, brilliancy. 4. splendour, magnificence. 5. (Braz.) vagrancy, idleness.

flamante adj. m. + f. 1. flaring, blazing. 2. glowing. 3. bright, brilliant. 4. splendid, ostentatious.

flamar, flambar v. to cauterize, asepticize, flame (by means of burning alcohol).

flambar (tech.) to buckle.

flame s. m. (vet.) fleam.

flamejante adj. m. + f. 1. flaming, blazing, ablaze, fiery. 2. flashy, flashing. 3. brilliant, bright. 4. ostentatious, pretentious. ‖ ~**mente** adv. flamingly, flashingly, etc.

flamejar v. 1. to flame, blaze. 2. to burn, glow. 3. to shine, glitter, sparkle. 4. to emit flames, flare, flash.

flamengo (I) s. m. (ornith.) flamingo.

flamengo (II) s. m. 1. Fleming: native or inhabitant of Flanders. 2. Flemish: Low-German language. ‖ adj. Flemish.

flâmeo s. m. (Roman hist.) flame-red veil worn by newlywed women. ‖ adj. flaming, bright, flamboyant.

flamífero, flamígero adj. 1. flamiferous, producing flame. 2. (fig.) brilliant, bright, sparkling.

flâmine s. m. (Roman hist.) flamen, pagan priest.

flamingo s. m. (ornith.) flamingo.

flamipotente adj. m. + f. (Roman hist.) flame-potent (epithet of Vulcan, god of fire).

flamispirante adj. m. + f. (poet.) flame-snorting, fiery, flame-sparkling.

flamívolo adj. (poet.) throwing flames, flying.

flamívomo adj. (poet.) flammivomous, vomiting flames.

flâmula s. f. 1. flammula, small flame. 2. pennant, streamer, pennon, bannerette, burgee, pendant.

flanar v. to lounge, stroll, saunter about.

flanco s. m. flank: 1. (mil.) flanker, wing, either side of a fortification, the sides of an army or fleet. 2. the side of anything. 3. (fig.) weak or vulnerable point. 4. side of an animal, thigh of man (plates C 12, G 1).
atacar o inimigo de ~ to attack (take) the flank of the enemy.

flandeiro s. m. tinsmith, tinworker.

flandre s. m. = **folha-de-flandres.**

flandres s. m., sg. + pl. 1. (Braz., pop.) tin can. 2. shortened form of **folha-de-flandres** tin plate.

flanela s. f. 1. flannel. 2. cotton fabric resembling flannel, swan-skin.

flanelógrafo s. m. a flannel-board, used as a teaching aid.

flange s. f. flange (plate C 1).

flanquear v. 1. to flank: a) attack the flank, take the enemy's flank. b) defend or guard the flank. c) border, march by the side of, by-pass, out-flank. d) pass around the flank of. 2. to make defensible.

flanqueador s. m. flanker.

flaqueirão adj. (pl. -**ões**) (S. Braz., pop.) meagre, lean.

flato s. m. 1. flatulence, flatulency, flatus. 2. hysteria, hysterism.

flatoso adj. flatulent, causing flatus.

flatulência s. f. 1. flatulence, flatulency, flatus. 2. wind, windiness, exhalation. 3. hysterism.

flatulento adj. flatulent, windy. ‖ -**amente** adv. flatulently.

flatuloso adj. flatulent.

flatuosidade s. f. flatulence, flatulency.

flatuoso adj. flatulent.

flauta s. f. 1. flute, fife, pipe, flue pipe. 2. (Braz.) indolence, vagrancy. 3. m. flutist, fifer.
levar tudo na ~ to take things easy. **tocar** ~ to pipe. ~ **pastoril** reed pipe, (hist.) syrinx.

flautado adj. fluted, fluty.

flautar v. 1. to flute, play the flute. 2. to make flutelike sounds. 3. (fig.) to speak with affectation.

flauteador s. m. 1. flute player, flutist. 2. (pop.) swindler, crook, sharper.

flautear v. 1. to flute, play on the flute. 2. to break one's word. 3. (pop.) to swindle, cheat. 4. to amuse o. s.
levar a vida flauteada to live a life of ease, to indulge in idleness.

flauteio s. m. 1. tootle. 2. (Braz., pop.) mockery, derision.

flauteiro s. m. flutist, flute player.

flautim s. m. (pl. -**ins**) (mus.) piccolo.

flautista s. m. + f. 1. flutist, flautist, flute player. 2. flute maker.

flava s. f. (bot.) sweet vernal grass.

flavescente adj. m. + f. flavescent: 1. turning yellow. 2. yellowish.

flavescer v. to turn yellow, become yellowish, take on a golden hue.

flavo adj. gold-yellow, flavid, flavescent.

flebectasia s. f. (med.) phlebectasis.

flébil adj. m. + f. (pl. -**eis**) 1. weeping, lachrymose. 2. mournful.

flebite s. f. (med.) phlebitis.

flebografia s. f. (anat.) phlebography.

flebólito s. m. (med.) phlebolite.

flebotomia s. f. (med.) phlebotomy, bloodletting, venesection.
praticar ~ to phlebotomize.

flebotômico adj. (med.) phlebotomic(al).

flebotomíneos s. m. pl. (zool.) a subfamily of dipterous insects.

flebotomista s. m. + f. (med.) phlebotomist, blood-letter.

flecha s. f. 1. arrow, dart, shaft, bolt. 2. (archit.) spire. 3. (archit.) rise of an arch. 4. (mech.) deflection set. 5. (mech.) sag, sagging (plate C 1). 6. (bot.) arrowleaf. 7. finger-post, sign-post, direction indicator, index.
cabeça de ~, **ponta de** ~ arrow-head. **em forma de** ~ arrow-shaped.

flechada s. f. (also **flechaço** m., **frechada** f.) arrow shot, arrow wound.

flecha-de-parto s. f. (pl. flechas-de-parto) Parthian shot: spiteful remark at leave-taking.
flechado adj. backswept.
flecha-peixe s. m. (pl. flecha-peixes) (ornith.) kingfisher.
flechar v. 1. to wound or pierce with an arrow, shoot an arrow. 2. to hurt someone's feelings, offend. 3. to flit, dart. 4. (Braz.) to come or to go in a straight line.
~ o arco to bend or draw a bow.
flecharia s. f. lots of arrows or darts.
flecheiro s. m. 1. archer, bowman. 2. bowyer.
flechilha s. f. (bot.) uva grass.
flechinha s. f. (bot.) twisted beard grass.
fle(c)tir v. to bend, flex.
flegma s. f. = fleuma.
flegmão, fleimão s. m. (med.) phlegmon: inflammation of the connective tissue.
flegmático adj. phlegmatic(al). ‖ flegmaticamente adv. phlegmatically.
fleima s. f. phlegm, apathy, calmness.
fleimão s. m. phlegmon.
fleimoso adj. (med.) phlegmonous.
fleme s. m. (Braz.) = flama.
flente adj. m. + f. 1. lachrymose, weeping. 2. mournful.
fleotripídeos s. m. pl. (zool.) an insect family of the order Thysanoptera (Thrips).
flertar v. to flirt, coquet, dally, jilt, philander, play at courtship, play around.
ela flertou com ele she flirted with him.
flerte (ê) s. m. flirt, flirtation, playful courtship.
flete s. m. (S. Braz., pop.) beautiful and richly harnessed horse.
fleuma s. m. + f. phlegm: 1. one of the four humours of the body (according to ancient pathology). 2. morbid or viscid mucus. 3. (fig.) apathy, imperturbability, indifference.
ele tem muita ~ he is rather phlegmatic.
fleumático adj. phlegmatic(al), apathetic(al), dull. ‖ fleumaticamente adv. phlegmatically, apathetically.
ela é muito -a she is a bad poke.
flexão s. f. (pl. -ões) 1. flexion, flection, bend(ing). 2. flexure, state of being bent. 3. curve, curvature. 4. (gram.) inflection, inflexion, form, accidence, number, declension.
ensaio de ~ a frio cold bend test.
flexibilidade s. f. 1. flexibility, flexibleness, suppleness, limberness, litheness. 2. pliability, pliancy. 3. manageableness, softness. 4. versatility, facility.
~ de condição flexibleness of mind or disposition.
flexibilizar v. to make flexible or pliable.
fléxil adj. m. + f. (pl. -eis) 1. (poet.) flexible, flexile. 2. pliable. 3. tractable. 4. versatile.
flexíloquo adj. flexiloquent, dubious.
flexional adj. m. + f. (pl. -ais) 1. (gram.) inflectional, inflexional. 2. flexional.
flexionar v. to inflect: 1. bend, deflect. 2. (gram.) vary by inflection, decline (a noun), conjugate (a verb).
flexionismo s. m. (gram.) the doctrine of accidence.
flexípede adj. m. + f. taliped(ic).
flexível adj. m. + f. (pl. -íveis) 1. flexible, pliable, pliant, limber, lithe, subtle. 2. bendable, elastic, distensible. 3. tractable, manageable, ductile. 4. corrigible. 5. yielding, submissive. 6. soft, weak. 7. versatile, facile. 8. deflective, inflective, flexional. 9. tough. ‖ flexivelmente adv. flexibly.
flexivo adj. (gram.) inflective, inflexional, inflectional (languages).
flexor s. m. (anat., also flexório) flexor, flexor muscle. ‖ adj. of, pertaining to or relative to a flexor.

flexuosidade s. f. flexuousness, flexuosity.
flexuoso adj. 1. flexuous, tortuous. 2. winding, sinuous.
flexura s. f. 1. (anat.) flexura, articulation. 2. flexure, flection. 3. flexibility. 4. (fig.) indolence, sluggishness.
flibustaria s. f. filibusterism.
flibusteiro s. m. 1. filibuster, freebooter, buccaneer, corsair. 2. (fig.): a) adventurer. b) thief, rover. ‖ adj. filibusterous.
flictena s. f. (med.) phlyct(a)ena: small vesicle or pustule.
floco s. m. 1. flake, chip, scale, flock. 2. fleck. 3. fuzz. 4. fluffy feathers, down, tuft. 5. vapour.
em ~s in flakes, flocky.
flocos s. m. (bot.) annual garden phlox.
flocosidade s. f. flakiness, flocculence, fuzziness.
flocoso adj. 1. floccose, flocculent, flocky. 2. flaky, flakelike. 3. tufty, tufted. 4. fuzzy. ‖ -amente adv. flakily.
flóculo s. m. little flake, flakelet, floccule.
floema s. m. (bot.) phloem, bast tissue, liber.
flogístico s. m. (old chem.) phlogiston, hypothetical principle of inflammability. ‖ adj. phlogistic.
flogopita s. f. (bot.) phlogopite.
flogose s. f. (min.) phlogosis, inflammation.
flor s. f. 1. flower, bloom, blossom. 2. grain-side, hair side of hides. 3. prime: a) the best or choicest part, cream, fat, elite. b) bloom of youth. c) freshness, vigour, beauty. 4. darling, pet. 5. fleuron, rosette. 6. flavour, bouquet (wine). 7. pureness, virginity. 8. (chem.) flowers. 9. down, fluff. 10. surface, superficies. 11. ~es pl. flowerage, foliage.
~ de laranja orange flower or blossom. ~ de lis lily. ~ de noz-moscada mace. ~ dos amores amaranth. ~es da primavera spring flowers. a fina ~ the pick. a ~ das tropas the elite troops. a ~ da nobreza the prime of nobility. ~ da sociedade the cream of society. coroa de flores wreath of flowers. jardim de flores flower garden. estar em flor to bear flowers, bloom. em plena ~ blown, in full flourish. perder as suas ~es to shed its blossoms. na ~ da mocidade in the pride of youth (or flower). ele morreu na ~ da idade he died in the prime of life. ela é uma ~ she is beautiful, charming. as ondas quebraram em ~ the waves broke in froth. flores de retórica flowers of speech. à ~ de even with, level with. à ~ da água even with the surface of water, awash. sem ~ (bot.) blind, flowerless. pede-se não enviar ~ (send) no flowers.
flora s. f. 1. Flora: a) (myth.) goddess of flowers. b) (astr.) the eighth planetoid. 2. flora: a) botany, plants or plant life of a region. b) systematic treatise on botany.
floração s. f. (pl. -ões) 1. blooming, blossoming, flowering, florescence, efflorescency, flowerage. 2. bloom.
florada s. f. 1. orange blossom comfit. 2. flower-shaped sweetmeat. 3. blooming of plants, flowerage.
florais s. m. pl. (Roman hist.) Floralia, festival in honor of Flora.
floral adj. m. + f. (pl. -ais) floral. ‖ ~mente adv. florally.
florão s. m. (pl. -ões) 1. (archit.) flowerwork, flowerlike ornament, rose, rosette, crocket, finial. 2. (her.) fleuron.
florar v. (Braz.) 1. to flower, bloom, blossom, flourish. 2. to adorn with flowers.
flor-da-cachoeira s. f. (pl. flores-da-cachoeira) (bot.) podostemad.

F 4

Floresta de árvores frondosas | Pinheiral | Bosque de salgueiros | Arvoredo parco | Floresta mista

Moita | Mato denso | Clareira | Alfobre florestal | **FLORESTA** | Vereda entre árvores | Quebra-ventos | Alfobre sementeiro

flor-d'água s. f. (pl. **flores-d'água**) (bot.) water lettuce.

flor-da-imperatriz s. f. (pl. **flores-da-imperatriz**) (bot.) water lily.

flor-da-paixão s. f. (pl. **flores-da-paixão**) (bot.) passion flower.

flor-das-almas s. f. (pl. **flores-das-almas**) (bot.) purple ragwort.

flor-da-verdade s. f. (pl. **flores-da-verdade**) (bot.) white hellebore.

flor-de-amor s. f. (pl. **flores-de-amor**) (bot.) 1. baby blue-eyes. 2. five-spot.

flor-de-baile s. f. (pl. **flores-de-baile**) (bot.) torch thistle, night blooming cereus, night queen.

flor-de-cachimbo s. f. (pl. **flores-de-cachimbo**) (bot.) Dutchman's-pipe, pipe vine.

flor-de-cetim s. f. (pl. **flores-de-cetim**) (bot.) lunary, perennial honesty.

flor-de-coral s. f. (pl. **flores-de-coral**) (bot.) 1. coral plant. 2. coral tree. 3. ceiba. 4. flame-of-the--woods.

flor-de-diana s. f. (pl. **flores-de-diana**) (bot.) mugwort.

flor-de-enxofre s. f. (pl. **flores-de-enxofre**) (chem.) flowers of sulphur, sulphur flour.

flor-de-lis s. f. (pl. **flores-de-lis**) 1. (bot.) Jacobean lily. 2. (her.) fleur-de-lis, flower-de-luce.

flor-de-noiva s. f. (pl. **flores-de-noiva**) (bot.) 1. ocean spray, arrowwood. 2. Italian May. 3. queen of the prairie. 4. meadowsweet.

flor-de-quaresma s. f. (pl. **flores-de-quaresma**) (bot.) Brazilian spiderflower.

flor-de-santo-antônio s. f. (pl. **flores-de-santo-antônio**) (bot.) self-heal, heal-all.

flor-de-são-joão s. f. (pl. **flores-de-são-joão**) (bot.) orange creeper.

flor-de-são-miguel s. f. (pl. **flores-de-são-miguel**) (bot.) 1. throatwort. 2. purple wreath.

flor-de-viúva s. f. (pl. **flores-de-viúva**) (bot.) 1. throatwort, coventry bell. 2. purple wreath.

flor-do-paraíso s. f. (pl. **flores-do-paraíso**) (bot.) 1. flamboyant, royal poinciana, peacock flower. 2. barbados pride.

flor-dos-tintureiros s. f. (pl. **flores-dos-tintureiros**) (bot.) woadwaxen, woodwaxen.

floreado s. m. 1. decoration, embellishment, flourish. 2. (mus.) variation, figuration, grace note. ‖ adj. 1. floriate(d), decorated with flowers, festooned, flowery, florid, flourishing. 2. figurative.

floreador s. m. flourisher.

floreal s. m. Floreal: eighth month of the year (French Revolution).

florear v. 1. to flourish: a) flower, bear or produce flowers. b) shine, become famous. c) (mus.) arpeggiate. 2. to cover or adorn with flowers, embellish. 3. to brandish, handle with dexterity (sword). 4. to show excellent horsemanship. 5. to cut a good figure. 6. (Braz., pop.) to grow tipsy. ~ **com a pena** to write with flourishes. ~ **o estilo** to adorn with figures of speech.

floreio s. m. 1. flourish, act of flourishing. 2. elegance of expression, floridness of literary style. 3. skill, dexterity (with blank arms). 4. (archit.) adornment, embellishment. 5. flower head.

floreira s. f. 1. flowerpot, flower vase, jardinière. 2. flower girl. 3. florist.

floreiro s. m. 1. florist, flower dealer. 2. flowerpot, jardinière.

florejar v. 1. to flower, bloom. 2. to cover or adorn with flowers. 3. to sprout vigorously, flourish. 4. to use a florid language.

florença s. f. florence: 1. a kind of cloth, florentine, variety of taffeta. 2. florin, English gold coin.

florense s. m. + f. native or inhabitant of the Flores Island (Azores, Port.). ‖ adj. of, pertaining to or relative to this island.

florente adj. m. + f. 1. flourishing, florid, flowery. 2. prosperous, vigorous.

florentim s. m. + f. (pl. **-ins**) Florentine: native or inhabitant of Florence. ‖ adj. Florentine.

florentino s. m. Florentine. ‖ adj. Florentine, of Florence.

flóreo adj. 1. floral, flowery, floreated. 2. flourishing.

florescência s. f. (also **florescimento** m.) florescence, efflorescence, inflorescence, floridness, bloom, blossom, flowerage, flowering time, acme. **em** ~ bloomingly.

florescente adj. m. + f. 1. florescent, flowering, bloomy, abloom, rank. 2. prosperous, vigorous, thriving, flourishing, palmy. 3. (com.) humming. ‖ ~**mente** adv. flourishingly, etc.

florescer v. 1. to bloom, blossom, effloresce, bud. 2. to flower. 3. to grow, prosper, thrive, flourish. 4. to gain renown or celebrity. 5. to distinguish o. s.

floresta s. f. 1. forest, wood, wildwood, woodland (plate F 4). 2. grove, 3. meadow. 4. (fig.) confusion, bewildering state of things.

~ **virgem** primeval or virgin forest. **uma clareira na** ~ a clearing in the wood. **uma** ~ **de mastros** a forest of masts.

florestal adj. m. + f. (pl. -ais) forest(al), sylvan, woodland.

ciência ~ science of forestry. **direito** ~ forest law. **guarda** ~ forest ranger. **horto** ~ forest reserve.

floreta s. f. 1. fleuret: floral ornament or decoration. 2. (arch.) dance step. 3. (shoemaking) upper part of the vamp.

florete s. m. 1. rapier, foil, blunt-edged sword. 2. (ichth.) spotted goby.

floreteado adj. 1. flowery, florid, floreate. 2. pointed, foil-like.

floretear v. 1. to adorn with flowers, flower. 2. to fence, practise fencing.

florético adj. (chem.) phloretic.

floretina s. m. + f. (chem.) phloretin.

florianismo s. m. (Braz., hist.) party that supported Marshal Floriano Peixoto.

florianista s. m. + f. (Braz., hist.) supporter of Marshal Floriano Peixoto's political party. ‖ adj. adherent to **florianismo**.

floricoroado adj. (poet.) crowned with flowers.

floriculo s. m. floret, floweret, little flower.

floricultor s. m. floriculturist, florist. ‖ adj. floricultural. ‖ ~**amente** adv. floriculturally.

floricultura s. f. floriculture.

florídeas s. f. pl. (bot.) Florideae, a class of red algae.

florido adj. 1. flowery, flowering, florescent. 2. blossomy, blooming, abloom. ‖ -**amente** adv. flowerily, etc.

flórido adj. 1. florid. 2. luxuriant. 3. adorned, decorated. 4. elegant, brilliant. 5. figurative. ‖ **floridamente** adv. floridly, etc.

florífago adj. floriphagous, feeding on flowers.

florífero, florígero adj. floriferous, producing flowers.

floriferto s. m. (Roman hist.) Cerealia, festival in honour of Ceres.

floriforme adj. m. + f. floriform.

florilégio s. m. 1. florilege, florilegium, collection of flowers. 2. (fig.) anthology, collection of literary works.

florim s. m. (pl. -ins) florin, guilder, a gold coin.

floríparo adj. (bot.) floriparous.

florir v. 1. to flower, bloom, blossom, flourish. 2. to develop, grow. 3. (Braz.) to adorn, decorate.

florista s. m. + f. 1. florist, flower seller. 2. flower girl. 3. manufacturer of artificial flowers.

florística s. f. floristics.

florístico adj. floristic(al).

floritura s. f. (mus.) fioritura; florid, melodic ornament, flourish.

florizina s. f. (chem.) phlor(h)izin.

floromania s. f. florimania, fondness for flowers.

flórula s. f. florula, flora of a small restricted area.

florzinha s. f. floret, small flower.

flósculo s. m. (bot.) floscule, floret, each of the small flowers in a cluster or compound inflorescence.

flosculoso adj. floscular, flosculous, flosculose.

flos-santório s. m. (pl. **flos-santórios**) (R. C.) Flos-sanctorum, book containing the biography of Saints.

flotilha s. f. flotilla, a small fleet, a fleet of small ships.

flox s. m. (bot.) phlox.

floxo adj. (S. Braz.) 1. lax, slack. 2. weak, feeble. 3. fearful. 4. poor (pastures).

fluência s. f. 1. fluency, flux(ion), flow(ing). 2. (fig.) abundance. 3. loquacity, fluidity of style. 4. facility. ~ **rio acima** profluence.

fluente s. m. (math.) fluent. ‖ adj. m. + f. 1. flowing, fluent. 2. fluid, liquid. 3. running. 4. easy, facile,

unlaboured. ‖ ~**mente** adv. fluently, fluidly, easily, etc.

estilo ~ fluent style.

fluidal adj. m. + f. (pl. -ais) (geol.) fluidal.

estrutura ~ **das rochas** fluidal structure of rocks.

fluidez s. f. fluidity, fluidness, fluency, flow(ingness).

fluídico adj. fluidic.

fluidificação s. f. fluidification.

fluidificar v. 1. to fluidify, convert into a liquid. 2. to dilute.

fluidificável adj. m. + f. (pl. -áveis) fluidifiable, liquefiable.

fluido s. m. 1. fluid, liquid. 2. gas. ‖ adj. 1. fluid, fluent, flowing (also fig.). 2. liquid. 3. thin. 4. gaseous. 5. gentle, soft, mild. 6. feeble.

~ **da alma** (theosophy) astral body.

fluir v. 1. to flow, run, stream. 2. to spring of, emanate, pour, flux, outflow, rill. 3. to proceed from.

flume, flúmen (pl. **flumens, flúmenes**) s. m. (poet.) stream, river.

fluminense s. m. + f. (Braz.) native or inhabitant of the state of Rio de Janeiro. ‖ adj. 1. fluvial. 2. of or pertaining to the state of Rio de Janeiro.

flumíneo adj. fluminous, fluvial.

fluobórico adj. (chem.) fluoboric.

flúor s. m. 1. (chem.) fluorine. 2. (med.) flux, catarrh.

fluorato s. m. (chem.) fluorate.

fluorescência s. f. (phys.) fluorescence.

fluorescente adj. m. + f. (phys.) fluorescent.

fluoreto s. m. (chem.) fluoride.

fluórico adj. (chem.) fluoric.

fluorídrico adj. (chem.) fluorhydric, hydrofluoric.

fluorita s. f. fluorite, fluor spar.

fluorítico adj. fluoric.

fluoroscopia s. f. fluoroscopy.

fluoroscópio s. m. fluoroscope.

fluossilicato s. m. (chem.) fluosilicate.

flutícola adj. m. + f. marine: living in the sea.

fluticolor adj. m. + f. sea-green.

flutígeno adj. fluctigenous, sea-born.

flutissonante adj. m. + f., **flutíssono** m. (poet.) fluctisonant, fluctisonous.

flutívago adj. (poet.) floating on the sea.

flutuabilidade s. f. buoyancy, fluctuability, floatage.

flutuação s. f. (pl. -ões) 1. fluctuation, heaving, surging (of waves), waft. 2. float(age). 3. waviness, ondulation. 4. wavering, indecision, hesitation. 5. inconstancy, fickleness. 6. instability (of prices or market conditions).

~ **de freqüência** (radio) swinging. -**ões do mercado** fluctuations of the market.

flutuador s. m. 1. float (of seaplanes). 2. floater, swimmer. 3. floating landing place.

flutuante adj. m. + f. 1. fluctuant, floating, afloat, natant, buoyant, water-borne. 2. fluctuating, wavering. 3. wavy. 4. flaunting. 5. pending. 6. (fig.) doubtful, uncertain. 7. (med.) amphibolic. ‖ ~**mente** adv. floatingly.

dívida ~ floating debt. **doca** ~ floating dock. **guindaste** ~ pontoon crane. **ponte** ~ pontoon bridge. **sua atitude** ~ his or her undecided attitude.

flutuar v. 1. to fluctuate, float. 2. to wave, heave, roll. 3. to swim, drift, stream, flow. 4. to undulate. 5. to flutter, flicker. 6. to sway, rock. 7. to waver, vacillate, hesitate. 8. to be uncertain.

~ **no ar** to hover. ~ **novamente** to refloat. **pôr um navio a** ~ to float a ship, set a ship afloat.

flutuável adj. m. + f. (pl. -áveis) 1. fluctuable, liable to fluctuation. 2. floatable. 3. navigable.

flutuosidade s. f. 1. fluctuosity, fluency. 2. uncertainty, undecidedness.

flutuoso adj. fluctuating: 1. floating, fluctuant. 2. wavering. 3. (fig.) doubtful, uncertain.

fluvial, fluviátil adj. m. + f. (pl. **-ais, -áteis**) 1. fluvial, fluviatic, fluviatile, riverine. 2. floatable.

fronteira ~ fluvial boundary. **plantas -ais** fluviatic plants. **paisagem** ~ waterscape.

flúvio-marinho adj. (pl. **flúvios-marinhos**) fluviomarine.

fluviômetro s. m. fluviometer.

flux s. m. used in the expressions:

a ~ abundantly. **ele tem todos os votos a** ~ he gets the totality of votes. **ele está a** ~ (at cards) he is flush.

fluxão s. f. (pl. **-ões**) (med.) fluxion, flux, catarrh.

fluxibilidade s. f. flexibility, fluxibleness.

fluxionário adj. fluxional, fluxionary.

fluxível adj. m. + f. (pl. **-íveis**) 1. fluxible. 2. transient, transitory. 3. instable.

fluxo s. m. (also **flux**) 1. flood, inflow of the tide. 2. high water. 3. ebb, flowing tide, issue, outflow. 4. (med.) flux, fluxion, (vet.) glanders. 5. flow, stream, current, gush, sweep. 6. (fig.) abundance, affluence. 7. vicissitude. 8. cold, catarrh. 9. soldering flux, flux medium. ‖ adj. 1. fluid, fluent, flowing. 2. transient, transitory.

o ~ **e o refluxo** 1. ebb and flow, rise and fall. 2. (fig.) the vagaries of life, ups and downs. **um** ~ **de palavras** a flood of words.

F. O. B. (com.) **posto a bordo** free on board.

foba s. m. + f. (N. Braz., pop.) lazybones, stupid, coward. ‖ adj. fearful, lazy, stupid.

fobar v. (Braz.) to win or lose all the money at gambling.

fobia s. f. 1. phobia, morbid fear. 2. aversion (to). **relativo à** ~ fobic.

fobó s. m. (Braz., pop.) poor or miserable individual. ‖ adj. (also **fobado**) poor, worthless, insignificant.

foboca s. f. (Braz., zool.) brocket.

fobofobia s. f. (psychiatry) phobophobia: fear of disease.

fobófobo s. m. phobophobiac.

foca (I) s. f. (zool.) 1. phoca, seal (m. bull seal, f. cow seal). 2. sea dog.

~ **nova** pup. **óleo de** ~s seal oil. **pele de** ~ sealskin.

foca (II) s. m. 1. miser, niggard, tightwad. 2. (Braz., sl.) greenhorn.

focagem s. f. (pl. **-ens**) (phot.) focalization, focus.

focal adj. m. + f. (pl. **-ais**) focal.

distância ~ focal length (or distance). **plano** ~ focal plane.

focalização s. f. focalization.

focalizar v. to focalize, focus.

focar v. 1. to focus, focalize. 2. to concentrate. 3. to bring into prominence, lay stress upon, emphasize.

focídeos s. m. pl. (zool.) Phocidae, the true seal family.

focinhada s. f. blow or thrust with the snout.

focinhar v. 1. to root, rout. 2. to thrust with the snout. 3. to snuffle, sniff. 4. to nose. 5. to fall upon one's face.

focinheira s. f. 1. muzzle, snout. 2. nose band, nosepiece (plates A 12, C 12).

focinho s. m. 1. muzzle, snout, muffle (plates C 12, G 1). 2. mouth. 3. nostril(s). 4. trunk. 5. (sl.) snoot, face, phiz, grimace, nose.

cair de ~ to fall upon one's face. **ele mete o** ~ **em tudo** he is nosing around. **ela torceu o** ~ she made a grimace, she puckered her mouth.

focinho-de-porco s. m. (pl. **focinhos-de-porco**) (ichth.) dorad.

focinhudo adj. 1. long-snouted, trunk-shaped. 2. sullen, sulky, morose.

foco s. m. focus: 1. focal distance or adjustment. 2. central or focal point, center of interest or attention. 3. (med.) nidus.

em ~ in focus. **ela estava em** ~ she was the center of attention. ~ **da infecção** the focus of infection.

foda s. f. (sl.) 1. copulation. 2. something difficult to perform or tolerate.

foder v. (sl.) to copulate, have sexual intercourse.

fofa (ô) s. f. (ant.) voluptuous Portuguese dance and the respective music.

fofar v. 1. to adorn with puffs. 2. to scarify (soil).

fofice s. f. 1. softness, flabbiness. 2. fluffiness. 3. conceit, infatuation. 4. boasting, ostentation.

fofo (ô) s. m. (pl. **fofos**) pad, bolster, puff (of a garment). ‖ adj. 1. light. 2. soft, smooth. 3. mild, gentle. 4. puffy, soufflé, spongy (bread). 5. dawny, cottony, fluffy. 6. vain, presumptuous. ‖ **fofamente** adv. lightly, spongily, etc.

fofoca s. f. (Braz., pop.) gossip, intrigue, malicious talk.

fofocar v. (Braz., pop.) to gossip, intrigue, spread rumors or scandal.

fogaça s. f. 1. big cake or loaf of bread. 2. (Braz.) diamondiferous formation of rock.

fogacho s. m. 1. little flame(s), low fire. 2. explosion, blast, discharge (as of dynamite in a stone quarry). 3. a) blushing. b) morbid suffusion of the cheeks. 4. fit of bad temper.

fogagem s. f. (pl. **-ens**) 1. (med., pop.) pimples, rash, pustules, wheal. 2. (bot.) leaf blister. 3. (fig.) irritation, anger. 4. bad temper.

fogal s. m. (pl. **-ais**) (ant.) hearth-tax.

fogaleira s. f. fire-shovel.

fogão s. m. (pl. **-ões**) 1. stove, hearth, kitchen-range, cooker, calefactor (plates C 20, F 3). 2. fireplace, fireside. 3. brazier. 4. touch-hole of a gun.

~ **revestido de azulejos** German stove, (U. S. A.) porcelain stove, cockle.

fogareiro s. m. little stove, cooker, burner, heater. ~ **de álcool** etna.

fogaréu s. m. 1. little flame, low fire. 2. cresset. 3. bonfire. 4. lampion. 5. (archit.) flamboyant stone ornament.

fogo s. m. 1. fire, blaze, conflagration. 2. light, flame, glow. 3. home, hearth, fire-place. 4. torture or death by fire. 5. cauterization. 6. warmth, heat. 7. ardour, fervour, enthusiasm, spiritedness, spunk. 8. energy, vigour. 9. violence, fierceness. 10. liveliness, brightness, brilliancy. 11. gunfire, firing volley. ‖ interj. (mil.) fire!

~ **cerrado** drumfire, running fire. ~ **de alegria** bonfire. ~**s de artifício** fireworks. ~ **de artilharia** gun-fire; (sl.) heavy stuff. ~ **de barragem** curtain fire. ~ **de bilbode** (mil.) running fire. ~ **do céu** lightning, thunderbolt. ~ **de flanco** (mil.) enfilade, flanking fire. ~**s de São João** (Braz.) bonfires and fireworks used in celebration of St. John's day (Midsummerday). ~ **indireto** (mil.) high-angle fire. **a** ~ **e a sangue** with fire and sword. **atiçar o** ~ to stir up the fire or the coals, (fig.) to stir up strife. **área sob** ~ **de artilharia** field of fire. **armas de** ~ fire-arms. **isto é bom para o** ~ that's good to throw away. **cessar o** ~ to cease fire. **cor do** ~ fire red, flame-coloured. **dar ou fazer** ~ (mil.) to give fire. **queira dar-me** ~ **(para o cigarro)** can you oblige me with a light (for the cigarette)? **debaixo de** ~ (mil.) under fire. **deitar lenha no** ~ to add fuel to the fire. **estar a** ~ **e a sangue com alguém** to be very angry at, bitterly hostile to s. o. **ele está entre dois** ~s he is between two fires. **fazer ou dar** ~ to fire, give fire. **lançar** ~ to sparkle, glitter. **fazer-se em** ~ to be all ablaze. **juntar o** ~ **e a pólvora** to leave two lovers alone. **manter o** ~ **aceso** to keep the fire burning. **eles mantiveram o** ~ **sagrado** they held up the holy flame, they did not give up their enthusiasm for the cause. **não há fumaça sem** ~ no smoke without fire. **pegar** ~ to inflame, ignite, to catch fire, flare up. **não é amor, é um** ~ **de palha!** it is not love, it is a strawfire. **pegar** ~ **novamente** to rekindle. **pôr** ~ to ignite. **pôr** ~ **numa casa** to set a house on fire. **porei as mãos no** ~ I would lay my life upon it. **sem** ~ fireless. **tição de** ~ fire-brand. **esta poesia tem vida e** ~ this poem has life and fire.

fogo-apagou s. f., sg. + pl. (ornith.) scaled dove.

fogo-central s. m. (pl. **fogos-centrais**) (Braz.) double- -barreled pistol.

fogo-de-bengala s. m. (pl. **fogos-de-bengala**) Bengal fire or light.

fogo-fátuo s. m. (pl. **fogos-fátuos**) ignis fatuus, fatu- ous fire, night-fire, friar's lantern, will-o'-the-wisp, corposant, marsh-fire, jack-o'-lantern.

fogo-grego s. m. (pl. **fogos-gregos**) Greek fire, Grecian fire, wildfire.

fogo-selvagem s. m. (Braz., med.) pemphigus foliaceus, inflammatory disease of skin or mucous mem- branes.

fogosidade s. f. 1. warmth, heat. 2. fieriness. 3. pas- sion, ardour, enthusiasm. 4. impetuosity, violence, vehemence. 5. fire, spirit, mettle.

fogoso adj. 1. hot, fiery. 2. flaming, burning. 3. ardent, enthusiastic, keen, passionate. 4. impetuous, vehe- ment. 5. hot-headed, hot-brained, fierce, high- -spirited. ‖ **-amente** adv. ardently, fierily passion- ately, etc.

cavalo ~ high-mettled horse.

foguear v. 1. to burn, build a fire. 2. to inflame, rouse. 3. to make blush. 4. to become glowing.

fogueira s. f. 1. bonfire, balefire. 2. pyre. 3. fire, flames, blaze. 4. stake. 5. fireplace, hearth. 6. home. 7. ardour, passion, exaltation. 8. (ichth.) candil. 9. (Braz.) braced framework of timbers, trestle.

ao lado da ~ at the fire. ~ **de acampamento** watch fire, campfire.

fogueiro s. m. (also **foguista**) stoker, fireman.

foguetada s. f. 1. noisy pyrotechnic display. 2. girandole(s). 3. (fig.) admonition, rebuke.

foguetão s. m. (pl. **-ões**) life rocket (carrying a lifeline to save shipwrecked crews).

foguete s. m. 1. rocket: a) skyrocket, girandole. b) jet engine. 2. (fig.) admonition, rebuke. 3. (fig.) vivacious, high-spirited or hot-tempered fellow. 4. (fig.) flirtatious girl. ‖ adj. m. + f. 1. lively, viva- cious. 2. high-spirited. 3. highhearted. 4. frivolous.

sair como um ~ to run like mad. **soltar os** ~**s antes da festa** to sell the bearskin before the hunt.

foguetear v. to discharge fireworks or rockets.

fogueteiro s. m. pyrotechnist: manufacturer, seller or maker of fireworks.

meter-se a ~ to pretend to understand a job (therefore bungling it).

foguetinho s. m. little rocket.

foguetório s. m. 1. display of fireworks, pyrotechnics. 2. a lot of rockets.

foguista s. m. stoker, fireman.

foiçada s. f. thrust with a scythe or sickle.

foiçar v. 1. to scythe, cut with a sickle. 2. to mow.

foice s. f. 1. scythe, sickle, hedgebill, reaping-hook. 2. (anat.) certain membranes shaped like the peritoneum.

~ **de ceifar** reaping-hook, sickle. ~ **podadeira** pruning hook. **meter a** ~ **em seara alheia** to thrust one's nose into other people's affairs. **a talho de** ~ intentionally, on purpose.

foiciforme adj. m. + f. falciform.

foicinha s. f. (also **foicinho** m.) small sickle, reaping- -hook.

foiteza s. f. courage, mettle, valour, boldness.

foito adj. courageous, mettlesome, valorous, bold.

fojo s. m. 1. pitfall, trap. 2. whirlpool, eddy. 3. very deep place in a river. 4. den, cavern. ~ **das minas** (min.) prospecting trench.

fola s. f. roaring of waves, heavy surge.

fólade s. f. (zool.) pholas, piddock.

folacho s. m. + f. weakling, soft or sickly person.

foladídeos s. m. pl. (zool.) Pholadidae, a family of molluscs of the order Pelecypoda.

folar s. m. Easter gift, Easter egg, Easter pudding.

folastria s. f. (Braz.) glee, mirth, excessive hilarity.

folclore s. m. (Braz.) folklore: traditional customs, tales, dances, music or songs of a people or the study of these.

folclórico adj. folkloric, folklorish, folkloristic.

folclorismo s. m. folklorism.

folclorista s. m. + f. folklorist.

folclorístico adj. folkloristic.

fole s. m. 1. bellows, wind-chest (plates F 3, M 3). 2. leather sack. 3. (fam.) stomach, belly.

máquina de ~ (phot.) camera with bellows (plate M 3). ~ **de cornamusa** windbag. **encher o** ~ to eat one's fill.

fôlego s. m. 1. breath, respiration, wind. 2. rest, relaxation, repose. 3. courage, valour, blast.

~ **curto** pursiness. **de** ~ **curto** pursy. **você precisa dar** ~ **ao seu cavalo** you must wind your horse. **dotado de grande** ~ long-winded. **falta de** ~ breathlessness, shortness of breath. **fiquei sem** ~ I was out of breath. **fiquei sem** ~ **com a corrida** I was winded by running. **perder o** ~ to lose one's wind. **ele tem bom** ~ he is in good wind. **ela tem** ~ **de gato** she has a considerable staying power. **tomar** ~ to gather breath. **ele tomou** ~ he got his wind. **sem** ~ windless. **ele trabalhou de um só** ~ he worked without interruption.

foleiro s. m. bellowsmaker, bellows vendor or bellows treader.

folga s. f. 1. temporary interruption of work, pause, respite, truce. 2. idleness, leisure. 3. rest, repose. 4. period or duration of a pause, (U. S. A.) recess. 5. (fig.) liberality. 6. (mech.) play, clearance, back- lash (gears). 7. space.

dia de ~ holiday, playday, free day. **ele está de** ~ he is off duty. **tomei um dia de** ~ I made a holiday of it. **a engrenagem tem bastante** ~ the gear has rather much play. **sem** ~ respiteless.

folgado adj. 1. broad, wide, ample, baggy, flyaway (dress). 2. loose, slack. 3. rested, restored. 4. calm, quiet. 5. easy, comfortable. 6. idle, lazy. ‖ **-amente** adv. freely, calmly, loosely, easily, lazily.

ele anda ~ he lives in plenty. **ela leva uma vida -a** she has an easy life. **ele usa sapatos** ~**s** he wears wide shoes.

folgança s. f. 1. rest, repose, fling. 2. leisure, recreation. 3. pastime, amusement, entertainment. 4. jest, joke, prank. 5. revelry, spree, frolic; frolicsomeness. 6. dalliance.

folgar s. m. amusement, play, merry-making. ‖ v. 1. to rest, repose, be free, be off duty. 2. to loosen, unlace, widen, slacken. 3. to be at ease. 4. to rejoice, like, cherish. 5. to take it easy, idle. 6. to amuse, divert or entertain o. s., play, make merry, rollick, frolic.

~ **do trabalho** to cease from labour. **folgo em ouvir** I am glad to hear. **folgo muito em conhecê-lo** I am delighted to have met you. **folgo muito com...** I am much pleased to...

folgaz adj. m. + f. cheerful, gay, merry, frolicsome.

folgazão s. m. (pl. **-ões**) (f. **-ona**) 1. revel(l)er. 2. merry fellow, backslapper, dallier, (sl.) card. 3. idler, loafer. ‖ adj. (also **folgador**) 1. merry, gay,

F 5

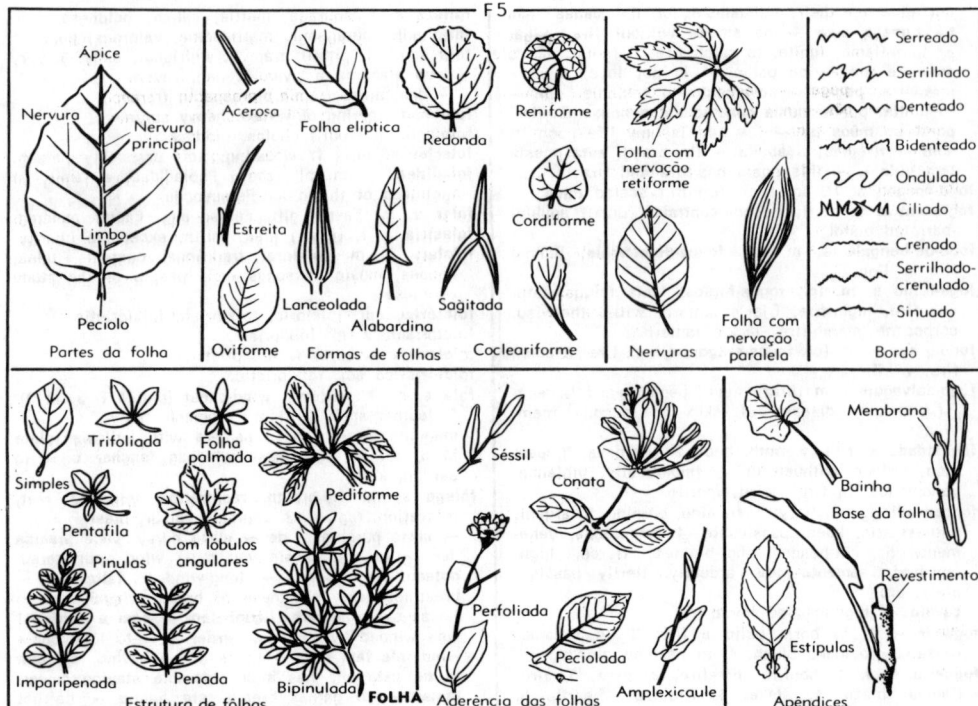

Partes da folha · Formas de folhas · Nervuras · Bordo · Estrutura de fôlhas · FOLHA · Aderência das folhas · Apêndices

2. playful, frolicsome, gamesome, jolly, diverting, fast. 3. idle, lazy.

folgazar v. less used form of **folgar**.

folgo (ô) s. m. (pl. **folgos**) = 1. **fôlego**. 2. **folgança**.

folguedo s. m. 1. rest, repose. 2. leisure, recreation. 3. pastime, amusement, entertainment, merry--making, play. 4. jest, joke, prank. 5. revelry, spree, frolic.

companheiro de ~s playmate.

folha (ô) s. f. 1. leaf: a) foliage, leaf or anything suggesting that (plates A 14, F 5). b) petal, sepal. c) sheet, plate, foil, lamina, shave. d) sheet of paper, interleaf. e) part of a door, gate, etc. 2. blade of an instrument or weapon (plate P 1). 3. journal, paper, newspaper, periodical. 4. list, report, register. 5. (typogr.) proof sheet. 6. payroll.

~ **clínica** (med.) case. ~ **corrida** certificate of conduct. ~ **de couve** cabbage leaf. ~ **de estanho** tin foil. ~ **de guarda** flyleaf. **de livro** leaf of a book. ~s **de louro** bay leaves. ~ **de ouro** gold leaf. ~ **de pagamento** payroll. ~ **de papel** sheet of paper. ~ **de porta ou janela** wing. ~ **de provas** proof sheet. ~ **de serra** saw blade, web. ~ **de trabalho** daily time ticket. ~ **em branco** blind sheet. **cair nas** ~s (Braz.) to flee, escape. **porta de duas** ~s folding doors. **novo em** ~ spick and span, brand-new. **roupa nova em** ~ brand-new clothes. **a** ~s **tantas...** at a given moment... **a notícia saiu nas** ~s the news appeared in the papers. **virou a** ~ **da fortuna** the tables turned.

folhada s. f. 1. fallen leaves, heap of dry leaves. 2. (bot.) green layer, sea lettuce. 3. (bot.) laurustine.

folha-da-fortuna s. f. (pl. **folhas-da-fortuna**) (bot.) life plant.

folha-de-flandres s. f. (pl. **folhas-de-flandres**) tin plate, white iron, tinned sheet iron.

folha-de-sangue s. f. (pl. **folhas-de-sangue**) (bot.) Christmas flower.

folhado s. m. 1. (cul.) puff, pastry, wafer puff paste. 2. foliage. 3. (bot.) laurustine. 4. foliation. || adj. 1. leafy. 2. leaf-shaped. 3. foliated, foliaged.

folha-dourada s. f. (pl. **folhas-douradas**) (bot.) star apple.

folhagem s. f. (pl. **-ens**) (also **folharia** f., **folhame** m.) 1. foliage: a) leafage, leafy branches, greens, greenery, umbrage. b) (archit.) leaf-work. 2. ornamental plants (conspicuous for their foliage).

folha-morta s. f. (aeron.) acrobacy in which the plane seems to fall like a loose leaf.

folhão s. m. (pl. **-ões**) 1. horse with an excrescence on its hoofs. 2. large leaf.

folhar v. 1. to leaf, put forth leaves, come into leaf, cover with leaves. 2. to decorate with leaves. 3. to paint or carve leaflike ornaments. 4. (carp.) to foliate, veneer. 5. to inlay.

folharada s. f. a lot of leaves, foliage.

folhato s. m. (Braz.) = **folhelho**.

folheação s. f. (bot.) foliation.

folheado s. m. 1. veneer, foil. 2. (bot.) foliation. || adj. 1. foliaged, foliate, in leaf, foliaceous, foliar. 2. veneered, plated. 3. (geol.) stratified.

folhear (I) adj. 1. foliar, foliaceous, foliaged. 2. foliicolous, living on leaves.

folhear (II) v. 1. to leaf, turn over the pages (of a book), read, skim (a book). 2. to study, peruse, consult with, examine (books). 3. to browse. 4. to cut into sheets. 5. (carp.) to veneer, plate, foil, foliate. 6. to decorate with leaves.

folheatura s. f. 1. foliature. 2. foliation. 3. vernation.

folheca s. f. snowflake(s).
folhedo s. m. foliage, leaves.
folheio s. m. the turning over of leaves (of a book).
folheiro (I) s. m. sheet metal worker, tinsmith.
folheiro (II) adj. (Braz., pop.) elegant, graceful, gay, lively, smart.
folhelho s. m. 1. hull, husk, shell, pod, cod, capsule (plate E 9). 2. chaff. 3. (geol.) stratified clayish rock.
folhento adj. leafy, abounding in leaves.
folheta s. f. thin metal sheet, veneer, gold foil, silver foil.
folhetaria s. f. 1. foliaceous artistic ornaments. 2. collection of pamphlets.
folhetear v. 1. to set, mount, foil (precious stones). 2. to veneer. 3. to cut into sheets.
folhetim s. m. (pl. **-ins**) 1. feuilleton. 2. serial (publication).
folhetinista s. m. + f. feuilletonist.
folhetinístico adj. feuilletonistic.
folhetista s. m. + f. pamphleteer: writer of pamphlets.
folheto s. m. 1. pamphlet, booklet, leaflet, prospectus. 2. sheet, fly-sheet. 3. bill, handbill. 4. chapbook. 5. brochure.
recebemos.~s de propaganda we received advertising matter.
folhinha s. f. 1. calendar (also tear-off calendar). 2. (R. C.) ordinal.
~ em bloco block calendar.
folho (ô) s. m. (pl. **folhos**) 1. frills, trimmings, ruche, flounce, furbelow, ruffle. 2. horny excrescence on the hoof.
folhoso s. m. omasum, psalterium. ‖ adj. leafy, leafed, full of leaves.
folhudo adj. leafy, foliate, full of leaves.
folia s. f. 1. gay entertainment, merry-making. 2. revelry, spree. 3. noisy racket, riot.
que ~! what a lark! what a fun! **andar na ~** to have one's fling.
foliação s. f. (pl. **-ões**) foliation: formation of leaves.
foliáceo adj. foliaceous, foliar, foliate.
foliado adj. 1. foliaceous, foliar, foliate. 2. foliated, veneered, plated.
foliador s. m. reveller, carouser.
foliagudo adj. lanceolate, cuspidate.
folião s. m. (pl. **-ões**) 1. buffoon, droll, jester. 2. reveller, carouser, merry-maker, larker. 3. (Braz.) carnival reveller.
foliar (I) v. 1. to revel, frolic, carouse, rollick. 2. to hop, leap, dance. 3. to amuse o. s.
foliar (II) adj. m. + f. foliar, folial.
folicular adj. m. + f. follicular, folliculate.
foliculário s. m. (depr.) poor journalist, pamphleteer.
folículo s. m. 1. (bot., anat.) follicle. 2. (anat.) crypt. 3. lamina. 4. pamphlet.
foliculoso adj. folliculous, follicular, folliculate(d).
folidólito s. m. (min.) pholidolite.
folidotos s. m. pl. (zool.) Pholidota, an order of edentate mammals (the pangolin).
folífago adj. foliphagous, leaf-eating.
folífero adj. foliferous.
foliforme adj. m. + f. 1. shaped like a leaf, foliate. 2. bellowslike, shaped like a bellows.
folilho s. m. (bot.) a concave pericarp.
fólio s. m. folio, folio book.
livro em ~ folio volume.
foliolado adj. (bot.) foliolate.
folíolo s. m. dim. of **folha** (bot.) foliole, leaflet, pinna, pinnule.
folioso adj. foliose, folious.
folpa s. f. 1. blister, vesicle. 2. bulge, fold (in a badly fitting dress). 3. ampoule.
folíparo adj. (bot.) foliparous.

folipo s. m. bulge, fold (in a badly fitting dress).
folote adj. 1. slack, feeble. 2. too wide.
folosa s. f. (ornith.) linnet.
fome s. f. 1. hunger, hungriness; (sl.) twist, collywobbles. 2. famine. 3. scarcity, want. 4. misery, penury. 5. (fig.) avidity, greed, greediness, esurience. 6. (path.) bulimia. 7. (fig.) violent desire.
~ canina canine appetite; (med.) bulimia. **tenho uma ~ canina** I have a rabid (ravenous) hunger, I am as hungry as a hunter. **ele tem ~, está com ~** he is hungry. **ela está fraca de ~** she is hunger-bitten. **eles entraram em greve de ~** they began a hunger strike. **cara de ~** starveling. **morrer de ~** to die of hunger, starve. **quem tem ~ tudo come** hunger is the best sauce. **pagamento de ~** sweating pay. **eles recebem salários de ~** they receive starvation wages. **eles passaram ~** they went hungry. **era o ano da ~ negra** it was the year of the great famine.
fomentação s. f. fomentation: 1. act of fomenting. 2. instigation, incitement, encouragement. 3. (med.) poultice, embrocation.
~ de guerras warmongering.
fomentador s. m. fomenter, promoter, supporter, encourager, developer, forwarder. ‖ adj. fomenting, encouraging.
~ de guerras warmonger.
fomentar v. to foment: 1. promote, advance, develop. 2. encourage, stimulate, harbour, nurse, foster, nourish. 3. incite, rouse up. 4. (med.) poultice, embrocate.
eles fomentam a amizade they further friendship. **ela fomenta o trabalho social** she is promotive of social work. **fomentamos a discórdia** we foment dissension.
fomentativo adj. fomenting, promotive.
fomento s. m. fomentation: 1. act of fomenting. 2. instigation, incitement, encouragement. 3. (med.) poultice, (warm) lotion. 4. (fig.) comfort, relief. 5. (fig.) protection, assistance, promotion, fosterage, furtherance.
fomitura s. f. (Braz., sl.) misery, penury.
fomo s. m. (Braz., pop.) manioc roaster: earthen or copper pan to roast manioc roots.
fona (I) s. m. 1. weakling, effeminate man. 2. last man of a procession or group. 3. m. + f. miser, niggard.
fona (II) s. f. 1. spark, sparkle. 2. haste, hurry, bustle.
andar numa ~ (pop.) to be on the move, to be in a hurry.
fonação s. f. (pl. **-ões**) phonation, formation of vocal sounds.
fonador adj. phonal, phonetic, phonic.
fonalidade s. f. tonality and character of speech sounds.
fonascia, fonástica s. f. phonascetics.
fonautógrafo s. m. (phys.) phonautograph.
fone s. m. phone, telephone receiver, telephone, headpiece, earpiece (plates M 9, T 4).
~ de ouvido ear-phone, headphone, headset.
fonema s. m. phoneme, phone, sound element of speech.
fonemática s. f. phonemics.
fonética s. f. phonetics, science of speech sounds, phonics.
foneticismo, fonetismo s. m. phoneti(ci)sm.
foneticista, fonetista s. m. + f. phonetician, phonetist, phoneticist.
fonético adj. phonetic(al). ‖ **foneticamente** adv. phonetically.
fonfom s. m. (onom.) toot(ing), blast of a horn.
fonfonar v. to toot, blow a horn.

fônica s. f. 1. art and science of harmony, harmonics. 2. phonetics, phonics.
fonice s. f. avarice, greed, meanness, niggardliness.
fônico adj. phonic.
fonocâmptico adj. phonocamptic, reflecting sound.
fonocinematografia s. f. sound film.
fonofobia s. f. (path.) phonophobia, morbid fear of speaking aloud.
fonófobo s. m. (med.) phonophobe.
fonóforo s. m. (electr.) phonophore.
fonogênico adj. phonogenic.
fonografar v. to phonograph.
fonografia s. f. phonography.
fonográfico adj. phonographic.
fonógrafo s. m. 1. phonograph. 2. recorder.
fonograma s. m. phonogram.
fonolítico adj. phonolitic.
fonólito s. m. (min.) phonolite, clinkstone.
fonologia s. f. phonology.
fonológico adj. phonologic(al). || **fonologicamente** adv. phonologically.
fonólogo s. m. phonologist.
fonometria s. f. (phys.) phonometry.
fonométrico adj. (phys.) phonometric(al).
fonômetro s. m. (phys.) phonometer.
fônon s. m. (phys.) phonon, a quantum of sound or vibratory energy.
fonopatia s. f. (med.) phonopathy.
fonoscópio s. f. (phys.) phonoscope.
fonospasmo s. m. (med.) phonatory spasm.
fontainha s. f. little fountain.
fontal adj. m. + f. (pl. -ais) fontal, original, primary.
fontana s. f. (arch.) fountain, spring.
fontanal adj. m. + f. (pl. -ais) fontal, original, causative.
fontanário s. m. public drinking fountain. || adj. fontal.
fontanela s. f. (anat., med.) fontanel(le).
fontano adj. fontal: pertaining to or relative to fountains.
fonte s. f. 1. fountain, spring(-head), headspring, well(-head), wellspring, (poet.) fount (plate F 7). 2. (surg.) fonticulus, drain. 3. (anat.) temple(s). 4. (fig.) origin, source, rise, beginning, root, cause. 5. original (literary work), authorship. 6. font, laver.
~ **batismal** font. ~ **de água mineral** spa. ~ **de água salgada** salt spring. ~ **de eletricidade** source of electric current. ~ **de energia** source of energy. ~ **de renda** source of revenue. ~ **de riqueza** source of one's wealth, (fig.) mine. ~ **mineral** mineral spring. ~ **submarina** submarine spring. ~ **termal** hot spring. ~ **vital** lifespring. **de boa** ~ on good authority. **de primeira** ~ from good hands. **eu sei disso de** ~ **segura** I have it on good authority. **o cântaro vai à** ~ **até quebrar** the pitcher goes to the well until it breaks. **ele foi à** ~ **limpa** he drew from the best source.
fontícula s. f., **fontículo** m. 1. little fountain. 2. (surg.) fonticulus drain, fontanelle.
fora s. m. (Braz.) 1. rejection, refusal. 2. elimination, exclusion. || adv. out, outside, outdoors, outlying, beyond, abroad, afield, forth, off, away. || prep. 1. expect, excepting, without. 2. besides. || interj. out!, get out! out you go!, off!, be off, be gone!, (U. S. A.) scram!
~! away with you! ~ **da compreensão de alguém** beyond one's grasp. ~ **de cogitação** out of question. ~ **de dúvida** beyond doubt. ~ **de foco** out of focus. ~ **de moda** out of fashion. ~ **de perigo** out of danger. ~ **de propósito** out of mind. ~ **do lugar** in the wrong place, out of place. ~ **do tempo** inopportune. **a cabeça** ~ **da água** the head above the water. **cai** ~! (Braz., sl.), **saia para** ~! go

out!, get out! **dar o** ~ to hop it. **dar o** ~ **em alguém** to give a p. the air, (sl.) to give a p. the mitten. **dê-lhe o** ~! give him the push! **de** ~ outside, outerly. **deitar** ~ to throw away. **deixar** ~ to outshut. **ele está** ~ **da casa** he is absent, he is away from home. **eu estou** ~ **de mim** I am beside myself. **ele está** ~ **de si** he is out of his wits, he is beside himself. **estar para** ~ to be away, to be travelling. **gente de** ~ strangers. **ir para** ~ to go on a journey. **jantar** ~ to dine out. **lá** ~ out there. **morar** ~ **da cidade** to live out of town. **por** ~ 1. besides. 2. part time. **pôr para** ~ to turn out, to show the door to. **portas a** ~ outdoors. **ele veio** ~ **de hora** he came ill-timed.
fora-da-lei s. m. + f., sg. + pl. outlaw (person). || adj. m. + f., sg. + pl. outlaw.
foragem s. f. (pl. -ens) minor court of justice.
foragido s. m. 1. fugitive, refugee, absconder. 2. immigrant. 3. outlaw. 4. vagrant. || adj. fugitive, flighty, erratic, hidden, persecuted, vagrant.
foragir-se v. to emigrate, take refuge, take shelter.
foral s. m. (pl. -ais) charter, register, privilege.
foraleiro adj. privileged.
forame, forâmen s. m. (pl. **foramens, forâmenes**) 1. (anat., bot., zool.) foramen, pl. foramina. 2. hole, pit, cave.
foraminíferos s. m. pl. (zool.) Foraminifera, an order of rhizopods.
foraminoso adj. foraminous, foraminate, foraminiferal.
foramontão adj. (pl. -ões) subject to a hunting tax.
forâneo adj. foreign, alien, strange.
foranto s. m. (bot.) phoranthium, clinanthium.
forasteiro s. m. foreigner, stranger, outlander. || adj. foreign, strange.
forata s. f. olive press.
forca (ô) s. f. 1. gallows, gibbet. 2. scaffold. 3. (fig.) noose, snare. 4. (fig.) humiliation. 5. pitchfork, hayfork.
a ~ **está esperando por ele** the gallows groans for him. **morrer na** ~ to die on the gibbet. **parece que caiu da** ~ he has a hanging look. **passar pelas** ~**s caudinas** to eat humble pie.
força (ô) s. f. 1. force, strength, power, (U. S. A.) vim. 2. energy, vigour, vigorousness. 3. robustness, stoutness, sturdiness. 4. fibre, pith, sinew, strain. 5. main, might. 6. raciness, virility. 7. (jur.) validity. 8. valour, courage. 9. motive, impulse. 10. cause. 11. compulsion, obligation. 12. great number. 13. plenty, abundance. 14. principal part or element. 15. body of soldiers, detachment.
~! stick it!, beef up! ~ **centrífuga** centrifugal power. ~ **aérea** 1. air force. 2. air service. ~ **combatente** striking power. ~ **da juventude** bloom of youth. ~ **de arranque** starting moment. ~ **de caráter** (fig.) backbone. ~ **de cisalhamento** shearing force. ~ **de espírito** strong-mindedness. ~ **de liga** setting strength. ~ **de sucção** suck, suction. ~ **de tração** pull, tensile stress. ~ **de vontade** strength of will, will-power. ~ **elétrica** electric power. ~ **eletromotriz** electromotive force. ~ **emissora,** ~ **irradiante** emissivity. ~ **legal** legal force. ~ **maior** force majeure, act of God. ~ **militar** effectives. ~ **motriz** driving power, driving force. ~**s naturais** physical agents. ~ **naval** naval force. ~ **vocal** lung power. **à** ~ forcedly. **à** ~ **de** by dint of. **as** ~**s aliadas** the allied forces. **as** ~**s do mal** the power of evil. **camisa de** ~ strait jacket. **é** ~ **que...** it is indispensable that... **falta de** ~ (jur.) unsubstantiality. **fazer entrar à** ~ to whip into. **isto ultrapassa minhas** ~**s** that is beyond my tether. **mediram as** ~**s entre si** they tried conclusions with each other. **na** ~ **do verão** in the middle of summer. **não pude resistir à** ~

do seu argumento I could not resist the force of his argument. **política de** ~ power politics. **por** ~ **de** by right of. **por** ~ **de vontade** by will-power. **sem** ~ unsubstantial. **sob a** ~ **de** under the thumb of. **tirar** ~ **da fraqueza** to make a virtue of necessity. **toda** ~ (mot.) throttle full open. **abalroar com toda a** ~ to run full tilt at. **à viva** ~ by main force.

forcada s. f. (pop.) bifurcation.

forcado s. m. fork, pitchfork, hayfork, manure-fork, pike (plates C 16, E 11, J 2, S 1). **arremessar com** ~ to hurl, pitch-fork.

forçado s. m. 1. shackle, fetter. 2. convict, galley--slave, criminal (sentenced to hard labour). ‖ adj. 1. compelled, obliged. 2. forcible, forced, compulsory. 3. unwilling, involuntarily, unspontaneous. 4. far--fetched. 5. artificial, unnatural, laboured. 6. imperative. 7. under restraint, fain. ‖ **-amente** adv. forcedly, compulsorily. **eles fizeram uma marcha -a** they made a quick march. **um sorriso** ~ a forced smile. **isto é uma comparação -a** this is a far-fetched parallel. **trabalho** ~ hard labour, penal servitude.

forçador s. m. forcer, coercer, ravisher.

forcadura s. f. 1. forkedness. 2. space between the prongs of a hayfork.

forçamento s. m. 1. act of forcing. 2. coercion, compulsion. 3. violence. 4. rape.

forçante adj. m. + f. coercive, forcible.

forção s. m. (pl. **-ões**) prop, stay.

forcar v. 1. to fork: spread out or turn over with a hayfork. 2. (arch.) to hang (by the neck).

forçar v. 1. to force, oblige, impel, compel, constrain. 2. to conquer, vanquish. 3. to win or obtain by force. 4. to break open, thrust, prong; pry or prize open (a lock); to break in; enter forcibly, ram. 5. to overcome, overpower. 6. to subdue, subject, subjugate. 7. to do violence, ravish, rape. 8. to remove, turn aside. 9. to twist, wring, distort, concuss, strain. 10. to misrepresent, misinterpret. 11. to put into force, enforce. 12. to strain, urge, rush, press on, drive. 13. to coerce. 14. ~**-se** to force, restrain or check o. s. ~ **uma decisão** to force an issue. ~ **a natureza** to force nature. ~ **para o serviço militar** to commandeer. ~ **o tempo** to sail against both the wind and the tide. ~ **a venda** to press the sale. **eles** ~**am a alta dos preços** they pushed up the prices. **ele forçou o cadeado** he prized (open) the lock. **eles** ~**am as leis** they perverted the laws. **eles** ~**am a passagem** they broke through. **ele forçou um sorriso** he forced a smile.

forcejar v. 1. to struggle, strive, endeavour. 2. to fight, strain every nerve. 3. to exert o. s. ~ **com as ondas** to struggle with the waves.

forcejo s. m. effort, exertion, struggle, endeavour.

fórceps s. m., sg. + pl., **fórcipe** m. (surg.) forceps, extractor.

forcipulados s. m. pl. (ichth.) Forcipulata, an order of starfishes.

forçoso adj. 1. forcible: a) forcibly, by force. b) strong. c) vigorous, energetic. 2. violent. 3. necessary, inevitable, fatal, imperative. 4. forceable. 5. obligatory. 6. cogent, stringent. ‖ **-amente** adv. forcibly, strongly, energetically, compulsorily, necessarily, needs, cogently, perforce. **isto é um argumento** ~ this is a strong argument.

forçudo adj. (Braz., pop.) strong, brawny, muscular, robust.

forçura s. f. 1. prop, stay. 2. (theat.) box, dress box.

fordeco s. m. (Braz., sl.) old Ford car, tin Lizzie.

fordo adj. (poet.) full, pregnant.

foreiro s. m. tenant, renter, copyholder, lessee. ‖ adj. tributary, rental, rent-paying.

forense adj. m. + f. 1. forensic(al), judicial, judiciary. 2. argumentative.

forésia s. f. (biol., zool.) phoresy.

forfalha s. f. crumb (of bread).

fórfex, fórfice s. m. (pl. of both **fórfices**) (surg.) forfex.

forficulinos s. m. pl. (ent.) insects of the order Forficula.

forficulídeo s. m. (ent.) earwig, specimen of the family Forficulidae. ‖ adj. 1. of, pertaining to or relative to the earwig. 2. forficate.

forja s. f. 1. forge. 2. open fireplace or furnace, (s)melting furnace. 3. blacksmith's shop, smithy, smithery. 4. foundry, shop of an ironworker. 5. (Braz.) pitfall. **estar na** ~ to be in preparation (in the melting pot). ~ **de cobre** copper works. ~ **para fiar ferro** bloomery, bloomary.

forjado adj. 1. forged, beaten, wrought. 2. counterfeit, apocryphal. ~ **à mão** hand-wrought. ~ **de uma peça** forged in the solid.

forjador s. m. forger: 1. blacksmith, smith, forgeman. 2. schemer, framer, concocter. 3. plotter, falsifier. ‖ adj. forging (also fig.).

forjadura s. f., **forjamento** m. 1. forging, a smith's work. 2. forgery. **forjamento em estampa** drop or die forging.

forjar v. 1. to forge: a) hammer, shape (head metal) with a hammer. b) form, fashion, produce, work, frame. c) imitate, fabricate, counterfeit, cook. 2. to invent, scheme, concoct, coin, trump-up.

forjável adj. m. + f. (pl. **-áveis**) forgeable.

forje s. m. (Braz.) pitfall, trap.

forjicar v. 1. to forge badly. 2. to arrange imperfectly, prepare negligently.

forma s. f. form: 1. appearance. 2. figure, shape (plates F 5, P 4). 3. figuration, configuration, conformation, contour. 4. make, structure, build, nature. 5. formation, characteristic disposition of parts or elements. 6. feature, semblance, aspect. 7. kind, sort, variety. 8. frame, model, mould, pattern, templet. 9. type, print. 10. state, condition, physical fitness. 11. habit. 12. (arts) style, expression, disposition. 13. (mil.) troop formation, rank, line. 14. way and manner, wise, means, system. 15. (gram.) inflectional aspects of a word. 16. (biol.) sporadic biotype. 17. (math.) quantic. ~ **de falar** manner of speaking. ~ **de governo** form of government, system, regime, polity. **apresentar sob nova** ~ to rehash. **argumentar em** ~ to argue in due form. **da melhor** ~ **possível** to the best of one's ability. **dar nova** ~ **a** to re-form. **de** ~ **alguma** in no case, on no terms, under no consideration, by no means, not at all, not by a long way, in no wise, nought. **de** ~ **bonita** well--shaped. **de** ~ **nenhuma vou fazê-lo** I just won't do it. **de qualquer** ~ 1. at any rate. 2. in any way, in any wise, howsoever. 3. at the least. **de qualquer** ~ **que queira** any way you please. **de tal** ~ **que** in such wise as to; so that. **ela nunca conseguirá fazê-lo desta** ~ she never will get it done that way. **em boa** ~ fit as a fiddle. **sua gratidão manifestou-se em** ~ **de um cheque** his gratitude took the form of a cheque. **em** ~ **de flecha** arrow-shaped. **em** ~ **de serra** ragged. **em** ~ **de "V"** V-shaped. **um anjo em** ~ **humana** an angel in human shape. **estar fora de** ~ to be out of training. **estar em** ~ to feel up to the mark. **na** ~ **que se segue** as follows. **que** ~ **tem isto?** of what shape is it? **tomar** ~ to take shape.

forma (ô) s. f. 1. last, form for the shoe uppers. 2. (typogr.) form(e). 3. hat block. 4. mould, baking mould, tin for baking (plates D 3, P 6). 5. cheese press.
~ **de sapato** shoe tree, last, stretcher. **escrever em letra de** ~ to write in print. **letra de** ~ type, print.

formação s. f. (pl. **-ões**) 1. formation: a) forming, building up, upbringing. b) origin, rise. c) arrangement. d) development. e) constitution, structure, conformation, shape. f) body of troops, unit, array. g) drawing up of troops. h) (geol.) system, series of beds or deposits of identical characteristics. 2. (bot.) plant association.
~ **carbonífera** carboniferous system. ~ **de batalha** battle array. ~ **de cabeça** (med.) gathering. ~ **de palavra** word-building. ~ **de trustes** trustification. ~ **dos preços** formation of prices.

formado adj. 1. formed, shaped, wrought, fashioned. 2. graduated, baccalaurean.
um corpo bem ~ a well-knit body. **não** ~ (fig.) unlicked, unformed.

formador s. m. former, moulder, pattern maker, fashioner, modeller, creator. ‖ adj. forming, formative, shaping, creative, constructive.

formadura s. f. 1. form, figure. 2. formation.

formal s. m. (pl. **-ais**) 1. (jur.) deed of division. 2. (jur.) house or residence within the limits of an emphyteutic property. ‖ adj. m. + f. 1. formal, conventional. 2. solemn, formulary. 3. state. 4. stiff, donnish. 5. stilted, starchy. 6. bookish. 7. evident. 8. positive. 9. decided, peremptory. 10. textual, exact, precise. ‖ ~**mente** adv. formally, evidently, categorically.
com palavras -ais in express terms. **causa** ~ formal cause. **ele é excessivamente** ~ he is as stiff as a poker.

formaldeído s. m. (chem.) formaldehyde.

formalidade s. f. formality: 1. ceremony. 2. tradition, etiquette. 3. conventionality, conventionalism. 4. form, red tape, established order, formal mode or method.
cheio de ~**s** red-tape. **falta de** ~ informality. **uma mera** ~ a mere form. **por** ~ for form's sake. **é apenas uma** ~ it is only a matter of form. **sem** ~**s** informal. **eles observaram todas as** ~**s legais** they complied with all legal formalities.

formalina s. f. (pharm.) formalin.

formalismo s. m. formalism: 1. formulism, formality, officialdom, conventionalism, strict adherence to order, rules, style or etiquette. 2. pedantry. 3. (philos.) philosophical system denying the existence of matter.

formalista s. m. + f. 1. formalist, Jack in office. 2. idealist. ‖ adj. formalistic, conventional.

formalizado adj. 1. formalized, formal. 2. offended, disgusted. 3. (fam.) finely dressed.

formalizador s. m. formalizer.

formalizar v. 1. to formalize, render formal. 2. to stand on formalities. 3. to take offence, become disgusted, take amiss.

formão s. m. (pl. **-ões**) chisel, former, firmer (plates F 2, M 4).

formar v. 1. to form: a) shape, fashion. b) model, mould, frame. c) conceive, create (idea). d) have the form of, resemble. e) establish, constitute. f) make, produce, construct, build. g) (mil.) put in rank and order, align. h) instruct, perfect. i) compose, compound. j) organize. k) construe. 2. to determine. 3. to promote, further. 4. ~**-se:** a) to be formed or made. b) to take shape, assume a form, emerge. c) to cultivate one's mind, train. d) to graduate, take a degree.

~ **cabeça de pus** to gather (of pustules). ~ **um convênio** to convene. ~ **dentes** to dent. ~ **em grão** to grain. ~ **novamente** to re-form, reshape, reframe. ~ **um projeto** to draw up or frame a plan. **no céu** ~**am-se nuvens** clouds formed in the sky. ~**am um cordão** they formed a cordon. **eles** ~**am as tropas para dar batalha** they ranged the troops in battle order. **ela formou um novelo de lã** she wound the wool into a ball. **ela formou-se em história** (U. S. A.) she majored in history.

formaria s. f. set of hat blocks or lasts.

formativo s. m. (gram.) formative. ‖ adj. formative, shaping, moulding, constituent. ‖ **-amente** adv. constitutively.

formato s. m. 1. format, shape, size. 2. make, outward, form.

formatura s. f. 1. formation: a) development. b) disposition, arrangement of parts or elements. c) array of troops or vessels. 2. graduation, commencement.

formeiro s. m. patternmaker, last maker.

formeno s. m. (chem.) methane, marsh-gas.

formiato s. m. (chem.) formate, formiate.

formica s. f. (med.) herpes miliaris.

fórmica s. f. (trademark) Formica.

formicação s. f. (pl. **-ões**) (med.) formication, itching.

formicante adj. (med.) formicant, formicating.

formicário s. m. (ornith.) Formicarius: a genus of ant thrushes. ‖ adj. formican, formicate.

formicida s. m. formicide: poison for killing ants.

formicídeos s. m. pl. (ent.) Formicidae, the ant family.

formicívoro adj. formicivorous.

fórmico adj. (chem.) formic.

formicular adj. m. + f. formican, formicate, antlike.

formidando adj. 1. dreadful, terrible. 2. tremendous, awe-inspiring. 3. immense, enormous.

formidável adj. m. + f. (pl. **-áveis**) 1. formidable; (sl.) corking, roaring, spanking, swell, snorting. 2. dreadful, fearful. 3. enormous. 4. terrible, horrible. 5. uncommon. 6. (Braz.) splendid, excellent. ‖ **formidavelmente** adv. formidably, screamingly, dreadfully.
pessoa ou coisa ~ crackerjack, topper. **isto é** ~ that thing is classy. **um carro** ~ a thumping great car. **a cantora é** ~ the diva is great.

formidoloso adj. 1. formidable. 2. dreadful, terrible. 3. awe-inspiring, terrifying. 4. afraid, fearful.

formiga s. f. 1. (ent.) ant, pismire; (arch.) emmet. 2. (fig.) an economical person. 3. person fond of sweets. 4. nose clamp (for bulls).
~ **branca** white ant, termite. ~ **obreira** worker ant. ~ **de fogo** black ant, myrmicid. **ele é uma** ~ **com catarro** he is talking very big. **semelhante a** ~ antlike.

formiga-açucareira s. f. (pl. **formigas-açucareiras**) (ent.) 1. Argentine ant. 2. red ant.

formiga-carregadeira, formiga-cortadeira s. f. (pl. **formigas-carregadeiras, formigas-cortadeiras**) (ent.) sauba ant.

formiga-leão s. f. (pl. **formigas-leão**) ant lion.

formigamento s. m. (med.) formication, puncture, prurigo, itching, tickling.

formigante adj. m. + f. itching, pruriginous, prurient, creepy, crawly.

formigão s. m. (pl. **-ões**) 1. large ant. 2. concrete.

formigar v. 1. formicate, to itch, tingle, prick(le). 2. to have in profusion, abound in. 3. to seethe, swarm (with). 4. (fig.) to work hard, try to make a living. 5. to accumulate, pile up.
meus dedos ~**am de frio** my fingers tingled from the cold. **o dedo me formiga** I feel a pricking in my finger.

formigueiro (I) s. m. 1. anthill, ants' nest or hole, formicary. 2. crowd, throng. 3. formication, itching. 4. impatience, restlessness. 5. (fig.) pins and needles.

formigueiro (II) s. m. wind from the south-east.

formigueiro (III) adj. pilfering.

formiguejar v. 1. to move or appear in a great number, seethe, teem, swarm. 2. to itch, tingle.

formiguilho s. m. horse thrush, disease on the feet of horses.

formilhão s. m. (pl. -ões) a hatter's brim form.

formilhar v. to apply the block in order to shape a hat.

formilho s. m. a hatter's block (that forms the dent in the crown of the hat).

formista s. m. 1. former, moulder, modeller. 2. pattern maker. 3. (typogr.) form maker.

formol s. m. (chem.) formaldehyde.

formosa-de-um-dia s. f. (pl. **formosas-de-um-dia**) (bot.) orange day lily.

formosear, formosentar v. 1. to beautify, embellish. 2. to adorn, decorate.

formoso adj. 1. beautiful, handsome. 2. pretty, fair, well-favoured, comely. 3. charming. pleasant. 4. splendid, brilliant. 5. perfect, pure. 6. harmonious.

formosura s. f. 1. beauty, handsomeness, beautifulness, fairness, sightliness. 2. prettiness, comeliness. 3. charmingness. 4. perfection, harmony. 5. beauty: beautiful thing or person.

fórmula s. f. 1. formula: a) set form or rule. b) prescription, recipe. c) (math.) general rule expressed in algebraic symbols. d) (chem.) chemical formula. e) (eccl.) formulary, ritual. 2. form (to fill in), (printed) blank.
~ **para registro** entrance form. ~ **de telegrama** telegraph form. **preencher uma** ~ to fill in a form.

formulação s. f. (pl. -ões) 1. formularization, formulating. 2. definition.

formulador s. m. formulator.

formular v. 1. to formulate: a) lay down, formul(ar)ize, reduce to or express in a formula. b) enounce, voice, express clearly or precisely. c) expound, put. 2. to prescribe, make out a prescription. 3. ~-se a) to take shape. b) to become manifest. c) to appear.
~ **um libelo** to article. **ela formulou uma pergunta** she asked a question. **isto é bem formulado** this is well said. **um tratado claramente formulado** a treatise conceived in plain terms. **uma frase bem formulada** a well-turned phrase.

formulário s. m. formulary: 1. collection of formulas. 2. ritual, book containing ceremonial forms. 3. form (to fill in), printed blank (more detailed than **fórmula** 2.)
~ **de imposto de renda** income-tax form.

formulismo s. m. formulism.

formulista s. m. + f. 1. formulist, person who conceives or uses formulas. 2. formalist, pedant. ‖ adj. formulistic.

fornaça s. f. furnace, grate.

fornada s. f. 1. batch, ovenful, baking. 2. (foundry and brickwork) charge. 3. (fig.) lot, throng (of people), batch (fig.) of books, letters, etc.
uma ~ **de pão** a batch of bread. **coser a** ~ to sleep o. s. sober.

fornalha s. f. 1. furnace, grate, firebox, stove, hearth (plates L 1. 3). 2. forge, smelting furnace. 3. kiln. 4. (fig.) a hot place, great heat.
boca de ~ (tech.) furnace mouth. ~ **com grelha de degraus** step grate furnace. ~ **com injeção de ar** furnace with blower. ~ **para carvão** coal furnace. ~ **para queima de refugos** destructor.

fornalheiro s. m. fireman, stoker.

fornear v. 1. to work as stoker or fireman. 2. to put a batch into the furnace.

fornecedor s. m. 1. furnisher. 2. supplier, contractor. 3. caterer, purveyor, victual(l)er, provisioner. 4. outfitter. ‖ adj. furnishing, supplying.
~ **da casa real** purveyor to the royal household. ~ **de provisões** contractor for provisions. ~ **de exército** army contractor.

fornecer v. 1. to furnish, supply. 2. to provide, purvey, cater. 3. to stock, store, equip, fit out. 4. to dispense, discharge, serve or hand out. 5. to give, serve, administer. 6. to make provisions for, victual. 7. to indue. 8. to produce. 9. ~-se to provide o. s. with.
~ **rações** to ration. **é fornecido em garrafas** it comes in bottles. **o país fornece minerais** the land affords minerals.

fornecimento s. m. furnishing, supply(ing), delivery, providing, provision, layout, ministration.
~ **de água** water supply. **modo de** ~ (com.) mode of delivery.

forneira s. f. oven-woman.

forneiro s. m. 1. ovenman, baker. 2. (Braz., ornith.) ovenbird.

fornejar v. 1. to work as a stoker. 2. to put a batch into the oven.

fornicação s. f. (pl. -ões) 1. fornication. 2. sexual intercourse.

fornicário s. m. fornicator.

fornicar v. 1. (sl., vulg.) to fornicate. 2. to importune, pester. 3. to afflict, bother, vex.

fórnice s. m. (archit.) arch, vault.

fornido adj. 1. furnished, provided, supplied. 2. strong, robust. 3. well-fed.
~ **de carne** fleshy, corpulent. **madeira bem -a** strong or resilient wood.

fornilho s. m. 1. little oven or furnace. 2. (mil.) contact mine. 3. pipe bowl (plate F 7).

fornimento s. m. 1. provisions, victuals. 2. robustness, sturdiness.

fornir v. 1. to feed well, satiate. 2. to make strong or robust. 3. to supply, provide, cater.

forno s. m. 1. oven, hearth (plates C 20, F 3, P 1). 2. stove. 3. kiln, furnace. 4. forge, smelting furnace. 5. (fig.) any hot place.
~ **de alimentação automática** self-feeding furnace. ~ **de bronze** melting furnace for bronze. ~ **de cal** lime kiln. ~ **de calcinar** (glassmaking) calcar. ~ **de cuba para cadinhos** shaft crucible furnace. ~ **de cúpula** cupola. ~ **de fundição** melting furnace. ~ **de revestimento** air furnace, reverberatory furnace. ~ **de tijolo** brick kiln. ~ **elétrico** electric furnace. **alto** ~ blast furnace. **pá de** ~ oven peel, oven shovel. **tratador de** ~ ovenman.

foro (I) s. m. forum.

foro (ô) (II) s. m. (pl. **foros**) 1. quitrent, groundrent. 2. freehold, tenancy. 3. rent, charge, obligation. 4. privilege, prerogative. 5. forum, court of justice, tribunal, judgement seat. 6. law. 7. immunity exemption. 8. pl. privilege, franchise, grant.
~ **civil** court of civil law. ~ **criminal** crime court. ~ **eclesiástico** ecclesiastical court. **ele tem** ~ **de cidadão** he has the freedom of the city. ~ **de fidalgo** patent of nobility.

foronídeos s. m. pl. (zool.) Phoronidae, a family of small marine wormlike animals.

foronomia s. f. (med.) phoronomy, phoronomics.

forqueadura s. f. (bi)furcation.

forquear v. to bifurcate.

forqueta s. f. 1. forked branch, crotch, fork. 2. divarication. 3. (Braz.) acute-angled confluence of rivers.
chave de ~ fork spanner.

forquilha s. f. 1. pitchfork with three prongs, trident. 2. crutch, crutchlike support, crotch. 3. fork (plate J 3). 4. rack. 5. (zool.) gapeworm. 6. (Braz., Amazonas) forked (punting) pole.
em forma de ~, forquilhado crotched.
forquilhar v. to fork, bifurcate.
forquilheiro s. m. (Braz., Amazonas) poler, boatsman handling a (punting) pole.
forquilhoso adj. forked, forky, furcate.
forra (l) s. f. (Braz., pop.) revenge, retaliation.
forra (ô) s. f. 1. (naut.) tabling. 2. wadding, padding. 3. buckram, lining.
forração s. f. (pl. -ões) furring, lining or casing.
forrado adj. lined, covered, padded.
forrador s. m. liner, lining stitcher.
forra-gaitas s. m. + f., sg. + pl. miser, niggard.
forrageador s. m. 1. forager. 2. forayer. || adj. foraging.
forrageal s. m. (pl. -ais) hayfield, clover field, meadow.
forragear v. 1. to forage, supply with fodder. 2. to cut fodder, harvest hay. 3. to search after, inquire into. 4. to glean. 5. to foray, ravage, spoil, ransack. 6. (fig.) to gather, collect (impressions, ideas).
forragem s. f. (pl. -ens) 1. fodder, feed, forage, green crop, greenfodder. 2. ensilage, hay, bedding.
~ seca provender.
forraginoso adj. rich in fodder, abounding in forage.
forramento s. m. furring, lining, covering, stuffing, reinforcement.
forrar v. 1. to face, line, cover with. 2. to paste paper, to case, plate. 3. to veneer, wainscot. 4. to fur 5. to save, lay by. 6. to reinforce with buckram. 7. to underlay. 8. **~-se:** a) to cloth or vest o. s. b) to recover, make up for. c) to avenge o. s., take revenge. 9. to free, liberate (slaves), buy the freedom of.
~ com madeira to timber, pane. **~ com tacos** to parquet. **~ novamente** to reline. **~ uma parede com mármore** to cover a wall with marble. **o céu forrava-se de nuvens** the sky became overcast. **ele não se forra com ninguém** he doesn't yield to anybody. **ele quer ~-se desta obrigação** he wants to get rid of this duty. **um tapete bonito forrava a parede** a beautiful carpet covered the wall.
forreta s. m. + f. miser, niggard.
forro (ô) s. m. (pl. **forros**) 1. doubling, lining, covering, casing (plates C 4, R 7). 2. padding. 3. ceiling. 4. wainscot, sheathing, veneer, liner. 5. backing. 6. (naut.) skin. || adj. 1. freed, enfranchised. 2. emancipated. 3. unencumbered. 4. free, independent, exempt. 5. well-off, wealthy.
~ de navio (copper) sheathing of a ship. **~ de parede** wallpaper. **~ de pele** fur lining. **~ lateral dos sapatos** side lining of shoes. **um escravo ~** an emancipated slave.
forró, forrobodó s. m. (Braz., sl.) nigger ball.
forróia s. f. (N. Braz.) old mare.
fortalecedor s. m. strengthener, reinforcer, invigorator, corroborator, annealer. || adj. (also **fortalecente** m. + f.) fortifying, strengthening, invigorating, corroborating.
fortalecer v. 1. to fortify, invigorate. 2. to strengthen, make strong or robust, to sinew. 3. to support, prop. 4. to toughen, innerve. 5. to encourage, animate. 6. to corroborate, confirm. 7. to anneal. 8. to consolidate.
fortalecido adj. fortified, strengthened, hardened.
fortalecimento s. m. 1. strengthening, invigoration. 2. encouragement. 3. fortification.
fortaleza s. f. 1. fort, fortress, fortification, stronghold. 2. bastion, bastille, citadel, hold, burg. 3. castle. 4. strength, force, vigour. 5. fortitude, courage, guts. 6. energy, power. 7. firmness, solidity.

ele revelou ~ extraordinária he gave evidence of extraordinary fortitude. **o inimigo atacou a ~ the** enemy assaulted the fortress.
fortalezar v. (rare) 1. to fortify. 2. to entrench, erect fortifications. 3. (fig.) to encourage.
forte s. m. 1. fort(ress), fortification, hold, sconce. 2. (mus.) forte. 3. talent, strong point. || adj. m. + f. 1. strong, athletic, vigorous, robust, hardy, tough. 2. fortitudinous, valiant, courageous. 3. sturdy, stout, stalwart. 4. solid, sound. 5. energical, energetical, forceful. 6. keen, ardent, eager, impetuous. 7. potent, powerful. 8. forcibly offensive. 9. (of liquors) nappy, heady, humming, rich in alcohol. 10. (mus.) forte, loud. 11. intense, acute. 12. spicy. 13. hot (colours). 14. tangy (smell). || adv. (mus.) forte, loudly, high-toned. || **~mente** adv. 1. strongly, vigorously. 2. valiantly. 3. sturdily, stoutly, corpulently. 4. eagerly. 5. energically. 6. impetuously. 7. powerfully. 8. firmly. 9. high.
um pequeno ~ a fortlet. **o ~ foi bem executado pela orquestra** the forte was well-played by the orchestra. **o vinho era ~** the wine was heady. **caixa-~** safe. **praça ~** stronghold. **razões ~s** strong reasons. **jogar ~** 1. to play violently. 2. to gamble for high stakes. **fazer-se ~** to fortify o. s. **ela é ~ de gênio** she is strongheaded, she is lively. **de espírito ~** strong-minded. **um ~ resfriado** a bad cold. **de cor ~** high-coloured. **ele é um homem de caráter ~** he is a strong-minded man. **ele não é ~ em gramática** grammar is not his strong point. **um homem ~** a well-set or strong-bodied man. **ele agiu com mão ~** he acted with a strong hand. **o rei governava com pulso ~** the king ruled with a high hand. **um homem com voz ~** a strong-voiced man. **ouviu-se uma voz ~** a high-toned voice was heard. **o vento soprou ~mente** the wind blew hard, there blew a gale. **choveu ~mente** it was raining fast. **um prato ~mente condimentado** a high-seasoned dish.
forteza s. f. (pop.) 1. force, strength. 2. boldness.
fortidão s. f. (pl. -ões) 1. thickness, grossness. 2. firmness, toughness. 3. solidity.
~ de caráter strength of character.
fortificação s. f. (pl. -ões) 1. fortification, fortress, fort. 2. hold, place, work, stronghold, bulwark, bastion, counterwork, gabionade, earthwork. 3. art of fortifying and defending a place.
~ de campanha (mil.) fieldwork. **eles erigiram -ões** (mil.) they erected defensive works.
fortificado adj. (mil.) fortified, fast.
uma praça -a a fast place.
fortificador s. m. 1. fortifier, military engineer or architect. 2. strengthener. 3. invigorator. 4. restorative. || adj. fortifying, strengthening, restorative.
fortificante s. m. restorative, analeptic, tonic, fortifier, invigorator, strengthener. || adj. m. + f. fortifying, invigorant, analeptic(al), restorative, (cor)roborant.
fortificar v. 1. to fortify, erect fortifications. 2. to encourage, brace up. 3. to strengthen, invigorate, vitalize. 4. to corroborate. 5. **~-se:** a) to surround o. s. with defensive works. b) to increase one's strength. c) to become strong, gather strength.
fortim s. m. (pl. -ins) fortlet, little fort, fortalice.
fortíssimo adj. abs. sup. of **forte** (mus.) fortissimo. || adv. fortissimo.
fortran s. m. (data processing) fortran: a computer system using mathematical notation, abbr. for(mula) tran(slation).
fortuidade s. f. fortuity, fortuitousness.
fortuito adj. 1. fortuitous, casual, accidental, random, chance, chanceful. 2. unforeseen, unexpected. || -amente adv. fortuitously, accidentally, casually, by cnance, unexpectedly, randomly, anyhow.

fortum s. m. rancid or foul smell, stench.
fortuna s. f. 1. fortune, good luck. 2. destiny, fate. 3. chance, hazard, casual event. 4. wealth, possessions, estate, money. 5. success, prosperity. 6. (myth.) Fortuna, goddess of fortune. 7. misfortune, vicissitude.
boa ~ fortunateness. **boa ou má** ~ good or bad luck. **ter** ~ to prosper. **lance de** ~ lucky strike or hit. ~ **inesperada** fluke. **filho da** ~ upstart. **ser autor de sua** ~ to be one's own carver. **ele adquiriu uma** ~ he made a fortune. **ele fez a sua** ~ he made his fortune, his pile. **ele herdou uma** ~ he came into a fortune. **correr** ~ to run a risk, to take a chance. **provar** ~ **em** to try one's luck at. **por** ~ fortunately.
fortunado adj. fortunate, lucky, successful.
fortunar v. to make happy, enrich, bless.
fortunoso adj. 1. fortunate, happy, lucky. 2. prosperous, successful. ‖ **-amente** adv. fortunately.
fórum s. m. 1. (Roman hist.) forum. 2. tribunal, court.
fosca s. f. 1. gesture, grimace. 2. disguise, pretence. 3. allurement.
foscar v. 1. to tarnish, dim. 2. to frost, make opaque.
fosco (ô) adj. (pl. **foscos**) 1. dim, tarnished. 2. lustreless, dull. 3. dark, murky. 4. opaque, mat, frosted. 5. clouded, obscured, darksome. 6. (fig.) coward(ly), weak.
vidro ~ frosted glass.
fosfagênio s. m. (biol.) phosphagene.
fosfatado, fosfático adj. (chem.) phosphated, phosphatic.
fosfato s. m. (chem.) phosphate.
~ **de cálcio** calcium phosphate, bone-ash.
fosfatúria s. f. (med.) phosphaturia.
fosfeno s. m. (physiol.) phosphene.
fosfeto s. m. (chem.) phosphid(e).
fosfina s. f. (chem.) phosphin(e).
fosfito s. m. (chem.) phosphite.
fosforado adj. (chem.) phosphorated.
fosforar v. to phosphorate, make phosphorescent.
fosforear v. to phosphoresce, gleam in the dark.
fosforeira s. f. matchbox.
fosforeiro s. m. 1. matchmaker, workman in a match factory. 2. match manufacturer.
fosforejante adj. m. + f. phosphorescent, gleaming.
fosforejar v. 1. to phosphoresce, gleam. 2. to flicker (like a burning match), flare. 3. to radiate.
fosfóreo adj. phosphoric(al), phosphorous.
fosforescência s. f. phosphorescence.
~ **do mar** phosphorescence (of the sea), sea fire.
fosforescente adj. m. + f. 1. phosphorescent, phosphorous, phosphoric. 2. (biol.) photogenic.
fosforescer v. to phosphoresce, gleam.
fosforeto s. m. (chem.) phosphid(e).
fosfórico adj. 1. (chem.) phosphoric(al). 2. phosphorescent. 3. (Braz., pop.) ignorant, illiterate.
fosforífero adj. phosphoriferous.
fosforíforo adj. partially phosphorescent (said of the body of certain animals).
fosforismo s. m. (med.) phosphorism, chronic phosphorous poisoning.
fosforita s. f. (min., petrog.) phosphorite.
fosforização s. f. (pl. **-ões**) 1. impregnation with phosphorus. 2. (chem.) phosphorylation. 3. (physiol.) phosphorolysis.
fosforizar v. to phosphorize, make phosphorescent.
fósforo s. m. 1. (chem.) phosphorus. 2. match, sulphur match. 3. fusee. 4. (sl.) ignorant. 5. intelligence. 6. (Braz.) intruder. ‖ adj. (Braz., sl.) 1. meddlesome, insolent. 2. ignorant.
~ **de segurança** safety match. ~ **de fricção** lucifer match. **riscar, acender um** ~ to strike a match.

fosforoscópio s. m. (phys.) phosphoroscope.
fosforoso adj. (chem.) phosphorous.
fosgênio s. m. (chem.) phosgene.
fosgenita s. f. (min.) phosgenite.
fósmea s. f. 1. confused or nonsensical idea. 2. blunder, absurdity.
fósmeo adj. 1. foolish, silly. 2. nonsensical, abstruse. 3. unintelligible, uncomprehensible. 4. undefinable.
fosquinha s. f. 1. gesture, grimace. 2. disguise.
fazer ~**s** 1. to pretend affection. 2. to make faces.
fossa s. f. 1. cesspool, cesspit, sinkhole, gully. 2. dimple(s). 3. (anat.) fossa, fosse, cavity, pit. 4. ditch, moat.
~ **comum, vala comum** general tomb, common grave. ~ **de fermentação** soaking pit. ~ **de fundição** teeming box. ~ **de mina** sump (plate M 10). ~ **nasal** nasal cavity. ~ **séptica** patent concrete cesspit.
fossado s. m. 1. (mil.) sally, sortie, raid. 2. ditch, trench.
fossador adj. fossorial.
fossar v. 1. to root, rout, nuzzle, turn up earth with the snout. 2. to dig: a) delve. b) work hard.
fossário s. m. 1. churchyard, cemetery. 2. gravedigger, sexton.
fosse (ô) v. (subj. imp. of **ser**).
se tu fosses if you were.
fosseta s. f. diminutive of **fossa**.
fossete s. m. dim. of **fosso**: fossette.
fóssil s. m. (pl. **-eis**) fossil: 1. (obs.) mineral or other object dug out of the earth. 2. petrified remains (of animals or plants) of past geological ages; typolite, toadstone, corallite, dendrolite. 3. (fig., pop.) antiquated person or thing. ‖ adj. m. + f. 1. fossil, fossillike, petrified. 2. old-fashioned, antiquated. 3. obsolete.
fossilífero adj. fossiliferous.
fossilificar v. to fossilize.
fossilismo s. m. fossilism, fondness for antiques.
fossilista s. m. + f. fossilist.
fossilização s. f. (pl. **-ões**) fossil(iz)ation, petrification.
fossilizar v. 1. to fossilize, petrify. 2. to become old-fashioned or antiquated.
fossípede adj. m. + f. fossorial, fossorious.
fosso (ô) s. m. (pl. **fossos**) 1. ditch, trench, fosse. 2. ravine, gully. 3. gutter, drain. 4. moat.
fossorial adj. fossorial.
foste s. m. (arch.) shaft, staff, stick, verge.
fot s. m. (phys.) phot.
fota s. f. Moorish turban.
fotelétrico adj. (also **fotoelétrico**) photoelectric(al).
célula -a photoelectric cell.
fotelétron s. m. (phys.) photoelectron.
foteliografia s. f. (astr.) photoheliography.
foteliográfico adj. (astr.) photoheliographic.
foteliógrafo s. m. (astr.) photoheliograph.
fótico adj. photic.
fotismo s. m. (physiol., psych.) photism, synesthesia.
foto s. f. abbr. of **fotografia**: photo, snapshot.
fotocarta s. f. photochart, photomap.
fotocélula s. f. (phys.) photoelectric cell.
fotocerâmica s. f. photoceramics.
fotocinesia s. f. (physiol.) photokinesis.
fotocópia s. f. photocopy.
~ **azul** blueprint.
fotocromia s. f. photocromy.
fotodesintegração s. f. (med. phys.) photodisintegration.
fotodinâmica s. f. photodynamics.
fotodoscópio s. m. (phys.) photoscope.
fotofilia s. f. (biol.) photophily.
fotófilo adj. (biol.) photophile, photophilous.

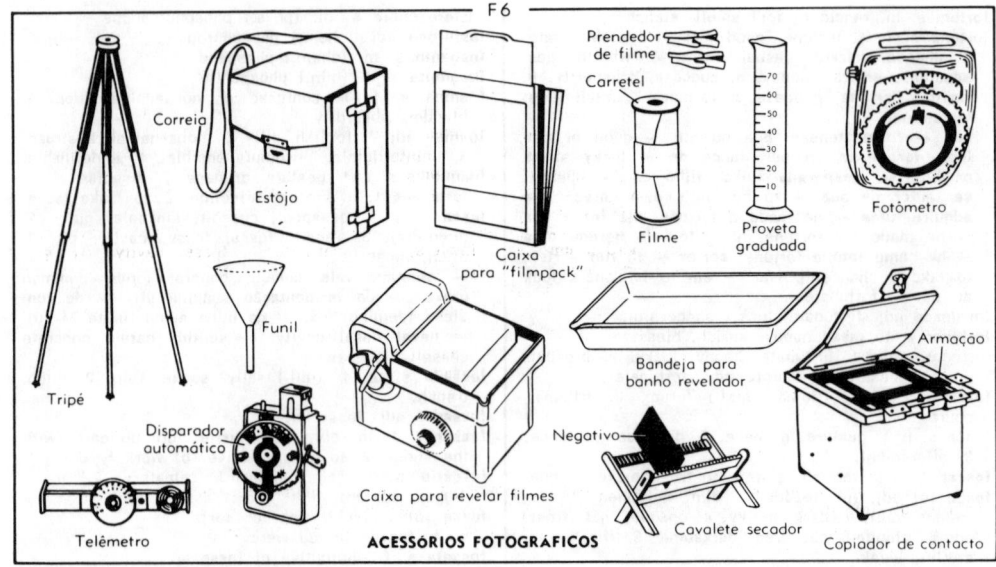

F 6

Tripé
Correia
Estôjo
Funil
Disparador automático
Telêmetro
Prendedor de filme
Carretel
Filme
Proveta graduada
Fotômetro
Caixa para "filmpack"
Bandeja para banho revelador
Negativo
Armação
Caixa para revelar filmes
Cavalete secador
Copiador de contacto

ACESSÓRIOS FOTOGRÁFICOS

fotofobia s. f. (med.) photophobia.
fotófobo s. m. photophobe.
fotogalvanografia s. f. photogalvanography.
fotogênico adj. photogenic.
fotogênio s. m. photogen(e).
fotografar v. 1. to photograph, take a photograph (snapshot) of, shoot. 2. (fig.) to relate or describe with full particulars.
  é difícil de ~ it photographs badly. **é bom para ser fotografado** it takes well.
fotografia s. f. 1. photography: a) the art of photographing. b) exact copy, replica. 2. photograph: a) photographic picture, (snap)shot. b) close description.
  ~ aérea air photograph, aerophoto. **a ~ não saiu** the photograph has not come. **álbum de ~s** photographic album. **tirar uma ~ de** to take a photo(graph) of. **mandei tirar uma ~ de mim** I had my photo(graph) taken. **~ em cores:** 1. colour-photography. 2. photochrome.
fotográfico adj. photographic(al).
fotógrafo s. m. photographer.
fotograma s. m. photogram.
fotogrametria s. f. photogrammetry, phototopography.
fotogravador s. m. photoengraver.
fotogravura s. f. photogravure, photoengraving, autotype.
foto-legenda s. f. main photograph on the front page (newspaper).
fotólise s. f. (chem.) photolysis.
fotolítico adj. photolytic.
fotolitografar v. to photolithograph.
fotolitografia s. f. 1. photolithography. 2. photolithograph.
fotolitográfico adj. photolithographic.
fotologia s. f. (phys.) photology, science of light, photics.
fotológico adj. (phys.) photologic(al).
fotomagnético adj. photomagnetic(al).
fotomecânico adj. photomechanical.
  cópia -a photoprint.
fotometria s. f. (phys.) photometry.
fotométrico adj. (phys.) photometric(al).

fotômetro s. m. photometer, lucimeter, exposure meter (plate F 6).
fotomicrografia s. f. 1. photomicrography. 2. photomicrograph.
fotomicrográfico adj. photomicrographic.
fotominiatura s. f. photominiature, miniature photography.
fotomontagem s. f. (pl. **-ens**) 1. photomontage, composite picture. 2. (cin.) dunning.
fóton s. m. (opt.) photon.
fotonovela s. f. a novel in pictures in a comic book.
fotopsia s. f. (med.) photopsia, photopsy.
fotoquímica s. f. (chem.) photochemistry.
fotoquímico adj. photochemist.
fotoscultura s. f. photosculpture.
fotosfera s. f. photosphere: 1. sphere of light. 2. (astr.) luminous envelope of the sun.
fotosférico adj. photospheric.
fotossensibilidade s. f. photosensitivity.
fotossíntese s. f. (chem., physiol.) photosynthesis.
fototáctico adj. (biol.) phototactic.
fototaxia s. f. (biol.) phototaxis, phototaxy.
fototelegrafia s. f. phototelegraphy.
fototelegráfico adj. phototelegraphic.
fototerapia s. f. (med.) phototherapy, phototherapeutics.
fototerápico adj. phototherapic, phototherapeutic.
fototérmico adj. photothermic.
fototipar v. to phototype.
fototipia s. f. phototypy.
fototípico adj. phototypic.
fotótipo s. m. phototype.
fototipografia s. f. phototypography.
fototipográfico adj. phototypographic.
fototopografia s. f. phototopography, photogrammetry.
fototopográfico adj. phototopographic, photogrammetric.
fototropismo s. m. (biol.) phototropism, heliotropism.
fotovoltaico adj. photovoltaic, photoelectric.
fotozincografia s. f. 1. photozincography (arts). 2. photozincograph (picture).
fotozincográfico adj. photozincographic.
fouçada s. f. (also **foiçada**) a stroke with the scythe

fouce s. f. (also **foice**) scythe.
foucear v. (also **foiçar**) to scythe.
foucinha s. f. (also **foicinha**) sickle.
fouquieráceas s. f. pl. (bot.) Fouquieriaceae, a family of thorny, deciduous plants (ocotillo).
fourierismo s. m. Fourierism (1772-1837): economic system based on cooperative socialism.
fouveiro adj. fallow, sorrel, bay.
cavalo ~ dun(-coloured) horse.
fóvea s. f. 1. fovea, pit, fossa. 2. (anat.) fovea centralis retinae, pit in the middle of the macula lutea.
fovente adj. m. + f. (poet.) favourable, propitious.
fovila s. f. (bot.) fovilla: contents of a pollen grain.
fovismo s. m. (paint.) Fauvism.
fox s. m. fox-terrier (plate C 3).
foxtrote s. m. foxtrot: a dance and the corresponding dance music.
foyer s. m. (Fr., theat.) foyer.
foz s. f. 1. mouth of a river, estuary, firth, outfall. 2. mountain gorge, narrow pass.
fracalhão s. m. (pl. **-ões**) (f. **-ona**) weakling, coward, feebling. ‖ adj. very weak, cowardly.
fração s. f. (pl. **-ões**) fraction: 1. act or process of breaking. 2. rupture, breach. 3. part, fragment, portion, share. 4. (math.) fractional number, an aliquot part of a unit. 5. quantum. 6. (theol.) the breaking of the Holy Host.
~ **algébrica** algebric fraction. ~ **decimal** decimal fraction. ~ **imprópria** improper fraction. ~ **ordinária** common or vulgar fraction. ~ **periódica** recurring decimal. ~ **própria** proper fraction. ~ **simples** simple fraction.
fraca-roupa s. m. + f. (pl. **fracas-roupas**) (pop.) ragamuffin, dirty or ragged fellow.
fracassado adj. unsuccessful, on the beach, stranded.
tentativa **-a** an abortive attempt.
fracassar v. 1. to shatter, burst apart. 2. to break, split in pieces. 3. to fail, meet with ill success, miscarry, strand, bust, fall through, go phut, prove abortive.
seus planos ~**am** they had their plans crossed. a revolução fracassou the revolution met with failure.
fracasso s. m. 1. crash, smash. 2. failure, ruin, miscarriage, unsuccessfulness, fiasco, cropper, washout, bloomer. 3. misfortune, disaster.
fracatear v. (Braz.) 1. to tire, weary, weaken. 2. to grow slack. 3. to fail.
fracionado adj. fractional.
fracionamento s. m. 1. fractionization, fragmentation. 2. division, separation into fractions.
fracionar v. 1. to shatter, fragment. 2. to divide, split. 3. to fraction(ate), fractionize.
fracionário adj. fractionary, fractional, partial. ‖ adv. fractionally.
fraco s. m. 1. weakling, feeble(-minded) creature, fainter. 2. weakness, foible, weak point or side. 3. trouble. 4. propensity, inclination. ‖ adj. 1. weak, feeble. 2. faint, faintish, fainting. 3. not resistant, frail, fragile. 4. languid, debile, sickly, shaky, rocky. 5. slim, slender, weedy. 6. deedless, lame, nerveless, spineless, pulseless. 7. powerless. 8. effeminate, unmanly. 9. cowardly, fainthearted. 10. soft, mild, meek. 11. thin, not dense, scanty, meager. 12. dilute, lacking in concentration, light, soft, watery (liquor, tea, coffee, etc.). 13. slack, sluggish, indolent, dull. 14. mediocre, ordinary, poor. 15. hardly hearable, almost soundless. 16. dim, dull, pale. 17. thready, rotten. 18. unimportant, insignificant. ‖ **-amente** adv. weakly, faintly, cowardly, etc.
-a consolação cold comfort. **-a razão** weak reason.
uma **desculpa -a** a sorry excuse. **memória -a** weak

or treacherous memory. **voz -a** weak voice. **ele apresentou uma desculpa -a** he proffered a thin excuse. **temos apenas -as esperanças** we have but slender hope. **escrever é o seu** ~ writing is his weakness. **gratidão não é o seu** ~ thankfulness is not his trouble. **ela tinha um** ~ **por música** she had a weakness for music. **vinho** ~ weak wine. **na minha -a opinião** in my poor opinion. **isto é o seu ponto (lado)** ~ this is his weak part (side, spot). **eu conheço o** ~ **dele** I have the blind side of him. **o sexo** ~ the gentle sex, the soft sex.
fracticipitos s. m. pl. (ent.) Fracticipta, a suborder of fleas.
fradalhada, fradaria s. f. (depr.) 1. monkship, friarship. 2. a lot of monks. 3. monkish demeanour or spirit.
fradalhão s. m. (pl. **-ões**) (depr.) corpulent monk.
fradar-se v. to become a friar or nun, take the vows.
frade s. m. 1. friar, monk, religious; Fra, Brother (title). 2. cornerstone. 3. (ichth.) black angelfish. 4. (ent.) mole-cricket. 5. (naut.) jack-stay.
~ **menor** Franciscan friar, Cordelier. ~**s pretos** Benedictine monks. **convento de** ~**s** monastery. ~ **leigo** lay brother.
frade-de-pedra s. m. (pl. **frades-de-pedra**) cornerstone.
ele mentiu de fazer corar um ~ he lied to make a cornerstone blush.
fradeiro adj. kindly disposed or friendly attached to monks.
fradejar v. to behave like a monk.
fradépio s. m. 1. (depr.) monk, friar. 2. cornerstone.
fradesco adj. friarly, monkish, monastic.
fradete s. m. part of a gunlock.
fradice s. f. monkishness.
fradicida s. m. person who kills a friar or a monk.
fradinho s. m. 1. (bot.) French or dwarf beans. 2. (ornith.) long-tailed titmouse. 3. (zool.) locust lobster.
fradinho-de-mão-furada s. m. (pl. **fradinhos-de-mão--furada**) goblin, hobgoblin, imp.
fraga s. f. 1. cliff, steep rock, crag. 2. pebbles, gravel.
fragal s. m. (pl. **-ais**) rocky place, rugged ground, cliff, precipice. ‖ adj. m. + f. craggy, precipitous.
fragalheiro s. m. 1. ragpicker. 2. ragman, rag-dealer.
fragalho s. m. rag, tatter.
fragalhotear v. to make merry, jest, frolic.
fragária s. f. (bot.) wild strawberry.
fragata s. f. 1. (naut.) frigate. 2. (Port.) lighter. 3. a stout woman.
fragateiro s. m. 1. master or crewman of a frigate. 2. longshoreman.
fragatim s. m. (pl. **-ins**) (nav.) brigantine.
frágil adj. m. + f. (pl. **-eis**) 1. fragile. 2. weak, frail, feeble. 3. brittle, brash, breakable, frangible. 4. not durable, transitory. 5. unstable, uncertain. 6. fallible. 7. delicate. 8. fine-spun, cobwebbed. ‖ **fragilmente** adv. fragilely, weakly, delicately, frailly, flimsy.
fragilariáceas s. f. pl. (bot.) Fragilariaceae, a family of diatoms.
fragilidade s. f. 1. fragility, infirmity. 2. frangibleness, brittleness. 3. weakness, shakiness. 4. frailty, delicateness, delicacy, daintiness. 5. lack of willpower, feebleness of character.
fragmentação s. f. (pl. **-ões**) fragmentation, shattering, act or process of breaking into fragments.
fragmentado adj. fragmented.
fragmentar v. 1. to break to little pieces, reduce to fragments, fractionize, fritter. 2. to split, divide, part, desintegrate. 3. to shatter, smash. 4. ~**-se** to break up.

fragmentário adj. 1. fragmentary, fragmental. 2 (geol.) clastic. ‖ **fragmentariamente** adv. fragmentarily.

fragmentista s. m. + f. collector of literary, artistic or antique fragments.

fragmento s. m. 1. fragment, fraction, scrap. 2. piece, part, portion, shive, wisp. 3. incomplete part (of a literary or artistic work). ~ **de gelo** brash. ~ **de tijolo** bat (plate A 7). **em** ~**s** apart.

fragmose s. f. (zool.) phragmosis.

frago s. m. (hunt.) 1. trail, scent. 2. droppings (of wild animals).

fragoído s. m. noise, clamour, din, crash.

fragor s. m. 1. crash, loud report, clatter(ing). 2. racket, din, uproar.

fragorar v. 1. to pound, produce a crashing sound. 2. to crack, crackle. 3. to roar, thunder.

fragoroso adj. 1. noisy, loud, clamorous. 2. overwhelming.

fragosidade s. f. (also **fragura**) 1. cragginess, craggedness. 2. inaccessibleness. 3. roughness.

fragoso adj. 1. craggy, rugged. 2. rocky, rock-bound, rough, jagged. 3. inaccessible, difficult to climb.

fragrância s. f. 1. fragrance, sweetness of smell. 2. agreeable odour, pleasant scent, odor(ifer)ousness. 3. balm(iness), bouquet, flavour. 4. aroma, perfume. **sem** ~ infragrant.

fragrante adj. m. + f. 1. fragrant, sweet-scented. 2. odoriferous, redolent, balmy. 3. odorous, perfumed, perfumy, aromatic(al). 4. (ironic) fetid, malodorous. ‖ ~**mente** adv. fragrantly.

frágua s. f. 1. forge, furnace. 2. (fig.) ardour, zeal. 3. intense heat, hotness. 4. bitterness, grief, distress.

fraguar v. 1. forge, shape by heating and hammering out. 2. to grieve, distress.

fraguedo s. m. 1. ridge, chain of rocks. 2. cliff, rock. 3. rocky ground.

fragueirice s. f. hardship, vicissitude.

fragueiro (I) s. m. 1. woodcutter, lumberjack. 2. mountainer, mountain peasant. ‖ adj. 1. dwelling in mountainous regions. 2. toilsome, wearisome. 3. hardy, inured. 4. rough, rude. 5. rustic, rural. 6. untiring, indefatigable. 7. independent.

fragueiro (II) s. m. 1. (ant.) shipbuilder. 2. (Braz.) river pilot.

fragueiro (III) s. m. shrub of the madder family (Dioidia prostrata Sw.). ‖ adj. ardent, fiery.

frajola adj. m. + f. (Braz., sl.) elegant.

fralda s. f. shirt tail, train (of a gown). 2. lap, inferior part. 3. brim. 4. swaddle, swaddling clothes, diaper (plate R 6). 5. flap, lappet. 6. foot of a mountain.
envolver em ~**s** to swaddle. **tirar as** ~**s** to unswathe. **ele anda em** ~**s de camisa** he is as poor as a church mouse. **cão de** ~ lap-dog. **deixar ver as** ~**s das cartas** to show one's cards, to make known one's intentions. ~**s do mar** strand, shore.

fraldão s. m. (pl. **-ões**) lappet of a mail armour, part of an armour below the waist.

fraldar v. to sew skirts or flaps on, garnish with lappets.

fraldar v. to skirt the foot of a mountain.

fraldejar v. 1. to skirt (mountain, etc.). 2. to show the hem of the petticoat (when going).

fraldelim s. m. (pl. **-ins**) underskirt petticoat.

fraldicurto adj. (poet.) short-skirted.

fraldilha s. f. leather apron.

fraldiqueira s. f. (depr.) pocket.

fraldiqueiro s. m. (also **fraldeiro**) mollycoddle, weakling. ‖ adj. 1. unmanly, effeminate. 2. of or relating to skirts.
cão ~ lap-dog.

fraldoso adj. 1. that has a long skirt, flap, or train. 2. verbose, long-winded.

framboesa s. f. raspberry (fruit) (plate B 1).

framboeseira s. f. **framboeseiro** m. raspberry (plant).

framboesia tropical s. f. (path). framboesia, yaws.

frâmea s. f. (hist.) halberd, javelin.

frança s. f. 1. self-conceited, flirtatious woman. 2. m. fop, dandy. ‖ adj. dandyish.

francalete s. m. buckled leather strap, holster strap.

franças s. f. pl. twigs (of a treetop).

francatripa s. f. puppet.

francear v. 1. to prune (tree). 2. to climb on the top of a tree.

francelho s. m. 1. (ornith.) kestrel. 2. pressing plate (of a cheese press). 3. person who apes French manners or usage. 4. chatterbox, talker.

francês s. m. (pl. **-eses**) (f. **-esa**) French: 1. Frenchman, Gaul. 2. the French language. ‖ adj. French, Gaulish, Gallic.
à francesa Frenchlike, after the French fashion. **falar** ~ to parley French; (fig.) to be rich. **ele falou** ~ 1. he spoke French. 2. he gave a generous gratuity. 3. he paid promptly. **ela fala** ~ **como uma vaca espanhola** she speaks French badly.

francesa s. f. Frenchwoman.

francesia s. f. Frenchification, affectation of French manners.

francesiar v. to speak French badly.

francesismo s. m. 1. Gallicism and its use. 2. aping of French ways and manners.

franchado adj. (her.) bendy, bended.

franchão adj. (pl. **-ões**) (f. **-ona**) ugly, repulsive.

franchinote s. m. 1. fop, dandy. 2. conceited or haughty fellow. 3. (depr.) Frenchy.

franchinótico adj. foppish, conceited, haughty.

frâncica s. f. (hist.) francisc: battle-ax(e).

frâncio s. m. (chem.) francium.

franciscana s. f. the Franciscan Order.

franciscano adj. Franciscan, friar of the Franciscan order, Grey friar, Capuchin. ‖ adj. 1. Franciscan, of or pertaining to the Franciscans. 2. (pop.) poor, miserable, wretched.

franciú s. m. (pop.) French language.

franco (I) s. m. franc: 1. old French silver or gold coin. 2. monetary unit in France, Belgium and Switzerland.
ele pagou 200 ~**s** he paid 200 francs (abbr. fr.).

franco (II) s. m. (hist.) Frank: native of the Frankish empire. ‖ adj. Frankish.

franco (III) adj. 1. frank, candid, outspoken, plain-spoken, unreserved, free-spoken, foursquare, open-hearted. 2. liberal, broad-minded. 3. sincere, straight, straightforward, direct. 4. honest. 5. pointblank, bluff, plump. 6. free, costless gratuitous. 7. unaffected, natural, candid, simple-minded. 8. generous. 9. spontaneous. 10. exempt from taxes, duty-free. ‖ **-amente** adv. 1. frankly, sincerely, blankly, richly. 2. freely, willingly. 3. liberally. 4. generously, richly. 5. openly, candidly.
~ **a bordo** free on board (FOB). ~ **a domicílio** free domicile. ~ **estação** free on rail. ~ **de porte** postpaid. **ele não é** ~ **para com você** he is not open with you. **você não foi inteiramente** ~ **comigo** you have not been entirely honest with me. **de modo** ~ **e correto** on the level. **seja** ~! be open-hearted. **-amente contra** strongly opposed.

franco-atirador s. m. (pl. **franco-atiradores**) sniper, partisan, franc-tireur, bushfighter.

franco-canadense s. m. + f. (pl. **franco-canadenses**) Franco-Canadian. ‖ adj. m. + f. Franco-Canadian.

francófilo s. m. Francophil(e). ‖ adj. Francophil(e).

francofobia s. f. Francophobia.

francófobo s. m. Francophobe. ‖ adj. Francophobe.

francolim s. m. (pl. **-ins**) (ornith.) francolin, black partridge.
franco-mação s. m. (pl. **franco-mações**) freemason.
franco-maçonaria s. f. freemasonry.
francônio s. m. Franconian: native or inhabitant of Franconia. ‖ adj. Franconian.
frandulagem s. f. (pl. **-ens**) 1. gang of ragamuffins. 2. rags. 3. trifles, knickknacks, trumpery.
franduleiro adj. (arch.) 1. foreign, alien. 2. trifling, insignificant, worthless.
franduno adj. 1. outlandish, strange. 2. presumptuous, conceited.
franga s. f. pullet, chicken.
~ **cevada** poulard.
frangainha s. f., **frangainho, franguinho, franganito** m. 1. chicken. 2. (fig.) cockerel, colt.
frangalhar v. to tear in rags and tatters.
frangalheiro s. m. ragamuffin, tatterdemalion, ragged or shabby fellow. ‖ adj. frumpish.
frangalho s. m. rag, tatter, frazzle.
frangalhona s. f. slut, slattern, frump.
frangalhote s. m. 1. cockerel. 2. (pop.) lad, (foolish) youngster.
frangão s. m. (pl. ~**s**) young cock, cockerel.
frangão-do-mar s. m. (pl. **frangões-do-mar**) (ichth.) bib.
frangelha s. f. cheese mould, cheese press.
franger v. 1. to fold, plait. 2. to gather in plaits, take out a tuck. 3. to knit one's brows. 4. to break.
frangibilidade s. f. frangibleness, frangibility, brittleness.
frangir v. = **franzir**.
frangível adj. m. + f. (pl. **-íveis**) frangible, breakable.
frango s. m. 1. chicken. 2. young cock, cockerel. 3. (Braz., ichth.) sharp-nosed shark. 4. (football sl.) blunder goal. 5. (Braz.) roasted corncob.
~ **assado** roast(ed) chicken. ~ **para assar na grelha** broiler. **ele está caçando** ~ he is drunk.
frango-d'água s. m. (pl. **frangos-d'água**) (ornith.) florida gallinule.
frangolho s. m. wheat meal porridge.
frangote s. m. 1. chicken. 2. lad, youngster, fledgling.
franguear v. to eat roasted corn.
franguinho s. m. small chicken.
frângula s. f. (bot.) thorn, berry-bearing alder, black dogwood.
franja s. f. 1. fringe, bullion, edging. 2. bangs, front (hair) (plate P 8).
franjado adj. 1. fringed, fringelike, fringy, laciniate. 2. (bot.) fimbriate. 3. conceited, affected, pretentious.
franjar v. 1. to fringe, trim or adorn with fringes. 2. to lace, adorn with a lace. 3. to decorate, make lively. 4. to unthread, unweave.
frankeniáceas s. f. pl. (bot.) Frankeniaceae.
franqueado adj. 1. patent. 2. prepaid, post-free, stamped (envelope).
franquear v. 1. to exempt, free, frank (from taxes or duties). 2. to facilitate. 3. to clear. 4. to prepay, pay the postage or transport of, stamp. 5. to concede, grant. 6. to overcome, get over (difficulty). 7. to open a port. 8. to remove (obstacle).
~ **as cartas** to prepay, stamp, pay postage. ~ **a passagem** to clear the way. ~ **ao público** to open to the public. **ela franqueou todas as dificuldades** she overcame all difficulties.
franqueável adj. m. + f. (pl. **-áveis**) clearable, exemptible, grantable, removable.
franqueira s. f. (Braz.) hunting knife, dagger.
franqueiro s. m. (S. Braz.) a race of sturdy cattle.
franqueza s. f. 1. frankness, candour. 2. liberality, broad-mindedness. 3. sincerity, openness, outspo-

kenness, unreservedness. 4. plain dealing, plain-spokenness, straightforwardness, foursquareness. 5. bluffness, plumpness. 6. explicitness, roundness. 7. honesty. 8. generosity. 9. franchise.
ele falou com ~ he was quite outspoken, (U. S. A. sl.) he talked turkey. **ele lhe falou com toda a** ~ he used plain language towards him. **usar de** ~ **com** to be plain with. **a sua** ~ **é surpreendente** his open-heartedness is surprising.
franquia s. f. 1. postage. 2. postage stamp. 3. franchise: a) exemption, immunity. b) privilege. c) asylum, refuge.
~ **postal** postage. **sem** ~ unstamped.
franquismo s. m. Francoism.
franzido s. m. folds, pleats, plaits, gathering, ruffle. ‖ adj. 1. plaited. 2. rugged, wrinkly, puckery.
franzimento s. m. 1. plaiting. 2. folds, plaits. 3. frown(ing). 4. pucker(ing).
franzino adj. 1. slender, slim. 2. weak, frail, flimsy. 3. delicate, fine. 4. tenuous, unsubstantial, thinnish.
franzir v. 1. (also ~**-se**) to wrinkle, pucker. 2. to fold, pleat, plait, crease, goffer, whip, ruffle, tuck, ruck, rill. 3. to frown, knit, draw, contract.
ele franziu as sobrancelhas (a testa) he frowned, he wrinkled up his brows, he scowled. **ele franziu os beiços** he curled his lips.
fraque s. m. morning coat, cutaway (plate R 7).
fraquear, fraquejar v. 1. to weaken, lose one's strength. 2. to lose courage. 3. to show signs of exhaustion, languish. 4. to go down on one's knees. 5. to yield, succumb. 6. to fail, dodder, fall.
fraqueira s. f. (fam.) weakness, debility.
fraqueiro adj. weak, tired, barren.
fraquete adj. weakly, frail.
fraqueza s. f. 1. weakness, feebleness. 2. powerlessness, impotence. 3. unsoundness. 4. peaked appearance, sickly look. 5. enervation, nervelessness. 6. debility, frailty. 7. despondency, dejectedness. 8. timidity, shyness. 9. defect, blemish, fault. 10. brittleness, fragility, infirmity. 11. faintness, languor, languishment. 12. weak point, foible, faillings, imperfections, shortcoming.
~ **da vista** weakness of the eyes. ~ **de espírito** feeble-mindedness. **fazer das** ~**s forças** to sum up pluck, take courage. **tirar forças da** ~ to make a virtue of necessity. **ela tem uma** ~ **por ele** she has a soft spot in her heart for him, she has a weakness for him. **ele sofre duma** ~ **do estômago** he suffers from a weak stomach.
frasca s. f. 1. kitchen utensils. 2. china, crockery. 3. provisions.
frascagem s. f. (pl. **-ens**) 1. lot of bottles. 2. kitchen utensils.
frascaria s. f. 1. lot of bottles or flasks. 2. (sl.) dissoluteness. 3. extravagance.
frascário adj. (pop.) 1. lewd, dissolute. 2. extravagant. 3. corrupt, licentious.
frasco s. m. bottle, flask, vial, phial, flagon, flacon, cruse.
~ **de boca larga** bocal, goblet. ~ **de pólvora** powder flask. **pôr em** ~ to bottle.
frase s. f. phrase: 1. sentence, proposition. 2. expression, locution. 3. part or piece of music, usually of four measures. 4. slogan:
~ **batida** commonplace. ~ **familiar** household word. ~ **feita** aphorism. ~ **inventada** coinage. ~ **musical** passage. ~ **trivial** hackneyed phrase. **fazer** ~**s** to make hollow phrases.
fraseado s. m. phrasing: 1. wording. 2. literary or rhetorical style, expression, way of expression. 3. mode of composing musical phrases. ‖ adj. formulated, expressed.

fraseador s. m. phrasemonger, gasbag, talker. ‖ adj. phrasal, phrasy, highfalutin(g), bombastic.

frasear v. to phrase: 1. express in words, esp. in a particular way. 2. (mus.) divide into phrases.

fraseologia s. f. phraseology: diction, phrase, idiomatic or peculiar style of phrasing.

fraseológico adj. phraseologic(al). ‖ **fraseologicamente** adv. phraseologically.

fraseólogo s. m., **frasista** m. + f. 1. phraseologist. 2. phrasemonger, gasbag.

frasqueira s. f. 1. bottle rack, cellaret, 2. bottle case or cellar. 3. wine cellar or vault. 4. (Braz.) demijohn of 6.5 gallons.

frasqueiro adj. 1. dissolute, lewd. 2. indecorous, unseemly. 3. rather décolleté.

frasqueta s. f. (typogr.) frisket.

frasquinho s. m. flasquet.

fraterna s. f. gentle reproof; brotherly reprimand.

fraternal adj. m. + f. (pl. -ais) 1. fraternal, brotherly, brotherlike. 2. (fig.) affectionate, devoted, fond. ‖ ~mente adv. fraternally, brotherly, affectionately.

fraternalismo s. m. fraternalism.

fraternidade s. f. 1. fraternity, brotherhood, brotherliness. 2. affection, friendship. 3. charity. 4. harmony. 5. union.

fraternização s. f. (pl. -ões) fraternization.

fraternizador s. m. fraternizer.

fraternizar v. to fraternize: 1. unite in friendship, form close fellowship with. 2. ally or unite like brothers.

fraterno adj. fraternal, brotherly.

caridade -a fraternal love, charity.

fratria s. f. (Greek hist.) phratry.

fratricida s. m. + f. fratricide: one who kills a brother (or sister). ‖ adj. 1. fratricidal. 2. of or relating to civil war.

fratricídio s. m. 1. fratricide: the act of killing a brother (or sister). 2. civil war.

fratura s. f. 1. fracture, break(ing), burst, disruption, (also med.), rupture, breach. 2. (geol.): a) fault, faulting, rock fissure. b) landslide.

~ **composta** compound fracture.

fraturar v. (also med. and geol.) to fracture, break.

fraudação s. f. (pl. -ões) 1. fraud, deceit. 2. defraudation. 3. trick, hoax. 4. malice, ill will.

fraudador s. m. 1. defrauder. 2. deceiver, cheat. 3. contrabandist, smuggler.

fraudar v. 1. to defraud. 2. to deceive, cheat, (U. S. A.) jew, fool, fob. 3. to pillage, plunder. 4. to smuggle. 5. (also ~-se) to deprive (o. s.) of.

fraudatório adj. fraudulent, deceitful.

fraudável adj. m. + f. (pl. -áveis) subject to fraud, deceptive.

fraude s. f. 1. swindle, deception, hoax 2. fraud, fraudulency, deceit. 3. trickery. 4. cheat, defraudation. 5. contraband, smuggling.

fraudulência s. f. fraudulence.

fraudulento, frauduloso, fraudento adj. fraudulent, cheating, dishonest, fallacious, wildcat, crooked, deceitful, deceptive, surreptious. ‖ -amente adv. fraudulently, deceivingly, deceitfully.

plano ~ rig.

frauta s. f. 1. (also **flauta**) flute. 2. (tech.) smoother, sleeker.

tocar ~ to play the flute.

frautar v. (rare) 1. to play the flute, to flute. 2. to produce a flutelike sound.

frauteiro s. m. (also **flauteiro**) flutist.

fraxinela s. f. (bot.) fraxinella, gas plant.

fraxíneo adj. ashen: 1. of or pertaining to the ash tree. 2. made of ash wood.

frear v. 1. to brake. 2. to repress, restrain, refrain. 3. to check, curb, control.

frecha s. f. 1. (also **flecha**) arrow. 2. (Braz.) frame of a handsaw. 3. guiding stick of a rocket.

de ~ straight on, directly.

frechada s. f. (also **flechada**) arrow shot.

frechal s. m. (pl. -ais) (carp.) 1. groundsill. 2. roof beam. 3. plate.

frechar v. (also **flechar**) 1. to hit, wound or pierce with an arrow. 2. to shoot an arrow. 3. to cffend, harrow. 4. to flit by, dart.

~ **o arco** to bend or draw the bow.

frecharia s. f. (also **flecharia**) a lot of arrows or darts.

frecheira s. f. loophole.

frecheiro s. m. 1. archer, bowman. 2. bowyer.

freeiro s. m. manufacturer of: 1. curb-bits. 2. brakes.

frega s. f. (Braz.) harlot, lewd woman.

fregatídeos s. m. pl. (ornith.) Fregatidae, the frigate bird family.

frege s. m. 1. quarrel, strife. 2. brawl, wrangle. 3. clamour. 4. a paltry feast. 5. shabby or dirty eating-house.

provocar ~ (Braz.) to provoke disorder, to riot.

frege-moscas s. m., sg. + pl. flyblown restaurant, dirty eating-house.

fregereba s. f. (ichth.) tripletail.

fregista s. m. keeper or attendant of a pothouse.

fregona s. f. kitchenmaid, charwoman.

freguês s. m. (pl. -eses) (f. -esa) 1. customer, client. 2. shopper. 3. habitual purchaser. 4. (U. S. A.), sl. proposition, patron. 5. hired (day) labourer. 6. fellow, chap. 7. parishioner.

adquirir fregueses to get customers. **angariar fregueses** to tout. **pessoa que cata fregueses** tout. **um** ~ **esquisito** a queer customer. **provável** ~ prospective customer.

freguesia s. f. 1. parish: 2. community, parishioners (collectively). 3. clientele, customers, patrons, patronage.

vá pregar noutra ~ tell it to the horse-marines.

frei s. m. 1. friar, monk. 2. (title) **Frei**: Father.

freijó, frei-jorge s. m. (pl. **freis-jorges**) (bot.) Brazilian walnut.

freima s. f. 1. impatience, restlessness. 2. prurigo, itching. 3. activity, action. 4. haste. 5. care, caution.

freimão s. m. (also **fleimão, flegmão**) phlegm, apathy, calmness.

freimático adj. 1. impatient, restless. 2. hasty. 3. prudent, cautious.

freio s. m. 1. bridle: a) (horse) bit, curb bit, bridoon (plate C 12). b) (anat., zool.) fr(a)enum. 2. check, curb, rein, repression, restraint. 3. brake, break. 4. skid, shoe. 5. vice jaw or vice cheek. 6. (fig.) submission. 7. (tech.) braking regulator, governor.

~ **a molinete** fan brake. ~ **a pedal** foot brake. ~ **de contrapedal (bicicleta)** back-pedalling brake, coaster brake. ~ **de disco** disk brake. ~ **de emergência** (railway) emergency brake, communication cord. ~ **de mão** parking brake. ~ **de pé** service brake. ~ **de segurança** safety brake. ~ **a vácuo** vacuum brake. ~ **hidráulico** hydraulic brake, pump brake. ~ **pneumático,** ~ **a ar comprimido** air brake. **colocar** ~ (horse) to bridle. **não dar pelo** ~ not to obey the rein, not to give in. **morder os** ~s to resist, not to submit. **ela pôs os s em suas ambições** she curbed her ambitions. **soltar ou largar os** ~s to give the reins (also fig.). **sem** ~ (horse) unruled. **tomar o** ~ **nos dentes** 1. (horse) to champ the bit, be unruly. 2. (fig.) to be carried away by one's passion.

freira s. f. 1. nun, religious, cloistress, sister; in titles: Mother. 2. (ichth.) pomfret. 3. ~s pl. (Braz., also **pipocas**) popcorn.

~ **leiga** lay sister. **à maneira de** ~**s** nunlike. **ela tornou-se** ~ she took the veil.

freiral adj. m. + f. (pl. **-ais**) conventual, monastic(al). nunlike.

freirar v. 1. to admit to a military or knighthood order. 2. to enter a convent, take the veil. 3. to become a monk or nun.

freiraria s. f. nuns (collectively), nunhood, a number of nuns.

freirático s. m. person favourably inclined or friendly attached to friars or nuns. ‖ adj. 1. monkish, nunlike. 2. monastic(al), conventual.

freire s. m. 1. monk, friar. 2. member of a military order, knight.

freiria s. f. nunnery, convent for nuns.

freirice s. f. nunlike behaviour.

freirinha s. f. 1. dim. of **freira**. 2. novice. 3. (Port., ornith.) greenfinch. 4. (zool.) calappid, box crab, calappian.

freix(i)al s. m. (pl. **-ais**) ash grove, forest of ash trees.

freixo s. m. ash (the tree and its wood). **de ou semelhante a** ~ ashen.

freme s. m. (Braz.) = **flame**.

fremebundo adj. m. **fremente** m. + f. 1. roaring, thundering. 2. excited, thrilled.

fremir v. 1. to roar, thunder. 2. to groan, moan. 3. to stir, fluster. 4. to tremble, shudder. 5. to vibrate, thrill.

frêmito s. m. 1. roar(ing), thunder. 2. crash, clangour. 3. shudder, shock, start. 4. thrill, shiver (of joy, fear). 5. murmur, whisper. 6. (med.) tremor.

frenação s. f. (pl. **-ões**) 1. brakeage, braking. 2. (fig.) moderation. 3. (fig.) check, restriction, curb.

frenar v. 1. to brake. 2. to scotch (wheel). 3. to snub (boat). 4. (fig.) to moderate. 5. (fig.) to check, curb, repress, restrict.

frendente adj. m. + f. gnashing.

frender v. 1. to gnash one's teeth. 2. to foam with rage. 3. to become annoyed or irritated.

frendor s. m. gnashing or grinding of teeth.

frenesi s. m. (less used **frenesim**) 1. frenzy, madness, distraction, 2. passion, rapture, franticness. 3. raving, rage, furore. 4. (med.) phrenitis. 5. impatience, eagerness. 6. impertinence. **com** ~ like mad.

frenesiar v. 1. to cause frenzy in, make frantic. 2. to behave like mad, be in a frenzy. 3. to get excited or upset. 4. to become impatient.

frenético adj. 1. frenetic(al), frantic(al), frenzied. 2. furious, angry, wild. 3. excited, flurried. 4. convulsed. 5. passionate. 6. impatient. ‖ **freneticamente** adv. 1. frenetically, frantically. 2. passionately. 3. furiously, wildly, ravingly. 4. impatiently.

frenicectomia s. f. (med.) phrenicectomy.

frênico adj. (anat.) phrenic, pertaining to the diaphragm.

frenite s. f. (med.) phrenitis: inflammation of the brain or the diaphragm.

frenologia s. f. phrenology.

frenológico adj. phrenologic(al).

frenologismo s. m. phrenologism, theories of phrenological studies.

frenologista s. m. + f., **frenólogo** m. phrenologist, phrenologer.

frenopata, frenópata s. m. + f. (med.) phrenopath.

frenopatia s. f. (med.) phrenopathy: any mental disease or disorder.

frenopático adj. (med. phrenopathic.

frente s. f. front: 1. façade. 2. front side, frontal part, frontage, fore, forefront (plate P 2). 3. face. 4. mien, demeanor, appearance. 5. (mil.) van, leading unit. advanced guard. 6. zone of conflict, line of battle. 7. movement (political, etc.). ~ **a** ~ opposite. ~ **única** a kind of bodice which leaves the back bare. ~ **tempestuosa** (meteor.) front of thunderstorms. **alteraram a** ~ they changed front. **a** ~ **do exército** the front of the army. **bem em** ~ straight ahead. **bem em** ~ **de** right against, straight in front of. **estar à** ~ **de alguém** to be in advance of s. o. **a casa faz** ~ **para o bosque** the house fronts the woods. **ele fez** ~ **a** he made head against. **ir à** ~ to go on ahead. **em** ~ **a** abreast of. **em** ~ **ao seu nariz** under your nose. **estar à** ~ to be ahead. **linha de** ~ front. **na** ~ **de** in advance, in front of, before, ahead. **para a** ~ 1. to the front. 2. onward. **para** ~**!** go ahead! **porta da** ~ front door. **saia da minha** ~ get out of my sight.

frentear v. (Braz.) to head off, round up (cattle).

frentista s. m. (archit.) façade finisher, stuccoworker, plasterer.

frenulados s. m. pl. (ent.) Frenatae, insects of the order Lepidoptera (butterflies, moths).

freqüência s. f. frequency: 1. act or practice of frequenting, attendance. 2. frequent repetition or occurrence, commonness, periodicity. 3. concourse. 4. (electr.) number of cycles, frequence. 5. (math., phys.) rate of occurrence. 6. crowd, multitude. 7. (classes) attendance. ~ **à escola** attendance at school. ~ **de pulso** pulse rate. ~ **musical** musical or audio frequency. ~ **portadora** (or **fundamental**) carrier frequency. ~ **radiofônica** radio frequency. ~ **supersônica** supersonic frequency. **ter boa** ~ to be much run after. **com** ~ frequently. **da mesma** ~ (electr.) synchronous.

freqüencímetro s. m. (electr.) frequency meter.

freqüentado adj. frequented, often visited. **pouco** ~ unfrequented. **não** ~ unvisited.

freqüentador s. m. frequenter, visitor, resorter, haunter. ‖ adj. frequenting, visiting. ~ **de cinema** filmgoer. ~ **de teatros** playgoer. ~ **de tavernas** bencher.

freqüentar v. 1. to frequent: a) visit repeatedly. b) be familiar with, resort to habitually. c) haunt, resort. d) associate. e) patronize. 2. to follow or take a course of lectures, attend a school or course. ~ **a casa de alguém** to frequent somebody's house, to keep company with somebody. **ela freqüenta a igreja** she goes regularly to church. **ele freqüenta a melhor sociedade** he moves in the best society. **eles** ~**am uma escola pública** they attended a public school.

freqüentativo adj. (gram.) frequentative.

freqüente adj. m. + f. 1. frequent, often. 2. recurrent, continual, repeated. 3. assiduous, diligent, constant. 4. untiring, indefatigable. 5. vulgar, common. ‖ ~**mente** adv. frequently, repeatedly, assiduously, commonly, continually, constantly, often, as often as not, again and again, time and again. **pouco** ~ unfrequent. **muito** ~ prolate. **visita** ~ a frequent caller. **ela escreveu** ~**mente** she wrote time and again. **ele viajou** ~**mente** he travelled more often than not.

fresa s. f. (tech.) 1. milling cutter (or tool). 2. milling machine, miller. ~ **cônica** angle cutter. ~ **de broquear** boring miller. ~ **de perfil** profile cutter. ~ **para fazer ranhuras** slot cutter.

fresar v. to mill.

fresca s. f. 1. breeze, cool breath of air. 2. fresh(ness), coolness.

à ~ in light clothes. **passear pela** ~ to take a walk in the cool of the day.

frescal adj. m. + f. (pl. **-ais**) 1. fresh, new, untainted. 2. saltish. 3. unspoilt, sound. 4. full of vigour, lively.

frescalhão adj. (pl. **-ões**) (f. **-ona**) 1. very fresh. 2. well-kept (in spite of age). 3. waggish.

frescata s. f. 1. walk, stroll or trip, esp. in the field. 2. pastime, amusement, frolic. 3. m. reveller, merrymaker.

fresco s. m. 1. fresh breeze, cool breath of air. 2. coolness, freshness. 3. (paint.) fresco. 4. (Braz., vulg.) passive pederast. ‖ adj. fresh: 1. new. 2. recent, novel. 3. vigorous, strong. 4. verdant, green, luxuriant. 5. healthy, wholesome. 6. brisk, lively. 7. sound, undamaged. 8. cool, refreshing. 9. not tinned, salted or pickled. ‖ **-amente** adv. freshly.

cor -a do rosto lively or ruddy complexion. **tinta -a** we paint. **a** ~ (paint.) in fresco. **pintura a** ~ fresco painting. **pintar a** ~ to paint in fresco. **ar** ~ fresh or cool air. **pão** ~ new bread. **peixe** ~ fresh fish. **tempo** ~ cool weather. **vento** ~ fresh gale. **está ainda muito** ~ **na minha memória** it is still fresh in my memory. **fazer jornada pelo** ~ to travel in the cool of the day. **guarde-o em lugar** ~ keep it in a cool place. **vamos sentar-nos num lugar** ~ let's sit in the cool.

frescor s. m. (also **fresquidão**) 1. freshness, cool(ness). 2. exuberance, verdure, verdancy, floridness. 3. breeze, cool wind. 4. liveliness, briskness, vigour, (fig.) greens. 5. brilliancy, resplendence.

frescura s. f. 1. = **frescor**. 2. (Braz., pop.) smutty or indecent sayings. 3. insolence, impudence.

frese s. f. (tech.) 1. milling cutter or tool. 2. miller, milling machine.

fresquinho adj. coolish.

fressura s. f. 1. pluck: heart, liver and lungs of slaughtered animals. 2. (of a pig) haslet, hasslet, pig's fry.

fressureiro s. m. pluck seller.

fresta s. f. 1. skylight, dormer-window, fanlight. 2. window slit, loophole, lunette. 3. opening, aperture. 4. breach, gap, slit, crack, crevice, interstice.
~ **nos dentes** gap in the teeth.

frestado adj. 1. having window slits. 2. cracked, chapped.

frestão s. m. (pl. **-ões**) French window, high sash window.

fretado adj. chartered.

fretador s. m. 1. charterer, freighter. 2. shipowner, ship broker.

fretagem s. f. (pl. **-ens**) freightage: 1. ship brokerage. 2. charges or fees. 3. freight.

fretamento s. m. freight(age): 1. transportation by ship. 2. (naut.) charter. 3. hiring or renting of a truck, etc.

fretar v. 1. to charter. 2. to freight, rent, hire (for freight). 3. to load, freight.

frete s. m. freight, freightage: 1. carriage, portage, cartage, transportation, truckage. 2. freight charges, drayage. 3. load, cargo, shipment.
~ **de ida e volta** freight out and home. ~ **extra** surplus freight, primage. ~ **marítimo** shipping charges. ~ **pagável à medida** freight payable on measurement. ~ **por distância percorrida** freight for distance run through. ~ **por reembolso** carriage forward, charges to be colleted on delivery.

freteiro s. m. (Braz.) herdsman, cattle drover.

fretejador s. m. porter, loader.

fretejar v. to run errands, carry loads, accept cargoes for transport.

fretenir v. to stridulate, chirp.

freto s. m. (poet.) arm of the sea, inlet, channel, strait(s).

freudiano s. m. Freudian ‖ adj. Freudian.

freudismo s. m. Freudianism.

frevo s. m. (Braz.) 1. bustle of carnival merriment, merry-making. 2. clamour, loud noise. 3. quarrel, brawl.

frexado adj. (N. Braz., pop.) famous, celebrated.

fria s. f. (Braz., sl.) pistol.

friabilidade s. f. 1. friability, friableness. 2. crumbliness, crispness.

friacho adj. fresh, cool, coldish.

friagem, frialdade s. f. 1. cold(ness). 2. chill(iness), coolness. 3. cold weather or wind. 4. (Braz.) frost blight. 5. (Braz., Amazonas) sudden drop of temperature. 6. (fig.) frigidity, indifference. 7. negligence, carelessness.

friável adj. m. + f. (pl. **-áveis**) friable, brittle, crisp(y), fragile, short, crump.

fricandó s. m. (Fr.) fricandeau.

fricassé s. m. (Fr.) fricassee.

fricativo adj. fricative, characterized by friction, affricative, spirant.
consoante -a 1. (gram.) fricative, fricative consonant. 2. (phon.) spirant.

fricção s. f. (pl. **-ões**) 1. friction, attrition, rub(bing), chafe, chafing, fret. 2. (med.) liniment, embrocation. 3. traction.
roda de ~ friction wheel.

friccionar v. 1. to rub, move or pass with friction, grit, embrocate, fret. 2. to scrub, abrade. 3. to apply a liniment, anoint.

fricote s. m. (Braz., sl.) 1. cunning, slyness. 2. vanity.

fricoteiro adj. (Braz.) cunning, cunningly, fussy.

frictor s. m. friction tube or primer.

frieira s. f. 1. kibe, chilblain. 2. eczema between the toes. 3. (fam.) glutton.
padecente de ~s affected with chilblains.

frieirão s. m. (pl. **-ões**) (f. **-ona**) timid or apathetic man, weakling, dull chap. ‖ adj. dull, timid, apathetic, weak.

friento adj. very sensitive to cold.

frieza s. f. (also **frigidez**) coldness: 1. frigidity, iciness, chill(iness), cold weather, coolness, frost(iness). 2. (fig.) indifference, coolness, callousness, hardheartedness, distance. 3. lack of animation or colour.

frigideira s. f. 1. pan, frying-pan, skillet, spider (plate C 20). 2. female frying cook. 3. (pop.) fried dish, fry. 4. m. + f.: a) braggart, boaster. b) morose or self-conceited person.
saltar da ~ **para as brasas** to fall out of the frying-pan into the fire.

frígido adj. frigid: 1. cold, chilly. 2. frosty, frozen, icy. 3. cool, indiferent. 4. callous, apathetic. ‖ **frigidamente** adv. frigidly.
zonas -as frozen zones.

frigífugo adj. that avoids or keeps off cold.

frígio s. m. (hist.) Phrygian: 1. native or inhabitant of ancient Phrygia. 2. language of the Phrygians. ‖ adj. Phrygian.

frigir v. 1. to fry, cook in hot fat, to roast, pan. 2. to harass with questions, pester. 3. to brag, boast, show off.

frigoria s. f. (phys.) refrigerating unit, (ant.) frigoric.

frigorífero, frigorífico s. m. 1. freezer, refrigerador, icebox. 2. cold-storage room (or building), frigorifico. 3. freezing mixture, coolant, cooling liquid. ‖ adj. frigorific(al): keeping or generating cold.
em frigorífico in cold-storage. **câmara frigorífica** cold store.

frigorificar v. 1. to produce or generate cold. 2. to keep cold. 3. to freeze or chill (food) for preservation.

frimáceas s. f. pl. (bot.) Phrymaceae, the lopseed family.

frimário s. m. (hist.) Frimaire: third month of the French Revolutionary calendar.

frincha s. f. fissure, rift, crack, chap, cleft.

fringilídeo s. m. (ornith.) a fringillid bird. ‖ adj. fringillid, fringilline, fringillaceous.

fringilídeos s. m. pl. (ornith.) Fringillidae, a family of passerine birds (canaries, finches, sparrows).

frio s. m. 1. cold: a) coldness, iciness, low temperature. b) cold weather, frost. c) chill(iness). 2. indifference, unconcern. 3. dejection, discouragement. 4. callousness, hardheartedness. ‖ adj. cold: 1. wintry, winterly, algid, icy, frosty, frigid, chilly, cool. 2. cooled, chilled, frozen. 3. Indifferent, unconcerned, harsh, distant. 4. insensible, callous. 5. insipid, flat, dull. ‖ **-amente** adv. coldly, frigidly, distantly, coldheartedly.
~ **e úmido** cold and moist, clammy. **um ~ intenso** a frostiness, keen cold. **estou (com) ~ I** feel cold. **está muito ~** it is very (or bitterly) cold. **excessivamente ~** overcold. **homem ~** 1. a coolheaded man. 2. a coldhearted man. **malhar em ferro ~** to lose one's labour. **morrer a ferro ~** to die by the sword. **morte de ~** death from exposure. **muito ~ gelid. sangue- ~** cold blood. **matar alguém a sangue- ~** to kill somebody in cold blood, cold-bloodedly. **sensação de ~** cold. **um sorriso ~** a wintry smile. **tempo ~** cold weather. **o tempo é bastante ~** the weather is on the cold side. **tremer de ~** to shiver with cold. **o ~ trouxe a neve consigo** the cold brought snow with it.

frioleira s. f. 1. lace used for trimming. 2. frivolity, trifle, bauble. 3. silliness, nonsense, flummery, frivolousness, falderal. 4. idle talk, chit-chat.

friorento adj. 1. very sensitive to cold. 2. chilly, shivery, acold.

frisa s. f. 1. frieze, fearnought, pilot-cloth: thick, coarse woollen cloth. 2. the nap of cloth. 3. cotton twist used for caulking. 4. (theat.) box, dress box.

frisado s. m. curled hair. ‖ adj. curled, curly, fuzzy, friz(z), frizzle, frizzly.

frisador s. m. frizzler.

frisagem s. f. (pl. **-ens**) 1. curling. 2. frizzling, frizziness. 3. (archit.) frieze.

frisante adj. m. + f. 1. fit(ting), appropriate, suitable. 2. exact, accurate. 3. significant, momentous. 4. decisive, categorical. 5. convincing. 6. (wine) effervescent.

frisão s. m. (pl. **-ões**) Frision: 1. Frieslander. 2. the language. ‖ adj. Frisian.

frisar v. 1. to (raise a) nap; frieze. 2. to frizz(le), curl, form locks. 3. (archit.) to furnish with a frieze. 4. to quote opportunely, cite appropriately. 5. to stress, emphasize, underline, accentuate, urge, make a point of. 6. to be similar to. 7. to touch almost, come very near. 8. ~**se**: a) to get crisp or curled (sea). b) to give a singe to one's hair.

friso s. m. (archit.) frieze: stringcourse, any longitudinal decorative feature, band, fillet or ledge.

frita s. f. frit(t) (of glass). 2. time required for melting it. 3. burning of mineral compounds to eliminate organic matter. 4. fried dish.

fritada s. f. fried or roasted food, poached eggs, fritter, fry.

fritalhada, fritangada s. f. (pop.) substantial but poorly prepared meal of roast meat or fish.

fritar v. 1. to fry, cook in hot fat, to frit, pan. 2. to roast, bake. 2. to harass with questions, pester. 4. to brag, boast, show off.

fritilária s. f. (bot.) guinea-hen flower, snake's-head, checkered lily.

fritilo s. m. dice-cup, dice-box.

frito s. m. fried food, fritter. ‖ adj. 1. fried. 2. (Braz., coll.) done for, cornered.
batatas fritas potato chips. **peixe ~** fried fish. **estamos ~s** (fig., pop.) we are in a tight corner, we are in a fix, we are on the rocks.

fritura s. f. any fried food, fritter, fry.

friúra s. f. = **friagem, frialdade.**

frivolidade, frivoleza s. f. 1. frivolousness, frivolity. 2. futility, uselessness. 3. idleness, emptiness. 4. trifling(ness), levity, lightness, fickleness, flightiness. 5. flippancy.

frívolo s. m. trifler. ‖ adj. 1. frivolous, wanton. 2. trifling, trivial. 3. futil. 4. superficial, fickle, featherbrained, flyaway, light(some), volatile, fast. 5. flippant. ‖ **frivolamente** adv. frivolously, superficially, paltrily, flightily, triflingly.

frocado s. m. flock trimming. ‖ adj. trimmed with flocks.

froco s. m. 1. snowflake, flake. 2. flock (of wool, cotton, etc.). 3. chenille.

frolo s. m. (Braz.) frou-frou, the rustling of a skirt or silk.

fronças s. f. twigs of a tree top.

froncil s. m. (pl. **-is**) pleated linen handkerchief.

fronda s. f. (hist.) Fronde: French political party during the reign of Louis XIV.

frondar v. (Braz.) to leaf, put on new foliage, frondesce.

fronde s. f. (bot.) frond. 2. frondage, leafage, foliage.

fronde(j)ar v. 1. to leaf, burst into leaves, frondesce. 2. to cover with leaves.

frondejante, frondente adj. m. + f., **frôndeo** m. 1. leafy, leafed. 2. fronded, frondescent.

frondescência s. f. frondescence, foliage, foliation, leafage.

frondescer v. to leaf, burst into leaves, frondesce.

frondícola adj. m. + f. growing or living on trees.

frondífero adj. (bot.) frondiferous: producing fronds or leaves.

frondista s. m. + f. (hist.) Frondist: member or supporter of the Fronde (1648-1653).

frondosidade s. f. 1. foliaceousness, leafiness. 2. luxuriant growth.

frondoso adj. 1. frondose, foliaceous. 2. foliate, frondescent, leafy, leaved. 3. branchy, bushy. 4. dense, thick.

fronha s. f. 1. pillowcase. 2. pillow. 3. (fig.) involucre, covering.

frontaberto adj. said of a horse that has a white spot on its forehead.

frontal s. m. (pl. **-ais**) 1. frontal: a) frontlet. b) (eccl.) antependium: cover or hanging for the front of an altar. c) (archit.) frontispiece or little pediment over a door or window. d) (anat., zool.) frontal bone, coronal bone (plate C 17). 2. (masonry) a quarter-brick wall. ‖ adj. m. + f. front, frontal: of or pertaining to the front or forehead. ‖ ~**mente** adv. frontally.
parede de ~ thin partition wall.

frontaleira s. f. altar cloth or hanging.

frontão s. m. (pl. **-ões**) (archit.) fronton, pediment, fable, frontal, frontispiece.

frontaria s. f. (archit.) 1. frontispiece. 2. façade, front. 3. frontage.

fronte s. f. 1. forehead, head. 2. (archit.): a) frontispiece. b) frontage, front or face. 3. front. 4. fore-rank.
~ **a ~** face to face. **curvar a ~** to yield, submit to.

frontear v. 1. to face, confront. 2. to be in front of, opposite to, to look towards.

fronteira s. f. frontier, bound, boundary, limit, border, mark, march, confine, extremity, ambit. **cidade ~** frontier town. **formar ~** to border.

fronteirar v. 1. to place in front of. 2. to border, bound. 3. to place on the frontier.

fronteiriço s. m. frontiersman, borderer, frontager. ‖ adj. 1. bordering upon, frontier, limitary, border line. 2. living on or near the frontier. 3. outland.

fronteiro s. m. (hist.) captain or commander of a frontier fortress. ‖ adj. 1. frontier, bordering. 2. facing, opposite, opposed.

frontino adj. (Braz.) said of a horse with a white spot on its forehead.

frontispício s. m. 1. (archit.) façade, front or face. 2. frontispiece: a) (archit.) pediment. b) title page of a book, front page (plate L 4). 3. (fig.) face, visage, appearance.

frota s. f. 1. fleet. 2. navy. 3. shipping. 4. (fig.) crowd, multitude. **~ mercante** merchant marine. **~ de caminhões** fleet of trucks.

frouva s. f. (ornith.) rook.

frouxel, froixel s. m. (pl. -éis) down, soft feathers.

frouxelado, froixelado adj. downy.

frouxeza, froixeza s. f. 1. weakness, faintness. 2. lack of energy. 3. slackness, sluggishness. 4. inertness, laziness. 5. negligence, remissness. 6. irresoluteness.

frouxidão, froixidão s. f. (also less used: **frouxidade, froixidade, frouxura, froixura**) 1. weakness, faintness. 2. lack of energy, languidness. 3. slackness, sluggishness, laxity, looseness. 4. inertness, laziness. 5. negligence, remissness. 6. irresoluteness, indecision, slowness. 7. dullness, flatness. 8. (med.) acedia.

frouxo s. m. flux, tide. ‖ adj. 1. weak, feeble, weak-kneed, faint, fainthearted. 2. lacking energy. 3. slack, sluggish, lax. 4. loose. 5. unfixed. 6. flaccid, floppy, flabby. 7. lazy, languid. 8. negligent, careless, easy. 9. irresolute, vacillating. 10. indolent. ‖ **-amente** adv. slackly, loosely, weakly, laxly, flabbily. **~ de riso** prolonged fit of laughter. **a ~** 1. abundantly. 2. unanimously.

frufru s. f. 1. froufrou, rustling of silken skirts. 2. whispering of leaves or of the wind. 3. murmuring, sough (of wind).

frufulhar, frufrutar v. to sough: make a rustling, murmuring sound.

frugal adj. m. + f. (pl. -ais) 1. frugal, sparing, thrifty, economical, provident, parsimonious. 2. moderate, not lavish. 3. close, canny, chary. 4. frugivorous. ‖ **~mente** adv. providently, frugally, thriftily, parsimoniously, sparely, sparingly.

frugalidade s. f. 1. frugality, frugalness. 2. parsimony, thrift(iness), sparingness, canniness. 3. economy, good husbandry. **regime de ~** spare diet.

frugífero adj. fructiferous, frugiferous.

frugivorista s. m. + f. frultarian.

frugívoro adj. frugivorous.

fruição s. f. (pl. -ões) fruition: 1. fulfilment, attainment. 2. realization, result. 3. enjoyment, satisfaction.

fruir v. 1. to be in possession of, own, hold down. 2. to usufruct, have the benefit of. 3. to find pleasure in, enjoy.

fruíta s. f. (also **fruito** m., ant. and pop.) fruit.

fruitivo adj. 1. fruitive. 2. agreeable, delicious, pleasant.

frulaniáceas s. f. pl. (bot.) a family of hepatic, rhizoid plants, including the liverwort.

frumentação s. f. (pl. -ões) foragement in wartime.

frumental adj. m. + f. (pl. -ais) 1. frumentaceous, frumentarious. 2. suitable for seeding.

frumentício adj. frumentaceous: of or relative to wheat.

frumento s. m. 1. the best quality of wheat. 2. cereals.

frumentoso adj. rich in wheat or cereals, fertile or abounding in corn.

fruncho, frunco, frúnculo s. m. (pop.) boil, furuncle.

frusseria s. f. small findings of gold and silver grains.

frusto adj. 1. worn out, defaced (coins, reliefs, sculptures). 2. (med.) benign, not malignant. 3. (Gall.) rude, impolite.

frustração s. f. (pl. -ões) frustration, failure, defeat, disappointment.

frustrado adj. 1. frustrate, failed, fruitless. 2. disappointed, balked. 3. incomplete, imperfect. 4. undeveloped. 5. defeated. ‖ **-amente** adv. vainly, frustrately. **ficar ~** to fall short of.

frustrador s. m. frustrater person or thing that frustrates, fails or disappoints. ‖ adj. frustrating, frustratory, failing.

frustrâneo adj. 1. frustraneous, frustrate. 2. vain, useless. 3. unproductive.

frustrar v. 1. to frustrate, foil, balk. 2. to baffle, thwart, defeat, disconcert. 3. to disappoint, disillusion(ize). 4. to spoil, nullify, render of no effect, confute, counteract, destroy, prevent. 5. to fail, meet with ill success. 6. to cheat, elude. **~am-se as nosssa esperanças** our hopes were shattered. **ele frustou meu intento** he put a spoke in my wheel.

frustratório adj. 1. frustratory, deceptive. 2. illusory, delusive. 3. useless, vain. 4. dilatory.

fruta s. f. fruit, fruitage. **~s cristalizadas** candied fruit. **~s de latada, ~s de parreira** wall fruit. **~s do tempo** fruits of the season. **~s secas** dried fruit. **~s temporãs** hastings, early fruit. **bolo de ~s** fruit cake. **casa de ~s** fruitery, fruit loft. **as primeiras ~s** the first fruit. **vendedor de ~s** fruiterer, costermonger.

fruta-de-arara s. f. (pl. **frutas-de-arara**) (bot.) anda.

fruta-de-conde s. f. (pl. **frutas-de-conde**) (bot., also **ata**) sweetsop.

fruta-de-condessa s. f. (pl. **frutas-de-condessa**) (bot.) biriba.

fruta-de-jacu s. f. (pl. **frutas-de-jacu**) (Braz., bot.) tropical lilac.

fruta-de-lobo s. f. (pl. **frutas-de-lobo**) (Braz., bot.) wild tobacco.

fruta-de-perdiz s. f. (pl. **frutas-de-perdiz**) (bot.) pearlberry, pearlfruit.

fruta-pão s. f. (pl. **frutas-pão, frutas-pães**) (Braz., bot.) breadfruit tree.

frutear v. 1. to bear fruit. 2. to yield good results. 3. to make fruitful or productive.

frutegar v. to cultivate, raise, plant trees.

fruteira s. f. 1. fruit tree. 2. female fruit peddler or costermonger. 3. fruit bowl or plate, centre piece.

fruteiro s. m. 1. fruit dealer, fruiterer, costermonger. 2. fruit bowl or plate. 3. fruit loft, fruitery. ‖ adj. 1. fruit-bearing, fruitful. 2. fond of fruit, feeding on fruit.

frutescência s. f. fructescence, fruitage, fructification, fruiting season.

frutescente adj. m. + f. 1. fructiferous, fructescent, fruticose. 2. arborescent.

frútice s. m. (bot.) frutex; shrub.

frutíceto s. m. orchard.

fruticoso adj. (bot.) fruticose, fruticous, shrubby.

fruticuloso adj. (bot.) fruticulose, resembling a small shrub.

fruticultor s. m. fruit grower or gardener, fruiter, pomologist, horticulturist.

fruticultura s. f. horticulture, fruit growing.

frutidor s. m. (hist.) Fructidor: the twelfth month of the French Revolutionary calendar (1794).

frutífero adj. 1. fructiferous, fruitful, fructuous. 2. fecund, fertile. 3. (fig.) useful, beneficial. 4. productive. 5. copious, bountiful, plenteous.

frutificação s. f. (pl. **-ões**) fructification: 1. (bot.) fruiting, forming or producing fruit, fruitage. 2. fertilization.

frutificar v. 1. to fructify: a) bear or produce fruit. b) fertilize, make fruitful. 2. (fig.) to yield good results, be profitable or advantageous.

frutificativo adj. fructificative.

frutifloro adj. (bot.) fructiflorous, having an inferior ovary.

frutiforme adj. m. + f. fructiform, fruitlike.

frutilha s. f. (S. Braz., pop.) strawberry.

frutívoro adj. (also **frutígero**) frugivorous, feeding on fruit.

fruto s. m. fruit: 1. fruitage. 2. offspring, progeny. 3. result, produce, product. 4. reward, profit, gain, revenue. 5. consequence, outgo. ~ **do matrimônio** offspring of the womb. ~ **proibido** the forbidden fruit. **dar** ~ 1. to fructify. 2. to show results. **dá** ~s it yields fruits. **tirar** ~ to profit from.

frutose s. f. fruit sugar, levulose, fructose.

frutuário adj. 1. of or relative to fruit(s). 2. fertile, fruitful. 3. that yields good results.

frutuoso adj. 1. rich in fruit, fruitful, fructuous. 2. prolific, fecund. 3. profitable, useful. ‖ **-amente** adv. fruitfully.

ftalato s. m. (chem.) phthalate.

ftaleína s. f. (chem.) phthalein.

ftálico adj. (chem.) phthalic.

ftiríase s. f. (med.) phthiriasis, pediculosis.

fu interj. ugh! phew! fie!

fuá s. m. (Braz.) intrigue, plot, machination. ‖ adj. m. + f. distrustful, suspicious.

fuão s. m. (pl. **fuãos, fuões**) (f. **fuã**) = **fulano**.

fubá s. m. (Braz.) maize flour, rice flour; samp, (U. S. A.) Indian meal, corn meal.

fubeca s. f. (Braz., sl.) defeat.

fubecar v. (Braz., sl.) to defeat.

fubica s. m. (Braz., pop.) 1. hop'-o'-my-thumb. 2. insignificant individual.

fuça s. f. (vulg.) nostril, nose, snout, face.

fucácea s. f. (bot.) specimen of the family Fucaceae.

fucáceo adj. (bot.) fucaceous.

fucícola adj. m. + f. that lives among fucuses.

fuciforme adj. m. + f. fuciform, fucoid.

fuco s. m. fucus: 1. (bot.) rockweed. 2. fucaceous dyestuff. 3. rouge. 4. fraud, dissimulation.

fucóide adj. m. + f. fucoid(al).

fúcsia s. f. (bot.) fuchsia.

fucsina s. f. fuchsin(e).

fueguino s. m. Fuegian: native or inhabitant of Fuegia or Tierra del Fuego. ‖ adj. Fuegian.

fueirada s. f. blow with a cart pole.

fueiro s. m. cart pole.

fúfia s. f. 1. haughtiness, conceit. 2. conceited and ridiculous woman. 3. (Braz.) ball, festivity. 4. m. + f. upstart.

fúfio adj. common, vulgar, low.

fuga s. f. 1. flight, escape(ment); (sl.) bolt, bunk, scuttle, skedaddle. 2. way out, means of escape.
3. retreat. 4. subterfuge. 5. venthole of a bellows. 6. leaking. 7. elopement. 8. (mus.) fugue. ~ **de um líquido** leakage. ~ **precipitada** stampede. **em** ~ in flight, (sl.) on the lam. **linha de** ~ (tech.) vanishing line. **pôr em** ~ to put to flight. **pôr-se em** ~ to take to flight, take to one's heels.

fugacidade s. f. 1. fugacity, fugaciousness, fugitiveness. 2. transitoriness. 3. rapidity, swiftness. 4. 5. flightiness, fickleness.

fugado adj. (mus.) fugato, fugued.

fugalaça s. f. riata, lariat.

fugar v. (mus.) to compose in the style of a fugue.

fugaz adj. m. + f. 1. fugacious. 2. transitory. 3. rapid, swift. 4. fleeing, fugitive, fleeting. 5. short-lived. 6. (fig.) meteoric. ‖ **~mente** adv. fugaciously.

fugente s. m. background (of a painting). ‖ adj. m. + f. (paint.) that seems to recede, forming the background.

fugida s. f. escape: 1. flight, running away; (sl.) bunk. 2. (fig.) evasion, subterfuge.

fugidiço, fugidio adj. 1. hard to be caught or detained. 2. fugitive, runaway. 3. fugacious, readily deserting or escaping. 4. evanescent, fleeting, transient, flying. ‖ **fugidiamente** adv. fugitively.

fugir v. 1. to flee, take to flight, run away, take to one's heels, run, escape, turn tail, withdraw. 2. to retreat. 3. to avoid by flight, shun. 4. to evade, elude. 5. to disappear, vanish. 6. to elope. 7. to free or extricate o. s. from. 8. to abandon, leave behind, eschew. 9. to abscond o. s., steal off. 10. (paint.) to fade into the background. 11. to be transient, fleeting, evanescent. ~ **à vista** to escape one's sight. ~ **com o corpo (a um golpe)** to avoid a blow. ~ **da justiça** to escape the law. ~ **de alguma coisa** to shun or avoid a thing, to sneak out of s. th. ~ **de pecados** to shun vice. ~ **de perigos** to flee from danger. ~ **do serviço militar** to desert. ~ **do trabalho** to be afraid of work. ~ **na surdina** to decamp. **ele fugiu** he skipped it. **eles** ~**am** they took to flight, they turned tail. **ele fugiu com a noiva** he carried off the bride. **ele fugiu da decisão** he side-stepped the issue. **fugiu da minha memória** it has slipped my memory. **eles** ~**am da obrigação** they skipped their duty. **não fuja do assunto** stick to the point. **ele fugiu para...** he made tracks for... **eles** ~**am para as florestas** they took to the forests. **ele fugiu à sua promessa** he went back from his promise. **fugiu o melro** (fig.) the bird is flown. **a lebre fugiu** the hare scuttled away. **o menino fugiu** the boy ran away.

fugitivo s. m. fugitive, exile, deserter, runaway, evader, levanter. ‖ adj. 1. fugitive, runaway, flying. 2. fleeing, fleeting. 3. deserting. 4. transitory, transient. 5. rapid, swift. 6. fugacious. 7. undecided, unclear, fallacious.

fuinha s. f. 1. (zool.) weasel, stone marten, beech marten. 2. (ornith.) nuthatch. 3. m. + f. miser, niggard. 4. lean person. 5. talebearer.

fuinhas s. m. + f., sg. + pl. niggard, miser.

fuinho s. m. (ornith.) spotted woodpecker.

fujão s. m. (pl. **-ões**) (f. **-ona**) habitual runaway, flyaway, fugitive, deserter. ‖ adj. prone to run away.

fujicar v. (N. Braz.) to sew, patch, repair superficially.

fula (I) s. f. 1. haste, hurry. 2. crowd. 3. cheek(s). 4. = **empola**. 5. fulling: a) felt preparation. b) mill. **à** ~ in a hurry.

fula (II) adj. m. + f. irritated, infuriated.

fulano s. m. (Mr.) So-and-So, such-and-such a man, thingamy; (U. S. A.) bugger. **Fulano de Tal** John Doe. **conheço aquele** ~ I know that bird (or bean). **Fulana de Tal** Jean Doe, a Miss, Mrs. So-and-So.

fular s. m. foulard.
fulcrado adj. (bot., zool.) fulcrate.
fulcro s. m. 1. fulcrum: a) prop, support. b) (tech.) point of support, center of motion, wedge. 2. (fig.) any expedient.
fulgência s. f. 1. fulgency, brilliancy. 2. brightness, radiance. 3. splendour. 4. glitter.
fulgente adj. m. + f., **fúlgido** m. 1. fulgent, fulgid. 2. shining, very bright. 3. brilliant, sparkling, glittering. 4. dazzling.
fulgentear v. to make fulgent or glittering, brighten.
fulgir v. 1. to make fulgent or brilliant. 2. to shine, glitter, fire. 3. to dazzle. 4. (fig.) to excel, outshine, surpass.
fulgor s. m. 1. fulgency, effulgence, fulgor. 2. brilliancy, (dazzling) brightness, splendour, fire, flame, blaze, corruscation. 3. flash of light.
fulgorídeos s. m. pl. (ent.) Fulgoridae, a family of homopterous insects.
fulguração s. f. (pl. -ões) 1. fulguration. 2. lightning, sheet-lightning. 3. gleam, flash of light. 4. injuries caused by flashes of lightning.
fulgural adj. m. + f. (pl. -ais) fulgurous.
fulgurância s. f. fulgor, dazzling brightness, splendour.
fulgurante adj. m. + f. 1. fulgurant, fulgurous, effulgent, flashing. 2. coruscant, sparkling, blazing. 3. vivid. 4. (med.) fulgurating, stabbing (pains). ‖ **~mente** adv. fulgurantly, fulgently.
fulgurar v. 1. to fulgurate, lighten, shine like lightning. 2. to sparkle, radiate, flare, glitter. 3. (fig.) to excel, surpass.
fulgurito s. m. (geol.) fulgurite.
fulguroso adj. fulgurous, fulgurant.
fulharia, fulheira s. f. swindle, cheat (at gambling).
fulheiro s. m. cardsharper, cheat. ‖ adj. sharping, swindling.
fuligem s. f. (pl. -ens) 1. soot, smoke-black, lamp--black. 2. smut, crock, grime.
cobrir com ~ to carbonize.
fuliginosidade s. f. 1. fuliginosity, sootiness. 2. smuttiness. 3. (med.) furring (tongue, gums, etc.).
fuliginoso adj. 1. fuliginous, sooty, smoky. 2. crocky, smutty. 3. (med.) furred (tongue, tooth, etc.).
fulista s. m. fuller, felt worker.
fulmilenho s. m. (chem.) nitrated wood cellulose, nitrocellulose.
fulminação s. f. (pl. -ões) fulmination, detonation, explosion.
fulminado adj. 1. thunderstruck, blasted, injured by lightning. 2. (fig.) astonished, amazed.
fulminador s. m. fulminator. ‖ adj. fulminatory.
fulminante s. m. 1. percussion cap. 2. fuse, quickmatch, ignition charge. 3. firecracker, toy torpedo. ‖ adj. m. + f. 1. fulminant, sudden. 2. fulminating, detonating. 3. thundering. 4. (fig.) terrible, ruthless, cruel.
fulminar v. 1. to fulminate, flash, lighten. 2. to hit, strike. 3. to injure, wound. 4. to punish, castigate. 5. to pull down, cause to collapse. 6. to destroy, extinguish, annihilate. 7. to kill instantaneously. 8. to threaten, decree, impose upon, inveigh against. 9. to explode, detonate. 10. to shine, sparkle.
ele fulminou ameaças he broke out in threats. **o juiz fulminou a sentença** the judge passed sentence. **ele morreu fulminado por uma faísca** he was struck by lightning.
fulminato s. m. (chem.) fulminate.
fulminatório adj. fulminatory.
fulmíneo adj. (also **fulminoso**) 1. fulmin(e)ous. 2. (fig.) dazzling, bright, brilliant. 3. (fig.) destroying, ravaging, terrible, dreadful.

fulmínico adj. (chem.) fulminic.
fulminífero adj. causing or attracting flashes of lightning.
fulminívomo adj. belching (flashes, fire or bullets).
fulo adj. 1. fulvous, bronze-coloured. 2. = **fula** (II).
ele ficou ~ **de raiva** he was burning with anger, wild with rage.
fulustreco s. m. (Braz., pop.) scamp.
fulverino s. m. dark colouring matter.
fulviana s. f. a diuretic herb.
fulvicórneo adj. (zool.) that has fulvous antennae.
fúlvido adj. fulvous, tawny.
fulvípede adj. m. + f. (zool.) tawny-footed.
fulvipene adj. m. + f. (zool.) with fulvous feathers.
fulvirrostro adj. (zool.) tawny-beaked.
fulvo adj. fulvous, tawny, dark-yellow.
fumaça s. f. 1. smoke. 2. fume, vapour, steam, reek. 3. whiff of tobacco smoke. 4. (fig.) vanity, pride, presumption.
cortina de ~ smoke-screen. **não há** ~ **sem fogo** no smoke without fire. **nuvem de** ~ whisp of vapour. **sem** ~ smokeless. **terminou em** ~ it ended in smoke. **ele tem** ~**s de artista** he prides (or fancies) himself an artist. **ele anda com** ~**s de rico** he puts on airs of being rich.
fumaceira s. f. dense smoke, mist or vapour.
fumada s. f. 1. smoke signal. 2. smoke, fume(s). 3. whiff of tobacco smoke.
fumador s. m. smoker, fumer. ‖ adj. fumaceous.
fumagem s. f. (pl.-ens) 1. fumage, hearth tax. 2. gilding of silverware. 3. smoking, fumigation, curing.
fumagina s. f. (plant path.) fumagine: dark-coloured, sooty mold on leaves.
fumal s. m. (pl. -ais) (Braz.) tobacco plantation.
fumante s. m. + f. smoker, puffer. ‖ adj. smoking, smoky, fumacious, fuming, fumigant.
cabina para ~**s** smoking compartment. **sala para** ~**s** smoking room.
fumar v. 1. to smoke: a) inhale or exhale tobacco smoke (plate F 7). b) cure with smoke. c) fumigate. d) move as smoke, throw off or emit fumes. 2. to fume. 3. to be in a rage, to be infuriated. 4. to fade away, evanesce, evaporate.
~ **demais** to oversmoke. **ele fuma charutos** he smokes cigars (or cheroots). **eles fumam presunto** they smoke ham. **ela fuma de raiva** she is in a rage. **vamos** ~**!** let's have a smoke!
fumaraça, fumarada s. f. 1. billows or volumes of smoke. 2. = **fumaça.**
fumarar v. to (emit) smoke, fume.
fumarento adj. smoky, fumy, vaporous, fumous.
fumária s. f. (bot.) fumitory.
fumarola s. f. 1. volcanic vapour or smoke. 2. (col.) blower.
fumatório adj. fumatory.
fumável adj. m. + f. (pl. -áveis) smokable.
fumega s. m. (Braz.) short or insignificant person.
fumegante adj. m. + f. smoking, fuming, fumigating.
fume(g)ar v. 1. to (emit) smoke. 2. to become inflamed, excited. 3. to foam, froth. 4. to exhale fumes or vapours, to lunt. 5. to exhale. 6. to besmoke.
fumeira s. f. (Braz.) tobacco-pouch.
fumeiro s. m. 1. chimney. 2. smoke flue, chimney pot, chimney flue, funnel (plate C 5). 3. billows of smoke. 4. smoking chamber, fumatory.
fúmeo adj. 1. smoky: a) smoking, emitting smoke. b) full of smoke, fumous. 2. fumiferous, producing smoke.
fumicultor s. m. (Braz.) tobacco planter.
fumicultura s. f. (Braz.) cultivation of tobacco.
fúmido, fumífero, fumífico adj. = **fumoso.**

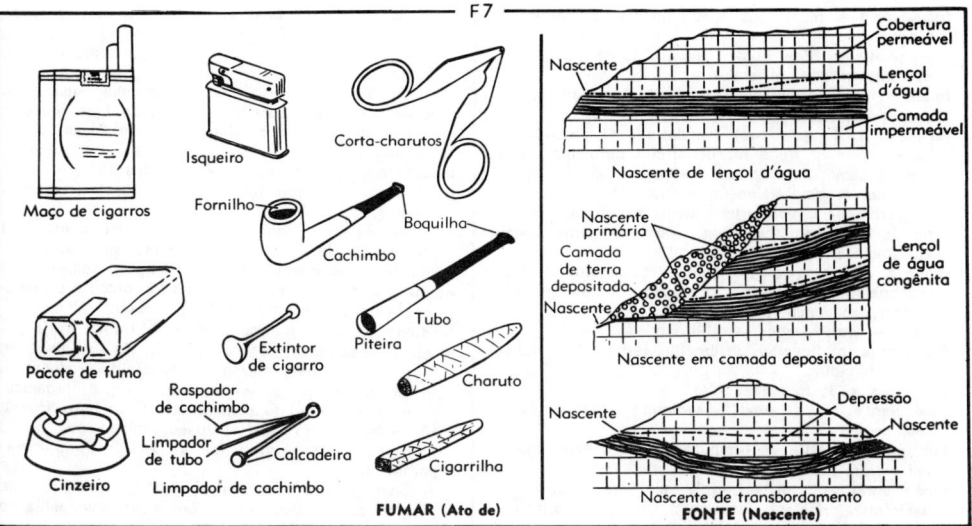

F 7

Maço de cigarros · Isqueiro · Corta-charutos · Fornilho · Boquilha · Cachimbo · Tubo · Pacote de fumo · Extintor de cigarro · Piteira · Raspador de cachimbo · Charuto · Cinzeiro · Limpador de tubo · Calcadeira · Limpador de cachimbo · Cigarrilha

FUMAR (Ato de)

Nascente · Cobertura permeável · Lençol d'água · Camada impermeável · Nascente de lençol d'água · Nascente primária · Camada de terra depositada · Nascente · Lençol de água congênita · Nascente em camada depositada · Nascente · Depressão · Nascente · Nascente de transbordamento

FONTE (Nascente)

fumiflamante adj. m. + f. 1. fuming, emitting smoke. 2. aflame, afire.

fumífugo s. m. fumifugist, smoke-consumer. ‖ adj. fumifugal.

fumigação s. f. (pl. -ões) fumigation.

fumigador s. m. fumigator, smoker (plate A 11).

fumigar v. 1. to fumigate: a) disinfect. b) cure. 2. to fume, smoke. 3. to pastil(le).

fumigatório s. m. fumigation. ‖ adj. fumigatory.

fumista s. m. + f. smoker.

fumívomo adj. smoky, smoking, emitting or producing smoke.

fumívoro adj. smoke-consuming, fumivorous. **instalação -a** smoke-consumer.

fumo s. m. 1. smoke, fume, vapour. 2. evaporation, vaporization. 3. mourning band, crape. 4. tobacco; (coll.) weed. 5. (fig.) vanity, pride. 6. evanescence, transitoriness. 7. lampblack. ~ **em corda** twist(ed) tobacco. ~ **para cachimbo** smoking tobacco. **~s de vinho** fumes of wine. **cheirar a** ~ to smell of smoke. **curado ao** ~ dried in smoke. smoked. **desfazer-se como** ~ to vanish into smoke, to come to nothing. **não há nem** ~ **disso** there is nothing left over. **secar ao** ~ to dry in smoke. **sem** ~ fumeless. **ter ~s** to be proud or haughty. **vendedor ou negociante de** ~ tobacconist.

fumo-agreste s. m. (pl. **fumos-agrestes**) (bot.) Syrian tobacco.

fumo-bravo s. m. (pl. **fumos-bravos**) (bot.) 1. woolly elephant's foot. 2. tobaccoweed. 3. devil's-grand-mother.

fumo-da-terra s. m. (pl. **fumos-da-terra**) (bot.) fumatory.

fumosidade s. f. 1. smokiness. 2. smoke, vapours, fumes.

fumoso adj. 1. smoky: a) smoking, emitting smoke. b) full of smoke, fumous. 2. fumiferous, producing smoke. 3. (fig.) conceited, vain.

funambulesco adj. funambulatory.

funambulismo s. m. funambulism, acrobatics.

funâmbulo s. m. funambulist: ropewalker, ropedancer, equilibrist, acrobat.

funca s. m. + f. (Braz., fam.) worthless person or thing. ‖ adj. bad, rotten.

funçanada, funçanata s. f. merrymaking, spree, frolic.

funçanista s. m. + f. pleasure hunter, reveller.

função s. f. (pl. -ões) 1. function: a) activity, action, normal operation. b) exercise of a faculty or office, service, duty. c) profession, occupation. d) ceremony, solemnity, public act. e) (math.) quantity whose value is dependent on the value of an independent variable. f) (chem.) characteristic behaviour of a compound in the presence of extraneous atoms. 2. use. 3. agency. 4. performance. 5. (Braz., pop.) ball, festivity, gay entertainment. ~ **de escrevente** clerkship. ~ **de cônsul** consulship. **em** ~ alive, (tech.) in gear, in operation, running.

funchal s. m. (pl. -ais) fennel plantation.

funchalense s. m. + f. native or inhabitant of Funchal (port of Madeira island). ‖ adj. of, pertaining to or relative to Funchal.

funcho s. m. (bot.) fennel.

funcho-bravo s. m. (pl. **funchos-bravos**) (bot.) dill.

funcho-de-porco s. m. (pl. **funchos-de-porco**) (bot.) hog's-fennel, sow fennel, brimstonewort.

funcho-marinho s. m. (pl. **funchos-marinhos**) (bot.) samphire, sea fennel.

funcho-selvagem s. m. (pl. **funchos-selvagens**) (bot.) poison hemlock.

funcional adj. m. + f. (pl. **-ais**) functional, functionary. ‖ **~mente** adv. functionally.

funcionalismo s. m. 1. functionalism. 2. functionarism, officialdom, officialism. 3. public functionaries (collectively). ~ **público** civil service.

funcionalista s. m. + f. functionalist.

funcionamento s. m. 1. functioning. 2. action, acting. 3. operation, running, work(ing), also play of a machine. 4. officiation: performance of official duties. ~ **de uma máquina** running or behaviour of a machine. **modo de** ~ working method, behaviour (machine). **ele põe o motor em** ~ he starts (or cranks) the engine.

funcionar v. to function: 1. perform, officiate, act. 2. work, operate, run smoothly and regularly. **meu aparelho de televisão não está funcionando** my television set is out of order. .

funcionário s. m. 1. public functionary. 2. employee, clerk.
~ **público** office holder, public functionary, civil servant, officer, official.

funda s. f. 1. sling(shot), catapult. 2. (med.) truss, suspender, bandage.

fundação s. f. (pl. **-ões**) foundation: 1. groundwork, base, basis. 2. fund for beneficial purposes, donation, legacy. 3. endowed institution or charity. 4. erection. 5. establishment, settlement.
~ **particular** private trust. **ele é beneficiário da** ~ he is on the foundation. **-ões de beneficência** charitable institutions.

fundado adj. 1. (well-)founded, established. 2. just, reasonable. 3. solid, grounded. ‖ **-amente** adv. solidly, reasonably.
bem ~ well-founded, well-grounded.

fundador s. m. founder, originator, father, establisher. ‖ adj. founding.

fundadora s. f. foundress.

fundagem s. f. (pl. **-ens**) 1. sediment, lees, dregs. 2. residues.

fundamentado adj. well-founded, established, based.
um relatório mal ~ an ill-grounded report.

fundamental adj. m. + f. (pl. **-ais**) fundamental: 1. basic(al), principal, elemental, basal, basilar. 2. essential, substantial, primordial, prime. 3. necessary. ‖ ~**mente** adv. fundamentally, basically.
não ~ insubstantial. **cores -ais** primary colours.

fundamentalismo s. m. fundamentalism.

fundamentalista s. m. + f. fundamentalist.

fundamentar v. 1. to found, lay the foundation of, ground. 2. to base, establish, set up. 3. to evidence, prove, justify, explain. 4. to confirm, validate.

fundamento s. m. 1. basis: a) base, bottom, ground. b) foundation, bed(ding), groundwork, basement. c) pedestal. d) fundamentals, principle, element, rudiment. e) support. f) starting point. 2. origin, motive, cause, reason. 3. justification.
~ **sólido** solid groundwork, hardpan. **com** ~ well--founded (hopes, suspicion), justified, reasonable (doubt). **falta de** ~ unfoundedness. **fazer** ~ **em alguém** to rely upon s. o. **lançar os** ~**s** to lay the foundation. **sem** ~ not a leg to stand on, unfounded, not justified, groundless(ly). **o boato não tem** ~ the rumour has no foundation.

fundão s. m. (pl. **-ões**) 1. whirlpool. 2. abyss, chasm. 3. (Braz.) out-of-the-way farmstead.

fundar v. 1. to found: a) lay the foundation, set up, establish. b) originate, create, institute. c) build, construct. d) ground. e) base. f) prove, offer reasons for. g) start. 2. to deepen, penetrate into the ground. 3. to rely on, depend upon. 4. to support. 5. ~**se** to be founded or based.
~ **uma igreja** to endow a church. ~ **a sua asserção** to justify one's assertion. **tornar a** ~ to refound.

fundeado adj. at anchor.
estar ~ to be (or ride) at anchor.

fundeadouro s. m. (naut.) roadstead, anchorage, anchoring place, berthage.

fundear v. (naut.) 1. to (cast) anchor, ride at anchor. 2. to touch the bottom. 3. to call at a port.

fundeiro (I) s. m. 1. truss maker. 2. sling maker.

fundeiro (II) adj. 1. deep, profound, abysmal. 2. of or pertaining to the bottom. 3. very deep or high.

fundente s. m. flux, soldering flux, melting medium. ‖ adj. m. + f. 1. melting, fusing. 2. solvent, flux.

fundiário adj. agrarian, landed; of, pertaining to or related to the soil or landed property.

fundibulário s. m. slinger: 1. one who slings. 2. soldier armed with a sling.

fundíbulo s. m. 1. sling. 2. (hist.) catapult.

fundição s. f. (pl. **-ões**) 1. foundry: a) act, process or art of casting metals. b) smeltry, forge. 2. melt(ing), cast(ing), fusion. 3. (fig.) project, plan, design, idea.
~ **de aço** steelworks. ~ **de chumbo** leadworks. ~ **de ferro** iron foundry. ~ **de tipos** type foundry. ~ **sob pressão** die casting. **caixa** (or **fossa**) **de** ~ teeming box.

fundido adj. 1. molten. 2. cast. 3. fusil(e).

fundidor s. m. founder, moulder, caster, melter, smelter.
~ **de estanho** tinner, tinman. ~ **de sinos** bell founder. ~ **de tipos** letter founder, type caster.

fundilhar v. to mend, patch up (trouser seats).

fundilho s. m. 1. seat of trousers. 2. patch for mending seats of trousers. 3. (sl.) breech.

fundinho s. m. 1. folding screen. 2. (min.) rutile.

fundir v. 1. to found, cast. 2. to melt, liquify, dissolve. 3. to smelt, fuse, merge. 4. to yield, produce. 5. to squander. 6. to unite, link. 7. to organize, arrange. 8. (com.) to consolidate. 9. to blow (fuse). 10. ~**se:** a) to get confused, mixed up. b) to interfuse, commix. c) to fall in, wreck. d) to incorporate, fuse.
~ **bem** (agric.) to yield a plentiful crop. ~ **um sino** to cast a bell. ~**se com outra companhia** to consolidate (unite) with another company. ~ **os minérios** to melt down from the ore. **o motor fundiu-se** the motor fused.

fundismo s. m. wool waste.

fundível adj. m. + f. (pl. **-íveis**) fusible, liquefiable, meltable, smeltable.

fundo s. m. 1. bottom (plates B 4, C 4). 2. remotest, profoundest or innermost part of a thing. 3. bottom of the sea, floor. 4. depth, deepness. 5. (stage) background, setting, rear, flat scene. 6. ground (paint, sea, river). 7. foundation, groundwork. 8. base, basis. 9. core, main point, essence (of a thing or affair). 10. fund(s), stock, pecuniary resources. 11. range of knowledge. 12. ~**s** pl. capital, finance. ‖ adj. 1. deep (plate Q). 2. fordless. 3. hollowed, sunken. 4. profound, unfathomable. 5. intimate, innermost. 6. inveterate, deep-rooted. 7. dense, compact. 8. thorough. 9. (Braz.) ironic.) ignorant, stupid.
~ **bom** good anchorage. ~ **de agulha** the eye of a needle. ~ **de areia** sandy ground. ~ **de barril** bottom piece of a cask. ~ **de cenário** (theat.) back scene, back cloth. ~ **de lama** muddy ground. ~ **de pedra** rocky bottom. ~ **de reserva** guarantee fund. ~ **duplo** false bottom, double bottom. ~ **monetário** treasury. ~ **movediço** shifting ground. ~ **musical** background music. ~**s em moeda estrangeira** stocks payable in foreign standard. ~**s públicos** public funds. **a** ~ thoroughly, fully. **conhecer a** ~ to have a thorough knowledge of. **ele mora nos** ~**s** he lives in the back-house. **o** ~ **da pintura é muito claro** the ground of the picture is very light. **o** ~ **de um navio** the bottom of a ship. **o** ~ **de um negócio** the main point of an affair. **o** ~ **do coração** the bottom of the heart. **o** ~ **do mar** the bottom of the sea, deep; (coll.) Davy Jone's locker. **alcançar o** ~ to bottom. **artigo de** ~ (newspaper) leading article. **dar** ~ to cast anchor. **do** ~ **do peito** breast-deep. **instituir** ~ **de reserva** to set up a reserve. **ir-se ao** ~ to sink. **no** ~ intrinsically. **no** ~ **do palco** on the backstage. **olhos** ~**s** sunken eyes. **prato** ~ soup plate. **sem** ~ bottomless. **servir de** ~ to back.

fundura s. f. 1. profundity, depth, deepness. 2. (Braz., sl.): a) ignorance. b) lack of skill.
meter-se em ~**s** to meet with or provoke difficulties.

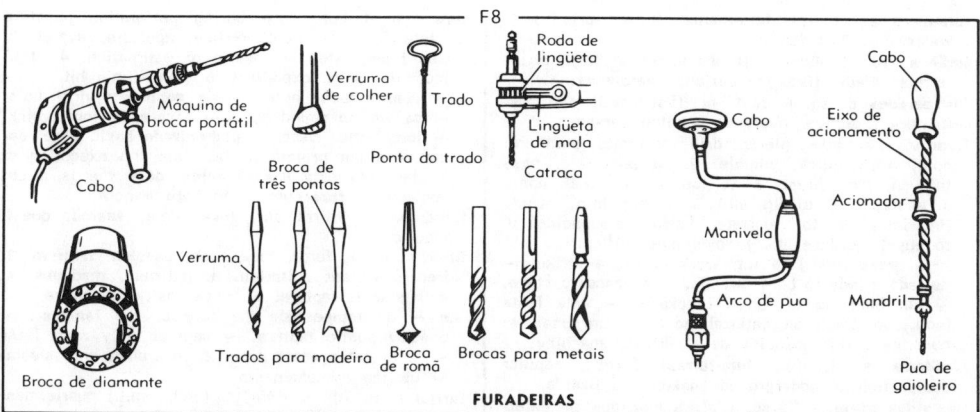

F8

Máquina de brocar portátil
Cabo
Verruma de colher
Trado
Broca de três pontas
Ponta do trado
Roda de lingüeta
Lingüeta de mola
Catraca
Cabo
Manivela
Arco de pua
Cabo
Eixo de acionamento
Acionador
Mandril
Verruma
Trados para madeira
Broca de romã
Brocas para metais
Broca de diamante
Pua de gaioleiro

FURADEIRAS

fúnebre adj. m. + f. (also **funéreo** m.) 1. funeral, mortuary. 2. lugubrious, dismal, macabre, sepulchral. 3. mournful, sad, doleful, funeral.
cerimônias ~s exequies. **oração** ~ funeral sermon. **pompa** ~ funeral pomp, obsequies.
funeral s. m. (pl. **-ais**) funeral, obsequies; funeral rites, burial service, exequies. ‖ adj. m. + f. funeral. **em** ~ in mourning, as a token of mourning. **levar as armas em** ~ to lower the arms (at a funeral).
funerário adj. funerary, funereal.
agente ~ (U. S. A.) mortician, undertaker. **levar em carro** ~ to hearse.
funestação s. f. (pl. **-ões**) 1. saddening. 2. mourning, sorrow, grief.
funestador s. m. cause of mourning or grief. ‖ adj. causing grief or mourning.
funestar v. 1. to make or become fatal, dire or funest. 2. to profane, desecrate. 3. to stigmatize, defame, slander. 4. to dishonour.
funesto adj. 1. funest, fatal. 2. dire, ill-boding, sinister, sinistrous. 3. unlucky, disastrous, calamitous, tragic(al). 4. mortal, deadly. 5. grievous, sorrowful, unhappy. 6. dismal, woeful, fateful. ‖ **-amente** adv. fatally, tragically, calamitously. **isto é muito** ~ that is very unfortunate.
funga s. f. (vet.) distemper (of dogs).
fungada s. f. sniff, snuff.
fungadeira s. f. (Braz., sl.) snuff box.
fungador s. m. snuffer.
fungão s. m. (pl. **-ões**) 1. fungus: a) (bot.) mushroom. b) (med.) spongy morbid growth. 2. (plant path.). ergot. 3. snuffer, snuff-taker. 4. (pop.) cry-baby. ‖ adj. snuffing, snuffy.
fungar v. 1. to snuff: a) snuffle, take snuff. b) sniff, breathe through the nose. 2. to grumble, mutter. 3. to weep, whimper.
fungicida s. m. fungicide. ‖ adj. fungicidal.
fúngico adj. fungal, fungoid.
fungícola adj. m. + f. fungicolous: living in or upon fungi.
fungiforme adj. m. + f. fungi(lli)form.
fungite s. f. fungite: a kind of fossil coral.
fungível adj. m. + f. (pl. **-íveis**) usable, consumable.
fungívoro adj. fungivorous.
fungo s. m. fungus: 1. fungal, plant of the group Fungi (mushrooms, molds, mildews, rusts, etc.). 2. (med.) proud flesh: spongy morbid excrescence on the skin. 3. sniffing.
fungóide adj. m. + f. agaric, fungoid.
fungosidade s. f. 1. fungosity: a) fungous quality. b) (med.) fungous excrescence. 2. sponginess.

fungoso adj. 1. fungous, funginous, fungoid, fungal, agaric. 2. spongy, porous, excrescent.
fungu s. m. (S. Braz.) witchcraft, black art.
funicular s. m. funicular, cable railway, cable car. ‖ adj. m. + f. funicular.
~ **aéreo** aerial railway, telpher.
funículo s. m. 1. funicle: small cord. 2. funiculus: a) (anat.) umbilical cord. b) (bot.) stalk of an ovule. c) hyphal cord.
funífero adj. (bot.) funiliferous: producing ropelike aerial roots.
funiforme adj. m. + f. funiform, like a rope or cord.
funil s. m. (pl. **-is**) 1. funnel, filler (plates F 3, 6). 2. anything so shaped.
~ **de enchimento** 1. hopper. 2. (foundry) ingate, trumpet. **em forma de** ~ funneled, infundibuliform. **ele bebe como um** ~ he drinks like a fish.
funilaria s. f. a tinsmith's (workshop).
funileiro s. m. tinsmith, tinker, tinman, brazier, plumber.
fúnquia s. f. (bot.) plantain lily, day lily.
fura s. f. (pop.) drill hole, chisel hole.
fura-barriga s. m. (pl. **fura-barrigas**) (ornith.) jacamar.
fura-bolo s. m. (pl. **fura-bolos**) (Braz., pop.) meddlesome fellow.
fura-bolos s. m., sg. + pl. (hum.) forefinger or index finger.
fura-buxo s. m. (pl. **fura-buxos**) (ornith.) Manx shearwater.
furacão s. m. (pl. **-ões**) 1. hurricane, ciclone, tornado, whirlwind, flaw. 2. any destructive power or element.
furacar v. (fam.) to˙pierce, make holes in.
furacidade s. f. thievishness, propensity to steal or rob.
furadeira s. f. (tech.) drill, drilling machine (plate F 8).
~ **elétrica** electric drill.
furado s. m. (Braz.) 1. hole, bore. 2. natural channel linking two rivers. 3. straight stretch of a river. ‖ adj. bored, pierced, flat, looped.
chapa -a perforated sheet. **tijolo** ~ perforated brick.
furador s. m. awl, bradawl, bodkin, perforator, punch(er), pricker, broach (plates A 5, M 4). ‖ adj. piercing.
~ **para papéis** paper perforator.
fura-festa s. m. (pl. **fura-festas**) person who goes to a party uninvited.
furagem s. f. (pl. **-ens**) boring, drilling.
fura-greve s. m. + f. (pl. **fura-greves**) strikebreaker, blackleg, rat, fink.

fura-mato s. m. (pl. **fura-matos**) (Braz., ornith.) 1. water rail. 2. tiriba.

furão s. m. (pl. **-ões**) 1. (zool.) ferret. 2. (fig.) prier, ferreter. ‖ adj. (Braz.) laborious, hard-working.

fura-paredes s. sg. + pl. 1. m. (bot.) wall pellitory. 2. m. + f. active, lively or cunning person.

furar v. 1. to bore, pierce, drill, perforate, puncture, hole, prick, stick, wimble. 2. to penetrate, pass through, jab, thrust. 3. to tap. 4. to break open. 5. to trepan. 6. to dig, sink. 7. to slip into, intrude (in, into). 8. to frustrate, baffle, disappoint. 9. to upset, confuse. 10. to overcome difficulties. ~ **a greve** (coll.) to rat: work during a strike. ~ **de lado a lado** to bore through. ~ **o casco** to stave. ~ **um bloqueio** to run a blockade. ~ **uma festa** (coll.) to crash an entertainment. ~ **um pneu** to puncture a tire. **máquina de** ~ drilling machine.

fura-terra s. f. (pl. **fura-terras**) (Braz.) popular designation of underground snakes and lizards.

fura-vidas s. m. + f., sg. + pl. industrious or enterprising person.

furbesco adj. roguish, crafty, deceitful, villainous.

furcífero adj. furciferous.

furco s. m. distance between the tips of the outstretched thumb and forefinger (about 6 ½").

fúrcula s. f. 1. (anat.) manubrium. 2. (zool.) furcula.

furdunçar v. (Braz., pop.) 1. to frolic, carouse, roister. 2. to brawl, promote disorder.

furdunceiro s. m. (Braz., pop.) 1. roisterer. 2. rioter, brawler. ‖ adj. 1. frolicsome. 2. riotous.

furdúncio, furdunço s. m. (Braz., pop.) 1. noisy feasting of the common people. 2. disorder, brawl.

furente adj. m. + f. furious, raging, furibund.

furfuráceo adj. 1. furfuraceous. 2. scaly, scurfy. 3. farinaceous.

furfuramido s. m. (chem.) furfuramide.

furfúreo adj. furfuraceous, branny.

furfurol s. m. (chem.) furfural, furfuraldehyde.

furgão s. m. (pl. **-ões**) (motor) delivery van, panel truck.

fúria s. f. 1. fury, furiosity, furiousness. 2. extreme anger, rage, angriness, raging, fierceness, rave, wrath. 3. enthusiasm, inspiration. 4. violent or impetuous action, vehemence. 5. precipitancy, impetuosity, rashness, rush, frenzy, furore. 6. furious person esp. woman, hag. 7. ~**s** pl. (Greek myth.) Furies, Erinyes. **num ataque de** ~ in a fit of rage.

furibundo adj. raging, frenzied, choleric.

furiosidade s. f. 1. furiosity, furiousness. 2. irritation, anger. 3. impetuosity. 4. enthusiasm.

furioso adj. 1. furious, mad, horn-mad, rageful, raging, wild, angry, fierce, berserk(er), red-hot, indignant, (poet.) wroth, wrathful. 2. frantic, frenitic, frenzied. 3. violent, vehement, rushing. 4. impetuous, rashly, dragonish. 5. enthusiastic, ardent, passionate. ‖ **-amente** adv. furiously, madly, angrily, ragingly, fiercely, wildly. **ele está** ~ he sees red. **estar** ~ to be in a rage, to be in a tantrum. **isso me deixa** ~ it gives me the wilds. **ele ficou** ~ he got his Irish up. **não fique** ~ **comigo** don't eat me. **tornamo-lo** ~ (fam.) we got his dander up.

furipterídeos s. m. pl. (zool.) Furipteridae, a family of the order Chiroptera.

furlana s. f. furlana, forlana: 1. Venetian dance. 2. the music for this dance.

furna s. f. 1. cavern, cave, grotto. 2. hole, pit. 3. den.

furnarídeos s. m. pl. (ornith.) Furnariidae, the family of the South American oven birds.

furo s. m. 1. hole, bore, boring, perforation, puncture (plate C 9). 2. vent, orifice, aperture, eyelet. 3. (fam.) peg, step or degree of estimation. 4. (fig.) loophole, shift, expedient. 5. journalistic hit. ~ **cônico** taper hole. ~ **de sondagem** drill hole. ~ **de violino** sound hole. ~ **escareado** countersink. ~ **jornalístico** beat. ~ **padronizado** basic bore. **dar um** ~ **a um projeto** to facilitate the execution of a plan. **ela está um** ~ **acima dele** she is a cut above him. **fazer um** ~ to bore a hole.

furoar v. to ferret out, investigate, search, quest, inquire.

furor s. m. 1. furor, fury, rage, passion, tantrum. 2. frenzy, violent agitation. 3. delirium, madness. 4. enthusiasm, rapture. 5. impetuosity, rashness. **o** ~ **da tempestade** the fury of the tempest. ~ **poético** poetic rapture. ~ **sagrado** holy zeal. **fazer** ~ 1. to cut a great dash. 2. to arouse enthusiasm. ~ **uterino** nymphomania.

furriel s. m. (pl. **furriéis**) 1. (arch., mil.) quartermaster. 2. (ornith.) grosbeak.

furta-cor s. m. (pl. **furta-cores**) 1. iridescent or chatoyant hue. 2. (zool.) a climbing snake (Philodryas mattogrossensis Karl). ‖ adj. m. + f. iridescent, chatoyant, tabby, changeable. **tafetá de furta-cores** shot taffety.

furtadela s. f. 1. pilfering, purloining. 2. concealment, dissimulation. **às** ~**s** clandestinely, stealthily.

furtado adj. 1. stolen, robbed. 2. hidden. 3. secret.

furta-fogo s. m. (pl. **furta-fogos**) dark lantern, bull's-eye.

furta-passo s. m. (pl. **furta-passos**) amble, ambling pace.

furtar v. 1. to steal, thieve. 2. to pilfer, purloin, filch, snitch, pick, finger, pinch, bone, pull. 3. to falsify, forge. 4. to cheat, defraud, swindle. 5. to rob. 6. to embezzle, peculate. 7. ~**-se:** a) to sneak away, escape, flunk. b) to avoid, shun. c) to hide out. ~ **alguma coisa** to make away with a thing. **furtar a alguém** to steal from s. o. ~ **horas ao sono** to deprive o. s. of sleep. ~ **o corpo ao golpe** to evade a blow. ~ **o vento à seta** to divert from a purpose. ~ **as voltas** to dodge a pursuer. **ele furtou-se de responsabilidade** he evaded responsibility. **não** ~**ás** thou shalt not steal.

furtivo adj. furtive: 1. stealthy, thieflike. 2. secret, clandestine, undercover, sly. ‖ **-amente** adv. furtively, stealthily, secretly, clandestinely.

furto s. m. 1. theft, thievery, stealing, larceny, pilferage, picking, filch. 2. robbery. 3. stolen goods. **a** ~ clandestinely, by stealth. **pegaram-no com o** ~ **na mão** they caught him red-handed. ~ **pequeno** crib. **furto comum** (jur.) simple larceny. ~ **qualificado** aggravated larceny.

furufuru s. m. (Braz.) foam of boiling molasses.

furuncular adj. m. + f. furuncular, furunculous.

furúnculo s. m. (med.) furuncle, boil.

furunculose s. f. (path.) furunculosis.

furunculoso adj. (med.) furunculous, furuncular.

fusa s. f. (mus.) demisemiquaver, thirty-second note (plate N 1).

fusada s. f. 1. blow with a spindle. 2. a spindleful. 3. a single turn of the spindle.

fusaiola s. f. spindle bearing.

fusão s. f. (pl. **-ões**) fusion: 1. (s)melting. 2. alloying, blend(ing), mixture, fluxion, amalgam. 3. union, association, coalescence. 4. conflation. 5. (phys.) liquefaction. 6. (nucl. phys.) a thermonuclear reaction in which light nuclei join to form heavier nuclei.

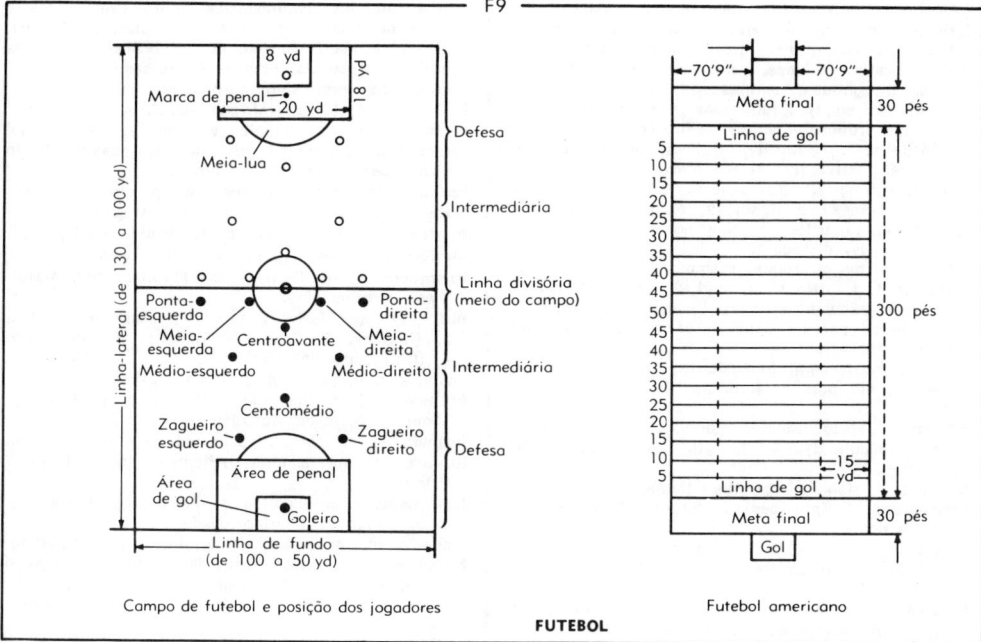

Campo de futebol e posição dos jogadores   Futebol americano

FUTEBOL

~ **de fusível elétrico** blowout. ~ **de empresas industriais** consolidation of industrial corporations.
fusário s. m. (bot.) Fusarium: a genus of fungi.
fúsaro s. m. (bot.) safflower, bastard saffron.
fuscalvo adj. (paint.) half-dark.
fuscicolo adj. (zool.) fuscous-necked.
fuscicórneo adj. (zool.) having fuscous antennae.
fuscipene adj. m. + f. **fuscipêneo** m. (zool.) fusco-
-pennate.
fuscirrostro adj. (zool.) fusco-rostrate.
fusco adj. 1. fuscous, dusky, dark(ish), tawny. 2. fuliginous. 3. pale. 4. (fig.) sad, melancholic.
entre a luz e o ~ at nightfall.
fusco-fusco s. m. (S. Braz.) twilight, dusk.
fuseira s. f. big spindle, arbor.
fuseiro s. m. spindle maker.
fusela s. f. (her.) fusil (figure of a spindle).
fuselado adj. (her.) fusiform, adorned with fusils.
fuselagem s. f. (pl. **-ens**) fuselage, the body of an airplane (plate A 3).
furar a ~ to hull.
fuselo s. m. (ornith.) redshank.
fusibilidade s. f. fusibility, liquescency, meltingness.
fusicórneos s. m. pl. (ent.) a family of lepidopterous insects.
fusiforme adj. m. + f. fusiform, spindle-shaped.
fúsil adj. m. + f. (pl. **-eis**) 1. fusible, meltable, liquefiable. 2. melted, molten.
fusionar v. 1. to fuse: a) melt. b) amalgamate, blend together. 2. to found, cast. 3. to coalesce. 4. to confound, confuse.
fusionista s. m. + f. (political) fusionist. ‖ adj. fusionist.
fusípede adj. m. + f. (zool.) having fusiform feet.
fusível s. m. (pl. **-íveis**) (Braz., electr.) (safety) fuse (plates E 3, M 5). ‖ adj. m. + f. fusile, fusible, (s)meltable.
o ~ **queimou** the fuse is blown.

fuso s. m. 1. (spinning) spindle, spool. 2. (mech.) screw, fusee, shaft, stud, arbor. 3. (naut.) jack-stay.
~ **do cabeçote** (tech.) trundle. ~ **do relógio** spring arbor of a watch. **cada terra com seu uso, cada roca com seu** ~ so many countries so many customs. **direito como um** ~ proud, stiff-necked. **ir direito como um** ~ to go straightforward or straightway.
fusório adj. of or pertaining to the art of (s)melting.
obra -a de ferro cast iron work.
fusta s. f. 1. (naut.) foist, pinnace, barge. 2. shawl.
fustalha s. f. many barges.
fustão s. m. fustian: 1. cotton cloth. 2. twilled cotton stuff, corduroy.
~ **listado** dimity. ~ **de algodão** (U. S. A.) jean.
fuste s. m. 1. shaft: a) pole. b) spear staff. c) verge, trunk, shank, main part of a column. d) (bot.) stem, stalk, trunk. 2. a goldsmith's little grip stick. 3. drum case. 4. shank (plate R 1).
fustete s. m. (bot.) 1. dwarf sumac. 2. smoke-tree. 3. Japanese wax-tree.
fustigação s. f. (pl. **-ões**) 1. fustigation. 2. punishment. 3. thrashing, beating, flogging. 4. maltreatment, ill-treatment. 5. vexation.
fustigador s. m. flogger.
fustigante adj. m. + f. vexatious.
fustigar v. 1. to fusticate, beat with switches, flog. 2. to punish, castigate. 3. to harass, harry. 4. to vex. 5. to maltreat, treat brutally.
fustigado por wrung with. **fustigado pelo inverno** winter-beaten. **fustigado pela peste** plague-stricken.
~ **cavalos** to whip horses.
fustigo s. m. blow with a whip or cudgel.
futebol s. m. (sport) football: 1. soccer (plate F 9). 2. Rugby. 3. American football (plate F 9).
~ **de acordo com as regras da liga internacional** association football, soccer.

futebolista s. m. + f. football player, footballer.
futicar v. (Braz.) to importune, bother, pester.
fútil adj. m. + f. (pl. **-eis**) 1. futile: a) trifling. b) frivolous, trivial, insignificant, unimportant. c) useless, chaffy, feckless, void, coxcombical. 2. heedless, thoughtless, careless. 3. windy, vaporous, frothy. 4. empty. ‖ **futilmente** adv. futilely, frivolously, worthlessly, voidly, triflingly, fecklessly.
futilidade s. f. 1. futility: a) insignificance. b) frivolousness, triviality. c) worthless thing or matter, trifle, trifling. d) uselessness, vainness, vanity. 2. thoughtlessness. 3. lightness, levity, frivolity.
futilizar v. to trifle: 1. talk nonsense, prattle. 2. treat lightly, disregard.
futre s. m. rascal, rogue, scamp.
futrica s. f. 1. little shop, stall. 2. pot-house, tavern. 3. trash, rubbish. 4. shaky wooden framework. 5. m. ill-bred person, common or ordinary man, the man in the street.
futricada, futricagem, futriquice s. f. (pop.) 1. trash, rubbish, old pots or furniture. 2. meanness, mean act.
futricar v. 1. to trade, barter. 2. to traffic. 3. to deal fraudulently. 4. to stir up, meddle with, interfere.
futura s. f. fiancée, betrothed (female) person.
futuração s. f. (pl. **-ões**) 1. futurity. 2. conjecture, supposition.
futurar v. 1. to foretell, predict. 2. to suppose, conjecture, prognosticate. 3. to prophesy a good future.
futurição, futuridade s. f. 1. futurity, future event. 2. the life hereafter, eternal life.
futurismo s. m. (arts) futurism.
futurista s. m. + f. (arts) futurist. ‖ adj. futurist(ic).
futuro s. m. 1. future: a) futurity, hereafter, time to come. b) (gram.) future tense. 2. destiny, fate. 3. fiancé, betrothed (male) person. ‖ adj. future, next to come, coming, forthcoming, ulterior. ‖ **-amente** adv. futurely, in or for the future, hereafter, in time to come, still.

o ~ **marido** the intended. **olhar para o** ~ to be provident. **-as contingências** future events. **ele é um homem de** ~ he is a rising star, coming up, a coming man. **ela tem um** ~ **brilhante** she has brilliant prospects. **sem** ~ futureless.
futuroso adj. promising, auspicious.
fuxicada s. f. (Braz.) intrigue, gossip.
fuxicar v. 1. to crumple, wrinkle. 2. to stir up, rummage. 3. (Braz.) to intrigue, gossip. 4. to baste, sew loosely. 5. to botch.
fuxico s. m. (Braz.) intrigue, gossip, plot.
fuxiqueiro s. m. (Braz.) intriguer, intrigant(e).
fuzarca s. f. (Braz., pop.) spree, frolic, revelry.
fuzarquear v. (Braz., pop.) to revel, frolic.
fuzarqueiro s. m. (Braz., pop.) reveller, merrymaker. ‖ adj. merrymaking.
fuzil s. m. (pl. **fuzis**) 1. link of a chain, metal ring. 2. flintlock. 3. flash of lightning. 4. gun, rifle. 5. (fig.) connexion, linking.
fuzilação s. f. (pl. **-ões**) flashing, flash of a gun.
fuzilada s. f. 1. fusillade, volley of guns. 2. firing, shooting. 3. sheet lightning.
fuzilado adj. 1. shot. 2. executed by a firing squad.
fuzilador s. m. shooter, rifleman. ‖ adj. shooting, firing.
fuzilamento s. m. shooting: 1. discharging of firearms. 2. execution by a firing-squad.
fuzilante adj. m. + f. sparkling, flashing, coruscating.
fuzilar v. 1. to shoot, fusillade. 2. to put to death by shooting. 3. to lighten, flash. 4. (fig.) to sparkle, scintillate. 5. to menace, become threatening.
fuzilaria s. f. 1. volley of rifleshots, fusillade. 2. shooting, fire, continuous firing. 3. (fig.) abundance, affluence.
fuzileiro s. m. (mil.) fusileer, rifleman.
~ **naval** marine, (sl.) leatherneck.
fuzilhão s. m. (pl. **-ões**) tongue of a buckle.
fuzuê s. m. (Braz., sl.) 1. noise, clamour. 2. feast, merrymaking. 3. brawl, noisy fight, wrangle.

G

G, g s. m. 1. the seventh letter of the Portuguese alphabet. 2. (mus.) the fifth note of the diatonic scale. ‖ adj. m. + f. 1. seventh (in a series or group). 2. (Medieval Roman numeral) 400, or, with a dash over it, 400,000.

gabação s. f. (pl. -ões) (also **gabadela**) praising, commendation, eulogy, boasting.

gabador s. m. 1. praiser, eulogizer, commender. 2. boaster, braggart. ‖ adj. boastful, bragging.

gabamento s. m. 1. laudation, commendation, praising. 2. boasting, bragging.

gabão s. m. (pl. -ões) 1. gaberdine: a) wool(l) or cotton cloth. b) rough cloth coat with sleeves and hood. 2. (f. **gabona**): a) praiser, eulogizer, commender. b) boaster, braggart. 3. (arch.) eulogy, praise.

fazer grandes -ões to promise mountains and marvels.

gabar v. 1. to praise, laud, emblazon. 2. to eulogize, extol. 3. to flatter, cajole. 4. ~-se de a) to boast (of), brag, show-off, vapour, flourish, vaunt, brave, gasconade, cut it fat. b) to pride o. s. on, to plume o. s. on.

gabo-lhe a confiança (ironic.) I'm much obliged for your confidence. **gabava-se de sua perícia** he plumed himself on his skill. **posso ~-me de** I flatter myself on. **ele gabava-se dos seus sucessos** he cut it fat. **ele se gaba de sua vitória** he talks big of his victory.

gabardina s. f. 1. gabardine (wool(l)en fabric). 2. raincoat (waterproof).

gabardo s. m. cloak with sleeves and hood.

gabaritado adj. qualified to hold a position (person).

gabarito s. m. (tech., also **gabari**) 1. mould, form, model. 2. templet, template, pattern. 3. gauge, instrument for measuring or testing (plates F 2, T 5). 4. jig. 5. rank, rate, qualification.

~ de carga loading gauge (plate E 12). **~ de carregamento** clearance loading gauge.

gabarola s. m. + f., **gabarolas** sg. + pl. boaster, braggart, swaggerer.

gabarolice s. f. 1. boast, brag, jactitation, swagger, rodomontade. 2. (U. S. A., coll.) splurge. 3. claptrap.

gabarote s. m. flatboat, small lighter.

gabarra s. f. 1. flat-bottomed barge for sailing and rowing. 2. drag-net, trawl-net.

gabarro s. m. abscess on the hoof of cattle or horses.

gabela s. f. (also **gavela**) sheaf, handful, bunch.

gabião s. m. (pl. -ões) 1. gabion, large basket of wickerwork. 2. (fort.) gabion(ade). 3. (agric.) hamper (for grape picking).

gabinardo s. m. gaberdine.

gabinete s. m. cabinet: 1. study, closet, den, chamber, private room or apartment. 2. office, consulting room, camarilla (plate D 1). 3. ministry, body of ministers. 4. cuddy.

~ de leitura reading-room. **o ~ deliberou** the cabinet deliberated. **~ do diretor** manager's room. **~ de imprensa** editorial office. **~ de toucador** lavatory compartment. **~ de física** physics laboratory (especially in schools).

gabionada s. f. (mil.) gabionade.

gabionar v. to provide with gabions.

gabirola s. f. (also **guabiroba**) (Braz.) popular name of several plants of the family Myrtaceae.

gabiru s. m. (Braz., sl.) 1. scoundrel. 2. hobbledehoy, awkward or clumsy person.

gabo s. m. 1. praise, eulogy. 2. boasting, bragging. 3. vanity.

gabola s. m. + f., **gabolas** sg. + pl. boaster, braggart, swaggerer, blow, swash-buckler. ‖ adj. blustering, vaunting.

gabolice s. f. bragging, boast, big talk, magniloquence, swagger, flapdoodle, swank.

gabona f. of **gabão** 2.

gabro s. m. (geol.) gabbro.

gaçaba s. f. (var. of **igaçaba**) jug, pitcher.

gacha s. f. 1. net covering the lateral planks of a fishing-boat. 2. (Port. fam.) hand.

gacheiro adj. (N. E. Braz., pop.) 1. narrow, tight. 2. crouched, squatting.

gacho s. m. 1. nape of a bull's neck. 2. (Port. pop.) bunch, cluster. ‖ adj. lowered, fallen.

gadanha s. f. 1. scythe (plate C 16). 2. ladle, soup ladle. 3. (pop.) hand. 4. a bricklayer's hammer.

gadanhada s. f. 1. a stroke with the scythe. 2. a grasping with the claws.

gadanhar v. 1. to cut with the scythe. 2. to scratch with claws. 3. to grasp firmly.

gadanheira s. f. (agric) mowing machine, corn-cutter, reaper, mower.

gadanho s. m. 1. claw, talon, pounce. 2. pitchfork. 3. (fam.) finger, hand. 4. scythe.

gadão s. m. (Braz.) cattle of superior race or quality.

gadaria s. f. (Braz.) 1. cattle, livestock. 2. herd of cattle. 3. cattle of a farm.

gadelha s. f., **gadelho** m. (Port. pop.) tuft or mop of hair, long tousled hair, tangled hair, mane.

gadelhudo adj. hairy, hirsute, long-haired.

gademar s. m. (Braz.) crossbreed of zebu and caracu (cattle).

gadídeo s. m. gadoid: fish of the family Gadidae (cod family). ‖ adj. gadoid.

gaditano s. m. native or inhabitant of Cádiz (Spain). ‖ adj. Gaditanian.

gado (I) s. m. 1. cattle, stock, livestock (plate G 1). 2. herd. 3. flock, drove. 4. beast. 5. (vulg.) prostitutes.

criação de ~ cattle raising, stock farming. **o ~ da fazenda** the livestock. **vagão de ~** (rail.) stock car. **manada de ~ grosso** a herd of great or big cattle. **rebanho de ~ miúdo** flock of small cattle (goats, sheep). **~ cerdoso** swine. **cão de ~** shepherd's dog. **~ de solta** cattle living free on pasture. **~ do rio** (N. Braz.) fresh-water turtle.

gado (II) s. m. (ichth.) cod, gadid.

gadolínio s. m. (chem.) gadolinium.

gadolinita s. f. (min.) gadolinite.

gadunhar v. (Braz.) to steal, pilfer, filch.

gaélico s. m. Gaelic, Gaelic language. ‖ adj. Gaelic.

gafa s. f. 1. (vet.) itch, scabies. 2. (med.) leprosy, mange. 3. (plant path.) mildew. 4. a kind of dark-coloured crab. 5. salt vat. 6. (Port., pop.) hunger. 7. (arch.) bending hook of a crossbow. 8. flood, high tide. 9. claw, gaff.

gafado adj. infected with scabies, mange, mildew or rot.

gafanhão s. m. (pl. -ões) 1. (ent.) meadow grasshopper. 2. native or inhabitant of Gafanha (Port.).

gafanhotão s. m. (pl. -ões) (ent.) lobe-crested locust.

gafanhoto s. m. (ent.) grasshopper, locust, jumper.

gafanhoto-de-arribação s. m. (pl. **gafanhotos-de-arribação**) (ent.) migratory locust.

gafar (I) s. m. (hist.) tribute exacted from Jews and Christians living under Turkish domination.

G1

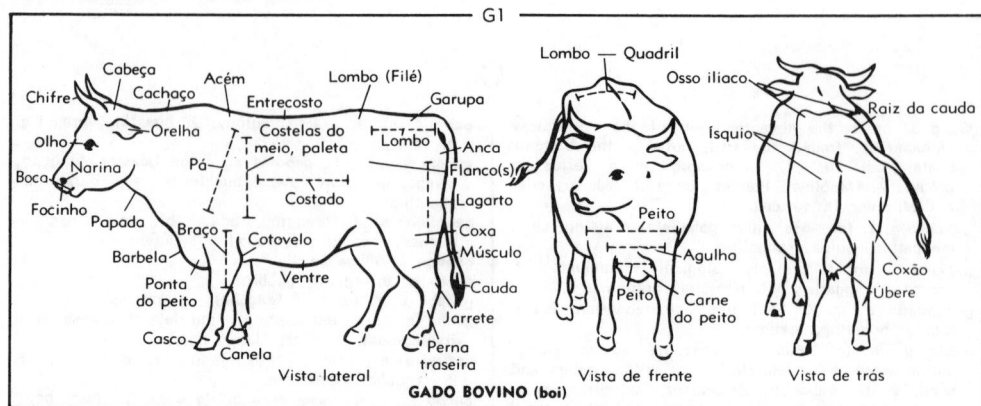

GADO BOVINO (boi)

Vista lateral — Vista de frente — Vista de trás

Labels: Chifre, Cabeça, Acém, Cachaço, Entrecosto, Lombo (Filé), Garupa, Olho, Orelha, Costelas do meio, paleta, Lombo, Anca, Boca, Narina, Pá, Flanco(s), Focinho, Papada, Costado, Lagarto, Braço, Cotovelo, Coxa, Barbela, Ventre, Músculo, Ponta do peito, Cauda, Casco, Canela, Jarrete, Perna traseira; Lombo, Quadril, Osso iliaco, Raiz da cauda, Ísquio, Peito, Agulha, Coxão, Peito, Carne do peito, Úbere

gafar (II) v. 1. to infect with itch, scabies or mange. 2. to contaminate, stain. 3. ~-se to become contaminated or corrupt. 4. (Gall.) to commit an indiscretion.
~-se de sarna to be infected with itch.
gafaria s. f. hospital or colony for lepers, leprosarium.
gafe s. f. (Gall.) gaffe: an involuntary indiscretion.
gafeira s. f. 1. (vet.) dog's distemper. 2. (vet.) measles, murrain, sheep-pox. 3. (med. obs.) leprosy.
gafeirento, gafeiroso, gafento adj. measled, measly, infected with scabies, itch or mange, leprous.
gafieira s. f. (Braz. sl.) 1. low dancing resort, gaff, honky-tonk. 2. dance festivity frequented by the populace.
gafo s. m. = **gafeira**. ‖ adj. 1. contaminated with scabies, itch or mange. 2. (fig.) corrupt, demoralized. 3. (Port.) full.
gaforina s. f. 1. tangled or dishevelled hair, mane. 2. long lock or curl. 3. toupee, small wig. 4. tousle, mop of hair. 5. curled hair of Negroes.
gaforinha s. f. (Braz., pop.) curled hair of Negroes.
gagá adj. m. + f. (Gall.) decrepit, enfeebled.
gagata s. f. (min.) jet, pitch-coal.
gago s. m. stutterer, falterer, stammerer. ‖ adj. stuttering, stammering, faltering. ‖ **-amente** adv. stammeringly.
ver-se ~ to be embarrassed.
gagosa s. f. word only used in the adverbial locution: **à** ~ without effort or expense, easy.
levar o bolo à ~ (gambling) to win the pool because all are passing.
gagueio s. m. stammer.
gagueira s. f. stutter, stammer, impediment of speech.
gaguejador adj. stammering.
gaguejar v. to stammer, stutter, falter in speech; hum and haw.
falar gaguejando to stammer.
gaguejo s. m. act of stuttering, stutter, stammer, impediment of speech, faltering.
gaguez, gaguice s. f. act of stuttering, stammer, stutter, impediment of speech.
gaiaco s. m. (bot.) pockwood, guaiacum tree, lignum vitae tree (Guaiacum officinale).
gaiacol s. m. (chem.) guaiacol, pyrocatechin, monomethylcatechol.
gaiado adj. 1. tufted (breast of a horse). 2. said of a horse having **gaias**.
gaial s. m. wild Indian bullock.
gaias s. f. pl. (horse breeding) feathery tuft of hair on the breast; feather, frizzling of hair.

gaiatada s. f. 1. gang of mischievous youngsters, young scamps, street urchins. 2. prank(s), mischievous trick(s).
gaiatar v. to play tricks like a scamp, to play pranks on s. o.
gaiatice s. f. 1. a street Arab's trick. 2. knavery, roguishness, drollery.
gaiato s. m. 1. street urchin, young scamp. 2. street Arab, lad. 3. wag. 4. rogue, rascal. ‖ adj. 1. gay, joyous, merry. 2. mischievous, naughty.
gaifona, gaifonice s. f. 1. grimace, wry faces. 2. pranks, monkey pranks.
gaifonar v. 1. to make grimaces or faces. 2. to play pranks.
gainambé s. m. (Braz. ornith.) bellbird, campanero.
gaio s. m. (ornith.) European jay. ‖ adj. jovial, merry, gay, cheerful.
verde-~ light green.
gaiola s. f. 1. cage: a) bird-cage; mew, coop, hutch (plate A 11). b) (fig.) prison, jail, lock-up. c) crate, wooden framework. d) framework of a house. e) elevator box (plate M 10). 2. (fig.) cramped quarters, small lodgings. 3. (rail.) open freight-car, truck, lorry. 4. m. (N. Braz.) small river steamer.
~ para pesagem de animais weighing cage.
gaioleiro s. m. cage maker or vendor.
gaiolim s. m. (pl. **-ins**) little (bird-)cage.
gaiolo s. m. bird's snare or trap. ‖ adj. crescent-shaped (horns).
gaita s. f. 1. shepherd's pipe or flute, reed. 2. **~s** pl. (zool.) branchial apertures of lampreys. 3. (Braz. sl.) money, tin, brass, chink(ers), jack, spondulics, dust. 4. mouth-organ. 5. depreciative name of anything.
~ de foles or **~ galega** bagpipe. **estar cheio da ~** (Braz. sl.) to be well-off. **estar de ~** to be merry or gay. **ir-se à ~** to go wrong, turn out crabs. **na primeira ~** at the first crowing of the cock. **não há ~** there is no money. **sabe a ~s** 1. it is a very exquisite dish. 2. it tastes good. **tocador de ~ de foles** bagpiper. **tocar a ~** 1. to play on the flute, bagpipe or mouth-organ. 2. (ironic.) to get tipsy. **tomar alguém como ~** to swindle somebody.
gaitada s. f. 1. blowing of a tune on a pipe or flute 2. (depr.) poor piece of music.
gaitear v. 1. to play on a pipe, mouth-organ, or flute. 2. to bagpipe, doodle.
gaiteira s. f. 1. (Port. pop.) instrument used to pick up sargasso weed. 2. (Braz. pop.): a) mangrove swamp. b) mangrove.

gaiteiro s. m. 1. bagpipe or mouth-organ player. 2. (Braz.) mangrove swamp. 3. (Braz.) mangrove. ‖ adj. 1. dandy, smart, lively. 2. merry, gay, jesting. 3. boastful, braggart.
gaiúta s. f. (naut.) companion.
gaiva s. f. rift or excavation caused in the ground by rain water.
gaivagem s. f. (pl. -ens) 1. deep ditch, trench. 2. drainage channel, gutter. 3. drainage, draining.
gaivão s. m. (pl. -ões) (ornith.) swift, martlet.
gaivar v. to dig a deep ditch.
gaivel s. m. (pl. -éis) wall whose thickness diminishes towards its top.
gaivina s. f. (also andorinha-do-mar) (ornith.) tern, sea swallow.
gaivota s. f. 1. (ornith.) gull, sea-gull, pewit-gull, mew (plate P 17). 2. (Braz., fam.) fool, simpleton.
gaivotão s. m. (pl. -ões) (ornith.) kelp gull.
gaivota-preta s. f. (pl. gaivotas-pretas) (ornith.) terutero, teruteru.
gaivota-rapineira s. f. (pl. gaivotas-rapineiras) (ornith.) 1. parasitic jaeger. 2. skua.
gaivotinha s. f. (Braz. bot.) spurge.
gajão s. m. (Braz. gypsies) master, sir.
gajeiro s. m. (naut.) lookout-man, top-watch, top-man. ‖ adj. well climbing.
gajeru s. m. (bot., also gajiru) 1. coco plum, cocoa plum. 2. carajura.
gajeta s. f. (S. Braz.) biscuit.
gajo s. m. 1. bully, brute. 2. (fam.) chap, fellow, guy. 3. rogue, rascal. ‖ adj. sly, cunning, roguish, crafty.
gajuru s. m. (bot.) = guajuru.
gala s. f. 1. festive dress, court-dress. 2. pomp, show, state, gala. 3. national festivity, celebration, solemnity. 4. rejoicing, delight. 5. boasting, bragging. 6. tread, cock-tread, fertilization speck in an egg. 7. sperm, seed. 8. (fig.) gracefulness, elegance.
dia de grande ~ national holiday. fazer ~ de to show off, to pride o. s. on. pôr-se de ~ to put on one's Sunday best. uniforme de ~ full-dress uniform. vestido de ~ gala dress, court-dress.
galã s. m. 1. (theat.) leading man, the romantic lead. 2. lover, admirer.
galação s. f. = galadura.
galacrista s. f. (bot.) yellow rattle.
galactagogo s. m. (med.) galactagogue, medicine which promotes the secretion of milk. ‖ adj. galactagogue, galactagoguic.
galáctico adj. galactic.
galactocele s. f. (med.) galactocele.
galactófago adj. galactophagous: feeding or subsisting on milk.
galactóforo adj. galactophorous: conveying milk, lactiferous.
galactologia s. f. galactology.
galactológico adj. galactologic.
galactômetro s. m. galactometer, lactodensimeter.
galactoposia s. f. (med.) milk cure or diet.
galactorréia s. f. (path.) galactorrhea, excessive flow of milk.
galactoscópio s. m. galactoscope.
galactose s. f. (chem.) galactose, lactose.
galactosúria s. f. (med. path.) galactosuria.
galactúria, galacturia s. f. (med.) galacturia, chyluria.
galadura s. f. gallature, tread.
galagala s. f. mixture of tar and resin used for calking.
galalau s. m. (Braz.) 1. tall person. 2. anything of gigantic size.
galalite s. f. galalith.
galana s. f. fight, brawl, row.

galane adj. gallant, chivalrous, polite, courteous.
galanear v. 1. to dress gaudily or elegantly, wear expensive or sumptuous garments.
galanga s. f. (bot.) galingale.
galanice s. f. 1. elegance, gracefulness. 2. civility, gallantry, polite attention to ladies. 3. courteous manners, smartness, grace.
galantaria s. f. 1. flirtation, courtship. 2. civility or polite attention to ladies. 3. gallantry, courteous behaviour, genteelness. 4. compliment, flattery. 5. gracefulness, niceness, elegance. 6. little present, gift. 7. jest, witticism, joke. 8. gallant person, beau.
galante s. m. + f. 1. gallant, suitor, beau. 2. gentleman, man of fashion. ‖ adj. 1. graceful, elegant, handsome. 2. gentle, nice, pleasant. 3. distinguished, notable. 4. civil, polite, attentive (to ladies). 5. funny, merry, witty. 6. gallant, courteous, amorous. 7. sparkish. ‖ ~mente adv. gallantly, politely, courteously.
um dito ~ a witty saying. ela é uma menina muito ~ she is a very graceful girl. não ~ ungallant.
galanteador s. m. gallant, cavalier, coquet, flirter, wooer, masher, philanderer, beau, suitor, admirer. ‖ adj. 1. gallant, courteous, polite. 2. flirtatious, amorous, amatory. 3. flattering, adulatory. ‖ ~amente adv. gallantly, flirtatiously.
galantear v. 1. to gallant, court, make love to, woo. 2. to flirt, coquet, pay gallant compliments. 3. to adorn, decorate. 4. to flatter, adulate. 5. to spark.
galanteio s. m. 1. gallantry, courtesy, politeness, attentions. 2. courtship, amour, love-making, wooing. 3. flirtation, dalliance. 4. flattery, adulation.
galanteria s. f. = galantaria.
galantina s. f. galantine: minced meat (fowl, veal, and other meat) in aspic.
galão s. m. (pl. -ões) 1. galloon, gold lace, silver lace, strap, cordon, orris; (mil.) stripe. 2. gilt brim of a glass. 3. (manège) croupade, curvet, prance. 4. gallon (Brit. 4.55 l., U. S. A. 3.78 l.).
galápago s. m. quitter: sore on the crown of the hoof (cattle, horses).
galapo s. m. 1. saddle pad. 2. bandage, ligature.
galar v. to tread, cover, copulate (of male birds).
galardão s. m. (pl. -ões) 1. premium, reward, recompense. 2. award, prize. 3. glory, honour, laurel, plume, crown, blue ribbon.
digno de ~ rewardable.
galardoador s. m. rewarder, awarder. ‖ adj. rewarding, honourable.
galardoar v. 1. to reward, recompense. 2. to compensate, remunerate. 3. to console, comfort. 4. to relieve, mitigate.
galarim s. m. (pl. -ins) 1. (gambling) doubling of stakes. 2. apex, summit, pinnacle. 3. wealth, opulence, influence. 4. worth, power. 5. high rank or station in life.
estar no ~ to command authority or influence, hold the reins.
gálata s. m. Galatian. ‖ adj. Galatian.
galáxia s. f. 1. (astr.) galaxy, the Milky Way. 2. a genus of iridaceous plants.
gálbano s. m. galbanum: 1. an evergreen plant (Ferula galbaniflua). 2. gum-resin obtained from this plant.
galbo s. m. (archit.) elegant profile or contour.
galbulídeos s. m. pl. (ornith.) Galbulidae, the jacamar family.
gálbulo s. m. (bot.) galbulus (of a cypress).
galdrope s. m. (naut.) tiller rope.
galé s. f. 1. galley: a) large open rowing-boat. b) printer's galley. 2. ~s pl. forced labour at galleys 3. m. galley slave.

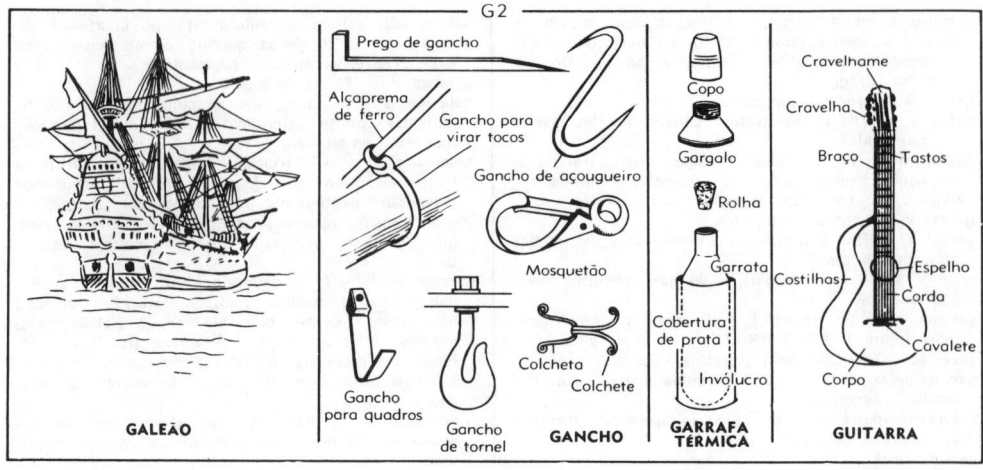

G 2

GALEÃO · GANCHO · GARRAFA TÉRMICA · GUITARRA

ele foi condenado às ~s he was sent to the galleys.

gálea s. f. helmet.

galeaça s. f. (naut.) three-masted galley.

galeado adj. 1. helmeted, covered with a helm. 2. (fig.) defensive. 3. shaped like a helm. 4. (bot.) galeate.

galeantropia s. f. (med.) galeanthropy, mental delusion that one has become a cat.

galeão s. m. (pl. **-ões**) 1. (naut.) galleon, carrack (plate G 2). 2. (typogr.) compositor's board.

galear (I) v. 1. to appear in full dress. 2. to dress elegantly. 3. (naut.) to toss, pitch, heave and set.

galear (II) v. 1. to balance, swing, rock, pitch (vessel). 2. to curvet, prance (horses). 3. to throw, fling, cast.

galeato adj. 1. helmeted, covered with a helm. 2. (fig.) defensive. 3. shaped like a helm. 4. (bot.) galeate(d).

galega s. f. (bot.) goat's-rue.

galegada s. f. 1. Galician saying or behaviour. 2. Galicians (natives of a Spanish province).

galego s. m. Galician: 1. native or inhabitant of Galicia (Spain). 2. language of the Galicians. 3. (Braz., depr.) Portuguese. ‖ adj. Galician.

galeiforme adj. m. + f. galeiform, galeate, helmet-shaped.

galeio s. m. (Braz.) rapid backward or sidewise movement with the body; recoiling, shrinking back.

perder o ~ to lose one's skill, become clumsy.

galena s. f. 1. (min.) galena, lead-glance, native sulphide of lead. 2. (radio) crystal set.

galênico adj. 1. (med.) Galenic(al), of or relative to Galen (famous ancient physician). 2. (chem.) galenic(al).

galenismo s. m. (med.) Galenism, Galenic system of medicine.

galenista s. m. + f. Galenist, follower or practitioner of Galenism.

galenita s. f. (min.) galenite, galena.

galeno s. m. physician.

galéola s. f. galleylike vessel.

galeonete s. m. (naut.) galliot, galiot(t).

galeopiteco s. m. (zool.) flying lemur, colugo.

galeota s. f. (naut.) small galley, galliot, galiot(t).

galeote s. m. 1. (naut.) small galley, galliot. 2. galley-slave, rower of a galley. 3. cloak (as used by galley-slaves).

galera s. f. 1. (naut.) two- or three-masted galley. 2. galley-furnace. 3. lorry, truck, freight-car, goods waggon.

galeria s. f. 1. gallery: a) picture or art gallery. b) long narrow room, passage. c) (theat.) tiers of seats in the upper circle; circus ring (plate T 3). d) covered passageway, ambulatory, piazza, balcony, veranda, porch. e) (mining) tunnel, drift-way, stulm, heading (plate M 10). 2. aisle. 3. aqueduct. 4. pelmet. 5. riverside forest. 6. ~s pl. spectators sitting in the gallery.

~ abobadada vault. **~ acústica** whispering-gallery. **~ de escoamento** culvert, drain gallery. **~ intermediária** (mining) sublevel. **~ transversal** (mining) crosscut. **para a ~** (to play) to the gallery.

galeriano s. m. galley-slave, rower of a galley. ‖ adj. of or relative to a galley-slave, slavish.

galerno s. m. soft breeze, gentle wind. ‖ adj. soft, gentle (of north-eastern winds).

galês s. m. 1. Welshman, Welsh, Cambrian, native or inhabitant of Wales. 2. Welsh language. ‖ adj. Welsh, Cymric.

os ~es the Welsh.

galeto s. m. (Braz.) 1. spring chicken. 2. roasted spring chicken, broiler, fryer.

galezia s. f. 1. trickery, deception. 2. fraud, deceit. 3. roguery, swindle.

galfarro s. m. 1. (pop.) bailiff, apparitor. 2. glutton, voracious, covetous or greedy person.

galga s. f. 1. greyhound bitch. 2. small anchor. 3. (pop.) lie, fib. 4. upper millstone (of an oil-mill).

galgar v. 1. to speed along, move along swiftly and elegantly. 2. to pass over or beyond, jump over, spring, leap or fly over. 3. to untwist, disentangle. 4. to reach (the age of). 5. to climb. 6. to rise rapidly, attain a better social or financial position. 7. to go through, traverse, cover a distance.

o menino galgou a parede the boy climbed over the wall. **ele ia ~ os quarenta anos** he was about to reach forty years of age.

galgaz adj. m. + f. slender, lean, meager.

galgo s. m. harrier, greyhound, courser (plate C 3).

correr como um ~ to race or rush along.

galguincho adj. (Braz.) emaciated, famishing.

galha s. f. 1. first dorsal fin. 2. gall(-nut).

galhada, galhadura s. f. 1. antlers. 2. branches.

galharda s. f. 1. galliard: lively dance. 2. music composed for such a dance.

galhardear v. 1. to show off, make a display. 2. to parade, vaunt. 3. to shine, glitter. 4. to excel, outshine, surpass. 5. to show courage, behave with grace.

galhardete s. m. pennant, pennon, banderole, streamer, banner.

galhardia s. f. 1. beauty, elegance, grace. 2. liveliness, spiritedness. 3. courage, valour, bravery. 4. (fig.) generosity. 5. gaiety, merriness.

galhardo s. m. (naut.) fore or aftcastle. ‖ adj. 1. handsome, elegant. 2. gay, merry. 3. graceful, elegant. 4. generous. 5. brave, courageous.

galhas s. f. pl. 1. antlers. 2. branches.

galheiro s. m. 1. (Braz.) stag with big antlers. 2. bonfire built of branches.

galheta s. f. cruet, vial, ampulla, caster.

galheteiro s. m. cruet stand, caster.

galho s. m. 1. branch (of trees), arm, twig, limb, offshoot, fescue, bough, sprig, stick (plate A 14). 2. ~s pl. brushwood, twiggery, trash. 3. prong, tine, knag (of antlers). ~ **pequeno** branchlet. **cada macaco no seu** ~ every jack to his trade! **pular de** ~ **em** ~ to find no rest, be restless. **qual é o** ~? what is the trouble? **quebrar o** ~ to shoot the trouble. **sem** ~**s** branchless. **dar um** ~ to cause trouble (a nuisance).

galhofa s. f. 1. jest, joke. 2. fun, merriment. 3. frolic, lark, whoopee. 4. friskness, playfulness. 5. idle life, leisure. **de** ~ cheerfully, frolicsomely. **fazer** ~ **de** to make fun at someone's expense, poke fun at.

galhofada s. f. (also **galhoferia**) big fun, carousing, loud revelry.

galhofar v. (also **galhofear**) 1. joke, jest. 2. to wanton, dally. 3. to frolic, make merry, disport. 4. to poke fun at, make game of a person.

galhofeiro s. m. jester, larker, revel(l)er, merry-maker, frolicker, dallier. ‖ adj. jesting, frolicsome, merry, rollicking, playful. ‖ **-amente** adv. playfully, merrily.

galhudo s. m. (Braz., ichth.) banner pompano. ‖ adj. 1. branchy, beamy. 2. antlered, pronged.

galicanismo s. m. (hist.) Gallicanism.

galicano s. m. (hist.) Gallican, adherent of Gallicanism.

galiciano s. m. Galician: native or inhabitant of Galicia (former crownland of Austria). ‖ adj. Galician.

galicínio s. m. 1. cock-crowing, crowing. 2. time of the first crowing, dawn.

galiciparla s. m. + f. person who talks or acts in a French manner.

galicismar v. to use Gallicisms.

galicismo s. m. Gallicism, French word or idiom (borrowed for use in another language).

galicista s. m. + f. Gallicizer, person fond of Gallicisms.

gálico s. m. (med. pop.) syphilis. ‖ adj. 1. Gallic, of or pertaining to Gaul (France). 2. (chem.) gallic. **ácido** ~ gallic acid.

galífero s. m. producing gall-nuts or galls.

galiformes s. m. pl. (ornith.) Galliformes, the order that comprises the domestic fowl.

galileu s. m. 1. Galilean, native or inhabitant of Galilee. ‖ adj. Galilean. **o Galileu** the Galilean (Jesus Christ).

galimatias s. m., sg. + pl. galimatias, nonsense, gibberish, jargon.

galináceo s. m. Gallinaceae, Gallinae, Galliformes; ~s pl. Rasores. ‖ adj. gallinaceous, gallinacean, rasorial.

galindréu s. m. (naut.) mooring ring.

galinha s. f. 1. hen, chicken, fowl, biddy. 2. (fig.) weakling, craven. 3. loose woman. 4. (fig.) titbit. 5. ill luck, misfortune. ~ **choca** 1. brooding hen. 2. (Braz.) incapable or restless person. ~ **poedeira** layer. **a** ~ **está a pôr** the hen is laying. **aquilo é** ~ **morta** that is dead easy. **cantar de** ~ to show the white feather. **ele deita-se com as** ~**s** he goes to bed with the sun, very early. **matar a** ~ **dos ovos de ouro** to kill the hen which laid the golden eggs. **muita** ~ **e poucos ovos** much cry and little wool. **quando as** ~**s tiverem dentes** when two Sundays come together, never.

galinha-anã s. f. (pl. **galinhas-anãs**) (ornith.) sand grouse.

galinha-arrepiada s. f. (pl. **galinhas-arrepiadas**) (Braz., bot.) anguria (Cucumis anguria), a gourd.

galinha-brava s. f. (pl. **galinhas-bravas**) (ornith.) black grouse.

galinhaça s. f., **galinhaço** m. chicken droppings, dung of hens.

galinha-choca s. f. (pl. **galinhas-chocas**) (bot.) Jamaica ironwood.

galinha-d'água s. f. (pl. **galinhas-d'água**) (ornith.) finfoot, water-hen.

galinha-da-guiné s. f. (pl. **galinhas-da-guiné**) (ornith.) guinea fowl.

galinha-da-índia s. f. (pl. **galinhas-da-índia**) (ornith.) guinea fowl.

galinha-d'angola s. f. (pl. **galinhas-d'angola**) (ornith.) guinea fowl, galeeny.

galinha-de-faraó s. f. (pl. **galinhas-de-faraó**) (ornith.) Egyptian vulture.

galinha-do-mato s. f. (pl. **galinhas-do-mato**) (ornith.) ant-thrush.

galinha-gorda s. f. (Braz., folkl.) children's play in which they contend for something belonging to another child.

galinha-morta s. f. (pl. **galinhas-mortas**) (Braz.) 1. popular tune. 2. weakling or coward. 3. bargain, rock-bottom prices. 4. trifle, insignificant object or matter. 5. sure easy thing, course of study or task, cinch, snap.

galinheiro s. m. 1. poulterer, poultry-dealer. 2. poultry yard, chicken roost, coop, pen, fowl run, hennery (plate C 11).

galinhola s. f. (ornith.) snipe, gallinule.

galinicultor s. m. poultry breeder, poulterer.

galinicultura s. f. breeding or keeping of poultry.

gálio s. m. 1. Gaul, native or inhabitant of ancient Gaul. 2. Gaulish, Celtic language of the Gauls, continental Celtic. 3. (chem.) Gallium. 4. any plant of the genus Gallium.

galipão s. m. (pl. **-ões**) (sl.) old-fashioned motor-car, tin can.

galiparla, galiparlista s. m. + f. person who talks or acts in a French manner.

galipina s. f. (bot.) galipine.

galipódio, galipote s. m. 1. galipot: the turpentine which concretes on the stem of certain pine trees. 2. Burgundy pitch.

galiré s. f. (Braz.) dwarf hen.

galispo s. m. little cock.

galista s. m. cocker: breeder or handler of fighting cocks.

galito s. m. (Braz., ornith.) yetapa: a fork-tailed flycatcher (Yetapa risivora).

galivar v. to mould, shape, give the right form.

galizia s. f. 1. cheat, trick, knavery. 2. complication, impertinency. 3. conceit, pride.

galo (l) s. m. 1. cock, (S. U. A.) rooster; chanticleer. 2. a genus of gallinaceous birds. 3. (eccl., Easter week) highest candle in a triangular sconce. 4. bump, protuberance, swelling on the forehead. **~ de briga** fighting cock. **~ doméstico** dung cock. **~ garnisé** (also **garnisé**) bantam: a chicken breed (the male of). **~·garnisé** (also **garnisé**) bantam: (fig.) small and quarrelsome person. **o ~ gaulês** the French cock (national symbol), France. **~ novo** (fig.) cockerel: a spirited youth. **~ pequeno** (fig.) cockalorum: a self-important little man. **~ silvestre** moor-cock, heath-cock, red grouse. **o ~ do terreiro** the cock of the roost. **ao cantar do ~** at daybreak, at dawn, very early. **ouvir cantar o ~ mas não saber onde** to have a very vague notion about a matter. **ele tem memória de ~** he has a very short memory. **outro ~ me cantaria** I should be better off if things took another turn. **salgar o ~** to have the first alcoholic drink of the day.

galo (II) s. m. Gaul: native or inhabitant of ancient Gaul. ‖ adj. Gaulish.

galocha s. f. galosh, rubber overshoe; (coll.) jemimas (plate B 16).

galocrista s. f. (bot.) yellow rattle.

galo-das-trevas s. m. (pl. **galos-das-trevas**) large ornamental candelabrum with thirteen candles.

galofobia s. f. Gallophobia, anti-French feeling.

galófobo s. m. Gallophobe. ‖ adj. Gallophobe.

galomania s. f. Gallomania: a mania for French fashions, literature, etc.

galomaníaco, galômano s. m. Gallomaniac.

galonar v. to adorn with gold-lace or silver-lace.

galopada s. f. 1. gallop. 2. gallopade. 3. running or riding at a gallop.

galopador s. m. galloper, loper. ‖ adj. galloping.

galopante adj. m. + f. galloping.

galopar v. 1. to gallop, run by leaps. 2. to ride at a gallop. 3. to cause to gallop. 4. to move or develop very fast. 5. to tittup.

galope s. m. 1. gallop: a) leaping gait of a horse or several other animals (plate C 12). b) gallopade. c) scamper. d) tittup. e) (fig.) rapidity, haste, hurry. 2. galop: a) sprightly dance. b) its music. **~ grande** (naut.) top-gallant mast with a long pole-head. **a ~, de ~** at a gallop; at full speed, in a hurry. **meio ~** canter. **ele saiu a ~** he struck a canter. **vir a todo ~** to come at full tilt. **~ de apresentação** canter.

galopeação s. f. (Braz.) = **galopada**.

galopeador s. m. galloper. ‖ adj. galloping.

galopear v. 1. (S. Braz.) to break in a colt. 2. = **galopar**.

galopim s. m. (pl. **-ins**) 1. lad. 2. street-boy. 3. errand-boy, messenger. 4. electioneer, canvasser, heeler. **~ de impressor** printer's devil.

galopinagem s. f. (pl. **-ens**) canvassing, electioneering.

galopinar v. to canvass, electioneer, solicit votes.

galpão s. m. (pl. **-ões**) (Braz.) hangar, shed, coach house, (railway) dock (plate A 4).

galponeiro adj. of, pertaining to or relative to an open shed.

galrão s. m. (pl. **-ões**) talker, prattler, chatterbox.

galrar v. 1. to prattle, babble, tattle. 2. to boast, brag, swagger.

galreador s. m. 1. talker, prattler, tattler. 2. boaster, braggart.

galrear v. (also **galrejar**) 1. to babble, prattle (like little children). 2. to brag, boast. 3. to chirp, twitter, warble.

galreiro, galrejador s. m. 1. talker, prattler. 2. boaster, braggart.

galrito s. m. (also **galricho**) 1. stake-net or hoop-net (for fishing). 2. trap, snare.

galucha s. f. (N. Braz.) cancerous boil.

galucho s. m. 1. raw recruit, newly enlisted soldier or sailor. 2. (fig.) novice, beginner. 3. greenhorn. 4. bashful or inexperienced fellow.

galvânico adj. (phys.) galvanic(al), voltaic.

galvanismo s. m. (phys.) galvanism, voltaism.

galvanização s. f. (pl. **-ões**) galvanization, plating, electro-deposition.

galvanizador s. m. galvanizer.

galvanizar v. 1. to galvanize. 2. to coat with metal. 3. to zinc. 4. to electroplate. 5. to stimulate, excite, reanimate, revive.

galvanocáustica s. f. galvanocauterization.

galvanocáustico adj. galvanocaustic.

galvanocautério s. m. (surg.) galvanocautery.

galvanografia s. f. galvanography.

galvanográfico adj. galvanographic(al).

galvanogravura s. f. galvano-engraving.

galvanomagnético adj. galvanomagnetic, electromagnetic.

galvanomagnetismo s. m. galvanomagnetism, electromagnetism.

galvanômetro s. m. galvanometer.

galvanoníquel s. m. (typogr.) nickeltype.

galvanoplastia, galvanoplástica s. f. galvanoplasty, galvanoplastics, electrotyping, electroplating.

galvanoplástico adj. galvanoplastic, electrotype.

galvanoscópio s. m. galvanoscope.

galvanostegia s. f. electroplating.

galvanoterapia s. f. galvanotherapy.

galvanoterápico adj. galvanotherapic.

galvanotipia s. f. galvanotype, electrotype.

galvanotípico adj. galvanotypic.

galvanotipista s. m. + f. (typogr.) electrotyper.

gama s. m. 1. gamma: third letter of the Greek alphabet. 2. (mus.) gamut, scale. 3. series or range (of ideas, theories, etc.). 4. (zool.) doe, fallow-deer. **~ de onda** range (radio).

gamação s. f. (Braz., sl.) passion, love.

gamacismo s. m. (med.) gammacism, guttural stammering.

gamado adj. hook-shaped, hooked. **cruz gamada** swastika, fylfot, gammadion.

gamão s. m. 1. backgammon (game). 2. backgammon board.

gamar v. (Braz., sl.) to love, to become enraptured.

gamarra s. f. martingale (plate C 12).

gamba s. f. (mus.) viola da gamba, bass viol.

gambá s. m. (zool.) opossum. **bêbedo como um ~** very tipsy. **comer ~ errado** to buy a pig in a poke, make a slip. **ele bebe como um ~** he drinks like a fish.

gambadonas s. f. pl. (naut.) rope windings around masts.

gambarra s. f. (N. Braz.) two-masted cattle barge.

gambérria s. f. 1. act of tripping up a person. 2. trick, snare. 3. quarrel, dispute.

gambeta, gambeteação s. f. (pl. **-ões**) (Braz.) 1. doubling or dodging (a pursuer). 2. craftiness. **fazer ~s** to double, make a sharp turn.

gambeteador s. m. (also **gambeteiro**) (Braz.) dodger, trickster. ‖ adj. dodging, trickish.

gambetear v. (Braz.) 1. to double, dodge, shun. 2. to escape or avoid (a blow).

gâmbia s. f. 1. (pop.) leg. 2. **~s**. pl. (fam.) pins. **dar às ~s** to run away.

gambiarra s. f. (theat.) stage lights, footlights (plate P 2).

gambito s. m. 1. feint, trick. 2. dodge, rose. 3. (chess) gambit.

gamboa s. f. a kind of sweet quince.

gamboeiro s. m. quince tree.

gamboína s. f. (pop.) swindling (at cards).

gambota s. f. (archit.) centering, wooden frame on which an arch or vault is built.

gamela s. f. 1. wooden trough, tray, kneading trough. 2. porringer, wooden bowl. 3. (Braz., pop.) lie. 4. little doe.
comer da mesma ~ to connive, conspire, be close friends; (fam.) to be as thick as thieves.

gamelada s. f. a troughful, contents of a trough or porringer.

gameleira s. f. (Braz.) any of various figs.

gamelo s. m. 1. wooden trough. 2. porringer. 3. (Braz., pop.) kite.

gamenhar v. 1. to dandify, dress or smarten (o. s.) up. 2. to behave like a dandy.

gamenho s. m. dandy, fop, beau, coxcomb. ‖ adj. dandified, decorated, smart.

gameta s. m. (biol.) gamete.

gametófito s. m. (bot.) gametophyte.

gametogênese s. f. (biol.) gametogenesis.

gâmico adj. gamic.

gamo s. m. (zool.) fallow-deer, buck, stag.
~ **novo** fawn.

gamocarpelar adj. m. + f. (bot.) gamocarpellary.

gamófilo adj. (bot.) gamophyllous.

gamologia s. f. gamology, treatise or discourse on marriage or matrimony.

gamológico adj. gamologic(al).

gamomania s. f. gamomania.

gamomaníaco s. m. gamomaniac. ‖ adj. gamomaniac(al).

gamopétalo adj. (bot.) gamopetalous.

gamossépalo adj. (bot.) gamosepalous.

gamostilo adj. (bot.) gamostyle.

gamote s. m. (naut.) scope, water shovel.

gana s. f. 1. hunger, appetite. 2. hate, grudge, ill will. 3. spite, rancour. 4. desire, wish, craving.
dar na ~ to have a liking to. **ter** ~ **de alguém** to be enraged at s. o.

ganacha s. f. lower jaw of a horse (plate C 12).

ganância s. f. 1. greed, greediness, rapacity, covetousness, acquisitiveness. 2. gain, profit. 3. advantage. 4. illicit lucre, usury.

gananciar v. to win, obtain, get (avariciously).

ganancioso s. m. greedy or ambitious fellow. ‖ adj. 1. greedy, avaricious, acquisitive. 2. profitable, lucrative. ‖ **-amente** adv. greedily, acquisitively.

ganchar v. to grapple, catch with a hook.

gancheado adj. hook-shaped, aduncous, uncinate, unciform.

gancheiro s. m. (N. Braz.) boat poler.

gancho s. m. 1. hook, grapple, crook, crotch, cramp, cleek, clasp (plates A 1, 2; C 4, 13; E 6; G 2, 5). 2. (tech.) dog. 3. hairpin, agraf(f)e. 4. angle, fish-hook. 5. holdfast. 6. odd job and earnings.
~ **de direita** right hook (boxing). ~ **de ferro** crampon. ~ **do telefone** receiver hook, receiver rest, cradle (plate T 4). ~ **de tornel** swivel-hook (plate G 2). ~ **de tração** draw-hook. **em forma de** ~ hamate. **prender com** ~ to fasten with a hook. **tirar a** ~ to get something with difficulty, in spite of ill will.

ganchorra s. f. 1. boat-hook, tackle-hook, grappling-iron. 2. (sl.) hand.

ganchoso adj. hooked, uncinal, hook-shaped, crooked.

gandaia s. f. 1. rag picking, rag gathering, bin picking. 2. (fig.) vagrancy, idleness. 3. dissolute life.
andar à ~ to mooch about, loaf about, gad about, lounge. **cair na** ~ (Braz., pop.) to go paint the town red.

gandaiar v. 1. to loiter, loaf about. 2. to roam, rove. 3. to abandon o. s. to a profligate life.

gandaieiro s. m. 1. vagrant, vagabond. 2. loafer, idler, lounger. 3. ragpicker.

gandarês adj. of, pertaining to or relative to wasteland and its inhabitants.

gandavo s. m. (N. Braz.) 1. storyteller. 2. (fig.) liar, impostor.

gandola s. f. (Braz.) capote.

gândara, gandra s. f. 1. barren land, wasteland. 2. moor, heath, sandy land.

gandular v. 1. to roam, ramble about. 2. to live at other people's expense. 3. to go begging or cadging.

gandulo s. m. 1. (Braz.) parasite, cadger. 2. mendicant, beggar. 3. (Port., pop.) swindler, sharper. 4. (Port.) street boy, urchin.

ganeira s. f. big branch of a tree.

ganga s. f. 1. (ornith.) hazel-hen, sand-grouse. 2. a species of African rhinoceros. 3. (min.) gangue. 4. native priest in Congo. 5. cotton cloth, jean. 6. (Port.) gentleness, caress.

gangana s. f. (Braz.) old woman.

gangão (I) s. m. (pl. **-ões**) (Braz.) rudimentary corncob.

gangão (II) s. m. used in the adverbial locution: **de** ~ in a hurry, without interruption.
levar alguém de ~ to drag somebody along.

gangarina s. f. (sl.) church.

gangarreão s. m. (pl. **-ões**) (Braz.) disorder, ailment, sickness.

gangético adj. Gangetic: of or pertaining to the Ganges river (India).

gangliforme adj. m. + f. gangliform, ganglioform.

gânglio s. m. 1. (anat.) ganglion(-cell): an aggregation of nerve-cells. 2. (path.) ganglion: globular tumour in the sheath of a tendon.

ganglioma s. m. (path.) ganglioma.

ganglionar adj. m. + f. (med.) ganglial, ganglionated, ganglionary, ganglionic.

ganglionite s. f. (med.) ganglionitis: inflammation of the ganglions.

gangolina s. f. (Braz., pop.) brawl, conflict.

gangolino s. m. (Braz., pop.) 1. slow payer. 2. rogue, rascal.

gangorra s. f. (Braz.) 1. seesaw, teeter (plate P 6). 2. manual cane-mill. 3. snare, trap. 4. bicycle.

gangosa s. f. (med.) gangosa, a mutilating rhinopharyngitis.

gangrena s. f. 1. (med.) gangrene, necrosis. 2. (fig.) cause of ruin or destruction. 3. moral decay.

gangrenado adj. 1. gangrenous. 2. (fig.) perverted, corrupt.

gangrenar v. 1. to gangrene, become gangrenous, canker. 2. to pervert, corrupt. 3. to be seized with gangrene.

gangrenoso adj. gangrenous, gangrenescent.

gângster s. m. gangster.

gangue s. f. (Braz., sl.) gang, group.

ganguês s. m. (N. Braz.) slight indisposition or ailment.

ganhadeiro s. m. day-labourer, journeyman. ‖ adj. earning, profiting.

ganha-dinheiro s. m. (pl. **ganha-dinheiros**) day-labourer, journeyman.

ganhador s. m. 1. bread-winner, earner. 2. winner, conqueror. 3. journeyman, day-labourer. 4. (Braz.) porter. ‖ adj. earning, profiting, winning.

ganhança s. f. 1. greed, covetousness. 2. gain, profit. 3. lucre, usury. 4. advantage.

ganhão s. m. (pl. **-ões**) 1. bread-winner. 2. journeyman, day-labourer. 3. workman. 4. earner.

ganha-pão s. m. (pl. **ganha-pães**) 1. livelihood, means of living, bread. 2. bread-winner. 3. journeyman.

ganha-perde s. m. (Port., in Braz. **perde-ganha**) game in which the loser wins.

ganhar v. 1. to acquire, earn. 2. to get, obtain, receive. 3. to procure, gain. 4. to win, secure, clear, carry. 5. to prevail, succeed. 6. to vanquish, get the better of, overcome. 7. to master, conquer, obtain by victory. 8. to profit, benefit. 9. to take advantage of, encroach upon. 10. to reach, arrive at, attain. 11. to seize, take possession, invade. 12. to deserve, become entitled to. 13. to attract, allure, captivate. 14. to exceed, excel. 15. to get one's due, receive one's pay. 16. to recover, regain, recuperate. 17. to conciliate. 18. to gather, pot. 19. to snatch. 20. to score. ~ **amigos** to acquire friends. ~ **uma batalha** to win a battle. ~ **a corrida com facilidade** (horse-race) to walk over the course. ~ **o cume da montanha** to gain the top of the mountain. ~ **a dianteira a alguém** to get the start of or forge ahead of s. o. ~ **dinheiro** to make or earn money, to draw. ~ **fama** to earn fame. ~ **graça** to grow in favour. ~ **o jogo** to win the game or match. ~ **de longe** to excel by far, to win with a fair margin. ~ **nome e reputação** to get a name and reputation. ~ **o pão de cada dia** to earn one's daily bread. ~ **um prêmio** to win a prize. ~ **tempo** to gain time. ~ **a vida** to earn one's livelihood, to make a living, keep the pot boiling. ~ **a vontade de alguém** to gain someone's friendship or good will. **ele ganha muito dinheiro** he is coining money. **ganhamos nosso dinheiro honestamente** we turned an honest penny by. **não ganhavam o bastante para viver** they paid not their way. **foi ganho arduamente** it was hard-earned. **não ganho muito** I do not earn much. **ganhou terreno** it gained ground. **o navio ganhou velocidade** the ship gathered speed. **o mal ganhado leva-o o diabo** ill-gotten gain never prospers. **quando** ~ **a sorte grande** when my ship comes home. **mas não arrastar** (also ~ **mas não levar**) to win, obtain a prize or victory, without enjoying or taking advantage of it. ~ **um processo** to win a lawsuit.

ganhável adj. m. + f. (pl. **-áveis**) gainable, attainable, obtainable.

ganho s. m. 1. profit, gain, acquisition. 2. advantage. 3. lucre, usury. 4. earnings. ‖ adj. gained, acquired. ~**s e perdas** profit and loss. ~ **de trabalho** mechanical advantage. ~ **de velocidade** increase in speed.

ganhoso adj. 1. greedy, covetous. 2. lucrative, profitable. 3. ambitious. 4. egoistic(al).

ganhuça s. f. (fam.) insignificant earnings or profit.

ganiçar v. Braz. to bark, yelp.

ganido s. m. yelping, yelp, bark, yap, yip, whine.

ganir v. to bark, yelp, yap, yip, whine.

ganja s. f. 1. ganjah, hashish. 2. (Braz.) vanity, pride, arrogance. ‖ adj. 1. conceited, vainglorious. 2. self-assertive.

ganjento adj. 1. vain, conceited. 2. arrogant, haughty.

ganóides s. m. pl. (ichth.) Ganoidei, an order that comprises the sturgeons and paddlefishes.

ganoina s. f. ganoin: bony tissue which produces the enamel-like luster on the scales of ganoid fishes.

gansão s. m. (pl. **-ões**) (also **ganso-do-norte**) (Braz., ornith.) flamingo.

ganso s. m. goose, gander. **ele apanhou** ~ he is quite drunk.

ganso-patola s. m. (pl. **gansos-patolas**) (ornith.) gannet, solan goose.

ganzá s. m. (N. Braz.) rattle (made of a sheet-metal box with little pebbles in it).

ganzepe s. m. (carp.) dovetail, splice joint.

gapinador s. m. (Braz.) native fisherman.

gapinar v. (N. Braz.) to fish, catch fish.

gapó s. m. (Braz., Amazonas) heath and woodland which is deluged in the rainy season.

gaponga s. f. (N. Braz.) ball made of manatee bones, dipped into the water to attract fish.

gapororoca s. f. (Braz., zool.) red brocket.

gapuia s. f. (Braz.) a catching of fish after poisoning the water with **timbó** (timbo).

gapuiar v. (Braz.) to fish (like an aborigine).

garabebel s. m. (ichth.) round pompano.

garabulha s. f. 1. confusion, disorder. 2. misunderstanding. 3. riot, uproar, brawl. 4. scrawling, scrawl. 5. m. intriguer.

garabulhar v. to scrawl, scribble, draw or write carelessly.

garabulhento adj. rough, rugged.

garafunhas s. f. pl. scrawl, scribble, doodle.

garagem s. f. (pl. **-ens**) garage, repair-shop for motor-cars.

garagista s. m. 1. garage man, worker of a garage. 2. proprietor of a garage.

garajau s. m. (Braz.) 1. hen-coop or basket. 2. basket for the transport of crockery.

garaldino adj. (typogr.) of or relating to the type known as old style Roman.

garalhada s. f. cawing of rooks.

garança s. f. 1. (bot.) madder. 2. dye obtained from this plant.

garançar v. to dye with madder.

garanceira s. f. madder field, madder plantation.

garancina s. f. garancin(e) (dyestuff obtained from madder residues).

garanhão s. m. (pl. **-ões**) 1. stallion, steed, stud-horse, sire. 2. (fig.) ladies' man, lady-killer.

garanjão s. m. (pl. **-ões**) (ironic.) very tall and stout fellow.

garante s. m. + f. guarantor, warrantor, guarantee.

garantia s. f. 1. guaranty, guarantee. 2. bail. 3. pawn, pledge, undertaking. 4. security, surety, gage, earnest, lien. 5. right. 6. responsibility. 7. warrant(y). 8. ~**s** pl. privileges. ~ **colateral** collateral security. ~ **por escrito** security in writing. ~ **solidária** joint security. ~ **verbal** verbal security. ~ **fidejussória** fidejussionary guaranty.

garantidor s. m. guarantor, warrantor. ‖ adj. warranting, warrantable.

garantido adj. 1. warranted, vouched for. 2. safe, secure. 3. infallible, assurable. 4. assured, made, pucka. **aquele negócio está** ~ that business is in the bag. **não** ~ unwarranted.

garantir v. 1. to guarantee, warrant, pledge. 2. to vouch for, be answerable for, accept the responsibility for. 3. to (make) secure, give security to. 4. to confirm, certify. 5. to protect, shield, forfend. 6. to affirm, asseverate, assure. 7. to ensure, insure. 8. to forewarn, caution. 9. to undertake. 10. to defend, free from. **a renda lhe foi garantida** the income was ensured to her. **ele garante a execução do programa** he is answerable for the execution of the program. **eles garantem as apostas** they are stake-holders. **ele garante o pagamento** he stands security for the payment. **garanto que você vai gostar da fita** I am sure you will like the film.

garapa s. f. (Braz.) 1. beverage made of the juice of sugar-cane mixed with a few drops of lemon. 2. refreshing drink made with fruit juice. 3. (bot.) squash. 4. (fig.) a cinch, snap. 5. a leguminous tree (Apuleia praecox). **é aquela** ~! it's so easy! it is dead sure!

garapeira s. f. (N. Braz.) a roadside hut selling garapa or fodder for animals.

garatéia s. f. (Braz.) 1. fishing-rod with three angle-hooks on a line. 2. stone anchor.

garatuja s. f. (also garavunha) 1. grimace, wry face. 2. scrawl, scribble, doodle, daub.

fazer ~s to scribble.

garatujar v. to scribble, scrabble, scrawl, doodle.

garatusa s. f. deceit, cheat, trick.

garavanço s. m. wooden winnowing fork or rake.

garavato, gravato s. m. 1. hook, pole with a hook (for picking fruit). 2. dry brushwood, faggot.

garavetar v. to gather dry brushwood.

garaveto (ê) s. m. dry brushwood, kindling, lop, wood chips.

garbo s. m. 1. elegance, garb, dress. 2. gracefulness. 3. distinction, stateliness. 4. nattiness. 5. debonairness. 6. dignity, nobility. 7. (fig.) valour, gallantry, bravery.

garbosidade s. f. 1. elegance, garb, gracefulness. 2. gallantry, valour.

garboso adj. 1. elegant, graceful, doggie, jaunty, dink, natty. 2. distinguished, stately. 3. perk. 4. noble-minded. 5. brave, courageous. ‖ -amente adv. elegantly, gracefully, jauntily.

garça s. f. (ornith.) heron.

garça-azul s. f. (pl. garças-azuis) (ornith.) little blue heron.

garça-bastarda s. f. (pl. garças-bastardas) (ornith.) lesser egret.

garça-branca s. f. (pl. garças-brancas) (ornith.) snowy egret.

garção (I) s. m. (pl. -ões) waiter; potman, garçon (plate R 5).

~ de navio ou trem steward. ~ chefe headwaiter.

garção (II) s. m. (pl. -ões) (ornith.) American egret.

garça-real s. f. (pl. garças-reais) (ornith.) common heron, greater egret.

garceiro s. m. (N. Braz.) secluded lagoon where herons gather, heronry. ‖ adj. heron hunting.

garço adj. light-blue, greenish blue, walleyed.

garçom s. m. = garção 1.

garçonete s. f. 1. waitress; barmaid (plate R 5). 2. stewardess.

garçota s. f. 1. (ornith.) lesser egret. 2. heron chick. 3. heron's feather, aigrette.

gardênia s. f. (bot.) gardenia.

gardingo s. m. (hist.) nobleman (among the Visigoths).

gardunho s. m. (zool.) stone marten, beech marten.

gare s. f. (Gall.) platform of a railway station.

garera s. f. (Braz.) earthen or metal bowl.

garfada s. f. a forkful.

garfar v. to fork, raise or pitch with a fork.

garfeira s. f. fork case.

garfete s. m. (tech.) guide fork (silk spinning machine).

garfiar v. to disappear, sneak away.

garfilha s. f. rim or edge of a coin.

garfo s. m. 1. fork (plates M 1, 8, T 1). 2. pitchfork. 3. saddle grafting, cleft grafting (of trees). 4. bicycle fork (plate B 11). 5. emigrating swarm (of bees, wasps, etc.). 6. (hist.) pronged torture instrument.

~ de telefone cradle. ~ de trinchar carving fork (plate M 1). almoçar de ~ to take a substantial meal. ele é um bom ~ he is a great eater, he plays a good knife and fork.

gargaçalada s. f. gurgling, gush or flow of a liquid (from the narrow mouth of a vessel).

gargajola s. m. lanky lad.

gargalaçada s. f. = gargaçalada.

gargalaçar v. to drink from the bottle.

gargaleira s. f. spigot of a cask or barrel.

gargalhada s. f. laughter, peals or burst of laughter, horse-laugh, shout, cackle, guffaw, cachinnation.

cair numa ~ to burst out laughing, break into a fit of laughter. eles caíram em estrondosa ~ they burst into a gale of laughter. eles o receberam com ~s they received him with roars of laughter. rir às ~s to laugh, outright.

gargalhadear, gargalhar v. to laugh loudly, burst into laughter.

gargalheira s. f. 1. neck-strap or neck-chain for slaves. 2. dog collar.

gargalho s. m. tough sputum.

gargalo s. m. neck of a bottle or pot (plate G 2).

garganta s. f. 1. (anat.) throat, larynx, weasand, throttle, (sl.) whistle (plate C 12). 2. gullet, gorge. 3. (fig.) voice. 4. defile, pass, ravine, abyss (plate M 11). 5. gulf, narrow, strait. 6. m. boaster, braggart, blower, roisterer, bladder. ‖ adj. boastful, swaggering.

ele é um ~ he is a big liar, a boaster. uma ~ blindada (ironic.) a drinker's throat. ele tem boa ~ he has a fine voice. estar com a corda na ~ to be in great straits. estar com dor de ~ to have a sore throat. pôr o cutelo na ~ de alguém to put the knife to somebody's throat. trazer alguém na ~ to be fed up with or to bear a grudge against somebody. molhar a ~ to have a drink.

garganta-de-ferro s. m. (pl. gargantas-de-ferro) (Braz.) 1. (ichth.) tomtate. 2. (ornith.) grand tanager.

gargantão s. m. (pl. -ões) voracious eater, glutton.

garganteação s. f. (pl. -ões) trill, warble.

garganteado s. m. warble, trill. ‖ adj. quavery, warbled.

garganteador s. m. 1. quaverer, warbler. 2. boaster, braggart.

gargantear v. 1. to quaver, warble, trill, shake. 2. to sing in a quavering or warbling manner. 3. (Braz.) to brag, boast, talk big, engross the conversation.

garganteio s. m. warble, trill, quaver.

gargantilha s. f. collar, collarband, neckband, necklace.

gargântua s. m. (fig.) enormous drunkard or glutton.

gargarejamento s. m. gargling.

gargarejar v. 1. to gargle, rinse the mouth or throat, to bubble. 2. (pop.) to court, make love (to a girl who is looking out of her window).

gargarejo s. m. 1. gargling. 2. gargle. 3. courting, love-making (at a window).

gargaúba s. f. (Braz.) yellow fruit of the size of a cherry.

garguitear v. to speak with a quavering voice, chant.

gárgula s. f. grotesque spout, water-spout, gargoyle.

gari s. m. (Braz.) street-sweeper.

garibáldi s. garibaldi: 1. f. loose shirt-waist worn by women and children. 2. f. short smock. 3. m. (tech.) differential pulley block, differential hoist.

garimpagem s. f. (pl. -ens) (Braz.) searching of a region for diamonds.

garimpar v. 1. to search for diamonds or other valuable mineral deposits, pan. 2. (fam.) to pick one's nose.

garimpeiro s. m. 1. diamond or gold seeker, prospector. 2. goldwasher. 3. worker in a gold or diamond mine. 4. clandestine prospector or miner. 5. (fig.) plagiarist.

garimpo s. m. 1. diamond mine, gold mine. 2. (min.) claim, prospect. 3. clandestine prospecting. 4. settlement of miners and prospectors.

gariteiro s. m. keeper of a gambling house.

garito s. m. gambling house.

garlindéu s. m. (naut.) cap (of a mast.)

garlopa s. f. jointer, jointing-plane, jack-plane, horse-plane, trying-plane (plate P 13).

garnacha s. f. robe, gown worn by judges, barristers, clergymen, etc.

garnacho s. m. gaberdine, cloak with sleeves and hood.

garnear v. to polish, burnish (leather).

garnimento s. m. trimmings, decoration, ornament.

garnir v. = guarnecer.

garnisé adj. (Braz.) 1. dwarfish (said of bantam fowl). 2. small and quarrelsome (person).

garo s. m. 1. variety of lobster. 2. pickles prepared from the guts of this crustacean.

garoa s. f. drizzle, mizzle, dribble.

garoar v. to drizzle, sprinkle, mizzle, dribble.

está garoando it is dew-dropping.

garoento adj. drizzling, sprinkling, misty, drizzly.

garota (ô) s. f. girl, lass, flapper; (U.S.A.) broiler, bobby-soxer.

garotada, garotagem s. f. (pl. ~s, -ens) 1. a lot of street boys, gang of street Arabs. 2. pranks and jargon of street boys.

garotar v. 1. to knock about the streets (like street Arabs). 2. to play mischievous tricks. 3. to stroll about, rove freely, prowl about.

garotice s. f. 1. life of a youngster or street Arab. 2. pranks, mischievous tricks, waggery. 3. vulgarism.

garoto (ô) s. m. 1. street Arab, urchin. 2. lad, youngster, kid, shaver. 3. (Braz.) boy. ‖ adj. waggish, mischievous.

garoupa s. f. (ichth.) 1. grouper. 2. serran.

garoupa-bexiga s. f. (pl. garoupas-bexiga) (ichth.) rock hind.

garoupa-rajada s. f. (pl. garoupas-rajadas) (ichth.) hamlet.

garoupa-são-tomé s. f. (pl. garoupas-são-tomé) (ichth.) red grouper.

garoupa-verdadeira s. f. (pl. garoupas-verdadeiras) (ichth.) guasa.

garoupeira s. f. trawling vessel.

garra s. f. 1. claw, talon, pounce, armature, ungula, nippers. 2. (joc.) nail, fingernail, finger, hand, paw, foot. 3. fetlock. 4. (fig.) gripe, clutch. 5. (fig.) tyranny. 6. (tech.) claw, clutch, pawl, grab, fang, grip (plates D 2, G 5). 7. seizure, act of grasping. ~ de acoplamento dent. ~ de correia belt clamp. embreagem de ~s shifting jaw. estar nas ~s de alguém to be in somebody's clutches. pela ~ se conhece o leão you know the lion by his claws. provido de ~s pounced, clawed, taloned. sem ~s fangless.

garrafa s. f. 1. bottle, carboy, flask (plates G 2, V 2). 2. contents of a bottle, a bottleful. ~ para água carafe. ~ bojuda flacon. ~ conta-gotas dropping bottle. ~ empalhada wicker bottle. ~ de Leyde Leyden jar. ~ de vidro cristal decanter. ~ de vinho wine-bottle. ~ térmica vacuum bottle, (Trademark) Thermos. beijar a ~ to crack a bottle. conversar com a ~ to be fond of the bottle, to tipple. vamos tomar uma ~ de cerveja? let us crack a bottle together?

garrafada s. f. 1. contents of a bottle, a bottleful. 2. medicine contained in a bottle. 3. stroke with a bottle.

garrafal adj. m. + f. (pl. -ais) 1. bottle-shaped. 2. ampullaceous. 3. thick, big-bellied.

garrafão s. m. (pl. -ões) large bottle, demijohn, carboy.

garrafaria s. f. 1. a lot of bottles. 2. bottle rack or bottle case. 3. wine-cellar.

garrafeira s. f. wine-cellar, cellaret.

garrafeiro s. m. 1. bottlemaker. 2. bottle dealer. 3. (Braz.) buyer of old bottles.

garrafinha s. f. vial.

garraiada s. f. 1. bullock fight, bullock baiting. 2. a number of bullocks.

garraio s. m. 1. bullock, yearling bull. 2. (fig.) greenhorn, inexperienced man.

garrona s. f. small but strong mare.

garranchada s. f. branches, boughs.

garranchento adj. 1. branched, full of boughs. 2. knotty, gnarled.

garrancho s. m. 1. malady of the hoof. 2. tortuous or gnarled branches. 3. brushwood. 4. cardplayer who passes.

garranchoso adj. gnarled, knotty, tortuous.

garrano s. m. 1. small but strong horse. 2. (fig.) sharper, scoundrel.

garrão s. m. (zool.) hock, tarsal joint in the hind limb (quadrupeds). afrouxar o ~ to become tired or discouraged, lose heart.

garrar v. 1. to loosen, untie, unfasten (shore-fast, mooring-chain). 2. to drift, float (ship). 3. to drag the anchor.

garrear v. (S. Braz.) to shear, clip (sheep).

garreio s. m. (S. Braz.) shearing.

garrida s. f. 1. little bell. 2. iron roller (for moving heavy stones).

garriça s. f. (ornith.) a wren (Troglodytes musculus).

garridice s. f., garridismo m. 1. dandyism, foppishness, foppery. 2. elegance, smartness, dressiness.

garrido adj. 1. dandyish, foppish, smug. 2. elegant, smart, dressy. 3. gallant, amorous. 4. ostentatious, showy. ‖ -amente adv. foppishly, ostentatiously, amorously.

garril s. m. (pl. -is) (Braz.) block or barricade across a road.

garrir v. 1. to resound, echo. 2. to chirp, warble. 3. to ring, clang. 4. to chatter, gossip. 5. to dress extravagantly, show off. 6. to shine, glitter. 7. to frolic, make merry.

garro s. m. 1. (med.) saburra, saburral deposit. 2. fur, tartar. ‖ adj. leprous, itchy.

garrocha s. f. goad, prod.

garrochada s. f. prodding, prick or blow with the goad.

garrochão s. m. (pl. -ões) big goad, prod.

garrochar v. 1. to prod, prick, goad (bulls). 2. to irritate.

garroeira s. f. (N. Braz., sl.) south wind.

garrota s. f. (Braz.) yearling heifer.

garrotada s. f. a lot of heifers.

garrotar v. (also garrotear) to garrote, execute or strangle with the garrote.

garrote s. m. 1. garrote, iron collar. 2. (fig.) agony, anguish.

garrotear v. = garrotar.

garrotilho s. m. 1. (med.) croup, membranous croup, true cough, quinsy. 2. (vet.) strangles.

garrucha s. f. 1. gaffle of a crossbow. 2. (hist.) strappado. 3. (naut.) bowline. 4. blunderbuss, old-fashioned short firearm.

garruchar v. (Braz.) to play overcautiously (at cards).

garruchismo s. m. (Braz.) miserliness, avarice.

garrular v. to chat, gossip, chatter, cackle.

garrulice s. f. 1. talkativeness, garrulity. 2. loquacity. 3. love of gossip. 4. cackle.

gárrulo s. m. chatterbox, prattler, gossip, cackler. ‖ adj. garrulous, talkative, loquacious, chattering, voluble.

garruncho s. m. (naut.) cringle, hank, grommet (plate B 10).

garua s. f. = garoa.

garuar v. = garoar.

garupa s. f. 1. croup, haunch, hindquarters (of a horse), crupper, buttocks, rump, hindleg (plate C 12). 2. saddle-bag.

ir na ~ **do cavalo** to ride pillion. **levar alguém na** ~ to carry a person pick-a-back.

garupada s. f. croupade (of a horse), curvet with the hind legs well under the belly.

garupeira s. f. (Braz.) leather or rawhide strips attached to the backside of the saddle.

garuva s. f. (Braz.) forest tree with a yellow wood.

gás s. m. 1. gas, vapour, fume. 2. (fig.) animation, liveliness. 3. (also ~**es** pl.) wind(iness), flatulence. ~ **de água** water gas. ~ **de combustão** stack gas. ~ **de escapamento** exhaust gas. ~ **de iluminação** lighting gas, coal gas. ~ **carbônico** carbon dioxide. ~ **combustível** fuel or power gas. ~ **hilariante** laughing gas. ~ **lacrimogêneo** tear gas. ~ **motriz** power gas. ~ **pobre** Dowson gas. **ela fechou (abriu) o** ~ she turned out (on) the gas. **bujão de** ~ gas container, gas bottle. **lâmpada de** ~ gas lamp.

gasalhado s. m. 1. shelter, lodging. 2. welcome, kind reception, hospitality. 3. clothes, bed-clothes. 4. (fig.) kindness, benevolence. **dar** ~ **a alguém** to take somebody in, accommodate somebody. **fazer bom** ~ **a alguém** to give a person a kind reception.

gasalhar v. 1. to shelter, lodge. 2. to warm. 3. to receive kindly, welcome. 4. to cover with clothes, wrap up.

gasalho s. m. 1. lodging, shelter. 2. welcome, kind reception. 3. act of clothing or wrapping up. 4. warm clothes, wrapper.

gasalhoso adj. hospitable, generous, kind.

gascão s. m. (pl. -**ões**) 1. Gascon, native or inhabitant of Gascony (France). 2. (fig.) gascon, boaster, braggart, vainglorious person. 3. -**ões** pl. part of a cannon bit.

gasconada s. f. gasconade.

gasear v. 1. to gasify. 2. to affect or treat with gas.

gaseificação s. f. gasification, transformation into gas.

gaseificar, gasificar v. to gasify, transform into gas.

gaseificável adj. m. + f. (pl. -**áveis**) gasifiable.

gaseiforme adj. gasiform, gaseous.

gasganete s. m. (pop.) throat, neck.

gasguita adj. f. (N. Braz.) screaming, shrieking (children or women).

gasista s. m. 1. streetlamp lighter, gaslamp lighter. 2. gas fitter, gas installer.

gasnate, gasnete s. m. (pop.) throat, neck.

gasoduto s. m. gas pipeline.

gasogênio s. m. gazogene, gasogene.

gosógeno s. m. gazogene. ‖ adj. gasogenic.

gasolina s. f. 1. petrol. 2. (U. S. A.) gas, gasoline, gasolene. 3. (sl.) juice. ~ **de avião** straight aviation gasoline. **bomba de** ~ petrol pump, filling station, (U. S. A.) gasoline pump. **motor a** ~ (Brit.) petrol engine; (U. S. A.) gasoline motor, gasoline engine.

gasometria s. f. gasometry, science or art of measuring gas.

gasométrico adj. gasometric(al).

gasômetro s. m. gasmeter, gasometer.

gasosa s. f. soda, soda water, fizz, soda lemonade.

gasoso adj. gaseous, gassy, aeriform, aerial. **estado** ~ gaseity. **água** -**a** aerated water.

gaspacho s. m. well-seasoned bread soup.

gasparinho, gasparino s. m. (Braz.) a smallest share of a lottery ticket.

gáspea s. f. vamp, upper front part of a shoe (plate B 16).

gaspeadeira s. f. (shoemaking) woman who sews the uppers.

gaspear v. to vamp, revamp, patch (shoes).

gastado adj. spent, worn out, used up, spoiled.

gastador s. m. 1. spendthrift, squanderer, prodigal, wastrel, waster, rounder, disburser, expender. 2. dis-

sipater, lavisher. ‖ adj. prodigal, wasteful, lavish, thriftless, extravagant, unthrifty.

gastalho s. m. holdfast, clamp, cramp, clasp.

gastamento s. m. = **gasto.**

gastar v. 1. to reduce in size, diminish. 2. to deteriorate, decay, spoil. 3. to consume, use up, work up. 4. to spend, defray, disburse, expend, dispose, outlay. 5. to destroy, ruin. 6. to wear out, off or down, scuff, batter, eat, devour. 7. to use, employ, apply. 8. to waste, dissipate, squander. 9. to efface, blot out. 10. to digest. 11. to tire, exhaust, enfeeble, sap. 12. ~-**se:** a) to get worn out, wear o.s. off. b) to be spent, worn away. c) to sell well, be in vogue. d) to become spoiled. ~ **cera com ruim defunto** to throw pearls before the swine. ~ **dinheiro de montão** to spend money like water. ~ **dinheiro rapidamente** to make money fly. ~ **em coisas inúteis** to trifle. ~ **em excesso** to overspend, dissipate. ~ **uma fortuna** to squander a fortune. ~ **mais do que ganha** to overrun the constable. ~ **a paciência de alguém** to exhaust somebody's patience. ~ **palavras** to speak in vain. **ela gasta seu dinheiro em jóias** she spends her money on jewels. **o dinheiro foi gasto em doces** the money went in sweets. **ela gasta muito tempo em seu trabalho** she spends much time on her work. **ele gastou dois pares de sapatos** he wore out two pairs of shoes. **nós não gastamos nessa venda** we do not buy in this shop. **dinheiro que se gasta em cigarros** money that goes on cigarettes.

gastável adj. m. +f. (pl. -**áveis**) 1. spendable, expendable. 2. applicable. 3. consumable, usable. 4. wastable. 5. soon used up or worn out.

gasto s. m. 1. expense, expenditure. 2. outlay, disbursement, cost. 3. loss, damage. 4. payment. 5. wear(ing), wear and tear, waste. 6. jadedness. 7. effeteness, consumption. ‖ ad. 1. spent, worn out, used up, jaded, bare, threadbare, shabby, battered. 2. broken-down. 3. tired, decrepit. ~**s imprevistos** incidental expenses. ~**s miúdos** petty charges. ~ **pelo tempo** time-worn, weather-worn. **fazer um grande** ~ to spend high. **fizeram** ~**s supérfluos** they made idle expenses. **nós temos muitos** ~**s** we have many expenses. **jogar para ver quem há de pagar os** ~**s** to play for the reckoning. **o terno é bem** ~ the suit is out at the elbows. **não** ~ 1. unspent. 2. unworn.

gastralgia s. f. (med.) gastralgia, pain in the stomach.

gastrálgico adj. (med.) gastralgic.

gastrectasia s. f. (path.) dilation of the stomach.

gastrectomia s. f. (surg.) gastrectomy.

gastrenterite s. f. (med.) gastroenteritis, inflammation of the stomach and the intestines.

gastrenterocolite s. f. (med.) gastroenterocolitis, inflammation of the stomach, small intestine and colon.

gastrenterologia s. f. gastroenterology.

gástrico adj. (med.) gastric, pertaining to the stomach. **úlcera** -**a** peptic ulcer.

gastrite s. f. (med.) gastritis, gastric fever, inflammation of the stomach.

gastro s. m. (hist.) big-bellied Roman vase.

gastroclínica s. f. (med.) a clinic for dyspeptic persons.

gastrocolite s. f. (med.) gastrocolitis, inflammation of the stomach and colon.

gastroconjuntivite s. f. (vet.) gastroconjunctivitis.

gastrodinia s. f. (med.) gastralgia, gastrodynia.

gastroduodenite s. f. (med.) gastroduodenitis.

gastrólatra s. m. + f. gastrolater, glutton.

gastrolatria s. f. gastrolatry.

gastrologia s. f. gastrology: 1. the science of matters pertaining to the stomach. 2. culinary art.

gastrológico adj. gastrologic.

gastrólogo s. m. gastrologist.

gastronomia s. f. gastronomy, art or science of good eating, epicurism.

gastronômico adj. gastronomic(al), epicurean.

gastrônomo s. m. gastronome, epicure, gourmet, gastronomist.

gastroperitonite s. f. (med.) gastroperitonitis.

gastrópode s. m. (zool.) gastropod, gasteropod: a large class of molluscs (snail, slug).

gastrorréia s. f. (med. gastrorrhea.

gastrose s. f. (med.) gastrosis.

gastrospasmo s. m. (med.) gastrospasm.

gastrozoário s. m. (zool.) gastrozooid.

gástrula s. f. (biol.) gastrula.

gastrulação s. f. (pl. -ões) (biol.) gastrulation, formation of a gastrula.

gastura s. f. (Braz.) 1. prurigo, itching. 2. affliction, tribulation. 3. nervous irritation. 4. shiver.

gata s. f. 1. cat. 2. (ichth.) spotted cat shark. 3. (naut.) mizzen top-sail. 4. catapult. 5. failure (in an examination).
~ **velha** grimalkin. **amarrar a** ~ to go out on a binge. **ela é a ~ borralheira da família** she is the Cinderella of the family, the domestic drudge. **tomar a** ~ to get tipsy. **a** ~**s** (Braz.) with great difficulties, almost not. **andar de** ~**s**, **pôr-se de** ~**s** to crawl on all fours. **chegar a** ~**s** to arrive exhausted. **mastro da** ~ mizzen-mast.

gatafunhar v. to scrawl, scribble.

gatafunho(s) s. m. scribble, scrawl.

gatão, gatarrão, gatarro s. m. big tomcat, big cat.

gata-parida s. f. (pl. **gatas-paridas**) (Braz.) a play of boys imitating the meowing of cats.

gataria s. f. a lot of cats.

gatárla s. f. (bot.) cat-mint, catnip.

gatázio s. m. 1. claw, talon. 2. (fam.) finger, hand.

gateado adj. (Braz.) 1. (of horses) reddish-yellow. 2. (of eyes) greenish-yellow.

gateador s. m. (Braz.) 1. sly hunter. 2. scoundrel.

gatear v. 1. to fasten with iron clamps. 2. to repair with clamps. 3 (hunt.) to approach stealthily.

gateio s. m. (Braz., hunt.) act or method of approaching the game stealthily.

gateira s. f. 1. small opening in a door or wall for a cat to creep in or out of the house. 2. window slit, dormer window. 3. (naut.) scuttle of a locker room, hatchway.

gateiro s. m. cat keeper, person fond of cats. ‖ adj. fond of cats.

gatesco adj. (obs.) catlike, catty.

gateza s. f. lightness, swiftness.

gaticida s. m. + f. cat killer.

gaticídio s. m. cat killing.

gatilho s. m. 1. trigger of a gun. 2. (tech.) dog-head. ~ **de desengate** releasing cam. ~ **de pouca pressão** hair-trigger.

gatimanhos s. m. pl. 1. ridiculous gesture, gesticulation. 2. beckon, nod, motion of the finger or hand.

gatina s. f. gattine, disease of the silkworm.

gatinha s. f. little cat, kitten, pussy.
andar de ~**s** to go or crawl on all fours.

gatinhar v. = engatinhar.

gato s. m. 1. cat, tomcat. 2. miauler. 3. (fig.) cunning fellow, crook. 4. hasp, clamp. 5. error, mistake. 6. (naut.) chain hook. 7. (Port. sl.) lie. 8. (Braz.) misprint, printer's error. 9. (tech.) dog. ~ **de corrente** chain-hook. ~ **de ferro** holdfast. ~ **do guindaste** crane hook. ~ **escaldado da água fria tem medo** a burnt child dreads the fire. ~ **escondido com o rabo de fora** an inadvertently disclosed secret. **isto é** ~ **de três cores** this is a very strange thing. **comer** ~ **por lebre** to be cheated. **cometer um** ~ to pull a boner. **comprar** ~ **por lebre** to buy a pig in a poke. **levar o** ~ **à água** to undertake a difficult task. **ter sete fôlegos como** ~ to be as tough as a cat. **viver como cão e** ~ to live like cat and dog, like hammer and tongs. **muito sabe o rato, porém mais sabe o** ~ every one meets with his match. **quando o** ~ **sai, folga o rato** when the cat's away the mice will play. **ele sabe onde está o** ~ he knows the gist of that trick. **de noite todos os** ~**s são pardos** at night all cats are grey.

gato-açu s. m. (pl. **gatos-açus**) (zool.) ocelot.

gato-de-botas s. m. (pl. **gatos-de-botas**) liar, story-teller.

gato-do-mato s. m. (pl. **gatos-do-mato**) (zool.) margay.

gato-dos-pampas s. m. (pl. **gatos-dos-pampas**) (zool.) pampas cat, pajero.

gato-mourisco s. m. (pl. **gatos-mouriscos**) (zool.) yaguarundi.

gato-pingado s. m. (pl. **gatos-pingados**) (pop.) 1. pall-bearer. 2. unimportant person.

gatorro s. m. big. tomcat.

gato-sapato s. m. contemptible matter or affair.
fazer ~ **de alguém** to make a fool of a person, to despise somebody.

gato selvagem s. m. (pl. **gatos selvagens**) (zool.) wildcat.

gatum adj. catlike, feline.

gatunagem s. f. (pl. -ens) 1. gang of robbers. 2. pilferage, swindling, cheating, robbery.

gatunar, gatunhar v. to steal, pilfer, finger, filch.

gatunice s. f. pilferage, theft.

gatuno s. m. thief, stealer, purloiner, robber, sharper, filch(er), prig.

gaturamo s. m. (ornith.) tanager.

gaturar v. (Braz.) 1. to seize, grasp. 2. to steal, pilfer.

gauchaço s. m. (S. Braz.) skilled horseman, daredevil.

gauchada s. f. (S. Braz.) a lot of gauchos.

gauchagem, gaucharia, gaucheria s. f. (S. Braz.) a gaucho's prowess, noble or daring feat, excellent horsemanship.

gauchar, gauchear v. (Braz.) 1. to lead the life of a gaucho. 2. to speak or behave like a gaucho.

gauchesco adj. (S. Braz.) of, pertaining to or relative to gauchos.

gauchismo s. m. (S. Braz.) idiom, custom or behaviour typical of gauchos.

gauchito s. m. (S. Braz.) little gaucho.

gaúcho s. m. gaucho: native or inhabitant of the pampas of South America.

gauda s. f. (bot.) base rocket, crambling rocket.

gauderiação s. f. (pl. -ões) vagrancy, vagabondage.

gauderiar v. 1. to lead a vagrant life, tramp or rove about. 2. to loaf, loiter or lounge about.

gaudério s. m. 1. merrymaking, feasting. 2. scamp, vagrant, vagábond. 3. (ornith.) cowbird. 4. (Braz.) parasite, toady.

gáudio s. m. 1. merrymaking, feasting. 2. rejoicing, jubilation. 3. merriness, hilarity, mockery.

gaulês s. m. 1. Gaul: native or inhabitant of ancient Gaul. 2. (loosely) Frenchman. 3. the language of ancient Gaul. ‖ adj. Gaulish.

gauro s. m. (zool.) gaur, wild ox of India.

gaussímetro s. m. (phys.) gauss meter.

gavarro s. m. (med.) whitlow, felon, agnail.

gávea s. f. (naut.) 1. topsail. 2. top.
cesto da ~ round top of a mast. **ter as** ~**s arriadas** to have the topsails lowered. **ter as** ~**s içadas** to have the topsails atrip.

gavela s. f. sheaf of grain, bundle of spikes of any cereal (plate C 16).

gaveta s. f. 1. drawer, locker (plates A 13, E 2, M 1, 2). 2. (tech.) slide valve, steam distributor. ~ de caixa (registradora) till. ~ de compensação (tech.) compensating chamber. ~ em D ou em concha (tech.) D-(slide) valve. é uma ~ de sapateiro it is all in a muddle. ele tem o negócio na ~ he is quite sure of this business. ~ do expulsor (typogr.) a sliding device that helps the ejector of the linotype.

gavetão s. m. (pl. -ões) large drawer.

gaveteiro s. m. a built-in chest of drawers.

gavetope s. m. (naut.) gaff-topsail.

gavial s. m. (pl. -ais) (zool.) gavial, Gangetic crocodile.

gavião s. m. (pl. -ões) 1. (ornith.) sparrow-hawk, martlet. 2. (bot.) tendril. 3. the canines or eye-teeth in the upper jaw of a horse. 4. buckle of a stirrup strap. 5. cutting edge of a chisel. 6. (Port.) curved cutting edge of pruning shears. 7. (Braz.) ladies' man, philanderer. 8. (Braz.) cunning individual.

gavião-belo s. m. (pl. gaviões-belos) (ornith.) black--necked falcon.

gavião-caboclo s. m. (pl. gaviões-caboclos) (ornith.) rufous-headed falcon.

gavião-de-coleira s. m. (pl. gaviões-de-coleira) (ornith.) femoral falcon.

gavião-de-penacho s. m. (pl. gaviões-de-penacho) (or- nith.) harpy eagle.

gavião-de-uruá s. m. (pl. gaviões-de-uruá) (ornith.) Everglades kite.

gavião-papa-peixe s. m. (pl. gaviões-papa-peixe) (Braz., ornith.) osprey.

gavião-podre s. m. (pl. gaviões-podres) (ornith.) black--necked falcon.

gavião-real s. m. (pl. gaviões-reais) (Braz., ornith.) 1. harpy eagle. 2. eagle hawk.

gavião-tesoura s. m. (pl. gaviões-tesoura) (Braz., or- nith.) swallow-tailed kite.

gaviãotinga s. m. (ornith.) rufous-headed falcon.

gavião-velho s. m. (pl. gaviões-velhos) (ornith.) black--necked falcon.

gaviete s. m. (naut.) anchor davit.

gavinha s. f. (bot.) tendril, clasper.

gavinhoso adj. (bot.) sarmentose, full of tendrils or claspers.

gaviola s. f. (Braz., sl.) 1. drawer, esp. of a cash register. 2. way of stealing money from a cash register.

gavionar v. (Braz.) 1. to fight shy of (speaking of horses). 2. (fig.) to tramp, rove about.

gavionice s. f. (Braz.) roguery, fraud, knavish tricks.

gavota s. f. gavotte, lively French dance and music.

gaxeta s. f. 1. (naut.) gasket, sennit. 2. (naut.) furling line, seizing. 3. (tech.) stuffing box, packing. caixa de ~ stuffing box.

gazão s. m. turf, sward, lawn.

gaze s. m. (also gaza f.) gauze, tissue. mecha de ~ (med.) tent.

gazeador s. m. 1. warbler, chirper. 2. truant, runaway.

gazeante adj. m. + f. 1. warbling. 2. truant.

gazear v. 1. to chirp, twitter, warble, carol. 2. to play (the) truant, shirk (a lesson or work). 3. to lounge about, loiter about.

gazeio s. m. 1. warbling, chirping, twittering. 2 truancy, shirking, vagrancy.

gazel s. m. (pl. -éis) (also gazal) gazel, ghazal: a type of Oriental lyric poem.

gazela s. f. (zool.) gazelle.

gázeo s. m. 1. light blue, greenish blue. 2. ~s pl. (pop.) eyes. ‖ adj. greenish.

gazeta s. f. 1. gazette, journal, newspaper. 2. truancy.

fazer ~ to play truant. pôr na ~ to make known, bring to public notice, air.

gazetal adj. m. + f. (pl. -ais), gazetário m. of, per- taining to or relative to a gazette or official journal.

gazetear v. 1. to play truant, shirk (a lesson or work). 2. to lounge or loiter about.

gazeteiro s. m. 1. (depr.) hack-writer, hack, mercenary journalist. 2. truant.

gazetilha s. f. 1. section of current events in a newspaper. 2. feuilleton. 3. literary supplement of a daily paper.

gazetilhista s. m. + f. gazetteer, feulletonist.

gazetismo s. m. power of the printed word, influence exerted by newspapers.

gazetista s. m. + f. journalist, gazetteer.

gazo s. m. (Braz. pop.) albino. ‖ adj. albinic.

gazua s. f. picklock, skeleton-key, false key, double key; (sl.) screw (plate F 1).

geada s. f. hoar, frost, hoar-frost, white frost, rime, freeze.
coberto de ~ rime-frosted.

gear v. 1. to frost, chill, freeze slightly. 2. to rime, cover with hoar-frost, form hoar-frost.

geba (ê) s. f. 1. hunch, hunchback, hump. 2. old hunchbacked woman.

gebada s. f. a crumpling or crushing of other people's hats (for fun during carnival).

gebar v. to crush or crumple hats.

gebo (ê) s. m. 1. scamp, ragged or shabby person, ragamuffin. 2. (zool.) zebu. ‖ adj. 1. shabby, ragged. 2. gibbous, humpbacked.

geboso adj. 1. shabby, ragged. 2. gibbous, hump- backed.

gecarcinídeos s. m. pl. (zool.) Gecarcinidae, the land crab family.

geconídeos s. m. pl. (zool.) Gekkonidae, the gecko family.

geena s. f. (bib.) Gehenna, hell.

geento adj. 1. rimy, frosty. 2. subject to hoar-frost.

geio s. m. act of freezing, state of being frozen, ice.

gêiser s. m. geyser, hot gushing spring.

gel s. m. (physical chem.) gel, colloid of jellylike consistency.

gelada s. f. 1. (bot.) ice-plant. 2. hoar-frost, rime. 3. dew. 4. vegetation covered with hoar-frost. 5. (Braz.) refreshing drink made of fruit juices, sherbet.

geladeira s. f. (Braz.) refrigerator, freezer, cooler, ice-safe, ice-chest, ice-box (plates A 2, C 20). na ~ in cold storage.

gelado s. m. 1. sherbet. 2. ice-cream. ‖ adj. 1. frozen, icy, glacial, gelid, algid. 2. frosty, wintry. 3. covered with ice.

gelador adj. freezing, chilly, frosty.

geladura s. f. damage done to the vegetation by hoar--frost.

gelar v. 1. to freeze, congeal, harden into ice. 2. to chill, make cool(er), rime. 3. (fig.) to curdle, cause fright or terror. 4. (Braz.) to deceive, dupe. 5. to be extremely cold, be frozen. 6. to lose one's enthusiasm. 7. to be benumbed by cold. 8. to become unfeeling, insensible, immovable.
o rio gelou the river is frozen over. o sangue me gelou nas veias my blood ran cold. fiquei gelado de pavor I froze with horror.

gelatina s. f. gelatin(e), jelly.

gelatiniforme adj. m. + f. gelatiniform, having the form or constitution of gelatin(e).

gelatinografia s. f. gelatin process.

gelatinoso adj. 1. gelatinous, resembling jelly, jellied. 2. sticky, gummy.

geléia s. f. fruit-jelly, marmalade.
~ **de carne** aspic. ~ **de frutas** jam (plate M 8). ~ **de laranjas** orange-marmalade. ~ **de mocotó** calf's foot jelly. **coberto de** ~ jellied.

geleificação s. f. (biol.) change in the cell wall, converting it into mucilage.

geleira s. f. 1. glacier, ice field, icecap. 2. ice-cave, ice pit. 3. freezing machine, freezer. 4. iceberg.

geleiro s. m. 1. ice manufacturer, ice vendor. 2. (geol.) glacier.

gelha s. f. 1. (rustic) withered grain or fruits. 2. wrinkle, crease, pucker. 3. fold, pleat.

gelidez s. f. icy cold, iciness, frostiness.

gélido adj. 1. very cold, gelid, icy, frosty. 2. frozen, congealed. 3. numb, paralysed. || **gelidamente** adv. gelidly, frostily, etc.

gelo (ê) s. m. 1. ice. 2. excessive cold-(ness), chill(iness). 3. (fig.) indifference, insensibility.
~ **flutuante** icedrift, pack-ice. ~ **movediço** floating ice. **barco quebra-~** (naut.) icebreaker. **um navio bloqueado pelo** ~ an icebound ship. **campo de** ~ ice-field. **chapa de** ~ **flutuante** ice-floe, ice-pack. **depósito de** ~ ice-house. **em** ~ in cold storage. **o** ~ **dos anos** the snow of old age. **o** ~ **do rio se desfaz** the river ice breaks up. **um pedaço de** ~ a piece of ice. **pingente de** ~ icicle. **pista de** ~ ice-rink. **ficar preso no** ~ to freeze in or up. **quebrar o** ~ (fig.) to break the ice. **o rompimento do** ~ the breaking of the ice. **pôr no** ~ to treat s. o. with indifference, give somebody the cold shoulder, ignore.

gelo-seco s. m. (pl. **gelos-secos**) dry ice: solidified carbon dioxide.

gelosia s. f. 1. slatted woodwork, latticework, trellis. 2. window blind, louvre-window, jalousie, Venetian shutter.

gelsêmio s. m. (bot.) Carolina jasmine.

gema s. f. 1. yolk of an egg, yellow, 2. shoot, germ, bud. 3. resin, rosin. 4. gem, precious stone, jewel. 5. (fig.) essential part, pith, vital point.
um inglês da ~ a thorough Englishman. **da** ~ genuine, pure. **ornar com** ~**s** to adorn with gems.

gemação s. f. 1. (biol.) gemmation. 2. act or process of budding. 3. formation or arrangement of buds.

gemada s. f. flip, egg-flip, egg-nog, drink of eggs beaten up with sugar, milk and sometimes an alcoholic liquor.

gemado adj. 1. yolk-coloured, luteous. 2. bejewelled, set with gems. 3. full of buds or germs.

gemagem s. f. (pl. **-ens**) the tapping of a tree (for resin, gum, etc.).

gemante adj. m. + f. bright, brilliant, sparkling.

gemar v. 1. to graft. 2. to prepare with yolks of eggs. 3. to sprout, bud, shoot.

gemebundo adj. groaning, wailing, moaning, sighing.

gemedor s. m. groaner, lamenter.

gemelhicar v. to wail, groan, moan.

gemelos s. m. pl. (anat.) twin muscles, gemelli.

gemente adj. groaning, wailing, moaning, sighing.

gêmeo s. m. 1. twin(s). 2. ~**s** pl. (astr.) Gemini. 3. a compound crystal. 4. span of the thumb and forefinger. || adj. 1. twin. 2 (fig.) identical, equal. **sua irmã -a** his twin sister. **irmão** ~ twin brother. **navio** ~ sister ship.

gemer v. 1. to groan, moan. 2. to wail, lament. 3. to bewail, bemoan. 4. to whimper, whine. 5. to sigh, sob. 6. to creak, squeak, grate, rattle (doors, windows, etc.). 7. to roar, whistle (waves, wind).

gemicar v. to wail, groan, moan.

gemido s. m. 1. groan, moan(ing.) 2. wailing, lamentation. 3. whimpering, whining, wail.
com ~ groaningly.

gemífero adj. gemmiferous: 1. containing or yielding gems. 2 (bot.) producing buds.

geminação s. f. (pl. **-ões**) 1. gemination, arrangement in pairs. 2. doubling. 3. (gram.) doubling of a consonant in the spelling of a word. 4. formation of a compound crystal.

geminado adj. 1. geminate, binate. 2. double, duplicate, twofold. 3. combined in pairs. 4. (bot.) geminous.

geminar v. 1. to geminate, double. 2. to arrange in pairs.

gemiparidade s. f. (biol.) gemmiparity.

gemíparo adj. (biol.) gemmiparous.

gemônias s. f. pl. 1. (Roman hist.) Gemonies. 2. (fig.) public opprobrium. 3. disgrace.

gêmula s. f. (bot.) gemmule.

genal adj. m. + f. (pl. **-ais**) pertaining to the cheek.

genciana s. f. (bot.) gentian.

genciana-amarela s. f. (pl. **gencianas-amarelas**) (bot.) yellow gentian (Gentiana lutea).

gencianácea s. f. plant belonging to the family Gentianaceae.

gencianáceo adj. gentianaceous.

genciana-dos-jardins s. f. (pl. **gencianas-dos-jardins**) (bot.) gentianella.

gendarmaria s. f. gendarmerie, gendarmery.

gendarme s. m. gendarme: 1. (hist.) knight or cavalier at arms, cavalryman. 2. policeman.

gene s. m. (biol.) gene: the factor in a gamete which determines the appearance of a hereditary characteristic.

genealogia s. f. genealogy, filiation.

genealógico adj. genealogical.
árvore -a genealogical tree, pedigree.

genealogista s. m. + f. genealogist.

genearca s. m. progenitor, founder of a family, progeny or species.

genebra s. f. gin, hollands, geneva.

genebrada s. f. gin-fizz, cordial gin.

genebrês, genebrino s. m. Genevan: native or inhabitant of Geneva. || adj. Genevan.

general s. m. (pl. **-ais**) 1. (mil.) general. 2. (fig.) leader, commander, chief. || adj. general.

generala s. f. 1. (fam.) a general's wife. 2. (mil.) a general drum or bugle call, alarm.

generalado, generalato s. m. 1. generalship. 2. (fig.) leadership, management.

general-de-brigada s. m. (pl. **generais-de-brigada**) brigadier-general.

general-de-divisão s. m. (pl. **generais-de-divisão**) major-general.

generalício adj. of or relative to a general.

generalidade s. f. 1. generality. 2. bulk, main body, greatest part. 3. vague statement or phrase. 4 commonness, commonplace. 5. ~**s** pl. rudiments, elementary principles.
sua conversa limitou-se a ~**s** their conversation confined itself to generalities.

generalíssimo s. m. generalissimo, commander in chief, supreme commander.

generalização s. f. (pl. **-ões**) generalization, generalizing, general inference.

generalizado adj. generalized.

generalizar v. 1. to generalize, treat generically. 2. to vulgarize, make commonplace. 3. to unravel, diffuse, spread about. 4. to form generalizations. 5. to universalize. 6. ~**-se** to be or become generalized, become widespread.
a doença generalizou-se the disease struck inwards. **uma opinião muito generalizada** a widespread opinion.

generante adj. m. + f. generant, generative.

generativo adj. 1. generative, procreative. 2. relative to procreation.

generatriz s. f. = geratriz.

genérico adj. 1. generic(al). 2. of or pertaining to a genus. 3. general, common. 4. characteristic, typical.

gênero s. m. 1. genus, class, order. 2. kind, sort, line. 3. (biol.) species, 4. (gram.) gender. 5. style, manner. 6. (philos.) fundamental notion. 7. (joc.) persuasion. 8. condition, quality. 9. ~s pl. goods, commodities, articles.
~s alimentícios foodstuff, edibles, groceries. o ~ humano humankind, humanity, men, our species. ~s principais (com.) staple commodities. uma mulher do seu ~ a woman of her stamp. gosto desse ~ de música I like this kind of music. ~ de vida manner, form of life.

generosamente adv. generously, liberally, nobly, unsparingly, bounteously, effusively openhandedly dar ~ to lavish.

generosidade s. f. 1. generosity, magnanimity. 2. liberality, munificence, bounteousness, ampleness. 3. large-heartedness, large-mindedness. 4. freeness. 5. openhandedness, largess(e). 6. unsparingness. 7. forgivingness.

generoso adj. 1. generous, magnanimous. 2. liberal, munificent. 3. noble, loyal. 4. daring, courageous. 5. fertile, fruitful (soil). 6. openhanded, free, freehanded, lavish, bounteous. 7. frank, freehearted. 8. large-hearted, noble-minded, high-souled. 9. unselfish. 10. charitable.
muito ~ unsparing. vinho ~ strong, sweet wine. ele foi ~ he came down handsome.

gênese s. m., Gênesis m. + f. 1. Genesis: the first book of the Pentateuch. 2. genesis, the coming into being. 3. birth, origin. 4. generation, procreation.

genesíaco, genésico adj. genetic(al), genic.

genética s. f. (biol.) genetics.

genético adj. genetic(al), genic.

genetlíaco s. m. genethliac. || adj. genethliac(al).

genetliologia s. f. astrology.

genetriz s. f. mother.

gengibirra s. f. (Braz.) ginger-ale or gingerbeer.

gengibre s. m. (bot.) ginger.

gengibre-amargo s. m. (pl. gengibres-amargos) (bot.) wild ginger.

gengibre-da-terra s. m. (pl. gengibres-da-terra) (bot.) butterfly lily.

gengiva s. f. gum, tissue which surrounds the necks of the teeth.

gengival adj. (pl. -ais) gingival.

gengivite s. f. (med.) gingivitis.

genial adj. m. + f. (pl. -ais) 1. ingenious, denoting genius, (fig.) brilliant. 2. (fig.) cheerful, jolly, gay.

genialidade s. f. 1. (creative) genius, originality. 2. geniality, kind disposition.

geniculação s. f. (pl. -ões) geniculation, geniculate formation.

geniculado adj. geniculate, geniculated.

gênio s. m. 1. genius. 2. good or evil spirit. 3. talent, natural capacity or skill. 4. nature, character, temper, temperament, humour. 5. intellectual power. 6. (Braz., fam.) irascibility.
~ d'água water sprite. ela é o seu bom ~ she is his good genius. o ~ do mal the devil, demon. mau ~ ill nature(dness), ill humour. de mau ~ bad-tempered, waspish. homem de mau ~ ill--humoured man, ill-natured man. ele tem ~ para a pintura he has talents for painting. ela tem um ~ ruim she is very bad-tempered. o ~ das trevas the prince of darkness.

genioso adj. ill-tempered, ill-natured, cross, surly, wayward.

genital adj. m. + f. (pl. -ais) genital, generative, reproductive, procreative.
órgãos -ais private parts, external genitals.

genitália s. f. genitalia, genitals.

genitivo s. m. genitive, the genitive case.

gênito adj. begotten, produced, created.

genitor s. m. genitor, father.

genitura s. f. 1. generation. 2. procreation, creation. 3. race. 4. origin.

geniturinário adj. (anat., med.) genito-urinary, urogenital.

genoblasto s. m. (biol.) genoblast.

genocídio s. m. genocide.

genoplastia s. f. plastic surgery of the face.

genótipo s. m. (biol.) genotype, the type species of a genus.

genovês, genoês s. m. Genoese: native or inhabitant of Genoa. || adj. Genoese.

genrear v. (Braz., pop.) to live at the expense of a father-in-law or mother-in-law.

genro s. m. son-in-law.

gentaça, gentalha s. f. rabble, mob, populace, riffraff, offscourings.

gentama s. f. (S. Braz.) throng of people, multitude, crowd.

gentarada s. f. (S. Braz.) multitude, crowd.

gente s. f. people, folk. 2. population, humanity. 3. domestics, hands, employees of an establishment. 4. nation, community, tribe. 5. family, clan, kindred, relations. 6. common people, populace. 7. congregation, community. 8. important people. 9. armed forces, men. 10. I, we (always preceded by a).
~ baixa the mob or rabble. ~ de bem honest people, persons of rank. ~ do mar sailors, mariners. ~ moça young people. ~ que não é ~ good-for--nothing people. ~ de trabalho workpeople. tem ~ chamando there is somebody calling. o direito das ~s the law of nations. você também já é ~? are you already somebody? falam como ~ grande they talk like grown-ups. muita ~ many people. ~ rica well-off people. da nossa ~ of our family. a ~ faz o serviço I, we do the job. também ser ~ to have the same rights. trabalhar como ~ grande to work like hell. ser ~ 1. to be somebody, be important. 2. to be a human being.

gentil adj. m. + f. (pl. -is) 1. genteel, well-bred. 2. gentle, noble, gentlemanlike. 3. pure, untainted. 4. pleasant, agreeable, charming. 5. delicate, pleasing. 6. kind, amiable. 7. (fig.) handsome, elegant. 8. soft, bland, tender. 9. meek, pigeon-livered. || ~mente adv. genteelly, gracefully, amiably, debonairly.

gentileza s. f. 1. gentility, genteelness, niceness. 2. courtesy, courteousness. 3. politeness, civility. 4. gracefulness, elegance. 5. chivalrousness. 6. gallantry, valour. 7. kindness. 8. noble or courageous deed. 9. amenity.
quer fazer a ~? will you do me the kindness (or the favour)?

gentil-homem s. m. (pl. gentis-homens) 1. gentleman, well-bred man. 2. nobleman, noble. || adj. elegant, distinguished, genteel, well-bred.

gentílico, gentilício adj. heathen, heathenish, pagan.

gentilidade s. f., gentilismo m. 1. paganism, heathenism, gentiledom. 2. pagan belief or faith. 3. pagans, pagan people.

gentilizar v. to paganize, make or become pagan, heathenize.

gentinha s. f. 1. low people, mob. 2. small fry.

gentio s. m. 1. pagan, heathen. 2. gentile. 3. idolater. 4. (pop.) mass of people, crowd. 5. savages. 6. infidel. || adj. 1. pagan, heathen. 2. idolatrous. 3. savage.

gentuça s. f. (pop.) common people, rable, mob.

genuense s. m. + f., genuês m. Genoese: native or inhabitant of Genoa. ‖ adj. Genoese.

genuflectir, genufletir v. to genuflect, bend the knees, kneel.

genuflector, genufletor adj. genuflecting, geniculate, crooked.

genuflexão s. f. (pl. -ões) genuflection, genuflexion.

genuflexo adj. 1. genuflexuous, bent. 2. kneeling.

genuflexório s. m. praying-chair, praying-stool, kneeler, kneeling board (plate B 2).

genuinidade s. f. genuineness, authenticity, unsophisticatedness, unsophistication.

genuíno adj. 1. genuine, authentic, original. 2. pure, unmixed, not adulterated, unmingled. 3. natural. 4. true, real, sincere, veritable, honest. 5. unsophisticated, unfeigned. 6. solid, entire. ‖ genuinamente adv. genuinely.

genuvalgo adj. (path.) knock-kneed.

genuvaro adj. (path.) bowlegged.

geobotânica s. .f. geobotanics, geographical botany.

geobotânico adj. geobotanical.

geocêntrico adj. (astr.) geocentric(al). ‖ -amente adv. geocentrically.

geociências s. f. pl. geoscience.

geodésia, geodesia s. f. geodesy.

geodésico, geodético adj. geodesic, geodetic.

geodinâmica s. f. geodynamics.

geofagia s. f. geophagy.

geófago s. m. geophagist.

geofísica s. f. geophysics.

geofísico adj. geophysical.

geogenia s. f. geogeny.

geogênico adj. geogenic(al).

geognosia s. f. geognosy.

geognóstico adj. geognostic(al).

geografar v. (Braz.) to describe geographically.

geografia s. f. geography.
~ física physical geography. ~ política political geography.

geográfico adj. geographic(al).

geógrafo s. m. geographer.

geo-história s. f. geo-history of the earth and its evolution.

geóide s. m. geoid.

geologia s. f. geology.

geológico adj. geologic(al).

geólogo s. m. geologist.

geomagnetismo s. m. geomagnetism.

geomancia s. f. geomancy.

geomante s. m. + f. geomancer.

geômetra s. m. + f. 1. geometer, geometrician. 2. (zool.) measuring worm.

geometral s. m. (pl. -ais) (math.) horizontal projection. ‖ adj. geometral, geometrical.

geometria s. f. 1. geometry. 2. textbook of geometry.

geométrico adj. geometric(al). ‖ geometricamente adv. geometrically.

geomorfologia s. f. geomorphology, physiography.

geonomástico adj. of or relative to the names of geographical localities.

geopolítica s. f. political geography.

geoquímica s. f. geochemistry.

georama s. m. georama: hollow globe on the inner surface of which a relief map is depicted.

georgiano s. m. Georgian: 1. one belonging to the Georgian period (England 1740-1830). 2. native or inhabitant of Georgia (Transcaucasian district). 3. language spoken in this district. 4. native or inhabitant of the State of Georgia (U. S. A.). ‖ adj. Georgian.

geórgica s. f. 1. treatise on agriculture. 2. Geórgicas pl. the Georgics of Virgil: a poem on agriculture and rural affairs.

geórgico adj. georgic; Georgian.

georgina s. f. (bot.) a kind of dahlia.

geoso adj. full of ice, cold, frosty, hoary.

geossauro s. m. Geosaurus: a genus of fossil saurians.

geossinclinal s. f. (geol.) geosynclinal, geosyncline: great depression in the earth's crust.

geostática s. f. geostatics.

geotermia s. f. geothermy: internal heat of the earth.

geotérmico adj. geothermic.

geotermômetro s. m. geothermometer.

geotrópico adj. geotropic.

geotropismo s. m. geotropism.

geração s. f. (pl. -ões) 1. creation, procreation. 2. offspring, progeniture, progeny, lineage. 3. generation, age or period of a generation. 4. descent, filiation. 5. genealogy. 6. kind, race, family. 7. formation. 8. prolification. 9. conception. 10. development, production. 11. origination.
~ espontânea autogenesis. a ~ vindoura the rising generation.

gerador s. m. generator, producer, creator, author. ‖ adj. generating, procreant, procreative, reproductive.
~ de gás (tech.) producer. ~ de corrente alternada (electr.) alternator.

geral s. m. (pl. -ais) 1. generality, majority. 2. bulk, main body. 3. commons. 4. (eccl.) general, chief of a religious order. 5. (Braz.) northeaster. 6. f. (theat.) gallery, gods. ‖ adj. m. + f. 1. common, usual. 2. generic. 3. general, universal. 4. sweeping. 5. overhead, gross, broad.
~ dos jesuítas the General of the Jesuits. conhecimentos -ais a general knowledge. correio ~ the General (Post Office). em ~ generally speaking. greve ~ general strike. um tópico de interesse ~ a topic of general interest. ele fez uma limpeza ~ he made a clean sweep of it. de um modo ~ generally speaking. opinião ~ current opinion. como regra ~ as a general rule. em termos -ais in general terms. ~ de circo circus gallery.

geralista s. m. + f. (Braz.) native or inhabitant of Minas Gerais (Central Brazil).

geralmente adv. 1. generally, usually, for the most part, ordinarily, more often than not, as often as not, commonly. 2. broadly. 3. universally.
supõe-se ~ que it passes for current that.

geraniácea s. f. plant of the order Geraniaceae.

geraniáceo adj. (bot.) geraniaceous.

gerânio s. m. (bot.) 1. geranium, crane's-bill. 2. crowfoot. 3. dove's-foot, pigeon-foot.

gerânio-hera s. m. (pl. gerânios-heras) (bot.) ivy geranium.

gerânio-rosa s. m. (pl. gerânios-rosas) (bot.) rose geranium, lady Washington geranium.

gerânio-sangüíneo s. m. (pl. gerânios-sangüíneos) (bot.) blood dock.

gerar v. 1. to beget, engender, father. 2. to generate, procreate. 3. to fecundate, fertilize. 4. to create, produce, develop, form. 5. to originate, cause. 6. to be born. 7. to spawn.
o vício gera a miséria vice produces misery.

geratriz s. f. 1. generator. 2. (math.) generatrix. ‖ adj. generating.

gerbão s. m. (pl. -ões) (bot.) bastard vervain.

gérbera s. f. (bot.) Transvaal daisy.

gerência s. f. 1. act or method of administrating a business enterprise. 2. management, managership, administration. 3. direction, control, supervision.

gerenciar v. 1. to manage, carry on business affairs. 2. to administer, administrate. 3. to direct, run, control, supervise. 4. to act as a manager.

gerente s. m. + f. 1. manager, administrator. 2. supervisor, director, conductor, executive, authority.

gergelim s. m. (pl. -ins) (bot.) sesame, benne. 2. sesame seeds. 3. sesame cake.

gergilada s. f. cookies made of flour, sugar and sesame.

geriatria s. f. (med.) geriatrics, subdivision of medicine which studies old age and its diseases.

gerifalte s. m. (ornith.) Iceland falcon.

geringonça s. f. 1. slang, jargon. 2. gibberish, gabble. 3. badly executed work. 4. misconceived plan.

gerir v. 1. to manage, administrate. 2. to direct, supervise. 3. to transact. 4. to regulate, bring under control.

germanar v. 1. to match, pair. 2. to make equal. 3. to join, unite. 4. ~-se: a) to identify o. s. with. b) to hold a meeting.

germânico s. m. Germanic, language of the Teutonic peoples. ‖ adj. 1. German. 2. Germanic, Teutonic.

germanidade s. f. (obs.) brotherhood or sisterhood, fraternity.

germânio s. m. (chem.) germanium.

germanismo s. m. Germanism, Teutonism: 1. a German idiom. 2. characteristic German behaviour, doctrines or thoughts. 3. imitation of German habits or traits. 4. special fondness for everything German.

germanista s. m. + f. Germanist.

germanização s. f. (pl. -ões) Germanization.

germanizar v. 1. to Germanize, render German. 2. to translate into German. 3. to Teutonize.

germano (I) s. m. 1. brother-german, sister-german, full brother or sister. ‖ adj. 1. german, sprung from the same father and mother. 2. (fig.) true, pure, whole.

irmão ~ blood brother.

germano (II) s. m. Teuton. ‖ adj. Teutonic, Germanic.

germanófilo s. m. Germanophile. ‖ adj. Germanophile.

germanófobo s. m. Germanophobe. ‖ Germanophobe.

germe, gérmen s. m. 1. the rudiments of any organism. 2. germ, embryo. 3. spore, germen, seed-bud. 4. cicatricle of an egg. 5. microbe. 6. (fig.) cause, origin, source. 7. undeveloped state, rudimentariness.

germicida s. m. germicide, substance capable of killing germs.

germinação s. f. (pl. -ões) 1. germination, beginning of vegetation or growth. 2. (fig.) evolution, slow development.

germinador s. m. germinator, apparatus for testing the germinating capacity of seeds. ‖ adj. germinating.

germinadouro s. m. germination room or cellar in a brewery.

germinal s. m. (pl. -ais) (hist.) Germinal, seventh month of the French Revolution. ‖ adj. germinal, germinative, pertaining to or constituting a germ.

germinante adj. m. + f. germinant, germinative, sprouting, developing gradually.

germinar v. 1. to germinate, bud, sprout, burgeon. 2. to begin to grow or develop. 3. to put forth shoots. 4. (fig.) to spring up, begin be born. 5. to generate, originate, produce. 6. to pullulate.

fazer ~ to bud. ~ **novamente** to regerminate.

germinativo adj. germinative, germinant, vegetative.

germiníparo adj. germiniparous, reproducing by germs.

germinista s. m. + f. believer in the germination theory. ‖ adj. germinative, germinant.

gerocomia s. f. (med.) gerocomy, gerocomia, hygiene of old age.

gerodermia s. f. (med.) geroderma, gerodermia, dystrophy of the skin, producing the appearance of old age.

gerontocracia s. f. gerontocracy: 1. government by old men. 2. predominance of older people in any social group.

gertrudes s. f. sg. + pl. (bot.) stone parsley.

gerundial adj. (pl. -ais) gerundial.

gerúndio s. m. (gram.) gerund.

gerundivo s. m. (L. gram.) gerundive.

gervão s. m. (pl. -ões) (bot.) bastard vervain.

gervão-verdadeiro s. m. (bot.) Jamaica vervain.

gesnéria s. f. Gesneria: a large genus of tropical American herbs.

gesneriácea s. f. plant of the family Gesneriaceae.

gesneriáceo adj. (bot.) gesneriaceous.

gessal s. m. (pl. -ais) (also **gesseira** f.) gypsum pit, chalk quarry.

gessar v. to plaster, cover with plaster, parget.

gesseiro s. m. plasterer, stucco-worker.

gesso (ê) s. m. 1. gypsum, plaster of Paris, parget. 2. plaster stone. 3. plaster cast, plaster image or bust. 4. stucco-work.

fazer ornatos em ~ to parget.

gesta s. f. 1. historical feat. 2. exploit, deed. 3. heroic or military deed.

gestação s. f. (pl. -ões) 1. gestation. 2. pregnancy. 3. (fig.) elaboration.

gestante s. f. 1. pregnant woman. 2. pregnancy. ‖ adj. pregnant, gravid.

gestão s. f. (pl. -ões) management, administration, conduct.

~ **dos negócios** management of business. ~ **presidencial** presidency.

gestatório adj. gestatory, of or pertaining to gestation or pregnancy.

cadeira -a gestatorial chair.

gesticulação s. f. (pl. -ões) 1. gesticulation. 2. gesture.

gesticulado s. m. = **gesticulação.** ‖ adj. gesticular, gesticulatory.

gesticulador s. m. gesticulator. ‖ adj. gesticulatory, gesticulating.

gesticular v. 1. to gesticulate, make gestures, to motion. 2. to express or represent by gestures. 3. to mimic, mime.

~ **impacientemente** to gesticulate impatiently.

gesto s. m. 1. gesture, gesticulation. 2. beckon, sign, suggestive motion with the head or limbs. 3. (fig.) look, appearance, expression. 4. air, mien. 5. grimace.

fazer ~s to gesticulate. **um** ~ **de amigo** a friendly turn. **um** ~ **generoso** a generous gesture.

gesto-chave s. m. (pl. **gestos-chave**) (theat.) conventional gestures by actors.

gestor s. m. manager, supervisor, director.

gestose s. f. (med.) gestosis.

geárdia s. f. (zool.) giardia.

giba s. f. 1. hunch, hunchback. 2. (naut.) jib, flying jib.

gibão s. m. (pl. -ões) short jacket, doublet, jerkin.

gibarra adj. m. + f. (Braz., sl.) enormous, very tall.

gibelino s. m. (hist.) Ghibelline.

gibosidade s. f. gibbosity, protuberance, convexity.

gibi s. m. (Braz.) litle Negro boy, street Arab.

gibizada s. f. gang of Negro boys, horde of street Arabs.

gibosidade s. f. gibbosity, protuberance, swelling, hump.

giboso adj. gibbous, gibbose, humped, hunched.

gibreiro s. m. (Braz.) labourer, field or farm hand.

giesta s. f. (bot.) woodwaxen, broom, dyer's weed.

giesta-das-serras s. f. (pl. **giestas-das-serras**) (bot.) Irish broom.

giesta-ordinária s. f. (pl. **giestas-ordinárias**) (bot.) Spanish broom.

giestal s. m. (pl. -ais) broom plantation.

giga s. f. flat and wide wicker basket.

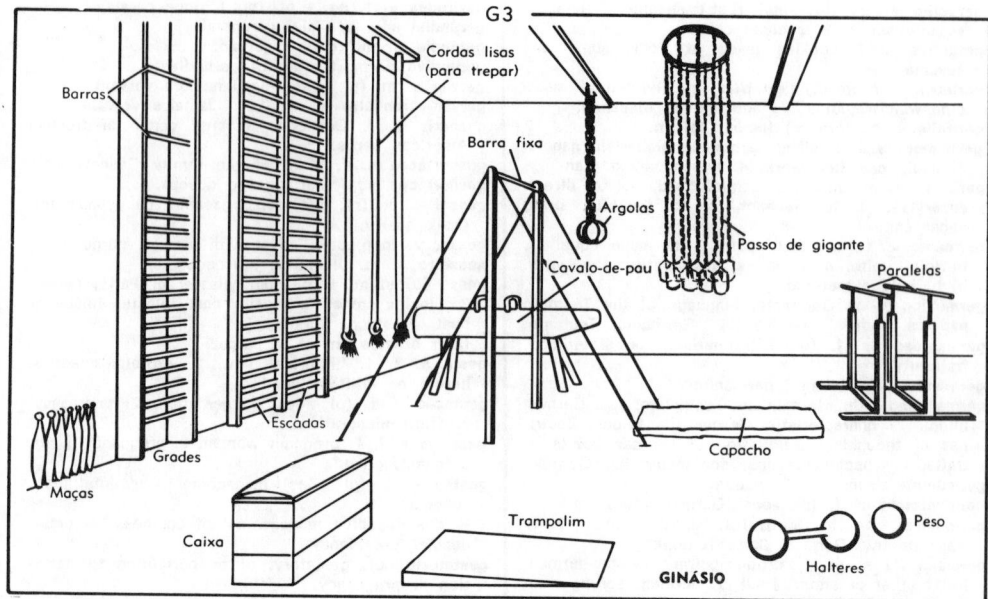

Barras · **Cordas lisas (para trepar)** · **Barra fixa** · **Argolas** · **Passo de gigante** · **Paralelas** · **Cavalo-de-pau** · **Escadas** · **Grades** · **Maças** · **Caixa** · **Capacho** · **Trampolim** · **Halteres** · **Peso** · **GINÁSIO** — G 3

gigantão s. m. (Braz., folkl.) any of the gigantic figures of men, women and boys, made of cardboard, for parading between Christmas and Carnival.

gigante s. m. 1. giant, colossus, titan. 2. (archit.) buttress. 3 .(bot.) girasol, sunflower. ‖ adj. m. + f. 1. giant, gigantic, enormous (plate Q). 2. (fig.): a) admirable, formidable. b) prodigious. c) sublime.

gigantear v. 1. to become gigantic. 2. to grow or thrive very fast. 3. to aggrandize.

gigânteo, gigantesco adj. 1. gigantic, gigantean. 2. enormous, huge; (U. S. A., coll.) jumbo. 3. (fig.) extraordinary. ‖ **-amente** adv. gigantically.

gigantil adj. m. + f. (bot.) giant (said of a variety of maize).

gigantismo s. m. giantism, gigantism.

gigo s. m. 1. wicker basket, hamper. 2. pannier. 3. branch full of fruit.

gigô, gigote s. m. a dish of minced meat.

gila(-caiota) s. f. (also **chila-caiota**) a kind of pumpkin, squash.

gilbarbeira s. f. (bot.) butcher's-broom.

gilete s. f. Gillette (trade name): 1. shaving tackle. 2. razor blade (plate B 7).

gília s. f. (bot.) gilia.

gilvaz s. m. cut or scar in the face, slash.

gilvicentesco adj. of or referring to the Portuguese poet Gil Vicente (1470-1540).

gim s. m. 1. (tech.) rail bender, rail bending machine. 2. gin, corn whisky.

gimnanto adj. (bot.) gymnanthous, having naked flowers.

gimnoblástico adj. (bot.) gymnoblastic.

gimnocarpo adj. (bot.) gymnocarpous.

gimnocaule adj. (bot.) gymnocaulus.

gimnocéfalo adj. (zool.) gymnocephalous.

gimnodermo adj. (zool.) gymnoderm.

gimnodonte adj. m. + f. (zool.) gymnodont.

gimnofiônios s. m. pl. (zool.) Gymnophiona, an order of Amphibia (the family Caeciliidae).

gimnofobia s. f. gymnophobia.

gimnógino adj. (bot.) gymnogynous.

gimnonecto s. m. (zool.) a specimen of the Gymnonectae (naked water animals).

gimnópode adj. m. + f. (zool.) gymnopod.

gimnosperma s. f. (bot.) a specimen of the Gymnospermae.

gimnospérmico, gimnospermo adj. (bot.) gymnospermal, gymnospermous, having naked seeds.

gimnosporado, gimnósporo adj. (bot.) gymnospore.

gimnossomo adj. (zool.) gymnosomous.

gimnuro s. m. gymnure, animal of the genus Gymnura.

gim-tônica s. m. (pl. **gins-tônicas**) (Braz.) gin and tonic.

ginantropo s. m. a hermaphrodite with more female characteristics.

ginasial adj. (pl. **-ais**) gymnasial.

ginasiano s. m. junior grade scholar.

ginásio s. m. gymnasium: 1. place or building for athletic exercises and competitions. 2. school for gymnastics (plate G 3). 3. secondary school.

ginasta s. m. + f. gymnast, teacher of gymnastics or athlete skilled in it.

ginástica s. f. gymnastics, physical exercises, drill(ing).

 ~ **terapêutica** hygienic gymnastics. **fazer** ~ **matutina** to make setting-up exercises. **maças para** ~ Indian clubs. **com** ~ gymnastically.

ginástico adj. gymnastic(al).

gincana s. f. gymkhana.

gineceu s. m. gynaeceum: 1. part of a Greek house reserved for women. 2. (bot.) gynoecium, apocarp.

ginecocracia s. f. 1. gynocracy, gynecocracy, government by women. 2. (fig.) female power or rule.

ginecocrata s. m. + f. gynecocrat, adherent of gynecocracy or government by women.

ginecoscrático adj. gynecocratic, gynecratic.

ginecofobia s. f. gynephobia, morbid aversion to the society of women.

ginecografia s. f. gynecography: 1. gynecology. 2. X-ray diagnosis in gynecology.

ginecográfico adj. gynecographic.

ginecologia s. f. (med.) gynecology.

ginecológico adj. gynecologic(al).

ginecologista s. m. + f. gynecologist.
ginecomania s. f. (med.) gynecomania, satyriasis.
ginecômano s. m. gynecomaniac.
ginecomastia s. f. (med.) gynecomastia.
ginecomasto s. m. man affected with gynecomastism.
ginecopatia s. f. (med.) gynecopathy, disease peculiar to women.
ginecoplastia s. f. plastic surgery (female genitals).
gineta (I) s. f. (zool.) genet: a kind of civet-cat.
gineta (II) s. f. method of riding with short stirrups. **montar à** ~ to ride with short stirrups.
ginetaço s. m. (S. Braz.) elegant and excellent horseman.
ginetário s. m. horseman skilled in riding with short stirrups.
ginete s. m. 1. jennet, small Spanish horse. 2. (hist.) cavalryman, rider. 3. (S. Braz.) rough cowboy saddle.
ginetear v. (Braz.) 1. to sit a horse well. 2. to ride a restive horse. 3. to let a horse prance or curvet.
ginga s. f. scull, oar used with twisting strokes over the stern of a boat.
gingação s. f. (pl. **-ões**) 1. pitching, lurch. 2. swing, swaying movement. 3. scull(ing).
gingador s. m. sculler.
gingante adj. m. + f. pitching, swaying, balancing.
gingão s. m. (pl. **-ões**) 1. loafer, idler. 2. brawler, rowdy. ‖ adj. pitching, swaying, balancing.
gingar v. 1. to roll, pitch. 2. to sway, swing. 3. to jig, jiggle. 4. to waddle. 5. to scull, propel a boat with a scull.
ginge s. m. (Braz. pop.) shivers, cold fits (due to emotional stress).
gingerlina s. f. camlet: fabric of wool with interwoven silk threads.
gínglimo s. m. (anat.) ginglymus, joint which allows motion in one plane only.
gingo s. m. 1. pitching, lurch. 2. swing, swaying movement.
ginitria s. f. (N. Braz.) excellent horsemanship.
ginja s. f. 1. morello, sour cherry. 2. beverage made of morellos. 3. emaciated old man.
ginjal s. m. morello grove.
ginjeira s. f. morello tree, dwarf cherry, morello cherry. **conhecer de** ~ to have a thorough knowledge of.
ginjeira-da-jamaica s. f. (pl. **ginjeiras-da-jamaica**) (bot.) Surinam cherry.
ginjeira-da-terra s. f. (pl. **ginjeiras-da-terra**) (bot.) Jerusalem cherry.
ginjinha s. f. brandy flavoured with mashed morellos.
ginobásico, ginobático adj. (bot.) gynobasic.
ginofobia s. f. gynophobia, aversion to or fear of women.
ginófobo s. m. gynophobe.
ginoforado adj. (bot.) gynophoric.
ginóforo s. m. (bot.) gynophore.
gimnotídeos s. m. pl. (ichth.) Gymnotidae, the electric eel family.
gio s. m. (naut.) transom.
gípseo adj. gyps(e)ous, resembling gypsum.
gipsífero adj. (min.) gypsiferous, bearing gypsum.
gipsita s. f. (min.) gypsum, hydrous calcium sulphate, plaster rock, parget.
gipsófila s. f. (bot.) gypsophila.
gipsografia s. f. gypsography.
gira s. f. 1. stroll, walk. 2. gyration, rotation. 3. m. crackbrained or fickle person. ‖ adj. (Braz.) cracked, queer, crazy; (sl.) balmy, pixilated. **ele é meio** ~ he has got a knock in the cradle.
giração s. f. (pl. **-ões**) gyre, gyration, revolving motion, rotation.
girador s. m. gyrator, swivel.

girafa s. f. 1. (zool.) giraffe. 2. (astr.) Camelopard. 3. (pop.) tall and long-necked person. **ela é uma** ~ she is a hop-pole.
girame s. m. = **gerânio**.
girândola s. f. girandole, catherine wheel, revolving firework.
girante adj. m. + f. gyrant, gyrating, gyral.
girão s. m. (pl. **-ões**) 1. hem, edge, border. 2. shred of cloth, tatter. 3. lappet. 4. long and narrow strip of cultivated land. 5. (her.) equilateral triangle in the center of an escutcheon. 6. (fig.) bosom, lap.
girar v. 1. to go, move, swing or turn (a)round. 2. to circle, move in a circle, spin round. 3. to revolve, gyrate, rotate, wheel, trundle. 4. to whirl, swirl, twirl. 5. to go up and down, walk from one side to the other. 6. to run, follow a course. 7. to shake, agitate. 8. to loiter, ramble about. 9. to labour, toil, work for a living. 10. (Braz.) to go mad, become crazy. 11. to circulate, be or put in circulation (money). 12. to circumscribe, encompass. 13. to traverse, pass through, circuit, travel over. 14. to trade, negociate.
~ **como um pião** to spin like a teetotum. **minha cabeça gira** my head swims. **fazer** ~ (com.) to bring into circulation.
girassol s. m. (pl. **-óis**) 1. (bot.) sunflower, helianthus. 2. (min.) girasol(e), fire-opal. 3. (chem.) litmus.
girassol-de-batatas s. m. (pl. **girassóis-de-batatas**) (bot.) Jerusalem artichoke.
girata s. f. 1. stroll, walk. 2. = **giro**.
giratório adj. 1. gyratory, gyrating, rotative, rotating, rotary. 2. circulatory. 3. whirling, revolving, spinning. 4. swinging. **articulação -a** swivel-joint. **ponte -a** turn (or swing swivel) bridge. **porta -a** revolving door.
girento adj. (N. Braz.) diligent, industrious, hardworking.
gíria s. f. 1. dialect, jargon. 2. lingo. 3. slang, cant, patois, argot. 4. (N. Braz.) interpreter, person who speaks native dialects.
~ **escolar** school-slang. ~ **dos malandros** thieves Latin, jargon. ~ **profissional** jargon.
girice s. f. (Braz.) craziness.
girino s. m. (zool.) tadpole, polliwog.
gírio adj. 1. dialectal, slangy, provincial. 2. pertaining to or relative to slang expressions and persons who use them. 3. (fig.) shrewd, cunning.
giro s. m. 1. rotation, revolution. 2. (mech.) turn. 3. circuit, circulation, circular motion. 4. (com.) turn-over. 5. (mech.) hinge. 6. foursome at billiards. 7. commerce, trade. 8. (fam.) stroll, walk, trip. 9. time, turn, occasion. 10. circumlocution, fuss. ‖ adj. (Port.) funny.
~ **de comércio** commercial intercourse. ~ **gigante** (gym.) slobber swing. **cada um por seu** ~ every one at his turn. **dar um** ~ to take a stroll, to go for a walk.
giro-horizonte s. m. (pl. **giros-horizonte**) (aeron.) gyro horizon.
girolas s. m. + f., sg. + pl. (Braz.) giddy-brained person.
gironda s. f. (zool.) full-grown wild sow.
girondino s. m. (hist.) Girondist. ‖ adj. Girondist.
giropiloto s. m. (aeron.) gyropilot, automatic pilot.
giroscópico adj. gyroscopic.
giroscópio s. m. 1. (phys.) gyroscope. 2. (naut.) gyro compass.
girosela s. f. (bot.) shooting star, American cowslip.
gitano s. m. Spanish gipsy; gypsy.
giz s. m. 1. chalk. 2. (chem.) carbonate of lime. 3. chalk-pencil or chalk-crayon.
~ **de alfaiate** French chalk.

gizar v. 1. to trace or mark with chalk, chalk out. 2. to determine, delineate, limit. 3. to project, plan. 4. (fig.) to indicate, suggest.

glabela s. f. (anat.) glabellum, space between the eyebrows.

glabriúsculo adj. (bot.) glabrescent, somewhat glabrous.

glabro adj. 1. glabrous, bald, hairless. 2. smooth.

glacê s. m. 1. glacé silk. 2. icing. || adj. 1. glossy, lustrous. 2. coated (with icing).

glaciação s. f. (pl. -ões) (geol.) glaciation, consequence of glacial action.

glacial adj. m. + f. (pl. -ais) 1. glacial, icy, freezing, frigid, algid. 2. (fig.) unresponsive, reserved, dispirited. || ~mente adv. icily, frigidly, reservedly, etc. mar ~ polar sea. período ~ ice age. vento ~ bleak wind.

glaciar s. m. glacier.

glaciário adj. of, pertaining to or relative to glaciers, glaciate.

período ~ glacial period.

glaciarista s. m. + f. glacialist.

gladiador s. m. (hist.) gladiator.

gladiar(-se) v. to fight one another with the sword.

gladiatório adj. gladiatorial, gladiatory.

gladiatura s. f. gladiatorship, gladiature, gladiatorism.

gladífero adj. (zool.) having an ensiform appendage.

gládio s. m. 1. two-edged sword. 2. daggerlike sword. 3. (fig.) power, energy, fighting spirit.

gladíolo s. m. (bot.) gladiolus, sword-lily.

glaiadina s. f. (chem.) glutinous substance (to make wine thicker and clearer).

glandado adj. (her.) glandarious.

glande s. f. 1. acorn, mast. 2. any glandiform object. 3. (anat.) glans.

glande-do-mar s. f. (pl. glandes-do-mar) (zool.) acorn barnacle.

glandífero adj. glandiferous, bearing acorns.

glandiforme adj. m. + f. glandiform, glandarious.

glândula s. f. 1. glandula, small gland. 2. (anat., bot.) any secretory organ or vessel.
~ lacrimal lachrymatory gland (plate O). ~ odorífera scent-gland. ~ oleífera oil-bag. ~ pituitária hypophysis, pituitary gland. ~ sudorípara sweat gland. ~ venenípara poison sac (snake).

glandulação s. f. (pl. -ões) glandulation: situation and structure of secretory vessels.

glandular adj. m. + f. glandular, resembling a gland, glandulous.

glandulífero adj. glanduliferous, bearing glands or glandulas.

glanduliforme adj. m. + f. glanduliform.

glanduloso adj. glandulous.

gláucico adj. 1. (chem.) glaucic. 2. glaucous, sea green, bluish green.

glauco adj. glaucous, bluish-green, greenish-blue.

glaucoma s. m. (med.) glaucoma.

glaucomatoso adj. (med.) glaucomatous.

glauconita s. f. (min.) glauconite.

gleba s. f. 1. soil, earth, turf. 2. clod of earth. 3. tract of farming land, glebe. 4. feudal estate. 5. mineral bearing ground.

gleiquênia s. f. (bot.) Gleichenia, a genus of leptosporangiate ferns.

glena s. f. (anat.) glenoid cavity.

glenodina s. f. a genus of Infusoria.

glenoidal, glenóide adj. m. + f., glenóideo m. glenoid(al).

gleucômetro s. m. glucometer: instrument for testing the percentage of sugar in wine or must.

glia s. f. (anat.) glia, neuroglia.

glicemia s. f. (path.) glucemia.

glicéria s. f. (bot.) floating fescue.

glicerina s. f. glycerin(e), glycerol.

glicerofosfatado adj. (chem.) glycerophosphoric, glycerophosphatic.

glicerol s. m. (pl. -óis) glycerol: scientific designation of glycerin(e).

gliceróleo s. m. (pharm.) glycerite: solution or mixture of a medicinal substance in glycerine.

glicínia s. f. (bot.) Chinese wistaria.

glicínia-da-américa s. f. (pl. glicínias-da-américa) (bot.) American wistaria.

glicínia-do-Japão s. f. (pl. glicínias-do-Japão) (bot.) Japanese wistaria.

glicocola s. f. (chem.) glycocoll, glycine.

glicofosfato s. m. (chem.) glycerophosphate.

glicogênese, glicogenia s. f. (path.) glycogenesis.

glicogênico adj. glycogenetic.

glicogênio s. m. (physiol.) glycogen.

glicógeno adj. glycogenic.

glicol s. m. (chem.) glycol.

glicólise s. f. (biochem.) glycolysis: hydrolytic decomposition of sugar.

glicolítico adj. (biochem.) glycolytic.

glicômetro s. m. glucometer, sugar-tester.

glicônico s. m. Glyconic verse. || adj. Glyconic.

glicosado adj. glucosic, pertaining to, of the nature of or producing glucose.

glicose s. f. 1. (biochem.) glucose, dextrose, dextroglucose. 2. grape sugar, corn syrup.

glicosido s. m. (chem.) glucoside, glycosid(e).

glicosúria, glicosuria s. f. (med.) glucosuria, presence of glucose in the urine.

glifo s. m. (archit.) glyph, vertical groove or channel (ornament).

glioma s. m. (path.) glioma, tumour occurring in the connective tissue of the brain, spinal cord, nerves and retina.

glíptica s. f. glyptics: the art of carving or engraving in gems, ivory, etc.

gliptodonte s. m. glyptodon: a genus of extinct American armadillos.

gliptogênese s. f. (geol.) formation of the relief of the earth's surface due to erosion and meteorological agents.

gliptografia, gliptologia s. f. glyptography: 1. art or technique of engraving gems. 2. study of antique engraved gems.

gliptoteca s. f. glyptotheca: building for the preservation of sculptures.

gliquemia s. f. (med., path.) glycemia, glycaemia, presence of glucose in the blood.

global adj. m. + f. (pl. -ais) global: 1. spherical. 2. pertaining to or involving the world. 3. all included. 4. entire, integral, total, over-all.

globicéfalo s. m. (zool.) blackfish.

globífero adj. (bot.) globiferous, bearing round fruit.

globifloro adj. (bot.) globiflorous, having globular flowers.

globo s. m. 1. sphere, ball, globe. 2. terrestrial globe. 3. celestial globe.
~ ocular eyeball, apple or bulb of the eye (plate O). ~ terrestre orb, earth, world, the terrestrial globe. em ~ in the lump, as a whole.

globo-do-sol s. m. (pl. globos-do-sol) (bot.) California poppy.

globosidade s. f. globosity, sphericity, orbicularity.

globoso adj. globose, globous, globular, spherical, round.

globular adj. m. + f. globular, globe-shaped, round, spherical, orbicular, conglobate.

globulária s. f. (bot.) globularia, globe daisy.

globulariácea s. f. plant of the family Globulariaceae.

globulariáceo adj. (bot.) globulariaceous.

globulina s. f. (biochem.) globulin.

globulito s. m. (min.) globulite.
glóbulo s. m. 1. globule, little globe or sphere. 2. (anat.) blood-disk, corpuscle.
globuloso adj. 1. globulous, globular. 2. round. 3. globule-shaped. 4. reduced to globules.
glomerar v. to agglomerate, heap up, gather.
glomérula s. f. fasciculation.
glomerulite s. f. (med.) glomerulitis: inflammation of the glomeruli of the kidney.
glomérulo s. m. 1. (bot.) glomerule, cymose inflorescence. 2. small ball. 3. (anat.) glomerulus.
glomerulonefrite s. f. (path.) glomerulonephritis.
glomo s. m. (path.) glomus.
glória s. f. 1. glory. 2. praise, honour, renown, honourable fame, (fam.) kudos. 3. magnificence, pomp. 4. brightness, splendour. 5. reverence, profound respect. 6. aureole, halo, gloriole. 7. pride, exultant elation. 8. variety of a game of dice. 9. (eccl.) gloria: a) hymn (Gloria in Excelsis Deo) played or sung at the beginning of mass. b) lauds at the end of each psalm.
~ a Deus nas alturas Glory to God in the highest. fazer ~ de to boast of. ir à ~ to lose all, go to pot (gambling). levar a banca à ~ to break the bank (gambling).
gloriabundo adj. ostentatious, vainglorious.
gloriar v. 1. to ascribe glory or honour to. 2. to cover o. s. with glory, win fame. 3. ~-se de to boast o. s. of, pride o. s. on, glory in.
glorificação s. f. (pl. -ões) 1. glorification, magnification, apotheosis. 2. praise, extol(l)ment, exaltation of honour or dignity. 3. canonization, beatification.
glorificador s. m. glorifier, praiser. ‖ adj. glorifying, laudatory.
glorificante adj. m. + f. glorifying, praising, laudatory.
glorificar v. 1. to glorify, extol, apotheosize. 2. to make glorious. 3. to honour, exalt, worship. 4. to bless, beatify, canonize. 5. ~-se to distinguish o. s., gain renown, become celebrated.
gloríola s. f. 1. gloriole, small glory. 2. unmerited esteem or standing.
gloriosa-dos-jardins s. f. (pl. gloriosas-dos-jardins) (bot.) glory lily.
glorioso adj. 1. glorious, illustrious. 2. splendid, bright, resplendent. 3. victorious. 4. honorable, praiseworthy. 5. proud. 6. vainglorious, conceited. ‖ -amente adv. gloriously, etc.
a gloriosa esquadra the glorious fleet.
glosa s. f. 1. gloss. 2. explanation, annotation. 3. comment, commentary. 4. criticism. 5. (poet.) a kind of rondel.
glosador s. m. 1. glossarist, glosser, glossographer. 2. commentator.
glosar v. 1. to comment, gloss. 2. to note down, annotate. 3. to make explanatory notes, interpret. 4. to criticize. 5. (poet.) to use the metric form of a gloss.
glossalgia, glossalgite s. f. (path.) glossalgia, neuralgia in the tongue.
glossantraz s. m. glossanthrax, malignant carbuncle in the mouth and especially on the tongue (horses, cattle).
glossário s. m. 1. glossary, collection of explanations or comments. 2. vocabulary or dictionary of limited scope.
glossarista s. m. + f. glossarist, commentator.
glossema s. f. (phon.) glosseme.
glossiano, glóssico adj. (anat.) glossal, pertaining to the tongue.
glossina s. f. Glossina: a genus of biting flies (e. g. the tsetse fly).
glossite s. f. (med.) glossitis, inflammation of the tongue.

glossocele s. f. (med.) glossocele: swelling and protrusion of the tongue.
glossofaríngeo adj. (anat.) glossopharyngeal, pertaining to the tongue and the pharynx.
glossografia s. f. glossography: 1. the writing of explanatory comments. 2. (anat.) description of the tongue.
glossográfico adj. glossographical.
glossógrafo s. m. glossographer.
glossoial s. m. (pl. -ais) (anat.) glossohyal: the hard basis of the tongue.
glossóide adj. m. + f. tonguelike, glossal.
glossologia s. f. glossology, linguistics, the science of language, glottology.
glossológico adj. glossological.
glossologista s. m. + f. glossologist.
glossópetra s. f. glossolite: tonguelike tooth of a fossilized fish.
glossotomia s. f. (surg.) glossotomy, glossectomy, excision of the tongue.
glote s. f. (anat.) glottis, opening at the top of the larynx.
gloterar v. to caw (like a stork).
glótica s. f. glottology, glossology, linguistics.
glótico adj. glottic, pertaining to the glottis.
glotologia s. f. glottology, linguistics, the science of language.
glotologista s. m. + f., glotólogo m. glottologist.
gloxínia s. f. (bot.) gloxinia.
glucínio s. m. (chem.) glucinum, beryllium.
gluglu s. m. 1. gobbling (of a turkey). 2. gurgling sound (made when emptying a bottle).
gluma s. f. (bot.) glume, a chafflike bract.
glumáceo adj. (bot.) glumaceous.
glumela s. f. (bot.) glume, a chaffy bract at the base of the spikelet of grasses.
glumélula s. f. (bot.) lodicule.
glumiflora s. f. Poales: an order of monocotyledonous plants (grasses and sedges).
glutão s. m. (pl. -ões) 1. glutton, gormandizer, hog-grubber, cormorant, devourer, guttler, (sl.) pig. 2. (zool.) glutton, carcajou. ‖ adj. voracious, gluttonous, edacious.
glute, glúten s. m. gluten: albuminous substance left in wheat-flour which has been washed in water.
glúteo adj. (anat.) gluteal, pertaining to the region of the gluteus muscle.
glutina s. f. (biochem.) gliadin, glutin(e), vegetable gelatin.
glutinar v. to glue, fasten with glue, conglutinate, stick fast, glutinate.
glutinativo adj. agglutinative.
glutinosidade s. f. glutinosity, glutinousness.
glutinoso adj. glutinous, viscid, sticky.
glutonaria, glutoneria, glutonia s. f. gluttony, gulosity, edacity, voracity.
glutônico adj. gluttonous, voracious, greedy.
gnafálio s. m. (bot.) gnaphalium.
gnaisse s. m. (min.) gneiss.
gnáissico adj. gneissic, gneissose.
gnatobdélidos s. m. pl. (zool.) Gnathobdelida, an order of leeches.
gnatodonte adj. m. + f. (zool.) gnathodont.
gnatoplastia s. f. restoring surgery of the maxillaries.
gnatoplegia s. f. (path.) chin paralysis.
gnetácea s. f. shrub or small tree of the family Gnetaceae.
gnetáceo adj. (bot.) gnetaceous.
gnoma s. f. gnome, proverb, aphorism, maxim.
gnômico adj. gnomic(al), containing a maxim.
gnomo s. m. gnome, goblin, sprite, kobold, elf.
gnomologia s. f. gnomology, compilation of or treatise on maxims.

gnomológico adj. gnomologic(al).
gnomólogo s. m. gnomologer, person who practices gnomology.
gnômon(e) s. m. gnomon, sun-dial (plate R 4).
gnomônica s. f. gnomonics, art and science of constructing gnomonic instruments.
gnomônico adj. gnomonic(al).
gnomonista s. m. + f. gnomonist.
gnose s. f. 1. gnosis. 2. science, superior knowledge. 3. mystical knowledge. 4. Gnosticism.
gnosiologia s. f. (philos.) gnosiology, epistemology.
gnosticismo s. m. (philos.) Gnosticism.
gnóstico s. m. gnostic(al).
gnu s. m. (zool.) gnu, wildebeest.
gobelino s. m. gobelin, famous French tapestry and upholstery.
gobo s. m. pebble, flintstone.
godé s. m. small pan of water-colour (plate P 12).
godeme s. m. 1. (Braz. sl.) a blow in the face. 2. nickname given to English people (corrupted from goddam).
goderar v. (N. Braz. pop.) 1. to grasp, get hold of. 2. to scrounge, cadge. 3. to begrudge, envy, watch s. o. eating.
godes adv. (N. Braz.) gratuitously, gratis.
godilhão s. m. (pl. -ões) 1. knot of entangled threads in a fabric. 2. clot of dough or flour (in the soup or any other dish).
godo s. m. pebble, small stone.
godo (ô) s. m. (hist.) Goth: one of an ancient Teutonic people. ‖ adj. Gothic.
goela s. f. 1. throat, gullet, esophagus, chap. 2. (tech.) throat of a blast furnace. 3. (fig.) talker, chatterbox. 4. gulf.
molhar a ~ to moisten one's throat. cair na ~ do lobo to be caught in a trap.
goela-de-pato s. f. (pl. **goelas-de-pato**) a kind of spaghetti in thin strings.
goelar v. 1. to cry out, scream. 2. to open the jaw. 3. to talk much.
goense, goês s. m. + f. Goan(ese): native or inhabitant of Goa. ‖ adj. Goanese.
gofrador s. m. instrument used to imprint the nervures of artificial flowers and leaves.
gofradura s. f. act or process of imprinting the nervures in artificial flowers and leaves.
gofrante s. m. upper part of the gofrador.
gofrar v. to stamp nervures into artificial flowers and leaves.
goga s. f. (N. Braz., pop.) boldness, pugnacity.
gogo (I) s. m. smooth pebble.
gogo (ô) (II) s. m. pip: disease of fowls marked by a scale on the tongue.
gogó s. m. (Braz.) Adam's apple.
gogoroba s. m. (Braz., sl.) drunkard.
gogoso, goguento adj. suffering from pip.
goiaba s. f. guava: fruit of the guava tree.
goiabada s. f. guava jam.
goiabal s. m. (pl. -ais) guava grove or plantation.
goiabeira s. f. (bot.) guava (tree).
goiaca s. f. (Braz.) belt, shoulder-strap.
goiamu(m) s. m. (Braz., zool.) crab.
goianzeiro s. m. (S. Braz.) thicket, underbrush, coppice.
goiano s. m. native or inhabitant of Goiás (Braz.). ‖ adj. of, pertaining to or relative to Goiás.
goiti s. m. (Braz.) pottery tree.
goiva s. f. (carp.) gouge, gouge chisel (plates F 2, M 4).
goivadura s. f. (carp.) gouge hole, gouge groove or furrow.
goivar v. 1. to cut with a gouge. 2. (fig.) to injure severely.

goiveiro s. m. (bot.) 1. stock, stock gillyflower. 2. ten-weeks stock. 3. wallflower.
goivete s. m. (carp.) fluting or grooving plane.
goivo s. m. (bot.) stock or gillyflower blossom.
gol s. m. (sports) goal; run-in (Rugby) (plate F 9).
gola s. f. 1. throat, gullet. 2. collar, shirt-collar (plate R 6). 3. throat-piece (of an armour or uniform). 4. (fort.) gorge, neck of a bastion. 5. (archit.) cornice, cyma, ogee. 6. (tech.) groove of a sheave.
pegaram-no pela ~ e atiraram-no para fora they collared him and threw him out.
golaço s. m. (Braz., ftb.) an extremely skillful goal.
golada s. f. 1. sound, narrow passage of water, gut. 2. navigation channel. 3. draught, sip, gulp.
golconda s. f. Golconda: a rich mine, source of wealth.
gole s. m. 1. gulp, draught, swallow. 2. sip, dram, sup, nip, tiff. 3. ~s pl. (her.) gules: red or vermillion colour.
de um ~ at a draught, holus-bolus. um ~ de água a drink of water. um ~ de cerveja a drain of beer. um golinho de uísque a spot of whisky. em grandes ~s in deep draughts. vamos tomar um ~ let's have a drink.
goleada s. f. (ftb.) great number of goals.
goleador s. m. (ftb.) player who scores many goals.
golear v. (ftb.) to score many goals.
goleiro s. f. (ftb.) goalkeeper (plate F 9).
golejar v. to drink by gulps.
golelha s. f. 1. oesophagus, esophagus, gullet. 2. babbling, prattle.
golelhar v. to chat, chatter, prate.
golelheiro s. m. talker, prattler, babbler.
goleta s. f. 1. inlet, creek, bay. 2. bar at the entrance of a harbour, navigation channel. 3. (naut.) schooner, barkentine.
golfada s. f. 1. gush, outpouring, violent emission of a liquid. 2. vomit, spew. 3. all that is vomited at one time. 4. (fig.) impetuosity, rush.
golfão, gólfão s. m. (pl. -ões) (bot.) fringed bog bean, fringed water-lily.
~ branco (bot.) water-fringe.
gólfão s. m. = golfo.
golfar v. (also golfejar) 1. to throw up, vomit, spew. 2. to gush out, spout out. 3. to expel, spurt. 4. to belch forth in great quantities. 5. to utter a violent tirade. 6. to emit, issue. 7. to run in spurts, rush. 8. to burst forth, appear impetuously.
golfe (ô) s. m. (sport) golf.
campo de ~ golf-links. taco para jogar ~ golf-club.
golfinho s. m. 1. (ichth.) dolphin, cow-fish, porpoise. 2. (mil. hist.) brass handles of a piece of ordnance (often formed like dolphins). 3. miniature golf.
golfista s. m. + f. golfer.
golfo (ô) s. m. 1. gulf, large open bay. 2. (bot.) water poppy.
Gólgota s. m. 1. (bib.) Golgotha. 2. (fig.) place of torment and suffering. 3. (fig.) anguish, pain.
goliardo s. m. regular frequenter of taverns, tippler, toper. ‖ adj. tavern-tainted, toping.
golinho s. m. 1. (fig.) thimbleful. 2. tot.
um ~ de uísque a spot of whisky.
golo s. m. (pop.) = gole.
golpada s. f. (pop.) 1. heavy blow, fierce stroke. 2. gush, spout.
golpe s. m. 1. blow, stroke. 2. wound, injury. 3. whack, beat, smite, knock, hit, lick, gash. 4. slash, incision. 5. stab, thrust. 6. shock, crisis. 7. misfortune, ill luck. 8. sip, draught. 9. impetus, rush.
~ acertado home-thrust. ~ de azar clap. ~ decisivo knockdown, knock-out. ~ de Estado coup d'état. ~ de mão surprise attack, coup de main. ~ de mar heavy sea (breaking over the deck). ~ de

mestre master-stroke. ~ **de vento** gust of wind, gale. ~ **do baú** marriage for economic interest. **acertar o** ~ **do baú** to strike home. **dar um** ~ to have a whack at. **de** ~ all at once, suddenly, at one dash. **desfechar um** ~ **mortal** to deal a mortal blow. **ele tem bom** ~ **de vista** he has a good (straight) eye. **com um** ~ **cruel** at one fell swoop. **num rápido** ~ **de vista** at a quick glance. **ele errou o** ~ he failed to hit, he missed his aim. **com** ~ **seguro** with sure touch. **de um só** ~ at one stroke. **queimar no** ~ to become angry. **um** ~ **de sorte** a lucky hit, a stroke of luck. **vir de** ~ to arrive unexpectedly.

golpeado adj. knocked down or out, struck.

golpeão s. m. (pl. **-ões**) (Braz.) 1. tracing saw. 2. deep draught of wine.

golpear v. 1. to strike, beat, knock, hit, clap, slog, thump, whack, smash, bang. 2. to wound, injure. 3. to cut, slash, stab. 4. to cut out. 5. to grieve, afflict, anguish.

golpelha s. f. 1. large basket made of esparto grass. 2. (obs.) she-fox, vixen.

goma s. f. 1. gum, latex. 2. (med.) gumma: a kind of tumor (syphilis). 3. starch. 4. starch-paste, glue, dextrine. 5. any clarifying agent for wine. 6. tapioca. 7. (plant path.) gummosis.

goma-arábica s. f. gum arabic.

goma de mascar s. f. (also **chicle**) chicle, chewing gum.

gomado adj. sticky.

gomador s. m. 1. paper gluer (person). 2. paper gluing machine.

goma-elástica s. f. India rubber, gum-elastic.

goma-laca s. f. shellac, French polish.

gomar v. 1. to starch, stiffen with starch. 2. to shoot, sprout.

goma-resina s. f. (pl. **gomas-resinas**) gum resin.

gombô s. m. (bot.) okra, gumbo.

gomeiro s. m. 1. gummaker or gum seller. 2. (Braz., pop.) boaster, braggart.

gomeleira s. f. (hort.) shoot from the roots, sucker, water shoot.

gomia s. f. crescent-shaped Moorish dagger.

gomiada s. f. thrust or stab with a Moorish dagger.

gomil s. m. (pl. **-is**) pitcher, narrow-mouthed jar.

gomo s. m. 1. (bot.) bud, shoot, gemma, button. 2. each pulpy segment of citrus fruits. 3. section. ~ **de alho** clove of garlic.

gomose s. f. (Braz., plant path.) gummosis.

gomosidade s. f. gummosity.

gomoso adj. 1. gummy, gummous. 2. segmented, divided into segments like citrus fruits.

gônada s. f. gonad (of human beings).

gonadia s. f. gonad (of animals).

gonalgia s. f. (med.) gonalgia, pain in the knee.

gonçalo-alves s. m., sg. + pl. (Braz., bot.) 1. ash leaf (Astronium fraxinifolium). 2. its wood (highly appreciated for cabinet works).

gôndola s. f. 1. gondola, Venetian boat (plate B 8). 2. (Braz., pop.) omnibus. 3. (Braz.) flatcar: a railway freight-car with low sides.

gondoleiro s. m. gondolier, man who rows a gondola.

gonete s. m. gimlet, auger, point.

gonfalão s. m. (pl. **-ões**) gonfalon, standard with two or tree streamers.

gonfocarpo s. m. Gomphocarpus: a large genus of asclepiadaceous herbs or shrubs.

gongar v. to gong (out).

gongilar adj. (bot.) 1. gongylar: of or relative to the gongyli. 2. gemmiparous.

gôngilo s. m. (bot.) gongylus.

gongo s. m. gong, disk-shaped instrument of percussion.

gongorar v. (N. Braz.) = **goderar**.

gongórico adj. (lit.) Gongoresque, gongoristic.

gongorismo s. m. Gongorism: affected style introduced into Spanish literature in imitation of the Spanish poet Góngora y Argote (1561-1627).

gongorista s. m. + f. (lit.) Gongorist.

gongorizar v. to imitate the style of the Spanish poet Góngora, write in a gongoristic manner.

gonguinha s. f. (Braz.) beverage made of sugar-cane juice mixed with manioc flour.

gonguito s. m. (Braz., ichth.) small variety of catfish.

gonialgia s. f. (med.) gonalgia: pain in the knee.

gonicele s. f. (med.) gonyocele: synovitis or tuberculous arthritis of the knee.

gonídia s. f. (bot.) gonidium.

gônio s. m. (anat.) gonion: the tip of the angle of the lower jaw.

goniógrafo s. m. goniograph: instrument for recording angles.

goniometria s. f. goniometry: science and method of measuring angles.

goniométrico adj. goniometric(al).

goniômetro s. m. goniometer: instrument for measuring angles.

gônis s. m. (ornith.) gonys: lower outline of the bill.

gonocele s. f. (med.) gonocele, spermatocele.

gonócito s. m. (biol.) gonocyte: primitive reproductive cell of the embryo.

gonococia s. f. (med.) infection and disease caused by gonococci.

gonocócico adj. (med.) gonococcal, gonococcic.

gonococo s. m. (med.) gonococcus.

gonocorismo s. m. (biol.) gonochorismus.

gonorréia s. f. (med.) gonorrhea, gonorrhoea; (sl.) clap, the claps.

gonorréico adj. (med.) gonorrheal, gonorrhoeal.

gonu s. m. plant of the family Cucurbitaceae.

gonzo s. m. hinge, gate hinge, joint, loop. **pino do** ~ pintle, joint pin. **fora dos** ~**s** off the hinges.

gorar v. 1. to miscarry, go wrong, end in failure, abort. 2. to frustrate, disappoint. 3. (also ~**-se**) to grow addle or rotten (eggs). 4. to be or become useless, make ineffectual.

gordacho, gordaço, gordalhaço, gordalhão, gordalhudo, gordalhufo, gordanchudo, gordão s. m. (Braz., pop.) fatty, pot-belly, paunch. ‖ adj. fubsy, chuffy, squab, roly-poly.

gordinho s. m. (Braz.) harvest fish. ‖ adj. fattish, plump.

górdio adj. (hist.) Gordian.

gordo s. m. 1. corpulent man, fatty. 2. any fatty substance. 3. lard, suet, tallow. ‖ adj. 1. obese, adipose, fat. 2. corpulent, plump(y), fleshy, squabby, rotund, gross, thick, stout (plate Q). 3. unctuous, oily, greasy, porky. 4. rich (soil). 5. (fig.) vigorous, courageous. 6. big, bulky, huge, considerable. 7. important. 8. dirty. 9. well-fed, high-fed, well-lined. **dia** ~ flesh-day. **domingo** ~ Shrove Sunday. **um dote** ~ a fat dowry. **leite** ~ whole milk. **nunca o tinha visto mais** ~ (fam.) I've never seen him in my life. **terra -a** fertile ground.

gorducho s. m. = **gordacho**.

gordura s. f. 1. obesity, adiposity. 2. corpulence, fatness, fleshiness, ful(l)ness, plumpness. 3. grease, fat, shortening. 4. fatty matter or substance, blubber. ~ **de leite** butterfat. ~ **de porco** lard. ~ **supérflua** (of horses) lumber. ~ **vegetal** vegetable fat, vegetable tallow. **sem** ~ fatless. **uma mancha de** ~ a grease-spot. **capim-**~ molasses grass.

gordural s. m. (pl. -ais) (Braz.) land covered with molasses grass.

gordurento adj. 1. unctuous, consisting of or containing fat. 2. fatty, greasy, oily. 3. covered or soiled with fat.

gorduroso adj. greasy, fatty, lardy, oily, oleaginous, sebaceous, adipose.

gorete s. m. (Braz.) a weakfish (Cynoscion petranus Mir. Rib.).

gorgolão s. m. (pl. -ões) 1. gush, gulp. 2. flow, bubbling. 3. small jet, blast. 4. morsel, bite, mouthful.

gorgolar v. 1. to pour out in gushes, spout. 2. to bubble, flow with a gurgling noise. 3. to eject in a jet.

gorgolejante adj. gurgling.

gorgolejar v. 1. to gurgle, utter gurgling sounds. 2. to drink noisily, gulp down.

gorgolejo s. m. 1. gurgling, gurgle. 2. act or sound of gurgling.

gorgoleta s. f. narrow-mouthed earthen pitcher.

gorgolhão s. m. = gorgolão.

gorgolhar v. = gorgolar.

gorgomila s. f., gorgomilo(s) m. (pl.) throat, gullet.

górgona, górgone s. f. 1. (Greek myth.) Gorgon. 2. (fig.) female monster, repulsive woman.

gorgôneo adj. (poe.) Gorgonian, Gorgonesque.

gorgônia s. f. (zool.) Gorgonia: a genus of polyps.

gorgonzola s. m. Gorgonzola (cheese).

gorgorão s.m. (pl. -ões) grosgrain, fabric of silk and wool.

gorgorejo s. m. guttural sound or utterance.

gorgulho s. m. (ent.) weevil.

gorila s. m. (zool.) gorilla (also gorilha).

gorja s. f. 1. throat, gullet. 2. (naut.) head of the keel.

mentir pela ~ to lie shamelessly.

gorjal s. m. (pl. -ais) gorget: neckpiece of an armour.

gorjala s. m. 1. (N. Braz., folklore) gigantesque sprite. 2. (fig.) big and gluttonous person.

gorjeador s. m. warbler, caroler, songster. ǁ adj. warbling, trilling.

gorjear v. 1. to warble, quaver, trill. 2. to sing, hum a tune. 3. to chirp, twitter. 4. to produce harmonious sounds.

gorjeio s. m. 1. warble, trill, quaver. 2. twitter, chirp. 3. (fig.) children's babble.

gorjeira s. f. lace or cloth for the neck worn by women.

gorjeta s. f. 1. drink-money, tip, gratuity, perquisite. 2. reward, gratification. 3. chisel.

dar ~ to tip.

gorjete s. m. shirt-front, (fam.) dickie.

gorne s. m. (naut.) sheave-hole in a pulley.

gornir v. (naut.) to draw the ropes through the sheave-holes.

gornope s. m. (N. Braz.) sip, dram, draught.

goro (ô) adj. 1. addle, rotten (egg). 2. (fig.) frustrate, vain, useless.

gororoba s. f. (Braz.) 1. (bot.) balaustre. 2. sluggard, idler. 3. coward. 4. poorly prepared meal.

gorovinhas s. f. pl. pleats, folds, creases, wrinkles.

gorra s. f. 1. cap, beret. 2. (Port.) bark of the spurge-laurel. 3. rope spun from esparto grass (used in rural districts to support the buckets of a conveyor).

meter-se de ~ to introduce upon, to connive, plot jointly against.

gorro s. m. cap, bonnet.

gorutubano s. m. offspring of Brazilian mestizos.

gosma s. f. 1. pip (disease of fowls marked by the formation of scales on the tongue). 2. strangles, inflammation of the respiratory mucous membranes

(of young horses). 3. (pop.) spittle, expectoration, gastrorrhea.

gosmar v. 1. to spit, expectorate. 2. to hawk up (the phlegm). 3. to cough up, clear one's throat coughing.

gosmento adj. 1. stopped up, obstructed (with phlegm). 2. spitting a lot, expectorating frequently. 3. weak, sickly.

gostador s. m. taster.

gostar v. 1. to relish, find palatable or savoury. 2. to consider tasteful or graceful. 3. to enjoy, feel pleasure, be pleased with. 4. to feel affection or friendship for, hold dear, be fond of, like, fancy, adore. 5. to approve, confirm. 6. to get on well with, be in accord with. 7. to be suitable or fit for. 8. to taste, try, prove. 9. to give pleasure to, delight. 10. to be attracted by, be captivated. 11. to sympathize with, be congenial to. 12. to like well.

~ da água to take to the water. ~ mais to like better. ~ muito to hold dear. ~ muito de alguma pessoa ou coisa to be fond of. ele gosta de ajudar he helps willingly. ela gosta das suas amigas she clings to her girl friends. é isto que a gente gosta de ouvir that is welcome news. ele gosta de velejar he goes in for sailing. as crianças gostam dele children take to him. você está gostando disso? does it meet with your approval? eu ~ia de dar um passeio I am game to go for a walk. eu ~ia de fazê-lo I am concerned to do it. eu ~ia que você viesse I should like you to come. gosto de jogar tênis I go in for tennis. gosto muito de frutas I adore fruit. ~ muito de ler to be very much given to reading. não gosto de ratos I cannot abide rats. você gostou do almoço? did you relish the dinner? ele fez cara de quem comeu e não gostou he looked as sour as verjuice.

gostável adj. m. + f. (pl. -áveis) 1. palatable, savoury, tasty. 2. tasteful, graceful. 3. agreeable, likeable. 4. appetizing, enticing, tempting.

gosto (ô) s. m. 1. taste, gustation. 2. flavour, relish, savour(iness), sapidity. 3. pleasure, enjoyment, fondness. 4. sympathy, liking, propensity. 5. spice. 6. raciness. 7. elegance, gracefulness. 8. good taste or manners. 9. character, style. 10. aesthetical discernment. 11. inclination, leaning, propensity. 12. skill, proficiency. 13. kindness, favour.

~ forte tang. ~ pelos livros bookishness. achar ~ em to take a liking to. a seu ~ to one's liking. bom ~ good taste. com ~ with pleasure, readily. dá ~ ver aquilo it is a real treat to see that. que falta de ~ what bad taste. ~s não se discutem there is no accounting for tastes, tastes differ. não há ~ sem desgosto no joy without annoy. levar em ~ to approve of. uma brincadeira de mau ~ a bad joke (or jest). muito a meu ~ much to my taste. sem ~ 1. in bad style. 2. insipid, tasteless. se é de seu ~ if it pleases you. tomar ~ por to get a taste for. o vinho tem ~ de rolha the wine tastes of the cork (is corked). sinto o ~ de pimenta I taste pepper in it. ter ~ de to taste of. virei com muito ~ I shall gladly come. viver a seu ~ to live at ease.

gostosão s. m. (pl. -ões) (Braz., sl.) 1. lover. 2. bus (Rio de Janeiro).

gostos-da-vida s. m. pl. a variety of plum.

gostoso adj. 1. tasty, savoury, flavourous. 2. appetizing, palatable, sapid. 3. tasteful. 4. delicious, pleasant, delightful. 5. pleasing, relishing. ǁ -amente adv. pleasantly, delightfully, etc.

este bolo é ~ this cake eats well. ele deu uma risada ~a he laughed heartily.

gostosura s. f. 1. great pleasure or enjoyment. 2. palatability. 3. (fig.) delightful thing or event.

gota (ô) s. f. 1. drop. raindrop, dewdrop. 2. minim. 3. blob. 4. tear. 5. (archit.) gutta, pendant spherical or cylindrical ornament. 6. (med.) gout. ~ **a** ~ by drops. ~ **das mãos** (med.) chiragra, gout in the hands. ~ **dos pés** (med.) podagra, gout in the feet. **uma** ~ **de sangue** a tear of blood. **eles beberam uma** ~ **de vinho** they had a drop of wine. **beber o cálice da amargura até a última** ~ to empty the bitter cup of sorrow. **parecer-se com duas** ~**s d'água** to resemble one another like two peas. **isto é uma** ~ **d'água num oceano** this is quite an insignificant matter, it is a mere drop in the ocean.

gota-coral s. f. (pl. **gotas-corais**) (med.) epilepsy.

gotado adj. 1. sprinkled with drops. 2. bedewed. 3. ornamented with drops. 4. guttate.

gota-serena s. f. (pl. **gotas-serenas**) (med.) amaurosis.

gotear v. = **gotejar.**

goteira s. f. 1. gutter, eaves. 2. gutter pipe. 3. leak, hole in the roof through which water drops. 4. drain. 5. drip, drip-moulding. ~ **em forma de "V"** arris-gutter.

gotejamento s. m. drip(ping), dropping, trickle.

gotejante adj. m. + f. dropping, dripping, trickling.

gotejar v. 1. to drip, trickle, drop. 2. to ooze. 3. to spill, pour, run out. 4. to distil.

gótico adj. Gothic: 1. of or pertaining to the Goths or their language. 2. (typogr.) black-letter. 3. (archit.) (also **ogival**) characterized by pointed arches.

gotinha s. f. droplet.

goto s. m. 1. (anat.) glottis, mouth of the windpipe. 2. a kind of Japanese lute. **dar no** ~ to go down the wrong throat.

gotoso adj. gouty.

governação s. f. (pl. **-ões**) 1. act or effect of governing. 2. government, administration. 3. management, guidance, direction.

governadeira s. f. good housekeeper, economical housewife.

governado adj. 1. directed, guided, conducted. 2. ruled, governed. 3. economical, frugal.

governador s. m. 1. governor, ruler, commander. 2. Lord-lieutenant. ‖ adj. governing.

governadora s. f. 1. governor's lady, female governor. 2. king's governess or female tutor. 3. (female) regent.

governamental s. m. (pl. **-ais**) supporter of a government. ‖ adj. governmental, civil.

governança s. f. = **governo.**

governanta s. f. (also **governante**) 1. female housekeeper. 2. nurse, governess, tutoress; (fig., hum.) dragon, chaperon, duenna.

governante s. m. potentate, ruler, governor.

governar v. 1. to govern, rule, command. 2. to exercise authority over, dominate. 3. to direct, guide. 4. to control, police. 5. (mus.) to conduct. 6. to administer, manage. 7. to regulate. 8. (naut.) to steer, navigate, take the helm. 9. ~**-se** to take care of one's interest or affairs, govern o. s., accommodate o. s. to. ~ **bem a sua casa** to be a good housekeeper. ~ **mal** to misgovern. ~ **um navio** to steer a ship. ~ **um negócio** to manage a business. ~ **paternalmente** to father. ~ **tiranicamente** to domineer. ~**-se por** to be determined by. ~**-se pelas circunstâncias** to act according to circumstances. **os que governam** the ins. **o navio governa bem** the ship steers well. **governa tua boca segundo tua bolsa** you must cut your coat according to your cloth. **ele é um homem que se governa pela mulher** he

is a henpecked man. **ela mesma governa sua vida** she shifts for herself.

governativo adj. governamental.

governatriz s. f. 1. managing, governing or ruling woman. 2. directress. ‖ adj. (f. of **governador**) 1. governable, guidable. 2. directive. **prudência** ~ sound policy, prudent conduct.

governável adj. m. + f. (pl. **-áveis**) 1. governable, guidable. 2. tractable, docile. 3. steerable.

governicho, governículo s. m. (Braz.) 1. inapt government. 2. (fam.) sinecure.

governismo s. m. 1. governmentalism. 2. authoritative government or rule, dictatorial administration.

governista s. m. + f. 1. governmentalist. 2. supporter of a government.

governo (ê) s. m. 1. act or effect of governing. 2. government, authority, domination. 3. superior administration, ministry, cabinet. 4. form of administration of public affairs. 5. (naut.) rudder, helm. 6. direction, guidance. 7. brake. 8. jurisdiction of a governor. 9. period of government. 10. command, control management. 11. regency, dominion. 12. rule of conduct, behaviour. 13. instruction. ~ **absoluto** autarchy, autocracy. ~ **autônomo** self--government. ~ **da casa,** ~ **doméstico** menage, household. ~ **mecânico** (tech.) mechanical action (or control). ~ **de um navio** steerage of a ship. **do** ~ government owned. **a queda do** ~ the overthrow of the government. **para o seu** ~ for your guidance. **sirva-lhe de** ~ take your measures in accordance.

gozação s. f. (Braz., pop.) the act of laughing at a person, a mockery.

gozada s. f. (Braz., pop.) a single act of laughing at a person.

gozado adj. (Braz., sl.) 1. comical, funny. 2. amusing, entertaining. 3. agreeable, pleasant.

gozador s. m. (Braz., fam.) enjoyer, idler. ‖ adj. happy-go-lucky, easy-going.

gozar v. 1. to derive pleasure from. 2. to enjoy o. s. 3. to take delight in. 4. to divert o. s. 5. to profit, benefit. 6. to take advantage of, avail o. s. of. 7. (vulg.) to come, achieve an orgasm. 8. ~**-se de** to find pleasure in. ~ **férias** to vacation, be on holiday, go on holiday. **ele** ~**á as férias em janeiro** he will take his vacation in January. **ele goza de boa saúde** he enjoys good health. **ele goza de má fama** he is in evil repute, he is under a cloud. **ele goza a estima dos amigos** he enjoys the esteem of his friends.

gozo (ô) s. m. 1. joy, enjoyment. 2. pleasure, delight. 3. satisfaction, contentment. 4. utility, usefulness. 5. (Braz., fam.) joke. 6. possession, usufrutc. 7. little street-dog, cur. **saltar de** ~ to leap for joy. **estar em pleno** ~ **de seus direitos** to be in full enjoyment of one's rights.

gozoso adj. 1. joyful, joyous. 2. merry, pleasant, delightful. 3. satisfied, content. 4. mirthful, jolly.

grã (I) s. f. 1. kermes; scarlet colour or dye. 2. kermes insect. 3. scarlet cloth. 4. (pop.) grain of wood.

grã (II) adj. abbr. of **grande** (used in compounds as: **Grã-Bretanha** Great Britain, United Kingdom. **Grã--Cruz** Grand Cross, etc.).

graal s. m. 1. grail. 2. (myth.) Holy Grail.

grabato s. m. miserable couch, plank bed, straw bed.

graça s. f. 1. favour, goodwill. 2. benevolence, kindness, sweetness. 3. pardon, mercy, clemency, indulgence. 4. affability, charm, loveliness, allurement. 5. beauty, handsomeness, prettiness. 6. elegance, gracefulness, genteelness, breeding. 7. Christian name. 8. wit, witticism, esprit, pleasantry.

9. humour. 10. drollery, jest, fun, joke. 11. grace, divine mercy or forgiveness. 12. ~s pl. thankfulness, thank(s). 13. (myth.) the (three) Graces. 14. dignity, distinction.
~ **de Deus** divine right. **~s a Deus** thanks be to God. **pela ~ de Deus** by the grace of God. ~ **ridícula** poor joke. **~s à sua bondade!** thanks to your kindness! **~s a ele enxergo de novo** thanks to him I can see again. **~s a sua recomendação** by virtue of his recommendation. **ação de ~s** thanksgiving. **no ano da ~ de** in the year of grace. **as ~s de uma língua** the beauties of a language. **de ~** without return, for nothing, gratis, gratuitous. **nem de ~** not even as a gift. **quase de ~** for next to nothing. **estar nas ~s de** to be in the grace of, to be in someone's favour. **não estar para ~s** to be in bad humour. **ele não é para ~s** he is not to be trifled with. **implorar a ~** to appeal to the mercy of. **obtive sua ~** I found favour with him. **perder a ~ de** to fall into disgrace. **por ~** for fun. **com pouca ~** rudely. **sem ~** graceless(ly), stale, barren. **qual é sua ~?** what's your name, please? I haven't the advantage of your name. **ela tem muita ~** she is very graceful. **isto não tem ~** that is no fun. **o livro não tem ~** the book has no guts in it. **trabalhei de ~** I worked for a song. **não vejo ~ nisto** I do not see the fun of it.
gracejador s. m. jester, joker. wag. ‖ adj. frolic.
gracejar v. to joke, jest, banter, crack jokes, droll, frolic, fun, trifle.
nunca se deve ~ de maneira que ofenda one must not carry a joke too far. **eu somente tencionava ~** I only intended to joke.
gracejo s. m. 1. mirth, merriness. 2. gracefulness. 3. jocundity, jocosity, good humour. 4. joke, jest, witticism, drollery, frolic, fun, waggery, play. 5. pleasantry.
fazer ~s to make fun. **ele gosta de fazer ~s** he likes his little jokes. **ela não gosta de ~s** she cannot take a joke. **isto passa de ~** that is past joking.
graceta s. f. bon-mot, jest, joke.
grácil adj. m. + f. (pl. **-eis**) 1. gracile, slender, slim. 2. delicate, fine. 3. weak, frail. 4. subtle.
gracilidade s. f. 1. gracility, slenderness, slimness. 2. delicateness, gracefulness. 3. weakness, frailty. 4. subtlety.
gracilifoliado adj. (bot.) angustifoliate.
gracilípede adj. m. + f. (zool.) gracilipede, slender-footed.
gracilirrostro adj. (zool.) gracilirostrate.
graciosidade s. f. 1. grace, gracefulness. 2. amenity, pleasantness. 3. elegance, beauty. 4. benevolence.
gracioso s. m. mocker, jester, joker. ‖ adj. 1. gracile, gracious, graceful, elegant, charming. 2. darling, cute, lovely, adorable. 3. pleasant, agreeable. 4. kind, benevolent, sweet. 5. witty, facetious, jocular. 6. gratuitous. ‖ **-amente** adv. charmingly, pleasantly, kindly, wittily, gratuitously, etc.
eles fizeram o serviço -amente they made the job without charge. **fazer-se ~** to ingratiate o. s. with.
graçola s. f. 1. bad joke, stupid jest. 2. m. scoffer, mocker.
graçolar v. to crack poor (bad) jokes, banter, scoff.
grã-cruz s. f. (pl. **grã-cruzes**) 1. designation of the highest rank in many orders of knighthood. 2. decoration indicating this rank. 3. m. dignitary wearing such a decoration.
gradação s. f. (pl. **-ões**) 1. gradation. 2. gradual increase or diminution. 3. continuous passage or transition. 4. degree or relative position in any series. 5. regular progress or advance.

gradador s. m. 1. harrower. 2. harrow, grader.
gradadura, gradagem s. f. act or process of levelling the ground with a harrow, harrowing.
gradar v. 1. to level (the ground), harrow, drag. 2. to increase (volume), grow. 3. to run to seed, form grains.
gradaria s. f. railing, grating, lattice-work or trellis-work, paling, pale-work.
gradativo adj. gradual, divided into steps, step by step, gradational, gradatory. ‖ **-amente** adv. gradually.
grade s. f. 1. rail(ing), barrier (plate R 8). 2. grille, grate. 3. grid, screen (plate P 2). 4. paling, trellis-work, grating. 5. locutory (of a convent or prison). 6. painter's easel. 7. harrow, grader. 8. tile mould. 9. (vet.) cauterizing or searing iron. 10. curry-comb.
~ **de manjedoura** hay-rack (plate E 11). ~ **de ripas** espalier. ~ **de vime** wattle. **fechar com ~** to wattle, rail. **finalmente foi posto entre as ~s** finally he was locked in jail. **ir para as ~s** to run in.
gradeado s. m. grating, screenwork. ‖ adj. enclosed, fenced in, grated.
gradeamento s. m. 1. act of effect of enclosing with a rail or paling. 2. = **gradeado.**
gradear v. 1. to fence in, bar, enclose with a rail or paling. 2. to shut in. 3. to cauterize a horse.
gradecer v. 1. to run to seed, form grains. 2. to increase (volume), grow. 3. to become well-developed or mature.
gradeira s. f. nun who chaperons lay-sisters in the locutory.
gradeza s. f. 1. quality of being well-developed or full of seed. 2. bigness, thickness.
gradiente s. m. (meteor.) gradient: 1. rate of alteration of a variable magnitude or the curve that represents it. 2. rate of change of a meteorological element.
gradil s. m. (pl. **-is**) (Braz.) low railing or fence, hoop edging.
gradim s. m. (pl. **-ins**) gradine, toothed chisel used by sculptors.
gradinada s. f. 1. cut or blow with a sculptor's chisel. 2. act of giving finishing touches with a gradine.
gradinar v. 1. to smooth, finish with a gradine. 2. to work with a sculptor's chisel.
grado s. m. will, wish, liking (frequently used in the adverbial locutions: **de bom ~** willingly, readily. **a seu mau ~** against his will. **mau ~** unwillingly. **mau ~ seu** in despite of you.
graduação s. f. (pl. **-ões**) (also **graduamento** m.) 1. graduation: a) division into degrees, arcs, circumferences). b) measurement of degrees. c) admission to a degree (college, university). 2. gradation scale. 3. social prominence, (high) standing. 4. hierarchy, rank, grade.
graduado adj. 1. arranged in steps or degrees. 2. high standing, distinguished. 3. superior. 4. graduate, having received an academic or professional degree. 5. honorary (title, rank). 6. graduated, marked with degrees (scale). 7. calibred. 8. shaded.
graduador s. m. graduator, scaler, grader, calibrator. ‖ adj. graduatory.
gradual s. m. (pl. **-ais**) (eccl.) gradual: 1. antiphon sung or read between the Epistle and the Gospel of the Mass. 2. office-book containing a collection of such responsories. ‖ adj. gradual, gradatory, successive, progressive, slow. ‖ **~mente** adv. gradually, successively, progressively, slowly.
graduando s. m. (Braz.) student who is about to graduate, commencer.

graduar v. 1. to graduate, calibrate, gauge. 2. to mark with degrees, divide into grades. 3. to classify, arrange in groups. 4. to compare, collate. 5. to change gradually. 6. to regulate or improve by degrees. 7. to nominate to a honorary rank or position. 8. to commence, confer a degree upon (college, university). 9. to proportionate, blend. 10. to gradate. 11. (mil.) to echelon. 12. ~-se to be graduated, receive an academic degree.
ele graduou-se advogado he was admitted to the bar (became a lawyer).

grã-ducado s. m. (pl. **grã-ducados**) grand-duchy. grand-dukedom.

grã-duque s. m. (pl. **grã-duques**) grand-duke.

grã-duquesa s. f. (pl. **grã-duquesas**) grand-duchess.

graeiro s. m. grain (corn, lead, etc.).

grafar v. 1. to express by letters, form letters or words by writing. 2. to spell or write correctly.

grafema s. m. (phon.) grapheme.

grafia s. f. 1. manner or style of writing. 2. spelling of a word. 3. orthography.

gráfica s. f. graphic art(s).

gráfico s. m. 1. graph; graphic representation of physical or sociological phenomena. 2. chart, plan, diagram. 3. typographer, printer. ‖ adj. graphic(al). ‖ **graficamente** adv. graphically.
oficina ~ printery, printing plant.

grafila, grafilha s. f. inscription on the border of a coin.

grã-finismo s. m. (pl. **grã-finismos**) Braz., pop.) 1. quality, act or habit of upper-class people. 2. snobbishness, snobbery.

grã-fino s. m. (pl. **grã-finos**) (Braz., pop.) 1. upper--class man, aristocrat. 2. snob. 3. would-be-gentleman, swell, high hat, dude (coll.). ‖ adj. spiffy, tony.

grafismo s. m. 1. manner of writing words. 2. peculiar manner of writing. 3. manner of tracing a line, of drawing.

grafista s. m. (Braz.) designer, draughtsman.

grafita s. f. graphite, black lead, plumbago.
mina de ~ black lead mine.

grafítico adj. graphitic, containing graphite, plumbaginous.

grafito s. m. (archeol.) graphite, graffito: rude inscription or drawing found on rocks, etc.

grafologia s. f. graphology.

grafológico adj. graphologic(al).

grafólogo s. m. graphologist.

grafômetro s. m. graphometer: instrument for measuring angles.

graforréia s. f. (path.) graphorrhea.

grafostática s. f. graphostatics: science applying graphic methods to the solution of statical problems.

grafoteca s. f. 1. museum of engravings. 2. engravings exhibition room (of a museum).

grainha s. f. kernel or stone of any fruit, pip.

graipu s. m. (Braz.) variety of bee.

grajau s. m. (Braz.) 1. hen-coop or basket. 2. basket for the transport of crockery.

grajéia s. f. 1. fondant, candy. 2. (pharm.) sugar--coated pill.

gral (I) s. m. mortar, pounder.
mão do ~ pestle of a mortar.

gral (II) s. m. 1. grail. 2. (myth.) Holy Grail.

gralha s. f. 1. (ornith.) carrion crow. 2. (typogr.) an inverted letter in the composition. 3. (fig.) chatterbox, blab, gossip (used exclusively with regard to women).

gralha-calva s. f. (pl. **gralhas-calvas**) (ornith.) rook.

gralha-cinzenta s. f. (pl. **gralhas-cinzentas**) (ornith.) hooded crow.

gralhada s. f. 1. cawing, croaking, chirping. 2. (fig.) din, racket, clamour. 3. chattering, prattle.

gralha-de-bico-vermelho s. f. (pl. **gralhas-de-bico-vermelho** (ornith.) Alpine chough.

gralhar v. 1. to caw, croak, chirp. 2. (fig.) to make much noise, shout, clamour. 3. to chatter, babble.

grama (I) s. f. (bot.) 1. grass. 2. grama, grama-grass. 3. carpet grass, Louisiana grass.
como ~ grassy. **cobrir de** ~ to sward. **coberto de** ~ swardy.

grama (II) s. m. gram, gramme: unit of mass and weight in the metric system.

grama-branca s. f. (pl. **gramas-brancas**) (bot.) 1. bent grass, marsh-bent. 2. concho grass.

grama-cheirosa s. f. (pl. **gramas-cheirosas**) (bot.) vetiver.

grama-da-praia s. f. (pl. **gramas-da-praia**) (bot.) seaside bent.

grama-da-terra s. f. (pl. **gramas-da-terra**) (Braz., bot.) French weed.

grama-de-adorno s. f. (pl. **gramas-de-adorno**) (bot.) spike grass.

gramadeira s. f. flax brake, swingle, hackle.

grama-de-jardim s. f. (pl. **gramas-de-jardim**) (bot.) 1. St. Augustine grass. 2. cloud grass.

gramado s. m. 1. lawn, turf, grass-plot. 2. grass, green. 3. sward, turf, sod. 4. football field. ‖ adj. 1. grassy, swardy. 2. scutched, beaten with a swingle.

gramagem s. f. (typogr.) = **gramatura**.

grama-inglesa s. f. (pl. **gramas-inglesas**) (bot.) St. Augustine grass.

grama-metro s. m. (pl. **gramas-metro**) grammetre.

grama-massa s. f. (pl. **gramas-massa**) (phys.) unit of mass.

gramão s. m. (bot.) dog's-tooth, Bermuda grass.

grama-pêlo-de-urso s. f. (pl. **gramas-pêlo-de-urso**) (bot.) snake's-beard.

gramar v. 1. to scutch, swingle, hackle, break hemp. 2. (fam.) to swallow, gulp down. 3. (pop.) to devour. eat hastily. 4. to suffer, endure, bear. 5. to scamper along, beat a path. 6. to plant grass, to sward, sod, turf. 7. (Port., pop.) to cry out, clamour.

grama-tapete s. f. (pl. **gramas-tapete**) (bot.) carpet grass.

gramática s. f. 1. grammar. 2. grammar book, treatise on grammar.

gramatical adj. m. + f. grammatic(al). ‖ ~**mente** adv. grammatically.

gramaticalismo s. m. exaggerated grammaticalness.

gramaticão s. m. (depr.) grammaticaster, petty grammarian.

gramaticar v. 1. to grammaticize. 2. to teach grammar. 3. to render grammatically correct.

gramático s. m. 1. grammarian, grammatist. 2. (depr.) grammaticaster. ‖ adj. grammatic(al).
~ **pedante** grammaticaster.

gramaticologia s. f. scientific examination of grammatical problems.

gramaticológico adj. grammatologic(al).

gramaticologo s. m. grammaticologer.

gramatiqueiro s. m. (Braz.) grammaticaster, petty grammarian.

gramatiquice s. f. grammaticism, grammatical subtility, grammatical rigorism.

gramatista s. m. grammatist, grammarian.

gramatologia s. f. treatise on grammatical fundamentals (letters, syllables, the alphabet, spelling, reading, writing).

gramatológico adj. of, pertaining to or relative to grammatical fundamentals.

gramatura s. f. (typogr.) basic weight of paper (indicated in grams per square meter).

grameal s. m. (pl. **-ais**) (N. Braz.) second-growth vegetation, brushwood.

gramínea s. f. gramineous plant, grass, specimen of the grass family.

gramíneo adj. gramineous, grasslike, grassy.

graminha s. f. (bot.) 1. rough meadow grass, bird grass. 2. carpet grass, Louisiana grass.

graminha-do-mato s. f. (pl. **graminhas-do-mato**) (bot.) ginger-grass.

graminhar v. to work with the marking gauge.

graminho s. m. (carp.) marking gauge (plate F 2).

graminícola adj. living on fields or camps.

graminifólio adj. (bot.) graminifolious.

graminiforme adj. m. + f. graminiform.

graminoso adj. rich in grass, grassy, covered with grass.

gramita s. f. (min.) amphibole.

gramofone s. m. gramophone, phonograph.

caixa de membrana de ~ sound-box.

gramômetro s. m. divider: instrument used by draughtsmen for dividing lines, etc.

grampeador s. m. stapler.

grampeadora s. f. (typogr.) stitcher: a stitching machine.

grampeamento s. m. (typogr.) the stitching of books with metallic wire.

grampear v. to fasten with clamps or staples, to clip, cramp.

máquina de ~ stapler, stapling machine.

grampo s. m. 1. cramp iron, clamp, cramp, clasp (plates M 4, P 15). 2. brace. 3. dog, crampon. 4. staple. 5. clip. 6. holdfast.

~ **para cabelo** hairpin, body pin (plate A 1).

grana s. f. (S. Braz., sl.) money.

granada s. f.: 1. (mil.) grenade, bomb, shell. 2. (min.) garnet. 3. garnet-red silk fabric.

~ **de mão** hand grenade, fireball, egg-bomb, tickler.

granadeiro s. m. 1. (mil.) grenadier. 2. (mil.) soldier on duty in the advanced guard. 3. (fig.) tall, stout man.

granadilho s. m. granadilla wood.

granadina s. f. 1. female native of Granaḍa. 2. grenadine, thin fabric or silk.

granadino s. m. Granadine: native or inhabitant of Granada. || adj. 1. Granadine. 2. garnet-red.

granador s. m. granulating machine (used in powder making).

granal adj. m. + f. (pl. **-ais**) granular, granulate.

granalha s. f. 1. granulation. 2. small shot, granulated metal. 3. coin-blank.

granar v. 1. to grain, granulate. 2. (Braz.) to produce seed grains (maize, etc.).

granatária s. f., precision balance, analytical balance. || adj. accurate, precise, exact (used with regard to balances).

grandalhão, grandão adj. (pl. **-ões**) huge, very large or tall, enormous.

grande s. m. 1. wealthy or influential person. 2. grandiosity, sublimeness. 3. grandee, Spanish or Portuguese nobleman. || adj. 1. great, large, bulky. 2. big. 3. long. 4. tall, high (plate Q). 5. vast, extensive, ample. 6. grown-up. 7. lasting, permanent. 8. powerful, mighty. 9. grave, serious. 10. ponderous. 11. heavy, weighty. 12. immoderate, excessive. 13. heroic(al). 14. abundant, plentiful. 15. intense. 16. magnanimous. 17. good, kind. 18. respectable. 19. eminent, grand. 20. famous, renowned. 21. (sl.) sparking, bally, bouncing, whacking || ~**mente** adv. greatly, generously, much, very much, etc.

~ **chuva** violent or heavy rain. ~ **coisa!** quite an event! **estive em** ~ **aperto** I was hard pressed.

estar em ~**s apuros** to be in a peck of troubles. **um** ~ **cientista** a fine scholar. **colheita muito** ~ bumper crop. **ela é** ~ **para a sua idade** she is tall for her age. **ele não é uma** ~ **luz** he does not exactly shine. **o cachorro é tão** ~ **quanto a raposa** the dog stands as high as the fox. **em** ~ **escala** in a large scale. **feito à** ~ magnificently made. **formato** ~ large size. **ganhar o** ~ **prêmio** to win the first prize. **um** ~ **livro** a remarkable book. **um livro** ~ a large book. **uma** ~ **mágoa** a sore trouble. **a** ~ **maioria** the great majority. **uma** ~ **paixão** a violent passion. **é um** ~ **prazer para ele** it is nuts for him. **saiu um pouco** ~ it came out on the large side. **há uma** ~ **surpresa à sua espera** there is a great surprise in store for you. **um** ~ **vento** a strong wind. **ela é uma** ~ **violinista** she is great on the violin.

grandeira s. f. flail or beetle for thrashing straw.

grandevo adj. long-lived, very old, of great age.

grandeza s. f. 1. largeness, bigness. 2. tallness, height. 3. greatness, ampleness. 4. length, extent. 5. size, bulk. 6. vastness, hugeness, enormousness. 7. grandeur, magnificence. 8. (math.) quantity, value. 9. power, might, mightiness, force. 10. dignity, eminence. 11. sublimity, loftiness. 12. grandeeship. 13. generosity, nobility, nobleness.

~ **de alma** greatness of the soul. **uma estrela de primeira** ~ a star of the first magnitude.

grandiloqüência s. f. grandiloquence; pompous eloquence; elevated, lofty language, loftiness of speech.

com ~ grandiloquently.

grandiloqüente adj. grandiloquent.

grandíloquo adj. grandiloquent.

grandiosidade s. f. 1. grandeur, greatness, grandiosity. 2. splendour, magnificence, pomp. 3. sublimity, loftiness. 4. heroic act.

grandioso adj. 1. grand, grandiose. 2. very great. 3. elevated, lofty, sublime. 4. strong, powerful. 5. pompous, magnificent. 6. gallant. 7. fabulous. noble, grand. || **-amente** adv. in grand style, majestically.

grandíssimo adj. superl. of **grande**: enormous, gigantesque, extremely big.

grandote adj. (Braz.) 1. somewhat tall or big. 2. nearly developed, already grown.

granear v. = **granar**.

granel s. m. (pl. **-éis**) 1. barn, granary, corn-loft. 2. (typogr.) parcel of type, letterboard.

a ~ by heaps, in great quantity; in bulk, mixed (with other material). **prova de** ~ (typogr.) slip-proof, galley-proof.

granido s. m. stippled drawing or engraving, stippling.

granidor s. m. (typogr.) contrivance used in the stipple-engraving process.

granífero adj. graniferous, grain-bearing, full of grains.

graniforme adj. m. + f. graniform, granular.

granilita s. f. tradename of a building material (sand, lime and concrete mixed with marble dust).

granir v. to stipple, draw or engrave by means of dots.

granita s. f. 1. globule formed of a soft substance. 2. goat or lamb droppings. 3. grape-stone, kernel.

granitar v. to granulate, form into grain, reduce to grains.

granítico adj. granitic, granitiform.

granitização s. f. (petrog.) granitization.

granito s. m. 1. (min.) granite. 2. little grain. 3. grape-tone, kernel.

granitóide adj. m. + f. (min.) granitoid.

granitoso adj. granitic, granitical.

granívoro adj. granivorous.

granizada s. f. 1. hailstorm, downpour of hail. 2. shower (also fig.).

granizar v. 1. to granulate, form into grains, reduce to grains. 2. to hail.

~ miúdo to sleet.

granizo s. m. hail: 1. hailstorm. 2. hailstone, sleet. 3. shower. 4. (fig.) shower of balls, stones, etc. temporal de ~ snow pellet shower.

granja s. f. 1. farm, grange, estate, ranch. 2. granary, corn-house. 3. shed, cow- or tool-shed.

~ leiteira dairy farm. ~ de avicultura poultry farm, fowl run, hennery.

granjaria s. f. granges or farms collectively.

granjeador s. m. farmer, granger. ‖ adj. of or pertaining to a grange.

granjear v. 1. to cultivate, farm. 2. to till the soil. 3. to acquire, obtain, procure, gain by one's·labour. 4. to attract, conquer. 5. to scrutinize, search thoroughly for. 6. ~-se to grow rich, gather wealth. ~ as simpatias de alguém to court a person's favours. ~ a vontade de alguém to gain one's good will or favour. sua originalidade granjeou-lhe admiradores his originality found him admirers. ~-se à custa alheia to grow rich at other people's expense.

granjearia s. f. 1. agriculture, farming. 2. tillage, cultivation. 3. grange, farm. 4. (fig.) profit, gain.

granjéia s. f. = grajéia.

granjeiro s. m. 1. act or method of farming. 2. agriculture, farming. 3. cultivation, tillage. 4. crop, harvest. 5. (fig.) profit, gain, earnings.

granjeira s. f. farmeress.

granjeiro s. m. farmer, cultivator, granger.

granjola s. m. + f. (pop.) thickset or corpulent person. ‖ adj. m. + f. fat, corpulent.

granoso adj. grainy, granulous, granular.

granulação s. f. (pl. -ões) 1. granulation, graining. 2. granulating, act of forming into grains. 3. (med.) granulation tissue.

de ~ fina fine-grained. de ~ grossa coarse-grained.

granulado adj. 1. granulated, granulative, ·grainy, grained. 2. pearl.

granulagem s. f. (pl. -ens) 1. granulation. 2. act of forming into grains. 3. process of being formed into grains.

granular v. to granulate, corn. ‖ adj. granular, granuliform, granulative.

granuliforme adj. m. + f. 1. granuliform. 2. (min.) having a granular structure. 3. (bot.) granular.

grânulo s. m. 1. granule, corn, small grain. 2. globule. 3. little pill. 4. any one of the small elevations on a granular surface.

granuloma s. m. (med.) granuloma, tumour made up of granulation tissue.

granulosidade s. f. granulosity, granularity, lumpiness.

granuloso adj. granular, grainy, lumpy, corny.

grão (I) s. m. grain: 1. cereals, corn, breadstuff, seed (plate E 9). 2. smallest unit of weight (150 mg) of the English weight system. 3. globule, globulet, minute globular particle. 4. grit. 5. (petrog.) granular tissue of rock and stone. 6. (phot.) particle of photosensitive material. 7. (sl.) testicle.

~ de chumbo pellet. ~ de cevada barley corn. ~ de saraiva hailstone. com ~ grained. em ~ gritty. pequeno ~ granule. formar em pequenos ~s to pearl. de ~ em ~ a galinha enche o papo little strokes fell great oaks, many a pickle makes a mickle.

grão (II) adj. great, grand.

grão-de-bico s. m. (pl. grãos-de-bico) (bot.) chick-pea.

grão-ducado s. m. (pl. grão-ducados) grand duchy.

grão-ducal adj. m. + f. (pl. grão-ducais) grand-ducal.

grão-duque s. m. (pl. grão-duques) 1. grand duke. 2. (ornith.) eagle owl.

grão-lama s. m. (pl. grão-lamas) Grand Lama, Dalai Lama.

grão-mestre s. m. (pl. grão-mestres) grand master.

grão-rabino s. m. (pl. grão-rabinos) chief rabbi.

grão-tinhoso s. m. (pl. grão-tinhosos) (pop.) Old Scratch, Old Nick, devil, fiend.

grão-turco s. m. (pl. grão-turcos) Grand Turk: the ruling sultan of Constantinople.

grão-vizir s. m. (pl. grão-vizires) grand vizier.

grapa s. f. (vet.) grapes, scratch.

graplapunha s. f. (Braz., bot.) squash.

grapirá s. m. (Braz., ornith.) frigate bird, man-of-war bird.

grapsídeos s. m. pl. (zool.) Grapsidae, a family of crustaceans.

grasnada, grasnadela s. f. (also grasno m.) 1. caw, croaking, clang, quack. 2. gaggle, cackle, jabber. 3. (fig.) bawling, crying, 4. screech, scream. 5. prattle, talk, gossip.

grasnado s. m. croak.

grasnador s. m. screamer, screecher, croaker, jabberer. ‖ adj. screaming, screeching.

grasnante adj. m. + f. screaming, screeching, jabbering.

grasnar v. (also grasnir) 1. to caw, croak, clang. 2. to gaggle, cackle, jabber. 3. to squawk, quack. 4. to scream, screech (birds.) 5. (fig.) to chatter, prattle, gossip.

grasneiro adj. screaming, screeching, cawing, croaking.

grasnido s. m. quack.

graspa s. f. brandy made from fermented wine dregs.

grassar v. 1. to develop gradually, penetrate little by little. 2. to rage, prevail.

está grassando a epidemia the epidemic is rife.

grassento adj. greasy, fat, oily, unctuous.

grasso adj. greasy, fat, oily, unctuous.

gratéia s. f. river bottom cleaning machine.

gratidão s. f. gratitude, gratefulness, thankfulness, thank(s), appreciation.

gratificação s. f. (pl. -ões) 1. gratification. 2. reward, recompense. 3. gratuity, tip, perquisite, cumshaw. 4. gift. 5. fee.

gratificador s. m. gratifier, rewarder. ‖ adj. gratifying, rewarding.

gratificar v. 1. to gratify, requite with gratitude. 2. to reward, recompense. 3. to tip, give gratuity to, remunerate, fee, pay. 4. to favour, humour, oblige. 5. to be grateful for.

gratificaram-no com 100 libras they made a settlement of £ 100 upon him.

gratífico adj. 1. grateful, thankful. 2. (fig.) delighted, pleased, gratified.

gratinado adj. (Fr., cul.) au gratin.

grátis adv. 1. gratis, gratuitously. 2. costless, free of charge, for nothing, without payment.

grato adj. 1. grateful, thankful. 2. gratifying, gratified. 3. agreeable, comforting. 4. pleasant, pleasing. 5. delightful, charming. ‖ -amente adv. gratefully, etc.

eu ficar-lhe-ia muito ~ I should take it kindly of him. sou-lhe muito ~ I am much obliged to you. eu ficar-lhe-ia ~ pelo livro I would thank you for the book. ficaremos ~s por uma pronta resposta an early reply will oblige. mostrar-se grato por to be thankful for.

gratuidade, gratuitidade s. f. gratuitousness.

gratuito adj. 1. gratuitous, gratis. 2. free, without payment, costless, frank. 3. for next to nothing. 4. freely bestowed, without regard to recompense. 5. spontaneous. 6. disinterested. 7. unfounded, groundless. ‖ -amente adv. gratuitously, graciously, spontaneously, for the asking, etc.

gratulação s. f. (pl. -ões) 1. congratulation, felicitation. 2. well-wishing.

gratular v. 1. to congratulate, felicitate. 2. to wish joy to. 3. to express pleasure at, rejoice at.

gratulatório adj. congratulatory, gratulatory.

grau s. m. 1. step, pace. 2. degree, grade. 3. measure, extent, length, dimension. 4. order, class, rating. 5. intensity, strength. 6. pitch. 7. hierarchy. 8. academical title or degree. 9. rank, position, office, title. 10. 360th part of the circumference of a circle. 11. unit of measurement of a scale or angle. 12. degree of kinship. 13. graduation, gradation 14. (math.) index, exponent of power, radical index.
~ centígrado centigrade degree. ~ de avanço stage of proceeding. ~ de doutor doctor's degree. ~ de parentesco degree of kindred, degree of consanguinity. ~ de umidade moisture contents. ~ intermediário intergrade. alguns ~s abaixo de zero some points below zero. até certo ~ to a certain degree. ele colou ~ he took his degree. de ~ em ~ from step to step, gradually. em alto ~ to a high degree, far, highly. ao mais alto ~ to the highest degree. o mais alto ~ de perfeição the perfection. por ~s by degrees. assassínio de primeiro ~ first degree murder. você subiu alguns degraus no meu conceito you have risen a few steps in my estimation.

grauçá s. m. (N. Braz.) albino.

graúdo adj. 1. great, distinguished. 2. grown, developed. 3. important. 4. full grained.

graúdos s. m. pl. the rich and/or influential people, the upper crust.

graúlho s. m. grape-stone, kernel, seed grain.

graúna s. f. (Braz.) bird of the family Icteridae (Cassidix orizivora Gm.).

gravação s. f. (pl. -ões) 1. engraving, intaglio (plate J 2). 2. canned music. 3. aggravation. 4. provocation, vexation, irritation. 5. insult, affront.
~ de som em fita tape-recording.

gravado adj. 1. engraved. 2. cut, incised. 3. (mus.) canned.

gravador s. m. engraver, chaser, graver, etcher. aparelho ~ de faixa sonora film recorder. ~ de fita (radio) tape recorder.

gravadora s. f. (Braz.) recording company.

gravame s. m. 1. gravamen. 2. molestation, bother. 3. vexation, irritation. 4. charge, office, commission. 5. onus, burden, obligation. 6. heavy tax or duty.

gravancear v. (Braz., sl.) to eat, have a meal.

gravanço s. m. 1. (bot.) chick-pea. 2. meal, food, victuals.

gravanzudo adj. (vet.) spavined.

gravar v. 1. to engrave, carve, sculpture, incise, cut, intaglio, (en)chase. 2. to stamp, print, imprint, impress. 3. to perpetuate, immortalize. 4. to mark, brand, character. 5. to oppress, burden. 6. to fix, fasten. 7. to record. 8. ~-se to become fixed, to engrain, infix, grave, leave a deep impression. 9. to aggravate. 10. to irritate. 11. to infuse.
~ a pontos to stipple. ~ em disco to record on a phonograph disk. ele grava em aço he engraves in steel. estava gravado na sua memória it was stamped on his mind.

gravata s. f. 1. (neck)tie, neckcloth, cravat, scarf (plate R 7). 2. neck strap, shoulder strap. 3. variegated feathers on the neck of certain birds. 4. (sport) stranglehold.
alfinete de ~ scarf-pin. ~ apertada (coll.) choker.

gravatá s. m. (bot.) long moss.

gravatá-açu s. m. (pl. gravatás-açus) bastard aloe.

gravata-borboleta s. f. (pl. gravatas-borboletas) (Braz.) bow tie.

gravata-de-couro s. m. (pl. gravatas-de-couro) (S. Braz., pop.) private, soldier.

gravatão s. m. (pl. -ões) pedant, prig, prattler.

gravataria s. f. 1. necktie workshop or shop. 2. a lot of neckties.

gravatazal s. m. (pl. -ais) (Braz.) long moss grove or plantation.

gravateador s. m. cutthroat, executioner.

gravatear v. to decollate, behead, decapitate.

gravateiro s. m. necktie manufacturer or retailer.

gravatilho s. m. (naut.) sail-hook, roping-needle.

gravatinha s. f. small necktie, narrow bow-tie.

gravato s. m. = garavato.

grave (I) s. m. ancient Portuguese silver coin.

grave (II) s. m. 1. the grave accent. 2 (mus.) grave: the slowest tempo in music. 3. sauterne, white variety of wine from the Bordeaux region. ‖ adj. 1. grave, serious. 2. heavy, weighty. 3. ponderous. 4. solemn, ceremonious. 5. important, consequential, portentous, momentous. 6. grievous. 7. distinguished, noble. 8. painful. 9. severe, austere. 10. tedious, dull. 11. (mus.) bass, deep, base, low in pitch, slow. 12. having an acute accent, paroxytone. 13. low, deep. ‖ ~mente adv. gravely, heavily, grievously, seriously, etc.
é uma doença ~ it is a serious illness. um erro ~ a gross error. um ~ negócio an important affair. ele é uma testemunha ~ he is a credible witness. as perspectivas são de caráter ~ the outlook is gloomy.

gravela s. f. 1. dry wine lees. 2. (med.) gravel, small calculous concretions in the kidneys.

gravelado adj. of, pertaining to or relative to the ashes of burnt lees.

gravéola s. f. = graviola.

graveolência s. f. offensive smell, stench.

graveolente, graveolento adj. malodorous, fetid, stinking.

graveta (ê) s. f. four-pronged gig used by codfishers.

gravetar v. to make firewood, make faggots.

graveto (ê) s. m. = garaveto.

graveza s. f. 1. gravity, seriousness. 2. importance. 3. danger, menace. 4. heaviness, weight. 5. grievance. 6. vexation, irritation. 7. injustice.

grávida adj. pregnant, with child, expectant, heavy. estar ~ to conceive, be in the family way.

gravidação s. f. (pl. -ões) (also gravidez) pregnancy.

gravidade s. f. 1. gravity, terrestrial gravitation. 2. seriousness, graveness, momentousness. 3. solemnity. 4. ponderation, prudence. 5. severity, danger, peril. 6. (med.) dangerous aggravation of an illness, crisis. 7. deepness (sound), gravity.
sem ~ weightless. o incidente se reveste de certa ~ the incident is of a serious nature. o centro de ~ the center of gravity.

gravidar v. 1. to make pregnant, fecundate. 2. to get into trouble.

gravidez s. f. pregnancy.

grávido adj. 1. gravid, pregnant, with child. 2. (fam.) in the family way. 3. (fig.) full, replete, heavy.

gravígrado adj. gravigrade: 1. walking with heavy steps. 2. (zool.) of, pertaining to or relative to the Gravigrada.

gravimetria s. f. gravimetry.

gravimétrico adj. gravimetric(al).

gravímetro s. m. gravimeter: instrument for determining the specific gravities of bodies (whether liquid or solid).

graviola s. f. 1. (bot.) cherimoya, custard apple. 2. slipway, building slip (for launching ships).

graviola-do-norte s. f. (pl. **graviolas-do-norte**) (Braz., bot.) soursop.

gravisco adj. 1. troublesome, annoying. 2. risky, dangerous. 3. serious, grave. 4. unsociable, untractable.

gravitação s. f. (pl. **-ões**) gravitation: 1. act of gravitating or its effect. 2. attraction between (celestial) bodies or acceleration of one toward another. 3. (fig.) prevailing tendency of forces. ~ **dos corpos** attraction of gravity. **relativo à** ~ gravitational.

gravitacional adj. m. + f. gravitational.

gravitante adj. m. + f. gravitational, gravitative.

gravitar v. to gravitate: 1. be affected by gravitation. 2. yield to the force of gravity. 3. (fig.) be strongly attracted, have a natural tendency toward, follow closely (person or thing).

graviton s. m. (phys.) graviton.

gravoso adj. 1. vexatious, annoying. 2. oppressive, onerous. 3. burdensome, bothersome. 4. exacting.

gravotear v. (carp.) to chalk or trace out (the cutting line on timber, boards).

gravura s. f. 1. engraving, carving, cut, plate, chalcograph. 2. art or process of engraving. 3. engraved copper plate or wooden block. 4. gravure, print, picture. ~ **em cobre** copper engraving, copper plate. ~ **a água-forte** etching. ~ **em aço** steel-engraving. ~ **a entalhe** intagliotype, a print from an intaglio plate. ~ **em relevo** embossed stamp.

graxa s. f. 1. shoe polish, blacking. 2. grease, axle-grease, fat, dope, slush. 3. (bot.) China rose. 4. (fam.) flattery. ~ **para sapato** shoeshine, shoeblack. ~ **de sapateiro** heelball. **passar uma boa** ~ (sl.) to grease well, sweeten.

graxear v. (Braz., sl.) to make love.

graxeiro s. m. oiler, lubricator, greaser.

graxento adj. 1. oily, greasy. 2. (fig.) fat, corpulent.

graxo adj. oily, greasy, fatty, sebaceous.

graxudo adj. (S. Braz.) fattened (cattle).

grazina s. m. + f. 1. prattler, chatterbox. 2. growler, grumbler. ‖ adj. 1. prattling, babbling. 2. grumbling.

grazinada s. f. clamour, noise, hubbub.

grazinador s. m. 1. chatterbox, prattler. 2. grumbler. ‖ adj. 1. prattling. 2. grumbling.

grazinar v. 1. to clamour, bawl, shout. 2. to pester, importune. 3. to grumble, growl. 4. to lament over, complain, bewail.

gré s. m. (N. Braz.) the last compartment of a fish rearing pond where grown fishes are kept.

grecânico, greciano s. m. Greek: 1. native or inhabitant of Greece. 2. language of the Greeks. ‖ adj. Greek, Gracian.

grecismo s. m. Gr(a)ecism: 1. a Greek idiom. 2. expression of Greek art or culture.

grecizar v. 1. to gr(a)ecise, Gr(a)ecise, give a Greek form or character. 2. to conform to Greek usage.

greco-latino adj. (pl. **greco-latinos**) Gr(a)eco-Latin.

grecomania s. f. Gr(a)economia, exaggerated admiration for the Greek language, art and culture.

greco-romano adj. (pl. **greco-romanos**) Gr(a)eco-Roman.

greda s. f. (min.) clay, potter's clay, argil, chalk. ~ **de pisoeiro** fuller's earth, smectite.

gredelém adj. gridelin, pale-purple, gray-violet.

gredoso adj. chalky, clayey, argillaceous, cretaceous.

grega s. f. fretwork, frets, Greek frets.

gregal adj. m. + f. (pl. **-ais**) 1. Greek, Grecian. 2. gregal, pertaining to a flock (also fig.), gregarious. 3. (Mediterranean region) north-east (wind). **soldado** ~ common soldier.

gregalada s. f. (Mediterranean region) north-easter.

gregário adj. gregarious, aggregative, living in flocks or herds, sociable, companionable. ‖ **gregariamente** adv. aggregatively. **o homem é um ser** ~ man is a gregarious being.

gregarismo s. m. 1. gregariousness. 2. (bot.) formation of open clusters.

grege s. f. = **grei**.

grego s. m. Greek: 1. Grecian, Hellene, native or inhabitant of Greece. 2. language of the Greek. 3. Argive. ‖ adj. 1. Greek, Grecian, Hellenic. 2. (fig.) obscure, unintelligible. 3. Argive. **isto para mim é** ~ that is Greek to me. **não falei** ~ I spoke clearly enough. **agradar a** ~**s e troianos** to please both sides. **ele viu-se** ~ he found himself in difficulties, he was at his wits' end.

gregoriano adj. Gregorian. **calendário** ~ Gregorian calender. **canto** ~ plain chant.

gregotins s. m. pl. scrawl, scribble.

greguejar v. (fam.) to talk Greek.

greguês adj. 1. Greek, Grecian. 2. of, pertaining to or relative to Greek fire.

grei s. f. 1. herd, flock. 2. (fig.) society group. 3. party, clique, faction. 4. parish, congregation. 5. (arch.) nation, people.

grela s. f. a kind of comb file.

grelação s. f. (pl. **-ões**) (Braz., sl.) 1. furtive look, glance. 2. courtship, love-making.

grelado adj. budding, sprouting.

grelador s. m. (Braz., sl.) 1. gaper, starer. 2. lady-killer, lover, beau.

grelar v. 1. to sprout, germinate. 2. to grow an ear, run to seed, put on buds. 3. to thrive, grow. 4. (Braz., sl.) to stare lovingly. 5. (Braz., gambling) to increase one's winnings.

grelha s. f. 1. grate, grill, fire or furnace grate, gridiron (plates C 5, F 3, L 1, P 1). 2. broiler, roaster, toaster. 3. barbecue. 4. (hist.) torture rack. **barra de** ~ fire bar. ~ **escalonada** step grate. ~ **de cadeia** chain grate. ~ **giratória** revolving grate. ~ **mecânica** stoker. ~ **sacudidora** rocking grate.

grelhado adj. grilled.

grelhar v. to broil, grill, fry.

grelheiro s. m. graterman, fire grate keeper.

grelo (ê) s. m. 1. sprout, shoot, sprig, tiller. 2. bulb. 3. acrospire.

gremial s. m. (pl. **-ais**) (eccl.) gremial: silk apron placed on a bishop's lap at certain religious ceremonies. ‖ adj. gremial.

grêmio s. m. 1. bosom. 2. lap. 3. community, society. 4. corporation. 5. assembly, fraternity, organization. 6. guild, club, circle.

grená s. m. grenadine red (colour). ‖ adj. of or relating to the colour of the pomegranate.

grenado adj. (Braz.) pugnacious, disposed to fight.

grenha s. f. 1. ruffled or tangled hair, mane. 2. shag. 3. dense foliage. 4. thicket.

grenho adj. (Braz.) dishevelled, entangled, rumpled.

grenhudo adj. (Braz., fam.) having dense dishevelled hair.

grás s. m. (min.) grès, sandstone, gritstone.

gresífero adj. bearing sandstone, arenitic.

gressório adj. gressorial.

greta (ê) s. f. 1. cleft, crack, fissure, hiatus, flaw. 2. cranny, chap, crevice. 3. chink, rift. 4. gap. 5. (geol.) joint.

gretado adj. chapped, cracked, cleft, split, creviced.

gretadura s. f. 1. chapping, cracking (hands, lips, etc.). 2. act or result of breaking into fissures.

gretar v. 1. to cleave, split. 2. to crack, fissure. 3. to chap. 4. ~**-se** to disintegrate, fall into pieces, burst asunder.

grevas s. f. pl. (hist.) greaves, jambeau: piece of armour protecting the front of the leg below the knee.

greve s. f. strike, turn-out; (sl.) walkout.
~ **branca** ca'canny. ~ **de fome** hunger-strike. ~ **de patrões** lockout. **entrar em** ~ to go on strike. **estar em** ~ to be on strike. **fazer** ~ to down tools, to strike work.

grevista s. m. + f. striker, workman on strike. **os** ~**s** the walkouts.

grifa s. f. 1. claw, talon, paw. 2. (myth.) female griffin.

grifado adj. (typogr.) italic, in italics.

grifar v. 1. to curl, roll into curls (hair). 2. to lay stress upon, emphasize. 3. to underline (words). 4. to italicize, print in italics.

grífico adj. 1. griffinish, griffinlike. 2. enigmatic, ambiguous.

grifínia s. f. a genus of bulbous plants of the family Amaryllidaceae.

grifo (I) s. m. 1. enigma, puzzle. 2. embarrassing question. 3. ambiguous speech, double talk.

grifo (II) s. m. 1. (myth.) griffin, griffon. 2. (ornith.) griffon vulture.

grifo (III) s. m. (typogr.) bastard type, italic type (plate L 4). || adj. 1. curled (hair). 2. italic (type), italicized. 3. having bristling feathers on the legs (chicken).

grigri s. m. (West Africa) gri-gri, gree-gree: 1. charm, amulet. 2. witchcraft, sorcery.

grilado adj. (Braz., sl.) 1. worried, troubled. 2. of or relating to a person having an obsession.

grilagem s. f. (pl. -ens) (Braz.) 1. illegal occupancy of landed property. 2. stratagems and organization of land-jumpers or claim-jumpers.

grilar v. 1. to worry, put s. o. in a state of obsession. 2. to confuse, spoil.

grileiro s. m. (Braz.) land-grabber, land-jumper or claim-jumper, squatter.

grilento adj. illegal or doubtful (title to landed property).

grilhagem s. f. (pl. -ens) chain made of metal rings, linkwork.

grilhão s. m. (pl. -ões) 1. metal chain, metal links. 2. fastening. 3. fetter, gyves. 4. golden chainlet. 5. (fig.) snare, bonds, captivity.

grilheta s. f. 1. fetter, chain, shackles, foot-irons. 2. m. convict, forced labourer.

grilo s. m. 1. (ent.) cricket; (coll.) grig. 2. (Braz., fam.) bobby, traffic patrolman. 3. (Braz.) landed property held without legal right or title.
o ~ **canta** the cricket chirps.

grilo-toupeira s. m. (ent.) mole cricket.

grima s. f. (arch.) 1. hatred, rage, fury. 2. antipathy, aversion.

grimaça s. f. grimace, wry face(s).

grimpa s. f. 1. movable part of a weathercock. 2. cock, weathercock, vane. 3. summit, ridge, crest, top. 4. (fig.) haughty bearing or voice. 5. (sl.) head. **ele é como a** ~ he is fickle, changeable like the weather. **levantar a** ~ to ride the high horse, to give o. s. great airs. **abaixar a** ~ to put a person down a peg or two, to humiliate s. o.

grimpado adj. 1. topped by a weathercock. 2. fickle, capricious. 3. (fig.) at the top, apogeal.

grimpar v. 1. to provide with a weathercock. 2. to attack, throw o. s. against. 3. to answer in a sharp, insolent or haughty manner. 4. to ascend, climb up.

grinalda s. f. 1. garland, wreath. 2. tiara, anadem. 3. (archit.) chaplet, festoon, cornice. 4. (naut.) stern-moulding, taffrail. 5. (fig.) anthology.
~ **de flores** chaplet. **sem** ~ wreathless.

grinalda-de-noiva s. m. (pl. **grinaldas-de-noiva**) (bot.) bridal wreath, St.-Peter's-wreath.

grindélia s. f. (bot.) Grindelia: a genus of asteroid herbs.

grinfar v. to warble.

gringada s. f. (also **gringalhada**; depr. among Latin Americans) a lot of gringos, a number of foreigners.

gringal s. m. (pl. -ais) a kind of fabric.

gringo s. m. (depr. among Latin Americans) gringo, dago, greenhorn, griffin.

gringolim s. m. (pl. -ins) (sl.) any intoxicating liquor.

gripado s. m. taken with grippe, seized with influenza (flu).

gripagem s. f. (pl. -ens) (tech.) seizing-up.

gripal adj. m. + f. (pl. -ais) grippal, of or relative to influenza.

gripar-se v. to be seized with grippe, taken ill with influenza.

gripe s. f. (med.) grippe, grip, catarrh, influenza (abbr.: flu).

gris s. f. miniver: squirrel fur. || adj. gray, blueish--grey.

grisado s. m. hatching.

grisalhar v. to turn grey, grow hoary.

grisalho adj. grey, greyish, grizzled, hoary, white, silver-haired.
ele tem cabelo ~ his hair is fleckered with grey. **tornar-se** ~ to grizzle.

grisão s. m. (pl. -ões) Grison: native or inhabitant of Grisons (largest canton of Switzerland).

grisar v. to grey, turn blueish-grey.

grise s. m. grise: a homespun cloth.

griseta s. f. 1. burner of oil lamps. 2. oil lamp.

grisete s. f. grisette: lively French girl of the working class.

griséu adj. griseous, grey, greyish.

grisu s. m. fire-damp, choke-damp, methane.

grita s. f. 1. cry, cries. 2. shouts, outcry. 3. clamour, noise.

gritada s. f. 1. cry, cries. 2. clamour, noise. 3. shouting, bawling. 4. altercation.

gritadeira s. f. bawling or squabbling woman.

gritador s. m. crier, shouter, yeller, bawler, squabbler. || adj. crying, shouting, yelling.

gritalhão s. m. (pl. -ões) shouter, bawler, screamer, barker.

gritalhona s. f. bawling or shouting woman.

gritante adj. chiding, crying; gross.

gritar v. 1. to cry, shout, clamour. 2. to bawl. 3. to exclaim. 4. to call. 5. to cry for help. 6. to scream, yell, screech, shriek, squeal. 7. to roar. 8. to how, yawl. 9. to scold, chide. 10. to complain, yammer. 11. to vociferate, thunder, storm. 12. to protest, raise objections.
~ **até ficar rouco** to shout o. s. hoarse. ~ **de alegria** to sing for joy. ~ **de dor** to wail, yell with pain. ~ **por socorro** to cry for help. **ele gritou comigo** he snarled at me. **ele gritou para mim** he shouted to me. **não grite comigo!** don't shout at me.

gritaria s. f. 1. crying, shouting. 2. bawling. 3. screaming, screech, shrieking. 4. vociferation, uproar. 5. clamour. 6. exclamation. 7. chiding.
~ **de gatos** caterwaul. **abafar com** ~ to howl down. **uma** ~ **dos diabos** an infernal din.

grito s. m. 1. shout, cry. 2. call. 3. yawp. 4. yell, squeal, shriek, screaming. 5. clamour, vociferation. 6. braying, screeching, mewing, crowing. 7. altercation, dispute. 8. clamour.
~ **de dor** wail, scream of pain. ~ **de guerra** war cry, battle cry; (U. S. A. Indians) war whoop. **soltar, um** ~ **agudo** to scream out. **eles deram um** ~ **de**

alegria they gave a whoop of joy. **um ~ chegou-me aos ouvidos** a cry fell on my ear.

groçaí-azeite s. m. (pl. **groçaís-azeite**) (Bras.) forest--tree of the family Leguminosae.

groenlandês s. m. Greenlander: native or inhabitant of Greenland. ‖ adj. Greenlandic, Greenlandish.

grogojó s. m. (Braz.) plant of the gourd family (Cucurbitacea ovoides).

grogotó interj. that's enough!, let me alone!

grogue s. m. grog: unsweetened mixture of spirit and water; toddy. ‖ adj. 1. groggy, tipsy. 2. staggering, faltering.

grolado s. m. (Braz.) sweetmeat made of unpeeled fruit.

groma (I) s. f. (Roman hist.) a surveyor's measuring rod.

groma (II) s. f. 1. merrymaking, rejoicing. 2. spree, revel.

gromática s. f. gromatics: science of surveying.

gromático adj. gromatic(al).

gronga s. f. (Braz.) 1. a piece of bad work. 2. sorcery through potions.

gronho s. m. a variety of pear.

grosa s. f. 1. gross: number of twelve dozen. 2 rasp file, rasp (plate L 3). 3. (tanning) dull shaving knife. 4. (arch.) slander, whispering, backbiting. **às ~s** by the gross.

grosar v. 1. to file with a rasp. 2. (arch.) to make comments or glosses.

groseira s. f. (Braz.) long line (used in dep-sea fishing).

groselha s. f. currant, gooseberry (plate B 1.) ‖ adj. currant-coloured.

de ou pertencente à ~ grossular.

groselheira s. f. red currant bush.

groselheira-da-índia s. f. (pl. **groselheiras-da-índia**) (bot.) star gooseberry.

groselheira-espinhosa s. f. (gl. **groselheiras-espinhosas**) (bot.) garden gooseberry.

groselheira-preta s. f. (pl. **groselheiras-pretas**) (bot.) black currant bush.

grossaria s. f. sack clott.

grosseira s. f. (Braz., med.) rash, hives.

grosseirão s. m. (pl. **-ões**) lout, boor, uncouth, clumsy or uneducated fellow. ‖ adj. 1. thick, stout. 2. ordinary, low. 3. coarse. 4. big. 5. important. 6. rude, uncouth, boorish.

grosseiro s. m. 1. lout, clumsy fellow, bumpkin. 2. rash, hives. ‖ adj. 1. coarse, crude, unpolished. 2. gross, rough, rustic. 3. common, of inferior quality. 4. badly executed. 5. rude, uncouth. 6. clumsy, lout(ish). 7. gruff, stern. 8. impolite, ill-mannered, uncivil, indelicate, tactless, boorish, churlish, vulgar. 9. immoral, loose. 10. unclean, dirty ‖ **-amente** adv. roughly, coarsely, rudely, boorishly, vulgarly, etc.

uma brincadeira -a a coarse joke. **um erro ~ a howler. de feições -as** horse-faced. **em linguagem -a** in strong terms. **uma mentira ~a** a bouncing lie. **fazer serviço ~** to do rough work. **um sujeito ~** a tough customer. **sumamente ~** most abusive.

grosseria s. f. 1. coarseness, roughness, rudeness. 2. uncivility, grossness, indelicacy, impoliteness, churlishness, boorishness. 3. rude expression. 4. harshness, uncouthness. 5. vulgarity, vulgarism. 6. horseplay.

dizer ~s a alguém to abuse a person.

grossidão s. f. = **grossura**.

grossista s. m. + f. wholesale dealer. ‖ adj. wholesale.

grosso s. m. main part, bulk, gross. ‖ adj. 1. bulky, big, gross, great. 2. coarse, crude. 3. dense, compact. 4. thick, stout, squat, stubby, stocky (plate

Q). 5. important, considerable. 6. rich, abundant. 7. violent, rough. 8. rude, uncouth. 9. curdy, semifluid.

algo ~ thickish. **dinheiro ~** large money. **erro ~** a gross mistake. **o ~ do exército** the body of the army **falar ~** to boss the show. **jogar ~** to play high. **gado ~** great cattle. **homem ~** stout man. **mar ~** rough sea. **fazer mar ~** to run high (sea). **tempo ~** stormy weather. **terra -a** fruitful soil. **fazer vistas -as** to shut one's eyes to. **voz -a** full voice.

grossulária s. f. 1. (arch.) currant bush. 2. (min.) grossular, garnet.

grossura s. f. 1. thickness, stoutness. 2. bigness, bulkiness. 3. grossness. 4. corpulence. 5. fat or grease of animals. 6. (fig.) abundance, fertility, fruitfulness.

~ de fio ou de corda grist. **duas polegadas de ~** two inches thick. **cinco pés de ~** five feet in thickness.

grota s. f. grotto, cavern, cave.

grotão s. m. (pl. **-ões**) 1. large cavern. 2. (Braz.) mountain gorge, hollow.

grotesco adj. grotesque, preposterous, ridiculous, eccentric, freakish, bizarre. ‖ **-amente** adv. grotesquely, etc.

grou (I) s. m. (ornith.) crane.

grou (II) s. m. Sudra, a Hindu who does the low work in Indian pagodas.

grua s. f. 1. (ornith.) female crane. 2. water crane, feeding pillar (plate E 12). 3. hoist crane, derrick.

grudado adj. glued, pasted together.

grudador s. m. gluer.

grudadouro s. m. tenter, drying rack or frame.

grudadura s. f. 1. gluing, pasting. 2. act or method of gluing.

grudar v. 1. to glue, paste. 2. to joint, unite. 3. to stick together, cling, bind. 4. to lead, fill or seal with lead. 5. (fig.) to agree on, come to terms, adhere.

grude s. m. 1. glue, size, paste. 2. cobbler's wax. 3. (Braz., sl.) plain meal.

~ de peixe isinglass.

grudento adj. sticky, gummy.

grueiro adj. of, pertaining to or relative to cranes. **falcão ~** falcon trained to chase cranes.

grugulejar v. to gabble, imitate the cry of a turkey--cock.

grugulhar v. (Braz.) 1. to boil, bubble. 2. to gobble, (like a turkey).

grugunzar v. (Braz.) to meditate, muse over.

grugutuba s. m. a variety of beans.

gruiformes s. m. pl. (ornith.) Gruiformes, birds of the crane order.

gruijuba s. f. (Braz.) = **gurijuba**.

gruir v. 1. to cry, trumpet, clang (like a crane). 2. (arch.) to run around, clamour, provoke a hubbub.

grulha s. m. + f. chatterbox, prattler, babbler.

grulhada s. f. 1. trumpeting of cranes. 2. (fig.) clamour, noise.

grulhar v. to chatter, babble, prattle.

grulho s. m. (S. Braz.) corn cob.

grumar v. 1. to form into clods, reduce to grumes. 2. to clot, coagulate. 3. to become grumous or clotted.

grumecência s. f. grumousness, clottedness.

grumecer v. 1. to clod, clot. 2. to form into clods, reduce to grumes. 3. to become grumous or lumpy.

grumetagem s. f. (naut.) cabin-boys, ship's-boys (collectively).

grumete s. m. (naut.) cabin-boy, sea-boy.

grumixá s. m. horny cocoons of insect larvae (order Thichoptera).

grumo s. m. 1. granule, small grain. 2. little ball of thread. 3. lump. 4. grume, clot. 5. concretion, coagulation.

grumoso adj. 1. granulated, lumpy. 2. grumous, clotted, clotty.

grúmulo s. m. little lump or clod, small particle.

gruna s. f. (Braz.) deep pit made by diamond miners, cave.

grunado s. m. (Braz.) subterraneous.

gruneiro s. m. (Braz.) diamond prospector or miner.

grunha s. f. a variety or pear.

grunhidela s. f. grunt, short deep guttural sound.

grunhido s. m. grunting, grunt, noise of a hog. **com** ~ gruntingly.

grunhidor s. m. grunter, growler, grumbler. ‖ adj. grunting, grumbling.

grunhir v. 1. to grunt. 2. (fig.) to grumble, growl.

grupal adj. m. + f. (pl. -ais) of, pertaining to or relative to a group.

grupado adj. in groups.

grupamento s. m. grouping, act or process of arranging in groups.

grupar v. 1. to arrange or dispose in groups. 2. to group, form groups.

grupelho s. m. (cont.) little group, insignificant faction.

grupeto s. m. (mus.) gruppetto: a musical turn.

grupo s. m. 1. group. 2. grouping, class, series. 3. party, clan, clique, ring. 4. set, cluster, bunch, batch, bundle, collection. 5. gang, band, flock. 6. division. 7. unit. ~ **escolar** public school. ~ **de ilhas** cluster of islands. ~ **sanguíneo** blood group. **um** ~ **de árvores** a cluster of trees. **seis** ~**s diferentes** six different groups. **um** ~ **étnico** an ethnical group. **um** ~ **de marujos** a gang of sailors. **em** ~**s** in troops. **vieram em** ~**s** they came trooping. ~ **social** social group.

gruta s. f. 1. grotto, grot. 2. cavern, cave. 3. den, lair.

grutesco s. m. grotto-work. ‖ adj. 1. of, pertaining to or relative to a grotto or grotto-work. 2. grotesque. 3. ridiculous, eccentric.

guabiru s. m. 1. (zool.) porcupine rat. 2. (fig.) thief.

guacari s. m. (Braz.) harness fish.

guache s. m. gouache.

guaco s. m. (bot.) 1. guaco. 2. climbing hempweed.

guaçu adj. m. + f. (Braz. word borrowed from the language of the Guaranis) large, great, big.

guaçubói s. m. (Braz., zool.) aboma.

guacuru s. m. (ornith.) black-crowned night heron.

guadameci, guadamecil, guadamecim s. m. hangings of gilt or painted leather.

guademã(o) s. m. (Braz.) = **gademar**.

guai interj. (arch.) oh! alas!, woe!

guaiaba s. f. guava: fruit of the guava tree.

guaiaca s. f. (S. Braz.) chamois leather belt or holster.

guaiacino adj. guaiacic.

guáiaco s. m. (bot.) guaiacum, pockwood, lignum-vitae.

guaiacol s. m. (chem.) guaiacol, pyrocatechin, monometylester.

guaiá-das-pedras s. m. (pl. **guaiás-das-pedras**) (Braz., zool.) mud crab.

guaiar v. 1. to moan, groan. 2. to complain, lament. 3. to cry, wail.

guaiara s. f. broad leather belt, sash.

guaíba s. f. (S. Braz.) doge swamp.

guaibira s. f. (Braz., ichth.) leather jack.

guaicuru s. m. + f. (Braz., bot.) biacuru.

guainumbiguaçu s. m. (Braz., ornith.) jacamar.

guaiúle s. m. (Braz., bot.) guayule.

guajuba s. m. (Braz., ichth.) yellow-tailed snapper.

gualdir v. (fam.) 1. to eat, eat up. 2. to consume, waste.

gualdo adj. yellow(ish).

gualdra s. f. handle, ring (on sliding drawers).

gualdrapa s. f. saddlecloth, caparison.

gualdripar v. to steal, pilfer.

gualdrope s. m. (naut.) tiller rope.

gualtéria s. f. (bot.) wintergreen, mountain tea, checkerberry.

guambu s. m. (bot.) bur marigold.

guampa s. f. (also **guampo** m.) 1. horn. 2. drinking cup or vessel made of horn.

guampaço s. m. (S. Braz.) beautiful, well-wrought drinking cup or vessel.

guampada s. f. 1. thrust with the horn(s). 2. contents of a drinking horn.

guampa-torta s. m. (pl. **guampas-tortas**) (S. Braz., col.) courageous fellow, bully.

guampear v. (S. Braz.) to fasten cattle at the horns.

guanabano s. m. (Braz., bot.) soursop.

guanabarino s. m. (Braz.) native or inhabitant of Rio de Janeiro. ‖ adj. of, pertaining to or relative to the Guanabara Bay (Rio de Janeiro).

guanaco s. m. (zool.) guanaco.

guancho s. m. aborigine of the Canary Islands.

guando, guandu s. m. (bot.) pigeon pea.

guano s. m. guano, excrements of seafowl used as fertilizer.

guante s. m. iron glove of an ancient armour.

guanxuma s. f. (Braz., bot.) Caesar weed.

guaparaíba s. f. (bot.) mangrove tree.

guapear, guapetonear v. 1. to show courage, valour, resistance. 2. to have a plucky spirit.

guapeza s. f. (S. Braz.) pluck, spirit, courage, resolution.

guapice s. f. 1. pluck, spirit, courage. 2. resolution. 3. handsomeness, elegance. 4. valour, prowess.

guapira s. f. (Braz.) dole, fountain-head.

guapo adj. 1. courageous, bold. 2. brave, valiant. 3. beautiful, graceful. 4. elegant. 5. slim, slender. 6. dapper.

guará s. m. (Braz.) 1. (ornith.) scarlet ibis. 2. (zool.) maned wolf, maned dog.

guarabu s. m. guarabu: one of several species of large trees.

guarambá s. m. (Braz., ichth.) horse-eye, horse-eyed jack.

guaraná s. m. (Braz.) guarana: 1. the Brazilian shrub (Paullinia sorbilis.) 2. (also ~**-pão**) paste prepared from the seeds of this shrub (for food or medicine). 3. soft drink flavoured with guarana.

guaranazal s. m. (pl. -ais) (Braz.) guarana shrub plantation.

guaranazeiro s. m. (Braz.) guarana planter or picker.

guarani s. m. (Braz.) Guarani: 1. Indian of a group of Tupian tribes. 2. language spoken by these Indians.

guaraniana s. f. (Braz.) designation of the region formerly occupied by the Guarani tribes.

guaranina s. f. (chem.) guaranine.

guaranítico adj. Guarani: of or pertaining to the Guaranis, or their language.

guarapu s. m. (Braz., zool.) red brocket, pita.

guaraúna s. f. (ornith.) white-faced glassy ibis.

guaraxaim, guaraxim s. m. (zool.) fox wolf.

guarda s. f. 1. guard: a) vigilance, watchfulness. b) care, concern. c) prudence, caution. d) basket of a sword. e) flyleaf (of a book, circular, etc.) f) anything that protects, fends, etc. (plates B 7), C 7, M 1). g) guard duty, watching. h) protection, safekeeping, custody, trust. i) protector. j) constable. k) m. watchman, ward(en), sentry, sentinel. 2.

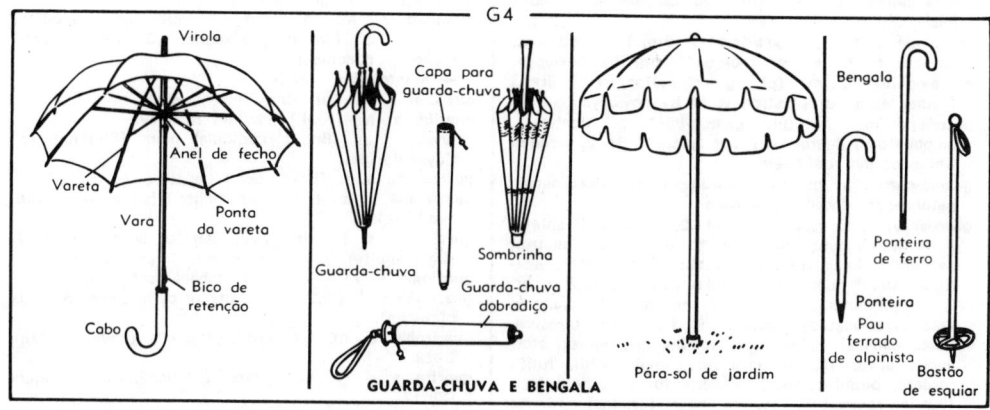

G 4

GUARDA-CHUVA E BENGALA

help, assistance. 3. kindness, benevolence. 4. (hort.) scion, graft. 5. flourish, paraph.
~ aduaneiro revenue officer. **~ avançada** outguard. **~ cívica** civic guard. **~ de comporta** lock keeper. **~s da fechadura** wards of a lock. **~ de honra** guard of honour. **~ nacional** national guard. **~ pessoal** bodyguard. **~ policial** policeman, (coll.) cop. **~s de uma ponte** parapet of a bridge. **~ de portaria** gate-keeper. **~ real** gentlemen-at-arms. **~ de trânsito** policeman on point-duty. **~ urbana** city militia. **anjo da ~** guardian angel. **cão de ~** house-dog, watchdog. **de ~** on the lookout. **dia de ~** holiday. **entrar de ~** to mount guard. **estar de ~** to keep guard. **oficial de ~** officer on duty. **render a ~** to relieve the guard. **sem ~** guardless. **tomar em sua ~** to take under one's guard. **tropas de ~** household troops. **vir da ~** to come off guard.

guarda-arnês s. m. (pl. **guarda-arneses**) harness-room, saddle-room.

guarda-bagagem s. m. (pl. **guarda-bagagens**) 1. baggage-room, parcel-room. 2. baggage checking office.

guarda-barreira s. m. (pl. **guarda-barreiras**) 1. excise officer, gate-clerk, pikeman. 2. (railway) line-keeper, lineman.

guarda-braço s. m. (pl. **guarda-braços**) brassart, armour for the arms.

guarda-caça s. m. (pl. **guarda-caças**) gamekeeper.

guarda-cadeira s. m. (pl. **guarda-cadeiras**) skirting board, baseboard.

guarda-calhas s. m. sg. + pl. (railway) cow-catcher.

guarda-cancela s. m. (pl. **guarda-cancelas**) (railway) line-keeper, signalman.

guarda-chapim s. m. (pl. **guarda-chapins**) banister, parapet.

guarda-chaves s. m. sg. + pl. 1. (railway) switch-man, shunter. 2. jailer.

guarda-chuva s. m. (pl. **guarda-chuvas**) umbrella, (sl.) brolly (plates G 4, R 7).

guarda-chuvada s. f. (pl. guarda-chuvadas) (fam.) scuffle with an umbrella.

guarda-civil s. m. (pl. **guarda-civis**) civil guard.

guarda-comida s. m. (pl. **guarda-comidas**) larder.

guarda-costas s. m. sg. + pl. 1. coast-guard vessel, revenue cutter. 2. bodyguard. **serviço de ~** (naut.) preventive service.

guardador s. m. warden, guardian, guard, watchman. ‖ adj. watching, on guard.

guardados s. m. pl. (Braz.) keepsakes.

guarda-espelho s. f. (pl. **guarda-espelhos**) (typogr.) type area flyleaf.

guarda-fato s. m. (pl. **guarda-fatos**) wardrobe.

guarda-fechos s. m. sg. + pl. leather cover for gun-locks.

guarda-fio(s) s. m. sg. + pl. (telegr., teleph.) section lineman, wireman.

guarda-florestal s. m. (pl. **guardas-florestais**) ranger, forester, fire-ward. **cargo ou função de ~** rangership.

guarda-fogo s. m. (pl. **guarda-fogos**) 1. firescreen, fender. 2. chimney-board.

guarda-freio(s) s. m., sg. + pl. 1. (railway) brake-man, braker. 2. streetcar-driver, conductor.

guarda-jóias s. m. sg. + pl. 1. jewel-case or safe, casket. 2. keeper of the crown jewels.

guarda-lama s. m. (pl. **guarda-lamas**) 1. fender, mudguard, dashboard, splashboard. 2. catch-pan of a manhole.

guarda-leme s. m. (pl. **guarda-lemes**) (naut.) stern-gun, stern-chaser.

guarda-linha s. m. (pl. **guarda-linhas**) (railway) line-keeper, lineman, switch-man.

guarda-livros s. m. + f., sg. + pl. book-keeper, accountant.

guarda-louça s. m. (pl. **guarda-louças**) cupboard, ambry; buffet; side-board.

guarda-lume s. m. (pl. **guarda-lumes**) = guarda-fogo.

guarda-mancebos s. m. pl. (naut.) mainropes of the bowsprit, ridge-line.

guarda-mão s. m. (pl. **guarda-mãos**) (mil.) 1. hand-guard. 2. basket-hilt.

guarda-marinha s. m. (pl. **guardas-marinha(s)**) ensign, midshipman.

guarda-mato s. m. (pl. **guarda-matos**) (mil.) trigger-guard.

guardamento s. m. 1. custody, guard. 2. preservation, safekeeping.

guarda-meta s. m. (pl. **guarda-metas**) 1. (cricket) wicketkeeper. 2. (Braz., ftb.) goalkeeper.

guarda-mor s. m. (pl. **guardas-mores**) 1. (Engl.) Lord High Steward. 2. inspector general of customs, havener. 3. commander of the guard, inspector, warden.

guardamoria s. f. (Braz.) 1. custom-house authorities. 2. revenue officers and police (collectively).

guarda-móveis s. m. sg. + pl. (Braz.) furniture warehouse or storehouse.

guardanapo s. m. table-napkin, serviette (plate M 1).

guarda-noturno s. m. (pl. **guardas-noturnos**) night watchman.

guarda-patrão s. m. (pl. guarda-patrões) (naut.) backboard.

guarda-pé s. m. (pl. guarda-pés) (Braz.) 1. petticoat, underskirt. 2. leather footgear worn by cowboys.

guarda-peito s. m. (pl. guarda-peitos) (N. Braz.) leather apron or plastron worn by cowboys.

guarda-pó s. m. (pl. guarda-pós) 1. dust-coat, smock-frock, duster, wrapper (plate R 6). 2. wooden lining of the roof-beam.

guarda-portão s. m. (pl. guarda-portões) doorkeeper, gatekeeper, doorman, warden.

guardar v. 1. to guard, protect. 2. to defend, shield. 3. to watch over, check. 4. to keep under control, set apart, keep, reserve, retain. 5. to watch, sentinel, stand guard. 6. to take care of, look after. 7. to preserve, care for. 8. to keep in custody, take into custody, secure. 9. to hoard, treasure, hide, conceal, stash. 10. to lay by, store, stow away, save. 11. to observe, comply with, fulfill (orders, promise, etc.). 12. not to lose, hold fast. 13. to remember. 14. to bear (grudge). 15. to destine to, designate. 16. ~se: a) to be cautious, be on one's guard. b) to abstain from, refrain. c) to keep clear of, avoid, shun.
~ a boca to keep one's tongue, keep silent. ~ a castidade to live in chastity. ~ em celeiro to barn up. ~ debaixo de chave to lock up. ~ a sete chaves to keep under lock and key. ~ a compostura to retain one's self-possession. ~ os dias santos to keep the holidays. ~ o gado to keep the cattle. ~ as leis to observe the laws. ~ o leito to lay up. ~ a palavra to keep one's word. ~ para sua filha to hold in trust for one's daughter. ~ em tapada to preserve (game). ~ numa urna to urn. ela guardou o dinheiro she tucked away her money. guardamos o emprego para ele we secured the post to him. ele guarda isso na memória he carries it with him. guardaram os móveis they stowed away their furniture. Deus o guarde! God have you in his keeping! Deus guarde o rei! God save the King! não lhe guardo rancor I hold no ill feelings for you. ela não soube ~ o segredo she could not keep the secret. eles guardaram seus tesouros they stored away their treasures.

guarda-raios s. m., sg. + pl. lightning conductor.

guarda-rede s. m. (pl. guarda-redes) goalkeeper.

guarda-rios s. m., sg. + pl. (ornith.) kingfisher.

guarda-roupa s. m. (pl. guarda-roupas) 1. wardrobe (plates A 13, D 4). 2. clothes-press. 3. dresser. 4. cloak-room. 5. keeper of a cloak-room or wardrobe. 6. (bot.) lavender cotton. 7. press.

guardas s. f. pl. wards (of a lock).

guarda-selos s. m., sg. + pl. 1. (Eng.) Lord Keeper of the Great Seal. 2. keeper of seal(s).

guarda-sol s. m. (pl. guarda-sóis) 1. sunshade, parasol, umbrella (plate P 17). 2. (bot.) Malabar almond.

guarda-soleiro s. m. (pl. guarda-soleiros) sunshade maker.

guarda-trem s. m. guard.

guarda-vala(s) s. m., sg. + pl. (ftb.) goalkeeper.

guarda-vassouras s. m., sg. + pl. skirting board.

guarda-vento s. m. (pl. guarda-ventos) windscreen, folding screen.

guarda-vestidos s. m., sg. + pl. wardrobe, clothes-press.

guarda-vinho s. m. (pl. guarda-vinhos) low wall which surrounds the winepress.

guarda-vista s. m. (pl. guarda-vistas) eyeshade.

guarda-voz s. m. (pl. guarda-vozes) sound-board of a pulpit.

guardear v. to keep watch over, set guards along (a line, frontier, etc.).

guardiania s. f. guardianship.

guardião s. m. (pl. -ões) 1. guardian, custodian, warden. 2. (sport) goalkeeper. 3. (Braz., bot.) creeping cucumber.
~ atento (fig.) argus.

guardim s. m. (pl. -ins) (naut.) vangs.

guariba s. m. (zool.) howling monkey.

guaribu s. m. (Braz.) medicinal plant (Silphium antidysenterica).

guaricanga s. f. (Braz., bot.) geonoma.

guaricema s. m. + f. (Braz., ichth.) horse-eye, horse-eyed jack.

guarida s. f. 1. lair, cave, den (of wild beasts). 2. (fig.) shelter, place of refuge. 3. protection.

guarimpe s. m. (N. Braz.) embankment, slope.

guariroba s. f. (Braz.) a variety of palm trees (Syagrus oleracea).

guarirobal s. m. (pl. -ais) (Braz.) a grove of palm trees.

guarita s. f. 1. sentry-box. 2. watch-tower, watch-turret.

guarnecedor s. m. 1. provider, furnisher. 2. trimmer, dresser. || adj. 1. providing, furnishing. 2. trimming, preparing.

guarnecer v. 1. to provide, supply, furnish, equip. 2 (mil.) to fortify, garrison. 3. (naut.) to rig. 4. to trim, garnish, adorn. 5. to hem, fringe. 6. to line, face. 7. to whitewash. 8. ~se to provide (o. s.) with.
~ um vestido de fitas to braid, ribbon. ~ de folhos ou babados to flounce.

guarnecido adj. faced, edged, ribboned.

guarnecimento s. m. 1. provision, supply. 2. decoration, ornament. 3. garrison.

guarnição s. f. (pl. -ões) 1. garrison, crew, personnel. 2. (mil.) post. 3. hilt and basket of a sword. 4. decoration, ornament, ornate, garniture, edging. 5. lining, facing. 6. embroidery or other trimming of a dress. 7. set of furniture. 8. gasket. 9. (cul.) garnish. 10. (tech.) armature.
~ da porta door lining, door furniture. ~ de amianto asbestos packing. anel de ~ packing-ring.

guatemalense s. m. + f. (also guatemalteco m.) Guatemalian, native or inhabitant of Guatemala. || adj. Guatemalian.

guaxima s. f. (Braz., bot.) 1. Caesar weed. 2. screw tree.

guaxima-do-mangue s. f. (pl. guaximas-do-mangue) (Braz., bot.) majagua.

guaximba-preta s. f. (pl. guaximbas-pretas) (Braz., bot.) amate.

guaxinim s. m. (Braz., zool.) crab-eating raccoon.

guazil s. m. (pl. -is) 1. bailiff. 2. a minor clerk of a court of justice.

gude s. m. (Braz.) = bilosca, birosca.

guebro s. m. (hist.) Gueber, Gheber: Parsee, a fire-worshipper.

guebuçu s. m. (Braz., ichth.) volador.

guedelha s. f., guedelho m. 1. tuft of hair. 2. tangled or dishevelled hair. 3. shag. 4. flock. 5. (fig.) profit, advantage.
~ de lã flock of wool.

guedelhudo adj. hairy, long-haired, shaggy.

guedre s. f. (bot.) elder flower.

gueixa s. f. geisha, Japanese singing and dancing girl.

guelfo s. m. (hist.) Guelf, Guelph: member of the papal party in medieval Italy. || adj. Guelfic, Guelphic.

guelra s. f. gills, branchiae (plate P 7).

guerra s. f. 1. war, warfare; (fig.) arms, sword. 2. campaign, military operation. 3. fight, conflict, strife, battle. 4. hostility, enmity. 5. art or science of war.

~ **civil** civil war or commotion. ~ **fria** cold war. ~ **de nervos** war of nerves. ~ **de posição** stationary war. ~ **nuclear** nuclear, atomic war. ~ **química** chemical warfare. ~ **relâmpago** lightning war. ~ **santa** holy war. ~ **total** total war. **ser arrastado para a** ~ to be drawn into the war. **nunca houve boa** ~ **ou má paz** there was never a good war or a bad peace. **eles declararam** ~ they declared war. **devastado pela** ~ war-ravaged. **fazer** ~ to wage war. **em** ~ **e paz** in war and peace. **em pé de** ~ on the warpath, belligerent. **ele estava em pé de** ~ **com** he was at war with. **as peculiaridades da** ~ the ways of war. **preparar-se para a** ~ to arm. **falaram em sorte da** ~ they spoke of the chance of arms.

guerreador s. m. warrior, fighter, combatant. || adj. warlike, martial.

guerrear v. 1. to war, make or wage war upon. 2. to fight, combat, struggle. 3. to persecute, show hostility to. 4. to oppose, be in opposition. 5. to oppress. 6. to invade, assail.

guerreiro s. m. 1. warrior, fighter, combatant. 2. soldier. 3. (hist.) thane. || adj. 1. warlike, martial. 2. combative, pugnacious, bellicose.

guerrilha s. f. 1. guer(r)illa: a) band of irregular soldiers or fighters. b) one who engages in irregular warfare. 2. gang of thieves. 3. group of indisciplined soldiers. 4. insurgent political faction.

guerrilhar v. 1. to engage in guerrilla warfare. 2. to lead he life of a guerrilla fighter.

guerrilheiro s. m. guerrilla fighter, partisan, bush--fighter; (U. S. A., sl.) jayhawker. || adj. guerrilla.

gueto s. m. ghetto: 1. (hist.) Jewish quarters in ancient Rome. 2. a district inhabited by Jews. 3. living quarters of a segregated racial group in a city.

guia s. f. 1. guidance, act or effect of guiding. 2. delivery bill. 3. pass bill, way bill, permit. 4. (letter of) safe-conduct. 5. official mail register. 6. vine--stake. 7. rein, bridle-strap (place C 12). 8. (tech.) guide (plate M 1). 9. channel stone, curb(ing). 10. m.: a) guide, leader, cicerone; (depr.) bellwether, b) conductor. c) guide-book, handbook. d) leadership, lead.

~ **comercial** commercial directory. ~ **da alfândega** custom-house permit. ~ **de bagagem** baggage--check. ~ **da dança** dance leader. ~ **de importação** bill of entry. ~ **de porto** portolano. ~ **de viagem** traveller's guide, guide-book, itinerary, road--book. **carneiro de** ~ bellwether. **sem** ~ guideless.

guiador s. m. 1. guide, leader. 2. conductor. 3. handle bar.

guiagem s. f. tax on the transportation of goods, cattle, etc.

guiamento s. m. guiding.

guião s. m. 1. banner, standard, guidon. 2. standard--bearer. 3. (mus.) custos.

guiar v. 1. to guide, lead. 2. to conduct, direct. 3. to orient(ate). 4. to advise, counsel. 5. to teach, instruct. 6. to protect. 7. to govern, rule. 8. to drive, steer, motor, truck. 9. to conduce, tend to. 10. to go, move forward. 11. to sail, helm, navigate. 12. to manage. 13. ~-**se** to be guided, be bound to or for.

~ **a toda velocidade** to drive at full speed. ~ **com imprudência (carro)** to hog. ~ **a dança** to lead the dance. ~-**se pelos conselhos de** to act in accordance with someone's counsels.

guichê s. m. 1. sliding window, ticket-office window, information counter (plate E 13). 2. booking-office, ticket-office. 3. service-hatch.

guidão, guidom s. m. handle bar (bicycle) (plates B 11, M 12.)

guieiro s. m. 1. leader, guide. 2. oxboy, boy who cares for a team of oxen. 3. street lamp. || adj. leading, guiding.

guiga s. f. (naut.) gig, outrigger.

guildas s. f. pl. guild(s), trade-corporations.

guilha s. f. 1. rich harvest of cereals, bumper crop. 2. (fig.) fraud, swindle.

guilherme s. m. rabbet, rabbet plane, grooving plane.

guilho s. m. pivot, pin, trunion, swivel.

guilhochês, guilochês s. m. pl. (archit.) guilloche: ornamental pattern composed of two or more bands of interlacing ribbons.

guilhotina s. f. 1. guillotine, machine for beheading condemned persons. 2. (tech.) guillotine-cutter, paper cutting machine. 3. sash-window.

guilhotinar v. to guillotine, behead.

guina s. f. 1. voracious appetite, wild hunger. 2. hate, anger. 3. fury, impetuosity, violence. 4. malice, viciousness.

guinada s. f. 1. (naut.) deflection, falling-off, yaw, leeway. 2. dodging leap (of a horse). 3. pitching of an airplane. 4. sudden sharp pain. 5. sudden impression. 6. attack.

guinar v. 1. to move by bounds and leaps. 2. to steer leeways, way. 3. (naut.) to tack, reel, laveer. 4. to dodge, evade (a blow). 5. to return rapidly.

guinchado s. m. 1. screaming, shrieking. 2. clamour. 3. squeaking.

guinchador, guinchante adj. squeaky.

guinchar v. 1. to scream, shriek, screech. 2. to squeal, squeak. 3. to ululate. 4. (Braz.) to hoist and tow disabled cars.

guincho (I) s. m. 1. (mot.) wrecker, breakdown-truck, tow-car. 2. winch, crab. 3. windlass, hoist. 4. (tech.) jack.

~ **simples** simple tackle. ~ **da âncora** (naut.) fish-tackle.

guincho (II) s. m. squeak, sharp cry, shriek, shrill, screech.

guincho (III) s. m. (ornith.) swift.

guincho-da-tainha s. m. (pl. **guinchos-da-tainha**) (ornith.) harrier eagle.

guinda s. f. rope for hoisting.

guindado adj. 1. affected, conceited, bombastic. 2. hoisted, lifted, elevated.

guindagem s. f. hoisting, winding up.

guindaleta s. f. rope of a winch or crane.

guindar v. 1. to lift, hoist, crane, wind, jack. 2. to be affected, be or become conceited. 3. (fig.) to elevate or raise to a high position.

guindaste s. m. crane, winch, hoist, derrick, crab, jack (plates E 12, G. 5, P 16).

~ **giratório** slewing-crane (plate G 5). ~ **de mastro** sheer-legs. ~ **de lança** jib-crane. ~ **móvel** travelling crane, jenny (plate G 5). ~ **flutuante** floating crane, pontoon crane (plate G 5).

guindável adj. (pl. **-áveis**) windable.

guindola s. f. (naut.) jury-mast.

guiné (I) s. f. (Braz., bot.) guinea-hen weed.

guiné (II) s. f. Guinea.

guineense s. m. + f. native or inhabitant of Guinea.

guinéu s. m. guinea: 1. former English gold coin, (worth 21 shillings). 2. goods, fees or sum of money worth a guinea.

guingão s. m. (pl. **-ões**) 1. guingham, a fine cotton fabric. 2. floss-silk, silk, waste. 3. fecal matter (from silkworms).

guipagem s. f. (pl. **-ens**) braided covering.

guipura s. f. guipure: a heavy decorative lace.

guiraponga s. f. (Braz., ornith.) bellbird, campanero.

guiratinga s. f. (Braz., ornith.) American egret.

guirlanda s. f. = grinalda.

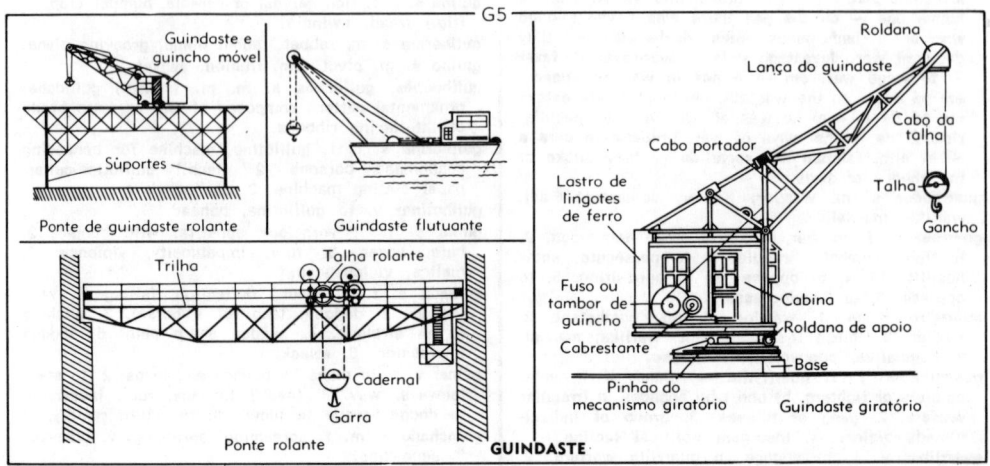

Guindaste e guincho móvel

Súportes

Ponte de guindaste rolante

Guindaste flutuante

Trilha　　Talha rolante

Cadernal

Garra

Ponte rolante

Roldana

Lança do guindaste

Cabo da talha

Cabo portador

Lastro de lingotes de ferro

Talha

Gancho

Fuso ou tambor de guincho

Cabina

Roldana de apoio

Cabrestante

Base

Pinhão do mecanismo giratório

Guindaste giratório

GUINDASTE

---

guisa s. f. mode, fashion. 2. manner, behaviour. 3. guise.
de ~ so that. à ~ de like, just as.
guisado s. m. 1. stew, ragout, hash, haricot. 2. (S. Braz.) minced or chopped meat. ‖ adj. stewed.
guisamento s. m. 1. ritual appointments for worship. 2. holy wafers and sacramental wine.
guisar v. 1. to dress or season (meat, fowl, etc.). 2. to stew, braise, dress, prepare by cooking. 3. to outline, trace. 4. to help. 5. to direct, conduct.
guita s. m. pack thread, string.
guitarra s. f. (mus.) guitar (plate G 2).
~ havaiana ukulele. **~ elétrica** electric guitar.
guitarrada s. f. guitar concert, guitar playing.
guitarrear v. to play on the guitar.
guitarreiro s. m. guitar maker.
guitarrista s. m. + f. guitar player, guitarist.
guizo (I) s. m. ball-bell, rattle.
pôr o ~ no pescoço da onça to bell the cat.
guizo (II) s. m. small globelike metal bell (like those on a foolscap).
guizo-de-cascavel s. m. (pl. **guizos-de-cascavel**) (bot.) 1. rattlebox. 2. yellow lupine.
gula s. f. 1. gluttony, voracity. 2. throat, gorge. 3. greed(iness), ravenousness. 4. (archit.) gula, cyma reversa, ogee. 5. (carp.) filletster plane.
guleima s. m. glutton.
gulodice s. f. 1. delicacy, titbit, dainty, sweetmeat, kickshaw. 2. lickerishness.
gulosar v. 1. to eat titbits or delicacies. 2. to eat daintily or sparingly.
guloseima, gulosice s. f. 1. dainties, sweets, sweetmeats. 2. delicacy, delicatessen, titbit, dainty morsel. 3. daintiness.
guloso s. m. glutton, sweet tooth, dainty feeder. ‖ adj. 1. gluttonous, fond of dainties, lickerish, liquorish. 2. cormorant.
ela é -a she has a sweet tooth.
gume s. m. 1. edge, knife-edge, cutting or sharp edge (plates P 1, T 1). 2. sharpness. 3. perspicacity, sagacity.

~ cego dull cutting edge. **~ afiado** a keen edge. **dar de ~** to strike with the edge of the sword. **espada de dois ~s** two-edged sword. **a faca não tem ~** the knife has no edge. **sem ~** edgeless.
gumífero adj. gummiferous, producing gum, resiniferous.
gunga s. m. (Braz.) magnate; boss.
gunjieiro s. m. (bot.) Indian licorice.
gurandi-azul s. m. (pl. **gurandis-azuis**) (Braz.) a bird of the family Fringillidae (Cyanocampsa cyanea).
guri s. m. (Braz.) child, little boy; (coll.) dot.
guria s. f. (Braz.) 1. little girl. 2. sweetheart.
guricema s. f. (Braz., ichth.) saurel.
gurita s. f. = **guarita.**
gurizada s. f. (Braz.) a lot of little girls and boys.
gurma s. f. (vet.) strangles.
gurupés s. m., sg. + pl. (naut.) bowsprit.
gurutuba s. f. a variety of beans.
gusa s. f. cast-iron, pig-iron.
gusano s. m. (zool.) shipworm, woodworm, borer, mite.
gusla s. f. gusla, gusle: simple musical instrument played in the Balkan, having a round body and one string.
gustação s. f. (pl. **-ões**) 1. act or faculty of tasting. 2. gustation.
gustativo adj. gustative, gustatory.
guta s. f. gutta, gamboge.
gutação s. f. (bot.) guttation.
guta-percha s. f. (pl. **gutas-perchas**) (bot.) gutta-percha.
gutiferácea, gutífera s. f. Guttiferae: a guttiferous plant.
gutiferáceo adj. (bot.) guttiferous.
gutífero adj. 1. guttiferous, yielding gum. 2. referring to or resembling gutta. 3. guttiform, forming drops.
gutural adj. m. + f. (pl. **-ais**) guttural, throaty. ‖ **~mente** adv. gutturally.
letra ~ guttural letter.
guturalidade s. f. gutturalness.
guturalização s. f. (pl. **-ões**) (phon.) gutturalization.
guturalizar v. (phon.) to gutturalize, speak gutturally.

H

H, h s. m. 1. the eighth letter and the sixth consonant of the Portuguese alphabet. 2. (mus.) si: the seventh note of the octave. 3. (chem.) H chemical symbol of hydrogen. ‖ adj. the eighth in order of place.

há see **haver.**

hã interj. exclamation of elucidation, reflection, admiration.

habanera s. f. (mus.) habanera: 1. dance of African origin, common in Cuba. 2. slow, rhythmic music written for this dance.

habeas-corpus s. m., sg. + pl. (jur.) habeas corpus.

habena s. f. (poet.) 1. reins, bridle. 2. whip.

hábil adj. m. + f. (pl. **-eis**) 1. skilful, skilled, apt, dexterous. 2. capable, able, fit. 3. fine. 4. intelligent, ingenious, subtle. 5. pert, clever, adroit. 6. competent. 7. (jur.) legally qualified. ‖ **habilmente** adv. skilfully, ably, ingeniously, cleverly, dexterously, subtly, artfully.

~ **advogado** clever lawyer. ~ **em** skilful at, skilled in. ~ **em prever o tempo** weather-wise. ~ **médico** skilful physician.

habilidade s. f. 1. aptitude, ability. 2. ingeniousness, intelligence, talent. 3. capacity, capability. 4. cleverness, skill. 5. dexterity, handiness, workmanship. 6. cunning, wit, artfulness. 7. ~**s** pl.: a) tricks. b) bodily suppleness and agility. c) sleights of hand, jugglery.

~ **oratória** readiness of speech. **ele tem a ~ de pular** he has the trick of jumping. **ele tem a ~ de lidar com rapazes** he understands boys. **exceder em ~** to outcraft. **falta de ~** ungainliness. **ter ~ para tudo** to be a good hand at everything.

habilidoso s. m. skilled worker or practitioner. ‖ adj. 1. skilful, skilled. 2. handy, dexterous. 3. clever, cunning. 4. witty, ingenious. 5. talented, able, inventive. ‖ **-amente** adv. cunningly, ingeniously, skilfully.

habilitação s. f. (pl. **-ões**) 1. habilitation, qualification, fitness. 2. (jur.) legal evidence. 3. capacity, competence. 4. **-ões** pl.: a) knowledge, culture. b) certificate(s), attestation. c) reference, character.

habilitado adj. 1. qualified, competent, entitled. 2. fit, able, capable.

habilitador s. m. qualifier, habilitator. ‖ adj. habilitating, qualifying.

habilitanço s. m. wager lent by one partner to another at gambling.

habilitando s. m. habilitator: one who is going to habilitate himself. ‖ adj. habilitating, qualifying.

habilitante s. m. + f. habilitator, litigator, (jur.) plaintiff. ‖ adj. qualifying, habilitating, litigant, contending in law.

habilitar v. 1. to habilitate, qualify. 2. to entitle, give a right to. 3. to prepare, make ready, fit out. 4. to authorize. 5. to make able, capable or fit. 6. (jur.) to submit evidence(s), prove, acquire certain necessary qualifications. 7. ~**-se:** a) to become able, capable or fit for. b) to habilitate o. s. c) to buy a lottery ticket. 8. to capacitate, empower, enable. **seus talentos habilitam-no para este trabalho** his talents fit him for this job. **ele habilitou-se para a herança** he prepared to enter upon the inheritance. **ele habilitou-se para professor** he entered upon a mastership.

habitabilidade s. f. habitableness, habitable state.

habitação s. f. (pl. **-ões**) 1. act of inhabiting, state of being inhabited. 2. quarters (pl.), abode, dwelling, lodging. 3. habitation, house. 4. domicile, residence.

~ **fixa** domicile. ~ **provisória** temporary (or emergency) dwelling.

habitacional adj. m. + f. (pl. **-ais**) habitational, habitative.

habitáculo s. m. poor or small dwelling place.

habitado adj. inhabited.

tornar ~ to people.

habitador s. m. 1. inhabitant, resident, tenant. 2. dweller, lodger. ‖ adj. inhabiting, habitable, dwelling, residing.

habitante s. m. + f. 1. inhabitant, habitant, resident. 2. inmate, dweller, lodger. 3. colonizer, colonist. 4. ~**s** pl. people. ‖ adj. 1. inhabiting, dwelling. 2. residing. 3. colonizing.

~ **das florestas** woodlander. ~ **de uma cidade** townsman.

habitar v. 1. to inhabit, lodge. 2. to reside, live in. 3. to populate, people, settle. 4. to occupy. 5. to frequent.

habitat s. m. (ecol.) habitat.

habitável adj. m. + f. (pl. **-áveis**) habitable, capable of being inhabited, tenantable.

habite-se s. m. a document which declares a construction in conditions of habitability.

hábito s. m. 1. custom, usage. 2. habit, frock. 3. natural condition, customary appearance. 4. dress, garment. 5. use, way, manner. 6. insignia and garb of religious or knightly orders. 7. (bot.) aspect, external appearance. 8. practice, folkway.

~**s da clientela (da freguesia)** buying habit. **o ~ de fazer** the habit of doing, wont, custom, practice. **o ~ faz o monge** fine feathers make fine birds. **o ~ não faz o monge** it is not the coat that makes the man. ~ **de fumar cigarros incessantemente** chain-smoking. **cavaleiros do ~ de Cristo** knights of Christ. **como é de seu ~** as it is his wont (or way) to write. **como era de seu ~** as was his habit (or custom). **um costume consagrado pelo ~** a habit rooted in custom. **falta de ~** unwontedness. **mau ~** vice. **privar do ~** (eccl.) to unfrock. **ele tinha como ~ fazer** he was by way of doing. **tomar o ~** to take the religious habit; nuns: to take the veil. **tornou-se-lhe um ~** it was with him a nature.

habituação s. f. (pl. **-ões**) habituation.

habituado adj. accustomed, used.

não estão ~**s à luz** they are not accustomed to light. **eu estava** ~ **a fazê-lo** I was used to do it.

habitual adj. m. + f. (pl. **-ais**) 1. habitual, customary. 2. usual, regular. 3. common, vulgar, ordinary. 4. frequent, chronic, inveterate. ‖ ~**mente** adv. habitually, regularly, frequently, normally, usually.

freguês ~ regular customer. **doença** ~ inveterate illness. **que não é** ~ unfamiliar. **vieram mais tarde do que** ~**mente** they came later than usual. **ele fazia este serviço** ~**mente** he did this job regularly.

habitualidade s. f. habitualness, customariness.

habitualismo s. m. habitualness, quality of being habitual, customariness.

habituar v. 1. to habituate, familiarize. 2. to accustom, get acquainted with. 3. to inure. 4. ~**-se a:** a) to take the habit of. b) to accustom o. s., become used to.

habituei-me a fazê-lo I got used to do it. **não estão habituados à luz** they are not accustomed to light. **eu estava habituado a fazê-lo** I was used to do it.

habitude s. f. 1. habitude, habitualness. 2. natural character, usual attitude. 3. usage, custom. 4. habitual practice or disposition.

habitudinário adj. 1. habitual, customary. 2. (fig.) incorrigible, incurable.

hacanéia s. f. ambler, pacer, palfrey.

hachura s. f. hachure.

hachurar v. to hachure.

Hades s. m. (Greek myth.) Hades: realm of the dead, underworld.

hadji s. m. hadji: a Moslem who has made his pilgrimage to Mecca.

hafalgesia s. f. (med.) haphalgesia: imaginary sensation of pain.

háfnio s. m. (chem.) hafnium.

hagiografia s. f. hagiography: 1. sacred literature or writings. 2. collection of biographies of saints.

hagiográfico adj. hagiographic, hagiographal.

hagiógrafo s. m. 1. hagiographer, writer of sacred books. 2. Hagiographa. ‖ adj. hagiographal, hagiographic.

hagiolatria s. f. hagiolatry.

hagiológico adj. hagiologic(al).

hagiológio s. m. hagiology: branch of literature which deals with the lives and legends of saints.

hagiólogo s. m. hagiologist.

hagiomaquia s. f. 1. hagiomachy. 2. holy war. 3. martyrology.

hagiômaco s. m. adept of hagiomachy.

haglura s. f. speck on the wing feathers or thighs of birds.

hahnemanniano adj. Hahnemannian: relating to Hahnemann, founder of the homoeopathic system of medicine.

haitiano s. m. Haitian: native or inhabitant of Haiti. ‖ adj. Haitian.

halali s. m. (hunt.) hallali, bugle-call, view-halloo, mort.

tocar o ~ (hunt.) to blow a mort, to sound the hallali.

halésia s. f. (bot.) Halesia: snowdrop or silverbell tree.

halial adj. m. + f. (pl. -ais) of, pertaining to or relative to the pollex.

haliêutica s. f. halieutics: the art or practice of fishing.

haliêutico adj. halieutic(al).

haliote s. m. (zool.) abalone: any of various species of ear shells.

halito s. m. rock-salt, halite.

hálito s. m. 1. breath, respiration. 2. smell, scent. 3. exhalation, emanation. 4. bad breath. 5. breeze, breath of air.

mau ~ (med.) haliotosis, bad or offensive breath.

halitose s. f. (med.) halitosis, bad breath.

halo s. m. 1. halo, aureole, corona. 2. rose-coloured ring around the nipple. 3. (fig.) glory, gloriole, nimbus.

formar ~ to halo.

halófilo adj. (bot.) halophilous, preferring or habitually growing in soil impregnated with salt.

halogêneo, halógeno s. m. (chem.) halogen, salt-former. ‖ adj. halogenous.

halogênico adj. (chem.) halogenous, generating saline compounds.

halografia s. f. halography, description of salts.

halógrafo s. m. expert in salts and their preparation.

halóide s. m. (chem.) haloid, saltlike, resembling salt. ‖ adj. haloid.

halologia s. f. treatise on salts and their preparation.

halomancia s. f. halomancy, divination by means of salt.

halomante s. m. halomancer.

halomântico adj. halomantic.

halometria s. f. (chem.) halometry: system and method of measuring the percentage of salt in brine.

halométrico adj. halometric(al).

halorragáceo adj. (bot.) haloragidaceous.

halotecnia s. f. (chem.) halotechny.

halotécnico adj. (chem.) halotechnical.

haltere, halter s. m. bar-bell, dumb-bell (plate G 3).

halterofilismo s. m. dumb-bell exercises.

halurgia s. f. (chem.) halurgy: art and science of preparing salt solutions.

hálux s. m. hallux: (anat., zool.) the first digit of the hind leg; (in man) the great toe.

hamadríade, hamadria, hamadríada s. f. 1. (Greek myth.) hamadryad: a wood nymph. 2. (zool.) sacred baboon.

hamamélia hamamélide, hamamélis s. f. (bot.) witch hazel.

hamamelidáceo adj. (bot.) hamamelidaceous.

hamburguês s. m. native or inhabitant of Hamburg.

hamélia s. f. a genus of tropical or subtropical shrubs (order Rubiaceae).

hâmulo s. m. (anat., bot., ornith.) hamulus, hamus, hooklet.

hangar s. m. shed, hangar, dock, lean-to.

hanoveriano, hanovriano s. m. Hanoverian, native or inhabitant of Hanover. ‖ adj. Hanoverian.

Hansa s. f. (hist.) Hanseatic league, Hanse or Hanseatic towns.

hanseático adj. Hanseatic.

hanseniano s. m. lazar, leper. ‖ adj. leprous.

haplografia s. f. haplography: a copyist's omission of a letter or word.

haplóide adj. m. + f. (biol.) haploid.

haplologia s. f. (phil.) haplology: contraction of a word by omission of one or more syllables in pronunciation, syllabic syncope.

haplológico adj. (phil.) haplologic.

haplotomia s. f. (surg.) haplotomy, simple surgical incision.

haraganear, haraganar v. (Braz.) 1. to run wild, rove at large (cattle). 2. (fig.) to loaf, idle.

haragano adj. (Braz.) 1. shy, wild (horse). 2. (fig.) idle, lazy, slothful.

haraquiri s. m. (Japan) hara-kiri: suicide by disembowelling.

haras s. m. stud, stud-farm, horse breeding establishment.

harém s. m. (pl. **-éns**) 1. harem, seraglio. 2. the occupants of a harem.

haríolo s. m. a guesser.

harmala s. f. (bot.) African rue, harmel.

harmonia s. f. 1. harmony, accord, consonance, concord. 2. (mus.) harmonics, rules of harmony, tonal laws. 3. smoothness and concordance of style. 4. agreement, consent. 5. due proportion, symmetry. 6. amity, friendship, understanding. 7. uniformity, unanimity. 8. harmoniousness, melodiousness.

Harmonia dos Evangelhos arrangement of the evangelic text in the form of a harmony. **a boa ~ entre nós** the good understanding between us. **eles viveram em ~ na mesma casa** they lived peacefully in the same house. **~ de cores** harmony of colours.

harmônica s. f. concertina, harmonica, accordion.

harmônico adj. 1. harmonic(al), tuneful. 2. concordant, consonant. 3. regular. 4. coherent. 5. proportionate, harmonious. ‖ **-amente** adv. harmonically, tunefully.

proporção -a harmonic proportion.

H

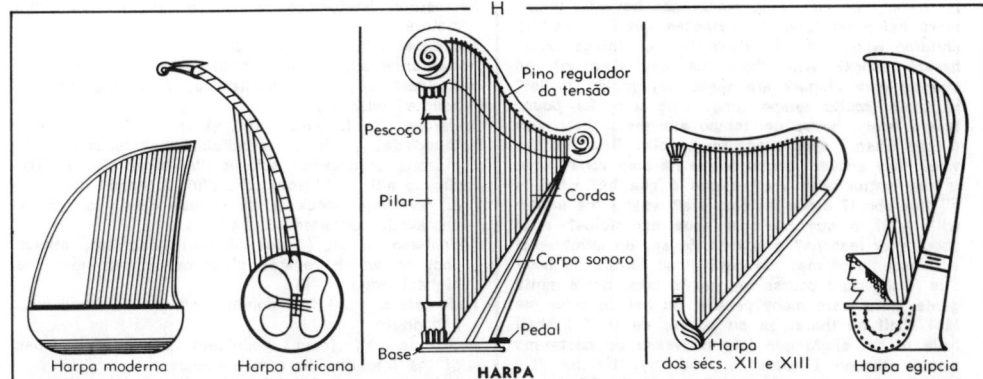

Harpa moderna • Harpa africana • Base • Pescoço • Pilar • Pino regulador da tensão • Cordas • Corpo sonoro • Pedal • Harpa dos sécs. XII e XIII • Harpa egípcia

HARPA

harmoniflute s. m. (mus.) harmoniphon.

harmônio s. m. (mus.) harmonium, orchestrion.

harmoniocordo s. m. (mus.; also **harmonicorde**) harmonichord.

harmonioso adj. 1. harmonious. 2. musical, melodious, sonorous, sweet-sounding. 3. concordant, consonant, accordant. 4. dulcet, symphonious. 5. aesthetic(al). ‖ **-amente** adv. harmoniously, melodiously, accordantly, concordantly, symphoniously.

harmonista s. m. + f. 1. harmonist, one skilled in the principles of musical harmony, musical composer. 2. (Braz.) harmonica or accordeon player.

harmonização s. f. (pl. **-ões**) harmonization, accomodation.

harmonizador s. m. 1. harmonizer, harmonist. 2. mediator. ‖ adj. harmonizing.

harmonizar v. 1. to harmonize. 2. to make harmonious, attune (to). 3. to be or arrange in musical harmony. 4. to conciliate, reconcile. 5. to agree, accord, concord. 6. (mus.) to set accompanying parts to (melody, tune). 7. to be in conformity. 8. to live in harmony with. 9. to blend. 10. to assort, coordinate. 11. to accommodate. **as idéias dele não se harmonizam com suas ações** his ideas are out of keeping (or harmony, tune) with his actions.

armonômetro s. m. harmonometer: instrument for measuring the harmonic relations of sounds.

arpa s. f. 1. harp (plate H). 2. (zool.) harp-shell. ~ **eólica** Aeolian harp.

árpaga s. f. a kind of catapult (ancient military engine).

arpear, harpar, harpejar v. 1. to harp, play on the harp. 2. to compose for the harp.

arpia s. f. 1. (myth.) harpy, winged monster. 2. (fig.) rapacious person. 3. (ornith.) harpy-eagle.

arpista s. m. + f. harpist, harper, harpress.

irto adj. 1. strong, vigorous. 2. robust, sturdy. ‖ adv. 1. superabundantly, in excess. 2. much, greatly. 3. more than enough, rather.

ısta s. f. 1. spear, lance. 2. pike, pole. 3. auction, public sale. **oferecer (ou vender) em ~ pública** to put up at auction.

ıste s. f. 1. staff, pole, long stick. 2. (bot.) stipe, stem, stalk. 3. young shoot, sprout. 4. peduncle, haulm. 5. (tech.) spindle, rod, shank, shaft (plates A 2, 6). 6. (mus.) tail of a note (plate N 1). ~ **de comando** (tech.) striker rod. ~ **de comando e balancim** (tech.) push-rod and rocker arm. ~ **ıe encontro** tappet-rod. ~ **de gramínea** spear of grass. ~ **de uma pena** rachis (pl. rachides). ~ **de válvula** valve stem. ~ **do êmbolo** piston rod (plates

B 14, C 11). ~ **do freio** brake-rod. ~ **do pára-lama** mudguard stay. ~ **do pavilhão** flagstaff. ~ **do trole** trolley-boom. **sem** ~ stemless.

hasteado adj. hoisted, pulled up, displayed.

hasteamento s. m. hoist, hoisting.

hastear v. 1. to stick at the end of a staff. 2. to hoist, pull up, heave. 3. to fly or display (a pennant or flag), unfurl. ~ **a bandeira** to fly the flag.

hastibranco adj. white with black tips (said of a bull's horns).

hastifino adj. slender-horned (bull or cattle).

hastifoliado adj. (bot.) hastate, lanceolate.

hastiforme adj. m. + f. spear-shaped, hastate.

hastil s. m. (pl. **-is**) 1. staff of a lance or halberd. 2. young shoot, sprout. 3. peduncle.

hastilha s. f. splint, splinter of wood.

hastiverde adj. having greenish horns (bulls).

hauinita s. f. (min.) azurite, blue carbonate of copper, copper-ore.

haurir v. 1. to drain, exhaust, draw off. 2. to suck, absorb. 3. (poet.) to drink, sip.

haurível adj. m. + f. (pl. **-íveis**) absorbable, drinkable.

hausto s. m. draught, gulp.

haustório s. m. haustorium, small roots, suckers (of parasitic plants or fungi).

havaiano s. m. Hawaiian: 1. native or inhabitant of Hawaii. 2. the Hawaiian language. ‖ adj. Hawaiian.

havana s. m. Havana (cigar). ‖ adj. Havana brown, light-brown.

havanês s. m. Havanese: native or citizen of Havana. ‖ adj. Havanese.

havano s. m. Havana cigar.

haver (I) s. m. (com.) 1. credit, outstanding debt. 2. **~es** pl. wealth, riches, fortune. ~ **de uma conta** credit of an account.

haver (II) v. 1. to have, possess, own. 2. to get, obtain, receive. 3. to attain, succeed in. 4. to consider, ponder. 5. to exist. 6. to judge, decide. 7. to happen, occur. 8. to elapse, pass (time). 9. to have on account or credit. 10. to proceed, continue to act. 11. to behave (o. s.), conduct (o. s.). 12. to agree. ~ **falta** to fail. ~ **por bem** 1. to deign. 2. to take in good part. **há algo de novo?** is there any news? **se houvesse algo** if there were anything, if aught there be. **há alguns bons e outros maus** there are good and bad ones. **havia ali uma janela** there used to be a window. **há seus altos e baixos na vida** there are ups and downs in life. **há anos** 1. years ago. 2. for years (back). **o primeiro dia livre desde há anos** the first free day for years. **há um ano** a year ago. **há muito tempo**

far back, long ago, long since. **não havendo tempo** there being no time. **há crianças que...** there are children who... **há tal coisa?** do such things exist? **haverá dança?** will there be any dancing? **há quartos para alugar?** are there any rooms to let? **há muito muito tempo** long, long ago. **há pouco tempo** lately. **houve um tempo em que...** there was a time when... **eles chegaram há oito dias** this day week they arrived. **o que é que há com você?** what is the matter with you? **o que é que há?** what is all this about? **o que há com ele?** what's the matter with him? **o que há com seus exercícios?** what about your lessons? **o que há de ser de mim?** what will become of me? **eis aqui como haveis de fazer** this is the right course for you to take. **havia muita gente** there were many people. **eu hei de achar-me lá** I shall be there. **se eu houver de ir** if I shall have to go. **ainda que isto houvesse de custar-me a vida** though I were to lose my life for it... **não há de que** don't mention it. **não há tempo** there is no time. **não haverá** there will not be. **isto nunca há de ser** that will never be. **caso não haja dificuldades** if there is no trouble. **não havia** there was not. **resolva as dificuldades que houver** dispose of what difficulties there are. **~ por bem** to decide; to make a resolution.

haxixe s. m. hashish, Indian hemp, marijuana.

heautognose s. f. (philos.) self-knowledge.

hebdômada s. f. hebdomad: 1. week, group of seven days. 2. sum of seven things or persons.

hebdomadário s. m. weekly publication, weekly. ‖ adj. weekly, hebdomadal.

hebdomático adj. hebdomadal, hebdomatical.

hebefrenia s. f. (path.) hebephrenia.

hebetação s. f., **hebetamento** s. m. 1. dullness, stupidity. 2. denseness, ignorance. 3. hebetation.

hebetar v. 1. to hebetate. 2. to dull, stupefy. 3. to become dull or obtuse.

hebetismo s. m. hebetude, dullness, lethargy, stupidity.

hebetizado adj. hebetudinous.

hebetude s. f. hebetude, dullness, obtuseness.

hebraico s. m. 1. Hebrew, Hebraist. 2. the Hebrew language. ‖ adj. Hebraic(al).

hebraísmo s. m. Hebraism: manner or custom peculiar to the Hebrews or to the Hebrew language.

hebraísta s. m. + f. Hebraist.

hebraizante adj. m. + f. Hebraizing.

hebraizar v. to Hebraize.

hebréia s. f. Jewess, Hebrew woman.

hebreu s. m. Hebrew: 1. an Israelite, a Jew. 2. language spoken by the Hebrews. 3. **~s** pl. collective designation of this people. ‖ adj. Hebrew, Hebraic, Jewish.

hecatombe s. f. hecatomb: 1. (myth.) sacrifice of a hundred oxen or other animals. 2. any sacrifice of victims. 3. (fig.) slaughter of human beings or animals.

hechor s. m. (S. Braz.) jackass (for breeding).

hectare s. m. hectare.

héctica, hética s. f. (med.) hectic (fever), consumption, phthisis.

hecticidade, heticidade s. f. (med.) hectic or consumptive state.

héctico, hético s. m. hectic or consumptive person. ‖ adj. 1. hectic(al), consumptive, phthisical. 2. (fig.) very lean.

hectoédrico adj. (min.) hectohedric.

hectografar v. to hectograph.

hectógrafo s. m. hectograph.

hectograma s. m. hectogram(me) (= 100 grams).

hectolitro s. m. hectoliter, hectolitre, 100 liters.

hectômetro s. m. hectometer, 100 meters.

hectostere, hectostéreo s. m. hectostere, 100 cubic meters.

hederáceo adj. (bot.) hederaceous.

hederiforme adj. m. + f. (bot.) hederiform.

hederígero adj. 1. hederiferous, producing ivy. 2. adorned with ivy.

hederoso adj. hederose, full of ivy.

hediondez(a) s. f. 1. dreadfulness, hideousness. 2. hideous or dreadful act, horrible deed. 3. atrocity.

hediondo adj. 1. hideous, dreadful. 2. horrid, horrible. 3. revolting, shocking. 4. vicious, foul, corrupt. 5. depraved, perverted. 6. hedonic.

hedonismo s. m. (Greek philos.) hedonism: ethical doctrine which regards pleasure or happiness the highest good in life.

hedonista s. m. + f. hedonist. ‖ adj. m. + f. hedonist, hedonistic.

hedrocele s. f. (med.) hedrocele: hernia or prolapse of the intestine through the anus.

hegelianismo s. m. (also **hegelismo**) Hegelianism: philosophical system of Georg Wilhelm Friedrich Hegel (1770-1831).

hegeliano s. m. Hegelian: adept of Hegelianism.

hegemonia s. f. 1. hegemony, predominance. 2. leadership. 3. preponderance. 4. peerlessness.

hegemônico adj. hegemonic(al).

hégira s. f. hejira: 1. flight of Mohammed from Mecca to Medina. 2. beginning of the Moslem era.

heiduque s. m. Haiduck, Heyduck: 1. Hungarian foot soldier. 2. attendant dressed in Hungarian semi-military costume.

hein (also **hem**) interj. hey!, hem!

helcologia s. f. (path.) helcology, treatise on ulcers.

helcose s. f. (med.) helcosis, ulceration.

heleborizar v. to purge with hellebore.

heléboro s. m. 1. (bot.) hellebore. 2. powdered root of the American hellebore.

heléboro-negro s. m. (pl. **heléboros-negros**) (bot.) black hellebore, Christmas rose.

heléboro-verde s. m. (pl. **heléboros-verdes**) (bot.) green hellebore, lingwort.

helênico adj. Hellenic.

helenismo s. m. Hellenism: 1. peculiarity of the Greek language. 2. spirit and influence characteristic of the Greek race, history or culture.

helenista s. m. + f. Hellenist: 1. one who adopted the Greek language, dress, customs, etc. 2. one who is learned in the Greek language and literature. ‖ adj. m. + f. Hellenistic.

helenístico adj. Hellenistic(al).

helenizar v. to Hellenize, make Hellenic or Hellenistic.

heleno s. m. 1. Hellene, Greek. 2. **~s** pl. Hellenic people, Greek nation. ‖ adj. Hellenic, Hellenistic, Greek, Grecian.

heliaco adj. (astr.) heliacal: closely connected with the sun.

helianto s. m. helianthus: a genus of plants containing the sunflower.

hélice s. m. + f. 1. (geom.) helix. 2. (aeron., naut.) airscrew, propeller (plates A 3, L 2, P 4). 3. (anat.) curved rim or margin of the outer ear. 4. (archit.) spiral, small volute. **~ dupla** (naut.) twin screw. **~ de duas pás** two-bladed airscrew. **~ de impulsão** impeller. **~ de transporte, ~ transportadora** worm-conveyer. **eixo da ~** propeller shaft. **pá de ~** propeller blade. **passo de ~** pitch of the screw.

helicite s. f. helicite: fossil snail-shell.

helicoidal adj. m. + f. (pl. **-ais**) helicoid(al), helical, screw-shaped, coiled like a helix. **engrenagem ~** spiral gear.

helicóide s. m. + f. helicoid, helicoidal surface. ‖ adj. m. + f. helicoid(al).

helicômetro s. m. helicometer: instrument for measuring the tractive force of propellers.
helicóptero s. m. helicopter, autogiro, autogyro, motor plane.
helícula s. f. little screw.
hélio s. m. (chem.) helium (symbol He).
heliocêntrico adj. heliocentric(al).
heliocromia s. f. (phot.) heliochromy, photography in natural colours.
heliocrômico adj. (phot.) heliochromic.
heliofilia s. f. heliophilia.
heliófugo adj. heliofugal.
heliografar v. to heliograph.
heliografia s. f. heliography: 1. description and mapping of the surface of the sun. 2. process of engraving by exposure to light.
heliográfico adj. heliographic(al).
   cópia ~a photographic printing. aparelho para cópias -as printing frame.
heliógrafo s. m. heliograph.
heliogravura s. f. heliogravure: 1. photo-engraving. 2. engraved plate or print.
heliolatria s. f. heliolatry.
heliométrico adj. heliometric(al).
heliômetro s. m. heliometer.
helionose s. f. generic designation of plant diseases caused by the action of sunrays.
helioscopia s. f. helioscopy: observation of the sun through the helioscope.
helioscópico adj. helioscopic.
helioscópio s. m. helioscope.
heliose s. f. heliosis: 1. (bot.) spots caused on leaves by the concentration of sunrays. 2. sunstroke.
heliostática s. f. heliostatics: doctrine of the planetary system held in equilibrium by its central force — the sun.
heliostático adj. heliostatic.
helióstato s. m. heliostat: instrument consisting of a mirror moved by clockwork by which a sunbeam is continuously reflected to one spot.
helioterapia s. f. (med.) heliotherapy.
helioterápico adj. (med.) heliotherapic.
heliotermômetro s. m. heliothermometer.
heliotipia s. f. heliotype.
heliotropia s. f. heliotropism, heliotropy.
heliotrópico adj. heliotropic(al).
heliotrópio s. m. 1. (bot. + physiol.) heliotrope. 2. (min.) blood-stone. 3. (chem.) litmus.
heliotropismo s. m. heliotropism, heliotropy.
hélix s. m. (anat.) helix: curved rim or margin of the outer ear.
helmíntico adj. helminthic.
helminto, helminte s. m. (zool.) helminth, intestinal worm.
helmintóide adj. m. + f. helminthoid.
helmintologia s. f. helminthology: the science of worms.
helmintologista s. m. + f. helminthologist.
helônia s. f. (bot.) swamp pink.
Helvécia s. f. Helvetia.
helvécio /s. m. Helvetian, Swiss. ‖ adj. Helvetic, Helvetian, Swiss.
helvético adj. Helvetian.
hem! interj. hem!, don't tell me! hey, what did you say!
   mas é, ~! tell me another!
hemal adj. m. + f. (pl. -ais) haemal.
hemácia, hematia s. f. erythrocyte, red blood corpuscle.
hemartrose s. f. (med.) hemarthrosis: hemorrhage in a joint.
hemastática s. f. hemastatics, haemastatics: the hydrostatics of the blood in living bodies.

hematêmese s. f. (med.) hematemesis, vomiting of blood.
hemático adj. haematic: of or pertaining to blood.
hematímetro s. m. hematimeter, hemacytometer.
hematina s. f. hematin, heme: a brown, amorphous pigment derived from hemoglobin.
hematita s. f. (min.) hematite, haematite: native red iron ore, native red oxide of iron, specular iron, blood-stone.
hematocéfalo s. m. (med.) 1. hematocephalus. 2. cerebral hematoma.
hematocele s. f. (med.) hematocelia, hematocoelia.
hematócrito s. m. hematocrit: a centrifugal device for determining the amount of blood-corpuscles.
hematode adj. m. + f. of the nature of blood, hematoid.
hematófago adj. (zool.) hematophagous.
hematofilo adj. (bot.) having blood-coloured leaves.
hematófilo adj. (zool.) hematophile, fond of blood.
hematofobia s. f. hematophobia.
hematófobo s. m. (med.) hematophobe.
hematóide adj. m. + f. hematoid.
hematologia s. f. (biol.) hematology.
hematológico adj. hematologic(al).
hematoma s. m. (med.) hematoma: a tumour containing effused blood.
hematônfalo s. m. (med.) umbilical hernia.
hematopoese s. f. hematopoiesis.
hematopoético adj. hematopoietic: pertaining to the formation of blood cells.
hematosar v. to arterialize, change venous into arterial blood.
hematose s. f. hematosis: formation or arterialization of blood.
hematóxilo s. m. logwood tree.
hematozoário s. m. (zool.) hematozoon, haematozoon.
hematúria, hematuria s. f. (med.) hematuria: the presence of blood in the urine.
   ~ do gado vacum e ovino (vet.) red-water.
hematúrico adj. hematuric, haematuric.
hemeralopia s. f. (med.) hemeralopia: day blindness.
hemeralópico adj. hemeralopic.
hemerocale s. f. (bot.) hemerocallis, day lilly.
hemerologia s. f. hemerology: art of composing a calender.
hemerológio s. m. hemerologium, a comparative calender.
hemeroteca s. f. hemerotheca: section of a library where daily papers are kept.
hemialgia s. f. (med.) hemialgia, megrim, neuralgia on one side only.
hemianopsia s. f. (med.) hemianopsia: blindness in one half of the field of vision in one or both eyes.
hemicarpo s. m. (bot.) hemicarp, half of a fruit which consists of two carpels.
hemicíclico adj. hemicyclic, semicircular.
hemiciclo s. m. hemicycle, semicircle, semicircular rows of seats.
hemicilíndrico adj. hemicylindrical.
hemicilindro s. m. hemicylinder, half of a cylinder (divided in the direction of its axis).
hemicrania s. f. (med.) hemicrania, hemialgia.
hemicrânico adj. (med.) hemicranic, hemicranial.
hemiedria s. f. (cryst.) hemihedry, hemihedrism.
hemiedro s. m. (cryst.) hemihedron, a hemihedral crystal or form.
hemiédrico adj. hemihedric, hemihedral.
hemimorfita s. f. (min.) hemimorphite, calamine.
hemioctaedro s. m. (geom.) tetrahedron.
hemiopia s. f. (med.) hemiopia, hemianopia, absence of visual power in one half of the retina.
hemiplegia s. f. (med.) hemiplegia: paralysis of one half of the body.

hemiplégico adj. hemiplegic.
hemiprismático adj. (cryst.) hemiprismatic.
hemíptero s. m. (zool.) 1. hemipter. 2. Hemiptera: an order of insects. ‖ adj. hemipteral, hemipterous.
hemisférico adj. hemispheric(al).
hemisfério s. m. hemisphere: 1. half of the celestial or terrestrial globe. 2. a half-sphere. 3. map or projection of the terrestrial or the celestial sphere.
hemisferoidal adj. (pl. -ais) hemispheroidal.
hemisferóide s. m. hemispheroid.
hemistíquio s. m. hemistich, half a verse or line.
hemiteria s. f. (med.) hemiteria, hemitery.
hemitríti(c)a s. f. (med.) a relapsing fever.
hemitropia s. f. hemitropism.
hemítropo adj. hemitropic, hemitropous.
hemocianina s. f. (zool.) hemocyanin, haemocyanin.
hemocitômetro s. m. (med.) hemocytometer: apparatus for counting the blood corpuscles.
hemocultura s. f. (med.) hemoculture: a bacteriological culture of blood.
hemodia s. f. (med.) hemodia: unusual sensitiveness of the teeth.
hemodinâmica s. f. (med.) hemodynamics: the science of blood pressure.
hemodinamômetro s. m. (med.) hemodynamometer: instrument for measuring the pressure of blood.
hemodromômetro, hemodrômetro s. m. (med.) hemodromometer: instrument for measuring the speed of blood.
hemofilia s. f. (med.) hemophilia: tendency to delayed clotting of blood.
hemoftalmia s. f. (med.) hemophtalmia: extravasation of blood within the eye.
hemoglobina s. f. hemoglobin, the oxygen carrying pigment of the red blood corpuscles.
hemoglobinúria, hemoglobinuria s. f. (med.) hemoblobinúria; presence of hemoglobin in the urine.
hemólise s. f. (med.) hemolysis: separation of the hemoglobin from the red blood corpuscles.
hemômetro s. m. (med.) hemometer, hemoglobinometer.
hemopatia s. f. (med.) hemopathy: any disease of the blood.
hemoplástico adj. (med.) hemoplastic: furthering the production of blood.
hemoptíico adj. (med.) hemoptysical.
hemoptise s. f. (med.) hemoptysis: spitting of blood.
hemorragia s. f. (med.) hemorrhage, copious bleeding, extravasation.
hemorrágico adj. hemorrhagic.
hemorrinia s. f. (med.) epistaxis, hemorrhage from the nose.
hemorroidal adj. m. + f. (pl. -ais) (med.) hemorrhoidal.
hemorroidário s. m. person suffering from piles. ‖ adj. hemorrhoidal.
hemorróidas, hemorróides s. f. pl. (med.) hemorrhoids, piles.
hemorroidoso s. m. (med.) hemorrhoidal.
hemospasia s. f. (med.) hemospasia: the drawing of blood, esp. by cupping or hemospasts.
hemospático adj. (also hemospásico) hemospastic.
hemóstase s. f. (med.) hemostasis: 1. stagnation of blood. 2. the checking of a hemorrhage.
hemostático s. m. hemostatic, styptic medicine, ergot. ‖ adj. hemostatic, styptic, stopping or preventing hemorrhage.
hemotexia s. f. (med.) dissolution of blood.
hemotórax s. m., sg. + pl. (med.) hemothorax: the presence of blood in a pleural cavity.
hena s. f. 1. (bot.) Egyptian privet. 2. dye or cosmetic made from the leaves of this plant. 3. red-brown, reddish or red-yellow hue.
hendecaedro s. m. (geom.) hendecahedron.

hendecágono s. m. (geom.) hendecagon: plane figure of eleven sides and angles.
hendecandro adj. (bot.) hendecandrous.
hendecassílabo s. m. (poet.) hendecasyllable.
hendíadis s. f., sg. + pl. (rhet.) hendiadys: figure of speech which consists in using two words to express a single idea, e. g. "by hook or by crook".
henequém s. m. (bot.) henequen, sisal hemp, silk grass.
heortônimo s. m. generic designation of popular feasts.
hep interj. (S. Braz. — used for animals) go on!
hépar s. m. hepar: 1. (anat.) liver. 2. (ancient chem.) collective designation of compounds of sulphur with metals.
hepatal adj. m. + f. (pl. -ais) (anat. + med.) hepatic.
hepatalgia s. f. (med.) hepatalgia: neuralgia of the liver.
hepatálgico adj. hepatalgic.
hepatargia s. f. (med.) hepatargy: auto-intoxication from defective liver action.
hepática s. f. (bot.) liverwort, hepatica, liver-moss, liver-leaf.
hepático adj. hepatic(al).
hepatismo s. m. (med.) hepatism: ill health due to a liver disease.
hepatita s. f. (min.) hepatite, liverstone.
hepatite s. f. (med.) hepatitis: inflammation of the liver.
hepatização s. f. (pl. -ões) hepatization: 1. transformation of organic tissue into a liverlike substance. 2. impregnation with hydrogen sulfide.
hepatizar-se v. to become hepatized.
hepatocele s. f. (med.) hepatocele: hernial protrusion of part of the liver.
hepatografia s. f. hepatography: description of the liver.
hepatologia s. f. hepatology: science of or treatise on the liver.
hepatológico adj. hepatologic.
hepatopatia s. f. hepatopathy: any disease of the liver.
hepatorréia s. f. (med.) hepatorrhea: morbidly excessive secretion of bile.
hepatotomia s. f. (surg.) hepatotomy: surgical incision of the liver.
heptacordo s. m. (mus.) heptachord: 1. instrument with seven strings. 2. diatonic series of seven tones. 3. interval of a major seventh.
heptadá(c)tilo adj. heptadactylo: having seven fingers.
heptaédrico adj. heptahedral: having seven faces.
heptaedro s. m. heptahedron: solid figure with seven faces.
heptafilo adj. (bot.) heptaphyllous, having seven leaves.
heptaginia s. f. Heptagynia: order of plants which have seven distinct styles.
heptágino adj. (bot.) heptagynious, heptagynian.
heptagonal adj. m. + f. (pl. -ais) heptagonal, septilateral.
heptágono s. m. heptagon, septangle.
heptâmetro s. m. (poet.) heptameter: verse of seven metrical feet.
heptandro adj. (bot.) heptandrous, heptandrian, heptandrious.
heptanemo adj. (zool.) having seven tentacles.
heptangular adj. heptangular.
heptanterado adj. (bot.) heptantherous.
heptapétalo adj. (bot.) heptapetalous.
heptarca s. m. heptarch, heptarchist: one of the rulers of a heptarchy.
heptarquia s. f. heptarchy: government of seven persons.

heptassépalo adj. (bot.) heptasepals.
heptassílabo s. m. (poet.) heptasyllabic verse. ‖ adj. heptasyllabic.
heptateuco s. m. (rel.) Heptateuch: the first seven books of the Old Testament.
heptátomo adj. (zool.) having seven articulations.
hera s. f. (bot.) ivy, English ivy.
coberto de ~ ivied.
heráclias s. f. pl. (Greek myth.) Heracleidan feasts, festival in honour of Heracles.
heráldica s. f. heraldry, heraldic art, armo(u)ry.
heráldico s. m. armo(u)rist, blazoner. ‖ adj. heraldic, armorial. ‖ **heraldicamente** adv. heraldically.
arte -a blazonry. **descrever heraldicamente** to blazon.
heraldista s. m. + f. person versed in heraldry, armo(u)rist.
heraldo s. m. herald.
herança s. f. 1. inheritance, heritage. 2. legacy, bequest. 3. family estate, hereditary property. 4. (physiol.) heredity, hereditariness. 5. heritage, birthright. 6. succession. 7. heirloom.
~ **em comum** parcenary, coinheritance. ~ **inalienável** entail. ~ **paterna** patrimony. **por** ~ by inheritance. **adir a** ~ to take into possession an inheritance. **imposto sobre** ~**s** death duty, legacy duty. **eles esperam uma** ~ (fam.) they wait for dead men's hoes. **inesperada** ~ **de bens de raiz** landfall. ~ **vacante, vaga** vacant legacy; vacant inheritance.
hera-terrestre s. f. (pl. **heras-terrestres**) (bot.) common ground ivy, ale-hoof.
herbáceo adj. herbaceous, herbescent.
herbanário s. m. 1. herb shop, herbalist's shop. 2. herb dealer.
herbário s. m. herbarium, collection of dry herbs systematically arranged.
herbático adj. herbal, herbaceous.
herbífero adj. herbiferous, producing vegetation.
herbívoro s. m. herbivore. ‖ adj. herbivorous, graminivorous, plantivorous.
herbolária s. f. herbwoman, sorceress who uses herbs and their decoctions.
herbolário s. m. herb gatherer, herbalist, herborist.
herbóreo adj. herbal.
herborista s. m. + f. herborist, herbalist.
herborização s. f. (pl. -ões) herborization, botanization.
herborizador s. m. herborist, herbalist.
herborizar v. to herborize, botanize.
herboso adj. herby, grassy, abounding with herbs, full of grass.
hercotectônica s. f. military architecture, fortification.
herculano adj. Herculean.
hercúleo adj. 1. Herculean. 2. (fig.) strong, vigorous, robust.
Hércules s. m. 1. (fig.) Hercules: man of extraordinary strength and courage. 2. (astr.) northern constellation between Corona Borealis and Lyra.
as colunas de ~ Pillars of Hercules. **trabalhos de** ~ Herculean labours; any difficult undertaking.
herdade s. f. 1. farm, estate, landed property. 2. homestead, country seat. 3. inheritance, heritage.
herdado adj. inherited, ancestral.
herdadola s. f. a small estate or rural property.
herdar v. 1. to inherit, get by succession. 2. to receive by transmission from ancestors, succeed by inheritance. 3. to come into a fortune. 4. to be vested with the right to a thing. 5. to bequeath, legate.
~ **as virtudes de seus pais** to inherit the virtues of one's ancestors. **bens que herdamos dos nossos avós** property which came to us from our grand-parents.
herdeira s. f. heiress, inheritress, inheritrix.

herdeiro s. m. 1. heir. 2. inheritor, successor. 3. legatee.
~ **direto** heir of the body. ~ **natural** heir-at--law. ~ **presuntivo,** ~ **provável** heir apparent, presumptive. ~ **testamentário** heir by will. ~ **universal** universal legatee. **ele é** ~ **de uma fazenda** he succeeds to an estate. **príncipe** ~ crown prince. **sem** ~ heirless.
hereditariedade s. f. 1. hereditariness. 2. hereditary succession. 3. hereditability, heritability. 4. (biol.) heredity, principles of hereditary descent or transmission.
hereditário adj. 1. hereditary. 2. heritable, descendable, hereditable. 3. ancestral, patrimonial, native. 4. passing naturally from parent to offspring. 5. possessed or claimed by right of inheritance. ‖ **hereditariamente** adv. hereditarily, heritably.
herege s. m. + f. 1. heretic. 2. dissenter, misbeliever. 3. sectary, sectarian. 4. nonconformist. ‖ adj. heretic(al), contrary to accepted standards (religious faith, political creed, etc.).
cara de ~ ill look. **a necessidade tem cara de** ~ necessity has no law.
heresia, heregia s. f. heresy, any opinion contrary to the accepted interpretation.
heresiarca s. m. + f. heresiarch, leader in heresy, chief of a sect of heretics.
herético s. m. 1. heretic. 2. dissenter, misbeliever. 3. sectary, sectarian. 4. nonconformist. ‖ adj. heretic(al), misbelieving, unorthodox. ‖ **hereticamente** adv. heretically.
heril adj. m. + f. (pl. **-is**) belonging to a master or lord, lordly, manorial.
herma s. f. herma: a statue of a head.
hermafrodita, hermafrodito s. m. hermaphrodite, epicene. ‖ adj. m. + f. hermaphrodite, hermaphroditic, epicene, bisexual, androgynous.
planta ~ androgynous plant.
hermafroditismo s. m. (also **hermafrodismo**) hermaphroditism, epicenism, androgyny.
hermatita s. f. (min.) specular iron.
hermeneuta s. m. + f. hermeneut, exegete.
hermenêutica s. f. hermeutics: art or science of interpretation or exegesis.
hermenêutico adj. hermeutic(al), explanatory, exegetical.
hermes s. m., s. + pl. statue of Hermes or Mercury.
hermeta, hermete s. m. column crowned with a hermes.
hermeticidade s. f. air-tightness.
hermético adj. hermetic: 1. of or pertaining to Hermes. 2. hermaic. 3. air-proof, air-tight. 4. (fig.) difficult to grasp, abstruse. ‖ **hermeticamente** adv. air-tightly, hermetically.
hermografia s. f. treatise on the planet Mercury.
hérnia s. f. (med.) hernia, rupture, breach.
~ **estrangulada** strangulated hernia. ~ **carnosa** fleshy rupture. **ele sofre de** ~ he suffers from hernia, he is ruptured.
hernial adj. m. + f. (pl. **-ais**) (med.) hernial.
herniário, hérnico adj. (med.) hernial.
hernioso s. m. person suffering from hernia. ‖ adj. hernial.
herniotomia s. f. (surg.) herniotomy.
hernuto s. m. (eccl.) Herrnhuter, one of the Moravian Brethren.
herói s. m. 1. hero, man of extraordinary courage, fortitude or greatness. 2. champion of a cause. 3. principal personage in a poem, play or story.
veneração dos ~**s** hero-worship. **ele é um verdadeiro** ~ **de salão** he is a real carpet-knight. **ele era o** ~ **do dia** he was the lion of the day. **ele agiu**

como um ~ de romance he acted like the hero of a penny novel.
heroicidade s. f. heroism, valour, heroicalness.
grau de ~ degree of heroism.
heróico adj. 1. heroic(al), noble. 2. bold, daring. 3. valiant, valorous. 4. courageous, fearless. 5. (poet) epic(al). 6. herolike, gallant. ‖ **heroicamente** adv. valiantly, heroically, valorously, epically.
feito ~ exploit. **poema ~** epic poem. **verso ~** heroic verse.
herói-cômico adj. (pl. **herói-cômicos**) heroicomic, mock-heroic.
heróide s. f. heroid: love poem in heroic verse.
heroificar v. 1. to heroify, make heroic, give heroic character to. 2. to glorify, exalt, heroize.
heroína (I) s. f. 1. heroess, heroine. 2. principal female character of a poem, play, story or romance.
heroína (II) s. f. (chem., pharm.) Heroin (originally a tradename of narcotic diacetyl-morphine).
heroísmo s. m. 1. heroism. 2. courage, intrepidity. 3. valour, valorousness. 4. prowess, gallantry. 5. heroic character or action.
ato de ~ exploit.
herpes s. m. pl. 1. herpes: skin disease. 2. (fig.) rot, decay, contamination.
~ labial fever blister, fever sore.
herpes-zoster s. m. shingles: a cutaneous disease.
herpético adj. herpetic(al).
herpetismo s. m. (med.) herpetism.
herpetografia s. f. herpetography, description of reptiles.
herpetográfico adj. herpetographic, herpetologic.
herpetógrafo s. m. herpetographer, herpetologist.
herpetologia s. f. herpetology: 1. (zool.) science of reptiles. 2. (med.) treatise on herpes.
herpetológico adj. herpetologic(al).
herpetologista s. m. + f. herpetologist, herpetographer.
hertziano adj. Hertzian.
ondas -as Hertzian waves, radio waves.
hesitação s. f. (pl. -ões) 1. hesitation, delay in acting, hesitance. 2. indecision, vacillation. 3. faltering, wavering. 4. indetermination. 5. pause. 6. stammering. 7. (pop.) dawdling, shilly-shally.
hesitante adj. m. + f. hesitant, wavering, pausing, irresolute, hesitating, faltering, vacillating, indecisive. ‖ **~mente** adv. hesitantly, waveringly, unreadily, vacillatingly.
hesitar v. 1. to hesitate. 2. to vacillate, waver. 3. to halt, linger, shilly-shally. 4. to be undecided. 5. to doubt. 6. to pause. 7. to tarry, falter. 8. to hum and haw, stammer, speak haltingly.
ele hesitou ao ouvir as palavras dela he paused upon her words. **hesitei a respeito** I was in two minds about it. **ele respondeu sem ~** he answered without flinching.
hesperídio adj. (bot.) hesperidate, hesperideous.
hespério adj. (poet.) Hesperian, Western.
hessocênico adj. (geol.) tertiary.
hester s. m. blackwood: dark-gray, dark-striped wood.
hesterno adj. (poet.) hestern, hesternal, of yesterday.
hetera, hetaira s. f. hetaera, courtesan.
heteracanto s. m. (bot.) heteracanth.
heterandra adj. (bot.) heterandrous.
heteria s. f. heteria: secret political society of Greeks.
heterismo s. m. hetaerism, open concubinage.
heterista adj. m. + f. of or relative to hetaeras, amorous, sensual.
heterobrânquio adj. (zool.) heterobranchiate.
heterocarpo adj. (bot.) heterocarpous.
heteróclito adj. 1. heteroclite, heteroclitic(al). 2. irregular, anomalous. 3. strange, peculiar. 4. (fam.) extravagant, ridiculous.

heterocromia s. f. (anat. + bot.) heterochromia.
heterócromo adj. heterochromous.
heterocronia s. f. (biol.) heterochrony.
heterócrono adj. (biol.) heterochronous.
heterodáctilo, heterodátilo adj. (zool.) heterodactyl(e), heterodactylous.
heterodinâmico adj. heterodynamic(al).
heteródino s. m. (radio) heterodyne. ‖ adj. heterodyne.
heterodoxia s. f. 1. heterodoxy, dissent. 2. heterodox opinion or doctrine.
heterodoxo adj. heterodox, unorthodox, misbelieving.
heterofilia s. f. (bot.) heterophylly, condition of having leaves different from the regular form.
heterofilo adj. (bot.) heterophyllous.
heterofonia s. f. heterophony: 1. (mus.) differentiation of the pitch of sound. 2. (phon.) different pronunciation of words written in the same way.
heterofônico adj. (mus., phon.) heterophonic.
heterófono s. m. heterophonic words.
heterogamia s. f. (bot.) heterogamy.
heterogâmico, heterógamo adj. (bot.) heterogamous.
heterogeneidade s. f. heterogeneity, dissimilarity.
heterogêneo s. m. (zool.) zoophyte. ‖ adj. 1. heterogeneous. 2. different in kind, unlike, dissimilar. 3. composed of unlike elements. 4. motley. ‖ adv. heterogeneously.
heterogenesia s. f. (biol.) heterogenesis: 1. alternation of generations. 2. spontaneous generation.
heterogenia s. f. (biol.) heterogeny, abiogenesis.
heterógono adj. (geom.) having different angles.
heterogradia s. f. (stat.) heterogradient classification: classification in accordance with the quantitative magnitude of an element in an aggregate.
heterógrado adj. (stat.) heterogradient, of or relative to heterogradient classification.
heteróide adj. m. + f. heteroideous, diversified in form.
heteroinfecção, heteroinfeção s. f. (pl. -ões) (med.) heteroinfection, exogenous infection.
heterologia s. f. (chem., med.) heterology, want or absence of homology, structural difference from normal standards.
heterólogo adj. heterologous.
heterômero adj. heteromerous: differing in number, form, or character of parts.
heteromorfia s. f. heteromorphy, heteromorphism.
heteromorfismo s. m. heteromorphism, deviation from a type or norm.
heteromorfo adj. heteromorphic, heteromorphous.
heteromorfose s. f. (biol.) heteromorphosis: malformation or malposition of tissues, organs or parts.
heteronímia s. f. (gram.) indication of the gender by a word of different root.
heterônimo s. m. fictitious name, pen name. ‖ adj. heteronymic.
heteronomia s. f. heteronomy.
heterônomo adj. heteronomous.
heteropatia s. f. heteropathy, allopathy.
heteropático adj. heteropathic(al), allopathic(al).
heteropétalo adj. (bot.) heteropetalous.
heteroplasia s. f. (biol., med.) heteroplasia: replacement of normal by abnormal tissue.
heteroplasma s. m. (biol.) heteroplasm: any heterologous tissue.
heteroplastia s. f. (surg.) heteroplasty: graft derived from other sources than the patient himself.
heteroplástico adj. (surg.) heteroplastical.
heterorexia s. f. (med.) bulimia, excessive appetite.
heteróscio s. m. heteroscian: person living on one side of the equator as compared with one living on the opposite side. ‖ adj. heteroscian.

heterotaxia s. f. (med.) heterotaxia: abnormal placement of viscera or parts.

heterotecnia s. f. heterotechnique: application of different methods and processes.

heterotérmico adj. heterothermic.

heterótomo adj. (bot.) heterotomous.

heterótropo adj. (bot.) heterotropal, heterotropous.

heterozigoto s. m. (biol.) heterozygote: progeny derived from parents possessing different genetic character.

heteu s. m. (hist.) Hittite, descendant of Heth.

hética s. f. (med.) hectic fever, phthisis.

heticidade s. f. (med.) hectic or consumptive state.

hético s. m. hectic or consumptive person. || adj. 1. hectic(al), consumptive. 2. (fig.) very lean.

heu s. m. 1. lamentation, wailing. 2. funeral chant, mourning song. || interj. how sad! what a pity!

heureca interj. eureka! I got it!

heurística s. f. heuristic, science or art of heuristic demonstration, heuretic.

hexacanto adj. (zool.) hexacanthous.

hexaciclo adj. (bot.) hexacyclic: having hexamerous whorls.

hexacorália s. f. (zool.) hexacorallan: hexamerous coral.

hexacordo s. m. (mus.) hexachord: 1. diatonic series of six tones. 2. interval of a major sixth. 3. instrument with six strings.

hexadáctilo, hexadátilo adj. hexadactylous: having six fingers or toes.

hexaédrico adj. hexahedral.

hexaedro s. m. hexahedron, polyhedron of six faces.

hexafilo adj. (bot.) hexaphyllous: having six leaves.

hexágino adj. (bot.) hexagynian, hexagynous.

hexagonal adj. m. + f. (pl. -ais) 1. hexagonal, sexangular, having six sides and six angles. 2. (min.) of or pertaining to the hexagonal system in crystallography. || ~mente adv. hexagonally, sexangularly.

hexágono s. m. sexagon, sexangle.

hexagrama s. m. hexagram.

hexalépide adj. m. + f. (bot.) hexalepid, having whorls formed of six scales.

hexâmero adj. (bot. + zool.) hexamerous.

hexâmetro s. m. hexameter, verse consisting of six feet. || adj. hexametral, hexametric.

hexandro adj. (bot.) hexandrous, having six stamens.

hexantéreo adj. (bot.) hexantherous.

hexaoctaedro s. m. hexaoctahedron, polyhedron delimited by 48 scalene triangles.

hexapétalo adj. (bot.) hexapetalous.

hexápode s. m. hexapod, six-footed insect. || adj. m. + f. hexapod, hecapodous.

hexaspermo adj. (bot.) hexaspermous, hexaspermal, having six seeds.

hexassépalo adj. (bot.) hexasepalous.

hexassílabo s. m. hexasyllabic word or verse. || adj. hexasyllabic.

hexastêmone adj. m. + f. (bot.) hexastemonous, having six stamens.

hexástico s. m. hexastich, verse or poem consisting of six lines. || adj. hexastichic.

hexastilo s. m. (archit.) hexastyle portico or temple.

híade s. f. Hyades: constellation of more than two hundred stars in the Head of Taurus.

hialino adj. hyaline, glassy, crystalline.

hialita s. f. (min.) hyalite, pellucid variety of opal.

hialite s. f. hyalitis: inflammation of the hyaloid membrane or of the vitreous matter of the eye.

hiálito s. m. hyalite, strong dark-coloured glass.

hialografia s. f. hyalography: art of painting on glass.

hialógrafo s. m. hyalograph: instrument for tracing designs on glass.

hialóide s. f. (anat.) hyaloid membrane. || adj. hyaloid, glassy, transparent.

hialóideo adj. (anat.) hyaloid, of, pertaining to or relative to the hyaloid membrane.

hialoplasma s. m. (biol.) hyaloplasm: the clear, fluid ground substance of protoplasm.

hialossomo adj. (zool.) having a transparent body.

hialotecnia s. f. hyalotechnique, art of working on glass.

hialurgia s. f. hyalurgy: art of manufacturing glass.

hialúrgico adj. hyalurgic(al).

hiante adj. m. + f. 1. gaping, open-mouthed. 2. cleft, split, fissured. 3. (fig.) hungry.

hiapuá s. m. (Braz.) wild manioc or cassava.

hiatizar v. to form a hiatus.

hiato s. m. hiatus: 1. opening, gap. 2. (anat.) foramen. 3. (gram., pros.) concurrence of two separate vowels which are to be distinctly pronounced. 4. interval, interruption. 5. (fig.) lacuna, break. 6. missing link in a chain of proof.

hibernação s. f. (pl. -ões) (zool.) hibernation, winter-leep.

hibernáculo s. m. 1. hot-house, glass-house, conservatory. 2. hibernacle, hibernaculum. 3. any part of a plant which protects an embryonic organ during winter. 4. (Roman., hist.) winter quarters of troops.

hibernal, hiberno adj. m. + f. (pl. -ais) hibernal, winterly, wintry, brumal.

hibernante adj. m. + f. hibernating.

hibernar v. (zool.) to hibernate, pass the winter in a torpid state, hole up.

hibérnico s. m. Gaelic, Old Irish language. || adj Hibernian, of or pertaining to Hibernia.

hibérnio s. m. Hibernian: native or inhabitant of Ireland.

hibisco s. m. (bot.) hibiscus, rose mallow, gumbo.

hibridação s. f. (pl. -ões) 1. hybridism, hybridity. 2. hybridation, cross-breeding.

hibridez s. f 1. hybridity, hybridism. 2. anomaly, irregularity.

hibridismo s. m. 1. hybridism, hybridity. 2. (gram.) word formed from two different languages.

híbrido s. m. 1. hybrid, half-breed, cross-breed. 2. (gram.) word of heterogeneous origin. || adj. hybrid, cross-bred, derived from heterogenous sources.

tornar ~ to hybridize. ~ **bigênero** bigener.

hidático adj. hydatidinous, hydatid, encysted.

hidátide s. f. hydatid: 1. (anat.) cystlike growth attached to an oviduct or testicle. 2. (path.) cyst, any cystlike structure. 3. (zool.) the encysted larvae of a tapeworm.

hidatidocele s. f. (med.) hydatidocele, tumour of the scrotum containing hydatids.

hidatiforme adj. m. + f. hydatiform, hydatidiform.

hidatismo s. m. (med.) hydatism, sound caused by the presence of a fluid in a cavity.

hidatódio s. m. any secreting organ of a plant.

hidatóide adj. m. + f. (anat.) hydatoid: of or pertaining to the aqueous humour of the eye.

membrana ~ hydatoid: membrane surrounding the aqueous humour of the eye.

hidatologia s. f. hydrology.

hidra s. f. 1. Hydra: a) (Greek myth.) monstrous serpent with nine heads, slain by Hercules. b) (astr.) southern constellation. 2. hydra: a) (fig.) evil arising from many sources. b) (zool.) genus of freshwater polyps. c) dogfish. d) water serpent of the family Hidrophidae.

hidrácido s. m. (chem.) hydracid: acid which contains no oxigen.

hidradenite s. f. (med.) hydr(o)adenitis.

hidragogo s. m. (med.) hydragogue, diuretic.

hidrante s. m. hydrant, fire-hydrant, plug (plate R 8).
hidrargírico adj. hydrargyrate, hydrargyric, mercurial.
hidrargírio s. m. hydrargyrum, mercury, quicksilver.
hidrargirismo s .m. (med.) hydrargyrism, mercurial poisoning.
hidrargirose s. f. (med.) mercurial friction.
hidrartrose s. f. (med.) hydrarthrosis, accumulation of water in a cavity of a joint.
hidraste s. f. (bot.) goldenseal.
hidrastina s. f. (chem.) hydrastin(e).
hidratação s. f. (pl. -ões) hydration, hydratation.
hidratado adj. hydrated, hydrous.
cal -a hydrated lime.
hidratante adj. hydrating.
hidratar v. to hydrate: 1. combine or impregnate with water. 2. form into a hydrate.
hidratável adj. (pl. -áveis) capable of being hydrated.
hidrático adj. having the qualities of a hydrate.
hidratiforme adj. (chem.) hydratiform.
hidrato s. m. (chem.) hydrate.
~ de amônio ammonium hydroxide. **~ de carbônio** carbo-hydrate. **~ de cloral** chloral-hydrate.
hidráulica s. f. hydraulics: branch of science which treats of liquids in motion, hydromechanics, hydrostatics.
~ fluvial fluviatic hydraulics. **~ marítima** maritime hydraulics.
hidráulico s. m. hydromechanical engineer. ‖ adj. hydraulic(al). ‖ **hidraulicamente** adv. hydraulically.
força -a hydraulic power. **energia -a** water power. **freio ~** hydraulic brake. **ligante ~** hydraulic cement. **macaco ~** hydraulic jack. **transmissão -a** fluid drive. **pressão -a** hydraulic pressure.
hidravião s. m. (pl. -ões) hydro-airplane, sea-plane, water-plane, flying boat.
hidrelétrico adj. hydroelectric(al).
usina -a hydroelectric power-station.
hidremia s. f. (med.) hydremia: excess of water in the blood.
hidreto s. m. (chem.) hydrid(e).
hídria s. f. (Roman hist.) hydria, water jug, pitcher.
hidriatria s. f. (med.) hydropathy, water-cure.
hídrico adj. hydric.
hidro- pref. hydro-, a combining form meaning water.
hidroa s. f. (med.) hydroa: skin disease marked by vesicular or bulbous eruptions.
hidroavião s. m. (less used form of **hidravião**) (pl. -ões) hydro-airplane, sea-plane.
hidróbio adj. hydrobic, hydrobial, living in water.
hidrocarbonato s. m. (chem.) hydrocarbonate, hydrated carbonate.
hidrocarboneto s. m. (chem.) hydrocarbon.
hidrocariáceo adj. hydrocaryaceous.
hidrocaritáceo adj. (bot.) hydrocharidaceous, of or pertaining to the family Hydrocharidaceae.
hidrocefalia s. f. (med.) hydrocephalus.
hidrocéfalo s. m. hydrocephalic patient. ‖ adj. hydrocephalous, hydrocephalic.
ele é ~ he has water in the brain.
hidrocele s. f. (med.) hydrocele.
hidrocélico s. m. person suffering from hydrocele. ‖ adj. of or pertaining to hydrocele.
hidrociânico adj. (chem.) hydrocyanic.
hidrocinética s. f. hydrokinetics.
hidrocinético adj. hydrokinetic.
hidrodinâmica s. f. hydrodynamics.
hidrodinâmico adj. hydrodynamic.
hidrófana s. f. (min.) hydrophane, semitranslucent opal that becomes transparent on immersion in water.
hidrófano adj. hydrophanous.
hidrofiláceo adj. (bot.) hydrophyllaceous.

hidrófilo adj. 1. hydrophil. 2. absorbing water. 3. (bot.) hydrophilous: pollinated by the agency of water.
hidrófito s. m. hydrophyte, plant which grows in water, aquatic plant.
hidrofitografia s. f. hydrophytography: treatise on hydrophytes.
hidrofitologia s. f. hydrophytology: branch of botany which treates of aquatic plants.
hidrofitológico adj. hydrophytologic.
hidrofobia s. f. 1. hydrophobia, morbid dread of water. 2. (vet.) rabies, canine madness, rabidness, rabidity.
hidrofóbico adj. hydrophobic(al).
hidrófobo s. m. person suffering from hydrophobia. ‖ adj. hydrophobic, rabid, mad.
hidróforo adj. hydrophorous, hydrophore, carrying water.
hidrofráctico adj. waterproof.
hidroftalmia s. f. (med.) hydrophthalmia.
hidrófugo adj. hydrofuge, repelling water.
hidrogenação s. f. (pl. -ões) hydrogenation, hydrogenization.
hidrogenado adj. hydrogenated.
hidrogenar v. (chem.) to hydrogenate, hydrogenize, cause to combine with hydrogen, form a hydrogen compound.
hidrogenia s. f. hydrology.
hidrogênio s. m. (chem.) hydrogen (chemical symbol H).
bomba de ~ hydrogen bomb, H-bomb. **tratar com ~** to hydrogenate. **~ fosforado** phosphine.
hidrogeologia s. f. hydrogeology, geology of water.
hidrogeológico adj. hydrogeologic.
hidrógono adj. (geol.) of or relative to rocks worn and rounded by the action of water.
hidrografia s. f. hydrography.
hidrográfico adj. hidrographic(al).
hidrógrafo s. m. hydrographer.
hidróide s. m. (zool.) hydroid: 1. a hydrozoon. 2. a hidropolyp.
hidrolato s. m. (pharm.) aromatic essence of flowers and herbs.
hidrólatra s. m. + f. hydrolater, worshipper of water.
hidrolatria s. f. hydrolatry, worship of water.
hidrólise s. f. (chem.) hydrolysis, chemical decomposition involving the addition of the elements of water.
hidrologia s. f. hydrology: science of water.
hidrológico adj. hydrologic(al).
hidrólogo s. m. hydrologist.
hidromania s. f. hydromancy, divination by water.
hidromecânico adj. hydromechanic(al).
hidromedusa s. f. (zool.) hydromedusa.
hidromel s. m. (pl. ~es, -éis) hydromel, mead.
hidrometra s. f. (med.) hydrometra: accumulation of watery fluid in the uterus.
hidrometria s. f. hydrometry, measurement of the specific gravity of a fluid.
hidrométrico adj. hydrometric(al).
hidrômetro s. m. hydrometer, water-meter.
hidromineral adj. m. + f. (pl. -ais) hydromineral, of or relative to mineral waters.
hidromotor s. m. hydromotor, motor driven by jets of water.
hidronefrose s. f. (med.) hydronephrosis: cyst formed by collection of urine in the pelvis of the kidneys.
hidrônio s. m. (chem.) hydrion, hydrogen ion.
hidropata, hidrópata s. m. + f. hydropathist.
hidropatia s. f. hydropathy, treatment of a disease by application of water.

hidropático adj. hydropathic(al).
estabelecimento para tratamento ~ hydropathic establishment.
hidropericárdio s. m. (med.) hydropericardium: accumulation of serous fluid in the pericardial cavity.
hidrópico s. m. (med.) endematous patient. || adj. hydropic, dropsical, endematous.
hidropírico adj. ejecting fire and water (volcanoes).
hidropisia s. f. (med.) hydropsy, dropsy.
hidroplano s. m. hydroplane, flying boat, water-plane.
hidropneumático adj. hydropneumatic.
hidrópota s. m. + f. water-drinker.
hidroquinona s. m. (chem.) hydroquinone, photographic developer.
hidroquisto s. m. (med.) hydrocyst, cyst with watery contents.
hidrorragia, hidrorréia s. f. (med.) hydrorrhea: copious watery discharge.
hidroscopia s. f. 1. divination by water. 2. art of locating subterraneous water.
hidróscopo s. m. 1. hydroscope, hydrometer. 2. water-finder. 3. hydromancer.
hidrose s. f. abundant perspiration.
hidrosfera s. f. (geogr.) hydrosphere.
hidrosférico adj. hydrospheric.
hidrossol s. m. (chem.) hydrosol(e), aquasol: aqueous colloidal solution.
hidrossolúvel adj. m. + f. (pl. -úveis) hydro-soluble, water-soluble.
hidrossulfato s. m. (chem.) hydrosulphate: hydrated salt of sulphuric acid.
hidrossulfito s. m. (chem.) hydrosulphite, hydrosulphurous acid, hydrated salt of sulphurous acid.
hidrossulfúrico adj. (chem.) hydrosulphuric.
hidrossulfuroso adj. (chem.) hydrosulphurous.
hidrostaquiácea s. f. Hidrostachiaceae: small family of aquatic herbs.
hidrostaquiáceo adj. (bot.) hidrostachiaceous.
hidrostática s. f. (phys.) hydrostatics, science of the pressure and equilibrium of fluids.
hidrostático adj. hydrostatic(al).
balança -a hydrostatic balance.
hidróstato s. m. hydrostat: 1. safety appliance to prevent the explosion of steam boilers. 2. device regulating the height of liquids in a reservoir.
hidrotecnia s. f. hydrotechnics.
hidrotécnico adj. hydrotechnic(al).
hidroterapia s. f. hydrotherapeutics, hydrotherapy, water-cure.
hidroterápico adj. hydrotherapeutic(al).
hidrotérmico adj. hydrothermal.
hidrótico adj. hydrotic(al), sudorific, diuretic.
hidrotimetria s. f. hydrotimetry, science and process of measuring the hardness of water.
hidrotímetro s. m. hydrotimeter, instrument used in the determination of the hardness of water.
hidrotórax s. m. (med.) hydrothorax, presence of an effused fluid in the pleural cavity.
hidrotropismo s. m. (bot.) hydrotropism, tendency of growing toward moisture.
hidrotrópico adj. (bot.) hydrotropic.
hidrovia s. f. (Braz.) waterway.
hidróxido s. m. (chem.) hydroxide: designation of basic compounds containing the OH group.
~ **de amônio** ammonium hydroxide. ~ **de sódio** sodium hydroxide.
hidroxílico adj. (chem.) hydroxy.
hidrúria, hidruria s. f. (med.) hydruria, excessive flow of watery urine.
hidrúrico adj. (med.) hydruric, characterized by hydruria.
hiemação s. f. (pl. -ões) hiemation, wintering.
hiemal adj. m. + f. (pl. -ais) hiemal, hibernal, wintry.

hiena s. f. (zool.) hyena.
hiena-escura s. f. (pl. **hienas-escuras**) (zool.) brown hyena.
hiena-malhada s. f. (pl. **hienas-malhadas**) (zool.) spotted hyena.
hiena-rajada s. f. (pl. **hienas-rajadas**) (zool.) striped hyena.
hieranose s. f. (med.) epilepsy.
hierarca s. m. hierarch, one who has authority.
hierarquia s. f. hierarchy: 1. power and authority of a hierarch. 2. body of ecclesiastical rulers. 3. organization in ranks and orders each subordinate to the one above. 4. (science, logic) series of systematic groups (kingdom, classes, orders, families, genera, species).
~ **militar** militar ranking.
hierárquico adj. hierarchic(al), hierarchal.
hierarquização s. f. (pl. -ões) act of hierarchizing.
hierarquizar v. to hierarchize: organize in conformity with hierarchical authority.
hierática s. f. (hist.) exceptional fine paper used for transcriptions of the Holy Writs.
hierático adj. hieratic(al), priestly, sacerdotal, religious.
hierofante, hierofanta s. m. 1. (hist.) hierophant, chief priest. 2. (fig.) seer, clairvoyant.
hieroglífico s. m. hieroglyph. || adj. hieroglyphic.
hieróglifo s. m. hieroglyph.
hierografia s. f. hierography, sacred writings.
hierográfico adj. hierographic.
hierograma s. m. hierogram, sacred or hieratic symbol.
hierogramático adj. hierogrammatic(al).
hierologia s. f. hierology: 1. science of Egyptian records. 2. scientific and comparative study of religions.
hierológico adj. hierologic(al).
hieronímico adj. Hieronymic: of or pertaining to St. Jerome.
hieronimita adj. Hieronymite, monk of the order of St. Jerome.
hierônimo s. m. collective designation of sacred or religious names (f. ex.: Jehovah, Allah, Nativity).
hierosolimita s. m. + f. (also **hierosolimitano** m.) Hierosolymitan: native or inhabitant of Jerusalem. || adj. Hierosolymitan.
hietômetro s. m. hyetometer.
hifa s. f. (bot.) hypha: one of the threadlike elements of the mycelium of a fungus.
hifema s. m. hyphema: hemorrhage into the anterior chamber of the eye.
hifemia s. f. hyphemia: oligemia or deficiency of the blood. /
hyfen s. m. hyphen, dash.
hifenizar v. to hyphenize; to hyphenate.
higidez s. f. state of health.
hígido adj. hygienic, sanitary.
higiene s. f. 1. hygienics, hygiene. 2. cleanliness, neatness.
tratado sobre ~ hygiology.
higiênico adj. 1. hygienic(al), sanitary. 2. healthy. 3. clean, neat. || **-amente** adv. hygienically, sanitarily.
não ~ insanitary, unhealthily.
higienista s. m. + f. hygienist.
higiologia s. f. hygiology, science of hygiene.
higróbio adj. hygrobic, living in moist earth.
higrófilo adj. (bot.) hygrophilous.
higrófito s. m. (bot.) hygrophyte.
higrógrafo s. m. (meteor.) hygrograph: instrument which registers the variations of moisture of the atmosphere.
higrologia s. f. hygrology, science which treats of the phenomena of humidity.

higrológico adj. hygrologic.

higroma s. m. (med.) hygroma, bursitis.

higrometria s. f. (phys.) hygrometry, science concerned with the determination of the humidity of bodies, especially of the air.

higrométrico adj. hygrometric.

higrômetro s. m. hygrometer.

higroscópico adj. hygroscopic(al).

higroscópio s. m. hygroscope, instrument for measuring the humidity of the air.

hílare adj. m. + f. 1. cheerful, gay. 2. glad. 3. smiling. 4. satisfied, content.

hilária s. f. Hilaria: a small genus of grasses.

hilaridade s. f. 1. hilarity, exhilaration. 2. joy, mirth, gaiety. 3. laughter. 4. jollity, high spirits.

hilariante adj. m. + f. hilarious, merry, gay, exhilarating, rip-roaring, sidesplitting.

hilário adj. (bot.) of, pertaining to or relative to the hilum.

hilarizar v. 1. to cheer (up), delight. 2. to exhilarate. 3. to animate, give vivacity to, enliven. 4. to evoke hilarity.

hiléia s. f. Hylea: name given by Alexander von Humboldt to the tropical rain forests of the Amazonas basin.

hilídeo s. m. (zool.) a specimen of the family Hylidae, tree-toad, tree-frog. ‖ adj. of or relative to the Hylidae.

hilo s. m. hilum: 1. (bot.) mark or scar of a seed produced by separation from its placenta. 2. (anat.) scar, mark, recess, opening.

hilófero s. m. (bot.) tegmen.

hiloformismo s. m. (philos.) Aristotelian doctrine which considers all objects a compound of two elements: form and substance.

hilogenia s. f. hylogenesis, the origin of matter.

hilota s. m. (Greek hist.) helot, (fig.) slave, serf.

hilozoísmo s. m. (philos.) hylozoism: doctrine that all matter is endowed with life.

hilozoísta s. m. + f. hylozoist, believer in hylozoism.

himantandrácea s. f. (bot.) a specimen of the family Himantandraceae.

himantandráceo adj. (bot.) of, pertaining to or relative to the Himantandraceae.

hímen s. m. (pl. ~s + ~es) 1. (anat.) hymen. 2. (fig., poet.) marriage, wedded state.

Himeneu (I) s. m. (Greek myth.) Hymen: god of marriage.

himeneu (II) s. m. hymen: marriage, wedding feast.

himênio s. m. (bot.) hymenium, hymenial layer.

himenocarpo adj. (bot.) hymenocarpous.

himenografia s. f. hymenography, description of membranes of animal bodies.

himenográfico adj. hymenographic(al).

himenologia s. f. hymenology, science or study of membranes.

himenológico adj. hymenologic(al).

himenópode adj. m. + f. (ornith.) web-footed.

himenóptero s. m. (zool.) hymenopter, hymenopteran, one of the Hymenoptera. ‖ adj. m. + f. hymenopteral, hymenopterous.

himenotomia s. f. (surg.) hymenotomy.

hinário s. m. hymn-book, service-book, hymnal.

hindi s. m. Hindi: Indo-Aryan language spoken in northern India.

hindu s. m. + f. Hindu, Hindo, Indian: member of one of the native races of India. ‖ adj. Hindu, Hindoo.

hinduísmo s. m. Hinduism, Hindooism: religious and social system of India.

hindustani s. m. Hindustan: most important dialect of Hindi. ‖ adj. m. + f. Hindustani, of or pertaining to Hindustan, its people or language.

hinista s. m. + f. hymnist, writer of hymns.

hino s. m. hymn, religious song, laud, anthem. ~ fúnebre dirge. ~ nacional national anthem. ~s da tarde vespers. cantar ~s to hymn. livro de ~s hymnal.

hinografia s. f. hymnography: 1. historical and technical study of hymns. 2. art and act of writing hymns.

hinógrafo s. m. hymnographer, hymn writer.

hinologia s. f. hymnology, science of hymns.

hinológico adj. hymnologic(al).

hinólogo s. m. hymnologist, hymnist.

hinterlândia s. f. hinterland, upland.

hioglosso s. m. (anat.) hyoglossus.

hióide s. m. (anat.) hyoid, tongue-bone, hyoidean bone. ‖ adj. hyoidean.

hióideo adj. hyoid, hyoidal, hyoidean.

hioscíamo s. m. (bot.) henbane, hyasciamine.

hip interj. exclamation used as a signal for applause, hip, hip, hurrah!

hipálage s. f. (rhet.) hypallage: inversion of syntactical relation between two terms.

hipanto s. m. hypanthium.

hipantódio s. m. (bot.) hypanthodium, syconium.

hipantropia s. f. (med.) hippanthropia: a condition in which the patient believes to be a horse.

hiperacidez s. f. (med.) hyperacidity, excessive degree of acidity.

hiperacusia s. f. (med.) hyperacusis, abnormally acute sense of hearing, painful sensitiveness to sounds.

hiperalbuminose s. f. (med.) hyperalbuminosis, excess of albuminoids in the blood.

hiperalgesia s. f. (med.) hyperalgesia, excessive sensitivity to pain, hyperalgia.

hiperalgésico, hiperálgico adj. (med.) hyperalgesic, hyperalgetic.

hiperatividade s. f. hyper-activity.

hipérbato(n) s. m. (rhet.) hyperbaton: transposition or inversion of words used principally for emphasis.

hiperbibasmo s. m. variable accent, shifting of accent from one syllable to another.

hipérbole s. f. 1. (rhet.) hyperbole: exaggeration, extravagant statement. 2. (geom.) hyperbola.

hiperbólico adj. hyperbolic(al).

hiperboliforme adj. m. + f. hyperboliform.

hiperbolismo s. m. hyperbolism.

hiperbolóide s. m. (geom.) hyperboloid, hyperbola of a higher order.

hiperbóreo adj. 1. hyperborean, situated or inhabiting the far north. 2. (fig.) very cold, frigid.

hipercataléctico, hipercatalético adj. hypercatalectic: having an additional syllable (Greek or Latin verse).

hipercatalecto s. m. hypercatalexis: excess of a final syllable or half foot (in classical peotry).

hiperceratose s. f. (med.) hyperkeratosis: 1. hypertrophy of the cornea. 2. hypertrophy of the corneous layer of the skin.

hipercrinia s. f. (med.) hipercrinia, hipercrinism: state caused by excessive secretion of an endocrine gland.

hipercrise s. f. (med.) hypercrisis, violent crisis.

hipercrítico s. m. hypercritic, captious censor, over--rigid critic. ‖ adj. hypercritic(al), ultracritical.

hipercromia s. f. (med.) hyperchromia, hyperchromatism.

hiperdiácrise s. f. (med.) hyperdiacrisis, excessive discharge of secretions.

hiperdulia s. f. (theol.) hyperdulia, worship offered to the Virgin Mary.

hiperemia s. f. (med.) hyperemia, hyperaemia: excess of blood in any part of the body.

hiperenterose s. f. (med.) intestinal hypertrophy.

hiperestesia s. f. (med.) hyperesthesia: excessive sensitiveness of the skin.
hipergenesia s. f. (med.) hypergenesis, excessive development, hypertrophy.
hipergenético adj. (med.) hypergenetic(al), congenital hypertrophy of parts or organs.
hiperglicemia s. f. (med.) hyperglycemia, abnormal concentration of glucose in the blood.
hipericão s. m. (bot.) St. John's-wort.
hiperidrose s. f. (med.) hyperhidrosis, excessive sweating.
hiperinose s. f. (med.) hyperinosis, hyperinosemia, excess of fibrin in the blood.
hipermetria s. f. (poet.) division of a compound word, remaining one part at the end of a line and the other at the beginning of the next.
hipérmetro s. f. (poet.) hypermeter: a verse or period with a redundant syllable at the end.
hipermétrico adj. hypermetrical.
hipermetrope adj. (med.) hypermetropic, far-sighted.
hipermetropia s. f. (med.) hypermetropia, hypermetropy far-sightedness.
hipermiopia s. f. (med.) hypermyopia, excessive short-sightedness.
hipermnésia, hipermnesia s. f. (med.) hypermnesia, extreme retentiveness of memory.
hiperosmia s. f. (med.) hyperosmia, morbid sensitiveness to odours.
hiperosteose s. f. (med.) hyperostosis: 1. morbid outgrowth of bone. 2. exostosis, abnormal increase of bony tissue.
hiperplasia s. f. (med.) hyperplasia, numeric hypertrophy, abnormal increase in the number of cells.
hipersarcose s. f. (med.) hypersarcosis: excessive formation of granulation tissue.
hipersecreção s. f. (pl. -ões) (med.) hypersecretion, excessive secretion.
hipersensibilidade s. f. sensibility, irritability, hypersensitiveness.
hipersensível adj. (pl. -íveis) hypersensitive.
hiperstênio s. m. (min.) hypersthene.
hiperstílico adj. (bot.) hyperstylar, inserted above the style.
hipertensão s. f. (med.) hypertension, abnormally high blood pressure.
hipertermia s. f. (med.) hyperthermia, abnormally high body temperature, fever.
hipértese s. f. (gram.) hyperthesis, metathesis, transposition of letters, sounds or syllables of a word.
hipertonia s. f. (med.) hypertonia: excessive tonicity, tension or activity.
hipertônico adj. (med.) hypertonic.
hipertrofia s. f. 1. (med.) hypertrophy: morbid enlargement or growth of an organ. 2. (fig.) excessive growth, exaltation.
hipertrofiado adj. hypertrophic(al).
hipertrofiar v. to hypertrophy, become hypertrophous.
hiperurbanismo s. m. excessive refinement of speech, and subsequent misusage of words.
hipiatria s. f. hippiatry, hippiatrics: art and science of curing diseases of horses.
hipiátrico adj. hippiatric(al).
hipiatro s. m. hippiater, horse-doctor, veterinarian.
hípico adj. hippic, equine.
hipismo s. m. horsemanship, equestrian tricks, art of horse-racing.
hipnoblepsia s. f. (med.) lucid somnambulism.
hipnofobia s. f. (med.) hypnophobia, morbid dread of falling asleep.
hipnófobo s. m. hypnophobe, one who suffers from hypnophobia.
hipnofone, hipnofono s. m. (med.) one who speaks during hypnotic sleep.

hipnógeno adj. (med.) hypnogenetic, producing sleep, hypnagogic.
hipnográfico adj. hypnographic(al).
hipnologia s. f. hypnology, the sum of knowledge concerning sleep and hypnotism.
hipnológico adj. hypnologic(al).
hipnose s. f. (med.) hypnosis: 1. inducement to sleep. 2. hypnotic state. 3. hypnotism.
hipnosia s. f. (med.) hypnosia, uncontrollable drowsiness.
hipnótico s. m. (med.) hypnotic: 1. opiate, soporific, hypnagogue. 2. individual subject to hypnotism. || adj. hypnotic: 1. producing sleep, soporific. 2. pertaining to or characterized by hypnotism. || hipnoticamente adv. hypnotically, soporifically, mesmerically.
hipnotismo s. m. hypnotism: 1. method or practice of inducing hypnosis. 2. hypnosis.
hipnotista s. m. + f. hypnotist.
hipnotização s. f. (pl. -ões) hypnotization.
hipnotizador s. m. hypnotist, hypnotizer, mesmerizer, fascinator.
hipnotizar v. 1. to hypnotize, induce hypnosis in. 2. to mesmerize. 3. to fascinate, entrance. 4. (fig.) to fix one's attentions or hopes on.
hipnotizável adj. m. + f. (pl. -áveis) hypnotizable.
hipnozigoto s. m. (bot.) hypnozygote.
hipo- pref. sub-, hypo-: prefix meaning under, beneath, down, below.
hipoalgesia, hipoalgia s. f. (med.) hypalgesia, hypalgia, diminished sensitiveness to pain.
hipobrânquio adj. (zool.) hypobranchial, situated below the gills, inferobranchiate.
hipocampo s. m. 1. (ichth.) hippocampus, sea-horse. 2. (myth.) sea-monster, half horse half fish.
hipocárpio s. m. (bot.) hypocarp, enlarged peduncle beneath certain fruits.
hipocastanácea s. f. plant of the order Hippocastanaceae.
hipocastanáceo adj. (bot.) hippocastanaceous.
hipocausto s. m. (archit.) hypocaust, fire-chamber, fire-place.
hipoclorina s. f. (chem.) solution of hypochlorous acid.
hipoclorito s. m. (chem.) hypochlorite, salt of hypochlorous acid.
~ de cal bleaching-powder.
hipocloroso adj. (chem.) hypochlorous.
hipocofose s. f. (med.) incomplete deafness.
hipocondria s. f. (med.) hypochondria, hypochondriasis: morbid anxiety as to one's health; spleen, melancholy, atrabiliousness.
hipocondríaco s. m. hypochondriac, person affected with hypochondria. || adj. hypochondriac(al), melancholic, atrabilious.
hipocôndrio s. m. (anat.) hypochondrium, upper lateral region of the abdomen.
hipocorístico s. m. pet name. || adj. hypocoristic(al).
hipocraniano adj. (anat.) hypocranial, below the cranium.
hipocrateácea s. f. plant of the family Hippocrateaceae.
hipocrateáceo adj. (bot.) hippocrateaceous.
hipocrático adj. Hippocratic(al), of or pertaining to Hippocrates.
hipocraz s. m. hippocras, old cordial made of spiced wine.
hipocrênico adj. (Greek myth.) Hippocrenian.
hipocrisia s. f. 1. hypocrisy, pharisaicalness. 2. falseness, dissimulation. 3. doubleness, double-dealing. 4. sanctimoniousness, sanctimony.
hipócrita s. m. + f. 1. hypocrite, pharisee. 2. false pretender, dissimulator. 3. double-dealer. 4. dissem-

bler. 5. tartuffe. 6. (coll.) sniveller, snuffler. ‖ adj. 1. hypocritic(al). 2. pharisaic(al). 3. double-faced. 4. snuffling, snivelling. ‖ **hipocritamente** adv. hypocritically, pharisaically.

hipodá(c)tilo s. m. hypodactylum, underside of the toe of a bird.

hipodermatomia s. f. (surg.) hypodermatomy, subcutaneous incision.

hipodérmico adj. 1. hypodermic, subcutaneous, under the skin. 2. (bot.) hypodermal, of or pertaining to the layer of cells just beneath the epidermis of a leaf. **injeção** -a hypodermic injection. **seringa** -a hypodermic syringe.

hipodromia s. f. 1. art of horse-racing. 2. skill of organizing races.

hipódromo s. m. hippodrome, race-course.

hipoema s. m. (med.) hypohemia, anemia.

hipoestesia s. f. (med.) hypoesthesia, hypesthesia, decreased sensibility to touch.

hipofagia s. f. hippophagy, act or practice of feeding on horse-flesh.

hipófago adj. hippophagous, feeding on horse-flesh.

hipófase s. f. (med.) condition in which nearly closed eyelids let only part of the sclera open.

hipófise s. f. (anat.) hypophysis, pituitary gland.

hipófora s. f. hypophora: 1. (rhet.) that part of the prolepsis in which the opponent's objections are stated. 2. (med.) deep sinuous ulcer.

hipofosfato s. m. (chem.) hypophosphate, salt of hypophosphoric acid.

hipofosfito s. m. (chem.) hypophosphite, salt of hypophosphorous acid.

hipofosfórico adj. (chem.) hypophosphoric.

hipofosforoso adj. (chem.) hypophosphorous.

hipogástrico adj. hypogastric.

hipogástrio s. m. (anat.) hypogastrium, lower part of the belly.

hipogeu s. m. 1. (archit.) hypogeum, underground vault, catacomb. 2. hypogeal growth of a plant, underground part of the stalk.

hipoginia s. f. (bot.) hypogyny.

hipógino adj. (bot.) hypogynous, situated beneath the pistil.

hipoglossa s. f. (bot.) a variety of asparagus.

hipoglosso s. m. 1. (anat.) hypoglossal nerve. 2. (ichth.) a) Hypoglossus: a genus of fishes. b) halibut. ‖ adj. hypoglossal, situated under the tongue.

hipognata adj. m. + f. (zool.) hypognathous.

hipógnato adj. (ornith.) hypognathous, having the lower mandible longer than the upper.

hipogrifo s. m. hippogriff, hippogryph; fabulous animal, half griffin half horse.

hipólito s. m. hippolith, concretion from the intestines of a horse; bezoar.

hipologia s. f. hippology, scientific study of the horse.

hipológico adj. hippologic(al).

hipólogo s. m. hippologist: student of hippology.

hipomania s. f. 1. hippomania, excessive passion for horses. 2. (vet.) fit of frenzy of horses.

hipomaníaco s. m. hippomaniac.

hipômetro s. m. instrument for measuring the height of horses.

hipopatologia s. f. (vet.) hippopathology.

hipopatológico adj. hippopathologic(al).

hipopétalo adj. (bot.) hypopetalous, hypogynous.

hipópio(n) s. m. (med.) hypopyon, accumulation of pus in the anterior chamber of the eye.

hipoplasia s. f. (med.) hypoplasia, defective or incomplete development.

hipópode s. m. + f. ungulate, a hoofed animal. ‖ adj. ungulate, hoofed, shaped like a hoof.

hipopotâmico adj. 1. (zool.) hippopotamic. 2. (fig.) stout, very fat, corpulent.

hipopótamo s. m. 1. (zool.) hippopotamus, river-horse. 2. (fig.): a) corpulent person. b) brutal person.

hiposcênio s. m. (theat.) hyposcenium.

hiposfagma s. m. (med.) ecchymosis of the eye, extravasation of blood in the eye.

hipospadia s. f. (med.) hypospadias, congenital opening of the urethra.

hipossistolia s. f. (med.) hyposystole, abnormal diminution of the systole.

hipossulfato s. m. (chem.) hyposulphate, salt of sulphuric acid.

hipossulfito s. m. (chem.) hyposulphite, salt of sulphurous acid.

hipossulfúrico adj. (chem.) hyposulphuric.

hipossulfuroso adj. (chem.) hyposulphurous.

hipóstase (I) s. f. (theol.) hypostasis: personal subsistence, as opposed to substance, of the Godhead.

hipóstase (II) s. f. (path.) 1. hypostatic congestion of the blood. 2. sediment in urine.

hipostático adj. hypostatic(al).

hipostenia s. f. (med.) hyposthenia, weakness, enfeebled state.

hipostênico adj. (med.) hyposthenic, hypostheniant, debilitant.

hipostilo adj. (archit.) hypostyle, having the roof supported by pillars.

hipotalássico adj. hypothalassic, submarine.

hipoteca s. f. 1. mortage, hypothec. 2. debt for which landed property is pledged as security. 3. instrument effecting the conveyance for a mortgage. **dar em** ~ to mortgage. **sem** ~ free and unencumbered. ~ **aérea** air mortgage. ~ **marítima** marine mortgage.

hipotecar v. 1. to mortgage, hypothecate. 2. to bond, pledge. 3. (fig.) to guarantee, vouchsafe.

hipotecado adj. bonded.

hipotecário adj. hypothecary.

hipotênar, hipótenar s. m. (anat.) hypothenar.

hipotensão s. f. (med.) hypotension, lowered blood pressure.

hipotenusa s. f. (geom.) hypotenuse, hypothenuse.

hipótese s. f. 1. hypothesis. 2. theory, assumption. 3. conjecture, supposition. **em** ~ **alguma** on (or upon) no account. **na melhor** ~ seen to advantage, at (the) best, if any. **em nenhuma** ~ no at all. **na** ~ **de** assuming that.

hipotético adj. hypothetic(al), assumed, suppositional. ‖ **hipoteticamente** adv. hypothetically, suppositionally.

hipotipose s. f. (rhet.) hypotyposis: vivid description of a scene or event.

hipotomia s. f. hippotomy: anatomy or dissection of horses.

hipotômico adj. hippotomical.

hipotonia s. f. (med.) hypotonia, hypotonus, hypotony, diminished tension or tonicity.

hipotônico adj. (med.) hypotonic(al).

hipotrofia s. f. (med.) hypotrophy: 1. deficient nutrition. 2. atrophy, undergrowth.

hipozóico adj. (geol.) hypozoic, situated beneath the strata that contains fossiliferous remains.

hippie s. m. + f. (Engl.) hippie.

hipsocéfalo adj. (anat.) hypsocephalous, having a high vertex.

hipsografia s. f. (geogr.) hypsography, branch of geography concerned with topographic relief.

hipsográfico adj. (geogr.) hypsographical.

hipsometria s. f. hypsometry: art of measuring heights with reference to the sea level.

hipsométrico adj. hypsometric(al).

hipsômetro s. m. hypsometer, Instrument for measuring heights by observing the boiling point of a liquid.

hipúria, hipuria s. f. (med.) hippuria: excess of hippuric acid in the urine.

hipúrico adj. hippuric.

hipurite s. f. (pal.) hippurite, fossil mollusc of the genus Hippurites.

hircina s. f. hircin, substance extracted from the suet of goats.

hircino adj. hircine: of or pertaining to a goat, goatlike, goatish.

hircismo s. m. (med.) hircismus, strong odour of the axillae.

hirco s. m. (poet.) he-goat, hircus.

hircoso adj. (bot., zool.) hircinous, smelling like a goat, having a hircine odour.

hirsutez s. f. hirsuteness, hairiness.

hirsuto adj. 1. hirsute, hairy. 2. shaggy, scraggly, rugged. 3. (bot., zool.) rough, bristly.

hirteza s. f. 1. rigidness, stiffness. 2. erectness, uprightness. 3. immobility. 4. crispness. 5. hirsuteness, hairiness.

hirto adj. 1. rigid, stiff. 2. erect, upright. 3. motionless. 4. crisp. 5. hirsute, hairy.

hirundino adj. hirundine, of or pertaining to the swallows, swallowlike.

hispalense s. m. + f. Sevillian, native or inhabitant of Sevilla. ‖ adj. m. + f. Sevillian.

hispânico adj. Hispanic: of or pertaining to Spain.

hispanismo s. m. Hispanicism: Spanish phrase or idiom.

hispanista s. m. + f. Hispanist: expert or student of Spanish philology, history, customs and modes of thought.

hispano-americano s. m. (pl. **hispano-americanos**) Hispano-American: native or inhabitant of one of the Spanish speaking countries of America. ‖ adj. Hispano-American.

hispano-árabe adj. m. + f. (pl. **hispano-árabes**) Spanish-Arabian.

hispar-se v. (Braz.) to bristle, set on end.

hispidar-se v. (Braz.) to bristle, set on end, become hirsute.

hispidez s. f. hirsuteness, hairiness, bristliness.

híspido adj. 1. bristly, shaggy. 2. hirsute. 3. bristling, standing up stiffly. 4. (bot., zool.) hispid.

hissom s. m. hyson: a variety of green tea from China.

hissopada s. f. aspersion, sprinkling with holy water.

hissopar v. to asperse, besprinkle with holy water.

hissope s. m. (eccl.) aspergillum, aspersorium.

hissopo (ô) s. m. (bot.) hyssop.

histeralgia s. f. (med.) histeralgia, neuralgia of the uterus.

histerálgico adj. (med.) hysteralgic, of, pertaining to or affected with hysteralgia.

histerândrico adj. (bot.) hysterandrous.

histeranto adj. (bot.) hysteranthous, putting forth leaves after the appearance of flowers.

histerese s. f. (phys.) hysteresis: lagging of one of two related phenomena behind the other.

histeria s. f. 1. (med.) hysteria, hysterics. 2. (coll.) wild emotion, excitement.

ela teve ataques de ~ she went into hysterics.

histérico s. m. hysteriac: one subject to hysteria. ‖ adj. hysteric(al), wildly emotional, excited.

histerismo s. m. (med.) hysteria.

histerocele s. f. (med.) hysterocele, partial or total uterine hernia.

histerofisa s. f. (med.) hysterophysa: distension of the uterus due to the accumulation of gases.

histerografia s. f. (med.) hysterography, roentgenological examination of the uterus.

histerográfico adj. (med.) hysterographic(al).

histerólito s. m. (med.) hysterolith, wombstone.

histerologia s. f. 1. (med.) hysterology: branch of medicine concerning the uterus. 2. (rhet.) hysteron-proteron, inversion of the natural or logical sequence of subjects in a speech.

histeromania s. f. (med.) hysteromania: 1. hysterical mania. 2. nymphomania.

histerômetro s. m. (med.) hysterometer: instrument for measuring the uterus.

histeroptose s. f. (med.) hysteroptosis: prolapse of the uterus.

histeroscópio s. m. (med.) speculum: instrument for dilating passages of the body, to facilitate inspection.

histerotomia s. f. (surg.) hysterotomy: incision of the uterus.

histofisiologia s. f. histophysiology: physiology of the minute elements of the tissues.

histofisiológico adj. histophysiologic(al).

histogêneo adj. (physiol.) histogenous, histogenetic, productive of organic tissue.

histogenia s. f. (physiol.) histogeny, histogenesis.

histografia s. f. (physiol.) histography: description of tissues.

histográfico adj. (physiol.) histographic(al).

histógrafo s. m. (physiol.) histographer.

histograma s. m. (statistics) histogram: diagram indicating frequency distribution.

histologia s. f. (med.) histology: the science of organic tissues.

histológico adj. (med.) histologic(al).

histologista s. m. + f. histologist: person learned in histology.

histoneurologia s. f. (med.) histoneurology: histology of the nervous system.

histoneurológico adj. (med.) histoneurologic(al).

histoneurologista s. m. + f. histoneurologist.

histonomia s. f. (med.) histonomy: laws of the formation of tissues.

histonômico adj. (med.) histonomic(al).

histoquímica s. f. (med.) histochemistry: chemistry of organic tissues and fluids.

história s. f. 1. history, systematic oral or written statement of past events. 2. branch of science that ascertains and records past facts. 3. story, tale, narration. 4. description. 5. biography. 6. fable, legend. 7. sham, fake, fabrication. 8. (coll.) rumour. ‖ interj. don't tell me!, fiddle-dee-dee!

~ da Antiguidade ancient history. **~ de amor** love-song. **~ do Far West** western. **~ natural** natural history. **~ universal** universal history. **contador de ~s** tale-teller. **é uma ~** it is a gib. **a isto liga-se uma ~** thereby hangs a tale. **isto é ~ para menino dormir sem ceia** that's empty talk. **é ~ da gente** it is the talk of the town. **ele meteu-se em ~s** he poked his nose into other people's business. **ela tinha uma ~ com a vizinha** she had a quarrel with her neighbour. **não conte ~s!** don't tell us tall tales! **qual ~!** what nonsense! **não me venha com ~s** don't come with any hanky-panky talk.

historiada s. f. rigmarole.

historiador s. m. historian, historiographer, chronicler.

historiar v. 1. to historize, chronicle. 2. to narrate, relate, tell. 3. to adorn with ornaments, embellish.

historicidade s. f. historicity, historicalness.

histórico s. m. 1. description, detailed report. 2. narration. 3. review. 4. biography. 5. (com.) abstract or statement of account. ‖ adj. 1. historical: of, pertaining to or related to history. 2. true,

veracious. 3. traditional. 4. noted or famous in history. || **historicamente** adv. historically.
os médicos discutiram o ~ do caso the physicians discussed the case history. **ele fez o ~ do clube** he talked about the club's historical development.
historieiro adj. (Braz.) unruly (horse).
historiento adj. (Braz., pop.) 1. impertinent, insolent. 2. exacting, hard to please. 3. = **cheio de histórias** complicated; fussy.
historieta s. f. 1. storiette, story. 2. tale, novel. 3. anecdote, feature.
~ em quadrinhos comic (strip). **~ humorística** funny.
historiografia s. f. 1. historiography: the art of writing history. 2. history. 3. historical and critical studies concerning historians and their work.
historiográfico adj. historiographical.
historiógrafo s. m. 1. historiographer, historian. 2. chronicler.
historíola s. f. historiette, short history or story, tale, yarn.
historiologia s. f. 1. historiology, storiology. 2. study or knowledge of history.
historismo s. m. historicism: philosophical doctrine which considers the progressive forms of civilization as consequence of a historical, spiritual process.
histrião s. m. 1. (pl. **-ões**) histrion. 2. clown, buffoon. 3. (fig.) humbug, impostor. 4. dissolute fellow.
histriônico adj. 1. histrionic(al), theatrical. 2. (fig.) feigned, unreal.
hitita s. m. + f. 1. Hittite: one of an ancient powerful people of northern Asia Minor. 2. language of the Hittite empire. || adj. Hittite.
hitlerismo s. m. Hitlerism.
hitlerista s. m. + f. Hitlerite. || adj. Hitlerite.
hiulco adj. (poet.) gaping, wide open.
hodierno adj. hodiernal, of this day, belonging to the present day.
hodometria s. f. hodometry, odometry: art and science of measuring the distances traversed by any means of conveyance.
hodométrico adj. hodometric(al), odometric(al).
hodômetro s. m. hodometer, odometer: instrument to measure the distance travelled by a vehicle.
hoje adv. 1. to-day, today, this day. 2. nowadays. 3. at the present time, actually.
~ em dia nowadays, at our days, in these days. **até o dia de ~** to this very day. **notícias de ~** today's news. **de ~ em diante** from this day on. **ainda ~** this very day. **faz ~ oito dias** a week ago. **de ~ a oito dias** in a week from this day, this day week.
holanda s. f. holland: cotton or linen fabric.
Holanda s. f. Netherlands, Holland.
holandês s. m. 1. Hollander, Netherlander, Dutchman, Batavian. 2. Dutch, language of the Netherlands. 3. (tech.) pulp engine. || adj. Hollandish, Dutch, Netherlandish.
holandilha s. f. buckram, coarse cloth of linen.
holicismo s. m. (phil.) expression common to several languages or dialects.
hólmio s. m. (chem.) holmium (symbol: Ho).
holobrânquio adj. (zool.) holobranchiate, having complete branchiae or gills (i.e. consisting of two rows of filaments).
holocausto s. m. holocaust: 1. (hist.) sacrifice or offering consumed by fire. 2. (fig.): a) sacrifice. b) destruction. c) carnage, slaughter. d) expiation, atonement.
holoedria s. f. (cryst.) holohedrism.
holoédrico adj. (cryst.) holohedral.
holoedro s. m. (cryst.) holohedron.

holofote s. m. 1. holophote. 2. projector, spotlight. 3. flashlight, searchlight (plate L 2). 4. floodlight.
hologênese s. f. hologenesis: biological theory asserting that every species originates new ones, whilst the original forms disappear.
holometabólico adj. holometabolic: including a complete metamorphosis in its cycle of development (insects).
holométrico adj. holometric.
holômetro s. m. holometer, pantometer: instrument for measuring angles and elevations.
holopetalar adj. m. + f. (bot.) holopetalous, transforming all essential parts of the inflorescence into petals.
holotúria s. f. (zool.) 1. Holothuria: a genus of sea-slugs. 2. holothurian: one of the Holothurioidea.
holoturióides s. m. (zool.) Holothurioidea: a class of echinoderms. || adj. holothurian.
hombridade s. f. 1. manliness, virility. 2. physique. 3. nobleness of character. 4. pride, haughtiness. 5. magnanimity.
homem s. m. (pl. **-ens**) 1. man. 2. human being. 3. manking, humanity. 4. male, husband, lover. 5. individual, person. 6. soldier, worker. 7. courageous or brave individual, one with manly qualities. 8. mortal. 9. (fam.) boy, fellow. 10. (sl.) bloke, chap. 11. **-ens** pl. menfolk.
~ autodidata autodidact. **~ bruto** brute. **~ carrancudo** (fig.) hedgehog. **um ~ da rua** he is a simple citizen. **~ de alta posição** man of high standing. **~ de bem** honest man, gentleman. **~ de convés** (naut.) deck-hand. **~ de Deus!** (coll.) man alive! **~ de duas caras** double-faced fellow. **~ de idade** old man. **~ de negócios** businessman. **~ de palavra** a man of his word. **~ do campo** countryman. **~ do leme** (naut.) steersman, helmsman. **~ do mar** seaman. **~ do mundo** man of the world. **~ do povo** commoner. **~ efeminado** jelly-bean. **~ esperto** sharp wit. **~ forte** strapper. **~ ilustre** a man of mark. **~ importante** bigwig. **~ inexperiente** green hand. **~ malcriado** ill-bred man. **~ moço** a young man. **~ prevenido vale por dois** forewarned is forearmed. **~ primitivo** cave-man. **~ recém-casado** benedick. **um ~ respeitado** a man of great account. **~ rico** rich man. **~ varonil** he-man. **que espécie de ~ é ele?** what kind of a person is he? **um grande ~** (coll.) a big noise. **ele é o meu ~** he is the right man (for the job). **ele é muito ~** he is a very aggressive fellow. **mas ele é outro ~** but he has changed considerably. **quantos -ens são?** what is their strength? **você já é ~** you are no longer a child. **você não é ~ para isto** you are not man enough to do that. **o ~ certo no lugar certo** the right man in the right place. **o ~ põe e Deus dispõe** man proposes, God disposes.
homem-chave s. m. (pl. **homens-chaves**) key man.
homem-de-palha s. m. (pl. **homens-de-palha**) 1. figure-head. 2. strawman, puppet.
homem-hora s. m. (pl. **homens-hora**) man-hour.
homem-rã s. m. (pl. **homens-rãs**) frogman.
homem-sanduíche s. m. (pl. **homens-sanduíche**) sandwich man, man carrying two advertising boards, one in front of his body, another behind.
homenageado s. m. 1. (feudal law) lord of tenure. 2. person to whom homage is paid. || adj. celebrated, honoured.
homenagear v. to homage, pay homage to.
homenagem s. f. (pl. **-ens**) 1. (feudal law) homage, fealty, allegiance. 2. respect, reverence. 3. tribute. 4. obeisance. 5. **-ens** pl. compliments.

dar ~ to do or to pay homage. **prestaram uma solene** ~ **ao velho casal** they paid a solemn homage to the old couple. **a** ~ **realizar-se-á no hotel** the celebration will take place at the hotel.

homenzarrão s. m. (pl. **-ões**) 1. tall, stout man. 2. (fig.) big shot, personality.

homenzinho s. m. 1. little man, dot, homunculus. 2. lad, young man. 3. man of no importance, nobody.

homeômero adj. homeomeric: having like parts.

homeopata s. m. + f. homeopath, homoeopathist.

homeopatia s. f. homeopathy.

homeopático adj. homeopathic(al).

homeoptoto s. m. (gram.) successive use of verbs in the same tense and person, or of nouns in the same case.

homérico adj. 1. (hist.) homeric(al). 2. (fig.) great, epic, resounding.
gargalhada -a epic laughter.

homérida s. m. (hist.) Homerid: rhapsodist who recited the Homeric poems.

homessa interj. 1. certainly not!, on the contrary! 2. don't say so!, indeed?! 3. that beats everything!

homicida s. m. + f. 1. murderer, slayer, homicide. 2. murderess. ‖ adj. murderous, homicidal, blood-guilty.

homicídio s. m. homicide, manslaughter, murder, assassination.

homilética s. f. homiletics: art of preaching.

homilético adj. homiletic(al).

homília, homilia s. f. homily: 1. elucidative sermon expounding the Scripture. 2. serious admonition upon morals and conduct.

homiliar v. 1. to compose homilies. 2. to sermonize. 3. to exhort, admonish.

homiliasta s. m. + f. homilist, composer of homilies, preacher.

hominal adj. m. + f. (pl. **-ais**) hominal, concerning man.

hominalidade s. f. 1. hominal character, hominal essence. 2. intrinsic property and power of human nature.

hominícola s. m. + f. admirer of homo sapiens.

hominídeo s. m. 1. hominid: one of the Hominidae. 2. **Hominídeos** pl. Hominidae: family of mammals, represented by the single genus Homo.

hominído adj. hominide, hominid.

homiziado s. m. fugitive, refugee. ‖ adj. hidden, concealed, fugitive.

homiziar v. 1. to conceal, hide. 2. to abscond. 3. to escape, run away from law. 4. to shelter. 5. to fall out with s. o., make an enemy of. 6. ~**se** to lie low, ensconce o. s.

homizio s. m. 1. shelter, lurking place, refuge. 2. concealment, hiding. 3. escape, getaway, lam.

homoblásteo adj. (bot.) homoblastic: arising from cells of the same kind.

homocêntrico adj. homocentric, concentric(al).

homocentro s. m. common center of several circles.

homoclamídeo adj. having identical floral leaves on the calyx and corolla.

homocromia s. f. homochromy, homochromatism.

homócrono adj. 1. (biol.) homochronous: appearing at the same period of evolution. 2. contemporaneous.

homofilo adj. (bot.) homophyllous: bearing leaves all of one kind.

homofonia s. f. homophony, sameness of sound.

homofônico adj. homophonous, homophonic: 1. of the same sound. 2. unisonant. 3. (phil.) agreeing in sound but differing in sense.

homófono s. m. homophonous words or syllables: words or syllables having the same sound in spite of different spelling. ‖ adj. homophonous.

homofonógrafo adj. homophonographic: having the same orthography and pronunciation but different sense and etymology.

homofonologia s. f. homophonology: study of homophonous words.

homofonológico adj. homophonologic(al).

homogamia s. f. homogamy: 1. (bot.) fertilization when stamens and pistils of a hermaphrodite flower mature at the same period. 2. (biol.) interbreeding of like with like.

homógamo adj. (biol.) homogamous.

homogeneidade s. f. 1. homogeneity, homogeneousness. 2. agreement in elements or character. 3. quality or state of being homogeneous.

homogeneização s. f. (pl. **-ões**) homogenization.

homogeneizar v. to homogenize, make homogeneous.

homogêneo adj. 1. homogeneous, congenial, uniform. 2. of the same kind or character. 3. consisting of similar parts and elements. 4. (math.): a) having the same degree. b) of the same nature and therefore comparable.

homogenesia s. f. (biol.) homogenesis: reproduction in which the successive generations are alike and have the same cycle of existence.

homogenia s. f. (biol.) homogeny: similarity due to descent from a common ancestor.

homografia s. f. (geom.) homography: interdependence of two figures (points, lines, planes, etc.).

homográfico adj. homographic(al).

homógrafo s. m. (phil.) homograph: words with the same spelling (orthography) but different origin and meaning.

homóica s. f. (bot.) parasitic plant which lives always on the same kind of host.

homóide adj. m. + f. 1. (bot.) similar in form to the involucre. 2. (zool.) descending from two races of the same species.

homologação s. f. (pl. **-ões**) 1. homologation. 2. (jur.) legal ratification. 3. confirmation. 4. accord, agreement.

homologar v. 1. to homologate. 2. (jur.) to ratify. 3. to confirm. 4. to agree. 5. ~**se** to resign o. s. to.

homologia s. f. 1. homology. 2. state or quality of being homologous, correspondence. 3. (rhet.) repetition of the same figure of speech.

homólogo adj. homologous.

homômero adj. homomeral: alike in all parts (two or more things).

homomerologia s. f. (anat.) study and treatise of organic systems.

homomorfismo s. m. homomorphism: adaptive or analogical resemblance.

homomorfo adj. homomorphous, analogous (not homologous) in form, superficially alike.

homonímia s. f. 1. homonymy, sameness of name. 2. (phil.) character of homophones.

homonímico adj. homonymic(al), homonymous.

homônimo s. m. 1. homonym, namesake. 2. (phil.) homophone. ‖ adj. homonymic, homonymous.

homopétalo adj. (bot.) homopetalous: having all the petals formed alike.

homoplasia s. f. homoplasy: agreement in form and structure without community of origin. ‖ adj. homoplasmic, homoplastic.

homoplástico adj. homoplastic, homoplasmic.

homóptero s. m. (zool.) 1. homopterous insect, homopteran. 2. ~**s** pl. Homoptera, order of insects.

homoptoto, homoptóton s. m. (gram.) successive use of verbs in the same tense and person or of nouns in the same case.

homorgânico adj. homorganic: 1. (med.) produced by the same or homologous organs. 2. (sounds of speech) produced by the same organs. 3. similarly organized.

homose s. f. 1. (rhet.) figure of speech in which a comparison is drawn. 2. (physiol.) assimilation of gastric juices.

homossexual s. m. (pl. **-ais**) homosexual. ‖ adj. homosexual.

homossexualidade s. f., **homossexualismo** m. homosexuality, eroticism for one of the same sex.

homotermal adj. m. + f. (pl. **-ais**) (phys.) homothermal, having the same temperature, isothermal.

homotesia, homotetia s. f. (math.) homothety, character of being homothetic, correspondence of similar figures, similarly placed.

homotético adj. (math.) homothetic: of or related to homothety.

homotipia s. f. (anat.) 1. homotypia, analogy of structure. 2. homotypy: structural correlation between any two organs of the body.

homotípico adj. (anat.) homotypic(al): of the same type, analogous.

homótipo adj. (anat.) homotypal, homotypic.

homótono adj. homotonous, monotonous: having the same tone.

homótropo adj. (bot.) homotropous, curved or turned in one direction.

homovalve adj. m. + f. (bot.) homovalvate: having similar valves.

homúnculo s. m. homunculus, little man, dwarf.

hondurenho s. m. Honduran, native or inhabitant of Honduras. ‖ adj. Honduran.

honestador s. m. 1. justifier, defender, advocate. 2. upholder of honour and decency.

honestar v. 1. to justify, defend. 2. to excuse, exculpate. 3. to honour. 4. to adorn, embellish. 5. **~-se** to proceed decently and honourably.

honestidade s. f. 1. honesty, honour. 2. uprightness, straightforwardness, squareness. 3. integrity, decency. 4. sincerity, truth. 5. good manners, deportment.

~ é a melhor política honesty is the best policy. **ele agiu com toda ~** he acted with all fairness. **seu procedimento fere os princípios de ~** their proceeding infringes the principles of fair play. **a ~ da menina é fora de dúvida** the fairmindedness of that girl is above doubt.

honestizar v. 1. to make honest, dignify. 2. to elevate, make noble.

honesto adj. 1. honest, honourable. 2. frank, sincere. 3. truthful, straight, square. 4. chaste, virtuous. 5. convenient, agreeable. 6. decent, proper, seemly. 7. straightforward, upright. 8. just, fair-minded, fair. 9. reputable. 10. competent, suitable, reliable. 11. well-mannered, refined. ‖ **-amente** adv. 1. honestly, honourably. 2. frankly, sincerely. 3. squarely. 4. virtuously. 5. uprightly. 6. rightly. 7. suitably. **preço ~** reasonable price. **condições -as** fair conditions. **ele é um homem ~** he is a true man. **ele ganha -amente o seu pão** he earns honestly penny by penny. **eles jogaram -amente** they played fair. **você precisa tentá-lo -amente** you have to play the game.

honor s. m. honour.

dama de ~ maid of honour.

honorabilidade s. f. honourableness, reputableness, reputability, worthiness.

honorário adj. 1. honorary, honorific. 2. conferring honour. 3. titular. 4. unpaid, unremunerative.

honorários s. m. pl. 1. honorarium, honorary. 2. income. 3. fee. 4. remuneration, pay.

honorificar v. to honourify, confer honour upon, honour.

honorificência s. f. mark of honour or distinction.

honorífico adj. honorific, honorary, unsalaried.

grau ~ honorary degree. **cargo ~** honorary office. **elegeram-no cidadão ~** they made him free of the city.

honra s. f. 1. honour, honor. 2. reputation, repute, good name. 3. respect, esteem, reverence. 4. probity, integrity, uprightness. 5. fame, glory. 6. culture, refinement. 7. dignity, distinction. 8. eminence, renown. 9. chastity, virtue. 10. **~s** pl.: a) courtesies rendered. b) special rank or distinction. c) honorific title. d) funeral ceremonies.

~ ao mérito honour to whom honour is due. **ele deu-me a ~ de sua visita** he did me the compliment of coming. **ele morreu no campo da ~** he died in battle. **código de ~** code of honour. **dama de ~** maid of honour. **um homem de ~** a man of honour. **lugar de ~** pride of place. **ele saiu sob palavra de ~** he left on parole. **isto é uma questão de ~** this is an affair of honour. **sentimento de ~** sense of honour. **em ~ de** in honour of. **em ~ dele** in his honour. **ele fez ~ ao churrasco** he did justice to the roast meat. **pela minha ~** on my honour. **ele é obrigado pela ~** he is bound in honour. **ele é uma ~ para mim** he is a credit to me. **sem ~** infamous. **ele recebeu as ~s** he had the credit of it. **ela foi recebida com ~s militares** she was received with military honours. **começaram as ~s fúnebres** the funeral solemnities began.

honrabilidade s. f. respectability, respectableness.

honradez s. f. 1. honour, probity. 2. character or state of being honourable, honourableness. 3. virtuousness. 4. righteousness, sincerity.

honrado adj. 1. honourable, reputable. 2. honest, sincere. 3. respected, worthy. 4. sound, straight, righteous. 5. virtuous, chaste. 6. trustworthy, reliable. 7. dignified. 8. straightforward. ‖ **-amente** adv. honourably, worthily, sincerely, righteously, virtuously.

gente -a worthy people. **não ~** unnoted. **dou-me por ~ com sua atenção** I consider myself honoured by your attention.

honrar v. 1. to honour, esteem. 2. to respect, revere. 3. to hold in honour, confer honours upon. 4. to dignify, glorify, ennoble. 5. to give credit to, believe in, rely on. 6. to flatter, adulate. 7. to exalt, elevate. 8. to grace, favour. 9. (com.) to accept and pay a bill. 10. **~-se:** a) to obtain honours and distinction. b) to become illustrious. c) to pride o. s. of.

ele o honrará he will do your credit. **ele me honra com sua amizade** he distinguishes me by his friendship. **ela nos honrou com sua presença** she honoured us with her presence.

honraria s. f. 1. distinction, eminence. 2. rank, elevated official standing. 3. honours. 4. mark or manifestation of esteem.

honrável adj. m. + f. (pl. **-áveis**) honourable, respectable, worshipful.

honroso adj. 1. honourable. 2. praiseworthy. 3. honest, fair. 4. decent. 5. creditable. ‖ **-amente** adv. honourably, reputably, honestly, decently.

a nomeação é muito -a para ele the appointment is very creditable for him.

hoplita s. m. (Greek hist.) hoplite: heavily armed foot soldier.

hóquei s. m. (sport) hockey.

hora s. f. 1. hour. 2. point of time indicated by a timepiece, time of day. 3. stroke of the clock, chiming of the hour. 4. opportunity, chance. 5. **~s** pl.: a) prayer-book. b) (eccl.) hours, prayers to be repeated at certain hours of the day. 6. last hour, fatal hour. 7. an hour's journey, measure of distance. **~s extras** overtime. **~ da morte** dying hour, death-

-hour. ~ **de chá** teatime. ~ **de dormir** beadtime. ~ **de encerramento do expediente na redação** copy-deadline. ~ **de estudo** prep (sl.). ~**s de grande movimento (trânsito, comércio)** rush hours. ~ **de jantar** dinner-time. ~ **de recolher** curfew. ~ **de recreio** playtime. ~ **de verão** summer time. **na** ~ **do começo** at the beginning. ~ **do crepúsculo** twilight. **a** ~ **do dia** the time of day. ~**s do expediente** business hours. **na** ~ **do levantar do sol** at sunrise. **na** ~ **do poente** at sunset. **ele voltou na** ~ **H** he came back at the eleventh hour. ~ **exata** high time. ~ **extra** overhour. **fazer** ~**s extraordinárias** to do overwork. ~ **média** mean time. ~ **oficial** standard time. **a** ~ **que lhe convém** in your own good time. ~ **vaga** free time, spare hours. **ele esperou até altas** ~**s** he waited until late at night. **ele apareceu em boa** ~ he arrived opportunely. **ele recolheu-se a boas** ~**s** he retired early. **ela contava as** ~**s até a colação de grau** she barely could abide the time until commencement day. **de** ~ **em** ~ from hour to hour. **ela esperou** ~**s e** ~**s** she waited a long time. **está na** ~ **de você ir** it is time for you to go. **fora de** ~ ill-timed. **chegou a** ~ the time has come. **chegou a hora da onça beber água** the critical moment has arrived. **chegou a** ~ **das orações** prayer time has come. **há uma** ~ an hour ago. **uma meia** ~ half an hour. **passar de** ~ **dormindo** to oversleep. **agora não é** ~ **para brincadeiras** this is no time for joking. **a sua** ~ **estava chegando** he was near his time. **eles não sabem esperar a sua** ~ they cannot watch their time. **não vejo a** ~ **que ele vá embora** I long for the moment of his departure. **ela escolheu bem a** ~ **da sua chegada** she timed her coming well. **o médico atendeu com** ~ **marcada** the physician attended at a fixed time. **mais ou menos às 9** ~**s** some time about nine. **um quarto de** ~ a quarter (of an hour). **que** ~**s são?** what time is it?, what's the time of the day? **pode dizer-me que** ~**s são?** can you tell me the right time? **por favor, diga-me que** ~**s são!** tell me the time, please! **dez** ~ **e meia** half past ten. ~ **média de Greenwich** Greenwich mean time. **os preços estão pela** ~ **da morte** the prices are disgustingly high.
horaciano adj. Horatian: of or pertaining to the Latin poet Horatius Flaccus.
horário s. m. time-table; school routine; schedule (plate E 13). ‖ adj. horal, hourly, horary.
o trem chegou no ~ the train arrived on scheduled time (on schedule). ~ **de verão** daylight saving, summer time.
horda s. f. horde, tribe of nomads. 2. troop, gang. 3. crew. 4. band, rout.
hordeáceo adj. (bot.) hardeaceous, barleylike.
hordeína s. f. (chem.) hordein, soluble protein found in barley seeds.
hordenina s. f. (chem.) hordenin(e), alkaloid extracted from barley.
hordéolo s. m. (med.) hordeolum, sty: inflamed swelling on the edge of the eyelid.
horista s. m. + f. hourly worker: a person who works by the hour. ‖ adj. m. + f. working by the hour.
horizontal s. f. (pl. -**ais**) horizontal line or surface. ‖ adj. m. + f. horizon: 1. parallel to the horizon, on a level (plate Q). 2. even, flat. ‖ ~**mente** adv. horizontally, evenly, flatly.
horizontalidade s. f. horizontality, state of being horizontal, horizontalness.
horizonte s. m. 1. horizon, visible horizon. 2. sky-line, sea-line (plate P 17). 3. (fig.) limit, range of perception, experience, intelligence. 4. (astr.) sensible horizon, celestial horizon.
~ **artificial** false or artificial horizon.

hormônio s. m. hormone: internal secretion of endocrine glands.
hornblenda s. f. (min.) hornblende.
horografia s. f. horography: art of constructing dials, account of the hours.
horográfico adj. horographic(al).
horologial adj. m. + f. (pl. -**ais**) horological: of or relative to the art of measuring time.
horoscopar v. to horoscope, elaborate a horoscope, foretell the future by observation of stars.
horoscópio s. m. horoscope.
horoscopista s. m. + f. horoscoper, horoscopist.
horoscopizar v. to horoscope.
horóscopo s. m. 1. horoscope, horoscopy. 2. (fig.) prediction, prophecy.
horrendo, horrente adj. 1. horrendous. 2. fearful, frightful. 3. horrible, horrid. 4. ugly. 5. heinous, monstrous. ‖ -**amente** adv. horrendously, frightfully, hideously, horribly.
crueldade -**a** abominable cruelty.
horribilidade s. f. 1. horribleness, horridness. 2. hideousness, gruesomeness. 3. dreadfulness, direness.
hórrido adj. 1. horrid. 2. fearful, frightful. 3. horrible, horrendous. 4. dreadful. 5. hideous, terrible.
horrífero, horrífico adj. horrific, causing horror.
horripilação s. f. (pl. -**ões**) horripilation, (fig.) goose--flesh, (fam.) shivers.
horripilante adj. m. + f. (also **horrípilo** m.) horrifying, hair-rising, terrifying, heinous, blood-curdling.
horripilar v. 1. to horripilate, horrify. 2. to produce horripilation in. 3. to shudder, shiver. 4. to feel horror.
horríssono adj. horrisonant, horrisonous.
horrível adj. m. + f. (pl. -**íveis**) 1. horrible, terrible, horrid. 2. dreadful, shocking. 3. hideous, grisly, grim. 4. frightful, awful, gruesome. ‖ **horrivelmente** adv. horribly, frightfully, shockingly, grimly, gruesomely.
horror s. m. 1. horror, terror. 2. hate. 3. repulsion, aversion. 4. suffering, pain, agony. 5. dread, heinousness. 6. barbarous crime. 7. abomination, detestation. 8. shudder(ing), shiver.
isto causa uma sensação de ~ **na gente** it gives you the creeps. **ele tem** ~ **ao crime** he abhors crime. **ele disse** ~**es dela** he said very nasty things about her.
horrorífico adj. 1. horrific, causing horror. 2. fearful, frightful. 3. horrible, horrid. 4. heinous, monstrous.
horrorizar v. 1. to horrify, terrify. 2. to feel horror. 3. to cause horror, frighten. 4. to be horrible. 5. to consternate, shock.
estou horrorizado com I am appalled at. **ela estava horrorizada** she stood aghast.
horroroso adj. 1. horrible, terrible, horrific. 2. fearful, frightful. 3. abhorrent, appalling. 4. dreadful, shocking. 5. hideous, monstrous.
horta s. f. kitchen-garden, market-garden, vegetable--garden.
hortaliça s. f. vegetable(s), potherb(s), green stuff, greenery.
hortar v. 1. to lay out a vegetable-garden. 2. to cultivate a market-garden. 3. to labour in a garden.
hortativo adj. 1. exhortative, admonitory. 2. hortative, encouraging.
hortelã s. f. (bot.) mint, garden mint, spearmint.
bala de ~ peppermint drops.
hortelã-brava s. f. (pl. **hortelãs-bravas**) (bot.) = **hortelã-do-brasil.**
hortelã-do-brasil s. f. (pl. **hortelãs-do-brasil**) (bot.) basilweed, identical to **hortelã-do-campo**, but with a shorter stalk.
hortelã-do-campo s. f. (pl. **hortelãs-do-campo**) (bot.) wild basil, basilweed.

hortelã-romana s. f. (pl. **hortelãs-romanas**) (bot.) = **balsamita**.

hortelão s. m. (pl. ~s, -ões) (f. **horteloa**) market--gardener.

hortelã-pimenta s. f. (pl. **hortelãs-pimenta**) (bot.) peppermint.
essência de ~ peppermint extract. **óleo de** ~ peppermint oil.

horteleiro s. m. (Braz.) market-gardener.

horteloa s. f. 1. a gardener's wife. 2. female gardener.

hortense adj. m. + f. hortensial, hortensian: pertaining to or produced in a garden.

hortênsia s. f. (bot.) hydrangea, hortensia.

hortícola adj. m. + f. horticultural.

horticultor s. m. horticulturist, plantsman.

horticultura s. f. horticulture, art and practice of gardening.

horto (ô) s. m. 1. little (kitchen-)garden. 2. plant nursery. 3. (fig.) place of suffering, calvary.
~ **florestal** tree farm.

hortulana s. f. (ornith.) ortolan, European bunting.

hosana s. m. 1. hosanna, shout of praise. 2. (fig.) praise, salutation.

hosco adj. (S. Braz.) deep brown, dark-coloured (cattle).

hóspeda s. f. 1. female guest. 2. hostess. 3. landlady.
fazer a conta sem a ~ to reckon without one's host.

hospedador s. m. host, landlord.

hospedagem s. f. (pl. -**ens**) 1. hospitality. 2. lodging, accommodation. 3. entertainment.
~ **sem comida** dry lodging.

hospedança s. f. (Braz.) group or reunion of guests.

hospedar v. 1. to receive or entertain as a guest. 2. to provide with a shelter. 3. to house, lodge, accommodate. 4. to entertain. 5. ~-**se** to be or become a guest, take up quarters in.

hospedaria s. f. 1. lodging-house, inn. 2. hotel, hostelry. 3. public-house, rest-house.

hospedável adj. m. + f. (pl. -**áveis**) hospitable, capable of receiving or being received as a guest.

hóspede s. m. (f. **hóspeda**) 1. guest, visitor. 2. paying guest, lodger (plate R 5). 3. chance-guest, sojourner. 4. stranger. 5. pilgrim. 6. host(ess), landlord, landlady. || adj. m. + f. 1. strange. 2. (fig.) ignorant, uninformed.
casa de ~s guest-house. **ele é** ~ **em sua casa** he is a diner-guest in his own home. **ela é** ~ **na matemática** she is not well versed in mathematics.

hospedeiro s. m. host: 1. landlord, innkeeper. 2. plant or animal in relation to a parasite usually dwelling on it. 3. entertainer. || adj. 1. of or relating to a guest or host. 2. hospitable.

hospício s. m. 1. hospice, hospitium, refuge for (poor) travelers. 2. asylum, almshouse. 3. lunatic asylum, madhouse.

hospital s. m. (pl. -**ais**) 1. hospital. 2. clinic, infirmary. 3. sanatorium. 4. lazaret(to).
~ **ambulante** ambulance. ~ **de emergência** field hospital. ~ **militar** infirmary, military hospital. **navio** ~ hospital-ship. ~ **de isolamento** isolation hospital.

hospitalar adj. m. + f. 1. of or pertaining to a hospital or hospice; nosocomial. 2. hospitable.

hospitalário s. m. hospital(l)er: 1. hospital inmate. 2. monk of the Order of Hospital(l)ers of St. John of Jerusalem. || adj. (also **hospitaleiro**) 1. of or pertaining to a hospital. 2. hospitable.

hospitaleira s. f. sister of a religious order devoted to the care of the sick and needy in hospitals.

hospitalidade s. f. hospitality, hospitableness, conviviality, entertainment.
falta de ~ inhospitableness.

hospitalização s. f. (pl. -**ões**) hospitalization: admission in a hospital for treatment.

hospitalizar v. to hospitalize, intern in a hospital for treatment.

hoste s. f. 1. host. 2. troop, army. 3. (fig.) gang, band. 4. enemy.

hóstia s. f. Host, holy bread or wafer, Eucharist.

hostiário s. m. box for the wafers not yet consecrated.

hostil adj. m. + f. (pl. -**is**) 1. hostile, inimical. 2. adverse, antagonistic. 3. belligerent, foelike. 4. aggressive, provocative. 5. contrary, opposed. 6. unfriendly (to), malevolent. || ~**mente** adv. hostilely, inimically, antagonistically, unfriendly, malevolently.

hostilidade s. f. 1. hostility, enmity. 2. hostile action. 3. inimical feeling. 4. antagonism, animosity. 5. opposition. 6. warfare, feud.
interromper as ~s to suspend hostilities.

hostilizar v. 1. to antagonize. 2. to show ill will, persecute. 3. to oppose. 4. to wound, hurt. 5. to wage war on. 6. ~-**se** to fight each other.

hotel s. m. (pl. -**éis**) 1. hotel (plate P 17). 2. inn, lodging house. 3. motel.
~ **para automobilistas** motel. **ele é o gerente do** ~ he is the hotel manager. **posso ter bilhetes para o carro-hotel?** may I have tickets for the hotel-car? **ele ficou no** ~ **para viajantes** he was staying in the transient hotel.

hoteleiro s. m. hotel-keeper, proprietor of a hotel.

hotentote s. m. + f. Hottentot, member of a South African native race.

hotentotismo s. m. Hottentotism: 1. characteristic of Hottentots. 2. (med.) defective speech.

hudu s. m. (Braz., ornith.) motmot.

huguenote s. m. (hist.) Huguenot, Calvinist.

hui! interj. ah! oh!, alas! oh dear me!

hulha s. f. coal, black coal, stone coal, mineral coal.
~ **gorda** cannel coal.

hulha-branca s. f. (pl. **hulhas-brancas**) water-power.

hulheira s. f. coal-mine, coal-pit.

hulhífero adj. carboniferous, producing or containing coal.

hum! interj. humph!, hem!, hum!

humanal adj. (pl. -**ais**) 1. human, of or relating to man. 2. humane, kind, benevolent. 3. gentle, affable.

humanar v. 1. to humanize, make human. 2. to refine, civilize. 3. to make kindly disposed, gentle or benevolent. 4. ~-**se** to become humane, be or become compassionate.

humanidade s. f. 1. humanity, condition or quality of being human. 2. human nature. 3. human beings collectively, mankind. 4. kindness, humaneness, benevolence. 5. ~s pl. human or classical learning.

humanismo s. m. humanism, study of humanities, study of classic languages and literature.

humanista s. m. + f. humanist, scholar of classic culture, languages and literature (esp. in the Renaissance period). || adj. m. + f. = **humanístico**.

humanístico adj. humanistic.
formação -a, educação -a humane learning, classical education.

humanitário s. m. humanitarian, philanthropist. || adj. humanitarian, humane, kind, benevolent, philanthropic(al).

humanitarismo s. m. humanitarianism, humanism: doctrines, principles and practices of humanitarians.

humanização s. f. (pl. -**ões**) humanization, assimilation to humanity, act of making human.

humanizar v. 1. to humanize, make human. 2. to render humane or gentle. 3. (fig.) to bring s.o. to his senses. 4. to make manageable. 5. to refine, civilize.

humanos s. m. pl. human beings, mankind. || **humano** adj. 1. human, of or belonging to man. 2. humane.

kind, benevolent. 3. gentle, affable. 4. humanitarian. 5. earth-born. ‖ **-amente** adv. humanly, kindly, humanely, gently.
o gênero humano the human race. **um ser humano** a human being. **na medida do discernimento humano** as far as human judgment goes. **humanamente possível** humanly possible. **-amente falando** humanly speaking.
húmico adj. (chem.) humic: of or derived from humus.
humificação s. f. (pl. **-ões**) humification, formation of humus.
húmil adj. m. + f. (pl. **húmiles**) (poet.) humble, modest.
humildação s. f. (pl. **-ões**) humiliation.
humildade s. f. 1. humbleness, humility. 2. modesty, meekness. 3. lowliness, lowness. 4. submission, submissiveness. 5. poverty, destitution. 6. inferiority.
humildar v. 1. to humble, humiliate, abase. 2. to mortify. 3. to subdue, subject, subordinate. 4. **~-se** to humble or abase o. s.
humilde adj. m. + f. (also **humildoso** m.) 1. humble, modest. 2. meek. 3. low(ly). 4. submissive. 5. common, vulgar. 6. unimportant, unpretending. 7. obscure. 8. poor, needy, shabby. 9. ignoble, contemptible. ‖ **~-mente** adv. humbly, lowly, meekly, obscurely, needily, contemptibly.
minha ~ pessoa my humble self. **ele é de descendência ~** he is of humble origin.
húmile adj. m. + f. (poet.) humble.
humilhação s. f. (pl. **-ões**) 1. humiliation, act of humbling. 2. mortification. 3. state of being humiliated. 4. shame. 5. abjection, abasement.
~ própria self-abasement.
humilhado adj. 1. humbled, abased, ashamed. 2. mean, destitute, poor.
ele foi ~ he lost face.
humilhante adj. m. + f. humiliating, humbling, depressing, mortifying.
humilhar v. 1. to humiliate, humble. 2. to mortify. 3. to debase, abase. 4. to lower, let down. 5. to shame, cheapen. 6. to treat contemptuously. 7. **~-se** to humble or abase o. s., eat humble pie, subject o. s. to, yield.
ele humilhou seu amigo he let his friend down. **elas humilharam o menino** they cropped the boy's feather. **eles ficaram humilhados** they ate humble pie. **eles o humilharam** they fetched him down.
humo s. m. humus, vegetable mould, earth.
humor s. m. humour: 1. moisture. 2. (arch.) bodily fluid. 3. condition of mind, mental state, mood,

disposition. 4. temper, feeling. 5. wit, fun. 6. jocoseness, jocularity.
de bom ~ good-humoured, in a good temper, in high spirits. **de mau ~** out of humour, in bad temper, cross, petulant, ill-humoured. **encontramo-lo de bom ~** we met him in a cheerful mood. **ela estava de mau ~** she was ill-disposed. **ele estava de mau ~** he was off-hand. **ele é um sujeito sem ~** he is a humourless chap. **os ~es do corpo humano** the fluids of the human body. **~ vítreo** vitreous humour (of the eye) (plate O). **ela está de ~ para cantar** she is in a mood to sing. **ela só segue o seu próprio ~** she is a fickle person. **~ negro** black or morbid humor, gallow's humour.
humorado adj. 1. humoured, tempered. 2. (med.) humoral, humorous. 3. funny, witty. 4. capricious, fickle.
humoral adj. m. + f. (pl. **-ais**) (med.) humoral: of or pertaining to the bodily humours.
humorismo s. m. humorism: 1. humorousness, jocoseness. 2. (path.) humoralism: doctrine that diseases have their origin in the humours of the body.
humorista s. m. + f. 1. humorist, humorous talker, or actor. 2. humoralist, adept of humoralism.
humorístico adj. 1. humoristic(al), funny, comical, witty. 2. (med.) of or related to humoralism. ‖ **humoristicamente** adv. 1. humoristically, comically, wittily. 2. humorally.
composição -a (mus.) humoresque, caprice. **assistir a um programa ~** to watch a humorous show.
humoroso adj. 1. (med.) humoral. 2. moist, humid. 3. humorous, funny, witty.
humoso adj. humous, rich in humus.
húmus s. m. humus, vegetable mould, earth, soil.
húngaro s. m. 1. Hungarian, Magyar. 2. Hungarian language. ‖ adj. Hungarian, Magyar.
huno s. m. (hist.) Hun, member of a barbarous Asiatic people that invaded Europe (in the fourth and fifth centuries). ‖ adj. Hunnish.
huri s. f. (rel.) 1. houri, nymph of the Mohammedan paradise. 2. woman of extraordinary beauty.
huroniano s. m. Huron: native of a tribe of Iroquoian Indians. ‖ adj. Huronian.
hurra! interj. hurrah!, hooray!, cheerio!
saudar com ~ to hurrah, applaud with cheers.
hússar, hussardo s. m. hussar: member of a class of light cavalry, cavalryman.
hussita s. m. + f. (rel., hist.) Hussite: follower of Huss. ‖ adj. m. + f. Hussite.

I

I, i s. m. (pl. is or ii) 1. ninth letter and third vowel of the Portuguese alphabet. 2. (chem.) symbol of iodine. 3. number one in the Roman notation. ‖ adj. ninth (in a group or series).
ele pôs os pontos nos ii he was quite outspoken. ela nunca esquece de pôr os pontos nos ii she is a very punctilious woman. o ponto no i the dot on the i. vamos pôr os pontos nos ii let us get that straight.
iá interj. 1. fie!, faugh!, what a shame!. 2. gee-ho!, gee-up! (urging draught animals).
iabá s. m. (N. Braz.) salted meat.
iaca s. f. (Braz.) offensive smell, rank odour.
iâmbico adj. (poet., pros.) iambic, consisting of iambics, of or pertaining to a iambus.
iambo s. m. 1. (poet., pros.) iamb(us). 2. (Fr. literat.) satire, sarcastic poem or prose.
iamologia s. f. (med.) iamatology: study or science of remedies.
iamológico adj. (med.) iamatologic(al), of or pertaining to iamatology.
iamotecnia s. f. (pharm.) iamatotechnique, the art of preparing remedies.
iamotécnico adj. (pharm.) iamatotechnical.
ianque s. m. + f. Yankee: native or inhabitant of (the northern part) of the U.S.A. ‖ adj. Yankee.
iansã s. f. (Braz.) nymph, deity of storms and tempests (worshipped by descendants of Negro slaves).
iaque s. m. yak: domesticated or wild Tibetan ox.
iara s. f. water-nymph of South American aborigines.
iatá s. f. (Braz.) a variety of a palm tree (Cocos syagrus).
iatagã s. m. yataghan, yatagan: short saber without crosspiece.
iate s. m. (naut.) yacht (plate B 10).
iatismo s. m. yachting.
iatralipta s. m. + f. physician who treats diseases by inunction and friction.
iatralíptica s. f. (med.) iatraliptics: treatment by inunction and friction.
iatralíptico adj. (med.) iatraliptic.
iátrica s. f. iatrics, surgery, medicine.
iatrologia s. f. iatrology, treatise on medicine or on physicians.
iatroquímica s. f. iatrochemistry: school of medicine which believes that all the phenomena of life are based on chemical action.
iatroquímico adj. (chem.) iatrochemical.
ibacurupari s. m. (Braz., Tupi) bacury: tropical South American timber tree.
ibapocaba s. f. (Braz., bot.) allamanda.
ibérico s. m. 1. Iberian, one of the primitive inhabitants of Spain and Portugal. 2. ancient Iberian language. ‖ adj. 1. of, pertaining to or relative to Iberia. 2. of or relating to the Iberic union.
ibérida s. f. (bot.) candytuft.
ibero s. m. Iberian: one of the primitive inhabitants of Spain and Portugal. ‖ adj. Iberian.
ibero-americano s. m. (pl. ibero-americanos) an individual of Spanish-American descent. ‖ adj. Spanish-American.
ibiboca s. f. (Braz., Tupi) coral snake.
ibicuíba s. f. (Braz., bot.) 1. becuiba tree. 2. becuiba nut.
ibijara s. f. (Braz., zool.) amphisbaenian.
ibirapiroca s. f. (Braz.) plant of the family Myrtaceae.
ibirapitanga s. f. (Braz., Tupi, bot.) brazilwood.
ibirataíba s. f. (Braz., bot.) Pernambuco jaborandi

íbis s. m. + f., sg. + pl. íbis: a bird of the family Ibididae.
íbis-branca s. f. (pl. íbis-brancas) (ornith.) 1. white ibis, Spanish curlew. 2. sacred ibis: object of religious veneration by the ancient Egyptians.
ibixuma s. f. (Braz., bot.) bastard cedar, bay cedar.
içá s. f. (Braz.) female sauba ant.
içabitu s. m. (Braz.) male sauba ant.
icacináceas s. f. pl. (bot.) Sapindaceae, flowering plants belonging to the soapberry family.
icacoré-catinga s. f. (pl. icacorés-catingas) (Braz., bot.) ardisia.
içado adj. 1. (naut.) aweigh, atrip. 2. hoisted.
içar v. 1. to hoist, hoist up. 2. to wind(lass). 3. to jack, lift. 4. to hitch up, sling up. 5. to crane, heave. 6. (naut.) to bowse, trice.
~ a bandeira to hoist the flag. ~ de vela arriba (naut.) to hoist away. eles ~am o escaler they hoisted the boat in.
ícaro s. m. 1. (Greek myth.) Icarus. 2. (fig.) person who insists upon a foolhardy or presumptuous enterprise.
icástico adj. 1. natural. 2. unvarnished, unadorned. 3. (fig.) vivid, expressive.
icebergue s. m. iceberg.
icéria s. f. (ent.) cottony-cushion scale, white scale.
ichneumonídeos s. m. pl. (zool.) (ent.) Ichneumonidae, a family of insects, the larvae of which are parasitic on caterpillars, etc.
ichó s. m. snare, trap (for rabbits, partridges, etc.).
icica(riba) s. f. (Braz.) icica, incense tree.
icipó s. m. (Braz.) red creeper (and several related plants).
icnêumone s. m. (zool.) 1. ichneumon, mongoose, Egyptian rat. 2. ichneumon fly.
icnografia s. f. (archit.) ichnography, ichnograph, ground plan.
icnográfico adj. ichnographic(al).
icnógrafo s. m. ichnographer, draughtsman.
icó s. m. (Braz., bot.) caper.
ícone s. m. icon: 1. image, portrait, picture. 2. (Eastern Church) painting, relief or mosaic of Christ, Our Lady or a saint.
icônico adj. iconic(al).
iconista s. m. + f. iconist, one skilled in the production of icons.
iconoclasmo s. m. iconoclasm, act of destroying icons.
iconoclasta s. m. + f. iconoclast, breaker or destroyer of images. ‖ adj. iconoclastic(al).
iconófilo s. m. iconophile, a lover of icons.
iconografia s. f. iconography: 1. study and description of paintings, sculptures, statues, etc. 2. the art of pictorial representation. 3. collection of such representations.
iconográfico adj. iconographic(al).
iconógrafo s. m. iconographer.
iconólatra s. m. + f. iconolater, image worship(p)er.
iconolatria s. f. iconolatry, idolatry, worship or adoration of images.
iconologia s. f. iconology: 1. science of emblematic representation. 2. study or description of emblematic figures. 3. study or history of artistic expression.
iconológico adj. iconologic(al).
iconologista s. m. + f., iconólogo m. iconologist, scholar of iconology.
iconômaco s. m. iconomachist, iconoclast.

iconomania s. f. iconomania, morbid interest in images.

iconoscópio s. m. (electronics) iconoscope, a television camera tube.

icor s. m. (med.) ichor: thin serous fluid from a wound.

icosaedro s. m. (geom.) icosahedron, polyhedron of twenty faces.

icosandria s. f. 1. icosander, plant having twenty or more stamens inserted in the calyx. 2. Icosandria: a class of icosandrous plants.

icosândrico, icosandro adj. (bot.) icosandrous, icosandrian.

icozeiro s. m. (Braz., bot.) caper.

i(c)terícia s. f. (med.) jaundice, icterus, (pop.) yellows. **medicamento contra a** ~ icteric.

i(c)térico adj. (med.) jaundice, icteric(al).

icterídeos s. m. pl. (ornith.) Icteridae, a large family of oscine birds.

íctero s. m. (med.) icterus, jaundice.

icterocéfalo adj. (zool.) icterocephalous, having a yellow head.

icteróide adj. (med.) icteroid, resembling jaundice.

ictíaco, ictíico adj. ichthyic, pertaining to fishes, piscine.

ictiocola s. f. fish glue, isinglass.

ictiodonte s. m. ichthyodont, fossil fish tooth.

ictiodorilite s. m. ichthyodorulite, fossilized spine of a fish.

ictiofagia s. f. ichthyophagy, practice of eating fish.

ictiófago s. m. ichthyophagist, fisheater, one who lives on a fish diet. ‖ adj. ichthyophagous.

ictiografia s. f. ichthyography, treatise on fishes, description of fishes.

ictiográfico adj. ichthyographic.

ictiógrafo s. m. ichthyographer, ichthyologist, person versed in ichthyography or ichthyology.

ictióide adj. m. + f. ichthyoid(al), resembling a fish.

ictióideo adj. ichthyoid(al).

ictiol s. m. (pharm.) ichthyol.

ictiologia s. f. (zool.) ichthyology.

ictiológico adj. ichthyologic(al).

ictiólogo s. m. ichthyologist, one versed in ichthyology.

ictiopsofose s. f. slight murmur produced by fishes swimming under water.

ictiose s. f. (med.) ichthyosis, fishskin disease.

ictiossauro s. m. (pal.) ichthyosaurus: 1. (capital letter) the chief genus of Ichthyosauria. 2. animal of this genus, ichthyosaur.

ictis s. m. ichthys: word formed by the initial letters of Christ's name in the Greek language (Jesus Christ, Son of God, Saviour).

id s. m. (psych.) id: fundamental self-preserving instincts, the true unconscious.

ida s. f. 1. departure, setting out. 2. starting, leaving. 3. journey. 4. travel, trip.
~ **por vinda** to go but to return immediately. ~**s e vindas** comings and goings. **ele comprou um bilhete de** ~ **e volta** he bought a ticket out and home, he bought a return ticket. **muitas** ~**s** frequent visits to a place.

idade s. f. 1. age. 2. time, lifetime. 3. epoch, century. 4. duration of existence, average life period. 5. stage of mental or physical development, maturity. 6. old age, decline of life. 7. historical or geological period. 8. great length of time, years. 9. seniority.
Idade da Pedra Stone Age. ~ **da razão** adulthood. ~ **de casar** marriage estate. ~ **de discrição** years of discretion or maturity. **Idade do Ferro** Iron Age. **Idade do Ouro** Gold Age. **Idade Média** Middle Ages, Dark Ages. ~ **viril do homem** age of man-

hood, man's estate. **a flor da** ~ the prime of life. **ela é de menor** ~ she is underage. **ela é de tenra** ~ she is of tender age. **ela tem mais de 18 anos de** ~ she turned eighteen. **ela tinha menos de 20 anos de** ~ she was in her teens. **ele alcançou setenta anos de** ~ he lived to threescore and ten. **ele é de** ~ **avançada** he is well advanced in years. **ele morreu na** ~ **avançada** he died at a ripe age. **ele não mostra a** ~ he does not look his age. **ele passou da** ~ he is overage. **ele tem a** ~ **dela** he is her age. **meninos da sua própria** ~ boys their own age. **na** ~ **grave** in old age. **na minha** ~ at my time of life. **os de sua** ~ his equals in age. **qual é a** ~ **que você lhe dá?** what age do you give him? **um homem de meia-** ~ a middle-aged man. **uma senhora de** ~ **não definida** a lady of a certain age. **você já está na** ~ **de obedecer** you are already old enough to obey.

idálico, idálio adj. 1. (hist.) of or relative to Idalium (ancient city in Central Cyprus consecrated to Venus). 2. (myth.) of or pertaining to Venus.

ideação s. f. (pl. -ões) 1. ideation, act or process of forming ideas. 2. idea. 3. notion, conception.

ideal s. m. (pl. -ais) 1. ideal. 2. conception that exceeds reality. 3. model, example. 4. standard of desire or perfection. ‖ adj. m. + f. 1. ideal(istic). 2. imaginary, conceptual. 3. of, pertaining to or consisting in ideas. ‖ ~**mente** adv. ideally, conceptually, notionally.
eles combinaram de maneira ~ they combined ideally. **eles comungaram nos mesmos ideais** they cherished the same ideals. **ela foi de uma beleza** ~ she was an ideal beauty.

idealidade s. f. 1. ideality, condition or quality of being ideal. 2. capacity of forming ideals. 3. state of being ideal or unreal. 4. idealism.

idealismo s. m. idealism: 1. philosophical theory that all reality is in its nature psychical. 2. spiritual or ideal conception of reality. 3. practice of forming ideals, and striving for their realization, pursuit of an ideal. 4. (art, literat.) tendency of depicting any motive in accordance with a preconceived ideal of beauty and perfection.

idealista s. m. + f. idealist: 1. supporter of the theory of idealism. 2. (art, literat.) artist who expresses idealism in his works. 3. imaginative, unpractical person, daydreamer. 4. doctrinaire. ‖ adj. idealistic(al).

idealístico adj. idealistic(al), Platonic.

idealização s. f. (pl. -ões) idealization, idealisation, act of making ideal or of forming an idea.

idealizador s. m. 1. idealizer, idealiser. 2. idealist. 3. creator, organizer.

idealizar v. 1. to idealize, idealise. 2. to Platonize, make ideal. 3. to form ideals. 4. to realize, organize. 5. to imagine, dream up.

idear v. 1. to ideate, idealize. 2. to form ideas, conceive. 3. to contrive, plan. 4. to invent, project. 5. to fancy, dream up. 6. to visualize.

ideário s. m. a set or system of political, social or economic ideas, etc.

ideativo adj. ideative, ideational.

ideável adj. m. + f. (pl. -áveis) conceivable, feasable, realizable.

idéia s. f. 1. idea, thought, notion. 2. mental conception, concept. 3. image, imagination. 4. perception, opinion, impression. 5. project, plan, scheme. 6. invention, inspiration. 7. model. 8. judgement, good sense. 9. memory, recollection. 10. fancy. 11. hint. **isto é uma** ~ **absurda** that's an absurd notion. **isto foi uma boa** ~**!** this was a happy thought. **eles andavam cheios de** ~**s** they were full of plans. **uma** ~ **brilhante** a brilliant idea, (coll.) a brain

wave. **isto foi uma ~ errônea** that was an erroneous idea. **creio que é uma ~ esquisita** I think it is a crotchet. **você não faz ~ disto** you have no idea of it. **tornou-se a sua ~ fixa** it became his obsession or the bee in his bonnet. **não é má ~ the** idea is not bad. **formar uma ~ de** to form an idea of. **foi uma ~ impraticável** it was an impracticable idea, (coll.) a pipe dream. **mudei de ~ I** changed my mind. **não tivemos a mínima ~** we had not the remotest idea. **que ~!** the idea! **sem ~** idealess. **troquei ~s com ele** I took counsel with him.
idem adj. ditto, same. ‖ adv. ditto, the same.
~ per ~ it is just the same.
idêntico adj. 1. identical, exactly alike. 2. equal. 3. similar, analogous. 4. same, selfsame. ‖ **-amente** adv. identically, equally, similarly.
quase ~ approximate.
identidade s. f. 1. identity, identicalness. 2. sameness, oneness, exactness. 3. individuality. 4. (math.) identical equation. 5. condition of being the very same (person or object).
documentos de ~ identity papers. **ficha ou talão de ~** identity tag. **ele apresentou o certificado de ~** he submitted the certificate of origin.
identificação s. f. (pl. **-ões**) 1. identification, act or process of establishing the identity. 2. (natural hist.) determination of a species.
ficha de ~ identification card. **chapa de ~** identification tag.
identificar v. 1. to identify: a) make identical. b) establish the identity of. c) recognize. d) make one, unite, combine. e) prove to be the same. 2. **~-se com** to identify o. s. with, habituate o. s. to.
identificável adj. m. + f. (pl. **-áveis**) identifiable, recognizable, capable of being identified.
ideogenia s. f. ideogeny, science of the origin of ideas.
ideogênico adj. ideogenic(al).
ideografia s. f. ideography, representation of ideas by graphic signs.
ideográfico adj. ideographic(al).
ideografismo s. m. 1. principles of representation of ideas by ideographic symbols. 2. ideographics.
ideógrafo s. m. ideographer, one versed in ideographics.
ideograma s. m. ideogram, ideograph.
ideologia s. f. ideology: 1. science of ideas or of mind. 2. (philos.) doctrine asserting that knowledge derives exclusively from sensations. 3. (sociol.) principles and aims of a widespread political, artistic, religious or social movement.
ideológico adj. ideologic(al).
ideólogo s. m. ideologist.
idílico adj. 1. idyllic(al), pleasing. 2. pastoral. 3. amorous. 4. suave, mild.
idílio s. m. idyl(l): 1. pastoral, rural poem. 2. (mus.) composition of sentimental character. 3. Platonic love affair.
idilista s. m. + f. idyl(l)ist, composer, painter or writer of idyls.
idioblasto s. m. (biol.) idioblast, biophore.
idiocromático adj. idiochromatic, coloured inherently (as certain metals).
idiófono adj. (mus.) ideophonous: said of a musical instrument made from a solid, naturally sonorous material, as a gong or glass harmonica.
idiógino adj. (bot.) idiogynous, having no pistil.
idiólatra s. m. + f. idiolater, self-worship(p)er.
idiolatria s. f. idiolatry, self-worship.
idioma s. m. 1. idiom. 2. tongue, language. 3. dialect, vernacular. 4. idiomatic expression.
~ da Pérsia Persian. **~ dos celtas** Celtic. **ele tem talento para ~s** he as the gift of tongues

idiomático adj. idiomatic(al), peculiar to a language. **expressões -as** idioms. **de modo ~** idiomatically.
idiomografia s. f. idiomography, science, classification and description of idioms.
idiomográfico adj. idiomographic(al).
idiomórfico adj. (min.) idiomorphic, having its own characteristic form, idiomorphous.
idiomorfo s. m. fossil that preserved its own peculiar form. ‖ adj. idiomorphic, idiomorphous.
idiopatia s. f. 1. (med.) idiopathy, morbid state not occasioned by a preceding disease. 2. peculiar affection, sympathy.
idiopático adj. idiopathic(al).
idioplasma s. f. (biol.) idioplasm, germ plasm.
idiossincrasia s. f. idiosyncrasy: 1. constitutional susceptibility. 2. inherent aversion, antipathy. 3. distinctive mental quality.
idiossincrático adj. idiosyncratic.
idiota s. m. + f. 1. idiot, cretin. 2. ignorant or simple person. 3. person afflicted with idiocy. 4. fool, simpleton. ‖ adj. idiotic(al), stupid, foolish, silly.
ele é um perfeito ~ he is a big fool.
idiotar v. 1. to make or render idiotic. 2. to become idiotic. 3. **~-se** to be absent-minded or inattentive.
idiotia s. f. idiocy, extreme intellectual deficiency, mental imbecility.
idiotice s. f. 1. foolishness, madness. 2. idiotic quality, utterance or act, nonsense.
idiótico adj. idiotic, foolish, stupid, senseless.
idiotismo s. m. idiotism: 1. idiocy, idioticalness. 2. foolishness, nonsense. 3. (phil.) idiom, peculiarity of speech.
idiotizar v. to idiotize, render idiotic.
ido adj. departed, past, gone.
em dias ~s in far-gone days.
idocrásio s. m. (min.) idocrase, vesuvianite.
idólatra s. m. + f. 1. idolater, idolatress, worship(p)er of idols. 2. pagan, heathen. 3. (fig.) great admirer, adorer. ‖ adj. idolatrous, pagan, heathen.
idolatrar v. 1. to idolize, worship as an idol. 2. to adore, admire. 3. to make an idol of, deify.
idolatria s. f. 1. idolatry, worship of idols. 2. idolism, paganism. 3. excessive love, wild passion.
idolátrico adj. idolatric(al), idolatrous, devoted to idols or the worship of idols.
ídolo s. m. 1. idol, image of a deity or saint, icon. 2. effigy. 3. object of passionate devotion or love. 4. heathen deity, pagan god. 5. (philos. — Bacon) fallacies, misleading conceptions and practices.
adoração de ~s idolization. **ele é o ~ das meninas** he is the favourite of the girls. **ele foi o ~ da torcida** he was the idol of football fans.
idoneidade s. f. 1. idoneousness. 2. aptitude, competence. 3. fitness, aptness. 4. capacity.
sem ~ incompetent, unfit.
idôneo adj. 1. idoneous. 2. apt, competent. 3. fit, capable. 4. suitable. 5. incorrupt, taintless.
uma letra de câmbio -a a fine bill.
idos s. m. pl. (Roman hist.) ides, the eight day after the nones.
idoso adj. old, aged, advanced in years.
de aspecto ~ looking old.
idumeu s. m. (f. **-éia**) Idumean, native or inhabitant of Idumea, Edomite. ‖ adj. Idumean.
iene s. m. yen: the monetary unit of Japan (divided into 100 sen).
igaçaba s. f. 1. (Braz., Tupi) earthen water pitcher. 2. funeral urn of South American Indians.
igaci s. m. (Braz., Tupi) main stream of a river.
igapará s. m. (Braz., Tupi) wide channel or branch of a river.
igapó s. m. (Braz., Tupi) periodically inundated parts of riverine woodland; swampland.

igara s. f. (Braz., Tupi), canoe, dugout.
igarapé s. m. (Braz., Tupi) narrow riverbank between two islands or between an island and the mainland.
igaratim s. m. (pl. **-ins**) (Braz.) canoe of Tupi chieftains.
igarité s. f. (Braz., Tupi) 1. dugout. 2. plank boat.
igariteiro s. m. (Braz., Tupi) boatsman, boatman.
igaraçu s. f. (Braz., Tupi) big canoe or dugout.
ignaro adj. 1. unlearned, uninstructed. 2. ignorant. 3. stupid.
ignávia s. f. idleness, slothfulness. 2. indolence. 3. weakness, feebleness. 4. cowardice, faintheartedness.
ignavo adj. 1. idle, lazy. 2. indolent. 3. weak, feeble. 4. cowardly.
ígneo adj. 1. igneous, fiery. 2. pyrogenic, pyrogenous. 3. resembling fire.
ignescência s. f. ignescent state or condition.
ignescente adj. m. + f. igneous, ignescent, inflammatory.
ignição s. f. (pl. **-ões**) 1. ignition, act of igniting. 2. ignescent state. 3. combustion.
~ **antecipada** early ignition. ~ **de bateria** coil ignition. ~ **espontânea** spontaneous combustion. ~ **retardada** retarded ignition. **bobina de** ~ ignition coil. **chave de** ~ ignition key or switch. **estopim de** ~ spark fuse.
ignícola s. m. + f. ignicolist, worshipper of fire.
ignífero adj. igniferous, producing fire.
ignificação s. f. (pl. **-ões**) combustion.
ignígeno adj. ignigenous, engendered in or by fire.
ignípede adj. m + f. (poet.) having fiery feet or hoofs, throwing off sparks.
ignipotente adj. m. + f. (poet.) ignipotent, ruling over the fire.
ignívomo adj. (poet.) ignivomous, vomiting fire.
ignívoro adj. ignivorous, eating fire.
ignizar-se v. 1. to catch fire, flare up. 2. to kindle, inflame. 3. to become inflamed.
ignóbil adj. m. + f. (pl. **-óbeis**) 1. ignoble, not noble. 2. base. 3. degrading, debasing. 4. mean, abject. 5. unworthy. ‖ **ignobilmente** adv. ignobly, debasingly, abjectly.
ignobilidade s. f. ignobleness, baseness, meanness, ignobility.
ignomínia s. f. 1. ignominy. 2. dishonour, disgrace. 3. discredit. 4. opprobrium, infamy.
ignominiar v. 1. to dishonour, disgrace. 2. to treat ignominiously. 3. to brand with infamy. 4. to bring shame upon.
ignominioso adj. 1. ignominious. 2. dishonourable, disgraceful. 3. base, mean. 4. infamous, shameful, opprobrious. ‖ **-amente** adv. ignominiously.
ignorado adj. unkown, obscure, unascertained.
ele foi ~ (fig.) he was left out in the cold.
ignorância s. f. 1. ignorance, want of knowledge. 2. illiteracy, illiterateness. 3. (fig.) darkness, blindness, emptiness. 4. witlessness, artlessness, nescience.
~ **crassa** gross ignorance. ~ **de direito** ignorance of the law. ~ **de fato** ignorance of the fact. **a** ~ **da lei não exime da culpa** ignorance of the law is no defence. **alegar** ~ to plead ignorance. **agir por** ~ to act from ignorance.
ignorantão s. m. (pl. **-ões**) blockhead, ignoramus, conceited fool. ‖ adj. very ignorant, stupid.
ignorante s. m. + f. 1. ignorant, ignoramus, illiterate. 2. idiot, know-nothing. 3. (coll.) ass, clodpate. ‖ adj. 1. ignorant. 2. unlearned, unlettered. 3. unschooled, unskilled. 4. witless, stupid, silly. 5. artless, simple-minded. ‖ ~**mente** adv. ignorantly, unlearnedly, artlessly, unconsciously.

ignorantinho s. m. Ignorantine: member of a religious order (Brethren of the Christian Schools). ‖ adj. of, pertaining to or related to this order.
ignorantismo s. m. (philos., rel.) ignorantism, obscurantism.
ignorantista s. m. + f. ignorantist, obscurantist, follower of ignorantism.
ignorar v. 1. not to know, be ignorant of. 2. to pass over, treat as if not known, cut, cold-shoulder. 3. to disregard. 4. not to be versed in, be a stranger to. 5. not to have or possess quality, talent, capacity, etc.).
ignoto adj. unknown, obscure, concealed, incognito.
igreja s. f. 1. church, House of God (plate A 4). 2. temple. 3. ecclesia, parish. 4. ecclesiastic authority. 5. religious community, sect. 6. (sociol.) believer(s). 7. minster, chapel.
Igreja Católica Romana Roman Catholic Church. ~ **grega ou ortodoxa** Byzantine Church. ~ **matriz** mother church, parish church. ~ **superior anglicana** High Church. **ele foi à** ~ he went to church. **ele freqüentou regularmente a** ~ he kept his chapels. **eles freqüentam a** ~ they attend service.
igrejário s. m. 1. little church, chapel. 2. churches of a diocese collectively.
igrejeiro s. m. 1. churchgoer, parishioner. 2. bigot, hypocrite. ‖ adj. churchly, ecclesiastical.
igrejinha s. f. 1. little church, chapel. 2. collusion. 3. trap. 4. intrigue. 5. group of plotters.
igrejório s. m. insignificant little church.
igual s. m. + f. (pl. **iguais**) equal, coequal, peer, fellow. ‖ adj. 1. equal, equable. 2. even, uniform. 3. identific(al), tantamount. 4. like, alike, same. 5. level. 6. (mus.) of equal temperament. 7. peer, match. 8. level, plane. ‖ ~**mente** adv. equally, identically, alike.
de tamanho ~ of equal size, of the same size. **estar em iguais condições** to be on equal footing. **já se ouviu coisa** ~? did you ever hear the like of it? **de** ~ **para** ~ between equals. **em partes iguais** in equal shares, (U. S. A., sl.) fifty-fifty. **por** ~ equally. **possibilidades iguais para todos** fair field and no favour. **é praticamente** ~ it is much the same. **quase** ~ nearly equal. **sem** ~ unequal(l)ed; incomparable, without rival, matchless. **isto é** ~ that is just as well. **é** ~ **a** it is tantamount to. **uma jarda é** ~ **a 36 polegadas** a yard contains 36 inches. **eles são iguais em força e idade** they are equal in strength and age. **cada qual com seu** ~ birds of a feather flock together. **com seus iguais** with his compeer. **este homem não tem o seu** ~ this man has not his fellow. **ele não tem** ~, **ele é sem-par** he is without equals.
igualação s. f. (pl. **-ões**) 1. equalization, equalizing, equation. 2. uniformization. 3. level(l)ing.
igualador s. m. equalizer.
igualamento s. m. 1. act of equalizing, equalization. 2. character of being equal, equalness. 3. level(l)ing.
igualar v. 1. to equalize, make equal. 2. to equal, be or become equal. 3. to match, cap, peer. 4. to even, level. 5. to fellow. 6. to equilibrate, assimilate, parallel. 7. to level, make flat. 8. to attain, raise to the same state. 9. to uniform. 10. to compare, conform. 11. ~**-se:** a) to compare o. s. with. b) to be on the level with. c) to be a match for. d) to pretend or suppose to be equal to. e) to adjust differences.
igualável adj. m. +f. (pl. **-áveis**) that can be equalized, attainable.
igualdade s. f. 1. equality, equalness. 2. equity. 3. (math.) equation, expression of equality. 4. uniformity, sameness. 5. levelness, flatness. 6. parity. 7. evenness.

~ **de condições** equality of condition, coordinateness, parity. **em** ~ **de circunstâncias** under the same circumstances. **ficar em condições de** ~ **com** to keep abreast of (or with). **pôr em pé de** ~ to put on the same level.
igualha s. f. 1. equality of rank. 2. identity of state or condition. 3. sameness.
ele não é de minha ~ he is not the likes of me. **pessoa de sua** ~ a person of the same station.
igualitário s. m. 1. equalitarian, egalitarian, follower of equalitarianism. 2. level(l)er. ‖ adj. equalitarian.
igualitarismo s. m. equalitarianism.
iguano s. m. (zool.) 1. iguana, guana. 2. (capital) typical genus of the family Iguanidae.
iguanodonte s. m. iguanodont, fossil reptile of the family Iguanodontidae.
iguaria s. f. 1. delicacy. 2. dish, food. 3. fare. 4. choice viands, cate. 5. custard.
ihi interj. oh!, oh!: exclamation of surprise, delight, irony, apprehension.
idiche s. m. Yiddish, High German dialect, spoken by Jews.
ilação s. f. (pl. **-ões**). 1. illation. 2. inference. 3. deduction, conclusion.
ilacerável adj. m. + f. (pl. **-áveis**) untearable.
ilacrimável adj. m. + f. (pl. **-áveis**) inexorable, implacable.
ilangue-ilangue s. m. (bot.) ilang-ilang.
ilapso s. m. 1. illapse, entrance as per permeation. 2. (rel., philos.) inspiration, divine influx.
ilaquear v. to illaqueate, insnare, entangle, entrap.
ilativo adj. illative, inferential, inferred, conclusive.
ileáceo adj. of, pertaining to or resembling holly.
ilegal adj. m. + f. (pl. **-ais**) 1. illegal, unlawful, lawless. 2. illicit, injudicial. 3. false, wrong. 4. unwarrantable. 5. illegitimate. ‖ ~**mente** adv. illegally.
tornar ~ to illegalize. **declarar** ~ to outlaw. **o seu procedimento foi** ~ his action was out of the straight.
ilegalidade s. f. 1. illegality, unlawfulness, lawlessness. 2. falseness, wrongfulness. 3. illicitness. 4. unwarrantableness.
ilegibilidade s. f. illegibility.
ilegitimidade s. f. 1. illegitimacy. 2. illicitness, unlawfulness. 3. spuriousness, bastardy.
ilegitimar v. to bastardize.
ilegítimo adj. 1. illegitimate, illegal. 2. unlawful, unauthorized. 3. unwarrantable. 4. spurious, bastard, unfathered, natural. 5. baseborn, born out of wedlock. ‖ **-amente** adv. illegitimately, unlawfully, spuriously, disorderly.
tornar ~ to illegitimize, illegitimate. **ele nasceu filho** ~ he was born on the wrong side of the blanket.
ilegível adj. m. + f. (pl. **-veis**) 1. illegible, unreadable, indecipherable. 2. scrawly, hard to read.
íleo s. m. (anat.) ileum, lowest part of the small intestine.
ileocecal adj. (pl. **ileocecais**) (anat.) ileocaecal, pertaining to both the ileum and the caecum.
ileso adj. 1. unhurt, uninjured. 2. sound and safe. 3. scarless, woundless. 4. unharmed, undamaged, unscathed.
ele escapou ~ he came off unhurt. **ele sempre sai** ~ he always comes off clear, (U. S. A., coll.) he gets away with murder.
iletrado s. m. illiterate, person unable to read or to write. ‖ adj. 1. illiterate, unlearned, unlettered. 2. unbookish. 3. rude, uncultured. ‖ **-amente** adv. illiterately, unlearnedly.
ilha s. f. island, isle, islet (plate M 11).
~ **fluvial** holm. ~ **de trânsito** island, street refuge (plate R 8). **transformar em** ~ to island.

ilhal s. m. (pl. **-ais**) flank(s) of an animal (horse, cattle).
ilhapa s. f. (S. Braz.) the strongest part of a lariat.
ilhar v. 1. to separate. 2. to isolate, insulate. 3. to confine, keep within limits, make incommunicable.
ilharga s. f. 1. flank, side (of an animal). 2. (fig.) support. 3. favourite. 4. counsel(l)or, supporter.
dor de ~ pain in the side. **de mão na** ~ with arms akimbo. **de** ~ laterally. **sempre está à minha** ~ he is always at my side. **rir até arrebentar as** ~s to split one's sides with laughing.
ilhava s‖ f. Portuguese fishing vessel.
ilhéu s. m. 1. islander, native or inhabitant of an island. 2. islet, small uninhabited island. 3. reef.
ilhó s. m. + f. (also **ilhós**; pl. **ilhoses**) 1. eyelet, eye, eyehole. 2. loop. 3. thimble, grummet.
ilhoa s. f. female islander.
ilhota s. f. islet, cay, key, reef.
ilíaco s. m. (anat.) ilium, thighbone. ‖ adj. iliac(al).
região -a (anat.) iliac region. **osso** ~ (anat.) hipbone.
ilíada s. f. (Greek myth.) Illiad, Greek epic poem, Ilyad(e)s.
ilibação s. f. 1. blamelessness, pureness, stainlessness. 2. rehabilitation.
ilibado adj. 1. blameless, unblemished. 2. untouched. 3. spotless, stainless. 4. undefiled, pure. 5. rehabilitated.
ilibar v. 1. to rehabilitate. 2. to restore pureness or stainlessness. 3. to free from guilt. 4. to justify, vindicate.
iliberal adj. m. + f. (pl. **-ais**) 1. illiberal, not liberal. 2. parsimonious, shabby. 3. mean, selfish. 4. narrow-minded, intolerant. ‖ ~**mente** adv. illiberally.
iliberalidade s. f. 1. illiberality. 2. parsimony, niggardliness. 3. meanness, selfishness. 4. narrow-mindedness.
iliberalismo s. m. illiberalism, illiberality.
iliçador s. m. cheat, impostor, swindler.
ilição s. f. (pl. **-ões**) fraud, deceit, swindle.
iliçar v. to cheat, deceive, swindle.
ilício s. m. fraud, deceit, swindle.
ilícito adj. 1. illicit, illegal. 2. unlawful, lawless. 3. illegitimate. 4. false, wrong, foul. 5. unauthorized, unlicensed. ‖ **-amente** adv. illicitly, unlawfully, illegitimately, foul.
dar um golpe ~ to hit s. o. foul.
ilídimo adj. 1. illegitimate, illegal. 2. unlawful, unauthorized. 3. spurious.
ilidir v. 1. to refute, repel. 2. to prove to be false. 3. to destroy, undo (by repeal).
ilidível adj. m. + f. (pl. **-íveis**) refutable, repealable.
ilimitado adj. 1. unlimited, limitless. 2. free. 3. unconfined, unrestrained, unrestricted. 4. boundless, spaceless, termless. 5. indefinite, indeterminate. 6. infinite, absolute, universal. ‖ **-amente** adv. unlimitedly.
ilimitável adj. m. + f. (pl. **-áveis**) illimitable, incapable of being limited, immeasurable.
ilínio s. m. (chem.) illinium, florentium.
ílio(n) s. m. (anat.) ilium, hipbone.
ilíquido, ilíqüido adj. 1. not liquid. 2. (com.) global, gross, total. 3. not ascertained, confuse.
iliterato s. m. illiterate, unlettered, uncultivated.
ilmenita s. f. (min.) ilmenite, titanic iron ore.
ilocável adj. m. + f. (pl. **-áveis**) unplaced, unplaceable.
ilógico adj. 1. illogical, irrational. 2. inconclusive, inconsequent. 3. absurd, incoherent. 4. unsound. 5. fallacious. ‖ **ilogicamente** adv. illogically, unreasoningly, nonsensically.
ilogismo s. m. illogicality, illogicalness.

iloricado adj. (zool.) illoricate(d), having no lorica (said of certain rotifers).

iludente adj. m. + f. 1. illusory, illusive. 2. deceptive, deceitful. 3. false.

iludir v. 1. to illude, deceive with false hopes. 2. to cheat, dupe. 3. to trick, bluf. 4. to mislead, mystify, delude. 5. to evade, elude. 6. to ensnare, insnare. 7. ~**se** to be wrong or mistaken.
~ **alguém em suas expectativas** to frustrate a person's expectations. ~ **as duas partes** to double-cross. **não deixar-se** ~ not to be deceived.

iludível adj. m. + f. (pl. **-íveis**) liable to err, deceptible, capable of being simulated.

iluminação s. f. (pl. **-ões**) 1. illumination. 2. act of illuminating, state of being illuminated. 3. display of light, decoration by means of many lights. 4. mental enlightenment. 5. pictorial ornamentation, illustration. 6. explication.
~ **elétrica** electric light.

iluminado s. m. 1. illuminate, illuminato, the inspired one. 2. prophet, seer. ‖ adj. 1. illuminated, lighted. 2. inspired, enlightened. 3. illustrated. 4. illustrious, famous.
~ **por muitas lâmpadas** bright with many lamps. ~ **pelo sol** sunny, sunlit.

iluminador s. m. illuminator, decorator (of books or manuscripts). ‖ adj. illuminating, illuminative.

iluminante adj. m. + f. illuminant, pertaining to illumination, giving light.

iluminar v. 1. to illuminate, illumine, light up, give light. 2. to decorate with many lights. 3. to enlighten, impart moral or intellectual light to. 4. to make luminous, brighten. 5. to elucidate, make clear. 6. to decorate in colour by hand, adorn with ornamental designs. 7. to inspire, stimulate.
seu rosto estava iluminado de alegria her (his) face was alight with joy. **ele iluminou-me o rosto com uma vela** he flared a candle at me. **eles iluminaram profusamente o campo** they floodlighted the field.

iluminativo adj. 1. illuminative, illuminating. 2. tending to give light. 3. enlightening. 4. inspiring.

iluminismo s. m. 1. illuminism, principles of the illuminati. 2. enlightenment.

iluminista s. m. + f. illuminist.

iluminura s. f. pictorial ornamentation, adornment of books or manuscripts by designs.

ilusão s. f. (pl. **-ões**) 1. illusion, illusiveness. 2. phantom, fantasy, fancy, mirage. 3. delusion, unreality, delusiveness. 4. fallacy. 5. error. 6. fleeting dream. 7. fraud, deceit.
entregar-se a -ões to delude o s. **eu não tenho -ões a respeito** I have no illusions about. **que grande** ~**!** what a delusion! **por uma** ~ **de óptica** by a trick of the eye.

ilusionismo s. m. 1. illusionism, prestidigitation, sleight of hand, jugglery.

ilusionista s. m. + f. 1. illusionist. 2. prestidigitator, legerdemainist. 3. juggler.

ilusivo adj. illusive, delusive, illusory, deceptive.

iluso adj. deluded, deceived, tricked.

ilusor s. m. 1. deceiver, deluder. 2. mocker, scoffer. 3. cheat.

ilusório adj. 1. illusive, illusory. 2. delusive, delusory. 3. deceitful, treacherous, deceptive. 4. phantasmal, phantasmic(al). 5. fallacious, false. 6. unreal. ‖ **ilusoriamente** adv. illusorily, illusively, etc.
aparência **-a** illusive appearance, hollow pretence.

ilustração s. f. (pl. **-ões**) 1. illustration. 2. knowledge, erudition, eruditeness. 3. culture. 4. enlightenment, elucidation. 5. magazine, illustrated periodical. 6. picture, figure, plate. 7. illustriousness.
em forma de ~ illustratively. **para** ~ as or for illustration.

ilustrado adj. 1. illustrated. 2. erudite, learned. 3. cultured. 4. enlightened. 5. illustrious. 6. pictorial.
álbum infantil ~ picture book.

ilustrador s. m. illustrator, person who draws pictorial illustrations.

ilustrar v. 1. to illustrate. 2. to illume, illuminate. 3. to elucidate, explain. 4. to enlighten, clarify. 5. to picture, picturize. 6. to dignify, make illustrious. 7. ~**-se** to distinguish o. s.

ilustrativo adj. illustrative, elucidative.

ilustre adj. m. + f. 1. illustrious, eximious. 2. worthy, honourable. 3. distinguished, eminent. 4. famous, egregious. 5. brilliant. ‖ ~**mente** adv. illustriously.
de descendência ~ of high birth.

ilustríssimo obs. sup. very illustrious, very famous or distinguished, most eminent.

ilutação s. f. (pl. **-ões**) (med.) illutation, treatment by mud baths.

ilutar v. (med.) to treat by mud baths, apply a mud bath.

ímã s. m. 1. magnet, loadstone. 2. bar magnet, horseshoe magnet. 3. (fig.) attractive person or thing.
~ **indutor** field magnet.

imaculabilidade s. f. immaculateness, spotlessness, purity, stainlessness.

imaculado adj. immaculate, spotless, unsoiled, stainless, pure. ‖ **-amente** adv. spotlessly, immaculately.
Imaculada Conceição (rel.) Immaculate Conception.

imaculatismo s. m. (R. C. Church) doctrine of the Immaculate Conception.

imaculável adj. m. + f. (pl. **-áveis**) that cannot be stained or defiled.

imagem s. f. (pl. **-ens**) 1. image. 2. drawing, painting, sketch. 3. likeness, semblance. 4. picture, sculpture, effigy, statue. 5. mental picture, contemplation. 6. reflection, mirage. 7. symbol. 8. beauty. 9. (rhet.) metaphor. 10. shape, apparition. 11. idol.
~ **viva** tableau vivant. **ele era a perfeita** ~ **de...** he was the very picture of... **o homem foi feito à** ~ **de Deus** man was created as God's image. **uma verdadeira** ~ **de miséria** a true picture of misery.

imaginação s. f. (pl. **-ões**) 1. imagination. 2. image in the mind. 3. formulated conception. 4. the act of scheming or planning. 5. idea, thought. 6. fantasy, fancy. 7. fantastic or illusory opinion. 8. superstition. 9. mania. 10. meditation, contemplation. 11. constructive or creative imagination. 12. wit, spirit. 13. conceit.
não passa de ~ **sua** it is all your imagination. **só existe na** ~ it is just imaginary. **não foi só** ~ it was not entirely imagination. **isto ultrapassa toda a** ~ it is just inconceivable.

imaginador s. m. imaginer, plotter, schemer. ‖ adj. imagining, scheming.

imaginante adj. m. + f. imagining, conceiving.

imaginar v. 1. to imagine, form a mental picture of. 2. to create or conceive in the mind. 3. to suppose, conjecture. 4. to invent. 5. to scheme, devise. 6. to fancy, presume. 7. to think, ponder. 8. to visualize, ideate, figure out.
imagine! just imagine! **ele fica imaginando coisas** he is under delusions. **ele imagina ser um grande sábio** he pretends to be a scholar. **eles imaginaram que** they had the theory that. **ele não o pode** ~ he can form no idea of it. **pode-se** ~ **que coisas assim acontecem** one can imagine such things happening. **não posso** ~ **o que ele pretende** I can't think what he means. **não posso** ~**-me em seu lugar** I can't put myself in his place. **não posso** ~ **nada melhor** I can conceive nothing better. **eu sempre imaginei que ele fosse inglês!** I always thought of him as an Englishman. **imagine só!**

just fancy!, fancy that!, just think! **imagine só, ela esqueceu!** fancy her having forgotten!

imaginária s. f. images, painted or embroidered pictures, human figures.

imaginário s. m. maker or carver of images. ‖ adj. 1. imaginary. 2. illusory, fantastic. 3. fictive, fictional. 4. not real, unreal. 5. fanciful, fancied. 6. chimeric(al), ideal. 7. romantic, poetic(al). 8. (math.) pertaining to an imaginary quantity. ‖ **imaginariamente** adv. unreally, imaginably, notionally, chimerically, fictionally.

imaginativa s. f. 1. imaginative power. 2. faculty of imagination. 3. imaginativeness.

imaginativo adj. 1. imaginative. 2. inventive, creative. 3. fanciful. 4. apprehensive, fearful. 5. conjecturable, realizable.

imaginável adj. m. + f. (pl. **-áveis**) imaginable, capable of being imagined or conceived, thinkable, contrivable.

o maior sucesso ~ the greatest success imaginable.

imagineiro s. m. maker of images.

imaginoso adj. imaginary, illusory, fanciful, fantastic.

imago s. f. imago: the final perfect stage of an insect (after metamorphosis).

imaleabilidade s. f. immalleability.

imaleável adj. m. + f. (pl. **-áveis**) immalleable, incapable of being extended by hammering.

imame s. m. imam, imaum: a spiritual leader of the Islam.

imanar v. to magnetize.

imane adj. m. + f. 1. huge, enormous. 2. excessive. 3. ferocious.

imanência s. f. immanence, immanency, condition of being immanent.

imanente adj. m. + f. immanent, intrinsic, inherent, indwelling.

imanentismo s. m. (phil.) immanentism: philosophical doctrine of immanence.

imanidade s. f. 1. hugeness, enormousness. 2. excessiveness. 3. cruelty, brutality.

imanização s. f. (pl. **-ões**) magnetization.

imanizar v. to magnetize, communicate magnetic properties to.

imantação s. f. (pl. **-ões**) magnetization.

imantar v. to magnetize.

imarcescibilidade s. f. 1. immarcescibleness, incorruptibility. 2. imperishableness.

imarcescível adj. m. + f. (pl. **-íveis**) immarcescible, incorruptible, imperishable.

imarginado adj. immarginate: 1. having no margin. 2. (bot.) destitute of a rim or border.

imaterial s. m. (pl. **-ais**) an immaterial thing. ‖ adj. m. + f. immaterial, not material, not consisting of matter, unsubstantial, incorporeal. ‖ ~**mente** adv. immaterially.

imaterialidade s. f. immateriality, immaterialness, incorporeity.

imaterialismo s. m. immaterialism: philosophical doctrine which maintains that the material world has no existence apart from conscious perception.

imaterialista s. m. + f. immaterialist.

imaterializar v. to immaterialize, make incorporeal, free from matter.

imaturidade s. f. 1. immaturity, unripeness. 2. incompleteness. 3. precocity. 4. untimeliness. 5. callousness, crudeness.

imaturo adj. 1. immature, unripe. 2. premature, precocious. 3. early. 4. unfinished. 5. abortive. 6. young, youthful. 7. green, tender, half-baked. 8. untimely, unseasoned. 9. crude, callous.

imba s. m. (Braz.) marble hole, immie hole (children's play).

imbaíba, imbaúba s. f. snakewood, trumpet tree.

imbatível adj. m. + f. unbeatable, insuperable, unsurpassable.

imbaubal s. m. (pl. **-ais**) snakewood grove.

imbé s. m. (Braz.) imbe plant.

imbecil s. m. + f. (pl. **-is**) 1. (med.) feeble-minded person. 2. idiot, imbecile. 3. fool, oaf. 4. featherbrain, loggerhead. ‖ adj. 1. feeble-minded, imbecile, soft-witted. 2. silly, stupid, idiotic(al). 3. oafish, foolish, featherbrained. ‖ **-mente** adv. imbecilely, feeble-mindedly.

imbecilidade s. f. 1. imbecility, feeble-mindedness. 2. stupidity, silliness. 3. weakness. 4. narrow-mindedness. 5. oafishness, dullness.

imbecilizar v. 1. to make imbecile, weaken. 2. to become feeble or imbecile. 3. to cretinize.

imbele adj. m. + f. 1. not fit for war, not warlike. 2. timid, fearful. 3. weak. 4. cowardly.

imberbe adj. m. + f. 1. beardless, unbearded. 2. young, youthful.

imbicar v. 1. to land, put into port. 2. to cast anchor. 3. to further, bring about. 4. to bring to an issue (business).

imbricação s. f. (pl. **-ões**) imbrication, overlapping of edges like that of tiles or shingles; imbricate ornamental designs.

imbricado adj. imbricate(d), scalelike, decorated with a pattern resembling overlapping tiles.

imbricante adj. m. + f. (bot.) imbricate.

imbricar v. to imbricate, overlap like tiles or scales of a fish, to lap.

imbrífero adj. (poet.) rainy, causing rainfall.

imbrífugo adj. dispelling rain.

imbróglio s. m. 1. imbroglio, intricate or perplexing situation. 2. misunderstanding. 3. entanglement. 4. confusion.

imbu s. m. ciruela: fruit of the Spanish plum tree or mombin.

imbuia s. f. (bot.) Brazilian walnut.

imbuir v. 1. to imbue, pervade. 2. to impregnate, soak, steep. 3. (fig.) to suggest, insinuate. 4. to inspire with, instil with. 5. ~**-se:** a) to be or become imbued with. b) to penetrate.

imbuído de orgulho imbued with pride.

imburana-de-cheiro s. f. (pl. **imburanas-de-cheiro**) (Braz., bot.) umburana.

imburi s. m. (Braz., bot.) miriti palm, ita palm.

imburizal s. m. (pl. **-ais**) (Braz.) grove of miriti palms.

imbuzada s. f. (Braz.) sweatmeat made from ciruelas.

imbuzeiro s. m. (Braz.) Spanish plum tree, mombin.

imediação s. f. (pl. **-ões**) 1. immediacy, immediateness. 2. neighbourhood, vicinity. 3. proximity.

imediatismo s. m. immediatism, quality of being immediate.

imediatar v. (Braz.) to serve as chief officer or first mate.

imediato s. m. (naut.) chief officer (second in command after the captain), first mate. ‖ adj. 1. immediate. 2. direct. 3. proximate, close. 4. near, contiguous. 5. instant, without delay. 6. urgent, prompt. ‖ **-amente** adv. 1. immediately. 2. proximately, directly. 3. instantly, at once, right away, straight away. 4. now, outright, readily.

virei -amente I shall come directly, I shall come right away. **-amente, senhor!** coming, Sir! **faça-o -amente!** do it this instant! **ela chegou -amente** she came in less than no time. **ele casou com ela -amente** he married her on the spot. **eles decidiram a questão -amente** they came to a decision then and there. **eles abandonaram a casa -amente sem aviso prévio** they left the house at a minute's warning. **mandaram o menino -amente de volta**

they hurried the boy back. **causa -a** proximity cause.

imedicável adj. m. + f. (pl. **-áveis**) incurable, immedicable, incapable of being healed.

imemorado adj. 1. unremembered, forgotten. 2. not yet reported.

imemorável adj. m. + f. (pl. **-áveis**) immemorial. ‖ **imemoravelmente** adv. immemorially.

imêmore adj. m. + f. (poet.) forgotten, unremembered.

imemorial, imemoriável adj. m. + f. (pl. **-ais, -áveis**) immemorial, long forgotten, extending far back beyond record or recollection.

imensidade, imensidão s. f. 1. immensity. 2. immeasurableness, boundlessness, vastness. 3. infiniteness, infinity. 4. very great amount, quantity, bulk or degree. 5. largeness, hugeness.

imenso adj. 1. immense. 2. immeasurable. 3. unlimited, boundless. 4. great, huge, vast, numerous, enormous, big. 5. infinite, interminable. 6. unfathomable, unbounded. ‖ **-amente** adv. immensely, etc. **sinto -amente** I am awfully sorry. **eles habitavam uma mansão -a** they were living in a huge mansion. **diverti-me -amente** I was hugely amused.

imensurabilidade s. f. immeasurability, immeasurableness, limitless, extent, immensurability.

imensurável adj. m. + f. (pl. **-áveis**) immeasurable, immense, limitless, incapable of being measured.

imerecido adj. 1. gratuitous. 2. unworthy. 3. unearned, undeserved, not merited. 4. undue, immerited. ‖ **-amente** adv. gratuitously, unworthily.

imergente adj. m. + f. immergent, immersing.

imergir v. 1. to immerge, immerse. 2. to plunge into. 3. to penetrate, enter. 4. to dip, submerge. 5. to dive, merge. 6. to douse.

imérito adj. unmerited, undeserved, immerited.

imersão s. f. (pl. **-ões**) 1. immersion, act of immersing, state of being immersed. 2. (fig.) absorption. 3. plunge. 4. ducking.

resistência de ~ (electr.) immersion boiling device.

imersível adj. m. + f. (pl. **-íveis**) immersible, capable of being immersed, submersible.

imersivo adj. immersive, suitable for immersion, involving immersion.

imerso adj. 1. immersed, submerged, deeply plunged into (a fluid). 2. (fig.) absorbed or engrossed in (thought, activity, vice, etc.).

eles viveram profundamente ~**s na miséria** they were living deeply steeped in misery.

imersor s. m. 1. immerger, one who immerges or dives. 2. immersionist, one who considers immersion essential to Christian baptism.

imido s. m. (chem.) imide.

imidogênio s. m. (chem.) 1. imidogen, the bivalent radical NH. 2. imido or imino group.

imigo s. m. (poet.) enemy, foe.

imigração s. f. (pl. **-ões**) immigration.

imigrado s. m. immigrant, person who has immigrated. ‖ adj. immigrant, immigrating.

imigrante s. m. + f. 1. immigrant. 2. incomer. ‖ adj. immigrant, immigrating.

~ **inexperiente** jackaroo, greenhorn.

imigrar v. 1. to immigrate, migrate. 2. to settle in a foreign country.

imigratório adj. immigratory, migratory.

iminência s. f. 1. imminence, quality or condition of being imminent. 2. impendency, impendence. 3. nearness.

na ~ **de** on the very edge of, on the brink of.

iminente adj. m. + f. 1. imminent, impending, pending. 2. threatening, menacing. 3. on the brink of. ‖ ~**mente** adv. imminently, impendingly.

estar ~ to impend.

imisção s. f. (pl. **-ões**) 1. mixture, mixing. 2. intromission, intermeddling. 3. intervention.

imiscibilidade s. f. immiscibility, quality of being immiscible.

imiscível adj. m. + f. ,pl. **-íveis**) immiscible, not capable of being mixed. ‖ **imiscivelmente** adv. immiscibly.

imiscuir-se v. 1. to meddle with, interfere, mix. 2. to intrude upon. 3. to participate, be involved in.

~ **na vida alheia** to poke one's nose in other people's business.

imisericórdia s. f. pitilessness, mercilessness.

imisericordioso adj. pitiless, merciless.

imissão s. f. (pl. **-ões**) 1. immission, act or process of sending in. 2. injection.

imitação s. f. (pl. **-ões**) 1. imitation, copy; act or process of imitating. 2. simulated reproduction or representation. 3. likeness, resemblance. 4. counterfeit. 5. sham, mock. 6. dummy.

~ **burlesca** travesty, parody. ~ **de moeda** counter (coin). ~ **fraudulenta** fake. **à** ~ **de** after the model of.

imitado adj. 1. imitated, imitative. 2. copied. 3. sham, mock, false. 4. counterfeit. 5. factitious.

imitador s. m. 1. imitator. 2. copier, copyist. 3. follower. 4. mimic. 5. echo, parroter. 6. emulator. ‖ adj. imitating, imitative.

imitadora s. f. imitatrix.

imitante adj. m. + f. imitation(al), artificial, apish.

imitar v. 1. to imitate. 2. to (make a) copy. 3. to mimic, pretend, assume the aspect of, simulate. 4. to use as a copy or model of. 5. to falsify, counterfeit. 6. to reproduce. 7. to personate. 8. to ape, echo. 9. to follow.

~ **a grã da madeira** to grain, vein. ~ **burlescamente** to travesty. **ele imitou o exemplo do seu irmão** (fig.) he took a leaf out of his brother's book. **esta pintura é imitada** this picture is copied.

imitativo adj. imitative, imitational, imitating, mimic, echoic.

imitável adj. m. + f. (pl. **-áveis**) imitable, capable of being imitated, worthy of imitation.

imitir v. to immit, send in, let in.

imizade s. f. enmity, hatred, hostility.

imo adj. 1. intimate. 2. inward, inmost.

imobiliário s. m. immovable, real estate, land or property fixed to the land. ‖ adj. of, pertaining to or relative to immovable property.

imobilidade s. f. 1. immobility, immovableness, immovability, steadfastness, fixedness. 2. serenity. imperturbability.

imobilismo s. m. immobilism: systematic opposition to progress.

imobilista s. m. + f. immobilist, adherent of immobilism, antiprogressionist.

imobilização s. f. (pl. **-ões**) immobilization, act or process of making immobile.

imobilizador adj. immobilizing.

imobilizar v. 1. to immobilize, fix. 2. to make immovable or stationary. 3. to oppose or hinder progress. 4. to impede, hamper, retain.

imoderação s. f. (pl. **-ões**) 1. immoderation, immoderacy, immoderateness. 2. lack of moderation, excess. 3. extravagance. 4. intemperance, inordinateness.

imoderado adj. 1. immoderate, not moderate. 2. excessive, exaggerated. 3. inordinate, unreasonable. 4. intemperate. 5. wild. ‖ **-amente** adv. immoderately, etc.

imodéstia s. f. 1. immodesty. 2. forwardness. 3. arrogance. 4. indecency, indelicacy. 5. impudence, shamelessness. 6. self-complacency.

imodesto adj. 1. immodest. 2. forward, importunate. 3. arrogant. 4. indecent, indelicate. 5. impudent, shameless. 6. selfish. || -amente adv. immodestly, etc.

imodicidade s. f. 1. immoderateness, excess. 2. intemperance. 3. licentiousness. 4. exaggeration, exorbitance.

imódico adj. 1. immoderate, excessive. 2. intemperate. 3. licentious. 4. exaggerated, exorbitant.

imodificável adj. m. + f. (pl. -áveis) unmodifiable, unchangeable, unalterable.

imolação s. f. (pl. -ões) immolation, act of immolating, sacrificial offering, sacrifice.

imolado adj. 1. sacrificed, immolated. 2 (fig.) damaged, wronged.

imolador s. m. immolator. || adj. immolating.

imolando adj. destined to be immolated or sacrificed, subject to immolation.

imolante adj. m. + f. immolating, sacrificial, immolate(d).

imolar v. 1. to immolate, sacrifice. 2. to kill in sacrifice. 3. to offer. 4. (fig.) to do damage or harm to. 5. ~-se to sacrifice o. s.

imoral s. m. + f. unprincipled or licentious person. || adj. 1. immoral, not moral. 2. vicious. 3. unprincipled, unwholesome. 4. dissolute, licentious, vile. 5. wanton, obscene. || ~mente adv. immorally, dissolutely.

imoralidade s. f. 1. immorality. 2. immoral thought or action. 3. wickedness, unwholesomeness. 4. vice. 5. dissoluteness, licentiousness. 6. wantonness, obscenity.

imoralismo s. m. immoralism: ethical system (Nietzsche) which opposes or fights traditional moral principles.

imorigerado adj. 1. unmannered, ill-mannered. 2. dissolute, licentious.

imorredouro adj. 1. immortal, deathless. 2. undecaying, imperishable.

imortal adj. m. + f. (pl. -ais) 1. immortal, not mortal. 2. undying, deathless. 3. undecaying, imperishable. 4. eternal. || ~mente adv. immortally.

imortalidade s. f. 1. immortality, eternity. 2. deathlessness, undyingness. 3. athanasia.

imortalização s. f. (pl. ões) immortalization.

imortalizador s. m. 1. one who makes (s. th.) immortal. 2. immortalizing feat. || adj. immortalizing, rendering immortal.

imortalizar v. 1. to immortalize, eternalize. 2. to become famous or celebrated. 3. ~-se to distinguish o. s. 4. to become perpetual.

imotiva adj. f. (bot.) germinating without deslocation of the episperm.

imoto adj. immotile, immovable, not moving, stationary.

imóvel s. m. (pl. imóveis) real estate, landed property. || adj. m. + f. 1. immovable, immobile. 2. motionless, unmoving. 3. steadfast, fixed, firm. 4. stationary, static(al). 5. quiet, still. || imovelmente adv. immovably, steadfastly, stationarily.
corretor de imóveis real estate agent. bolsa de imóveis property market. ela ficou ~ de surpresa she stood aghast.

impaciência s. f. 1. impatience. 2. eagerness. 3. restlessness, restiveness. 4. anxiety. 5. hastiness. 6. touchiness, irritability. 7. covetousness.

impacientar v. 1. to exhaust someone's patience. 2. to grow impatient. 3. to importune, irritate. 4. ~-se: a) to fidget, fret. b) to be or become angry.

impaciente adj. m. + f. 1. impatient. 2. eager. 3. restless, restive. 4. hasty, quick. 5. touchy, snappish, irritable. 6. fidgety, fretful. || ~mente adv. impatiently, etc.
ficar ~ to grow impatient.

impacto s. m. 1. impact. 2. discharge, shot. 3. shock, hit. 4. crash. || adj. impelling, impelled, impacted, driven by sheer force.

impagável adj. m. + f. (pl. -áveis) 1. impayable, not payable. 2. inestimable, priceless, precious. 3. ridiculous, funny, comic.
essa é ~! that is capital!

impalpabilidade s. f. impalpability, quality or state of being imperceptible by touch.

impalpável adj. m. + m. f. (pl. -áveis) 1. impalpable. 2. immaterial, unsubstantial. 3. intangible. 4. (fig.) incomprehensible, that cannot be grasped by the intellect.

impaludação s. f. (pl. -ões) infection with malaria.

impaludar v. to infect with malaria.

impaludismo s. m. (med.) impaludism, malarial cachexia, paludism.

impar v. 1. to breathe with difficulty, pant. 2. to weep convulsively, sob. 3. to eat immoderately, glut. 4. to behave in an arrogant or contemptuous manner.

ímpar adj. m. + f. 1. odd, uneven. 2. unique. 3. unpaired. 4. unrival(l)ed, unparalleled. 5. unmatchable.

imparcial adj. m. + f. (pl. -ais) 1. impartial, not partial. 2. just, equitable. 3. unbiased, fair. 4. dispassionate, disinterested. 5. even, equal. 6. objective, judicial. 7. independent, indifferent. || ~mente adv. impartially, equitably, evenly, fairly, dispassionately.
ele agiu ~mente he acted without fear or favour.

imparcialidade s. f. 1. impartiality. 2. justness, justice, equitableness. 3. fairness, fair-mindedness. 4. dispassionateness, disinterest. 5. equity, objectiveness, neutrality, evenness. 6. indifference.

imparcializar v. (obs.) to render impartial.

imparidade s. f. 1. imparity. 2. inequality, disproportion. 3. quantitative or numerical unevenness, oddness.

imparinervado adj. (bot.) imparinervate.

imparipenada s. f. (bot.) imparipinnate.

imparissilábico, imparissílabo adj. imparisyllabic.

impartível adj. m. + f. (pl. -íveis) impartable, indivisible.

impasse s. m. 1. impasse. 2. predicament, dilemma, plight. 3. trouble, difficulty. 4. obstacle.

impassibilidade s. f. 1. impassibility, impassibleness. 2. impassiveness, phlegm. 3. dispassion, stolidness.

impassibilizar v. to make impassible, make or be insensible to pain.

impassível adj. m. + f. (pl. -íveis) 1. impassible, impassive. 2. insensible to pain and harm. 3. insensitive, phlegmatic, apathetic. 4. dispassionate, unperturbed, unaffected. 5. unrepining. 6. unmoved, unemotional. 7. stoical.
ele foi um pecador ~ he was a hard-boiled sinner. ela persistia numa atitude ~ her attitude was not to be shaken.

impatriótico adj. unpatriotic.

impavidez s. f. 1. boldness, daring. 2. courage, valour. 3. intrepidity, bravery.

impávido adj. 1. impavid, undaunted. 2. fearless. 3. courageous, brave, intrepid.

impeachment s. m. (Engl.) impeachment: the formal accusation of improper conduct by a public official.

impecabilidade s. f. impeccability, character of being impeccable, sinlessness.

impecável adj. m. + f. (pl. -áveis) 1. impeccable, not subject to sin. 2. faultless, flawless, perfect. 3. immaculate, pure, sinless. 4. irreproachable,

unimpeachable. 5. spotless. ‖ **impecavelmente** adv. impeccably, faultlessly, flawlessly, irreproachably.
impedância s. f. (electr.) impedance, apparent increase of resistance due to induction in a circuit. ~ **de entrada** (radio) input impedance.
impedição s. f. (pl. **-ões**) 1. impedition, hindering. 2. impediment, hindrance. 3. obstacle, obstruction.
impedido s. m. 1. orderly. 2. (Braz.) soldier on barrack duty. ‖ adj. 1. hindered. 2. obstructed, blocked. 3. (ftb.) offside. 4. suppressed, fettered.
impedidor s. m. hinderer, obstructor. ‖ adj. hindering, obstructive, impeding.
impediência s. f. impediment, hindrance.
impediente adj. m. + f. 1. impeditive, impeding. 2. impedimental, obstructive. 3. hindering, deterrent.
impedimento s. m. 1. impediment, hindrance. 2. block, obstruction. 3. embargo, stoppage. 4. obstacle, check. 5. stumbling block. 6. (ftb.) offside. 7. inhibition. 8. counteraction, countercheck. 9. restraint, retardation, determent. 10. fetter, shackle. 11. difficulty. 12. opposition. 13. (pol.) impeachment. ~ **de trânsito** traffic jam. ~ **do crescimento** stunt. **em** ~ (ftb.) offside.
impedir v. 1. to impede, hinder. 2. to hamper, obstruct. 3. to block, check, bar. 4. to countercheck, counteract. 5. to restrain, encumber, deter. 6. to fetter, shackle. 7. to thwart. 8. to inhibit. 9. to intercept, interfere. 10. to prevent. 11. to oppose. 12. to discourage.
a chuva impediu sua vinda the rain prevented his (her, their) coming. **impedimos que ele o fizesse** we kept him from doing it. **assim ~am o crescimento da planta** thus they stunted the plant.
impeditivo adj. impeditive, obstructive, impeding, preventive.
impelente adj. m. + f. impellent, driving forward.
impelir v. 1. to impel, drive forward. 2. to push on, force on, whip on. 3. to throw, thrust. 4. to incite, stir up, spur on. 5. to stimulate, encourage, animate. 6. to hurry on, urge, rush. 7. to embarrass, constrain, coerce.
os motivos que o ~am para o feito the reasons that prompted him to this action. **eles o ~am à ruína** they drove him to ruin. **ela impeliu o barco com a vara** she punted the boat.
impendente adj. m. + f. impendent, impending, imminent, threatening.
impender v. 1. to impend, be imminent, threaten. 2. to overhang, be ready to fall. 3. to be incumbent on, concern.
impene adj. m. + f. plumeless, without feathers.
impenetrabilidade s. f. 1. impenetrability, impenetrableness. 2. imperviousness. 3. (fig.) inscrutableness.
impenetrado adj. 1. not penetrated, impenetrable. 2. unexplored.
impenetrável adj. m. + f. (pl. **-áveis**) 1. impenetrable, not penetrable. 2. impervious. 3. fathomless, unfathomable. 4. unexplorable, unsearchable. 5. inscrutable. ‖ **impenetravelmente** adv. impenetrably, unsearchably, fathomlessly.
impenhorável adj. m. + f. (pl. **-áveis**) unseizable, undistrainable.
impenitência s. f. 1. impenitence, impenitency. 2. obduracy. 3. hardheartedness.
impenitente adj. m. + f. 1. impenitent. 2. unrepentant, unconverted. 3. not contrite, obdurate. ‖ ~**mente** adv. impenitently.
impensado adj. 1. thoughtless, heedless. 2. wild. 3. unintended, unpremeditated. ‖ **-amente** adv. thoughtlessly, headlessly, wildly.
impensável adj. m. + f. (pl. **-áveis**) unthinkable, inconceivable.

imperador s. m. 1. emperor, imperator. 2. Caesar, Kaiser.
imperante s. m. + f. sovereign, ruler. ‖ adj. reigning, ruling, commanding.
imperar v. 1. to reign, rule. 2. to command. 3. to govern. 4. to dominate, predominate, prevail.
imperativo s. m. 1. imperative. 2. (gram.) imperative mood. ‖ adj. 1. imperative, peremptory. 2. imperatorial. 3. absolute. 4. binding, obligatory. ‖ **-amente** adv. imperatively, peremptorily, obligatorily.
imperatório adj. 1. imperatorial, imperative. 2. categorical, absolute. ‖ **imperatoriamente** adv. imperatorially.
imperatriz s. f. empress, imperatrix.
impercebível adj. m. + f. (pl. **-íveis**) imperceptible, imperceptive, invisible.
imperceptibilidade s. f. 1. imperceptibility, imperceptibleness. 2. indiscernibleness. 3. inconspicuousness.
imperceptível adj. m. + f. (pl. **-íveis**) 1. imperceptible, unperceivable. 2. undiscernable, inconspicuous. 3. insensible, subsensible. 4. evanescent, fleeting, faintish. 5. invisible. ‖ **imperceptivelmente** adv. imperceptibly, etc.
imperdível adj. m. + f. (pl. **-íveis**) unlosable.
imperdoável adj. m. + f. (pl. **-áveis**) unpardonable, inexcusable, unforgivable, unwarrantable.
de modo ~ beyond all pardon, unpardonable.
imperecedouro adj. 1. imperishable, indestructible. 2. fadeless, unfading. 3. eternal, everlasting, undying. 4. immortal.
imperecível adj. m. + f. (pl. **-íveis**) 1. imperishable, indestructible. 2. unfading, fadeless. 3. eternal, everlasting. 4. undying, undecaying. 5. immortal, eternal. ‖ **imperecivelmente** adv. imperishably.
imperfectibilidade s. f. imperfectibility: state or condition of being imperfectible.
imperfectível adj. m. + f. (pl. **-íveis**) imperfectible, incapable of being made perfect.
imperfeição s. f. (pl. **-ões**) 1. imperfection, imperfectness. 2. defectiveness, faultiness. 3. fault, defect, flaw. 4. deficiency, failing, frailty. 5. blemish. 6. incorrectness, incompleteness. 7. inadequacy, inadequateness.
imperfeiçoar v. to imperfect, render imperfect, impair.
imperfeito s. m. (gram.) imperfect tense, past continuous tense. ‖ adj. 1. imperfect, not perfect. 2. defective, faulty. 3. deficient, flawy. 4. crude, rough. 5. incomplete, incorrect. 6. frail, weak. 7. bad. 8. inadequate. ‖ **-amente** adv. imperfectly, inadequately, deficiently, faultily, incorrectly, badly.
trabalho muito ~ poorly done work. **escreva a frase no pretérito** ~ write this sentence in the imperfect tense. **ele tem um estilo** ~ he has a vicious style.
imperfuração s. f. (pl. **-ões**) 1. imperforation. 2. (med.) occlusion.
imperfurado adj. imperforate, imperforated.
imperfurável adj. m. + f. (pl. **-áveis**) imperforable, incapable of being perforated.
imperial adj. m. + f. (pl. **-ais**) 1. imperial, pertaining to an empire or emperor. 2. majestic, regal. 3. sovereign, supreme, august. 4. haughty, proud. 5. commanding, authoritative. ‖ ~**mente** adv. imperially, imperiously.
política ~ imperial policy.
imperialismo s. m. imperialism: 1. system of imperial government. 2. policy to form an empire. 3. policy of territorial extension.
imperialista s. m. + f. imperialist. ‖ adj. imperialistic.
imperícia s. f. 1. unskilfulness. 2. incompetence. 3. incapacity, ineptitude. 4. inadequacy.

império s. m. 1. empire, imperium. 2. monarchy, country ruled by an emperor. 3. power, authority, command. 4. sovereignty, realm, domain. 5. government, rule.

imperiosidade s. f. 1. imperiousness. 2. domineeringness, haughtiness, arrogance. 3. urgency.

imperioso adj. 1. imperious. 2. commanding, masterful. 3. haughty, arrogant. 4. peremptory, absolute, dictatorial. 5. urgent, pressing. ‖ **-amente** adv. imperiously, haughtily, etc.

imperito adj. 1. inexpert. 2. unskilled, unskilful. 3. inexperienced. 4. ignorant.

impermanência s. f. 1. impermanence, impermanency. 2. inconstancy. 3. instability.

impermanente adj. m. + f. 1. impermanent. 2. not enduring, inconstant. 3. instable. ‖ ~**mente** adv. impermanently.

impermeabilidade s. f. 1. impermeability, impenetrability. 2. (water)tightness.

impermeabilização s. f. (pl. **-ões**) act or process of making impermeable, (water)proofing.

impermeabilizante s. m. proofing.

impermeabilizado adj. waterproof, impervious.

impermeabilizar, impermear v. to render impermeable, make waterproof.

impermeável s. m. (pl. **-áveis**) rain-coat. ‖ adj. m. + f. 1. impermeable, not permeable. 2. impervious, impenetrable. 3. rain-tight, waterproof. 4. stanch, tight. ‖ **impermeavelmente** adv. impermeably. ~ **ao ar** air-tight. **a tampa é** ~ the cover is dampproof.

impermissível adj. m. + f. (pl. **-íveis**) unallowable, not permissible.

impermisto adj. unmixed, unalloyed, pure.

impermutabilidade s. f. impermutability.

impermutável adj. m. + f. (pl. **-áveis**) impermutable.

imperscrutável adj. m. + f. (pl. **-áveis**) imperscrutable, unsearchable, untraceable, unfathomable.

impersistente adj. m. + f. impersistent, not enduring.

impersonalidade s. f. impersonality, absence of personality.

impertérrito adj. fearless, intrepid.

impertinência s. f. 1. impertinence, impertinency. 2. irrelevance, insolence. 3. petulance, petulancy, peevishness. 4. bother, annoyance. 5. flippancy, testiness. **que** ~**!** what a cheek! **ele agiu com** ~ he acted with assurance.

impertinente s. m. + f. impertinent or importune person. ‖ adj. 1. impertinent, irrelevant. 2. insolent, petulant. 3. peevish, pettish. 4. importune. 5. flippant, spleenful. 6. rude. ‖ ~**mente** adv. impertinently.

imperturbabilidade s. f. imperturbability, steadfastness, calmness, serenity.

imperturbado adj. 1. unperturbed, undisturbed. 2. untouched. 3. untroubled. 4. calm.

imperturbável adj. m. + f. (pl. **-áveis**) 1. imperturbable, unshak(e)able. 2. steadfast, steady. 3. unabashed, unembarrassed. 4. calm, cool, cold-livered. 5. unerring. 6. unemotional, unmoved. ‖ **imperturbavelmente** adv. imperturbably, unerringly.

impérvio s. m. trackless, wild region. ‖ adj. 1. impervious, not pervious. 2. impermeable. 3. impenetrable. 4. impassable.

impessoal adj. m. + f. (pl. **-ais**) impersonal, not personal, objective. ‖ ~**mente** adv. impersonally.

impessoalidade s. f. impersonality.

impetar v. to throw, fling, hurl.

impeticar v. to implicate, involve, entangle.

impetigem s. f. (med.) impetigo, pustulous skin disease.

impetiginoso adj. impetiginous.

impetigo s. m. (med.) impetigo.

ímpeto s. m. 1. impetus, momentum. 2. impulse. 3. force, vehemence, impetuosity. 4. mettle, punch, élan. 5. rashness, haste, rushing. 6. emotion, excitement, agitation. 7. fury. 8. fierceness, fieriness, frenzy.

impetra s. f. 1. impetration, procurement. 2. supplication. 3. petition.

impetrabilidade s. f. impetrability.

impetração s. f. (pl. **-ões**) 1. impetration, act of obtaining. 2. entreaty, supplication. 3. petition.

impetrante s. m. + f. supplicant, suppliant, petitioner. ‖ adj. supplicatory, supplicant, entreating.

impetrar v. 1. to impetrate, obtain by petition. 2. to supplicate, entreat for. 3. to petition.

impetrativo, impetratório adj. impetrative, supplicatory, impetratory.

impetrável adj. m. + f. (pl. **-áveis**) 1. impetrative, obtainable by prayer or petition. 2. persuasive.

impetuosidade s. f. 1. impetuosity, impetuousness. 2. fury, anger. 3. violence, forcefulness, vehemence. 4. mettlesomeness, sharpness, eagerness. 5. fierceness, wildness. 6. exuberant vivacity.

impetuoso adj. 1. impetuous. 2. furious, angry. 3. violent, forceful, vehement. 4. mettlesome, sharp, fierce, brash. 5. hasty, precipitate. 6. temperamental, warm-blooded. 7. passionate, fiery. ‖ **-amente** adv. impetuously, etc. **ele tem um temperamento** ~ he has a hasty temper.

impiedade s. f. 1. impiety. 2. ungodliness, irreligion. 3. unrelentingness. 4. wickedness, cruelty. 5. irreverence. 6. pitilessness, mercilessness.

impiedosidade s. f. impiousness, impiety.

impiedoso adj. 1. impious, ungodly. 2. pitiless, void of pity. 3. merciless, unmerciful. 4. unrelenting, unsparing. 5. cruel. 6. irreverent. ‖ **-amente** adv. pitilessly, mercilessly, unrelentingly, cruelly, irreverently.

impigem s. f. (med.) tetter, eczema, ringworm, dartre.

impingidela s. f. 1. impingement. 2. deception, imposition. 3. mean trick, base action.

impingir v. 1. to impinge. 2. to strike, dash. 3. to encroach. 4. to force, enforce. 5. to foist, palm on (or upon). 6. to fob off, trick. **impingiram-no a ele** they foisted it on him.

ímpio s. m. impious man, heretic. ‖ adj. 1. impious, ungodly. 2. profane, irreligious. 3. wicked. 4. inhuman, cruel. 5. pagan. 6. merciless. 7. graceless, prayerless. ‖ **impiamente** adv. impiously, mercilessly, wickedly.

implacabilidade s. f. 1. implacability, implacableness. 2. irreconcilable enmity. 3. relentlessness. 4. inexorability, inflexibility. 5. insensibility.

implacável adj. m. + f. (pl. **-áveis**) 1. implacable, unappeasable. 2. irreconcilable, inexorable, inexpiable. 3. relentless, merciless, unmerciful. 4. inflexible, immovable. 5. insensible. 6. ruthless. 7. mortal, deadly. ‖ **implacavelmente** adv. implacably, etc.

implacidez s. f. unrest, lack of placidness, disquietude, commotion.

implantação s. f. (pl. **-ões**) implantation, act of implanting, state of being fixed firmly in place.

implantador s. m. implanter, planter.

implantar v. 1. to plant, implant. 2. to introduce, establish. 3. to insert, instil. 4. to enroot, ingraft. 5. to inseminate. 6. ~**-se** to fix o. s. firmly, take root.

implante s. m. implantation.

implantodontia s. f. (odont.) the technique used for implanting or reimplanting teeth.

implantologia s. f. (med.) the branch of medicine which studies the phenomena related to the grafting of organs.
implausível adj. m. + f. (pl. -íveis) unplausible.
implemento s. m. 1. implement. 2. accessory. 2. tool, utensil, instrument. 4. apparel, gear. 5. fulfilment, execution.
implexo adj. 1. implex, intricate, entangled. 2. complicated.
implicação s. f. (pl. -ões) 1. implication, act of implicating. 2. involution, involvement. 3. inference. 4. complication. 5. incompatibility. 6. contraction.
implicado adj. entangled, involved, implied.
não ~ unconcerned.
implicância s. f. 1. implication, involvement. 2. incompatibility. 3. annoyance, trouble. 4. malevolence.
implicante s. m. + f. 1. captious or quarrelsome person. 2. (logic) implicate, implicant. || adj. implicating, implicative, involving, captious. || ~mente adv. implicatingly, implicatively, involvingly, captiously.
ele é muito ~ he is a fault-finder, he is a quarrelsome person. ela deu uma resposta ~ she gave a captious answer.
implicar v. 1. to implicate. 2. to involve, entangle. 3. to embarrass, encumber. 4. to imply, hint, express by inference. 5. to perplex. 6. to include, comprise. 7. to cause, give raise to. 8. to ask for, require. 9. to be incompatible, to irreconcile. 10. to quarrel, contend.
isto não implica que this does not imply that. está implicado em it is implicated in. ele está implicado no crime de... he is involved in the crime of...
implicativo, implicatório adj. implicative, implicatory, connotative. || -amente, implicatoriamente adv. implicatively, implicatorily, connotatively.
implícito adj. 1. implicit. 2. implicate, implicative. 3. tacit, implied, inferred. 4. involved, entangled. 5. constructive. || implicitamente adv. implicitly.
imploração s. f. (pl. -ões) imploration, act of imploring, supplication.
implorador s. m. implorer, implorator. || adj. imploring, beseeching.
implorante s. m. + f. implorer, implorator. || adj. imploring, beseeching.
implorar v. 1. to implore. 2. to entreat, petition with urgency. 3. to beseech. 4. to supplicate. 5. to pray, beg for earnestly. 6. to invoke, conjure.
ele implorou perdão he cried mercy. implorei-lhe que me ouvisse I entreated of him to hear me.
implorativo adj. imploring, entreating, beseeching, supplicatory, appealing. || -amente adv. imploringly.
implorável adj. m. + f. (pl. -áveis) implorable.
implume adj. m. + f. 1. featherless, plumeless. 2. unfledged. 3. bald, callow.
implúvio s. m. (Roman hist.) impluvium, basin for the rain-water in the middle of the atrium.
impolidez s. f. impoliteness, rudeness, coarseness, incivility.
impolido adj. 1. impolite. 2. ill-mannered, rude. 3. uncivil, discourteous, disrespectful. 4. unrefined, unpolished. || -amente adv. impolitely, uncivilly, rustically.
impolítica s. f. 1. impolicy, incivility. 2. inexpediency. 3. unsuitableness.
impolítico adj. 1. impolitic, unpolitic(al). 2. inexpedient, injudicious. 3. impolite, discourteous. || impoliticamente adv. impolitically, injudiciously, impolitely.
impoluível adj. m. + f. (pl. -íveis) 1. that cannot be defiled or polluted, impollutable. 2. immaculate, unblemished.

impoluto adj. 1. impolluted, unsullied, undefiled. 2. immaculate. 3. virtuous.
imponderabilidade s. f. imponderability.
imponderado adj. 1. inconsiderate, heedless. 2. precipitate, rash. 3. thoughtless. 4. unweighed, unweighing.
imponderáveis s. m. pl. imponderables, imponderable things or elements.
imponderável adj. m. + f. (pl. -áveis) imponderable, not capable of being weighed, inappreciable, very subtle.
imponência s. f. 1. imposingness, portliness, stateliness. 2. majesty. 3. pride, arrogance. 4. authoritativeness. 5. magnificence.
imponente adj. m. + f. 1. imponent, imposing. 2. portly, stately. 3. majestic. 4. proud, arrogant, authoritative, commanding. 5. grand, grandiose. 6. superb, sightly. 7. fearful. 8. noble, gallant. || ~mente adv. imposingly.
um efeito final muito ~ a clever curtain.
impontual adj. m. + f. (pl. -ais) unpunctual, not punctual, inexact.
impontualidade s. f. impunctuality, neglect of punctuality.
impopular adj. impopular, unpopular. || ~mente adv. unpopularly.
impopularidade s. f. unpopularity.
impor v. 1. to impose. 2. (eccl.) to lay on, set on (hands in ordination or confirmation). 3. to lay on, encumber, burden. 4. to levy, assess, tax, exact. 5. to restrain, curb. 6. to establish, institute. 7. to determine, decide. 8. to command, direct. 9. to force, enforce. 10. to fix upon, impute, charge (falsely). 11. inflict, afflict, trouble. 12. to inspire, instil. 13. to oblige to accept. 14. to trick, illude, deceive. 15. to palm off, foist, pass off. 16. to oblige, subject. 17. to give a name, surname. 19. ~-se to impose o. s., presume, obtrude.
~ condições to condition. ~ um imposto to assess a tax. ~ recurso to appeal. o sacerdote impôs as mãos the priest laid his hands on. eles se impuseram aos vizinhos they took advantage of their neighbours. o professor impôs silêncio aos alunos the teacher reduced the pupils to silence. eles impuseram-se they won their way. ela impôs sempre sua vontade she carried her point all the time. impuseram-lhe a obrigação de estudar they fastened upon him the obligation to study. impusemos um plano de trabalho we established a working program.
importação s. f. (pl. -ões) 1. importation, act or practice of importing. 2. entry, influx (of goods from another country). 3. import(s), merchandise imported.
falta de ~ nonimportation. eles pagaram direitos de ~ they paid import duties.
importador s. m. importer. || adj. importing.
importância s. f. 1. importance. 2. momentousness, consequence. 3. concernment. 4. consideration, regard. 5. social standing, dignity. 6. pretentiousness, pompousness. 7. emphasis, stress. 8. preciousness, valuableness. 9. influence, authority. 10. significance, value, account. 11. weight, moment. 12. repute, fame. 13. presumption, arrogance. 14. interest. 15. seriousness, ponderosity. 16. amount, quantity. 17. cost. 18. sum, total. 19. urgency.
um assunto de ~ vital a thing of vital concernment; a matter of great weight. um assunto de grande ~ a matter of great concern. pagável até a ~ de payable to the extent of. eles dão ~ ao assunto they attribute importance to the subject. eles dão demasiada ~ à questão they overmeasure the question. ela não dá ~ a she makes no matter of. eles não dão a mínima ~

they do not care a straw. **ele se deu ares de** ~ he put on airs. **não dou** ~ **a suas queixas** I attach no importance to his complaints. **ele o excede em** ~ he outranks him. **ele deve a** ~ **global de** he owes the lump sum of. **não ligo a mínima** ~ I don't care a pin. **isto é de pouca** ~ **para mim** this is a trifling circumstance with me. **uma pessoa sem** ~ a person of no account. **sem** ~ of no consequence; weightless; insignificant; unessential. **ele é de** ~ he imports to something. **isto é de somenos** ~ this is but of little importance. **ele deu ao trabalho somenos** ~ he made light of his work. **não tem** ~ it does not matter, never mind, that does not count, it is no great matter. **ela pagou uma** ~ **considerável** she paid a good round sum. **este assunto tem mais** ~ **que qualquer outro** this topic is paramount to any other.

importante s. m. important act, fact or person. ‖ adj. m. + f. 1. important. 2. indispensable, essential. 3. serious, earnest, significant. 4. (Braz., ironic.) overbearing, presumptuous. 5. pretentious, pompous. 6. momentous, weighty. 7. considerable, capital. 8. consequential, influential. 9. eminent, distinguished. 10. grave, pregnant, substantial. ‖ ~**mente** adv. in an important manner, essentially, seriously, momentously.

dar-se ares de ~ to ride the high horse. **é** ~ **que eu faça isto agora?** is it a point that I do it now? **ele é** ~ he is somebody. **ele julga-se** ~ he thinks himself somebody. **é um assunto muito** ~ it is a vital topic. **isto não é** ~ this is of no importance. **ele é a pessoa mais** ~ **na firma** he is the most important person in the firm, (sl.) he is tops in the firm. **ela não é nada de** ~ she is no person of consequence; (coll.) she is no great shakes. **não há nada de** ~ there is nothing of importance to write home about. **ele bancou o** ~ he did it grand. **ela falou sobre a questão mais** ~ she spoke the uppermost question.

importar v. 1. to import, introduce from abroad, bring from a foreign country. 2. to bring into practice or play. 3. to cause, occasion. 4. to produce, bring about. 5. to amount to, aggregate. 6. to come to, total up. 7. to interest, concern. 8. to be useful, matter. 9. to be significant, be of consequence. 10. to indicate, imply. 11. to correspond to.

aquilo importa muito that matters very much. **isto não me importa** that is indifferent to me, it is not my affair. **daqui a cem anos ninguém mais se importará** it will be all the same in a hundred years. **não me importo absolutamente** I don't care a fig for it. **não se importe com coisa alheia** go about your own business. **o tempo não importa** time is no consideration. **ele não se importa** he doesn't care. **que importa?** what does it matter? **não me importo em absoluto!** I don't care a rap (or damn)! **em quanto importa a conta?** what does the bill run to? **o preço importava em 32 dólares** the price amounted to 32 dollars. **as despesas importaram em...** the expenses total(l)ed...

importável adj. m. + f. (pl. -áveis) importable, that may be imported.

importe s. m. 1. sum, total amount. 2. cost, price, cost price.

importunação s. f. (pl. -ões) 1. importunity, importunateness. 2. molestation, bother, annoyance. 3. forwardness, obtrusiveness. 4. tease. 5. troublesomeness.

importunador s. m. importuner, disturber, teaser, troublesome or importunate person. ‖ adj. thoublesome or importunate person. ‖ adj. thoublesome, vexatious, importunate, offensively persistent.

importunar v. 1. to importune. 2. to require urgently, beg for persistently, pester. 3. to annoy, molest. 4. to embarrass, hinder. 5. to disturb, derange. 6. to tease, vex. 7. to incommode, trouble. 8. to interrupt.

ela importunou a amiga com perguntas she plied her friend with questions. **eles o** ~**am até consentir** they teased him into consenting. **sinto importuná-lo** I am sorry to trouble you.

importunidade s. f. 1. importunateness, importunity. 2. cumbersomeness. 3. obtrusiveness. 4. persistent solicitation. 5. bother, annoyance, molestation. 6. disturbance, inconvenience.

importuno s. m. 1. annoyer, molester, plaguer. 2. obtruder. 3. pesterer. ‖ adj. 1. importunate, importune. 2. worrisome, troublesome. 3. obtrusive, impertinent. 4. disturbing, pesterous, cumbersome. 5. insupportable. ‖ -**amente** adv. importunately, worrisomely, troublesomely, obtrusively, disturbingly. **ele não é** ~ he is quite unobtrusive. **você foi muito** ~ **com o chefe** you were bothering the boss.

imposição s. f. (pl. -ões) 1. imposition. 2. placing, laying on. 3. assessment, tax, tribute. 4. rule, order. 5. infliction, punishment. 6. trick, deception, imposture. 7. bestowal of the insignia of an order, investiture.

impositivo adj. imposing, commanding, authoritative.

impossibilidade s. f. 1. impossibility. 2. incapability, helplessness. 3. impossible matter or thing.

impossibilitar v. 1. to make impossible. 2. to weaken, enfeeble. 3. to incapacitate, disable. 4. to deprive of force or aptitude. 5. ~**-se** to become unable.

impossível s. m. (pl. -íveis) impossibility. ‖ adj. m. + f. 1. impossible, not possible. 2. very difficult. 3. unfeasible, unattainable. 4. impracticable. 5. insupportable, intolerable. 6. extravagant, odd. ‖ **impossivelmente** adv. impossibly, intolerably.

não posso fazê-lo, é ~ I cannot possibly do it. **ele é um homem** ~ he is an eccentric man. **uma história** ~ an incredible story. **eles pedem o** ~ they ask for the impossible, cry for the moon.

imposta s. f. (archit.) impost, abutment, springer (plate A 12).

impostação s. f. correct pronunciation of sounds.

impostar v. to pronounce sounds correctly.

imposto s. m. 1. imposition. 2. tax, duty, tribute. 3. excise, impost. 4. ~**s** pl. taxation, revenue. ‖ adj. forced, enforced.

~ **de diversões** entertainment tax. ~ **de lucros extraordinários** excess profits duty. ~ **de renda** income tax. ~ **de selo** stamp-duty. **aumentaram o** ~ **predial** they upped the house tax. **ele requereu isenção de** ~ he requested tax exemption. **eles pagaram** ~ **de consumo** they paid excise duty. **este artigo é livre de** ~ this article is untaxed. **introduziram um** ~ **sobre o capital** they established a capital levy. **isento de** ~ tax-free, taxless, tax-exempt. **lançar** ~**s** to levy taxes. **o governo impôs um** ~ **a** the government imposed a tax on. **o** ~ **sobre o salário é muito alto** the tax on wages is very high. **o** ~ **de vendas** the turnover tax. **pagaram um pesado** ~ **territorial** they paid a heavy land tax. **a sonegação de** ~**s é um crime** tax avoidance is a crime.

impostor s. m. 1. impostor, imposer. 2. deceiver, cheat, fraud. 3. counterfeit, charlatan, humbug. ‖ adj. impostrous, deceptive, deceitful.

impostoria s. f. (Braz.) 1. imposture, deceit, deception. 2. vanity, conceit, pride. 3. haughtiness, presumption.

impostura s. f. 1. imposture, imposition. 2. deceit, fraud. 3. false pretense, farce, take-in. 4. conceit, presumption 5. slander, calumny.

imposturar v. 1. to deceive, cheat. 2. to boast, brag. 3. to palm off, pass off.

impotabilidade s. f. impotability.

impotável adj. m. + f. (pl. **-áveis**) impotable, unfit for drinking.

impotência s. f. impotence, impotency: 1. physical or intelecctual feebleness. 2. weakness, inability, disability. 3. powerlessness. 4. sexual incapacity in the male.

impotente s. m. impotent: feeble or impotent male. ‖ adj. impotent: 1. lacking strength or vigour. 2. feeble, week. 3. powerless, helpless. 4. unable, inefficacious. ‖ **~mente** adv. impotently.

impraticabilidade s. f. impracticability, impracticableness.

impraticável adj. m. + f. (pl. **-áveis**) 1. impracticable. 2. inexecutable, unrealizable. 3. impossible, unworkable. ‖ **impraticavelmente** adv. impracticably.

imprecação s. f. (pl. **-ões**) 1. imprecation, malediction. 2. curse, profanity. 3. (ironic.) blessing. 4. ban.

imprecar v. 1. to imprecate. 2. to invoke, pray for. 3. to call down some evil upon. 4. to maledict, curse, swear. 5. to use profane language.

imprecatado adj. 1. unaware(s), unwary. 2. unprepared, unguarded. 3. incautious. 4. unforeseen.

imprecativo adj. imprecatory, maledictory.

imprecatório adj. imprecatory, maledictory, invoking evil.

imprecaução s. f. (pl. **-ões**) lack of precaution, imprudence, carelessness.

imprecisão s. f. imprecision, inexactness, inaccuracy, inaccurateness.

impreciso adj. 1. inaccurate, inexact, incorrect. 2. undetermined, vague.

impreenchível adj. m. + f. (pl. **-íveis**) unfillable, unaccomplishable.

impregnação s. f. (pl. **-ões**) 1. impregnation, permeation. 2. infusion, saturation. 3. fecundation.

impregnado adj. impregnate(d), saturated, imbued.

impregnar v. 1. to impregnate. 2. to fecundate, fertilize. 3. to imbue, saturate. 4. to percolate, permeate. 5. to steep, soak. 6. to fill up. 7. **~-se** to be impregnated, become imbued.

impremeditação s. f. (pl. **-ões**) unpremeditation.

impremeditado adj. 1. unpremeditated, not deliberately, unintentional. 2. instinctive, spontaneous.

imprensa s. f. 1. printing press. 2. machine by which pressure is applied, winepress, clothespress. 3. art, process and business of printing, typography. 4. press: newspapers and periodicals collectively. 5. personnel employed in the newspaper business. 6. printing establishment. 7. opinion or critical comment published by the press.
~ ordinária gutter press. **~ sensacionalista** the yellow press. **ele tem uma queda para a ~** he is cut out for journalism. **o livro que está na ~** the book that is in the press. **o poder da ~** the power of the press. **reservado para a ~** (place) reserved for the members of the press, press box. **sufocar a ~** to muzzle the press. **tinta de ~** printer's ink.

imprensado adj. pressed, printed, marked by pressing.

imprensador s. m. pressman, calenderer.

imprensadura s. f. act or result of pressing.

imprensar v. 1. to press, compress. 2. to print, imprint. 3. to stamp, squeeze, subject to pressure, impact.

impresciência s. f. imprescience, want of foresight or prescience.

imprescindível adj. m. + f. (pl. **-íveis**) vital, necessary, indispensable.

imprescritibilidade s. f. imprescriptibility.

imprescritível adj. m. + f. (pl. **-íveis**) imprescriptible, not subject to prescription.

impressão s. f. (pl. **-ões**) 1. impression, pression, state of being impressed. 2. print, imprint. 3. art of printing, typography, presswork. 4. edition, whole number of copies printed at once. 5. stamp, mark. 6. impact, shock. 7. feeling, sensation. 8. vague idea, notion. 9. opinion, belief. 10. illusion. 11. emotional shock, thrill. 12. draft, rough sketch, colour sketch. 13. critique.
a ~ causada era bem clara the percept was quite clear. **ela causou muita ~** she cut a dash. **os fatos causaram forte ~** the facts produced a deep impression. **nós lhes causamos má ~** we made an unfavourable impression upon them, (U. S. A., coll.) we got in wrong with them. **ele causou má ~** he impressed unfavourably. **ele causou a ~ de estar doente** he gave the impression of being sick. **~ a cores** colour printing. **ele deixou -ões** he left some tracks. **eles procuraram -ões digitais** they were looking for fingerprints. **compararam os méritos da ~ em talho doce e em relevo** they compared the advantages of copperplate and surface printing. **tratava-se de um erro de ~** it was a misprint. **eles queriam uma ~ litográfica em cores** they wanted a chromolithography. **ele agiu sob a ~ de** he acted impressed with the idea. **sob a ~ dos acontecimentos recentes** in the light of the recent events. **sob a ~ da novidade** under the novelty. **tenho forte ~ de que** I feel strongly that. **combinaram uma troca de -ões** they agreed on an exchange of views.

impressionabilidade s. f. impressionability, sensibility, sensitivity, sensitiveness.

impressionado adj. impressed, shocked, troubled.
ele ficou bem ~ com he was favourably impressed by. **fiquei muito mal ~** I was quite shocked. **ela ficou -a com a idéia** she was impressed with the idea. **ela ficou profundamente -a** she was deeply impressed.

impressionante adj. m. + f. 1. impressing, striking. 2. moving, touching. 3. forcible, penetrative. 4. awful, terrific. 5. solemn. 6. effective.
mostraram um filme ~ they gave a thriller.

impressionar v. 1. to impress. 2. to mark, stamp in. 3. to affect deeply, move, touch. 4. (phot.) to expose. 5. **~-se** to be impressed, get excited, become nervous.
isto não me impressiona I am not impressed by that. **foi o que o impressionou** that is what weighed on him. **o artigo impressionou-me** the article took a hold on me. **ele não impressiona bem** he does not impress favourably, (sl.) he cuts no ice. **elas se ~am com o filme** they were thrilled by the movie.

impressionável adj. m. + f. (pl. **-áveis**) 1. impressionable, impressible. 2. sensitive, receptive, susceptible. 3. capable of receiving impressions.

impressionismo s. m. 1. impressionability, great sensibility. 2. (arts) impressionism.

impressionista s. m. + f. impressionist. ‖ adj. impressionist(ic), impressionary.

impressivo adj. 1. impressive. 2. susceptible, impressible. 3. imposing, commanding. 4. moving, touching. ‖ **-amente** adv. impressively.

impresso s. m. 1. printed matter, printed papers. 2. impression, copy. 3. book-post. 4. book, folder, program. ‖ adj. printed.
~ para faturas billhead. **prova de ~** advance copy. **o livro está sendo ~** the book is printing. **o folheto saiu ~** the folder appeared in type.

impressor s. m. 1. printer, pressman. 2. presser, pressworker.
aprendiz de ~ printer's devil.

impressório s. m. (phot.) printer, printing frame (with a hinged back).

imprestável s. m. + f. (pl. -áveis) dud, good for nothing. ‖ adj. 1. useless, worthless. 2. unfit, unserviceable, unsuitable. 3. wretched, dud, rotten. ‖ -imprestavelmente adv. uselessly, unsuitably, wretchedly.

impreterível adj. m. + f. (pl. -íveis) 1. not to be put off. 2. unsurpassable. 3. unconditional, implicit. 4. indeclinable, unfailing. 5. indispensable, essential. ‖ impreterivelmente adv. unfailingly; without any further delay.

imprevidência s. f. improvidence, imprudence, incautiousness, unwariness.

imprevidente adj. m. + f. 1. improvident. 2. careless, shortsighted. 3. unthrifty, wasteful. 4. unwary, happy-go-lucky, imprudent.

imprevisão s. f. (pl. -ões) 1. improvidence. 2. unexpectedness. 3. imprudence, carelessness. 4. thriftlessness. 5. negligence.

imprevisível adj. m. + f. (pl. -íveis) unexpected, unforeseeable.

imprevisto s. m. unexpected thing. ‖ adj. 1. unforeseen, unexpected. 2. unanticipated, unlooked-for. 3. unthought of, surprising. 4. unprovided.

imprimação, imprimadura s. f. priming, first coating of paint.

imprimar v. to prime a canvass, to lay on the first coat of paint.

imprimir v. 1. to print, imprint. 2. to impress. 3. to stamp, enstamp. 4. to inculcate, implant. 5. to publish in the press. 6. to transmit, communicate, transcribe. 7. to engrave. 8. to produce, cause. 9. ~-se to become impressed or fixed into.
ele mandou ~ o livro he sent the book to the press, he has a book printed. ele imprimiu maior velocidade ao carro he sped on the car. foi impresso como separata it was offprinted.

improbabilidade s. f. improbability, unlikelihood, unlikeliness, implausibility.

improbidade s. f. 1. improbity, lack of rectitude. 2. dishonesty, infamy. 3. characterlessness. 4. wickedness, baseness.

ímprobo adj. 1. dishonest, infamous. 2. characterless. 3. wicked, base, foul. 4. unfair.

improcedência s. f. 1. unfoundedness, groundlessness. 2. illogicalness, want of basis, irreverency. 3. unfairness, injustice.

improcedente adj. m. + f. 1. unfounded, groundless. 2. illogical, irrelevant. 3. unfair, unjust.

improdutível adj. m. + f. (pl. -íveis) unproducible, incapable of being produced.

improdutividade s. f. unproductiveness, fruitlessness.

improdutivo adj. 1. unproductive, nonproductive. 2. unfruitful, barren. 3. unprofitable. 4. useless. 5. unemployed. ‖ -amente adv. unproductively.

improferível adj. (pl. -íveis) 1. unutterable, unpronounceable. 2. (phon.) explosive.

improficiência s. f. improficience, improficiency, incompetence.

improficiente adj. m. + f. improficient, incompetent, inefficient, not versed or skilled.

improfícuo adj. 1. unprofitable, gainless. 2. fruitless. 3. useless, in vain. 4. ineffectual. 5. unthrifty. ‖ improficuamente adv. unprofitably, fruitlessly.

improgressivo adj. improgressive, unprogressive.

improlífico adj. unprolific, unproductive, infertile.

impronúncia s. f. (Braz., jur.) rejection of an accusation or complaint.

impronunciar v. (Braz., jur.) to reject an accusation.

improperar v. 1. to reproach, reprimand, upbraid. 2. to insult, abuse, affront. 3. to slander, defame.

impropério s. m. 1. affront, insult, outrage. 2. baseness, vulgarity. 3. invective(s).

impropriar v. 1. to make improper. 2. to apply wrongly or in an improper manner. 3. ~-se to become unfit.

impropriedade s. f. 1. impropriety. 2. unseemliness, indelicacy. 3. incorrectness. 4. unsuitableness, unfitness. 5. irrelevance. 6. inadequateness, inadequacy.

impróprio adj. 1. improper, inappropriate. 2. inexact, inaccurate. 3. incorrect, wrong. 4. inadequate, unsuitable. 5. inconvenient, inopportune. 6. incapable, unapt, unfit. 7. indecorous, unseemly, unbecoming. 8. untimely, unpropitious. 9. troublesome, wearisome. 10. undue, malapropos. ‖ impropriamente adv. improperly, etc.
ele agiu de modo ~ he acted in an improper way. ele contou uma piada -a he told an off-colour joke. isto acontece em tempo ~ this happens out of season. restou uma fração -a there remained an improper fraction. o seu comportamento foi ~ para uma moça (senhora) her behaviour was unmaidenly (unladylike).

improrrogabilidade s. f. impossibility of being prorogued, protracted or delayed.

improrrogável adj. m. + f. undelayable, unpostponable, fatal.

impróspero adj. 1. unprosperous. 2. unfortunate, unhappy. 3. portentous, threatening.

improvar v. 1. to disapprove. 2. to censure, reproach. 3. to blame.

improvável adj. m + f. (pl. -áveis) 1. improbable, unlikely. 2. unprovable. 3. implausible, unthinkable. 4. problematic. 5. remote. 6. (coll.) fishy. ‖ improvavelmente adv. improbably.
é muito ~ que ele o faça he is most unlikely to do it.

improvidência s. f. 1. improvidence, lack of caution or foresight. 2. imprudence, carelessness. 3. thriftlessness.

improvidente adj. m. + f. 1. improvident, wanting caution or foresight. 2. imprudent, careless. 3. unthrifty. 4. inconsiderate. ‖ ~mente adv. improvidently, without caution or foresight.

impróvido adj. improvident, careless, unthrifty. ‖ improvidamente adv. improvidently.

improvisação s. f. (pl. -ões) 1. improvisation, extemporization. 2. (mus.) impromptu.

improvisado adj. 1. improvised, improvisate. 2. unprepared, unstudied. 3. extempore, extemporaneous. 4. unpremeditated. 5. off-hand, impromptu. ‖ -amente adv. unexpectedly, extemporaneously.
composição -a impromptu.

improvisador s. m. improviser, improvisator, extemporizer. ‖ adj. improvisatory.

improvisar v. 1. to improvise, improvisate. 2. to extemporize. 3. to do or perform in an off-hand way. 4. to compose verses or music extemporaneously.

improviso s. m. improvisation, impromptu, extemporization. ‖ adj. 1. sudden, precipitate. 2. unexpected. 3. fortuitous. 4. improvised, unprepared. 5. extempore, extemporaneous. ‖ -adamente adv. extemporaneously, suddenly, fortuitously, impromptu.
ele agiu de ~ he acted off-hand. a atriz falou de ~ the actress spoke out of hand. ele falou de ~ he extemporized freely.

imprudência s. f. 1. imprudence, want of caution. 2. rashness, heedlessness. 3. indiscretion. 4. foolhardiness. 5. imprudent act. 6. inconvenience. 7. improvidence.

imprudente s. m. + f. imprudent person. ‖ adj. 1. imprudent, not prudent. 2. rash, precipitate. 3. thoughtless, headless. 4. incautious, unwary. 5. indiscreet, injudicious. 6. improvident. 7. unwise, foolish. 8. ill-advised. 9. foolhardy. ‖ ~mente adv. imprudently, foolhardily, etc.

impuberdade s. f. impuberty.
impúbere s. m. + f. adolescent, person below the age of puberty. ‖ adj. impubic, impuberal, impubescent, under age.
impubescência s. f. impuberty, immatureness, immaturity.
impubescente s. m. + f. person below the age of puberty, adolescent. ‖ adj. impubic, impuberal, impubescent.
impublicável adj. m. + f. (pl. -áveis) unprintable.
impudência s. f. 1. impudence, impudency. 2. brazenness, shamelessness. 3. impudent act or saying. 4. insolence, barefacedness. 5. affrontery. 6. (coll.) gall, cheek, cockiness.
foi uma ~ perfeita it was an unmitigated impudence. **ele teve a ~ de fazê-lo** he had the face to do it.
impudente adj. m. + f. 1. impudent, shameless. 2. insolent, grossly disrespectful. 3. immodest. 4. bold, bold-faced, brazen. 5. cocky, cheeky. 6. rude, indelicate. 7. blushless, brash. 8. presumptuous. ‖ ~mente adv. impudently, shamelessly, brazenly, cockily, rudely.
impudicícia s. f. 1. impudicity, shamelessness. 2. unchastity, lewdness. 3. impurity. 4. meretriciousness. 5. immodesty. 6. (coll.) nerve.
impúdico adj. 1. shameless, impudent. 2. wanton, unchaste, lewd. 3. impure, unclean. 4. immodest. 5. meretricious. 6. impertinent. ‖ -amente adv. impudently, shamelessly, lewdly, meretriciously.
impudor s. m. 1. impudence, impudency. 2. brazenness, shamelessness. 3. impudent act or saying. 4. insolence, affrontery. 5. impertinence, cheek. 6. immodesty.
impueira s. f. (Braz.) seasonal pools and swamps which border the course of a river (after high water).
impugnabilidade s. f. refutability.
impugnação s. f. (pl. -ões) 1. impugnation, impugnment. 2. refutation, contestation. 3. gainsay. 4. opposition, contradiction.
impugnador s. m. impugner, contester, opposer.
impugnar v. 1. to impugn, refute. 2. to contradict, contest. 3. to defy, withstand. 4. to assail, attack. 5. to oppose, call in question.
impugnativo adj. impugnative, tending to contradict or contest.
impugnável adj. m. + f. (pl. -áveis) impugnable, capable of being refuted or opposed.
impulsão s. f. (pl. -ões) 1. impulse, thrust, push. 2. impulsion, propulsion, impelling force or action. 3. (fig.) stimulation, incentive, spur.
impulsar v. 1. to give impulse, impel. 2. to throw, thrust. 3. to push, force on, drive. 4. (fig.) to encourage, stimulate.
impulsionar v. 1. to animate, stimulate. 2. to urge, boast. 3. to push, propel, drive forward. 4. to impel, actuate.
impulsividade s. f. 1. impulsiveness, impulsivity, impetuosity, impetuousness. 2. hastiness, rashness. 3. irritableness, petulance.
impulsivo adj. 1. impulsive. 2. hasty, rash. 3. impetuous, precipitate. 4. irritable, petulant. 5. quick, sudden. ‖ -amente adv. impulsively.
impulso s. m. 1. impulse. 2. impelling force, drive, thrust, push. 3. impulsion, propulsion. 4. impetus, force, urge. 5. stimulation, incentive, spur. 6. incitation, boast.
tomar um pequeno ~ to take a short run (for jumping). **ele obedeceu a um ~ natural** he was guided by his instinct. **registrou-se um ~ no comércio** there was an upswing in the trade. **trata-se dum ~ instintivo do indivíduo** it is a reaction

of his id. **levado por um ~ poético, ele escreveu o drama** carried away by his afflatus he wrote the drama. **ele agiu sob um ~ repentino** he acted on the spur of the moment.
impulsor s. m. impeller, propulsor, propeller, propellent. ‖ adj. impelling, impulsive, driving, boasting.
impune adj. m. + f. 1. unpunished, with impunity. 2. unavenged, unbeaten. 3. (coll.) scot-free. 4. unrequited. ‖ ~mente adv. without punishment, with impunity.
ele saiu ~ he left scot-free.
impunidade s. f. impunity, exemption from punishment or penalty.
impunido adj. unpunished, impune. ‖ -amente adv. impunely.
impunível adj. m. + f. (pl. -íveis) impunible, unpunishable.
impureira s. f. = **impueira**.
impureza s. f. 1. impurity, impureness. 2. uncleanness. 3. muddiness, filthiness. 4. dirt, filth. 5. lees, dregs, sediment. 6. foulness, pollutedness. 7. unchasteness, lewdness. 8. grossness, vulgarity.
impuridade s. f. impurity, impureness.
impurificar v. 1. to make impure, soil, dirty. 2. (fig.) to defile.
impuro adj. 1. impure, tainted. 2. foul, feculent. 3. dirty, filthy. 4. unclean. 5. contaminated, polluted. 6. unchaste, lewd, sensual. 7. sordid, profane. 8. improper, vulgar. ‖ -amente adv. impurely, uncleanly.
imputabilidade s. f. imputability, imputableness.
imputação s. f. (pl. -ões) 1. imputation. 2. attribution, ascription. 3. accusation, charge. 4. censure, reproach.
imputador s. m. imputer, accuser, reproacher. ‖ adj. imputative.
imputar v. 1. to impute. 2. to attribute, ascribe. 3. to charge with, accuse. 4. to consider wrong or chargeable. 5. to blame, reproach. 6. to slur, slander.
~am o crime ao menino they fastened the crime upon the boy. **~am a responsabilidade à professora** they laid the blame on the teacher. **naturalmente ~am a culpa a mim** naturally they laid the blame on my door.
imputável adj. m. + f. (pl. -áveis) 1. imputable, imputative. 2. ascribable, attributable. 3. chargeable. ‖ **imputavelmente** adv. imputatively.
imputrescibilidade s. f. imputrescibility, incorruptibility.
imputrescível adj. m. + f. (pl. -íveis) imputrescible, incorruptible.
imudável adj. m. + f. (pl. -áveis) immutable, unchargeable, unalterable.
festas -veis immoveable feasts.
imundícia s. f. 1. uncleanness, uncleanliness. 2. foulness, filthiness. 3. (Braz.) slum district. 4. sloppiness. 5. carrion, ordure. 6. dinginess, dirtiness. 7. sordidness. 8. any troublesome insect.
imundície s. f. 1. = **imundícia**. 2. (Braz., coll.) rabbit hunting.
imundo adj. 1. dirty, filthy. 2. unclean, foul, feculent. 3. impure, tainted. 4. indecent, indecorous. 5. immoral, obscene, lewd. 6. corrupt.
imune adj. m. + f. immune, exempt, protected (from disease), not susceptible.
imunidade s. f. 1. immunity, exemption. 2. freedom from contagion or infection. 3. (sociol.) franchise, franchisement, particular privilege.
imunização s. f. (pl. -ões) immunization.
imunizado adj. immune, mithridatic.
imunizador s. m. immunizing agent. ‖ adj. immunizing.

imunizar v. 1. to immunize, render immune. 2. to protect from (disease, penalty, charges, etc.).

imutabilidade s. f. 1. immutability, immutableness. 2. unchangeableness. 3. constancy. 4. quiescence, quiescency.

imutação s. f. (pl. -ões) immutation, change, transformation, substitution of one thing for another.

imutar v. to immute, change, transform, substitute one thing for another.

imutável adj. m. + f. (pl. -áveis) 1. immutable, unchangeable, unalterable. 2. not subject to mutation. 3. steady, steadfast. 4. stationary, constant.

inabalável adj. m. + f. (pl. -áveis) 1. unshak(e)able, unshaken. 2. unwavering, unswerving. 3. immoved. 4. constant, firm, steady. 5. unfaltering, unflinching. 6. inexorable. 7. (fig.) fearless, brave. 8. unbreakable. ‖ **inabalavelmente** adv. unshakably, unflinchingly.

inabdicável adj. m. + f. (pl. -áveis) inabdicable, incapable of being abdicated, unrelinquishable.

inábil adj. m. + f. (pl. **inábeis**) 1. unapt, unfit. 2. incapable. 3. unqualified, unskilled. 4. artless. 5. incompetent. 6. bungling. ‖ **inabilmente** adv. bungingly, unaptly, shiftlessly.

inabilidade s. f. 1. inability, incapacity. 2. unskilfulness, unhandiness. 3. inaptness. 4. incompetence, inefficiency.

inabilitação s. f. (pl. -ões) disablement, incapacitation, disqualification.

inabilitado adj. unqualified, disqualified.

inabilitar v. 1. to incapacitate, disable. 2. to make incapable. 3. to disincline, indispose. 4. to reject (at an examination). 5. ~-se: a) to become unapt or unfit. b) to disqualify. c) to fail (of promotion).

inabitado adj. 1. uninhabited. 2. unoccupied, untenanted (house). 3. deserted.

inabitável adj. m. + f. (pl. -áveis) uninhabitable.

inabordável adj. m. + f. (pl. -áveis) 1. inaccessible, unapproachable. 2. (fig.) uncommunicative.

inacabado adj. 1. unfinished, uncompleted. 2. undone. 3. unachieved, unaccomplished.

inacabável adj. m. + f. (pl. -áveis) unaccomplishable, unfinishable, interminable.

inação s. f. (pl. -ões) 1. inaction, inactivity. 2. idleness, inertness. 3. indecision. 4. dormancy. 5. indolence. 6. rest.

inaceitável adj. m. + f. (pl. -áveis) unacceptable, inadmissible.

inacessibilidade s. f. 1. inaccessibility. 2. imperviousness. 3. unapproachableness.

inacessível adj. m. + f. (pl. -íveis) 1. inaccessible. 2. unapproachable, unattainable. 3. impervious. 4. exclusive, reserved. 5. unsociable. 6. (fig.) incomprehensible, unintelligible. ‖ **inacessivelmente** adv. inaccessibly.

inacesso adj. (poet.) inaccessible.

inácia s. f. (Braz., mil., sl.) routine, rut.

inaclimável adj. m. + f. (pl. -áveis) unacclimatizable.

inacreditável adj. m. + f. (pl. -áveis) 1. incredible, unbelievable. 2. doubtful. 3. extraordinary, unheard of. 4. impossible. ‖ **inacreditavelmente** adv. incredibly.

inacusável adj. m. + f. (pl. -áveis) unaccusable, irreproachable, unimpeachable.

inadaptação s. f. (pl. -ões) 1. inadaptation, inadaptability. 2. inadequacy.

inadaptável adj. m. + f. (pl. -áveis) inadaptable, unadaptable, unsuitable.

inadequabilidade s. f. unsuitability, inadequateness.

inadequado adj. 1. inadequate. 2. improper, inappropriate. 3. unfit, unsuitable, unqualified. 4. unsatisfactory. 5. unseemly, indecent, unbecoming.

6. unserviceable, unemployable. 7. unseasonable. 8. out of place. ‖ **-amente** adv. inadequately.

inaderente adj. m. + f. inadherent, inadhesive.

inadestrado adj. unschooled, untrained.

inadestrar v. to abstain from teaching or training.

inadiável adj. m. + f. (pl. -áveis) 1. undelayable. 2. pressing, urgent. 3. unavoidable.

inadimplemento s. m. (jur.) breach of contract.

inadimplir v. to fail to carry out a contract or a condition thereof within the stipulated term.

inadmissão s. f. (pl. -ões) nonadmission, exclusion.

inadmissibilidade s. f. inadmissibility, unpermissibility.

inadmissível adj. m. + f. (pl. -íveis) inadmissible, unpermissible, unallowable.

inadvertência s. f. 1. inadvertence, inadvertency. 2. incautiousness, unwariness. 3. inconsiderateness. 4. improvidence.

inadvertido adj. 1. inadvertent. 2. headless, careless. 3. inattentive. 4. unintentional. 5. inconsiderate, rash. ‖ **-amente** adv. inadvertently.

inafiançável adj. m. + f. (pl. -áveis) unbailable.

inajá s. m. (bot.) inaja palm (Maximiliana regia).

inalação s. f. (pl. -ões) 1. inhalation, act of inhaling, drawing in of air. 2. (pharm.) inhalant: preparation intended to be inhaled.

inalado adj. wingless.

inalador s. m. 1. inhaler: a) person who inhales. b) apparatus for inhaling vapours. 2. inhalant: preparation intended to be inhaled. ‖ adj. inhaling, inhalant.

inalante adj. m. + f. inhalant.

inalar v. to inhale, breathe in, draw air into the lungs.

inalbuminado adj. 1. unalbuminated, lacking albumin. 2. (bot.) unalbuminous, lacking an endosperm.

inalcançado adj. unique, unmatched.

inalcançável adj. m. + f. (pl. -áveis) 1. unattainable, unachievable. 2. unapproachable.

inaliável adj. m. + f. (pl. -áveis) 1. unalliable, that cannot be allied. 2. unalloyable, that cannot be alloyed.

inalienabilidade s. f. inalienability, indefeasibility.

inalienação s. f. (pl. -ões) condition or state of inalienability.

inalienado adj. not alienated.

inalienar v. 1. not to be alienated or alienable. 2. to entail.

inalienável adj. m. + f. (pl. -áveis) inalienable, indefeasible. ‖ **inalienavelmente** adv. inalienably.

inalterabilidade s. f. inalterability, unalterableness, immutability.

inalterado adj. 1. unaltered, unchanged. 2. unmodified, unconverted. 3. true, same. 4. pure. 5. undisturbed, unmoved. 6. unimproved.

seu estado é praticamente ~ she is much the same.

inalterável adj. m. + f. (pl. -áveis) 1. inalterable, unalterable. 2. unchangeable, imperturbable. 3. constant. ‖ **inalteravelmente** adv. inalterably, unchangingly, unalterably.

inamável adj. m. + f. (pl. -áveis) 1. unamiable, not lovable. 2. unfriendly. 3. discourteous, ill-mannered, impolite. ‖ **inamavelmente** adv. unamiably.

inambu s. m. (ornith.) tinamou, ynambu.

inambulação s. f. (pl. -ões) 1. act of walking up and down. 2. gesticulation.

inamissibilidade s. f. inamissibleness, character of being inamissible or unlosable.

inamissível adj. m. + f. (pl. -íveis) inamissible, unlosable.

inamistoso adj. 1. unfriendly, unamiable. 2. adverse. 3. hostile.

inamolgável adj. m. + f. (pl. -áveis) undeformable, uncrushable.

inamovibilidade s. f. irremovability.
inamovível adj. m. + f. (pl. **-íveis**) 1. irremovable. 2. undeposable, not subject to removal or discharge. 3. stable, permanent. 4. inflexible, unyielding.
inamu s. m. (Braz., ornith.) tinamou, ynambu.
inane adj. m. + f. 1. inane. 2. empty, void. 3. vain, futile. 4. senseless, silly. 5. trifling, frivolous.
inânias s. f. pl. trifles, baubles, gewgaws.
inanição s. f. (pl. **-ões**) 1. ination. 2. starvation, famishment. 3. weakness from lack of nourishment.
inanidade s. f. 1. inanity, emptiness, vacuity. 2. futility. 3. silliness, senselessness. 4. frivolity.
inanimado adj. 1. inanimate. 2. lifeless, dead. 3. inert, inactive. 4. spiritless, dull. 5. soulless. 6. insentient. ‖ **-amente**, adv. inanimately, lifelessly.
inânime adj. m. + f. inanimate, lifeless, spiritless.
inanir v. to inanitiate, exhaust by lack of nourishment, famish.
inantéreo adj. (bot.) inantherate.
inapacanim s. m. (pl. **-ins**) (Braz., ornith.) eagle hawk.
inapagável adj. m. + f. (pl. **-áveis**) ineffaceable.
inapelabilidade s. f. inapellability, irrepealability.
inapelável adj. m. + f. (pl. **-áveis**) inappellable, unappealable.
inapendiculado adj. inappendiculate: 1. (zool.) not provided with appendages. 2. (bot.) not appendaged.
inaperto adj. (bot.) inapertous, not open.
inapetência s. f. inappetence, inappetency, lack of appetite.
inapetente adj. m. + f. inappetent.
inaplicabilidade s. f. inapplicability, unsuitableness, irrelevancy.
inaplicado adj. inattentive, negligent, indolent, lazy.
inaplicável adj. m. + f. (pl. **-áveis**) inapplicable, unsuitable, irrelevant.
inapreciável adj. m. + f. (pl. **-áveis**) 1. inappreciable. 2. insignificant. 3. inestimable.
inapresentável adj. m. + f. (pl. **-áveis**) unpresentable.
inapropriado adj. 1. improper, unbecoming, indecorous. 2. inadequate.
inaproveitado adj. unused, waste.
inaproveitável adj. m. + f. (pl. **-áveis**) 1. useless, unserviceable. 2. ineffectual, inefficient. 3. inapplicable, unworkable. 4. unpractical. ‖ **inaproveitavelmente** adv. uselessly, unpractically.
inaptidão s. f. (pl. **-ões**) 1. inaptness, inaptitude. 2. unfitness, inability. 3. incapacity, incapableness. 4. inefficiency. 5. unhandiness. 6. stupidity.
inapto adj. 1. inapt, unfit. 2. unable, incapable. 3. inefficient. 4. unsuitable, inappropriate. 5. unskilful, unhandy.
inaquídeos s. m. pl. (zool.) Inachidae, a family of the Decapoda order of crustaceans, including crabs, lobsters, shrimps, etc.
inarmonia s. f. inharmoniousness, dissonance, discord.
inarmônico, inarmonioso adj. 1. inharmonious, inharmonic(al). 2. unmusical. 3. dissonant, discordant. 4. (fig.) conflicting, disagreeing.
inarrável adj. m. + f. (pl. **-áveis**) 1. indescribable, inexpressible. 2. ineffable, unspeakable.
inarrecadável adj. m. + f. (pl. **-áveis**) uncollectable.
inarticulado adj. inarticulate, incapable of expressing thought in speech.
inarticulados s. m. (pl.) (zool.) Inarticulata, a class of nonarticulated brachyuran crustaceans comprising the true crabs.
inarticulável adj. m. + f. (pl. **-áveis**) unutterable, unpronounceable.
inartístico adj. inartistic, unartistic, unskilful, rude.
inascível adj. m. + f. (pl. **-íveis**) innascible.
inassiduidade s. f. want of assiduity or diligence.

inassimilável adj. m. + f. (pl. **-áveis**) nonassimilable, inassimilable.
inassinável adj. m. + f. (pl. **-áveis**) unsignable.
inatacabilidade s. f. unimpeachableness.
inatacável adj. m. + f. (pl. **-áveis**) unimpeachable, unassailable, incontestable.
inatendível adj. m. + f. (pl. **-íveis**) unable or unworthy of receiving attention.
inatingido adj. unachieved, unequal(l)ed.
inatingível adj. m. + f. (pl. **-íveis**) unattainable, unachievable, inaccessible.
inatividade s. f. 1. inactivity, inertness. 2. passiveness, passivity. 3. idleness, sluggishness. 4. retirement.
inativo adj. 1. inactive, inert. 2. passive. 3. idle, indolent. 4. unemployed, unplaced. 5. retired, withdrawn from active duty or business. 6. slow. 7. motionless, stagnant. 8. paralytic. ‖ **-amente** adv. inactively.
inato adj. 1. innate, native. 2. inborn. 3. connate, connatural, congenital. 4. by nature, organic. 5. untaught. 6. inherent. 7. unborn.
inatural adj. m. + f. (pl. **-ais**) unnatural, non-natural.
inaturalidade s. f. unnaturalness.
inaturável adj. m. + f. (pl. **-áveis**) insufferable, insupportable, intolerable.
inaudito adj. 1. unprecedented. 2. unheard of. 3. beyond example. 4. extraordinary.
inaudível adj. m. + f. (pl. **-íveis**) inaudible. ‖ **inaudivelmente** adv. inaudibly.
inauferível adj. m. + f. (pl. **-íveis**) inherent, intrinsic, that cannot be taken away.
inauguração s. f. (pl. **-ões**) 1. inauguration, initiation. 2. beginning, opening.
inaugurador s. m. inaugurator. ‖ adj. inauguratory.
inaugural adj. m. + f. (pl. **-ais**) inaugural, inauguratory, initial.
inaugurar v. 1. to inaugurate. 2. to initiate, begin, commence. 3. to institute, establish. 4. to open, start.
~am o novo edifício they consecrated the new building.
inauspicioso adj. 1. inauspicious. 2. unpromising, unfavourable. 3. unfortunate, unlucky. 4. unpropitious. 5. unlikely.
inautenticidade s. f. unauthenticity.
inautêntico adj. unauthentic, not genuine, untrue.
inavaliável adj. m. + f. (pl. **-áveis**) unappreciable.
inavegabilidade s. f. unnavigability.
inavegável adj. m. + f. (pl. **-áveis**) unnavigable, incapable of being navigated.
inca m. + f. Inca: Indian of the dominant tribe in Peru previous to the Spanish conquest. ‖ adj. Incan: of or pertaining to the Incas.
incabível adj. m. + f. (pl. **-íveis**) irrelevant, unreasonable.
incaico adj. Incan: of or pertaining to the Incas of Peru.
incalcinável adj. m. + f. (pl. **-áveis**) incalcinable.
incalculável adj. m. + f. (pl. **-áveis**) 1. incalculable, incomputable. 2. incommensurable. 3. innumerous, innumerable.
incameração s. f. incameration.
incandescência s. f. 1. incandescence, incandescency. 2. glowing heat, white heat. 3. (fig.) fervour, ardour, fervency. 4. passion, exaltation.
incandescente adj. m. + f. 1. incandescent. 2. red hot, white hot. 3. aglow. 4. fervent, ardent. 5. exalted, passionate.
lâmpada ~ incandescent lamp.
incandescer v. 1. to incandesce, glow with heat. 2. to be or become incandescent.

incansável adj. m. + f. (pl. **-áveis**) 1. tireless, untiring. 2. unweariable. 3. fatigueless, indefatigable. 4. assiduous, unremitting. 5. laborious, industrious. ‖ **incansavelmente** adv. tirelessly.
ele é um homem ~ he is an indefatigable man, (coll.) he is a hustler.
incapacidade s. f. incapacity: 1. inability, incapableness. 2. inaptitude, disablement, disability. 3. incompetence, inefficiency, unfitness. 4. impotence, impotency. 5. disqualification.
incapacitar v. 1. to incapacitate: a) make incapable. b) unfit, disable. c) deprive of a right or privilege. 2. to cripple. 3. ~-**se** to become unable, disqualified.
incapacitável adj. m. + f. (pl. **-áveis**) 1. impossible of being capacitated. 2. inconvincible, unpersuadable.
incapaz adj. m. + f. (pl. **-es**) 1. incapable: a) inapt, unfit. b) incompetent, inefficient. c) unable. d) unserviceable. e) unqualified. 2. ignorant, stupid. 3. impotent.
ela é ~ **perante a lei** she is incapable of acting in law. **ela foi** ~ **de mentir** she shrank from telling a lie.
inçar v. 1. to crowd, overcrowd, swarm (insects or other animals which fill a place to capacity). 2. to contaminate, infect. 3. to propagate, disseminate. 4. to proliferate, multiply.
incara(c)terístico adj. uncharacteristic(al), confoundingly.
incásico adj. Incan: of or pertaining to the Incas of Peru.
incasto adj. 1. unchaste: a) lewd, shameless, incontinent. b) immodest. 2. unclean. 3. dishonest.
incauto s. m. incautious man, dupe. ‖ adj. 1. incautious: a) unwary, heedless. b) imprudent, careless. 2. improvident. 3. credulous, guillible. 4. ingenuous, artless, simple. ‖ -**amente** adv. incautiously.
incender v. 1. to light, kindle. 2. to inflame, set on fire. 3. to burn. 4. to redden. 5. to stimulate, animate. 6. to arouse enthusiasm. 7. ~-**se**: a) to be inflamed, braze up. b) to be or become enthusiastic. c) to become irritated or excited.
incendiado adj. afire.
incendiar v. 1. to ignite, enkindle, emblaze. 2. to set on fire, burn down. 3. to inflame, excite. 4. (fig.) to irritate. 5. ~-**se**: a) to catch fire, be on fire. b) to be or become enthusiastic. c) to become irritated.
~**am a fazenda** they laid the farm in ashes. ~**am a efígie** they committed the image to the flames. **a cidade foi incendiada** the town went up in flames.
incendiário s. m. 1. incendiary, arsonist. 2. (coll.) fire-bug. 3. fire-brand, agitator. ‖ adj. 1. incendiary. 2. inflammatory. 3. inciting.
bomba -a incendiary bomb. **projetil** ~ incendiary bullet. **ele fez um discurso** ~ he delivered an inciting address.
incendimento s. m. 1. incension, act or effect of setting on fire. 2. incendiarism, malicious burning.
incêndio s. m. 1. conflagration, great fire. 2. burning, incension. 3. incendiary fire, arson. 4. (fig.) calamity, disaster. 5. enthusiasm.
houve um ~ a fire broke out. **ele foi acusado de** ~ **culposo** he was accused of arson. **alarma de** ~ fire alarm. **o** ~ **florestal causou grandes prejuízos** the forest fire caused great losses. **extintor de** ~ fire extinguisher.
incensação (pl. **-ões**), **incensadela** s. f. 1. incensation, burning of incense. 2. perfuming with incense. 3. flattery, adulation.

incensador s. m. 1. incenser. 2. incensorium. 3. flatterer. ‖ adj. incensing.
incensar v. 1. to incense, perfume with incense. 2. to offer incense to, worship. 3. to flatter, fawn.
incensário s. m. (also **incensório**) incense burner, incensorium, thurible.
incenso s. m. 1. incense, aromatic fumes. 2. perfume. 3. homage, worship. 4. flattery, adulation.
queimar ~ **a alguém** (fig.) to grease a person.
incensurável adj. m. + f. (pl. **-áveis**) 1. uncensurable. 2. correct, right. 3. unpolluted.
incentivar v. 1. to animate, estimulate. 2. to encourage. 3. to incite.
incentivo s. m. 1. incentive, impulse. 2. incitement, stimulant. 3. encouragement. ‖ adj. incentive, stimulative, provocative, inciting.
incentor s. m. 1. stimulator, inciter, rouser. 2. incendiary, arsonist.
incerimonioso adj. 1. unceremonious, informal. 2. off-hand(ed), casual. ‖ -**amente** adv. unceremoniously.
incerta s. f. 1. (mil. sl.) a surprise review of troops. 2. a surprise visit or act performed without prior warning or agreement.
a ~ **do governador pegou todo mundo com a mão na massa** the surprise visit of the governor caught everybody red-handed.
incerteza s. f. 1. uncertainness, uncertainty, incertitude. 2. hesitance, hesitation. 3. doubt, doubtfulness, dubiety. 4. unreliableness, insecurity, vagueness. 5. (coll.) quandery, tossup, if.
eles estavam num estado de ~ they were in a situation of touch and go. **ela o manteve na** ~ she kept him in suspense. **ficaram na** ~ they were left in the dark.
incerto adj. 1. uncertain. 2. hesitating. 3. doubtful, dubious. 4. unreliable, undependable. 5. insecure, unsure, vague. 6. equivocal, ambiguous. 7. problematic(al). 8. floating, fluctuating. 9. unsettled, unsteady, unfixed. 10. (fig.) treacherous, slippery. 11. variable. 12. fickle, inconstant. 13. capricious, fitful. 14. inexplicit, indeterminate. 15. unclear. 16. aimless. ‖ -**amente** adv. uncertainly, dubiously, unreliably, vaguely, variably, equivocally, unsteadily, aimlessly.
esse negócio é bem ~ that business is up in the air. **isto é um caso** ~ this is a doubtful case.
incessante adj. m. + f. 1. incessant, unceasing. 2. continuous, perpetual, constant. 3. unremitting, unending. 4. eternal. ‖ ~**mente** adv. 1. incessantly. 2. constantly. 3. unremittingly.
incessibilidade s. f. untransferability, unalienability.
incessível adj. m. + f. (pl. **-íveis**) untransferable, inalienable.
incestar v. 1. to defile by incest. 2. to pollute, profane. 3. to commit incest.
incesto s. m. incest, incestuousness. ‖ adj. infamous, base.
incestuoso adj. incestuous.
inchação s. f. (pl. **-ões**) (also **inchamento** m.) 1. (med.) swelling, morbid, protuberance, tumour, tumefaction. 2. (vet.) warble. 3. (pop.) lump, bulge. 4. (fig.) vanity, pride, arrogance.
ele tem uma ~ **na junta do dedão** he has a bunion on the first joint of the great toe.
inchaço s. m. (pop.) swelling, lump, bump.
inchado adj. 1. swollen, turgescent, turgid. 2. bloated, inflated, blubbery, bulgy. 3. proud, haughty. 4. elated, exalted. 5. (Braz.) not yet fully ripened (fruits).
inchar v. 1. to swell, intumesce. 2. to inflate, distend. 3. to bulge, puff up, balloon. 4. to rise. 5. to belly,

bunt (sails). 6. to grow proud or haughty. 7. to elate, exalt, flush with success.

incicatrizável adj. m. + f. (pl. **-áveis**) unhealable.

incidência s. f. 1. incidence, incidency. 2. incidental occurrence. 3. rate or scope of an occurrence. 4. act, effect or manner of falling upon.

ângulo de ~ angle of incidence.

incidentado adj. 1. chanceful, casual, incidental. 2. full of incidents.

incidental adj. m. + f. (pl. **-ais**) incidental, accidental. ‖ ~**mente** adv. incidentally; by way of parenthesis.

incidir (I) v. 1. to happen, occur. 2. to fall on or upon. 3. to arise, turn up. 4. to supervene, incur. 5. to coincide, concur.

um raio solar incidiu sobre a superfície da água a sunray struck the surface of the water.

incidir (II) v. (med.) 1. to cut into, incise. 2. to disperse, mitigate. 3. to separate.

incineração s. f. (pl. **-ões**) 1. incineration, cineration. 2. cremation. 3. burning to ashes.

incinerador s. m. 1. cinerator, incinerator. 2. crematory. ‖ adj. incinerating.

incinerar v. to incinerate, cremate, burn to ashes.

incipiente adj. m. + f. 1. beginning, initial. 2. incipient. 3. inchoate. 4. crude. ‖ ~**mente** adv. incipiently.

incircunciso s. m. uncircumcised male. ‖ adj. uncircumcised.

incircunscritível adj. m.+f. (pl. **-íveis**) uncircumscribable.

incircunscrito adj. 1. uncircumscribed. 2. unlimited, limitless, boundless.

incisa adj. (bot., zool.) incised, having marginal slits or notches.

incisão s. f. (pl. **-ões**) 1. incision, cut. 2. act of cutting. 3. separation, division (by cutting). 4. notch, kerb, nick.

incisar v. 1. to incise, cut into. 2. to notch, nick.

incisivo s. m. (anat., zool.) incisor, foretooth. ‖ adj. 1. incisive, cutting. 2. sharp, keen. 3. (fig.): a) decisive, conclusive. b) efficient. c) precise, acute (style of speech or writing). ‖ **-amente** adv. incisively.

inciso s. m. 1. interpolated proposition. 2. (rhet.) each clause of a sentence. 3. each element of a musical phrase. ‖ adj. incised, cut.

incisor s. m. 1. (anat., zool.) incisor, foretooth. 2. cutter. ‖ adj. incisive, incisorial, cutting.

incisório adj. incisorial, cutting, incisive.

incisura s. f. 1. incision, cut. 2. act of cutting. 3. separation, division (by cutting). 4. notch, kerb, nick.

incitabilidade s. f. 1. excitability, irritability. 2. (physiol.) susceptibility to the action of stimulants.

incitação s. f. (pl. **-ões**) 1. incitation, stimulation. 2. encouragement, impulsion. 3. fomentation. 4. sedition.

incitador s. m. 1. inciter, instigator. 2. prompter, rouser. 3. provoker. ‖ adj. inciting, stimulating, rousing.

incitamento s. m. 1. incitement, incitation. 2. prod, incentive, encouragement. 3. excitement, excitation. 4. provocation. 5. fomentation.

incitante adj. m. + f. incitant, inciting, inflammatory, stimulative. ‖ ~**mente** adv. incitingly.

incitar v. 1. to incite, stimulate. 2. to inspire, encourage. 3. to excite, arouse, stir. 4. to instigate. 5. to provoke, challenge. 6. to prod, set on, goad. 7. to move, impel. 8. to urge, prompt, egg on. 9. ~-**se**: a) to be or become enthusiastic. b) to become irritated or furious.

~**am-no a esforçar-se ao máximo** they put him

on his mettle. **inicitamo-los a tomar providências** we urged them to take steps. ~**am o professor ao máximo** they put the teacher to his trumps. **ele incitou as massas** he stirred up the crowd. **estas palavras** ~**am o seu interesse** these words roused his interest, (coll.) set him agog.

incitativo adj. incitive, stimulative, hortative, hortatory, stirring up.

incitável adj. m. + f. (pl. **-áveis**) incitable, liable to incitement.

incivil adj. m. + f. (pl. **-is**) 1. incivil. 2. discourteous, disrespectful. 3. ungentle, unrefined. 4. rude, rough. ‖ ~**mente** adv. uncivilly, disrespectfully, disobligingly.

incivilidade s. f. 1. incivility. 2. discourtesy, discourteousness, disrespect. 3. ungentleness, ill breeding. 4. rudeness.

incivilizado adj. 1. uncivilized. 2. uncultured. 3. rude, rough. 4. savage, barbarous, wild. 5. uncivil, unpolished, impolite.

incivilizável adj. m. + f. (pl. **-áveis**) incapable of being civilized, uneducable.

inclassificável adj. m. + f. (pl. **-áveis**) 1. unclassifiable, unclassable. 2. untidy, disorderly. 3. reprehensible, censurable. 4. unqualifiable.

inclemência s. f. 1. inclemency, mercilessness. 2. asperity, severity (weather). 3. sternness, rigour. 4. harshness, rudeness.

sofreram sob a ~ **do tempo** they suffered under the inclemency of the weather.

inclemente adj. m. + f. 1. inclement, merciless. 2. cruel, hard. 3. severe, rigorous (frequently used with reference to weather or climate). 4. disagreeable. 5. rude, rough. ‖ ~**mente** adv. rigorously.

inclinação s. f. (pl. **-ões**) 1. incline, inclination. 2. bow, nod. 3. bending. 4. vocation, disposition. 5. tendency, leaning, penchant. 6. fondness, liking, affection. 7. partiality, bias, propensity, proclivity. 8. (geom.): a) angle of inclination. b) declivity, falling gradient. 9. (astr.) inclination of an orbit. 10. (naut.): a) list. b) sheer. c) pitch. 11. slant, slope.

-ões para o vício vicious proclivities. **descobri nele uma** ~ **para a melancolia** I discovered a vein of melancholy in his character. **ela não tem** ~ **para isto** she has no bend that way. **ela não tem** ~ **para a música** she has no relish for music. **ele mostrou uma** ~ **forte para a moça** he disclosed a strong passion for the girl. **ele tem** ~ **para a bebida** he is given to drink. **um homem com** ~ **para a técnica** a person with a technical bent.

inclinado adj. 1. inclined, inclinatory, at an angle (plate Q). 2. bowed, bent. 3. well-inclined, well-disposed. 4. apt, predisposed, tending, leaning. 5. prone to, subject to, addicted. 6. fond of, liking. 7. partial, biased. 8. sloping, aslope. 9. pitching, slanting. 10. deflexed, atilt, lopsided

~ **para o mal** ill-natured. **a caixa estava num plano** ~ the box stood on an inclined plane. **a tampa estava em posição -a** the lid is at a tilt. **ele estava** ~ **a ir** he was ready to go. **o avião estava** ~ **lateralmente** the plane was in bank. **ela não estava -a a ceder** she was undisposed to yield.

inclinar v. 1. to incline, recline. 2. to bow, bend. 3. to have a bent or tendency, be well-disposed toward. 4. to be fond, like. 5. to be partial or biased. 6. to slant, slope. 7. to let hang, droop. 8. to prepare, make compliant. 9. to tip, tilt. 10. to deflect, deviate. 11. ~-**se**: a) to become inclined, bent or tilted. b) to be or become compliant. c) to bow, stoop. d) to agree to (or with).

o pai inclinou-se sobre o filho adormecido the father bent over his sleeping son. **a balança in-**

clinou-se a seu favor the balance preponderated in favour of him. **os talos ~am-se ao vento** the stalks swayed in the wind.
inclinável adj. m. + f. (pl. **-áveis**) inclinable.
ínclito adj. 1. egregious, prominent, eminent. 2. distinguished, renowned. 3. celebrated, famous.
incluído adj. 1. implicate, implicative. 2. included, enclosed, involved. 3. comprehended, comprised.
incluir v. 1. to include, enclose. 2. to comprise, comprehend. 3. to contain, add in, fall under. 4. to involve, implicate. 5. to insert, introduce. 6. to embody, embrace, encompass. 7. to cover.
inclui todos os casos it covers all cases. **os preços incluem todas as despesas** the terms are inclusive. **com as bebidas incluídas** including drinks, with drinks thrown in.
inclusão s. f. (pl. **-ões**) 1. inclusion, inclosure, enclosure. 2. incorporation, embodiment. 3. comprehensiveness, comprisal. 4. subsumption. 5. (petrog.) inclusion: foreign matter enclosed in minerals.
inclusivo adj. 1. inclusive, included, including. 2. comprehensive, comprisable. ‖ **-amente** adv. inclusively, comprehensively.
~ segunda-feira Monday inclusive.
incluso adj. included, enclosed.
incoação s. f. (pl. **-ões**) beginning, inchoation.
incoado adj. inchoate, recently or just begun.
incoadunabilidade s. f. incompatibility.
incoadunável adj. m. + f. (pl. **-áveis**) incompatible.
incoagulável adj. m. + f. (pl. **-áveis**) incoagulable.
incoativo s. m. inceptive verb. ‖ adj. inchoative, recently or just begun.
incobrável adj. m. + f. (pl. **-áveis**) uncollectible, uncoverable.
incoercibilidade s. f. incoercibility.
incoercível adj. m. + f. (pl. **-íveis**) incoercible, irrepressible.
incoerência s. f. 1. incoherence, incoherency, incongruity. 2. inconsequence. 3. contradiction.
incoerente adj. m. + f. 1. incoherent, noncoherent. 2. unconnected, disjointed. 3. inconsequential, illogical. 4. contradictory. 5. inconsistent. ‖ **~mente** adv. incoherently.
incoesão s. f. (pl. **-ões**) incohesion, incoherence.
incogitado adj. 1. thoughtless, heedless. 2. incogitant. 3. inconsiderate. 4. unthought.
incogitável adj. m. + f. (pl. **-áveis**) incogitable, unthinkable.
incógnita s. f. 1. (math.) unknown quantity. 2. unknown or disguised woman.
temos uma equação com duas ~s we have there an equation of two unknown quantities.
incógnito s. m. 1. incognito. 2. unknown or disguised man. 3. assumed name. 4. concealment. ‖ adj. incognito, unknown, disguised.
ele agiu em ~ he acted under an alias. **o príncipe viajou ~** the prince travelled incognito. **puseram em perigo o seu ~** his incognito was endangered.
incognoscibilidade s. f. incognoscibility.
incognoscível adj. m. + f. (pl. **-íveis**) incognoscible, unknowable.
íncola s. m. + f. (poet.) inhabitant.
incolor adj. m. + f. hueless, colourless, uncoloured, blank.
incólume adj. m. + f. 1. safe and sound. 2. unhurt, scarless. 3. uninjured, undamaged. 4. entire, whole.
incolumidade s. f. 1. safety, security. 2. freedom from danger. 3. well-being, soundness.
incombente adj. m. + f. bent downwards, incumbent.
incombustibilidade s. f. incombustibility.
incombustível adj. m. + f. (pl. **-íveis**) incombustible, unburnable, fire-proof.
incombusto adj. unburnt.

incomensurabilidade s. f. incommensurability, incommensurateness, incommensurableness.
incomensurável adj. m. + f. (pl. **-áveis**) 1. incommensurable, incommensurate. 2. unmeasurable, measureless. 3. unfathomable. 4. vast, immense. ‖ **incomensuravelmente** adv. immeasurably, incommensurately.
incomível adj. m. + f. (pl. **-íveis**) uneatable.
incomodada adj. f. (Braz.) menstruating, undergoing monthly courses.
incomodador s. m. troubler, importuner, botherer. ‖ adj. troubling, importunate, bothersome.
incomodante adj. m. + f. troubling, importunate, bothersome.
incomodar v. 1. to incommode, inconvenience. 2. to trouble, disturb. 3. to annoy, importune. 4. to plague, harass. 5. to be troublesome. 6. to vex, bother. 7. to ail, molest. 8. **~-se** to become irritated or tired.
não me incomodava de andar seis horas por dia I thought nothing of walking six hours a day. **tinha de incomodá-lo** I had to put you to the trouble. **não se incomode** don't trouble, never mind! **eu não me incomodo com coisa alguma** I do not care a pin. **não se incomode comigo!** never mind me. **não me incomodo** I don't mind. **não o incomode!** let him alone.
incomodativo adj. troubling, importunate, bothersome.
incomodidade s. f. 1. incommodity, incommodiousness. 2. inconvenience, disturbance. 3. indisposition. 4. uncomfortableness, uneasiness.
incômodo s. m. 1. indisposition, disease. 2. discomfort, trouble, disturbance. 3. menstruation. 4. nuisance, bother, plague. 5. fatigue, exhaustion. 6. labour, toil. ‖ adj. 1. troublesome, bothersome. 2. inconvenient. 3. cumbersome, exasperating. 4. uncomfortable, disagreeable. 5. unhandy, bulky. 6. uneasy, disturbing. 7. irksome, burdensome. ‖ **-amente** adv. disturbingly, troublesomely.
sinto causar-lhe tanto ~ I am sorry to give you so much trouble. **se não for muito ~** if it isn't too much trouble.
incomparabilidade s. f. incomparableness, matchlessness.
incomparável adj. m. + f. (pl. **-áveis**) 1. incomparable. 2. matchless, unmatched. 3. peerless. 4. unparalleled, unequaled, unrival(l)ed. ‖ **incomparavelmente** adv. incomparably, matchlessly.
ele é um orador ~ he is unparalleled as an orator.
incompassível adj. m. + f. (pl. **-íveis**) incompassionate, pitiless, merciless.
incompatibilidade s. f. incompatibility, unconformity, unsuitability.
incompatibilizar v. to make incompatible or irreconcilable.
incompatível adj. m. + f. (pl. **-íveis**) 1. incompatible, incapable of agreeing. 2. unconformable, discordant. 3. inconsistent. 4. contradictory. 5. repugnant. ‖ **incompativelmente** adv. incompatibly.
incompensado adj. unrewarded.
incompensável adj. m. + f. (pl. **-áveis**) irreparable, irrecoverable, that cannot be made right or good.
incompetência s. f. 1. incompetence, incapacity, inability, unfitness.
incompetente s. m. + f. incompetent, unfit or legally unqualified person. ‖ adj. 1. incompetent. 2. unfit, unable, incapable. 3. unqualified. ‖ **~mente** adv. incompetently, unqualifiedly.
incomplacência s. f. incompliance, unyieldingness.
incomplacente adj. m. + f. incompliant, unyielding.
incompleto adj. 1. incomplete, uncompleted. 2. fragment, fragmentary. 3. unachieved, unaccomplished.

4. unfinished, undone. 5. deficient, defective. 6. imperfect. || **-amente** adv. incompletely, fragmentarily.
Incomplexidade s. f. incomplexity, simplicity, artlessness.
Incomplexo adj. 1. incomplex. 2. simple, uncompounded. 3. artless. 4. plain, not intricate.
Incomportável adj. m. + f. (pl. **-áveis**) 1. insupportable, incomportable. 2. intolerable, unbearable.
Incompreendido adj. incomprehended, misunderstood.
Incompreensão s. f. (pl. **-ões**) 1. incomprehension, lack of understanding. 2. misunderstanding. 3. unreason, irrationality.
Incompreensibilidade s. f. incomprehensibility, incomprehensibleness, inconceivability.
Incompreensível adj. m. + f. (pl. **-íveis**) 1. incomprehensible, inconceivable. 2. inapprehensible, incredible. 3. unknowable, impenetrable. 4. inexplicable, unintelligible. 5. marvellous, transcendental, enigmatical. || **Incompreensivelmente** adv. incomprehensibly, inconceivably.
isto é ~ para mim this is beyond my grasp. **aquilo me é completamente ~** I cannot make head or tail of it. **o procedimento dela é ~** her behaviour doesn't make any sense. **o seu raciocínio é ~** his reasoning is past comprehension.
Incompreensivo adj. unappreciative.
Incompressibilidade s. f. incompressibility, incompressibleness.
Incompressível adj. m. + f. (pl. **-íveis**) 1. incompressible. 2. (fig.) inflexible, uncompromising, unyielding.
Incomprimido adj. not compressed.
Incompto adj. 1. artless, unadorned. 2. plain, primitive. 3. rough.
Incomputável adj. m. + f. (pl. **-áveis**) incomputable.
Incomum adj. m. + f. 1. uncommon, unusual. 2. abnormal. 3. scarce, rare. 4. unaccustomed.
Incomunicabilidade s. f. incommunicability, incommunicableness.
Incomunicável adj. m. + f. (pl. **-áveis**) incommunicable, noncommunicable. || **Incomunicavelmente** adv. incommunicably.
Incomutabilidade s. f. incommutability, incommutableness.
Incomutável adj. m. + f. (pl. **-áveis**) incommutable. || **Incomutavelmente** adv. incommutably.
Inconcebível adj. m. + f. (pl. **-íveis**) 1. inconceivable, incomprehensible. 2. unthinkable. 3. extraordinary. || **Inconcebivelmente** adv. inconceivably.
Inconcepto adj. (poet.) inconceivable.
Inconcessível adj. m. + f. (pl. **-íveis**) unconcessible, unpermissible.
Inconcesso adj. illicit, forbidden, not permitted or allowed.
Inconciliabilidade s. f. irreconcilability, irreconcilableness.
Inconciliação s. f. (pl. **-ões**) irreconciliation, irreconcilement.
Inconciliável adj. m. + f. (pl. **-áveis**) irreconcilable, incompatible. || **Inconciliavelmente** adv. irreconcilably.
Inconcludente adj. m. + f. 1. inconclusive, indeterminate. 2. illogical.
Inconclusivo adj. inconclusive.
de maneira -a inconclusively.
Inconcluso adj. unfinished, incomplete.
Inconcordável adj. m. + f. (pl. **-áveis**) irreconcilable, unconcordable, uncorresponding, incompatible.
Inconcusso adj. 1. firm, unmoved. 2. unshaken, inconcussible. 3. incorruptible. 4. incontestable, indubitable. 5. (fig.) austere.
Incondicionado s. m. the infinite, absoluteness. || adj. inconditional, absolute, unconditioned.

Incondicional adj. m. + f. (pl. **-ais**) 1. unconditional, without qualification or limitation. 2. absolute, categorical. 3. termless. || **~mente** adv. unconditionally.
renderam-se ~mente they surrendered unconditionally.
Incondicionalidade s. f. unconditionality, unconditionalness, absoluteness.
Incondicionalismo s. m. doctrine or existence of unconditional power, absolutism, despotism.
Incôndito adj. 1. incondite. 2. disorderly, disarranged, irregular. 3. confused. 4. ill constructed. 5. unpolished, rude.
Inconexão s. f. (pl. **-ões**) inconnexion, inconnection, disconnection.
Inconexo adj. 1. unconnected, disconnected. 2. disengaged, detached. 3. independent. 4. inharmonic, discordant.
Inconfessado adj. 1. unconfessed, unadmitted. 2. unconfessant.
Inconfessável adj. m. + f. (pl. **-áveis**) unconfessable.
Inconfesso adj. unconfessed, unacknowledged.
Inconfidência s. f. 1. unconfidence, lack of confidence. 2. infidelity, treachery. 3. disloyalty. 4. distrust.
Inconfidência Mineira (hist.) revolutionary movement against the Portuguese colonialism in Brazil.
Inconfidente s. m. (Braz., hist.) partisan of the **Inconfidência Mineira**. || adj. m. + f. 1. disloyal. 2. unfaithful, false. 3. treacherous. 4. indiscreet.
Inconformado s. m. a person not in agreement, unresigned. || adj. in disagreement, unresigned.
Inconfortável adj. m. + f. (pl. **-áveis**) uneasy, uncomfortable. || **Inconfortavelmente** adv. uncomfortably.
Inconfundível adj. m. + f. (pl. **-íveis**) 1. unconfoundable, unmistakable. 2. distinctive, distinct. || **Inconfundivelmente** adv. unconfoundably, distinctly.
Incongelado adj. not congealed or frozen.
Incongelável adj. m. + f. (pl. **-áveis**) incongealable, uncongealable.
Incongruência s. f. 1. incongruence, incongruity. 2. inconsistency. 3. unsuitableness. 4. inconsequence. 5. incompatibility.
Incongruente adj. m. + f. 1. incongruent, incongruous. 2. inconsistent. 3. unsuitable, contradictory. 4. incompatible. || **~mente** adv. incongruously.
Incongruidade s. f. incongruity, incongruousness.
Incôngruo adj. incongruous, inconsistent, unsuitable. || **~amente** adv. incongruously.
Inconho adj. (bot.) coalescent.
Inconivente adj. m. + f. unconniving.
Inconjugável adj. m. + f. (pl. **-áveis**) unconjugable.
Inconquistabilidade s. f. unconquerableness.
Inconquistado adj. 1. unconquered. 2. (fig.) unsubmissive.
Inconquistável adj. m. + f. (pl. **-áveis**) unconquerable, unsubduable, invincible.
Inconsciência s. f. 1. unconsciousness. 2. (med.) coma. 3. (fig.) inconsiderateness, unscrupulousness.
Inconsciencioso adj. 1. unconscientious. 2. unscrupulous. || **-amente** adv. unconscientiously, unscrupulously.
Inconsciente s. m. + f. 1. person acting unconsciously or unknowingly. 2. m. (psych.) the unconscious. || adj. 1. unconscious, unknowing. 2. senseless. 3. (psych.) automatic. 4. unwitting. 5. unaware. || **~mente** adv. unconsciously, unknowingly, unwittingly.
ofendemo-lo ~mente we offended him unwittingly.
Incônscio adj. 1. unconscious, unknowing. 2. insensible, senseless. 3. (psych.) automatic. 4. unwitting. 5. unaware.

inconseqüência s. f. 1. Inconsequence. 2. Inconclusiveness. 3. Incongruence. 4. Inconnection, Inconnexion. 5. contradiction. 6. (logic) Inconsequent illations.
inconseqüente adj. m. + f. 1. Inconsequent(ial). 2. inconsistent. 3. inconclusive. 4. disconnected, incoherent. 5. contradictory. || ~**mente** inconsequently, inconsequentially.
inconsideração s. f. (pl. -ões) 1. inconsideration, inconsiderateness. 2. thoughtlessness, carelessness. 3. indiscretion, indiscreetness. 4. rashness, precipitation.
inconsiderado adj. 1. inconsiderate. 2. thoughtless, careless. 3. indiscreet. 4. rash, precipitate. 5. inconstant, unreliable. || -**amente** adv. inconsiderately.
inconsiderável adj. m. + f. (pl. -áveis) inconsiderable, unimportant, trivial.
inconsistência s. f. 1. inconsistence, inconsistency. 2. incongruity, discrepancy. 3. contrariety, contradiction. 4. instability (physical or moral). 5. incoherence.
inconsistente adj. m. + f. 1. inconsistent, not consistent. 2. incongruous, discrepant. 3. contradictory. 4. unstable (in physical or moral sense). 5. incoherent.
inconsolado adj. unconsoled, uncomforted.
inconsolável adj. m. + f. (pl. -áveis) inconsolable, disconsolate. || **inconsolavelmente** adv. inconsolably, disconsolately.
inconsonância s. f. inconsonance, discordance, want of harmony.
inconsonante adj. m. + f. inconsonant, inharmonious.
inconstância s. f. 1. inconstancy. 2. unstableness, unsteadiness. 3. instability, impermanency. 4. fickleness, uncertainty. 5. variability, changeability. 6. mutability, mutation.
inconstante adj. m. + f. 1. inconstant, not constant. 2. unstable, unsteady. 3. fickle, capricious, uncertain. 4. variable, changing, changeable, mutable. 5. unfaithful, disloyal, untrue. 6. wavering, shifty. || ~**mente** adv. inconstantly, unstably, variably.
inconstitucional adj. m. + f. (pl. -ais) unconstitutional, unstatutable. || ~**mente** adv. unconstitutionally.
inconstitucionalidade s. f. unconstitutionality.
inconsulto adj. 1. unconsulted. 2. unconsulting, unadvised, rash. 3. thoughtless, inconsiderate.
inconsumível adj. m. + f. (pl. -íveis) inconsumable, inconsumptible. || **inconsumivelmente** adv. inconsumably.
inconsunto adj. unconsumed, undestroyed.
inconsútil adj. m. + f. (pl. -úteis) 1. seamless. 2. whole, of one piece.
incontaminado adj. 1. unpolluted, undefiled. 2. incontaminate. 3. not adulterated. 4. pure.
incontável adj. m. + f. (pl. -áveis) 1. uncountable, countless. 2. innumerable, numberless. 3. untold, incalculable.
incontentável adj. m. + f. (pl. -áveis) uncontentable, unsatisfiable.
incontestabilidade s. f. incontestability, indisputableness, undeniableness, incontrovertibility.
incontestado adj. 1. uncontested, undisputed. 2. unrefuted, uncontradicted.
incontestável adj. m. + f. (pl. -áveis) 1. incontestable, indisputable. 2. unquestionable, undeniable, undubitable. 3. certain, valid, sure. || **incontestavelmente** adv. incontestably, undoubtedly.
a alegação é ~ the assertion is beyond dispute.
inconteste adj. m. + f. uncontested, undisputed.
incontido adj. 1. uncurbed, unrestricted. 2. unconstrained. 3. not included.

incontinência s. f. 1. incontinence, incontinency. 2. lack of restraint. 3. unchasteness, licentiousness.
incontinente s. m. + f. licentious person. || adj. 1. incontinent, unrestrained. 2. unchaste, licentious. 3. immediate, prompt. || ~**mente** adv. incontinently.
incontinenti adv. immediately, incontinently, forthwith.
incontingência s. f. 1. certainty, surety. 2. necessity.
incontingente adj. m. + f. 1. not contingent, certain. 2. necessary.
incontinuidade s. f. incontinuity, incontinuousness.
incontínuo adj. incontinuous.
incontrastável adj. m. + f. (pl. -áveis) 1. firm, stable. 2. irresistible. 3. irrevocable.
incontrito adj. unrepentant, unrepenting.
incontrolável adj. m. + f. (pl. -áveis) 1. uncontrollable. 2. unruly, ungovernable. 3. unworkable. 4. unmoved, unshaken. || **incontrolavelmente** adv. uncontrollably.
incontroverso adj. 1. uncontroverted, undisputed. 2. incontestable. 3. exact, accurate.
incontrovertível adj. m. + f. (pl. -íveis) incontrovertible, undisputable.
inconvencível adj. m. + f. (pl. -íveis) unconverted, unconvincible.
inconveniência s. f. 1. inconvenience, inconveniency. 2. unseemliness, impolicy. 3. inexpediency. 4. incommodiousness, incommodity. 5. unworthiness.
inconveniente s. m. 1. inconvenience, embarrassment. 2. trouble, nuisance. || adj. m. + f. 1. improper, unseemly, unbecoming. 2. unsuitable, inopportune. 3. rude, impolite. 4. unworthy. || ~**mente** adv. unseemly, inopportunely.
inconversível, inconvertível adj. m. + f. (pl. -íveis) inconvertible. || **inconversivelmente** adv. inconvertibly.
inconvicto adj. unconvinced, not persuaded.
incoordenação s. f. (pl. -ões) incoordination, lack of coordination.
incorporação s. f. (pl. -ões) 1. incorporation, embodiment. 2. grouping, assembly. 3. affiliation. 4. annexation.
incorporado adj. incorporated, consolidate.
incorporador s. m. incorporator.
incorporar v. 1. to incorporate. 2. to form into a body, embody. 3. to combine, joint, unite. 4. to connect, link up. 5. to consolidate, merge (two or more corporations). 6. to congregate, assemble. 7. to affiliate, attach, associate. 8. ~**-se**: a) to be or become incorporated. b) to partake of, share in.
incorporeidade s. f. incorporeity, immateriality.
incorpóreo adj. 1. incorporeal. 2. immaterial, unsubstantial. 3. unfleshly, bodiless. 4. spiritual.
incorreção s. f. (pl. -ões) 1. incorrection, incorrectness. 2. inaccuracy. 3. error, mistake. 4. uncivility, impoliteness.
incorrer v. 1. to incur. 2. to run into, fall within. 3. to become liable to (through one's own actions), bring upon o. s. 4. to occur, come to pass, pass. **~ sempre no mesmo erro** to fall always into the same error. **eles ~am na multa de...** they incurred into the fine of...
incorreto adj. 1. incorrect, not correct. 2. faulty, wrong. 3. inaccurate. 4. erroneous. 5. improper, impolite, uncivil. 6. false, untrue. 7. unfair, unjust. || -**amente** adv. incorrectly, wrong(ly), impolitely, untruly.
incorrigibilidade s. f. incorrigibility, incorrigibleness.
incorrigível adj. m. + f. (pl. -íveis) 1. incorrigible. 2. incurable, hopeless. 3. unregenerate, indurate. 4. unimprovable. 5. engrained, confirmed. || **incorrigi-**

velmente adv. Incorrigibly, unregenerately, confirmedly.

um beberrão ~ a sad drunkard. **ele é um tolo** ~ he is no end of a fool.

incorrimento s. m. 1. incurrence. 2. incursion, attack.

incorrutibilidade, incorruptibilidade s. f. 1. incorruptibility, incorruptibleness. 2. integrity, honesty, uprightness. 3. austerity.

incorrutível, incorruptível adj. m. + f. (pl. -íveis) 1. incorruptible. 2. not easily impaired or spoiled. 3. unbribable. 4. untainted. 5. undecayable. 6. just, fair. 7. righteous. ‖ **incorru(p)tivelmente** adv. incorruptibly.

incorrutivo, incorruptivo adj. incorruptive, not liable to corruption or decay.

incorruto, incorrupto adj. incorrupt, unspoiled, undefiled.

incredibilidade s. f. incredibility, incredibleness.

incredulidade s. f. 1. incredulity. 2. ungodliness, faithlessness. 3. unbelief, disbelief. 4. distrust, doubt. 5. skepticism.

incrédulo s. m. skeptic, agnostic, unbeliever. ‖ adj. 1. incredulous. 2. faithless, ungodly. 3. unbelieving. 4. skeptical, impious. 5. distrustful. ‖ **incredulamente** adv. incredulously, unbelievingly.

incrementar v. to develop, augment, increase, swell.

incremento s. m. 1. increment, incrementation. 2. development. 3. increase, growth. 4. swell, flush. 5. boom.

increpação s. f. (pl. -ões) increpation, rebuke, censure, reprimand.

increpador s. m. reprimander, rebuker, reprover.

increpante adj. m. + f. reprimanding, rebuking.

increpar v. to chide, rebuke, reprimand.

incréu s. m. skeptic, agnostic, unbeliever.

incriado adj. uncreated, self-existent.

incriminação s. f. (pl. -ões) incrimination, accusation, imputation.

incriminar v. 1. to incriminate. 2. to accuse, criminate. 3. to charge, inculpate. 4. to consider as a crime.

eles o ~**am falsamente** they falsely incriminated him.

incriticável adj. m. + f. (pl. -áveis) uncriticisable, above critic.

incristalizável adj. m. + f. (pl. -áveis) uncrystallizable.

incrível adj. m. + f. (pl. -íveis) 1. incredible, not credible. 2. unbelievable, inconceivable. 3. extraordinary, remarkable, marvellous. 4. inexplicable. 5. strange, eccentric. ‖ **incrivelmente** adv. incredibly, remarkably.

é ~ it is incredible. **foi uma** ~ **bobagem** it was an unutterable nonsense. **ele contou uma história** ~ he told us an incredible story, a cock-and-bull story. **está doendo incrivelmente** it hurts unbelievably, like hell.

incruento adj. bloodless, without bloodshed.

incrustação s. f. (pl. -ões) 1. incrustation, crustation. 2. crust, coat. 3. inlay. 4. (geol.) efflorescence. 5. deposit(s).

incrustador s. m. inlay worker, intarsist. ‖ adj. incrusting, incrustive.

incrustante adj. m. + f. incrustate, incrusting, incrustive.

incrustar v. 1. to incrust, encrust. 2. to plate, coat. 3. to inlay, work in intarsia.

incubação s. f. (pl. -ões) incubation: 1. hatching, brooding. 2. (fig.) elaboration, preparation. 3. (med.) interval between infection and the development of its first symptoms.

incubador s. m. 1. brooding animal or bird. 2. brooder, incubator. ‖ adj. brooding, hatching, incubative.

incubadora s. f. 1. incubator, brooder. 2. hatchery.

incubar v. 1. to incubate, hatch, sit upon eggs. 2. (fig.) to contrive, scheme. 3. to draw plans, project.

íncubo s. m. 1. incubus, cacodemon. 2. nightmare. ‖ adj. oppressive, nightmarish.

incude s. f. (anat., poet.) anvil.

inculca s. f. 1. inculcation. 2. implantation. 3. (fig.) suggestion. 4. search, quest. 5. research. 6. information, inquiry.

inculcadeira s. f. inculcatrix, female go-between or telltale.

inculcador s. m. inculcator.

inculcar v. 1. to inculcate. 2. to implant, instil. 3. to indoctrinate, drum into. 4. to indicate, point out. 5. to propose, propound. 6. to advise. 7. ~**-se**: a) to offer or present itself. b) to impose itself as advantageous. c) to ingratiate o. s.

ele inculca latim aos alunos he grinds Latin into his pupils. **inculcou-se na alma dela** it was engraved in her soul.

inculpabilidade s. f. inculpableness, unimpeachableness, blamelessness.

inculpação s. f. (pl. -ões) 1. inculpation, imputation. 2. charge, accusation, incrimination.

inculpado adj. inculpable, innocent, blameless.

inculpar v. 1. to inculpate. 2. to expose to blame, incriminate. 3. to censure, reprimand. 4. to charge, accuse. 5. ~**-se** to incriminate o. s.

inculpável adj. m. + f. (pl. -áveis) inculpable, faultless, innocent, unimpeachable. ‖ **inculpavelmente** adv. inculpably, unimpeachably.

inculpe adj. m. + f. blameless, inculpable, guiltless, innocent.

inculposo adj. guiltless, inculpable.

incultivável adj. m. + f. (pl. -áveis) 1. uncultivable, untillable. 2. unproductive.

inculto adj. 1. uncultivated, uncultured. 2. unreclaimed, untilled, fallow, unlaboured. 3. rude, rough, rugged. 4. untaught, untutored, uninstructed, unschooled. 5. desert. 6. wild, savage. 7. natural.

incultura s. f. inculture, lack of culture, wildness.

incumbência s. f. 1. incumbency. 2. duty, responsibility, obligation. 3. task, commission, charge. 4. undertaking, mission. 5. errand. 6. commendation.

uma ~ **inauspiciosa** an unlikely errand.

incumbido adj. entrusted.

incumbir v. 1. to encharge, charge with. 2. to undertake, engage in. 3. to entrust, commission with. 4. to task, assign a duty to. 5. to be incumbent upon. 6. to be one's duty. 7. ~**-se** to take upon o. s., take charge of.

ele se incumbiu da tarefa he took this task upon himself.

incunábulo s. m. incunabulum, any book printed before 1500 A.D.

incurabilidade s. f. incurability, incurableness.

incurável adj. m. + f. (pl. -áveis) 1. incurable, not curable. 2. irremediable, past cure. 3. hopeless. 4. irreparable, incorrigible. ‖ **incuravelmente** adv. incurably.

incúria s. f. 1. negligence, neglect. 2. carelessness, thoughtlessness. 3. inertia, sluggishness. 4. disregard.

incurial adj. m. + f. (pl. -ais) irregular, unlawful.

incurialidade s. f. irregularity, infraction of legal rules.

incuriosidade s. f. incuriosity, incuriousness.

incurioso adj. 1. incurious, deficient in interest. 2. careless, negligent. 3. indifferent. 4. indolent.

incursão s. f. (pl. -ões) 1. incursion, invasion. 2. raid, foray. 3. attack, inroad. 4. infection, contamination.

incurso s. m. incursion, invasion. ‖ adj. subject to a penalty or fine.

ser ~ to incur a penalty.

incurvado adj. incurvate, curved inward or upward.
incuso adj. incuse, stamped on one side only.
incutir v. 1. to infuse, instil. 2. to inspire, rouse. 3. to suggest. 4. to inculcate. 5. to imbue.
incutiu-o à força no menino he inculcated it on the boy, flogged it into the boy.
inda adv. (poet.) still, yet.
indagação s. f. (pl. -ões) 1. searching, search. 2. indagation. 3. quest, inquiry. 4. investigation. 5. examination.
~ da opinião pública survey of public opinion, (U. S. A.) canvass, straw poll.
indagador s. m. searcher, inquirer, querist.
indagar v. 1. to enquire, inquire. 2. to indagate. 3. to pry into, poke about, ferret out. 4. to investigate. 5. to query, question, quest. 6. to search.
ele indagou o caminho he inquired the way. eles ~am as horas they asked for the time. ~am a verdade they inquired into the truth.
indaiá s. m. (Braz., bot.) pindova palm.
indébito adj. 1. undue. 2. not demandable, not owing. 3. not right, unjust. 4. unfair.
indecência s. f. 1. indecency. 2. indecorousness, impropriety, indelicacy. 3. obscenity, immorality. 4. dishonesty. 5. trouble, inconvenience.
indecente adj. m. + f. 1. indecent. 2. indecorous, improper, indelicate. 3. obscene, immoral. 4. dishonest. 5. inconvenient. 6. shameful. || ~mente adv. indecently, shamefully.
indecidido adj. 1. undecided. 2. unsettled. 3. wavering, vacillating. 4. unresolved.
indecifrável adj. m. + f. (pl. -áveis) 1. indecipherable, undecipherable, illegible. 2. (fig.) intricate, obscure.
indecisão s. f. (pl. -ões) 1. indecision, irresolution. 2. wavering, vacillation. 3. hesitation. 4. indecisiveness, indetermination. 5. doubt.
indeciso adj. 1. undecided, indecisive. 2. wavering, vacillating. 3. hesitant, hesitative. 4. unconfirmed. 5. dubious, doubtful, unsure. 6. drawn. 7. unresolved. || -amente adv. undecidedly.
estou ~ I have not made up my mind. ela estava -a she was undecided, (coll.) she sat (stood) on the fence. o jogo estava ~ the game (match) was drawn. a questão continuou -a the question hung at poise.
indeclarável adj. m. + f. (pl. -áveis) 1. undeclarable. 2. unexplicable. 3. unspeakable.
indeclinabilidade s. f. indeclinability, inevitability, irrecusability.
indeclinável adj. m. + f. (pl. -áveis) indeclinable, inevitable, irrecusable. || indeclinavelmente adv. indeclinably.
indecomponível adj. m. + f. (pl. -íveis) indecomposable.
indecoro s. m. 1. indecorum, indecorousness. 2. unseemliness, impropriety. 3. indecency. 4. shamelessness.
indecoroso, indécoro adj. 1. indecorous. 2. unseemly, improper, unbecoming. 3. indecent. 4. shameless. 5. unworthy. || -amente adv. indecorously.
indefectibilidade s. f. indefectibility.
indefectível adj. m. + f. (pl. -veis) indefectible, unfailable, not liable to failure or decay.
indefensável, indefensível adj. m. + f. (pl. -áveis, -íveis) indefensible, unsustainable. || indefensavelmente adv. indefensibly.
indefensabilidade, indefensibilidade s. f. indefensibility, indefensibleness.
indefenso adj. 1. undefended. 2. defenceless, unprotected. 3. unarmed. 4. (fig.) weak.
indeferido adj. 1. rejected, refused. 2. not granted. 3. undispatched.

indeferimento s. m. 1. denial, refusal. 2. rejection (of a request).
indeferir v. to refuse, reject a demand or petition, not to grant.
indeferível adj. m. + f. (pl. -íveis) ungrantable.
indefeso adj. 1. undefended. 2. defenceless, unprotected. 3. unarmed. 4. (fig.) weak.
indeficiente adj. m. + f. 1. indeficient, not deficient. 2. enough. 3. unfailing, everlasting.
indefinido s. m. indefiniteness, vagueness, uncertainty. || adj. 1. indefinite, not defined. 2. vague, uncertain. 3. generic. 4. indeterminate, inexplicit. 5. unlimited. 6. uncertain in number (of floral whorls). 7. (gram.) not defining or determining (article, pron., etc.). || -amente adv. indefinitely, vaguely, unlimitedly.
tomaram em consideração os fatores ~s they took into consideration the imponderables.
indefinito adj. indefinite, vague, indeterminate.
indefinível adj. m. + f. (pl. -íveis) indefinable, undefinable, vague.
indeiscência s. f. (bot.) indehiscence.
indeiscente adj. m. + f. (bot.) indehiscent, not opening spontaneously when mature.
indelebilidade s. f. indelibility, undelebility, quality of being indelible.
indelével adj. m. + f. (pl. -éveis) indelible, indeleble, ineffaceable, incapable of being obliterated. || indelevelmente adv. ineffaceably.
tinta ~ marking ink.
indeliberação s. f. (pl. -ões) indeliberation, irresolution, inertia.
indeliberado adj. 1. indeliberate, unpremeditated. 2. irresolute, inert. || -amente adv. indeliberately.
indelicadeza s. f. 1. indelicacy. 2. incivility, tactlessness. 3. unkindness. 4. disregard. 5. unfriendliness.
indelicado adj. 1. indelicate, indecent. 2. impolite, tactless. 3. unkind, rough. 4. disrespectful, gross. 5. unfriendly, ungenial. || -amente adv. indelicately, unkindly, tactlessly.
indelineável adj. m. + f. (pl. -áveis) vague, indistinct, undelineative.
indemissível adj. m. + f. (pl. -veis) undismissible, undismissable.
indemonstrável adj. m. + f. (pl. -áveis) undemonstrable.
indene adj. m. + f. undamaged, unhurt, safe and sound.
indenidade s. f. 1. indemnity. 2. indemnification. 3. reparation, reimbursement. 4. (fig.) forgiving.
indenização s. f. (pl. -ões) 1. indemnity, indemnification. 2. compensation, restitution, reparation.
~ por desemprego unemployment compensation.
indenizador s. m. indemnitor, indemnifier, reimburser. || adj. indemnifying.
indenizar v. 1. to indemnify (from), secure against loss. 2. to compensate, repay. 3. to redeem, recoup. 4. to recompense.
~ por uma perda to make up for a loss. ~am-lhe as despesas they repaid his expenses.
indenizável adj. m. + f. (pl. -áveis) subject to reparation or indemnification.
independência s. f. 1. independence, independency. 2. freedom, liberty. 3. autarky, autonomy.
dia da ~ Independence Day (U. S. A.: July 4th; Brazil: September 7th).
independente s. m. 1. one who acts independently. 2. (rel.) Congregationalist. || adj. m. + f. 1. independent, not dependent. 2. free, unattached. 3. autonomous. 4. liberal. 5. sovereign. 6. unrestricted. 7. (rel.) Congregational. 8. (coll.) rich, well-to-do. || ~mente adv. independently, autonomically.

ele é ~ he is independent, he stands on his own legs, (coll.) he paddles his own canoe.
indesatável adj. m. + f. (pl. -áveis) that cannot be untied or unfastened, indissoluble.
indesconfiável adj. m. + f. (pl. -áveis) (Braz., pop.) unsuspecting.
indescritibilidade s. f. indescribableness, indescribability.
indescritível adj. m. + f. (pl. -íveis) 1. indescribable. 2. unutterable, unspeakable. 3. extraordinary, remarkably. ‖ **indescritivelmente** adv. indescribably, unspeakably.
indescritivelmente belo too beautiful for words.
indesculpável adj. m. + f. (pl. -áveis) inexcusable, unpardonable, unjustifiable, culpable.
indesejado adj. undesired, unwished, uncalled for.
foi bastante ~ it was very unwelcome, it came as a great blow.
indesejável s. m. + f. (pl. -áveis) 1. undesired person, undesired foreigner. 2. undesirability. ‖ adj. 1. undesirable, undesired. 2. unwished for, unwelcome.
indestronável adj. m. + f. (pl. -áveis) undethronable.
indestrutibilidade s. f. indestructibility, indestructibleness.
indestrutível adj. m. + f. (pl. -íveis) undestructible, undestroyable.
indeterminação s. f. (pl. -ões) 1. undetermination, indeterminateness. 2. hesitation, wavering. 3. inertia. 4. irresoluteness.
indeterminado s. m. indeterminate thing or person. ‖ adj. 1. indeterminate, indetermined. 2. indefinite, vague. 3. irresolute, vacillating, wavering. 4. (math.) indefinite (as to the number of solutions or values). 5. uncertain in number (of floral whorls). 6. unresolved. ‖ -amente adv. indeterminately.
indeterminar v. 1. to make indetermined, uncertain or vague. 2. ~-se to be irresolute, not to come to a resolution.
indeterminável adj. m. + f. (pl. -áveis) indeterminable, undefinable, unascertainable. ‖ **indeterminavelmente** adv. indeterminably.
indeterminismo s. m. (philos.) indeterminism: doctrine that actions are not exclusively determined by antecedent causes.
indevassável adj. m. + f. (pl. -áveis) inaccessible, unpenetrable.
indevido adj. 1. undue, not due. 2. improper. 3. unjustified. 4. inconvenient. ‖ -amente adv. unduly, wrong(ly).
indevoção s. f. (pl. -ões) indevotion, impiety, irreligion.
indevoto adj. undevout, irreligious, impious.
índex (I) s. m. Index Librorum Prohibitorum: catalogue of books which Roman Catholics were formerly forbidden to read.
pôr no ~ to forbid something, to point out as dangerous. eles o puseram no ~ they blacklisted him.
índex (II) s. m. (pl. índices) index-finger, forefinger. ‖ adj. of or referring to the index-finger.
indez s. m. 1. nest-egg. 2. (fig.) very sensitive or touchy person. 3. naughty or bawling child.
indiada s. f. (Braz.) group of South American Indians.
indianismo s. m. Indianism: 1. word or phrase peculiar to Indian languages. 2. characteristic Indian custom or mode of thought. 3. study and science of Indian culture. 4. (Braz.) literature on the American Indian(s).
indianista s. m. + f. 1. student of the languages and history of India. 2. (Braz.) ethnologist devoted to the study of history and customs of American Indians.

indiano s. m. 1. Indian: native or inhabitant of India. 2. American Indian: aboriginal native of North and/or South America. ‖ adj. Indian.
andaram em fila ~a they walked in single file (or Indian file).
indicação s. f. (pl. -ões) 1. indication, act of pointing out. 2. manifestation, symptom. 3. sign, token, evidence. 4. information, hint, suggestion.
ele forneceu uma ~ incompleta he made an incomplete statement.
indicado adj. well-timed, right, convenient.
conforme ~ embaixo as under.
indicador s. m. 1. index-finger, forefinger. 2. indicator (plate E 12). 3. (mech.) dial, gauge, recorder, pointer (plate B 4). 4. guide-book. 5. advertising page of a newspaper. ‖ adj. 1. indicatory, indicative. 2. of or relative to the index-finger.
~ de lugar (movie theatre, etc.), also (sl.) lanterninha, vaga-lume usher. ~ de nível de óleo oil gauge. ~ de velocidade speedometer. ~ do destino de trens destination board. poste ~ finger post, handpost.
indicana s. f. (chem.) indican, uroxanthin.
indicante adj. m. + f. indicant, indicatory.
indicar v. 1. to indicate, outpoint. 2. to denote, demonstrate, show. 3. to reveal, disclose, hint. 4. to determine, decide. 5. to enumerate. 6. to propose, propound. 7. to guide, advise. 8. to evince, betoken.
indicamo-lo para o cargo we proposed him for the office. ~emos a função de cada elemento we shall point out the function of each element.
indicativo s. m. 1. mark, sign. 2. indication. 3. (gram.) indicative mode. ‖ adj. 1. indicative, indicant. 2. expressive. ‖ -amente adv. indicatively.
indicção s. f. (pl. -ões) 1. indiction. 2. (hist.) ecclesiastical fiscal period of 15 years. 3. declaration, proclamation. 4. rule, principle. 5. prescription.
índice s. m. 1. table, index. 2. table of contents. 3. catalogue, register. 4. report. 5. (mech.) pointer, hand, needle, indicator. 6. alphabetical list. 7. enumeration.
~ de endereços comerciais commercial directory. ~ de mortalidade death rate. ~ de octana octane number or rating. ~ de preços price index. ~ pluviométrico precipitation or rainfall indicator.
indiciado s. m. the accused, defendant.
indiciação s. f. (pl. -ões) circumstantial evidence.
indiciador s. m. informer, accuser.
indiciar v. 1. to denounce, inform against. 2. to accuse. 3. to arraign, indict. 4. to point out indicia or circumstantial evidence in a criminal process.
indiciativo adj. adumbrative. ‖ -amente adv. adumbratively.
indício s. m. 1. indicium (pl. indicia). 2. indication. 3. clue, trace, vestige. 4. evidence, proof. 5. symptom. 6. sign, mark, token.
índico adj. Indian: of, pertaining to or relating to India.
indículo s. m. 1. little or insignificant index. 2. inventory. 3. report, enumeration.
indiferença s. f. 1. indifference, indifferency. 2. unconcern, aloofness. 3. negligence, carelessness. 4. coldness, apathy. 5. impassiveness, stoicism. 6. scorn, contempt. 7. insensitiveness, morbid inconscience. 8. (phys.) inertia.
indiferente s. m. + f. dispassionate, irresponsive or cold-hearted person, indifferentist. ‖ adj. 1. indifferent, unconcerned. 2. negligent, careless. 3. cold, apathetic(al). 4. impassive, unresponsive. 5. scornful, contemptuous. 6. (chem.) neutral. 7. insensitive. ‖ ~mente adv. indifferently, etc.
ela lhe deu um olhar ~ she gave him a cold

look. **isso para mim é** ~ that's all the same to me, that leaves me cold, (U. S. A., sl.) I don't care a cuss. ~ **ao perigo, ele saiu** regardless to danger he went out. **sou** ~ **à política** I am unconcerned with politics.

indiferentismo s. m. indifferentism, adiaphorism.

indiferentista s. m. + f. indifferentist, adiaphorist.

indifusível adj. m. + f. (pl. **-íveis**) indiffusible.

indígena s. m. + f. native, indigene, aboriginal, aborigine, autochthon. || adj. indigenous, native, aboriginal, inlandish.

tratava-se de plantas ~s they were autochthon plants. **ela viveu como os** ~s she went native.

indigência s. f. 1. indigence. 2. poverty, poorness. 3. penury, want, need. 4. misery.

indigente s. m. + f. pauper, beggar, poor. || adj. 1. indigent, poor. 2. needy, wretched. 3. poverty-stricken. 4. necessitous, penurious. || ~**mente** adv. indigently.

indigerível adj. m. + f. (pl. **-íveis**) indigestible, indigestive. || **indigerivelmente** adv. indigestibly.

indigestão s. f. (pl. **-ões**) indigestion, dyspepsia, surfeit.

indigestar v. to suffer from indigestion, be affected by indigestion.

indigesto adj. 1. indigestible, indigestive. 2. raw. 3. (fig.) incomprehensible. 4. (fig.) unendurable.

foi um livro ~ it was a book hard to digest.

indígete s. m. venerated hero, demigod.

indigitar v. 1. to indigitate, indicate. 2. to point out, show. 3. to designate. 4. to suggest, recommend.

indignação s. f. (pl. **-ões**) 1. indignation, vexation. 2. resentment, wrath. 3. anger. 4. abhorrence.

indignado adj. 1. indignant, vexed. 2. provoked, exasperated. 3. angry. || **-amente** adv. indignantly, unworthily, despicably.

aquilo me deixou muito ~ it just sickened me. **a multidão -a avançou** the angry crowd pushed ahead.

indignar v. 1. to cause indignation. 2. to provoke, make angry. 3. to offend. 4. ~**-se** to be offended, angry with.

indignidade s. f. 1. indignity. 2. unworthiness, shamelessness. 3. disrespect, slight. 4. offense, insult. 5. contemptuous or dishonourable conduct, nefariousness. 6. degradation.

indigno adj. 1. unworthy, worthless. 2. unmerited, undeserving. 3. base, ignoble. 4. inconvenient. 5. despicable. 6. shameful. || **-amente** adv. unworthily. ~ **de ser mencionado** not worth mentioning.

índigo s. m. indigo, anil, Indian blue.

índigo-do-brasil s. m. (pl. **índigos-do-brasil**) indigo-plant (Solanum indigoferum) cultivated in Brazil for indigo.

indigófera s. f. Indigofera: genus of shrubs including several species of indigo-plants.

indiligência s. f. 1. lack of diligence, indiligence. 2. slothfulness. 3. negligence.

indiligente adj. m. + f. indiligent, idle, slothful, negligent.

índio (I) s. m. 1. Indian: a) native or inhabitant of India. b) aboriginal native of North or South America. 2. (Braz., pop.): a) farm-hand. b) daredevil.

~ **da América do -Norte** Red, Red Indian.

índio (II) s. m. (chem.) indium (symbol In).

indireta s. f. (Braz.) allusion, hint, slant.

dar ~**s** to become personal.

indireto adj. 1. indirect, not direct. 2. (gram.) oblique. 3. disguised, simulated. 4. circuitous, roundabout, ambagious. 5. mediate. || **-amente** adv. 1. indirectly. 2. (gram.) obliquely. 3. ambagiously. 4. circuitously. 5. mediately.

causa -a secondary cause. **caminho** ~ indirect way. **fogo** ~ (mil.) high-angle fire. **citação -a** indirect speech.

indirigível adj. m. + f. (pl. **-íveis**) unmanageable, ungovernable, not dirigible.

indiscernível adj. m. + f. (pl. **-íveis**) undiscernible, indiscernible, undistinguishable, imperceptible.

indisciplina s. f. 1. indiscipline. 2. insubordination, disobedience. 3. disorder. 4. rebellion, insurrection.

indisciplinabilidade s. f. indisciplineness.

indisciplinado adj. 1. undisciplined, indisciplined. 2. insubordinate, disobedient. 3. ungovernable, unruly, 4. seditious.

indisciplinar v. 1. to destroy the discipline. 2. to rouse to revolt. 3. to demoralize. 4. ~**-se** to revolt or turn against.

indisciplinável adj. m. + f. (pl. **-áveis**) indisciplinable.

indiscreto s. m. indiscreet or unfaithful person. || adj. 1. indiscreet. 2. imprudent, injudicious. 3. unfaithful. 4. prattling, chattering. || **-amente** adv. indiscreetly, injudiciously, pryingly.

indiscrição s. f. (pl. **-ões**) 1. indiscreetness, indiscretion. 2. imprudence, injudiciousness. 3. faithlessness, treachery.

indiscriminado adj. 1. indiscriminate, indiscriminating. 2. promiscuous. 3. undistinguishing. 4. confused. || **-amente** adv. indiscriminately.

indiscriminável adj. m. + f. (pl. **-áveis**) that cannot be discriminated, undistinguishable.

indiscutibilidade s. f. indisputableness, indisputability.

indiscutido adj. unquestioned.

indiscutível adj. m. + f. (pl. **-íveis**) 1. undiscussable. 2. unquestionable, incontestable. 3. indubitable. 4. certain, positive. || **indiscutivelmente** adv. unquestionably, undeniably.

indisfarçado adj. undisguised, frank.

indisfarçável adj. m. + f. (pl. **-áveis**) unconcealable, undisguisable.

indispensabilidade s. f. indispensability, indispensableness.

indispensável s. m. (pl. **-áveis**) a lady's handbag. || adj. m. + f. 1. indispensable. 2. infallible. 3. essential, necessary. 4. needful. || **indispensavelmente** adv. indispensably.

indisponibilidade s. f. quality or state of being inalienable or untransferable.

indisponível adj. m. + f. (pl. **-íveis**) inalienable, unavailable, untransferable.

indispor v. 1. to indispose: a) render unfavourable, disincline. b) make ill, cause illness in. c) make unfit or unable. d) disaffect, set against. 2. to irritate, annoy.

indisposição s. f. (pl. **-ões**) 1. indisposition: a) malaise, slight illness or ailment. b) aversion, dislike. c) hostility, animosity. 2. quarrel, discord.

indisposto adj. indisposed: 1. unwell, sick, poorly. 2. ill, ailing. 3. averse, disliking. 4. hostile. 5. unwilling, disinclined.

ele sente-se ~ he feels bad. **ela anda muito -a** she is always ailing. **ele estava bem** ~ he was quite out of humour. **ele bebeu demais e agora está** ~ he drank too much and now he is indisposed, (U. S. A., coll.) he is under the weather.

indisputabilidade s. f. indisputability, indisputableness, incontrovertibleness.

indisputado adj. undisputed, unquestioned, uncontested.

indisputável adj. m. + f. (pl. **-áveis**) 1. indisputable, incontestable. 2. incontrovertible, unquestionable. 3. evident, true. || **indisputavelmente** adv. indisputably, incontrovertibly.

indissimulável adj. m. + f. (pl. **-áveis**) that cannot be dissimulated.

indissolubilidade s. f. indissolubility, indissolubleness.
indissolução s. f. (pl. **-ões**) fact or state of being undissolved.
indissolúvel adj. m. + f. (pl. **-úveis**) indissoluble, not dissolvable, indiscerptible. ‖ **indissoluvelmente** adv. indissolubly.
indistinção s. f. (pl. **-ões**) 1. indistinction, indistinctness. 2. indiscrimination, indiscriminateness.
indistinguível adj. m. + f. (pl. **-íveis**) indistinguishable, indistinctive. ‖ **indistinguivelmente** adv. indistinguishably, indistinctively.
indistinto adj. 1. indistinct, not clearly distinguishable. 2. wavering, undecided. 3. vague, uncertain. 4. indiscriminate, promiscuous. 5. confused, undefined. 6. unclear, blurry, dim. 7. out of focus. ‖ **-amente** adv. indistinctly, vaguely, indiscriminately, dimly.
inditoso adj. unfortunate, unlucky, wretched.
individuação s. f. (pl. **-ões**) individuation, individual character or singularity.
individuador s. m. individualizer. ‖ adj. individualizing.
individual adj. m. + f. (pl. **-ais**) 1. individual, peculiar to one single person or thing. 2. personal, private, particular. 3. separate. 4. single, singular. ‖ **~mente** adv. individually, singly, separately, singularly.
    isto é a sua opinião ~ this is your (his, her, their) private opinion. **é uma qualidade ~ desta raça** it is a peculiar quality of this race.
individualidade s. f. 1. individuality. 2. distinctive character. 3. identity. 4. personality. 5. person.
individualismo s. m. individualism: 1. individuality. 2. principle of free independent action. 3. doctrine of pure egoism. 4. egoism.
individualista s. m. + f. individualist. ‖ adj. individualistic.
individualização s. f. (pl. **-ões**) individualization.
individualizar v. 1. to individualize. 2. give a distinctive character to. 3. to distinguish, specify.
individuante adj. m. + f. individuant, characteristic.
individuar v. 1. to individuate, make individual. 2. to mark as distinct. 3. to individualize. 4. to treat or expound in an individual manner.
indivíduo s. m. 1. being, individual, person. 2. single organism. 3. indivisible entity. 4. (coll.) customer, fellow, party. 5. (Braz. and Açores, sl.) castaway. ‖ adj. 1. individual. 2. single. 3. particular. 4. indivisible.
    ele é um ~ aborrecido he is an annoyer. **~ estúrdio** Bohemian. **os direitos do ~** the individual rights.
indivisão s. f. (pl. **-ões**) indivision, quality or state of being undivided.
indivisibilidade s. f. indivisibility, indivisibleness.
indivisível s. m. (pl. **-íveis**) indivisible, infinitely small particle. ‖ adj. m. + f. indivisible, impartible.
indiviso adj. undivided, whole.
indizível adj. m. + f. (pl. **-íveis**) unutterable, inexpressible, unspeakable, unnam(e)able. ‖ **indizivelmente** adv. unspeakably.
indo-britânico adj. Indo-Briton.
indócil adj. m. + f. (pl. **-óceis**) 1. indocile, unmanageable, unpliant. 2. unteachable. 3. stubborn, unruly. 4. vicious. ‖ **indocilmente** adv. ungovernably, unmanageably.
indocilidade s. f. 1. indocility, intractability. 2. ungovernableness. 3. viciousness.
indocilizar v. 1. to render indocile or stubborn. 2. to run wild.
indo-europeu s. m. (pl. **indo-europeus;** f. **indo-européia,** pl. **indo-européias**) Indo-European. ‖ adj. Indo-European.

indo-germânico adj. (pl. **indo-germânicos**) Indo-Germanic, Indo-European.
índole s. f. 1. natural disposition, nature. 2. temper, character. 3. propensity, bent, proclivity.
    de acordo com a sua ~ true to his (her, their) character. **ela mostrou a sua verdadeira ~** she unmasked her true nature. **um menino de boa ~** a fair-conditioned (good-natured) boy. **ele revelou má ~** he showed his ill nature, the cloven foot. **por causa de sua ~ vingativa (pacífica)** due to her (his) vindictiveness (peaceableness).
indolência s. f. 1. indolence, indolency. 2. insensibility, apathy. 3. negligence. 4. laziness, slothfulness, inertness.
indolente adj. m. + f. 1. indolent. 2. insensible, apathetic. 3. negligent. 4. lazy, slothful, idle. 5. slack, slow. 6. listless. ‖ **~mente** adv. indolently, idly, listlessly, supinely.
indolor adj. m. + f. 1. painless, pangless, free from pain. 2. (fig.) easy.
indomado adj. 1. untamed, undomesticated. 2. wild. 3. unruly, disobedient.
indomável adj. m. + f. (pl. **-áveis**) 1. indomitable, untam(e)able. 2. irreducible. 3. unconquerable, invincible. 4. implacable, relentless. 5. unruly, uncontrollable. ‖ **indomavelmente** adv. uncontrollably, indomitably.
indomesticado adj. undomesticated.
indomesticável adj. m. + f. (pl. **-áveis**) (also **indoméstico** m.) 1. untamed, undomesticated. 2. wild, ferocious. 3. savage.
indômito adj. 1. untamed. 2. unvanquished. 3. wild. 4. uncontrolled, uncurbed. 5. (fig.) arrogant, haughty. ‖ **-amente** adv. indomitably, wildly, unruly.
indonésio s. m. Indonesian: native or inhabitant of the East Indian islands. ‖ adj. Indonesian.
indouto adj. 1. unlearned, ignorant. 2. inapt, foolish.
indubitabilidade s. f. doubtlessness.
indubitado adj. undoubted.
indubitável adj. m. + f. (pl. **-áveis**) 1. undoubted, unquestionable. 2. incontestable, indisputable. 3. certain, assured. ‖ **indubitavelmente** adv. undoubtedly, unquestionably, assuredly.
indução s. f. (pl. **-ões**) 1. induction. 2. act of inducting or bringing in. 3. introduction. 4. (logic) process of drawing a general conclusion from particular facts. 5. suggestion. 6. electrical induction or influence.
    corrente de ~ induction current. **~ magneto-elétrica** magnetoelectric induction.
indúcias s. f. pl. 1. truce, armistice. 2. (com.) moratorium. 3. (jur.) respite given to debtors.
indúctil adj. m. + f. (pl. **-úteis**) inductile.
inductilidade s. f. inductility.
indulgência s. f. 1. indulgence. 2. clemency, lenity. 3. tolerance. 4. remission of sin or punishment, pardon. 5. forgivingness, absolution. 6. kindness, mildness.
indulgenciar v. 1. to treat with indulgence. 2. to pardon, forgive.
indulgente adj. m. + f. 1. indulgent. 2. clement, lenient. 3. tolerant, broad-minded. 4. pardoning, forgiving. 5. kind, gentle. ‖ **~mente** adv. indulgently, forbearingly, charitably, kindly, gently.
indultado s. m. person favoured by an indult or pardon.
indultar v. 1. to grant an indult or exemption. 2. to exempt, free from. 3. to pardon. 4. to indulge.
indultário s. m. beneficiary of an indult. ‖ adj. exempt, pardoned.
indulto s. m. 1. indult. 2. permission, grant. 3. pardon, remission. 4. privilege. 5. grace, favour.

indumentária s. f. 1. art of dressing. 2. history of dresses, their styles and fashion, garb. 3. clothing, apparel, garments. 4. (theat.) stage properties.
indumentário adj. of, pertaining to or relative to clothes, their styles and history.
indumento s. m. 1. garment(s), clothes. 2. covering, lining. 3. integument. 4. indumentum, skin, rind, outer layer of a plant which forms a coating.
induplicado adj. (bot.) induplicate, having the edges rolled inward (said of floral parts of a bud).
indúsia s. f. indusium: 1. protective covering of the fruit dots in ferns. 2. protective covering which encloses the stigma of flowers.
indústria s. f. 1. industry. 2. manufacture, productive labour. 3. works. 4. application, diligence. 5. activity, laboriousness.
~ **alimentícia** provision industry. ~ **base** key industry. ~ **da pesca** fishery. ~ **de automóveis** automotive industry. ~ **de papel** paper manufacturing. **cavalheiro de** ~ confidence man. **ele trabalhava com** ~ he was working industriously.
industriador s. m. 1. elaborator. 2. instructor, trainer. || adj. elaborating, training, instructing.
industrial s. m. + f. (pl. **-ais**) industrial, manufacturer, producer. || adj. manufacturing, industrial. || **~mente** adv. industrially.
cidade ~ industrial town. **conselho** ~ industrial council. **escola de aprendizagem** ~ industrial school.
industrialismo s. m. industrialism: 1. devotion to industrial pursuits. 2. predominance of industry in the economic structure of a nation. 3. organization of industries.
industrialista s. m. + f. 1. industrial, industrialist. 2. adherent of industrialism. || adj. industrialist, of or relative to industrialism.
industrialização s. f. (pl. **-ões**) industrialization.
industrializar v. 1. to industrialize. 2. to devote to industrialism. 3. to give industrial character to.
industriar v. 1. to elaborate. 2. to teach, instruct, train. 3. to prime. 4. to make profitable by industrial organization.
industriário s. m. industrial worker, industrial employee.
industrioso adj. 1. industrious. 2. diligent, laborious. 3. skilful, apt. 4. clever, shrewd. || **-amente** adv. industriously.
indutância s. f. inductance.
indutar v. 1. to cover, coat. 2. to furnish with, garnish.
indutivo adj. 1. inductive. 2. inducing, persuasive. 3. (electr.) operating or produced by induction. 4. introductory.
induto s. m. = **indumento**.
indutor s. m. inductor: 1. person who inducts. 2. any part of an electrical apparatus acting inductively.
indúvia s. f. induviae (pl.): withered leaves which remain on the stems of some plants.
induviado adj. (bot.) induviate, covered with induviae.
induvial adj. m. + f. (pl. **-ais**) (bot.) induvial, of or relative to the induviae.
induzido s. m. (electr.) armature.
induzidor s. m. inducer, instigator, persuader.
induzimento s. m. 1. inducement. 2. incentive. 3. persuasion, intigation. 4. introductory explanation.
induzir v. 1. to induce. 2. to incite, entice. 3. to infer, deduce. 4. to conclude. 5. to persuade. 6. to instigate. 7. to motivate. 8. (electr.) to produce by induction.
~ **alguém a desistir de alguma coisa** to cajole someone out of something. ~ **com lisonjas** to wheedle. ~ **em erro** to lead into error. **induzido a roubar** tempted to theft.

inebriante adj. m. + f. inebriant, intoxicant, intoxicating.
agente ~ intoxicant.
inebriar v. 1. to inebriate, intoxicate. 2. to make drunk, fuddle. 3. to fluster, exhilarate. 4. **~-se** to become intoxicated.
inédia s. f. inedia: 1. abstinence from food. 2. starvation.
ineditismo s. m. quality of being unpublished.
inédito s. m. unpublished works, inedita (pl.) || adj. inedited, unpublished.
inefabilidade s. f. ineffability, unspeakableness, inexpressibility, inexpressibleness.
inefável adj. m. + f. (pl. **-áveis**) 1. ineffable. 2. incapable of being expressed, inexpressible. 3. unspeakable. 4. (fig.) fascinating, charming. || **inefavelmente** adv. ineffably.
ineficácia s. f. 1. inefficacy, lack of efficacy. 2. ineffectualness, ineffectiveness, inoperativeness. 3. powerlessness. 4. uselessness.
ineficaz adj. m. + f. 1. inefficacious, not efficacious. 2. ineffectual, ineffective, inoperative. 3. powerless. 4. feeble. 5. useless. 6. inconvenient. || **~mente** adv. ineffectually, inefficaciously.
ineficiência s. f. inefficiency, incompetency, powerlessness.
ineficiente adj. m. + f. 1. inefficient, inefficacious. 2. ineffective. 3. incompetent. 4. deficient, poor. 5. powerless. || **~mente** adv. inefficiently.
inegável adj. m. + f. (pl. **-áveis**) 1. undeniable. 2. indisputable, incontestable. 3. evident. 4. positive. || **inegavelmente** adv. undeniably.
inegociável adj. m. + f. (pl. **-áveis**) unnegotiable, unmarketable.
inelegância s. f. inelegance, inelegancy.
inelegante adj. m. + f. inelegant, ungraceful, unrefined.
inelegibilidade s. f. ineligibility.
inelegível adj. m. + f. (pl. **-íveis**) ineligible, unworthy of choice, unsuitable. || **inelegivelmente** adv. ineligibly.
inelutável adj. m. + f. (pl. **-áveis**) 1. ineluctable, unavoidable. 2. inescapable. 3. irresistible. 4. incontestable, indisputable.
inembrionado adj. (bot.) inembryonate.
inenarrável adj. m. + f. (pl. **-áveis**) incapable of being narrated or told, inenarrable.
inépcia, ineptidão s. f. (pl. **-ões**) 1. ineptness, ineptitude. 2. unfitness, unsuitableness. 3. stupidity, foolishness. 4. nonsense, absurdity.
inepto adj. 1. inept, not apt. 2. unfit, unsuitable. 3. unpractical. 4. stupid, foolish. 5. absurd, nonsensical. || **-amente** adv. ineptly, inaptly, unpractically.
inequipalpos s. m. pl. (ent.) Inaequipalpia, a suborder of insects having unequal maxillary feelers.
inequivalve adj. m. + f. (zool.) inequivalve, having unequal valves (bivalve molluscs).
inequívoco adj. inequivocal, unmistakable, unambiguous. || **inequivocamente** adv. unequivocally, unmistakably.
inércia s. f. 1. inertion, inertness. 2. inaction, inactivity. 3. laziness, sluggishness. 4. indolence. 5. torpidity, torpidness. 6. lethargy. 7. (phys.) inertia. **lei da** ~ (phys.) law of inertia. **momento de** ~ moment of inertia.
inerciar v. to make inert.
inerência s. f. 1. inherence, inherency. 2. state of being inherent. 3. inhesion.
inerente adj. m. + f. 1. inherent. 2. intrinsic(al). 3. native, inborn. 4. connate, ingrained. 5. organic, constitutional. 6. indigenous. || **~mente** adv. inherently, constitutionally.
inerir v. to inhere, belong intrinsically, be innate.

inerme adj. m. + f. unarmed, defenceless.
inerradicável adj. m. + f. (pl. **-áveis**) ineradicable.
inerrância s. f. inerrancy, freedom from error, inerrability.
inerrante adj. m. + f. inerrant, unerring.
inerte adj. m. + f. 1. inert. 2. inactive, passive. 3. lazy, sluggish. 4. indolent, dull. 5. torpid, drowsy, lethargic. ‖ ~**mente** adv. inertly.
inervação s. f. (pl. **-ões**) innervation: 1. (physiol.) supply of nervous energy to any part of the nervous system. 2. arrangement and disposition of the nervous filaments in the body.
inervar v. (physiol.) to innervate, give nervous influence to.
inérveo adj. (bot.) veinless.
inescrupuloso adj. 1. unscrupulous. 2. unprincipled, unconscientious. ‖ **-amente** adv. unscrupulously.
inescrutabilidade s. f. inscrutability, inscrutableness, impenetrableness.
inescrutável adj. m. + f. (pl. **-áveis**) inscrutable, impenetrable, undiscoverable. ‖ **inescrutavelmente** adv. inscrutably.
inescurecível adj. m. + f. (pl. **-íveis**) 1. that cannot be obscured or blotted out. 2. memorable. 3. evident.
inescusável adj. m. + f. (pl. **-áveis**) inexcusable, unpardonable, indefensible.
sua conduta é ~ your (his, her, their) conduct is inexcusable.
inesgotabilidade s. f. unfailingness.
inesgotado adj. unspent, unexhausted.
inesgotável adj. m. + f. (pl. **-áveis**) 1. unfailing. 2. inexhaustive. 3. copious, abundant.
inesperado adj. 1. unexpected, unforeseen, unlooked for. 2. sudden, abrupt. 3. surprising. 4. accidental. ‖ **-amente** adv. unexpectedly, suddenly, accidentally, surprisingly.
ele o fez -amente he did it without warning. ela surgiu -amente she popped upon them. isto se passou -amente it happened all of a sudden.
inesquecível adj. m. + f. (pl. **-íveis**) unforgettable, that cannot be forgotten. ‖ **inesquecivelmente** adv. unforgettably.
isto me será ~ I shall never forget it. um acontecimento ~ an event never to be forgotten.
inestendível adj. m. + f. (pl. **-íveis**) inextensible.
inestimável adj. m. + f. (pl. **-áveis**) 1. inestimable, invaluable. 2. precious, priceless. 3. inappreciable. ‖ **inestimavelmente** adv. inestimably.
inevidência s. f. inevidence, lack of evidence, obscurity.
inevidente adj. m. + f. 1. inevident, not clear. 2. obscure.
inevitabilidade s. f. inevitability, inevitableness, unavoidableness.
inevitável adj. m. + f. (pl. **-áveis**) 1. unavoidable, unpreventable. 2. inevitable, ineluctable. 3. fatal. 4. infallible. ‖ **inevitavelmente** adv. unavoidably, inevitably, infallibly.
inexatidão s. f. (pl. **-ões**) 1. inexactness, inexactitude. 2. inaccuracy, incorrectness. 3. mistake, error. 4. falseness, wrongness. 5. negligence.
inexato adj. 1. inexact. 2. inaccurate, incorrect. 3. untrue, false. 4. negligent. ‖ **-amente** adv. inexactly, inaccurately.
inexaminável adj. m. + f. (pl. **-áveis**) unexaminable.
inexaurível adj. m. + f. (pl. **-íveis**) 1. unfailing. 2. inexhaustive, inexhaustible. 3. abundant. ‖ **inexaurivelmente** adv. inexhaustively.
inexausto adj. inexhausted, unexhausted.
inexcedível adj. m. + f. (pl. **-íveis**) unexceedable.
inexcitabilidade s. f. inexcitability.

inexcitável adj. m. + f. (pl. **-áveis**) 1. inexcitable. 2. impassible, imperturbable.
inexecutável adj. m. + f. (pl. **-áveis**) 1. inexecutable. 2. unaccomplishable, unachievable. 3. (mus., sport) unplayable. 4. impracticable.
inexeqüibilidade s. f. 1. inexecutableness. 2. non-execution, inexecution. 3. impracticability.
inexeqüível adj. m. + f. (pl. **-íveis**) 1. inexecutable. 2. unachievable. 3. unworkable. 4. impracticable.
inexigível adj. m. + f. (pl. **-íveis**) unclaimable.
inexistência s. f. 1. inexistence, non-existence. 2. (fig.) want, need. 3. nothingness.
inexistente adj. m. + f. 1. inexistent, non-existent. 2. not being. 3. absent.
inexorabilidade s. f. 1. inexorability, inexorableness. 2. inflexibility. 3. relentlessness.
inexorado adj. unasked for, unbidden, unrequested.
inexorável adj. m. + f. (pl. **-áveis**) 1. inexorable. 2. inflexible, unyielding. 3. merciless, unpitying. 4. relentless. ‖ **inexoravelmente** adv. inexorably.
inexperiência s. f. 1. inexperience, want of experience. 2. rawness, youngness. 3. unskilfulness.
inexperiente adj. m. + f. 1. inexperienced, unexperienced, unconversant. 2. rawish, fresh, young. 3. unpractised, unskilled, artless. 4. (pop.) green, half-baked. ‖ ~**mente** adv. inexpertly, unskilfully, rawly.
ele é muito ~ he is very inexperienced, he is very green. ele é ~ neste negócio he is young in this business.
inexperto adj. inexpert, unskilled, unpractised, unexperienced.
inexpiado adj. inexpiate, not appeased or atoned.
inexpiável adj. m. + f. (pl. **-áveis**) 1. inexpiable, not to be expiated or atoned. 2. not to be satisfied or appeased. 3. implacable. ‖ **inexpiavelmente** adv. inexpiably.
inexplicabilidade s. f. inexplicability, unaccountability.
inexplicável adj. m. + f. (pl. **-áveis**) 1. inexplicable. 2. unaccountable, undecipherable. 3. incomprehensible. 4. obscure. ‖ **inexplicavelmente** adv. inexplicably, unaccountably.
inexplícito adj. inexplicit. ‖ **inexplicitamente** adv. inexplicitly.
inexplorado adj. unexplored, untrod, untravelled.
inexplorável adj. m. + f. (pl. **-áveis**) inexplorable, incapable of being explored or discovered.
inexpressividade s. f. inexpressiveness, expressionlessness.
inexpressivo adj. 1. inexpressive, expressionless. 2. meaningless, featureless. 3. inexpressible. 4. vacuous, vacant. ‖ **-amente** adv. inexpressively, meaninglessly, vacuously.
inexprimível adj. m. + f. (pl. **-íveis**) inexpressible, unutterable, unspeakable. ‖ **inexprimivelmente** adv. inexpressibly, unspeakably.
inexpugnabilidade s. f. invincibility, insuperableness, impregnability.
inexpugnável adj. m. + f. (pl. **-áveis**) 1. inexpugnable. 2. invincible, insuperable. 3. impregnable. ‖ **inexpugnavelmente** adv. inexpugnably.
inextensão s. f. (pl. **-ões**) inextension, lack of extension.
inextensível adj. m. + f. (pl. **-íveis**) inextensible.
inextenso adj. unextended, without extension.
inexterminável adj. m. + f. (pl. **-áveis**) inexterminable, incapable of being exterminated.
inextinguibilidade s. f. inextinguishableness.
inextinguível adj. m. + f. (pl. **-íveis**) 1. inextinguishable. 2. imperishable. 3. unquenchable. 4. indestructible. ‖ **inextinguivelmente** adv. inextinguishably.
inextinto adj. inextinct, inextinguished.

inextirpável adj. m. + f. (pl. -áveis) inextirpable.
inextricabilidade s. f. inextricability, inextricableness.
inextricável adj. m. + f. (pl. -áveis) 1. inextricable, that cannot be freed from intricacy. 2. involved, entangled. ‖ inextricavelmente adv. inextricably.
infactível, infatível adj. m. + f. (pl. -íveis) impracticable, unfeasible, irrealizable.
infalibilidade s. f. 1. infallibility, unfailingness. 2. unerringness. 3. certainty. 4. inevitability.
infalível adj. m. + f. (pl. -íveis) 1. infallible, not fallible. 2. unerring, inerrable. 3. unfailing. 4. certain, sure. 5. inevitable. ‖ infalivelmente adv. infallibly, unfailingly, inerrably, doubtlessly.
  claro, isto é ~ of course, that is sure as death. ele infalivelmente vai ganhar he will not fail to win.
infalsificável adj. m. + f. (pl. -áveis) unfalsifiable, unadulterable.
infamação s. f. (pl. -ões) 1. defamation, calumny. 2. infamy. 3. detraction, slander.
infamado adj. defamed, made infamous.
infamador s. m. defamer, degrader, calumniator.
infamante adj. m. + f. 1. defamatory, injurious. 2. ignominious. 3. opprobrious.
infamar v. 1. to defame, infamize. 2. to render ignominious. 3. to dishonour, discredit. 4. to slander, calumniate. 5. to pollute, defile. 6. ~-se to disgrace or discredit o. s.
infamatório adj. defamatory, infamous, ignominious, opprobrious.
infame adj. m. + f. 1. infamous. 2. of ill fame, odious. 3. shameful, disgraceful. 4. wicked, heinous. 5. base, nefarious, ignominious. 6. disreputable, discreditable. ‖ ~mente adv. infamously, disreputably.
infâmia s. 1. infamy. 2. evil fame, disrepute. 3. dishonour, discredit. 4. disgracefulness, shamefulness. 5. wickedness, villainy. 6. ignominy, opprobrium.
infamiliaridade s. f. unfamiliarity.
infância s. f. 1. infancy, earliest childhood, babyhood. 2. nonage, minority. 3. early period (of an institution, art, etc.).
  ela é uma amiga de ~ she is a childhood friend. na ~ in tender age, in early life. desde a ~ from a child. ele está na segunda ~ he is in his dotage. assistência à ~ infant welfare.
infando adj. infandous, unspeakable, odious, nefarious, horrible.
infanta s. f. infanta: 1. Spanish or Portuguese princess (except the eldest) of royal blood. 2. wife of an infante.
infantado s. m. an infant's demesne or estate.
infantaria, infanteria s. f. infantry, foot soldiers, foot (of an army).
  ~ ligeira light infantry.
infante s. m. 1. (Spain, Portugal) infante: younger prince of royal blood (their heir apparent is called: prince). 2. child, infant. 3. infantryman, foot soldier.
infanticida s. m. + f. infanticide, murderer of a child. ‖ adj. infanticidal.
infanticídio s. m. infanticide, murder of an infant.
infantil adj. m. + f. (pl. -is) 1. infantile, infantine. 2. childish, puerile. 3. innocent. 4. (fig.) young, tender. ‖ ~mente adv. childishly.
  literatura ~ juvenile literature. mortalidade ~ infant mortality. um livro ~ a book for the young, a children's book.
infantilidade s. f. 1. childlike nature or behaviour. 2. childishness, boyishness, girlishness. 3. infantile act or saying.
infantilismo s. m. (med.) infantilism, puerilism.

infantilizar v. 1. to make infantile, give a childlike character to. 2. to act in a childish or silly manner. 3. ~-se to be or become puerile.
infanto-juvenil adj. m. + f. (pl. infanto-juvenis) relating or belonging to children and youths.
infarto s. m. (also enfarte, enfarto) (med., pathol.) infarct.
infatigabilidade s. f. indefatigability, indefatigableness, tirelessness.
infatigável adj. m. + f. (pl. -áveis) 1. indefatigable. 2. untiring, unflagging, unremitting, unwearying. 3. zealous, assiduous. ‖ infatigavelmente adv. indefatigably, unremittingly, assiduously.
infausto adj. 1. unlucky, unfortunate. 2. fatal. 3. calamitous, disastrous. 4. wretched. ‖ -amente adv. unfortunately, calamitously.
infecção, infeção s. f. (pl. -ões) 1. infection, contagion, contamination. 2. (fig.) corruption, taint.
infeccionado, infecionado adj. 1. infected, contaminated. 2. tainted, corrupt.
infeccionar, infecionar v. 1. to infect, contaminate. 2. to corrupt: a) taint. b) (fig.) pollute, defile. 3. ~-se to be or become infected.
infeccioso, infecioso adj. 1. infective, infectious. 2. contagious, contaminative. 3. catching, communicable. 4. corrupting, defiling.
infecundidade s. f. 1. infecundity, sterility. 2. barrenness, unfruitfulness. 3. (fig.) unproductiveness.
infecundo adj. 1. infecund, sterile. 2. barren, fruitless. 3. (bot.) acarpous. 4. (fig.) unproductive.
infelicidade s. f. 1. infelicity, unhappiness. 2. misfortune, mischance. 3. adversity, calamity.
  para completar a ~ to make matters worse. uma série de ~s a run of ill luck. isto traz ~ this brings misfortune. nem tudo é ~ it is an ill wind that blows nobody any good. por ~ ele tinha saído the misfortune was that he had left.
infelicitador s. m. person who brings ill luck or makes unhappy. ‖ adj. causing unhappiness, infelicific.
infelicitar v. 1. to make unhappy or miserable. 2. to cause unhappiness to.
infeliz s. m. + f. unfortunate person, unlucky chap, wretch. ‖ adj. 1. unhappy, unfortunate, unlucky. 2. ill-fated, disastrous. 3. miserable, wretched, distressful. 4. unsuccessful. ‖ ~mente adv. unfortunately, unhappily, unluckily, unsuccessfully.
  uma expressão ~ an infelicitous expression. ela é ~ she is unlucky. que dia ~! alas the day! naquele dia ele foi mesmo ~ on that day he was really out of luck. ~mente é verdade unfortunately it is true, sad to say, but it is true. é esse o seu serviço? sim ~mente! is this your work? I am afraid it is!
infenso adj. 1. hostile, inimical. 2. adverse, contrary to. 3. irate, angry.
inferaxilar adj. m. + f. (bot.) infra-axillary.
inferência s. f. 1. inference. 2. conclusion, deduction. 3. induction. 4. consequence. 5. corollary.
inferior s. m. inferior: 1. person or thing classed lower than others. 2. subordinate. 3. underling. ‖ adj. inferior: 1. of poorer quality, less capacity or merit, of lower rank. 2. low(er), downmost. 3. lesser, smaller. 4. after, behind. 5. second, secondary. 6. ordinary, common. 7. cheap, poor. 8. mediocre, second-rate. 9. subordinate, subaltern. 10. (mil.) non-commissioned. 11. base, mean. ‖ -mente adv. inferiorly, in an inferior manner, position or relation.
  ele é um oficial ~ he is a non-commissioned officer. ele não é ~ a ninguém he is second to none. o material não é em nada ~ the material is in no

way inferior to. **tratava-se duma peça teatral** ~ it was a third-class play.
inferioridade s. f. 1. inferiority. 2. disadvantage. 3. ordinariness, commonness. 4. poorness.
inferiorizar v. 1. to make inferior. 2. to abash, degrade. 3. ~-se to become inferior.
inferir v. 1. to infer. 2. to deduce, conclude. 3. to imply. 4. to presume, guess.
infermentescibilidade s. f. unfermentability.
infermentescível adj. m. + f. (pl. -íveis) unfermentable, unsusceptible to fermentation.
infernal adj. m. + f. (pl. -ais) 1. infernal. 2. hellish, diabolical. 3. atrocious, cruel. 4. terrible, horrible. 5. furious, raging. || ~amente adv. infernally, diabolically.
um barulho ~ a hell of a noise.
infernalidade s. f. infernality.
infernar v. (also **infernizar**) 1. to doom to hell. 2. to afflict, torment. 3. to harass, importune. 4. ~-se to despair, fret.
inferneira s. f. 1. confusion, disorder. 2. great noise, clamour, din. 3. tumult, turmoil.
inferno s. m. 1. (myth.) infernal regions, Stygian shore, Hades. 2. hell, underworld, inferno. 3. (fig.) perdition. 4. despair, torment.
o ~ **verde** the Amazon jungle. **o caminho para o** ~ **está calçado com boas intenções** the way to hell is paved with good intentions. **vá para o** ~ go to hell! go to perdition! **fizeram de sua vida um** ~ they worried out his life.
ínfero s. m. inferno, hell. || adj. inferior.
inferovariado adj. (bot.) inferovarian.
infértil adj. m. + f. (pl. -eis) 1. infertile, not fruitful. 2. sterile, barren. 3. unproductive.
infertilidade s. f. 1. infertility, unfruitfulness. 2. barrenness, sterility. 3. unproductiveness.
infertilizar v. 1. to make infertile. 2. to sterilize.
infestação s. f. (pl. -ões) infestation, molestation.
infestado adj. infested.
infestador s. m. infester. || adj. infesting.
infestante adj. m. + f. infesting.
infestar v. 1. to infest. 2. to attack, molest. 3. to swarm over. 4. to plague.
~ **de parasitas** to parasitize.
infesto adj. 1. offensive, hostile. 2. troublesome, annoying. 3. prejudicial, harmful, pernicious.
infetante, infectante adj. m. + f. infecting, infectious.
infetar, infectar v. 1. to infect, taint with disease. 2. to contaminate. 3. to pollute, defile.
infeto, infecto adj. 1. infected, contaminated. 2. pestilential. 3. fetid, malodorous. 4. degenerate, depraved.
infetuoso, infectuoso adj. infectuous, contagious.
infibulação s. f. (pl. -ões) infibulation.
infibulador s. m. infibulator. || adj. infibulating.
infibular v. to infibulate, clasp or confine with a buckle.
inficionação s. f. (pl. -ões) infection, contamination.
infidelidade s. f. 1. infidelity, disloyalty. 2. unfaithfulness. 3. falseness, treachery. 4. faithlessness, incredulity, unbelieve.
infido adj. (poet.) unfaithful, infidel.
infiel s. m. + f. (pl. -éis) infidel, apostate, misbeliever, unbeliever. || adj. 1. infidel, unfaithful. 2. disloyal, dishonest. 3. false, treacherous. 4. apostate, unbelieving. 5. inexact, inaccurate. || ~mente adv. unfaithfully, disloyally.
infiltração s. f. (pl. -ões) 1. infiltration: a) act or process of infiltrating. b) (med.) accumulation of extraneous matter in a tissue. c) gradual penetration of foreign elements (ideas, principles, troops, etc.). 2. seepage, pervasion. 3. imbibition.
infiltrador adj. infiltrating, pervasive.

infiltrar v. 1. to infiltrate, infilter. 2. to filter, seep, sift in. 3. to percolate, penetrate. 4. to imbibe, soak in. 5. (fig.) to penetrate gradually (ideas, thoughts, principles), edge in, worm in.
ínfimo adj. 1. lowermost, undermost. 2. inferior. 3. insignificant.
os preços são ~s the prices are rock-bottom.
infindável adj. m. + f. (pl. -áveis) 1. endless, unending. 2. permanent. 3. boundless. 4. interminable.
infindo adj. 1. endless, unending. 2. infinite. 3. unlimited, boundless. 4. innumerable, countless.
infinidade s. f. 1. infinity, infiniteness. 2. boundlessness. 3. endlessness. 4. immensity. 5. innumerableness, numberlessness. 6. (fig.) world.
infinitésima s. f. (math.) infinitesimal, immeasurably small quantity.
infinitesimal adj. m. + f. (pl. -ais) infinitesimal, minute, infinitely small.
infinitésimo s. m. = **infinitésima**. || adj. infinitesimal.
infinitivo s. m. (gram.) infinitive mood. || adj. infinitive.
infinito s. m. 1. infinite, infinity. 2. (gram.) infinitive mood. || adj. 1. infinite, infinitive. 2. boundless, limitless. 3. endless, interminable. 4. timeless, termless. 5. immeasurable. 6. numberless, innumerable. 7. indefinite. 8. eternal. || -amente adv. 1. infinitely. 2. boundlessly. 3. endlessly. 4. immeasurably. 5. eternally.
até o ~ ad infinitum.
infirmar v. 1. to weaken, enfeeble. 2. (fig.) to invalidate, annul. 3. to revoke.
infirmativo adj. infirmative, weakening.
infirme adj. m. + f. 1. infirm, not firm. 2. faltering, feeble, weak. 3. voidable.
infixidez s. f. unfixedness, inconsistency.
infixo adj. (gram.) affix, infix.
inflação s. f. (pl. -ões) inflation: 1. swelling, inflating. 2. pride. 3. haughtiness, conceit. 4. excessive increase of paper currency.
inflacionista s. m. + f. inflationist, inflater, one who favours the increased issue of paper-money. || adj. inflating.
inflado adj. 1. inflated. 2. swollen, puffy. 3. conceited, haughty, proud.
inflador s. m. (S. Braz.) bicycle pump, air pump.
inflamabilidade s. f. inflammability, inflammableness, combustibility.
ponto de ~ flush point.
inflamação s. f. (pl. -ões) 1. inflammation: a) ignition, act of inflaming. b) (med.) morbid condition characterized by swelling, redness and pain, phlogosis. 2. enthusiasm, passion.
~ **do duodeno** (med.) duodenitis. ~ **espontânea** spontaneous combustion.
inflamado adj. inflamed: 1. ablaze, afire. 2. fiery, glowing. 3. vehement, ardent. 4. passionate, enthusiastic. 5. irritated, angry.
inflamador s. m. inflamer. || adj. inflammatory.
inflamar v. 1. to inflame. 2. to ignite, kindle, set on fire. 3. to excite, stimulate. 4. (med.): a) to cause an inflammation. b) to become inflamed. c) to fester, rankle. 5. to incense. 6. to rouse. 7. ~-se to take fire, flame, glow.
inflamativo adj. inflammative, inflammatory.
inflamatório adj. inflammatory, phlogistic.
inflamável adj. m. + f. (pl. -áveis) 1. inflammable, ignitable. 2. combustible. 3. piceous, fiery.
inflar v. 1. to inflate, swell with air or gas. 2. to puff up, bloat. 3. to become proud or haughty.
inflatório adj. inflatory.
inflectir, infletir v. 1. to inflect. 2. to bend, curve. 3. to incline, slant. 4. (gram.) to vary a word by inflection. 5. to modulate (sound, voice).

inflexão s. f. (pl. -ões) 1. inflection, inflexion. 2. bending, curving. 3. (gram.) grammatical inflection, conjugation. 4. variation, modulation. 5. slant, inclination.

inflexibilidade s. f. 1. inflexibility, incapability of being bent. 2. stiffness, rigidity. 3. (fig.) unrelentingness, implacability, inexorability. 4. perseverance, stubbornness.

inflexível adj. m. + f. (pl. -íveis) 1. inflexible. 2. unpliant, unbending. 3. stiff, rigid. 4. unrelenting, implacable, inexorable. 5. adamant, stern. 6. unyielding, die-hard. 7. unmerciful. || **inflexivelmente** adv. inflexibly, etc.

inflexivo adj. inflective, deflecting, inflectional.

inflexo adj. 1. inflexed. 2. (bot.) bent inwards. 3. inclined. 4. (gram.) uninflected, flexionless.

inflição s. f. (pl. -ões) infliction.

infligir v. 1. to inflict. 2. to impose punishment, penalize.

inflitivo adj. inflictive.

inflorescência s. f. inflorescence.

influência s. f. 1. influence. 2. a flowing in, influx. 3. ascendancy over. 4. authority, power, action. 5. importance, prestige. 6. (coll.) drag, pull, hold. 7. interest. 8. electrical induction. 9. occult power attributed to stars and constellations. 10. (med.) contagion, influenza.
estar sob a ~ de to be under the influence of. **fazer valer as suas ~s** to put one's influences into action. **um nome de máxima ~** a most influential name, a name to conjure with. **ele não possui ~ na cidade** he has no interest in the town. **um homem de ~** a man of some concernment. **ela tem grande ~ sobre as crianças** she exercises a great influence on the children. **sua ~ secreta deu resultado** the use of his secret influence proved successful, (coll.) his wire-pulling turned the trick. **ele é uma pessoa sem ~** he is an uninfluential person.

influenciado adj. influenced, affected, interested.
não ~ uninfluenced, untouched, unswayed.

influenciar v. 1. to influence, exercise influence upon. 2. to act on, sway over 3. to modify, affect. 4. to touch, impress. 5. to actuate, (also electr.) induce.
~ contra to prejudice against. **~ favoravelmente** to influence favourably, prepossess. **ele o influenciou** he influenced him, worked up on him.

influente s. m. + f. influencer, big-wig, big shot. || adj. 1. influential, influent. 2. powerful, important. 3. weighty. || **~mente** adv. influentially, powerfully.
gente ~ influential people, people of consequence. **ter um amigo ~** to have an influential friend, have a friend at court.

influenza s. f. 1. (med.) influenza, flue, grippe. 2. (vet.) pinkeye.

influição s. f .(pl. -ões) 1. influx, act of flowing in. 2. influence.

influído adj. (Braz.) 1. enthusiastic, animated, lively. 2. flirtatious.

influidor s. m. influencer. || adj. influential.

influir v. 1. to flow into. 2. to influence, exercise power over. 3. to implant, instil with. 4. to make enthusiastic or animated. 5. to excite, inspire. 6. to impel, actuate. 7. to prevail upon. 8. to communicate with. 9. **~-se** to become enthusiastic, be or become delighted.

influxo s. m. 1. influx. 2. act of flowing in, inflow. 3. infusion, intromission. 4. influence, power. 5. high or full tide, instreaming, inrush.

in-fólio s. m. (typogr.) folio. || adj. folio (said of a sheet once folded, making two leaves or four pages).

informação s. f. (pl. -ões) 1. information. 2. intelligence, report. 3. act or effect of informing. 4. communication, notice. 5. news. 6. advice. 7. inquiry. 8. authoritative opinion, decision or request, judgement. 9. investigation.
~ de jornal (news) item. **~ falsa** misinformation. **dar boas -ões** to give good references. **dar -ões sobre alguém ou alguma coisa** to supply information about a person or thing. **guichê de -ões** information desk (plate E 13). **pedimos -ões** we made inquiries. **pedir -ões sobre** to request information. **ele recebeu uma ~ secreta** he received a secret information, (coll.) got a tip. **serviço de -ões** intelligence service. **tirar -ões** to gather information. **uma ~ errada** a misinformation.

informado adj. 1. informed. 2. aware, knowing. 3. wise, initiated. 4. forewarned.
bem ~ well-informed. **não ~** uninformed, unposted. **pessoa bem -a** well-informed person, insider. **ele foi ~ em tempo** he was informed in time, he got wind of it. **ela é mal -a** she is ill-advised. **manter alguém bem ~** to keep a person well-informed, keep a person posted.

informador s. m. 1. informer, informant. 2. enlightener. 3. warner. 4. detractor. || adj. informant, informative, informational.

informante s. m. + f. 1. informer, informant. 2. reporter, notifier. || adj. informant, informative, informational.

informar v. 1. to inform, impart information. 2. to instruct, teach. 3. to confirm. 4. to tell, mention. 5. to communicate, notify. 6. to report. 7. to apprise, advise. 8. to disclose, reveal, divulge. 9. to warn. 10. to advertise, publish. 11. to brief. 12. to notify, intimate. 13. to tip. 14. to inspire, animate. 15. **~-se** to inquire, make an investigation or examination.
ele informou-me a respeito he informed me of it, (U. S. A.) put me wise to it. **ele informou-se sobre o meu estado de saúde** he inquired after my health. **sentimos informá-los de que** we are sorry to inform you that. **~ alguém de alguma coisa** to inform a person of s. th., break a thing to a person.

informativo adj. informative, instructive, informatory.

informe (I) s. m. 1. information, intelligence. 2. advice. 3. report.

informe (II) adj. 1. unformed. 2. formless, shapeless. 3. clumsy, crude, rough. 4. deformed. 5. enormous, monstrous. || **~mente** adv. formlessly, clumsily, enormously.

informidade s. f. 1. shapelessness. 2. deformity. 3. informality.

infortificável adj. m. + f. (pl. -áveis) unfortifiable, that cannot be fortified.

infortuna s. f. 1. misfortune, unfortunateness. 2. unhappiness. 3. misery, distress.

infortunado adj. 1. unfortunate, fortuneless. 2. unhappy. 3. miserable, wretched. 4. ill-fated. || **-amente** adv. unfortunately, miserably, unsuccessfully.

infortunar v. to make unhappy, cause unhappiness to.

infortúnio s. m. 1. misfortune, infelicity, unhappiness. 2. misery, distress. 3. casualty, disaster. 4. ill luck, mishap, mischance. 5. adversity, woe.

infortunística s. f. part of the forensic medicine which studies labour risks, as well as industrial accidents and infirmities.

infortunoso adj. unhappy, unfortunate, ill-fated, disastrous.

infração, infracção s. f. (pl. **-ões**) 1. infraction, infringement. 2. transgression, contravention. 3. breach. 4. (sports) foul, foul play.
~ **no cumprimento do dever** violation of duty.
infra-escrito adj. undermentioned, named below.
infra-estrutura s. f. 1. substructure. 2. groundwork or bed.
infrajurássico adj. (geol.) infra-Jurassic, situated under Jurassic rocks.
infrangível adj. m. + f. (pl. **-íveis**) infrangible, unbreakable.
infra-oitava s. f. (pl. **infra-oitavas**) sequence of eight days following a religious feast day.
infrato, infracto adj. 1. broken, worn out. 2. dejected, depressed, broken-hearted.
infrator, infractor s. m. 1. infractor. 2. infringer, transgressor. 3. violator. 4. defaulter. 5. forfeiter.
infravermelho s. m. infra-red. ‖ adj. infra-red.
infrene adj. m. + f. unrestrained, immoderate. 2. unbridled, uncontrolled. 3. unruly.
infreqüência s. f. 1. infrequence, infrequency. 2. rarity.
infreqüentado adj. unfrequented, not visited.
infreqüente adj. m. + f. 1. infrequent, unfrequent. 2. scarce, rare. 3. uncommon. ‖ ~**mente** adv. infrequently.
infringir v. 1. to infringe. 2. to commit an infraction, infract. 3. to transgress, violate, break, contravene. 4. to disobey. 5. to overpass, trespass.
infringível adj. m. + f. (pl. **-íveis**) infringible, that can be infringed, breakable.
infrutescência s. f. fructescence, fruiting of a plant.
infrutífero adj. 1. unfruitful, fruitless. 2. barren. 3. unproductive, unsuccessful. 4. futile, vain. 5. profitless. ‖ **infrutiferamente** adv. unfruitfully, fruitlessly, unproductively.
infrutuosidade s. f. infructuosity, unfruitfulness.
infrutuoso adj. 1. unfruitful, fruitless. 2. infructuous. 3. useless, futile, vain. 4. barren. 5. unproductive. ‖ **-amente** adv. fruitlessly, unfruitfully, infructuously.
infuca s. f. (Braz.) 1. attempt, endeavour. 2. plot, intrigue. 3. knotty problem; rub.
infulminável adj. m. + f. (pl. **-áveis**) that cannot be fulminated.
infumável adj. m. + f. (pl. **-áveis**) unsmokable.
infundado adj. 1. unfounded, baseless. 2. ungrounded, groundless. 3. causeless, unsolid. ‖ **-amente** adv. unfoundedly, baselessly, footlessly, causelessly.
pretensão -a false claim.
infundibuliforme adj. m. + f. 1. (also bot., ent.). infundibular, infundibulate, infundibuliform. 2. (bot.) funneliform.
infundíbulo s. m. 1. (anat., zool.) infundibulum. 2. funnel.
infundiça, infundice s. f. a kind of lye made of urine (used to soak and wash very dirty clothes).
infundir v. 1. to infuse. 2. to pour in or into. 3. to spill, shed. 4. to implant, instill. 5. to steep, soak. 6. to impress, inculcate. 7. ~**-se** to slip in, sneak in, introduce o. s.
infunicar v. (sl.) 1. disfigure, deform. 2. to disguise.
infusa s. f. pitcher, earthen pot.
infusação s. f. (pl. **-ões**) (Braz., coll.) impoverishment, pauperization.
infusado s. m. (Braz., coll.) impoverished person. ‖ adj. impoverished, poor, indebted.
infusão s. f. (pl. **-ões**) 1. infusion: a) act of infusing or pouring in. b) instilling, imbuing. c) act of steeping a vegetable substance in a liquid in order to obtain an extraction of its active principles. d) liquid extract thus obtained, as tea, essence, etc. 2. (pharm.) maceration.

infusar v. (Braz., coll.) to impoverish, become indebted.
infusibilidade s. f. infusibility.
infusível adj. m. + f. (pl. **-íveis**) infusible, incapable of being dissolved or melted.
infuso s. m. 1. infusion, liquid extract, essence. 2. liquid used for steeping. ‖ adj. infused, macerated.
infusórios s. m. pl. (zool.) Infusoria, protozoans of the Ciliata or Ciliophora classes.
infustamento s. m. musty smell in old wine barrels or casks.
infusura s. f. (vet.) laminitis.
ingá s. m. 1. inga tree, cocowood and several other related shrubs. 2. inga; a genus of tropical plants. 3. fruit of these trees.
ingazeira s. f., **ingazeiro** m. inga: common name of several tropical shrubs and trees of the mimosa family (genus Inga).
ingênito adj. 1. innate, inborn. 2. inbred. 3. congenital, hereditary.
ingente adj. m. + f. vast, large, huge, enormous.
ingênua s. f. (theat.) 1. ingénue: artless, innocent girl. 2. actress who fills such a role.
ingenuidade s. f. 1. ingenuity, ingenuousness. 2. naiveness, simplicity. 3. frankness, openheartedness. 4. candour, sincerity. 5. innocence.
ingênuo s. m. 1. ingenuous, artless person. 2. (Braz.) freeborn child of slaves (after abolition of slavery). ‖ adj. 1. ingenuous. 2. naive, simple. 3. frank, open-hearted. 4. candid, sincere. 5. innocent, unartful. 6. gullible, unsuspicious. 7. free(born). ‖ **-amente** adv. ingenuously, open-heartedly, credulously, naively.
ingerência s. f. 1. interference, act of interfering, interposition. 2. meddling, intermeddling. 3. intervention.
ingerir v. 1. to swallow, ingest. 2. introduce, insert. 3. to meddle, intermeddle with. 4. to interfere in.
ingestão s. f. (pl. **-ões**) 1. ingestion. 2. swallowing, deglutition.
Inglaterra s. f. England, Great Britain, Britannia.
inglês s. m. 1. Britisher, Englishman. 2. the English language, English. ‖ adj. English.
~ **básico** basic English. ~ **mal falado** broken English. **ele fala o** ~ **básico** he talks basic English. **o povo** ~ the British, (coll., ironic.) John Bull. **isto é só para** ~ **ver** that's only eyewash; that's merely for show.
inglesa s. f. English woman.
café à ~ coffee with a little milk. **vamos à** ~ each one pays for himself.
inglesada s. f. (depr.) group of English people.
inglesar v. 1. to Anglicize, render conformable to English usages. 2. adopt English behaviour and customs.
inglório adj. inglorious, obscure, renownless.
inglorioso adj. inglorious. ‖ **-amente** adv. ingloriously.
ingluvial adj. m. + f. (pl. **-ais**) (zool.) ingluvial, of or pertaining to the ingluvies.
inglúvias s. f. pl. (zool.) ingluvies: 1. (ornith.) crop, craw. 2. dilatation of the digestive tube (situated before the true stomach).
inglúvio s. m. (ornith.) craw.
ingovernável adj. m. + f. (pl. **-áveis**) 1. ungovernable, unmanageable. 2. uncontrollable, indisciplinable. 3. unruly, unsubmissive.
ingranzéu s. m. 1. great noise, clamour. 2. confusion. 3. gibberish.
ingratão, ingratalão s. m. (pl. **-ões**) ungrateful man.
ingratidão s. f. (pl. **-ões**) 1. ingratitude, ungratefulness. 2. unthankfulness.
tratado com ~ ill-requited.

ingrato s. m. ungrateful person, ingrate. ‖ adj. 1. ungrateful, ingrate. 2. unthankful, thankless. 3. (fig.) sterile, barren. 4. (fig.) unproductive. 5. disagreeable, unpleasant. 6. troublesome, annoying. ‖ **-amente** adv. ungratefully, thanklessly. **uma tarefa -a** a thankless task.

ingrediente s. m. ingredient, component part of a compound or mixture.

íngreme adj. m. + f. 1. steep, sheer (plate Q). 2. abrupt, proclivous, precipitous. 3. acclivitous, uphill. 4. craggy, cragged. 5. (fig.) arduous, difficult.

ingremidade, ingremidez s. f. steepness, precipitousness, craggedness, cragginess.

ingresia s. f. 1. gibberish. 2. great noise, clamour. 3. gibberish.

ingressar v. to enter, ingress, go in.

ingresso s. m. 1. ingression, ingress. 2. entry, entrance, act of entering. 3. admission, admittance. 4. ticket.
~ gratuito pass. **bilhete de ~** admission ticket. **preço de ~** admission.

ingriba s. f. (S. Braz.) quarrel, dispute.

íngua s. f. (med.) inguinal bubo, bubo of the groin.

inguinal adj. m. + f. (pl. **-ais**) inguinal, of or pertaining to the groin.

ingurgitação s. f. (pl. **-ões**), **ingurgitamento** m. 1. ingurgitation act of swallowing greedily. 2. (med.): a) cramming. b) infarct, infarction.

ingurgitar v. 1. to ingurgitate, engorge. 2. to swallow. 3. to glut, cram. 4. to swell up. 5. to suffer from an infarction.

ingurunga s. f. (N. Braz.) uneven piece of land.

inhaca (I) s. m. (Port., Africa) king, supreme lord.

inhaca (II) s. f. (Braz., coll.) bad or rank smell, rank body odour.

inhaíba s. f. Brazilian forest tree (Nectandra mollis N.).

inhambu s. m. (Braz.) = **inambu.**

inhame s. m. (bot.) yan, sweet potato.

inhapa s. f. (S. Braz.) little gift offered to a purchaser as a token of regard.

inhenho s. m. timid, foolish or decrepit man. ‖ adj. stupid, foolish, imbecile.

inibição s. f. (pl. **-ões**) 1. inhibition, act of inhibiting. 2. prohibition. 3. restraint, (jur.) embargo. 4. (med.) lowering or suspension of the function of an organ.

inibidor s. m. inhibiter, inhibitor. ‖ adj. inhibiting.

inibir v. 1. to inhibit. 2. to check, repress. 3. to forbid, prohibit. 4. to interdict. 5. to obstruct, hinder.

inibitivo adj. inhibitive, inhibitory.

inibitória s. f. 1. difficulty. 2. hindrance, obstruction. 3. (jur.) writ which forbids a judge any further proceeding. 4. inhibition.

inibitório adj. inhibitory.

iniciação s. f. (pl. **-ões**) 1. initiation. 2. beginning, start. 3. formal admission into an association.

iniciado s. m. initiate, adept.

iniciador s. m. 1. initiator, founder. 2. starter, beginner. ‖ adj. initiating, initiatory.

iniciadora s. f. initiatrix.

inicial s. f. (pl. **-ais**) initial: first letter of a word (plate L 4). ‖ adj. m. + f. 1. initial, initiatory. 2. original, primordial. 3. primitive. 4. young. 5. inaugural.

iniciar v. 1. to initiate. 2. to begin, start, commence. 3. to inaugurate. 4. to introduce, induct. 5. to give preliminary instructions. 6. to enter. 7. to launch. 8. to open. 9. to admit. 10. to inform, advise.
~ o trabalho to start work. **~ uma briga** to pick up a quarrel. **~am uma conversa** they entered upon a conversation. **ela iniciou uma ação judicial** she took action. **ele não sabe como iniciá-lo** he doesn't know how to set about it.

iniciativa s. f. 1. initiative. 2. introductory step, leading action. 3. ability for original conception, gumption. 4. enterprise, activity. 5. diligence.
faço isto por ~ própria I do this of my own accord. **ele é um homem de ~** he is a man of enterprise. **tomar a ~** to take the initiative. **por ~ de** at the suggestion of. **ter muita ~** to be enterprising. **~ particular** private enterprise. **de quem foi a ~?** whose initiative was it? **por ~ própria** on one's own.

iniciativo adj. initiative, initial, initiatory.

iniciatório adj. initiatory, introductory.

início s. m. 1. beginning, start, commencement. 2. inauguration. 3. outset, origin, leadoff. 4. opening. 5. dawn, rise, infancy. 6. rudiment, prime.
dar ~ to lead off. **ter ~** to commence. **de ~** at first, to begin with. **desde o ~** from the start.

inidôneo adj. not idoneous.

inigualável adj. m. + f. (pl. **-áveis**) 1. unequal(l)ed, unmatchable. 2. peerless, unique, unrival(l)ed. ‖ **inigualavelmente** adv. matchlessly, uniquely, peerlessly.

iniludível adj. m. +f. (pl. **-íveis**) 1. undeceivable. 2. undoubtful, evident.

inimaginável adj. m. + f. (pl. **-áveis**) unimaginable, inconceivable, unthinkable.

inimbó s. m. (Braz., bot.) bonduc (Caesalpina bonducella).

inimicícia s. f. enmity, hatred, hostility.

inimigo s. m. 1. enemy, adversary. 2. (mil.) foe. 3. opponent. 4. antagonist. ‖ adj. inimical, averse, hostile, foelike. ‖ **-amente** adv. inimically.
~ da sociedade wrongdoer of the people. **~ de morte** sworn enemy, mortal foe. **~ mortal** archenemy. **~ principal** archfiend. **ele é o seu próprio ~** he is his own enemy. **não o faça um ~ seu** don't make an enemy of him. **um ~ temido** a dreaded foe. **desertar para o lado ~** to desert to the enemy. **eu sou ~ destas coisas** I am opposed to these things. **tornar-se ~ de alguém** to fall out with s. o. **isto torna-os ~s** it sets them at variance, it sets them by the ears. **cair nas mãos do ~** to fall into the hands of the enemy.

inimistar v. 1. to make an enemy of, set at variance. 2. **~-se** to become someone's enemy.

inimitabilidade s .f. inimitability, inimitableness.

inimitável adj. m. + f. (pl. **-áveis**) inimitable, surpassing imitation. ‖ **inimitavelmente** adv. inimitably.

inimizade s. f. 1. enmity, hostility. 2. ill will, bad blood. 3. animosity, disaffection. 4. hatred.
cair em ~ to fall out with. **causar ~** to alienate. **estar em ~ com** to be at enmity with. **fomentar ~s** to sow the seeds of hatred.

inimizar v. 1. to make an enemy of, set at variance. 2. to antagonize, provoke the hostility of.

ininteligente adj. m. + f. unintelligent, unreasonable, unwise, witless. ‖ **~mente** adv. unintelligently, unreasonably, unmeaningly.

ininteligível adj. m. + f. (pl. **-íveis**) 1. unintelligible, inapprehensible. 2. obscure, mysterious. ‖ **ininteligivelmente** adv. unintelligibly.

inintencional adj. b. + f. (pl. **-ais**) unintentional, unpremeditated.

ininterrupção s. f. (pl. **-ões**) 1. continuity, ceaselessness. 2. sequence, consecutiveness. 3. uninterruptedness.

ininterrupto adj. 1. uninterrupted. 2. unbroken, undivided. 3. constant, ceaseless, continuous. 4. non--stop. ‖ **-amente** adv. uninterruptedly, etc.

ínio(n) s. m. (anat.) inion, external occipital protuberance.

iniqüidade s. f. 1. iniquity. 2. wickedness, wrongfulness. 3. unjustness, unrighteousness. 4. perversity.

iníquo adj. 1. iniquous, iniquitous. 2. wicked, wrongful. 3. unjust, unrighteous, perverse. 4. unequal, unfair. ‖ **iniquamente** adv. iniquitously, unrighteously, wrong(ly).

injeção s. f. (pl. **-ões**) injection: 1. act or effect of injecting. 2. substance injected. 3. enema. 4. (med.) cappillary hyperemia, congestion. 5. (geol.) intrusion of magma between rocks.
~ de pasta de cimento para reforço grouting. **~ hipodérmica** hypodermic injection, hypodermic. **~ intramuscular** intramuscular injection. **~ intravenosa** intravenous injection. **~ subcutânea** subcutaneous injection.

injetado adj. injected.

injetar v. 1. to inject, treat by injection, syringe. 2. to introduce, force in (liquids into a cavity). 3. to insert.

injetor s. m. injector, spray nozzle, blower.

injucundo adj. disagreeable, unpleasant.

injudicioso adj. injudicious, imprudent, ill-judged, ill-advised.

injunção s. f. (pl. **-ões**) 1. injunction. 2. command, order. 3. admonition. 4. imposition, dictate.

injungir v. 1. to oblige, force. 2. to impose an obligation. 3. to inflict. 4. to command, order. 5. to enjoin.

injuntivo adj. obligatory, imperative, commanding.

injúria s. f. 1. injuria, violation of rights. 2. affront, offense. 3. wrong. 4. invective, insult, outrage, vituperation. 5. damage, harm. 6. slander, detraction. 7. attack, aggression.
ele lançou ~s contra he broke out into invectives against.

injuriador s. m. injurer, inveigher.

injuriar v. 1. to injure. 2. to do harm, hurt. 3. to affront, offend. 4. to wrong. 5. to insult, outrage, 6. to slander. 7. to attack, assail. 8. **~-se** to be offended, take as an insult.
ela o injuriou she offended him, she called him names.

injurídico adj. injudicial, not according to the forms of law.

injurioso adj. 1. injurious. 2. harmful, hurtful. 3. offending, affronting. 4. wrong. 5. outrageous, insulting, invective. 6. defamatory. 7. offensive. 8. reproachful. ‖ **-amente** adv. injuriously, etc.

injustiça s. f. injustice, unjustness. 2. inequity, unfairness, unrighteousness. 3. wrong, harm. 4. iniquity, offense, foul play.
não lhe faça ~ don't do him wrong. **corrigir uma ~** to right a wrong. **uma ~ indisfarçável** a crying injustice. **fazer ~ a alguém** to do s. o. an injustice. **sou vítima de uma ~** I am wronged. **ele cometeu uma ~ para comigo** he did me wrong. **reparar uma ~** to right a wrong.

injustiçoso adj. 1. unjust, unfair. 2. dishonest. 3. unrighteous. 4. inequitable.

injustificabilidade s. f. unjustifiableness.

injustificado adj. unjustified, unlicensed.

injustificável adj. m. + f. (pl. **-áveis**) 1. unjustifiable, unjustified. 2. unwarrantable, not defensible. 3. unjust, illegal. ‖ **injustificavelmente** adv. unjustifiably, unwarrantably, unjustly.

injusto s. m. unjust man, wrongdoer. ‖ adj. 1. unjust, unfair. 2. dishonest. 3. unrighteous. 4. inequitable. 5. iniquitous, wrongful. 6. foul. ‖ **-amente** adv. unjustly, unrighteously, inequitably, wrongfully, iniquitously.
somos ~s para com ele we wrong him. **justamente ou injustamente** rightly or wrongly. **ele é um juiz ~** he is an inequitable judge.

inobediência s. f. disobedience, insubordination.

inobediente adj. m. + f. disobedient.

inobliterável adj. m. + f. (pl. **áveis**) unobliterable, ineffaceable.

inobscurecível adj. m. + f. (pl. **-íveis**) unobscurable, that cannot be obscured or hidden.

inobservado adj. 1. unobserved, unregarded. 2. unperceived, unwitnessed. 3. unseen.

inobservância s. f. inobservance, inobservancy, non-observance.

inobservante adj. m. + f. 1. inobservant, not attentive. 2. not careful to comply with (laws, rules, customs, etc.).

inobservável adj. m. + f. (pl. **-áveis**) 1. unobservable, incapable of being observed. 2. unaccomplishable.

inocência s. f. 1. innocence, innocency. 2. harmlessness, guilelessness. 3. cleanness, purity. 4. guiltlessness. 5. simplicity. 6. immaculateness.

inocentar v. 1. to pronounce not guilty, acquit. 2. to justify, warrant. 3. to excuse, pardon.

inocente s. m. + f. (fig.) child, baby. ‖ adj. 1. innocent. 2. inoffensive, unoffending, harmless. 3. guiltless, blameless. 4. simple, ingenuous. 5. chaste, pure, immaculate. 6. unsophisticated. 7. undeserving. ‖ **~mente** adv. innocently, guiltlessly, harmlessly, ingenuously.
~ como uma criança innocent as a lamb. **declarar-se ~ de** to wash one's hands of. **ele foi declarado ~** he was found innocent.

inocuidade s. f. innocuity, innocuousness, harmlessness, innoxiousness.

inoculabilidade s. f. inoculability.

inoculação s. f. (pl. **-ões**) inoculation, vaccination, ingrafting.

inoculador s. m. inoculator.

inocular v. 1. to inoculate. 2. to graft by budding. 3. to insert. 4. (fig.) to transmit, transfuse. 5. (fig.) to diffuse, divulge. 6. to contaminate.

inoculável adj. m. + f. (pl. **-áveis**) inoculable, inoculative.

inocultável adj. m. + f. (pl. **-áveis**) that cannot be concealed, hidden or dissimulated.

inócuo, inóxio adj. 1. innocuous, innoxious. 2. harmless, hurtless. 3. innocent, inoffensive.

inodoro adj. inodorous, scentless, odourless.

inofensivo adj. 1. inoffensive, unoffending. 2. harmless, hurtless. 3. innocent, innocuous. 4. undesigning. ‖ **-amente** adv. inoffensively, innocuously.

inoficioso adj. 1. inofficious. 2. without consideration of duty or natural obligation. 3. prejudicial.
testamento ~ inofficious testament or will (in which natural heirs are disregarded).

inolvidável adj. m. + f. (pl. **-áveis**) unforgettable.

inominado adj. innominate, having no name.

inominável adj. m. + f. (pl. **-áveis**) 1. unnamable, undescribable. 2. nameless. 3 (fig.) base, abject, revolting.

inoperante adj. m. + f. inoperative, inert, destitute of effect.

inoperável adj. m. + f. (pl. **-áveis**) inoperable, that cannot be operated.

inópia s. f. 1. want, poverty, penury. 2. (fig.) poorness of intellect. 3. (fig.) defect, flaw.
confessar a sua ~ to confess one's fault.

inopinado adj. (also **inopino**) 1. unexpected, unforeseen. 2. unawares. 3. extraordinary. 4. accidental. ‖ **-amente** adv. unexpectedly, accidentally.
eles surgiram -amente they turned up.

inopinável adj. m. + f. (pl. **-áveis**) inopinable: 1. unforseeable, unexpected. 2. unappreciable.

inopioso adj. poor, needy, indigent.

inoportunidade s. f. 1. inopportuneness, inopportunity. 2. untimeliness, unseasonableness. 3. inconvenience. 4. impertinence.

inoportuno adj. 1. inopportune, not opportune. 2. unseasonable, untimely. 3. inconvenient, inappropriate. 4. ill-timed, amiss. 5. impertinent, importunate. ‖ **-amente** adv. inopportunely, untimely, inconveniently.

é um tanto ~ it is rather out of season. **isto vem muito** ~ this comes in very awkwardly.

ignorgânico adj. inorganic: 1. not organic. 2. unorganized. 3. (chem.) said of compounds which do not contain carbon.

inorganizado adj. unorganized, inorganized; inorganic.

inospitaleiro adj. inhospitable, inimical to foreigners, affording no shelter. ‖ **-amente** adv. inhospitably.

inospitalidade s. f. inhospitableness, inhospitality.

inóspito adj. 1. inhospitable. 2. barren, wild. 3. affording no shelter or subsistence.

inovação s. f. (pl. **-ões**) 1. innovation, introduction of new things or methods. 2. change, alteration. 3. newness, novelty.

inovador s. m. innovator, introducer of changes. ‖ adj. innovatory.

inovar v. 1. to innovate. 2. to change or alter by introducing something new. 3. to renew, renovate. 4. to repair.

inoxidável adj. m. + f. (pl. **-áveis**) 1. inoxidable, inoxidizable. 2. rustproof, stainless.

inóxio adj. 1. innoxious, innocuous. 2. inoffensive, harmless. 3. innocent. 4. undamaged, unhurt.

input s. m. (Engl.) input. 2. (econ.) data entering into a calculation. 2. (ind.) materials and energy entering into a process.

inqualificável adj. m. + f. (pl. **-áveis**) 1. unqualifiable, incapable of being qualified. 2. ambiguous, equivocal. 3. unworthy, base, vile.

inquebrantável adj. m. + f. (pl. **-áveis**) 1. infrangible, unbreakable. 2. inflexible, unyielding. 3. unflagging, untiring. 4. indestructible.

inquebrável adj. m. + f. (pl. **-áveis**) unbreakable, nonbreakable, adamantine, infrangible.

vidro ~ safety glass.

inquerideira s. f. pack cinch, pack strap.

inquerir v. to tighten the straps of a packsaddle.

inquérito s. m. 1. inquiry, search for truth or information. 2. question, probe. 3. examination. 4. inquest. 5. investigation.

~ **judicial** assize, trial.

inquestionável adj. m. + f. (pl. **-áveis**) 1. unquestionable. 2. indubitable, doubtless. 3. indisputable, incontestable.

inquietação s. f. (pl. **-ões**) 1. inquietude, unquietness. 2. unrest, disturbance. 3. uneasiness, anxiety, apprehension, peacelessness, embarrassment, concern. 4. tumult, commotion. 5 (med.) jactitation.

provocou -ões it caused uneasiness.

inquietador s. m. disquieter, disturber, agitator. ‖ adj. disturbing, troubling, irritative.

inquietante adj. m. + f. 1. disturbing, troubling. 2. alarming, irritative, vexatious. 3. worrisome. 4. uneasy. ‖ ~**mente** adv. uncomfortably, alarmingly, worrisomely.

é muito ~ it is quite disturbing. **uma época** ~ an anxious time. **uma nova** ~ alarming news.

inquietar v. 1. to disquiet. 2. to disturb, trouble. 3. to alarm, vex, agitate. 4. to worry, molest. 5. to stir, disconcert. 6. ~**se** to be uneasy, fret, fuss, fidget.

ela inquietou-se de she took alarm at. ~**-se por** to put o. s. about for. **eles** ~**am-se** they toook alarm at.

inquieto adj. 1. unquiet, disquiet. 2. disturbed, unrestful. 3. uneasy, vexed. 4. anxious, restive, peace-

less. 5. troublesome, turbulent. 6. busy, solicitous. 7. apprehensive. ‖ **-amente** adv. unquietly, uneasily, vexedly, turbulently.

estou ~ my mind is not at ease. **ele ficou** ~ **por causa** he was alarmed at. **ela estava muito -a** she was ill at ease.

inquietude s. f. 1. inquietude, unquietness. 2. unrest, disturbance. 3. uneasiness, apprehension. 4. tumult, commotion.

inquilinato s. m. tenancy, tenantry.

~ **rescindível pelo proprietário** tenancy at will.

inquilinismo s. m. (bot., zool.) inquiline: cotenancy of plants or animals without causing harm to the host.

inquilino s. m. 1. tenant. 2. lodger, occupant. 3. housemate.

ela tem ~**s** she keeps lodgers.

inquinação s. f. (pl. **-ões**), **inquinamento** m. 1. inquination. 2. act of defiling. 3. pollution, contamination. 4. corruption.

inquinar v. 1. to inquinate. 2. to defile. 3. to pollute, contaminate. 4. to corrupt.

inquirição s. f. (pl. **-ões**) 1. inquest, inquiry. 2. inquisition. 3. strict search, investigation. 4. examination.

inquiridor s. m. inquisitor, inquirer, investigator. ‖ adj. inquiring, inquisitorial, prying. ‖ ~**amente** adv. inquiringly, pryingly, inquisitorially.

inquirimento s. m. 1. inquest, inquiry. 2. inquisition. 3. strict search, investigation. 4. examination.

inquirir v. 1. to inquire, ask for information. 2. to question, interrogate, query. 3. to investigate, probe. 4. to pry into, examine.

inquisição s. f. (pl. **-ões**) 1. inquisition, investigation, inquiry. 2. (hist.) Inquisition, the Holy Office.

inquisidor s. m. inquisitor.

inquisitivo adj. inquisitive, prying, eagerly curious, nosey.

inquisitorial adj. m. + f.(pl. **-ais**), **inquisitório** m. 1. inquisitorial, inquisitional. 2. vexatious. 3. inhuman, cruel. ‖ ~**mente** adv. inquisitorially, vexatiously.

irestaurável adj. m. + f. (pl. **-áveis**) unrestorable.

insaciabilidade s. f. insatiability, insatiableness.

insaciado adj. not satiated, unsated.

insaciável adj. m. + f. (pl. **-áveis**) 1. insatiable, insatiate. 2. unappeasable, unquenchable. 3. greedy, avid for, voracious. 4. (fig.) avaricious, ‖ **insaciavelmente** adv. insatiably.

insadio adj. unsound, unhealthy. ‖ **-amente** adv. unsoundly.

insalivação s. f. (pl. **-ões**) (physiol.) insalivation: mixing of the saliva with the food.

insalivar v. to insalivate, salivate, mix with saliva.

insalubre adj. m. + f. 1. insalubrious, unhealthy. 2. unwholesome, diseased, unsound. 3. noxious, unsanitary. ‖ ~**mente** adv. insalubriously, unhealthily, noxiously.

insalubridade s. f. 1. insalubrity, unhealthfulness. 2. unwholesomeness, unsoundness. 3. noxiousness. 4. unsanitariness.

insalutífero adj. unwholesome, insalutary.

insanabilidade s. f. incurability, incurableness, irremediableness.

insanável adj. m. + f. (pl. **-áveis**) incurable, irremediable, irreparable.

insânia s. f. insanity, madness, lunacy.

insanidade s. f. insanity, insaneness.

insano adj. 1. insane, deranged, crazy. 2. demented, maniacal. 3. mad. 4. foolish. 5. excessive, exhaustive. 6. expensive.

é um trabalho ~ it's a hell of a work.

insaponificável adj. m. + f. (pl. **-áveis**) unsaponifiable.
insatisfação s. f. (pl. **-ões**) unsatisfactoriness, dissatisfaction.
insatisfatório adj. unsatisfactory, poor, wrong, insufficient.
insatisfeito adj. dissatisfactory, dissatisfied, discontented, ungrateful.
insaturável adj. m. + f. (pl. **-áveis**) unsaturable.
insciência s. f. 1. inscience. 2. ignorance, nescience. 3. incapacity, ineptitude.
insciente adj. m. + f. inscient, ignorant, unskilful.
íscio adj. (poet.) inscient, ignorant.
inscrever v. 1. to make an inscription, inscribe. 2. to engrave. 3. to register, book. 4. to enrol, matriculate, enlist. 5. to record. 6. to write.
~-se na lista to enrol o. s.
inscrição s. f. (pl. **-ões**) 1. inscription. 2. lettering, legend. 3. matriculation, enlistment, enrolment. 4. registration, registry, register. 5. record. 6. epigraph, epitaph.
inscritível adj. m. + f. (pl. **-íveis**) inscribable.
inscrito adj. 1. inscribed. 2. engraved. 3. registered, enrolled. 4 (geom.) circumscribed.
insculpir s. 1. to engrave, carve. 2. to inscribe.
inscultor s. m. engraver.
inscultura s. f. 1. art of engraving. 2. carving, engraving.
insecável adj. m. + f. (pl. **-áveis**) undryable.
inseduzível adj. m. + f. (pl. **-íveis**) unseducible.
insegurança, inseguridade s. f. 1. insecurity. 2. unsafety, unsafeness. 3. unreliableness, unstableness. 4. (fig.) doubt, apprehension.
inseguro adj. 1. unsecure, unsafe. 2. unsure, unreliable. 3. unstable. 4. unsound. 5. shaky. 6. (fig.) uncertain, doubtful. || **-amente** adv. unsecurely, unsafely, unreliably.
inseminação s. f. (pl. **-ões**) insemination.
~ arficial artificial insemination.
insensatez s. f. 1. insensateness, foolishness. 2. madness. 3. stupidity. 4. absurdity, absurdness. 5. senselessness.
não é ~ dele fazer isto? is it not unwise for him to do that?
insensato adj. insensate: 1. unreasonable, irrational. 2. foolish, unwise. 3. demented, mad. 4. absurd. || **-amente** adv. 1. foolishly, unwisely. 2. senselessly. 3. dementedly.
insensibilidade s. f. 1. insensibility, unfeelingness. 2. indifference. 3. impassibility, apathy. 4. cold-heartedness, unkindliness. 5 (fig.) hardness, stoniness; callousness.
insensibilização s. f. (pl. **-ões**) insensibilization.
insensibilizar v. 1. to insensibilize, render insensible. 2. to dull, deaden, numb. 3. to drug. 4. **~-se** to harden o. s. against.
insensitivo adj. insensitive.
insensível adj. m. + f. (pl. **-íveis**) 1. insensible, insensate. 2. hard, callous. 3. indifferent, impassible. 4. dull, torpid. 5. senseless. 6. unfeeling, unkind, cold-hearted. 7. unconscious. 8. ruthless, implacable. 9. imperceptible. || **insensivelmente** adv. insensibly, insensately, etc.
inseparabilidade s. f. inseparability, inseparableness.
inseparado adj. inseparate.
inseparável adj. m. + f. (pl. **-áveis**) inseparable, undisjoinable. || **inseparavelmente** adv. inseparably.
insepulto adj. unburied.
inserção s. f. (pl. **-ões**) 1. insertion. 2. implantation. 3. inset. 4. (anat., bot.) place and mode of attachment of an organ.
inserir v. 1. to insert. 2. to introduce, put in. 3. to implant, inoculate. 4. to interpolate, intercalate. 5. to advertise, publish.

~ uma cláusula to add a clause. **~ um dia** to fit in a day.
inserto adj. insert, put or set in, placed in among other things.
inservível adj. m. + f. (pl. **-íveis**) unserviceable, useless, unsuitable, unfit.
insetarrão s. m. (Braz., pop.) big insect.
inseticida s. m. insecticide, vermin-killer, insect-powder. || adj. m. + f. insecticidal.
inseticídio s. m. insecticide: killing of insects.
insetífero adj. infested with insects.
insetífugo adj. repelling insects, insectiferous.
insétil, inséctil adj. m. + f. (pl. **-eis**) indivisible, incapable of being sectionalized.
insetívoro s. m. (zool., bot.) insectivore: 1. an insectivorous animal or plant. 2. any mammal of the Insectivora order, comprising moles, shrews, hedgehogs, etc. || adj. insectivorous.
planta -a (bot.) carnivore.
inseto s. m. 1. (zool.) insect. 2. (fig.) insignificant or importune person. 3. pest, vermin.
insetologia s. f. insectology, entomology, science of insects.
insetológico adj. insectological, entomologic(al).
insetologista s. m. + f. insectologer, entomologist.
insexual adj. m. + f. (pl. **-ais**) unsexual.
insexualidade s. f. unsexuality, sexlessness.
insídia s. f. 1. ambush, ambuscade. 2. stratagem. 3. perfidy, treachery.
insidiador s. m. insidiator, waylayer, corrupter.
insidiar v. to insidiate, waylay.
insidioso adj. 1. insidious. 2. lying in wait. 3. deceitful, sly, treacherous. 4. subtle. || **-amente** adv. insidiously, subtly, treacherously.
insight s. m. (Engl., psychol.) insight, a sudden understanding, usually intuitive, of one's own attitudes and behaviour.
insigne adj. m. + f. 1. notable, famous. 2. renowned, distinguished. 3. remarkable, eminent. 4. excellent. 5. extraordinary.
insígnia s. f. 1. sign, mark. 2. token, symbol. 3. emblem, badge. 4. (her.) cognizance. 5. **~s** pl. insignia.
~s da dignidade real regalia. **~ militar** colours.
insignificância s. f. 1. insignificance, insignificancy. 2. unimportance. 3. triviality, trivialness, pettiness, trifle.
insignificante s. m. + f. insignificant person. || adj. 1. insignificant, meaningless. 2. unimportant, inconsiderable. 3. trivial, trifling. 4. paltry, petty. **uma pessoa ~** a nobody. **este ramalhete ~!** this apology for a bouquet! **por uma moeda ~** for one paltry shilling.
insignificativo adj. insignificative.
insimular v. 1. to accuse, denounce. 2. reproach. 3. to slander.
insinceridade s. f. 1. insincerity. 2. untruthfulness. 3. deceitfulness, duplicity. 4. dissimulation.
insincero adj. 1. insincere. 2. untruthful. 3. deceitful, double-faced. 4. fast, underhand.
insinuação s. f. (pl. **-ões**) 1. insinuation. 2. act of insinuating or ingratiating. 3. hint, suggestion. 4. allusion, innuendo. 5. charge, allegation. 6. intimation. 7. warning. 8. (jur.) lodging of an alleged will for registration.
~ velada innuendo. **uma leve ~** a delicate hint.
insinuador s. m. insinuator.
insinuante adj. m. + f. 1. insinuating, insinuative. 2. ingratiating, engaging. 3. suggestive.
insinuar v. 1. to insinuate. 2. to hint, suggest. 3. to ingratiate. 4. to charge, allege. 5. to intimate, warn. 6. (jur.) to register an alleged will or other public documents. 7. to persuade, induce. 8. to

advise, counsel. 9. to introduce gradually, worm in. 10. to work o. s. into a person's favour. ~ **casualmente** to drop a hint.
insinuativa s. f. art or talent of being insinuative.
insinuativo adj. insinuative, insinuating.
insipidez s. f. 1. insipidity, tastelessness. 2. flatness, vapidity, drabness. 3. (fig.) inconvenience, annoyance. 4. bad taste. 5. monotony.
insípido adj. 1. insipid, tasteless. 2. drab, vapid, flat. 3. flavourless, unsavoury. 4. (fig.) inconvenient, disagreeable. 5. of bad taste, distasteful. 6. pointless, monotonous. ‖ **insipidamente** adv. insipidly, vapidly, unsavourily, distastefully, monotonously.
insipiência s. f. 1. insipience, lack of wisdom. 2. foolishness, folly. 3. ignorance. 4. want of understanding. 5. senselessness.
insipiente adj. m. + f. insipient, unwise, foolish, senseless, nonsensical.
insistência s. f. 1. insistence, perseverance. 2. persistence, pertinacy. 3. urgency. 4. obstinacy. 5. importunity.
   recomendaram-lhe com ~ they urged upon him. **a** ~ **vence!** perseverance triumphs, it's dogged does it!
insistente adj. m. + f. 1. insistent, insisting upon. 2. urgent, pressing. 3. vivid, intense. 4. obstinate. 5. importunate. ‖ ~**mente** adv. insistently, urgently, pressingly.
insistir v. (**em, sobre**) 1. to insist, stand upon. 2. to persist, urge on, press hard. 3. to assert emphatically, argue. 4. to be or become obstinate.
   ~**am em que ele cantasse** he was urged to sing. **ele insiste em obter o livro** he perseveres in obtaining the book. **ele insiste em sua opinião** he sticks to his opinion. **eu insisto em meus direitos** I am tenacious of my rights. **insisto em sua vinda** I insist on your coming. **ele vai** ~ **em seu direito** he will make a stand for his right.
ínsito adj. innate, inborn, natural.
insóbrio adj. intemperate.
insociabilidade s. f. unsociability, unsociableness.
insocial adj. m. + f. (pl. -**ais**) unsocial, reserved, unsociable.
insociável adj. m. + f. (pl. -**áveis**) 1. unsociable, not sociable. 2. untractable, ungovernable. 3. misanthropical. ‖ **insociavelmente** adv. unsociably.
insofismável adj. m. + f. (pl. -**áveis**) unsophisticated, simple, artless.
insofrido adj. 1. impatient. 2. restless. 3. stormy, turbulent, boisterous.
insofrimento s. m. impatience, restlessness, intolerance.
insofrível adj. m. + f. (pl. -**íveis**) insufferable, insupportable. ‖ **insofrivelmente** adv. insufferably.
insolação s. f. (pl. -**ões**) 1. insolation: a) (path.) sunstroke, heatstroke. b) (med.) treatment by exposure to the sun's rays, sun bath, siriasis. 2. (meteor.): a) daily time of clear solar radiation. b) rate of solar energy spent.
insolar v. to insolate, expose to the rays of the sun.
insolência s. f. 1. insolence, impertinence. 2. arrogance, presumption. 3. rudeness, affrontery. 4. insult, offense. 5. insolent act or saying.
   com muita ~ with much impudence, (coll.) with a face of brass. **ele agiu com extrema** ~ he acted as cool as a cucumber, with extreme insolence. **ele tinha a** ~ **de perguntar** he had the audacity to ask, (coll.) he had the cheek to ask.
insolente adj. m. + f. 1. insolent, impertinent. 2. arrogant, haughty, presumptuous. 3. rude, forward, uncivil. 4. insulting, offensive. 5. cocky, petulant. ‖ ~**mente** adv. insolently, etc.

não seja ~**!** don't be impertinent, (coll.) none of your cheek! **ele é um sujeito** ~ he is an insolent fellow, a whipper-snapper, a cool customer.
insolidariedade s. f. lack of solidarity.
insolidez s. f. unsubstantiality.
insólito adj. 1. uncommon, unusual. 2. remarkable, extraordinary. 3. arrogant, haughty. 4. contrary to custom or usage. ‖ **insolitamente** adv. uncommonly, unsually, haughtily.
insolubilidade s. f. insolubility, insolubleness, indiscerptibility.
insolúvel adj. m. + f. (pl. -**eis**) 1. insoluble, indissolvable. 2. unsolvable, incapable of being solved or explained. 3. inextricable. 4. (com.) unrecoverable.
insolvabilidade s. f. (com.) insolvency, bankruptcy.
insolvável adj. m. + f. (pl. -**áveis**) insolvable, insolvent.
insolvência s. f. 1. (com.) insolvency, bankruptcy, inability to pay. 2. failure.
insolvente s. m. + f. bankrupt, insolvent, debtor who is unable to meet his liabilities. ‖ adj. insolvent, nonsolvent, insolvable, bankrupt.
insolvível adj. m. + f. (pl. -**íveis**) insolvable, incapable of being paid, unredeemable.
insondabilidade s. f. 1. unfathomableness, impenetrability. 2. unsearchableness. 3. (fig.) inexplicableness.
insondado adj. 1. unfathomable, impenetrable. 2. unsounded, unplumbed. 3. unexamined. 4. unknown.
insondável adj. m. + f. (pl. -**áveis**) 1. unfathomable, fathomless. 2. impenetrable, unsoundable. 3. unsearchable. 4. bottomless, abysmal. ‖ **insondavelmente** adv. fathomlessly, unsearchably, abysmally.
insone adj. m. + f. 1. insomnious, sleepless, slumberless. 2. restless. 3. wakeful.
insônia s. f. 1. insomnia, sleeplessness. 2. restlessnes. 3. wakefulness. 4. vigilance, vigil.
insonioso adj. insomnious, sleepless.
insonolência s. f. insomnolence, insomnia, sleeplessness.
insonoro adj. soundless, unvoiced.
insonte adj. m. + f. guiltless, innocent.
insopitável adj. m. + f. (pl. -**áveis**) unappeasable, unquenchable.
insossar v. 1. to prepare without salt or seasoning. 2. to make insipid or tasteless.
insosso (ô) adj. 1. saltless, tasteless. 2. flat. 3. dull, spiritless. 4. mortarless (said of brickwork erected without mortar).
inspeção s. f. (pl. -**ões**) 1. inspection, critical examination. 2. survey, supervision. 3. perlustration. 4. controlment, review. 5. overhaul. 6. inspectorship, superintendence. 7. fiscalization. 8. visitation, visit.
   ~ **de cadáveres** coroner's inquest. ~ **geral** a general check-up. ~ **médica** medical examination. **serviço de** ~ inspection duty.
inspecionar v. 1. to inspect, scrutinize, examine. 2. to survey, supervise. 3. to control, review. 4. to overhaul, look into. 5. to perlustrate. 6. to fiscalize. 7. to visit. 8. to check, go over. 9. (mil.) to reconnoitre.
inspetar v. 1. to inspect, scrutinize. 2. to review, survey. 3. to guard, watch over.
inspetor s. m. 1. inspector, supervisor. 2. superintendent. 3. viewer. 4. surveyor. 5. overseer, controller.
   ~ **de disciplina** (university) proctor. ~ **do quartel** (mil.) barrack-master.
inspetoria s. f. inspectorate, inspectorship.
inspiração s. f. (pl. -**ões**) 1. inspiration: a) act of inspiring or breathing in. b) creative impulse, awakening of thought, intellectual exaltation. c)

(rel.) divine afflatus or influence. 2. instinct. 3. suggestion.

uma ~ súbita a sudden inspiration, (coll.) a brain wave. seguindo uma ~ repentina on the spur of the moment. levado pela ~ poética enraptured by poetic fire.

inspirado adj. inspired.

inspirador s. m. inspirer, stimulator, animator. ‖ adj. inspired, inspiring, animating, dynamic(al), inspiriting.

inspirar v. to inspire: 1. inhale, breathe in. 2. breathe into. 3. imbue, infuse. 4. animate, inspirit. 5. suggest, instil. 6. ~-se get enthusiastic about, feel inspired.

isto não inspira confiança this does not command confidence. ele a inspirou com nova coragem he inspired her with new courage.

inspirativo, inspiratório adj. inspirational, inspiring, inspiratory.

inspirável adj. m. + f. (pl. -áveis) inspirable.

inspissação s. f. (pl. -ões) inspissation, incrassation, thickening.

inspissar v. to inspissate, incrassate, thicken.

instabilidade s. f. 1. instability, instableness. 2. unsteadiness, inconstancy. 3. impermanence. 4. fluctuation, mutability. 5. shakiness, frailty.

instabilizar v. to unsettle, make unstable or inconstant.

instalação s. f. (pl. -ões) 1. installation, instal(l)ment. 2. erection, construction. 3. plant. 4. fittings, fixture(s), equipment.

~ de água quente hot water connections. ~ de tratamento de água waterworks. ~ de vapor steam installation. a ~ elétrica the electric fittings, the wiring.

instalado adj. installed, settled.

ele estava confortavelmente ~ numa poltrona he was comfortably installed in an easy chair. comodamente ~ snugly installed, snug as a bug in a rug.

instalador s. m. installer, fitter. ‖ adj. installing.

~ eletricista wireman.

instalar v. 1. to instal(l). 2. to place in a seat. 3. to erect, construct. 4. to fit out, equip. 5. to settle. 6. to instate, invest. 7. ~-se to settle down.

~ máquinas to mount machines. ~ na presidência (de uma sociedade) to chair.

instaminado adj. (bot.) unstamened, having no stamens.

instância s. f. 1. instance, instancy. 2. quality or state of being instant. 3. urgency, insistence. 4. jurisdiction, law court(s). 5. (jur.) stages of a lawsuit. 6. entreaty, request. 7. repeated solicitation.

a primeira ~ first hearing of a cause; court of first instance. segunda e terceira ~ second and third instance. em última ~ without further appeal. à ~ da parte at the solicitation of the party. por ~ de at the instance of.

instantaneidade s. f. instantaneousness, instantaneity.

instantâneo s. m. 1. instantaneous photograph, snapshot. 2. (phot.) instantaneous exposition. ‖ adj. 1. instantaneous. 2. rapid. 3. momentary, immediate. 4. unhesitating. ‖ -amente adv. instantaneously, momentarily.

instante s. m. 1. instant, moment. 2. minute, second. 3. flash, twinkling. ‖ adj. m. + f. instant, pressing, urgent, imminent. ‖ ~mente adv. instantly, immediately.

num ~! in a jiffy!, in a second!, in a flash!, in a hand's turn!, in a trice! vejamos, um ~ just a moment, let me see. ela voltou num ~ she came back in no time. naquele ~ at that instant. no primeiro ~ in the first moment. espere um ~! wait a minute! no último ~ at the last moment. a cada

~ every minute, continually. ela muda de opinião de ~ a ~ she changes her mind from moment to moment. ele telefonou neste ~ he called up a moment ago.

instar v. 1. to ask insistently, urge. 2. to press, drive. 3. to insist upon, persist. 4. to enforce.

instei com ela para que ficasse I urged her to stay.

instauração s. f. (pl. -ões). 1. instauration. 2. beginning, start, opening. 3. renewing, restoration.

~ de processo institution of proceedings, prosecution.

instaurador s. m. 1. founder. 2. restorer, renewer.

instaurar v. 1. to begin, initiate. 2. to establish, found. 3. to renew, restore, repair.

~ processo to prosecute. ele instaurou processo contra seu sócio he proceeded against his partner.

instável adj. m. + f. (pl. -áveis) 1. unstable, unsettled. 2. inconstant, changeable, fluctuating. 3. baffling, fickle. 4. shaky, sandy. 5. astatic, labile. 6. precarious. ‖ instavelmente adv. unstably, inconstantly, astatically.

instigação s. f. (pl. -ões) 1. instigation, incitement. 2. prompting, provocation. 3. suggestion. 4. inducement, enticement. 5. fomentation.

por ~ sua at your instigation.

instigado adj. instigated, induced, set on.

~ pelo irmão at the instigation of his brother.

instigador s. m. instigator, setter-on, inducer, inveigher, prompter.

~ do crime (jur.) accessory before the fact.

instigar v. 1. to instigate. 2. to goad on, urge, spur. 3. to prompt, provoke. 4. to induce, entice. 5. to foment.

ele o instigou a fazê-lo he put him up to it. ela o instigou para um maior esforço she egged him on to a greater effort.

instilação s. f. (fl. -ões) instillation, instil(l)ment, act of instilling.

instilar v. to instil(l), pour in by drops, infuse.

instintivo adj. 1. instinctive, prompted by nature. 2. conative, natural. 3. spontaneous, impulsive. 4. intuitive. ‖-amente adv. instinctively.

instinto s. m. 1. instinct, intuition. 2. flair. 3. libido. 4. natural propensity, innate tendency (essential for the preservation of existence). 5. natural affection or aversion. 6. (fig.) inspiration.

~ de preservação instinct of self-preservation. agir por ~ to act on instinct.

institor s. m. institor, manager, head clerk, agent.

instituição s. f. (pr. -ões) 1. institution, act of instituting. 2. establishment, investment. 3. creation, constitution. 4. established custom or usage. 5. appointment of an heir. 6. -ões pl. fundamental rules, first principles. 7. institute.

~ de caridade charitable institution. -ões beneficentes charities.

instituidor s. m. institutor, establisher, founder, erector.

instituir v. 1. to institute, set up, establish. 2. to found, create. 3. to appoint as heir. 4. to instruct, educate. 5. to constitute, organize. 6. to settle. 7. to originate, begin. 8. to nominate, designate.

institutos s. f. pl. (jur.) institutes: 1. collection of established laws, rules and principles. 2. Justinianian Code.

instituto s. m. 1. institute, institution. 2. established rule or principle. 3. order, regulation, precept. 4. constitution or fundamental rules of a religious order.

~ correcional house of correction. ~ de beleza beauty parlour. ~ Nacional de Saúde National Health Institute. ~ tecnológico technological institute.

instrução s. f. (pl. -ões) instruction: 1. act of teaching. 2. education, schooling. 3. tutelage, tuition.

4. coaching, training. 5. indoctrination. 6. knowledge, information. 7. direction, order, discipline. 8. (jur.) program of proceedings in a lawsuit. ~ **da demanda** (jur.) preliminary instructions for the prosecution. ~ **primária** elementary education. ~ **pública** public instruction. ~ **secundária** secondary education. **ela não tem** ~ she is unschooled. **eles receberam -ões de serviço** they were briefed on their duties. **falta de** ~ illiteracy. **juiz de** ~ examining judge. **-ões de manejo** operating instructions (plate T 4).

instruído adj. 1. learned, educated. 2. informed. 3. initiat(ed). 4. sage, wise.

instruir v. to instruct: 1. teach. 2. educate, school. 3. train, drill, coach. 4. indoctrinate. 5. inform, enlighten, acquaint. 6. prepare particulars of prosecution in a lawsuit.

instrumentação s. f. (pl. **-ões**) instrumentation, (mus.) scoring.

instrumental s. m. (pl. **-ais**) 1. the different instruments of an orchestra collectively. 2. (gram.) instrumental case. ‖ adj. m.+ f. instrumental, instrumentary.

instrumentar v. (mus.) to instrument, score.

instrumentista, instrumentalista s. m. + f. instrumentalist, player.

instrumento s. m. instrument: 1. means, agency. 2. tool, implement, utensil (plate M 7). 3. contrivance, engine, machine. 4. (mus.) apparatus for producing musical sounds, organ, clavier. 5. (jur.) deed, factum, grant, patent. 6. human tool, medium, creature. ~ **de corda** (mus.) stringed instrument. ~ **de contrato** contract. ~ **de percussão** percussion instrument. ~ **de sopro** (mus.) wind instrument. **o** ~ **da ira divina** vessel of wrath. **distribuição dos** ~**s** instrument layout. **ser o** ~ **de** to be instrumental in. **você toca algum** ~? do you play an instrument?

instrutivo adj. 1. instructive, instructional. 2. educative, didactic, preceptive. 3. informative, informatory. 4. edificatory. ‖ **-amente** adv. instructively.

instrutor s. m. 1. instructor, teacher. 2. trainer, coach, drillmaster. 3. tutor, don, preceptor.

instrutora s. f. instructress, preceptress.

instrutura s. f. (archit., constr.) structure of a building, construction, frame.

insua s. f. little river island, islet.

insuave adj. m. + f. 1. insuave, lacking suavity. 2. unpleasant, disagreeable.

insuavidade s. f. insuavity.

insubmergível, insubmersível adj. m. + f. (pl. **-íveis**) insubmergible, unsinkable.

insubmissão s. f. (pl. **-ões**) unsubmissiveness, disobedience, mutinousness.

insubmisso s. m. unsubmissive, disobedient, ungovernable. **ele é** ~ (mil.) he is a deserter.

insubordinação s. f. (pl. **-ões**) insubordination, subversion, mutiny, rebellion, insurrection.

insubordinado s. m. insubordinate, disobedient or unsubmissive person. ‖ adj. 1. insubordinate. 2. unruly, disobedient. 3. disorderly. 4. mutinous.

insubordinar v. 1. to revolt, rebel. 2. to instigate to revolt, incite against. 3. ~**-se** to commit an insubordination, raise (in arms) against.

insubordinável adj. m. + f. (pl. **-áveis**) 1. incapable of subordination. 2. unruly, disobedient. 3. rebellious. 4. indocile, intractable. 5. incorrigible, inveterate.

insubornável adj. m. + f. (pl. **-áveis**) incorruptible, unbribable.

insubsistência s. f. 1. lack of support. 2. inability to subsist. 3. instability, inconstancy.

insubsistente adj. m. + f. 1. unable to subsist, unstable, inconstant. 2. ineffectual.

insubstancial adj. m. + f. (pl. **-ais**) 1. unsubstantial, insubstantial. 2. not strengthening. 3. illusive. ‖ ~**mente** adv. unsubstantially.

insubstancialidade s. f. unsubstantiality.

insubstituível adj. m. + f. (pl. **-íveis**) irreplaceable, irretrievable, that cannot be substituted.

insucesso s. m. ill success, failure, unsuccessfulness.

insueto adj. 1. unusual, uncommon. 2. disused.

insuficiência s. f. 1. inufficience, insufficiency. 2. inadequacy, inadequateness. 3. poorness, paucity. 4. deficiency. 5. incapacity, inaptitude, incompetence. ~ **cardíaca** (med.) cardiac insufficiency.

insuficiente adj. m. + f. 1. insufficient, wanting. 2. inadequate, unsatisfactory. 3. poor, scanty. 4. deficient. 5. unfit, incapable, incompetent. ‖ ~**mente** adv. insufficiently, poorly, scantily, deficiently. **com tripulação** ~ ill-manned.

insuflação s. f. (pl. **-ões**) 1. insufflation, act of breathing on or into, blowing. 2. (fig.) inspiration. ~ **divina** afflatus.

insuflador s. m. (med.) insufflator: apparatus used in performing insufflation. ‖ adj. insufflating.

insuflar v. to insufflate: 1. blow into, breathe upon. 2. (med.) treat by insufflation. 3. (fig.) suggest, insinuate. 4. inspire. 5. incite, provoke.

ínsula s. f. (poet.) island, islet.

insulação s. f. (pl. **-ões**), **insulamento** m. 1. insulation. 2. act of insulating, detachment, segregation. 3. isolation. 4. seclusion, solitude.

insulano s. m. islander. ‖ adj. insular.

insular (I) s. m. + f. islander. ‖ adj. insular. **situação** ~ insularity.

insular (II) v. 1. to set apart, separate. 2. to give an insular character to. 3. to live secludedly, shut o. s. off from society. 4. to isolate, insulate.

insulcado adj. 1. not furrowed, untilled. 2. (fig.) never previously navigated.

insulina s. f. (pharm.) insulin: specific for diabetes.

insulso adj. insipid: 1. saltless. 2. insipid, tasteless, flat. 3. stale. 4. (fig.) uninteresting, dull, tedious. ‖ **-amente** adv. insulsely, insipidly, dully.

insultado adj. insulted, offended.

insultador s. m. offender, insulter, reviler. ‖ adj. insulting, insultant.

insultante s. m. + f. offender, insulter. ‖ adj. 1. insultant, insulting. 2. abusive. 3. sacrilegious. 4. contumelious. ‖ ~**mente** adv. insultingly, affrontingly. **ele achou-o** ~ he considered it as insultant. **linguagem** ~ abusive language.

insultar v. 1. to insult. 2. to abuse, affront. 3. to offend, wound. 4. to outrage, revile. **isto é** ~ **além de injuriar** that's adding insult to injury.

insulto s. m. 1. insult. 2. abuse, affront. 3. offence, offense, slur, affrontery. 4. revilement. 5. (med.) sudden attack, fit, seizure.

insultor s. m. insulter, offender.

insultuoso adj. = **insultante (insultante** with respect to persons; **insultuoso** to qualify actions or things).

insumo s. m. (econ.) input, referring to data; raw materials or supplies entering into a calculation or process.

insuperabilidade s. f. insuperability.

insuperável adj. m. + f. (pl. **-áveis**) 1. insuperable, impassable. 2. unsurmountable. 3. unexcelled, unmatched. 4. invincible, unconquerable. 5. peerless. ‖ **insuperavelmente** adv. insuperably, unconquerably, unsurmountably. **ele é** ~ he takes the highest ranks.

insuportável adj. m. + f. (pl. -áveis) 1. insupportable. 2. insufferable, intolerable, unbearable. 3. annoying, bothersome. ‖ **insuportavelmente** adv. insupportably, unendurably, beyond endurance.
que pessoa ~! what an insupportable being! **aquele sujeito é ~** I cannot bear the sight of that chap. **o insulto é ~** the insult is not to be tolerated. **a dor era ~** the pain was beyond bearing.
insuprimível adj. m. + f. (pl. -íveis) insuppressible.
insuprível adj. m. + f. (pl. -íveis) 1. that cannot be supplied or replaced. 2. irreplaceable.
insurdescência s. f. deafness.
insurgente s. m. + f. 1. insurgent, rebel. 2. traitor. ‖ adj. insurgent, rebellious, seditious, mutinous.
insurgir v. (also **insurrecionar**) 1. to rise against, revolt, rebel. 2. to engage in an uprising, become insurgent. 3. to stir up to insurrection. 4. to emerge, appear, come into view. 5. **~-se** to rise in arms, resist, protest.
insurrecionado adj. insurgent, rebellious.
insurrecional adj. m. + f. (pl. -ais) insurrectional, insurrectionary.
insurreição s. f. (pl. -ões) 1. insurrection, insurgency. 2. (up)rising. 3. rebellion, revolt. 4. disobedience. 5. vigorous opposition.
insurreto s. m. insurgent, insurrectionist, rebel. ‖ adj. insurgent, rebellious.
insuspeição s. f. (pl. -ões) unsuspiciousness, unsuspicion, unsuspectingness.
insuspeito adj. 1. unsuspicious, unsuspected. 2. impartial, equitable. ‖ **-amente** adv. insuspectingly, impartially.
insustentabilidade s. f. untenability.
insustentável adj. m. + f. (pl. -áveis) 1. unsustainable. 2. untenable, unmaintainable. 3. baseless. 4. not subsistent.
uma posição ~ an unsustainable position.
intã s. f. (N. Braz.) stone ornament (found in funeral urns of ancient aborigines).
intaipaba, intaipava s. f. (Braz.) rapids.
intangibilidade s. f. intangibility.
intangível adj. m. + f. (pl. -íveis) intangible, untouchable. ‖ **intangivelmente** adv. intangibly.
intanha s. f. (Braz.) a species of tropical toads with a hornlike process over the eyes (family Cystignathidae).
intátil, intáctil adj. m. + f. (pl. -eis) intangible, impalpable, unsubstantial.
intatilidade, intactilidade s. f. intangibility, impalpability.
intato, intacto adj. 1. intact, untouched. 2. whole, entire, complete. 3. sound, woundless. 4. (fig.) unspoiled, pure.
inté prep. (pop.) till, until.
integérrimo adj. (sup. of **íntegro**) most upright, correct or honourable.
íntegra s. f. 1. totality, a whole. 2. completeness, entireness. 3. full text, word for word (of a letter, law, paragraph, etc.).
o texto na ~ the verbatim text.
integrabilidade s. f. integrality, entireness.
integração s. f. (pl. -ões) integration: 1. act of integrating. 2. (math.) operation of finding the integral of a function.
integracionista s. m. + f. a supporter of racial integration. adj. m. + f. referring to racial integration.
integrador s. m. integrator.
integral adj. m. + f. (pl. -ais) 1. integral. 2. total, whole. 3. unimpaired, unabridged. 4. entire, complete. 5. intrinsic(al). 6. (math.) pertaining to or produced by integration. ‖ **~ mente** adv. integrally, fully, soundly.

eles pagam a importância ~ they pay the whole sum. **pão ~** whole bread. **forma uma parte ~ do engenho** it forms an essential part of the apparatus. **cálculo ~** (math.) integral calculus. **ela vai pagar ~mente** she will pay in full.
integridade s. f. completeness, integrality.
integralizar v. to integrate, complete, complement.
integrante adj. m. + f. integrant, integral, component, constituent.
é parte ~ de seu caráter it is an important trait of her (his, their) character. **esta mola faz parte ~ do mecanismo** this spring is an essential part of the mechanism.
integralismo s. m. 1. the full application of a doctrine or system. 2. (Braz.) a right-wing political movement, similar to Fascism.
integrar v. 1. to integrate. 2. to make into a whole, aggregate. 3. to complete, total. 4. (math.) to find the integral of.
integrável adj. m. + f. (pl. -áveis) integrable, capable of being integrated.
integridade s. f. 1. integrity. 2. entireness, completeness. 3. integrality, intactness. 4. (fig.) rectitude, honesty. 5. (fig.) incorruptibility, incorruptibleness. 6. fairness, impartiality.
a ~ de seu caráter está acima de qualquer dúvida his trustworthiness is above doubt.
integrifólio adj. (bot.) integrifolious.
integripaliados s. m. pl. (zool.) Integropalliata, a suborder of molluscs.
íntegro adj. 1. complete, entire. 2. intact, inviolate. 3. righteous, honest. 4. incorruptible. 5. fair, impartial. 6. virtuous. 7. irreproachable.
inteirado adj. perfectly acquainted, well-informed, initiate(d).
estou ~ disso I am aware of it.
inteirar v. 1. to make entire, complete. 2. to integrate. 3. to acquaint, inform. 4. to initiate. 5. to fulfill, accomplish. 6. to make known. 7. to pay (the rest of a debt). 8. **~-se** a) to inquire about s. th. b) to inform o. s. in detail.
você precisa inteirá-lo de todos os fatos you have to bring all the facts to his notice. **ele inteirou a quantia** he made up the full amount. **inteire-se de seus deveres!** acquaint yourself with your duties!
inteireza s. f. 1. integrity. 2. entireness, completeness. 3. righteousness, honorability, probity. 4. incorruptibility. 5. severity, rigour.
inteiriçado adj. rigid, stiff.
~ de frio stiff or benumbed with cold.
inteiriçar v. 1. to stiffen, benumb. 2. **~-se** to become stiff or rigid. 3. to make stiff.
inteiriço adj. 1. entire, whole, of one piece. 2. stiff, rigid. 3. inflexible.
inteiro s. m. (math.) whole number, integer. ‖ adj. 1. entire: a) whole, unbroken, of one piece. b) exact, perfect. c) intact, uninjured. d) complete, full, total. e) (math.) whole. f) undiminished. g) uncastrated (animals). h) (fig.) honest, upright, righteous. 2. sound, safe. 3. uncorruptible. 4. resolute, firm. 5. all. ‖ **-amente** adv. 1. entirely, all, altogether, etc.
um retrato de corpo ~ a whole-length picture. **esperei duas semanas -as** I waited for two whole weeks. **número ~** (math.) whole number. **uma hora -a** a whole hour, (coll.) a solid hour. **ele pagou a conta -a** he paid in full. **durante o dia ~** throughout the whole day. **a doença se espalhou no país ~** the disease spread all over the country. **a família -a foi para Santos** the whole family went to Santos. **a conta está -amente errada** the account is quite wrong. **ele reconheceu -amente o perigo** he recognized the danger to its full extent.

intelecção s. f. (pl. -ões) 1. intellection, comprehension, understanding. 2. meaning, sense.
intelectivo adj. 1. intellective, rational. 2. mental, intellectual.
intelecto s. m. 1. intellect. 2. understanding. 3. faculty of perceiving and discerning. 4. intelligence, brains, mind.
intelectual s. m. + f. (pl. -ais) 1. intellectual. 2. pl. the educated people of a country collectively, intelligentsia. ‖ adj. 1. intellectual, of or pertaining to the intellect. 2. spiritual. 3. mental. 4. intelligential.
intelectualidade s. f. intellectuality, intellectual faculties, power of intellect.
intelectualismo s. m. intellectualism: 1. devotion to intellectual pursuits. 2. doctrine that the fundamental principle of all reality is intellect.
intelectualista s. m. + f. intellectualist. ‖ adj. intellectualistic.
intelectualizar v. to intellectualize, develop the intellect, give intellectual character to.
inteligência s. f. 1. intelligence: a) mental acuteness, sagacity, pertness. b) understanding, comprehension. c) knowledge, aptitude, intellect. d) intelligent being. e) sharpness, wit, cleverness. f) correspondence, mutual communication. 2. interpretation, elucidation (of a text). 3. (fig.) conspiration, collusion. 4. harmony, concord of opinions or interests.
falta de ~ unwisdom. quociente de ~ intelligence quotient (abbr. I. Q.). elas trocaram olhares de ~ they exchanged knowing (warning) looks. que falta de ~! how foolish! ele nunca criará ~! he will never grow wise. segundo a própria ~ according to one's lights. eles representam a ~ da cidade they are the talent of the town. será que você não tem ~? is it possible that you have no wits at all?
inteligente adj. m. + f. intelligent: 1. acute, sagacious, wise. 2. intellectual, knowing, learned. 3. apt, skilful. 4. clever, smart, cute. 5. talented, bright. 6. understanding, comprehensive. 7. shrewd, sharp-witted. ‖ ~mente adv. 1. intelligently, understandingly, wisely. 2. aptly, cleverly, cutely. 3. shrewdly, artfully.
ela é uma moça ~ she is a clearheaded girl. ela é uma moça bonita e, aiém disso, ~ she is a nice girl and clever withal. ele é muito ~ he has plenty of brains. ele não é lá muito ~ he hasn't cut his wisdom tooth yet.
inteligibilidade s. f. intelligibility, comprehensibleness.
inteligível adj. m. + f. (pl. -íveis) 1. intelligible, comprehensible, understandable. 2. clear, plain, perspicacious. ‖ inteligivelmente adv. intelligibly, apprehensibly.
intemente adj. m. + f. unfearing, undaunted.
intemerato adj. 1. pure, undefiled. 2. incorruptible. 3. righteous, honest. 4. (frequently misused instead of intimorato) unshrinking, fearless, intrepid.
intemperado adj. 1. intemperate, immoderate. 2. hard-drinking. 3. inordinate, unrestrained. 4. excessive.
intemperança s. f. 1. intemperance, intemperancy. 2. gluttony, debauchery. 3. insobriety, drunkenness. 4. inordinateness. 5. excess.
intemperante adj. m. + f. intemperate, unsober, immoderate, dissolute. ‖ ~mente adv. intemperately.
intempérie s. f. bad weather, inclemency of meteorological or climatological conditions.
intempestividade s. f. intempestivity, untimeliness, unseasonableness.
intempestivo adj. intempestive, untimely, unseasonable. ‖ -amente adv. intempestively, unseasonably.

intemporal adj. 1. timeless, eternal, perennial, not temporary or transitory. 2. not worldly or profane; spiritual.
intenção s. f. (pl. -ões) intention: 1. intent, purpose, aim. 2. design. 3. determination, deliberation. 4. notion, animus.
com má ~ with evil intentions, (jur.) with malice prepense. com a melhor das -ões with the best intentions. com a ~ de with a view to. ele tem más -ões he is bent on mischief, he is ill-disposed. não denunciar suas -ões to keep one's counsel. descobri as -ões dele I found out his intentions, (U. S. A., sl.) I've got his number. com firme ~ with determination. ele agiu com segundas -ões he had second motives. eu tenho a ~ de my intention is. fi-lo com a ~ de agradar-lhe I did it with a view to please him. uma missa por ~ de sua alma a mass for the repose of his soul. revelaram suas -ões they revealed their intentions, showed their colours. ela não tem a menor ~ de fazê-lo she hasn't a notion of doing it; she has no thought of doing it. não tinha más -ões I meant no harm.
intencionado adj. intentioned, disposed, affected.
~ a iludir o público calculated to deceive the public. ele está bem-~ a seu respeito he means well by you. ela é uma moça bem- -a she is a well-meaning girl.
intencional (pl. -ais), intencionável (pl. -áveis) adj. m. + f. 1. intentional, done with purpose. 2. intended, designed. 3. deliberate. 4. wanton, willful. ‖ ~mente adv. intentionally, purposely, consciously, willfully, deliberately.
ela contou uma mentira ~ she told a deliberate lie. não foi ~ it was undesigned. ela não o fez ~mente she did it unwittingly.
intencionalidade s. f. intentionality, willfulness, designedness.
intencionalismo s. m. (scholastic logic) doctrine which maintains that the intention is the characteristic end product of a process of thought.
intencionar v. to plan, aim at, have the intention of. o que ele intencionou com isto? what did he intend by it? what is the big idea of it?
intendência s. f. 1. intendancy, office or duties of an intendant. 2. administration. 3. stewardship. ~ militar commissariat.
intendente s. m. intendant, superintendant, manager, administrator, steward.
intender v. 1. to superintend. 2. to administrate, manage. 3. to watch over, inspect, control.
intensão s. f. (pl. -ões) 1. intensity, intenseness. 2. vehemence. 3. increase in intensity (or density).
intensar v. 1. to make intense. 2. to enliven, invigorate. 3. to increase. ‖ ~-se to become intense.
intensidade s. f. 1. intensity, intenseness. 2. degree of action or effect. 3. high degree. 4. vehemence, violence. 5. strength, force, power. 6. profoundness, depth.
~ do som volume of sound. ~ em velas candle-power. ~ do campo (electr.) field intensity, field strength. ela trabalhava com menor ~ she was working with relenting forces.
intensificação s. f. (pl. -ões) 1. intensification, act of intensifying. 2. enhancement.
intensificar v. 1. to intensify. 2. to enhance. 3. to amplify, deepen, heighten. 4. to exalt. 5. to concentrate. 6. to aggravate.
a luta intensifica-se the struggle thickens.
intensivo adj. 1. intensive, intensifying. 2. adding intensity or force. 3. active, lively. 4. vehement, violent. 5. (gram.): a) expressing action. b) serving

to give emphasis. 6. (agric.) of or relative to intensive cultivation.

intenso adj. 1. intense, intensive. 2. active, vivid, lively. 3. vehement, violent. 4. energetic, strong. 5. excessive, extreme. 6. ardent, fervent. 7. acute, penetrating, profound. ‖ **-amente** adv. intensely, acutely, ardently, violently.

ele sentiu uma fome -a he felt a poignant hunger. **o frio era ~** the cold was piercing. **ela tinha uma -a dor de cabeça** she had an intense headache, (coll.) a splitting headache.

intentar v. 1. to intend, design. 2. to attempt, endeavour. 3. to aim at. 4. to scheme. 5. to undertake. 6. (jur.) to bring an action against.

~am ação judicial contra o vizinho they brought an action against their neighbour.

intento s. m. 1. intention, intent. 2. plan, project, design. 3. aim, purpose. ‖ adj. 1. attentive. 2. dedicated, devoted.

conseguiram o seu ~ they attained their purpose, carried their point. **trabalharam com o ~ de** they were working with a view to. **frustrou-se o seu ~** their project miscarried.

intentona s. f. 1. conspiracy, complot. 2. wild scheme, extravagant intention or project.

interação s. f. (pl. **-ões**) interaction, interplay.

interacionismo s. m. (philos.) interactionism.

interalveolar adj. (anat., zool.) interalveolar.

interamericano adj. inter-American.

interanular adj. m. + f. interanular.

interarticular adj. m. + f. (anat., zool.) interarticular, situated in a joint.

intercadência s. f. 1. interruption, intermission. 2. (med.) intercadence, irregularity of the pulse.

intercadente adj. m. + f. 1. intermittent. 2. irregular. 3. alternating. 4. (med.) intercadent.

dia ~ (med.) intercadent day.

intercalação s. f. (pl. **-ões**) intercalation, interspersion, insertion.

intercalado adj. intercalar, intercalary, parenthetic(al).

intercalar (I) adj. m. + f. intercalar(y), inserted.

intercalar (II) v. 1. to intercalate, intersperse. 2. to insert between, interpolate. 3. to interlay. 4. **~-se** to intermingle, intermix.

~ folhas em branco to interleave. **~am um dia de descanso** they fitted in a day of rest.

intercambiar v. to interchange, exchange, trade.

intercâmbio s. m. 1. interchange, reciprocal exchange. 2. barter. 3. intercommunion. 4. reciprocity. 5. communication, dealing.

intercedente adj. m. + f. interceding, pleading.

interceder v. 1. to intercede. 2. to mediate, plead for. 3. to pray for. 4. to intervene.

intercedi com ele a seu respeito I interceded with him in your behalf.

intercelular adj. m. + f. intercellular.

intercepção, interceptação s. f. (pl. **-ões**) 1. interception. 2. interruption. 3. obstruction, hindrance. 4. intervention.

interceptar v. 1. to intercept, seize by the way. 2. to interrupt, break off, cut off. 3. to obstruct, hinder. 4. to stop, bring to a stand.

intercepto adj. intercepted.

interceptor s. m. interceptor. ‖ adj. intercepting.

intercervical adj. m. + f. (pl. **-ais**) (anat.) intercervical, situated between the cervical vertebrae.

intercessão s. f. (pl. **-ões**) 1. intercession. 2. mediation, entreaty in behalf of. 3. intercessory prayer. 4. solicitation, advocation. 5. interposition. 6. intervention.

graças à sua ~ through your (his, her, their) mediation.

intercessor s. m. intercessor, interceder, pleader. ‖ adj. intercessory, intercessorial.

interciso adj. 1. cut in halves, cut through. 2. cut to pieces, truncated. 3. interrupted.

interclavicular adj. m. + f. (anat.) interclavicular.

intercolegial adj. m. + f. (pl. **-ais**) intercollegiate, between colleges.

campeonato ~ de xadrez intercollegiate chess championship.

intercolonial adj. m. + f. (pl. **-ais**) intercolonial, between colonies.

comércio ~ intercolonial trade.

intercolunar adj. m. + f. intercolumnar, between columns.

intercolúnio s. m. (archit.) intercolumniation, space between columns.

intercomunicação s. f. (pl. **-ões**) 1. intercommunication, reciprocal intercourse. 2. anastomosis.

intercondral adj. m. + f. (pl. **-ais**) (anat.) intercartilaginous, interchondral.

intercontinental adj. m. + f. (pl. **-ais**) intercontinental.

intercorrência s. f. 1. intercurrence. 2. incident. 3. variation, modification.

intercorrente adj. m. + f. 1. intercurrent. 2. coming and taking place between. 3. intervening. 4. (med.) breaking into and modifying the course of an already existing disease.

intercostal adj. m. + f. (pl. **-ais**) (anat.) intercostal.

intercurso s. m. intercourse, communication, reciprocal dealing, interchange.

intercutâneo adj. subcutaneous.

interdependência s. f. interdependence, interdependency, mutual dependence.

interdição s. f. (pl. **-ões**) 1. interdiction, authoritative prohibition. 2. interdict, prohibitory order. 3. (jur.) estoppel. 4. ban, veto.

interdigital adj. m. + f. (pl. **-ais**) interdigital.

interditar v. 1. to interdict. 2. to forbid, prohibit. 3. (jur.) to estop, preclude. 4. to proscribe, embargo. 5. to restrain.

a piscina está interditada the use of the swimming pool is interdicted.

interdito s. m. interdict, interdiction, ban. ‖ adj. 1. interdicted. 2. forbidden, prohibited. 3. interdictive.

interdizer v. 1. to interdict. 2. to prohibit, forbid. 3. to debar, preclude. 4. to cut off from ecclesiastical privileges.

intereletródico adj. (electronics) referring to phenomena occurring between two or more electrodes.

interescolar adj. interscholastic.

interessado s. m. 1. profit-sharing employee, sharer. 2. partner, party. 3. prospect, prospective customer. ‖ adj. 1. interested. 2. concerned. 3. being a part-owner. 4. biased, not impartial. 5. selfish, covetous. ‖ **-amente** adv. interestedly, concernedly, selfishly.

ele está ~ na aviação he is an air-minded man. **ele não está muito ~** he is not particularly interested in. **ela é muito -a em novidades políticas** she is very much alive to political news. **encontraram-se as partes -as** the parties concerned met. **ela olhou -amente para** she cast on interested eye at.

interessante adj. m. + f. 1. interesting. 2. entertaining, engaging. 3. important. 4. sympathetic. ‖ **~mente** adv. interestingly.

ela está em estado ~ she is in the family way.

interessar v. 1. to interest: a) concern, affect, be of interest to. b) engage the attention of. c) call someone's attention to, attract. d) excite the interest or curiosity of. e) arouse concern, stimulate. 2. to be profitable to. 3. to cause to participate, give a share in. 4. ~-se to interest o. s. in, take a share in, concern o. s. with, be involved in.

interesso-me por I interest myself in. **não se ~ por** to take no interest in. **a quem possa ~ to** whom it may concern. **não me interesso por estas coisas** I have no concern for such things. **isso não me interessa** I take no interest in that, that is not my line. **isto não interessa!** that is of no consequence! **eu me interessei muito por ele** (fig.) I helped him a lot. **isto lhe interessa** that concerns you.

interesse (ê) s. m. 1. interest: a) benefit, advantage. b) profit, gain. c) sympathetic attention, personal concern, regard. d) participation in advantages, benefits or profits. e) payment for the use of borrowed money. f) share, stake. g) proprietory right, business control. h) influence, authority. 2. selfishness, covetousness.

ele tem ~ no negócio he is interested in the business. **ela toma ~ pela criança** she is concerned for the child. **em meu ~** in my interest. **ele demonstrou grande ~ pelo meu caso** he showed a great interest for my case. **ela está bem dentro do seu campo de ~** she is quite in her sphere. **no ~ de** on account of. **ele mostrou seu ~ pela aviação** he disclosed his air-mindedness. **demonstraram ~ particular por** they showed peculiar interest for. **prejudicaram os ~s da comunidade** they prejudiced the interests of the community. **o assunto é sem ~ algum** it is a barren topic. **é no seu ~** it is to your advantage. **ele tem um ~ pessoal nisso** his personal concerns are in question. **ele tem ~ no projeto** he has a stake in the project. **um vivo ~** a keen interest. **ele perdeu o ~ por completo** he lost all his interest.

interesseiro adj. 1. self-seeking, selfish. 2. calculating, mercenary. 3. covetous.

ele é muito ~ he is very selfish, he takes care of number one.

interestadual adj. m. + f. (pl. **-ais**) interstate.

comércio ~ interstate commerce.

interestratificado adj. (geol.) interstratified.

interfacial adj. m. + f. (pl. **-ais**) interfacial.

interfalangiano adj. (anat.) interphalangeal.

interestelar adj. m. + f. interstellar, existing among stars.

interferência s. f. 1. interference, act of interfering. 2. intervention. 3. obstruction, restriction. 4. (radio) jamming. 5. (phys.) interaction of different wave strains (light, sound, electricity, etc.) 6. meddlesomeness.

interferente adj. m. + f. interfering, interferential.

interferir v. 1. to interfere. 2. to collide, clash. 3. to intervene. 4. to interpose. 5. (phys.) to influence or counteract mutually. 6. (radio) to jam. 7. to meddle (in, with). 8. to obstruct, restrict, clog.

tenho de ~ I must intervene, I must get my hand in. **melhor não ~!** it is better not to interfere, better to let it be!

interfixo adj. having the fulcrum between the weight and the power.

interfoliáceo adj. (bot.) interfoliaceous.

interfoliar (I) adj. m. + f. (bot.) of or relative to the space between leaves.

interfoliar (II) v. to interfoliate, interleave.

interfone s. m. interphone, intercommunication system.

intergaláctico adj. (astr.) intergalactic, occurring or existing between galaxies.

interfrontal adj. m. + f. (pl. **-ais**) (anat.) interfrontal.

interglaciário adj. (geol.) interglacial, between two glacial periods.

interglobular adj. m. + f. interglobular, situated between globes.

interim s. m. (pl. **-ins**) interim, the meantime, intervening time, interval.

no ~ in the meantime, meanwhile.

interinado s. m. interimistic office or position.

interinidade s. f. interimistic state, provisional arrangement, provisionality.

interino s. m. interimistic worker or official. || adj. 1. interim. 2. provisional. 3. temporary, conditional.

interinsular adj. m. + f. interinsular.

interior s. m. 1. interior. 2. inland, country, countryside. 3. inward, inside. 4. entrails, intestines. 5. heart, soul. 6. province. 7. inner or private life. 8. internal affairs of a nation. || adj. m. + f. 1. interior. 2. upcountry, midland. 3. inner, inward. 4. intrinsical. 5. internal. 6. (fig.) secret, hidden, intimate. || ~mente adv. internally, intimately.

Ministério do Interior Home Department. **moramos no ~** we live in the country. **ele foi para o ~** he went into the country. **o ~ de uma casa** the inner rooms of a house. **só Deus conhece o ~** God alone knows the heart of a man.

interiorano s. m. provincial. || adj. provincial.

interioridade s. f. 1. provincialism. 2. interiority, inwardness.

interjacente adj. m. + f. interjacent, lying or being between.

interjecional adj. m. + f. (pl. **-ais**) interjectional, interjected. || ~mente adv. interjectionally, by way of an interjection.

interjeição s. f. (pl. **-ões**) interjection: 1. act of throwing in, interjecting. 2. exclamation, utterance. 3. (gram.) exclamatory word.

interjetivo adj. interjectional, interjectory.

interlinear adj. m. + f. interlineal, interlinear.

tradução ~ interlinear translation.

interlingüística s. f. the comparative study of interlanguages, or universal languages such as Esperanto, Ido, Interlingua.

interlobular adj. m. + f. (anat.) interlobular.

interlocução s. f. (pl. **-ões**) interlocution, dialogue, interchange of speech.

interlocutor s. m. interlocutor, prolocutor, speaker.

interlocutora s. f. interlocutress, interlocutrix.

interlocutória s. f. (jur.) interlocution, interlocutory order or decree.

interlocutório s. m. interlocutory order, decree or injunction. || adj. interlocutory.

interlope s. m. 1. smuggler, runner. 2. (fig.) adventurer.

interlúdio s. m. (arts, mus.) interlude.

interlunar adj. m. + f. interlunar, interlunary.

interlúnio s. m. interlunar period, new moon.

intermaxilar adj. m. + f. intermaxillary.

intermediar v. 1. to intermediate. 2. to intervene. 3. to interpose. 4. to intermix.

intermediário s. m. 1. intermediate, intermediary. 2. broker, commission agent. 3. mediator, middleman. || adj. intermediate, intervening, interposed, mean, middle, agential.

transmissão -a (tech.) intermediate gearing. **eixo ~** intermediate shaft. **exame ~** intermediate examination.

intermédio s. m. 1. intermediary, intermediate. 2. agent, go-between. 3. mediator. 4. intervention. 5. interlude, interval, interim. 6. means, way. || adj. intermediate, intervening, interposed.

recebi o livro por ~ da firma I received the book through the company. **recebi a carta por ~ do meu primo** I received the letter by my cousin's hand. **enviaram a notícia por outro ~** they sent their news through another channel.

intermeter v. 1. to interpose, place between. 2. to interfere, intervene.

intermezzo s. m. (It., arts., mus.) intermezzo.
interminado adj. unaccomplished, unfinished.
interminável adj. m. + f. (pl. **-áveis**), **intérmino** m.
1. interminable. 2. endless, unending. 3. enormous,
vast, widespread. 4. tardy. 5. limitless. 6. infinite.
‖ **interminavelmente** adv. interminably, without
end.
um discurso ~ an endless speech. **viram então
uma planície** ~ then they saw a vast plain.
intermissão s. f. (pl. **-ões**) 1. intermission. 2. interruption. 3. pause, interval. 4. respite.
trabalharam sem ~ they worked without intermission.
intermitência s. f. 1. intermittence, intermittency. 2.
(med.) intermission: temporary cessation between
two paroxysms.
intermitente adj. m. + f. 1. intermittent, intermitting.
2. ceasing at intervals, spasmodic(al). ‖ ~**mente**
adv. intermittingly.
febre ~ (med.) intermittent fever, quartan fever.
o pulso está ~ the pulse is intermittent.
intermitir v. 1. to intermit. 2. to suspend, interrupt.
3. to abate. 4. to stop or pause at intervals.
intermundial adj. m. + f. (pl. **-ais**) intermundane,
intercontinental, lying between worlds.
intermúndio s. m. 1. intermundium, space between
worlds. 2. (fig.) solitude, loneliness.
intermural adj. m. + f. (pl. **-ais**) intermural, between
walls.
intermuscular adj. m. + f. (anat.) intermuscular: lying
between or separating muscles.
internação s. f. (pl. **-ões**) 1. internation, internment,
(in a camp, hospital, etc.). 2. placement (in a
boarding school).
internacional s. f. (pl. **-ais**) international association.
‖ adj. m. + f. international, pertaining to or concerning different nations.
direito ~ international law. **política** ~ foreign
policy.
internacionalidade s. f. internationality.
internacionalismo s. m. internationalism.
internacionalista s. m. + f. internationalist. ‖ adj.
of or relative to internationalism.
internacionalização s. f. (pl. **-ões**) internationalization.
internacionalizar v. to internationalize, make international, make known among several nations.
internado s. m. 1. intern, resident physician in a
hospital. 2. inpatient. 3. boarder, inmate of a
school. 4. internee. 5. boarding school. ‖ adj. in-
terned.
internamento s. m. internment, confinement, restraint.
internar v. 1. to intern. 2. to confine, cause to reside
in an interior locality (without permission to leave
it). 3. to introduce, insert, put into. 4. ~**-se**: a) to
confine o. s.; isolate o. s. b) (fig.) to become
absorbed in, plunge into.
a vítima foi internada no hospital the victim was
hospitalized.
internato s. m. boarding school, children's home,
orphanage.
interno s. m. 1. intern. 2. inmate of a boarding
school. ‖ adj. 1. intern, internal. 2. interior, inside,
inward, inner. 3. intimate. 4. domestic(al). ‖ **-amente**
adv. internally, inwardly, intimately, domestically.
antena -a indoor aerial. **assuntos -s de um país**
domestic affairs of a country. **consumo** ~ home
consumption. **diâmetro** ~ inside diameter. **filete** ~
female thread (of a screw). **médico** ~ intern. **medida -a** inside dimension. **o paciente** ~ the inpatient. **a parte -a da casa** the interior of the
house. **a natureza -a do assunto** the internal nature
of the problem. **pista -a** inside track.

internódio s. m. (bot.) internode, space between two
leaf knots.
internúncio s. m. 1. internuncio, papal representative at a minor court. 2. messenger, mediator.
interoceânico adj. interoceanic.
interocular adj. m. + f. interocular, interorbital.
interoposição s. f. (pl. **-ões**) 1. interposition. 2. intervention. 3. interruption.
interósseo adj. (anat.) interosseal, interosseous.
interparietal adj. m. + f. (pl. **-ais**) (anat.) interparietal.
interpartidário adj. among parties, between parties.
interpeciolar adj. m. + f. (bot.) interpetiolar(y).
interpelação s. f. (pl. **-ões**) 1. interpellation. 2. verbal
interference (as in a debate). 3. judicial summons
or citation. 4. (parl.) formal demand for official
explanations.
interpelador s. m. interpellator.
interpelante s. m. + f. interpellant. ‖ adj. interpellant.
interpelar v. 1. to interpellate. 2. to question, interrogate. 3. to summon, cite. 4. (parl.) to demand
official explanations. 5. to interrupt.
interpenetração s. f. (pl. **-ões**) interpenetration.
interpenetrar v. to interpenetrate.
interpeninsular adj. m. + f. interpeninsular.
interplanetário adj. interplanetary.
foguete ~ interstellar craft.
interpolação s. f. interpolation: act of interpolating,
interpolated matter.
interpolado adj. interpolated, intercalar(y).
interpolador s. m. interpolator. ‖ adj. interpolating.
interpolar (I) adj. m. + f. interpolar, situated between
poles.
interpolar (II) v. 1. to interpolate. 2. to insert, introduce. 3. to foist in (spurious or unauthorized text).
4. to interrupt, interfere. 5. (theat.) to gag.
interpontuação s. f. (pl. **-ões**) interpunctuation, inter-
punction, points or periods between words.
interpor v. 1. to interpose. 2. to cause to intervene.
3. to place between. 4. to oppose, contend against.
5. to mediate. 6. to interrupt, break in upon. 7. to
interfere, intervene, intercede. 8. to intercalate,
insert. 9. to obstruct.
~ **um recurso** to lodge an appeal.
interporto s. m. intermediate port.
interposição s. f. (pl. **-ões**) 1. interposition, interloca-
tion. 2. interruption, interference. 3. intervention.
interpositiva s. f. (gram.) middle vowel of a triphthong.
interposto (I) s. m. emporium, trading post, store,
warehouse.
interposto (II) adj. intermediary, interposed, interjacent.
pessoa -a mediator.
interpotente adj. m. + f. (mech.) having the point of
application between the fulcrum and weight (lever).
interprender v. 1. to undertake, engage in. 2. (mil.)
to take by surprise, assault, attack.
interpresa (ê) s. f. 1. enterprise, undertaking. 2.
surprise attack, assault.
interpretação s. f. (pl. **-ões**) 1. interpretation, act of
expounding. 2. explanation, elucidation, explication.
3. translation, version. 4. exposition, exegesis. 5.
play, rendition, rendering.
~ **errônea** misinterpretation. ~ **individual** individual understanding **o trecho admite duas -ões** the
passage admits two constructions.
interpretador s. m., **interpretante** m. + f. interpreter.
‖ adj. interpretative, interpreting.
interpretar v. 1. to interpret, expound. 2. to explain,
explicate, elucidate. 3. to translate, construe. 4. to

act as an interpreter. 5. (theat., mus.) to play, enact, render. 6. to decipher.
ela interpretou mal as nossas palavras she misinterpreted our words. **eu interpreto aquilo como relaxamento** I put it down to negligence. **interpretemos da melhor forma seu ato** let us put the best construction on his deed. **ele interpretou erroneamente minhas palavras** he put a false construction on my words. **interpretei suas palavras como recusa** I construed his words to mean a refusal. ~ **um sonho** to read a dream.
interpretativo adj. interpretative, hermeneutic. ‖ **-amente** adv. interpretatively.
interpretável adj. m. + f. (pl. **-áveis**) interpretable, definable, construable.
intérprete s. m. + f. 1. interpreter, translator. 2. expositor, construer. 3. performer, singer. 4. prolocutor.
interregno s. m. interregnum.
inter-resistente adj. m. + f. having the weight between the fulcrum and the power.
interrogação s. f. (pl. **-ões**) 1. interrogation, question. 2. interrogatory. 3. inquiry. 4. question mark.
interrogado adj. questioned, interrogated.
não ~ unquestioned, untried.
interrogador s. m., **interrogante** m. + f. interrogator, (jur.) examining magistrate.
interrogar v. 1. to interrogate. 2. to inquire, put questions. 3. to examine, cross-examine. 4. to ask, question.
~ **um aluno** to ask a pupil questions. ~ **testemunhas** to question witnesses. **deixe de** ~**-me** stop asking me questions. **ele me interrogou minuciosamente** he interrogated me thoroughly, he picked my brains. **eles o** ~**am severamente horas a fio** they interrogated him severely for hours, (coll.) they grilled him for hours.
interrogativo adj. interrogative, interrogatory. ‖ **-amente** adv. interrogatively.
interrogatório s. m. 1. interrogatory. 2. interrogation, question. 3. inquiry. 4. questioning, examination. 5. hearing, trial. ‖ adj. interrogative, interrogatory.
chamaram-no para um novo ~ they called him for a rehearing. **submeter a um** ~ **contraditório** to cross-question.
interromper v. to interrupt: 1. discontinue, cease, break off. 2. stop, desist, suspend. 3. cut short, cut in (conversation). 4. disturb. 5. break in upon.
~ **a viagem** to interrupt the journey, (coll.) stop off. ~ **no meio o telefonema** to hang up on s. o. **ele me interrompeu** he cut me short. **ela interrompeu a viagem em Nova York** she interrupted her journey in New York. **ela se interrompeu** she made pause. **não me interrompa tão rudemente** don't interrupt me so rudely, don't jump down my throat.
interrompido adj. interrupted, discontinued, cut off, suspended. ‖ **-amente** adv. interruptedly, with interruption.
o julgamento foi ~ the judgement was arrested. **o jogo foi** ~ **pela chuva** the match was interrupted by rain. **a ligação telefônica foi -a** the telephone connexion was cut off.
interrupção s. f. (pl. **-ões**) 1. interruption, act of interrupting. 2. cessation, intermission. 3. suspension, discontinuance. 4. distraction. 5. stoppage, stop.
trabalhavam sem ~ they were working through, they were working without intermission. ~ **de viagem** stopover. ~ **de corrente** (electr.) break. ~ **temporária do fornecimento** suspension of delivery.
interrupto adj. interrupted, suspended, broken off. ‖ **-amente** adv. interruptedly.

interruptor s. m. 1. interrupter. 2. (electr.) cutout, contact-breaker, circuit breaker, switch (plates D 4, M 5). ‖ adj. interrupting.
~ **automático** arrester. ~ **a tração** pull switch (plate M 5). ~ **rotativo** rotary switch (plate M 5).
interse(c)ção s. f. (pl. **-ões**) intersection: 1. cutting, dividing. 2. crossing, crossover. 3. (geom.) point of intersection.
intersecional, interseccional adj. m. + f. intersectional, intersectant.
interserir v. to insert, interpose.
intersexualidade s. f. (biol.) intersexuality, the possession of sexual characteristics intermediate between male and female.
interstelar adj. m. + f. interstellar.
intersticial adj. m. + f. (pl. **-ais**) interstitial.
interstício s. m. 1. interstice. 2. chink, crevice, crack, cranny. 3. interval of time.
intertrigem s. f. (pl. **-ens**) (med.) intertrigo.
intertropical adj. m. + f. (pl. **-ais**) intertropical.
interurbano s. m. (Braz.) long-distance call or telephone connexion. ‖ adj. interurban, between cities.
intervalar (I) adj. m. + f. intervallic, spaced at intervals.
intervalar (II) v. 1. to interval, space. 2. to form an interval. 3. to separate or interrupt at intervals.
intervalo s. m. 1. interval. 2. space between two points or objects. 3. intermittence, intermission. 4. space between two or more facts, epochs, etc. 5. (phys.) interrelation between frequencies, vibrations, etc. 6. interact, interlude. 7. recess, pause. 8. intermediate space. 9. (mus.) bar of rest.
~ **de segunda maior** (mus.) whole step. **no** ~ during the interval. **no** ~ **para o café** at the coffee break. **plantaram árvores no** ~ **de dez metros** they set trees at intervals of ten meters. **por** ~**s** now and then. **sem** ~ pauseless.
intervenção s. f. (pl. **-ões**) 1. intervention. 2. interposition, interference. 3. mediation, intermediation. 4. (com.) agency, procurement.
não ~ non-intervention. ~ **cirúrgica** surgical operation.
intervencionismo s. m. interventionism.
intervencionista s. m. + f. interventionist.
interveniente s. m. + f. intervenient: (com.) endorser of a bill of exchange, mediator. ‖ adj. intervenient, intervening, coming between.
interventivo adj. interventive.
interventor s. m. interventor, temporary governor or administrator, mediator, intervener.
interversão s. f. (pl. **-ões**) inversion, alteration of the natural order.
intervertebral adj. m. + f. (pl. **-ais**) (anat.) intervertebral.
interverter v. to intervert, invert.
intervindo adj. intervening, intervenient.
intervir v. 1. to intervene. 2. to interfere, intercede. 3. to interpose. 4. to intermediate. 5. to intermeddle. 6. to happen incidentally.
ele interveio na contenda he interfered in the dispute. **por favor, não intervenha nos meus negócios** please, do not interfere in my affairs.
intervocálico adj. (phon.) intervocal(ic).
intestado adj. intestate, without a will.
morrer ~ to die intestate.
intestável adj. m. + f. (pl. **-áveis**) intestable, legally unqualified to make a will.
intestinal adj. m. + f. (pl. **-ais**) intestinal, enteric.
intestino s. m. intestine, bowel(s), entrails, gut. ‖ adj. 1. intestine. 2. internal. 3. intimate, inward. 4. (fig.) national, domestic.
~ **cego** (med.) caecum.

intimação s. f. (pl. **-ões**) 1. announcement, notification. 2. citation. 3. summons, writ, subpoena. ~ **para servir como jurado** venire. **recebi uma** ~ a writ was served upon me.
intimador s. m. intimater, summoner.
intimar v. 1. to summon, cite, convoke. 2. to subpoena. 3. to notify, inform. 4. to order, urge. 5. (jur.) to garnish. ~ **a ordem** to give an order. ~ **a pagar** to summon to pay. **fui intimado a comparecer** (jur.) I was summoned.
intimativa s. f. 1. overbearing gesture or manner. 2. authoritative statement, energetic declaration. 3. arrogance.
intimativo adj. energetic, authoritative, imperious.
intimidação s. f. (pl. **-ões**) 1. intimidation, threat. 2. state of being intimidated.
intimidade s. f. 1. intimacy, intimity. 2. privacy, familiarity. 3. nearness, closeness. 4. friendship. **tomar** ~ **com** to make friends with. **eles têm muita** ~ they are close friends. **permitir-se** ~**s com** to take freedoms with.
intimidado adj. frightened, scared, awe-struck, intimidated. **não** ~ undaunted. **ele ficou muito** ~ he was put out of countenance.
intimidador s. m. intimidator. ‖ adj. intimidating, intimidator.
intimidar v. 1. to intimidate. 2. to frighten, cow. 3. to threaten, browbeat, bully. 4. to scare, discourage. 5. ~**se** to become discouraged or intimidated, be disheartened. ~**am-no até ceder** they cowed him into submitting.
íntimo s. m. 1. intimate friend, intimate, familiar. 2. soul. 3. pith, heart, core. ‖ adj. 1. intimate. 2. inner, internal. 3. innermost, inmost. 4. near, close. 5. familiar. 6. confidential. 7. cordial, hearty. ‖ **intimamente** adv. intimately, familiarly, inwardly, affectionately, confidentially. **eles são muito** ~**s** they are very intimate, (coll.) they are hand and glove. **ele é um amigo** ~ he is an intimate friend, (sl.) he is a great pal. **ela conhece os meus pensamentos** ~**s** she knows my inmost thoughts. **ele é** ~ **de** he is an intimate of, he rubs elbows with... **tornaram-se amigos** ~**s** they became fast friends.
intimorato adj. fearless, bold, intrepid.
intina s. f. (bot.) intine.
intinção s. f. (pl. **-ões**) (eccl.) intinction.
intitulação s. f. (pl. **-ões**) intitulation, act of conferring a title, titling.
intitulado adj. entitled.
intitular v. 1. to intitule, give a right or title to. 2. to entitle, title. 3. to address. 4. ~**se** to call o. s.
intocável s. m. (pl. **-áveis**) (India) untouchable, one of the lowest cast.
intolerância s. f. 1. intolerance, intolerancy. 2. intransigence, intransigency. 3. impatience, hastiness. 4. bigotry.
intolerante s. m. + f. intolerant, intransigent, impatient, bigot(ed). ‖ ~**mente** adv. intolerantly.
intolerantismo s. m. intolerance, dogmatism, doctrinaire unwillingness to tolerate contrary opinions.
intolerável adj. m. + f. (pl. **-áveis**) 1. intolerable. 2. unbearable, unendurable. 3. insupportable. ‖ **intoleravelmente** adv. intolerably, unbearably.
intonação s. f. (pl. **-ões**) intonation, tone, modulation of tone.
intonso adj. unshaven, hirsute.
intorção s. f. (pl. **-ões**) (bot.) intortion.
intoxicação s. f. (pl. **-ões**) (med.) intoxication, poisoning, toxication. ~ **alimentar** botulism, food poisoning.

intoxicado adj. (med.) intoxicated (not drunk).
intoxicante s. m. poison. ‖ adj. poisoning.
intoxicar v. 1. to poison. 2. to make poisonous.
intra- pref. intra-: within, in the interior.
intra-abdominal adj. m. + f. (pl. **intra-abdominais**) (anat.) intra-abdominal.
intracelular adj. m. + f. intracellular.
intracraniano adj. (anat.) intracranial, situated within the cranium.
intradilatado adj. (bot.) intradilated.
intradorso s. m. (archit.) intrados (plate A 12).
intraduzível adj. m. + f. (pl. **-íveis**) untranslatable, inexpressible.
intrafegável adj. m. + f. (pl. **-áveis**) impassable, untransitable.
intrafólio adj. (bot.) intrafoliaceous.
intragável adj. m. + f. (pl. **-áveis**) 1. unpalatable, uneatable. 2. (fig.) unreadable. ‖ **intragavelmente** adv. unpalatably.
intra-hepático adj. (pl. **intra-hepáticos**) (anat.) intrahepatic, situated or occurring within the liver.
intramarginal adj. m. + f. (pl. **-ais**) intramarginal.
intramedular adj. m. + f. (anat.) intramedullary.
intramuscular adj. m. + f. (anat.) intramuscular.
intramuros adj. m. + f. intramural, within the walls or boundaries.
intranqüilidade s. f. 1. intranquility. 2. unquietness, uneasiness. 3. fidget, restlessness.
intransferível adj. m. + f. (pl. **-íveis**) untransferable.
intransigência s. f. 1. intransigence, intransigency. 2. irreconcilableness. 3. intolerance. 4. austerity.
intransigente s. m. + f. 1. intransigent, irreconcilable. 2. intolerant. 3. (fig.) austere, strict.
intransitivo adj. 1. (gram.) intransitive. 2. not transitive, intransmissible. ‖ **-amente** adv. intransitively. **verbo** ~ (gram.) intransitive, verb which does not require an object.
intransitabilidade s. f. impassability, impassableness, untransitableness.
intransitável adj. m. + f. (pl. **-áveis**) 1. impassable, untransitable. 2. pathless, invious. 3. (fig.) untractable. ‖ **intransitavelmente** adv. impassably, impenetrably.
intransmissibilidade s. f. untransmissibleness, incapacity of being transmitted.
intransmissível adj. m. + f. (pl. **-íveis**) intransmissible, untransferable, not negotiable.
intransplantável adj. m. + f. (pl. **-áveis**) not transplantable.
intransponível adj. m. + f. (pl. **-íveis**) unsurmountable, unbridgeable, that cannot be transposed or overcome.
intransportável adj. m. + f. (pl. **-áveis**) untransportable.
intra-ocular adj. m. + f. (pl. **intra-oculares**) (anat.) intraocular.
intrapeciolar adj. m. + f. (bot.) intrapetiolar.
intrapulmonar adj. m. + f. (anat.) intrapulmonary.
intrário adj. (bot.) of or relative to an embryo situated within the endosperm.
intratabilidade s. f. intractableness, intractability.
intratado adj. 1. untreated (illness, injury). 2. untried, unattempted.
intratável adj. m. + f. (pl. **-áveis**) 1. intractable, unmanageable. 2. stubborn, dogged. 3. haughty. 4. unsociable, reserved, unapproachable. ‖ **intratavelmente** adv. intractably, untowardly. **ele é uma pessoa** ~ he is an intractable person **que sujeito** ~! what a crab!
intravascular adj. m. + f. (anat.) intravascular.
intravenoso adj. (anat.) intravenous. **por via -a** intravenously.

intrêmulo adj. 1. unshaking, untrembling. 2. (fig.) fearless, intrepid.
intrepidez s. f. 1. intrepidity. 2. boldness, daring. 3. courage, braveness. 4. fearlessness, dauntlessness.
intrépido s. m. dare-devil, darer, bold or reckless fellow. ‖ adj. 1. intrepid. 2. bold, daring. 3. courageous, brave. 4. fearless, dauntless. 5. venturous, adventurous. ‖ **intrepidamente** adv. intrepidly, fearlessly.
intricado adj. (also **intrincado**) 1. intricate. 2. obscure. 3. complicated, complex, difficult. 4. entangled, crabbed. 5. puzzling. ‖ **-amente** adv. intricately, complicatedly.
intricar v. (also **intrincar**) 1. to intricate. 2. to make perplexing or obscure. 3. to confound, confuse. 4. to complicate, render (more) difficult. 5. to enmesh, entangle. 6. to embarrass, disconcert. 7. to puzzle. 8. to ensnare, entrap. 9. ~-se to become complicated or confused, get entangled in.
intrico s. m. (Braz., pop.) 1. intricacy, complication. 2. embarrassment. 3. unintelligibility.
intriga s. f. 1. intrigue, plot, scheme. 2. conspiracy. 3. snare, trap. 4. gossip. 5. disloyalty.
ela sempre faz ~ she is always plotting.
intrigado s. m. (Braz., sl.) rival, adversary.
intrigalhada s. f. 1. intriguery. 2. cabal. 3. gossip, slander.
intrigante s. m. + f. intrigant(e), intriguer, schemer, troublemaker. ‖ adv. 1. intriguing, scheming. 2. meddling. 3. cunning, artful.
de maneira ~ intriguingly.
intrigar v. 1. to intrigue. 2. to involve, entangle. 3. to plot for, scheme. 4. to ensnare. 5. to gossip, slander. 6. to rouse the interest of.
isto me intriga that puzzles me.
intriguista s. m. + f. intrigant(e), schemer, troublemaker. ‖ adj. 1. intriguing, scheming. 2. meddlesome. 3. cunning, artful.
intrínseco adj. 1. intrinsic(al). 2. inherent, innate. 3. internal, inward. 4. intimate. 5. real, true. 6. essential. ‖ **intrinsecamente** adv. intrinsically.
intro- pref. within, into, in.
introdução s. f. (pl. **-ões**) 1. introduction. 2. act of bringing in or inserting. 3. act of bringing into practice. 4. importation. 5. preface, foreword, preamble. 6. (mus.) prelude. 7. preliminary studies.
ele tinha uma carta de ~ he had a letter of introduction. **foi a** ~ **para** it was the prologue to. **ela escreveu a** ~ she wrote the foreword.
introdutivo adj. 1. introductive, introductory. 2. preliminary, prefatory. 3. initiative. 4. preparatory.
introdutor s. m. introducer, announcer, usher, presenter. ‖ adj. introductory, introductive.
introdutório adj. 1. introductory, introductive. 2. preliminary, prefatory. 3. initiatory. 4. preparatory. 5. (mus.) preludial.
introduzir v. 1. to introduce. 2. to lead or bring in. 3. to show in, usher in. 4. to import. 5. to bring into practice, establish. 6. to initiate, begin with. 7. to put in, insert. 8. to inoculate, inject. 9. to invite to enter, let in. 10. to intrude, penetrate, infiltrate. 11. to announce. 12. ~-se to introduce o. s., edge in, slip in. 13. (mus.) to prelude.
ele introduziu-o no clube he got him into the club. **ela introduziu-se à força** she wedged herself in. **ele tentou** ~ **o aparelho no mercado** he tried to put the gadget on the market. ~**am várias novidades** they started several innovations.
intróito s. m. 1. beginning, commencement. 2. introduction. 3. (rel.) introit.
intrometer v. 1. to introduce, insert. 2. to intercalate. 3. to intromit, allow to enter, admit. 4. ~**-se:** a)

to interfere, intermeddle. b) to butt in, (sl.) pry into. c) to intrude.
~**-se em assuntos alheios** to intermeddle in other people's affairs, (coll.) to poke one's nose in other people's business. ~**-se em um negócio** to have a finger in the pie. ~**am-se vagarosamente** slowly they horned themselves in. **ele se intromete em tudo** he meddles in everything, puts his nose into everything. **não se intrometa em meus negócios** don't pry into my affairs. **não se intrometa em coisas que você não entende** don't tamper with things you don't understand.
intrometido s. m. 1. meddler, busybody. 2. eavesdropper. 3. intruder. ‖ adj. 1. meddlesome, intrusive. 2. importunate. 3. impertinent. 4. snoopy, prying.
ele é muito ~ he is an awful meddler.
intrometimento s. m. act of interfering, meddling or intruding.
intromissão s. f. (pl. **-ões**) 1. intromission, introduction. 2. interference, meddlesomeness. 3. obtrusion, officiousness.
introrso adj. (bot.) introrse, turned or facing inward (applied to anthers whose valves are turned toward the style).
introsca s. m. + f. (Braz., sl.) busybody, meddlesome person.
introspecção, introspeção s. f. (pl. **-ões**) 1. introspection. 2. self-contemplation, self-examination.
introspectivo, introspetivo adj. introspective.
de modo ~ introspectively.
introversão s. f. (pl. **-ões**) introversion, self-contemplation, concentration of interest upon our inner life.
introvertido adj. introverted, introversive.
intrujão s. m. (pl. **-ões**) 1. intruder. 2. deceiver, cheater. 3. impostor. 4. receiver of stolen goods, fence.
intrujar v. 1. to intrigue, plot. 2. to dupe, deceive, delude. 3. to tell fibs. 4. to trick each other.
intrujice s. f. 1. fraud, cheat. 2. humbug, hoax. 3. trickery.
intrujir v. (sl.) to twig, catch on, understand.
intrusão s. f. (pl. **-ões**) 1. intrusion, act of intruding. 2. encroachment. 3. trespass, wrongful entry. 4. (geol.) intrusive rocks.
intrusivo adj. intrusive.
intruso s. m. 1. intruder, trespasser. 2. encroacher. 3. interloper, meddler. ‖ adj. intruded, intrusive, meddling. ‖ **-amente** adv. obtrusively.
intubação (pl. **-ões**), **intubagem** (pl. **-ens**) s. f. (med.) intubation.
intubar v. (med.) to intubate.
intuição s. f. (pl. **-ões**) 1. intuition, instinctive knowledge or perception. 2. feeling, anticipation. 3. (coll.) hunch.
intuitivismo s. m. (philos.) intuitivism.
intuitivo adj. intuitive, perceived by the mind. ‖ **-amente** adv. intuitively.
intuito s. m. 1. design, intention. 2. plan, scheme. 3. aim, purpose.
escrevo no ~ **de...** I write for the purpose of...
intumescência s. f. (med., also **intumescimento** m.) intumescence, tumidity, swelling.
intumescente adj. m. + f. intumescent, tumescent, swelling up.
intumescer v. to intumesce, swell up, become tumid, tumefy.
intumescido adj. swollen.
inturgescência s. f. turgescence, turgidity.
inturgescente adj. m. + f. turgescent, swollen.
inturgescer v. to become turgid, swell up.
intuspecção, intuspeção s. f. (pl. **-ões**) self-observation, self-knowledge.

intuspectivo, intuspetivo adj. of or relative to self--observation and self-knowledge.

intussuscepção s. f. (also intuscepção) (pl. -ões) (biol., med.) intussusception, introsusception.

inúbia s. f. (Braz.) Indian (Tupi) war horn.

inúbil adj. m. + f. (pl. -úbeis) not nubil, not marriageable.

inubo adj. unmarried, single.

ínula s. f. (bot.) inula, elecampane.

inulina s. f. (biochem.) inulin.

inulto adj. unavenged, unpunished.

inultrapassável adj. m. + f. (pl. -áveis) unsurpassable.

inumação s. f. (pl. -ões) inhumation, burial, interment.

inumanidade s. f. inhumanity, cruelty, barbarity.

inumano adj. inhuman, cruel, brutal, merciless.

inumar v. to inhume, bury.

inumerabilidade s. f. innumerability, innumerableness.

inumerável adj. m. + f. (pl. -áveis) innumerable, unnumbered, countless. || inumeravelmente adv. innumerably.

estrelas -eis stars without number.

inúmero adj. innumerable, numberless, countless, untold.

-as dificuldades a host of difficulties. -as pessoas a lot of people, a power of people. -as preocupações no end of trouble. -as vezes ever so many times.

inundação s. f. (pl. -ões) 1. inundation, flood. 2. cataclysm. 3. (fig.) overflow, superfluous aboundance. 4. crowd, throng of people. 5. invasion.

inundado s. m. flood victim. || adj. flooded, awash.

inundante adj. m. + f. inundant, overflowing.

inundar v. 1. to inundate, flood. 2. to overflow. 3. to submerge, deluge. 4. to swamp. 5. to fill inordinately. 6. to invade. 7. ~-se to be covered with water.

~ o mercado to overstock the market. fui inundado de cartas I was flooded with letters.

inundável adj. m. + f. (pl. -áveis) floodable, subject to inundations.

inupto adj. unmarried, single.

inurbano adj. inurbane, uncivil, impolite, rude.

inusitado adj. 1. unused, not used. 2. not worn, new. 3. strange, unusual. 4. unaccustomed. 5. unknown.

inútil s. m. + f. (pl. -úteis) worthless person, good--for-nothing, ne'er-do-well. || adj. inutile: 1. useless. 2. unserviceable, unnecessary, superfluous. 3. effectless, unproductive. 4. worthless. 5. unprofitable, infructuous. 6. vain, empty, idle. 7. unneeded, unhelpful. 8. thwarted, frustrated. || inutilmente adv. uselessly, ineffectively, vainly, unavailingly, worthlessly.

é ~ com ele it is wasted on him. é ~ perguntar it is no good asking. é completamente ~ it is purposeless. o seu trabalho é ~ his work is of no avail. eles se esforçaram inutilmente they tried hard to no effect.

inutilidade s. f. 1. inutility, uselessness. 2. worthlessness. 3. unproductiveness, fruitlessness. 4. unprofitableness.

inutilizar v. 1. to make useless or unserviceable. 2. to frustrate, nullify. 3. to render effectless. 4. to incapacitate.

inutilizável adj. m. + f. (pl. -áveis) unavailable, unserviceable.

invacilante adj. m. + f. unvacillating, unwavering.

invadeável adj. m. + f. (pl. -áveis) unfordable, unwad(e)able.

invadir v. 1. to invade, enter by force, raid. 2. to conquer. 3. to trespass, encroach on. 4. to usurp. 5. to spread over. 6. to dominate.

o inimigo invadiu o país the enemy invaded the country.

invaginação s. f. (pl. -ões) 1. (bot.) invagination. 2. (med.) intussusception.

invaginante adj. m. + f. invaginating.

invaginar v. to invaginate, suffer from an intussusception.

invalescer v. to grow strong, strengthen, invigorate.

invalidação s. f. (pl. -ões) invalidation, cancellation, annulment.

invalidade s. f. invalidity, voidness, nullity, illegitimacy.

invalidar v. 1. to invalidate, render invalid. 2. to deprive of legal force, nullify, annul. 3. to make useless or unserviceable. 4. to discredit. 5. ~-se to become invalid or void.

invalidez s. f. 1. invalidity, infirmity. 2. invalidism.

inválido s. m. invalid, disabled person. || adj. 1. infirm, disabled. 2. invalid. 3. void, null, without effect. || invalidamente adv. invalidly.

invar s. m. invar: nickel-steel alloy (36/64).

invariabilidade s. f. invariability, invariableness, unchangeableness.

invariável adj. m. + f. (pl. -áveis) 1. invariable, unchangeable, unalterable. 2. constant, firm. 3. even. 4. uniform. || invariavelmente adv. invariably, constantly, changelessly, uniformly; always.

invasão s. f. (pl. -ões) invasion, incursion, inroad, raid.

invasivo adj. 1. invasive. 2. aggressive. 3. hostile.

invasor s. m. invader, forayer.

invectiva s. f. 1. invective, diatribe, tirade. 2. abuse, vituperation.

invectivador s. m. invectivist, vituperator, inveigher.

invectivar v. 1. to inveigh against, rail at. 2. to vituperate. 3. to attack or denounce verbally. 4. to rebuke, censure.

invectivo adj. 1. invective, abusive. 2. aggressive. 3. vituperative. 4. hostile. || -amente adv. invectively, aggressively.

inveja s. f. 1. envy, enviousness. 2. jealousy. 3. rivalry, emulation.

morder-se de ~ to be eaten with envy. causar ~ a alguém to excite a person's envy. ele olhou com ~ he looked enviously, he looked askance.

invejar v. 1. to envy, feel envious of. 2. to begrudge, grudge. 3. to desire, long after, covet.

não lhe invejo a posição I don't envy him his position. não há razão de ~-lhe o progresso there is no reason to begrudge their (his, her) progress.

invejável adj. m. + f. (pl. -áveis) 1. enviable, covetable. 2. desirable. 3. valuable. 4. appreciable. || invejavelmente adv. enviably.

invejoso s. m. envier, grudger. || adj. envious, jealous, grudging. || -amente adv. envyingly, jealously, enviously.

invenção s. f. (pl. -ões) 1. invention: a) act or process of inventing. b) that which is invented. c) device, contrivance, gadget. d) faculty of inventing, ingeniousness. e) (arts) creative imagination. f) fabrication, framing, forgery. g) discovery. 2. shrewdness. 3. (mus.) fantasia, study. 4. subterfuge, evasion.

de ~ própria out of one's own head. a ~ da Santa Cruz the Invention of the Cross. não passa de ~ (fig.) it's nothing but a rumour.

invencibilidade s. f. 1. invincibility, invincibleness. 2. insuperability, unconquerableness.

invencionar v. to adorn artfully.

invencioneiro s. m. habitual liar or impostor. || adj. 1. prim, affected, formal. 2. mendacious, deceitful 3. extravagant, capricious. 4. cunning, artful.

invencionice s. f. 1. lie, falsehood. 2. cunning, craft ruse, artifice, trick.

invencível adj. m. + f. (pl. -íveis) 1. invincible, insuperable. 2. indomitable, unconquerable. 3. irresistible. 4. unsubduable. ‖ **invencivelmente** adv. invincibly, unconquerably, insuperably.

invendável, invendível adj. m. + f. (pl. -íveis) 1. unsalable, unmarketable. 2. unalienable. 3. unrealizable. 4. unconvertible.

inventado adj. 1. invented. 2. found out. 3. made up, fabled, feigned.

a história toda é -a the whole story is a fabrication.

inventar v. 1. to invent, ideate. 2. to create, devise, contrive. 3. to fabricate, fake, forge. 4. to manufacture. 5. to discover, originate. 6. to frame, mint.

~ **uma mentira** to frame a lie. **~emos alguma coisa** let us think up s. th. **ele não inventou a pólvora** he will never set the Thames on fire. **certamente não foi ele quem inventou o trabalho** he is no glutton for work.

inventariação s. f. (pl. -ões) inventorying, act of registering in an inventory.

inventariante s. m. + f. executor or administrator who compiles an inventory or takes stock. ‖ adj. inventorying.

inventariar v. to inventory, catalogue, take stock, register.

inventário s. m. 1. inventory. 2. detailed list of property (esp. that one left by deceased persons). 3. schedule, register. 4. stock. 5. act of inventorying or taking stock.

fazer um ~ to take stock.

inventiva s. f. inventiveness, ingeniousness, faculty of creative imagination.

inventividade s. f. inventiveness.

inventivo adj. inventive, imaginative, creative, ingenious.

invento s. m. = **invenção.**

inventor s. m. 1. inventor. 2. discoverer. 3. author, originator. 4. framer, fabricator. 5. (coll.) liar.

inventora s. f. inventress, creatress.

inverdade s. f. untruth, untruthfulness.

inverídico adj. untrue, untruthful, inexact, false.

inverificável adj. m. + f. (pl. -áveis) unverifiable.

invernação s. f. (pl. -ões) (Braz.) practice of wintering cattle on pastures.

invernada s. f. 1. hard winter, winter season. 2. rainy weather. 3. (Braz.) winter pasture (for fattening cattle).

invernador s. m. (Braz.) stock-farmer, cattle fattener, grazier.

invernadouro s. m. 1. place to pass the winter. 2. winter pasture. 3. greenhouse, hothouse.

invernagem s. f. (pl. -ens) 1. wintering. 2. professional stock-feeding on winter pastures.

invernal adj. m. + f. (pl. -ais) hibernal, winterly, wintry.

invernar v. 1. to winter, pass the winter. 2. to hibernate. 3. to drive cattle to winter pastures. 4. (fig.) to visit and stay beyond the proper time.

invernia s. f. hard winter, cold weather, winter season.

invernista s. f. (Braz.) stock-farmer, cattle fattener, grazier.

inverno s. m. 1. winter, winter season, wintertide. 2. (Braz.) rainy period. 3. cold weather. 4. (fig.) old age.

num dia de ~ one winter's day. **fustigado pelo** ~ winter beaten. **lavra de** ~ winter fallow. **no meio do** ~ in the depths of winter.

invernoso adj. 1. winterly, wintry. 2. rainy, wet. 3. cold, snowy. 4. stormy.

inverossímil adj. m. + f. (pl. -ímeis) improbable, unlikely, unplausible.

inverossimilhança s. f. improbability, unlikeliness, unlikelihood.

inversa s. f. inverted state or condition.

inversão s. f. (pl. -ões) 1. inversion. 2. reversion, reversal. 3. transposition, metathesis. 4. investment. ~ **de capitais** investment of capital. ~ **de marcha de uma máquina** reversal of an engine.

inversivo adj. inversive.

inverso s. m. 1. contrary, reverse. 2. inverse. 3. (geom.) geometrical inversion. 4. (math.) inverse proportion. 5. (gram., logic) inverted state or condition. ‖ adj. inverted, inverse, retrograde, transposed, reciprocal. ‖ **-amente** adv. inversely, reciprocally.

na razão -a de in the inverse ratio to.

inversor s. m. invertor, reverser. ‖ adj. inverting, inversive.

invertebrado s. m. 1. invertebrate animal. 2. ~**s** pl. Invertebrata (pl.): division of the animal kingdom. ‖ adj. invertebrate, without backbone.

inverter v. 1. to invert: a) turn in an opposite direction, reverse. b) transpose. c) (electr.) commutate. 2. to change, transform, modify. 3. to exchange. 4. to invest (capital).

~ **a ordem das coisas** to put the cart before the horse.

invertido s. m. invert. ‖ adj. inverted, inverse, reverse, upside-down. ‖ **-amente** adv. invertedly.

invertina s. f. (biochem.) invertase, invertin.

invertível adj. m. + f. (pl. -íveis) invertible.

invés s. m. 1. reverse side, wrong side. 2. opposite. **ao** ~ on the contrary. **ao** ~ **de:** 1. contrary to, opposite to. 2. instead of, in lieu of, in the place of.

investida s. f. 1. attack, assault. 2. charge, sally. 3. rush, onrush. 4. (fig., fam.) raillery.

investido adj. vested.

investidura s. f. investiture, formal bestowal of a right, office or estate.

investigação s. f. (pl. -ões) 1. investigation. 2. inquiry. 3. study, research, examination. 4. search.

investigador s. m. investigator, detective, researcher. ‖ adj. investigating, investigative, investigatory.

investigante adj. m. + f. investigating.

investigar v. 1. to investigate. 2. to search into, inquire. 3. to examine, scrutinize. 4. to probe into. 5. to trace, ferret out.

~ **alguma coisa** to search into or go behind s. th. ~ **o íntimo** to search one's heart. ~ **profundamente** (fig.) to touch bottom. ~**am os seus atos e caminhos** they investigated his doings and dealings, they spied on him. **ele investigou o assunto** he inquired into the thing. **vou** ~ **o caso** I'll look into the matter. **investigamos o assunto profundamente** we sifted it to the bottom. **vamos** ~ **o assunto!** let's investigate the thing or spy into the thing.

investigável adj. m. + f. (pl. -áveis) investigable.

investigativo adj. investigative, investigatory.

investimento s. m. 1. attack, assault. 2. vesture, investiture. 3. investment.

investir v. 1. to attack, assault. 2. to vest, enrobe. 3. to install (in office). 4. to invest, lay out (capital in business). 5. to fall upon, rush at.

~ **capital em** to invest capital in. ~ **contra o inimigo** to fall on the enemy. **ele o investiu de todos os poderes** he invested him with full powers.

inveterado adj. 1. inveterate. 2. deep-rooted, obstinate, deep-seated. 3. confirmed. 4. ingrained, incarnate. 5. chronic(al). ‖ **-amente** adv. inveterately.

pecador ~ obdurate sinner.

inveterar v. to make inveterate, render chronic, establish by force of habit.
inviabilidade s. f. unviability, unfeasibility, impracticableness.
inviável adj. m. + f. (pl. **-áveis**) 1. unviable, unfeasible, impracticable. 2. trackless.
invicto adj. unvanquished, unconquered, unbeaten.
invídia s. f. (poet.) envy.
ínvido adj. (poet.) envious.
invigilância s. f. want of vigilance, unvigilance.
invigilante adj. m. + f. 1. unvigilant, inattentive. 2. careless, negligent.
ínvio adj. 1. pathless, trackless. 2. untrodden. 3. (of roads) impassable.
inviolabilidade s. f. inviolability, inviolableness.
inviolado adj. 1. inviolate, unviolated. 2. pure. 3. whole, unhurt.
inviolável adj. m. + f. (pl. **-áveis**) inviolable, sacred, sacrosanct. || **inviolavelmente** adv. inviolably, sacredly.
inviolentado adj. unforced, not coerced or violated.
inviscerar v. 1. to penetrate deeply, implant deeply. 2. **~-se** to take root.
invisibilidade s. f. invisibleness, invisibility.
invisível s. m. (pl. **-íveis**) 1. the invisible, the unseen. 2. fine hairnet (for ladies). 3. fine hairpin. || adj. m. + f. invisible, unseen, unsighted. || **invisivelmente** adv. unsightedly, invisibly.
  cerzidura ~ invisible mending. **tinta ~** sympathetic ink. **ele se torna ~** (fig.) he makes himself scarce.
inviso adj. (poet.) 1. unseen, never seen before. 2. envied. 3. hated.
invitar v. to invite.
invitatório s. m. 1. invitatory psalm (the Venite). 2. (poet.) invocation. || adj. invitatory.
invite s. m. 1. invitation. 2. (gambling) act of doubling the stakes.
invito adj. unwilling, forced, against one's own wish or heart, involuntary.
invocação s. f. (pl. **-ões**) 1. invocation. 2. act of calling for help. 3. prayer invoking divine blessing, supplication.
  sob a ~ de todos os maus espíritos with the invocation of all the evil spirits.
invocador s. m. invoker, supplicant. || adj. invoking, invocatory.
invocar v. 1. to invoke, invocate. 2. to call for protection or aid. 3. to implore, supplicate. 4. to pray to or for. 5. beseech.
  ~ a proteção dos santos to invoke the Saints. **~ o auxílio de amigos** to evoke the assistance of friends. **ele invocou a ira do céu contra mim** he called down curses upon me.
invocativo adj. invocative, invocatory.
invocatória s. f. invocation.
invocatório adj. invocative, invocatory.
invocável adj. m. + f. (pl. **-áveis**) invocable.
involução s. f. (pl. **-ões**) 1. (biol.) retrogressive development, degeneration. 2. (math.) involution. 3. complication, entanglement.
involucelado adj. (bot.) involucellate.
involucelo s. m. (bot.) involucel.
involucral adj. m. + f. (pl. **-ais**) (bot.) involucral.
involucriforme adj. m. + f. (bot.) involucriform.
invólucro s. m. 1. (anat., bot., zool.) involucre. 2. wrapping, wrappage. 3. envelope, jacket. 4. cover, case (plate G 2).
involuntário adj. 1. involuntary. 2. unwilling, unwilled. 3. unintended, unintentional. || **involuntariamente** adv. involuntarily, unwittingly.
  ele o fez involuntariamente he did it against his desire.
involuto adj. (bot.) involute.

involutório s. m. wrapper, covering.
invulgar adj. m. + f. 1. invulgar. 2. rare. 3. unusual, uncommon. 4. exceptional, unique. || **~mente** adv. unusually, uncommonly.
invulnerabilidade s. f. invulnerability.
invulnerado adj. invulnerate, unhurt, without wound.
invulnerável adj. m. + f. (pl. **-áveis**) 1. invulnerable, incapable of being hurt or harmed. 2. (fig.) irrefutable. || **invulneravelmente** adv. invulnerably.
inzona s. f. (Braz., pop.) trick, hoax, intrigue.
inzonar v. (Braz., pop.) to trick, cheat, intrigue.
inzoneiro adj. (Braz., pop.) intriguer, liar, cheat.
iodar v. 1. to iodize, cover or mix with iodine. 2. (med.) to treat with iodine.
iodato s. m. (chem.) iodate.
iodeto s. m. (chem.) iodide.
iódico adj. (chem.) iodic.
iodismo s. m. (med.) iodism, iodine poisoning.
iodo (ô) s. m. (chem.) iodine.
  tintura de ~ tincture of iodine. **intoxicação pelo ~** iodism. **tratar com ~** to iodize.
iodofórmio s. m. (chem.) iodoform.
iodoterapia s. f. (med.) iodotherapy.
iodureto s. m. (chem.) iodide.
ioga s. f. (Hinduism) yoga.
iogue s. m. + f. yogui, ascetic.
ioiô s. m. 1. yoyo, disk-shaped toy. 2. (Braz.) Negro corruption of the word **senhor:** master.
iogurte s. m. yoghurt, yogurt.
iole s. f. jolly-boat, yawl, dinghy (plate B 10).
íon, iônio, ionte s. m. (chem., phys.) ion.
iônico adj. (hist.) Ionic, of or pertaining to the Ionians or their country.
iônio s. m. 1. (hist.) Ionic dialect. 2. (poet.) Ionic foot or meter. 3. (chem.) ionium: radioactive isotope of thorium.
ionização s. f. (pl. **-ões**) (chem., phys.) ionization.
ionizar v. (chem., phys.) to ionize.
ionona s. f. (chem.) ionone.
ionosfera s. f. (radio) ionosphere.
iorubano s. m. Yoruban: native or inhabitant of Yoruba (Africa). || adj. Yoruban.
iota s. m. iota: letter "i" of the Greek alphabet.
iotacismo s. m. iotacism, excessive use of the letter iota or of its sound.
ipadu s. m. (Braz.) coca plant, coca shrub.
ipê s. m. common name of several Brazilian trees and shrubs (Caesalpinia, Bignonia and Boraginaceae).
ipecacuanha s. f. (Braz., bot.) feverroot, ipecacuanha, ipecac.
ipecacuanha-falsa s. f. (pl. **ipecacuanhas-falsas**) (Braz., bot.) goitcho.
ipecacuanha-preta s. f. (pl. **ipecacuanhas-pretas**) (Braz., bot.) black ipecac.
ipecu s. m. (Braz.) common name of several birds of the woodpecker family.
ipecuacamirá s. m. (Braz., ornith.) lineated woodpecker.
ipecuati s. m. (Braz., ornith.) a woodpecker (Celeus flavescens).
ipecumirim s. m. (pl. **-ins**) (Braz., ornith.) lesser black woodpecker.
ipecupará s. m. (Braz., ornith.) a woodpecker (Veniliornis spilogaster).
ipecutauá s. m. (Braz., ornith.) a woodpecker (Crocomorphus flavu).
ipequi s. m. (Braz., ornith.) sun grebe.
ipíneos s. m. pl. (ent.) Ipidae, a subfamily of insects comprising the bark beetles and the coffee borer.
I.P.M. abbr. of Military Police Inquiry.
ipoméia s. f. (Braz., bot.) morning glory.

744 ipsilóide — iridemia

ipsilóide adj. m. + f. ypsiliform, Y-shaped.
ípsilon s. m. upsilon, wye.
ipu s. m. (Braz.) 1. moorland. 2. (angling) a wire to protect a fishhook. 3. (ent.) andrena.
ipuã s. f. (N. Braz., Amazonas) island.
ipuaçu s. m. extensive tract of moorland.
ipuada s. f. (N. Braz.) hut, cottage.
ipueira s. f. (N. Braz.) 1. ponds and pools left by receding flood waters. 2. swamp. 3. puddle, small lake.
ipuruna s. f. (Braz.) starch extracted from malpighiaceous plants.
ir v. 1. to go: a) walk. b) march, run. c) move, pass about, proceed. d) depart, leave, go away. e) row, sail, float. f) travel, be bound for. g) (time) pass, elapse. h) withdraw, retire. i) work, operate. j) present o. s. at. k) lead, guide to. 2. (health) to be well (ill, so-so). 3. to concur, participate. 4. to aim at, strive. 5. to let go, enter or pass. 6. (gambling) to bet, wager. 7. ~-se: a) to go away, be off, go out. b) to depart, set out. c) (time) to slip away, elapse. d) to disappear, vanish. e) to die, pass away.
~ **a bordo** to go aboard. ~ **abaixo** to go down, (fig.) to fail. ~ **acabando** (fig.) to decline. ~ **a cavalo** to go on horseback. ~ **à cidade** to go down-town. ~ **adiante** to go ahead; succeed. ~ **água abaixo** (fig.) to go to the dogs. ~ **a leilão** to be put up at auction. ~ **além de** to overdoo, go beyond. ~ **ao ar fresco** to take an airing. ~ **ao encontro de** 1. to go to meet. 2. to face, clash. ~ **a passo lento** to walk slowly. ~ **a pé** to go on foot. ~ **a pique** to founder, sink. ~ **a Roma e não ver o Papa** to let slip by a favourable opportunity, to waste one's time. ~ **às pressas** to hurry. ~ **até o fim** (fig.) to go to the limit. ~ **atrás** to go behind, go after. ~ **bem** to be well, be all right. ~ **buscar lã e sair tosquiado** to go for wool and return shorn. ~ **com Deus** to go in peace. ~ **com o tempo** to yield to modern trends. ~ **com pressa** to go in a hurry. ~ **contra a corrente** to swim against the tide. ~ **de mal a pior** to go from bad to worse. ~ **de avião** to fly. ~ **de bonde** to go by tram. ~ **de vento em popa** to run before the wind, (fig.) proceed under favourable conditions. ~ **dormir** to retire. ~ **embora** 1. to go away, leave. 2. to pass away, die. ~ **em férias** to vacation. ~ **longe** to go far. ~ **mal de saúde** to be in poor health. ~ **nas pegadas** to follow in the footsteps. ~ **no encalço de** to pursue s. o. ~ **para a escola** to go to school. ~ **para o céu** to go to heaven. ~ **primeiro** to go first. ~-**se** to be on one's way. ~-**se embora** to vacate, depart. ~ **ver** to visit. **tenho de** ~ **embora** I must depart, I have got to run along. **tenho de** ~ I must be gone. **as coisas têm ido mal** things have been going on badly, (U. S. A., coll.) it's been tough going lately. **como vai indo?** how are you getting along? **as coisas estão indo bem** things are going on well. **ele irá** he'll go. **deixar as coisas irem o seu caminho** to let things slide. **ele foi revezado** he came off duty. **ele foi para o interior** he went to the country. **por fim foi-se** at last he went his way. **eles foram para a universidade** they went up to the university. **esperávamos que ele fosse** we expected him to go. **não vá atrás disto!** you can't go by that! **não vá ainda!** don't go yet! **não vá se esquecer!** don't forget it! **vá vê-lo!** go see him! have a look at it! **por onde vás, como vires, assim farás!** with foxes one must play the fox! **ide!** go on! **como vai?** how do you do? **devagar se vai longe** easy does it. **você vai apanhar** (fig.) you will have it (spanking).

ele vai melhor he is feeling better. **ele vai com a maioria** he sides with the majority, (fig.) he floats with the current. **o sol vai deitar-se** the sun goes down. **vai-te embora** be off with you. **isto vai longe demais** this is going too far. **isto vai longe** that goes far. **ele vai mendigar** he goes begging. **vai-te embora!** get along with you! (coll.) toddle off! **você vai ver!** you will see! **parece que vai chover** it looks like rain. **este vestido me vai bem** this dress suits me well. **daí não vai sair nada de bom** no good will come of it. **vamos!** let us go!, come on! (coll.) make it snappy! **vamos depressa!** let's hurry! **vamos ao assunto!** let's come to the point! **vamos ao que interessa** let us proceed to business. **vamos desistir?** shall we give up? **como é que vamos sair desta?** how can we get out of this? **vamos ver!** let us see! **já lá vão dois anos** it is already two years. **lá vão eles** there they go. **não vão bem um com o outro** they don't get along well. **já vou!** I'm coming! **não vou bem** I am not well. **obrigado, vou indo bem** thanks, I am getting on well. **eu vou sempre lá** I visit there. **eu também vou para este lado** I am going that way myself. **hoje vou ter com ele** I am going to meet him.

ira s. f. 1. anger, rage. 2. wrath, ire. 3. fretfulness. 4. exasperation. 5. passion. 6. indignation.
acesso de ~ fit of rage. **ele provocou sua** ~ put him in a passion.
irá s. m. (ent.) a ground nesting bee, andrena.
iracúndia s. f. choleric character, irascibility.
iracundo adj. 1. iracund, angry. 2. irritable, irascible. 3. passionate.
irado adj. 1. irate, ireful. 2. angry, furious. 3. choleric, irascible. 4. wrathful. ‖ **-amente** adv. irefully, wrathfully.
iraniano, irânico s. m. Iranian. ‖ adj. Iranian.
irapuá, irapuã s. m. a species of small stingless bees.
irapuru s. m. (Braz., ornith.) opalmanikin.
iraquiano s. m. Iraqi, Iraki. ‖ adj. Iraquian.
irar v. 1. to make angry, enrage. 2. to irritate, provoke. 3. ~-se: a) to grow angry, fly into a passion. b) to feel angry, to rage.
irara s. f. (zool.) tayra (Tayra barbara).
irascibilidade s. f. 1. irascibility, irascibleness. 2. irritability. 3. choleric character.
irascível adj. m. + f. (pl. -íveis) 1. irascible, susceptible to anger. 2. irritable, choleric. 3. quarrelsome, short-tempered. 4. passionate.
iratauá s. m. (Braz.) collective name of several marsh blackbirds of the family Icteridae.
iraúna s. f. = **graúna**.
iraxim s. f. (pl. -ins) (Braz., also **iratim**) a species of wild bees.
irenista s. m. adept of the irenical theology.
irerê s. m. (Braz., ornith.) a kind of tree duck (Dendrocygna viduata).
iri s. f. (Braz.) a palm tree (Astrocaryum ayri).
iriante adj. m. + f. iridescent.
iriar v. 1. to make iridescent, iridize. 2. to brighten, enliven. 3. to shimmer with rainbow colours.
iriártea s. f. Iriartea: a genus of palm trees.
iricurana s. f. (Braz., bot.) alchornea.
iricuri s. m. (Braz., bot.) urucury, urucuri palm.
iridáceas s. f. pl. (bot.) Iridaceae, a family of plants belonging to the subclass Monocotyledoneae, allied to the lilies.
iridectomia s. f. (surg.) iridectomy.
iridectopia s. f. (med.) abnormal position of the iris.
iridemia s. f. (med.) iridemia, hemorrhage from the iris.

irideremia s. f. (med.) irideremia, congenital absence of the iris.
iridescência s. f. iridescence.
iridescente adj. m. + f. iridescent, shimmering with rainbow colours.
iridiano adj. (anat.) iridian, of or pertaining to the iris of the eye.
irídico adj. (chem.) iridic, of or pertaining to iridium.
iridífero adj. iridiferous, yielding or containing iridium.
irídio s. m. (chem.) iridium (Ir).
iridite s. f. (med.) iritis, inflammation of the iris of the eye.
iridoplegia s. f. (med.) iridoplegia, paralysis of the iris.
iridoplégico adj. (med.) iridoplegic.
iridosmina s. f. (min.) iridosmine, iridosmium.
iridotomia s. f. (surg.) iridotomy.
irimirim s. f. (Braz.) a palm tree (Bactris vulgaris).
íris s. f. 1. iris: a) rainbow. b) (phys.) the solar spectrum. c) (myth.) Iris: goddess of the rainbow. d) (bot.) the yellow flag. e) (anat.) the pigmented membrane behind the cornea (plate O). f) (min.) rock-crystal with iridescent properties. 2. (fig.): a) hopefulness. b) peace. c) good fortune.
irisação s. f. (pl. **-ões**) irisation.
irisar v. = **iriar**.
iritataca s. f. (Braz., zool.) a badgerlike skunk (Conepatus suffocans).
irite s. f. (med.) iritis, inflammation of the iris.
iritinga s. f. (Braz., ichth.) a sea catfish (Tachysurus proops).
iriz s. m. (Braz.) (phytology) epiphytotic disease of the coffee tree.
irizar v. to be blighted by an epiphytotic disease.
irlandês s. m. 1. Irish, Irishman. 2. the Irish language. || adj. Irish.
irmã s. f. sister.
~ **colaça** foster sister. ~ **de caridade** Sister of Charity. ~ **germana** full sister. **meia** ~ half sister. **sem** ~ sisterless.
irmanar v. 1. to fraternize, fellow. 2. to couple, match, pair. 3. to unite, join, link.
irmandade s. f. 1. brotherhood, sisterhood. 2. fraternity, sodality. 3. sorority.
~ **religiosa** religious order, friary.
irmão s. m. (pl. **~s**) 1. brother. 2. fellow member, coreligionary. 3. equal, partisan, follower. || adj. 1. alike, similar. 2. equal. 3. brotherly.
~ **colaço** foster brother. ~ **de armas** brother in arms. ~ **gêmeo** twin brother. ~ **germano** brother german, full brother. ~ **uterino** brother on the mother's side. **ele o tratou de** ~ he brothered him. **meio** ~ half brother, stepbrother.
irmão-da-opa s. m. (sl.) drunkard.
iró s. f. a sort of eel.
ironia s. f. 1. irony, mockery. 2. sarcasm. 3. ironical act or saying.
~ **do destino** the irony of fate.
irônico adj. 1. ironic(al). 2. sarcastic(al). 3. sneering, derisive. || **-amente** adv. ironically, sarcastically, jeeringly.
ironista s. m. + f. ironist, ironical writer or orator.
ironizar v. 1. to speak or write ironically. 2. to render ironical. 3. to use ironically. 4. to pretend to be pleased.
iroquês s. m. Iroquois.
iroso adj. 1. irascible. 2. angry, furious. 3. turbulent, violent.
irra interj. zounds!, confound it!, fie!
irracional s. m. (pl. **-ais**) 1. irrational being. 2. lower animal. 3. brute. || adj. m. + f. 1. irrational. 2. unreasonable, illogical. 3. senseless, preposterous.

4. (math.) surd. || **~mente** adv. irrationally, unreasonably.
irracionalidade s. f. irrationality, unreason, unreasonableness.
irracionalismo s. m. irrationalism.
irracionável adj. m. + f. (pl. **-áveis**) 1. irrational, unreasonable. 2. illogical. 3. absurd.
irradiação s. f. (pl. **-ões**) 1. irradiation. 2. irradiance, irradiancy. 3. radiation, emission. 4. (radio) broadcasting, sending.
irradiado adj. irradiated.
irradiador adj. irradiating.
irradiante adj. m. + f. irradiant, emitting rays, radiative.
força ~ emissivity.
irradiar v. 1. to irradiate. 2. to shed light on. 3. to emit rays, shine. 4. to radiate. 5. (radio) to broadcast, telecast. 6. (fig.) to spread, diffuse, disperse.
irré s. m. (Braz., ornith.) tyrant flycatcher.
irreal adj. m. + f. (pl. **-ais**) 1. unreal, illusive. 2. unsubstantial, chimeric(al), fanciful. 3. visionary. 4. fictive. || **~mente** adv. unreally, chimerically, fictively.
irrealidade s. f. 1. unreality. 2. unsubstantiality. 3. artificialness. 4. falseness.
irrealizado adj. unrealized, unmaterialized.
irrealizável adj. m. + f. (pl. **-áveis**) 1. unrealizable, unachievable. 2. inoperable. 3. illusory.
isto é ~ this will never answer.
irreclamável adj. m. + f. (pl. **-áveis**) irreclaimable, irredeemable.
irreconciliabilidade s. f. irreconcilability, irreconcilableness.
irreconciliado adj. unreconciled.
irreconciliável adj. m. + f. (pl. **-áveis**) 1. irreconcilable, reconcileless. 2. incompatible. 3. implacable, unappeasing. 4. conflicting. || **irreconciliavelmente** adv. irreconcilably.
irreconhecível adj. m. + f. (pl. **-íveis**) irrecognizable, unrecognizable.
irrecorrível adj. m. + f. (pl. **-íveis**) unappealable, unavoidable.
irrecuperável adj. m. + f. (pl. **-áveis**) irrecoverable, irretrievable, irreclaimable. || **irrecuperavelmente** adv. irrecoverably.
irrecusável adj. m. + f. (pl. **-áveis**) irrecusable, not to be rejected or refused.
irredentismo s. m. irredentism: underground movement against foreign occupation or oppression.
irredento adj. unredeemed.
irredimível adj. m. + f. (pl. **-íveis**) irredeemable, irreclaimable.
irredutibilidade s. f. irreducibility, irreducibleness.
irredutível, irreduzível adj. m. + f. (pl. **-íveis**) 1. irreducible, incapable of being reduced. 2. invincible, indomitable. 3. unbending. 4. indecomposable. 5. (math.): a) divisible by no whole number (except itself). b) of or referring to an irreducible equation.
irreelegível adj. m. + f. (pl. **-íveis**) incapable of being reelected.
irrefletido adj. m. (also **irreflexivo**) 1. irreflective, thoughtless. 2. unreasoning, unwary. 3. unpremeditated. 4. inconsiderate. 5. rash, precipitate. || **-amente** adv. irreflectively, unthinkingly, unwarily, foolhardily.
irreflexão s. f. (pl. **-ões**) 1. irreflection. 2. thoughtlessness. 3. imprudence. 4. light-mindedness. 5. inconsiderateness.
irreflexo adj. not reflexive.
irreformável adj. m. + f. (pl. **-áveis**) irreformable.
irrefragável adj. m. + f. (pl. **-áveis**) irrefragable, undeniable, indisputable, unquestionable. || **irrefragavelmente** adv. irrefragably.

irrefrangível adj. m. + f. (pl. -íveis) irrefrangible, inviolable.
irrefreável adj. m. + f. (pl. -áveis) uncontrollable, unrestrainable.
irrefutabilidade s. f. 1. irrefutability. 2. incontestability, unquestionableness. 3. cogency.
irrefutado adj. not refuted, uncontested.
irrefutável adj. m. + f. (pl. -áveis) irrefutable, incontestable, unquestionable, cogent. ‖ **irrefutavelmente** adv. irrefutably, unanswerably.
irregenerado adj. unregenerate, impenitent.
irregenerável adj. m. + f. (pl. -áveis) unregenerable, incorrigible.
irregressível adj. m. + f. (pl. -íveis) 1. unregressive, that cannot come back. 2. lacking the possibility of return.
irregular s. m. + f. 1. irregular soldier, volunteer, insurgent. 2. (eccl.) persons excluded from clerical office due to a canonical impediment. ‖ adj. 1. irregular, not regular. 2. lawless, illegal. 3. unruly, disorderly. 4. abnormal, anomalous. 5. variable, changeable. 6. (mil.) not belonging to a regular army. 7. (gram.) strong (verbs). 8. unsystematic, unmethodical. 9. erratic. ‖ ~mente adv. irregularly.
ele tem uma vida ~ he leads an irregular life. seu procedimento é bem ~ his behaviour is quite out of square.
irregularidade s. f. 1. irregularity. 2. unevenness. 3. inordinateness. 4. laxity. 5. (eccl.) canonical impediment to reception of orders. 6. anomaly, abnormality.
~ de forma malformation.
irreligião s. f. irreligion, impiety.
irreligiosidade s. f. irreligiosity, impiety.
irreligioso adj. irreligious, impious, atheistic, ungodly. ‖ -amente adv. irreligiously.
irremediável adj. m. + f. (pl. -áveis) 1. irremediable, incapable of being cured. 2. incurable. 3. inevitable, fatal. 4. irreparable, past mending. ‖ **irremediavelmente** adv. irremediably.
irremissibilidade s. f. irremissibility.
irremissível adj. m. + f. (pl. -íveis) 1. irremissible. 2. unpardonable. 3. irremediable, incurable. 4. fatal, inevitable. ‖ **irremissivelmente** adv. irremissibly.
irremitente adj. m. + f. unremitting, not abating.
irremível adj. m. + f. (pl. -íveis) unredeemable, irreclaimable.
irremovível adj. m. + f. (pl. -íveis) 1. irremovable, unremovable. 2. inevitable. 3. firm, stable. ‖ **irremovivelmente** adv. irremovably.
irremunerado adj. unremunerated, unrewarded, unrecompensed, unpaid.
irremunerável adj. m. + f. (pl. -áveis) irremunerable, incapable of being rewarded or paid.
irrendabilidade s. f. unproductiveness.
irreparabilidade s. f. irreparableness, irreparability.
irreparável adj. m. + f. (pl. -áveis) irreparable, irretrievable, beyond remedy or repair. ‖ **irreparavelmente** adv. irreparably, irretrievably.
uma perda ~ an irrecoverable loss.
irrepartível adj. m. + f. (pl. -íveis) indivisible, infrangible.
irreplicável adj. m. + f. (pl. -áveis) unrepliable, incapable of being answered.
irrepreensibilidade s. f. irreprehensibleness, unblamableness, irreproachability, faultlessness.
irrepreensível adj. m. + f. (pl. -íveis) 1. irreprehensible. 2. blameless, faultless. 3. reproachless. 4. impeccable. ‖ **irrepreensivelmente** adv. irreprehensibly, unblamably, impeccably.
procedimento ~ conduct above reproach.

irrepresentável adj. m. + f. (pl. -áveis) irrepresentable, not admitting representation.
irreprimível adj. m. + f. (pl. -íveis) irrepressible, incapable of being restrained, uncontrollable. ‖ **irreprimivelmente** adv. irrepressibly.
irreprochável adj. m. + f. (pl. -áveis) irreproachable, impeccable, free from blame.
irreproduzível adj. m. + f. (pl. -íveis) irreproducible, incapable of being reproduced.
irrequieto adj. 1. unquiet, not quiet. 2. restless, ill at ease. 3. fidgety, fussy. 4. turbulent, agitated. 5. sleepless.
irresgatável adj. m. + f. (pl. -áveis) unredeemable.
irresignável adj. m. + f. (pl. -áveis) unrenounceable, that cannot be relinquished, incapable of being resigned.
irresistência s. f. nonresistance.
irresistente adj. m. + f. unresisting, not opposing.
irresistibilidade s. f. irresistibility, irresistibleness.
irresistível adj. m. + f. (pl. -íveis) 1. irresistible, resistless. 2. cogent. 3. charming. 4. overwhelming. ‖ **irresistivelmente** adv. irresistibly, uncontrollably, overwhelmingly, cogently.
irresolução s. f. (pl. -ões) 1. irresolution, irresoluteness. 2. indecision, vacillation. 3. faltering. 4. doubtfulness. 5. uncertainty.
irresoluto adj. 1. irresolute. 2. undecided, vacillating, hesitant. 3. unsure. 4. uncertain, doubtful. 5. unsettled, unresolved. ‖ -amente adv. irresolutely, etc.
irresolúvel adj. m. + f. (pl. -úveis) insoluble, irresoluble.
irrespirabilidade s. f. quality or state of being irrespirable.
irrespirável adj. m. + f. (pl. -áveis) irrespirable, unfit for respiration.
irrespondível adj. m. + f. (pl. -íveis) unanswerable, irrefutable, unquestionable.
irresponsabilidade s. f. 1. irresponsibility, irresponsibleness. 2. unwarrantableness.
irresponsável adj. m. + f. (pl. -áveis) 1. irresponsible. 2. unwarrantable, unaccountable, unanswerable. ‖ **irresponsavelmente** adv. irresponsibly, unaccountably.
irrestringível adj. m. + f. (pl. -íveis) unrestrictable, unrestrainable.
irrestrito adj. 1. unrestricted, unrestrained. 2. unlimited. 3. unconfined, unbounded. 4. unfettered. 5. free. ‖ -amente adv. unrestrictedly, unlimitedly, free(ly).
irretorquível adj. m. + f. (pl. -íveis) unanswerable, irrefutable.
irretratável adj. m. + f. (pl. -áveis) 1. irrevocable. 2. not retractable. 3. unchangeable.
irrevelado adj. unrevealed.
irreverência s. f. 1. irreverence, disrespect. 2. flippancy. 3. insolence, profanity. 4. disrespectfulness.
irreverencioso adj. irreverent, disrespectful, insolent.
irreverente adj. m. + f. irreverent, disrespectful, flippant, insolent. ‖ ~mente adv. irreverently.
irreversível adj. m. + f. (pl. -íveis) irreversible, reverseless.
irrevogabilidade s. f. (also **irrevocabilidade**) 1. irrevocability, irrevocableness. 2. irrepealability. 3. unavoidableness.
irrevogável, irrevocável adj. m. + f. (pl. -áveis) 1. irrevocable. 2. irrepealable, unrepealable. 3. unavoidable. 4. unalterable, unchangeable. ‖ **irrevogavelmente** adv. irrevocably, irrepealably, unavoidably.
irrigação s. f. (pl. -ões) irrigation, watering.
irrigador s. m. irrigator, syringe, sprinkler. ‖ adj. irrigating, irrigational.
irrigar v. to irrigate, water, moisten.

irrigatório adj. irrigative.
irrigável adj. m. + f. (pl. -áveis) irrigable.
irrisão s. f. (pl. -ões) 1. irrision. 2. derision, sneering. 3. scorn, contempt. 4. mockery.
irrisor s. m. derider, scoffer, mocker.
irrisório adj. 1. derisive, scornful. 2. ridiculous. 3. flouting, sneering. ‖ irrisoriamente adv. derisively, ridiculously, floutingly.
irritabilidade s. f. 1. irritability, irritableness. 2. soreness, touchiness. 3. emotionality, excitableness. 4. (physiol.) responsiveness of living matter (cells, nerves, muscles, etc.) to external stimuli.
irritação s. f. (pl. -ões) (also irritamento m.) 1. irritation. 2. anger, enragement. 3. excitement, agitation. 4. stimulation. 5. inquietude. 6. exasperation. 7. (physiol.) act of evoking reactions in living matter by chemical, physical or pathological agents.
irritadiço adj. petulant, querulous, peevish.
irritado adj. 1. irritated. 2. angry, furious. 3. edgy, snappish. 4. excited. ‖ -amente adv. irritatedly, angrily, excitedly.
   ela estava muito -a she was very angry, (coll.) she was up in the air; her back was up. eles estavam terrivelmente ~s they were in a terrible mood.
irritador s. m. irritant. ‖ adj. irritant, irritative, irritatory.
irritante s. m. irritant. ‖ adj. m. + f. 1. irritant, irritative. 2. provoking, vexatious. 3. annoying. 4. exasperating. ‖ ~mente adv. irritatively, provokingly, annoyingly.
irritar (I) v. 1. to irritate. 2. to anger, annoy, vex. 3. to enrage, madden. 4. to excite. 5. to provoke, incite. 6. to exasperate. 7. ~-se to be or become irritated, grow angry.
   ~ uma pessoa to make a person angry, (coll.) to rub a person the wrong way. ~am-me they exasperated me. isto me irrita this irritates me. irrita--me os nervos it grates on my nerves. aquilo irritou-o muito that rose his anger. deixaram-no muito irritado they made him very angry, they got his back up. ele se irrita por pouco he is short-tempered. eles o ~am they angered him, they roughed him up.
irritar (II) v. to annul, make void, cancel.
irritativo adj. irritative, irritant.
irritável adj. m. + f. (pl. -áveis) 1. irritable. 2. irascible, petulant. 3. touchy, short-tempered, bilious. 4. fretful, peevish. 5. querulous. ‖ irritavelmente adv. irritably, touchily, testily, querulously.
   ela tem um gênio ~ she is a high-strung girl. que sujeito ~! what a petulant fellow!
írrito adj. 1. invalid, null. 2. useless, vain. 3. ineffectual.
irrivalizável adj. m. + f. (pl. -áveis) unequalable, inimitable, peerless.
irrogação s. f. (pl. -ões) imposition, infliction (of a burden, duty, penalty).
irrogar v. to impose upon, inflict, cause to suffer.
irromper v. 1. to rush in, urge forward. 2. to break out. 3. to burst forth, penetrate. 4. to emerge, appear suddenly, come into view. 5. to sprout.
   ~ em aplausos to break into applause. ~ em chamas to burst into flame. ~ em lágrimas to burst into tears. ~ numa gargalhada to burst out laughing. irrompeu a peste the plague broke out. irrompeu uma crise a crisis has arisen. ele irrompeu na sala he plunged into the room.
irroração s. f. (pl. -ões) irroration, bedewing, sprinkling.
irrorar v. to bedew, moisten, sprinkle, irrorate.
irrupção s. f. (pl. -ões) 1. irruption. 2. sudden incursion, invasion. 3. foray, raid. 4. outburst.

irruptivo adj. irruptive.
isabel (I) s. f. a variety of vines.
isabel (II) adj. m. + f. isabel(l)e-coloured, dun, drab.
isagoge s. f. isagoge, introduction.
isagógico adj. isagogic, introductory.
isandro adj. (bot.) isandrous.
ísatis s. f. (bot, also ísate) woad, dyer's weed.
isatina s. f. (chem.) isatin.
isbá s. f. blockhouse, log-hut.
isca (I) s. f. 1. bait, lure, (plate P 9). 2. tinder. 3. (fig.) allurement, enticement.
   ~ artificial fishing fly. ~ viva live bait (plate P 9). morder a ~ to take the bait. prover com ~ to bait.
isca (II) interj. (Braz.) yoicks!
iscado adj. baited.
iscar v. 1. to bait. 2. to infect, contaminate. 3. to allure, entice. 4. (Braz.) to set on (dogs).
iscnofonia s. f. weakness of the voice.
iscnóceros s. m. pl. (ent.) Ischnocera, a suborder of mallophagous insects lacking maxillary feelers, typified by bird lice.
iscurético adj. (med.) ischuretic.
iscúria, iscuria s. f. (med.) ischuria: suppression or retention of the urine.
isenção s. f. (pl. -ões) 1. exemption, act of exempting, state of being exempt. 2. freedom, independence. 3. immunity, franchise. 4. impartiality. 5. abnegation. 6. disinterestedness.
   ~ de imposto tax exemption.
isentar v. 1. to exempt, free from. 2. to release, dispense. 3. to privilege. 4. to except. 5. to excuse. 6. to affranchise.
isento adj. 1. exempt. 2. free, unrestrained, independent. 3. excused. 4. released from, dispensed. 5. immune.
   ~ de selo free of postage. ~ de culpa free from guilt. ~ de dívidas debtless. ~ de taxa scot--free. ~ de direitos aduaneiros free of custom duties.
islã, islame s. m. (rel.) Islam.
islado adj. surrounded by water.
islamismo s. m. (rel.) Islam, Islamism, Mahometanism.
islamita s. m. + f. (rel.) Mohammedan, Islamite.
islamítico adj. (rel.) Islamitic, Islamic.
islandês s. m. 1. Icelander. 2. Icelandic: the language of the Icelanders. ‖ adj. Icelandic.
islão s. m. (rel.) Islam.
islenho, isleno s. m. islander. ‖ adj. insular.
ismaeliano s. m. (rel.) Ismailian, Ismaelian.
ismaelismo s. m. (rel.) Ismaelism.
ismaelita s. m. + f. (rel.) Ismailite, Ismaelite. ‖ adj. Ismaelitic, Ismailitic.
ismaelítico adj. (rel.) Ismailitic, Ismaelitic.
isóbare adj. m. + f. isobare, isobaric, indicating equal atmospheric pressure.
isobárico adj. isobare, isobaric.
isobarométrico adj. isobarometric.
isóbaro s. m. (chem., phys.) isobar.
isocarpo daj. (bot.) isocarpous.
isoclinais s. f. pl. (geol.) isoclinal, isocline strata of equal inclination or dip.
isóclino, isoclino adj. (geol.) isoclinal.
isócolo, isocólon adj. (gram., rhet.) isocolic.
isocromático adj. isochromatic, of the same colour.
isocromia s. f. lithochromy.
isocrômico adj. isochromatic.
isocrônico adj. isochronic, isochronous.
isocronismo s. m. isochronism.
isócrono adj. isochronic, isochronous.
isodáctilo, isodátilo adj. (zool.) isodactylous.
isodiáfero s. m. (nucl. phys.) isodiaphere. ‖ adj. referring to the isodiaphere.

isodinâmico adj. (phys.) isodynamic.
isodonte adj. m. + f. (zool.) isodont.
isoédrico adj. (min.) isohedric, isohedral.
isoetácea s. f. plant of the family Isoetaceae, the quillworts.
isoetáceo adj. (bot.) isoetaceous.
isoetinas s. f. pl. (bot.) Isoetales, a class of pteridophytous plants typified by the ferns.
isofilo adj. (bot.) isophyllous.
isófono, isofono adj. isophone.
isogamia s. f. (biol., bot.) isogamy, conjugation of two gametes of similar form.
isógino adj. (bot.) isogynous, isocarpous.
isógono adj. isogonal, isogonic.
isografia s. f. isography, exact reproduction of hand-writing.
isográfico adj. isographic.
isolação s. f. (pl. -ões) isolation, state of being isolated or alone.
isolacionismo s. m. isolationism.
isolado adj. 1. isolated, isolate. 2. separate, disconnected. 3. alone, secluded, withdrawn. 4. segregate. seclusive. 5. insulated. ‖ **-amente** adv. separately, singly, lonely.
  a casa fica um tanto -a the house is rather solitary. **viver ~** to keep to oneself.
isolador s. m. insulator, dielectric (plates A 10, C 1). ‖ adj. isolating, insulating.
isolamento s. m. 1. isolation, separation. 2. separateness, lonesomeness. 3. solitude. 4. insulation. 5. isolation hospital.
  eles vivem em completo ~ they live completely secluded.
isolante s. m. insulating material. ‖ adj. m. + f. isolating, insulating.
  fita ~ adhesive tape.
isolar v. 1. to isolate, set or place apart. 2. to detach, separate. 3. to segregate. 4. to let alone, stand alone. 5. to insulate. 6. **~-se** to immure o. s., retire from, withdraw.
  ela isolou-se do mundo she sequestered herself from the world.
isólogo adj. isologous.
isômere adj. m. + f. (bot., chem., also **isômeris**) isomeric, isomerous.
isomeria s. f. (chem.) isomerism, isomery.
isomérico adj. isomeric, isomerous.
isomerismo s. m. (chem.) isomerism.
isômero s. m. (chem.) isomer.
isômeros s. m. pl. (nucl. phys.) isomeric nuclides.
isométrico adj. isometric(al).
isomórfico adj. isomorphic, isomorphous.
isomorfismo s. m. isomorphism, similarity of crystalline forms.
isomorfo adj. isomorphous, isomorphic.
isonomia s. f. isonomy, equality before the law.
isônomo adj. (min.) isonomous.
isopata, isópata s. m. + f. (med.) isopathist.
isopatia s. f. (med.) isopathy.
isopático adj. (med. isopathic.
isoperimétrico adj. (math.) isoperimetrical.
isopétalo adj. (bot.) isopetalous.
isópiro s. m. Isopyrum: a small genus of plants (order Ranunculaceae).
isópode s. m. (zool.) ‖ adj. m. + f. isopodous.
isóptero s. m. (entom.) ‖ adj. isopterous.
isoquímeno adj. (phys.) isochimal, isocheimonal.
isóscele(s) adj. m. + f., sg. + pl. (geom.) isosceles.
isosférico adj. isospherical.
isosmose s. f. (phys.) isosmosis.
isospôndilos s. m. pl. (ichth.) Isospondyli, an order of fishes (herring, salmon).
isosporado adj. (bot.) isosporous, homosporous.

isóstase s. f. isostasy.
isostático adj. isostatic.
isostêmone adj. m. + f. (bot.) isostemonous.
isotérmico adj. isothermal, isotherm.
  curva -a isothermal curve, isotherm.
isotermo adj. isotherm.
isótero adj. (phys.) isotheral.
isotonia s. f. (phys.) isotonia.
isotônico (phys.) isotonic: having the same osmotic pressure.
isótopos s. m. pl. isotopes.
isotropia s. f. isotropism, isotropy.
isotrópico, isótropo adj. isotropic, isotropous.
isqueiro s. m. lighter, fire-lighter (plate F 7).
isquial adj. m. + f. (pl. -ais) (anat., med.) ischial, ischiatic.
isquiático adj. (anat., med.) ischiatic.
ísquio, ísquion s. m. (anat.) ischium, pinbone (plate G 1).
israelita s. m. + f. Israelite, Hebrew, Jew. ‖ adj. Israelitish, Jewish.
israelítico adj. Israelitic, Israelitish.
isso demonstrative pron. that.
  ~ mesmo, exatamente (coll.) that's just it! **~ não é nada** never mind, that does not matter. **~ não importa** that doesn't matter. **~ não me interessa** that does not interest me, that's not my business. **a ~** thereto. **com ~** therewith. **nem por ~** 1. not so much as... 2. don't mention it. **por ~** 1. therefore, hence. 2. by it. **apesar de tudo ~** for all that. **que é ~?** what is that, what does it mean? **não quero nada disso** I don't want anything of that. **apesar disso** nevertheless. **por ~ mesmo** for that very reason. **eu não disse ~** I didn't say that.
ístmico adj. isthmian.
istmo s. m. isthmus, strait.
isto demonstrative pron. this.
  ~ é that is. **~ é outra história** that is another story. **~ está liquidado** that is settled, (coll.) and that was that. **a ~** hereto. **além disto** besides. **para ~** to it. **que quer dizer ~?** what does it mean? **diga-me só ~** tell me this much. **conversamos sobre ~ e aquilo** we talked about this, that and the other. **é ~ que eu queria saber** that's all I wanted to know. **eu esperava que chegasse a ~** I hoped it would come to that. **justamente ~** this of all things! **não é bem ~ que se deve fazer** that is not quite the thing to do. **você é responsável por ~** you are responsible for that. **tudo ~** all this.
isurídeos s. m. pl. (ichth.) Isuridae, a family of elasmobranch fishes, including the makerel sharks.
itá s. f. (Braz.) Tupi-Guarani word meaning rock or metal, used as a prefix in forming compound words.
itã s. f. (Braz.) 1. polished stone ornaments found in funeral urns. 2. (zool.) a species of bivalvular shells.
itabirito s. m. (min.) itabirite.
itacolumito s. m. (min.) itacolumite.
itacurua s. f. (Braz.) cooking trivet made of three rocks.
itacuruba s. f., **itacurumbi** m. pebbly soil, pebble pit.
itaimbé s. m. (Braz., also **itambé**) steep mountain, ridge, peak, precipice.
itaipaba, itaipava s. f. (Braz.) rapids.
italianidade s. f. Italianity, Italianism.
italianismo s. m. Italianism.
italianização s. f. (pl. -ões) Italianization.
italianizar v. to Italianize.
italiano s. m. Italian: 1. native of Italy. 2. the Italian language. ‖ adj. Italian.
italianófilo s. m. Italophile.

italianófobo s. m. Italophobe.
itálico s. m. italics: an italic letter or type. ‖ adj. italic.
imprimir em tipos ～s to italicize.
italiota s. m. + f. (hist.) Italiote: native or inhabitant of Italy before the Roman domination.
ítalo s. m. Italian. ‖ adj. Italian, Roman, Latin.
itamaca s. f. (N. Braz.) fishing-net.
itaoca s. f. (Braz.) cave, cavern, den.
itapanhoacanga s. f. (Braz.) iron ore, native iron oxide.
itapeba, itapeva s. f. (Braz.) rock shelf forming the banks of a river.
itapecerica s. f. (Braz.) granite mountain with gentle slopes.
itapema s. f. (Braz., ornith.) swallow-tailed kite.
itapicuim s. m. (pl. -ins) (Braz., ent.) termite, white ant.
itapiri s. m. (Braz.) rude hut or shelter.
itapitanga s. f. (Braz., bot.) a kind of rockweed.
itapuá s. m. (Braz.) a kind of fish-spear.
itaquatiara s. f. (N. Braz.) rude drawings, paintings or engravings on rocks or cavern walls.
itararé s. m. (Braz.) subterranean river-channel.
itaúba s. f. (Braz.) common name of three timber trees of the laurel family (Ocotea megaphylla, Silvia itauba, Silvia Duckei).
itaúba-branca s. f. (pl. itaúbas-brancas) (Braz., bot.) bebeeru.
itaúna s. f. (Braz.) popular designation of dark or black rocks (basalt, diorite, etc.).
ité adj. m. + f. (Braz., pop.) insipid, tasteless.
item s. m. (pl. itens) item, article, separate particular of an enumeration. ‖ adv. item, also, likewise, further.
especificar por itens to itemize.

iteração s. f. (pl. -ões) iteration, repetition.
iterar v. to iterate, repeat.
iterativo adj. iterative.
itérbio s. m. (chem.) ytterbium.
itericia s. f. = icterícia.
itérico adj. = ictérico.
itinerante s. m. + f. itinerant, tramp. ‖ adj. itinerant, peripatetic.
itinerário s. m. itinerary, regular course, route, schedule. ‖ adj. itinerary.
itomídeos s. m. pl. (ent.) Itomidae, a family of lepidopterous insects (Hessian fly, clover-seed midge).
itororó s. m. (Braz.) chute, small waterfall.
ítria s. f. (chem.) yttria, yttrium oxide.
ítrio s. m. (chem.) yttrium.
itu s. m. (Braz., bot.) ironwood.
ituá s. m. = ituaá.
ituá-açu s. m. (pl. ituás-açus) (Braz., bot.) a kind of jointfir (Gnetum urens).
ituí s. m. (Braz.) a fresh-water fish (Sternopygus carapus).
ituituí s. m. (Braz., ornith.) the coloured plover (Charadius collaris).
itupava, itupeba, itupeva s. f. (Braz., also itoupava) small waterfall, chute.
iucá s. f. yucca: a genus of liliaceous plants.
iuçá s. m. (Braz., pop.) itch, itching.
iugoslavo s. m. Yugoslav, native or inhabitant of Yugoslavia. ‖ adj. Yugoslav.
iva s. f. (bot.) yellow bugle, ground pine.
ivantiji s. m. (Braz., bot.) the common whiptree.
ivirapema, ivirapeme s. m. (Braz.) Indian club (cudgel).
ixe interj. (Braz., pop.) don't tell me!
ixodídeos s. m. pl. (ent.) Ixodidae, the tick family.
ixora s. f. ixora: a genus of rubiaceous plants.

J

J, j s. m. tenth letter of the Portuguese alphabet. ‖ adj. tenth of a series, order or class.

já adv. 1. now, at once, immediately, this minute, without delay. 2. presently. 3. beforehand. 4. then. ‖ conj. already, since, once.
~ **agora** even now. ~ **assim** so, in this way. **desde** ~ at once, immediately, now. ~ **então** even then. ~ **estou entendendo** now I understand it. ~ **se vê** it is evident. ~ **não** no longer, no more. ~ **foi para Santos?** have you ever been in Santos? ~ **que** since, whereas, seeing that. ~ **há muito tempo** for a long time, it has been a long time. ~, ~ immediately. ~ **para fora!** out with you! ~ ... ~ now ... then.

jaaraboá s. m. (Braz.) a sort of kidney bean.

jabá s. m. (Braz.) dried meat, jerked beef.

jabaculê s. m. (Braz., sl.) 1. a tip. 2. money.

jabiraca s. f. (Braz.) 1. ugly woman, hag, shrew. 2. old or badly sewn clothes, rags.

jabô s. m. (Braz.) jabot.

jaborandi s. m. (Braz.) 1. (bot.) jaborandi. 2. drug obtained from it.

jabre s. m. (Braz.) large hole.

jaburu s. m. 1. (ornith.) jabiru stork. 2. ugly fellow.

jabuti s. m. (Braz.) 1. land turtle. 2. cotton-gin: device to separate the seed from the cotton.

jabuticaba s. f. (Braz.) fruit of the **jabuticabeira.**

jabuticabal s. m. (pl. **-ais**) grove of **jabuticabeiras.**

jabuticabeira s. f. jaboticaba: tree of the myrtle family, bearing cherrylike fruit on the stem.

jaca (I) s. m. native ruler in Africa.

jaca (II) s. f. 1. jack: fruit of the **jaqueira.** 2. (Braz.) top hat.

jacá s. m. (Braz.) pannier: pair of baskets used as a packsaddle.

jaça s. f. 1. spot or fault in a precious stone. 2. (vulg.) dungeon, calaboose; bed.

jacamar s. m. (ornith.) jacamar.

jacamim s. m. (pl. **-ins**) (Braz., ornith.) trumpeter, agami.

jaçanã s. f. (Braz.) jacana: wading bird.

jacanídeos s. m. pl. (ornith.) Jacanidae, the jacana family.

jacarandá s. m. (Braz., bot.) jacaranda: 1. any of the tall tropical trees of the bignoniaceous genus Jacaranda. 2. their fragrant ornamental wood.

jacarandá-da-baía s. m. (pl. **jacarandás-da-baía**) (Braz., bot.) Brazilian rosewood (Dalbergia nigra).

jacaré s. m. 1. jacare, alligator, cayman. 2. a bricklayer's pointing trowel. 3. cork roller. 4. frog of railway switch. 5. (sl.) young man who awaits his girl at the church door.
deixe estar, ~, **a lagoa há de secar** never mind, the day of reckoning will come.

jacazinho s. m. basket to start coffee seedlings in.

jacente s. m. 1. girder of a bridge. 2. **~s** pl. shallows, reefs. ‖ adj. m. + f. 1. jacent, lying, resting, recumbent. 2. (jur.) abeyant, stationary.
herança ~ abeyant inheritance.

jacina s. f. a kind of dragonfly.

jacintino adj. 1. hyacinthine. 2. of a violet or purple colour.

jacinto s. m. hyacinth: 1. (bot.) liliaceous plant. 2. (min.) reddish-orange variety of zircon.

jacitara s. f. (Braz.) jacitara palm.

jacobeu s. m. (f. **-éia**) 1. member of a political and religious organization founded in Portugal during the reign of D. João V (18th century). 2. (fig.) hypocrite. ‖ adj. hypocritical, sanctimonious.

jacobice s. f. hypocrisy.

jacobina s. f. (N. Braz.) brushland not suitable for agriculture.

jacobinismo s. m. 1. Jacobinism. 2. radicalism. 3. revolutionary trends.

jacobino s. m. 1. Jacobin. 2. (Braz.) nationalist, enemy of foreigners. ‖ adj. Jacobinic(al).

jacobita s. m. + f. (Engl. hist.) Jacobite: partisan of James II.

já-começa s. f. (Braz., fam.) itch(ing).

jactação s. f. (pl. **-ões**) (med.) (also **jatação**) jactitation: restless tossing of the body.

jactância s. f. (also **jatância**) 1. vanity, self-love. 2. pride, boastfulness. 3. arrogance, haughtiness. 4. bragadoccia.

jactanciosidade s. f. (also **jatanciosidade**) boastfulness, braggartism.

jactancioso adj. (also **jatancioso**) 1. vain, ostentatious. 2. vaunting, arrogant. 3. braggart, boastful. ‖ **-amente** adv. vainly.

jactante adj. m. + f. (also **jatante**) 1. suffering from jactation. 2. = **jactancioso.**

jactar-se v. (also **jatar-se**) to brag, boast, swagger, vaunt, bounce, gasconade.

jacto s. m. (also **jato**) 1. cast, hurl, throw. 2. jet, gush, flush, outpour, stream, rush, spout (plate T 6). ~ **de areia** sandblast. ~ **de luz** flash. ~ **de vapor** spout of steam. **avião a** ~ jet plane. **de um** ~ at one stretch, at one go. **motor a** ~**-propulsão** turbo jet.

jacu s. m. (Braz., ornith.) jacu, guan.

jacuba s. f. (Braz.) dish made of water, tapioca and honey.

jaculação s. f. (pl. **-ões**) 1. jaculation, range of artillery. 2. shot. 3. space covered by a shot. 4. throwing.

jacular v. to jaculate, throw, cast, hurl, dart.

jaculatória s. f. ejaculatory prayer.

jaculatório adj. 1. jaculatory, tending to or fit to eject, cast. 2. expelling jets. 3. ejaculatory.

jacumã s. m. (Braz., Amazonas) a sort of fishtrap.

jacuru s. m. (Braz.) puffbird.

jacutinga s. f. (Braz., ornith.) piping guan.

jade s. m. (min.) jade(ite), nephrite.
verde-~ jade green.

jadeíta s. f. (min.) jadeite.

jaez s. m. 1. harness, caparison. 2. quality, sort. 3. character, temperament.
do mesmo ~ of the same kind.

jaezar v. to harness, caparison.

jafético adj. Japhetic, descendent from Japheth, third son of Noah.

jaga s. f. 1. drain hole of a boat. 2. stopper to close that orifice.

jágara, jagra s. f. dark brown Indian sugar.

jagodes s. m., sg. + pl. 1. (pop.) simpleton, nincompoop, dunce. 2. (Braz.) large china figure representing a fat Chinese, whose mouth is the opening of a leter-box. 3. clumsy fellow.

jaguané adj. m. + f. (Braz.) said of any oxen with a white belly and white spine-line and red or black sides.

jaguar s. m. (also **onça-pintada**) jaguar, large spotted feline. 2. (by extension) a feline.

jaguareçá s. m. (Braz.) squirrel-fish.

jaguarundi s. m. (Braz., zool.) yaguarundi.

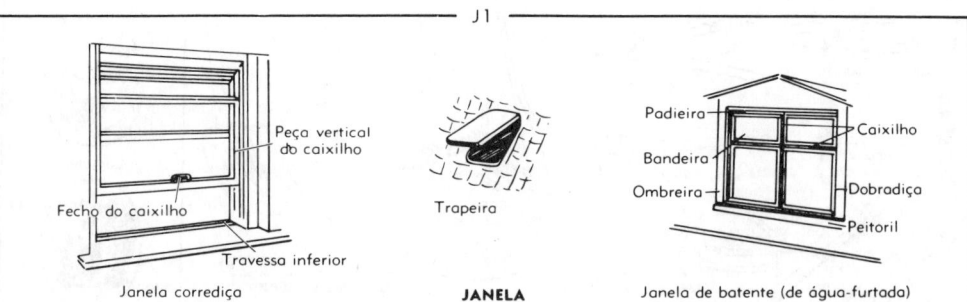

J 1

Peça vertical do caixilho

Fecho do caixilho

Travessa inferior

Janela corrediça

Trapeira

Padieira

Bandeira

Ombreira

Caixilho

Dobradiça

Peitoril

JANELA

Janela de batente (de água-furtada)

jagunçada s. f. (also **jagunçaria**) (Braz.) ruffians, (hired) assassins.

jagunço s. m. (Braz.) 1. (also **capanga**) hired rowdy, gunman, assassin. 2. goad.

jaibradeira s. f. (Braz.) croze: a cooper's tool to cut furrows in the stave of a barrel.

jaibro s. m. (Braz.) 1. furrow, groove, notch. 2. croze. 3. hole, opening.

jalapa s. f. jalap, any of the plants of the jalap (morning-glory) family. 2. its dried root (as purgative). 3. (Port.) bad or sour wine.

jaleca s. f. 1. short jacket. 2. fatigue-dress. 3. (Braz.) nickname for Portuguese.

jaleco s. m. 1. a short jacket. 2. an undress uniform. 3. (Braz., depr.) Portuguese (see **galego**). 4. a small anteater (Myrmecophaga tetradactyla).

jalne adj. m. + f. (also **jalde, jaldinino** m.) golden or bright yellow.

jalofo adj. rude, rough, barbaric.

jamaiquinho s. m. (Braz.) bantam domestic fowl.

jamais adv. 1. never, ever, at no time. 2. (pop.) especially, mainly.

~ **feito** original, never done before. ~ **outra coisa a não ser preocupações** never anything but sorrows.

jamanta s. f. 1. (ichth.) devilfish, large manta ray. 2. unkempt person. 3. (mot.) semi-trailer. 4. (Braz.) slipper.

jamba s. f. (Braz.) 1. jamb: a vertical piece forming the side of a doorway, window, or the like. 2. each of the folds of folding-doors.

jambé s. m. (Braz.) dish made of amaranth.

jâmbico adj. 1. iambic. 2. (Braz.) ironic, sarcastic, satyric.

jambo s. m. 1. iambus. 2. (bot.) jambo.

jamboeiro s. m. (Braz., bot.) jambo.

jamegão s. m. (Braz., sl., pop.) signature, "John Hancock".

jamelão s. m. (pl. **-ões**) (Braz., bot.) jambolan.

janeirinho adj. of or referring to January.

janeiro s. m. 1. January, the first month of the year. 2. ~s pl. years of age.

janela s. f. 1. window (plates B 15, D 4, E 7, J 1, V 4). 2. (geol.) hole produced by erosin exposing older geological layers. 3. (pop.) any opening, hole, tear, rip. 4. ~s pl. (fig.) eyes.

~ **corrediça,** ~ **de correr** sash window, sliding window (plate J 1). ~ **de sacada** bay window. **caixilho da** ~ window-frame. **peitoral da** ~ window sill. **deitar pela** ~ **fora** to throw out of the window. **estar à** ~ to be at the window. **olhar pela** ~ to look out of the window. **a** ~ **dá para a rua** the window looks upon the street. ~s **da alma** eyes.

janelar v. to keep at the window constantly.

janeleira adj. f. 1. flirtatious. 2. given to stay at the window.

janeleiro s. m. individual who habitually stays at the window. ‖ adj. given to stay at the window.

jangada s. f. 1. raft. 2. sailing raft used especially on the N. Braz. coast for fishing. 3. float of planks to save the shipwrecked.

~ **do alto** oceangoing sailing raft.

jangadeiro s. m. 1. owner or fisherman of a **jangada**. 2. raftsman.

jângal (pl. **-ais**), **jângala** s. m. jungle.

jangalamarte, jangalamaste s. m. seesaw.

janicéfalo s. m. janiceps: two-headed monster.

janízaro s. m. 1. (hist.) janizary. 2. satellite of a tyrant. 3. Turkish infantryman. 4. ~s pl. troops employed with great violence against people.

janota s. m. dandy, fop, coxcomb, dude, swell. ‖ adj. 1. foppish, dandyish, dapper. 2. elegant.

janotada s. f. (also **janotaria**) 1. group of dandies. 2. dandyism.

janotar v. to dress with excessive care, play the gallant, play the dude.

janotice s. f., **janotismo** m. dandyism, excessive care in dressing, foppery.

jansenismo s. m. (eccl., hist.) Jansenism.

jansenista s. m. + f. (eccl., hist.) Jansenist. ‖ adj. Jansenistic.

janta s. f. (pop.) dinner.

jantar s. m. dinner, main meal of the day. ‖ v. to dine, have one's dinner.

~ **dançante** dinner dance. ~ **fora** to dine out. ~ **mal** to dine poorly. **o** ~ **está na mesa** dinner is served. **hora de** ~ dinner-time. **sem** ~ dinnerless. **sala de** ~ dining room.

jantarão s. m. (pl. **-ões**) opulent dinner, banquet.

jante s. f. (Braz., mot.) the rim of a car wheel.

na ~ in a bad financial situation; stone-broke.

japa s. f. (S. Braz.) tip, gratuity.

japá s. m. (N. Braz.) mat of palm leaves.

Japão s. m. 1. Japan. 2. (pl. **-ões**) (f. **japoa**) Japanese: native or inhabitant of Japan. ‖ adj. Japanese.

japara s. f. (N. Braz.) sandy land at the seaside flooded in winter.

japecanga s. f. (Braz., bot.) a sarsaparilla.

japona s. f. 1. short jacket. 2. (Braz.) nickname of the Portuguese.

japonês s. m. Japanese: 1. native or inhabitant of Japan. 2. language spoken in Japan. ‖ adj. Japanese.

japonizar v. (also **japonesar**) to give Japanese traits to something or to assume Japanese habits.

jaqueira s. f. jack: a species of the breadfruit tree.

jaqueta s. f. 1. short jacket for men reaching to the waist only. 2. (Braz.) old-fashioned fellow.

jaquetão s. m. (pl. **-ões**) double-breasted coat (plate R 7).

jará s. f. (bot.) piassava palm.

jaraquá s. m. (Braz.) forage grass.

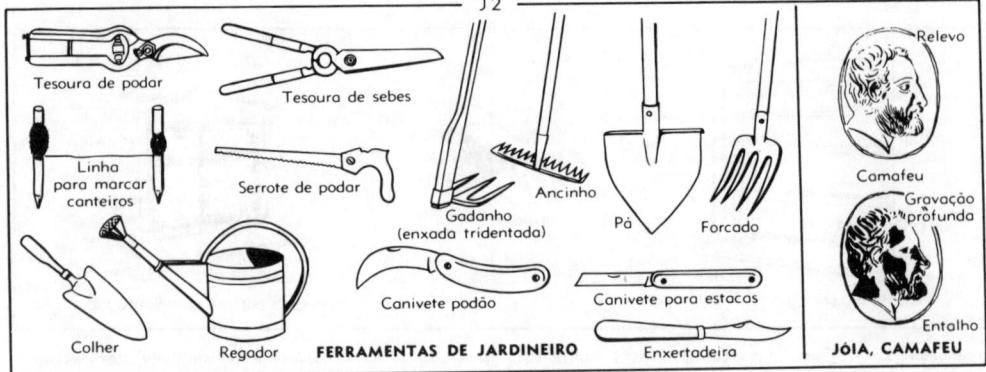

Tesoura de podar

Tesoura de sebes

Linha para marcar canteiros

Serrote de podar

Gadanho (enxada tridentada)

Ancinho

Pá

Forcado

Colher

Regador

Canivete podão

Canivete para estacas

FERRAMENTAS DE JARDINEIRO

Enxertadeira

Relevo

Camafeu

Gravação profunda

Entalho

JÓIA, CAMAFEU

jararaca s. f. 1. venomous snake of the genus Bothrops, jararaca. 2. (fig.) venomous or spiteful woman.

jararacuçu s. m. (Braz.) jararacussu: very dangerous pit viper (Bothrops jararacussu).

jarda s. f. yard: common unit of linear measurement used in English speaking countries (36 inches; 0.9144 m).

jardim s. m. (pl. **-ins**) 1. garden, flower-garden (plate A 4). 2. fertile, well-cultivated country. 3. stern gallery of a ship.
~ **botânico** botanical garden. ~ **da infância** kindergarten. ~ **público** public park. ~ **zoológico** zoological garden, zoo. **fazer um** ~ to lay out a garden.

jardinagem s. f. (pl. **-ens**) gardening.

jardinar v. to garden, cultivate or work in a garden.

jardineira s. f. 1. table or other piece of furniture used to hold flowers, plants or other decorative objects. 2. jardiniere (also cul.) 3. woman gardener. 4. (Braz.) station wagon. 5. old dance.

jardineiro s. m. gardener.

jardinista s. m. + f. person fond of gardens.

jarê s. m. (N. Braz.) fetishistic dance.

jargão s. m. 1. slang. 2. jargon, gibberish; uncomprehensive foreign language. 3 (min.) red variety of zircon.

jarra s. f. 1. pitcher, jar. 2. vase, flowerpot. 3. (naut.) water keg, water container.

jarreta (ê) s. m. + f. 1. person dressed badly or in an old-fashioned manner. 2. ridiculous person.

jarretar v. 1. to hamstring. 2. to cripple, maim, disable. 3. to destroy, annihilate. 4. to frustrate, render impossible.

jarrete (ê) s. m. 1. (anat.) hollow of the knee, ham (plate C 18). 2. (zool.) hamstring; hock; hough plates C 12, G 1).

jarreteira s. f. garter (plate R 7).
cavalheiros da ~ knights of the Garter.

jarro s. m. (dim. **jarrinho**) pitcher, jar, jug (plate V 2).

jarmim s. m. (pl. **-ins**) jasmin(e), jessamin(e): 1. the flower. 2. its essence.

jasminácea s. f. plant of the genus Jasminum.

jasmineiro s. m. jasmin(e) shrub.

jaspe s. m. jasper: a compact, opaque, often highly coloured, cryptocrystalline variety of quartz.

jaspear v. to speckle, mottle, give the colour or appearance of jasper.

jaticá s. m. (N. Braz.) long-stemmed harpoon to spear turtles.

jaú s. m. (Braz.) Amazon catfish.

jaula s. f. cage, esp. for wild beasts.

javali s. m. (f. **javalina**) wild boar (Sus scrofa).
caçar ~ to hunt wild boar.

javanês s. m. (pl. **-neses**) Javanese. ‖ adj. Javanese, pertaining to Java.

javardo s. m. 1. wild boar. 2. (fig.) brute, ruffian, rough fellow. ‖ adj. nauseating, filthy.

javevó adj. m. + f. (S. Braz.) ugly, badly dressed, of disagreeable appearance.

já-vi-ontem s. m., sg. + pl. (Braz., pop.) the leftovers from a previous meal, served without any alteration.

javradeira s. f. croze: a cooper's tool to make notches, furrows.

javrar v. (cooper) to croze: make notches, furrows.

javre s. m. croze, notch, furrow (in the staves of a barrel).

jazer v. 1. to lie, be stretched out, rest. 2. to be dead, or like dead. 3. to be buried. 4. to be serene, calm, quiet. 5. to stay, continue. 6. to be situated, located.
aqui jaz here lies (used in epitaphs).

jazida s. f. 1. resting-place, bed, couch. 2. act of resting, lying. 3. (Braz.) natural deposit of ores, mine. 4. (fig.) quietness, calmness.

jazigo s. m. 1. grave, sepulcher, tomb, vault, burial monument. 2. mine, bed. 3. (fig.) deposit, shelter.
~ **de família** family vault.

jazz s. m. (Engl.) jazz.

jazz-band s. m. (Engl., mus.) jazz band.

jazzista s. m. + f. 1. a jazz music composer. 2. an admirer of jazz.

jazzístico adj. pertaining or relative to jazz.

jebu s. m. (N. Braz.) defective explosion of a firecracker.

jeca s. m. (sl.) rube, hayseed, rustic; countryman. ‖ adj. awkward, clumsy, uncouth.

jeca-tatu s. m. (pl. **jecas-tatus**) name (and symbol) of the simple Braz. countryman or hillbilly.

jecoral adj. m. + f. (pl. **-ais**) (anat.) jecoral.

jegue s. m. (N. Braz.) donkey, ass.

jeguedê s. m. (Braz.) Negro dance of African origin.

jeira s. f. 1. yoke of land (varying from 19 to 36 hectares). 2. (ant.) land ploughed by a couple of oxen in one day. 3. a day's work of a journalist. 4. a day's wages.
à ~ by the day, daily.

jeito s. m. 1. aptitude, aptness. 2. dexterity, adroitness, skill, knack, propensity. 3. way, manner. 4. kind. 5. appearance.
~ **de uma coisa** the hang of a thing. **dar um** ~ to manage, to engineer. **dei mau** ~ **no pé** I strained my foot. **de qualquer** ~ at any rate, any old way. **de todo** ~ at all events. **ela sempre dá um** ~ **de ficar mais bonita do que as outras** she always manages to look prettier than the others. **ela tem um** ~ **especial de lidar com crianças** she

has a way with children. **ele tem de dar um ~ nesta sua vida** he's got to do something about that life he leads. **ele tem ~ para poeta** he has the stuff of a poet. **estou sem ~ de pedir o seu carro emprestado outra vez** it embarrasses me to borrow your car again. **falta de ~** awkwardness, left-handedness. **fiquei sem ~** I felt awkward, embarrassed. **isso é o ~ dela mesmo** that's the way she is, that's her way. **não tenho ~ para línguas** I have no talent for languages. **qual, não tem ~ mesmo** no doubt, it is hopeless; might as well give up. **sem ~** awkward.

jeitoso adj. 1. skillful, adroit, dexterous. 2. handy, manageable. 3. versatile. 4. comely, graceful. ‖ **-amente** adv. skillfully, adroitly.
    meu cabelo não é ~ my hair is unmanageable.

jejé s. m. (Braz.) prison, jail, clink, gaol.

jejuador s. m. person who fasts, faster. ‖ adj. fasting.

jejuar v. 1. to fast. 2. (fig.) to abstain from something. 3. to ignore, be ignorant.
    ~ depois de farto to fast with a full belly.

jejum s. m. (pl. **-uns**) 1. fasting, abstinence from food (and fig. from anything else). 2. a time of fasting. 3. (fam.) lack of knowledge of certain things.
    dia de ~ fast day. **em ~** fasting. **quebrar o ~** to break one's fast.

jejuno s. m. (anat.) jejunum, the middle part of the small intestine between the duodenum and ileum. ‖ adj. fasting.

jenipapada s. f. (Braz.) sweet or dessert made of genipap.

jenipapeiro s. m. (Braz., bot.) genipap tree (Genipa americana).

jenipapo s. m. (Braz.) 1. genipap: the fruit of the rubiaceous genipap tree. 2. the juice of the fruit used by the Indians to blacken their faces and by the people of N. Braz. to make wine. 3. dark spot on the lower part of the back of children, taken as the sign of mixed blood.

jenneriano adj. relative to Jenner, discoverer of the smallpox vaccine.

jenolim s. m. yellowish colour used in painting.

Jeová s. m. Jehova, God.

jeovismo s. m. Jehovism, Judaism.

jeovista adj. Jehovistic: characterized by the use of the name of Jehova for God.

jequi s. m. (N. Braz.) a sort of eel-buck, fishtrap. ‖ adj. tight.
    botar o ~ to get (somebody) into a fix.

jequiá s. m. (Braz.) open basket.

jequice s. f. (Braz.) boorishness; behaviour befitting a hillbilly or rube.

jequitibá s. m. (Braz.) (bot.) jequitiba.

jerarquia s. f. (also **hierarquia**) hierarchy.

jereba s. m. (Braz.) 1. worn-out nag, mare or jade. 2. harness. 3. f. awkward or sloppy person.

jeremiada s. f. jeremiad, prolonged lamentation, lugubrious complaint.

jeremiar v. to whine, blubber; lament, complain.

jereré s. m. 1. (Braz.) itch, prurigo. 2. (S. Braz.) long, drizzly rain. 3. (N. Braz.) long-handled hoop net to catch shrimps.

jericada s. f. 1. group of donkeys. 2. stupidity, nonsense.

jerico s. m. donkey, ass.

jerimu(m) s. m. (N. Braz.) pumpkin.

jerivá s. m. (S. Braz.) 1. a variety of palm tree. 2. (fig.) tall and thin person.

jeróglifo s. m. = **hieróglifo**.

jeropiga s. f. 1. beverage of unfermented fruit juice, brandy and sugar. 2. poor wine.

jerosolimita, jerosolimitano adj. = **hierosolimita**.

jerra s. f. (S. Braz.) picnic.

jérsei s. m. jersey (wool, silk or cotton knitted fabric.)

jesuíta s. m. Jesuit: member of a R. C. order. ‖ adj. 1. Jesuitical. 2. (fig.) cunning, fanatical.

jesuítico adj. Jesuitic(al).

jesuitismo s. m. 1. Jesuitism. 2. Jesuitry.

Jesus s. m. (rel.) Jesus.

jetatura s. f. evil eye, bad omen.

jetica s. f. (Braz.) sweet potato.

jetton s. m. (Fr.) 1. jetton. 2. a chip which is later exchanged for pay. 3. the pay (in 2.).

jevura s. m. (Braz.) name given to beans planted in February and March, the dry months.

jia s. f. (Braz., zool.) bullfrog.

jibóia s. f. boa constrictor: a nonvenomous snake.

jiboiar v. (Braz.) to digest resting, to sleep off a large meal.

jiçuí adj. m. + f. (N. Braz.) painful; hispid.

jiga s. f. jig, lively dance.

jigajoga s. f. 1. old card game. 2. (fig.) scorn, mockery. 3. passing, evanescent thing.
    andar numa ~ to go from pillar to post.

jiló s. m. fruit of the **jiloeiro**.

jiloeiro s. m. (Braz.) plant of the family Solanaceae (Solanum melangena).

jingoísmo s. m. jingoism: patriotism favouring a bellicose and blustering foreign policy.

jingoísta s. m. + f. jingoist: supporter of an aggressive foreign policy. ‖ adj. jingoistical.

jingoto s. m. 1. long rod, switch. 2. whip.

jinjibirra s. f. ginger beer.

jinriquixá s. m. jinrikisha, rickshaw, ricksha.

jipe s. m. (mot.) jeep.

jiquipanga s. f. (N. Braz.) recreation, amusement; fun, spree.

jiquitaia s. f. (Braz.) 1. pepper sauce. 2. any hot sauce or juice. 3. dried and powdered pepper. 4. a species of ant.

jirau s. m. 1. raised indoor platform to keep pots and pans, kitchen utensils, vegetables, etc. on. 2. wooden structure on which houses are built to protect them from water or humidity. 3. crude bed made out of wooden rods. 4. (fig.) old house, ruin.

jiribana s. f. (N. Braz.) braided lasso of thin leather strips.

jiribanda s. f. violent reproof, admonition, scolding.

jirigote s. m. rascal, crook, cheat, scoundrel.

jiritana s. f. (Braz., bot.) a variety of bean.

jirote s. m. (sl.) lazybones, loafer, idler.

jitirana s. f. (Braz., bot.) scarlet starglory.

jito s. m. sow: channel through which melted metal is led into the mold. ‖ adj. (N. Braz.) small, tiny.

jiu-jitsu s. m. (also **jujutsu**) jiu-jitsu.

joalharia, joalheria s. f. jeweller's shop, jewelry store.

joalheiro s. m. jewel(l)er.

joanete s. m. 1. bunion: swelling on the first joint of the big toe. 2. (naut.) topgallant sail.

joaninha s. f. 1. ladybird, ladybug. 2. safety pin.

joanino adj. 1. (hist.) of or referring to D. João I and III. 2. of or referring to (São) João (St.) John.
    estilo ~ architectural style of the time of D. João III of Portugal. **festas -as** feasts in honour of St. John (June 24).

joão-de-barro s. m. (pl. **joões-de-barro**) ovenbird (family Furnariidae) that makes his nest out of clay.

joão-de-pau s. m. (pl. **joões-de-pau**) 1. thorn-bird (family Furnariidae). 2. (N. Braz.) oar of a boat tied to the stern.

joão-fernandes s. m. (pl. **joões-fernandes**) s. m. country-dance, fandango.

joão-ninguém s. m. (pl. **joões-ninguém**) a nobody.

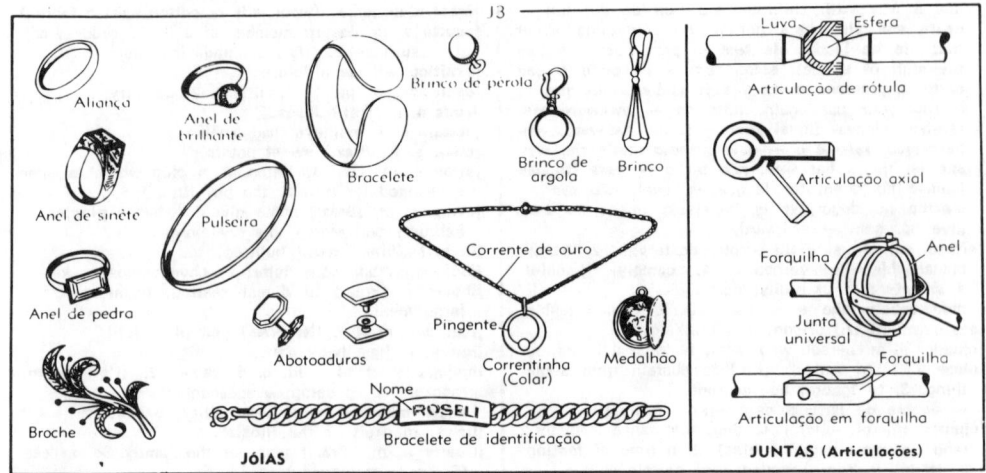

Aliança

Anel de brilhante

Anel de sinête

Pulseira

Anel de pedra

Broche

Abotoaduras

Bracelete

Brinco de pérola

Brinco de argola

Brinco

Corrente de ouro

Pingente

Nome

Correntinha (Colar)

Medalhão

Bracelete de identificação

JÓIAS

Luva — Esfera

Articulação de rótula

Articulação axial

Forquilha — Anel

Junta universal

Forquilha

Articulação em forquilha

JUNTAS (Articulações)

joão-pestana s. m. (pop.) sleep.

joça s. f. (Braz.) 1. mess. 2. any old thing, thrash, rubbish.

joçal s. m. (pl. -ais) (Braz.) hairy coat of sugar cane leaves.

joco-sério adj. (pl. **joco-sérios**) half serious, half joking.

jocosidade s. f. joviality, jocosity, jocoseness, facetiousness, cheerfulness, playfulness.

jocoso adj. jesting, jovial, merry, playful, funny, droll, waggish.

joeira s. f. large sieve, winnowing basket, winnowing machine, screen (plate E 11).

joeiramento s. m. winnowing, sieving, screening (grain).

joeirar v. to sift: 1. winnow, fan. 2. (fig.) separate carefully, select.

joeireiro s. m. winnower, sifter, screener.

joelhada s. f. hit or stroke with the knee.

joelheira s. f. 1. (armour) kneepiece. 2. wooden bench with two depressions into which the knees are set to do certain jobs, like washing. 3. baggy knees of pants. 4. wounded knees of beasts. 5. kneepad (Braz. also for football).

joelheiro adj. reaching to the knees, knee-high, knee-deep.

joelho s. m. 1. knee (plate C 12, 18). 2. joint.
ação de ~ (tech.) knee action. cair de ~s to fall on one's knees. dobrar os ~s 1. to bend one's knees. 2. (fig.) to yield. pôr-se de ~s to fall on one's knees.

joelhudo adj. having thick or heavy knees; big-kneed.

jogada s. f. 1. play, game. 2. (in a game) throw, cast, move, hit, shot, stroke.
bela ~! good shot! well played!

jogado adj. 1. played, gambled. 2. thrown. 3. (Braz.) prostrate, half dead, abandoned.
~ aos dados exposed to imminent danger.

jogador s. m. 1. (sport) player. 2. gambler, gamester. ‖ adj. 1. playing. 2. gambling.
~ de primeira classe first-rate player. um ~ a mais an odd player.

jogar v. 1. (sport) to play. 2. to take part in a game. 3. to make a move in a game. 4. to gamble, stake, risk, venture. 5. to lose money. 6. to throw, hit, fling, cast. 7. (naut.) to lurch, roll. 8. (vehicle) to toss. 9. to observe jocosely. 10. to have fun, to frolic, enjoy o. s.

~ bridge, futebol, cartas, etc. to play bridge. football, cards, etc. ~ água no mar to carry coals to Newcastle. ~ armas to wield arms. ~ água na fervura to pour oil on troubled waters. ~ com malícia to play foul. ~ com pau de dois bicos to hunt with the hounds and run with the hare. ~ os dados to play at dice. ~ limpo to play fair. ~ para cima to toss. ~ para fora to throw out. ~ a última cortada to sink or swim. ~ uma partida to play a game.

jogata s. f. game, set.

jogatina s. f. habit or vice of gambling.

jogo (ô) s. m. 1. game, match; play, amusement; sport; pastime. 2. bet, gamble, stake. 3. cheat, trick. 4. vice of gambling. 5. (mech.) play, looseness. 6. set, equipment, collection (plate B 3). 7. scorn. 8. fancing.
~ de água fountain. ~ de azar game of chance. ~ de empurra (fig.) passing the buck. ~ de mão jugglery, legerdemain. ~ de palavras play on words, pun. ~ de salão parlour game. ~s olímpicos Olympic games. casa de ~ gambling house. eu conheço o seu ~ I know your little game. esconder o ~ (fig.) to hide one's game. estar em ~ to be at stake. jogar o ~ to play the game, play fair. pôr em ~ a carreira to risk one's career. um ~ de copos a set of glasses. você quer entrar no ~? will you join us in the game? a direção do carro tem muito ~ the steering of the car has too much play.

jogral s. m. (pl. -ais) jester, scoffer, buffoon.

jogralesco adj. of or pertaining to a jester; playful, jesting, droll.

joguete (ê) s. m. 1. plaything, toy. 2. jest, mockery. 3. laughing-stock, fool.

joguetear v. 1. to play, jest, make sport. 2. to play at fencing.

jóia s. f. 1. jewel, trinket, gem (plate J 2, 3). 2. entrance fee for new club members. 3. (fig.) person or thing of great esteem and value. 4. prize. 5. ~s pl. jewelry.
minha ~ my darling.

joio s. m. (bot.) darnel.
separar o ~ do trigo to separate the wheat from the tares.

joliz adj. m. + f. (anat.) amiable, pleasant, merry.

jongar v. to dance the **jongo**.

jongo s. m. dance and song of African origin.

jongueiro s. m. (Braz.) person fond of jongo dancing.
jônico adj. Ionic: 1. referring to Ionia. 2. (archit.) pertaining to one of the Greek orders of architecture.
jônio s. m. Ionian: 1. native or inhabitant of Ionia. 2. language spoken on the Ionian Islands. ‖ adj. Ionian.
jóquei s. m. jockey.
jorna s. f. 1. (pop.) daily wage. 2. (S. Braz.) booze, soaks, binge.
tomar uma ~ to get drunk.
jornada s. f. 1. distance travelled in one day. 2. trip overland. 3. military action. 4. expedition. 5. (N. Braz.) singing at the Christmas manger. 6. a day's work.
jornadear v. to travel, go on a trip; make a day's journey.
jornal s. m. (pl. -ais) 1. daily pay or wages. 2. newspaper, journal (plate E 3). 3. diary, daybook. 4. newsreel.
banca de -ais newsstand. ~ da manhã morning paper.
jornaleco s. m. badly written newspaper, paper of no consequence.
jornaleiro s. m. 1. day labourer, journeyman, worker paid by the day. 2. news vendor, newboy (plate E 13). ‖ adj. daily, per day; consecutively.
jornalismo s. m. journalism, press.
jornalista s. m. + f. journalist; newspaperman; news editor.
jornalístico adj. journalistic.
jorra (ô) f. 1. pitch. 2. (met.) dross. 3. (Port.) wine.
jorrão s. m. (pl. -ões) lorry or sort of low lorry to haul heavy rocks or earth.
jorrar v. 1. to gush, spout out, (out)pour, spring forth, spurt. 2. to bubble forth. 3. to belly or bulge out. 4. to tar, cover with pitch.
jorro s. m. (also jorramento) outpour, gush, jet, rush, spout, stream.
corre em jorros it spouts out. a jorros in torrents.
jota s. m. 1. tenth letter of the Portuguese alphabet. 2. f.: a) Spanish dance. b) the music for this dance.
joule s. m. (electr.) joule: a unit of work or energy.
jovem s. m. + f. (pl. -ens) young person, youth. ‖ adj. young, youthful, juvenile.
uma ~ bonita a beautiful girl.
jovial adj. m. + f. (pl. -ais) jovial, merry, gay, jolly, convivial, jocose, jocund.
jovialidade s. f. joviality, merriment, jollity, gaiety, cheerfulness, facetiousness, good humour.
jovializar v. 1. to make jovial, cheer, enliven. 2. to be jovial or cheerful.
juá s. m. (Braz., bot.) jujube.
juazeiro s. m. (Braz., bot.) jujube tree.
juba s. f. a lion's mane.
jubado adj. maned.
jubilação s. f. (pl. -ões) 1. jubilation, exultation, great joy, rejoicing. 2. retirement of a professor.
jubilar v. 1. to rejoice, exult, jubilate. 2. to retire. 3. to pension off. ‖ adj. of or referring to a jubilee.
jubileu s. m. jubilee: 1. (eccl.) indulgence proclaimed by the Pope. 2. 50th anniversary (service, wedding, etc.).
júbilo s. m. jubilation, exultation, joy, satisfaction.
jubiloso adj. jubilant, rejoicing, exultant, elated, joyful.
juçana s. f. (Braz.) bird snare.
juçapé s. m. (Braz.) sape grass.
jucubaúba s. m. (Braz.) steersman, helmsman of a row-boat.
jucundidade s. f. jocundity, jocundness, mirth, cheerfulness, gaiety.
jucundo adj. jocund, merry, cheerful, blithe, gay.

judaico adj. Jewish, Judaic.
judaísmo s. m. 1. Judaism, religion of the Jews. 2. the Jews collectively.
judaizante s. m. + f. Judaizer, observer of Jewish rituals or ways. ‖ Judaizing, observing Jewish rituals or ways of living.
judaizar v. to Judaize, observe Jewish rituals and ways of life.
judas s. m., sg. + pl. 1. (fig.) traitor, false friend. 2. puppet which is burned on Easter Saturday. 3. (Braz.) badly dressed person.
judeu s. m. (f. -ia) 1. Jew. 2. member of the Hebrew state Israel. 3 (pop.) bargainer. 4. (Braz.): a) dish of beans. b) kind of corn cake. 5. (N. Braz.) name given to Syrian and oriental people. ‖ adj. Jewish.
judiação s. f. (pl. -ões) torment, ill-treatment; perversity, cruelty; meanness, baseness.
judiar v. 1. to torment, hurt; mistreat, pester. 2. to mock.
judiaria s. f. 1. large quantity of Jews. 2. ghetto, Jewish quarter in a city. 3. (fig.) cruelty, ill-treatment; mockery, derision.
judicativo adj. judicative, judging, judicial.
judicatório adj. judicatory.
judicatura s. f. judicature: 1. power of judging, jurisdiction. 2. court of judges. 3. judgeship, a judge's office. 4. judiciary.
judicial adj. m. + f. (pl. -ais) judicial, juridical, forensic, judiciary. ‖ ~mente adv. judicially.
judiciar v. to judge, decide judicially, pass judgement.
judiciário adj. judiciary, judicial, forensic.
judicioso adj. 1. judicious, sensible, discerning, clear-sighted, wise. 2. cautious, prudent, discreet.
jugada s. f. yoke of land, portion ploughed by a team of oxen in one day.
jugadeiro s. m. owner or cultivator of a yoke of land. ‖ adj. referring to a yoke of land.
jugador s. m. iron instrument to kill sheep in a slaughterhouse.
jugal adj. m. + f. (pl. -ais) nuptial, matrimonial.
jugar v. to slaughter (heifers) by breaking their neck.
juglandáceas s. f. pl. (bot.) Juglandaceae, the walnut tree family.
juglandales s. f. pl. (bot.) Juglandales.
jugo s. m. 1. yoke. 2. a team of oxen. 3. submission, oppression. 4. servitude, bondage.
sacudir o ~ to shake off the yoke. sob o ~ romano dominated by the Romans.
jugoslavo s. m. + adj. = iugoslavo.
jugular v. 1. to strangle; cut the throat. 2. to murder. 3. to dominate, suffocate. ‖ adj. m. + f. jugular.
juiz s. m. 1. judge, member of a court of judges. 2. referee, umpire. 3. arbiter, arbitrator.
~ de direito district judge. ~ de fato juryman. ~ de linha (also bandeirinha, ftb.) linesman. ~ de paz justice of the peace. ~ de primeira instância judge of a lower court. ~ do supremo tribunal judge of the supreme court. ser ~ em causa própria to be the judge and party.
juíza s. f. 1. female judge. 2. wife of a judge.
juizado s. m. judgeship.
juízo s. m. 1. judgement; trial. 2. wits, good sense, brains, intelligence. 3. discernment, understanding, reason, discretion, opinion. 4. prediction.
~ de Deus trial by ordeal. ~ de Salomão to judge according to one's instinct rather than the law. ~ temerário rash, precipitated judgement. chamar a ~ to summon to court. criar ~ to settle down, become reasonable. veja se consegue dar ~ a esta menina see if you can put some sense into her. dar volta ao ~ to go mad. dia do ~ judgement day. dia do ~ final doomsday. estar em ~ perfeito

to have one's senses. **você perdeu o ~?** have you lost your mind? **tenha ~** be sensible. **não ter ~** to be a little wanting (foolish). **ela não tem ~ bastante para deixá-lo** she has not enough sense to leave him.

jujuba s. f. (Braz., bot.) jujube.

julepo s. m. julep, soothing drink.

julgado s. m. 1. territory or borough under the jurisdiction of a judge. 2. judicial district, judgeship. ‖ adj. 1. judged, sentenced. 2. thought of, considered.

julgador s. m. 1. judge(r), arbiter. 2. critic. ‖ adj. judging.

julgamento s. m. 1. judgement, verdict, sentence, decision. 2. opinion, understanding. 3. examination, discrimination, discernment. 4. appreciation. 5. court session, trial.
ela será submetida a um ~ she will have to stand trial. **~ em público** open trial.

julgar v. 1. to judge, try, pass sentence on. 2. to think, suppose, imagine, deem, believe. 3. to decide, conclude. 4. to criticize, censure. 5. to consider, regard, hold, account.
~ os outros por si to judge others by o. s. **~-se feliz** to consider o. s. happy. **~-se grande coisa** to have a (too) high opinion of o. s. **~-se no dever** to feel obliged to; to feel it one's duty. **julgo que farei isto** I think I shall do this. **julgo que ele o fará** I believe he will do it. **não cabe a mim ~ os seus atos** it is not for me to judge his actions.

julho s. m. July, seventh month of the year.

juliana s. f. julienne, clear soup containing vegetables cut into thin strips or small pieces. ‖ adj. 1. of or referring to this soup. 2. julienne.

julianiáceas s. f. pl. (bot.) a family of dicotyledonous plants.

juliano adj. Julian: referring to the calendar established by Julius Caesar in 46 B.C.

júlidas s. m. pl. (ent.) Julidae, a family of myriapods.

júlio adj. Julian, of or pertaining to Julius Caesar.

jumentada s. f. stupidity, foolishness, dumbness, nonsense.

jumento s. m. donkey, ass.

junça s. f. (bot.) the chufa, flatsedge.

juncáceas s. f. (bot.) Juncaceae, the rush family.

juncada s. f. (bot.) large quantity of rushes.

juncal s. m. (pl. **-ais**) a growth os rushes.

junção s. f. (pl. **-ões**) junction: 1. act of joining. 2. point of union. 3. connection, linking. 4. joint.

juncar v. 1. to cover with rushes. 2. to cover, strew all over with leaves or flowers. 3. (fig.) to spread, cover, scatter.

junco s. m. 1. rush (Juncaceae): plant with a thin, long, and flexible stem used for wickerwork and canes. 2. Chinese junk.
bengala de ~ rat(t)an, cane.

jundu s. m. zone near the beach or dunes covered by a xerophilous and sclerophilous vegetation (also **nhundu**).

jungir v. 1. to yoke, harness with a yoke. 2. to unite, couple, join, link. 3. to tie. 4. to submit, enslave.

junho s. m. June, sixth month of the year.

junino adj. of or pertaining to June.

júnior (abbr. jr.) s. m. junior. ‖ adj. 1. younger. 2. (sport) of the younger set.

junípero s. m. (bot., also **zimbro**) juniper.

junqueira s. f. (Braz.) a variety of strong, fat cattle bred in Goiás.

junta s. f. 1. junction, juncture, union. 2. pair, yoke, team. 3. commission, junta. 4. council, assembly, board. 5. plane, line or point at which two or more

things join. 6. joint: a) (anat. + tech.) articulation, knuckle (plate J 3). b) (carp.) junction (plate C 9). c) (constr.) slit between two bricks (plate A 7). d) (tech.) hinge. 7. (geol.) joint: more or less sharply defined fracture which cuts the rocks independently of stratification layers. 8. seam. 9. designation for various plants.
~ administrativa administrative council. **~ articulada** swivel joint. **~ de ângulo** end lap. **~ de bois** a yoke of oxen. **~ de cruzeta** cross lap. **~ de espiga e encaixe** tenon joint. **~ de expansão** expansion joint. **~ de meia-esquadria** miter joint. **~ de meio** middle lap. **~ do comércio** board of trade. **~ hermética** hermetic joint. **~ municipal** common council. **~ sobreposta** lap joint. **~ universal** (mot.) universal joint.

juntar v. 1. to join, connect. 2. to collect, heap up, pile up. 3. to annex, adjoin, attach. 4. to meet, come together. 5. to unite, assemble. 6. to associate, couple. 7. to occur at the same time or successively.
~ em parelha to team (oxen). **~ firmemente** to clench. **~ forças** to join forces. **~ pouco a pouco** to scrape together. **juntei-me a eles** I joined them. **ele juntou-se aos seus antepassados** he was gathered to his fathers. **ela juntou seu destino ao meu** she threw in her lot with mine.

junteira s. f. jointer, small plane to make rabbets.

junto adj. 1. united, joined. 2. near, next to, close, adjoining, contiguous, adjacent (plate Q). ‖ adv. (also **-amente**) together, jointly, closely, adjoining. **~ a** near, by (plate P 18). **~ à praia** alongshore. **mandarei as batatas ~ com as cenouras** I'll send the potatoes along with the carrots. **pôr ~ a** to put next to. **todos ~s** all together. **todos ~s temos mil cruzeiros** we have thousand cruzeiros between us. **-amente, nossa lista de preços** (com.) enclosed, our price list (in letters).

juntoura s. f. (also **juntoira**) 1. = **junteira**. 2. perpend, bonder, bond-stone, header (plate A 7).

juntura s. f. 1. junction. 2. joint, articulation. 3. union. 4. line of junction.

jupará s. m. (Braz., zool.) kinkajou.

jupati s. m. (Braz., bot.) jupati, raffia palm.

jupiá s. m. (N. Braz.) whirlpool (in a river).

jupindá s. m. (Braz., bot.) spiderflower.

Júpiter s. m. Jupiter: 1. the planet. 2. (myth.) father of the gods.

jupiteriano adj. haughty, proud; domineering.

juquiraí s. m. (Braz.) seasoning of ground pepper and salt (Indian seasoning).

juquiri s. m. (Braz.) any of the trees or shrubs of the genus Mimosa.

jura s. f. 1. oath, vow. 2. curse, imprecation, blasphemy.
fazer ~s to swear, curse.

jurado s. m. juror, member of the jury, juriman. ‖ adj. 1. sworn to, solemnly declared. 2. (Braz.) threatened.
inimigo ~ sworn enemy. **primeiro ~** foreman.

jurador s. m. 1. swearer, curser, blasphemer. 2. a habitual swearer. ‖ adj. swearing, cursing.

juramentar v. (also **ajuramentar**) 1. to pledge by oath. 2. to make somebody take an oath, to administer an oath.

juramento s. m. 1. oath, vow. 2. imprecation, curse.
~ à bandeira color oath. **debaixo de ~** under oath. **prestar ~** to take an oath, swear in.

jurão s. m. (pl. **-ões**) (Braz.) pilework, house on piles or stilts to protect it from floods.

jurar v. 1. to swear, confirm by oath, take one's oath. 2. to vow, pledge. 3. to invoke, appeal to. 4. to declare, affirm. 5. to curse, blaspheme.

~ **abstenção do jogo** to forswear gambling. ~ **falso** to perjure. ~ **por tudo que é sagrado** to swear by all that is sacred. **juro que sim (não)** I swear it is (not) so.

jurássico adj. (geol.) Jurassic, pertaining to a mid--Mesozoic period.

jurema s. f. (Braz., bot.) an acacia.

juremal s. m. (pl. **-ais**) (bot.) grove of acacias.

juremeiro s. m. (N. Braz.) witch doctor.

jureminha s. f. (Braz., bot.) a mimosa.

júri s. m. jury: 1. a body of persons selected according to law and sworn in to render a verdict. 2. a body of persons chosen to adjudge prizes, etc. ~ **ordinário** petty jury.

jurídico adj. juridical, judicial, forensic, of or pertaining to the administration of justice; legal. ‖ **juridicamente** adv. juridically. **assassínio** ~ judicial murder.

jurisconsulto s. m. jurisconsult, person authorized to give legal advice.

jurisdição s. f. (pl. **-ões**) jurisdiction: 1. the right, power, or authority to administer justice. 2. (fig.) power, authority, right, control. 3. the extent or range of judicial or other authority. 4. the territory over which authority is exercised. 5. competence, legal capacity.

jurisdicional adj. m. + f. (pl. **-ais**) jurisdictional.

jurisperito s. m. jurisprudent, jurist, expert in law.

jurisprudência s. f. jurisprudence: 1. the science of law. 2. a body or system of laws.

jurisprudencial adj. m. + f. (pl. **-ais**) jurisprudential.

jurisprudente s. m. + f. jurisprudent.

jurista (I) s. m. + f. 1. jurist, jurisconsult, lawyer. 2. student of law.

jurista (II) s. m. + f. 1. moneylender, usurer. 2. bondholder.

juriti s. f. (Braz., ornith.) a field dove.

juro s. m. 1. interest (on money). 2. (fam.) reward, compensation, profit. ~ **de mora** interest on deferred payment. **~s atrasados** back interest. **~s compostos** compound interest. **dar dinheiro a** ~ to put money to interest. **tabela de ~s** table of interest.

jurubeba s. f. (Braz., bot.) a nightshade.

jurubita s. f. (Braz., pop.) sugar cane brandy.

jurupari s. m. (Braz.) demon (Tupi tribe).

juruparipiruba s. f. (Braz., Amazonas) a medicinal plant.

jururu adj. m. + f. (Braz.) sad, melancholic, moody, dejected, discouraged.

jus s. m. right. **fazer** ~ **a** to be entitled to, have a right to, merit.

jusante s. f. low tide, low water, reflux, ebb. **a** ~ downstream.

jussivo adj. (gram.) jussive, expressing a command.

justa (I) s. f. 1. joust, tournament, tilting, combat between two armoured knights or men-at-arms, usually on horseback. 2. fight, combat. 3. dispute, controversy.

justa (II) s. f. (ant.) cup or vessel into which the wine for each guest was poured.

justador s. m. 1. (hist.) jouster, tilter. 2. rival, competitor. ‖ adj. 1. (hist.) jousting. 2. (fig.) competing, rival.

justafluvial adj. m. + f. (pl. **-ais**) riverine, marginal, riparian.

justalinear adj. m. + f. line by line. **tradução** ~ line by line translation.

justamente adv. 1. just, precisely, exactly, rightly. 2. fairly, rightfully. ~ **isto!** this of all things! ~ **no meio** in the very middle.

justapor v. to juxtapose: place in close proximity or side by side.

justaposição s. f. (pl. **-ões**) 1. juxtaposition, contiguity, proximity. 2. apposition.

justaposto adj. juxtaposed, side by side, contiguous.

justar v. 1. to joust, tilt. 2. to fight. 3. to compete. 4. to fence. 5. to adjust, ascertain (price). 6. to hire for wages.

justeza s. f. 1. justness, righteousness, lawfulness, correctness. 2. accuracy, exactitude.

justiça s. f. 1. justice. 2. rightness, justness, fairness, equity. 3. right. 4. the law, bar, jurisdiction, administration of law. 5. lawyers, magistrates. 6. court personnel. ~ **eqüitativa** retributive justice. **fazer** ~ to do justice. **fazer** ~ **pela própria mão** to take the law into one's own hand. **fugir à ação da** ~ to abscond, to flee justice. **levar à** ~ to bring to trial. **obter** ~ (jur.) to come to one's own. **com** ~ rightly. **oficial da** ~ a court employee. **ouvir alguém de** ~ to listen to a person's reason. **por** ~ by rights. **ele o tratou com** ~ he did him justice.

justiçado s. m. 1. executed person. 2. punished or judged person. ‖ adj. 1. executed. 2. punished.

justiçar v. 1. to inflict capital punishment, to execute. 2. to sue at law.

justiceiro, justiçoso adj. 1. just, righteous. 2. severe, inflexible. 3. impartial. 4. incorruptible.

justificação s. f. (pl. **-ões**) 1. justification. 2. excuse. 3. defense plea, vindication. 4. rehabilitation, state of being justified. 5. cause, reason.

justificado adj. justified. ‖ **-amente** adv. rightly.

justificador s. m. justifier, one who or that which justifies; vindicator. ‖ adj. justifying; vindicative.

justificante s. m. warrant, justification. ‖ adj. m. + f. justifying.

justificar v. 1. to justify. 2. to prove, warrant. 3. to vindicate. 4. to defend or uphold as right or blameless. 5. to absolve, clear from guilt, acquit, exculpate. 6. to explain, set right. 7. to rehabilitate. ~ **a ausência** to explain one's absence. **o fim justifica os meios** the end justifies the means. **você pode** ~ **a sua conduta?** can you explain your conduct? **o tempo justificou a sua ação** his action was vindicated by events.

justificativa s. f. justification; apology.

justificativo adj. justificatory, serving to justify.

justificável adj. m. + f. (pl. **-áveis**) justifiable; accountable.

justilho s. m. tight bodice, corselet.

justo s. m. fair, correct, righteous person. ‖ adj. 1. just, fair, equitable, right, righteous, honest. 2. legitimate. 3. deserved, fairly earned. 4. reasonable. 5. narrow, right, close-fitting. 6. perfect, just, right, correct, exact. **a** ~ exactly. **é** ~ **para ambas as partes** it cuts both ways. **uma parte -a** a fair share. **uma recompensa -a** a fair reward. **ele só pede o que é** ~ he only asks what is fair. **fazer o** ~ to hit the head on the nail. **este vestido é muito** ~ this dress is too tight. **isto é mais que** ~ this is more than fair.

justura s. f. 1. adjustment. 2. form and shape given to a horseshoe.

juta s. f. jute (plant and its strong fiber).

juvenil adj. m. + f. (pl. **-is**) juvenile, young, adolescent, youthful. ‖ **~mente** adv. juvenilely.

juvenília s. f. juvenilia: works, especially writings, produced in youth.

juvenilidade s. f. 1. juvenescence, juvenility, youth. 2. young persons collectively.

juventude s. f. 1. youth, adolescence, boyhood, girlhood. 2. young people. **conservar a** ~ to keep one's youthfulness.

K

K, k s. m. letter used in Portugal and Brazil only in internationally known symbols and abbreviations and in foreign words adopted by the Portuguese language.

K (chem.) symbol for potassium.

kaiser s. m. emperor: Germanized form of the Latin word Caesar.

kantismo s. m. Kantism: the philosophy of Immanuel Kant, the founder of the Critical System of Philosophy.

kantista s. m. + f. Kantian: one who adopts the theories of Kant. ‖ adj. Kantian: of or pertaining to Kant or Kantism.

kart s. m. (Engl., mot.) kart, a small vehicle with automatic clutch, consisting only of a chassis, with neither gear-box nor suspension.

karting (Engl., mot.) kart races.

kartista s. m. + f. a kart pilot.

kartódromo s. m. a kart racing track.

kc abbr. of kilocycle.

kepleriano adj. Keplerian: of or pertaining to Johannes Kepler, the German astronomer.

kg abbr. of kilogram.

kibutz s. m. kibbutz, a Jewish small community farm.

kilt s. m. (Engl.) 1. kilt. 2. a women's skirt, resembling a wilt (fashion).

kirsch s. m. cherry brandy (in German).

kl abbr. of kiloliter.

km abbr. of kilometer.

km² abbr. of square kilometer.

km³ abbr. of cubic kilometer.

kodachrome s. m. picture in colours and permeable to light (trademark).

Kr (chem.) symbol for krypton.

kümmel s. m. kümmel: alcoholic beverage aromatized with cumin.

kv abbr. of kilovolt.

kw abbr. of kilowatt.

kwh abbr. of kilowatt-hour.

L

L, l s. m. 1. the eleventh letter of the Portuguese alphabet. 2. Roman numeral for fifty. ‖ adj. eleventh, in order or class. ‖ **l** abbr. of **litro**.

La (chem.) symbol of lanthanum.

la personal pron. f. third person singular used after verbal forms ending in **r, s** or **z**; after the pron. **nos** and **vos** and after the adverb **eis**. **ei·~!** there she is! **eu não pude vê·~** I could not see her.

lá (I) s. m. (mus.) la, a: the sixth tone of the diatonic scale in solmization.

~ **bemol (sustenido)** (mus.) a flat (sharp). ~ **maior (menor)** (mus.) a major (minor).

lá (II) adv. 1. there, yonder. 2. beyond. 3. in that place. 4. on the other side. 5. thither.

~ **dentro** in there, inside there. ~ **embaixo** down there, downstairs. ~ **em cima** upstairs, up there. ~ **fora** out there. ~ **mesmo** in that very place. ~ **se foi tudo** all is lost. **até** ~ till then, by then. **cá e** ~ here and there, hither and thither. **de** ~ thence, from that place. **diga** ~, **você veio a pé?** I say, did you walk it? **para** ~ over there, to that place. **para** ~ **e para cá** hither and thither, backwards and forwards, to and fro. **sei** ~! heaven knows! **vá até** ~ **e volte!** go there and come back! **viemos de** ~ we came from there.

lã s. f. 1. wool. 2. fleece (sheep). 3. woolen fabric (or cloth). 4. (Braz.) raw cotton.

~ **de aço** steel wool. ~ **de camelo** mohair, camlet. ~ **de carneiro** fleece. ~ **de cordeiro** lamb's wool. ~ **de vidro** glass wool. ~ **mineral** silicate wool. ~ **para bordar** Berlin wool, crewel. **artigos de** ~ worsted articles, woolen goods. **de** ~ woolly. **fardo de** ~ woolpack. **ir buscar** ~ **e sair tosquiado** to go for wool and return shorn. **meias de** ~ worsted stockings.

labaça s. f. 1. (bot.) dock. 2. (Port.) voluble tongue, well-oiled tongue, good flow of language.

labaçal s. m. (pl. **-ais**) dock plantation.

labareda s. f. 1. braze, flame, flare; fire. 2. (fig.) vivacity; impetuosity; enthusiasm, ardour; fervour. 3. m. very busy man.

lábaro s. m. 1. (Roman emperors) labarum: imperial standard. 2. standard, flag.

labelado adj. labellate, shaped like lips.

labelo s. m. 1. liplet, little lip. 2. (bot.) labellum: one of the three divisions of an orchidaceous corolla.

labéu s. m. 1. blot, blur, spot on a reputation. 2. blemish. 3. disgrace. 4. shame. 5. dishonour.

lançar o ~ **de covarde em alguém** to brand a person a coward.

lábia (I) s. f. 1. cunning, craftiness, guile. 2. astuteness. 3. fine words. 4. well-oiled tongue. 5. power of persuasion.

ter ~ to have the gift of gab, the power of convincing or persuading.

lábia (II) s. f. (Port.) reliquary.

labiada s. f. labiate: any plant of the mint family. ‖ adj. labiate.

labiado adj. lipped, liplike, labiate.

labial s. f. (pl. **-ais**) (phon.) labial (consonant). ‖ adj. m. + f. labial: 1. of or pertaining to lips. 2. (phon.) articulated by the lips, labialized. ‖ **~mente** adv. labially.

labialização s. f. (pl. **-ões**) labialization: act of labializing.

labializar v. (phon.) to labialize: 1. make labial, round. 2. to pronounce with the lips.

lábil adj. m. + f. (pl. **lábeis**) 1. labile (also geol., chem., phys.). 2. transitory, unstable. 3. weak. 4. slippery: liable or apt to slip or lapse.

lábio s. m. (anat.) 1. lip, labium: a) one of the two edges of the mouth. b) the inner folds of the vulva. 2. **~s** pl. the lips, mouth. 3. lobule.

~ **leporino** harelip. **~s ressequidos** parched lips. **morder os ~s** to bite one's lips.

labiodental adj. m. + f. (pl. **-ais**) (phon.) labiodental. **consoante** ~ labiodental consonant.

labionasal adj. m. + f. (pl. **-ais**) (phon.) labionasal.

labioso adj. 1. (also **beiçudo**) big-lipped, blobber-lipped. 2. crafty, wily, cunning, smooth-tongued.

labiríntico adj. m. **labirintiforme** m. + f. labyrinthine, labyrinthiform: having the form of a labyrinth.

labirinto s. m. 1. labyrinth: a) maze, place with many intricate passages. b) (anat., zool.) the internal ear. c) (fig.) intricate or entangled affairs. 2. (fig.) very difficult situation; embarrassment. 3. (N. Braz., also **crivo**) embroidery.

labor s. m. labour, work; toil, task; handiwork.

laboração s. f. (pl. **-ões**) 1. labouring, toil, working. 2. activity.

laborão s. m. (Braz.) hard work.

laborar v. 1. to labour, work, toil. 2. to operate, function. 3. to plough, till.

laboratório s. m. laboratory: place of (chemical or other) experimental study.

laboratorista s. m. + f. laboratory technician.

laboriosidade s. f. 1. laboriousness, toilsomeness. 2. diligence, industriousness. 3. effort.

laborioso adj. 1. laborious: a) toilsome, difficult, arduous. b) devoted to labour. c) hard-working, diligent, industrious, sedulous. 2. irksome, fatiguing. ‖ **-amente** adv. laboriously.

laborista adj. m. + f. of or referring to the Labour Party.

laboro (ô) s. m. (pl. **laboros**) (N. Braz., pop.) 1. (also **labor**) labour, work. 2. hurry, bustle.

laborterapia s. f. (psych.) occupational therapy.

labradorita s. f. (min.) labradorite: a triclinic feldspar.

labreado adj. (N. Braz., pop.) soiled, dirty, sully.

labrear v. (N. Braz., pop.) to soil, dirty.

labrego s. m. 1. boor, yokel, rustic person. 2. peasant, villager. 3. (fig.) rough, rowdy, ruffian. 4. (Port.) the devil. 5. a kind of plow. ‖ adj. 1. rustic, boorish. 2. coarse, uncouth, rough.

labrídeos s. m. pl. (ichth.) Labridae, a family of percoid fishes.

labro s. m. labrum: the upper lip of mammals or insects.

labroso adj. (zool.) labrose: having thick lips.

labrosta s. m. (also **labrego**) 1. boor, yokel, rustic person. 2. peasant, villager. ‖ adj. rude, rustic, coarse, uncouth.

labrusco s. m. 1. ruffian, brutal fellow. 2. boor, uncouth person. ‖ adj. 1. rude, brutal, coarse. 2. boorish, uncouth. 3. Alpine, from the mountains. 4. wild, sylvan.

laburno s. m. laburnum: small leguminous tree (Cytisus laburnum).

labuta, labutação s. f. 1. drudgery, (hard) work, toiling, struggling, exertion. 2. labour, task.

labutador s. m. toiler, drudger, person who works hard.

labutar v. 1. to struggle, drudge. 2. to labour, toil and moil, plod. 3. to work hard, strive. 4. to make efforts, take pains. 5. to strive diligently. 6. (fig.) to live, support, endure.
~ **pela vida** to scrub for a living.
labuzar v. = **lambuzar.**
laca s. f. 1. lac: resinous substance extracted from some leguminous trees. 2. (also **goma-laca**) shellac, lacquer.
laçaço s. m. (S. Braz.) flick with a lasso; lassoing.
laçada s. f. 1. bowknot, slipknot, running knot. 2. tie, loop.
peruca de ~ tie-wig, bag-wig.
laçador s. m. (Braz.) lassoer: person skilled in the use of a lasso.
lacaiada s. f. 1. actions proper of lackeys or footmen; base language. 2. flunkeydom, flunkeyism. 3. a group of lackeys; lackeys collectively.
locaiar v. (Braz.) to lackey: 1. attend as a lackey. 2. act servilely.
lacaiesco adj. 1. of or pertaining to lackeys, flunkeyish. 2. proper of lackeys.
lacaio s. m. 1. lackey, footman, valet; flunk(e)y. 2. (fig.) vile or servile person.
lacambeche s. m. (N. E. Braz.) an ancient flintlock shotgun.
laçar v. 1. to lasso: catch with a lasso. 2. to lace, tie, bind. 3. ~-**se** to hang o. s. 4. (fig.) to entangle; catch, snare.
laçarada s. f. a lot of ornamental ribbons.
laçaria s. f. 1. festoon, garlands, flowerwork. 2. (archit.) tracery, flourish. 3. a lot of laces.
laçarotes s. m. pl. bows, furbelows, ornamental slipknots, knots of ribbons.
laçarrão s. m. (pl. -ões) big knot or tie.
lacedemônio s. m. Lacedemonian, Spartan. || adj. Spartan, Lacedemonian.
laceração s. f. (pl. -ões) (also **dilaceração**) laceration: 1. act of lacerating. 2. wound caused by laceration.
lacerador s. m. (also **dilacerador**) person who lacerates, tearer. || adj. (also **dilacerador** m., **lacerante, dilacerante** m. + f.) 1. (di)lacerating, tearing, harrowing. 2. afflictive, cruel.
lacerar v. (also **dilacerar**) 1. to lacerate, harrow, afflict, rend, tear. 2. (fig.) to torture, torment. 3. to defame, slander, discredit. 4. ~-**se**: to hurt o. s.
lacerável adj. m. + f. (pl. -áveis) (also **dilacerável**) (di)lacerable: capable of being lacerated.
lacerdinha s. m. (Braz., ent.) a thrips (Gynaikothrips ficorum).
lacertiforme adj. m. + f. lacertiform: shaped like a lizard.
lacertílio s. m. (zool.) lacertilian: one of the Lacertilia (lizards, chameleons, etc.), saurian.
lacete s. m. 1. small lace or bow. 2. S curve (of a road). 3. stone layer of a macadamized road.
lacínia s. f. (bot.) lacinia.
laciniado adj. (bot.) laciniate(d), irregularly cut into narrow lobes.
laço s. m. 1. (also **laçada** f.) bowknot, slipknot, running or sliding knot, noose. 2. bow, tie, knot; loop, sling (plates C 5, R 6, 7). 3. snare, trap. 4. tie, bond. 5. (Braz.) lasso. 6. (fig.): a) stratagem, trick, cheat, treason. b) chain, link. c) alliance.
~**s de amizade** ties of friendship. **cair no** ~ to fall into a trap.
lacolito s. m. (geol.) laccolith: mass of igneous rock.
lacônico s. m. Laconian; Spartan: native or inhabitant of Laconia. || adj. 1. Laconian, Spartan: pertaining to Laconia. 2. laconic, concise, brief, terse. || -**amente** adv. laconically.
laconismo s. m. laconism, sententiousness, conciseness, pointed brevity of speech or expression.

laconizar v. 1. to laconize, render laconic, short or concise. 2. to speak concisely.
laços-espanhóis s. m. pl. (Braz., bot.) gaillardia.
lacrador s. m. sealer: person who seals or plumbs.
lacraia s. f. (Braz., ent.) centipede: any of the division Chilopoda of the Myriapoda.
lacrainha s. f. (Braz., ent.) 1. dim. of **lacraia.** 2. earwig: insect of the family Forficulidae.
lacranar v. (S. Braz., also **lacerar**) to lacerate, rend.
lacrar v. 1. to seal (up) with sealing-wax. 2. to plumb (seal with lead).
lacrau s. m. (ent., pop.) scorpion.
lacre s. m. 1. sealing-wax: resinous substance used to seal letters, documents, etc. 2. (Braz., bot.) bloodwood.
lacreada s. f. ornament made of lacquer.
lacrear v. to lacquer.
lacrecanha s. f. (Braz.) an old toothless woman.
lacrimação s. f. (pl. -ões) lachrymation, emission or shedding of tears.
lacrimal s. m. (pl. -ais) 1. (anat., zool.) lachrymal (bone) (plate C 17). 2. (Braz.) spring, fountain. || adj. m. + f. lachrymal, lacrimal: 1. of or pertaining to tears. 2. designating the organs producing tears.
glândula ~ lachrymal gland.
lacrimante adj. m. + f. (also **lacrimoso** m.) lachrymose.
lacrimatório s. m. (Roman hist.) lachrymatory: vessel (supposedly for tears). || adj. lachrymatory, lachrymal: of or pertaining to tears.
lacrimável adj. m. + f. (pl. -áveis) lamentable, deplorable, mournful, tearful.
lacrimejante adj. m. + f. shedding tears, tearful.
lacrimejar v. (also **lagrimejar**) to shed tears.
lacrimogêneo adj. lachrymatory: causing or provoking tears.
gás ~ tear gas.
lacrimoso adj. (also **lagrimoso**) 1. lachrymose, tearful, weeping. 2. afflicted. 3. pitiful, sad. || -**amente** adv. tearfully.
lacrimotomia s. f. (surg.) incision into a tear-duct.
lactação s. f. (pl. -ões) lactation: 1. the formation or secretion of milk. 2. act of giving suck.
lactante adj. m. + f. 1. lactific(al), lactiferous: producing or yielding milk. 2. sucking, giving milk, nursing.
lactar v. 1. to suckle, give suck, nurse, lactate. 2. to suck.
lactário s. m. dispensary (of milk) for children. || adj. lactary, lactiferous, yielding milk.
lactase s. f. (chem.) lactase.
lactato s. m. (chem.) lactate: salt of lactic acid, or the acid of sour milk.
lactente s. m. + f. sucking baby, infant. || adj. sucking.
lácteo, láteo adj. lacteal, milky, lacteous: pertaining to or resembling milk.
lactescência, latescência s. f. lactescence, lactescency, milkiness.
lactescente, latescente adj. m. + f. lactescent: 1. secreting milk, lactiferous. 2. milky, like milk.
lacticínio, laticínio s. m. 1. milk-food, food made of or with milk. 2. dairy, creamery. 3. ~**s** pl. dairy products.
lacticinoso adj. lacteal, milky, lacteous.
láctico, lático adj. (chem.) lactic.
ácido ~ lactic acid.
lacticolor adj. m. + f. milky, milk-hued; having the colour of milk.
lactífago adj. feeding on milk.
lactífero adj. lactiferous: 1. secreting milk, yielding milk. 2. conveying milk.

lactífugo adj. lactifugal: serving to check or stop the secretion of milk.
lactígeno adj. lactigenic: lactiferous, producing milk.
lactobutirômetro s. m. lactobutyrometer.
lactômetro s. m. lactometer: instrument to verify the purity of milk.
lactoridáceas s. f. pl. (bot.) a family of dicotyledonous plants, consisting of the Lactoris fernandeziana.
lactoscópio s. m. lactoscope.
lactose s. f. lactose, milk sugar.
lactucário s. m. (chem.) lactucarium.
lacuna s. f. 1. lacuna: a) gap, hiatus. b) omission, neglect, default. c) (biol.) intercellular space. 2. vacuum, void, empty space.
    preencher uma ~ to fill or stop a gap.
lacunar adj. m. + f. lacunal, lacunary: having lacunae.
lacunário s. m. (archit.) lacunar.
lacunoso adj. 1. (also **lacunar**) lacunary. 2. lacunose: a) full of or having lacunae. b) marked by gaps. 3. deficient, failing, incomplete.
lacustre adj. m. + f. lacustrine: 1. of or pertaining to a lake. 2. living on or in a lake.
    habitações ~s lake dwellings. **paisagem** ~ waterscape.
lacustres s. m. pl. lake dwellers.
lacuteio s. m. (N. Braz., pop.) 1. noise, brawl, agitation. 2. confusion, mess.
lada s. f. 1. watercourse, the navigable part of a river parallel to its margins. 2. (bot.) rockrose.
ladainha s. f. 1. litany: liturgical prayer of invocations and supplications. 2. (fig.) tiresome recital, rigmarole, rambling talk.
    ~ **de Nossa Senhora** (R. C. Church) Litany of Loreto. ~ **de Todos os Santos** (R. C. Church) Litany of the Saints. ~ **do Coração de Jesus** (R. C. Church) Litany of the Most Holy Name of Jesus. **pare com essa** ~! stop with this rigmarole.
ladairo s. m. 1. procession of penitence. 2. prayer of supplications.
ladanífero adj. ladanigerous: yielding labdanum.
ládano s. m. labdanum, ladanum: a resinous juice from a rockrose (Cistus ladanum and C. creticus).
ladeamento s. m. 1. turning aside. 2. (fig.) deviation. 3. shift, subterfuge. 4. act or fact of siding.
ladear v. 1. to flank: a) skirt, border. b) attack the flank of. 2. to go side by side; accompany; escort. 3. to be situated or run alongside. 4. to surround. 5. to evade, shift, dodge, tergiversate; avoid. 6. to sidestep (horse).
    ~ **a questão** to evade the question (subject, matter).
ladeira s. f. 1. declivity, slope, gradient. 2. slope of a roof. 3. hillside, acclivity, ascent. 4. steep street.
    ~ **abaixo** downhill. ~ **íngreme** chute. **ir** ~ **acima** 1. to go uphill. 2. (fig.) to swim against the stream. **na metade da** ~ half-way up the slope.
ladeirento adj. (also **ladeiroso**) steep, declivitous, sloping, sloped, inclined, slanting.
ladeiro adj. 1. sloped, declivous; side(ways). 2. alongside.
ladinaza, ladinice s. f. 1. cleverness, smartness. 2. adroitness. 3. slyness, cunning, wiliness.
ladino s. m. smart, foxy, astute person. ‖ adj. 1. (Braz., hist.) intelligent, skilled (said of domesticated Negro slaves or Indians). 2. astute, cunning, artful; wily, sly, clever.
lado s. m. 1. side: a) the right or left part of a body, flank (plate C 4). b) face or surface of an object. c) a boundary line of a geometrical figure. d) (fig.) party. 2. direction, position, way. 3. aspect, form. 4. site, place.
    ~ **a** ~ side by side. ~ **da cama** bedside. ~ **inferior** underside. ~ **posterior** backside. **andar de um** ~

para outro to walk to and fro, up and down. **ao** ~ 1. by the side, next door, close by. 2. apart. **ao** ~ **de** beside, at the side of. **ao** ~ **paterno** by the father's side. **de** ~ 1. aside. 2. sideways. **de** ~ **a** ~ throughout, from side to side; entirely. **de ambos os** ~s on or from either side. **de dois** ~s 1. two-sided, double-sided. 2. from two sides. **de muitos** ~s 1. many-sided. 2. from many sides. **de todos os** ~s from all directions. **de um e outro** ~ on both sides. **deste** ~ on this side. **do** ~ **errado** offside, on the wrong side. **deixaram-no de** ~ they gave him the cold shoulder. **ela se mantém de** ~ she keeps out of the way. **em cada** ~ **de** on each side of. **o** ~ **agradável** the bright side. **o** ~ **direito** the right side. **o** ~ **de dentro** 1. the seamy side. 2. the inside. **o** ~ **esquerdo** the left side. **o** ~ **fraco** the weak side, the weak point. **moramos no outro** ~ **da rua** we live across the street. **olhar alguém de** ~ to look down upon somebody, to look askance at s. o. **pôr de** ~ to put aside. **por outro** ~ otherwise, on the other hand. **por todos os** ~s all around. **a contenda virou para o** ~ **ruim** the strife took a bad turn.
ladra s. f. woman who steals, a female thief. ‖ adj. concerning a female thief.
ladrado s. m. 1. bark(ing), bay. 2. (fig.) evilspeaking, backbite.
ladrante adj. m. + f. 1. barking. 2. like the barking of dogs.
ladrão s. m. (pl. **-ões**) 1. thief, stealer, burglar, robber. 2. highway-man. 3. bandit, outlaw, gangster, swindler. 4. pilferer; (fam.) light-fingered fellow. 5. (fig.) scoundrel, despicable man. 6. (pop.) loafer. 7. (bot.) sucker. 8. (mech.) overflow pipe (plate B 3). ‖ adj. thievish, stealing, robbing.
    ~ **de estrada** knight of the road, highway-man. ~ **de gado** cattle-lifter, rustler. ~ **não rouba** ~ don't set a thief to catch a thief. **a ocasião faz o** ~ opportunity makes the thief. **pega** ~! stop thief!
ladrar v. 1. to bark, bay. 2. to bow-wow. 3. (fig.) to cry or shout without necessity.
    ~ **à lua** to bark at the moon. **cão que ladra não morde** barking dogs seldom bite.
ladravaz, ladravão s. m. (pl. **-azes, -ões**) an arrant thief; arch-villain.
ladriço s. m. fetter, shackle for the feet of a horse.
ladrido s. m. (also **latido**) bark(ing), yelping, baying.
ladrilhado adj. tiled, paved with tiles or bricks.
ladrilhador s. m. tile paver, tile setter; bricklayer. ‖ adj. pertaining to tile setting.
ladrilhar v. 1. to tile, pave floors or cover walls with tiles. 2. to work as a tile setter.
ladrilheiro s. m. tilemaker; brickmaker.
ladrilho s. m. 1. (paving-)tile, floor tile; brick. 2. a rectangular piece of quince marmalade. 3. (Port., sl.) pilferer, thief.
    ~ **vidrado** encaustic tile, glazed tile.
ladro s. m. 1. thief, stealer, larcener. 2. (zool.) crab-louse. 3. bark(ing), yelping, baying. ‖ adj. 1. thievish, stealing, larcenous. 2. concerning the crab-louse (piolho ~).
ladroaço s. m. an arrant thief; knave, arch-scoundrel.
ladroagem s. f. (pl. **-ens**) 1. (also **ladroeira**) thievery, robbery, stealing. 2. thieves collectively.
ladroar v. to steal, rob, pilfer.
ladroeira s. f. (also **ladroíce**) 1. thievery, robbery, stealing, theft. 2. extortion. 3. embezzlement. 4. swindle. 5. den of robbers.
ladroeirar v. to steal, scrounge; cheat, swindle.
ladroeiro s. m. sucker; sprout or shoot harmful to a plant.
ladrona s. f. (also **ladra**) woman who steals, female thief. ‖ adj. thievish (speaking of a woman).

ladronaço s. m. = **ladrão**

lady s. f. (Engl.) lady, as a title of nobility or referring to a woman of high social standing.

lagalhé s. m. (also **joão-ninguém**) nobody: person of no importance or consequence.

lagamar s. m. 1. chasm, abyss, a pit at the bottom of the sea or river; deepest part of a river. 2. lagoon; bay; lake of salt water. 3. harbour, haven.

lagar s. m. press: 1. fruit-press, machine to press fruit. 2. place where such a press is operated.
~ **de azeite** olive-press. ~ **de vinho** wine-press.

lagarada s. f. pressful.

lagaragem s. f. (pl. **-ens**) 1. fruit-pressing. 2. retribution, in species, to the owner of a fruit press.

lagareiro s. m. 1. person who works at a fruit press, pressman. 2. owner of a fruit press.

lagariça s. f. small fruit press.

lagariço adj. of or pertaining to a fruit press.

lagarta s. f. caterpillar: 1. (ent.) the wormlike larva of a moth or butterfly; grub. 2. (mech.) track of a tractor (plate D 2).

lagarta-aranha s. f. (pl. **lagartas-aranhas**) (Braz., ent.) sluglike caterpillar.

lagarta-de-fogo s. f. (pl. **lagartas-de-fogo**) (Braz., ent.) caterpillar of the flannel moth (also **taturana**).

lagarta-rosada s. f. (pl. **lagartas-rosadas**) (Braz., ent.) pink bollworm.

lagartear v. (Braz.) to bask in the sun, warm o. s. in the sun, sun o. s. (as a lizard).

lagarteiro adj. 1. clever, smart, cunning. 2. astute, wily, crafty.

lagartinho s. m. small lizard.

lagartixa s. f. 1. (zool.) any small harmless lizard as the gecko or sand lizard. 2. (Braz., sl.) hiker, mountain climber. 3. slender woman.

lagarto s. m. 1. (zool.) lizard: any reptile of the order Lacertilia; saurian. 2. (fig.) biceps. 3. small cork press, cork softener (in a shop). 4. a certain cut of beef.

lagarto-do-mar s. m. (pl. **lagartos-do-mar**) lizard fish.

lagena s. f. lagena: 1. bottle-shaped vase. 2. (Roman ant.) wine vase, amphora; eared vase of earthenware.

lageniforme adj. m. + f. bottle-shaped.

lagênula s. f. small flask or vase.

lago s. m. lake: 1. inland sea. 2. small pond as an ornament of a park. 3. pool of anything (also fig.) 4. (fig.) flood.
~ **artificial** an ornamental water. **Os Grandes Lagos** The Great Lakes.

lagoa s. f. 1. lagoon, pond, pool, small lake, lakelet (plate A 4). 2. mud puddle, marsh, swamp, moor.
~ **de patos** duck pond.

lagoão s. m. (pl. **-ões**) large and deep lagoon or lake.

lagocéfalo adj. (zool.) harelipped.

lagoeiro s. m. 1. rain puddle, pool, pond. 2. ground covered with water, drenched or soaked ground.

lagomorfos s. m. pl. (zool.) Lagomorpha, an order comprising the rabbits and hares.

lagópode s. m. (zool.) lagopode, ptarmigan, a snow grouse. || adj. m. + f. lagopodous, hare-footed.

lagosta s. f. 1. lobster: large marine macrural crustacean esteemed for food. 2. red-cheeked person.

lagosta-comum s. f. (pl. **lagostas-comuns**) (zool.) spiny lobster, sea crayfish.

lagosta-gafanhoto s. f. (pl. **lagostas-gafanhoto**) (zool., also **tamarutaca**) squilla; a large mantis crab.

lagostim s. m. (pl. **-ins**) (zool.) 1. small lobster. 2. Norway lobster. 3. crawfish.

lágrima s. f. 1. tear: a) drop of saline liquid secreted by the lachrymal glands. b) drop. c) any object like a tear or drop. 2. ~s pl. crying, weeping; lament.

~ **sabéia** incense. ~**s de alegria** tears of joy. ~**s de crocodilo** crocodile tears, false or affected tears. **chorar** ~**s de sangue** to weep bitterly. **com olhos marejados de** ~**s** with the eyes filled with tears. **debulhado em** ~**s** bathed in tears. **derramar** ~**s** to shed tears. **enxugar as** ~**s de alguém** to wipe somebody's tears away, to console him. **inundar de** ~**s** to work the tear-pump. **obscurecido por** ~**s** tear-dimmed. **sem** ~**s** tearless. **torrente de** ~**s** burst of tears.

lagrimação s. f. (pl. **-ões**) (also **lacrimação**) secretion of tears.

lágrima-de-moça s. f. (pl. **lágrimas-de-moça**) (Braz., bot.) common ginger lily.

lágrima-de-nossa-senhora, lágrima-de-santa-maria s. f. (pl. **lágrimas-de-nossa-senhora, lágrimas-de-santa--maria**) (Braz., bot.) Job's-tears (grass).

lagrimal s. m. (pl. **-ais**) (also **lacrimal**) lachrymal (bone). || adj. m. + f. (also **lacrimal**) lachrymal.

lagrimante adj. m. + f. (also **lacrimante**) lachrymose.

lagrimejar v. (also **lacrimejar**) 1. to shed tears; weep, cry. 2. to lament; whine, whimper.

lagrimoso adj. = **lacrimoso**.

laguna s. f. 1. lagoon, lagune: shallow lake separated from the sea by a sandbank. 2. shallow estuary or firth.

lai s. m. lay, ballad.

laia s. f. 1. quality, kind, nature, race. 2. ilk, sort. 3. figure, shape. 4. manner. 5. (sl.) silver.
à ~ **de** in the manner of, like. **da mesma** ~ of the same kind. **gente da mesma** ~ birds of a feather. **outros da sua** ~ others of his kind.

laical adj. m. + f. (pl. **-ais**) laic(al): of or pertaining to a layman, secular.

laicalidade s. f. laicality.

laicalismo s. m. laic procedure.

laicidade s. f. laity: the state of being a layman.

laicificar, laicizar v. to laicize, secularize.

laico adj. laic, lay, secular: belonging to the laity or people (distinguished from the clergy).

laissez-aller s. m. (Fr.) disregard; negligence.

laissez-faire s. m. (Fr.) laissez-faire.

laivar v. to dirty, soil, sully, spot, stain.

laivo s. m. 1. spot, blot, spek, blotch; (fig.) stain. 2. mark. 3. (fig.) tincture, vestige. 4. ~s pl. smattering, superficial knowledge.
ele tem ~**s de poeta** he has something of a poet.

laje, lájea, laja s. f. 1. flag(stone), flagging. 2. cement slab. 3. gravestone, slate. 4. (archit.) table, flat.
~ **de fundação** (archit.) ground plate. ~ **de pedra** slabstone.

lajeado s. m. (also **lajedo**) 1. flagged floor, flagging, slab covering. 2. (Braz.) creek in a rocky bed. || adj. flagged.

lajeador s. m. flagger, paver, person who lays flags.

lajeamento s. m. 1. flagging, paving with stones or slabs. 2. = **lajeado**.

lajear v. to flag, pave with flagstones.

lajeiro s. m. (Braz.) 1. large flat rock surface. 2. = **lajeado**.

lajota s. f. small flagstone.

lama (I) s. f. 1. mud, mire, dirt, slime, slop, sludge, slush. 2. clay. 3. (fig.) blot, blemish, dishonour, disgrace.
~ **de carvão** coal sludge. **arrastar alguém pela** ~ to fling or throw dirt at s. o. **sair da** ~ **e meter-se no atoleiro** to jump out of the frying pan into the fire. **salpicar alguém de** ~ to fling dirt at a person, to insult him or her. **tirar da** ~ to raise somebody from a low or humble condition. **viver na** ~ to live in poverty.

lama (II) s. m. lama: priest of Lamaism.

lama (III) s. m. (zool.) llama: South American ruminant.
lamaçal s. m. (pl. -ais), lamaceira f., lamaceiro m. 1. slough, muddy place. 2. marsh, swamp, bog, mire.
tirar-se do ~ to overcome a difficult situation.
lamacento adj. 1. muddy, full of mud; miry. 2. dirty.
lamaico adj. Lamaistic: of or pertaining to Lamaism.
lamaísmo s. m. Lamaism: a corrupted form of Buddhism prevailing in Tibet.
lamaísta s. m. + f. Lamaist: person professing Lamaism.
lamarão s. m. (pl. -ões) 1. a large slough. 2. mud flat. 3. large tracts of muddy shore land.
lamarckiano adj. (biol.) Lamarckian: of or pertaining to Lamarckianism.
lamarckismo, lamarckianismo s. m. Lamarckism, Lamarckianism.
lamarckista s. m. + f. Lamarckian.
lamartiniano adj. concerning the French poet Lamartine or his works.
lamaseria s. f. lamasery.
lamba s. m. (Braz.) used in the idiomatic phrase: passar ~ to lead a dog's life, to have a hard time.
lambada s. f. 1. blow (with a stick or whip). 2. stroke, lash, rap. 3. beating. 4. drub. 5. reproach, rebuke. 6. (sl.) a swig or cup of an alcoholic beverage. 7. piece or strip of something.
lambaio s. m. (Braz.) 1. mop: a broom made of an old piece of cloth or tow. 2. scullion: servant of very low station.
lambamba s. m. (N. Braz.) drunkard, sot, toper.
lambança s. f. 1. anything that can be licked. 2. anything eatable. 3. (Braz.) boast, swagger, vaunt, brag. 4. discussion, debating, recrimination. 5. unmotivated quarrel, wrangling. 6. entanglement. 7. vagabondage, laziness, indolence. 8. fib, lie. 9. deceptive adulation, fawning, flattery, blarney. 10. intrigue, plot.
muita chança e pouca ~ much ado about nothing.
lambancear v. (Braz.) 1. to intrigue, plot. 2. to talk too much.
lambanceiro s. m. (Braz.) 1. intriguer, plotter. 2. idle talker. ‖ adj. 1. intriguing, plotting. 2. flattering, fawning.
lambão s. m. (pl. -ões) (f. -ona) 1. person without manners at table, slobberer. 2. glutton, gormandizer, gorger. 3. (fig.) fool, booby. 4. botcher, bungler. ‖ adj. 1. slobbery. 2. gluttonous, greedy. 3. foolish, idiotic.
lambar v. (Braz.) to lash, whip, scourge, flog, switch.
lambarão s. m. (pl. -ões) (Braz., also lambuzão) a dirty and shabby fellow.
lambarar v. 1. to eat sweetmeats. 2. to be fond of sweets.
lambareiro s. m. 1. = lambão. 2. sweet-toothed or dainty person. 3. talebearer, gossip. 4. (naut.) anchor cable. ‖ adj. 1. = lambão. 2. gossipy, gossiping.
lambari s. m. (Braz.) 1. name of several fishes of the family Characinidae. 2. a saw with a very narrow blade.
lambarice s. f. 1. greediness, gluttony. 2. ~s pl. sweetmeats, dainties, titbits, goodies.
lambaz s. m. mop (plate E 8). ‖ adj. m. + f. 1. gluttonish, gluttonous, greedy. 2. sloppy, slobbery.
lambazar v. to swab, mop (deck or floor).
lambda s. m. lambda: the eleventh letter of the Greek alphabet.
lambdacismo s. m. lambdacism: 1. an imperfect pronunciation of the letter r making it sound like l. 2. frequent use or misuse of the letter l; lallation.
lambda-zero s. m. (nucl. phys.) lambda-zero.

lambedeira s. f. 1. feminine of lambedor. 2. (Braz., pop.) a kind of bowie-knife, a long and thin knife. ‖ adj. licking, lambent (feminine form).
lambedine s. m. (fam.) 1. sweetmeat, dainty. 2. titbit.
lambedor s. m. 1. licker: person who licks or laps up. 2. (Braz.) flatterer, fawner, cajoler, wheedler. lickspittle. ‖ adj. 1. licking, lambent. 2. flattering, fawning.
lambedura s. f. = lambidela.
lambe-esporas s. m. + f., sg. + pl. (Braz.) flatterer, fawner, cajoler, lickspittle.
lambeiro s. m. 1. (also lambão) glutton, gormandizer. 2. licker. 3. (fig.) flatterer, cajoler, wheedler. ‖ adj. 1. gluttonous. 2. licking, lambent. 3. (fig.) flattering, toadying.
lambel s. m. (pl. -éis) 1. strip, band, belt. 2. striped cloth (with which benches were covered).
lambe-lambe s. m. (pl. lambe-lambes) (Braz., pop.) 1. an ambulant photographer. 2. the front row in a vaudeville theater.
lambe-olhos s. f., sg. + pl. (Braz.) a stingless bee (Melipona duckei).
lambe-pratos s. m. + f., sg. + pl. glutton, plate-licker.
lamber v. 1. to lick, pass the tongue over. 2. to touch slightly. 3. to polish, refine; finish off, file. 4. to devour, engulf. 5. to swallow. 6. ~-se to rejoice, delight in.
~ a poeira (sl.) to kick the bucket; die. ~ os beiços to lick one's lips. ~ os pés de alguém to lick someone's boots.
lambeta s. m. + f. (also lambeteiro m.) (Braz.) 1. intriguer, intrigant. 2. accuser, denouncer. 3. (fig.) flatterer, adulator. ‖ adj. 1. intriguing. 2. denouncing. 3. flattering.
lambetear v. 1. to intrigue, plot, scheme. 2. to accuse, denounce. 3. to flatter, cajole.
lambição s. f. (pl. -ões) (Braz.) adulation, flattery, blarney, cajolery.
lambida, lambidela s. f. 1. licking, a lick. 2. flattery, blandishment, soft soap. 3. bargain. 4. tip.
lambido adj. 1. overrefined (painting, poetry), excessively soft. 2. (Braz.) ungraceful, unhandsome. 3. ungainly.
cabelo ~ slicked-down hair. vestido ~ ungraceful dress.
lambiscador s. m. (Braz.) 1. gormandizer, nibbler, dainty eater. 2. greedy person, gourmand. ‖ adj. 1. nibbling. 2. fond of dainties. 3. greedy.
lambiscar v. to nibble, gormandize, eat in small bits, eat daintily or sparingly.
lambiscaria s. f. (Braz.) dainty, choice dish, titbit.
lambisco s. m. morsel: 1. titbit, small quantity. 2. little bit of food, mouthful.
em um ~ (pop.) in a trice. por um ~ (pop.) by the fraction of an inch.
lambisgóia s. f. 1. haughty arrogant woman. 2. meddler, busybody. 3. meager person; insipid, dull person.
lambisqueiro s. m. 1. sweet-toothed person. 2. nibbler, gormandizer. ‖ adj. 1. sweet-toothed, fond of dainties. 2. nibbling.
lamborada s. f. (Braz., also lambada) lashing, whipping, flogging, blow with a whip.
lambrequim s. m. (pl. -ins) lambrequin.
lambrequinado adj. adorned with lambrequins.
lambril (pl. -is), lambrim (pl. -ins) s. m. wainscot-(t)ing: a lining of wood on the walls of a room.
lambrisamento s. m. (Braz.) act of wainscot(t)ing.
lambrisar v. (Braz.) to wainscot (wall).
lambujar v. 1. (also lambarar) to eat sweetmeats, be fond of sweets. 2. (Braz.) to give a handicap (in a game or wager).

lambujeiro s. m. person fond of sweets. ‖ adj. lickerish, liquorish; dainty.

lambujem s. f. (pl. **-ens**) 1. sweetmeat; dainty. 2. greediness. 3. (fig.) gain, small profit. 4. (Braz.) odds, bisque, handicap, advantage.
dar ~ to give advantage to another. **isto fica de** ~ (scornful) you can keep that over and above.

lambuzada s. f. 1. lick(ing). 2. stain, dirty spot. 3. anything that stains or dirties; soil.

lambuzadela s. f. 1. lick(ing). 2. stain, spot. 3. smattering, superficial knowledge. 4. thin coat of paint.

lambuzão adj. (f. **-ona**) (Braz.) 1. shabby, untidy, threadbare, careless. 2. unclean, greasy, dirty.

lambuzar v. 1. to dirty, soil, stain; daggle. 2. to (be)smear. 3. ~-se to eat without manners: smear one's face or soil one's clothes with food.
a criança lambuzou-se toda the child dirtied himself all over (esp. with food).

lamecha s. m. infatuated person. ‖ adj. infatuate, enamoured, languishing.

lameirão s. m. (pl. **-ões**) very large swamp or slough.

lameiro s. m. (also **lameira** f.) 1. slough, slush, bog. 2. marsh(land), moorland, swamp, quagmire. 3. pasture (land). ‖ adj. said of a horse that is a good runner on wet tracks.

lamela s. f. lamella: 1. thin plate or blade. 2. (bot., zool.) thin plate, layer or leaf. 3. (anat.) platelike organ.

lamelação s. f. (pl. **-ões**) lamellation.

lamelado adj. lamellated, foliated.

lamelar v. 1. to dispose in lamellas. 2. to laminate. ‖ adj. m. + f. lamellose, lamellar.

lamelibrânquios s. m. pl. (zool.) Lamellibranchia, a class of molluscs including the clams, oysters and mussels.

lamelicórneos s. m. pl. (ent.) Lamellicornia, a superfamily of beetles.

lamelífero adj. m. **lameliforme** m. + f. lamellose, lamellar, lamelliform.

lamelirrostro s. m. lamellirostral: lamellirostral bird (goose, duck). ‖ adj. lamellirostral, having a lamellose bill.

lameloso adj. lamellose, lamellar, lamellate; provided with lamellae.

lamentação s. f. (pl. **-ões**) 1. lamentation, lament, wailing. 2. mourning, outcry, weeping. 3. sorrow, complaint. 4. funeral song.
as -ões (bib.) the Lamentations of Jeremiah.

lamentador s. m. lamenter: person who laments or mourns; wailer; complainer. ‖ adj. 1. lamenting, mournful. 2. complaining.

lamentar v. 1. to lament: a) express sorrow, feel sorry for, regret. b) deplore, bewail, bemoan. c) moan for, wail. d) mourn. e) afflict, distress. f) grieve over. g) feel hurt. 2. ~-se: a) to complain of. b) to cry, weep (over).
lamento dizer I am ashamed to say. **ele lamentou a morte de seu amigo** he lamented the death of his friend. **lamento estarmos atrasados** I am sorry we are late.

lamentável adj. m. + f. (pl. **-áveis**) lamentable: 1. mournful, doleful, grievous. 2. pitiable. 3. deplorable, regrettable. 4. sorrowful. 5. distressful. 6. miserable, poor; pitiful, wretched. 7. sad. ‖ **lamentavelmente** adv. lamentably.
é profundamente ~ it's a thousand pities. **isto é** ~ it is to be regretted, it is too bad. **um acidente** ~ **a** deplorable accident.

lamento s. m. 1. lament: a) expression of grief or sorrow. b) lamentation. c) dirge, elegy or the music for an elegy. 2. complaint, grievance. 3. moan, groan, wail(ing). 4. (fig.) weeping, tears.

lamentoso adj. 1. lamentable, mournful, sad. 2. deplorable, pitiable, wretched. 3. plaintive. 4. tearful, weeping. 5. querulous. 6. elegic(al). ‖ **-amente** adv. 1. lamentably. 2. querulously. 3. elegiacally. 4. deplorably.

lâmia s. f. lamia: 1. (Gr. and Roman myth.) monster who charmed children. 2. (fig.) witch, vampire.

lâmina s. f. 1. lamina: a) thin plate or sheet; slab, foil; flake, scale. b) (bot.) limb, leaf blade. 2. blade (plates S 2, T 1). 3. strip(e). 4. splinter, sliver. 5. slide (for microscope).
~ **de barbear (gilete)** razor blade (plate B 7). ~ **de cortar** shearing blade, knife blade. ~ **de espada** sword blade. ~ **de metal** metal plate. ~ **de mola** spring leaf. ~ **de serra** saw blade. **mola de** ~ flat spring.

laminação s. f. (pl. **-ões**) (also **laminagem**) 1. lamination: a) act or process of laminating. b) state of being laminated. 2. rolling (mill).
~ **de aço** rolling of steel. ~ **a frio** (tech.) cold rolling.

laminado adj. 1. laminate. 2. plated. 3. rolled (steel).

laminador s. m. (tech.) 1. rolling mill. 2. flatting mill. 3. roller. ‖ adj. rolling, laminating.
~ **de arames** wire mill. ~ **universal** slabbing mill.

laminar (I) adj. m. + f. laminar, lamellose, lamellar, laminate(d): 1. provided with laminas. 2. composed of laminas.

laminar (II) v. to laminate, roll, form into laminas.
~ **a frio (quente)** to cold-roll (hot-roll).

laminária s. f. (bot.) laminaria: a genus of kelps.

laminoso adj. (also **lameloso**) laminous, laminate, lamellar.

lamínula s. f. 1. a little lamina, slab, sheet or blade. 2. slide (for microscopy).

lâmio-branco s. m. (pl. **lâmios-brancos**) (bot.) white archangel, white dead nettle.

lamiré s. m. (also **alamiré**) 1. diapason; tuning fork. 2. (fig.) starting signal. 3. (pop.) reprehension, reprimand, scolding, chiding.

lamoja s. f. a lye made of water and clay.

lamoso adj. = **lamacento**.

lampa (I) s. f. China silk.

lampa (II) s. f. 1. fruit gathered in a midsummer's night. 2. a variety of fig-tree. 3. = **lâmpada**.
levar as ~**s a alguém** to get the better of.

lâmpada s. f. 1. lamp: a) vessel with a wick and an inflammable liquid to produce artificial light. b) any contrivance that gives light. 2. (also **elétrica**) bulb, electric lamp (plates D 1, E 11, 12, L 1). 3. (fig.) light.
~ **de arco voltaico** arc lamp. ~ **de cabeceira** bedside lamp. ~ **de luz ultravioleta** sun lamp. ~ **de mesa** table lamp. ~ **de mineiro**, ~ **de segurança** safety lamp. ~ **de querosene** kerosene lamp. ~ **de pé** standard lamp. ~ **elétrica** electric lamp. ~ **fluorescente**, ~ **néon** fluorescent lamp, neon lamp (plates P 10, 19). ~ **incandescente** incandescent lamp. ~ **para "flash"** photoflash lamp. ~ **pendente** swing lamp. ~ **piloto** pilot lamp. ~ **tubular** tubular lamp. ~ **ultravioleta** ultraviolet lamp. **não ter azeite na** ~ (fig.) to have no strength left, be very weak. **prover com** ~**s** to lamp.

lampadário s. m. 1. candelabrum, chandelier. 2. candlestick.

lampadeiro s. m. 1. lampmaker. 2. candlestick: support for candles.

lampadejar v. 1. to shine, beam; flash up. 2. to emit light. 3. to flare, flicker, flutter.

lampana s. f. 1. lie. 2. slap (in the face); box on the ear.

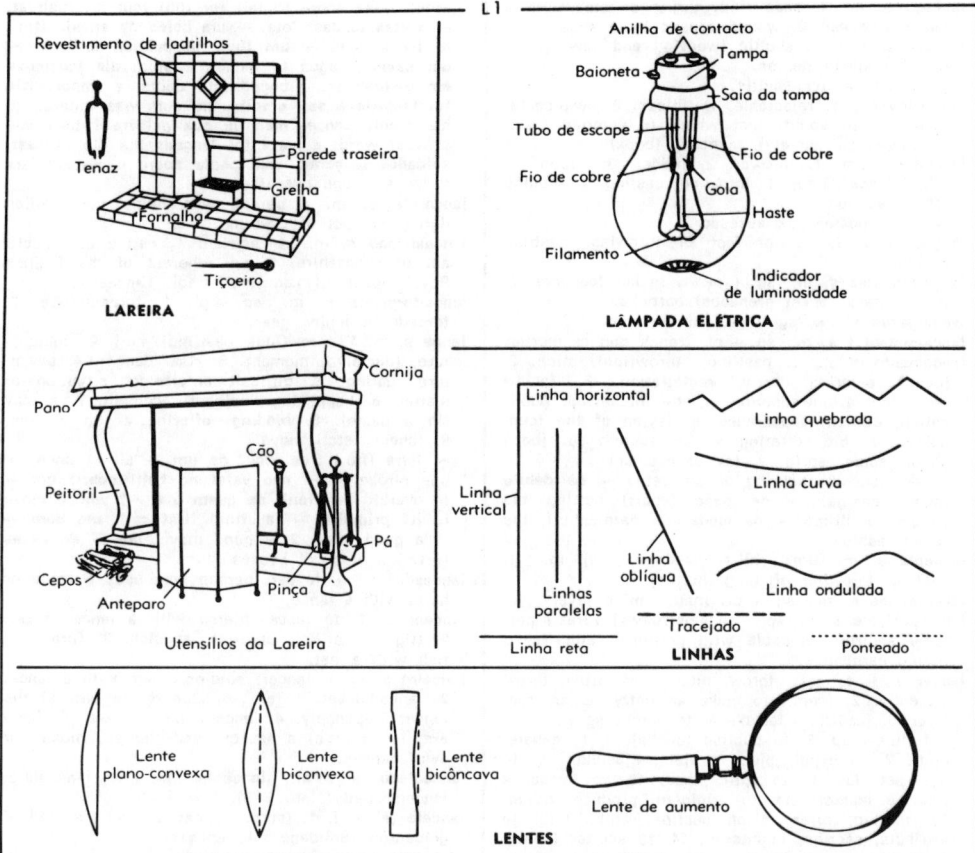

L 1

LAREIRA

Revestimento de ladrilhos
Tenaz
Parede traseira
Grelha
Fornalha
Tiçoeiro

LÂMPADA ELÉTRICA

Anilha de contacto
Tampa
Baioneta
Saia da tampa
Tubo de escape
Fio de cobre
Fio de cobre
Gola
Haste
Filamento
Indicador
de luminosidade

Cornija
Pano
Cão
Peitoril
Pá
Cepos
Pinça
Anteparo

Utensílios da Lareira

LINHAS

Linha horizontal
Linha quebrada
Linha curva
Linha
vertical
Linha
oblíqua
Linha ondulada
Linhas
paralelas
Tracejado
Linha reta
Ponteado

LENTES

Lente
plano-convexa
Lente
biconvexa
Lente
bicôncava
Lente de aumento

lamparina s. f. 1. small night lamp, night light, oil lamp. 2. (pop.) slap, cuff or box on the ear. 3. (mech., also ~ **de soldar**) blowtorch.

lampeiro adj. 1. untimely, premature, unseasonable. 2. meddlesome, intrusive; forward, bold. 3. hurried, hasty, quick. 4. alert, lively.

lampejante adj. m. + f. glittering, flashing; sparkling, flaring; shining.

lampejar v. 1. to sparkle, glitter, coruscate. 2. to flash, flare, flicker, flutter. 3. to scintillate.

lampejo s. m. 1. flash of light. 2. lightening. 3. glitter, flare. 4. (fig.) sudden inspiration. ~ **de engenho** a flash of wit. ~ **de gênio** a flash of genius.

lampião s. m. (pl. -ões) 1. lantern, large lamp. 2. street lamp; gas lamp (plate R 8).

lampinho adj. beardless.

lampíride s. f., **lampírio, lampiro** m. (ent.) firefly, glowworm.

lampo adj. premature, precocious; early ripe.

lampreia s. f. (ichth.) lamprey; catfish.

lampreia-dos-rios s. f. (pl. **lampreias-dos-rios**) (ichth.) freshwater lamprey.

lamprômetro s. m. instrument to mesure the intensity of light.

lampsana s. f. (bot.) nipplewort.

lamúria s. f. 1. lamentation, complaint, jeremiad. 2. wailing, whimpering.

lamuriador s. m. lamenter; whiner. ‖ adj. lamenting, plaintive.

lamuriante adj. m. + f. 1. lamenting. 2. complaining, plaintive, querulous. 3. weeping, crying.

lamuriar v. 1. to lament: a) wail, weep. b) mourn. c) (be)moan. d) express sorrow. 2. to complain. 3. to whine. 4. to whimper, cry.

lamuriento, lamurioso adj. whimpering, whining, whiningly.

lana-caprina s. f. insignificance, trifle. **uma questão de** ~ a trifling matter.

lanada s. f. sponge, swab, drag: mop to clean cannon bores.

lanar adj. m. + f. lanigerous, woollen, woolly.

lança s. f. 1. lance: a) spear. b) javelin. c) (fig.) lancer. 2. pole or shaft of a carriage. 3. jib, boom, beam of a crane (plate G 5). ~ **farpada para pescar** fish spear. **à ponta de** ~ (fig.) to the utmost. **em forma de** ~ spear-shaped. **medir** ~s **com alguém** to enter the lists against s. o. **meter uma** ~ **em África** 1. to perform a difficult task. 2. to obtain a great advantage. **quebrar** ~s **por alguém** to take up the cudgels on someone's behalf.

lança-bombas s. m., sg. + pl. (mil.) 1. bomb-thrower. 2. bomb-release mechanism.

lança-chamas s. m., sg. + pl. (mil.) flame-thrower.

lançaço s. m., **lançada** f. 1. thrust or stab with a lance or spear. 2. wound caused by a spear.

lançadeira s. f. 1. shuttle (weaving and sewing). 2. (pop.) restless person.
~ **cilíndrica** long-shuttle.

lançadiço adj. 1. rejectable, worthless. 2. despicable.

lançado s. m. vomit, that which is vomited. ‖ adj. introduced (in society), launched (book).

lançador s. m. 1. thrower. 2. bidder. 3. caster. 4. (obs.) lancer. ‖ adj. 1. throwing, casting. 2. bidding (at an auction).
~ **de impostos** tax assessor.

lançadura s. f. act or fact of throwing, casting, hurling.

lança-foguetes s. m., sg. + pl. 1. rocket launcher. 2. (for antitank rocket grenades) bazooka.

lança-gases s. m., sg. + pl. gas thrower.

lança-granadas s. m., sg. + pl. trench gun or mortar.

lançamento s. m. 1. cast(ing), throw(ing), pitch. 2. (com.) entering, entry, registration. 3. (naut.) launching. 4. introduction on the market. 5. publication, edition, appearance. 6. laying of the foundation. 7. bid, offering at an auction. 8. (bot.) shoot, scion, sprig. 9. tax assessment.
~ **de concreto** pouring of concrete. ~ **de débito** (com.) charge. ~ **de peso** (sport) putting the weight. **o último** ~ **da moda** the dernier cri, the latest fashion.

lançante s. m. (Braz.) hillside, slope. ‖ adj. m. + f. casting, throwing, flinging, hurling.

lança-minas s. m., sg. + pl. (naut.) mine layer.

lança-perfume s. m. (pl. **lança-perfumes**) (Braz.) perfume squirter: ampoule with perfumed ether used during carnival.

lançar v. 1. to cast, throw, pitch, hurl; fling, throw violently. 2. (com.) to make an entry, enter, register. 3. (naut.) to launch. 4. to vomit, spew, belch out, throw up. 5. to publish (books). 6. to exhale, emit. 7. to expel, eject, project, ejaculate. 8. to put, set, lay. 9. to spill, shed. 10. to introduce (on the market). 11. to originate, produce, cause. 12. to bid, offer at an auction, outbid. 13. to attribute, ascribe, impute to. 14. to scatter (seed), sow, disseminate. 15. to impose taxes. 16. to shoot, sprout. 17. ~-se: a) to throw o. s. b) to hurl o. s.; whirl. c) to dare, venture. d) to flow (into), discharge.
~ **à água** to launch (a vessel). ~ **água ao mar** to carry coals to Newcastle. ~ **alguma coisa na cara de alguém** to tell s. o. a thing to his face, hit s. o. in the teeth with s. th. ~ **âncora**, ~ **ferro** (naut.) to cast anchor. ~ **a soma (ao crédito ou ao débito)** (com.) to make the entry of a sum. ~ **ao chão** to fling down. ~ **bombas** to drop bombs. ~ **com ímpeto** to hurl, dart. ~ **contribuição sobre** to assess. ~ **à conta de alguém** to charge to someone's account. ~ **de si** to repel, repulse. ~ **em fuga** to put to flight. ~ **fora** to throw off, turn away, disgorge. ~ **a luva a alguém** (fig.) to challenge. ~ **luz sobre** to throw light on, flash at. ~ **mão de** to lay hold of, make use of, seize upon, resort to. ~ **na balança** to weigh, ponder, consider. ~ **no diário** (com.) to enter the day-book, journalize. ~ **no mercado** to introduce on the market. ~ **os alicerces de uma casa** to lay the foundations of a house. ~ **olhares furiosos** to cast furious looks at s. o. ~ **poeira nos olhos de** to throw dust in the eyes of, deceive. ~ **por terra** to throw down, prostrate. ~ **raios** to ray. ~ **raízes** to take root. ~ **a rede** to throw the net. ~ **sobre** to throw on. ~-**se aos pés de alguém** to throw o. s. at the feet of. ~ **suspeitas sobre** to cast suspicion on. ~-**se nos braços de alguém** to fling o. s. into someone's

arms. ~-**se sobre** to fall (or run) foul of, rush at. ~ **sortes** to cast lots. ~ **um balão de ensaio** (fig.) to fly a kite. ~ **um livro** to publish a book. ~ **um navio à água** to launch a ship. **ela lançou-se em dívidas** she plunged into debts. **a importância foi lançada a seu crédito** the sum was entered to his credit. **lancei mão de sua palavra** I took you at your word. **a sorte foi lançada** the die is cast. **soldados lançaram uma ponte sobre o rio** soldiers threw a bridge over the river.

lançarote s. m. a person who helps the stallion during the act of covering.

lancastriano s. m. Lancastrian: 1. native or inhabitant of Lancashire. 2. an adherent of the English Royal House of Lancaster. ‖ adj. Lancastrian.

lança-torpedos s. m., sg. + pl. 1. torpedo-tube. 2. torpedo launching gear.

lance s. m. 1. throw(ing), cast(ing), hurl. 2. conjuncture, (decisive) moment. 3. risk, danger. 4. adventure, daring. 5. difficult enterprise, situation or matter. 6. happening, incident, accident. 7. a play (in a game). 8. bidding, offering at an auction. 9. (chess, etc.) move.
~ **livre** (ftb.) free kick. **de um** ~ all at once, in one stroke. **o** ~ **não vale!** no ball! **cobrir um** ~ to overbid (auction). **de quem é o** ~? whose move is it? **primeiro** ~ (auction) first call. **um bom** ~ 1. a good offer. 2. a good move. **um** ~ **de casas** (Braz.) a block of houses.

lanceador s. m. lancer: person who uses a lance or hurts with a lance.

lancear v. 1. to lance, pierce with a lance; spear. 2. (fig.) to afflict, distress, anguish. 3. (Braz.) to fish with a net.

lanceiro s. m. 1. lancer: soldier armed with a lance. 2. lance-bucket: a rest to support the butt of the lance. 3. panoply. 4. lance maker. 5. ~s pl. lancers, lanciers: a) a set of quadrilles. b) music for such dances.

lanceolado adj. m., **lanceolar** m. + f. lanceolate, lance-shaped (plate F 5).

lanceta (ê) s. f. 1. (surg.) lancet. 2. (bot.) a kind of goldenrod (Solidago microglossa).
~ **para vacinação** vaccine-point.

lancetada s. f. cutting or piercing with a lancet.

lancetar v. to lance: 1. open or cut with a lancet. 2. pierce with a lance.

lanceteira s. f. riffler, bow file.

lancha s. f. 1. motor-boat (plate L 2). 2. launch, barge, ship's boat. 3. fisherboat. 4. (Braz., fam.) distorted and heavy shoes. 5. (Braz., fig.) big, huge foot.
~ **aduaneira** revenue cutter. ~ **de desembarque** landing barge. ~ **patrulheira** vedette boat. ~ **rápida** speed-boat.

lanchada s. f. load of a motor-boat; boatful.

lanchão s. m. (pl. **-ões**) lighter: a large boat or barge.

lanchar v. 1. to eat or take a snack. 2. to breakfast.

lancha-torpedeira s. f. (pl. **lanchas-torpedeiras**) patrol torpedo boat, gunboat.

lanche s. m. snack; sandwich or the like between meals (as for school children).

lanchonete s. f. (Braz.) snack bar.

lancil s. m. (pl. **-is**) large hewn stone for paving.

lancinante adj. m. + f. 1. lancinating, stabbing, twinging, painful. 2. afflictive, harrowing, heart-rending. 3. pungent, poignant.
um grito ~ a piercing cry.

lancinar v. 1. to lancinate, pierce, stab. 2. to twinge. 3. to torment, torture; afflict, distress.

lanço s. m. 1. throw(ing), cast(ing), act of hurling. 2. bid(ding), offer(ing) (at an auction). 3. netful or draught of fishes. 4. series, range, row (houses).

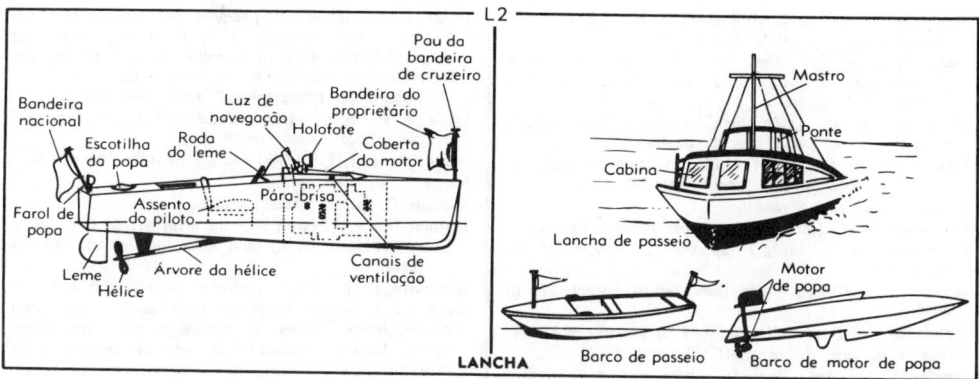

L 2

Pau da bandeira de cruzeiro

Bandeira nacional
Luz de navegação
Bandeira do proprietário
Escotilha da popa
Roda do leme
Holofote
Coberta do motor
Farol de popa
Assento do piloto
Pára-brisa
Leme
Árvore da hélice
Hélice
Canais de ventilação

Mastro
Ponte
Cabina
Lancha de passeio
Motor de popa

LANCHA   Barco de passeio   Barco de motor de popa

5. stretch (of a road, wall, etc.); distance, extent. 6. a turn of a shuttle. 7. flight (of stairs); landing. 8. (Braz.) posture, position.
~ **de dados** a cast of dice. ~ **de olhos** a glance. ~ **de rede** a cast of the net. **cobrir o seu** ~ 1. to outbid (auction). 2. (fig.) to supplant.
landa s. f. heath, tract of wasteland.
landau s. m. (also **landô**) landau: four-wheeled carriage with a foldable top of two parts.
lande s. f. 1. acorn: fruit of the oak. 2. wasteland; extensive heath.
landeira s. f. forest or grove of oaks.
landgrave s. m. landgrave: a title assumed by some German counts in the 12th century; later the title of certain German princes.
landuá s. f. (Braz.) 1. rumour, false report. 2. hand-fishnet used to catch shrimps and small fishes.
langanho s. m. (Braz.) 1. (ichth.) a kind of jellyfish. 2. meat of inferior quality. 3. any soft and repugnant thing.
langor s. m. (also **languidez** f.) languor.
langoroso adj. 1. languorous, languid. 2. weak, feeble. 3. dull. 4. enervate.
langue, languente adj. m. + f. languid.
languenho s. m. (Braz.) piece of (low quality) meat.
languento adj. 1. sickly, ailing, unhealthy. 2. fussy, finicky. 3. silly.
languescente adj. m. + f. languishing, that languishes.
languescer v. to languish: 1. become languid. 2. grow weak. 3. lose strength or animation. 4. droop, fade, pine. 5. fall sick, become ill, ail.
languidez s. f. 1. languidness, languour. 2. weakness, faintness. 3. sluggishness, indolence, lassitude, inertia. 4. looseness, slackness. 5. prostration; spiritlessness; dullness, listlessness. 6. weariness.
lânguido, lângüido adj. 1. languid, languishing: a) sluggish, dull. b) ailing, sickly, weakened, feeble, debilitated, faintish, without force; drooping, listless. c) prostrate. d) voluptuous. 2. morbid, unhealthy. 3. loose, slack. ‖ **-amente** adv. languidly, languishingly; weakly; listlessly.
languinhento adj. 1. clammy, viscous, ropy. 2. soft and wet. 3. weak, feeble.
languir v. (also **languescer**) to languish: 1. lose force, strength or vitality. 2. grow dull. 3. long, pine.
lanhar v. 1. to wound, hurt, injure; bruise. 2. to rip, tear up. 3. to embowel. 4. to gut, draw (fish). 5. to mistreat, ill-treat. 6. to afflict, trouble, grieve. 7. to adulterate, alter, modify.
lanho s. m. 1. slash, cut, incision. 2. (Braz.): a) lard, bacon in strips. b) slice of meat.
lanífero adj. laniferous: bearing or producing wool; fleecy.

lanifício s. m. 1. woollen fabric or cloth. 2. ~**s** pl. woollen goods. 3. factory of woollen goods.
lanígero adj. 1. lanigerous, laniferous. 2. lanuginous: covered with or bearing wool (animal).
gado ~ sheep.
lanolina s. f. lanolin(e), wool-fat.
lanosidade s. f. woolliness, fleeciness.
lanoso adj. woolly: 1. woollen, fleecy: of, pertaining to or like wool. 2. bearing wool.
lansquenê, lansquenete s. m. lansquenet: 1. one of a class of mercenary German foot-soldiers of the 15th century. 2. a game at cards.
lantânio s. m. (chem.) lanthanum.
lantejoula, lantejoila s. f. = **lentejoula, lentejoila.**
lanterna s. f. lantern: 1. a translucent case inclosing a light and protecting it from wind and rain; lamp (plates C 15, M 12). 2. (archit.) an upright structure on a roof or dome to give light and air to the interior. 3. clerestory.
~ **de bolso** spotlight. ~ **furta-fogo** dark lantern. ~ **mágica** magic lantern.
lanterna-de-aristóteles s. f. (pl. **lanternas-de-aristóteles**) (zool.) Aristotle's lantern.
lanterneiro s. m. 1. lantern maker. 2. lantern bearer. 3. lamplighter, lighthouseman.
lanternim s. m. (pl. **-ins**) 1. (archit.) clerestory, clearstory. 2. lantern-wheel, lantern-pinion.
lanterninha s. f. 1. a small lantern. 2. (mot.) tail-lamp, tail-light. 3. (Braz., sport) m. club or team occupying the last place in a series of competitions. 3. m. + f. (movie theater) usher (also **vaga-lume** m.).
lanudo adj. (also **lanoso**) woolly: 1. woollen, fleecy. 2. bearing wool.
lanugem s. f. (pl. **-ens**) down: 1. fine soft hair of the face; lanugo. 2. (bot.) fuzz, fluff, pubescence. 3. nap, pile.
lanugento adj. downy, lanuginous.
lanuginoso adj. 1. woolly: of the nature of wool. 2. lanuginous, downy.
lanzinha s. f. bunting: very thin woollen fabric.
lanzudo s. m. rustic, boor, brute, stupid person. ‖ adj. 1. woolly, woollen. 2. rustic, coarse, stupid.
lapa s. f. 1. a natural shelter formed by an overhanging stone. 2. cave, den, grotto. 3. (zool.) limpet (Patella vulgata). 4. drift or gallery of a mine. 5. (Port., prov.) stone. 6. (pop.) slap in the face, box on the ear.
lapáceo adj. (bot.) lappaceous, echinate.
lapada s. f. 1. (Braz.) beating, lashing, thrashing. 2. slap in the face, box on the ear. 3. a stone's cast or throw.

lapantana s. m. + f. 1. simpleton. 2. idiot, blockhead, imbecile. ‖ adj. foolish, stupid, imbecile.

lapão (I) s. m. (pl. -ões) Lapp: 1. Laplander: native or inhabitant of Lapland. 2. the language of this people. ‖ adj. Lappish.

lapão (II) s. m. (also -ões) 1. (sl.) boor, churl, bumpkin. 2. a large natural shelter.

laparão s. m. (pl. -ões) (path.) 1. lymphangitis. 2. (zool.) a large limpet (genus Patella).

láparo s. m. young rabbit.

laparocele s. f. (med.) laparocele: lumbar hernia.

laparotomia s. f. (surg.) laparotomy: abdominal incision.

lapear v. (N. Braz.) 1. to lash, whip, switch. 2. to walk.

lapedo s. m. place full of caves or natural shelters.

lapela s. f. lapel (of a coat) (plates R 6, 7).

lapidação s. f. (pl. -ões) 1. cutting and polishing of gems. 2. lapidation: execution by stoning. 3. (fig.): a) improvement, perfecting. b) polishing, refining. c) education.
~ de diamantes diamond-cutting.

lapidar v. 1. to lapidate: stone, kill by stoning. 2. to cut and polish gems. 3. (fig.) to polish, refine; improve; educate. 4. to engrave upon gems. ‖ adj. m. + f. 1. lapidary: a) or pertaining to the cutting of gems. b) engraved upon stones. 2. concise, terse. 3. perfect, artistic.

lapidaria s. f. art of cutting and polishing precious stones.

lapidária s. f. science that studies the deciphering of old inscriptions on monuments and the like.

lapidário s. m. 1. lapidary, stone-cutter, person who cuts, polishes or engraves precious stones. 2. jeweller. ‖ adj. lapidary: of or pertaining to the art of deciphering old inscriptions on monuments.

lápide s. f. (also lápida) 1. gravestone, tombstone, ledger. 2. any engraved stone.

lapídeo adj. stony, lapideous; consisting of or like stone.

lapidescente adj. m. + f. petrifying, turning to stone.

lapidícola adj. m. + f. (zool.) lapidicolous.

lapidificação s. f. lapidification, petrifaction: 1. act of petrifying. 2. state of being petrified.

lapidificar v. to petrify, lapidify: 1. convert into stone. 2. ~-se: become stony.

lapidífico adj. lapidific(al).

lapidoso adj. stony, rocky.

lapiga s. m. (Braz.) meager, lean bullock.

lapijar v. to pencil: mark or draw with a pencil.

lapíli s. m. pl. (geol.) lapilli: small stony volcanic fragments.

lapinha s. f. 1. small grotto. 2. (N. Braz.) grotto with the Nativity scene (for Christmas).

lápis s. m., sg. + pl. 1. pencil. 2. any pencil-shaped object.
~ de carvão charcoal pencil. ~ de cor coloured pencil. ~ de desenho crayon. ~ vermelho (azul, etc.) red (blue, etc.) pencil. apontador de ~ pencil sharpener. desenhar a ~ to draw with a pencil.

lapisada s. f. trace with a pencil.

lapiseira s. f. pencil-case, port-crayon.
~ automática propelling pencil.

lápis-lazúli s. m., sg. + pl. lapis lazuli, lazulite, azure-stone.

lápis-cópia s. m., sg. + pl. ink-pencil.

lápis-tinta s. m., sg. + pl. indelible pencil.

lapo s. m. (Braz.) 1. leather-stripe on the end of a whip. 2. piece, fragment, bite, chunk. 3. slash. 4. a whip lash.

lapônio s. m. boor, churl, bumpkin, yokel. ‖ adj. coarse, rough, uncouth, boorish, rude.

lapso s. m. lapse: 1. passage or portion of time. 2. slip error, mistake. 3. fault, wrong, oversight, slight offence. 4. slip, stumble. 5. slip of the pen or memory. ‖ adj. guilty of; in default.
~ tipográfico typographical error, misprint.

lapuz s. m. boor, churl, rustic, yokel. ‖ adj. m. + f. coarse, rough, rude, uncouth.

laqueação s. f. (pl. -ões) (surg.) ligature (of arteries).

laquê s. m. hair spray.

laquear (I) s. m. tester, canopy.

laquear (II) v. 1. (surg.) to tie arteries, to ligature. 2. (Braz.) to lacquer: a) coat with lacquer. b) enamel. c) japan.

laqueário s. m. (hist.) gladiator armed with a noose.

lar s. m. 1. hearth, fireplace, fireside. 2. (fig.) home: a) residence; house. b) native country, fatherland. c) the family, household. 3. ~es pl. (Roman gods) lares.
eles dissolveram o seu ~ they dissolved their household.

laracha s. f. 1. jest, joke; raillery, mockery. 2. m. jester, wit.

larada s. f. 1. embers. 2. spot, stain. 3. spilt liquid.

larafi s. m. (Braz.) purgatory of the malês.

laranja s. f. 1. orange (fruit). 2. (fig.) simpleton, naive person; nobody. ‖ adj. orange, orange-coloured. casca de ~ orange peel. espremedor de ~s orange squeezer. suco de ~s orange juice.

laranja-amarga (pl. laranjas-amargas), laranja-azeda (pl. laranjas-azedas), laranja-da-terra (pl. laranjas-da-terra) s. f. (Braz., bot.) bitter orange, Seville orange.

laranja-cravo s. f. (pl. laranjas-cravo) (Braz., bot.) mandarin orange, tangerine.

laranjada s. f. 1. orangeade: beverage made of orange juice, water and sugar. 2. a heap of oranges. 3. throw with an orange.

laranja-da-baía s. f. (pl. laranjas-da-baía) (Braz., bot.) navel orange.

laranjal s. m. (pl. -ais) orangery, orange orchard or grove.

laranja-pêra s. f. (pl. laranjas-pêra) small, oblong variety of the common orange (Citrus sinensis).

laranjarana s. f. (bot.) mangrove.

laranjeira s. f. (bot.) orange (tree).
flor de ~ orange blossom.

laranjeiro s. m. (Braz.) 1. orange grower. 2. orange dealer or seller.

laranjinha s. f. 1. small orange. 2. (Braz.) sugar-cane rum with orange peel.

laranjo adj. (Braz.) said of orange-coloured cattle.

larapiar v. to purloin, pilfer, filch, steal.

larápio s. m. pilferer, fingerer, filcher, stealer, thief.

larário s. m. (Roman hist.) Lararium: small shrine in private houses used to worship the lares.

lardeadeira s. f. larding-needle, larding-pin.

lardear v. 1. to lard: a) stuff with bacon or pork. b) smear with lard. 2. to intermix, interlace, interlard.

lardiforme adj. m. + f. lardaceous: resembling lard.

lardívoro adj. feeding on lard.

lardo s. m. 1. lard, bacon. 2. (fig.) condiment, seasoning. 3. ornament.

laré s. m. used in the adv. locution: andar ao ~ 1. to loiter, idle. 2. to be bad off.

lardizabaláceas s. f. pl. (bot.) Lardizabalaceae, a family of woody vines of the order Ranales.

lareira s. f. fireplace, hearth (plate L 1).

lareiro adj. 1. of or pertaining to a hearth or fireplace. 2. homely.

larga s. f. 1. giving up, setting free, loosening. 2. relaxation, abandonment, relinquishment. 3. liberty.

freedom, unrestraint. 4. largess. 5. width. 6. (Braz.) open country. 7. holdfast, clamp. **à ~:** 1. freely, loosely. 2. abundantly. 3. generously. **dar ~s a** to give free rein to. **dar muitas ~s a alguém** to give too much liberty to a person. **estar à ~** to be at ease. **gastar à ~** to spend freely. **viver à ~** to live in clover, to be well-off.

largada s. f. 1. act of releasing. 2. (sport) start. 3. (naut.) departure, sea-going. 4. joke, wisecrack. 5. (S. Braz.) feat, prowess, stunt.

largado adj. (Braz.) 1. abandoned. 2. despised. 3. (fig.): a) turbulent, tumultuous, unruly (horse). b) incorrigible. c) faint, unconscious.

largar v. 1. to release, set at liberty, let go, free. 2. to relax, slacken, ease. 3. to leave, give up, abandon, forsake, put or leave aside. 4. to cede, yield, give up. 5. to emit, discharge. 6. to utter, pronounce. 7. to unfurl (flag). 8. to start, leave, go away; set sail. 9. **~-se:** a) to give o. s. over to. b) to separate, desunite.
~ a presa to let go one's hold. **~ as rédeas** to give a horse the bridle; give free reins to. **~ as velas ao vento** to unfurl, set sails. **~ (mão) de** to stop, desist from, renounce. **~ todo o pano** (naut.) to pack on sail. **larga-me** let me alone. **vou ~ de fumar** I am going to stop smoking.

largífluo adj. (poet.) flowing copiously.

largo s. m. 1. breadth, width. 2. public square, plaza. 3. (naut.) high sea; offing. 4. (mus.) largo movement or piece. ‖ adj. 1. broad: a) large, wide, ample (plate Q). b) extensive, vast. c) spacious, roomy. d) generous, liberal. e) detailed. 2. important, relevant, momentous. 3. considerable. 4. long, of great extent in time. 5. (fig.) plentiful, abundant, copious. ‖ adv. 1. broadly. 2. (mus.) largo, very slow. ‖ **-amente** adv. 1. broadly. 2. largely, abundantly. 3. liberally, generously.
-a margem de lucros ample profits. **~s anos** long (many) years. **ao ~** (naut.) afar, in the offing. **a passos ~s** hurriedly. **com -as mãos** copiously. **duas polegadas de ~** (Port.) two inches broad. **fazer-se ao ~** (naut.) to put off, sail, gain an offing. **passar de ~ sobre** (fig.) not to care much about. **por -a margem** by a wide margin. **por ~s anos** for many years.

largueador s. m. lavisher, spendthrift. ‖ adj. lavish, prodigal, liberally.

larguear v. to spend liberally, lavish, squander.

largueirão adj. (pl. -ões), (f. -ona) very large, broad or wide.

largueza s. f. 1. breadth, width; broadness, wideness; spaciousness. 2. (fig.): a) generosity, largess, liberality. b) dissipation, lavishness.

largura s. f. 1. breadth, width; wideness, broadness (plate E 6). 2. amplitude, extensiveness. 3. extension.
que ~ tem? how wide is it? **tem 90 cm de ~** it has a width of 90 cm.

lariço s. m. (bot.) 1. Larix: a genus of coniferous trees. 2. the larch.
~ dos E.U.A. (bot.) tamarack. **~ americano** (bot.) hackmatack.

larídeos s. m. pl. (ornith.) Laridae, a family comprising gulls and terns.

lariformes s. m. pl. (ornith.) Lariformes, an order of birds comprising the gulls.

laringalgia s. f. (med.) laryngeal neuralgia.

laringe s. m. + f. (anat., zool.) larynx: 1. the upper part of the windpipe. 2. the organ of voice (in man).

laríngeo, laringiano adj. laryngeal, laryngic, laryngean.

laringite s. f. laryngitis: inflammation of the larynx.

laringografia s. f. description of the larynx.

laringologia s. f. laryngology: treatise on the larynx and its diseases.

laringologista s. m. + f. (med.) laryngologist: person (practitioner) devoted to laryngology.

laringoscopia s. f. laryngoscopy: inspection of the larynx by means of a laryngoscope.

laringoscópio s. m. laryngoscope: instrument for examining the larynx.

laringotomia s. f. (surg.) laryngotomy: the operation of incising the larynx.

laroz s. m. (archit.) jack rafter.

larva s. f. (zool.) larva: 1. the early form of any insect, a grub. 2. worm.

larváceos s. m. pl. (zool.) Larvacea, an order of pelagic tunicates.

larvado adj. insidious; masked; atypic.

larval adj. m. + f. (pl. -ais) larval: of or pertaining to a larva.

larviforme adj. m. + f. larviform.

larvíparo adj. larviparous.

lasanha s. f. (It. cul.) lasagne: flat, large, rectangular strips of pasta, baked with meat, cheese, tomatoes and oil.

lasca s. f. 1. splint, splinter. 2. chip(ping), shaving; shard. 3. flake, sliver. 4. (fig.) morsel, slice, scrap, bit, fragment; piece.

lascado adj. 1. split, splintered. 2. chipped; cracked. 3. mutilated.
o prato está ~ the plate has got a chip.

lascar v. 1. to splinter, crack, chip. 2. to cleave, split. 3. to break into pieces. 4. to strike. 5. **~-se:** a) to sliver, spall. b) to be broken into fragments.

lascívia s. f. 1. lasciviousness, wantonness, lewdness, lechery. 2. sensuality, libidinousness.

lascivo adj. 1. lascivious, wanton, lewd, luxurious. 2. sensual, bestial. 3. uncontrolled. 4. playful, frolic, gay. ‖ **-amente** adv. 1. lasciviously. 2. playfully.

láser s. m. (Engl.) laser.

lassar v. 1. to grow weary, become tired. 2. to slacken, loose.

lassidão (pl. -ões), **lassitude** s. f. 1. lassitude: a) weariness, fatigue, tiredness. b) languor, lethargy. 2. looseness, slackness.

lasso adj. 1. weary, tired, worn out, fagged. 2. lax, loose, slack; flabby. 3. dissolute, lewd.

lástima s. f. 1. compassion, pity. 2. pain, heartache. 3. lamentation, complaint, wail, weeping, moan. 4. grief, sorrow. 5. misery. 6. (fig.) worthless or troublesome person or thing.
ele é uma ~ 1. he is a problem. 2. he is hard to handle. 3. he is a good-for-nothing. 4. he is a poor wretch. **é uma ~!** that is too bad. **que ~!** what a pity!

lastimado adj. (S. Braz.) wounded, bruised.

lastimador s. m. lamenter, complainer, whiner. ‖ adj. 1. pitiful, distressful, sad. 2. complaining.

lastimadura s. f. (S. Braz.) bruise, wound, contusion.

lastimar v. 1. to deplore, regret, lament. 2. to bemoan, bewail. 3. to grieve, worry, hurt. 4. to pity, feel sorrow for, commiserate. 5. (S. Braz.) to wound, bruise. 6. **~-se:** to complain o. s. dolefully.

lastimável adj. m. + f. (pl. -áveis) 1. pitiable, pitiful. 2. lamentable, deplorable. ‖ **lastimavelmente** adv. 1. pitiably. 2. lamentably.
seu estado é ~ he is in a pitiful condition.

lastimoso adj. 1. pitiful, doleful. 2. lamentable, mournful. 3. wailing. ‖ **-amente** adv. 1. pitifully. 2. wailingly.

lastração s. f. (pl. -ões) (also **lastramento** m.) (the act of) ballasting.

lastrador s. m. ballaster. ‖ adj. ballasting.

lastragem s. f. (pl. -ens) (Braz.) ballasting: the act of providing ballast for a railroad bed.

lastrar v. to ballast: 1. furnish with ballast. 2. lay or pack with ballast. 3. (fig.) steady.

lastreamento s. m. ballasting.

lastro s. m. 1. ballast: a) weight carried in a ship or balloon to steady or control it. b) broken rock or gravel for the bed of a road or railroad. 2. (fig.): a) house. b) appetizer. 3. (Braz., railroad) switch engine.

lata (I) s. f. 1. tin: a) tin plate. b) tin box, canister. c) tin can (plate P 12). 2. (Braz., sl.) a) face. b) refusal of a lover. ~ de conservas tin of preserves, canned goods. ~ de gasolina petrol can, (U. S. A.) gasoline can. ~ de lixo dust-bin, waste-bin, refuse-bin, garbage pail. ~ de tintas paint-box. ~ para chá tea-caddy. ~ velha jalop(p)y. abridor de ~ tin opener, (U. S. A) can opener. dar a ~ a to dismiss (a lover). meter a mão na ~ de alguém to slap a person's face.

lata (II) s. f. lath, strip of wood.

latada s. f. 1. a blow on or a noise with a tin can. 2. espalier, trellis, latticework.

latagão s. m. (pl. -ões) (f. -ona) strong and tall fellow.

latâneo adj. (obs.) lateral, situated at the side.

latão s. m. 1. brass: an alloy of copper and zinc. 2. (pl. -ões) large can. ~ de leite churn, milk can. ~ em bruto wrought brass. ~ fundido cast brass.

latear v. to adorn with brass or tin ornaments.

lategada s. f. a slash with a whip or scourge.

lategar v. to whip, lash, scourge.

látego s. m. 1. whip, scourge, rawhide. 2. (fig.): a) punishment, reprimand. b) flagellum. c) stimulus.

latejante adj. m. + f. palpitant, pulsating, beating, throbbing.

latejar v. to palpitate, pulsate, pulse, beat, throb; pant.

latejo s. m. 1. throbbing, pulsation, beat. 2. (Braz.) agitation, tumult; sound of voices.

latência s. f. latency: the state of being latent or concealed.

latente adj. m. + f. 1. latent: a) occult, hidden, concealed. b) not visible or apparent. c) implied. d) (med.) slow, lingering. 2. (fig.) disguised, dissembled. ‖ ~mente adv. latently.

later v. to palpitate, pulsate, throb.

lateral adj. m. + f. (pl. -ais) 1. lateral or pertaining to the side; situated at the side. 2. transversal, transverse. ‖ ~mente adv. laterally. entrada ~ side entrance. linha ~ 1. touch-line. 2. (sport) side-line. nave ~ da igreja side aisle. porta ~ side-door. vista ~ side-view.

lateranense adj. m. + f. of or pertaining to the Lateran (palace or basilica).

laterício adj. latericeous: of brick.

laterita s. f. (geol.) laterite: a red residual of rock decay.

látex, látice s. m. latex: a milklike fluid, as of the rubber tree, found in many plants.

latíbulo s. m. 1. hiding place. 2. heaven. 3. the abode of the gods.

laticífero adj. laticiferous: bearing or containing latex.

laticlávio s. m. (Roman hist.) wearer of a laticlave.

laticlavo s. m. (Roman hist.) laticlave: a broad purple stripe worn on the front of the tunic of senators.

laticolo adj. large-necked, broad-necked.

laticórneo adj. broad-horned.

latido s. m. 1. bark(ing), yelp(ing), bay(ing). 2. (fig.): a) remorse. b) nonsense, silly talk.

latifloro adj. (bot.) large-flowered.

latifólio adj. (bot.) latifoliate, broad-leaved.

latifundiário s. m. the owner of a latifundium.

latifúndio s. m. latifundium: large landed estate.

latílabro adj. (zool.) thick-lipped.

latim s. m. 1. Latin: the language of ancient Latium and of Rome. 2. (fig.) thing difficult to understand. ~ bárbaro garden Latin. ~ macarrônico dog Latin. perder o seu ~ to waste one's breath.

latímano adj. (zool.) large-handed, broad-handed.

latinada s. f. 1. mistake in Latin. 2. speech in Latin.

latinar v. 1. to speak or write Latin. 2. to Latinize, translate into Latin.

latinice s. f. presumption of knowing Latin.

latinidade s. f. Latinity: 1. use of the Latin language. 2. rules for speaking or writing Latin. 3. the Latin peoples.

latinismo s. m. Latinism.

latinista s. m. + f. Latinist.

latinização s. f. (pl. -ões) Latinization.

latinizar v. to Latinize: 1. convert into Latin forms. 2. speak Latin or use Latin words or phrases.

latino s. m. Latin: native or inhabitant of ancient Latium or of Rome. ‖ adj. 1. Latin: a) of or pertaining to Latium, its people and language. b) of or pertaining to the R. C. Church. 2. (naut.) lateen. ‖ -amente adv. according to Latin usage, like the Latins.

latino-americano s. m. (pl. latino-americanos) Latin-American. ‖ adj. Latin-American.

latinório s. m. 1. dog Latin, bad Latin. 2. ecclesiastical Latin.

latípede adj. m. + f. (zool.) large-footed, broad-footed.

latipene adj. m. + f. (zool.) having broad feathers.

latir v. 1. to bark, yelp, bay. 2. to howl. 3. (fig.): a) to clamour, make a noise. b) to throb, palpitate. o cachorro latiu the dog gave mouth. cão que late não morde barking dogs do not bite.

latirismo s. m. (med.) lathyrism.

latirrostro adj. (ornith.) latirostral, broad-billed.

latitude s. f. 1. latitude: a) distance on the earth's surface northward or southward from the equator, measured in degrees on the respective meridian. b) breadth. c) scope, extent, range. 2. climate.

latitudinal adj. m. + f. (pl. -ais) latitudinal: relating to latitude. ‖ ~mente adv. latitudinally.

latitudinário adj. latitudinarian: 1. broad, liberal. 2. wide, extensive.

lato adj. (L.) wide, broad, large, ample, vast, diffuse. ‖ -amente adv. amply, in a broad, wide sense.

latoaria s. f. a tinsmith's shop.

latoeiro s. m. (also funileiro) tinner, tinman, tinsmith, tinker.

latomia s. f. (Braz.) 1. noise, clamour, hoots and jeers. 2. loud weeping. 3. idle talk.

latria s. f. (R. C. Church) 1. latria: supreme worship to be offered to God only. 2. (fig.) adoration, worship.

latrina s. f. latrine, privy, water-closet (plate A 7).

latrinário adj. 1. that lives in latrines. 2. concerning latrines. 3. (fig.) sordid, squalid; filthy, repugnant.

latrineiro s. m. cleaner of a latrine.

latrocinar v. to rob, take by force.

latrocínio s. m. armed robbery, a taking away by violent means; hold-up, highway robbery.

lauda (I) s. f. 1. a page of a book. 2. each side of a sheet of paper.

lauda (II) s. f. (R. C. Church) laud: music or song in praise of God.

laudabilidade s. f. laudability, laudableness, praiseworthiness.

laudanidina s. f. (chem.) laudanidine.

laudanina s. f. (chem.) laudanine, laudanin.

laudanizado adj. containing laudanum; narcotized.

L 3

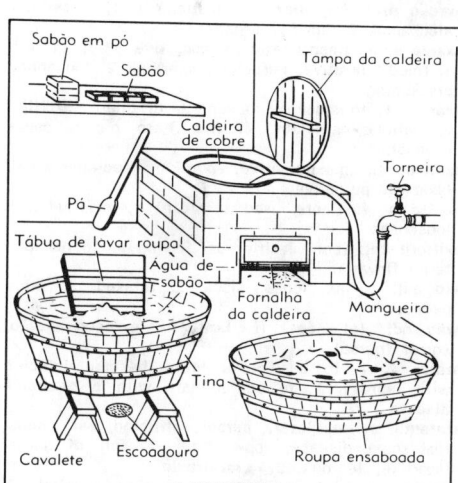

Sabão em pó
Sabão
Tampa da caldeira
Caldeira de cobre
Torneira
Pá
Tábua de lavar roupa
Água de sabão
Fornalha da caldeira
Mangueira
Tina
Cavalete
Escoadouro
Roupa ensaboada

LAVANDERIA

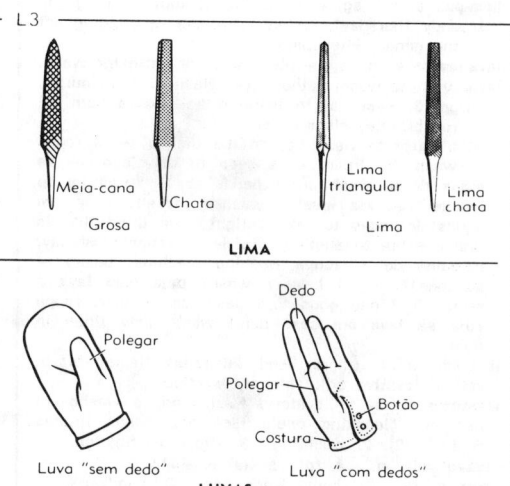

Meia-cana
Grosa
Chata
Lima triangular
Lima
Lima chata

LIMA

Dedo
Polegar
Polegar
Botão
Costura
Luva "sem dedo"
Luva "com dedos"

LUVAS

laudanizar v. to prepare or mix with laudanum or opium; narcotize.

láudano s. m. laudanum: 1. any preparation of opium. 2. a tincture of opium.

laudatício, laudativo, laudatório adj. laudative, laudatory, containing or expressing praise.

laudável adj. m. + f. (pl. **-áveis**) laudable, praiseworthy, commendable, worthy of being lauded.

laudel s. m. (pl. **-éis**) buffcoat.

laudes s. m. pl. lauds: religious service, canonical hours after matins.

laudo s. m. 1. award: the decision of arbitrators, report of experts. 2. finding, the verdict of an umpire.

lauráceas s. f. pl. (bot.) Lauraceae, a family of dicotyledonous trees and shrubs.

láurea s. f. laurel: 1. crown of laurel. 2. (fig.) honour, homage; reward, prize, premium.

laureado s. m. laureate. ‖ adj. laureate.

poeta ~ poet laureate.

laurear v. 1. to laureate: crown with a wreath of laurel. 2. praise, applaud. 3. to reward. 4. to mash, ogle, make advances to women.

laureio s. m. laureation: the act of crowning with laurel.

laurel s. m. (pl. **-éis**) laurel: 1. crown of laurel. 2. (fig.) honour, homage; reward, prize, premium.

laurentino, láureo adj. of, pertaining to or consisting of laurel.

lauréola s. f. 1. laurel, crown of laurel. 2. aureole, glory, halo. 3. any plant of the genus Laurus.

lauréola-fêmea s. f. (pl. **lauréolas-fêmeas**) (bot.) mezereon, paradise plant.

lauréola-macha s. f. (pl. **lauréolas-machas**) (bot.) copse spurge, wood laurel.

láurico adj. (chem.) lauric.

ácido ~ lauric acid.

laurícomo adj. (poet.) laureate, crowned with laurel.

laurífero adj. (also **laurígero**) 1. laureate, crowned with laurel. 2. lauriferous: producing or carrying laurel.

laurifólio adj. (bot.) laurel-leaved.

lausperene s. m. (R. C. Church) continual adoration of the Blessed Sacrament in some churches.

lauto adj. 1. sumptuous, magnificent, splendid, luxurious. 2. plentiful, abundant, copious. ‖ **-amente** adv. 1. sumptuously. 2. plentifully.

laúza s. f. (Braz., sl.) confusion, disorder.

lava s. f. 1. lava: molten rock which issues from a valcano during an eruption, slag (plate M 11). 2. (fig.): a) torrent. b) flame, fire.

lavabo s. m. 1. (eccles.) lavabo: a) the priest's ritual washing of his hands in the Mass. b) the verses he recites in doing so. c) the towel he uses after the washing. 2. any wash-basin.

lava-bunda s. m. (pl. **lava-bundas**) (Braz., ent.) dragonfly.

lavação s. f. (pl. **-ões**) wash: act of washing.

lavada s. f. a kind of fishing-net.

lavadaria s. f. = **lavanderia**.

lavadeira s. f. 1. laundress, laundrywoman, washerwoman. 2. washing-machine.

lavadela s. f. slight washing.

lava-dente s. m. (pl. **lava-dentes**) (pop.) drink.

lavado adj. washed.

lavador s. m. washer, person who washes.

lavadouro s. m. (also **lavadoiro**) 1. washboard; washtub. 2. place for washing clothes.

lavadura s. f. 1. washing, lavation. 2. dish-wash, dish-water.

lavagem s. f. (pl. **-ens**) 1. wash, act or fact of washing, lavation; ablution, cleansing. 2. placer mining. 3. payment for a washing. 4. hogwash, swill for hogs. 5. (Braz., sl.): a) clyster, enema. b) reprehension, rebuke. c) (ftb.) victory by a large score.

~ **do chão** a washing up. ~ **química**, ~ **a seco** dry cleaning.

lavamento s. m. wash(ing).

lavanda s. f. (bot.) lavender.

água de ~ lavender water. **óleo de** ~ lavender oil.

lavandeira s. f. (also **lavadeira**) 1. washerwoman, laundress. 2. (Braz., ornith.) sandpiper, plover; waterchat.

lavanderia s. f. (also **lavandaria**) laundry, place where laundering is done, wash-house (plate L 3).

~ **a vapor** steam laundry.

lava-pé s. m. (pl. **lava-pés**) (bot.) blueweed, viper's bugloss.

lava-pés s. m., sg. + pl. 1. (eccl.) foot washing (on Maundy Thursday). 2. (ent.) fire ant: a stinging ant of the genus Solenopsis.

lava-pratos s. m., sg. + pl. (Braz., bot.) stinking weed.

lavar v. 1. to wash, bathe, lave; cleanse. 2. to purify, purge. 3. ~-se: a) to bathe o. s., take a bath. b) to rehabilitate, clear o. s.
~ a louça to wash up, do the dishes. ~ a roupa to wash the linen. ~ a seco to dry-clean. ~ as mãos de to wash one's hands of. ~ e passar to launder. eu me lavei I washed myself. ~-se em águas de rosas to take delight in a thing that is disagreeable to another. dia de ~ roupa wash-day. máquina de ~ roupa washing machine. posso ~ as mãos? may I have a wash? uma mão lava a outra (fig.) one good turn deserves another. roupa suja se lava em casa don't wash dirty linen in public.

lavareda s. f. (more used **labareda**) flame, blaze.

lavático, lavativo adj. abluent, laxative.

lavatório s. m. 1. lavatory, washstand; a washbasin esp. for cleansing one's face and hands (plates B 3, P 19). 2. wash(ing). 3. (fig.) purification.

lavável adj. m. + f. (pl. **-áveis**) washable.

lavor s. m. 1. labour, work, task. 2. handwork. 3. fancy needlework, embroidery. 4. fretwork, work in relief, carved work. 5. superficial cristallization in a saltern.

lavorar v. 1. to labour, work. 2. to work in relief, carve, chisel. 3. = **lavrar**.

lavoso adj. lavatic, lavic: consisting of, relating to or resembling lava.

lavoura s. f. (also **lavoira**) 1. farming, agriculture, husbandry. 2. ploughing, plowing, tillage, cultivation of land, field work.

lavra s. f. (also **lavrada**) 1. cultivation, husbandry, tillage. 2. mining: mine work. 3. fabrication, production. 4. (Braz.) a mine. 5. (Braz.) cultivation of cotton.
obras de sua ~ books written by him. de minha ~ of my own making.

lavradeira s. f. 1. woman who works on a farm, female farm hand. 2. peasant woman, country-woman. 3. needle-woman, woman who does fancy needlework.

lavradeiro adj. ploughing (animal).

lavradio s. m. farming, tillage. || adj. arable, plough-able, tillable.

lavrado s. m. 1. needlework. 2. tilled land. 3. (Braz.) jewel of pure gold. || adj. 1. wrought, worked. 2. ploughed, plowed, tilled. 3. embroidered. 4. chased, carved. 5. drawn up (of documents).
terra -a ploughed land.

lavrador s. m. 1. tiller, husbandman, farmer; peasant. 2. agricultural worker, farm hand; ploughman, plowman. 3. landowner. 4. owner of a saltern. 5. (pop., depr.) clodhopper.

lavradorita s. f. (min.) labradorite.

lavragem s. f. (pl. **-ens**) 1. tillage, cultivation. 2. ploughing, plowing, farming. 3. woodworking.

lavramento s. m. 1. ploughing, tillage. 2. coinage. 3. engraving, carving.

lavrante s. m. + f. goldsmith, silversmith. || adj. 1. ploughing, tilling. 2. engraving, carving.

lavrar v. 1. to cultivate, till. 2. to plough, plow. 3. to chisel, engrave, carve, work. 4. to chase. 5. (carp.) to plane, smooth. 6. to cut, polish (stones), hew.
~ a terra to till the soil. ~ em ata to draw up the minutes; to draft the report; to commit to paper.

lavratura s. f. (Braz.) drafting, engrossment (of a document, etc.).

lavrita s. f. (Braz., min.) carbon diamond, black diamond.

laxação s. f. (pl. **-ões**) 1. laxation, laxity, lassitude, slackness. 2. (med.) purgation.

laxante s. m. (med.) laxative, purgative. || adj. m. + f. 1. (med.) laxative, purgative, aperient. 2. loosening, slackening.

laxar v. 1. to slacken, loosen. 2. to dilate. 3. (fig.) to relieve, alliviate. 4. (med.) to purge, cause evacuation.

laxativo s. m. purgative, purging medicine. || adj. laxative, purgative.

laxidão s. f. (more used **lassidão**) 1. lassitude. 2. looseness.

laxifloro adj. (bot.) laxiflorous: having loose or scattered flowers.

laxo adj. 1. lax, loose, slack. 2. relaxed. 3. unimpeded.

lazão adj. (pl. **-ões**) (f. **lazã**) (more used **alazão**) sorrel (horse).

lazarar v. 1. to become a lazar, become infected with leprosy. 2. to contaminate with a repulsive disease.

lazarento s. m. lazar, person afflicted with some loathsome disease; leper. || adj. 1. full of sores, lazarlike, leprous. 2. = **lazeirento**.

lazareto s. m. 1. quarantine: isolation hospital. 2. lazaret, lazaretto, pesthouse.

lazaria s. f. (Braz.) epizooty of swine.

lazarina s. f. (Braz.) fowling piece.

lazarista s. m. + f. (R. C. Church) Lazarist: member of the order of St. Vincent de Paul.

lázaro s. m. 1. lazar: person infected with a repulsive disease. 2. a leper.

lazarone s. m. (It.) 1. beggar. 2. vagabond, vagrant.

lazeira s. f. 1. misery, poverty. 2. misfortune, ill luck. 3. leprosy. 4. (pop.) hunger, starvation.

lazeirento adj. 1. miserable, poor. 2. hungry, starveling.

lazer s. m. 1. leisure, laziness. 2. spare time. 3. recreation.
momentos de ~ leisure time.

lazulita s. f. (min.) lazulite, lapis lazuli, azure stone.

lazurita s. f. (min.) lazurite, azurite.

lé s. m. word used only in the expression: ~ com ~, cré com cré birds of a feather flock together.

leal s. m. (pl. **leais**) ancient Portuguese coin. || adj. m. + f. 1. loyal, faithful, true, devoted. 2. sincere, honest, frank. || ~mente adv. loyally, faithfully.
ser ~ a to keep faith with.

lealdação s. f. (pl. **-ões**) (also **lealdamento**) 1. legalization. 2. declaration at the custom-house.

lealdade s. f. 1. loyalty, faithfulness, fidelity, allegiance. 2. sincerity, honesty.

lealdado adj. very clean (sugar).

lealdador s. m. customs official.

lealdar v. 1. to legalize. 2. to declare at the custom-house.

lealdoso adj. (more usually **leal**) loyal.

leão s. m. (pl. **leões**) (f. **leoa**) 1. lion: a) (zool.) carnivorous animal of the cat family (Felis leo). b) Leão Lion: the constellation Leo. c) (fig.) very courageous or cruel man; lionheart. 2. (coll.) heartbreaker, lady-killer.
a parte do ~ the lion's share.

leão-marinho s. m. (pl. **leões-marinhos**) (zool.) sea-lion.

leãozete, leãozinho s. m. lionet, young lion.

lebracho s. m. leveret, bunny.

lebrada s. f. hare stew, jugged hare.

lebrão s. m. (pl. **-ões**) male hare.

lebre s. f. 1. (zool.) hare: mammal of the genus Lepus. 2. (astr.) the constellation Lepus.
comprar gato por ~ to buy a pig in a poke. levantar a ~ (fig.) to raise a question. passar gato por ~ to sell a gold brick.

lebré s. m. hunting dog especially trained for hares.
lebreiro adj. hunting hares (dog).
lebrel (pl. -éis), lebréu s. m. harrier: dog used to hunt hares.
lebre-marinha s. f. (pl. lebres-marinhas) (ichth.) blenny, butterfly fish.
lecanicefalóideos s. m. pl. (zool.) Lecanicephaloidea, an order of platyhelminth worms.
lecheguana s. f. (Braz.) a social wasp.
lechetrez s. m. (bot.) euphorbia, spurge.
lechia s. f. 1. litchi: tree of the soapberry family (Litchi chinensis). 2. its fruit.
lecionando s. m. pupil, student, disciple. || learning, taking lessons.
lecionar v. 1. to teach, lecture. 2. to (in)doctrinate. 3. to explain, instruct. 4. to study, learn, take lessons.
ele leciona inglês he teaches English.
lecionário s. m. (eccl.) lectionary: the book of the saints.
lecionista s. m. + f. private teacher; tutor.
lecitidáceas s. f. pl. (bot.) Lecythidaceae, a family of tropical trees of the order Myrtales.
lecitina s. f. (biochem.) lecithin: nitrogenous substance found in nerve tissues and yolk of eggs.
leco s. m. (obs.) 1. young man. 2. lackey. || adj. (Braz.) 1. weak. 2. forsaken, abandoned.
lecre s. m. (Braz., ornith.) royal flycatcher.
lectocéfalo s. m. microcephalus. || adj. microcephalic, microcephalous.
ledice s. f. 1. joyfulness, merriment, gaiety. 2. ~s pl. gallantry, facetiousness, quips.
ledo adj. 1. joyful, merry, gay, happy, glad. 2. smiling. 3. jovial. || -amente adv. joyfully; merrily.
ledor s. m. reader, peruser: person fond of reading. || adj. reading.
lega s. f. (Braz.) instrument for extracting latex.
legação s. f. (pl. -ões) legation: a) the office and dignity of a legate; legateship. b) diplomatic mission inferior in rank to an embassy. c) personnel belonging to a legation. d) place of business or the official residence of a legate. 2. bequest, legacy.
legacia s. f. legateship, legation: office or dignity of a legate.
legado s. m. 1. legate: a) ambassador, envoy. b) papal nuncio. 2. legacy, bequest.
legal adj. m. + f. (pl. -ais) 1. legal, lawful. 2. (Braz., pop.) right, correct, O.K., true. || ~mente adv. 1. legally, lawfully. 2. (Braz., pop.) correctly.
herdeiro ~ true heir. está ~ it's all right.
legalidade s. f. legality, lawfulness; conformity to law.
legalismo s. m. legalism: strict adherence to law.
legalista s. m. + f. legalist: person who insists on strict adherence to law. || adj. legalist; lawful.
legalização s. f. (pl. -ões) legalization: the act or fact of legalizing.
legalizar v. 1. to legalize: make legal, render conformable to law. 2. to authenticate, validate; certify. 3. to justify.
legar v. 1. to delegate, send as a legate, depute. 2. to bequeath: give or leave by will, devise, transmit. ~ alguma coisa a alguém to will s. th. to s. o.
legatório s. m. legatee: person to whom a legacy is bequeathed; heir; devisee. || adj. legatorial.
legenda s. f. legend: 1. story of the life of saints. 2. inscription, lettering; motto. 3. title, heading. 4. (typogr.) caption. 5. myth; fable.
~s das ilustrações (typogr.) captions.
legendário s. m. 1. legendist: writer of legends. 2. legendry: legends collectively. || adj. legendary: 1. of or pertaining to a legend or legends. 2. fabulous: of or pertaining to fables.

legião s. f. (pl. -ões) legion: 1. (ancient Rome) a body of soldiers. 2. any distinct military force or organization comparable to a Roman legion. 3. a great number, multitude, host.
~ estrangeira foreign legion.
legionário s. m. legionary: member of a legion. || adj. legionary: of or pertaining to a legion.
legislação s. f. (pl. -ões) legislation: 1. the laws enacted by the legislators. 2. lawmaking. 3. act of legislating.
legislador s. m. legislator, lawgiver, lawmaker, a member of a legislative assembly. || adj. legislating, lawgiving, lawmaking.
legisladora s. f. legislatress.
legislar v. to legislate: 1. make or enact laws. 2. exercise the function of legislator.
legislativo s. m. legislative: the legislative power. || adj. legislative: of or pertaining to legislation, lawmaking.
legislatório adj. legislatorial; lawful.
legislatura s. f. legislature: body of men authorized to make, change or repeal the laws of a country or state.
legislável adj. m. + f. (pl. -áveis) liable to become lawful.
legisperito s. m. jurisconsult: person skilled in law, jurist.
legista s. m. + f. legist, jurist, legal expert, lawyer.
legítima s. f. 1. (jur.) legitime: the children's obligatory share of an inheritance. 2. division of a saltern.
legitimação s. f. (pl. -ões) legitimation, legitimization: legalization, authentication, attestation.
legitimado s. m. legitimized child. || adj. legitimate(d) (child).
legitimador s. m. person who legitimates or legalizes. || adj. legitimating.
legitimar v. 1. to legitimate: a) make legitimate (a child). b) legalize, make lawful; authenticate, attest. 2. to justify. 3. ~-se to prove one's identity.
legitimidade s. f. 1. legitimacy, legitimateness. 2. legality, lawfulness; rightness. 3. authenticity, genuineness. 4. legitimism.
legitimismo s. m. legitimism; the doctrine of the Legitimists.
legitimista s. m. + f. 1. (Fr. hist.) supporter of the claim to the throne of the elder branch of the Bourbons. 2. by extension: supporter of legitimate authority. || adj. legitimistic.
legítimo adj. 1. legitimate: a) lawful, legal. b) rightful. c) true, genuine, real, authentic. d) lawfully begotten, born in wedlock. 2. reasonable, justified. || legitimamente adv. legitimately, lawfully.
-a defesa self-defense. filho ~ legitimate child. herdeiro ~ heir apparent. ouro ~ true gold.
legível adj. m. + f. (pl. -íveis) legible, readable: that may be read easily; written plainly. || legivelmente adv. legibly.
ter letra ~ to write a clear hand.
legra s. f. 1. (surg.) xyster, raspatory. 2. a mason's jointer.
legração s. f. (pl. -ões), legradura (surg.) scraping of bones.
legrar v. (surg.) to scrape a bone.
legre s. m. (S. Braz.) a horseshoer's knife.
légua s. f. league, measure of distance (in Portugal equal to 6,179.74 meters; in Brazil equal to 6,000 meters = 3.72 miles).
~ de sesmaria (Braz.) measure equal to 6,600 meters. ~ marítima marine league (in Braz. equal to 5,555 meters = 3.45 miles).
leguelhé s. m. (Braz.) a nobody.

leguleio s. m. 1. stickler. 2. pettifogger, trickster. 3. pettifogging lawyer.

legume s. m. (bot.) 1. legume: a) any edible vegetable. b) fruit of the leguminous plants, as string--beans. 2. ~s pl. (Braz.) pot-herbs, vegetables, greens. ~s frescos green vegetables. ~s em conservas preserved vegetables.

legumina s. f. legumin: globulin obtained from legumes.

leguminário adj. (bot.) leguminous: bearing legumes.

leguminiforme adj. m. + f. (bot.) leguminiform: having the form of legumes.

leguminívoro adj. feeding on legumes; vegetarian.

leguminosas s. f. pl. (bot.) Leguminosae, a large order of dicotyledonous plants.

legumista s. m. + f. a legume grower, person who grows vegetables.

lei s. f. 1. law: a) (jur.) rule of conduct prescribed by the authorities; jurisprudence. b) decree, edict. c) commandment. d) control of law. 2. norm, standard, rule, statute, settled principle. 3. (fig.) religion, doctrine, principle.
~ **agrária** agrarian law. ~ **civil** civil law. ~ **criminal** criminal law. ~ **da guerra** rules of war. ~ **da necessidade** law of necessity. ~ **das nações** law of nations. ~ **de Deus** testimony. ~ **de Lynch** lynch law. ~ **de oferta e procura** the law of supply and demand. ~ **de talião** talion, retaliation. ~ **divina** divine law. ~ **do imposto** finance bill. ~ **do selo** stamp act. ~ **do trabalho** statute of labourers. ~ **fundamental** basic law. ~ **marcial** martial law. ~ **militar** military law. ~ **moral** moral law. ~ **seca** dry law. à ~ **de** according to general usage. dar a ~ (fig.) to boss the show; to bully. impor a ~ to inforce, lay down the law. fora da ~ unlawful. fora-da-lei outlaw (person). madeira de ~ hardwood. a necessidade não tem ~ necessity has no law. obediente à ~ law-abiding. ouro de ~ solid (standard) gold. passar a ~ (um projeto) to go or pass into law (a bill). por ~ by law. sem ~ lawless. transgressor da ~ lawbreaker.

leiaute s. m. layout.

leicenço s. m. phlegmon, furuncle, felon.

leigaço s. m. very ignorant person. || adj. very ignorant.

leigal adj. m. + f. (pl. -ais) laic(al): of or pertaining to a layman.

leigar v. (obs.) 1. to laicize, secularize. 2. ~-se to become laical.

leigo s. m. 1. layman, laic. 2. outsider, person who does not belong to a particular profession. || adj. 1. laic(al), lay, secular. 2. unprofessional, not expert. || -amente adv. laically.

leiguice s. f. laical procedure; laicality.

leilão s. m. (pl. -ões) auction: public sale, outcry. pôr em ~ to sell by (at) auction. ser vendido em ~ to come under the hammer. vender em ~ to auction off.

leiloamento s. m. auctioning.

leiloar v. to auction, outcry, auctioneer, sell by auction.

leiloeiro s. m. auctioneer: 1. person who sells at auctions. 2. organizer of an auction.

leira s. f. 1. parterre or bed of a garden. 2. ridge between two furrows.

leirão s. m. (pl. -ões) (N. Braz., agric., hort.) a large bed.

leirar v. (agric., hort.) to divide into beds.

leishmaniose s. f. (med.) leishmaniasis, leishmaniosis.

leita s. f. fish milt.

leitado adj. that produces a milky sap (as a fig).

leitão s. m. (pl. -ões) (f. leitoa) a sucking pig, shoat. em ~ (Port.) stark-naked.

leitar v. to yield a milky sap (as a fig). || adj. milky, white like milk.

leite s. m. 1. milk. 2. (bot.) the white juice of some plants.
~ **coalhado** sour milk. ~ **condensado** condensed milk. ~ **de cal** milk of lime. ~ **de pato** (fig.) a no-stakes game. ~ **desnatado** skim milk. ~ **em pó** powdered or dried milk. ~ **integral**, ~ **gordo** rich milk. ~ **magro** skim milk. ~ **materno** mother's milk, suck. a ~ **de pato** (Braz., fig.) without gain. criar sem ~ **materno** to dry-nurse, bring up by hand. dente de ~ milk tooth. frango de ~ (Braz.) young chicken. irmão de ~ foster-brother. tirar o ~ **de uma vaca** to milk a cow. tirar leite de vaca morta (S. Braz., pop.) to cry over spilt milk.

leite-de-cachorro s. m. (pl. leites-de-cachorro) (bot.) milkweed.

leite-de-galinha s. f. (pl. leites-de-galinha) (bot.) star--of-Bethlehem, sleepy dick.

leitegada s. f. (pop.) a litter of pigs.

leiteira s. f. 1. milkmaid, dairy woman. 2. a milkman's wife. 3. milk jug (plate M 8). 4. (bot.) a species of milkwood (Sapium aucuparium).

leiteiro s. m. 1. milkman: man who sells milk. 2. (bot.) cow milk. || adj. 1. milky. 2. yielding milk.

leitelho s. m. buttermilk.

leitento adj. milky, lacteous: 1. yielding milk. 2. yielding a milklike sap (plant).

leiteria s. f. (also leitaria) dairy, creamery: 1. place where cheese and butter are made. 2. establishment where milk and milk products are sold.

leitneriáceas s. f. pl. (bot.) Leitneriaceae, a family of dicotyledonous plants of the order Leitneriales.

leito s. m. 1. bed: bedstead; berth, cot, couch, bunk, anything to sleep or rest on. 2. frame. 3. (archit., tech.) substructure.
~ **de estrada** road bed. ~ **de morte** death-bed. ~ **de rio** river-bed. ~ **de um córrego** watercourse. ~ **inferior (superior)** lower (upper) berth. guardar o ~ to keep the bed, be bedridden.

leitoa s. f. female sucking-pig.

leitoada s. f. 1. (also leitegada) a litter of pigs. 2. meal consisting mainly of the meat of sucking--pigs.

leitoado adj. 1. fat, obese. 2. sleek, glossy.

leitor s. m. 1. reader: person who reads; lecturer. 2. lector: an ecclesiastic in minor orders. || adj. reading.
~ **de provas** proof-reader, press corrector, press reader.

leitorado s. m. 1. readership, lectureship: office or function of a reader. 2. time spent in reading. 3. (eccl.) lectorate: office of a lector.

leitoso adj. milky: resembling milk, lacteal, lactescent.

leitura s. f. reading: 1. act, practice or art of one who reads. 2. perusal, lection. 3. lecture. 4. (fig.) knowledge, scholarship. 5. material intended to be read.
~ **da ata** reading of the minutes. ~ **em voz alta** reading aloud. ~ **labial** lip-reading. sala de ~ reading-room.

leiva s. f. 1. ploughed land, land under cultivation. 2. furrow (plate C 13). 3. ridge between furrows. 4. field, glebe.

leixamento s. m. (obs.) forsaking; distress.

leixão s. m. (pl. -ões) 1. cliff. 2. islet.

leixar v. (obs.) to abandon, forsake, leave.

lelé s. m. (Braz., sl.) nuts, silly person. || adj. m. + f. silly, crazy, nutty, insane.

lelê s. m. (Braz., pop.) 1. confusion, disorder. 2. intrigue, plot.

lema s. m. 1. lemma: auxiliary proposition used in the demonstration of an other proposition; premise. 2. (fig.) motto, device, saying, epigraph.

lemático adj. 1. of or concerning a lemma. 2. (fig.) of or pertaining to a motto.

lembradiço s. m. person with a good memory. ‖ adj. retentive (memory).

lembrado adj. 1. mindful. 2. remembered, unforgotten. 3. memorable. 4. retentive (memory).

digno de ser ~ noteworthy, worth while to be remembered. estar ~ to remember. se eu estou bem ~... if I remember rightly...

lembrador s. m. reminder, rememberer. ‖ adj. remindful, remembering.

lembrança s. f. 1. remembrance, recollection. 2. relic; memento, memorial, souvenir. 3. gift, keepsake, present. 4. memory, mind. 5. reminder. 6. advice, counsel, hint. 7. admonition. 8. ~s pl. regards, greetings, compliments.

~s à família! give my kindest regards to your family!, remember me to the folks! segundo a minha ~ as far as I can remember. trazer à ~ to remind.

lembrar v. 1. to remind. 2. to suggest, prompt, advise, advert. 3. to recollect. 4. to recall to mind. 5. to occur. 6. ~-se to remember, recollect, bear in mind.

lembra-se de suas palavras? can you recall his words? lembrei-me vagamente disto I sort of remembered it. lembre-se do que eu lhe disse mind what I have told you. lembrei-o de sua promessa I put him in mind of his promise. lembre-se de que... bear in mind that... isto me faz ~ que... that reminds me that... não me lembrei disto I did not think of it. não me lembro de mais nada I don't remember anything more. não me lembro do nome dele I cannot think of his name. você se lembra daquilo? do you remember it?

lembrete s. m. 1. memorandum, note. 2. (fam.) admonition, reprimand, rebuke, remonstrance.

leme s. m. 1. rudder, helm (plates A 3, B 8, L 2). 2. (fig.) government, direction, control. 3. steerage.

~ de inclinação (aeron.) aileron. ~ de profundidade 1. (aeron.) elevator (plate A 3). 2. (naut.) depth rudder. ~ horizontal (aeron.) tailplane (plate A 3). ir ao ~ to steer, guide, direct. perder o ~ (fig.) to lose one's head. sem ~ helmless, rudderless. ter o ~ to govern, direct, control.

lemingue s. m. (zool.) lemming.

lemiste s. m. very fine woollen black fabric.

lemna s. f. (bot.) lemna, duckweed.

lemnáceas s. f. pl. (bot.) Lemnaceae, the duckweed family.

lemniscata s. f. (geom.) lemniscate: curve of the general form of a figure 8.

lemnisco s. m. lemniscus: 1. (Roman hist.) fillet or ribbon. 2. the character ÷ employed by ancient textual critics.

lempa s. f. a pearl fished off some Braz. islands.

lemural adj. m. + f. (pl. -ais) (zool.) lemuroid: of or referring to lemurs.

lêmure s. m. 1. (zool.) lemur: a monkeylike animal of the family Lemuridae. 2. ~s pl. spirits, spectres.

~ de Madagáscar (zool.) aye-aye. ~ volante (zool.) flying lemur.

lemuriano s. m. (zool.) lemur. ‖ adj. lemuroid.

lemuróides s. m. pl. (zool.) Lemuroidea, a suborder of Primates comprising the lemurs, lorises, and tarsiers.

lena s. f. bawd, procuress.

lençaria s. f. 1. factory where handkerchiefs or neckerchiefs are made. 2. store where handkerchiefs or neckerchiefs are sold; a linen draper's shop. 3. great quantity of handkerchiefs. 4. linen, white goods.

lenço s. m. 1. handkerchief (plate R 7). 2. neckerchief; neckcloth. 3. kerchief: piece of cloth worn as a covering for the head.

lençol s. m. (pl. lençóis) sheet: a broad piece of linen or cotton used as a covering for a bed (plate C 7). ~ d'água, ~ freático ground water (plate F 7). ele estava branco como um ~ he was white as a sheet. ele está em maus lençóis he is in deep water, things are at a low ebb with him; he is in a fix. isto me deixa em maus lençóis that puts me in a bad spot.

lenda s. f. 1. legend, folk-tale. 2. myth, fable, fiction. 3 (fig.): a) lie, made up story. b) a tiresome story.

lendário adj. 1. legendary. 2. fabulous, mythical. 3. traditional.

lêndea s. f. 1. nit: the egg of a louse. 2. fragment; piece, insignificance.

lendeaço s. m. a great quantity of nits.

lendeoso adj. nitty: infested with nits.

lene adj. m. + f. smooth, soft, suave.

lêneo adj. Bacchic: of Bacchus, concerning Bacchus.

lengalenga s. f. 1. prolix discourse, tedious narrative or recital. 2. idle talk, balderdash. 3. rigmarole, rambling talk.

vamos parar com essa ~! let us come to an end with this silly talk!

lengalengar v. to speak monotonously.

lenha s. f. 1. firewood; fuel. 2. (fam.) beating, blow with a stick.

deitar ~ ao fogo to add fuel to the fire. entrar na ~ (Braz., fig.) to be beaten with a stick. levar ~ para o mato to carry coals to Newcastle. pôr ~ na fogueira to pour oil on the flames.

lenha-branca s. f. (pl. lenhas-brancas) plant of the staff tree family.

lenhador s. m. (also lenhateiro) woodcutter, log man; lumberman, woodman.

lenhar v. 1. to cleave or cut wood or logs. 2. to cut firewood.

lenheira s. f. (S. Braz.) place in woods from which firewood is cut.

lenheiro s. m. 1. woodcutter, woodman. 2. dealer in firewood. 3. (Braz.) woodbin: bin for holding firewood.

lenhificar v. to lignify: become woody.

lenho s. m. 1. xylem: woody tissue. 2. wood, log, trunk, stem. 3. timber. 4. bough. 5. (fig.) ship, vessel.

~ da cruz the cross of Jesus. Santo Lenho the Holy Cross.

lenhoso adj. ligneous, woody: 1. of the nature of wood. 2. consisting of or resembling wood.

lenidade, leniência s. f. lenity, leniency, softness, mildness, gentleness.

leniente adj. m. + f. lenient, softening, lenitive.

lenificar v. 1. to lenify, soften. 2. to assuage, mitigate.

lenimento s. m. 1. lenitive: a) palliative medicine to ease pain. b) anything which softens or mitigates. 2. liniment.

leninismo s. m. (pol.) Leninism.

lenir v. 1. to lenify, soften, soothe. 2. to assuage, mitigate, ease, alleviate.

lenitivo s. m. 1. lenitive, palliative, liniment, balsam, balm. 2. (fig.) mitigation. 3. relief, easement. 4. consolation. ‖ adj. 1. lenitive, emollient, softening. 2. mitigating, soothing.

lenoáceas s. f. pl. (bot.) Lennoaceae, a family of dicotyledonous, tubiflorous plants.

lenocínio s. m. panderage, pimpery.

lenqüência s. f. (N. Braz., pop.) talk, discourse, speech, eloquence.

lentar v. (also **lentescer**) 1. to moisten, damp. 2. to grow moist.

lente (I) s. f. lens (plates B 13, E 5, L 1, M 9). ~ **bicôncava** double-concave lens. ~ **bifocal** bifocal lens. ~ **de aumento** magnifying glass (plate L 1). ~ **de lanterna** bull's eye (lantern). ~ **divergente** diverging lens. ~ **para leitura** hand glass, reading glass (plate L 1).

lente (II) s. m. + f. 1. university professor. 2. teacher, master. 3. (obs.) lecturer, reader. ‖ adj. lecturing; reading.

lenteiro s. m. 1. a watery tract of land. 2. marsh, swamp, slough.

lentejar v. 1. to moisten, damp, wet. 2. to refresh. 3. to become moist.

lentejoula s. f. (also **lantejoula, lantejoila, lentejoila**) spangle, sequin: ornamental metal disk for dresses.

lentejoular v. (also **lentejoilar**) to spangle: adorn with a spangle or sequin.

lentescente adj. m. + f. 1. humid, moist, wet. 2. sticky, clammy, viscous.

lentescer v. 1. to moisten, damp. 2. to grow moist.

lenteza s. f. 1. slowness, lentitude. 2. dampness, moistness.

lenticela s. f. lenticel: one of the cortical pores in the stems of woody plants through which respiration takes place.

lentícula s. f. lenticula: small lens.

lenticular s. m. instrument to pierce the hoof of a horse. ‖ adj. m. + f. 1. lenticular: a) of or pertaining to a lens. b) resembling a lentil in size or form. c) having the form of a double-convex lens (as some seeds). 2. said of two ossicles of the ear.

lentidão s. f. 1. slowness, lentitude. 2. sluggishness. 3. delay, long wait. 4. moistness, dampness.

lentiforme adj. m. + f. lentiform, lenticular.

lentigem s. f. (pl. **-ens**) (also **lentigo** m.) lentigo: a freckly pigmentation of the skin.

lentiginoso adj. lentiginous, freckly.

lentígrado adj. slow-gaited, walking slowly.

lentilha s. f. 1. lentil: a) the annual leguminous plant of the pea family (Lens esculenta). b) its seeds. 2. carbuncle, anthrax.

lentilha-d'água s. f. (pl. **lentilhas-d'água**) (bot.) 1. duckweed. 2. water lettuce.

lentilhoso adj. abounding in lentils.

lentiscal s. m. (pl. **-ais**) (also **lentisqueira** f.) lentisk grove.

lentisco s. m. (bot.) lentiscus, mastic tree.

lento adj. 1. slow. 2. laggard, sluggish, tardy, dilatory, lingering. 3. lazy, indolent. 4. prolongued. 5. damp, moist. 6. loose, slack; dull. 7. flabby, remiss. 8. (mus.) lento. ‖ **-amente** adv. slowly, laggardly.
fogão de combustão -a slow-combustion stove. **marcha -a** (mec.) slow running. **muito ~ as** slow as a tortoise.

lentor s. m. = **lentidão**.

lentura s. f. 1. slowness. 2. moisture, dampness, humidity. 3. dew. 4. night air. 5. (pop.) sweat.

leoa s. f. 1. (zool.) lioness: female lion. 2. (fig.): a) shrew, termagant. b) an elegant woman.

leocádio s. m. (N. Braz.) chandelier.

leonado adj. lion-coloured, tawny.

leônculo s. m. lionet.

leoneira s. f. 1. a lion's den or cavern. 2. a lion's cage.

leonês s. m. (pl. **-esses**) (f. **-esa**) Leonese: native or inhabitant of the province or city of León in Spain. ‖ adj. Leonese: of or pertaining to the ancient kingdom of León in Spain.

leônico adj. 1. lionesque. 2. (anat.) sublingual (veins).

leonino adj. 1. leonine: a) pertaining to or resembling a lion. b) lionlike. c) (pros.) consisting of metrical Latin hexameters. 2. lionesque. 3. (fig.) perfidious, treacherous; fraudulent. **verso ~** leonine verse.

leontíase s. f. (med.) leontiasis. ~ **óssea** leontiasis ossea.

leopardo s. m. leopard: a large and wild spotted cat (Felix pardus).

lepas s. m. (zool.) goose barnacle.

lépido adj. 1. gay, merry, cheerful. 2. jovial, jolly, pleasant, sprightly. 3. jaunty. 4. jocose. 5. quick, swift. 6. lively, spry. ‖ **lepidamente** adv. 1. pleasantly. 2. quickly. 3. livelily.

lepidodendro s. m. Lepidodendron: a common fossil plant.

lepidóideo adj. lepidoid, like scales, flaky.

lepidólita s. f. (min.) lepidolite: lithia mica.

lepidópteros s. m. pl. (ent.) Lepidoptera, an order of arthropod insects (butterflies and moths).

lepidossirene s. f. (ichth.) lepidosiren.

leporídeo s. m. leporid: a hare or rabbit of the family Leporidae. ‖ adj. leporid: of or pertaining to the Leporidae.

leporino adj. leporine: of, pertaining to or like a hare. **lábio ~** (med.) harelip.

leporíneos s. m. pl. (icht.) a group of fresh-water fishes inhabitating S. American rivers (genus Leporinus).

lepra s. f. 1. (med.) (also **morféia, mal de Hansen**) leprosy: a chronic endemic infectious disease, also called Hansen's disease. 2. dog mange. 3. (fig.) moral corruption. 4. (S. Braz.) scoundrel.

leprologia s. f. leprology.

leprologista s. m. + f., **leprólogo** m. leprologist.

leprosaria s. f., **leprosário** m. leprosery, leprosarium: hospital for the treatment of leprosy.

leproso s. m. 1. (also **lazarento, hanseniano**) leper, lazar. 2. (fig.) nasty person. ‖ adj. 1. leprous: infected with leprosy. 2. (fig.) nasty, loathsome, repugnant.

leptinito s. m. (petrog.) leptynite.

leptocárdios s. m. pl. (zool.) Leptocardii, a class of Chordata.

leptodonte adj. m. + f. (zool.) small-toothed.

leptofilo adj. (bot.) leptophyllous, slender-leaved.

leptologia s. f. leptology: minute and detailed speech or description.

leptomedusas s. f. pl. (zool.) Leptomedusae, an order of hydrozoans.

leptomórfico adj. (geol.) leptomorphic.

leptoprosopo adj. (physiol.) leptoprosopic: having a long narrow face.

leptorrino s. m. (physiol.) leptorrhinian. ‖ adj. leptorrhine.

leque s. m. 1. fan: device to make a current of air. 2. fanlike curve in a stair. 3. (Braz., zool.) mollusc of the family Pectinideae (as the scallop) (Pecten nodosus). ~ **de aluvião** (geol.) fan delta. **antena em ~** fan aerial.

lequéssia s. f. (N. Braz.) 1. drunkenness. 2. idleness, loafing.

ler v. 1. to read, peruse. 2. to interpret, give a certain meaning to (a text). 3. to recite, rehearse. 4. to lecture, give a lesson on. 5. to learn, study. ~ **a sorte de** to tell or read the fortune of. ~ **de cadeira** to master a subject completely. ~ **correntemente** to read fluently. ~ **demais** to overread o. s. ~ **do princípio ao fim** to read over or through. ~ **em voz alta** to read aloud, call over. ~ **entre**

as linhas to read between the lines. ~ **mal** to misread. ~ **música** to read music. ~ **para si** to read to o. s. ~ **por alto** to read superficially, skim over. ~ **por cima** to read without spelling. ~ **provas** to read proofs. ~ **repetidamente** to read repeatedly, con. **este livro é agradável de** ~ this book reads well. **eu li um bom livro** I read a good book. **tornar a** ~ to read over again.

lerca s. f. 1. a lean cow. 2. ~**s** pl. wrinkled skin; dewlap.

lerdaço adj. foolish, slow-witted, dull.

lerdeador adj. (Braz.) phlegmatic, sluggish; slow-paced.

lerdear v. (Braz.) 1. to loiter, delay, retard, dillydally. 2. to be slow. 3. to walk slowly.

lerdeza, lerdice s. f. (Braz.) slowness, tardiness, sluggishness, slothfulness.

lerdo adj. 1. slow, laggard. 2. dull, torpid, stupid, slow-witted, blunt. 3. clumsy, awkward, boorish. 4. shy, timid. ‖ **-amente** adv. 1. slowly. 2. dully. **ele é muito** ~ he is a dawdler.

leréia, léria s. f. 1. rigmarole. 2. idle talk, idle chatter, tawdle. 3. smooth talk. 4. verbosity. 5. fallaciousness.

lero-lero s. m. (pl. **lero-leros**) (Braz., sl.) tawdle, idle talk.

lés s. m. word used in the expression: **de** ~ **a** ~ from end to end, from side to side.

lesado adj. 1. injured, wounded; hurt. 2. damaged. 3. tarnished (as in reputation). 4. aggrieved. 5. (N. Braz.) forgetful, slightly touched.

ele foi ~ **em duzentos cruzeiros** he was cheated out of 200 cruzeiros.

lesa-majestade s. f. (jur.) lese majesty.

lesante s. m. + f. injurer, person who causes damages to another or tarnishes his reputation. ‖ adj. injuring, hurting.

lesão s. f. (pl. **-ões**) 1. lesion: a) hurt, wound, injury, detriment. b) (med.) any morbid change in the structure of organs. 2. financial loss, prejudice. 3. (jur.) wrong, grievance, offense.

lesa-pátria s. f. (pl. **lesas-pátrias**) a crime or offense commited against the country.

lesar v. 1. to injure, hurt, wound. 2. to damage. 3. to bruise, batter. 4. to aggrieve, wrong. 5. to cheat, rook. 6. to prejudice. 7. (Braz.): a) to twaddle. b) to roam, wander.

lesbianismo s. m. Lesbianism: homosexual relations between women.

lesbiano, lésbico adj. Lesbian: 1. of or pertaining to Lesbos. 2. of or referring to Lesbianism.

lésbio s. m. Lesbian: native or inhabitant of Lesbos. ‖ adj. Lesbian: 1. of or pertaining to Lesbos. 2. of or referring to Lesbianism.

lesco-lesco s. m. (pl. **lesco-lescos**) (Braz., sl.) chore, a day-to-day tedious work.

leseira s. f. (N. Braz.) 1. idiotism, foolishness, stupidity. 2. m. + f. fool, simpleton, numskull.

lesivo adj. injurious: 1. hurtful, prejudicial. 2. offensive.

lesma (ê) s. f. (zool.) 1. any of the terrestrial pulmonate gastropods, snail. 2. a slow-moving person, sluggard.

com a velocidade de ~ at a snail's pace.

lesma-do-mar s. f. (pl. **lesmas-do-mar**) (zool.) holothurian, sea cucumber.

lesmar v. 1. to dawdle, loaf. 2. to saunter lazily.

lés-nordeste s. m. east-northeast.

leso adj. 1. injured, hurt, wounded. 2. offended, wronged. 3. damaged. 4. cheated. 5. (Braz.) foolish, crazy. 6. paralytic.

lés-sueste s. m. east-southeast.

leste s. m. 1. east: a) the direction of sunrise; eastward. b) the Orient. 2. east wind.

a (para) ~ easterly, eastward. **ao** ~ **de** in the east of. **vento do** ~ east wind.

lesto adj. 1. light, quick, agile, nimble. 2. rapid, fast. 3. active, spry, alert, brisk.

letal adj. m. + f. (pl. **-ais**) lethal, deadly, fatal, mortal. ‖ ~**mente** adv. deadly, mortally.

letalidade s. f. lethality, deadliness.

letão s. m. 1. (pl. **-ões**) Lett. 2. Lettish: language spoken by the Letts. ‖ adj. Lettish, Lettic.

letargia s. f. 1. (med.) lethargy: morbid drowsiness, profound sleep. 2. apathy, dullness, inactivity, indifference. 3. stupor, torpor.

letargiar v. to lethargize.

letárgico adj. 1. lethargic(al): of or pertaining to lethargy, drowsy. 2 (fig.) indolent. 3. apathetic, torpid, dull. ‖ **letargicamente** adv. lethargically.

letargo s. m. lethargy.

leteu adj. (f. **letéia**) Lethean, infernal.

lético s. m. Lettish: the language of the Letts. ‖ adj. Lettish: of or pertaining to the Letts or their language.

letífero adj. lethiferous, lethal, mortiferous, deadly.

letificante adj. m. + f. gladsome, causing joy, cheerful, frolicsome.

letificar v. 1. to gladden. 2. to rejoice. 3. to cheer up.

letífico adj. 1. lethal, lethiferous, deadly, mortal. 2. gladsome, causing joy.

letivo adj. concerning (school) teaching or a period of learning.

ano ~ school year.

letomania s. f. morbid mania of suicide.

letra s. f. 1. letter: a) an alphabetical character or symbol. b) written communication. c) handwriting. d) (typogr.) type. 2. literal meaning. 3. the word's of a tune. 4. inscription. 5. (com.) promissory note. 6. ~**s** pl. literature, art, culture, learning.

~ **a** ~ word by word, literally. ~ **à vista** (com.) sight-bill, bill payable on sight. ~ **de câmbio** bill of exchange, draft. ~ **de forma** printing type, block-letter, round hand. ~ **gótica** Gothic letter, black-letter. ~ **maiúscula** capital letter, upper case letter (plate L 4). ~ **minúscula** minuscule, lower case letter (plate L 4). ~ **morta** a written promise which has not been kept. ~**s vencidas** due bills. **à** ~, **ao pé da** ~ literally. **em** ~**s gregas** in Greek characters. **homem de** ~**s** man of letters, literary man. **ter boa** ~ to have a good handwriting, write a good hand. **tomar ao pé da** ~ to take literally.

letradete adj. half-learned.

letradice s. f. 1. presumption of learnedness. 2. empty talk. 3. swagger.

letrado s. m. 1. man of letters, scholar, savant. 2. lawyer. 3. literate. ‖ adj. 1. lettered, learned. 2. erudite. 3. literate, literary. ‖ **-amente** adv. learnedly.

letreirista s. m. + f. (Braz., typogr.) 1. poster artist. 2. a worker who mounts posters.

letreiro s. m. 1. lettering. 2. label, ticket. 3. inscription, title. 4. (fig.) poster, placard.

letrilha s. f. a little poem to be sung.

letrista s. m. + f. (Braz.) 1. (typogr.) letterer, lettering artist. 2. sign painter.

léu s. m. 1. time; leisure, idleness. 2. opportunity, occasion, chance.

ao ~ aimlessly, at leisure. **com a cabeça ao** ~ bareheaded, hatless.

leucanto adj. (bot.) leucanthous, white-flowered.

leucemia s. f. (med.) leuk(a)emia.

leucina s. f. (biochem.) leucin(e).

leucita s. f. (min.) leucite (a potassium aluminium silicate).

leucito s. m. (bot.) leucoplast.
leucocarpo adj. (bot.) leucocarpous: producing white fruit.
leucocéfalo adj. (zool.) white-headed.
leucócito s. m. leucocyte: a white corpuscle of the blood.
leucócomo adj. 1. white-haired. 2. (bot.) white-leaved.
leucodonte adj. m. + f. (zool.) white-toothed.
leucoma s. m. (med.) leucoma, albugo: a white opacity in the cornea of the eye.
leucomaína s. f. (biochem.) leucomaine: alkaloid substance produced in the living animal body.
leucopatia s. f. leucopathy, albinism.
leucopático adj. leucopathic, albinistic.
leucorréia s. f. (med.) leucorrh(o)ea: a white mucous discharge from the vagina.
leucorréico adj. leucorrh(o)eal: of or referring to leucorrh(o)ea.
leuquemia s. f. (med., also **leucemia**) leuk(a)emia: morbid condition caused by an excess of leucocytes.
leuquêmico adj. leuk(a)emic: pertaining to or affected with leuk(a)emia.
leva s. f. 1. (naut.) the weighing of the anchor; hence: departure. 2. recruitment, levy of troops. 3. lot (soldiers, prisioners), batch; convoy of prisoners. 4. (pop.) pace, gait.
uma nova ~ de soldados partiu para a frente a new batch of soldiers left for the front.
levação s. f. (pl. **-ões**) 1. swelling. 2. malignant tumour. 3. height, elevation.
levada s. f. 1. a taking or carrying off or away. 2. leat, mill-stream, mill-race, sluice. 3. (Braz.) slope; hill, elevation.
de ~ overhasty.
leva-dente s. m. (pl. **leva-dentes**) (pop.) 1. bite, tooth marks. 2. rebuke, reprehension.
levadia s. f. (Braz.) swelling of the sea.
levadiça s. f. (Braz.) drawbridge: a bridge that can be lifted, lowered or moved to one side.
levadiço adj. 1. movable, mobile. 2. capable of being lifted or lowered.
levadio adj. said of the roof which has loose tiles.
levado adj. (Braz.) 1. mischievous, impish, rompish, naughty. 2. unquiet, fidgety. 3. undisciplinated, disobedient, wayward.
ele é um menino ~ da breca he is a mischievous boy. **uma mocinha ~a** a chit of a girl.
levador s. m. transporter, conveyer. ‖ adj. carrying, conveying, transporting.
levadoura s. f. (also **levadoira**, naut.) a vessel with transshipment appliances.
leva-e-traz s. m. + f., sg. + pl. (Braz.) talebearer, intriguer.
levamento s. m. 1. taking away. 2. theft, stealing.
levantada s. f. 1. act of lifting. 2. rising; getting up, uprising.
levantadiço adj. 1. unruly, disobedient. 2. unquiet, restless, turbulent, refractory, rebellious. 3. careless, heedless. 4. unreasoning, thoughtless.
levantado adj. 1. upright, erect. 2. up, out of bed. 3. lifted, raised. 4. high, elevated, sublime, noble, lofty. 5. rough, heavy (sea). 6. uprisen, insurgent. 7. riotous, seditious. 8. heedless, rash.
levantador s. m. (surg.) levator: 1. instrument to raise depressed parts of the skull. 2. (anat.) lifting muscle. ‖ adj. 1. lifting, raising. 2. seditious, rebellious.
levantadura s. f., **levantamento** m. 1. lifting, raising. 2. elevation, rise; erection. 3. survey (land). 4. insurrection, rebellion. 5. a gathering or collecting of facts.
~ de mapas ordnance survey.

levantante adj. m. + f. (her.) rampant: reared up.
levantar s. m. rising, getting up, uprising. ‖ v. 1. to lift (up), raise (up), elevate. 2. to rise, set upright. 3. to stand or get up, get on one's legs. 4. to erect, build, construct. 5. to hoist, heave, run up. 6. to pick up, take up. 7. to heighten. 8. to levy, recruit. 9. to ennoble; dignify, give a push to. 10. to draw (money). 11. to close, conclude (a session). 12. to survey (land). 13. **~-se:** a) to rise. b) to arise, get or stand up. c) to upraise. d) to rebel. e) to get excited, exalt o. s. f) to arrive, be successful. g) to surge, appear (stars).
~ acampamento to break camp, pull up stakes. **~ a caça** to spring the game. **~ o cerco ou sítio** (mil.) to raise the siege. **~ a crista** (fig.) to show arrogance, defy. **~ dúvidas** to raise doubts. **~-se contra** to stand up against. **~-se de repente** to jump up. **~ falso testemunho** to accuse one falsely, calumniate. **~ ferro** (naut.) to weigh anchor. **~ fervura** to begin to boil. **~ a mão contra** to raise (one's) hand against. **~ a mesa** to clean the table. **~ objeções** to object. **~ os ombros** to shrug one's shoulders. **~ o pano** to raise the curtain, to ring up. **~ poeira** to raise dust. **~ -se com o pé esquerdo** (fig.) to get out of the bed on the wrong side, get up in a bad humour. **~ um brinde** to raise a toast. **~ uma lebre** to start a hare. **~ uma queixa contra** to bring an accusation against. **~ uma questão** to put a question. **~ um protesto** to enter a protest. **~ vôo** (aeron.) to take off, take the air. **~ a voz** to lift the voice. **a ave levantou vôo** the bird took flight. **a névoa matinal levanta-se dos prados** the morning mist arises from the meadows. **a que horas se levanta?** at what time do you get up? **ela levantou-se** she sat up. **ela já pode ~-se** she is getting about again. **ele levantou as mãos** he threw up his hands. **ele levantou-se com esforço** he struggled to his feet. **ele não pode ~(-se) da cama** he can't stir from his bed. **eles se levantaram** they stood up. **levantaram os copos** they clicked glasses. **levantei-me da cama** I rose from my bed. **levanto-me às seis** I get up at six o'clock. **levantou-se uma tempestade** a storm rose. **o pássaro levantou vôo céu adentro para o ninho** the bird winged the sky, to its nest. **o avião deve ~ vôo às 12 horas** the plane is timed to take off at 12. **o senhor levanta-se muito cedo** you get up very early.
levante s. m. 1. East, Orient. 2. the Levant. 3. (fig.) mutiny, insurrection. 4. (Braz., bot.) horsemint.
de ~ 1. headlessly. 2. ready to leave.
levantino s. m. Levantine: native or inhabitant of the Levant. ‖ adj. (also **levântico**) Levantine: of or pertaining to the Levant.
levanto s. m. starting or springing of game.
levar v. 1. to carry, take (away), bear, remove. 2. to convey, transport, drive. 3. to lead, guide, conduct; (fig.) to induce. 4. to kill (sickness). 5. to push, drag (away) (of water). 6. to obtain, get, receive, gain, win. 7. to seize, steal, snatch away. 8. to hold, contain (as a vessel). 9. to need, require (time). 10. to spend, pass (life).
~ a cabo to realize, accomplish. **~ a efeito** to make it true, realize. **~ à força** to take by force. **~ alguma coisa consigo** to carry about s. th. with one. **~ a mal** to take amiss, be displeased at. **~ à mão** to carry by hand. **~ a melhor** to get the better of. **~ ao desespero** to reduce to despair. **~ a palma** to surpass, exceed; win the prize. **~ a pior** to get the worst of. **~ (do mar) à praia** to wash ashore. **~ à sepultura** to lead to the grave. **~ a sua avante** to get one's way. **~ a vida (na moleza)** (fig.) to take things easy. **~ avante** to

go ahead with. ~ **boa vida** to lead a jolly good life. ~ **com paciência** to bear patiently. ~ **de vencida** to overcome, defeat. ~ **de volta** to take back. ~ **em conta** 1. to consider, regard. 2. to discount. ~ **na cabeça** (fig.) to get it in the neck. ~ **o diabo** to dissappear, vanish. ~ **para dentro** to carry in. ~ **para um passeio** to take out for a walk. ~ **pau** (fig.) to flunk (in an examination). ~ **por bem** to treat gently. ~ **um prejuízo** to suffer a loss. ~ **um recado** to go an errand. ~ **tempo** to require or take time. ~ **uma vida miserável** to eke out a miserable existence. ~ **vantagem** to exceed, surpass; have the advantage over. ~ **vida de cachorro** to lead a dog's life. **a água levou-o embora** the water washed it away. **a história nos leva até o presente** the story takes us up to present day. **aquilo vai ~ um fim mau** that will end badly. **deixar-se ~** to be prevailed upon, yield to. **é preciso ~ em conta a sua idade** you must consider his age. **ela sabe como levá-lo** she knows how to take him. **ele levou as dele** he got his spanking. **ele me levou no bico** (fig.) he coaxed it out of me. **ele sabe ~ o público** he has the right sense for the public. **ele se deixa levar muito à toa** he is to be influenced or prevailed upon very easily. **este caminho leva para o mal** this way leads to perdition. **eles foram levados do convés pelas ondas** they were washed overboard. **isto leva a crer em erro** this admits the possibility of an error. **levamo-lo ao seu conhecimento** we put it up to him. **levaram o dinheiro dele na conversa** (Braz.) they talked him out of his money. **levaram a sua parte** they came in for a share. **levaremos o negócio até o fim** we'll see the thing out. **leve esta carta ao correio** take this letter to the post office. **levei comigo o meu paletó** I took my coat along with me. **não leve a mal se eu lhe digo** excuse my saying so. **quanto tempo leva?** how long does it take? **que fim levou ele?** what ever happened to him? **que o leve o diabo** the devil take him. **saber ~ a água a seu moinho** to care for the interest of number one; to know how to bring grist to one's mill.

leve adj. m. + f. 1. light, (almost) weightless (plate Q). 2. nimble, quick, agile. 3. easy. 4. slight(ly). 5. flighty. 6. (eccl.) venial. 7. trivial. 8. fickle, inconstant. 9. thin, delicate, fine (cloth). 10. indistinct, faint. 11. gentle. || ~**mente** adv. lightly.
~ **esperança** faint hope. ~ **como uma pena** light as a feather. **de ~** 1. lightly. 2. superficially. **óleo ~** thin oil. **tocar de ~** to touch lightly. **ter sono ~** to be a light sleeper. **um ~ resfriado** a slight cold.

levedação s. f. (pl. -ões) leavening: act of exciting fermentation in anything; fermentation.
levedar v. to leaven: 1. ferment, yeast. 2. cause to ferment.
lêvedo s. m. yeast: 1. (bot.) a fungi of the family Saccharomycetaceae. 2. leaven: any substance used to produce alcoholic fermentation. || adj. leavened, fermented.
levedura s. f. (also **fermento** m.) leaven, yeast, ferment: a fermentation agent.
bolo de ~ barmbrack.
leves s. m. pl. lights: lungs of animals (esp. birds).
leveza s. f. lightness: 1. state of being light. 2. levity, imprudence. 3. quickness, nimbleness, delicacy. 4. fineness (cloth).
leviandade s. f. 1. levity, thoughtlessness, improvidence, imprudence. 2. frivolity, folly, flippancy.
leviano adj. 1. flighty, thoughtless. 2. frivolous, flippant. 3. fickle. 4. imprudent, improvident, incon-

siderate. 5. precipitate, rash. 6. (Braz., pop.) light, not heavy. || -**amente** adv. flightily; frivolous.
pessoa -a harum-scarum, rattlebrain.
leviatã s. m. (bib.) leviathan: an aquatic monster mentioned in the Old Testament.
levidade s. f. (also **leveza**) 1. lightness, levity, want of weight. 2. (fig.) agility, quickness, nimbleness, easiness.
levidão s. f. (pl. -ões) 1. (obs.) lightness. 2. frivolity, thoughtlessness.
levigação s. f. (pl. -ões) levigation: the reduction of a solid substance to a fine impalpable powder.
levigar v. to levigate: to reduce to powder or paste.
levípede adj. m. + f. (poet.) levipede: light-footed, smooth-footed.
levirato s. m. (bib.) levirate.
levita s. m. 1. (Jewish hist.) Levite: a) descendant of Levi. b) an assistant to the priest. 2. (fig.) deacon; priest.
levitação s. f. (pl. -ões) (spiritualism) levitation, table-lifting: a rising by annulling the effects of gravity.
levitar-se v. to levitate: rise or cause to rise into the air by levitation.
Levítico s. m. 1. (bib.) Leviticus: the third book of the Pentateuch. 2. (bot.) lovage, sea parsley. || adj. levitical.
levogiro adj. (physic.) levogyrate, levorotatory.
levulose s. f. levulose, fructose, fruit sugar.
lexical adj. m. + f. (pl. -ais) lexical: 1. of or pertaining to a lexicon or lexicography. 2. relating to the vocabulary of a language.
léxico s. m. (also **léxicon**) lexicon; dictionary.
lexicografia s. f. lexicography: the art or process of making a dictionary.
lexicográfico adj. lexicographic(al): of or pertaining to lexicography. || **lexicograficamente** adv. lexicographically.
lexicógrafo s. m. (also **dicionarista** m. + f.) lexicographer: 1. author of a dictionary. 2. person who compiles a vocabulary.
lexicologia s. f. lexicology: the science of words.
lexicológico adj. lexicologic(al): relating to lexicology.
lexicólogo s. m. lexicologist: person versed in lexicology.
lezíria s. f. a tract of marshy land alongside a river.
lha contr. of the personal pron. **lhe** and the demonstrative pron. or the article **a** f. (pl. ~**s**).
as cartas? já lhas entreguei the letters? I handed them over already to you, him or her.
lhama (I) s. f. lamé: a rich fabric woven from gold or silver threads.
lhama (II) s. m. (zool.) llama: an Andean ruminant of the family Camelidae.
lhaneza s. f. 1. plainness, sincerity, frankness, plain-dealing, honesty. 2. simpleness. 3. kindness, affability.
lhano adj. 1. sincere, frank, plain. 2. honest. 3. kind, gracious. 4. unpretentious, simple, unaffected. 5. affable. || -**amente** adv. sincerely, kindly.
lhanos s. m. pl. (S. Am.) llanos: extensive plains.
lhanura s. f. 1. sincerity, frankness. 2. plainness, smoothness.
lhe personal pron. 1. to him, her or it. 2. to you. 3. ~**s** pl. for them, to you.
dei-~ I gave you, him or her. **eu ~ direi** I'll tell you, him or her. **eu já ~ disse** I have told you, him or her.
lho contr. of the personal pron. **lhe** and the demonstrative pron. or the article **o** m. (pl. ~**s**).
os livros? já lhos dei! the books? I gave them already to you, him or her.
lia s. f. lees, dregs, sediment, feces; mother of wine.

liaça s. f. straw packings or covers for bottles or glasses; packing straw.

liação s. f. (pl. -ões) joining, binding, splicing, act of tying.

liadouro s. m. (also **liadoiro**) bondstone, bonder: a stone going through a wall.

liamba s. f. (Braz., bot., also **diamba**) cannabis, hemp (Cannabis sativa).

liame s. m. 1. bond, tie. 2. connection. 3. (naut.) strengthening pieces; cordage, rigging.

liana s. f. (bot.) liana, liane.

liança s. f. 1. band, tie. 2. ligature, bandage. 3. (also **aliança**) alliance, union.

liar v. 1. to bind, fasten, tie. 2. to link, connect, bond; attach. 3. to join.

libação s. f. (pl. -ões) libation: 1. a pouring out of a liquid (as wine) in honour of a deity. 2. potation, drinking.

libanês s. m. (pl. -eses) (f. -esa) Lebanese: native or inhabitant of Lebanon. ‖ adj. Lebanese.

libar v. 1. to sip, drink. 2. to suck, imbibe. 3. to taste. 4. to libate: make a libation.

libelinha s. f. (ent.) dragonfly.

libelista s. m. + f. (law) libel(l)ant.

libelo s. m. 1. booklet. 2. (law) lampoon; bill of indictment, charge sheet.

libélula s. f. dragonfly: insect of the order Odonata.

libente adj. m. + f. 1. agreeable, pleasant. 2. kind, officious, willing.

líber s. m. (bot.) liber, phloem, bast of exogens.

liberação s. f. (pl. -ões) liquidation, discharge, acquittance (of debts or obligations); release.

liberal s. m. + f. (pl. -ais) liberal(ist): 1. a follower of liberalism. 2. person of liberal principles. ‖ adj. liberal: 1. generous, open-handed, bountiful. 2. munificent. 3. broad-minded, large-minded. 4. befitting a free man. 5. favourable to personal, political and religious liberty. ‖ ~mente adv. liberally.

liberalão s. m. (pl. -ões) person who makes a show of liberal opinions, a great liberalist.

liberalidade s. f. liberality: 1. generosity, open-handedness, bountifulness. 2. munificence. 3. large-mindedness.

liberalismo s. m. liberalism: 1. liberal principles and theories. 2. the principles of liberalists.

liberalista s. m. + f. liberalist: person of liberal principles, follower of liberalism. ‖ adj. liberalistic: relating to liberalism.

liberalizar v. 1. to liberalize: make or become liberal. 2. to lavish.

liberar v. 1. to discharge, liquidate, settle (a debt). 2. to set free (from an obligation). 3. to release; liberate.

liberativo adj. 1. that which frees (from an obligation or debt); acquitting. 2. liberating.

liberatório adj. 1. tending to set free, tending to acquit. 2. relating to a liquidation (of debts or obligations).

liberdade s. f. 1. liberty: a) freedom. b) free will. c) permission, licence, leave. 2. frankness. 3. boldness. 4. exemption. 5. ~s pl.: a) liberties, immunities. b) special privileges. c) rights. d) undue familiarities.
~ **civil** civil liberty. ~ **de consciência** freedom of conscience. ~ **de culto** freedom of worship. ~ **de ensino** freedom of education. ~ **de palavra** freedom of speech. ~ **individual** individual freedom. ~ **natural** natural freedom. ~ **política** political freedom. **dizer** ~s to talk licentiously. **ele foi posto em** ~ he was set free. **em** ~ free, at liberty. **estar em** ~ to be at liberty. **pôr em** ~ to set at liberty. **o senhor tem toda a** ~ **de ir** you are free

to go, (fig.) you are welcome to go. **ter, tomar** ~s **com alguém** to be free with s. o. **tomar a** ~ to take the liberty. **vagar em** ~ to wander at large.

liberiano s. m. Liberian: native or inhabitant of Liberia. ‖ adj. 1. Liberian: of or pertaining to Liberia. 2. (bot.) concerning the liber (bast or inner bark of exogens).

libertação s. f. (pl. -ões) 1. liberation: act of liberating or setting free, restitution, release. 2. delivery, deliverance. 3. acquittal, discharge.

libertador s. m. liberator; deliverer. ‖ adj. liberating, delivering, releasing.

libertar v. 1. to liberate: a) set free. b) set at liberty, deliver, save, rescue. c) release. d) discharge, unbind. e) disengage, exempt, disembarrass. 2. ~-se: to get free, free o. s. of (de), escape from, get rid of.

libertário s. m. libertarian: person who maintains the doctrine of the freedom of will. ‖ adj. libertarian.

liberticida s. m. + f. liberticide: a destroyer of liberty. ‖ adj. liberticidal, liberticide.

liberticídio s. m. liberticide: the destruction of liberty.

libertinagem s. f. (pl. -ens) 1. libertinism: a) licentiousness, lewdness. b) debauchery. 2. irreligiousness.

libertino s. m. libertine, lecher, rake, debauchee. ‖ adj. libertine, licentious; dissolute, debauched.

libertista s. m. + f. libertarian: person who advocates the doctrine of free will; indeterminist. ‖ adj. libertarian: advocating the doctrine of free will.

liberto s. m. 1. a manumitted slave. 2. freedman. ‖ adj. 1. manumitted, released from slavery. 2. free, at liberty; independent. 3. loose.

líbico s. m. Libyan; native or inhabitant of Libya. ‖ adj. Libyan.

libidibi s. m. dividivi: tree of the family Leguminosae (Caesalpinia coriaria).

libidinagem s. f. (pl. -ens) libidinousness: 1. lustfulness, wantonness, lewdness. 2. sensuality, voluptuousness.

libidinoso s. m. libidinous person, lecher. ‖ adj. libidinous: 1. lustful, lewd, lascivious. 2. sensual, voluptuous. 3. dissolute. ‖ -amente adv. libidinously.

libido s. f. (psych.) libido: the sex instinct.

líbio s. m. Libyan: native or inhabitant of Libya. ‖ adj. Libyan.

libita s. f. (Braz.) a kind of tunic without sleeves.

líbito s. m. (free) will, choice, voluntariness.

libra s. f. 1. pound: the unit of weight and the monetary unit. 2. (also **libra esterlina**) pound sterling. 3. (astr.) Libra: a zodiacal constellation also called Balance.
~ **padrão** standard pound.

libração s. f. (pl. -ões) libration: 1. act of librating, balancing. 2. (astr.) an apparent oscillatory motion. ~ **da lua** libration of the moon.

librar v. 1. to librate: a) move as a balance. b) weigh. c) hold in equipoise; be poised. 2. to support, prop. 3. ~-se: a) to ground, found upon. b) to hover, stay almost on the same place in the air.

libratório adj. libratory.

libré s. f. 1. livery. 2. (fig.) attire; appearance, uniform.

libretista s. m. + f. librettist: writer of a libretto, as of an opera.

libreto s. m. libretto: 1. book containing the words of an extended musical composition like an opera. 2. the text of an opera.

librina s. f. (Braz., pop.) 1. fog, mist, haze. 2. drizzle, mizzle.

librinar v. (Braz., pop.) 1. to mist, grow misty, dim. 2. to drizzle, mizzle.

liça s. f. 1. lists: a) tilting field, barrier. b) an arena, a ring. 2. (fig.) fight, combat, contest. 3. (Braz.) the heddle of a loom.
chamar às ~**s** (fig.) to challenge. **entrar nas** ~**s** to enter the lists (for).
licanço s. m. (zool.) glass snake (Ophiodes striatus), a limbless anguidean lizard.
licantropia s. f. lycanthropy: madness in which the patient supposes himself to be a wolf.
licantropo s. m. lycanthrope, lycanthropist: person affected with lycanthropy.
lição s. f. (pl. -ões) 1. lesson: a) (course of) instruction. b) school-exercise, task, school-work. c) explanation. d) lecture; reading; lection. 2. (fig.) experience, example. 3. reprimand, admonition, punishment.
~ **de leitura** reading lesson. ~ **de piano** piano lesson. ~ **prática** object lesson. **dar uma** ~ **a alguém** (fig.) to teach s. o. a lesson. **que isto lhe sirva de** ~! let that be a warning to you! **dar -ões** to give lessons.
liceal adj. m. + f. (pl. -ais) concerning a lyceum.
liceidade s. f. licitness, lawfulness.
licença s. f. license, licence: 1. permission, authority. 2. consent. 3. licentiousness, liberty. 4. leave, furlough. 5. right, authorization, permit.
~! allow me! ~ **de motorista** driver's license. ~ **de obras** building permit. ~ **poética** poetic license. **com** ~ 1. excuse me! 2. pardon me! by your leave! **de** ~ on leave. **dê-lhe** ~ give him permission. **pedir** ~ to ask for leave (of absence). **sem** ~ unlicensed. **uma** ~ **para sair a** leave to take off.
licença-prêmio s. f. (pl. **licenças-prêmios**) (Braz.) a premium vacation acquired chiefly through assiduity.
licenciado s. m. licentiate: person holding a university degree between bachelor and doctor, young barrister. ‖ adj. 1. licensed, permitted. 2. on leave. 3. (mil.) discharged.
licenciamento s. m. 1. licensing. 2. permission. 3. discharge.
licenciar v. 1. to licence: a) permit, authorize, allow. b) give a licence to, furlough. 2. to dismiss, disband (from service). 3. to discharge, muster out. 4. ~**-se**: a) to take leave. b) to take liberties. c) to take the degree of licentiate.
ele licenciou-se em Direito he obtained a lawyer's license.
licenciatura s. f. licentiateship: the condition or office of a licentiate.
licenciosidade s. f. licentiousness, libertinism, dissoluteness.
licencioso adj. licentious, dissolute, profligate, libertine. ‖ -**amente** adv. licentiously.
liceu s. m. lyceum: 1. a manual arts training school. 2. a secondary school.
lichi s. m. (bot.) litch (Litchi chinensis).
liciatório s. m. slay, sley: a weaver's reed.
lício s. m. (bot.) boxthorn.
licitação s. f. (pl. -ões) bidding at an auction.
licitador s. m., **licitante** m. + f. bidder or seller at an auction. ‖ adj. bidding or selling at an auction.
licitar v. 1. to bid at an auction. 2. to auction: sell at an auction.
lícito s. m. that which is licit or allowed. ‖ adj. 1. licit, lawful, allowed, legal. 2. just. ‖ **licitamente** adv. licitly, lawfully.
licnomancia s. f. lychnomancy.
licnomante s. m. + f. a practiser of lychnomancy.
liço s. m. warp threads.
licopodiáceas s. f. pl. (bot.) Lycopodiaceae, the club moss family.
licopódio s. m. 1. lycopod(ium) club moss, plant of the family Lycopodiaceae. 2. lycopodium powder.

licor s. m. 1. liqueur: a spirituous drink usually sweet and flavoured with aromatic substances, a cordial. 2. liquor: any liquid substance.
~ **de cereja** cherry-brandy. ~**es puros** raw spirits.
licoreira s. f., **licoreiro** m. a liqueur service.
licorista s. m. + f. person who makes or sells liqueur.
licorne s. m. unicorn: a fabulous animal like a horse with one horn.
licoroso adj. sweet and fortified (wine).
licosídeos s. m. pl. (zool.) Lycosidae, the wolf spider family.
licranço s. m. (zool.) slow-worm, blind-worm.
li(c)tor s. m. lictor: a civil officer among ancient Romans.
li(c)tório adj. of or pertaining to lictors.
licuri s. m. (Braz.) urucuri iba (a palm tree).
lida s. f. 1. work, drudgery, toil, chore, fag. 2. hurry, bustle, ado, trouble.
tanta ~ **para pouca vida** so much pain for so little gain. **de muita** ~ toilsome.
lidador s. m. drudger, toiler, worker; fighter, combatant. ‖ adj. working, drudging; fighting.
lidar v. 1. to struggle, strive, toil, drudge. 2. to work, labour. 3. to fight (bulls). 4. to make efforts. 5. (fig.) to dispute; cope, deal (with).
~ **com muita gente** to have to deal (or do) with many persons. ~ **com a morte** to struggle against death. **ela sabe** ~ **com ele** she knows how to deal with him; she keeps on the right side of him. **ele não é fácil de se** ~ he is not easy to deal with. **não é fácil** ~ **com ela** she is not easy to get along with.
lide s. f. 1. work, toil. 2. contest, fight, struggle. 3. dispute. 4. bullfighting.
líder s. m. leader: 1. chief, commander. 2. conductor, guide, head.
liderança s. f. 1. leadership: the office of a leader. 2. lead.
estar na ~ to be in the lead.
liderar v. to lead: guide, conduct, be a leader.
lidimar v. to legitimate.
lídimo adj. 1. legitimate, legal. 2. authentic. 3. vernacular.
lídio s. m. Lydian: native or inhabitant of Lydia. ‖ adj. Lydian: of or pertaining to Lydia.
lidita s. f. (min.) touchstone.
lidite s. f. lyddite: a high explosive.
lido adj. 1. read. 2. studied, well-read. 3. erudite. **homem** ~ well-read man.
lienal adj. m. + f. (pl. -ais) (anat.) splenic: of or pertaining to the spleen.
lienite s. f. (med.) splenitis: inflammation of the spleen.
lienteria s. f. (med.) lientery: diarrhea in which the aliments are discharged undigested.
lientérico s. m. person affected with lientery. ‖ adj. lienteric: relating to or affected with lientery.
liga s. f. 1. league, alliance, union, coalition. 2. (also **ligação**) binding, fastening. 3. alloy (of metals), fusion. 4. garter.
~ **de alumínio e bronze** (tech.) albronze. ~ **de cobre** (tech.) copper alloy. ~ **permeável** (tech.) permalloy. **Liga das Nações** League of Nations.
ligação s. f. (pl. -ões) 1. ligation, binding, fastening, joining. 2. junction, union, connection, relation, coupling. 3. coherence. 4. liaison. 5. bond, tie. 6. (fig.) friendship, familiarity, acquaintance.
~ **à terra** (radio) ground connection. ~ **cruzada** cross connection. ~ **em paralelo** (electr.) parallel connection. ~ **em série** (electr.) tandem connection. ~ **errada** (tech.) faulty control. **caixa de** ~ terminal box, junction box. **cano de** ~ service-pipe. **não consigo** ~ I can't get through (telephone).

ligado adj. joint, united, connected; close, intimate. **eles são muito ~s** they cling together. **estar ~ a** to be attended with. **este assunto está ~ à matéria** this matter is germane to our subject. **riscos ~s ao meu trabalho** risks contingent to my work.
ligadura s. f. (also **ligatura**) ligature: 1. tie, bandage. 2. (mus.) curve that connects notes, slur. 3. (med.) string or thread to tie an artery.
ligame s. m., **ligâmen** (pl. **ligamens** and **ligâmenes**) 1. connection, relationship. 2. bonds, ties. 3. obstacle to marriage.
ligamento s. m. 1. ligament: a) bandage, bond. b) (anat.) band of connective tissue. 2. vinculum, tie.
ligamentoso adj. ligamentous, ligamentary; fibrous.
ligar (I) v. 1. to tie, bind, fasten. 2. to bandage. 3. to attach, fix. 4. to link, connect. 5. to alloy, amalgamate (metals). 6. to switch (turn) on (electric appliances). 7. (anat.) to ligate. 8. to pay attention to, attach importance to. 9. (mus.) to slur. 10. **~-se:** a) to league, confederate, associate. b) to join, unite. c) to combine with.
ligue para o meu escritório telephone to my office, call me up at my office. **liguei o ferro elétrico (na tomada)** I plugged in the electric iron. **ligue o rádio!** turn on the radio! **ela não liga para o namorado** she doesn't care at all for her boyfriend. **não consegui ~ para ela, o telefone estava sempre ocupado** I couldn't get through to her, the phone was always busy. **por favor, ligue-me com...** please, put me through to...
ligar (II) v. to be in luck.
ligeira s. f. 1. lightness. 2. facility, ease.
à ~ quickly.
ligeireza s. f. (also **ligeirice**) 1. quickness, swiftness, rapidity. 2. lightness, nimbleness. 3. promptness, readiness. 4. agility. 5. fickleness, unsteadiness, levity. 6. (Braz.) villainy; trickery.
~ de mãos legerdemain.
ligeirias s. f. pl. gibe, scoff, taunt, jests, drolleries, jokes.
ligeiro s. m. 1. quick, swift, agile, nimble; alert. 2. fast, speedy, rapid; light-legged. 3. light. 4. slight, superficial. 5. inconstant, unsteady, fickle. 6. light-minded. 7. (Braz.) fraudulent, deceitful, dishonest, slippery. || **-amente** adv. 1. fastly. 2. lightly. 3. slightly, superficially.
andar ~ to speed, walk fast. **um resfriado ~ a** slight cold.
liglídeos s. m. pl. (zool.) Liglidae, a family of crustaceans.
lígio s. m. liege man. || adj. liege.
lígneo adj. ligneous, woody: of, pertaining to or like wood.
lignificação s. f. (pl. **-ões**) lignification: process of becoming or of making woody.
lignificar-se v. to lignify: convert into or become woody.
ligniforme adj. m. + f. ligniform: like or resembling wood.
lignina s. f. (chem.) lignin: the essential substance of woody tissue.
lignite s. f. (min., also **linhite**) lignite: a dark brown kind of coal.
lignívoro s. m. (zool.) xylophagan, xylophage. || adj. lignivorous, xylophagous: eating wood.
lígula s. f. 1. (zool.) ligula. 2. (bot.) ligule.
liguláceo adj. resembling a ligula.
ligulado adj. (bot., also **ligurífero**) ligulate.
ligulifloro adj. (bot.) liguliflorous, ligulate-flowered.
liguliforme adj. m. + f. (bot.) liguliform.
liguloso adj. (bot.) ligulate.
ligúrio s. m. Ligurian: native or inhabitant of Liguria.
ligústica s. f. (bot.) lavage, sea parsley.

lila s. f. Lille lace.
lilás, lilá s. m. (pl. **lilases**) lilac: 1. a shrub of the genus Syringa. 2. the colour of lilac flowers. || adj. m. + f. lilac: of the colour lilac.
lilás-da-índia s. m. (pl. **lilases-da-índia**) (bot.) chinaberry tree (Melia azedarach), also called **cinamomo**.
lili s. m. (N. Braz.) fetish, numbo-jumbo; evil eye.
liliáceas s. f. pl. (bot.) Liliaceae, a large family of monocotyledonous plants.
lilifloro adj. having leaves like a lily.
liliforme adj. m. + f. liliform, lily-shaped.
liliputiano s. m. Lilliputian: inhabitant of the imaginary kingdom of Lilliput. || adj. Lilliputian: of or pertaining to Lilliput.
lima (I) s. f. (mech.) file: steel instrument used for cutting and smoothing metals (plates F 1, L 3).
~ chata flat file (plate L 3). **~ de desbastar** rough file. **~ murça** smooth file. **~ paralela** blunt file. **~ pontiaguda** taper file. **~ arredondada** round file. **~ triangular** triangular file, three-square file.
lima (II) s. f. 1. filing: act of cutting or smoothing with a file. 2. perfecting, last touch, finish.
lima (III) s. f. (bot.) 1. sweet lime. 2. its fruit.
limacídeo s. m. (zool.) any pteropod of the family Limacidae (as slugs). || adj. (zool.) limacine.
limacomorfos s. m. pl. (zool.) Limacomorpha, an order of Chilognatha.
limada s. f. (Braz.) limeade: beverage made of sweet lime, water and sugar.
lima-de-cheiro s. f. (pl. **limas-de-cheiro**) (Braz.) paraffin or rubber ball filled with perfumed water (used formerly during carnival).
limador s. m. filer. || adj. filing.
limadura s. f. 1. filing: act of smoothing or cutting with a file. 2. finishing up, last touch.
limagem s. f. (pl. **-ens**) operation of filing.
limalha s. f. filings, file dust.
~ de aço steel filings.
limantrídeos s. m. pl. (ent.) Lymantriidae, the tussock moth family.
limão s. m. (pl. **-ões**) lemon: the acid fruit of the lemon tree.
suco de ~ lemon juice.
limão-canudo s. m. (pl. **limões-canudo**) (Braz.) a stingless bee (Melipona limão).
limão-cravo s. m. (pl. **limões-cravo**) (Braz.) lemon tree of the family Rutaceae.
limão-de-cheiro s. m. (pl. **limões-de-cheiro**) (N. Braz.) = **lima-de-cheiro**.
limão-doce s. m. (pl. **limões-doces**) (Braz., bot.) sweet lime.
limão-francês s. m. (pl. **limões-franceses**) (bot.) lime-berry.
limão-galego s. m. (pl. **limões-galegos**) (Braz., bot.) citron (Citrus medica).
limãorana s. f. (Braz., bot.) the old fustic.
limãozinho s. m. diminutive of **limão**: a small lemon.
limar (I) v. 1. to file: a) smooth or cut with a file. b) remove with a file. 2. to polish, elaborate, refine, perfect, correct. 3. (fig.) to corrode, waste gradually, wear down.
limar (II) v. to flavour with lemon and oil.
limatão s. m. (pl. **-ões**) round or coarse file.
límbico adj. limbic: of or pertaining to a limbus.
limbífero adj. limbiferous.
limbo s. m. 1. limb: a) edge, border. b) (bot.) leaf blade (plate F 5). c) (math.) the graduated semicircular edge of a protractor. 2. (R. C. Church) limbo: abode of souls of unbaptized infants and of the souls of just men who died before Christ.
limeira s. f. (bot.) sweet lime (Citrus limetta).
limenho s. m. Limean: citizen of Lima (Peru). || adj. Limean: of or pertaining to Lima.

limiar s. m. 1. threshold, doorsill. 2. (fig.) doorway, entrance; beginning.
o ~ **da consciência** the threshold of consciousness.
limiforme adj. m. + f. filelike, rough like a file.
liminar s. m. = limiar. ‖ adj. 1. at or of the threshold. 2. (fig.) preliminary, introductory.
limitação s. f. (pl. -ões) 1. limitation: a) act of setting limits. b) restriction, restraint; check. 2. limiting, bounding, confinement.
~ **de natalidade** birth control.
limitado adj. 1. limited: a) limitary. b) confined within limits, circumscribed, narrow; poor. 2. (fig.) stinted. ‖ -amente adv. limitedly.
companhia -a limited company. **pedido** ~ (com.) stop order.
limitar v. 1. to (de)limit, circumscribe, set bounds. 2. to restrict, restrain, restringe. 3. to fix, appoint. 4. to border on. 5. to retrench. 6. ~-se: a) to keep o. s. back, withhold o. s., refrain from, limit o. s. b) to adjoin.
ele limitou-se a generalidades he confined himself to generalities. **o Brasil limita com quase todos os países sul-americanos** Brazil borders on most of the South American countries.
limitativo adj. limitative, limiting; restrictive.
limitável adj. m. + f. (pl. -áveis) limitable, confinable.
limite s. m. 1. limit: a) border line, boundary, line of demarcation, border. b) confine. c) utmost extent. 2. frontier. 3. end, aim, purpose.
~ **de alcance** load limit. ~ **máximo de velocidade** speed limit. **ele se manteve dentro dos ~s** he kept within compass. **passar dos ~s** to go too far, overshoot, outreach.
limítrofe adj. m. + f. 1. limitrophe, frontier, adjacent. 2. confining, adjoining.
limnantáceas s. f. pl. (bot.) Limnanthaceae, the false-mermaid family.
limneídeos s. m. pl. (zool.) Lymneidae, a family of freshwater snails.
limnímetro s. m. limnometer.
limnófilo adj. (zool.) limnophilous: living in ponds or pools.
limnografia s. f. description of lakes.
limnologia s. f. limnology: the study of lakes.
limnológico adj. limnologic(al).
limnologista s. m. + f., **limnólogo** m. limnologist.
limnomedusas s. f. pl. (zool.) an order of animals of the class Hydrozoa to which belongs the microhydra (Craspedacusta sowerbii), a minute Brazilian freshwater hydrozoan medusa.
limnômetro s. m. limnometer.
limo s. m. 1. (bot.) alga of the genus conferva. 2. (fig.) slime, ooze, sludge; mud, mire.
limoado adj. lemon-coloured.
limoal s. m. (pl. -ais) lemon orchard.
limoctônia s. f. death by starvation.
limoeiro s. m. (bot.) lemon tree (Citrus limonum).
limoeiro-bravo (pl. limoeiros-bravos), **limoeiro-do-mato** (pl. limoeiros-do-mato) s. m. (bot.) torolillo.
limonada s. f. lemonade: a beverage made of lemon juice, water and sugar.
~ **gasosa** lemon soda water. ~ **purgativa** purgative consisting of citrate of magnesia. **soda** ~ lemon-squash.
limonadeiro s. m. limonade maker or vendor.
limonete s. m. (bot.) lemon-scented verbena.
limônio s. m. (bot.) sea-lavender.
limonito s. m. (min.) limonite, brown hematite, peanut ore.
limosela s. f. (bot.) mudweed.
limosidade s. f. sliminess, ooziness, muddiness.
limoso adj. slimy, oozy, muddy.
limote s. m. a triangular file.

limpa s. f. 1. cleaning. 2. (N. Braz.) sugar-cane brandy or rum.
limpação (pl. -ões), **limpadela** s. f. cleaning.
limpa-chaminés s. m., sg. + pl. chimney-sweeper.
limpado s. m. (Braz.) a tract of land cleared for cultivation.
limpador s. m. 1. cleaner: a) person who cleans. b) any device for cleaning (plate F 7). 2. corn sheller. 3. wiper.
~ **de pára-brisa** windshield wiper. ~ **de rua** street sweeper.
limpadura s. f. 1. cleaning. 2. rubbish, table scraps.
limpamento s. m. 1. act of cleaning. 2. a cleaning (up).
limpa-penas s. m., sg. + pl. a penwiper.
limpa-pés s. m., sg. + pl. foot scraper, door scraper.
limpa-pratos s. m., sg. + pl. (fig.) glutton.
limpar v. 1. to clarify, clean (up), cleanse. 2. to purify, cure. 3. to wipe off, wash. 4. to winnow, fan. 5. to lop, prune, trim. 6. to sweep. 7. to expurge. 8. to empty entirely (glass, plate). 9. to steal (from), purloin. 10. to make a partner (of a game) lose his last penny. 11. to clear up. 12. ~-se: a) to wash, clean o. s. b) to become clean.
~ **a chaminé** to sweep the chimney. ~ **esfregando** to wipe away. **ela limpou o nariz** she wiped her nose.
limpa-trilhos s. m., sg. + pl. (railway) cowcatcher; fender; track cleaner, rail guard.
limpeza s. f. 1. cleanness, cleanliness. 2. neatness. 3. cleansing, cleaning. 4. sweep, washing. 5. purity; perfection; honesty, fairness.
~ **de mãos** (fig.) honesty, integrity; fidelity. ~ **total** cleanup.
limpidez s. f. 1. limpidity, limpidness: a) clearness. b) transparency. c) lucidity, clarity. 2. brightness. 3. pureness. 4. serenity. 5. ingenuousness.
límpido adj. 1. limpid: a) clear, transparent. b) lucid; brigth. 2. clean, neat. 3. pure; fair. 4. polite, courteous. 5. cloudless. 6. ingenuous. ‖ **limpidamente** adv. limpidly.
água -a clear water. **o céu está** ~ the sky is cloudless.
limpo s. m. (Braz.) a tract of land without vegetation. ‖ adj. 1. clean(ly), neat, unsoiled. 2. trim, tidy, spruce. 3. clear, bright. 4. cloudless. 5. bare. 6. pure, chaste, stainless, spotless. 7. immaculate, incorrupted. 8. (Braz.) moneyless, broke. ‖ -amente adv. cleanly, neatly.
de mãos -as clean-handed. **estar com a consciência -a** to have a clear conscience. **ficar** ~ (fig.) to have no money left. **passar a** ~ to make a fair copy of. **pôr em pratos ~s** (fig.) to lay the cards on the table; to dot the i's and cross the t's. **quem tem a consciência -a dorme tranqüilo** a clear conscience makes a soft pillow.
limusine s. f. limousine (automobile).
linária s. f. (bot.) toadflax.
lince s. m. (zool.) lynx: a wildcat of the family Felidae (Felis lynx).
linchamento s. m. lynching: act of punishing by lynch law.
linchar v. to lynch.
linda s. f. 1. landmark, boundary. 2. limit, border. 3. pattern, standard.
lindaço adj. (S. Braz.) very beautiful.
linda-flor s. f. (pl. lindas-flores) (Braz.) coreopsis: plant and flower.
lindar v. 1. to demarcate, delimit, fix the limits of. 2. to border.
lindeira s. f. 1. doorpost. 2. sidepiece of a window-frame. 3. lintel.

lindeiro adj. 1. referring to a landmark. 2. limitrophe, bordering.

lindeza s. f. (also Braz., pop. **lindura**) 1. beauty, prettiness, fineness. 2. grace(fulness); handsomeness. 3. (fig.) perfection.

lindo adj. 1. pretty, beautiful, nice, fair, handsome. 2. elegant, fine, graceful. 3. agreeable, pleasing. 4. (fig.) good, perfect. || **-amente** adv. prettily, finely.
-a menina pretty girl. **que** ~! how beautiful!

lineamento s. m. 1. trace; tracing. 2. ~s pl. lineaments; a) features. b) outlines. c) contours of the face.

linear adj. m. + f. (also **lineal**) linear, lineal: 1. of or pertaining to a line or lines. 2. like a line. || ~**mente** adv. lineally.
equação ~ (math.) linear equation.

líneo adj. linen.

lineolar adj. m. + f. (bot.) lineolate(d): marked with fine lines.

linfa s. f. (physiol.) lymph: the fluid of the lymphatic vessels.

linfangioma s. m. (med.) lymphangioma: tumour composed of lymphatic vessels.

linfangite s. f. (med.) lymphangitis: inflammation of the lymphatic vessels.

linfático adj. lymphatic: of, pertaining to or containing lymph.
vasos ~s lymphatic vessels, lymphatics.

linfatismo s. m. lymphatism, lymphatic temperament.

linfoma s. m. (med.) lymphoma.

linfotomia s. f. (surg.) lymphotomy: dissection of the lymphatics.

linga s. f. 1. sling rope to hold or hoist cargo. 2. (myth.) linga(m).

lingada s. f. the quantity of things hoisted at a time by a sling.

lingar v. to sling: hoist cargo in a sling.

lingote s. m. ingot.
~ **de ferro** iron ingot, pig iron.

lingoteira s. f. a mould for ingots.

língua s. f. 1. tongue: a) (anat., zool.) the movable organ in the mouth, in man also called organ of speech. b) (fig.) speech. c) language, idiom. d) anything like a tongue. 2. m. interpreter.
~ **afiada** sharp tongue. ~ **comprida**, ~ **de palmo** (fig.) slanderer. ~ **de palmo e meio** chatterbox. ~ **extinta** extinct language. ~ **materna** mother tongue. ~ **morta** dead language. ~ **portuguesa** Portuguese language. ~ **viva** living language. ~ **suja** (med.) dirty, furred tongue. **dar com a** ~ **nos dentes** to blab. **dobrar a** ~ to retract. **ele põe sua** ~ **para fora** he puts out his tongue. **ela tem uma** ~ **solta** she knows all the answers. **na** ~ **da minha terra** in my mother tongue. **saber na ponta da** ~ to have at one's finger tips. **uma** ~ **venenosa** a spiteful tongue.

língua-cervina s. f. (pl. **línguas-cervinas**) (bot.) heart's-tongue.

língua-de-boi s. f. (pl. **línguas-de-boi**) (bot.) bugle.

língua-de-cão s. f. (pl. **línguas-de-cão**) (bot.) hound's-tongue.

língua-de-cobra s. f. (pl. **línguas-de-cobra**) (bot.) adder's-tongue.

língua-de-mulata s. f. (pl. **línguas-de-mulata**) (Braz., ichth.) tonguefish.

língua-de-ovelha s. f. (pl. **línguas-de-ovelha**) (bot.) sheep's fescue.

língua-de-trapos s. m. + f. (pl. **línguas-de-trapos**) 1. a child who does not speak yet. 2. a stammering or faltering person.

língua-de-vaca s. f. (pl. **línguas-de-vaca**) (bot.) bugloss, oxtongue.

linguado s. m. 1. a long blade. 2. a copy of type-written matter for a newspaper. 3. (ichth.): a) sole. b) flounder.

linguafone, linguafono s. m. a modern recorder used for the study of languages.

linguagem s. f. (pl. **-ens**) 1. language: idiom, tongue, dialect. 2. speech; style; diction.
~ **pedante** inkhorn terms.

língua-geral s. f. (Braz.) língua geral, Tupi.

linguajar s. m. 1. talk, speech, dialect. 2. mode of speech. || v. to talk, speak, prattle.

lingual adj. m. + f. (pl. **-ais**) lingual: of, pertaining to or like a tongue.

linguará, linguaral s. m. (Braz.) an interpreter between whites and Indians.

linguarado, linguarão (pl. **-ões**) (f. **-ona**), **linguareiro** s. m. 1. prattler; chatterbox: gossip. 2. backbiter. || adj. 1. talkative. 2. slanderous.

linguaraz s. m. + f. + adj. m. + f. = **linguarado**.

linguarudo s. m. 1. chatterbox. 2. slanderer. 3. gabbler, prattler. || adj. 1. talkative, loquacious, windy. 2. slanderous. 3. gabbling, long-tongued.

lingüeirão s. m. (pl. **-ões**) 1. big tongue. 2. (zool.) a razor clam.

lingüeta s. f. 1. a little tongue. 2. languet. 3. click, ratchet pawl (plate F 8). 4. catch, stop pawl. 5. reed, stop. 6. ramp of a pier. 7. tongue of a shoe (plate B 16). 8. bolt of a lock (plate F 1).
~ **e ranhura** tongue and groove (plate C 9).

lingüiça s. f. an inferior variety of sausage (plate A 2).

lingüífero adj. provided with a tongue or with tongue-shaped organs.

lingüiforme adj. m. + f. linguiform, tongue-shaped.

lingüinha s. m. + f. (Braz., pop.) stutterer.

lingüista s. m. + f. linguist: person versed in linguistics.

lingüística s. f. linguistics: the science of languages, philology.

lingüístico adj. linguistic(al): of or pertaining to linguistics. || **lingüisticamente** adv. linguistically.

lingulado adj. lingulate(d): tongue-shaped.

linguodental adj. m. + f. (pl. **-ais**) linguadental, dentilingual.
consoante ~ dentilingual consonant.

linha s. f. 1. line: a) sewing thread. b) rope, string, cord (plates J 2, P 12). c) lineage. d) track, rail. e) fishing line. f) row, file, rank. g) bound, limit, mark, border. h) a regular transportation service between two places. i) (typogr.) a row of printed letters or words. j) a telephone or telegraph line (plate E 3). k) (geom.) the path of a moving point (plate L 1). l) stroke with a pen, dash (plate N 1). 2. ~s pl. (Braz., pop.) letter.
~ **aérea** 1. airline, airway. 2. (electr.) overhead line, overhead wire (plate C 1). ~ **agônica** agonic line. ~ **curva** curved or crooked line (plate L 1). ~ **d'água** 1. watermark. 2. (naut.) water-line. ~ **de barquilha** log-line. ~ **de bonde** streetcar line, tramway (plates B 15, C 1, R 8). ~ **de bordar** embroidery thread. ~ **de combate** the front line (mil.). ~ **de composição** (typogr.) setting-rule. ~ **de flutuação** (naut.) a ship's water-line. ~ **de fundo** 1. (fishing) bottom-line. 2. (Braz., ftb. also ~ **de gol**) goal line (plate F 9). ~ **de luz** lighting connection. ~ **de mira** bearing line. ~ **de montagem** (tech.) assembly line. ~ **de pescar** fishing line (plate P 9). ~ **de prumo** plumb line. ~ **de sonda** fathom-line. ~ **de tiro** range. ~ **de transmissão** power line. ~ **dianteira** (ftb.) forward line. ~ **do destino** fate-line of the hand. ~ **férrea** railway. ~ **final** bottom-line. ~ **horizontal** horizontal line (plate L 1). ~ **interurbana** (teleph.) trunk-line. ~ **média**

(ftb.) line of halfbacks. ~ **ondulada** winding curve. ~ **quebrada** broken line (plate L 1). ~ **reta** straight line (plate L 1). ~ **tracejada** dotted line (plate L 1). ~**s suplementares** (mus.) leger lines. ~, **por favor!** (teleph.) give me a line, please! **a ~ de conduta** line of conduct. **a ~ ferroviária Paris--Lille** the Paris-Lille railway. **em toda a ~** all along the line. **entrar na ~** 1. to fall into line. 2. to range o. s. **ficar em ~** to toe the line. **fora da ~** out of line. **juiz de ~** (ftb.) linesman. **manter em ~** to keep in line. **perder a ~** to lose one's decorum. **tirar uma ~ com** to make eyes at s. o.
linhaça s. f. linseed, flaxseed.
linhada s. f. (Braz.) 1. throwing of a fishing line. 2. a peep, a look. 3. a flirt from afar, by looks, etc.
linhagem s. f. (pl. **-ens**) 1. lineage, genealogy. 2. race, progeny. 3. pedigree. 4. (fig.) social position. 5. coarse linen fabric.
~ **antiga** ancient or old family. **de alta ~** highborn.
linhagista s. m. + f. genealogist: one who studies the descent of persons or families.
linhal s. m. (pl. **-ais**) flax field.
linheira s. f. 1. woman who prepares flax for spinning. 2. woman who sells linen.
linheiro s. m. 1. a dealer in flax. 2. person who sells threads. ‖ adj. 1. linear, lineal. 2. slender, fine, thin.
linhite s. f. (min.) lignite, brown coal.
linho s. m. 1. flax: any plant of the family Linaceae (Linum usitatissimum). 2. linen: cloth made of flax.
~ **bravo** toad-flax. ~ **para encadernação** binder's cloth. **cardador de ~** flax-dresser. **fiação de ~** flax-mill. **semente de ~** linseed, flax-seed.
linho-da-nova-zelândia s. m. (pl. **linhos-da-nova-zelândia**) (bot.) New Zealand flax.
linhol s. m. (pl. **-óis**) cobbler's thread.
linho-purgante s. m. (pl. **linhos-purgantes**) (bot.) purging flax.
linhoso adj. flaxen: pertaining to or resembling flax or its fibers.
linhote s. m. (constr.) joist, girder, beam.
linifício s. m. 1. manufacture of linen fabrics, linen industry. 2. linen goods.
linígero adj. clad in linen.
linimento s. m. (med.) liniment: a liquid preparation for external application.
linneano adj. Linn(a)ean: pertaining to the naturalist Karl von Linné.
linóleo s. m. linoleum: a kind of floor-cloth anointed with linseed-oil.
linotipista s. m. + f. linotypist: an operator of a linotype.
linotipo s. m. linotype.
lintel s. m. (pl. **-éis**) (archit.) lintel.
lio s. m. bundle, faggot.
liocéfalo adj. leiocephalous.
liócomo adj. leiotrichous: having straight hair.
liodermo adj. (zool.) leiodermatous.
liofilo adj. (bot.) leiophyllous.
liômeros s. m. pl. (ichth.) Lyomeri, an order of deep-sea fishes.
liomioma s. m. (med.) liomyoma.
lionês s. m. (pl. **-eses**) (f. **-esa**) Lyonese. ‖ adj. Lyonese.
lionetídeos s. m. pl. (ent.) Lyonetidae, a family of moths of the order Lepidoptera.
liótrico adj. (zool.) leiotrichous: having straight hair.
líparo s. m. 1. (ent.) tussock moth. 2. (ichth.) sea snail.
liparocele s. f. (med.) liparocele, lipoma.
lípase s. f. (biochem.) lipase.

lipitude s. f. (med.) lippitude, blearedness.
lipograma s. f. lipogram.
lipogramático adj. lipogrammatic.
lipogramatista s. m. + f. lipogrammatist.
lipóide adj. m. + f. lipoid(al), lipoidic, fatlike.
lipoma s. m. (med.) lipoma: a tumour formed of fatty tissue.
lipomatoso adj. lipomatous: pertaining to or of the nature of a lipoma.
liposo adj. bleary, blear-eyed.
lipossolúvel adj. m. + f. (pl. **-úveis**) fat-soluble.
lipotimia s. f. (med.) lipothymy, lipothymia: fainting, faint, swoon, syncope.
liquação s. f. (pl. **-ões**) liquation: separation of metals by liquefaction.
liquefação s. f. (pl. **-ões**) liquefaction: act or process or liquefying.
liquefativo adj. liquefactive: producing liquefaction.
liquefazer v. to liquefy: 1. reduce to a liquid. 2. ~**-se** become liquid.
liquefeito adj. 1. liquefied. 2. molten, melted.
líquen s. m. (pl. **liquens, líquenes**) (bot., path.) lichen.
liquenáceo adj. lichenous.
líquen-da-islândia s. m. (pl. **liquens-da-islândia**) (bot.) Iceland moss.
liquenografia s. f. (bot.) lichenography.
liquenográfico adj. lichenographic(al).
liquescer v. to liquesce: become liquid.
liquidação, liqüidação s. f. (pl. **-ões**) 1. liquidation: a) act of liquidating. b) settlement of debts. 2. a special sale of merchandise; clearing, clearance; sell-out. 3. (fig.) extinction.
~ **total** clearance sale. **em ~ de** in payment of.
liquidado adj. 1. liquidated. 2. finished, extinct. 3. (fig.) done for.
ele está ~ (fig.) his goose is cooked. **estou ~** (fig.) I'm done for.
liquidador s. m. liquidator. ‖ adj. promoting liquidation.
liquidâmbar s. m. (bot.) liquidambar.
liquidar, liqüidar v. 1. to liquidate: settle, adjust, square (accounts). 2. (fig.) to annihilate, destroy. 3. to sell out, clear, dump. 4. to shut, cease, close (firm, business, shop).
~ **uma conta** to settle an account. ~ **uma dívida** to cancel or pay a debt. **Pedro liquidou as dívidas de Paulo** Peter squared Paul's debts. **eu o liquidei** (fig.) I cooked his goose.
liquidatário s. m. liquidator. ‖ adj. liquidating.
liquidável adj. m. + f. (pl. **-áveis**) liquidable: capable of being liquidated or settled.
liquidez s. f. liquidness: state or quality of being liquid.
liquidificação s. f. (pl. **-ões**) liquefaction: act of liquefying.
liquidificador s. m. liquefier.
liquidificante adj. m. + f. liquefacient: that which liquefies or serves to liquefy.
liquidificar v. to liquidify.
liquidificável adj. m. + f. (pl. **áveis**) liquefiable: capable of being liquefied, melted, or changed to a liquid state.
líquido, líqüido s. m. 1. liquid, solution. 2. drink. ‖ adj. 1. liquid, fluid. 2. net. 3. clear, evident. ‖ **liquidamente** adv. liquidly; clearly.
~ **de Dakin** (pharm.) Dakin's solution. **lucro ~** net produce.
lira (I) s. f. 1. lyre: a) (mus.) a stringed instrument used by ancient Greeks. b) Lyre: the constellation Lyra. 2. (fig.) Lyrics. 3. (ornith.) lyre bird.
lira (II) s. f. lira: the monetary unit of Italy.
lirado adj. (bot.) lyrate, lyre-shaped.

lirial s. m. (pl. **-ais**) (Braz.) place where lilies grow. || adj. m. + f. lily: resembling a lily in purity or colour.
lírica s. f. 1. lyric poem or composition. 2. collection of lyric poems.
lírico s. m. a lyric poet; composer of lyrical poetry. || adj. 1. lyric: a) of or pertaining to a lyre. b) of or pertaining to lyric poems. 2. (fig.) sentimental. 3. operatic. || **liricamente** adv. lyrically.
liriforme adj. m. + f. lyriform, lyre-shaped.
lírio s. m. lily: 1. plant of the family Liliaceae. 2. its flower.
lírio-ácaro-bastardo s. m. (pl. **lírios-ácaro-bastardos**) (bot.) yellow iris, yellow flag, corn flag.
lírio-amarelo-do-brejo s. m. (pl. **lírios-amarelos-do-brejo**) (bot.) butterfly lily.
lírio-branco s. m. (pl. **lírios-brancos**) (bot.) 1. white lily, madonna lily. 2. trumpet lily.
lírio-convale s. m. (pl. **lírios-convales**) (bot.) lily of the valley.
lírio-cravinho s. m. (pl. **lírios-cravinhos**) (bot.) scorpion iris.
lírio-d'água s. m. (pl. **lírios d'água**) (bot.) water lily.
lírio-da-índia s. m. (pl. **lírios-da-índia**) (bot.) chinaberry tree (Melia azedarach).
lírio-da-pérsia s. m. (pl. **lírios-da-pérsia**) (bot.) Persian iris.
lírio-das-areias s. m. (pl. **lírios-das-areias**) (bot.) sea daffodil.
lírio-de-petrópolis s. m. (pl. **lírios-de-petrópolis**) (bot.) common garland flower.
lírio-do-amazonas s. m. (pl. **lírios-do-amazonas**) (bot.) Amazon lily.
lírio-do-brejo s. m. (pl. **lírios-do-brejo**) (bot.) common garland flower.
lírio-dos-tintureiros s. m. (pl. **lírios-dos-tintureiros**) (bot.) dyer's-weed, weld, woad, yellow weed.
lírio-do-vale s. m. (pl. **lírios-do-vale**) (bot.) lily of the valley.
lírio-fétido s. m. (pl. **lírios-fétidos**) (bot.) fetid iris.
lirióide adj. m. + f. lily-shaped.
lírio-roxo s. m. (pl. **lírios-roxos**) (bot.) Portugal iris.
lírio-roxo-dos-montes s. m. (pl. **lírios-roxos-dos-montes**) (bot.) German iris.
lírio-verde s. m. (pl. **lírios-verdes**) (bot.) meadow saffron, autumn crocus.
lírio-vermelho s. m. (pl. **lírios-vermelhos**) (bot.) orange day lily.
lirismo s. m. lyricism: quality of being lyric.
lirista s. m. + f. 1. lyrist: person who plays on a lyre. 2. lyrical poet.
lis s. m. (bot.) lily.
lisboano, lisboês (pl. **-eses**) (f. **-esa**) s. m., **lisboeta** m. + f. native or inhabitant of Lisbon. || adj. of or pertaining to Lisbon.
lisim s. m. (pl. **-ins**) a layer of stone in a quarry.
lisimáquia s. f. (bot.) common loosestrife.
lisímetro s. m. lysimeter.
lisina s. f. (biochem.) lysin(e).
lísio adj. resulting from chemical dissolution.
liso adj. 1. smooth, even, sleeky (plate Q). 2. lank. 3. soft. 4. plane, flat. 5. plain; simple; sincere. 6. (Braz., pop.) moneyless, pennyless. || **-amente** adv. 1. smoothly. 2. plainly.
~ **como enguia** slippery as an eel. **cabelo** ~ straight hair. **chumaceira -a, mancal** ~ (tech.) plain bearing.
lisol s. m. (pl. **-óis**) lysol.
lisonja s. f. flattery, wheedling, coaxing, adulation, blarney, soft soap, cajolery. 2. (fig.) caress.
lisonjaria s. f. flattery, adulation, cajolery.
lisonjeador s. m. flatterer, cajoler, toady, fawner. || adj. flattering, fawning, cajoling.
lisonjear v. 1. to flatter, court, fawn, softsoap, cajole, wheedle, adulate. 2. to please, satisfy, gratify. 3. **~-se** to delight in; evanesce; be pleased.
ela sabia lisonjeá-lo she knew to fawn on him. **ele procurou lisonjear-me** he curried favour with me. **ele sentiu-se lisonjeado com suas palavras** he felt flattered by your words.
lisonjeiro s. m. flatterer, adulator. || adj. 1. flattering, adulatory. 2. smooth-tongued, smooth-spoken. 3. pleasing. 4. satisfactory, satisfying, agreeable. || **-amente** adv. 1. flatteringly. 2. satisfactorily.
lissencéfalo adj. (anat.) lissencephalous, lissencephalic.
lissocarpáceas s. f. pl. (Braz., bot.) a dicotyledonous family of the order Ebenales, which comprises only the Amazonian tree Lissocarpa benthami.
lissofobia s. f. (med.) lyssophobia: nervous state produced by a morbid dread of having contracted rabies.
lissótrico adj. lissotrichous, smooth-haired.
lista s. f. 1. list: a) roll, roster. b) catalogue. c) strip (of cloth, paper, etc.) ribbon, band, slip. 2. schedule. 3. bill of fare, menu, wine list (plate R 5). 4. line, stripe.
~ **de endereços comerciais** commercial directory. ~ **de preços** price list; statement of prices. ~ **de contribuições** subscription list. ~ **de estoque** statement of goods. ~ **negra** black book, black-list. ~ **telefônica** telephone book, directory (plate T 4).
listão s. m. (pl. **-ões**) 1. a large ribbon. 2. long and broad stripe. 3. strip. 4. carpenter's rule. 5. wake of a ship. || adj. striped.
listel s. m. (pl. **-éis**) (archit.) listel: a narrow fillet.
listra s. f. stripe (in a cloth).
listrado adj. 1. striped. 2. ribboned.
listrão s. m. (pl. **-ões**) a broad stripe.
listrar v. to stripe: adorn with stripes.
lisura s. f. 1. smoothness; softness. 2. (fig.): a) sincerity, frankness, openness, candour. b) honesty, fairness, plain dealing. c) good faith.
litagogo s. m. lithagogue: a medicine supposed to expel small calculi from the bladder. || adj. lithagogue.
litania s. f. (more used **ladainha**) litany.
litão s. m. (pl. **-ões**) a small dried dogfish.
litargírio s. m. litharge, protoxide of lead, lead monoxide.
liteira s. f. litter: couch with shafts, sedan (chair).
liteireiro s. m. litter carrier.
literal adj. m. + f. (pl. **-ais**) literal: 1. according to the letter. 2. following the exact words (translation). 3. exact, true. 4. expressed by letters. || **~mente** adv. literally.
tradução ~ verbal translation. **não é o sentido** ~ **da palavra** it is not the exact meaning of the word.
literalismo s. m. literalism.
literalista s. m. + f. literalist.
literário adj. 1. literary: of or pertaining to letters or literature. 2. lettered: of or pertaining to learning.
obra -a a literary work.
literata s. f. 1. authoress. 2. bluestocking: a literary woman.
literataço s. m. a pretentious man of letters.
literatagem s. f. (pl. **-ens**) (depr.) literati: men of letters.
literateiro s. m. (depr.) = **literatiço.**
literatejar v. to scribble: 1. write carelessly. 2. to be a writer of inferior matter.
literatice s. f. 1. bad writing, trashy literature. 2. mania of writing or mania for literature.
literatiço, literatiqueiro s. m. (also **literatelho**) scribbler: a writer of worthless or inferior matter. || adj. half-learned.
literatismo s. m. mania of writing.

literato s. m. 1. literate: a learned or literary person. 2. a man of letters.

literatura s. f. 1. literature, learning, letters, production of literary work. 2. literary production as a collective body. 3. men of letters. 4. literary life or profession. 5. bibliography. 6. any kind of printed matter. ~ **de cordel** worthless literature. ~ **de ficção** fiction, novels. ~ **de vanguarda** avant-garde literature. **ele especializou-se no ramo da literatura** he makes literature his special study.

lítia s. f. (chem.) lithia, lithium oxide.

litíase s. f. (med.) lithiasis: formation of stony deposits of any kind in any part of the body.

lítico adj. lithic: 1. (med.) of or pertaining to stone (calculi). 2. (chem.) uric (acid). 3. (Braz., coll.) genuine, authentic, pure.

litigante s. m. + f. litigant, litigator. ‖ adj. litigant.

litigar v. to litigate: 1. contend or suit at law. 2. plead (a cause).

litigável adj. m. + f. (pl. **-áveis**) litigable, disputable, contestable.

litígio s. m. 1. litigation, lawsuit. 2. dispute, contest, discussion. 3. pleadings.

litigioso adj. 1. litigious, contentious. 2. disputable, controvertible. ‖ **-amente** adv. litigiously.

litina s. f. (chem.) hydroxide of lithium.

lítio s. m. (chem.) lithium.

litispendência s. f. (jur.) the time during which a lawsuit is going on.

litobiomorfos s. m. pl. (zool.) Lithobiomorpha, an order of centipeds.

litocarpo s. m. fossilized fruit.

litóclase s. f. (geol.) lithoclase.

litoclasia, litoclastia s. f. (surg.) lithoclasty, lithotrity: breaking of stones in the bladder.

litoclasto s. m. lithoclast: an instrument used for crushing stones in the bladder.

litocromia s. f. lithochromatics, chromolithography.

litocrômico adj. lithochromatic, lithochromic.

litocromista s. m. + f. an expert in lithochromatics.

litófago adj. (zool.) lithophagous.

litofilo s. m. lithophyl(l): fossil leaf or impression of a leaf.

litófilo adj. lithophilous: growing on rocks.

litogenesia s. f. lithogenesis, petrogenesis.

litogenético adj. of or pertaining to lithogenesis.

litoglifia s. f. lithoglyptics: art of engraving on stone.

litóglifo s. m. lithoglypher: person who engraves precious stones.

litografar v. to lithograph: reproduce by means of lithography.

litografia s. f. 1. lithography: a printing process. 2. lithograph: a print made by lithography. 3. lithographical plant.

litográfico adj. lithographic(al): of or pertaining to lithography. ‖ **litograficamente** adv. lithographically.

litógrafo s. m. lithographer: person who practises lithography.

litóide adj. m. + f. lithoid(al): resembling stone.

litólatra s. m. + f. litholatrous person.

litolatria s. f. litholatry: the worship of stones of particular shapes.

litologia s. f. lithology: 1. (geol.) the study of rocks. 2. (med.) the study and treatment of calculi found in the human body.

litológico adj. lithologic(al): of or pertaining to lithology.

litologista s. m. + f. lithologist: person versed in lithology.

litólogo s. m. lithologist.

litomancia s. f. lithomancy: divination by means of stones.

litomarga s. f. (min.) lithomarge.

litômetro s. m. instrument for measuring stones.

litontríptico adj. lithontriptic.

litoral s. m. (pl. **-ais**) littoral: region lying along the coast; coastland, seaside, seaboard. ‖ adj. m. + f. (also **litorâneo, litóreo** m.) littoral, coastal.

litorina s. f. (Braz.) diesel-electric railway unit.

litorinídeos s. m. pl. (zool.) Litorinidae, a family of marine snails.

litosfera s. f. lithosphere: the crust of the earth.

litospermo adj. (bot.) lithospermous: having hard and stonelike seeds.

litotes s. f., sg. + pl. (rhet.) litotes: a figure in which an affirmative is expressed by the negative of the contrary.

litotomia s. f. (surg.) lithotomy: the operation, art, or practice of cutting for stones in the bladder.

litotomista s. m. + f. lithotomist: surgeon who removes stones from the bladder.

litotrícia s. f. (surg.) lithotrity: operation of crushing stones in the bladder.

litóxilo s. m. lithoxyl(e).

litráceas s. f. pl. (bot.) Lythraceae, a family of herbs, shrubs and trees of the order Myrtales.

litragem s. f. (pl. **-ens**) quantity expressed in liters.

litro s. m. 1. liter, litre: the unit of capacity in the metric system. 2. a bottle holding a liter.

lituano s. m. Lithuanian: 1. native or inabitant of Lithuania. 2. language of the Lithuanians. ‖ adj. Lithuanian.

litura s. f. 1. erasure. 2. obliterated word(s).

liturgia s. f. (eccl.) liturgy: public rites of the Christian Church; ritual.

litúrgico adj. liturgical: of or pertaining to liturgy. ‖ **liturgicamente** adv. liturgically.

liturgista s. m. + f. liturgist: person versed in liturgy.

livel s. m. (pl. **livéis**) (more frequently used **nível**) level.

livelar v. (also **nivelar**) to level.

lividez s. f. (also **livor** m.) lividity, lividness: the state of being livid.

lívido adj. livid: 1. black and blue, like a contusion. 2. ashy, pale. 3. wan(nish). ‖ **lividamente** adv. lividly.

livra interj. (Braz.) 1. look out!, beware! 2. heaven forbid!

livrador s. m. liberator, deliverer. ‖ adj. liberating, delivering.

livranhada s. f. (Braz.) a pile, heap or lot of books.

livramento s. m. 1. liberation, release; discharge. 2. delivery, deliverance, redemption, rescue. ~ **condicional** release on parole.

livrança s. f. 1. = **livramento**. 2. written order for payment.

livrar v. 1. to liberate, release, free, set at liberty, let go. 2. to save, rescue, deliver. 3. to protect, shield. 4. to exempt from. 5. **~-se**: a) to get rid of, escape from. b) to be free from. c) to free o. s. of. d) to shake off. **~-se de alguém** to get rid of s. o. ~ **uma propriedade de hipoteca** to clear an estate. **livramo-nos disso em boa hora** we got rid of it in time. **livrei-me à força (de)** I wrenched myself (from). **não é possível ~-se disto** there's no getting away from it. **não podia ~-me do meu resfriado** I could not throw off my cold. **Deus me livre!** God forbid!, Heaven preserve me!

livraria s. f. 1. bookshop, bookstore. 2. library; a collection of books.

livre adj. free: 1. at liberty, independent. 2. absolved, liberated, released. 3. unoccupied, unengaged, disengaged. 4. exempt, clear. 5. unimpeded, loose. 6. unmarried. 7. unlimited, boundless. 8. licentious, dissolute. 9. not literal. ‖ **~-mente** adv. freely.

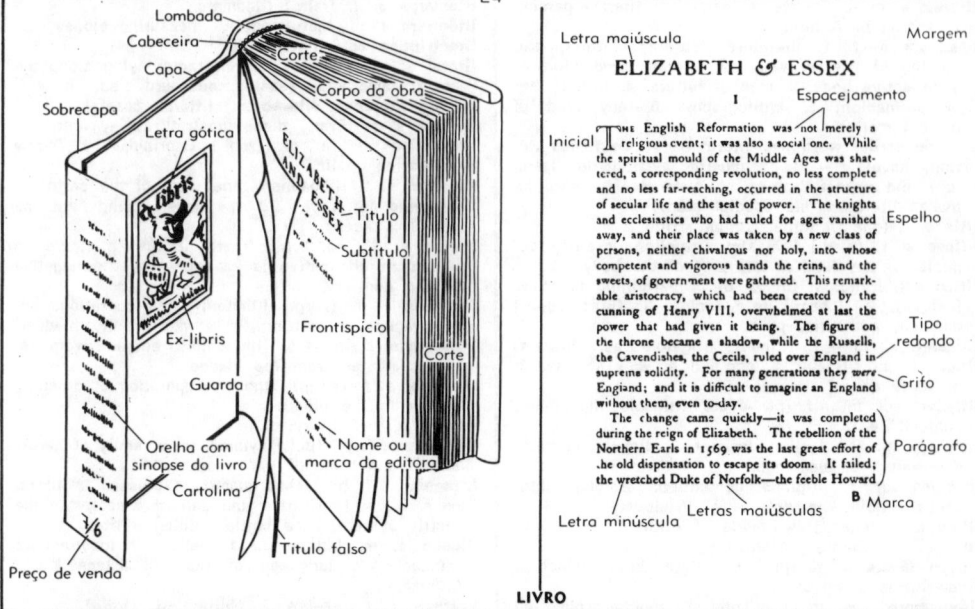

~ **de** free from, free of; innocent of, without. ~ **de dívidas** clear of debt. ~ **de doença** free from disease. ~ **de porte** free of postage. ~ **de restrições** free from restraint. ~ **sob fiança** out on bail. **ao ar** ~ out of doors. **de minha** ~ **e espontânea vontade** of my own free will. **ficamos** ~**s dele** we got clear of him. **você está** ~? are you disengaged?

livre-arbítrio s. m. (pl. **livres-arbítrios**) (philos.) free will.

livre-câmbio s. m. (pl. **livres-câmbios**) (also **livre-troca**) free trade.

livre-cambismo s. m. the policy of free trade.

livre-cambista s. m. + f. (pl. **livre-cambistas**) free trader.

livreco s. m. a worthless book.

livre-cultismo s. m. (pl. **livre-cultismos**) religious freedom, free worship.

livre-cultista s. m. + f. (pl. **livre-cultistas**) adherent of religious freedom.

livre-docência s. f. (pl. **livres-docências**) the professorship of a **livre-docente**.

livre-docente s. m. + f. (pl. **livres-docentes**) a college or university teacher contracted to eventually substitute a university professor. ‖ adj. m. + f. relating to a substitute college teacher.

livreiro s. m. bookseller.

livre-pensador s. m. (pl. **livres-pensadores**) freethinker.

livre-pensamento s. m. freethinking, freethought.

livresco adj. bookish: 1. of or pertaining to books. 2. fond of, or learned in books.

livrete s. m. (also **livreta** f.) 1. booklet: a little book. 2. notebook.

livre-troca s. f. (pl. **livres-trocas**) free trade.

livrilho s. m. liber.

livrinho s. m. diminutive of **livro**: booklet.

livro s. m. 1. book: a) a written or printed work (plate L 4). b) a literary or scientific composition. c) (fig.) anything that may be studied like a book. 2. (zool.) tripe, omasum, psalterium. 3. volume; writing; work.

~ **caixa** cash book, book of account. ~ **de apon-** tamentos agenda. ~ **de apostas** betting book. ~ **de bolso** pocketbook. ~ **de bordo** (naut.) logbook. ~ **de consulta** reference book. ~ **de endereços** directory. ~ **de leitura** reader, reading-book. ~ **de orações** prayer-book. ~ **de ponto** time-book, time--card, time-sheet. ~ **de salmos** psalm-book. ~ **em branco** blankbook. ~ **em quarto** a quarto book. ~ **escolar** school-book. ~ **estoque** stock-book. ~**s infantis** children's books. ~ **razão** ledger. ~**s sagrados** Holy Scriptures. **arrumar os** ~**s** to keep the books. **o** ~ **foi bem recebido** the book had a favourable acception. **venda de** ~**s** bookselling.

livrório s. m. (depr.) a very large, but worthless book.

lixa s. f. 1. sandpaper, glasspaper. 2. shagreen. 3. (ichth.) dog-fish.

~ **de esmeril** emery-cloth. ~ **de unha** emery-board.

lixação s. f. (pl. **-ões**) act of sandpapering.

lixadeira s. f. sander: sandpapering machine.

lixador s. m. sander: 1. person who sands, paperer. 2. a sandpapering machine. ‖ adj. sanding.

lixar v. 1. to sandpaper, to paper, rub with sand-paper. 2. to smooth, polish. 3. (sl.): a) to grow angry. b) to turn out badly.

lixeira s. f. (Braz., bot.) chaparro, sandpaper tree.

lixeiro s. m. (Braz.) 1. garbage collector. 2. dustman.

lixento adj. dirty, filthy.

lixívia s. f. lixivium, lye.

lixiviação s. f. (pl. **-ões**) lixiviation: act of leaching; percolation.

lixiviador s. m. lixiviator.

lixiviar v. to lixiviate, leach: separate by washing.

lixivioso adj. lixivial, lixivious.

lixo s. m. 1. garbage, trash. 2. refuse, waste, sweepings. 3. dirtiness, filthiness. 4. (fig.) rabble, mob.

lixoso adj. dirty, filthy.

lo (I) archaic form of the masculine definite article **o**.

lo (II) personal pron. m. third person singular used after verbal forms ending in **r**, **s**, or **z**, after the pron. **nos** and **vos**, and after the adv. **eis**.

ei-~! there he is! **ele no-**~ **pediu** he asked us

for it. **eu não pude vê-~** I could not see him.
fi-~ I did it.
ló s. m. 1. a kind of gauze. 2. (naut.) luff.
loa s. f. 1. prologue of a play. 2. laudatory speech.
3. (fig.) lie, swaggering, brag. 4. **~s** pl. popular
song in honour of the saints; carols.
loasáceas s. f. pl. (bot.) Loasaceae, a family of
dicotyledonous plants of the order Parietales.
loba (l) s. f. tumour on the breast of horses.
loba (ll) (ô) s. f. 1. she-wolf. 2. (obs.) harlot, strumpet. 3. cassock.
lobacho s. m. (also **lobato**) wolf cub.
lobado adj. (bot.) lobate(d), lobed.
lobal adj. m. + f. (pl. **-ais**) 1. wolfish: of or referring
to wolves. 2. (fig.) bloodthirsty, sanguinary.
lobão s. m. = **loba** (l).
lobaz s. m. a large wolf.
lobecão s. m. (pl. **-ões**) a crossbreed between a wolf
and a dog.
lobeiro s. m. wolf hunter: person who hunts wolves.
‖ adj. 1. wolf-hunting. 2. wolflike, wolfish.
lobélia s. f. 1. lobelia: plant of the family Lobe-
liaceae. 2. blue cardinal-flower.
lobinho s. m. 1. a little wolf. 2. (Braz.) cub: boy
scout of less than ten years of age. 3. a subcutaneous cyst, wen.
lobisomem s. m. (pl. **-ens**) (in folklore) werwolf: person who can change into a wolf.
lobo s. m. 1. (anat.) lobe: a rounded and globular
projection or part. 2. a sort of children's game.
lobo (ô) s. m. 1. (zool.) wolf: any of the doglike
animals of the genus Canis lupus. 2. (astr.) the
constellation Lupus. 3. (fig.) sanguinary person,
bloodthirsty man.
entre o ~ e o cão at twilight. **ele é um ~ em
pele de carneiro** he is a wolf in sheep's clothing.
lobo-cerval s. m. (pl. **lobos-cervais**) (zool.) the common European lynx (Lynx lynx).
lobo-do-mar s. m. (pl. **lobos-do-mar**) 1. sea-wolf: a)
(ichth.) wolf-fish. b) (zool.) sea-lion. c) (zool.) elephant seal. 2. (fig.) sea-dog, an experienced sailor.
lobo-marinho s. m. (pl. **lobos-marinhos**) (zool.) seal;
sea-wolf.
lôbrego adj. 1. dark, gloomy, dismal, moody. 2. sad,
mournful, lugubrious. 3. frightful.
lobrigador s. m. person who catches a glimpse of.
‖ adj. catching a glimpse of.
lobrigar v. 1. to catch a glimpse of. 2. to see for
an instant or faintly. 3. to perceive. 4. to descry,
discern, distinguish.
lobulado adj. lobulate(d): having small lobed divisions, lobate(d).
lobular adj. m. + f. lobular: having the form of a
lobule.
lóbulo s. m. lobule: a little lobe (plate F 5).
~ da orelha ear-lap, lappet.
lobuloso adj. lobulate(d).
loca s. f. 1. hiding place of fish under a stone. 2.
(Braz.) a little den or grotto.
locação s. f. (pl. **-ões**) location: 1. situation, place.
2. staked area. 3. letting, leasing, renting; hiring.
contrato de ~ location contract.
locador s. m. lessor: person who grants a lease, hirer.
local s. m. (pl. **-ais**) 1. place, spot, site, premises,
locality. 2. f. local news. ‖ adj. m. + f. local: of
or pertaining to a particular place. ‖ **~mente** adv.
locally.
cor ~ local colour. **~ de descoberta** site of discovery. **~ de diversão** place of amusement. **~ de
entrega** place of delivery. **~ de origem** point of
origin. **no ~** on the premises.
localidade s. f. 1. locality, place; situation. 2. settlement, small village.

localismo s. m. localism, sectionalism.
localista s. m. + f. writer or editor of local news. ‖
adj. m. + f. local: of or pertaining to a particular
place.
localização s. f. (pl. **-ões**) localization: act of localiz-
ing and the state of being localized.
localizado adj. seated, situated, localized.
localizar v. to localize, locate: 1. to fix the place of.
2. to determinate the situation or limits of. 3. to
make local. 4. **~-se** to be localized or situated.
localizável adj. m. + f. (pl. **-áveis**) localizable.
locanda s. f. 1. low tavern. 2. inn, lodging house.
3. small shop.
locandeiro s. m. 1. taverner. 2. innkeeper, innholder,
publican. 3. shopkeeper.
loção s. f. (pl. **-ões**) 1. lotion: a) washing. b) (med.)
ablution and the liquid therefore. 2. (Braz.) a
perfumed hair lotion.
locar v. 1. to let, lease, hire, rent. 2. to localize;
locate. 3. to mark out.
locatário s. m. 1. lessee: person to whom a lease is
granted. 2. tenant, renter. 3. lodger.
locativo s. m. (gram.) the locative case. ‖ adj. 1. tenantable. 2. (gram.) locative.
locomobilidade s. f. locomobility.
locomoção s. f. (pl. **-ões**) locomotion: act or effect
of moving from place to place.
locomotiva s. f. locomotive(-car), train engine.
~ a vapor steam engine. **~ diesel** diesel engine.
~ elétrica electric engine.
locomotividade s. f. locomotivity: power of locomotion.
locomotivo adj. locomotive: of or pertaining to locomotion.
locomotor adj. locomotor.
locomotriz adj. feminine form of **locomotor**.
locomóvel s. m. (pl. **-óveis**) locomobile, locomotive. ‖
adj. m. + f. 1. locomobile, locomotive: able to
move from place to place. 2. self-propelling.
locomover-se v. to move about, move from place to
place; to locomote.
locução s. f. (pl. **-ões**) 1. locution: a) form or mode
of speaking. b) phraseology, phrase. 2. expression.
3. language.
loculado adj. loculate: having loculi or cells (also
bot.).
locular adj. m. + f. (also bot.) locular: having one
or more loculi.
loculicida adj. m. + f. (bot.) loculicidal: dehiscing
through the back of the loculus.
lóculo adj. loculate: provided with loculi.
locupletar v. 1. to enrich, make rich. 2. to satiate.
3. **~-se:** a) to grow rich. b) to satiate o. s. c) to
get one's fill.
locusta s. f. 1. (zool.) locust: any grasshopper of the
family Acridiidae or Lacustidae. 2. (bot.) locusta:
a spikelet.
locustário adj. locustlike.
locustídeos s. m. pl. (ent.) Locustidae, Acridiidae,
the grasshopper family.
locutor s. m. speaker, radio announcer.
~ de televisão telecaster.
locutório s. m. parlour, locutory (esp. at a monastery); parlatory.
lodaçal s. m. (pl. **-ais**) 1. bog, swamp. 2. (fig.): a)
dissolute life. b) place of perdition.
lodaças s. f. pl. (Braz., pop.) 1. wheedling. 2. cute-
ness, artfulness. 3. boasting, bragging; audacity.
lódão s. m. (pl. **lódãos**) (bot.) 1. lotus. 2. nettle tree,
tree lotus.
lodeira s. f., **lodeiro** m. mudhole, quagmire, marsh,
swamp.
lodícula s. f. (bot.) lodicule.

lodo (ô) s. m. 1. mud, mire, dirt, slop, slush. 2. loam, clay. 3. silt; slime. 4. (fig.) ignominy, disgrace, dishonour, degradation.

lodoso adj. (also lodacento) 1. muddy, miry. 2. slimy. 3. sloppy. 4. dirty, turbid.

loendro s. m. (bot.) oleander, rosebay.

loess s. m. (geol.) loess.

lofobrânquios s. m. pl. (ichth.) Lophobranchii, an order of fishes that includes the sea horse.

loganiáceas s. f. pl. (bot.) Loganiaceae, a family of herbs, shrubs and trees of the order Gentianales.

logarítmico adj. logarithmic(al).

logaritmo s. m. (math.) logarithm.

lógica s. f. logic: 1. the science of reasoning; dialectics. 2. ratiocination, argumentation. 3. coherence. ele pensa com ~ he thinks coherently. falta de ~ illogicality.

logicar v. (obs.) to logicize.

lógico s. m. logician: person versed in logic. || adj. 1. logical: a) of or pertaining to logic. b) according to the principles of logic. 2. rational. 3. coherent, consistent. || logicamente adv. logically. coisa ~a an understood thing.

logística s. f. 1. logistics. 2. symbolic logic.

logo adv. 1. immediately, betimes, at once, right away, directly. 2. soon, before long. 3. later on. || conj. therefore, consequently, hence, so, ergo. ~ ~ (Braz.) forthwith. ~ após thereupon. ~ atrás hard after; soon after. ~ depois soon after. ~ ele é que fez isso! he, of all people, did that! ~ hoje é que foi chover it had to rain today of all days! ~ mais before long, at an early date. ~ mais eu vou ao cinema I'm going to the movies later. ~ no começo at the very beginning. ~ que as soon as. ~ que possa at your earliest convenience. até ~! so long! see you soon! desde ~ from that moment on. eu lhe disse ~ I told you so. farei isso ~ que receber instruções I will do it as soon as I have received instructions. penso, ~ existo I think, therefore I am. tão ~ que for possível as soon as possible.

logografia s. f. 1. logography. 2. stenography, shorthand.

logógrafo s. m. 1. logographer. 2. stenographer.

logográfico adj. logographic.

logogrifo s. m. 1. logogriph: a word puzzle. 2. (fig.) an obscure matter.

logomaquia s. f. logomachy: 1. contention about words. 2. a war of words.

logomáquico adj. logomachic(al): of or pertaining to logomachy.

logorréia s. f. (Braz.) logorrhea: excessive talkativeness, incoherent talk.

logotecnia s. f. the knowledge of words and their usage.

logotipo s. m. (typogr.) logotype.

logração s. f. (pl. -ões) 1. cheating, fraud; artifice, snare. 2. enjoyment, possession.

logradeira s. f. a female swindler or cheater.

logrador s. m. swindler, cheater, defrauder, crook, sharper. || adj. swindling, cheating, fraudulent.

logradouro s. m. (also logradoiro) public park; playground; common ground.

logramento s. m. cheating, fraud, swindle.

logrão s. m. (pl. -ões) cheater, swindler, crook.

lograr v. 1. to cheat, trick, deceive, defraud, swindle, gyp, dupe, take in, entrap, cozen, hoodwink. 2. to obtain, get, attain, acquire, win. 3. to enjoy, profit. 4. to succeed in, achieve. 5. to make a fool of; befool. 6. ~-se: a) to take advantage of. b) to increase. ~ êxito to meet with success. lograram-no no pri-

meiro de abril they made an April fool of him. não ~ êxito to come off badly.

logrativo adj. cheating, swindling, fraudulent.

logreiro s. m. (obs.) speculator; usurer. || adj. defrauding, cheating.

logro (ô) s. m. 1. cheat, swindle, fraud, trick, gyp, bamboozlement. 2. enjoyment, fruition, possession. 3. humbug; prank, hoax. 4. success, achievement. ele caiu no ~ he was trapped up.

loiça s. f. = louça.

lóio s. m. friar of the order of St. John the Evangelist. || adj. pertaining to this order.

loiro s. m., adj. = louro.

loja s. f. 1. ground floor. 2. shop: a) store; baza(a)r. b) workshop. 3. freemason's lodge. 4. (bot.) each division of an anther. ~ de artigos para homens shop for gentlemen's articles, haberdashery. ~ de doces sweetshop. ~ de ferragens hardware shop. ~ de miudezas (Braz.) notion shop. ~ de secos e molhados grocery. ~ de varejo retail shop. eles abriram uma ~ they set up a shop. eles têm uma ~ they keep a shop. ladrão de ~s shoplifter.

lojeca s. f. 1. shoplet. 2. small tavern.

lojista s. m. + f. shopkeeper: person who keeps a shop.

loligídeos s. m. pl. (zool.) Loliginidae, the squid family.

lólio s. m. (bot.) darnel (Lolium temulentum).

lomba s. f. 1. ridge or brow of a hill, crest. 2. tableland, elevated plain. 3. slope. 4. (Port.) indolence, laziness.

lombada s. f. 1. range of hills, mountain-chain. 2. mountain-ridge. 3. rump (animal, esp. ox). 4. back of a book, spine (plate L 4).

lombar adj. m. + f. lumbar: of or pertaining to the loins. região ~ lumbar region.

lombarda s. f. (also couve ~) savoy (cabbage).

lombardo s. m. Lombard: native or inhabitant of Lombardy. || adj. 1. Lombardic. 2. black with brown spots on the rump (bull).

lombear v. (Braz.) 1. to gall (the back of a horse). 2. ~-se: a) to curve the back (horse). b) to become lazy. c) to procrastinate, defer, delay, put off.

lombeira s. f. (Braz.) 1. feebleness, listlessness. 2. indolence, laziness.

lombeiro s. m. skin or hide of the rump of some animals. || adj. lumbar: of or pertaining to the loins.

lombilheiro s. m. (Braz.) person who makes or sells a species of saddle called lombilho.

lombilho s. m. 1. (Braz.) a kind of saddle. 2. tenderloin.

lombinho s. m. 1. tenderloin (beef or pork). 2. smoked tenderloin (of pork).

lombo s. m. 1. loin, reins, back (of an animal) (plates C 12, G 1). 2. pork loin (smoked or roasted). 3. back of a book. 4. (fig.) any curved surface. ~ de boi sirloin, loin of beef. encadernação com cantos e ~ de couro half-binding. endurecer o ~ to sulk.

lombrical adj. m. + f. (pl. -ais) of, pertaining to or like the roundworms.

lombricóide s. m. lumbricoid: the worm Ascaris lumbricoides. || adj. m. + f. lumbricoid.

lombriga s. f. roundworm, Ascaris lumbricoides.

lombrigueira s. f. pinkroot: plant of the family Longaniaceae (Spigelia anthelminthica).

lombrigueiro s. m. (Braz.) anthelmintic, vermifuge.

lombrosiano adj. Lombrosian.

lombudo adj. strong-backed.

lona s. f. 1. canvas, sailcloth; tarpaulin (plate T 2). 2. (fig.): a) nonsense. b) lie, fib. ~ **de freio** brake lining. ~ **para acondicionamento** packing-sheet.

lonca s. f. (S. Braz.) 1. half of a horse's back. 2. stripes of rawhide.

londrino s. m. Londoner: native or inhabitant of London. || adj. of or pertaining to London.

longada s. f. (obs.) a long journey. **de** ~ travelling.

longal adj. m. + f. (pl. **-ais**) longish; dilated, wide, enlarged.

longamira s. f. spyglass, telescope.

longana s. f. (Braz.) longan: plant of the family Sapindaceae (Nephelium longana).

longânime adj. m. + f., **longânimo** m. 1. longanimous, forbearing, patient, tolerant, long-suffering. 2. magnanimous, generous.

longanimidade s. f. longanimíty, forbearance, long--suffering, patience.

longarina s. f., **longarino** m. 1. stringer: longitudinal piece of a bridge (as a girder). 2. longitudinal bar of an automobile chassis. 3. spar, longeron (of an airplane).

longe adj. m. + f. remote, distant, far away, far off. || adv. 1. far, far off, at a great distance, afar. 2. to a great degree, by a great deal. || interj. by no means! ~ **da vista** out of sight. ~ **de** away, distant from. ~ **de fazer alguma coisa** far from doing anything. ~ **daqui** a long way from here. ~ **demais para ser ouvido** out of hearing. ~ **de mim!** far be it from me! ~ **disso** far from it. ~ **de alvo** wide of the mark. ~ **dos olhos,** ~ **do coração** out of sight, out of mind; long absent, soon forgotten. **ao** ~ at a distance, far off. **bem** ~ a good way off. **de** ~ : 1. from afar. 2. by far. **de** ~ **em** ~ at intervals; from time to time. **devagar se vai ao** ~ more haste, less speed. **ela está** ~ **de ser forte** she is far from strong. **ela mora um pouco mais** ~ she lives a little farther away. **ele está** ~ **do seu lar** he is far away from home. **ele leva sua independência** ~ **demais** he carries his independence too far. **ele mora bem** ~ **daqui** he lives far away from here. **estamos** ~ **de casa** we are far from home. **estou** ~ **de pensar que** I am far from thinking that. **estender-se** ~ to cover much ground. **mais** ~ farther, beyond. **muito** ~ very far away, way off. **não precisa procurar** ~ **daqui** you have not far to seek. **para** ~ far away. **tão** ~ **assim?** as far as that? **tão** ~ **quanto a vista alcança** as far as the eye can reach.

longerão s. m. (pl. **-ões**) a lateral beam of a loco-motive frame.

longes s. m. pl. 1. background. 2. slight resemblance. 3. great distance (in time or space).

longevidade s. f. longevity: 1. long life. 2. length or duration of life.

longevo adj. 1. longevous, macrobian: long-lived. 2. of advanced age.

longicaule adj. m. + f. (bot.) long-stemmed.

longilobado adj. divided into alongated lobules.

longimano adj. longimanous: long-handed.

longimetria s. f. longimetry: measurement along a line.

longínquo adj. distant, far-away, far-off, remote.

longipalpo adj. (zool.) having long feelers.

longípede adj. m. + f. long-footed.

longipétalo adj. (bot.) having long petals.

longirrostro adj. (zool.) longirostral, longirostrate, long-beaked.

longitude s. f. 1. (geog.) longitude. 2. distance.

longitudinal adj. m. + f. (pl. **-ais**) longitudinal. || ~**mente** adv. longitudinally, lengthwise, endways.

longo adj. 1. long, lengthy. 2. prolix, diffuse, pro-tract. || **-amente** adv. 1. for a long while or time. 2. at lenght, extensively. **a** ~ **prazo** long-dated. **ao** ~ **de** along of, along-side, along. **ao** ~ **da costa** along the coast. **de** ~ **a** ~ at full length. **vôo de -a distância** long-dis-tance flight.

longobardo s. m. (hist.) Lombard. || adj. Lombardic.

longor s. m. 1. lenght. 2. (fig.) delay.

longrina s. f. 1. longitudinal beam or girder. 2. lon-gitudinal stringer.

longueirão s. m. (pl. **-ões**) (zool.) razor clam. || adj. very long.

longueiro adj. (obs.) long, lasting a long time.

longuidão s. f. (pl. **-ões**) length: quality or state of being long.

longura s. f. 1. length. 2. protraction, delay.

lonjura s. f. great distance.

lonquear v. to scrape leather and cut it into stripes which are used for plaitwork, lassos or the like.

lontra s. f. (zool.) otter (Lutra platensis).

lontra-do-mar s. f. (pl. **lontras-do-mar**) (zool.) sea otter.

loquacidade s. f. loquaciousness, loquacity, talkative-ness, garrulity.

loquaz adj. m. + f. 1. loquacious, talkative, chatter-ing, garrulous. 2. eloquent. || ~**mente** adv. loqua-ciously.

loque s. m. (pharm.) lohock, lohoch, linctus.

loqüela s. f. 1. speech, talk, the faculty of speech. 2. verbosity, verbal nimbleness, gift of the gab.

loquete s. m. 1. padlock. 2. (door) bolt.

loquial adj. m. + f. (pl. **-ais**) (med.) lochial: of or pertaining to lochia.

lóquios s. m. pl. (med.) lochia: discharge from the uterus and vagina which follows childbirth.

lorantáceas s. f. pl. (bot.) Loranthaceae, the mistletoe family.

loranto s. m. (bot.) loranthus.

lordaça s. m. (N. Braz., coll.) foreigner.

lordaço adj. (N. Braz.) wealthy, rich.

lorde s. m. 1. lord: an English title of noblemen. 2. (fig.) a man who leads an ostentatious and luxu-rious life. || adj. ostentatious, lordly.

lordose s. f. (med.) lordosis: abnormal forward cur-vature of the spinal column.

lorica s. f. (bot.) testa, episperm.

loricados s. m. pl. (zool.) Loricata, a suborder of metazoan animals.

loriga s. f. loriga: a Roman cuirass.

lóris s. m. (zool.) loris.

lornhão s. m. (pl. **-ões**) (opt.) lorgnon, lorgnette: eyeglasses with a handle.

loro s. m. 1. stirrup leather, stirrup strap (plate S 2). 2. lore: the part of a bird's head between the eyes and the bill. **encurtar os** ~**s** (Braz., pop.) to be quiet, hold one's tongue, shut up.

lorota s. f. (Braz., pop.) 1. fib, lie. 2. idle talk, non-sense. 3. bragging, bunk, twaddle. **ele contou uma** ~ he told a fib.

lorotagem s. f. (pl. **-ens**) (Braz., pop.) 1. lies. 2. a lot of nonsense.

lorotar v. 1. to lie, fib. 2. to tell tales. 3. to brag, boast, gabble.

loroteiro s. m. lier, fibber. || adj. lying, false.

lorpa s. m. + f. 1. imbecile, nitwit, numskull. 2. dolt, loggerhead. 3. fool, simpleton. || adj. 1. imbecile, silly, foolish. 2. doltish.

lorpice s. f. silliness, foolishness.

losango s. m. (geom.) lozenge: a plane figure with four equal sides having two acute and two obtuse angles; also called diamond.

losna s. f. (bot.) wormwood.

losna-do-algarve s. f. (pl. **losnas-do-algarve**) (also **losna-menor**, pl. **losnas-menores**) (bot.) a wormwood (Artemisia arborescens), common in Algarve (Port.).

losna-maior s. f. (pl. **losnas-maiores**) (bot.) common wormwood (Artemisia absinthum).

lota s. f. a place where fish are sold by auction.

lotação s. f. (pl. **-ões**) 1. allotment, division into parcels. 2. capacity (of a room, vehicle, etc.). 3. estimate, valuation, estimated cost. 4. tonnage (of a ship). 5. blending of wine. 6. m. (Braz.) a jitney vehicle.

lotado adj. 1. full, filled, replete. 2. crowded (as a bus).

lotador s. m. 1. apprizer, estimator, valuer. 2. man who divides land into parcels.

lotar v. 1. to allot: a) distribute by lots. b) distribute in portions. 2. to divide into parcels. 3. to fix the number of, calculate. 4. to blend wine.

lotaria s. f. less used form of **loteria**.

lote s. m. 1. lot, allotment, portion, share, parcel. 2. quality, sort. 3. tonnage (of a ship). 4. a plot of land, lot. 5. quantity of articles sold at a time.

loteamento s. m. (Braz.) division of land into parcels or lots.

lotear v. (Braz.) to divide land into parcels or lots.

loteca s. f. (Braz., pop.) popular name for **loteria esportiva**.

loteria s. f. lottery: 1. a method of allotting prizes by chance. 2. (fig.) an affair of chance.
~ **esportiva** official lottery in which win they who guess the winning team of thirteen preestablished soccer games. ~ **federal** official lottery controlled by the federal government.

lotérico adj. concerning lotteries or lottery tickets.

loto (I) s. m. (bot.) lotus (Nelumbo nucifera).

loto (II) s. f. (Braz.) a number lottery in which one must guess five numbers in one hundred (from 01 to 00) in order to gain the jackpot.

loto (ô) s. m. lotto, keno.

loto-sagrado-do-egito s. m. (pl. **lotos-sagrados-do--egito**) (bot.) Egyptian lotus.

lótus s. m., sg. + pl. (bot.) lotus.

louça s. f. (also **loiça**) 1. chinaware, dishware. 2. earthenware, crockery, ceramics.

louçainha s. f. 1. pomp, display. 2. gala dress; ornament, attire. 3. finery.

louçainho adj. 1. ornamented, adorned. 2. chic, elegant.

louçania s. f. 1. pomp, showiness, elegance. 2. elegant bearing.

loução adj. (pl. **louçãos**) (f. **louçã**) 1. smart, stylish, fashionable, elegant, fine. 2. gracious, kind. 3. rank, lusty.

louçaria s. f. (also **loiçaria**) 1. chinaware shop, crockery shop. 2. an amount of crockery.

louceira s. f. 1. a woman who makes or sells chinaware. 2. cupboard for china, china closet.

louceiro s. m. 1. dealer in chinaware or crockery. 2. cupboard for china, china closet.

louco s. m. 1. mad, crazy or insane person, a maniac, madman, lunatic. 2. (bot.) climbing plumbago (Plumbago scandens). ‖ adj. 1. mad, lunatic, crazy, insane, maniacal. 2. extravagant. 3. bold, daring. 4. infatuated. 5. rash. 6. furious, enraged, wild. 7. (fig.) foolish, silly. ‖ **-amente** adv. 1. madly, crazily, maniacally. 2. boldly, daringly.
~ **de alegria** mad with joy, as pleased as Punch. ~ **de raiva** frantic with anger, as mad as a hatter. ~ **varrido** stark crazy. **cada** ~ **com sua mania**

each to his own taste. **ele está** ~ **atrás disto** he is spoiling for it. **ele está** ~ **por ela** he is madly in love with her, he is struck on her. **eles estavam** ~**s para me ver** they were wild to see me. **estou** ~ **para dar um tapa nele** my fingers itch to box his ears. **isto me deixa** ~ it makes me quite mad. **não me faça ficar** ~**!** don't drive me mad!

loucura s. f. (also **louquice**) 1. madness, craziness, insanity. 2. folly, nonsense, foolishness. 3. extravagance. 4. (Braz., bot.) crape myrtle.

louquejar v. to act crazily or foolishly.

loura s. f. (also **loira**) 1. blond woman or girl. 2. (fam.) sovereign, gold coin.

louraça s. m. + f. 1. flaxen-haired person. 2. (fig.) simpleton.

loureira s. f. (also **loireira**) 1. wanton woman. 2. strumpet, whore, prostitute. 3. coquette, seducteress.

loureiral s. m. (pl. **-ais**) (also **loireiral**) laurel grove.

loureiro s. m. (also **loireiro**) (bot.) laurel (tree), bay--tree (Laurus nobilis).

loureiro-cereja s. m. (pl. **loureiros-cereja**) (bot.) cherry-laurel (Prunus laurocerasus).

lourejante adj. m. + f. yellowing: 1. growing yellow. 2. making yellow.

lourejar v. (also **lourecer**) to yellow: 1. become yellow. 2. make yellow.

louro (I) s. m. (also **loiro**) 1. (bot.) laurel tree, bay--tree. 2. laurel. 3. ~**s** pl. (sl.) triumph, glory.

louro (II) s. m. (also **loiro**) (fam.) parrot.

louro (III) adj. (also **loiro**) 1. yellow. 2. blond, fair (-haired).

louro-amarelo s. m. (pl. **louros-amarelos**) (bot., also **loiro-amarelo**) the onion cordia (Cordia alliodora).

louro-branco s. m. (pl. **louros-brancos**) (bot., also **loiro-branco**) the white-laurel ocotea (Ocotea guianensis).

louro-cravo s. m. (pl. **louros-cravo**) (Braz., bot., also **loiro-cravo**) pinkwood (Dicypellium caryophyllatum).

louro-vermelho s. m. (pl. **louros-vermelhos**) (Braz., bot., also **loiro-vermelho**) loblolly whitewood (Ocotea rubra).

lousa s. f. 1. slate. 2. frame tablet of slate. 3. gravestone, tombstone. 4. (Braz.) blackboard.

louva-a-deus s. m., sg. + pl. (ent.) mantis, praying mantis (Mantis religiosa).

louvação s. f. (pl. **-ões**) (also **louvamento** m.) 1. laudation, praise, praising. 2. eulogy. 3. valuation, appraisement.

louvado s. m. 1. umpire, arbiter, judge. 2. valuer, appraiser. ‖ adj. praised. ‖ **-amente** adv. with praise.
~ **seja Deus** praise be to God!, God be praised!

louvador s. m. praiser, lauder, eulogizer. ‖ adj. praising, laudatory.

louvaminha s. f. flattery, adulation, fawning, coaxing, cajolery.

louvaminhar v. to flatter, coax, wheedle, cajole.

louvaminheiro s. m. flatterer, coaxer, cajoler. ‖ adj. flattering, coaxing, wheedling.

louvar v. 1. to laud, eulogize, praise, extol. 2. to exalt, ennoble. 3. to glorify, bless. 4. to approve, applaud, commend. 5. to value, rate. 6. ~**-se** to boast, swagger.
~**-se em alguém** to accept the opinions or the judgement of somebody else, submit a case to the judgement of others.

louvável adj. m. + f. (pl. **-áveis**) laudable, commendable, praiseworthy. ‖ **louvavelmente** adv. laudably, commendably.

louvor s. m. 1. praise, laudation, laud, encomium, eulogy. 2. glorification. 3. applause.
digo-o em seu ~ I say it to praise him.

loxodromia s. f. loxodromics, loxodromy.

loxodrômico adj. loxodromic(al).

loxodromismo s. m. loxodromism.
lua s. f. 1. moon. 2. (fig.) month. 3. (coll.) bad humour, neurasteny. 4. (pop.) menses.
~ **cheia** full moon. ~-**de-mel** honeymoon. ~ **nova** new moon. **hoje ele está de** ~ he is ill-humoured today.
luar s. m. moonlight, moonshine.
luarento adj. moonlit.
lubambeiro adj. (Braz., pop.) 1. disorderly, rowdy. 2. scheming, intriguing.
lubambo s. m. (Braz., pop.) 1. noise, row, riot. 2. entanglement. 3. scheme, intrigue.
lubricar v. to lubricate.
lubricidade s. f. 1. lubricity, smoothness, slipperiness. 2. (fig.) lasciviousness, lewdness, lechery, sensuality.
lúbrico adj. 1. slippery, lubricous. 2. (fig.) lascivious, sensual, lecherous, lewd. ‖ **lubricamente** adv. lasciviously.
lubrificação s. f. (pl. -**ões**) lubrication: act of lubricating.
~ **sob pressão** (mech.) forced lubrication.
lubrificador s. m. lubricator (plate E 1). ‖ adj. lubricational.
lubrificante s. m. lubricant. ‖ adj. m. + f. lubricative, lubricating.
lubrificar v. 1. to lubricate: a) make smooth or slippery. b) grease, oil. 2. to become smooth or slippery.
luca s. f. (zool.) tree toad.
lucanário s. m. space between girders of a building.
lucão s. m. (pl. -**ões**) a variety of fishing-net.
lucarna s. f. lucarne, dormer, dormer-window, garret window, skylight.
lucerna s. f. 1. lucerne: a small light. 2. (obs.) skylight.
lucescente adj. m. + f. (poet.) 1. beginning to shine. 2. shining.
luchar v. (Port.) to soil, dirty.
lúcia-lima s. f. (pl. **lúcias-lima**) (bot.) lemon verbena (Lippia citriodora).
lucidar v. to pounce or trace (a drawing).
lucidez s. f. lucidity, lucidness: 1. brightness, clearness. 2. clearheadedness. 3. perceptibility, perspicality, perspicuity.
lúcido adj. lucid: 1. shining, bright. 2. clear, pellucid. 3. clearheaded, perspicaceous, discerning. ‖ **lucidamente** adv. lucidly; clearheadedly.
Lúcifer s. m. (pl. **Lucíferes**) Lucifer: 1. Satan. 2. (astr.) Venus, morning star.
luciferário s. m. candle bearer at a procession.
luciferino adj. (also **luciferiano, luciférico**) 1. Luciferian, Satanic. 2. diabolic, devilish.
lucífero adj. (poet.) luciferous, illuminating, giving light.
lucífugo adj. lucifugous, avoiding light.
lucilação s. f. (pl. -**ões**) glimmer(ing).
lucilante adj. m. + f. glimmering, gleaming.
lucilar v. 1. to glimmer, gleam, glitter, flicker. 2. to sparkle, twinkle.
luciluzir v. (Braz.) to sparkle, twinkle (firefly).
lucímetro s. m. lucimeter.
lucina s. f. (poet.) the moon.
lucinídeos s. m. pl. (zool.) Lucinidae, a family of bivalve molluscs.
lúcio s. m. (ichth.) pike.
lucipotente adj. m. + f. (poet.) 1. intensely bright. 2. illuminating everything.
lucivelo, lucivéu s. m. (Braz.) lampshade.
luco s. m. (obs.) wood, forest.
lucrar v. 1. to profit, benefit. 2. to gain, earn, reap. 3. to take advantage of.
lucrativo adj. 1. lucrative, profitable, gainful. 2. advantageous. ‖ -**amente** adv. lucratively, gainfully.
ser ~ to make or obtain good returns.

lucro s. m. 1. profit, gain, returns, earning. 2. advantage(ousness), utility. 3. lucre.
~ **líquido** clear gain. ~**s e perdas** profits and losses. **com um** ~ **de** at a profit of. **deixa** ~ it leaves a profit. **obtiveram** ~ **disto** they made a profit on it. **participação nos** ~**s** profit-sharing.
lucroso adj. 1. = **lucrativo**. 2. making profit.
luctífero, lutífero adj. (poet.) 1. mournful, sorrowful, saddening. 2. disastrous, calamitous.
luctíssono, lutíssono adj. (poet.) sounding mournfully.
lucubração s. f. (pl. -**ões**) (also **elucubração**) lucubration: 1. work or study done during the night. 2. close meditation; careful consideration. 3. too elaborate a composition.
lucubrar v. to lucubrate: 1. study or work earnestly or laboriously (esp. at night). 2. meditate, think closely.
lúcula s. f. (astr.) granule.
luculento adj. (poet.) luculent, bright, shining.
luculiano adj. Lucullan, Lucullian.
ludâmbulo s. m. (Braz.) tourist.
ludar s. m. (bot.) lodebark.
ludibriante adj. m. + f. 1. deceiving, cheating. 2. sham. 3. mocking, derisive. 4. ridiculing.
ludibriar v. 1. to deceive, cheat, illude. 2. to mock, deride, scorn. 3. to ridicule.
ludíbrio s. m. 1. mockery, scorn. 2. laughing-stock, butt. 3. subject of mockery. 4. (fig.) fool.
ludibrioso adj. 1. mocking, derisive, scornful. 2. jeering. 3. injurious.
ludo s. m. ludo: a kind of pachisi.
ludoterapia s. f. (therapeutics) the treatment of mental patients by means of toys, entertainment and games (including sports).
ludreiro s. m. 1. mudhole. 2. slough, quagmire.
lúdrico adj. ludicrous, ridiculous, funny, sportive, droll.
ludro, ludroso adj. 1. dirty. 2. coarse (of wool). 3. turbid (of liquids).
lues s. f. (med.) lues, syphilis.
luético adj. (med.) luetic, syphilitic.
lufa s. f. 1. high wind, gust. 2. (fig.) ado, fuss, bustle, hurry, flurry.
lufada s. f. flurry, gust of wind, blast, squall.
lufa-lufa s. f. 1. fuss, ado, bustle. 2. great haste, hurry.
andar numa ~ to wear o. s. out. **muita** ~ much ado.
lufar v. 1. to blow violently (wind). 2. to pant, puff, gasp, breathe with difficulty.
lugar s. m. 1. place, room, space. 2. spot, site, locality. 3. village, town. 4. position, office, employment, post. 5. passage of a book. 6. opportunity, occasion, time. 7. (theat., school, etc.) seat.
~ **de honra** place of honour. ~ **de partida** (turf) starting-gate, starting-post. ~ **geométrico** locus. ~ **público** public place. ~ **santo** holy place. **dar** ~ **a** 1. to yield, give place to. 2. to cause; occasion. **deixe um** ~ **para mais uma cadeira** leave room for another chair. **ela está em qualquer** ~ **do jardim** she is about the garden. **ela sabe o** ~ **que lhe compete** she knows her place. **ele ocupou seu** ~ he took his place. **em algum** ~ in some place, somewhere. **em** ~ **de** instead of, in place of. **em primeiro** ~ in the first place. **em qualquer** ~ anywhere. **em seu** ~ in his place. **irei em** ~ **de meu pai** I shall go in my father's stead. **não queria estar no seu** ~ (fig.) I should not like to be in your (his) shoes. **naquele mesmo** ~ (ou **instante**) on the spot. **no** ~ **certo** in (the right) place. **o homem adequado no** ~ **que lhe compete** the right man in the right place. **o** ~ **da capa é no armário** the coat goes in the wardrobe. **o teatro tem 900**

~es the theatre seats 900. **ter** ~ to take place, be realized. **tomem seus ~es!** take your seats!

lugar-comum s. m. (pl. **lugares-comuns**) commonplace, cliché.

lugarejo s. m. small village, hamlet.

lugar-tenente s. m. (pl. **lugar-tenentes**) locum tenens, substitute.

lugdunense s. m. + f. Lyonese: native or inhabitant of Lyon. || adj. Lyonese: of or pertaining to Lyon.

lugente adj. m. + f. plaintive, mournful, doleful.

lugre s. m. 1. lugger: a vessel carrying a lugsail or lugsails. 2. (ornith.) siskin, aberdevine.

lúgubre adj. m. + f. 1. lugubrious, mournful, doleful, sad. 2. gloomy, dark. 3. dreadful, direful, terrible. 4. frightful, sinister. || **lugubremente** adv. 1. lugubriously. 2. frightfully.

lugubridade s. f. 1. lugubriousness, mournfulness. 2. frightfulness.

luís s. m. louis d'or: a French gold coin.

lula s. f. (zool.) squid, calamary.

lumaquela s. f. lumachel(la) (limestone).

lumaréu s. m. 1. bonfire, camp-fire. 2. little flame.

lumbágico adj. lumbaginous: of, pertaining to or affected with lumbago.

lumbago s. m. (med., also **lumbagem** f.) lumbago: rheumatic pain in the lumbar region.

lumbrical adj. m. + f. (pl. **-ais**) (also **lumbricário** m., **lombrical** m. + f.) lumbrical.

lumbricida adj. m. + f. (med.) anthelmintic, vermicide: destroying intestinal worms.

lume s. m. 1. fire, flame. 2. light. 3. candle. 4. spark. 5. brightness, splendour. 6. (fig.) insight, penetration.

~ **de água** water level, surface of water. **acender o** ~ to light the fire. **dar a** ~ to publish. **ter** ~ **de alguma coisa** to have a slight knowledge about something. **ter** ~ **no olho** to be clever. **tirar a** ~ to bring to light, make known.

lumeeira s. f. 1. torch. 2. candlestick. 3. skylight. 4. dormer-window. 5. gleam of light. 6. (ent.) glowworm, firefly.

lumeeiro s. m. 1. star. 2. source of light. 3. light shaft. 4. (ent.) firefly.

lúmen s. m. (pl. **lumens**) lumen: unit of light.

luminar s. m. 1. track, trail, trace. 2. illustrious person. || adj. m. + f. illuminating.

luminária s. f. 1. luminary: a) a body that gives light. b) an artificial light. 2. small lantern. 3. candle. 4. luminaire. 5. (fig.) very illustrious person. 6. ~s pl. festive illumination.

luminescência s. f. luminescence: an emission of light otherwise than from incandescence.

luminescente adj. m. + f. luminescent: pertaining to luminescence.

luminosidade s. f. luminosity: quality of being luminous.

luminoso adj. 1. luminous: a) shining, bright, brilliant, radiant. b) light, bright. c) (fig.) enlightened, perspicacious, keen, intelligent. 2. clear, evident. 3. beautiful.

anúncios ~s illuminated ads.

lumpo s. m. (ichth.) lumpfish.

lunação s. f. (pl. **-ões**) lunation: the period between two successive new moons.

lunar s. m. mole, spot on the skin; birthmark. || adj. m. + f. lunar: of or pertaining to the moon.

mês ~ lunar month.

lunária s. f. (bot.) lunary, perennial honesty.

lunário s. m. lunar calendar.

lunático s. m. a lunatic, madman. || adj. lunatic, mad, crazy, moonstruck.

lundu(m) s. m. (Braz.) a dance of African origin.

luneta s. f. 1. eyeglasses, spectacles, pince-nez. 2. field-glass, spy-glass. 3. (archit.) lunette; small, round or half-round window; skylight. 4. in a guillotine the hole for the victim's head.

~ **de torno** (mech.) back rest (lathe).

lunícola s. m. + f. selenite: hypothetical inhabitant of the moon. || adj. concerning the selenites.

luniforme adj. m. + f. luniform.

lunissolar adj. m. + f. lunisolar: pertaining to the moon and the sun.

lúnula s. f. 1. (astr.) a satellite. 2. (geom.) lune. 3. (anat., zool.) lunule: mark at the base of a fingernail.

lupa s. f. magnifying glass.

lupulina s. f. 1. (bot.) black medic (Medicago lupulus). 2. lupulin, lupulite.

lúpulo s. m. hop: plant of the family Moraceae (Humulus lupulus).

lúpus s. m. (med., also **lupo**) lupus.

lura s. f. burrow: hole dug in the ground by rabbits (or other animals) for refuge or shelter.

lurar v. 1. to burrow: dig a hole in the ground. 2. to excavate, hollow out.

lúrido adj. 1. lurid, wan, pale, dismal. 2. (poet.) dark.

lusco adj. 1. squint-eyed, cross-eyed. 2. one-eyed.

entre ~ **e fusco** at twilight. **ir entre** ~ **e fusco** to act without precise instructions.

lusco-fusco s. m. twilight, dusk, nightfall.

ao ~ in the dusk of the evening.

lusíada s. m. + f. 1. Lusitanian, Portuguese. 2. **Lusíadas** pl. (lit.) Lusiads. || adj. Lusitanian, Portuguese.

lusismo s. m. a word, expression or grammatical construction peculiar to Portugal.

lusitânico, lusitano s. m. (also **luso**) Lusitanian, Portuguese: native or inhabitant of ancient Lusitania or of modern Portugal. || adj. Lusitanian, Portuguese.

lusitanismo s. m. 1. the quality of being Portuguese. 2. a word, or expression peculiar to Portugal.

lustração s. f. (pl. **-ões**) 1. polishing, shining. 2. (fig.) lustration; purification. 3. varnish.

lustradela s. f. a slight polishing, glossing or shining.

lustrador s. m. polisher, glosser, shiner, burnisher. || adj. polishing, glossing.

lustral adj. m. + f. (pl. **-ais**) 1. lustral: used in purification. 2. used in polishing.

lustrar v. 1. to polish, gloss, shine, burnish. 2. to purify, lustrate. 3. to varnish. 4. to illustrate, instruct.

lustre s. m. 1. luster, lustre: a) brightness, gloss, shine. b) glory, splendour. c) fame, reputation, renown. 2. chandelier, candelabrum. 3. pendant lamp.

dar ~ **a** to give (new) luster to.

lustrina s. f. lustring: a lustrous silk fabric.

lustro s. m. 1. lustrum, quinquennium (a period of five years). 2. lustre, shine; polish.

lustroso adj. 1. lustrous, shining. 2. glossy, polished. 3. magnificent, noteworthy.

luta s. f. 1. fight, contest, combat. 2. conflict, war, battle. 3. struggle, effort, pains, toil and moil.

~ **corpo a corpo** hand to hand fight. ~ **de classes** class-conflict. ~ **de morte** war to the knife. ~ **final** final battle, show-down. ~ **livre** catch as catch can. ~ **romana** wrestling. ~ **séria** stand-up fight. **a** ~ **pela vida** the struggle for life. **atirar-se na** ~ to fling o. s. into the fray. **aceitar a** ~ to accept combat. **disputa de** ~ **romana** wrestling match.

lutador s. m. fighter, wrestler, contender. || adj. combative, fighting, pugnacious.

lutar (I) v. 1. to fight, contend, combat. 2. to wrestle. 3. to struggle, strive.

~ **contra a maré** to stem the tide. ~ **contra pre-**

conceitos to battle with prejudice. ~ até o fim to fight to the bitter end. ~ corpo a corpo to come to grips. ~ por to fight for. ~ pela vida to struggle for life. ~ vigorosamente to make a fight of it, to lay about. ele luta com grandes dificuldades he is hard up. ele luta por isto he fights for it. eles ~am ombro a ombro they fought shoulder to shoulder. pronto para ~ ready for battle.

lutar (II) v. to lute, close or seal with lute.

lutécio s. m. (chem.) lutecium.

luteicórneo adj. (zool.) having yellow horns or antennae.

luteína s. f. (chem.) lutein.

luteolina s. f. (chem.) luteolin.

luteranismo s. m. Lutheranism: the doctrines and ecclesiastical system of the Lutheran Church.

luterano s. m. Lutheran: 1. disciple or follower of Luther. 2. a member of the Lutheran Church.

lutjanídeos s. m. pl. (ichth.) Lutjanidae, a family of percoid fishes which includes the snapper.

luto (I) s. m. 1. mourning, lamentation. 2. sorrow, grief, affliction, sadness. 3. mourning dress. 4. crape.

~ fechado deep mourning. estar de ~ por alguém to be in mourning for a person. meio ~ half mourning. tirar o ~ to come out of mourning. vestir ~ to go into mourning.

luto (II) s. m. (chem.) lute.

lutulência s. f. lutulence, muddiness.

lutulento adj. lutulent, muddy, miry.

lutuoso adj. 1. in mourning. 2. mournful, sad, doleful, grievous.

luva s. f. 1. glove (plates L 3, R 6, 7). 2. (mech.) pipe coupling, sleeve; socket (plate E 10). 3. ~s pl. handsel, earnest-money; extra payment, advance money or premium (as for a contract).

~ de acoplamento (mech.) coupling-sleeve. ~ de junta (mech.) double socket. ~ de redução (mech.) reducing socket. ~ móvel (mech.) clutch sleeve. ~ roscada (mech.) screw coupling. ~s de boxe boxing gloves. assentar como uma ~ to fit like a glove. atirar a ~ to defy, challenge. dar com ~ de pelica to retort an insult gently. ela estava procurando suas ~s she was hunting for her gloves.

luvaria s. f. 1. glover's shop. 2. factory where gloves are made.

luveiro s. m., luvista m. + f. glover: person who makes or sells gloves.

lux s. m. lux: unit of illumination.

luxação s. f. (pl. -ões) (med.) 1. luxation, dislocation (of joints). 2. sprain, wrench.

luxar v. 1. (med.): a) to luxate, dislocate (joints). b) to disarticulate, disjoint. c) to wrench, sprain. 2. to show off, flaunt, display ostentatiously. 3. (Braz.) to refuse (drink, food) for form's sake.

luxaria s. f. (Braz.) 1. superfluity. 2. fancy-goods.

luxemburguês s. m. (pl. -eses) (f. -esa) Luxemburger: native or inhabitant of the duchy of Luxemburg. || adj. Luxemburgian: of or pertaining to Luxemburg.

luxento adj. (Braz.) 1. fussy, cerimonious, finical. 2. pretentious; ostentatious.

luxo s. m. 1. luxury, splendour, magnificence. 2. luxuriance, exuberance, luxuriousness. 3. ostentation, pomp. 4. (Braz.): a) airs, affectation. b) mock-refusal; a standing on ceremonies.

apartamento de ~ state room. dar-se ao ~ de to permit o. s. the luxury of. de ~ de luxe. deixar-se de ~ to stop being formal. eles vivem com todo ~ they live luxuriously, like fighting-cocks. cheio de ~ (fig.) fussy, pretentious.

luxuriosidade s. f. luxuriousness; ostentation, pomp.

luxuoso adj. 1. luxurious, sumptuous. 2. ostentatious, showy. 3. splendid, magnificent. || -amente adv. 1. luxuriously. 2. ostentatiously.

luxúria s. f. 1. luxuriance, exuberance. 2. luxury. 3. luxuriousness, sensuality, voluptuousness, lechery, lasciviousness. 4. libertinism, extravagance. 5. dissolution, corruption.

luxuriante adj. m. + f. 1. luxuriant, rank; plenty, copious. 2. sensual, lascivious.

luxuriar v. 1. to luxuriate, grow exuberantly. 2. to indulge in luxury. 3. to be lewd.

luxurioso adj. 1. luxuriant, rank, exuberant. 2. sensual, licentious, lewd.

luz s. f. 1. light; illumination, luminosity. 2. source of light, anything that furnishes light (as a lamp, candle, etc.). 3. radiance, shining, clearness, brightness. 4. (fig.) knowledge, understanding, instruction, enlightenment, elucidation. 5. publicity. 6. ~es pl. (fig.): a) science. b) progress. c) notions, information.

~ alta (mot.) highway lights. ~ artificial artificial light. ~ baixa (mot.) dimmed light or low headlights. ~ branca white light. ~ da gávea (naut.) top-light. ~ de breque, ~ "pare" (mot.) stop light (plate V 3). ~ de navegação navigation light (plate L 2). ~ do dia daylight. ~ elétrica electric light. ~ fluorescente fluorescent light. ~ solar sunshine, sunlight. ~ traseira (mot., aeron.) tail-light, tail-lamp (plate M 12). ~ ultravioleta ultraviolet light à meia ~ between the lights, darkly. dar à ~: 1. to give birth to. 2. to publish. ela deu à ~ um filho she was confined of a son. resistente à ~ fast to light. sem ~ lightless. transmitir as ~es da instrução to hand on the torch of learning. vir à ~ to come to light.

luzecu, luzecuco s. m. (Braz.) glowworm, firefly.

luzeiro s. m. 1. luminary: a (strong) source of light. 2. lighthouse. 3. a bright star. 4. illustrious person. 5. clearness, brightness. 6. ~s pl. (fig.) the eyes.

luze-luze s. m. (pl. luze-luzes) (pop.) glowworm, firefly.

luzente adj. m. + f. luminous, bright, shining.

luzerna s. f. 1. light, flash, bright light. 2. skylight. 3. lucarne, garret window. 4. (bot.) lucerne, alfalfa.

luzerna-arborescente s. f. (pl. luzernas-arborescentes) (bot.) tree medic.

luzerneira s. f. lucerne field, alfalfa field.

luzica s. m. (Port.) glowworm, firefly.

luzidio adj. bright, glittering, shining.

luzido adj. 1. pompous, showy. 2. splendid, sumptuous.

luziluzir v. (Braz.) to twinkle, flicker, glimmer, sparkle.

luzimento s. m. splendour, brightness, magnificence, pomp.

luzincu s. m. (Port.) glowworm, firefly.

luzio s. m. 1. (hum.) eye. 2. lantern.

luzir v. 1. to shine, light, emit light, radiate. 2. to gleam, glitter. 3. to brighten, reflect light. 4. (fig.) to be conspicuous.

nem tudo que reluz é ouro all is not gold that glitters.

M

M, m s. m. 1. twelfth letter of the Portuguese alphabet. 2. **M** 1000 in Roman numerals. 3. **m** abbr. of meter or meters in the metric system and for masculine in grammar.

ma contraction of the pronoun **me** and the article (or pronoun) **a**: to me.
a garrafa? dê-ma! the bottle? give it to me!

má s. f. (also **arrieira**) tumour. ‖ adj. feminine form of **mau.**
~ **fama** ill repute. ~-**fé** unfairness. ~ **língua** an evil tongue. **ação** ~ misdeed. **de** ~ **vontade** unwillingly.

mabaça s. m. + f. (also **babaça**) twin brother or sister. ‖ adj. twin.

maca s. f. 1. canvas cot, litter. 2. stretcher, a sailor's hammock. 3. (N. Braz.) leather bag (for clothes) usually carried on horseback.
meter na ~ (fig.) to cheat, swindle, take in.

maça s. f. 1. bat, club, mace, cudgel (plate G 3). 2. beetle, rammer, tamper.

maçã s. f. 1. apple. 2. (fig.) anything like an apple. 3. (Braz.) variety of sugar-cane.
~-**de-adão, pomo-de-adão** Adam's apple. ~ **do peito** (Braz.) brisket. ~ **do rosto** cheekbone.

macabro adj. 1. macabre, gruesome, ghastly. 2. lugubrious, mournful.
dança -a the dance of death, infernal dance.

macaca s. f. 1. female monkey. 2. ugly woman. 3. bad luck, continuous ill fortune. 4. (S. Braz.): a) grippe, influenza. b) whip with a short trick handle. 5. (N. Braz.) cow without calf.
pegar no rabo da ~ to have continuous bad luck or to insist despite of it. **ele está com a** ~ he is full of excitement.

macacada s. f. 1. band of monkeys 2. (Braz., pop.) folks, the members of one's family.

macacão s. f. (pl. **-ões**) 1. big monkey. 2. dodger, shifty person. 3. (Braz.) workers' overalls, dungaree (plate R 7). 4. (Braz.) ugly and grotesque person.

macaca-de-auditório s. f. (pl. **macacas-de-auditório**) (Braz., pop.) a female fan of any singer that frequents radio or television auditoriums with persistence.

macacar v. = **macaquear.**

macacaria s. f. 1. tribe or band of monkeys. 2. monkeyishness, monkey trick.

macaco s. m. 1. monkey, ape; common name for all simians. 2. jack, hoist. 3. monkey hammer. 4. (Braz.) paving stone. 5. (Braz.) pillar of two bricks per layer. 6. (N. Braz.) a cowboy's helper. ‖ adj. dark-coloured like a monkey (horse).
~ **velho** (Braz.) sly, cunning, astute person. ~**s me mordam se ...** I'll be damned if ... ~ **de rosca** jackscrew, screw jack. ~ **de tesar** rigging screw.
morrer de morte -a to meet with a sudden death.

macaco-barrigudo s. m. (pl. **macacos-barrigudos**) (zool.) a woolly monkey (genus Lagothrix).

macaco-cabeludo s. m. (pl. **macacos-cabeludos**), (also **parauaçu**) (Braz., zool.) monk saki (Pithecia monachus).

macaco-da-meia-noite s. m. (pl. **macacos-da-meia-noite**) (zool.) a kinkajou.

macacoa s. f. (fam.) slight illness.

maçada s. f. 1. blow with a mace or club. 2. (fig.) row, quarrel. 3. fishpond on the sea-shore. 4. cheat, fraud, deceit. 5. drudgery, nuisance. 6. tiresome talk.
uma bela ~ a pretty kettle of fish. **eles fizeram uma bela** ~ **daquilo** they made sad work of it.
ele está numa ~ he is in a jam.

macadame s. m. macadam, a macadamized road or pavement.

macadamização s. f. (pl. **-ões**) macadamization.

macadamizar v. to macadamize, construct a road by laying and rolling successive layers of broken stone.

maçadiço adj. 1. easily bored. 2. insensible, dull. 3. accustomed to be beaten by everybody.

maçador s. m. 1. teaser, pesterer. 2. bore, tedious person, pest. ‖ adj. tiresome, boring, importunate, stupid.
ele é ~ he is a nuisance. **que sujeito** ~ what a bore.

maçadoria s. f. nuisance, bother.

maçadura s. f. 1. bruise, contusion. 2. methodical compression as a surgical means. 3. beating of flax.

macaense s. m. + f. (also **macaísta**) Macanese: inhabitant of Macao. ‖ adj. Macanese: of or pertaining to Macao.

maçagem s. f. (pl. **-ens**) beating or dressing of flax.

macaguã s. m. (Braz., ornith.) laughing falcon.

macaia s. f. (Braz., also **macaio** m.) tobacco of inferior quality.
pitar ~ to kick the bucket, die.

maçal s. m. (pl. **-ais**) whey: milk serum, separated as a watery liquid from the curd after coagulation.

macamã s. m. (Braz., hist.) runaway Negro slave.

macamba s. m. + f. (Braz.) 1. name given to their customers by greengrocers. 2. (hist.) name used by the slaves for their fellows on the same farm or of the same owner.

maçambará s. m. Johnson grass.

macambira s. f. (Braz., bot.) a common bromeliad.

macambiral s. m. (pl. **-ais**) (Braz.) growth of bromeliads.

macambúzio adj. 1. sullen, morose. 2. sad, melancholic, downcast.

macambuzismo s. m. (Braz., also **macambuzice**) 1. sadness, melancholy. 2. sullenness, sulkiness. 3. hypochondria.

macaná s. m. heavy wooden club (used by Brazilian Indians).

maçaneta (ê) s. f. (pl. **maçanetas**) 1. knob, pommel. 2. door handle, doorknob (plate F 1). 3. saddle pommel (plate S 2).

maçanetar v. to shape like a knob, handle or pommel.

maçangana s. f. (N. Braz.) sugar-cane brandy.

maçanilha s. f. small apple.

macanjice s. f. roguishness.

macanjo s. m. (pop.) 1. rascal, rogue. 2. false coin. ‖ adj. knavish, roguish.

maçante s. m. + f. (also **maçador** m.) bore, pesterer. ‖ adj. dull, boring, weary, plaguesome.

macanudo adj. (S. Braz.) 1. mighty, strong, powerful. 2. formidable, noteworthy, excellent. 3. admired.

mação s. m. 1. (pl. ~**s**) Freemason. 2. (pl. **-ões**) large mallet.

maçapão s. m. (pl. **-ães**) marzipan, marchpane, sweetmeat of almonds and sugar.

macaqueação s. f. (pl. **-ões**) mockery; monkeyshine.

macaqueador s. m. ape, person who monkeys around, mimic, mimicker. ‖ adj. apish, monkeyish.

macaquear v. 1. to monkey around, ape, mimic. 2. to mock, imitate ridiculously.

macaqueiro s. m. 1. worker who cuts and shapes paving stones. 2. (N. Braz.) worker in a cocoa plantation. ‖ adj. apish, monkeyish.

macaquice s. f. 1. foolishness, foolery, apishness, monkey tricks, monkey business; monkeyshine. 2. flattery. 3. apple-polishing, the buttering up of a person.

macaquinho s. m. little monkey.

ele tem ~s no sótão he has bats in the belfry.

maçar v. 1. to strike with a club or mace. 2. to beat, pound. 3. (fig.) to rehash topics of conversation; to bore, weary. 4. to pester.

macaréu s. m. bore, eagre, tidal flood (also known as pororoca on the Amazon).

maçarica s. f. small hare.

maçarico s. m. 1. torch, blowtorch. 2. blowpipe. 3. (ornith.) kingfisher, halcyon.

~ de soldar welding torch. canelas de ~ or pernas de ~ long and thin legs.

maçarico-das-rochas s. m. (pl. maçaricos-das-rochas) (ornith.) sandpiper.

maçariqueiro s. m. person who works with a blowtorch.

maçaroca s. f. 1. spindleful, thread twisted around a spindle. 2. an ear of corn. 3. bundle, sheaf. 4. curl or ringlet of hair resembling an ear of corn. 5. (Braz.) entangled hair of a horse's mane or tail. 6. (N. Braz.) hairy extremity of an oxtail. 7. (S. Braz.) gossip, intrigue. 8. quantity of small objects heaped together haphazardly.

maçarocar v. 1. to entangle, twist, snarl. 2. to fill a spindle with thread.

maçaroco s. m. strand of hair curled by an iron.

maçaroqueira s. f. (Braz., textile industry) rover (machine and operator).

macarrão s. m. 1. macaroni. 2. (Braz.) spaghetti: rubber or plastic tubing for insulating electrical wires. 3. (S. Braz., fig.) soft-spoken individual, wishy-washy person.

macarronada s. f. dish essentially of macaroni.

Macarrone s. m. (Braz.) nickname given to Italians in various states.

macarrônea s. f. literary effort in the macaronic style.

macarroneiro s. m. (S. Braz.) macaroni manufacturer.

macarronete s. m. thin macaroni.

macarrônico adj. macaronic(al): 1. burlesque. 2. designating a language pronounced wrongly.

latim ~ dog Latin.

macarronismo s. m. macaronic style.

macarronista s. m. + f. writer in the macaronic style.

macau s. m. (Braz.) a certain breed of pig.

macaxeira, macaxera s. f. (N. Braz.) sweet cassava.

macaxeiral s. m. (pl. -ais) (N. Braz.) sweet cassava plantation.

mácea s. f. a pig's trough.

macedônia s. f. macédoine: 1. mixture of vegetables or fruit served as a salad or otherwise. 2. medley of subjects and styles in a literary composition.

macedônio s. m. Macedonian. ‖ adj. (also macedônico) Macedonian.

macega s. f. 1. weed. 2. (Braz.) high and dry grass that makes passing through difficult. 3. (S. Braz.) ordinary bush on inferior lands.

macegal s. m. (pl. -ais) (S. Braz.) growth of weeds.

macegoso, maceguento adj. (Braz.) weedy, full of weeds.

maceió s. m. (Braz.) coastal pool or puddle resulting from high tide or heavy rainfall.

maceioense s. m. (Braz.) native or inhabitant of Maceió. ‖ adj. of or pertaining to Maceió.

maceiro s. m. verger, mace bearer, beadle.

macela s. f. (bot. also macela-do-campo) camomile.

macelão s. m. wild camomile.

macerá s. m. (N. Braz.) a kind of fish trap, hollow cylinder of wood set up like a snare.

maceração s. f. (pl. -ões) 1. maceration. 2. softening, soaking, steeping. 3. (fig.) mortification.

macerado s. m. liquid resulting from maceration. ‖ adj. 1. macerate(d). 2. soaked; softened. 3. mortified.

maceramento s. m. maceration.

macerar v. 1. to macerate. 2. to soften by steeping, to steep, soak. 3. (chem.) to digest. 4. (fig.) to mortify, torture, torment.

macéria s. f. stone wall without clay.

maceta (ê) s. f. 1. iron mallet. 2. drumstick. 3. muller (implement for grinding pigments, powders, etc., on a slab of stone or the like). 4. (ant.) cuspidor. ‖ adj. having sore fetlocks.

macetação s. f. (pl. -ões) (Braz.) separation of plant fibers by beating.

macetada s. f. (Braz.) stroke with a beetle or mallet.

macetar v. 1. to strike with a beetle or mallet, ram. 2. (S. Braz.) to cause the horse to have sore fetlocks due to trips on stony roads.

macete (ê) s. m. little wooden mallet (plates M 4, 5). ~ de calafate calking mallet. ~ de cartas small stack of letters. todo ofício tem seu ~ (Braz., sl.) every craft has its tricks.

macetear v. (Braz., sl.) to work the stiffness out of a riding horse by leading it through rough paths.

macetudo adj. 1. suffering very badly from sore fetlocks. 2. (fig.) old, worthless (person or animal).

machacá s. m. 1. (Braz.) badly castrated ox. 2. (N. Braz.) a sort of rattle for Negro dances.

machacaz s. m. 1. heavy, brutish and clumsy man. 2. sly and crafty person. ‖ adj. sly, crafty, cunning, foxy.

machada s. f. hatchet, small ax, chopper (plate A 2).

machadada s. f. stroke or blow with an ax.

machadar v. 1. to work or hit with an ax, wield an ax. 2. to split wood with an ax.

machadeiro s. m. (Braz.) 1. individual hired to cut down trees. 2. wood chopper for the charcoal industry.

machadinha s. f. small ax, hatchet (plate F 2).

machadinho s. m. 1. small ax, hatchet. 2. (Braz.) brand stamped on the ears of cattle resembling an ax. 3. (Braz.) rubber plantation worker.

machado s. m. ax, hatchet (plate T 5).

feito ao ~ (fig.) bungled.

machador s. m. (Braz.) individual who divides the body of killed swine into two halves with an ax.

macha-fêmea s. f. (pl. machas-fêmeas) 1. hinge and/or joint. 2. hermaphrodite. ‖ adj. hermaphroditic.

machão s. m. (pl. -ões) 1. (pop., f. machoa, machona) virago, termagant. 2. stupid fellow. 3. (pop.) tall, robust man.

bancar o ~ (Braz., sl.) to play a macho.

macharrão s. m. (pl. -ões) 1. large male. 2. (Braz.) adult male leopard (also onça f. jaguar).

machatim s. m. (pl. -ins) (obs.) 1. pantomimist. 2. farceur, joker. 3. pantomime representing battles, etc.

macheado s. m. pleat, plait. ‖ adj. (N. Braz.) said of cornfields where male flowers predominate.

machear v. 1. to plait, pleat, fold. 2. to copulate, mate, pair (animals). 3. (carp.) to mortise, dovetail.

machego s. m. (pop.) male (animal) of poor quality.

macheiro adj. (N. Braz.) said of the bull and stallion whose offspring are predominantly male.

machete s. m. 1. an artillerist's two-edged sabre. 2. small guitar or ukelele. 3. machete. 4. popular song.

macheza s. f. (Braz.) = machismo.

machial s. m. (pl. -ais) 1. uncultivated land used as pasture. 2. barren land; chaparral.

machiar v. (agric.) 1. to dry. 2. to degenerate, turn barren.

machila s. f. palanquin.

machim s. m. (pl. **-ins**) 1. (N. Braz.) ukelele. 2. fetlock joint.

machinho s. m. 1. (Braz.) fetlock (plate C 12). 2. young donkey.

machio s. m. mating, pairing, copulation (animals).

máchio adj. dried, withered, stunted (tree).

machismo s. m. machismo: 1. acts or manners of a **macho**. 2. the belief in the superiority of the human male.

macho s. m. 1. male animal. 2. mule. 3. box pleats, flute. 4. (mech.) part that fits into another as in: male and female plug, hook and eye, mortise and tenon, over tile and under tile (plate T 5). 5. (foundry) molding core. 6. a large eel. 7. (vulg.) lover. ‖ adj. 1. masculine. 2. (pop.) strong, virile. ~ **cônico** taper tap. ~ **de tarraxa** screw tap (plate F 1). ~ **do leme** rudder pintle. ~ **de torneira** plug (tap).

machorra adj. sterile, barren (female).

machuca, machucação s. f. (pl. ~**s, -ões**) 1. wound, bruise. 2. wounding, bruising.

machucador s. m. wounder, injurer. ‖ adj. hurting, wounding, injuring.

machucadura s. f. 1. wound, injury, bruise, contusion. 2. pounding, crushing. 3. grinding, trituration. 4. threshing.

machucão s. m. (pl. **-ões**) (Braz.) bruise, contusion.

machucar v. 1. to wound, bruise, hurt, injure. 2. to crush, smash, grind, crumble. 3. to thresh. 4. to offend.

machucho (I) s. m. 1. sly, cunning, crafty individual. 2. rich or influential person. ‖ adj. 1. sly, cunning, astute, crafty. 2. rich, influential.

machucho (II), **machuchu, chuchu** s. m. (bot.) chayote (Sechium edule).

machudo adj. daredevil.

maciço s. m. 1. dense forest. 2. (geol.) massif: a) compact portion of a mountain range (plate M 11). b) band or zone of the earth's crust raised or depressed as a unit and bounded by faults. 3. (constr.) solid piece of stonework or masonry. 4. throng. ‖ adj. 1. massive, compact, massy, solid. 2. bulky, weighty. 3. (fig.) important, appreciable. **ouro** ~ solid gold.

macieira s. f. apple tree.

macieira-da-china s. f. (pl. **macieiras-da-china**) (bot.) Chinese flowering crab-apple.

macieira-de-boi s. f. (pl. **macieiras-de-boi**) (bot.) bull apple.

macieira-ordinária s. f. (pl. **macieiras-ordinárias**) (bot.) common apple.

maciez, macieza s. f. 1. softness, smoothness. 2. sleekness. 3. suppleness, flexibility. 4. mildness.

macilência s. f. emaciation, haggardness, gauntness.

macilento adj. 1. emaciated, pale and thin, peaked. 2. lean, meagre, cadaverous.

macio adj. 1. soft, smooth. 2. sleek. 3. supple, flexible. 4. mild. 5. agreeable, mellow.

maciota s. f. easygoingness. **na** ~ 1. smoothly, softly. 2. slowly.

macis s. m. mace (spice).

macla s. f. macle: twin crystal.

maço s. m. 1. mallet (plate A 7). 2. bundle, bunch, wad. 3. pile, heap, stack. 4. pack (cigarettes). 5. (Braz.) stacked deck of cards. ~ **de calceteiro** ram.

maçom s. m. mason, Freemason.

maçonaria s. f. 1. Freemasonry. 2. (ant., gall.) masonry.

maconha s. f. (Braz.) 1. marijuana. 2. (bot.) hemp.

maçônico adj masonic: of or pertaining to the Freemasons.

macorongo s. m. (S. Braz.) lover who exploits the woman, pimp.

maçorral adj. = **mazorral**.

macota s. m. (Braz.) 1. local personality, big shot, man of prestige and influence. 2. f.: a) bad luck. b) leprosy. ‖ adj. m. + f. 1. great, powerful. 2. beautiful. 3. superior in any respect.

macoteiro s. m. (Braz.) 1. = **macota**. 2. (pop.) the biggest and best of them all.

macotena s. m. + f. (Braz., pop.) leper, lazar. ‖ adj. leprous.

macouba s. f. maccaboy: snuff smelling like roses.

macramé s. m. macramé lace.

macranto adj. (bot.) large-flowered.

má-criação s. f. (pl. **más-criações**) 1. ill breeding, bad manners. 2. rudeness, discourtesy, coarseness.

macrobia s. f. macrobiosis, old age, longevity.

macróbio s. m. Methuselah: person of advanced age. ‖ adj. macrobian, macrobiotic: long-lived.

macrobiótica s. f. macrobiotics: study to prolong life.

macrocefalia s. f. macrocephaly.

macrocefálico adj. macrocephalic.

macrocéfalo s. m. individual with an abnormally large head. ‖ adj. macrocephalic.

macrocerco adj. (zool.) long-tailed.

macrócero adj. (zool.) long-horned.

macrócomo adj. having long hair or long filaments.

macrocosmo s. m. macrocosm: the great world or universe.

macrodáctilo adj. 1. macrodactylous: long-fingered. 2. having prolongations in form of fingers.

macroeconomia s. f. (econ.) macroeconomics.

macrofilo adj. macrophyllous: said of plants with large leaves.

macrogameta s. m. (biol.) macrogamete: the female and larger of two conjugating gametes.

macrologia s. f. macrology: prolix style, long and wordy speech.

macrópode adj. m. + f. having long feet, peduncles or fins.

macropsia s. f. (path.) macropsia: morbid state of mind during which objects appear excessively large to the eye.

macróptero adj. (zool.) macropterous: having large wings or winglike membranes.

macrorrinco adj. having a long beak or snout.

macrorrizo adj. large-rooted.

macróscio adj. macroscian: referring to those inhabitants of the globe who, being hit by the sunrays at noon very obliquely, project a very long shadow.

macroscópico adj. (min.) macroscopic, visible to the naked eye.

macruro s. m. (zool.) macruran crustacean. ‖ adj. macruran, having a long tail.

macuca s. f. 1. coin used among the Negroes of Angola. 2. wild pear-tree. 3. (also **macuco**) bird of the genus Tinamus.

macucar v. (S. Braz.) 1. to speak angrily to o. s. 2. to get angry.

maçudo adj. 1. club-shaped. 2. (fig.) monotonous, dull, weary, boring, tedious.

mácula s. f. 1. macula, spot, stain, blemish, taint. 2. (fig.) dishonour, discredit, disgrace.

maculado adj. 1. maculate, spotted, stained. 2. impure. 3. defiled, dishonoured.

macular v. 1. to maculate, stain, spot. 2. to pollute. 3. (fig.) to shame, dishonour, discredit, blemish.

maculatura s. f. 1. (typogr.) spoilage. 2. wastepaper.

maculável adj. m. + f. (pl. **-áveis**) 1. stainable. 2. apt to dirty o. s. 3. discreditable, disreputable, disgraceful.

maculífero adj. maculiferous.

maculiforme adj. m. + f. like a small macula, stain or spot.

maculirrostro adj. (ornith.) having a speckled beak.

maculo s. m. (Braz., hist.) diarrheic disease of new slaves.

macuma s. f. (Braz., hist.) female slave working as a woman's companion.

macumba s. f. (Braz.) 1. fetichist ceremony of Negro origin with Christian inflection, accompanied by dances, songs, and drums. 2. sorcery, witchcraft; fetichism.

tem ~ neste negócio there is some witchcraft in this business.

macumbeiro s. m. macumba adept; fetichist.

macuquinho s. m. (Braz., ornith.) the sharp-tailed creeper.

macuru s. m. (N. Braz.) a sort of hanging basket to put babies in and leave them to themselves.

macutena s. f. (Braz.) 1. leprosy. 2. (fig.) unlucky person.

madagascarense s. m. + f. Madagascan. || adj. Madagascan.

madama s. f. 1. madam, polite formal address to a woman. 2. (pop.) wife. 3. mistress of the house. 4. (Braz., vulg.) prostitute. 5. (Braz., fam.) seamstress. 6. midwife.

madamismo s. m. (fam.) 1. assembly of ladies. 2. ladies.

madapolão s. m. 1. madapollam: cloth, originally of Indian make. 2. (N. Braz.) duck: cotton cloth.

madeficar v. 1. to moisten, dampen. 2. to bathe. 3. to wet.

madeira s. f. 1. wood, timber, lumber. 2. (N. Braz.) rubber tree (term used by rubber plantation men). 3. (pop.) cane, walking-stick.

~ branca softwood, any timber of inferior quality regardless of its colour. ~ de lei, ~ dura hardwood, timber of good quality. ~ compensada plywood (plate C 9).

Madeira s. m. Madeira: a rich strong white wine.

madeiramento s. m. 1. heap of wood. 2. timberwork, framework of a construction. 3. timber, framing, woodwork (also of a roof).

madeirar v. 1. to set up a wooden frame. 2. to work with wood. 3. to adjust the timber frame of a construction. 4. to plank, timber.

madeireiro s. m. 1. wood or lumber merchant. 2. woodworker. 3. woodcutter, lumberjack.

madeirense s. m. + f. Madeiran: native or inhabitant of Madeira. || adj. Madeiran: of or pertaining to Madeira.

madeiro s. f. 1. log, trunk or thick block of wood, timber. 2. (fig.) the cross of the Lord. 3. (N. Braz.) horns of cattle. 4. (pop.) stupid fellow.

madeixa s. f. 1. small skein. 2. skein of silk, wool, etc. 3. (fig.) tress, lock or strand of hair; braid.

madeixar-se v. to cover o. s. with hair locks.

mádido adj. 1. moistened, dampened; dewy. 2. drenched, soaked, wet.

Madona s. f. Madonna: 1. the Virgin Mary. 2. a picture or statue representing her. 3. Italian title of respect for a woman.

madorna, madorra s. f. = modorra.

madraçal s. m. (pl. -ais) (ant.) primary school.

madraçaria s. f. (also madracice) lazyness, sloth, truantship, sluggishness, aversion against work.

madraceador s. m. lazy, vagrant person; lazybones, vagabond, truant.

madracear v. to be lazy, saunter, loiter, play truant, idle, lounge, loaf.

madraceirão s. m. (pl. -ões) great truant, loiterer. || adj. very lazy.

madraço s. m. 1. vagrant. 2. truant, sluggard, idler, vagabond. 3. drone. || adj. 1. very lazy. 2. loitering, sluggish, idle, indolent.

madrasta s. f. 1. stepmother. 2. (fig.) unloving and harsh mother and wife.

madrasto s. m. (N. Braz.) = madapolão.

madre s. f. 1. mother, professed nun, mother superior. 2. (anat.) uterus, womb. 3. (carp.) joist. 4. mold, matrix of metals. 5. mother of vinegar or wine, mucilaginous substance produced during fermentation. 6. river bed.

~ do leme (naut.) main piece of the rudder.

madrepérola s. f. mother-of-pearl, nacre.

madrépora s. f. madrepore (stony corals).

madreporário s. m. (zool.) madreporarian: any of various corals.

madrepórico adj. (zool.) madreporic.

madreporífero adj. producing madrepores.

madreporiforme adj. m. + f. madreporiform: shaped like a madrepore.

madreporite s. f. madreporite: fossil madrepore.

madressilva s. f. (bot.) honeysuckle, woodbine.

madria s. f. whitecaps, crested waves.

madrigal s. m. (pl. -ais) madrigal: 1. short, gallant poem. 2. a lyric poem suited for musical setting. 3. pastoral poem. 4. musical composition for voices with or without accompaniment.

madrigalesco adj. madrigalian: having the character of a madrigal.

madrigalista s. m. + f. madrigalist, author or singer of a madrigal. || adj. m. + f. composing madrigals.

madrigalizar v. to produce madrigals.

madrigaz s. m. thin, peaked, cadaverous individual.

madrija s. f., madrijo m. (Braz.) mother whale.

madrileno, madrilês s. m. madrilense m. + f., native or inhabitant of Madrid. || adj. of or pertaining to Madrid.

madrinha s. f. 1. godmother. 2. (female) witness at a marriage. 3. (fig.) sponsor, protector, patroness, well-wisher. 4. (Braz.) mare or mule guiding a band of mules.

~ de casamento maid or matron of honour. ser ~ to stand godmother to a child.

madrinhar v. (S. Braz., also amadrinhar) to lead a band of pack-horses (animal).

madrinheiro s. m. (Braz.) fellow riding the leading mare in order to set the speed.

madrugada s. f. 1. dawn(ing), day-break. 2. (fig.) precocity.

de ~ at dawn, at day-break. às quatro horas da ~ at four o'clock in the morning.

madrugador s. m. early riser; person who is always on the spot, early bird. || adj. rising early; early, preceding.

madrugar v. 1. to get up early in the morning, to be up at the crack of dawn. 2. to act before the proper time has come. 3. to precede somebody in an action. 4. to speak up prematurely. 5. to show up before the proper hour or too early.

a quem madruga, Deus ajuda early to bed and early to rise, makes a man happy, healthy and wise.

maduração s. f. 1. ripening, maturation. 2. (med.) suppuration.

madurador adj. that which fosters ripening.

madurar v. 1. (also fig.) to mature, ripen; to come to maturity. 2. (med.) to reach complete suppuration.

madureza s. f. ripeness: 1. maturity, matureness. 2. (fig.) prudence, circumspection.

exame de ~ (Braz.) final examination covering the curriculum of all four years of the gymnasial course.

maduro s. m. (N. Braz.) a fermented drink. ‖ adj. 1. ripe, mature, mellow, perfect. 2. full-blown, full- -fledged. 3. getting on in years. 4. (fig.) prudent, circumspect. 5. (vulg.) odd, queer.

mãe s. f. 1. mother. 2. mother of vinegar. 3. (fig.) cause, reason, source, origin. 4. (fig.) charitable and protective woman. 5. (Braz., pop., ftb.) player who, playing badly, gives the other team too many chances. ‖ adj. m. + f. (pop.) excessively large. **ele estava num sono ~** ~ he was fast asleep. **ele levou uma surra** ~ he took quite a walloping. **ficar como a ~ de São Pedro** to end waif and stray. **nossa ~!** gosh!, good heavens!

mãe-benta s. f. (pl. **mães-bentas**) (Braz.) a small cookie made of wheat flour and eggs.

mãe-d'água s. f. (pl. **mães-d'água**) (Braz.) 1. fabulous water nymph also known as **uiara, iara.** 2. fountain, spring, wellhead. 3. (fig.) a person who cries easily.

mãe-de-santo s. f. (pl. **mães-de-santo**) fetishistic sorceress.

mãe-do-fogo s. f. (pl. **mães-do-fogo**) (Braz.) 1. tree trunk aglow for many days. 2. piece of wood aglow until the next day to relight the fire (southern ranches).

mãe-do-ouro s. f. (pl. **mães-do-ouro**) (S. Braz.) fabulous being believed to guard the gold mines.

mãe-do-rio s. f. (pl. **mães-do-rio**) (Braz.) river-bed.

maenga s. m. (N. Braz.) 1. policeman, constable, cop. 2. person of no consequence, a nobody.

maestria s. f. = **mestria.**

maestrina s. f. (mus.) female conductor or composer.

maestrino s. m. composer of light music.

maestro s. m. 1. (mus.) maestro: conductor of an orchestra. 2. composer.

mafabé adj. (S. Braz.) good-for-nothing.

mafamético adj. Mohammedan.

mafarrico s. m. devil, demon.

máfia s. f. mafia, maffia.

mafioso adj. mafioso.

mafuá s. m. (Braz.) amusement park.

maga s. f. female magician, witch, sorceress.

magana s. f. 1. antique music. 2. loose or lascivious woman. ‖ adj. 1. jovial, flirty. 2. concupiscent, lustful.

maganagem s. f. (pl. **-ens**) 1. group of jovial persons. 2. group of rogues. 3. trick, roguery. 4. agglomeration of insignificant things or persons.

maganão s. m. (pl. **-ões**) 1. scoundrel, rogue. 2. jovial fellow, droll. 3. mischievous or facetious person. ‖ adj. 1. roguish, scoundrelly. 2. frollicsome, prankish.

maganeira, maganice s. f. 1. joviality. 2. prank, practical joke. 3. wanton play.

magano s. m. 1. rogue, rascal, scoundrel. 2. wag. 3. person of low social standing. ‖ adj. 1. jovial. 2. funny. 3. roguish, base, riotous.

magarefe s. m. 1. butcher: person who kills and skins oxen in the slaughterhouse. 2. (fig.) unskilled or inferior surgeon.

magazine s. m. (Engl.) magazine: 1. periodical with miscellaneous articles and usually illustrated. 2. store specialized in fashions. 3. deposit for casting type of the Linotype.

magia s. f. 1. magic. 2. sorcery, witchcraft. 3. hidden forces of nature, occult power. 4. enchantment, fascination.

~ imitativa imitative magic (imitation of the desired thing). **~ simpática** magic control over a person or a distant object, of which one has a part. **~ negra** black magic.

magiar s. m. + f. Magyar, Hungarian. ‖ adj. Hungarian.

mágica s. f. 1. magic, sorcery. 2. legerdemain. 3. enchantment. 4. sorceress.

lanterna ~ magic lantern. **passe de** ~ sleight-of- -hand trick. **truque de** ~ magician's trick.

magicar v. 1. to brood, think. 2. to worry. 3. to ruminate.

mágico s. m. 1. magician. 2. juggler, conjurer. 3. wizard, sorcerer, necromancer. ‖ adj. 1. magic(al). 2. (fig.): a) enchanting. b) extraordinary.

maginação s. f. pop. form of **imaginação.**

maginar v. pop. form of **imaginar** and **magicar.**

magismo s. m. 1. magics. 2. religion of the Magi.

magister s. m. (lat., fam.). 1. magister, master. 2. sententious person.

magistério s. m. 1. professorship, mastership, teachership. 2. the class of teachers, teachers collectively. 3. scholastic profession.

magistrado s. m. magistrate: 1. civil officer charged with administration of law, having authority. 2. judge.

magistral adj. m. + f. (pl. **-ais**) 1. magisterial. 2. masterly. 3. (fig.) perfect, complete, exemplary, excellent.

foi o seu gesto ~ it was his (her) masterly gesture.

magistralidade s. f. 1. magistracy. 2. magisterial manner. 3. (fig.) pedantry.

magistrando s. m. candidate to a master's or professor's degree.

magistrático adj. magisterial.

magistratura s. f. magistrature, magistracy: 1. dignity or function of a magistrate. 2. class of the magistrates. 3. office period of a magistrate.

magma s. m. (geol.) magma: molten material beneath the solid crust of the earth, from which igneous rock is formed.

magna-carta s. f. 1. Magna Charta, the charter of the English liberties forced from King John by the English barons at Runnymede, June 15, 1215. 2. the constitution of rights of a country.

magnanimidade s. f. magnanimity: 1. greatness of mind, forbearance. 2. generous act, generosity.

magnânimo adj. magnanimous: 1. noble, high-minded. 2. generous and free of petty feelings.

magnata, magnate s. m. magnate: 1. important and illustrious person. 2. grandee, nobleman. 3. tycoon.

magnésia s. f. magnesia, magnesium oxide and hydroxide used medically as laxative and purgative and against acidity.

magnesiano, magnésico adj. magnesian, magnesic: referring to or containing magnesium.

magnésio s. m. (chem.) magnesium: metallic element which burns with a dazzling white light (symbol Mg).

magnesita s. f. magnesite: native magnesium carbonate.

magnete s. m. 1. magnet: magnetized iron or steel, which attracts iron. 2. loadstone.

magnético adj. magnetic(al): 1. of or pertaining to a magnet or magnetism. 2. attracting like a magnet. 3. (fig.) attractive, enchanting, entrancing. **agulha -a** magnetic needle.

magnetismo s. m. magnetism: 1. attractive power of magnets. 2. the influence of the willpower of one person on the other's. 3. (fig.) attraction, power of attracting, enchantment.

magnetita s. f. (min.) magnetite; black iron oxide, loadstone.

magnetização s. f. (pl. **-ões**) magnetization.

magnetizador s. m. magnetizer. ‖ adj. magnetizing.

magnetizar v. to magnetize: 1. communicate magnetic properties. 2. (fig.): a) dominate the willpower of somebody. b) influence. c) attract, enchant, captivate.

magnetizável adj. m. + f. (pl. **-áveis**) magnetizable, that may be magnetized.

magneto s. m. (electr., mot.) magneto (plate M 12). ~ **de ignição** ignition magneto. ~ **de partida** starting magneto, booster magneto.

magnetogenia s. f. the study of magnetic phenomena.

magneto-gerador s. m. (pl. **magnetos-geradores**) (electr.) magnetogenerator.

magnetógrafo s. m. magnetograph.

magnetóide adj. m. + f. (phys.) magnetoid.

magnetologia s. f. treatise on magnets and their properties; study of magnetism.

magnetômetro s. m. magnetometer: instrument to measure the attractive power of a magnet or magnetic forces.

magnéton s. m. (phys.) magneton.

magnetoquímica s. f. magnetochemistry.

magnificação s. f. (pl. **-ões**) magnification: 1. act or effect or magnifying; state of being magnified; apparent enlargement. 2. magnifying power. 3. laudation, extolment.

magnificar v. to magnify: 1. cause to look more important. 2. exaggerate, overstate. 3. exalt, laudate, extol, praise, commend. 4. enlarge, augment.

magnificatório adj. magnifying.

magnificência s. f. magnificence: 1. sumptuosity, pomp, show, splendour, grandeur. 2. magnanimousness, broadmindedness.

magnificente adj. m. + f. magnificent: 1. extraordinary, fine; superb, grand, sumptuous, majestic. 2. sublime. 3. noble. 4. liberal.

magnífico adj. magnificent: 1. superb, grand, magnific, sublime. 2. excellent. 3. beautiful. 4. wonderful.

magniloqüência s f. magniloquence: pompous and grandiose way of speaking.

magniloqüente adj. m. + f. magniloquent.

magníloquo adj. eloquent; pompous.

magnitude s. f. magnitude: 1. size, extent, greatness, largeness. 2. great amount. 3. (fig.) importance, consequence.

magno adj. great, grand, important.

magnólia s. f. magnolia: any plant of the genus Magnolia.

magnoliáceo adj. (bot.) magnoliaceous.

mago s. m. Magus: 1. each of the three wise men who came to Bethlehem to do homage to the child Jesus. 2. ancient or medieval astrologer or charlatan. 3. magus: sorcerer, magician, wizard. || adj. 1. enchanting, magic(al), charming. 2. delicious. 3. seductive.

mágoa s. f. 1. bruise, sore, blue spot, hurt. 2. (fig.) injury, wrong, sorrow, grief, anguish, sadness. 3. ~s pl. lamentation, complaint.

quem canta, suas ~s espanta he who sings, chases away his sorrows.

magoado adj. 1. hurt, sore. 2. sad, woeful, rueful, heart-sick, unhappy. 3. anguished, afflicted. 4. offended. || **-amente** adv. sadly, afflictedly.

magoar v. 1. to hurt, wound, bruise. 2. (fig.): a) to harrow, upset, afflict, grieve, trouble. b) to sadden, depress. 3. to offend, distress.

magoei o braço I hurt my arm. **magoaram-no** they offended him.

magoativo adj. 1. hurting, hurtful, bruising. 2. pungent. 3. grievous, afflictive.

magote s. m. 1. group of persons, crowd of people. 2. lot of things. 3. multitude. 4. big pile, heap.

magra s. f. (Braz., pop.) 1. (also **magrinha**) pulmonary tuberculosis. 2. death.

magrelo s. m. (Braz.) very lean person. || adj. very lean.

magrém s. f. (pl. **-éns**) (Braz.) 1. (also **magreza**) leanness. 2. dry season in the Northeast.

magrete adj. m. + f. (fam.) somewhat thin, lean.

magreza s. f. thinness, leanness, gauntness, slenderness, meagerness.

magricela s. m. + f. lean person. || adj. m. + f. lean.

magriço s. m. 1. knight or champion of the ladies. 2. ridiculous defender of silly and futile things.

magrinha s. f. (Braz., pop.) 1. pulmonary tuberculosis. 2. low caliber rifle.

magriz s. m. very thin person. || adj. thin as a rail.

magrizel s. m. (pl. **-éis**), **magrizela** m. + f. (also **magrelo** m., **magricela** m. + f., **magruço** m.) pale and skinny person.

magro adj. 1. thin, skinny, lean, meager, bony, slim (plate Q). 2. (fig.) unprofitable. 3. (fig.) insignificant, scarce.

dia ~ fasting day. dias ~s meager days. carvão ~ hard coal.

magusto s. m. 1. fire to roast chestnuts. 2. roasted chestnuts.

maia s. f. (Port.) 1. old popular feast, celebrated during the first days of May. 2. (fig.) woman dressing and making up with poor taste.

maiêutica s. f. maieutic: Socratic method to use questions to develop a latent idea.

mainça s. f. 1. handful. 2. the ring on a spindle.

mainel s. m. (pl. **-éis**) rail, handrail.

maio s. m. May, the fifth month of the civil year.

maiô s. m. bathing suit (plate B 3).

maiólica s. f. (also **majólica**) majolica: Italian pottery, esp. of the Renaissance period.

maionese s. f. (Gall.) mayonnaise: a dressing consisting of oil, vinegar or lemon juice, egg yolks, and seasoning.

maior s. m. + f. person of full or mature age. || adj. 1. comparative of **grande**: larger, higher, bigger, etc. (in size, space, intensity, or number). 2. adult, of age. 3. (mus.) major.

~ **do que** larger or bigger than. **os nossos ~es** our forebears. **você é o** ~ you are the greatest. **dó** ~ C major. **na** ~ **parte** mostly. **a** ~ **parte** the lion's share. **força** ~ force majeure. **estado-** ~ (mil.) general staff. || ~**mente** adv. (also **mormente**) principally, especially.

maioral s. m. (pl. **-ais**) 1. the head; chief, boss, big shot. 2. (fig.) the largest, biggest, greatest. 3. (Braz.) coachman. 4. headman of a farm or group of riders or horses. 5. bell-wether.

maioria s. f. majority, the greater number, portion or part.

maioridade s. f. 1. majority, full legal age. 2. (fig.) emancipation.

maiorquino s. m. native or inhabitant of Majorca. || adj. of or pertaining to Majorca.

maiorzinho adj. somewhat greater, slightly larger.

maiozinho adj. 1. referring to the month of May. 2. (bot.) appearing during the month of May.

maipoca s. f. (N. Braz.) replantation of a manioc (cassava) field.

mair s. m. (Braz., hist.) name given to the French by the Indians.

mais s. m. 1. more; greater part. 2. the rest, remnant, surplus. 3. something else. || adj. m. + f., sg. + pl. 1. more. 2. further. || adv. 1. more. 2. also. 3. besides. 4. over. 5. preferentially. 6. further. 7. moreover.

~ **cinco anos** another five years. ~ **detalhes** further particulars. ~ **e** ~ more and more. ~ **hoje,** ~ **amanhã** sooner or later. ~ **ou menos** more or less. ~ **ou menos no dia 10** around the 10th. ~ **quero** ser pobre, a ser bajulador I'd rather be poor than a flatterer. ~ tarde later on. a ~ more than necessary. às ~ das vezes mostly, usually. de ~ a ~ besides, moreover. é o ~ que eu posso fazer it is the most I can do. fizeram o ~ que puderam they did their utmost. não posso esperar ~ I cannot wait any longer. o ~ do caminho era pedregulhento the rest of the way was stony. os ~ dos homens the majority of men. por ~ que however much. nunca ~ never again. quanto ~, quanto melhor the more the better. quanto ao ~ as for the rest. sem ~ nem menos without reason, without much ado. tanto ~ so much the more. um pouco ~ a bit more. ela está ~ para lá do que para cá she is more dead than alive, on the brink of the grave.

maisena s. f. maizena (trademark), corn starch prepared to be used as food.

maisquerer v. 1. to prefer. 2. to love more.

mais-valia s. f. rise, increase of the value of a piece of merchandise.

maitaca s. f. 1. = **baitaca.** 2. (Braz.) gossip.

maiúscula s. f. capital letter.
   tecla para ~s (typewriter) shift key (plate M 2).
   fixador de ~s (typewriter) shift lock (plate M 2).

maiusculizar v. to capitalize: to begin a phrase with a capital letter.

maiúsculo adj. capital.
   letra -a capital letter.

majestade s. f. majesty: 1. excellency, magnificence. 2. royal power. 3. noble, regal appearance. 4. crucifix of precious metal worn at the neck. 5. title of a sovereign, sovereignty. 6. imposing character. 7. stateliness, grandeur.

majestoso adj. 1. majestic. 2. august, regal, imperial. ‖ **-amente** adv. majestically.

majólica s. m. = **maiólica.**

major s. m. (mil.) major.

majoração s. f. (pl. **-ões**) (Braz.) rise, augment, increase.
   a ~ dos preços da carne the rise in meat prices.

majorana s. f. marjoram.

majorar v. to rise, raise, increase, augment.

majoria s. f. (mil.) majorate, majority, majorship: rank or dignity of a major.

majoritário adj. (Braz.) relative to majority.
   partido ~ (pol.) majority party.

mal s. m. (pl. **~es**) 1. evil, ill. 2. maleficence. 3. disease, illness. 4. pain. 5. hurt, wrong, harm. 6. vice. 7. misfortune, calamity. 8. (Braz.) rabies, hydrophobia. ‖ adj. 1. bad. 2. evil. ‖ adv. (also **~mente**) 1. scarcely, hardly. 2. wrong, wrongly, amiss. 3. badly, with difficulty. 4. ill. ‖ conj. 1. hardly. 2. no sooner.
   ~ de Hansen leprosy. ~disposto ill-disposed; indisposed. ~-educado ill-mannered. ~ o conheço I hardly know him. ~parecido ill-looking, ugly. ~-reputado ill-favoured. ~ eu tinha saído, começou a chover I had hardly left when it started to rain. acabará ~ com ele it will come to a bad end with him. de dois ~es o menor of two evils choose the least. de ~ a pior from bad to worse, out of the frying pan into the fire. ele andou muito ~ (fig.) it was very wrong of him. ele está menos ~ he is fairly well. estar ~ com alguém to be on bad terms with somebody. estar ~ to be badly off, feel ill. estar ~ de saúde to be sick or ill. falar ~ de alguém to speak evil of somebody. fazer ~ 1. to do harm. 2. to disagree (food.) fazer por ~ to do it from pure spite. há ~es que vêm para bem it's an ill wind that blows nobody any good. ir ~ to go badly or wrong. levar alguma coisa a ~ to be offended at s. th. não faz ~ it doesn't matter. não lhe faz ~ algum it doesn't hurt you

(him, her). para grandes ~es, grandes remédios desperate diseases require desperate remedies. parecer ~ to look bad. por bem ou por ~ by hook or by crook. pôr-se de ~ com alguém to fall out with s. o. proceder ~ to behave ill. querer ~ a alguém to bear one a grudge. tomar por ~ to take offense. um vestido que fica ~ an unbecoming dress.

mala s. f. 1. bag, handbag, valise. 2. trunk, box, suitcase, portmanteau (plates E 13, V 3). 3. (vulg.) stomach. 4. (Braz.) wrong or faulty hit in a ball game. 5. (S. Braz., vulg.) testicles. 6. m. snake charmer. ‖ interj. get out! you are no good!
   ~ aérea air mail. ~ de garupa saddlebag. ~s do correio mail bags. fazer as ~s to pack one's bags or trunks.

malabar s. m. + f. 1. native or inhabitant of Malabar. 2. breed of cattle. ‖ adj. m. + f. 1. referring to Malabar and its inhabitants. 2. said of extravagant and difficult positions and movements of the body in games.

malabarismo s. m. (also **jogos malabares** pl.) juggling, conjuring tricks.

malabarista s. m. + f. juggler, conjurer, trickster.

malaca s. f. (S. Braz.) illness, ailing.

mal-acabado adj. (pl. **mal-acabados**) (Braz.) 1. said of a queer person with a badly developed body. 2. badly finished.

malacacheta s. f. (Braz.) = **mica.**

malacafento adj. (N. Braz.) sick, indisposed.

malacara s. m. (S. Braz.) 1. horse with a blaze except for a black horse, which is then called **picaço**. 2. (Braz.) any animal with a blaze. ‖ adj. having a blaze.

malacênico adj. (geol.) pertaining to the Cenozoic era.

malacia s. f. 1. calm, dead calm. 2. (fig.) debility, weakness, feebleness.

malacodermo adj. (zool.) malacodermous: soft-skinned.

malacologia s. f. malacology, science and study of the molluscs.

mal-acondicionado adj. (pl. **mal-acondicionados**) 1. ill-conditioned. 2. badly packed.

mal-aconselhado adj. (pl. **mal-aconselhados**) ill-advised, imprudent.

malacopterígio adj. malacopterygian: of or pertaining to a division of soft-finned teleost fishes.

malacostráceo s. m. malacostracan: crustacean belonging to the Malacostraca (a subclass, including lobsters, shrimps, crabs, etc.) ‖ adj. malacostracan.

malacozoário s. m. mollusc. ‖ adj. molluscan.

maladia s. f. 1. (obs.) malady. 2. (ant.) manor seat, manor house. 3. feudal mansion.

malafaia s. f. (Braz.) an ochnaceous tree.

mal-afeiçoado adj. (pl. **mal-afeiçoados**) 1. ill-looking, ugly. 2. ill-disposed.

mal-afortunado adj. (pl. **mal-afortunados**) unfortunate.

málaga s. m. Malaga: wine produced in the province of Malaga, Spain.

malagma s. m. medication of external use to soften the tissue; cataplasm, poultice.

mal-agourado adj. (pl. **mal-agourados**) ill-omened.

mal-agradecido s. m. (pl. **mal-agradecidos**) ungrateful person. ‖ adj. ungrateful.

malaguenha s. f. malaguena: a Spanish folk tune and dance.

malaguenho, malaguês s. m. (pl. **-eses**) native or inhabitant of Malaga. ‖ adj. of or pertaining to Malaga, Spain.

malagueta s. f. malagueta pepper also known as **pimenta-malagueta**.

malaiala s. m. language spoken in Malabar.

malaio s. m. 1. Malay, Malayan: a) member of the Malayan race. b) the Malayan language. 2. Malaysian: native of Malaysia. ‖ adj. Malay, Malayan. Malaysian.

mal-ajambrado adj. (pl. **mal-ajambrados**) (Braz.) said of a badly dressed person of disagreeable and ungainly appearance.

mal-ajeitado adj. (pl. **mal-ajeitados**) badly disposed, badly arranged.

mal-amanhado adj. (pl. **mal-amanhados**) 1. badly arranged. 2. badly dressed. 3. shabby, untidy, disorderly. 4. awkward, clumsy.

mal-americano s. m. (pl. **males-americanos**) syphilis.

malamba s. f. (N. Braz.) 1. disgrace, unhappiness. 2. lament.

malambeiro s. m. (N. Braz.) person enjoying to tell over and over his mishaps. ‖ adj. lamenting.

malampança s. f. (Braz.) variation of **manampança.**

malandante s. m. (ant.) 1. vagabond. 2. highwayman. ‖ adj. m. + f. (obs.) unhappy.

malandra s. f. 1. roguish woman. 2. idle good-for--nothing woman.

malandraço, malandrão s. m. great scoundrel, great vagabond.

malandragem s. f. (pl. **-ens**) 1. roguery, trickery 2. nasty or mean purpose. 3. group of rascals. 4. vagrant life, vagabondage.

malandrar v. 1. (Braz.) to wander around, rove, loaf. 2. to lead the life of a vagabond. 3. to misuse.

malandres s. m. pl. malanders: transverse wound on the knee joint of a riding animal.

malandrice s. f. 1. vagrancy, idleness. 2. roguery, rascality, scoundrelism.

malandrim s. m. (pl. **-ins**) (pop.; also **malandrete, malandrino**) 1. lazy-bones, scamp, vagrant, vagabond, loiterer, idler. 2. thief. 3. rascal.

malandrino s. m. = **malandrim.** ‖ adj. acting like or having the habits of a vagrant or vagabond.

malandro s. m. (also **malandréu**) 1. scoundrel, rogue, rascal, gallows bird. 2. vagrant, hooligan. 3. thief. ‖ adj. 1. roguish. 2. vagrant. 3. scampish.

mala-posta s. f. (pl. **malas-postas**) mail-coach, stage--coach.

malaquês s. m. (also **malaqueiro**) native or inhabitant of Malacca. ‖ adj. of or pertaining to Malacca.

malaquita s. f. (min.) malachite.

malar (I) s. m. (anat.) malar, malar bone, cheekbone. ‖ adj. of or pertaining to the cheekbone.

malar (II) v. (Braz.) to err in a ball game.

malária s. f. (med.) malaria: a febrile disease.

malárico adj. (med.) malarial; malarious.

malarífero adj. containing the germ of malaria.

malarígeno adj. producing malaria.

malariologia s. f. (med.) malariology.

malariologista s. m. + f. malariologist.

malarioterapia s. f. therapy consisting in inoculating the patient with the malaria protozoa to fight certain diseases, especially on overall paralysis.

mal-arrumado s. m. (pl. **mal-arrumados**) (Braz.) land covered by large chunks of rock making transit rather difficult. ‖ adj. untidy.

malas-artes s. m. + f. 1. awkward person. 2. f. pl. confusion, mess. ‖ adj. m. + f. 1. awkward, unhappy (person). 2. mischievous, tricksy (person).

mal-assada s. f. 1. omelet. 2. (Braz.) a poultice made of medicinal plants.

mal-assombrado s. m. (pl. **mal-assombrados**) (Braz., also **mal-assombração**) ghost, spook, spectre, apparition. ‖ adj. haunted, spooky.

mal-aventurado adj. (pl. **mal-aventurados**) unfortunate, unhappy.

mal-avindo adj. (pl. **mal-avindos**) = **desavindo.**

mal-avinhado adj. (pl. **mal-avinhados**) 1. quarrelsome when drunk. 2. that turns wine sour or bad-flavoured. 3. pessimistic.

mal-avisado adj. (pl. **mal-avisados**) ill-advised.

malaxação s. f. (pl. **-ões**) malaxation: 1. act of reducing to a soft mass by kneading or rolling. 2. form of massage. 3. (med.) mollification, act of mollifying.

malaxadeira s. f., **malaxador** m. 1. butter kneader. 2. mixing mill.

malaxar v. 1. to malax: a) massage. b) (pharm.) soften, reduce to a paste. c) beat, knead or stir strongly to make compact. 2. to tire.

mal-azado adj. (pl. **mal-azados**) 1. awkward, clumsy. 2. unfavourable, unpropitious.

malbaratador s. m. 1. dissipator, spendthrift, squanderer, wastrel, prodigal. 2. poor businessman, underseller.

malbaratar, malbaratear v. 1. to sell at a loss, undersell. 2. to dissipate, squander, waste. 3. to make bad use of.

~ **os seus esforços** to bark up the wrong tree.

malbarato s. m. 1. sale at a loss, underselling. 2. wasteful expenditure, squandering. 3. depreciation. 4. disdain, contempt.

mal-caduco s. m. (Braz., pop.) epilepsy.

malcasado (I) s. m. (Braz.) type of pancake made of tapioca and the milk of a coconut and wrapped up in a banana leaf. Also known as **malcassá.**

malcasado (II) adj. 1. ill-matched, unhappily married. 2. married to a person of inferior social standing.

malcheiroso adj. malodorous, stinking, fetid.

malcomido adj. ill-fed, undernourished, thin.

malcontentadiço adj. difficult to satisfy, hard to please.

malcontente adj. m. + f. malcontent.

malcozinhado adj. badly cooked, underdone.

malcriadez s. f. ill breeding, bad manners, rudeness.

malcriado adj. ill-bred, ill-mannered, rude, uncivil, impolite, uncouth.

maldade s. f. 1. badness, wickedness. 2. bad action. 3. malice. 4. iniquity; cruelty. 5. naughtiness, mischief (of children). 6. (S. Braz.) pus, pus of an ulcer.

maldadoso adj. = **maldoso, maléfico.**

mal-da-praia s. m. (Braz., path.) erysipelas.

maldar v. (Braz.) 1. to have a wrong opinion of something or somebody. 2. to suspect the worse.

mal-das-montanhas s. m. (path.) mountain sickness.

mal-da-terra s. m. (S. Braz.) ancylostomiasis, hookworm disease.

mal-de-ano s. m. (Braz.) epidemic disease of cattle.

mal-de-cuia s. m. (S. Braz., pop.) leprosy.

mal-de-engasgo, mal-de-engasgue s. m. (Braz.) affliction of the esophagus characterized by swallowing troubles.

mal-de-escancha s. m. (N. Braz., also **mal-das-ancas, mal-de-cadeiras, mal-dos-quartos**) epizootic disease attacking horses in swamp regions ruining them.

mal-de-garapa s. m. (Braz.) trypanosomiasis: a disease of horses.

mal-de-lázaro s. m. leprosy.

maldelazento s. m. (Braz.) leper. ‖ adj. leprous.

mal-de-pott s. m. tuberculosis of the vertebrae.

mal-de-são-lázaro s. m. leprosy.

mal-de-secar s. m. (Braz.) pulmonary tuberculosis.

mal-de-vaso s. m. (S. Braz.) wound at the root of the hoof of horses and asses.

maldição s. f. (pl. **-ões**) malediction, curse, imprecation.

maldiçoar v. (also **amaldiçoar**) to curse.

maldisposto adj. 1. ill-humoured, sullen, cross. 2. indisposed, slightly ill.

maldita s. f. 1. persisting dermatitis, tetter. 2. malignant pustule. 3. (Braz. pop.) erysipelas.

maldito s. m. 1. (Braz., pop.) devil. 2. cursed person. ‖ adj. confounded, cursed, darned, damned, execrable, blasted.
~ **o dia!** woe the day!

malditoso adj. (pop.) unhappy, unfortunate, unlucky, ill-fated.

maldizente s. m. + f. (also **maldizedor** m.) slanderer, defamer, backbiter. ‖ adj. slanderous, defamatory, calumnious.

maldizer s. m. slander, backbiting, calumny. ‖ v. 1. to slander, defame, backbite. 2. to curse, ban, execrate. 3. to swear. 4. to beshrew.

mal-do-sangue s. m. leprosy.

mal-dos-aviadores s. m. airsickness.

mal-dos-cascos s. m. (Braz.) vulgar name for the hoof and mouth disease.

mal-dos-chifres s. m. (Braz.) epizooty of the cattle attacking the base of the horns making them fail out.

mal-dos-mergulhadores s. m. (also **mal-das-ensecadeiras**) caisson disease, marked by paralysis and other nervous symptoms, caused by the high pressures to which the body is subjected in diving.

maldoso adj. 1. wicked, bad, spiteful. 2. malign, pernicious. 3. (fig.) malicious, mischievous. ‖ **-amente** adv. wickedly.

mal-dos-peitos s. m. (Braz., pop.) tuberculosis.

malê s. m. + f. (Braz.) Mussulman of African origin, of which there are small nuclei in Rio de Janeiro and Bahia. ‖ adj. relative or pertaining to the **malês**.

maleabilidade s. f. malleability, malleableness.

maleáceo adj. malleiform.

maleador s. m. hammerer. ‖ adj. hammering.

malear v. 1. to laminate. 2. to distend metal through hammering. 3. (fig.) to soften, make pliable, render docile.

maleável adj. (pl. **-áveis**) malleable: 1. capable of being distended through hammering or by rollers. 2. (fig.): a) pliant, pliable. b) adaptable. c) soft, docile.
ferro ~ soft iron.

malebra s. m. + adj. (S. Braz.) = **maleva**.

maledicência s. f. slander, detraction, calumny, defamation.

maledicente s. + adj. m. + f. = **maldizente**.

mal-educado adj. (pl. **mal-educados**) ill-bred, impolite, rude.

maleficência s. f. maleficence, mischievous temper, malignancy.

maleficiar v. 1. to do evil, harm. 2. to bewitch, fascinate. 3. to hurt, damage, prejudice.

malefício s. m. 1. malefaction, misdeed. 2. witchcraft, sortilege, spell.

maléfico adj. (abs. superl. **maleficentíssimo**) 1. malefic, malign, evil. 2. with bad intentions. 3. prejudicial, harmful, detrimental. 4. criminal.

maleiforme adj. m. + f. malleiform.

maleiro s. m. 1. person who makes or sells suitcases, trunks, valises. 2. (Braz.) name given to the natives of Bahia in the diamond mining district.

maleita s. f. (also ~**s** pl.) malaria.

maleita-brava s. f. severe and malign malaria.

maleiteira s. f. (bot.) euphorbia.

maleitoso adj. malarial, malarious: of, referring to or subject to malaria.

mal-e-mal adv. barely, scarcely.

mal-empregado adj. (pl. **mal-empregados**) ill-used, misused.

mal-encarado adj. (pl. **mal-encarados**) 1. ill-favoured, looking cross. 2. revealing poor character. 3. badly accepted. 4. bearish.

mal-enjorcado adj. (pl. **mal-enjorcados**) (Braz.) badly or improperly dressed.

mal-ensinado adj. (pl. **mal-ensinados**) unmannered, unmannerly, uncivil.

mal-entendido s. m. (pl. **mal-entendidos**) (gall.) misunderstanding: 1. disagreement or dissension. 2. failure to understand, mistake as to meaning. ‖ adj. misunderstood: 1. improperly interpreted. 2. unappreciated.

maleolar adj. (anat.) malleolar: pertaining to a malleolus.

maléolo s. m. (anat.) malleolus: bony protuberance of the ankle.

mal-estar s. m. (pl. **mal-estares**) 1. moral or physical indisposition. 2. unrest, uneasiness. 3. illness, slight ailment.

mal-estreado adj. (pl. **mal-estreados**) 1. ominous, ill-omened. 2. awkward.

maleva s. m. (also **malevo**) bandit, evil-doer, malefactor. ‖ adj. m. + f. (S. Braz., pop.) 1. malevolent, bad, evil. 2. perverse. 3. ill-tempered. 4. mean. 5. said of a horse, that for any reason rears.

malevão s. m. (pl. **-ões**) (augm. of **maleva**) archrogue. ‖ adj. very wicked.

malevolência s. f. 1. malevolence, malignity, ill will. 2. grudge, spite, hatred.

malevolente adj. m. + f., **malévolo** m. 1. malevolent, unwilling, unkind. 2. ill-natured, malignant, spiteful. 3. mean.

malfadado s. m. unlucky, unhappy person. ‖ adj. 1. ill-fated, ill-starred, ill-omened. 2. accursed. 3. disgraced. 4. unlucky, fatal. ‖ **-amente** adv. ill-starredly.

malfadar v. 1. to make unhappy. 2. to disgrace. 3. to curse, invoke evil upon. 4. to foredoom.

malfalante s. + adj. m. + f. = **maldizente**.

malfamado adj. ill-famed.

malfazejo adj. (also **malfazente** m. + f.) maleficent, doleful, malignant, harmful, pernicious; mischievous.

malfazer v. 1. to do mischief, evil, wrong. 2. to hurt, harm.

malfeito (I) adj. 1. ill-done, badly finished. 2. batched, bungled. 3. deformed. 4. (fig.) bad, evil. 5. (fig.) unjust, undeserving.

malfeito (II) s. m. 1. (Braz., ant.) = **malfeitoria**. 2. (S. Braz.) witchcraft, sorcery.

malfeitor s. m. 1. malefactor, evil-doer. 2. criminal, villain. ‖ adj. maleficent.

malfeitoria s. f. malefaction, delict, misdeed, offense.

malfeliz adj. m. + f. (obs.) = **infeliz**.

malferido adj. badly or mortally wounded.

malferir v. 1. to hurt mortally. 2. to shed blood εs in a combat.

malformação s. f. (pl. **-ões**) malformation.

malformado adj. malformed.

mal-francês s. m. (pl. **males-franceses**) syphilis.

malga s. f. glazed, white or coloured bowl.

malgalante adj. m. + f. discourteous with the ladies, unchivalrous.

mal-gálico s. m. syphilis.

malgastar v. 1. to misspend, squander, lavish, waste, dissipate. 2. to sell at a loss.

malgaxe s. m. + f. Madagascan. ‖ adj. Madagascan.

mal-germânico s. m. (pl. **males-germânicos**) syphilis.

malgovernar v. 1. to govern badly. 2. to spend more than one has.

malgrado prep. notwithstanding, in spite of.

malha s. f. 1. mesh (net). 2. stich in knitting. 3. mail of an armour. 4. spot, speckle: fleck in the coat of an animal. 5. discoloured patch in the vegetation of an area. 6. hut. 7. (also **mealha**) old coin. 8. metal disk used in a game called

jogo de ~ (resembling quoits). 9. (naut.) bowline knot. 10. act of threshing grain. 11. beating, walloping. 12. snare, trap.
~ **de lã** sweater, cardigan. ~**s caídas de meia** a run in a stocking, ladder. **agulha de** ~ knitting needle. **cota de** ~ armour, coat of mail. **de pequenas** ~**s** fine-meshed. **escapar pela** ~ **rota** to slip the collar. **levantar uma** ~ to take up a stitch in knitting. **passar pela** ~ 1. to go through the mesh (a fish). 2. (fig.) to slip out of one's memory.

malhada s. f. 1. act of threshing. 2. threshing-floor, place where the threshing takes place. 3. stroke with a mallet, hammer or with a flail. 4. hut of a shepherd. 5. corral, enclosure for cattle. 6. flock of sheep, sheepfold. 7. (Braz.) shady place under large trees where the cattle seek shelter from the greatest heat. 8. (N. Braz.) small tobacco plantation. 9. area planted with grass for cutting. 10. cast, throw (at quoits). 11. (N. Braz.) damp valley. 12. plot, story.
cor ~ brindle, piebald. **estar na** ~ to protect o. s. from the sun and the heat.

malhadeiro s. m. 1. flail. 2. pestle. 3. scapegoat, laughing-stock. ‖ adj. 1. = **malhadiço**. 2. stupid. 3. rude.

malhadiço adj. 1. kicked about, used to a beating. 2. insolent, having a nerve. 3. incorrigible.

malhado adj. 1. mailed, speckled, spotted, patchy, brindle, piebald. 2. threshed or beaten with a flail, hammered, beaten with a mallet or hammer.

malhador s. m. 1. thresher. 2. hammerer, cudgeller. 3. (Braz.) plane and shady area sought by the cattle as resting place. ‖ adj. 1. disorderly. 2. fond of beating or threshing.

malhadouro s. m. (also **malhadoiro**) threshing floor, threshing place.

malhal s. m. (pl. -ais) wooden cross-piece of a winepress or fruit press.

malhão s. m. 1. high shot, throw or cast in a ball game. 2. ball used therefore. 3. = **malhal**. 4. popular Portuguese song and dance.
de ~ 1. at one throw. 2. (fig.) at random, rashly, inconsiderately.

malhar v. 1. to thresh, flail. 2. to hammer, beat with a mallet or hammer, batter, maul. 3. to spank, pelt. 4. to make fun of, scorn. 5. to seek protection from the sun (cattle). 6. to fall into the trap. 7. to mottle. 8. to pester.
~ **em ferro frio** to make ropes out of sand. ~ **o ferro enquanto está quente** to strike the iron while it is hot. ~ **o piano** to pound the piano.

malheirão s. m. boys' game similar to hopscotch.

malhetar v. to mortise, dovetail, fit one piece of metal or wood into the other.

malhete (ê) s. m. 1. mortise, mortise and tenon joint. 2. small mallet (plate M 6).

malho s. m. 1. sledgehammer (plate M 5). 2. flail. 3. maul. 4. beetle. 5. mallet (plate A 7). 6. rattle.

malhó s. m. (less used form of **maiô**) bathing suit.

malhoada s. f. 1. conspiracy, intrigue. 2. plot.

mal-humorado adj. (pl. **mal-humorados**) 1. ill-humoured. 2. sickly. 3. (fig.) angry, ill-tempered, hard to handle, irritable, fretful, peevish.

malícia s. f. 1. malice, evil intention. 2. ill will, maliciousness, spite, spitefulness. 3. animosity. 4. malevolence. 5. astuteness. 6. wantonness. 7. malicious interpretation. 8. humorous finesse; sarcastic humour.
deitar ~ to twist a person's words deliberately, misinterpret the intents.

maliciar v. 1. to impute malice to somebody, to be suspicious. 2. to misconstrue, interpret maliciously. 3. to suspect maliciously. 4. (rel.) to misjudge.

malicioso s. m. (also **maliciador**) 1. person full of malice. 2. person given to malicious gossip. 3. wanton. 4. rascal. 5. one who uses words of double and doubtful meaning. ‖ adj. 1. malicious, malevolent. 2. artful, crafty, catty, foxy. 3. wanton. 4. prankish, mischievous. 5. spiteful. ‖ -**amente** adv. maliciously.

málico adj. (chem.) malic.
ácido ~ malic acid.

maligna s. f. 1. malignant fever, typhoid. 2. (Braz.) malaria.

malignar v. 1. to turn bad or malign. 2. to vitiate, become a vice addict. 3. to corrupt, pervert. 4. to have a strong and malign relapse of an illness. 5. to slander.

malignidade s. f. malignity, malignancy, malignance, malevolence, malice, spite.

maligno s. m. (Braz.) the devil. ‖ adj. 1. malign, pernicious. 2. baleful. 3. malevolent, spiteful. 4. ill-natured, wicked. 5. (path.) malignant, deadly, tending to produce death, fatal, virulent. 6. malicious. ‖ -**amente** adv. malignantly, with ill intention.
espíritos ~**s** malign spirits. **febre -a** malignant fever. **tumor** ~ malignant tumour, cancer.

malina s. f. (mar.) spring tide.

malinar v. (Braz.) to prank, frolic (children).

malineza s. f. (N. Braz., pop.) 1. badness. 2. prank.

má-língua s. (pl. **más-línguas**) 1. m. + f. slanderer, backbiter. 2. f. slanderousness.

malinha s. f. 1. small valise, suitcase. 2. (N. Braz.) rattle looking like a tiny suitcase used by folk singers.

malinidade s. f. (Braz., variation of **malignidade**) 1. malevolence. 2. perversity.

malino s. m. (Braz., pop.) devil. ‖ adj. 1. (ant., pop.) malign. 2. (Braz., pop.) prankish, playful. 3. lazy (of children).

mal-intencionado adj. (pl. **mal-intencionados**) having bad intentions, evil-minded, perfidious.

maljeitoso adj. (pl. **maljeitosos**) 1. awkward, clumsy. 2. unskilful.

malmequer s. m. (bot.) marigold.

malnascido adj. 1. lowborn. 2. born under an unlucky star, ill-starred. 3. ill-natured.

maloca s. f. (Braz.) 1. Indian hut for several families. 2. Indian village. 3. a roundup of cattle to be lead to the corrals. 4. bunch of untrustworthy persons or bandits. 5. hiding place.
uma ~ **de ciganos** a band of gipsies.

malocado adj. (Braz.) (Indian) living in a village or settlement.

malocar v. (Braz.) to settle down in villages (Indians).

malograr v. 1. to frustrate, fail, spoil, wreck. 2. to render of no effect; overthrow. 3. to thwart. 4. to waste. 5. ~-**se**: a) to come a cropper, miscarry. b) to lag. c) to be lost prematurely.

malogro (ô) s. m. (pl. **malogros**). 1. frustration. 2. failure. 3. poor luck. 4. premature end.

maloio s. m. 1. villager. 2. peasant, boor.

maloqueiro s. m. (Braz.) 1. street Arab. 2. badly dressed individual without education. 3. (S. Braz.) member of a gang of bandits.

malotão s. m. (pl. -ões). 1. large suitcase, cabin trunk. 2. large package.

malote s. m. 1. small suitcase, bag. 2. oil-cloth for a soldier's cape.
enviar correspondência pelo ~ to send correspondence through own mail service.

mal-ouvido adj. (pl. **mal-ouvidos**) (Braz.) 1. disobedient. 2. heedless. 3. unruly.

malparado adj. 1. running a lopsided risk. 2. precarious, insecure. 3. in bad hands.

malparar v. 1. to risk. 2. to venture. 3. to subject to a poor future.
malparição s. f. (pl. -ões) (Braz.) induced abortion.
malparir v. 1. to give birth under unfortunate circumstances. 2. to miscarry.
malpinguinho s. m. (N. Braz.) tobacco imported from the Southern states.
mal-polaco s. m. (pl. **males-polacos**) syphilis.
malpropício adj. 1. unpropitious, improper. 2. inadequate, unsuitable.
malquerença s. f. 1. malevolence. 2. ill will. 3. animosity, aversion; hate.
malquerer s. m. 1. animosity. 2. aversion. 3. enmity. ‖ v. 1. to wish ill to; hate, detest. 2. to bear one a grudge.
malquistar v. 1. to cause somebody to be disliked. 2. to estrange, set at variance. 3. to indispose. 4. to produce or cause enmities or animosities. 5. ~-**se**: a) to render o. s. odious. b) to make enemies. ~-**se com alguém** to fall out with s. o., to break with s. o.
malquisto adj. 1. disliked. 2. hated, detested. 3. at variance, estranged.
malregido adj. misgoverned, mismanaged.
malroupido s. m. 1. badly dressed individual. 2. tatterdemalion. ‖ adj. 1. shabby, badly dressed. 2. tattered. 3. down at the heels.
malsão adj. (pl. ~s) (f. **malsã**) 1. unhealthful, unhealthy, unsalubrious, unwholesome. 2. sickly. 3. convalescent.
malsim s. m. (pl. **-ins**) 1. customs official. 2. internal police inspector. 3. police agent. 4. informer; (U. S. A.) stool pigeon. 5. denouncer. ‖ adj. disclosing, calumniating.
malsinação s. f. (pl. **-ões**) 1. information against s. o., denunciation, slanderous information or report. 2. intentional misinterpretation.
malsinar v. 1. to denounce (said of an official or agent). 2. to delate. 3. to spy upon s. o. 4. to slander. 5. to misconstrue, twist the meaning of something. 6. to censure. 7. to condemn. 8. to attribute a bad character to somebody. 9. to vaticinate a bad fate.
malsoante, malsonante adj. m. + f. 1. ill-sounding. 2. inharmonious, jarring, grating. 3. (fig.) shocking.
malsofrido adj. 1. impatient, disquiet. 2. unresigned.
malsonância s. f. dissonance.
malsorteado adj. unlucky, ill-fated.
malta (I) s. f. (also **maltesaria, maltesia**) 1. rabble, mob. 2. gang, pack. 3. group of itinerant farm labourers. 4. life of a vagabond. 5. vagrancy.
malta (II) s. f. (min.) maltha: a viscous asphalt resembling tar.
maltagem s. f. (pl. **-ens**) malting: preparation of malt.
maltar v. to malt: transform barley into malt.
malte s. m. malt: germinated barley, used in brewing.
maltês s. m. (pl. **-eses**) (f. **-esa**; pl. **-esas**) 1. Maltese: a) native or inhabitant of Malta. b) language spoken in Malta. 2. knight of the order of Malta. 3. vagrant farm labourer. ‖ adj. 1. Maltese: of or pertaining to Malta. 2. bluish grey (like a Maltese cat).
malthusianismo s. m. Malthusianism (doctrine that the growth of the population should be checked).
maltose s. f. (chem.) maltose: sugar obtained by the action of diastase on starch.
maltrapido, maltrapilho s. m. ragamuffin, tatterdemalion. ‖ adj. ragged, tattered, torn, shabby.
maltratado adj. 1. maltreated, abused. 2. hurt. 3. whipped, beaten. 4. unkindly received. 5. insulted. 6. hurt by the saddle (horse).
maltratar v. 1. to maltreat, treat badly, mishandle. 2. to receive badly. 3. to insult. 4. to vex. 5. to destroy, damnify, damage, spoil. 6. to hurt physically. 7. to beat, whip. 8. to abuse. 9. to wrong. **eles o** ~**am** they maltreated him, (coll.) played the devil with him.
mal-triste s. m. (Braz.) sickness of the cattle transmitted through ticks.
malucagem, maluqueira, maluquice s. f. 1. state of insanity. 2. an insane or crazy act. 3. eccentricity. 4. foolishness.
mal-turco s. m. (pl. **males-turcos**) syphilis.
malucar v. 1. to fool around. 2. to say or do crazy things. 3. to be pensive, moody. 4. to speak or brood like a madman.
maluco s. m. 1. nuts, crackpot. 2. fool. 3. extravagant person. ‖ adj. 1. wacky, nutty. 2. crazy. **deixar alguém** ~ to drive somebody nuts. **você está** ~ you're nuts, you are out of your mind.
maludo s. m. (Braz.) stallion. ‖ adj. valiant, brave, courageous.
malungo s. m. 1. companion. 2. comrade (among African slaves of the same transport). 3. (Braz.) foster brother, milk brother.
mal-usar v. 1. to use badly, make ill use of. 2. to abuse.
malva s. f. mallow(s): plant of hte family Malvaceae.
malvácea s. f. a malvaceous plant.
malváceo adj. malvaceous: pertaining to the Malvaceae.
malvadez(a) s. f. 1. meanness, baseness. 2. perversity, wickedness; malice.
malvada s. f. (Braz., pop.) (literally: the bad one) vulgar name for **cachaça** sugar-cane brandy.
malvado s. m. 1. (Braz., pop.) devil. 2. knave; mean, perverse person. ‖ adj. 1. mean, wicked. 2. perverse. 3. evil. ‖ **-amente** adv. meanly.
malvaísco, malvavisco s. m. (bot.) marsh mallow (Althaea officinalis), a medicinal herb of the family Malvaceae.
malvar s. m. ground where the Malvaceae grow.
malvasia s. f. malvasia: 1. malmsey: a variety of grapes. 2. the wine made out of these grapes.
malventuroso adj. (also **mal-aventurado**) ill-fated, ill-starred.
malversação s. f. 1. malversation: fraudulent handling of an official job or public money. 2. maladministration.
malversado adj. mishandled, misused.
malversador s. m. person who perpetrates malversation. ‖ adj. guilty of malversation.
malversar v. 1. to handle badly; to misuse, embezzle. 2. to dilapidate.
malvisto adj. 1. disliked. 2. suspected, distrusted. 3. near-sighted.
mama s. f. 1. mamma, female breast, udder, teat. 2. milk sucked from the mother's or wet-nurse's breast.
mamã s. f. (also **mamãe**) 1. mamma, mammy: mother in baby talk. 2. affectionate term for the mother, used by adults. 3. (Braz.) wet-nurse.
mamadeira s. f. 1. nursing bottle. 2. (S. Braz.) popular name given to the **muçurana** mussurana, a snake (Pseudoboa cloelia), in the assumption that it sucks the milk from cows.
mamado adj. 1. (vulg.) disappointed, disillusioned. 2. deceived, duped, illusioned. 3. (S. Braz., sl.) half-drunk, tipsy.
mamadura s. f. (also **mamada**) 1. lactation, act of sucking. 2. time required for nursing or giving suck.
mama-em-onça s. m. (pl. **mama-em-onças**) (Braz., pop.) 1. coveter, egoist, self-interested person. 2. fortune hunter. 3. man married to an ugly woman.

mamãezada s. f. (N. Braz.) 1. corruption and lack of morality in public services and government. 2. political patronage, political or administrative nepotism. 3. dishonesty. 4. intrigue. 5. perfidy. **deixe de** ~ cut out the false complication.
mamalogia s. f. mammalogy: study of or treatise on mammals.
mamalógico adj. mammalogical.
mamalogista s. m. + f. mammalogist.
mama-na-égua s. m., sg. + pl. (Braz., pop.) 1. coward. 2. simpleton. 3. inept, miserable person.
mamangaba s. f. (Braz., ent.) bumblebee: any social bee of the genus Bombus, also called **mangangá** and **mamangava**.
mamão s. m. (pl. **-ões**) 1. papaya: fruit of the papaw. 2. one year old donkey; unweaned calf. 3. (bot.) sucker. ‖ adj. 1. unweaned, still sucking. 2. sucking an awful lot.
mamão-macho s. m. (pl. **mamões-machos**) (also **cara--de-mamão-macho**) term for a person with a very long or very thin face.
mamar v. 1. to suck, take the breast. 2. (fig.) to suck something. 3. to learn in the cradle. 4. (S. Braz., pop.) to get drunk. 5. to obtain, extort. 6. (Braz., fig.) to mismanage private or public funds. **dar de** ~ to suckle, nurse, give suck. **dar de** ~ **à enxada** (N. Braz., pop.) to lean on the handle of the hoe. ~ **com o leite** (fig.) to imbibe from the earliest infancy. **ele mamou no erário público** he drew money out of the public purse.
mamário adj. (also **mamal**) mammary: of or pertaining to the breast or mamma.
mamarracho s. m. bad painter.
mamarreis s. m. (Braz., ichth.) a silverside.
mamata s. f. (Braz.) 1. shady business, theft. 2. pap. 3. enterprise, company or public administration of which favoured persons take pecuniary advantages.
mamaurana s. f. (N. Braz.) two kinds of trees, whose filamentous pulp is used to make rope and to calk ships.
mambembe s. m. (Braz.) lonely, solitary place. ‖ adj. mediocre, inferior, bad.
mambira s. m. + f. (S. Braz.) peasant; gaucho. ‖ adj. 1. rustic, rural. 2. rude.
mambirada s. f. (S. Braz.) group of gauchos.
mamelado adj. 1. mamillared. 2. covered with rounded hillocks.
mamelão, mamilão (pl. **-ões**) s. m. 1. a rounded hillock. 2. breast nipple.
mameluco s. m. (also **mamaluco**) 1. Mameluke: a) member of an Egyptian military class. b) slave in Mohammedan countries. 2. (Braz.) mestizo, son of an Indian and a white person.
mamífero s. m. mammal, mammifer, mammalian. ‖ adj. mammalian, mammiferous: having breasts.
mamiforme adj. m. + f. mammiform, mammillary: shaped like a breast or nipple.
mamilar s. m. corselet or brassière. ‖ adj. mammilary: shaped like or pertaining to the nipple.
mamilho s. m. metallic protuberance in a gun-barrel.
mamilo s. m. mammilla, nipple (plate C 18).
mamiloso adj. mammillated: having a nipple or being nipple-shaped.
maminha s. f. 1. nipple. 2. small breast. 3. breast nipple of a man.
mamite s. f. inflammation of the nipple.
mamoeiro s. m. 1. papaya tree, papaw tree. 2. (N. Braz.) habitual drunkard.
mamona, mamoneira s. f. **mamoneiro** m. 1. castor--oil plant. 2. castor bean. 3. name given by miners to magnetite dust.
mamoso adj. 1. mammillated. 2. mammiform. 3. big--breasted.

mamota s. m. + f. awkward person, lout.
mamote s. m. 1. a child that is breast feeding at an advanced age. 2. (Braz.) grown animal still sucking. ‖ adj. (ant.) ridiculous, silly.
mampar v. (S. Braz., coll.) to eat.
mamparra s. f. 1. simulated work, dawdling. 2. gang, mob. 3. (Braz.) laziness. 4. indolence. 5. (N. Braz.) small theft. 6. swindle, fraud. 7. rascality. 8. ~**s** subterfuges, evasions.
mamparreação s. f. (pl. **-ões**) (Braz.) 1. waste of time. 2. lingering, löitering. 3. evasion of issues. 4. fraudulent prolongation of due terms. 5. laziness, lounge.
mamparreador s. m. (Braz.) 1. waster of time. 2. lingerer, loiterer. 3. tergiversator, evader of issues. 4. fraudulent prolonger of due terms. 5. lazy-bones, lounger. ‖ adj. 1. dawdling. 2. lingering, loitering. 3. lazy, lounging. 4. evasive. 5. fraudulently dilatory.
mamparrear v. (Braz.) 1. to waste time. 2. to linger, loiter. 3. to evade issues, shuffle, temporize, tergiversate. 4. to prolong due terms fraudulently. 5. to be lazy, sit around.
mamparreiro s. m. lazy-bones, sluggard. ‖ adj. lazy, slothful, dawdling.
mamposta s. f. 1. reserve troops. 2. arrest, imprisonment or act of taking somebody to jail. **de** ~ on purpose.
mamposteiro s. m. (ant.) 1. procurator, substitute. 2. alms collector for prisoners.
mamposteria s. f. (ant.) office of a procurator or alms collector for prisoners.
mamudo adj. large-breasted.
mamujar v. to suck slowly, reluctantly and without appetite.
mâmula s. f. (anat.) excrescence, excrescency.
mamulengo s. m. (N. Braz.) puppet-show.
mamulo s. m. (S. Braz.) large breast.
mamute s. m. mammoth.
mana (I) s. f. sister.
mana (II) s. f. influence of spirits on an object or a person (Melanesia).
maná s. m. manna: 1. food miraculously bestowed upon the children of Israel in the desert. 2. resinous juice of some plants. 3. (fig.) delicious food. 4. excellent thing. 5. an exudate of the flowering ash, Fraxinus ornus, used in medicine.
manacá s. m. (Braz.) ornamental and medicinal shrub belonging to the family Solanaceae.
manação s. f. = **emanação**.
manada s. f. 1. herd of cattle. 2. (S. Braz.) group of forty or fifty she-asses following a stallion.
manadio adj. 1. of or pertaining to a herd of cattle or she-asses. 2. moving in herds.
manaíba s. f. (Braz.) 1. manioc cutting ready to be planted. 2. manioc seedlings.
manajeiro s. m. 1. overseer of the harvest. 2. foreman. 3. chief. 4. worker in saltbeds.
manalvo adj. white-spotted on its forelegs (horse).
manampança s. f. (Braz.) a sort of confection or cake made of manioc.
manancial s. m. (pl. **-ais**) (also **manadeira** f., **manadeiro** m.) 1. fountainhead, spring. 2. source, fountain. 3. abundant well. ‖ adj. m. + f. flowing, running incessantly; inexhaustible.
mananga s. m. (N. Braz.) medicine man.
manangüera s. m. + f. (S. Braz.) thin and withered person. ‖ adj. lean and thin.
manante adj. m. + f. 1. running, flowing. 2. emanant.
manantial s. m. (pl. **-ais**) (S. Braz.) swamp, moor, mire.
manápula s. f. (also **manopla**) large and ugly hand.
manaquim s. m. (pl. **-ins**) (ornith.) manakin.

manar v. 1. to emanate. 2. to flow continuously and abundantly. 3. to produce, bring forth, give rise to; to origin. 4. to bud, flower. 5. to proceed, 6. to come from. 7. to issue. 8. to ooze. 9. to shed.

manata s. m. 1. rogue. 2. thief. 3. dandy. 4. important person, big shot. 5. magnate.

manatídeo s. m. (zool.) one of the sirenians, as the manatee. ‖ adj. of or pertaining to the mammals of the order of the sirenians.

manatim s. m. (pl. **-ins**) (Braz., zool.) manatee, one of the sirenians (better known as **peixe-boi**).

manauê s. m. (Braz., also **manuê**) cake made out of sugar, honey, corn meal and other ingredients.

manauense s. m. + f. (Braz.) native of Manaus (capital of Amazonas). ‖ adj. of or referring to Manaus.

mancada s. f. (Braz., coll.) mistake or lapse; blunder. **dar ~ em alguma coisa** to bungle s. th.

mancador s. m. (S. Braz.) 1. lame horse. 2. bad horseman who rides his horse lame. ‖ adj. lame (horse).

mancal s. m. (pl. **-ais**) 1. (mech.): a) bearing. b) pillow. 2. (electr.) bushing. 3. door hinge.
~ aquecido hotbox. **~ extremo** outbearing. **~ do munhão** trunnion. **~ oscilante** swing bearing. **~ de pé** pivot bearing. **~ de pressão** thrust bearing. **~ reto** pillow block, plummer block. **caixa de ~** axle bed.

mancar (I) v. 1. to limp, hobble, go lame. 2. to be, become, or render limp, lame. 3. to cripple, maim.

mancar (II) v. (Braz.) 1. to fail, fail somebody; to break one's word, not to keep one's promise. 2. to let one down.

mancarrão s. m. (pl. **-ões**) (S. Braz.) jade, old worthless horse. ‖ adj. jadish, old, worthless (horse).

manceba s. f. 1. girl, lass. 2. mistress, concubine.

mancebia s. f. 1. liaison, concubinage. 2. dissolute life. 3. brothel. 4. (obs.) youth, the young ones.

mancebo s. m. 1. lad, boy, youth. 2. (obs.) lover, paramour. 3. ordinary seaman. 4. servant. 5. (Braz.) clothes hanger, clothes tree. 6. (S. Braz.) wooden stick to hang small lamps on. ‖ adj. (obs.) juvenile.

mancenilha s. f. (also **mancinela, mancenilheira**) (bot.) 1. manchineel: a tropical tree of the family Euphorbiaceae (Hippomane mancinella), with a milky, highly caustic, poisonous sap. 2. the fruit of this tree.

mancha s. f. 1. spot, stain, speck, fleck, blotch. 2. blemish, disgrace, reproach, tarnish on the reputation. 3. flaw, defect. 4. brush stroke. 5. den, sleeping place of the wild boar. 6. (Braz.) tobacco disease. 7. carbuncle of the cattle.
~ negra epizooty of the cattle. **~ solar** sun spot.

mancha-de-ferro s. f. (pl. **manchas-de-ferro**) a sphere fungus harmful to coffee plantations.

manchado adj. 1. stained, spotted. 2. soiled. 3. piebald, mottled. 4. discredited.

manchão s. m. (pl. **-ões**) (Braz.) 1. coloration of alluvial diamond ground. 2. (pop.) rubber patch of a tire.

manchar v. 1. to spot, blot, stain. 2. to blemish. 3. to soil, defile, dirty. 4. (fig.) to dishonour, discredit; scar, tarnish.
~ de sangue to stain with blood.

manchear v. (Braz.) to cause the fermentation of cocoa.

manchego adj. 1. of or pertaining to La Mancha, Spain. 2. said of the Cervantes' character Don Quixote, a nobleman of La Mancha.

mancheia s. f. (also **mão-cheia**) wisp, handful.
a ~s prodigally. **de ~** splendid. **uma ~ de palha** a wisp of straw.

manchete s. f. 1. head-line. 2. streamer (newspaper).
~ de jornal banner, head-line.

manchil s. m. (pl. **-is**) 1. cleaver, a butcher's chopping knife. 2. scythe. 3. (hist.) war weapon.

manchilha s. f. (Braz.) epizooty of the cattle.

mancho adj. (Braz.) lame, defective (usually applied to the gait of a horse).

manchu s. m. + f. Manchurian: native or inhabitant of Manchuria. ‖ adj. Manchurian: of or pertaining to Manchuria.

mancinismo s. m. (**canhotismo** is more frequently used) left-handedness, predominant use of the left hand.

mancípio s. m. 1. (obs.) slave. 2. (fig.) dependent person or thing.

manco s. m. lame person; cripple. ‖ adj. 1. lame; hobbling. 2. maimed, mutilated, crippled, unable to use a limb. 3. defective, incomplete, imperfect. 4. (fig.): a) shy, awkward. b) ignorant. c) lazy, sluggish.
estar ~ to be lame. **não ser ~ nem coxo** to be no fool.

mancomunação s. f. (pl. **-ões**) 1. adjustment, combination. 2. plot, conspiracy, collusion, connivance.

mancomunado adj. 1. adjusted, engaged. 2. combined, agreed. 3. conjured, plotted, conspired, colluded.

mancomunar v. 1. to adjust, contract. 2. to combine, agree. 3. to plot, conspire, collude, connive, make common cause with, act in concert.

mancornar v. to grab the horns of a bull throwing him on the ground.

mancueba s. m. (Braz., also **cuba**) 1. powerful or influential person. 2. individual versed in witchcraft.

manda s. f. 1. note of reference, reference mark. 2. (obs.) legate, testamentary disposition. 3. m. short for **mandachuva**: big shot.

mandaçaia s. f. (Braz., also **manaçaia**) a bee (Melipona anthidioides) that produces excellent honey.
conhecer o rigor da ~ (S. Braz., pop.) to suffer acute punishment, to learn the hard way.

mandachuva s. m. 1. bigwig, big shot. 2. boss. 3. influential person. 4. political leader in the interior of Brazil. 5. magnate.

mandada s. f. (Braz.) act of dealing cards.

mandadeiro s. m. 1. messenger, errand runner. 2. one who carries out orders. ‖ adj. referring to a message, order or command.

mandado s. m. 1. order or command. 2. court order, judicial writ; mandate; commission. 3. message, errand. 4. (S. Braz., also **~-de-deus**) lightning. ‖ adj. 1. sent. 2. ordered.
a ~ de by order of. **~ judicial** a judge's order. **~ de prisão** warrant of arrest. **~ de segurança** a court injunction.

mandalete s. m. (S. Braz.) person (usually a child or an old person) doing light work on a farm or acting as a messenger.

mandamento s. m. 1. command, order. 2. word of command. 3. commandment, precept of the Decalogue, precept of the church. 4. (ant.): a) district, circumscribed territory. b) jurisdiction. c) parish.
os dez ~s the Ten Commandments.

mandante s. m. + f. 1. person who stimulates certain acts, leader of a plot, instigator of a crime. 2. orderer, person giving orders. ‖ adj. ordering, commanding.
roda ~ (tech.) driving wheel.

mandão s. m. (pl. **-ões**) (f. **mandona**) 1. despot. 2. boss, bully. 3. haughty, domineering or imperious person.

mandar v. 1. to order, command; bid. 2. to rule, govern; to lay down the law. 3. to lead and direct.

4. to dominate. 5. to send, remit, forward, ship. 6. to throw, hurl. 7. to depute. 8. to authorize. 9. to ordain. 10. to nominate. 11. to exile. ~ **às favas,** ~ **para o inferno** to send to hell. ~ **bugiar** to sack with contempt and anger. ~ **buscar** to send for. ~ **de lá para cá** to send about. ~ **desta para a melhor** to kill. ~ **embora** to sack, throw out, send away. ~ **entrar** to show in. ~ **e desmandar** to exercise total authority. ~**-se dizer** (S. Braz.) to speak well on a certain topic. ~**-se dizer na estrada** to run away, flee. ~ **um cabograma** to send a cable. **ela quer** ~ she wants to manage, (sl.) to run the show. **ele manda dizer que** he wants me to tell you that. ~**am-no para fora** they sent him out. **mande lembranças a ele** give him my kind regards, remember me to him. **mande-me notícias** let me hear from you. **mande-o falar comigo** tell him to see me.

mandarim s. m. (pl. **-ins**) mandarin, member of any of the nine ranks of public officials in Imperial China.

mandarina s. f. 1. wife of a mandarin. 2. mandarin, tangerine: a variety of citrus fruit.

mandarinado, mandarinato s. m. mandarinate: 1. quality or function of a mandarin. 2. (fig.) privileged class, the influential people.

mandatário s. m. 1. mandatary, nation or person holding a mandate. 2. executive of mandates. 3. representative, solicitor, proxy, attorney.

mandato s. m. 1. mandate. 2. power of attorney, power of procuration. 3. commission. 4. prescript, order, precept. 5. charge. injunction. 6. delegation. 7. trust. 8. (eccl.) maundy: ceremony of feet washing.

mandchu s. + adj. m. + f. = **manchu.**

mandembe, mandengo s. m. (Braz.) nearly inaccessible place, full of dense forest.

mandi s. m. any of a species of Brazilian catfishes.

mandiba s. f. (Braz.) a variety of manioc (cassava).

mandíbula s. f. mandible: 1. jaw, jawbone, inferior maxillary (plate 17). 2. the lower jaw of animals. 3. each of the two parts of the beak of birds. 4. one of the first pairs of the hard and movable mouth-appendages of certain insects. 5. (tech.) each of two grasping parts of some tools (plates B 16, T 1).

mandibular adj. m. + f. mandibular: of or pertaining to the mandible.

mandigüera s. m. (Braz.) weak and runtish piglets, that are usually killed to give the other pigs of the litter a better chance to become big and fat.

mandil s. m. (pl. **-is**) 1. (kitchen) apron. 2. cleaning rag. 3. thick cloth used on the waxer. 4. horse cloth (for rubbing down horses).

mandileiro s. m. (Braz.) = **mandrião.**

mandinga s. 1. f. (Braz.) witchraft, sorcery. 2. m. + f. Mandingo, any member of a number of Negro tribes of West Africa, who suffered a Mahometan influence. They were considered to be masters at sorcery. 3. m. the language spoken by the Mandingos. ‖ adj. m. + f. of or pertaining to the Mandingos.

mandingar v. 1. to bewitch. 2. to use sorcery.

mandingaria s. f. (Braz.) witchcraft, practice of sorcery.

mandingueiro, mandinguento s. m. sorcerer, charmer.

mandioca s. f. 1. cassava, manioc. 2. (N. Braz.) name of a political party and its followers during the time of the Empire.

a conversa rendeu que nem ~ **de várzea** it became an unending conversation.

mandiocaba s. f. (N. Braz.) pap or gruel of sweetened rice with manioc juice.

mandioca-doce s. f. (pl. **mandiocas-doces**) (Braz.) sweet cassava (Manihot dulcis).

mandiocal s. m. (pl. **-ais**) (Braz.) manioc plantation.

mandiola s. f. (N. Braz.) 1. revolution, revolt. 2. disorder. 3. noisy demonstration.

mandioqueiro s. m. (Braz.) small scale tenant farmer growing almost exclusively manioc.

mandiva s. f. (Braz.) = **mandiba.**

mando s. m. 1. the power of ordering. 2. power, authority. 3. command. 4. right.

mandolim m., **mandolina** f. mandolin: stringed musical instrument with a pear-shaped body and a fretted neck.

mandolinete s. m. small Italian mandolin.

mandonismo s. m. (Braz.) 1. habit and misuse of ordering; bossing. 2. tyranny, despotism. 3. pre-eminent power or influence.

mandora, mandola s. f. (mus) mandola, mandora, mandore: a 16th century lute, the forerunner of the modern mandolin.

mandraca s. f. (Braz.) 1. witchcraft, sorcery. 2. magic potion.

mandraco s. m. (S. Braz.) amulet, old coin or any other object, worn by gamblers, or carried along in the pockets.

mandrágora s. f. mandragora, mandrake root (used extensively in witchcraft in the Middle Ages).

mandrana s. m. + f. loiterer, drone.

mandranice s. f. (also **mandriíce**) idleness, laziness, quality or habits of a loiterer.

mandraqueiro adj. (Braz.) bewitching, magical.

mandraquice s. f. (Braz.) wittchcraft, sorcery.

mândria s. f. (also **mandriíce**) 1. laziness, idleness, slothfulness. 2. indolence.

mandrião s. m. (pl. **-ões**) (f. **-ona**) 1. lazy-bones, idler, loiterer, lounger, sluggard, drone. 2. short and light coat worn by women and children (in the house). ‖ adj. lazy, loitering, sluggish, slothfull, indolent.

mandriar v. (also **mandrianar**) to idle, loiter, lounge, loaf, dawdle.

mandril (I) s. m. (pl. **-is**) (tech.) 1. chuck: cutter block (plate F 8). 2. mandrel, drift. 3. expander. 4. broach, reamer. 5. boaring bit. 6. metal thread used in injection needles to keep them clean.

mandril (II) s. m. (zool.) mandrill, large baboon.

mandrilar v. (tech.) to ream, broach.

mandu s. m. + f. (Braz.) simpleton, ninny, booby. ‖ adj. silly, dumb.

manducação s. f. (pl. **-ões**) (coll.) chewing, eating.

manducar v. (coll.) to manducate, eat, chew.

mandureba s. f. (N. Braz.) sugar-cane brandy.

mandurim s. f. (pl. **-ins**) (Braz.) a certain stingless bee.

mané s. m. (Braz. + Port., prov.) 1. nincompoop. 2. lazy, sluggish, untidy individual. 3. fool.

maneador s. m. leather curb on a horse's harness.

manear v. 1. = **manejar.** 2. (Braz.) to hobble, fetter (horse).

maneável adj. (pl. **-áveis**) 1. soft, tractable. 2. that can be handled easily.

mané-coco s. m. (pl. **manés-coco**) fool, idiot.

mané-gostoso s. m. (pl. **manés-gostosos**) 1. (N. Braz.) folklore character. 2. stilted person. 3. puppet, marionette. 4. badly dressed person.

maneia s. f. (Braz.) fetter, clog; hobble, strap used to hobble a horse's legs.

maneio s. m. 1. direction, management, act of managing. 2. administration of capital. 3. manual work, handwork. 4. handling, manipulation. 5. activity. 6. (ant.) gain, profit. 7. ~**s** pl. fat of cattle.

maneira s. f. 1. way, manner, form. 2. make, kind. 3. fashion. 4. opportunity, possibility. 5. style of an artist or writer. 6. aspect, view, look. 7. behav-

iour, manners; use, custom, habit. 8. (Braz., Port., prov.) placket: lateral opening of a skirt at the waist.
~ **de andar** bearing, carriage. ~ **de falar** way of speech, mere talk. ~ **de pensar** way of thinking, mental attitude, mentality. **à** ~ **de** in the way of, like, as. **de** ~ **alguma** not in the least, in no way. **de** ~ **que** thus; so that. **de** ~ **superior** in the best way. **de muitas** ~s in many ways. **de qualquer** ~ anyhow, anyway. **de que** ~ how? **desta** ~ thus, in this manner. **de uma** ~ **ou de outra** some way or the other. **não há** ~ **de fazer isto** there is no possibility to do it.
maneirar v. (Braz., sl.) 1. to relieve temporarily an embarrassment or problem. 2. to accommodate shrewdly.
maneirismo s. m. mannerism.
maneirista s. m. + f. mannerist: 1. artist who adheres excessively to a peculiar style. 2. person sporting affected manners of dress and speech.
maneiro adj. 1. easy to be handled, handy, easily managed, manageable. 2. portable. 3. light, requiring little force. 4. manual. 5. comfortable, graceful. 6. polite, mannerly. 7. tame, domestic, brought up by hand, used to eat out of the hand.
maneiroso adj. 1. well-mannered, mannerly, polite, civil. 2. amiable. || **-amente** adv. politely; amiably.
manejador s. m. tugger, plyer.
manejar v. 1. to handle: a) move, carry out or direct, or work with the hands; manipulate; wield. b) manage, govern, direct. c) deal with. d) treat. e) trade. f) pratice. 2. (horsemanship) to execute correct movements with the feet (horse).
~ **a agulha** to work with a needle, sew. ~ **mal** to mishandle. ~ **negócios** to handle affairs.
manejável adj. m. + f. (pl. **-áveis**) 1. manageable, workable. 2. feasible. 3. handy.
manejo s. m. 1. management. 2. administration. 3. attendance. 4. manège, training, breaking in. 5. (mil.) manoeuvre. 6. handling, wielding. 7. ~s pl. machinations, intrigues.
de fácil ~ handy, easily managed.
manelo s. m. 1. handful. 2. management. 3. manipulation, handling.
manema s. m. (Braz.) coarse manioc flour.
manemolência s. f. (N. Braz.; pop.) 1. laziness, sluggishness. 2. indisposition. 3. weakness. 4. continuous bad luck.
manengüera adj. m. + f. (Braz.) 1. weak, feeble. 2. thin, frail. 3. wilted.
manequim s. m. (pl. **-ins**) 1. manikin, mannequin: a) tailors' dummy (plate A 5). b) lay figure (plate V 5). c) model: woman employed to display gowns. 2. (fig.): a) fop, dandy. b) milksop, puppet, person without own will.
manes s. m. pl. manes: 1. spirits of dead persons. 2. tutelary deities. 3. lower gods invoked by the Romans on the graves.
maneta s. m. + f. one-handed or one-armed person. || adj. one-handed, one-armed.
manete s. m. (aeron.) accelerator.
manetear v. (S. Braz.) to become deprived of the use of one hand or arm.
manga s. f. 1. sleeve: a) part of a garment (plates R 6, 7). b) (tech.) socket, bushing; journal (car.) 2. filtering bag, straining bag. 3. waterspout. 4. lamp-chimney. 5. (Braz.) extreme part of a fisher's net where the ropes are pulled. 6. detachment of troops. 7. (N. Braz.): a) walls of a fish corral. b) corridor, sort of chute, used to guide cattle on board a ship. 8. (bot.) mango.
arregaçar as ~**s** to pull up the socks; to build up disposition. **dar** ~**s** to offer chances. **ser** ~ **de**

colete to be scarce or rare. **dinheiro aqui é** ~ **de colete** (sl.) we have no money at all. **em** ~**s de camisa** in one's shirt sleeves. **não ter pano para** ~ (fig.) to be unable to launch out. **ter a** ~ **larga** to have a lawyer's conscience.
mangaba s. f. (Braz.) fruit of the mangabeira.
mangabal s. m. (pl. **-ais**) (Braz.) mangabeira grove.
mangabar v. (Braz.) to extract latex from the mangabeira.
mangabeira s. f. (Braz., bot.) mangabeira: a treelet (Hancornia speciosa) of the family Apocynaceae yielding latex.
mangabeiro s. m. (Braz.) person who extracts latex from the mangabeira.
mangação s. f. (pl. **-ões**) mockery, derision, sport, jesting, jeer, kidding, ribbing, railery, banter.
mangaço s. m. (Braz.) stroke with a whip.
manga-d'água s. f. (pl.) **mangas-d'água** violent shower, cloud-burst.
manga-de-alpaca s. f. (pl. **mangas-de-alpaca**) (Braz.) white-collar worker; public employee.
mangador s. m. mocker, banterer, scoffer, duper, kidder. || adj. mocking, jeering.
mangagá adj. m. + f. (Braz.) enormous, very large, huge.
mangal s. m. (pl. **-ais**) (Braz.) a growth of mangroves.
mangalaça s. f. 1. vagrancy, idling. 2. brothel, bawdy-house.
mangalaço adj. 1. lazy, idling, slothful. 2. vagrant. 3. villain, scoundrel.
mangalho s. m. (N. Braz., usually pl.) products of small-scale farming and home industry sold on the markets.
mangalô s. m. (Braz., bot.) jack bean (Canavalia ensiformis), used for forage.
manganato s. m. (chem.) manganate.
manganês s. m. manganese, chemical element.
manganésico, mangânico adj. manganic.
mangangá s. m. (Braz.) 1. (ichth.) common name of various fishes of the family Scorpaenidae (also called **beatinha, beatriz** f.). 2. (ent.) bumþlebee: any social bee of the genus Bombus.
mangânico adj. manganic: of or containing manganese, usually in the trivalent state.
manganífero adj. manganiferous: containing or yielding manganese.
manganilha s. f. sleight: 1. cheat, trick, artifice. 2. subtleness of the hands, legerdemain.
manganita s. f. manganite: 1. mineral hydrous manganese oxide, one of the minor manganese ores. 2. salts containing tetravalent manganese.
manganoso adj. (chem.) manganous.
mangão s. m. (pl. **-ões**) (f. **mangona**) 1. joker, mocker, ribber. 2. very ample and large sleeve. || adj. ribbing extensively, derisive, mocking.
mangar v. 1. to joke, rib, kid, deride, mock, make game of. 2. to scorn. 2. to cheat, dupe, defraud, dodge. 4. (S. Braz.) to idle, delay, be slow.
mangará s. m. (N. Braz.) flowering extremity of a banana stalk formed by the bracts.
mangarataia s. f. (Braz.) (bot.) ginger.
mangarito s. m. (Braz., also **mangará-mirim**) plant of the family Araceae producing edible tubercles.
mangaua s. m. + f. (Braz.) 1. mutual relationship between children and foster children; the name they give each other. 2. foster brother.
mango s. m. 1. handle of a flail. 2. (Braz. + Port., prov., sl.) **mil-réis** former monetary unit; a thousand réis. 3. (S. Braz.) whip consisting of a wooden handle and an unbraided broad leather strip.
mangoça, mangofa s. f. (N. Braz., pop.) scorn, derision.

mangona s. f. 1. indolence, slothfulness, idleness, laziness. 2. f. of mangão. 3. m. lazy man.

mangonar, mangonear, mangolar v. 1. to idle, be lazy, dawdle. 2. to loiter, loaf.

mangonga s. m. (ichth.) sand shark.

mangorra s. f. (S. Braz.) sadness, melancholy; the blues.

mangorrear v. (S. Braz.) 1. to betray, cheat. 2. to bore, pester.

mangostão s. m. (pl. -ões) mangosteen: 1. East-Indian guttiferous tree. 2. its fruit.

mangra s. f. 1. mildew. 2. blight, rust. 3. (ant.) any disease.
~ do trigo dust-brand.

mangrado adj. 1. mildewy, blighted. 2. emaciated, stunted.
comprar a grado e ~ to buy in or by the lump, by the bulk.

mangrar v. 1. to mildew, blight. 2. to stunt, hamper the development of. 3. to render useless. 4. to frustrate. 5. to get lost. 6. to weaken, wilt. 7. (fig.) to perish, decay.

mangrueiro adj. (S. Braz., pop.) impertinent, demanding, provoking.

mangrulho s. m. high military observation post made out of wood.

manguá, mangual s. m. (pl. ~s, -ais) 1. flail. 2. lash, whip.

mangualada s. f. 1. stroke with a flail. 2. (fig.) the jump of a snake.

manguapa adj. (Braz.) having fine gaits (horse).

manguara s. f. (Braz.) 1. coarse walking stick. 2. a sort of cudgel or club: mace. 3. pole, rod. 4. wooden bar used for the transportation of fowl, whose feet are tied together and slid over the bar. 5. m. + f. (fig.); also manguarão m.) tall and thin person, hop-pole.

manguari s. m. (Braz., also galalau) very tall man.

mangue s. m. 1. mangrove. 2. swamp area covered with mangroves, marsh, morass.

mangueação s. f. (pl. -ões) (S. Braz.) 1. act of guiding cattle through rivers or towards the corral. 2. deceit, fraud.

mangueador s. m. 1. one who guides cattle through a river or to the corral. 2. cheat, swindler, impostor, sharper. || adj. deceiving, fraudulent.

manguear v. (S. Braz.) 1. to guide cattle through a river, or to the corral. 2. to deceive with tricks and artifices, cheat, fraud, swindle.

mangueira s. f. 1. rubber or canvas hose (plate R 3). 2. (S. Braz.) corral or pen near the main building of a farm. 3. mango tree.
~ de incêndio fire hose.

mangueiral s. m. (pl. -ais) mango grove.

mangueirão s. m. (pl. -ões) (S. Braz.) large corral.

mangueiro s. m. (Braz.) 1. small corral, or pen. 2. small and round ironing-board used to iron sleeves. || adj. (pop.) 1. wily, guileful, crafty. 2. stubborn, pigheaded. 3. slow.

manguerana s. f. (Braz.) a guttiferous shrub.

manguezal s. m. (pl. -ais) (Braz.) = mangal.

manguito s. m. 1. mitt. 2. (obs.) fur muff. 3. obscene gesture esp. of contempt, consisting in raising the closed hand (also known as banana). 4. small sleeve.

mangusto s. m. mongoose; a mammal of India that kills snakes.

manha s. f. 1. slyness, artfulness, cunningness, shrewdness; malice. 2. dexterity. 3. trick, artifice. 4. vice, bad habit. 5. whim. 6. complaining. 7. (Braz. fam.) whining, crying of kids. 8. ~s pl. (obs.) manners, habits.
o bebê está fazendo ~ the baby is whining.

manhã s. f. 1. morning, forenoon. 2. dawn. 3. early hours of the day. 4. (fig.) beginning, dawn.
à ~, de ~, pela ~ in the morning. amanhã de ~ tomorrow morning. ontem de ~ yesterday morning. todas as ~s every morning. uma ~ maravilhosa a wonderful morning.

manhãzinha s. f. (dim. of manhã) the early morning.

manheirar v. (S. Braz.) 1. to trick. 2. to fake illness. 3. to dawdle, work slowly and reluctantly. 4. to try to run away (cattle).

manheirento adj. 1. sly, cunning. 2. cheating. 3. stubborn. 4. whimsical. 5. vicious (horse).

manheiro, manhento adj. (S. Braz.) 1. whimsical. 2. artful, deceiving. 3. wilful. 4. said of tobacco that burns slowly. 5. said of a drawn out tough business.

manho adj. 1. (obs.) great. 2. confused, bewildered, perplexed. 3. foolish, idiotic.

manhoso adj. 1. foxy, cunning, crafty, shrewd. 2. smart, clever, sly. 3. whimsical. 4. whining. 5. vicious, jadish (horse). || -amente adv. smartly, whimsically, foxily, etc.
um político ~ a foxy politician.

mania s. f. 1. mania, form of insanity. 2. whim, kink, excentricity. 3. obsession, passion, wild craze, fad, rage. 4. addiction, vice, bad habit. 5. hobby. 6. fixed idea.
~ da perseguição persecution mania. ele tem a ~ da grandeza he is possessed by megalomania.

maníaco s. m. maniac, madman, lunatic. || adj. maniac, maniacal, raving with madness.

maniatado adj. 1. handcuffed, tied. 2. (fig.) constrained.

maniatar v. 1. to manacle, fetter, handcuff, tie the hands of. 2. to trammel. 3. (fig.): a) to constrain; check, restrict; submit. b) to deprive of liberty. c) to tie, bind.

manicaca s. m. (N. Braz.) a weak, spineless, timid, cowardly individual (same as macufa and mutanje).

manicla s. f. (S. Braz., also manica) the smallest of the three stones of the bolas of a lasso, which is kept in the hand.
como bolas sem ~ aimlessly.

maniçoba s. f. (Braz.) 1. leaf of the manioc plant. 2. (also maniçobeira) plant of the family Euforbiaceae, from which rubber is extracted. 3. food made out of manioc shoots mixed with meat and/or fish and seasoned with salt and pepper.

maniçobal s. m. (pl. -ais) (Braz.) a maniçoba plantation or growth.

manicômio s. m. lunatic asylum, mad-house.

manicora s. f. architectural ornament representing an animal with a snake's head and tail and a spherical body.

manicórdio s. m. ancient musical instrument resembling a clavichord.

manicuera s. f. (N. Braz.) 1. manioclike plant. 2. its sweet juice.

manicujá s. m. (N. Braz.) hole made to plant a cassava cutting.

manícula s. f. 1. forefoot of a mammal. 2. leather glove used by shoemakers and leatherworkers. 3. (Braz.) crank, winch handle.

manicura s. f. 1. manicure. 2. manicurist.

manicuro s. m. manicurist.

manicurto adj. 1. short-handed. 2. (fig.) tight-fisted, avaricious.

manidestro adj. (also mandestro) right-handed; using habitually and preferentially the right hand.

manietar v. = maniatar.

manifestação s. f. (pl. -ões) manifestation: 1. act of manifesting. 2. state of being manifested. 3.

demonstration of the people to show their opinions. 4. in spiritualism a materialization.

manifestante s. m. + manifestant, manifester, demonstrator. ‖ adj. manifesting, demonstrative, displaying.

manifestar v. to manifest: 1. make public, reveal, disclose, express, make known. 2. show plainly, display, exhibit. 3. list the goods carried by a ship for the customs officials or other authorities; to declare, state.

~ **sua opinião** to voice one's opinion. **ele manifesta por toda parte a sua decepção** he airs his disappointment everywhere. **seus preconceitos manifestam-se em seu relato** his report reveals his prejudices.

manifesto s. m. manifest: 1. public declaration or explanation of reasons. 2. political, religious or other program. 3. list of goods transported or sold and subject to taxes. ‖ adj. 1. manifest, evident, obvious, plain. 2. public, broad. ‖ **amente** adv. plainly, manifestly.

~ **de mercadorias embarcadas** a ship's list of the cargo. **dar ao** ~ to declare goods. **mentira -a a flat lie.**

maniflautista s. m. + f. person who produces flutelike sounds with his hands.

maniforme adj. m. + f. shaped like a hand.

manigância s. f. 1. prestidigitation: sleight-of-hand. 2. mysterious operation. 3. black magic. 4. manoeuvre, artifice; underhand dealing.

manigânciar v. (Braz.) to use witchcraft, black magic, prestidigitation, artifices.

manilha s. f. 1. bracelet, armlet. 2. foot ring among some African tribes. 3. shackle, fetter, manacle. 4. a certain card game. 5. glazed clay pipes used in canalization. 6. variety of tobacco.

papel ~ Manila paper: a strong light-brown paper made originally out of Manila hemp.

manilhar v. 1. to adorn with rings or bracelets. 2. to canalize with glazed clay pipes.

manilheiro s. m. 1. producer of glazed clay pipes. 2. player of the **manilha** card game.

manilúvio s. m. bath of the hands, ordinarily hot.

manimolência s. f. (N .Braz.) = **manemolência.**

manina adj. f. (Braz., also **maninha**) barren (of cows).

maninelo s. m. 1. fool, idiot. 2. effeminate man. ‖ adj. 1. idiotic, foolish. 2. effeminate, womanish.

maninha s. f. (also **manina**) a raw material used for making ropes. ‖ adj. f. = **manina.**

maninhado adj. uncultivated, untilled, fallow.

maninhar v. to let the land lie uncultivated.

maninhez s. f. barrenness, infecundity, infertility, sterility.

maninho s. m. 1. uncultivated land, waste. 2. ~s pl. legacy of a deceased without children. ‖ adj. 1. barren, sterile, infecund, unfruitful, unproductive. 2. desert, wild, waste.

manino adj. tiny, very little, trifling, petty.

maniota s. f. trammel, fetter, shackle.

manipanso s. m. 1. African idol, fetish. 2. (hum.) very fat person.

manipresto adj. (also **prestímano**) nimble-gingered, neat-handed, handy, dexterous, deft, skilful.

manipuçá s. m. (Braz.) fruit and tree of the family Melastomaceae.

manipueira or **manipuera** s. f. (Braz.) milky, poisonous juice pressed from the ground manioc.

manípula s. f. handle, knob, crank.

manipulação s. f. (pl. -ões) 1. manipulation, handling. 2. (chem.) laboratory operations.

manipulado adj. manipulated; processed, handled.

manipulador s. m. 1. manipulator, handler, operator. 2. sending key, Morse key.

manipular (I) v. 1. to manipulate, handle, process, work. 2. to prepare medicine. 3. to invent, imagine, think up. 4. to manage through artful skill. 5. to organize.

manipular (II) s. m. soldier of an ancient Roman maniple. ‖ adj. m. + f. of or pertaining to a maniple.

manipulário s. m. commander of a Roman maniple.

manipulatório adj. manipulatory, manipulative.

manípulo s. m. 1. handful. 2. wisp, bundle, sheaf, faggot, which can be spanned with one hand. 3. maniple: a) (eccl.) ornamental band worn by the priest on his left wrist when saying mass (plate P 5). b) subdivision of a Roman legion. 4. standard of Roman troops. 5. (tech.) handle, lever, arm (plate P 4).

maniqueísmo s. m. 1. Manichaeism: religious doctrine of Mani (or Manichaeus), widely spread in Asia from the 3rd to the 5th century. 2. any doctrine founded on the principle of the two opposite forces, the good and the evil.

maniqueísta s. m. + f. Manichaean: believer in Manichaeism. ‖ adj. Manichaean.

maniquete s. m. lace that trims the sleeve of the alb of a Roman Catholic priest.

maniqueu s. m. Manichaean: adherent of Manichaeism. ‖ adj. Manichaean.

manirroto adj. spendthrift, prodigal, wasteful, lavish.

manistério s. m. = **manutério.**

manita s. f. 1. (fam.) little hand. 2. (chem.) mannitol: hexavalent alcohol, manna sugar. 3. m + f. = **maneta.** ‖ adj. m. + f. = **maneta.**

manitó, manitu s. m. manitu, manitou.

maniva s. f. (N. Braz.) manioc, cassava (Manihot utilissima) also known as **maniveira** and **manaíba.**

manival s. m. (pl. **-ais**) (Braz., also **mandiocal**) manioc plantation.

manivela s. f. 1. handle, crank, winch (plate F 8). 2. (tech.) crank.

~ **de eixo** centre crank. ~ **forjada** forged crank. ~ **propulsora** driving crank. **dar à** ~ to crank.

manivelar v. 1. to crank. 2. (fig.) to promote.

manivérsia s. f. (pop.) swindle, cheating, mean trick.

manja s. f. 1. act of eating, meal. 2. (Braz.) children's game, a sort of hide and seek, known also as **tempo-será.**

manjado adj. (Braz., sl.) broadly known.

manjaleco s. m. (N. Braz.) = **marmanjo.**

manja-léguas s. m. + f., sg. + pl. person walking a lot, eating up the miles.

manjaléu s. m. (N. Braz.) bogey, hobgobble, bugbear, usually quoted to frighten children.

manjar s. m. 1. any foodstuff. 2. tidbit, dainty, choice morsel, delicious and appetizing specialty. 3. custard, pudding. 4. (fig.) a feast or treat to the eye or the mind. ‖ v. 1. to eat. 2. (Braz., sl.): a) to spy, get a peep of. b) to twig, get it, perceive.

ele manja do assunto he understands about the subject. ~**es finos** delicatessen.

manjar-branco s. m. (pl. **manjares-brancos**) blancmange.

manjedoura s. f. (also **manjedoira, manjadoura**) manger, crib (plate E 11).

manjelim s. m. (bot.) red sandalwood.

manjericão s. m. 1. (bot.) basil. 2. (N. Braz.) low woods seen at the horizon.

manjerioba s. f. (Braz., bot.) coffee senna, stinking weed: a medicinal plant (Cassia occidentalis).

manjeriobas-grande s. f. (pl. **manjeriobas-grandes**) ringworm bush.

manjerona s. f. (bot.) marjoram (Glechon spathulata).

manjola s. f. (Braz.) = **mangual.**

manjolão s. m. (pl. **-ões**) (N. Braz.) tall, lanky individual.

manjolinho s. m. (Braz.) hut, log cabin.

manjuba, manjuva s. f. (Braz., also **pititinga** or **pipitinga**) 1. sea fish of the family Engraulidae. 2. food, meal.

mano s. m. 1. (fam.) brother, brother-in-law; friend, buddy. 2. **~s** pl. brothers and sisters. 3. f. (ant.) hand (still used in phrases like ~ a ~ hand in hand. **de ~ a ~** from hand to hand). ‖ adj. very friendly, intimate, inseparable.

manobra s. f. maneuver: 1. tactical military exercise. 2. movement or evolution in mliitary tactics. 3. art or act of directing the movements of the navy or air forces. 4. shunting: a) the changing of position of waggons to compose a train. b) switching (of a train). 5. (tech.) control. 6. a skillful move. 7. artful, shady procedure, machination.

locomotiva de ~s pony engine, switching engine. **~s aeronavais** maneuvers of the navy and air force.

manobrar v. to maneuver: 1. perform maneuvers. 2. direct the movements of troops, vessels, vehicles. 3. shunt (tráins). 4. manipulate, handle, direct skillfully. 5. manage artfully, scheme. 6. function, work. 7. direct, conduct.

~ melhor que to outmaneuver.

manobreiro s. m. 1. maneuverer: a) person directing maneuvers. b) manipulator. c) schemer. 2. (Braz.) railway yardman, switchman. 3. handbook on nautical maneuvers.

manobrista s. m. + f. maneuverer: an expert in maneuvers of boats.

manoca s. f. (N. Braz.) bundle of five or six tobacco leaves.

manocagem s. f. (pl. **-ens**) (N. Braz.) bundling of tobacco leaves.

manocar v. (N. Braz.) to bundle tobacco leaves.

manojo s. m. (also **manolho**) handful, bunch, bundle which can be spanned with one hand.

mano-juca s. m. (pl. **manos-jucas**) (S. Braz.) 1. (also **caipira**) a rustic. 2. person of unpolished manners.

manômetro s. m. manometer, pressure gauge: instrument to determine the pressure of gases, vapours or liquids (plate C 5).

~ de ar air pressure gauge (plate B 15).

manopla s. f. 1. gauntlet, iron glove. 2. a coachman's long whip. 3. (fig.) big and ugly hand.

manoseado adj., **manoseador** s. m., **manosear** v. (S. Braz.) = **amanonsiado, amanonsiador, amanonsiar.**

manoseio s. m. (S. Braz.) the breaking of a horse without riding it.

manotaço s. m. (S. Braz.) 1. a horse's kick or pawing when pursued or constrained. 2. slap, stroke with the hand.

manoteador adj. (S. Braz.) 1. kicking or pawing habitually (horse). 2. used to slapping.

manotear v. (S. Braz.) 1. to kick. 2. to slap. 3. to grasp, clutch.

manotudo adj. (Braz., pop.) large-handed.

manquecer v. to become lame.

manqueira s. f. 1. lameness, hobble, limp, halt. 2. (fig.) defect, fault, flaw. 3. (Braz.) epizooty of the cattle and horses in form of carbuncles.

manquejante adj. m. + f. limping, lame.

manquejar v. 1. (also but less frequent **manquetear, manquitar, manquitolar**) to limp, hobble, lame. 2. (fig.) to be defective. 3. to err, commit a blunder. 4. to falter. 5. to give in, become weak.

manquitola s. m. (Braz., pop., also **manquitó,** obs.) lame or limping person, cripple. ‖ adj. lame, limping.

mansão s. f. (pl. **-ões**) 1. mansion: a) a luxurious, imposing and stately house. b) a manor-house. 2. (fig.) situation.

mansarda s. f. (archit.) 1. mansard, attic, garret. 2. door or window opening out on the roof.

mansarrão s. m. (pl. **-ões**) (f. **mansarrona**) a very quiet, meek, gentle or somewhat sluggish individual; very tame animal. ‖ adj. 1. quiet, meek, gentle, sluggish, unexcitable. 2. tame.

mansidão s. f. (pl. **-ões**) (also **mansuetude**) 1. tameness, meekness, gentleness, submissiveness, docility. 2. slowness or sluggishness of speech.

mansinho adj. dim. of **manso**: 1. tame, domesticated. 2. meek, gentle, docile, peaceful, quiet.

de ~ softly, gently, lightly, low, slowly, by little and little, step by step. **ele foi embora de ~** he went away unnoticed.

manso s. m. 1. stretch of a river with water flowing slowly. 2. (Braz.) experienced rubber extractor; person given to the customs of the Amazon region. ‖ adj. 1. tame, domesticated. 2. meek, gentle, docile, tractable, submissive, peaceful, even-tempered, sweet-tempered, quiet. 3. cultivated (vegetable). 4. (hort.) grafted. 5. (Braz.) low (said of a hill). ‖ **-amente** adv. tamely, peacefully, etc.

~ como um cordeiro meek as a lamb. **~ de baixo** (S. Braz.) said of a horse which, though tamed, does not tolerate a rider. **~ de em pêlo** (S. Braz.) tame horse which can be ridden without saddle or bridle. **falar ~** to speak low. **fogo ~** slow fire.

manta s. f. 1. manta. 2. blanket, travelling rug. 3. shawl, wrap. 4. kerchief worn by men as tie. 5. horsecloth. 6. furrow for (vine) cuttings. 7. layer of fallen leaves in woods. 8. (fort.) mantelet. 9. screen or blanket spread underneath the olive trees at harvest time. 10. (Braz.) sun-dried large piece of meat or fish. 11. (S. Braz.) meat of the breast or ribs of cattle. 12. cheat, swindle. 13. loss at business. 14. shoal of fishes. 15. absurd speech. 16. (ichth.) manta ray.

~ de retalhos 1. patchwork quilt. 2. patchwork: composition formed of verses or passages from various authors. **~ de toicinho** flitch of bacon. **pintar a ~** to paint the town red. **tomar uma ~** (Braz.) to be cheated.

mantar v. to dig furrows for the plantation of vine cuttings.

manteação s. f. (pl. **-ões**) blanketing: tossing in of a blanket.

mantear v. 1. to blanket: toss in a blanket. 2. (fig.) to annoy, pester, bother somebody. 3. (Braz.) to fool around. 4. to cheat. 5. to cut up cattle.

mantearia s. f. 1. (hist.) house or store for the implements of the royal table. 2. position of the person in charge of it.

manteeiro s. m. (hist.) official who took care of the linen of the royal table.

manteiga s. f. 1. butter. 2. (obs.) designation for some metallic chlorides. 3. a variety of beans. 4. (pop.) flattery. 5. (N. Braz.) any animal or vegetable oil. 6. (sl.) handicap.

~ derretida (fam.) a whiny child. **~ de tartaruga** (Braz.) oily substance made out of the yolk of turtle eggs. **~ em venta de gato, ~ em focinho de cachorro** something which doesn't last long, which is soon used up. **dar ~** to butter up.

manteigaria s. f. dairy, place where butter is made or sold.

manteigoso adj. (also **manteiguento**) 1. buttery. 2. tasting of butter. 3. fatty.

manteigueira s. f. buttter dish (plate M 8).

manteigueiro s. m. buttermaker, buttter merchant; butterman. ‖ adj. fond of butter.

manteiro s. m. blanketmaker or blanket seller.

mantel s. m. (pl. mantéis) 1. table-cloth. 2. altar cloth. 3. pl. (obs.) table linen.

mantelado adj. (her.) mantled: having a mantling or mantle.

manteler s. m. (her.) mantle, mantling.

mantelete s. m. 1. mantelleta: short, sleeveless cloak worn by ecclesiastic dignitaries. 2. manta; mantilla; ladies' short, light cape trimmed with lace. 3. (fort.) mantelet.

mantém s. m. table-cloth.

mantença s. f. (also manutenção) maintenance, subsistence.

mantenedor s. m. (also mantedor) 1. maintainer. 2. defender (esp. of a champion's title). 3. (hist.) principal knight of a tournament.

manter v. 1. to maintain: a) keep, sustain, support, pay for. b) affirm, sustain, support by reasoning or argument; assert. c) uphold. d) conserve, keep from change, carry on, continue. e) obey, observe the rules. f) bear bravely. g) keep in repair or proper condition. 2. ~-se to hold out, carry on, keep up.
~ a calma to remain calm, weep one's hair on. ~ a ordem to keep order. ~ em estoque to keep in stock. ~ correspondência com to correspond with. ~ na expectativa to keep in suspense. ~ o preço to maintain the price. ~-se afastado, alheio to keep aloof, to stand aside. ~-se de to live by. ~-se fiel a to stick by. ~-se firme to hold one's own. ~ sua palavra to stand by one's word. ~ um segredo to keep a secret. ~ uma decisão to abide by one's decision. ele mantém vivas as tradições he keeps alive the traditions.

mantéu s. m. 1. cape with a collar used by monks. 2. ruff: fluted collar or collar with hanging edges. 3. slim skirt. 4. place where oracles were consulted.

manteúdo adj. 1. kept (said of a woman or concubine). 2. (Braz.) robust, strong (said of a horse or oxen which so keeps despite of age and hard work).

mântica s. f. small sack.

manticostumes s. m. maintenance of usages and customs.

mantídeo s. m. mantis, praying mantis. || adj. of or pertaining to the genus Mantis.

mantilha s. f. 1. mantilla: silk or lace scarf worn on the head. 2. mantelet.

mantimento s. m. 1. maintainance. 2. provisions, supply, food, victuals. 3. expenses.

mantissa s. f. mantissa, decimal part of logarithms.

manto s. m. 1. mantle: a) cloak, robe. b) (fig.) cover of something. c) fleshy part covering the body of certain molluscs. 2. veil, worn by women in Portugal. 3. old-fashioned wide cape with train. 4. habit of certain orders of nuns. 5. (fig.) darkness. 6. superior part of the body of some animals, especially of birds when it distinguishes itself by its colour from the rest of the body. 7. tapestry.
o ~ da hipocrisia the veil of hypocrisy.

mantô s. m. (Fr.) manteau, a ladies' mantle or cloak.

manto-do-diabo s. m. (pl. mantos-do-diabo) (Braz., bot.) wild lily.

mantopaque s. m. (Braz.) river fish of the family Siluridae (catfish).

manual s. m. (pl. -ais) manual: 1. handbook. 2. summary. 3. ritual, book of rites. || adj. m. + f. 1. manual: a) of or pertaining to the hand. b) done by hand or referring to work done by hand. 2. handy, manuable, easily handled. 3. light, portable. || ~-mente adv. manually, etc.
habilidade ~ handicraft. trabalho ~ manual labour.

manubial adj. m. + f. (pl. -ais) resulting from the plunder of an enemy.

manúbrio s. m. manubrium: 1. (zool.) any bone, cell, or segment shaped like a handle. 2. (anat.): a) the uppermost part of the sternum. b) a process of the malleus.

manucódio s. m. (ornith.) manucode.

manudução s. f. manuduction: guidance by the hand.

manuê s. m. (Braz.) var. of manauê.

manuel-de-abreu, manuel-de-breu s. m. (pl. manuéls-de-abreu) (Braz.) a variety of cinnamon-coloured bees (Trigona varia).

manuelino adj. of or pertaining to Manuel, referring especially to the architectural style of Portugal developed under the reign of D. Manuel I.

manuel-magro s. m. (pl. manuéis-magros) (Braz., ent.) walking stick, an orthopterous insect of slow movements (also mané-magro, maria-seca and bicho-pau).

manufator s. m. manufacturer: one who runs or owns a manufacturing plant. || adj. manufacturing: of or pertaining to manufacture.

manufatura s. f. 1. manufacture: a) the making of goods by hand or machinery, esp. on large scale. b) work done by hand. 2. manufactory, factory, plant. 3. product of a manufacturing plant; manufactures.

manufaturado adj. 1. handmade. 2. manufactured, produced.

manufaturar v. 1. to make by hand. 2. to manufacture, produce. 3. to work up.

manufatureiro adj. manufacturing: of or pertaining to manufacture.

manuleio s. m. (Braz.) political collusion.

manumissão s. f. (pl. -ões) manumission: releasement from slavery.

manumisso adj. manumitted: released from slavery.

manumissor s. m. manumitter.

manumitente adj. releasing.

manumitir v. to manumit: release from slavery.

manuscrever v. to write by hand.

manuscrito s. m. manuscript; document, letter, book written by hand. || adj. written by hand.

manusdei s. m. (pharm., obs.) healing plaster.

manuseação s. f., (pl. -ões) manuseamento, manuseio m. 1. handling, management. 2. act of turning over the pages of a book, leafing.
de fácil manuseio easy to handle.

manusear v. 1. to handle, manage. 2. to touch, feel. 3. to crumple with the hands. 4. to soil. 5. to turn over the pages of a book; to thumb.
~ desajeitadamente to paw; to handle clumsily.
livro manuseado a thumbed book.

manutenção s. f. (pl. -ões) 1. maintenance: a) sustenance, support. b) (tech.) upkeep. 2. administration, management. 3. (mil.) bakery.

manutenir v. (Braz., jur.) to concede a mandate of maintenance to.

manutenível adj. m. + f. (pl. -íveis) maintainable.

manutérgio s. m. (eccl.) napkin used by the priest to wipe his hands during the mass at the lavabo.

manzanza s. m. + f. adj. m. + f., manzanzar v. = mazanza, mazanzar.

manzape s. m. (Braz.) 1. maize or manioc cake. 2. badly done cake. 3. (N. Braz.) stick or whip used for punishment.

manzorra s. f. large hand.

mão s. f. (pl. mãos) 1. hand: a) (anat.) grasping organ of man and ape (plate C 18) (augm.: manzorra or mãozorra, manopla, manápula; dim.: mãozinha, mãozita, manita). b) forefoot of a quadruped. c) dexterousness of the hands. d) style, trait, touch. e) lead in a game of cards. f) handful. g) (Braz.) side: each of the directions of the traffic. h) side, part. i) help, assistance. j) hand of a clock or watch. k)

handwriting. 2. cut of meat. 3. claws of some birds. 4. power, authority, influence, control, domination. 5. handle. 6. coat of paint or whitewash. 7. completed throw, pass in a game. 8. suction cup of a creeping plant. 9. smal comb used on wool or fur. 10. pestle. 11. (N. Braz.) stick with which the manioc press is turned. 12. (Braz.) corn measure varying from 24 to 64 cobs according to the part of the country. 13. linear measure in Goa. 14. old Indian weight.
~ **certa** a sure hand at throwing, etc. ~ **de linho** twelve strikes of flax. ~ **de verniz** coat of varnish. ~ **do martelo** handle of a hammer. ~ **por baixo,** ~ **por cima** cautiously. ~ **por** ~ conjointly or concurrently. ~**s ao alto!** hands up! ~**s à obra!** let's set to work! ~**s de anéis** delicate hands. ~**s de fada** hands of woman skilful in sewing. ~**s limpas** clean hands, honesty, integrity. ~**s postas** hands raised for prayer, with joint palms. **à** ~ by hand. **à** ~ **direita (esquerda)** on or at the right (left) hand. **abrir, largar** ~ **de** to put by, to leave off. **andar com as** ~**s nas algibeiras** to idle. **andar nas** ~**s de alguém** to be in the hands of, go through the hands of. **apertar a** ~ **a alguém** to shake hands with s. o. **aperto de** ~ handshake. **às** ~**s cheias** liberally, plentifully, largely. **assentar a** ~ to become skilled, sure of o. s. **assentar a** ~ **em alguém** to strike s. o. **as** ~**s do relógio** the hands of the clock. **cair em boas** ~**s** to fall into good hands. **cair nas** ~**s de alguém** to fall into someone's hands. **coisa em primeira** ~ first-hand article. **coisa em segunda** ~ handed down, second--hand article. **com** ~ **de gato** slyly. **com ambas as** ~**s** with both hands, with pleasure. **com pés e** ~**s** with all one's power. **comprar de primeira** ~ to buy at first-hand. **com** ~ **armada** by force of arms. **com as** ~**s fechadas** with clenched fists. **com as** ~**s cruzadas** with clasped hands. **correr a** ~ **por** to pass one's hand over. **cruzar as** ~**s** to clasp one's hands. **dar a** ~ **a** to shake hands with, to give a hand. **dar a** ~ to help, to lend a helping hand. **dar a última** ~ to put the finishing hand to something. **dá-lhe a** ~ **e ele tomará o braço** give him an inch and he will take an ell. **dar a** ~ **a alguém** 1. to marry s. o. 2. to help, assist s. o. 3. to give s. o. the lead (at cards). **dar as** ~**s à palmatória** to confess one's error. **dar de** ~ **beijada** to give gratuitously. **de** ~ **cheia** masterly, excellent, perfect. **de** ~ **em** ~ from hand to hand. **de boa** ~ from good authority. **debaixo de** ~ underhand, privately. **deitar** ~ **a** to set about a thing, to lay hold of. **entregar-se nas** ~**s de alguém** to throw o. s. into the hands of. **escolhido a** ~ hand-picked. **estar à** ~ to be on hand, at one's elbow. **estar com as** ~**s na massa, ter entre as** ~**s** to be working on. **estar de** ~**s dadas** to be hand in hand. **estar na** ~ **de** to be in the power of. **estar em boas** ~**s** to be in good hands. **estar atado de pés e** ~**s** to be tied hand and foot. **espelho de** ~ hand mirror. **estar na minha** ~ it is in my power. **fazer** ~ **baixa em** to steal. **feito por** ~ **de mestre** very well done. **feito à** ~ done, or made by hand, handmade. **ficar na** ~ to be cheated, to be stood up. **fora de** ~ out of the way, on the wrong side of the way. **fugir das** ~**s** to slip out of one's hands, to escape. **ir à** ~ to put a stop to, to restrain, impede, hinder. **jogar de** ~ 1. to be first to play. 2. to kick with the front legs (horse). **lançar** ~ **de todos os recursos** to use all possible means. **lançar** ~ **de alguma coisa** to make use of s. th. **lavar as (suas)** ~**s de** to wash one's hands of. **levar a** ~ **ao chapéu** to touch one's hat. **levar pela** ~ to lead by the hand. **mais vale um pássaro**

na ~ **que dois voando** a bird in the hand is worth two in the bush. **meter a** ~ **na consciência** to examine o. s. **meter a** ~ **à espada** to draw one's sword. **meter os pés pelas** ~**s** to fumble, to get muddled. **meter ou pôr** ~**s à obra** to set out to work cheerfully. **meter a** ~ **em cumbuca** (Braz.) to fall into the snare. **não ter** ~**s a medir** to have one's hands full of business, to have much on one's hands. **não ter** ~ **de si** not to contain one-self. **não saber qual é a sua** ~ **direita** not to know one's left hand from one's right hand, to be stupid. **palma da** ~ the palm. **passar de** ~ **em** ~ to go from hand to hand. **passar a** ~ **em** (Braz.) to seize. **passar para as** ~**s de** to pass over to. **pedir a** ~ **de** to ask for the hand of. **pôr as** ~ **na cinta** to set one's arms akimbo. **por baixo da** ~ underhand, secretly. **por** ~ **própria, por suas** ~**s** by one's own hand. **pôr as** ~**s no fogo por alguém** to swear for someone's integrity. **reconheço nesta obra a sua** ~ I recognize your style in this work. **ser ou jogar de** ~ to be first at play, to be elder hand. **ter a** ~ **em algum negócio** to have a hand in a business. **ter à** ~ to have at hand. **ter boa** ~ to be handy or skilful, to have a lucky hand. **ter** ~ 1. to be careful. 2. to help. **ter a** ~ **leve** (fig.) to be quick to spank. **ter** ~**s em** to have influence in. **tire a** ~ hands off. **uma** ~ **lava a outra** one hand washes the other. **uma** ~ **feliz** a happy touch. **untar as** ~**s a alguém** (fig.) to bribe s. o. **vir à** ~ to come to hand. **vir às** ~**s** to fight, to come to blows. **vir às** ~**s de** to fall into the hands of. **viver de suas** ~**s** to live by one's hands. **voltar com as** ~**s vazias** to return empty-handed.

mão-aberta, s. m. + f. (pl. **mãos-abertas**) (Braz.) 1. prodigal, spendthrift. 2. liberal, generous person.

mão-cheia s. f. (pl. **mãos-cheias**) (also **mancheia**) handful.

mão-curta s. m. (pl. **mãos-curtas**) (Braz.) a variety of deer.

mão-de-branco s. f. (pl. **mãos-de-branco**) plant of the genus Amaryllis.

mão-de-cabelo s. m. (pl. **mãos-de-cabelo**) (Braz.) fantastic creature of superstition, shaped like a man with hands made out of long hair.

mão-de-ferro s. f. (pl. **mãos-de-ferro**) iron hand, tyranny, oppression.

mão-de-gato s. f. (pl. **mãos-de-gato**) (Braz.) plant of the family Connaraceae.

mão-de-obra s. f. (pl. **mãos-de-obra**) 1. manual work on a product or job. 2. the expense resulting from this work.

mão-de-onça s. f. (pl. **mãos-de-onça**) (Braz.) shrub of the family Marcgraviaceae.

mão-francesa s. f. (pl. **mãos-francesas**) strut, brace.

maoísmo s. m. (China, pol.) Maoism.

maometanismo s. m. (also **maometismo**) Mohammed-anism, Mohammedism.

maometano s. m. Mohammedan, Mahomedan, Mahometan. ‖ adj. (also **maomético**) Mohammedan.

mão-pelada s. m. (pl. **mãos-peladas**) (Braz., zool.) crab-eating racoon (Procyon cancrivorus).

mão-pendente s. f. (pl. **mãos-pendentes**) (Braz.) corrupting influence, bribery.

mão-posta s. f. (pl. **mãos-postas**) 1. something reserved for a special occasion. 2. combination, agreement. 3. premeditation.

maori s. m. + f. Maori: Polynesian and New Zealand natives. ‖ adj. Maori: of or pertaining to the Maoris.

mãos-atadas s. m. + f., sg. + pl. shy, timid person.

mãos-largas s. m. + f., sg. + pl. generous, open-handed person.

mãos-rotas s. m. + f., sg. + pl. prodigal.

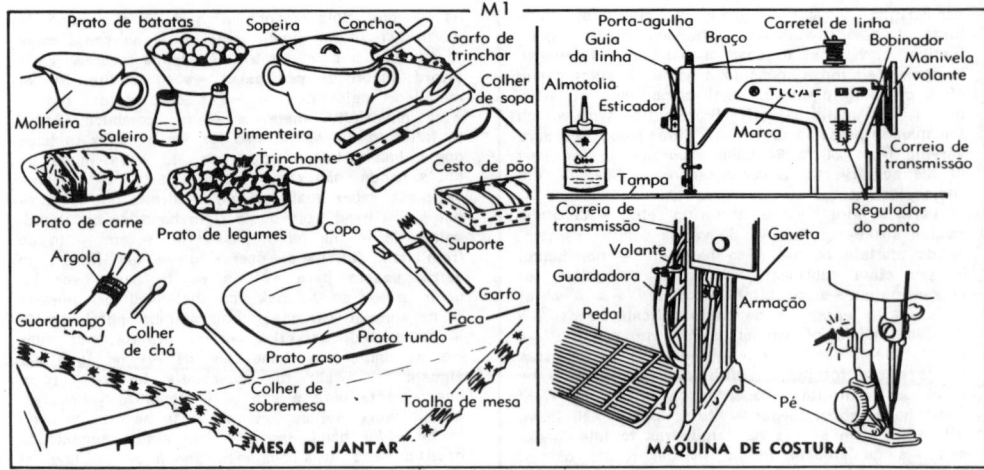

M 1

Prato de batatas — Sopeira — Concha — Garfo de trinchar — Colher de sopa — Molheira — Saleiro — Pimenteira — Trinchante — Cesto de pão — Prato de carne — Prato de legumes — Copo — Suporte — Argola — Garfo — Guardanapo — Colher de chá — Faca — Prato tundo — Prato raso — Colher de sobremesa — Toalha de mesa

MESA DE JANTAR

Porta-agulha — Guia da linha — Braço — Carretel de linha — Bobinador — Manivela volante — Almotolia — Esticador — Marca — Correia de transmissão — Tampa — Correia de transmissão — Volante — Gaveta — Regulador do ponto — Guardadora — Armação — Pedal — Pé

MÁQUINA DE COSTURA

mão-tenente, mão-tente s. f. point-blank distance. **à mão-tenente** 1. point-blank, close, at a small distance. 2. firmly, tightly, with a firm hand.

mãozada s. f. 1. (pop.) a strong handshake. 2. lot of things held in one hand.

mãozinha s. f. 1. small hand. 2. m. + f. (N. Braz., pop.) one-handed person.

mãozinha-preta s. m. (Braz.) (pl. **mãozinhas-pretas**) a fabulous being, the product of popular belief.

mãozudo adj. large-handed.

mapa s. m. 1. map, chart, graph. 2. list. **tirar um** ~ (Braz., pop.) to observe.

mapã s. m. (Braz.) euphorbiaceous plant.

mapa-do-brasil s. m. (pl. **mapas-do-brasil**) (Braz., pop.) old, wrinkled person.

mapa-múndi s. m. (pl. **mapas-múndi**) map of the world.

mapará s. m. (Braz., also **mapurá**) fish of the catfish family (Siluridae).

maparajuba s. f. (Braz.) tree of the family Sapotaceae.

mapareíba s. f. (Braz.) mangrove variety (also known as **mangue-vermelho**).

mapati s. m. (Braz.) plant belonging to the mulberry family.

mapear v. (Braz.) to map.

maperoá s. m. (Braz.) tree of the family Sterculiaceae (Basiloxylon rex).

mapiação (pl. **-ões**), **mapiagem** (pl. **-ens**) s. f. (Braz., pop.) talk, chatter, gossip.

mapiador s. m. chatterer, chatterbox, talkative person. ‖ adj. chatty, idle, talkative.

mapiar v. (Braz., also **pautear**) 1. to talk rubbish, to chew the rag. 2. to chatter, gossip.

mapinguari s. m. (Braz.) legendary giant of the Amazon folklore, wearing an armour made out of tortoise shell.

mapironga s. f. (N. Braz.) pimple, boil.

mapixi s. m. (Braz.) plant of the family Myrtaceae.

mapoão s. m. (Braz.) poisonous plant out of which the Indians make their arrow poison.

mapoteca s. f. collection of maps.

mapuche s. m. a Chilean Indian.

mapurá s. m. (Braz.) = **mapará**.

maqueira s. f. (N. Braz.) hammock made out of a palm tree fiber.

maqueiro s. m. stretcher-bearer, ambulance man.

maqueta s. f. maquette: clay or wax model of a building, statue, etc.

maqui s. m. maqui: terrain covered with heather and bushes in Corsica.

maquia s. f. 1. old grain measure corresponding to 4.5 l. 2. a miller's fee or toll taken in kind. 3. (fig.): a) money. b) profit. c) tip.

maquiadura s. f. 1. measurement with a maquia. 2. subtraction of part of s. th.; fraudulent taking. 3. collection of the miller's fee or toll in kind.

maquiar v. 1. to measure with a maquia. 2. (fig.) to subtract part of, take fraudulently. 3. to collect the miller's fee or toll in kind.

maquiavelice s. f. Machiavellism: an act worthy of Machiavel; slyness, craftiness, astuteness.

maquiavélico adj. Machiavellian: 1. pertaining to or like Machiavellism. 2. astute, sly, cunning, tricky.

maquiavelismo s. m. Machiavellism: 1. political system described by Machiavelli in his book "The Prince". 2. politics which places expediency above morality. 3. sly, cunning, wily procedures.

maquiavelista s. m. + f. Machiavellian: person adopting ideas or methods of Machiavelli.

maquiavelizar v. to procede in a Machiavellian manner.

maquiçapa s. m. (Braz.) a spider monkey.

maquidum s. m. (pl. **-uns**) (Braz.) seat, chair.

maquilado adj. painted (face).

maquilagem s. f. (pl. **-ens**) make-up.

maquilar v. to make up.

máquina s. f. 1. machine: a) apparatus used to perform some kind of work. b) engine, mechanical apparatus. c) (mech.) a device which modifies or transmits forces. d) any instrument or implement. e) ingenious contrivance. 2. (fig.) puppet: person devoid of own ideas, carrying out work like an automaton. 3. (Braz.) car, automobile. 4. important and solid construction. 5. complex agency or operating system. 6. organism. 7. locomotive. 8. (sl.) revolver, pistol.

~ **acabadora** finishing machine. ~ **acepilhadora** planing machine, planer, surfacer. ~ **agrícola** agricultural machine (plate C 11). ~ **auxiliar** auxiliary engine. ~ **bobinadora** winding machine. ~ **cardadeira** carding machine. ~ **centrífuga** centrifugal machine. ~ **copiadora** copying machine. ~ **cortadora** cutting machine. ~ **de adicionar** adding machine. ~ **de afiar (ou amolar) ferramentas** tool grinding or sharpening machine. ~ **de amassar e misturar** kneeding and mixing machine, kneeder and mixer. ~ **de aparar papel** trimming or cutting machine. ~ **de aplainar** planing machine, planer.

M 2

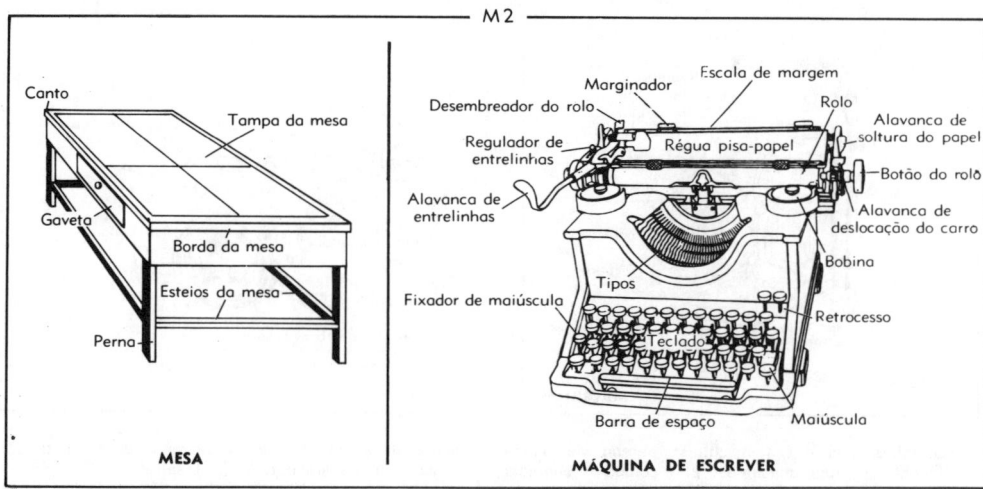

Canto · Tampa da mesa · Gaveta · Borda da mesa · Esteios da mesa · Perna

Desembreador do rolo · Marginador · Escala de margem · Rolo · Alavanca de soltura do papel · Regulador de entrelinhas · Régua pisa-papel · Botão do rolô · Alavanca de entrelinhas · Alavanca de deslocação do carro · Bobina · Tipos · Fixador de maiúscula · Retrocesso · Teclado · Barra de espaço · Maiúscula

MESA   **MÁQUINA DE ESCREVER**

~ **de apontar lápis** pencil sharpening machine. ~ (or **motor**) **de ar quente** hot-air engine, hot-air motor. ~ **de arrancar batatas** potato digger. ~ **de aveludar** napping machine, nap lifting machine. ~ **de brocar** (or **furar**) drilling machine, boring machine (plate F 8). ~ **de calcular** calculating machine. ~ **de contabilidade** accounting machine. ~ **de costura** sewing machine (plate M 1). ~ **de debulhar** threshing machine, thresher. ~ **de endereçar** addressing machine. ~ **de engarrafar** bottling machine. ~ **de ensamblar** jointer, jointing machine. ~ **de escanelar** grooving machine. ~ **de escrever** typewriter (plate M 2). ~ **de estirar** drawing machine. ~ **de fazer moldes**, ~ **de moldar** moulding machine. ~ **de forjar** forging machine. ~ **de gravar** punch cutting machine. ~ **de impressão plana** flat-bed printing press. ~ **de imprimir** printing machine. ~ **de lavar garrafas** bottle washer, cleanser or washing machine. ~ **de lavar louça** dishwasher (plate C 20). ~ **de lavar roupa** washing machine, washer (plate C 20). ~ **de lustrar** or **polir** polishing machine. ~ **de passar** (**roupa**) ironer, press machine (plate C 20). ~ **de pautar** ruling machine. ~ **de precisão** precision machine. ~ **de projeção** projecting machine. ~ **de prova** testing machine. ~ **de puncionar** (hole) punching machine. ~ **de rebitar** riveter, riveting machine. ~ **de rebordear** crimping machine. ~ **de retificar** rectifying machine. ~ **de revirar** (or **remanchar**) bordos beading machine. ~ **de riscar** scratching machine. ~ **de triturar** crushing machine, crusher. ~ **de serrar** power or machine saw, sawing machine. ~ **de soldar** welding machine. ~ **de somar** adding machine. ~ **distribuidora** (typogr.) automatic distributing machine. ~ **ensacadora** sacking machine. ~ **escavadora, escavadeira** excavator (plate D 2). ~ **fotográfica** camera (plate M 3). ~ **infernal** infernal machine. ~ **operatriz** machine tool. ~ **para coser a arame** stapling machine, wire stitching machine. ~ **para coser livros** stitching machine. ~ **para cravar ilhós** eyeletting machine. ~ **para desempenar chapas** straightening machine. ~ **para dobrar** folding machine. ~ **para dobrar cartão** cardboard bending machine. ~ **para encalcar e soldar** upsetting and bending machine. ~ **para endireitar** straightening machine. ~ **para engomar** gumming machine. ~ **para fazer machos** tonguing and grooving machine. ~ **para fazer espigas** ten-

oning machine. ~ **para fazer rodas dentadas** gear cutting machine. ~ **para fotografia aérea** aerial camera, air photographic camera. ~ **para fotografia aérea noturna** aerial night camera. ~ **para fotografias em série** aerial survey camera. ~ **para fundir letras** type casting machine. ~ **para fundir por linhas** line casting machine. ~ **para gravar** engraving machine. ~ **para impressão a duas cores** two-colour printing press. ~ **para impressão "off--set"** off-set machine. ~ **para imprimir em relevo** relief printing machine. ~ **para lavrar** (**trabalhar**) **madeira** woodworking machine. ~ **para fabricar envelopes** envelope machine. ~ **para moer tintas** ink grinding mill, colour grinding machine. ~ **para numerar, numeradora** numbering machine. ~ **para paginar, paginadora** paging machine. ~ (**bomba**) **pneumática** air pump. ~ **rotativa** rotary press. ~ **saca-bocados** punching machine. ~ **tipográfica de platina** flat-bed press. ~ **a vapor** steam engine.
máquina-ferramenta s. f. (pl. **máquinas-ferramenta**) machine tool.
maquinação s. f. (pl. **-ões**) machination: 1. act and effect of machinating; intrigue, crafty scheme, evil plot. 2. frame-up.
maquinador s. m. machinator; one who machinates, plotter, schemer. ‖ adj. machinating.
maquinal adj. m. + f. (pl. **-ais**) 1. of or pertaining to machines, mechanical. 2. (fig.) automatic. 3. (fig.) unconscious. ‖ ~**mente** adv. mechanically, etc.
maquinar v. to machinate, plot, scheme, intrigue, contrive.
máquina-registradora s. f. (pl. **máquinas-registradoras**) cash register.
maquinaria s. f. 1. machinery. 2. work and skill of a machinist.
maquiné s. m. (N. Braz., also **bicudo-maquiné**) bird belonging to the Fringillidae, the finch family, which includes sparrows, canaries, etc.
maquineta s. f. 1. sacrarium or sanctuary in which the sacrament is exposed on the altar. 2. small oratory, shrine. 3. ornate glass shrine containing the image of a saint. 4. wardrobe.
maquinismo s. m. 1. mechanism, machinery, works, gear. 2. any machine or apparatus capable of producing motion. 3. any organism working on its own. 4. any articulation of the body. 5. (theat.) stage appliances and machinery. 6. machine, apparatus, instrument.

M3

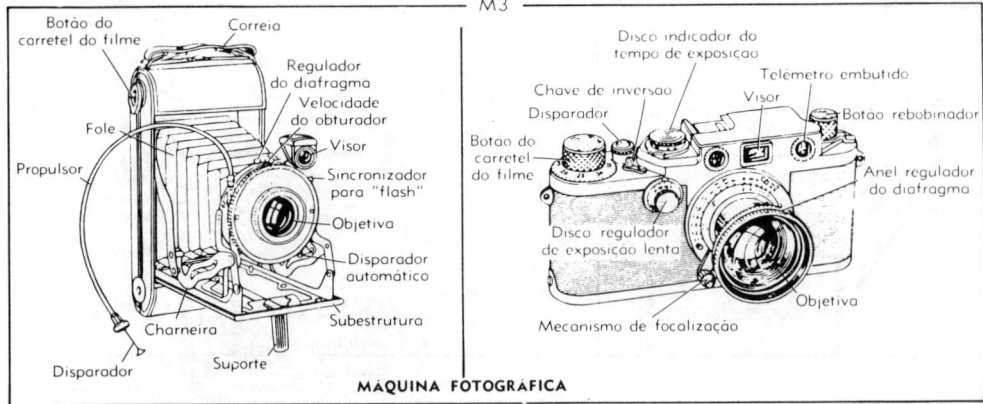

Botão do carretel do filme / Correia / Regulador do diafragma / Velocidade do obturador / Fole / Visor / Propulsor / Sincronizador para "flash" / Objetiva / Disparador automático / Charneira / Subestrutura / Disparador / Suporte

Disco indicador do tempo de exposição / Chave de inversão / Telémetro embutido / Disparador / Visor / Botão rebobinador / Botão do carretel do filme / Anel regulador do diafragma / Disco regulador de exposição lenta / Objetiva / Mecanismo de focalização

MÁQUINA FOTOGRÁFICA

maquinista s. m. + f. 1. machinist: person who builds, invents, or runs machines. 2. locomotive engineer, locomotive driver. 3. person who builds or operates theatrical decor or machinery. 4. (sl.) man who lives on his wife's income.

mar s. m. 1. sea, ocean. 2. (fig.) large quantity. 3. profundity, depth, abyss, immensity. 4. title of a Maronite (old Syriac liturgy) bishop.
~ **alto** high sea. ~ **banzeiro** gently agitated sea. ~ **chão** smooth sea. ~ **crespo, encrespado** rippled sea. ~ **de cabeças** a sea of faces. ~ **cavado,** ~ **encapelado** hollow, stormy sea. ~ **de leite** very calm sea. ~ **de rosas** 1. calm sea. 2. (fig.) pink cloud, happiness. ~ **do Sul** South sea. ~ **grosso** heavy sea. ~ **interior** land-locked, inland sea. ~ **largo** open sea. ~ **Mediterrâneo** the Mediterranean. ~ **picado** choppy sea. ~ **tempestuoso** tempestuous sea. ~ **tormentoso** tempestuous sea. **açoitado pelo** ~ sea-beaten. **água do** ~ sea water. **alga do** ~ seaweed. **banhado pelo** ~ washed by the sea, sea-bathed. **cair ao** ~ to fall overboard. **costa do** ~ seacoast, seashore. **de** ~ **a** ~ totally. **deitar ao** ~ to throw overboard. **deitar cargas ao** ~ to be seasick, throw up. **deitar água ao** ~ to carry coals to Newcastle. **em alto** ~ at sea. **escuma do** ~ meerschaum: 1. silicate of magnesium, a white claylike substance light enough to float on water, when dry. 2. tobacco-pipe with a bowl made of this material. **fazer-se ao** ~ to sail, put to sea. **fazer-se na volta do** ~ to leave the shore behind. **homem do** ~ seaman, mariner. **homem ao** ~! man overboard! **monstro do** ~ sea monster. **nem tudo ao** ~, **nem tudo à terra** neither too much, nor too little. **o** ~ **brame** the sea roars. **o** ~ **quebra nos rochedos** the sea breaks on the rocks. **percorrer os** ~**es** to sail the seas. **porto de** ~ seaport. **praia do** ~ seabeach, strand. **por** ~ **e por terra** by sea and land. **um** ~ **de sangue** a sea of blood. **risco do** ~ sea-risk. **um** ~ **de tribulações** a sea of trouble. **viagem por** ~ voyage. **verde** ~ sea green. **nem tanto ao** ~ **nem tanto à terra** without extremes; neither do nor die, somewhere in between.

mará s. m. 1. (zool.) mara, pampas hare: a South-American rodent. 2. (Braz.) rowing pole which, stuck in the earth, serves to fasten the boat.

marabá s. m. 1. (Braz.) offspring of a Frenchman and an Indian. 2. offspring of a white and an Indian. 3. (N. Braz.) child of an unknown father.

marabu s. m. 1. (ornith.) marabou, African stork. 2. (rel.) marabout: a Mohammedan hermit or saint. 3. ~**s** pl. trimming made out of marabou feathers.

marabuto s. m. 1. (rel.) = **marabu.** 2. rural temple used by a marabout. 3. (sl.) sailor.

maracá s. m. 1. (Braz.) rattle made of a dry gourd, used by the Indians in their religious and war ceremonies. 2. rattle, a child's toy. 3. f. rattlesnake.

maracajá s. m. (Braz.) margay: a wildcat.

maracanã s. m. (Braz.) bird of the parrot family.

maracatiara s. m. (Braz.) ship's captain.

maracatim s. m. (pl. **-ins**) (N. Braz.) old form of Indian boat.

maracatu s. m. (N. Braz.) group of people dancing at carnival to the sounds of a percussion band.

maracauim s. m. (pl. **-ins**) (Braz.) crustacean, also known as **chama-maré.**

marachão s. m. (pl. **-ões**) 1. dike, embankment. 2. sandbank.

maracotão s. m. (pl. **-ões**) melocoton: a variety of peach.

maracoteiro s. m. melocoton: peach tree grafted onto a quince tree.

maracujá s. m. maracock (fruit).

maracujazeiro s. m. (Braz.) maracock: plant of the passion-flower family (Passiflora incarnata).

marafa s. f. (Braz.) dissolute life, libertinism.
viver na ~ to lead a licentious life.

marafo s. m. (Braz., sl.) = **cachaça.**

marafona s. f. 1. rag doll. 2. prostitute, slut.

marafonear v. to deal with prostitutes.

marafunda s. f. (Braz., pop.) tumult, confusion, uproar.

maragatada s. f. (S. Braz.) group of revolutionaries (see **maragato**).

maragatagem s. f. (pl. **-ens**) (S. Braz., also **maragatice**) actions of the **maragatos.**

maragatear v. (S. Braz.) to act politically like a revolutionary of the **maragato** party.

maragatismo s. m. (S. Braz.) 1. = **maragatagem.** 2. party of the **maragatos.**

maragato s. m. (S. Braz., hist.) 1. revolutionary of 1893 fighting the politics of Júlio de Castilhos. 2. federalist, adept of Gaspar da Silveira Martins.

maragojipe s. m. (Braz.) a variety of coffee. ‖ adj. said of a certain variety of coffee.

marajá s. m. 1. maharaja(h). 2. f. (Braz.) a palm tree also called **tucumã.**

marajatina s. f. (Braz.) grove of **marajá** palms.

marajó s. m. (N. Braz.) wind blowing in the afternoon across the Guajará bay coming from the isle of Marajó, an island in the mouth of the Amazon.

marajoara s. m. (N. Braz.) 1. wind that blows through the woods of the Marajó island. 2. m. + f. native or inhabitant of the Marajó Island. ‖ adj. of or pertaining to the Isle of Marajó.

marambala s. m. (Braz., naut., sl.) 1. half-hearted sailor who would much rather stay on land. 2. flirty sailor.

marambaiar v. (Braz., naut., sl.) to live and act like a **marambaia**.

marandová s. m. (Braz.) 1. big larva of certain butterflies. 2. ill-tempered individual.

maranduba, maranduva s. f. (Braz.) 1. war or travel tale. 2. unlikely story, big tale. 3. lie.

maranha s. f. 1. entangled, interwoven threads or fibres. 2. woollen cloth before it is fulled. 3. (fig.) plot, story. 4. intricate business, confusion, entanglement. 5. slyness. 6. (N. Braz.) artfulness. 7. act of shying away from work, vagrancy.

maranhar v. = **emaranhar**.

maranhense s. m. + f. (Braz.) native or inhabitant of the state of Maranhão. ‖ adj. of or pertaining to Maranhão.

maranho s. m. 1. giblet gravy. 2. special dish made out of sheep's pluck with rice, chicken, etc.

maranhoso adj. 1. telling big stories or lies, mendacious. 2. intriguing. 3. gossipy.

maranta s. f. Maranta: a genus of plants typifying the family Marantaceae.

marantácea s. f. maranta: plant of the genus Maranta.

marantáceo adj. (bot.) marantaceous: of or pertaining to the genus Maranta.

marapajuba s. f. (Braz., bot.) a sapotaceous tree (Mimusops paraensis).

marapuama, marapuana s. f. (Braz.) a medicinal herb.

marasca s. f. marasca: a wild cherry from which maraschino is distilled.

marasmar v. to cause marasmus or to become marasmic.

marasmático adj. marasmic.

marasmo s. m. 1. marasmus: a gradual loss of strength and weight, due to old age, malnutrition, etc., rather than to an organic disease. 2. (fig.) moral apathy, indifference, melancholy.

marasmódico adj. marasmic: pertaining to or similar to marasmus.

marasquino s. m. maraschino: a liqueur or cordial made out of marasca cherries.

marata s. m. + f. 1. Mahratta (Maratha): member of a Hindu people of central and western India. 2. m. Mahratti (Marathi): the language spoken by the Mahrattas. ‖ adj. of or pertaining to the Mahrattas.

maratimba s. m. + f. (Braz.) = **caipira**.

maratona s. f. marathon, marathon race.

marato s. m. fennel.

marau s. m. 1. wise fellow. 2. rascal, rogue, swindler.

maraunita s. f. (Braz.) light coloured tertiary peat, very rich in volatile matters, found in Maraú, Bahia.

maravalhas s. f. pl. 1. ribbands, wood shavings, kindling wood. 2. (fig.) trifles.

maravedi, maravedil s. m. (also **maravidil**) old Gothic coin formerly used in Portugal and Spain.

maravilha s. f. 1. marvel, wonder, marvellous thing, prodigy. 2. extraordinary person: surprising fact or thing. 3. (Braz.) (bot.) marigold. 4. a kind of pastry. **as sete ~s do mundo** the seven wonders of the world. **às mil ~s, à ~** marvellously, admirably well. **fazer ou dizer ~s** to do or say extraordinary or strange things, to perform wonders.

maravilha-do-sertão s. f. (pl. **maravilhas-do-sertão**) (Braz.) very tasty tea made out of the leaves of an euphorbiaceous plant.

maravilhado adj. amazed.

maravilhador s. m. one who causes marvels or admiration. ‖ adj. amazing, wondrous, causing admiration.

maravilhamento s. m. amazement, admiration, surprise, wonder.

maravilhar v. 1. to cause admiration, marvel. 2. to amaze, astound, astonish. 3. to enrapture, enchant, dazzle. 4. **~-se** to wonder, be surprised, astonished. 5. **~-se com** to marvel at.

maravilhoso s. m. wonder, marvel. ‖ adj. wonderful, marvellous, admirable, amazing, dazzling. ‖ **-amente** adv. wonderfully, etc.

passamos uma temporada -a we had a grand time.

maraximbé s. m. (Braz.) a tree of the family Icacinaceae (Emmotum fagifolium).

marca s. f. 1. mark: a) brand, type, make. b) seal, stamp, token. c) signature, impression. d) limit, demarcation, boundary (also in games). e) clothes mark. f) sign, indication of quality, character, etc. g) bruise, blemish. h) external signs left by a disease. i) stigma. 2. category. 3. branding iron; apparatus to mark something. 4. blaze, sign to indicate trees to be chopped down. 5. step or development of a dance. 6. scoreboard.

~ de acerto remarque. **~ do fabricante** maker's mark, maker's stamp (plate L 1). **~ registrada** registered trade-mark. **de ~** excellent, remarkable. **de ~ maior** (Braz.) uncommon, beyond measure, first-rate. **passar (d)as ~s, ultrapassar (exceder) as ~s** to go too far, to exceed all bounds. **sair de ~ quente** (S. Braz.) to leave suspiciously.

marcação s. f. (pl. **-ões**) 1. act or effect of marking. 2. (naut.) taking of the bearings. 3. (theat.) booking of places. 4. (S. Braz.) branding with an iron. **estar de ~, ter ~ com** to keep somebody under persecution.

marca-de-judas s. m. + f. (pl. **marcas-de-judas**) (N. Braz., pop.) short person.

marcado s. m. (S. Braz.) cheater (especially in business). ‖ adj. 1. marked. 2. deceitful. 3. (fig.) distinctive, distinguished, remarkable.

marcador s. m. 1. marker, scorer, scoreboard. 2. piece of cross-stitch canvas (used by little girls to learn to embroider). ‖ adj. marking, scoring.

marçagão s. m. (pl. **-ões**) rough and nasty March.

marca-grande s. m. (pl. **marcas-grandes**) (Braz.) well--to-do farmer.

marçalino adj. pertaining to the month of March.

marca-mês s. m. pl. **marca-meses**) (N. Braz., pop.) tear-off calendar.

marçano s. m. 1. cashier's apprentice. 2. apprentice, beginner.

marcante adj. m. + f. 1. marking. 2. remarkable. ‖ **~mente** adv. remarkably.

marcapasso s. m. (med.) pacemaker.

marca-pés s. m. sg. + pl. (Braz.) clay used in the purifying process of sugar.

marcar v. 1. to mark, brand, seal, label. 2. to indicate, determine, designate, fix. 3. to book. 4. to stamp (silver, etc.). 5. (mus.) to beat time. 6. (naut.) to take the bearings of the land. 7. to stain, spot. 8. to calculate, appraise. 9. to limit, ascertain. 10. to brand (cattle). 11. to blaze (trees). 12. to bruise. 13. to mark clothes with initials or signs. 14. to watch somebody and try to prevent him from making mistakes or to point out errors. **~ a data** to set a date. **~ o compasso** (mus.) to beat the time. **~ passo** to mark time. **~ uma hora** to fix an appointment, a time. **~ um encontro** to make a date. **~ um lugar com uma cruz** to mark a spot with a cross. **~ um prazo** to set a time. **estou marcando o meu irmão desde muito tempo** I've been watching my brother for a long time. **o termômetro marca 35° C** the thermometer reads 35° C (95° F).

marcassita s. f. (min.) marcasite: white iron pyrites.

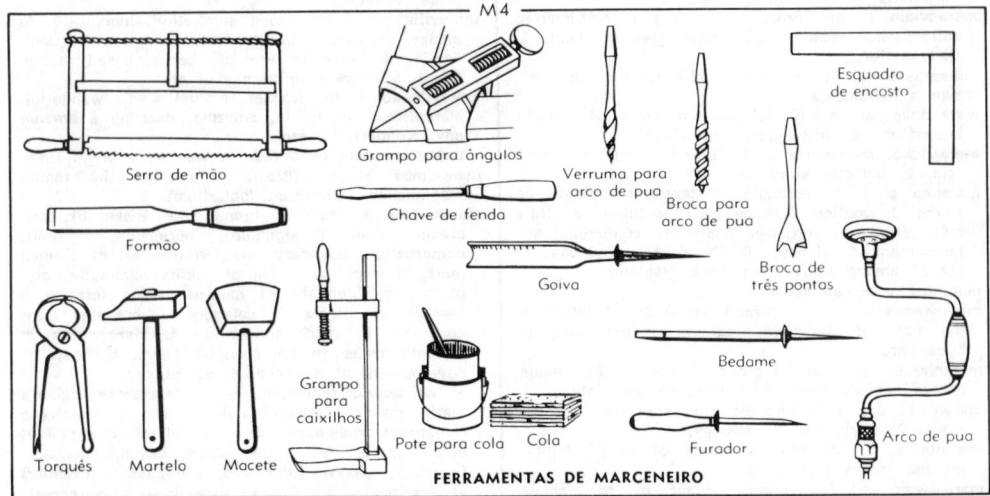

M 4

Serra de mão · Grampo para ângulos · Verruma para arco de pua · Broca para arco de pua · Esquadro de encosto · Chave de fenda · Formão · Goiva · Broca de três pontas · Grampo para caixilhos · Pote para cola · Cola · Bedame · Furador · Arco de pua · Torquês · Martelo · Macete

FERRAMENTAS DE MARCENEIRO

marcenaria s. f. shop or art of a cabinet-maker, joinery, a joiner's trade and work.
marceneiro s. m. cabinet-maker, joiner.
 ferramenta de ~ a joiner's tools (plate M 4).
marcescência s. f. marcescence.
marcescente adj. m. + f. (bot.) 1. marcescent: withering without falling off. 2. said of the calyx which remains on the fruit after the flower has wilted.
marcescível adj. m. + f. (pl. -íveis) (bot.) that which withers or may wither without falling off.
marcha s. f. 1. march: a) act of marching. b) regular and measured advance, progress. c) walk, gait. d) route, journey. e) a piece of music suitable to accompany marching. f) dance, musical rhythm. 2. (tech.) running, velocity. 3. gear of an automobile. ~ **avante** headway, ahead motion. ~ **dos negócios** run of business. ~ **surda** noiseless march. **a** ~ **dos acontecimentos** the march of events. **a** ~ **do progresso** the march of progress. **estar em** ~ 1. to be in progress. 2. (tech.) to be running, working. 3. (mil.) to be marching. **ordem de** ~ marching order. **pôr em** ~ 1. to set going, in motion. 2. to start. 3. (mil.) to set to march. **pôr-se em** ~ to begin to march, set forward, move, start. ~ **à ré** the reverse gear.
marchador s. m. 1. (Braz.) the one who foots the bill. 2. pacer (horse). ‖ adj. pacing.
marchantaria s. f. trade in cattle for slaughter.
marchante s. m. 1. cattle dealer, esp. for slaughterhouse. 2. (ant.) merchant. 3. (N. Braz.) owner or employee of a butchery. 4. (S. Braz.) keeper of a mistress. 5. the one who foots the bill.
marchar v. 1. to march, walk with a regular and measured gait. 2. (mach.) to run, turn, work. 3. to progress. 4. (Braz., pop.) to foot the bill.
marcha-rancho s. f. pl. (Braz.) slow march music composed specially for carnival.
marche-marche s. m. (mil.) 1. double time, double. 2. command for this pace.
 a ~ **on the double.** ~**!** double (the pace)!
marcheta (ê) s. f. 1. part of the mantle or mantilla where the ribbons are fastened. 2. = **marchete.**
marchetado s. m. inlaid work. ‖ adj. 1. inlaid. 2. imitating inlaid work. 3. (fig.) variegated; shadowed.

marchetar v. 1. to inlay, incrust, tesselate. 2. to veneer. 3. to variegate. 4. to set off.
marchetaria s. f. marquetry, tesselation, inlaying.
marchete (ê) s. m. each of the pieces which form the pattern of an inlaid work.
marcheteiro s. m. inlayer.
marcial adj. m. + f. (pl. -ais) (also **márcio** m.) martial, military. ‖ ~**mente** adv. martially.
 lei ~ martial law.
marciano, marciático s. m. Martian: hypothetical inhabitant of Mars. ‖ adj. Martian: pertaining to Mars.
márcido adj. wilted, withered, limp, without vigour.
marco s. m. 1. mark: a) boundary, limit. b) landmark, demarcation, sign. c) monetary unit of Germany. 2. window frame, pylon. 3. (ant.) weight of 8 ounces.
 ~ **quilométrico** milestone.
março s. m. March: third month of the civil year.
marcomano s. m. member of the Marcomanni: an ancient Germanic tribe. ‖ adj. of or pertaining to this tribe.
maré s. f. 1. tide. 2. (fig.) ups and downs in human affairs. 3. (fig.) reason, opportunity, occasion, disposition. 4. (N. Braz.) distance which can be covered between two tides on river voyages.
 ~ **alta,** ~ **cheia** high tide. ~ **baixa,** ~ **vazia** low tide. ~ **de carvoeiro** 1. (N. Braz.) a transitory difficulty. 2. opportunity. ~ **enchente** flood tide. ~ **vazante** ebb tide. ~ **viva** spring tide. **a** ~ **enche** the tide is rising. **a** ~ **vaza** the tide is falling. **perder a** ~ to slip the occasion. **recuar contra a** ~ to oppose in vain to s. th., to struggle in vain. **remar contra a** ~ to go against the tide.
mareação s. f. (pl. -ões) the act of steering and controlling a ship, seafaring.
 gente de ~ seafarers.
mareado adj. 1. seasick. 2. (S. Braz.) slightly under the weather.
mareagem s. f. (pl. -ens) 1. = **mareação.** 2. tackle, rigging, cordage. 3. route followed by a ship.
mareante s. m. seaman, mariner, sailor. ‖ adj. m. + f. sailing, making or being seasick, marring, spotting, etc.
marear v. 1. to steer a ship, navigate, be at sea. 2. to make seasick. 3. to stain, mar, dull, oxidize.

4. to discredit. 5. to daze a bull in bullfighting. 6. to travel by boat. 7. to control and restrain o. s. 8. to be troubled, become seasick. 9. ~-se: a) orient o. s. on sea. b) to lose lustre, become dull. **agulha de** ~ compass. **carta de** ~ log, sea-card.

marechal s. m. (pl. **-ais**) marshal: 1. (ant.) rank in the army. 2. supreme commander of the army in case of war.

marechal-de-campo s. m. (pl. **marechais-de-campo**) field-marshal.

marechal-do-ar s. m. (pl. **marechais-do-ar**) air-marshal.

marechalado, marechalato s. m. marshalry.

mareiro s. m. sea-breeze. ‖ adj. 1. blowing in from the sea (wind). 2. favourable for navigating. **vento** ~ a wind from the sea.

marejada s. f. (also **marulho**) light agitation of the sea.

marejar s. 1. to exude a liquid through the pores. 2. to bubble up. 3. to trickle, ooze out. 4. ~-se to fill, cover with tears.

marel s. m. (pl. **-éis**) sire: male beast kept for breeding. ‖ adj. siring. **touro** ~ bull kept for breeding.

marema s. f. maremma: unhealthy swampland, as on the Italian coast.

maremático adj. referring to maremma, esp. in connection with swamp fevers.

maré-me-leva-maré-me-traz s. m. + f., sg. + pl. (Braz.) weak and irresolute person.

maremoto s. m. seaquake.

mareografista s. m. person in charge of a tide-gauge.

mareógrafo, mareômetro s. m. (also **marégrafo, marêmetro**) tide-gauge: instrument that registers automatically the height of the tide.

maresia s. f. 1. bad smell of the sea at low tide. 2. rollers, breakers. 3. whitecaps. 4. corrosive sea air.

mareta s. f. 1. small wave. 2. river wave.

marfado adj. 1. ill-humoured, angry, vexed, disgusted. 2. rabid, hydrophobic.

marfar v. 1. to offend, hurt. 2. to annoy, make angry, infuriate, vex.

marfim s. m. (obs. also **marfi**) (pl. **-ins**) 1. ivory. 2. (also **itapeuá**) an apocynaceous plant. 3. (sl.) money. ‖ adj. ivory: looking like or having the colour of ivory. **deixar correr o** ~ to let things take their course.

marfim-vegetal s. m. (pl. **marfins-vegetais**) (Braz.) 1. vegetable ivory: endosperm of the ivory nut. 2. jarina, ivory-nut palm (Phytelephas macrocarpa) that yields the ivory nut.

marfinizar-se v. to take on the aspect of ivory.

marga s. f. marl: clay containing much calcareous matter (much used as a fertilizer).

margagem s. f. (pl. **-ens**) marling: fertilization with marl.

margar v. to marl: fertilize with marl.

margarida s. f. (bot.) daisy, marguerite. ~ **anual,** ~ **do campo** Spanish daisy.

margarina s. f. margerine: butter substitute composed of vegetable and animal oils and fats.

margarita s. f. 1. margarite: a) pearl. b) mineral. 2. (bot.) daisy. 3. (zool.) Margarites: a genus of molluscs that produce pearls.

margaritáceo adj. margaritaceous: said of the molluscs that produce pearls.

margaritífero adj. producing pearls; pearl-bearing.

margaritita, margaritite s. f. old denomination for a fossil pearl.

margeador s. m. (typogr.) layer-on, feeder.

margeante adj. m. + f. marginal.

margear v. 1. to marginate: a) provide with a margin. b) border. 2. to follow along a margin. 3. to write, draw, etc. on the margin. 4. to go along on or to edge the margin. 5. (typogr.) to lay on, feed.

margem s. f. (pl. **-ens**) 1. margin: a) border, unprinted edge around the pages of a manuscript, book, etc. (plate L 4). b) limit, borderline. c) bank, shore. d) brim, rim, edge. e) (fig.) opportunity, facility. f) possibility, cause. 2. enclosure. 3. balk of land between two furrows. ~ **de velocidade** speed limit, range. **dar** ~ to occasion, to cause. **deitar à** ~, **lançar à** ~ to discard, abandon. **notas à** ~ marginal notes. **pôr à** ~ to lay aside.

marginado adj. marginate(d): 1. having a margin. 2. written on the margin of a page. 3. (ent.) having a distinctly coloured margin.

marginador s. m. 1. (typogr.) = **margeador**. 2. margin stop (typewriter) (plate M 2).

marginal s. m. + f. (Braz.) outlaw (person). ‖ adj. m. + f. (pl. **-ais**) marginal; criminal. **homem** ~ marginal man: person living on the margin of two cultural groups without being able to identify himself with either one. **nota** ~ marginal note. **terras -ais** riverside territory.

marginalidade s. f. condition of a marginal man.

marginalizar v. to keep someone apart from society, groups, or public life.

marginar v. 1. = **margear**. 2. to make marginal notes.

marginiforme adj. m. + f. similar to a border.

margoso adj. marly, marlaceous.

margrave s. m. 1. margrave. 2. **margravina** f. margravine.

margraviado, margraviato s. m. margraviate.

margueira s. f. marlpit.

margueiro s. m. marl digger.

mari s. m. the spring andira: a leguminous and medicinal plant.

Maria s. f. Mary: proper name. **há mais ~s na terra** she is not, you are not the only pebble on the beach.

maria-anjica s. f. (pl. **marias-anjicas**) (Braz.) the larva of a certain beetle: a sugar-cane plague.

maria-branca s. f. (pl. **marias-brancas**) (Braz.) 1. bird of the family Tyrannidae, also known as **pombinha-das-almas**. 2. (Braz., sl.) = **cachaça**.

maria-caraíba s. f. (pl. **marias-caraíbas**) (Braz.) = **atingaçu**.

maria-cavaleira s. f. (pl. **marias-cavaleiras**) (Braz., ornith.) fierce flycatcher.

maria-com-a-vovó s. f. (pl. **marias-com-a-vovó**) (Braz., ornith.) Pará spinetail.

maria-da-serra s. f. (pl. **marias-da-serra**) (Braz.) river fish of the family Callichthyidae (Corydoras barbatus).

maria-da-toca s. f. (pl. **marias-da-toca**) (Braz.) river fish of the family Gobiidae (Gobiosoma molestum).

maria-de-barro s. f. (pl. **marias-de-barro**) = **joão-de-barro**.

maria-é-dia s. f., sg. + pl. (Braz.) bird of the family Troglodytidae (Elaenia flavogaster) also known as **maria-já-é-dia, marido-é-dia** and **maridedia**.

maria-faceira s. f. (pl. **marias-faceiras**) (Braz.) bird of the family Ardeidae (Lyriqma sibilatrix).

maria-farinha s. f. (pl. **marias-farinha**) (Braz.) ocypode: a crab of the family Ocypodidae (Ocypode albicans).

maria-fumaça s. m. + f. (pl. **marias-fumaça**) (Braz., pop.) 1. smoker: a steam locomotive. 2. a heavy smoker.

maria-gomes s. f. (pl. **marias-gomes**) (Braz., bot.) puchero. Variation: **mariangombe**.

maria-judia s. f. (pl. **marias-judias**) (Braz.) = **tico-tico**.

marial adj. m. + f. (pl. -ais) Marian: relating to the Virgin Mary.

marialva s. m. good horseman. ‖ adj. m. + f. pertaining to the rules of horsemanship established by the Marquis of Marialva.

maria-macumbé s. f. (S. Braz.) game of hide-and-seek.

maria-mole s. f. (pl. marias-moles) (Braz.) 1. tree of the family Nyctaginaceae (Pisonia inermis) also known as maria-preta and baraúna. 2. fish belonging to the family Sciaenidae (Cynoscion striatus). 3. a wading bird (Butorides striatus striatus). 4. sweet made mainly out of the white of egg, ground coconut meat and sugar.

maria-mucanguê s. f. (Braz.) a children's game (hide-and-seek).

maria-mulata s. f. (pl. marias-mulatas) (Braz.) bird of the family Tyrannidae (Knipolegus nigerrimus Vieill).

maria-nagô s. f. (pl. marias-nagô) (Braz.) a croaker: sea fish belonging to the family Sciaenidae.

marianinha s. f. (Braz.) bird of the parrot family (Pionites leucogaster), known also as periquito-d'anta.

marianismo s. m. elevated cult to the Virgin Mary.

marianita s. m. + f., adj. m. + f. = marista.

mariano s. m. member of the order of the barefooted Carmelites. ‖ adj. = marial.

maria-pereira s. f. (pl. marias-pereira or maria-pereiras (Braz.) tree of the family Rubiaceae (Posoqueria macrocarpus).

maria-preta s. f. (pl. marias-pretas) (Braz.) 1. bird of the family Tyrannidae (Knipolegus comatus). 2. (also mocitaíba, tarumã, maria-mole) name of several plants belonging to various families, especially to the Borraginaceae and the Compositae.

maria-rendeira s. f. (pl. marias-rendeiras (Braz.) = rendeira.

maria-rita s. f. (pl. marias-rita or maria-ritas) (Braz.) name of two kinds of wasps (Polistes versicolor and Polistes canadensis).

maria-rosa s. f. (pl. marias-rosa or maria-rosas) (Braz.) a variety of palm (Cocos procopiana).

mariato s. m. signalling flags (Navy).

maria-vai-com-as-outras s. m. + f., sg. + pl. (Braz.) person without own will doing what the others do.

maribondo s. m. (Braz.) = marimbondo.

maricá s. m. (Braz., bot.) a mimosa.

maricagem s. f. (pl. -ens) (Braz.) actions and habits of a milksop.

maricas s. m., sg. + pl. (also maricão, mariquinha m.) 1. sissy, milksop. 2. man doing a womans's work. 3. coward. 4. (N. Braz.) marihuana pipe.

maricazal s. m. (pl. -ais) (S. Braz.) terrain where maricá (mimosa) grows abundantly.

maridagem (pl. -ens) maridança s. f. married life.

maridar v. 1. to marry, take for one's husband. 2. to join, interlace. 3. ~-se to marry, get married (woman).

marideia s. f. (Braz.) = maria-é-dia.

marido s. m. husband, consort, spouse.
~ governado pela mulher hen-pecked husband.

marido-é-dia s. f., sg. + pl. = maria-é-dia.

marigüi s. m. (Braz.) name of a mosquito.

marimacho s. m. mannish woman, virago.

marimba s. f. 1. marimba: a kind of xylophone originated in Africa. 2. (Braz.) lousy piano. 3. any piano.

marimbá s. m. (Braz., ichth.) sargo: a sea fish of the family Sparidae (Diplodus argenteus).

marimbar v. 1. to win at the marimbo card game. 2. to play the marimba. 3. (fig., vulg.) to cheat.

marimbau s. m. (Braz., ichth.) = marimbá.

marimbo s. m. name of a card game.

marimbondo s. m. (Braz.) 1. a variety of wasp. 2. nickname given to the Brazilians by the Portuguese during the independence days. 3. nickname given to the people of Pernambuco during the revolt of 1852.

marimbondo-caçador s. m. (pl. marimbondos-caçadores) (ent.) hornet.

marimbu s. m. (Braz.) swamp area along a river.

marimonda s. m. (Braz.) spider monkey (Ateles).

marinas s. f. pl. sea plants, seaweed.

maringá adj. m. + f. (Braz.) said of a cow with a light coloured and black speckled hide.

marinha s. f. 1. navy, marine. 2. naval force. 3. naval service. 4. beach, shore, coast. 5. saline. 6. seascape. 7. (Braz.) coastland.
~ de guerra navy. ~ mercante merchant marine, mercantile marine. arsenal de ~ dock yard. oficial da ~ naval officer. soldado da ~ marine.

marinhagem s. f. (pl. -ens) (also maruja) 1. the crew of a ship. 2. bunch of sailors. 3. seamanship.

marinhar v. 1. to man a ship. 2. to navigate. 3. to climb.

marinharesco adj. seamanlike, relating to mariners or to the navy.

marinheiraria s. f. 1. seamanship. 2. the practical part of nautics.

marinheiro s. m. 1. sailor, mariner, seaman; seafarer. 2. person directing a boat. 3. marine: person serving in the navy. 4. (Braz.) nickname given to the Portuguese in some states and esp. in the north. 5. name of a crustacean also known as aratu. 6. plant belonging to the Meliaceae. 7. grain of corn which escaped processing in the machines. 8. (sl.) individual with plenty of money claiming that he has none. ‖ adj. sailorly.
~ de água doce fairweather-sailor, land-lubber. ~ de primeira viagem beginner.

marinho adj. (also marino) marine: of or pertaining to the sea.
azul-~ navy blue. cavalo-~ sea-horse.

marinismo s. m. marinism: affected literary style.

marinista s. m. + f. marinist.

mariola s. m. 1. messenger. 2. porter, carrier. 3. villain, knave, rogue. 4. f. block of a sweet made out of banana. ‖ adj. 1. mean, infamous, of bad character. 2. roguish, cheating.

mariolada s. f. knavish act, roguery.

mariolagem s. f. (pl. ~ens) 1. = mariolada. 2. rogues collectively.

mariolar v. 1. to act like a rogue. 2. to lead the life of a scoundrel.

marionete s. f. marionette, puppet.

mariposa s. f. 1. moth. 2. butterfly. 3. butterfly-shaped jewel. 4. (S. Braz.) a type of dredge to remove earth with and drawn by horses or oxen. 5. (S. E. Braz., pop.) nightwalker (a hooker).

mariposar v. to fly about like a butterfly.

mariquice s. f. effeminacy, womanish behaviour.

mariquinha (I) s. m. (also mariquina f., mariquinhas m. sg. + pl.) (Braz.) = mono.

mariquinha (II) s. f. (Braz.) 1. mobile tripod used in the kitchen. 2. (pop.) lie, big tale. 3. = maricas.

mariquita s. f. (Braz.) 1. name for two serranoid sea fishes (Serranus flaviventris and Dules auriga). 2. a variety of butterfly (Heliconius eucrates). 3. wooden tripod to hang the kettle over the fire.

mariscador s. m. (N. Braz.) 1. individual who fishes with a casting net. 2. person who catches shellfish. 3. person skilled in hunting and fishing.

mariscar v. 1. to catch shellfish. 2. to hunt or fish. 3. to pick up shellfish or insects along the strand (birds). 4. (N. Braz.) to fish with a casting net.

marisco s. m. 1. shellfish. 2. (Braz.) clawlike or spoonlike instruments for pulping halved coconuts. 3. person doing the pulping. 4. a variety of wildcat.

marisma s. f. marshy area on the seashore.

marisqueira s. f. 1. sea fish of the family Sciaenidae (Micropogon opercularis). 2. female shellfish dealer.

marisqueiro s. m. 1. shellfish gatherer or seller. 2. = **martim-pescador.** ‖ adj. fishing, hunting.

marista s. m. + f. (eccl.; also **marianita**) Marist: member of the Society of Mary. ‖ adj. pertaining to the Marists.

marital adj. m. + f. (pl. **-ais**) marital. ‖ ~**mente** adv. maritally.

maritataca, maritafede s. f. (Braz., zool.) the S. American hog-nosed skunk (Conepatus chilensis amazonicus).

mariticida s. f. mariticide: woman who kills her husband.

mariticídio s. m. mariticide: crime of a woman killing her husband.

marítimo s. m. sailor, mariner. ‖ adj. maritime, marine.

cidade -a a sea town.

marlota s. f. short cape with a hood used by the Moors.

marlotar v. 1. to give a wrinkled appearance to something. 2. to crush, line, wrinkle.

marma s. f. marver: iron with which glass is rounded and polished in factories.

marmanjada s. f. (depr.) 1. group of young men or rough boys. 2. gang of rascals.

marmanjaria s. f. roguery: doings of rascals or rogues.

marmanjo s. m. (depr.) 1. adult male, awkward young man. 2. brute, bully man. 3. rogue, rascal, mean character.

corja de ~**s** gang of rascals.

marmelada s. f. 1. marmalade made out of quinces. 2. (sl.) advantage, bargain. 3. (Braz., sport., sl.) fixed game. 4. a variety of grass.

marmelada-brava s. f. (pl. **marmeladas-bravas**) a rubiaceous plant (Amajoua guianensis).

marmelada-de-cavalo s. f. (pl. **marmeladas-de-cavalo**) (also **carrapicho** m.) (Braz., bot.) beggar's-lice.

marmeladeiro s. m. (Braz.) vendor of quince marmalade.

marmeleiral s. m. (pl. **-ais**) (Braz.) quince tree grove.

marmeleiro s. m. quince tree.

marmeleiro-da-china s. m. (pl. **marmeleiros-da-china**) (Braz.) tree of the family Rosaceae (Cydonia sinensis).

marmeleiro-do-campo s. m. (pl. **marmeleiros-do-campo**) tree of the family Euphorbiaceae (Maprounea brasiliensis).

marmelo s. m. quince.

marmita s. f. 1. marmite, marmit: a metal can with a lid, fitting three or four in a metal frame for carrying food. 2. a soldier's chow pan.

marmita-de-gigante s. f. (pl. **marmitas-de-gigante**) cylindrical depression in a river bed.

marmiteiro s. m. (Braz.) 1. person distributing to homes food furnished by boardinghouses. 2. (sl.) worker who brings his own food from home in a marmit to eat at work during lunch time.

marmo adj. (N. Braz.) big, excellent.

roçado ~ large piece of cleared land.

marmoraria s. f. establishment where marble is cut; marble industry or works.

marmorário s. m. (also **marmoreiro, marmorista** m. + f.) marble cutter. ‖ adj. marble: of or pertaining to marble.

mármore s. m. 1. marble. 2. something cold, hard, and white like marble. 3. (fig.) indifferent person devoid of feelings. 4. indifference, insensibility.

marmorear v. to marble.

marmoreira s. m. marble quarry.

marmóreo adj. marmoreal, marmorean: 1. similar or pertaining to marble. 2. made out of marble. 3. coloured like marble. 4. (fig.) unfeeling, indifferent.

marmorização s. f. (pl. **-ões**) 1. transformation of limestone into marble. 2. marbling: process or act of staining like marble. 3. (path.) state of an organ showing veins and threads on its external surface.

marmorizar v. 1. to turn into marble. 2. to marble, marbleize: stain or vein like marble.

marmota s. f. 1. (zool.) marmot: a small rodent of the genus Marmota. 2. (N. Braz.) (pop.) mirage, spook, ghost.

marna s. f. = **marga.**

marnota s. f. 1. marshland along rivers and the sea. 2. salt pan: graduation (of a saline).

marnoteiro, marnoto s. m. worker in a saline.

maro s. m. (bot.) cat thyme, herb mastic.

marola s. f. (S. Braz.) 1. comber, beachcomber (wave). 2. agitated, rough sea.

marolinho-do-campo s. m. (pl. **marolinhos-do-campo**) plant of the family Annonaceae (Rollinia geraensis).

marolo s. m. (Braz.) a custard-apple tree (Annona crassifolia).

maroma s. f. 1. rope, cable. 2. tightrope. 3. (N. Braz.) stilts on which houses are built along the rivers. 4. the entire house plus the stilts.

andar na ~ 1. to walk on the rope. 2. (fig.) to be engaged in a dangerous enterprise.

maromba s. f. 1. a ropedancer's pole. 2. (fig.) predicament. 3. (Braz.) dubious questionable attitude of somebody waiting for the coming events. 4. slyness, artfulness. 5. (Braz.) cable of a ferryboat (to pull it from one side of the river to the other). 6. (Braz.) place where cattle is kept during floods. 7. (N. Braz.) float used for the transport of cattle. 8. (N. Braz.) herd of oxen. 9. (Braz.) machine to make bricks with. 10. (S. Braz.) a variety of large sardines.

marombado adj. N. Braz., pop.) lying, bigmouthed.

marombar v. (Braz.; South also **marombear**) 1. to try to keep the balance, try to keep o. s. up. 2. (S. Braz.) to pull a ferryboat across a river using a cable. 3. (fig.): a) to cheat, shy away from work, simulate. b) to hesitate between two possibilities always looking for a personal advantage. c) to complicate and embarrass things purposely.

marombeiro adj. 1. flattering, apple-polishing. 2. (sl.) sly.

marombista s. m. + f. 1. person avoiding responsibilities, appointments, etc. 2. opportunist. ‖ adj. evasive.

maronita s. m. + m. Maronite: member of a Catholic group from Lebanon. ‖ adj. Maronite: pertaining to this group.

marosca s. f. plot, trick, trap.

marotagem s. f. (pl. **-ens**) 1. = **maroteira.** 2. gang of rascals.

marotear v. 1. to behave like a rascal or rogue. 2. to lead a loose life.

maroteira s. f. rascality, roguery, knavery.

maroto s. m. 1. rascal, rogue, person of poor character. 2. (affectionate) waggish person, naughty child. 3. (Braz.) nickname given to the Portuguese especially in Bahia after the declaration of Independence. ‖ adj. 1. malicious, artful. 2. lascivious. 3. waggish.

seu ~ you rascal! (of children).

marouço s. m. (also **maroiço**) (S. Braz.) 1. agitated sea with whitecaps. 2. ~s pl. beachcomber, large whitecaps, billow, breaker.

marqueiro s. m. (S. Braz., also **marcador**) person in charge of heating the branding irons.

marquês s. m. (pl. **-eses**) marquis.

marquesa s. f. 1. marchioness, marquise. 2. woman owning a marquisate. 3. sofa with a cane seat.

marquesado s. m. marquisate.

marquesinha s. f. 1. ladies' parasol. 2. officers' tent in a camp. 3. (archit.) marquise, marquee.

marra s. f. 1. weeding tool. 2. sledge hammer, esp. used by stone-masons. 3. ditch alongside the road. 4. clearing in wine and olive plantations. 5. boys' game.

na ~ 1. by force or violence. 2. at any cost.

marrã s. f. 1. a weaned young sow. 2. (N.E. Braz.) fresh pork. 3. ewe lamb.

marraco s. m. marrock.

marrada s. f. 1. butt, thrust (with a horn). 2. unexpected meeting with somebody. 3. a beating of the head against something.

marrafa s. f. 1. forelock. 2. each of the sides of parted hair. 3. (N. Braz.) small ornamental comb.

marralhar v. 1. to insist, be obstinate. 2. to try persistently to convince somebody in an argument. 3. to idle, loiter.

marralheiro adj. 1. crafty, cunning, artful. 2. idle, indolent, lazy.

marralhice s. f. 1. shyness, artfulness. 2. indolence, idleness, laziness.

marrana s. m. + f. 1. hunchback. 2. f. = **marrã**.

marrano s. m. 1. excommunicated person. 2. impure person. 3. (Braz.) poor cattle. ‖ adj. 1. excommunicated. 2. impure. 3. said of poor cattle.

marrão s. m. (pl. **-ões**) 1. weaned hog. 2. a stone-mason's hammer. 3. (S. Braz.) wild, untamed cattle. 4. (Braz. = **chimarrão**. ‖ adj. untamed, wild (of cattle).

marrar v. 1. to horn, butt. 2. to strike with the head. 3. to run against, come across, hit upon. 4. to beat with a stone-mason's hammer. 5. to become turbid (wine).

marraxo s. m. 1. old playful cat. 2. large shark of the Atlantic and Indian Ocean. ‖ adj.= **matreiro**.

marreca s. f. (Braz., ornith.) mareca: name of various wild ducks including the widgeon.

marreca-apaí s. f. (pl. **marrecas-apaí**) (Braz.; also **marreca-piadeira, marreca-viúva**) widow duck.

marreca-assobiadeira s. f. (pl. **marrecas-assobiadeiras**) (Braz.) the whistling teal.

marreca-cabocla s. f. (pl. **marrecas-caboclas**) (Braz.) black-bellied tree duck.

marreca-caneleira s. f. (pl. **marrecas-caneleiras**) (Braz.; also **marrecapeba**) fulvus tree duck.

marreca-carijó s. f. (pl. **marrecas-carijó**) (Braz., ornith.) a spotted teal (Querquedula versicolor).

marreca-grande-de-marajó s. f. (pl. **marrecas-grandes-de-marajó**) = **marreca-cabocla**.

marrecão s. m. (pl. **-ões**) (Braz.) two birds of the duck family (Neochen jubata and Metopiana peposaca).

marrecarana s. f. = **marrequinha**.

marreca-toicinho s. f. (pl. **marrecas-toicinho**) (Braz.) Bahaman pintail.

marreco s. m. teal. ‖ adj. 1. hunchbacked. 2. (Braz., ant., fig.) astute, sly, cunning.

marreco-do-pará s. m. (pl. **marrecos-do-pará**) (Braz.) = **chega-e-vira**.

marrequém-de-igapó s. f. (pl. **marrequéns-de-igapó**) (Braz.) bird of the parrot family (Pyrrhura picta amazonum).

marrequinha s. f. (Braz., ornith.) (also **marrecarana** f., **paturi** m.) masked duck (Nomonyx dominicus).

marrequinho-do-brejo s. m. (pl. **marrequinhos-do-brejo**) (Braz.) grass wren.

marrequinho-do-campo s. m. (pl. **marrequinhos-do-campo**) (Braz.) gray teal.

marreta (ê) s. f. 1. small stone-mason's hammer, hammer for breaking stones. 2. (Braz.) nickname given to the Portuguese at the time of the Independence movement. 3. name given to a political party and its adepts in Pernambuco. 4. (sl.) shoe.

marretada s. f. 1. blow, stroke with a stone-mason's hammer. 2. (Braz., sl.) sexual intercourse.

marretar v. (Braz.) 1. to strike with a stone-mason's hammer. 2. to beat. 3. to ruin, lose, waste.

marreteiro s. m. 1. (Braz.) worker who drives in the mining drills with a stone-mason's hammer. 2. (S. Braz.) peddler, hawker, huckster.

marroada s. f. 1. stroke with a stone-mason's hammer. 2. herd of weaned hogs.

marroaz s. m. Asiatic boat. ‖ adj. stubborn, obstinate.

marrom s. m. (pl. **-ons**) brown colour. ‖ adj. m. + f. (pl. **-ons**) brown, hazel.

marroquim s. m. (pl. **-ins**) Morocco (leather).

marroquinar v. to convert into Morocco.

marroquino s. m. native or inhabitant of Morocco. ‖ adj. of or pertaining to Morocco.

marrote s. m. (S. Braz.) young pig not yet castrated; shote, shoat.

marroteiro s. m. 1. foreman in a saline. 2. =-**marroteiro**.

marroxo s. m. 1. rest, refuse, waste. 2. = **marrufo**.

marruá s. m. (Braz.) 1. untamed calf, yearling. 2. easily cheated person. 3. novice, inexperienced person.

marruás s. m. (Braz.) 1. bull. 2. = **marruá**.

marruco s. m. (Braz.) breeding bull.

marrueiro s. m. (N. Braz.) tamer or breaker of bulls.

marrufo s. m. (ant.) 1. lay brother. 2. rogue, rascal.

marselhês s. m. (pl. **-eses**) (f. **-esa**, pl. **-esas**) native or inhabitant of Marseilles. ‖ adj. of or pertaining to Marseilles.

marselhesa s. f. Marseillaise: national anthem of France.

marsília s. f. Marsilea: a genus of plants that grow in stagnating waters.

marsiliácea s. f. the marsilea, a cryptogamic plant.

marsiliáceo adj. marsileaceous: pertaining to the clover ferns.

marsipobrânquio s. m. (ichth.) marsipobranch.

marsupial s. m. (pl. **-ais**) marsupial: animal pertaining to the Marsupialia order of mammals, including the kangaroo. ‖ adj. m. + f. marsupial, relating to the Marsupialia.

marsúpio s. m. marsupium: abdominal pouch in which marsupials carry and nurse their youngs.

marta s. f. marten.

martagão s. m. (pl. **-ões**) (bot.) martagon, a variety of lilies.

martaréu s. m. (naut.) topgallant.

marte s. m. 1. Mars: a) ancient Roman god of war. b) planet. 2. (fig.): a) war. b) bellicose person.

marteiro s. m. (ant.) = **martírio**.

martel s. m. (pl. **-éis**) drinking cup in rural taverns.

martelada s. f. 1. blow or stroke with a hammer. 2. constant hammering.

martelador s. m. hammerer.

martelagem s. f. (pl. **-ens**) hammering.

martelão s. m. (Braz., sl.) blockhead: person who only learns through persistent repetition.

martelar v. 1. to hammer, pound, beat (plate C 16). 2. to bother, annoy. 3. to insist, pursue stubbornly. 4. to produce laboriously.

~ **a frio** to cold-draw with a hammer.

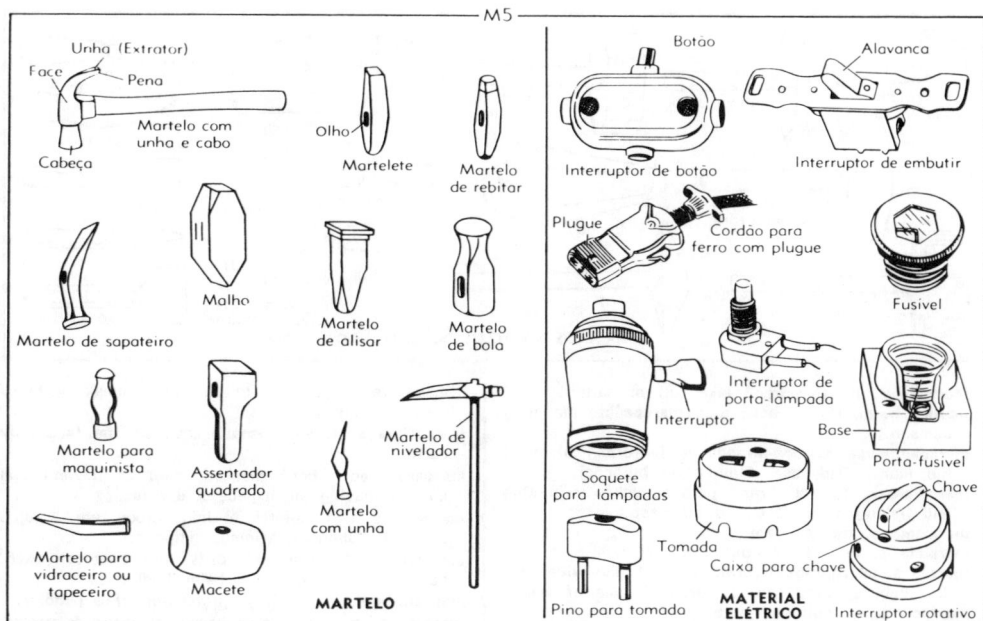

M5

MARTELO

MATERIAL ELÉTRICO

martelete s. m. 1. small hammer, light hammer (plate M 5). 2. Moorish spur.

martelinho s. m. 1. small hammer (plate M 5). 2. cup holding about half a pint.

martelo s. m. 1. hammer (plates F 1, M 5, 6). 2. (anat.) malleus. 3. (zool.) hammerhead shark. 4. hammer of a piano. 5. (fig.) pursuer of evil who tries to end with it. 6. inopportune person. 7. (Braz.) wriggler: larva of the mosquito that transmits yellow fever. 8. liquid measure corresponding to 0,165 l. 9. musical and poetic style of northeast Brazil. 10. instrument to tune a piano. 11. a species of mollusc.
~ **a vapor** steam hammer. ~ **de alisar** face hammer. ~ **de aplainar** planishing hammer, smoothing hammer. ~ **de bola** ball pane hammer (plate M 5). ~ **de carne** meat tenderer (plate C 20). ~ **de duas faces** double-faced hammer. ~ **de marceneiro** joiner's hammer (plate M 4). ~ **de orelhas**, ~ **de unha** claw hammer. ~ **de queda** drop-hammer. ~ **de rebitar** riveting hammer (plate M 5). ~ **de ripamento** lath hammer (plate T 5). ~ **mecânico** tilt hammer. **a** ~ 1. with a hammer. 2. (fig.) by force. **arremessar o** ~ (sport) to throw the hammer. **estar entre a bigorna e o** ~ to hold a wolf by the ears.

martilhar v. (S. Braz.) 1. to set the trigger of a gun. 2. to get a horse ready for a fast spurt. 3. to get ready.

martim-pescador s. m. (pl. **martins-pescadores**) (Braz., ornith., also **martim**, **martim-cachá**, **martim-cachaça**, **martim-grande**, **matraca**, **flecha-peixe**, **pica-peixe**, **ariramba-grande**) kingfisher.

martinete s. m. 1. steam hammer; pile-driver. 2. hammer of a piano. 3. pin of a sun dial. 4. (zool.): a) long-winged swallow; martin, swift. b) hawk. 5. panache of a grouse. 6. (bot.) cockscomb.

martiniáceas s. f. pl. Martyniaceae: a family of dicotyledoneous plants.

martiniáceo adj. (bot.) martyniaceous.

martinica s. f. (N. Braz.) 1. a type of wide pants used by the simple people in Maranhão. 2. any type of pants in Piauí.

mártir s. m. + f. martyr: 1. person who suffered for the Christian beliefs. 2. one who suffers for his views and beliefs. 3. sufferer.

martírio s. m. martyrdom: 1. the suffering of a martyr. 2. extreme sufferings. 3. (bot.) the passion-flower.

martirizador s. m. martyrizor. ‖ adj. tormenting, torturing.

martirizar v. to martyrize: 1. make a martyr of. 2. torment.

martirológio s. m. martyrology: book of martyrs and their sufferings.

martirologista s. m. + f. martyrologist: author or authoress of a martyrology.

martita s. f. iron sesquioxide.

marubá s. m. (Braz., bot.) simaruba.

marufle s. m. potent glue, lining paste.

marufo s. m. fermented sap of a leguminous tree, much appreciated by Africans.

maruim (pl. -**ins**), **maruí** s. m. (Braz., also **miruim**, **muruim**, **meruim**) Amazonian mosquito.

maruja s. f. = **marinhagem**.

marujada s. f. 1. seamen collectively. 2. crowd of sailors.

marujo s. m. sailor, mariner, salt.

marulhado adj. touched or covered by sea waves.

marulhar v. 1. to surge, form waves, toss (the sea). 2. to roar like the stormy sea or breakers.

marulheiro adj. storming, arousing the sea.

marulho s. m. (also **marulhada** f.) 1. agitation, tossing, rearing of the sea. 2. (fig.) noise, confusion, tumult.

marulhoso adj. 1. billowy, surgy. 2. murmurous. 3. roaring.

marumbé s. m. (Braz.) variety of bean.

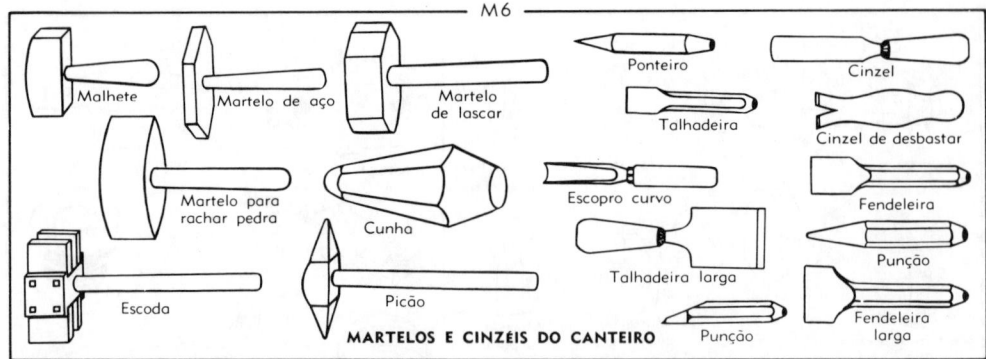

MARTELOS E CINZÉIS DO CANTEIRO

marumbi s. m. (N. Braz.) lake full of cattail.
marupá s. m. (Braz., bot.; also **marupaúba**) mountain damson.
marupapiranga, marupá-piranga s. f. (Braz.) plant of the family Tridaceae (Eleutherine bulbosa).
marupiara s. m. (N. Braz.) person lucky in hunting and fishing or in love and business.
marxismo s. m. Marxism.
marxista s. m. + f. Marxist. ‖ adj. Marxist.
marzão s. m. (pl. **-ões**) (Braz., pop.) 1. the wide sea. 2. rough, agitated sea. 3. large masses of water.
marzoco s. m. buffoon, jester.
mas s. m. 1. objection, restriction, obstacle, hindrance. 2. defect, fault. ‖ adv. indeed, yes. ‖ conj. but, only, however, still, yet, even. ‖ contr. of the personal pron. **me** and the personal pron. **as.** ~ **claro!** ~ **sim** why yes! **não só vadio** ~ **também malcriado** not only lazy but also ill-mannered. **nem** ~ **nem meio** ~ but me no buts! **sempre tens um** ~ **para meus desejos** you always have a but to set against my wishes.
mascador s. m. 1. chewer. 2. cock that fights with his beak and not with his claws. ‖ adj. 1. chewing. 2. said of the cock fighting with his beak rather than with his claws.
mascar v. 1. to chew (tobacco, gum). 2. to mumble, swallow the words. 3. to mutter, grumble. 4. (fig.) to insinuate. 5. to ruminate, plan, think (up), meditate. 6. (N. Braz., pop.) to cheat, obtain through dubious ways.
goma de ~ chewing gum.
máscara s. f. 1. mask: a) a cover for the face to disguise and conceal it. b) a cover for the face to protect it as in fencing, fights, etc. c) (fig.) disguise. d) pretence, dissimulation. e) death mask. f) characteristic expression or countenance. g) m. + f. masker, masked person. 2. blinds of an animal.
~ **contra gases** gas mask. ~ **de oxigênio** oxigen mask. **baile de** ~s fancy dress ball. **largar, tirar a** ~ to throw off the mask. **tirar a** ~ to unmask (also fig.)
mascarada s. f. masquerade, fancy dress ball.
mascarado s. m. 1. mask, masked person. 2. masquerade. 3. (Braz., sport, sl.) a lousy but popular player. ‖ adj. 1. masked. 2. disguised. 3. said of an army camouflaged in the bushes. 4. said of a horse or cow having a white face or a large white spot on its face. ‖ **-amente** adv. disguisedly.
mascarão s. m. (pl. **-ões**) mascaron: stone mask used as an architectural ornament.
mascarar v. 1. to mask. 2. to disguise, hide. 3. to give a false appearance to. 4. to masque. 5. to

masquerade. 6. ~**-se** to put on a mask, a fancy dress; to disguise o. s.
mascarilha s. f. small mask covering the face only partly.
mascarino adj. (bot.) masked: said of flowers and corollas having the aspect of a mask.
mascarra s. f. 1. splotch of ink, carbon, etc. 2. dirt. 3. (fig.) dishonour, stigma, disgrace.
mascarrar v. 1. to splotch, dirty, soil, besmear, daub, begrime. 2. to write or paint badly.
mascataria s. f. peddlery: profession of a peddler.
mascate s. m. (Braz., also known as **turco da prestação**) 1. peddler, pedlar, hawker. 2. (Braz., hist.) derisive nickname given to the Portuguese in Olinda (Pernambuco).
mascateação (pl. **-ões**), **mascateagem** (pl. **-ens**) s. f. (Braz.) peddlery, pedlary.
mascatear v. (Braz.) to peddle, hawk.
mascavado adj. 1. unrefined (sugar). 2. (fig.) impure, bad, adulterated.
açúcar ~ brown sugar, unrefined sugar.
mascavar v. 1. to separate white sugar from that of a lesser quality. 2. (fig.) to adulterate, falsify. 3. to speak or write incorrectly.
mascavinho s. m. sugar slightly lighter in colour than brown sugar.
mascavo s. m. purification, refining of sugar. ‖ adj. = **mascavado.**
mascotar v. 1. to crush, pound with a stamper. 2. to chew, masticate.
mascote s. f. 1. mascot. 2. plant of the family Cucurbitaceae (Gurania malacophylla).
mascoto s. m. stamper, large hammer, mallet, stamp, pestle.
masculifloro adj. (bot.) masculiflorous: having male flowers.
masculinidade s. f. masculinity, virility.
masculinizar v. 1. to make masculine. 2. to attribute the masculine gender or masculine forms to. 3. (fig.) to make things look masculine. 4. to adopt masculine ways and manners.
masculino adj. masculine: 1. male. 2. manly, virile. 3. strong-minded. 4. (gram.) of the masculine gender.
gênero ~ masculine gender.
másculo adj. 1. pertaining to the male sex. 2. virile, manly. 3. energetic, strong. ‖ **masculamente** adv. energetically, etc.
masdeísmo s. m. (also **mazdeísmo**) Mazdaism: ancient Persian religion.
masdevália s. f. (Braz., bot.) Masdevallia: a genus of orchids.
maser s. f. (Engl.) (phys.) maser.

masmarro s. m. (sl.) 1. lay brother. 2. hermit with a friar's gown. 3. stout, self-interested friar. 4. rough man.

masmorra s. f. 1. subterraneous prison, dungeon. 2. (fig., fam.) cold and somber place or room.

masoquismo s. m. masochism: sexual perversion in which maltreatment causes sensual gratification.

masoquista s. m. + f. masochist. ‖ adj. masochistic.

massa s. f. 1. dough, bread paste (plate P 1). 2. soft or pulverized substance. 3. mass of like things. 4. totality. 5. (constr.) mortar. 6. ground manioc for the fabrication of manioc meal or cakes. 7. excellent wine from the neighbourhood of Naples. 8. amorphous mass. 9. (phys.) mass. 10. fermenting husks of grapes. 11. (pop.) money, dough. 12. ~s pl. masses of people, multitude, the lower classes. ~ de pão kneaded dough. ~ de vidraceiro glaziers' putty. ~ falida bankrupt person's estate. ~ folhada puff paste. ~ podre short paste. ~s alimentícias noodles. da mesma ~ of the same quality. estar com as mãos na ~ to have something in hand, to be about a thing. estar na ~ do sangue. to be bred in the bone. levantar-se em ~ to rise in a body, in mass. meter as mãos na ~ to poke one's nose into something. ~ cinzenta (Braz.) intelligence, brains.

massa-bruta s. m. + f. (pl. massas-brutas) (Braz., coll.) 1. a brute. 2. a rude person.

massacrar v. to massacre, kill cruelly, butcher.

massacre s. m. (Gall.) massacre, carnage, butchery.

massagada s. f. 1. confusion, bedlam. 2. jumble of things.

massagear v. to massage.

massagem s. f. (pl. ~ens) massage.

dar ~ a to massage.

massagista s. m. + f. masseur, masseuse.

massame s. m. 1. stone work at the bottom of a well. 2. base for a tiled floor. 3. (naut.) cordage.

massamorda s. f. 1. bread crumbs soaked in water and cooked with oil and garlic. 2. confusion, mixture. 3. badly cooked food.

massapê s. m. (N. Braz., or massapé in the South) very fertile soil for cane growing, usually almost black in colour.

massaroco s. m. sour dough, fermenting dough.

massau s. m. (N. Braz.) any of the Amazonian saky monkeys.

masseira s. f. 1. kneading trough. 2. channel to convey the water of a well. 3. wooden lid of a manioc press.

masseter s. m. (anat.) masseter: masticatory muscle which raises the lower jaw.

masseterino, massetérico adj. (anat.) masseteric: pertaining to the masseter.

massificar v. to guide or influence the individual through mass communication.

massilha s. f. papier maché.

massinha s. f. 1. soup noodles. 2. = massilha.

massoca s. f. (Braz.) manioc past produced in Maranhão.

massorá s. f. Masorah: the Hebrew tradition as to the exact form of the Scriptures.

massoreta s. m. Masorete: each of the contributers to the Masorah.

massudo adj. 1. massive, bulky, compact, thick, crude. 2. doughy, doughlike.

mastaréu s. m. (naut.) handmast, topmast (plate) B 10).

~ da gata mizen-topmast. ~ de gávea topmast. ~ de joanete topgallant-mast. ~ de velacho fore topmast.

masticatório s. m. (med.) masticatory: medicinal substance chewed to induce the flow of saliva.

mastigação s. f. (pl. -ões) mastication, chewing.

mastigado adj. 1. masticated, chewed. 2. (fig.) well--prepared, well-planned.

mastigadouro s. m. (also mastigadoiro) bit facilitating the mastigation of horses.

mastigar v. 1. to chew, masticate. 2. (fig.) to ponder, examine, think over, ruminate, meditate. 3. to repeat, re-use (words). 4. to mumble, talk between the teeth, mutter. 5. to talk back, grumble.

mastigóforo s. m. (also flagelado) flagellated protozoarian.

mastim s. m. (pl. -ins) 1. mastiff (plate C 3). 2. cur, tyke. 3. (fig.) gossip, heckler. 4. police agent.

mástique s. m. (also mástica f.) mastic: resin from a Mediterranean tree, used for varnish.

~ asfáltico asphalt mastic.

mastite s. f. (med.) mastitis: inflammation of women's breasts.

mastodinia s. f. (med.) mastodynia: pain in the mammary glands.

mastodonte s. m. 1. mastodon: elephantoid fossil animal. 2. (fig.) very heavy person.

mastóide adj. m. + f. mastóideo m. mastoid: formed like a woman's breast.

mastoidite s. f. (med.) mastoiditis: inflammation of the mastoid apophysis.

mastoquino s. m. short blade used by sailors.

mastozoário s. m. mammal. ‖ adj. mammalian, mammiferous.

mastozoologia s. f. study of mammals.

mastozoológico adj. referring to the study of mammals.

mastozoótico adj. said of a terrain containing fossils of mammals.

mastreação s. f. (pl. -ões) 1. masts, mastings. 2. the setting of masts.

mastrear v. to set the masts of a ship, supply with masts.

mastro s. m. 1. mast of a ship (plates B 10, L 2). 2. flagpole. 3. climbing pole.

~ da antena aerial mast (plate A 10). ~ de bandeira flagstaff, flagpole. ~ de cocanha greasy pole. ~ da gata, da mezena mizen-mast (plate B 10). ~ do traquete, da proa foremast. ~ grande mainmast (plate B 10).

mastruço, mastruz s. m. (also mentruz) bitter cress.

masturbação s. f. (pl. -ões) masturbation, onanism.

masturbar-(se) v. to masturbate, practise onanism.

mata s. f. 1. wood, forest, jungle, thicket, copse. 2. (fig.) sea of masts, poles or similar objects. 3. (Braz.) geographical zone of the north-eastern states, between the beach and the barren area, characterized by great fertility and abundant vegetation. 4. (Braz.) southwestern coffee zone of the state of Minas Gerais. 5. = matadura. 6. (sl.) secondhand dealer.

~ virgem wild forest, deep jungle.

mata-bicho s. m. (pl. mata-bichos) 1. dram of white rum or another alcoholic beverage. 2. (sl.) tip, gratuity. 3. (pop.) = cachaça.

mata-boi s. m. (pl. mata-bois) (S. Braz.) 1. leather strip joining the axle of an oxcart to the platform. 2. leather strip for joining the beam of an oxcart to the yoke.

mata-borrão s. m. (pl. mata-borrões) 1. blotting paper (plate E 2). 2. (Braz., fig., sl.) drunkard, alcoholic.

mata-burro s. m. (pl. mata-burros) (Braz.) cattle-guard at gates or crossings, consisting of a bridge of isolated planks.

mata-cachorro s. m .(pl. mata-cachorros) 1. (N. Braz., also cachimbo, gafonha, galo-enfeitado, macaco, meganha, morcego) nickname of a policeman. 2. name of two plants of the family Connaraceae (Bernardinia fluminensis and Connarus cymosus).

matacalado s. m. plant of the family Flacourtiaceae (Patrisia acuminata).

matacão s. m. (pl. -ões) 1. small stone. 2. large slice or piece. 3. sideburns or beard that leaves the chin uncovered. 4. (Braz.) large loose stone coming from a decomposing rock, boulder.

mata-cão s. m. (pl. **mata-cães**) aconite.

mata-cavalo s. m. (pl. **mata-cavalos**) (also **cavalo-de-cão**) 1. plant of the nightshade family (Solanum ciliatum).

a ~s at full speed, galloping.

mataco s. m. (Braz.) buttocks.

mata-cobra s. m. (pl. **mata-cobras**) 1. cudgel. 2. a variety of ants (Euponera marginata).

matado adj. (Braz.) 1. badly done, badly finished, without value, bad. 2. harvested before ripened and then ripened artificially (fruit). 3. full of riding sores (horse).

matador s. m. 1. killer, assassin, murderer. 2. matador (bullfights). 3. (fig.) tedious, tiresome person. 4. (S. Braz.) irresistible man, lady-killer, charmer. 5. **~es** pl.: a) principal trumps. b) all means necessary for the obtainment of some purpose. || adj. killing, murderous, deadly.

matadora s. f. 1. murderess. 2 (S. Braz.) fascinating woman. || adj. f. killing.

matadouro s. m. (also **matadoiro**) 1. packing house, shambles, butchery, slaughterhouse. 2. unhealthy place.

matadura s. f. 1. (also **mata**) riding sore, gall, blister (horses). 2. (fig.) moral defect.

mata-fome s. m. (pl. **mata-fomes**) (Braz.) common name of two vegetables with edible fruits (Paulinia sp. and Cordia sellowiana).

matagal s. m. (pl. -ais) 1. jungle, dense forest, underwood, thicket, brushwood, brake. 2. anything resembling a jungle or brake.

mata-gato s. m. (pl. **mata-gatos**) (Braz.) river fish of the family Caracinidae (Brycon falcatus).

matagoso adj. copsy, brushy, overgrown with brushes.

mata-junta s. f. (pl. **mata-juntas**) (constr.) batten: wooden lath used to cover up the space between boards.

mata-leopardos s. m., sg. + pl. aconite.

matalotado adj. provisioned: supplied with provisions (ship).

matalotagem s. f. (pl. -ens) 1. provisions, food supply for a ship, victuals. 2. (fig.) bunch of sundry things. 3. amalgam.

matalote s. m. 1. sailor, mariner. 2. fellow traveller, travelling companion. 3. working companion, fellow worker. 4. ship that precedes another serving as a mark for her maneuvers. 5. (ant.) cunning, sly person; rascal.

matamatá s. m. (zool.) matamata; bearded tortoise.

matambre s. m. (S. Braz.) rib beef, meat sitting on the ribs of an ox and the first to be stripped after the hiding.

matame s. m. (Braz.) 1. scallops: angular cuts in the extremity of pleats, women's shirts, bed sheets, etc. 2. meat which after the skinning remains on the hide.

mata-mosquito s. m. (pl. **mata-mosquitos**) (Braz.) employee of the Sanitary and Hygiene Department who kills mosquito larvae and destroys their breeding places.

mata-mouros s. m., sg. + pl. (also **mata-moiros**) braggart, bully.

matança s. f. 1. killing. 2. massacre, bloodshed(ding). 3. slaughter, butchery of animals. 4. violent or brutal game, tough playing. 5. (fig., fam.) = **afã**. 6. (N. Braz.) slaughterhouse.

mata-negro s. f. (pl. **mata-negros**) (Braz.) a variety of manioc.

matão s. m. (pl. -ões) (Braz.) 1. a variety of rice. 2. unfair jockey who tries to crowd the others during the race.

mata-olho s. m. (pl. **mata-olhos**) (Braz.) tree of the family Euphorbiaceae (Ophtalmoblapton pedunculare) (also known as **árvore-de-santa-luzia**, **olho-de-santa-luzia**, **grumaré**).

mata-pasto s. m. (pl. **mata-pastos**) (Braz., also known as **caquera** f.) 1. coffeeweed, fetid cassia. 2. Christmas bush. 3. ringworm bush.

mata-pau s. m. (pl. **mata-paus**) (Braz.) name given to various plants of the families Bombacaceae, Guttiferae and Moraceae.

matapi s. m. (N. Braz.) basket made of a palm fibre with an opening at the base (used for fishing).

mata-piolho s. m. (pl. **mata-piolhos**) (pop.) thumb.

matar v. 1. to kill, murder. 2. to destroy, annihilate. 3. to slaughter, butcher. 4. to extinguish, eliminate, end, put out, quench, satiate, wither, wash out. 5. to ruin, discredit. 6. to win, bag (games). 7. to do s. th. fast and badly, to botch. 8. (fig.) to annoy, pester. 9. to satisfy, quench (hunger, thirst). 10. **~-se**: a) to commit suicide. b) to ruin one's health. c) to kill o. s. working. d) to sacrify o. s. **~ a fome** to appease the stomach, the hunger. **~ à** or **de fome** to famish. **~ alguém** to kill s. o. **~ a sede** to quench one's thirst. **~ a tiro** to shoot (dead), to kill by a shot. **~ de amores** to inspire a great passion. **~ de inveja** to turn green with envy. **~ dois coelhos com uma só cajadada** to kill two birds with one stone. **~ o bicho** to have a drink. **~ o tempo** to dally, waste time, kill time, while away the time, to dawdle one's time away. **~ o tempo cavaqueando** to talk away. **~-se por** to pine for, yearn after. **bater a ~** to beat to death. **comer a ~** to eat o. s. to death. **o calor matou as plantas** the heat has withered the plants. **o trabalho mata-o** the work is getting him down. **que me matem se...** I'll be shot if... **você se mata trabalhando** you toil yourself to death. **~ as aulas** to play truant.

matarana s. f. 1. (Braz.) mace with sharp edges on one extremity and a point on the other. 2. plant of the family Zingiberaceae (Renealmia sylvestris).

mata-ratos s. m., sg. + pl. (Braz., also **mata-rato**) 1. rat poison. 2. wine, cigar, or cigarrete of cheap and inferior quality. || adj. adequate to kill rats.

mataria s. f. (Braz.) great stretch of woods.

mataru s. m. (Braz.) clay jar used in fish oil making.

mata-sanos s. m., sg. + pl. (also **mata-sano**) 1. witch doctor. 2. quack.

matassa s. f. 1. raw silk. 2. silk before it is spun.

mate s. m. 1. checkmate. 2. casting off (of meshes at knitting). 3. = **remate**. 4. maté, mate, Paraguay tea: plant and beverage. || adj. dim, opaque, marred, dull.

~ chimarrão mate without sugar. **~ de armada curta** very hot mate. **aquentar água para o ~ dos outros** to slave for the benefit of others.

mateador s. m. (S. Braz., also **matista**) person very fond of maté.

matear v. (S. Braz.) 1. to drink maté. 2. to run around in the woods, spend the day in the woods.

mateiro s. m. 1. forest keeper, forester. 2. (Braz.) feller, woodman. 3. explorer of forests. 4. person who guides himself through forests without compass, through mere instinct. 5. (zool.) brocket: a small S. American deer (Mazama americana). 6. (N. Braz.) person opening up seringa paths in the forest. 7. (N. Braz.) inhabitant of the Zona da

Mata in the state of Bahia. 8. = **caipira**. 9. exploiter of maté.

matejar v. 1. to ramble through the woods. 2. to cut wood, fell trees.

matemática s. f. mathematics. ~s **aplicadas** applied mathematics. ~s **puras** pure mathematics.

matemático s. m. mathematician. ‖ adj. 1. mathematical. 2. (fig.) exact, correct. ‖ **matematicamente** adv. mathematically.

mateologia s. f. mateology: 1. the useless study of things above human comprehension. 2. meaningless speech.

mateológico adj. pertaining to the study of mateology.

mateologista s. m. + f. person occupied with mateology.

mateotecnia s. f. mateotechny: useless, fantastic science.

matéria s. f. 1. matter: a) substance, stuff, material. b) subject, topic. c) pus. d) subject-matter of a message, news, etc. e) subject-matter in school. 2. opportunity, chance. 3. pretext, cause. ~ **corante** colouring matter. ~ **de ensino** discipline. ~ **orgânica** organic matters. **entrar na** ~ to get down to business.

material s. f. (pl. **-ais**) 1. material: a) stuff, matter, substance. b) building material. 2. household, school or any other utensils or implements; material. ‖ adj. m. + f. 1. material: a) solid. b) perceptible to the senses or one particular sense. c) crude, raw. d) sensual. e) corporeal, bodily, incarnate. 2. occasional. ‖ ~**mente** adv. materially, etc. ~ **de construção** building material. ~ **elétrico** electrical fittings (plate M 5). ~ **rodante** (railway) rolling stock.

materialão s. m. (pl. **-ões**) (f. **materialona**) gross materialist. ‖ adj. 1. materialistic. 2. bestial.

materialeira s. f. (hum.) something material and crude.

materialidade s. f. 1. materiality. 2. stupidity. 3. vile sentiments.

materialismo s. m. materialism.

materialista s. m. + f. 1. materialist. 2. (Braz.) dealer in construction materials. ‖ adj. m. + f. materialistic.

materialização s. f. (pl. **-ões**) materialization.

materializar v. 1. to materialize. 2. to become crude, stupid. 3. to become corporeal.

matéria-prima s. f. (pl. **matérias-primas**) raw material.

matério-espiritual adj. m. + f. (pl. **matério-espirituais**) (Braz.) half material, half spiritual.

maternal adj. m. + f. (pl. **-ais**) maternal, mother(ly), motherlike. ‖ ~**mente** adv. maternally, motherly. **amor** ~ mother love.

maternidade s. f. maternity: 1. motherhood. 2. maternity ward, lying-in-hospital.

Vossa Maternidade dear Reverend Mother: form of addressing mother superiors of a sisterhood.

materno adj. 1. maternal: a) motherly. b) related on the mother's side. 2. kind, sweet, charitable. **avô** ~ grandfather from the mother's side. **língua** -a native language.

matesiologia s. f. mathesis: science of general teaching and education.

matetê s. m. (N. Braz.) thick broth enriched with seasoning and flour.

maticar v. (only used in the third person) to bay, give a sign by barking (hounds).

matidez s. f. quality of a low deadened sound.

matilha s. f. 1. pack of hounds. 2. (fig.) gang of rascals.

matimpererê s. m. (Braz.) = **saci-pererê**, **saci**.

matina s. f. daybreak, dawn.

matinada s. f. 1. dawn, daybreak. 2. rising at dawn. 3. matins. 4. noise, crash, hubbub. 5. morning performance. 6. racket, charivari.

matinador adj. (Braz., pop.) 1. talkative, loquacious, verbose. 2. noisy, brawling, boisterous. 3. untruthful, mendacious, lying.

matinal adj. m. + f. (pl. **-ais**) 1. matinal, matutinal, matutine. 2. rising early.

matinar v. 1. to awaken betimes. 2. to rise early. 3. to sing the matins. 4. (fig.) to train, break in (animals). 5. to try insistently to convince s. o.; to importune. 6. to instruct, exercise. 7. (Braz.) to fancy something, brood over something.

matinas s. f. pl. matins.

matinê s. f. 1.ᵃ matinée. 2. house coat worn by women.

matineiro s. m. 1. (ant.) the matin prayer book. 2. ~s pl. confraternity which sings the matins. ‖ adj. said of the matin prayer book.

matintapereira, matintaperera s. m. (Braz., also **matitaperê**) the striped cuckoo.

matirão s. m. (pl. **-ões**) (ornith.) yellow-crowned night heron.

matista s. m. + f. (S. Braz.) person fond of mate.

matiz s. m. 1. tint, tincture, tinge, tone, hue, shade. 2. delicate gradation of colours, nuance. 3. blending of colours. 4. (fig.) colouring in style. 5. (fig.) political colour, party.

matização s. f. (pl. **-ões**) shading, tinting, variegation.

matizado adj. 1. variegated, many-coloured, multicoloured, party-coloured, shaded. 2. iridescent, opalescent, versicoloured, toned.

matizar v. 1. to variegate, give diverse hues, shade. 2. to adorn, embellish. 3. ~-**se** to take diverse colours.

mato s. m. 1. wood, brush, brushwood, thicket, jungle, forest (plate F 4). 2. (Braz.): a) the country in opposition to the city. b) (sl.) great quantity. ~ **bom** woods with a rich vegetation indicating fertile soil, good for cultivation. ~ **grosso** (Braz.) dense wood, forest. ~ **mau** (S. Braz., also **catanduva**) woods with poor soil unsuited for agriculture. ~ **ralo** thin forest. **a caça saiu do** ~ the game broke cover. **botar no** ~ (N. Braz.) to throw out, discard. **dinheiro no bolso dele é** ~ (pop.) he is loaded with dough. **estar ou ficar no** ~ **sem cachorro** (Braz., pop.) to be in a tight spot. **ganhar o** ~ (Braz., fig., pop.) to run away, disappear. **ser** ~ (pop.) to exist in abundance.

mato-grossense s. m. + f. (pl. **mato-grossenses**) (Braz.) native or inhabitant of Mato Grosso. ‖ adj. of or pertaining to Mato Grosso.

matolão s. m. (pl. **-ões**) (N. Braz.) leather satchel used (by the inlanders) for clothes and travel utensils.

matombo s. m. (Braz.) = **matumbo**.

matoso adj. covered with wood, brushy, full of brush; jungly, jungled.

matraca s. f. 1. rattle. 2. (fig.) kidding, ribbing, mockery, jeering, scoffing. 3. (ornith.) = **martim-pescador**. 4. (Braz., fam.) eloquent, talkative fellow, prattler.

matracar v. 1. to insist impertinently on something. 2. to harp on, repeat monotonously. 3. to bore, annoy, plague.

matracolejante adj. m. + f. rattling, clattering, chattering.

matracolejar v. to rattle, clatter, chatter.

matraqueado adj. 1. experienced, shrewd. 2. sly, knowing.

matraqueador s. m. 1. scoffer, jeerer. 2. experienced person. 3. knowing guy.

matraquear v. 1. to rattle. 2. to boo, jeer, scoff, rail. 3. to mutiny. 4. to teach, educate, train.

matraz s. m. matrass: retort, glass vase for chemical operations.

matreirar, matreirear v. 1. to become restive, having run away into the woods; stray (animal). 2. (fig.) to be furtive, sly, knowing. 3. to evade business, deals, contracts, to shift.

matreirice s. f. slyness, smartness, shrewdness, craftiness, sagaciousness, artfulness, cunning, astuteness.

matreiro adj. 1. sly, artful, smart, shrewd, crafty, sagacious, cunning, astute. 2. (S. Braz.) furtive, dodgy, shy. 3. feline.

matriarca s. f. matriarch.

matriarcado s. m. matriarchy.

matriarcal adj. m. + f. (pl. **-ais**) matriarchal, matriarchic.

matricária s. f. (bot.) chamomile, camomile (Matricaria chamomilla).

matricida s. m. + f. matricide: murderer of one's own mother.

matricídio s. m. matricide: murder of one's own mother.

matrícula s. f. 1. registration. 2. matriculation fee. 3. matriculation book, register, roll, roster.

matriculado adj. 1. matriculated, registered, enrolled. 2. (pop.) experienced, knowing, capable, cut out for the job.

matricular v. to matriculate, register, enroll. **ele matriculou-se na universidade** he entered the university.

matrilinear adj. m. + f. pertaining to the female line of succession.

matrilocal adj. m. + f. (pl. **-ais**) (ethn.) matrilocal: pertaining to the institution according to which a husband has to follow his wife to her house, village, etc.

matrimonial adj. m. + f. (pl. **-ais**) matrimonial, nuptial, conjugal, spousal, connubial. ‖ **~mente** adv. matrimonially.

matrimoniar v. to unite in matrimony, to marry, wed.

matrimônio s. m. matrimony, marriage, wedlock. **~ dissolvido** dissolved marriage. **~ clandestino** clandestine marriage. **~ consumado** consummated marriage. **~ morganático** left-handed or morganatical marriage. **~ rato** legal marriage not consummated. **contrair ~** to contract marriage, to marry. **filhos do primeiro, do segundo ~** children of the first, of the second wife or husband.

matrinxão s. m. (pl. **-ões**) (Braz.) a characinid river fish, also known as **mamuri.**

mátrio adj. pertaining to the mother.

matritense s. m. + f., adj. m. + f. = **madrileno.**

matriz s. f. 1. matrix: a) uterus, womb. b) (math.) matrix of a determinant. c) origin, spring, source. d) (typogr.) mat, mold for casting type. 2. main house, main office. ‖ adj. m. + f. 1. original, primitive, primordial. 2. main, principal. **~ coronária** coronary matrix (plate C 9). **~ predial** register of real estate, cadastre. **~ quadrada** (math.) square matrix of n² constituents, disposed in n columns and n rows. **~ retangular** (math.) matrix of mn constituents, disposed in m columns and n rows. **igreja ~** mother church.

matroca s. f. word used in the expression: **à ~** by chance, at random, haphazard, in vain.

matrona s. f. (fam.) 1. matron: woman respected due to age, estate, conduct. 2. mother of a family. 3. old or elderly lady. 4. (fam.) woman of manly manners, virago.

matronaça s. f. (fam.) fat and husky woman.

matronal adj. m. + f. (pl. **-ais**) matronly.

matrucar v. (Braz.) to cut up slaughtered cattle.

matruco s. m. (Braz., Rio) 1. hind quarters of slaughtered cattle. 2. meat train.

matruqueiro s. m. (Braz.) butcher who cuts up slaughtered cattle.

matula s. f. 1. gang, rabble, mob. 2. (Braz.) travelling provisions carried in the knapsack.

matulagem s. f. (pl. **-ens**) 1. gang of vagrants or tramps. 2. vagrants or tramps collectively. 3. idleness, vagrancy.

matulão s. m. (pl. **-ões**) (f. **matulona**) (also **matolão**) 1. lazybones, vagrant, vagabond, good-for-nothing. 2. tall and sturdy youth.

matumbo s. m. elevation between furrows.

matungada, matungama s. f. (S. Braz.) herd of worthless horses.

matungão s. m. (pl. **-ões**) (S. Braz.) large unspirited horse.

matungo s. m. 1. (S. Braz.) oud, worthless horse, jade. 2. horse of poor breed. 3. (Braz., São Paulo) good, strong horse. (In S. Braz. there is a tendency to call any horse a **matungo**).

matupá s. m. 1. (N. Braz.) large masses of fluvial grass at the river banks. 2. (N. Braz., also **pariatã, periantã**) floating banks covered with vegetation.

matupiri s. m. (Braz.) common name for a group of river fishes of the family Characinidae.

maturação s. f. maturation: 1. ripening. 2. maturing. 3. (med.) formation of suppuration.

maturado adj. 1. ripe, mature, seasoned. 2. (fig.) said of a person matured through study, work, experience.

maturar v. to mature: 1. ripen. 2. (fig.) become mature through study, work, experience; to reach maturity, full development.

maturativo adj. maturative: 1. helping maturation. 2. (med.) promoting suppuration.

maturescência s. f. maturescence: quality or state of maturity.

maturi s. m. 1. peduncle of the unripe cashew. 2. the green unripe cashew before the evolution of the peduncle.

maturidade s. f. 1. maturity, matureness, ripeness, mellowness. 2. (fig.) maturity of spirit. 3. (fig.) perfection. **chegar à ~** to come of age.

maturo adj. = **maduro.**

maturrangada s. f. 1. (S. Braz.) herd of worthless horses. 2. fault in horsemanship. 3. badly carried out field-work, as if done by an unskilled farm hand.

maturrango s. m. 1. (S. Braz., also **maturrengo**) 1. poor rider. 2. field-worker unable to handle cattle and horses.

maturrão s. m. (pl. **-ões**) (S. Braz.) old or blind beast of burden, useless for work.

maturranguear v. (also **maturrangar, maturenguear**) (S. Braz.) to do things worthy of a **maturrango.**

maturu s. m. (Braz.) clay jar used in the production of fish-oil.

matusalém s. m. (fam.) Methuselah: very old person, macrobiote.

matusalêmico adj. (Braz.) long-living, long-lived, macrobiotic.

matusquela s. m. + f. (S. E. Braz., sl.) balmy, crazy person.

matutada s. f. (N. Braz.) bunch of rustics, yokels, backwoodsmen.

matutagem s. f. (pl. **-ens**) 1. (Braz.) = **matutice.** 2. (N. Braz., pop.) = **matalotagem.** **fazer ~** to slaughter cattle, usually for festive occasions.

matutar v. 1. (pop.) to think, brood, muse, meditate, reflect, ponder. 2. to plan, try, essay. **~ em** to muse on.

matutice s. f. 1. appearance, manners, or actions of a boor or bumpkin. 2. mania, whim.

matutinário s. m. (also matineiro) book of matutines.
matutino s. m. 1. morning newspaper. 2. ~s pl. (obs.) = matinas. ‖ adj. (also matutinal m. + f.) matutinal, early, pertaining to or occurring in the morning, rising early.
matuto s. m. 1. (N. Braz.) fieldworker, boor, backwoodsman, bushwhacker. 2. hillbilly. 3. rustic and naive person (see caipira). ‖ adj. 1. living in the woods, in the interior; rustic, peasant, boorish. 2. (N. Braz.) timid, shy, untrusting, awkward. 3. (fam.) sly, crafty, cunning.
mau s. m. 1. bad, evil. 2. person of bad character. ‖ adj. (f. má; abs. superl. malíssimo, péssimo) 1. bad, evil, harmful, noxious, pernicious. 2. mean, perverse, vicious, malicious, mischievous, malignant, ill-natured, wicked, naughty, ill-mannered. 3. wrongful. 4. poor. ‖ interj. expressing reproval. ‖ mamente adv. (pop.) malevolently.
~ caráter bad character. ~ cheiro bad smell. ~ condutor bad conductor. ~ jeito wrick. ~ negócio bad bargain. ~ pagador bad payer. ~ procedimento misbehaviour. ~s modos bad manners. ~ tempo bad weather. ~ trato maltreatment. de ~ agouro ill-omened. de ~ humor ill-tempered, bilious. estamos em ~s lençóis we are in a nice fix. estar em ~ estado to be in a poor condition. más línguas evil tongues. às más inimically; by force. não é ~ it is not bad. ter ~ coração to be hardhearted. ser ~ to be bad, evil.
mauari s. m. (Braz.) = maguari, baguari.
maúba s. f. (Braz.) tree of the family Lauraceae (Licaria mahuba).
maueza s. f. (Braz., pop., see also maldade) badness, perversity.
maújo s. m. (naut.) ravehook, ripping iron.
maula adj. (S. Braz.) bad, cowardly (of man and horse).
maunça s. f. 1. handful. 2. the thin part of a spindle.
mau-olhado s. m. (pl. maus-olhados) evil eye.
mauresco, mauriense adj. = mourisco.
mauritânia s. f. (bot.) sweet william.
mauritano s. m. Mauretanian: native or inhabitant of Mauretania. ‖ adj. Mauretanian: of or pertaining to Mauretania.
mauro s. m. Moor. ‖ adj. Moor, Moorish.
mausoléu s. m. 1. mausoleum. 2. Mausoleum: sepulchral monument of Mausolus, one of the seven wonders of the world.
maviosidade s. f. 1. tenderness, gentleness. 2. sonority, melodiousness.
mavioso adj. 1. affectionate, tender, suave. 2. compassionate. 3. moving, touching. 4. full of harmony, melodious. ‖ -amente adv. affectionately.
mavórcio, mavórtico adj. 1. pertaining to Mars. 2. belligerent.
maxambeta s. f. (Braz., pop.) lie, false tale.
maxambomba s. f. (Braz.) 1. a shaky vehicle. 2. trolley used in the harbours of the Taquari river to load and unload the boats.
maxicote s. m. mortar, made of sand, lime, earth and water.
maxila s. f. 1. maxilla: jaw, jawbone, maxillary bone. 2. maxilla inferior, lower jaw, chin (plate C 17).
maxilar s. m. maxillary. ‖ adj. m. + f. maxillary: pertaining to the jaw or jawbone.
~ superior superior maxillary, upper jaw. ~ inferior inferior maxillary, lower jaw, mandible of vertebrates.
maxilite s. f. infection of the maxilla.
maxiloso adj. having large maxillas.
máxima s. f. 1. maxim, precept, aphorism, axiom, principle. 2. (math.) maxima. 3. (ant.) musical figure.

maximalismo s. m. (pol.) maximalism: former radical socialism in Russia.
maximalista s. m. + f. (pol.) maximalist: adherent of maximalism. ‖ adj. maximalistic.
maximalizar v. to maximize.
maximário s. m. collection of maxims.
máxime adv. principally.
máximo s. m. maximum: the greatest quantity or highest degree attainable in a given case. ‖ adj. maximum, greatest, highest, best, etc. ‖ maximamente adv. principally, to the highest degree.
até o ~ to the utmost. carga -a peak load. com o ~ prazer with the utmost pleasure. com velocidade -a at maximum speed, at top speed. ele trabalhou até o ~ de suas forças he worked to the top of his bent. isto é o ~ que você pode exigir this is the most you can ask. no ~ at the utmost. tirar o ~ proveito de algo to make the most of a thing.
maxissaia s. f. maxiskirt.
maxixar v. to dance the maxixe.
maxixe s. m. 1. maxixe, Brazilian maxixe: a dance which originated in the city of Rio de Janeiro. 2. fruit of the anguria.
maxixeiro s. m. 1. anguria (plant). 2. person fond of the maxixe dance. ‖ adj. liking the maxixe.
mazagrã s. m. cold, watered coffee, served in a glass.
mazagrã s. m. a species of American deer.
mazanza s. m. + f. (Braz., also manzanza) lazybones, idler, sluggard. ‖ adj. lazy, idle, indolent.
mazanzar v. (Braz., also manzanzar) 1. to idle, loiter. 2. to dawdle, take all the time to carry out a job. 3. to become foolish.
mazela s. f. 1. wound, sore, bruise, gall (horse). 2. (fam.) infirmity, illness. 3. (fig.) stain on the reputation, blemish, infamy. 4. deficiency, defect.
mazelar v. 1. to wound, bruise, hurt, gall. 2. to molest. 3. to afflict. 4. to stain, blemish, defile. 5. to feel hurt; to resent; to brood bitterly.
mazeleiro adj. full of sores, wounds, bruises.
mazelento adj. bruised, hurt, stained.
mazombo s. m. (depr.) Brazilian of foreign (esp. Portuguese) parents. ‖ adj. sombre, melancholic, sullen, gloomy, sulky.
mazorca s. f. (Braz.) disorder, turmoil, commotion.
mazorqueiro s. m. (Braz.) person who provokes disorder, rioter. ‖ adj. provoking disorders, riotous.
mazorral adj. m. + f. (pl. -ais) crude, uncivil, rude.
mazorro s. m. crude, uncivil person, ruffian. ‖ adj. 1. crude, uncivil. 2. lazy. 3. sombre.
mazurca s. f. Polish dance and music.
mbacaiá s. m. (Braz.) plant of the family Zingiberaceae (Costus spicatus).
mbaiá s. m. (Braz., also caçada de ~) a method of hunting where the hunter disguises himself as a bush and thus tries to fool the animals.
mbatará s. m. (Braz.) common name of several birds of the family Formicariidae.
mbuí s. m. (Braz.) plant of the composite family (Solidago polyglossa).
me pers. pron. me, to me, myself, to myself (oblique form of the pronoun eu, united with the verb by a hyphen when placed behind it).
ele não ~ disse he did not tell me.
meação s. f. (pl. -ões) 1. halving. 2. division of a wall or fence in two parts, each belonging to a different owner. 3. joint property, the right of co-ownership of one or more objects by two neighbours.
meada s. f. 1. skein: a) coil of yarn. b) tangle. 2. (fig.) plot, intrigue, gossip.
o fio da ~ the clue to the puzzle.

meadeira s. f. (Braz.) reel: machine that makes skeins.

meado s. m. middle, mean. ‖ adj. 1. halved. 2. middle, mean, medial.

no ~ do mês in the middle of the month.

mealha s. f. 1. doit: a) former coin. b) (fig.) bit, spot, touch. 2. crumb.

mealheiro s. m. 1. money box, treasure chest. 2. saved money, savings; lot of doits. ‖ adj. consisting of doits or little money.

meandrar v. to meander, form meanders.

meândrico adj. meandrous, meandering, winding. ‖ **meandricamente** adv. meanderingly.

meandro s. m. meander: 1. winding, turning. 2. entanglement, intrigue.

~ do rio bend of the river.

meante adj. m. + f. 1. halved. 2. in the middle, towards the middle.

mês ~ middle of the month, nearing the middle of the month.

meão s. m. (pl. **meões**) (f. **meã**) 1. (mech.) hub, nave of a wheel. 2. knob on a lid. ‖ adj. 1. mean, median, middle, middling. 2. mediocre. 3. (N. Braz.) relating to a horse that sticks to a medium gait.

mear v. 1. to halve. 2. to reach the middle; to put in the middle.

meato s. m. 1. small canal, passage, passageway. 2. orifice of a canal. 3. (anat.) meatus, foramen, duct.

~ **auditivo** auditory passage.

mecânica s. f. mechanics: 1. science of machinery. 2. branch of physics, comprising kinetics, statics and kinematics.

~ **de precisão** precision mechanics. ~ **aplicada**, ~ **prática** applied, practical mechanics. ~ **dos corpos líquidos** hydromechanics. ~ **dos corpos rígidos** mechanics of rigid bodies. ~ **dos fluidos** mechanics of fluids. ~ **ondulatória** wave mechanics.

mecânico s. m. 1. mechanic, mechanician. 2. person versed in mechanics. ‖ adj. 1. mechanic, mechanical. 2. automatical. ‖ **mecanicamente** adv. mechanically, etc.

~ **de aviação** aircraft mechanic. ~ **de bordo**, ~ **de vôo** (av.) air mechanic, flight mechanic.

mecanismo s. m. 1. mechanism, gear, device, machinery, work; motion (plates M 3, 10). 2. organization.

~ **de acionamento** driving gear. ~ **de alimentação** feeding, feed mechanism. ~ **de avanço** feed gear, feed mechanism. ~ **de comando** head mechanism, controlling mechanism, driving-gear. ~ **de desembreagem** disengaging mechanism. ~ **de desengate** uncoupling mechanism. ~ **de desligar**, ~ **de disparo** releasing mechanism. ~ **de distribuição** (mot.) timing device, timing gear, valve mechanism. ~ **de engate** coupling gear. ~ **de engrenagem** gear, motion. ~ **de governo** control gear. ~ **de inversão de marcha** reversing gear. ~ **de mudança de velocidade** speed change gear. ~ **de propulsão** driving gear. ~ **de relógio** clock work. ~ **de travamento** locking gear, stop gear. ~ **irreversível** irreversible. ~ **reversível**, ~ **de inversão de marcha** reversing gear. ~ **motor** driving gear.

mecanização s. f. (Braz.) mechanization.

mecanizar v. to mechanize.

mecanografia s. f. mechanography.

mecanógrafo s. m. mechanograph.

mecanoterapia s. f. mechanotherapy.

mecanoterápico adj. mechanotherapeutic.

meças s. f. pl. 1. measuring. 2. comparison.

pedir ~ 1. to ask for a verification. 2. to ask for an explanation or satisfaction. 3. to be unafraid of any comparison.

mecê pers. pron. (Braz., pop.) abbr. form of **vossemecê**.

mecenas s. m., sg. + pl. (fig.) Maecenas: protector and fosterer of the arts and sciences.

mecha s. f. 1. fuse, lunt, match. 2. sulphurized paper or rag. 3. wick of a lamp, stove, etc. 4. (med.) tent. 5. (carp.) tenon, tongue, feather (plate C 9).

mechar v. 1. to provide with a wick. 2. to light a fuse. 3. to tent. 4. to fumigate a cask with a sulphurized rag.

mechoação s. m. (bot.) mechoacan: convolvulaceous plant of purgative properties.

meco s. m. (sl.) 1. fellow, chap, individual. 2. libertine, debauchee, rake, lecher. 3. slyboots. 4. cheeky person.

mecômetro s. m. surgical instrument to measure the length of a fetus.

mecônio s. m. 1. meconium: first faeces of a newborn child. 2. juice of poppies.

mecópode adj. m. + f. long-footed.

meda s. f. 1. stack, rick. 2. heap, pile.

~ **de carvão** charcoal-kiln, charcoal pile. ~ **de feno** haystack (plate A 4).

medalha s. f. medal.

~ **comemorativa** commemorative medal. ~ **de honra** prize medal. **o reverso da** ~ the reverse of the medal. **o rosto da** ~ the face of the medal.

medalhão s. m. (pl. **-ões**) 1. medallion. 2. locket (plate J 3). 3. (fig., pop.) VIP, toff. 4. (fig., depr.) stuffed shirt.

medalhar v. 1. to engrave on a medal. 2. to commemorate by issuing medals.

medalhário s. m. cabinet for medals.

medalheiro s. m. 1. collection of medals, place where medals are kept. 2. medalist.

medalhista s. m. + f. person versed in medals.

médão s. m. (pl. **-ãos**) dune along the coast.

medeixes s. m. (pl. (Braz., fam.) 1. excuses. 2. simulated, feigned disdain.

mede-léguas s. m., sg. + pl. (Braz.) (zool.) a nighthawk.

mede-palmos s. m., sg. + pl. common name of various lepidopterous larvae of the geometric moth.

média s. f. 1. mean, medium, average. 2. (Braz.) cup of coffee with milk.

~ **aproximativa** rough average. ~ **aritmética** arithmetic mean. ~ **geométrica** geometric mean. ~ **ponderada** weighted mean, weighted average. ~ **proporcional** mean proportional. **em** ~ as a rule, on the average. **produzir, vender em** ~ to average. **tirar a** ~ to strike an average. **fazer** ~ (Braz.) to wheedle, coax.

mediação s. f. (pl. **-ões**) 1. mediation, intervention, interposition. 2. culmination point of a star.

mediador s. m. (also **medianeiro** and **mediatário**) mediator, intermediary, interposer, interceder, go-between, arbiter. ‖ adj. mediatory, mediatorial, mediating, arbitrating.

servir de ~ to go between.

medial s. f. (pl. **-ais**) medial, medial linguistic element. ‖ adj. m. + f. medial, in the middle of the word.

mediana s. f. (also **valor mediano** m.) median: 1. (geom.) straight line joining the vertex of a triangle to the middle of the opposite side. 2. (stat.) central value or number in a given series.

mediania s. f. 1. median quality. 2. middle term. 3. mediocrity. 4. mean between richness and poverty. 5. (fig.) moderation.

mediano adj. 1. average, mean, median, medium, mesial. 2. mediocre, middling, ordinary.

homem de estatura -a a middle-sized man.

mediante s. m. interim, meantime. ‖ adj. m. + f. intermediary. ‖ prep. by means of, by the aid of, through, against.

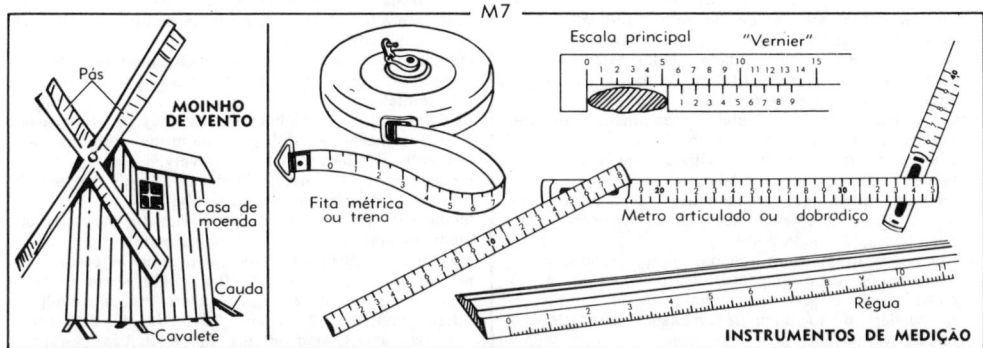

M7

MOINHO DE VENTO — Pás, Casa de moenda, Cauda, Cavalete

Fita métrica ou trena

Escala principal — "Vernier"

Metro articulado ou dobradiço

Régua

INSTRUMENTOS DE MEDIÇÃO

~ os bons ofícios de through the kind offices of. ~ pagamento à vista against cash payment.

mediar v. 1. to halve. 2. to mediate, act as an arbiter. 3. to interfere, intervene, interpose, intercede. 4. to be in the middle, lie between. 5. to be. or happen between two eras. 6. to diverge, be away from.

mediastinite s. f. infection of the tissue of the mediastinum.

mediastino s. m. (anat.) mediastinum: space between the pleurae, at the median line of the thorax.

mediato adj. indirect, mediate. ‖ **-amente** adv. mediately, indirectly.

mediatriz s. f. (geom.) mediatrix.

médica s. f. 1. feminine of **médico**, female physician, lady-doctor. 2. medic: a variety of clover; lucerne.

medicação s. f. (pl. **-ões**) medication, medical treatment.

medical adj. m. + f. (pl. **-ais**) medical: relating to medicine. ‖ **~mente** adv. medically.

medicamentação s. f. (pl. **-ões**) 1. = **medicação**. 2. medical treatment.

medicamentar v. 1. to medicate. 2. to administer medicaments.

medicamento s. m. medicine, medicament, remedy, drug.

medicamentoso adj. medicamental, medicinal.

medição s. f. (pl. **-ões**) measurement, measuring, measuration.
instrumentos de ~ instruments for measuring (plate M 7).

medicar v. 1. to practise medicine. 2. to administer medicaments. 3. to medicate. 4. to take medicaments.

medicastro s. m. quack.

medicativo adj. medicative, medicinal.

medicatriz s. f. substance of medicamental properties. ‖ adj. curing, healing, medicinal.

medicável adj. m. + f. (pl. **-áveis**) medicable, curable.

medicina s. f. 1. medicine: a) medicament. b) science of preserving health and curing diseases. 2. (fig.) remedy for an evil.
~ legal legal medicine.

medicinal adj. m. + f. (pl. **-ais**) medicinal: relating to medicine. ‖ **~mente** adv. medically.

medicinar v. to practise medicine, medicate.

medicineiro s. m. medicinal bush of the family Euphorbiaceae (Jatropha officinalis).

médico s. m. 1. physician, medico, doctor, practitioner. 2. (fig.) remedy. ‖ adj. medical, medicinal.
~ assistente 1. physician who regularly attends a person. 2. assistant surgeon. ~ da família family doctor. ~ de clínica geral general practitioner. ~ de senhoras specialist for women's diseases. ~

escolar school doctor. ~ **espiritual** confessor. ~ **interno** house physician. ~ **legista** coroner. ~ **operador** surgeon. ~ **psiquiatra** alienist. **consultar um** ~ to see a doctor. **mandar chamar o** ~ to send for the doctor. **tratamento** ~ medical treatment.

medida s. f. 1. measure, standard of measurement. 2. an instrument for measuring. 3. measuring, measurement, admeasurement. 4. measure, extent, dimension, size. 5. gauge. 6. degree. 7. proportion, limit, range. 8. means to an end. 9. standard. 10. computation, calculation. 11. measure, step. 12. moderation. 13. order, just measure. 14. judgment, circumspection. 15. musical measure, metre.
~ **acertada** right move. ~ **de capacidade** measure of capacity, liquid or dry measure. ~ **de comprimento** long measure. ~ **de superfície** square measure. ~ **de volume** cubic measure. ~ **padrão** standard. ~s **anticoncepcionais** contraception, birth control. ~s **de urgência** emergency steps. ~s **extremas** extreme measures, extremities. **ele tomou** ~s **extremas** he went to extremities. **à** ~ **de** in proportion to. **feito sob** ~ tailor-made, made to order. **não estar com meias** ~ not to take half measures. **sem** ~ without measure, immoderate, beyond all bounds. **tirar a** ~ **de** to take the measurements of. **tomar as devidas** ~s to take measures accordingly. **encher as** ~s 1. to satisfy completely. 2. to exceed all bounds. ~ **de segurança** a security measure.

medidagem s. f. (pl. **-ens**) 1. work of measuring. 2. a measurer's fee in kind.

medidor s. m. measurer, meter (plate E 3). ‖ adj. measuring.
~ **de água** water meter (plate E 3). ~ **de gás** gas-meter (plate E 3).

medieval adj. m. + f. (pl. **-ais**) (also **mediévico**) medieval: pertaining to the Middle Ages.

medievalismo s. m. (also **medievismo**) 1. medievalism: a) ideas and practices of the Middle Ages. b) civilization of the Middle Ages. c) predilection for medieval ideas and practices. 2. designation for modern schools of thought which try to revive the ideals of the Middle Ages.

medievalista s. m. + f. (also **medievista**) medievalist: 1. person versed in matters of the Middle Ages. 2. adherent of medievalism. ‖ adj. m. + f. relating to medievalism.

medievo adj. medieval.

medimarímetro s. m. instrument used to determine the medial level of the sea.

médio s. m. (ftb.) halfback (plate F 9). ‖ adj. mean, medium, mesial, middle, average, intermediate, median.
~ **direito** right halfback (plate F 9). ~ **esquerdo**

left halfback (plate F 9). **classe -a** middle class. **com a velocidade -a de noventa quilômetros por hora** at an average of ninety kilometres an hour. **dedo** ~ middle finger. **Idade Média** Middle Ages. **vida -a** (stat.) average lifetime. **vida -a ao nascer** expectation of life at birth.

mediocracia s. f. 1. social predominancy of the middle classes. 2. middle class.

medíocre s. m. something without much merit or value. ‖ adj. m. + f. mediocre, average, mean, medium, middling, commonplace, second-rate, ordinary. ‖ **mediocremente** adv. in a mediocre manner, tolerably, moderately.

medir v. 1. to measure, gauge, mete, survey. 2. to measure up to a standard. 3. to appraise. 4. to consider. 5. to eye provokingly. 6. to refrain. 7. to ponder. 8. to compete, measure strength and forces with, fight. ~ **alguém dos pés à cabeça** to measure a person with one's eyes. ~ **as palavras** to weigh one's words. ~ **as suas forças com alguém** to try one's strength against s. o. ~ **os outros por si** to judge of another's actions by our own. ~ **todos pela mesma bitola** to measure all by the same yardstick. **não** ~ **esforços** to grudge no pains. **não ter mãos a** ~ to have much on one's hands.

meditabundo adj. (also **meditativo**) pondering, meditating, contemplative, pensive, reflective, melancholic, ruminative, thoughtful, musing.

meditação s. f. (pl. **-ões**) meditation: 1. thought, cogitation, ponderation, rumination, contemplation, reflection, musing. 2. contemplation: deep reflection on religious things.

meditador s. m. meditator. ‖ adj. meditating, meditative.

meditar s. m. meditation. ‖ v. to meditate, cogitate, muse, think, ponder, ruminate, reflect, contemplate, brood.

meditativo adj. (also **meditabundo**) meditative.

meditável adj. m. + f. (pl. **-áveis**) worth meditation.

mediterrâneo s. m. Mediterranean. ‖ adj. Mediterranean, midland.

mediterrânico adj. Mediterranean.

médium s. m. + f. (pl. **médiuns**) spiritualistic medium.

mediúnico adj. referring to a medium, mediumistic.

mediunidade s. f. mediumism, mediumship.

medo s. m. 1. Mede: native or inhabitant of Media. 2. = **medão**. ‖ adj. Median: of or pertaining to Media.

medo (ê) s. m. fear, fright, dread, awe, terror.

medonho s. m. a bird, also known as **mandrião**. ‖ adj. awful, frightful, horrible, forbidding, dreadful, fearful, dreary, hideous. ‖ **-amente** adv. awfully, etc.

medra s. f. (also **medrança**) 1. prosperity, progress, thriving. 2. growth, development. 3. growing, increase, augmentation.

medrar v. 1. to prosper, progress, thrive, flourish. 2. to grow, develop. 3. to augment, increase. 4. to improve, meliorate. 5. to promote, foster.

medrica s. m. + f. chickenhearted person.

medronhal s. m. (pl. **-ais**) strawberry tree grove.

medronheiro s. m. strawberry tree (Arbutus unedo).

medronho s. m. fruit of the strawberry tree. ‖ adj. said of a screw having the shape of this fruit.

medroso adj. 1. fearful, frightful, timid, timorous, chickenhearted, fainthearted, frightened. 2. timid. 3. awful. ‖ **-amente** adv. fearfully, etc.

medula s. f. 1. medulla: a) (anat.) marrow, inner part of some organs (kidney), pith (hair). b) (bot.) pith. 2. (fig.) the most intimate part, pith, essence, substance.

~ **óssea** bone marrow. ~ **espinhal** spinal marrow. ~ **supra-renal** soft marrowlike centre of the suprarenal. **até a** ~ to the quick.

medular v. (ant.) to run through, penetrate to the medulla. ‖ adj. m. + f. 1. medullary, pithy. 2. essential.

meduloso adj. 1. medullose, marrowy. 2. term used to designate the ability to paint or sculpture well a soft, flexible object. 3. velvety.

medusa s. f. 1. (myth.) Medusa. 2. ugly woman. 3. (zool.) medusa, sea-nettle, jellyfish.

medusário adj. medusan; pertaining to the jellyfish.

medúseo, medúsico adj. horrible, awful.

meeira s. f. (Braz.) the second picking of cotton.

meeiro s. m. 1. person having half a share in business or interest. 2. (agric.) share cropper. ‖ adj. 1. half; divisible. 2. equally divided into two parts. 3. (N. Braz.) said of the horse that sticks to a medium gait.

mefistofélico adj. Mephistophelian, diabolic, sarcastic.

mefítico adj. mephitic, noxious, pestilential.

mefitismo s. m. 1. mephitis. 2. caused by mephitis. 3. paludism.

megaciclo s. m. (radio) megacycle.

megafone s. m. megaphone.

megalanto adj. (bot.) having large flowers.

megalegoria s. f. pompous style.

megálito s. m. megalith: prehistoric monumental stone or stone monument.

megalítico adj. megalithic: relating to megaliths.

megalocefalia s. f. megalocephaly.

megalocéfalo adj. megacephalic, megacephalous: large-headed.

megalógono adj. said of crystals whose sides form very obtuse angles.

megalografia s. f. megalography: descriptions or paintings of very important and noteworthy facts.

megalomania s. f. megalomania: 1. delusion of grandeur. 2. mania for big or great things.

megalômano s. m. megalomaniac: person suffering from megalomania. ‖ adj. (also **megalomaníaco**) megalomaniac.

megalopia s. f. = **macropsia**.

megalópole s. f. megalopolis.

megalóporo adj. having large pores.

megalossauro s. m. megalosaurus, megalosaur: extinct genus of gigantic terrestrial carnivorous reptiles.

megâmetro s. m. megameter: 1. instrument to measure angular distances between the stars. 2. instrument to determine nautical longitudes.

megascópico adj. megascopic(al): 1. macroscopic(al), perceptible without the aid of a microscope. 2. enlarged (said of images).

megascópio s. m. megascope: 1. (phot.) enlarging camera. 2. sort of magic lantern.

megatério s. m. megathere, megatherium: genus of extinct huge slothlike animals.

megera s. f. 1. (myth.) Megaera. 2. cruel woman, shrew, vixen, termagant, grimalkin. 3. cruel mother.

megistocéfalo adj. megacephalous: large-headed.

meia s. f. 1. stocking, hose, sock, knitwork (plate R 6). 2. old Portuguese measure for liquids. ~ **elástica** elastic stocking. ~s **curtas** half hose, socks. (plate R 6). ~s **de lã** worsted stockings. **estar de** ~s to be stockinged. **fazer pé de** ~ to build up savings. **um par de** ~s a pair of stockings. **ponta da** ~ toe. **ponto de** ~ stocking stitch. **cerzidor de** ~s stocking darner.

meia-água s. f. (pl. **meias-águas**) one plane roof, lean-to roof.

meia-calça s. f. (pl. **meias-calças**) pantyhose.

meia-cana s. f. (pl. **meias-canas**) (archit.) 1. flute. 2. concave frame. 3. half-round file (plate L 3). **de** ~ channelled, fluted, grooved.

meia-canha s. f. (pl. **meias-canhas**) (S. Braz.) square dance danced to the tune of a polka.

meia-cara s. m. + f. (pl. **meias-caras**) 1. slave imported secretly when traffic was already forbidden. 2. individual without importance. **de** ~ (Braz.) gratis, clandestine.

meia-colher s. m. (pl. **meias-colheres**) (Braz.) a bricklayer's assistant, hodman.

meia-confecção s. f. (pl. **meias-confecções**) half ready--made garment.

meia-direita s. m. (pl. **meias-direitas**) (ftb.) inside right (plate F 9).

meia-esquadria s. f. (pl. **meias-esquadrias**) 1. line dividing the right angle in the middle. 2. miter joint, miter square.

meia-esquerda s. m. (pl. **meias-esquerdas**) (ftb.) inside left (plate F 9).

meia-idade s. f. 1. middle age: period of life between thirty and fifty. 2. (Port.) Middle Ages. **homem de** ~ middle-aged man.

meia-laranja s. f. (pl. **meias-laranjas**) 1. (Braz.) gentle, rounded hill. 2. (naut.) companion hatch.

meia-lona s. m. (pl. **meias-lonas**) coarse linen fabric.

meia-lua s. f. (pl. **meias-luas**) 1. half-moon. 2. crescent. 3. half-moon of the nail. 4. (naut.) yoke of a rudder. 5. (S. Braz.) sign of the form of a crescent on the forehead of some animals. 6. (N. Braz.) fishing boat whose bow and stern end in a point.

meia-nau s. f. middle and longitudinal line of a ship, equidistant of the gunwhales. **a** ~ (naut.) amidship, amidships.

meia-noite s. f. (pl. **meias-noites**) midnight.

meia-praça s. m. (pl. **meias-praças**) (N. Braz.) diamond or gold miner who receives provisions and works on half-share.

meia-rédea s. f. (pl. **meias-rédeas**) gait of the horse faster than a canter and slower than a fast gallop.

meia-rotunda s. f. (pl. **meias-rotundas**) semicircular construction.

meias s. f. pl. half-shares, contract dividing equally gains and losses between the two contractants. **trabalhar a** ~ to work on a fifty-fifty basis.

meia-tigela s. f. used only in the adv. phrase **de** ~ of no value, of no importance, mediocre, vulgar, second-rate.

meia-tinta s. f. (pl. **meias-tintas**) half-tint, demitint: 1. shading of colours. 2. hue of a colour between light and dark. 3. mezzotint: process of engraving.

meigo adj. sweet, tender, suave, gentle, meek, mild, tenderhearted, affable, insinuating, amiable, affectionate, kind. ‖ **-amente** adv. tenderly, caressingly.

meiguice s. f. 1. tenderness, gentleness, mildness, meekness, sweetness, affability, kindness. 2. ~**s** pl. caresses, affectionate words, endearments.

meijoada s. f. nightwork.

meiminho s. m. the little finger. ‖ adj. pertaining to the little finger.

meio s. m. 1. middle, centre, intermediate position, midst. 2. medium, expedient, means, agent, manner, way, course, possibility. 3. ambiency, environment, element, milieu. 4. sphere, moral or social atmosphere. 5. way of life. 6. (math.) mean. 7. ~**s** pl.: a) means, riches, property, wealth, resources, wherewithal, ways and means. b) centre beams of a sailing raft. ‖ adj. 1. half, mean, middle, intermediate. 2. undecided, irresolute. 3. evasive. ‖ adv. mean, half, not entirely, almost. ~ **anticoncepcional** contraceptive. ~ **assado** half--baked. ~ **caminho** halfway, middle of the way.

~ **de transporte** means of transportation. ~ **de vida** livelihood, means of subsistence. ~ **do mundo** (N. Braz.) solitary faraway place. ~ **familiar** familiar surroundings. ~ **fechado** partly closed. ~ **irmão** half brother. ~ **luto** half mourning. ~ **morto** half--dead. ~ **quarto** (naut.) dog-watch. ~ **sangue** half breed. ~ **soldo** half pay. ~ **tempo** (ftb.) half time. ~**s e possibilidades** means and possibilities. ~**s escassos** narrow means. ~**s legais** legal means. ~**s pecuniários** pecuniary resources. ~**s próprios** own means. **-a dúzia** half a dozen. **-a entrada** half price (ticket). **-a hora** half an hour. **-a lauda** (typogr.) column. **-a sola** half sole. **-a volta** (mil.) about-face. **-a volta, à direita** (mil.) right about! **-a volta, à esquerda** (mil.) left about! **-a volta, volver!** (mil.) about-face! **-as palavras** allusions, hints, equivocal words. **a -a voz** in an undertone. **a** ~ **caminho** halfway. **de -a cara** gratis. **de** ~ **a** ~ entirely, thoroughly. **do** ~ **de** from among. **ele está fora de seu** ~ he is out of his element. **ele está** ~ **cansado** he is sort of tired. **encadernação** ~ **linho** half cloth (binding). **encontrar-se no seu** ~ to be in one's element. **estar bem de** ~**s** to be well-off. **estar em** ~ to be half-finished, be in operation or progress. **estar sem** ~**s** to be resourceless. **ficar em** ~ to remain unfinished. **lei de** ~**s** (pol.) (law of) budget. **não haver** ~ to be quite impossible. **neste** ~ **tempo** meanwhile, in the meanwhile. **no** ~ in the middle. **no** ~ **da luta** in the thick of the fight. **no** ~ **da noite** in the depth of the night. **no** ~ **de** in the midst of, amid, amidst, between, among. **morar paredes -as com alguém** to live in a house contiguous to that of somebody else. **paredes -as** partition-wall. **por este** ~ by this means, by this agency. **por** ~ **de** by means of, by dint of, through. **por** ~ **disto** by this (means), hereby. **por qualquer** ~ by any means. **retrato de** ~ **corpo** half-length picture. **tirar alguém do seu** ~ to take s. o. out of his sphere. **um e** ~, **uma e** -a one and a half. **uma hora e -a** 1. one hour and a half. 2. (time of day) half past one. **vamos fazer o negócio** ~ **a** ~ let us go by halves. **vez e -a de largura** half as broad again. ~ **a** ~ fifty-fifty.

meio-busto s. m. (pl. **meios-bustos**) bust, head and shoulders done in sculpture.

meio-copeiro adj. (pl. **meios-copeiros**) (N. Braz.) said of the sugar engine working with a water wheel.

meio-corpo s. m. (pl. **meios-corpos**) superior part of the human body, bust.

meio-dia s. m. (pl. **meios-dias**) 1. midday, noon. 2. south. **antes do** ~ in the forenoon, ante meridiem (abbr. a. m.) **ao** ~ at noon.

meio-fio s. m. 1. curb (plate R 8). 2. groove; notch; rabbet. 3. rabbet plane. 4. (naut.) pouch, shifting boards.

meio-relevo s. m. (pl. **meios-relevos**) bas-relief, low relief.

meiose s. f. (biol.) meiosis: diminution of the number of chromosomes in the nuclei of germinal cells.

meio-soprano s. m. 1. mezzo-soprano. 2. mezzo--soprano singer.

meio-termo s. m. (pl. **meios-termos**) 1. middle term, medium, mean. 2. (fig.) modesty. 3. eclectism.

meio-tom s. m. (pl. **meios-tons**) half note, half-tone, demitone.

meirinhado s. m. office or jurisdiction of a bailiff.

meirinho s. m. 1. (ant.) bailiff, apparitor. 2. name of several small jumping spiders. ‖ adj. designating cattle that grazes in the mountains in the summer and in the planes in the winter and the wool of this cattle.

meiru-de-preto s. m. (pl. meirus-de-preto) (Braz.) plant of the family Annonaceae.

meizinha s. f. (N. Braz.) (ant. also mezinha) remedy.

mel s. m. (pl. meles and méis) 1. honey. 2. (fig.) sweetness, candor. ~ cabaú (Braz.) the syrup left over from the sugar production, also known as mel de tanque. ~ de dedo not very sweet honey. ~ de engenho sugar-cane juice after cooking. ~ de furo (Braz.) treacle from sugar-refining moulds. ~-de-pau (N. Braz.) honey produced by bees that live in hollow trees. ~ de toicinho (N. Braz.) syrup made of molasses and bacon. ~ silvestre wild honey. ~ virgem virgin honey. cair a sopa no ~ something very much to the point. dez réis de ~ coado worthless sum of money, trifle. ficar sem ~ nem cabaça, perder ~ e cabaça (Braz., fig.) to lose two things at once, or: none of the things hoped for came true. mais doce do que o ~ very sweet. não há ~ sem fel honey is sweet, but the bee stings. lua de ~ honeymoon. passar ~ pelos beiços de alguém to butter a person up, to wheedle or cajole a person. palavras de ~ words sweet as honey. ser de ~ com alguém to be exceedingly friendly to s. o.

mela s. f. 1. blight, mildew. 2. omission, blank in a writing. 3. (fig.) illness. 4. loss of hair, partial baldness. 5. malnutrition. 6. (Braz.) drunken brawl. 7. (S. Braz.) hiding, flogging.

melaceiro s. m. vendor of molasses.

melaço s. m. molasses, sugar-cane syrup, treacle.

meladinha s. f. (N. Braz.) drink made out of honey and sugar-cane brandy.

melado s. m. 1. (Braz.) sugar-cane syrup thickened almost to sugar. 2. (S. Braz.) thick broth made out of molasses served as dessert. 3. (sl.) blood. ‖ adj. 1. honey-coloured. 2. sweetened with honey. 3. sweet like honey. 4. (Braz.) spotted with honey or some other sticky substance. 5. (N. Braz.) said of a honey-coloured horse. 6. (S. Braz.) said of an albino animal or man. 7. (Braz.) blond. 8. empty, hollow, abortive, withered (fruit, vegetable). 9. (N. Braz.) having a faulty, dull edge. 10. said of a sweet sob sister story. 11. (N. Braz.) drunk. 12. blighted, mildewed.

melador s. m. (Braz.) extractor of wild honey from the woods.

meladura s. f. boilerful of sugar-cane juice.

meláfiro s. m. (geol.) melaphyre: porphyritic rock.

melafólio s. m. (archit. and bot.; also acanto) acanthus.

melambo s. m. Winter's bark (Drimys winteri): tree of the magnolia family. 2. the bark of this tree, used in medicine.

melâmpiro s. m. (bot.) melampyre, cowwheat.

melampódio s. m. (bot.) melampod, black hellebore.

melanagogo s. m. (med., ant.) melanagogue: medicament supposed to expel black bile or melancholy. ‖ adj. relating to this medicament.

melananto adj. having black flowers.

melança s. f. honey harvest.

melancia s. f. 1. watermelon. 2. a variety of apple.

melancia-da-praia s. f. (pl. melancias-da-praia) (N. Braz.) plant of the family Solanaceae (called babá in Bahia and arrebenta-cavalo in the middle states of Brazil).

melancia-de-cobra s. f. (pl. melancias-de-cobra) (bot.) snake mellon.

melancial s. m. (pl. -ais) 1. watermelon plantation, patch or bed. 2. production of watermelons.

melancieira s. f. 1. watermelon plant. 2. watermelon vender (female).

melancolia s. f. 1. (med.) melancholy, melancholia: mental disorder. 2. melancholy, gloom, dreariness,

dismalness, low spirits, spleen, atrabiliousness, sombreness, dumps.

melancólico adj. melancholic, melancholy, gloomy, dreary, sombre, atrabilious, low-spirited. ‖ melancolicamente adv. melancholically.

melancolizar v. to become or turn melancholic or melancholy.

melanésio s. m. Melanesian: native of Melanesia. ‖ adj. Melanesian: relating to Melanesia.

melangástreo adj. (zool.) black-bellied.

melania s. f. 1. darkness, somberness. 2. (ant.) moreen.

melanina s. f. melanin: 1. dark pigment of the skin and hair. 2. black matter secreted by cephalopods.

melanismo s. m. (med.) melanism: abnormal darkness of the skin, hair or tissue.

melanita s. f. (min.) melanite: black variety of garnet.

melanocarpo adj. (bot.) yielding black fruit.

melanocéfalo adj. (zool.) melanocephalic: black-headed.

melanocéraso s. m. old name for belladonna.

melanócero adj. (zool.) having black horns or antennae.

melanocrático adj. melanocratic: quality of black eruptive rocks.

melanodermia s. f. (med., also melasmo m.) melanodermia, melanoderma-melasma: skin disease characterized by excess of black pigment.

melanoftalmo adj. 1. black-eyed. 2. having spots circled in black resembling an eye.

melanografita s. f. rock or stone showing black lines resembling a drawing.

melanoma s. m. (med.) melonoma: tumour formed by cells containing dark pigment.

melanope adj. m. + f. (zool.) black-eyed.

melanóptero adj. (zool.) having black wings or elytrons.

melanose s. f. (path.) melanosis: disease characterized by the deposition of black pigment in the tissues.

melanospermo adj. (bot.) melanospermous: having black seeds or spores.

melanóstomo adj. (zool.) black-mouthed.

melanótico s. m. (med.) melanotic: person affected by melanosis. ‖ adj. melanotic: affected by melanosis.

melanótrico adj. melanotrichous: black-haired.

melanoxanto adj. black and yellow.

melântemo s. m. old name for camomile.

melantéria s. f. 1. sort of pitch used by ancient ropemakers. 2. kind of argil with which shoes were dyed black.

melanterita s. f. melanterite: hydrated ferrous sulphate.

melanúria, melanuria s. f. (med.) melanuria: presence of a black or dark-blue pigment in the urine.

melanuro adj. (zool.) black-tailed.

melão s. m. (pl. -ões) melon, melon plant.

melão-caboclo s. m. (pl. melões-caboclos) (Braz.) cassabanana.

melão-de-são-caetano s. m. (pl. melões-de-são-caetano) (Braz.) balsam apple.

melar v. 1. to cover or sweeten with honey. 2. to sweeten. 3. to give the colour of honey to. 4. (N. Braz.) to stain or smear with honey or any sticky substance. 5. (Braz.) to make honey. 6. to become coloured or sweet like honey. 7. to search for honey in the woods. 8. to blight, mildew. 9. to become hollow, abortive, to wither. 10. to make dents in. 11. to cut, cut up, dice. 12. (Braz.) to get drunk.

melasmo s. m. malasma, melanodermia, melanoderma.

melastomatácea s. f. specimen of the family Melastomaceae, dicotyledonous plants.

melastomatáceo adj. melastomaceous, pertaining to the family Melastomaceae.

melatrofia s. f. (med.) atrophy of a member.

melcatrefe s. m. + adj. = **mequetrefe**.

melcochado s. m. shot silk: silk with a changeable colour.

mel-de-anta s. m. (pl. **méis-de-anta**) (Braz.) a species of meliponine bee (Melipona flavipennis).

mel-de-pau s. m. (Braz.) 1. meliponine bees that make their nests in trees. 2. (N. Braz.) something complicated, mysterious, not well-known.

mel-de-sapo s. m. (pl. **méis-de-sapo**) a species of meliponine bee (Melipona fuscipensis).

melê s., m. (Braz.) diamond of inferior quality.

meleca s. f. (Braz., pop.) dried nasal secretion.

meleira s. f. (Braz.) 1. smudge of honey or some other sticky oily substance. 2. dirt, filth. 3. (S. Braz.) nest of wild bees.

meleiro s. m. 1. person who sells honey. 2. (Braz.) honey extractor. 3. (N. Braz.) vender of sugar-cane syrup. 4. (S. Braz., ornith.) a species of woodpecker.

melena s. f. 1. long hair. 2. long, loose and unkempt hair. 3. dejection of blood.

melenudo adj. hairy, having dense hair.

méleo adj. (poet.) mellifluous, sweet.

meleta s. m. (Braz., zool.) the little ant-eater.

melga s. f. gnat, midge.

melgaço adj. (N. Braz.) blond, reddish blond.

melgueira s. f. 1. beehive with honeycombs. 2. (fig.) secretly hoarded money. 3. (pop.) bargain.

melhor s. m. 1. the best. 2. the wise or clever thing to do. ‖ adj. m. + f. better, superior, preferable, best. ‖ adv. better, preferably. ‖ interj. so much the better!
~ **que** better than. **à falta de** ~ for want of better. **cada vez** ~ better and better. **ela é a minha** ~ **amiga** she is my very best friend. **ele fará o** ~ **que puder** he will do his best. **ele está** ~ he is doing better. **fazer o** ~ **possível** to do the utmost. **levar a** ~ to get the better of. **não há nada** ~ there is nothing better. **o** ~ the best. **o** ~ **a fazer** the best thing to do. **o** ~ **meio** the best way. **o** ~ **que eu puder** as best I can. **tirar o** ~ **partido de** to make the best of. **sinto-me** ~ I feel better. **tanto** ~! so much the better! **passar** ~ to be better. **um tanto** ~ rather better.

melhora s. f. (also **melhoria**) improvement, mending, amelioration, change for the better, recovery.
estimo as suas ~**s** I am glad at his recovery.

melhorado adj. better, bettered, perfected, improved, ameliorated, corrected.

melhorador s. m. improver, reformer, amender. ‖ adj. improving, perfecting.

melhoramento s. m. 1. = **melhora**. 2. advance, progress. 3. enrichment, profit, benefit. 4. improvement, amelioration (of lands, buildings, etc.).

melhorar v. 1. to improve, better, ameliorate. 2. to reform, amend, mend. 3. to prosper, enrich. 4. to convalesce, amend, get better, recover. 5. to perfect. 6. to repair. 7. to cultivate. 8. to clear up (weather).
~ **de posição** to better o. s. ~ **de saúde** to grow better, amend. **o gado foi melhorado por cruzamento** the cattle was graded up. **o tempo está melhorando** the weather is clearing up.

melhorável adj. m. + f. (pl. **-áveis**) improveable.

melhoria s. f. advance, improvement, amelioration, betterment, superiority, perfection, progress.
~ **de vencimentos** raising of salary. **a caminho da** ~ on the mend.

meliácea s. f. a specimen of the family Meliaceae.

meliáceo adj. meliaceous: relating to the family Meliaceae.

meliana s. f. variety of earth used by painters to preserve the paint on their pictures. ‖ adj. relating to this earth.

meliantácea s. f. specimen of the Melianthaceae, family of dicotyledoneous plants.

meliantáceo adj. melianthaceous: of or pertaining to the family Melianthaceae.

meliante · s. m. scoundrel, vagrant, rascal, cheat, thief.

melicéris, melicéride s. f. encysted tumour containing a yellow liquid.

melícia s. f. sweet made out of almonds, lard, sugar, cinnamon, etc.

mélico adj. 1. musical, melodious, harmonious, soft. 2. of or referring to honey.

melieiro adj. 1. tender, sweet. 2. flattering, especially out of interest, honey-tongued.

melífago adj. melliphagous.

melífero adj. (also **melífico**) melliferous: producing honey.

melificação s. f. (pl. **-ões**) mellification: honey production; transformation into honey.

melificador s. m. vessel in which the honeycombs are heated to release the honey.

melificar v. 1. to turn into honey. 2. to sweeten with honey. 3. to produce honey.

melífico adj. (also **melífero**) melliferous.

melifluidade s. f. 1. mellifluousness, mellifluence. 2. (fig.) unctuousness. 3. mildness, softness.

melifluo adj. 1. mellifluous, mellifluent: flowing like honey. 2. (fig.) soft, tender, harmonious. 3. (fig.) unctuous, smooth-tongued, honey-tongued. ‖ **melifluamente** adv. mellifluously, etc.
voz -a mellifluous voice.

meliloto s. m. (bot.) sweet clover.

melindrar v. 1. to hurt the feelings of; to pique, wound, offend. 2. to shock, scandalize. 3. ~**-se** to take offence, be scandalized, feel hurt.
~ **alguém** to hurt someone's feelings.

melindre s. m. 1. politeness. 2. sensitivity, susceptibility, squeamishness, resentfulness. 3. coyness, prudery, bashfulness, primness, affectation, affected manners or ways. 4. a kind of balsam. 5. (Braz., bot.) asparagus. 6. a honey cake.

melindrice s. f., **melindrismo** m. sensitivity, coyness, touchiness.

melindrosa s. f. (Braz.) affected girl with exaggerated manners and ways of clothing.

melindroso adj. 1. delicate; susceptible, squeamish, resentful, touchy. 2. coy, prudish, prim, finical, affected. 3. innocent. 4. dangerous, risky, ticklish. ‖ **-samente** adv. delicately, etc.
assunto ~ a ticklish affaire.

melinita s. f. melinite: explosive containing picric acid.

meliorativo adj. meliorative: improving.

meliorismo s. m. meliorism: doctrine that the world must and can bee improved.

melipona s. f. a genus of hymenopterous insects.

melisma s. m. 1. melisma: vocal embellishment in the Gregorian chant. 2. any melodious embellishment.

melissa s. f. (bot.) lemon balm (Melissa officinalis).

melissografia s. f. 1. treatise on bees. 2. description of the habits of bees.

melissugo adj. mellisugent, sucking honey.

melito s. m. any pharmaceutical preparation containing honey, instead of sugar.

meliturgia s. f. apiculture.

melitúria, melitura s. f. 1. melituria, glucosuria: morbid expelling of sugar in the urine. 2. diabetes mellitus.

melívoro adj. (zool.) mellivorous: feeding on honey.

meloa s. f. large melon.

meloal s. m. (pl. **-ais**) melon plantation.

melodia s. f. 1. melody, tune, air. 2. tunefulness. 3. (fig.) sweetness in singing, writing, speaking. ~ **acompanhada** harmonious accompaniment of a melody. ~ **infinita** freely developing melody.

melodiar v. (mus.) to melodize, harmonize.

melódica s. f. 1. melodics. 2. melodeon, a kind of organ with metallic reeds. 3. music box. 4. musical theory.

melódico adj. melodious, melodic. ‖ **melodicamente** adv. melodiously.

melodioso adj. melodious, harmonious, sweet. ‖ **-amente** adv. melodiously.

melodista s. m. + f. melodist: composer of melodies.

melodizar v. 1. to melodize, make melodious. 2. to sing or play melodiously.

melodrama s. m. melodrama.

melodramático adj. melodramatic.

meloeiro s. m. melon plant.

melofone, melofono s. m. melophone: wind instrument, resembling in shape a guitarre.

melografia s. f. the art of writing music.

melógrafo s. m. 1. writer or copier of music. 2. melograph: instrument adapted to the piano or organ to register the notes (of an improvisation or a piece) played.

melomania s. f. melomania: inordinate love for music.

melomaníaco, melômano s. m. melomaniac: music maniac. ‖ adj. melomanic: crazy for music.

melômele s. m. monster having supplementary members inserted into the ordinary members.

melomelia s. f. monstruosity consisting in supplementary members.

melonídeo adj. m., **meloniforme** m. + f. (bot.) melon-like, melon-shaped.

melopéia s. f. 1. musical accompaniment of a recital of verse or prose. 2. declamation agreeable to the ear. 3. monotonous tune.

meloplastia s. f. (med.) plastic surgery of the face.

melosa s. f. orange plague.

melose s. f. (Med.) act of exploring with a probe or catheter.

meloso adj. 1. sticky, syrupy. 2. sweet like honey.

melote s. m. a sheep's hide with the wool.

melrão s. m. (pl. **-ões**) (Braz., ornith.) the rice grackle.

melro s. m. (f. **mélroa** and. **melra**) 1. (ornith.): a) blackbird. b) ouzel. 2. (fig.) sly, cunning fellow.

meloterapia s. f. (med.) musicotherapy.

melro-pintado s. m. (pl. **melros-pintados** (ornith.) a Brazilian maizebird (Pseudoleistes guiarahuro).

melroado adj. of the colour of a blackbird.

melúria s. f. 1. (pop.) habitual or sly complaint. 2. (Braz.) flattery. 3. m. + f. (pop.) feigning person.

membeca s. f. a gramineous plant (Paspalum repens). ‖ adj. m. + f. (Braz.) soft, tender.

membi s. m. (Braz.) 1. war horn of the Indians. 2. a leguminous tree (Cassia apoucouita).

membrado adj. (her.) said of the birds, represented on shields, with legs in a different colour.

membrana s. f. (anat., bot.) membrane, tunic (plate F 1). ~ **hidatóide** hydatoid: membrane surrounding the humour of the eye. ~ **mucosa** mucous membrane. ~ **natatória** natatory membrane. ~ **sinovial** (anat.) synovial membrane: membrane lining the articular cavities.

membranáceo adj. membranaceous: having the form or consistency of a membrane.

membraniforme adj. m. + f. membraniform.

membranoso adj. membranous: having membranes or being of their nature.

membrânula s. f. small membrane.

membro s. m. member: 1. limb of the body. 2. fellow, associate. 3. associate of a corporation. 4. member of a jury. 5. (gram.) a constituent of a sentence. 6. (math.) member of an equation. 7. penis (also ~ **genital**). ~ **do clube** member of the club. ~ **do Parlamento** Member of Parliament. ~ **honorário** honorary member.

membrudo adj. 1. strong-limbed. 2. vigorous.

membura, membira s. f. (Braz.) each of the lateral beams of a sailing raft.

memento s. m. 1. memento, reminder. 2. either of two prayers, for the living and the dead, in the canon of Mass. 3. notebook or paper for writing memoranda on. 4. booklet giving the essential parts of a dispute.

memorando s. m. memorandum, memorial, notification; note, record; summary of the state of a question. ‖ adj. worth remembering, memorable, noteworthy.

memorar v. 1. to memorize. 2. to remind, bring back to the memory. 3. = **comemorar**.

memorativo adj. = **comemorativo**.

memorável adj. m. + f. (pl. **-áveis**) memorable, notable, remarkable. ‖ **memoravelmente** adv. memorably.

memória s. f. 1. memory: a) faculty of remembering. b) recollection, remembrance, reminiscence. c) reputation, fame of a person or thing particularly after death. 2. commemorative monument. 3. record, report, account, memorial. 4. diplomatic note. 5. scientific, literary or artistic paper to be presented to the government, a corporation, academy, etc. 6. notes made to remember something. 7. vestige. 8. (ant.) commemorative ring. 9. (Braz.) ring. 10. (S. Braz.) jewelry. 11. ~**s** pl.: a) report of a witness on historic events. b) memoirs. **de** ~ from memory, by heart. **de boa** ~, **de feliz** ~ of blessed memory. **digno de** ~ memorable, notable. **em** ~ **de** in memory of. **conservar na** ~ to keep in mind. **ficar gravado na** ~ to be stamped on one's memory. **fugir da** ~ to slip, escape one's memory. **sua** ~ **vai muito longe** she remembers a long way back. **ter boa** ~ to have a good memory. **ter de** ~ to remember. **trazer à** ~ to call to mind. **uma** ~ **como peneira** a head like a sieve. **varrer da** ~ to sweep out of one's memory. **vir à** ~ to come back to mind. ~ **de anjo** excellent memory. ~ **de elefante** extraordinary memory. ~ **de galo** weak memory. ~ **visual** visual memory.

memorial s. m. (pl. **-ais**) 1. memorial: a) written record. b) monument or something to preserve the memory of a person or event. c) petition, petitionary letter. 2. memorandum book, note book. ‖ adj. m. + f. memorial, commemorative, memorable, remarkable.

memorialista s. m. + f. memoirist: writer of memoirs.

memorião s. m. (pl. **-ões**) (fam.) 1. good memory. 2. facility in learning by heart.

memoriar v. 1. to reduce something to a report or relation. 2. to write a memorial (or memoir) on. 3. to inscribe.

memorioso adj. 1. retentive (memory). 2. memorable.

memorista s. m. + f. author of academic dissertations.

memorização s. f. (pl. **-ões**) memorization.

memorizar v. to memorize.

mênade s. f. maenad: 1. bacchante: priestess of Bacchus. 2. dissolute woman.

menagem s. f. (pl. **-ens**) 1. house arrest under bail. 2. (ant.) = **homenagem.**
torre de ~ keep, donjon: the main tower of a medieval castle.
menálio adj. 1. pertaining to the Menalus (mountain). 2. (poet.) bucolic, pastoral.
menção s. f. (pl. **-ões**) 1. mention, reference, citation, incidental remembrance. 2. gesture indicating a purpose.
~ **favorável** commendation. ~ **honrosa** honourable mention. **fazer** ~ **de** 1. to make mention of. 2. to set about doing a thing.
mencheviquismo, menchevismo s. m. Menshevism, Minimalism.
mencionar v. 1. to mention, refer to, cite, name. 2. to narrate, expose.
abaixo -do undermentioned. **acima -do** above-mentioned. **o acima -do** the above-named. **ele não deseja ser -do** he wishes to be unnamed. **fica sem ser -do** it shall be left unsaid. **sem** ~ without mentioning.
mendacidade s. f. mendacity, mendaciousness.
mendáculo s. m. (Braz.) moral defect, fault.
mendaz adj. + f. (also **mendace**) mendacious, lying, false, deceitful. (abs. sint. sup. **mendacíssimo**).
mendelismo s. m. (biol.) Mendelism..
mendicante s. m. + f. mendicant, beggar. || adj. begging; mendicant.
mendicidade s. f. (also **mendigagem, mendicância, mendigaria**) mendicity, mendicancy, beggary.
estar reduzido à ~ to be reduced to mendicancy. **viver da** ~ to live on alms.
mendigação s. f. (pl. **-ões**) mendicancy, begging.
mendigar v. 1. to beg, go begging, ask alms, cadge. 2. (U. S. A., sl.) to panhandle.
mendigo s. m. 1. beggar, mendicant, cadger, pauper, almsman. 2. (U. S. A.), sl.) panhandler.
mendubi, mendubim, menduí s. m. (Braz.) less used forms for **amendoim:** peanut.
mendubirana s. f. (Braz.) a leguminous plant (Cassia Diphylla).
meneador s. m. waggler, flounderer, shaker; wielder. || adj. waggling, floundering; shaking; wielding.
menear v. 1. to waggle, flounder, wriggle. 2. to handle, wield. 3. to brandish, flourish. 4. to shake, toss. 5. to direct, manage.
~ **a cabeça** to shake one's head. **o cão meneava a cauda** the dog was wagging its tail.
meneável adj. m. + f. (pl. **-áveis**) 1. handy, manageable. 2. (fig.) flexible.
menecma s. m. double: person who has a great physical resemblance with another.
meneio s. m. 1. wagging, waggling; shaking, tossing, movement of the body or part of it. 2. handling, management. 3. movement, gesture, nod, hint. 4. slyness. 5. preparation. 6. employment, use. 7. cost of labour. 8. (com.) turnover, business done. 9. (fig.) machination, trick, knack. 10. way of life.
menestrel s. m. (pl. **-éis**) minstrel, bard.
mengar v. (Braz., vulg.) to make erotic motions with the body.
menicaca s. m. + f. (pop.) stuck-up person ridiculously made-up.
menina s. f. 1. girl, maiden, young woman, miss. 2. familiar and affectionate term for a person of the feminine sex, adult or child.
~ **casadoura** marriageable girl. ~ **do olho** pupil (of the eye). ~ **de cinco olhos** ferule. ~ **dos meus olhos** (fig.) the apple of my eye.
meninada s. f. boys and girls collectively; a group of boys and girls.
menina-moça s. f. (pl. **meninas-moças**) 1. a teen-age girl. 2. a girl reaching puberty.

menineiro adj. 1. boyish, puerile. 2. loving children.
meninges s. f. (pl. (anat.) meninges: the three membranes enclosing the cerebrospinal apparatus.
meningite s. f. (med.) meningitis: inflammation of the meninges.
meningose s. f. (anat.) meningosis: the union of two bones through membranes.
meninice s. f. 1. childhood, infancy. 2. childish behaviour, action or speech.
segunda ~ second childhood, extreme old age.
meninico s. m. (N. Braz.) dish made out of the viscera of a sheep.
meninil adj. m. + f. relative to boyhood; infantile, puerile.
menino s. m. 1. boy, infant; lad. 2. (coll.) sonny, old boy. || adj. childlike, childish.
~ **de coro** choir boy. **desde** ~ ever since a boy.
meninório s. m. (Braz.) childish person.
meninota s. f. (Braz.) half-grown girl, teen-ager.
meninote s. m. half-grown boy, stripling, lad, teen-ager.
menir s. m. menhir: prehistoric upright monumental stone.
menisco s. m. meniscus: 1. (anat.) a fibrous cartilage (as of the knee). 2. a concavo-convex lens. 3. curved surface of a liquid in a capillary tube. 4. crescent-shaped body.
meniscóide adj. m. + f. **meniscóideo** m. meniscoid.
menispermácea s. f. menisperm: plant of the family Menispermaceae.
menispermáceo adj. menispermaceous: pertaining to the family Menispermaceae.
menológio s. m. menology: martyrology of the Greek Church.
menopausa s. f. menopause: end of menstruation.
menor s. m. + f. 1. minor, person under legal age. 2. ~**es** m. pl. minute details. || adj. 1. little, small, smaller, lesser, younger. 2. minor. 3. ~**es** pl. concerning underwear. 4. inferior.
ele é (de) ~ he is underage. **frade** ~ Franciscan monk. **idade** ~ minority. **nem a** ~ **possibilidade** not the ghost of a chance. **sem a** ~ **paciência** with no patience whatever. **trajes** ~**es** underclothes, undergarments, underclothing. **tribunal de** ~**es** Juvenile Court.
menoridade s. f. minority: 1. nonage, state of being under legal age. 2. smaller number.
menorista s. m. clergyman of a minor order.
menorita s. m. Menorite: Franciscan friar.
menorítico adj. concerning the Menorites.
menorragia s. f. menorrhagia: excessive menstrual flux.
menorréia s. f. menstrual flux.
menos s. m. 1. the least, smallest quantity. 2. that of the least importance. || adj. m. + f., sg. + pl. 1. (ant.) minor. 2. less, fewer, least, lesser, minus, wanting, lacking. || adv. less, least. || prep. but, save, except, less, lest.
~ **mal** not so bad, so so. ~ **que** under, below. **a** ~, **de** ~ too little, short. **a** ~ **que** except, unless. **ao** ~, **pelo** ~ at least. **cada vez** ~ less and less. **coisa de** ~ a trifle, a thing of no importance or value. **dez cruzeiros a** ~ ten cruzeiros short. **ele faria tudo com isto, menos...** he would do anything with it rather than... **é o** ~ **que se pode fazer** it is the least thing one can do. **em** ~ **de uma hora** in less than an hour. **isto é o** ~ **que se esperaria** this is the least one would expect. **mais ou** ~ more or less. **muito** ~ **um outro** let alone anyone else. **nada** ~ **de** nothing less than. **nada** ~ **de dez** not fewer than ten. **nem mais nem** ~ neither more nor less. **o** ~ the least, the least thing. **o** ~ **possível** as little as possible. **pelo** ~ at least.

por ~ for less. **por** ~ **disso não o faço** I shall not do it for less. **pouco mais ou** ~ a little more or less, about, nearly. **quanto** ~ **dinheiro, tanto** ~ **amigos** the less money, the fewer friends. **quanto** ~, **melhor** the fewer, the better. **tudo** ~ **isso** anything but (not) this.

menoscabador s. m. slighter, belittler, disparager, despiser, depreciator. ‖ adj. slighting, despising, belittling.

menoscabar v. 1. to slight, belittle, disparage, despise, disdain, depreciate, lessen, revile, discredit, slander. 2. to undervalue, underestimate. 3. to make imperfect, leave incomplete.

menoscabo s. m. 1. contempt, detriment, disdain, slight, dispargement, depreciation. 2. undervaluing.

menosprezador s. m. despiser, disparager, scorner, slighter, person who looks down on others. ‖ adj. despising, depreciating.

menosprezar v. (also **menospreçar**) 1. to despise, scorn, contemn, slight, disdain, disparage. 2. to look down on, hold cheap. 3. to underestimate, underrate, undervalue.

ele não é de ~ he is not to be trifled with.

menosprezível adj. m. + f. (pl. **-íveis**) despisable, despicable.

menosprezo (ê) s. m. 1. despite, contempt, disdain, scorn. 2. depreciation, underestimation, slight, disregard.

menostasia s. f. menostasia: holding back or retention of the menstruation.

mensageiro s. m. 1. messenger, envoy, emissary, errand-boy. 2. announcer, herald, harbinger. 3. person who, or thing that presages. ‖ adj. carrying or taking messages; annunciative.

mensagem s. f. (pl. **-ens**) 1. message, communication. 2. dispatch, presidential speech. 3. summons, errand. 4. the essence of a thought, school, style, culture, etc.

mensal adj. m. + f. (pl. **-ais**) monthly. ‖ ~**mente** adv. monthly, every month.

mensalidade s. f. 1. monthly fee, salary or dues. 2. monthly allowance.

mensário s. m. monthly (publication). ‖ adj. pertaining to the table or to what is eaten at the table.

menso adj. (N. Braz.) 1. pending. 2. crooked, lame.

menstruação s. f. (pl. **-ões**) menstruation: period of menstrual discharge.

menstruada s. f. menstruating woman or one who has the menses regularly. ‖ adj. menstruant, menstruous.

menstrual adj. m. + f. (pl. **-ais**) menstrual: relating to menstruation.

menstruar v. to menstruate.

mênstruo s. m. 1. menstrual discharge, catamenia, menses, monthlies. 2. (chem.) menstruum, solvent.

mensual s. m. (pl. **-ais**) (S. Braz.) employee, salary receiver. ‖ adj. m. + f. monthly.

mensura s. f. 1. (ant.) = **medida**. 2. (mus.) measure, time.

mensurabilidade s. f. mensurability, measurability.

mensuração s. f. (pl. **-ões**) mensuration: act of measuring.

mensurador s. m. measurer ‖ adj. measuring.

mensurar v. to measure.

mensurável adj. m. + f. (pl. **-áveis**) measurable, mensurable.

menta s. f. (bot.) mint.

mentado adj. remembered, thought of.

mentagra s. f. mentagra: dermatosis of the beard.

mental adj. m. + f. (pl. **-ais**) mental: 1. concerning the mind, intellectual, spiritual. 2. of or pertaining to the chin. ‖ ~**mente** adv. mentally.

cálculo ~ mental calculation. **doença** ~ mental

disease, insanity. **esforço** ~ mental effort. **fraqueza** ~ feeble-mindedness, mental weakness. **oração** ~ mental prayer. **restrição** ~ mental restriction.

mentalidade s. f. mentality.

mentalizar v. to mentalize.

mentário s. m. inventory.

mentastro, mentastre s. m. (also **mentrasto, mentraste**) (bot.) wild mint.

mente s. f. 1. mind, intellect. 2. spirit, disposition. 3. intention, intent, purpose, design. 4. tension, emotional strain. 5. intuition.

de boa ~ with pleasure, willingly. **de má** ~ unwillingly. **ter em** ~ 1. to keep in mind. 2. to have a mind to.

mentecapto s. m. madman, fool. ‖ adj. 1. idiotic, mad, insane. 2. stupid, foolish, ignorant. 3. = **alienado**.

mentideiro s. m. cradle of rumours. ‖ adj. (ant.) lying, untruthful.

mentido adj. false, vain, illusive.

mentir v. 1. to lie, tell a lie. 2. to illude, deceive. 3. to convey a false impression. 4. to induce into error. 5. to err, fall flat, to fall short.

~ **descaradamente** to lie impudently. ~ **fogo** (Braz.) 1. to fail to fire, renege fire. 2. to let down, fail a person. ~ **a alguém** to tell s. o. a falsehood; to deceive s. o. by lies.

mentira s. f. 1. lie, untruth, falseness, fabrication. 2. deceit. 3. error, illusion, misjudgement.

uma ~ **assombrosa** a rousing lie. ~ **de rabo e cabeça** whopper, monstrous lie. ~ **inocente** white lie. ~ **oficiosa** officious untruth. **espalhar uma** ~ to broach a lie. **parece** ~ it is almost incredible.

mentira-carioca s. f. (pl. **mentiras-cariocas**) (Braz. cul.) a doughnut-like tapioca flour biscuit.

mentirola s. f. petty lie, fib.

mentirolar v. to tell a lot of petty lies.

mentiroso s. m. 1. liar. 2. false, betraying person. ‖ adj. lying, untruthful, mendacious, false. ‖ **-amente** adv. lyingly, falsely.

mento s. m. 1. chin. 2. (archit.) cyma.

mentol s. m. (med.) menthol: solid alcohol obtained from peppermint oil.

mentolado adj. mentholated: containing menthol.

mentor s. m. mentor: guide, counsellor.

~ **intelectual** an intellectual adviser.

mentorear v. (Braz.) to be a mentor of.

mentrasto, mentraste s. m. = **mentastro**.

mequetrefe s. m. (vulg.) 1. meddler, busybody, intriguer. 2. villain, scoundrel, rascal.

mera s. f. juniper oil.

merca s. f. buy, purchase: act of buying or thing bought.

mercadejar v. (also **mercanciar**) 1. to negotiate, barter. 2. to traffic, carry on commercial deals. 3. to sell. 4. to obtain illicit profits.

mercadinho s. m. 1. small market. 2. (S. Braz.) small store selling vegetables, fruit and cereals; greengrocery. 3. (Braz.) suburban market.

mercadizar v. to merchandize.

mercado s. m. 1. market, market-place, fair. 2. emporium. 3. trading centre, commercial centre. 4. trade, commerce.

~ **abastecedor** provision market. ~ **animador** encouraging market. ~ **desanimador** discouraging market. ~ **financeiro** money-market. ~ **firme** steady market. ~ **frouxo** slack market. ~ **livre de valores** curb market. ~ **negro** black market.

mercador s. m. 1. merchant, trader, dealer. 2. cloth dealer. 3. (Braz., ichth.) black angelfish.

fazer orelhas de ~ to turn a deaf ear to.

mercadoria s. f. 1. merchandise, goods, commodities, ware. 2. (N. Braz.): a) common name for diamond,

carbonade and black diamonds. b) a lot of such stones.
~ **avariada** damaged goods. ~ **de contrabando** smuggled goods. ~ **estrangeira** foreign goods. ~**s em consignação** consignment.

merca-honra s. m. + f. **merca-honras** sg. + pl. person who traffics in other people's honour.

mercancia s. f. 1. = **mercadoria**. 2. trade, commerce, traffic, business.

mercanciar v. = **mercadejar**.

mercante s. m. + f. = **mercador**. ‖ adj. commercial, trade, mercantile.
navio ~ merchant ship, merchantman, trader. **marinha** ~ mercantile marine, merchant navy.

mercantil adj. m. + f. (pl. **-is**) 1. mercantile, commercial. 2. (fig.) mercenary, self-interested, covetous. 3. ambitious.

mercantilidade s. f. quality of being mercantile.

mercantilismo s. m. (also **mercantilagem** f.) mercantilism, commercialism, shopocracy.

mercar v. 1. to buy, purchase. 2. to buy and sell. 3. to barter. 4. to acquire through hard work. 5. (N. Braz.) to cry, advertise by outcry.

merca-tudo s. m., sg. + pl. 1. dealer in almost anything. 2. junk dealer. ‖ adj. 1. dealing in any trade. 2. junk, secondhand.

mercável adj. m. + f. (pl. **-áveis**) marketable, negotiable.

mercê s. f. 1. indult, grace, mercy. 2. favour. 3. benefit, reward, retribution. 4. gift. 5. payment, fee, wages, salary.
~ **de** thanks to, owing to. **à** ~ **de** at the mercy of. **direitos de** ~ payment for the use of honorary titles. **vossa** ~ old polite form of address, later contracted to **vossemecê** and **você**. **estar à** ~ **de alguém** to be at someone's mercy, in someone's power or hands.

mercearia s. f. 1. a grocer's shop, grocery store. 2. trade of little consequence or store where such trade takes place. 3. (ant.) hostelry, asylum. 4. ~**s** pl. groceries.

merceeiro s. m. 1. grocer. 2. (ant.) person with certain spiritual obligations in return for lodging and board.

mercenário s. m. mercenary, hireling. ‖ adj. mercenary, venal, self-interested, covetous. ‖ **mercenariamente** adv. mercenarily.
tropas -**as** mercenary troops.

mercenarismo s. m. mercenariness: mercenary spirit.

merceologia s. f. science of commerce and trade.

mercerização s. f. (pl. **-ões**) mercerization.

mercerizado adj. mercerized.

mercerizar v. to mercerize: give a silky lustre to cotton threads or fabric.

mércia s. f. (vulg.) 1. shady underhand business. 2. secret flirt.

mercurial s. (pl. **-ais**) 1. f. (bot.) herb mercury (also **urtiga-morta**). 2. f. (fam.) reprehension. 3. m. mercurial: medicament containing mercury. ‖ adj. m. + f. mercurial: pertaining to or containing mercury.

mercurialismo s. m. (path.) mercurialism: morbid condition due to the abuse of mercury.

mercúrico adj. (chem.) mercuric: containing divalent mercury.

mercúrio s. m. 1. (also **azougue**) mercury, quicksilver (plate B 4). 2. Mercury: a) (astr.) planet. b) (myth.) a god. 3. (fig. fam.) messenger of love, go-between, procurer.

mercúrio-do-campo s. m. (pl. **mercúrios-do-campo**) (Braz.) (bot.) Jamaica ironwood.

mercúrio-dos-pobres s. m. (pl. **mercúrios-dos-pobres**) (Braz.) medicinal plant of the family Cucurbitaceae (Wilbrandtia verticillata).

mercurocromo s. m. (chem.) mercurochrome.

mercuroso adj. mercurous.

merda s. f. (vulg.) 1. excrement. 2. shit. ‖ interj. of disgust and nausea: shit!
cheio de ~ (Braz.) fussy, finicky.

merdívoro adj. merdivorous: feeding on excrements.

merecedor adj. meritorious, worthy, deserving.
ser ~ **de** to deserve, be worthy of. **tornar-se** ~ **de** to become entitled to.

merecer v. 1. to earn, deserve. 2. to have a right to. 3. to merit, be worthy of.
~ **atenção** to deserve attention. ~ **bem de alguém** to deserve well of a person. ~ **consideração especial** to deserve attention. ~ **confiança** to be deserving of trust, trustworthy. ~ **crédito** to be worthy of credit. ~ **ser castigado** to deserve punishment. ~ **ser louvado** to be deserving of praise, praiseworthy. ~ **uma boa nota** to deserve a good mark. ~ **uma recompensa** to deserve a reward. **ele bem o mereceu** (U. S. A., fam.) he had it coming to him. **ele merece bem o que ganha** he is well worth what he gains.

merecido adj. merited, deserved, just, condign, due. ‖ -**amente** adv. deservedly.
bem ~ well-earned; well-deserved. **castigo** ~ condign punishment. **recompensa** -**a** deserved reward.

merecimento s. m. 1. merit, desert, worthiness, worth. 2. value, importance, superiority.
homem de ~ a man of merit.

merejar v. (Braz., pop.) var. of **marejar**.

merencório adj. = **melancólico**.

merenda s. f. snack: 1. afternoon lunch. 2. packed luncheon to be eaten on a trip or excursion, or by children at school.
~ **escolar** a meal for school children, distributed by governmental institutions.

merendar v. to have a snack, take one's afternoon lunch.

merendeira s. f. roll or bun suitable for a snack.

merendeiro s. m. 1. = **merendeira**. 2. person accustomed to a snack. 3. basket or the like to carry the snack along. ‖ adj. said of the bread or basket used for a snack.

merendiba s. f. (Braz.) tree of the family Combretaceae (Forminalia brasiliensis) also known as **mirindiba**.

merengue, merenque s. m. 1. meringue: cake of white of eggs, sugar, etc. (plate D 3). 2. (Braz.) nickname for the French.

merepeiro adj. (N. Braz., pop.) 1. roughish, cunning, sly. 2. said of a pacer (horse).

merequém s. m. (pl. **-éns**) (ornith.) a Brazilian parrot.

mererê s. m. (Braz.) 1. disk fish. 2. lansquenet (game at cards). 3. any game of hazard.

meretriciar-se v. to become a harlot.

meretrício s. m. 1. prostitution. 2. prostitutes. ‖ adj. of or pertaining to prostitutes, lewd, whorish.

meretriz s. f. prostitute, harlot, strumpet, whore.

merganso s. m. merganser, goosander.

mergulhador s. m. 1. diver, plunger. 2. pearl diver. 3. (Braz., ornith.) diver. ‖ adj. diving.

mergulhante adj. m. + f. diving.

mergulhão s. m. (pl. **-ões**). 1. a long dive. 2. big splash. 3. (agric.) layer. 4. (ornith.) diver, plungeon, colymbus, grebe, didapper, finfoot, dabchick, ember-goose, loon. ‖ adj. said of a variety of diving goose.

mergulhar v. 1. to dive, plunge, sink, duck. 2. to immerse, submerge, dip. 3. to hide, disappear. 4. (agric.) to layer, provine. 5. to sound.

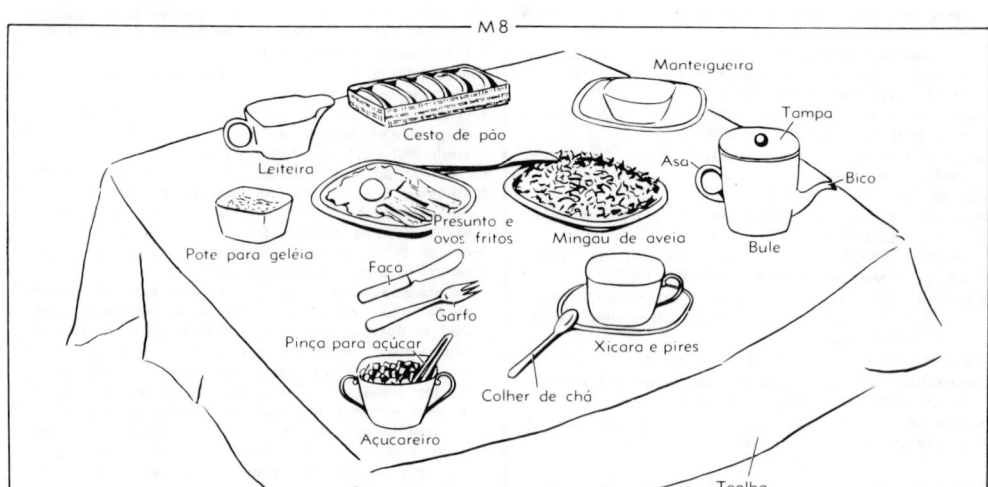

MESA DE CAFÉ

(labels in figure:) M 8 · Manteigueira · Cesto de pão · Tampa · Leiteira · Asa · Bico · Presunto e ovos fritos · Mingau de aveia · Bule · Pote para geléia · Faca · Garfo · Xícara e pires · Pinça para açúcar · Colher de chá · Açucareiro · Toalha

~ **as vides** to layer vines. ~ **nas trevas** to disappear into darkness. ~ **o quarto na escuridão** to plunge the room into darkness. **ele está mergulhado em meditação** he is lost in meditation.
mergulhia s. f. (agric.) layering.
mergulho s. m. 1. dive, plunge. 2. (aeron.) dive, nose-dive. 3. (geol.) dip. 4. (agric.) layer.
   dar um ~ to take a dive.
mericarpo s. m. (bot.) mericarp, hemicarp.
mericismo s. m. (med.) abnormal regurgitation of food in man.
mericologia s. f. study of the ruminants.
meridiana s. f. 1. meridian line: intersection of a meridional plane with the plane of the horizon or any other plane. 2. sundial. 3. (Braz.) = **sesta**.
meridiano s. m. 1. (astr., geogr.) meridian. 2. (geom.) intersection of a surface of revolution by a meridional plane. ‖ adj. meridian: 1. relating to a meridian. 2. relating to midday.
   plano ~ (geom.) plane that passes through the axis of a surface of revolution. ~ **de Greenwich** (geogr.) prime meridian.
merídio adj. meridional: pertaining to midday or noon.
meridional s. m. (pl. **-ais**) meridional, inhabitant of the south of Europe. ‖ adj. m. + f. meridional, austral, south, southern, midday, noonday.
merinaque s. m. farthingale, hoop skirt.
merino s. m. (Braz., also **merinó**) cloth made out of merino wool. ‖ adj. merino.
merisma s. m. division of a subject into distinct parts.
merismático adj. (bot.) meristematic.
meristema s. m. (bot.) meristem: 1. vegetable tissue, not yet partitioned within. 2. embrionary tissue.
meriti s. m. (bot.) miriti palm.
meritíssimo adj. most worthy, most deserving (form of addressing judges).
mérito s. m. 1. = **merecimento**. 2. aptitude, superiority.
   sócio de ~ honorary member. **isso não tem ~ nenhum** there is no merit at all in that, anyone can do that.
meritório adj. meritorious, praiseworthy. ‖ **meritoriamente** adv. meritoriously, worthily.

merlão s. m. (pl. **-ões**) (fort.) merlon: the solid part separating two embrasures or crenelles.
merlim s. m. (pl. **-ins**) 1. (naut.) marline, tarred rope. 2. foundation, gauze. 3. ax used to chop wood. 4. (fig.) artful fellow, slyboots.
merma s. f. (S. Braz.) breakage, loss, diminution, loss in the weight of merchandise.
mermar v. (S. Braz.) to lose value, diminish, decrease.
mero s. m. (ichth.) jewfish. ‖ adj. mere, sheer, simple, pure, sole. ‖ **meramente** adv. merely, solely, only.
   -a coincidência mere coincidence. **um ~ subterfúgio** a mere subterfuge.
merocele s. f. (med.) merocele: femoral hernia.
merologia s. f. treatise on the elementary principles of any science.
merovíngio adj. (hist.) Merovingian.
meru s. m. 1. (bot.) achira: canna edulis. 2. (zool.) sambar, sambur.
merua s. f. (Braz.) bush of the family Rubiaceae (Spermococe longifolia).
meruanha s. f. (N. Braz., also **beruanha**) stable fly.
meruim, meruí s. m. (Braz.) = **maruim**.
meruquiá s. f. (Braz.) plant of the family Graminaceae (Eragrostis Vahli).
mexuringa s. f. (Braz.) a variety of small fly.
mês s. m. (pl. **meses**) 1. month. 2. wage for a month's work.
   ~ **lunar** lunar month. ~ **solar** solar month. **a três meses da data** in three months time. **de hoje a um** ~ a month from today. **no** ~ **passado** last month. **no próximo** ~ next month. **todos os meses** monthly, every month. **do** ~ **corrente** (com.) instant.
mesa s. m. 1. table (plates D 1, 4, M 2, 14, P 1, R 5). 2. board, board of assembly, board of directors, committee, jury. 3. sum of money at stake in games, bets, etc. 4. common name for various custom offices. 5. communion altar. 6. (fig.) food, fare, board. 7. (Braz.) session of witchcraft or sorcery. 8. (N. Braz.) comedy. 9. (geol.) mesa (plate M 11).
   ~ **da enxárcia** (naut.) chain, wale. ~ **de café** breakfast table (plate M 8). ~ **de cozinha** kitchen table. ~ **de desenho** drawing table. ~ **de jantar** dining table (plate M 1). ~ **de jogo** gambling table, card table (plate M 14). ~ **de raposa** (naut.) bill-

board. ~ **dobradiça** folding table (plate M 14). ~ **elástica** expandable table. ~ **eleitoral** polls. ~ **franca** open table, open house. ~ **para o ponto** (theat.) prompt desk (plate P 2). ~ **-redonda** 1. round table. 2. table d'hote. **à** ~ at the table. **cama e** ~ board and lodging. **ela pôs a** ~ she laid the table. **ela pôs a sopa na** ~ she served up the soup. **pôr as cartas na** ~ 1. to put all one's cards on the table. 2. (fam.) to show down. **roupa de** ~ table linen. **sentar-se à** ~ to sit down to table. **servir à** ~ to wait at table. **ter boa** ~ to keep a good table. **tirar a** ~ to clear the table.

mesa-de-cabeceira s. f. (pl. **mesas-de-cabeceira**) bedside table.

mesada s. f. monthly allowance.

mesário s. m. board member.

mesatocéfalo adj. mesaticephalic: said of a cranium halfway between a dolichocephal and brachycephal.

mescla s. f. 1. mixture, variety of colours, miscellany, 2. admixtures. 3. (weaving) melange, mixed cloth. 4. (fig.) grouping.

mesclar v. 1. to mix, mingle, variegate. 2. to add, intercalate. 3. to amalgamate. 4. to join. 5. to mix blood through marriage.
~ **alguma coisa a** (or **com**) to mix something (with).

mesencéfalo s. m. (anat.) mesencephalon: midbrain.

mesentérico adj. (anat.) mesenteric: relating to the mesentery.

mesentério s. m. (anat.) mesentery: fold of the peritonium investing the small intestines.

mesenterite s. f. mesenteritis: inflammation of the mesentery.

meseta s. f. (geol.) smal plateau.

mesmeriano s. m. mesmerist: sectary of mesmerism. ‖ ad. mesmeric.

mesmerismo s. m. mesmerism: doctrine of animal magnetism.

mesmíssimo adj. the very same.

mesmo s. m. 1. the same thing. 2. **-a** f.; a) the same state; the same circumstances. b) inalterated state. ‖ adj. same, equal, identical. ‖ adv. exactly, precisely, even, yet. ‖ pron. same, identical, like, equal.
~ **assim** even so. **agora** ~ just now. **ainda** ~ **que** although, even if, notwithstanding. **ao** ~ **tempo** at the same time. **assim** ~ 1. precisely so. 2. even thus. **da -a data** of even date. **da -a maneira** in the same manner, likewise. **de si** ~ by itself. **é isso** ~ it is just the thing. **ela -a** she herself. **hoje** ~ this very day. **isso** ~ quite so. **isso vem a dar no** ~ it comes to the same thing. **na -a** inaltered, unchanged. **deixar ficar na -a** to leave things as they were. **ficar na -a** to come to the same, to be all the same. **o doente continua na -a** the state of the patient is unchanged. **nem** ~ not even. **o** ~ **que** the same as. **por isso** ~ for that very reason. **quase o** ~ much the same. **você não parece o** ~ **esta noite** you are not quite yourself tonight.

mesnada s. f. (ant.) troop of mercenary soldiers.

mesnadaria s. f. (ant.) pay of a mercenary soldier or captain.

mesnadeiro s. m. (ant.) 1. mercenary soldier. 2. leader of a group of mercenary soldiers.

mesocárpico adj. (bot.) pertaining to the mesocarp.

mesocarpo s. m. (bot.) mesocarp: middle layer of a pericarp.

mesocefalia s. f. mesocephaly.

mesocéfalo s. m. (anat.) mesocephalon: middle part of the brain. ‖ adj. mesocephalic: mesaticephalic.

mesóclise s. f. (gram.) tmesis.

~ **pronominal** collocation of the pronoun in the middle of the verb or verbal expression.

mesocracia s. f. mesocracy: predominance of the middle classes in the government.

mesocrânio s. m. mesocranium: middle of the forehead.

mesocrático adj. mesocratic: relating to a middle class government.

mesocuneiforme adj. m. + f. concerning the middlemost of the three cuneiform bones, of the tarsus.

mesocúrtico adj. (stat.) said of a frequency curve with a flatness equal to that of the curve of Gauss.

mesoderma s. m. (bot., embriol.) mesoderm.

mesodiscal adj. m. + f. (pl. **-ais**) said of the plants with the stamen inserted into the upper surface of the disc.

mesofalange s. f. (anat.) mesophalanx: middle part of the finger.

mesofilo s. m. (bot.) mesophyll: 1. inner tissue of a leaf. 2. parenchyma.

mesófito s. m. (bot.) mesophyte: line of demarcation between the internode and the petiole.

mesófrio s. m. (anat.) part of the face between the brows.

mesogástrio s. m. (anat.) mesogastrium: 1. umbilical region. 2. mesentery of the stomach.

mesolábio s. m. old instrument used to find two mean proportionals between two given lines.

mesolítico adj. (geol.) mesolithic: intervening between the neolithic and the palaeolithic periods of the Stone Age.

mesolóbulo s. m. (anat.) mesolobe: callous part between the two spheres of the brain.

mesologia s. f. mesology: science of the relationship between beings and their environment.

mesológico adj. mesological: pertaining to mesology.

mesopotâmia s. f. region between rivers.

mesorrino, mesorrine s. m. mesorrhinium: part of a bird's beak between the external nostrils. ‖ adj. mesorrhine: having a medium-sized nose.

mesotenar s. m. (anat.) muscle of the hand.

mesotórax s. m., sg. + pl. mesothorax: 1. (anat.) middle part of the breast. 2. (zool.) second of the divisions of the thorax of insects.

mesozóico s. m. (geol.) Mesozoic (period.) ‖ adj. Mesozoic: secondary; belonging to the second great geological epoch.

mesquinhador s. m. (S. Braz.) horse that refuses to be bridled. ‖ adj. concerning such a horse.

mesquinhar v. 1. to be stingy, to grudge, skimp, scrimp, deal in a niggardly manner. 2. (S. Braz.) to refuse to be bridled (horse). 3. to evade an issue or run away from something, to be evasive.
~ **alguma coisa a alguém** to grudge something to s. o.

mesquinharia, mesquinhez s. f. 1. avarice, stinginess, niggardliness, paltriness, shabbiness, meanness, indigence. 2. wretchedness. 3. insignificance.

mesquinho s. m. niggard, skinflint, codger, curmudgeon, miser. ‖ adj. 1. stingy, niggardly, paltry, skimpy, mean, shabby. 2. insignificant, petty, little. 3. pitiful, indigent, poor, wretched. 4. barren. 5. narrow, narrow-minded. 6 (S. Braz.) refusing to be bridled (horse). 7. (fig.) intractable, coy, mistrustful. ‖ **-amente** adv. stingily.
ele é exageradamente ~ he skins a flint.

mesquita s. f. mosque: Mohammedan temple.

messageiro s. m. (ant.) = **mensageiro**.

messalina s. f. immoral woman.

messe s. f. 1. standing crop. 2. harvest, crop. 3. (fig.) acquisition, conquest. 4. officer's mess (Army and Navy). 5. (fig.) conversion of souls.

messiado s. m. Messiahship: function or mission of a Messiah.

messiânico adj. Messianic: relating to the Messiah.

messias s. m., sg. + pl. Messiah: 1. Christ. 2. anxiously awaited saviour. 3. (fig.) social reformer.

esperar pelo ~ to hope for the impossible.

messidor s. m. Messidor: tenth month of the French Revolutionary calendar.

mestiçagem s. f. (pl. **-ens**), **mestiçamento** m. crossing of races or individuals of different races.

mestiçar-se v. to cross one race with another creating mestizos.

mestiço s. m. 1. mestizo, half-caste, half-breed, half-blood. 2. (Braz., ichth.) variety of sheatfish. ‖ adj. 1. mestizo. 2. crossbred, mongrel.

mesto adj. (poet.) sad, afflicted, melancholic, causing sadness.

mestra s. f. (m. **mestre**) 1. schoolmistress, female teacher, preceptress. 2. (fig.) chief, principal. 3. ~s pl. cones of solid earth left in a terrain where earth is removed, in order to enable the measurement of the work done. ‖ adj. main, principal (see **mestre**).

mestraço s. m. (also **mestrão**) a master in his field.

mestrado s. m. 1. mastership of a military order. 2. exercise of such a mastership.

mestral adj. m. + f. (pl. **-ais**) referring to a military master.

mestrança s. f. 1. arsenal of war material. 2. deposit for boat material. 3. (pop.) group of the best masters of a trade.

mestre s. f. (f. **mestra**) 1. master, teacher, instructor. 2. learned man, expert. 3. boss, foreman, headman. 4. skipper. 5. (naut.) petty officer, boatswain. 6. master mason. 7. (S. Braz.) master pole of a fence. ‖ adj. (Braz.) main, principal.

~ **de obras** architect, surveyor, master-builder. **abelha** -a queen bee. **chave** -a (electr.) main switch. **estrada** -a main road. **livro** ~ ledger. **parede** -a main wall. **raiz** ~ tap-root.

mestre-cuca, ~**-cuco** s. m. (pl. **mestres-cuca**, ~**-cuco**) cook.

mestre-de-armas s. m. (pl. **mestres-de-armas**) fencing master.

mestre-de-cerimônias s. m. (pl. **mestres-de-cerimônias**) master of ceremonies.

mestre-escola s. m. (pl. **mestres-escola**) (f. **mestra--escola**) primary school teacher, schoolmaster.

mestre-sala s. m. (pl. **mestres-sala**) master of ceremonies.

mestrear v. (Braz.) to talk or act like a master.

mestria s. f. mastership, mastery, masterliness, perfection, great knowledge.

mesura s. f. reverence, bow, curtsy.

fazer ~ to bow, curtsy.

mesurado adj. 1. prudent, wise, measured, grave, circumspect, cautious, sedate. 2. revered. 3. = **mesureiro**. ‖ **-amente** adv. gravely, sedately.

mesurar v. 1. to bow. 2. to court. 3. ~**-se** to restrain o. s.; to act with moderation, circumspection; to keep one's temper.

mesureiro adj. 1. cerimonious, courteous. 2. servile, obsequious, fawning.

mesurice s. f. 1. courteousness. 2. fawning, exaggerated politeness.

meta s. f. 1. mark, limit, barrier. 2. hurdle. 3. aim, goal. 4. (sport) wicket, tee, goal, end zone (plate F 9).

metábole s. f. (rhet.) metabola, figure of speech in which words are repeated in different order, or ideas in different words.

metabólico adj. metabolic: relating to metabolism or metabola.

metabolismo s. m. (physiol.) metabolism: the transformations suffered by substances in biological economy.

~ **basal** or **básico** basic metabolism.

metábolo adj. undergoing metamorphosis (insects.)

metabologia s. f. (med.) part of medicine dealing with metabolic diseases.

metabologista s. m. + f. (med.) specialist in metabolism.

metacárpico adj. metacarpal: relating to the metacarpus.

metacarpo s. m. metacarpus: part of the hand between the wrist and the fingers.

metacentro s. m. metacenter: point whose position determines the stability of fluctuating bodies.

metacismo s. m. metacism: 1. too frequent repetition of the phoneme m. 2. fault in pronouncing the letter m.

metacrítica s. f. criticism of a criticism.

metacromatismo s. m. metachromatism: change of colour of hair, skin or feathers, according to age or due to morbid conditions.

metacronismo s. m. metachronism: chronological error committed by postdating an event.

metade s. f. half, moiety.

cara ~ better half, wife. **fazer as coisas pela** ~ to do things by halves.

metafalange s. f. metaphalanx (anat.): phalangette, distal phalanx.

metáfase s. f. (biol.) metaphase: second phase of caryocinetic cellular division.

metafísica s. f. metaphysics: science of transcendental, supersensual and supernatural things.

metafisicar v. 1. to become or turn metaphysical. 2. to subtilize.

metafísico s. m. metaphysician. ‖ adj. metaphysical, transcendental, supernatural. ‖ **metafisicamente** adv. metaphysically.

metafonia s. f. (gram.) metaphony.

metafônico adj. metaphonical.

metáfora s. f. (rhet.) metaphor, trope: figurative use of words.

metafórico adj. metaphoric, figurative, tropical. ‖ **metaforicamente** adv. metaphorically.

metaforista s. m. + f. metaphorist: person using metaphores.

metaforizar v. to express metaphorically.

metáfrase s. f. 1. metaphrase: literal interpretation of a figurative phrase or an original writer. 2. paraphrase.

metafrasta s. m. + f. metaphrast: 1. a figurative phrase of an original writer. 2. paraphrase.

metagênese s. f. (bot. metagenesis: alternation of asexual and sexual generation.

metagenético adj. metagenetic: relating to metagenesis.

metageometria s. f. metageometry: non-Euclidean geometry which studies threedimensional spaces.

metagoge s. f. (rhet.) figure of speech lending a soul to inanimate things.

metagrama s. m. = **metaplasmo**.

metajurídico adj. said of certain juridical questions that cannot be analysed by juridical methods.

metal s. m. 1. metal. 2. brass. 3 (fig.) money. 4. timbre of a voice. 5. **-ais** pl.: a) brass instruments. b) kitchen utensils. c) (N. Braz.) common name for diamonds and carbonados.

~ **amarelo** brass. ~ **branco** Babbit metal. ~ **patente** patent metal. ~ **precioso** precious metal. ~ **sonante** hard cash. **o vil** ~ money, filthy lucre.

metalepse s. f. (rhet.) metalepsis: substitution by metonymy of one figurative sense for another.

metalepsia s. f. (chem.) metalepsy: theory of substitutions.

metaléptico adj. metaleptic: relating to metalepsis.

metalescência s. f. quality of having metallic tones.

metalescente adj. m. + f. said of a surface with metallic tones.

metalicidade s. f. state of being metallic, properties characterizing metals.

metálico adj. metallic(al): of, pertaining to or made of a metal. ‖ **metalicamente** adv. metallically.
não ~ nonmetallic. **som** ~ metallic sound.

metalífero adj. metalliferous: containing or producing metal, yielding metals.

metalificação s. f. metallification: 1. act or effect of reducing a substance to metal. 2. natural formation of metals in the earth.

metaliforme adj. m. + f. metalliform: having the form or qualities of a metal.

metalino adj. 1. metalline: pertaining to or resembling a metal. 2. metallic.

metalista s. m. + f. metallist, metallurgist: worker in metal.

metalização s. f. (pl. **-ões**) metallization: act of metallizing, state of being metallized.

metalizar v. 1. to metallize, metalize: a) convert into a metal. b) impart metallic qualities. c) coat, impregnate with a metal. 2. to purify a metal. 3. to reduce to metal (circulating money).

metalografia s. f. metallography: 1. description of metals. 2. science of metals. 3. printing process, using metal plates instead of stones.

metalográfico adj. metallographic: relating to metallography.

metalógrafo s. m. metallographist: 1. writer on metallography. 2. person engaged in metallography.

metalóide s. m. metalloid: element having both metallic and nonmetallic properties. ‖ adj. m. + f. metalloid: resembling a metal.

metalosfera s. f. (astron.) the central nucleum of the planets.

metaloterapia s. f. metallotherapy: treatment of a disease by applying metal plates to the body.

metalurgia s. f. metallurgy: 1. science of metals. 2. the art of extracting metals from their ore.

metalúrgico s. m. metallurgist: 1. person versed in the science of metallurgy. 2. person engaged in extracting metals. ‖ adj. metallurgic: relating to metallurgy. ‖ **metalurgicamente** adv. metallurgically.

metameria s. f. (chem.) metamerism, isomerism: state of being metameric.

metâmero s. m. metamere: (zool.) each of the segments of the earth-worm and other animals. ‖ adj. metameric, isomeric: of the same composition but different structure and properties.

metamórfico adj. metamorphic: 1. (zool.) relating to the metamorphosis of insects. 2. (geol.) relating to rocks that have undergone metamorphism.

metamorfismo s. m. metamorphism: 1. change of form. 2. (geol.) mineralogical recomposition of rock.

metamorfose s. f. metamorphosis: 1. transformation of one being into another. 2. (fig.) considerable change in the appearance, character, etc. of a person.

metamorfosear v. 1. to metamorphose: transform, change the form or character of. 2. ~-se to be transformed or changed into.

metaplasmo s. m. (gram.) metaplasm: change in a word by alteration of a letter or syllable.

metaplástico adj. metaplasmic: relating to metaplasm.

metapsíquica s. f. metapsychics: study of abnormal psychic phenomena, like clairvoyance, telepathy, etc.

metara s. f. (Braz., Indians) labret, earplug, etc.

metástase s. f. 1. (rhet.) figure of speech in which the orator holds somebody else responsible for what he affirms. 2. (med.) metastasis: transference of the seat of a disease.

metastático adj. metastatic: relating to metastasis.

metasterno s. m. (anat.) metasternum: superior extremity of the breast-bone.

metatársico adj. metatarsal: relating to the metatarsus.
osso ~ cannon bone (plate C 12).

metatarso s. m. (anat.) metatarsus: instep.

metátese s. f. (gram.) 1. metathesis: transposition of letters or sounds in a word. 2. (logic) transposition of terms in a reasoning.

metatético adj. metathetic: relating to or containing a metathesis.

metatipia s. f. change of type in the animal or vegetal nature.

metátomo s. m. (archit.) metatome: space between two dentils.

metazoário s. m. (zool.) metazoan: multicellular organisms. ‖ adj. metazoan, metazoal.

metazóico adj. metazoic: that was formed after the apparition of animals.

meteco s. m. (hist.) 1. stranger who lived in Athens. 2. any stranger domiciled in a country, resident foreigner.

metediço adj. = **intrometido**.

metedor s. m. 1. (naut.) cloth wrapped around the mast to keep it dry. 2. (N. Braz.) worker in a sugar factory who puts the cane into the mill.

metempsicose s. f. metempsychosis: transmigration of souls.

meteórico adj. meteoric: 1. relating to or resembling a meteor. 2. atmospheric, meteorologic.

meteorismo s. m. meteorism: flatulent distention of the abdomen.

meteorito s. m. meteorite: fallen meteor.

meteorizar v. to meteorize: 1. cause meteorism in. 2. (chem.) sublimate. 3. ~-se to distend flatulently, suffer from meteorism.

meteoro s. m. meteor, bolide, shooting star.

meteorografia s. f. meteorography: description of meteors.

meteorográfico adj. meteorographic: of or pertaining to the description of meteors.

meteorógrafo s. m. meteorograph: 1. instrument for meteorological observations. 2. person who writes about meteors.

meteorólito s. m. meteorolite, meteorite, meteoric stone.

meteorologia s. f. meteorology: science of atmospheric phenomena or of meteors.

meteorológico adj. meteorologic(al): relating to meteorology.
boletim ~ weather forecast. **observatório** ~ meteorological observatory.

meteorologista s. m. + f. meteorologist: person versed in meteorology.

meteoronomia s. f. study of the laws of the meteors.

meteoroscópio s. m. meteoroscope: instrument used in meteorology.

meter v. 1. to put. 2. to put into, introduce. 3. to place, lay, set, set down. 4. to include. 5. to dip, submerse, engulf. 6. to deposit. trust, keep. 7. to cause, inspire. 8. ~-se: a) to put, lay, set o. s. b) to thrust o. s. into, intrude, get or creep in, hide. c) to penetrate, enter into, pierce, plunge, dive, inquire. d) to meddle, intermeddle, interfere. e) to provoke.
~ **a cara** to enter, attack. ~ **alguma coisa na cabeça de alguém** to put s. th. into someone's

head. ~ **a mão** to sell very dear, extort. ~ **a mão em** 1. to slap. 2. to lend a helping hand. ~ **a mão na consciência** to examine one's conscience, to go over one's acts. ~ **a mão no fogo por alguém** to lay one's hand into the fire for s. o. ~ **a pata** (S. Braz.) to break in on a conversation. ~ **a pique** to sink (a ship). ~ **a ronca,** ~ **a taca** (Braz., fam.) to speak ill of someone, to criticise harshly. ~ **as botas em alguém** to speak ill of s. o., censure s. o. severely. ~ **dentro** to put in, to bring or get into. ~ **em boas** to let in for. ~ **em ferros** to chain, put in fetters, fetter. ~ **em perigo** to endanger, expose to danger or risk. ~ **mãos à obra** to set to work. ~ **na cabeça** to suggest, influence or put into one's head. ~ **medo a alguém** to frighten, scare s. o. ~ **no bolso** to pocket. ~ **num chinelo** to put someone's nose out of joint. ~ **o arco** to run. ~ **o nariz em** to meddle, interfere with. ~ **os pés pelas mãos** to be befuddled, awkward. ~ **respeito a alguém** to strike s. o. with awe. ~**-se a caminho** to set out. ~**-se alguma coisa na cabeça** to take s. th. into one's head. ~**-se a** to pretend to be, set up for. ~**-se a fazer alguma coisa** to meddle with s. th. ~**-se a sábio** to set up for, pretend to be a scholar. ~**-se com alguém** to provoke s. o., to meddle with s. o.; to join with s. o. ~**-se consigo** to mind one's own business. ~**-se de gorra com alguém** to creep into someone's favour, to join with s. o. in an enterprise. ~**-se de posse** to take possession. ~**-se em dificuldades** to run into trouble. ~**-se em um negócio** to engage in a business. ~**-se nas encolhas,** ~**-se nas encóspias** to be quiet, draw in one's horns, give no sign of o. s. ~**-se no mato** to hide in the wood. ~**-se no meio** to intervene, intercede, interfere. ~**-se numa camisa de onze varas** to get in too tight a spot. ~**-se onde não se é chamado** to meddle with other people's affairs. ~**-se para dentro** to enter, retire. **meta-se com a sua própria vida** mind your own business. **não saber onde se há de** ~ not to know where to hide.
meticulosidade s. f. meticulosity: meticulousness.
meticuloso adj. meticulous: overcareful, painstaking, scrupulous, punctilious, finical, fearful, timid, cautious. || **-amente** adv. meticulously.
metido adj. 1. meddling. 2. busy. 3. familiar with. 4. audacious.
~ **com** in close friendship with, intimate with. ~ **consigo** self-absorbed, reserved. **estar** ~ **em** 1. to stick, lie, sit in. 2. (fig.) to have a hand in. **ele é** ~ **a besta** (pop.) he is a pedant.
metilo s. m. (chem.) methyl: monovalent hydrocarbon radical CH_3.
metim s. m. satinet for linings.
metódico adj. 1. methodic(al). 2. systematical, orderly, circumspect, pondering. || **metodicamente** adv. methodically.
metodismo s. m. Methodism: evangelical denomination founded by John Wesley.
metodista s. m. + f. methodist: 1. strict observer of a method. 2. routinist. 3. Methodist: follower of Methodism.
metodizar v. to methodize: systematize, organize, arrange, coordinate.
método s. m. 1. method, system, mode, form, manner, style. 2. (fig.) circumspection, prudence. 3. art, process, procedure.
sem ~ at random.
metodologia s. f. methodology: 1. science of method in scientific procedure. 2. treatise on methods.
metodológico adj. methodological.
metonímia s. f. (rhet.) metonymy: figure consisting in change of words.

metonímico adj. metonymic(al): relating to metonymy. || **metonimicamente** adv. metonymically.
metonomásia s. f. substitution of a proper name for its translation into another language.
métopa, métope s. f. (archit.) metope: space between the triglyphs of a Doric frieze, often adorned with sculptures.
metópio s. m. (anat.) medial point of the forehead between the two frontal lobes.
metopopagia, metopagia s. f. monstruosity consisting in the formation of two bodies for one head only.
metopópago, metópago s. m. monster with two bodies and one head. || adj. of or pertaining to this monster.
metragem s. f. (pl. **-ens**) (Braz.) length in meters, length.
filme de longa-~ feature film.
metralgia s. f. (med.) metralgia: pain in the womb.
metrálgico adj. metralgic: relating to metralgia.
metralha s. f. 1. grapeshot, shrapnel, case shot, canister shot. 2. (fig.) shower of bullets, missiles. 3. (fig.) large portion. 4. all the means leading to one end. 5. (Braz.): a) filling of rubblework. b) rubble from demolition of buildings.
metralhada s. f. shrapnel fire, machine gun fire.
metralhador s. m. machine gunner. || adj. 1. machine--gunning. 2. referring to machine gun fire.
metralhadora s. f. machine gun.
metralhar v. to machine-gun; to attack, hurt with machine gun fire.
métrica s. f. metrics: art of versification: prosody.
métrico adj. metric: 1. relating to the meter, based on the meter. 2. relating to versification.
cadeia -a surveyor's chain. **fita -a** tape measure. **sistema** ~ metric system.
metrificação s. f. (pl. **-ões**) versification.
metrificador s. m. metrist, versifier, poet. || adj. versifying, rhyming.
metrificar v. to put into metric verse, make metric verses.
metrite s. f. (med.) metritis: inflammation of the uterus.
metro s. m. 1. meter: unit of length in the metric system, 39.37 inches. 2. meter stick. 3. measure of a verse.
~ **corrente,** ~ **corrido** running meter, lineal meter. ~ **cúbico** cubic meter, 35.314850 cu. ft. ~ **dobra-diço** folding rule, carpenter's rule (plate M 7). ~ **quadrado** square meter, 10.7639 sq. ft. **ao** ~ **by** the meter. ~ **padrão** standard meter.
metrô s. m. underground railway; (U. S. A.) subway.
metrocele s. f. (med.) metrocele: hernia of the uterus.
metrodinia s. f. (med.) metrodynia: pain in the uterus.
metrografia s. f. treatise on metrology.
metrologia s. f. metrology: science of weights and measures.
metrológico adj. metrologic(al): relating to metrology.
metrologista s. m. + f. metrologist: person versed in metrology.
metromania s. f. 1. metromania: mania for making verses. 2. (med.) uterine delirium.
metrômano adj. metromaniac: having metromania.
metrônomo s. m. (mus.) metronome: instrument for marking time.
metrópole s. f. metropolis: 1. principal town or capital of a country. 2. archiepiscopal church or seat in relation to the suffragan churches or dioceses. 3. mother country. 4. centre of civilization or commerce, emporium.
metropolita s. m. metropolite: metropolitan prelate.
metropolitano s. m. 1. metropolitan: metropolitan prelate in relation to his suffragans. 2. subway,

underground railway. ‖ adj. metropolitan: pertaining to a metropolis.

metroptose s. f. (med.) metroptosis: sagging of the uterus.

metrorragia s. f. (med.) metrorrhagia: uterine hemorrhage.

metrorréia s. f. 1. (med.) metrorrhea: morbid discharge of mucus from the uterus. 2. (depr.) prolific verse-making, mongery.

metrotomia s. f. (surg.) metrotomy: incision into the uterus.

metuendo adj. frightening, terrifying, terrible.

meu adj. (f. **minha**) my, mine. ‖ pron. mine, my. ~ **irmão** my brother. **minha irmã** my sister. ~ **chapéu** my hat. ~ **velho!** old chap! **a ~ ver** in my opinion. **este chapéu é ~** this hat is mine. **não tenho nada de ~** I have nothing of my own. **os ~s estão bem** my family is well. **os ~s são maiores que os seus** mine are larger than yours. **um amigo ~** a friend of mine.

meuâ s. m. (N. Braz.) nasty face, grimace. **fazer ~** to make faces to intimidate.

meuê-meuê adv. (N. Braz.) more or less.

mexeção s. f. (Braz., fam.) stiring, fidgeting, meddling.

mexediço adj. 1. busy, fidgety, bustling, unsetled, lively, restless. 2. movable.

mexedor s. m. 1. bustler, active person. 2. intriguer, busybody, agitator. 3. stirrer, mixer, shaker (object). ‖ adj. moving, bustling.

mexedura s. f. moving, stirring, mixing, shaking, churning.

mexer v. 1. to move, stir, shuffle, shake. 2. to fidget, wriggle, stir uneasily, budge. 3. to touch. 4. to meddle. 5. to rummage. 6. to mix, mix up. 7. ~-**se** to stir, move, budge. ~ **céu e terra** to move heaven and earth. ~ **com** 1. to annoy, pester, provoke. 2. to put one's foot in with a person. ~ **em** to stir in, touch. ~ **o café** to stir one's coffee. ~ **os pauzinhos** to do everything exactly right to get what one wants. ~ **num vespeiro** to stir up a hornets' nest. **ela não mexeu nem um dedo** she didn't lift a finger. **mexa-se!** get going! keep yourself busy! **não mexa** leave it alone. **não se mexa** don't budge. **põe-te a ~!** clear out! **quem mexeu nesta gaveta?** who rummaged this drawer?

mexerica s. f. (Braz.) tangerine.

mexericar v. 1. to gossip, intrigue, twaddle. 2. ~-**se** to become evident; to expose o. s.

mexerico s. m., **mexericada** f. 1. gossip, intrigue, chit-chat, tattle. 2. (S. Braz.) confusion, disorder, mess.

mexeriqueira s. f. (Braz.) tangerine tree.

mexeriqueiro s. m. 1. gossip, talebearer, intriguer, tattler, busybody, newsmonger. 2. (N. Braz., also **periquito**) small oil lamp made out of tin-plated metal. ‖ adj. gossiping, intriguing.

mexerucar v. to fiddle, meddle, fumble, touch continuously.

mexerufada s. f. 1. food for pigs. 2. (pop.) meddley, confusion, mix-up, embroilment.

mexicana s. f. Mexican: Mexican Dollar (silver coin).

mexicano s. m. Mexican: native or inhabitant of Mexico. ‖ adj. Mexican.

mexida s. f. 1. confusion, disorder, mix-up, jumble. 2. disagreement. 3. bustle, stir, noise. 4. meddley. 5. gossip, intrigue.

mexido s. m. 1. sweet made out of grated bread, syrup, honey and lemon peel. 2. twisting and turning in certain dances. 3. intrigue, gossip. 4. (Braz.) dish made out of manioc flour, beans, bacon, and vegetables. 5. dish made out of beans or cut up meat prepared with manioc flour. ‖ adj.

1. astir, busy, active, lively. 2. agitated, restless. 3. touched, turned, revolved. 4. stirred, mixed. **ovos ~s** scrambled eggs.

mexilhão s. m. (pl. **-ões**) (f. **-ona**) (zool.) mussel, muscle. ‖ adj. 1. said of a person touching and fingering everything. 2. playful, riotous, mischievous.

mexilho s. m. pin (of a plough).

mexinflório s. m. (S. Braz.) 1. something worthless, useless. 2. confusion, mix-up. 3. plot, intrigue.

mexoalho s. m. manure of foul crabs and seaweeds.

mexonada s. f. 1. irregular movement of things in disorder. 2. = **mexida.**

mezanelo s. m. clinker, hard and glazed brick used for stairs, paving, etc.

mezanino s. m. (archit.) mezzanine: 1. entresol. 2. small window in an entresol. 3. cellar window.

mezana s. f. (naut.) mizen, mizen-sail: sail of the mizen-mast. **mastro de ~** mizen-mast: aftermost mast of a three-master.

mezereão s. m. (bot.) mezereon: spurge flax, spurge-laurel.

mezinha, meizinha s. f. 1. clyster. 2. household medicine, family remedy.

mezinhar v. to apply household medicine; to medicate.

mezinheiro s. m. 1. person who makes or applies household medicine. 2. quack, charlatan. 3. person always medicating himself.

mezinhice s. f. 1. household medicine. 2. medicaments or practices of a quack.

mi s. m. (mus.) mi, E: third note of the diatonic scale. ‖ pron. old form of **mim. ~ bemol** E flat.

miada s. f. 1. mewing of many cats. 2. (fig.) howler, mistake, error.

miadela s. f. each mew of a cat.

miado s. m. mew, mewing of a cat.

miador s. m. mewer, miauler. ‖ adj. mewing, miauling.

miadura s. f. continuous mewing.

mialgia s. f. (med.) myalgia: pain in the muscles.

miar v. to mew, miaul, miaow.

miasma s. m. miasma: 1. mephitic exhalation. 2. exhalation from putrescent plants or animals.

miasmático adj. miasmatic, miasmal: producing miasmas, resulting from miasmas.

miau s. m. 1. (onom.) miaow, mew. 2. chinese pagoda or temple.

mica s. f. 1. (min., also **malacacheta**) mica. 2. small portion, bit, morsel. 3. (Port., prov.) goat.

micáceo adj. micaceous: 1. containing mica. 2. pertaining to or resembling mica.

micado s. m. mikado: 1. emperor of Japan. 2. ancient title of the supreme Japanese religious authority.

micageiro adj. making faces, grimacing.

micagem s. f. (pl. **-ens**) nasty face, act of pulling faces like a monkey, grimace.

miçanga s. f. 1. bead, glass pearl. 2. ornament made out of beads. 3. (typogr.) pearl. 4. trifles.

micante adj. m. + f. brilliant, shining, glittering.

micção s. f. (pl. **-ões**) urination.

micélio s. m. mycelium: vegetative and filamentous part of fungi.

micetografia s. f. study, description and history of fungi.

micha s. f. 1. bread made out of mixed flours. 2. (Braz., thieves's sl.): a) false note, counterfeit money. b) picklock. ‖ adj. m. + f. (sl.) 1. insignificant, of no value. 2. sloppy.

michar v. (sl.) 1. to fail. 2. to miscarry. 3. to make or become ineffectual.

michole s. m. (Braz.) fish of the family Serranidae (Haliperca radialis).

mico s. m. (Braz.) name for various monkeys of the genera Cebus (~-**comum** Cebus negrivittatus; ~-**de-topete** Cebus nigritus; ~-**pardo** Cebus apella; ~-**peludo** Cebus vellerosus).

destripar o ~ (Braz., pop.) to vomit. **quero ser um ~ se...** strike me ugly if...

micoderma s. m. mycoderma: fungus that forms on the surface of fermented liquors and sugary juices.

micologia s. f. (also **micetologia**) micology, mycetology: 1. science of fungi. 2. treatise on fungi.

micológico adj. (also **micetológico**) mycologic: relating to mycology.

micólogo s. m. mycologist: person versed in mycology.

micótico adj. mycotic: caused by fungi.

micracústico adj. micracoustic: serving to reinforce low sounds.

micranto adj. (bot.) having small flowers.

microbial adj. m. + f. (pl. -ais), **microbiano** m., microbial, microbian, microbic: relating to microbes.

microbicida s. m. microbicide. ‖ adj. m. + f. destroying microbes.

micróbio s. m. microbe: microorganism, bacterium.

microbiologia s. f. microbiology: science of or treatise on microbes.

microbiológico adj. microbiological: relating to microbiology.

microbiologista s. m. + f. microbiologist: person versed in microbiology.

microcefalia s. f. microcephalia, microcephaly: condition presented by an abnormally small head.

microcefálico adj. microcephalic, microcephalous: having an abnormally small head.

microcéfalo s. m. microcephalous: 1. microcephalic person. 2. (fam.) idiot. ‖ adj. 1. microcephalic. 2. unintelligent.

micrócero adj. (zool.) microceratous: having short antennae.

micrococo s. m. micrococcus: a genus of minute spherical bacteria.

microcósmico adj. microcosmic: relating to the microcosm.

microcosmo s. m. microcosm: 1. miniature cosmos. 2. man as an epitome of the universe.

microcosmologia s. f. microcosmology: description of man as a microcosm.

microdáctilo, microdátilo adj. (zool.) short-fingered.

microdonte adj. m. + f. (zool.) microdont: small-toothed.

microeconomia s. f. (econ.) microeconomics.

microfilmar v. to microfilm.

microfilme s. m. microfilm: cinematograph film of documents or book pages for recording purposes.

microfilo adj. (bot.) microphylous: having small leaves.

micrófita s. f., **micrófito** m. microphyte: extremely small plant.

microfítico adj. microphytic: relating to microphytes.

microflora s. f. (bot., bact.) microflora: flora constituted of microscopic vegetals.

microfone, micrófono s. m. microphone: instrument for augmenting low sounds (plate M 9).

microfonia s. f. (med.) microphony: weakness of the voice.

micrófono s. m. instrument for detecting low sounds. ‖ adj. microphonic: 1. weak-voiced. 2. weakening (a sound).

microfotografia s. f. 1. microphotography: photography on a very small scale. 2. microphotograph: microscopic photograph.

microftalmia s. f. microphthalmy: abnormal smallness of the eye.

microgameta s. m. (biol.) microgamete: smaller gamete of a heterogamous organism.

microglosso adj. (zool.) short-tongued.

micrognatia s. f., **micrognatismo** m. (zool.) micrognathia.

micrógnato adj. (zool.) having small jaws.

micrografia s. f. micrography: description of microscopically small objects.

microlepidóptero s. m. microlepidopteron: one of the smaller moths.

microlítico adj. microlithic: pertaining to or characterized by microliths.

micrólito s. m. (min.) microlith, microlite: microscopic acicular crystals in igneous rocks.

micrologia s. f. micrology: science of, or treatise on microscopic bodies.

micrológico adj. micrologic: relating to micrology.

micrólogo s. m. 1. micrologist: person versed in micrology. 2. short speech. 3. finical person.

micrômato adj. small-eyed (invertebrate animal).

micrômego s. m. mathematical instrument to measure land.

micromelia s. f. (path.) micromelia: monstruosity characterized by the excessive smallness of a limb.

micrômero adj. having thin members and appendages.

micrometria s. f. micrometry: 1. measurement with a micrometer. 2. art of measuring with a micrometer.

micrométrico adj. micrometrical: pertaining to, or made with the aid of a micrometer. ‖**micrometricamente** adv. micrometrically.

micrômetro s. m. micrometer: instrument for very small and precise measurements (plate M 9).

micromicete s. m. 1. micromycete: cryptogamic plant which produces alcoholic fermentation. 2. yeast.

mícron, micromilímetro s. m. micron, micromillimeter: thousandth part of a millimeter.

micronemo adj. (zool.) having small tentacles.

microondas s. m. (pl. (phys.) microwaves: electromagnetic waves of very small length.

microônibus s. m. (Braz.) microbus: a small motor bus.

micrópila s. f. (bot.) micropyle: orifice of an ovule through which the tube of the pollen penetrates.

micróporo adj. (biol.) having excessively small pores.

micropsia s. f. (path.) micropsia: visional defect causing things to appear smaller than they really are.

micropsiquia s. f. 1. weakness of spirit. 2. pusillanimousness.

micropterígio adj. (zool.) micropterigian: small-finned.

micróptero adj. (zool.) micropterous: small-winged.

microrganismo s. m. microorganism: microscopic organism, microbe.

microscopia s. f. microscopy: art of using the microscope.

microscópico adj. microscopic(al): 1. visible only with the help of a microscope. 2. made with the help of a microscope. 3. sharp-sighted.

microscópio s. m. microscope (plate M 9).

microscopista s. m. + f. microscopist: person versed in microscopy.

microsficto adj. (med.) having a weak pulse.

microspermo s. m. (bot.) microsperm: a series of monocotyledonous plants characterized by numerous very small seeds.

microssomatia, microssomia s. f. abnormal smallness of the body.

microssomático, microssômico adj. abnormally small (body).

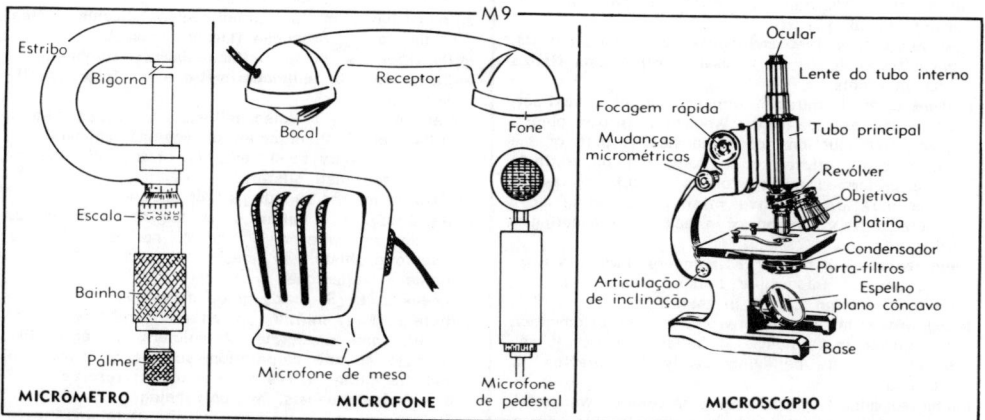

M9

MICRÓMETRO — Estribo, Bigorna, Escala, Bainha, Pálmer

MICROFONE — Receptor, Bocal, Fone, Microfone de mesa, Microfone de pedestal

MICROSCÓPIO — Ocular, Lente do tubo interno, Focagem rápida, Mudanças micrométricas, Tubo principal, Revólver, Objetivas, Platina, Condensador, Porta-filtros, Espelho plano côncavo, Base, Articulação de inclinação

microssomo adj. abnormally small.

micróstomo adj. (zool.) microstomatous: small-mouthed.

micrótomo s. m. microtome: instrument for cutting very thin slices of tissue for microscopic examination.

microzoário s. m. microzoarian: microscopic animal-cule, infusory.

micruro adj. (zool.) small-tailed.

micterismo s. m. (neol.) tight face, sour face, low spirit.

mictório s. m. public convenience, urinol. ‖ adj. diuretic.

micturição s. f. (pl. **-ões**) micturition: morbidly frequent urination.

micuim s. m. (pl. **-ins**) (Braz., zool.) small tick.

micurê s. m. (Braz., zool.) opossum.

midríase s. f. (med.) mydriasis: morbid dilation of the pupil of the eye.

mielencefálico adj. myelencephalic: cerebrospinal.

mielencéfalo s. m. myelencephalon: the brain and spinal cord as a whole.

mielina s. f. myelin: substance of the medulary sheath of a nerve.

mielite s. f. myelitis: inflammation of the spinal cord or marrow.

mielócite s. m. myelocyte: marrow cell.

mielóide adj. m. + f. myeloid: medullary.

mieloma s. m. (med.) myelome: sarcoma formed by marrow cells.

mielomalacia s. f. (med.) myelomalacia: softening of the spinal cord.

mielossarcoma s. m. (med.) myelosarcoma: sarcoma of the marrow of the bones.

miga s. f. = **migalha.** ‖ **~s** pl. bread soups.

migado adj. minced, sliced.

migalha s. f. 1. crumb. 2. bit, small portion. 3. (fig.) doit, wee, little bit. 4. **~s** pl. leftovers, scraps.

migalhar v. = **esmigalhar.**

migalheiro s. m. punctilious person, stickler. ‖ adj. punctilious, fussy.

migalhice s. f. insignifance, bagatelle, something not worth mentioning.

migar v. 1. to break into little pieces, crumble. 2. to crumbe bread into a broth.

migração s. f. (pl. **-ões**) migration: 1. wandering, emigration, immigration, change of residence of people. 2. (zool.) periodical change of habitat.

animais de **~** migratory animals. em **~** wandering.

migrante adj. m. + m. migrant: that migrates.

migrar v. to migrate.

migratório adj. migratory: relating to migration.

miguelismo s. m. (Port., hist.) political party of D. Miguel de Bragança.

miguelista s. m. (Port., hist.) 1. affiliate of the party of D. Miguel de Bragança. 2. (Braz.) name given to the conservative party of Pernambuco and its adepts in 1848. ‖ adj. m. + f. of or pertaining to these parties.

miguim s. m. (pl. **-ins**) (Braz., ornith.) vermillion flycatcher.

miiocéfalo s. m. (med.) staphyloma forming a small round and dark tumour.

miiodopsia s. f. (med.) (pop. also **moscas volantes**) myiodesopsia: visual disturbance characterized by the seeing of floating spots.

miiologia s. f. entomology of the flies.

miiológico adj. of or pertaining to the study of flies.

mijacão s. m. (pl. **-ões**) (Braz., also **mijicão**) 1. toad-stool: parasol-shaped fungus growing in the excrements or areas drenched by the urine of animals. 2. (S. Braz.) tumour on the sole or between the toes, which popular belief attributes to the contact with the urine of horses.

mijada s. f. (vulg.) the urine produced at one urination.

dar uma **~** to piss, piddle.

mijadeiro s. m. 1. chamber pot. 2. = **mijadouro.**

mijadela s. f. 1. stream of urine. 2. stain caused by urine.

mijadouro s. m. (also **mijadoiro**) pissing place, piss corner.

mija-fogo s. f. (pl. **mija-fogos**) (Braz.) a variety of wild bee.

mija-mija s. f. (pl. **mijas-mijas** or **mija-mijas**) (Braz.) marine mollusc of the family Cardiidae (Cardium muricatum).

mijão s. m. (pl. **mijões**) (f. **mijona**) person who urinates frequently; bed wetter. ‖ adj. urinating frequently.

mijar v. 1. to piss, piddle; stale (horse). 2. to urinate unwillingly. 3. **~-se:** a) to wet o. s. with urine. b) (fig.) to show fright.

~ fora do caco (Braz., vulg.) to keep away from one's duties. **~ fora do penico** 1. to retreat from an assumed obligation. 2. to do otherwise than expected.

mijo s. m. (vulg.) urine, piss; stale of a horse.

mijuba s. f. (N. Braz.) yellow manioc.

mijuí s. m. (Braz.) small black bee.
mil s. m. 1. thousand. 2. multitude, great number, undetermined quantity.
~ **vezes** 1. a thousand times. 2. a thousandfold.
um entre ~ one in a thousand. **Mil e uma Noites** Arabian Nights.
milagre s. m. 1. miracle, wonder, marvel. 2. extraordinary success. 3. (Braz.) wooden or waxen object, mostly reproductions of some healed part of the human body, offered to a saint out of gratitude for a performed miracle or as an offering asking for a miracle. 4. votive offering consisting of a picture or reproduction of a scene representing a miracle.
ele realizou ~**s** he worked wonders. **fazer** ~**s** (fig.) to do almost impossible things. **olha o** ~! (fig.) there is nothing clever in that!
milagreiro s. m. 1. wonder-worker. 2. miraclemonger. 3. believer in miracles. 4. believer in occult sciences. || adj. 1. believing easily in miracles. 2. credulous.
milagroso adj. 1. miraculous, marvelous, wonderful. 2. extraordinary, stupendous. || **-amente** adv. miraculously, etc.
milanês s. m. (pl. **-eses**) (f. **-esa**, pl. **-esas**) Milanese: native or inhabitant of Milan. || adj. Milanese.
míldio s. m. mildew: parasitic fungus growing on plants.
milefólio s. m., **mil-folhas** f., sg. + pl., **mil-em-rama** f. (bot.) milfoil, yarrow.
milenário s. m. millenary. || adj. 1. consisting or pertaining to a thousand years. 2. millenarian, millenial: relating or pertaining to a millenium.
milênio s. m. millenium: 1. chiliad: period of a thousand years. 2. millenial period of righteousness on earth, before the end of the world.
milésima s. f. millesimal: a thousandth part.
milésimo s. m. (also **milésima** f.) millesimal.
milésio s. m. Milesian: native or inhabitant of Mileto, ancient city of Lesser Asia. || adj. Milesian.
mil-flores s. m., sg. + pl. essence of many different flowers.
mil-folhas s. m., sg. + pl. 1. (Braz., cul.) a puff paste with cream filling. 2. (bot.) = **milefólio.**
milfurado adj. with numerous holes.
milha s. f. mile.
~ **marítima**, ~ **náutica** sea-mile, nautical mile (Braz. 6,076.1 feet.)
milhã s. f. (bot.) crab grass.
milhado adj. 1. (S. Braz.) sick from eating too much maize (horse). 2. (fig.) drunk.
milhagem s. f. mileage.
milhal s. m. (pl. **-ais**) (also **milharal, milheiral**) maize field.
milhão s. m. (pl. **-ões**) 1. million. 2. (augm. of **milho**) maize.
milhar s. m. 1. thousand, chiliad. 2. great undetermined number. 3. = **milhal.** || v. to give corn to. ~**es de** thousands of. **aos** ~**es** by thousands.
milharada s. f. 1. great quantity of maize. 2. = **milhal.**
milharas s. f. pl. 1. (hard) roe of fish. 2. seeds of a fig.
milheiro s. m. 1. maize plant. 2. a thousand in the counting of fruits, vegetables, etc. 3. tooth of a horse.
milhenta s. f. childish version of a number above a thousand. || adj. more than a thousand.
milhete s. m. a variety of maize with very small kernels.
milho s. m. 1. maize, corn, Indian corn. 2. (Braz.) plant of the family Rosaceae. || adj. said of the outer leaves and the flour of maize; corn.

dinheiro como ~ lots of money. **farinha de** ~ maize meal, (U. S. A.) Indian meal, corn meal.
milho-cozido s. m. (pl. **milhos-cozidos**) licania: a tree of the family Rosaceae (Licania incana).
milho-zaburro s. m. (pl. **milhos-zaburros**) sorghum.
miliamperômetro, miliamperímetro s. m. (electr.) milliammeter.
miliar adj. m. + f. (also **milheal**) 1. shaped like a millet kernel. 2. of small dimensions (animals).
febre ~ miliary fever: eruption of the skin characterized by small blisters.
miliare s. m. thousandth part of an are.
miliário adj. 1. = **miliar.** 2. pertaining to miles. 3. marking the miles of a road. 4. marked, noticeable (events of history or eras).
marco ~ milestone.
milicada s. f. (S. Braz.) group of soldiers.
milícia s. f. 1. militia: citizen army, national guard. 2. life and discipline of soldiers. 3. army life country. 4. any corporation subject to army life and discipline. 5. ~**s** pl. trainbands; reserve.
a ~ **celeste** angels, heavenly beings.
miliciano s. m. militiaman. || adj. pertaining to a militia.
milico s. m. (S. Braz.) soldier.
miligrama s. m. milligramme: one thousandth part of a gramme.
mililitro s. m. milliliter: one thousandth part of a liter.
milímetro s. m. millimeter: one thousandth part of a meter.
milímodo adj. infinitely variable.
milionário s. m. millionnaire. || adj. very rich.
milionésima s. f. millionth part.
milionésimo s. m. = **milionésima.** || adj. (ordinal number) millionth.
milionocracia s. f. (Braz.) plutocracy: rule of wealth.
milípede adj. m. + f. myriapod, myriapodan: 1. having many feet. 2. pertaining to the Myriapoda.
milistéreo s. m. the thousandth part of a stere.
militança s. f. 1. militancy: quality of being militant. 2. military profession. 3. soldiers.
militante adj. m. + f. militant: 1. fighting. 2. combative, warlike.
militar s. m. soldier || v. 1. to serve as a soldier. 2. to fight, militate. 3. to be in a party. 4. to oppose. || adj. m. + f. military. || ~**mente** adv. militarily: in a military manner.
disciplina ~ military discipline. **serviço** ~ military service, active duty. **ordens** ~**es** military orders.
militarismo s. m. militarism: 1. military spirit. 2. military policy.
militarista s. m. + f. militarist: partidary of militarism. || adj. militaristic: relating to militarism.
militarização s. f. (pl. **-ões**) militarization: preparation in a military manner.
militarizar v. to militarize: prepare in a military manner.
milite s. m. (poet.) soldier.
militofobia s. f. (neologism) horror of or aversion to everything military.
milonga s. f. 1. (S. Braz.) sorrowful and melancholic music sung to the sound of a guitar. 2. ~**s** pl. (Braz.): a) gossip. b) artfulness, craftiness. c) affectation, coyness. d) lame excuses.
milongueiro s. m. 1. (S. Braz.) singer of **milongas.** 2. artful individual, braggart. || adj. 1. singing **milongas.** 2. artful, sly; boastful. 3. affected, coy.
milorde s. m. 1. milord. 2. big, important man.
mil-réis s. m., sg. + pl. former Brazilian monetary unit. || adj. having white and reddish hair (horse).
miltônia s. f. a genus of orchids.
mílvio s. m. (poet.) **milhafre.**

M10

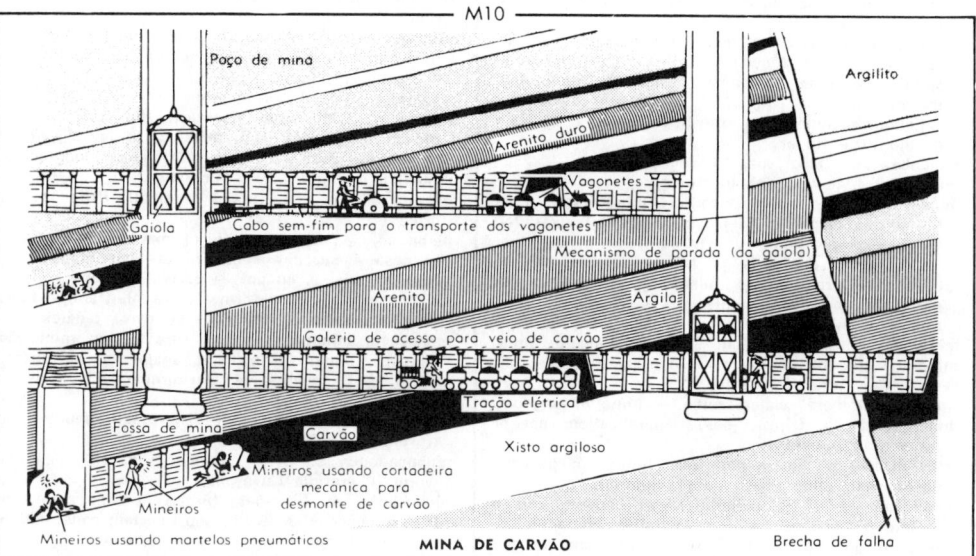

Poço de mina
Argilito
Arenito duro
Vagonetes
Gaiola
Cabo sem-fim para o transporte dos vagonetes
Mecanismo de parada (da gaiola)
Arenito
Argila
Galeria de acesso para veio de carvão
Tração elétrica
Fossa de mina
Carvão
Xisto argiloso
Mineiros usando cortadeira mecânica para desmonte de carvão
Mineiros
Mineiros usando martelos pneumáticos
MINA DE CARVÃO
Brecha de falha

mim pers. pron. me.
a ~ to me. **de** ~ of me, from me. **ai de** ~! woe to me! woe is me. **de** ~ **para** ~ to myself. **para** ~ for me, to me. **por** ~, **quanto a** ~ as for me, for my part. **que será de** ~? what will become of me?

mimaça s. f. 1. excessive fondling. 2. much indulgence with children.

mimalhice s. f. behaviour peculiar to a spoiled child.

mimalho, mimanço s. m. fondling, darling, pet, spoiled brat, minion. ‖ adj. spoiled, fondled, spoon- -fed.
ele é o ~ **da família** he is the pet of the family.

mimar v. 1. to pet, fondle, cocker, cosset, pamper. spoil. 2. to mimic.

mimburas s. f. pl. (N. Braz. also **mumburas**) the two extreme logs or boards of raft.

mimeografar v. (Braz.) to mimeograph: reproduce by means of a mimeograph.

mimeógrafo s. m. mimeograph: duplicating apparatus for typewritten matter.

mimese s. f. (rhet.) mimesis: imitation of voice, gestures and words of another person.

mimetismo s. m. (zool.) mimetism, mimicry: simula- tion, imitation (as of surroundings).

mimetizar v. (bot., zool.) to mimic.

mímica s. f. mimic(king), art of miming, imitation.

mímico s. m. mimic, mimicker. ‖ adj. mimical, mimic. ‖ **mimicamente** adv. mimically.

mimo s. m. 1. delicate gift, offering, present. 2. tenderness, sweetness, daintiness. 3. caress, pet- ting, fondling. 4. delicacy. 5. neatness. 6. mime, jester, buffoon. 7. (ant.) burlesque, farce.
dar ~**s** to spoil (children), pamper. **que** ~! how sweet! how lovable!

mimo-do-céu s. m. (pl. **mimos-do-céu**) mountain rose.

mimo-de-vênus s. m. (pl. **mimos-de-vênus**) (bot.) China rose (Hibiscus rosa-sinensis).

mimodrama s. m. dramatic pantomime.

mimografia s. f. treatise on mimics.

mimográfico adj. pertaining to the study of mimics.

mimologia s. f. mimicry, mimicking, imitation of the voice or speech habits of s. o.

mimológico adj. imitating the voice or speech habits of s. o.

mimologismo s. m. 1. word formed by imitation. 2. onomatopoeia.

mimólogo s. m. 1. person mimicking s. o.; mimicker. 2. person versed in onomatopoeia.

mimosa s. f. (bot.) mimosa.

mimosácea s. f. a specimen of the Mimosaceae.

mimosáceo adj. mimosaceous: belonging to the Mimo- saceae.

mimosear v. 1. to pet, fondle, pamper. 2. to give presents, favour. 3. ~-**se** to insult each other.

mimoso s. m. 1. tenderling, fondling. 2. one tenderly loved, darling. 3. favourite of fortune. 4. (N. Braz.) pasture where the gramineous plant **mimoso** or **capim-mimoso** is abundant. ‖ adj. 1. tender, sweet, exquisite, dainty, loveable, gentle, soft, delicate. 2. prim, finical, pampered, effeminate. ‖ **-amente** adv. tenderly.
fubá ~ corn starch, (U. S. A.) corn flour.

mina s. f. 1. mine, quarry, pit. 2. (mil.) mine. 3. (fig.) source of richness, wealth. 4. (Braz.) natural growth of mate plants in the woods. 5. black lead of pencil. 6. m. + f. Negro originary from the Sudan. ‖ adj. of or pertaining to these Negroes.
~ **de carvão** coal-mine, coal-pit (plate M 10). ~ **submarina** submarine mine. ~ **terrestre** land-mine. **campo de** ~**s** mine field. **engenheiro de** ~**s** mining engineer.

minador s. m. 1. miner, hewer. 2. sapper, underminer. 3. (Braz.) = **minadouro**.

minadouro s. m. (Braz., also **minadoiro**) well, spring, fountain, usually source of a brook.

minar v. 1. to mine, excavate. 2. to explore furtively. 3. (fig.) to undermine, sap, corrode, honeycomb. 4. to subvert. 5. to torment, annoy, hurt secretly. 6. to spread; rage. 7. (mil.) to lay mines. 8. to leak.
a doença latente minava-o the latent sickness tormented him. **o incêndio minando nos porões do navio** the fire raging in the holds of the ship.

neste lugar mina água this place is leaking with water.

minarete s. m. minaret: turret of a mosque.

minaz adj. m. + f. (poet.) (absolute superl. **minacíssimo**) minacious, minatory, menacing, frightening, threatening.

mindinho, minguinho s. m. the little finger. ‖ adj. said of the little finger.

minduba s. f. (Braz., pop.) = **cachaça.**

mineira s. f. terrain rich in mines.

mineiro s. m. 1. miner, collier, mineowner (plate M 10). 2. sapper. 3. discoverer of an unexploited and unexplored mate growth. 4. (Braz.) native or inhabitant of the state of Minas Gerais. ‖ adj. 1. mining. 2. relating to mines. 3. (Braz.) of or pertaining to Minas Gerais.

região -a mining region.

mineração s. f. 1. mining. 2. purification of ores.

mineral s. m. (pl. **-ais**) mineral: inorganic body. ‖ adj. m. + f. mineral, inorganic.

água ~ mineral water. **reino** ~ mineral kingdom.

mineralização s. f. (pl. **-ões**) mineralization: act or process of mineralizing.

mineralizador s. m. mineralizer: liquid or gaseous agent that mineralizes. ‖ adj. mineralizing.

mineralizar v. 1. to mineralize: a) convert into a metal. b) change from a metallic character to that of an ore. 2. to look for minerals in the earth.

mineralogia s. f. mineralogy: science of minerals.

mineralógico adj. mineralogical: relating to mineralogy. ‖ **mineralogicamente** adv. mineralogically.

mineralogista s. m. + f. mineralogist: person versed in mineralogy.

mineralurgia s. f. applied mineralogy, especially metallurgy.

mineralúrgico adj. of or pertaining to applied mineralogy.

minerar v. to work in mines, to mine, exploit mines.

minério s. m. ore.

~ **de ferro** iron ore.

minerografia s. f. description and study of ores.

minerográfico adj. of or pertaining to the study of ores.

minerógrafo s. m. specialist in the study of ores.

minerva s. f. small printing press.

minerval s. m. (pl. **-ais**) fee paid in some countries to the teacher by outpupils. ‖ adj. m. + f. of or pertaining to Minerva.

minestra s. f. (Braz.) artifice or expedient through which one tries to obtain certain things.

minestre s. m. (Braz.) person skilful in the use of his resources to get what he wants.

mingacho s. m. gourd filled with water to keep fish alive in (for some time).

mingau s. m. (Braz.) 1. wheat or manioc pap. 2. (fig.) something very watery or sloppy.

~ **de aveia** porridge.

mingau-das-almas s. m. (pl. **mingaus-das-almas**) the mucous substance which is formed in the mouth, after several hours of sleeping.

mingo adj. (S. Braz., pop.) small, little, smallest.

o dedo ~ the little finger.

mingolas s. m. + f., sg. + pl. (Braz.) stingy, avaricious person; miser.

mingu s. m. (Braz.) tree whose wood is much appreciated for marquetry.

míngua s. f. 1. lack, need, want of the most necessary things. 2. scarcity, shortage. 3. wane, decrease, diminution. 4. defect, deficiency.

à ~ de for want of. **morrer à ~** to starve.

minguado adj. 1. destitute, unprovided, poor, needy. 2. scarce, limited, short.

minguamento s. m. 1. lack, want. 2. decrease, diminution.

minguante s. m. decadence, decay, decline, diminution. ‖ adj. m. + f. waning, decreasing, diminishing, declining, lacking.

quarto ~ (astr.) last quarter.

minguar v. 1. to wane, decrease, diminish, dwindle, reduce. 2. to lack, fail, miss. 3. to lower, fall. 4. to decline, decay. 5. to belittle, lessen, depreciate.

minguinho s. m. + adj. = **mindinho.**

minguta adj. m. + f. (Braz.) 1. small, little. 2. dry, dried up.

minha adj. + poss. pron. (f. of **meu**) mine, my.

~ **casa é sua** my house is at your disposal. ~ **irmã** my sister. **eu por** ~ **parte** I for one.

minhoca s. f. 1. earthworm. 2. ~**s** pl. (fam.) whims, crotchets, manias, ridiculous believes, fancies.

minhocaçu, minhocuçu s. m. (Braz., also **minhocão**) fabulous being having the shape of a gigantic worm and capable of performing all sorts of miracles.

minhocal s. m. (pl. **-ais**) (N. Braz.) country untraversable in the rainy season.

minhoca-louca s. f. (pl. **minhocas-loucas**) annelidan worm (Pheretima Lawayana).

minhocão s. m. (pl. **-ões**) (Braz.) 1. large eathworm. 2. = **minhocaçu.** 3. (Braz., pop.) certain constructions or mechanisms, having a great extension.

minhoteira s. f. small wooden bridge.

minhoto s. m. native or inhabitant of the Portuguese province of Minho. ‖ adj. of or pertaining to the Minho.

miniatura s. f. 1. miniatura: a) painting or portrait of very small dimensions. b) anything represented on a greatly reduced scale. c) red initial letters in ancient manuscripts. 2. résumé, summary, abstract.

miniaturar, miniaturizar v. to miniature: portray in miniature, on a small scale.

miniaturista s. m. + f. miniature painter. ‖ adj. painting miniatures.

minigâncias s. f. pl. (S. Braz., pop.) trifles, knick-knacks, trinkets.

mínima s. f. (mus.) minim, half note (plate N 1).

minimalista s. m. + f. Minimalist: member of the moderate section of the former Social Revolutionary party in Russia. ‖ adj. Minimalistic: relating to the Minimalists.

minimalizar v. (math.) to minimize.

mínimo s. m. 1. minimum: the least. 2. the little finger. ‖ adj. 1. minimal, least, very little. 2. remote, faint.

reduzir os gastos ao ~ to reduce one's expenses to a minimum. **eu não tenho a -a idéia** I haven't the faintest idea. **salário** ~ minimum wage.

mínio s. m. 1. minium: red lead oxide. 2. vermillion, cinnabar.

minissaia s. f. miniskirt.

ministerialismo s. m. ministerialism: political trend of inconditional support of the ministry in office.

ministério s. m. 1. ministry, cabinet, state department. 2. office or service of a minister. 3. charge, office, profession, post, position, function. 4. = **mister.**

~ **da Aeronáutica** air ministry. ~ **da Agricultura** ministry of agriculture. ~ **do altar,** ~ **da Igreja** the priestly office. ~ **de Educação e Saúde** ministry of public instruction and health. ~ **da Fazenda** ministry of finance; exchequer, treasury. ~ **da Guerra** ministry of war. ~ **da Justiça e dos Negócios Interiores** ministry of justice and home affairs. ~ **da Marinha** ministry of naval affairs. ~ **público** prosecuting counsel. ~ **das Relações Exteriores** ministry of foreign affairs. ~ **de Trabalho e Comércio** ministry of labour and commerce. ~ **de Viação e Obras Públicas** ministry of communications and public works.

ministra s. f. 1. wife of a minister or ambassador. 2. ministress, ambassadress. 3. revolving compartment through which food was passed into the refectory of a convent. 4. arbitress. 5. type of Italian soup, minestrone.

ministrador s. m. ministrant, one who ministers. ‖ adj. ministrant, ministering.

ministral adj. m. + f. (pl. **-ais**) ministral: relating to ministers.

ministrante s. m. ministrant, acolyte, altar boy. ‖ adj. m. + f. ministering.

ministrar v. 1. to minister. 2. to render aid, service or attendance. 3. to furnish, give, administer, supply, dispense, give medicine. 4. to suggest, confer. 5. to contribute as to comfort, happiness, etc. 6. to serve as a minister.

ministrículo s. m. insignificant minister.

ministro s. m. 1. minister: a) minister of state. b) diplomatic representative in rank under an ambassador. c) aide. d) (rel.) clergyman, priest (plate P 5). 2. (Braz.) member of the Supreme Court or Supreme Military Court, and the Audit Department of the Exchequer.
~ **da Aeronáutica** air minister. ~ **da Agricultura** minister of agriculture. ~ **do altar,** ~ **da Igreja** priest. ~ **de Educação e Saúde** minister of public instruction and health. ~ **do Evangelho** minister of the gospel. ~ **da Fazenda** minister of finance. ~ **da Guerra** minister of war. ~ **da Justiça e dos Negócios Interiores** minister of justice and home affairs. ~ **da Marinha** minister of naval affairs. ~ **das Relações Exteriores** minister of foreign affairs. ~ **de Trabalho e Comércio** minister of labour and commerce. ~ **de Viação e Obras Públicas** minister of communications and public works.

minivestido s. m. minidress.

minjoada s. f. 1. (N. Braz.) fishing with a fixed rod without the presence of the fisherman. 2. (S. Braz.) large fishing-net.

minjolinho s. m. (Braz.) = **bico-rasteiro.**

minoração s. f. (pl. **-ões**) 1. decrease, diminution, lessening, reduction, abatement. 2. softening, assuagement, mitigation.

minorar v. 1. to decrease, diminish, lessen, reduce, abate. 2. to soften, alleviate, ease, assuage.

minorativo s. m. laxative. ‖ adj. lessening, softening, diminishing, soothing, gentle (laxative).

minoria s. f. minority: minor part in number.
a ~ 1. the few. 2. (pol.) the minority.

minorquino s. m. native or inhabitant of Minorca. ‖ adj. of or pertaining to Minorca.

minuana s. f. (S. Braz.) name of three plants of the genus Oenothera (Oenothera affinis, Oenothera indecora and Oenothera mollissima).

minuano s. m. (S. Braz.) cold and dry southwestern winter wind.
~ **sujo** extremely disagreeable cold wind accompanied by a drizzly rain.

minúcia s. f. 1. minute, detail, nicety. 2. insignificance, trifle. 3. particularity. 4. **~s** pl. minutiae: trivial particulars.
fazer questão de ~s to stand up to niceties.

minuciar v. to detail.

minuciosidade s. f. 1. minuteness, circumstantiality, particularity. 2. accuracy, exactness. 3. conscientiousness, scrupulosity. 4. (depr.) meticulousness, punctiliousness.

minucioso adj. 1. minute, circumstantial, particular. 2. conscientious, scrupulous. 3. (depr.) finical,

hairsplitting. ‖ **-amente** adv. minutely, etc.
~ **em excesso** hairsplitting. **detalhes ~s sobre** full details about.

minudência s. f. minuteness. 2. minute, detail, trifle. 3. (fig.) scrupulous observation.

minudencioso, minudente adj. fussy, exacting, finical.

minuendo s. m. (Braz.) = **diminuendo.**

minuete, minueto s. m. minuet: 1. slow stately dance. 2. music for this dance.

minuir v. = **diminuir.**

minúscula s. f. minuscule: small letter.

minusculizar v. to turn insignificant.

minúsculo adj. minuscule, tiny, insignificant.
letra -a small letter, lower case letter.

minuta s. f. 1. minute, draft of a document. 2. sketch. 3. (Braz.) in restaurants, a dish prepared within a minute.
à ~ prepared immediately (meal).

minutador s. m. minuting person, recording secretary. ‖ adj. minuting.

minutar v. 1. to minute: write or dictate a minute. 2. to draft, sketch.

minuto s. m. 1. minute: a) sixtieth part of an hour. b) (math.) sixtieth part of a degree. 2. moment, instant. ‖ adj. minute, tiny.
espere um ~ wait a minute.

mio s. m. miaow, mewing.

miocárdio s. m. (anat.) myocardium: muscular part of the heart.

miocele s. f. myocele: muscular tumour.

mioceno s. m. (geol.) Miocene: middle section of the Tertiary period. ‖ adj. Miocenic: relating to the Miocene.

miodinia s. f. (med.) 1. muscular pain. 2. muscular rheumatism.

miografia, miologia s. f. (anat.) myography: description of muscles.

miográfico, miológico adj. relating to myography.

miógrafo s. m. myograph: instrument which represents graphically the contraction of muscles.

mióide adj. m. + f. myomatous: said of a tumour consisting of muscular tissue.

miolada s. f. 1. brains. 2. sweetbread.

mioleira s. f. 1. brains. 2. (fig.) sense, brains.

miolema s. m. (anat.) myolemma.

miolo s. m. 1. brain. 2. medulla. 3. soft part of bread. 4. pulp of some fruit. 5. kernel of a walnut. 6. the interior of anything. 7. (fig.) sense, savvy.
cabeça sem ~s empty-headed fellow. **dar no ~** to come into one's head.

mioloso, mioludo adj. rich in pulp (fruit) or brains.

mioma s. m. (med.) myoma: tumour consisting of muscular tissue.

miomalacia s. f. softening of the muscles.

mio-mio s. m. (pl. **mios-mios** or **mio-mios**) (S. Braz.) poisonous composite plant (Baccharis cordifolia).

míope s. m. + f. 1. myopic person. 2. (fig.) nearsighted person, person of little intelligence. ‖ adj. myopic: 1. nearsighted, shortsighted. 2. (fig.) of low intelligence.

miopia s. f. myopia. 1. nearsightedness, shortsightedness. 2. lack of perspicacity or intelligence.

miopraxia, miopragia s. f. (med.) insufficiency or inferiority of an organ.

miose s. f. (med.) myosis: contraction of the pupil of the eye.

miosótis s. f., sg. + pl. (bot., also **não-te-esqueças-de-mim**) myosotis, forget-me-not.

miótico adj. myotic: relating to myosis.

miotomia s. f. myotomy: dissection of muscles.

miotômico adj. myotomic: relating to myotomy.

miquear v. (Braz., pop.) to ruin, impoverish.

miqueletes s. m. pl. 1. little flags, a surveyor's poles, aiming posts. 2. (fig.) indications, signs.

mira s. f. 1. sight (fire-arms). 2. aim, bourn(e), mark, scope, end, design, purpose. 3. desire, wish. 4. a surveyor's pole. 5. fish of the family Serranideae (Epinephelus ruber). **à ~** on guard. **cruz de ~** cross wires, spider lines. **linha de ~** sight line. **ponto de ~** foresight, frontsight. **pôr a ~ em** to aim at, to fix one's glance upon. **ter a ~ em** to watch closely.

mirabanda s. f. (Braz.) large fly.

mirabolante adj. m. + f. showy, ridiculously pompous, gaudy.

miracídio s. m. miracidium: first larval form of heterogenetic trematodes.

miraculado s. m. a person who has been subject to a miracle. ‖ adj. of or relating to such a person.

miraculoso adj. = **milagroso.**

mira-falante s. f. (pl. **miras-falantes**) (topogr.) self--reading rod.

miragem s. f. (pl. **-ens**) 1. mirage, optical illusion, fata morgana. 2. (fig.) illusion, deception.

miralmuminim, miramolim s. m. (pl. **-ins**) calif: commander of the faithful (Mussulmans).

miramar s. m. belvedere with a view of the sea.

mirante s. m. (also **miradouro, miradoiro**) mirador: belvedere, building set up to provide a beautiful view.

mirão s. m. = **mirone.**

mira-olho s. m. (pl. **mira-olhos**) a variety of peach. ‖ adj. appetizing, inviting, good-looking.

mirar v. 1. to eye, examine, stare at, look at. 2. to see, discern. 3. to aim, take aim, aim a gun. 4. to have in mind, plan, consider. 5. to observe, observe secretly. 6. **~-se** to look at o. s. in the mirror.

miri, mirim s. m. (Braz.) plant of the family Sapotaceae (Bumelia nigra), of medicinal properties.

miríade, miríada s. f. myriad: 1. ten thousand. 2. (fig.) a very great number of people or things; indeterminate enormous quantity.

miriagrama s. m. myriagramme: 10 kilogrammes.

mirialitro s. m. myrialiter: ten thousand liters.

miriápode s. m. (zool.; also **milípede**) myriapod: millepede. ‖ adj. m. + f. myriapod: having numerous legs.

miriare s. m. myriare, ten thousand ares.

miricácea s. f. a species of the Myricaceae, family of dicotyledonous plants.

miricáceo adj. (bot.) myricaceous: of or pertaining to the family Myricaceae.

mirificar v. 1. to render mirific. 2. to cause marvel, admiration. 3. to cause fright.

mirífico adj. mirific, marvellous, excellent, wonderful, magnificent.

mirim s. m. (pl. **-ins**) (Braz.) 1. = **miri.** 2. name of various small bees of the genus Melipona. ‖ adj. m. + f. small.

mirim-guaçu s. f. (pl. **mirins-guaçus**) a certain bee whose honey has medicinal properties.

mirindiba s. f. (Braz.) tree of the family Lythraceae (Lafoensia replicata).

mirinzal s. m. (pl. **-ais**) (Braz.) place where the sapotaceous plant **miri** or **mirim** grows abundantly.

mirioftalmo adj. (zool.) having many eyes.

miriquiná s. m. (Braz.) night ape (Nyctipith felinus).

miristicácea s. f. a member of the Myristicaceae, family of dicotyledonous plants.

miristicáceo adj. (bot.) myristicaceous: of or pertaining to the family Myristicaceae.

mirmecófago adj. (zool.) myrmecophagous.

mirmecófilo adj. myrmecophile: living with ants.

mirmidão s. m. (pl. **-ões**) 1. a cook's assistant, scullion. 2. companion.

mirolho (ô) s. m. a person who has very good aim (marbles).

mirone s. m. (fam.) spectator, onlooker, bystander; (U. S. A., sl.) kibitzer.

mironga s. f. (Braz., pop.) disagreement, quarrel.

miroró s. m. (Braz.) a species of fish known also as **mororó** and **tororó.**

mirra s. f. 1. myrrh. 2. myrrh gum. 3. m. + f.: a) (fam.) skinny person. b) miser, niggard.

mirrado adj. dried up, withered, wizened, skinny; lean; faded.

mirrar v. 1. to prepare with myrrh. 2. to dry up, wither, wizen, emaciate, waste. 3. to lose energy or strength. 4. to drain the strength of somebody or something gradually. 5. to diminish, disappear. 6. to reduce (weight) enormously. 7. **~-se:** a) to humiliate o. s. b) to flee. c) to hide o. s.

mírreo adj. (poet.) perfumed with myrrh.

mirsinácea s. f. one of the Myrsinaceae, family of dicotyledonous plants.

mirsináceo adj. (bot.) of or pertaining to the family Myrsinaceae.

mirtácea s. f. plant of the family Myrtaceae.

mirtáceo adj. myrtaceous: relating to or resembling the myrtle.

mirtal, mirtedo s. m. myrtle grove.

mírteo adj. 1. of or pertaining to the myrtle. 2. made out of myrtle. 3. said of a place where myrtles grow.

mirtiforme adj. m. + f. myrtiform, like myrtle.

mirtilo s. m. (bot.) whortleberry, blueberry (plate B 1).

mirto s. m. = **murta.**

mirtóide adj. m. + f. myrtaceous: resembling the myrtle.

mirtoso adj. containing myrtle.

miruim s. m. (Braz.) = **maruim.**

misantropia s. f. misanthropy: aversion to mankind, unsociableness.

misantrópico adj. misanthropic(al): relating to misanthropy.

misantropo s. m. 1. misanthrope, misanthropist: man--hater, unsociable person. 2. melancholic person. ‖ adj. misanthropic; cynical; farouche.

míscaro s. m. mushroom growing habitually under pine trees.

miscelânea s. f. 1. miscellanea, miscellany: collection of miscellaneous literary pieces. 2. miscellany: (fig.) mixture, confusion, medley, odds and ends, salmagundi.

miscibilidade s. f. miscibility.

miscigenação s. f. miscigenation: interracial crossing.

miscigenar v. to mix races, to crossbreed.

miscível adj. m. + f. (pl. **-íveis**) miscible: capable of being mixed.

miseração s. f. (pl. **-ões**) commiseration, compassion, pity.

miserando adj. deplorable, pitiable, miserable, wretched.

miserar v. 1. to disgrace, make miserable, unhappy. 2. **~-se** to feel sorry for o. s., to lament, complain.

miserável s. m. + f. (pl. **-áveis**) 1. miserable, wretch. 2. miser, skinflint. 3. infamous person, villain. ‖ adj. 1. unhappy, miserable, wretched, pitiful, woeful. 2. niggard, stingy, sordid, shabby. 3. mean, infamous, despisable, abject. ‖ **miseravelmente** adv. miserably.

miserê s. m. (Braz., pop.) situation of extreme misery.

miséria s. f. 1. misery, unhappiness, wretchedness, distress. 2. poverty, indigence, penury, calamity

3. avarice, niggardliness, miserliness. 4. meanness, sordidness. 5. mere trifle, bagatelle. 6. human imperfection.

as ~s da vida humana the miseries of human life. **cair na** ~ to come to poverty. **estar na** ~, **passar ~s** to be hard up, to bear calamity. **ficar reduzido à** ~ to be reduced to poverty. **ganhar uma** ~ to earn a pittance. **viver na** ~ to live in extreme poverty.

misericórdia s. f. 1. mercy, compassion, commiseration, pity. 2. pardon, clemency, forgiveness. 3. charity, charitable institution. 4. (ant.) misericord: dagger with which knights killed their foes if they did not plead for mercy. 5. cry pleading for mercy. **por ~!** for mercy's sake. **golpe de** ~ finishing stroke. **pedir** ~ to beg for mercy. **Santa Casa de Misericórdia** hospital for indigent persons.

misericordioso adj. merciful, clement, compassionate, pitiful. ‖ **-amente** adv. mercifully.

mísero adj. (abs. superl. **misérrimo**) 1. disgraced, miserable, wretched, unhappy, pitiable. 2. (fig.) scarce. 3. stingy, niggard.

misofobia s. f. mysophobia: morbid terror of contacts for fright of contamination or dirt.

misófobo adj. terrified of contacts.

misogamia s. f. misogamy: hatred of marriage.

misógamo s. m. misogamist: hater of marriage. ‖ adj. misogamic: hating marriage.

misoginia s. f. (med.) misogyny: hatred of women.

misógino s. m. misogynist: woman-hater. ‖ adj. miso-, gynic(al), misogynous: hating women.

misologia s. f. misology: aversion to reason or of knowledge.

misólogo s. m. misologist: hater of reason or of knowledge.

misoneísmo s. m. misoneism: hatred of novelties (ideas, customs, etc.).

misoneísta s. m. + f. misoneist: hater of novelties. ‖ adj. misoneistic.

misopedia s. f. misopedia: a hatred for children.

mispíquel s. m. (Braz., min.) mispickel: arsenopyrite.

missa (I) s. f. 1. (Church) mass. 2. (ant.) any religious festivity.

~ calada, rezada, particular low mass. **~ campal** field mass. **~ cantada** high mass. **~ das almas, ~ de defunto, ~ fúnebre** mass for the deceased. **~ de réquiem** requiem mass. **~ de três em renge** mass celebrated by more than one priest and with organ music. **~ do galo** midnight mass at Christmas. **~ do trigésimo dia** month's mass. **~ pontifical** pontifical mass. **~ solene** high mass. **ajudar à** ~ to serve at mass. **celebrar a** ~ to say mass. **ir à** ~ to go to mass. **ouvir** ~ to hear mass, to attend mass. **não ir à ~ com alguém** to dislike s. o. **não saber da** ~ **a metade** to be badly informed. **~ concelebrada** a concelebrated mass.

missa (II) s. m. (N. Braz.) nickname given to the adepts of Protestant sects.

missado adj. having the orders of a presbyter.

missagra s. f. 1. hinge. 2. (naut.) block, moor's head.

missal s. m. (pl. **-ais**) 1. missal, mass-book. 2. (typogr.) missal letter.

missão s. f. (pl. **-ões**) mission: 1. the act of sending. 2. delegation. 3. incumbence, commission, errand. 4. calling, vocation. 5. body of missionaries. 6. a missionary's field of action. 7. missionary station. 8. religious services for rousing spiritual interest. 9. diplomatic mission, legation. 10. propaganda. 11. obligation. 12. m. (ant.) postillion, mailman, mail.

missar v. to say or hear mass.

miss, misse s. f. (Engl.) miss, a title obtained in a beauty contest.

misseiro s. m. person devoted to mass. ‖ adj. devoted to mass.

missionar v. 1. to evangelize, preach the gospel. 2. to carry on missionary work.

missionário s. m. 1. missionary: person sent to carry on missionary work. 2. propagator.

missioneiro s. m. (S. Braz.) native or inhabitant of the Missões region. ‖ adj. of or pertaining to this region.

missiva s. f. missive: written message, letter, epistle, dispatch.

missivista s. m. + f. (Braz.) person who writes or takes a missive.

missivo adj. 1. missive: that can or may be sent. 2. missile, that can be cast, flung, hurled.

missúri s. m. a variety of tobacco from Missouri (U. S. A.).

mistagogia s. f. mystagogy: initiation into divine mysteries.

mistagogo s. m. 1. mystagogue: person who initiates into divine mysteries. 2. initiator, mentor.

mistela s. f. (pop.) 1. badly prepared and evil tasting food or drink. 2. = **mixórdia**.

mister s. m. 1. occupation, employment, office, business. 2. service, work, incumbence. 3. urgency, necessity, want, need.

haver ~, ser ~ to be necessary. **há ~** it is necessary.

mistério s. m. 1. mystery, enigma, secret. 2. (rel.) mystery of the sacral rite, eucharistic elements, etc. 3. secret rite known only to those iniciated. **fazer ~ de alguma coisa** to make a mystery of a thing.

misterioso adj. mysterious, enigmatic, secret, obscure. ‖ **-amente** adv. mysteriously, etc.

mística s. f. study of divine or spiritual things.

misticidade s. f. mysticity: mystical quality.

misticismo s. m. mysticism: 1. doctrine of direct communion of the soul with God, by contemplation. 2. belief in supernatural things.

místico s. m. mystic: believer in mysticism. ‖ adj. 1. mystic: a) pertaining to mysticism. b) spiritual, allegorical, emblematical. c) occult, esoteric, mysterious. 2. (obs.): a) mixed. b) annexed, joined. c) pertaining to a miscellany.

mistificação s. f. (pl. **-ões**) mystification: act or fact of mystifying.

mistificado adj. mystified, illuded.

mistificador s. m. mystifier: person who mystifies, deceiver, cheater. ‖ adj. mystifying, deceiving.

mistificar v. 1. to mystify, puzzle, bewilder, hoax, play on a person's credulity. 2. to impose upon, deceive, cheat.

mistifório s. m. miscellany, mix-up, confusion, medley, jumble, hodge-podge.

mistilíneo adj. (geom.) mixtilineal, mixtilinear.

mistinérvio adj. (bot.) said of leaves with veins going in various directions.

misto s. m. 1. mixture. 2. set, a whole. ‖ adj. 1. mixed. 2. variegated. 3. confused. 4. (math.) consisting of a fractionary and a whole part. **colégio** ~ mixed school, coed school. **número** ~ mixed number. **trem** ~ mixed train, train taking both pasengers and cargo.

misto-quente s. m. (pl. **mistos-quentes**) (Braz.) a hot ham and cheese sandwich.

mistral s. m. mistral: cold and dry northwestern wind in the south-east of France.

mistura s. f. 1. mixture, blend. 2. chemical mixture.

misturada s. f. 1. mix-up, confusion, medley, jumble, hodge-podge. 2. miscellany. 3. (Braz.) the mixture of white rum with another drink. 4. (N. Braz.)

dark girl between mulatto and Indian in colouring. 5. (S. Braz.) final dance at a ball.
tomar uma ~ to have the above described drink.
misturador s. m. concrete mixer, mixer.
misturar v. 1. to mix, blend, mingle. 2. to shuffle, confound, confuse. 3. to cross (breeding). 4. to intermarry. 5. ~-se to intrude, unite, join.
misturável adj. m. + f. (pl. -áveis) mixable, miscible, blendable, confusable.
mísula s. f. 1. (archit.) console, corbel, supporting bracket. 2. (naut.) brackets supporting the afterdeck.
mitene s. f. mit, mitten: ladies' fingerless gloves.
mítico adj. mythical: relating to myth, fabulous, legendary.
mitificação s. f. (pl. -ões) act or effect of mythicizing.
mitificar v. to mythicize, mythify; turn into a myth, turn mythical.
mitigação s. f. (pl. -ões) mitigation; alleviation, assuagement.
mitigador s. m. mitigator: one who or that which mitigates. ‖ adj. mitigative, mitigatory: that mitigates, relieves.
mitigar v. to mitigate, alleviate, slacken, moderate, soften, soothe, assuage, quench.
~ **a sede** to quench one's thirst.
mitigativo adj. mitigative, mitigant, lenitive, assuasive.
mitigável adj. m. + f. (pl. -áveis) mitigable: that can be mitigated.
mitismo s. m. mythology: science of myths.
mito s. m. 1. myth: ancient historical legend. 2. (fig.) something unbelievable, incredible.
mitografia s. f. mythography: description of myths.
mitográfico adj. of or pertaining to mythography.
mitógrafo s. m. mythographer, mythographist: person who describes myths.
mitologia s. f. mythology: 1. system of myths. 2. science of myths.
mitológico adj. mythologic(al): relating to mythology. ‖ **mitologicamente** adv. mythologically.
mitólogo s. m. mythologer, mythologist: person versed in mythology; writer on mythology.
mitomania s. f. mythomania: morbid tendency for lying.
mitômano s. m. mythomaniac: person suffering from mythomania.
mitose s. f. (biol.) mitosis: indirect cell division.
mitra s. f. 1. miter, mitre: official headdress of a bishop (plate P 5). 2. dignity of a bishop. 3. paper hood that covered the heads of the condemned during the Inquisition. 4. (pop.) tail-end of birds. 5. (S. Braz.) slyness, cunningness. 6. m.: a) (S. Braz.) vicious, stubborn animal. b) (N. Braz.) miser. ‖ adj. 1. = **mitrado**. 2. vicious stubborn (animal). 3. stingy.
mitração s. f. (pl. -ões) (S. Braz.) slyness, cunningness, roguery.
mitrado adj. 1. mitered, mitred: entitled to wear or wearing a miter. 2. having a natural headdress like a miter (animals). 3. sly, cunning, astute, lively.
mitral adj. m. + f. (pl. -ais) (anat.) mitral.
válvula ~ mitral valve (of the heart).
mitridatismo s. m. mithridatism: 1. method of acquiring immunity against a poison by taking gradually increased doses of it. 2. the immunity thus acquired.
mitridatizado adj. mithridatic: immunized by mithridatism.
mitridatizar v. to mithridatize: immunize by mithridatism.

mitriforme adj. m. + f. mitral, mitriform: resembling a miter.
mitu, mitua s. m. (Braz.) = **mutum**.
miúça s. f. 1. small portion or fragment. 2. (N. E. Braz., also **miunça**) common name for goats and sheep. 3. ~s pl. small tithes paid to the Church.
miuçalha s. f. **miuçalho** m. 1. (obs.) = **miúça**. 2. (Braz.) gang of children, fry. 3. ~s pl. trifles, fry.
miudagem s. f. (pl. -ens) (Braz.) 1. lots of little things, trifles. 2. leftovers in stock after a sale. 3. small cattle. 4. fry, bratts, bunch of children. 5. pluck, giblets.
miudear v. 1. to tell, narrate something giving full details. 2. to give a blow by blow account. 3. to detail, particularize.
miudeiro s. m. (N. Braz.) seller of pluck and giblets.
miudeza s. f. 1. minuteness, smallness. 2. (fig.) exactingness, rigorousness. 3. (fig.) careful observation, exactitude, strictness, nicety. 4. punctiliousness, paltriness, meanness. 5. ~s pl.: a) particularities, details. b) pluck, giblets. c) trifles, small wares, odds and ends. d) novelty shop for small wares.
miudinho s. m. (Braz.) popular dance. ‖ adj. (dim. of **miúdo**) tiny.
miúdo s. m. 1. pastern part of an animal's leg where the fetters are fastened. 2. (S. Braz., fam.) boy. 3. ~s pl.: a) change (money). b) giblets and pluck. ‖ adj. 1. minute, small, little. 2. circumstantial, particular, detailed. 3. frequent. 4. (fig.) precise, rigorous, scrupulous, punctilious, mean, stingy. ‖ **miudamente** adv. 1. in little pieces. 2. strictly, exactly. 3. detailedly, circumstantially.
caça -a lesser, lower chase. **chumbo** ~ small shot. **gado** ~ small cattle. **a** ~ frequently, often. **troco** ~ small change. **vender por** ~ to sell by retail.
miul, miúlo s. m. hub (of a wheel).
miunça s. f. = **miúnça**.
miúro adj. (med.) gradually weakening (pulse).
miúva s. f. (Braz.) medicinal plant of the family Melastomataceae.
miva s. f. medicinal preparation containing fruit and meat juices.
mixanga s. m. (S. Braz.) backwoodsman, rustic, boor.
mixar v. = **michar**.
mixe adj. m. + f. (S. Braz.) 1. of little value, small, insignificant, small in size. 2. said of dull parties.
mixedema s. m. (med.) mixedema: sickness caused by thyroid insufficiency.
mixila s. f. (Braz., zool.) a four-toed anteater (Myrmecophaga tetradactyla).
mixilanga s. f. (N. Braz.) 1. drunken brawl. 2. mixture of drugs.
mixira s. f. (N. Braz.) preserve of a manatee or young turtle in its own oil.
mixórdia s. f. 1. confusion, mix-up, medley, jumble, hotchpotch, gallimaufry, mishmash. 2. intrigue. 3. poor, spoiled wine.
mixorne s. m. fish of the family Cichlidae (Crenicichla lacustris).
mixuango s. m. (Braz., also **muxuango**) backwoodsman, rustic, boor.
mizocéfalo adj. having a head formed like a cupping glass.
mnemônica s. f. mnemonics: system for aiding the memory.
mnemônico adj. 1. mnemonic: relating to or aiding the memory. 2. according to mnemonics.
mnemonização s. f. (pl. -ões) mnemonization: act of turning mnemonic.
mnemonizar v. to mnemonize: make mnemonic.
mnemonizável adj. m. + f. (pl. -áveis) 1. that can be mnemonized. 2. easily remembered.

mnemotecnia s. f. mnemotechny: art of developing the memory.

mnemotécnico adj. mnemotechnic: relating to mnemotechny.

mo contr. of the pronouns **me** and **o**.
ele deu-mo he gave it to me. **ele disse-mo** he told me of it. **ele vendeu-mos** he sold them to me.

mó s. f. 1. millstone. 2. grindstone, whetstone. 3. (Port., prov.) large quantity, masses.

moafa s. f. (pop.) drunken brawl.

moagem s. f. (pl. **-ens**) 1. grinding, milling. 2. grist.
fábrica de ~ flour mill. **indústria de** ~ milling industry.

mobica s. m. + f. (N. Braz.) freed slave.

móbil s. m. (pl. **móbeis**) (also **móvel**) 1. cause, motive, spring. 2. motor. ‖ adj. m. + f. movable, mobile.

mobilador s. m. furnisher. ‖ adj. furnishing.

mobilar, mobilhar, mobiliar v. (Braz.) to furnish, provide with furniture.
~ **uma casa** to fit up a house. **quarto mobiliado** furnished room.

mobília s. f. furniture.

mobiliário s. m. 1. furniture. 2. movables. ‖ adj. of or pertaining to furniture or movables.

mobilidade s. f. 1. mobility, movableness. 2. (fig.) inconstancy. 3. (sociology) mobility.

mobilização s. f. (pl. **-ões**) mobilization: act of mobilizing.

mobilizar v. to mobilize: 1. render mobile. 2. put in motion or circulation. 3. make armed forces ready for war.

moca s. m. 1. superior quality of coffee coming originally from Arabia. 2. (Braz.) coffee. 3. f. (pop.): a) mace, club, cudgel. b) (Braz.) mockery, joke. c) lie. d) nonsense.

moça s. f. 1. young woman, girl, lass, gal. 2. (Port., prov.) maid, maid-servant. 3. concubine, mistress, prostitute.

moça-branca s. f. (pl. **moças-brancas**) 1. (Braz.) a variety of honeybee (Melipona angustata). 2. (Braz.) = **cachaça**.

mocada s. f. stroke with a mace or cudgel.

moçada s. f. (S. Braz.) group of youngsters.

mocamau s. m. (Braz., hist., also **quilombeiro**) fugitive Negro living in the woods.

mocambeiro s. m. (Braz.) 1. = **mocamau**. 2. evildoer who took a refuge in the woods. ‖ adj. 1. living in a hiding-place in the woods. 2. hiding in the woods, stray, runaway (cattle).

mocambo s. m. (Braz., hist.) 1. refuge of slaves in the woods. 2. (N. Braz.) hiding-place of cattle in the woods. 3. (also **mocambinho**) hut, cabin, shelter.

moçame s. f. (also **moceiro**) (Braz., fam.) group of girls.

mocanquice s. f. (Braz., fam.) = **moganga** 2.

moção s. f. (pl. **-ões**) motion: 1. movement. 2. commotion, agitation, instigation. 3. proposition in an assembly.

moçar s. m. (ant.) heap of stones, ruin. ‖ v. 1. to deflower. 2. ~**-se** to become a prostitute.

moçárabe s. m. + f. Mozarab: Spanish Christian who lived under the Moorish regime. ‖ adj. Mozarabic: of or pertaining to such a person.

moças-e-velhas s. f. (pl. (Braz., bot.) zinnia.

mocetão s. m. (pl. **-ões**) (f. **mocetona**) big, strong, husky fellow; strapping fellow.

mocetona s. f. strong, well-shaped or pretty girl; strapping girl.

mocha (ô) s. f. (pl. **mochas**) (Braz., pop.) fire-arm without a cock.

mochadura s. f. the act or effect of cutting off the horns.

mochar v. 1. to cut off a member, esp. the horns, to maim, mutilate. 2. to prune trees. 3. (Braz.): a) to cheat, jilt. b) to hide, keep from. 4. to fall back on one's word.

mocheta s. f. (archit.) bead, beading, fillet.

mochila s. f. 1. rucksack, knapsack, haversack. 2. (fig.) hunchback.

mocho (ô) s. m. (pl. **mochos**) 1. nocturnal bird of prey smaller than an owl. 2. (fig.) misanthrope. 3. stool (plate C 2). ‖ adj. 1. hornless, polled, devoid of a member, esp. the horns; mutilated, maimed. 2. (Braz.) without cock (fire-arm). 3. mastless. 4. pruned.
gado ~ polled cattle.

mocica s. f. jerk, shake, trembling.

mocidade s. f. youth: a) youthfulness, youthful age. b) young people. c) (fig.) imprudence, lack of sense and ponderation.

mocinho s. m. (dim. of **moço**) 1. young man. 2. (Braz.) name given to the hero in cowboy and adventure films by the children.

mocitaíba s. f. (Braz., also **moçutaíba**) leguminous tree (Swartzia crocea) with very hard wood.

mocô, mocó s. m. (N. Braz.) 1. charm, amulet. 2. sorcery.

mocó s. m. (Braz.) 1. rock cavy: rodent resembling a guinea pig. 2. (N. Braz.) bag with a shoulder-strap used for papers, lunch, etc. 3. a variety of cotton much appreciated for the length and silkiness of its fibers. 4. = **mocô**.

moço s. m. 1. young man. 2. servant. ‖ adj. 1. young, youthful. 2. (fig.) inexperienced.
~ **de fretes** porter, carrier. ~ **de recados** errand-boy.

moçoila s. f. dim. of **moça**.

mocorongo s. m. (Braz.) backwoodsman, rustic, boor, lout.

mocororó s. m. (Braz.) 1. name of various soft drinks made out of rice, manioc or cashew. 2. limonite found in the gold region of Bahia. 3. diamond chips.

mocotó s. m. (Braz.) 1. wild plant of the family Acanthaceae (Elytroria alagoana). 2. calf's foot without hoof used for food. 3. (vulg.) leg.
geléia de ~ gelatine made out of calve's feet.

mocozal s. m. (pl. **-ais**) (N. Braz.) place with high stone walls full of holes in which the rock cavy lives.

mocureiro s. m. (S. Braz.) person of little skill or knack for his trade.

moda s. f. 1. manner, fashion, vogue, mode, custom, usage. 2. way, method. 3. (sociology) style undergoing changes during the course of history. 4. (stat.) mode. 5. song, aria. 6. ~**s** pl. feminine fashion and apparel.
à ~ fashionable. **à** ~ **francesa** after the French fashion. **andar à** ~ to follow the fashion. **à sua** ~ in his own way. **a última** ~ the latest fashion. **desfile de** ~**s** fashion show. **estar fora de** ~ to be out of fashion. **entrar em** ~ to come into fashion. **canção da** ~ hit song. **estar na** ~ to be in fashion. **este estilo passou da** ~ this style has gone out of fashion. **loja de** ~**s** millinery shop. **ser** ~ to be in fashion. **vestir-se à** ~ to follow the fashion.

modal adj. m. + f. (pl. **-ais**) modal: relating to the mode or form.

modalidade s. f. modality: 1. manner, way. 2. form. 3. kind, sort. 4. condition.

modelação s. f. (pl. **-ões**) modelling, moulding.

modelador s. m. modeller, moulder, patternmaker. ‖ adj. modelling.

modelagem s. f. (pl. **-ens**) modelling, moulding.

modelar v. 1. to model, shape, mould, form. 2. to take as a model. ‖ adj. m. + f. model, exemplary, perfect.
modelismo s. m. model(l)ing.
modelista s. m. + f. model(l)ist: maker of models.
modelo (ê) s. m. (pl. **modelos**) model: 1. mould, pattern, standard. 2. (fig.) ideal, example. 3. mannequin. 4. person who poses for a painter or sculptor. **servir de** ~ to serve as an example. **tomar a alguém por** ~ to follow the example of s. o.
moderação s. f. (pl. **-ões**) 1. moderation, restraint, temperance, forbearance. 2. prudence, sense. 3. the middle term, medium, mean.
moderado adj. 1. moderate, temperate, restrained, prudent. 2. middling, mediocre.
moderador s. m. moderator. ‖ adj. moderating.
moderante adj. m. + f. moderating.
moderantismo s. m. 1. act or quality of being moderate. 2. moderatism: principles of moderation in politics or religion.
moderar v. 1. to moderate, mitigate, temper. 2. to diminish, lessen. 3. to restrain, refrain, repress, subdue, control, govern, regulate. 4. **~-se** to act with moderation, avoid excesses, restrain o. s., keep one's temper.
moderativo adj. moderating, that moderates.
moderável adj. m. + f. (pl. **-áveis**) that can be moderated.
modernice s. f. 1. mania for modern things or innovations. 2. exaggerated use of the latest styles.
modernidade s. f. modernity, modernness.
modernismo s. m. 1. = **modernice**. 2. modernism: a) tendency to accept modern ideas and practices. b) generic designation of various modern literary and artistic styles. c) (rel.) tendency to harmonize religion with science.
modernista s. m. + f. modernist: adherent of modernism. ‖ adj. pertaining to one of the trends of modernism.
modernização s. f. (pl. **-ões**) modernization.
modernizar v. 1. to modernize: render modern, accommodate to modern usages. 2. **~-se** to accommodate o. s. to modern usages.
moderno adj. 1. modern, new, of the latest style of our days, recent, actual, new-fashioned. 2. (N. Braz.) young, juvenile. 3. (Azores) moderate, gentle. 4. (N. Braz., pop. and Port., prov.) calm, quiet, easygoing. 5. (N. Braz., pop.) said of a light, soft colour. ‖ **-amente** adv. modernly, in modern times. **arte -a** modern art. **estilo** ~ modern style. **vida -a** modern life. **viver à -a** to live after the latest style.
modernos s. m. pl. men of today.
modéstia s. f. modesty: 1. unpretentiousness, humbleness, simplicity. 2. chastity.
modesto adj. modest: 1. unpretentious, moderate, humble, simple, frugal, of little means. 2. discreet, reserved. 3. decorous, chaste. ‖ **-amente** adv. modestly.
modicar v. 1. to moderate, render moderate, limit, refrain, restrain. 2. to diminish, lessen. 3. to soften.
modicidade s. f. moderateness; smallness, insignificance, lowness, inexpensiveness.
módico adj. small, slight, moderate, low, insignificant, reasonable. **preços ~s** low prices.
modificação s. f. (pl. **-ões**) modification, alteration, change.
modificador s. m. modifier. ‖ adj. modifying.
modificar v. 1. to modify, change, alter. 2. to moderate, refrain, restrain. 3. **~-se** to suffer a modification.

modilhão s. m. (pl. **-ões**) (archit.) modillion: ornamental bracket beneath a cornice.
modilhar v. to sing arias.
modilho s. m. light music, aria. ‖ adj. following exaggeratedly fashions and styles.
modinatura s. f. (archit.) framework of a construction.
modinha s. f. (also **modilho**) popular song, glee, tune.
modíolo s. m. (archit.) space between modillions.
modismo s. m. idiom, idiotism of language.
modista s. f. 1. dressmaker, fashion designer. 2. (Braz.) m. + f. singer of **modinhas** (popular songs).
modo s. m. 1. mode, manner, fashion, style, form, method, way, custom. 2. disposition, humour, temper, state of mind. 3. quality. 4. decency, propriety. 5. (gram.) mode, mood. 6. (mus.) mode. 7. **~s** pl. manners, behaviour.
~ de agir mode of proceeding. **~ de andar** gait. **~ de escrever** manner of writing, style. **~ de falar** manner of speaking; mere words. **~ de pensar** mode of thinking, point of view. **~ de ver** point of view. **~ de vida** way of living, trade, profession. **~ maior**, **~ menor** (mus.) major mode; minor mode. **ao ~ de** like, as. **a seu ~** in his way. **de ~ a** so as to. **de ~ algum** under no circumstances. **de ~ geral** altogether. **de ~ nenhum** in no way; not at all. **de ~ que** so that. **de certo ~** in a way. **de outro ~** in another manner, otherwise. **de qualquer ~** by some means. **deste ~** thus. **de tal ~** in such a manner. **de um ~ ou de outro ~** by some way or other. **do ~ seguinte** in the following way. **do mesmo ~** in the same manner. **isto é ~ de falar** that is a way of saying it without meaning it. **isto não é ~ de agir** this is no way of doing. **levar por bons ~s** to use gentle means. **maus ~s** bad manners. **pelo ~ como ele age** from the way he acts. **pelos ~s** apparently, evidently, obviously. **por nenhum ~** by no means. **por todos os ~s** by all means. **quarto de ~** (naut.) middle watch. **tratar alguém com bons ~s** to treat s. o. politely.
modorra (ô) s. f. (pl. **modorras**) 1. morbid prostration. 2. sleepiness, somnolence, drowsiness, doziness. 3. sturdy, staggers (in sheep). 4. (fig.) lethargy, apathy, indolence.
modorral adj. m. + f. (pl. **-ais**) 1. causing sleep. 2. drowsy, lethargic, sleepy, indolent.
modorrar v. 1. to make sleepy, drowsy, lethargic. 2. to stun. 3. to drowse, doze.
modorrento, **modorro** (pl. **modorros**) adj. 1. sleepy, drowsy, lethargic. 2. (fig.) stupid. ‖ **-amente** adv. drowsily.
modulação s. f. (pl. **-ões**) 1. modulation, variation, inflection of voice. 2. (fig.): a) melody. b) softness.
modulador s. m. modulator. ‖ adj. modulating.
modular v. to modulate, inflect, sing melodiously. ‖ adj. m. + f. modular: pertaining to a module or modulus.
módulo s. m. 1. (archit.) module: unit of architectonic proportions. 2. (math.) modulus: a) absolute value. b) coefficient: positive value of a function or property. 3. (mus.) modulation. 4. diameter of medals and coins. 5. unit of any measure. ‖ adj. melodious.
moeda s. f. coin, token, money.
~ corrente currency. **~ de cálculo** or **imaginária** imaginary coin, money. **~ falsa** false coin, counterfeit money. **~ ouro** gold standard. **~ sonante** hard cash. **casa da ~** the mint. **direção da ~** foreign exchange superintendence. **papel-~** paper money, bills. **pagar na mesma** ~ to give tit for tat.
moedagem s. f. (pl. **-ens**) 1. coinage, mintage. 2. wage paid for coining.

moedeira s. f. 1. instrument to grind enamel in a goldsmithery. 2. (fig.) fatigue, weariness, fatiguing work. 3. (pop.) constant ache or pain.

moedeiro s. m. coiner, minter, mintman. ~ **falso** counterfeiter.

moedela s. f. beating, thrashing.

moedor s. m. grinder, miller, pounder. ‖ adj. 1. grinding. 2. impertinent, boring. ~ **de carne** meat grinder, mincer (plate C 20).

moedura s. f. grinding, milling.

moega s. f. 1. mill hopper. 2. store-room of an import and export warehouse.

moela s. f. gizzard: second stomach of birds.

moelà-de-mutum s. f. (pl. **moelas-de-mutum**) (Braz.) plant of the family Aurinaceae (Lacunaria jenmani).

moenda s. f. 1. millstone, millwork. 2. any grinding equipment. 3. grinding, trituration. 4. a miller's fee.

moendeiro s. m. 1. millowner, miller. 2. (N. Braz.) workers who feed the sugar cane into the mill.

moente s. m. pivot, gudgeon (plate C 15). ‖ adj. m. + f. 1. grinding. 2. ready for any use or application.

moenza s. f. (Braz.) tree the wood of which is used for boats and clogs.

moer v. 1. to grind, crush, triturate, bray, press, press out. 2. to chew. 3. to think something over and over again. 4. to tire, fatigue, wear out. 5. to bother. 6. to beat, cudgel. 7. to repeat, grind (studying), harp on the same string. 8. to hurt, crush, bruise. 9. to grind in a mill. 10. to worry, molest, harass, vex, plague. 11. ~-**se**: a) to drudge, slave. b) to be afflicted, worry, fret. ~ **com pancadas** to beat soundly.

mofa s. f. mockery, derision, scorn. **fazer** ~ **de** to scoff at.

mofador s. m. scoffer, mocker, derider, jeerer, flouter. ‖ adj. scornful, derisive, mocking.

mofar v. 1. to mock, scorn, scoff, deride, flout, jeer, fleer, ridicule. 2. to grow mouldy; to mould. ~ **de** to jeer at, laugh at.

mofatra s. f. fraud, feigned purchase or sale.

mofatrão s. m. (pl. **-ões**) trickster.

mofento s. m. (Braz., pop.) = **diabo** ‖ adj. (also **mofoso**) 1. mouldy, musty. 2. (fig.) fatal, disastrous.

mofeta s. f. mofette: exhalation of noxious gases from the earth.

mofina s. f. 1. unhappiness, misfortune, bad luck. 2. unhappy, shy woman. 3. (fig.) avarice, stinginess, miserliness, niggardliness. 4. (Braz.) anonymous diffamatory article. 5. ancylostomiasis; hookworm disease.

mofineiro s. m. (Braz.) writer of anonymous diffamatory articles.

mofino s. m. 1. unhappy or shy individual. 2. miser. 3. importunate, turbulent person. 4. (Braz.) coward. 5. sickly individual. 6. (Braz., pop.) = **diabo**. ‖ adj. 1. unhappy, infortunate, wretched, miserable. 2. shy. 3. miserly. 4. importunate. 5. turbulent, troublesome. 6. cowardly. 7. sickly, indisposed.

mofo (ô) s. m. (pl. **mofos**) 1. mould, mildew, must, frowst. 2. gratuitous vantage. **cheirar a** ~ to smell musty. **criar** ~ to mould, grow mouldy. **de** ~ without paying; at other people's expenses.

mofofô s. m. (Braz., pop.) bug that lives in rotten wood.

mofumbal s. m. (pl. **-ais**) (Braz.) hidden place, place for hiding.

mofumbar v. (N. Braz.) to hide, conceal.

mofumbo s. m. (Braz.) 1. leguminous plant (Viborgia polygaliformis) also known as ~-**da-beira-do-rio**. 2. = **mofumbal**.

mofungo s. m. (Braz.) climbing plant of the family Amaranthaceae (Chamissoa rubrocaulia).

moganga s. f. 1. a variety of pumpkins. 2. (Braz., also **moganguice**) grimaces; pranks. 3. endearments, caresses. 4. highfalutin, big and empty words. ‖ adj. said of a variety of pumpkins.

mogangar v. to grimace.

mogangueiro, moganguento s. m., **moganguista** m. + f. 1. grimacing individual, prankster. 2. soft-spoken, bigmouthed individual. ‖ adj. 1. grimacing, jesting. 2. flattering.

mogiganga s. f. 1. burlesque dance. 2. trifles, gewgaws. 3. ~**s** pl. grimaces.

mogigrafia s. f. (med.) mogigraphy: writer's cramp.

mogilalismo, mogislalismo s. m. mogilalism: 1. habit of mispronouncing or difficulty in pronouncing the p and b. 2. stuttering, stammering. 3. (med.) difficulty of speech.

mogno, mógono s. m. mahogany: tree of tropical America yielding excellent wood.

mogorim s. m. (pl. **-ins**) (Braz.) Japanese rose, camelia.

moicano s. m. Mohican.

moído adj. 1. ground, crushed. 2. beat, dead tired, fatigued. 3. bothered, harassed. 4. slightly tainted (meat, fish).

moimento s. m. (ant.) mausoleum, monument.

moinante s. m. + f. 1. joker, party boy, merrymaker. 2. idler, vagrant, sluggard. 3. rascal. ‖ adj. 1. merrymaking, funny, joking. 2. lazy, sluggish. 3. not good, sly.

moinha s. f. 1. chaff. 2. powder to which any dry substance is reduced or triturated.

moinho s. m. mill, flour-mill, water-mill, grinding works. ~ **d'água** water-mill. ~ **de café** coffee-mill, coffee grinder. ~ **de mão** hand-mill. ~ **de vento** windmill (plate M 7). **isto é água para o seu** ~ it's grist to his mill. **levar água ao seu** ~ to bring grist to one's mill.

moio s. m. old measure of volume corresponding to 828 l.

moita s. f. thicket, coppice, copse, scrub, brake brush, bush, tuft. ‖ interj. designating silence, especially when one waits for an answer: not a word!

moitão, moutão s. m. (pl. **-ões**) 1. (naut.) block, single block. 2. (also **moitedo, moutedo**) bush, thickets. ~ **de amura** tack-block. ~ **de braços** jewel-block, life-block. ~ **de dente** shoulder-block. ~ **de gancho** hook-block. ~ **duplo** sister-block. ~ **de rabicho** tail-block. ~ **de retorno** leading-block.

moitar v. (Braz., sl.) 1. to stay mum. 2. not to answer a question, despite knowing it.

mojica s. f. (N. Braz.) 1. fish broth thickened with fish meal. 2. thickening of a broth with any starch.

mola s. f. 1. (tech.) spring (plates B 4, 11, C 15), F 1). 2. (fig.) motive, incentive. 3. (med., vet.) mole: tumour of the uterus. ~ **amortecedora de choque** buffer spring. ~ **de fechadura** lock spring (plate F 1). ~ **de lâmina** leaf spring (plate V 3). ~ **de relógio** watch spring (plate R 4). ~ **de válvula** valve spring. ~ **espiral** spiral spring (plate B 4). ~ **hidatiforme** (med.) hydatiform mole. ~ **mestra** master spring. ~ **real** main spring, master spring. ~ **vesicular** (vet.) vesicular mole. **colchão de** ~ spring mattress (plate C 4). **fecho de** ~ spring catch. **gancho com** ~**s** spring hook. **ter boas** ~**s** to be springy. **ter pancada na** ~ (fig.) to have a bee in one's bonnet.

molada s. f. 1. portion of paint ground at one time. 2. water contained in the grinding box.

molagem s. f. (pl. -ens) gratuitous advantage; cheat: used only in the expressions:
de ~ payable by somebody else. comer de ~ to eat at another's expenses.

molambento, molambudo s. m. (Braz.) run-down, ragged individual, ragamuffin. || adj. run-down, ragged, dirty.

molambo s. m. (Braz.) 1. rag, tatter. 2. (fig.) weak character, weakling.

molancas s. m. + f., molangueirão m. (also molanqueirão, molanqueiro) spineless, sluggish, indolent individual; mollycoddle.

molar adj. m. + f. 1. molar, grinding, that which is ground easily. 2. (anat.) molar. 3. soft, brittle. 4. (med.) pertaining to a tumour of the placenta.
dente ~ molar tooth. prenhez ~ molar pregnancy.

molariforme adj. m. + f. 1. molariform. 2. (bot.) having something like teeth on the surface (as some fungi).

molarinha s. f. (bot., also fumária) fumatory.

molassa s. f. wood grinder (paper industry).

molasso s. m. 1. (geol.) Molasse: fossiliferous sedimentary deposits of the Miocene. 2. ~s pl. intestinal worm, helminth with a gelatinous transparent body.

moldação s. f. (pl. -ões) moulding, casting.

moldado s. m. (archit.) mould, moulding, plasterwork. || adj. moulded.

moldador s. m. 1. moulder. 2. (archit.) instrument for carving ornamental mouldings. || adj. moulding.

moldagem s. f. (pl. -ens) 1. moulding. 2. type of sculpture. 3. (geol.) fossile impression.

moldar v. 1. to mould. 2. to cast. 3. to make moulds for casting. 4. (fig.) to shape, frame, form, model. 5. to adapt, accommodate, direct the development of. 6. ~-se to a) to accommodate o. s., adapt o. s. b) to take shape.
~ em barro to mould out of clay.

moldávia s. f. (bot.) Moldavian balm.

molde s. m. 1. mould, casting mould. 2. pattern. 3. norm, model, example. 4. printing mold.
~ de fundição casting mould. de ~ on purpose, as one might wish.

moldura s. f. 1. frame, borders (plates B 2, C 2, 4, P 2). 2. (archit.) moulding, panel, wainscot (plate A 13).

molduragem s. f. (pl. -ens) framing, moulding.

moldurar v. (also emoldurar) 1. to frame. 2. to make mouldings.

moldureiro s. m. 1. producer of picture frames. 2. picture framer. 3. (archit.) maker of mouldings.

mole s. f. 1. enormous volume, bulk. 2. shapeless mass. 3. construction of great proportions. || adj. m. + f. 1. soft, limp. 2. lazy, sluggish, spineless. 3. effeminate, weak.
mole mole slowly, little by little.

molear v. 1. to render limp or soft. 2. (Braz.) to become limp or soft.

moleca s. f. (Braz.) young black girl.

molecada s. f. gang of young boys.

molecagem s. f. (pl. -ens) (Braz., also molequeira) actions of a moleque, a boyish trick.

molecar, molequear v. (Braz.) to act like a moleque.

molecório s. m. (Braz.) gang of moleques.

molecote s. m. (Braz.) stout, tall boy.

molécula s. f. 1. (chem.) molecule. 2. minute particle of matter.

molécula-grama s. f. (pl. moléculas-grama) (chem.) gram molecule.

molecular adj. m. + f. molecular: relating to molecules.

moledo s. m. (Braz.) decomposing rock forming pebbles or gravel.

moleira s. f. 1. wife of a miller, woman owning a mill, woman working in a mill. 2. (anat.) fontanel.

moleirão s. m. (pl. -ões) (Braz.) = molengão.

moleiro s. m. 1. miller: a) owner of a mill. b) worker in a mill. 2. (Braz.) bird of the family Psitacidae.

moleirona s. f. indolent, lazy, sloppy woman.

moleja s. f. 1. vulgar name of the thymus gland. 2. (pop.) pancreas of animals. 3. birds' dung.

molenga, molengue s. m. + f., molengo m. lazy-bones, slowcoach. || adj. lazy, sluggish, indolent.

molengão s. m. (pl. -ões) (f. -ona; also moleirão) lazy-bones, sluggard.

molengar v. to act lazily, indolently.

moleque s. m. 1. little Negro. 2. frivolous and unreliable person. 3. (Braz.) young boy, urchin. 4. (N. Braz.) = ~-de-assentar. 5. (Braz.) magnetic separator for separating iron from powdered gold. || adj. funny, jocund, mocking.
~ de rua street Arab, gutter snipe.

moleque-de-assentar s. m. (pl. moleques-de-assentar) (N. Braz.) strickle for levelling the sugar in the boxes of a sugar-mill.

molestador s. m. molester, harasser, teaser. || adj. molesting.

molestamento s. m. molestation, harassment.

molestar v. 1. to molest, disturb, trouble, bother, importune, annoy, harass, tease. 2. to hurt, ill-treat. 3. to damage, prejudice. 4. to pinch (shoe). 5. to offend, disgust. 6. to affect, attack (illness). 7. to meddle with. 8. to oppress. 9. ~-se to grieve over, worry, be annoyed, take offense.

moléstia s. f. 1. disease, sickness, malady, illness, affection. 2. disturbance, uneasiness; pain. 3. (Braz.) rabies.

moléstia-magra s. f. (pl. moléstias-magras) (N. Braz., pop.) tuberculosis.

molesto adj. 1. molesting, troublesome, bothersome, annoying, vexatious, importunate, offensive. 2. indisposed, sick. 3. burdensome, laborious, tiresome.

moleta s. f. 1. muller: stone to grind colouring matters with. 2. (her.) mullet: star-shaped figure with an empty center.

moleza s. f. 1. softness, weakness. 2. languidness, slackness, indolence. 3. lack of colour in a work of art.

molhada s. f. 1. large bundle. 2. lots of bundles.

molhadela s. f. (also molha, molhadura) 1. wetting, moistening, drenching, soaking. 2. bath. 3. tip, gratuity, drink money.
apanhar uma ~ to get wet through.

molhado s. m. 1. place wetted by an overturned or spilled liquid. 2. ~s pl. (Braz.) wine, oil, and other liquids sold in a store. || adj. 1. wet, moist. 2. (N. Braz., pop., fig.) drunk.
armazém de secos e ~s grocery, emporium.

molhamento s. m. 1. = molhadela. 2. immersion, ducking.

molhança, molhanga s. f. a lot of sauce or gravy.

molhar v. 1. to wet, dampen, moisten. 2. to soak, douse, water, drench. 3. to splash, sprinkle, spray. 4. ~-se to get wet.
~ a garganta, ~ a goela (Braz.) to moisten one's throat, to have a drink. ele molhou a comida he washed his food down. ~ a mão de to tip, to give a gratuity.

molhe s. m. mole, breakwater, pier, jetty (plate P 16).

molheira s. f. sauce-boat, butter-boat.

molhe-molhe s. m. drizzle, mizzle.

molho s. m. 1. bundle, faggot, sheaf. 2. handful.
~ de chaves bunch of keys. ~ de lenha faggot of sticks. ~ de trigo sheaf of wheat. em ~s in bundles, in faggots.

molho (ô) s. m. 1. sauce, gravy. 2. soak: liquid in which anything is soaked. **~ branco** white sauce. **pôr de ~** to soak (clothes). **ficar de ~** 1. to stay inactive for a period of time. 2. to be bedridden, sick.

mollana s. f. 1. reprehension, reproof. 2. plant of the family Vochysiaceae (Salvertia convallariaedora). **cantar (a alguém) a ~** to rate s. o. soundly, scold, rail at.

molibdênio s. m. molybdenum: metallic element.

molição s. f. (pl. -ões) great effort to reach an end.

molície, molícia s. f. 1. weariness, lethargy. 2. idleness. 3. rest.

moliço s. m. 1. algae used as dung. 2. thatch used to cover roofs.

molificação s. f. (pl. -ões) 1. mollification, emollition, sóftening. 2. enervation, relaxation. 3. assuagement.

molificante adj. m. + f. mollifying, softening, assuaging, appeasing.

molificar v. 1. to mollify, soften. 2. to mitigate, appease. 3. to calm. 4. to weaken, enervate.

molificativo adj. emollient, mollifying.

molime, molímen s. m. (pl. **molimens, molímenes**) (mech.) molimen: impulsive force of a body in movement.

molinete s. m. 1. moulinet: a) turnstile. b) (naut.) windlass. c) circular swing of a sword or stick around one's body. 2. reel (fishing). 3. hydrometric propeller, current meter. 4. windmill anemometer.

molinha s. f. 1. (also **molhe-molhe, molinheiro**) drizzle, mizzle. 2. dim. of **mola**: small spring.

molinhar v. 1. to grind little by little, with frequency. 2. to operate a mill. 3. to rain in thin drops.

molinheira s. f. 1. large mill. 2. persisting drizzle.

molinheiro s. m. drizzle.

molinhoso adj. drizzly, mizzly.

molinilho s. m. 1. handmill. 2. twirling stick for chocolate, chocolate beater.

molinismo s. m. Molinism: doctrine of the Spanish Jesuit Molina.

molinosismo s. m. Molinism: quietism, doctrine of the Spanish theologian Molinos.

molinote s. m. 1. sugar mill, sugar-cane mill. 2. horse gear for running a sugar-cane mill with beasts in case of water shortage.

molípede adj. m. + f. (zool.) having soft or tender feet.

molito adj. (S. Braz.) 1. soft, boneless. 2. lascivious.

moloca s. f. (N. Braz.) stretch of forest.

molóide s. m. + f. = **molenga**. || adj. = **molenga**.

molongó s. m. plant of the family Apocynaceae (Ambelania grandiflora) and others of the genus Zschokkeae. || adj. (N. Braz.) 1. weak, indisposed, sickly. 2. lazy, sluggish. 3. silly.

molosso s. m. 1. mastiff. 2. (fig.) bold, turbulent fellow.

molugem s. f. (pl. -ens) (bot., also **solda**) wild madder, infant's breath, white bedstraw.

molulo s. m. a composite plant (Piptocarpha macropoda) much used to make carbon for gunpowder.

molúria s. f. 1. = **moleza**. 2. copious dew. 3. open air. 4. m. shy man.

molusco s. m. mollusc, shellfish.

mombaca s. f. acid fruit, used in Brazil for seasoning food.

momboiaxió s. f. (Braz.) a sort of mouth-organ used by countrymen.

momentâneo adj. momentary, transitory, instantaneous, rapid. || **-amente** adv. momentarily.

momento s. m. 1. moment, instant. 2. circumstance. 3. consequence, importance, weight. 4. opportune moment. 5. (phys.) momentum. 6. (mech.) moment. || adj. grimacing, joking. **~ de inércia** moment of inertia. **~s depois** some moments after. **a cada ~** at every moment. **até este ~** up to this moment. **conseqüências de grande (pouco) ~** consequences of great (little) importance. **desde este ~** from this moment. **espere um ~** wait just a second. **neste ~** at this moment. **no ~** at present. **no ~ oportuno** at the proper moment. **no ~ próprio** at the right time. **num ~** in a twinkling. **o ~ que passa** the present moment. **por ~s** for a few moments. **por um ~** for a moment.

momentoso adj. grave, serious, important, momentous, weighty. || **-amente** adv. momentously.

momices s. f. pl. antics, pranks, grimaces, mummery.

momo s. m. 1. Momus. 2. pantomime, farce. 3. actor of a farce, mime, mimic, buffoon.

mona s. f. 1. she-monkey, she-ape. 2. (vulg.) drunkenness. 3. (fam.) ill humour. 4. rag doll.

monacal adj. m. + f. (pl. -ais), **monástico** m. monachal, monastic, monkish.

monacanto adj. (ichth.) monacanthid, monacanthous: having a single row of spines.

monacato s. m. monachism, monasticism: monastic condition of life.

monada s. f. 1. monkey tricks, pranks, foolery. 2. monkeyishness, monkeyism. 3. lots of apes.

monadário s. m. (zool.) monad: flagellate protozoans typified by the genus Monas. || adj. monadic: relating to or like a monad.

mônade s. f. (also **mônada**) monad: 1. (philos.) elementary particle of the universe. 2. (biol.) elementary single-celled organism.

monadelfia s. f. Monadelphia: class of plants with monadelphous flowers.

monadelfo adj. (bot.) monadelphous: having the filaments of the stamens united.

monadismo s. m. monadism: theory that the universe is a composite of monads.

monadista s. m. + f. monadist: adherent of monadism.

monadologia s. f. monadology: Leibniz's doctrine of monads.

monândrico, monandro adj. (bot.) monandrous: having only one stamen.

monantero adj. (bot.) monantheridial: having but one anther.

monanto adj. (bot.) monanthous: one-flowered.

monantropia s. f. system of anthropology admitting only one original race of men.

monarca s. m. 1. monarch, sovereign. 2. (fig.) dominating, domineering person or thing. 3. (S. Braz.) gaucho riding elegantly and proudly. 4. elegant, proud horse. || adj. (Braz., pop.) 1. of the time of the monarchy. 2. of ancient habits, ancient. 3. very large.

monarquia s. f. 1. monarchy. 2. (S. Braz.) life of an elegant, proud gaucho.

monarquiação s. f. (pl. -ões) (S. Braz.) act of riding gracefully.

monarquiar v. (S. Braz.) 1. to ride a horse gracefully. 2. to walk gracefully (horse). 3. to dominate.

monárquico s. m. (Port.) monarchist. || adj. monarchistic, monarchic(al).

monarquismo s. m. monarchism: political system of a monarchy.

monarquista s. m. + f. monarchist.

monastério s. m. monastery, convent.

monástico adj. = **monacal**. || **monasticamente** adv. monastically.

monatômico adj. (chem.) monatomic.

monaxífero adj. (bot.) monaxial (inflorescence).

monazita s. f. (min.) monazite.

monazítico adj. monazitic: relating to or containing monazite.
areia -a monazitic sand.
monção s. f. (pl. -ões) 1. monsoon: a) periodical wind in S. W. Asia and the region of the Indian Ocean. b) any periodical wind. 2. opportunity, proper moment. 3. (hist.) fluvial expedition to explore the interior of Brazil.
moncar v. to blow the nose, clean the nose.
monchão s. m. (pl. -ões) (Braz.) stretch of ground with diamond deposits.
monco s. m. 1. mucus of the nose. 2. (vulg.) snot, snivel.
~ **de peru** wattle of a turkey.
moncoso adj. 1. running (nose). 2. (vulg.) snotty. 3. (fig.) sordid, despisable.
monda s. f. 1. weeding. 2. the proper time for weeding (fields).
mondadeira s. f., **mondadeiro** m. weeder.
mondador s. m. 1. = mondadeiro. 2. weending tool, weeding hoe. ‖ adj. weeding.
mondadura s. f. 1. weeding. 2. the weeds cleared out.
mondar v. 1. to weed, weed out. 2. to prune. 3. to correct. 4. to eliminate, cut. 5. to clean, purge.
mondé(u) s. m. (Braz.) = mundéu.
mondego s. m. (ichth., N. Braz.) small specimen of grey mullet.
mondonga s. f. sloppy, filthy woman; slattern.
mondongo s. m. 1. pluck, giblets of some animals. 2. dirty and sloppy person. 3. (N. Braz.) swamp, bog covered with aquatic plants.
mondongudo adj. (S. Braz., depr.) poor horse for racing.
mondongueiro s. m. 1. pluck vendor, tripeman, tripe seller. 2. (fig.) person engaged in dirty deals.
mondrongo s. m. (Braz.) 1. shapeless individual, fat and awkward person. 2. (N.) swelling.
monécia s. f. Monoecia: class of plants with the stamens and pistils in distinct flowers.
monera s. f. (zool.) Monera.
monésia s. f. (Braz.) medicinal plant of the family Sapotaceae (Chrysophyllum glycocyphoeum).
moneta s. f. (naut.) auxiliary sail.
monetário s. m. 1. collection of coins. 2. book on numismatics. ‖ adj. monetary.
circulação -a circulation of money. **sistema** ~ coinage, system of coinage, standard of coinage.
monete s. m. 1. long unruly hair. 2. scarce hair. 3. lock of a lady's hair-do.
monetizar v. to monetize: 1. coin. 2. give a currency standard (to metal).
monge s. m. (f. **monja**) 1. monk, friar. 2. anchorite, recluse. 3. (S. Braz.) person living, apparently at least, the life of an anchorite.
mongil s. m. (pl. -is) 1. habit of a nun. 2. long tunic of a woman. 3. mourning clothes for a woman other than a widow. ‖ adj. m. + f. monkish.
mongol s. m. + f. (pl. -óis) Mongol: native or inhabitant of Mongolia. ‖ adj. Mongol, Mongolian.
mongólico adj. Mongolian.
mongolóide adj. m. + f. Mongoloid, xanthous: 1. proper to the Mongolian race. 2. of the Mongolian type.
monguba s. f. (Braz.) 1. = mongubeira. 2. fruit of the munguba tree.
mongubeira s. f. munguba: Brazilian silk cotton tree.
monha s. f. 1. dressy bow worn by bulls in fights. 2. rosette worn on the back of the head by toreros. 3. fashion or hairdresser's lay figure, dummy.
monho s. m. 1. false tuft of hair, false chignon worn by ladies. 2. natural roll, bun of hair. 3. bow to adorn or hold a hair-do.

mônica s. f. (Braz.) manioc variety.
moniliforme adj. m. + f. moniliform: 1. of the form of a rosary or necklace. 2. tortulous.
monimiácea s. f. specimen of the Monimiaceae, a family of dicotyledonous plants.
monimiáceo adj. monimiaceous: of or pertaining to the Monimiaceae.
monir v. 1. = admoestar. 2. to give evidence.
monismo s. m. (philos.) monism: theory that all things or activities may be reduced to one primary matter or principle.
monístico adj. monistic: relating to monism.
monitor s. m. monitor: 1. person who advises, admonishes, warns. 2. war vessel. 3. prepositor: senior pupil appointed to care for order and discipline. 4. any of the large lizards of the genus Varanus.
monitória s. f. 1. monitory. 2. notice to everybody to tell everything they know about a crime. 3. advice. 4. (fam.) admonition, reproof, warning.
monitorizar v. to monitor.
monjoleiro s. m. (Braz.) 1. thorny, prickly tree. 2. (S. Braz.) person in charge of a water-driven corn pounder.
monjolo s. m. 1. (Braz.) simple water-driven engine used to pound corn, peel coffee, etc. 2. (N. Braz., also **mujolo**) a hornless calf. 3. old designation for certain slaves.
mono s. m. 1. (also **mariquinha, mariquinhas, mariquina**) ape, monkey. 2. (fig.) ugly and stupid fellow, booby, grumbler, growler. 3. unsalable article, dead stock.
pregar um ~ **a alguém** to put a thing over to a person; to impose upon a person.
monobafia s. f. quality of being monochromatic.
monobásico adj. (chem.) monobasic.
monoblepsia s. f. (med.) monoblepsia: disease where vision is normal only when but one eye is used.
monocarpelar adj. m. + f. (bot.) monocarpellary: consisting of a single carpel.
monocarpiano, monocárpico adj. monocarpian, monocarpic: bearing fruit once.
monocarpo adj. monocarp: monocarpic plant.
monocarril s. m. monorail.
monocásio s. m. (bot.) monochasium: cymose inflorescence with only one main axis.
monocefalia s. f. monstruosity characterized by two bodies with one head.
monocéfalo s. m. a monster with two bodies and one head. ‖ adj. relating to this monster.
monocelular adj. m. + f. (bot., zool.) monocellular: unicellular.
monócero adj. 1. (zool.) monocerous: one-horned. 2. (bot.) having one prolongation only in form of a horn.
monoceronte s. m. monoceros, unicorn.
monociclo s. m. monocycle: one-wheeled velocipede.
monoclamídeo adj. (bot.) monochlamydeous: having a single floral envelope but no corolla.
monoclínico adj. (geol.) monoclinic: having one oblique intersection of the axis (crystal).
monoclino adj. (bot.) monoclinous: hermaphroditic.
monocórdio s. m. monochord: musical instrument with one string only. ‖ adj. monotonous.
monocotilar adj. m. + f. (zool.) having one trunk or sucker only.
monocotiledônea s. f. monocotyledon: a monocotyledonous plant.
monocotiledôneo adj. (bot.) monocotyledonous: having a single cotyledon.
monocrômico, monocromático adj. monochrome, monochromic(al): painted or made with a single colour.
monocromo adj. monochromatic: of one colour.

monóculo s. m. monocle: single eyeglass. ‖ adj. monocular: single-eyed, one-eyed.

monodáctilo, monodátilo adj. (zool.) monodactylous: having only one finger.

monodelfo s. m. monodelphian.

monodia s. f. monody: air sung by a single voice; funeral song.

monodiar v. to sing a monody, bewail, bemoan.

monódico adj. monodic(al): relating to monody.

monodonte adj. m. + f. monodont: having only one tooth.

monofásico adj. (electr.) monophase.

monofilo adj. (bot.) monophyllous: composed of a single leaf.

monofisismo s. m. monophysitism: doctrine that there is only one nature in the person of Christ.

monofisita s. m. + f. monophysite: adherent of monophysitism. ‖ adj. monophysitic: relating to monophysitism.

monófito adj. (bot.) comprising but one species.

monofobia s. f. monophobia: morbid dread of being alone.

monófobo adj. suffering from monophobia.

monoftalmo adj. monophthalmic: one-eyed.

monogamia s. f. monogamy: 1. marriage with but one person at a time. 2. (zool.) pairing with a single mate.

monogâmico adj. monogamic: relating to monogamy.

monogamista s. m. + f. monogamist: person who practices or upholds monogamy. ‖ adj. monogamistic: practicing or upholding monogamy.

monógamo s. m. 1. monogamist. 2. animal having but one mate. 3. (bot.) containing only unisexual flowers. ‖ adj. monogamous: 1. having but one wife. 2. (zool.) having but one mate.

monogástrico adj. (zool.) monogastric: having but one stomach.

monogenésico adj. (zool.) monogenetic: relating to monogenesis.

monogenia s. f. monogenesis: asexual reproduction.

monogênico adj. monogenic: reproducing in one way only.

monogênico adj. (zool.) appearing to be of one and the same genus.

monografar v. to monograph: 1. write a monograph. 2. treat of in a monograph.

monografia s. f. monograph: treatise on a particular subject.

monográfico adj. monographic: relating to a monograph.

monógrafo s. m. monographer, monographist: author of a monograph. ‖ adj. monographic(al): treating of only one subject.

monograma s. m. monogram: interwoven initials of a name.

monogramático adj. monogrammatic: relating to a monogram.

monogramista s. m. + f. 1. person who makes monograms. 2. artist signing his work not with his full name but with his initials or monogram.

monogramo adj. 1. said of a painting or drawing consisting of lines and contours only. 2. (philos.) abstract, not palpable.

monóico adj. monoecious: having male and female flowers on the same plant.

monoideísmo s. m. monoideism: mental state where one idea dominates the whole psychic organism.

monóilo adj. (zool.) having a body formed of a homogenous mass.

monolépide adj. m. + f. (zool.) having one scale only.

monolítico adj. monolithic: relating to or resembling a monolith.

monólito s. m. monolith: 1. tall stone. 2. monument consisting of a tall single stone.

monologar v. 1. to monologize, monologue, soliloquize, recite monologues. 2. to speak to o. s.

monólogo s. m. monologue, monolog, soliloquy.

monomania s. f. monomania: derangement of a single faculty of the mind or with regard to a particular subject.

monomaníaco s. m. monomaniac: person affected with monomania. ‖ adj. monomaniacal.

monômero adj. monomerous: having single-jointed tarsi (insects).

monometalismo s. m. monometallism: single metallic standard.

monométrico adj. 1. monometric(al): pertaining to, or consisting of a monometer. 2. (min.) monometric: isometric.

monômetro s. m. monometer: rhythmical series of a single meter.

monômio s. m. monomial: algebraic expression of one term.

mononeuro adj. (zool.) having one nervous system only.

monoperiantado, monoperiânteo adj. (bot.) monoperianthial: having but one perianth.

monopétalo adj. (bot.) monopetalous: having but one petal.

monoplano s. m. monoplane: aeroplane with one supporting plane.

monoplástico adj. monoplastic: made of one piece.

monoplegia s. f. (med.) monoplegia: paralysis of a single limb or part.

monopneumôneo adj. (zool.) monopneumonian, monopneumonous: having one lung or airsac only.

monopodia s. f. monopodium: state of being one--footed.

monopódio s. m. one-footed table.

monópode adj. m. + f. monopode: one-footed.

monopólio s. m. monopoly: exclusive possession of a trade or right of trading in some article or on a given market.

monopolista s. m. + f. monopolist: person who has a monopoly or who monopolizes.

monopolização s. f. (pl. -ões) monopolization: act or fact of monopolizing.

monopolizador s. m. monopolizer: person who monopolizes.

monopolizar v. to monopolize: 1. obtain or possess a monopoly. 2. engross the whole of.

monopse adj. m. + f. one-eyed.

monóptero s. m. (archit.) monopteral temple. ‖ adj. monopteral: having one row of columns only.

monoquíni s. m. (Braz.) a topless bathing suit.

monórquido adj. monorchid: having one testicle only.

monorrefringente adj. m. + f. of single refraction.

monorrimo adj. monorhyme: having but one rhyme.

monospermo adj. (bot.) monospermous: having only one seed.

monósporo adj. (bot.) monosporous, monospored: having a single spore.

monossépalo adj. (bot.) monosepalous, gamosepalous: having the sepals united.

monosseriado adj. forming one series only.

monossilábico adj. monosyllabic: 1. consisting of one syllable. 2. formed of words of one syllable.

monossílabo s. m. 1. monosyllable: word of one syllable. 2. ~s pl. incomplete expression. ‖ adj. monosyllabic.

falar por ~s to be sparing of words; to throw out hints.

monossitia s. f. habit of having one meal per day only.

—— M 11 ——

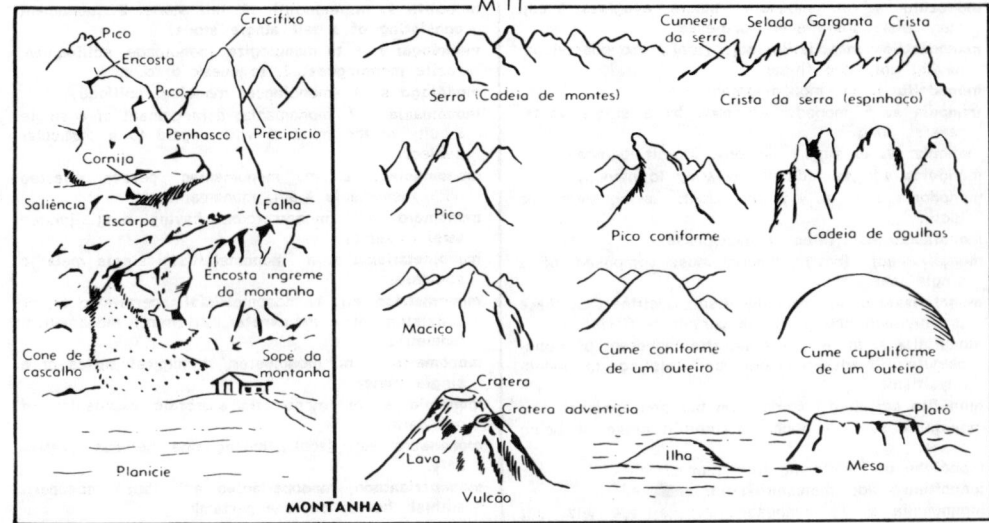

MONTANHA

Pico, Crucifixo, Encosta, Pico, Penhasco, Precipicio, Cornija, Saliência, Escarpa, Falha, Encosta ingreme da montanha, Cone de cascalho, Sope da montanha, Planicie, Serra (Cadeia de montes), Pico, Macico, Cratera, Cratera adventicia, Lava, Vulcão, Cumeeira da serra, Selada, Garganta, Crista, Crista da serra (espinhaço), Pico coniforme, Cadeia de agulhas, Cume coniforme de um outeiro, Cume cupuliforme de um outeiro, Ilha, Mesa, Platô

monossomo adj. said of two monsters having one body.

monóstico s. m. monostich: poem of one verse. ‖ adj. monostich: consisting of one verse.

monostigmatia s. f. condition of a plant with only one stigma.

monostilo adj. (bot.) monostylous: having a single style.

monóstrofe s. f. poem with only one strophe.

monóstrofo adj. composed of one strophe.

monotálamo adj. (zool.) monothalamous: one-chambered (conch).

monotéico adj. (also **monoteístico**) monotheistic: pertaining to monotheism.

monoteísmo s. m. monotheism: the belief or doctrine of the existence of one God only.

monoteísta s. m. + f. monotheist: follower of monotheism. ‖ adj. monotheistic: believing in one God only.

monotipar v. (typogr.) to set by monotype.

monotipo s. f. monotype: typesetting machine which casts separate types.

monótipo adj. (bot.) monotypic: having only one species (genus).

monótiro adj. said of shells or clams having one valve only.

monotongo s. m. (gram.) monophthong: vocalic group representing only one sound.

monotonia s. f. monotony, monotonousness: 1. disgusting uniformity of sound. 2. sameness, uniformity, want of variety.

monótono adj. monotone: 1. unisonous. 2. unvarying. 3. dull, tedious, wearisome. ‖ **monotonamente** adv. monotonously.

monotremo s. m. (also **monotrêmato**) monotreme: specimen of the Monotremata, group of aplacental, oviparous mammals with a cloaca.

monovalente adj. m. + f. (chem.) monovalent, univalent.

monóxilo s. m. monoxylon, monoxyle: pirogue, dugout. ‖ adj. cut out of one log.

monozoicidade s. f. (zool.) quality of having an individual and isolated life.

monozóico adj. (zool.) having an individual and isolated life.

monquilho s. m. disease of the laniferous cattle.

monroísmo s. m. Monroe Doctrine.

monsenhor s. m. 1. (R. C. Church) Monsignor: title of honour conferred to some prelates. 2. (Braz.) chrysanthemum.

monsenhorado s. m. dignity of a Monsignor.

monstrengo s. m. = **mostrengo**.

monstro s. m. monster: 1. abnormal being, freak, abortion. 2. fabulous being of the imagination or myth. 3. abnormally large animal or person. 4. prodigy. 5. (fig.) cruel, horrible person. ‖ adj. (Braz.) very large.

monstruosidade s. f. monstrosity, monstrousness, enormity, abortion.

monstruoso adj. monstrous: 1. abnormal, unnatural, huge. 2. frightful, horrible, heinous. 3. excessively bad or ugly.

monta s. f. 1. amount, sum, importance. 2. estimation, calculation. 3. cost.

coisa de pouca ~ a thing of little importance or value. **posto (estação) de** ~ stud farm, station keeping excellent male breeding stock to improve the livestock of the surrounding farms.

monta-cargas s. m., sg. + pl. 1. an equipment used for transporting artilery parts. 2. (Braz.) an elevator for goods.

montada s. f. 1. riding, mounting. 2. mount (of a soldier). 3. horse and rider. 4. curb-bit of a bridle.

montado s. m. oak grove where hogs feed. ‖ adj. 1. mounted, astride on horseback. 2. established. 3. (tech.) assembled.

engorda de ~ mast of acorns, pannage. **estar** ~ to be mounted on, to sit astride on.

montador s. m. (tech.) erector, fitter.

~ **de máquinas** engine fitter.

montagem s. f. (pl. **-ens**) mounting, erecting, erection, assembly, fitting up.

~ **de máquinas** assembly, erection, fitting up of machines. **linha de** ~ assembly line.

montanha s. f. 1. mountain (plate M 11). 2. large heap, pile. 3. large volume.

cadeia de ~s mountain range. **mal-das-**~s mountain sickness.

montanha-russa s. f. (pl. **montanhas-russas**) roller coaster, switchback.

montanheira s. f. 1. = **montado**. 2. pannage, mast of acorns.

montanhês s. m. (pl. -eses) (f. -esa, pl. -esas) moun-taineer, highlander. ‖ adj. living in the mountains.
montanhesco adj. 1. mountainous. 2. alpine. 3. wild, rough.
montanhismo s. m. mountain climbing.
montanhoso adj. mountainous, alpine.
região -a highlands, mountainous country.
montanística s. f. science studying the extraction and fusion of metals.
montano adj. 1. montane. 2. rude, rough.
montante s. m. 1. amount, sum. 2. post, pillar, upright. 3. (math.) sum of the capital plus the produced interest. 4. rising tide, high tide. 5. two--handed sword. ‖ adj. m. + f. rising; upstream.
a ~ upstream. no ~ de to the amount of.
montão s. m. (pl. -ões) 1. heap, disorderly pile. 2. lot, accumulation.
aos -ões in heaps, by heaps. de ~, em ~ pell-mell, all of a jumble.
montar v. 1. to mount: a) ride (horse). b) erect, set up, assemble, fit up. c) furnish, provide with every-thing necessary. d) set, encase (gem). e) amount to, reach a certain sum. f) ascend, climb. 2. to represent, signify, be worth. 3. ~-se to straddle, bestride.
~ a to total, to amount to; to figure up to. ~ a cavalo to mount, ride or go on horseback; to mount a horse. ~ à gineta to ride with short stirrups. ~ a guarda to mount guard. ~ bem a cavalo to be a good horseman; to sit a horse well. ~ em pêlo to ride bareback. ~ um andaime, uma tenda to erect, put up a scaffolding, a tent. ~ uma casa to fit up a house. ~ uma fábrica to set up a factory. ~ uma máquina to fit up an engine. ~ uma peça (theat.) to stage a play. ~ um negócio to set up a business.
montaraz s. m. 1. forest guard, forester. 2. person granting asylum to bandits. ‖ adj. m. + f. montane, rough, wild.
montaria s. f. 1. big game hunting(-ground). 2. moun-tain hunting. 3. = montaraz. 4. (hunt.) battue. 5. (fig.) mischievous armed gang. 6. persecution by a crowd, hooting. 7. remount horses or mules, re-mount cavalry. 8. riding horse, mule. 9. ladies' saddle. 10. ladies' riding habit. 11. (N. Braz.) small dugout, boat.
fazer a ~ a alguém to hoot a person.
monte s. m. (augm. montão, dim. montinho, mon-tículo) 1. mount, hill. 2. portion, heap, pile, ac-cumulation. 3. the bulk of an inheritance. 4. a game of hazard. 5. pool (in a game).
~-de-socorro pawn shop. ~ de Vênus (anat.) mons veneris. a ~ at random, by the bulk. andar a ~ to live absconding in the wilderness. por ~s e vales up hill and down dale. aos ~s in heaps. 2. plentiful.
monteada s. f. 1. = montaria. 2. mountain hunting.
monteador s. m. 1. huntsman (esp. in the mountains). 2. forester, forest guide or guard.
montear (I) v. 1. to hunt in the mountains. 2. to heap up.
montear (II) v. (archit.) to plan, sketch.
montéia s. f. 1. plan of a construction giving dimen-sions and elevations. 2. space occupied by a build-ing.
monteira s. f. 1. huntress (esp. of the mountains). 2. hood of a mountaineer.
monteiria s. f. 1. position of a forest warden or ran-ger. 2. the quarter-rangers' share in the fine paid by poachers.
monteiro s. m. 1. hunter in the mountains. 2. (hunt.) beater. 3. forest warden, ranger. 4. person giving asylum to bandits. ‖ adj. 1. of or pertaining to a

mountain ranger or forest warden. 2. proper for hunting in the mountains.
montenegrino s. m. Montenegrin(e): native or inhabi-tant of Montenegro. ‖ adj. Montenegrin(e): of or pertaining to Montenegro.
montepio s. m. 1. widows' fund. 2. the pension paid by such an institution.
montês adj. m. + f. (pl. -eses) (f. -esa, pl. -esas) 1. montane, of the mountains. 2. crude, rustic, wild.
cabra ~ chamois. cabrito ~ ibex.
montesinho, montesino adj. 1. montane. 2. wild, sylvan. 3. rustic, simple, ignorant.
montevideano s. m. native or inhabitant of Mon-tevideo. ‖ adj. of or pertaining to Montevideo.
montevidéu s. m. (S. Braz.) scar received in a fight or war.
montícola s. m. + f. person or animal living in the mountains. ‖ adj. living in the mountains.
montículo s. m. monticle, monticule, hillock, mound.
montígeno adj. produced in the mountains.
montívago adj. strolling or roaming through the mountains.
montoeira, montureira s. f. (Braz.) 1. heap of stones showing where diamonds were dug for. 2. large quantity. 3. dunghill.
montra s. f. showcase of a store, shopwindow.
montuava s. f. (Braz., pop., also cachaça) white rum.
montuoso adj. = montanhoso.
montureiro s. m. ragpicker.
monturo s. m. 1. dunghill, scrap heap, rubbish heap, dust heap. 2. (fig.) pile of repulsive things.
monumental adj. m. + f. (pl. -ais) monumental, mag-nificent, extraordinary, enormous. ‖ ~mente adv. monumentally.
monumento s. m. 1. monument. 2. beautiful, majestic building. 3. mausoleum, memorial. 4. notable and noteworthy work. 5. memory, recollection.
moponga s. f. (N. Braz.) primitive method of fishing by stirring and beating the water to drive the fish into a weir.
moquear v. 1. to grill. 2. to beat meat. 3. to dry meat on a grill. 4. (pop.) to kill.
moqueca s. f. (Braz.) 1. fish or mussels simmered in oil and pepper (poqueca in Pará). 2. (N. Braz.) fish thus prepared wrapped up in a leaf. 3. cat-aplasm of mango and tobacco leaves used against headache.
moquecar-se v. (Braz.) 1. to crouch, squat. 2. to make o. s. as unnoticed as possible.
moquém s. m. (pl. -éns) (Braz.; also moqueteiro) grill to fry or dry meat or fish.
moquenca s. f. simmered beef with vinegar, garlic, pepper, etc.
moquenco, moquenquo s. m. 1. lazybones, idler. 2. big talker. 3. grimacer. ‖ adj. 1. indolent, lazy. 2. grimacing. 3. wheedling, coaxing.
moquenquice s. f. 1. cajolery, wheedling, coaxing. 2. grimaces. 3. idleness, laziness.
moquiço s. m. (N. Braz.) hut, small house, shack, shanty.
mor adj. m. + f. short or syncopated form of maior.
mora s. f. 1. delay, respite. 2. prolongation of a term or deadline.
morabitino s. m. = maravedi.
morábito s. m. (also marabuto) marabout: Moham-medan ascetic.
morácea s. f. (bot.) specimen of the Moraceae, the mulberry family.
morada s. f. residence, dwelling, dwelling place, hab-itation, abode, domicile, home, quarters, lodgings.
a última ~ the grave.
moradia s. f. 1. = morada. 2. (obs.) pension of the noblemen.

moradilho s. m. wood of a purple-brownish hue.
morado adj. mulberry-coloured.
morador s. m. 1. inhabitant, dweller. resident, tenant, lodger. 2. (N. Braz.) farm hand living on a rural property. 3. person who belongs to a household but not to the family. ‖ adj. dwelling.
moral s. f. 1. (philos.) moral philosophy, morals, ethics. 2. morality. 3. m. morale: mental condition. ‖ adj. m. + f. (pl. **-ais**) moral, ethical. ‖ **~mente** adv. morally, in a moral sense.
moralidade s. f. 1. morality. 2. moral of a story.
moralismo s. m. moralism: philosophic system of morality.
moralista s. m. + f. moralist: 1. writer on or professor of morals. 2. person who advocates moral principles. ‖ adj. moralizing, moralistic.
moralização s. f. (pl. **-ões**) moralization.
moralizador s. m. moralizer: moral preacher. ‖ adj. moralizing.
moralizar v. to moralize: 1. censure. 2. render moral, improve the moral of. 3. teach morality to.
moranga s. f. 1. (Port.) variety of grape. 2. (Braz.) variety of squash. ‖ adj. (Port.) relating to the **moranga** (grape or squash).
morangal s. m. (pl. **-ais**) strawberry plantation.
morango s. m. strawberry (plant or fruit) (plate B 1).
morangueiro s. m. 1. strawberry plant. 2. strawberry vendor.
morar v. 1. to live, dwell, inhabit, reside, abide, lodge. 2. to remain, stay, find o. s. 3. (Braz., sl.) to understand.
eles moram no interior they live in the interior (hinterland). **ir ~ para** to move over to. **moramos nos confins do diabo** we live at the end of the world (far away). **onde ele mora?** where does he live? (Braz., sl.) **ele morou no assunto** he understood it, he got the message.
moratória s. f. moratorium: authorization for delay of payment.
moratório adj. moratory, delaying, deferring.
morbidez, morbideza s. f. 1. morbidness, morbidity, sickness. 2. languidness. 3. (arts) morbidezza: delicacy and softnes of colours in the representation of flesh.
morbidizar v. to become or turn morbid.
mórbido adj. 1. morbid, diseased, sickly, unhealthy, unsound. 2. languid, peccant. 3. enervating. 4. (paint. or sculp.) soft, delicate. ‖ **morbidamente** adv. morbidly.
morbífico, morbígeno, morbígero, morbíparo, morboso adj. morbific(al), morbiferous, morbiferal, causing disease.
morbo s. m. morbus, illness, pathological state.
morcegar v. (Braz.) 1. to explore, exploit. 2. (N. Braz.) to jump up or down from a streetcar, bus, etc., in movement.
morcego (ê) s. m. (pl. **morcegos**) 1. (zool.) bat, flicker-mouse, flittermouse. 2. (fig.) person leaving the house only at night. 3. (N. Braz.) = **mata-cachorro.** 4. boy riding railroads, streetcars, etc., without ever paying for it. 5. paper kite.
morcegueira s. f. (Braz.) cabbage tree.
morcela, morcilha s. f. (S. Braz.) 1. blood pudding, black pudding. 2. a kind of sweet sausage.
mordaça s. f. 1. muzzle, gag. 2. (fig.) repression of the liberty of press and speech. 3. (S. Braz., also **sovador**) stick split longitudinally to the middle used to soften the cordage.
~ de torninho (mech.) vice clamps.
mordaçar v. (engr.) to mordant.
mordacidade s. f. 1. mordacity, mordancy, corrosiveness, causticity, acridity. 2. evil talk. 3. sarcasm, very severe criticism. 4. piquancy, piquant taste.

mordaz adj. m. + f. (absolute sup. **mordacíssimo**) 1. biting, snappish. 2. corrosive, pungent, caustic, scorching. 3. piquant, acrid, mordaceous, satirical, sarcastic, saucy, cutting, sharp.
um estilo ~ a caustic style. **uma língua ~** a sharp tongue. **uma observação ~** a cutting remark.
mordedor s. m. 1. biter. 2. (Braz., sl.) person asking his friends continuously for money, sponger. ‖ adj. biting, caustic.
mordedura s. f. (also **mordedela, mordidela, mordimento** m., **mordida**) 1. bite, teethmark. 2. (fig.) painful reminder, offense.
morde-e-assopra s. m. +f., sg. + pl. (Braz., pop.) hypocrite, double-dealer.
mordente s. m. 1. (paint.) mordant, stain, fixative. 2. (print.) visorium: instrument used to fix the lines to be copied. 3. (mus.) mordent. 4. (mech.) vice jaw or cheek (plate P 4). ‖ adj. m. + f. 1. biting, mordant, mordacious. 2. caustic, corrosive. 3. provoking.
morder v. 1. to bite, snap, nip, hurt with the teeth, sink the teeth into, put a toothmark into. 2. to hurt, torment, disgust, afflict. 3. to waste, corrode, burn. 4. to penetrate into, cling to. 5. to stimulate, instigate. 6. to carp at, backbite, speak evil of. 7. to borrow money habitually from. 8. to be piquant. 9. to itch. 10. **~-se:** a) to bite o. s. b) to despair, grow angry, worry.
~ a areia to bite the ground; to die. **~ a batata** (N. Braz., pop.) to have an alcoholic drink. **~ a isca** to bite; take the bait. **~ a língua** to bite one's tongue, to hold one's peace. **~ o freio** to bite on the bit. **~ o pó** to bite the dust. **~-se de inveja** to be eaten up with envy.
mordexim s. m. (med.) cholera.
mordicação s. f. (pl. **-ões**) 1. nibble, gnawing. 2. biting, smarting, prickle, pinching.
mordicante adj. m. + f. (also **mordicativo** m.) nibbling, pinching, prickling.
mordicar, mordiscar v. 1. to nibble, gnaw, pick at. 2. to bite, smart, prickle. 3. to stimulate.
mordida, mordidela s. f. (Braz., fam.) = **mordedura.**
mordido adj. 1. bitten. 2. (Braz., pop., fig.) drunk.
ele está ~ he has contracted a venereal disease.
mordimento s. m. 1. = **mordedura.** 2. (fig.) remorse.
mordomado s. m. 1. position of a majordomo or steward. 2. time the stewardship lasts. 3. taxes paid by those having a mordomo.
mordomar v. to act as a majordomo or steward.
mordomia s. f. stewardship, office of a majordomo.
mordomo s. m. 1. majordomo, steward. 2. butler.
~ da igreja churchwarden, vestry-man. **~ de uma irmandade** chief manager of a confraternity.
moréia s. f. moray: fish of the family Muraenidae. 2. (agric.) shock (of sheaves).
moréia-comum s. f. (pl. **moréias-comuns**) (ichth.) European moray.
moreira s. f. plant of the family Moraceae (Bagassa guianensis).
moreiredo s. m. mulberry grove.
morena s. f. 1. (geol.) moraine. 2. (Braz.) dance accompanied by singing. 3. (Braz.) name given by hunters to either a paca or a partridge. 4. (Braz.) brunette. 5. (Braz.) country girl.
morenado adj. browned, tanned.
moreno s. m. brunet. ‖ adj. brunet, brown, dark, tanned, tawny, swarthy.
moreota s. m. + f. native or inhabitant of Morea, Greece. ‖ adj. of or pertaining to Morea, Greece.
morerê s. m. (Braz.) pompadour fish.
morféia s. f. leprosy.
morfema s. f. morpheme: linguistic element which expresses the relations between ideas.

morfético s. m. (Braz.) leper. ‖ adj. 1. pertaining to Morpheus. 2. sleepy. 3. leprous.

morfina s. f. (pharm.) morphine, morphia.

morfinismo s. m. morphinism: morphine habit.

morfinizar-se v. to use or abuse of morphine; become a morphine addict.

morfinomania s. f. morphinomania, morphiomania: morbid craving for morphine.

morfinômano s. m. morphinomaniac, morphomaniac.

morfogenia s. f. (biol.) morphogenesis, morphogeny: production or evolution of morphological characters.

morfogênico adj. morphogenetic: relating to morphogenesis.

morfologia s. f. morphology: 1. (biol.) science of form and structure of organisms. 2. (phil.) branch of grammar dealing with form and transformation of words.

~ social study of the structures or forms of life of society.

morfológico adj. morphologic: relating to morphology.

morfologista s. m. + f. morphologist: scientist engaged in morphology.

morfólogo s. m. expert in morphology, morphologist.

morfose s. f. morphosis: act of taking or giving form.

morfozoário s. m. any animal of a distinct form.

morgada s. f. 1. wife or widow of an entail owner. 2. woman owning an entail.

morgadio s. m. 1. majorat. 2. entail, tail. ‖ adj. relating to entail.

morgado s. m. 1. first-born son or heir to an owner of an entail. 2. oldest or only son. 3. entail, tail. 4. heir of an entail. 5. (fig.) very lucrative thing. 6. ~s pl. a kind of pastry.

morganático adj. morganatic, left-handed (marriage).

morganho s. m. mouse.

morgue s. f. morgue, mortuary.

moribundo s. m. moribund, dying person. ‖ adj. moribund, dying, expiring, on the verge of extinction.

morigeração s. f. (pl. -ões) 1. moralization, moderation of customs. 2. good customs or habits; moderation, modesty.

morigerado adj. (also morígero) well-mannered, well-bred, moderate, modest.

morigerar v. 1. to moralize, moderate the customs of. 2. to teach, educate. 3. to teach moral principles. 4. ~-se to acquire good manners, mend one's ways.

morim s. m. (also madapolão, madrasto) longcloth.

morinda s. f. (bot.) Indian mulberry.

moringa, moringue s. f. (S. Braz.) clay jar to keep the drinking water cool.

moringácea s. f. specimen of the Moringaceae, a family of dicotyledonous plants.

moringáceo adj. (bot.) of or pertaining to the family Moringaceae.

morioplastia s. f. (med.) surgical substitution of any part of the human organs.

mormaceira s. f. sweltry, sultry, weather; sultriness.

mormacento adj. (alto fig.) sultry, muggy, sweltry.

mormaço s. m. 1. = mormaceira. 2. (N. Braz.) flirt.

mormente adv. mainly, chiefly, principally.

mormo s. m. (vet.) glanders, equinia: contagious disease of equine animals.

mórmon s. m. (pl. mórmons, mórmones) Mormon: a member of the Latter-day Saints.

mormonismo s. m. Mormonism: religious system of the Mormons, a North American denomination.

mormoso adj. (vet.) glandered, glanderous: affected with glanders.

mornança s. f. (N. Braz.) slowness, sluggishness, delay.

mornar v. 1. = amornar. 2. (N. Braz.) to delay, retard, hold up the works.

mornidão s. f. 1. lukewarmness, tepidity. 2. (fig.) laxness, halfheartedness, indifference.

morno (ô) adj. (pl. mornos) 1. lukewarm, tepid. 2. (fig.) lax, insipid, dull, monotonous, indifferent, halfhearted. 3. (fig.) serene.

de água -a indifferent, insignificant, worthless.

morocho s. m. (S. Braz.) 1. back-country man. 2. mestizo. 3. brunet.

mororó, miroró s. m. (Braz. also pé-de-boi, unha-de--boi, unha-de-vaca) leguminous tree of the family Caesalpinaceae (Bauhinia forficata).

estar de ~ (N. Braz.) to be confined to bed.

morosidade s. f. 1. moroseness. 2. slowness, tardiness, slackness, sluggishness, laxity, laxness.

moroso adj. 1. morose, glum, gloomy, ill-humoured. 2. slow, lax, tardy, slack, sluggish, lagging. ‖ -amente adv. morosely, slowly.

morotó s. m. (Braz., also tapuru, bicho-de-coco) larvae of flies, maggot.

morototó s. m. (Braz.) plant of the family Araliaceae (Didymoparax morototoni).

morra interj. down with!

morraca s. f. tinder made from rags.

morraça s. f. 1. natural manure from mud or swamps; mire. 2. wine of inferior quality.

morrão s. m. (pl. -ões) 1. match, lunt. 2. snuff (of a wick). 3. grain rotted in the ear before ripened.

morraria s. f. ridge of hills.

morrediço adj. 1. about to die, dying, short-lived. 2. = mortiço.

morredor s. m. (Braz.) 1. finishing line of a race. 2. place where something ends or dies. 3. place from which the game can hardly escape. 4. fish corral. ‖ adj. 1. = morredouro. 2. (N. Braz., pop.) cowardly.

morredouro s. m. (also morredoiro) 1. unhealthy place where many deaths occur. 2. = morredor. ‖ adj. 1. dying, mortal, perishable, short-lived. 2. decrepit, fragile, transitory.

morremorrer v. (Braz.) to die slowly, die away.

morrente adj. m. + f. = morrediço, mortiço.

morrer s. m. dying, death. ‖ v. 1. to die, perish, decease, expire, pass away. 2. to end, terminate, vanish, disappear, become extinct, cease, stop. 3. to fade, decay, wither, die away, succumb. 4. to go out (light, fire). 5. to become numb, torpid or paralysed. 6. to be forgotten. 7. to suffer, go through agonies. 8. to long, crave for.

~ de 1. to die of (from). 2. to suffer badly of. ~ de fome 1. to perish from starvation. 2. to be very hungry. ~ de frio to freeze to death; to die (perish) from cold. ~ de morte natural to die a natural death, in one's bed. ~ de morte violenta to die a violent death. ~ de riso to die of laughing. ~ de velhice to die of old age. ~ no campo de honra to die on the field of honour. ~ para o mundo to die to the world. ~ por 1. to die for. 2. to have a great affection for, to have a yearn for. ~ sem ser vovó (N. Braz.) to suffer a fiasco without a consolation. estar para ~ to be about to die. ~ de rir to burst with laughter. lindo de ~ extremely beautiful. ~ na conta (Braz., sl.) 1. to satisfy a debt. 2. to pay the bill.

morrião s. m. (pl. -ões) 1. pimpernel. 2. morion: ancient helm without a visor.

morrinha s. f. 1. (vet.) epidemic mange. 2. murrain. 3. slight illness. 4. (Braz.) offensive body odour of a person or animal. 5. sadness, melancholy, lassitude, prostration. 6. (Port., prov.) mizzle, drizzle.

morrinhar v. (Braz.) to become displeased, weary, disgusted, tedious or bored.

morrinhento adj. 1. (vet.) affected with mange or sufferring of murrain. 2. weakened, fatigued, prostrated, sickly. 3. (Braz.) stinking, smelling. 4. sad, languid, melancholic. 5. drizzly, overcast, lowering, murky, dreary, gloomy. **chuva -a** drizzly rain. **dia** ~ gloomy day.

morro s. m. 1. mount, mound, hill. 2. quarry. ~ **pelado** (N. Braz.) hill with sparse or no vegetation.

morsa s. f. 1. (zool.) morse, walrus, sea horse. 2. (also **torninho**) (mech.) vice, vise, bench vice, (bench vise), screw vice, (screw vise), screw clam (plates F 1, P 4).

morsegão s. m. (pl. **-ões**) 1. bite, piece bitten off. 2. pinch.

morsegar v. 1. to bite off. 2. to nibble. 3. to indent, dint, pinch.

morso s. m. 1. bite. 2. bite of a bridle.

mortadela s. f. large Italian sausage.

mortagem s. f. (pl. **-ens**) (carp.) mortise, mortice.

mortal s. m. (pl. **-ais**) 1. human being. 2. pl. humanity. ‖ adj. m. + f. mortal: 1. lethal, deadly, deathly, deathful, fatal, moribund. 2. transitory, transient. 3. implacable. ‖ ~**mente** adv. mortally, deadly. ~**mente ferido** mortally wounded. **doença** ~ fatal illness. **inimigo** ~ mortal enemy. **ódio** ~ deadly hatred. **os restos -ais de** the mortal remains of. **pecado** ~ mortal sin.

mortalha s. f. 1. hearse cloth, winding-sheet, shroud. 2. cigarette paper.

mortalidade, mortandade s. f. mortality: 1. quality of being mortal, deadliness. 2. death rate.

mortalizar v. to mortalize: 1. to become or make mortal. 2. to destroy, annihilate.

mortandade s. f. 1. = **mortalidade**. 2. slaughter, blood shed, massacre, carnage.

morte s. f. 1. death, decease, dying, demise. 2. destruction, extinction, end. 3. Death: the imaginary being who takes away life. ~ **civil** (jur.) civil death. ~ **moral** depravation, loss of all sentiments of honour. **a** ~ **em pé** a walking skeleton. **de** ~ mortally. **de má** ~ of bad character. **estar às portas da** ~ to be at death's door. **estar pela hora da** ~ to be very dear. **leito de** ~ deathbed. **perigo de** ~ danger of life. **tão certo como a** ~ as sure as death. **você é de** ~ (sl.) you are the limit.

morte-cor, morta-cor, morta-luz s. f. (paint.) dead colouring.

morteirada s. f. 1. shot of a mortar. 2. hit, stroke. 3. hit with the head.

morteiro s. m. 1. mortar: a) short cannon. b) device for firing pyrotechnic shells. c) a bowl in which substances are pounded with a pestle. 2. that which is ground in a mortar. 3. (naut.) binnacle, compass box.

morticínio s. m. slaughter, massacre, bloodshed.

mortiço adj. 1. dying (light, fire). 2. dim, about to go out. 3. dull, spiritless, lifeless. **olhos** ~**s** dull eyes.

mortífero adj. mortal, murderous, lethal, deadly, deathful, causing death.

mortificação s. f. (pl. **-ões**) mortification: 1. humiliation. 2. torment, affliction, chagrin. 3. grief, trouble, vexation. 4. the act of subduing the flesh by abstinence and prayer. 5. (med.) partial paralysis.

mortificado adj. mortified, humiliated, tormented, troubled, vexed.

mortificador s. m. mortifier. ‖ adj. mortifying.

mortificante adj. m. + f. (also **mortificador, mortificativo** m.) mortifying, grievous.

mortificar v. to mortify: 1. humiliate. 2. torment, afflict, disgust, trouble. 3. torpify, benumb. 4. affect with gangrene or necrosis. 5. destroy. 6.

macerate by penitential discipline. 7. torture. 8. efface, obliterate, extinguish. 9. dissipate. 10. ~-**se** to mortify one's flesh; to grieve, be afflicted. ~ **as paixões** to subdue one's passion.

morto s. m. 1. dead, deceased, departed; defunct, corpse, cadaver. 2. (S. Braz.) retaining post of a wire fence. ‖ adj. 1. dead, deceased, killed. 2. wilted, withered, faded, dried (vegetable). 3. extinct, gone, finished, disappeared, forgotten, obsolete. 4. paralysed, benumbed, torpid, stiff. 5. stagnant. 6. obliterated. 7. tarnished, dull, inexpressive. 8. superfluous, unnecessary. 9. inert, lifeless, inanimate. 10. dead tired. ~ **e vivo** (N. Braz.) phantom, vision. **água -a** stagnant water. **cair** ~ to drop down dead. **criança nascida -a** stillborn child. **dinheiro** ~ dead capital. **estação -a** dead season. **estar** ~ **por** to long after. **estou** ~ **de fome** I am famished. **nem** ~ **nem retalhado** on the hoof, alive. **ponto** ~ dead center. **quase** ~ all but dead. **ser** ~ **e vivo num lugar** (N. Braz.) to frequent a place constantly.

mortório s. m. 1. funeral. 2. decease. 3. funeral procession. 4. void patches in a seed plot. 5. (N. Braz.) idleness, rest. 6. disuse, oblivion.

mortualha s. f. 1. funeral. 2. heap of corpses.

mortuárias s. f. (pl. (also **mortulhas;** obs.) portion of a deceased parishioner's fortune paid to the church.

mortuário adj. mortuary, funerary.

mortuório s. m. funeral, exequies.

morubixaba s. m. (Braz., also **murumuxaua, muruxaua, tuxaua, cacique, curaca**) temporal chief of Indian tribes.

mórula s. f. 1. slight delay. 2. (embryol.) morula: globular aggregate resulting from the segmentation of an ovum.

morupeteca s. f. (N. Braz.) legionary ant.

morzelo s. m. black horse. ‖ adj. mulberry-coloured (horse).

mosaicista, mosaísta s. m. + f. mosaicist, mosaist: person working on mosaics. ‖ adj. working on a mosaic.

mosaico (I) s. m. 1. mosaic, tesselation. 2. (fig.) miscellany. 3. (plant path.) mosaic disease.

mosaico (II) adj. Mosaic: of or pertaining to Moses.

mosca (ô) s. f. 1. fly. 2. (fig.) bothersome, importunate person. 3. tiny beard below the underlip. 4. beauty spot. 5. patch for reinforcement of seams, pleats, etc. ~ **artificial** fly (for fishing). ~ **dos cavalos** horse fly, breeze, gadfly. ~ **de Espanha** Spanish fly, cantharis. ~**s volantes** muscae volitantes. **andar às** ~**s** to idle, fiddle around. **comer** ~**s** to be cheated, to be left out, not to understand what is going on. **estar com a** ~ to be restless or fidgety. **estar às** ~**s** not to be frequented, be empty, without clients or spectators. **pagar** ~**s** to stand gaping about, be fooled.

mosca-da-madeira s. f. (pl. **moscas-da-madeira**) dipterous insect of the family Pantophitalmideae (Pantophtalmus pictus).

mosca-berneira s. f. (pl. **moscas-berneiras**) = **mosca--do-berne**.

mosca-das-frutas s. f. (pl. **moscas-das-frutas**) fruit fly.

mosca-de-fogo s. f. (pl. **moscas-de-fogo**) (N. Braz.) firefly.

moscadeira s. f. (bot.) nutmeg tree.

moscadeiro s. m. fly-flap.

mosca-do-berne s. f. (pl. **moscas-do-berne**) (Braz., ent.) a botfly (Dermatobia hominis).

moscado adj. aromatic, musky. **noz -a** nutmeg.

mosca-morta s. f. (pl. **moscas-mortas**) 1. underhand person, sneak. 2. slowcoach.

moscão s. m. (pl. -ões) 1. large fly, blowfly, bluebottle. 2. (fig.) sly, crafty person.

moscar v. 1. to run away from flies (cattle). 2. (fig.) to run away, take off, blow.

moscardo s. m. 1. = moscão, tavão. 2. (N. Braz., sl.) secret police.

moscaria s. f. (also fam., mosquedo) large quantity of flies.

moscatel s. m. (pl. -éis) 1. muscatel. 2. a variety of figs, pears and apples. ‖ adj. m. + f. said of the muscat grape.

moscatelina s. f. (bot.) moschatel.

mosca-varejeira s. f. (pl. moscas-varejeiras) (Braz., ent.) . a blowfly (Callitroga hominivorax) whose larvae, the screwworms, parasitize the flesh of mammals including man.

mosco (ô) s. m. 1. little fly. 2. mosquito.

moscóvia s. f. Russian leather.

moscovita s. m. + f. Muscovite: native or inhabitant of Moscow, Russian. ‖ adj. Muscovite: of Moscow, Russian.

moslêmico adj. Moslem.

moslemita s. m. + f. Christian who became a Moslem.

moslim s. m. (pl. -ins) Moslem: Mohammedan. ‖ adj. Moslem: Mohammedan.

mosqueado adj. spotted, dotted, speckled, flecked, dapple; (bot.) guttate.

cavalo ~ dapple grey, piebald horse.

mosqueador adj. (S. Braz.) restlessly shying away the flies with its tail (cattle).

mosquear v. 1. to speckle, spot, fleck, dot, mottle, dapple. 2. (S. Braz.) to shy away the flies with the tail (cattle). 3. to flip, turn the tail (horse) when feeling the spurs or the whip.

mosquedo s. m. 1. = moscaria. 2. = mosqueiro.

mosqueiro s. m. 1. place infested with flies. 2. fly-trap, fly-paper, fly-net, fly-flap. 3. (N. Braz.) shack, filthy hovel.

mosqueta s. f. 1. musk-rose. 2. Arabian jasmine (Jasminum sambac).

mosquetaço s. m. musket shot.

mosquetada s. f. 1. = mosquetaço. 2. wound caused by a musket shot.

mosquetão s. m. (pl. -ões) 1. snap hook, spring hook (plate G 2). 2. (Braz., mil.) carbine.

mosquetaria s. f. 1. musketry. 2. fire from small arms.

mosquete s. m. 1. musket. 2. (N. Braz.) small, fast horse.

mosquetear v. 1. to shoot. 2. to shoot a musket.

mosqueteiro s. m. musketeer.

mosquitada s. f. (Braz.) lots of mosquitoes.

mosquitador s. m. (Braz.) 1. merchant of small diamonds or mosquitos. 2. smalltime buyer of diamonds or precious stones.

mosquiteiro s. m. 1. mosquito-curtain, mosquito-net. 2. = mosqueiro. 3. (Braz.) tree of the family Leguminosae-Papilionaceae (Machaerium ɾngustifolium). 4. (S. Braz.) outdoor onlookers at a house party.

mosquitinho s. m. 1. dim. of mosquito. 2. (Braz.) small black earth bee.

mosquito s. m. 1. mosquito. 2. small diamond. 3. (N. Braz.) (fireworks) serpent.

mosquito-do-mangue s. m. (pl. mosquitos-do-mangue) = maruim.

mosquito-palha s. m. (pl. mosquitos-palha), mosquito-pólvora (pl. mosquitos-pólvora) (Braz., also birigui, maruim) punkie, midge.

mosquito-prego s. m. (pl. mosquitos-prego) mosquito of the family Culicideae.

mossa s. f. 1. dent, dint, jag, indentation, notch. 2. bruise. 3. notch in a yoke. 4. (fig.) moral impression. 5. (S. Braz.) notch in the ear of cattle as a mark.

mossegar v. = morsegar.

mossoró s. m. (N. Braz.) periodic wind from the N.

mostaço s. m. large quantity of must (new wine).

mostárabe m. + f., adj. = moçárabe.

mostarda s. f. 1. mustard: a) the plant. b) the seed. c) the powder. 2. (fig.) stimulant. 3. shooting, fighting, scuffle. 4. m. (Braz.) small shot.

subir a ~ ao nariz to have a fit of rage.

mostardal s. m. (pl. -ais) mustard field.

mostardeira s. f. 1. mustard (plant). 2. mustard pot.

mostardeiro s. m. 1. mustard seller. 2. mustard pot.

mosteiro s. m. convent, monastery.

mostífero adj. yielding must.

mosto s. m. 1. must, new wine. 2. swarm of bees.

mostra s. f. 1. show, exhibition, display. 2. ~s pl. gestures, signal, outside appearances.

à ~ bare, uncovered, visible. dar ~s de to show, give proofs of. fazer ~ de to seem to be on the point of doing. pôr à ~ to bring forward, show, exhibit.

mostrador s. m. 1. dial-plate, hour-plate, face of a clock (plate R 4). 2. counter, showcase. ‖ adj. 1. showing. 2. indicatory (finger). 3. tell-tale.

mostrar v. 1. to show, exhibit, display, present. 2. to signify, denote, mean. 3. to signalize, point out, indicate. 4. to simulate. 5. to teach, show, demonstrate. 6. to prove. 7. ~-se to manifest, reveal itself, to show o. s., to appear.

~ as cartas to show down. ~ boa cara to take it well. ~ as costas to turn one's back on s. o. ~ com (or de) quantos paus se faz uma canoa (Braz.) to teach somebody a lesson. ~ o caminho to show the way to somebody. ~ os dentes to show one's teeth, to snarl. ela mostrou bom porte she carried herself well. mostramo-nos à altura da situação we rose to the occasion. mostre que é homem show yourself a man.

mostrengar v. to become a fat, awkward, and ugly person.

mostrengo s. m. 1. fat, awkward, and ugly person. 2. scarecrow. 3. good-for-nothing, scapegrace.

mostruário s. m. (Braz.) showcase, collection; book or set of samples.

mota s. f. 1. mound of earth around a tree. 2. rampart, dam, dike. 3. (S. Braz., also inhapa) earnest-money, extra, tip.

motacu s. f. (Braz.) a variety of palm tree (Attalea princips).

mote s. m. 1. heraldic motto, heraldic device. 2. idea in a distich or verse. 3. theme. 4. epigraph. 5. = motejo.

motejador s. m. 1. scoffer, mocker, flouter. 2. jester, banterer. ‖ adj. scoffing, mocking.

motejar v. 1. to scoff, mock, deride, jeer, flout, ridicule. 2. to criticize, censure. 3. to joke, jest, banter, chaff, rally. 4. to make mottoes, epigraphs.

motejo s. m. 1. scorn, flout. 2. jest, joke, quib, raillery, banter. 3. piquant or off-coloured remarks.

motete s. m. 1. mot: funny or satyrical saying. 2. (mus.) motet.

motevo s. m. (Braz., pop.) nutty fellow.

motilidade s. f. motility, motive power.

motim s. m. (pl. -ins) 1. mutiny, revolt, uproar, insurrection, rebellion, sedition. 2. disorder, tumult, riot, fray.

promover um ~ to stir up a rebellion.

motivação s. f. (pl. -ões) motivation: 1. argumentation, reasoning. 2. inducement.

motivado adj. motivated: 1. properly explained, well supported. 2. caused, originated, induced.

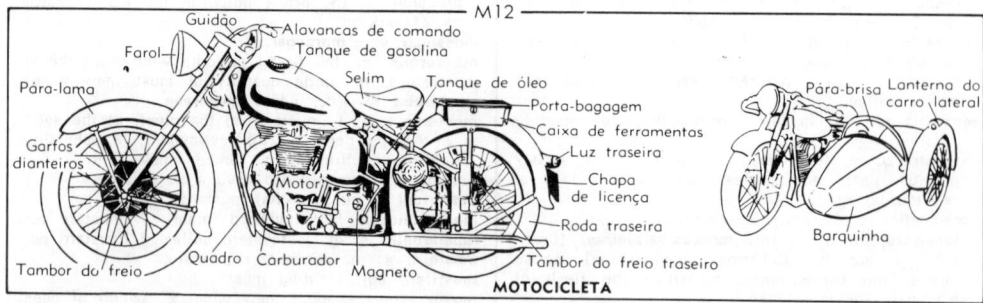

MOTOCICLETA

motivador s. m. causer, motivating thing, person, thought, etc. ‖ adj. 1. giving a motive or reason. 2. moving, impelling, inducing.

motivar v. to motivate: 1. give the motive, reason, cause of. 2. cause, occasion, induce, give motive.

motivo s. m. 1. motive, ground, cause, reason. 2. intent, purpose. 3. end, aim, object. 4. scope. 5. (mus.) theme. ‖ adj. motive, motor, moving.

por ~ de by reason of, on account of. **sem ~** groundless, groundlessly.

moto s. m. 1. motion, movement, impulse. 2. musical theme, movement. 3. knightly motto, device. 4. f. reduced form of **motocicleta:** motorcycle.

de ~ próprio spontaneously, of one's own accord.

motocicleta s. f. (also **motociclo m., moto** f.) motorcycle (plate M 12).

motociclista s. m. + f. motorcyclist.

motogodile s. f. (Braz.) small boat with an outboard motor.

motoqueiro s. m. (Braz.) motorcyclist.

motor s. m. 1. motor, engine (plates M 12, 13, V 3). 2. mover: person or thing causing or imparting motion; motive force. ‖ adj. (f. **motora, motriz**) motor, motive, moving.

~ a dois, a quatro tempos two-stroke, four-stroke engine. **de um só ~** monomotor. **~ de partida** starter (motor) (plate M 13). **~ de popa** outboard motor (plate L 2). **~ Diesel** Diesel engine. **~ elétrico** electromotor (plate D 1). **o ~ falhou** the motor stalled. **desligar o ~** to stop the engine. **inspecionar o ~** to check the motor. **ligar o ~** to start the engine.

motoreiro, motorneiro s. m. (Braz.) motorneer, motorman.

motório adj. motory, motorial.

motorista s. m. + f. motorist. 2. (railroad) engineer. 3. driver of any motor vehicle.

~ de praça taxi driver, taximan.

motorização s. f. motorization.

motorizado adj. motorized.

motorizar v. to motorize.

motoro s. m. (Braz., ichth.) ray.

motricidade s. f. 1. motricity: a quality of motive power. 2. (physiol.) motor function of certain nervous cells.

motriz s. f. that which causes motion. ‖ adj. motive, motor, motory, moving.

força ~ motive power. **roda ~** traction wheel.

moucarrão adj. stone-deaf.

mouchão s. m. (pl. **-ões**) 1. small river island. 2. small wood in a marsh.

mouco s. m. deaf person. ‖ adj. deaf, hard or dull of hearing, deafish.

fazer ouvidos ~s to play deaf.

mouquice, mouquidão s. f. deafness; hard hearing.

moura-encantada s. f. (pl. **mouras-encantadas**) (also **moira-encantada**) fabulous brunette who, according to Portuguese popular belief, lived in the rivers and wells, always dressed in red, always combing her hair.

mourama s. f. (also **moirama**) 1. the land of the Moors. 2. a multitude of Moors. 3. the Moors. 4. (S. Braz.) = **mouronada**.

mourão (I) s. m. (pl. **-ões**) (also **moirão**) 1. vine stake. 2. stake, post, pole. 3. (Braz.) heavy pole to which cattle is tied. 4 (Braz.) moorage post for boats.

mourão (II) s. m. (pl. **-ões**) horseman riding at the left in a game called **canas**.

mourar v. (also **moirar**) 1. to become a Moor, a Moslem. 2. to practise the Moslem religion. 3. to dress or act like a Moor.

mouraria s. f. (hist., also **moiraria**) quarter where the Moors lived.

moura-torta s. f. (pl. **mouras-tortas**) (also **moira-torta**) evil-doing fabulous being of the Portuguese folklore, the opposite of the **moura-encantada**.

mourejado adj. (also **moirejado**) obtained through hard work.

mourejar v. (also **moirejar**) 1. to work hard, toil, fag, moil, drudge, moider, plod, slave. 2. to work constantly.

mourejo s. m. (Braz., also **moirejo**) toil, pain, struggle.

mourescos s. m. pl. (also **moirescos**) Moresque ornates in goldsmithry. ‖ **mouresco** adj. Moorish.

mouriscos s. m. pl. (also **moiriscos**) = **mourescos**. ‖ **mourisco** adj. 1. Moorish. 2. (N. Braz.) dark-grey with lighter undertones (cat).

mourisma s. f. (also **moirisma**) 1. religion of the Moors. 2. = **mourama**.

mourizar c. (also **moirizar**) to turn into a Moor, become a Moslem.

mouro s. m. (also **moiro**) 1. Moor, Saracen. 2. faithless, unbeliever. 3. (Braz.) slaving man. 4. **~s** pl. game representing a naval battle between Moors and Christians. ‖ adj. 1. Moorish. 2. faithless, unchristened. 3. dark-coated speckled with white (horse).

mouronada s. f. (also **moironada, mourama**) (S. Braz.) a lot of poles, posters or stakes.

movediço adj. 1. movable. 2. unstable. 3. (fig.) fickle.

areia ~ a- quicksand, drifting sand.

movedor s. m. mover, contriver; that which moves. ‖ adj. moving.

móvel s. m. (pl. **-eis**) 1. cause, motive, moving force. 2. piece of furniture. 3. projectile. 4. **-eis** pl.: a) movables, movable property. b) furniture. ‖ adj. m. + f. movable, moveable, changeable, variable.

móveis estofados upholstered furniture (plate C 2). **bens -eis** movables, movable property. **festas -eis** movable feasts.

movelaria s. f. (Braz.) furniture store.

moveleiro s. m. (Braz.) 1. furniture maker. 2. furniture dealer.

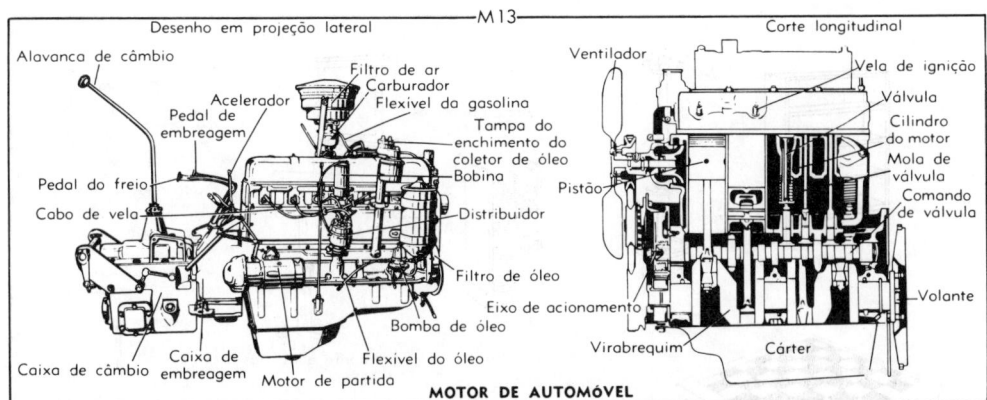

─────M 13─────

Desenho em projeção lateral — Corte longitudinal

Alavanca de câmbio
Acelerador
Pedal de embreagem
Pedal do freio
Cabo de vela
Caixa de câmbio
Caixa de embreagem
Motor de partida
Filtro de ar
Carburador
Flexível da gasolina
Tampa do enchimento do coletor de óleo
Bobina
Distribuidor
Filtro de óleo
Bomba de óleo
Flexível do óleo
Ventilador
Pistão
Eixo de acionamento
Virabrequim
Cárter
Vela de ignição
Válvula
Cilindro do motor
Mola de válvula
Comando de válvula
Volante

MOTOR DE AUTOMÓVEL

movente adj. m. + f. moving, changeable.
mover v. 1. to move: a) put in motion, cause to change place or position. b) advance, progress. c) persuade, induce, incite, influence, cause, stimulate. d) stir, budge. e) perturb. f) alter, change. g) touch, affect, strike, impress strongly. h) (coll.) get going, blow. i) keep in motion. j) promote, provoke, excite, prompt. k) stir up. l) rouse. 2. to miscarry, have an abortion. 3. ~se: a) to be in motion; to move o. s., go from one place to another; to stir, start, set out; to move itself. b) to be moved, touched, affected. c) to be prevailed on or upon. d) to let o. s. convince.
~ ação judicial to sue. ~ as pernas to get some exercise for one's feet, to walk. ~ às lágrimas to move to tears. ~ guerras to promote wars. fazer ~ to sway. não se mova! don't budge! ~ céus e Terra to move heaven and earth.
movido adj. 1. moved, impelled, taken, caused. 2. (Braz.) rachitic, underdeveloped.
movimentação s. f. (pl. -ões) movement, moving.
movimentar v. 1. to move, put into motion. 2. to stir. 3. to enliven, animate.
movimento s. m. 1. movement: a) motion, moving, changing of position, dislocation, displacement (plate P 18). b) constant motion. c) stir, agitation, trouble, emotion. d) gesture. e) activity, liveliness, animation. f) (mus.) movement, time. g) evolution of ideas. h) (mil.) movement of troops or ships. i) (astr.) movement of the stars. 2. turnover, business. 3. sedition, uproar. 4. traffic.
~ comercial business turnover. pôr em ~ to set in motion, start, throw into gear. pôr-se em ~ to move, start, set out. rua de muito ~ busy street.
móvito s. m. (med.) 1. premature birth. 2. abortion, miscarriage.
movongo s. m. (N. Braz.) canyon.
moxa s. f. flaming surgical cotton to cauterize the skin.
moxama s. f. dried and salted fish.
moxamar v. to smoke fish.
moxameiro s. m. 1. person who prepares or sells dried fish. 2. place where fishes are dried.
moxar v. to fume fish.
moxinifada s. f. medley, mixture, confusion, miscellany.
mozabita s. m. + f. member of a mixed race of Turks and Moors. ‖ adj. of or pertaining to this race.
mozeta s. f. mozzetta: short cape worn by prelates.
mu, mulo s. m. mule.
muafo s. m. (N. Braz.) 1. old rag. 2. ~s pl. old clothes, old rags; junk.

muamba (I) s. f. 1. African transport basket. 2. (N. Braz.): a) a knapsack. b) all the military outfit.
muamba (II) s. f. (Braz.) 1. theft of things from anchored ships and custom stores. 2. smuggling, contraband, buying and selling of stolen goods. 3. fraud, theft, knavery.
muambeiro s. m. (Braz.) smuggler, dealer in stolen goods.
muar s. m. + f. mule. ‖ adj. of or pertaining to mules; mulish.
mubu s. m. (Braz.) = membi.
mucajá s. m. (also macaíba) (N. Braz.) a variety of palm tree.
mucama, mucamba s. f. (Braz., hist.) 1. female household slave. 2. coloured wet nurse.
muçambé, muçambê s. m. (Braz.) medicinal plant of the family Capparidaceae (Cleome heptaphylla).
muçarete s. m. (Braz.) a marine snail.
mucedíneo adj. mucedinaceous, mucedinous.
muchacha s. f. (fam.) girl, esp. a smart and sly one.
muchachada s. f. (S. Braz.) 1. group of youths. 2. frolic, prank of a youth. 3. fun, play.
muchacharia s. f. (fam.) a large group of young men.
muchacho s. m. boy, young man.
muchão s. m. (pl. -ões) a species of marshland mosquito.
mucica s. f. (N. Braz.) 1. nervous tick. 2. jerk applied to the fishing line when the fish starts to bite. 3. jerk with which the cowboys throw the cattle down. 4. jerk at the line of a kite.
muciforme adj. mucinoid.
mucilagem s. f. (pl. -ens) 1. mucilage: turbid, slimy substance found in some vegetables. 2. viscous and gummous liquid.
mucilaginoso adj. mucilaginous, slimy, viscous, mucous.
mucina s. f. mucin: proteic substance found in mucus.
mucíparo adj. producing mucus.
mucívoro adj. mucivorous: feeding on mucilage.
muco s. m. mucus, slime; phlegm.
mucol s. m. (pl. -óis) mucilage used in pharmacy as an excipient.
mucor s. m. mucor: a variety of mucedinous fungi.
mucosa s. f. (anat.) mucosa: mucous membrane.
mucosidade s. f. 1. mucus. 2. mucosity.
mucoso adj. 1. mucous, slimy, viscous. 2. said of the fever accompanying an infection of the mucous membrane.
mucro, múcron s. m. (anat.) 1. xiphisternum, xiphoid process; appendix of the sternum. 2. any sharp-pointed appendix.

— M14 —

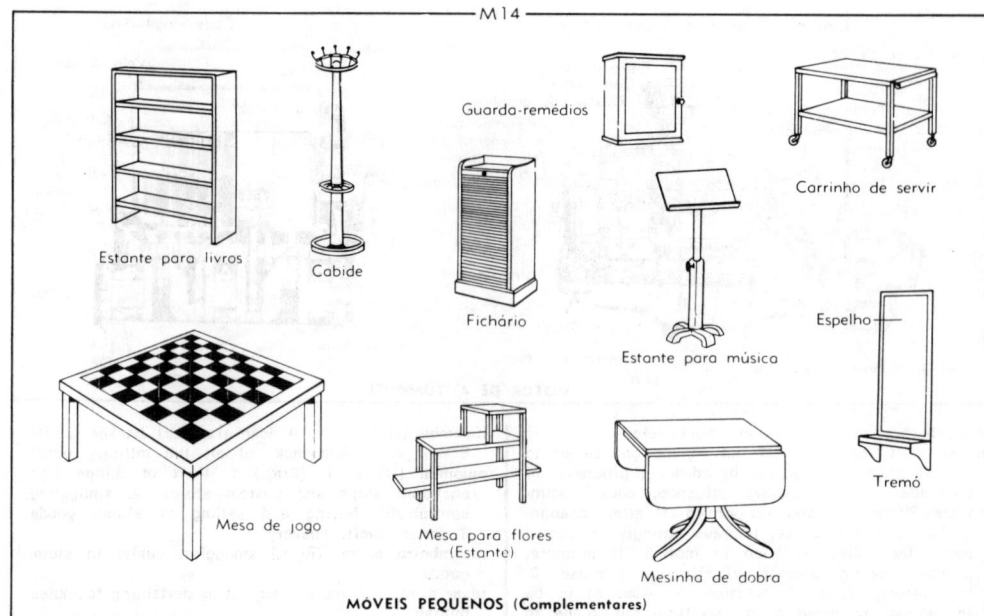

Estante para livros

Cabide

Guarda-remédios

Fichário

Estante para música

Carrinho de servir

Espelho

Tremó

Mesa de jogo

Mesa para flores (Estante)

Mesinha de dobra

MÓVEIS PEQUENOS (Complementares)

mucronado adj. mucronated, mucronate: ending in a sharp point.

mucruará s. m. (N. Braz.) swamp, bog.

muçuã s. m. (N. Braz.) small turtle (Cinosternon scorpioides) of very tasty meat.

mucuaxe s. m. (N. Braz.) meat of stolen cattle.

mucuaxeiro s. m. (N. Braz.) cattle thief.

mucubu s. m. (N. Braz.) haunch of a cow.

mucudo adj. (Braz., sl.) muscular.

mucufa s. m. (N. Braz.) 1. coward. 2. nincompoop. 3. f. very dirty house. ‖ adj. m. + f. 1. ordinary. 2. cowardly.

mucufo s. m. (Braz.) 1. = **mucufa**. 2. = **caipira**. 3. ~s pl.: a) old household furniture. b) old rags. ‖ adj. = **mucufa**.

mucuim s. m. (pl. **-ins**) (Braz.) small arachnid (Tetranychus molestissimus) producing a horrible itch.

mucujê s. m. (Braz.) tree of the family Apocynaceae (Couma rigida).

muçulmanismo s. m. Mussulmanism; Mohammedanism.

muçulmano s. m. Mussulman: Mohammedan. ‖ adj. Moslem, Mohammedan.

muçulmim, muçulmuí, muçurmuni s. m. (N. Braz.) Moslem Negro.

muçum s. m. (pl. **-uns**) (also **muçu**) (Braz.) name for two eels of the order Symbranchidae.

mucumbagem s. f. (pl. **-ens**) (Braz.) old rags, old furniture, junk.

mucumbu s. m. (Braz., pop.) 1. utensils, things, old furniture, junk, lumber. 2. coccyx.

mucunã, mucuna, mucuná s. f. mucuna: various leguminous plants, to which belongs the cowhage.

muçunga, muçungão s. m. (Braz.) pinch, nip with the fingerpoints.

mucungo s. m. (Braz.) = **mutamba**.

muçununga s. f. (Braz.) sandy, fluffy and damp earth.

mucuoca s. f. (N. Braz.) fishgarth to which the Indians drive the fish by agitating and beating the waters at a distance.

mucura s. m. (Braz., zool.; also **gambá, cassaco**) opossum.

mucuracaá s. m. (Braz.) two medicinal plants of the Amazon region, of the family Phytolacaceae (Petiveria tetrandra and Petiveria alliacea).

mucurana s. m. + f. (Braz.) = **muquirana**.

muçurana s. f. (Braz.) 1. (zool.) mussurana: a nonvenomous snake (Pseudoboa cloelia) feeding on venomous snakes. 2. (Braz.) rope with which the Indians tied their prisoners.

muçurango s. m. (Braz.) smal river fish of the family Gobiidae.

mucuraxixica s. m. philander: opossum of N. Braz.

mucureca s. f. (S. Braz.) shack, cabin, hut, tent of Indians.

mucuri s. m. (Braz.) tree producing a yellow peachlike fruit.

mucuta s. f. (Braz.) purse, bag with a shoulder strap.

mucutaia s. f. (also **caneleira-do-mato**) lauraceous plant (Nectandra canescens).

muda s. f. 1. change, shift. 2. move, the act of moving. 3. change of horses, relay. 4. moult of birds and animals. 5. moulting season. 6. seedling, scion. 7. breaking of the voice. 8. mute, dumb woman. 9. clothes, change of clothes. 10. silent or taciturn woman.

canário de uma ~ só or **canário sem ~** (Braz.) person wearing always the same clothes.

mudadiço adj. = **mudável**.

mudado adj. 1. different, altered, changed. 2. moved, displaced. 3. removed.

mudador s. m. 1. mover, remover. 2. (Braz.) place of relay of horses. ‖ adj. changing, moving.

mudança s. f. 1. change, exchange, substitution. 2. move. 3. removal, transfer, displacement. 4. alteration, modification, transformation, variation. 5. move, change of abode. 6. variety.

~ de velocidade (mot.) change of gear. **~s de temperatura** atmospheric change. **caminhão de ~** pantechnicon, furniture van.

mudar v. 1. to change, shift. 2. to move. 3. to exchange, substitute. 4. to dispose differently. 5. to alter, modify, vary. 6. to remove. 7. to move from one house or one city to another. 8. to pass, disappear. 9. to take turns, shift. 10. to slough. 11. ~-se: a) to remove, change one's lodgings. b) to be transformed. c) to pass, disappear. d) to change one's clothes. ~ a camisa 1. to shift one's shirt. 2. (N. Braz., sl.) to have a (alcoholic) drink. ~ a cena to shift the scene. ~ a sorte to turn the tables. ~ de casa to change one's lodgings. ~ de conversa to change the subject of a conversation. ~ de cor to change colour. ~ de parecer to change one's opinion. ~ de roupa to change clothes. ~ de vida to amend. ~ para melhor to change for the better. ~ para pior to change for the worse. ~-se para to remove to. as coisas ~am the tide has turned. ela mudou a roupa da cama she changed the linen.

mudável adj. m. + f. (pl. -áveis) 1. changeable, mutable, alterable. 2. unsteady. || **mudavelmente** adv. changeably, etc.

mudéjar s. m. + f. 1. Mudejar: Moor who stayed on in Spain or Portugal after the reconquest by the Christians. 2. m. Mudejar style of architectonic ornamentation. || adj. Mudejar: relating to these Moors or their style; Moorish.

mudez, mudeza s. m. (obs.) 1. dumbness, muteness, mutism, speechlessness. 2. silence. 3. serenity.

mudo s. m. 1. speechless, mute person. 2. a kind of game. || adj. 1. dumb, mute, speechless, voiceless. 2. silent. 3. (fig.) taciturn. || **mudamente** adv. dumbly, etc.

ficar ~ to grow dumb, remain speechless, be struck dumb.

muezim s. m. (pl. -ins) (also **almuadem**) muezzin: Mohammedan crier of the hour of prayer.

mufla s. f. 1. ornament in form of a muffle. 2. muffle furnace.

mufti s. m. mufti: doctor of Mohammedan law.

mugido s. m. moo, mooing, low, lowing of a cow.

mugir v. 1. to moo, low. 2. to low or bellow like a cow. 3. (fig.) to bellow. 4. to roar, howl.

mugunzá s. m. (Braz.) = **munguzá, mungunzá**.

mui adv. short form of **muito** employed together with tetrasyllabic adjectives or long adverbs.

muiracaua s. f. (Braz.) tree of the family Rutaceae (Rhabdodendron paniculatum).

muiracutaca s. f. (Braz.) leguminous tree of the family Caesalpiniaceae (Swartzia acuminata).

muirajuba s. f. (Braz.) leguminous tree (Apuleia molaris).

muirajuçara s. f. (Braz.) tree of the family Apocynaceae (Rauwolfia pentaphylla).

muirapaxiúba s. f. (Braz.) leguminous tree (Cassia adiantifolia).

muirapinima s. f. (Braz., bot.) snakewood (Brosimum guianensis).

muirapiranga, murapiranga s. f. (Braz. 1. = **pau--brasil**. 2. (N. Braz.) a leguminous tree (Eperua bijuga). 3. satiné and another tree of the family Moraceae (Brosimum paraense).

muirapuama s. f. (Braz.) three medicinal plants of the family Olacaceae (Liriosma ovata, Ptychopetalum olacoides and Ptychopetalum uncinatum).

muirapuamina s. f. (Braz.) alkaloid extracted from the **muirapuama**.

muiraquatiara, muiracatiara s. f. (Braz.) tree of the family Anacardiaceae (Astronium Le-Cointei).

muiraqueteca s. f. (Braz.) = **cipó-caboclo**.

muiraquitã s. m. (also **pedra-verde** and **pedra-das--amazonas**) (N. Braz.) amulet carved out of jade having the shape of serpents, frogs, etc.

muiraximbé s. f. (Braz.) plant of the family Icacinaceae (Emmotum fagifolium).

muísca s. + adj., m. + f. = **chibcha**.

muitá s. m. (N. Braz.) = **mutá, mutã**.

muito s. m. large quantity. || adj. 1. much, plenty, very, a good deal, a great deal. 2. ~s pl. many, a great many, a good many, too many. || adv. very, most, considerably, much, too, too much, very much.

~ **acima** far above. ~ **barato** very cheap. ~ **bem!** very well! bravo! well done! ~ **bom** very good. ~ **cedo** very early, too soon. ~ **diferentemente** far otherwise. ~ **dinheiro** much money. ~ **divertido** jolly good fun. ~ **doente** very ill. ~ **longe** a great way off. ~ **mais** much more. ~ **menos** much less. ~ **obrigado** many thanks. ~ **pequeno** very little. ~ **pouco** too little, not enough. ~ **prudente** most wise, very wise. ~ **tarde** very late. -a **gente** many people. -as **vezes** many times, frequently, often. ~s **poucos fazem um** ~ many a little makes a mickle. **de** ~ by far, for a long time. **de -as maneiras** in many ways. **falta** ~ it wants a lot. **gostar** ~ **de** to be very fond of. **há** ~ long ago. **há** ~ **para comer** there's plenty to eat. **não** ~ not much. **não é** ~ **agradável** it is none too pleasant. **não há** ~ not long since; but lately. **não importa** ~ it is no great matter. **não ser** ~ **de** not to be much of. **nem pouco nem** ~ neither too much, nor too little. **por** ~ **bonito que seja** however beautiful it may be. **quando** ~ at most. **sacrificar pouco para ganhar** ~ to throw a sprat to catch a herring. **viver** ~ to live long.

muiúna s. m. (Braz.) whirlpools at the banks of the Amazon during the rainy season.

mujanguê, mujanguê s. m. (N. Braz.) dish consisting of turtle or sea gull eggs with sugar and flour.

mujique s. m. moujik, muzhik: Russian peasant.

mujolo s. m. (N. Braz.) = **monjolo**.

mula s. f. 1. she-mule, she-hinny. 2. bubo of venereal origin. 3. heap of salt of the form of a triangular prism and ending in half-cones.

mulada s. f. (S. Braz.) troop of mules.

mulador s. m. dunghill.

muladeiro s. m. (S. Braz.) muleteer: mule driver.

mulata s. f. 1. mulatto woman. 2. variety of potato appropriate for baking. 3. (ichth.) yellow-tailed snapper.

mulataria s. f. large group of mulattoes.

mulateira s. f. she-ass breeding with a horse.

mulateiro s. m. 1. stud-ass breeding with mares. 2. (Braz.) tree of the Amazon region known also as **pau-mulato**.

mulatinha s. f. 1. dim. of **mulata**. 2. vulgar name of a variety of honey-bee (Melipona basalis).

mulatinho s. m. 1. small mulatto. 2. a variety of beans. 3. plant of the family Rubiaceae (Rudgea dahlgrenii).

mulato s. m. 1. mulatto. 2. dark-coloured fellow. 3. mule. 4. (N. Braz.) cattle with orange-coloured back and the rest black.

mulato-velho s. m. (pl. **mulatos-velhos**) (Braz. Rio de Janeiro) salted and dried catfish.

mulembá s. m. (Braz.) name given to the Ficus doloria while in the epiphytic state.

muleta s. f. 1. crutch. 2. (fig.) anything lending support. 3. stick used by a matador to hold up the cape. 4. crank of a barrel organ. 5. small fishing boat.

muletada s. f. 1. blow with a crutch. 2. herd of mules.

muleteiro s. m. 1. muleteer: mule driver. 2. person who takes care of mules.

muletim s. m. (pl. -ins) sail of a boat called **muleta**.

mulher s. f. (augm. **mulherão, mulheraça, mulherona**) 1. woman. 2. wife.
~ **à-toa,** ~ **da rua,** ~ **da vida,** ~ **pública** prostitute. ~ **casada** married woman, (law) feme covert. ~ **solteira** single woman, (law) feme sole.
mulheraça (also **mulherão, mulherona**) s. f. tall and strong woman, virago.
mulherengo s. m. 1. milksop. 2. dangler after women, ladies' man. ‖ adj. 1. womanish, unmanly, effeminate. 2. mad after women.
mulherico adj. 1. effeminate. 2. weak. 3. coward.
mulherigo s. m. effeminate man.
mulheril adj. m. + f. (pl. **-is**) 1. womanish, effeminate. 2. womanlike, womanly.
mulherinha s. f. (fam.) 1. dim. of **mulher.** 2. ordinary, crude, badly behaved woman, hussy. 3. gossip.
mulherio s. m. (Braz., also **mulherada** f., **mulherio** m.) great number of women, womankind, womenfolk.
muliado adj. 1. monstrous. 2. hybrid. 3. (fig.) opposite to what it should be or would be convenient.
mulita s. f. (S. Braz.) 1. (zool.) mule armadillo. 2. (fig.) swindle, cheat.
passar ~ to swindle, cheat.
mulo s. m. = **mu.**
mulso s. m. hydromel, mead.
multa s. f. 1. mulct, fine, penalty, forfeiture, amercement, pecuniary penalty. 2. (fig.) condemnation.
apanhar uma ~ to be fined.
multar v. 1. to mulct, fine. 2. (fig.) to condemn.
ele foi multado em Cr$ 100,00 he was fined to Cr$ 100,00.
multiangular adj. m. + f. (math.) multiangular: having many angles.
multiaxífero adj. (bot.) multiaxial: having many axis.
multicapsular adj. m. + f. (bot.) multicapsular: having many capsules.
multicaudo adj. (zool.) having many taillike prolongations.
multicaule adj. m. + f. (bot.) multicauline: having many stalks or stems.
multicelular adj. m. + f. (bot.) multicellular: many--celled.
multicolor, multicor adj. m. + f. multicoloured: many--coloured, motley.
multidão s. f. (pl. **-ões**) 1. multitude: a) crowd, throng. b) the people, masses. c) heap. d) abundance. 2. (sociol.) heterogenous group of people reacting to the same stimulus in a similar manner.
multifário adj. multifarious: of many aspects, varied, manifold.
multifido adj. (bot.) multifid, multifidous: divided into many segments.
multifloro adj. (bot.) multiflorous: having many flowers.
multifoliado adj. (bot.) multifoliate: having many leaflets.
multiforme adj. m. + f. multiform: having many forms, diversified.
multifuro adj. having many holes.
multígeno adj. comprising many species or genera.
multilátero adj. (math.) multilateral: many-sided.
multilobado adj. multilobular, multilobate: many--lobed.
multilocular adj. m. + f. multilocular, multiloculate: having many loculi or chambers.
multíloquo adj. multiloquent, multiloquous, loquacious, talkative.
multilustroso adj. bright, shining very much.
multimâmio adj. (zool.) multimammate: having more than two breasts or teats.
multimilionário s. m. multimillionaire. ‖ adj. possessing several millions.

multimodo adj. multiform, multifarious, diversified.
multinérveo adj. (bot.) multinervate: having many veins (leaves of plants.)
multiparidade s. f. (biol., med.) multiparity: quality of being multiparous.
multíparo adj. multiparous: 1. (zool.) bringing forth more than one young. 2. (med.) having born more than one child.
multipartido adj. (bot.) multipartite: divided into many parts.
multípede adj. m. + f. (zool.) multiped: having many feet.
multiplicação s. f. (pl. **-ões**) 1. multiplication, increase in number, growth, reproduction. 2. (arith.) multiplication.
multiplicador s. m. (arith.) multiplier, coefficient. ‖ adj. multiplying.
multiplicando s. m. (arith.) multiplicand: the number to be multiplied.
multiplicar v. 1. to multiply, increase in number. 2. (arith.) to multiply. 3. ~**se:** a) to propagate, have offspring. b) to augment, grow in number. c) to develop extraordinary activity.
~ **por** to multiply by.
multiplicativo adj. multiplicative, multiplying.
multiplicável adj. m. + f. (pl. **-áveis**) multipliable: that may be multiplied.
multíplice adj. m. + f. 1. multiplex, varied, manifold. 2. copious. 3. appearing under many aspects.
multiplicidade s. f. multiplicity, manifoldness, great number.
múltiplo s. m. (orith.) multiple. ‖ adj. multiple: 1. consisting of or involving many individual parts, manifold. 2. (arith.) said of a number containing another number two or more times.
mínimo ~ **comum** smallest common multiple.
multipontoado adj. speckled, having many spots or dots.
multisciente adj. m. + f., **multíscio** m. knowing much.
multissecular adj. m. + f. having many centuries.
multíssono adj. multisonous: producing many or various sounds.
multívago adj. multivagant, multivagous: wandering, vagrant.
multivalve adj. m. + f. (biol., bot.) multivalve: having many valves.
multivalvular adj. m. + f. (bot.) multivalvular: having many valvules.
multívio adj. multivious: having many ways.
multívolo adj. multivolent: having many desires, exacting, ambitious.
mulundu s. m. (Braz.) a Negro dance.
mulungu, murungu s. m. (also **corticeira**) Braz., bot.) coral tree.
mulungu-crista-de-galo s. m. (pl. **mulungus-crista-de--galo**) (Braz., bot.) ceibo.
mumbaca s. f. (Braz.) name of two plants of the palm family (Astrocaryum humile and Astrocaryum mumbaca).
mumbanda s. f. (N. Braz.) 1. young favourite female slave. 2. = **mucama.** 3. any especially favoured servant-maid.
mumbava s. m. (S. Braz.) 1. favourite. 2. parasite. 3. hired ruffian.
mumbavo s. m. (also **xerimbabo**) (S. Braz.) any domestic animal.
mumbica s. f. (N. Braz.) small, thin, rachitic calf. ‖ adj. m. + f. (Braz.) 1. bad. 2. badly dressed, unbecoming. 3. badly bridled, having a poor gait (horse).
mumbuca s. f. (Braz., also **mambucão, papa-terra**) honey-bee (Melipona capitata).

múmia s. f. 1. mummy: a) corpse preserved by embalming. b) (fig.) very thin shrivelled person. 2. (Braz.) person without drive or energy.

mumificação s. f. mummification: 1. process of mummifying. 2. state of being mummified.

mumificador s. m. mummifier. ‖ adj. mummifying.

mumificar v. 1. to mummify, mummy, embalm. 2. (also ~-se): a) to lose weight. b) to dry up mentally.

mumificável adj. m. + f. (pl. -áveis) which can be mummified.

mumuca s. m. + f. (S. Braz.; also papão) a bugbear, hobgoblin.

munã s. f. (N. Braz.) mare.

mundana s. f. 1. dissolute, fast woman. 2. whore.

mundanalidade s. f. 1. earthliness. 2. wordliness, wordly-mindedness. 3. dissolute life.

mundanismo s. m. mundaneness, mundane life, worldly-mindedness.

mundano adj. (also mundanal m. + f.) mundane: 1. wordly, earthly, terrestrial, temporal. 2. wordly-minded. ‖ -amente adv. mundanely.
vida -a the great social life.

mundão s. m. (Braz.) 1. vast expanse. 2. great multitude of persons or things. 3. (N.) very far-away place.

mundaréu s. m. (Braz.) 1. great world. 2. = mundão.

mundaú s. m. (also carrapato-do-mato, cabuim) (Braz.) an euphorbiaceous bush (Cicca inflata).

mundeiro s. m. (S. Braz.) vagabond, tramp. ‖ adj. wandering, vagrant.

mundéu, mundé s. m. (Braz.) 1. hunting trap. 2. (fig.) any rickety house or thing threatening to collapse and being a hazard. 3. large quantity. 4. (N.) name given to a wild hog in some areas.
cair no ~ to fall into a trap, into the pit.

mundial adj. m. + f. (pl. -ais) world-wide, general. ‖ ~mente adv. world-widely.
fama ~ world-wide reputation. guerra ~ world war. ~mente conhecido known all over the world. ~mente famoso world-famous.

mundiar v. (N. Braz.) to enchant, drug or magnetize.

mundiça s. f. (N. Braz., pop.) 1. = piolho-de-galinha. 2. scum, mob.

mundícia (I), mundície s. f. cleanliness, love for cleanliness.

mundícia (II), mundice s. f. (Port., prov.) 1. pigs. 2. herd of sheep or goats.

mundificação s. f. (pl. -ões) mundification: purification, cleansing.

mundificante adj. m. + f. (also mundificativo m.) mundificant: cleansing, cleaning, detergent.

mundificar v. to mundify: 1. clean, deterge. 2. purify. 3. ~-se become clean, undergo purification.

mundo s. m. 1. earth, world, universe, terraqueous globe. 2. humanity, mankind. 3. present life. 4. social class, society. 5. the wordly pleasures. 6. (Braz.) large quantity, great many, great number. ‖ adj. clean, pure.
~ aberto sem porteiras (Braz., pop.) vast spaces. assim é o ~ that's the way of the world. cair no ~ (Braz., pop.) to flee. desde que o ~ é ~ since the world was. despachar para o outro ~ (Braz., pop.) to dispatch, kill. enquanto o ~ for ~ as long as the world lasts. enfiar a cara no ~ to run away, flee. eu daria o ~ para saber I'd give anything to know. homem do ~ man of the world, gentleman. meio ~ all the world and his wife. o antigo ~ the Old World. o novo ~ the New World. o ~ que corre our age, the world we live in. o ~ todo the whole world. outro ~ the next world. pessoa ou coisa do outro ~ (Braz., pop.) splendid, excellent person or thing. pôr a boca no ~ to yell, shout. por nada neste

not for my life. prática do ~ knowledge of the world. prometer ~s e fundos to make extraordinary promises. todo o ~ all the world, everybody. um ~ de dificuldades a world of troubles. um ~ de gente an enormous crowd of people. velho como o ~ old as the hills. ver o ~ to see the world, travel. no ~ da lua daydreaming, absent-minded, completely distracted. vir o ~ abaixo 1. the occurrence of catastrophic rains or winds. 2. great disorder or tumult. a notícia correu ~ the news spread all over. ela azulou no ~ she ran off and disappeared.

mundrunga s. f. (N. Braz.) sorcery, witchcraft, enchantment, magic.

mundrungo s. m. (N. Braz.) jade, ordinary horse.

mundrungueiro s. m. (N. Braz.) sorcerer, magician.

munduri s. m. (Braz.) wild honey-bee (Melipona marginata).

munduru s. m. (N. Braz.) 1. mound, hillock. 2. large fish trap made of a palm fiber with an opening at the bottom.

mungida, mungidura s. f. 1. act of milking. 2. quantity of milk drawn.

mungir v. 1. to milk. 2. (fig.) to exploit, squeeze.

mungunzá, munguzá s. m. (also mugunzá) (N. Braz.) a specialty made out of corn grains cooked in sugar syrup and sometimes in milk or coconut milk.

munhão s. m. (pl. -ões) 1. trunnion of a cannon. 2. axle journal, gudgeon.
~ do eixo stub axle (plate E 1).

munhata s. f. (S. Braz.) sweet potato.

munheca s. f. 1. wrist. 2. (Braz.) fern leaves when they start to sprout and have the form of a crosier. 3. (S. Braz.) hand.

munheca-de-cutia s. f. (pl. munhecas-de-cutia) (Braz.) whip with a handle made out of the foot of a coati.

munheca-de-samambaia s. m. + f. (pl. munhecas-de-samambaia) (Braz.) miser.

munhecar v. (Braz., sl.) to grasp, hang on to.

munhoneira s. f. trunnion plate.

munição s. f. (pl. -ões) 1. ammunition. 2. fortification. 3. (fig.) defense. 4. munitions, military stores. 5. preventive, preservative. 6. small shot; bird shot.
pão de ~ (mil.) ammunition bread.

municiar v. to ammunition.

munício s. m. 1. ammunition bread. 2 (S. Braz.) cattle taken along as food for the troops. 3. rations taken along by a driver of pack animals (mules).

municionamento s. m. munitionment, provisioning, supply of provisions or ammunition.

municionar v. to munition: provide with munitions.

municionário s. m. commissary of stores.

municipal s. m. (pl. -ais) (Braz., pop.) municipal theatre. ‖ adj. m. + f. municipal.
câmara ~ town hall.

municipalidade s. f. 1. municipality: municipal district, urban community. 2. town hall. 3. city council, aldermanry.

municipalismo s. m. municipalism: theory or system of decentralization of government through municipal autonomy.

munícipe s. m. + f. citizen of a municipality. ‖ adj. of or pertaining to a municipality.

município s. m. 1. municipality, municipal district, urban community. 2. city council.

munificência s. f. munificence, generosity, liberality.

munificente adj. m. + f. munífico m. munificent, generous, magnanimous, liberal.

munir v. 1. to munition, provide with munition. 2. to provide, supply, furnish. 3. to strengthen, fortify.

4. to defend. 5. to warn. 6. to replenish, provide.
7. ~-se to provide o. s. with.
~-se de paciência to arm o. s. with patience.
munpiú s. m. (Braz.) plant of the family Euphorbiaceae (Sapium euphorbium).
múnus s. m., sg. + pl. charge, function, duties.
munzuá s. m. (Braz.) fish trap made out of lattice
of bamboo.
mupéua s. f. (N. Braz.) shallow canal on shoals or
extensive beaches.
mupicar v. (N. Braz., also **mupucar**) 1. to row rapidly
with swift little strokes. 2. to mark the way through
the woods by breaking off twigs.
mupunga s. f. (N. Braz.) word used in the expression:
bater ~ to beat the water to make all fish turn
towards a weir where they are caught.
muque s. m. (Braz., sl.) muscles, muscular force,
biceps.
a ~ by force, violently.
muquinhar v. (S. Braz.) to loaf, wander aimlessly.
muquira s. m. + f. (N. Braz.) niggard, skinflint.
muquirana s. f. (also **mucurana**) 1. (Braz.) body louse.
2. m. + f. = **muquira**.
murada s. f. horizontal row of stitches in a net.
muradal s. m. (pl. **-ais**) heap of rubbish.
murador adj. hunting mice or rats (cat).
murajuba s. f. (Braz.) 1. parrot of the Amazon region.
2. leguminous tree (Apuleia molaris).
mural adj. m. + f. (pl. **-ais**) mural: relating to a
wall.
muralha s. f. wall, battlement.
muralhar v. to wall (in).
muramento s. m. walling, enclosure, fortification.
murapiranga s. f. (Braz.) = **muirapiranga**.
murar v. 1. to wall, immune, fence in, enclose. 2. to
fortify, strengthen. 3. to protect against assaults.
4. to mouse, to watch mice to catch them (cat).
5. ~-se: a) to fortify, defend o. s.; b) to fence,
cover o. s., take shelter. c) to arm o. s. with.
~-se de paciência to arm o. s. with patience.
murça s. f. 1. (eccl.) pallium. 2. smooth-cut file.
murceiro s. m. person who makes or sells pallia.
murcha s. f. (Braz.) wilt: plant disease characterized
by the drying up of all succulent parts.
murchar v. 1. to wilt, wither, wizen, sear, dry up,
shrivel. 2. (fig.) to take away the strength from.
3. ~-se: a) to lose the freshness, colour, brightness.
b) to languish. c) to wilt, wither, fade, dwindle,
decay. d) to become sad.
murchecer v. = **emurchecer**.
murchidão s. f. 1. witheredness, fadedness. 2.
languidness.
murcho adj. 1. wilted, withered, wizened, seared,
shrivelled, faded. 2. (fig.) sad, pensive, languid. 3.
dull, lacking colour, brilliance, etc.
murciana s. f. a variety of cabbage. ‖ adj. said of
this cabbage.
murciano s. m. native or inhabitant of Murcia, Spain.
‖ adj. of or pertaining to Murcia.
mureira s. f. dunghill.
muremuré s. m. (Braz.) = **murmuré**.
mureru s. m. (Braz.) 1. (also **mururé-redondinho**) plant
of the water-shield family (Calomba aquatica). 2.
water hyacinth (Eichhornia crassipes).
murganho s. m. small brownish rat.
murianha, murinhanha s. f. (Braz., ent.) stable fly
(Stomoxys calcitrans).
muriático adj. (chem.) muriatic: hydrochloric.
muriato s. m. (chem., obs.) muriate: chloride.
murici, muricizeiro s. m. (Braz.) 1. tree of the genus
Byrsonima, the most common being **murici-cascudo**,
murici-da-praia, murici-de-lenha. 2. fruit of this
tree.

muricizal s. m. (pl. **-ais**) (Braz.) terrain where the
murici grows abundantly.
muriçoca, muruçoca s. f. (also **meruçoca**) (N. Braz.,
ent.) mosquito.
murídeo s. m. specimen of the Muridae (rodents as
rats and mice). ‖ adj. pertaining to the Muridae.
muriqui s. m. (also **macaco-vermelho**) (Braz., zool.)
spider monkey.
muriquina s. f. (Braz.) night ape (Aotus azare).
muriti, muritim (pl. **-ins**) s. m. (Braz., also **buriti**)
muriti palm.
muritizal, muritinzal s. m. (pl. **-ais**) (Braz., also
buritizal) a growth of muriti palms.
murixaba s. f. (also **muruxaba**) (N. Braz., pop.)
prostitute, whore, concubine.
murmulhante adj. m. + f. (Braz.) rustling, rippling.
murmulhar v. 1. to rustle (tree), ripple (waves). 2. to
whisper, mutter.
murmulho s. m. 1. rippling (of waves). 2. rustling (of
leaves).
múrmur s. m. (also **murmúrio**) murmur, purl, rippling.
murmuração s. f. (pl. **-ões**) 1. murmur(ing), whispering.
2. gossiping. 3. grumbling, muttering.
murmurador adj. 1. whispering, gossiping. 2. mumbling. 3. murmuring, grumbling, muttering.
murmurante adj. m. + f. 1. murmuring, murmurous.
2. grumbling, muttering. 3. rustling, whispering.
murmurar v. 1. to murmur, whisper. 2. to mumble.
3. to grumble, mutter. 4. to buzz a secret. 5. to
complain, bicker. 6. to gossip; to spread rumours,
slander. 7. to form a wrong idea about a person
or thing. 8. to rustle (leaves). 9. to whisper (wind),
to ripple (waves).
~ de alguém to slander s. o.
murmurativo adj. murmurous.
murmuré s. m. (also **muremuré** and **murumuré**) (Braz.)
musical instrument made out of bones and used
by the Indians.
murmurejar v. 1. to murmur. 2. to gossip. 3. to rustle,
ripple.
murmurinhar v. 1. = **murmurejar**. 2. to produce a low
murmuring sound.
murmurinho s. m. (also **murmúrio**) 1. low murmur of
voices. 2. rustling of leaves, whispering of the
wind, purl of a brook. 3. confusing medley of soft
sounds.
murmúrio s. m. 1. murmur of many voices. 2. rustling
of leaves, purl of a brook, ripple of waves. 3. sound
of low talk. 4. whispered gossip. 5. mutter, grumble.
múrmuro adj. (poet.) = **murmurante**.
murmuroso adj. murmurous.
muro s. m. 1. wall: a) brick or stone enclosure of a
yard, garden, etc. b) (fig.) defence. 2. (Braz.)
enclosure for beehives. 3. (Port., prov.) rat.
~ de arrimo (archit.) retaining wall. ~ de fornalha
(naut.) fire bridge.
murra s. f. scorch on the skin.
murraça s. f. tremendous punch, blow.
murro s. m. punch, blow, slug, fisticuff.
dar ~ em ponta de faca to insist on the practically
impossible. **dar o** ~ to work very hard.
murta, murteira s. f., **murteiro, mirto** m. myrtle and
its fruit.
murta-de-cheiro s. f. (pl. **murtas-de-cheiro**) name of
two rutaceous plants (Murraya exotica and Murraya paniculata).
murta-do-mato s. f. (pl. **murtas-do-mato**) (also **quina,
quinaquina, quinquina**) a medicinal rubiaceous plant
(Coutarea hexandra).
murtal s. m. (pl. **-ais**) myrtle grove.
murtinho s. m. 1. berry of a myrtle. 2. various plants
of the myrtle family (Eugenia arenaria, Eugenia
ovatifolia, Eugenia insipida, etc.).

murua s. f. (Braz.) name of an Indian dance.

muruanha s. f. (Braz.) = murianha.

muruchi s. m. (Braz.) plant of the family Malpighiaceae (Banisteria dispar).

muruci s. m. (Braz.) = murici.

murucu s. m. (N. Braz.) lance made out of red wood with a poisoned tip.

murucututu s. m. (also coruja-do-mato) (Braz.) a nocturnal bird.

murugem s. f. (pl. -ens) (bot.) field myosotis.

murumuré s. m. (Braz.) = murmuré.

murumuru s. m. a variety of palm tree (Astrocaryum murumuru).

murumuruzal s. m. (pl. -ais) (Braz.) group of murumuru trees.

murumuxaua s. m. (Braz.) = morubixaba.

murundu s. m. (Braz.) 1. small hill. 2. large heap. 3. = munduru.

murungu s. m. (Braz.) = mulungu.

murupita s. f. (Braz.) name of various euphorbiaceous trees (genus Sapium).

mururé s. m. (Braz.) 1. name of two moraceous plants (Brasimpsis acutifolia and Brasimpsis obovata). 2. = mureru.

mururu s. m. (Braz.) 1. habitual indisposition, intermittent disease. 2. megrim. 3. an urticaceous plant (Bichetea officinalis).

muruti s. m. (Braz.) = buriti.

murutizeiro s. m. (Braz.) = buritizeiro.

muruxaua s. m. (Braz.) = morubixaba.

mus s. m., sg. + pl. (S. Braz.) a card game.

não dizer chus nem ~ to remain silent, shut up.

musa (I) s. f. 1. muse. 2. poetical inspiration. 3. poetry.

musa (II) s. f. 1. Asiatic banana tree. 2. common banana.

musácea s. f. specimen of the Musaceae, family of plants typified by the banana tree.

musáceo adj. 1. musaceous: pertaining to the Musaceae. 2. relating to or resembling a banana tree.

musal adj. m. + f. (pl. -ais) pertaining to the muses.

muscadínea s. f. (bot.) muscadine.

muscardina s. f. muscardine, calcino: infectious disease of the silkworm.

muscari s. m. muscary, grape hyacinth, grapeflower.

muscarina s. f. (chem.) muscarine.

muscícola adj. m. + f. (zool.) muscicolous: living among mosses.

muscínea s. f. division of cryptogamic plants comprising the Musci and Hepaticae.

muscíneo adj. of or pertaining to the Musci or Hepaticae.

muscoso adj. = musgoso.

muscovita s. f. (min.) muscovite: common mica.

musculação s. f. (pl. -ões) 1. the whole muscular activity. 2. muscular exercise.

musculado adj. muscled, sinewy, brawny.

muscular adj. m. + f. muscular: relating to the muscles.

musculatura s. f. 1. musculature, muscularity. 2. way of painting the muscles in art.

musculina s. f. 1. preparation of raw beef without fat. 2. musculin, substance found only in the muscles.

músculo s. m. 1. (anat.) muscle. 2. one of the cuts of meat at the butcher's.

~ constritor (anat.) constrictor. ~ contrator (anat.) contractor. ~ extensor (anat.) extensor. ~s escalenos (anat.) scalene muscles. ter ~ be strong. ~ glossofaríngeo (anat.) glossopharyngeal muscle.

musculosidade s. f. musculature, muscularity.

musculoso adj. 1. muscular, sinewy. 2. brawny, sturdy.

museologia s. f. museology.

museu s. m. 1. museum. 2. (fig.) collection of curiosities. 3. miscellany.

~ de cera waxworks.

musgo s. m. moss.

musgoso, musguento adj. (also muscoso) mossy.

música s. f. 1. music. 2. melody, harmony. 3. musical execution. 4. any musical composition. 5. band, orchestra, philharmonic. 6. any pleasing sound. 7. (fig.) any series of sounds.

~ de câmara chamber music. ~ de dança dance music. ~ de programa programme music. ~ pura purely instrumental music. ~ sacra church music. caixa de ~ music box. dançar conforme a ~ to act according to the circumstances (to dance to the music).

musical adj. m. + f. (pl. -ais) musical, tuneful, melodious. || ~mente adv. musically.

musicalidade s. f. musicality, musicalness.

musicar v. (also musiquear) to sing, make music, set to music.

musiquei o seu poema I set your poem to music.

musicata s. f. (fam.) 1. fanfare. 2. philharmonic. 3. musical execution.

musicista s. m. + f. (Braz.) 1. lover of music, amateur musician. 2. connoisseur of music.

músico s. m. 1. musician, artist, performer, player. 2. composer, bandsman. 3. (ornith.) organ bird. || adj. musical, harmonious.

galo ~ name of certain cocks that crow in a very peculiar and particular way.

musicografia s. f. musicography: 1. the art of musical notation. 2. treatise on music.

musicógrafo s. m. musicographer: 1. (musical) notator. 2. writer on music. 3. instrument to notate music.

musicologia s. f. musicology: 1. art of music. 2. treatise on music.

musicólogo s. m. musicologist: writer on music.

musicomania s. f. musicomania: excessive love or mania for music.

musicômano s. m. music maniac. || adj. said of a music maniac.

musiqueta s. f. 1. small musical composition. 2. second-rate music.

musiquim s. m. (pl. -ins) 1. awkward musician, scraper, fiddler. 2. ambulant musician.

musselina s. f. muslin.

~ de lã delaine.

mussitar v. 1. to mumble. 2. to whisper.

mussiú s. m. (Braz., pop.) playful nickname given to the French.

mustelídeo s. m. specimen of the Mustelideae, a family of weasel-like mammals. || adj. musteline: pertaining to or resembling the Mustelideae.

mutá, mutã s. m. (N. Braz.; also muitá) 1. crude ladder to climb the rubber trees. 2. platform in the trees used to wait for and hunt animals.

mutabilidade s. f. mutability, mutableness, changeability, volatility.

mutação s. f. (pl. -ões) 1. mutation: a) change, alternation, variation, substitution. b) (biol.) change in the heritable characteristics. 2. volubility, inconstancy. 3. shifting of scenes in theatres.

mutacismo s. m. mytacism: abusive repetition or wrong use of the letter m.

mutamba s. f., mutambo m. (Braz., bot., also ibixuna, mucungo) bastard cedar.

mutanje s. m. (N. Braz.) coward. || adj. coward.

mutapa s. f. (N. Braz.) island taken along by the current.

mutatório adj. mutatory, mutative, shifting, mutable.

mutável adj. m. + f. (pl. -áveis) (also mudável) mutable, changeable, inconstant.

mutelina s. f. (also **funcho-dos-alpes**) medicinal, umbelliferous plant (Meum mutelina).

mútico adj. (bot. + zool.) mutic: smooth, without edges or spines.

mutilação s. f. (pl. **-ões**) mutilation, maiming, defacement.

mutilado s. m. mutilated person. ‖ adj. mutilated, maimed, diminished.

mutilador s. m. mutilator. ‖ adj. mutilating.

mutilar v. 1. to mutilate, maim, cripple, disable, mangle, disfigure. 2. (fig.) to cut off a part. 3. to destroy a part of. 4. to diminish, reduce. 5. to diminish the value of. 6. ∼-**se** to mutilate o. s.

mutirão s. m. (pl. **-ões**) 1. (Braz.) bee: gratuitous work (esp. in rural regions) of all the neighbours for the benefit of one who foots the bills on that day (also **muxirão**). 2. (N. Braz.) bird of the family Ardeidae (Nyctanassa violacea).

mutirom, mutirum s. m. (N. Braz.) = **muxirão**.

mutismo s. m. mutism, muteness, dumbness, speechlessness, taciturnness, silence.

mutreita s. f. (S. Braz.) excessive fat on cattle.

estar de ∼ to be very fat (either the meat or the animal).

mútua s. f. (Braz.) loan company.

mutuação s. f. (pl. **-ões**) 1. mutuality, mutualization, permutation, reciprocation. 2. lending. 3. borrowing.

mutualidade s. f. mutuality, reciprocity, permutation, exchange.

mutualista s. m. + f. person partaking in a mutual insurance company or benefit society. ‖ adj. mutualist.

mutuante s. m. + f. loaner, lender. ‖ adj. loaning, lending, contracting a loan.

mutuar v. 1. to mutualize. 2. to exchange. 3. to loan, lend. 4. to borrow. 5. ∼-**se** to interchange.

mutuário s. m. person receiving a loan, borrower.

mutuca s. f. (Braz.) 1. horse-fly. 2. (N.) oarsman of a whaleboat. 3. (pop.) spur. ‖ adj. (Braz.) 1. said

of a battered and frightened fighting cock. 2. (N.) coward. 3. said of a poor fighting cock.

mutucacaba s. f. (Braz.) general name for the wasps of the genus Parachartegus.

mútulo s. m. (archit.) mutule: square modillion on a Doric cornice.

mutum s. m. (pl. **-uns**) (Braz., ornith.; also **mitu, mitua, urumutum**) curassow.

mutum-cavalo s. m. (pl. **mutuns-cavalo**) (Braz., ornith.) mitu.

mutum-de-assobio s. m. (pl. **mutuns-de-assobio**) (Braz., ornith; also **boicenim-açu**) globose curassow.

mutumporanga s. m. (Braz., ornith.) crested curassow.

mútuo s. m. 1. loan, insurance. 2. permutation, exchange. 3. reciprocity, mutuality. ‖ adj. mutual, reciprocal, interchangeable. ‖ **mutuamente** adv. mutually, each other.

mutuqueiro s. m. (S. Braz.) beginner in cockfighting.

muxarabiê s. m. Moorish balcony protected by a wooden grating.

muxiba s. f. (Braz.) 1. lean meat for dogs. 2. lean folds of flesh. 3. hag.

muxibento adj. (Braz.) 1. wrinkly, rugate. 2. lean (meat).

muxicão s. m. (pl. **-ões**) (N. Braz., fam.) 1. thrust, sudden violent push. 2. pinch.

muxicar v. (N. Braz., fam.) 1. to thrust, push suddenly. 2. to pinch.

muxinga s. f. (Braz.) 1. whip, flag. 2. (fig.) whipping, hiding, beating.

muxirã s. f., **muxirão** m. (Braz.) = **mutirão**.

muxoxar v. 1. to give kisses. 2. to caress, fondle.

muxoxear v. (Braz.) to click or smack (one's tongue), snap.

muxoxo (ô) s. m. (pl. **-oxos**) (Braz.) 1. smack, kiss, caress. 2. smacking of the tongue and lips, sometimes accompanied by an interjection to express disgust or scorn.

muxuango s. m. (Braz., also **mixuango**) = **caipira**.

muxurundar v. (Braz., pop.) to spank.

N

N, n s. m. thirteenth letter of the Portuguese alphabet. ‖ adj. thirteenth in a series. ‖ abbr. of **nossa, nosso, norte;** (chem.) N **nitrogênio.**

na contraction of the prep. **em** with the article **a.** ‖ enclitic form of the pron. **a** after a nasal sound: her, it.
~ **chuva** in (the) rain. ~ **escola** at school. ~ **esperança** in hopes. ~ **guerra** at war. ~ **miséria** in adversity. ~ **ocasião** hereat. ~ **sexta-feira** on Friday. **ponha isto** ~ **luz** put it to the light. **ela mora** ~ **casa da Sra. Smith** she lives at Mrs. Smith's. **viram-na** they saw her.

nababesco adj. rich, opulent.

nababia s. f. 1. nabobism, nabobery. 2. a nabob's territory.

nababo s. m. nabob: 1. vice governor of the Mogul Empire. 2. viceroy in India. 3. rich or important foreigner in the East. 4. million(n)aire; opulent, rich person.

nabada s. f. dish of turnips.

nabal s. m. (pl. **-ais**) turnip plantation, turnip field.

nabiça s. f. turnip leaf or turnip rootlet.

nabiçal s. m. (pl. **-ais**) field with turnip rootlets.

nabo s. m. 1. (bot.) turnip. 2. stupid, ignorant. 3. thicker part of a fence post.
~**-selvagem** (bot.) jack-in-the-pulpit. **comprar** ~**s em sacos** to buy a pig in a poke.

nabuco adj. (Braz.) tailless; bobtail.

naca, nacada s. f. (also **naco** m.) piece, chop, lump, slice.

nação s. f. (pl. **-ões**) 1. nation: a) country, land, state, polity. b) people, race, folk. 2. nationality. 3. sort, species. 4. origin. 5. (bib.) heathen.
Liga das Nações League of Nations.

nácar s. m. 1. nacre, mother-of-pearl. 2. carmine. 3. pink (colour).

nacarado adj. (also **nacarino**) 1. nacreous, pearly. 2. carmine. 3. pink.

nacarar v. 1. to give a nacreous appearance to. 2. to redden, make or become pink.

nacela s. f. 1. (archit.) moulding in the base of a column. 2. (aeron.) nacelle.

nacional s. m. national. ‖ adj. m. + f. 1. national, inlandish, domestic. 2. vernacular. ‖ ~**mente** adv. nationally.
bandeira ~ national flag. **de âmbito** ~ nationwide. **de fabricação** ~ home-made. **economia** ~ home economy. **hino** ~ national anthem. **poder** ~ national power. **problema** ~ national problem. **produto** ~ **bruto** gross national product.

nacionalidade s. f. nationality: 1. nation. 2. national status. 3. national character.

nacionalismo s. m. nationalism: 1. patriotism. 2. nationalistic policy. 3. devotion to national interests.

nacionalista s. m. + f. nationalist. ‖ adj. nationalistic.

nacionalização s. f. (pl. **-ões**) 1. naturalization. 2. nationalization.

nacionalizar v. 1. to naturalize. 2. to nationalize. 3. (fig.) to acclimate, acclimatize. 4. to socialize.

nacional-socialismo s. m. Nazism.

naco s. m. large piece, lump, chop, slice, portion, hunk, chunk.
~ **de fumo** plug (tobacco).

nada s. m. 1. nothing: a) nothingness, nought, nil. b) inexistence, nonentity. 2. insignificance, trifle, wisp. 3. uselessness. ‖ adv. 1. nothing. 2. not at all.

~ **de importância** nothing to make a song about. ~ **disso!** nothing of the kind! no such matter! ~ **feito** nothing doing. ~ **mais** nothing else. ~ **sobrou** there is nothing left on hand. **acabar em** ~ to end in smoke. **antes de mais** ~ first of all. **do** ~, ~ **se faz** a dead bee makes no honey. **ele não faz** ~ he does nothing. **não há** ~ **de novo** there are no news. **nem por** ~ not for anything, not for a pension. **ou isso ou** ~ have this or go without. **por** ~ **neste mundo revelaria isto** wild horses shall not drag it from me. **quase** ~ next to nothing. **não quer mais** ~? don't you want anything else? **ele não tem** ~ he has not a shirt to his back. **não tenho** ~ **a ver com isso** I have nothing to do with it. **não vale** ~ it is not worth a whoop. **ele não vale** ~ he is good for nothing. **muito obrigado! de** ~! thank you very much! don't mention it! **isto não é** ~ that is nothing.

nadadeira s. f. fin, flipper; paddle.

nadador s. m. swimmer. ‖ adj. swimming, notatory.
~ **de costas** back swimmer. **ave** ~**a** swimming bird, palmiped.

nadante adj. m. + f. natant, swimming, floating.

nadar v. to swim: 1. move in the water using arms, legs, fins. 2. float. 3. bathe, be immersed. 4. be or become wet. 5. wallow, have plentifully.
~ **em dinheiro** to wallow in money, to roll in wealth. ~ **(pelo sistema) crawl** to crawl. ~ **como uma pedra** to swim like a stone. ~ **a favor da correnteza** (fig.) to swim with the tide. **fui** ~ I took a swim. **vamos** ~? let's go for a swim? **você sabe** ~? can you swim? **ficou a** ~ (fig.) he was at a loss. **filho de peixe sabe** ~ such a father such a son. ~ **em sangue** to take a bloodbath; wallow in gore, cause a carnage.

nádega s. f. buttock: 1. crupper, rump (plate C 12). 2. ~**s** pl. seat, backside, posteriors; (sl.) bum (plate C 18).

nadegada s. f. (also **nalgada**) blow on the buttock.

nadegudo adj. having large buttocks.

nadegueiro adj. of or pertaining to the buttocks.

nadir s. m. nadir: 1. opposite to the zenith. 2. (fig.) the lowest point; depression.

nadível adj. (obs., pl. **-íveis**) that may be crossed by swimming.

nado s. m. 1. swim, act or fact of swimming. 2. distance that may be covered by swimming. ‖ adj. born.
a ~ 1. swimming. 2. afloat. **atravessar a** ~ to swim across.

nafé s. m. a medicinal plant of the mallow family, Arabian in origin.

náfego s. m. horse with unequal hindquarters. ‖ adj. having unequal hindquarters; lame, limping (horse).

nafta s. f. naphta.

naftalina s. f. naphthalene, naphtalin(e).

naftol s. m. naphtol.

nagã, nagão s. m. (pl. **-ãs, -ões**) (Braz.) large army (cavalry) pistol.

nagibe s. m. (Braz.) (sl.) Turk.

nágua s. f. (also **anágua**) petticoat, slip.

naia, náiada, náiade s. f. naiad, water-nymph.

náilon s. m. nylon.

naipada s. f. suit of cards.

naipar v. (Braz.) to play the cards of a suit.

naipe s. m. 1. (cards) suit (plate B 5). 2. each of the groups of instruments of an orchestra. 3. (fig.) quality, class, group.

~ **de paus** (cards) club. **não reconhecer o** ~ (cards) to renounce.

naira s. f. woman of the Nair (Malabar coast).

naire s. m. Nair: one of a military caste of the Malabar coast.

naja s. f. 1. (zool.) cobra, spectacled cobra, hooded snake. 2. spittoon, cuspidor.

nalga s. f. (also **nádega**) buttock.

nalgada s. f. (also **nadegada**) blow on the buttock.

nambi s. m. (Braz.) ear. ‖ adj. m. + f. 1. tailless (animal). 2. (Braz.) earless. 3. drop-eared (horse).

nambiju adj. (S. Braz.) said of fulvous-eared cattle.

nambiuvu s. m. (vet.) haemorrhage of dogs'· ears.

namoração s. f. (pl. -ões) (also **namoro** m.) flirt(ing).

namorada s. f. sweetheart, ladylove, flame; sweet, fair; lassie, gal. ‖ adj. 1. loved, beloved. 2. enamoured, in love.

sua ~ his young lady.

namoradeira s. f. coquette, flirtatious woman, flirt, jilt. ‖ adj. flirtatious, coquettish.

namoradeiro, namoradiço adj. flirtatious, fond of love-making.

namorado (I) s. m. (also pop. **pequeno**) 1. sweetheart, lover, admirer, beau, fiancé. 2. boy friend, flame, honey, follower. ‖ adj. 1. courted, beloved. 2. meek, sweet. 3. enamoured, amorous.

namorado (II) s. m. (Braz., ichth.) a large Atlantic gamefish (Pseudopercis numida).

namorador s. m. flirter, gallant, lady-killer, amorist. ‖ adj. flirtatious.

namorar v. 1. to make love to, court, woo, philander, coquet. 2. to want eagerly, long for, covet. 3. to captivate, attract, seduce.

~ **uma moça** to court a girl, (sl.) mash a girl. ~ **por divertimento** to dally. **ele a namora** he plays the wanton with her. **ele namora a filha dela** he carries on with her daughter. ~ **altos postos** to crave, aspire to high office.

namoricar v. (also **namorichar, namoriscar**) to flirt, ogle, jilt.

namorice s. f. (also **namorico, namorilho** m.) calf-love, flirtation, puppy love.

namoro s. m. 1. love-making, courtship, wooing. 2. (sl.) entanglement, crush, carryings-on. 3. wooed person, sweetheart. \

estar de ~ **com** to have an affair with, keep company with. **romper o** ~ to jilt.

nana s. f. lullaby.

fazer ~ to lull to sleep.

nanã s. f. = **nhanhã, iaiá**.

fazer ~ (Braz., children) to sleep.

nanar v. (children) to sleep.

nanico adj. dwarfish, stunted.

naniquice s. f., **naniquismo, nanismo** m. dwarfishness, stuntedness.

nanocefalia s. f. (med., also **microcefalia**) microcephaly.

nanocefálico adj. (med., also **microcefálico**) microcephalous.

nanocéfalo s. m. (med., also **microcéfalo**) microcephalus.

nanomelia s. f. (med.) micromelia.

nanquim s. m. 1. China ink, Indian ink. 2. nankeen, nankin: a brownish cloth.

nanzuque s. m. nainsook: thin cotton cloth.

não s. m. 1. no. 2. refusal, denial. ‖ adj. no, nay. ‖ adv. no, not. ‖ pref. non-.

~ **é tanto assim** it is not so very much. ~ **faça caso** never mind. ~ **há café** there is no coffee. ~ **há dúvida** no doubt. ~ **incomodar,** ~ **interferir** to leave alone. ~ **obstante** in spite of, none the less. ~ **posso** I cannot. ~ **posso trabalhar mais** I can work no more. ~ **que eu gostasse** not that I

should like it. ~ **sei** I do not know. ~ **se sabe o que vai acontecer** there is no knowing what will happen. ~ **somente queremos, mas fazemos questão de ir** we are willing, nay eager to go. ~ **tenha medo** never fear. ~ **vir** to fail to come. **a** ~ **ser que** except, unless. **ainda** ~ not yet. **creio que** ~ I do not think so. **é ou** ~ **é?** is it so or not? **isto** ~ **está bem** that is not right. **já** ~ **há mais** there are not any more. **quem** ~ **arrisca,** ~ **petisca** nothing venture, nothing have. **um** ~ **seco** a downright no. **vem conosco? pois** ~! will you come with us? certainly, why not!

não-agressão s. f. (pl. **não-agressões**) nonaggression.

não-alinhamento s. m. (pl. **não-alinhamentos**) nonalignment.

não-combatente s. m. (pl. **não-combatentes**) non--combatant.

não-conformista s. m. (pl. **não-conformistas**) non--conformist.

não-euclidiano adj. (pl. **não-euclidianos**) (geom.) non-Euclidean.

não-me-deixes s. m., sg. + pl. (bot.) growndsel.

não-metal s. m. (pl. **não-metais**) (chem.) nonmetal.

não-me-toques s. m., sg. + pl. (bot.) touch-me-not.

napa s. f. Napa leather.

napáceo adj. turnip-rooted.

napéia s. f. napaea, wood nymph.

napeiro adj. indolent, slothful, sleepy.

napelo s. m. (bot.) monk's-hood.

napeva adj. m. + f. (S. Braz.) short-legged (poultry, dogs).

napiforme adj. m. + f. = **napáceo**.

napoleão s. m. (pl. -ões) napoleon: former French gold coin.

napoleônico adj. Napoleonic.

napoleonismo s. m. Napoleonism.

napoleonista s. m. + f. Napoleonist.

napolitano s. m. Neapolitan. ‖ adj. Neapolitan.

naquele, naquilo contraction of the prep. **em** and the adj. **aquele** or **aquilo**. 1. at that, thereat. 2. in that, therein. 3. on that, thereon.

naquela direção thitherward. **naquele tempo** at that time. **ficou naquilo** there the matter ended.

narandiba s. f. (Braz.) orange grove, orange garden.

narceína s. f. (chem.) narceine: an alkaloid found in opium.

narceja s. f. (ornith.) snipe.

narcisamento s. m. pride in o. s., in one's own beauty.

narcisar-se v. 1. to pride o. s. upon one's own beauty. 2. to adorn o. s. excessively. 3. to take pleasure in looking at o. s. in a mirror.

narcisismo s. m. narcissism.

narciso s. m. 1. (bot.) narcissus, pheasant's-eye. 2. young man infatuated with his own beauty.

narcisóides s. m. pl. (bot.) species of the narcissus. ‖ **narcisóide** adj. m. + f. like the narcissus.

narcose s. f. 1. narcosis. 2. narcotism.

sob ~ under chloroform.

narcótico s. m. 1. narcotic, drug; (U. S. A.) stuff. 2. (sl.) dope. 3. (fig.) dull, fatiguing person. 4. opiate. ‖ adj. narcotic.

narcotina s. f. (chem.) narcotine.

narcotismo s. m. narcotism.

narcotização s. f. narcotization.

narcotizador adj. narcotizing, causing narcosis.

narcotizar v. 1. to narcotize: a) subject to a narcotic drug. b) (fig.) stupefy, cause indifference, soothe to unconsciousness. 2. to bore, fatigue, annoy.

nardino adj. (bot.) nardine.

nardo s. m. (bot.) nard, spikenard.

narguilé, narguilhé s. m. narg(h)ile, hookah, kalian.

narícula s. f. 1. nostril. 2. ~**s** pl. nose.

narigada s. f. 1. a blow with the nose. 2. a pinch of snuff.

nariganga s. f. = **narigão**.

narigão s. m. (pl. **-ões**) 1. large nose. 2. (also **narigudo**) large-nosed person. ‖ adj. (also **narigudo**) large-nosed, nos(e)y, conky.

narina s. f. nostril; blowhole (plate C 12).

nariz s. m. (pl. **~es**) 1. nose (plates C 12, 18). 2. (sl.) smeller, pecker. 3. (fig.) peak, point, prow (as the nose of an airplane, ship).
~ **arrebitado** snub-nose, pug-nose, (coll.) snub, pug. ~ **grande (narigão)** (sl.) conk. **ficar de ~ comprido** to lose out, not attain one's objective. **cair de ~** to fall on one's nose. **dar com o ~ na porta** to find closed doors. **de ~ vermelho** red-nosed. **saber onde tem o ~** to be expert, competent; to know what's what. **limpar o ~** to blow one's nose. **meter o ~ onde não é chamado** to poke one's nose into other people's business. **torcer o ~** to turn up one's nose.

nariz-de-cera s. m. (pl. **narizes-de-cera**) 1. commonplace. 2. emphatic introduction.

narração s. f. (pl. **-ões**) narration: 1. narrating. 2. narrative. 3. story, tale, yarn. 4. description, report, relation.
~ **minuciosa** recountal, recountment. ~ **por escrito** write-up. **a história não perdeu pela ~** the story lost nothing in the telling.

narrado s. m. report, narrative. ‖ adj. reported, told.

narrador s. m. 1. narrator, narrater. 2. describer. 3. retailer, relater. ‖ adj. narrative, descriptive.

narrar v. 1. to narrate. 2. to relate, report, describe, picture.
~ **detalhadamente** to recount, detail. ~ **novamente** to retell.

narrativa s. f. 1. narrative, narration. 2. tale, story. 3. report, account, description.

narrativo adj. 1. narrative. 2. descriptive, expository.

narval s. m. (pl. **-ais**) narwhal(e), narwal; unicorn fish.

nasal s. m. (pl. **-ais**) nasal: 1. (anat.) nasal bone. 2. f. nasal sound. ‖ adj. m. + f. nasal: 1. of or pertaining to the nose; rhinal. 2. (phon.) spoken through the nose. ‖ ~**mente** adv. nasally.

nasalação, nasalização s. f. (pl. **-ões**) nasalization.

nasalar, nasalizar v. to nasalize.

nasalidade s. f. nasality.

nascediço adj. nascent, being born.

nascedouro s. m. (also **nascedoiro**) 1. birthplace. 2. (anat.) orifice of the uterus.

nascença s. f. 1. nascency, birth. 2. origin, beginning; source.
de ~ by birth.

nascente s. f. 1. fountain: a) source. b) origin, beginning, rise. c) spring, well, wellhead, fountainhead, riverhead (plate F 7). 2. east, orient. ‖ adj. m. + f. 1. nascent, being born. 2. beginning. 3. rising.

nascer s. m. rising, uprising. ‖ v. 1. to be born, see the light; fall (certain animals). 2. to come to light. 3. to issue, originate. 4. to rise, grow. 5. to spring, head, well. 6. (bot.) to shoot, germinate. 7. to dawn.
nasceu-lhe um filho he had a son born to him. **ele nasceu** he came into the world. **ele nasceu em Nova York** he saw the light in New York. **ele nasceu de novo hoje** he had a narrow escape today. **não ter nascido ontem** not to be born yesterday. **ao ~ do dia** at dawn. **ao ~ do sol** at sunrise. ~ **em berço de ouro** to be born with a silver spoon in one's mouth.

nascida s. f. boil, swelling, abscess.

nascidiço adj. natural, native.

nascido s. m. = **nascida**. ‖ adj. born.
-a née, nee. **bem ~** well-off, well-born. ~ **de pais pobres** low-born, base-born. ~ **morto** stillborn.

nascimento s. m. 1. birth, nativity. 2. origin, source. 3. rise, formation.
~ **de criança morta** (pop. **insucesso**) still birth. **antes do ~ de Cristo** before the Christian era. **ter ~** to be highborn.

nascituro s. m. unborn child; embryo. ‖ adj. unborn; embryonal.

nascível adj. m. + f. (pl. **-íveis**) that may be born.

nasicórneo s. m. (zool.) nasicorn. ‖ adj. nasicornous.

nassa s. f. eel-buck.

nassada s. f. 1. a lot of eel-bucks. 2. quantity of fish caught in an eel-buck.

nata s. f. cream: 1. the rich, fatty part of milk, butterfat. 2. (fig.): a) the choicest part. b) the pick, plum, prime.

natação s. f. natation, swimming.
aula de ~ swimming lesson.

natadeira s. f. basin or dish to curdle milk in.

natado adj. creamy.

natal s. m. (pl. **-ais**) 1. birthday. 2. Christmas, Noel. ‖ adj. m. + f. natal, native.
Natal de Jesus Cristo the Nativity. **árvore de ~** Christmas tree. **dia de ~** Christmas day. **época de ~** Christmastide, Yuletide. **véspera de ~** Christmas eve. **a terra ~** one's native land.

natalício adj. natal, or of or referring to the birthday.
aniversário ~ birthday.

natalidade s. f. natality, birth-rate.

natalino adj. referring to Christmas.

natátil adj. m. + f. (pl. **-eis**) floatable, natant, able to remain on the surface of the water.

natatório s. m. 1. natatorium, swimming place, swimming pool. 2. aquarium. ‖ adj. natatory, natatorial: of, referring to or for swimming.
a arte -a the art of swimming.

nateirado adj. 1. creamy. 2. slimy, muddy.

nateiro s. m. mud, slime.

natento adj. 1. = **nateirado**. 2. covered with cream or slime. 3. fertile.

natimorto adj. stillborn.

natio s. m. place with uncultivated growth of plants.

natividade s. f. 1. nativity, birth. 2. Nativity: the birth of Christ.

nativismo s. m. nativism: 1. (Braz.) aversion against foreigners, esp. Portuguese. 2. doctrine of inborn ideas.

nativista s. m. + f. nativist. ‖ adj. nativistic.

nativo s. m. native, home-born. ‖ adj. native: 1. indigenous. 2. national, home-bred, home-born. 3. inborn. 4. vernacular. 5. original. 6. unaffected. **água -a** spring water. **língua -a** native language, vernacular.

nato adj. 1. born. 2. native. 3. living, alive. 4. innate.

natrão s. m. (chem.) natron.

nátrio s. m. (chem.) (obs.) designation of sodium.

natura s. f. 1. (poet.) nature. 2. (fig.) species.

natural s. m. (pl. **-ais**) 1. native, home-born. 2. nature, character. 3. reality. 4. something natural. ‖ adj. m. + f. natural: 1. of or pertaining to nature. 2. native. 3. according to nature. 4. after the nature. 5. spontaneous. 6. instinctive. 7. unaffected, genuine, true. 8. unadulterated. 9. inborn, congenital, inherent. 10. original. 11. not cultivated, not artificial; unlaboured, raw. 12. usual, normal. 13. human. 14. elemental. ‖ ~**mente** adv. naturally. ‖ interj. indeed! of course! well, to be sure!
~ **de S. Paulo** born in S. Paulo. **uma coisa ~ a** matter of course. **é ~ que eu vou** of course I shall go. **em estado ~** crude. **fora do ~** extraordinary. **história ~** natural history. **isto é ~** that is understood. **não ~** laboured. **ao ~** ungarnished, referring

to foodstuff in a natural, unaltered state. **~mente teve que fazer barulho!** he would make a noise!

naturaleza s. f. (obs.) = **natureza**.

naturalidade s. f. 1. naturalness. 2. simplicity, artlessness. 3. ease, unaffectedness, unconstraint. 4. lifelikeness. 5. nationality, nativeness.

naturalismo s. m. 1. naturalism. 2. materialism, positivism. 3. realism.

naturalista s. m. + f. naturalist: 1. person versed in natural science. 2. person who adheres to naturalism. || adj. naturalistic.

naturalização s. f. (pl. **-ões**) naturalization; nationalization.

naturalizado s. m. naturalized person, denizen. || adj. naturalized.

naturalizando adj. that is about to be naturalized.

naturalizar v. 1. to naturalize, nationalize, denizen. 2. to familiarize, acclimatize.

naturalizável adj. m. + f. (pl. **-áveis**) that may be naturalized.

naturalmente adv. naturally.

natureza s. f. nature: 1. all beings of nature. 2. the universe. 3. forces of nature. 4. primitive form of life. 5. natural disposition. 6. character, temper, mood. 7. type, sort, grain. 8. constitution. 9. substance. 10. (Braz.) genitals (esp. of a man). **~ felina** felineness, felinity. **de má ~** ill-natured, disagreeable. **~ humana** 1. human nature. 2. humanity. **~ morta** (arts) still life. **contra a ~** against the grain. **de ~** innate(ly). **segundo a ~** true to nature.

naturismo s. m. naturalism.

naturista s. m. + f. naturalist. || adj. naturalistic.

nau s. f. 1. (large) vessel, ship; man-of-war. 2. crew.

náufico adj. = **náfego**.

naufragado adj. 1. (ship)wrecked. 2. (fig.) on the beach.

naufragante s. m. + f. shipwrecked person. || adj. shipwrecked.

naufragar v. 1. to wreck, shipwreck, (also wrack). 2. to fail, frustrate, miscarry. 3. to go to wreck and ruin. **o navio naufragou** the ship has been wrecked. **quase a ~** waterlogged. **ele naufragou** he suffered shipwreck.

naufragável adj. m. + f. (pl. **-veis**) subject to shipwreck, sinking; capable of failure.

naufrágio s. m. 1. wreck, shipwreck. 2. failure, frustration, miscarriage; ruin, loss.

náufrago s. m. 1. shipwrecked person. 2. derelict person; castaway. || adj. 1. (ship)wrecked. 2. (fig.) failed; ruined; castaway.

naufragoso adj. 1. causing shipwreck. 2. (fig.) dangerous.

naumaquia s. f. (Roman hist.) naumachy: mock naval battle.

naumáquico adj. of or referring to a naumachy.

naupatia s. f. sea-sickness.

nauscopia s. f. nauscopy: the pretended art of finding out land or ships at a great distance.

náusea s. f. nausea: 1. (sea-)sickness, qualm, queasiness, surfeit. 2. (fig.) repugnance, repulse; loathing, disgust.

nauseabundo adj. (also **nauseante** m. + f., **nauseativo**, **nauseoso** m.) 1. nauseous, nauseating. 2. repulsive, repugnant. 3. loathsome. 4. unpalatable.

nausear v. 1. to nauseate, sicken. 2. to repugnate. 3. to disgust, bore. 4. to feel sick about.

nauseento adj. propensive to nauseas, squeamish.

nauseoso adj. (also **nauseabundo**) nauseous. || **-amente** adv. nauseously.

nauta s. m. sailor, mariner, seaman.

náutica s. f. navigation, nautics, seamanship.

náutico adj. nautical, navigational, marine, naval. || **nauticamente** adv. nautically.

nautilídeo, nautilóide adj. (zool.) nautiloid.

náutilo s. m. (zool.) nautilus (mollusc).

nautografia s. f. (neologism) description of a ship's instruments and their use.

nava s. f. plain surrounded by mountains.

naval adj. m. + f. (pl. **-ais**) naval, marine, maritime. **base ~** naval base. **batalha ~** naval engagement, sea-fight. **política ~** naval, marine policy. **supremacia ~** thalassocracy, naval supremacy.

navalha s. f. 1. razor. 2. (fig.) venomous person, viper. 3. intense cold. 4. pocket-knife, clasp-knife. **o fio da ~** the razor's edge.

navalhada s. f. 1. stroke or slash with a razor. 2. slash or wound caused by a stroke with a razor.

navalhão s. m. (pl. **-ões**) large razor or knife.

navalhar v. to wound or slash with a razor.

navalhista s. m. + f. person who slashes with a razor.

navarra s. f. a certain figure in bullfighting.

navarro, navarrês s. m. native or inhabitant of Navarra (Spain). || adj. of or referring to Navarra.

nave s. f. 1. (archit.) nave. 2. (fig.) temple, church. 3. (obs.) vessel, ship. **~ de igreja** (archit.) aisle. **~ espacial** spaceship.

navegabilidade s. f. 1. navegability, navigableness. 2. seaworthiness. **~ aérea** airworthiness. **em mau estado de ~** unseaworthy.

navegação s. f. (pl. **-ões**) 1. navigation, seafaring; sailing, shipping. 2. maritime commerce. 3. voyage. 4. nautics. 5. (Braz.): a) ship. b) launch, barge. c) river boat. **~ aérea** air navigation. **~ costeira** coasting, cabotage. **~ fluvial** internal navigation. **agência de ~** shipping office. **companhia de ~** shipping company. **~ mercante** merchant shipping.

navegado adj. navigated, plyed (waterway).

navegador s. m. 1. navigator, seafarer, seaman, sailor. 2. person who makes a long journey by sea. || adj. 1. navigating, seafaring. 2. expert in navigation.

navegar v. 1. to navigate: a) manage a vessel. b) travel by sea. c) engage in navigation. 2. to transport by ship. 3. to sail, steam. 4. (fig., pop.): a) to go (on). b) to prosper, be successful. **~ ao redor** (naut.) to double. **~ com lastro** to be in ballast. **~ com o vento de popa** to sail before the wind. **~ contra o vento** to sail into the wind's eye. **~ em iate** to yacht. **~ perto da costa** to hug the coast. **~ rio abaixo** (naut.) to drop. **~ sob bandeira falsa** to sail under false colours. **incapaz de ~** unseaworthy.

navegável adj. m. + f. (pl. **-áveis**) 1. navigable, passable, voyageable. 2. floatable.

naveta s. f. 1. navicula: incense-boat. 2. (tech.) shuttle. 3. small vessel, ship.

naviarra s. f. (obs.) large vessel, boat.

navícula s. f. navicular part or organ.

navicular, naviforme adj. m. + f. navicular, boat-shaped.

navífrago adj. (poet.) shattering ships.

navígero adj. (poet.) = **navegável**.

navio s. m. 1. ship, vessel, craft; boat, bark. 2. (poet.) prow, keel, sail. **~ alvo** target ship. **~ abastecedor** (navy) victualler. **~ a vapor** steam vessel, steamer, steamship. **~ capital** capital ship. **~ cargueiro** cargo ship, freighter. **~ carvoeiro** coal-ship. **~ corsário** privateer, pirate. **~ costeiro** coasting vessel. **~ de bloqueio** blockader. **~ de carga** cargo ship, cargo vessel. **~ de guerra** warship. **~ de linha** ship of the line. **~-escola** training ship. **~ farol**

light ship. ~ **guarda-costas** guard ship. ~ **hospital** hospital ship. ~ **mercante** merchantman, merchant ship. ~ **negreiro** slave ship, slaver. ~ **quebra-gelos** icebreaker, iceboat. **~-tanque** tank-ship, tank--steamer. **~-transporte de tropas** trooper, troopship. **casco de** ~ hull. **construtor de** ~**s** shipwright. **dentro do** ~ inboard. **é um** ~ **rápido** she is a good sailer. **ficar a ver** ~**s** to be too late in the field.

nazarena s. f. (S. Braz.) large-sized spur.

nazareno s. m. Nazarene: a) native or inhabitant of Nazareth. b) **Nazareno:** Christ. || adj. Nazarene.

nazismo s. m. Nazi(i)sm.

nazi(sta) s. m. + f. Nazi, nazi. || adj. Nazi, nazi.

neblina s. f. 1. mist, haze, fog, gauze, vapour. 2. (fig.) cobwebs.
~ **amarela londrina** peasoup fog. ~ **baixa** ground fog.

neblinar v. 1. to be foggy, mist. 2. to drizzle.

nebrina s. f. less used form of **neblina**.

nebulento adj. = **nevoento**.

nebulização s. f. (the act of) spraying.

nebulizador s. m. sprayer.

nebulizar v. to spray (paint, insecticide, perfume).

nebulosa s. f. (astr.) nebula.

nebulosidade s. f. nebulosity, mistiness, haziness, fogginess, cloudiness.

nebuloso adj. 1. misty, foggy, hazy, cloudy, vaporous. 2. (fig.) obscure, vague, indistinct. 3. sad, dreary. 4. mysterious.

necear v. to talk nonsense, act foolishly.

necedade s. f. 1. (also **nescidade**) ignorance, stupidity, nescience. 2. foolishness, nonsense. 3. contraction of **necessidade:** necessity.

necessária s. f. (fam.) latrine, privy.

necessário adj. necessary, indispensable, requisite, exigent, essential, needful. || **necessariamente** adv. necessarily, of necessity.
é ~ **um homem honesto para...** it takes an honest man to... **se for** ~ if need be. **não é** ~ there is no occasion (need) for it. **as coisas -as à vida** the necessaries of life.

necessidade s. f. 1. necessity, necessitousness, necessariness, must, needfulness. 2. want, need. 3. privation, hardship, distress, poverty. 4. exigence, requirement. 5. (com.) demand.
a ~ **desconhece a lei** necessity knows no law. **uma** ~ **premente** a felt want. **artigo de** ~ commodity. **em caso de** ~ in case of need. **fazer as suas** ~**s** to relieve nature. **nós temos poucas** ~**s** we have few wants. **ter** ~ **de** to stand in need of. **ele tinha premente** ~ **de dinheiro** he was in urgent need of money. **gêneros de primeira** ~ essential commodities. **nós passamos muita** ~ we kept the wolf from the door. **é na** ~ **que se conhece o amigo** a friend in need is a friend indeed.

necessitado s. m. needer, indigent person. || adj. necessitous, needful, poor, poverty-stricken, destitute. || **-amente** adv. necessitously.
~ **de dinheiro** pressed for money.

necessitar v. 1. to necessitate, want, need. 2. to demand, require. 3. to be necessary, obligatory, essential. 4. to be destitute of, be needy, poor, indigent. 5. to suffer distress.

necessitoso adj. necessitous.

necrobiose s. f. (path.) necrobiosis.

necrófago s. m. necrophagous person or animal feeding on carrion. || adj. necrophagous.

necrofilia s. f. (path.) necrophilia.

necrofobia s. f. necrophobia.

necrologia s. f. necrology; obituary.

necrológico adj. necrological; obituary.

necrológio s. m. necrology: brief history of a deceased person.

necrologista s. m. + f., **necrólogo** m. necrologist: person who writes necrologies.

necromancia s. f. (also **nigromancia**) necromancy, conjuration, gramarye.

necromante s. m. + f. (also **nigromante**) necromancer, sorcerer, conjurer, fetisheer.

necromântico adj. (also **nigromântico**) necromantic.

necrópole s. f. necropolis, cemetery.

necropsia s. f. necropsy, autopsy.

necrópsico adj. necropsic(al).

necrosar v. to cause necrosis.

necroscopia s. f. necroscopy, necropsy.

necrose s. f. necrosis, sphacelation.

necrotério s. m. dead-house, mortuary, morgue.

necrótico adj. necrotic.

néctar s. m. (pl. **néctares**) nectar: 1. (myth.) the drink of the gods. 2. any delicious drink. 3. (fig.) anything delicious. 4. sweet liquid of certain plants gathered by bees.

nectáceo adj. (also **nectário**) nectarean, nectareous.

nectarífero adj. nectariferous.

nectarina s. f. (S. Braz.) nectarine, a variety of peach.

nectário s. m. (bot.) nectary.

nectópode adj. (zool.) web-footed.

nediez s. f. sleekness, plumpness.

nédio adj. sleek; well-fed, fat, plump.

neerlandês s. m. (pl. **-eses;** f. **-esa**) Netherlander. || adj. Netherlandish.

nefando adj. 1. nefarious, heinous. 2. abominable, execrable. 3. wicked, profligate. || **-amente** adv. nefariously.

nefário adj. 1. = **nefando**. 2. villainous.

nefasto adj. 1. disastrous, disgraceful, tragic, fatal. 2. ill-omened.

nefelibata, nefelíbata s. m. + f. nepheliad, dreamer. || adj. (day)dreaming.

nefelinito s. m. (petrog.) nephelinite.

nefelita, nefelina s. f. (min.) nephelite, nepheline.

nefelóide adj. m. + f. nepheloid, cloudy.

nefoscopia s. f. (meteor.) nephoscopy.

nefralgia s. f. (path.) nephralgia.

nefrálgico adj. (path.) nephralgic.

nefrite s. f. (path.) nephritis; Bright's disease.

nefrítico s. m. (path.) person suffering from nephritis. || adj. nephritic.

nefroflegmasia s. f. (path.) nephritis. || adj. nephritic.

nefróide adj. m. + f. nephroid, reniform.

nefrólito s. m. (path.) nephrolith, renal calculus.

nefrolitotomia s. f. (med.) nephrolithotomy.

nefrologia s. f. (med.) nephrology: study of renal diseases.

nefrologista s. m. + f. (med.) nephrologist.

nefroma s. m. (path.) nephroma, a tumour of the kidney tissue.

nefrose s. f. (path.) nephrosis.

nefrotomia s. f. (med.) nephrotomy.

nega s. f. 1. denial. 2. lack of inclination, calling, talent.

negaça s. f. 1. enticement, allurement. 2. bait, decoy. 3. provocation. 4. feint. 5. take-in, trap. 6. mistake.

negação s. f. (pl. **-ões**), **negamento** m. negation: 1. negative. 2. denial. 3. disavowal. 4. lack of some positive quality.
~ **de um fato** (jur.) traverse. **ele é uma** ~ **completa** he is a complete wash-out.

negaceador s. m. (also **negaceiro**) enticer, allurer, decoyer, swindler, cheat. || adj. enticing, alluring, taking in.

negacear v. 1. to entice, allure. 2. to bait, decoy. 3. to provoke. 4. to take in, cheat.

negador s. m. 1. denier. 2. (jur.) traverser. ‖ adj. 1. denying. 2. falling.

negalho s. m. 1. piece of thread, of sewing cotton. 2. (fig.): a) small quantity of anything. b) small person.

negar v. 1. to deny, say no. 2. to negate. 3. to contradict, controvert. 4. to disavow. 5. to gainsay, forbid. 6. to abandon, betray, let down, abnegate. 7. to refuse, reject, repudiate. 8. (jur.) to traverse. 9. to withhold. 10. ~-se to deny o. s. ~ um favor to deny a favour. ~ fogo to hang fire (fire-arm). ~ a autoridade a to disallow. ele negou tê-la visto he denied having seen her. não se pode negar-lho you've got to hand it to him, you cannot deny it to him.

negativa s. f. negative: 1. a negative term or proposition. 2. a negative reply, refusal, negation.

negatividade s. f. negativity, negativeness.

negativismo s. m. negativism.

negativista s. m. + f. negativist. ‖ adj. negativistic.

negativo s. m. (phot.) negative (plate F 6). ‖ adj. 1. negative (also chem., math., phot., phys.). 2. contrary (result), not positive. 3. null. ‖ -amente adv. negatively.

negatório adj. denying.

negável adj. m. + f. (pl. -áveis) deniable.

negligência s. f. negligence: 1. neglect. 2. laziness, indolence. 3. carelessness, indifference, disregard. 4. barratry, thoughtlessness. ~ do dever dereliction of duty.

negligenciado adj. neglectful, neglected.

negligenciar v. 1. to neglect, disregard. 2. to pretermit, leave out of account. 3. to omit, fail to do, oversee. ele negligenciou o seu trabalho he failed in his work.

negligente adj. m. + f. 1. negligent, neglectful. 2. lazy, indolent, idle, lax, slack. 3. careless, indifferent, thoughtless. 4. easy-going. 5. untidy, slipshod. ‖ ~mente adv. negligently, etc.

negociabilidade s. f. negotiability.

negociação s. f. (pl. -ões) 1. negotiation, transaction. 2. treaty. 3. deal. 4. trading.

negociador s. m. 1. negotiator. 2. transactor, speculator. 3. merchant, trader. 4. businessman.

negociante s. m. + f. 1. merchant, merchandiser. 2. trader, tradesman, dealer. 3. shopkeeper, retailer. 4. businessman, businesswoman. ‖ adj. negotiating. ~ de meias e roupas de malha hosier. ~ de tecidos woollen draper. ~ de vinhos vintner. ~ em artigos de papelaria stationer. ~ em lã wool stapler.

negocião s. m. a good stroke of business, an especially profitable deal.

negociar v. 1. to negotiate. 2. to trade or deal in, traffic. 3. to do business. 4. to transact, buy or sell, job, bargain. ~ em lãs to trade in wool. ~ um empréstimo to negotiate a loan. ~ em pequena escala to dicker.

negociarrão s. m. (pl. -ões) splendid transaction, deal or business.

negociata s. f. 1. somehow suspicious or unfair business or deal. 2. swindle. ele faz ~s he works swindles.

negociável adj. m. + f. (pl. -áveis) negotiable, marketable, sellable.

negócio s. m. 1. business. 2. commerce, trade, traffic. 3. transaction, deal(ing). 4. bargain; pennyworth. 5. (com.) shop, establishment. 6. affair, matter, concern; any subject. 7. enterprise. ~ a prazo time-bargain. ~ à vista cash business. ~ arriscado (com.) adventure. ~ a varejo retail business. ~ da China fine bargain. ~ de ocasião a bargain, a good value. ~ de corretagens e

consignações factorage. ~ de estado state affair. ~ de ocasião bargain. ~ de pai para filho (fig.) a deal between pals. ~ perdido lost business. o ~ todo the whole business, the whole shebang. o ~ não é tão simples there are some strings attached to it. o ~ deles foi muito bem they drove a roaring business. ele arrumou o ~ he did the trick. falta de ~ (com.) inanimateness. fazer bom ~ to do a good stroke of business. ele faz bons ~s he does a good trade. fazer mau ~ to drive a bad bargain. homem de ~s businessman. em matéria de ~ in the way of business. não quero saber de ~s com ele I do not want to have anything to do with him. ele saiu a ~s meus I sent him on errands. sem negócios (com.) inanimate. tratar de diversos negócios ao mesmo tempo to have many irons in the fire.

negocioso adj. 1. doing a lot of business. 2. busy, occupied. 3. active, diligent. 4. careful.

negocista s. m. + f. (Braz.) 1. person fond of business; businessman. 2. person fond of shady business; adventurer. 3. jobber.

negra s. f. 1. Negress; blacky. 2. female slave. 3. decider (of a game).

negrada s. f. 1. group of Negroes. 2. group of brawlers. 3. company, gang.

negral adj. m. + f. (pl. -ais) 1. almost black. 2. black.

negralhada, negraria s. f. (also negrada) group or lot of Negroes.

negregado adj. 1. unlucky, disgraceful, unhappy. 2. toilsome, difficult.

negregoso adj. very black.

negreiro s. m. slaver: person who trades slaves. ‖ adj. of or pertaining to (black) slaves. navio ~ slave ship.

negrejante adj. m. + f. 1. blackish, dark. 2. gloomy. 3. threatening.

negrejar v. - 1. to be or look black. 2. to be sad or gloomy. 3. to be or look threatening.

negridão s. f. (pl. -ões) (also negrura) 1. blackness, darkness, obscurity, gloom. 2. (fig.): a) perversity, rudeness, roughness. b) crime, black deed.

negrilho s. m. 1. young Negro. 2. ~s pl. black glass trinkets.

negrinha s. f. 1. Negro girl. 2. (ornith.) titling.

negrinho s. m. 1. Negro boy. 2. (Braz., São Paulo) small coffee grains.

negrito s. m. (typogr., also negrita f.) blackface, boldface. ‖ adj. black-faced, bold-faced, heavy.

negritude s. f. Negritude.

negro s. m. 1. Negro, black (person), nigger, African; (sl.) blackamoor, blacky, darky. 2. (black) slave. ‖ adj. 1. black, dark, dark-skinned; ebon(y). 2. sullen, gloomy. 3. African. ~ animal bone black. ~ australiano blackfellow. ~ como azeviche pitchy. ~-de-fumo lampblack. ~-de-marfim ivory black. ~-de-platina platinum black. tráfico de ~s slave-trade. ver tudo ~ to take a gloomy view of things.

negrofilia s. f. Negrophilism.

negrófilo s. m. Negrophile; abolitionist. ‖ adj. friendly towards Negroes; abolitionist.

negróide s. m. + f. Negroid. ‖ adj. Negroid.

negror s. m. 1. darkness, obscurity. 2. (Braz.) agitation in the water caused by a pursued whale.

negrote s. m. (Braz.) young Negro, Negro boy.

negrume s. m. 1. darkness, obscurity. 2. fog, mist, haze. 3. sadness, gloom.

negrura s. f. = negridão.

nela contr. of em + ela in her, in it; on her, on it.

nele contr. of em + ele in him, in it; on him, on it. encontrei ~ um amigo I found a friend in him.

nelore s. m. variety of cattle from Nelore (India).

nem adv. + conj. neither, nor, not even. ~ **assim** ~ **assado** neither this way nor that. ~ **mais** ~ **menos** neither more nor less. ~ **mesmo me ouviu com atenção** he never even listened to me. **ela não tomou providências** ~ **mesmo me avisou que saía** she made no arrangements nor even told me she was going. ~ **peixe** ~ **carne** neither fish nor fowl. ~ **por bem** ~ **por mal** neither the soft nor the rough way. ~ **por isso deixei de ir** I went just the same. ~ **por nada** not for all the world. ~ **sequer** not even, not so much. ~ **sempre** not always. ~ **todos** not all. **sem pé** ~ **cabeça** without rhyme or reason.
nematelmíntio s. m. (zool.) roundworm.
nematócero s. m. (zool.) nematoceron.
nematociste s. f. (zool.) nematocyst.
nematóide s. m. (zool.) nematode, thread worm. ‖ adj. m. + f. nematode.
nembo s. m. (archit.) solid masonry work (between open spaces).
nemeu adj. (archaeol.) Nemean.
nemoral adj. m. + f. (pl. -ais) of or pertaining to the woods.
nemoroso adj. 1. shaded by trees. 2. woody, abounding in woods.
nena s. f. (fam.) doll, puppet.
nenê s. m. (Braz., also **neném**) baby, newborn or a few months old child.
nenhum adj. (pl. -ns) 1. null, void, of no consequence. 2. neither, any, no. ‖ -**amente** adv. in no wise, on no account, by no means. ‖ pron. none, no one, nobody, not any, neither. ~ **de nós** none of us, neither of us. **de modo** ~ on no account, by no means, not at all. **de** ~**a utilidade** of no use. **em** ~**a parte** nowhere. **não tive chance** ~**a** I had no chance whatsoever. **ela tem pouco dinheiro, talvez** ~ she has little money if any. **uma pessoa, como** ~**a outra competente para dizer** no person more competent to have the say about.
nenhures adv. nowhere.
nênia s. f. epicedium, elegy, dirge.
nenúfar s. m. (pl. ~**es**) (bot.) nenuphar, nuphar, water-lily.
neocatolicismo s. m. neo-Catholicism.
neocatólico s. m. neo-Catholic.
neoclássico adj. neoclassic.
neocriticismo s. m. (philos.) neocriticism.
neodímio s. m. (chem.) neodymium, neodidymium.
neófito s. m. 1. neophyte, proselite, convert. 2. novice. 3. beginner.
neofobia s. f. neophobia: aversion against new things or progress.
neófobo s. m. neophobic person.
neofonema s. m. (phil.) a phonemic neologism.
neoformação s. f. (pl. -ões) neoformation.
neografia s. f. a written neologism.
neogrego adj. neo-Greek.
neolatino adj. neo-Latin.
neolítica s. f. Neolithic period.
neolítico adj. Neolithic.
neologia s. f. neology, neologism.
neológico adj. neologic.
neologismo s. m. 1. neologism: a) use of a new word or sentence. b) new meaning of an old word. 2. new doctrine.
neologista s. m. + f. neologist. ‖ adj. neologistic.
neon, neônio s. m. (chem.) neon. **lâmpada** ~ neon lamp. **luz** ~ neon light (plate P 19).
neoplásico adj. (path.) of or referring to neoplasm.
neoplasma s. m. (path.) neoplasm, tumour, growth.
neoplastia s. f. (surg.) neoplasty.

neoplástico adj. (surg.) neoplastic.
neoplatônico adj. Neoplatonic.
neoplatonismo s. m. Neoplatonism.
neorama s. m. panorama of the interior of a building.
neórnites s. f. pl. (ornith.) Neornithes, a subclass comprising all true birds.
neotérico adj. neoteric, novel, new.
neotínea s. f. (zool.) neoteinea.
neótipo s. m. (biol.) neotype.
neotomismo s. m. (philos.) Neo-Thomism.
neotrópico adj. (geogr.) Neotropic.
neozelandês s. m. (pl. -eses; f. esa) New Zealander.
neozóico s. m. (geol.) Neozoic (period). ‖ adj. Neozoic.
neotropical adj. (geogr.) Neotropical, referring to Tropical America (South and Central America, the Caribean and Mexico till South of Rio Grande).
nepentáceas s. f. pl. (bot.) Nepenthaceae.
nepentáceo adj. (bot.) nepenthaceous.
nepente s. f. nepenthe: drug formerly supposed to kill pains and sorrows.
nepote s. m. 1. the pope's nephew. 2. favourite.
nepotismo s. m. 1. nepotism. 2. favouritism.
nepotista s. m. + f. nepotist.
nequícia s. f. wickedness, malice; perversity.
nereida, nereide s. f. Nereid, sea nymph.
neres adv. (Braz. sl.) nothing. ~ **de** ~, ~ **de pitibiriba** nothing whatsoever.
neroniano adj. (hist.) Neronian: of or pertaining to Nero.
nervação s. f. (pl. -ões) (bot. + zool.) nervation, venation, veining.
nervado adj. nervate, veined, ribbed.
nerval adj. m. + f. (pl. -ais) (also **nervoso** m.) nerval, neural.
nervino s. m. nervine: tonic for the nerves. ‖ adj. (also **nerval** m. + f., **nérveo** m.) nerval.
nervo s. m. 1. nerve: a) (anat.) filamentous tissue. b) (anat.) sinew, tendon. c) strength, power, force, vigour. d) (bot. + zool.) vein, nervure. 2. (archit.) rib. ~ **ciático** sciatic nerve. ~ **óptico** optic nerve (plate O). ~ **radial** radial nerve. **um ataque de** ~**s** a fit of nerves. **meus** ~**s estão abalados** my nerves are shattered. **ela é uma pilha de** ~**s** she is but a bundle of nerves.
nervosa s. f. (Braz., pop., also **nervoso** m.) any nervous malady.
nervosidade s. f. 1. nervousness. 2. nervous energy.
nervosismo s. m. 1. nervousness, jumpiness, nerves; excitability. 2. willies; (sl.) jim-jams. 3. flutter, flurry.
nervoso s. m. any nervous malady, nervousness, hysterics. ‖ adj. 1. nervous: a) of or referring to the nerves. b) that has nerves. c) (bot. + zool.) nervate, nervy, veined, ribbed. d) energetic, spirited. e) vigorous, sinewy. 2. excited, on edge. 3. excitable, irritable. 4. jumpy, fussy. 5. apprehensive. 6. suffering from the nerves. ‖ -**amente** adv. excitedly, etc. **crise -a, esgotamento** ~ nervous breakdown. **ela está -a** she is on edge. **estar** ~ to be nervous, (U. S. A. sl.) be jittery. **muito** ~ high-strung. **sistema** ~ nervous system, autonomic system.
nervudo adj. 1. strong-nerved, strong, robust, sinewy. 2. wiry. 3. nervous.
nervura s. f. 1. nervure: a) (bot.) vein, rib (plate F 5). b) (zool.) rib of an insect's wing. 2. (archit.) rib. 3. rib on the back of a book. ~ **da abóbada** (archit.) groin. **sem** ~ veinless.
nescidade s. f. (also **necedade**) nescience.
néscio s. m. ignoramus, stupid person, fool. ‖ adj. ignorant, stupid, nescient, witless. ‖ **nesciamente** adv. nesciently, etc.

nesga s. f. 1. gore: a) small (triangular) piece of land. b) small (triangular) piece of cloth, gusset. 2. small space, nook, corner, plot.

nesografia s. f. description of isles.

nêspera s. f. loquat (fruit).

nespereira s. f. (bot.) loquat, Japanese medlar (tree) (Eriobothria japonica).

nesse contr. of **em esse** (f. **em essa = nessa**) in that, on that.

nessas circunstâncias in these circumstances.

neste contr. of **em este** (f. **em esta = nesta**) in that, on that.

nestas condições under these circumstances. ~ **mundo** herebelow. **visite-me** ~s **dias** come over sometime.

nestoriano s. m. (eccl. hist.) Nestorian.

neta s. f. granddaughter; grandchild.

neto s. m. 1. grandson; grandchild. 2. ~s pl. descendants, posterity.

netuniano, netunino, netúnio adj. Neptunian.

Netuno s. m. (astr. + mytol.) Neptune.

neuma s. m. (hist. of mus.) neume (symbol formerly used).

neural adj. m. + f. (pl. -ais) neural: of or referring to the nerves or the nervous system.

neuralgia s. f. (med.) neuralgia.

neurálgico adj. (med.) neuralgic.

neurastenia s. f. 1. (med.) neurasthenia. 2. (pop.) ill humour; irritability.

neurastênico adj. (med.) neurasthenic.

nêurico adj. neural.

neurilema s. m. (anat.) neurilemma.

neurilidade s. f. (physiol.) neurility.

neurite s. f. (med.) neuritis.

neurítico adj. (med.) neuritic.

neurocirurgia s. f. (med.) neurosurgery.

neurografia s. f. (anat.) neurography: description of the nerves.

neurologia s. f. (med.) neurology.

neurológico adj. (med.) neurologic.

neurologista s. m. + f. (med.) neurologist.

neuroma s. m. (path.) neuroma: tumour developed from a nerve.

neurônico adj. (anat.) neuronic.

neurônio s. m. (anat.) neuron(e).

neuropata, neurópata s. m. + f. neuropath: person suffering from neuropathy.

neuropatia s. f. (path.) neuropathy.

neuropático adj. (path.) neuropathic.

neuropatologia s. f. (med.) neuropathology.

neurose s. f. (path.) neurosis: nervous disorder without functional lesion.

~ **de guerra** war neurosis.

neurótico s. m. (med.) neurotic (person). || adj. neurotic.

neurotomia s. f. (med.) neurotomy.

neutral adj. m. + f. (pl. -ais) 1. neutral, neuter. 2. impartial, unbiassed. 3. indifferent. 4. non-belligerent. || ~mente adv. neutrally.

ser ou ficar ~ to be or remain neutral.

neutralidade s. f. 1. neutrality. 2. impartiality. 3. indifference.

~ **armada** armed neutrality.

neutralização s. f. (pl. -ões) neutralization.

neutralizador s. m. neutralizer.

neutralizar v. 1. to neutralize. 2. to counteract. 3. to kill. 4. to destroy.

neutro s. m. (gram.) neuter. || adj. 1. (gram.) neuter. 2. (also biol., chem., electr.) neutral. 3. impartial. 4. non-belligerent. 5. inert, inactive.

neutrófilo s. m. (anat.) neutrophil(e).

nêutron s. m. (chem. + phys.) neutron.

nevada s. f. 1. snow-fall; flurry of snow. 2. snow. 3. hoar-frost.

nevado s. m. névé, firn. || adj. 1. snowy: a) covered with snow. b) snow-white. 2. cold, icy.

nevar v. 1. to snow. 2. to cover with snow. 3. to whiten. 4. to cool, freeze.

nevasca s. f. snow-storm, blizzard, drift.

neve s. f. 1. snow. 2. (fig.): a) whiteness. b) white hair. c) extreme coldness.

~ **aguada (semiderretida)** snow-broth. **amontoado de** ~ wreath of snow, snow-drift. **cercado de** ~ snow-bound. **coberto de** ~ snow-capped. **cobrir de** ~ to oversnow, snow in, snow up. **floco de** ~ snowflake. **limite das** ~s **perpétuas** or **eternas** snow-line. **soterrar sob a** ~ to snow under.

neviscar v. to snow slightly.

nevo s. m. nevus, birthmark.

névoa s. f. 1. mist, fog, vapour. 2. film, gauze (eyes). 3. obscurity, darkness.

nevoaça s. f. = **nevoeiro.**

nevoado adj. (also **enevoado**) 1. foggy, misty, cloudy. 2. dimly, blurry.

nevoar-se v. 1. to become foggy, misty, obscure. 2. to darken.

nevoeiro s. m. 1. mist, fog (bank), vapour. 2. haze. 3. (fig.) obscurity.

nevoento adj. 1. misty, foggy, mistful, vaporous. 2. (fig.) obscure.

nevoso adj. 1. snowy. 2. full of snow. 3. = **nevoento.**

nevralgia, etc. = **neuralgia,** etc.

newtoniano s. m. Newtonian. || adj. Newtonian.

nexo s. m. connection, nexus, link, tie.

sem ~ incoherent.

nhá s. f. (Braz., pop. for **iaiá**) miss, missy.

nhambu s. m. 1. (ornit.) (= **inhambu**) tinamou, common name for any of several birds of the family Tinamidae, found in South and Central America. 2. (bot.) (= **jambu**) a herbaceous plant (Spilanthes acmella) of the family Compositae.

nhamdu s. m. (Braz., ornith.) nandu.

nhanhã s. f. (Braz., pop.) affectionate form of **nhá:** miss, missy.

nhenhenhém s. m. (pl. -éns) (Braz., coll.) 1. grumbling. 2. talk, gossip.

nhô s. m. (Braz., pop. **ioiô**) mister, master or more properly **massa.**

nhô Chico massa Frank.

nhoque s. m. (cul.) gnocchi, dumplings.

nhor não (sim) adv. locution (Braz., pop.) no (yes) sir.

nica s. f. 1. impertinence. 2. puerility. 3. trifle. 4. (obs.) swindle, fraud.

nicada s. f. 1. pecking. 2. (S. Braz.) striking of one marble against another.

nicar v. 1. to peck. 2. (S. Braz.) to strike one marble against the other.

nicaraguano s. m. Nicaraguan. || adj. Nicaraguan.

nicho s. m. 1. niche (plate C 7). 2. break, recess(ion). 3. fenestella. 4. alcove. 5. small home. 6. sinecure, easy money.

nicles adv. (coll.) nothing whatsoever.

nicociana s. f. nicotiana: tobacco-plant.

nicociâneo adj. of or referring to the nicotiana.

nicol s. m. (pl. -óis). Nicol prism.

nicótico adj. of or referring to tobacco.

nicotina s. f. nicotine: a poisonous alkaloid occurring in tobacco.

nicotínico adj. nicotinic.

nicotinismo s. m. (med.) nicotinism.

nicotino adj. 1. nicotin. 2. soporiferous.

nictação s. f. (pl. -ões) nictation, winking, blinking.

nictagináceas s. f. pl. (bot.) Nictaginaceae (the four-o'clock family).

nictalope s. m. + f. nyctalope: person who can see only during the night.
nictalopia s. f. (med.) nyctalopia.
nictalópico adj. (med.) nyctalopic.
nictêmero s. m. a day and a night, twenty-four hours.
nictitante s. f. nictitating membrane (of birds).
nictobata, nictóbata s. m. + f. sleepwalker, somnambulist.
nictofobia s. f. (path.) nyctophobia: morbid dread of the night.
nictúria, nicturia s. f. (path.) nycturia, nocturia.
nidícola adj. m. + f. (ornith.) nidicolous.
nidificação s. f. (pl. -ões) nidification, nesting.
nidificar v. to nidificate, nidify, nest.
nidífugo adj. nidifugous (bird).
nidor s. m. halitosis, offensive breath.
nidoroso adj. bad-smelling, stinking, musty.
nietzschiano adj. Nietzschean.
nietzschista s. m. + f. Nietzschean.
nigela s. f. 1. niello (decoration), niellowork. 2. (bot.) love-in-a-mist.
nigelador s. m. niellist.
nigelagem s. f. (pl. -ens) nielloing.
nigelar v. to niello, decorate with niello.
nigérrimo adj. very black.
nigrícia s. f. land of Negroes.
nigrípede adj. m. + f. (zool.) black-footed.
nigripene adj. m. + f. (zool.) black-winged.
nigrirrostro adj. (zool.) 1. black-billed. 2. that has a black trunk or snout.
nigromancia s. f., **nigromante, nigromântico** adj. = necromancia, necromante, necromântico.
niilismo s. m. 1. (philos.) nihilism. 2. entire disbelief.
niilista s. m. + f. nihilist; destructionist. ‖ adj. nihilistic.
nílico, nilótico adj. Nilotic.
nilo adj. (S. Braz.) white-headed (cattle).
nimbar v. to glorify, to give a nimbus to.
nimbífero adj. (poet.) bringing rain, rainy.
nimbo s. m. nimbus: 1. (meteor.) rain cloud (plate N 2); light rain. 2. aureole, halo, gloriole.
nimbo-estrato s. m. (pl. **nimbos-estratos**) (meteor.) nimbostratus, a formless rain cloud.
nimboso adj. rainy; covered with nimbus.
nimiedade s. f. excessiveness.
nímio adj. excessive, overmuch.
nina s. f. 1. (tech.) washer. 2. short for **menina**: girl.
ninar v. 1. to lull to sleep, rock asleep. 2. to sleep (children).
ela ninava sua criança she sang her child to sleep.
ninfa (I) s. f. nymph: 1. divinity of waters, mountains etc., siren, dryad. 2. beautiful girl or woman. 3. (zool.) intermediate form between a larva and an insect.
ninfa (II) s. f. (anat.) nympha: each one of the inner labia.
ninfeácea s. f. (bot.) the water-lily family.
ninféia s. f. (bot.) water-lily. ‖ adj. (f. of **ninfeu**) nymphal.
ninfeu adj. nymphal, nymphean.
ninfóide adj. m. + f. nymphlike.
ninfômana s. f. (path.) nymphomaniac.
ninfomania s. f. (path.) nymphomania.
ninfomaníaco adj. (path.) nymphomaniac.
ninfose s. f. (zool.) nymphosis.
ningres-ningres s. m., sg. + pl. (pop.) 1. shy person. 2. a nobody.
ninguém pron. nobody; no one, no man, no person.
ele não vê ~ he sees nobody. ser um joão-ninguém to be a nobody. não há ~? isn't there anybody?
ninhada s. f. 1. nide, clutch, nest(ful), covey. 2. fall, litter. 3. progeny. 4. (fig.) hotbed.

uma ~ de leitões farrow: a litter of pigs. uma ~ de pintos a brood of chicken.
ninhal s. m. (pl. -ais) (Braz.) a flight of birds.
ninharia s. f. insignificance, trifle, nonentity; (sl.) fiddle-faddle, fingle-fangle, flea-bite.
apenas uma ~ a mere trifle. ocupar-se de ~s to peddle: occupy o. s. with trifles.
ninhego adj. taken out of the nest.
ninho s. m. 1. nest. 2. hole, den, lair. 3. (fig.) hiding-place, breeding place, hotbed; comfortable retreat.
~ de águia aerie, aery. ~ de metralhadoras machine-gun nest. ~ de rato (Braz.) an untidy drawer. saíram do ~ they were flown out.
ninivita s. m. + f. (bib.) Ninevite. ‖ adj. Ninevitical.
nióbico adj. (chem.) niobic, niobous.
nióbio s. m. (chem.) niobium, columbium.
niple s. m. (tech.) nipple (plate E 3).
nipônico s. m. Nipponese, Japanese. ‖ adj. Nipponese, Japanese.
níquel s. m. (pl. -eis) nickel (metal and coin).
estou sem um ~ I am broke, pennyless.
niquelagem s. m. (pl. -ens) nickel-plating.
niquelar v. to nickel(-plate).
niqueleira s. f. (S. Braz.) purse, nickel-purse.
niquelífero adj. nickelous, containing nickel.
niquento adj. fussy, paltry, punctilious, pedantic.
niquice s. f. punctiliousness, pedantry, fussiness, peevishness.
nirvana s. m. (rel.) nirvana.
nissei, nisei s. m. + f. Nisei, nisei.
nisso contr. of **em isso** at, in or on that, thereat, therein, thereon, thereby.
nisto contr. of **em isto** at, in or on this, hereat, herein, hereon, hereby.
~ você tem razão in that you are right. não há nada ~ there is nothing in t. onde está a piada ~? where does the joke come in?
nitente adj. m. + f. 1. bright, shining. 2. resistant. 3. clear, distinct.
niteroiense s. m. + f. (Braz.) native or inhabitant of Niterói (former state capital of Rio de Janeiro). ‖ adj. of or referring to Niterói.
nitescência s. f. brightness, splendour.
nitidez s. f. 1. clearness, distinctness. 2. brightness, brilliance. 3. (phot.) sharpness. 4. (memory) vividness. 5. articulateness. 6. nicety.
nítido adj. 1. clear. 2. distinct(ive), well-marked; clear-cut, sharp. 3. explicit, articulate. 4. clean, neat, fair. 5. vivid (memory). 6. brilliant, shining, blazing. ‖ **nitidamente** adv. clearly, etc.
memória -a a fresh memory. ele escreve muito nitidamente he writes a very clear hand, his writing is like a copperplate.
nitrado adj. (chem.) nitrated.
nitrato s. m. (chem.) nitrate.
~ de prata cristalizado lunar caustic.
nitreira s. f. 1. saltpetre mine or works. 2. cesspool; compost heap.
nítrico adj. (chem.) nitric.
ácido ~ nitric acid.
nitrido s. m. neigh, act or sound of neighing.
nitridor s. m. neighing animal. ‖ adj. neighing.
nitrificação s. f. (pl. -ões) (chem.) nitrification.
nitrificar v. (chem.) to nitrify.
nitrir s. m. neigh(ing). ‖ v. to neigh.
nitrito s. m. (chem.) nitrite.
nitro s. m. (chem.) nitre; nitrate; saltpetre.
nitrobactérias s. f. pl. (bact.) nitrobacteria.
nitrogenado, nitrogenoso adj. nitrogenous.
nitrogênio s. m. (chem.) nitrogen, azote.
nitroglicerina s. f. nitroglycerin(e).
nitrômetro s. m. (chem.) nitrometer.

nitroso adj. (chem.) nitrous.
niveal adj. m. + f. (pl. **-ais**) nival: 1. blooming in winter. 2. growing or living in the snow.
nível s. m. (pl. **-eis**) level: 1. water-level, balance level, gauge-glass. 2. horizontality, levelness. 3. plane. 4. level surface; plain. 5. height. 6. (fig.) situation, position, standard, degree; par.
  ~ **de água** water-level. ~ **de bolha de ar** spirit level, air level (plate A 7). ~ **de prumo** plumb rule, plummet. ~ **de retenção** height of swell. ~ **de vida** standard of living. ~ **do lençol de água** water table. ~ **do mar** sea-level. (o) ~ **mais alto** summit level. ~ **perfeito** dead level. **ao** ~ levelly, flush. **passagem de** ~ (plate V 4) level crossing, grade crossing. **este livro é de um** ~ **muito alto** the standard of this book is very high. ~ **social** social level, position.
nivelação s. f. (pl. **-ões**) levelling, grading.
nivelado adj. even, level, flush, flat.
nivelador s. m. leveller, grader, evener. || adj. levelling, grading.
nivelamento s. m. 1. levelling; grading. 2. equalizing, flattening.
nivelar v. to level: 1. grade. 2. equalize, flush. 3. even, flatten. 4. be or put on the same level. 5. raze, destroy.
níveo adj. 1. snowy, white. 2. of or referring to snow.
nivoso s. m. Nivose: sixth month of the French revolutionary calendar. || adj. snowy, covered with or abounding in snow.
no 1. contr. of the prep. **em** and the article **o**: in the, on the. 2. enclitic form of the pron. **o** after a nasal sound: him.
  ~ **jantar** at dinner. ~ **sul** at or in the South. ~ **que me concerne** as far as I am concerned. **jogue-o** ~ **chão** throw him to the ground. **respeitam-**~ they respect him.
nó s. m. knot: 1. knurl, knarl, knag, burl. 2. knob, protuberance. 3. (bot.) node. 4. (fig.) rub, difficulty, problem. 5. (fig.) tie; union. 6. (naut.) division of the log line. 7. knuckle, joint, articulation. 8. bow (ribbon, etc.).
  ~ **cego** love-knot. ~ **corrediço** noose, running knot. ~ **da garganta** Adam's Apple. ~ **na garganta** a lump in the throat. **dar** ~ to tie. **não dar ponto sem** ~ to act on the safe side. **aí é que está o** ~ **da questão** there is the rub. **senti um** ~ **na garganta** I had a lump in my throat. **ter** ~**s pelas costas** to be artful, tricky.
noa s. f. (eccl.) nones.
nobiliário s. m. peerage book. || adj. nobiliary.
nobiliarista s. m. + f. person versed in peerage books or blazonry.
nobiliarquia s. f. 1. peerage book. 2. treatise on blazonry.
nobiliárquico adj. of or referring to blazonry.
nobilitação s. f. ennoblement.
nobilitante adj. m. + f. dignifying; ennobling.
nobilitar v. 1. to ennoble, raise to nobility. 2. to dignify. 3. to glorify, exalt, praise, render illustrous. 4. to aggrandize.
nobre s. m. noble, nobleman, aristocrat; peer, baron, thane; lord. || adj. m. + f. noble: 1. high-bred, aristocratic. 2. knightly, lordlike. 3. generous, chivalrous, gallant. 4. great, grand; high, elevated. 5. dignified. 6. illustrous, honourable. 7. renowned, famous. || ~**mente** adv. nobly.
  o ~ **colega** (in a speech) the honourable gentleman. **de sangue** ~ of aristocratic blood.
nobreza s. f. nobility: 1. aristocracy, gentility; baronage, peerage. 2. nobleness, noble-mindedness. 3. honour, dignity. 4. illustrousness. 5. distinction.

~ **da província** country nobility. ~ **de sentimentos** nobility of sentiments, noble-mindedness.
noção s. f. (pl. **-ões**) notion: 1. idea. 2. conception, impression. 3. inclination, fancy. 4. whim. 5. cognizance, perception. 6. view.
  ~ **esquisita** whims(e)y. **noções superficiais, rudimentares** elements, isagogics.
nocaute s. m. (sport) knock-out.
nocautear v. to knock out (one's opponent in boxing), to render unconscious (by violence).
nocente adj. m. + f. harmful, noxious.
nocional adj. m. + f. (pl. **-ais**) notional. || ~**mente** adv. notionally.
nocividade s. f. noxiousness, harmfulness, perniciousness, ruinousness, badness.
nocivo adj. 1. noxious, harmful, bad, ruinous, malign, pernicious, baneful. 2. poisonous. 3. foul. || **-amente** adv. noxiously.
noctambulação s. f. (pl. **-ões**) (path.) noctambulation.
noctambulismo s. m. (path.) noctambulism, somnambulism, sleep-walking.
noctâmbulo s. m. (path.) noctambulist, somnambulist, sleep-walker. || adj. somnambulistic, noctambulous.
nocticolor adj. m. + f. dark, somber, black.
noctífero adj. (also **noctígeno**) that causes somberness.
noctifloro adj. (bot.) noctiflorous.
noctilúcio s. m. (also **noctiluca** f.) noctiluca. || adj. noctilucal, noctilucent, noctilucous.
noctívago s. m. night-walker. || adj. noctivagant, noctivagous, nocturnal.
noctívolo adj. that flies at night.
nodal adj. m. + f. (pl. **-ais**) nodal.
  ponto ~ nodal point.
nó-de-adão s. m. (pl. **nós-de-adão**, also **pomo-de--adão**) Adam's apple.
nodo s. m. node: 1. (anat.) swelling. 2. (zool.) knot-like part. 3. (astr.) point of intersection of a planet's orbit and the ecliptic.
nódoa s. f. 1. blot, blur, fleck, spot, stain, mark. 2. blemish; dishonour. 3. ignominy; offence.
nodoar v. (also **enodoar**) to spot, stain.
nodosidade s. f. nodosity; knottinèss, kinkiness.
nodoso adj. nodose; knotty; knurly, gnarled; torous; burled.
nódulo s. m. nodule, node, nodus, knot.
noduloso adj. nodular, nodulous, knotty.
noete s. m. umbrella runner.
nogada s. f. 1. blossom of a walnut tree. 2. sweetmeat of nuts. 3. sauce containing nuts.
nogado s. m. 1. nougat. 2. cake made of nuts.
nogueira s. f. walnut: a) the tree. b) its wood.
nogueirado adj. walnut-coloured.
nogueiral s. m. (also **nogal**) (pl. **-ais**) walnut grove, walnut plantation.
nogueira-pecã s. f. (pl. **nogueiras-pecã**, bot.) pecan.
noitada s. f. (also **noutada**) 1. a night's period. 2. vigil, watch. 3. sleeplessness. 4. a night's carousal, night-out. 5. a night of work.
noitão s. m. late hours of the night.
noite s. f. (also **noute**) night: 1. time between dusk and dawn; nighttime, evening. 2. darkness, obscurity. 3. (fig.) ignorance; sadness; period of affliction.
  à ~, **ao anoitecer** in the evening. **à** ~ **ela costumava ler para mim** of an evening she would read to me. **à alta** ~ late at night. **ao cair da** ~ at dusk, at nightfall. **boa-**~! 1. good evening! 2. good night. **de** ~ in the night; nocturnally; at night. **durante a** ~ overnight. **esta** ~, **hoje à** ~ to-night, tonight; this evening. **fazer-se** ~ to become dark, grow late. **horas mortas da** ~ the

dead of night. **passar uma ~ em claro** to have a sleepless night. **passar uma ~ em festa** to make a night of it. **pela calada da ~** in the dead of night. **pela ~ afora** far into the night. **uma ~ em festa** a night out.

noitibó s. m. (ornith., fig.) nighthawk.

noitezinha, noitinha s. f. (also **noutinha**) late afternoon, dusk, nightfall.

noiva s. f. 1. fiancée, girl promised in marriage, betrothed. 2. bride. 3. woman who has just or recently married.
ela ficou ~ de she engaged herself with, she got engaged to. **de ~** bridal. **vestido de ~** bridal dress, wedding dress. **véu de ~** bridal veil.

noivado s. m. 1. wedding day. 2. wedding feast. 3. wedlock, matrimony, espousals. 4. period of engagement; betrothal.
anel de ~ wedding ring. **ela rompeu o seu ~** she broke off her engagement.

noivar v. 1. to become engaged. 2. to court, woo. 3. to honeymoon. 4. to become a bridegroom. 5. to make a marriage settlement.

noivinha s. f. dim. of **noiva**.

noivo s. m. 1. fiancé, betrothed man. 2. bridegroom, groom. 3. man who has just or recently married. 4. **~s** pl. a) engaged couple. b) newlyweds.

nojado adj. (also **anojado**) 1. sad. 2. disgustful; disgusted.

nojento adj. 1. nauseating, sickening. 2. repulsive, repugnant; sordid. 3. loathsome, tedious. 4. disgusting. ‖ **-amenet** adv. repulsively, disgustingly, etc.

nojo s. m. 1. nausea, qualm. 2. repulsiveness, repugnance. 3. loathing. 4. cause of nausea or vomit. 5. disgust, annoyance. 6. sorrow, grief; sadness. 7. mourning.
causar ou dar ~ to sicken. **sentir ou ter ~ de** to feel sick about, to keck at. **é de dar ~** it is enough to make one sick, gives one the pip. **tomar ~** to go into mourning.

nojoso adj. 1. qualmish, sickening. 2. disgustful, loathsome. 3. in mourning.

nolição s. f. (pl. **-ões**) unwillingness.

no-lo contr. of the personal pronouns **nos** and **lo**.
é um bom livro; o professor no-lo deu it is a good book; the teacher gave it to us.

noma s. m. (med.) noma.

nômada, nômade s. m. 1. nomad. 2. **~s** pl. nomad tribes. ‖ adj. m. + f. 1. nomad(ic), wandering, vagrant, errant. 2. vagabond.

nomadismo s. m. nomadism.

nomancia s. f. divination by the letters of a proper name.

nomarca s. m. (hist.) nomarch.

nomarcado s. m. a nomarch's government or function.

nomarquia s. f. nomarchy: province of modern Greece.

nome s. m. name: 1. title of a thing or person; designation, appelation, denomination (plates C 5, L 4, V 4). 2. reputation, fame, renown. 3. lineage, family, clan, descent. 4. (gram.) noun, substantive. 5. nickname.
~ de batismo Christian name. **~ de família** surname. **~ próprio** (gram.) proper name. **~ de guerra** popular name or nickname for business purposes. **bom ~** reputation. **chamar ~s** to call names. **dar novo ~ a** to rename. **dar ~** 1. to name. 2. to nickname. 3. to make famous. **de ~** 1. adj. named. 2. by name. 3. from hearsay. **conheço-o de ~** I know him by name. **em ~ da lei!** in the name of the law. **o advogado age em ~ de seu cliente** the lawyer acts for his client. **qual é o seu ~?** what is your name? **sem ~** 1. nameless. 2. unspeakable, infamous.

nomeação s. f. (pl. **-ões**) 1. nomination, appointment, appointing, calling. 2. right to nominate or appoint. **de, relativo ou sujeito a ~** appointive. **nova ~** reappointment. **~ efetiva** effective appointment.

nomeada s. f. good name, reputation, renown, fame.

nomeado adj. 1. nominated, appointed, designated. 2. named.

nomeador s. m., **nomeante** m. + f. appointer, designator, nominator. ‖ adj. appointing, designating.

nomear v. 1. to name, give a name, denominate. 2. to call (by name). 3. to institute, create, constitute. 4. to designate, appoint, nominate, assign. 5. **~-se** to entitle o. s.
nomeamo-lo diretor we made him manager. **~ cavalheiro** to knight. **~ um professor** to appoint a master.

nomenclador s. m. nomenclator: person who classifies things and gives them names. ‖ adj. denominating or classifying.

nomenclar v. to classify and give names to.

nomenclatura s. f. 1. nomenclature. 2. terminology (plate N 1). 3. list, catalogue.

nomenclaturar v. to nomenclature, to classify and/or give names to.

nômina s. f. 1. little bag to keep an amulet in; phylactory. 2. amulet (in form of a written piece of paper). 3. brass stud.

nominação s. f. (pl. **-ões**) coining or giving a name to, denomination.

nominal adj. m. + f. (pl. **-ais**) nominal: 1. of or referring to a name or names. 2. existing in name only. 3. not actual, unreal. ‖ **~mente** adv. nominally.
valor ~ (com.) face value. **cheque ~** nominal check made out in the name of the payee.

nominalismo s. m. (philos.) nominalism: doctrine that denies the existence of the universals.

nominalista s. m. + f. (philos.) nominalist. ‖ adj. nominalistic.

nominativo s. m. (gram.) nominative.

nomo s. m. nome: a province of modern Greece or ancient Egypt.

nomografia s. f. nomography: the art of drafting laws or a treatise on it.

nomográfico adj. nomographic(al).

nomograma s. m. (math.) nomogram.

nomologia s. f. nomology.

nona s. f. 1. verse of nine lines. 2. (obs.) sister, member of a sisterhood. ‖ adj. ninth.

nonada s. f. (also **ninharia**) trifle, bagatelle, nonentity.

nonagenário s. m. nonagenarian. ‖ adj. nonagenarian.

nonagésimo s. m. ninetieth. ‖ adj. ninetieth, nonagesimal.

nonas s. f. pl. (eccl.) nones.

nó-nas-tripas s. m. (med., pop.) (pl. **nós-nas-tripas**) volvulus.

nonato s. m. (S. Braz.) a slaughtered cow's foetus.

nongentésimo, noningentésimo adj. nine hundredth.

nônio s. m. nonius, vernier.

nono s. m. (obs.) friar, monk. ‖ adj. ninth.
em ~ lugar ninthly.

nônuplo s. m. ninefold quantity. ‖ adj. ninefold.

nopal s. m. (pl. **-ais**) (bot.) nopal.

noque s. m. (Braz., also **anoque**) place or vessel where hides are tanned.

nora s. f. 1. daughter-in-law. 2. noria, scoop-wheel, kibble chain.
~ de rosário (tech.) chaplet.

norça s. f. (bot.) bryony.

nordestal adj. m. + f. (pl. **-ais**) northeasterly.

nordeste s. m. 1. northeast. 2. northeastern Brazil. 3. northeaster (wind).

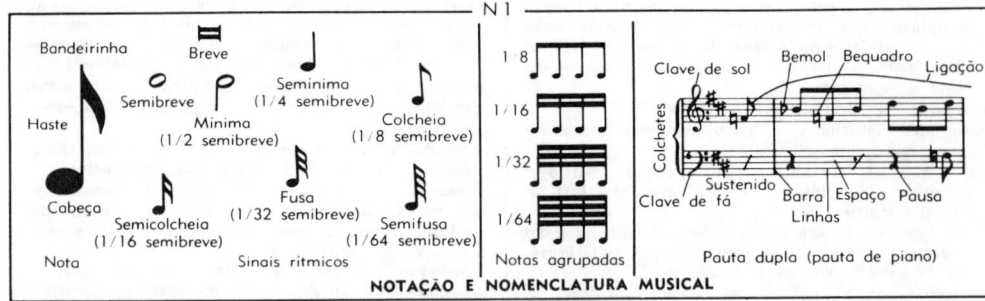

NOTAÇÃO E NOMENCLATURA MUSICAL

do ~, **para o** ~ northeastwardly. **em direção ao** ~ northeastward. **no** ~ northeastern.

nordestear v. to steer or point (needle) northeastward.

nordésteo adj. of the northeast, northeastern.

nordestia s. f. cold northeast wind.

nordestino s. m. native or inhabitant of northeastern Brazil.

nórdico s. m. Nordic; Northman. ǁ adj. Nordic.

nórico s. m. Noric. ǁ adj. Noric.

norma s. f. norm: 1. principle, direction. 2. precept, rule. 3. type, standard. 4. pattern, form, model. ~ **prática** rule of thumb. ~ **vigente** regime. ~ **de conduta,** ~ **de ação** standard of conduct, rule of behaviour.

normal s. m. (pl. **-ais**) normal: 1. one who or that which is normal. 2. f. (geom.) perpendicular line. ǁ adj. m. + f. normal, regular, natural. ǁ **~mente** adv. normally, in an ordinary way. **escola** ~ normal school. **pressão** ~ (med.) normal pressure.

normalidade s. f. normality, normalness.

normalista s. m. + f. pupil of a normal school. ǁ adj. said of pupils or the courses of a normal school.

normalização s. f. (pl. **-ões**) normalization; adjustment.

normalizar v. 1. to normalize; adjust. 2. to make according to a norm. 3. to return to normal.

normando s. m. 1. Norseman. 2. Norman: a) native or inhabitant of Normandy. b) the language there spoken (Norman-French). ǁ adj. Norman.

normativo adj. normative, preceptive, standard.

normócito s. m. (med.) normocyte.

normógrafo s. m. device to draw letter(ing)s.

nor-nordeste s. m. north-northeast. ǁ adj. north-northeast.

nor-noroeste s. m. north-northwest. ǁ adj. north-northwest.

noroeste s. m. northwest: 1. direction between north and west. 2. wind from that direction, northwester. **a** ~ northwestward. **do** ~ northwestwardly, northwestern, northwesterly. **habitante do** ~ (U. S. A.) northwester. **para o** ~ northwestward(ly).

noroestear v. to steer or point (needle) northwestward.

norreno adj. (also **nórdico**) Nordic.

nortada s. f. cold north wind.

norte s. m. 1. north. 2. northward. 3. northern regions. 4. pole-star. 5. (fig.) guide, rule, direction. ǁ adj. north; northward; northern. **do** ~ northern, boreal. **em direção ao** ~, **para o** ~ northwardly, northwards. **mais ao** ~ northernmost. **latitude** ~ north latitude. **perder o** ~ (fig.) to lose one's head. **vento** ~ norther.

norteador adj. guiding, directing.

norteamento s. m. guidance, direction, orientation.

norte-americano s. m. (pl. **norte-americanos**) North American, native of the U. S. A. ǁ adj. North American.

nortear v. 1. to indicate the north, point or steer northwards. 2. to guide, direct, lead.

norte-europeu s. m. (pl. **norte-europeus**) a North European (person). ǁ adj. North European, referring to North Europe.

nortista s. m. + f. 1. northerner. 2. (Braz.) native of the north, from Bahia upwards, esp. Maranhão, Pará and Amazonas. 3. (U. S. A., hist.) Copperhead. ǁ adj. of or pertaining to the north.

noruega s. f. 1. (S. Braz.) cool and moist hillside. 2. cold wind. 3. **Noruega:** Norway.

noruegal s. m. (pl. **-ais**) (S. Braz.) an extensive **noruega** (sense 1).

norueguês s. m. (pl. **-eses**) (f. **-esa**) Norwegian: 1. native or inhabitant of Norway. 2. language of the Norwegians.

nos contr. of the prep. **em** and the article m. pl. **os:** at, in the, in the, on the. ǁ pron. complement of the first person pl. (to) us, ourselves. ǁ enclitic form of the pron. **os** after a nasal sound: them. ~ **livros** in the books. ~ **telhados** on the roofs. **visitaram-~** they came to see us. **mandam-~ trabalhar** they send them to work.

nós pron. 1. we. 2. us. ~ **mesmos** (we) ourselves. ~ **nos ferimos** we hurt ourselves. ~ **todos** all of us. ~ **três** the three of us. **entre** ~ between us. **olhamos em redor de** ~ we looked about us.

nosocômico adj. (also **nosocomial** m. + f., pl. **-ais**) nosocomial.

nosocômio s. m. hospital.

nosofobia s. f. (path.) nosophobia: fear of diseases.

nosófobo s. m. (med.) person suffering from nosophobia.

nosogenia s. f. 1. development of diseases. 2. its study.

nosografia s. f. (med.) nosography.

nosologia s. f. (med.) nosology.

nosológico adj. (med.) nosological.

nosologista s. m. + f., **nosólogo** m. (med.) nosologist.

nosomania s. f. (path.) nosomania.

nossa-amizade s. f. (Braz., joc.) old chap, chum.

nosso adj. our, ours. ǁ pron. our, ours. ~ **pão de cada dia** our daily bread. **Nossa Senhora** Our Lady, Madonna. **o tempo é** ~ the time is ours. **os ~s** our relatives, our folks. **ele é dos ~s** he is a friend of ours.

nostalgia s. f. homesickness, nostalgia. **estou com** ~ I am sick for home. **sofrer** ~ to be homesick.

nostálgico adj. homesick, nostalgic.

nota s. f. note: 1. act or fact of noting. 2. distinctive mark or sign. 3. reminder. 4. annotation; chit. 5. attention, heed. 6. mark, grade. 7. notice, observation. 8. notification, short informal letter. 9. diplomatic memorandum. 10. comment, explanation. 11. bill (restaurant), account. 12. bank-note; (sl.) yellow boy. 13. printed acknowledgement of debt. 14. musical sign (plate N 1); melody, tune; voice. 15. reputation, fame. ~ **de despacho** forwarding note. ~ **falsa** counterfeit bill. ~ **fundamental** (mus.) fundamental. ~ **marginal** side-note. ~ **ornamental** (mus.) grace note. ~ **promissória** note of hand, promissory note, bill. ~ **tônica** (mus.) keynote. **de boa (má)** ~ of good (evil) reputation. **digno de** ~ noteworthy. **preciso tomar** ~ **disto** I must write this down. **tomar** ~ to (make a) note, commit to paper. ~ **fiscal** a formal bill of sale.

notabilidade s. f. notability: 1. noteworthiness, remarkableness, conspicuousness. 2. remarkable person, person of note.

notabilizar v. to fame, make or become notable, renowned; to shine.

notação s. f. (pl. **-ões**) notation: representation by signs, figures, ect. (also mus.) (plate N 1).

notado adj. 1. noted. 2. notable. 3. remarkable, conspicuous. ‖ **-amente** adv. notedly.

notador s. m. noter: person who notes or observes. ‖ adj. noting, observing.

notalgia s. f. (path.) notalgia: pain in the back.

notar v. 1. to note: a) mark, provide with marks. b) notice, observe, remark. c) mind. d) make a notice of, set down in writing. 2. to find strange or odd. 3. to rebuke, censure, reproach. 4. to record. 5. to enter into public register. **note bem!** for notice! **eu bem notei a observação** I well noticed the remark. **precisamos** ~ **que** we must have in mind that. **eu notei a sua ausência** I missed him.

notariado s. m. office or profession of a notary; conveyancing.

notarial adj. m. + f. (pl. **-ais**) notarial: of or referring to a notary.

notário s. m. notary (public); conveyancer.

notável adj. m. + f. (pl. **-áveis**) 1. notable. 2. noticeable. 3. noteworthy. 4. considerable, remarkable. 5. important, famous. 6. (socially) prominent, eminent. 7. conspicuous. 8. great, wonderful. 9. strange, amazing. ‖ **notavelmente** adv. notably, etc. **um homem** ~ a man of consequence. **pessoa** ~ notable.

notícia s. f. 1. news, piece of news, information, tidings. 2. report, word, notice. 3. knowledge. 4. note, annotation. 5. summary. 6. memory, remembrance. 7. biography. **ser** ~ to be newsworthy. **~s comerciais** city news. **~s de primeira mão** first-hand news. ~ **exagerada** (Engl.) canard. ~ **falsa** misintelligence. **~s infundadas** false report. **as ~s espalham-se rapidamente** the news run like wildfire. **as ~s são boas** the news is good. **agência de ~s** news agency. **aguardamos as suas breves ~s** (com.) we are looking forward to your early good news. **boas ~s sobre** glad tidings of. **conforme ~s** as per advice. **dar ~s (de, sobre)** to inform about. **mandou ~s** he wrote word. **más ~s** bad news, Job's post. **quais são as ~s** what is the news? **trazer ~s** to bring word.

noticiador s. m. informer, reporter. ‖ adj. informative.

noticiar v. 1. to notify, inform, give word. 2. to notice. 3. to announce. 4. to publish. 5. to advertise. 6. to report.

noticiário s. m. 1. news section of a newspaper. 2. news, news service (also for broadcasting, television).

noticiarismo s. m. (Braz.) the class of newsmen or reporters.

noticiarista s. m. + f. reporter, news writer.

noticioso adj. 1. of or referring to news. 2. informative. 3. (coll.) newsy. **agência -a** press bureau, news agency.

notificação s. f. (pl. **-ões**) 1. notification, notice, communication. 2. announcement. 3. summons, citation. 4. warning. ~ **do imposto de renda** income tax notification. ~ **compulsória** compulsory notification.

notificador s. m. notifier, informer. ‖ adj. (also **notificante** m. + f.) notifying, informative.

notificar v. 1. to notify, communicate, inform. 2. to make known. 3. to summon, intimate; garnish. 4. to warn. 5. to bill. **prazo para** ~ **a cessação** term for giving notice.

notificativo, notificatório adj. informative, that notifies.

notificável adj. m. + f. (pl. **-áveis**) notifiable.

noto s. m. notus, south wind. ‖ adj. notorious, known.

notocórdio s. m. (anat.) notochord.

notoriedade s. f. 1. notoriety, notoriousness. 2. publicness, publicity, patency. 3. prominency, egregiousness.

notório adj. notorious, widely known, public. ‖ **notoriamente** adv. notoriously. **uma injustiça -a** a crying wrong. **tornar-se** ~ to become known, come into notice. **um patife** ~ an arrant scoundrel.

nótula s. f. brief note, notice or commentary.

noturnal adj. m. + f. (also **nocturnal**, pl. **-ais**) nocturnal.

noturno s. m. (also **nocturno**) 1. (Catholic liturgy) part of the evening service. 2. (mus.) nocturne. 3. (ent.) moth. 4. (ornit.) night bird. 5. (Braz.) night train. ‖ adj. nocturnal, nightly; wandering or moving at night ‖ **-amente** adv. nocturnally. **carta telegráfica -a** night letter. **escola -a** night-school. **trabalho** ~ night-work. **guarda-~** night watchman.

nova s. f. (also **notícia, novidade**) news; tidings. **boas (más) ~s** good (bad) news.

novação s. f. (pl. **-ões**) 1. renewal (contract). 2. change, innovation.

novador s. m. news bringer; innovator. ‖ adj. innovating.

nova-iorquino s. m. New Yorker.

nova-seita s. f. (pl. **novas-seitas**) (N. E. Braz.) protestant.

novato s. m. 1. beginner, novice; greenhorn. (sl.) tenderfoot, Johnny Raw. 2. apprentice. 3. (university) freshman. 4. (Braz., hist.) nickname of newly arrived Portuguese. 5. new-comer. 6. (fig.) fledgling. ‖ adj. inexperienced, raw, untrained, ingenuous; youngish.

nove s. m. nine. ‖ adj. nine. ~ **de copas** nine of hearts (plate B 5). **o** ~ **de ouros** (cards) nine of diamonds, (sl.) the curse of Scotland. ~ **vezes mais** ninefold.

novecentos adj. nine hundred.

novedio s. m. shoot, sprout, sprig, bud. ‖ adj. young.

nove-horas s. f. pl. (Braz., coll.) airs; ceremonies; ado. **cheio de** ~ full of airs; standing on ceremonies; fussy; overpolite.

novel adj. m. + f. (pl. **novéis**) 1. new. 2. fresh. 3. beginning. 4. inexperienced, without training, raw.

novela s. f. 1. novel. 2. narration, tale, story. 3. plot; fabrication. ~ **de rádio,** ~ **de televisão** soap opera. ~ **emocionante** thriller. ~ **policial** detective story; (sl.) whodunit.

novelar v. to write novels.

noveleiro s. m. 1. novelist. 2. newsmonger, telltale. ‖ adj. 1. novelistic. 2. telltale.

novelesco adj. novelistic, novellike.

novelista s. m. + f. novelist. ‖ adj. scheming, plotting, intriguing.

novelo (ê) s. m. 1. ball (of yarn), clue, hank, skein. 2. (fig.) mess, hodgepodge; intrigue. 3. (bot.) guelder rose.

novelo-da-china s. m. (pl. **novelos-da-china**) (bot.) hortensia.

novembro s. m. November.

novena s. f. 1. space of nine days. 2. (R. C. rel.) novena: prayer or devotion repeated during nine days. 3. a group of nine (persons or objects). 4. (Braz., hist.) nine-day flogging of slaves.

novenal adj. m. + f. (pl. -ais) of or referring to a **novena.**

novenário s. m. (R. C., rel.) prayer book containing novenae.

novênio s. m. space of nine years.

noveno adj. ninth (referring to day of sickness).

noventa s. m. ninety. ‖ adj. ninety.

noviciado s. m. 1. novitiate, noviciate. 2. apprenticeship. 3. duration of the novitiate or apprenticeship.

noviciar v. 1. (rel.) to be a novice. 2. to be an apprentice. 3. to start, begin, try out.

noviciaria s. f. (rel.) novitiate, noviciate: section of a convent where novices live or are instructed.

noviciário adj. of or referring to novices.

noviço s. m. novice: 1 (eccl.) person on probation in a religious house. 2. apprentice, beginner, tyro. 3. probationer. 4. freshman. 5. neophyte. ‖ adj. inexperienced, new, unfledged, green.

novidade s. f. 1. newness; recentness; youngness. 2. novelty; new fangle. 3. news, tidings. 4. latest fashion. 5. (Braz.) unforessen trouble, mishap. 6. new fruit of the season. 7. harvest, crop. 8. agitation.
cheio de ~s (Braz.) full of airs. **há alguma ~?** anything doing?, any news? **sem ~** in good order. **a última ~** the latest thing. **uma ~** a piece of news.

novidadeiro s. m. 1. newsmonger, gossiper. 2. telltale, intriguer.

novilha s. m. heifer.

novilhada s. f. 1. group or quantity of bullocks. 2. bullfight.

novilho s. m. bullock; steer.

novilunar adj. m. + f. novilunar.

novilúnio s. m. new moon.

novíssimos s. m. pl. (eccl.) man's ultimate purpose. ‖ **novíssimo** adj. (abs. sup. of **novo**) newest, latest.

novo (ô) s. m. 1. new. 2. coming (next) crop. 3. **~s** pl. young (people). ‖ adj. 1. young. 2. new, recent, novel. 3. fresh; green. 4. original. 5. strange. 6. unused, not worn. 7. inexperienced. ‖ **-amente** adv. again, once more, newly, afresh, over, over and again; yet.
~ em folha fire-new, brand new, spick-and-span. **o Novo Mundo** the New World. **começar de ~** to make a new start. **de ~** anew, over again, afresh. **Novo Testamento** (rel.) New Testament. **lua -a** new moon. **que há de ~?** what's cooking? what is the news? **sempre de ~** time and again. **voltar de ~** to come again. **fazer tudo -amente** to do all over again. **tentar -amente** to try once more.

novocaína s. f. (pharm.) novocaine.

novo-rico s. m. (pl. **novos-ricos**) new rich.

nóxio adj. noxious.

noz s. f. nut; walnut.
~ branca butternut. **~ de caju** cashew-nut. **casca de ~** nutshell.

noz-moscada s. f. (pl. **nozes-moscadas**) nutmeg.

noz-vômica s. f. (pl. **nozes-vômicas**) nux vomica, poison nut.

nu s. m. (arts.) nude. ‖ adj. 1. nude, naked, undressed, uncovered. 2. bare, barren. 3. crude. 4. simple; sincere. 5. plain, without ornaments, artless. 6. unsheathed, drawn (sword). ‖ **nuamente** adv. nudely, etc.
~ em pêlo stark-naked.. **a olho ~** with the naked eye. **~ artístico** (artistic) nude. **pôr a ~** uncover, unveil, disclose. **verdade nua e crua** the naked truth.

nuança s. f. nuance, hue, shade.

nubente s. m. + f. betrothed. ‖ adj. betrothed.

nubífero adj. (poet.) nubiferous, bringing clouds, cloudy.

nubífugo adj. (poet.) dissolving clouds.

nubígeno adj. (poet.) cloud-born.

núbil adj. m. + f. (pl. **núbeis**) marriageable, nubile. **não ~** unmarriageable.

nubilar s. m. wheat barn.

nubilidade s. f. marriageability, marriageableness, nubility.

nubiloso adj. cloudy, foggy, misty.

núbio s. m. Nubian. ‖ adj. Nubian.

nubívago adj. (poet.) 1. travelling in the clouds. 2. (fig.) sublime.

nublado adj. 1. cloudy. 2. dark, obscure, somber. 3. overcast, skyless. 4. sad, gloomy. 5. uneasy, anxious. 6. blurred.

nublar v. to cloud: 1. become cloudy, cover with clouds, overcloud. 2. darken, obscure; shadow. 3. sadden, render sullen.

nubloso adj. clouded, cloudy: 1. covered with clouds, overcast, misty. 2. gloomy, sullen, sad.

nuca s. f. neck; nape; scruff (plate C 12, 18).
agarrar pela ~ to take by the neck.

nucal adj. m. + f. (pl. -ais) of or referring to the neck or nape.

nução s. f. (pl. -ões) 1. assent, acquiescence. 2. discretion.

nucela s. f. (bot.) nucellus.

nuciforme adj. m. + f. nuciform, nut-shaped.

nucífrago adj. nut-cracking.

nucívoro adj. nucivorous, nut-eating.

nucleal adj. m. + f. (pl. -ais) (also **nuclear**) nuclear.

nuclear v. to nucleate. ‖ adj. m. + f. nuclear, nucleated.
ciência ~ nucleonics. **engenharia ~** nuclear engineering. **física ~** nuclear physics.

nucleário adj. nucleary.

nucleífero adj. nucleiferous.

nucleiforme adj. m. + f. nucleiform.

núcleo s. m. 1. nucleus. 2. center, middle, essential part. 3. core, kernel. 4. seat. 5. pick, choicest part. **~ atômico** atomic nucleous. **~ social** social nucleus.

nucleolado adj. nucleolated.

nucléolo s. m. nucleolus.

núcleon s. m. (nucl. phys.) nucleon.

nucleoproteína s. f. nucleoprotein.

nuclídeo s. m. (nucl. phys.) nuclide.

núcula s. f. nutlet.

nucular adj. m. + f. 1. of or referring to nuts. 2. that contains a nut.

nudação s. f. (pl. -ões) 1. undressing, stripping. 2. nakedness, nudity.

nudez(a) s. f. 1. nakedness, nudity, nudeness, bareness. 2. (fig.): a) simplicity. b) dryness. c) barrenness. d) privation, want, poorness.

nudibrânquio adj. (zool.) nudibranch.

nudicaule adj. m. + f. (bot.) nudicaul.

nudípede adj. m. + f. nudiped.

N 2

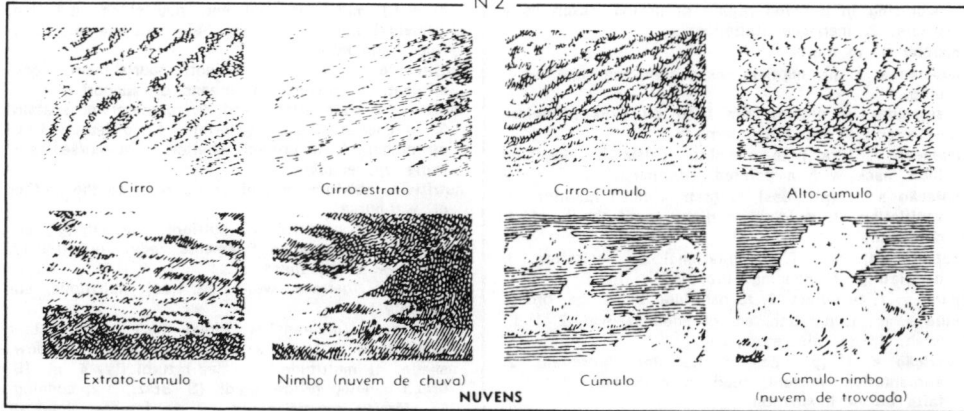

Cirro · Cirro-estrato · Cirro-cúmulo · Alto-cúmulo

Extrato-cúmulo · Nimbo (nuvem de chuva) · Cúmulo · Cúmulo-nimbo (nuvem de trovoada)

NUVENS

nudismo s. m. nudism: cult of the nude, practice of going naked.

nudista s. m. + f. nudist: person who practises nudism.

nuelo adj. 1. new-born. 2. unfeathered, unfledged.

nuga s. f. trifle.

nugá s. m. nougat: candy made of nuts.

nugação s. f. (pl. **-ões**) 1. ridiculous sophism. 2. vain argument.

nugacidade s. f. 1. futility; trifle. 2. frivolity. 3. joke.

nugativo, nugatório adj. 1. trifling, futile, trivial. 2. worthless, vain, frivolous. 3. ridiculous.

nulidade s. f. 1. nullity. 2. voidness, invalidity. 3. inaptitude; negation. 4. unimportant person, non-entity, nobody. 5. insignificancy, nothingness.

nulificação s. f. (pl. **-ões**) nullification.

nulifacador adj. nullifying.

nulificar v. to nullify, annull, cancel.

nulo adj. 1. null, void, invalid. 2. unable, inept. 3. vain, effectless, useless, worthless. 4. zero, none, nought. 5. frivolous. ‖ **nulamente** adv. voidly, vainly, etc.

tornar ~ to nullify.

num(a) contr. of the prep. **em** and **um(a):** at a (one), in a (one), on a (one).

num abrir e fechar de olhos in two shakes of a duck's tail, in a twinkling. **num baile** at a ball. **numa parede** on a wall.

numária s. f. numismatics: science of coins and medals.

numário adj. numismatic(al).

nume s. m. 1. (ancient Rome) numen. 2. deity. 3. (poet.) genius, inspiration.

~ **tutelar** tutelary spirit.

númeno s. m. (metaphysics) noumenon.

numeração s. f. (pl. **-ões**) 1. numeration: art of forming, writing and reading numbers. 2. numbering. 3. enumeration. 4. foliation.

numerado adj. 1. numbered. 2. in numerical order. **não** ~ 1. numberless. 2. unnumbered.

numerador s. m. 1. numberer, numerator. 2. numbering machine. ‖ adj. numerative.

numeral s. m. (gram., pl. **-ais**) numeral. ‖ adj. m. + f. numeral, numeric(al).

numerar v. 1. to number: provide with or indicate by numbers. 2. to enumerate; numerate. 3. to expose, explain. 4. to count. 5. to figure.

numerário s. m. money, cash; coin; specie(s). ‖ adj. nummary: of or referring to money or coins.

numerável adj. m. + f. (pl. **-áveis**) numerable.

numérico adj. numeric(al), numeral. ‖ **numericamente** adv. numerically.

número s. m. number: 1. cypher, mark, figure (plate E 13). 2. quantity, index, amount. 3. abundancy, multitude. 4. numeral. 5. series. 6. unity. 7. volume (of a periodical). 8. number of a show or vaudeville act; event. 9. size. 10. (gram.) singular or plural. 11. harmony of style and verse.

~ **atômico** atomic number. ~**s arábicos** Arabic numerals or figures. ~ **atrasado (de revista, jornal, etc.)** back number. ~ **cardinal** cardinal number. ~ **composto** composite number. ~ **de ordem** reference number. ~ **de página** page number. ~ **fracionário** fractional number. ~ **ímpar** odd number. ~ **misto** mixed number. ~ **múltiplo** composite (number). ~ **ordinal** ordinal (number). ~ **par** even number. ~ **quadrado** square (number). ~ **redondo** round (number). **fazer** ~ (fig. + coll.) to fill the number; to be an "also". **sem-**~ countless, uncountable. **ele é mesmo um** ~ (fig. + coll.) he really is a funny guy.

numerosidade s. f. numerousness.

numeroso adj. 1. numerous, plentiful, copious, abounding. 2. rhyming, harmonious, melodious.

númida s. m. + f. Numidian. ‖ adj. Numidian.

numiforme adj. m. + f. (also **numismal, numular**) coin-shaped.

numismata s. m. + f. numismatist; mintman.

numismática s. f. (also **numulária**) numismatics: science of coins, medals, etc.

numismático adj. numismatical.

numismatografia s. f. numismatography.

numismatógrafo s. m. numismatologist.

nunca adv. 1. never, ne'er, at no time; ever. 2. no. ~ **farei isto!** catch me doing this! ~ **mais** never more. ~ **se pode saber** you can never tell. **mais do que** ~ more than ever. **quase** ~ hardly ever. **seria um** ~ **acabar** there would be no end to it.

núncia s. f. female messenger, harbinger.

nunciativo adj. bearing news.

nunciatura s. f. 1. nunciature, dignity of a nuncio. 2. residence of a nuncio. 3. (eccl.) tribunal subordinate to a nuncio.

núncio s. m. 1. (eccl.) nuncio; legate. 2. messenger; harbinger.

nuncupação s. m. nuncupation.

nuncupativo, nuncupatório adj. nuncupative, nuncupatory: (of wills) oral, not written.

nunes s. m. odd number. ‖ adj. m. + f., sg. + pl. odd (not even).

nupcial adj. m. + f. (pl. **-ais**) nuptial, bridal, spousal.

nupcialidade s. f. 1. marriage rate, the marriages occurring in a given region or period, taken as a whole. 2. marriage statistics.

nupciar v. to marry.

núpcias s. f. pl. nuptials, espousals, marriage, wedding. **segundas** ~ digamy. **um filho de suas primeiras** ~ a son of his first marriage.

nuquear v. (Braz.) to slaughter cattle by punching their neck with a pointed iron bar.

nutação s. f. (pl. -ões) 1. (astr. + bot.) nutation. 2. vacillation. 3. nodding or drooping of the head. 4. dizziness.

nutante adj. m. + f. 1. nutational. 2. hesitating. 3. oscillating. 4. nodding; drooping .

nutar v. 1. to nutate. 2. to oscillate. 3. to nod, droop.

nuto s. m. 1. nutation, act of nodding, nod. 2. (fig.) wish, desire, discretion.

nutrição s. f. (pl. -ões) 1. nutrition, nutriment. 2. alimentation, nurture, feed, nourishment. **falta de** ~ innutrition.

nutrício adj. = **nutritivo.**

nutricionismo s. m. the systematic study of nutritional problems.

nutricionista s. m. + f. nutritionist. ‖ adj. nutritional.

nutrido adj. 1. fed, well-fed, nourished. 2. robust, strong, corpulent. 3. continued, continual (fire, combustion).

nutridor s. m. nourisher, feeder. ‖ adj. (also **nutriente** m. + f.) nutritious, nutrient, nourishing, nutritive.

nutrimental adj. m. + f. (pl. -ais) nutrimental, nutritious, alimental.

nutrimento s. m. 1. nutriment, nourishment; food, aliment. 2. sustenance; means of support.

nutrir v. 1. to nourish, feed. 2. to maintain, sustain. 3. to cherish, foster, entertain. 4. to fatten. 5. to strengthen. 6. to protect, shelter. 7. to nurse, rear, bring up, educate.

nutrício, nutrítico adj. of or referring to the mother or wet-nurse.

nutritivo adj. nutritious, nutrient, nourishing, alimental, alimentative. ‖ **-amente** adv. nutritiously. **poder** ~ nutritiveness.

nutriz s. f. fostress, wet-nurse. ‖ adj. nutritious, alimentary.

nuvem s. f. (pl. -ens) 1. cloud; haze, mist, pother (plate N 2). 2. (fig.): a) gloom, sadness. b) shadow, shade. c) multitude. 3. (med.) turbidity. 4. m. (S. Braz.) cunning fellow. ‖ adj. (S. Braz.) sly, cunning. ~ **atômica** atomic cloud. ~ **de fumaça** cloud of smoke, trail of steam. ~ **pequena, nuvenzinha** cloudlet. **-ns de neblina** streaks of mist. **cair das -ns** to be flabbergasted. **coberto de -ns** overcast, cloudy. **ir às -ns** (fig.) to give vent, explode. **em brancas ~s** 1. to live in ease and comfort. 2. to pass unnoticed (event).

nuvioso adj. overcast, cloudy.

O

O, o s. m. 1. the fourteenth letter of the Portuguese alphabet. 2. the fourteenth of an order or class. 3. zero, cipher. 4. (minuscule) symbol for degree. ‖ article (m.) the. ‖ pron. 1. it, him, to him. 2. you, to you.
eu ~ avisei mas ele não me atendeu I warned him but he didn't care.
ó interj. o!, oh!, wo!, hallo!
~ garção, traga-me o café! waiter, bring me the coffee! **~ de casa!** hello in there!, anybody home?
oanaçu s. m. (Braz., bot.) curua (palm).
oaristo s. m. 1. intimate chat (esp. of man and wife). 2. intercourse.
oasiano s. m. native or inhabitant of an oasis. ‖ adj. (also **oásico**) oasitic.
oásis s. m., sg. + pl. oasis: 1. fertile spot in a waste or desert. 2. (fig.) resting place, comfort.
oba interj. whoopee!
obarana s. f. (Braz., ichth.) ladyfish.
obcecação s. f. (pl. -ões) 1. blindness. 2. (fig.) contumacy, obduracy, stubbornness, persistency in the error; delusion.
obcecado adj. 1. incomprehensive, unreasoning; blind. 2. contumacious, stubborn. 3. bewildered.
obcecante adj. m. + f. blinding, dazzling, detrimental to good judgement.
obcecar v. 1. to blind. 2. to obscure, obfuscate, confuse. 3. to bewilder, fascinate. 4. to obsess. 5. to root in error.
obcláveo adj. (bot., zool.) obclavate, inversely clavate.
obcônico adj. obconical, inversely conical.
obcordado adj., **obcordiforme** m. + f. (bot.) obcordate, inversely heart-shaped.
obducto adj. 1. covered. 2. hidden, secret.
obduração s. f. (pl. -ões) 1. obduracy, obdurateness. 2. obstinacy, persistency.
obdurar v. 1. to obdurate, harden. 2. to persist. 3. to indurate, make or become unfeeling.
obeba s. f. (Braz., ichth.) cabezon, a croaker (Larinus breviceps).
obedecer v. 1. to obey. 2. to execute, comply with (order, request). 3. to subordinate, submit. 4. to follow, mind. 5. (fig.) to listen. 6. to yield.
~ cegamente to obey blindly. **ele me obedece** he obeys me. **o menino já não obedece ao professor** the boy has got beyond his master's control. **~ a um regulamento** to obey a regulation.
obediência s. f. 1. obedience, submission, subordination, compliance, submissiveness. 2. allegiance, dependence, subservience. 3. duteousness, dutifulness. 4. humility.
obediente adj. m. + f. (also **obedecedor**) 1. obedient, submissive, compliant. 2. allegiant, observant. 3. dutiful. 4. biddable, docile, amenable. 5. humble, meek. ‖ **~mente** adv. obediently, obeyingly.
~ à lei law-abiding. **o Zezinho é um menino ~** Joey is an obedient nice boy.
obélio(n) s. m. (anat.) obelion.
obeliscal adj. m. + m. (pl. -ais) obeliscal.
obelisco s. m. 1. obelisk. 2. obelisklike object.
óbelo s. m. obelus: mark for doubtful passages in old manuscripts.
oberado adj. 1. indebted, overloaded with expenses. 2. pawned, mortgaged.
oberar v. 1. to run into debt, burden with debts. 2. to impose obligations.
obesidade s. f. 1. obesity, obeseness; fatness, corpulence. 2. paunchiness, plumpness.

obeso adj. 1. obese, fat, corpulent. 2. paunchy. ‖ **-amente** adv. obesely.
obfirmado adj. 1. firm, resolute. 2. contumacious, pertinaceous.
obfirmar v. 1. to persist, persevere, be constant. 2. to be obstinate, stubborn.
óbice s. m. hindrance, impediment, obstacle.
óbito s. m. obit, death, decease.
coluna de ~s agony column. **atestado de ~** death certificate.
obituário s. m. 1. obituary. 2. death rate. ‖ adj. obituary, necrological.
objeção s. f. (pl. -ões) 1. objection, opposition. 2. contestation, disapproval. 3. obstacle. 4. reply.
~ insignificante trivial objection. **fazer -ões** to argue. **eu não tenho ~ a...** I have no objection to. **você faz -ões a que eu vá?** do you object to my going? **não há -ões a fazer** there is no objection.
objetar v. 1. to object, oppose. 2. produce an argument against. 3. to refute. 4. to contest, disapprove.
~ contra o casamento to forbid the banns.
objetiva s. f. objective: 1. (optics) lens, a system of lenses; object glass (plates B 13, M 3, 9). 2. aim, purpose, end, goal, object.
~ ortocromática orthochromatic objective lens.
objetivação s. f. (pl. -ões) objectification.
objetivar v. 1. to objectify. 2. to materialize. 3. to pretend, purpose, have in view, aim.
objetividade s. f. objectiveness, objectivity.
objetivismo s. m. objectivism.
objetivo s. m. 1. objective, object, end, aim, purpose, intent. 2. (philos.) outer. ‖ adj. objective: 1. of or referring to an object. 2. not subjective, phenomenal. 3. impartial. 4. (gram.) accusative, objective. ‖ **-amente** adv. objectively.
ele conseguiu o seu ~ he gained his ends. **sem ~** objectless, aimlessly.
objeto s. m. 1. object, concrete thing. 2. (gram.) word toward which the action of the verb is directed. 3. subject, matter, topic. 4. motive, reason. 5. intention, end, aim, purpuose.
~s de arte objects of artistic worth or curiosity. **~ direto (indireto)** (gram.) direct (indirect) object. **~ de estimação** a prized possession. **~ final** final aim. **~s perdidos** lost property. **~s roubados** stolen objects, (sl.) swag. **~s de trabalho** (econ.) objects or natural materials transformed into marketable products.
objurgação s. f. (pl. -ões) 1. objurgation, reproof. 2. censure, blame, reproach, rebuke.
objurgado adj. objurgated, chided, reproached, berated.
objurgar v. 1. to objurgate, reproof, chide, censure, blame. 2. to reproach, rebuke, upbraid. 3. to argue. 4. (fig.) to fling into a person's teeth.
objurgatória s. f. objurgation.
objurgatório adj. objurgatory, reprehensive, reproachful, upbraiding, rebuking. ‖ **objurgatoriamente** adv. objurgatorily.
oblação s. f. (pl. -ões) oblation: 1. offering (to God), immolation. 2. gift, donation.
oblata s. f. 1. oblation, offering (to God), immolation. 2. (rel.) mass, altarage. 3. charitative or pious gift or donation. 4. (rel.) oblate (sister).
oblativo adj. oblatory, oblational.
oblato s. m. (rel.) oblate (priest).
oblíqua s. f. (geom.) oblique (line).

obliquângulo adj. (geom.) oblique-angled.
triângulo ~ (geom.) oblique-angled triangule.
obliquar v. 1. to oblique, slant. 2. (mil.) to move forward obliquely. 3. to disguise, dissemble, use shifts. 4. to skew.
obliqüidade s. f. 1. obliquity, obliqueness. 2. slanting position.
oblíquo adj. 1. oblique: a) slanting, sideways. b) not perpendicular, diagonal, skew. c) sloping, a-slope. d) bias, aslant. 2. (gram.) referring to the oblique case. 3. cross-eyed, asquint, awry. 4. ambiguous. 5. (fig.) indirect, crooked, underhand, malicious. ‖ **obliquamente** adv. obliquely.
obliteração s. f. (pl. **-ões**) 1. obliteration, extinction, effacement. 2. destruction. 3. obstruction, plugging, closing.
obliterado adj. obliterated, forgotten, unremembered, extinguished, effaced.
obliterar v. 1. to obliterate, erase, efface. 2. to blot out of memory. 3. to destroy, extinguish. 4. to obstruct, plug, close. 5. to exclude. 6. **~-se:** a) to become extinct. b) to fall into oblivion.
obliterável adj. m. + f. (pl. **-áveis**) capable of being obliterated, effaceable.
oblívio s. m. oblivion, forgetfulness, unmindfulness.
oblongo adj. 1. oblong, elongated. 2. oval, elliptic(al).
obnóxio adj. 1. obnoxious. 2. punishable. 3. submissive, servile. 4. offensive, objectionable. 5. inauspicious, doleful, fatal.
obnubilação s. f. (pl. **-ões**) (med.) obnubilation, mental derangement.
obnubilar v. to obnubilate, (over)cloud, obscure, darken.
oboé s. m. oboe, hautboy: 1. wind-instrument of wood played through a double reed. 2. organ reed stop.
oboísta s. m. + f. oboist, hautboyist.
óbolo s. m. 1. obol: ancient Greek silver coin. 2. (fig.) alms, donation.
obóveo adj. (also **obova(ado), obovóide**) obovoid, obovate.
obra s. f. 1. work, workmanship, job. 2. handwork. 3. opus: literary or musical composition. 4. painting, artistic creation. 5. production, treatise. 6. tractate. 7. act, deed. 8. brickwork, repairs (of a building) (plate A 7). 9. defecation. 10. (Braz.) pretty person or thing.
~ **clássica** classic (work). ~ **de arte** work of art. ~ **de caridade** works of mercy, charity. ~ **de consulta** a reference work. ~ **de empreitada** a contract job. ~ **de fancaria** shoddy work. ~ **dramática** drama. **~s mortas** (naut.) upper works. ~ **de referência** reference work. **~s vivas** (naut.) quickwork. **~s póstumas** (lit.) remains. **~s públicas** public works. ~ **de fachada** window dressing, an undertaking (public work) mainly for show but of little value. **uma ~ em três volumes** a work in three volumes. **uma ~ de Miguel Ângelo** a work of Michelangelo. **fé e boas ~s** faith and works. **as ~s de Deus** the works of God. **ter ~s de muitos autores** to have many authors on one's shelves. **mãos à ~!** let's get to work!
obrador s. m. (also **obreiro**) workman, worker, laborer, artisan. ‖ adj. working.
obrage s. f. (S. Braz.) sawmill; logging.
obrageiro s. m. (S. Braz.) logger.
obragem s. f. (pl. **-ens**) work, labour.
obra-prima s. f. (pl. **obras-primas**), also **obra-mestra** s. f. (pl. **obras-mestras**) masterpiece, work of art; chief work of an author.
obrar v. 1. to make, do, execute. 2. to realize, put into practice. 3. to work, operate, act. 4. to per-

form, act, proceed. 5. to produce, manufacture; build. 6. to take effect (medicine). 7. (fig.) to defecate.
obréia s. f. wafer: 1. (eccl.) thin and round unleavened bread used in the Eucharist. 2. adhesive disk of dry paste for sealing letters, documents, etc.
obreira s. f. 1. workwoman. 2. working-bee.
obreiro s. m. worker, wright, workman, labourer. ‖ adj. laborious, working.
ob-repção s. f. (pl. **ob-repções**) 1. obreption, surreption. 2. fraud, cunning.
ob-reptício adj. obreptitious; fraudulent.
obrigação s. f. (pl. **-ões**) 1. obligation, duty. 2. necessity, need. 3. charge, responsibility, astriction. 4. rule, commandment, precept. 5. imposition. tax, onus. 6. engagement, bond. 7. debenture, liability. 8. gratitude, indebtedness. 9. task, occupation, work, function. 10. (pop.) household, family, wife and children.
cumpra primeiro as suas -ões first do your duty. ~ **civil** purely personal obligations between individuals or between individual and state. **ter a ~ de** to be obliged to. **ela lhe deve muitas -ões** she is under an obligation to him. **devo-lhe -ões** I owe him a debt of gratitude. **lembrar alguém de suas -ões morais** to put s. o. by one's honour. **primeiro a ~, depois a devoção** duty before pleasure.
obrigacional adj. m. + f. (pl. **-ais**) obligational. ‖ **-mente** adv. obligationally.
obrigacionário s. m. obrigacionista m. + f. bondholder.
obrigado adj. 1. obligated, obliged, compelled. 2. imposed, forced, obligatory. 3. bound (in duty). 4. thankful, grateful. 5. necessary, inevitable. 6. indebted, mortgaged. ‖ Interj. thanks!, thank you! **muito ~!** many thanks!, thank you very much! **fico-lhe muito ~** I am indebted to him. **fico-lhe ~ por isto** I am obliged to you for this. **ficamos muito ~s** we are much obliged. **sou ~ a** I am under the necessity of. **não, ~!** no, thank you! **fui ~ a falar** I was forced to speak.
obrigar v. 1. to oblige. 2. to obligate, put under an obligation, engage. 3. to incite, urge. 4. to force, impose. 5. to compel, constrain. 6. to do a favour to. 7. to render grateful. 8. to astrict, bind. 9. to subject. 10. **~-se** to assume an obligation.
~ **alguém ao cumprimento de uma promessa** to pin someone down to his promise. **obrigaram-no, pela fome, a obedecer** they starved him into obedience. **obrigaram-no a concordar** they forced him to agree.
obrigatário s. m. (also **obrigacionário**) bondholder.
obrigatoriedade s. f. obligatoriness, compulsiveness, compulsoriness.
obrigatório adj. 1. obligatory, forceable. 2. compulsory, compulsive. 3. binding. ‖ **obrigatoriamente** adv. obligatorily, compulsorily.
ob-rogação s. f. (pl. **ob-rogações**) derogation.
ob-rogar v. to derogate.
obscenidade s. f. 1. obscenity, obsceneness, bawdiness. 2. smuttiness, ribaldry, indecency. 3. lewd picture 4. dirt, ordure, filth. 5. lewdness, unchastity.
obsceno adj. 1. obscene, bawdy, indecent, filthy. 2. impure, vile, fescennine, sensual, lewd. 3. gross, vulgar. 4. dirty, foul. 5. ribald, smutty, pornographic. ‖ **-amente** adv. obscenely, bawdily.
um livro ~ a pornographic book.
obscurante s. m. + f. (also **obscurantista**) obscurant(ist). ‖ adj. darkening, obscuring.
obscurantismo s. m. obscurantism.
obscurantista s. m. + f. obscurant(ist). ‖ adj. obscurant(ist).

obscurantizar v. 1. to lead towards obscurantism or become an obscurant. 2. to prevent or hinder enlightenment, progress, knowledge.

obscurecer v. 1. to (become) osbcure, fog, (be)dim, darken. 2. to confuse, bewilder. 3. to overcast. adumbrate. 4. to perturb, haze 5. to conceal, disguise, hide. 6. to dishonour. 7. to afflict, trouble. 8. to shade, cloud. 9. ∼-se to be extinguished; to sadden; to dusk.
sua fama obscureceu his fame faded away.

obscurecido adj. 1. dark, cloudy, overcast, obscure(d). 2. obfuscated. 3. (fig.) forgotten, unknown.

obscurecimento s. m. obscuration, darkening, obfuscation, adumbration; darkness.

obscuridade s. f. (also **obscureza**) 1. obscurity, obscureness, darkness, dimness, murkiness. 2. confusion, vagueness, unintelligibility. 3. sombreness, haziness, cloudiness. 4. namelessness. 5. seclusion. **na** ∼ (fig.) in the background. **em completa** ∼ in perfect obscurity or darkness.

obscuro adj. 1. obscure, dark, dim. 2. somber, shady, dusky, murky. 3. cloudy, foggy, hazy, misty. 4. unknown, enigmatic, unintelligible, vague, ambiguous, doubtful. 5. solitary, retired, secluded. ‖ **-amente** adv. obscurely, darkly, etc.

obsecração s. f. (pl. **-ões**) obsecration: 1. the act of imploring. 2. supplication, entreaty. 3. earnest prayer.

obsecrar v. to obsecrate, beseech, supplicate.

obsedante adj. m. + f. (Braz.) obsessive, importunate, annoying, persistent.

obsedar, obsediar v. 1. to obsess, importune with pertinacious demands. 2. to annoy, pester, molest, harass. 3. to haunt, beset.

obsediante adj. m. + f. 1. = **obsedante**. 2. = **obsessor**.

obseqüente adj. m. + f. 1. docile, tractable, compliant. 2. obedient, submissive, obsequious, serviceable. 3. suitable, favourable.

obsequiador s. m. obliger, complier, kind person. ‖ adj. obliging, kindly, friendly.

obsequiar v. 1. to oblige, captivate. 2. to do a favour, render a service, accommodate, meet the wishes of. 3. to give a present to.
ele o fez para obsequiá-lo he did it to accommodate you.

obséquias s. f. pl. (obs.) obsequies, funeral rites.

obséquio s. m. 1. favour, obligation, courtesy, kindness, complaisance. 2. goodwill; service; politeness. **faça-me o** ∼**!** do me the favour! **quer fazer-me um** ∼**?** will you do me a favour? **por** ∼**, onde fica a Rua Tito?** can you, please, tell me where Rua Tito is?

obsequiosidade s. f. 1. benevolence, kind(li)ness, affability, obligingness. 2. courtesy, complaisanse. 3. helpfulness, accommodation.

obsequioso adj. 1. obliging, serviceable. 2. courtly, kind, polite, courteous. 3. accommodating, complaisantly.

observação s. f. (pl. **-ões**) 1. observation, remark, comment. 2. notice, note, annotation. 3. study, examination, investigation. 4. admonition, warning. 5. watchfulness.
estar sob ∼ to be under restraint.

observador s. m. 1. observer, watcher. 2. spectator, onlooker, beholder. 3. noter, regarder. 4. astronomer, weather observer. ‖ adj. observant, watchful, regardful.

observância s. f. 1. observance, execution, keeping. 2. accomplishment, fulfilment. 3. application, practice. 4. discipline. 5. penitence, contrition.

observante s. m. + f. 1. observer, spectator. 2. m. (R. C. Church) Observant(ine): a Franciscan order also called Observant Friars. ‖ adj. 1. observant,

watchful. 2. obedient, attentive. 3. loyal, constant, militant.

observar v. 1. to observe, watch, look at, notice, perceive. 2. to examine, investigate, study, view. 3. to spy. 4. to fulfil, accomplish, execute. 5. to consider, respect, pay attention to, keep. 6. to obey, comply, follow (a rule). 7. to practise, perform. 8. to remark, advise, call a person's attention to. 9. ∼-se to observe o. s.
∼ **a criança** to keep an eye on the child. ∼ **as regras** to observe the rules.

observatório s. m. 1. (astr.) observatory. 2. turret. 3. belvedere. 4. = **observação**.
∼ **meteorológico** weather station.

observável adj. m. + f. (pl. **-áveis**) observable.

obsessão s. f. (pl. **-ões**) 1. obsession, fixed idea, mania. 2. impertinence, insolence, vexation. 3. persecution, harassment.

obsessivo adj. = **obsessor**.

obsesso s. m. person possessed or beset by an evil spirit. ‖ adj. obsessive, importuned, vexed, tormented, harassed, haunted.

obsessor s. m. 1. obsessor: one who obsesses. 2. importuner, annoyer. ‖ adj. (also **obsessivo**) obsessive, troublesome, vexatious.

obsidente s. m. + f. besieger. ‖ adj. besieging, besetting, obsessive.

obsidiana s. f. (petrog.) obsidian: dark-coloured vitreous lava.

obsidiar v. 1. to besiege, beset, surround, encompass. 2. (fig.) to spy, watch (on a person). 3. to importune, molest, annoy; haunt, harass.

obsidional adj. m. + f. (pl. **-ais**) obsidional, besetting, besieging.

obsolescência s. f. obsolescence.

obsoletar v. to obsolesce: be, become or render obsolete.

obsoletismo s. m. obsoletism, obsoleteness.

obsoleto adj. obsolete: 1. out of use or date, archaic, antiquated, outmoded. 2. (bot., zool.) aborted, atrophied.

obstaculizar v. to raise difficulties, impede, embarrass, hinder.

obstáculo s. m. 1. obstacle, hindrance, obstruction. 2. embarrassment, entanglement. 3. difficulty, opposition, objection. 4. inconvenience, drawback. 5. impediment, holdback, balk. 6. barrier. 7. (fig.) stop. 8. (sport). jump, hurdle.
corrida de ∼**s** obstacle race. **passar sobre um** ∼ (fig.) to hurdle. **sem** ∼ unopposed. **ele removeu todos os** ∼**s** he removed all obstacles. **o cavalo tomou o** ∼ the horse took the jump.

obstância s. f. (Braz.) difficulty, obstacle, trouble.

obstante adj. m. + f. (also **obstativo**) hindering, obstructive, impeding.
não ∼ 1. nevertheless, in (de)spite of. 2. however, notwithstanding, albeit. **não** ∼ **a sua resistência** notwithstanding his resistance. **não** ∼ **isso** for all that.

obstar v. 1. to oppose, thwart, resist, withstand. 2. to impede, prevent, hinder, bar.
nada obsta a que aquilo se faça there is nothing to prevent its being done.

obstativo adj. (also **obstante** m. + f.) obstructive, hindering.

obstétrica, obstetrícia s. f. (med.) obstetrics, midwifery: science of parturition.

obstetrício, obstétrico adj. obstetric(al): of or pertaining to midwifery or childbirth.

obstetriz s. f. obstetrix, midwife, obstetrician.

obsticidade s. f. (path.) inclination of the head towards one of the shoulders due to rheumatism.

obstinação s. f. (pl. -ões) 1. obstinacy, pigheadedness, obduracy. 2. pertinacity, persistence, stubbornness. 3. refractoriness, contumacy. 4. stubborn perseverance. 5. tenacity, hardness, tenaciousness.
obstinado adj. 1. obstinate, dogged, pigheaded. 2. pertinacious, persistent, contumacious. 3. firm, resolute, obdurate, unyielding. 4. headstrong, stubborn, forward. 5. refractory, intractable. ‖ -amente adv. obstinately.
a criança está bem -a hoje the child is quite contrary today.
obstinar v. 1. to become obstinate. 2. to persevere, persist (in error). 3. to be stubborn.
obstipação s. f. (pl. -ões) (med.) obstipation, extreme costiveness.
obstipar v. to cause obstipation.
obstringir v .1. (med.) bind, tie; press, compress. 2. to constrain, compel, oblige, obstringe; stanch.
obstrito adj. constrained, bound, forced, obliged.
obstrução s. f. (pl. -ões) obstruction: 1. hindrance, stoppage, impediment. 2. (fig.) opposition, counteraction. 3. = **obstrucionismo**. 4. (also med.) block-(age), engorgement, obstruent.
~ **intestinal** (med.) intestinal obstruction.
obstrucionismo s. m. obstructionism: retardation of progress, dilatory methods in parliament.
obstrucionista s. m. + f. obstructionist, filibuster. ‖ adj. obstructionistic: of or pertaining to obstructionists.
obstruir v. 1. to obstruct, block up, engorge, oppilate. 2. to shut, close. 3. to stop up, choke up, clog. 4. to nonplus, hinder, embarrass. 5. to bar, impede. 6. ~-**se** to be or become obstructed.
~ **uma passagem** to obstruct a passage. **a chaminé está obstruída de fuligem** the chimney is foul.
obstrutivo adj. obstructive: causing or tending to cause obstruction. ‖ -amente adv. obstructively.
obstrutor s. m. obstructor, hinderer, obstructant. ‖ adj. obstructing, hindering, obstructive.
obstupefação s. f. (pl. -ões) 1. astonishment, amazement, surprise. 2. stupefaction.
obstupefato adj. 1. amazed, astonished. 2. stupefied.
obstúpido adj. astonished, amazed, surprised.
obtemperação s. f. (pl. -ões) obedience, compliance, submission.
obtemperar v. 1. to obtemper, reply mildly. 2. to ponder, consider. 3. to obey, agree, acquiesce. 4. to subject o. s. 5. to submit to, comply with (orders or instructions).
obtenção s. f. (pl. -ões) 1. obtainment, obtention. 2. attainment, acquisition, acquirement. 3. conquest.
obtenível adj. m. + f. (pl. -íveis) obtainable, procurable.
obtentor s. m. obtainer, acquirer, gainer. ‖ adj. obtaining.
obter v. 1. to obtain, gain, win, achieve. 2. to get, catch. 3. to attain, take, secure. 4. to acquire, buy, purchase. 5. (fig.) to steal.
~ **fiança** to find bail. ~ **informações** to get information. ~ **posse de alguma coisa** to obtain possession of s. th. ~ **por força** to obtain by force, compel. ~ **um emprego** to get (coll. land) a job. **obtive isto por uma ninharia** (coll.) I picked up the thing for a song, I got the thing for a trifle. **ele obteve o grau de...** he proceeded to the degree of... **de onde obteve isto?** how did you come by it? **nós obtivemos influência sobre ele** we gained influence with him, we won (up)on him. **queriam** ~ **minha colaboração** they wanted to gain me over. **eles obtiveram a mais irrestrita admiração de todos** they won golden opinions.
obtestação s. f. (pl. -ões) obtestation.

obtestar v. to obtest: 1. call to witness. 2. protest, insist. 3. supplicate, adjure, beseech. 4. incite, provoke.
obtido adj. obtained, attained, gained, achieved, got.
obtundente adj. m. + f. obtunding, blunting, deadening, obtundent.
obtundir v. 1. to obtund, dull, blunt, deaden. 2. to beat, drub, thrash.
obturação s. f. (pl. -ões) obturation, stopping, plugging, filling (of a tooth), closing (of a cavity).
obturador s. m. 1. obturator (also anat.); stopper, plugger, filler. 2. (phot.) obturator.
obturante s. m. + f. obturator. ‖ adj. obturator.
obturar v. 1. to obturate, close, stop, plug. 2. to fill (a tooth).
o dentista obtura dentes cariados the dentist fills decayed teeth.
obtusado adj. obtuse: rounded at the extremity (leaf, sepal or petal).
obtusângulo adj. obtuse-angled, obtuse-angular (triangle).
obtusão s. f. (pl. -ões) 1. obtusity, obtuseness, dullness. 2. unintelligence, stupidity.
obtusidade s. f. 1. obtusity, obtuseness. 2. dullness, bluntness.
obtusífido adj. (bot.) obtusifid.
obtusifoliado, obtusifólio adj. (bot.) obtusifolious: having obtuse leaves.
obtusilobulado adj. (bot.) obtusilobous: having obtuse lobes.
obtusirrostro adj. (zool.) obtusirostrate: having obtuse rostra.
obtuso adj. obtuse: 1. (geom.) greater than a right angle. - 2. not pointed or acute, blunt, rounded (plate Q). 3. stupid, dull, foolish. ‖ -amente adv. abtusely.
ângulo ~ obtuse angle.
obumbração s. f. (pl. -ões) (also **obumbramento** m.) the act of darkening or obscuring; shade; (obs.) obumbration.
obumbrado adj. obumbrated, overcast, shady.
obumbrar v. 1. to shade, overshadow. 2. to overcast, darken. 3. to cloud, become cloudy. 4. to dim. 5. to disguise, dissimulate, occult.
obus s. m. (artillery) howitzer.
obuseiro adj. said of the ship armed with a howitzer.
obvenção s. f. (pl. -ões) incidental gain or advantage.
obverso s. m. obverse.
obviar v. 1. to obviate. 2. to forestall, prevent. 3. to remedy, improve. 4. to intercept, oppose, intervene, counteract. 5. to hinder, check, resist.
óbvio adj. 1. obvious, plain, evident, unmistakable. 2. manifest, not to be doubted. 3. visible, patent, clear. ‖ **obviamente** adv. obviously, plainly.
obvir v. 1. to accrue, come to (by law, right, etc.). 2. to escheat.
oca s. f. 1. game played with counters on a board. 2. (min.) ocher, ochre. 3. shanty, hut (of Indians). 4. (Braz.) hub (in a wheel of an oxcart).
ocapi s. m. okapi: animal of the giraffe family.
ocar v. 1. to excavate, hollow, dig out. 2. to empty.
ocarina s. f. ocarina: musical instrument of terra--cotta, giving a mellow whistling sound.
ocarinista s. m. + f. 1. ocarina player. 2. person who makes ocarinas.
ocasião s. f. (pl. -ões) 1. occasion, conjuncture, opportunity. 2. motive, cause, reason. 3. place, space, ground. 4. time at one's disposal, spare time. 5. instance, circumstances.
aproveitar a ~ **favorável** to strike while the iron is hot. **a** ~ **faz o ladrão** opportunity makes the thief. **em outra** ~ at another time. **em todas as -ões** on all occasions, at all times. **deixar escapar uma** ~

to slip a fair opportunity. **esta não é a** ~ **propicia** there is no occasion for it. **na** ~ **oportuna** in due time. **negócio de** ~ 1. a rare business opportunity. 2. bargain. **por** ~ **de** on the occasion of. **quando se der a** ~ when the opportunity presents itself. **os amigos conhecem-se nas -ões de necessidade** a friend in need is a friend indeed.

ocasionado adj. 1. occasioned, caused. 2. (Braz., pop.) exasperated, confused.

ocasionador s. m. causer.

ocasional adj. m. + f. (pl. **-ais**) occasional, casual, eventual, contingent. ‖ ~**mente** adv. occasionally, opportunely, sometimes.

serviços -ais contingent services.

ocasionalismo s. m. occasionalism: the doctrine of the occasional causes.

ocasionar v. 1. to occasion, cause. 2. to originate, create, begin, give rise to, bring about, provoke, produce. 3. to occur, happen, take place.

ocaso s. m. 1. sunset. 2. west, occident. 3. (fig.) decline, decay, end, death.

occipício s. m. (anat., also **occipúcio**) occiput, hindhead, back of the head (plate C 18).

occipital s. m. (pl. **-ais**) (anat.) = **occipício**. ‖ adj. m. + f. occipital: of or referring to the hindhead.

oceânico adj. 1. oceanic: a) belonging, inhabiting or relating to the ocean, marine. b) wide or extensive as the ocean. 2. Oceanian: of or pertaining to Oceania.

oceânides s. f. (pl. Greek myth.) Oceanids: nymphs of the ocean.

oceano s. m. 1. ocean, sea, flood. 2. high seas, main. 3. (fig.): a) great extension, vastness, imensity. b) great quantity, great deal.

Oceano Antártico, Ártico, Atlântico, Índico, Pacífico Antarctic, Artic, Atlantic, Indian, Pacific Ocean. **ele é um** ~ **de virtudes** he is a paragon of virtues.

oceanografia s. f. oceonography.

oceanográfico adj. oceanographic(al).

oceanografista s. m. + f. oceanographist.

oceanógrafo s. m. oceanographer.

ocelado adj. ocellate(d): marked by or having ocelli.

océleo adj. (zool.) ocellar.

ocelifero adj. (bot.) ocelliferous.

ocelo s. m. (zool.) ocellus: little eye, eyespot, stemma.

ocidental adj. m. + f. (pl. **-ais**) occidental, western: of or pertaining to the occident or west.

na parte ~ in the west of.

ocidentalidade s. f. occidentality.

ocidentalismo s. m. occidentalism.

ocidentalizar v. to occidentalize, westernize.

ocidente s. m. occident, west: the region of the setting sun; Western Hemisphere.

o Ocidente the West.

ocíduo adj. (poet.) setting (star, sun).

ocimo s. m. (bot.) Ocimum: a genus of labiate herbs and shrubs.

ócio s. m. 1. leisure, rest (time). 2. tranquillity, immobility, inactivity. 3. laziness, idleness, indolence, sloth.

entregar-se ao ~ to live in idleness.

ociosidade s. f. 1. laziness, idleness, indolence, inoccupation. 2. truancy, loaf, vagrancy.

a ~ **é a mãe de todos os vícios** idleness is the root of all evil.

ocioso s. m. lazybones, truant, loafer, idler. ‖ adj. lazy, idle, indolent, do-nothing. ‖ **-amente** adv. lazily, idly.

estar ou andar ~ to idle.

oclocracia s. f. ochlocracy, mobocracy, mob rule.

oclocrático adj. ochlocratic(al): relating to ochlocracy or government by the mob.

oclusão s. f. (pl. **-ões**) occlusion: 1. shutting up, closing. 2. (phys., chem.) absorption of a gas. 3. (med.) obstruction.

~ **intestinal** obstruction of the intestine.

oclusivo adj. (also **oclusor**) occlusive.

ocluso adj. 1. obstinated, occluded. 2. shut, closed.

oco s. m. (pl. **ocos**) (Braz.) hollow, excavation, hole, emptiness. ‖ adj. 1. hollow, addle, deep, empty. 2. (fig.): a) futile, vain, void, insignificant, trivial. b) cavernous. ‖ **ocamente** adv. hollowly, chimerically.

cabeça oca dunderhead.

ocorrência s. f. 1. occurrence, incident, event, fact, happening. 2. chance. 3. casuality, eventuality. 4. occasion.

ocorrente adj. m. + f. 1. occurring, happening, occurrent. 2. convergent, incident.

ocorrer v. 1. to occur, happen, befall, take place. 2. to appear, come out. 3. to present itself, come to mind. 4. to concur, happen at the same time. 5. to help, assist, aid, succour. 6. to remedy, correct, redress.

ocorreu-me que... it occurred to me that... **não me ocorreu que...** it did not occur to me that.

ocra s. f., **ocre** m. (min.) ocher, ochre.

ocráceo adj. ocherous, ochreous.

ócrea s. f. (bot.) ocrea.

ocreoso adj. ocherous.

ocricórneo adj. (zool.) having yellow antennae.

ocrocéfalo adj. (zool.) having a yellow head.

ocrodermia s. f. (path.) paleness or yellowing of the skin.

ocrópode adj. m. + f. (zool.) having yellow feet.

ocróptero adj. (zool.) having yellow wings.

octaédrico adj. octahedral: having eight equal surfaces or faces.

octaedrita s. f. (min.) octahedrite, anatase.

octaedro s. m. (geom.) octahedron: a solid bounded by eight faces.

octaetéride s. f. octaeterid, octaeteris: period of eight years.

octandro adj. (bot.) octandrous: having eight stamens.

octangular adj. m. + f. (also **octogonal**) octangular, octagonal.

octateuco s. m. Octateuch: the first eight books of the Old Testament.

octeto s. m. (mus.) octet: 1. a composition for eight voices or instruments. 2. an ensemble of eight voices or instruments.

octil adj. m. + f. (pl. **-is**) (astr.) octantal.

octilhão, octilião s. m. (pl. **-ões**) octillion: number denoted by a unity followed by 27 ciphers in Brazil, U. S. A. and France, and by 48 ciphers in England and Germany.

octingentésimo s. m. eighthundredth. ‖ adj. eighthundredth.

octocórneo adj. (zool.) having eight horns.

octodáctilo adj. (zool.) octodactyle: having eight digits.

octogenário s. m. octogenarian: person of more than eighty and less than ninety years. ‖ adj. octogenarian: aged between eighty and ninety years.

octogésimo s. m. eightieth. ‖ adj. eightieth.

octógino adj. (bot.) octogynous: having eight pistils.

octogonal adj. m. + f. (pl. **-ais**) octagonal: having eight sides.

octógono s. m. 1. (geom.) octagon: figure of eight angles and eight sides. 2. octagonal building. ‖ adj. (also **octogonal**) octagonal.

octonado adj. in groups of eight.

octonário s. m. octonarius: verse of eight feet. ‖ adj. octonary: consisting of eight feet (verse).

octópode s. m. (zool.) octopod, octopus. ‖ adj. m. + f. octopod: having eight feet or limbs.

octorum s. m. + f., **octoruno** m. octoroon.

octossilábico adj. octosyllabic: consisting of eight syllables.

octossílabo s. m. octosyllable: line or word of eight syllables. ‖ adj. (also **octossilábico**) octosyllabic.

octuplicar v. to octuple, make eighfold.

óctuplo s. m. octuple. ‖ adj. octuple, eightfold.

oculação s. f. (pl. -ões) the grafting of a bud to a tree.

oculado adj. (also **oculoso**) oculate: 1. eyed, having eyes. 2. (bot.) having spots resembling eyes, ocellate(d), spotted.

ocular s. f. ocular, the eyepiece of an optical instrument as of a telescope or microscope (plates B 13, M 9). ‖ adj. m. + f. ocular: of or pertaining to the eye, visual. ‖ ~mente adv. ocularly.
  globo ~ eyeball. **testemunha** ~ eyewitness. **eu fui testemunha** ~ **do seu acidente** I had ocular demonstration of his accident.

oculífero adj. (zool.) oculiferous: bearing an eye or eyes.

oculiforme adj. m. + f. oculiform, eyelike in shape or appearance.

oculista s. m. + f. 1. oculist, ophtalmologist, eye doctor, eye specialist. 2. optician: person who makes or sells optical glasses or instruments. ‖ adj. oculistic.

oculística s. f. (med.) ophthalmology: science which deals with the eye, its anatomy and function, in health and disease.

óculo s. m. 1. spy-glass. 2. eyeglass. 3. circular or eyed window. 4. ~s pl. spectacles, glasses.
  ~**s de alcance** spy-glass. ~**s de proteção** goggles. ~**s escuros contra o sol** sun-glasses, sun-goggles (plate R 6).

ocultação s. f. (pl. -ões) occultation, act or fact of hiding.

ocultador s. m. concealer. ‖ adj. concealing.

ocultar v. 1. to occult, hide; ensconce. 2. to conceal, enshroud. 3. to cover, eclipse. 4. to be quiet, keep secret. 5. to disguise, dissemble, (dis)simulate. 6. ~-**se** to hide o. s.
  ~ **a verdade** to hold back the truth. **não oculte seu candeeiro debaixo do alqueire** don't hide your light under a bushel. **não se nos ocultou nada** nothing was concealed from us. **por que ele lhe ocultou esta novidade?** why has he withheld this news from you?

ocultas s. f. pl. used only in the adv. loc.: **às** ~ secretly, clandestinely, in an underhand manner.

ocultismo s. m. occultism: belief in mysterious powers, outside ordinary knowledge; its study or investigation.

ocultista s. m. + f. occultist: person who adheres to occultism. ‖ adj. occultist.

oculto adj. 1. occult, hidden, concealed. 2. covered, veiled, eclipsed. 3. secret. 4. unknown, esoteric(al). 5. invisible, supernatural. 6. mysterious, cryptic(al), mystic(al), transcendental. ‖ -**amente** adv. occultly, secretly.
  manter-se ~ to keep out of sight. **seus objetivos** ~s his ulterior objects. **ciências** -**as** occult sciences.

ocupação s. f. (pl. -ões) occupation: 1. act of occupying or taking. 2. occupancy, possession, tenure. 3. business, employment, job. 4. trade, work, office; pursuit, concern.
  uma ~ **rotineira** a routine business.

ocupado adj. + p. p. of **ocupar** 1. occupied, busy, engaged. 2. taken, seized. ‖ **ocupadíssimo** obs. sup. up to the elbows (in work).
  a casa está -**a por dois inquilinos** the house is taken up by two lodgers. **estar** ~ **com uma coisa** to be concerned about a thing. **estou** ~ **em escrever** I am engaged in writing. **muito** ~ **pelo trabalho** tied down by much work. **o telefone estava sempre** ~ the phone was always busy. **todos os lugares na sala estão** ~s all the seats in the room are occupied. **este lugar está** ~? is this place taken? **estar ocupadíssimo** to have many calls on one's time.

ocupador s. m., **ocupante** m. + f. 1. occupant, occupier. 2. inmate, tenant. 3. bearer. 4. squatter. ‖ adj. occupying.

ocupar v. to occupy: 1. possess, take possession of. 2. live in, tenant, reside, lodge, inhabit. 3. take up, seize, capture. 4. invade, encroach upon. 5. employ, engage, keep busy, discharge (a function). 6. fill. 7. hold. 8. ~-**se** to do, ply, devote o. s. to.
  ~ **lugar de destaque** to run foremost, rank high. ~ **um lote de terreno** to occupy a lot of ground. ~-**se com alguma coisa** to occupy o. s. with. s. th. ~-**se com ninharias** to fiddle-faddle. **ele ocupa um bom lugar** he holds a good position. **ocupem seus lugares!** take your seats! **deixe que me ocupe com os meus assuntos** let me attend to my business. **ele se ocupa de ilusionismo nas horas vagas** he dabbles in prestidigitation in his spare hours. **a mesa ocupa muito lugar** the table takes up too much room. **os soldados** ~am **as ruas** the soldiers lined the streets.

odalisca s. f. odalisque, odalisk: a female slave in the harems of the East; concubine.

ode s. f. ode: 1. a lyric poem in symmetrical form. 2. the music to which it is set.

odeão, odeon s. m. (Gr. hist.) odeum: theatre especially for musical performances.

odiar v. 1. to hate, detest, dislike. 2. to abhor, disgust, loathe. 3. to abominate, execrate. 4. to intrigue, make an enemy of. 5. ~-**se** to hate o. s. **eles odeiam-se** they hate each other.

odiento adj. hateful, odious, spiteful, rancorous, invidious.

ódio s m. 1. hatred, odium. 2. aversion, enmity. abhorrence. antipathy, detestation. 3. anger, fury, rage. 4. rancour, hostility, spite.
  ~ **enraigado** inveterate hatred, riveted hatred. **ele reanimou o** ~ (fig.) he blew the coals.

odiosidade s. f. hatefulness, odiousness, detestableness.

odioso s. m. person who or thing which causes hatred. ‖ adj. 1. hateful, odious. 2. spiteful, rancorous. 3. abominable, hatable, detestable. 4. invidious, malign. ‖ -**amente** adv. hatefully, odiously.

Odisséia s. f. Odyssey: 1. epic poem attributed to Homer. 2. (fig.) long wandering or a series of adventures and vicissitudes.

odometria s. f. odometry.

odômetro s. m. odometer, perambulator: an instrument for measuring distances travelled.

odonato s. m. dragonfly: pseudoneuropterous insect of the order Odonata.

odontalgia s. f. (med.) odontalgia, toothache.

odontálgico adj. (med.) odontalgic.

odontíase s. f. (med.) odontiasis: 1. dentition, teething. 2. any disorder caused by dentition.

odontite s. f. (med.) odontitis, inflammation of a tooth.

odontoceto s. m. (zool.) odontocete: a toothed cetacean, as a sperm whale.

odontogenia s. f. (med.) odontogeny: the origin and histogenesis of the teeth.

odontografia s. f. (med.) odontography: a treatise on teeth.

odontográfico adj. (med.) odontographic.

odontógrafo s. m. odontograph.

odontóide adj. m. + f., **odontóideo** m. odontoid, like a tooth.

odontolando s. m. senior student of odontology.

odontólite s. f. tartar (of the teeth).

odontolitíase s. f. (med.) odontolithiasis: presence of tartar on the teeth.

odontologia s. f. odontology, dentistry: the science which treats of the teeth, their structure, development and diseases.

odontológico adj. odontologic(al): of or pertaining to odontology.

odontologista s. m. + f. odontologist, dentist: a specialist in odontology.

odontoma s. m. (med.) odontoma: toothlike tumour.

odor s. m. 1. smell, odo(u)r. 2. aroma, sweet smell, fragrance. 3. perfume, scent.

odorante adj. m. + f. odorous, odoriferous, aromatic(al), sweet-smelling, fragrant, scented, perfumed.

odorar v. 1. to emit odour. 2. to perfume, scent.

odorífero, odorífico, odoroso adj. = **odorante** odoriferous. ‖ **odoriferamente** adv. odoriferously.

odre s. m. 1. leather bottle, leather pipe, wineskin. 2. (fig.): a) fat person. b) drunkard.

odreiro s. m. person who makes leather bottles or wineskins.

oés-noroeste s. m. west-north-west.

oés-sudoeste s. m. west-south-west.

oeste s. m. 1. (abbr. **W** or **O**) west; occident. 2. west wind. ‖ adj. m. + f. west, western, westerly, of or pertaining to the west; blowing from the west (wind). ‖ a ~ adv. westerly.

o vento vem do ~ the wind is in the west. **a** ~ **de** to the west of. **eles foram para o** ~ they went west.

ofegante adj. m. + f. 1. panting, gasping, breathless, puffing, wheezing. 2. tired, fatigued, exhausted. 3. (fig.) anxious, uneasy.

ofegar v. 1. to pant, puff, gasp, wheeze. 2. to thirst for, be anxious about, yearn after.

ofego s. m. 1. pant, gasp, wheeze, breathlessness, difficulty in breathing. 2. fatigue, tiredness.

ofendedor s. m. offender.

ofender v. 1. to offend, insult, huff, hur, pique, displease. 2. to sin, transgress, wrong, disrespect. 3. to counteract, oppose. 4. to affront, provoke. 5. to scandalize, outrage. 6. to strike, wound, harm, injure. 7. ~-**se** to resent, take ill, feel hurt, take offence.

~ **a honra** to dishonour. **não o ofenda** dont't offend him, don't tread on his corns. **não havia intenção de** ~ no offence was meant.

ofendículo s. m. hindrance, obstacle, snag.

ofendido s. m. offended person. ‖ adj. (also **ofenso**) 1. offended, insulted. 2. wounded, sore, hurt.

sinto-me ~ I feel hurt.

ofensa s. f. 1. offense, outrage, insult, affront. 2. wound, hurt. 3. injustice, lesion, tort. 4. sin, wrong, trespass, transgression. 5. disrespect, impoliteness. 6. resentment. 7. disdain, underestimation. 8. ~**s** pl. bad words.

desforrar-se de uma ~ to pay off or settle a score.

ofensiva s. f. 1. offensive, aggression, assault; position or attitude of attack. 2. attack (also sport).

tomar a ~ to take the offensive.

ofensivo adj. offensive: 1. giving offense, insulting. 2. hurting, injurious. 3. aggressive, attacking. 4. revolting, shocking. ‖ -**amente** adv. offensively.

ofensor s. m. offender, wounder, injurer. ‖ adj. offending, hurting.

oferecedor s. m. offerer, offeror. ‖ adj. offering.

oferecer v. 1. to offer, proffer, tender, give. 2. to proportion, afford. 3. to present with. 4. to expose, exhibit. 5. to propose, proffer, suggest. 6. to bid

(as a price). 7. to consecrate, devote, dedicate. 8. ~-**se** to present itself or o. s.

~ **garantia** to stand security. ~ **perspectivas de êxito** to promise well. ~ **resistência** to stand against, make a stand. **o quarto oferece uma vista bonita** the room commands a fine view. **ofereceram-me dinheiro** I was offered money. **ofereci-lhe um sorvete** I treated him to an ice. **ele lhe oferecerá seus préstimos** he will offer you his services.

oferecido adj. 1. offered, proffered, tendered, given. 2. exposed, exhibited. 3. -**a** f. said of an apparently easy woman.

oferecimento s. m. 1. offer(ing), proffer, proposal. 2. presentation. 3. tender. 4. dedication (inscription). ~ **de paz** peace offering.

oferenda s. f. 1. offer(ing), proffer. 2. sacrifice, oblation, corban.

oferendar v. 1. to offer, present. 2. to make an offering.

oferente s. m. + f. + adj. = **oferecedor**.

oferta s. f. 1. offer(ing), proffer. 2. donation, gift, present. 3. tender, overture. 4. oblation, sacrifice. 5. (eccl., also **ofertório**) offertory. 6. promise. 7. (poet.) envoy. 8. bid(ding). 9. (fig.) bargain, deal. ~ **e procura** (com.) supply and demand. **fazer uma** ~ **para** to make a tender for.

ofertante s. m. + f. profferer, presenter, offerer. ‖ adj. offering.

ofertar v. 1. to give, present, bestow. 2. to offer, proffer. 3. to tender. 4. to bid. 5. ~-**se** 1. to volunteer. 2. to present itself.

ofertório s. m. (eccl.) offertory: 1. part of the Mass at which bread and wine are offered to God. 2. any collection of gifts for a church festival.

oficalcito s. m. (petrog.) ophicalcite: crystalline marble with greenish veins.

oficiador s. m. officiator, officiant. ‖ adj. officiating.

oficial s. m. (pl. -**ais**) 1. (mil.) officer. 2. artisan, skilled workman, artificer. 3. craftsman, journeyman. 4. official (person who holds an office). ‖ adj. m. + f. 1. official. 2. standard, formal, authentic. 3. authorized, authoritative. 4. solemn, important. ‖ ~**mente** adv. officially, authoritatively.

~ **da justiça** a minor court official, peace-officer. ~ **de alfaiate** journeyman tailor. ~ **de dia** officer of the day, orderly officer. ~ **de ligação** liaison officer. ~ **do Estado-Maior** general staff officer, field-officer. ~ **reformado** retired officer, half-pay officer. ~ **subalterno** non-commissioned officer. **hora** ~ standard time.

oficialato s. m. officership: position or dignity of an officer.

oficial-de-sala s. m. (pl. **oficiais-de-sala**) (Braz., bot.) bastard ipecac, bloodflower.

oficial-de-gabinete s. m. (pl. **oficiais-de-gabinete**) (Braz.) private secretary to an official.

oficialidade s. f. a body or staff of officers, officiality.

oficialismo s. m. 1. officialism, officialdom, bureaucracy. 2. (Braz.) the class of officials.

oficialização s. f. officialization: act of making official.

oficializado adj. officially established or recognized.

oficializador s. m. person who officializes. ‖ adj. officializing.

oficializar v. to officialize, approve, sanction.

oficial-maior s. m. (pl. **oficiais-maiores**) (Braz.) a deputy notary public, one who is authorized to perform the functions of a notary public.

oficiante s. m. + f. (eccl.) officiant, celebrant, person who officiates a religious service. ‖ adj. officiant, officiating.

oficiar v. 1. to officiate (at Mass). 2. to serve at Mass. 3. to address official letters or dispatches to.
oficina s. f. 1. workshop, shop. 2. machine shop. 3. the offices or necessary conveniences of a house or convent, as a pantry, scullery, wash-house, store-rooms, etc. 4. ~s pl. factory. ~ **de conserto** repair shop. ~ **de encadernação** bookbindery, bookbinders' workshop. ~ **de ferreiro** forge (shop), smithy.
oficinal adj. m. + f. (pl. **-ais**) 1. (pharm.) officinal. 2. of or relating to a workshop.
ofício s. m. 1. art, workmanship. 2. position, office, post, charge. 3. function, profession, employment. 4. occupation, trade, business, craft. 5. duty, obligation. 6. service, job, work. 7. (eccl.) office, rites. 8. official letter (esp. on government business). ~ **divino** divine office, church service, the Mass. ~ **da Santa Comunhão** communion service. ~ **das trevas (na Semana Santa)** (eccl.) tenebrae. **artes e ~s** arts and crafts. **Santo Ofício** Holy Office. **cada um no seu** ~ everyone to his trade. **é do seu** ~ it's his line. **papel** ~ legal cap: legal-sized paper (22 × 33 cm). **pedimos seus bons ~s** we would ask for your kind cooperation. **são ossos do** ~ it's all in a day's work.
oficiosidade s. f. officiousness.
oficioso adj. 1. obliging, accommodating. 2. kind, polite, obsequious. 3. serviceable, willing. 4. self--denying, unselfish. 5. officious, unofficial, informal, semi-official. || **-amente** adv. officiously. **em caráter** ~ unofficially. **advogado** ~ lawyer apointed by a court. **mentira -a** white lie.
oficlide s. m. (mus.) ophicleide.
ofídico adj. ophidian: of or pertaining to snakes.
ofídio s. m. 1. ophidian, snake. 2. ~s pl. the Ophidia (snakes). || adj. ophidian, snakelike.
ofidismo s. m. 1. snake poisoning. 2. study of the poison of snakes.
ofiocéfalo adj. ophiocephalous: having a triangular head like snakes.
ofiofagia s. f. habit of feeding on snakes.
ofiófago adj. ophiophagous, snake-eating.
ofioglossácea s. f. (bot.) a specimen of the Ophioglossaceae.
ofioglossáceo adj. (bot.) ophioglossaceous.
ofioglosso s. m. (bot.) ophioglossum: adder's tongue.
ofiografia s. f. ophiography: a description of or a treatise on serpents.
ofióideo adj. ophioid: pertaining to or like snakes.
ofiólatra s. m. + f. ophiolater, serpent worshipper.
ofiolatria s. f. ophiolatry, serpent worship, snake worship.
ofiólito s. m. (petrog.) 1. ophiolite, serpentine. 2. ophicalcite.
ofiologia s. f. ophiology: that part of zoology which deals with serpents.
ofiológico adj. (zool.) ophiologic: pertaining to ophiology.
ofiologista s. m. + f. ophiologist: snake expert.
ofiomancia s. f. ophiomancy: the art of divining or predicting events by means of serpents.
ofiomante s. m. + f. practitioner of ophiomancy.
ofiomântico adj. of or referring to ophiomancy.
ofiomórfico, ofiomorfo adj. ophiomorphic, serpentiform, formed like a snake.
ofítico adj. ophitic.
ofito s. m. (also **ofita** f.) ophite: 1. (petrog.) serpentine marble. 2. (rel., hist.) a member of a gnostic sect.
Ofiúco s. m. (astr.) Ophiuchus: Serpent Bearer, Serpentarius.
ofiuróides s. m. pl. Ophiuroidea: an order of achinoderms of the class Stellerida or starfishes.

ófrio(n) s. m. (craniology) ophryon.
ófris s. f., sg. + pl. (bot.) ophrys, listera: a genus of terrestrial orchids of the family Ophrydeae.
ofsete s. m. (typogr.) offset: 1. a printing system. 2. strongly sized, fuzz-free paper for offset printing.
oftalgia, oftalmalgia s. f. ophthalmalgia: pain in or about the eye.
oftalmálgico adj. ophthalmalgic: relative to ophthalmalgia.
oftalmia s. f. ophthalmia: inflammation of the eyeball or of the conjunctiva.
oftálmico s. m. ophthalmiac: person affected with ophthalmia. || adj. (med.) 1. ophthalmic: of or pertaining to the eyes, ocular. 2. of or referring to ophtalmia.
oftalmologia s. f. ophthalmology: the science which treats of the structure, function and diseases of the eye.
oftalmológico adj. ophtalmologic(al): of or pertaining to ophthalmology.
oftalmologista s. m. + f., **oftalmólogo** m. ophthalmologist: eye specialist.
oftalmomalacia s. f. (med.) ophthalmomalacia.
oftalmômetro s. m. (opt., med.) ophthalmometer: an instrument for measuring the eye, especially the curvature of the cornea.
oftalmoplegia s. f. (med.) ophthalmoplegia: paralysis of the eye muscles.
oftalmoscopia s. f. ophthalmoscopy.
oftalmoscópio s. m. ophthalmoscope: perforated mirror used in inspecting the interior of the eye.
oftalmóstato s. m. ophthalmostat: instrument for holding the eye steady during an operation.
oftalmoteca s. f. (ent.) ophthalmotheca.
oftalmotomia s. f. (med.) ophthalmotomy: incision of the eyeball.
oftalmotorrinolaringologista s. m. + f. eye, ear, nose and throat specialist.
ofuscação s. f. (pl. **-ões**) 1. obfuscation, darkness, dimness, obscuration. 2. dazzlement. 3. (fig.) concealing, hiding; bewildering.
ofuscado adj. obfuscated; blear, dim.
ofuscante adj. m. + f. blinding, flaring, dazzling.
ofuscar v. 1. to obfuscate, obscure, darken, dim. 2. to cloud, overcast. 3. to occult, eclipse, hide. 4. to dazzle, daze. 5. (fig.) to confuse, bewilder. 6. to blind, blear. 7. to lower the prestige of, discredit, disparage, throw into shade. 8. ~-se to grow or become obscure, dark, etc.
ogano adv. (obs.) in this year.
ogiva s. f. (archit.) ogive: 1. diagonal rib of a vault. 2. pointed or Gothic arch.
ogival adj. m. + f. (pl. **-ais**) ogival.
ogra s. f. ogress.
ogro s. m. ogre, bugbear.
oh interj. o!, oh!, ay (my)!, ah!
ohm s. m. ohm: the unit of electrical resistance.
ôhmico adj. (electr.) ohmic.
ohmímetro, ohmômetro s. m. (electr.) ohmmeter: instrument for measuring the resistance of a conductor.
oi interj. (N. E. Braz.) hallo!, hoy!
oídio s. m. (bot.) Oidium: genus of fungi containing the mildews.
oiro, oiro-de-gato, etc. (Port.) = **ouro, ouro-de-gato,** etc.
oitante s. m. octant: 1. an arc of 45 degrees. 2. (naut.) instrument for measuring angles, with a graduated arc of 45 degrees. 3. (astr.) position of a heavenly body (45 degrees distant from another).
oitão s. m. (pl. **-ões**) (contr.) side wall of a building.
oitava s. f. 1. octave: a) (mus.) the eighth note above or below a given tone. b) church festival of eight

days or its eighth day. c) any group of eight. 2. stanza of eight lines. 3. ancient weight whose value was the eighth part of an ounce.

oitava-de-final s. f. (pl. **oitavas-de-final**) (Braz., ftb.) in competitive sports, the round preceding the quarterfinals, with the participation of eight competitor teams.

oitavado adj. (also **octogonal**) octagonal, eigh-sided.

oitavão s. m. (pl. **-ões**) octoroon: person having one eighth Negro blood, mustee. ‖ adj. having one eighth Negro blood.

oitavar v. 1. to make eight-sided. 2. to divide into eight equal parts. 3. (mus.) to octave, play in octaves.

oitavário s. m. (R. C. Church) 1. festival of eight days. 2. octavarium: book of the rituals for the octave.

oitavo s. m. the eighth part, eighth. ‖ adj. eighth. **décimo ~** eighteenth. **em ~ lugar** eighthly.

oiteira s. f. Brazilian mahogany.

oitenta s. m. eighty, fourscore. ‖ adj. eighty. **~ vezes** eightyfold. **é oito ou ~** it's all or nothing.

oitentão s. m. (pl. **-ões**) (f. **-ona**) octogenarian: person of eighty years of age.

oiti s. m. (Braz. also **oitizeiro, oiti-da-praia**) pottery tree.

oiticica s. f. oiticica tree (Liconia rigida) whose seeds yield oiticica oil.

oitiva s. f. ear, hearing. **de ~** by hearsay.

oito s. m. eight. ‖ adj. eight. **~ de copas** (cards) eight of hearts (plate B 5). **~ vezes** eightfold. **tomar um ~** (Braz.) to have one's fill (of drink).

oitocentos adj. eight hundred.

ojeriza s. f. 1. ill will, grudge. 2. antipathy, detestation, aversion.

ojerizar v. (Braz.) 1. to dislike, have a dislike to, detest (another person). 2. to feel antipathy towards.

olá interj. hallo(o)!, holla!, (a)hoy!, whoops!, hey!, hello! **~ você!** you there!

olada s. f. (S. Braz.) 1. occasion, chance, right moment, opportunity. 2. good luck. **estar de ~** to be in luck.

olaia s. f. (bot., also **olaeira**) Judas tree, redbud.

olaria s. f. 1. pottery, factory where earthenware is made. 2. brickyard, brick factory. 3. tilery.

olé interj. = **olá!**

oleáceas s. f. pl. (bot.) Oleaceae (olive family).

oleáceo adj. 1. (bot.) oleaceous: of or pertaining to the Oleaceae. 2. oleaginous.

oleado s. m. 1. oilcloth; floorcloth; linoleum. 2. oilskin. 3. tarpaulin, cerecloth. ‖ adj. oily, greasy, containing oil.

oleagíneo adj. 1. of or relative to the olive tree. 2. = **oleaginoso**.

oleaginoso adj. oleaginous: 1. having the qualities of oil. 2. oily, unctuous.

oleandro s. m. (bot.) oleander.

olear v. to oil: 1. to smear or rub over with oil. 2. to anoint with oil.

olearia s. f. oil factory, place where oil is made.

oleastro s. m. (bot., also **zambujeiro**) oleaster.

olecrânio s. m. (anat.) olecranon: projection of the elbow.

oleento adj. = **oleoso**.

oleícola adj. m. + f. of or relative to the culture of olive trees and olive-oil commerce.

oleicultor s. m. olive grower.

oleicultura s. f. (also **olivicultura**) olive growing, olive-oil industry.

oleídeo adj. oillike, oily.

oleífero, oleificante adj. oleiferous: producing or yielding oil. **glândula oleífera** oil-bag.

oleína s. f. (chem.) olein.

oleiro s. m. 1. brickmaker; tiler, potter, person who makes earthenware. 2. (ornith., also **joão-de-barro**) baker or oven-bird (so called on account of its ovenlike nest of clay).

olência s. f. fragrance.

olente adj. m. + f. fragrant, sweet-smelling, odorous.

óleo s. m. oil. **~ bruto ou cru** crude oil. **~ canforado** camphorated oil. **~ de caroço de algodão** cotton-seed oil. **~ de amendoim** peanut oil. **~ de baleia** whale-oil. **~ de fígado de bacalhau** cod-liver oil. **~ de lavanda** lavander oil. **~ de oliva** olive-oil, sweet-oil. **~ de palma** palm-oil. **~ de rícino** castor oil. **~ lubrificante** lubricating oil. **~ mineral** petroleum. **~ santo** chrism, consecrated oil. **~ sicativo** drying oil. **~ volátil** essential oil. **copo de ~** oil-cup. **gás de ~** oil-gas. **máquina a ~** oil-engine. **pintura a ~** oil-painting. **reservatório de ~** oil chamber, oil tank. **tinta a ~** oil-colo(u)r, oil-paint. **pôr ~ na fogueira** to pour oil into the fire. **os Santos ~s** (eccl.) the extreme unction.

oleoduto s. m. pipe-line, oleoduct.

oleografia s. f. oleograph(y).

oleográfico adj. oleographic.

oleogravura s. f. imitation oil painting produced by colour lithography on canvas-textured paper, generally completed by hand-painting and varnishing.

oleômetro s. m. oleometer: instrument to measure oil densities.

óleo-pardo s. m. (pl. **óleos-pardos**) (Braz., bot.) cabreuva (Myrocarpus frondosus).

oleosidade s. f. oiliness, oleaginousness, greasiness, unctuousness.

oleoso adj. 1. oily, unctuous. 2. greasy, fat, oleaginous. 3. lardy, pinguid. ‖ **-amente** adv. oilily, oleaginously.

oleráceo adj. oleraceous: 1. of the nature of a pot-herb. 2. esculent, edible.

olericultor s. m. olericulturist, person versed in olericulture. ‖ adj. olericultural.

olericultura s. f. olericulture: the culture of esculent vegetables, esp. pot-herbs.

olfação s. f. olfaction: the sense or process of smelling.

olfativo adj. olfactive, olfactory.

olfato s. m. smell, scent, the sense of smell.

olga s. f. 1. a strip of cultivated land. 2. plain between hills.

olha (ô) s. f. (pl. **olhas**) 1. hotchpotch, stew, olio. 2. (meat)pot.

olhada, olhadela s. f. 1. eye, look, squint. 2. peep, glimpse, (side) glance. 3. flash of the eye. **dar uma ~ em** to take a keek at. **dei uma ~ no livro** I cast an eye over (on) the book. **dê uma ~ nisto** have a look at it.

olhado s. m. (also **mau-olhado**, pl. **maus-olhados**) evil eye, bewitching, spell. ‖ adj. looked at, seen, noticed, eyed. **bem ~** appreciated, esteemed. **deitar mau-~ a, dirigir mau-~ sobre** to cast an evil eye on, overlook. **mal ~** disliked, hated.

olhador s. m. seer, looker, observer, overseer, spectator. ‖ adj. seeing, looking.

olhal s. m. (pl. **-ais**) 1. archway, arch of a bridge, span. 2. (naut.) eye, ring (to fasten ropes) (plates E 5, P 9). 3. touchhole of former cannons.

olhalva s. f. field that yields two crops a year.

olhalvo s. m. **olhalva**. ‖ adj. white-eyed.

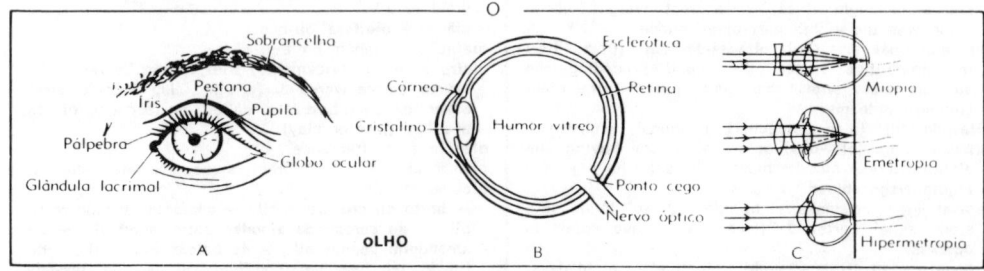

OLHO

olha-podrida s. f. (pl. **olhas-podridas**) olla: 1. Spanish stew, olio. 2. (fig.) miscellany, mixture; mess.

olhar s. m. 1. look, glance. 2. expression of the eyes (or face), countenance, mien. ‖ v. 1. to look; eye, stare at, gaze. 2. to view, sight, behold. 3. to consider. 4. to keep vigil, watch. 5. to care for, protect, look after. 6. to feel interested. 7. to pay (or give) attention to. 8. to observe, contemplate. 9. to study, inspect, examine. 10. to face, front. 11. to scan. 12. (Braz., bot.) to bud, sprout. 13. **~-se** to look at o. s. (in the mirror) or at each other.
~ amoroso ogle. **~ fixo** stare. **~ através** to look through. **~ ao longe** to look afar, look into the future. **~ com bons olhos** to look upon with favo(u)r. **~ com desprezo** to look at with disdain. **~ de cima** to overlook, look down on. **~ de esguelha** to look askance. **~ para fora** to look out, stick out. **~ para o dia de amanhã** (fig.) to look out for rainy days. **~ pelo rabinho dos olhos** to glance sideways at. **~ por** to care for, mind. **~ rapidamente** to blink. **~ sonhador** far-away look. **de ~ abatido** tired-looking, worn-looking. **de ~ aquilino** eagle-eyed. **~es significativos** telltale looks. **lançar um ~ furtivo** to steal a glance at. **ela olhou em redor de si** she looked round her. **ela olhou-me** she gave me a look. **ele olhou apaixonadamente para ela** he gave her the glad eyes. **ele olhou demoradamente para o quadro** he gazed at the picture. **ele olhou para o seu relógio** he consulted his watch. **ele olhou para** he glanced his eye at. **não olhe para ela com ~es lânguidos** don't cast sheep's eyes at her. **ela lhe lançou ~es (meigos)** she made eyes at him. **a cavalo dado não se olham os dentes** beggars must be no choosers, look not a gift horse in the mouth. **sentido! ~ à direita, à esquerda!** (mil.) attention! eyes front, right, left! **olhe! lo!, behold! ele me olhou dos pés à cabeça** he eyed me from top to toe.

olheiras s. f. pl. shadows under or around the eyes.
olheirento adj. having shadows under the eyes (for lack of sleep).
olheiro s. m. 1. foreman, overseer. 2. superintendent, inspector. 3. informer. 4. spring, fountain, jet of water. 5. (Braz.) public guard of parked cars.
olhento adj. eyed; porous, bored, full of holes.
olhete s. m. 1. little eye or opening. 2. kink (in a rope).
olhiagudo adj. sharp-eyed, piercing.
olhibranco adj. (also **olhalvo**) white-eyed.
olhimanco adj. 1. squint-eyed. 2. one-eyed.
olhinegro, olhipreto adj. black-eyed.
olhirridente adj. m. + f. gay-eyed.
olhitouro, olhitoiro adj. having eyes like a bull's.
olhizaino adj. 1. squint-eyed, cross-eyed. 2. one-eyed.
olhizarco adj. blue-eyed.
  cavalo ~ walleyed horse.

olho (ô) s. m. 1. eye, vision (plates C 12, 15, G 1, O). 2. eyesight. 3. sight, view, look. 4. care, attention. 5. (bot.): a) button, bud. b) knothole. 6. (typogr.) face (of a type) (plate T 6). 7. eye of a tool, needle (plates A 1, 6, M 5). 8. hole (cheese). 9. bunghole.
~ clínico clinical eye. **~ da rua** the middle of the street. **~ de agulha** ear, the eye of a needle. **~ de tipo** (typogr.) face. **~ de vidro** glass eye. **~ estrábico** cross-eye, walleye. **~ por ~** tit for tat, an eye for an eye, claw me and I'll claw you. **~ por ~, dente por dente** an eye for an eye, a tooth for a tooth. **~ preto** black eye. **a ~ nu** with naked eye. **abaixar os olhos** to cast down the eyes. **abrir os olhos** to awaken, look out for. **abrir os olhos a** (fig.) to undeceive s. o. **arregalar os olhos** to open wide one's eyes, stare. **bons olhos o vejam!** well! met! **com olhos estreitos** slit-eyed. **com os olhos encovados** hollow-eyed. **com outros olhos** with other eyes. **custar os olhos da cara** to be excessively expensive. **de olhos azuis** blue-eyed. **de olhos pequenos** small-eyed. **de olhos abertos (fechados)** with the eyes open (shut). **deitar poeira nos olhos** to throw dust into someone's eyes. **diante dos meus olhos** before my face. **ela está de ~ nele** she sets her cap at him. **ela ficou de ~ nele** she kept her eyes peeled. **enquanto o diabo esfrega um ~** in the twinkling of an eye. **faz lacrimejar os olhos** it makes your eyes water. **fechar os olhos a** to connive at. **fique de ~ nele!** keep an eye on him! **isto me custou os olhos da cara** it cost me awfully much. **levantar os olhos** to look up. **longe dos olhos, longe do coração** out of sight, out of mind. **menina do ~** (fig.) apple of an eye, darling. **não ver com bons olhos** to take a dim view of. **nós ficamos de olhos abertos** we had our eyes wide open. **num abrir e fechar de olhos** in the twinkling of an eye. **pelos seus lindos olhos** for his fair face. **o patrão o pôs no ~ da rua!** his boss threw him out, gave him the kick. **ponha-se no ~ da rua!** get out of here! **o que os olhos não vêem o coração não sente** what you don't know won't hurt you. **quatro olhos vêem mais que dois** two heads are better than one. **seus olhos foram maiores do que a boca** your eyes were bigger than your belly. **ter bom ~ clínico** (med.) to be a good diagnostician. **ela tinha os olhos rasos de lágrimas** her eyes were flooded with tears. **a olhos vistos** visibly, plainly, obviously. **~ mágico** 1. a small spyglass set in a door to identify would-be visitors. 2. (electronics) a visual radio tuning device.
olho-d'água s. m. (pl. **olhos-d'água**) water spring.
olho-de-boi s. m. (pl. **olhos-de-boi**) 1. (tech., naut., archit.) bull's-eye, deck light. 2. the first Brazilian postage stamp. 3. (ichth.) yellowtail, amber jack. 4. (bot.) oxeye (bean).
olho-de-cabra s. m. (pl. **olhos-de-cabra**) 1. an early Brazilian postage stamp. 2. (bot.) a kind of rib grass.

olho-de-cão s. m. (pl. **olhos-de-cão**) catalufa, bigeye: a marine spiny-finned fish (Priacanthus arenatus).

olho-de-fogo s. m. (pl. **olhos-de-fogo**) (Braz.) 1. (pop.) albino. 2. (ichth.) queriman.

olho-de-gato s. m. (pl. **olhos-de-gato**) 1. plant of the family Caesalpiniaceae, bonduc, nicker tree. 2. (pop.) rear-light (motorcycle); reflector (bicycle). 3. (min.) cat's-eye.

olho-de-peixe s. m. (pl. **olhos-de-peixe**) 1. (min.) white chalcedony. 2. (Braz., pop.) corn, callus.

olho-de-perdiz s. m. (pl. **olhos-de-perdiz**) 1. (bot.) bird's-eye, pheasant's-eye, garden pink. 2. (fig.) a small corn on the toe.

olho-de-pombo s. m. (pl. **olhos-de-pombo**) (Braz., bot.) jequirity.

olho-de-vidro s. m. (pl. **olhos-de-vidro**) (Braz., ichth.) a squirrel fish.

olho mágico s. m. (pl. **olhos mágicos**) (radio) cathodic eye, tuning eye, tunoscope.

olhudo adj. big-eyed, ox-eyed, goggle-eyed.

olíbano s. m. olibanum, frankincense: fragrant gum resin used as incense.

oligarca s. m. oligarch: member or follower of an oligarchy.

oligarquia s. f. oligarchy: 1. form of government by a small exclusive class; government by a few. 2. the group thus governing.

oligárquico adj. oligarchic(al).

oligisto s. m. (min.) oligist: specular iron ore.

oligoceno s. m. (geol.) Oligocene: period between the Eocene and Miocene (Tertiary series).

oligoclasita s. f. (min.) oligoclase: a soda-lime triclinic feldspar.

oligocolia s. f. (med.) oligocholia: a lack or deficiency of the bile.

oligocronômetro s. m. oligochronometer: instrument to measure very small time intervals.

oligodacria s. f. (med.) deficient tear secretion.

oligoemia s. f. (also **anemia**) oligohemia, deficiency of the blood volume.

oligofilo adj. (bot.) oligophyllous: having few leaves.

oligofrenia s. f. (med., also **oligopsiquia**) oligophrenia: mental deficiency.

oligoqueto s. m. (zool.) earthworm (the popular name is **minhoca**).

oligoquilia s. f. (med.) oligochylia: deficiency of chyle.

oligospermia s. f. (med.) oligospermia: deficiency of semen.

oligospermo adj. (bot.) oligospermous: having few seeds.

oligossialia s. f. (path.) oligosialia: diminished secretion of saliva.

oligotriquia s. f. (med.) oligotrichia: congenital thinness of hair growth.

oliguresia, oligúria, oliguria s. f. oliguria, oliguresis: diminished secretion of urine.

oligúrico s. m. one who suffers from oliguria. ‖ adj. oliguretic.

olimpíada, olimpíade s. f. Olympiad: 1. (Gr. hist.) period of four years from one celebration of the Olympic games to the next. 2. (also **~s**, sport) the quadrennial celebration of modern Olympic games.

olimpiano s. m. (myth.) Olympian: a dweller in Olympus, one of the deities.

olímpico adj. 1. Olympic: a) (Gr. hist.) of or pertaining to Olympia. b) (Gr. myth.) pertaining to the Olympus. 2. (fig.) divine, pompous.

Olimpo s. m. Olympus: 1. (Gr. myth.): a) the abode of gods. b) the gods. 2. (fig., poet.) heaven.

oliniáceo adj. (bot.) oliniaceous.

olissiponense adj. m. + f. of or referring to Lisbon.

oliva s. f. 1. (more usual: **azeitona**) olive. 2. (also **oliveira**) olive tree. 3. (zool.) an olive shell.

óleo de ~ olive oil.

oliváceo adj. olivaceous, olive-green (colour).

olival s. m. (pl. **-ais**) (also **oliveiral, olivedo**) olive-yard, olive grove.

olivar adj. m. + f. **olivário** m. olivary: resembling an olive, olive-shaped, oliviform.

oliveira s. f. olive tree.

ramo de ~ olive-branch.

oliveiral s. m. (pl. **-ais**) (also **olival**) olive-yard.

olíveo adj. (poet.) of or referring to the olive tree.

olivicultor s. m. (also **oleicultor**) olive grower.

olivicultura s. f. (also **oleicultura**) olive growing, cultivation of olive trees.

olivina s. f. (min.) olivine, chrysolite: a green-coloured, translucent, orthorhombic mineral.

olmedal s. m. (pl. **-ais**) **olmedo** s. m. an elm grove.

olmeira s. f. (also **ulmária**) (bot.) goat's-beard, meadow-sweet.

olmeiro, olmo s. m. elm: tree of the genus Ulmus.

olor s. m. (poet.) aroma, fragrance, perfume, balminess, scent, odour.

oloroso adj. aromatic, fragrant, odorous.

olvidamento s. m. forgetting.

olvidar v. 1. to forget, fail to remember, slip one's memory. 2. to be unable to remember. 3. to omit, neglect, leave out. 4. **~-se** to forget o. s.

olvidável adj. m. + f. (pl. **-áveis**) forgettable.

olvido s. m. 1. forgetfulness, oblivion. 2. (fig.) rest, repose, tranquillity.

omagra s. f. omagra: gout in the shoulder.

omalgia s. f. omalgia: pain in the shoulder.

ombrear v. 1. to shoulder, bear (a burden). 2. to equal, compare, match, be on a par with. 3. to rival with.

ele não chega a se ~ **com** (fig.) he cannot hold a candle to.

ombreira s. f. 1. shoulder piece (clothes). 2. door-case, door-post, door-jamb (plates J 1, P 10).

ombro s. m. 1. shoulder (plates C 6, 18). 2. (fig.) robustness, strength; diligence, effort.

~ **a** ~ side by side. ~ **armas!** (mil.) shoulder arms! **de ~s largos** square-built (person). **encolher os ~s** (also fig.) to shrug one's shoulders. **olhar alguém por cima do** ~ to look down upon, despise, disdain (a person). **tenho em meus ~s a preocupação de cuidar de suas crianças** I have the care for his children on my back.

ômega s. m. omega: 1. the last letter of the Greek alphabet. 2. (fig.) the end; the last of a series.

omeleta s. f. omelet (obs. in Brazil).

omelete s. f. (Braz.) omelet: dish of beaten eggs with cheese, ham, etc.

ominar v. (also **agourar**) 1. to augur ill. 2. to portend, foreshow, presage.

ominoso adj. 1. ominous, inauspicious, portentous, bodeful. 2. baneful, detestable, hateful. ‖ **-amente** adv. ominously.

omissão s. f. (pl. **-ões**) 1. omission, neglect, oversight, negligence. 2. lacuna, default, failure, fault. 3. preterition, elimination. 4. (jur.) nonfeasance. 5. forgetfulness.

salvo erro ou ~ errors and omissions excepted.

omisso adj. 1. omissive. 2. negligent, careless. 3. remiss, neglectful. 4. deficient, incomplete.

omitido adj. suppressed, omitted, undone.

omitir v. 1. to omit, overlook, neglect. 2. to overslip, leave out, pretermit. 3. to default, fail. 4. to forget. 5. to expurge, eliminate, suppress. 6. to skip, pass without notice.

omófago adj. omofagic, omophagous, eating raw meat.

omoplata s. f. (anat.) omoplate: the shoulder-blade or scapula (plate C 18).
omotocia s. f. (med.) premature delivery or labour.
onagra s. f. (bot.) evening-primrose.
onagrácea s. f. (bot.) the evening primrose family.
onagráceo adj. (bot.) onagraceous.
onagro s. m. (zool.) onager: a wild ass.
onanismo s. m. masturbation, onanism, sexual self--abuse.
onanista s. m. + f. onanist, masturbator. ‖ adj. onanistic.
onanizar-se v. to masturbate, practise onanism or sexual self-abuse.
onça (I) s. f. ounce: 1. old unit of weight about 1/16th of a **libra** (28.69 gr); also the ounce avoirdupois (1/16th of a pound or 28.3495 gr). 2. Spanish double doubloon (coin).
onça (II) s. f. 1. (zool.) jaguar (Panthera onca). 2. (fig.) ugly person. 3. (fig.) very strong and corageous man; daredevil. ‖ adj. corageous, bold, daring.
ele é amigo da ~ (Braz.) he is a false friend. **do tempo da** ~ very old, old-fashioned, from way back.
onça-d'água s. f. (pl. **onças-d'água**) (Braz., zool.) a kind of otter.
onça-parda s. f. (pl. **onças-pardas**) (Braz., zool.) cougar, puma.
onça-pintada s. f. (pl. **onças-pintadas**) (Braz., zool.) jaguar.
onceiro s. m. (Braz.) hound used in the chase of the jaguar.
oncologia s. f. oncology: the study and knowledge about tumours.
oncotomia s. f. (surg.) oncotomy: the incision into or an excision of a tumour.
oncotômico adj. of or relating to oncotomy.
onda s. f. 1. wave: a) billow, comber, surge, a moving ridge or swell of water, undulation, roughness of the sea (plate C 19). b) (phys., radio) vibration, oscillation. 2. (fig.) agitation, moving, tumult, confusion.
~ **amortecedora** damping wave. ~ **de arrebentação** breaker (plate P 17). ~ **de calor** heat wave. ~ **de frio** cold wave, a cold snap. ~**s curtas** (radio) short waves. ~**s encrespadas** skipper's daughters. ~**s etéreas** (radio) ether waves. ~**s longas** (radio) long waves. ~**s médias** (radio) medium waves. ~**s ultra-curtas** ultra-short waves. ~ **sonora** sound wave. ~**s hertzianas** Hertzian waves. **atacaram em** ~**s sucessivas** they attacked in waves. **ao sabor das** ~**s** at the mercy of the waves, afloat, adrift. **ir na** ~ to be cheated, to be taken in, be badly left. **uma** ~ **de gente** a rush of people.
ondada s. f. many waves.
onda-maré s. f. (pl. **ondas-marés**) tide wave.
onde adv. where. ‖ pron. wherein, in which.
~ **ele viu isto?** where did he see that? ~ **posso encontrar um médico?** whereabouts can I find a doctor? ~ **quer que seja** no matter where, wheresoever, wherever. ~ **você está?** where are you? **de** ~? (= **donde?**) (from) whence? **de** ~ **em** ~ now and then, here and there. **de** ~ **você vem?** where do you come from? **diga-me o lugar de** ~ **você vem** tell me the place from whence you come. **o** ~ **e o como** the where and the how. **para** ~ **estão indo eles?** wherever are they going? **para** ~ **foram eles?** which way did they go? **por** ~? which way? **você está** ~ **quis estar** you are where you wished to be.
ondeado s. m. undulation. ‖ adj. (also **ondulado**) 1. wavy, billowy, undulate(d). 2. rippled, crisp. 3. corrugated.
ondeante adj. m. + f. (also **ondulante**) 1. undulating, undulant, waving, billowing. 2. (bot.) undate(d).

ondear v. 1. to wave, sway, billow. 2. to undulate, ripple. 3. to flow, fluctuate, float. 4. to agitate, rock. 5. to move in spirals, to serpentine. 6. to wimple, dimple.
ondina s. f. (Nordić myth.) undine: a female water spirit.
ondômetro s. m. (radio) ondometer: an instrument for measuring Hertzian waves.
ondulação s. f. (pl. **-ões**) 1. undulation, fluctuation, waving. 2. waviness. 3. curling, corrugation. 4. wave, vibration.
~ **permanente** permanent waves. **seu cabelo perdeu a** ~ her hair went out of curl.
onduladeira s. f. (papermaking) corrugator (machine).
ondulado adj. (also **ondeado**) wavy, ondulate, crisp (plate F 5).
cabelo ~ wavy hair.
ondulante adj. m. + f. (also **ondeante**) waving, undulant, curling.
ondular v. (also **ondear**) to wave, undulate.
~ **os cabelos** to give a (permanent) wave to the hair.
ondulatório adj. undulatory: 1. of or pertaining to undulation. 2. wavy, having the form of a series of waves.
onduloso adj. (also **ondeante**) undulous, undulating, wavy, waving, undulant.
oneração s. f. (pl. **-ões**) burdening or oppressing financially or legally; taxation.
onerado adj. 1. overburdened, oppressed, taxed. 2. liable to an onus or tax.
onerar v. 1. to burden, tax, encumber, load. 2. to oppress. 3. to subject o. s. to an onus.
onerosidade s. f. onerousness, burdensomeness, oppressiveness.
oneroso adj. 1. onerous, burdensome. 2. weighty, heavy. 3. oppressive. 4. disgusting, vexatory. ‖ **-amente** adv. onerously, burdensomely.
onfacita s. f. (min.) omphacite: leek-green mineral related to pyroxene.
onfálico adj. (anat.) omphalic, umbilical: pertaining to the navel.
onfalite s. f. (med.) omphalitis: inflammation of the navel.
ônfalo s. m. omphalos: 1. (anat.) navel. 2. (Gr. myth.) sacred stone in the temple of Apollo.
onfalóptico adj. (opt.) biconvex (lens).
onfalorragia s. f. (med.) omphalorrhagia: hemorrhage from the navel.
onfalotomia s. f. (surg.) omphalotomy: the cutting of the umbilical cord.
onglete s. m. (en)graver, burin.
ônibus s. m., sg. + pl. omnibus, bus (plate V 3).
ponto de ~ bus stop. ~ **elétrico** troll(e)ybus.
onicofagia s. f. onychophagy: habit or vice of biting the nails.
onicopatia s. f. (path.) onychopathy: generic designation of ailments of the nails.
onilíngüe adj. m. + f. omnilingual.
onímodo adj. omnimode, omnimodous.
oniomania s. f. mania to acquire anything, prodigality.
oniômano s. m. spendthrift, prodigal, extravagant. ‖ adj. prodigal.
oniparente adj. m. + f. omniparient, omniparous.
onipotência s. f. omnipotence, almightiness, plenitude of power.
onipotente s. m. God himself, the Omnipotent, the Almighty. ‖ adj. m. + f. omnipotent, almighty, all--powerful.
onipresença s. f. omnipresence, ubiquity.
onipresente adj. m. + f. omnipresent, ubiquitary, ubiquitous.
onírico adj. oneiric: of or referring to dreams.

onirismo s. m. (med.) oneirism: a dreamlike, waking hallucination.
onirocricia s. f. oneirocritics: analysis and interpretation of dreams.
onirocrítico adj. oneirocritical: referring to the interpretation of dreams.
oniromancia s. f. oneiromancy, oneirocritics, oneirocritism: art of interpreting dreams.
oniromante s. m. + f. (also **onirocrita**) oneiromancer, oneirocritic: interpreter of dreams, dream-reader.
onisciência s. f. omniscience, infinite knowledge.
onisciente adj. m. + f. omniscient, all-knowing: having infinite or universal knowledge.
somente Deus é ~ God only is omniscient.
onívoro adj. omnivorous, all-devouring, eating foods of every kind indiscriminately.
ônix s. m., sg. + pl. onyx: a variety of quartz closely allied to agate of different shades of colour.
onixe s. m. (med., also **unha encravada** f.) ingrowing nail.
onofrita s. f. (min.) onofrite: lustrous black mineral; mercury sulphide and selenide.
onomástica s. f. 1. onomasticon: vocabulary or collection of proper names. 2. their explanation.
onomástico s. m. = **onomástica**. ‖ adj. onomastic: of or pertaining to proper names.
onomático adj. of or pertaining to the name.
onomatomancia s. f. onomatomancy, divination by names.
onomatomania s. f. (med.) onomatomania: mania of repeating words.
onomatômano s. m. (med.) person who has the mania of repeating words. ‖ adj. suffering of onomatomania.
onomatopéia s. f. (phil.) onomatopoeia: formation of words in imitation of natural sounds.
onomatopéico, onomatópico adj. onomatopoeic(al): of or pertaining to onomatopoeia.
onomatópose s. f. pseudonym, pen-name, nickname.
ontem s. m. yesterday. ‖ adv. yesterday: 1. on the day before today. 2. at a time not long past, recently.
~ **à noite** last night. ~ **eu fui ao cinema** yesterday I went to the movies.
ontogênese s. f. (biol.) ontogenesis: origin and development of the individual organism.
ontogenético adj. ontogenetic; of or pertaining to ontogenesis.
ontogenia s. f. ontogeny, ontogenesis, embryology.
ontogênico adj. ontogenic: of or pertaining to ontogeny; embryological.
ontologia s. f. ontology: the science of the form and characteristics of being.
ontológico adj. ontological, referring to the science of being.
ontologismo s. m. (philos.) ontologism.
ontologista s. m. + f. ontologist: person versed in ontology.
ônus s. m., sg. + pl. 1. onus, burden, charge. 2. obligation, responsibility. 3. heavy taxes.
onusto adj. overburdened, (sur)charged, overloaded, full.
onze (I) s. m. eleven (also sport). ‖ adj. eleven.
o ~ **brasileiro** (ftb.) the Brazilian team.
onze (II) s. m. + f. procurer, pander, pimp.
onze-horas s. f., sg. + pl. (bot.) sun flower, rose moss.
onze-letras s. m. + f., sg. + pl. pander(ess).
onzena s. f. 1. (math., com.) eleven percent interest. 2. usury. 3. (obs.) portion or quantity of eleven things.
onzenar v. 1. to lend money at illegal interest, practise usury. 2. to tell tales.

onzenário s. m. money jobber, usurer, money-lender. ‖ adj. usurious.
onzeneiro s. m. 1. = **onzenário**. 2. telltale, intriguer. ‖ adj. 1. gossiping, intriguing, telling tales. 2. usurious.
onzenice s. f. 1. intrigue, plot. 2. tittle-tattle, gossip.
onzeno adj. eleventh.
oogônio s. m. oogonium: the female sexual organ of some cryptogamic plants.
oolítico adj. oolitic: of or pertaining to an oolite.
oólito s. m. (min.) oolite: a limestone made up of roelike grains of sand.
oologia s. f. oology: the study of or a treatise on birds' eggs.
oológico adj. oological: referring to the study of birds' eggs.
oosfera s. f. (biol.) oosphere.
oósporo s. m. (bot.) oospore.
opa (I) s. f. 1. (eccl., also **oba**) sleeveless surplice worn by clergymen. 2. (sl.) mockery.
opa (II) interj. oh!, wow!, whoop!
opacidade s. f. 1. opacity, opaqueness. 2. obscurity, darkness. 3. denseness, shadows.
opaco adj. 1. opaque, not transparent, dull. 2. obscure, dark, not clear. 3. shadowy, dim, turbid. ‖ **-amente** adv. opaquely.
opado adj. 1. swollen, swelled. 2. fluffy, puffed up.
opala s. f. 1. (min.) opal: mineral consisting of silica. 2. a kind of fine muslin.
~ **nobre** noble opal. ~ **xilóide** wood opal.
opalanda s. f. long loose ecclesiastical surplice.
opalescência s. f. opalescence, a milky iridescence.
opalescente adj. m. + f., **opalino** m. opalescent, opaline, of milky iridescence.
opalina s. f. 1. opaline, milk glass. 2. any object made of opaline.
opalizar v. 1. to opalesce, give a play of colours like an opal. 2. to opalize, make opalescent.
opar v. to swell, puff up.
opção s. f. (pl. **-ões**) option, choice, the liberty of choosing, selection.
opcional adj. m. + f. optional, subject to choice.
open market s. m. (Eng., fin.) open market.
ópera s. f. 1. (mus.) opera. 2. opera-house.
ópera-bufa s. f. (pl. **óperas-bufas**) opera buffa.
operação s. f. (pl. **-ões**) operation: 1. act or fact of operating, working; action, execution. 2. surgical procedure on a patient's body. 3. (math.) the process of adding, dividing, etc. 4. (com.) business transaction. 5. a series of military movements.
~ **cesariana** (surg.) Caesarean operation. ~ **militar** military operation. **mesa de -ões** operating table. **sala de -ões** operating room. **as quatro -ões** (math.) the four species. **submeter-se a uma** ~ to undergo an operation.
operacional adj. m. + f. 1. operating, operational. 2. ready to operate.
ópera-cômica s. f. (pl. **óperas-cômicas**) comic opera (it contains spoken dialogues and ends happily).
operado s. m. person who has been operated. ‖ adj. operated.
operador s. m. operator, surgeon. ‖ adj. operative, operating.
~ **cinematográfico** cinematographer, projectionist.
operante adj. m. + f. (also **operativo** m.) operative, operating.
operar v. 1. to produce, work, function. 2. to accomplish. 3. to operate, perform a surgical operation. 4. to act, produce, effect. 5. to take place.
ele operou um milagre he worked a miracle.
operariado s. m. the workers, working classes, proletariat.
operária s. f. feminine factory worker.

operário s. m. 1. worker, workman. 2. artisan, (handi)-craftsman. 3. labourer, factory-hand. || adj. operating.
~ **especializado** skilled workman. **sindicato** ~ trade union, (U. S. A.) labor union.

operatório adj. (also surg.) operative, operating.

operável adj. m. + f. (pl. -áveis) (also surg.) operable.

operculado adj. (bot., zool.) opercular, operculate(d).

opercular adj. m. + f., **operculífero** m. operculiferous: having opercula.

operculiforme adj. m. + f. operculiform.

opérculo s. m. 1. operculum: a) (bot.) lid, cover, calix. b) (zool.) gill-cover (plate P 7). c) (zool.) protecting plate on the foot of some gastropods.

opereta s. f. operetta: short humorous opera with dialogues.

operosidade s. f. operoseness, laboriousness.

operoso adj. 1. laborious, operose, active, productive. 2. difficult, irksome.

opiáceo, opiado adj. opiate: 1. of or pertaining to opium. 2. consisting of opium. 3. narcotic.

opiar v. to opiate, mix or compound with opium; narcotize.

opiato s. m. (pharm.) opiate: medicine containing opium, a narcotic.

opífero adj. (poet.) aiding, helpful.

opífice s. m. (obs.) artificer, workman.

opifício s. m. work, labour, workmanship.

opilação s. f. 1. oppilation, obstruction. 2. (Braz.) ancylostomiasis, hookworm disease.

opilado s. m. person affected with the hookworm disease. || adj. suffering from hookworm disease.

opilar v. 1. to oppilate, obstruct (liver, intestines, etc.). 2. to hinder, block, obstruct.

opilência s. f. (med.) = **epilepsia.**

opilião s. m. (pl. -ões) (zool.) opilio: a harvestman.

opimo adj. 1. excellent, eminent. 2. rich, fruitful, fertile, abundant, productive.

opinante s. m. + f. person who holds an opinion. || adj. m. + f. holding an opinion, opining.

opinar v. 1. to judge, opine, deem. 2. to think, consider, suppose. 3. to vote, give or express an opinion about. 4. to estimate. 5. to express o. s.

opinativo adj. 1. opinionative. 2. arbitrary, despotic.

opinável adj. m. + f. (pl. -áveis) conjectural; problematic; susceptible to dispute.

opinião s. f. (pl. -ões) 1. opinion, view, judg(e)ment. 2. impression, notion, mind, feeling. 3. thinking, idea, thought. 4. conjecture, point of view. 5. reputation, credit. 6. (Braz., fig.) freak, caprice.
~ **pública** public opinion. **da mesma** ~ like-minded, at one with. **de acordo com a** ~ **geral** by all accounts. **dar a sua** ~ to speak one's mind. **ele deu a sua** ~ **a respeito** he passed his verdict upon it. **ele dá muito valor à sua** ~ he sets great store by her opinion. **ele é da minha** ~ he is of my way of thinking. **mudar de** ~ to sway, change one's mind. **na minha** ~ in my opinion (or view), to my thinking, as I take it. **ninguém pediu sua** ~ your criticism was not called for. **qual é a sua** ~? what is your opinion? **qual é a sua** ~ **a respeito?** what is your slant about it?, what do you think about it? **sou de** ~ **que** I hold the opinion that. **ser da mesma** ~ to be of the same mind. **sou inteiramente da sua** ~ I am quite of your mind.

opiniático adj. opinionated, self-conceited, arrogant.

opinioso adj. 1. opinionative, opinionated. 2. stubborn, headstrong, contumacious. 3. (Braz.) self-willed, whimsical.

ópio s. m. opium: narcotic derived from the unripe capsules of the opium poppy.

opiofagia s. f. opium-eating.

opiófago s. m. opium-eater.

opiomania s. f. opiumism, opium habit.

opiômano, opiomaníaco s. m. opium-eater, opium-smoker. || adj. opium-eating, opium-smoking.

opíparo adj. magnificent, sumptuous, abounding.

opístio s. m. (anat.) opisthion.

opistódomo s. m. (archit.) opisthodome.

opistogástrico adj. (anat.) opisthogastric: behind the stomach.

opistoglifa s. f. opisthogliphous snake.

opistógrafo s. m. opisthograph: manuscript with writing on both sides. || adj. opisthograpihc: written on both sides.

opodeldoque s. m. (pharm.) opodeldoc: a camphorated liniment or balm.

opoente, oponente s. m. + f. opponent, antagonist, adversary, rival. || adj. opponent, opposing, adversative.

opopânace, opópanax s. m. opopanax: 1. the plant. 2. the perfume.

opor v. 1. to oppose: a) hinder, prevent. b) place in front. c) make a stand, refuse, resist. d) place in opposition, set against; to object to, counter, thwart; to offer resistance, withstand, resist, be opposed to. 2. to refuse, gainsay; to antagonize, contradict. 3. to impugn, contravene.
~-**se a projeto de lei** to block (a law). ~-**se tenazmente** to set one's face against. **ele opôs resistência** he offered resistance, showed fight.

oportunidade s. f. opportunity, favourable occasion, chance, convenience, turn, vantage.
aproveitar a ~ to take an opportunity. **cada qual tem a sua** ~ everyone has his chance, every dog has his day. **dê-lhe** ~ **de fazê-lo** put him in the way of doing it. **vamos dar-lhe uma** ~ let us give him a chance. **ele esperou sua** ~ he watched his opportunity. **na primeira** ~ at the first opportunity. **perder a** ~ to miss the opportunity. **uma boa** ~ a lucky chance, good innings.

oportunismo s. m. opportunism.

oportunista s. m. + f. opportunist, timeserver, temporizer. || adj. opportunistic, timeserving.

oportuno adj. opportune: 1. auspicious, propitious. 2. favourable, convenient, suitable. 3. promising. 4. well-timed, timely, handy. || -**amente** adv. opportunely, on occasion, apropos, seasonably.
no momento ~ in the nick of time. **na ocasião -a** at the proper time.

oposição s. f. (pl. -ões) opposition: 1. the act of opposing, resistance. 2. antagonism. 3. impediment, obstacle, hindrance. 4. contrast. 5. the political party opposed to the ministry. 6. (astr.) situation of a celestial body.
em ~ **a** in opposition to, against. **o líder da** ~ the leader of the opposition. **encontrar** ~ to meet with opposition.

oposicionismo s. m. oppositional attitude or behaviour.

oposicionista s. m. + f. oppositionist: member of the opposition. || adj. oppositional, opposing.

opositivo adj. oppositive, opposable, opposed.

opositor s. m. 1. opponent, opposer, antagonist. 2. candidate, aplicant, competitor (for a job). || adj. opposing, opponent.

oposto s. m. 1. the opposite, contrary. 2. opponent. || adj. 1. opposite, over against, facing. 2. contrary, adverse, antagonistic. 3. contradictory. || -**amente** adv. oppositely.
o sexo ~ the opposite sex.

opoterapia s. f. (med., also **organoterapia**) organotherapy: treatment by medicine from animal extracts.

opressão s. f. (pl. -ões) 1. oppression, oppressiveness: a) act of oppressing. b) hardship, pressure. c) tyranny, cruelty, persecution. 2. vexation, shame. 3. suffocation, stifling.

opressivo adj. oppressive, tyrannical, burdensome.

opressor s. m. oppressor, despot, tyrant. ‖ adj. (also **oprimente** m. + f.) oppressing, oppressive.

oprimido s. m. oppressed person. ‖ adj. (also **opresso**) oppressed, persecuted.

oprimir v. to oppress: 1. suppress. 2. persecute, molest, torment. 3. overweigh, (over)burden. 4. hold down, overpower, abuse. 5. tyrannize, enslave. 6. vex, humiliate, scourge.
aquilo a oprimia it preyed on her mind. **está oprimindo-o muito** it sits heavy (up)on him. **oprimiu-o bastante** it weighed on him.

opróbrio s. m. opprobrium: 1. ignominy, disgrace. 2. contumely, insult. 3. dishonour, violation, infamy, shame.

oprobrioso adj. opprobrious: 1. shameful, disgraceful. 2. held in dishonour. 3. defamatory, injurious. 4. base, vile.

optar v. to opt, choose, make a choice, prefer, decide for, select.

optativo adj. optative: indicative of or expressing desire or choice (also gram.).

óptica, ótica s. f. optics: the science treating of light, vision and sight.

opticista s. m. + f. opticist: person skilled or engaged in the study of optics.

óptico, ótico s. m. 1. opticist, oculist. 2. optician: person who makes or sells optical glasses and instruments. ‖ adj. optic: 1. of or pertaining to the eye or vision. 2. optical, pertaining to optics.

optimacia, otimacia s. f. aristocracy, government by the optimates.

optimates, otimates s. m. pl. optimates: 1. (hist.) the Roman aristocracy. 2. the nobles, aristocrats, magnates.

optimismo, optimista = otimismo, otimista.

optometria s. f. optometry: measurement of the power of vision.

optômetro s. m. optometer: instrument for measuring the refractive powers of the eye.

opugnação s. f. (pl. **-ões**) 1. oppugnancy, opposition, adversity, resistance, antagonism. 2. assault, attack.

opugnador s. m. oppugner: 1. opposer, opponent. 2. person who attacks or assails; fighter. ‖ adj. oppugnant, opposing, contrary; combative, fighting.

opugnar v. to oppugn: 1. oppose, conflict with. 2. to attack, assail. 3. to impugn, combat. 4. to refuse, reject, resist. 5. to contradict.

opulência s. f. opulence: 1. opulency, riches; affluence. 2. wealth. 3. plentifulness, abundance. 4. corpulence.
viver em ~ (fig.) to live on the fat of the land.

opulentar v. to become opulent; enrich; be plentiful.

opulento adj. opulent: 1. rich, affluent, wealthy. 2. plentiful, abundant, profuse, luxurious. 3. (fig.) splendid.

opus s. m. (L., mus.) opus: work or composition, usually numbered in order of publication.

opuscular adj. m. + f. opuscular.

opúsculo s. m. 1. opuscule: small literary or musical work. 2. pamphlet.

ora (I) adv. now, at present. ‖ conj. but, nevertheless, however. ‖ interj. well!, why!, pooh!, bah!
~ bem, ~ mal sometimes well, sometimes badly. **~, certamente!** why, to be sure! **~, ela pode ter razão** why, yes, she may be right. **~ essa!** well, I'm sure!, well now! **~ este, ~ aquele** now this, now that. **por ~** for the present. **~ tibe!** what a bore!

ora (II) s. f. Greek measure of length.

oração s. f. (pl. **-ões**) 1. (rel.) prayer, supplication, rogation. 2. (rel.) sermon. 3. oration, speaking, formal speech or discourse. 4. (gram.) clause, sentence, proposition.
~ jaculatória ejaculatory prayer. **casa de ~** place of worship. **livro de -ões** prayer-book. **ela fez as suas -ões** she said her prayers.

oracional adj. m. + f. (pl. **-ais**) (gram.) clausal, propositional.

oracular v. to oracle, oraculate, speak oracularly. ‖ adj. m. + f. oracular; oraculous.

oráculo s. m. oracle.

orada s. f. (pop.) 1. oratory, place for prayer. 2. wayside chapel.

orador s. m. 1. orator, public speaker. 2. preacher, sermonizer.

oradora s. f. oratress.

orago s. m. 1. patron or tutelary saint of a church. 2. oracle.

oral adj. m. + f. (pl. **-ais**) oral: 1. of or pertaining to the mouth. 2. spoken, by word of mouth, verbal, vocal. ‖ **~mente** adv. orally, verbally.
exame ~ oral examination (college, university).

oralidade s. f. orality.

orangista s. m. + f. (Engl., hist.) Orange(man). ‖ adj. of or pertaining to Orange or the Orangemen.

orangotango s. m. (zool.) orangutan, orangoutang.

ora-pro-nóbis s. m., sg. + pl. (bot.) Barbados gooseberry.

orar v. 1. to pray, supplicate, beseech. 2. to preach, sermonize. 3. to orate, make an oration or speech.
~ a Deus to pray to God.

orate s. m. mad, insane, lunatic, crazy.
casa de ~s bedlam, madhouse, lunatic asylum.

oratória s. f. oratory: the art of public speaking, eloquence, rhetoric.

oratoriano s. m. priest of the Oratory Congregation. ‖ adj. of or pertaining to the Oratory Congregation.

oratório s. m. 1. oratory: a) place for private prayers, small chapel, shrine. b) (R. C. Church) Oratory Congregation of priests. 2. (mus.) oratorio. ‖ adj. oratorical: of or pertaining to oratory or an orator; rhetorical. ‖ **oratoriamente** adv. oratorically.

orbe s. m. 1. orb: a) sphere, globe. b) roundness. 2. (fig.) the world, earth.

orbícola adj. m. + f. cosmopolitan.

orbicular s. m. (anat.) orbicularis. ‖ adj. m. + f. orbicular: 1. formed like an orb or orbit. 2. circular, round, spherical.

órbita s. f. 1. orbit: a) (astr.) the path of a heavenly body. b) (anat., zool.) the bony cavity of the eye, eye socket (plate P 7). c) the ring around the eye of a bird. 2. (fig.) range or sphere of action, scope.

orbitar v. to orbit (around something); to describe an orbit.

orbitário adj. (also **orbital** m. + f., pl. **-ais**) 1. (astr.) of or relating to an orbit. 2. (anat., zool.) of or pertaining to the orbit of the eye.

orbitelo adj. orbitelar (said of a spider's orbicular web).

orca s. f. (zool.) grampus, killer whale.

orça s. f. 1. guess, calculation, estimate. 2. (naut.) bowline.
andar à ~ (naut.) to go windward, take the weather side.

orçado adj. calculated, estimated.

orçador s. m. estimator. ‖ adj. estimative.

orçamental adj. m. + f. (pl. **-ais**) (also **orçamentário**) adj. budgetary: of or relating to a budget.

orçamentista s. m. + f. (Braz.) budgeter, estimator.

orçamento s. m. 1. budget. 2. calculation, cost estimate, valuation.
fazer um ~ to draw up an estimate. **equilibrar um ~** to balance a budget.

orçaneta s. f. (bot.) alkanet.

orçar v. 1. to calculate, rate, compute, reckon; estimate, apprize. 2. to budget for. 3. (naut.) to luff, sail into the wind. 4. to match, equal. 5. to reach, attain (a number of).
aquilo orça em milhões it comes up to millions.

orchata s. f. orgeat: a sirup or drink made from sugar and almonds, crushed melon seeds or barley.

orco s. m. (poet.) hell, Hades, the abode of the dead.

ordálio s. m. ordeal: trial to determine guilt or innocence.

ordeiro adj. 1. orderly: a) methodical, systematic. b) peaceful, peaceable. 2. conservative.

ordem s. f. (pl. **-ens**) 1. order: a) disposition, regularity, method. b) tidiness, neatness. c) rule, law, edict. d) command(ment), bidding, word, mandate. e) rank, grade, degree. f) sort, kind. g) class, category, group. h) direction, prescription, regulation. i) arrangement, array. j) (R. C. Church) one of the seven sacraments, the sacrament of ordenation. k) religious order, brotherhood. 2. peace, discipline, harmony. 3. succession, sequence. 4. (jur.) writ.
~ cronológica chronological order. **~ de seqüestro** writ of assistance. **~ de despejo** (jur.) eviction notice. **~ de execução** death warrant. **~ de pagamento** banker's order. **~ de prisão** writ of attachment, warrant for arrest. **~ do dia** order of the day. **~ do Banho** Order of the Bath. **~ judicial** (jur.) precept. **~ judicial de pagamento** writ of execution. **~ religiosa** religious order. **~ social** social order. **~ terceira** (R. C. Church) third order of Saint Francis. **-ns maiores** (R. C. Church) the major orders. **-ns menores** (R. C. Church) the minor orders. **chamar à ~** to call to order. **até novas (segundas) -ns** until further orders. **da ~ dos 100** (fig.) of about hundred. **de primeira ~** first-rate, a one. **ele deu a ~ para vir** he gave the word to come. **ele executou uma ~** he discharged a commission. **em perfeita ~** in due (fig., apple-pie) order, shipshape. **está em ~** it is in order, (U. S. A. coll.) it is there, it's jack. **fora de ~** out of order, untidy. **manter em ~** to keep in order. **pôr em ~** to put (or set) to right, tidy, array. **por ~ de** by order (direction or authority) of. **às -ns de** under the order of. **às suas -ns** at your service. **estou às suas -ns** I am at your command. **dar -ns** to lay down the law. **eu não estou sob as suas -ns** I am not under your orders. **execute minhas -ns!** carry out my wishes! **não recebo -ns de você** I will not be dictated to by you. **receber -ns** to be dictated to. **sob as -ns de** under the commands of.

ordenação s. f. (pl. **-ões**) (also **ordenamento** m.) 1. ordering. 2. ordinance, law, regulation, rule. 3. ordination: a) (R. C. Church) the rite of consecration to the ministry. b) arrangement, disposition, order. c) act of tidying.

ordenada s. f. (geom.) ordinate.

ordenado s. m. salary, pay(ment), stipend, wage. ‖ adj. orderly: 1. in good shape or order, arranged. 2. methodical, systematical. 3. (eccl.) ordained.

ordenador s. m. 1. orderer. 2. ordainer. ‖ adj. 1. ordering. 2. ordaining.

ordenamento s. m. 1. act or effect of arranging or placing in order. 2. method to be followed in forestry and forest exploitation.

ordenança s. 1. f.: a) ordinance, authoritative rule, order, command. b) (obs.) army, military forces. 2. m. + f. (mil.) orderly: a soldier who attends on a superior officer to carry orders or messages.

ordenar v. 1. to order: a) array, dispose, assort, put in good order or shape, arrange, organize, tidy.

b) rule, regulate. c) (eccl.) ordain. d) command, bid, enjoin. 2. to prepare. 3. to consecrate. 4. **~-se:** a) to take (holy) orders. b) to prepare o. s. to.
~ a batalha to array troops for battle. **~ que seja feita alguma coisa** to command s. th. to be done. **ele ordenou-se sacerdote em 1958** he took the holy orders in 1958. **ordeno que lhe seja dito!** I command that he should be told.

ordenável adj. m. + f. (pl. **-áveis**) 1. orderable: capable of being ordered, biddable. 2. ordainable.

ordenha s. f. milking.

ordenhador s. m. milker.

ordenhadora s. f. milkmaid.

ordenhar v. to milk, draw milk from the udder.

ordinal adj. m. + f. (pl. **-ais**) (gram.) ordinal.
número ~ ordinal.

ordinando s. m. ordinand: person about to be ordained or to receive the holy orders. ‖ adj. ordaining.

ordinária s. f. 1. (daily, monthly or yearly) expenses. 2. food allowance; fare.

ordinário s. m. ordinary: 1. common way or practice, custom. 2. high Church official. 3. (R. C. Church) order of the Mass. ‖ adj. 1. ordinary: a) habitual, customary, usual, common, everyday. b) commonplace, mediocre. c) regular, normal. d) frequent, general. 2. bad, of poor quality. 3. vulgar, low. 4. coarse, rough. 5. impolite, gross. 6. (Braz.) characterless, base. 7. wretched, shabby. ‖ **ordinariamente** adv. 1. ordinarily, commonly, vulgarly, usually. 2. basely.
fração -a (math.) vulgar fraction. **de ~ usually.

ordinarismo s. m. (Braz.) baseness, characterlessness.

oréade s. f. (Gr. myth.) oread: a mountain nymph.

orear v. (Braz.) 1. to dry in the sun or wind (washing, meat). 2. to air, go for an airing.

orégão s. m. (pl. **-ões**) (bot.) origan(um), sweet marjoram.

orelha s. f. 1. (anat., also **ouvido**) ear: a) the organ of hearing. b) the external ear (plates C 12, 18). 2. (archit.) volute (of a Corinthian capital). 3. (fig.): a) tongue (of a shoe). b) wing (of a chair). 4. (naut.) lug (of an anchor). 5. **~s** pl.: a) plowshares. b) claws (of a hammer).
~ de um livro flap (of a dust-jacket) (plate L 4). **andar de ~ em pé** to be on the lookout, wary. **até as ~s** up to the ears, over head and ears. **estar com a pulga atrás da ~** to smell a rat, to be uneasy or anxious. **ficar de ~s murchas, baixar as ~s** to come down a peg or two, eat humble pie. **Pedro e João batem ~s na estupidez** Peter and John run neck and neck in stupidity. **protetor de ~s** ear-cap. **ele é trazido pela ~** he is lead by the nose. **torcer as ~** to repent. **fazer ~s de mercador** to turn a deaf ear.

orelha-de-burro s. f. (pl. **orelhas-de-burro**) (bot., also **orelha-de-onça**) rough comfrey.

orelha-de-cabra s. f. (pl. **orelhas-de-cabra**) (bot.) round-head plantain.

orelha-de-gato s. f. (pl. **orelhas-de-gato**) (Braz., bot.) St.-John's-wort.

orelha-de-judas s. f. (pl. **orelhas-de-judas**) (bot.) jew's-ear.

orelha-de-lebre s. f. (pl. **orelhas-de-lebre**) (bot.) rose--campion, mullein pink.

orelha-de-rato s. f. (pl. **orelhas-de-rato**) (bot.) forget--me-not, field scorpion grass.

orelha-de-urso s. f. (pl. **orelhas-de-urso**) (bot.) bear's--ear, auricula primula.

orelhudo adj. eared.

orelhador s. m. (Braz.) person who holds a horse, etc. by the ears, to help the tamer to mount it.

orelhão s. m. (pl. -ões) 1. the act of pulling s. o. by the ears. 2. (med.) parotitis, mumps. 3. (Braz., pop.) public street telephone.

orelhar v. (Braz.) to hold a horse by the ears (for the tamer to mount it).

orelheira s. f. 1. animal's (esp. pig's) ears. 2. earflap.

orelhudo s. m. 1. (zool., also morcego) bat. 2. donkey. 3. (fig.) dunce, stupid. ‖ adj. 1. long-eared, big-eared. 2. (fig.): a) stupid, ignorant. b) obstinate, stubborn.

oreognosia, oreognóstico, etc. = orognosia, orognóstico, etc.

orexia s. f. (med.) orexis, voracity of appetite.

orfanado adj. orphaned.

orfanar v. 1. to orphan, bereave of parents. 2. (fig.) to deprive of.

orfanato s. m. 1. orphanage: a) orphan asylum. b) the state of being an orphan. 2. (fig.) destitution, abandonment.

orfandade s. f. 1. orphanhood, orphanage. 2. orphans collectively. 3. (fig.) forlornness; privation, helplessness, destitution.

orfanologia s. f. legislation concerning orphans.

orfanológico adj. of or pertaining to orphans.

órfão s. m. (pl. ~s) (f. órfã) orphan: child bereaved of one or both parents. ‖ adj. 1. orphan: bereft of parents, fatherless, motherless. 2. (fig.) deprived, bereft of protection.

~ de pai (mãe) fatherless (motherless).

orfeão s. m. 1. choral society, (U. S. A.) glee club. 2. orpharion, a little musical instrument. 3. singing school.

orfeico adj. musical, orphean.

orfeônico adj. choral: pertaining to or sung by a chorus.

orfeonista s. m. + f. orpheonist: member of a choral society.

órfico adj. Orphic: of or pertaining to Orpheus or his doctrines.

organdi s. m. organdie, organdy: very thin and transparent muslin.

organeiro s. m. organ-builder.

organicismo s. m. (med., phil., sociol.) organism.

orgânico adj. organic(al): 1. of or pertaining to the organism. 2. of, pertaining to or affecting an organ or organs. 3. fundamental, basic. ‖ -amente adv. organically, fundamentally.
química -a organic chemistry.

organismo s. m. 1. organism: a) (organized, corporate) body. b) organic structure. 2. constitution, formation, arrangement, organization. 3. temperament. 4. (Port.) authority.

organista s. m. + f. organist: person who plays the organ (esp. pipe organs).

organização s. f. (pl. -ões) 1. organization: a) act of organizing. b) the state of being organized; arrangement, order. c) organism. d) organic structure. 2. (fig.) institution.

organizado adj. 1. organized. 2. organically structured. 3. (Braz.) methodic(al), orderly, systematical.
um rapaz bem ~ a methodic, orderly lad.

organizador s. m. organizer, organiser: person who organizes. ‖ adj. organizing.

organizar v. to organize, organise: 1. to form organically, make organic, give organic structure to. 2. to arrange, put in order, dispose. 3. to systematize, establish. 4. ~-se: a) to become organic, unite into an organic whole. b) to assume organic structure. c) to get organized.
eu organizei uma festa I promoted a party.

organizável adj. m. + f. (pl. -áveis) organizable, arrangeable.

organogenesia, organogenia s. f. organogenesis: development of organs.

organogenésico, organogênico adj. organogenic: of or pertaining to organogenesis.

organografia s. f. (biol.) organography: description of the organs.

organográfico adj. (biol.) organographic(al), describing organs.

organograma s. m. (Braz.) organization chart.

organologia s. f. (biol.) organology: study of the organs.

organometálico adj. (chem.) organometallic: of or pertaining to a compound of metal and carbon.

organopatia s. f. (med.) organopathy: disease of an organ or organs.

organoscopia s. f. organoscopy, phrenology.

organoterapia s. f. organotherapy: treatment of diseases by medicines from animal extracts.

organsim, organsino s. m. organzine (silk thread).

organsinar v. to organsine (silk).

órgão s. m. (pl. ~s) organ: 1. (mus.) pipe organ. 2. any part of an organism. 3. instrument, means. 4. newspaper. 5. part (of a mechanism). 6. agency for communication. 7. (mus., pop.) harmonium, reed-organ.
~s genitais private parts. os ~s visuais the organs of vision.

orgasmo s. m. orgasm: culmination of sexual excitement.

orgástico adj. orgastic: referring to the orgasm.

orgia s. f. 1. orgy, riot, revelry; debauch; bacchanals. 2. anarchy, disorder, confusion. 3. lavishness, squandering.

orgíaco, orgiástico, órgio adj. orgiastic: bacchanal, anarchic.

orgulhar v. 1. to make proud of, cause to be haughty. 2. ~-se: a) to pride o. s. on, be proud (of). b) to become boastful.
~-se de to be proud of, take a pride in. disto você pode ~-se it's s. th. for you to be proud of, that is a feather in your cap. ele orgulhou-se do seu trabalho he took a pride in his work. ele orgulhou-se muito de sua prudência he valued himself upon his discretion.

orgulho s. m. pride: 1. vanity, conceit. 2. self-respect. 3. arrogance, superciliousness, hauteur, haughtiness, loftiness.
ele é o ~ de sua classe he is the pride of his class. ele está inchado de ~ he is puffed up with pride. encheram-no de ~ they did him proud. você é o ~ dele you are his very pride. ~ próprio self-pride: one's own pride.

orgulhoso adj. 1. proud. 2. vainglorious. 3. arrogant, haughty, supercilious, lofty, conceited. ‖ -amente adv. proudly.
~ como um pavão proud as a peacock. muito ~ as proud as a turkey cock.

oricalco s. m. (Gr.) orichalch.

orientação s. f. (pl. -ões) 1. orientation: act of orientating. 2. (fig.): a) direction, course. b) impulse, impetus. 3. guidance, beacon.
~ vocacional professional guidance. para sua ~ for your information, for your guidance. ~ educacional educational guidance.

orientador s. m. 1. person who (or thing which) guides, directs, or orientates. 2. (fig.) guide, leader. ‖ adj. orienting, guiding, directing.
~ escolar school guidance counsellor.

oriental s. m. + f. (pl. ~ais) (more usually in the pl.) Oriental. ‖ adj. 1. Oriental: of or pertaining to the Orient or East. 2. Eastern, Oriental.
hemisfério ~ the Eastern Hemisphere.

orientalidade s. f. Orientality.

orientalismo s. m. Orientalism: knowledge of the Oriental languages, literature, etc.

orientalista s. m. + f. Orientalist: person versed in the languages and literature of Oriental peoples.

orientar v. 1. to orient, orientate: to find or determine the position of s. th. in respect to the east. 2. to guide, direct, give directions to. 3. ~-se: a) to find one's way, get one's bearings. b) to orient o. s.

ele orientou-se pelo sol he oriented himself by the sun.

oriente s. m. 1. orient, east. 2. **Oriente** the Orient, the eastern countries (Asia). 3. the Asiatic peoples. 4. the right side of a geographical chart.

o Oriente Médio the Middle East. **o Oriente Próximo** the Near East. **o Extremo Oriente** the Far East.

orifício s. m. 1. orifice, opening, hole (plates B 4, 12, 14; E 3, 10). 2. small aperture, boring. 3. (mus.) vent(age) (of a flute).

~ de lubrificação oil-hole.

oriflama s. f. oriflamme: the early royal flag of France.

oriforme adj. m. + f. oriform: shaped like a mouth.

origem s. f. (pl. -ens) 1. origin: a) source, provenance. b) ancestry, ascendance, descent, extraction. c) cause, reason, rise, motive, root. d) beginning, principle. 2. fatherland, home.

a ~ de todos os males the root of all evil. **de ~ obscura** of uncertain origin.

originador s. m. originator. ‖ adj. originative, originating.

original s. m. (pl. -ais) original: 1. archetype; pattern, model. 2. that from which anything is derived (literature or artistic works); manuscript. 3. the language in which a book is first written. 4. (fam.) singular or eccentric person. ‖ adj. m. + f. original: 1. of or pertaining to the origin or beginning. 2. creative, inventive, not imitative. 3. primitive, primary. 4. novel, new, fresh. 5. (fig.) singular, eccentric. 6. odd, queer. ‖ ~mente adv. originally.

ele é um ~ he is quite a character. **pecado ~** original sin. **um desenho ~ de Rafael** an authentic drawing by Raphael. **este é o ~ da obra** this is the original of the book (work).

originalidade s. f. originality.

originar v. 1. to originate: a) cause, rise, start. b) occasion, produce, bring about. c) create. 2. ~-se: a) to arise, stem (from). b) to proceed, result (from). c) to derive, descend.

~ novas idéias to give rise to new ideas. **esta época originou o movimento** this period gave birth to the movement.

originário adj. 1. primitive, original, originary. 2. derived, arising (from). 3. descended, descending. 4. native, natural (of). 5. originating (in). ‖ **originariamente** adv. originally.

ele é ~ do Amazonas he is a native of Amazonas.

orilha s. f. 1. border, edge, rim. 2. (goldsmithery) fillet.

Órion s. m. (astr.) Orion.

oriundo adj. (also **originário**) 1. derived, arising (from). 2. native, natural (of). 3. originating in. 4. resultant.

orixá s. m. (Braz.) a pagan African divinity or idol.

orizicultor s. m. (also **rizicultor**) rice grower. ‖ adj. rice growing.

orizicultura s. f. (also **rizicultura**) rice growing.

orizívoro adj. oryzivorous: feeding on rice (animals).

orizófago adj. oryzivorous: feeding on rice (man).

orizóideo adj. (bot.) resembling rice.

orla s. f. 1. skirt, border (plate P 2). 2. edge, rim. 3. margin. 4. fringe. 5. hem, welt. 6. (archit.) orle, fillet.

~s douradas (de livro) gilt edges (book).

orlado adj. bordered.

orladura s. f. 1. edging, binding, hemming. 2. fringe, border.

orlar v. 1. to border; skirt. 2. to, edge. 3. to hem. 4. to outline. 5. to fringe.

orleã s. f. a light fabric of wool and cotton or silk.

orleanista s. m. + f. (Fr. hist.) Orleanist. ‖ adj. Orleanist.

orlom s. m. Orlon: commercial name of a synthetic textile fiber.

ornado adj. ornate(d), ornamented, decorated, adorned.

ornador s. m. ornamenter, decorator. ‖ adj. ornamenting, decorating.

ornamentação s. f. (pl. -ões) ornamentation: act or fact of adorning; decoration, adornment.

ornamentado adj. ornamented, decorated.

ornamental adj. m. + f. (pl. -ais) ornamental, decorative, adorning.

ornamentar v. 1. to ornament, adorn, decorate, attire, garnish. 2. ~-se to embellish o. s. (with ornaments)

ela ornamentou o altar com rosas she adorned the altar with roses.

ornamentista s. m. + f. ornament(al)ist, interior decorator: person who makes a business of decorating rooms or houses.

ornamento s. m. 1. ornament, decoration, adornment. 2. embellishment, trim(ming). 3. (fig.): a) eminent person. b) honour.

ornar v. 1. to adorn, ornament, decorate, attire. 2. to embellish, beautify. 3. to bedeck, embroider, trim, garnish. 4. to illustrate (with pictures). 5. ~-se: to embellish o. s., dress o. s. up, preen o. s.

ornato s. m. 1. ornament. 2. garnishment, decoration. 3. embellishment.

ornear, ornejar v. (also **zurrar**) to bray, heehaw (ass).

orneio, ornejo s. m. (also **zurro**) bray(ing), heehaw.

ornejador s. m. brayer. ‖ adj. braying.

ornis s. m. an Indian muslin.

ornitodelfo s. m. (ornith.) ornithodelphian, monotreme.

ornitófilo s. m. 1. ornithophile, bird-lover. 2. (bot.) plant fertilized by birds. ‖ adj. ornithophilous: 1. bird-loving. 2. (bot.) pollinated by birds.

ornitofonia s. f. imitation of the cry or song of birds.

ornitóideo adj. ornithoid, birdlike, resembling birds.

ornitologia s. f. ornithology: 1. the branch of zoology which relates to birds. 2. treatise on birds.

ornitológico adj. ornithologic(al): pertaining to the study of birds.

ornitologista s. m. + f., **ornitólogo** m. ornithologist, bird expert, person who studies birds.

ornitomancia s. f. ornithomancy: divination based upon a bird's song or flight.

ornitomântico adj. ornithomantic.

ornitorrinco s. m. (zool.) ornithorhynchus, duckbill, platypus.

ornitotomia s. f. ornithotomy: the art or practice of dissecting birds.

órobo s. m. (bot.) 1. Sudan cola-nut. 2. bitter vetch.

orogenia s. f. (geol.) orogeny: the formation of mountains by folding of the crust of the earth.

orogênico adj. (geol.) orogenic: of or pertaining to the formation of mountains.

orognosia s. f. (also **orologia**) orology: the scientific description of mountains.

orognóstico adj. (also **orológico**) orological: of or referring to the description of the mountains.

orografia s. f. (also **oreografia**) orography, orology: the branch of physiography treating of mountains and mountain systems.

orográfico adj. (also **oreográfico**) orographic(al): referring to orography.

orógrafo s. m. orologist: a person versed in orography.

oroneta s. f. (Levant) net to catch flying fish.

oropa s. f. (Braz.) bee that swarmed from the hive and lives in trees.

orosfera s. f. (also litosfera) lithosphere: solid part of the earth's surface.

orosférico adj. pertaining to the solid surface of the earth.

orquestra s. f. orchestra: 1. a band of musicians. 2. the music they perform. 3. (theat.) orchestra pit, the place before the stage for the musicians (plates P 2, T 3).
~ de cordas string-band. ~ de jazz jazz band. ~ sinfônica symphony orchestra.

orquestração s. f. (pl. -ões) orchestration: arrangement of music for an orchestra.

orquestral adj. m. + f. (pl. -ais) orchestral: 1. of or pertaining to an orchestra. 2. resembling an orchestra.
arranjo ~ orchestration, orchestral arrangement.

orquestrador s. m. orchestrator. || adj. orchestrating.

orquestrar v. to orchestrate: 1. compose or arrange music for an orchestra. 2. combine harmoniously.

orquidácea s. f. plant of the family Orchidaceae.

orquidáceo adj. (bot.) orchidaceous: of or pertaining to the family Orchidaceae.

orquidário s. m. place where orchids are cultivated, exhibited or sold.

orquídea s. f. orchid, orchis: any plant of the family Orchidaceae.

orquiectomia s. f. (surg.) orchiectomy: excision of one or both testicles.

orquiocele s. f. (med.) 1. tumour of a testicle. 2. scrotal hernia.

orquite s. f. orchitis: inflammation of the testicle.

orquítico adj. (med.) orchitic: of, pertaining to or affected with orchitis.

orreta s. f. narrow valley between mountains.

ortita s. f. (min.) orthite: variety of allanite.

ortivo adj. 1. ortive: relating to the rising of a star. 2. eastern, oriental.

orto s. m. (astr.) rising of a star.

ortoclásio s. m. (min., also ortósio) orthoclass, ice-par.

ortocrômico, ortocromático adj. (phot.) orthochromatic.

ortodontia s. f. (med.) orthodontia.

ortodoxia s. f. orhtodoxy: orthodox practice.

ortodoxo adj. 1. orthodox, according to established rules, precepts, etc. 2. Orthodox, conforming to the faith of the Eastern Church.
Igreja -a Eastern Church.

ortodromia s. f. orthodromy: 1. (naut.) great-circle arch (of the terrestrial globe). 2. (topogr.) the shortest distance between two points.

ortoépia, ortoepia s. f. (gram.) orthoepy: 1. the art of correct pronunciation. 2. that part of grammar which treats of pronunciation.

ortoépico adj. orthoepic(al).

ortofonia s. f. orthophony: the art of correct speaking.

ortogonal adj. m. + f. (pl. -ais) (also ortógono) orthogonal, right-angled.

ortografar v. (gram.) to spell correctly (or according to the usage).

ortografia s. f. orthography: 1. (gram.) correct spelling. 2. (geom.) drawing in correct architectural projection.
erro de ~ misspelling.

ortográfico adj. orthographic(al): relating to orthography. || ortograficamente adv. orthographically.

ortógrafo s. m. orthographer, orthographist.

ortolexia s. f. correct expression.

ortometria s. f. exact measure.

ortopedia s. f. (surg.) orthopedics, orthopaedics, art of curing, correcting or preventing deformities (esp. of children).

ortopédico adj. orthop(a)edic(al).

ortopedista s. m. | f. orthop(a)edist.

ortopnéia s. f. (path.) orthopnoea, orthopnea, difficult or painful breathing except in an upright position.

ortóptero s. m. (ent.) orthopteran. || adj. orthopterous, orthopteral.

ortorrômbico adj. (cryst.) orthorhombic.

ortósio s. m. (min.) = ortoclásio.

orvalhada s. f. 1. morning dew. 2. dewfall, dewiness.

orvalhado adj. dewy.

orvalhar v. 1. to bedew, dew. 2. to drop moisture. 3. to besprinkle (liquids). 4. to drizzle, rain in scattering drops. 5. ~-se: a) to mist, cover or cloud with mist, become dewy. b) to wet, moisten. 6. (fig.) to gladden.
está orvalhando dew is falling.

orvalheira s. f. (Braz., pop.) heavy dew.

orvalhinha s. f. (bot.) roundleaf sundew.

orvalho s. m. 1. dew. 2. mist, drizzle.

orvalhoso adj. dewy, misty, drizzly.

oscilação s. f. (pl. -ões) 1. oscillation: a) act of oscillating. b) swinging like a pendulum. c) vibration. d) fluctuation, variation. 2. (fig.): a) vacillation, unsteadiness. b) perplexity, doubt.

oscilador s. m. oscillator. || adj. oscillating.
~ de provas (radio) oscillograph.

oscilante adj. m. + f. oscillating, oscillatory, swinging.
ferramenta ~ floating tool. mancal ~ swing-bearing. peneira ~ shaking sieve. polia ~ (mech.) floating sheave.

oscilar v. 1. to oscillate: a) swing, sway. b) move back and forward. c) vibrate. d) (fig.) waver, fluctuate. 2. (fig.): a) to vacillate. b) to hesitate. 3. to rock, see-saw.
~ entre esperança e medo to stick between hope and fear. ~ entre o medo e o amor to be torn between fear and love.

oscilatório adj. oscillatory, oscillating.

oscilógrafo s. m. (phys., radio) oscillograph.

osciloscópio s. m. (phys.) oscilloscope.

óscines s. m. pl. (ornith.) Oscines: a suborder of passerine birds.

oscitação s. f. (pl. -ões) (med., also bocejo m.) yawn(ing), gaping.

oscitar v. (med., also bocejar) to yawn, gape.

osculação s. f. (pl. -ões) osculation: 1. kiss(ing). 2. (geom.) contact of two osculating curves.

osculador s. m. 1. kisser. 2. (geom.) osculating line. || adj. osculating, osculatory; kissing.

oscular v. to osculate, kiss.

osculatório s. m. (R. C. Church) osculatory, pax. || adj. osculatory, osculating.

ósculo s. m. 1. kiss. 2. osculum: one of the apertures in sponges.

osfresia s. f. osphresis, sense of smell.

osfrésico adj. osphretic: of or pertaining to the sense of smell.

osga s. f. 1. (zool.) gecko. 2. (pop.) profound aversion.

osmandi s. m. Turkish: the language of Turkey, Osmanli.

osmanli s. m. Osmanli, Ottoman Turk.

ósmico adj. (chem.) osmic: referring to osmium.

ósmio s. m. (chem.) osmium.

osmologia s. f. osmology.

osmológico adj. osmologic.

osmômetro s. m. osmometer: instrument to measure the velocity of the osmotic force.

osmose s. f. osmosis, osmose.

osmótico adj. osmotic.

osmunda s. f. (bot.) osmund, flowering fern.

ossada s. f. 1. heap of bones. 2. skeleton. 3. ruins, mortal remains. 4. carcass. dar a ~ (Braz., pop.) to die, (sl.) kick the bucket.

ossamenta s. f. skeleton (animal).

ossaria s. f., ossário m. 1. heap of bones. 2. bone house, ossuary, charnel house.

ossatura s. f. 1. bones of an animal. 2. skeleton, frame. 3. ossature.

osseína s. f. (biochem.) ossein, ostein.

ósseo adj. osseous: pertaining to, of the nature of, or containing bones, bony.

ossiânico adj. Ossianic: pertaining to or characteristic of Ossian or his poems.

ossicos s. m. pl. (zool.) vomer.

ossiculado adj. having ossicles or bones.

ossículo s. m. (anat., zool.) ossicle: 1. small bone. 2. ~s the small bones in the tympanic cavity of the ear.

ossificação s. f. (pl. -ões) ossification.

ossificar v. to ossify: 1. convert or be converted into bone. 2. harden like a bone.

ossívoro adj. feeding on or eating bones.

osso s. m. 1. (anat.) bone. 2. (fig.) difficulty, rub, nut. 3. (sl.) sweetheart, lover, paramour. || adj. (Braz., sl.) 1. valiant, brave. 2. competent. ~ frontal frontal bone (plate A 14). ~ ilíaco whirl-bone, ilium, hip-bone (plate G 1). ~ maxilar jaw-bone (plate P 7). ~ molar cheek-bone. ~ nasal nasal bone (plate C 17). ~ occipital occipital bone (plate C 17). ~ temporal temporal bone. ~s do ofício the seamy side of a job. até os ~s to the very bones. carne sem ~ (fig.) profit without pain. eu tenho um ~ duro de roer I have a hard nut to crack. sem ~s boneless. ser pele e ~ to be nothing but skin and bones. ~ calcâneo calcaneum: the heel bone.

osso-do-pai-joão s. m. (pl. ossos-do-pai-joão) (joc.) tail bone, cocyx.

ossuário s. m. ossuary, charnel house, bone house.

ossudo adj. big-boned, bony, rawboned.

ostaga s. f. (naut.) halliard, halyard: rope to hoist sails, flags, etc.

ostealgia s. f. (med.) pain in the bone.

osteíctes s. m. pl. (ichth.) Osteichthyes.

osteíte s. f. (med.) osteitis: inflammaiton of bone.

ostensivo adj. (also ostensível) ostensive, ostensible: 1. exhibiting, demonstrative. 2. conspicuous.

ostensor s. m. exhibitor: person who shows off; (sl.) blowhard. || adj. ostensive, exhibiting.

ostensório s. m. (R. C. Church) monstrance, ostensorium.

ostentação s. f. (pl. -ões) ostentation: 1. show(ing), display. 2. splurge, dash, flaunt. 3. pomp(osity), array. 4. vainglory, vanity, pride. 5. magnificence, luxury. 6. swank. 7. boastfulness, fanfare. 8. pretension, pretence. ela não tem ~ her manner is free of pretence.

ostentador s. m. ostensive or ostentatious person; displayer, flaunter, boaster. || adj. ostentatious, ostensive.

ostentar v. 1. to exhibit, make a show of, display, parade. 2. to splurge, flaunt. 3. to swank, boast, swagger. 4. ~-se: a) to show off. b) to pride o. s. in.

ostentativo adj. (also ostensivo) ostentatious, ostensive, boastful.

ostentoso adj. 1. ostentatious, showy, displaying, gaudy. 2. magnificent, splendid, excellent. 3. flashy. || -amente adv. ostentatiously, showily.

osteoblasto s. m. (biol.) osteoblast: bone-forming cell.

osteodermo adj. osteodermatous: having a bony skin.

osteogênese s. f. (biol.) osteogenesis, ossification: formation of bone.

osteogenético adj. (biol.) osteogenetic: referring to the formation of bones.

osteografia s. f. (med.) osteography: description of bones.

osteográfico adj. of or pertaining to osteography.

osteólito s. m. (min.) osteolite.

osteologia s. f. (anat.) osteology: the science which treats of the bones.

osteológico adj. osteological: referring to the study of the bones.

osteólogo s. m. osteologist: specialist in the study of bones.

osteoma s. m. (med.) osteoma: tumour of bony tissue.

osteomalacia s. f. (med.) osteomalacia.

osteometria s. f. (anthr.) osteometry.

osteomielite s. f. (med.) osteomyelitis: inflammation of the bone marrow.

osteonecrose s. f. (med.) osteonecrosis: necrosis of bone.

osteoplastia s. f. (surg.) osteoplasty: a plastic operation by which a loss of bone is remedied.

osteoplástico adj. (surg.) osteoplastic: pertaining to osteoplasty.

osteose s. f. (also calcificação) (physiol.) calcification.

ostiário s. m. (R. C. Church) ostiary: doorkeeper of a church, porter of a monastery.

ostíolo s. m. (bot.) ostiole, small opening, little orifice.

ostra s. f. (zool.) oyster. 2. (fig.) sticker-on, bore; shadow. ~ -americana (zool.) Virginia oyster. ~ perolífera pearl-oyster. banco de ~s oyster-bed. pescador de ~s, vendedor de ~s oysterer. vendedora de ~s oysterwoman. ~ verdadeira (zool.) the true oyster.

ostráceo adj. oysterlike.

ostracismo s. m. ostracism: 1. (Gr. hist.) banishment by popular vote. 2. banishment in general, expulsion, relegation. condenar ao ~ to ostracize.

ostracista s. m. + f. person who adheres to ostracism.

ostracite s. m. ostracite: fossil oyster.

ostracologia s. f. the division of natural history studying shellfish.

ostraria s. f. heap or accumulation of oysters.

ostreário adj. (zool.) living in an oystershell.

ostreicultor s. m. (also ostricultor) oyster farmer, oyster-culturist.

ostreicultura s. f. (also ostricultura) oyster farming, oyster culture.

ostreídeos s. m. pl. Ostreidae, the oyster family.

ostreiforme adj. m. + f. oysterlike, shaped like an oyster.

ostreira s. f. 1. oyster-bead, oyster-bank. 2. oyster-woman.

ostrífero adj. ostriferous: producing oysters.

ostrogodo s. m. Ostrogoth: one of the East Goths. || adj. Ostrogothic.

ota (Braz.) interj. meaning more ore less: what a. ota, cachorro brabo! what a fierce dog!

otalgia s. f. (med.) otalgia, earache, neuralgia of the ear.

otálgico adj. otalgic, referring to earache.

otarídeos s. m. (zool.) Otaridae, the sea lion family.

otário s. m. (Braz., sl.) sucker, dull, gull, dupe, foolish fellow.

ótica, ótico, otimacia, otimates = óptica, óptico, optimacia, optimates.

ótico adj. (anat.) otic.

otimismo s. m. (also optimismo) optimism: belief that everyting is ordered for the best.

otimista s. m. + f. (also optimista) optimist: 1. person who believes in the doctrine of optimism, i. e.

that all is as good as possible. 2. person of hopeful, confident disposition who sees only the bright side of things. ‖ adj. optimistic(al), hopeful, confident.

otimização s. f. (stat.) optimization: process of determining the optimum value of a quantity.

otimizar v. to optimize: to determine the optimum value of a quantity.

ótimo adj. (abs. sup. of **bom**) 1. excellent, very good, surpassing. 2. best. 3. grand. 4. fine. ‖ interj. fine!, excellent!, swell! ‖ **otimamente** adv. fine(ly), excellently.

estar com -a disposição to be in the pink. **seu trabalho está** ~ your work is very good. **ele arranjou um** ~ **emprego** he got himself a good job.

otite s. f. (med.) otitis: inflammation of the ear.

otologia s. f. (med.) otology: the study of the ear and its diseases.

otológico adj. (med.) otological: referring to the ear and its ailments.

otomana s. f. ottoman: 1. upholstered, backless and armless sofa. 2. heavy corded silk.

otomano s. m. Ottoman, Turk. ‖ adj. Ottoman, Turkish.

otorrino s. m. + f. (Braz.) short for **otorrinolaringologista** or **oftalmotorrinolaringologista**.

otorrinolaringologia s. f. (med.) otorhinolaryngology: study of the ear, nose and throat.

otorrinolaringológico adj. otorhinolaryngologic.

otorrinolaringologista s. m. + f. otorhinolaryngologist: ear, nose and throat specialist.

otoscópio s. m. (med.) otoscope, ear speculum.

ou conj. or, either.

~ **então** or else. ~ **oito** ~ **oitenta** all or nothing. ~ **você** ~ **ele** either you or he. ~ **você** ~ **seu irmão está enganado** either you or your brother is wrong. **comporte-se** ~ **vá embora!** behave or else you may go! **é um erro** ~ **então uma imprudência** it is a mistake or else it is an imprudence.

ouça s. f. (also **oiça**) ear.

ouçum s. m. (pl. **-ões**) (ent.) cheese-mite.

oura s. f. (also **oira**) dizziness, giddiness, vertigo.

ourama s. f. (also **oirama**) heap of gold.

ourana s. f. (bot.) willow (Salix martiana Leyb).

ourar (I) v. (also **oirar**) to endow (a bride) with gold.

ourar (II) v. (also **oirar**) 1. to become dizzy, giddy. 2. to hallucinate.

ourela s. f. 1. list, selvedge (fabrics). 2. border, edge. 3. margin.

ourelo s. m. 1. strip (of heavy cloth). 2. = **ourela**.

ouricana s. f. (Braz., zool.) arboreal pit viper.

ouriçar v. (also **oiriçar**) 1. to bristle, frizzle. 2. to ruffle. 3. ~**-se** to become echinate; to become frizzly (hair).

ouriço s. m. (also **oiriço**) 1. chestnut bur. 2. (zool.) hedgehog: insectivorous mammal with stout spines on its back and sides.

ouriço-cacheiro s. m. (pl. **ouriços-cacheiros**) (Braz., zool.) coendou, a hedgehog.

ouriço-do-mar s. m. (pl. **ouriços-do-mar**) (Braz., zool.) (also **pindá**) sea-urchin, sea hedgehog.

ourinque, ouringue s. m. (naut.) buoy rope.

ourives s. m., sg. + pl. 1. goldsmith, worker in gold. 2. jeweler, dealer in jewelry.

ourivesaria s. f. 1. goldsmithery, jewelry. 2. jewelry store.

ouro s. m. (also **oiro**) 1. gold: a) (min.) precious metallic element of yellow colour (symbol Au), yellow metal. b) any golden coin. c) (fig.) gilding, golden-yellow colour. d) (pop.) wealth, riches, money. 2. ~**s** pl. (cards) diamond (plate B 5).

~ **bruto** native gold. ~ **de lei** standard gold. ~ **em folha** leaf gold. ~ **em pó** gold-dust. ~ **puro** fine (pure) gold. **a preço de** ~ at a very high price.

ele vale seu peso em ~ he is worth his weight in gold. **ele tem um coração de** ~ he has a heart of gold. **imitação de** ~ talmi-gold. **mina de** ~ gold-mine. **naipe de** ~**s** (cards) suit of diamonds. **nem tudo que reluz é** ~ all is not gold that glitters. **prometer montes de** ~ to promise wonders. ~ **branco** white gold: a gold alloy containing 20 to 50% nickel and sometimes palladium.

ouro-de-gato s. m. (pl. **ouros-de-gato**) (min.) a kind of yellow mica.

ouro-fio adv. (also **oiro-fio**) likewise, equally.

ouro-negro s. m. (pl. **ouros-negros**) (Braz.) black gold: 1. Amazon rubber. 2. petroleum.

ouropel s. m. (pl. **-éis**) 1. tinsel, brass. 2. pinchbeck, ormolu, gew-gaw, bauble. 3. tawdriness. 4. anything spurious, sham, flaunt.

ouro-pigmento s. m. (pl. **ouros-pigmento**) (min.) arsenic sulphide.

ouro-pretano s. m. (pl. **ouro-pretanos**) (also **ouro-pretense** m. + f.) native or inhabitant of the Braz. city Ouro Preto in the State of Minas Gerais. ‖ adj. of or pertaining to Ouro Preto.

ousadia s. f. 1. daring, boldness. 2. courage, audacity, effrontery. 3. gallardy, bravery. 4. shamelessness, insolence, impudence. 5. temerity. 6. (fam.) nerve, face, cheek.

ele tem a ~ **de fazê-lo** he has the nerve (crust) to do it. **ele tem a** ~ **de falar com ela** he ventures to speak to her.

ousado adj. 1. bold, audacious. 2. courageous, valiant, brave, forward. 3. daring, intrepid, venturous. 4. insolent, impudent. ‖ **-amente** adv. audaciously, courageously.

ousar v. 1. to dare, make bold. 2. to be courageous. 3. to brave, venture. 4. to risk, attempt. 5. to have the courage or audacity for; to have the nerve or cheek to.

outão s. m. (pl. **-ões**) = **oitão**.

outar v. 1. to screen, sift. 2. to fan, winnow (grain). 3. to separate the wheat from the chaff.

outeiro s. m. (also **oiteiro**) hillock, small hill or mound, knoll.

outo s. m. heap of chaff.

outonada s. f. 1. autumnal harvest, rowen. 2. autumn.

outonal adj. m. + f. (pl. **-ais**) autumnal, fall: of, pertaining to or like autumn.

outonar v. 1. to spend the autumn (at a seaside), take a vacation. 2. to sprout or grow in autumn. 3. to water (land) with the first rains of autumn.

outoniço adj. 1. autumnal. 2. growing in autumn. 3. past the middle years.

outono s. m. autumn: 1. the third season of the year between summer and winter; fall. 2. harvest (season). 3. (fig.) decline of human life.

outorga s. f. 1. grant: act of granting. 2. bestowal. 3. warrant. 4. charter.

outorgado s. m. (jur.) grantee. ‖ adj. granted, authorized.

outorgante s. m. + f. (jur.) grantor. ‖ adj. granting; bestowing, authorizing.

outorgar v. 1. to approve, sanction. 2. (jur.) to grant, allot to. 3. to award. 4. to bestow, vouchsafe, confer. 5. to warrant. 6. to allow, consent, concede. 7. to declare by deed. 8. ~**-se** to declare or confess o. s.

ele outorgou plenos poderes a he conferred full powers to.

output s. m. (Engl., econ.) output: product or result of production.

outrem pron. 1. somebody else, another person. 2. other people.

não devemos desejar os bens de ~ we ought not to covet other people's goods.

outro adj. other, another: 1. different, not the same. 2. opposite, contrary. 3. different. 4. following, next after, second. ‖ pron. 1. other, another. 2. ~s pl. others, other people. **-a coisa** another thing. **-a pessoa não o faria** nobody else would do it. **-a vez** again, once more. **~ dia** 1. the other day. 2. another day. **~ qualquer** any other. **~ tanto** twice as much, as much more. **~ delito como este o levará à cadeia** another such misdemeanour will land him in jail. **a -a vida** the life to come. **de um ou ~ modo** some way or other. **do ~ lado de** beyond. **ela pediu -a xícara** she asked for a fresh cup. **em -a parte** somewhere else. **isto é -a coisa** this is another thing. **o ~ mundo** the beyond, the other world. **ou por -a** otherwise, this means, that is to say... **que dirão os ~s?** what will people say? **um ~ Daniel** another Daniel. **um ao ~** each other, one another. **em -a ocasião** then, at another time.

outrora adv. formerly, of old, yore; long ago, in former times, before now.

outrossim adv. also, likewise, moreover, further; besides.

outubro s. m. October: the tenth month of the year.

ouvido s. m. 1. audition, the sense of hearing. 2. ear. 3. sound-hole of an instrument. 4. (artil.) touch-hole.
~ externo external ear. **~ interno** inner ear. **~ médio** middle ear. **chegar aos ~s de** to reach the ears of. **de ~** by ear. **dor de ~** earache. **de ~ fino** (fig.) open-eared. **entrar por um ~ e sair pelo outro** in at one ear and out at the other. **fazer ~ de mercador** to turn a deaf ear. **as paredes têm ~s** walls have ears. **ser duro de ~** to be hard of hearing. **ser todo ~s** to be all ears. **tapar (cerrar) os ~s** to close the ears. **ter ~ para música** to have a good ear for music. **não dê ~s a isso** don't give ear to it.

ouvidor s. m. 1. listener, auditor, hearer. 2. special magistrate. 3. (colonial Braz.) a sort of justice of the peace.

ouvinte s. m. + f. 1. listener, hearer. 2. auditor (at school). 3. hearkener.
amigos ~s! listeners! (to an auditory).

ouvir v. 1. to hear, listen (to), harken. 2. to pay attention to, attend to, heed. 3. to understand, perceive (by hearing). 4. to lend an ear.
~ em confissão (eccl.) to confess. **~ mal** to mishear. **~ missa** to hear mass. **~ rádio** to listen in (radio). **ouça-me** lend me an ear. **ouça o que lhe digo!** mark my words! **fazer-se ~ (no palco)** to take the floor. **eu ouvi dizer que...** I heard it said that... **não há pior surdo do que aquele que não quer ~** there is none so deaf as he who will not listen. **por ~ dizer** by hearsay. **nós não queremos ~ nada a respeito** we won't have any words about it. **ouve-se facilmente sua voz no outro lado do salão** his voice carries well to the other end of the hall.

ova s. f. s. fish ovary. 2. ~s pl. roe, spawn, eggs of fishes. ‖ **uma ~!** interj. fiddlesticks!, nuts!

ovação (I) s. f. (pl. **-ões**) ovation: 1. enthusiastic public homage, applause. 2. (eccl.) triumphal honour.

ovação (II) s. f. (pl. **-ões**) roe, the spawn of fishes.

ovacionar v. (Braz.) to acclaim, applaud enthusiastically, cheer, homage.

ovado s. m. 1. (archit.) echinus, ovolo, the principal moulding of a Doric capital. 2. (her.) oval coat of arms. ‖ adj. ovate, egg-shaped.

oval s. f. (pl. **ovais**) (geom.) oval curve. ‖ adj. m. + f. oval, ovate, egg-shaped, oviform.

ovalar v. to ovalize, make oval.

óvalo, óvano s. m. (archit.) ovolo, convex moulding.

ovante adj. m. + f. triumphant, exultant, jubilant, rejoicing.

ovar v. 1. to lay eggs (birds.) 2. to spawn, deposit roe (fishes).

ovariano, ovárico adj. (anat., zool.) ovarian: of or pertaining to the ovary.

ovariectomia s. f. (surg.) ovariotomy: excision of the ovary.

ovário s. m. ovary, ovarium: 1. (anat., zool.) organ in which the ova or eggs are produced. 2. (bot.) portion of the pistil in which the ovules are contained.

ovariocele s. f. (med.) tumour in the ovary.

ovariotomia s. f. (surg.) ovariotomy: the removal of the ovary or of a tumour from it.

oveiro s. m. 1. bird ovary. 2. egg-cup. 3. (Braz., pop.) oviduct of a hen.

ovelha s. f. 1. (zool.) ewe, (female) sheep. 2. (fig.) member of a spiritual flock.
~ desgarrada stray sheep. **a ~ negra da família** the black sheep of the family. **cada ~ com sua parelha** every cat to her kind. **uma ~ má põe o rebanho a perder** one rotten apple spoils the barrel.

ovelhada s. f. flock of sheep.

ovelheiro s. m. 1. shepherd, person who keeps or herds sheep. 2. sheep-dog.

ovelhum adj. m. + f. (pl. **-ns**) 1. ovine, of or pertaining to sheep. 2. woolly, laniferous, bearing wool.

ovém s. m. (pl. **-éns**) (naut.) shroud, lateral support rope of the mast.

óveo adj. 1. having eggs. 2. oval, ovate, egg-shaped.

oveva s. f. (Braz., ichth) = **obeba**.

oviário s. m. 1. = **ovil**. 2. flock of sheep.

ovidiano adj. Ovidian: belonging to or characteristic of the Latin poet Ovid.

oviduto s. m. (anat., zool.) oviduct: 1. tube through which the ovum or egg is transported from the ovary. 2. (in mammals) Fallopian tube.

oviforme adj. m. + f. (also **oval**) oviform, egg-shaped (plate F 5).

ovil s. m. (pl. **ovis**) sheepfold, pen for sheep.

ovino adj. ovine, sheeplike.

ovinocultor s. m. sheepman, sheep breeder.

ovinocultura s. f. sheep raising, sheep breeding.

oviparidade s. f., **oviparismo** m. oviparity, oviparousness.

ovíparo adj. (zool.) oviparous, laying eggs.

ovipositor s. m. ovipositor: in many insects, an organ by which eggs are deposited.

ovissaco s. m. (anat.) ovisac, a Graafian vesicle.

ovívoro adj. ovivorous, feeding on eggs.

ovo (ô) s. m. (pl. **ovos**) ovum, egg, a cell formed in the ovary.
~ choco ou podre rotten egg. **~ fresco** new-laid egg. **ovos cozidos** hard eggs. **ovos duros** hard-boiled eggs. **ovos estrelados** fried eggs. **ovos mexidos** scrambled eggs. **ovos escaldados** poached eggs. **ovos quentes** soft-boiled eggs. **batedor de ovos** egg beater. **a clara do ~** the white of the egg. **a gema do ~** the yolk of the egg. **~ de páscoa** Easter egg. **pisar em ~s** to walk on eggs, tread on thin ice, behave cautiously.

ovo-de-peru s. m. (pl. **ovos-de-peru**) freckle.

ovóide adj. m. + f. (also **oval**) ovoid, egg-shaped.

ovologia s. f. (ornith., also **oologia**) oology: the study of birds' eggs.

ovológico adj. (ornith., also **oológico**) oologic(al) of or pertaining to oology.

ovovivíparo adj. (zool.) ovoviviparous: producing eggs that are incubated and hatched within the parent's body.

ovulação s. f. (pl. -ões) ovulation: the formation and discharge of the ova.

ovulado adj. ovulate: having or bearing ovules.

ovular adj. m. + f. (pl. ~es) resembling an egg.

ovuliforme adj. m. + f. ovule-shaped.

óvulo s. m. ovule: 1. small ovum. 2. (anat., zool.) ovum, egg-cell. 3. (bot.) seed-bud.

oxácido s. m. (chem.) oxyacid: an acid containing oxygen.

oxalá interj. would to God!, may it please God! ~ assim seja! I hope so!, that's what I hope!, let's wait for the best! ~ (assim) fosse! would that it were so! ~ tudo vá bem! may all go well!

oxalato s. m. (chem.) oxalate, salt and ester of oxalic acid.

oxálico adj. (chem.) oxalic.
ácido ~ oxalic acid.

oxalidácea, oxalídea s. f. (bot.) a specimen of the Oxalidaceae or Oxalideae.

oxalidáceo, oxalídeo adj. (bot.) oxalidaceous: of or pertaining to the family Oxalidaceae or Oxalideae.

oxalúria, oxaluria s. f. (med.) oxaluria: presence of crystallized oxalate of lime in the urine.

oxalúrico s. m. person who suffers from oxaluria. || adj. referring to oxaluria.

oxicedro s. m. (bot.) sharp cedar, prickly juniper.

oxicrato s. m. oxycrate: a mixture of water and vinegar.

oxidabilidade s. f. oxidability: convertibility into oxid.

oxidação s. f. (pl. -ões) oxidation: 1. (chem.) the act or process of combining (a substance) with oxygen; oxidization. 2. (phys.) addition of an electronegative element to a compound or the deduction of an electropositive one. 3. act of rusting.

oxidante adj. m. + f. oxidizing.

oxidar v. to oxidize, oxidate: 1. combine (a substance) with oxygen. 2. ~-se cause the oxidation of; rust, make or become rusty. 3. add an electronegative element to, or decrease by an electropositive one.

oxidase s. f. oxidase.

oxidável adj. m. + f. (pl. -áveis) oxidizable: capable of being oxidized.

óxido s. m. (chem.) oxid(e): compound of oxygen with another element.
~ de cálcio calcium oxide. ~ de carbônio carbonic oxide. ~ de estanho stannic oxide.

oxidrilo s. m. (chem.) hydroxyl: the radical consisting of one atom of oxygen and one of hydrogen.

oxidulado adj. (chem.) oxidulated.

oxigenação s. f. (pl. -ões) oxygenation: act or process of oxygenating.

oxigenado adj. 1. oxygenated: combined with oxygen. 2. treated with oxygenated water.
água -a oxygenated water. loura -a peroxide blonde.

oxigenar v. 1. to oxygenate: a) treat, combine or impregnate with oxygen. b) (also ~-se) oxidize. 2. (fig.) to fortify, invigorate, strengthen.

oxigênio s. m. (chem.) oxygen: gaseous element (symbol O), occurring free in the atmosphere.

oxigeusia s. f. (med.) oxygeusia: morbid acuteness of the sense of taste.

oxígono adj. (geom.) oxygon(i)al, acute-angled.

oximel s. m. (pl. -éis) oxymel: mixture of vinegar and honey.

oximetria s. f. (also acidimetria) acidimetry.

oxiopia s. f. (med.) oxyopia: abnormal acuteness of sight.

oxítono s. m. (gram.) oxytone: a word which has the acute accent on the last syllable. || adj. oxytone: having the acute accent on the last syllable.

oxiúro s. m. (med.) pinworm.

oxoniano adj. Oxonian: of or pertaining to Oxford (Engl.) or to its university.

oxum s. m. (Braz.) African divinity of the waters, goddess of the African Oxum river.

ozena s. f. (med.) ozena: fetid smelling ulceration of the nose.

ozênico adj. ozenic: referring to ozena.

ozenoso s. m. person suffering from ozena. || adj. suffering from ozena.

ozocerite s. f. ozocerite: mixture of natural paraffins.

ozonide s. m. (chem.) ozonide.

ozônio s. m. (chem., also ozone) an allotropic form of oxygen.

ozonização s. f. act of ozonizing.

ozonizador s. m. ozonizer: apparatus for generating ozone.

ozonizar v. to ozonize, treat or combine with ozone.

ozonometria s. f. ozonometry: act of measuring the amount of ozone in the atmosphere.

ozonométrico adj. ozonometric: referring to ozonometry.

ozonômetro s. m. ozonometer: instrument for measuring the amount of ozone in the atmosphere.

ozonoscópico adj. ozonoscopic: indicating the presence of ozone.

ozonoscópio s. m. ozonoscope: instrument for indicating the presence of ozone.

ozostomia s. f. (med.) ozostomia, foulness of breath, bad breath, halitosis.

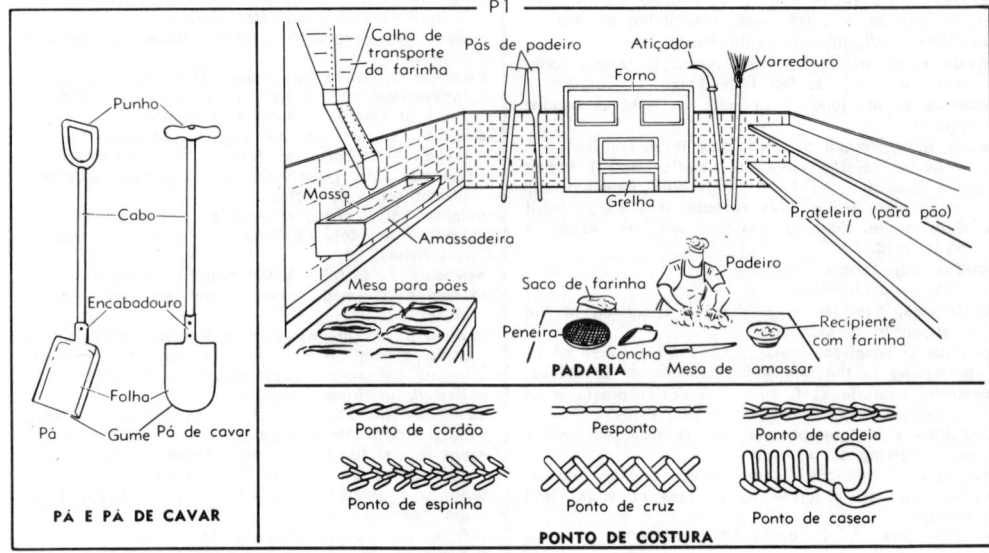

P 1

Calha de transporte da farinha — Pás de padeiro — Atiçador — Varredouro — Forno — Massa — Grelha — Prateleira (para pão) — Amassadeira — Mesa para pães — Saco de farinha — Padeiro — Peneira — Concha — Recipiente com farinha — Mesa de amassar

PADARIA

Punho — Cabo — Encabadouro — Folha — Pá — Gume — Pá de cavar

PÁ E PÁ DE CAVAR

Ponto de cordão — Pesponto — Ponto de cadeia — Ponto de espinha — Ponto de cruz — Ponto de casear

PONTO DE COSTURA

P

P, p s. m. 1. fifteenth letter of the Portuguese alphabet. 2. abbr. for: a) **padre** priest. b) (mus.) **piano** piano. c) **pp.**, **próximo passado** immediately precedent; (com.) last month.

pá s. f. 1. spade, shovel, scoop (plates J 2, L 1, P 1, 6). 2. peel: a) rudder-blade (plates B 8, 9). b) ovenpeel. 3. shoulder of an ox (plate G 1). 4. shoulder-blade of a horse. 5. scoop.
~ **direita,** ~ **de cavar** spade (plates P 1, 6). ~ **de lixo** dustpan. ~ **de hélice** propeller blade (plate P 4). ~ **do forno** ovenpeel. ~ **de remo** peel. ~ **para carvão** coal shovel. **roda de** ~ paddle-wheel. **da** ~ **virada** (Braz.) brash, rash, hotheaded, impetuous, headstrong.

paaguaçu s. m. (Braz., ornith.) the black skimmer (Rhynchops nigra).

pabola s. m. + f. (N. Braz.) 1. braggart, boaster. 2. liar. ‖ adj. 1. boasting. 2. untruthful.

pabulagem s. f. (pl. **-ens**) (Braz.) 1. fatuity, vainglory, pride. 2. boasting, swaggering. 3. trick, deceit.

pabular(-se) v. 1. to swagger, boast, bluster. 2. to talk big, pride o. s. on.

pábulo s. m. 1. pabulum: a) means of sustenance. b) food. 2. (Braz.) braggart, boaster. ‖ adj. boasting, blustering.

paca s. f. 1. (zool.) paca (Cuniculus paca). 2. bale, package. 3. m. simpleton, nincompoop. ‖ adj. inexperienced, ingenuous.

pacalho s. m. (Braz.) used in the adv. phrase: **virar** ~ to come to nothing, fall a cropper.

pacará s. m. (N. Braz.) a variety of basket.

pacarana s. f. (Braz., zool.) pacarana, false paca, long-tailed paca (Dinomys branckii).

pacari s. m. (Braz.) tree of the family Lythraceae (Lafoensia densiflora).

pacatez s. f. peaceableness, peacefulness, tranquility, placidity.

pacato s. m. peaceable or quiet person. ‖ adj. 1. peaceable, peaceful, pacific. 2. tranquil, placid, serene. ‖ **-amente** adv. peacefully, tranquilly.

pacau s. m. 1. (Braz.) a kind of card game. 2. (Braz., sl.) stick, reefer, a marijuana cigarette. **bater o** ~ (S. Braz., sl.) to die.

pacavira s. f. (Braz.) plant of the family Musaceae (Heliconia pendula).

paceiro s. m. courtier. ‖ adj. courtly.

pacejar v. (obs.) to jest, joke.

pachecada s. f. (Braz.) foolishness, nonsense, absurdity.

pachola s. m. 1. idler, loafer. 2. well-dressed person. ‖ adj. m. + f. 1. proud, boastful, swanky. 2. well-dressed, elegant.

pacholar v. 1. to swagger, boast. 2. to live elegantly.

pacholice s. f. **pacholismo** m. 1. idleness. 2. pleasantry. 3. boasting. 4. foolishness.

pachorra s. f. 1. phlegm, sluggishness of temperament, apathy, impassivity. 2. slowness.

pachorrento adj. 1. phlegmatic, sluggish, apathetic. 2. slow. 3. easy, easy-going, leisurely.

pachouchada s. f. 1. nonsense, absurdity. 2. coarse expression. 3. an obscene remark.

paciência s. f. 1. patience: a) state or quality of being patient. b) resignation. c) long-suffering, forbearance. d) name of several card games (usually a form of solitaire). 2. persistence, pertinacity. 3. (bot.) patience dock (Rumex patientia). ‖ interj. easy!, take it easy!, calm down!
~ **de Jó** Job's patience. **acostumar-se a ter** ~ **to** school o. s. to patience. **ele me aborrece a** ~ he gets on my nerves. **minha** ~ **está no fim** my patience is worn out, my withers are wrung. **perder a** ~ to lose one's patience. **tenha** ~ **com ele!** have patience with him. **uma** ~ **de santo** the patience of a saint.

pacientar v. 1. to have patience. 2. to be patient.

paciente s. m. + f. patient: 1. a person under treatment, a sick person. 2. (gram.) the object or recipient of an action. ‖ adj. patient: 1. resigned. 2. persevering, persistent. 3. forbearing, long-suffering. ‖ ~mente adv. patiently.
o leitor ~ the gentle reader.
pacificação s. f. (pl. -ões) 1. pacification: a) act of pacifying or reducing to a state of peace. b) reconciliation. 2. tranquility.
pacificador s. m. pacifier, pacificator, peacemaker: person who pacifies. ‖ adj. pacifying, peacemaking, pacificatory.
pacificar v. 1. to pacify, pacificate: a) make to be at peace, allay. b) tranquilize, calm. c) conciliate, appease. 2. ~-se to become peaceful.
pacificidade s. f. (Braz.) quality of being pacific.
pacífico s. m. a peaceable person. ‖ adj. pacific(al): 1. peacemaking, conciliatory, peaceable. 2. peaceful, tranquil, calm. ‖ **pacificamente** adv. pacifically; peacefully.
Oceano Pacífico Pacific Ocean.
pacifismo s. m. pacifism: policy of settling international disputes by peaceful means without recourse to war.
pacifista s. m. + f. pacifist: an advocate of pacifism. ‖ adj. pacifistic: pertaining to pacifism.
paco s. m. (Braz.) a parcel simulating a parcel of paper money (used by swindlers).
paço s. m. 1. palace, residence (royal or episcopal). 2. (fig.): a) the court. b) courtiers.
pacoba, pacova s. f. (Braz., also **banana**) banana.
pacobal, pacoval s. m. (pl. -ais) (Braz., also **bananal**) banana plantation.
pacobeira, pacoveira s. f. (Braz., also **bananeira**) banana tree.
pacoca s. f. (Braz.) rapid: part of a river where the current moves with great swiftness, almost a fall.
paçoca s. f. (Braz.) 1. a dish made of meat with manioc meal. 2. roasted and crushed peanuts mixed with sugar and manioc flour. 3. (fig.) hodgepodge, mixture, jumble, confusion.
paco-catinga s. f. (pl. **paco-catingas**) (Braz., bot.) spiralflag (Costus pisonis).
pacolé s. m. (Braz.) a variety of cotton plant.
paco-seroca s. f. (pl. **paco-serocas**) (Braz., bot.) = **pacová**.
pacote s. m. 1. package, packet, pack, parcel, bundle (plate F 7). 2. swindle, trick. 3. ~s pl. (Braz., sl.) money, a pile or heap of money.
ele está cheio dos ~s he has heaps of money.
fazer ~s to pack.
pacotilha s. f. 1. luggage or the like a passenger Is allowed to take with him without paying. 2. shoddy work; poor quality articles. 3. (Braz., sl.) a gang of bandits.
pacotilheiro s. m. (Braz.) person who deals in low quality articles.
pacova s. 1. f. (Braz.) = **pacoba**. 2. m. + f.: a) lazybones. b) fool, nincompoop. ‖ adj. m. + f. 1. lazy. 2. very foolish.
pacová s. f. (Braz.) a medicinal plant of the family Zingiberaceae (Renealmia exaltata).
pacóvio s. m. imbecile, blockhead, dunce, simpleton. ‖ adj. imbecile, stupid, foolish.
pactório s. m. party that joins in a pact. ‖ adj. participant of a pact.
pacto s. m. pact, agreement, compact; concordat; alliance.
ter ~ **com o diabo** to have the devil's own luck.
pactuante s. m. + f. person who makes a pact with. ‖ adj. pact-making.
pactuar v. 1. to make a pact with; join in a pact. 2. to agree (with), covenant.

pactuário s. m. 1. pact maker, covenanter. 2. covenantor: a party to a covenant, pact or agreement.
pacu s. m. (Braz., ichth.) a sort of snapper of the genus Prochilodus (family Lutjanidae).
pacuçu s. m. (Braz.) the male paca.
pacuera s. m. (Braz.) viscera (of cattle).
pada s. f. 1. a small bread. 2. (fig.) small thing or quantity.
padaria s. f. bakery: 1. place where bread, cakes, etc. are made (plate P 1). 2. a baker's or breadseller's shop.
pá-de-cavalo s. f. (pl. **pás-de-cavalo**) power shovel.
padecedor s. m. sufferer: person who suffers. ‖ adj. suffering.
padecente s. m. + f. sufferer. 2. person condemned to death. ‖ adj. suffering, ailing.
padecer v. to suffer: 1. undergo or endure pain of body or mind; ail. 2. tolerate, bear, put up with.
padecimento s. m. suffering, affliction, distress; pain; illness.
padeiro s. m. baker: 1. person who makes bread, cakes, etc. (plate P 1). 2. breadseller, breadman.
padejador s. m. 1. shoveller, person who works with a shovel or spade. 2. baker. ‖ adj. shovelling.
padejar v. 1. to shovel, spade, work with a shovel or spade. 2. to work with the peel (baker). 3. to work as a baker.
padejo s. m. 1. act of shovelling. 2. the work of a baker, bakery.
padieira s. f. 1. lintel (plates J 1, P 10). 2. door-frame, window-frame.
padiola s. f. handbarrow, litter, stretcher.
padioleiro s. m. (Braz.) stretcher-bearer.
padixá s. m. Padishah: Turkish, Persian or Indian title.
padralhada s. f. (depr.) 1. priests collectively, priesthood. 2. a great number of priests.
padrão s. m. (pl. -ões) 1. standard: rule of measure and weight; gauge. 2. model, pattern, sample. 3. guidance, precept. 4. stone monument the Portuguese erected in the territories descovered by them. 2. monolithic monument. 3. landmark. 4. inscription on stone.
~ **de vida** standard of living. ~ **ouro** gold standard, gold currency. ~ **prata** silver standard, silver currency.
padrar-se v. to take holy orders, become a priest.
padrasto s. m. (f. **madrasta**) stepfather: the husband of one's mother by a subsequent marriage.
padre s. m. 1. priest, father (plate P 5). 2. reverend. 3. Padre Father: a) the first person of the Trinity. b) title of a priest: **Padre Antônio** Father Antônio.
o Santo Padre the Holy Father (the pope). **ele tornou-se** ~ he took holy orders.
padreação s. f. (pl. -ões) act of covering (stallion).
padreador s. m. studhorse. ‖ adj. stud.
padrear v. to cover (stallion).
padreco s. m. (depr.) priestling.
padre-cura s. m. (pl. **padres-curas**) parish priest.
padre-mestre s. m. (pl. **padres-mestres**) 1. a teaching priest. 2. (fig.) wiseacre.
padre-nosso s. m. (pl. **padre-nossos, padres-nossos**) Pater Noster (Our Father), the Lord's Prayer.
ensinar o ~ **ao vigário** to teach one's grandmother to suck eggs.
padre-santo s. m. (pl. **padres-santos**) Holy Father, the pope.
padresco adj. (depr.) of or pertaining to priests.
padrinho s. m. (f. **madrinha**) 1. (eccl.) godfather, sponsor (at a baptism). 2. best man; bridesmaid

(at a wedding). 3. second (of a duel). 4. para-nymph. 5. (fig.) patronizer, protector.

ele serviu de ~ **para meu filho** he stood sponsor to my child.

padroado s. m. ecclesiastical patronage, advowson: the right to present a candidate to an ecclesiastical benefice.

padroeira s. f. patroness.

padroeiro s. m. patron: 1. patron saint. 2. the owner of the advowson. 3. protector, sponsor. ‖ adj. patronal.

padrófobo s. m. (Braz.) an enemy of priests.

padronizar v. to standardize: set the standard of; gauge.

padu s. m. (Braz.) the Amazonian coca shrub or treelet (Erythroxylum cataractum).

paduano s. m. Paduan: native or inhabitant of Padua (Italy). ‖ adj. Paduan: of or pertaining to Padua.

paga s. f. 1. pay(ment): act of paying; wages, remuneration, salary. 2. (fig.) reward.

a ~ **do pecado é a morte** the wage of sin is death. **em** ~ in reward.

pagador s. m. payer, paymaster: person in charge of payments. ‖ adj. paying: that pays.

ele é bom ~ he is good pay.

pagadoria s. f. 1. pay-office, a paymaster's office. 2. any place of disbursement of money.

pagadouro adj. (also **pagadoiro**) payable.

pagamento s. m. (also **paga** f.) 1. payment: act of paying. 2. instalment payment.

~ **adiantado** payment in advance. ~ **à vista** payment in cash, sight payment. ~ **em prestações** payment by instalments. ~ **inicial** first instalment. ~ **integral** payment in full. ~ **pontual** ready payment. ~ **por conta** payment on account. **condições de** ~ terms of payment. **contra** ~ **à vista** against payment. **dia de** ~ pay-day. **em** ~ **de** in discharge of. **folha de** ~ pay-roll. **mediante** ~ **de** on payment of. **hoje vamos receber** ~ today is our pay-day.

paganais s. f. pl. (Roman hist., also **paganálias**) paganalia: a festival celebrated in honour of Ceres.

paganal adj. m. + f. (pl. -**ais**) pagan: 1. of or pertaining to pagans. 2. heathen, irreligious.

paganismo s. m. paganism: 1. the religion and worship of pagans. 2. idolatry, heathenism.

paganização s. f. (pl. -**ões**) paganization: return to paganism.

paganizador adj. paganizing.

paganizar v. to paganize, heathenize: 1. become pagan. 2. return to paganism, turn pagan or heathen.

pagante s. m. + f. payer: person who pays. ‖ adj. paying: said of a person who pays.

pagão s. m. (pl. **pagãos**) (f. **pagã**) pagan: 1. heathen, irreligious person, gentile. 2. idolater, worshipper of idols. ‖ adj. pagan: 1. of or pertaining to pagans. 2. heathen, irreligious. 3. idolatrous.

pagar v. 1. to pay: a) remunerate, reimburse, discharge, make a payment. b) repay, compensate, retaliate. c) recompense, reward. 2. to expiate, atone for.

~ **a prestações** to pay in instalments. ~ **à vista** to pay cash down, pay at sight. ~ **adiantado** to prepay. ~ **as dívidas** to pay one's debts, quit scores. ~ **caro** to pay dear. ~ **caução** to give bail. ~ **demais** to overpay. ~ **em espécie** to pay in kind. ~ **integralmente** to pay off. ~ **na mesma moeda** to pay s. o. in his own coin, do like for like, return like for like, turn the tables upon. ~ **o bem com o mal** to render good for evil. ~ **uma visita** to pay a visit (to). **ele pagará o pato** he is in for it. **ele pagará por isso** he shall pay

for this. **ele teve de** ~ **por sua negligência** he had to pay the forfeit for his carelessness. **eu mesmo pago minha despesa** I pay for myself. **isto você pagará** (fig.) you can't get away with that. **não resta outra alternativa senão** ~ there is nothing for it but to pay. **pagarei o almoço** I'll pay for the dinner. **pago-lhe uma garrafa** I'll stand you a bottle. **pague-lhe a conta** pay her bill. **você me paga!** I'll get even with you!

pagável adj. m. + f. (pl. -**áveis**) payable: 1. that can be paid. 2. that is to be paid, due.

~ **ao portador** payable to the bearer. **ser** ~ to become due, fall due.

página s. f. page: 1. one side of a leaf of a book, manuscript, etc. 2. an event.

~ **de rosto** title page of a book. ~ **em branco** (also fig.) blank page. **a** ~**s tantas** at a certain moment, at a certain point. **na** ~ **9** at page 9.

paginação s. f. (pl. -**ões**) pagination, paging: 1. act of paging. 2. arrangement of pages.

paginador s. m. pager: person who pages books, etc.

paginadora s. f. paging machine.

paginar v. to paginate, page: arrange or number the pages (of a book, manuscript or the like).

pago s. m. pay, wages, remuneration; retribution. ‖ adj. 1. paid. 2. rewarded, retributed. 3. satisfied, gratified.

~ **com a morte** blood-bought. ~ **na mesma moeda** paid in the same coin. **bem** ~ well-paid. **já está** ~ it has been paid for.

pagode s. m. 1. pagoda: a towerlike temple in Asia; joss-house. 2. frolic, spree, revel(ry). 3. (Braz.) mockery, jesting.

de ~ (Braz., pop.) in great quantity or intensity: a great deal, very much.

pagodear v. 1. to revel, make merry. 2. (Braz.) to jeer, make fun of, mock.

pagodeira, pagodice s. f. (pop.) frolic, revelry.

pagodista s. m. + f. reveller, merrymaker.

pagodita s. f. (min.) pagodite, agalmatolite.

pagos s. m. pl. birthplace: place where one was born.

paguro s. m. (zool.) pagurian: a hermit-crab of the genus Pagurus.

pai s. m. (f. **mãe**) 1. father: a) man who has begotten a child. b) a male parent. c) **Pai** Father: the first person of the Trinity. d) forefather, progenitor. 2 (fig.) author. ~**s** pl. parents.

~ **adotivo** foster-father. ~ **da mentira** the devil. ~ **da pátria** a national political leader (as a deputy, senator, etc.). ~ **de família** family man. **o** ~**-nosso** the Lord's Prayer. **como um** ~ fatherly. **o seu** ~ **está em casa?** is your father within? **tal** ~, **tal filho** like father, like son. **sem** ~ unfathered.

paíba adj. m. + f. (Braz., coll.) awkward, clumsy, disastrous; unable.

pai-das-queixas s. m. (pl. **pais-das-queixas**) (N. Braz., pop.) a chief of police.

pai-d'égua s. m. (pl. **pais-d'égua**) a studhorse.

pai-de-mel s. m. (pl. **pais-de-mel**) (Braz.) a variety of honey-bee.

pai-de-santo s. m. (pl. **pais-de-santo**) (Braz.) (also **pai-de-terreiro, babalorixá, babaloxá, babá**) witch-doctor, medicine-man.

pai-de-todos s. m. (pl. **pais-de-todos**) (fam.) the middle finger.

pai-dos-burros s. m. (pl. **pais-dos-burros**) (Braz., fam.) a dictionary.

paié s. m. (Braz.) = **pajé**.

pai-gonçalo s. m. (pl. **pais-gonçalos**) (Braz., pop.) a hen-pecked husband; home-bird.

pai-luís s. m. (pl. **pais-luíses, pai-luíses**) (Braz.) weeds, wild growth.

pai-mané s. m. (pl. **pais-manés**) dunce; an ignorant person.

paina s. f. kapok, floss, vegetable silk, silk cotton.

paina-cipó s. f. (pl. **painas-cipó**) (Braz.) the white bladder flower (Araujia sericifera).

paina-de-seda s. f. (pl. **painas-de-seda**) = **paineira**.

painça adj. f. of or relating to husk or flour of millet.

painço s. m. 1. (bot.) Italian millet. 2. its edible grain.

paineira s. f. (Braz.) silk-cotton tree: plant of the family Bombacaceae (Chorisia speciosa).

painel s. m. (pl. **-éis**) 1. panel: a) framed picture; painting. b) pane, a rectangular piece of wood as a frame forming a compartment of a door, window, wainscot, etc. 2. (fig.) spectacle, show, sight. ~ **de instrumentos** (mot., aeron.) instrument panel (plate V 3).

paio s. m. (Braz.) 1. a variety of pork sausage. 2. fool, nincompoop; a gullible person. ‖ adj. 1. very foolish. 2. excessively credulous, gullible.

paiol s. m. (pl. **paióis**) 1. a magazine for military stores. 2. corn crib. 3. storehouse. 4. (ship's) hold; bunker. ~ **de pólvora** (mil.) powder magazine.

paioleiro s. m. storekeeper: one in charge of stores (esp. military).

pairar v. 1. to scud, lie to (a ship); tack. 2. to hover (over); brood. 3. to soar slowly. 4. to float. 5. to impend, be imminent. 6. to hesitate, vacillate. **paira sobre nós o perigo de uma epidemia** we are in danger of an epidemic.

pairo s. m. hover: act of hovering.

país s. m. (pl. **países**) 1. country: a) nation, land. b) fatherland. c) region. 2. landscape. ~ **das maravilhas** wonderland. **comércio ativo de um** ~ a country's own trade. **em todo o** ~ all over the country. **neste** ~ in this country. **os países com padrão ouro** the countries on gold standard.

paisagem s. f. (pl. **-ens**) landscape: 1. a view or scenery on land. 2. a picture with a land scene. ~ **marinha** seascape, waterscape.

paisagista s. m. + f. landscape painter, landscapist: person who paints a land scene.

paisagístico adj. of or referring to a landscape.

paisanada s. f. (deprec.) civilians.

paisano s. m. 1. compatriot, fellow citizen, fellow countryman, patrician. 2. civilian. ‖ adj. 1. compatriotic. 2. civilian. **à -a** in civilian clothes, in plain clothes; (mil.) in mufti.

Países-Baixos s. m. pl. Low Countries.

paixão s. f. (pl. **-ões**) passion: 1. love, ardent affection, infatuation. 2. strong feeling (as hate, love, joy). 3. intense emotion. 4. vehemence, ardour. 5. zeal. 6. wrath. 7. martyrdom; suffering; affliction. 8. (also **Paixão de Cristo**) the suffering of Christ. **domingo da Paixão** Passion Sunday. **a leitura é a** ~ **dele** reading is a passion with him. **ela tem** ~ **por música** she has a passion for music. **semana da Paixão** Passion Week.

paixoneta s. f. (fam.) passing love affairs; a slight passion.

paixonite s. f. (Braz., fam.) a crush, infatuation.

pajamarioba s. m. (Braz., bot.) coffee senna (Cassia occidentalis).

pajé s. m. (Braz.) 1. peai, shaman. 2. witch doctor, medicine man.

pajear v. 1. to nurse: serve as a nurse. 2. to page: act as a page.

pajem s. m. (pl. **-ens**) 1. page, attendant. 2. f. nursemaid, baby-sitter. 3. (naut.) swabber.

pajeú s. m. (Braz.) plant of the family Polyganaceae.

pala s. f. 1. visor, peak. 2. setting for a gem. 3. eyeshade. 4. (eccl.) pall: a linen-covered cardboard lid for the chalice. 5. yoke (of a dress). 6. (tail.) flap of a pocket. 7. tong, flap of a shoe. 8. (mot.) visor. 9. (her.) pale. 10. (S. Braz.) light poncho. **boné de** ~ peaked cap.

palacete s. m. 1. a small palace. 2. stately house.

palaciano s. m. courtier. ‖ adj. 1. palatial: of or pertaining to a palace. 2. aristocratic. 3. (Braz., pop.) polite, courteous.

palácio s. m. palace: 1. the official residence of a sovereign. 2. a stately house. 3. a large public bulding, edifice. ~ **da justiça** courthouse.

paladar s. m. palate: 1. the roof of the mouth. 2. sense of the taste. 3. taste, flavour, savour. ~ **agradável** toothsomeness, zest.

paladínico adj. of or pertaining to a paladin or champion.

paladino s. m. (also **paladim**) paladin: 1. in the Charlemagne romances, one of the knightly champions. 2. a champion; knight-errant. 3. strenuous defender.

paládio s. m. 1. (hist.) Palladium: a statue of Pallas Athena. 2. palladium: a) safeguard. b) (chem.) palladium: a rare metallic element.

palado s. m. (her.) paly.

palafita s. f. (archaeol.) palafitte: a lake dwelling, lacustrine hut built on piles.

palafrém s. m. (pl. **-éns**) (ancient hist.) palfrey: a saddle horse; esp. a woman's saddle horse.

palafreneiro s. m. (ancient hist.) palfrenier: a stable servant who had charge of palfreys, groom.

palagonita s. f. (min.) palagonite.

palamalhar, palamalho s. m. pall-mall (game).

palamedeídeos s. m. pl. (Braz., ornith.) Palamedeidae, the horned screamer family.

palamenta s. f. 1. (naut.) gear. 2. (mil.) everything necessary for serving a cannon.

pálamo s. m. web: membrane uniting fingers or toes (as in many water-birds and amphibians).

palanca s. f. 1. a structure of piles. 2. lever.

palanco s. m. (naut.) tackle.

palanfrório s. m. = **palavreado**.

palangona s. f. 1. a platter for roasts. 2. a large bowl.

palanque s. m. 1. stand, scaffold, raised platform (esp. at the open air) whence spectacles may be viewed. 2. (S. Braz.) post for tieing up a horse.

palanquear v. (S. Braz.) to tie to a post (a colt to break it in or dress its verminous sores).

palanqueiro s. m. person who raises platforms.

palanquim s. m. (pl. **-ins**) palanquin, palankeen: an enclosed litter.

palatal adj. m. + f. (pl. (also **palatinal**) palatal: 1. of or pertaining to the palate. 2. (gram.) uttered with the aid of the palate.

palatalização s. f. (pl. **-ões**) (also **palatização**) palatalization: act of palatalizing (sound).

palatalizar v. (also **palatizar**) to palatalize: make palatal (sound).

palatina s. f. palatine: a womans's fur tippet.

palatinado s. m. palatinate: 1. territory of a palatine. 2. dignity of a palatine. 3. Polish province, voivodeship.

palatino s. m. palatine: 1. lord or master of a palace. 2. officer of an imperial palace. 3. palsgrave. 4. voivode: governor of a province in Poland. 5. (anat.) a palatine bone. ‖ adj. palatine: 1. of or

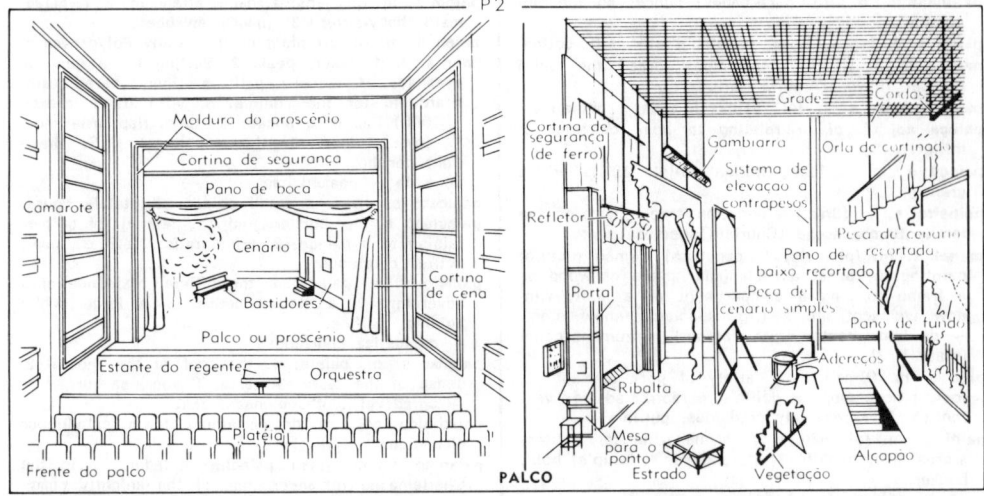

P 2

Moldura do proscénio
Cortina de segurança
Pano de boca
Camarote
Cenário
Bastidores
Cortina de cena
Palco ou proscénio
Estante do regente
Orquestra
Platéia
Frente do palco

Grade
Cordas
Cortina de segurança (de ferro)
Gambiarra
Orla de cortinado
Sistema de elevação a contrapesos
Refletor
Peça de cenário recortada
Pano de baixo recortado
Peça de cenário simples
Portal
Pano de fundo
Ribalta
Aderecos
Mesa para o ponto
Estrado
Vegetação
Alçapao

PALCO

pertaining to a palace. 2. said of persons holding office in a royal palace. 3. of or pertaining to the palate; palatal.

palatite s. f. (med.) palatitis: inflammation of the palate.

palato s. m. palate: 1. the roof of the mouth. 2. sense of the taste. 3. taste, flavour, savour.

palatofaríngeo adj. palatopharyngeal: of or pertaining to the palate and the pharynx.

palatolabial adj. m. + f. (pl. **-ais**) palatolabial: of or pertaining to the palate and the lips.

palatolingual adj. m. + f. (pl. **-ais**) palatolingual: of or pertaining to the palate and the tongue.

palavra s. f. 1. word: a) that which is said. b) term, expression, vocable, utterance. c) promise, warrant, declaration. 2. permission to talk. 3. faith, doctrine. **~!** (I give you) my word! **~ composta** compound word. **~ de Deus** the Word of God. **~ de honra** word of honour. **~ de honra!** upon my honour! upon my word! **~ de ordem** word of command. **~ divina** divine word. **~ empenhada** pledged word. **~ familiar** household word. **~ por ~** word for word. **~ que não sei** honestly, I don't know. **~ quebrada** broken promise. **~s cruzadas** crossword puzzle. **~s acaloradas** high (or hot) words. **~s mágicas** magic words. **~s pesadas** offensive language. **~s pomposas** big words. **~s sem nexo** meaningless words. **acreditei cegamente em suas ~s** I took his word for it. **a bom entendedor meia ~ basta!** a word to the wise is sufficient. **briga de ~s** wordy warfare. **com ~ elogiosas** in terms of praise. **dar a ~** to give one's word. **dar a ~ a** to give s. o. permission to speak. **dou-lhe a minha ~** I give you my word for it. **em outras ~s** stated another way, in other words. **em poucas ~s** in a few words. **estou com a ~ na ponta da língua** I have the word on the tip of my tongue. **faltar com a ~** to break one's word. **guardar a sua ~** to keep one's word. **ele cumpre bem a sua ~** he is as good as his word, he keeps his word. **ele deu (quebrou, cumpriu) sua ~ de vir** he gave (broke, kept) his word to come. **ele ouviu atentamente as suas ~s** he hung on her words. **fazer uso da ~, usar da ~ (numa reunião)** to address a meeting, (parl.) address the house. **foi-lhe concedida a ~** he was given permission to speak, (parl.) he

caught the speaker's eye. **formação de ~s** word-building. **formule-o em ~s** put it into words. **homem de ~** a man of his word. **homem de poucas ~s** a man of few words. **jogo de ~s** word-play. **nas ~s de Shakespeare** in the words of Shakespeare. **não dizer sequer uma ~** not to say a word. **não entender uma ~** not to understand anything. **nem uma ~ de verdade** not a syllable of truth. **ordem das ~s** word order. **sob minha ~** upon my word. **suas ~s não me saíram da cabeça** his words ran in my head. **ter a ~** (parl.) to have the ear of the house. **ter ~** to keep one's promise. **tirar a ~ da boca de alguém** to take the word out of another's mouth. **tomar a ~** to begin to speak, (parl.) take the floor. **tomar a ~ a** to interrupt a person's speach. **a última ~ em chapéus** the last word in hats. **a última ~ está com você** the last word lies with you. **últimas ~s** dying words. **uma ~ apenas!** a word with you! **uma ~ em segredo** a word in your ear. **uma ~ irada** an angry word.

palavração s. f. a method to learn word by word.

palavrada s. f. 1. a dirty or obscene word, swear-word. 2. insulting language; bad words. 3. coarse language or expression.

palavrão s. m. (pl. **-ões**) insulting word, four-letter word.
   dizer -ões to swear, sling the language, use base language.

palavreado s. m. (also **palavrório**) 1. idle talk, chatter; rigmarole. 2. loquacity, talkativeness.

palavreador s. m. 1. chatterer. 2. talker. ‖ adj. chattering.

palavrear v. 1. to talk idly, chatter, palaver. 2. to be loquacious. 3. to talk.

palavrório s. m. = **palavreado**.

palavroso adj. 1. having much words, prolix. 2. loquacious, talkative.

palco s. m. stage: 1. (theat.) the raised flooring where plays are enacted (plates P 2, T 3). 2. (fig.) scenary of an event.

pálea s. f. 1. (eccl.) pall: a linen cloth for covering the chalice. 2. **~s** pl. (bot.) paleae: the bracts or scales of certain grasses.

paleáceo adj. (bot.) paleaceous, chaffy.

paleantropologia s. f. paleoanthropology: study of prehistoric man.

paleantropológico adj. paleoanthropologic: of or pertaining to prehistoric man.
palear v. 1. to manifest, make known. 2. (Braz.) to shovel, use a shovel. 3. (Port.) to chatter, talk idly.
palearqueologia s. f. the scientific study of the material remains of prehistoric man.
paleetnologia s. f. palaeethnology: the science of the most primitive peoples or races.
paleetnológico adj. palaeethnologic(al): of or pertaining to the science of palaeethnology.
paleetnólogo s. m. palaeethnologist: person versed in palaeethnology.
paleiforme adj. m. + f. (bot.) paleiform: having the appearance of chaff.
paleio s. m. (N. Braz.) 1. joke, noise, merrymaking. 2. fun. 3. idle talk, chatter. 4. act of shoveling.
palejar v. (Braz.) to pale, blanch; lose colour.
paleoacantocéfalos s. m. pl. (zool.) Palaeacanthocephala: an order of parasites.
paleobotânica s. f. palaeobotany: the study of fossil plants.
paleofitologia s. f. palaeophytology: the study of fossil plants.
paleofitológico adj. palaeophytologic(al): of or pertaining to palaeophytology.
paleofitólogo s. m. palaeophytologist.
paleogêneo adj. (geol.) Palaeogene.
paleogeografia s. f. palaeogeography: the geography of prehistoric age.
paleografia s. f. palaeography: the science or art of deciphering ancient documents or writings.
paleográfico adj. palaeographic(al): relating to palaeography.
paleógrafo s. m. palaeographer: person versed in palaeography.
paleognatas s. f. pl. (ornith.) Palaeognathae: a superorder that includes the ostrich.
paléola s. f. (bot.) paleola: a diminute palea.
paleolífero adj. (bot.) having paleolae.
paleolítica s. f. (geol.) palaeolith: a stone implement of the Palaeolithic period.
paleologia s. f. palaeology: the study of antiquities (esp. ancient languages).
paleólogo s. m. palaeologist: person who studies the ancient languages. || adj. versed in palaeology.
paleonemertinos s. m. pl. (zool.) Palaeonemertini: an order of nemertean worms.
paleontografia s. f. palaeontography: the description of fossils.
paleontologia s. f. palaeontology: the science or study of fossil organisms and especially of fossil animals.
paleontológico adj. palaeontologic(al): of or pertaining to palaeontology.
paleontólogo s. m. palaeontologist: person versed in palaeontology.
paleopterígeos s. m. pl. (ichth.) Palaeopterygii: bony fishes of the class Osteichthyes.
paleozóico s. m. (geol.) Palaeozoic era. || adj. Palaeozoic: of or pertaining to the Palaeozoic era or group.
paleozoologia s. f. palaeozoology: the study of fossil animals.
paleozoológico adj. palaeozoological: relating to fossil animals.
paleozoologista s. m. + f. palaeozoologist: person versed in palaeozoology.
palerma s. m. + f. idiot, fool, imbecile, blockhead; loggerhead. || adj. foolish, idiotic, silly, dull, stupid.
palermar v. to behave like a fool.
palermice s. f. idiotism, foolishness, imbecility.
palescência s. f. paleness, pallor; lack of colour.
palestesia s. f. (med.) pallesthesia: sensibility to vibrations.

palestina s. f. (typogr.) double small pica.
palestino s. m. Palestinian: native or inhabitant of Palestine. || adj. Palestinian: of or pertaining to Palestine.
palestra s. f. 1. conversation, talk. 2. chatter. 3. (Gr. hist.) palestra: public place appropriated to exercises.
palestrador s. m. (Braz.) 1. chatterer. 2. talker. || adj. 1. chattering. 2. talking.
palestrar, palestrear v. 1. to converse, talk. 2. to chat.
paleta s. f. 1. palette (of painters or sculptors) (plate P 12). 2. (anat., zool.) shoulder-blade (plate C 12). 3. m. + f. (sl.) intruder; kill-joy.
paletada s. f. (Braz.) attack, thrust.
paletear v. 1. to spur a horse. 2. to poke one's nose into other people's business, meddle, interfere.
paletó s. m. 1. a man's coat; jacket (plate R 7). 2. paletot.
~ **de pijama** pajama jacket. ~ **esporte** sports jacket.
palha s. f. straw: 1. stalks or stems of grain after drying. 2. dry grass. 3. a hollow tube for sucking up beverages. 4. (fig.) trifle, bagatelle.
~ **de aço** steel wool. ~ **de madeira** wood wool. ~ **de milho** corn husk. **chapéu de** ~ straw hat. **boneco de** ~ jack straw. **coberto de** ~ straw-thatched. **muita** ~ **e pouco grão** much cry and little wool, much noise about nothing. **por dá cá aquela** ~ (to lose one's temper) for nothing.
palhabote s. m. a two-masted schooner.
palha-brava s. f. (pl. **palhas-bravas**) (bot.) melic grass.
palhaçada s. f. 1. buffoonery, clowning. 2. slapstick comedy. 3. group of buffoons.
palhaço s. m. 1. buffoon, clown, jester. 2. (fig.) funny person. || adj. dressed in or made of straw.
bancar o ~ to play the giddy goat.
palhada s. f. 1. fodder: coarse food for cattle. 2. boring talk.
palha-de-arroz s. f. (pl. **palhas-de-arroz**) (Braz.) the cyanite crystals found in diamond beds.
palha-de-penacho s. f. (pl. **palhas-de-penacho**) (bot.) pampas grass.
palhagem s. f. (pl. **-ens**) heap of straw.
palhal (pl. **-ais**), **palhar** s. m. thatched hut.
palharesco adj. of or like straw.
palhegal s. m. (pl. **-ais**) grassy land.
palheirão s. m. (pl. **-ões**) 1. a large hayloft. 2. (f. **-ona**) a very prolix and confusing speaker. 3. a book full of incomprehensible or useless things.
palheireiro s. m. 1. person who sells straw. 2. person who makes chair bottoms of cane.
palheiro s. m. 1. hayloft: place for keeping straw or hay. 2. haystack.
procurar agulha em ~ to look for a needle in a haystack.
palhento adj. strawy.
palheta (ê) s. f. 1. reed (of musical instruments). 2. slat: the thin narrow bar of wood of a Venetian blind. 3. straw hat. 4. blade, vane (of a turbine, etc.) (plate T 6).
palhetada s. f. stroke with a bat.
em duas ~**s** quick and without trouble.
palhetão s. m. (pl. **-ões**) bit of a key (plate C 6).
palhetar v. to rejoice in, delight in.
palhete (ê) s. m. = **palhetão**. || adj. 1. straw-coloured. 2. of straw.
vinho ~ claret (wine).
palhetear v. to banter, pull a person's leg.
palhiço s. m. 1. craff, bits or fragments of straw. 2. chopped straw. || adj. made of straw.
palhinha s. f. 1. a small straw. 2. cane splints for chair-bottoms. 3. m. (N. Braz.) straw hat.

palhoça s. f. 1. (also palhota f., palhote m.) thatched hut: a hut covered with straw. 2. straw cape.

páli s. m. Pali: a dialect used in Buddhist sacred writings.

paliação s. f. (pl. -ões) palliation, extenuation; alleviation.

paliador s. m. palliator: person who palliates. ‖ adj. palliative.

paliar v. 1. to palliate: a) extenuate, excuse. b) mitigate, alleviate. c) cloak, disguise. 2. to moderate.

paliativo s. m. a palliative medicine. ‖ adj. palliative: serving to palliate, mitigating.

paliçada s. f. 1. palisade: a fence of stakes or pales. 2. stockade.

palidez s. f. paleness: the character or condition of being pale; wanness, pallor, colourlessness.

pálido adj. pale, shallow, wan, colourless, pallid; faint. ‖ palidamente adv. palely, wanly.
cara-pálida pale-face.

palificação s. f. (pl. -ões) palification: act of enclosing with pales or stakes.

palificar v. to pale: enclose with pales or stakes; fence.

palilho s. m. a small stick used by dyers.

palilogia s. f. palilogy: repetition of a word or words.

palimpséstico adj. of or pertaining to palimpsest.

palimpsesto s. m. palimpsest: a parchment from which one writing has been rubbed out to make room for another.

palindromia s. f. (med.) palindromia: the recurrence of a disease.

palíndromo s. m. palindrome: a word, verse or sentence that reads the same either from. left to right or from right to left. ‖ adj. palindromic: that reads the same either forward or backward.
verso ~ palindromic verse.

palingenesia s. f. palingenesis: a new or second birth or production; rebirth, regeneration.

palingenético adj. palingenetic: of or pertaining to palingenesis.

palinódia s. f. palinode: 1. poem or song retracting a former poem. 2. recantation, a formal retraction.

palinódico adj. palinodic: relating to a palinode.

palinodista s. m. + f. palinodist: a writer of palinodes.

pálio s. m. (R. C. Church) a canopy carried over the Sacrament in processions.

palissandra s. f. (Braz.) palisander: plant of the family Bignoniaceae (Jacaranda mimosaefolia).

palitar v. to pick the teeth (with a toothpick).
ele palitou seus dentes he picked his teeth.

paliteira s. f. (bot.) bishop's weed, Spanish toothpick.

palito s. m. 1. toothpick. 2. (pop.) a match. 3. (sl.) a very thin person.
jogar ~s to draw cuts.

paliúro s. m. (bot.) Paliurus, Christs'-thorn (Paliurus australis).

palma s. f. 1. palm: a) palm leaf. b) (also ~ da mão) palm of the hand (plate C 18). c) sole (of a hoof) (plate C 9). 2. (fig.) victory, triumph. 3. ~s hand clapping; applause.
bater ~s to clap hands. ele o conhece como a ~ da mão he knows the highways and byways of it. ganhar a ~ to win the day. levar a ~ to carry off the palm. óleo de ~ palm-oil.

palmáceas s. f. pl. (bot.) Palmae: the palm family.

palma-crísti s. f. (pl. palmas-crísti) castor-oil plant.

palmada s. f. slap, rap, cuff, smack.

palma-de-santa-rita s. f. (pl. palmas-de-santa-rita) (bot.) gladiolus, sword lily.

palma-de-são-josé s. f. (pl. palmas-de-são-josé) (bot.) Bermuda lily.

palmado adj. (bot.) palmate.
folha -a palmate leaf (plate F 5).

palmar (I) s. m. a grove of palm trees; palmery. ‖ adj. m. + f. 1. palmar: of or pertaining to the palm of the hand. 2. that is a span long. 3. (fig.) big.

palmar (II) v. (also empalmar) 1. to palm: hide in the hand (as in sleight-of-hand tricks); grasp. 2. to pilfer, filch, snatch.

palmares s. m. pl. (N. Braz.) name of an extensive region covered with palms.

palmatífido adj. (bot.) palmatifid: cleft in a palmate manner.

palmatiforme adj. m. + f. (bot.) palmatiform: said of the leaves whose ribs are arranged in a palmate form.

palmatilobado adj. (bot.) palmatilobate: lobed in a palmate manner.

palmatinérveo adj. (bot.) palmatinerved: nerved in a palmate manner.

palmatoar v. (also palmatoriar) to pandy, punish by striking the palm of the hand.

palmatória s. f. 1. a pandy, ferule or palmer formerly used for striking school children on the palm of the hand. 2. (bot.) a prickly pear.
dar a mão à ~ to see one's error, acknowledge one's mistake. ser a ~ do mundo to be a highly self-righteous person.

palmeador s. m. 1. traveller. 2. excursionist. 3. explorer.

palmear v. (also palmejar) 1. to clap hands, applaud. 2. to tramp, travel on foot. 3. to crumble (tobacco) in the palm of the hand.

palmeira s. f. palm tree: any tree of the family Palmae.

palmeira-bambu s. f. (pl. palmeiras-bambu) the yellow butterfly palm.

palmeira-das-vassouras s. f. (pl. palmeiras-das-vassouras) (bot.) fan-palm, hemp-palm.

palmeiral s. m. (pl. -ais) a grove of palm trees, palmery.

palmeira-real s. f. (pl. palmeiras-reais) (Braz., bot.) royal palm.

palmeirim s.' m. (pl. -ins) palmer, pilgrim.

palmeiro s. m. = palmeirim. ‖ adj. that is a span long.

pálmer s. m. (pl. pálmeres) micrometer gauge (plate M 9).

palmeta s. f. 1. spatula (to spread salves, plasters). 2. auxiliary iron wedge used in splitting rocks. 3. insole: thin sole inside of a shoe.

palmífero adj. palmiferous: bearing or producing palms.

palmiforme adj. m. + f. palmiform: resembling a palm.

palmilha s. f. 1. insole: the inside sole of a shoe. 2. sole of a stocking.

palmilhadeira s. f. a woman who mends stockings.

palmilhar v. 1. to provide (a shoe) with an insole. 2. to mend stockings. 3. to tread, tramp on. 4. to go on foot.

palminervado adj. (bot.) palminerved: palmately nerved.

palminhas s. f. pl. used in the locution trazer nas ~ to take great care of.

palminho s. m. used in the phrase ~ de cara cutie (girl or child).

palmípede adj. m. + f. (zool.) palmiped(e): broad-footed, web-footed.

palmira s. f. (bot.) palmyra palm.

palmital s. m. (pl. -ais) = pindobal.

palmitato s. m. (chem.) palmitate: a salt of palmitic acid.

palmítico adj. (chem.) palmitic (acid).

palmitina s. f. (chem.) palmitin.

palmito s. m. 1. palm cabbage: the edible terminal bud of some palm trees. 2. palm leaf.

palmo s. m. 1. span (of the hand). 2. palm: a lineal measure.

~ a ~ inch by inch, foot by foot. **não enxergar um ~ adiante do nariz** to be a very ignorant.

palmoura s. f. (also **palmoira**) webfoot: foot having the toes connected by a web (as that of a goose).

palomar s. m. a sailmaker's twine. ‖ v. to stitch sails.

palomba s. f. (naut.) 1. bolt-rope. 2. hank.

palombeta, palometa s. f. (Braz., ichth.) pompano: a carangoid fish (Trachinotus carolinus).

palonço s. m. numskull, fool, imbecile. ‖ adj. stupid, foolish.

paior s. m. (also **palidez**) paleness, pallor, wanness.

palpação (pl. -ões), palpadela s. f. (usually **apalpação**) palpation: act of touching, feeling, or fumbling.

andar às palpadelas to feel one's way.

palpar v. (usually **apalpar**) to palpate, feel, grope.

palpatores s. m. pl. (ent.) Palpatores, a suborder of beetles.

palpável adj. m. + f. (pl. -áveis) 1. palpable, touchable. 2. (fig.) evident, obvious. ‖ **palpavelmente** adv. palpably.

pálpebra s. f. (anat.) palpebra: eyelid (plate O).

palpebrado adj. palpebrate: having eyelids.

palpebral adj. m. + f. (pl. -ais) palpebral: of or pertaining to eyelids.

palpebrite s. f. (med.) palpebritis: inflammation of the eyelids.

palpígrados s. m. pl. (zool.) Palpigradi, Microthelyphonida, an order of minute Arachnida.

palpiforme adj. m. + f. (zool.) palpiform.

palpígero adj. (zool.) palpigerous.

palpitação s. f. (pl. -ões) palpitation: 1. rapid pulsation of the heart. 2. act of palpitating.

palpitante adj. m. + f. 1. palpitant, palpitating, pulsating visibly. 2. thrilling.

palpitar v. 1. to palpitate: a) beat rapidly, pulsate, pulse. b) flutter; throb; quiver. 2. to be moved. 3. to conjecture, guess.

palpite s. m. 1. = **palpitação**. 2. suggestion. 3. tip (as at horse racing).

~ **acertado** straight tip. ~ **bom** hot tip. **dar ~ to tip. dar-lhe-ei alguns ~s** I'll give him some tips, (coll.) put him up to a wrinkle or two.

palpiteiro s. m. tipster, tout. ‖ adj. used to give tips or suggestions.

palpitoso adj. (Braz., pop.) desirous, eager.

palpo s. m. 1. (zool.) palpus. 2. (ent.) feeler.

estar em ~s (or **papos) de aranha** to be in a very difficult situation.

palra s. f. (also **palraria**) 1. speech, talk; chatter, babble. 2. garrulity, talkativeness.

palrador s. m. prattler, chatterer, tattler, rattler, gabbler. ‖ adj. (also **palradeiro, palreiro**) garrulous, chattering.

palrar v. 1. to jabber, chatter. 2. to converse, talk. 3. to disclose, reveal.

palratório s. m. 1. locutory. 2. conversation. 3. chatter, idle talk.

palrice s. f. chattiness, babble.

paludamento s. m. paludamentum: the cloak worn by an ancient Roman general in command of an army.

palude s. m. 1. lagoon, pool. 2. marsh, swamp.

paludial adj. m. + f. (pl. -ais) paludal, marshy: of or pertaining to marshes or fens.

paludícola adj. m. + f. paludicole: inhabiting or fond of marshes.

paludismo s. m. paludism, malarial poisoning.

paludoso adj. marshy, swampy, paludous.

palurdice s. f. stupidity, nonsense.

palúrdio s. m. blockhead, fool, nincompoop. ‖ adj. stupid, foolish.

palustre adj. m. + f. swampy, marshy, paludal.

febre ~ malarial fever.

pamonha s. f. 1. a sweetish concoction of which green corn paste is the chief ingredient, rolled and baked in fresh corn husks. 2. m.: a) fool, nincompoop. b) loafer. c) softy.

pampa s. m. pampas: vast treeless plains in South America. ‖ adj. m. + f. white-faced (horses).

pâmpano s. m. 1. vine shoot. 2. (ichth.) pompano.

pamparra adj. m. + f. (Braz., fam.) 1. excellent. 2. great. 3. tasteful, delicious; succulent.

pampeiro s. m. (Braz.) 1. pampero: wind from the pampas. 2. (sl.) conflict, quarrel.

pampiano adj. pampean: of or pertaining to the pampas of South America.

pampilho s. m. 1. goad. 2. (bot.) a chrysanthemum.

pampilho-das-searas s. m. (pl. **pampilhos-das-searas**) (bot.) corn-marigold.

pampilho-ordinário s. m. (pl. **pampilhos-ordinários**) (bot.) crown daisy, garland chrysanthemum.

pamplo, pampo s. m. (ichth.) pompano (Trachinotus carolinus).

pamprodá(c)tilo adj. pamprodactylous: having all four toes turned forward (birds).

panabásio s. m. (min.) panabase: tetrahedrite, gray copper ore.

panaca s. m. (Braz., pop.) simpleton, fool, silly person. ‖ adj. m. + f. simple, silly.

panacarica s. f. (N. Braz.) straw canopy on a canoe.

panacéia s. f. 1. panacea: a remedy for all diseases, a cure-all. 2. (bot.) alheal.

panacheiro s. m. plant of the family Myrtaceae (Callisthemon speciosus).

panaço s. m. blow with a sword or sabre.

panacu(m) s. m. (Braz.) a large wicker basket.

panado adj. breaded.

panal s. m. (pl. -ais) 1. cloth, shroud. 2. round woods to roll a boat into the water.

panamá s. m. Panama hat.

panamenho s. m., panamense m. + f. Panamanian: native or inhabitant of Panama. ‖ adj. Panamanian: of or pertaining to Panama.

pan-americanismo s. m. Pan-Americanism: political alliance of all the states of America.

pan-americano adj. (pl. **pan-americanos**) Pan-American: of or pertaining to all Americas.

panapaná s. m. (Braz.) an extensive swarm of butterflies.

panar v. to bread: cover with bread crumbs. ‖ adj. m. + f. of or pertaining to bread.

panaria s. f. storehouse, barn, granary.

panarício, panariz s. m. (med.) panaris, panonychia, whitlow.

panascal s. m. (pl. -ais) (also **panasqueira** f.) a growth of parsnips.

panasco s. m. (bot.) parsnip (Pastinaca silvestris).

panasqueiro s. m. 1. (bot.) parsnip. 2. coarse and rough person.

panatenéias s. f. pl. Panathenaea: the chief national festival of ancient Athenians.

panázio s. m. (pop.) 1. kick. 2. box on the ear, blow in the face. 3. blow with a sword or sabre. 4. blast of a firearm. 5. large portion.

panca s. f. 1. a wooden lever. 2. (fig.) style, mode of expression.

pança s. f. 1. (zool.) rumen: the first stomach of ruminants. 2. (pop.) paunch, belly, potbelly.

pancada s. f. 1. blow, knock, bang, hit. 2. shock, collision, impact. 3. pulsation. 4. drubbing. 5. (fig.) presentiment. 6. (pop.) mania. 7. flurry, hailstorm.

8. m.: a) crazy, lunatic person. b) brute, stupid man.

pançada s. f. a bellyful.

pancadão s. m. (pl. **-ões**) (Braz., sl.) buxom woman.

pancadaria s. f. 1. scuffle, fray, brawl, row. 2. beating, drubbing. 3. (mus.) percussion instruments.

pancárpia s. f. wreath of flowers.

panclastite s. f. panclastite: an explosive compound.

pancrácio s. m. simpleton, fool, idiot.

pâncreas s. m., sg. + pl. (anat.) pancreas.

pancreatalgia s. f. (med.) pancreatalgia: a pain in the pancreas.

pancreatectomia s. f. (surg.) pancreatectomy: excision of the pancreas.

pancreático adj. (med.) pancreatic: of or pertaining to the pancreas.

pancreatina s. f. pancreatin.

pancreatite s. f. (med.) pancreatitis: inflammation of the pancreas.

pancromático adj. (phot.) panchromatic: sensitive to light of all colours (plate or film).

pançudo s. m. sponger, parasite. ‖ adj. big-bellied, paunchy, potbellied.

panda (I) s. f. 1. cork float of a fishing-net. 2. (bot.) Panda: a genus of dicotyledonous trees. 3. (bot.) panda: the tree itself (Panda oleosa).

panda (II) s. m. (zool.) common name of two bearlike carnivores: **panda pequeno** lesser panda (Ailurus fulgens), of the Himalayas, and **panda grande** giant panda (Ailuropoda melanoleuca), of Tibet and southern China.

pandáceas s. f. pl. (bot.) Pandaceae, the panda family.

pandacosta s. m. (Braz.) a bright shawl used formerly by Negro women.

pandanáceas s. f. pl. (bot.) Pandanaceae, the screw--pine family.

pandano s. m. pandanus: a screw-pine of the genus Pandanus (Pandanus utilis).

pandarecos s. m. pl. chips, splinters, slivers, fragments, scraps.

em ~ (fig.) off the hinges.

pandear v. 1. to belly, swell out. 2. to distend, expand.

pandecta s. f. 1. pandect: an encyclopedic treatise. 2. ~s pl. Pandects: a collection of Roman civil laws.

pândega s. f. 1. spree, folly, revelry. 2. feast with excessive eating.

andar na ~ to have a jolly good time. **que** ~! what a lark!

pandegar v. 1. to revel: engage in boisterous festivities. 2. to make merry.

pândego s. m. 1. revel(l)er, carouser. 2. merrymaker. 3. funny person. ‖ adj. 1. revel(l)ing, carousing. 2. merrymaking. 3. amusing, funny. ⁾

pandeireiro s. m. 1. person who makes tambourines or timbrels. 2. tambourine player.

pandeireta s. f. a small tambourine.

pandeiro s. m. tambourine: a musical instrument with jingles in the rim; a timbrel.

pandemia s. f. (med.) pandemia, pandemy.

pandêmico adj. pandemic: widely epidemic.

pandemônio s. m. pandemonium: 1. the infernal regions, hell. 2. (fig.) a riotous uproar, tumult.

pandiculação s. f. (pl. **-ões**) pandiculation: act of stretching o. s.

pandilha s. f. 1. complot for the purpose of deceiving other people. 2. a gang of evil-doers. 3. m.: a) gangster, hoodlum. b) scoundrel, rogue.

pandilhar v. 1. to swindle, live by cheating. 2. to loaf.

pandilheiro s. m. 1. rogue. 2. gangster, hoodlum.

pândita s. m. pundit (Brahman).

pando adj. 1. full, replete. 2. inflated. 3. broad, wide.

velas -as full sails.

pandora s. f. 1. pandore, bandore: an old lutelike musical instrument. 2. (Gr. myth.) Pandora.

pandorga s. f. (also **pandorca**) 1. discordant and out of tune music. 2. confused noise of many instruments. 3. obese woman. 4. (S. Braz.) paper kite. 5. m. (Braz.) fool, dullard, blockhead.

pandulho s. m. 1. sinker: a weight for sinking a fishing-net. 2. a stone used to anchor a fishing--net. 3. (Braz., also **bandulho**) belly.

panduriforme adj. m. + f. panduriform, pandurate: fiddle-shaped (leaves).

pane s. f. failure or breakdown of the motor of an airplane, automobile or motorcycle.

panegirical adj. m. + f. (pl. **-ais**) panegyric(al): elaborately eulogistic or laudatory.

panegírico s. m. panegyric: 1. a formal public eulogy. 2. encomium, eulogium. ‖ adj. panegyrical.

panegirista s. m. + f. panegyrist: person who makes a panegyric.

paneiro s. m. 1. pannier, basket, hamper. 2. seats for passengers in a boat. 3. a wicker carriage. 4. (Braz., theat.) curtain handler. 5. street peddler (of clothes).

panejamento s. m. 1. act of draping. 2. flapping (sails).

panejar v. 1. to drape: make the drapery of a figure (as in painting). 2. to flap (sails).

panela s. f. 1. pot, pan: vessel for kitchen use (plate C 20). 2. the underground nest of ants.

~ **de pressão** pressure cooker; digester. **quebrar a** ~ or **quebrar a tigela** to use s. th. for the first time. **ela comprou um chapeuzinho novo e quebrou a** ~ **logo em seguida** she bought a brand-new little hat and put it on immediately.

panelada s. f. 1. potful, panful. 2. many pots.

panelinha s. f. 1. a small pot or pan. 2. caucus: political insiders. 3. literary clique. 4. (fig.) intrigue, plot.

ser da mesma ~ to be in the plot.

panema s. m. + f. (N. Braz.) 1. unlucky person. 2. unsuccessful hunter or fisherman. 3. a victim of persistent bad luck. ‖ adj. 1. unlucky. 2. unsuccessful.

pan-eslavismo s. m. Pan-Slavism.

pan-eslavista s. m. + f. (pl. **pan-eslavistas**) Pan--Slavist. ‖ adj. Pan-Slavistic, Pan-Slavic.

panfletário s. m. pamphleteer: person who writes pamphlets. ‖ adj. 1. pamphletary, pamphletic: referring to a pamphlet. 2. passionate (in speech).

panfletista s. m. + f. pamphleteer: person who writes a pamphlet.

panfleto s. m. pamphlet: 1. booklet in paper covers, brochure. 2. a brief treatise.

panfobia s. f. pantophobia: fear of everything.

pangaio s. m. reveller, merrymaker; loafer.

pangarave adj. (Braz., pop.) 1. despicable. 2. vile. 3. miserable.

pangaré s. m. 1. a somewhat dark-red horse having usually a clearer muzzle and belly. 2. unruly or indocile horse. ‖ adj. m. + f. said of such a horse.

pangenético adj. (biol.) pangenetic.

pangermanismo s. m. Pan-Germanism: the principle of assembling all German peoples in one political organization.

pangermanista s. m. + f. Pan-Germanist. ‖ adj. Pan--Germanic: of or pertaining to Pan-Germanism.

pangolim s. m. (pl. **-ins**) (zool.) pangolin: an Asiatic mammal (Manis pentadactyla).

pan-helênico adj. (pl. **pan-helênicos**) Panhellenic: of or pertaining to Panhellenism.

pan-helenismo s. m. Panhellenism: the movement for political union of all Greeks.

paníceo adj. panic: of, pertaining to or resulting from a sudden and contagious terror or fear.
pânico s. m. panic: a sudden and unreasonale fear; terror, sudden alarm. ‖ adj. panic: of, pertaining to or resulting from a panic or fear.
em ~ panic-driven.
paniconografia s. f. paniconography: a photozincography.
panícula s. f. (bot.) panicle: a compound racemose inflorescence.
paniculado adj. m., panicular m. + f. paniculate, panicled: 1. having or forming panicles. 2. arranged in panicles.
paniculite s. f. (med.) panniculitis: inflammation of the panniculus adiposus.
panículo s. m. (anat.) panniculus.
~ adiposo panniculus adiposus.
panífero adj. (poet.) producing cereals.
panificação s. f. (pl. -ões) panification: 1. breadmaking. 2. conversion into bread.
panificador s. m. baker, breadmaker, breadman.
panificadora s. f. (Braz.) bakery: establishment for baking bread, cakes, etc.
panificar v. to convert into bread (flour).
paniguado adj. adherent, sectarian, attached to.
paninho s. m. 1. diminutive of pano (cloth). 2. a fine cotton cloth.
panléxico s. m. universal dictionary.
pano s. m. 1. cloth: a) a woven fabric of wool, silk, cotton, linen. b) cover (of cloth) (plate L 1). 2. (naut.) sail. 3. (pop.) a mole on the body, spot in the face, skin blemish. 4. (theat.) curtain.
~ cru unbleached cloth. ~ da chaminé manteltree of a chimney. ~ de boca stage curtain (plate P 2). ~ da cozinha torchon. ~ de fundo back-cloth (plate P 2). ~ de mesa table-cloth, table-cover. ~s quentes (fig.) mollifications, silencings. ~ verde green cloth. a todo o ~ 1. under full sail. 2. with full speed. cai o ~ (theat.) the curtain comes down. dar ~ para mangas to set tongues wagging. fecha-se o ~ the scene closes. por baixo do ~ (fig.) under the counter. saia de quatro ~s a four-gore skirt. ter ~ para mangas to be amply provided with anything.
panóplia s. f. 1. panoply: the complete equipment of a warrior. 2. armour.
panorama s. m. panorama: 1. scene, scenery; view. 2. landscape.
panorâmico adj. panoramic(al): of or pertaining to a panorama.
panqueca s. f. 1. pancake: a thin batter cake fried in a pan; a griddle cake. 2. (fig.): a) rest, repose. b) idleness, laziness.
panri s. m. (bot.) orange jessamine.
pânria s. f. 1. indolence, laziness; idle life. 2. m. + f. idler, loafer.
pansexual adj. m. + f. pansexual.
pansofia s. f. pansophy: 1. a system embracing all human knowledge. 2. a complete knowledge.
pansófico adj. pansophic(al): referring to pansophy.
panspermia s. f. (biol.) panspermy.
panspérmico adj. panspermic: referring to panspermy.
pantafaçudo adj. 1. fat-cheecked, chubby-faced. 2. (fig.) monstrous.
pantagruélico adj. Pantagruelian, Pantagruelic.
pantagruelismo s. m. Pantagruelism: the theories and practices of Pantagruel.
pantagruelista s. m. + f. Pantagruelist. ‖ adj. Pantagruelistic.
pantalão s. m. (pl. -ões) 1. Pantaloon: an old dotard wearing a certain kind of tight-fitting trousers. 2. pantaloon: an imbecile or feeble old man, buffoon. 3. trousers.

pantalha s. f. 1. lamp shade. 2. screen.
pantalonada s. f. buffoonery.
pantalonas s. f. pl. pantaloons, trousers.
pantana s. f. (fam.) ruin, squandering.
dar em ~ to run to ruin, go broke.
pantanal s. m. (pl. -ais) 1. swampland; large pool or swamp. 2. (Braz.) the lowlands of Mato Grosso.
pântano s. m. swamp, marsh, bog, morass; quagmire, mudhole.
pantanoso adj. swampy, marshy, boggy.
panteão s. m. 1. pantheon: a mausoleum or temple resembling the Roman Pantheon. 2. (Roman hist.) Pantheon: a circular temple dedicated to all the gods.
pantear v. 1. to mock, jeer. 2. to speak nonsense.
panteísmo s. m. pantheism: the doctrine which holds that the self-existent and self-developing universe, conceived as a whole, is God.
panteísta s. m. + f. pantheist: sectarian of pantheism. ‖ adj. pantheistic: of or pertaining to pantheism.
pantelefone s. m. pantelephone: device for the reception of sounds of very feeble intensity.
pantelegrafia s. f. pantelegraphy: facsimile telegraphy.
pantelégrafo s. m. pantelegraph: a facsimile telegraph.
panteônico adj. pantheonic: of or pertaining to a pantheon.
pantera s. f. 1. (zool.) panther: a large feline carnivore; leopard. 2. (fig.) a cruel person.
pantim s. m. small night lamp of clay or bronze.
pantofagia s. f. habit of eating very much.
pantófago adj. eating very much.
pantofobia s. f. pantophobia: fear of everything.
pantófobo s. m. person affected with pantophobia.
pantoftalmídeos s. m. pl. (ent.) Pantophthalmidae, a family of two-winged flies.
pantografia s. f. pantography.
pantográfico adj. pantographic(al): of or referring to a pantograph.
pantógrafo s. m. pantograph: an instrument for copying a drawing or diagram.
pantólogo s. m. pantologist, encyclopedist.
pantômetro s. m. pantometer: instrument for measuring angles and determining elevations, distances, etc.
pantomima s. f. (also pantomina) 1. pantomime: a) series of actions or gestures used to express ideas. b) any play in which the actors express their meaning by actions without dialogues. 2. (fig.) fraud, swindle; farce.
pantomimar v. 1. to pantomime. 2. (fig.) to trick, cheat, deceive.
pantomimeiro, pantomimo s. m. pantomimist.
pantomímico adj. pantomimic(al): of or referring to pantomime.
pantomórfico adj. pantomorphic: able to assume any shape.
pantopolista adj. m. + f. cosmopolitan: common to all the world.
pantoscópio s. m. (phot.) pantoscope: a very wide-angled lens.
pantufa s. f. 1. = pantufo. 2. (fig.) an obese and dressed up woman.
pantufo s. m. 1. slipper, pantofle. 2. (fig.) an obese man. 3. young male termite.
pantum s. m. pantum: a short extemporaneous Malay poem.
panturra s. f. 1. belly, paunch. 2. (fig.) vainglory, haughtiness.
panturrilha s. f. calf of the leg.
paó s. m. (Braz., ornith.) (also pavó, pavô) fruit-crow (Pyroderus scutatus).
pão s. m. (pl. pães) 1. bread. 2. our daily bread, (plate P 3) food in general, sustenance. 3. cereals. 4. loaf (plate P 3). 5. Host, the consecrated wafer.

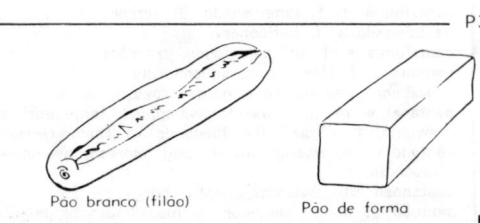
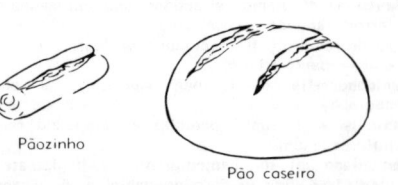

Pão branco (filão)

Pão de forma

Pãozinho

PÃO

Pão caseiro

~ **amanhecido** yesterday's bread. ~ **ázimo** unleavened bread. ~ **bento** holy bread. ~ **branco** white bread. ~ **caseiro** home-made bread. ~ **com manteiga** bread and butter. ~ **de açúcar** sugar-loaf. ~ **de cada dia,** ~ **cotidiano** daily bread. ~ **de centeio** rye bread, brown bread. ~ **de forma** sandwich loaf (plate P 3). ~ **de gengibre** brandy-snap. ~ **de milho** maize cake, Johnny cake, hoe-cake. ~ **do céu** the consecrated host. ~ **do espírito** (fig.) knowledge, wisdom. ~ **integral** whole bread, coarse bread. ~ **nosso de cada dia** our daily bread. ~ **torrado** toast. **comer o** ~ **seco** to eat dry bread. **ganhar o** ~ to earn a living. **miolo de** ~ bread crumb. **sem** ~ breadless. **viver a** ~ **e água** to live on bread and water.

pão-de-ló s. m. (pl. **pães-de-ló**) sponge-cake (plate D 3).

pão-de-pobre s. m. (pl. **pães-de-pobre**) (Braz., pop.) manioc (plant).

pão-durismo s. m. (pl. **pão-durismos**) (Braz., fam.) niggardlines, avariciousness.

pão-duro s. m. (pl. **pães-duros**) (Braz., fam.) niggard, miser, stingy person.

pãozeiro s. m. (N. Braz.) breadman.

pãozinho s. m. (pl. **pãezinhos**) dim. of **pão**: little bread, roll (plate P 3).

papa s. m. (f. **papisa, papesa**) pope: the bishop of Rome; supreme pontiff.

papa s. f. pap: any soft food for babies; mush, gruel. ~ **de aveia** flummery. **não ter** ~**s na língua** to be outspoken.

papá s. m. papa, dad(dy), father.

papa-arroz s. m. (pl. **papa-arrozes**) (ornith.) 1. bobolink, reedbird. 2. cowbird.

papa-capim s. m. (pl. **papa-capins**) (Braz., ornith.) the lined seed-eater (Sporophila lineola).

papa-ceia s. m. + f. (pl. **papa-ceias**) (Braz., pop.) Vesper: the evening star.

papada s. f. double chin; gills; dewlap (plate G 1).

papa-defuntos s. m., sg. + pl. (Braz., zool.) armadillo.

papado s. m. papacy: 1. the dignity, office or jurisdiction of the pope; pontificate. 2. period of a pontificate.

papa-figo s. m. (pl. **papa-figos**) 1. (naut.) the mainsail and the foresail. 2. bogeyman. 3. (ornith.) golden oriole, figpecker.

papa-filas s. m., sg. + pl. (Braz.) a very long bus for many passengers.

papa-fina s. m. (pl. **papas-finas**) ridiculous person. ‖ adj. m. + f. 1. savoury, tasty, delicious. 2. excellent.

papa-formigas s. m., sg. + pl. (Braz.) ant birds of the family Formicariidae.

papagaiada s. f. hum of voices, noisy chatter.

papagaiado adj. parrot-toed, pidgeon-toed (horses).

papagaial adj. m. + f. (pl. **-ais**) of, pertaining to or referring to parrots.

papagaiar v. to parrot: 1. repeat words as a parrot. 2. talk idly; talk nonsense.

papagaieira s. f. (Braz., bot.) a poinsettia.

papagaio s. m. 1. parrot: a) (ornith.) any of certain birds of the order Psittaciformes. b) a person who repeats or imitates as a parrot. 2. paper kite. 3. (aeron.) kite. 4. (bot.) Christmas flower. 5. (ichth.) ladyfish. 6. (coll., com.) a bill of exchange; a kite. ~! heavens! good heavens! **falar como um** ~ to chatter like a parrot.

papagaio-grego (pl. **papagaios-gregos**), **papagaio-real** (pl. **papagaios-reais**), **papagaio-verdadeiro** (pl. **papagaios-verdadeiros**) s. m. (Braz., ornith.) a yellow-winged parrot (Amazona aestiva).

papa-gente s. m. + f. (pl. **papa-gentes**) phantasm, hobgoblin.

papagueador s. m. parroter: person who repeats or imitates without understanding (as a parrot). ‖ adj. parroting.

papaguear v. to parrot: 1. repeat words mechanically as a parrot. 2. talk idly, talk nonsense. 3. chatter.

papa-hóstias s. m. + f., sg. + pl. (depr.) sanctimonious or very devout person.

papai s. m. (fam.) papa, dad(dy), father, pappy. **Papai Noel** Santa Claus.

papaia s. f. papaya: 1. (also **papaieira**) the American papaw tree (Carica papaya). 2. its yellow melonlike fruit.

papaína s. f. (biochem.) papain: a vegetable enzyme contained in the milk of papaya fruit.

papa-jantares s. m. + f., sg. + pl. parasite, sponge.

papal adj. m. + f. (pl. **-ais**) papal, pontifical: of or pertaining to the papacy or the pope.

papa-lagartas s. m., sg. + pl. (Braz.) a bird of the family Cuculidae (Coccyzus melacoryphus).

papalino s. m. a papal soldier. ‖ adj. papal: of or pertaining to the papacy or to the pope.

papalvice s. f. 1. silliness, gullibility. 2. simpletons collectively.

papalvo s. m. simpleton, fool, silly person.

papa-mel s. f. (pl. **papa-méis**) (Braz., zool.) tayra (Eira barbara).

papa-mico s. m. (pl. **papa-micos**) (Braz., ornith.) the tyrant hawk-eagle (Spizaetus tyrannus).

papa-missas s. m. + f., sg. + pl. (depr.) sanctimonious or very devout person.

papa-moscas s. m., sg. + pl. 1. flycatcher: a bird of the family Tyrannidae (Muscipipra vetula). 2. a jumping spider of the family Attidae. 3. m. + f. (fig.) simpleton, silly person.

papança s. f., **papandórico** m. much eating; grub; food.

papangu s. m. (N. Braz.) 1. masquerader. 2. lazy person; fool.

papa-novenas s. f., sg. + pl. (depr.) sanctimonious woman.

papão s. m. (pl. **-ões**) 1. bugbear, hobgoblin, bugaboo. 2. a monster.

papa-ovo s. m. (pl. **papa-ovos**) 1. (zool.) cribo. 2. (ornith.) ant shrike (Mackenziaena leachii).

papa-peixe s. m. (pl. **papa-peixes**) (Braz., ornith.) a kingfisher (Ceryle torquata).

papar v. (fam.) 1. to eat; gabble (food). 2. to cheat, deceive. 3. to extort. 4. to obtain by unfair means.
paparicar v. to nibble, pick at (food), eat on the sly.
paparicos s. m. pl. 1. careful nursing (as of sick). 2. caresses. 3. titbits.
paparriba adv. on one's back, idle.
paparrotada, paparrotagem (pl. -ens) s. f. 1. boasting, swagger; vainglory. 2. food for pigs, hogwash.
paparrotão s. m. (pl. -ões) (also **paparreta**) 1. (fam.) impostor, deceiver. 2. braggart. ‖ adj. 1. vain, conceited, haughty. 2. boastful.
paparrotear v. to boast, brag.
paparrotice s. f. swagger, bragging; imposture; vainglory.
papa-santos s. m. + f., sg. + pl. (depr.) a sanctimonious person.
papata s. f. unclean deal, business or gains; professional swindling.
papa-tabaco s. m. (pl. **papa-tabacos**) 1. stargazer: a marine fish. 2. a user of snuff.
papa-taoca s. f. (pl. **papa-taocas**) (Braz., ornith.) an antbird of the family Formicariidae (Pyriglena leucoptera).
papa-terra s. m. (pl. **papa-terras**) (Braz.) 1. (bot.): a) bitterblain: herb of the family Scrophulariaceae (Vandelia diffusa). b) name of three plants of the family Rubiaceae (Basanacantha spinosa, Chomelia anisomeris and Posoqueria latifolia). 2. (ichth.) king whiting (Menticirrhus americanus L.). 3. (also **mumbuca** f.) a stingless bee (Melipona capitata). 4. m. + f. geophagist, dirt eater.
papável adj. m. + f. (pl. -áveis) papable: eligible to the papacy (Cardinal).
papaveráceas s. f. pl. (bot.) Papaveraceae, the opium poppy family.
papaverina s. f. (chem.) papaverine: a crystalline alkaloid obtained from opium.
papazana s. f. much eating, substantial meal.
papeá-guaçu s. m. (pl. **papeás-guaçus**) (bot.) whiptree (Luhea speciosa).
papear v. 1. to chatter, jabber. 2. to tittle-tattle, gossip. 3. to trill, warble, chirp.
papeata s. f. (Braz.) ridiculous and hypocritical demonstration of compassion.
papeira s. f. 1. (med.) parotitis, mumps. 2. (vet.) the actinomycosis of cattle. 3. a shrub of the family Boraginaceae (Tournefortia lucidaphylla).
papeiro adj. (Braz.) affected with parotitis.
papel s. m. (pl. **papéis**) 1. paper. 2. (theat.) role, rôle: a part taken by an actor. 3. paper money. 4. **papéis** pl. documents.
~ **acetinado** glazed paper. ~ **almaço** foolscap paper. ~ **brilhante** (phot.) glossy paper. ~ **carbônio**, ~ **carbono** carbon paper. ~ **cartucho**, ~ **de embrulho** wrapping paper. ~ **chupão** blotting paper. ~ **couché** art paper. ~ **de carta** letter paper. ~ **de (escrever a) máquina** typing paper. ~ **de impressão** printing paper. ~ **de seda** tissue paper. ~ **em branco** blank paper. ~ **fantasia** fancy paper. ~ **de filtro** filter paper (plate F 3). ~ **heliográfico** dyeline paper. ~ **higiênico** toilet paper (plate P 19). ~ **impermeável** greaseproof paper, oil-paper. ~ **indicador** test paper. ~ **manilha** manilla paper. ~ **mata-moscas** flypaper. ~ **mate** (phot.) mat paper. ~ **milimetrado** millimeter paper. ~ **para cópias** copy (duplicating) paper. ~ **para desenho** drawing paper. ~ **de escrever** or ~ **para escrever** writing paper. (plate C 10). ~ **para rascunho** scrap paper. ~ **pautado** ruled paper. ~ **pega-moscas** flypaper. ~ **pergaminho** parchment paper. ~ **queimado** (fig.) a married man. ~ **químico** carbon paper. ~ **relativo** test paper. ~ **selado** stamped sheet of paper.

~ **usado** waste paper. **desempenhar o** ~ **de** to play the part of. **ele não está dentro do seu** ~ he is out of his character. **fábrica de** ~ paper mill. **fabricante de** ~ papermaker. **fazer** ~ **de bobo** to play the fool. **fazer o** ~ **de** to play the role of. **folha de** ~ a sheet of paper. **molde de** ~ paper pattern. **o** ~ **aceita tudo** paper does not blush. **saco de** ~ paper bag, paper sack. **tira de** ~ wisp of paper.
papelada, papelagem (pl. -ens) s. f. a lot of papers or documents, a heap of papers.
papelão s. m. (pl. -ões) 1. cardboard: pasteboard used for making cards, boxes. 2. (fig.) fool, nincompoop. 3. fiasco, failure; sorry sight.
~ **alcatroado** roofing felt (plate T 5).
papelaria s. f. stationer's shop: place where writing materials in general (papers, pens, pencils, ink) are sold.
papeleira s. f. standing desk.
papeleiro s. m. 1. papermaker. 2. stationer: person who sells writing materials.
papelejo s. m. a piece of paper; paper of no importance.
papeleta s. f. 1. edict. 2. bill, placard, poster, notice. 3. identification paper or tag. 4. patient's chart.
papelete, papelico, papelinho s. m. 1. a small piece of paper. 2. paper of no importance.
papelismo s. m. (Braz.) inflationary policy of issuing large amounts of currency.
papelista s. m. + f. 1. person busy in searching old papers, documents. 2. archivist, filing clerk. 3. person who favours inflation. ‖ adj. 1. favouring inflation. 2. cunning, artful.
papel-moeda s. m. (pl. **papéis-moeda**) paper currency.
papelório s. m. (Braz.) 1. an amount of papers, documents, etc. 2. a sorry figure; fiasco.
papelotes s. m. pl. papillotes: curl-papers (for the hair).
papelucho s. m. 1. paper of no importance. 2. a piece of paper. 3. wrapping paper.
papesa s. f. popess: a female pope.
papelzinho s. m. any small piece of paper.
papila s. f. papilla: 1. (anat.): a) nipple of the mammary gland. b) any nipplelike process of connective tissue. 2. (bot.) nipple-shaped protuberance on a flower or leaf.
papilar adj. m. + f. papillary: 1. having papillae. 2. resembling papillae.
papilha s. f. a cock's barbel.
papiliforme adj. m. + f. papilliform: having the form of a papilla.
papilionáceas s. f. pl. (bot.) Papilionaceae, Leguminosae, the leguminous plants family.
papilionídeo s. m. any butterfly of the family Papilionidae. ‖ adj. papilionid: of or pertaining to the Papilionidae.
papilionídeos s. m. pl. (ent.) Papilionidae, the butterfly family.
papiloma s. m. (med.) papilloma: a morbid growth on the skin (as corns, warts or mucous tubercles).
papilomatose s. f. (med.) papillomatosis: the development of papillomas.
papiráceo adj. papyraceous, papery, resembling paper.
papíreo adj. papyraceous: made of papyrus.
papiri s. m. (N. Braz.) thatched hut or shed.
papiro s. m. papyrus: 1. a plant of the sedge family (Cyperus papyrus). 2. writing paper of the ancient Egyptians. 3. ancient manuscript written on papyrus.
papironga s. f. fraud, swindle.
papisa s. f. popess: a female pope.
papismo s. m. papism: 1. papal system. 2. Roman Catholicism.

papista s. m. + f. papist: 1. an adherent of papacy. 2. a Roman Catholic. ‖ adj. papistic(al).

papo s. m. 1. crop, pouch, craw (of birds). 2. (pop.) stomach. 3. goiter, goitre: a morbid enlargement of the thyroid gland. 4. (fig.) arrogance, pride. 5. (bot.) pappus.

bater ~ to chatter, talk, chat. **de grão em grão a galinha enche o** ~ little strokes fell great oaks. **estar em** ~**s** (or **palpos) de aranha** to be in a tight corner, be in hot water. **ficar de** ~ **para o ar** to lead an idle life, sit with folded hands.

papocar v. to pop, crackle.

papoco (ô) s. m. (pl. **papocos**) pop, crackling.

papo-roxo s. m. (pl. **papos-roxos**) (ornith.) robin, redbreast.

papoula s. f. (also **papoila**) poppy: any plant of the genus Papaver.

papoula-da-califórnia s. f. (pl. **papoulas-da-califórnia**) (bot.) California poppy.

papoula-do-são-francisco s. f. (pl. **papoulas-do-são--francisco**) (Braz., bot.) brown Indian hemp, ambary hemp (Hibiscus cannabicus).

papoula-rubra s. f. (pl. **papoulas-rubras**) (bot.) corn poppy, redweed (Papaver rhoeas).

papua s. m. + f. Papuan: native or inhabitant of Papua (New Guinea). ‖ adj. Papuan: of or pertaining to Papua or the Papuan people.

papudo adj. 1. goitrous. 2. arched. 3. prominent. 4. (Braz.) boastful, swaggering, puffed up.

pápula s. f. papule, pimple: a small protuberance on the skin.

papuloso adj. papulous, pimply.

paquebote s. m. packet boat.

paqueiro s. m. dog trained for hunting **pacas**. ‖ adj. trained for hunting pacas.

paquera s. (Braz., sl.) flirt: 1. f. flirtation. 2. m. + f. a person who flirts.

paquete (ê) s. m. 1. packet: a) steamship for conveying mail and passengers. b) a small package, parcel. 2. (Braz., coll.) menses. ‖ adj. (Braz.) elegant.

paquevira s. f. (Braz., bot.) heliconia (Heliconia pendura).

paquicefalia s. f. pachycephaly: exceptional thickness of the skull.

paquicéfalo adj. pachycephalic, pachycephalous: having an abnormally thick skull.

paquiderme s. m. (zool.) pachyderm: any of certain thick-skinned mammals. ‖ adj. m. + f. pachydermous, thick-skinned.

paquidérmico adj. pachydermatous, pachydermous: 1. of or referring to the pachyderms. 2. thick-skinned.

paquimeningite s. f. (med.) pachymeningitis: inflammation of the dura mater.

paquímetro s. m. 1. (phys.) pachymeter: an instrument for measuring thickness. 2. calliper rule, sliding calliper (plate F 1).

paquinha s. f. 1. a little paca. 2. (ent.) mole cricket.

paquítrico adj. (zool.) pachytrichous.

par s. m. 1. pair, couple, brace (plate V 4). 2. peer. 3. two of a kind. 4. partner: one of two persons united in some enterprise (as marriage, dance, game). ‖ adj. m. + f. 1. equal, like, similar, equivalent. 2. even.

~ **e ímpar** even and odd. **a** ~ **de:** 1. informed about. 2. along with. **ao** ~ at par. **aos** ~**es** in pairs. **acima do** ~ above par. **abaixo do** ~ below par, under par. **colocar a** ~ to par. **dispor em** ~**es** to pair off. **ele não tem** ~ he is without equals. **eles saíram aos** ~**es** they paired off. **estar a** ~ **de** to be informed about, be in the know. **estar abaixo do** ~ to be at a discount. **estar ao** ~ (com.) to be at par. **estas meias não são do mesmo** ~ these stockings are not fellows. **não estar a** ~ **de** not

to be informed about, be outside the rope. **onde está o** ~ **deste sapato?** where is the fellow of this shoe? **um** ~ **de luvas** a pair of gloves.

para prep. 1. for, to, towards, at, in(to) (plate P 18). 2. about to, on the point, in order to.

~ **baixo** downward. ~ **cima** upward. ~ **diante** forward. ~ **lá e** ~ **cá** to and fro, hither and thither. ~ **onde ele foi?** where did he go? ~ **o futuro** for the time to come. ~ **o meu gosto** to my taste. ~ **o meu sentimento** to my feeling. ~ **quê?** what for? ~ **sempre** forever. ~ **todo o ano** for the whole year. ~ **trás** backward. ~ **a vida ou a morte** come life, come death. **deixamos o livro em cima da mesa** ~ **que ele o achasse** we left the book on the table, so that he could find it. **ele foi um amigo** ~ **mim** he was a friend to me. **ela lê bem** ~ **a sua idade** she reads well for her age. **ele parou** ~ **que pudesse ver** he stopped that he might see. **ele vai** ~ **Londres** he goes to London. **livros** ~ **crianças** books for children. **minha contribuição** ~ **as despesas** my contribution towards the expenses. **nosso dever** ~ **com** our duty to. **pronto** ~ **o combate** ready for action. **o que significa isto** ~ **ele?** what's that to him? **ser bastante ajuizado** ~ **não proceder assim** to be wiser than to do so. **temos um presente** ~ **você** we have a present for you. **tome cuidado** ~ **não perder o seu dinheiro** be careful lest you lose your money. **trem** ~ **Londres** train for London. **3 está** ~ **6 assim como 9 está** ~ **18** 3 is to 6 as 9 is to 18. **tudo** ~ **você** all for yourself.

pára interj. 1. stop! 2. whoa!

parábase s. f. parabasis: that part in ancient Greek comedy consisting of an address from the poet to the audience.

parabélum s. f. (Braz.) Parabellum: name given to the German Luger automatic pistol.

parabéns s. m. pl. congratulations, felicitations.

dar os ~ to congratulate. **queira aceitar os meus** ~ accept my congratulations.

parablasto s. m. parablast: the yolk of a meroblastic ovum. ‖ adj. parablastic.

parábola s. f. 1. parable: a short narrative with a moral or religious point; allegory. 2. (geom.) parabola: a conic section arising from the cutting of a cone by a plane parallel to one of its sides.

as ~**s de Cristo** the parables of Christ. **representar por** ~**s** to parable.

parabólico adj. parabolic(al): 1. (geom.) pertaining to or having the form of a parabola. 2. of or pertaining to a parable. ‖ **parabolicamente** adv. parabolically.

parabolismo s. m. parabolicalism.

parabolóide s. m. (geom.) paraboloid: a surface or solid generated by the rotation of a parabola about its axis. ‖ adj. m. + f. paraboloidal: having the form of a parabola.

pára-brisa s. m. (pl. **pára-brisas**) (mot.) wind-screen, windshield (plates B 15, L 2, M 12, V 3).

limpador de ~ windshield wiper.

paração s. f. (pl. **-ões**) round-up: the bringing together of cattle.

paracatas s. f. pl. clodhoppers: large, heavy shoes (as those of a plowman).

paracelsista s. m. + f. a follower of the Swiss physician Paracelsus.

paracentese s. f. (surg.) paracentesis: puncture of a cavity; tapping.

paracentral adj. m. + f. (pl. **-ais**) (anat.) paracentral: near a center.

pára-chispas s. m., sg. + pl. spark arrester.

pára-choque s. m. (pl. **pára-choques**) 1. (mot.) bumper: a guard to attenuate the shock of collision (plate V 3). 2. (railway) buffer, (U. S. A.) bumper (plates E 13, V 1).

paraciânico adj. (chem.) fulminic.

paracianogênio s. m. (chem.) paracyanogen: a polymer of cyanogen.

paraciesia s. f. (med.) paracyesis: extrauterine pregnancy.

paráclase s. f. (geol.) fault: a displacement or break in the continuity of rock masses.

paracletear v. to help (as the Holy Spirit).

Paracleto s. m. 1. Paraclete: the Holy Spirit. 2. **paracleto** paraclete: mentor; interceder; advocate, helper.

paracorola s. f. (bot.) paracorolla: a corona or other appendage of a corolla.

pára-costas s. m., sg. + pl. (fort.) parados.

paracusia s. f. (med.) paracusia: any desorder in the sense of hearing.

parada s. f. 1. parade: a) a marshal(l)ing and maneuvering of troops for display or official inspection. b) ostentation, display, pomp. c) pompous show. 2. stop; pause, rest. 3. halt, standstill. 4. stop, stopping place (as for a bus). 5. bet, stake, (at games). 6. (railway) flag-station. 7. (fig.) adventure, hazard. 8. m. (Braz.) fanfaron, swaggerer. ~ **de gala** dress parade. ~ **musical** hit parade. **agüentar a** ~ to stick it out; to face the music. **dia de** ~ field day. **ela é uma** ~ (coll.) she is a smasher. **ponto de** ~ stopping place, halting place. **vou descer na próxima** ~ I shall get down at the next stop.

paradear v. to bluster, swagger, boast.

paradeiro s. m. 1. stopping place. 2. whereabouts: place where a person or thing is. **nós não sabemos o seu** ~ we don't know his whereabouts.

paradigma s. m. paradigm: 1. (gram.) a model or table for the inflection of a class of words (as of a conjugation). 2. a pattern, model.

paradigmal adj. m. + f. (pl. **-ais**) paradigmatic(al): referring to a paradigm.

paradisíaco, paradísico adj. paradisiac(al), paradisaic(al): of or pertaining to the paradise; celestial.

parado adj. 1. still; motionless. 2. quiet. 3. spiritless. 4. immovable. 5. stagnant. ~**!** interj. ease all! **água -a** backwater. **estar** ~ to be at a stand;

parador s. m. 1. a round-up cowboy. 2. (mech.) backstop.

paradouro s. m. (also **paradoiro**) place where cattle rest at night.

paradoxal adj. m. + f. (pl. **-ais**) paradoxical: of the nature of a paradox.

paradoxar v. (Braz.) to paradox: 1. show a paradox in. 2. utter paradoxes.

paradoxo s. m. paradox: self-contradictory statement.

paraense s. m. + f. (Braz.) native or inhabitant of the State of Pará. ‖ adj. of or pertaining to Pará.

paraestatal adj. m. + f. (pl. **-ais**) (Braz.) partially controlled by the state (certain institutions).

parafernais s. m. pl. (jur) paraphernalia: the personal belongings or possessions of a wife. ‖ adj. (also sg. **parafernal**) paraphernal.

parafina s. f. paraffin: a solid mixture of hydrocarbons. **cera de** ~ paraffin wax.

parafinar v. to paraffin(e): 1. to treat with paraffin. 2. to apply paraffin to.

paráfise s. f. (bot.) paraphysis: a slender sterile filament of many cryptogamic plants.

pára-fogo s. m. (pl. **pára-fogos**) fire-screen.

paráfrase s. f. paraphrase: free translation of a passage of a work; exposition.

parafrasear v. to paraphrase: express, interpret, or translate paraphrastically.

parafrasta s. m. + f. paraphrast, paraphraser: person who paraphrases.

parafrástico adj. paraphrastic(al).

parafusador s. m. screwer: person who screws. ‖ adj. screwing.

parafusar v. 1. to screw: tighten or fasten with a screw. 2. to cogitate, think about, meditate. 3. to speculate on, ponder.

parafuso (I) s. m. 1. screw (plates B 4, C 11, P 4, R 4). 2. spindle of a press. 3. bolt. ~ **com porca alada** butterfly screw. ~ **de ajustamento** adjusting screw. ~ **de aperto** pressure screw, clamping screw (plate P 4). ~ **de cabeça chata** flat-head screw. ~ **de cabeça quadrada** square-head screw. ~ **de cabeça redonda** round-head screw (plate P 4). ~ **de fenda** wood screw. ~ **de fixação** hold-down screw, fastening screw. ~ **de porca** bolt with nut. ~ **de regulação** regulating screw, adjusting screw (plates P 4, R 4). ~ **de travação** check-bolt. ~ **embutido** dormant bolt. ~ **micrométrico** micrometer screw. ~ **sem cabeça** grub screw (plate P 4). **apertar com** ~ to screw tight. **apertar um** ~ to tighten a screw. **chave de** ~ screw driver. **encosto de** ~ screw dolly. **o** ~ **soltou-se** the screw became loose. **rosca de** ~ screw thread. **ter um** ~ **solto** (fig.) to be wrong in the upper storey.

parafuso (II) s. m. spin: the downward spiral motion of an airplane about a vertical axis.

paragão s. m. (pl. **-ões**) paragon: resemblance, similarity; comparison.

paragata s. f. (Braz., pop.) a sort of simple footwear with a sole of hemp and canvas uppers.

paragem s. f. (pl. **-ens**) 1. stopping, stoppage. 2. whereabouts.

parageusia s. f. parageusia, parageusis: abnormality of the sense of taste.

paragoge s. f. (gram.) paragoge: the addition of a sound or syllable at the end of a word.

paragógico adj. (gram.) paragogic(al).

paragonar v. to paragon: compare with; be similar.

paragonita s. f. (min.) paragonite.

paragrafação s. f. (pl. **-ões**) arrangement in paragraphs.

paragrafar v. to paragraph: arrange into paragraphs.

paragrafia s. f. paragraphia: a symptom of mental disorder in which the patient writes wrong letters or words.

parágrafo s. m. paragraph: 1. a short passage in a written or printed discourse. 2. a short article. 3. a mark (§) used to indicate where a paragraph begins. 4. (jur.) a clause.

paraguaio s. m. Paraguayan: native or inhabitant of Paraguay. ‖ adj. Paraguayan: of or pertaining to Paraguay.

paraíba s. f. 1. (Braz.) a tree of the genus Simaruba (Simaruba parahyba). 2. non-navigable stretch of a river.

paraibano s. m. (Braz.) native or inhabitant of the State of Paraíba. ‖ adj. of or pertaining to the State of Paraíba.

paraíso s. m. paradise: 1. the garden of Eden. 2. heaven. 3. any delightful place or situation.

paraláctico, paralático adj. parallactic(al): of or referring to a parallax.

paralalia s. f. (med.) paralalia: any defect in the faculty of speech.

pára-lama s. m. (pl. **pára-lamas**) mudguard, automobile fender, dashboard, splashboard (plates B 11, C 15, M 12, V 3).

paralaxe s. f. (astr.) parallax: angular measurement of the difference between the position of a heav-

P 4

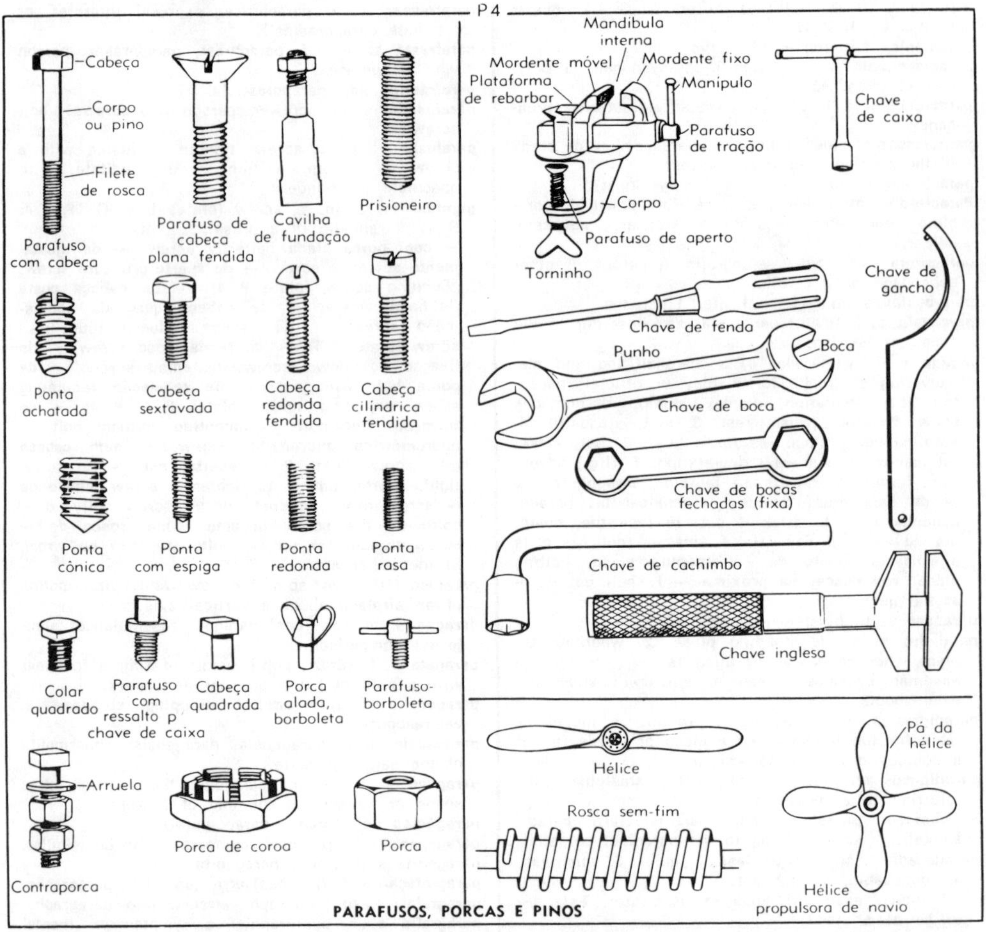

PARAFUSOS, PORCAS E PINOS

enly body as viewed from a station on the earth's surface and as it would be if seen from the center of our planet.

paraldeído s. m. (chem.) paraldehyde: a transparent liquid formed by the action of sulfuric acid on acetic aldehyde.

paralela s. f. 1. parallel: a line extending in the same direction and being equidistant at all points from another line. 2. ~s pl. (gymnastic) parallel bars (plates G 3, P 6).

paralelepipedal adj. m. + f. (pl. **-ais**) parallelepipedal: of, pertaining to or resembling a parallelepiped.

paralelepípedo s. m. 1. parallelepiped: a prism whose six faces are parallelograms. 2. (Braz.) paving stone (shaped like a parallelepiped).

paralelígero adj. (zool.) having the eyes in rows disposed parallelly (of certain spiders).

paralelismo s. m. parallelism, parallel position.
~ **psicofísico** (philos.) psychophysical parallelism.

paralelo s. m. 1. (geogr.) parallel. 2. confrontation, comparison. ‖ adj. 1. parallel. 2. collateral. ‖ **-amente** adv. parallelly.
correr ~ **a** to run parallel to. **ligação em** ~ (electr.) parallel connection. **lima -a** parallel file. **sem** ~ without parallel, unparalleled. **ser** ~ **a** to be parallel to. **traçar um** ~ to draw a parallel.

paralelogrâmico adj. parallelogrammic(al): shaped like a parallelogram.

paralelogramo s. m. parallelogram: a four-sided plane figure whose opposite sides are parallel.

parálico adj. (geol.) paralic.

paralipômenos s. m. pl. (bib.) paralipomena: writings added as a supplement.

paralipse s. f. paralipsis: a pretended suppression of what is really said.

paralisação s. f. (pl. **-ões**) 1. paralyzation: a) an attack of paralysis. b) weakness, enfeeblement. 2. interruption, suspension, stoppage.
~ **de empresas** shutdown.

paralisar v. 1. to paralyze: a) strike with paralysis. b) weaken. 2. to make torpid, benumb. 3. to neutralize. 4. ~**se** to become paralyzed or paralytic.

paralisia s. f. 1. paralysis, palsy: partial or complete loss of the power of voluntary motion. 2. (fig.) marasmus, numbness, torpor.
~ **geral** (path.) general paralysis. ~ **infantil** (path.) infantile paralysis, poliomyelitis.

paralítico s. m. paralytic: person subject to or suffering from paralysis. ‖ adj. paralytic: pertaining to or affected with paralysis.

paralógico adj. paralogical: referring to paralogism.

paralogismo s. m. paralogism: a fallacy in reasoning.

P 5

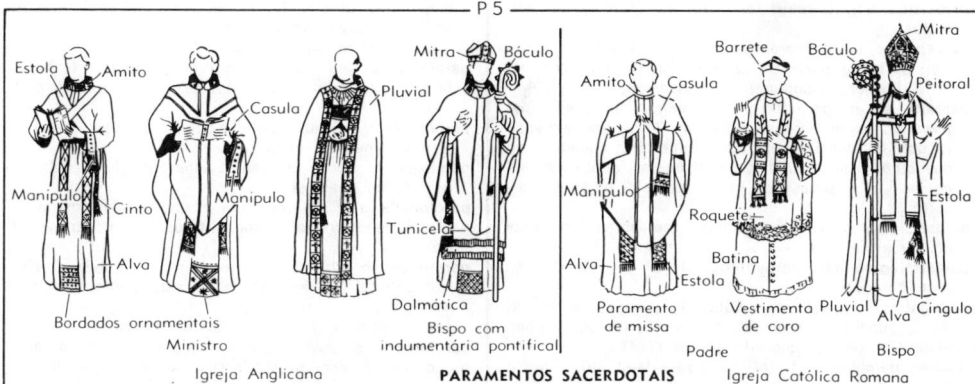

Igreja Anglicana   **PARAMENTOS SACERDOTAIS**   Igreja Católica Romana

pára-luz s. m. (pl. **pára-luzes**) lamp shade.

paramagnético adj. paramagnetic: having magnetic polarity in the same direction as the magnetizing force.

paramagnetismo s. m. (phys.) paramagnetism.

paramentado adj. 1. wearing liturgical vestments. 2. adorned, ornamented, decorated. 3. vested.

paramentar v. 1. to adorn, ornament. 2. to vest. 3. ~**-se**: a) (eccl.) to clothe o. s. with liturgical vestments (as a priest). b) to dress o. s. up.

paramenteiro s. m. tailor who makes liturgical vestments.

paramento s. m. 1. canonicals, liturgical vestments. 2. ornament, adornment. 3. vest. 4. (archit.) facing. ~ **de missa** mass vestment (place P 5). ~**s sacerdotais** clergical vestments (plate P 5).

paramétrico adj. (math.) parametric: of or referring to a parameter.

parametrite s. f. (med.) parametritis: pelvic cellulitis.

parâmetro s. m. (math.) parameter.

paramilitar adj. m. + f. semimilitary, pseudomilitary.

paramnésia, paramnesia s. f. paramnesia: distortions of the memory.

páramo s. m. 1. paramo: high region in the Andes. 2. desert plain. 3. firmament, sky.

paramorfismo s. m. paramorphism: the change of one mineral into another.

paraná s. m. (Braz.) arm of a large river separated by an island from the main course.

paranaense s. m. + f. (Braz.) native or inhabitant of the State of Paraná. ‖ adj. of or pertaining to the State of Paraná.

parança s. f. 1. stopping, a stop. 2. rest, repose.

paranéfrico adj. (anat.) paranephric: of or pertaining to paranephros.

paranefro s. m. (anat.) paranephros: the suprarenal capsule or gland.

parangona s. f. (typogr.) paragon: a size of type.

paraninfar v. 1. to sponsor. 2. to act as a paranymph.

paraninfo s. m. 1. paranymph: groomsman. 2. sponsor. 3. spokesman of a graduating class. 4. (fig.) protector.

paranista s. + adj., m. + f. = **paranaense**.

paranóia s. f. (med., also **paranéia**) paranoia: a chronic mental disorder or psychosis characterized by monomania, systematized delusions of persecution.

paranóico s. m. (also **paranéico**) paranoiac: person affected with paranoia. ‖ adj. paranoiac: of, pertaining to or affected with paranoia.

parapará s. m. (Braz., bot.) fotui.

parapeitar v. to make or form the parapet of.

parapeito s. m. parapet: 1. a low wall about the edge of a roof, terrace, bridge, fortification. 2. window sill. 3. breastwork.

parapétalo adj. (bot.) parapetalous.

paraplegia s. f. (med., also **paraplexia**) paraplegia: paralysis of the lower half of the body.

paraplégico s. m. paraplegic: person suffering from paraplegia. ‖ adj. paraplegic: pertaining to or affected with paraplegia.

parapodário adj. (zool.) parapodial: of or pertaining to the parapodia.

parápodes s. m. pl. (zool.) parapodia.

parapsicologia s. f. parapsychology.

parapsocidos s. m. pl. (ent.) psocids, insects of the order Corrodentia, suborder Psocidae: book lice.

pára-quedas s. m., sg. + pl. parachute: an umbrella--shaped contrivance for retarding the speed of a falling body (especially from an airplane). **colete de** ~ parachute harness. **saltar de** ~ to parachute. **salto com** ~ parachute jump.

pára-quedismo s. m. parachutism.

pára-quedista s. m. + f. (pl. **pára-quedistas**) parachutist.

parar v. 1. (also ~**-se**) to stop: a) cease to move, come to an end. b) pause, halt. c) discontinue. d) make a stand. 2. to stop: a) stay, check. b) clog, intercept. 3. to parry, ward off. 4. to wager, bet. 5. to remain in. ~ **de repente** to stop short. ~ **quieto** to be quiet. **eles pararam** they came to a stop. **fazer** ~ **um trem (com bandeira)** to flag a train. **mandar** ~ to call a halt. **pára com isso!** have done! **parei de ler** I finished reading. **ninguém pára aqui** (fig.) nobody can live here. **onde vai** ~ **o vosso discurso?** what is the end of your discourse? **o relógio parou por falta de corda** the clock (or watch) has run down. **sem** ~ without interruption, continuously.

pára-raios s. m., sg. + pl. 1. lightning-conductor, lightning-rod: device used to protect buildings from lightnings (plate C 11). 2. lightning-arrester.

parari s. m. a pigeon of the genus Zenaida (Zenaida auriculata virgata Bertoni).

parascéve s. f. parasceve: 1. the day before the Jewish Sabbath. 2. (R. C. Church) Good Friday.

parasita s. m. + adj. m. + f. = **parasito**.

parasitar v. (also **parasitear**) 1. to live like a parasite. 2. to sponge.

parasitário adj. parasitic(al): of, pertaining to or resembling a parasite.

parasiticida s. m. parasiticide: any agent that destroys parasites. ‖ adj. m. + f. parasiticide, parasiticidal: efficacious for destroying parasites.

parasítico adj. parasitic(al): of or referring to parasites.
parasitismo s. m. parasitism: 1. the state or condition of being parasitic. 2. the condition or conduct of a fawner, sycophant or hanger-on.
parasito s. m. parasite: 1. an animal or plant that lives on or in another organism at whose expense it obtains nourishment. 2. hanger-on, sponger: an obsequious sycophant who lives at another's expense. ‖ adj. parasitic: of or pertaining to a parasite.
parasitologia s. f. parasitology: the scientific study of parasites.
parasitológico adj. parasitological: of or referring to parasitology.
pára-sol s. m. (pl. **pára-sóis**) 1. parasol: a small, light sunshade (carried by women). 2. garden umbrella, beach umbrella (plate G 4).
pára-sol-da-china s. f. (pl. **pára-sóis-da-china**) Chinese parasol tree (Sterculia platanifolia).
parasselene, parasselênio s. m. paraselene: a mock moon appearing on a lunar halo.
parassematografia s. f. heraldry: the science of blazoning.
parassematográfico adj. heraldic: of or pertaining to heraldry.
parassematógrafo s. m. person versed in heraldry.
parassífilis s. f., sg. + pl. parasyphilis, metasyphilis.
parassimpático s. m. the parasympathetic system of nerves.
parassintético adj. parasynthetic: pertaining to parasynthesis or parasyntheta.
parati s. m. 1. a variety of **cachaça**. 2. (ichth.) white mullet (Mugil carema).
paratifo s. m. (med.) parathyphoid fever.
paratireóide s. f. parathyroid gland. ‖ adj. f. parathyroid: pertaining to or designating one of several (usually four) small glands on the inner side near the back of each lobe of the thyroid.
paratropa s. f. (mil.) paratroop, parachute troop.
paratudo s. m. (Braz., bot.) 1. balloon vine, heart pea. 2. Winter's bark tree. 3. cedron, rattlesnake bean.
paraturá s. m. (Braz.) 1. plant of the family Cyperaceae (Remirea maritima). 2. a cord grass (Spartina brasiliensis).
parauaçu s. m. (Braz., zool.) monk saki (Pithecia monachus).
parável adj .m. + f. (pl. **-áveis**) that is easily obtained.
párᴾ-vento s. m. (pl. **pára-ventos**) wind-screen.
parazoários s. m. pl. (zool.) Parazoa, metazoans.
parca s. f. (myth.) one of the three Fates called Parchae.
parceirada s. f. (Braz.) a group of partners.
parceiro s. m. partner: associate, copartner, person sharing in some enterprise. ‖ adj. similar, like, equal.
parcel s. m. (pl. **parcéis**) reef, shelf, shoal.
parcela s. f. 1. parcel, portion. 2. an indefinite number. 3. fragment. 4. quota. 5. item, entry. 6. any number of an addition.
vender em pequenas ~s to sell in small lots.
parcelado adj. 1. full of shoals. 2. made in parcels. ‖ -adamente adv. by piece, in parcels.
parcelar v. to parcel: divide into parts or parcels. ‖ adj. m. + f. parcel: divided into parts.
parceria s. f. 1. partnership, copartnership. 2. association. 3. cahoot. 4. (Braz.) a couple of composers of popular music.
parcial s. m. + f. (pl. **-ais**) partisan, sectarian, co-religionist. ‖ adj. partial: 1. pertaining to or involving a part only, not complete. 2. favouring one side, unfair, influenced, prejudiced. ‖ ~mente adv. partially, partly; unfairly.
~mente feito partly done.
parcialidade s. f., **parcialismo** m. partiality: 1. party, faction. 2. unfairness, bias, prejudice, unjust preference.
parcializar v. 1. to render partial. 2. (also ~-se) to join a group or party.
parciário s. m. 1. partisan: adherent of a party. 2. participant; partner.
parcimônia s. f. 1. parsimony: undue sparingness in the expenditure of money; frugality; meanness. 2. economy.
parcimonioso adj. parsimonious, frugal, sober, thrifty; economic(al). ‖ -amente adv. parsimoniously, economically.
ser ~ com to be very economical with.
parcioneiro s. m. (obs.) 1. accomplice. 2. partner.
parco adj. 1. economic(al), sparing. 2. frugal, thrifty. 3. scanty, poor. ‖ -amente adv. economically; frugally.
pardacento, pardaço adj. (also **pardento, pardusco**) brownish, greyish, dark grey.
pardal s. m. (pl. **-ais**) (f. **pardoca, pardaloca, pardaleja**) (ornith.) sparrow (Passer domesticus).
pardalada s. f. a flight of sparrows.
pardavasco s. m. mulatto: person having one white and one Negro parent. ‖ adj. mulatto.
pardieiro s. m. decayed house; the ruins of a house.
pardilho s. m. (obs.) a kind of brown cloth. ‖ adj. brownish.
pardo s. m. 1. mulatto. 2. (obs.) pard, leopard. ‖ adj. brown, dusky, dark grey; drab.
párea s. f. (also **pareia**) a gauge for barrels, tuns, casks.
parear v. 1. to keep posted, informed. 2. to gauge barrels, tuns, casks.
páreas s. f. pl. (anat., also **secundinas**) afterbirth, secundines.
parece-mas-não-é s. f., sg. + pl. (Braz., bot.) poinsettia (Euphorbia pulcherrima).
parecença s. f. 1. resemblance, similarity, likeness. 2. affinity, analogy.
parecente adj. m. + f. similar, like, resembling.
parecer s. m. 1. appearance, aspect. 2. semblance; look, mien. 3. opinion, concept, idea. 4. point of view. ‖ v. 1. to appear, seem, look. 2. ~-se (com): a) to resemble, be similar to. b) to figure as; look like.
~ de perito expert's report. **ele deu o seu ~ sobre meu serviço** he passed sentence (up)on my work. **emitir o seu ~** to speak one's sentiment. **sou do ~ que** I am of the opinion that. **a título de ~** by way of an opinion. **alguma coisa parecia estar perto de mim** I felt as if something were near me. **ao que parece** seemingly. **o ar parece quente** the air feels warm. **ela parece-se com a mãe** she looks like her mother. **ele parece mais moço do que é** he does not look his age. **ele parecia estar zangado** he seemed angry. **isto parece fraude** this bears semblance to a fraud. **parece-me esquisito que...** it strikes me as strange that... **parece-me impossível** it seems impossible to me. **parece-me que a campainha está tocando** I seem to hear the bell ringing. **parece-me que sim (não)** I should (not) think so. **parece que vai chover** it looks like rain. **parece que você não me conhece** you appear not to know me. **parece ser diferente** it looks the other way. **parece um sonho** it seems like a dream. **que lhe parece?** what do you think? **queria ~-me que...** it seemed to me that... **a sua filha parece-se muito com a senhora** your daughter takes after you. **você parece desapontado** you look disappointed.

parecido adj. similar, like, resembling.
~s como dois ovos as like as two peas.
paredão s. m. (pl. **-ões**) 1. a very thick and high wall. 2. high bank, steep slope.
parede s. f. 1. wall (plates A 7, C 9, D 4, P 16, 19). 2. (by extension) barrier, fence. 3. (fig.) strike (work stoppage).
~ de pau-a-pique a wall of wattles and mud, cob-wall. **~ de tábuas** partition (made of boards). **~ divisória** partition wall. **~s-meias com** next door to. **~ sem janelas ou portas** dead wall. **dar com a cabeça na ~** to butt one's head against a wall. **as ~s têm ouvidos** walls have ears. **encostaram-no à ~** they drove him to the wall. **entre quatro ~s** between four walls. **falar às ~s** to talk to a brickwall. **fazer ~** to strike (cease work). **fechar com ~** to wall up. **ele foi encostado à ~** he got the wall.
paredismo s. m. (Braz.) striking: ceasing of work.
paredista s. m. + f. striker. ‖ adj. striking.
paredro s. m. 1. director. 2. representative. 3. important person. 4. political boss.
paregoria s. f. act or fact of soothing.
paregórico adj. paregoric, soothing.
parelha s. f. 1. team, yoke (of horses, oxen) (plates C 16, S 1). 2. pair, couple, brace. 3. match. 4. anything perfectly like another. 5. running mate. **correr ~ com** (also fig.) to run neck-and-neck with. **fazer ~s** to match well. **sem ~** matchless. **uma ~ de bois** a yoke of oxen.
parelheira s. f. (S. Braz.) any snake of the family Colubridae.
parelheiro s. m. race horse: a horse bred and trained for contests of speed.
parelho s. m. a man's suit (coat and trousers). ‖ adj. 1. similar, like, equal. 2. matched.
parélio s. m. (astr.) parhelion: a mock sun, often coloured, appearing in connection with solar halos.
parêmia s. f. proverb, saying, a brief allegory.
paremiologia s. f. a set of proverbs.
parencéfalo s. m. (anat.) parencephalon: the cerebellum.
parencefalocele s. f. (med.) parencephalocele: hernia of the cerebellum.
parênese s. f. parenesis, persuasion, exhortation.
parenética s. f. holy eloquence.
parenético adj. parenetic(al): of or pertaining to parenesis.
parênquima s. m. parenchyma: 1. (anat., zool.) the proper tissue or substance of any part or organ, as distinguished from the connective tissue which it contains. 2. the fundamental cellular tissue of plants.
parenquimatoso adj. (anat., zool., bot.) parenchymatous: of or referring to the parenchyma.
parenta s. f. kinswoman.
parental adj. m. + f. (pl. **-ais**) parental: of or pertaining to a parent (father or mother).
parentalha s. f. = **parentela**.
parente s. m. 1. relative, kinsman. 2. **~s** pl. relatives, kinsfolk, kindred, folk (of a family). ‖ adj. related, kin.
~ consangüíneo blood-relation. **~ longínquo** a distant relative. **~ por afinidade** a relation by marriage (in-laws). **~ por parte de mãe** cognate. **~ próximo** a close relative. **ele é meu ~ por parte de pai** he is a relation on my father's side. **gosto dos ~s de minha mulher** I like my in-laws. **ela é minha ~** she is a connection of mine. **eles são ~s dela** they are akin to her. **meus ~s** my folks. **sem ~s** kinless. **um ~ afastado** a remote relative.
parentear v. to be related to.

parenteiro s. m. 1. person who protects his relations. 2. person who is very partial to his kindred. ‖ adj. partial to his kindred.
parentela s. f. kindred, relations, relatives, kinsfolk.
parenteral adj. m. + f. (pl. **-ais**), **parentérico** m. (med.) parenteral: pertaining to or designating a mode of assimilation other than through the alimentary canal.
parentesco s. m. 1. kinship, relationship, kinsfolk; blood. 2. connection, alliance. 3. similarity.
parêntesis s. m. (also **parêntesis** sg. + pl.) parenthesis: 1. a clause inserted in a sentence that is grammatically complete without it, separated usually by brackets. 2. (also **parênteses** m. pl.) either or (parentheses) both of the brackets ( ) so used. **pôr entre ~s** to parenthesize.
parentético adj. parenthetical: 1. pertaining to a parenthesis. 2. abounding in parenthesis.
páreo s. m. 1. horse race. 2. running match. 3. prize of a race or course.
parergo s. m. parergon: embellishment, adornment.
paresia s. f. (med.) paresis: partial paralysis affecting muscular motion but not sensation.
parestatal adj. m. + f. of or relating to autarchical enterprises or institutions.
parestesia s. f. (med.) paresthesia: 1. abnormal or perverted sense of touch. 2. a sensation of itching or prickling of the skin.
parga s. f. 1. stack of straw; heap of corn. 2. pile, heap, stack.
pargasita s. f. (min.) pargasite: a dark-green crystallized variety of amphibole.
pargata s. f. (Braz., usually **alparcata, alpargata**) a sort of sandal with a sole of hemp.
pargo s. m. (ichth.) red porgy (Pagrus pagrus).
pari s. m. (N. Braz.) fish weir.
pária, pariá s. m. pariah: 1. (Hindustan) one of the lowest class of inhabitants who are not included in any caste. 2. a social outcast.
pariambo s. m. (also **pirríquio**, poet.) pyrrhic: a foot of two short syllables.
pariatã s. f. (N. Braz., also **matupá**) a large floating island with vegetation on it.
pariato s. m. peerage: 1. the rank or dignity of a peer. 2. the body of peers.
parição s. f. (pl. **-ões**) 1. parturition: bringing forth of young. 2. (Braz.) yearly increase of cattle.
parida s. f. a woman in childbed; animal recently delivered of young.
paridade, parilidade s. f. 1. parity, equality; par. 2. resemblance, likeness; analogy.
~ de câmbio par of exchange. **na ~ de** at the parity of.
parídeos s. m. pl. (ornith.) Paridae, a family of passeriform birds: chickadees, titmice.
parietal s. m. (pl. **-ais**) (anat.) a parietal bone (plate C 17). ‖ adj. m. + f. mural: 1. pertaining to or supported by a wall. 2. resembling a wall.
parietário adj. 1. parietal. 2. growing on walls (plants).
pariforme adj. m. + f. of the same form, equal.
pariparoba s. f. (Braz.) plant of the family Piperaceae (Piper macrophyllum).
paripenada adj. f. (bot.) paripinnate (leaves).
parir v. 1. to bring forth, give birth to, deliver (of animals). 2. (fig.) to produce, cause.
pariri s. f. (Braz., ornith., also **jurutipiranga**) partridge dove.
parisiense s. m. + f. Parisian: a native or inhabitant of Paris. ‖ adj. Parisian: of or pertaining to the city of Paris.
parissílabo adj. (gram.) parisyllabic(al): having the same number of syllables.
paritá s. m. (Braz.) fish weir.

paritário adj. relative to parity: 1. formed of paired elements (for equalling purposes). 2. (jur.) on the same level (of voting members in labour judicial cases, and, by extension, of the judging courts).

parkeriáceas s. f. pl. (bot.) Parkeriaceae, a family of ferns.

parla s. f. talk, conversation, palaver.

parlamentação s. f. (pl. -ões) parleying, negotiations for a truce.

parlamentar (I) s. m. + f. parliamentary: member of a parliament. ‖ adj. parliamentary: 1. of, pertaining to or characterized by a parliament. 2. according to the rules of Parliament.

parlamentar (II) v. (also **parlamentear**) to parley, treat, negotiate a truce.

parlamentário s. m. person who negotiates a truce. ‖ adj. parleying.

parlamentarismo s. m. parliamentarism, parliamentary system.

parlamentarista s. m. + f. an adherent of parliamentarism.

parlamento s. m. parliament: 1. legislative body. 2. a national legislature.

parlapassada s. f. prior agreement.

parlapatão s. m. (pl. -ões) (f. **parlapatona**) 1. liar. 2. vain person, braggart. 3. impostor, deceiver.

parlapatear v. 1. to talk big. 2. to boast, brag.

parlapatório s. m. (Braz.) babbling, verbosity, loquacity.

parlar v. to jabber, chatter.

parlatório s. m. 1. parlatory (visiting room as of a convent), parlour. 2. locutory. 3. loquacity, verbosity.

parlenda, parlenga s. f. 1. speech; conversation. 2. idle talk. 3. annoying discussion. 4. quarrel.

parma s. f. (Roman hist.) a circular shield, buckler.

parmesão s. m. (pl. -ões) 1. Parmesan: native or inhabitant of Parma (Italy). 2. (also **queijo** ~) Parmesan cheese. ‖ adj. Parmesan: of or pertaining to Parma.

parnaibano s. m. (Braz.) native or inhabitant of the city of Parnaíba (Piauí). ‖ adj. of or pertaining to the city or Parnaíba.

parnasianismo s. m. Parnassianism.

parnasiano s. m. Parnassian: a representative of a school of poetry founded in France about the middle of the 19th century. ‖ adj. Parnassian: of or pertaining to poetry.

Parnaso s. m. Parnassus: 1. a mountain in central Greece, formerly regarded as sacred to Apollo and the Muses. 2. a collection of poems or literary works.

pároco s. m. parish priest, vicar, rector, curate.

paródia s. f. parody: 1. a literary composition imitating and ridiculing some serious work. 2. travesty, burlesque imitation.

parodiar v. 1. to parody: make a parody of; imitate, travesty. 2. to mimic.

parodista s. m. + f. parodist: person who makes a parody.

parol s. m. (pl. **paróis**) (Braz.) manger trough.

parola s. f. (also **paroleira**) 1. loquacity, talkativeness. 2. chatter, palaver. 3. m. (also **parolador**) = **paroleiro**.

parolagem s. f. (pl. -ens), **parolamento** m. prate, idle talk; palavering, babbling, chattering.

parolar, parolear v. 1. to chatter, prate, prattle, babble. 2. to palaver: talk much and idly.

paroleiro s. m. 1. talker, babbler: person who talks much and idly. 2. cheater, impostor, liar. ‖ adj. talkative, loquacious.

parolice s. f. loquacity, talkativeness; gossip.

parolim s. m. (pl. -ins) paroli.

paronímia s. f. paronimy.

parônimo s. m. paronym: a cognate word, a word having the same root as another. ‖ adj. (also **paronímico**) paronymic, paronymous.

paroníquia s. f. 1. (med., also **panarício, panariz** m.) paranychia, whitlow: an inflammatory tumour (esp. on the terminal phalanx of a finger). 2. (bot.) whitlow grass.

paronomásia s. f. paronomasia: a play upon homophonous words.

paropsia s. f. (med.) paropsis: a disorder of the sense of sight.

paróquia s. f. (R. C. Church) parish: 1. the district whose jurisdiction is confined to a church. 2. a parish church.

~ **rural** outparish. **receber auxílio da** ~ to be on the parish.

paroquial adj. m. + f. (pl. -ais) 1. parochial: pertaining to a parish. 2. of or pertaining to a parish priest.

escola ~ parochial school. **junta** ~ parish council. **registro** ~ parish register.

paroquiano s. m. parishioner: a member of a parish. ‖ adj. parochial.

paroquiar v. to be in charge of a parish.

parótico adj. (anat.) parotic: situated near the ear.

parótida, parótide s. f. parotid: a salivary gland below the ear.

parotídeo adj. parotid: referring to the parotid gland.

parotidite s. f. (med.) paroti(di)tis, mumps: Inflammation of the parotid gland.

paroxísmico adj. (also **paroxístico**) paroxysmal, paroxysmic: relating to a paroxysm.

paroxismo s. m. 1. paroxysm, fit of a disease. 2. ~**s** pl. (med.) death rattle.

paroxítono s. m. paroxytone word. ‖ adj. paroxytone: having the acute accent on the penultimate syllable.

párpado s. m. (obs.) = **pálpebra**.

parque s. m. park: 1. public square, garden. 2. a large área containing natural curiosities for public enjoyment. 3. game preserve. 4. an enclosure where guns, trucks, etc., are placed for safety; an artillery park.

~ **de diversões** amusement park. ~ **infantil** playground (plate P 6). ~ **nacional** forest preserve.

parquete s. m. parquetry: wooden mosaic used especially for floors; inlaid floor.

parra s. f. vine leaf.

parrado adj. 1. full of vine leaves. 2. trellised vine.

parrafar v. (obs.) to divide into paragraphs.

párrafo s. m. (ob.) paragraph.

parrana s. m. + f. badly dressed person; ragamuffin. ‖ adj. badly dressed; tattered.

parranda s. f. (S. Braz.) 1. a gang of thieves. 2. robbery, extortion.

parrar-se v. to grow leaves, spread (as trellised vines).

parreira s. f. 1. trellis, trellised vine. 2. (bot.) vine.

parreira-brava, parreira-do-mato s. f. (pl. **parreiras-bravas, parreiras-do-mato**) velvetleaf: a tropical climbing shrub of the family Menispermaceae (Cissampelos pareira).

parreiral s. m. (pl. -ais) arbour, trellised vines.

parricida s. m. + f. parricide: person who has killed a parent. ‖ adj. parricidal.

parricídio s. m. parricide: murder of a parent.

parruda s. f. (Braz., sl.) maiden, virgin.

parrudo adj. 1. squat, dumpy. 2. short and fat.

parse s. m. + f. Parsi, Parsee: 1. a Zoroastrian. 2. the Iranian dialect of the Parsi. ‖adj. Parsic.

parsec s. m. (astron.) parsec, a unit of measure for interstellar space, equivalent to 3.26 light-years.

parsismo s. m. (rel.) Parsism, Parseeism.

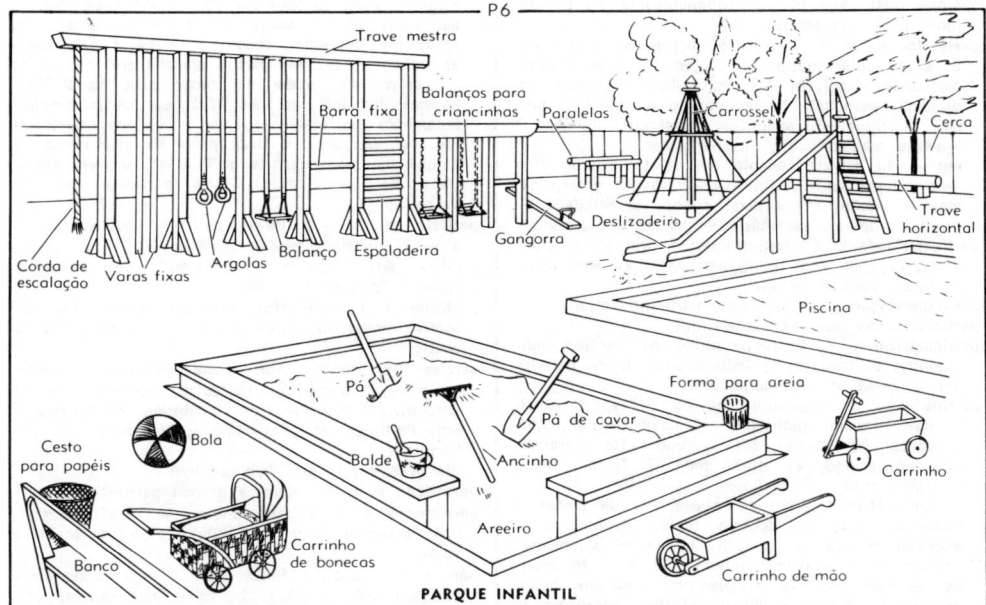

PARQUE INFANTIL

P6 — Trave mestra — Balanços para criancinhas — Barra fixa — Paralelas — Carrossel — Cerca — Deslizadeiro — Trave horizontal — Gangorra — Corda de escalação — Varas fixas — Argolas — Balanço — Espaladeira — Piscina — Pá — Forma para areia — Cesto para papéis — Bola — Balde — Pá de cavar — Ancinho — Carrinho — Areeiro — Banco — Carrinho de bonecas — Carrinho de mão

parte s. f. 1. part: a) portion, piece, fraction. b) region, place, spot. c) member, particle. d) side, party. e) lot, share. f) (mus.) the melody intended for a single voice or instrument in a concerted piece. 2. (oral or written) communication or information. 3. rôle, character. 4. ~s: a) qualities, accomplishments, talents. b) genitals. c) (Braz.) insinuations. d) cunning. e) coyness.
  ~ **dianteira** front end. ~ **interna** inside (plate R 4). **~s componentes** or **integrantes** component parts. ~ **traseira** rear end, tail piece. **à ~** apart; by itself; aside. **à ~ de** along with; aside from. **à ~ os inconvenientes** apart from any inconvenience. **a maior ~ das vezes** the most of the time. **as ~s autorizadas** the parties entitled. **cumpra a ~ que lhe couber** do your part. **da ~ de** on the part of, from, at the hand of. **da minha ~** from me; on my part; in my name. **dar ~** to report; impart. **de minha ~ farei tudo** I shall not be wanting for my part. **de outra ~** elsewhere. **de sua ~** on his (her) part. **de uma só ~** unipartite. **ele só obteve uma ~ daquilo que queria** he got only a fraction of what he wanted. **em ~** in part, in a measure, partly. **em ~ alguma** nowhere. **em alguma ~** somewhere. **em grande ~** in large part, largely. **em qualquer ~** anywhere. **em toda ~** all about, everywhere. **fazer ~ de** to be constituent of. **a maior ~** the great(er) part. **na maior ~** in the main, for the main. **não quero ter ~ nisto** I'll be no party to it. **nesta ~** in this quarter. **por ~ de** on the part of. **por toda ~** everywhere, around, all over. **isso representa uma ~ de** it forms a part of. **ter ~ com** to have dealings with. **tomar ~ em** to participate.
parteira s. f. midwife, accoucheuse: a woman who assists at childbirth.
parteiro s. m. obstetrician: a medical and surgical specialist in childbirth. ‖ adj. referring to such a specialist.
partejamento s. m. midwifery: act of assisting at childbirth.

partejar v. 1. to deliver (a woman) of a child, assist in childbirth. 2. to give birth to. 3. to act as a midwife.
partejo s. m. 1. assistance at childbirth. 2. midwifery, obstetrics.
partenogênese s. f. (zool., bot.) parthenogenesis: reproduction by means of unfertilized eggs or seeds.
partenogenético adj. parthenogenetic: of or pertaining to parthenogenesis.
partenologia s. f. (med.) parthenology.
partição s. f. (pl. **-ões**) partition, division, partitionment.
participação s. f. (pl. **-ões**) 1. communication, notification, advice. 2. participation, partnership, copartnership.
  ~ **de noivado** notice of engagement. ~ **em mina** mining share. ~ **nos lucros** profit sharing.
participador s. m., **participante** m. + f. 1. informer, communicator. 2. participant, partaker. ‖ adj. 1. informing, communicating. 2. participant.
participar v. 1. to communicate, announce, make known. 2. to impart, inform, report. 3. to participate in, partake of, take part in, share in.
  ~ **da mesma sorte com** to cast (or throw) in one's lot with. ~ **de um jogo** to take part in a play. **ele participou da minha sorte** he shared his luck with me. **ele participou no negócio** he embarked in (upon) the enterprise.
participável adj. m. + f. (pl. **-áveis**) capable of being announced, communicated, imparted.
partícipe s. m. + f. 1. informer, communicator. 2. participant. ‖ adj. 1. informing. 2. participant.
participial adj. m. + f. (pl. **-ais**) (gram.) participial: of or pertaining to a participle.
particípio s. f. (gram.) participle: a form of verb that permits its use either verbally or adjectively or both verbally and adjectively.
  ~ **passado** past participle.
partícula s. f. particle: 1. a minute part, piece or portion of any material; atom, element. 2. (gram.) any uninflected word. 3. (R. C. Church): a) the

small host used for lay communicants. b) a fragment of a consecrated host.

particular s. m. 1. a private person, an individual.
2. a particular matter or subject. 3. ~es details,
particulars. ‖ adj. m. + f. particular: 1. private, individual, personal. 2. peculiar to a specified person or thing. 3. specific. 4. minute, detailed. ‖
~mente adv. privately, in particular.
em ~ in private. **escola** ~ private school. **fins**
~es private ends. **iniciativa** ~ private enterprise.
meu ~ **amigo** my special friend. **propriedade** ~
private property. **secretária** ~ private secretary.

particularidade s. f. particularity: 1. the state, character, or quality of being particular. 2. peculiarity.
3. circumstance, detail.

particularização s. f. (pl. -ões) particularization.

particularizador adj. particularizing.

particularizar v. 1. to particularize: a) mention individually. b) specify. c) individualize, make individual. 2. ~-se to distinguish o. s.

partida s. f. 1. departure, leaving. 2. (sport) start.
3. party, social gathering. 4. game, match, set.
5. parcel (of goods); lot, shipment (of merchandize). 6. a body of armed men. 7. (com.) entry.
8. (fam.) trick, prank, hoax.
~ **automática** (mech.) self-starter. ~ **de cartas** a
game at cards. ~ **dobrada** (com.) double entry.
anunciar a sua ~ to give notice of departure.
contato de ~ starting contact. **dar a** ~ to start.
escrituração por ~s **simples ou dobradas** bookkeeping by single or double entries. **ponto de** ~
starting-point. **pregar uma** ~ **(em alguém)** to play
a trick (on s. o.). **uma** ~ **de futebol** a (soccer)
football game. **uma** ~ **de xadrez** a game of chess.
válvula de ~ starting valve.

partidão s. m. (pl. -ões) (fam.) 1. fine marriage. 2.
good position, swell job.

partidário s. m. 1. adherent, member of a party,
sectarian, correligionist. 2. backer. ‖ adj. 1. adherent; party; sectarian. 2. partisan.
~ **político** party liner. **máquina -a** party machinery.

partidarismo s. m. partisanship; proselytism.

partido s. m. 1. party: a) political organization. b) a
body of persons united for some common purpose;
a faction. 2. handicap given. 3. side, part. 4. expedient, shift. ‖ adj. broken; fractured.
Partido Agrário Country Party. **Partido Democrático**
Democratic Party. **Partido Trabalhista** Labour Party.
ele é um ótimo ~ he is an excellent match. **ele
mudou de** ~ he changed sides. **o** ~ **no poder e
a oposição** the ins and outs. **tomar** ~ **contra** to
discriminate against. **tirar o melhor** ~ **duma situação difícil** to make the best of a bad situation.
tomar o ~ **de** to make common cause with. **tomar
o** ~ **dos seus amigos** to rally to the side of one's
friends. **tomo o seu** ~ I take his part.

partidor s. m. 1. divider, sharer; distributer. 2. (S.
Braz.) starting-point for a horse-race. ‖ adj. apportioning.

partilha s. f. 1. partition, apportionment. 2. division,
sharing (of profits). 3. repartition. 4. portion, share,
allotment.

partilhar v. 1. to partition, apportion. 2. share with,
partake of, participate in. 3. to divide. 4. to distribute, allot.

partimento s. m. 1. division, distribution, partition.
2. departure, leave.

partir v. 1. to break (up), shatter, split, cleave. 2. to
separate, sever, disunite. 3. to fracture **(um osso**
a bone). 4. to part, divide, share. 5. to depart, leave
(para for, **de** from), go away. 6. to arise from,
emanate. 7. to start from. 8. ~-se: a) to break.
b) to become divided.

~ **(em avião)** to take the air. ~ **em expedição** to
set forth on an expedition. **a** ~ **de hoje** from
today on, beginning today. **a** ~ **de 1.º de maio**
as from May 1st. **ela partirá amanhã** she will leave
tomorrow. **ele acaba de partir para Nova York**
he has just left for New York. **ele partiu precipitadamente** he made a flying start. **nós partimos**
we took our way. **o trem parte às oito horas da
manhã** the train departs at 8 a. m. **o trem partiu**
the train went off. **o jarro partiu-se** the jug
broke up.

partista adj. m. + f. (Braz., coll.) 1. touchy, full of
airs. 2. skittish; easily frightened.

partitivo adj. partitive: 1. separating into parts. 2.
(gram.) designating a part.

partitura s. f. partitur(a), partition, score: the collective notes in which a musical composition is
written.

partível adj. m. + f. (pl. -íveis) partible, divisible.

parto s. m. 1. parturition, childbirth, delivery. 2. (fig.)
product. 3. Parthian: an inhabitant of Parthia. ‖
adj. Parthian: of or pertaining to Parthia or the
Parthians.
ela teve um ~ she was confined.

parturição s. f. (pl. -ões) a normal parturition.

parturiente s. f. a parturient woman. ‖ adj. parturient: bringing forth or about to bring forth a
young.

paru s. m. (Braz.) 1. tonka bean: a leguminous plant
(Coumarouna adorata). 2. (also **paru-rajado**) (pl.
parus-rajados) butterfly fish (Chetodon paru).

paru-de-pedra s. m. (pl. **parus-de-pedra**) (Braz., ichth.)
black angelfish (Pomacanthus ruthboni).

paru-dourado s. m. (pl. **parus-dourados**) (Braz., ichth.,
also **paru-doirado**) harvest fish.

parúlide s. f. (med.) (also **parúlia, parúlida**) gumboil:
a small boil or abscess formed on the gum.

parva s. f. 1. breakfast: a light snack before lunch.
2. a small sum of money. 3. (S. Braz.) haystack.

parvajola s. m. + f. numskull; fool.

parvalhão s. m. (pl. -ões) (f. -ona) a big fool.

parvalhice s. f. foolishness, silliness; idiotic behaviour.

parvidade s. f. 1. smallness, littleness. 2. stupidity,
silliness.

parvo s. m. (f. **parva, párvoa**) 1. numskull, blockhead.
2. fool, stupid person. ‖ adj. 1. small, little, skimpy.
2. idiotic, foolish, silly.

parvoeirão s. m. (pl. -ões) (f. -ona) big fool, very
foolish person.

parvoejar v. to talk or behave like a fool.

parvoíçada s. f. 1. idiotic behaviour. 2. nonsense.

parvoíce s. f. 1. folly, nonsense, absurdity, silly talk.
2. imbecility, stupidity.

parvolina s. f. (chem.) parvolin(e).

parvulez(a) s. f. 1. childhood. 2. puerility, childishness. 3. foolishness; a childish trick.

párvulo s. m. child. ‖ adj. childish; tiny, wee.

pascacice s. f. 1. silly talk. 2. idiotic behaviour.

pascácio s. m. fool, imbecile.

pascal adj. m. + f. (pl. -ais) (also **pascoal**) paschal:
of or pertaining to Easter or to the Jewish Passover.
comunhão ~ Easter Communion. **tempo** ~ Passion-
tide.

pascentar v. (usually **apascentar**) to lead to a
pasture.

pascer v. 1. to pasture, graze, browse. 2. to delight.
3. to divert, cheer. 4. ~-se: a) to take pleasure
in. b) to feed on. c) to amuse. o. s. with.

pascigo s. m. pasture, grassland, grazing.

Páscoa s. f. 1. (R. C. Church) Easter: a festival commemoration of the resurrection of Christ. 2. the

Jewish Passover. 3. (Braz.) a collective communion (at Easter).

ovo de ~ Easter egg. **véspera de** ~ Easter eve.

pascoar v. 1. to celebrate Easter. 2. to take the sacrament.

pascoela s. f. the eighth day after Easter, Low Sunday.

pascoinha s. f. (bot.) honey coronilla (Coronilla glauca).

pasigrafia s. f. pasigraphy: any of various systems of writing proposed for universal use.

pasmaceira s. f. 1. amazement, stupefaction. 2. apathy, melancholy.

pasmado s. m. an old fence post. ‖ adj. 1. amazed, astonished, stupefied. 2. fatuous, foolish, stupid, witless. ‖ **-amente** adv. 1. amazedly. 2. witlessly. **ele ficou** ~ **de horror** he was transfixed with horror.

pasmar v. 1. to amaze, astonish, surprise, stupefy. 2. to admire, wonder. 3. to stare at. 4. **~-se:** a) to be amazed, astonished or surprised. b) to be flabbergasted.

pasmo s. m. 1. -amazement, astonishment, stupefaction. 2. surprise, admiration, wonder. ‖ adj. (Braz.) amazed.

pasmoso adj. 1. amazing. 2. admirable, wonderful.

paspalhão s. m. (pl. **-ões**) (f. **-ona**) 1. fool, stupid person. 2. numskull. ‖ adj. foolish, stupid.

paspalhice s. f. 1. foolishness, silliness. 2. idiotic behaviour.

paspalho s. m. 1. fool, stupid person. 2. dunce. 3. scarecrow.

pasquim s. m. (pl. **-ins**), **pasquinada** f. 1. pasquin(ade:) an abusive or coarse personal satire posted in a public place; lampoon. 2. cheap newspaper.

pasquinagem s. f. (pl. **-ens**) lampoonery: writing of satires to bring a person into ridicule.

pasquinar v. to pasquinade, lampoon: satirize, attack or ridicule in pasquinades or lampoons.

pasquineiro s. m. pasquinader, lampooner.

passa s. f. raisin: a dried grape.

passa-culpas s. m. + f., sg. + pl. a very indulgent person.

passada s. f. 1. pace, footstep, stride. 2. **~s:** a) diligences. b) efforts.

dar uma ~ **de pano** to whisk off.

passadeira s. f. 1. stepping-stones. 2. filter, strainer, colander. 3. ring for a necktie. 4. runner, staircarpet. 5. (Braz.) a machine for pressing clothes. 6. (mil.) shot gauge.

passadiço s. m. 1. passageway; corridor, gallery. 2. sidewalk. 3. (naut.) bridge. ‖ adj. transitory, passing.

passadio s. m. daily feeding or ration.

passadista s. m. + f. person who lives in the past. ‖ adj. of or pertaining to the past.

passado s. m. 1. the past. 2. **~s** pl. ancestors. 3. (gram.) preterit. ‖ adj. 1. past, gone, bygone. 2. ended, finished. 3. former. 4. old-fashioned. 5. overripe (fruits). 6. last, latter. 7. amazed, astonished. 8. (Braz.) clever, cute.

ano ~ last year. **bem** ~ (beef) done to a turn, well-done. **como tem ~?** how have you sped? **do** ~ onetime. **em tempos ~s** beforetime. **esqueça o ~!** let bygones be bygones, wipe off the slate! **mal** ~ (beef) underdone. **isto são coisas do** ~ these are things of the past. **morto e** ~ dead and gone. **não falemos mais no** ~ let bygones be bygones. **a noite -a** last night. **no tempo** ~ formerly, in former times. **particípio** ~ (gram.) past participle. **um homem de** ~ **duvidoso** a man with a past. **um filé bem** ~ a rare steak.

passador s. m. 1. passer: a) person who passes. b) transporter; person who carries or conveys from one place to another. 2. smuggler. 3. receiver and passer of stolen goods, counterfeit money. 4. colander, strainer. 5. misleader. ‖ adj. passing.

passadouro s. m. (also **passadoiro**) passage, way, passing.

passageira s. f. (Braz.) a sort of river ferry.

passageiro s. m. passenger: 1. traveller. 2. passer-by. ‖ adj. 1. transitory, momentary, temporary. 2. passing, fleeting. 3. ephemeral ‖ **-amente** adv. 1. transitorily. 2. fleetingly.

~ **clandestino** stowaway. ~ **de avião** air passenger. ~ **de convés** deck passenger.

passagem s. f. (pl. **-ens**) 1. passage: a) act of passing. b) passageway: way by which a person or thing may pass; way of entrance or exit. c) (**-ens** pl.) a happening, a series of events, episode; incident. d) (mus.) a portion of a musical composition; a run or series of short notes. 2. fare; ticket. 3. a separate portion of a book. 4. communication.

~ **de nível** level or grade crossing (plate V 4). ~ **de volta** passage home, return ticket. ~ **direta** through passage. ~ **elevada** overpass. ~ **para pedestres** crossing for pedestrians, (U. S. A.) crosswalk (plate R 8). ~ **reduzida** half price (fare). ~ **subterrânea** subway, tunnel (plate E 13). **comentar de** ~ to remark parenthetically. **compramos as -ens** we took our passage. **de** ~ (in) passing, by the way. **eles reservaram suas -ens** they booked their passages. **ele trabalhou em troca da sua** ~ he worked his passage out. **quanto custa a ~?** what is the fare?

passajar v. to repair (clothes) by sewing.

passamanar v. 1. to lace: adorn with lace. 2. to trim: adorn with trimming.

passamanaria s. f. 1. lacemaking, lacework 2. passementerie: trimming for dresses.

passamaneiro s. m. lacemaker or lace seller.

passamanes s. m. pl. passementerie, trimming for dresses, lace, braid.

passamento s. m. 1. passing, death. 2. death rattle.

passa-moleque s. m. (pl. **passa-moleques**) (Braz.) perfidy; fraud, swindle.

passanito s. m. (Braz.) (fam.) 1. a nobody, person of no importance. 2. any person.

passante s. m. + f. passer-by. ‖ adj. passant, passing. ~ **de** surpassing.

passa-piolho s. m. (pl. **passa-piolhos**) (pop.) spade beard.

passaporte s. m. 1. passport, a safe-conduct, pass. 2. (fam.) full permission.

passar v. 1. to pass. a) pass over, cross, traverse. b) go (by, over, around, beyond, through). c) convey, carry, transport. d) enact, decree. e) spend, employ, elapse (time). f. endure, bear, suffer. g) (ftb.) kick (the ball) to another player of one's own side. h) omit, leave out. 2. to exceed, surpass. 3. to leave behind. 4. to transpierce. 5. to circulate, be current. 6. to be accepted. 7. to filter, percolate. 8. to sift. 9. to enjoy, delight in. 10. to legate, bequeath. 11. to thread. 12. to administer, minister to. 13. to vanish, fade away. 14. to expire, cease. 15. to die. 16. to escape. 17. to be enacted. 18. to send (as a telegram). 19. to elapse, pass away, slide away. 20. (Braz.): a) to become overripe (fruits). b) to be approved in an examination. 21. to dry (fruits). 22. **~-se:** a) to happen, take place, occur. b) to direct one's steps to.

~ **adiante** to hand on. ~ **a ferro** to press (clothes). ~ **a limpo** to write out fair, make a clean copy of. ~ **a mão em** (fig.) to steal. ~ **a noite em claro** to spend a sleepless night. ~ **a noite fora** to stay over. ~ **ao fio de espada** to put to the sword. ~ **ao longo de** to pass along. ~ **a perna em** to trick, outwit (s. o.). ~ **apertado** to scrape through. ~ **apressadamente por** to hasten past. ~ **a prova** to stand the test. ~ **as raias** to overpass the bounds. ~ **bem** to live well. ~ **correndo** to speed by. ~ **das medidas** (fig.) to exceed o. s. ~ **de boca em boca** to spread (news) from person to person. ~ **de mão em mão** to hand round or about. ~ **depressa por cima de alguma coisa** to hurry over s. th. ~ **despercebido** to go unnoticed. ~ **desta vida para outra** to die, pass from the present life to another. ~ **dos limites** (fig.) to exceed o.s. ~ **em revista as tropas** to take the salute of the troops. ~ **fome** to go hungry. ~ **mal** 1. to scrape one's living. 2. to be sick. ~ **na frente** to surpass, take down. ~ **o dia com alguém** to get through the day with s. o. ~ **o fim de semana em** to weekend in. ~ **o tempo** to pass, while away the time. ~ **para** to pass to; go over to. ~ **para baixo** to hand down. ~ **por** to pass by (for), overpass. ~ **por alto** to omit, overlook. ~ **por baixo de uma ponte** to pass under a bridge. ~ **por cima** to pass over; slide over. ~ **por uma inspeção** to muster. ~ **raspando (no exame)** (Braz., coll.) to scrape through (in an examination). ~**-se para outro partido** to change to another party. ~ **uma mão de cal sobre** to wash over. ~ **um telegrama** to send a telegram. **o bilhete (passagem) passou da data** the ticket is expired. **deixar** ~ to let pass. **deixar** ~ **uma oportunidade** to let slip a fair opportunity. **ela passa sua vida com tristeza e aflição** she frets her life away. **ela passou a noite lendo** she spent the evening in reading. **ela passou dos trinta** she is past thirty. **ela passou pó-de-arroz** she made up her face. **ela passou rapidamente** she flitted by. **ele não passa sem vinho** he can't abstain from wine. **ele passou no exame** he got through the examination. **ele passou um barbante em volta do pacote** he passed a string around the parcel. **ele passou uma temporada agradável** he had a nice time. **eles passaram** they walked by. **estou passando bem!** I am quite all right! **faça o favor de me** ~ **a manteiga!** pass me the butter, please! **fizemo-nos** ~ **por ricos** we passed ourselves off as rich. **isto não passa de um sonho** it is only a dream. **isto passa das minhas forças** this is beyond my strength. **isto passa de minha compreensão** it is above me. **já passa de meio-dia** it is past twelve. **não** ~ **de ano (na escola)** to be left back (at school). **não passemos daqui** let us stop here. **não passe os limites!** don't carry things too far! **não posso** ~ **sem isso** I can't make shift without it. **não sei o que me passou pela cabeça** I can't imagine what I was thinking of. **os dias passam** the days go by. **passamos em frente da porta** we went past the door. **passamos por Londres** we passed through London. **passe bem!** good-bye! **passe o livro adiante a...** pass the book on to... **passei a carta rapidamente para ela** I slipped the letter into her hand. **passei a noite a jogar** I passed the night at play. **passei-lhe um pito** (fig.) I gave him a snuff. **passei muito mal** I fared badly, felt very ill. **passei pelo pior do trabalho** I broke the back of my work. **passemos a outro assunto** let's pass on to s. th. else. **passou a chuva** the rain is over. **a propriedade passará para seu irmão** the property goes to his brother. **quero** ~ **um cabograma para Lisboa** I would like to send a cable to Lisbon. **a tempestade passou** the storm subsided.

pássara s. f. (Braz., coll.) turkey hen.

passarada s. f. (also **passaredo** m.) 1. a flock or crowd of birds. 2. birds collectively.

passarão s. m. (pl. **-ões**) 1. a great bird. 2. (Braz., ornith.) wood ibis (Mycteria americana).

passareira s. f. aviary: a birdhouse.

passarinha s. f. the spleen of an animal.

passarinhada s. f. 1. a crowd or flock of birds. 2. sudden buckjump of a mettlesome horse.

passarinhagem s. f. (pl. **-ens**) a bird hunting, bird trapping.

passarinhar v. 1. to bird: trap or shoot birds. 2. to loaf; dawdle. 3. (Braz.) to be startled (horse).

passarinheiro s. m. 1. birdcatcher; bird trapper; fowler. 2. fancier: a breeder and seller of birds. 3. mettlesome horse.

passarinho s. m. 1. any small bird, birdie. 2. passerine: any songbird.

pássaro s. m. 1. bird; any passerine bird. 2. (fig.) a cunning fellow.

mais vale um ~ **na mão que dois voando** a bird in the hand is worth two in the bush.

pássaro-angu s. m. (pl. **pássaros-angu**) (Braz., ornith.) black-capped mocking thrush (Donacobius atricapillus).

passaroco s. m. (Braz., pop.) sorrow, melancholy, the blues.

passarola s. f. 1. any large bird. 2. (Braz.) name given to the airship invented by the Brazilian Jesuit Bartolomeu Lourenço de Gusmão (1675-1724).

pássaro-preto s. m. (pl. **pássaros-pretos**) (Braz., ornith.) a cowbird of the genus Molothrus.

passatempo s. m. pastime: 1. amusement, diversion, entertainment, recreation. 2. sport, play.

~ **favorito** favourite pastime. **jogar por** ~ to play for love. **por** ~ as a pastime; for fun.

passavante s. m. pursuivant: an attendant upon a herald.

passável adj. m. + f. (pl. **-áveis**) passable, tolerable, not too bad, allowable, so-so, pretty good.

passe s. m. pass: 1. permit to pass, permission. 2. pass bill. 3. a ticket giving one free admission: free ticket. 4. (sport) action of passing the ball between players at a game. 5. ~**s** pl. (spiritualism) passes of the hands.

passeador s. m. 1. promenader, person fond of walking. 2. stroller. ‖ adj. walking for amusement, much given to promenading.

passeadouro s. m. promenade: 1. place for walking or promenading. 2. the act of walking for amusement.

passeante s. m. + f. 1. a promenader, stroller. 2. vagrant, idler, loafer. ‖ adj. 1. promenading. 2. idling.

passear v. 1. to promenade: walk for amusement or pleasure. 2. to go for a walk. 3. to walk, stroll. 4. to ride. 5. to take for a walk. 6. to show, exhibit ostentatiously. 7. to journey, tour about. ~ **de carro** to drive. **mandar** ~ to send s. o. about his business. **vamos** ~? let's go for a walk?

passeata s. f. 1. stroll: a leisure walk. 2. (Braz.) a public parade of protest.

passeio s. m. 1. walk, promenade, stroll, jaunt. 2. a trip; excursion; tour. 3. side-walk, promenade (plate P 17).

~ **a cavalo** ride. ~ **ao ar livre** airing. **barco de** ~ pleasure boat. **dar um** ~ to go for a walk. **eu não sou muito amigo de** ~**s** I am not much of a walker. **vamos dar um** ~ let's take a walk, let's go for a walk.

passeira s. f. place where grapes are spread to dry.

passeiro s. m. (S. Braz.) a ferryman: person who transports (goods or passengers) by boat or ferry across a river. ‖ adj. 1. walking. 2. (fig.): a) slow b) negligent, careless. 3. pacing (horse).

passento adj. pervious, permeable (paper, cloth).

passe-partout s. m. (Fr.) passe-partout.

passe-passe s. m. (pl. **passes-passes, passe-passes**) prestidigitation, sleight-of-hand.

passeriforme s. m. (ornith.) passeriform, passerine.

passibilidade s. f. possibility, passibleness: the quality of being passible.

passiflora s. f. (bot.) the genus Passiflora (comprising the passionflower).

passifloráceas s. f. pl. Passifloraceae: the passion-flower family.

passilargo adj. wide-paced.

passinho s. m. diminutive form of **passo**.
    cada ~ (Braz., pop.) at each step; at every moment.

passional (pl. **-ais**), **passionário, passioneiro** s. m. passional: a book describing the passion of Christ and the sufferings of saints and martyrs. ‖ adj. m. + f. passional: of or pertaining to passion.

passista s. m. + f. (Braz.) 1. (N. E.) a frevo dancer. 2. (S. E.) a person who dances the samba with much agility and grace.

passiva s. f. (gram.) passive voice.

passivar v. 1. to render passive. 2. (gram.) to change a verb to the passive. 3. to make indifferent.

passível adj. m. + f. (pl. **-íveis**) passible; susceptible. ~ **de** liable to, subject to.

passividade s. f. passivity, passiveness: quality of being passive.

passivo s. m. (com.) liabilities. ‖ adj. passive: 1. acted upon or receiving impression from external agents or causes. 2. not vitally or mentally active. 3. inactive, inert. 4. indifferent. 5. (gram.) of or pertaining to the passive voice. ‖ **-amente** adv. passively.
    resistência -a passive resistance. **voz -a** (gram.) passive voice.

passo s. m. 1. pace, step, footstep. 2. walk, gait; manner of walking (plate C 12). 3. march. 4. passage, narrow pass. 5. (fig.) action, measure. 6. (in dancing) chassé. 7. juncture. 8. pitch (of a screw). ~ **a** ~ step by step, foot by foot. ~ **acelerado** (mil.) double time, double quick. ~ **de gigante** (gym.) giant stride (plate G 3). ~ **errado** misstep. ~ **largo** stride, long step. ~ **lento** jog, snail's pace. **a** ~ slowly. **a** ~**s largos** at a great pace. **a cada** ~ at every step. **acompanhar os** ~**s de** to keep pace with. **a dois** ~**s** at two steps from. **andamos a** ~ **moderado** we went at a walk. **andar com** ~**s curtos** to trip along. **ângulo de** ~ (tech.) pitch angle. **ao** ~ **que** while, as. **apertar o** ~ to step out. **com** ~**s de gigante** rapidly. **dar o primeiro** ~ (fig.) to break ground. **dar um** ~ to take a step. **de** ~ **lento** slow-paced. **ele deu dois** ~**s em sua direção** he took two paces up to him. **ele deu o primeiro** ~ he made the first move. **ele não queria ceder nenhum** ~ he would not yield an inch. **em** ~ **acelerado** at a quick, round pace. **este** ~ **está sendo planejado** this step is being considered. **mantive o** ~ **com ele** I kept up with him. **marcar o** ~ to mark time. **perder o ritmo dos** ~**s** to get out of step. **tenciono fazer este** ~ I have this step in contemplation. ~ **passo** to mark time.

pasta s. f. 1. paste. 2. dough. 3. pulp. 4. portfolio: a) folder, binder, briefcase. b) a position in the cabinet of the President.
    ~ **de esmeril** flour of emery. ~ **dentifrícia**, ~ **de dente**, ~ **dental** toothpaste. ~ **mata-borrão** blotting-pad (plate E 2). ~ **para escrever** writing-pad. ~ **para soldar** flux paste for soldering.

pastagem s. f. (pl. **-ens**) pasture, pasturage: 1. grazing ground, feeding ground. 2. herbage: grass and herbage for cattle.

pastar v. 1. to pasture, graze, browse. 2. to feed, give or take food. 3. (fig.) to be delighted, enjoy, feast on.
    o gado está pastando the cattle is on the feed.

pastaria s. f. (Braz.) pasturage, grazing ground.

pastejar v. 1. = **pastar**. 2. to herd, graze, put to graze.

pastel s. m. (pl. **-éis**) 1. turnover, pastry, pie (of meat, cheese) enclosed and baked in a crust of pastry. 2. (typogr.) a mixture of types. 3. (drawing) pastel: a) a coloured crayon (plate P 12). b) the art of drawing with coloured crayons. 4. (fig.) indolent person.

pastelão s. m. (pl. **-ões**) a big pie.

pastelaria s. f. pastry shop.

pastel-dos-tintureiros s. m. (pl. **pastéis-dos-tintureiros**) a plant of the mustard family (Isatis tinctoria).

pasteleiro s. m. pastryman, pastry-maker, pastry-cook.

pastelista s. m. + f. (arts) pastellist.

pasteurização s. f. (pl. **-ões**) pasteurization: sterilization (as milk) by heating from 60° to 70° C.

pasteurizadeira s. f. pasteurizer: an apparatus for pasteurizing liquids.

pasteurizador s. m. pasteurizer: one who pasteurizes.

pasteurizar v. to pasteurize: sterilize (as milk) by heating from 60° to 70° C.

pastichar v. to make a pasticcio or a pastiche.

pasticho s. m. 1. pasticcio: a medley of fragments of works (esp. lit. or mus.) 2. pastiche: an imitation or caricature of another work.

pastifício s. m. (Braz.) paste factory: place where macaroni is made.

pastilha s. f. pastille, lozenge: a small medicated or sweetened tablet, troche.
    ~ **expectorante** pectoral lozenge.

pastinha s. f. diminutive form of **pasta**.

pastio s. m. ground abounding in grass, grazing.

pasto s. m. 1. pasture, pasturage: a) grazing. b) grass and herbage for cattle. 2. (fig.): a) food. b) joy, delight.
    casa de ~ eating-house, cheap restaurant.

pasto-natural s. m. (pl. **pastos-naturais**) timothy grass.

pastor s. m. (pl. **pastores**) 1. herdsman, shepherd. 2. pastor, minister, clergyman, vicar (of a Protestant Church). 3. (fig.) parish priest. 4. studhorse.
    cão ~ **alemão** German shepherd dog.

pastora s. f. shepherdess.

pastorador s. m. (N. Braz.) pasture, pasturage, grazing.

pastoral s. f. (pl. **-ais**) 1. pastoral: a) pastoral letter. b) eclogue, idyl: a pastoral poem. c) a simple melody in a rustic style. 2. pastorale: a cantata or operetta on a rustic theme. ‖ adj. m. + f. 1. pastoral: pertaining to the life of shepherds and rustics. 2. bucolic.
    terra ~ pasture land.

pastorar v. 1. = **pastorear**. 2. (N. Braz.) to watch, keep an eye on.

pastoreação s. f. (pl. **-ões**) act of pasturing, grazing.

pastoreador s. m. 1. herder, grazier: person engaged in grazing or pasturing cattle. 2. pasture, grazing.

pastorear v. 1. to pasture, herd, graze, put to graze. 2. (fig.) to guide, direct, lead.

pastoreio s. m. (also **pastorejo**) 1. pasturing (business). 2. (Braz.) pasture, grazing.

pastoreiro, pastorejador s. m. (Braz.) = **pastorador**.

pastorejar v. 1.(S. Braz.) = **pastorear**. 2. (fig.) to woo, court.

pastorela s. m. (mus.) pastorale, eclogue.

pastorício adj. pastoral: of or pertaining to shepherds.

pastoril s. m. (pl. **-is**), (also **pastorinhas** f. pl., N. Braz.) a certain outdoor folk play. ‖ adj. m. + f.

pastoral: 1. of or pertaining to shepherds or rustics and their work. 2. rural in spirit or sentiment. 3. rustic, bucolic.

poesia ~ eclogue.

pastorizar c. (usually **pasteurizar**) to pasteurize.

pastoso adj. 1. pasty, viscous, gummy. 2. syrupy. 3. husky (voice).

pastrano s. m. rustic, coarse person. ‖ adj. rustic, coarse, uncouth.

pata s. f. 1. (female) duck. 2. paw, pad (plate R 2). 3. foot. 4. (sl.) a big foot. 5. (naut.) fluke of an anchor. 6. (ichth.) shovelhead.

~ **dianteira (traseira)** fore-foot (hind-hand). **meter a** ~ to interfere in a conversation.

pataca s. f. (Braz.) 1. an old silver coin worth 320 réis. 2. riches, money.

meia ~ (fam.) 1. a pittance. 2. a trifle.

patacão s. m. (pl. **-ões**) 1. an ancient Portuguese copper coin of 40 réis. 2. (Braz.) an ancient silver coin of two mil-réis. 3. (fig.) a large and old--fashioned pocket watch.

patacho s. m. 1. a two-masted pinnace. 2. a large knife.

pata-choca s. m. (pl. **patas-chocas**) (depr.) 1. sacristan. 2. (Braz., pop.) soldier from the old National Guard. 3. heavy car. 4. fat and slow woman.

pataco s. m. 1. = **patacão**. 2. (fig.) stupid person.

pataço s. m. (S. Braz.) a backward kick.

patacoada s. f. 1. absurdity, nonsense, fudge. 2. braggadocio. 3. (Braz.) idle talk; lie.

patacudo adj. (Braz.) (sl.) moneyed, rich.

patada s. f. 1. a kick, stamping with the paws or feet. 2. (fig.) blunder, foolishness.

dar ~ (fam.) 1. to commit an ungracious or gross act. 2. to be boorish, rude. **levar** ~ (fam.) 1. to be the victim of an ungracious or gross act. 2. to be treated boorishly, rudely.

pata-d'água s. f. (pl. **patas-d'água**) (Braz., ornith.) cormorant.

patágio s. m. (zool.) patagium: the wing membrane of a bat.

patagônio s. m. (also **patagão**; pl. **-ões**) Patagonian: native or inhabitant of Patagonia. ‖ adj. Patagonian: of or pertaining to Patagonia.

patalear v. to kick, stamp with the paws or feet.

pataluco s. m. (bot.) cursed crowfoot (Ranunculus sceleratus).

patamar s. m. 1. landing, platform interrupting a flight of stairs (plate E 7). 2. even stretch of a railway line.

patamaz s. m. (sl.) 1. sanctimonious person. 2. big fool. ‖ adj. 1. sanctimonious. 2. very foolish.

patão s. m. (pl. **-ões**) (Braz.) merganser (Mergus octosetaceus).

pataqueiro s. m. (Braz.) 1. rich person. 2. cheap actor. ‖ adj. 1. common, ordinary, poor. 2. cheap, low-priced.

pataquinha s. f. (Braz.) a variety of pigeon.

patarata s. f. 1. harmless fib, white lie. 2. ridiculous ostentation. 3. m. + f. boaster, swaggerer.

pataratar, pataratear v. 1. to fudge. 2. to tell white lies. 3. to boast, brag.

patarateiro s. m. fibber, person who tells white lies. ‖ adj. boastful, braggart.

pataréu s. m. = **patamar** 1.

patarrás s. m. (naut.) shroud, back-rope.

patau s. m. 1. numskull. 2. fool, simpleton. 3. ignorant person.

patavina s. f. nothing.

eu não entendo ~ I don't understand anything.

patavino s. m. Paduan: native or inhabitant of Padua (Italy). ‖ adj. Paduan: of or pertaining to the city of Padua or to Paduans.

patchuli s. m. patchouli, patchouly: 1. plant of the mint family (Pogostemon patchouly). 2. the perfume obtained from it.

patchwork adj. m. + f. (Engl.) of or referring to patchwork.

pate adj. (chess) pat, stalemated (plate X).

pateada, pateadura s. f. 1. stamping with the feet (in contempt). 2. hooting, hissing.

patear v. 1. to stamp with the feet. 2. to express disapproval by stamping with the feet; to hoot, hiss. 3. to succumb. 4. to admit defeat. 5. to be unsuccessful.

patego s. m. 1. simpleton, fool, blockhead. 2. yokel, coarse person. ‖ adj. 1. foolish, stupid. 2. coarse.

pateguice s. f. stupidity, nonsense.

pateiro s. m. 1. gooseherd; person who keeps geese or ducks. 2. (fam.) lay brother (in a monastery). 3. retriever dog.

patejar v. (also **patinhar**) to splash, dabble (in water).

patel s. m. (pl. **patéis**) (Braz., chess) pate.

patela s. f. 1. (anat.) patella, kneecap. 2. quoits (the game). 3. quoit: the disk used in quoits.

patelar adj. + f. patellar: of or pertaining to the patella.

patelha s. f. (naut.) pintle: iron bolt on which the rudder or helm of a ship moves.

patena, pátena s. f. (eccl.) paten: a plate for the Eucharistic bread.

patente s. f. 1. patent: a) governmental protection of an invention. b) privilege. c) exclusive grant. 2. military rank. ‖ adj. m. + f. 1. patent: a) evident, clear, manifest. b) open. c) unequivocal, obvious. 2. frank.

altas ~**s do exército** high-ranking army officers. **concessionário de** ~ patent holder, patentee. **concessor de** ~**s** patentor. **metal** ~ patent metal. **receber** ~ **de oficial** (mil.) to receive one's commission. **registro de** ~**s** patent office. **requerer** ~ **de invenção para...** to take out a patent for...

patentear v. 1. to patent (an invention). 2. to manifest, make evident or patent. 3. to frank. 4. ~**-se** to become evident.

pátera s. f. patera: a shallow platelike vessel used by the Romans for libations.

paternal adj. m. + f. (pl. **-ais**) paternal, fatherlike, fatherly. ‖ ~**mente** adv. paternally.

paternalismo s. m. paternalism: paternal care or control.

paternidade s. f. paternity, fatherhood, fathership.

atribuíram-lhe a ~ they fathered the child on him.

paterno adj. 1. paternal: a) fatherly. b) hereditary. 2. of or pertaining to one's fatherland.

casa -a father's house, home.

patesca s. f. (naut.) snatch block.

pateta s. m. + f. dotard, simpleton, fool, stupid fellow.

patetar, patetear v. 1. to behave like a dotard. 2. to speak nonsense.

patetice s. f. dotage, stupidity; nonsense.

patético s. m. 1. something moving or touching. 2. commotion. ‖ adj. pathetic(al): 1. touching, moving, stirring. 2. arousing compassion. ‖ **pateticamente** adv. pathetically.

patibular adj. m. + f. 1. of or relating to a gallows. 2. criminal, mien.

patíbulo s. m. gallows, gibbet, scaffold.

pático adj. 1. libidinous, lascivious. 2. libertine.

patifão s. m. (pl. **-ões**) a big rascal or scoundrel.

patifaria s. f. knavery, scoundrelism, rascality, villainy.

patife s. m. rascal, villain, rogue, scoundrel, rotter. ‖ adj. 1. scoundrel, knavish. 2. coward, pusillanimous. 3. impudent.

patilha s. f. 1. (saddle) cantle (plate S 2). 2. (bicycle) brake.

patim s. m. (pl. **-ins**) 1. skate (ice or roller). 2. runner of a sledge (sleigh) (plate T 6). 3. small stair landing.
~ **de freio** brake-shoe. **-ins de gelo** ice skates. **-ins de roda** roller skates. ~ **da cauda** (aeron.) tail skid (of an airplane).

pátina s. f. patina: the green layer on ancient bronzes, copper coins, medals.

patinação s. f. (pl. **-ões**) (Braz.) 1. skating. 2. (also **rinque de** ~) skating-rink.

patinador s. m. skater: person who skates. ‖ adj. skating.

patinar v. 1. to skate: glide or move over ice on skates. 2. to roller-skate. 3. (fig.) to slid, skid (as wheels in the mud).

patinete s. m. toy scooter.

patinhar v. 1. to splash, dabble, paddle; play in the water. 2. to skid (as the wheels of a locomotive).

patinho s. m. 1. duckling: a young duck. 2. (fig.) fool, simpleton.
cair como um ~ 1. to be had. 2. to be taken in. 3. to swallow the bait.

patinho-d'água s. m. (pl. **patinhos-d'água**), **patinho--de-igapó** (pl. **patinhos-de-igapó**) (Braz., ornith.) sun-grebe, sun bittern, finfoot (Heliornis fulica).

pátio s. m. 1. courtyard: an enclosed yard adjoining a building or surrounded by buildings to which it gives access; patio. 2. court. 3. vestibule.
~ **de armazenagem** storage yard. ~ **de desvios** (railway) siding yard. ~ **de estrada de ferro** railway yard. ~ **de fazenda** farmyard (plate C 11). ~ **de manobra** (railway) marshalling yard (plate E 12). ~ **de recreio** playground.

patioba s. f. (Braz., herpet.) a venomous pit viper (Bothrops bilineata).

patível adj. m. + f. (pl. **-íveis**) tolerable, bearable.

pato s. m. -1. (ornith.) duck, drake. 2. (pop.) simpleton. 3. (Braz.) a bad player.
~ **novo** duckling. **pagar o** ~ to pay the piper.

patoá s. m. patois, a dialect.

pato-arminho s. m. (pl. **patos-arminho**) (Braz., ornith.) a swan of the family Anatidae (Cygnus melanocoryphus).

patofobia s. f. (med.) pathophobia: a morbid fear of diseases or of being sick.

patogênese, patogenesia s. f. (med.; also **patogenia**) pathogenesis, pathogeny.

patogenético adj. pathogenetic, of or relating to pathogenesis.

patogênico adj. pathogenic, causing diseases.

patognomônico adj. (med.) pathognomonic, symptomatic of certain diseases.

patola s. f. 1. claw of a crab and some other crustaceans. 2. (naut.) can hook. 3. (Braz., sl.) hand. 4. m. + f. simpleton, fool. ‖ adj. m. + f. foolish, stupid, silly, ignorant.

patolar v. to buttonhole: seize (a person) by the lapels.

patologia s. f. pathology: the science which treats of diseases.

patológico adj. pathologic(al): pertaining to pathology.

patologista s. m. + f. pathologist: person skilled in pathology.

pato-marinho s. m. (pl. **patos-marinhos**) (Braz., ornith.; also **pingüim**) penguin (Spheniscus magellanicus).

patos s. m. pathos.

patota s. f. (Braz.) 1. robbery. 2. swindle, gyp. 3. cheating, fraud.

patotada s. f. (Braz.) a series of swindles.

patoteiro s. m. 1. swindler, cheat. 2. cardsharp. ‖ adj. swindling, cheating.

pato-trombeteiro s. m. (pl. **patos-trombeteiros**) (ornith.) shoveller.

patranha s. f. 1. fib: a petty falsehood. 2. a great lie. 3. untruthful story.
contar ~**s** to tell tales.

patranhada s. f. a series of fibs.

patranheiro s. m. 1. fibber. 2. story-teller. 3. liar. ‖ adj. lying.

patrão s. m. (pl. **-ões**) (f. **patroa**) 1. master: a) boss, employer; foreman. b) chief. 2. landlord. 3. protector, patron. 4. coxswain, cockswain; skipper.

patrazana s. m. 1. any fellow. 2. a fat and easygoing person.

pátria s. f. 1. native country, fatherland, motherland. 2. (fig.) home(-land).
rumo à ~ homeward bound.

patriarca s. m. patriarch: 1. (ancient hist.) head of a family (among Hebrews). 2. the founder of a religious order. 3. (R. C. Church) a bishop of the highest rank. 4. a chief of the Greek Church.

patriarcado s. m. patriarchate: the office, dominion or residence of a patriarch.

patriarcal s. f. patriarchal see. ‖ adj. m. + f. (pl. **-ais**) 1. patriarchal: a) of or pertaining to a patriarch. b) governed by a patriarch. c) venerable, respectable. 2. peaceful. 3. kind.

patriciado, patriciato s. m. patriciate: 1. the patricians as a class. 2. the nobility. 3. dignity of a patrician.

patrício s. m. 1. (ancient Rome) patrician, aristocrat. 2. fellow-countryman. ‖ adj. 1. patrician: a) pertaining to the Roman aristocracy. b) aristocratic. 2. distinct. 3. elegant, graceful.

patrilinear adj. m. + f. (ethnology) patrilineal: derived from or descending through the male line.

patrimoniado adj. having a patrimony.

patrimonial adj. m. + f. (pl. **-ais**) patrimonial.

patrimônio s. m. patrimony: 1. an inheritance from a father or ancestor. 2. family estate. 3. an endowment.
~ **hereditário** birthright.

pátrio adj. 1. of or relating to one's country; native. 2. paternal, of or pertaining to one's father.
~ **poder** paternal power (in relation to the children). **língua -a** native language.

patriota s. m. + f. 1. patriot: person who loves his country. 2. patrician, countryman. ‖ adj. patriotic.

patriotada s. f. (Braz.) 1. (depr.) a show of patriotism. 2. a number of patriots.

patrioteiro s. m. (depr.) an overpatriotic person, a chauvinist. ‖ adj. chauvinistic.

patriotice s. f. (depr.) 1. chauvinism: exaggerated patriotism. 2. false patriotism.

patriótico adj. patriotic: 1. characterized by patriotism. 2. of or pertaining to a patriot. ‖ **patrioticamente** adv. patriotically.

patriotismo s. m. patriotism: devotion to one's country.

patrístico adj. patristic(al): of or pertaining to the fathers of the Christian church or to their writings.

patrizar v. to behave like a patriot.

patroa s. f. mistress: 1. matron, housekeeper. 2. madam. 3. (pop.) a married woman or wife.

patrocinador s. m. 1. patronizer: sponsor. 2. supporter. 3. protector. ‖ adj. 1. patronizing. 2. supporting, favouring. 3. protecting.

patrocinar v. 1. to patronize (also com.) 2. to protect, favour, support. 3. to defend.

patrocínio s. m. (also **patronagem** f.) 1. patronage, protection, favour. 2. support, aid, help. 3. sponsorship.
sob o ~ **de** under the auspices of.

patrologia s. f. (eccl.) patrology: the study of the doctrines and writings of the fathers of the Christian church.

patrona s. f. 1. patroness, a female patron. 2. cartridge box.

patronal adj. m. + f. (pl. **-ais**) patronal: of or relating to patrons.

patronato s. m. (also **patronado**) 1. patronage, advowson. 2. the authority of a patron. 3. asylum for children.

patronear v. 1. to patronize: a) act as a patron to. b) favour, support. 2. to sponsor. 3. to take airs of a boss.

patronesse s. f. (Fr.) patroness, a woman who organizes or sponsors a charity festival or campaign.

patronímico s. m. patronymic: a name derived from an ancestor, a family name. ‖ adj. patronymic: 1. formed after one's father's name. 2. referring to or derived from a family name.

patrono s. m. patron: 1. protector, defender, advocate, patronizer. 2. a patron saint. 3. sponsor. 4. (ancient Rome) master of a freed slave maintaining certain rights over him.

patrulha s. f. patrol: 1. a patrolling. 2. the soldiers or policemen patrolling a district.

rádio ~ radio patrol.

patrulhar v. to patrol: 1. walk around in order to guard or inspect. 2. go the rounds.

patuá s. m. (Braz.) 1. a basket of straw. 2. leather bag.

patudo adj. broad-footed, big-pawed.

patuléia s. f. (fig.) mob, rabble.

pátulo adj. patent, evident, open, clear.

patureba s. m. 1. dried and salted catfish. 2. m. + f. (pop.) simpleton, silly person. ‖ adj. m. + f. simple, silly.

patuscada s. f. 1. banquet: a sumptuous feast. 2. merrymaking, revelry. 3. mirth, frolic.

patuscar v. to make merry, revel.

patusco s. m. 1. feaster, banqueter. 2. merrymaker. 3. ridiculous person. ‖ adj. merrymaking, ridiculous.

pau s. m. 1. stick, cudgel. 2. timber. 3. wood. 4. lath. 5. beam, girder. 6. beating. 7. (Braz.) horn. 8. (Braz., pop.): a) failure in an examination. b) cruzeiro, escudo. 9. ~s pl. (cards) clubs (plate B 5). ‖ adj. (Braz.) importunate, obstrusive, boresome. ~ **de bandeira** flagpole, flagstaff. ~ **da bandeira de cruzeiro** jack staff (plate L 2). ~ **ferrado de alpinista** (also **alpenstock**) alpenstock, mountaineering stick (plate G 4). ~ **para toda obra** jack-of-all-trades. ~ **podre** touchwood, spunk. **aqui ou é** ~ **ou é pedra** here you can only do either one thing or the other. **dar por** ~**s e por pedras** to do crazy things. **a dar com** ~ a great deal. **de** ~ wooden. **jogar com** ~ **de duas pontas** to run with the hare and hunt with the hounds. **levar** ~ (Braz., pop.) to flunk an examination. **meio** ~ half-mast. **meter o** ~ **em** 1. to beat. 2. (Braz., sl.) to speak ill of. 3. to squander. **meteu o** ~ **no dinheiro** he spent all the money. **mostrar com quantos** ~**s se faz uma canoa** (fig.) to teach s. o. a lesson. **naipe de** ~**s é trunfo** clubs are trumps.

pau-a-pique s. m. (pl. **paus-a-pique**) mud wall, lath-and-plaster, stud and mud.

pau-bala s. m. (pl. **paus-bala**) (Braz.) tree of the family Meliaceae (Guarea trichilioides).

pau-bálsamo s. m. (pl. **paus-bálsamo**) myrocarpus: tree of the family Leguminosae (Myrocarpus frondosus).

pau-brasil s. m. (pl. **paus-brasil**) brazilwood, Pernambuco wood, redwood (Caesalpinia echinata).

pau-caixeta s. m. (pl. **paus-caixeta**) Brazilian cork-tree.

paucifloro adj. (bot.) pauciflorous: having few flowers.

paucirradiado adj. (bot.) pauciradiated.

pau-cravo s. m. (pl. **paus-cravo**) (Braz., bot.) pink-wood (Dicypellium caryophyllatum).

pau-d'água s. m. (pl. **paus-d'água**) (Braz.) 1. copalyé tree (Vochysia thyrsoidea). 2. (pop.) drunkard, boozer.

pau-d'arco s. m. (pl. **paus-d'arco**) (Braz., bot.) fiddlewood, roble (Tecoma heptaphylla).

paul-de-arrasto s. m. (pl. **paus-de-arrasto**) (S. Braz.) wooden clog for a grazing horse.

pau-de-balsa s. m. (pl. **paus-de-balsa**) (Braz.) balsa, tropical American corkwood (Ochroma lagopus).

pau-de-cabeleira s. m. (pl. **paus-de-cabeleira** (Braz., pop.) 1. pander, pimp. 2. mediator between lovers.

pau-de-caixa s. m. (pl. **paus-de-caixa**) (Braz.) tree of the family Vochysiaceae (Vochysia tucanorum).

pau-de-cangalha s. m. (pl. **paus-de-cangalha**) (Braz.) tree of the family Symplocaceae (Symplocos parviflora).

pau-de-carga s. m. (pl. **paus-de-carga**) boom (plate D 2).

pau-de-curtume s. m. (pl. **paus-de-curtume**) (Braz., bot.) locustberry, bay-bay.

pau-de-cutia s. m. (pl. **paus-de-cutia**) (Braz.) plant of the family Rutaceae (Esenbeckia grandiflora).

pau-de-formiga s. m. (pl. **paus-de-formiga**) (Braz.) ant tree (Triplaris noli-tangere).

pau-de-guiné s. m. (pl. **paus-de-guiné**) tree of the family Annonaceae (Annona acutiflora).

pau-de-jangada s. m. (pl. **paus-de-jangada**) (Braz., bot.) tiburbou (Apeiba tibourbou).

pau-de-novato s. m. (pl. **paus-de-novato**) (Braz.) ant tree (Triplaris americana).

pau-de-pente s. m. (pl. **paus-de-pente**) (Braz., bot.) pereira bark.

pau-de-pernambuco s. m. (pl. **paus-de-pernambuco**) (Braz., bot.) brazilwood, redwood.

pau-de-porco s. m. (pl. **paus-de-porco**) (Braz., bot.) either of two caesalpinias (Caesalpinia gardneriana and Caesalpinia pyramidalis).

pau-de-rosas s. m. (pl. **paus-de-rosas**) (Braz.) a lauraceous tree (Aniba rosaeodora).

pau-de-sapã s. m. (pl. **paus-de-sapã**) (bot.) sapanwood.

pau-de-sebo s. m. (pl. **paus-de-sebo**) (Braz.) 1. greasy pole. 2. (bot.) Chinese tallow-tree (Sapium sebiferum).

pau-de-seda s. m. (pl. **paus-de-seda**) (Braz., bot.) silkwood (Matingia calabura).

pau-de-tamanco s. m. (pl. **paus-de-tamanco**) Brazilian cork-tree.

pau-de-tingui s. m. (pl. **paus-de-tingui**) (Braz., bot.) tingui, tinguy (Magonia pubescens).

pau-de-viola s. m. (pl. **paus-de-viola**) (Braz., bot.) fiddlewood (Citharexyon cinereum).

pau-de-virar-tripa s. m. (pl. **paus-de-virar-tripa**) (pop.) skinny person.

pau-ferro-da-índia s. m. (pl. **paus-ferro-da-índia**) (bot.) ironwood, rose-chestnut.

pau-forquilha s. m. (pl. **paus-forquilha**) (Braz., bot.) pereira bark (Geissospermum vellosii).

paul s. m. (pl. **pauis**) marsh, swamp, quagmire.

paulada s. f. blow with a cudgel; drabbing, beating with a stick.

paulama s. f. (Braz.) 1. heap of sticks, trunks. 2. brush, branches, half-burned tree trunks.

paulatino adj. slow, by degrees, made little by little. ‖ **-amente** adv. gradually; slowly.

paulificação (pl. **-ões**), **paulificância** s. f. (Braz.) irksome task, importunity.

paulificante adj. m. + f. (Braz.) 1. tedious, boring. 2. importunate, inopportune.

paulificar v. (Braz.) to importune, bore.

paulista s. m. + f. 1. Paulista: (Braz.) native or inhabitant of the State of S. Paulo. 2. Paulist: (R. C. Church) a member of the Congregation of the missionary priests of St. Paul the Apostle. 3. (fig.) insistent or obstinate person. ‖ adj. of or pertaining to the State of S. Paulo.

paulistano s. m. (Braz.) native or inhabitant of the city of S. Paulo. ‖ adj. of or pertaining to the city of S. Paulo.

paulito s. m. peg (as in quoits).

pau-mandado s. m. (pl. **paus-mandados**) (coll.) tool, servile person.

pau-mulato s. m. (pl. **paus-mulatos**) mulatto calycophyllum: tree of the family Rubiaceae (Calycophyllum spruceanum).

pau-pereira s. m. (pl. **paus-pereira**) pereira bark: tree of the family Apocynaceae (Geissospermum vellosii).

pauperismo s. m. pauperism: 1. poverty. 2. the poor.

paupérrimo abs. sup. of **pobre**: very poor.

pau-preto s. m. (pl. **paus-pretos**) (bot.) blackwood (Dalbergia latifolia).

paurópodes s. m. pl. (zool.) Pauropoda, a subclass cf arthropods.

pau-rosa s. m. (pl. **paus-rosa**) (Braz., bot.) 1. rosewood, tulipwood (Dalbergia cearensis). 2. kingwood.

pau-rosado s. m. (pl. **paus-rosados**) (Braz., also **pau-brasil**) brazilwood.

pausa s. f. 1. pause: a) a cessation or intermission of action, a stop, interval, interruption. b) hesitation. c) (mus.) a rest. 2. rose, sprinkling nozzle.

pausado adj. 1. paused. 2. slow(-moving). 3. leisurely. ‖ -amente adv. pausingly.

pau-santo s. m. (pl. **paus-santos**) (bot.) 1. holy wood. 2. guaiacum, lignum vitae.

pausar v. to pause: 1. make a pause. 2. suspend action. 3. stop temporarily, rest. 4. delay.

pauta s. f. 1. (mus.) stave, staff, space-line (plate N 1). 2. list, roll, register. 3. guide lines. 4. ruled lines. 5. tariff.

pautação s. f. (pl. **-ões**) ruling: making of ruled lines.

pautado adj. 1. ruled (paper). 2. correct, regular; methodic; measured.

pautador s. m. ruler: anything that rules lines, as a ruling machine.

pautal adj. m. + f. (pl. **-ais**) customary, liable to dues.

pautar v. 1. to rule: mark with straight parallel lines. 2. to list, enroll (customs, dues). 3. to methodize.

pau-tartaruga s. m. (pl. **paus-tartaruga**) (bot.) snakewood.

pauteação s. f. (pl. **-ões**) talkativeness; idle talk.

pautear v. (Braz.) to jabber, chatter, talk idly.

pauzama s. f. (Braz., pop.) a pile of sticks, trunks or pieces of wood.

pauzinho s. m. 1. a little stick, small piece of wood. 2. plot; intrigue; mischief-making.

pavana s. f. pavan(e): a slow, stately Italian dance.

pavão s. m. (pl. **-ões**) (f. **pavoa**) peacock: a gallinaceous crested bird (genus Pavo).

pavão-bode s. m. (pl. **pavões-bodes**) (ornith.) crimson tragopan.

pavão-de-java s. m. (pl. **pavões-de-java**) (ornith.) Javan peacock.

pavão-do-mar s. m. (pl. **pavões-do-mar**) (ornith.) ruff.

pavão-do-mato s. m. (pl. **pavões-do-mato**) (ornith.) umbrella bird (Cephalopteros ornatus).

pavê s. m. (Fr., cul.) a sweet made of French sticks usually soaked in liqueur.

paveia s. f. wisp: small bunch of hay or straw.

pavena adj. (S. Braz.) skittish, turbulent.

pavês s. m. (pl. **paveses**) pavese: a large shield.

pávido adj. 1. pavid, timid, afraid, fearful. 2. amazing.

pavilhão s. m. (pl. **-ões**) 1. pavillion: a) dismountable structure for temporary shelter or dwelling. b) summer-house, bower. c) a large tent. d) (anat.) the external ear. e) canopy. f) division of a hospital, in a separate building. 2. flag, pennant, standard. 3. ensign.

pavimentação s. f. (pl. **-ões**) paving: act or effect of laying a pavement.

pavimentar v. 1. to pave: a) lay pavements. b) cover with asphalt, gravel, concrete (as a road). 2. to floor: provide with a floor.

pavimento s. m. 1. pavement: a hard covering for a road. 2. paving. 3. floor (of a building); story.

pavio s. m. wick: a band of a candle. ~ **de lampião** lampwick. ~ **de vela** wick of a candle. **de fio a** ~ from the beginning to the end.

pá-virada s. f. (pl. **pás-viradas**) reckless or wild person.

pavó, pavô s. m. (Braz., ornith.) fruit crow (Pyroderus scutatus.)

pavonaço adj. of the colour violet, brownish red.

pavonada s. f. 1. spreading of the tail (peacock). 2. (fig.) boasting, vainglory, self-conceit.

pavonear v. 1. to peacock: a) make a display of. b) (also ~-se) prance, strut about vainly. 2. to flaunt. 3. to adorn with gay colours and ornaments. 4. ~-se: a) to become proud or haughty. b) to pride o. s. on.

pavor s. m. 1. great fear, fright, dread. 2. terror, horror, consternation.
ter ~ to be in great fear.

pavorosa s. f. a horrifying news, report or rumour.

pavoroso adj. 1. dreadful, terrible, horrific. 2. frightful, fearful. 3. appalling, causing fear. ‖ -amente adv. dreadfully; frightfully; appallingly.

pavulagem s. f. (pl. **-ens**) fatuity, vainglory.

pávulo s. m. 1. fanfaron, blusterer. 2. pedant. 3. boaster, braggart. ‖ adj. 1. blustering, swaggering. 2. pedantic.

pavuna s. f. (Braz.) steep and deep valley.

paxá s. m. pasha: a Turkish honourable title.

paxalato s. m. pashalik, pashalic: the province or jurisdiction of a pasha.

paxiúba s. f. (Braz., bot.) rasp palm (Iriartea exorrhiza).

paxiúba-manjerona s. f. (pl. **paxiúbas-manjeronas**) a sort of palm tree (Martinezia cayotaefolia).

pax-vóbis s. m., sg. + pl. a simple and peaceful person.

paz s. f. (pl. **pazes**) peace: 1. tranquillity, calm, repose, rest. 2. agreement, concord, harmony. 3. absence or cessation of war. 4. silence, quiet. ~ **à sua alma** peace to his soul. ~ **aos homens de boa vontade** peace to the men of good will. ~ **de Deus** truce of God, peace of God. **cachimbo da** ~ peace pipe. **deixe-o em** ~ leave him in peace, leave him alone. **descansar em** ~ to rest in peace. **fazer as** ~**es** to make peace. **juiz de** ~ justice of the peace.

pazada s. f. 1. a shovelful; spadeful. 2. a blow with a shovel.

pazear v. to peace: establish peace or harmony.

paziguar v. to pacify, conciliate.

pé s. m. 1. foot: a) (anat., zool.) terminal segment of the leg (plate C 18). b) ancient linear measure of 33 centimetres. c) (Engl.) 12 inches. d) pedestal, base, foundation, bottom, short leg of furniture (plate C 7). 2. dregs, sediment. 3. pretext. 4. occasion. 5. state (of business). 6. (bot.) stalk, stem. 7. a single plant. 8. (zool., bot.) peduncle. 9. paw. 10. footing. 11. leg (plate A 13).
~ **ante** ~, **nas pontinhas dos** ~**s** foot by foot, on tiptoe. ~ **chato** flatfoot. ~ **chato e torto** splay-

foot. ~ **d'água** shower, heavy downpour, spill. ~ **de abacate** avocado tree. ~ **de alface** head of lettuce. ~ **de anjo** (Braz., fam.) big foot. ~**-de- -cobra** crowbar. ~**-de-galinha** crow's-foot, crow's- -feet. ~ **de porco** pettitoes. ~ **dianteiro** forefoot. ~ **direito (esquerdo)** right (left) foot. ~ **na tábua!** (mot.) step on it! ~**s da cama** foot end of a bed (plate C 7). **a** ~ afoot, on foot. **abrir o** ~, **dar no** ~ to run away. **andar com os** ~**s em duas canoas** to hunt with the hounds and run with the hare. **ao** ~ at (the) foot. **ao** ~ **da letra** with fidelity, literally. **ao** ~ **de** near, beside, beneath. **aos pés dele** at his feet. **apertar o** ~ to hasten one's steps. **arrastar os** ~**s** (fam.) to dance. **bater o** ~ to put one's foot down. **a cidade dos** ~**s juntos** (fam.) the cemetery. **debaixo do(s)** ~**(s)** underfoot. **de** ~ standing, on foot, unseated. **o dia inteiro em** ~ on the foot all day. **do** ~ **para a mão** in a very short time, unexpectedly. **dos** ~**s à cabeça** from head to foot, from one end to another. **ele está com um** ~ **na sepultura** he has (already) one foot in the grave. **ele fez seu** ~- -**de-meia** (fig.) he made his pile. **em** ~ erect, on foot, standing, upright (plate Q). **em** ~ **de guerra** on the warpath. **estar com o** ~ **no estribo** (fig.) to have one foot in the stirrup. **estar de** ~ to be well. **estar em** ~ 1. to be standing. 2. to bristle (hair). **estive de** ~ **toda a noite** I sat up all night. **entrar com o** ~ **direito** to begin (or start) luckily. **fazer** ~ **firme** to withstand. **ficar de** ~ to stand up, remain standing. **hoje levantei-me com o** ~ **esquerdo** today I got up on the wrong side of the bed. **ir a** ~ to leg it. **irei com um** ~ **lá e outro cá!** I'll be back in a minute! **lamber os** ~**s de alguém** to fawn upon s. o. **não tornarei a pôr os** ~**s aqui!** you will have seen the last of me! **neste lugar o rio não dá** ~ here the river is not wadable. **no dia seguinte ponho-me em** ~ **às 5 horas** on the following day I get up at 5 o'clock. **passar o** ~ **adiante da mão** to go too far in. **passar o** ~ **em alguém** to trip a person up. **peito do** ~ instep. **perder o** ~ to lose one's footing. **ponta do** ~ tiptoe. **pôr-se em** ~ to stand up. **prendi o** ~, **fiquei com o** ~ **preso** I caught my foot. **prostrar-se aos** ~**s de outrem** to cast o. s. at the feet of another. **sem** ~ **nem cabeça** not a leg to stand on. **sob os** ~**s** under foot. **um** ~ **de meia** a single stocking. **virar os** ~**s para dentro** to toe in. **você não chega aos** ~**s dele** you are not able to hold a candle to him, you are far beneath him.

peã s. m. paean: 1. song of praise honouring Apollo. 2. any song of joy or exultation.

peagem s. f. (pl. -ens) pontage, toll.

peal s. m. (pl. -ais) a woollen sock; pump.

pealar v. 1. to lasso (an animal). 2. (fig.) to lay a trap for; deceive.

pealo s. m. 1. a lasso, cattle rope. 2. lassoing.

peanha s. f. a small pedestal (as for supporting a statue).

peão s. m. (pl. peões) 1. walker, pedestrian. 2. foot- -soldier, footman. 3. (chess) pawn (plate X3. 4. a plebeian. 5. (Braz.) farm hand, peon; roughrider.

pear v. 1. to fetter or clog an animal. 2. to embar- rass, hinder, impede.

pé-atrás s. m. (Braz.) mistrust, precaution.

peba s. f. m. (Braz., zool.) peludo, payou: a variety of armadillo.

pegar um ~ (Braz.) to tumble, take a spill.

pebado adj. (Braz., pop.) frustrated, unsuccessful.

peça s. f. 1. piece: a) separated part. b) fragment. c) portion. d) division; section. e) firearm. f) (theat.) drama, play. g) (mus.) a musical composi- tion. h) (chess) man (plate X). 2. a piece of fur-

niture. 3. room of a house. 4. document. 5. (fig.): a) fraud, hoax, prank, trick. b) a practical joke; jest. ~ **curta** (theat.) playlet. ~ **de artilharia** (mil.) a piece of ordnance, a cannon. ~ **de campanha** (mil.) field-piece, field-gun. ~ **em T** T piece, T joint, tee junction, tee (plate E 3). ~ **de roupa** wearable, garment. ~ **em um ato** (theat.) one-act play. ~ **por** ~ piece by piece. ~ **teatral** play, review. ~ **vertical de caixilho** stile (plate A 13, J 1). **a** ~ **foi encenada no ano passado** the play was produced last year. **ele me pregou uma** ~ he played a trick on me, he played me a dirty trick. **mercadorias vendidas por** ~ piece goods. **por** ~ by the piece, apiece. **pregar uma** ~ **em alguém** to play a trick on s. o. **uma** ~ **de mobília** a piece of furniture.

pecadilho s. m. peccadillo: a slight or trifling sin.

pecado s. m. sin: 1. offense, misdead. 2. transgres- sion of a rule. 3. fault, error, wrong. 4. debt. ~ **costumeiro** besetting sin. ~ **mortal** mortal sin. ~ **original** original sin. ~ **venial** venial sin. **come- ter um** ~ to commit sin.

pecador s. m. 1. sinner, offender, wrongdoer. 2. peni- tent. ‖ adj. sinful, sinning.

pecadora s. f. 1. sinner, sinful woman. 2. prostitute.

pecadoraço s. m. a great sinner.

pecaminoso adj. sinful: consisting in, suggestive of, or tainted with sin. ‖ **-amente** adv. sinfully.

pecante s. m. + f. sinner. ‖ adj. peccant, sinful.

pecar v. 1. to sin: a) commit sin. b) transgress the divine law. c) err. d) trespass. e) offend. 2. to incur. 3. to commit a fault. 4. (bot.) to wither. ~ **contra a decência** to fly into the face of de- cency. ~ **contra as regras do jogo** (fig.) to hit below the belt. ~ **por ignorância** to do wrong from igno- rance. **ele pecou perante Deus** he did evil in the sight of the Lord. **você peca contra o bom senso** you sin against light.

pecari s. m. (zool.) peccary: a wild pig of America.

pecável adj. m. + f. (pl. -áveis) peccable: liable to sin.

pecém adj. (pl. -éns) unbalanced, hanging.

peceta s. f. 1. a small piece. 2. m. crook, rascal.

pecha s. f. defect, failing, foible; blemish.

pechada s. f. 1. collision, shock. 2. fraud, swindle. 3. a touch (request) for money.

pechar v. (S. Braz.) 1. to collide with, crash. 2. to touch for money. 3. ~**-se** to meet up with.

pechblenda s. f. pitchblende.

pechincha s. f. 1. unexpected profit. 2. bargain: a) an advantageous transaction. b) an article bought or offered at a low price.

pechinchar v. 1. to profit unexpectedly. 2. to bar- gain: a) make an advantageous transaction. b) buy or offer (articles) at a low or advantageous price. 3. to barter; haggle (over).

pechincheiro s. m. bargainer, chafferer. ‖ adj. fond of bargains; bartering.

pechiringar v. (Braz.) 1. to bet or wager little. 2. to grudge: give in a niggardly way.

pechisbeque s. m. pinchbeck: an alloy of copper, zinc and tin, forming a cheap imitation of gold; tombac.

pechoso adj. 1. finding fault with everything. 2. capricious, whimsical, difficult to satisfy. 3. scru- pulous.

pecilocrômico, pecilocromático adj. variegated: paint- ed in different colours or tints; polychromatic.

peciolado adj. (bot.) petiolate(d): having petiole (plate F 5).

peciolar adj. m. + f. (bot.) 1. petiolar: referring to the petiole. 2. petiolate(d).

pecíolo s. m. (bot.) petiole: the foot-stalk of a leaf, leaf-stalk (plate F 5).
peciólulo s. m. (bot.) petiolule: a small petiole.
peco (ê) s. m. blight of plants. ‖ adj. (pl. pecos) (f. -eca) 1. emaciated, wasted. 2. (bot.) stunted. 3. nescient, ignorant, stupid.
peçonha s. f. 1. poison, venom. 2. (fig.) wickedness, malice, ill will.
peçonhento adj. poisonous, venomous, full of poison.
pécora s. f. 1. a despicable woman. 2. a prostitute.
péctico adj. (chem.) pectic: said of an acid found in many fruits.
pectina s. f. (biochem.) pectin: a substance obtained from ripe fruits.
pectíneo adj. pectinal, pectinate(d), comblike.
pectinibrânquio adj. (zool.) pectinibranch: having pectinate branchiae.
pectinibrânquios s. m. pl. (zool.) Pectinibranchia, a large order of Gastropoda.
pectinicórneo adj. (zool.) pectinicorn: having pectinate antennae.
pectoral adj. m. + f. (pl. -ais) (also peitoral) pectoral.
pectoriloquia s. f. (med.) pectoriloquy: pathologic resonance of the voice through the thorax so that it is heard distinctly with the stethoscope.
pectoríloquo adj. (med.) pectoriloquial: of the nature of pectoriloquy.
pecuária s. f. cattle breeding, cattle raising: art of raising cattle.
pecuário s. m. cattleman: person who raises cattle. ‖ adj. of or pertaining to cattle.
pecuarista s. m. + f. person skilled in cattle raising.
peculador, peculatário s. m. peculator: person who peculates.
peculato s. m. peculation: embezzlement of public money or goods.
peculiar adj. m. + f. peculiar: 1. one's own, pertaining to one. 2. special, individual, proper. 3. singular, uncommon.
peculiaridade s. f. peculiarity, peculiarness: the state of being peculiar.
pecúlio s. m. peculium: 1. private property. 2. private purse. 3. money reserves.
pecúnia s. f. money.
pecuniário adj. pecuniary: consisting of or relating to money; monetary.
pecunioso adj. pecunious: 1. full of money, rich, moneyed. 2. opulent, wealthy.
pedaço s. m. 1. piece, bit, fragment. 2. fraction. 3. bite, slice (plate D 3). 4. portion, parcel, chunk, bit. 5. (pop.) comely and attractive woman. 6. long space of time.
~ de sabão brick of soap. aos ~s brokenly, by snatches. ele o quebrou em mil ~s he broke it to a thousand bits, (coll.) knocked it to smithereens. cair em ~s to fall into pieces. em ~s in pieces, in tatters. estou em ~s I am very tired. fazer em ~s to break, rend to pieces. você é um ~ de asno you are a great fool.
pedados s. m. pl. (zool.) Pedata, a division of the Holothurioidea.
pedágio s. m. (Braz.) toll; passage money.
pedagogia s. f. pedagogy: 1. the science or profession of teaching. 2. the theory or the technics of how to teach.
pedagógico adj. pedagogic: pertaining to the science of teaching. ‖ pedagogicamente adv. pedagogically.
pedagogismo s. m. pedagogism.
pedagogista s. m. + f. pedagogist: expert in the science of pedagogy.
pedagogo s. m. pedagog(ue): a teacher of children, a schoolmaster.
pé-d'água s. m. (pl. pés-d'água) shower, a heavy rain.

pedal s. m. (pl. -ais) pedal: 1. a lever operated by the foot (plates D 1, H). 2. treadle, foot lever (plate M 1).
~ da embreagem (mot.) clutch pedal (plate V 3). ~ de bicicleta pedal of a bicycle (plate B 11). ~ do freio (mot.) brake pedal (plate M 13). ~ forte (mus.) sustaining pedal (plate P 10). ~ pequeno (de surdina) (mus.) soft pedal (plate P 10).
pedalada s. f. act of using a pedal, a pushing with a pedal.
pedalar v. 1. to pedal: a) operate by pedals. b) use the pedals. 2. to ride on a bicycle.
pedaleiro s. m. the pedals of a velocipede.
pedaliáceas s. f. pl. (bot.) Pedaliaceae, a family of tropical herbs.
pedâneo adj. 1. said of an itinerant judge in small localities. 2. illiterate.
pedantaria s. f. pedantry: the manners, acts, or character of a pedant, pedantism.
pedante s. m. + f. a pedant. ‖ adj. 1. pedantic, exhibiting pedantry. 2. priggish. 3. (fig.) deceitful. 4. ostentatious, pretentious, arrogant.
pedantear v. to pedantize: 1. be a pedant. 2. use pedantic expressions.
pedantesco adj. pedantic(al): 1. marked by pedantry. 2. affected. ‖ -amente adv. pedantically.
pedantismo s. m. pedantry, pedantism: the manners, acts, or character of a pedant.
pedantocracia s. f. (neologism) pedantocracy: the government or sway of a pedant or of pedants.
pedantocrático adj. of or pertaining to the government or sway of pedants.
pedarquia s. f. (ironic) the government of children.
pedatrofia s. f. (med.) mesenteric atrophy.
pé-de-alferes s. m. (pl. pés-de-alferes) (fam.) courtship, love-affair.
pé-de-altar s. m. (pl. pés-de-altar) altar fees (as for marriage or baptism).
pé-de-bezerro s. m. (pl. pés-de-bezerro) a tropical plant of the arum family (Colocasia antiquorum).
pé-de-boi s. m. (pl. pés-de-boi) 1. old-fashioned person, slowcoach. 2. (Braz.) a hard-working man.
pé-de-cabra s. m. (tech.) 1. crowbar. 2. (Braz., pop.) the devil.
pé-de-cana s. m. (pl. pés-de-cana) (Braz., fam.) drunkard.
pé-de-cavalo s. m. (pl. pés-de-cavalo) (bot.) Indian pennywort.
pé-de-chumbo s. m. (pl. pés-de-chumbo) scarlet sage (Salvia splendens).
pé-de-galinha s. m. (pl. pés-de-galinha) 1. (bot.) feather grass. 2. (bot.) low spear-grass. 3‖ crow's-feet, wrinkles at the outer corner of the eye.
pé-de-galo s. m. (pl. pés-de-galo) hop (Humulus lupulus).
pé-de-ganso s. m. (pl. pés-de-ganso) (bot.) nettle-leaved goosefoot.
pé-de-gato s. m. (pl. pés-de-gato) (bot.) cat's-foot (Antennaria dioica).
pé-de-meia s. m. (pl. pés-de-meia) money-box, savings.
pé-de-moleque s. m. (pl. pés-de-moleque) (Braz.) a sweet made with candy and peanuts.
pé-de-pato s. m. (pl. pés-de-pato) (Braz., pop.) the devil.
pé-de-pau s. f. (pl. pés-de-pau) (Braz.) a variety of honey-bee (Melipona nigra).
pé-de-poeira s. m. (pl. pés-de-poeira) (N. Braz.) a man of low station, a plebeian.
pederasta s. m. a pederast: person addicted to pederasty.
pederastia s. f. pederasty, sodomy, homosexualism.

pedernal s. m. (pl. -ais) plint, firestone. ‖ adj. m. + f. rocklike, petrean.

pederneira s. f. flint, firestone.

pedestal s. m. (pl. -ais) pedestal: 1. socle: base or support for a column, statue or vase (plate E 9). 2. any foundation or basis.

pedestre s. m. + f. pedestrian: person who walks or journeys on foot, a walker. ‖ adj. pedestrian: 1. moving on foot, walking. 2. pertaining to common people.

estátua ~ pedestrian statue.

pedestrianismo s. m. pedestrianism: pedestrian exercise, practice of traveling on foot.

pé-de-vento s. m. (pl. pés-de-vento) a blast of wind.

pediatra s. m. + f. pediatrist, pediatrician: a specialist in children's diseases.

pediatria s. f, pediatrics: medical or hygienic treatment of children.

pediátrico adj. pediatric: of or pertaining to pediatrics.

pedicelado adj. (bot.) pedicellate: provided with a pedicel or pedicels.

pedicelo s. m. pedicel: (bot.) the ultimate division of a peduncle.

pediculados s. m. pl. (ichth.) Pediculati, an order of marine teleost fishes: the batfish, the frogfish.

pediculídeos s. m. pl. (ent.) Pediculidae, the true louse family.

pedículo s. m. (bot.) pedicle, pedicel, peduncle.

pedicuro s. m. pedicure: 1. person whose business is the surgical care of the feet (corns, bunions, etc.). 2. a chiropodist.

pedido s. m. 1. petition, demand. 2. request, solicitation, act of asking for. 3. supplication, prayer. 4. (com.) order; commission.

~ **de graça** appeal for clemency. ~ **de indulto** petition for clemency. ~ **de falência** petition in bankruptcy. **a** ~ 1. on demand. 2. upon (or by) request. **a** ~ **de** 1. at the request of. 2. as suggested by. 3. on behalf of. **conforme** ~ as requested. **ele fê-lo a meu** ~ he did it at my desire. **em atenção a seu** ~ in response to your request. **fazer um** ~ (com.) to place an order. **talão de** ~**s** (com.) order-book.

pedidor s. m. 1. demander. 2. applicant, petitioner. 3. beggar, person who begs alms. ‖ adj. begging.

pediforme adj. m. + f. pediform: foot-shaped, foot-like, having the form of a foot (plate F 5).

pedilúvio s. m. foot-bath.

pedímano s. m. pedimane. ‖ adj. (zool.) pedimanous: having all four feet like hands.

pedímanos s. m. pl. (zool.) Pedimana, Didelphidae, the opossum family.

pedimento s. m. petition: 1. request, suit, solicitation, demand. 2. supplication.

pedincha s. f. act of asking or begging insistently.

pedinchão s. m. (pl. -ões) (also **pedintão**) 1. person who is always asking or begging. 2. importunate petitioner or beggar. ‖ adj. begging insistently.

pedinchar v. 1. to be always begging. 2. to ask importunately.

pedintaria s. f. begging, beggary, mendicity.

pedinte s. m. beggar, mendicant: person who asks for alms; panhandler. ‖ adj. m. + f. mendicant: begging, depending on alms for a living.

pedioso adj. pedate: resembling or having the function of a foot.

pedipalpo s. m. pedipalp: an arachnid of the order Pedipalpida.

pedir v. 1. to ask, beg, demand. 2. to claim, appeal, cry, call in. 3. to pray, beseech, implore, supplicate, entreat. 4. to request, solicit. 5. to require. 6. (com.) to order.

~ **alguém em casamento** to ask s. o. in marriage. ~ **coisas impossíveis** to ask impossibilities, cry for the moon. ~ **esmolas** to beg charity (alms). ~ **encarecidamente** to demand earnestly. ~ **explicações** to call to account, call over the coals. ~ **licença** (mil.) to take leave. ~ **por alguém** to intercede, pray in behalf of s. o. **ele a pediu em casamento** he sought her in marriage. **ele pediu demissão** he sent in his resignation, (sl.) chucked up his job. **ele pediu-me emprestado** he asked me to lend him, (sl.) tapped me for. **escrever pedindo dinheiro** to write for money. **fui ter com ele para pedir-lhe um conselho** I called upon him for advice. **pedi e dar-se-vos-á** ask, and it shall be given you. **peça-lhe que venha aqui** ask him round. **peço desculpas** I apologize. **peço que não me interrompa** I beg I may not be interrupted. **pediram-me que ajudasse** I was called upon to help. **pedi o seu conselho** I asked his advice. **pedi a sua permissão** I asked his permission. **preciso** ~-**te um favor** I must request a favour of you. **você tem de pedi-lo por escrito** you must write and ask for it.

pé-direito s. m. (pl. pés-direitos) (archit.) 1. height of a room (from ceiling to roof). 2. pillar or pier of an arch.

peditório s. m. 1. the begging of alms (for charity). 2. importunate begging.

pedologia s. f. pedology: 1. the study of children. 2. the science that treats of the nature and properties of soils.

pedológico adj. pedologic: of or pertaining to the study of children.

pedômetro s. m. pedometer: instrument that measures distances covered on foot.

pedotrofia s. f. pedotrophy.

pedra s. f. 1. stone. 2. gravel. 3. hail. 4. man, piece, figure (as of chess). 5. flint. 6. pebble. 7. (Braz., pop.) draught beer mug. 8. tombstone. 9. (med.) calculus.

~ **angular** corner-stone. ~ **argilosa** clay-stone. ~ **britada** broken stone, road metal (plate V 4). ~ **de amolar** whetstone. ~ **de moinho** millstone. ~ **de toque** touch-stone. ~ **especular** mirror stone. ~ **fedorenta** stink-stone. ~ **fundamental** foot-stone, keystone. ~ **preciosa** precious stone, gem. ~ **filosofal** philosopher's stone. ~ **refratária** firestone. ~**s sedimentares** sedimentary rocks. **água mole em** ~ **dura tanto dá até que fura** (fig.) constant dropping will wear down a stone. **dormir como uma** ~ to sleep like a log. **de** ~ **e cal** (fig.) firm, solid. **duro como uma** ~ hard as stone. **Idade da Pedra** Stone Age. **muro de** ~ stone wall. **não deixaram** ~ **sobre** ~ they left no stone standing. **quem tem telhado de vidro não atire** ~**s no do vizinho** people in glass houses shouldn't throw stones. **ser de** ~ to be insensible, be stone-hearted. **pôr uma** ~ **em cima de** to put an end to, to put a stop to.

pedra-braba s. m. + f. (pl. pedras-brabas) rascal, evil person.

pedrada s. f. 1. throw of a stone, blow with a stone. 2. (fig.) insult, offence.

pedra-da-lua s. f. (pl. pedras-da-lua) adularia.

pedra-de-águia s. f. (pl. pedras-de-águia) aetite, eaglestone.

pedra-de-anil s. f. (pl. pedras-de-anil) (Braz., min.) lazulite.

pedra-de-fogo s. f. (pl. pedras-de-fogo) firestone, flint.

pedra-de-raio s. f. (pl. pedras-de-raio) aerolite.

pedrado adj. 1. rock-paved. 2. spotted with black and white.

pedra-do-sol s. f. (pl. pedras-do-sol) sunstone.

pedra-ímã s. f. (pl. pedras-ímãs) loadstone.

pedra-infernal s. f. (pl. pedras-infernais) lunar caustic.

pedral s. m. (Braz.) (pl. **-ais**) place in a river where many stones impede navigation. ‖ adj. m. + f. 1. stony. 2. spotted with black and white.

pedra-lipes s. f. (pl. **pedras-lipes**) bluejack, blue vitriol.

pedranceira s. f. a hill or heap of stones.

pedra-olar s. f. potstone, steatite, massive talc.

pedra-pomes s. f. (pl. **pedras-pomes**) pumice(-stone).

pedraria s. f. 1. a large quantity of ashlars or building stones. 2. jewels, precious stones.

pedra-sabão s. f. (pl. **pedras-sabão**) steatite, soapstone.

pedra-ume s. f. (pl. **pedras-umes**) alum.

pedregal s. m. (pl. **-ais**) a place full of stones.

pedregoso adj. stony, full of stones.

pedregulhento adj. full of gravel, gravelly.

pedregulho s. m. 1. gravel, gravel stone. 2. big stone; block of rock, boulder.

pedreira s. f. quarry, stone-pit, stone-quarry.

pedreirinho s. m. (ornith.) bank-swallow (Cotyle riparia).

pedreiro s. m. 1. mason: a) bricklayer (plate A 7). b) stonecutter. 2. trebuchet. 3. (ornith.): a) (Braz.) ovenbird. b) swift.

pedreiro-livre s. m. (pl. **pedreiros-livres**) Freemason.

pedrento adj. 1. resembling stone. 2. stony: abounding in stone.

pedrês adj. m. + f. (pl. **-eses**) spotted with black and white.

pedrinha s. f. (dim. of **pedra**) a little stone.

    estar com a ~ no sapato (fig.) to be unquiet.

pedrisco s. m. hail, a shower of stones, sleet.

pedroso adj. stony: 1. pertaining to, like or characteristic of stone. 2. consisting of stone.

pedrouço s. m. a heap of stones.

pedunculado adj. pedunculate: provided with a pedicel, having a peduncle.

peduncular adj. m. + f. peduncular: of or pertaining to a peduncle.

pedúnculo s. m. peduncle: 1. (bot.) stalk or support of an inflorescence. 2. (zool.) a little foot or footlike part.

pedunculoso adj. 1. pedunculate(d). 2. having a long peduncle.

pé-duro s. m. (pl. **pés-duros**) (Braz.) 1. rustic. 2. ill-bred person.

pé-fresco s. m. (pl. **pés-frescos**) 1. plebeian. 2. barefoot man.

pé-frio s. m. (pl. **pés-frios**) (Braz., pop.) 1. an ill-starred, unlucky person. 2. (S. Braz.) a person with cold feet: timid, coward.

pega (I) s. f. 1. (bullfight) act of taking the bull by the horns. 2. discussion, quarrel, falling out. 3. ear, handle (as of a pot). 4. (Braz.) fraud, swindle. 5. hardening of mortar. 6. m. (Braz.) quarrel, violent dispute; great noise.

pega (II) s. f. fetters for fugitive slaves.

pega (ê) s. f. 1. (ornith.) magpie. 2. prating woman, chatterbox. 3. (naut.) cap.

pegada s. f. 1. (ftb.) act of catching (goalkeeper). 2. footstep, footprint, footmark; track, trace, vestige.

    nas ~s de on the track of. **seguir as ~s de alguém** to follow in someone's footsteps.

pegadiço adj. 1. clammy, viscous. 2. (fig.): a) contagious, catching. b) importunate.

pegadilha s. f. 1. disorder, dispute, debating. 2. quarrel, provocation.

pegadio s. m. (N. Braz.) affection, fondness; friendship.

pegado adj. 1. near to, close, contiguous; touching, joined, adjoining, nearby. 2. befriended, fond of, close. 3. (Braz., fam.) drunken.

pegador s. m. 1. catcher: one who or that which catches. 2. tag: a juvenile sport. 3. (ichth.) remora. ‖ adj. catching, that which catches.

pegadouro s. m. handle: that part of an object which is held in the hand.

pega-fogo s. m. (pl. **pega-fogos**) (S. Braz.) a hop, rural dance.

pegajoso adj. (also **pegajento, peganhento, peguenhento** and **peguento**) 1. clammy, viscous, adhesive. 2. contagious, catching. 3. (fig.) tedious, troublesome, importunate. ‖ **-amente** adv. viscously.

pega-ladrão s. m. (pl. **pega-ladrões**) 1. a gadget which fastens tiepins, brooches, to clothes, to keep them from being stolen. 2. an electric or mechanical alarm device.

pega-mão s. m. (pl. **pega-mãos**) (S. Braz.) valise, handbag.

pegamassa s. f. (bot.) lesser burdock, cockle-bur (Lappa tomentosa).

pegamasso s. m. 1. anything that is viscous; paste, loam. 2. importunate fellow.

pegão s. m. (pl. **-ões**) 1. (archit.) butment: a support or end of a bridge. 2. arc-boutant: a flying buttress. 3. a gust of wind; wind spout, whirlwind.

pega-pega s. m. (pl. **pegas-pegas, pega-pegas**) (Braz.) 1. a bur: prickly flower head. 2. conflict, quarrel.

pega-pra-capar s. m., sg. + pl. (Braz., pop.) brawl, row, rumpus, wrangle.

pegar v. 1. to glue, fasten together; unite, join. connect. 2. to adhere, stick. 3. to catch, hold, grasp. 4. to bind, tie. 5. to take, lay hold. 6. to confine with, be near to. 7. to be _contagious, contaminate, infect. 8. to diffuse, become generalized; produce an effect; begin. 9. to take or catch fire. 10. **~-se:** a) to stick to. b) to come together with. c) to adhere to. d) to become attached to. e) to be contiguous with.

    ~ fogo to catch fire. **~ de** to take hold of. **~ no sono** to fall asleep. **~ nas armas** to take up arms. **~-se com alguém** to pick a quarrel with. **~ um peixe** to land a fish. **agora o peguei** I have got you. **agora você me pegou** you've got me there. **aí pude pegá-lo** there I had him. **ele foi pego desprevenido** he was thrown off his guard. **ele pegou-a pela mão** he took her by the hand. **ele pegou no sono** he fell asleep. **eles pegaram em armas** they rose in arms. **estas desculpas não pegam** these excuses won't go down with me. **o gato não deixa de ~ o rato** cats will catch mice. **o motor não pega** the motor does not start up. **não se consegue pegá-lo** he is not to be got at. **pegaram-no como Judas** he is in for it. **pegaram-no numa mentira** he was found out fibbing. **pegá-lo-ei pela palavra** I'll take you on at that! **a planta pegou bem** the plant took on well.

pega-rapaz s. m. (Braz., pop.) (pl. **pega-rapazes**) a lock of hair on the forehead (of women).

pegas (ê) s. m., sg. + pl. pettifogger, lawmonger, an ignorant lawyer.

pégaso s. m. Pegasus: 1. (myth.) a winged horse. 2. (astr.) a northern constellation.

pegativo adj. contagious, catching, that catches easily.

pegmatito s. m. (petrog.) pegmatite: a coarsely crystallized granite.

pego s. m. 1. pool, a deep place in a stream. 2. the sea, main sea, ocean. 3. (fig.) abyss; swirl, vortex.

pegomancia s. f. pegomancy: divination by the agency of fountains.

pegomântico adj. of or pertaining to pegomancy.

pegueiro s. m. person who manufactures or deals in pitch.

peguilha s. f. a cause for or beginning of a dispute.

P 7

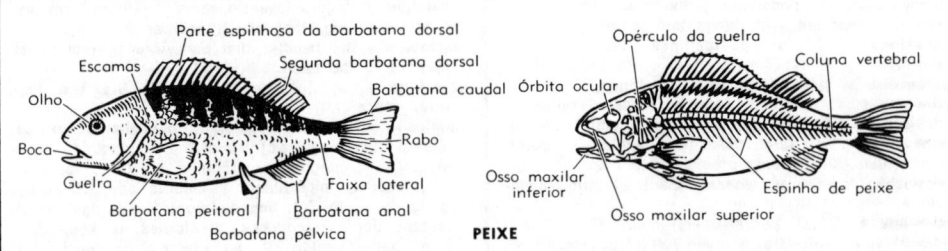

PEIXE

peguilhar v. to provoke a dispute or quarrel.
peguilhento adj. quarrelsome.
peguilho s. m. 1. any sticky thing. 2. obstacle, hindrance, difficulty. 3. (fig.) motive, pretext for quarrel.
peguinhar v. 1. to trample; treat scornfully. 2. (fig.): a) to contravene, counteract. b) to provoke; implicate, involve.
pegural adj. m. + f. (pl. **-ais**) pastoral: of or pertaining to a shepherd.
pegureiro s. m. 1. shepherd: a keeper or herder of sheep. 2. a shepherd dog. 3. a hunting dog.
pela s. f. 1. fetters for horses, tedders, tether. 2. (fig.) obstacle, hindrance, impediment. 3. whip. 4. a strap of leather.
peia-boi s. m. (pl. **peia-bois**) a whip.
peita s. f. 1. bribe: a gift or money given or promised to suborn a person. 2. an ancient duty or tribute.
peitada s. f. (Braz.) a blow on the chest.
peitar v. 1. to bribe: give, offer or promise bribes; suborn. 2. (in ancient times) to pay a duty or tribute. 3. (Port.) to offend, vex (morally).
peitaria s. f. (vulg.) big breasts (of women).
peiteira s. f. (Braz.) breastband.
peiteiro s. m. briber. ‖ adj. paying duties or tributes.
peitica s. f. 1. (Braz.) = **saci**. 2. (N. Braz.) impertinence, insolence; petulance. 3. m. + f. a troublesome person.
peitilho s. m. bosom: the part of a dress, shirt, etc., worn upon the breast.
~ **da camisa** shirt bosom, (stiff) shirt front (plate R 7).
peito s. m. 1. breast, chest, bosom (plates C 12, 18, G 1). 2. breast of a woman. 3. thorax. 4. heart. 5. courage, valour, resolution. 6. strong voice.
~ **de pombo** pigeon breast. ~ **de prova** breastplate. ~ **do pé** instep. **bater nos** ~**s** to repent. **criança de** ~ sucking child. **doente do** ~ a tuberculous person. **amigo do** ~ bosom friend. **homem de** ~ a man of courage. **de** ~ **aberto** sincerely. **meter os** ~**s** (Braz., pop.) to put one's shoulder to the wheel. **tomar alguma coisa a peito** 1. to take s. th. to heart. 2. to work at s. th. with might and main.
peito-de-forno s. m. (pl. **peitos-de-forno**) a hash of turtle meat spiced with lemon, salt and pepper.
peito-de-moça s. f. (pl. **peitos-de-moça**) macaw tree, turkeyberry.
peitogueira s. f. 1. a cough. 2. hoarseness.
peito-largo s. m. (pl. **peitos-largos**) (Braz.) 1. (mil. sl.) orderly. 2. bodyguard.
peitoral s. m. (pl. **-ais**) 1. pectoral: a) any medicament for ailments of the chest. b) (also **cruz** ~) pectoral cross (plate P 5). 2. breastband (harness) (plate A 12). ‖ adj. m. + f. pectoral: 1. of or pertaining to the breast or thorax. 2. curing diseases of the lungs or chest.

peitoril s. m. (pl. **-is**) parapet: a low wall about the edge of a roof, terrace, bridge or fortification.
~ **de janela** window sill (plate J 1).
peito-roxo s. m. (pl. **peitos-roxos**) a parrot (Amazona vinacea).
peitudo s. m. a good singer. ‖ adj. 1. having a big and strong chest. 2. big-bosomed (woman). 3. valiant, brave, intrepid.
peiú adj. m. + f. (Braz.) 1. swollen. 2. full of wind. 3. arrogant, self-conceited.
peixada s. f. a stew of fish.
peixão s. m. (pl. **-ões**) 1. a big fish. 2. fine, shapely woman.
peixaria s. f. establishment where fishes are sold.
peixe s. m. 1. fish (plate P 7). 2. (fig.) a comely girl.
~ **assado** fried fish. ~ **de água doce** freshwater fish. ~ **de mar** sea fish. ~ **salgado** salt fish. **eles tiveram** ~ **para o jantar** they had fish for dinner. **não ser nem** ~ **nem carne** to be a fence-sitter. **viveiro de** ~**s** fishpond.
peixe-agulha s. m. (pl. **peixes-agulha**) 1. tanglefish. 2. needlefish. 3. balao.
peixe-anjo s. m. (pl. **peixes-anjo, peixes-anjos**) (ichth.) 1. angelfish, mongrel skate (Squatina vulgaris). 2. isabelita.
peixe-aranha s. m. (pl. **peixes-aranha**) (ichth.) 1. greater weever, stingbull. 2. lesser weever (Trachinus vipera).
peixe-boi s. m. (pl. **peixes-boi**) (Braz.) manatee, cowfish (Trichechus inunguis).
peixe-borboleta s. m. (pl. **peixes-borboleta**) butterfly fish (Gasteropelecus stellatus).
peixe-briga s. m. (pl. **peixes-briga**) Siamese fighting fish (Betta splendens), frequently kept in aquariums.
peixe-cabra s. m. (pl. **peixes-cabra**) (ichth.) red gurnard, red crooner.
peixe-cavalo s. m. (pl. **peixes-cavalo**) moonfish.
peixe-cobra s. m. (pl. **peixes-cobra**) (Braz., ichth.) snake eel.
peixe-coelho s. m. (pl. **peixes-coelho**) (Braz., ichth.) rabbit fish.
peixe-da-china s. m. (pl. **peixes-da-china**) goldfish.
peixe-elétrico s. m. (pl. **peixes-elétricos**) (Braz., ichth.) electric eel.
peixe-espada s. m. (pl. **peixes-espada**) 1. swordfish. 2. cutlass fish.
peixe-folha s. m. (pl. **peixes-folha**) (Braz., ichth.) leaf fish.
peixe-galo s. m. (pl. **peixes-galo**) (Braz., ichth.) 1. moonfish. 2. john dory.
peixeira s. f. 1. fish-woman, fish-wife. 2. a knife used for cutting and scaling fishes.
peixeirada s. f. (N. Braz.) a blow with a knife called **peixeira**.
peixeiro s. m. fishmonger: a seller of or dealer in fishes.

peixe-lua s. m. (pl. peixes-lua) ocean sunfish (Mola mola).

peixe-macaco s. m. (pl. peixes-macaco) (Braz., ichth.) blenny.

peixe-martelo s. m. (pl. peixes-martelo) (ichth.) hammerhead (Sphyrna zygaena).

peixe-morcego s. m. (pl. peixes-morcego) (Braz., ichth.) batfish.

peixe-pau s. m. (pl. peixes-pau) (ichth.) dragonet (Callianymus lira).

peixe-pena s. m. (pl. peixes-pena) (ichth.) sheepshead porgy (Calamus penna).

peixe-piolho s. m. (pl. peixes-piolho) (icth.) remora.

peixe-porco s. m. (pl. peixes-porco) hogfish (Monocanthus hispidus).

peixe-rei s. m. (pl. peixes-rei) (ichth.) atherine.

peixe-sapo s. m. (pl. peixes-sapo) (Braz., also piracururu, piacururu) toadfish (Pseudopimelodus zungaro).

peixe-serra s. m. (pl. peixes-serra) (Braz., also espadarte) saw-fish.

peixe-voador s. m. (pl. peixes-voadores) flying fish (Exocoetus volitans).

peixinho s. m. fishlet, fry.

peixota s. f. (ichth.) hake, sea luce.

peja s. f. (N. Braz.) stopping of the work (in a sugar mill).

pejado adj. 1. bashful, shamefaced, modest, timid. 2. encumbered, overcharged, replete. 3. -a f. pregnant (woman).

pejamento s. m. 1. encumbrance, hindrance. 2. stoppage.

pejar v. 1. to fill (up), charge. 2. to embarrass, obstruct. 3. to impregnate. 4. to cause shame. 5. ~-se: a) to be ashamed, be bashful. b) to become full, charged or embarrassed. c) to debase o. s. d) to hesitate.

pejo s. m. 1. encumbrance, hindrance, embarrassment. 2. shame, shamefacedness, bashfulness, pudicity, modesty. 3. shyness, timidity.

pejorar v. 1. to make or render worse. 2. to depreciate, underrate. 3. to lower, debase.

pejorativo adj. (also gram.) pejorative, giving a low or bad sense to, depreciative. ‖ -amente adv. pejoratively.

pejoso adj. 1. shameful, ashamed, shamefaced. 2. timid, bashful.

pela contr. of the prep. per with the archaic f. article la by, through, at, in the, for the.

~ mesma razão for the same reason. ~ minha parte as for me, for my part. ~ rainha by the queen. ~ razão de because. ~ rua through or in the street. ~ última vez for the last time. aí ~s três horas at three o'clock more or less. ele entrou ~ porta, mas saiu ~ janela he got in at the door, but he got out at the window. eles morreram ~ pátria they died for their country. comprei ~ metade do preço I bought at half the price.

péla s. f. 1. ball, playing ball (as a tennis-ball). 2. ball, bullet. 3. (fig.) toy, plaything. 4. the bark of a cork tree.

pelada s. f. 1. (med.) alopecia. 2. (Braz.) football played by boys.

pelado s. m. (fig.) poor, moneyless person. ‖ adj. 1. bald, without hair, hairless. 2. skinless: destitute of skin. 3. (Braz.) stark naked.

pelador s. m. 1. person who removes hair. 2. skinner: person who strips the skin from. ‖ adj. 1. removing hair. 2. skinning: stripping the skin from.

peladura s. f. 1. act of removing hair. 2. skinning: act of stripping the skin from.

pelagem s. f. (pl. -ens) pelage: the hair, fur, wool, or other soft covering of a mammal.

pelagianismo s. m. Pelagianism: the doctrines of Pelagius.

pelagiano s. m. Pelagian: a follower of Pelagius.

pelágico, pelágio adj. pelagic: of or inhabiting the deep or open sea; marine, oceanic.

pélago s. m. 1. the sea, main sea, ocean. 2. abyss, chasm. 3. profundity, deepness.

pelagoscopia s. f. art of examining the deep parts of bodies of water.

pelagoscópio s. m. pelagoscope: an instrument for examining or observing the deep parts of bodies of water.

pelagra s. f. (med.) pellagra: a disease characterized by gastric disturbances, skin eruptions and nervous derangements.

pelagroso s. m. person who suffers from pellagra. ‖ adj. pellagrous: 1. of or pertaining to pellagra. 2. affected with pellagra.

pelame s. m. 1. = pelagem. 2. a heap of pelts.

pelanca s. f. (also pelanga(na), pelhanca). 1. wrinkled skin, loose folds of skin. 2. very lean and skinny flesh or meat.

pelanco s. m. (N. Braz.) 1. a young bird. 2. (fig.) overgrown boy; child, brat.

pelar v. 1. to pull or scrape off the hair. 2. to peel, bark. 3. to make bald. 4. to skin: strip the skin from, flay. 5. to strip (all the money of a person) by fraud. 6. ~-se: a) to lose hair; become bald. b) to come off in peels. c) (fig.) to be crazy about.

a água está pelando (Braz., fig.) the water is boiling.

pelargônio s. m. pelargonium: a herb or shrub of the family Geraniaceae (Pelargonium grandiflorum).

pelaria s. f. 1. many hides. 2. peltry: a) pelts collectively. b) place for keeping or storing pelts. 3. a furrier's shop; a furrier's trade.

pelásgico adj. Pelasgic: of or pertaining to the Pelasgians or Pelasgi.

pelasgo s. m. Pelasgian: a member of the Pelasgi, a primitive people who inhabited the coasts of Greece.

pele s. f. skin: 1. (anat., zool.) the covering of the body, epidermis. 2. pelt, hide, fur. 3. leather (plates B 4, E 9). 4. (bot.) peel, hull, rind, shell, pod, husk. 5. wineskin.

caça de ~s e penas fur and feather. de ~ branca white-skinned. defender a sua ~ to stand in defence of one's life. ele é só ~ e osso he is nothing but skin and bones. enxerto de ~ skingrafting. não queria estar em sua ~ I shouldn't like to be in his skin, I would not stand in his shoes. salvar a ~ to save one's skin.

peleador s. m. a quarrelsome or turbulent person; ruffian. ‖ adj. quarrelsome; turbulent; ruffian.

pelear v. (S. Braz.) 1. to fight, quarrel, contend. 2. to argue.

pelechar v. to molt, shed the hair (animals).

pelecho s. m. act of shedding the air (animals).

pelecípodes s. m. pl. (zool.) Pelecypoda, a class of bivalve molluscs.

pelega s. f. (Braz.) bill (paper money).

pelego s. m. a sheepskin used over the saddle.

peleia s. f. quarrel, fight, dispute, combat.

peleiro s. m. (also peleteiro) furrier, a dealer in furs or fur goods, skinner.

peleja s. f. 1. fight, battle, combat. 2. conflict, quarrel. 3. disagreement, dissension. 4. discussion, debating, controversy. 5. (Braz.) play, game (as football).

pelejador s. m. fighter, combatant. ‖ adj. fighting, battling, ready to combat.

pelejar v. 1. to fight, combat, struggle with. 2. to contend, dispute, quarrel. 3. to disagree, differ, dissent. 4. to discuss, argue. 5. to make a battle. 6. to insist.

pelerine s. f. pelerine: a long cape worn by women.

peletaria, peleteria s. f. (Braz.) = **pelaria**.

pé-leve s. m. (pl. **pés-leves**) (Braz.) loafer, vagrant, idler.

pele-vermelha s. m. + f. Red Indian, Redskin: a North American Indian. ‖ adj. redskin: pertaining to or characteristic of the North American Indians.

peliagudo adj. (S. Braz.) dangerous, risky.

pelica s. f. kid (leather), used to make gloves, shoes.

peliça s. f. pelisse: a garment made of or lined with fur.

pelicanídeos s. m. pl. (ornith.) Pelecanidae, the pelican family.

pelicaniformes s. m. pl. (ornith.) Pelecaniformes: an order of totipalmate fish-eating birds.

pelicano s. m. pelican: 1. (ornith.) a large piscivorous natatorial bird of the family Pelecanidae. 2. an instrument for extracting teeth.

peliceiro s. m. (obs.) tanner.

película s. f. pellicle: 1. a thin skin, cuticle. 2. epidermis. 3. film, motion picture.

pelicular adj. m. + f. (bot.) pellicular: having the character or quality of a pellicle.

pelintra s. m. + f. poor but pretentious fellow. ‖ adj. 1. poor but self-important. 2. (Braz.): a) well--dressed. b) mischievous, prankish. c) effeminate.

pelintrão s. m. (pl. **-ões**) (pop.) ragamuffin, a very poor man.

pelintrice s. f. meanness; poverty, misery.

peliqueiro s. m. a dealer in kid leather.

pelítico adj. (geol.) pelitic: composed of fine sediment or mud (as many rocks).

pelmatozoários s. m. pl. (zool.) Pelmatozoa: a subphylum of Echinodermata; crinoids, cystoids, blastoids.

pelo (l) contr. of the prep. **per** and the archaic m. article **lo** by, through, of, at, for the, in the, toward the. ~ **amor de Deus** for God's sake. ~ **contrário** on the contrary, per contra. ~ **mesmo preço** at the same price. ~ **menos** at least. ~ **motivo de** because of. ~ **que dizem** as they say. ~ **que você diz** from what you say. ~ **que sei** so far as I know.

pêlo (ê) (II) s. m. hair, down, flue, pile. ~ **de camelo** camel's hair. **em** ~ naked. **montar em** ~ to ride a horse without saddle.

pelória s. f. peloria: abnormal regularity in the structure of normally irregular flowers.

peloso adj. hairy, shaggy, furry.

pelota s. f. 1. bullet: a) any small ball. b) a cannon ball. 2. a pellet used for a slingshot. 3. a football.

pelotada s. f. (Braz., ftb.) a kick at the ball.

pelotão s. m. (pl. **-ões**) platoon: 1. a subdivision of a company, troop, or other military unit. 2. a company of people.

pelote s. m. a jerkin made of sheepskin.

pelotear v. 1. to whip, lash, scourge. 2. to mistreat, maltreat.

pelotica s. f. 1. a little ball of a juggler. 2. sleight of hand.

pelotiqueiro s. m. 1. juggler. 2. mountebank.

pelourada s. f. a shot with a ball or bullet.

pelourinho s. m. (also **peloirinho**) pillory: a framework in which an offender was fastened by the neck and wrists and exposed to public scorn; whipping-post.

pelouro s. m. (also **peloiro**) 1. ball, musket ball, cannon ball. 2. (obs.) ballot.

pelta s. f. pelta: a small and light buckler.

peltada adj. f. (bot.) peltate: having the petiole inserted into the lower surface of the lamina.

peltiforme adj. m. + f. (bot.) peltiform: peltate in form, shield-shaped.

peltinérveo adj. (bot.) peltinerved: having nerves rediating from a point at or near the center (said of a leaf).

pelúcia s. f. plush: a pile fabric of silk, rayon or mohair having a deeper pile than velvet; shag.

peludo s. m. 1. (zool.) peludo. 2. a circus employee who removes the objects used by the artists. 3. tipsiness. ‖ adj. 1. hairy, shaggy. 2. inexperienced, unfledged. 3. timid, shy. 4. mistrustful, suspicious. 5. (Braz.) habitually (undeservedly) lucky in games.

pelugem s. f. (pl. **-ens**) 1. a mass of hair (esp. that which grows upon the head). 2. down, flue, fluff, fuzz.

peluginoso adj. hairy, shaggy; downy; fuzzy.

pelve s. f. (anat., also **pélvis**) pelvis: the basinlike structure of the skeleton.

~ **renal** (anat.) pelvis of the ureter.

pélvico adj. (anat.) pelvic: of or pertaining to the pelvis.

pelviforme adj. m. + f. pelviform: shaped like a shallow cup or basin.

pelvimetria s. f. (med.) pelvimetry: measurement of the pelvis.

pelvímetro s. m. pelvimeter: instrument for measuring the diameter of the pelvis.

pena s. f. 1. (ornith.) feather, plume, quill; calamus. 2. pen, nib (place C 11). 3. composition, writing, style. 4. penman, writer, author. 5. (naut.) the end of the yard that supports the mizzen-sail. 6. punishment, penalty. 7. suffering, affliction, pain. 8. sorrow, pity; compassion. 9. pane of a hammer (plate M 5).

~ **de aço** steel-pen. ~ **de água** water gauge. ~ **de morte** capital punishment, pain of death. ~**s pecuniárias e de reclusão** pains and penalties. ~ **tetriz** (ornith.) wing-covert. **caça de pêlo e de** ~**s.** fur and feather. **desenho a bico-de-**~ pen-and-ink drawing. **é** ~ **it is a pity, that is too bad. é** ~ **que ele nos deixa** it is a thousand pities that he leaves us. **leve como uma** ~ light as a feather. **não vale a** ~ it is not worth the candle, it is not worth-while. **que** ~**!** what a pity! **sem** ~**s** featherless. **sob** ~ **de morte** under pain of death. **tenho** ~ **dela** I am sorry for her. **ter** ~ **de** to feel sorry for.

penação s. f. (pl. **-ões**) suffering, pain, affliction, enduring.

penáceo adj. (ornith., bot.) pennaceous: resembling a feather.

penacho s. m. 1. panache: plume or bunch of feathers (used as an adornment). 2. a crest. 3. plume of a helmet. 4. (fig.) government, administration.

apanhar ~ to take over the lead or power.

pé-na-cova s. m. (pl. **pés-na-cova**) (Braz., hum.) 1. a pale and skinny person. 2. a monthly preretirement allowance paid by the government after 30 years of active work.

penada s. f. 1. penful: a) a dip of ink. b) as much as a pen will hold. 2. as much as one can write with one dip of ink. 3. a stroke of the pen. 4. (bot.) a pinnate leaf.

penado adj. 1. feathered, plumed. 2. afflicted, troubled, painful.

folha -a (bot.) pinnate leaf (plate F 5).

penagris s. m. a brown down or fuzz.

penal s. m. (pl. -ais) a case for keeping pencils, pens, rubbers. ‖ adj. m. + f. penal, inflicting punishment, punitive.
código ~ penal code.
penalidade s. f. penalty, punishment, castigation.
~ máxima (ftb.) penalty (kick).
penalizar v. 1. to pain, afflict, distress, grieve. 2. to torment, torture. 3. ~-se to feel pity or sorrow for; be afflicted.
penalogia s. f. penology: the study of punishment for crime.
penalógico adj. penological: of or pertaining to penology.
penalogista s. m. + f. penologist: an expert in penology.
penálogo s. m. (Braz.) penologist.
pênalti s. m. (Braz., ftb., pop.) penalty (kick).
penamar adj. m. + f. rough, without luster (pearl).
penante s. m. (sl.) hat.
penão s. m. (pl. -ões) penon, pennant, pendant.
penar v. 1. to pain, torment, torture. 2. to suffer, endure. 3. to grieve, distress, afflict. 4. to castigate, punish. 5. ~se: a) to feel sorrow. b) to be afflicted.
penaroso adj. 1. (S. Braz.) painful, grievous. 2. pungent. 3. sorry, sorrowful.
penates s. m. pl. 1. Penates: the household gods. 2. (fig.) home, family.
penatífido adj. (bot.) pinnatifid: cleft in a pennate manner, with the incisions half-way down.
penatilobado adj. (bot.) pinnatilobed.
penatuláceos s. m. pl. (zool.) Pennatulacea: an order of Alcyonaria.
penca s. f. 1. stalk, stem of some plants (as lettuce, banana). 2. bunch (of bananas or grapes). 3. (fig.): a) a long or big nose. b) (Braz.) great quantity.
em ~ in a great quantity.
pence s. f. tuck: a fold sewn in a garment to make it shorter or smaller.
pencudo adj. having a long or big nose.
pendanga s. f. 1. anything frequently made use of. 2. job, petty work, accessory occupation.
pendão s. m. (pl. -ões) 1. banner, standard, pennon, flag, pennant, labarum. 2. (bot.) panicle.
~ do milho blossom of corn.
pendência s. f. 1. quarrel, dispute, squabble. 2. scuffle, fight, fray. 3. (jur.) pendency or duration of a suit.
pendenciador s. m. a quarrelsome person. ‖ adj. quarrelsome; pugnacious, rowdy.
pendenciar v. to quarrel, dispute, disagree; fight, come to blows.
pendenga s. f. 1. quarrel, dispute, squabble, wrangle. 2. discussion, debating, controversy. 3. war of words.
pendente s. m. pendant, ear-ring. ‖ adj. m. + f. 1. hanging, depending, pendent, suspended. 2. pending. 3. inclined, slanting, sloping. 4. in abeyance, abeyant. 5. imminent.
pender v. 1. to hang, be suspended or hanging. 2. to lean, slope, tilt, slant. 3. to incline, bend, be inclined. 4. to drop. 5. to decline, fall. 6. to depend on. 7. to be imminent. 8. to be favourably disposed to. 9. to be pending (a lawsuit). 10. to verge, tend. 11. to lean back, recline.
a cor pende para o vermelho the colour verges on red. a sua vida pende por um fio his life hangs upon a thread.
penderica s. f., penderico m. pendant, fripperies, gewgaws.
pendericalho, penderucalho s. m. = penduricalho.
pendoado adj. (Braz.) said of the corn which puts forth tassels or inflorescences.
pendoar. v. to put forth tassels.

pendor s. m. 1. declivity, slope, incline, bent. 2. inclination, disposition, propensity, propension. 3. obliquity.
pêndula s. f. pendulum clock.
pendular adj. m. + f. pendular: of or pertaining to a pendulum; oscillatory.
pêndulo s. m. 1. pendulum (plate R 4). 2. (fig.) equilibrium, equipoise. ‖ adj. hanging, pendulous.
prumo de ~ pendulum bob. regulador de ~ pendulum governor. serra de ~ pendulum saw.
pendura s. f. 1. hanging: act of suspending. 2. suspended thing.
estar na ~ (Braz., pop) to be without money.
pendurado adj. dangling, hanging down, hung, suspended, pending.
pendural s. m. (pl. -ais) kingpost (roof).
pendurar v. 1. to hang, suspend. 2. (fig.) to fix (eye, attention) on. 3. ~-se: a) to be suspended. b) to depend.
penduricalho s. m. 1. ear-ring, pendant. 2. ~s pl. gewgaws, fripperies. 3. (sl.) condecoration, medal, badge.
peneáceas s. f. pl. (bot.) Penaeaceae: a family of S. African evergreen shrubs.
penedia s. f., penedio m. a rocky place.
penedo s. m. 1. a great stone. 2. a rock. 3. (geol.) boulder.
penego s. m. a pillow or cushion made with feathers.
peneira s. f. 1. bolter, sieve, riddle, screen, strainer (plates A 7, E 11, F 3, P 1). 2. (pop.) drizzle, light rain. 3. (coll.) straw hat. 4. spark arrester: a device for catching sparks, as on a locomotive.
peneiração s. f. (pl. -ões) bolting, sifting, screening.
peneirada s. f. 1. = peneiração. 2. quantity sifted at a time.
peneirador s. m. sifter: person who sifts or bolts. ‖ adj. screening, sifting.
peneiramento s. m. 1. screening, bolting, sifting. 2. selection, classification.
peneirar v. 1. to sift, bolt, screen, sieve. 2. to winnow. 3. to drizzle, rain in fine drops. 4. ~-se to shake the hips (in walking).
peneireiro s. m. 1. a sieve maker. 2. person who sells sieves. 3. person who operates with a sieve.
peneiro s. m. a big sieve used in some bakeries.
penejar v. to write, draw or sketch with pen and ink.
penela s. f. hillock; a little rock.
peneplanície s. f. (geol.) peneplain, a surface reduced by erosin nearly to the condition of a plain.
penetra s. m. + f. 1. insolent person. 2. (Braz., sl.) uninvited guest; intruder; gate crasher.
penetrabilidade s. f. penetrability.
penetração s. f. (pl. -ões) 1. penetration: act of penetrating or piercing. 2. (fig.) mental acuteness, discernment; sagacity, perspicacity.
penetrais s. m. pl. penetralia: 1. the most retired or hidden part of an edifice. 2. innermost. 3. hidden things.
penetrante adj. m. + f. (also penetrador, penetrativo m.) 1. penetrant, piercing, penetrative. 2. pungent, acute; deep. 3. discerning, sagacious, astute, perspicacious. ‖ ~mente adv. penetrantly.
frio ~ sharp or pinching cold. um olhar ~ a piercing look.
penetrar v. 1. to penetrate, invade, enter, go in, come in. 2. (fig.) to crash, enter without being invited or without paying any admission charge. 3. to cross over, pass through. traverse. 4. to repass. 5. to pierce. 6. to dive into. 7. to apprehend, understand. 8. to discover, reveal, uncover. 9. ~-se to be convinced, convince o. s. that.
~ fundo em to reach far into. ~ no interior de um país to go a great way into the country. ~

na propriedade de alguém to trespass on some-one's property. ~ **no assunto** to see into the subject. **o corante penetrou no material** the dye worked into the stuff. **ele penetrou** he edged himself into.

penetrável adj. m. + f. (pl. **-áveis**) penetrable: capable of being penetrated or of penetrating.

pênfigo s. m. (med.) pemphigus: a skin disease characterized by watery vesicles successively formed on various parts of the body.

pengó s. m. (N. Braz.) 1. fool, blockhead, stupid person. 2. badly dressed person, ragamuffin.

penha s. f. rock, cliff, bluff.

penhasco s. m. a high and steep rock or cliff; crag (plate M 11).

penhascoso adj. rocky, cragged, cliffy, full of rocks.

penhasqueira s. f. (also **penhascal** m., pl. **-ais**) a series of crags or high rocks.

penhoar s. m. (Fr.) peignoir: a woman's loose negligee or dressing gown.

penhor s. m. 1. pawn, pledge. 2. mortgage. 3. token, proof. 4. security, guaranty, bail.

cautela de ~ pawn ticket. **casa de penhores** pawn-shop. **dar em** ~ to pawn, give something in pledge.

penhora s. f. (jur.) distraining, distress, seizure, attachment (as of a property).

alvará de ~ warrant of distress. **mandado de** ~ writ of extent.

penhorado adj. 1. seized, distrained. 2. pledged, engaged. 3. obliged, grateful, thankful.

~**s, agradecemos a sua gentileza** we are most grateful for your kindness.

penhorante adj. m. + f. 1. pledging. 2. engaging, obliging. 3. kind; deserving acknowledgement.

penhorar v. 1. to distrain, seize, confiscate. 2. to pledge, pawn; give in pawn, put in a pledge, mortgage. 3. to oblige, engage. 4. to oblige one to keep his word. 5. to captivate, fascinate. 6. to guarantee, warrant, vouch for. 7. ~**-se** to feel obliged.

penicilina s. f. penicillin: a very powerful antibiotic made from a penicillium mold.

penico s. m. (vulg.) chamber pot, chamber utensil. **pedir** ~ (Braz., sl.) to show the white flag.

pênico s. m. Punic: native or inhabitant of Carthage, Carthaginian ‖ adj. Punic: of or pertaining to Carthage or the Carthaginians.

penífero adj. (also **penígero**) feathered, having feathers, penniferous.

peniforme adj. m. + f. (nat. hist.) penniform: having the form of a feather.

peninervado adj. penninerved, penninervate.

península s. f. peninsula, spit (plate C 19).

a Península Ibérica the Peninsula, Iberia.

peninsular s. m. + f. peninsular: a native or inhabitant of a peninsula. ‖ adj. peninsular: of, pertaining to or resembling a peninsula.

penipotente adj. m. + f. having strong wings.

pênis s. m., sg. + pl. penis: the copulatory and urethral organ.

peniscar v. 1. to eat little bits, eat daintily. 2. to nibble, numble.

penisco s. m. seed of the pine tree.

penisqueiro adj. eating daintily; nibbling.

penitência s. f. penitence: 1. state of being penitent. 2. regret for sin. 3. contrition, repentance. 4. penance: a) the penalty or discipline imposed by the priest in the confession. b) self-punishment expressive of penitence.

penitencial s. m. (pl. **-ais**) (R. C. Church) penitential: a book of rules relating to penance and the reconciliation of penitents. ‖ adj. m. + f. penitential: pertaining to or expressing penitence.

penitenciar v. 1. to penance: inflict a penance upon. 2. ~**-se:** a) to make penance; be penitent. b) to repent, regret.

penitenciária s. f. penitentiary; prison.

penitenciário s. m. (R. C. Church) 1. penitentiary: one who prescribes or superintends penances. 2. a convict confined in a penitentiary. ‖ adj. penitentiary: 1. of or referring to penance. 2. relating to or used for the punishment and discipline of criminals.

penitencieiro s. m. (R. C. Church) 1. a Grand Penitentiary. 2. a confessor.

penitente s. m. + f. (R. C. Church) 1. penitent: person who confesses his sins to a priest and submits himself to the penance prescribed. 2. ~**s** pl. the Franciscans. ‖ adj. penitent, contrite, repentant. ‖ ~**mente** adv. penitently, contritely.

peno s. m. + adj. = **cartaginês.**

pé-no-chão s. m. (pl. **pés-no-chão**) (Braz.) a rustic, backwoodsman.

penol s. m. (pl. **penóis**) (naut.) arm of a yard.

penosa s. f. (sl.) very lean hen or chicken.

penoso adj. 1. painful, dolorous, grievous. 2. difficult, hard, arduous. ‖ **-amente** adv. 1. painfully. 2. arduously.

uma morte -a a hard death. **viver -amente** to make but a poor shift.

pensabundo adj. = **pensativo.**

pensado adj. thought of, considered, deliberate, studied.

bem ~ well-thought. **de caso** ~ deliberately, on purpose.

pensador (I) s. m. 1. thinker. 2. philosopher. ‖ adj. thinking, thoughtful.

pensador (II) s. m. person who dresses and bandages a wound. ‖ adj. dressing (wound).

pensadura s. f. 1. swaddling clothes. 2. act of cleaning, swaddling and feeding a child.

pensamento s. m. 1. thought. 2. act of thinking. 3. imagination, fancy. 4. idea. 5. mind, spirit. 6. meaning, notion.

adivinhador de ~ thought-reader. **eu pagaria para saber os seus** ~**s** a penny for his thoughts. **seu único** ~ **foi escutar isto** his one thought was to hear it. **transmissão de** ~ thought-transference.

pensante adj. m. + f. thinking, thoughtful.

pensão s. f. (pl. **-ões**) pension: 1. periodical allowance. 2. a boarding school. 3. a boarding house.

pensar (I) s. m. 1. thinking. 2. opinion. 3. judgement, prudence. ‖ v. (also but rare **pensament(e)ar** 1. to think. 2. to reflect, ponder, meditate. 3. to imagine, fancy; suspect. 4. to ratiocinate, reason. 5. to intend. 6. to cogitate. 7. to consider, judge, study. 8. to suppose, believe. 9. to attend.

~ **como** to think how. ~ **em vantagem própria** to consult one's own advantage. ~ **melhor** to come round. **conte-lhe o que você pensa (sobre)** tell him your thoughts about. **depois de** ~ **bem** on second thoughts. **ele estava pensando em voz alta** he was thinking aloud. **é exatamente o que eu pensei** I thought as much. **ele não pensou mais nisso** he dismissed the question from his thought. **ele nunca pensou nisso** it never entered his thoughts. **eu pensava que ela fosse minha amiga** I fancied her to be my friend. **jamais pensei em semelhante coisa** I never dreamt of such a thing. **modo de** ~ way of thinking. **não pense que...** don't think that..., don't run away with the idea that... **não sei o que** ~ **a respeito** I make neither head nor tail of it. **eu nunca pensaria em fazer isto** I should never think of doing that. **pensamos nisto** we gave a thought to that. **pensando bem** on further consideration, when all is said. **pensa que sou trouxa?**

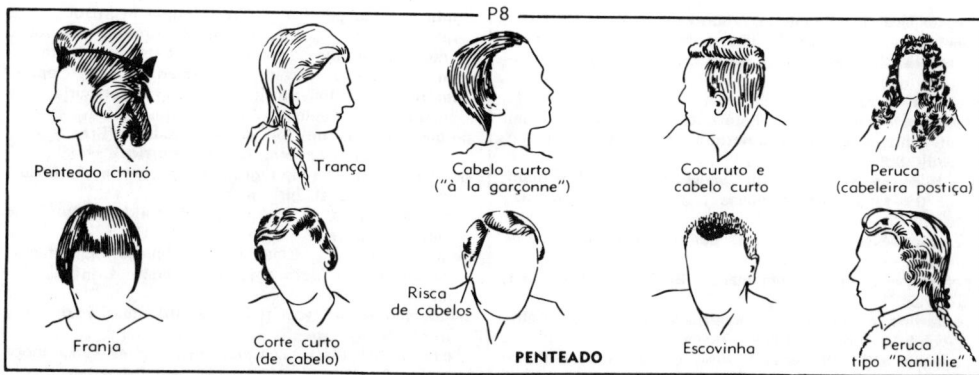

P8

Penteado chinó

Trança

Cabelo curto
("à la garçonne")

Cocuruto e
cabelo curto

Peruca
(cabeleira postiça)

Franja

Corte curto
(de cabelo)

Risca
de cabelos

PENTEADO

Escovinha

Peruca
tipo "Ramillie"

do you see any green in my eye? **pense bem antes de agir** think twice before you act, look before you leap. **pensei que devia dizer alguma coisa** I felt called upon to say something. **pensei que devíamos ir** I thought we should go. **pense no futuro!** look ahead! **penso que...** what I say is..., I have an idea that... **que é que está pensando?** what's the big idea? **que pensa que eu sou?** what do you take me for? **o que você pensa sobre Haydn?** what do you say to Haydn? **só em ~ fico com arrepios** I shudder at the bare idea. **você deve ~ bem sobre isto** you must think it over. **você pode ~ o que quiser!** (ironic.) you are welcome to your own opinion!

pensar (II) v. 1. to dress (a wound). 2. to clean, swaddle and feed a child.

pensativo adj. 1. musing, meditative, pensive. 2. contemplative. 3. wistful. 4. melancholic, sad. ‖ **-amente** adv. pensively, musingly.

pênsil adj. m. + f. (pl. **pênseis**) hanging, suspended, pensile. **ponte ~** suspension-bridge.

pensionar v. 1. to pension, grant or pay a pension. 2. to impose a burden. 3. to overload with work.

pensionário s. m. = **pensionista**. ‖ adj. of or referring to pension.

pensioneiro adj. lodger of a boarding house.

pensionista s. m. + f. 1. pensioner: one in receipt of a pension. 2. boarder: a) person who regularly takes his meals at the house of another. b) person who is boarded and lodged at a boarding house or school. ‖ adj. 1. pensionary. 2. who is a boarder.

penso s. m. 1. attendance, care, nursing (of children). 2. food ration (as for cattle). 3. dressing of a wound. ‖ adj. (Braz.) inclined, slanting, sloping.

pentacarpo adj. (bot.) pentacarpellary: composed of five carpels.

pentacórdio, pentacordo s. m. (mus.) pentachord: an instrument of five strings.

pentadáctilo, pentadátilo adj. pentadactyl(e): having five fingers or toes.

pentadecágono s. m. (geom.) pentadecagon: a plane figure with fifteen sides and angles.

pentadelfo adj. pentadelphous: (bot.) grouped together in five sets.

pentaedro s. m. (geom.) pentahedron: a solid figure having five faces.

pentafiláceas s. f. pl. (bot.) Pentaphylacaceae, a family of Chinese flowering plants.

pentafilo adj. (bot.) quinquefoliate (plate F 5).

pentagonal adj. m. + f. (pl. **-ais**) (geom.) pentagonal: having five corners or angles.

pentágono s. m. (geom.) pentagon: a figure of five sides and five angles.

pentagrafia s. f. pantography: art of using a pantograph.

pentágrafo s. m. pantograph: instrument for copying a drawing or diagram.

pentagrama s. m. 1. (mus.) staff. 2. pentagram: a) a figure having five points. b) pentacle.

pentâmero s. m. (ent.) a pentamerous beetle. ‖ adj. pentamerous: composed of five similar parts.

pentâmeros s. m. pl. (ent.) Pentamera, a great division of beetles.

pentâmetro s. m. pentameter: a verse containing five units or feet. ‖ adj. pentameter: having five metrical feet.

pentandro adj. (bot.) pentandrous: having five stamens with distinct filaments not connected with the pistil.

pentangular adj. m. + f. pentangular: having five angles.

pentapétalo adj. (bot.) pentapetalous: having five petals.

pentápole s. f. pentapolis: a group or confederation of five cities.

pentarquia s. f. pentarchy: a government administered by five joint rulers.

pentaspermo adj. (bot.) pentaspermous: containing five seeds.

pentassílabo adj. pentasyllabic: having five syllables.

pentastilo s. m. pentastyle portico or building.

pentastomídeos s. m. pl. (zool.) Linguatulida, a subclass of wormlike, pseudosegmented parasites; tongue worms.

Pentateuco s. m. Pentateuch: the first five books of the Bible.

pentatlo s. m. (Gr. hist.) pentathlon: an athletic contest of five events: leaping, running, wrestling, throwing the discus and hurling the spear.

pentavalente adj. m. + f. pentavalent: (chem.) having a valence or combining value of five.

pente s. m. 1. comb. 2. card: a wire-toothed brush for combing wool. 3. reed of a loom. 4. (mil.) clip. 5. pubis. 6. **~s** pl. pecten: the comblike organs behind the posterior legs of a scorpion.
~ carregador (mil.) ammunition clip. **~ fino** tooth-comb. **escova para limpar ~** a comb-brush.

penteadeira s. f. dressing-table (with a mirror).

penteadela s. f. a careless, hasty combing.

penteado s. m. hairdressing, hairdo, coiffure: style of dressing the hair (plate P 8).

penteador s. m. 1. comber; hairdresser. 2. combing cloth. 3. peignoir, dressing gown (plate R 6). ‖ adj. combing.

penteadura s. f. combing, hairdressing.

pentear v. 1. to comb, dress the hair. 2. to disentangle. 3. ~-se: a) to comb one's hair. b) to prepare o. s.
~ lã to card or comb wool.

Pentecostes s. m. pl. Pentecost: the Christian feast of Whitsunday, commemorating the descent of the Holy Spirit.

pente-de-macaco s. m. (pl. **pentes-de-macaco**) a plant of the family Bignoniaceae (Pithecoctenium echinatum).

pente-dos-bichos s. m. (pl. **pentes-dos-bichos**) tooth-comb.

penteeiro s. m. 1. combmaker. 2. person who sells combs.

pente-fino s. m. (pl. **pentes-finos**) (Braz.) 1. tooth-comb. 2. crook, slicker, rascal.

penugem s. f. (pl. **-ens**) 1. down: a) the first feathering of a bird. b) the soft hair that first appears on the human face. c) soft and short hair. 2. fuzz, pubescence of certain plants, fluff.

penugento adj. 1. downy, covered with soft feathers or hair. 2. pubescent (plants).

penujar v. to become downy or pubescent.

pênula s. f. (obs.) a short, thick, napped coat of wool or leather.

penúltimo adj. last but one, penultimate.

penumbra s. f. 1. (astr.) penumbra. 2. partial shadow, shade. 3. half-light. 4. (fig.) insulation; withdrawal.

penumbrar v. (Braz.) to make shadowy, produce shade.

penumbroso adj. 1. (astr.) penumbral, penumbrous. 2. producing shade; shadowy.

penúria s. f. penury: extreme poverty or want, beggary, misery, indigence, pauperism; need, destitution; mendicancy.

penurioso adj. needy, indigent, very poor, destitute.

peoa, peona s. f. (S. Braz.) f. of **peão.**

peonada s. f. a great number of peons.

peonagem s. f. (pl. **-ens**) 1. a group of peons or farm workers. 2. foot soldiers, orderlies.

peônia s. f. peony: plant of the crowfoot family (Paeonia officinalis).

pepé s. m. + f. (S. Braz., pop.) a cripple. ‖ adj. lame, crippled.

peperômia s. f. peperomia: plant of the family Piperaceae (Peperomia sandersii).

pepinal s. m. (pl. **-ais**) a place where cucumbers grow; plantation of cucumbers.

pepinar v. (Braz.) 1. to cut into small pieces. 2. to pierce. 3. to nibble (at food).

pepineira s. f. 1. field of cucumbers. 2. = pepineiro. 3. spree, revel. 4. plant nursery. 5. (fig.) bargain; find; a profitable sinecure.

pepineiro s. m. cucumber (the plant, Cucumis sativus).

pepino s. m. 1. cucumber. 2. = pepineiro.

pepita s. f. nugget, lump (esp. of a precious metal, as gold).

pepitória s. f. chicken giblets.

peplo s. m. peplum, peplos: in ancient Greece an elaborate shawl or upper garment worn by women.

pepolim adj. (pl. **-ins**) (obs.) lame, crippled.

peponídeo adj. said of the fruit of the gourd family, with hardened rind and numerous enclosed seeds, as the squash, cucumber, pumpkin, melon.

pepônio s. m. pepo: a fruit like that of the gourd.

pepsia s. f. (med.) digestion.

pepsina s. f. (biochem.) pepsin(e): the proteolytic ferment found in the gastric juice.

péptico adj. peptic: promoting digestion, dietetic, digestive.

peptizante adj. m. + f. peptizing.

peptizar v. to peptize: convert into a hydrosol.

peptona s. f. peptone: a soluble protein compound into which the albuminous substances contained in food are converted when acted upon by pepsin.

peptonúria, peptonuria s. f. (med.) peptonuria: the presence of peptones in the urine.

pé-quebrado s. m. (pl. **pés-quebrados**) (Braz., pop.) a poetic composition, usually satirical.

pequena s. f. 1. (pop.) girl, young woman. 2. (Braz.) girl, one's best girl, sweetheart.

pequenada s. f. 1. a group of children. 2. large family, spawn.

pequenez s. f. 1. smallness, littleness. 2. infancy, childhood. 3. pettiness, scantiness. 4. (fig.) humility.

pequenino s. m. (young) boy, a little one. ‖ adj. very little; teeny, wee.
os ~s the little ones, the little tinies. **uma moça** -a a wisp of a girl.

pequenito adj. very small.

pequenitote s. m. a little child. ‖ adj. = pequenino.

pequeno s. m. 1. child, boy, young man. 2. boy friend. 3. ~s pl. the common people. ‖ adj. (dim. menor; augm. maior) 1. small, little (plate Q). 2. short. 3. trifling, petty. 4. mean, low.
-as despesas petty charges or expenses. -as necessidades small demand. ele é dos ~s he is on the small side. os ~s e os grandes the little and the great ones.

pequenote s. m. young man; boy, lad, youngster. ‖ adj. rather small, smallish.

pequerrucho s. m. baby, little child. ‖ adj. very little; wee.

pequetito adj. (Braz.) very little; teeny, tiny, wee.

pequi s. m. (Braz.) a tree of the genus Caryocar (C. brasiliense).

pequiá-amarelo s. m. (pl. **pequiás-amarelos**) (Braz.) a tree of the family Apocynaceae (Aspidosperma sessiliflorum).

pequice s. f. 1. nonsense, stupidity. 2. foolishness, fatuity.

pequinês s. m. (pl. **-eses**) (f. **-esa**) Pekingese, Pekinese: 1. native or inhabitant of Peking. 2. a Pekingese dog. ‖ adj. Pekingese, Pekinese: of or pertaining to Peking.

pequito s. m. 1. (Braz.) child, baby. 2. (Port.) = periquito.

per prep. (obs. form of **por**) by, for.
de ~ si by itself.

pêra s. f. (pl. **peras**) 1. pear (fruit). 2. pear-shaped electric switch. 3. goatee.

pé-rachado s. m. (pl. **pés-rachados**) (S. Braz., pop.) = pé-rapado.

perada s. f. 1. conserve of pears. 2. perry, pear wine.

peragração s. f. (pl. **-ões**) (astr.) peragration.

peral s. m. (pl. **-ais**) an orchard of pear-trees. ‖ adj. of, pertaining to or resembling a pear.

peralta s. m. + f. 1. fop, dandy, coxcomb. 2. chattering person. 3. mischievous or naughty child. 4. idler, vagrant. ‖ adj. 1. foppish, dandyish. 2. mischievous, naughty, prankish (child). 3. idle, lazy; vagrant.

peraltar, peraltear, peralvilhar v. to behave like a vagrant, be mischievous.

peraltice, peralvilhice s. f. 1. foppery, coxcombry. 2. michievousness. 3. mischievousness.

peraltismo s. m. 1. = peraltice. 2. mischievousness.

peralvilho s. m. 1. fop, coxcomb. 2. chattering person. 3. vagrant.

perambeira s. f. precipice, crag; abyss, chasm.

perambulação s. f. (pl. **-ões**) (Braz.) perambulation: act of perambulating.

perambular v. 1. to perambulate, walk through or over. 2. to walk about. 3. to take for a walk. 4. to roam, wander.

perambulatório adj. (Braz.) perambulatory.

perante prep. in the presence of, before. ~ **o juiz** in the presence of the judge. ~ **mim** before me. **ele se viu** ~ **dificuldades** he was up against difficulties.

pé-rapado s. m. (pl. **pés-rapados**) very poor person, poor devil, underdog.

perca s. f. (pop.) 1. loss, damage, waste. 2. financial loss, misfortune.

percal s. m. (pl. **-ais**) (also **percale**) percale: a closely woven cotton fabric without gloss.

percalço s. m. 1. profit, gain, benefit. 2. perquisite. 3. disturbance, trouble.

percalina s. f. percaline: a glossy cotton cloth.

percebe (ê) s. m. (pl. **percebes**) = **perceve.**

perceber v. 1. to perceive: a) have knowledge of (through the medium of the senses). b) know. c) discern, understand, apprehend, note. d) discry. 2. to hear, listen. 3. to feel, sense. 4. to receive (salary).
ela percebeu as suas artimanhas she saw through or was up to his tricks. **fazer-se percebido** to make o. s. conspicuous, show the flag. **logo percebi suas intenções** I saw through him at once.

percebimento s. m. act of perceiving; perception.

percentagem s. f. (pl. **-ens**) percentage: 1. rate per hundred or proportion in a hundred parts. 2. (com.) duty or interest in a hundred.

percepção s. f. (pl. **-ões**) 1. perception: act or process of perceiving. 2. understanding, comprehension, apprehension, perceptivity. 3. feeling. 4. outsight, view.

perceptibilidade s. f. perceptibleness, perceptibility: the state or property of being perceptible; sensibleness.

perceptível adj. m. + f. (pl. **-íveis**) (also **percebível**) perceptible, perceivable, sensible, noticeable. || **perceptivelmente** adv. perceptibly.

perceptivo adj. perceptive, perceiving, perceptional.

percesoces s. m. pl. (ichth.) Percesoces, a suborder of Percomorphi: gray mullets, barracudas, silversides.

perceve s. m. (zool.) a kind of barnacle.

percevejo s. m. 1. (ent.) bedbug (Cimex lectularius or rotundatus). 2. thumbtack: a broad-headed tack.

percevejo-da-cama s. m. (pl. **percevejos-da-cama**) a common bedbug.

percha s. f. 1. (gym.) perch, pole. 2. stake, a long stick. 3. short for **guta-percha.**

percherão s. m. (pl. **-ões**) Percheron: a) native or inhabitant of Perche (France). b) a breed of horses. || adj. Percheron: of or pertaining to Perche.

perclorato s. m. (chem.) perchlorate: salt of perchloric acid.

percloreto s. m. (chem.) perchloride: chloride having a large proportion of chlorine.

perclórico adj. perchloric: said of an acid formed when potassium perchlorate is distilled with sulphuric acid.
ácido ~ perchloric acid.

percluso adj. maimed, crippled, lamed, unable to move about.

percóide adj. m. + f. (ichth.) percoid, perchlike.

percolação s. f. (pl. **-ões**) percolation: act of percolating, filtration; act of passing through small interstices.

percolador s. m. percolator: percolating apparatus, especially for preparing coffee.

percomorfos s. m. pl. (ichth.) a class of freshwater and marine teleost fishes: perches, mackerels, gobies, basses.

percorrer v. 1. to pass or run through. 2. to go through. 3. to visit or travel all over. 4. to traverse, cross. 5. to explore. 6. to investigate, examine, scrutinize, search. 7. to observe, glance over.
ele percorreu o campo com os olhos his eyes travelled over the field. **eles percorreram o país** they roamed about the country. **percorremos cinco milhas** we covered five miles. **percorremos o trecho de carro** we cabbed the distance. **percorri toda a rua de porta em porta** I went from door to door through the whole street, (coll.) I called the whole street.

percuciente adj. m. + f. 1. percutient, percussive, striking. 2. acute, penetrating.

percurso s. m. 1. passage, course, route, way. 2. trajectory, journey. 3. circuit. 4. act of passing along a given route.

percussão s. f. (pl. **-ões**) percussion: 1. the sharp striking of one body against another, collision. 2. the shock or vibration produced by collision.
espoleta de ~ percussion fuse. **granada de** ~ percussion shell. **instrumento de** ~ percussion instrument. **parafuso de** ~ percussion screw. **potência de** ~ percussion power.

percussor s. m. (also **percutidor**) 1. percussor: a) one who or that which strikes. b) an instrument of percussion. 2. firing pin. || adj. striking, percussive.

percutâneo adj. (med.) percutaneous: passed, done, or effected through or by means of the skin.

percutir v. 1. to percuss, strike, beat. 2. to wound, injure. 3. to touch.

perda s. f. 1. loss. 2. damage, prejudice, detriment. 3. misfortune, calamity. 4. destruction, ruin. 5. disappearance. 6. casualty.
~s e danos (com.) indemnity for loss and damage. ~ **por trabalho improdutivo (máquina)** loss by waste. ~ **total** a dead loss. **sem** ~ **de tempo** out of hand, immediately. **sofrer uma** ~ to meet with a loss. **tivemos grandes ~s em mortos** we had to pay a heavy toll of killed. **uma grande** ~ **de tempo para mim** a great tax upon my time.

perdão s. m. (pl. **-ões**) 1. pardon, forgiveness. 2. pardoning; amnesty. 3. remission of sin, indulgence. 4. indult. 5. excuse.
perdão! I am sorry!, excuse me! **foi-lhe concedido** ~ he was pardoned.

perde-ganha s. m. (also **ganha-perde**) a sort of game at cards or draughts in which the loser wins.

perder v. 1. to lose: a) miss. b) be deprived or bereaved of. c) fail. d) ruin, bring to ruin. e) cause to perish. f) deprave, vitiate, disgrace, corrupt. g) waste, squander. h) fail to gain or win. i) forget. 2. **~-se** to lose o. s.: a) lose one's way. b) become confused. c) be lost. d) disappear. 3. to bring misfortune upon. 4. to lose merit or value.
~ **a cabeça** to lose one's head, forget o. s. ~ **a batalha** to lose the battle. ~ **a coragem** to lose heart. ~ **a esperança** to lose hope. ~ **as cores** to lose its colours. ~ **as estribeiras** to lose one's temper. ~ **a oportunidade** to miss the opportunity. ~ **a paciência** to lose patience. ~ **de vista** to lose sight of, disappear. ~ **a vida** to lose one's life. ~ **o caminho** to lose one's way, go astray. ~ **o fôlego** to get out of breath. ~ **o passo** to get out of step. ~ **o trem** to miss the train. ~**-se em minúcias** to split hairs. ~ **sem demonstrar contrariedade** to bear a loss. ~ **tempo** to lose one's time. ~ **tempo à toa** to idle away the time. ~ **tempo falando** to talk away the time, make almanacs for last year. ~ **a terra de vista** to lay the land. ~ **terreno** 1. to fall behind. 2. to lose ground. **deitar a** ~ to vitiate, deprave. **ele está**

se perdendo no terreno da fantasia he is losing his grip on reality. ele não tem nada a ~ he has no venture. ele nunca perde a coragem his courage never yields. ele perdeu a cabeça he is off his head. ele perdeu o caminho he lost his way. ele perdeu a fala the word stuck in his throat. ele perdeu até as calças no jogo (fig.) he lost his shirt. ele perdeu-se he went to the bad. ele perdeu seu dinheiro no jogo he gambled away his money. ele está se perdendo he goes to loss. fazer alguém ~ a cabeça de medo to frighten one out of his wits. não há tempo a ~ it is high time. não perca tempo! run along! não perdemos a calma we did not lose our self-possession. para não perdê-lo for fear of losing it. perdemo-lo de vista we lost track of him. perdeu velocidade it lost way. perdi o caminho I wandered out of my way. quase perdi a coragem I came near losing my courage. o que perde sempre sofre o escárnio the laugh is always against the loser.

perdição s. f. (pl. -ões) 1. perdition: a) damnation, loss of one's soul and the joys of heaven; eternal death. b) ruin, destruction. 2. misfortune, calamity. 3. dishonour, disgrace. 4. irreligiousness. é uma ~ it is a great pity.

perdíceo adj. resembling a partridge.

perdida s. f. 1. = perda. 2. prostitute, harlot. 3. (Braz.) branching off; wrong road.

perdidiço adj. easily lost.

perdido s. m. any lost thing. ‖ adj. 1. lost. 2. dispersed, scattered. 3. disappeared, gone. 4. ruined, destroyed. 5. shipwrecked. 6. infatuated, desperately in love. 7. immoral, licentious, depraved. 8. puzzled, perplexed. ‖ -amente adv. desperately; extremely.
~ como foi ganho light come, light go. ~ em meditações absorbed in thought. dar por ~ to give it up. ele está ~ he is done for, it is all over with him, (sl.) his jig is up. ele está ~ de amor por ela he is madly in love with her. um caso ~ a hard case.

perdidoso adj. prejudicial.

perdigão s. m. (pl. -ões) the male of the tinamou or partridge.

perdigoteiro s. m. person who sputters (in speaking). ‖ adj. sputtering.

perdigoto s. m. (pl. perdigotos) 1. young (male) partridge. 2. (pop.) sputter: saliva emitted in speaking.

perdigueiro s. m. (also cão ~) setting-dog, pointer, setter (plate C 3). ‖ adj. hunting partridges.

perdimento s. m. = perdição.

perdível adj. m. + f. (pl. -íveis) losable: capable of being lost.

perdiz s. f. (orniht.) 1. partridge. 2. (Braz.) tinamou.

perdoador s. m. pardoner, forgiver. ‖ adj. forgiving, pardoning.

perdoar v. 1. to pardon, forgive, excuse, exculpate. 2. to remit. 3. to let off. 4. to justify, condone. 5. to exonerate, absolve. 6. ~-se: a) to forgive o. s. b) to spare o. s.
estou perdoado? am I forgiven? perdoai as nossas dívidas forgive us our trespasses... perdoa-lhe! show him mercy! perdoaram-lhe o imposto he was excused the tax. perdoe-me I beg your pardon. seu erro foi-lhe perdoado his was forgiven his fault. todos os seus erros lhe podem ser perdoados he can be excused all his errors. a morte não perdoa a ninguém death spares nobody.

perdoável adj. m. + f. (pl. -áveis) forgivable, pardonable, excusable.

perdoe s. f. (Braz.) a straw purse used by mendicants to collect alms.

perdulário s. m. prodigal, spendthrift, lavisher. ‖ adj. prodigal, lavish, wasteful, pound-foolish, large-handed, unthrifty.

perduração s. f. (pl. -ões) duration, perdurability, perdurableness, continuance, length.

perdurar v. to perdure, continue (for a long time), last forever; persist, endure; remain.

perdurável adj. m. + f. (pl. -áveis) 1. perdurable, very durable, lasting, enduring, abiding. 2. eternal. ‖ perduravelmente adv. 1. perdurably. 2. eternally.

pereba s. f. (Braz.) 1. aposteme, abscess, boil. 2. itch, scabies, mange.

perebagem s. f. (pl. -ens) (N. Braz.) a lot of sores.

perebento adj. (Braz.) covered with sores; mangy.

perecedor, perecedouro adj. 1. perishable, decaying, fading. 2. endable, terminable. 3. mortal, deadly, dying.

perecer v. 1. to perish, die, decay. 2. to come a cropper. 3. to end, finish, terminate. 4. to be ruined.
~ de fome to perish by hunger.

perecimento s. m. 1. perishing. 2. extinction. 3. emaciation.

perecível adj. m. + f. (pl. -íveis) 1. perishable. 2. endable, terminable.

peregrinação s. f. (pl. -ões) 1. pilgrimage. 2. peregrination, travelling about, journey, wandering. em ~ on the tramp.

peregrinador s. m., peregrinante m. + f. 1. pilgrim. 2. peregrinator, wanderer, traveller. ‖ adj. 1. wandering, travelling. 2. going on a pilgrimage, peregrinating.

peregrinar v. 1. to go on a pilgrimage. 2. to travel, wander, peregrinate.

peregrinismo s. m. 1. foreign word or expression; foreignness. 2. rareness. 3. use of foreign words.

peregrino s. m. (also peregrim, obs.) 1. pilgrim. 2. peregrinator, traveller, wanderer. ‖ adj. 1. pilgrim. 2. peregrine, travelling. 3. foreign. 4. rare, extraordinary, uncommon. 5. excellent.

pereira s. f. (bot.) pear-tree (Pirus communis).

pereira-do-japão s. f. (pl. pereiras-do-japão) a variety of quince (Cydonia japonica).

pereiral s. m. (pl. -ais) = peral.

pereirina s. f. (chem.) pereirine.

perempção s. f. (pl. -ões) (jur.) prescription.

perempto adj. (jur.) extinct, null, void, prescriptive.

peremptório adj. peremptory: 1. decisive; absolute. 2. terminating, conclusive, final. 3. absolute. ‖ peremptoriamente adv. peremptorily; formally.

perendengues s. m. pl. (Braz.) gewgaws, fripperies, pendants.

perene adj. m. + f. (also perenal) perennial, unceasing, incessant, continual, permanent, perpetual, eternal, enduring, lasting. ‖ ~mente adv. perennially, perpetually.
fontes ~s perennial fountains.

perenidade s. f. perenniality, eternity, perpetuity.

perenizar v. to perennate: perpetuate; make eternal.

perequê m. m. (S. Braz., pop.) 1. discussion, debating. 2. quarrel, disturbance, rumpus, noise.

perequeté adj. m. + f. (also prequeté) (Braz., pop.) 1. given to self-display. 2. elegant.

perereca s. f. (Braz.) 1. a tree-frog of the family Hylidae. 2. m. + f. dwarf, a small person or animal. ‖ adj. dwarfish, like a dwarf. :

pererecar v. 1. to go about, move to and fro. 2. to be bewildered, giddy. 3. to become confused, flounder. 4. (S. Braz.) to leap (top).

perereco s. m. (Braz., pop.) a noisy quarrel, conflict, riot, fracas.

pererento adj. (Braz.) 1. mottled (white and black). 2. white-speckled.

pereva s. f. (Braz.) = **pereba**.
perfazer v. 1. to perfect, finish, conclude, complete. 2. to accomplish, execute, perform, do. 3. to supply, fill up, make up. 4. to amount to.
perfazimento s. m. finishing, perfecting, completion.
perfectibilidade s. f. perfectibility.
perfectível adj. m. + f. (pl. -íveis) perfectible, perfective; tending to make perfect.
perfectivo adj. perfecting, finishing.
perfeição s. f. (pl. -ões) 1. perfection, accomplishment, excellence. 2. completeness, finishing. 3. beauty, attractiveness. 4. faultlessness, purity. 5. refinement, height, acme (of perfection).
a ~ adquire-se com a prática practice makes perfect. **a mais alta ~** the pink of perfection.
perfeiçoar v. (also **aperfeiçoar**) 1. to perfect, bring to perfection. 2. to improve, ameliorate, make better.
perfeito adj. perfect: 1. complete(d). 2. finished, accomplished. 3. correct, entire. 4. faultless, spotless. 5. sinless. 6. fine, divine, excellent. 7. beautiful. ‖ **-amente** adv. perfectly; completely; rightly; well.
~! fine!, very true! **ele foi um marinheiro ~** he was a thoroughbred seaman. **entendemo-nos -amente** we got along excellently together, got on swimmingly together. **eu compreendo isto -amente** I am fully aware of it. **pretérito ~** (gram.) preterit indicative.
perficiente adj. m. + f. perfect, complete.
perfídia s. f. perfidy: 1. perfidiousness, faithlessness. 2. treacherousness, treachery. 3. foul play. 4. disloyalty, falseness. 5. apostasy.
pérfido adj. perfidious, unfaithful, faithless, false, disloyal, treacherous. ‖ **perfidamente** adv. perfidiously, treacherously.
perfil s. m. (pl. -is) 1. profile, sideface. 2. outine or contour of a building. 3. (fig.) aspect, appearance. 4. (mil.) align(ment). 5. rough sketch.
~ do solo soil profile. **resistência de ~** (aeron.) profile drag. **retrato de ~** a picture in profile.
perfilar v. 1. to profile: a) draw the profile of. b) outline. c) draw in section. 2. to draw up in a line (soldiers). 3. to stand, straighten up. 4. **~-se** to become straight.
perfilhação s. f. (pl. -ões) adoption, affiliation.
perfilhador s. m. adopter. ‖ adj. adoptant.
perfilhar v. 1. to adopt, affiliate. 2. (fig.) to protect, defend. 3. to shoot (plants).
perfluxo s. m. fluxion or flow of humours.
perfolhado, perfoliado adj. (bot.) perfoliate (plate F 5).
performance s. f. (Engl.) performance.
perfulgência s. f. refulgence, splendour, brilliant radiance.
perfulgente adj. m. + f. brilliant, splendid, refulgent, very bright.
perfumado adj. perfumed, odorous, odoriferous, fragrant, sweet-smelling. ‖ **-amente** adv. fragrantly, odoriferously.
perfumador s. m. perfumer; censer, perfuming pan. ‖ adj. perfuming.
perfumar v. 1. to perfume: a) render odorous; aromatize. b) scent. 2. to embalm. 3. **~-se** to put on perfume.
perfumaria s. f. 1. perfumery: a) perfumes in general. b) a place where perfumes are manufactured. 2. a perfumer's shop. 3. (coll.) soft drinks.
perfume s. m. 1. perfume: a) pleasant odour, fragrance. b) an artificial fragrant substance. c) scent 2. (fig.) sweetness, pleasantness. 3. balm.
borrifador de ~s perfume sprayer.

perfumista s. m. + f. perfumer: person who makes or deals in perfumes.
perfumoso adj. perfumed, aromatic, fragrant, odoriferous, sweet-smelling.
perfunctório, perfuntório adj. 1. perfunctory: a) done merely for the sake of routine. b) superficial. c) careless, negligent. 2. slight. ‖ **perfunctoriamente** adv. perfunctorily.
perfuração s. f. (pl. -ões) 1. perforation: act of boring into or piercing through. 2. drill(ing).
~ de poço well-sinking.
perfurador s. m. 1. perforator. 2. borer, boring machine. 3. stabber. 4. drill. ‖ adj. perforating, perforatory.
perfurante adj. m. + f. perforating, piercing, penetrant, perforative.
perfurar v. 1. to perforate, bore, drill. 2. to enter, penetrate, pierce, stab.
perfuratriz s. f. drilling machine, borer, drill.
pergamináceo, pergaminháceo adj. pergamineous, pergamentaceous, like parchment.
pergaminharia s. f. the making of parchment.
pergaminheiro s. m. 1. parchment-maker. 2. person who sells parchment.
pergaminho s. m. 1. parchment: a) the skin of sheep or goats prepared for use as writing material. b) a formal writing on parchment. c) a college graduation diploma. d) vegetable parchment. 2. **~s** pl. honours, titles.
pérgula s. f. pergola: an arbour or trelliswork of a structural nature, covered with vegetation or flowers.
pergunta s. f. 1. question, interrogation, asking. 2. inquiry, interrogatory.
~ de algibeira a difficult or tricky question. **a ~ atinge todos os fatos** the question raises the whole issue. **a ~ é sem importância** the question does not arise. **fazer ~s** to ask questions.
perguntador s. m. 1. questioner, interrogator. 2. inquirer, querist. ‖ adj. 1. questioning. 2. inquiring. 3. curious, inquisitive.
perguntante s. m. + f. questioner: person who asks questions.
perguntar v. 1. to ask, question, interrogate, query. 2. to inquire, ask about. 3. to ask for.
~ por to ask after. **~ por alguém** to ask for s. o. **~ pelo caminho** to ask one's way of s. o. **ele perguntou por moedas raras** he inquired after rare coins. **perguntei-lhe muitas coisas** I asked him many quesitons. **posso ~?** may I ask? **se alguém ~ por mim** if I am asked for.
peri s. m. 1. (Persian myth.) peri: a fairy or elf. 2. (Braz.) gully: a ravine or channel cut in the earth by running water.
periambo s. m. = **períquio**.
periândrico adj. surrounding the stamens of a flower.
periantado adj. (bot.) perianthial, periantheous: provided with a perianth.
perianto s. m. (bot.) perianth: the floral envelopes, whether calyx or corolla or both.
periblema s. m. (bot.) periblem: the primary cortex between the dermatogen and the plerome in a growing point.
períbolo s. m. space between a building and the wall that surrounds it.
pericardiário adj. situated at or forming on the pericardium.
pericardial adj. pericardial: of or pertaining to the pericardium.
pericárdio s. m. (anat.) pericardium: the membranous sac which surrounds and protects the heart.
pericardite s. f. (path.) pericarditis: inflammation of the pericardium.

pericarpial adj. m. + f. (pl. **-ais**) (bot.) pericarpial: developing in the pericarp.

pericárpico adj. (bot.) pericarpic: of or pertaining to the pericarp.

pericárpio, pericarpo s. m. (bot.) pericarp: the wall of the ripened ovary or seed vessel.

pericentral adj. m. + f. (pl. **-ais**) pericentral: situated about a center or central body.

pericêntrico adj. (bot.) pericentric.

perícia s. f. 1. skill, ability, dexterity, cleverness, know-how, expertness. 2. perfection, art. 3. mastership, masterfulness.
com ~ skillfully.

pericial adj. m. + f. skillful, cleverly.

periciclo s. m. pericycle: the outer portion of the central or fibrovascular cylinder in plants, capable of active growth.

pericistite s. f. (path.) pericystitis: inflammation of the tissues around the bladder.

pericliniforme adj. m. + f. (bot.) having the form of a periclinium.

periclinita s. f. (min.) pericline: a variety of albite.

periclino s. m. (bot.) periclinium: the involucre of the capitulum in the Compositae.

periclitante adj. m. + f. running a risk or hazard. 2. in a dangerous situation. 3. exposed to danger.

periclitar v. 1. to run a risk or hazard. 2. to be in danger. 3. to endanger.

pericondrite s. f. (path.) perichondritis: inflammation of the perichondrium.

pericondro s. m. (anat.) perichondrium: membrane which covers the surface of a cartilage.

pericote s. m. topknot: a type of feminine hairdo.

pericrânio s. m. (anat.) pericranium: the cranial periosteum.

periculosidade s. f. (jur.) condition of one who or that which constitutes or offers danger.

perididimo s. m. (anat.) perididymis: the tunica vaginalis testis.

perídio s. m. (bot.) peridium: the outer coat of an angiocarpous fungus.

peridotito s. m. (petrog.) peridotite: a granular igneous rock composed essentially of olivine.

peridoto s. m. (min.) peridot: a yellowish-green gem, variety of olivine.

perídromo s. m. (archit.) peridrome: the open space or passage around a building.

periecos s. m. pl. perioeci: inhabitants of the earth who live on the same parallels of latitude, but on opposite meridians.

periélio s. m. perihelion, perihelium: that point of the orbit of a planet or comet where it is nearest the sun.

periergia s. f. periergia, periergy: excessive care or refinement of language.

periferia s. f. periphery: 1. (geom.): a) the perimeter of a curvilinear figure. b) circumference. c) the surface of a body. 2. a surrounding region, country or area; circuit, suburb.

periférico adj. peripheric(al), peripheral: 1. of, belonging to or situated on the periphery. 2. (bot.) denoting an embryo curved so as to surround the albumen.

periforântio, periforanto s. m. (bot.) periphoranthium, periclinium: the involucre of the capitulum in the Compositae.

perífrase s. f. periphrasis, circumlocution: 1. roundabout way of speaking. 2. a roundabout phrase or expression.

perifrasear v. to periphrase: express by periphrasis or circumlocution.

perifrástico adj. periphrastic: of the nature of or involving periphrasis, circumlocutory.

perigador adj. dangerous, perilous.

perigalho s. m. thin flap of skin under the chin of very old or lean persons.

perigar v. 1. to be in danger. 2. to peril, expose to danger, put in peril.

perigeu s. m. perigee: the point in the orbit of the moon where it is nearest the earth.

periginia s. f. (bot.) the state or condition of being perigynous.

perígino adj. (bot.) perigynous: denoting stamens borne on the calyx.

perigo s. m. 1. danger, hazard, peril. 2. risk. 3. jeopardy. 4. seriousness. 5. (Braz., sl.) a seductive woman. 6. (Port.) involuntary abortion. 7. (fig.) flash of lightning.
~ **de incêndio** fire risk. **correr** ~ to run a risk or hazard. **ele está fora de** ~ he is out of danger, (coll.) out of the wood. **em** ~ **de** in peril of. **em** ~ **iminente** in imminent danger, on the top of a volcano. **estar em** ~ to be in danger. **evitar o** ~ to keep out of harm's way. **expor-se ao** ~ to expose o. s. to danger. **não há** ~ no fear. **não há** ~ **de que ele esqueça** there is no fear of his forgetting. **pôr em** ~ to put in a risk, bring into danger.

perigônio s. m. (bot.) perigone, perianth.

perigosa s. f. (Braz., pop., also **cachaça**) white rum, booze.

perigoso adj. 1. dangerous, hazardous, perilous. 2. fatal. 3. exposed to danger. ‖ **-amente** adv. dangerously.
no ponto mais ~ at the hottest.

perígrafo s. m. (anat.) perigraph: fibrous impressions on the straight muscle of the abdomen, resulting from tendinous intersections.

perilha s. f. ornament having the form of a pear.

perilinfa s. f. perilymph: the clear fluid contained within the osseous labyrinth of the ear, surrounding the membranous labyrinth.

perilo s. m. (archit.) pyramidal capital.

perimetria s. f. (geom.) perimeter: measure of a perimeter.

perimétrico adj. perimetrical: of or pertaining to a perimeter.

perímetro s. m. perimeter: 1. the circumference, border or outer boundary of a superficial figure. 2. the sum of the sides of a plane figure.

perimir v. (jur.) to annul, cancel (as an indictment).

perimísio s. m. (anat.) perimysium: the delicate sheath of connective tissue surrounding a muscle.

perineal adj. m. + f. (pl. **-ais**) perineal: of or pertaining to the perineum.

perinefrite s. f. (path.) perinephritis: inflammation of the perinephrium.

períneo s. m. (anat., also **perineu**) perineum: the region of the body between the genital organs and the rectum.

perineocele s. f. (med.) perineocele: hernia in the perineum.

perineuro s. m. (anat.) perineurium: the sheath of connective tissue surrounding a peripheral nerve.

periodicidade s. f. periodicity, periodicalness, periodic character.

periodicista s. m. + f. periodicalist: person who writes for or publishes a periodical.

periódico s. m. periodical: a publication appearing at regular intervals. ‖ adj. periodic(al): 1. of, pertaining to or of the nature of a period; cyclic. 2. happening or occurring at regular intervals of time. 3. published at regular intervals (as a magazine). ‖ **periodicamente** adv. periodically.
dízima -a (math.) periodic decimal.

periodiqueiro s. m. (depr.) person who writes for a periodical.
periodismo s. m. 1. journalism. 2. periodicalness: the state of being periodical.
periodista s. m. + f. periodicalist: person who writes for or publishes a periodical.
periodização s. f. (pl. -ões) act of dividing into periods.
periodizar v. 1. to divide into periods. 2. to produce periodically. 3. to bring into periods.
período s. m. period: 1. circuit. 2. a lapse of time. 3. age, era, epoch, series of years or days. 4. term. 5. (gram.) a complete sentence. 6. circle. ~ **de atracação** (naut.) lay days. ~ **de função** term of office. ~ **de mandato** tenure of office. ~ **de sorte** streak of luck. ~ **de trabalho noturno** swing shift. ~ **de vida** period of life. ~ **glacial** glacial period. ~ **solar** the solar period. **neste** ~ **de vida** at this stage of life. ~ **posterior** after ages. **um** ~ **de infelicidade** a run of bad luck. **um** ~ **de mau tempo** a spell of bad weather.
periodontite s. f. (path.) periodontitis: alveolar periostitis.
perioftálmico adj. periophthalmic: surrounding the eye; orbital.
periórbita s. f. (anat.) periorbita: the periosteum of the orbit of the eye.
periost(e)al adj. m. + f. (pl. -ais) periosteal: of or pertaining to the periosteum.
periosteíte s. f. (path., also **periostite, periostose**) periostitis: inflammation of the periosteum.
periósteo s. m. (anat., also **periôneo**) periosteum: a nervous, vascular membrane that surrounds and nourishes the bones.
perióstraco s. m. (zool.) periostracum.
periovular adj. m. + f. surrounding the ovule.
periparoba s. f. (Braz.) = **pariparoba**.
peripatético s. m. Peripatetic: a disciple of Aristotle. ‖ adj. Peripatetic: pertaining to the philosophy of Aristotle.
peripatetismo s. m. Peripateticism: the philosophical doctrines of Aristotle.
perípato s. m. the philosophy of the Peripatetics.
peripécia s. f. 1. peripetia: that part of a drama in which the plot is unraveled or the whole situation changes unexpectedly. 2. (fam.) an incident, an event (esp. an unexpected one).
peripiema s. m. (med.) peripyema: suppuration surrounding a part of a tooth.
períplo s. m. periplus, circumnavigation.
peripneumonia s. f. (path.) peripneumonia: inflammation of the lungs.
peripneumônico s. m. person affected with peripneumonia. ‖ adj. peripneumonic.
periproctite s. f. (path.) periproctitis: inflammation of the tissues surrounding the rectum.
peripterado adj. surrounded by a wing or thin border (fruit).
períptero s. m. (archit.) peripteros, periptery: building having a peristyle of a single range of columns.
periquitar v. to walk with the feet turned inward.
periquitinho s. m. (Braz., ornith.) lovebird.
periquito s. m. (Braz.) 1. parakeet, parrakeet: name of various species of birds of the family Psittacidae. 2. a plant of the family Amaranthaceae (Alternanthera paronichioides). 3. a topknot.
perísclos s. m. pl. (geog.) Periscii: the inhabitants of the polar circles.
periscópio s. m. periscope (as of submarines).
perispérmico adj. (bot.) perispermic: provided with or characterized by perisperm.
perispermo s. m. (bot.) perisperm: tissue surrounding the embryo sac in an ovule.
perisporângio s. m. (bot.) perispore: the outer membrane or covering of a spore.
perissístole s. f. (physiol.) perisystole.
perissodáctilo, perissodátilo s. m. (zool.) perissodacty(e): a member of the Perissodactyla.
perissodáctilos, perissodátilos s. m. pl. (zool.) Perissodactyla, an order of huge mammals: horse, tapir, rhinoceros.
perissologia s. f. perissology: needless amplification in writing or speaking.
peristalse s. f. (physiol., also **peristaltismo** m.) peristalsis: the peculiar, involuntary muscular movement of various hollow organs of the body.
peristalse s. f. (physiol., also **peristaltismo** m.) peristalsis.
perítase s. f. the complete and detailed subject of a discourse.
peristilo s. m. peristyle: a circular arrangement of columns.
perístole s. f. peristole.
perístomo s. m. peristome: 1. (bot.) the fringe of delicate hairlike appendages around the mouth of the capsule of a moss. 2. (zool.) the mouthparts in general.
peritécio s. m. (bot.) perithecium.
peritiflite s. f. (path.) perityphlitis: inflammation of the peritoneum surrounding the cecum.
perito s. m. 1. expert, skilled person. 2. specialist. 3. technician. 4. an official appraiser. 5. connoisseur. ‖ adj. 1. skilful, expert, proficient, versed. 2. dexterous, apt, adroit. 3. masterful. 4. specialist. 5. experienced. **ele é um** ~ **de gado vacum** he is a good judge of cattle. **um** ~ **de arte** an art expert.
peritoneal adj. m. + f. (pl. -ais) peritoneal: pertaining to the peritoneum.
peritônio s. m. (also **peritoneu**) (anat.) peritoneum: the serous membrane lining the abdominal walls and investing the viscera.
peritonite s. f. (path.) peritonitis: inflammation of the peritoneum.
peritríqueos s. m. pl. (zool.) Peritricha, an order of Ciliophora.
perituro adj. perishable: liable to perish, mortal.
perjurar v. to perjure: 1. forswear; make guilty of perjury. 2. bear false witness. 3. take a false oath.
perjúrio s. m. perjury: 1. false oath. 2. oath-breaking, violation of an oath.
perjuro s. m. perjurer, forswearer, oath-breaker. ‖ adj. perjuring; perjured, forsworn.
perlar v. (also **perolar**) to pearl: 1. adorn with pearls. 2. cause to resemble pearls. 3. make into or become like a pearl.
perlasso s. m. pearlash: crude potassium carbonate.
perlavar v. to purify, cleanse, clean; wash entirely.
perlenda, perlenga s. f. (pop.) idle talk, palaver, nonsense.
perleúdo adj. (depr.) well-read, erudite, learned.
perlífero adj. that produces pearls (shell).
perliquitete adj. 1. lively, spirited. 2. presumptuous, pretentious.
perlonga s. f. delay postponement.
perlongar v. 1. to lengthen, elongate. 2. to prolong, extend. 3. to delay unduly, retard. 4. to adjourn, postpone. 5. to move along. 6. to follow (the coast).
perlongo s. m. sloping side of a roof.
perlustração s. f. (pl. -ões) act of observing or examining thoroughly.
perlustrador s. m. observer, examiner. ‖ adj. observing, examining.
perlustrar v. 1. to observe, look at, look into. 2. to search, scan, scrutinize, examine thoroughly, survey.

perluxidade s. f. prolixity, prolixness.
perluxo adj. 1. prolix, diffuse, tedious. 2. presumptuous, conceited.
permanecente adj. m. + f. permanent: 1. enduring, durable, lasting, abiding, constant. 2. fixed, stable, unchangeable. ‖ ~**mente** adv. permanently.
permanecer v. 1. to stay, continue, stand. 2. to remain, endure, last. 3. to maintain. 4. to persist, persevere, insist. 5. to delay, retard. 6. to be durable.
~ **por mais tempo** to stop on. ~ **sem ser vendida (mercadoria)** to lie on one's hands (goods). **o roubo permaneceu impune** the robbery went unrequited.
permanência s. f. permanence, permanency: 1. the state of being permanent. 2. durability. 3. fixity, stability, stableness. 4. persistence, constancy. 5. stay.
permanente s. m. 1. (Braz.) a ticket or fare which grants its owner free admission during a certain length of time. 2. f. permanent wave. ‖ adj. m. + f. permanent: 1. lasting, durable, enduring, abiding, constant. 2. continuous. 3. fixed, stable, unchangeable, invariable, unchanging. 4. persistent. ‖ ~**mente** adv. permanently.
ondulação ~ permanent wave. **via** ~ permanent way.
permanganato s. m. permanganate: a dark purple salt of permanganic acid.
permangânico adj. permanganic.
ácido ~ permanganic acid.
permeabilidade s. f. permeability: the quality of being permeable.
permear v. 1. to permeate, penetrate. 2. to enter into. 3. to traverse. 4. to pierce. 5. to interpose, place between. 6. to supervene.
permeável adj. m. + f. (pl. -**áveis**) permeable, pervious, allowing passage. ‖ **permeavelmente** adv. permeably.
permeio adv. used in the adv. locution **de** ~ 1. inwardly. 2. in the middle of, among, between.
permiano s. m. Permian: 1. native or inhabitant of Perm (Russia). 2. the language. ‖ adj. Permian: of or pertaining to the city or government of Perm.
permissão s. f. (pl. -**ões**) permission: 1. allowance, permit. 2. consent, leave, licence, liberty. 3. formal authorization.
com ~ **de** by authority of.
permissível adj. m. + f. (pl. -**íveis**) permissible, admissible, allowable; licit. ‖ **permissivelmente** adv. permissibly.
permissivo adj. permissive: 1. that permits, granting permission. 2. that is permitted.
permissão s. f. (pl. -**ões**) mixture, blend, confusion.
permisto adj. mixed, blended, confused.
permitir v. to permit: 1. allow, consent. 2. empower. 3. make possible. 4. authorize, give permission. 5. let, licence. 6. admit, concede, grant. 7. tolerate, indulge.
~ **o casamento de** to give s. o. permission for marriage, give s. o. in marriage. ~ **fiança** to allow bail. **o corredor era tão baixo que não permitia ficar em pé** the corridor was so low that it did not permit of standing upright. **não lhe foi permitido ir** he was forbidden to go. **permita-me perguntar-lhe as horas** may I trouble you to tell me the time? **permita-me segurar-lhe o guarda-chuva?** may I hold the umbrella for you? **permita-me um aparte** let me get in a word. **permite-me!** allow me! **se o tempo** ~ time permitting.
permocarbonífero adj. (geol.) Permocarboniferous.
permuta s. f. 1. exchange, truck, barter; interchange. 2. transposition, substitution.

permutabilidade s. f. permutability, permutableness: the condition or character of being permutable, exchangeable or interchangeable.
permutação s. f. (pl. -**ões**) permutation: 1. the act of permuting. 2. interchange, exchange, barter. 3. (math.) linear arrangement of objects resulting from a change of their order.
permutador s. m. person who exchanges. ‖ adj. exchanging, interchanging.
permutar v. to permute: 1. exchange, interchange, truck, barter, change. 2. substitute.
permutável adj. m. + f. (pl. -**áveis**) permutable: capable of being permuted; exchangeable, interchangeable.
perna s. f. 1. leg: a) a limb of man or animal (plates C 12, 18). b) something resembling a leg. 2. branch. 3. prong, shank of an instrument (plates P 11, T 1). 4. each side of a rafter. 5. stroke of letters. 6. the foot of a pair of compasses. 7. anything that gives support (plates B 2, E 6, 7).
~ **da calça** trouser leg. **pernas de pau** (also **andas**) stilts. ~**s arqueadas**, ~**s em O** bandy legs; **de** ~**s em O** bandy-legged. ~**s em X** (knock-kneed; **de** ~**s em X** knock-kneed. ~ **torta** bowleg. ~ **traseira** hind leg (plate G 1). **barriga da** ~ calf of the leg. ~**-fina** dude, coxcomb. **com as** ~**s às costas** easily, with the greatest of ease. **dar à** ~ to walk fast. **dar às** ~**s** to take to one's heels, turn away; set up a good pair of heels. **de** ~**s cruzadas** cross-legged. **de** ~**s para o ar** upside down. **de** ~**s tortas** bowlegged. **ele deu às** ~**s** he fled, (sl.) he hared it. **estirar as** ~**s** to stretch one's legs. **passar a** ~ **em** 1. to get ahead of. 2. to trick, outwit s. o.
pernaça s. f. (pop.) a large or thick leg.
pernada s. f. 1. a kick, spurn. 2. a large or big stride. 3. (Braz.): a) a long and tiring walk. b) trip: a sudden catch, especially of the legs and the feet. 4. first strong branches of a tree.
perna-de-pau s. m. **pernas-de-pau** (Braz.) 1. (ornith.) Hudsonian curlew, jack curlew. 2. (pop.) a bad football player. 3. a wooden-legged person, peg leg, (Brit., col.) timber-toes.
perna-de-xis s. m. (pl. **pernas-de-xis**) (Braz., pop.) a bowlegged (person or animal).
pernaltas s. f. pl. (zool.) waders, wading birds.
pernalto adj. (also **pernalteiro, pernaltudo**) long-legged.
pernambucana s. f .(Braz.) a sharp pointed knife.
pernambucano s. m. (Braz.) native or inhabitant of the State of Pernambuco. ‖ adj. of or pertaining to the State of Pernambuco.
pername s. m. (Braz., pop.) (also **pernão**) a fat or thick leg.
perné s. m. (Braz.) a kind of fishing boat.
pernear v. (also **pernejar**) 1. to kick or shake one's legs. 2. to jump, leap, skip.
pernegudo adj. (Braz.) long-legged.
perneira s. f. 1. a disease which attacks the legs of oxen. 2. ~**s** pl. leggings.
perneta s. f. 1. dim. of **perna**: little or small leg. 2. m. (Braz.) one-legged person. ‖ adj. m. + f. one-legged, wooden-legged.
pernetear v. 1. to kick the legs. 2. (Braz.) to limp, hobble.
pernibambo adj. slack-legged.
pernície s. f. destruction, prejudice, ruin.
pernicioso adj. 1. pernicious, destructive, bad, noxious. 2. perverting, ruinous, malign. 3. perilous, dangerous. ‖ **-amente** adv. perniciously; dangerously.
pernicurto adj. short-legged.
pernigrande adj. m. + f. big-legged.

pernil s. m. (pl. **-is**) 1. thighbone of a quadruped. 2. ham (plate A2). 3. a thin leg.
esticar o ~ (pop.) to kick the bucket; die.
pernilongo s. m. 1. (Braz., ent.) common name of the mosquito. 2. (ornith.) European stilt. ‖ adj. long--legged.
~-rajado (ent.) yellow-fever mosquito (Aedes aegypti).
perno s. m. bolt, pin, stud.
~ central (tech.) kingbolt. **~ de manilha** clevis bolt. **~s dos moitões** (naut.) pins of the blocks.
pernoita s. f., **pernoitamento** m. (also **pernoite, pernoute**) an overnight stay.
pernoitar v. (also **pernoutar**) 1. to stay overnight, pass the night anywhere. 2. to sleep.
pernosticismo s. m. 1. presumptuousness, arrogance, insolence. 2. vainglory, bumptiousness.
pernóstico adj. (Braz., pop.) 1. presumptuous, arrogant. 2. affected, pretentious. 3. bumptious. 4. pedantic, priggish.
pernudo adj. long-legged, big-legged.
pero (ê) s. m. (pl. **peros**) pearmain: a sort of apple.
peroba s. f. 1. (bot.) peroba (Aspidosperma polyneuron). 2. (fig.) m. + f. a tiresome person. 3. (Braz., pop.) a large object. ‖ adj. m. + f. tedious, boring.
perobal s. m. (pl. **-ais**) place where peroba trees grow.
perobeação s. f. (Braz., sl.) importunity, nuisance, tediousness.
perobear v. (Braz., sl.) 1. to bore, weary. 2. to be tedious. 3. to importune.
perobinha s. f. a medicinal leguminous plant (Sweetia elegans).
pero-botelho s. m. (N. E. Braz.) the devil.
pérola s. f. 1. pearl. 2. bead. 3. a kind person. 4. dewdrop. 5. tear. 6. anything resembling a pearl. ‖ adj. of the colour of a pearl.
~ apingentada a kind of long pearl as of a drop at women's ears. **branco de ~** pearl-powder. **não deite ~s a porcos** cast not pearls before swine. **pescador de ~s** pearl-fisher.
pérola-vegetal s. f. (pl. **pérolas-vegetais**) a plant of the genus Euphorbia (Phyllantus nobilis).
peroleira s. f. a sort of earthen vessel to keep olives in.
perolífero adj. producing pearls (shells).
ostra -a pearl oyster.
perolino adj. pearl: of pearl.
perolizar v. to pearl: 1. cause to resemble pearls (in colour and shape). 2. be or become like pearls.
peroneal adj. m. + f. (pl. **-ais**) peroneal: of or pertaining to the fibula.
perônio s. m. (anat.) (also **peroneu**) fibula: the calf bone.
peroração s. f. (pl. **-ões**) peroration, epilogue: the conclusion of a discourse, poem or symphony.
perorador s. m. orator, haranguer. ‖ adj. perorating.
perorar v. to perorate: 1. make a peroration. 2. make a speech, esp. a grandiloquent one.
peroxidar v. to peroxidize: oxidize to the utmost degree.
peróxido s. m. (chem.) peroxide: an oxid having a larger proportion of oxygen than any other oxide of the same series.
perpassar v. 1. to pass by. 2. to graze, touch lightly. 3. to move. 4. to come to pass. 5. to pretermit, pass over.
perpassável adj. m. + f. (pl. **-áveis**) passable: 1. capable of being passed. 2. tolerable.
perpendicular s. f. perpendicular (line). ‖ adj. m. + f. perpendicular: said of a line being at a right angle to the plane of the horizon. ‖ **~mente** adv. perpendicularly.

perpendicularidade s. f. perpendicularity: the state of being perpendicular.
perpendículo s. m. perpendicle: plumb-line.
perpetração s. f. (pl. **-ões**) perpetration: 1. act of perpetrating. 2. act of committing an evil action. 3. an evil action.
perpetrador s. m. perpetrator: person who perpetrates. ‖ adj. perpetrating.
perpetrar v. to perpetrate: do, execute or commit (as a crime).
perpétua s. f. an everlasting (plant and flower) (Helichrysum lancifolium).
perpetuação s. f. (pl. **-ões**) (also **perpetuamento** m.) perpetuation: the act of perpetuating or making perpetual.
perpetuador s. m. perpetuator: person who perpetuates something. ‖ adj. perpetuating.
perpetuar v. 1. to perpetuate: a) cause to be continued or to endure indefinitely. b) make perpetual. 2. to immortalize, gain immortal fame. 3. to propagate. 4. to conceive. 5. **~-se**: a) to remain in the memory. b) to endure. c) to become immortal. d) to eternize.
perpétua-roxa s. f. (pl. **perpétuas-roxas**) (bot.) globe--amaranth, bachelor's-buttons.
perpetuidade s. f. perpetuity: the state or character of being perpetual; endless duration.
perpétuo adj. 1. perpetual, perennial, ceaseless, constant, continuous, continual, incessant, uninterrupted, endless. 2. eternal, immortal, everlasting. 3. unalterable, unchangeable. 4. lifelong. ‖ **perpetuamente** adv. perpetually; eternally; unalterably.
moto ~ perpetual motion.
perpianho s. m. perpend: a stone header extending through a wall so that one end appears on each side of it; perpend stone.
perplexidade s. f. (also **perplexão, perplexidez**) perplexity: 1. amazement, astonishment, confusion, bewilderment. 2. irresolution, indecision, hesitation.
perplexo adj. perplexed, uncertain, irresolute; confused, embarrassed.
deixar ~ (fig.) to knock down. **ele ficou ~** he was flabbergasted. **isso me deixa ~** that upsets me.
perquirição s. f. (pl. **-ões**) minute investigation, search or examination; search, quest, scrutiny.
perquiridor adj. investigating, scrutinizing, inquiring.
perquirir v. 1. to investigate minutely, examine, scrutinize. 2. to inquire or search into.
perquisição s. f. (pl. **-ões**), **perquisidor** adj. = **perquirição, perquiridor**.
perquisitivo adj. inquisitive, sifting.
perra s. f. bitch: the female of a dog.
perraria s. f. spite, affront, insult, outrage, spiteful taunt.
perreiro s. m. (Braz.) doorman: one who whips the dogs out of the churches.
perrengar v. (Braz.) 1. = **perrenguear**. 2. to show o. s. weak, feeble, coward or dispirited.
perrengue adj. 1. weak, feeble. 2. coward. 3. dull, stupid. 4. bad, poor, inferior. 5. loose, slack. 6. dispirited. 7. sullen, sulky. 8. lame, crippled (animal).
perrenguear v. 1. to make or become ill or sick. 2. to weaken.
perrexil s. m. (pl. **-is**) 1. (bot.) parsley. 2. appetizer: anything that excites the appetite or gives relish.
perrice s. f. 1. pertinacy, stubbornness. 2. aversion, antipathy.
perro s. m. 1. dog. 2. (depr.) rascal, vile person. ‖ adj. 1. hardy. 2. stubborn, pertinacious, dogged.
persa s. m. + f. Persian: 1. native or inhabitant of Persia. 2. the language of Persia. ‖ adj. Persian: of or pertaining to Persia.

perscrutação s. f. (pl. **-ões**) minute search or inquiry.

perscrutador s. m. observer; investigator: person who scrutinizes and searches with diligence. ‖ adj. searching, scrutinizing.

perscrutar v. 1. to search, scrutinize, scan, examine. 2. to probe, ransack, sound out, sift. 3. to investigate, inquire into. 4. to peer into the future. 5. to analize, study.

perscrutável adj. m. + f. (pl. **-áveis**) that can be investigated.

persecutório adj. demandable, demandative.

perseguição s. f. (pl. **-ões**) (also **persecução**) 1. persecution, oppression, vexation. 2. pursuit, chase, chasing. 3. castigation. 4. follow(ing).

perseguidor s. m. 1. persecutor: person who persecutes. 2. pursuer, chaser. ‖ adj. 1. persecuting. 2. pursuing, chasing, pursuant.

perseguir v. 1. to persecute: a) treat in an injurious or afflictive manner. b) harass, oppress, worry, hunt. c) annoy, importune. 2. to pursue: a) follow persistently (for seizing). b) chase, hunt. c) run after. d) follow closely.

perseidade s. f. inherency: the condition of being inherent per se (by itself).

persentir v. to feel deeply sorry for.

pérseo adj. = persa.

persevão s. m. (pl. **-ões**) footrest in a coach.

perseverança s. f. perseverance: 1. the act of persevering. 2. persistence. 3. constancy. 4. steadiness, resolution.

perseverante adj. m. + f. persevering, constant, steady, firm; diligent; tenacious; persistent. ‖ **~mente** adv. perseveringly.

perseverar v. 1. to persevere, persist, continue, go on. 2. to remain, stay. 3. to last, endure. 4. to be persistent. 5. to be constant, steadfast or unflinching.

persiana s. f. Persian blinds, persiennes, Venetian blinds (plate C 20).

persicária s. f. (bot.) persicary (Persicaria hydropiper).

persigal s. m. (pl. **-ais**) 1. hog cote, hogsty. 2. corral, barnyard. 3. pigsty, pigpen. 4. a herd of swine.

persignação s. f. (pl. **-ões**) act of one who crosses himself on the forehead, mouth and chest.

persignar-se v. to cross o. s. (making three crosses with the thumb) on the forehead, mouth and chest.

persistência s. f. 1. persistence, perseverance, constancy, permanence, steadfastness. 2. stability, firmness.

persistente adj. m. + f. 1. persistent, persisting. 2. lasting. 3. persevering, constant, firm, steady. 4. insistent, obstinate. ‖ **~mente** adv. persistently; perseveringly; insistently.

persistir v. 1. to persist, continue, persevere. 2. to insist. 3. to subsist, last, endure, remain, perdure.

persolver v. 1. to pay off, pay all. 2. to free o. s. of obligation.

personado adj. (bot.) personate, masklike.

personagem s. m. + f. (pl. **-ens**) personage: 1. a man or woman of importance or rank. 2. a role played. 3. a character (in a novel, poem or play).

persona-grata s. f. (L.) persona-grata: an acceptable person.

personalidade s. f. personality, personal existence, a person, individuality, character.

expressão da própria **~** self-expression.

personalismo s. m. personalism: 1. the character of being personal. 2. individualism.

personalização s. f. (pl. **-ões**) personalization, personalizing, personification.

personalizar v. 1. to personalize: a) personify. b) make personal. 2. to name persons. 3. to make offensive allusions.

personificação s. f. (pl. **-ões**) 1. personification, embodiment, impersonation. 2. (rhet.) prosopopoeia.

personificar v. 1. to personify: a) attribute human qualities to. b) represent (as a person), symbolize. c) be the embodiment of. d) exemplify, typify. 2. to express, manifest.

perspéctico, perspético adj. (also **perspectivo, perspetivo**) perspective: pertaining to the art of perspective.

perspectiva, perspetiva s. f. 1. perspective. 2. outlook. 3. representation or picture of objects in perspective. 4. view, prospect, vista, panorama. 5. appearance, aspect.

~ aérea aerial perspective. **~ linear** linear perspective. **cliente ou comprador em ~** prospective customer, prospective buyer. **ele tem boas ~s de êxito** he is in a fair way to succeed. **em ~** in perspective. **está em ~** it lies in prospect.

perspectivação, perspetivação s. f. (pl. **-ões**) act of putting in perspective.

perspectivar, perspetivar v. to put in perspective.

perspicácia s. f. perspicacity, perspicaciousness, acuteness of sight, quick-sightedness; discernment, astuteness, sagacity.

perspicaz adj. m. + f. perspicacious: 1. keenly discerning. 2. quick-eyed, quick-sighted, keen-sighted, sharp-sighted. 3. sagacious, astute. 4. acute, discerning. 5. penetrating, penetrant. 6. talented. ‖ **~mente** adv. perspicaciously, quick-sightedly.

perspicuidade s. f. perspicuity, transparency, clearness, distinctness, lucidity.

perspícuo adj. perspicuous, transparent, clear, lucid, distinct, manifest, obvious.

perspiração s. f. (pl. **-ões**) perspiration: sweating; the functional excretion of sweat.

perspirar v. to perspire, sweat.

perspiratório adj. (med.) perspiratory: of or pertaining to perspiration.

persuadir v. 1. to persuade; influence, convince, induce. 2. to counsel, advise. 3. **~-se:** a) to persuade o. s. b) to be convinced, persuaded or assured of.

ele o persuadiu a fazer he prevailed on him to do. **ele procura persuadi-la a gastar dinheiro** he argues her into spending money. **nós o persuadimos a escrever** we wooed him to write. **o vendedor persuadiu-a a comprar o vestido** the salesman wheedled her into buying the dress.

persuadível adj. m. + f. (pl. **-íveis**) (also **persuasível**) persuadable, persuadible.

persuasão s. f. (pl. **-ões**) (also **persuadimento** m., **persuadição** f.) 1. persuasion: act of persuading. 2. persuasiveness. 3. conviction.

persuasiva s. f. persuasive power or talent; persuasiveness.

persuasivo adj. (also **persuasível** m. + f., **persuasório, persuasor, suasivo, suasório** m.) persuasive: 1. tending to persuade. 2. persuading.

persuasor s. m. persuader: person who persuades. ‖ adj. persuading.

persuasória s. f. inducement, that which persuades; means of persuasion.

persulfato s. m. (chem.) persulphate.

persulfeto, persulfureto s. m. (chem.) persulphide, persulphid.

persulfúrico adj. (chem.) persulphuric.

pertença s. f. 1. anything pertaining or belonging to, appurtenance. 2. attribution, attribute. 3. domain. 4. accessory, part, fitting.

com suas ~s with all accessories.

pertence s. m. 1. = **pertença**. 2. (jur.) appurtenance, appendage. 3. **~s** pl.: a) belongings. b) property.

pertencente adj. m. + f. 1. pertaining, belonging. 2. proper, relating to, concerning. 3. appurtenant.

pertencer v. 1. to pertain, appertain, belong to, be owned by. 2. to relate to, concern, be due to. 3. to be fitting to. 4. to be one's duty. 5. to be pertinent to.
este livro me pertence this book belongs to me, this book is mine. **ele pertence ao grupo de rapazes** he is among the boys.

pértiga s. f., **pértigo** m. long stick, pole, perch.

pertinácia s. f. pertinacity, pertinaciousness, obstinateness, obstinacy, stubbornness.

pertinaz adj. m. + f. pertinacious: 1. unyielding, persistent, tenacious, dogged. 2. obstinate, stubborn. ‖ ~mente adv. pertinaciously.

pertinência s. f. 1. pertinence, pertinency. 2. appurtenance.

pertinente adj. m. + f. pertinent.

perto adj. near, close, not distant, toward, proximate. ‖ adv. 1. near(by), close(-by). 2. nearly, towardly. 3. about, almost. 4. nigh.
~ **da casa** near the house. ~ **da igreja** near the church. ~ **de** near, by, beside, nearly, closely, at hand (plate P 18). ~ **de vinte homens** about twenty men. **chegue mais** ~ **de mim** come nearer to me. **conhecer alguém de** ~ to know s. o. thoroughly. **de** ~ nearly, at hand, closely. **ela veio** ~ **das seis horas** she came at about six o'clock. **ele mora aqui** ~ he lives near here. **estar** ~ **de alguém** to be near s. o., be within call. **eu estava justamente** ~ **dela** I was just up her way. **ficar** ~ **de** to stick close to. **muito** ~ next, close by.

pertos s. m. pl. close-ups.

pertransido adj. pierced through.

perturbação s. f. (pl. **-ões**) 1. perturbation, perturbance, commotion, trouble, disturbance. 2. disorder, confusion, disarrangement. 3. unquietness, disquiet. 4. mental uneasiness. 5. dizziness. 6. jitters, agitation.

perturbado adj. 1. perturbed, upset, troubled. 2. embarrassed. 3. unquiet, restless. 4. uneasy.
fiquei ~ **com o barulho** I was thrown out by the noise.

perturbador s. m. 1. perturbator, disturber, disquieter. 2. troubler; rioter. ‖ adj. 1. disturbing, perturbing. 2. turbulent. 3. troublesome. 4. irritating.

perturbar v. 1. to perturb: a) disturb, molest. b) disquiet, agitate. c) confuse, put into confusion. d) disorder, disconcert, disarrange. e) upset. 2. to embarras, worry, trouble, vex. 3. to put out of countenance. 4. to stun, daze. 5. ~-se: a) to be or become disordered, disquiet, troubled or confused, feel uneasy. b) to get mixed up or tangled. c) to be puzzled. d) to inconvenience o. s.
~ **o sossego** to disturb the peace. **ele o perturbou com o seu olhar** he stared him out of countenance. **esta fatalidade lhe perturbou a mente** this misfortune has sent him out of his mind. **isto não me perturba** I am not bothered about it.

perturbativo adj. perturbative, perturbing, disturbing.

perturbatório adj. 1. = **perturbativo**. 2. oscillatory.

perturbável adj. m. + f. (pl. **-áveis**) perturbable: capable of being perturbed, agitated or disquieted.

pertuso adj. (bot.) pertuse: having holes or slits, as a leaf.

peru s. m. 1. turkey, turkey cock (Meleagris gallopavo). 2. (coll.) kibitzer. 3. a large embarkation.
~ **novo (pequenino)** turkey poult.

perua s. f. 1. turkey hen. 2. (mot.) station wagon. 3. (pop.) drunkenness. 4. (Braz., sl.) prostitute, harlot.

peruano s. m. (also **peruviano**) Peruvian: native or inhabitant of Peru. ‖ adj. Peruvian.

peruar v. 1. to kibitz (in a game). 2. to woo.

peruca s. f. wig, periwig, peruke (plate P 8).

peru-de-festa s. m. (pl. **perus-de-festa**) (fam.) social butterfly, a person fond of parties.

peru-do-mato s. m. (pl. **perus-do-mato**) (ornith.) piping guan.

pérula s. f. (bot.) perule: a scale (as of a leaf bud).

peruruca s. f. (Braz.) a variety of Indian corn.

pervagante adj. m. + f. 1. roving, wandering. 2. travelling. 3. crossing.

pervagar v. 1. to traverse, travel all over. 2. to cross. 3. to roam, wander.

pervencer v. to overpower, subdue; (sl.) floor.

perversão s. f. (pl. **-ões**) perversion, corruption, depravity, depravation.

perversidade s. f. perversity, perverseness, depravation, wickedness; ferociousness, atrocity.

perversivo adj. perversive, perverting; corruptible.

perverso adj. 1. perverse, wicked, bad. 2. evil, devilish. 3. feral, brutal. 4. vicious, corrupted, malicious. ‖ **-amente** adv. 1. perversely; badly. 2. treacherously.

perversor, pervertedor s. m. perverter, corrupter. ‖ adj. perverting, perversive.

perverter v. 1. to pervert: a) make perverse, mislead, lead astray. b) alter the worth. c) misrepresent, distort. d) corrupt, deprave, pervert, e) adulterate, falsify. 2. to overturn, disturb. 3. to disparage, minimize. 4. ~-se: a) to become perverted or corrupt. b) to demoralize o. s.

pervertido adj. 1. perverted, corrupt, depraved, wry. 2. demoralized. ‖ **-amente** adv. pervertedly, wry.

pervicácia s. f. pertinacity, obstinacy.

pervicaz adj. m. + f. pertinacious, obstinate, stubborn, positive.

pervígil s. m. + f. (pl. **-eis**) vigilant person.

pervinca s. f. (bot.) periwinkle (Vinca disformis).

pérvio adj. 1. pervious, permeable, open. 2. passable. 3. frank, sincere. 4. patent.

pesa-álcool s. m. (pl. **pesa-álcools**) alcoholometer.

pesa-cartas s. m., sg. + pl. letter-balance, letter-weight.

pesada s. f. that which is weighed at one time.

pesadão adj. (pl. **-ões**) (f. **-ona**) 1. very weighty or heavy. 2. slouch, awkward, slow-moving (said of heavy persons).

pesadelo s. m. 1. nightmare. 2. (fig.) a troublesome fellow; a bore, an impertinent person.
o ~ **da pobreza** the pinch of poverty.

pesado adj. 1. weighty, heavy (plate Q). 2. hard, troublesome. 3. laborious, difficult, onerous. 4. molestful. 5. irksome, boresome, tedious. 6. slow, sluggish, slow-moving; ungainly. 7. coarse, rough, rude. 8. offensive, insulting, injurious. 9. muggy (weather). 10. (Braz., sl.) unlucky, luckless, out of luck. ‖ **-amente** adv. heavily; slowly; soundly.
chuva -a fast rain. **de andar** ~ heavy-gaited. **dizer palavras -as a alguém** to speak hard to one. **dormir -amente** to sleep soundly. **peso** ~ (sport) heavy-weight. **sono** ~ heavy or sound sleep. **trabalho** ~ hard work.

pesador s. m. weigher: one who or that which weighs. ‖ adj. weighing.

pesadume s. m. 1. heaviness, weight. 2. sourness, bitterness. 3. sorrow, trouble. 4. ill will, grudge.

pesagem s. f. (pl. **-ens**) 1. weighing, weighage. 2. (turf) weighing-in place.

pesa-leite s. m. (pl. **pesa-leites**) milk gauge, lactometer.

pesa-licores s. m., sg. + pl. alcoholometer.

pêsames s. m. pl. (also **pêsame**) condolences, condolement, condoling.
dar os ~ **a** to condole with. **dei-lhe os** ~ **pela morte**

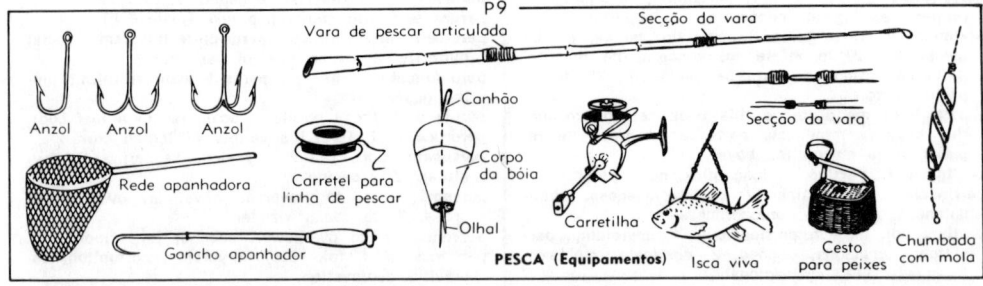

Vara de pescar articulada — P9 — Secção da vara

Anzol   Anzol   Anzol

Rede apanhadora

Canhão

Carretel para linha de pescar

Corpo da bóia

Olhal

Carretilha

Secção da vara

Gancho apanhador

PESCA (Equipamentos)   Isca viva

Cesto para peixes

Chumbada com mola

de seu pai I expressed my condolence with her (him) on the death of her (his) father.

pesar s. m. sorrow, regret, grief; sadness. ‖ v. 1. to weigh, poise, balance. 2. to scrutinize, examine. 3. to consider, ponder. 4. to influence. 5. to grieve, cause sorrow. 6. ~-se: a) to poise o. s. b) to be sorry. c) to feel sorry for, condole with.
~ as suas palavras to weigh one's words. ~ (o jóquei) antes (depois) de uma corrida (racing) to weigh in (out). apesar dos ~es notwithstanding. com grande ~ with great grief or sorrow. ele pesa-me muito no bolso he is a great drain on my means. para ~ nosso to our regret. quanto pesa isto? how much does it weigh? ~ sobre to hang on. o vitelo pesa 56 kg the calf scales 56 kg.

pesaroso adj. 1. sorrowful, grievous, sorry. 2. condoling. 3. mournful, sad. 4. unhappy. 5. rueful. ‖ -amente adv. sorrowfully; condolingly; mournfully.

pesca s. f. 1. fishing, fishery (plate P 9). 2. quantity of fish caught. 3. (fig.) search, investigation, examination.
~ com isca de minhoca worm-fishing. ~ da truta trout-fishing. ~ de baleia whale-fishing. vara de ~ fishing rod. andar à ~ (fig.) to angle or fish for. aparelho de ~ fishing tackle.

pescada s. f. a codlike fish; hake, sea luce.

pescada-polacha s. f. (ichth.) (pl. **pescadas-polacha**) pollack, pollock.

pescada-preta s. f. (pl. **pescadas-pretas**) (ichth.) black-fish.

pescadaria s. f. fish market.

pescadinha s. f. a weakfish (genus Cynoscion).

pescado s. m. 1. quantity of fish caught. 2. any eatable fish.

pescador s. m. fisherman, fisher (plate P 17). ‖ adj. fishing.
~ de bacalhau banker. ~ de ostras dredger. ~ de pérolas pearl-fisher.

pescadora s. f. fisherwoman.

pesca-em-pé s. m., sg. + pl. (Braz., ornith.) lesser yellowlegs.

pescar v. 1. to fish, catch fish; net, entrap, ensnare, bag (fish). 2. to work as a fisher. 3. to catch, seize. 4. to obtain by cunning. 5. to perceive, see, understand. 6. to have some knowledge of. 7. to hit, strike. 8. to sound, investigate, discover. 9. to cheat (at examinations). 10. to nap, nod.
~ com isca viva to live-bait. ~ elogios to fish compliments. ~ em águas turvas to fish in troubled water. ~ ostras to dredge. ~ pérolas to pearl. ela o pescou she hooked him. ele não pesca nada de latim he does not understand a word in Latin. o rio é bom para ~ the river fishes well. vamos ~ let's go fishing, (coll.) let's have a fish.

pescaria s. f. 1. fishery, fishing. 2. fish trade, fishing industry. 3. a great quantity of fish.

pescoçada s. f., **pescoção** (pl. -ões) m. 1. a blow on the neck. 2. a slap.

pescoceador s. m. horse that tosses its head. ‖ adj. = pescoceiro.

pescocear v. 1. to toss the head rapidly (horse). 2. to go back on one's obligations.

pescoceiro adj. (also **pescoceador**) 1. given to tossing its head (horse). 2. going back on his obligations.

pescocinho s. m. 1. a small neck. 2. a collar (as of a clergyman).

pescoço s. m. 1. neck; throat (plates C 12, H). 2. nape. 3. bottleneck.
pôr no ~ to put around the neck. ~ de cervo ewe neck (horse) (plate C 12). ~ de cisne swan-neck (plate C 12). ~ taurino bullneck (plate C 12). ele pegou-o pelo ~ he got him by his throat.

pescoçudo adj. thick-necked, long-necked.

pés-de-lebre s. m. pl. switches: the movable sections of railroad tracks.

pesebre s. m. a manger, crib, cratch or rack for cattle, horses.

pesepelo, pês e pelo adv. barefoot.

peseta s. f. Spanish silver coin.

pesga (ê) s. f. a covering or lining with pitch (the inside of jars).

pesgar v. to cover or line with pitch (the inside of wine jars).

peso (ê) s. m. (pl. **pesos**) 1. weight: a) heaviness. b) piece of metal used to weigh. c) gravity. d) ponderousness. e) a particular standard or system for weighing. f) pressure load. g) oppression, onus, burden. h) (fig.) importance, power, influence. i) (sport) iron ball to be thrown (plate G 3). 2. peso (coin). 3. (Braz., sl.) bad luck.
~ atômico atomic weight. ~ bruto gross weight. ~ de relógio clock weight (plate R 4). ~ líquiao neat or net weight. ~ normal standard weight. ~ para segurar papéis letter-weight. ~s e medidas weights and measures. arremesso de ~ (sport) putting the weight. ele é um grande ~ para ela he is a drag on her. em ~ entire; in a body. homem de ~ man of importance.

peso-galo s. m. (pl. **pesos-galo**) (box) bantamweight (up to 53.45 kg).

peso-leve s. m. (pl. **pesos-leves**) (box) lightweight (up to 61.15 kg).

peso-médio s. m. (pl. **pesos-médios**) (box) middle-weight (up to 72.48 kg).

peso-meio-médio s. m. (pl. **pesos-meio-médios**) (box) light middleweight (up to 66.59 kg).

peso-meio-pesado s. m. (pl. **pesos-meio-pesados**) (box) light heavyweight (up to 79.27 kg).

peso-mosca s. m. (pl. **pesos-mosca**) (box) flyweight (up to 50.74 kg).

peso-pena s. m. (pl. **pesos-pena**) (box) featherweight (up to 57.08 kg).

peso-pesado s. m. (pl. **pesos-pesados**) (box) heavy-weight (above 79.27 kg).

pespegar v. 1. to strike, hit. 2. to impose, apply, lay on. 3. ~-**se** to fix; settle; spread.

pespego (ê) s. m. (pl. **pespegos**) impediment, encumbrance, hindrance, obstacle, difficulty.

pespontar, pespontear v. 1. backstitch, quilt, stitch. 2. to presume, suppose.

pesponto s. m. quilting stitch, backstitch.

pesporrência s. f. haughtiness.

pesqueira s. f. 1. place for fishing. 2. fishing gear, fishing tackle.

pesqueiro s. m. 1. fish hatchery. 2. fishing ground. 3. line and hook for fishing. **estragar o** ~ to upset.

pesquisa s. f. 1. search, inquiry, examination, diligence, investigation. 2. sounding. 3. (min.) prospecting. ~ **de mercado** market research. **ele se ocupa com** ~**s** he is engaged in researches.

pesquisador s. m. searcher, examiner, inquirer, investigator, researcher. ‖ adj. searching, examining, investigating.

pesquisar v. 1. to search, inquire, examine, scrutinize. 2. to investigate. 3. to inquire about. 4. to research.

pessário s. m. (med.) pessary: 1. instrument introduced into the vagina, to support the uterus, in cases of prolapsus. 2. diaphragm, a contraceptive device.

pessegada s. f. peach preserves.

pessegal s. m. (pl. -**ais**) peachery, peach grove: a place where peach-trees are cultivated.

pêssego s. m. peach: the fruit of the peach-tree.

pessegueiro s. m. peach-tree (Prunus persica).

pessegueiro-da-índia s. m. (pl. **pessegueiros-da-índia**) (bot.) amaga.

pessimismo s. m. pessimism: a disposition to take a gloomy view of affairs.

pessimista s. m. + f. pessimist: 1. adherent of the doctrine of pessimism. 2. person who exaggerates the evils of life. ‖ adj. pessimistic: pertaining to, characterized by, or of the nature of pessimism.

péssimo adj. (abs. of **mau**) very bad. ‖ **pessimamente** adv. very badly, detestably.

pessoa s. f. person: 1. individual, personage, human being. 2. individuality. 3. (gram.) one of the three relations of the subject or object. 4. ~**s** pl. people. ~ **importante** important person, a great gun. **jurídica** artificial person. ~ **maleável** wax in one's hand (person). ~ **sem importância** person of no importance, a nobody. **aparecer em** ~ to appear in person. **boa** ~ a good person, a good egg. **é o diabo em** ~ he (or that) is the very devil. **em** ~ in person, personally. **qualquer** ~ **que seja** whosoever. **as três** ~**s da Santíssima Trindade** the three persons of the blessed Trinity. **uma** ~ **sensata** a matter-of-fact person. **vossa real** ~ your royal self.

pessoal s. m. 1. personnel: persons collectively, esp. employees, workers; staff. 2. folks. ‖ adj. m. + f. (pl. -**ais**) personal: of or pertaining to a particular person; not general or public, private, individual. ‖ ~**mente** adv. personaly, individually, in person. **alusões -ais** personal remarks. **pronome** ~ personal pronoun. **seção do** ~ personnel department. **tornar-se** ~ to make personal remarks.

pessoalidade s. f. personality, individuality.

pessoalizar v. to personalize, personify.

pessoalizável adj. m. + f. (pl. -**áveis**) capable of being personified.

pessoeiro s. m. (obs.) chief of a family.

pestana s. f. 1. eyelash (plate O). 2. flap of a garment. 3. vegetation along a river bank. 4. (mus.) nut (of a string instrument) (plate V 5). **queimar as** ~**s** to fag at one's book (at study). **tirar uma** ~ to nap, snooze.

pestanejante adj. m. + f. twinkling, winking (with the eyes).

pestanejar v. (also **pestanejar**) 1. to twinkle, wink (with the eyes). 2. to blink. 3. to scintillate (stars). **sem** ~ without wincing; without turning a hair.

pestanejo s. m. 1. twinkling, winking. 2. blink.

pestanudo adj. that has great eyelashes.

peste s. f. 1. plague, pest: a) a violent epidemic pestilence. b) pestilential disease. c) a pernicious or vexatious person or thing; bane. 2. ill smell. 3. a vile person. ~ **bovina** rinderpest, cattle plague. ~ **bubônica** bubonic plague. **este garoto é uma** ~ this boy is a devil. **marca de** ~ plague spot.

pestear v. 1. to plague, visit with plague. 2. to contaminate. 3. to be infected with a plague (animals).

pesteira s. f. (S. Braz.) disease, chronic ailment.

pestífero s. m. person affected with plague. ‖ adj. pestiferous: 1. carrying pestilence. 2. pernicious, malign.

pestilença, pestilência s. f. 1. pestilence, plague, pest. 2. contagion.

pestilencial (pl. -**ais**), **pestilente** adj. m. + f., **pestilencioso, pestilento** m. pestilent, pestilential; pernicious, baneful.

pestilo s. m. 1. knocker of a door. 2. latch of a door.

pestoso s. m. person affected with plague (esp. the bubonic plague). ‖ adj. pestiferous.

peta (ê) s. f. 1. lie, story, humbug, fib. 2. the part that juts out like a little hatchet on a pruning-hook. 3. a spot in a horse's eye. **pregar uma** ~ to tell a lie.

pétala s. f. petal: each leaf of a corolla.

petalado adj. petal(l)ed, petalous: provided with a petal or petals.

petalhada s. f. a lot of lies.

petaliforme adj. m. + f. (bot.) petaliform, petaline, shaped like a petal.

petalino adj. petaline: 1. of or pertaining to a petal. 2. petaliform, shaped like a petal.

Petalismo s. m. petalism: a form of banishment by public vote in ancient Syracuse, with olive leaves for ballots.

petalita s. f. (min.) petalite.

petalóide adj. m. + f. (bot.) petaloid: like or consisting of petals.

petalomania s. f. (bot.) petalody, petalomania: a condition frequent in flowers, in which other organs assume the appearance of petals.

petar (I) v. to fib, lie, prevaricate.

petar (II) v. to part into smal bits.

petardar, petardear v. to blow up with a petard.

petardeiro s. m. (obs.) petardeer, petardier: 1. person who makes petards. 2. soldier who employs petards.

petardo s. m. 1. petard. 2. bomb.

peteca s. f. (Braz.) 1. a sort of shuttlecock: a leather pad stuck with feathers; it is struck with the palm of the hand. 2. laughing-stock; plaything.

petecada s. f. a blow with the open hand to send off the **peteca**.

petecar v. to adorn or dress up exaggeratedly.

petegar v. to cut with a pruning-knife.

peteiro s. m. liar, fibber, shuffler. ‖ adj. lying, untruthful.

peteleca s. f. a hard slap in the face.

peteleco s. m. (Braz.) 1. slap, rap. 2. ear-pulling. 3. thrashing.

petequear v. (Braz.) to play with a **peteca**.

petequial adj. m. + f. (pl. **-ais**) petechial: of the nature of petechiae or livid spots.

petéquias s. f. pl. (med.) petechiae, livid spots.

petição s. f. (pl. **-ões**) 1. petition, request, solicitation, suit, appeal. 2. entreaty. 3. formal petition, petitionary letter. 4. supplication.
　dirigir uma ~ a alguém to make an application to s. o. **ele fez uma ~ para...** he made an appeal to...

peticego s. m. very shortsighted person. ‖ adj. near-sighted, very shortsighted.

peticionar v. to petition, present a petition to.

peticionário s. m. petitioner, applicant.

petiço s. m. (S. Braz.) (dim.: **petiçote**) 1. pony: a very small horse. 2. a small person.

petigris s. m. gray squirrel.

petimetre s. m. dandy, beau, fop, petit-maître. ‖ adj. dandyish, foppish.

petinga s. f. 1. a small fish. 2. a small fish used as a bait.

petinho s. m. a bird of the genus Turdus (Turdus iliacus).

petintal s. m. (pl. **-ais**) 1. shipbuilder, shipwright. 2. calker.

petipé s. m. 1. scale. 2. measuring scale. 3. map--scale.

petisca s. f. a boyish play; it consists in throwing pebbles at a coin; the boy who hits it is the winner.

petiscador s. m. nibbler, dainty feeder, dainty person. ‖ adj. nibbling, fond of dainties.

petiscar v. 1. to nibble, pick at food. 2. to taste, eat without appetite. 3. to eat dainties or tidbits. 4. to smatter. 5. to strike fire.

petisco s. m. 1. tidbit, dainty, morsel, delicacy. 2. steel, flint and tinder. 3. (fig.) ridiculous person.

petisqueira s. f. 1. tidbit, delicacy. 2. = **petisqueiro**.

petisqueiro s. m. cupboard, food closet.

petisquice s. f. (fam.) choiceness.

petisseco adj. (pop.) 1. withered, wilted. 2. half-dry, parched (trees). 3. stunted, wizened.

petitório s. m. petition. ‖ adj. 1. petitionary: of or pertaining to a petition. 2. (jur.) petitory: claiming the property of a thing.

petiz s. m. boy, child. ‖ adj. little, small.

petizada s. f. kids, boys (collectively), the little ones.

peto (I) s. m. used in the adv. locution **de ~** purposely, on purpose.

peto (ê) (II) s. m. 1. (ornith.) woodpecker. 2. (obs.) tobacco.

peto (ê) (III) adj. 1. cross-eyed. 2. tedious, boring.

peto-galego s. m. (pl. **petos-galegos**) (ornith.) lesser spotted woodpecker.

peto-malhado s. m. (pl. **petos-malhados**) (ornith.) great spotted woodpecker.

peto-verde s. m. (pl. **petos-verdes**) (ornith.) green woodpecker.

petrechar v. to furnish, provide, equip, prepare, supply.

petrechos s. m. pl. 1. ammunition. 2. equipment, accoutrement, gear. 3. tools, implements. 4. supplies.

petrel s. m. (pl. **-éis**) (ornith.) petrel.

pétreo adj. 1. rockey, stony, petrous. 2. insensible. 3. inhuman.

petrificação s. f. (pl. **-ões**) 1. petrification. 2. silicification.

petrificador adj. petrifying.

petrificar v. 1. to petrify: a) change to stone. b) (fig.) shock, dumbfound, paralyze. 2. **~-se** to

become petrified: a) turn into stone, become stony. b) be or become shocked, stunned.

petrífico adj. petrific, petrifying.

petrina s. f. 1. chest. 2. waist. 3. belt.

petrografia s. f. petrography: the study of rocks.

petrográfico adj. petrographic(al): of or pertaining to petrography.

petrolaria s. f. oil refinery.

petroleiro s. m. 1. (naut.) tanker. 2. pétroleur. ‖ adj. petrolic, of or pertaining to petroleum.

petróleo s. m. petroleum, coal oil.

petrolífero adj. petroliferous, bearing oil.
　campo ~ oil-field. **poço ~** oil-well.

petrologia s. f. (geol.) petrology: the science of the origin, structure, constitution and characteristics of rocks.

petrológico adj. petrologic: of or pertaining to petrology.

petrologista s. m. + f., **petrólogo** m. petrologist.

petromizonte s. m. (zool.) petromyzont, a cyclostome of the family Petromyzontidae: the lamprey.

petrópolis s. m., sg. + pl. (Braz., sl.) heavy walking--stick.

petropolitano s. m. (Braz.) native or inhabitant of the city of Petrópolis. ‖ adj. of or pertaining to the city of Petrópolis.

petroso adj. = **pétreo.**

petulância s. f. petulance, insolence, sauciness, forwardness, immodesty.

petulante adj. m. + f. 1. petulant, saucy, forward, pert, fretful, insolent, flippant. 2. shameless, brazen(-faced). ‖ **~mente** adv. petulantly.

petúnia s. f. (bot.) petunia.

peucédano s. m. (bot.) brimstone, sow fennel, hog's fennel (Peucedano officinale).

peúga s. f. 1. buskin: a) half-boot. b) cothurnus. 2. sock, anklet (plate R 6).

peugada s. f. 1. track, footprint. 2. vestige, sign, trace, trail.

peúva s. f. (bot.) trumpetbush (Tecoma speciosa).

peuvação s. f. (pl. **-ões**) (N. Braz.) irksome task, tedious talk.

pevide s. f. 1. kernel (of an apple, orange, melon). 2. pip (a disease in fowls). 3. (sl.) rum.

pevidoso adj. full of kernels.

pevitada s. f. crushed kernels.

pexorim s. m. (pl. **-ins**) (Braz.) = **pixurim.**

pexotada s. f. bad playing, bungle, clumsy performance, a botch.

pexote s. m. 1. bad gambler or player. 2. novice, beginner, tyro. 3. bungler: a clumsy or awkward workman. 4. simpleton, ignorant person.

pez s. m. 1. pitch, resin, rosin. 2. tar, bitumen, asphalt.
　untar com ~ to cover with pitch.

pez-de-borgonha s. m., sg. + pl. Burgundy pitch.

pezenho adj. pitchy, pitch-coloured.

pezudo adj. big-footed.

pezunho s. m. 1. pig's foot. 2. large foot.

phot s. m. (phys.) phot, the cgs unit of illumination.

pia s. f. 1. kitchen sink, lavatory basin, wash basin, (plate E 3). 2. (naut.) keelson.
　~ batismal baptismal font.

piá s. m. (Braz.) 1. a young Indian. 2. a half-bred lad. 3. boy from the country.

piã s. m. (med.) yaws, pian.

piaba s. f. (Braz.) 1. (also **piava**) a small freshwater fish (Leporinos copelandi). 2. a thing of no importance, trifle.

piabar v. 1. not to risk much. 2. to wager but little. 3. to borrow money in a game.

piaçá, piaçaba s. f. (Braz.) 1. piassava palm (Attalea funifera). 2. a brush made with piassava fibers.

P 10

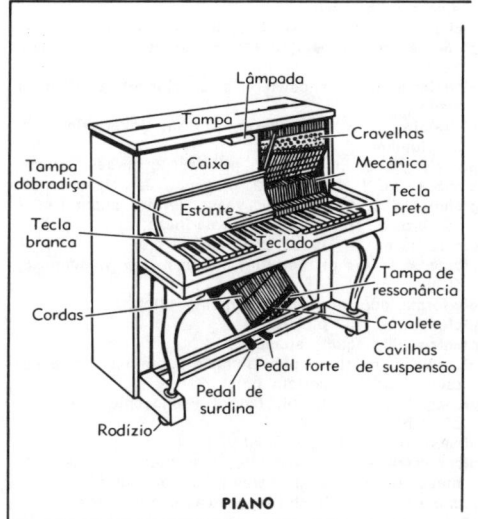

PIANO

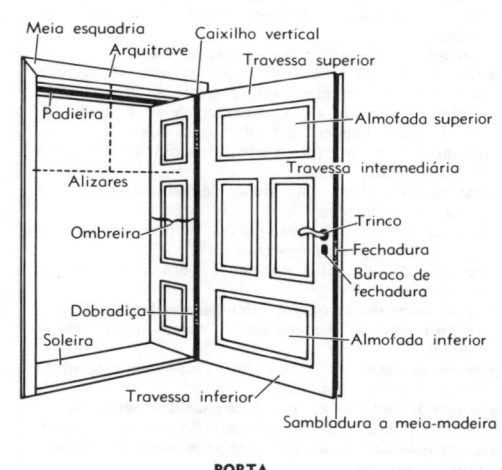

PORTA

piaçabal s. m. (pl. -ais) (Braz.) place where piassava palms grow.

piaçoca s. f. (Braz., ornith.) jaçana (Parra jacana).

piacular adj. m. + f. (obs.) piaculus, expiatory.

pláculo s. m. (obs.) expiatory or propitiatory sacrifice.

piada s. f. 1. peep, chirp, bird call, whistle. 2. anecdote; joke, quip, gag; jeer, jest.
~ **batida** Joe Miller. **isto é** ~**!** you are joking! **uma boa** ~ a delicious joke. **uma** ~ **estrondante** a capital joke. **uma** ~ **forte** a spicy joke.

piadeira s. f. the yellow-billed teal (Nettion flavirostre).

piadeiro s. m. (ornith.) wryneck (Yunz torquilla).

piadinha s. f. (pop.) a little joke.

piadista s. m. + f. wisecracker, jester. || adj. jocose, jocular.

piado s. m. peep, chirp, bird call.

pia-máter s. f. (pl. **pias-máter**) (anat.) pia mater: the delicate inner vascular membrane that covers the brain and spinal cord.

piançar v. (Braz.) to crave, yearn, long for.

pianino s. m. pianette, a little piano.

pianíssimo adj. (mus.) pianissimo, very soft.

pianista s. m. + f. pianist: person who plays on the pianoforte; piano player.

pianística s. f. art of playing piano.

pianístico adj. pianistic; of or pertaining to a piano.

piano s. m. 1. piano, pianoforte (plate P 10). 2. a pianist. || adv. (mus.) piano: softly, with slight force. ~ **de cauda** grand piano. ~ **vertical**, ~ **de armário** upright piano. **ao** ~ at (on) the piano. **recital de** ~ piano recital. **tocar** ~ to play the piano.

pianola s. f. pianola: 1. mechanical piano player. 2. piano played by such apparatus.

pião s. m. (pl. -ões) 1. top (toy). 2. a sort of pull candy.
fazer virar o ~ to spin a top. **girar como um** ~ to spin like a teetotum.

pia-pouco s. m., sg. + pl. (Braz., ornith.) the red--billed toucan.

piar s. m. a chirp, peep. || v. to peep (like a chicken), chirp, whistle, cheep.

piara s. f. 1. multitude. 2. band, gang. 3. herd, drove.

piastra s. f. piaster, piastre (coin).

piau s. m. (Braz., coll., pop.) fraud, swindle, trick.

piauiense s. m. + f. (Braz.) native or inhabitant of the State of Piauí. || adj. of or pertaining to the State of Piauí.

piava s. f. (Braz.) = **piaba**.

pica s. f. 1. ancient lance; pike. 2. (sl.) the penis. 3. (Port.) injection.

picaço adj. (Braz.) said of a dark horse that has a white face and white feet.

picada s. f. 1. (also **picadela, picadura**): a) sting (as of a bee). b) bite (of an insect). c) peck (with the beak). d) prick (of a pin or needle). e) puncture (as of an epidermic needle). 2. (Braz.) a narrow trail in a forest. 3. peak, summit. 4. dive (plane).
~ **de pulga** fleabite.

picadão s. m. (pl. -ões) (Braz.) a large trail in a forest.

picadeira s. f. 1. pickaxe. 2. brick hammer.

picadeiro s. m. 1. a riding-school. 2. circus ring. 3. (naut.) stocks upon which the keel of a ship is laid during building.

picadinho s. m. minced meat, hash. || adj. touchy, easily offended or hurt.

picado s. m. 1. minced meat, hash. 2. hopping dance. || adj. 1. pricked. 2. pinked (like cloth). 3. punctured. 4. choppy (sea). 5. sourish. 6. minced, like meat. 7. piqued, hurt.

picador s. m. 1. riding-master, horse-master. 2. (bullfighting) picador. 3. a ticket punch. 4. pricker. 5. person who opens a trail through a forest. || adj. pricking, stinging, piercing.

pica-flor s. m. (pl. **pica-flores**) (ornith.) colibri.

pica-folhas s. f. (pl. **pica-folhas**) (bot.) holly.

pica-fumo s. m. (pl. **pica-fumos**) (Braz., sl.) 1. a coarse pocketknife. 2. a miser. || adj. avaricious.

picamento s. m. act of stinging, pricking, pecking.

pica-milhos s. m., sg. + pl. 1. a seller of corn bread. 2. person fond of corn bread. 3. (fig.) vulgar person.

picana s. f. oxgoad.

picancilho s. m. (ornith.) 1. lesser spotted woodpecker. 2. tree creeper.

picanço s. m. (ornith.) 1. woodchat. 2. great spotted woodpecker.

picante s. m. whet, appetizer; a stimulant of appetite. ‖ adj. m. + f. 1. appetizing. 2. piquant, pungent (taste). 3. (fig.): a) biting, sharp, bitter, caustic, tart. b) piercing, pricking, stinging. c) malicious, spiteful.
anedota ~ a risky joke, a risqué story.

picão s. m. (pl. **-ões**) 1. pick: a sort of pointed hammer used in stonecutting (plate M 6). 2. pick, pickaxe (plate E 4). 3. weeding hoe. 4. goad. 5. (Braz., bot.) beggar-ticks (Bidens pilous).

picão-branco s. m. (pl. **picões-brancos**) (Braz., bot.) French weed.

picão-da-praia s. m. (pl. **picões-da-praia**) (Braz., bot.) sheep bur, Paraguay bur.

pica-osso s. m. (pl. **pica-ossos**) (ornith.) cinereous vulture (Aegypius monachus).

pica-pau s. m. (pl. **pica-paus**) (Braz., ornith.) a woodpecker.

pica-pau-amarelo s. m. (pl. **pica-paus-amarelos**) (Braz., ornith.) yellow woodpecker (Crocomorphus flavus flavus).

pica-pau-cinzento s. m. (pl. **pica-paus-cinzentos**) (Braz., ornith.) nut-hatch.

pica-pau-dourado s. m. (pl. **pica-paus-dourados**) (Braz., ornith.) flicker, yellow hammer (Piculus aurulentus).

pica-pau-pequeno s. m. (pl. **pica-paus-pequenos**) (Braz., ornith.) piculet.

pica-peixe s. m. (pl. **pica-peixes**) (ornith.) a kingfisher.

pica-ponto s. m. (pl. **pica-pontos**) a sort of awl.

picar v. 1. to sting, (as a bee). 2. to bite. 3. to prick, pierce with a pin; puncture, needle. 4. to peck. 5. to bite (the fish at the bait). 6. to mince meat, hash, chop. 7. to goad, spur, prick, stimulate, incite, excite, animate, stir. 8. to molest, annoy. 9. to provoke, tease, exasperate. 10. to punch. 11. to perforate. 12. to reduce to pieces. 13. to raise (prices). 14. to dive (plane). 15. to become sour (as a wine). 16. **~-se:** a) to take offence, feel hurt, be offended; be angry. b) to prick o. s.
~ o cavalo to clap spurs to the horse.

picarço adj. (pop.) grizzly, gray-coloured.

picardia s. f. 1. knavery, rascality, crookedness, roguery. 2. meanness, baseness. 3. maliciousness. 4. foolish stubbornness.

picardo s. m. Picard: 1. a Frenchman of Picardy. 2. the Picard dialect. ‖ adj. Picard: of Picardy.

picaresco adj. 1. burlesque, incongruous. 2. comic(al), funny, jocose. 3. ridiculous, farcical.

picareta s. f. 1. pick, pickax(e), pick mattock (plate E 4). 2. (fig.) straw hat. 3. (Braz., sl.) chiseler.

picaretagem s. f. (Braz., sl.) chiseling; cheating or swindling.

picaria s. f. 1. horsemanship, equestrian art. 2. riding-school.

pícaro adj. 1. cunning, artful, astute. 2. rascally, knavish, roguish, crooked, scoundrelly, mean. 3. ridiculous.

picaroto s. m. vertex, top, summit.

piçara s. f. (also **piçarro** m.) slate, gravel, shale, clay rock, quarry.

piçarral s. m. (pl. **-ais**) a place full of pebbles or gravel.

piçarro adj. (N. Braz., sl.) famous, notable.

piçarroso adj. 1. full of pebbles. 2. slaty. 3. gravelly. 4. stony.

picatoste s. m. stuffing made with mutton, eggs, and bread.

píceo adj. pitchy, piceous; black as pitch.

pichador s. m. person who covers, smears or paints with pitch.

pichamento s. m. act of covering, coating or smearing with pitch.

pichar v. to pitch, tar: cover, coat, paint, line or smear with pitch.

piche s. m. pitch, tar; betumen, asphaltum.

pichel s. m. (pl. **-éis**) a sort of pewter or silver tankard.

pichelaria s. f. a pewterer's or tinsmith's shop or trade.

picheleiro s. m. 1. pewterer, tinman, tinker, tinsmith. 2. plumber.

pichelingue s. m. (obs.) 1. pilferer. 2. corsair, pirate.

picho s. m. 1. + **pichel**. 2. clay pot. 3. chignon, bun.

pichorra s. f. 1. a pewter, vessel with a spout like a tankard. 2. (fig.) laziness, weariness.

picica s. m. (N. Braz., pop.) child, brat.

picídeos s. m. pl. (ornith.) Picidae, the woodpecker family.

piciforme adj. m. + f. resembling pitch.

picles s. m. pl. pickles.

pícnico adj. squat, stumpy.

picnídio s. m. (bot.) pycnidium: a spore-bearing receptacle found in certain fungi.

picnogônidas s. m. pl. (zool.) Pycnogonida, a class of arthropods.

picnometria s. f. pycnometry.

picnômetro s. m. pycnometer: a bottle or flask to measure the specific gravity as of fluids.

picnostilo s. m. (archit.) pycnostyle colonnade.

pico s. m. 1. peak, apex, summit, top (plate M 11). 2. sharp point. 3. prickle, thorn. 4. a little, small quantity. 5. (fig.) malice; sharpness, acidity.
uma semana e ~ a week and a bit.

picola s. f. a small chisel used in stonecutting.

picolé s. m. (Braz.) popsicle.

picolina s. f. (chem.) picolin, picoline.

picoso adj. 1. peaked, pointed. 2. sharp-pointed. 3. piercing, pricking.

picota s. f. 1. post, stake. 2. pillary. 3. rod of a pump. 4. (Braz.) guinea fowl.

picotagem s. f. (pl. **-ens**) 1. perforation (of papers). 2. punching (of tickets).

picotar v. 1. to perforate (papers). 2. to punch (tickets). 3. to prick off.

picote s. m. 1. a sort of coarse cloth. 2. picot, purl, pearl stitch. 3. (Braz., philately) perforation.

picotilho s. m. a sort of cloth.

picoto (ô) s. m. 1. peak, the pointed top of a high mountain; pinnacle. 2. geodesic pyramid.

pícrico adj. (chem.) picric (acid).

pictografia s. f. pictography: art of representing and expressing an idea by pictures or hieroglyphs.

pictográfico adj. pictographic: of or pertaining to pictography.

pictórico adj. (also **pictorial** m. + f., pl. **-ais**) pictorial: pertaining to or concerned with pictures or painting. ‖ **pictoricamente** adv. pictorially.

picuá s. m. (Braz.) 1. round wicker basket, hamper. 2. a horn or a segment of bamboo used to keep rough diamonds in. 3. **~s** pl. household utensils or pieces of furniture.

picuaba s. f. (N. Braz.) a coloured mortar for imitating stonework.

picuí-caboclo s. m. (Braz.) (pl. **picuís-caboclos**) the talpacoti dove.

picuinha s. f. (also **picueta(da)**) s. f. 1. cheep, chirp, peep. 2. jest. 3. twit, gibe, taunt.

picuipeba s. f. (Braz., ornith.) cinerous dove (Peristera cinerea).

picuipiúma s. m. (Braz., ornith.) scaled dove.

picum s. m. (pl. **-uns**) (Braz.) peak, top, summit.

picumã s. m. scoot, grime, smut, cobweb.

pidão (pl. **-ões**; f. **-ona**), **pidonho** (Braz.) s. m. begging fellow, person who always wants something. ‖ adj. constantly begging.

piedade s. f. 1. piety, devotion, religiousness; piousness. 2. pity, compassion, mercy, mercifulness, commiseration.
exercícios de ~ exercises of devotion, spiritual exercises. **por ~!** for mercy's sake, for pity's sake! **sem dó nem** ~ pitilessly. **Senhor, tende** ~ **de nós** Lord, have mercy on us.
piedoso adj. 1. pious, religious, godly, devout. 2. merciful, compassionate, pitiful, piteous. 3. prayerful. || **-amente** adv. piously; pitifully.
plegas s. m. + f., sg. + pl. fussy fellow, piddler; ridiculous person. || adj. 1. fussy, caring too much for trifles. 2. scrupulous, tricklish. 3. ridiculous.
pleguice s. f. 1. fussiness, mush, slush. 2. scrupulousness, niceness. 3. punctiliousness; pedantry. 4. ridiculousness, ridiculous sentimentality. 5. extravagance.
pleira s. f. whistling sound, wheeze, wheezy breathing.
piela s. f. (pop.) drunken spree; drunkenness.
pielite s. f. (med.) pyelitis: inflammation of the pelvis and calyxes (outlets) of the kidney.
piemia s. f. (path.) pyemia: a poisonous infection of the blood due to the absorption of vitiated pus into the circulation.
piêmico adj. (med.) pyemic.
piemontita s. f. (min.) piedmontite.
piérides s. f. pl. Pierides, the Muses.
pierídeos s. m. pl. (ent.) Pieridae: the cabbage and sulphur butterfly family.
piério adj. Pierian: of or pertaining to the Muses.
pierrete s. f. pierrete: a female pierrot.
pierrô s. m. pierrot: 1. a character of French pantomimes. 2. a buffoon dressed like a pierrot.
pietismo s. m. Pietism: a religious awakening in the Lutheran Church of Europe during the later decades of the 17th century.
pietista s. m. + f. Pietist: an adept of Pietism. || adj. Pietistic(al): of or pertaining to Pietism.
piezeletricidade s. f. piezoelectricity: electric phenomenon resulting from pressure upon certain bodies esp. crystals.
piezômetro s. m. piezometer: an instrument for determining pressure (esp. an apparatus for measuring the compressibility of liquids).
pifão s. m. (pl. **-ões**) drunkenness; a drinking spree.
pífaro s. m. (also **pífano**) (fife(r); a small shrill-toned flutelike instrument.
pífio adj. (pop.) 1. poor, inferior, vulgar. 2. coarse, rough. 3. vile, mean.
pigarço adj. speckled (horse).
pigarra s. f. (Braz.) chicken pip.
pigarrar, pigarrear v. 1. to clear the throat, cough up. 2. to hawk, hem.
ele pigarreou he cleared his throat.
pigarrento adj. raucous, thick.
pigarro s. m. raucousness, hoarseness, a frog in the throat, roup.
pigídio s. m. pygidium: the terminal or posterior segment as of an insect.
pigmentação s. f. (pl. **-ões**) pigmentation, coloration.
pigmentado adj. pigmented: containing pigment.
pigmentar v. to pigment.
pigmentário adj. pigmentary: producing, secreting or containing pigment.
pigmento s. m. pigment: 1. colouring matter. 2. (biol.) a substance that imparts colour to animal or vegetable tissues.
pigmeu s. m. 1. Pigmy: a member of a people of equatorial Africa, much below the average size of men. 2. pigmy, pigmean: a dwarf. || adj. pigmy, diminutive, dwarfish.
pignoratício adj. pignorative.
pigostílio s. m. (ornith.) pygostyle.

piguancha s. f. 1. (Braz.) Indian woman or girl. 2. hussy.
piina s. m. pyin: a protein compound contained in pus.
pijama s. m. pyjama, pajama (plates R 6, 7).
pila s. m. (Braz., pop.) 1. bread (money). 2. one buck.
ele me deve cem ~s he owes me hundred bucks.
pilado adj. 1. brayed, bruised, pounded. 2. peeled, hulled.
pilador s. m. bruiser, pounder, crusher. || adj. bruising, pounding, crushing.
pilantra s. m. + f. (Braz., sl.) 1. one who, without means, likes to present a good appearance. 2. a scoundrel, rascal, bad egg. || adj. of or relating to such persons.
pilão s. m. (pl. **-ões**) 1. pestle, stamper, crusher, beetle; a large wooden mortar for pounding or peeling rice, corn, etc. 2. conic sugar-loaf. 3. a weight with which the Roman balance is equilibrated. 4. (pop.) trotting horse.
pilar (I) s. m. 1. pillar, column, pier, post (plates C 11, E 7, H, P 15). 2. prop, sustainer.
pilar (II) v. 1. to pound, bray, bruise, beat (grains). 2. to peel, take off the peel (as in a mortar).
pilarete s. m. pillaret, a little pillar.
pilarte s. m. an ancient Portuguese silver coin.
pilastra s. f. (archit.) pilaster, a square pillar (esp. when it forms part of a wall from which it projects somewhat).
pilcha s. f. (S. Braz.) 1. money; jewels. 2. (fig.) harness.
pilchudo adj. (S. Braz.) well-to-do, well-off, wealthy.
pilé s. m. a sort of granulated or rock sugar.
pileca s. f. (pop.) jade, worn-out horse.
pilecado adj. (Braz.) drunken.
píleo s. m. pileus: 1. (ancient Rome) a pointed hat or brimless felt cap. 2. (eccl.) a sort of cap worn by bishops. 3. (bot.) the umbrella-shaped part of a mushroom.
pileque s. m. (Braz.) 1. (pop.) drunkenness, drinking spree. 2. a rubber ring.
tomar um ~ to get drunk.
pileta s. f. (S. Braz.) wash-basin, sink.
pilha (I) s. f. 1. pile, heap, stack (plate A 7). 2. electric battery; dry battery.
~ **elétrica** electric cell. ~ **seca** dry pile. ~ **termelétrica** thermopile.
pilha (II) s. f. 1. plunder, pillage. 2. a sort of card game.
pilhagem s. f. (pl. **-ens**) plunder(ing), pillage: 1. sacking, act of pillaging, maraud. 2. robbery. 3. that which is pillaged, booty.
pilhante s. m. + f. plunderer, pillager, marauder. || adj. plundering.
pilhar v. 1. to plunder, pillage, maraud, sack, loot, rob, steal. 2. to catch, seize.
~ **alguém** to take or catch one in the very act.
ele foi pilhado quando furtava chumbo he was caught stealing lead. **pilharam a cidade** they put the town to sack.
pilheira s. f. 1. place where things are heaped up. 2. place wherein ashes are thrown.
pilheiro s. m. a great reservoir of water.
pilhéria s. f. 1. quip, jest, flash of wit, witticism. 2. a knavish trick, joke; prank.
pilheriador s. m. person fond of joking, a jester. || adj. jocose.
pilheriar v. 1. to jest, gag, trifle, joke. 2. to play jokes.
pilhérico adj. sportive, jesting, playful, mocking.
pilheta s. f. wooden trough, tub or vessel.
pilífero adj. (bot.) piliferous: bearing hairs.

piliforme adj. m. + f. piliform: having the form of hair.
pilípede adj. m. + f. having hairy feet.
pilo s. m. pile: (Roman hist.) a heavy dart.
piloada s. f. stroke with a pestle.
pilocarpina s. f. (chem.) pilocarpine: a white crystalline alkaloid.
pilóia s. f. white rum.
pilono, pilone s. m. pylon, gateway, esp. a monumental gateway of an Egyptian temple or edifice.
pilorada s. f. (N. Braz.) a blow with a stick.
pilórico adj. (anat.) pyloric: of or pertaining to the pylorus.
piloro s. m. (anat.) pylorus: the opening between the stomach and the intestine.
pilosela s. f. (bot.) mouse-ear, mouse-ear hawkweed.
pilosela-alaranjada s. f. (pl. **piloselas-alaranjadas**) (bot.) orange hawkweed.
pilosela-dos-muros s. f. (pl. **piloselas-dos-muros**) (bot.) wall hawkweed.
pilosidade s. f. pilosity, hairiness.
pilosismo s. m. pilosis, pilosism: excessive or abnormal growth of hair.
pilosina s. f. (chem.) pilosine, pilosin.
piloso adj. pilose, pilous, hairy, covered with hair (esp. soft hair).
pilota s. f. fatigue, tiredness. 2. rout, defeat. 3. critique.
pilotagem s. f. (pl. **-ens**) pilotage: 1. act or business of piloting a vessel or aircraft. 2. a pilot's fee.
pilotar, pilotear v. to pilot: 1. steer or direct the course of a vessel or aircraft. 2. act as a pilot.
piloto (ô) s. m. 1. pilot: a) steersman (of a ship). b) flyer, aviator, airplane pilot. c) guide, director. 2. (ichth.) pilot-fish (Naucrates ductor). 3. pilot burner. 4. (Braz.) one-eyed person. ‖ adj. (Braz.) one-eyed.
~ **de provas** test pilot. **balão** ~ pilot balloon. **barcaça de** ~ pilot-boat. **lâmpada** ~ pilot lamp.
piloura s. f. (N. Braz., pop.) 1. dizziness. 2. insanity, crazy action.
pilrete s. m. homunculus.
pilriteiro s. m. (bot.) hawthorn (Crataegus oxyacantha).
pilrito s. m. haw, hawthorn berry.
pílula s. f. 1. a pill. 2. (fig.) unpleasant thing. 3. (pop.) fraud, swindle.
dourar a ~ to gild a bitter pill. **ele tem de engolir a** ~ he must swallow the pill.
pilulador s. m. (pharm.) pillmaker, pillmachine.
pilular adj. m. + f. pilular, pertaining to or like pills.
pilureiro s. m. (Braz.) 1. a device in which pills are made, pillmachine. 2. pillmaker.
pilungo s. m. (S. Braz.) plug, a broken-down or worn-out horse.
pimelose s. f. (med.) pimelosis, fatness, obesity.
pimenta s. f. 1. pepper: a plant of the genus Capsicum or its fruit entire or powdered. 2. eroticism. 3. unquiet person. 4. peppery person.
pimenta-cumari s. f. (Braz.) (pl. **pimentas-cumari**) (bot.) bird pepper (Capsicum fructescens).
pimenta-d'água s. f. (pl. **pimentas-d'água**) (Braz., bot.) water pepper, lakeweed, smartweed.
pimenta-da-jamaica s. f. (pl. **pimentas-da-jamaica**) (bot.) allspice tree (Pimenta officinalis).
pimenta-das-paredes s. f. (pl. **pimentas-das-paredes**) (bot.) English wall pepper, stonecrop, bird's bread.
pimenta-de-cheiro s. f. (pl. **pimentas-de-cheiro**) (Braz., bot.) cherry pepper.
pimenta-de-galinha s. f. (pl. **pimentas-de-galinha**) (bot.) nightshade.
pimenta-do-reino s. f. (pl. **pimentas-do-reino**) 1. (bot.) black pepper (Piper nigrum). 2. its fruit (entire or powdered).

pimental s. m. (pl. **-ais**) place where pepper grows.
pimenta-malagueta s. f. (pl. **pimentas-malaguetas**) (bot.) Spanish pepper, chilli, spur pepper.
pimentão s. m. (pl. **-ões**) 1. (bot.) pimiento, Spanish paprika. 2. its fruit.
pimentão-comprido s. m. (pl. **pimentões-compridos**) (bot.) long pepper.
pimentão-doce s. m. (pl. **pimentões-doces**) Jerusalem-cherry, bonnet pepper (Solanum pseudocapsicum).
pimenteira s. f. 1. pepper shrub, pepper tree, pepper plant. 2. pepperbox, pepper caster (plate M 1).
pimenteiro s. m. pepper plant, hemp (Vitex agnus-castus).
pimpão s. m. (pl. **-ões**) (f. **-ona**) 1. ruffian. 2. braggart, swaggerer, boaster. 3. fop, dandy. ‖ adj. 1. swaggering. 2. haughty, proud. 3. dandyish, foppish.
pimpar (I) v. 1. to flaunt, show off. 2. to figure, appear. 3. to enjoy o. s.
pimpar (II) v. to beat.
pimpilim s. m. (pl. **-ins**) long pepper.
pimpinela s. f. (bot.) anise (Pimpinella anisum).
pimpleu s. m. (bullfighting) a small dart decked with ribbons.
pimpolhar v. to sprout, grow, proliferate.
pimpolho (ô) s. m. 1. young tender shoot of a vine. 2. sarmentum, runner. 3. (fig.) a robust youngster.
pim-pom s. m. = **pingue-pongue** ping-pong.
pimponar, pimponear v. to swagger, show off.
pimponete s. m. (fam.) fop, dandy.
pina s. f. felloe, felly (of a wheel).
pinaça s. f. 1. (naut.) pinnace. 2. rope of a pile driver.
pinácea s. f. one of the Pinaceae, a pinaceous plant.
pinacoteca s. f. pinacotheca: a picture gallery.
pináculo s. m. pinnacle: 1. the top of an edifice, gable. 2. the highest or topmost point; peak. 3. summit. 4. ((fig.) the utmost degree.
pinafres s. m. pl. (N. Braz.) engine trouble, failure.
pinante s. m. (Braz.) boy, youngster.
pinar v. (Braz.) to set pins.
pinatifido adj. (bot.) pinnatifid, divided in a pinnated manner (leaf).
pinázio s. m. cross-bar of a window-frame.
pinça s. f. 1. tweezers (plate P 11). 2. (surg.) nippers. 3. tongs (plate L 1).
~ **para açúcar** sugar-tongs (plate M 8).
pinção s. m. (pl. **-ões**) = **pinçote**.
píncaro s. m. pinnacle, apex, peak, summit.
os ~**s de uma carreira** the prizes of a profession.
pincel s. m. (pl. **pincéis**) 1. brush. 2. a painter's brush (plates E 8, P 12). 3. way of painting. 4. a painter. 5. shaving-brush (plates B 7, E 8).
~ **de caiar** a plasterer's brush.
pincelada, pincelagem s. f. (pl. **-ens**) a stroke with a brush.
pincelar v. to paint or daub with a brush.
pinceleiro s. m. 1. brushmaker. 2. seller of brushes. 3. small tin case to wash pencils or brushes in.
pincha s. f. cruet, phial.
pinchar v. 1. to throw (out or away), cast, hurl, fling, pitch. 2. to push. 3. to thrust aside. 4. to toss. 5. to leap, spring (from).
pincho (I) s. m. 1. toss, thrust. 2. leap, jump.
pincho (II) s. m. (Braz.) 1. crowbar, a pinch bar. 2. ruffian.
pinçote s. m. (naut.) whipstaff of the helm.
pinda s. f. (sl.) lack of money, pennylessness.
pindá s. m. 1. (Braz.) Indian name for fishhook. 2. (zool.) sea urchin.
pindaíba s. f. (Braz.) 1. palm-fiber rope. 2. lack of money. 3. plant of the family Annonaceae (Xylopia muricata).
estar na ~ to be broke, pennyless.

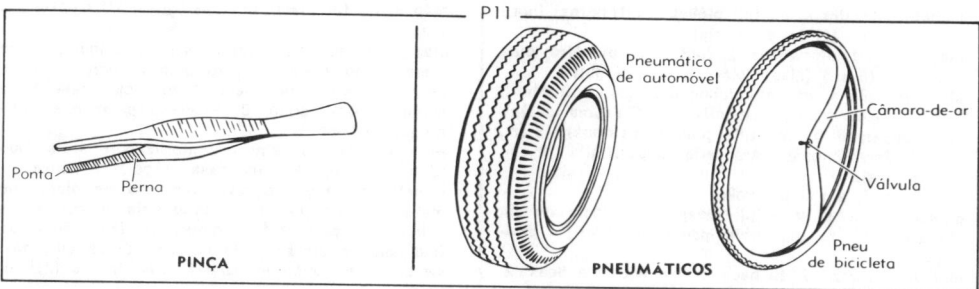

P 11

Ponta

Perna

PINÇA

Pneumático
de automóvel

Câmara-de-ar

Válvula

Pneu
de bicicleta

PNEUMÁTICOS

pindárico adj. 1. Pindaric: of or pertaining to Pindar. 2. (fam.) excellent, magnificent.
pindarismo s. m. the Pindaric (poet.) style.
pindarizar v. 1. to laud exaggeratedly. 2. to write in the complex style of Pindar.
pindoba s. f. (also pindova) (Braz.) pindova palm (Attalea compta).
pindobal s. m. (pl. -ais) (Braz., also pindoval) place where pindova palms grow.
pindonga s. f. (Braz.) a woman who keeps much company, who is frequently out of her home.
pindongar v. to be out frequently, keep much company (woman).
pindorama s. m. region or country of the palms (said of Brazil by some of its neighbours).
pineal adj. m. + f. (pl. -ais) pineal: 1. (anat., zool.) designating an appendage of the brain. 2. shaped like a pine cone.
glândula ~ (anat., zool.) pineal body, pineal gland.
píneno s. m. (chem.) pinene.
píneo adj. (poet.) of pine, of pine wood.
pinéu s. m. (Braz., coll.) tailor.
pinga s. f. 1. a drop. 2. (Braz.) rum, white rum; booze. 3. (pop.) gulp, swallow. 4. (Braz., pop.) roof gutter. 5. (fam.) penniless person.
vamos tomar uma ~ let's take a drop, (U. S. A. coll.) let's take a horn. estar na ~ to be drunk.
pingaço s. m. (S. Braz.) a very beautiful horse.
pingadeira s. f. 1. a dripping-pan: the pan into which the fat of roasting meat falls. 2. small but continuous receipts. 3. constant expense. 4. (Braz., pop.): a) menses. b) (med.) gonorrhea.
pingado adj. 1. besprinkled, bespattered, full of drops. 2. (Braz.) said of the coffee to which a little milk has been added, or vice versa. 3. drunk.
pinga-fogo s. m. (pl. pinga-fogos) 1. (Braz.) a sort of large wasp. 2. braggart, bully, troublesome person. ‖ adj. troublesome, tormenting.
pingalim s. m. (pl. -ins) a long and thin whip.
pingante s. m. (sl.) a pauper, a poor fellow. ‖ adj. m. + f. dripping.
pingão s. m. (pl. ões) a poor and dirty fellow, tatterdemalion, ragamuffin.
pingar (I) v. (also pingotear) 1. to drip, fall in drops. 2. to sprinkle. 3. to trickle, dribble. 4. to drizzle, rain slightly. 5. to yield continually small profits. 6. to leak, ooze.
pingar (II) v. (Port., prov.) to drop one's head, nap, be sleepy.
pingente s. m. 1. bob, drop, pendant (plate J 3). 2. earring. 3. trinket. 4. (Braz.) hanger-on (bus, tramway). 5. ~s gewgaws, fripperies.
pingo s. m. 1. a drop. 2. dripping: fat which drops from roasting meat. 3. fat. 4. snivel, mucus. 5. a little bite. 6. (S. Braz.) a very beautiful horse.
nem um ~ not a particle, not one jot. um ~ de

esperança a flicker of hope. um ~ de verdade an element of truth.
pingo-d'água s. m. (pl. pingos-d'água) name the prospectors give to the colourless pebbles or hyalites.
pingoso adj. dripping, drippy.
pinguço s. m. (Braz., pop.) drunkard. ‖ adj. (Braz., pop.) drunk(en).
pingue s. m. dripping, fat. ‖ adj. m. + f. 1. fat. 2. fruitful, fertile. 3. profitable.
pingueiro s. m. (Braz.) an alcoholic, a drunkard. ‖ adj. drunk(en).
pinguela s. f. 1. a little stick used in a bird snare. 2. a plank used as a footbridge.
pinguelear v. to jump, leap from one side to the other as a monkey on a tree.
pinguelim s. m. (pl. -ins) = pingalim.
pinguelo s. m. 1. = pinguela. 2. (Braz.) trigger.
pingue-pongue s. m. (pl. pingue-pongues) ping-pong.
pingüim s. m. (pl. -ins) 1. (ornith.) penguin (Sphenicus magellanicus). 2. (Braz., bot.) pinguin (Bromelia pinguin).
pinguinho s. m. (Braz., fam.) 1. a tiny bit, small quantity. 2. insignificance, a trifle.
pinguruto s. m. (N. Braz.) top, summit.
pinha s. f. 1. pine cone. 2. (Braz., bot.) sweetsop, sugar apple. 3. crowd, bunch, heap.
pinhal s. m. (pl. -ais) a wood or grove of pine trees, pine forest.
pinhão s. m. (pl. -ões) 1. piñon, the edible pine seed. 2. (tech.) pinion (gear) (plates B 13, G 5). 3. (bot.) physic nut (Jatropha curcas). ‖ adj. said of a dark-red horse.
pinhão-de-purga s. m. (pl. pinhões-de-purga) (bot.) physic nut.
pinhé s. m. (Braz., ornith.) chimachima: a sort of hawk.
pinheira s. f. sweetsop: a tropical American tree (Annona squamosa).
pinheiral s. m. (pl. -ais) (Braz., bot.) = pinhal (plate F 4).
pinheirinho s. m. a plant of the family Podocarpaceae (Podocarpus Lambertii).
pinheiro s. m. (bot.) pine tree.
pinheiro-baboso s. m. (bot.) (pl. pinheiros-babosos) sundew, flycatcher.
pinheiro-branco s. m. (pl. pinheiros-brancos) (bot.) white pine.
pinheiro-branco-do-canadá s. m. (pl. pinheiros-brancos-do-canadá) (bot.) Weymouth pine.
pinheiro-bravo s. m. (pl. pinheiros-bravos) (bot.) pinaster.
pinheiro-manso s. m. (pl. pinheiros-mansos) (bot.) stone pine, parasol pine.
pinheiro-marítimo s. m. (pl. pinheiros-marítimos) (bot.) cluster pine, star pine, sea pine (Pinus laricio).

pinheiro-silvestre s. m. (pl. **pinheiros-silvestres**) (bot.) Scotch pine (Pinus silvestris).

pinho s. m. 1. pinewoods. 2. (bot., also **pinheiro**) pine tree. 3. (Braz.) (also **violão**) a sort of guitar.

pinho-do-brejo s. m. (pl. **pinhos-do-brejo**) (Braz., bot.) tree of ₒthe family Magnoliaceae (Talauma ovata).

pinho-do-paraná s. m. (pl. **pinhos-do-paraná**) (Braz., bot.) Paraná pine (Araucaria angustifolia or A. brasiliana).

pinhola s. f. a wooden yoke.

pinicada s. f., **pinicão** (pl. **-ões**) m. a pinch; twitch.

pinica-pau s. m. (pl. **pinica-paus**) (N. Braz.) = **pica-pau**.

pinicar v. (Braz.) 1. to peck, strike with the beak. 2. to pinch, nip. 3. to spur. 4. to wink. 5. (pop.) to run away.

pinico s. m. (Braz.) 1. a sharp point. 2. beak.

pinífero adj. (poet.) piny.

piniforme adj. m. + f. piniform.

pinígero adj. (poet.) piny, producing pine trees.

pinima s. f. (Braz., sl.) 1. plague, scourge. 2. pig-headedness.

pinípede s. m. (zool.) a pinnipedian. ‖ adj. m. + f. pinniped: of or pertaining to the Pinnipedia (seals, walruses).

pinípedes s. m. pl. (zool.) Pinnipedia.

pino s. m. 1. a wooden peg used by shoemakers. 2. pin, peg, bolt (plates H, V 3). 3. the highest point, highest degree, top, summit, apex. 4. pivot (plate T 1).
~ **cônico** taper pin. ~ **de articulação** link-pin. ~ **de êmbolo** (tech.) wrist pin. ~ **de manivela** crank-pin (plate E 2). ~ **mestre** kingbolt, king-pin (plate E 1). ~ **de tomada** (electr.) plug (plates A 6, M 5). ~ **roscado** tap bolt. **a ~** upright, perpendicular. **no ~ do dia** exactly at noon. **no ~ do inverno** in the midst of the winter.

pinóia s. f. 1. an elegant but too easygoing woman. 2. (Braz.): a) a worthless thing. b) fraud, swindle. 3. m. weak person or person of no importance. ‖ adj. m. without importance (person).

pinote s. m. 1. jump, leap, bound, caper. 2. curvet.

pinotear v. 1. to jump, leap, bound. 2. to curvet (horse).

pinta s. f. 1. spot. 2. mole (on the body), mark. 3. pip (at cards). 4. countenance, appearance, expression (of the face), complexion. 5. (Braz., sl.) perilous person. 6. young pullet. 7. an ancient Portuguese measure.
conhecer pela ~ to know or recognize immediately.

pinta-brava s. m. + f. (pl. **pintas-bravas**) (Braz.) a suspect person, a scoundrel; (sl.) a louse, a bad hat, a crook.

pinta-cega s. f. (pl. **pintas-cegas**) 1. nighthawk. 2. m. (Braz.) shortsighted person.

pintada s. f. 1. a Guinea fowl. 2. (Braz., also **onça-~**) jaguar.

pintado adj. 1. painted. 2. coloured. 3. spotted (birds). 4. (fig.) exactly alike, speckled.
não quero vê-lo nem ~! I definitely do not want to see it (or him)!

pintagol s. m. (pl. **~óis**) (ornith.) a cross between a canary and a goldfinch.

pintainho s. m. young chicken (esp. one whose feathers are not yet grown).

pintalegrete s. m. 1. dandy, fop, coxcomb. 2. conceited person. ‖ adj. 1. foppish, dapper. 2. vain, conceited.

pintalgado adj. 1. spotted, speckled, flecked. 2. variegated.

pintalgar v. 1. to spot, speckle, freckle. 2. (of colours) to variegate.

pinta-monos s. m., sg. + pl. dauber: unskilful painter, bad painter.

pintão s. m. (pl. **-ões**) 1. chickling, small chicken. 2. fop.

pintar v. 1. to paint, draw, set in colours. 2. to tinge. 3. to speckle. 4. to picture, portray. 5. to depict, describe, represent. 6. to trick, cheat. 7. to surge, appear, arise. 8. **~-se** to paint o. s., use rouge, make-up.
~ **a aquarela** to paint in water-colours. ~ **a óleo** to paint in oil. ~ **uma casa** to paint a house. ~ **o sete** to paint the town red. **ela se pinta** she makes up. **ele pintou o retrato dela do natural** he painted her portrait from nature. **o diabo não é tão feio como o pintam** it is not as bad as they say. **vir ao ~** to come in handy; come in the nick of time.

pintassilgo s. m. (Braz., ornith.) goldfinch (Spinus magellanicus ictericus).

pintassilgo-verde s. m. (pl. **pintassilgos-verdes**) (ornith.) siskin.

pinteiro s. m. 1. (Braz.) a cover for sheltering young chickens. 2. (N. Braz.) filcher, pilferer.

pintinho s. m. a young chicken; poult.

pinto s. m. 1. (young) chicken. 2. an ancient Portuguese coin. 3. (Braz., sl.) youngster, kid.
estar como um ~ to be wet to the skin.

pinto-calçudo s. m. (pl. **pintos-calçudos**) (Braz., fam.) boy who begins to use long trousers.

pinto-d'água s. m. (pl. **pintos-d'água**) (Braz., ornith.) = **frango-d'água**.

pinto-do-mato s. m. (pl. **pintos-do-mato**) (Braz., ornith.) ant-thrush.

pintor s. m. painter: 1. artist who paints pictures. 2. workman who covers, coats or decorates surfaces with paint.
~ **de cenários** scene-painter. ~ **em miniatura** a miniature-painter.

pintora s. f. paintress, lady painter.

pintura s. f. 1. painting: a) the act of painting, art or work of a painter. b) a picture; figure, image. 2. paint. 3. face make-up. 4. (fig.) description. 5. a beautiful person. 6. (fam.) colour.
~ **a esmalte** enamel painting. ~ **a óleo** oil-painting. **belo como uma ~** beautiful like a picture. **camada de ~** coat of paint.

pinturesco adj. picturesque.

pínula s. f. pinnule: 1. a plate pierced with a peephole or sighthole. 2. (bot.) a division of a pinnate leaf (plate F 5).

pinulado adj. pinnulate(d): having pinnules.

pio (I) s. m. peep, cheep; chirp(ing) of birds; bird call (also the whistle).

pio (II) adj. 1. pious, godly, religious, devout. 2. charitable.
obras -as works of piety.

pioca s. m. + f. (Braz.) backwoodsman, rustic.

piocada s. f. (Braz.) a group of **piocas**.

piodermite s. f. (med.) pyodermitis: a pustular skin inflammation.

pioemia s. f. pyohaemia.

piogênico adj. pyogenic: producing pus.

piogênese s. f. pyogenesis: the formation or secretion of pus.

piola s. f. (S. Braz.) twine, string.

piolhada, piolhama s. f. a great quantity of lice.

piolhar v. to be infested with lice.

piolharia s. f. 1. = **piolhada**. 2. (fig.) extreme poverty.

piolheira s. f. 1. lousiness. 2. a swarm of lice. 3. (bot.) lousewort. 4. (fig.) filthy, dirty house or a lot of dirty things. 5. (pop.) a lousy business.

piolhento adj. lousy, infested with lice.

piolho s. m. 1. (ent.) louse. 2. a tree of the family Flacurtiaceae (Casearia parvifolia).·

Tento (apóia-mão)

Tijolo de tinta

Paleta de aquarela

Paleta de tempera

Linha de guia

Godé de tinta

Pastel

Godé

Paleta dobradiça

Tubo de tinta

Lata de tinta

Copo

Broxa para pontilhar

Cavalete dobradiço

Espátula

Escova de aço

Pincel redondo

Estojo de tintas

Rolo

Pincel chato

Broxa — Pincel

Raspadeira

Revólver de pintura

Balde

Régua

Espátula de vidraceiro

Estampa

Broxa ou pincel de cerdas

Espátula de pintor

Trincha chata

Pincel bífido com argola de cobre

Pincel para estencil

Espátula de moldador

PINTURA

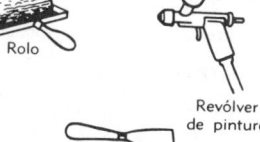

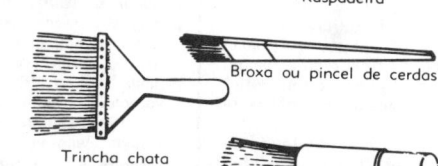
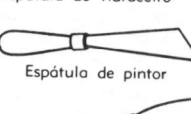

piolho-da-cabeça s. m. (pl. **piolhos-da-cabeça**) (ent.) head louse.

piolho-das-aves s. m. (pl. **piolhos-das-aves**) (ent.) bird louse.

piolho-das-virilhas s. m. (pl. **piolhos-das-virilhas**) (ent.) crab louse.

piolho-de-galinha s. m. (pl. **piolhos-de-galinha**) chicken louse.

piolhoso adj. lousy, infested with lice.

pioneiro s. m. 1. pioneer, explorer. 2. precursor. **ser o ~ de alguma coisa** to be a pioneer in a thing.

piongo adj. dejected, unhappy.

pior s. m. the worst. ‖ adj. m. + f. worse, worst. ‖ adv. (also **~mente**) worst, in the worst manner, worse. **~ a emenda que o soneto** the remedy is worse than the disease. **cada vez ~** worse and worse. **coisa ~ não se pode narrar** worse cannot be told. **de mal a ~** from bad to worse. **ele está em ~ situação que antes** he is worse off than he was. **ele está preparado para o ~** he is prepared for the worst. **ele não é ~ que os outros** he might pass in a crowd. **escolher o ~** to choose the worst. **estou ~ assim?** am I the worse for it? **eu me saí o ~ de todos** I got the worst of it. **ir de mal a ~** to grow worse and worse. **não faço ~ juízo dele se...** I think none the worse of him if... **não o olhe de seu lado ~** don't see him at his worst. **(não) estar ~ (not)** to be worse. **na ~ das hipóteses** at the worst. **o ~ ainda está para vir** the worst is yet to come. **o ~ de todos** the worst of all. **para ~** backward. **muito ~ ainda** farther and far worse. **se o ~ acontecer** if the worst comes to the worst. **tanto ~** more's the pity. **uma mudança para ~** a change for worse.

piora s. f., **pioramento** m. worsening, a growing worse; aggravation.

piorar v. 1. to worsen: make or become worse. 2. to aggravate, complicate. 3. to exasperate. **o cinema tem piorado** the cinema has gone off.

pioria s. f. 1. a worsening or state of being worse. 2. aggravation. 3. exasperation.

piorno s. m. (bot.) a variety of woodwaxen.

pioró s. m. (Braz.) a bird of the family Fringillidae (Pyrrhocoma ruficeps).

piorra s. f. whirligig, top.

piorréia s. f. (med.) pyorrh(o)ea: a loosening of the teeth accompanied by inflammation of their lining membrane; the Riggs' disease.

piorréico adj. (med.) pyorrh(o)eal, pyorrh(o)eic.

piose s. f. (med.) pyosis, suppuration.

pipa s. f. 1. barrel, cask, pipe, hogshead. 2. (pop.) a short and fat person. 3. (zool.) Surinam toad. 4. (Braz.) a kind of kite. 5. (pop.) drunkard.

pipal s. m. (pl. **-als**) pipal: a tree of the family Moraceae (Ficus indica).

piparote s. m. fillip, flick.

piparotear v. to fillip.

piperáceas s. f. pl. (bot.) Piperaceae, the pepper family.

piperazina s. f. piperazine: a crystalline substance formed by the action of aniline on ethylene bromide.

piperina s. f. piperine: a crystalline alkaloid contained in peper.

pipeta s. f. pipette.

pipi (I) s. m. 1. children's name for chickens or pullets. 2. (Braz., bot.) a phytolacaceous garlic--scented herb (Petiveria alliacea).

pipi (II) s. m. a child's penis or vulva.

fazer ~ (children) to piddle, make water.

pipia s. f. a sort of whistle children make of a cornstalk.

pipiar s. m. (also **pipilar, pipitar**) chirp, peep(ing). || v. to chirp, pip, peep.

pipilante adj. m. + f. peeping, chirping.

pipio s. m. (also **pipilo, pipito**) 1. act of chirping. 2. (Braz.) young chicken.

pipira s. f. (N. Braz.) factory girl (esp. in a textile factory).

pipiri s. m. (Braz.) plant of the family Cyperaceae (Rhynchospora storea).

pipo s. m. 1. a small barrel, cask, keg. 2. suction pipe or tube.

pipoca s. f. 1. popcorn. 2. (Braz., fig.) a wart.

pipocar, pipoquear v. 1. to pop, burst or cause to burst (as corn), to crackle. 2. to boil, bubble.

pipoco (ô) s. m. (N. Braz.) disorder, tumult, riot.

pipoqueamento s. m. (S. Braz.) 1. act of popping. 2. burst, explosion, crack.

pipoqueiro s. m. (Braz.) a popcorn seller.

pique s. m. 1. pike (weapon). 2. piquancy: piquant taste. 3. (Braz.) hide-and-seek (children's game). 4. a cut. 5. prick, puncture. 6. earmark (of cattle). 7. (Braz.) spite, grudge; slight anger or displeasure. 8. sarcasm.

a ~ vertically, perpendicularly. **a** ~ **de** in danger of. **ir a** ~ 1. to sink, founder (a ship). 2. (fig.) to go down. **meter a** ~ to sink a ship. **por** ~ purposely, intentionally.

piqueiro s. m. 1. pikeman: a soldier armed with a pike. 2. (bullfight) picador.

piquenique s. m. picnic: an outdoor pleasure party.

piqueta (ê) s. f. picket: a pointed post or stake.

piquetagem s. f. (pl. **-ens**) act of picketing.

piquetar v. to picket: mark, enclose, secure with pickets.

piquete (ê) s. m. 1. picket: a) body of soldiers (as on an advanced post). b) a number of men set by a trade union to watch a shop, or factory (during a strike). 2. a shift of workmen.

piquira s. f. 1. small horse; pony. 2. a small fish. 3. insignificant person. || adj. 1. small. 2. insignificant.

pira s. f. 1. pyre: pile of wood for burning a dead body. 2. (fig.) a severe test or trial. 3. Tupian name of fish.

~ **funerária** funeral pile; funeral pyre.

pirá-andirá s. m. (pl. **pirás-andirás**) a fresh-water fish (Raphiodon vulpinus).

piracajara s. f. a fluvial fish (Platystoma perdale).

piracanjuba, piracanjuva, piracanjuvira s. m. (Braz.) a fish of the family Characinidae (Brycon).

piracanto s. m. (bot.) fire thorn, pyracanth.

piracema s. f. (Braz.) 1. shoal of fish. 2. spawning time (of fish). 3. period when the shoals of fish go upstream to deposit their eggs.

piracicaba s. f. (Braz.) place where a waterfall does not permit the fishes to go upstream (hence a good place for fishing).

piracirica s. m. (Braz., ichth.) sand whiting.

piracuí s. m. a meal of dried fish.

pirágua s. f. (S. Braz.) piragua: a canoe made of planks used to transport maté.

piraguara, piriguara s. f. (Braz., zool.) an aglyphous snake (Helicops leopardina).

piraí s. m. (Braz.) a scourge or whip made of rawhide.

piraíba s. m. (Braz.) a fresh-water fish (Bagrus reticulatus).

pirajá s. m. (Braz.) an unexpected rainfall of short duration.

pirambeira s. f. (Braz.) 1. steep bluff. 2. precipice, cliff.

pirambóia s. f. (Braz.) a lungfish (Lepidosirem paradoxus).

piramidal adj. m. + f. (pl. **-ais**) pyramidal: 1. pyramid-like. 2. (fig.) colossal, huge, extraordinarily great.

pirâmide s. f. (monument and geom.) pyramid.

as ~**s do Egito** the Pyramids of Egypt.

piramido s. m. (chem., also ~**na** f.) pyramidon.

piramidografia s. f. the description of pyramids.

piranema s. f. (Braz., ichth.) catalufa, bigeye (Priacanthus arenatus).

piranga (I) s. m. + f. 1. pauper. 2. stingy person. 3. f. poverty, want, lack of money. || adj. 1. poor, miserable. 2. stingy.

ele anda na ~ he is broke, penniless.

piranga (II) s. m. (Braz.) red clay. || adj. m. + f. (Braz., coll.) red.

piranga (III) s. f. (Braz.) a plant of the family Bignoniaceae from which Indians extract a tattooing pigment.

pirangar v. (Braz., pop.) to beg (alms).

pirangueiro s. m. fisher. || adj. 1. poor, shabby; ridiculous; despicable. 2. (Braz.) fond of or skilled in fishing with hook and line.

piranha s. f. 1. (Braz.) piranha, caribe: an extremely voracious fresh-water fish of the family Characinidae (Serrasalmus scapularis). 2. (Braz., sl.) a loose woman; wanton.

piranheira s. f. (Braz.) a plant of the family Euphorbiaceae (Piranhea trifoliata).

pirão s. m. (pl. **-ões**) (Braz.) 1. mush or meal of manioc flour boiled in water. 2. (pop.) a very beautiful girl or woman.

pirapanema s. m. (Braz.) a place in a river where there are but a few fish.

pirapema s. f. (Braz.) a fresh-water fish (Megalope thrissoides).

pirapeua, pirapeuaua s. f. (Braz.) a fish of the family Siluridae (Platystomatichthys sturio).

piraquara s. m. + f. (Braz.) 1. name given to the inhabitants of the banks of the Paraíba River. 2. m. (fig.) a fisherman.

piraqüera s. f. (N. Braz.) a fishing at night, esp. with a spear.

pirar v. (sl.) to steal away, slip away, beat it, be gone, make o. s. scarce.

pirarucu s. m. (Braz.) pirarucu, one of the largest fresh-water fishes, it belongs to the family Osteoglossidae (Arapaima gigas).

pirata s. m. + f. 1. pirate, corsair, sea-robber, buccaneer. 2. (by extension) thief, robber. 3. (Braz.): a) philanderer; seducer, lady-killer. b) loafer, rascal.

piratagem s. f. (pl. **-ens**) (also **pirataria**) piracy, robbery on the sea.

pirá-tamanduá s. m. (pl. **pirás-tamanduá**) (Braz.) a fresh-water fish of the family Siluridae (Conorhynchus conirostris).

pirataria s. f. 1. piracy. 2. (by extension) robbery, extorsion; fraud. 3. (Braz.) rascality.

piratear v. to pirate, rob like a pirate, commit piracy.

pirático adj. piratical: of or pertaining to a pirate.

piratiningano s. m. (Braz.) a native or inhabitant of the State of São Paulo. || adj. of or pertaining to the State of São Paulo.

pirauxi s. m. (Braz.) plant of the family Rosaceae (Couepia paraensis).

pireliômetro s. m. pyrheliometer: an instrument for measuring the heat and energy of the sun.

pirenaico, pireneu adj. Pyrenean: of or pertaining to the Pyrenees.

pirenóide adj. m. + f. (bot.) pyrenoid: resembling a drupe stone.

pirento adj. mangy.

pires s. m., sg. + pl. saucer (plate M 8).

pirético adj. (med.) pyretic, febrile, feverish.

piretologia s. f. pyretology: a treatise on fevers.

piretológico adj. of or pertaining to pyretology.

piretoterapia s. f. (med.) pyretotherapy: treatment of a disease by raising the patient's temperature.

píretro s. m. 1. (bot.): a) pellitory of Spain, bertram. b) painted lady. 2. (pharm.) Pyrethrum.

pirexia s. f. pyrexia: fever, feverish condition.

piri s. m. (N. Braz.) a plant of the family Cyperaceae, (Rhynchospora cephalotes).

pírico adj. of or referring to fire.

pirífora s. f. (Braz.) firefly, glowworm.

piriforme adj. m. + f. pyriform, pear-shaped.

piriguara s. f. (Braz.) a climbing shrub of the family Violaceae (Anchietea salutaris).

pirilampear, pirilampejar v. (Braz.) to glow (as a firefly).

pirilâmpico adj. phosphorescent; emitting light as a firefly.

pirilampo s. m. (also **vaga-lume**) (ent.) glowworm, firefly.

piriquiti s. m. (Braz.) a plant of the family Cannaceae (Canna glauca).

piriri s. m. (Braz.) an euphorbiaceous plant (Mabea occidentalis).

piririca (I) s. f. (Braz.) 1. a small waterfall. 2. ripple: the ruffling of the surface of water.

piririca (II) adj. m. + f. (Braz.) 1. rough, coarse. 2. restless, fidgety.

piriricar v. (Braz.) 1. to ripple: (said of the surface of a river). 2. (fig.) to frown, wrinkle one's brows. 3. to touch, move, thrill, affect.

pirita s. f. pyrites, sulphide of iron.

piritífero, piritoso adj. pyritiferous: containing pyrites.

piroca adj. m. + f. (Braz.) bald, hairless.

pirocar v. to grow bald; lose hair or the skin.

pirofobia s. f. pyrophobia: abnormal dread of fire.

piróforo s. m. pyrophorus: a substance taking fire spontaneously on exposure to the air. ‖ adj. pyrophorous; inflammable.

piroga s. f. 1. piragua, pirogue, a dugout canoe (plate B 9). 2. canoe with outrigger.

pirogalato s. m. (chem.) pyrogallate: a salt or ether of pyrogallol.

pirogálico adj. (chem.) pyrogallic (acid).

pirogênese s. f. (phys.) pyrogenesis: production of heat.

pirogênico adj. pyrogenic: produced by heat.

pirogravura s. f. pyrogravure; pyrography: a design in wood or leather made by means of fire.

piroláceas s. f. pl. (bot.) Pyrolaceae, a family of evergreen herbs of temperate regions.

pirólatra s. m. + f. pyrolater, a fire worshi(p)per.

pirolatria s. f. pyrolatry, fire worship.

pirologia s. f. pyrology: the science of heat.

pirometria s. f. pyrometry: art of measuring high temperatures.

pirométrico adj. pyrometric: of or pertaining to pyrometry.

pirômetro s. m. pyrometer: an instrument for measuring high temperatures.

piropo s. m. 1. (min.) pyrope: a deep red variety of garnet. 2. the colour of fire.

piroscópio s. m. pyroscope.

pirose s. f. (med.) heartburn.

pirosfera s. f. pyrosphere: the hot central portion of the earth.

pirosômido s. m. (zool.) pyrosome, an ascidian of the order Pyrosomida.

pirote s. m. topknot.

pirotecnia s. f. pyrotechnics: 1. the art of making fireworks. 2. pyrotechny: application of fire in science and art.

pirotécnico s. m. pyrotechnist: person who makes or displays fireworks. ‖ adj. pyrotechnic: of or pertaining to pyrotechnics.

pirótico s. m. pyrotic: a caustic medicine. ‖ adj. pyrotic, caustic.

piroxênio s. m. (min.) pyroxene: a name used for a group of silicates of lime, magnesium or manganese.

piroxilina s. f. pyroxylin, gun-cotton, explosive cotton.

pirraça s. f. roguish trick, dog's trick, spite, impertinence, ill will.

por ~ purposely, spitfully, out of spite.

pirraçar v. 1. to play roguish tricks. 2. to spite thwart, hinder purposely.

pirraceiro s. m. person fond of mischievous or roguish tricks. ‖ adj. teasing.

pirralhada s. f. (Braz.) kids, group or lot of children.

pirralho s. m. (Braz.) 1. kid, boy, youngster, brat. 2. a very small person.

pírrica s. f. pyrrhic: an ancient Grecian martial dance.

pirríquio s. m. (pros.) Pyrrhic foot.

pirronice s. f. 1. Pyrrhonism; suspiciousness. 2. stubbornness.

pirrônico s. m. Pyrrhonist; sceptic. ‖ adj. 1. Pyrrhonic, sceptic(al). 2. obstinate, stubborn.

pirronismo s. m. 1. Pyrrhonism. 2. absolute scepticism. 3. stubbornness.

pírtiga s. f. a long stick, pole, shaft.

pírtigo s. m. swiple or swingle of a flail.

pirueta (ê) s. f. pirouette: 1. a whirling or turning on one or both feet. 2. a sudden short turn of a horse.

piruetar v. to pirouette, perform a pirouette.

pirulito s. m. 1. lollypop, lollipop (on a stick). 2. (fig.) a very thin person.

pirupiru s. m. (ornith.) oyster catcher (Haematopus ostralegus palliatus).

piruruca s. f. (Braz.) coarse sand or gravel on the bottom of a river.

pisa s. f. 1. treading, stamping (as of grapes). 2. (fig.) a beating, spanking, thrashing.

pisada s. f. 1. footstep, track, trace. 2. treading of grapes.

seguir as ~s de alguém to follow a person's footsteps.

pisadela s. f. treading, stamping, trampling.

pisado adj. 1. trodden, stepped on, stamped. 2. aggrieved, bruised, hurt.

pisador s. m. 1. treader: person who treads or stamps. 2. winepress. ‖ adj. 1. treading, trampling. 2. pounding, braying.

pisadura s. f. 1. footstep. 2. trampling, treading. 3. bruise, contusion. 4. wrong(ing).

pisa-flores s. m., sg. + pl. 1. beau, fop, high-stepper. 2. lady-killer.

pisa-mansinho s. m., sg. + pl. pussyfoot, sly or wily person, sneaking fellow. ‖ adj. sneaking, sly, wily.

ele é um ~ he is a bit of a sneak.

pisão (I) s. m. (pl. -ões) fulling-mill.

pisão (II) s. m. = **pisada, pisadela**.

pisar v. 1. to tread on, trample. 2. to step on. 3. to pass or walk through or over. 4. to offend, hurt. 5. to press (down), oppress. 6. to conquer, subjugate. 7. to despise. 8. to crush, squash, grind. 9. to stamp, pound, bray. 10. to bruise, contuse. ~ aos pés 1. to trample down. 2. (fig.) to despise. ele pisou-me o pé he trod on my foot.

pisca s. f. a very small thing, particle, granule, pinch; spark.

piscadela s. f. (also piscação f., pl. -ões, piscado, piscamento m.) wink(ing), blink; twinkling.

pisca-pisca s. m. + f. (pl. pisca-piscas) 1. (path). person who winks constantly. 2. (electr.) flasher (as of a display sign). 3. blinker (of a car).

piscar s. m. a wink, blink. ‖ v. 1. to wink, blink: a) close and open the eyelids quickly. b) give a sign by such a motion of the eyelids. 2. to twinkle, sparkle (as the light). ele piscou para ela he cocked his eyes at her. pisquei para ela I winked at her. num ~ de olhos in the twinkling of an eye.

piscatória s. f. poetical composition portraying piscatory life.

piscatório adj. piscatory, piscatorial: belonging to fishing.

písceo adj. piscine: of or pertaining to fishes.

Pisces s. m. pl. Pisces, the Fishes: twelfth sign of the Zodiac.

piscicultor s. m. pisciculturist, fish breeder.

piscicultura s. f. pisciculture: fish breeding.

pisciforme adj. m. + f. pisciform, fishlike.

piscina s. f. 1. swimming pool, basin, swimming bath (plates B 3, P 6). 2. pond, vivary. 3. reservoir of water. 4. watering-place. 5. (eccl.) piscina, baptismal font.

piscinal adj. m. + f. that lives in a pond.

piscívoro adj. piscivorous: fish-eating, feeding on fish.

pisco s. m. (ornith.) bullfinch. ‖ adj. 1. winking (the eyelids). 2. half-open (eye).

píscola s. f. two or more ploughs working at a time.

piscoso adj. fishy: abounding in fish.

pisgar-se v. to run away, make o. s. scarce.

pisiforme adj. m. + f. pisiform: having the form or size of a pea.

piso s. m. 1. floor, level ground, paving, pavement. 2. manner of walking, gait. 3. tread (of a stair) (plate E 7).
~ de linóleo linoleum floor (plate C 20).

pisoador s. m. (also pisoeiro) fuller.

pisoagem s. f. (pl. -ens), pisoamento m. fulling.

pisoar v. to full cloth.

pisolítico adj. (petrog.) pisolitic: pertaining to, characteristic of, or having the structure of pisolite.

pisotear v. (S. Braz.) 1. to treat harshly. 2. to humble, humiliate. 3. to trample upon (also fig.).

pisoteio s. m. (S. Braz.) 1. a trampling on or upon. 2. a harsh treatment.

pisqueiro adj. (Braz.) winking, blinking.

pisquila s. m. + f. (Braz.) slender and small person.

pissasfalto s. m. píssasphalt, mineral tar.

pista s. f. 1. track: a) racecourse, race track, cinder track, running track b) trace, foiling. c) footprint. d) clue, trail, vestige. 2. (at an airport) runway.
~ de corridas racecourse, race ground. a ~ está boa the going is good. desviamo-lo da ~ we threw him off the scent. estar na ~ de uma coisa do be on the scent of an affair. seguir a ~ de to track down. você está na ~ errada you are on the wrong scent.

pistácia s. f. (also pistacha f., pistache f., pistacho m.) a plant of the family Anacardiaceae (Pistacia vera, Pistacia lentiscus).

pistão s. m. (pl. -ões) 1. (mech., also êmbolo) piston (plate M 13). 2. (mus.) cornet.

pistilar adj. m. + f. (bot.) pistillary.

pistilo s. m. (bot.) pistil.

pistiloso adj. pistillate: having a pistil.

pistola s. f. 1. pistol: a short firearm. 2. Roman candle: a kind of firework consisting of a tube that shoots out balls of fire. 3. pistole: an ancient gold coin.
~ automática automatic pistol. ~ de lubrificação grease-gun.

pistolaço s. m., pistolada f. pistol-shot.

pistolão s. m. (pl. -ões) 1. big shot, big-wig, an influential person. 2. Roman candle.

pistoleiro s. m. pistoleer, bandit, gunman.

pistoleta s. f., pistolete m. pistolet: a little pistol.

pita s. f. pita: a fiber obtained from the common century plant.

pitada s. f. 1. a pinch of snuff. 2. a small quantity of a thing (as of salt).
dar uma ~ (Braz.) to smoke a pipe. uma ~ de sal a relish of salt.

pitadear v. to take a pinch of snuff.

pitador s. m. (Braz.) smoker (esp. a pipe smoker).

pitagórico s. m. Pythagorist, Pythagorean. ‖ adj. Pythagoric(al), Pythagorean: of or pertaining to Pythagoras.

pitagorismo s. m. Pythagorism, Pythagoreanism: the philosophic doctrine founded by Pythagoras.

pitagorista s. m. + f. Pythagorist, Pythagorean: a follower of Pythagoras.

pitança s. f. pittance: 1. small allowance of food. 2. (at the Mass) alms.

pitanceiro s. m. pittancer: (in religious houses) the administrator of pittances.

pitanga s. f. Surinam cherry (fruit).

pitanguá s. m. (Braz., ornith.) pitangua.

pitangueira s. f. Surinam cherry (tree) (Eugenia uniflora).

pitar v. to smoke (esp. a pipe). eu pitei o meu cachimbo I puffed at my pipe.

pitauá s. m. (Braz., coll.) = bem-te-vi.

pitecóide adj. m. + f. pithecoid: of or pertaining to monkeys.

piteira s. f. 1. the common century plant (Agave americana). 2. cigar-holder, cigarette-holder (plate F 7). 3. a fig brandy. 4. (fig.) drunkenness.

piteireiro s. m. drunkard. ‖ adj. drunken.

pitéu s. m. (fam.) dainty, tidbit, delicacy.

pítia s. f. Pythia: the priestess and prophetess of Apollo at Delphi.

pitiático adj. of or pertaining to hysteria.

pítico adj. Pythian, Pythic: 1. of or pertaining to Apollo or his priestess at Delphi. 2. referring to the Pythic games.

pitimbóia s. f. (Braz.) an apparatus used to catch shrimp.

pitiríase s. f. (med.) pityriasis: name of various skin diseases characterized by branny scales.

pitiú s. m. (Braz.) 1. the odour of fish (esp. dried codfish). 2. name of various species of chelonians.

pito s. m. (Braz.) 1. a fish of the family Loricariidae (Loricaria Kronei). 2. pipe (for smoking). 3. reprimand, scolding.
ela lhe passou um ~ she gave him a good scolding.

pitoco adj. (Braz.) bobtailed; having a short tail.

píton s. m. python: 1. (Gr. myth.) a gigantic serpent slain by Apollo. 2. (f. pitonisa) necromancer, soothsayer.

pitônico adj. pythonic, oracular; necromantic; diabolic.

pitonisa, pitonissa s. f. pythoness, witch, (female) fortune-teller or soothsayer.

pitoresco s. m. picturesque; picturesqueness. ‖ adj. picturesque, pictorial. ‖ -amente adv. picturesquely.

pitorra s. f. 1. a little top, whirligig. 2. m. + f. a small, thick-set person.

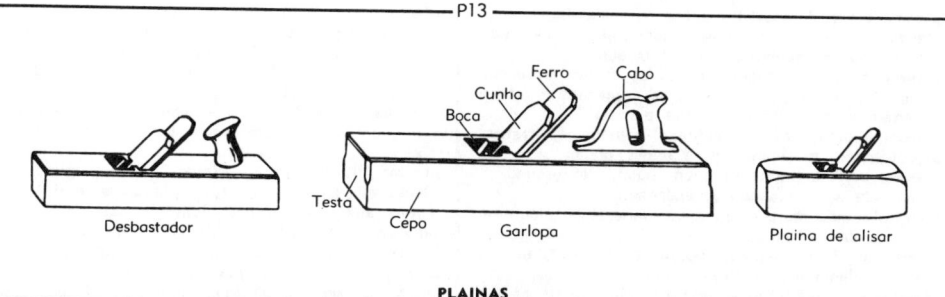

PLAINAS

Desbastador — Testa — Cepo — Garlopa — Boca — Cunha — Ferro — Cabo — Plaina de alisar

P13

pitosga s. m. + f. 1. short-sighted person. 2. person who blinks. ‖ adj. 1. short-sighted. 2. blinking.

pitosporáceas pl. (bot.) Pittosporaceae, a family of shrubs and trees (order Rosales).

pitósporo s. m. pittosporum: a plant of the family Pittosporaceae (Pittosporum tobira).

pitu s. m. (Braz.) a large prawn (Bithynis acanthurus).

pituá s. m. a sort of fine-haired brush.

pituba s. m. (Braz.) horse thief. ‖ adj. m. + f. coward.

pituí, pituim s. m. 1. fetid body odour. 2. the rank smell of a billy-goat.

pituíta s. f. pituite, phlegm, mucus.

pituitária s. f. 1. pituitary (body). 2. pituitary membrane.

pituitário adj. pituitary: containing or secreting mucus.

pituitoso adj. pituitous: full of mucus.

pituitrina s. f. pituitrin: a compound hormone secreted by the posterior lobe of the pituitary gland.

plúca s. f. (S. Braz.) very dry piece of wood; a half--burned trunk.

plum s. m. (pl. **-uns**) (N. Braz.) a very small mosquito.

plúria, pluria s. f. (med.) pyuria: the presence of pus in the urine.

pivete s. m. 1. aromatic substance, burned as an incense. 2. smart child. 3. (Braz.) a youthful accomplice of a thief.

piveteiro s. m. perfuming pan.

pivô s. m. 1. pivot: a) pin. b) central factor. 2. pin tooth.

pivotante s. f. (bot.) tap-root.

pixaim, pixainho s. m. (Braz.) kinky and woolly hair of Negroes. ‖ adj. crisp, kinky, curly (hair).

pixé s. m. (N. Braz.) bad smell, malodour. ‖ adj. tasting of smoke.

píxide s. f. 1. (eccl.) pyx: a covered vessel in which the Host is kept; ciborium. 2. (bot.) pyxidium.

pixoxó s. m. (Braz., ornith.) a seedeater.

pixuá s. m. (Braz.) 1. a plant of the family Euphorbiaceae (Euphorbia portucaloides). 2. a bad and strong tobacco.

pixuna s. f. a sort of small rat.

pixurim s. m. (pl. **-ins**) 1. Brazilian sassafras: plant of the family Lauraceae (Acrodiclidium puchury major). 2. its fruit, the pichurim bean.

pizicato s. m. (mus.) pizzicato. ‖ adj. (mus.) pizzicato, plucked.

pizza s. f. (It.) pizza.

plá s. m. (Braz., sl.) 1. piece of information; a lead. 2. chatter, conversation.

placa s. f. 1. plate: a) flat, thin piece of metal, slab, sheet of any material (plates A 8, B 4, E 8). b) a piece of metal with an inscription (as a doorplate). 2. plaque; brooch; decoration. 3. a branched candlestick, sconce. 4. (electr.) anode.
~ **comemorativa** memorial tablet. ~ **do construtor**

builder's sign (plate A 7). ~ **de licença** (mot.) licence plate (plate V 3). **circuito de** ~ (radio) plate circuit, anode circuit.

placabilidade s. f. placability, placableness, appeasableness.

placar (I) s. m. 1. placard, poster bill. 2. plaque, decoration.

placar (II) v. (also **aplacar**) to placate, appease.

placável adj. m. + f. (pl. **-áveis**) placable, appeasable, reconciliable.

placenta s. f. placenta: 1. (anat.) the organ that nourishes the foetus (in the higher mammals). 2. that part of the ovary which holds the ovules.

placentação s. f. (pl. **-ões**) (anat., zool., bot.) placentation.

placentário s. m. placentary. ‖ adj. placental: of or pertaining to the placenta.

placidez s. f. placidity, placidness, serenity, tranquillity, quiet, calmness.

plácido adj. placid, quiet, tranquil, serene, calm, peaceful. ‖ **placidamente** adv. placidly.

plácito s. m. 1. sanction, approval, consent. 2. a vow of chastity made by the bishops.

placóide adj. placoid: platelike (scales).

plaga (I) s. f. (poet.) region, country, land.

plaga (II) s. f. (mus.) plagal tone.

plagal adj. m. + f. (pl. **-ais**) (mus.) plagal (tone).

plagiar v. to plagiarize; commit plagiarism.

plagiário s. m. (also **plagiador**) plagiary, plagiarist: person who commits plagiarism. ‖ adj. plagiaristic.

plagiato, plágio s. m. plagiarism, literary theft.

plagiocéfalo adj. plagiocephalic.

plagioclásio s. m. (petrog.) plagioclase: triclinic feldspar.

plagióstomo s. m. (ichth.) any of the Plagiostomi. ‖ adj. (zool.) plagiostome, plagiostomous.

plagióstomos s. m. pl. (ichth.) Plagiostomi, a group of cartilaginous fishes.

plaina s. f. (carp.) plane (plate P 13).
~ **de alisar** smoothing plane (plate P 13). ~ **de desbastar, desbastador** jack-plane (plate P 13). **ferro de** ~ plane iron, cutting iron.

plaino s. m. prairie, plain, level land. ‖ adj. = **plano**.

plana s. f. 1. category, class. 2. reputation, fame.

planador s. m. glider: an airplane without an engine; sailing plane.

planáltico adj. marked by plateaus; upland(ish).

planalto s. m. plateau, elevated plain, tableland, upland.

planar v. to plane, glide.

plancha s. f. (also **prancha**) plank.

plancto, plâncton s. m. plankton: the minor animal and plant organisms that float in the water.

planear, planejar v. 1. to project, plan. 2. to intend. 3. to trace, draw, sketch, scheme. 4. to calculate.

planejador s. m. planner, schemer.

planejamento s. m. projection, planning, scheming.

planeta (I) s. f. (eccl.) planeta, a chasuble.
planeta (ê) (II) s. m. planet: any one of the heavenly bodies revolving about the sun.
planetário s. m. planetarium: an apparatus representing the planetary system. ‖ adj. planetary: of or pertaining to a planet or the planets.
roda -a planet wheel. **sistema** ~ planetary system.
planetóide s. m. planetoid, a minor planet.
planeza s. f. a plain, an even, open, flat ground.
plangência s. f. plangency, sadness.
plangente adj. m. + f. plangent, mourning, mournful; pitiful, sad.
planger v. 1. to lament, mourn. 2. to beat, toll or sound plangently (bells).
planície s. f. plain: level or flat ground (plate M 11).
planiço s. m. (Braz.) 1. = **planície**. 2. a large stretch of grassy land.
planificação s. f. (pl. -ões) planning.
planificar v. to design, delineate.
planifólio adj. (bot.) planifolious: having flat leaves.
planiforme adj. m. + f. planiform, flat, level.
planimetria s. f. planimetry: the measurement of plane surfaces.
planimétrico adj. planimetric(al): of or pertaining to planimetry.
planímetro s. m. planimeter: an instrument for measuring the area of plane surfaces.
planipenes s. m. pl. (ent.) Planipennia, a suborder of neuropterous insects.
planirrostro adj. (zool.) planirostral.
planisférico adj. planispheric(al): of or pertaining to a planisphere.
planisfério s. m. (also **planiglobo**) planisphere: a projection or representation of a sphere on a plane (esp. a map).
plano s. m. 1. plain, plane, level ground. 2. a plan: a) drawing of a building. b) a scheme, delineation, diagram, project. c) outline. 3. intention, intent, purpose, design. ‖ adj. 1. plane, even, smooth, flat, level (plate Q). 2. (fig.) clear, evident, manifest.
~ **aerodinâmico** (mot.) airfoil. ~ **côncavo** (opt.) plano-concave. ~ **convexo** (opt.) plano-convex. ~ **de incidência** (opt.) plane of incidence. ~ **de mira** (mil.) plane of sight. ~ **de projeção** (geom.) plane of projection. ~ **de refração** plane of refraction. ~ **inclinado** slide-way, inclined plane. **ângulo** ~ (math.) plane angle. **conforme os** ~**s** according to plans. **curva -a** (geom.) plane curve. **ela transtornou os seus** ~**s** she upset his plans, his apple-cart. **ele auxiliou seus** ~**s** he played her game. **espelho** ~ plane mirror. **estabelecer um** ~ **de trabalho** to draw up a programme. **forjamos** ~**s** we made plans. **geometria -a** plane geometry. **no primeiro** ~ in the foreground. **o** ~ **falhou** the plan has been unsuccessful, the game is up. **último** ~ background.
planografia s. f. planography.
planta s. f. 1. a plant. 2. plan (building, town). 3. (anat.) (also ~ **do pé**) sole of the foot (plate C 18).
~ **medicinal** medicinal herb. **vaso de** ~**s** flowerpot.
plantação s. f. (pl. -ões) 1. plantation, planting. 2. planted ground.
plantador s. m. planter, grower. ‖ adj. planting.
plantagináceas s. f. pl. (bot.) Plantaginaceae, a family of dicotyledonous plants.
planta-misteriosa s. f. (pl. **plantas-misteriosas**) (bot.) sacred bamboo (Nandina domestica).
plantão s. m. (pl. -ões) 1. the duty of an orderly or the orderly himself. 2. duty, service, attendance (esp. as on free saturdays, sundays or at night in an office, hospital or the like).
de ~ on duty. **enfermeiro de** ~ hospital orderly on duty. **médico de** ~ physician on duty.

plantar (I) v. 1. to plant; scatter seed. 2. to cultivate. 3. to propagate. 4. to fix firmly into the ground. 5. to found, build, establish, settle. 6. to lay, place. 7. to infiltrate, inculcate, implant. 8. ~**-se** to plant, set, place or put o. s.
~ **bananeira** to do a handstand. ~**-se diante de** to plant o. s. before. **vá** ~ **batatas!** go chase yourself! go to the devil!
plantar (II) adj. m. + f. (anat., zool.) plantar.
planta-telégrafo s. f. (pl. **plantas-telégrafo**) (bot.) telegraph plant (Desmodium gyrons).
plantear v. to make the plan of a building.
plantel s. m. (pl. -éis) (Braz.) breeding stock.
plantígrado s. m. a plantigrade animal. ‖ adj. plantigrade: walking on the whole sole of the foot.
plantígrados s. m. pl. (zool.) Plantigrada.
plantio s. m. = **plantação**.
plânfula s. f. plantule, an embryo plant.
planura s. f. = **planície**.
plaquê s. m. 1. plated metal. 2. plated goods or ornaments.
plaqueta s. f. a small volume with only a few pages.
~ **sanguínea** (anat.) blood platelet.
plasma s. m. plasma: 1. (anat.) the liquid part of blood or lymph. 2. (min.) a green, faintly translucent variety of quartz. 3. (biol.) protoplasm.
plasmado adj. shaped, produced, molded, formed.
plasmar v. to mold, shape, model (as in clay).
plásmase s. f. (biochem.) plasmase, fibrin ferment.
plasmático adj. plasmatic, plasmic: of or pertaining to plasm.
plasmodesmas s. m. pl. plasmodesm.
plasmódio s. m. plasmodium: a multinucleate continuous mass of protoplasm.
plasmodromos s. m. pl. (zool.) Plasmodroma, a subphylum of protozoans.
plasta s. f. lazy or slothful person.
plástica s. f. 1. plastic art; model(l)ing, molding. 2. plastic surgery. 3. the general conformation of the human body.
plasticidade s. f. plasticity: quality of being plastic.
plasticizar v. to plasticize: 1. render plastic. 2. give shape to.
plástico s. m. plastic. ‖ adj. 1. plastic: a) having the power of molding. b) capable of being modelled, moldable. 2. pertaining to plastics.
argila -a plastic clay. **cirurgia -a** plastic surgery. **matéria -a** plastic (material).
plastídios, plastídulos s. m. pl. (biol.) plastid.
plastificar v. to plasticize, plastify: to make or become plastic.
plastilina s. f. (also **plasticina**) plasticine, plastilina: a variety of modelling clay.
plastômetro s. m. plastometer.
plastrão s. m. (pl. -ões) 1. a sort of large tie. 2. plastron: a) a padded leather shield worn by fencers to protect the breast. b) a shirt-front.
plataforma s. f. 1. platform: a) any flat surface raised above the adjoining level (plate P 4). b) a landing-stage. c) a raised pavement at a railway station (plate E 13). d) (fort.) a basis to mount guns on. e) (fig.) a political programme. 2. (railway) flatcar, platform car. 3. terrace, roof terrace (plate B 13). 4. (pop.) simulacrum, pretense.
~ **de embarque** (railway) loading ramp (plate E 12). ~ **giratória** (railway) turntable (plate E 12). ~ **para saltos ornamentais** diving tower (plate P 17).
plataleídeos s. m. pl. (ornith.) Plataleidae, the spoonbill family.
platanácea s. f. a platanaceous plant.
platanáceo adj. (bot.) platanaceous: belonging to the Platanaceae.

plátano s. m. plátan(e): plane tree (Platanus orientalis).

platéia s. f. (theat.) 1. pit, auditorium (plate P 2). 2. the audience.

ela arrebata a ~ she holds the stage. poltronas de ~ pit stalls (plate T 3).

platelmintos s. m. pl. (zool.) Platyhelminthes: the flatworms.

platense s. m. + f. + adj. = platino.

platibanda s. f. 1. (archit.) platband. 2. a border of flowers (in a garden). 3. wall or railing of a terrace.

platicefalia s. f. platycephaly.

platicéfalo adj. platycephalic, platycephalous: flat-headed.

platicopos s. m. pl. (zool.) Platycopa, an order of crustaceans.

platicúrtico adj. (stat.) platykurtic: said of a curve that is flatter than the Gaussian curve.

platidáctilo, platidátilo adj. (zool.) platydactyl(e): having flat digits.

platielminte, platielmíntio s. m. platyhelminth: any of the Platyhelminthes.

platilobulado adj. (bot.) platylobate.

platina (I) s. f. (chem.) platinum.

platina (II) s.) f. stage of a miscrocope (plate M 9). 2. shoulder-strap.

platinado s. m. (mot.) platinum-point, platinum-contact. ‖ adj. platinated, platinized.

platinagem s. f. (pl. -ens) platinization, platinum coating.

platinar v. to platinize.

platino s. m. Platine: native or inhabitant of the region bordering the River Plate. ‖ adj. Platine: bordering the River Plate.

platinotipia s. f. platinotype: a process of photographic print in which a platinum salt is employed.

platípode adj. m. + f. (zool.) platypod, broad-footed.

platirrinia s. f. platyrrhiny.

platirrínico, platirrínio adj. platyrrhinian: having a short broad nose.

platirrino s. m. 1. a platyrrhinian person. 2. (zool.) a monkey of the order Platyrrhina.

platirrinos s. m. pl. (zool.) Platyrrhina: a division of S. American monkeys.

platispermo s. m. a flat seed.

platô s. m. 1. plateau (plate M 11). 2. balance spring collet (of a watch).

platônico adj. 1. Platonic: of or pertaining to Plato or his philosophy. 2. Platonic. a) professing Platonic love. b) theorical; ideal, mental.

amor ~ Platonic love.

platonismo s. m. 1. Platonism: the philosophy of Plato. 2. (fig.) quality of being Platonic.

plausibilidade s. f. plausibility, plausibleness.

plausível adj. m. + f. (pl. -íveis) 1. plausible; specious. 2. reasonable, sensible. ‖ plausivelmente adv. plausibly.

play-boy s. m. (Engl.) playboy.

play-ground s. m. (Engl.) playground.

plebe s. f. the common people, mob, rabble, populace, riffraff.

plebeidade s. f. the state of being a plebeian.

plebeísmo s. m. plebeianism: 1. the conduct or the character of plebeians. 2. vulgarity, vulgarism.

plebeizar v. to plebeianize: turn into or become a plebeian.

plebeu s. m. (f. plebéia) plebeian: one of the common people. ‖ adj. plebeian: pertaining to the common people; vulgar.

plebiscitário adj. plebiscitary: of or pertaining to a plebiscite.

plebiscito s. m. plebiscite, a direct vote, referendum.

plectógnato s. m. plectognath: a fish of the order Plectognathi.

plectógnatos s. m. pl. (ichth.) Plectognathi, an order of bony fishes.

plectro s. m. 1. plectrum: a small implement of ivory to pluck the strings of a lyre. 2. (fig.) poetry.

plêiade s. f. (also plêiada) 1. Pleiad: a) any of the Pleiades. b) a group of illustrious or brilliant persons. 2. Plêiades pl. (astr.) the Pleiades.

pleiofilia s. f. (bot.) pleiophylly.

pleiteador s. m., pleiteante m. + f. pleader, litigant, demandant, complainant. ‖ adj. pleading; disputing, demanding.

pleitear v. 1. to go to law, plead. 2. to dispute, contest, demand, litigate. 3. to vie with; strive.

pleito s. m. 1. lawsuit, process, plea, prosecution. 2. contest, dispute; discussion.

plenário s. m. (Braz.) plenary assembly; court, jury. ‖ adj. plenary, full, complete, entire; absolute.

indulgência -a plenary indulgence. sessão -a plenary sitting.

plenificar v. to fill; fill in or out; complete.

plenilunar adj. m. + f. plenilunal, plenilunar(y).

plenilúnio s. m. plenilune: a full moon.

plenipotência s. f. plenipotence, full power.

plenipotenciário s. m. plenipotentiary: an ambassador with full powers to act. ‖ adj. plenipotentiary, invested with full powers.

ministro ~ plenipotentiary minister.

plenitude s. f. plenitude, fullness; completeness, abundance.

~ de graça plenitude of grace. ~ do poder absolute power.

pleno adj. 1. full, entire, absolute, plenary. 2. complete, perfect. ‖ -amente adv. fully, quite, completely, entirely, wholly, absolutely.

-a ignorância absolute ignorance. dar ~s poderes to invest with full powers. ele tem -a liberdade it is open to him. em -a luz do dia in full daylight. em -a rua in the open street. em ~ andamento in full swing. ter -a liberdade de freqüentar uma casa to go in and out.

pleonasmo s. m. (gram.) pleonasm: redundance of expression in speaking or writing.

pleonástico adj. pleonastic, redundant.

pleroma s. m. (bot.) plerome: the portion of meristem in the growing ends of stems and roots which gives rise to the stele.

plerose s. f. (med.) plerosis: the restoration of lost tissue.

plesiossauro s. m. Plesiosaurus.

plessometria s. f. (also plessimetria) pleximetry: art of using the pleximeter.

plessométrico adj. (also plessimétrico) pleximetric.

plessômetro s. m. (med., also plessímetro) pleximeter: a plate used in the examination of the chest by mediate percussion.

pletora s. f. plethora: 1. (path.) excessive fullness of blood. 2. superabundance.

pletórico adj. plethoric.

pleura s. f. (anat.) pleura: a thin membrane that covers the lungs.

pleural adj. m. + f. (pl. -ais) pleural: of or pertaining to pleura.

pleuris s. m., pleurisia, pleurite f. (med.) pleurisy, pleuritis: inflammation of the pleura.

pleurítico s. m. person affected with pleurisy. ‖ adj. pleuritic.

pleurodinia s. f. (path.) pleurodynia: chronic rheumatism of the chest walls.

pleurodínico adj. of or pertaining to pleurodynia.

pleurodonte adj. m. + f. (zool.) pleurodont.

pleuronecto s. m. pleuronectid: a fish of the genus Pleuronectidae; a flat-fish.

pleuropneumonia s. f. (path.) pleuropneumonia: pleurisy complicated with pneumonia.

plévia s. f. (S. Braz.) rabble, mob, the masses.

plexo s. m. (anat.) plexus: 1. network of veins, nerves, or fibres. 2. (fig.) a network, a complication.

plexo-coróide s. m. choroid plexus.

plica s. f. 1. accent. 2. plica, fold.

plicar v. to plicate, fold.

plicatura s. f. plication, plicature, fold.

plinto s. m. plinth: 1. (archit.) the lower square part of the base of a column or pedestal. 2. pedestal, socle of a statue (plate E 9).

pliocênico, plioceno adj. (geol.) Pliocene: referring to the most modern Tertiary deposits.

plissagem s. f. (pl. **-ens**) pleating, crimping.

plissar v. to pleat, crimp, tuck, fold.

plistocênico, plistoceno adj. (geol.) Pleistocene.

ploceídeos s. m. pl. (ornith.) Ploceidae, the weaverbird family.

plugue s. m. (electr.) plug.

pluma s. f. 1. plume: a) a feather (esp. a large one). b) a tuft or bunch of feathers (for ornament). 2. writing quill.

plumaceiro s. m. plumassier: person who works or deals in feathers.

plumacho, plumaço s. m. 1. = **plumagem**. 2. ornamental tuft or feathers on a horse.

plumagem s. f. (pl. **-ens**) 1. plumage, feathers, the entire feathery covering of a bird. 2. plume (of feathers); crest.

plumão s. m. (pl. **-ões**) plume or bunch of feathers.

plumar v. to plume, adorn with a plume or feathers.

plumbagina s. f. (min.) plumbago, graphite, blacklead.

plumbaginácea s. f. plumbago: a plumbaginaceous plant.

plumbagináceas s. f. pl. (bot.) Plumbaginaceae.

plumbaginales s. f. pl. (bot.) Plumbaginales, an order of plants comprising solely the family Plumbaginaceae.

plumbear v. to give a leaden appearance or colour to.

plúmbeo adj. plumbeous: 1. leaden. 2. lead-coloured.

plâmbico adj. (chem.) plumbic: of or containing lead.

plumbífero adj. plumbiferous: yielding or containing lead.

plumboso adj. plumbous: containing lead.

plumeiro s. m. a plume or bunch of feathers.

plúmeo adj. plumose, feathered, having feathers.

plumetis s. m. + f. plumetis.

plumicolo adj. having a feathered neck.

plumilha s. f. plumelet, small plume.

plumista s. m. + f. plumist: person who deals in ornamental plumes or feathers.

plumoso adj. plumose, plumous, feathery; feathered; adorned with feathers.

plúmula s. f. plumule: the bud of the ascending axis of a plant while still in the embryo.

plumuliforme adj. m. + f. (bot.) featherlike.

plural s. m. (pl. **-ais**) plural. ‖ adj. m. + f. plural.

pluralidade s. f. plurality.

a ~ **dos votos** the plurality of votes.

pluralismo s. m. (philos.) pluralism: doctrine that there is more than one ultimate principle in the universe.

pluralização s. f. (pl. **-ões**) pluralization: act of pluralizing.

pluralizar v. 1. to pluralize. 2. to multiply.

pluricelular adj. m. + f. (bot.) pluricellular.

plurifloro adj. (bot.) pluriflorous: having many flowers.

plurilíngüe adj. m. + f. plurilingual: speaking several languages.

pluripartido adj. (bot.) pluripartite.

plurisseriado adj. pluriseriated.

plurivalve adj. m. + f. (bot., zool.) plurivalve, multivalve.

Plutão s. m. (astr.) Pluto.

plutarco s. m. (fig.) a biographer. ‖ adj. Plutarchian: of or pertaining to the Greek biographer Plutarch.

plúteo s. m. (archit.) pluteus: a wall or parapet between columns.

plutocracia s. f. plutocracy: rule or dominion of wealth or of the rich.

plutocrata s. m. + f. plutocrat: an adherent of plutocracy.

plutocrático adj. plutocratic: of or pertaining to plutocracy.

plutônico adj. (geol.) plutonic.

plutônio s. m. (chem., phys.) plutonium. ‖ adj. Plutonian: of or pertaining to Pluto.

plutonismo s. m. Plutonism: the Plutonic theory.

plutonista s. m. + f. Plutonist: an adherent of the Plutonic theory. ‖ adj. Plutonist, Plutonic.

plutonomia s. f. plutonomy, political economy.

pluvial s. m. (pl. **-ais**) (eccl.) cope, pluvial (plate P 5). ‖ adj. m. + f. (also **pluviátil**, pl. **-áteis**) pluvial: of or pertaining to rain, rainy.

pluviômetro s. m. pluviometer: an instrument for measuring rainfall.

pluvioso s. m. Pluviôse: the fifth month of the French Revolutionary calendar. ‖ adj. (poet.) pluvial, rainy, pluvious.

pneu s. m. (short for **pneumático**) tyre, tire (plates B 11, P 11, R 2).

~ **antiderrapante** non-skid tyre (plate V 3). ~ **balão** balloon tyre. ~ **sobressalente** spare tyre, stepney, step wheel (plate V 3).

pneuma s. m. pneuma, breath, spirit, soul.

pneumática s. f. pneumatics: the science which deals with the physical properties of gases.

pneumático s. m. (also **pneu**) tyre, tire (plate P 11). ‖ adj. pneumatic: of or pertaining to air.

pneumatologia s. f. pneumatology: the science of spiritual existence.

pneumatológico adj. pneumatological: of or pertaining to pneumatology.

· **pneumatologista** s. m. + f., **pneumatólogo** m. pneumatologist.

pneumatose s. f. (med.) pneumatosis: abnormal presence of air in any part of the body.

pneumectomia s. f. (surg.) pneumectomy: the excision of lung tissue.

pneumocele s. f. (path.) pneumatocele: hernial protrusion of the lung tissue.

pneumococia s. f. (med.) pneumococcosis: infection with pneumococci.

pneumococo s. m. (bact.) pneumococcus: the microbe (Diplococcus pneumoniae) which causes labor pneumonia.

pneumoconiose s. f. (med.) pneumoconiosis: a chronic fibrous reaction in the lungs to the inhalation of dust.

pneumogástrico adj. pneumogastric: pertaining to the lungs and stomach.

pneumólise s. f. pneumo(no)lysis: the operation of stripping the pleura from the fascia of the thoracic wall in order to allow the lung to collapse.

pneumolitíase s. f. (med.) pneumolithiasis: the presence of concretions in the lungs.

pneumologia s. f. pneumology: the study of the respiratory organs.

pneumológico adj. pneumological: of or pertaining to pneumology.

pneumonalgia s. f. a pain in the lungs.

pneumonia s. f. pneumonia: inflammation of the lungs.

~ **aguda** (or **fibrinosa**) fibrinous or lobar pneumonia.

pneumônico s. m. person affected with pneumonia. ‖ adj. pneumonic: pertaining to pneumonia.

pneumoperitônio s. m. (med.) pneumoperitoneum: the presence of air in the peritoneal cavity.

pneumopleurisia s. f. (med.) pneumopleuritis: inflammation of the lungs and pleura.

pneumorragia s. f. pneumorrhagia: hemorrhage from the lungs.

pneumorrágico adj. of or pertaining to pneumorrhagia.

pneumotomia s. f. (surg.) pneumonotomy.

pneumotórax s. m., sg. + pl. pneumothorax: accumulation of gas in the pleural cavity.

~ **artificial** artificial pneumothorax.

pó s. m. 1. powder. 2. dust.

~**-de-arroz** rice powder. ~ **de ouro** gold dust. **aspirador de** ~ vacuum cleaner. **leite em** ~ powdered milk. **levantar** ~ to raise the dust. **reduzir a ou fazer em** ~ to reduce to dust. **tu és** ~ **e em** ~ **te hás de tornar** dust thou art, and to dust shalt thou return.

poa s. f. (naut.) bridle.

~**s de bolinha** (naut.) the bridles of the bow line.

poalha s. f. a little cloud of fine dust.

pobre s. m. + f. pauper, beggar, a poor man or woman. ‖ adj. 1. poor, indigent, needy. 2. unhappy, wretched. 3. unprofitable, worthless. 4. scanty, meagre. 5. barren, unproductive (soil). 6. pitiable. ‖ ~**mente** adv. poorly; badly.

~ **como Jó** as poor as a church mouse. ~**-diabo!** poor devil!, poor fellow! ~ **de mim!** poor me! ~ **homem** poor fellow, poor man. **bem-aventurados os** ~**s de espírito, porque deles é o reino dos céus** blessed are the poor in spirit, for theirs is the kingdom of heaven. **ele é um homem** ~ he is a penniless person. **os** ~**s** the poor.

pobre-diabo s. m. (pl. **pobres-diabos**) a sad sack: 1. wretched fellow. 2. inoffensive person, without personality.

pobrerio s. m. (S. Braz.) the poor collectively.

pobretão s. m. (pl. **-ões**) 1. a poor person, wretch. 2. person who asks for alms without being poor.

pobrete s. m. a poor fellow. ‖ adj. rather poor.

pobreza s. f. 1. poverty, poorness, indigence, want, need, penury, destitution. 2. the poor.

~ **não é vileza** poverty is no crime. **a** ~ **da terra** the nakedness of the land. **extrema** ~ extreme poverty. **reduzir à** ~ to reduce to poverty.

poca s. f. a sort of bamboo used in basketry.

poça s. f. 1. plash, puddle (of water). 2. pool.

~ **de sangue** a pool of blood.

poção (I) s. f. (pl. **-ões**) potion: a drink, a draught (esp. of medicine); a dose.

poção (II) s. m. (pl. **-ões**) a deep place in a river.

poceiro s. m. 1. a digger of wells. 2. a large basket used for washing wool.

pocema s. f. (Braz.) 1. war cry. 2. hullabaloo, uproar, clamour. 3. murmur.

pochade s. f. (arts) pochade: a rough or quickly executed sketch or study.

pocilga s. f. 1. sty, pigsty, pigpen (plate E 11). 2. (fig.) a filthy house or room.

poço s. m. 1. well. 2. shaft of a mine, pit (plate M 10). 3. (naut.) height of a ship from the hold to the deck. 4. abysm, chasm. 5. deepest part of a river or lake.

~ **artesiano** artesian well. ~ **de elevador** elevator shaft, lift shaft (plate E 2). ~ **de escoamento**

dumb-well. ~ **de inspeção** man-hole (plate R 8). ~ **de petróleo,** ~ **petrolífero** oil-well. **água de** ~ well-water.

poçoca s. f. (N. Braz., pop.) lie.

poçuca s. m. + f., **poçuqueador** m. (S. Braz.) cadging person.

poçuquear v. (S. Braz.) to cadge, sponge.

poda s. f. (also **podadura**) pruning, lopping of trees. **fazer a** ~ **a alguém** to speak ill of one. **tempo da** ~ the pruning season.

podadeira s. f. pruning shears; pruning hook, pruning knife (plate J 2).

podador s. m. pruner: person who prunes. ‖ adj. pruning.

podagra s. f. podagra, gout.

podágrico adj. podagric: pertaining to or affected with gout.

podal adj. m. + f. (pl. **-ais**) pedal: of or pertaining to the foot.

podão s. m. (pl. **-ões**) 1. pruning-hook, pruning-knife, vine-knife. 2. pruning-shears. 3. (fig.) a clumsy awkward man.

podar v. 1. to prune, lop, trim; dress (vines). 2. (fig.) to cut.

~ **as árvores** to tip the trees.

podengo s. m. setting dog, rabbit hound.

poder s. m. 1. power: a) might. b) strength, force, vigour, potency, energy. c) authority, dominion, command, sway, influence. d) ability, faculty, possibility, capacity. e) sovereignty. f) government. g) political ascendency. 2. efficacy. 3. possession, keeping. 4. means. 5. ~**es** pl. procuration. ‖ v. 1. to be able to. 2. can. 3. may. 4. to have authority or influence. 5. to have power to. 6. ~**-se** to be possible or permitted.

~ **absoluto** absolute power. ~ **andar** to be able to walk. ~ **executivo** executive power. ~ **explosivo** explosive force. ~ **legislativo** legislative power, legislature. **cair em** ~ **de alguém** to fall into someone's hands. **ela não pode com ele** she is no match for him, (sl.) she is not in it with him. **ele pode chegar a qualquer momento** he may come this moment. **ele podia tê-lo feito** he could have done it. **eles se apossaram do** ~ they seized the power. **em que lhe posso ser útil?** what can I do for you? **estar no** ~ to be in (power). **estava em seu** ~ it was in his (your) possession. **eu posso** I can. **isso pode ser** it is possible. **isto se pode fazer** this may be done. **logo que puder, ajudá-lo-ei** when I get a chance, I'll help you. **não está em meu** ~ it is without my power. **não podemos ir porque está chovendo** we can't go because it is raining. **não posso** I cannot. **não posso deixar de fazer isso** I can't but do it. **não posso senão ir** I can't but go. **não se pode viver com ela** there is no living with her. **no** ~ in power. **o** ~ **das circunstâncias** the force of circumstances. **os** ~**es das trevas** the powers of darkness. **plenos** ~**es** full powers. **pode bem ficar com ele** you may have it for your own. **pode estar certo!** you may be sure of it!, (U. S. A.) I'll tell the world! **pode ser** it may be. **posso entrar?** may I come in? **posso ficar?** may I stay? **salve-se quem puder!** every man for himself! **sua vida está em meu** ~ his (your) life lies in my hands. **ter o** ~ **nas mãos** to be in authority.

poderio s. m. 1. power, might, force. 2. authority. 3. jurisdiction.

poderoso adj. 1. powerful, mighty. 2. efficacious, potent. 3. intense, vigorous, energetic. 4. influential. 5. forceful. ‖ ~**-amente** adv. powerfully.

Deus todo-poderoso God Almighty.

podestade s. m. podestà: (in Italy) a chief magistrate in medieval towns and republics.
pódice s. m. podex, anal region.
podicipedídeos s. m. pl. (ornith.) Podicipedidae, Colymbidae, the grebe family.
pódio s. m. (zool.) podium, the tube foot of the Echinoderma.
podoa s. f. a gardener's knife, pruning knife, vine knife (plate J 2).
podobrânquia s. f. (zool.) podobranch(ia).
podocarpo s. m. podocarp: a plant of the genus Podocarpus.
pododáctilo, pododátilo s. m. (anat.) toe.
podofilo s. m. (bot.) May apple (Podophyllum peltatum).
podométrico adj. pedometric(al).
podômetro s. m. pedometer: an instrument that measures the distance covered on foot, registering the number of the steps.
podospermo s. m. (bot.) podosperm, a funicle.
podostemonácea s. f. podostemad: a podostemaceous plant.
podrão adj. (pl. -ões) (f. -ona) (N. Braz., pop.) very bad.
podre s. m. 1. a rotten or putrid part of a thing 2. ~s pl. blemishes, vices, defects, imperfections, bad habits. ‖ adj. m. + f. 1. rotten, putrid, carious. 2. fetid. 3. (fig.) perverted. depraved, corrupt. ~ **de rico** rich as Croesus, very rich. **maçã** ~ rotten apple. **saber os** ~**s de alguém** to know a person's faults.
podredouro s. m. (also **podredoiro**) 1. place where things rot easily. 2. garbage dump. 3. (fig.) place of corruption.
podricalho s. m. anything rotten. ‖ adj. lazy, slothful; weak.
podrida s. m. = **olha-podrida.**
podridão s. f. (pl. -ões) 1. rottenness, putridity, putridness; putrefaction. 2. (fig.) corruption, licentiousness, demoralization.
podrido adj. 1. putrefied, putrid. 2. useless.
podrigueira s. f. (Braz.) 1. place of corruption. 2. = **podridão.**
podrura s. f. 1. (obs.) putridity. 2. (N. Braz., fig.) a very lazy person.
poedeira s. f. laying hen; ‖ adj. f. laying (hen). **galinha** ~ 1. laying hen. 2. hen that lays many eggs.
poedouro s. m. (also **poedoiro**) place where hens lay.
poeira s. f. 1. dust (raised by the wind). 2. powder. 3. (fig.) noise, disorder, trouble. 4. (fam.) presumption, self-conceit.
dar ~ (Braz.) to overpass (said of a car which overtakes another on the road). **deitar** ~ **nos olhos dos outros** to throw dust into people's eyes. **levantar (fazer)** ~ 1. to kick up dust. 2. (fig.) to make a noise.
poeirada s. f. a cloud of dust, dust cloud.
poeirento adj. dusty, covered with dust.
poejo (I) s. m. (bot.) pennyroyal, pudding grass (Mentha pulegium).
poejo (II) s. m. the finest powder of flour.
poema s. m. poem.
~ **épico** heroic or epic poem.
poemeto s. m. a little poem.
poente s. m. 1. the west, occident. 2. the setting of the sun. ‖ adj. m. + f. 1. setting: said of the sun. 2. laying.
poento adj. = **poeirento.**
poesia s. f. poesy, poetry: 1. the art of metrical composition. 2. poetical work, verse, poem. 3. poetic quality. 4. poetic spirit or feeling.
~ **lírica** lyric poetry.

poeta s. m. (f. **poetisa**) poet: person who composes poetry; bard.
~ **laureado** poet laureate.
poetaço s. m. poetaster, inferior poet.
poetagem s. f. (pl. -ens) loquacity, talkativeness.
poetar v. to poetize, poeticize: 1. make poetry or verses. 2. express in poetic form.
poetastro s. m. poestaster, inferior poet, versemaker.
poética s. f. 1. poetics: art of composing verses. 2. theory of poetry.
poético adj. poetic(al): 1. having the qualities of poetry. 2. of or pertaining to poetry. 3. characteristic of or befitting a poet. ‖ **poeticamente** adv. poetically.
engenho ~ poetic talent.
poetisa s. f. poetess, poetress, a female poet.
poetismo s. m. the poets collectively.
poetização s. f. (pl. -ões) act of poeticizing.
poetizar v. (also **poetificar**) to poeticize, poetize: 1. make poetic. 2. write poetry.
pogoníase s. f. pogoniasis: 1. excessive growth of a beard. 2. the growth of a beard in a woman.
poia s. f. a large flat loaf (of bread).
póia s. m. (Braz.) slug, sluggard, lazybones.
poial s. m. (pl. -ais) 1. a stone bench near a house. 2. place where something is usually put.
poiar v. 1. to place, put. 2. to dispose, arrange. 3. to lean on.
pois conj. since, because, whereas, therefore, as, for, so; moreover.
~ **bem** well then. ~ **é isso mesmo!** that's just it! ~ **é, meu caro, a situação não está boa** that's it, friend, things don't look so good. ~ **não!** of course!, certainly! ~ **se ele mesmo disse que viria!** but he himself said he would come! ~ **sim!** (also ironically) oh, sure!
poita s. f. (also **pouta**) a stone or the like used by fishermen instead of an anchor.
poitar v. (also **poutar**) to stop a boat by means of a **poita.**
poja s. f. (naut.) claw of a sail.
pojadouro s. m. (also **pojadoiro**) top round (of beef).
pojante adj. m. + f. (naut.) going before the wind.
pojar (I) v. to land, touch land, cast anchor; disembark.
pojar (II) v. 1. to elevate, raise. 2. to intumesce, swell up.
pojo (ô) s. m. landing-place.
pola (ô) s. f. branch, sprout.
póla s. f. a beating, thrashing.
polaca s. f. 1. Polish woman. 2. polonaise (music and dance). 3. (pop.) a prostitute. 4. (naut.) polaca: three-masted vessel.
polaciúria, polaciuria s. f. (med.) unduly frequent emiction.
polaco s. m. Pole: native or inhabitant of Poland. ‖ adj. Polish: of Poland.
polainas s. f. pl. gaiters, spatter-dash, leggings.
polar adj. m. + f. polar, of the pole.
círculo ~ polar circle. **estrela** ~ polar star, North-star.
polaridade s. f. (phys.) polarity.
polarímetro s. m. (phys.) polarimeter: an instrument for showing the phenomena of polarized light.
polarização s. f. (pl. -ões) (phys.) polarization.
polarizador s. m. polarizer. ‖ adj. polarizing.
polarizar v. to polarize: 1. give polarity to. 2. cause polarization in.
polarizável adj. m. + f. (pl. -áveis) polarizable.
polca s. f. polka: a lively round dance of Bohemian origin and a piece of music for this.
polcar v. to polka, dance a polka.

pôlder s. m. (pl. **pôlderes**) polder: a tract of land (esp. in the Netherlands) reclaimed from the sea and protected by dikes.

poldra s. f. 1. filly. 2. (also **alpondra**) stepping-stone.

poldro s. m. a colt, young horse.

polé s. f. 1. a pulley. 2. (obs.) strappado.

poleá s. m. (also **polear**) pariah.

poleame s. m. (naut.) all the blocks or pulleys of a ship, tackle.

polear v. to strappado.

poleeiro s. m. person who makes or sells pulleys.

polegada s. f. 1. ancient linear measure equal to 2.75 cm. 2. inch: 2.54 cm
~ **quadrada** square inch.

polegar s. m. 1. thumb (plates C 18, L 3). 2. the big toe. ‖ adj. of or pertaining to the thumb or to the big toe.
pequeno ~ hop-o'-my-thumb. **unha do** ~ thumbnail.

poleiro s. m. 1. roost, perch; hen-roost. 2. (fig.) domineering position. 3. (pop., theat.) pigeonhole, peanut gallery (the top gallery).

polemarco s. m. (Gr. hist.) polemarch: a military commander-in-chief.

polêmica s. f. polemic(s), controversy, discussion, dispute, debate.

polemicar v. to polemize: engage in polemics.

polêmico adj. polemic(al): of or pertaining to polemics, controversial.

polemista s. m. + f. polemist, controversialist. ‖ adj. given to polemics.

polemizar v. to polemize.

polemoniáceas s. f. pl. (bot.) Polemoniaceae, a family of herbaceous plants.

pólen s. m. (pl. **polens, pólenes**) (bot., also **polem**) pollen.

polenta s. f. polenta: a kind of porridge made of maize meal (a common food in Italy).

pólex s. m. pollex, thumb.

polha s. f. 1. chicken; pullet. 2. (fig.) young girl.

polhastro s. m. 1. a big chicken. 2. (fig.) a tall young man. 3. rascal, scoundrel.

polia (I) s. f. (mech.) pulley, sheave.
~ **escalonada** step-cone pulley. ~ **louca** loose pulley; idle pulley. ~ **motriz** driving pulley. ~ **oscilante** floating sheave.

polia (II) s. f. (Braz., ent.) the bristly larva of the larder beetle.

poliacanto adj. polyacanthus, thorny, having many thorns.

poliadelfia s. f. (bot.) polyadelphia.

poliadelfo adj. polyadelphous: having stamens united in more than two bundles.

poliandra s. f. 1. polyandrous woman. 2. polyandrous plant. ‖ adj. polyandrous: 1. having more than one husband at a time. 2. (bot.) having numerous stames.

poliandria s. f. polyandry: system of marriage with several husbands.

poliândrico adj. polyandric: of or pertaining to polyandry.

poliandro adj. (bot.) polyandrous: having many stamens inserted on the receptacle.

poliantéia s. f. polyanthea, an anthology.

polianto adj. polyanthous: producing many flowers.

poliarquia s. f. polyarchy: government by many.

poliatômico adj. (chem.) polyatomic.

policárpico, policarpo adj. (bot.) polycarpous: producing much flowers or fruits.

pólice s. m. pollex, thumb.

policêntrico adj. polycentric (spiral).

Polichinelo s. m. 1. punchinello, Punch: the chief character in a puppet-show of Italian origin. 2. buffoon, ridiculous person.

polícia s. f. 1. police (force, organization or department). 2. civilization. 3. polity. 4. m. a policeman.
~ **marítima** coast-guard. ~ **militar** military police. ~ **secreta** secret service. **comissário de** ~ police commissioner. **inspetor de** ~ police inspector. **oficial de** ~ police officer. **tribunal de** ~ police court.

policiado adj. 1. policed. 2. civilized. 3. moderate.

polícia-inglesa s. f. (pl. **polícias-inglesas**) the Cayenne red-breasted blackbird.

policial s. m. (pl. **-ais**) policeman. ‖ adj. m. + f. police: of or pertaining to the police.
cão ~ police dog. **romance** ~ detective story.

policiamento s. m. police supervision, policing, patrolling.

policiar v. 1. to police: a) maintain order by means of police. b) provide with police. c) patrol; guard. 2. to keep vigil. 3. to take care of. 4. to civilize. 5. ~-**se** to control, refrain, check o. s.

policitação s. f. (pl. **-ões**) pollicitation: 1. a promising or a promise. 2. an informal promise not yet accepted by the promisee.

policitemia s. f. (med.) polycythemia: excess of the number of red corpuscles in the blood.

policlínica s. f. polyclinic: 1. a clinic or hospital treating diseases of many sorts. 2. the practice of general medicine. 3. dispensary for outpatients in a hospital.

policlínico s. m. physician for general medicine. ‖ adj. polyclinic.

polícomo adj. having much hair.

policônico adj. polyconic: having many cones.

policórdio, policordo s. m. polychord: a viol-shaped instrument of ten strings.

policresto adj. polychrestic: serving for many purposes (as a remedy).

policromático adj. (also **policrômico**) polychromatic.

policromia s. f. 1. (med.) polychromy: excessive pigmentation. 2. polychromasia: quality of being polychromatic or multicoloured.

policromo adj. polychromatic, multicoloured: having many colours.

policultura s. f. (agric.) mixed farming.

polidáctilo, polidátilo adj. polydactil(e): having many fingers.

polidesmóideos s. m. pl. (zool.) Polydesmoidea, an order of diploid millipeds.

polidez s. f. politeness, courtesy, urbanity, elegance of manners, civility.

polidípsia s. f. (med.) polydipsia: excessive thirst.

polido adj. 1. polished, smoothed; varnished. 2. shining, bright. 3. polite, genteel, accomplished, civil, well-bred, elegant, well-mannered, courtly, urbane. ‖ **-amente** adv. 1. smoothly, brightly. 2. politely.

polidor s. m. polisher, burnisher. ‖ adj. polishing.

poliédrico adj. polyhedral, polyhedric, polyhedrous, relating to a polyhedron.

poliedro s. m. (geom.) polyhedron: a solid figure having many faces.

poliéster s. m. (chem.) polyester.

polifagia s. f. polyphagia: 1. excessive or voracious eating. 2. craving for all kinds of food.

polífago adj. polyphagous: 1. having a voracious appetite. 2. living on many kinds of food.

polifásico adj. polyphase.

polifilo adj. polyphyllous: having many leaves.

polífagos s. m. pl. (ent.) Polyphaga, a suborder of Coleoptera.

polifiodonte s. m. (zool.) polyphyodont: animal with several sets of teeth (as a shark).

polifonia s. f. (mus.) polyphony, polyphonic composition.

polifônico adj. polyphonic: of or pertaining to polyphony.
polígala s. f. (bot.) milkwort (Polygala senega).
poligaláceas s. f. pl. (bot.) Polygalaceae, the milkwort family.
poligamia s. f. polygamy: practice or condition of having more than one wife or husband at the same time.
poligâmico adj. polygamous, of or pertaining to polygamy.
polígamo s. m. polygamist. ‖ adj. polygamous.
poligarquia s. f. polyarchy: government by many.
poligástrico adj. polygastric: having more than one stomach.
poligenia s. f. polygenesis.
polígeno adj. polygenous.
poliginia s. f. polygyny: the state or practice of having several wives at the same time.
poligino adj. polygynous: 1. having more than one wife at the same time. 2. (bot.) having many pistils.
poliglota s. m. + f. polyglot: 1. person who knows several languages. 2. a book or writing with the same text in several languages. ‖ adj. poliglot: 1. knowing several languages (person). 2. written in several languages (as a book).
poliglótico adj. polyglottal, polyglottic: 1. of or pertaining to a polyglot. 2. written in many languages.
poliglotismo s. m. polyglottism.
poligonáceas s. f. pl. (bot.) Polygonaceae, a family of herbs, shrubs and trees (order Polygonales).
poligonal adj. m. + f. (pl. -ais) polygonal: having the form of a polygon.
polígono s. m. (geom.) polygon: a plane figure having many (more than four) angles and sides.
poligrafia s. f. 1. polygraphy, a collection of different scientific or literary works. 2. knowledge, versatility of thought.
poligráfico adj. polygraphic.
polígrafo s. m. 1. polygraph. 2. polygrapher.
poligrama s. m. polygram.
polilépide adj. m. + f. (bot.) polylepidous, many-scaled.
polimastiginos s. m. pl. (zool.) Polymastigina, an order of flagellates.
polilha s. f. 1. fine dust. 2. a clothes moth.
comido de ~s moth-eaten.
polímata, polímate s. m. 1. polyhistor, polyhistorian, polymath. 2. polygraph.
polimatia s. f. polymathy.
polimático adj. polymathic.
polimento s. m. 1. act or result of polishing. 2. polish, burnish, shine. 3. finish. 4. varnish. 5. varnished leather.
polímere s. m. (chem.) polymer, polymeric compound.
polimérico adj. (chem.) polymeric.
polimerismo s. m. (chem.) polymerism.
polimerização s. f. (pl. -ões), (chem.) polymerization.
polimerizar v. (chem.) to polymerize.
polímero adj. (chem.) polymeric.
polimignita s. f. (min.) polymignite.
polímnico adj. rhetorical.
polimórfico adj. polymorphic, polymorphous.
polimorfismo s. m. (biol., cryst.) polymorphism.
polimorfo adj. polymorphic, polymorphous, multiform, various.
polinário adj. (bot.) pollinar.
polinésico s. m. Polynesian: the language of the Polynesians. ‖ adj. Polynesian.
polinésio s. m. Polynesian, Kanaka, Maori: native or inhabitant of Polynesia. ‖ adj. Polynesian.
polineurite s. f. (med., also polinevrite) polyneuritis.
polineurítico adj. (med.) also polinevrítico) polyneuritic.

polínia s. f. (bot.) pollinium.
polínico adj. (bot.) pollinic(al), pollinar.
polinífago adj. (zool.) polliniphagous.
polinífero adj. (bot.) polliniferous.
polínio s. m. (bot.) pollinium.
polinização s. f. (pl. -ões), (bot.) pollination.
praticar a ~ cruzada (biol.) to cross-pollinate.
polinizar v. to pollinate.
polinômico adj. (math.) polynomic, polynomial.
polinômio s. m. (math.) polynomial, polynomial expression.
pólio s. m. (bot.) poly, bastard hyssop.
poliomielite s. f. (med.) poliomyelitis.
poliônimo adj. polyonymous, having several names.
poliope s. m. (med.) polyopic person.
poliopia s. f. (med.) polyopia, multiple vision.
poliorama s. m. polyorama.
poliorcética s. f. (mil.) poliorcetics, art of conducting sieges.
poliorcético adj. (mil.) poliorcetic(al).
poliose s. f. 1. discolouring or bleaching of hair. 2. (chem.) polyose, polysaccharide.
polipeiro s. m. (zool.) 1. polyparia, polypary. 2. a group of polyps.
polipétalo adj. (bot.) polypetalous, choripetalous.
polipiforme adj. m. + f. polypiform, shaped like a polyp.
poliplacóforos s. m. pl. (zool.) Polyplacophora, an order of molluscs: the chitons.
pólipo s. m. polyp: 1. (zool.) an invertebrate animal belonging to the Coelenterata. 2. (zool.) an octopus. 3. (med.) polypus, a pedunculate tumour of the mucous membrane.
polipodiácea s. f. (bot.) 1. polypody. 2. ~s pl. Polypodiaceae: a family of ferns.
polipódio s. m. 1. (zool.) polypod, polypod animal. 2. (bot.) polypody, adder's-foot, oak fern. ‖ adj. polypod.
polipóide adj. m. + f. polypous, polypoidal.
poliporáceas s. f. pl. (bot.) Polyporaceae: a family of spore-bearing fungi (order Agaricales).
políporo s. m. (bot.) Polyporus: a genus of fungi (Polyporaceae).
políporo-da-isca-de-couro s. m. (pl. políporos-da-isca-de-couro), (bot.) hard tinder fungus.
poliposo adj. (zool., med.) polypous, polypose, polypoid(al).
poliprisma s. m. (phys.) poliprism.
poliprotodontes s. m. pl. (zool.) polyprotodontia: carnivorous marsupials.
poliptoto, poliptóton s. m. (rhet.) polyptoton: repetition of the same word in different inflections (in the same phrase).
poliqueta s. m. (zool.) 1. polychaete. 2. ~s pl. Polychaeta: an order of the class Chaetopoda (marine worms).
polir v. 1. to polish: a) make glossy or smooth. b) furbish, brighten, burnish. c) varnish. d) refine, civilize. e) become brilliant or polished. 2. ~-se to become polite.
~ novamente to repolish. uma frase bem polida a well-turned phrase.
polirrítmico adj. polyrhythmic(al).
polirrizo adj. polyrhizous, polyrhizal.
poliscópio s. m. (phys.) polyscope.
polispermia s. f. (biol., med.) polyspermy, polyspermia.
polispermo adj. polyspermic, polyspermal, polyspermous.
polísporo adj. (bot.) polysporous, polysporic.
polissacarídeo s. m. (chem.) polysaccharide.
polissemia s. f. (polysemy, multiplicity of meanings.
polissialia s. f. (med.) excessive salivary secretion.
polissilábico adj. polysyllabic(al).

polissilabismo s. m. polysyllabism.
polissílabo s. m. polysyllable, polysyllabic word. ‖ adj. polysyllabic(al).
polissíndeto, polissíndeton s. m. (rhet.) polysyndeton.
polissíntese s. f. polysynthesis.
polissintético adj. polysynthetic(al).
polissulfeto, polissulfureto s. m. (chem.) polysulphide.
polistilo s. m. (archit.) polystile. ‖ adj. polystile.
polistireno s. m. (chem.) polystyrene.
polistomo s.m. (zool.) polystome: a trematode worm.
Politburo s. m. (pol.) Politburo.
politeama s. m. a theatre which presents various kinds of plays.
politécnica s. f. polytechnic, polytechnical school.
politécnico s. m. polytechnical student. ‖ adj. polytechnic(al).
politéico adj. polytheistic.
politeísmo s. m. polytheism.
politeísta s. m. + f. polytheist, one who believes in many gods. ‖ adj. polytheistic(al).
política s. f. 1. the art of ruling. 2. political science, politics, statecraft. 3. (fig.) cunning, artifice. 4. sagacity. 5. politeness. 6. agility or smoothness of action, cleverness.
   a honestidade é a melhor ~ honesty is the best policy. a ~ de boa vizinhança the comity of nations, the policy of good neighbourhood. discutir questões de ~ to talk politics. ~ administrativa interna domestic policy. ~ externa foreign policy.
politicagem, politicalha s. f. (pl. -ens, s) 1. pursuit of personal interest in politics. 2. petty politics, petty politician. 3. politicaster.
politicalhão s. m. (pl. -ões), (depr.) politicaster.
politicalheiro adj. given to petty politics.
politicalho s. m. (depr.) politicaster, petty politician.
politicante s. m. + f. (depr.) politicaster, petty politician. ‖ adj. dabbling in politics, politicizing.
politicão s. m. (pl. -ões) party big shot, important politician.
politicar v. to politicize, discuss, or take part in politics.
politicastro s. m. (depr.) politicaster.
político s. m. 1. politician. 2. statesman. 3. (depr.) politicaster. ‖ adj. 1. of or relative to public affairs. 2. politic(al). 3. cunning, artful. 4. delicate, diplomatic. ‖ politicamente adv. politically.
   aritmética -a political arithmetic. direito ~ public or political law. economia -a political economy. orador ~ platform speaker, stump orator. por motivos ~s for political reasons.
politicóide s. m. (depr.) politicaster.
polítipo adj. (bot.) polytypical.
politiqueiro s. m. (depr.) politicaster, petty politician. ‖ adj. given to petty politics, politizing, unfair, corrupt.
politiquete s. m. political nonentity, unimportant politician.
politiquice s. f. (depr.) 1. pursuit of private interests in politics. 2. act of petty politics. 3. party politics.
politiquilho s. m. (depr.) politicaster.
politiquismo s. m. (depr.) petty politics.
politômico adj. polytomous.
politonalidade s. f. (mus.) polytonality, polytony.
politonar v. (mus.) 1. to use simultaneously two or more tonalities in a musical composition. 2. to sing in two different voices.
polítrico s. m. (bot.) maidenhair spleenwort. ‖ adj. (zool.) polytrichous, having much hair.
politrofia s. f. (med.) excessive nutrition.
poliúria, poliuria s. f. (med.) polyuria.
poliúrico adj. (med.) polyuric.
polivalente adj. m. + f. (chem.) polyvalent, multivalent.

políxeno s. m. (min.) crude native platinum.
polizoário s. m. (zool.) polyzoan. ‖ adj. polyzoan.
polizoicidade s. f. (zool.) quality of being polyzoic.
polizóico adj. (zool.) polyzoic.
polizonado adj. polyzonal.
polmaço s. m. dense fog, heavy mist.
polmão s. m. (pl. -ões), (pop.) 1. swelling. 2. tumour. 3. boil, phlegmon.
polme s. m. pap, pulp.
polmo s. m. cloudiness of a liquid.
pólo (I) s. m. 1. North Pole, South Pole. 2. polar region. 3. the positive or negative terminal (pole) of a magnet or an electric cell. 4. (fig.) guide, leader. 5. the North.
   ~ ártico (antártico) Arctic, North Pole (Antarctic, South Pole). ~ magnético magnetic pole. aí estão os dois ~s da controvérsia these are the antithetical points of the debate.
pólo (II) s. m. (sport) polo.
   ~ aquático water polo.
pôlo s. m. a yearling hawk or falcon.
polografia s. f. (astr.) an astronomical description of the sky.
polonês s. m. (pl. -eses) Polish: 1. native or inhabitant of Poland. 2. the Polish language. ‖ adj. Polish.
polonesa s. f. 1. Polish woman. 2. (mus.) polonaise. 3. polonaise, a woman's garment worn over the skirt, robe after a Polish fashion. 4. redingote.
polônio (I) s. m. (chem.) polonium (symbol Po).
polônio (II) s. m. Polish citizen, native or inhabitant of Poland. ‖ adj. Polish.
polonizar v. to Polonize.
polpa s. f. 1. pulp. 2. the meat of fruits or roots. 3. pap, squash. 4. flesh. 5. marrow. 6. (fig.) importance. 7. (fig.) worthiness, prestige.
   ~ de madeira wood pulp. ~ dentária dental pulp.
polpação s. f. (pl. -ões) act or process of reducing to pulp.
polposo adj. pulpy, pultaceous, macerated.
polpudo adj. 1. pulpy, pultaceous. 2. macerated. 3. fleshy. 4. mellow, succulent. 5. (fig., pop.) very profitable.
poltrão s. m. (pl. -ões, f. -ona) coward, poltroon, a mean-spirited wretch. ‖ adj. cowardly, mean, craven, yellow.
poltrona s. f. 1. easy chair, armchair, elbow chair (plate C 2). 2. a saddle with low bows. 3. orchestra seat (plate T 3).
   ~ de orelhas wing chair (plate C 2). ~ de platéia (theat.) pit stall (plate T 3).
poltrona-cama s. f. (pl. poltronas-camas) chair bed.
poltronaria s. f. poltroonery, cowardice.
poltronear v. to act poltroonishly, show cowardice.
poltronear-se v. 1. to lean back in an easy chair, lounge. 2. to live in idleness.
poltronice s. f. poltroonery.
polução s. f. (pl. -ões) 1. pollution. 2. desecration, defilement. 3. dirt, filth. 4. (med.), also ~ noturna nocturnal emission, wet dream: involuntary emission of semen.
poluição s. f. = poluição 1, 2, 3.
poluído adj. polluted.
poluidor s. m. polluter.
poluir v. 1. to pollute. 2. to defile, desecrate. 3. to soil, dirty, stain. 4. to corrupt. 5. to contaminate. 6. to profane. 7. to tarnish, taint, blot.
poluível adj. m. + f. (pl. -íveis) that may be polluted, subject to pollution, corruptible.
poluto adj. polluted, foul, corrupted, tainted, soiled.
polvadeira s. f. 1. a cloud of dust, a lot of dust. 2. m. a bragging coward, bully, ruffian.
polvarim s. m. (pl. -ins) a very fine gun-powder.

polvarinho s. m. powder horn, powder flask.

polvilhação s. f. (pl. -ões) powdering, spraying, dusting.

polvilhar v. 1. to cover with dust. 2. to powder, dust. 3. to sprinkle, spray. 4. to flour.

polvilheiro s. m. manufacturer of powder(s), manioc flour, gunpowder, etc.

polvilho s. m. 1. any fine powder. 2. manioc flour. 3. white hairpowder. 4. starch (for linen).

polvo s. m. (zool.) octopus, polypus.

pólvora s. f. 1. gunpowder, blasting-powder. 2. powder. 3. gunpowder tea.
ele não descobriu a ~ (pop.) he surely has not invented the gunpowder, he is rather dull. está como uma ~ he is quick-tempered. fábrica de ~ powder-mill. gastar a ~ em salvas to waste one's powder on sparrows, toil in vain.

polvorada s. f. 1. explosion of gunpowder. 2. gunpowder smoke.

polvorento adj. powdery, pulverulent.

polvorim s. m. (pl. -ins) 1. very fine gunpowder. 2. powder dust.

polvorinho s. m. powder-horn, powder-flask.

polvorista s. m. + f. gunpowder manufacturer.

polvorosa s. f. 1. hectic activity. 2. uproar, hubbub. 3. disorder, confusion. 4. agitation, commotion.

polvoroso adj. powdery, dusty, covered with dust.

poma s. f. 1. a woman's breast. 2. teat, nipple, mammila. 3. sphere, globe, ball.

pomada s. f. 1. (pharm.) salve, ointment. 2. pomade, pomatum. 3. unction. 4. cream. 5. balsam, balm. 6. vanity. 7. presumption. 8. (fig.) flattery.
~ de óxido de zinco zinc ointment.

pomadear v. 1. to be presumptuous or conceited. 2. to show off. 3. to flatter, wheedle round, fawn upon.

pomadista s. m. + f. 1. pedantic or vain person. 2. liar. 3. flatterer, adulator. || adj. pedantic, vain, wheedling.

pomar s. m. orchard (plate A 4).

pomarada s. f. a group of orchards.

pomareiro s. m. orchardist, orchardman, orchard keeper, fruitgrower. || adj. of, pertaining to or relative to an orchard.

pomátomo s. m. (ichth.) bluefish.

pomba s. f. 1. (ornith.) female dove, pigeon. 2. a large copper vessel used in sugar mills. 3. any bird belonging to the order Columbiformes. 4. a term of endearment: my dove! 5. a very sweet, innocent or meek person.   o
~ nova dovelet.

pomba-amargosa s. f. (pl. pombas-amargosas), (ornith.) the plumbeous pigeon (Columba plumbea plumbea).

pomba-cabocla s. f. (pl. pombas-caboclas), (ornith.) partridge dove.

pomba-cascavel s. f. (pl. pombas-cascavel), (ornith.) scaled dove.

pomba-de-arribação, pomba-de-bando s. f. (pl. pombas-de-arribação, pombas-de-bando), (ornith.) the Paraguayan eared dove.

pomba-de-santa-cruz, pomba-do-ar s. f. (pl. pombas-de-santa-cruz, pombas-do-ar), (ornith.) the rufous pigeon (Columba rufina).

pomba-do-cabo s. f. (pl. pombas-do-cabo), (ornith.) pintado, the Cape pigeon.

pomba-do-sertão, pomba-espelho s. f. (ornith.) = pomba-de-arribação.

pomba-galega s. f. (pl. (pombas-galegas), (ornith.) the rufous pigeon.

pombal s. m. (pl. -ais) dove-cot, pigeon house, pigeon loft, pigeonry (plate C 11).

pomba-legítima s. f. (pl. pombas-legítimas), (ornith.) rufous pigeon.

pombalino adj. of, pertaining to or relative to the first Marquis of Pombal and his epoch.

pomba-pararu s. f. (pl. pombas-pararu), (ornith.) the Paraguayan eared dove.

pomba-trocal s. f. (pl. pombas-trocal), (ornith.) scaled pigeon.

pombear v. (Braz.) 1. to trade with Indians. 2. to snoop, spy out. 3. to act as a stool pigeon.

pombeira s. f. (Braz.) anchor.

pombeiro (I) s. m. (Braz.) person who trades with Indians, emissary who takes up contact with Indians.

pombeiro (II) s. m. chicken or pigeon peddler, hawker, fish peddler.

pombeiro (III) s. m. stool pigeon.

pombeiro (IV) adj. designating a variety of Indian corn.

pombinha s. f. 1. dim. form of pomba. 2. dovelet. 3. the flesh around the tail and buttocks of cattle. 4. (pop.) the female pudenda.

pombinha-cascavel s. f. (pl. pombinhas-cascavel), (ornith.) scaled dove.

pombinha-das-almas s. f. (pl. pombinhas-das-almas) a bird of the flycatcher family (Taenioptera nengeta).

pombinho (I) s. m. a little dove or pigeon.

pombinho (II) adj. designative of a variety of wheat.

pombo s. m. dove, pigeon, any bird belonging to the order Columbiformes.
criador de ~s, pigeon fancier. ~ bravo a wild pigeon. ~ de barro (sport) clay pigeon.

pombo-anambé s. m. (pl. pombos-anambé), (ornith.) a cotingid.

pomboca s. m. + f. 1. a lazy fellow. 2. good-for-nothing. || adj. lazy, idle, loafing.

pombo-correio s. m. (pl. pombos-correios), (ornith.) carrier pigeon, homing pigeon, homer.

pombo-da-rocha s. m. (pl. pombos-da-rocha), (ornith.) rock dove, rock pigeon, blue rock.

pombo-de-leque s. m. (pl. pombos-de-leque), (ornith.) fantail.

pombo-gravatinha s. m. (pl. pombos-gravatinhas), (ornith.) jacobin.

pombo-torcaz s. m. (pl. pombos-torcazes) ring-dove.

pombo-volteador s. m. (pl. pombos-volteadores), (ornith.) tumbler.

pomear v. to pumice.

pomeraniano s. m. Pomeranian: 1. native or inhabitant of Pomerania. 2. a small long-haired dog. || adj. Pomeranian.

pomicultor s. m. pomiculturist, fruitgrower, orchardist.

pomicultura s. f. pomiculture, orcharding, fruitgrowing.

pomífero adj. pomiferous, fruit-bearing.

pomo s. m. 1. fruit, any pomelike fruit. 2. pome. 3. pommel. 4. (poet.) a woman's breast. 5. apple.
~ de discórdia apple of discord, a bone of contention. o ~ vedado the forbidden fruit.

pomo-de-adão s. m. (pl. pomos-de-adão) the Adam's apple (plate C 18).

pomologia s. f. pomology: the art of fruitgrowing.

pomológico adj. pomologic(al).

pomólogo s. m. pomologist, fruitgrower.

pomona s. f. (Roman myth.) Pomona, the goddess of gardens, trees and fruits.

pompa s. f. 1. pomp, splendour. 2. pageantry. 3. ostentation, display of riches and luxury, showiness. 4. royalty, state, stateliness. 5. magnificence. 6. gala, parade. 7. array(al). 8. vanity.
~ fúnebre funeral pomp.

pompadouriano adj. Pompadour, pompadoured.

pompeante adj. m. + f. 1. ostentatious. 2. pompous. 3. high-flown, bombastic. 4. vainglorious, boastful.

pompear v. 1. to be pompous, act pompously. 2. to strut. 3. to show off, display riches. 4. to flaunt.

pompeiano s. m. (hist.) Pompeian: an inhabitant or citizen of Pompeii. ‖ adj. Pompeian.

pompilídeos s. m. pl. (ent.) Pompilidae: the spider wasp or tarantula killer family.

pompom s. m. (pl. **-ons**) 1. pompon, a tuft or ball (of silk, wool, etc.). 2. powder puff, puff. 3. (bot.) a lion's ear.

pomposidade s. f. 1. pomposity, pompousness. 2. ostentatiousness. 3. pontificality.

pomposo adj. 1. pompous. 2. ostentatious. 3. grandiose, magnificent. 4. showy, garish. 5. sententious, consequential. 6. solemn, sumptuous, splendid. 7. (of language) sounding, inflated, bombastic, windy. ‖ **-amente** adv. pompously, spectacularly, showily, grandiosely, magniloquently.

pômulo s. m. cheek-bone, malar.

ponchaço s. m., **ponchada** f. 1. a blow with the poncho (cloak). 2. a great lot of things, lots of money.

ponche (I) s. m. punch: a strong drink made of tea, sugar, brandy or rum and lime juice; cobbler, bishop.

ponche (II) s. m. (Port., prov.) tub.

poncheira s. f. punch bowl.

poncho s. m. poncho, a blanket with a slit in the middle for the head.

poncho-pala s. m. (pl. **ponchos-pala**) a light poncho worn in summer.

ponçó s. m. a vivid fiery red colour.

ponderabilidade s. f. ponderability, deliberativeness.

ponderação s. f. (pl. **-ões**) 1. act of pondering, ponderation. 2. consideration. 3. deliberation, judiciousness. 4. reflection. 5. advisability, advisableness.

coisa de ~ a matter of consequence. ~ **de prós e contras** the weighing of issues.

ponderado adj. 1. weighed. 2. considerate, deliberate. 3. well-advised, wary. 4. cool, objective, judicious. ‖ **-amente** adv. deliberately, advisedly.

média -a (stat.) weighted average. **sua opinião bem -a** his advised opinion.

ponderador s. m. ponderer. ‖ adj. pondering.

ponderal adj. m. + f. (pl. **-ais**) ponderal.

ponderar v. 1. to ponder. 2. to weigh, cogitate. 3. to reflect, think over. 4. to deliberate. 5. to consider, contemplate. 6. to examine carefully, study. 7. to mull over, chew, revolve in mind. 8. to meditate.

ponderativo adj. ponderative.

ponderável adj. m. + f. (pl. **-áveis**) ponderable.

ponderoso adj. 1. weighty, heavy. 2. ponderous. 3. important. 4. notable, significant. 5. worthy of consideration. 6. convincing. ‖ **-amente** adv. massively, ponderously, convincingly, notably.

pondra s. f. (pop.) steppingstone.

pônei s. m. pony, a small horse.

ponente s. m. 1. sunset. 2. unforeseen event, chance happening. ‖ adj. m. + f. setting, going down (sun).

ponga s. f. (Braz.) a game of dice.

pongar v. (Braz.) to jump on a tramway-car in movement.

pongo (I) s. m. a chimpanzee.

pongo (II) s. m. a stretch of river flowing through a canyon.

pongó s. m. + f. booby, stupid or silly person. ‖ adj. foolish, stupid, silly.

pongueró s. m. (bot.) coral-tree.

ponjê s. m. pongee.

ponjô adj. (S. Braz.) foolish, stupid.

ponta s. f. 1. point: a) the sharp end of anything (plates A 1, 2, C 12, P 11, 15). b) peak, top. c) extremity (plates C 12, G 4, P 4). d) barb, tine, nib, jag. 2. the beginning or end of a row or series. 3. corner. 4. small quantity. 5. horn, feeler of an insect. 6. fag-end of a cigar or cigarette. 7. toe (of a boot) (plate B 16). 8. head. 9. small group of animals. 10. stretch of a river where the passage is difficult. 11. evidence. 12. ostentation. 13. (theat.) insignificant part in a play.

~ **cortante de ferramenta** bit. ~ **da flecha** arrow-head. ~ **de cornadura** prong. ~ **de espada** sword tip. ~ **de Paris** wire nail (plate P 15). ~ **do molhe** pierhead. ~**s de agulhas** (railway) blades of a point (switch) (plate V 4). **colocar** ~ to tip. **com** ~ **de aço** steel-headed. **de** ~ on end. **de** ~ **a** ~ from end to end. **foram colocados de modo a se tocarem com as** ~**s** they were placed end to end. **na** ~ **da língua** on the tip of the tongue. **saber alguma coisa na** ~ **da língua** to have s. th. at one's fingertips. **sem** ~ edgeless, unpointed.

ponta-cabeça s. f. used in the locution: **de ponta-cabeça** head over heels, head-on, headlong.

pontaço s. m. stab, thrust or blow with a pointed weapon.

pontada s. f. 1. stab, jab. 2. stitch. 3. pang. 4. twinge.

estou com ~**s no lado** my side twinges.

ponta-direita s. m. (pl. **pontas-direitas**), (ftb.) outside-right (plate F 9).

pontado adj. 1. basted, stitched. 2. pointed.

ponta-esquerda s. m. (pl. **pontas-esquerdas**) (ftb.) outside-left (plate F 9).

pontal s. m. (pl. **-ais**) 1. (naut.) depth of the hold, depth. 2. tongue of land, small point of land (on a seashore or riverside). 3. wooden prop or shoring. ‖ adj. designating a kind of large nail or iron spike.

pontaletar v. to prop up, shore, brace.

pontalete (ê) s. m. 1. prop, supporting timber pole. 2. stay, brace, stanchion. 3. shoring.

pontão (I) s. m. (pl. **-ões**) 1. punt, flatboat. 2. pontoon (plate P 14). 3. float bridge. 4. viaduct, small highway bridge. 5. projecting part of a forest.

pontão (II) s. m. (pl. **-ões**) 1. prop, stay. 2. brace. 3. support.

pontapé s. m. 1. kick, blow with the foot. 2. spurn. 3. (fig.) offence, insult. 4. disaster, calamity.

dar ~**s** to boot, hack.

pontapear v. to kick, give a kick, give a blow with the foot.

pontar (I) v. (naut.) to provide with a bridge.

pontar (II) v. (theat.) to work as a prompter.

pontar (III) v. to point, indicate.

pontarelo s. m. a long or clumsily made stitch.

pontaria s. f. 1. act of aiming (with a gun). 2. aim, sight. 3. target. 4. aiming, sighting.

dormir na ~ to take slow aim. **fazer** ~ to aim. **sem** ~ aimless. **superar na** ~ to outshoot.

ponta-seca s. f. (pl. **pontas-secas**) 1. etching needle. 2. etching produced with this instrument. 3. the leg of a pair of compasses which holds the pencil (or drawing pen).

pontavante s. f. (naut.) the forepart of the deck.

ponte s. f. 1. bridge (plate P 14). 2. a ship's bridge, deck (plate L 2). 3. (dent.) dental bridge, bridgework. 4. overpass.

~ **basculante**, ~ **de báscula** bascule bridge (plate P 14). ~ **de arcos** arch bridge (plate P 14). ~ **de arco com cantilever** cantilever arched bridge (plate P 14). ~ **de atracação** pier. ~ **de cavaletes** trestle bridge. ~ **de desembarque** landing pier. ~ **de guin-**

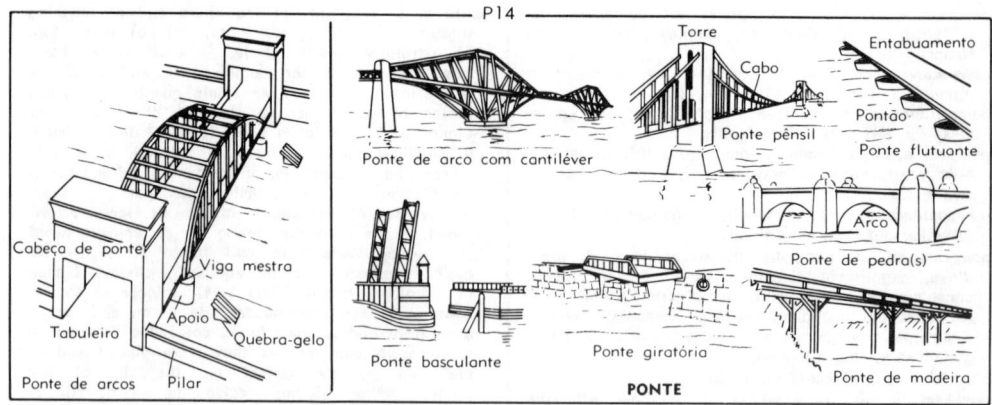

P14

Ponte de arco com cantiléver

Torre
Cabo
Ponte pênsil
Entabuamento
Pontão
Ponte flutuante

Arco
Ponte de pedra(s)

Cabeça de ponte
Viga mestra
Apoio
Tabuleiro
Quebra-gelo
Ponte de arcos   Pilar

Ponte basculante

Ponte giratória

Ponte de madeira

PONTE

daste volante gantry (plate G 5). **~ de madeira** timber bridge, wooden bridge (plate P 14). **~ esconsa** slew-bridge. **~ pênsil** chain bridge, suspension-bridge (plate P 14). **~ em treliça, ~ treliçada** truss bridge. **~ flutuante** pontoon bridge (plate P 14). **~ giratória** pivotal bridge, swivel bridge, swing-bridge, turn-bridge (plate P 14). **~ levadiça** drawbridge **~ volante** flying bridge.

ponteado s. m. stipple, dotted drawing. ‖ adj. dotted, pointed (plate L 1).

pontear (I) v. 1. to mark with points. 2. to baste, stitch. 3. to dot. 4. to sew. 5. to finger a musical instrument. 6. to play (a string instrument).

pontear (II) v. to ride at the head of a herd of cattle.

ponte-de-água s. f. (pl. **pontes-de-água**) a strong current in a river bend.

pontederiáceas s. f. pl. Pontederiaceae: a family of aquatic plants.

ponteira s. f. 1. metal tip of a cane or stick, ferrule (plate G 4). 2. the removable tip of a cigarette holder, a cigarette holder. 3. the last cotton harvest. 4. a piece of cord or lash fixed to the end of a whip (to increase the sound of the crack).

ponteiro (I) s. m. 1. fescue, a teacher's pointer. 2. indicator. 3. point, point chisel, puncheon (plate M 6). 4. style. 5. (mus.) plectrum. 6. hand (of several instruments). 7. cowboy who rides at the head of a drove of cattle. 8. pointer, hunting dog. 9. (fig.) a bad adviser.
~ da tabela (sport) the leader of a championship. **~ de relógio** watch hand (plate R 4). **~ dos minutos** minute-hand (plate R 4).

ponteiro (II) adj. 1. contrary (wind). 2. disobedient (hunting dog). 3. poorly balanced (gun).

ponteiro (III) adj that aims well.

pontel s. m. (pl. **-éis**) punty, pontee.

ponte-suela s. f. (pl. **pontes-suelas**) a metal ornament on the sides of the bit of a bridle.

pontiagudo adj. pointed, sharp, acuminate(d), acerose, acerous, tined, edged, cuspidal, peaky.

pôntico adj. (geogr.) Pontic: of or pertaining to Pontus (the Black Sea) and its region.

pontícula s. f. a small bridge, a narrow wood bridge.

pontículo s. m. punctule.

pontificado s. m. 1. pontifical authority or dignity. 2. pontificate, pontificality. 3. popedom. 4. papacy.

pontifical s. m. (pl. **-ais**) pontifical book (containing the forms for rites). ‖ adj. m. + f. 1. pontifical. 2. papal. 3. episcopal. 4. (fig.) pompous. ‖ **~mente** adv. pontifically.

pontificante s. m. pontifical priest, bishop. ‖ adj. m. + f. pontificating, pontifying, pontifical.

pontificar v. 1. to pontify, pontificate. 2. to officiate as a pontiff, celebrate a pontifical mass. 3. to speak or write bombastically. 4. to teach, indoctrinate.

pontífice s. m. 1. pontiff, pontifex. 2. hierarch. 3. bishop, prelate. 4. the Pope. 5. the spiritual leader of a sect, school of thought or philosophical system.
Sumo Pontífice (R. C.) Pontifex Maximus, the Pope.

pontifício adj. pontificial, pontificious.

pontilha s. f. 1. sharp point, sharp end. 2. a fine gold or silver purl. 3. spikelet.

pontilhado adj. 1. spotted. 2. dotted. 3. (bot., zool.) punctate.

pontilhão s. m. (pl. **-ões**) a small bridge.

pontilhar v. 1. to stipple, dot. 2. to mark with fine points. 3. to sprinkle. 4. to baste.

pontilheiro s. m. banderillero (in bullfights).

pontilhoso adj. 1. punctilious, scrupulous. 2. demanding, exacting. 3. easily offended.

pontinha s. f. 1. dim. form of **ponta**. 2. small point or peak. 3. trifle. 4. quarrel. 5. antipathy, aversion. **da ~!** (Braz. sl.) splendid! excellent!, delicious!

pontinho s. m. 1. dim. form of **ponto**. 2. fleck, speck. 3. a special stitch used in glovemaking. 4. punctule. 5. **~s** pl. (typogr.) ellipsis.

pontino adj. (geogr.) Pontine, of or pertaining to a marshy, region between Rome and Naples.

ponto s. m. 1. point, tittle, dot. 2. punctuation mark, full stop, period. 3. speck, spot. 4. stitch (plate P 1). 5. prick. 6. the twelfth part of a line (ancient measure: about 0.19 mm). 7. limit or intersection of lines. 8. place. 9. matter, question, subject. 10. end, conclusion. 11. (theat.) prompter. 12. moment. 13. the subdivisions of a measuring stick. 14. stand. 15. stop (tramway, railway, etc.). 16. item. 17. notch. 18. a bit of adhesive plaster or stitch applied in order to close a wound. 19. **~s** pl. score (of a game). 20. spike. 21. fret (of a guitar, etc.).
~ aberto, ~ ajour hemstitch. **~ cardeal** cardinal point. **~ cego** blind spot in the retina (plate O). **~ culminante** culminating point. **~ de acionamento** driving point. **~ de alimentação** (tech.) feeding point. **~ de apoio** point of support, (tech.) bearings. **~ de cadeia** looped stitch, chain stitch (plate P 1). **~ de caseado, de casear** buttonhole stich (plate P 1). **~ de condensação** dew point. **~ de congelamento** freezing point. **~ de contato** point of contact. **~ de cruz** cross-stitch (plate P 1). **~ de divergência**

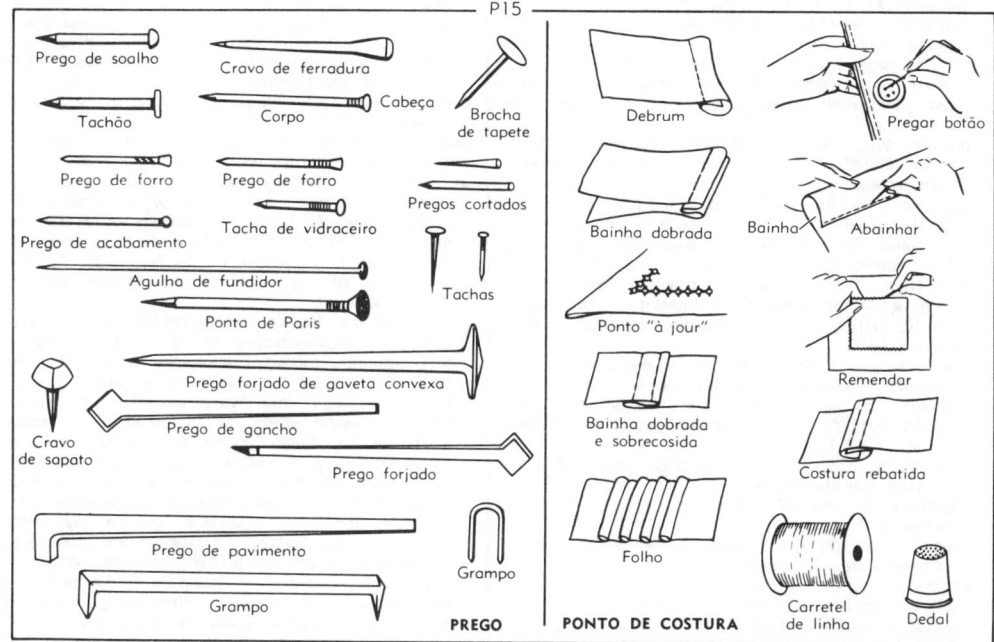

P15

Prego de soalho

Cravo de ferradura

Tachão — Corpo — Cabeça

Brocha de tapete

Prego de forro — Prego de forro

Pregos cortados

Prego de acabamento — Tacha de vidraceiro

Agulha de fundidor

Tachas

Ponta de Paris

Prego forjado de gaveta convexa

Cravo de sapato — Prego de gancho

Prego forjado

Prego de pavimento

Grampo

Grampo

PREGO

Debrum — Pregar botão

Bainha dobrada — Bainha — Abainhar

Ponto "à jour" — Remendar

Bainha dobrada e sobrecosida

Costura rebatida

Folho

Carretel de linha — Dedal

PONTO DE COSTURA

point of controversy. ~ **de ebulição** boiling point. ~ **de encontro** point of convergence. ~ **de espinha** herringbone-stitch (plate P 1). ~ **de exclamação** point or sign of exclamation. ~ **de fixação** sticking place, sticking point. ~ **de fração decimal** decimal point. ~ **de fusão** melting point, flashing point. ~ **de interrogação** point of interrogation, sign of interrogation, (U. S.A.) question mark. ~ **de intersecção** point of intersection. ~ **de parada** station, stop, stopping place. ~ **de partida** starting point. ~ **de referência** point of reference, station. ~ **de reunião** place of assembly. ~ **de táxi** cab-stand, taxi-rank. ~ **de tomada elétrica** tap. ~ **de vista.** 1. point of view, viewpoint. 2. standpoint. 3. aspect. 4. angle. 5. opinion, belief. 6. position. ~ **essencial** substantial matter, essentiality, center. ~ **e vírgula** semicolon. ~ **final** 1. (gram.) full stop. 2. (bus, tramway) end stop, terminus. 3. ultimate. ~ **fraco** weak point, failing, foible. ~ **mais alto** culminating point, culmination. ~ **mais importante** crux. ~ **morto** (tech.) dead center. ~ **morto inferior (superior)** (tech.) lower (upper) dead center. ~ **múltiplo** (geom.) multiple point. ~ **nevrálgico** punctilio. ~ **por** ~ from point to point, point by point. ~ **principal** cardinal point. ~ **principal de acusação** (jur.) gravamen. ~ **reverso** (knitting) purl, inversion of stitches. ~ **saliente** feature. ~**s equinociais** equinoctial points. **a** ~ **de partir** ready to depart. **as coisas chegaram a tal** ~ matters have come to such a pass that... **até certo** ~ up to a certain point, to a certain extent. **até certo** ~ **concordo com ele** in a sense I agree with him. **à uma hora em** ~ upon the stroke of one. **baixar de** ~ to decline, diminish, **chegar ao** ~ **da questão** to come to the point. **chegar a um** ~ **morto** to come to a deadlock. **dar uns** ~**s** to stitch up. **defender o seu** ~ **de vista** to hold the ground. **de um** ~ **de vista superior** from a higher point of view, from a new angle. **dois** ~**s** colon. **ela provou seu** ~ **de vista** she

proved her point. **ela chegou ao** ~ **de afirmar** she went so far as to say. **ele fez um** ~ (billiards) he pocketed a ball. **estar a** ~ **de** to be about to... **eu estava a** ~ **de fazê-lo** I was on the point of doing it. **falando de um** ~ **de vista prático** practically speaking. **isto me serve sob todos os** ~**s de vista** that suits me down to the ground. **mesa para o** ~ (theat.) prompt desk. **o vencedor por** ~**s** the winner on points. **perder por** ~**s** to lose on points. **por favor, venha às três horas em** ~ please, come at three o'clock sharp. **pôr os** ~**s nos ii** to dot the i's, make things clear, be quite outspoken. **sob todos os** ~**s de vista** in every regard, in all respects. **temos** ~**s de vista diferentes!** our points of view differ! **trabalho de** ~ **à jour** thread-drawing.
pontoada s. f. a blow with the edge of any instrument.
pontoar v. 1. to mark with points. 2. to dot, point. 3. to baste, stitch. 4. (gram.) to punctuate correctly.
ponto-limite s. m. (pl. **pontos-limites**), (math.) limit point.
pontoneiro s. m. pontoneer, pontoon builder.
pontoso adj. 1. punctilious. 2. scrupulous. 3. sensible with regard to questions of honour. 4. proud, self-respecting.
pontuação s. f. (pl. **-ões**) 1. (gram.) punctuation, interpunctuation. 2. act of marking with dots. 3. pointing. 4. (bot., zool.) punctation.
pontuado adj. punctate(d), punctuate, dotted.
pontual s. f. (pl. **-uais**), (math.) a series of points in a straight line. ‖ adj. m. + f. 1. punctual. 2. exact, accurate. 3. strict. 4. sharp, pointed. 5. prompt. 6. precise. ‖ ~**mente** adv. punctually, accurately, duly.

~ **como um relógio** like clockwork. **ela é** ~ she keeps time. **ele chegou** ~**mente** he arrived in due time. **ele foi rigorosamente** ~ he came to the moment. **ele paga** ~**mente** he pays promptly, (coll.) he pays to the tick.

pontualidade s. f. 1. punctuality, punctualness. 2. accuracy, exactitude, preciseness. 3. promptitude, promptness.

~ **no pagamento** readiness in paying.

pontuar v. 1. (gram.) to punctuate, interpunctuate, use punctuation marks. 2. to point, dot, mark with points.

pontudo adj. 1. pointed, peaked (plate Q). 2. tined, sharp-pointed.). spiky, pricked. 4. (fig.) agresssive, offensive.

ponxirão s. m. (pl. -ões), (Braz., pop.) 1. bee, neighbourly gathering in order to help in the execution of some work. 2. the food and drink offered by the beneficiary.

popa (I) s. m. (Roman hist.) a priest of low standing who had to take care of the interior of the temple.

popa (ô) (II) s. f. (naut.) stern poop, (tech.) afterbody.

à ~ **astern**, abaft. **a vela de** ~ the aftersail. **cabina de** ~ after-cabin. **canhão da** ~ (naut.) stern-chaser. **de** ~ aft, after. **em direção à** ~ aft, astern. **farol de** ~ poop lantern. **painel de** ~ stern frame.

pope s. m. (Orthodox Church) pope: the bishop or patriarch of Alexandria.

popeiro s. m. pilot of a canoe.

popelina s. f. poplin.

poperi s. m. (Braz.) a shack in which the newly gathered latex is smoked.

póplite s. m. (anat.) popliteus.

poplíteo, poplítico adj. (anat.) popliteal.

popocar v. to crack, crackle, burst open, explode (as firecrakers).

popuca adj. m. + f. 1. fragile, brittle. 2. rotten, corrupt. 3. offering no resistance, weak.

populaça s. f. 1. the masses, common people. 2. populace, rabble. 3. herd. 4. mob.

população s. f. (pl. -ões) 1. population. 2. inhabitants. 3. the number of inhabitants of a certain region. 4. class, category. 5. (fig.) a lot of animals.

populacho s. m. 1. populace. 2. mob, rabble. 3. vulgar herd. 4. plebs, plebes. 5. crowd.

popular s. m. a man of the people, common citizen. ‖ adj. m. + f. 1. popular. 2. public, common. 3. of or pertaining to the common people. 4. communal. 5. agreeable, lik(e)able, sympathetic(al), well-liked. 6. democratic. 7. demotic. 8. enchorial. 9. exoteric(al). 10. folkloristic(al). ‖ ~**mente** adv. popularly.

ela é uma moça ~ she is a popular girl.

popularidade s. f. 1. popularity. 2. vogue.

gozar de ~ to enjoy popularity, (coll.) be on the band wagon. **perder a** ~ to lose one's popularity, efface o. s.

populário s. m. (Braz.) folklore.

popularismo s. m. popularism: 1. a school of modern poetry which tries to imitate folkloric poems. 2. vulgarism.

popularização s. f. (pl. -ões) popularization.

popularizar v. 1. to popularize, make popular. 2. to divulge, make public. 3. to make accessible (scientific matter) to the untrained mind. 4. to vulgarize. 5. to become popular. 6. ~-**se** to make o. s. well--liked or beloved, ingratiate o. s with.

populeão s. m. (pl. -ões), (pharm.) unguent, ointment (in the composition of which enters belladonna and poppy leaves).

populéo adj. (poet.) poplar, of or pertaining to the poplar or tulip tree.

populina s. f. (chem.) populin.

populismo s. m. (pol.) Populism.

populista s. m. + f. (pol.) Populist, member of the people's party. 2. a friend of the people. 3. writer who describes favourably the life of the humble people. 4. a book written on this subject. ‖ adj. 1. Populist, Populistic(al). 2. of or relative to a certain school of literature which describes the life of the humble people.

populoso adj. 1. populous, abounding in people. 2. crowded, filled.

poqueca s. f. (Braz.) a well-seasoned fish stew.

pôquer s. m. poker (a card game).

por (I) prep. 1. at, by, for, from, in, per, pro, to, through, via, with. 2. because of, on account of. 3. by means of, through the agency of. 4. for the sake of. 5. in order to. 6. out of. 7. in place of, instead of. 8. in behalf of, in favour of. 9. with permission of, by order of. 10. in the capacity of. 11. towards.

~ **acaso** by chance, unexpectedly. ~ **aí** thereabout. ~ **algum tempo** for a while. ~ **ali** in that direction, there. ~ **alto** superficially. ~ **amor de** for love of, for the sake of. ~ **ano** per year, yearly. ~ **aqui** this way, around here, hereabout. ~ **assim dizer** so to speak. ~ **atacado** wholesale. ~ **baixo** underneath, below. ~ **bem** willingly, freely. ~ **causa de** through, because of, on account of, for. ~ **certo** certainly. ~ **cima** above, over, over and above. ~ **conseguinte** consequently, therefore. ~ **conta e risco do consignatário** for account and at the risk of the consignee. ~ **costume** usually, habitually. ~ **dentro** within. ~ **desprezo** in contempt. ~ **Deus!** in God's name! ~ **enquanto** pro tempore, for the time being. ~ **escrito** in writing. ~ **essas razões** for these reasons. ~ **exemplo** for example, for instance. ~ **extenso** in full, unabridged. ~ **falar em** with respect to, apropos, speaking about. ~ **falta de** for want of. ~ **fás ou** ~ **nefas** by hook or by crook. ~ **fim** lastly, at last. ~ **fora**. 1. outside, without. ~ **força** by force, unwillingly. ~ **gosto** gladly. ~ **graças de Deus** by the grace of our Lord. ~ **herança** by inheritance, hereditarily. ~ **hoje** for today. ~ **intenção de** in honour of, in favour of. ~ **intervalos** at intervals. ~ **inveja** out of envy. ~ **isso** for that reason, therefore, hereby. ~ **isso mesmo** for that very reason. ~ **mais que eu faça...** whatever I may do... ~ **mar** by sea. ~ **medo de** for fear of. ~ **meio de** by means of, thereby, with. ~ **meios indiretos** indirectly, by circuitous roads. ~ **mim!** well then!, for my sake! ~ **muito** by long odds. ~ **muito que** no matter how long (or much). ~ **nada** 1. for nothing. 2. (in reply to thanks) don't mention it. 3. quasi. ~ **natureza** by nature. ~ **ora** for the present, for the time being. ~ **ordem de** by order of, on behalf of. ~ **outro lado** on the other hand. ~ **perto** near to. ~ **pouco** well--nigh, nearly, quasi, almost. ~ **pouco ele pereceu afogado** he was all but drowned. ~ **procuração** per procuration (abr.: per pro or p. p.). ~ **qualquer preço** at any price. ~ **quanto tempo?** for how long? ~ **quê?** why? how? how come? ~ **que isso?** why so? ~ **que ele não veio?** why did he not come? ~ **que não?** why not? ~ **que tanta pressa?** why do you hurry so? where is the fire? ~ **rico que seja...** however rich he may be... ~ **seca e meca** from place to place, from post to pillar. ~ **si per se**. ~ **si mesmo** in itself. ~ **sua conta** at your cost. ~ **sua vez** in his turn. ~ **terra** by land. ~ **toda parte** throughout, everywhere. ~ **toda a vida** for life. ~ **turno** by turns. ~ **uma pechincha** for a song. ~ **um lado** on one side. ~ **um triz eu teria sido atropelado** I had a narrow escape from being run over. ~ **ventura** by chance. ~ **via de** by means of, through. ~ **via marítima** per ship. ~ **volta** around, about (in time). ~ **voltas** circuitous. **anseio** ~ **um descanso**

I long for a rest. **à razão de vinte** ~ **cento** at the rate of twenty percent. **comprei o livro** ~ **duzentos cruzeiros** I bought the book for two hundred cruzeiros, **duas vezes** ~ **ano ele faz a viagem** twice a year he makes the trip. **e assim** ~ **diante** and so forth. **ele é reputado** ~ **sábio** he is looked upon as a wise man. **ele foi condenado** ~ **ter furtado** he was punished for stealing. **eles votaram** ~ **Roosevelt** they voted for Roosevelt. **escapamos** ~ **pouco** we had a narrow escape. **está** ~ **fazer** it is not yet done, it has to be done yet. **ele está** ~ **partir** he will depart, he is about to leave. **eu tenho-o** ~ **meu amigo** I consider him as my friend. **foi** ~ **pouco** it was a tight fit. **nem** ~ **isso** nevertheless, for all that, hardly. **nem** ~ **isso deixamos de divertir-nos** in spite of all that we had a good time. **oitenta milhas** ~ **hora** eighty miles per hour. **palavra** ~ **palavra** word for word. **queira dar-me o sal,** ~ **favor** may I ask you to pass me the salt? **sim,** ~ **certo!** yes, certainly! **temos de passar** ~ **muitos perigos** we must pass through many dangers. **trocaram vinagre** ~ **vinho** they exchanged vinegar for wine. **um momento,** ~ **favor!** just a moment, please! **um xelim** ~ **libra** a shilling in a pound. **uma vez** ~ **todas** once for all.

pôr (II) v. 1. to place, put. 2. to lay, set. 3. to bring into some particular state or condition. 4. to cause to be. 5. to inculcate, instil. 6. to deposit. 7. to add. 8. to impute, attribute. 9. to render or translate into. 10. to include. 11. to lay down. 12. to put on, wear. 13. to lay eggs. 14. ~**-se:** a) to put, lay or set o. s., place o. s. in a definite position. b) (astr.) to disappear again, set, go down again. c) to dress o. s , outfit o. s. ~ **a bandeira a meio pau** to halfmast. ~ **a carroça adiante dos bois** to put the cart before the horse. ~ **a casa em ordem** to set one's house in order. ~ **a coberto** to shelter. ~ **a culpa em** to lay the blame on. ~ **à disposição de** to place at s. one's disposal. ~ **alguém em dificuldades** to get s. o. into a predicament, (pop.) to put s. o. in a hole. ~ **a mesa** to set the table, lay the tablecloth. ~ **à morte** to put to death. ~ **a par** to inform, initiate. ~ **à prova** to put to test. ~ **a prumo** to plumb. ~ **as cartas na mesa** to put one's cards on the table. ~ **as esperanças em alguma coisa** to fasten one's hopes upon s. th. ~ **à venda** to put to sale. ~ **à vista** to disclose, expose. ~ **à vontade** to relax. ~ **carga em** to charge. ~ **casa** to set up one's household. ~ **cobro a** to put an end to a thing, put a stop to. ~ **cuidado em** to take care of. ~ **data** to date. ~ **de acordo** to bring to an agreement, dispose. ~ **de baixo** to put, set or lay underneath. ~ **defronte de** to oppose, put in front of. ~ **de lado** to set aside, neglect, doff, do away with, discard, set apart, put away, put by. ~ **de molho** 1. to steep, soak. 2. (fig.) to consult with the pillow. ~ **de pé** to raise. ~ **distante** to distance. **o**~**-do-sol** sundown, sunset. ~ **em ação** to put in practice, put in motion, animate. ~ **em campo** to put in the field. ~ **em cena** (theat.) to stage a play, enact. ~ **em conta** to allow (for). ~ **em contato** to contact. ~ **em contingência** to chance, risk. ~ **em debandada** to disperse, disband. ~ **em depósito** to deposit. ~ **em desalinho** to dishevel. ~ **em desordem** to dissarray, confuse, put out of order, strike all of a heap. ~ **em dieta** to put to diet. ~ **em dúvida** to put in doubt, call in question, doubt, controvert. ~ **em efeito** to put into effect. ~ **em estoque** to lay in. ~ **em evidência** to make clearly visible, call the attention to. ~

em execução to carry out, put to practice. ~ **em fila** to rank, put in line, ordinate. ~ **em fuga** to put to flight. ~ **em funcionamento** to install, put in motion. ~ **em jogo** to jeopardize. ~ **em leilão** to put up at auction. ~ **em lugar de outrem** to put in the place of another. ~ **em movimento** to put in motion, set going, gear, bestir. ~ **em obra** to set on foot. ~ **em ordem** to put in order, straighten, ordinate, regulate. ~ **em palavras** to conceive, put in words. ~ **em posição** to put or bring in position, emplace. ~ **em perigo** to expose to danger, put in danger, endanger. ~ **em prática** to put into practive. ~ **em relevo** to stress, emphasize. ~ **em risco** to risk. ~ **em serviço** to put in service, commission. ~ **em terra** to debark, unload. ~ **à venda** to offer for sale, set to sale. ~ **em versos** to turn into verse. ~ **em vigor** to put in force. ~ **fim a** to put an end to, decide. ~ **fogo** to lay fire, set fire to. ~ **fora** to throw out. ~ **fora de ação** to put out of action. ~ **fora de perigo** to bring out of danger, save, assure. ~ **freio em** to curb, restrain. ~ **lado a lado** to lay together. ~ **mãos à obra** to lay hands on, put one's hand to the plow. ~ **meia sola** to half-sole. ~ **na cadeia** to confine in jail. ~ **na cama** to put to bed, put to sleep. ~ **na rua** to put on the street, throw out, fire. ~ **no berço** to cradle. ~ **no bolso** to pocket. ~ **no chão** to put on the ground, to ground. ~ **no prego** (pop.) to put up the spout, hock, pawn. ~ **no seguro** to insure. ~ **num curral** to corral. ~ **o chapéu** to put on the hat, cover o. s. ~ **o preço** to set a price. ~ **ovos** to lay eggs, oviposit, ovulate. ~ **para fora** to throw out, squander. ~ **para o lado** to put aside. ~ **por terra** to throw over, destroy. ~**-se a...** to be about to... ~**-se a falar** to begin to speak, be about to speak. ~**-se a caminho** to get under way. ~**-se a salvo** to run away, run for it, save one's skin. ~**-se bem com** to come to friendly terms with, make up to, reconcile o. s. with. ~**-se em campo** to take the field. ~**-se em contato com** to get in contact with. ~**-se em evidência** to distinguish o. s., (coll.) fill the bill. ~**-se em movimento** to begin to go, start out. ~ **sinal em** to mark. ~ **termo a** to make an end to. ~ **versos em música** to set a poem to music. **ponha isto na minha conta** charge it to my account. **pusemos mãos à obra** we turned our hands to it. **puseram-no a ferros** they put him in irons. **ela põe a mesa** she spreads the cloth. **ele põe o dedo no nariz** he picks his nose. **ele pôs-se a escrever** he settled down to writing. **não sei onde pus aquela carta** I don't know where I have put that letter. **o homem põe e Deus dispõe** man proposes, God disposes.

poracá s. m. a big hamper used for fishing.
poracé s. m. + f. (Braz.) a native Indian dance.
poranduba s. f. (Braz.) 1. story, history. 2. notice, information. 3. report.
poranga s. f. (Braz.) a tyrannid bird (Grypturellus variegatus).
porangaba s. f. (Braz., bot.) a cordia (Cordia salicifolia).
porão s. m. (pl. -ões) 1. (naut.) hold of a ship, bilge, stowage. 2. cellar, basement.
no ~ 1. belowstairs. 2. in the hold (of a ship). ~ **do palco** (theat.) trap cellar.
poraquê s. m. (Braz., ichth.) electric eel, gymnotus.
porca s. f. 1. f. of **porco**, sow. 2. nut, screw-nut (plate P 4). 3. (fig.) a dirty woman, slattern.
~ **acastelada,** ~ **de coroa** castellated nut (plate P 4). ~ **alada,** ~ **borboleta,** ~ **de orelhas** wing nut, butterfly nut, thumb nut (plate P 4). ~ **com colar** flanged nut. ~ **de aperto** clasp nut. ~ **de**

parafuso screw nut. ~ **de segurança** check nut, jam nut, lock nut. ~ **interna** female screw, inside screw. ~ **não roscada** blank nut. ~ **quadrada** square nut. ~ **sextavada** hexagon nut. ~ **tensora** adjusting nut.

porcada s. f. 1. a herd of swine. 2. dirt, filth. 3. filthiness. 4. nastiness, indecency. 5. bungled work, any job badly done.

porcalhão s. m. (pl. **-ões**) (f. **porcalhona**) 1. a very dirty person. 2. (coll., fig.) pig, hog. 3. bungler, botcher. ‖ adj. dirty, filthy, nasty.

porca-marinha s. f. (pl. **porcas-marinhas**), (ichth.) hogfish.

porção s. f. (pl. **-ões**) 1. portion, part, piece. 2. snack, bit. 3. slice, whack. 4. helping, serving. 5. dose. 6. share, lot, allotment. 7. heap, pile. 8. amount, quantum. 9. proportion(s). 10. interest. 11. dole, pittance. 12. dividend, allowance.

~ **legítima** (jur.) legitimate portion. **dividir em -ões** to portion.

porcaria s. f. 1. filthiness, dirtiness. 2. swinishness, nastiness. 3. dirt, filth, rubbish. 4. dirty work, patchwork, botchery. 5. an offensive word or expression, term of invective.

porcariço s. m. swine-herd.

porcelana s. f. 1. porcelain. 2. fine chinaware, dishware. 3. earthenware. 4. (bot.): a) portulaca (Portulaca oleracea). b) green purlane.

porcelana-argosinha s. f. (pl. **porcelanas-argosinhas**), (zool.) argus shell.

porcelânico adj. porcellaneous.

porcelanita s. f. (petrog.) porcellanite.

porcentagem s. f. (pl. **-ens**) percentage.

porcino adj. porcine.

porcionário s. m. 1. portioner, one who has or receives a share. 2. (eccl.) portionist, joint incumbent of a benefice.

porcionista s. m. + f. portionist, college student who has a certain academical allowance (for food, upkeep, fees).

porciúncula s. f. 1. a small portion. 2. a feast of the Franciscan order.

porco s. m. 1. (zool.) swine, pig, hog. 2. porker, grunter. 3. pork. 4. a very dirty or indecent fellow. ‖ adj. 1. swinish, hoggish. 2. dirty, filthy. 3. foul. 4. obscene, indecent. 5. base, vulgar. ‖ **-amente** adv. swinishly, piggishly, indecently.

~ **castrado** barrow, barrow hog. ~ **cevado** a fattened pig, fat sow or hog. **lançar pérolas aos** ~**s** to throw pearls before swine. **rabo de** ~ pigtail.

porco-bravo s. m. (pl. **porcos-bravos**), (zool.) a peccary.

porco-da-terra s. m. (pl. **porcos-da-terra**), (zool.) aardvark.

porco-do-mato s. m. (pl. **porcos-do-mato**), (zool.) white-lipped peccary (Tayassu pecari).

porco-espim, porco-espinho s. m. (pl. **porcos-espim, porcos-espinhos**), (zool.) porcupine, porky.

porco-marinho s. m. (pl. **porcos-marinhos**), a blackfish (Globicephalus melaena).

porco-montês s. m. (pl. **porcos-monteses**), (zool.) wild boar (Sus scrofa).

porco-selvagem s. m. (pl. **porcos-selvagens**), (zool.) razorback hog.

porco-sujo s. m. (pl. **porcos-sujos**), (pop.) the devil.

porco-veado s. m. (pl. **porcos-veado**), (zool.) babirussa, babiroussa.

porejar v. 1. to sweat out, perspire. 2. to expel through the pores. 3. to exude, ooze out. 4. to distil.

porém conj. 1. but, yet. 2. notwithstanding, nevertheless. 3. however. 4. still. 5. only. 6. even so.

porfia s. f. 1. discussion, argument, debate. 2. contention. 3. quarrel, strife, dispute. 4. challenge. 5. perseverance, pertinacity. 6. obstinacy.

à ~ in rivalry, in competition with.

porfiada s. f. seam of a fishing net.

porfiado adj. 1. obstinate, stubborn. 2. pertinacious. 3. disputed, eagerly sought after. 4. challenged.

porfiador s. m. 1. challenger. 2. a stubborn or tenacious fellow. ‖ adj. 1. stubborn, obstinate. 2. persistent, persisting. 3. enduring. 4. contumacious.

porfiar (I) v. 1. to discuss, debate. 2. to argue, dispute. 3. to interrogate, question persistently. 4. to challenge, contend. 5. to insist on, persist in. 6. to be obstinate. 7. to rivalize. 8. to compete with, vie with.

porfiar (II) v. to strengthen with a seam (fishing nets).

pórfido s. m. (min.) red porphyry of Egypt, porphyrite.

porfioso adj. 1. contentious, quarrelsome. 2. fond of picking quarrels. 3. obstinate, stubborn. 4. persevering. 5. constant, continuous.

porfirião s. m. (pl. **-ões**), (ornith.) the purple water hen.

porfírico, porfirítico adj. (min.) porphyritic.

porfirito s. m. (min.) porphyrite.

porfirização s. f. (pl. **-ões**) transformation into porphyry.

porfirizar v. 1. to porphyrize, convert into porphyry. 2. to pulverize. 3. to destroy. 4. to refute.

pórfiro s. m. (min.) porphyry.

porfiróide adj. m. + f. (petrog.) porphyroid, porphyritic.

poricida adj. m. + f. (bot.) poricidal.

porífero s. m. (zool.) 1. a sponge, poriferan. 2. ~**s** pl. Porifera: a class of animals constituted by the sponges. ‖ adj. poriferous, poriferal, poriferan.

poriforme adj. m. + f. poriform, resembling a pore.

porisma s. m. (geom.) porism.

porístico adj. (geom.) poristic(al).

pormenor s. m. 1. particularity, particular. 2. minutiae. 3. detail. 4. ~**es** pl. circumstances.

pormenorização s. f. (pl. **-ões**) 1. act or result of particularizing. 2. detailing. 3. a detailed report. 4. circumstantiation.

pormenorizado adj. detailed, particularized, circumstantial. ‖ **-amente** adv. circumstantially, in detail, minutely.

pormenorizar v. 1. to describe in detail, particularize. 2. to relate the particulars of.

pornéia s. f. licentiousness, debauchery.

porneu s. m. 1. brothel, bawdyhouse. 2. licentiousness.

porno s. m. (naut.) treenail.

pornô s. f. (Braz., pop.) abr. of **pornografia** pornography. ‖ adj. m. + f. abr. of **pornográfico** pornographic.

filme ~ blue movie, skin flick.

pornocracia s. f. pornocracy, decisive influence of profligate noblemen or women on government.

pornocrático adj. pornocratic(al).

pornografar v. 1. to write pornographies. 2. to describe in an obscene or indecent manner. 3. to describe, paint or reproduce obscene acts.

pornografia s. f. pornography: 1. a treatise on prostitution. 2. collection of pornographic writings, paintings or pictures. 3. obscene character of a publication. 4. licentiousness.

pornográfico adj. pornographic(al), obscene, licentious, libidinuos, lascivious.

pornógrafo s. m. pornographer, pornographist.

poro s. m. 1. pore, a minute foramen. 2. each one of the hypothetical interstices between the molecules or particles of a body. 3. a minute orifice in the membranous surface of a plant.

porocele s. f. (med.) porocele, a hardening of the hernial sac.

porócito s. m. (zool.) porocyte, ampula of a sponge.

porongo s. m. (bot.) the common calabash gourd (Lagenaria vulgaris).

porongudo adj. having a bony outgrowth on the joints of the leg (said of horses).

porongueiro s. m. (bot.) the calabash gourd.

pororoca (I) s. f. a great tidal wave; (Braz.) tidal wave which enters a river, a bore, eagre.

pororoca (II) s. f. (pop.) popcorn.

pororoca (III) s. f. (bot.) ironwood (Dialium divaricatum).

pororocar v. 1. to produce great tidal waves. 2. to be subject to the effects of the pororoca.

pororom s. m. (pl. **-ons**) 1. a stunted or misformed fruit. 2. a fruit of inferior quality.

porosidade s. f. porosity, poroseness, porousness. **falta de ~** imporosity.

poroso adj. 1. porous, having pores. 2. foraminiferal, foraminiferous. 3. cavernous. 4. full of interstices. **não ~** imporous.

porquanto conj. as, when, while, since, whereby, in view of the fact that, considering that, whereas, because, because of, by reason of, inasmuch as.

porque conj. because, since, as, in as much as, considering that, seeing that. (Not to be confounded with the adverb **por que** why. **por que você fez isso?** why did you do that?.)

fi-lo ~ o achei justo I did it for I thought it right. **não vim ~ estava doente** I did not come because I was ill. **se escrevo, é ~...** if I write, it is that...

porquê s. m. the cause or reason, the why, the wherefore.

porqueira s. f. 1. pig pen, pigsty, shed for pigs. 2. (fig.) a dirty place or house. 3. a female swineherd. 4. (pop.): a) intrigue. b) quarrel.

porqueiro s.m. swineherd, swine-keeper. || adj. designative of a certain kind of gourd and a variety of cabbage.

porquete s. m. (naut.) strengthening beams.

porquice, porquidade s. f. dirt, filth, filthiness.

porquinho s. m. 1. dim. form of porco piglet, gruntling. 2. a sheaf of flax or hemp.

porquinho-da-índia s. m. (pl. **porquinhos-da-índia**) guinea pig.

porráceo adj. porraceous, leek-green.

porrada (I) s. f. (sl.) a blow with a cudgel, clubbing, hit, knock.

porrada (II) s. f. any kind of stew in which leeks are used.

porrado adj. (pop.) drunk.

porral s. m. (pl. **-ais**) a leek plantation, a bed or field of leeks.

porrão s. m. (pl. **-ões**) 1. a pot-bellied earthen vessel with a narrow neck. 2. a thickset fellow.

porre s. m. (pop.) 1. a gulp of brandy, swing, swallow. 2. a drinking bout, binge.

ele tomou um ~ he got drunk.

porretada s. f. (sl.) a blow with a truncheon.

porrete s. m. 1. club, cudgel, truncheon, stick. 2. (pop.) efficient remedy or cure.

porrigem s. f. (pl. **-ens**) (med.) porrigo.

porriginoso adj. (med.) porriginous.

porrista s. m. + f. person who indulges frequently and habitually in intoxicating drinks, drunkard. || adj. given to drinking, dipsomaniacal.

porro s. m. 1. (bot.) leek (Allium porrum). 2. (med., surg.) callus, a bony outgrowth which forms around the fragments of a broken bone.

porrudo s. m. a freshwater fish (Schizodon nasutus).

porta s. f. 1. door (plates B 15, C 11, P 10, V 3). 2. entry, entrance. 3. leaf of a door. 4. gate, gateway. 5. (fig.) access. 6. (fig.) expedient.

~ corrediça sliding door. **~ da fornalha** furnace door, stokehole (plate C 5). **~ da rua** street door. **~ de duas folhas** folding doors. **~ de emergência** emergency door. **~ de entrada** street door. **~ de saída de uma fortaleza** sally-port. **~ dos fundos** back-door, (fig.) loophole, means of escape. **~ falsa** (fort.) postern. **~ giratória** revolving door (plate R 5). **~ levadiça** portcullis. **~ principal** portal, main gate or door. **~ secreta** jib-door. **~ vaivém** swing door. **almofada da ~** door-panel. **arrombar uma ~ aberta** (fig.) to force an open door. **bater com a ~** to slam the door. **dar com a ~ na cara de alguém** to shut the door into someone's face. **de ~s a dentro** indoors, privately. **de ~ em ~** from door to door. **esta ~ fica fechada para nós** this escape is closed to us. **estar às ~s da morte** to be at the point of death. **ganhar pela ~ traseira** to get by unlawful means. **por ~s travessas** by foul practices, by illicit means.

porta- prefix which serves to form compounds, with the meaning "holder, rest, carrier", etc. as in **porta-copo** glass-holder (plate P 19), **porta-chicote** whip rest (plate C 15).

porta-aviões s. m., sg. + pl. aircraft carrier, sea-plane carrier.

porta-bagagens s. m., sg. + pl. 1. parcel rack, rack, luggage carrier (of a bicycle, etc.) (plates B. 11, M 12, V 1). 2. parcel room.

porta-bandeira s. m. (pl. **porta-bandeiras**) 1. standard-bearer, flag-bearer, ensign. 2. ensignship.

porta-cabos s. m., sg. + pl. rope gun, apparatus which hurls a life-line to ships or people in distress.

porta-cartas s. m., sg. + pl. mailbag.

porta-chapéus s. m., sg. + pl. 1. hatbox. 2. hatrack.

porta-chaves s. m., sg. + pl. key-ring, key holder.

porta-cigarros s. m., sg. + pl. cigarette case.

porta-cocheira s. f. (pl. **porta-cocheiras**) porte cochere, a large gateway or entrance door.

porta-colo s. m. (pl. **porta-colos**) 1. a student's satchel. 2. protocol, original copy of a document.

porta-cossinetes s. m., sg. + pl. (mech.) screw stock.

portada s. f. 1. portal. 2. the principal or main door of a building. 3. frontispiece, façade.

portador s. m. 1. porter, carrier. 2. messenger. 3. bearer, holder (of titles or offices). 4. conveyor. 5. (fig.) vehicle, instrument of conveyance. || adj. carrying, conveying.

~ de doença carrier of disease. **~ de germes** carrier of germs. **~ de clava** club-man. **~ de más novas** messenger of ill tidings. **~ de uma licença** permittee.

porta-enxerto s. m. (pl. **porta-enxertos**) stock for grafting.

porta-espada s. m. (pl. **porta-espadas**) sword-belt, shoulder-belt.

porta-estandarte s. m. + f. (pl. **porta-estandartes**) 1. standard-bearer, flag-bearer, ensign. 2. guidon.

porta-ferramenta s. m. (pl. **porta-ferramentas**), (mech.) tool-holder.

porta-frasco s. m. (pl. **porta-frascos**) the belt or string on which the powder horn hangs.

porta-fusível s. m. (pl. **porta-fusíveis**) (electr.) fuse holder (plate P 2).

portageiro s. m. toll collector, exciseman.

portagem s. f. (pl. **-ens**) 1. toll. 2. toll gate, toll bridge, toll road. 3. toll house.

porta-janela s. f. (pl. **porta-janelas**) French window.

porta-jóias s. m., sg. + pl. jewel case.

portal s. m. (pl. **-ais**) 1. portal. 2. the principal or main door of a building. 3. frontispiece, façade. 4. (theat.) tormentor (plate P 2).

porta-lanterna s. m. (pl. **porta-lanternas**) lamp holder.

porta-lápis s. m., sg. + pl. 1. pencil case. 2. pencil rack. 3. port-crayon.

portalegrense s. m. + f. native or inhabitant of Porto Alegre (Braz.). ‖ adj. of, pertaining to or relative to this city and its inhabitants.

portaló s. m. (naut.) 1. gangway, gangplank. 2. entering port(-hole). 3. loading port.

porta-maça s. m. (pl. **porta-maças**) mace bearer, beadle.

porta-machado s. m. (pl. **porta-machados**) ax bearer, sapper.

porta-malas s. m., sg. + pl. (mot.) luggage compartment, luggage space (plate V 3).

porta-marmita s. f. (pl. **porta-marmitas**) 1. a soldier's mess kit. 2. a portable metal container used to transport food to soldiers in the field.

portamento s. m. (mus.) portamento.

porta-microfone s. m. (pl. **porta-microfones**) microphone holder.

portamira s. m. (land surveying) rodman.

porta-mitra s. m. (pl. **porta-mitras**), (eccl.) miter bearer.

porta-níqueis s. m., sg. + pl. purse, porte-monnaie.

porta-novas s. m. + f., sg. + pl. newsmonger.

portante adj. m. + f. 1. carrying, bearing, bringing. 2. (naut.) loose (said with regard to an anchor at the bottom of the sea).

portanto adv. consequently, therefore, hence, thus, so. ‖ conj. ergo, as, in as much as, in so far as. ~ **conclui-se que...** thence it follows that...

portão s. m. (pl. **-ões**) 1. a large door, portal (plate C 11). 2. gate, gateway, yard gate (plates A 4, C 11). 3. entrance. 4. (Braz.) a steep bank of a river. ~ **coberto** lich gate, lych gate (plate A 4).

porta-objeto s. m. (pl. **porta-objetos**) stage of a microscope.

porta-papel s. m. (pl. **porta-papéis**) toilet-roll holder (plate P 19).

porta-paz s. m. (pl. **porta-pazes**), (R. C. Church) pax, osculatory.

porta-penas s. m., sg. + pl. penholder.

porta-pneumático s. m. (pl. **porta-pneumáticos**) spare tire holder.

portar (I) v. 1. to enter a port, land. 2. to lead or bring to a certain place. 3. to arrive.

portar (II) v. 1. to take away, carry off. 2. to proceed, go on, carry on. 3. ~**-se** to behave, act correctly, conduct o. s. correctly.

porta-rede s. m. (pl. **porta-redes**) the boat that carries the net (of a fishing fleet).

porta-rédeas s. m., sg. + pl. terret (plate A 12).

porta-relógio s. m. (pl. **porta-relógios**) watch holder, watch case.

portaria (I) sã f. 1. the principal door of a convent. 2. vestibule or hall of a convent. 3. a doorkeeper's desk, box or lodge. 4. entrance. 5. portal.

portaria (II) s. f. 1. a governmental decree, order or regulation. 2. official diploma or document.

portaria (III) s. f. office or room of a doorkeeper.

porta-seios s. m., sg. + pl. bust bodice, brassière.

porta-sementes s. m., sg. + pl. 1. a seed plant. 2. seed tree, mother tree.

porta-tarraxa s. m. (pl. **porta-tarraxas**), (mech.) die head.

portátil adj. m. + f. (pl. **-eis**) 1. portable. 2. easily borne or transported. 3. handy, small. 4. light. 5. manual. **armas -eis** small arms. **máquina de escrever** ~ portable typewriter. **órgão** ~ portative organ. **rádio** ~ portable radio. **telégrafo** ~ field telegraph.

porta-toalhas s. m., sg. + pl. towel rack.

porta-voz s. m. (pl. **porta-vozes**) 1. speaking tube, megaphone. 2. (fig.) spokesman, voice.

porte s. m. 1. act of transporting or bringing. 2. transport, conveyance. 3. load, burden. 4. charge, transport fee. 5. loading capacity (of a ship), tonnage. 6. postage. 7. deportment, bearing. 8. air, gait. 9. behaviour, conduct. 10. poise, tact. 11. importance, consequence. ~ **de arma** gun licence. **coisa de** ~ matter of consequence. **com** ~ **pago** post-paid, post-free.

portear v. 1. to stamp, put a stamp on a letter. 2. to pay postage, prepay.

porteira s. f. 1. a doorkeeper's wife. 2. portress, female doorkeeper (esp. in a convent). 3. barrier at a railroad crossing. 4. yard gate, gate, low wooden farm gate.

porteiro (I) s. m. 1. doorman, doorkeeper (plate R 5). 2. janitor, warden. 3. gate-keeper. 4. usher. 5. porter. 6. auctioneer, crier.

porteiro (II) s. m. (ant.) royal tax collector.

portela s. f. 1. portal, gate. 2. a sharp bend in a road. 3. a narrow passage between mountains. 4. (archit.) a small door or gate.

portenho s. m. native or inhabitant of Buenos Aires (Argentine). ‖ adj. of, pertaining to or relative to Buenos Aires and its inhabitants.

portento s. m. 1. a wonderful thing or event, marvel. 2. prodigy. 3. person of outstanding qualities or intelligence. 4. wonder, miracle.

portentoso adj. 1. significant. 2. wonderful, marvellous. 3. amazing, surprising. 4. uncommon, unusual. 5. rare. ‖ **-amente** adv. amazingly, unusually, wonderfully.

pórtico s. m. 1. (archit.) portico, colonnade. 2. portal. 3. principal or main door of a palace. 4. entrance hall, lobby, entry. 5. porch, varanda.

portilha s. f. 1. (archit.) portal, large opening in a wall. 2. embrasure, loophole.

portilhão s. m. (pl. **-ões**) aperture in a wall, breach.

portilho s. m. a small port or harbour.

portinhola s. f. 1. a little door, small carriage door. 2. flap of a pocket (plate R 7). 3. fly of a garment. 4. wicket. 5. (naut.): a) porthole, scuttle. b) gun-port.

porto (ô) (I) s. m. 1. port, harbour, haven (plate P 16). 2. (fig.) refuge, retreat. 3. (fig.) shelter, asylum. 4. harbourage. ~ **de baldeação** transshipment port. ~ **de destino** port of destination. ~ **de escala** port of call. ~ **de pesca** fishing harbour (plate P 16). ~ **de saída** port of clearance. ~ **para abastecimento de navios com carvão** coaling station. **capitão do** ~ port captain, harbour captain.

porto (ô) (II) s. m. port (wine).

porto-alegrense s. m. + f. (pl. **porto-alegrenses**) native or inhabitant of Porto Alegre (Braz.). ‖ adj. of, pertaining to or relative to this city and its inhabitants.

porto-franco s. m. (pl. **portos-francos**) free port.

porto-riquenho s. m. (pl. **porto-riquenhos**) Puerto Rican, native or citizen of Puerto Rico (Central America). ‖ adj. Puerto Rican, Porto Rican.

porto-seco s. m. (pl. **porto-secos**) a big store, storehouse.

portuário s. m. dock worker, longshoreman. ‖ adj. of, pertaining to or relative to a port or harbour. **direitos** ~**s** port charges, port dues. **taxas -as** quayage.

portucha s. f. (naut.) reef hole.

portuchar v. (naut.) to reef in, reef sails.

portuchos s. m. pl. the orifices of a goldsmith's drawplate.

P 16

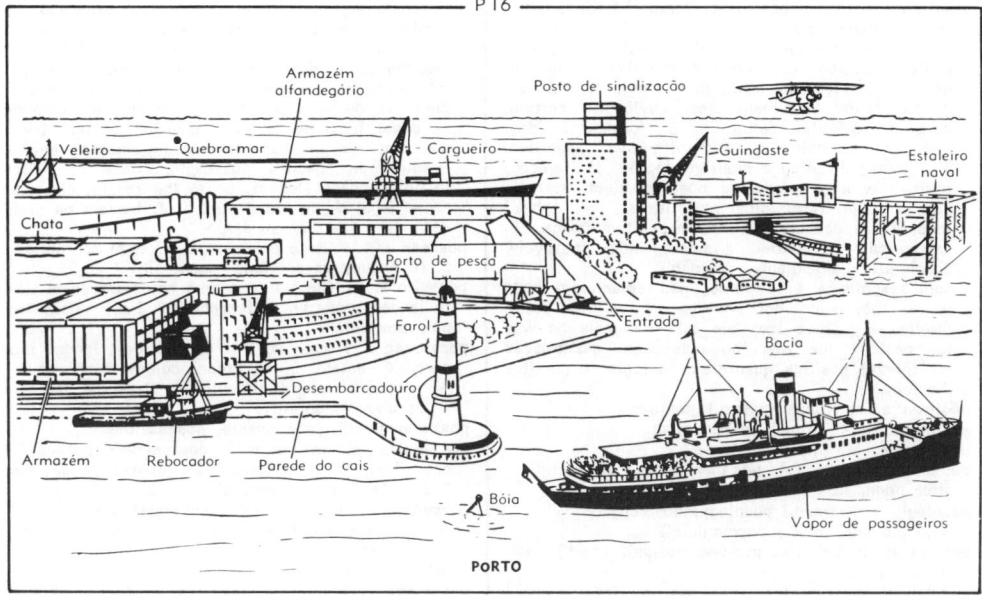

Veleiro — Quebra-mar — Armazém alfandegário — Cargueiro — Posto de sinalização — Guindaste — Estaleiro naval — Chata — Porto de pesca — Farol — Entrada — Bacia — Desembarcadouro — Armazém — Rebocador — Parede do cais — Bóia — Vapor de passageiros

PORTO

portuense s. m. + f. native or inhabitant of Oporto (Port.). ‖ adj. of, pertaining to or relative to Oporto.

portuga s. m. (Braz., sl. or depr.) Portuguese.

português s. m. (pl. ~es) Portuguese: 1. a native or inhabitant of Portugal. 2. the language spoken by Portuguese and Brazilians. ‖ adj. Portuguese.

portuguesismo s. m. 1. Portuguese behaviour and mannerism. 2. Portuguese way of thinking. 3. Portuguese idiom or peculiar expression.

portulaca s. f. (bot.) portulacca.

portulacáceas s. f. pl. Portulacaceae: a family of herbs (order Chenopodiales).

portulano s. m. portolano, port and sailing directory with charts for navigators.

portuoso adj. having many seaports or harbours.

poruca s. f. (Braz.) a large sieve used for the sifting of coffee-beans.

porunga s. f. (Braz.) a leather bag used for the transport of liquids.

poruti s. m. (ornith.) a swift (Cypselus squamatus).

porventura adv. 1. perchance, by chance. 2. perhaps, possibly.

porvindouro s. m. 1. the future. 2. ~s pl. the newcomers, the coming generations. ‖ adj. future, coming hereafter.

porvir s. m. 1. time to come, future. 2. destiny.

pós prep. post, after, behind. ‖ pref. post.

posar v. 1. to pose, assume a pose. 2. to posture, attitudinize. 3. to sit for (as a model).
ela posa para um pintor she sits to an artist. **ele posa para um retrato** he sits for his portrait.

pós-boca s. f. (pl. **pós-bocas**) the back of the mouth.

poscefálico adj. (anat.) postcephalic.

poscéfalo s. m. (anat.) postcephalic part of the head.

poscênio s. m. (theat.) postcenum, backstage.

pós-data s. f. (pl. **pós-datas**) 1. postdate, date affixed to a document later than the actual date. 2. false date.

pós-datar v. to postdate, date after the day of writing.

pós-diluviano adj. postdiluvian, postdiluvial.

pós-dorsal adj. m. + f. (pl. **-ais**), (anat.) postcostal, postcostate.

pose s. f. 1. pose. 2. position, posture. 3. posing (as a model). 4. (phot.) time exposure, still. 5. physical or mental attitude.

pós-escolar adj. (pl. **pós-escolares**) postschool.

pós-escrito s. m. (pl. **pós-escritos**) postscript. ‖ adj. written at the end, written as a postscript.

posfácio s. m. postface.

pós-glacial adj. m. + f. (pl. **-ais**), (geol.) post-glacial.

pós-graduação s. f. postgraduate work.

posição s. f. (pl. **-ões**) position: 1. place occupied by a person or thing, situation. 2. attitude, posture (place C 12). 3. disposition. 4. circumstance(s). 5. state, social standing, rank, class. 6. public office. 7. appointment. 8. (mil.) position suitable for an attack or defense. 9. location, station.
~ das velas (naut.) the trim of sails. **~ de cadete** cadetry, cadetship. **~ de um terreno** the lay of the land. **~ defensiva** guard. **~ social** station, rank. **~ vantajosa** vantage ground. **~ zero** (tech., mil.) zero position. **ângulo de ~** angle of position. **ela está numa ~ difícil** she is in a fix. **ele procura uma melhor ~** he is looking for a better post. **o inimigo foi expulso de sua ~** the enemy was dislodged. **não estive em ~ de** I was not in a position to... **ocupar ~ preeminente** to hold a leading position, play the first fiddle. **ocupar uma ~ firme** to take a firm stand. **tomar ~** to take one's stand.

positivar v. 1. to make positive. 2. to ascertain definitely. 3. to prove, evidence.

positividade s. f. 1. positiveness, positivity. 2. definitiveness. 3. assertiveness. 4. (phys.) any nucleus charged with positive electricity.

positivismo s. m. 1. (phil.) positivism, Comtism. 2. religious sect founded by Auguste Comte. 3. positivistic conception of life. 4. (fig.) practical life.

positivista s. m. + f. positivist, Comtist. || adj. positivist, positivistic(al).
positivo s. m. positive: 1. certainty, reality. 2. (gram.) positive degree. 3. (phot.) a positive picture or print. 4. categorical affirmation. || adj. 1. positive. 2. real, actual. 3. evident, clear, obvious. 4. certain, sure. 5. definite, definitive. 6. formal. 7. dogmatic(al). 8. objective. 9. affirmative, assertive. 10. (gram.) denoting a positive degree. 11. (electr.) charged with or producing positive electricity. 12. greater than zero, plus. 13. literal. 14. (phot.) revealing or capable to reveal a positive image. 15. categorical. 16. distinct. || **-amente** adv. positively, absolutely, indisputably, decidedly.
com respeito a este ponto, não adiantaram nada de ~ they were not positive as to this point. **direito** ~ positive law. **ele foi** ~ **demais** he was too positive, he was too outspoken. **quantidades -as** (math.) positive quantities. **teologia -a** positive theology.
pósitron s. m. (phys., chem.) positron.
poslimínio s. m. (jur.) postliminium.
poslúdio s. m. (mus.) postlude.
pós-meridiano adj. (pl. **pós-meridianos**) postmeridian, after noon, in the afternoon (abbr., p. m.).
posologia s. f. (med.) posology, dosology.
posológico adj. (med.) posologic(al).
pós-operatório adj. (pl. **pós-operatórios**), (med.) postoperative.
pós-palatal adj. m. + f. (pl. **-ais**) 1. (anat., zool.) postpalatine. 2. (phon.) postpalatal.
pós-palato s. m. (pl. **pós-palatos**), (anat., zool.) postpalatine bone.
pospasto s. m. dessert, after-dinner course or dish.
pospelo s. m. 1. direction against the fur or the grain. 2. (fig.) violent reaction.
a ~ 1. against the grain, against the fur. 2. (fig.) in a wrong way or manner. 3. (fig.) untimely.
pós-perna s. f. (pl. **pós-pernas**), (anat.) upper thigh (of a horse or bovine animal).
pospontar v. to backstitch.
posponto s. m. backstitch, quilting stitch.
pospor v. 1. to place after or behind. 2. to postpone, defer, put off, delay. 3. to omit. 4. to neglect. 5. to procrastinate. 6. to set aside. 7. to disregard, despise. 8. to esteem less. 9. to adjourn.
posposição s. f. (pl. **-ões**) 1. act or result of postponing. 2. postposition, a placing after. 3. postponement.
pospositiva s. f. 1. the second particle of a diphthong, the third of a triphthong. 2. a postpositive word or word element.
pospositivo adj. 1. postpositive. 2. placed after s. th. else. 3. (gram.) postpositional (said of particles or words which are placed behind or at the end of another word).
posposto adj. 1. postpositive. 2. placed after or behind. 3. omitted. 4. deferred. 5. disregarded, spurned, despised, slighted. 6. neglected, set aside.
pós-romano adj. (pl. **pós-romanos**), (hist.) post-Roman, after the decline of the Roman empire.
possança s. f. 1. power, might. 2. force, strength. 3. bravery, courage. 4. (geol.) the thickness of a layer of sedimentary rocks or of a series of strata.
possante adj. m. + f. 1. powerful, mighty. 2. vigorous, potent. 3. strong. 4. majestic, grand. 5. wealthy.
posse s. f. 1. holding or fruition of a property or right. 2. ownership. 3. ~s pl. possessions, wealth, riches, property. 4. (jur.) tenure. 5. occupancy. 6. ability, capacity. 7. appropriation, legal title to land. 8. initiation. 9. the act of taking office. 10. grasp.

~ **conjunta** commonage. ~ **de um benefício** incumbency. ~ **de um cargo** entrance into office. ~ **imediata** (jur.) vacant possession. ~ **prévia** (jur.) prepossession. **dar** ~ 1. to give possession to, put into someone's possession. 2. to invest (in office), enthrone. **de** ~ in possession, tenurial. **ele está de** ~ **deste livro** he is in possession of this book. **ele tem** ~**s** he has independent means. **em** ~ **irrestrita** in absolute possession. **estar de** ~ **de** to be in possession of, be in the receipt of. **estar na** ~ **legal de** to stand seized of. **homem de grandes** ~**s** a man of substance.
possear v. 1. to take possession of. 2. to appropriate. 3. to occupy vacant land, squat on.
posseiro s. m. (jur.) 1. one who holds the legal title to landed property. 2. leaseholder. || adj. possessional, proprietary.
possessão s. f. (pl. **-ões**) 1. possessions, landed property. 2. estate. 3. dominion, colony, territory.
~ **conferida** tenure at will. ~ **ilegítima** detinue. ~ **secular** temporality.
possessível adj. possessable, possessible.
possessivo s. m. (gram.) possessive, possessive case. || adj. 1. proprietary. 2. (gram.) possessive. || **-amente** adv. possessively.
possesso s. m. demoniac, one possessed by evil spirits, passions, fixed ideas, etc. || adj. possessed, demoniac(al), mad, crazy.
tornar ~ to make distracted.
possessor s. m. 1. possessor. 2. tenant. 3. (Roman hist.) designation of a colonist endowed with conquered land. || adj. possessive, possessory.
possessório s. m. (jur.) possessory judge or magistrate. || adj. 1. possessive, possessory. 2. proprietary. 3. (jur.) of or relative to a possessory court, magistrate or action. || **possessoriamente** adv. possessorily.
possibilidade s. f. 1. possibility. 2. contingency. 3. feasibility, verisimilitude. 4. chance, odds, peradventure. 5. ~**s** pl.: a) means, possessions, wealth. b) prospects, potentialities. 6. capacity. 7. the wherewith(al).
~ **de alteração** alterability, alterableness. ~ **de defesa** defensibleness, defensibility. ~ **de prevenir** preventibility. ~ **de transporte** transportability. **acima de suas posses e** ~**s** above his means and possibilities, above his weight. **ele deu ordens levando em conta a** ~ **de um avanço** he gave orders on the chance of advancing. **ele não tem qualquer** ~ he has no chance whatever, he has not a dog's chance, he is out of the running. **fora de** ~ impossible, out, past. **sua** ~ **de vida é limitada** his tenure of life is a precarious one. **uma** ~ **remota** an off-chance.
possibilismo s. m. (pop.) possibilism.
possibilista s. m. + f. (pol.) possibilist.
possibilitar v. 1. to make possible. 2. to enable. 3. to allow.
possível s. m. (pl. **-íveis**) 1. the possible. 2. a possibility. 3. effort, zeal. || adj. m. + f. 1. possible. 2. attainable, feasible. 3. contingent. 4. conceivable. 5. eventual. 6. verisimilar, believable. 7. practicable. 8. earthly. || **possìvelmente** adv. possibly, maybe, feasibly, perchance.
é ~ **que** it might be that. **é** ~ **que ele venha hoje** he may come today. **fazer o** ~ to do one's best. **fazer todo o** ~ to do one's utmost. **fizemos todo o** ~ we left nothing undone. **ele tentou todo o** ~ he tried everything possible, he explored every avenue. **o mais cedo** ~ as soon as possible. **se for** ~ if it is at all possible. **será** ~?! is it possible?! indeed?! **tanto quanto é** ~ as much (far) as possible.

possuído s. m. property; ~s pl. wealth, means, riches. ‖ adj. (and p. p. of **possuir**) 1. possessed. 2. haughty, lofty, overbearing. 3. vain, self-satisfied.
possuidor s. m. owner, possessor, master. ‖ adj. possessing.
~ **de direitos autorais** copyrighter.
possuir v. 1. to possess. 2. to have, hold (property). 3. to own. 4. to occupy, inhabit. 5. to enjoy. 6. to perform, exercise. 7. to contain, comprise. 8. to imbue. 9. to have fruition of 10. to possess, make one's own carnally. 11. ~-se: a) to convince o. s. of. b) to master one's passions. c) to be dominated by.
~ **ações** to hold shares. **ele está possuído desta idéia** he is a slave to this idea. **ele possui as qualidades necessárias** he is endowed with the necessary qualities, he's got what it takes. **não ~ nada** to own nothing, be out of all.
posta (I) s. f. 1. a slice of fish. 2. piece, slice, cut, chop. 3. portion, share. 4. (fam.) a lucrative job. 5. (pop.) a lazy person.
~ **sem osso nem espinho** (fam.) a profit or advantage without trouble.
posta (II) s. f. 1. post office or administration. 2. mail. 3. post relay station. 4. diligence, stage-coach. 5. postrider, postboy, courier.
postal s. m. (pl. -**ais**) postal card. ‖ adj. m. + f. postal.
agência ~ post office. **mala** ~ mail. **selo** ~ postage stamp, stamp.
postalista s. m. + f. postal clerk.
postar v. 1. to post, send or dispatch by the post. 2. to put in the mailbox. 3. to station, position. 4. to dispose. 5. ~-se: a) to place o. s. b) to remain for a long time in a certain place or position.
posta-restante s. f. (pl. **postas-restantes**) poste restante.
estar confiado à ~ to be called for.
poste s. m. 1. stake, stud. 2. pillar. 3. post. 4. mast, pylon, standard (plates C 1, R 8). 5. pillory, whipping post. 6. jamb, upright.
~ **de amarração** (naut.) bollard. ~ **de chegada** winning post. ~ **de iluminação** lamppost. ~ **indicador** finger-post, sign-post, guide-post, way-post (plate C 8). ~ **itinerário** index. ~ **de portão** gate post. ~ **telegráfico** telegraph pole (plate V 4). ~ **de partida** starting post.
posteirada s. f. (S. Braz.) the watchmen, guards or herdsmen of a fazenda, collectively.
posteiro s. m. (S. Braz.) watchman, guard, herdsman.
postejar v. to cut into slices, cut up, slice.
postema s. f. (med.) aposteme.
postemão s. m. (pl. -**ãos**) (surg., vet.) bistouri.
pós-temporada s. f. (pl. **pós-temporadas**) after-season.
postergação s. f. (pl. -**ões**) 1. postponement. 2. act of putting off or neglecting. 3. disdain, contempt. 4. carelessness. 5. transgression.
postergar v. 1. to postpone. 2. to put off, set aside, pass over. 3. to omit, leave undone. 4. to despise, disregard. 5. to neglect. 6. to transgress.
posteridade s. f. 1. posterity, posteriors. 2. the future generations, descendants. 3. the coming ages or times. 4. offspring, issue. 5. fame or glorification in the future.
posterior s. m. (pop.) the behind, seat, backside, posterior. ‖ adj. m. + f. 1. posterior. 2. later (in time). 3. behind, hinder. 4. ulterior. 5. after. 6. hindmost. ‖ ~**mente** adv. posteriorly, subsequently, afterward(s).
efeito ~ aftereffect.
posterioridade s. f. posteriority.
póstero s. m. 1. the future. 2. ~**s** pl. the coming generations. ‖ adj. coming, future, hereafter.

póstero-dorsal adj. m. + f. (pl. **póstero-dorsais**), (anat.) posterodorsal.
póstero-exterior adj. m. + f. (pl. **póstero-exteriores**) posteroexternal.
póstero-inferior adj. m. + f. (pl. **póstero-inferiores**) posteroinferior.
póstero-interior adj. m. + f. (pl. **póstero-interiores**) posterointernal.
póstero-superior adj. m. + f. (pl. **póstero-superiores**) posterosuperior.
postiço adj. 1. false, counterfeit. 2. artificial. 3. that can be put on or taken off. 4. imitated. 5. superadded, additional. 6. dummy.
cabelos ~**s** false hair, wig. **dentes** ~**s** a set of artificial teeth, false teeth.
postigo s. m. 1. a small door. 2. a small opening in a door or window, peephole. 3. wicket. 4. hatch, scuttle. 5. shutter.
~ **da cozinha** service hatch. ~ **da janela** window shutters. ~**s da câmara:** 1. (naut.) deadlights. 2. skylights.
postila s. f. 1. a student's copybook with explanatory notes. 2. explanations offered by the professor during the lesson and collected by students. 3. commentary. 4. postil. 5. marginal notes, class notes.
postilar v. 1. to write marginal notes, annotate. 2. to take down in writing the lecture and explanations of a professor. 3. to dictate a lecture.
postilhão s. m. (pl. -**ões**) 1. postil(l)ion, postboy. 2. messenger, courier. 3. a railroad mail clerk.
postimária s. f. end.
postimeiro adj. 1. last, hindmost. 2. ultimate, final. 3. extreme.
postliminio s. m. (jur.) postliminium.
posto (ô) (I) adj. (and p. p. of **pôr**) 1. put, put in place. 2. (of sun, moon, stars) set. 3. disposed, arranged. ‖ **posto, posto que** conj. although, though, even though, even if, notwithstanding that.
depois do sol ~ after sunset. **não** ~ unset. **o cenário da história é** ~ **em Nova York** the scene of the story is laid in New York. ~ **no costado do navio** (com.) free alongside ship (abbr. FAS).
posto (ô) (II) s. m. 1. post. 2. place, position. 3. station, stand. 4. (mil.) military post, police station. 5. office, duty. 6. rank, grade. 7. dignity, authority. 8. employment.
~ **avançado** outpost. ~ **comercial** trading post. ~ **de alarma** alarm post. ~ **de bombeiros** fire-station. ~ **de gasolina** filling station, gas station (plate B 2). ~ **de general** generalship. ~ **de observação** observation post. ~ **de pedágio** pike, turnpike, tollgate. ~ **de pronto-socorro** first aid station, dressing station. ~ **de salvamento** lifeguard (plate P 17). ~ **de sinalização** signal station (plate P 16). ~ **de telefone público** public call-box, telephone booth, kiosk (plate T 4). ~ **meteorológico** weather station. ~ **militar** cantonment. ~ **naval** naval station. ~ **policial** police post, police station. **ele tem o** ~ **de major** he ranks with major.
postônico adj. (gram.) posttonic: after the stressed vowel.
postre s. m. (also **postres** pl.) dessert.
postreiro, postremeiro, postremo adj. last, extreme, terminal, final; ultimate.
postrídio s. m. the following day.
postulação s. f. (pl. -**ões**) 1. postulation, supplication, prayer. 2. petition, application.
postulado s. m. postulate, postulation, principle, assumption.
postulante s. m. + f. 1. postulant, applicant, petitioner, candidate. 2. (eccl.) person who wants to take up the novitiate. ‖ adj. postulating.

postular v. to postulate: 1. solicit, require, claim. 2. assume, take for granted.

póstumo adj. posthumous: 1. born after the death of the father. 2. appearing after the death of the author. ‖ **postumamente** adv. posthumously.

postura s. f. 1. posture: a) position, situation, state. b) attitude, pose, gesture. c) disposition, deportment, carriage. 2. (Port.) make-up (cosmetic). 3. laying of eggs, egging, quantity of eggs laid. 4. a municipal order.

postureiro s. m. seller of rouge and cosmetics.

pós-verbal adj. m. + f. (pl. **pós-verbais**) (gram.) postverbal.

potaba s. f. (N. Braz.) 1. gift, present, donative. 2. a sort of bait.

potabilidade s. f. potability, potableness.

potagem s. f. (pl. **-ens**) potage, pottage, soup.

potâmide s. f. river nymph.

potamita adj. m. + f. living in rivers; potamic.

potamogetonáceas s. f. pl. (bot.) Potamogetonaceae, the pondweed family.

potamografia s. f. potamography.

potamologia s. f. potamology: 1. science of rivers. 2. treatise on rivers.

potamológico adj. potamological, of or pertaining to potamology.

potassa s. f. potash, potass. **~ cáustica** (chem.) caustic potash. **~ do comércio** lump potash. **cianeto de ~** prussiate of potash.

potássio s. m. (chem.) potassium, kalium.

potável adj. m. + f. (pl. **-áveis**) potable, drinkable.

pote s. m. 1. pot; vessel (of earth, iron or aluminium) (plates C 20, M 4, C 2). 2. water jug, pitcher. 3. an ancient measure of capacity. 4. (pop.) squat person. 5. (N. Braz., pop.) jail, prison.

potéia s. f. putty, a powder of tin oxid used in polishing glass and steel.

potência s. f. 1. potency: the quality of being potent; power, strength. 2. might, authority, sovereignty, influence. 3. (phys.) working power, force. 4. faculty. 5. a world power, great nation. 6. (math.) potence. **~ calorífica** calorific power, heating power, calorific value. **~ desenvolvida** output. **~ efetiva** effective power. **~ em velas** (electr.) candlepower. **carga de ~** performance load, power loading. **curva de ~** performance curve. **elevar à segunda ~** (math.) to raise to the second power. **equilíbrio de ~** balance of power. **fator de ~** (electr.) power factor. **as grandes ~s** the Great Powers. **segunda ~** (math.) square power. **quarta ~** biquadrate. **na quarta ~** biquadratic. **quinta ~** sursolid.

potenciação s. f. (pl. **-ões**) potentiation.

potencial s. m. (pl. **-ais**) potential. ‖ adj. m. + f. potential: 1. powerful, mighty, potent. 2. (phys.) existing in a positional form. ‖ **~mente** adv. potentially. **~ decrescente** falling potential. **energia ~** potential energy.

potencialidade s. f. potentiality, potency.

potenciar v. (math.) to involve, raise to a power.

potenciômetro s. m. (electr.) potentiometer, an instrument for measuring electromotive force.

potentado s. m. potentate, monarch, ruler, sovereign.

potente adj. m. + f. 1. potent, potential, powerful, mighty. 2. strong, vigorous, dynamic. 3. rough, violent. ‖ **~mente** adv. potently.

potentéia s. f. (her.) potent. **cruz ~** cross potent.

potentilha s. f. (bot., also **cinco-em-rama**) potentilla, five-finger, cinquefoil.

potério s. m. (bot.) burnet.

poterna s. f. postern, a back-door or back-gate.

potestade s. f. 1. power, authority, strength. 2. divine power. 3. **~s** pl. the second hierarchy of angels.

poti s. m. (Braz.) shrimp, prawn.

potiche s. m. porcelain vase, esp. of China or Japan.

potici s. m. (Braz.) abundance, plenty, overfulness.

potiúna s. m. (Braz.) a kind of dark shrimp.

poto s. m. (poet.) drink, potion.

potó s. m. (Braz., ent., also **potó-pimenta**) rove beetle.

potoca s. f. (Braz.) lie, falsehood.

potocar v. to lie, deceive.

potoqueiro s. m., **potoquista** m. + f. (Braz.) liar. ‖ adj. untruthful, lying.

potosi s. m. (fig.) treasures, wealth, source of wealth.

potra s. f. 1. filly, foal. 2. (med.) hernia, rupture. 3. (pop.) good luck, fortune. 4. haughtiness, arrogance, pride. 5. (bot.) node, joint.

potrada s. f. (S. Braz., also **potraria**) a herd of colts or foals.

potranca s. f. (Braz.) female colt of two years.

potrancada s. f. (Braz.) a herd of colts.

potranco s. m. (Braz.) a colt of less than two years.

potreação (pl. **-ões**), **potreada** s. f. (S. Braz.) herding, roundup (colts, horses).

potreador s. m. (S. Braz.) herder. ‖ adj. herding, rounding up.

potrear v. 1. to herd, round-up (colts, horses). 2. (fig.): a) to grow angry. b) to pick up a quarrel.

potréia s. f. nauseous drink, bad potion.

potreiro s. m. 1. horse-dealer, trader in cattle. 2. (S. Braz.) pen, hurdle, corral, paddock.

potril s. m. (pl. **-is**) (also **poldril**) paddock for colts.

potrilha s. m. + f. 1. person affected with hernia. 2. (pop.) poor devil.

potrilhada s. f. (S. Braz.) a herd of colts.

potrilho s. m. (S. Braz.) colt (of less than two years).

potro s. m. 1. colt, foal, young horse. 3. (hist.) instrument of torture. 2. (S. Braz.) untamed horse.

potroso adj. afflicted with hernia, ruptured.

potrudo adj. (S. Braz.) lucky, auspicious, fortunate.

poucachinho, poucochinho s. m. (also **poucadinho**) a little bit. ‖ adj. very little.

pouca-vergonha s. f. (pl. **poucas-vergonhas**) sauciness, shamelessness; knavery, rascality, trickery.

pouco s. m. a little, trifle, small quantity, somewhat, something. ‖ adj. 1. little. 2. **~s** pl. few. ‖ adv. little, insufficiently, not much; rather, about, nearly. **~ a ~**, **~ e ~** little by little, by degrees. **~ adiante** a little further on. **~ antes** a little before. **~ caso** disregard. **-a coisa** a small matter, trifling. **~s dias depois** a few days after. **-a gente** few people. **~ menos** somewhat less, almost, about. **~ se me dá** I don't care a pin. **~ talentoso** poorly gifted. **~ tempo atrás** a short time ago. **-as vezes** seldom, rarely. **a -a distância** near. **aos ~s** little by little, by fits and starts, by inches, inch meal, by inch meal. **um ~ de felicidade** a crumb of happiness. **um ~ úmido** somewhat moist. **uns ~s a** few. **ainda há ~** a while ago. **acostumar-se aos ~s** to slide into the habit. **afastar aos ~s** to inch out. **apreciar ~** to set little by. **dar aos ~s** to inch out. **dá-me um ~ de café** give me some coffee. **dentro de ~ tempo** in a short time, soon, in a little while. **durar ~** to go a little way, be short-lived. **eu não tenho mais nem um ~ de respeito para com ele** I have not a vestige of respect left for him. **fazer ~ caso** to minimize, belittle. **há ~s espectadores** spectators are few. **homem para ~** an insignificant fellow. **isto é ~ provável** that is hardly probable. **julgamo-lo de ~ valor** we think poorly of it. **mais um ~ de chá?** some more tea? **melhor ~ do que nada** half a loaf is better than no bread. **muitos ~s fazem muito** many a pickle makes a mickle.

nem um ~ not a little, not a fraction. **para dizer** ~ to say the least of it. **pareceu um ~ esquisito** it seemed a trifle odd. **perder um ~ da sua importância** to lose somewhat of its (one's) importance. **por** ~ about, almost. **por** ~ **que** never so little, if ever so little. **por** ~ **que morreu afogado** he was within a hair's breadth of being drowned. **tão** ~ so little. **todo o assunto em -as palavras** the long and the short of it. **uma criança** ~ **desenvolvida** a backward child.

poupa s. f. 1. (ornith.) hoopoe. 2. crest (feather), tuft, cop. 3. toupet, toupee.

poupado adj. 1. spared, saved. 2. saving, economical, frugal; forehanded, canny. || **-amente** adv. sparingly. **vintém** ~, **vintém ganhado** penny saved, penny earned.

poupador s. m. a saving person. || adj. saving, economical, thrifty.

poupança s. f. (also **poupa**) 1. economy, parsimony, thriftiness. 2. providence, forehandedness. **medidas de** ~ economy measures.

poupão s. m. (pl. **-ões**) lazy fellow, work-shy person. || adj. work-shy, lazy.

poupar v. 1. to economize, spare, save, husband, lay up. 2. to preserve, reserve, hold, retain. 3. ~**-se** to care for o. s. ~ **o seu dinheiro** to spare one's money. ~ **a ninguém** to spare nobody. **poupe-lhe aquela pena!** save him that grief. **poupe-me tudo isto!** spare me all this! **ela não se poupa** she does not take care of herself. **ele não poupou elogios** he was ungrudging in praise. **não** ~ **nem esforços nem dinheiro** to spare neither trouble nor money.

poupinha s. f. (ornith.) crested titmouse.

poupudo adj. tufted, crested (feathers).

pouquidade, pouquidão s. f. (pl. **-ões**) 1. smallness, littleness, small quantity or portion. 2. small matter, trifle.

pouquinho s. m. a little bit, trifle, snatch. **um** ~ **de** a sprinkle of. **um** ~ **escuro demais** a thought too dark. **nem um** ~ not a iota. **você precisa ser um** ~ **mais amável** you got to be a bit friendlier.

pouquíssimo adj. little, precious little.

pousa s. f. (also **poisa**) 1. stop(ping). 2. resting-place, inn, lodge, lodging.

pousada s. f. (also **poisada**) 1. stopping, resting. 2. inn, lodging. 3. (Braz.) place for passing a night. **falar com coração de** ~ to speak without passion.

pousadia s. f. (also **poisadia**) retirement, lodging.

pousar v. (also **poisar**) 1. to put, set, lay down. 2. to rest, stop, stay, halt, pause. 3. to lodge, spend the night at. 4. to dwell. 5. to perch, repose, alight. 6. to land (plane). 7. to rest upon. 8. ~**-se** to be at ease, repose. ~ **fora de casa** to outlie.

pousio s. m. (also **poisio**) fallow ground. || adj. fallow, uncultivated.

pouso s. m. 1. resting place. 2. tree on which birds perch. 3. landing (plane). 4. (naut.): a) anchorage, anchoring place. b) slip, slipway. 5. the nether millstone. **tomar** ~ to cast anchor.

pouta s. f. (also **poita**) a stone that substitutes the anchor (fishermen).

poutar v. (also **poitar**) to throw the anchor stone (**pouta**).

povaréu, poviléu s. m. = **povoléu**.

povo s. m. 1. people, folk; nation, race. 2. village, settlement. 3. multitude, crowd. 4. mob, rabble. 5. (fig.) large quantity. 6. (Braz., pop.) family. **o** ~ **americano** (fig.) Jonathan. **o** ~ **inglês** (fig.) John Bull. ~ **miúdo** mob, common people. **chamar o**

~ **às urnas** to appeal to the country. **isto é caviar para o** ~ that's caviar to the general. **procurar agravar ao** ~ to play for the gallery.

póvoa s. f. small village.

povoação s. f. (pl. **-ões**) 1. population, inhabitants; settlement, village. 2. (N. Braz.) a group of rubber trees in the forest.

povoado s. m. settlement, village, place. || adj. populated, populous. **densamente** ~ close-peopled. **não** ~ unsettled.

povoador s. m. populator, colonist, peopler. || adj. populating.

povoamento s. m. 1. population, process of populating or peopling. 2. part of a forest (reserved for cutting).

povoar v. 1. to populate, people, colonize, settle. 2. to stock, fill. 3. ~**-se**: a) to establish o. s. b) to become populated.

povoeiro s. m. (S. Braz.) townsman, villager.

povoléu s. m. mean or low people, rabble.

pozeira s. f. (Braz.) powder box, puff box.

pozolana s. f. (petrog.) pozzuolana, pozzolana, a volcanic substance found first at Pozzuoli (Italy).

pozolânico adj. pozzuolanic.

praça s. f. 1. square, market-place. 2. the merchants of a town. 3. fortified place, fortress. 4. (mil.) garrison. 5. a soldier. 6. enrollment, enlistment (for service). 7. bluster, show. 8. (pop.) scoundrel. ~ **de armas** (naut.) gun-room. ~ **do comércio** exchange, trading center. ~ **forte** ward, fortress, citadel. ~ **de manobra** (aeron.) apron. ~ **pública** plaza, square. ~ **de touros** bull ring. **carro de** ~ taxi, taxi car. **fazer, abrir** ~ to make way. **sentar** ~, **assentar** ~ to enter the service, engage in the army.

pracear v. to sell by auction, auction off.

praceiro adj. local; public; known.

pracejar v. to boast, show off, make a show of.

praciano s. m. (Braz.) townsman. || adj. dwelling in the town; well-bred, having fine manners.

pracista s. m. + f. 1. salesman. 2. countryman with city manners. 3. (S. Braz.) name given to the townspeople by the countrymen.

pracuuba s. f. (Braz.) Amazonian timber tree.

pradaria s. f. prairie, level grassy land; meadow.

prado s. m. 1. meadow, plain, pasture ground, grassy land. 2. (Braz.) hippodrome, race-course.

pradoso adj. rich in meadows or pasture; grassy.

prafrentex adj. m. + f., sg. + pl. (sl.) with it, in, modern.

praga s. f. 1. imprecation, curse, malediction, malison; damnation. 2. blasphemy, profanity. 3. calamity, plague. 4. (fig.) misfortune, affliction. 5. (Braz.) noxious weeds. **boca de** ~**s** slanderer, backbiter. **rogar** ~**s** to curse, imprecate evil on s. o.

pragal s. m. (pl. **-ais**) steppe, heath, wasteland.

pragana s. f. (bot.) awn, beard.

praganoso adj. (bot.) awned, bearded.

pragmática s. f. 1. rules and prescriptions for state and eccl. ceremonies. 2. (by extension) etiquette (social life).

pragmático adj. 1. pragmatic(al), officious. 2. usual, customary.

pragmatismo s. m. (philos.) pragmatism.

pragmatista s. m. + f. (philos.) pragmatist. || adj. pragmatic, pragmatist.

praguedo s. m. a series of execrations.

praguejado adj. (Braz.) 1. plagued. 2. imprecated. 3. sickly, morbid.

praguejador s. m. curser, blasphemer, swearer. || adj. cursing

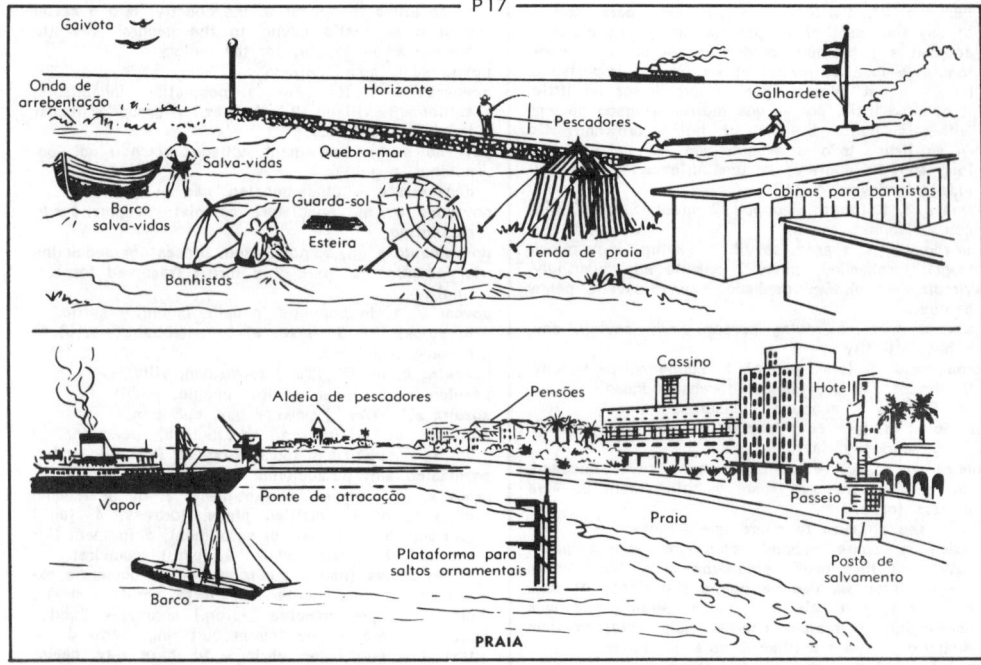

P 17

Gaivota
Onda de arrebentação
Horizonte
Galhardete
Pescadores
Salva-vidas
Quebra-mar
Barco salva-vidas
Guarda-sol
Cabinas para banhistas
Esteira
Tenda de praia
Banhistas

Aldeia de pescadores
Pensões
Cassino
Hotel
Vapor
Ponte de atracação
Passeio
Praia
Plataforma para saltos ornamentais
Posto de salvamento
Barco

PRAIA

praguejamento s. m. imprecation, cursing, swearing.
praguejar v. 1. to curse, imprecate, blaspheme, swear; beshrew. 2. to be infested with noxious weeds. 3. (fig.) to fling dirt on a person, revile.
~ **excessivamente** to swear like a trooper, to swear like a bargee.
praguento adj. 1. cursing, imprecatory. 2. calumnious, slanderous, detractory. ‖ **-amente** adv. calumniously.
praia s. f. beach, sea-shore, coast, strand (plates C 19, P 17).
à ~, na ~ ashore. **passar as férias na** ~ to spend the holydays on the seaside. **pôr na** ~ to beach.
praiano s. m. inhabitant of the seaside, person dwelling near the beach. ‖ adj. of or pertaining to the seaside or beach.
praieiro s. m. 1. = **praiano**. 2. (Braz.) name of the rebels of the revolution in Pernambuco in 1848. ‖ adj. said of the liberal party of those rebels.
praíno s. m. (S. Braz.) plain, esp. a low plain near a water(course).
prajá s. m. (Braz.) sweetmeat prepared of molasses and eggs.
pralina s. f. praline, confection prepared of almonds and boiled sugar.
prancha s. f. 1. plank, board, deal. 2. gangway, gang-plank. 3. flat side of a sword. 4. circular of one freemason's lodge to another. 5. printed picture. 6. (Braz., sl.) large foot. 7. (Braz., pop.) refusal of a proposal of marriage.
pranchada s. f. 1. stroke with the flat side of a sword. 2. cap over the touch-hole (of a gun), apron.
pranchão s. m. (pl. **-ões**) large plank, thick board.
pranchar v. (Braz.) to strike with the flat side of a sword.
pranchear v. (Braz., Port. prov.) to fall at full length.
prancheiro s. m. (Braz.) rower, oarsman.

prancheta s. f. 1. thin or small board (plate A 13). 2. small metal plate. 3. a surveyor's table.
prândio s. m. (poet.) banquet, dinner.
pranteadeira s. f. hired female mourner.
pranteador s. m. mourner, weeper. ‖ adj. mourning, wailing, weeping.
prantear v. 1. to mourn, lament; weep, cry, deplore, wail. 2. ~-**se** to complain (o. s.).
ela o pranteou she wept for him.
pranto s. m. (N. Braz., also **prantina** f.) weeping, lamentation, wailing; cry.
em ~ in tears, tear-stained.
prásino s. m. emerald (stone). ‖ adj. leek-green, porracious.
prásio s. m. (min.) prase, a leek, green variety of massive quartz.
prasiodímio s. m. (chem.) praseodymium.
prasmar v. (obs.) to reprehend, blame, censure, criticize.
prasmo s. m. (obs.) censure, blame, reprehension.
prata s. f. silver: 1. the metallic element. 2. any silver coin. 3. silverware. 4. (fig.) money, argent.
~ **de lei** sterling silver. ~ **dourada** silver gilt. ~ **em barras** silver bars. ~ **em folhas** silver foil. ~ **viva** quicksilver. **banho de** ~ silver bath. **bodas de** ~ silver wedding. **cobertura de** ~ silver-plating. **falar é** ~, **calar é ouro** speech is silver, silence is gold. **fio de** ~ silver wire. **liga de** ~ silver alloy. **nitrato de** ~ silver nitrate. **ourives de** ~ silversmith. **pessoa com língua de** ~ an eloquent person. **veia de** ~ silver vein. **voz de** ~ clear voice, silver voice.
pratada s. f. plateful, plate.
pratalhada s. f. plateful (food).
pratalhaz s. m. (also **pratarraz**) a full plate.
prataria (I) s. f. silver plate, silverware, silver jewelry.
prataria (II) s. f. a lot of plates.

prateação s. f. (pl. -ões) process of silvering.

prateado adj. silvered, plated with silver; silver-grey, silvery, argenteous.
as ondas -as the silvery waves. **papel** ~ silver paper. **raposa -a** silver fox.

prateador s. m. silversmith, silverer, plateworker. ‖ adj. plating with silver.

pratear v. to silver, cover or plate with silver; electroplate; make silvery.

prateira s. f. closet for silverware.

prateiro s. m. silversmith, silver plater.

prateleira s. f. (also **prateleiro** m.) 1. shelf, rack, bracket (plates A 13, P 1, T 4). 2. ~s pl. shelving. ~ **para garrafas** bottle rack. ~ **para livros** bookshelf. **colocar sobre** ~ to rack.

prateleiro (I) s. m. (Braz.) cymbaler, cymbalist.

prateleiro (II) s. m. (Port. prov.) silversmith, silver plater.

pratense adj. pratincolous, living in meadows.

pratibu s. m. (N. Braz., ichth.) any mullet.

prática s. f. 1. practice: a) action, exercise, performance, doing. b) habit, usage, custom, form. c) drill, training, function. d) experience, skill, dexterity. e) knowledge. 2. conversation, familiar discourse, exhortation; speech.
~ **no magistério** experience in teaching. **a** ~ **faz o mestre** practice makes perfect. **conservar a** ~ to keep one's hand in. **falta de** ~ inexperience. **manter** ~ to converse, maintain a conversation. **na** ~ in practice. **pôr em** ~ to actualize, apply, put into practice. **sem** ~ unskilled, out of practice, inexperienced. **ter grande** ~ to have great skill. **ter perdido a** ~ to have one's hand out.

praticabilidade s. f. practicability, practicableness, availability, feasibility, workability.

praticagem s. f. (naut.) piloting, pilotage.

praticante s. m. + f. practitioner, practiser, probationer; apprentice. ‖ adj. practising, performing.
~ **de um culto** cultist. **estudantes** ~s **nos hospitais** walkers of the hospitals.

praticar v. 1. to practice, practise: a) put into practice, execute, perform, enact, profess, prosecute. b) use; exercise, train, drill. 2. ~-se to be in practice. 3. to talk, converse; discourse; preach. ~ **um crime** to commit a crime. ~ **esporte** to go in for sport. ~ **ao piano** to practise on the piano. **pratica e serás mestre** practice makes perfect. **os estudantes (de medicina) praticam nos hospitais** the students walk the hospitals.

praticável adj. m. + f. (pl. -áveis) practicable, workable, exercisable, performable, feasible, possible; attainable, available.

prático s. m. 1. (naut.) pilot. 2. practician, practiser; adept. ‖ adj. practical, skilled, experienced; functional; operative. ‖ **praticamente** adv. practically. ~ **da costa** coasting pilot. **aula -a** practicum. **espírito** ~ practical mind. **indivíduo** ~ businesslike person. **médico** ~ practising physician. **não** ~ unpractical.

pratícola adj. m. + f. 1. pratincolous, living in meadows. 2. relating to the culture of meadows or pastures.

praticultor s. m. cultivator of meadows or pastures.

praticultura s. f. the culture of meadows or pastures.

pratilheiro s. m. (mus.) cymbaler, cymbalist.

pratinho s. m. 1. small plate or dish, caster (plate R 5). 2. (fig.) laughing-stock, object of laughter.

pratiqueira s. f. (Braz., ichth.) white mullet.

prato (I) s. m. 1. plate, dish (plates M 1, 8, R 5). 2. dish, mess, food, meal. 3. pan (scales). 4. ~s pl. (mus.) cymbals.
um ~ **de ameixas** a plate of prunes. ~ **fundo** soup-plate (plate M 1). ~ **raso** dinner plate (plate M 1).

~ **de toca-disco** (phonograph) turntable. **do** ~ **à boca se perde a sopa** there is many a slip between the cup and the lip. **fazer** ~ **de alguém** to have a fling at one. **lavadeira de** ~s scullery maid. **pôr em** ~s **limpos** to clear up a matter. **refeição de dois** ~s two-course meal.

prato (II) adj. flat.

pravidade s. f. pravity, perverseness, depravity.

pravo adj. depraved, wicked, perverse.

praxe s. f. practice, praxis, use, wont, habit, custom. ~ **judicial** judicial usages. **de** ~ habitual, wonted, customary, usual. **é** ~ it is the rule. **uso e** ~ use and wont.

praxista s. m. + f. 1. stickler. 2. person familiar with judicial usages, attorney, pleader. ‖ adj. conventional, traditional, ceremonious.

prazentear v. 1. to flatter, praise falsely. 2. to jest, joke.

prazenteio s. m. flattery, blandishment.

prazenteiro adj. festive, pleasant, amusing, merry, gay; sportive, jovial, likable; obsequious. ‖ -amente adv. jovially, obsequiously.

prazer s. m. 1. pleasure, joy, contentment, delight, satisfaction, complacence. 2. amusement, diversion, fun, sport. ‖ v. to please.
~es **fúteis** hollow joys. **o** ~ **de um é o desgosto de outro** it as an ill wind that blow nobody any good. **com** ~ with pleasure. **com** ~ **sempre novo** with unwearying delight. **dá-me grande** ~ it gives me great joy. **dar** ~ **a** to pleasure. **é um grande** ~ **para ele** it gives him great pleasure. (sl.) **it is nuts for him. é um** ~ **ouvi-la** it's a pleasure to hear her. **foi um** ~ **ouvir** it was a treat to hear it. **isto foi um** ~ **sem amargura** this was a joy without alloy. **muito** ~ **em conhecê-lo** happy to meet you. **a peça proporcionou-me enorme** ~ the play afforded me endless entertainment. **quer dar-nos o** ~ **de uma recitação?** will you favour us with a recital? **ter o** ~ **de dizer** to be glad to say. **tenho** ~ **em ensiná-lo** I do not grudge teaching him. **virei com todo o** ~ I shall be delighted (charmed) to come.

prazeroso adj. (Braz.) pleasant, zestful, joyful, cheerful, merry. ‖ -amente adv. pleasantly, lief.

prazimento s. m. delight, pleasure.

praz-me s. m., sg. + pl. (obs.) consent.

prazo s. m. 1. term, time, stated period, appointed day. 2. delay.
~ **de entrega** time of delivery. ~ **de vencimento** term. **a** ~ on account (instalment). **ao** ~ **de um ano** at a prompt of a year. **alargar o** ~ to extend, prolong the time. **fim de** ~ closing date. **a longo** ~ at long date. **com** ~ **de três meses** at three months' credit. **seguro a** ~ **fixo** terminable assurance. **transação a** ~ transaction on credit.

prazo-dado s. m. (pl. **prazos-dados**) appointment (meeting); interview.

pré s. m. (mil.) daily pay.

preá s. f. Braz. 1. (zool.) opossum, cavy. 2. m. (N.) sponger, parasite.

preaca s. f. (Braz.) leathern whip.

preacada s. f. (Braz.) lash, stroke with a whip.

pré-adamita s. m. + f. (pl. **pré-adamitas**) pre-Adamite: person who lived before Adam. ‖ adj. pre-Adamic.

pré-agônico adj. (med.) preagonal.

prealegar v. to quote or allege before.

preamar s. f. flood, high water, high tide.
é ~ the tide is up. **nível de** ~ high-water mark. **sinal de** ~ floodmark.

preambular (I) adj. m. + f. preambular(y), introductory.

preambular (II) v. to preamble, precede, preface; serve as a preamble or introduction.

preâmbulo s. m. preamble, preface, prologue, introduction, prelude.
sem mais ~s without delay.
preanunciação s. f. (pl. **-ões**) preannouncement.
preanunciar v. to preannounce, announce before.
preaquecedor s. m. extraction heater, economizer.
prear v. to prey, take, snatch, catch.
prebenda s. f. 1. prebend, prebendary, stipend, benefice. 2. (fig.) sinecure, well-paid office with little or no responsibility.
prebendado s. m. prebendary, person who holds a prebend. ‖ adj. prebendal.
prebendar v. to prebendate, confer a prebend.
prebendaria s. f. prebendship, the office of a prebendary.
prebendeiro s. m. prebendary.
prebixim s. m. (pl. **-ins**) (Braz., ornith.) a magpie.
prebostado s. m. rank of a provost.
prebostal adj. m. + f. (pl. **-ais**) provostal, relating to a provost.
preboste s. m. provost.
pré-cabraliano adj. (pl. **pré-cabralianos**) (Braz.) before the discovery of Brazil by Pedro Álvares Cabral.
precação s. f. (pl. **-ões**) supplication, entreaty.
precâmbrico adj. (geol.) pre-Cambrian.
precantar v. to vaticinate in verses.
precariedade s. f. precariousness, uncertainty, unsafeness.
precário adj. precarious, uncertain, insecure, unstable, unsafe; risky, doubtful; dangerous, hazardous. ‖ **precariamente** adv. precariously.
preçário s. m. price list.
precatado adj. cautious, wary, circumspect, chary. ‖ **-amente** adv. warily.
precatar v. 1. to precaution, warn, forewarn, caution beforehand. 2. to avoid, provide against. 3. **~-se** to take care, be on one's guard, beware.
quando mal me precato when I least think of it.
precatória s. f. (jur.) mandamus. ‖ adj. relating to a mandamus.
precatório s. m. precatory letter, petition. ‖ adj. precatory, suppliant, beseeching.
precaução s. f. (pl. **-ões**) precaution, caution, foresight, care, alertness, provision.
a título de ~ by way of precaution. **tomar -ões** to take precautions, guard.
precaucionar-se v. to take precautions, be on one's guard, take care.
precautório adj. precautional, precautionary, preventive.
precaver v. (also **precautelar**) 1. to prevent, obviate. 2. to provide against, forewarn. 3. **~-se** to be cautious, stand upon one's guard, beware.
precavido adj. precautious, wary; vigilant, canny.
prece s. f. 1. prayer. 2. petition, invocation.
~s matinais morning prayers.
precedência s. f. precedence, priority, anteriority, preeminence.
dar ~ a alguém to give precedence to a person.
ter ~ sobre to take rank before.
precedente s. m. + f. (also jur.) precedent. ‖ adj. precedent, preceding, going before (in order of time, place or rank), antecedent, anterior, previous, former; prevenient. ‖ **~mente** adv. precedently, hereinbefore.
criar um ~ to set a precedent. **sem ~** without precedent, unexampled.
preceder v. 1. to precede, go before in order of time, place or rank. 2. to antedate, anticipate. 3. to surpass, excel, exceed, prevail. 4. to have precedence or preference. 5. **~-se** to take precedence of.
a corrução da moral precede o crime corruption of morals precedes crime.

preceito s. m. precept: 1. principle, maxim, rule, formula. 2. teaching, instruction. 3. commandment, prescription.
de acordo com ~s estabelecidos according to received notions.
preceituar v. to prescribe, order, establish.
preceituário s. m. collection of directions or precepts.
precentor s. m. precentor.
preceptivo adj. preceptive, instructive.
preceptor s. m. preceptor, teacher, instructor, tutor, mentor.
preceptora s. f. preceptress, mistress, governess.
preceptoral adj. m. + f. (pl. **-ais**) preceptoral, preceptorial, relating to a preceptor.
preceptoria s. f. preceptory, preceptorate.
precessão s. f. (pl. **-ões**) precession, precedence, anticipation, advance.
~ dos equinócios (astr.) precession of the equinoxes.
precingir v. to gird, girdle, lace; enclose, encircle.
precinta s. f. 1. band, strip. 2. (naut.) wale, strap for covering ropes.
precintar v. to strap up, fasten with a strap.
precinto s. m. precinct, inclosure; peribolus.
preciosidade s. f. 1. preciousness, valuableness, worth, costliness; anything of great value. 2. **~s** pl. treasure.
preciosismo s. m. preciosity, fastidiousness, excessive refinement.
precioso adj. 1. precious, valuable, costly. 2. magnificent, splendid, excellent. 3. (fig.) affected, over-refined. 4. beloved, dear. ‖ **-amente** adv. preciously.
precipício s. m. 1. precipice, abyss, abrupt descent (plate M 11). 2. (fig.) ruin, danger, perdition.
cair num ~ to fall down a precipice.
precipitação s. f. (pl. **-ões**) precipitation: 1. precipitancy, haste, rush, hurry, rashness, abruptness. 2. (chem.) process of subsiding, subsidence.
precipitado s. m. 1. precipitator. 2. (chem.) precipitate: deposition, sediment. ‖ adj. precipitate: 1. headlong, plunging down. 2. heedless, hasty, rash, hurried; sudden, abrupt. 3. ill-judged, inconsiderate. ‖ **-amente** adv. precipitately.
fuga -a head over heels flight. **tirar conclusões -as** to jump at conclusions.
precipitante s. m. (chem.) precipitant, an agent which causes the precipitation of a solution. ‖ adj. m. + f. precipitant, precipitative.
precipitar v. 1. to precipitate: a) deposit, extract, subside, fall as a sediment. b) cast down headlong, hurl down. c) hasten, hurry up, fly, speed 2. **~-se** to precipitate o. s., throw o. s. into; (fig.) put the cart before the horse.
~-se para a porta to make a rush for the door.
ela precipitou-se enfurecidamente para fora da sala she flounced out of the room in rage. **ele precipitou-se sobre isto** he went for it.
precípite adj. m. + f. 1. precipitate, hasty, speedy, hurried. 2. dangerous.
precipitina s. f. (immunology) precipitin, coagulin.
precipitoso adj. 1. precipitous, steep, declivitous. 2. (fig.) rash, inconsiderate, abrupt, sudden.
precípuo s. m. (jur.) right to a preferential share. ‖ adj. essential, foremost, chief, main.
precisado adj. needy, poor, destitute.
precisão s. f. (pl. **-ões**) 1. precision, preciseness, exactness, accuracy, correctness. 2. distinctness, nicety. 3. need, want; poverty. 4. necessity.
~ de trabalho working accuracy. **balança de ~** precision balance. **falta de ~** vagueness. **de grande ~** pinpoint. **torno de ~** precision turning-lathe.
precisar v. 1. to need, necessitate, want. 2. to require, demand. 3. to particularize, exact, fix. 4. **~-se** to be necessary, be required.

precisa-se de um criado servant wanted. **precisa-se trabalhar para viver** one must work to live. **precisa ser já?** need it be at once? **ora preciso de descanso** I stand in need of repose. **preciso ir** I must go, I need to go. **ele precisa cortar o cabelo** his hair wants cutting. **isto precisa ser feito** it wants doing. **não precisa escrever** don't trouble to write. **precisamos de um empregado** we are in want of an employee. **você precisa pagar** you must pay, you have to pay. **o negócio precisa muita atenção** the business requires great attention.

preciso adj. 1. precise, exact, just, definite. 2. nice, distinct. 3. correct, accurate. 4. necessary, indispensable, needful, requisite, wanted.

é ~ que você saiba I would have you know. **se ~ for** if required. **se for ~** if need be, if necessary. **não é ~** it is not necessary. **ser ~** to be necessary.

precitado adj. mentioned before, aforesaid.

precito s. m. reprobate; scoundrel. ‖ adj. reprobate, corrupt, vitious; guilty, culpable; damned.

preclaro adj. 1. preclare, preclair, noble, brave, famous, illustrious, renowned. 2. fine, beautiful, brilliant.

pré-clássico adj. preclassic(al).

preclusão s. f. (pl. -ões) preclusion, a pursing of the lips to produce a sound as b or p.

preço s. m. price: 1. worth, value, estimation. 2. cost, expense, charge, rate. 3. prize, award, recompense. 4. esteem, reputation.

~ de assinatura subscription price. **~ bruto** gross price. **~ de custo** cost price. **~ do dia** spot price. **~ excessivo** overcharge, costliness, fancy price. **~ de fábrica** manufacturer's price. **~ de fatura** billing cost, invoice price. **~ fixo** fixed price. **~ global** all-round price. **~ de inauguração** starting price. **~ líquido** net price. **~ máximo**, **~ teto** ceiling price. **~ de ocasião** bargain price. **~ de pechincha** underprice. **~ de resgate** ransom, redemptory price. **~ com tudo incluído** inclusive terms. **~ de varejo** retail price. **~ de venda** selling price. **a ~s elevados** at high charges. **a ~s reduzidos** at reduced prices. **ao ~ da sua vida** at the cost of his life. **a qualquer ~** at all costs. **cobrar um ~ baixo** to make a small charge. **elevar os ~s** to drive up the prices. **estabelecer ~** to fix the price. **lista de ~s** price list. **oferecer a ~ inferior** to undersell. **pagar um ~ exorbitante** to pay an exorbitant price, pay through the nose. **pelo ~ mais baixo** at the lowest price. **por bom ~** cheap. **pôr um ~ em** to put a price on. **sem ~ fixo** unpriced. **vou fazê-lo a qualquer ~** I will do it at any price.

precoce adj. m. + f. 1. precocious, premature. 2. untimely, early. 3. unripe. ‖ adj. precociously.

criança ~ precocious child, prodigy. **ela é ~ para sua idade** she is forward for her age.

precocidade s. f. precocity, precociousness, prematurity; forwardness.

precogitar v. to precogitate, consider beforehand, premeditate, plan, scheme, contrive.

precógnito adj. known before, known by anticipation.

pré-colombiano adj. (pl. pré-colombianos) pre-Columbian, prior to the time of Christopher Columbus, prior to the discovery of America.

preconceber v. to preconceive, plan beforehand.

preconcebido adj. preconceived, premeditated; deliberate, intentional, prepense.

preconceito s. m. 1. preconceit, preconception, foregone conclusion. 2. superstition, prejudice, bias, preopinion.

sem ~ unprejudiced. **ter um ~ contra alguém** to have a prejudice against s. o.

preconício s. m. (Braz.) advertising, propaganda.

preconização s. f. (pl. -ões) preconization, a public proclamation, esp. the public confirmation of an ecclesiastic dignity.

preconizador s. m. preconizer. ‖ adj. preconizing.

preconizar v. to preconize: 1. profess, proclaim, summon publicly. 2. confirm an ecclesiastical appointment. 3. extol, praise, commend.

pré-consciente s. m. (pl. pré-conscientes) (psychoanalysis) preconsciousness, a state anterior to consciousness.

precordial adj. m. + f. (pl. -ais) (nat.) precordial, situated in front of the heart.

região ~ precordial region, epigastric region.

precordialgia s. f. (med.) precordial pain.

pré-cristão adj. (pl. pré-cristãos) pre-Christian(ic), before the Christian era.

precursor s. m. 1. precursor, forerunner, predecessor, pioneer. 2. harbinger, herald; omen, sign. ‖ adj. precursory, preceding; introductory, indicative.

o ~ de Cristo the Precursor of Christ, John the Baptist.

predador s. m. predator.

pré-datar v. to predate; to antedate.

predatório adj. predatory, predatorious; plundering, thievish.

predecessor s. m. predecessor, precursor, antecessor.

predefinição s. f. (pl. -ões) predefinition, definition in advance, predetermination, an appointing beforehand; prognostication, prediction.

predefinir v. to predefine, predetermine, define beforehand.

predestinação s. f. (pl. -ões) predestination, foreordination, predetermination, election; fate, destiny.

predestinacionismo s. m. (philos.) predestinarianism, the doctrine of predestination.

predestinacionista s. m. + f. (philos.) predestinarian, person who believes in the doctrine of predestination.

predestinado s. m. (theol.) elect. ‖ adj. predestinate(d), foreordained, fated, selected, predetermined. ‖ -amente adv. fatefully.

predestinar v. to predestinate, predestine, foreordain, foredoom, predetermine.

predeterminação s. f. (pl. -ões) predetermination, preordination, foreordainment; previous resolution.

predeterminante adj. m. + f. predetermining.

predeterminar v. to predetermine, preordain, foreordain, appoint beforehand, preorder.

predial adj. m. + f. (pl. -ais) predial, praedial.

imposto ~ house tax.

prédica s. f. preaching, preachment, sermon.

predicação s. f. 1. preaching, sermon. 2. assertion. 3. (gram.) predication.

predicado s. m. 1. quality, property, character, attribute. 2. talent, faculty, aptitude, capacity. 3. (gram.) predicate.

predicador s. m. preacher. ‖ adj. preaching.

predical adj. m. + f. (pl. -ais) predicatory, pertaining to preaching.

predicamental adj. m. + f. (pl. -ais) predicamental, of or pertaining to predicaments.

predicamentar v. to classify, place in a category, grade.

predicamento s. m. predicament, class, category; order, degree; state, condition.

predicante s. m. + f. predicant, preacher; preaching friar; Protestant preacher. ‖ adj. preaching.

predição s. f. (pl. -ões) prediction, prophecy, prognostication, presage, vaticination, forecast.

predicar v. to preach, admonish, counsel.

predicativo s. m. (gram.) predicate. ‖ adj. predicative.

predicatório adj. encomiastic, eulogiastic, flattering.

predileção s. f. (pl. **-ões**) predilection: 1. favour, preference, partiality. 2. attachment, addiction, inclination.
ter ~ por to feel attached to; prefer.
predileto s. m. favourite, darling, minion. ‖ adj. beloved, favourite, dear.
Pedro é o ~ dela Peter is her favourite. **o gênero ~ de leitura dele são biografias** his preference in reading are biographies. **minha flor -a é a rosa** my favourite flower is the rose.
prédio s. m. 1. estate, landed property, farm. 2. building, construction, edifice, house.
predisponência s. f. predisponency, predisposition.
predisponente adj. m. + f. predisponent, predisposing, predetermining.
predispor v. 1. to predispose, predetermine, predestine. 2. to prepossess, prejudice. 3. to prepare, prearrange.
uma experiência infeliz o predispôs contra todas as mulheres one unhappy experience prejudiced him against all women.
predisposição s. f. (pl. **-ões**) predisposition, tendency, inclination, liability, susceptibility, proneness; vocation.
predisposto adj. predisposed, prone; prejudiced.
predito adj. 1. aforesaid, above-mentioned. 2. predicted, prophesied.
preditor s. m. predictor, one who or that which predicts.
predizer v. to predict: 1. foretell, forecast. 2. prophesy, presage, divine, vaticinate, betoken, soothsay.
predominação s. f. (pl. **-ões**) predomination, prevalence, superiority, ascendency.
predominador s. m. person who predominates. ‖ adj. predominating, predominant.
predominância s. f. predominance, predominancy, domination, preponderance, superiority, prevalence, ascendency; influence, advantage.
predominante adj. m. + f. predominant, prevailing, ruling, preponderant; superior. ‖ **~mente** adv. predominantly.
predominar v. to dominate, preponderate, rule, prevail, dominate; be superior, surpass.
predomínio s. m. predominancy, supremacy, dominion; power, superiority, preponderance, reign.
pré-eleger v. to pre-elect, elect or chose beforehand.
pré-eleição s. f. (pl. **-ões**) pre-election, previous choice or election.
ter a ~ to have the right of chosing first.
pré-eleitoral adj. m. + f. (pl. **-ais**) (Braz.) pre-election.
preeminência s. f. pre-eminence, superiority, distinction, precedence.
preeminente adj. m. + f. pre-eminent, superior, distinguished, remarkable; honourable. ‖ **~mente** adv. pre-eminently.
preempção s. f. (pl. **-ões**) pre-emption, orestallment, the right to purchase before others.
cláusula de ~ clause of pre-emption. **sujeito a ~** pre-emptible.
preencher v. to fulfil, accomplish, comply with, perform; supply, fill.
~ um cheque to fill out a cheque. **~ uma vaga** to fill a vacancy. **não preenchido** unfilled.
preenchimento s. m. 1. act of filling out. 2. fulfilling, accomplishment, performance.
preensão s. f. (pl. **-ões**) prehension, seizing; apprehension, understanding.
preênsil adj. m. + f. (pl. **-eis**) prehensile, seizing, grasping, holding.
pré-escolar adj. m. + f. preschool, precollege.
preestabelecer v. to pre-establish, order or arrange previously, settle beforehand.

preestabelecido adj. pre-established, settled beforehand.
pré-estréia s. f. (Braz.) preview, trade show.
preexcelência s. f. superior grade of excellence.
preexcelente adj. m. + f. most excellent, superexcellent.
preexcelso adj. sublime, grand, eminent.
preexistência s. f. pre-existence, previous existence.
preexistente adj. m. + f. pre-existent, preceding, existing before.
preexistir v. to pre-exist: 1. exist before another. 2. exist in a previous state.
pré-fabricação s. f. (pl. **pré-fabricações**) prefabrication.
pré-fabricado adj. prefabricated.
pré-fabricar v. to prefabricate.
prefaciador s. m. prefacer, prologizer, writer of a preface.
prefacial adj. m. + f. (pl. **-ais**) prefatorial, prefatory, introductory.
prefaciar v. to preface, preamble, prelude, prologue, prologize.
prefácio s. m. (also **prefação** f.) preface: 1. preamble, introduction, preludo, prologue, foreword, prolegomenon. 2. (liturg.) the section before the canon.
prefeito s. m. 1. prefect. 2. mayor, chief magistrate. 3. provost.
prefeitoral adj. m. + f. (pl. **-ais**) prefectoral, prefectorial, prefectural.
prefeitura s. f. 1. prefecture, the office, state or jurisdiction of a prefect. 2. town hall, city hall.
preferência s. f. preference: 1. choice, selection, election, option, alternative. 2. predilection, favouritism, distinction, liking. 3. priority, precedence. 4. (traffic) right of the way. 5. (jur.) privilege.
~ pela aviação air-mindedness. **com ~** by preference, preferably. **dar ~ a alguém** to throw the handkerchief to s. o. **de ~ a** before. **é de grande ~ geral** it is all the vogue, it is in full vogue. **ter ~ em geral** to tend to be privileged.
preferencial adj. m. + f. (pl. **-ais**) preferential, preferred, favoured.
ação ~ priority share. **tarifa ~** preferential duty.
preferente s. m. + f. preferrer. ‖ adj. preferring, preferential.
preferido adj. favoured, preferred, elected, chosen.
preferir v. 1. to prefer, give preference to, like better; select, choose, opt. 2. to be preferred.
prefiro cerveja a vinho my preference is for beer rather than wine. **eu preferiria** I had rather. **preferimo-lo a tudo** we prefer it to everything.
preferível adj. m. + f. (pl. **-íveis**) preferable, better. ‖ **preferivelmente** adv. preferably, rather, first.
prefiguração s. f. (pl. **-ões**) prefiguration, prefigurement, foreshadowing.
prefigurar v. to prefigure, foreshow, foreshadow, presage; adumbrate.
prefinir v. to fix a time or term, set down, determine, appoint.
prefixação s. f. (pl. **-ões**) 1. prefixation, prefixion. 2. (gram.) use of prefixes.
prefixado adj. 1. settled beforehand, appointed in advance. 2. (gram.) prepositive, prefixed.
prefixal adj. m. + f. (pl. **-ais**) prefixal.
prefixar v. to prefix: 1. appoint in advance, settle beforehand. 2. (gram.) add as a prefix.
prefixo s. m. (gram.) prefix, affix: a word or syllable put at the beginning of a word. ‖ adj. prefixed, settled beforehand.
~ musical signature tune.
prefloração s. f. (pl. **-ões**) (bot.) prefloration, estivation.
prefoliação s. f. (pl. **-ões**) (bot.) prefoliation, foliation, vernation.

preformação s. f. (pl. **-ões**) preformation.
pré-formar v. to preform, form beforehand.
prefulgente adj. m. + f. outshining, very bright.
prefulgir v. to sparkle, be very bright, be resplendent.
prega s. f. 1. pleat, plait, gather, fold (plate R 6). 2. crease, rumple, pucker (plate R 7).
~ **do cotovelo** (anat.) apron.
pregação s. f. (pl. **-ões**) 1. preachment, preaching, sermon. 2. (fig.) pulpit. 3. act of nailing.
pregada s. f. (N. Braz., pop.) wound inflicted by a piercing instrument.
pregadeira s. f. pincushion, pincase.
pregado adj. 1. nailed, fastened with nails. 2. fastened, fixed. 3. (Braz.) overtired, worn out, exhausted. 4. (N., pop.) drunk.
pregador (I) s. m. 1. nailer; fastener. 2. (S. Braz., sl.) liar. ‖ adj. nailing; fastening, fixing.
pregador (II) s. m. 1. preacher, predicant; clergyman. 2. scolder. ‖ adj. preaching; scolding.
~ **ambulante** itinerant preacher. **frades** ~**es** predicant friars (Dominicans).
pregadura, pregagem s. f. (pl. ~**s**, **-ns**) nailwork.
pregalhas s. f. pl. prayers, preces.
pregalho s. m. (naut.) halyard, hoist rope.
pregão s. m. 1. divulgation, proclamation, cry, street cry. 2. **-ões** pl. bans of marriage.
os -ões dos vendedores ambulantes the cries of the street venders.
pregar (I) v. 1. to nail, fasten with nails. 2. to fix, fasten; spring, peg. 3. (Braz.) to be exhausted. 4. to lie. 5. (N.) ~**-se** to get drunk.
~ **com um alfinete** to pin. ~ **um bofetão** to box a person's ears. ~ **um botão** to sew on a button (plate P 15). ~ **na memória** to imprint in one's memory, keep in mind. ~ **os olhos em alguém** to fix one's eyes upon s. o. ~ **uma peça a alguém** to play a trick on s. o. ~ **um prego** to drive a nail in, start a nail. ~ **um quadro numa parede** to nail a picture to a wall. **não pude** ~ **os olhos toda a noite** I could not sleep a wink all night.
pregar (II) v. = **preguear**.
pregar (III) v. 1. to preach, predicate, sermonize. 2. to publish, divulge; proclaim. 3. to exhort.
~ **no deserto** to cry out in the desert. ~ **um sermão a alguém** to lecture a person, give a person a pi-jaw.
pregar (IV) v. (obs.) to pray for, implore, beseech, beg.
pregaretas s. f. pl. Dominican nuns.
pregaria s. f. 1. a lot of nails. 2. nail work. 3. nail factory.
pré-glacial adj. (pl. **pré-glaciais**) (geol.) preglacial, prior to the glacial period.
prego s. m. 1. nail, sprig (plates G 2, P 15). 2. (obs.) hatpin. 3. (pop.) spout, a pawnbroker's shop. 4. (N. Braz., zool.) a species of monkey. 5. (pop.) lie. 6. exhaustion.
~ **cortado** cut nail (plate P 15). ~ **de acabamento** finishing nail (plate P 15). ~ **de arame** wire nail (plate P 15). ~ **de assoalho** flooring nail (plate P 15). ~ **de ferro** casing nail (plate P 15). ~ **de gancho** clasp nail (plate P 15). ~ **de pavimento** floor brad (plate P 15). ~ **forjado** wrought nail (plate P 15). ~ **fundido** cast nail. ~ **sem cabeça** brad, clout nail. **dar o** ~ to become exhausted, feel unable to go on. **fechar com** ~**s** to nail down. **no** ~, **na pendura** up the spout. **pôr no** ~ to pawn.
pregoamento s. m. crying, proclamation.
pregoar v. to cry, proclaim; publish, divulge; praise.
prego-cachorro s. m. (pl. **pregos-cachorro**) (Braz.) dog spike.
prego-dourado s. m. (pl. **pregos-dourados**) (N. Braz., pop.) fair-haired boy.

pregoeiro s. m. crier, proclamer, divulger; auctioneer.
~ **público** town crier.
pregresso adj. previous, preceding, prior, antecedent, former, foregoing.
preguari s. m. (Braz., zool.) a mollusc of the genus Strombus.
pregueadeira s. f., **pregueador** m. crisping-iron, crimper, ruffler, tucker.
pregueado s. m. pleat, folding. ‖ adj. pleated, tucked.
preguear v. 1. to tuck, plait, pleat, gather, fold. 2. to ruffle, crimp, crease.
pregueiro s. m. 1. nail manufacturer. 2. seller of nails. ‖ adj. nail-making, selling nails.
preguiça s. f. 1. indolence, sluggishness, laziness, idleness, slothfulness, slowness, dullness. 2. (zool.) sloth.
~ **é a chave da pobreza** laziness is the key to poverty.
preguiça-pequena s. f. (pl. **preguiças-pequenas**) (Braz., zool.) two-toed sloth.
preguiçar v. to idle, lounge, laze.
preguiceira s. f. hammock-chair, easy chair, deck chair.
preguiceiro s. m. (Braz.) couch, lounge, sofa. ‖ adj. lazy, idle.
preguiçosa s. f. 1. deck chair (plate C 2). 2. (ent.) a stingless honeybee.
preguiçoso s. m. idler, lazy-bones, lie-a-bed, scalawag, do-nothing. ‖ adj. (also **preguicento**) lazy, idle, indolent, laggard, dronish, work-shy, sluggish, slothful. ‖ **-amente** adv. lazily, indolently.
preguilha, preguinha s. f. 1. a small nail. 2. a small pleat or tuck.
pregustação s. f. (pl. **-ões**) pregustation, tasting beforehand, foretaste.
pregustar v. to taste before, foretaste.
pré-helênico adj. pre-Hellenic.
pré-história s. f. prehistory.
pré-histórico adj. prehistoric(al).
período ~ prehistoric period. **raças -as** prehistoric races.
preia s. f. = **presa**.
preia-mar s. f. = **preamar**.
preignição s. f. (pl. **-ões**) preignition.
pré-incaico adj. (pl. **pré-incaicos**) pre-Incan.
preitear, preitejar v. to do, pay or render homage, homage.
preito s. m. 1. homage, reverence, respect. 2. (obs.) agreement, contract, solemn promise.
prejeraba s. f. (ichth.) tripletail, black grunt.
prejudicado adj. prejudiced, damaged, injured, aggrieved, impaired; hurt, wronged.
prejudicador s. m. impairer, mischief-maker. ‖ adj. damaging, impairing, injuring.
prejudicar v. 1. to prejudice, damage, hurt, wrong, impair, injure, aggrieve, harm. 2. to annul, cancel, make null and void. 3. ~**-se** to come to harm. **ele mesmo se prejudicou** he prejudiced himself, cut his own throat. **isto prejudica meu mérito** it takes from my merit.
prejudicial adj. m. + f. (pl. **-ais**) 1. prejudicial, disadvantageous. 2. hurtful, harmful, ill, evil, bad. 3. mischievous. ‖ ~**mente** adv. prejudicially.
prejuízo s. m. prejudice: 1. prejudgement, prepossession, bias, leaning. 2. damage, wrong, hurt, loss, impairment, disadvantage, harm, injury; mischief.
causar ~ to cause damage. **com** ~ at a sacrifice. **compensar um** ~ to make good a loss. **não sofreram** ~ **por causa dele** they were none the worse for him. **qual é o** ~? what's the damage? **recuperar** ~**s** to recover damages. **sem** ~ without prejudice. **vender com** ~ to sell to disadvantage.

prejulgamento s. m. prejudgement, forejudgement, foregone conclusion.

prejulgar v. to prejudge, judge beforehand, decide in anticipation.

prelação s. f. (pl. -ões) prelation, preference, preferment.

prelacia s. f. (obs.) prelacy, prelateship, dignity or office of a prelate.

prelacial adj. m. + f. (pl. -ais) prelatial, prelatical, episcopal.

prelada s. f. prelatess, abbess, prioress.

preladia s. f. prelacy, prelature.

prelado s. m. prelate, superior of a convent or monastery.

prelatício adj. prelatic(al), prelatial, relating to prelacy.

prelatura s. f. prelacy, prelature, dignity or office of a prelate.

preleção s. f. (pl. -ões) prelection, reading, lecture; public discourse, sermon; dissertation.
fazer uma ~ sobre to give a lecture on.

prelecionador s. m. prelector, lecturer, teacher.

prelecionar v. to prelect, lecture, read a lecture, give a lesson, teach.

prelegado s. m. prelegacy.

preletor s. m. prelector, lecturer.

prelevar v. 1. to raise, surmount. 2. to excuse, exculpate.

prelibação s. f. (pl. -ões) prelibation, foretaste; anticipation.

prelibador s. m. foretaster. ‖ adj. foretasting.

prelibar v. to foretaste, taste beforehand.

preliminar s. m. preliminary; introduction, preface; prelude. ‖ adj. m. + f. preliminary, precursory, introductory, preparatory, prefatory, prolegomenary. ‖ ~mente adv. preliminarily.
inquérito ~ preliminary inquiry. julgamento ~ preliminary judgement.

preliminarista s. m. + f. (S. Braz.) pupil of a preliminary course.

prélio s. m. (poet.) battle, fight, combat, conflict.

prelo s. m. printing press, press.
dar um livro ao ~ to give a book in print. ir para o ~ to go to the press. no ~ in the press.

prelucidação s. f. (pl. -ões) preliminary explication, previous elucidation.

prelúcido adj. extremely brilliant, very clear.

preludiar v. 1. (mus.) to prelude: play a prelude, introduce by a prelude. 2. preface, introduce, serve as an introduction. 3. foreshadow, prepare; announce; begin.

prelúdio s. m. prelude: 1. preludium, introduction, preface, presage, preliminary. 2. (mus.) ouverture, an introductory piece.

preluzir v. to be very bright, shine brightly.

prema s. f. constraint, oppression, compulsion.

premar v. to oppress, mistreat; trouble, annoy, harass, aggrieve.

prematurar v. to do s. th. prematurely, precipitate, cause to hasten.

prematuridade s. f. (also **prematuração**) prematureness, prematurity, earliness, precociousness, precocity; untimeliness.

prematuro adj. premature, untimely, immature, precocious; too early; unripe. ‖ -amente prematurely.

premedeira s. f. treadle (of a weaver's loom).

pré-médico adj. premedical.

premeditação s. f. premeditatedness, premeditation, forethought, precogitation.

premeditado adj. premeditate(d), deliberate; studied. ‖ -amente adv. deliberately.
~ com intenção criminosa with malice aforethought.

premeditar v. to premeditate, precogitate, plan, scheme.

premência s. f. (Braz.) pressure, urgency.

premente adj. m. + f. pressing, urgent, exigent.
uma necessidade ~ a crying need.

premer v. (also **premir**) 1. to press, squeeze; express. 2. to oppress. 3. to urge, hasten. 4. to beseech, entreat.

premiado adj. rewarded, distinguished.

premiador s. m. rewarder. ‖ adj. rewarding.

premiar v. to premiate, reward, remunerate, recompense, give a prize to.

premiável adj. m. + f. (pl. -áveis) awardable.

prêmio s. m. 1. premium, reward, recompense, prize, award. 2. remuneration, gain, profit, interest, bonus.
~ de consolação booby prize. ~ de loteria prize in the lottery. ~ honorífico honorary reward. ~ monetário purse, pewter, cash prize. ~ de seguro de vida premium of assurance. concurso com ~s prize competition. conquistar o ~ to take the prize, get the prize. detentor de ~ prizeman.

premissa s. f. premise, premiss, reason, sumption, supposition.
~ maior major premise. ~ menor minor premise.

premoção s. f. (pl. -ões) (theol.) premotion, premovement, previous motion.

pré-molar s. m. (pl. pré-molares) (anat., zool.) premolar, milk molar (tooth). ‖ adj. premolar.

pré-moldado s. m. (pl. pré-moldados) prefabricated concrete block. ‖ adj. premolded: 1. that was previously cast in a mold. 2. prefabricated.

premonitório adj. premonitory, premonitive, precursory.

premonstratense s. m. Premonstratensian, Premonstrant: a religious order, founded by St. Norbert at Prémontré, observing St. Austin's rules.

premorso adj. (bot.) premorse, having the end irregularly truncate.

premunição s. f. (pl. -ões) premonition, forewarning.

premunir v. 1. to premonish, forewarn. 2. to prevent, avert. 3. ~-se to look out, be on one's guard.

pré-natal adj. m. + f. (pl. -ais) prenatal, previous to birth.

prenda s. f. 1. present, gift, favour. 2. talent, dexterity, ability. 3. token, proof, pledge. 4. bad person. 5. ~s pl. accomplishments, endowments.
~ de fidelidade pledge of fidelity. ~s de mão embroidery, needlework. jogo de ~s game of forfeits. pessoa de grandes ~s a person of great talents.

prendado adj. gifted, talented, accomplished.

prendar v. 1. to make or give a present to, gift. 2. to endow, indue. 3. to render dexterous.

prendedor s. m. 1. arrester, seizer. 2. fastener; staple; clasp, clip (plate F 6). ‖ adj. arresting, seizing, fastening; stapling; hooking.
~ de roupa clothes-peg, clothes-pin.

prender v. 1. to fasten, tie, bind, fix. 2. to seize, apprehend, take, grasp, grip. 3. to catch capture, take hold of. 4. to arrest, incarcerate, imprison, lock in, lay by the heels. 5. captivate, attract, fascinate, charm. 6. to attach. 7. to enlink. 8. to adhere, stick to. 9. ~-se: a) to be connected. b) to become entangled. c) to become attached to. d) to get caught, be captivated. e) to engage o. s., promise marriage, marry.
~ o ladrão em flagrante to catch the thief in the very act. ela se prende a ele como um carrapato she sticks to him like wax. eu prendi o dedo na porta I caught my finger in the door. o livro prendeu toda minha atenção the book engrossed my attention. não quero prendê-lo por mais tempo don't let me keep you any longer. o temor lhe prendeu a língua the fright struck him dumb.

prenhe adj. m. + f. (Braz., also **prenha** f.) 1. gravid, pregnant, parturient, heavy. 2. (of animals) breeding, big with young. 3. (fig.) full, replete.
andar ou estar ~ to be with child, be in the family way. **ficar** ~ to conceive.
prenhez s. f. pregnancy, gestation.
~ **molar** hydatiform mole.
prenoção s. f. (pl. **-ões**) prenotion, preconception, preliminary notion, foreknowledge.
prenome s. m. first name, Christian name, prenomen, praenomen.
prenominar v. to give a first name or call by the first name.
prenotar v. to note beforehand, mention previously, designate before.
prensa s. f. 1. press (plate C 16). 2. printing press. 3. printing frame.
~ **de algodão** cotton press. ~ **de enfardar** bundle press. ~ **de estampar** stamping press. ~ **de garganta** throated press. ~ **de parafuso** screw press. ~ **hidráulica** hydraulic press. ~ **para extração de óleo** oil press. ~ **de vinho** winepress.
prensado adj. pressed, squeezed.
cartão ~ pressboard.
prensador s. m. presser, pressman.
prensagem s. f. (pl. **-ns**) pressing, squeezing.
prensar v. to press, compress, crush, squeeze.
prenseiro s. m. (N. Braz.) presser, workman of a press.
prenunciação s. f. (pl. **-ões**) prenunciation, prophecy, prediction.
prenunciador s. m. foreshadower, foreteller. ‖ adj. prognostic, foretelling, foreshowing.
prenunciar v. to foretell, foreshadow; prophesy, predict; adumbrate.
prenunciativo adj. prenuncious, presaging, adumbrative.
prenúncio s. m. adumbration, presage, foretoken, sign, prognostic; prediction.
preocupação s. f. (pl. **-ões**) 1. preoccupation, prepossession. 2. apprehension, anxiety, trouble, worriment, concern, care.
com grande ~ with deep concern.
preocupado adj. preoccupied, troubled, worried, heavy-hearted, uneasy, concerned, unhappy. ‖ **-amente** adv. anxiously, uneasily.
~ **com** anxious for, troubled about. ~ **por causa de** alarmed at. **estar muito** ~ **com alguma coisa** to be worried about s. th. **um olhar** ~ a troubled look.
preocupante s. m. + f. preoccupier. ‖ adj. preoccupying, taking possession beforehand.
preocupar v. 1. to preoccupy: a) prepossess, pre-engage, engross in advance. b) take possession before another. 2. to trouble, worry, bother, grieve. 3. ~**-se** to be worried, become anxious.
~**-se com alguma coisa** to trouble about s. th. **não se preocupe demais com isto!** don't take on so much about that. **preocupo-me** I worry myself.
pré-operatório adj. (surg.) preoperative.
preopérculo s. m. (ichth.) preopercle, praeoperculum.
preopinação s. f. (pl. **-ões**) preopinion, opinion previously formed.
preopinante s. m. + f. preceding or previous speaker. ‖ adj. speaking before.
preopinar v. to express one's ideas or speak before another.
preordenação s. f. (pl. **-ões**) preordination, foreordination, predetermination, predestination.
preordenar v. to preordain, ordain beforehand, foreordain, predetermine, pre-establish.
preparação s. f. (pl. **-ões**) (also **preparamento** m.) preparation: 1. preparing, making ready, training. 2. that which is prepared. 3. formation, confection, manufacture.

preparado s. m. (chem., pharm.) preparation. ‖ adj. 1. prepared, ready. 2. educated.
~ **químico** chemical preparation. ~ **para lustrar** polisher (substance). **bem** ~ well-prepared.
preparador s. m. 1. preparer. 2. preparator, prosector. 3. (Braz.) assistent who prepares subjects of natural history for study in secondary schools. ‖ adj. preparatory, preparing.
~ **de estudantes para o exame** coach, crammer, grinder.
preparar v. 1. to prepare: a) make ready, provide, arrange; adapt. b) instruct, teach. c) fit, fit out, equip. d) dispose, predispose. e) form, compound, make. 2. ~**-se** to prepare o. s., make o. s. ready, take care of o. s.
~ **a arma** to cock the gun. ~ **um combate** to embattle. ~ **medicamentos** to dispense medicines. ~ **o menino para o colégio** to coach the boy for college. ~ **para publicação** to redact. **preparei o caminho para ele** (fig.) I paved the way for him. **ele preparou uma emboscada** he laid an ambush. **ela preparou sua lição** she prepared her lesson. **o cozinheiro vai** ~ **uma refeição** the cook will fix a meal. **estar preparado para a viagem** to stand ready for the trip. **estou preparado para sair** I am prepared to go. **eles estão preparando uma festa** they are getting up a party.
preparativos s. m. pl. preparatives, preparatories. ‖ **preparativo** adj. preparative, preparatory.
preparatoriano s. m. (Braz.) pupil of a preparatory course.
preparatórios s. m. pl. preparatories. ‖ **preparatório** adj. preparatory, preparative. ‖ **preparatoriamente** adv. preparatorily, preparatively.
curso de ~**s** preparatory of school.
preparo s. m. 1. preparation. 2. (Braz.) education, refinement; competence, ability, capableness. 3. ~**s** pl.: a) notions for dressmaking. b) (S. Braz.) gear, riding accessories.
preponderância s. f. preponderancy, preponderance, predominance, superiority, supremacy; ascendence, prevalence; advantage; overweight, overbalance.
preponderante adj. m. + f. preponderant, superior, predominant, prevalent, ascendant. ‖ ~**mente** adv. preponderantly.
preponderar v. to preponderate: 1. overbear, overweigh, overbalance. 2. predominate, prevail, exceed in influence or power.
preponente s. m. + f. undertaker, enterpriser; proposer. ‖ adj. proposing; undertaking, enterprising.
prepor v. 1. to preplace. 2. to prefer. 3. (gram.) to prepose, prefix. 4. to appoint.
preposição s. f. preposition: 1. a preposing. 2. (gram.) a word that expresses the relation of two other words (plate P 18).
preposicional adj. m. + f. (pl. **-ais**) prepositional.
prepositiva s. f. prepositive, a word or particle put before another word.
prepositivo adj. prepositive, placed before, prefixed.
prepósito s. m. 1. purpose, intention. 2. (obs.) provost, superior of a religious order.
prepositura s. f. prepositure, provostship.
preposteração s. f. (pl. **-ões**) preposterousness, unreasonableness, absurdity.
preposterar v. to preposterate, invert, pervert, reverse.
preposteridade s. f. preposterousness.
prepóstero adj. preposterous: 1. inverted, perverted, reversed. 2. silly, foolish, unreasonable, absurd, stupid. ‖ **preposteramente** adv. preposterously.
preposto (I) s. m. institutor, agent.
preposto (II) adj. put or placed before; preferred.

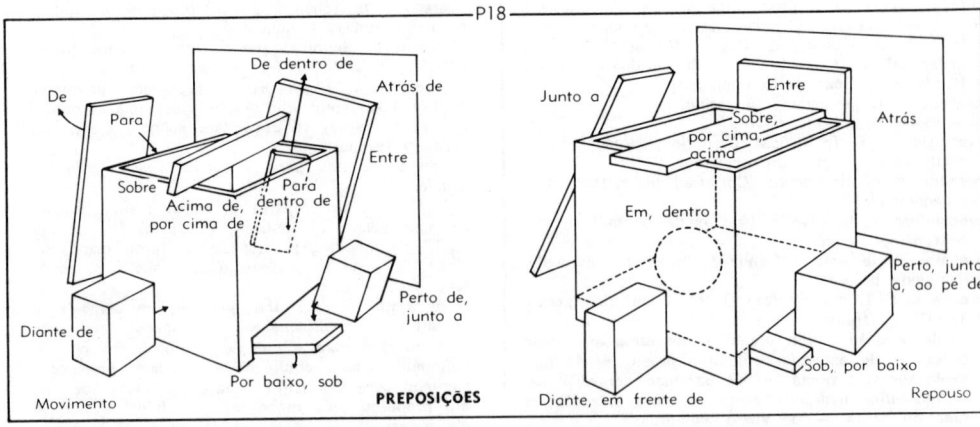

prepotência s. f. prepotence, prepotency, predominance, superiority, prevalence; despotism, absolutism.

prepotente adj. m. + f. prepotent, all-powerful, predominant, preponderant; overbearing; despotic.

pré-primário adj. preschool.

prepucial adj. m. + f. (pl. -ais) (anat.) preputial, of or pertaining to the prepuce.

prepúcio s. m. (anat.) prepuce, foreskin.

prequeté (I) s. f. sandal used by the Amazonian Indians.

prequeté (II) adj. m. + f. (Braz.) elegant, dandy, foppish (person).

pré-rafaelismo s. m. Pre-Raphaelism, Pre-Raphaelitism, style of painting prevailing before Raphael.

pré-rafaelista s. m. + f. Pre-Raphaelite. ‖ adj. Pre--Raphaelite.

pré-rafaelita adj. m. + f. Pre-Raphaele.

pré-renascentista adj. m. + f. pre-Renaissance.

pré-romano adj. pre-Roman, prior to the Roman domination.

pré-romantismo s. m. pre-romanticism.

prerrogativa s. f. prerogative, privilege, advantage; precedence.

presa (ê) (I) s. f. 1. capture, seizure, catch, catchment. 2. prey, plunder, booty, loot, ravin. 3. captive, prisoner (woman).

presa (ê) (II) s. f. fang; tusk, claw, prong, clutch. sem ~s fangless.

presador s. m. person who captures, seizes, catches. ‖ adj. that captures.

presar v. = apresar.

presbiopia s. f. presbyopia, long-sightedness, far--sightedness.

presbita s. m. + f. presbyope, presbyte, long-sighted person. ‖ adj. presbyopic, far-sighted. ‖ ~mente adv. far-sightedly.

presbiterado s. m. presbyterate, office or dignity of a presbyter.

presbiteral adj. m. + f. (pl. -ais) presbyter(i)al, relating to a presbyter or presbytery.

presbiterato s. m. presbyterate.

presbiterianismo s. m. Presbyterianism, Presbyterism.

presbiteriano s. m. Presbyterian. ‖ adj. Presbyterian.

presbitério s. m. 1. presbytery: a) an assembly of presbyters. b) parsonage, manse. c) chancel of a church. 2. eldership.

presbítero s. m. presbyter, elder, priest.

presbitia s. f., presbitismo m. presbyopia, far-sightedness.

presciência s. f. prescience, foreknowledge, foresight, prevision.

presciente adj. m. + f. prescient, foreknowing.

prescindir v. 1. to prescind, dispense, leave out or aside. 2. to renounce, do without, give up.

prescindível adj. m. + f. (pl. -íveis) prescindent, dispensable.

prescrever v. to prescribe: 1. order the use of. 2. ordain, lay down as a precept. 3. fix, appoint, establish. 4. direct, assign, dictate. 5. lapse, become void. 6. fall into disuse, exist no more.

prescribente adj. m. + f. prescriptive.

prescrição s. f. (pl. -ões) prescription: 1. order, command, instruction. 2. precept, recipe. 3. lapse, forfeiture.
ato de ~ prescription act. duque por ~ duke by prescription. título por ~ title by prescription. conforme ~ by precept.

prescritível adj. m. + f. (pl. -íveis) prescriptible, depending on a prescription.

prescrito adj. prescribed, ordained, ordered, appointed, set down.

presença s. f. presence, act or fact of being present. 2. aspect, appearance. 3. carriage, port, mien, air, demeanor. 4. stature.
~ de espírito presence of mind, wittiness, ready tongue. na ~ de in the presence of. pessoa de boa ~ person of fine carriage.

presencial adj. m. + f. (pl. -ais) of or pertaining to a present person or thing; done in the presence of somebody.

presenciar v. to be present, witness, observe.

presentação s. f. (pl. -ões) = apresentação.

presentâneo adj. ready, quick, immediate, momentary; efficacious. ‖ -amente adv. immediately, instantly.

presentar v. = apresentar.

presente s. m. 1. present, actuality. 2. present person or persons. 3. (gram.) present tense. 4. gift, donative. ‖ adj. m. + f. 1. present, not absent. 2. actual, instant, being, not future or past. 3. at hand. 4. in question (case). ‖ ~mente adv. presently.
~ de aniversário birthday present. ~ de Natal Christmas box. presente! (interj.) here! dar de ~ to offer, present as a gift. está ~ em minha memória it is fresh in my memory. estar ~ to appear, assist. isto sempre me é ~ I always think of it. no tempo ~ at the present time, now. todos os ~s the whole room. vimos informá-los pela ~ we herewith wish to inform you that (in letters).

presenteador s. m. presenter. ‖ adj. presenting, offering.

presentear v. to present, offer as a gift, give a present.

presepada s. f. (N. Braz.) boasting, bragging, swaggering, ostentation.

presepe (I) s. m. 1. stable, stall. 2. crib, manger.

presepe (II) s. m. (N. Braz.) puppet show.

presepeiro s. m. 1. person who mounts Nativity scenes or figurines. 2. boaster, swaggerer, braggard, bully.

presépio s. m. 1. stable, stall. 2. crèche, the cradle of Christ, Nativity scene.

preservação s. f. (pl. -ões) preservation, conservation, keeping.

~ **da própria vida** self-preservation.

preservador s. m. preserver, conservator; preservative. ‖ adj. preserving; conservative.

preservar v. to preserve: 1. protect, guard, defend, save. 2. retain, uphold, keep, maintain.

preservativo s. m. prophylactic, preventive, preservative. ‖ adj. preservative, conservative, keeping safe.

preservatório s. m. preservative. ‖ adj. preservatory, conservatory.

presidência s. f. presidency, presidentship; chairmanship.

ocupar a ~ to be in the chair.

presidencial adj. m. + f. (pl. -ais) presidential, presiding.

presidencialismo s. m. presidentialism.

presidenta s. f. 1. presidentess, female president; chairwoman. 2. a president's wife.

presidente s. m. 1. president. 2. chairman, manager, superior. ‖ adj. m. + f. presiding, ruling.

eles dirigiram-se ao ~ they addressed the chair.

presidente-da-porcaria s. f. (pl. **presidentes-da-porcaria**) (Braz., ornith.) an ovenbird (Lochmias nematura).

presidiar v. to garrison, defend.

presidiário s. m. criminal condemned to do service in a presidio or fortress; prisoner. ‖ adj. presidiary, presidial.

presídio s. m. 1. presidio. 2. fortress; fortified military place; garrison. 3. the forces therein. 4. penitentiary.

presidir v. to preside, manage, direct, administer, guide.

presigo s. m. anything eaten along with bread (as ham, bacon, etc.).

presilha s. f. 1. loop. 2. staple. 3. fastening belt; strap, strip (plate R 7). 4. cleat. 5. hook and eye fastener.

~ **para calça** trouser strap. **sentar-se na** ~ (S. Braz., fig.) to be refractory, oppose.

presilheiro s. m. slyboot, dodger.

preso (ê) s. m. (pl. **presos**) prisoner, captive, jailbird. ‖ adj. captive, imprisoned, arrested, taken, jailed, fast, confined, trammeled.

~ **a sete chaves** under lock and key. ~ **em sua própria armadilha** hoisted with his own petard. ~ **pelo mau tempo** weather-bound. **ele foi** ~ he was thrown into prison. **ele será** ~ he will be taken in charge. **fuga de presos** jail-break.

pressa s. f. 1. velocity, speed, celerity, alacrity. 2. haste, hurry. 3. expedition, dispatch. 4. urgency, impatience. 5. embarrassment, dilemma, affliction.

a ~ **é a inimiga da perfeição** haste makes waste. **às** ~**s** in full career. **a toda** ~ with all speed. **com** ~ in haste. **com muita** ~ in a tearing hurry. **em** ~ **louca** in a whirl. **entrar às** ~**s** to hurry in. **estou com** ~ I am in a hurry, I'm pressed for time. **não há** ~ there is no hurry. **não tenha** ~ take your time. **tinham muita** ~ they were hard pressed for time. **umas linhas às** ~**s** a few hasty lines. **vesti-me às** ~**s** I slipped into my dress.

pressagiador s. m. presager; foreboder, foreshadower. ‖ adj. foreboding; ominous.

pressagiar v. 1. to presage, forebode. 2. to foretell, predict, prophesy, adumbrate. 3. to vaticinate, prognosticate, omen, presignify.

eles ~**am sucesso** they augured success.

presságio s. m. 1. presage, omen, sign, shadow, augury. 2. prognostic, prediction. 3. presentiment.

de mau ~ ill-omened.

pressagioso, pressago adj. presagious, presageful, ominous, foreboding. ‖ **-amente** adv. presagiously.

pressama s. f. (Braz., pop.) cutaneous inflammation.

pressão s. f. (pl. -ões) 1. pression, pressing, pressure. 2. compulsion. 3. oppressiveness; opression. 4. stress, strain, tension.

~ **de água** water pressure. ~ **alta** high pressure. ~ **atmosférica** air pressure. ~ **de corrente de ar** blast pressure. ~ **dinâmica** dynamic pressure. ~ **hidrostática** fluid pressure. ~ **nos pneus** inflation pressure. ~ **de recalque** driving pressure. ~ **sanguínea** blood pressure. ~ **terminal** final pressure. ~ **do vapor** steam tension. **botão de** ~ push button. **cabina de** ~ pressure cabin. **caldeira de** ~ pressure boiler. **câmara de** ~ pressure chamber. **grau de** ~ pressure stage. **lubrificação sob** ~ pressure-fed lubrication. **panela de** ~ pressure cooker. **regulador de** ~ pressure govèrner. **sob a pressão das circunstâncias** under the stress of circumstances.

pressentido adj. 1. foreseen. 2. presentient, perceiving beforehand, having a presentiment or foreboding. 3. suspicious.

pressentimento s. m. presentiment, foreboding, apprehension;. suspicion; (U. S. A. coll.) hunch.

pressentir v. 1. to have a presentiment or foreboding; foresee, perceive or understand beforehand, anticipate. 2. to surmise, think; suspect.

eu pressinto o desastre I foresee the disaster.

pressirostro adj. (ornith.) pressirostral, having a compressed beak.

pressupor v. to presuppose, suppose beforehand, assume, take for granted.

pressuposição s. f. (pl. -ões) presupposition, surmise, conjecture; postulation, prerequisite.

pressuposto s. m. 1. = **pressuposição**. 2. pretext; purpose, project, plan. ‖ adj. presupposed, assumed, projected.

pressuroso adj. 1. speedy, swift, quick, prompt. 2. hasty, hurried, busy. 3. impatient, eager, keen.

prestação s. f. (pl. -ões) 1. payment by instalments. 2. service rendered; contribution. 3. m. (Braz.) nickname for a hawker or pedlar.

prestacionar v. to pay in instalments; sell on account.

prestadio, prestador adj. 1. serviceable, obliging. 2. usable, useful. 3. profitable, advantageous.

prestamento s. m. usefulness; fitness.

prestamista s. m. + f. 1. moneylender. 2. usufructer of debentures or bonds. 3. person who buys on monthly instalments.

prestança, prestância s. f. 1. utility, usefulness; advantageousness, convenience. 2. kindness; serviceableness. 3. excellence.

prestante adj. m. + f. 1. useful, fit, proper. 2. efficacious. 3. profitable, advantageous. 4. excellent.

prestar v. 1. to lend, loan. 2. to render, give, afford, perform. 3. to be useful, be good or proper for. 4. ~**-se** to be of service, be useful; be obliging. ~ **atenção** to listen, lend an ear, take account of, give attention. ~ **auxílio** to afford assistance. ~ **bons serviços** to render good services. ~ **contas** to render account. ~ **exame** to go in for examination. ~ **juramento** to take an oath. ~ **homenagem** to homage, pay reverence. **ele se presta para tudo** he can turn his hand to anything. **não presta para**

nada it is good for nothing. **você pode prestar esclarecimentos a respeito?** can you account for it?
prestativo adj. serviceable, useful, helpful.
prestável adj. m. + f. (pl. **-áveis**) serviceable, subservient; useful.
prestemente adv. speedily, quickly, readily.
prestes adj. m. + f., sg. + pl. 1. ready, prompt; prepared. 2. about to, on the point of. 3. quick, speedy, swift. ‖ ~**mente** adv. readily, quickly, promptly.
~ **a chegar** about to arrive. ~ **a dar à luz** quick with child. ~ **a virar** on the turn. **ele está** ~ **a sair** he is about to go. **fazer** ~ to get ready.
presteza s. f. 1. rapidity, celerity, quickness. 2. readiness, promptness, promptitude. 3. forwardness, towardness. 4. dispatch. 5. activity, agility.
prestidigitação s. f. prestidigitation, magic, jugglery, wizardry; sleight of hand.
prestidigitador s. m. (also **prestigiador**) prestidigitator, juggler, magician, palmer, wizard.
truque de ~ sleight of hand.
prestidigitar v. to perform sleight of hand tricks.
prestigiação s. f. (pl. **-ões**) prestidigitation; witchcraft.
prestigiar v. 1. to give prestige to, esteem, render important. 2. to esteem.
prestígio s. m. 1. illusion, juggling trick. 2. fascination, charm, imposture. 3. prestige, reputation, influence, credit.
prestigioso adj. prestigious: 1. magic, deluding; illusory, deceptive. 2. important, influential.
prestimanear v. to deceive, get by means of tricks.
prestímano s. m. = **prestidigitador.**
préstimo s. m. 1. utility, usefulness. 2. serviceableness. 3. fitness. 4. service. 5. merit, worth.
prestimônio s. m. prestimony, fund or revenue for the support of a priest.
prestimoso adj. useful; serviceable.
prestíssimo adj. m. (mus.) prestissimo: an extremely fast passage. ‖ adv. prestissimo.
préstito s. m. procession, train, cortège.
presto s. m. (mus.) presto. ‖ adj. 1. (mus.) presto, 2. quick, speedy, swift; prompt, ready. ‖ adv. quickly, soon, immediately.
presumido s. m. flaunter, self-conceited person. ‖ adj. self-conceited, self-satisfied, presumptuous, arrogant, haughty, vain; saucy, bold. ‖ **-amente** adv. presumptuously.
presumidor s. m. presumer, one who presumes. ‖ adj. 1. presuming. 2. presumptuous, arrogant, proud.
presumir v. 1. to presume, suppose, surmise, suspect, think, conjecture, imagine. 2. ~**-se** to be presumptuous or arrogant.
presume-se que ele saiba he is presumed to know.
presumível adj. m. + f. (pl. **-íveis**) presumable, probable, surmisable, presumptive, supposable. ‖ **presumivelmente** adv. presumably.
o autor ~ **do crime** the probable author of the crime.
presunção s. f. (pl. **-ões**) presumption: 1. supposition, conjecture, guess. 2. presumptuousness, arrogance, pride, affectation, vanity, priggishness, vainglory, self-conceit, conceit(edness), self-importance.
presunçoso adj. presumptuous, vainglorious, arrogant, proud, self-conceited, uppish, assumptive. ‖ **-amente** adv. presumptuously.
presunho s. m. (zool.) dewclaw.
presuntivo adj. presumptive, probable, a priori.
herdeiro ~ heir presumptive.
presunto s. m. ham, gammon (plate M 8).
presúria s. f. dam, dike, embankment.
preta s. f. Negro woman, Negress.
pretalhada s. f. (also **pretaria**; depr.) Negroes collectively, crowd of Negroes.
pretalhão s. m. (pl. **-ões**; f. **-ona**) tall or stout Negro.

pretejar v. 1. to blacken, begrime, turn black. 2. (Braz.) to be crowded (a street).
pretendedor s. m. pretender, claimer, claimant, demander, applicant, aspirant, suitor. ‖ adj. pretending, claiming.
pretendente s. m. + f. 1. pretender, candidate. 2. m. suitor. ‖ adj. pretending, claiming, contemplating, expecting.
~ **ao trono** pretender to the crown (throne).
pretender v. 1. to pretend: a) claim, demand, come in for. b) aspire, wish, aim at, stand for, expect. c) intend, contemplate, purpose, think, mean, assume. 2. to assert, affirm. 3. ~**-se** to pass o. s. off for.
~ **uma mulher** to suit, woo, court a woman. **ele pretende viajar amanhã** he expects to leave to-morrow. **o que é que ele pretende?** what is he driving at? **você pretende ficar?** do you intend to stay? **você sabe o que pretende fazer?** do you know what you are about?
pretendida s. f. bride, fiancée.
pretendido adj. claimed, pretended, intended.
pretensão s. f. (pl. **-ões**) 1. pretension, pretence, claim, demand. 2. intention, assumption. 3. design, aim. 4. arrogation, ambition. 5. pretext.
pretensioso s. m. smatterer, prig, wiseacre. ‖ adj. pretentious, arrogant, ambitious, snobbish; affected; finical. ‖ **-amente** adv. pretentiously, ostentatiously.
pretenso adj. assumed, supposed, alleged, presumed, false, putative.
~ **cavalheiro** would-be gentleman.
pretensor s. m. pretender, claimer; suitor. ‖ adj. pretending, claiming.
preterição s. f. (pl. **-ões**) 1. preterition, a passing over or by. 2. postponement, deferment. 3. (rhet.) paraleipsis.
preterir v. 1. to pretermit, pass over, omit, neglect, slight. 2. to defer, postpone.
ele me preteriu he passed me by.
pretérito s. m. (gram.) the preterit tense. ‖ adj. (gram.) preterit, past, bygone.
~ **imperfeito** the imperfect tense. ~ **perfeito** (gram.) preterperfect, past-perfect. ~ **mais que perfeito** (gram.) pluperfect.
preterível adj. m. + f. (pl. **-íveis**) that may be pretermitted.
pretermissão s. f. (pl. **-ões**) pretermission, passing over, omission, preterition.
pretermitir v. to pretermit: 1. let pass. 2. omit, disregard, overlook, neglect.
preternatural adj. m. + f. (pl. **-ais**) preternatural, supernatural, miraculous.
pretexta s. f. (Roman hist.) pr(a)etexta.
pretextar v. to pretext, use as an excuse or pretext, allege as an pretext; pretend, feign.
pretexto s. m. pretext, pretence, pretension, excuse, cover, cloak, feint, allegation, subterfuge.
um ~ **para resmungar** a peg to hang a nagging on. **com** ~ **de** under colour of. **é fácil achar um** ~ it is easy to find a pretext, a stick to beat a dog. **sob o** ~ **do dever** under the semblance (pretence, plea) of duty. **usar como** ~ to make a pretext of.
pretidão s. f. (pl. **-ões**) blackness, black colour.
pretinha s. f. 1. little Negress. 2. (Braz.) common black tourmaline.
preto (ê) s. m. (pl. **pretos**) (f. **preta**) 1. Negro, black-a-moor. 2. black (colour). 3. a black suit. ‖ adj. 1. Negro. 2. black, dark; jet, scooty. 3. sombre, sad, mournful.
~ **no branco** (pop.) in cold print. ~ **como carvão** coal-black, as black as ink. **ficar** ~ to blacken. **frades** ~**s** monks of the order of St. Benedict.

pôr o ~ no branco to set down in black and white. tornar ~ to black. vestir ~ to wear black.
preto-aça s. m. (pl. pretos-aças) albino among Negroes.
pretor s. m. (Roman hist.) pr(a)etor, judge.
pretoria s. f. pretorship, office or dignity of a pretor.
pretória s. f. session hall (of a convent).
pretoriano s. m. (Roman hist.) pr(a)etorian, a soldier of the pr(a)etorian guard (the emperor's guard). ‖ adj. pr(a)torian: 1. relating to a praetor. 2. belonging to the emperor's body-guard.
pretório (I) s. m. 1. in ancient Rome: a general's tent; pr(a)etorian tribunal. 2. law court.
pretório (II) adj. pr(a)etorian, relating to a pr(a)etor.
pretume s. m. (N. Braz., pop.) darkness, blackness.
prevalecente adj. m. + f. prevalent, prevailing, current, general.
prevalecer v. 1. to prevail: a) be superior, dominate, b) predominate, preponderate, overbalance. 2. ~-se to take advantage, avail o. s.
~-se da oportunidade to take the opportunity, avail o. s. of. ~-se da situação desvantajosa de alguém to take s. o. at a disadvantage. nosso argumento prevaleceu our argument prevailed.
prevalecido adj. (S. Braz.) impertinent, despotic, presumptuous.
prevalência s. f. prevalence, predominance, superiority.
prevaricação s. f. (pl. -ões) prevarication, malversation, embezzlement, forfeiture; equivocation, shift.
prevaricador s. m. prevaricator, shuffler, quibbler, transgressor. ‖ adj. prevaricatory, transgressing.
prevaricar v. to prevaricate: 1. transgress, violate (a law). 2. sin. 3. quibble, swerve (from the truth). 4. pervert, abase, deviate from the proper way.
prevenção s. f. (pl. -ões) 1. prevention, precaution, arrangement, preventive measure. 2. preconception, prejudice, prepossession. 3. warning.
prevenido adj. (also prevento) 1. advised, forewarned, informed. 2. provident, cautious, on one's guard. ‖ -amente adv. advisedly.
fomos ~s de que não é permitido usar o novo caminho we have been warned off the new way. seja ~! be advised.
preveniente adj. m. + f. 1. prevenient: anticipative, precedent. 2. preventive.
graça ~ prevenient grace.
prevenir v. 1. to prevent: a) avert, forestall, hinder, impede. b) alarm, alert, forewarn, premonish, caution. 2. ~-se to provide against, take measures beforehand, be on one's guard.
~ alguém to tip s. o. off. deixamo-nos ~ por we took warning by. mais vale ~ do que remediar a stitch in time saves nine, prevention is better than cure.
preventivo s. m. preventive. ‖ adj. 1. preventive. 2. provident, cautious.
prisão -a preventive detention.
preventório s. m. preventive service.
prever v. 1. to foresee, foreknow, anticipate. 2. calculate, reckon, suppose, expect.
previdência s. f. 1. providence, precaution; provision. 2. foresight, forethought, prevision.
~ social social welfare. caixa de ~ provident fund.
previdenciário s. m. (Braz.) employee of a social welfare institution.
previdente adj. m. + f. 1. provident, foreseeing, cautious, thoughtful; prudent, economical, calculative. 2. far-seeing. ‖ ~mente adv. providently.
prévio adj. previous, precedent, prior, former, foregoing, anterior, earlier; preliminary.
exame ~ pre-examination. notícia -a previous notice. questão -a previous question.

previsão s. f. (pl. -ões) 1. prevision, foresight; forecast. 2. foreknowledge, prescience.
~ divina providence. ~ do tempo weather forecast.
~ depois do acontecimento não requer inteligência after-wit is everybody's wit. em ~ de against.
previsibilidade s. f. previsibility.
previsível adj. m. + f. (pl. -íveis) previsible, foreseeable, foreknowable.
previso s. m. (obs.) sorcerer. ‖ adj. foreseen.
previsor adj. (Braz.) = previdente.
previsto adj. foreseen, anticipated; expected.
~ pela lei due to the law. isto está ~ that is in the arrangement. não ~ unforeseen.
pré-vocacional adj. m. + f. (pl. -ais) prevocational.
prezado adj. esteemed, dear.
~s senhores Dear Sirs; Gentlemen (address).
prezador s. m. person who esteems, respects. ‖ adj. who esteems.
prezar v. 1. to esteem, value, respect, honour, appreciate, hold dear, prize. 2. ~-se to boast of, give o. s. airs.
prezável adj. m. + f. (pl. -áveis) estimable, respectable, praiseworthy.
priaca s. f. (N. Braz.) hunting pouch.
priapismo s. m. (med.) priapism.
priapulídeo s. m. (zool.) priapulid: a marine worm of the group Priapuloidea.
priapulóides s. m. pl. (zool.) Priapuloidea: a group of marine worms, the priapulids.
prima (I) s. f. (female) cousin.
~ em quarto grau cater-cousin.
prima (II) s. f. 1. treble string, first string of some instruments. 2. (eccl.) prime (first canonical hour).
primacial adj. m. + f. (pl. -ais) primatial, primatical, of or belonging to a primate.
primado s. m. 1. primacy, primateship, pre-eminence, priority, first rank or place. 2. (eccl.) primate.
prima-dona s. f. (pl. prima-donas) prima donna, première.
primagem s. f. (pl. -ens) (naut.) primage.
primar v. to rank first, excel, surpass, transcend, top; be superior; distinguish o. s.
primário s. m. primitive person. ‖ adj. 1. primary, principal, fundamental. 2. (Braz.) narrow-minded, restrained, limited.
enrolamento ~ (electr.) prime winding. escola -a primary school, elementary school. pilha -a primary cell.
primata, primate s. m. (zool.) one of the primates, the order of primatic mammals (as the monkey).
primavera s. f. 1. spring, springtime. 2. (fig.) youth. 3. (bot.): a) primrose. b) bougainvillaea. 4. ~s pl. years, age.
primavera-de-flores s. f. (pl. primaveras-de-flores) a sort of silk cloth.
primavera-dos-jardins s. f. (pl. primaveras-dos-jardins) (bot.) oxlip, paigle, polyanthus.
primaveral, primaveril adj. m. + f. (pl. -ais, -is), primavero m. vernal.
dia ~ a spring day. flores -ais spring flowers.
primaverar v. to enjoy the spring(time).
primaz s. m. (eccl.) primate, archbishop. ‖ adj. m. + f. prime, first in rank.
primazia s. f. primacy, primateship, superiority, priority; precedency, preference; rivalry.
primeira s. f. a certain game at cards.
primeiranista s. m. + f. 1. student of the first year in any school. 2. abecedarian (elementary school).
primeiras-águas s. f. pl. (N. Braz.) the first rains after the summer season.
primeiro s. m. the first, top-dog. ‖ adj. 1. first, prime, foremost. 2. principal, main, chief. 3. primitive

original. 4. former, earliest. 5. first-born. ‖ -amente adv. first(ly), mainly, primely.
~ andar first floor. -a dama dum país first lady. -a mão (de tinta) ground colour, dead-colouring. ~-ministro prime minister. -a notícia primeur. ~ plano foreground. ~ prêmio first prize. -a rua à esquerda first turning at the left. ~s sintomas (med.) premonitive symptoms. ~s socorros first aid. ~ tenente first lieutenant. -a vez the first time. ~ vem a pele, depois a camisa near is my shirt, but nearer is my skin. à -a vista at the first glance, at first blush. as -as horas após meia-noite the small hours. ele chegou ~ he was the first to come. carne de -a quality meat. de -a ordem first-rate, first grade. de -a qualidade high-class, classic. ele foi um dos ~s compositores italianos he was one of the earliest Italian composers. em ~ lugar in the first place. estar entre os ~s to rank among the first. quem ~ vem, ~ mói first come, first served. senhoras e crianças em ~ lugar ladies and children first. ser o ~ da classe to be at the top of the class. tomarei o ~ trem I shall take the first train that comes. viajar em -a classe to travel first--class, go first.
primevo adj. primeval, primitive, original.
primicério s. m. 1. the first (in rank or dignity). 2. (obs.) choir leader, precentor.
primícias s. f. pl. 1. firstlings, primitiae: the first fruits. 2. (fig.) first production, work or composition.
primigênio, primígeno adj. primigenial, primogenial, first-born; primary, primordial.
primigesta s. f. (med.) woman pregnant for the first time.
primina s. f. (bot.) primine.
primípara adj. (med.) primiparous, bearing a child for the first time.
primitiva s. f. (pop.) the ancient times; origin, beginning.
primitivismo s. m. primitivism: 1. primitiveness, the state of being primitive, primitivity. 2. the doctrine of primitive life. 3. rudeness.
primitivo adj. primitive: 1. original, early, first. 2. simple, rudimental; rude, barbaric. 3. (biol.) primordial, inceptive. 4. old-fashioned. 5. (gram.) said of a word from which another one is derived. 6. (geol.) pertaining to the earliest formation.
circunferência -a (tech.) pitch circle. verbo ~ primitive verb.
primo (I) s. m. cousin.
~ coirmão or ~ germano first cousin. ~s cruzados relationship of male and female cousins, who are children of a brother and a sister. ~s de segundo grau second cousins, cousins twice removed.
primo (II) adj. 1. first, prime. 2. excellent, perfect, accomplished. 3. (arith.) indivisible except by unity or by itself.
matéria -a raw material. número ~ prime number. obra -a masterwork, masterpiece.
primogênito s. m. the first-born, firstling, the eldest born. ‖ adj. first-born, eldest.
primogenitor s. m. primogenitor, forefather, ancestor.
primogenitura s. f. primogeniture, seniority by birth.
direito de ~ the right of the first-born, primogenitureship.
primoponendo adj. that must be put in the first place.
primor s. m. 1. beauty, nicety, delicacy. 2. excellence, perfection, accuracy.
com ~ nicely, meticulously. ~ de arte masterpiece feito com ~ high-wrought.
primordial adj. m. + f. (pl. -ais) primordial, original, primeval, prime, primitive. ‖ ~mente adv. primordially, at the beginning.

primórdio s. m. primordium, beginning, origin.
primoroso adj. 1. beautiful, nice. 2. excellent, perfect, accurate. 3. exquisite. 4. genteel, graceful, magnificent. ‖ -amente adv. excellently, perfectly; nicely.
prímula s. f. (bot.) primula, primrose.
primuláceas s. f. pl. (bot.) Primulaceae, a family of herbs widely distributed in temperate regions.
primulina s. f. primulin(e), a substance obtained from the root of the primula.
princês s. m. (pl. -eses) 1. prince (depr.). 2. (Braz.) fancy dress of a prince.
princesa s. f. princess: 1. a woman of princely rank, daughter of a sovereign or consort of a prince. 2. (fig.) the first, most excellent lady of her group.
~ real princess royal.
principado s. m. 1. princedom, dignity, sovereignty of a prince. 2. principality, the territory of a prince. 3. ~s pl. principalities, the seventh order of angels.
principal s. m. (pl. -ais) 1. principal: a) main thing. b) chief, leader. c) superior of a religious community or college. d) capital (of a debt), fund. 2. magnate. ‖ adj. m. + f. principal, chief, main, essential, leading. ‖ ~mente adv. mainly, principally.
alimento ~ staple food. ator ~ leading man (actor). canção ~ theme song. eixo ~ (mech.) principal axis. motivo ~ prime motive. oração ~ principal clause. papel ~ leading part. pessoa ~ top manager. rua ~ high street, avenue. questão ~ the grand question, pivotal question. via ~ through street. o ~ é entrar the great thing is to get in.
principalidade s. f. principalness, fundamentality; pre--eminence.
príncipe (I) s. m. 1. prince: member of a royal family, title of nobility, dynast. 2. (Braz., ornith.) vermilion flycatcher.
~ consorte prince consort. ~ herdeiro crown prince. ~ da Igreja prince of the church, bishop. ~ da Paz Prince of Peace, the Messiah. ~ de sangue real prince of royal blood. ~ das trevas prince of darkness, devil.
príncipe (II) adj. principal, prime, first.
edição ~ first edition.
principelho s. m. princelet, princekin: 1. little prince. 2. an inferior prince.
principesco adj. princely, stately, magnificent. ‖ -amente adv. in a princely manner.
principiado adj. begun, inchoated.
principiador s. m. beginner, initiator. ‖ adj. beginning, initiating.
principiante s. m. + f. principiant, beginner, tyro, novice, apprentice, probationer, commencer, inceptor; (sl.) tenderfoot, griffin, greenhorn, Johnny Raw. ‖ adj. m. + f. beginning, inceptive.
principiar v. to begin, initiate, commence, start, set in motion.
principículo s. m. (depr.) = principelho.
princípio s. m. 1. beginning, start, commencement. 2. origin, source. 3. the first cause, principle. 4. element, ingredient, fundamental substance. 5. maxim, axiom, fundamental doctrine. 6. ~s pl. first principals, rudiments.
~s ativos active principles (spirit, oil and salt). ~s passivos passive principles (water and earth). o ~ do fim the beginning of the end. adotar como ~ to take as principle. basear-se nos mesmos ~s to be on common ground. bom ~ é a metade do serviço a good beginning is half the work done. do ~ ao fim from start to finish. em ~ in principle. estabelecer um ~ to lay down a principle. homem de sãos ~s a man of sound principles. no ~ do ano at the beginning of the year. por ~ by principle. todos os ~s são penosos all beginnings are difficult.

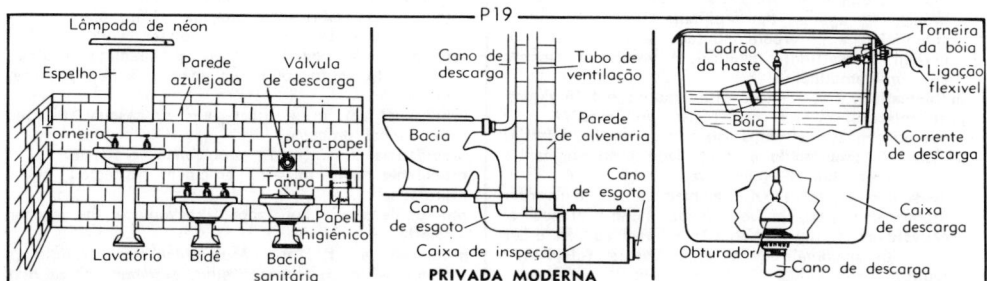

PRIVADA MODERNA

prino s. m. (bot.) mountain holly.

prior s. m. 1. prior, rector. 2. the head of a convent, abbot.

priora s. f. prioress.

priorado s. m. (also **priorato**) priorate, priorship: 1. the rank or dignity of a prior. 2. the period of a priorship.

prioral adj. m. + f. (pl. **-ais**) pertaining to a prior or to a priorship.

prioresa s. f. prioress, abbess.

prioridade s. f. priority, preference, primacy; precedence.

  direito de ~ the prior claim. **lista de artigos de** ~ priority list. **ter** ~ **sobre** to take priority to.

prisão s. f. 1. prison, jail, ward, gaol, prison-house. 2. capture, apprehension, imprisonment, detention, confinement, seizure. 3. fetter, chain, shackle.

  ~ **perpétua** lifelong imprisonment. ~ **de ventre** constipation, obstipation. **entregar-se à** ~ to render o. s. prisoner. **ordem de** ~ warrant of arrest, writ of attachment. **pôr na** ~ to put into prison. **procurar com ordem de** ~ to take a warrant against.

prisca s. f. (S. Braz.) cigarette end.

priscador s. m. (S. Braz.) dodger. || adj. dodging.

priscar v. (S. Braz.) to dodge.

prisco (I) s. m. (S. Braz.) dodge, jump, leap.

prisco (II) adj. pristine, ancient.

prisional adj. m. + f. (pl. **-ais**) relating to a prison.

prisioneiro s. m. 1. prisoner, captive. 2. (mech.) stud, stud bolt (plate P 4).

  ~ **de guerra** prisoner of war. ~ **político** prisoner of state. **dez soldados caíram** ~s ten soldiers were taken prisoners.

prisma s. m. prisma (plate B 13).

prismático adj. prismatic(al).

  cores -as prismatic colours, the colours of the rainbow.

prismatóide adj. m. + f. prismatoidal.

prismóide adj. m. + f. prismoidal.

pristídeos s. m. pl. (ichth.) Pristidae, the sawfish family.

prístino adj. pristine, primeval, former, first, original, primitive.

prítane s. m. (ancient Greece) prytanis, member of the Senate of Five Hundred.

pritaneu s. m. (ancient Greece) prytaneum, a public hall where the prytanes were entertained at public charges.

privação s. f. (pl. **-ões**) 1. privation, want, destitution; bereavement, dispossession, debarment. 2. **-ões** pl. hardships.

privada s. f. privy, water-closet; toilet, lavatory, bathroom (plates E 10, P 19).

privado s. m. favorite, secret or intimate friend. || adj. 1. private, particular, not public, familiar, personal. 2. deprived, wanting, destituted.

  conselho ~ privy counsellor, privy councillor. **ele**

recolheu-se à vida -a he retired to private life. **selo** ~ privy seal. **vida -a** personal life.

privança s. f. favour, intimacy, closeness.

  ter grande ~ **com alguém** to be in favour with.

privar v. 1. to prive, deprive, bereave, debar, disseise, divert, curtail. 2. to prohibit, forbid, hinder. 3. to be in favour, be very intimate with. 4. **~-se** to deprive o. s. of, abstain from, abnegate.

privativo adj. privative, private, proper, peculiar, particular; exclusive. || **-amente** adv. privatively, exclusively.

privilegiado s. m. privileged person, grantee. || adj. privilegèd, favoured; prerogative.

  a classe -a the privileged class. **os** ~s the elect.

privilegiar v. 1. to privilege, grant a privilege, exempt, free. 2. to favour, invest with peculiar rights. 3. **~-se** to be favoured.

privilégio s. m. 1. privilege, exclusive right, advantage, prerogative. 2. immunity, patent. 3. priority, precedence.

  ~ **gracioso** privilege granted without any respect to the merit of the person. **tínhamos o** ~ **de pertencer a** we were privileged to belong to.

pró s. m. pro, advantage, reason. || adv. pro, for, in favour of.

  os ~s **e os contras** the pros and cons. **nem** ~ **nem contra** neither for nor against, indifferent.

proa s. f. 1. (naut.) stem, prow, bow, nose, steerage (plate B 8). 2. the forepart of anything. 3. (fig.) presumption, pride, arrogance, vanity.

  de ~ **à popa** from stem to stern. **pôr a** ~ **a** to steer or bear towards. **ter alguém pela** ~ to have an adversary.

proar v. to steer for, head for.

  ~ **em terra** to land, set on shore.

probabilidade s. f. probability; 1. likeliness, likelihood. 2. expectancy, chance, prospect.

  cálculo da ~ theory of probability. **com toda** ~ in all probability. **quais são as minhas** ~s? what are my prospects? **ter boas** ~s to stand a good chance.

probabilismo s. m. probabilism, the theory of probability.

probabilista s. m. + f. probabilist, adherent to probabilism. || adj. probabilistic.

probante adj. m. + f. probative, authentic, convincing, evidential.

  em forma ~ in an authentic form.

probático adj. said of the pool Bethesda at Jerusalem.

probatório adj. probatory, probational, serving as a proof or trial.

probidade s. f. probity, honesty, integrity, uprightness, virtue, trustworthiness, rectitude.

problema s. m. problem: 1. (math.) proposition. 2. any question put for decision. 3. doubt, quiz.

  ~ **complicado** a knotty problem, great problem. **há um** ~ **nisso** there is a catch to it. **levantar**

1016   problemático — procurado

~s to problemize. **vimo-nos diante do** ~ we were brought up against the problem.

problemático adj. problematic(al), questionable, uncertain, unsettled, doubtful. ‖ **problematicamente** adv. problematically.

problematizar v. to render problematic; put in doubt.

problemista s. m. + f. problemist, problematist.

probo adj. honest; virtuous, good, trustworthy, faithful.

probóscida, probóscide s. f. 1. (zool.) an elephant's trunk, proboscis. 2. (ent.) weevil.

proboscídeo s. m. (zool.) a mammal of the order Proboscidea. ‖ adj. proboscidean, having a proboscis.

proboscídeos s. m. pl. (zool.) Proboscidea, an order of large mammals with a proboscis (elephants, tapirs).

procacidade s. f. procacity, impudence, petulance, insolence, pertness.

procaína s. f. (pharm.) procaine.

procâmbio s. m. (bot.) procambium.

procaz adj. m. + f. procacious, pert, petulant, saucy, insolent.

procedência s. f. 1. origin, derivation, provenance, source. 2. genealogy, antecedence.

procedente adj. m. + f. 1. proceeding, coming from, derived. 2. consequent, logical. 3. descended.

proceder s. m. procedure, manner of acting, conduct. ‖ v. to proceed: 1. go on. 2. come, arise or spring from. 3. result, be derived, originate. 4. behave, conduct o. s., act, deal. 5. take legal action.
~ **com cuidado** to proceed carefully. ~ **de boa fé** to act in good faith. ~ **contra alguém** to proceed against s. o. ~ **honestamente** to play fair. **eles procedem sem chance de sucesso** they play a loosing game.

procedimento s. m. 1. proceeding, procedure; operating, dealing, transaction. 2. derivation. 3. behaviour, carriage, conduct. 4. process, judicial proceedings. ~ **condenável** foul practices. ~ **correto** round dealing. ~ **franco, leal** plain dealing. ~ **processual** practice of the court.

procefálico adj. (zool.) procephalic, of or pertaining to the fore part of the head.

procela s. f. 1. storm at sea, tempest. 2. (fig.) agitation, disturbance.

procelária s. f. (ornith.) storm-bird, petrel.

procelária-do-cabo s. f. (pl. **procelárias-do-cabo**) cape pigeon.

procelarídeos s. m. pl. (ornith.) Procellariidae, a family of pelagic birds.

procelariformes s. m. pl. (ornith.) Procellariiformes, an order of pelagic birds (albatross, petrel, shearwater, fulmar).

proceleusmático adj. proceleusmatic.

proceloso adj. procellous, stormy, tempestuous. ‖ **-amente** adv. tempestuously.

prócer s. m. (pl. **próceres**) 1. magnate, chief, head. 2. ~es pl. proceres, the nobles, lords, grandees.

proceridade s. f. procerity, tallness, height of stature, loftiness.

prócero adj. procere, hight, ta.l, lofty; important.

processamento s. m. processing.

processão s. f. (pl. **-ões**) 1. proceeding, origin. 2. procession.

processar v. to carry on a lawsuit; to process, law, go to law, sue, prosecute, pursue, indict, take action.

processional adj. m. + f. (pl. **-ais**) processional, pertaining to a procession.

processionário s. m. a processional book.

processo s. m. 1. process, legal proceedings, lawsuit. 2. the papers or documents of a case or lawsuit. 3. method, procedure, manner of proceeding. 4. course, cycle. 5. (chem.) operation.

~ **civil** civil suit. ~ **disciplinar** disciplinary proceeding. ~ **de fabricação** process of manufacture. ~ **de júri** trial by jury. ~ **do serviço** working order. **instaurar** ~ **contra** to take proceedings against. **ir a** ~ to go to court. **um novo** ~ a new process, departure.

processual adj. m. + f. (pl. **-ais**) processual, relating to a legal process.

procidência s. f. (med.) procidence, prolapse.

procidente adj. m. + f. procident: affected by a prolapse.

procionídeos s. m. pl. (zool.) Procyonidae, the raccoon family.

procissão s. f. (pl. **-ões**) procession (religious). **ir em** ~ to go in procession. **passamos pelas ruas em** ~ we processioned the street.

proclama s. m. ban, banns; publishment, proclamation.

proclamação s. f. (pl. **-ões**) proclamation: 1. publication, pronunciation, announcement. 2. ban, publishment. 3. declaration, edict, ukase.

proclamador s. m. proclaimer, trumpeter. ‖ adj. proclaiming.

proclamar v. 1. to proclaim: a) to promulgate, announce, publish. b) declare, call or cry out publicly. 2. ~-se to proclaim o. s.
~ **a lei marcial** to establish martial law. ~ **a paz** to proclaim peace. ~ **alguém rei** to proclaim s. o. king.

proclamas s. m. pl. (eccl.) banns.

proclamatório adj. proclamatory.

próclise s. f. (gram.) proclisis.

proclítico adj. (gram.) proclitic.

proclive adj. m. + f. proclive, proclivous, inclined.

proclividade s. f. proclivity, inclination.

procônsul s. m. (pl. **procônsules**) proconsul.

proconsulado s. m. proconsulate, proconsulship, the office of a proconsul.

proconsular adj. m. + f. proconsular, proconsulary.

procotó s. m. the bloodsucking barber bug.

procrastinação s. f. (pl. **-ões**) procrastination, delay, deferment, putting off; dilatoriness.

procrastinador s. m. procrastinator, a dilatory person. ‖ adj. procrastinating, dilatory.

procrastinar v. to procrastinate: 1. defer, postpone. 2. delay, retard, protract. 3. be dilatory.

procriação s. f. (pl. **-ões**) procreation, generation, breeding.

procriador s. m. procreator. ‖ adj. procreative, progenitive, breeding.

procriar v. 1. to procreate, beget, engender, generate, produce (young). 2. to bud, burgeon, germinate.

procronismo s. m. prochronism, antedating.

proctite s. f. (path.) proctitis, inflammation of the rectum.

procumbente adj. (bot.) procumbent, prostrate.

procumbir v. 1. to fall down wounded or dead; to prostrate. 2. ~-se to prostrate o. s.

procura s. f. 1. search, quest, pursuit. 2. demand (com.).
~ **e oferta** demand and supply. **estar à** ~ **de** to be on the outlook for, search. **não há** ~ **para** there is no call for.

procuração s. f. (pl. **-ões**) procuration: 1. management of another's affairs. 2. mandate, power or letter of attorney, proxy.
por ~ by attorney.

procuradeira s. f. curious and intriguing woman.

procurado adj. demanded, sought after, récherché.
ele está sendo ~ he is wanted. **empregos** ~s situations wanted. **este artigo é muito** ~ this article is much called for. **muito** ~ in demand, in great request. **não** ~ unsought, unvisited.

procurador s. m. procurator, proctor, proxy, solicitor, attorney, assignee, mandatary, trustee.
~ **geral** universal agent, Attorney-General.
procuradora s. f. female procurator.
procuradoria s. f. 1. procuracy, procuratorship. 2. a procurator's fees.
procurar v. 1. to look for, seek, search. 2. to try, attempt. 3. to endeavour, aim at. 4. to see, visit, call on. 5. to solicit, quest. 6. to be or act as a procurator or attorney; administer, manage.
~ **agradar** to be studious to please. ~ **agulha em palheiro** to seek a needle in a haystack. ~ **briga** to be out for disorder. ~ **conselho** to have advice. ~ **o sono** to court sleep. **procura-se um guarda** watchman wanted. **diga-lhe que quem o procurou foi o Davi** tell him David called. **é isto que eu estou procurando** that is what I am seeking after, that is the stuff I need. **ela estava procurando suas luvas** she was hunting for her gloves. **ele procurou a amizade dela** he ingratiated himself with her. **ele procurou dormir** he wooed to sleep. **não procure encrenca comigo!** don't pick a quarrel with me! **um certo Sr. Ferreira procurou-o a** Mr. Ferreira called for you. **ele procurou sarna para se coçar** he looked for trouble.
procuratório adj. procuratory, pertaining to a procurator or a procuration.
prodiagnóstico s. m. anticipated diagnosis.
prodição s. f. (pl. -ões) treason.
prodigalidade s. f. 1. prodigality, lavishness. 2. profusion, abundance. 3. extravagance, wastefulness.
prodigalizador s. m. prodigal, spendthrift, waster. ‖ adj. prodigal, profuse, lavish, wasteful.
prodigalizar, prodigar v. to prodigalize, waste, squander, dissipate, lavish.
prodígio s. m. 1. prodigy, marvel, portent. 2. sign, wonder, miracle, phenomen.
prodigioso adj. prodigious, portentous, marvelous. 2. extraordinary, wonderful, miraculous. ‖ -amente adv. prodigiously.
pródigo s. m. 1. prodigal, spendthrift, waster, wastrel, squanderer. 2. (naut.) riders. ‖ adj. prodigal: 1. wasteful, lavish, extravagant. 2. profuse, unthrifty, bountiful.
~s **do berço** the spurs of the cradle. **filho** ~ prodigal son.
pródito adj. treacherous, betrayed.
proditor s. m. traitor, betrayer.
proditório adj. proditorious, treacherous, perfidious, traitorous. ‖ **proditoriamente** adv. proditoriously.
prodrômico adj. prodromal, preliminary.
pródromo s. m. (med.) prodrome: 1. prodromus: a) (med.) prodromal symptom. b) prodromal or preliminary book. 2. forerunner, harbinger. 3. (fig.) first work of an author.
produção s. f. (pl. -ões) production: 1. producing, manufacturing; work. 2. produce, product. 3. yield, output, outturn. 4. work done.
~ **de energia elétrica** production of current. ~ **insuficiente** underproduction. ~ **em série** mass production. **controle de** ~ production control. **custos de** ~ production costs. **linha de** ~ production line. **planejamento de** ~ production scheduling.
producente adj. m. + f. 1. producing, causing. 2. conclusive.
produtibilidade s. f. productiveness, productivity.
produtível adj. m. + f. (pl. -íveis) producible.
produtividade s. f. productivity, productiveness, creativeness.
produtivo adj. productive, generative; efficient; fertile, fruitful, fecund. ‖ -amente adv. productively.

produto s. m. product: 1. production, proceeds, produce. 2. output, yield. 3. fruit. 4. (also math.) result.
~ **acabado** end product. ~ **agrícola** produce of the country. ~ **básico** basic product. ~ **da nossa época** a child of our time. ~s **nacionais** domestic goods. ~ **secundário** by-product. ~s **da terra** the fruits of the earth. **o homem é o** ~ **do seu ambiente** man is the product of his surroundings.
produtor s. m. producer, creator, manufacturer. ‖ adj. producing, productive, creative.
produtora s. f. productress, creatress.
produzir v. to produce: 1. bring forth. 2. bear, yield, generate. 3. cause, effect, bring about, afford. 4. make, manufacture, work, create, form. 5. beget, engender.
~ **efeito** to act or tell upon, take effect. ~ **semente** to run to seed. ~ **vapor** to get up steam.
produzível adj. m. + f. (pl. -íveis) producible.
proeiro s. m. bowman, bow oarsman.
proejar v. 1. to steer towards, head for. 2. (fig.) to struggle against difficulties.
proembrião s. m. (pl. -ões) (bot.) proembryo.
proemial adj. m. + f. (pl. -ais) proemial, introductory, prefatory, preliminary.
proemiar v. to preface, make a preamble.
proeminência s. f. (also **prominência**) prominence: 1. salience, protuberance. 2. conspicuousness, distinction, notoriety.
proeminente adj. m. + f. proeminent: 1. jutting, protuberant. 2. conspicuous, eminent, distinguished.
proêmio s. m. proem, preface, introduction, preamble; prefatory discourse.
proeza s. f. 1. prowess, bravery, courage, valor; feat of valor. 2. exploit, achievement. 3. scandal.
profanação s. f. (pl. -ões) profanation, desecration, pollution, sacrilege; violation.
profanador s. m. profaner, desecrator, sacrilegist, defiler. ‖ adj. profanatory, sacrilegious.
profanar v. to profane, desecrate, unhallow, pollute; revile, abuse.
profanidade s. f. profanity, profaneness, blasphemy.
profano s. m. profane or irreligious person; layman. ‖ adj. profane: unconsecrated, secular, blasphemous, irreligious, irreverent, unholy, worldly, vulgar.
prófase s. f. (biol.) prophase, mitosis.
profecia s. f. prophecy, prediction, forecast, presage, vaticination.
profectício, profetício adj. profectitious, derived from an ancestor.
bens ~s profectitious goods.
proferir v. to pronounce, utter, speak, say.
~ **sentença** to give judgement, pass judgement upon s. o. ~ **um discurso** to make a speech, to give an address. **sem** ~ **uma palavra** without saying one word.
professar v. 1. to profess, declare openly, avow, acknowledge, affirm. 2. to teach, instruct, educate. 3. to take the veil. 4. ~-**se** to confess, declare o. s.
~ **a religião cristã** to profess the Christian religion.
professo s. m. 1. professed person (as a monk or a nun). 2. an expert. ‖ adj. professed, avowed, declared.
professor s. m. (pl. **professores**) 1. professor, teacher, master, instructor, educator, pedagogue. 2. expert, skilled person. 3. (mus.) maestro.
~ **assistente** assistant professor, usher. ~ **catedrático** full professor. ~ **de dança** dancing master. ~ **de desenho** art master, drawing master. ~ **de línguas** language master. ~ **particular** domestic tutor.
professora (ô) s. f. school mistress, woman teacher, instructress.

professorado s. m. 1. professorship, professorate. 2. body of professors, teaching staff.

professoral adj. m. + f. (pl. **-ais**) professorial.

professorando s. m. (Braz.) student about to obtain his mastership.

professorar v. to teach, be a teacher, educate, instruct.

profeta s. m. 1. prophet, predictor, foreteller, soothsayer, seer. 2. (Braz., pop.) lamplighter.

ninguém é ~ na sua terra no prophet is believed in his own country.

profético adj. prophetic(al), predictive, presageful, pythonic.

profetisa s. f. prophetess, pythoness, sibyl.

profetismo s. m. prophetism.

profetista adj. m. + f. prophetic(al).

profetizador s. m. prophesier, predictor, foreteller. ‖ adj. prophesying, prophetizing.

profetizar v. (also **profetar**) to prophetize, prophesy, predict, foretell, soothsay, presage, vaticinate.

proficiência s. f. proficiency, adeptness, progress, expertness, skill.

proficiente adj. m. + f. proficient, adept, skilled, qualified, competent. ‖ **~mente** adv. proficiently.

proficuidade s. f. utility, usefulness, profitableness, profitability, advantageousness.

profícuo adj. useful, advantageous, profitable. ‖ **proficuamente** adv. usefully.

profiláctico, profilático adj. (med.) prophylactic, preventive.

profilaxia s. f. prophylaxis, prophylaxy, preventive medicine.

profissão s. f. (pl. **-ões**) profession: 1. occupation, metier, office, employment. 2. vocation, calling. 3. career. 4. confession of faith; avowal, declaration.

~ de fé profession of faith, creed. **de ~** by occupation. **errar a ~** to mistake one's vocation. **sem ~** unprofessional.

profissional s. m. + f. (pl. **-ais**) (Braz.) professional. ‖ adj. professional, occupational.

profissionalismo s. m. professionalism.

profitente adj. m. + f. professing.

profligação s. f. (pl. **-ões**) profligacy, shamelessness; overthrowing; defeat, rout.

profligador s. m. destroyer, depraver. ‖ adj. defeating, destructive, corruptive.

profligar v. 1. to defeat, drive away, disperse, overcome, rout. 2. to destroy, ruin, corrupt.

prófugo adj. fugitive; deserter; vagrant, vagabond.

profundador s. m. scrutinizer, a person who examines a thing thoroughly; one who digs deep. ‖ adj. 1. deepening. 2. examining thoroughly.

profundar v. 1. to deepen, make deep or deeper. 2. to sink, force, drive down. 3. to examine thoroughly, explore; probe, fathom, sound. 4. **~-se:** a) to grow deeper. b) to go into details.

~ as raízes to take root.

profundas s. f. pl. the depths; inferno, hell.

profundidade s. f. (also **profundez, profundeza, profundura**) 1. profundity, depth, deepness, abyss. 2. (fig.) depth of knowledge; thoroughness.

a ~ de seus estudos the thoroughness of his studies. **um poço com 20 metros de ~** a well that has a depth of 20 meters.

profundo s. m. profundity, depth; (fig.) hell; sea. ‖ adj. 1. deep, profound. 2. impenetrable, fathomless, unfathomable, inscrutable, obscure. 3. thorough, complete, intense. ‖ **-amente** adv. profoundly; thoroughly; soundly.

~ silêncio deep silence. **~ sono** sound, fast sleep. **conhecimentos ~s** profound knowledge. **desmaio ~** dead faint. **com os olhos ~s** hollow-eyed. **em -a**

meditação immersed in meditation. **ele lhe fez uma -a reverência** he swept her a low bow. **ela está dormindo -amente** she is sound asleep.

profusão s. f. (pl. **-ões**) profusion, prodigality, lavishness, abundance, exuberance, plenty.

profuso adj. profuse, prodigal, wasteful, lavish, extravagant, exuberant. ‖ **-amente** adv. profusely.

progênie s. f. (also **progenitura**) 1. offspring, issue, progeny. 2. lineage, parentage; race.

progenitor s. m. progenitor, ancestor, forefather, father, sire, parent.

progenitora s. f. progenitress, progenitrix, female ancestor or parent, mother.

proglote, proglótide s. f. proglottid, proglottis.

prognatismo s. m. prognathism.

prógnato s. m. prognathic person, person with protrusive jaws. ‖ adj. (also **prognático**) prognatic, prognathous.

progne s. f. (poet.) 1. swallow. 2. (fig.) spring.

prognose s. f. (med.) prognosis.

prognosticação s. f. (pl. **-ões**) prognostication.

prognosticar v. 1. to prognosticate, foretell, predict, prophesy. 2. to judge from symptoms, make a prognosis.

isto prognostica adversidade this augurs ill.

prognóstico s. m. 1. prognostic, omen, presage. 2. prognostication, prediction. 3. (med.) prognosis; sympton.

progoniados s. m. pl. (zool.) Progoneata, a subclass of Arthropoda.

programa s. m. program(me): 1. edict, schedule, plan. 2. card, bill.

~ das corridas race card. **~ do governo** programme of government. **~ de serviço** program of work. **~ teatral** play-bill. **~ de televisão** telecast. **música de ~** programme-music. **pôr em ~** to bill. **qual é o ~ de rádio?** what's on the air?

programação s. f. (pl. **-ões**) programming.

programador s. m. programmer, programmist. ‖ adj. programmistic.

programar v. to program(me), plan, schedule.

programático adj. programmatic.

progredimento s. m. progress, advance, advancing.

progredir v. 1. to progress, proceed, advance. 2. to make progress, improve.

~ na vida to get on in life. **fazer ~** to advance. **não ~** to remain stationary. **ele está progredindo** he is getting on, he is on the upgrade. **o navio não conseguiu ~ contra o vento** the ship could not make head against the wind.

progressão s. f. (pl. **-ões**) 1. (also math.) progression. 2. progress, progressing, advancing.

~ aritmética arithmetical progression. **~ geométrica** geometrical progression. **~ gradual** graduation. **~ musical** musical progression. **~ para o norte** northing.

progressista s. m. + f. progressist, progressionist. ‖ adj. progressive, favouring progress.

progressivo adj. progressive, advancing, making progress, onward, active, ascensive. ‖ **-amente** adv. progressively.

progresso s. m. progress: 1. a proceeding or going forward. 2. advance, advancement, proficiency, improvement. 3. growth, development.

cidade em ~ a thriving town. **ele tem acusado ~** he has been making progress. **fazer ~** to make headway, get on. **sem ~** unprogressive.

pró-homem s. m. (pl. **pró-homens**) important person in a certain period of history.

proibição s. f. (pl. **-ões**) prohibition, interdiction, forbidding, forbiddance, debarment, ban; veto.

proibicionismo s. m. prohibitionism.

proibicionista s. m. + f. prohibitionist. ‖ adj. favouring prohibition.

proibido adj. prohibited, forbidden; unlawful, unauthorized; taboo.
é ~ fumar neste recinto smoking is not allowed here. **foi-lhe ~ fumar** he was forbidden smoking. **o fruto ~** the forbidden fruit.

proibidor s. m. prohibiter, interdicter, forbidder. ‖ adj. prohibiting, forbidding.

proibir v. to prohibit, inhibit, forbid, disallow, deny, ban, veto, debar.
proibi-lhe entrar em minha casa I forbade him my house. **~ um livro** to suppress a book.

proibitivo adj. prohibitive, prohibitory; interdictory. ‖ **-amente** adv. prohibitively.

proiz s. m. (naut.) painter, rope.

projeção s. f. (pl. **-ões**) (also **projetação**) 1. projection, plan, delineation, scheme. 2. prominence. 3. projecting, impelling, throwing forward. 4. protuberance, overhang, bulge.
~ horizontal ground plan. **~ ortográfica** orthographic projection. **movimento de ~ projectile** motion. **sala de ~** projection room.

projetar v. 1. to project: a) throw out, cast forth, shoot, propel. b) protrude, bulge, stand out. c) scheme, plot, contrive, plan, devise. d) sketch, outline, delineate. 2. **~-se** to be thrown; protrude.

projetil, projétil s. m. (pl. **-is, -éteis**) projectile, missile, bullet, bomb. ‖ adj. projectile, forward.
~ dirigido guided missile. **~ foguete** rocket missile. **~ luminoso** tracer.

projetista s. m. + f. projector, schemer, delineater, planner, deviser.

projetivo adj. projective, projecting.

projeto s. m. project: 1. plan, scheme, design. 2. sketch, draft, draught, delineation.
~ contrário counterproject. **~ de lei** bill. **em ~** in plan. **fazer passar um ~ de lei** to carry a motion. **fazer um ~** to draw up a plan.

projetor s. m. projector, searchlight.
~ cinematográfico bioscope. **~ de teto** (aeron.) ceiling projector.

projetura s. f. projection, projecture, a jutting or standing out.

prol s. m. + f. (pl. **próis**) advantage, benefit.
em ~ de in favour of, for. **homem de ~** an able man.

prolábio s. m. (anat.) prolabium.

prolação s. f. (pl. **-ões**) 1. prolation, utterance, pronunciation. 2. (mus.) colorature.

prolapso s. m. (med.) prolapse, prolapsus.
sofrer ~ to prolapse.

prole s. f. issue, offspring, progeny, descendants.

prolegômenos s. m. pl. prolegomenon, preliminary observation, introductory part, preface.

prolepse s. f. (rhet.) prolepsis, a figure by which objections are anticipated.

proléptico adj. proleptic(al).

proletariado s. m. proletariat(e), the proletarian class.

proletário s. m. proletarian, proletary. ‖ adj. proletarian: 1. relating to the lower class; poor. 2. (obs.) mean, vulgar.

proletarização s. f. (pl. **-ões**) proletarization, proletarianization.

proletarizar v. to proletarize, proletarianize, make proletarian.

proliferação s. f. (pl. **-ões**) 1. proliferation, rapid growth by multiplication of cells, 2. (bot.) prolification.

proliferar v. to proliferate, reproduce, grow rapidly and profusely.

prolífero adj. prolific, proliferous; fertile, fruitful, fecund. ‖ **proliferamente** adv. prolifically.

prolificação s. f. (pl. **-ões**) prolification.

prolificar v. to proliferate, breed, produce offspring, generate.

prolífico adj. prolific, productive, fruitful, fertile, generative, procreant. ‖ **prolificamente** adv. proliferously.

prolígero adj. proligerous, generative, productive.

prolixidade s. f. prolixity, prolixness, diffuseness; extension, length, verbosity, wordiness.

prolixo adj. prolix, diffuse, tedious, long-winded, spun-out, prolonged, lengthy; tiresome, wearisome. ‖ **-amente** adv. prolixly, at great length.

prologar v. to prologue, prologize, preface.

prólogo s. m. prologue, preface, preamble, introduction.

prolonga s. f. 1. (mil.) prolonge. 2. delay, deferment, retardation, protraction.

prolongação s. f. (pl. **-ões**) prolongation, elongation, extension, protraction; delay, postponement.

prolongado adj. 1. prolonged: a) delayed, protracted, lengthened. b) long-drawn, extended. 2. longish, ablong. ‖ **-amente** adv. extendedly, lengthily.

prolongador s. m. prolonger, protractor. ‖ adj. prolonging, protracting, extending.

prolongamento s. m. prolongation, lengthening, extension; protraction, delay.

prolongar v. 1. to prolong, lengthen. 2. to delay, postpone, put off, defer. 3. (naut.) to lay alongside of. 4. **~-se** to continue, go on; last.

prolongável adj. m. + f. (pl. **-áveis**) prolongable.

proloquial adj. m. + f. (pl. **-ais**) relating to a maxim, sentence or axiom.

prolóquio s. m. maxim, axiom, proverb.

prolusão s. f. (pl. **-ões**) prolusion, prelude, introduction.

promanar v. to emanate, proceed, issue, come from.

promécio s. m. (chem.) promethium.

promessa s. f. promise, assurance, word, parole; pledge, vow, engagement.
~ de auxílio promise of help. **~ de casamento** engagement, betrothal. **~ solene** solemn promise, vow. **fazer uma ~** to make a vow, be under a vow. **sob ~ de sigilo** under pledge of secrecy.

prometedor s. m. promiser ‖ adj. promising, expectant, hopeful.

prometéico adj. Promethean.

prometer v. 1. to promise, make a promise, assure, pledge, give hopes. 2. to presage, predict. 3. to vow, swear. 4. to betroth, engage, affiance.
~ auxílio to promise help. **~ êxito** to frame well. **~ a filha a alguém** to betroth one's daughter to s. o. **~ mundos e fundos** to promise mountains and marvels, promise wonders. **ela lhe prometeu a mão** she said yes to him. **eles cumprem o que prometem** they do what they preach.

prometida s. f. fiancée.

prometido s. m. 1. thing promised. 2. fiancé. ‖ adj. promised, pledged; vowed; engaged.
o ~ é devido promise is binding.

prometimento s. m. promise, promising.

promiscuidade s. f. promiscuity, promiscuousness, confusion, indiscriminate mixture.

promiscuir-se v. to mingle with, blend with.

promíscuo adj. promiscuous, mingled, indiscriminate, confused.

promissão s. f. (pl. **-ões**) promise, promising.
terra da ~ Promised Land, Holy Land.

promissária s. m. (jur.) promisee.

promissivo adj. promissive, promissory.

promissor s. m. promiser. ‖ adj. promising, flattering.

promissória s. f. promissory note.

promissório adj. promissory.

promitente s. m. + f. promiser. ‖ adj. promissory.

promoção s. f. (pl. **-ões**) promotion, preferment, preference; advance, elevation, rise, graduation; progress.
~ **de venda** sales promotion.
promombó s. m. (Braz.) a kind of fishing by torchlight that makes the fish jump into the boat.
promontório s. m. (geol.) promontory, headland, rocky cape (plate C 19).
promotor s. m. (also **promovedor**) promoter, supporter, sponsor; inciter, exciter, instigator. ‖ adj. promoting, promotive.
~ **público** prosecutor, attorney.
promotoria s. f. office of a prosecutor or attorney.
promover v. 1. to promote: a) further, foster, forward. b) elevate, raise, advance. c) foment, encourage. 2. to prosecute.
~ **a agricultura** to promote the interest in agriculture. ~ **uma tempestade num copo d'água** to make an affair of nothing.
promovido adj. promoted, preferred, advanced.
ele foi ~ **a capitão** he was promoted captain. **ela foi -a de classe** she was promoted at school, she was graduated.
promulgação s. f. (pl. **-ões**) promulgation, publication, proclamation, declaration.
promulgador s. m. promulgator, publisher. ‖ adj. promulgating, proclaiming, publishing.
promulgar v. to promulgate, publish, proclaim, announce, declare, make known.
pronação s. f. (pl. **-ões**) 1. pronation: movement of the hand turning the palm downward. 2. act or fact of lying with the face downward, a lying flat.
pronador s. m. (anat.) pronator, muscle of the forehand. ‖ adj. of or pertaining to the pronatory muscle.
pronau s. m. (archit.) pronaos.
prônefro s. m. (embryol.) pronephros, pronephron.
prono adj. prone, inclined, propense, tending to.
pronome s. m. (gram.) pronoun, a word used instead of a noun.
~ **demonstrativo** demonstrative pronoun. ~ **interrogativo** interrogative pronoun. ~ **pessoal** personal pronoun. ~ **possessivo** possessive pronoun. ~ **reflexivo** reflexive pronoun. ~ **relativo** relative pronoun.
pronominal adj. m. + f. (pl. **-ais**) (gram.) pronominal, belonging to a pronoun. ‖ ~**mente** adv. pronominally.
pronóstico adj. (pop.) presumptuous, pretentious, petulant, immodest, affected, exigent.
pronoto s. m. pronotum, the anterior division of an insect's notum.
prontidão s. f. (pl. **-ões**) 1. promptitude, promptness, readiness, quickness, alacrity; willingness. 2. (pop.) pennylessness. 3. m. (Braz.) policeman on duty.
prontificar v. 1. to make ready, prepare. 2. ~**-se** to offer o. s., volunteer, be ready or willing to do s. th.
ele prontificou-se a ajudar-me he offered to help me.
pronto s. m. 1. (Braz., pop.) person without money, starveling. 2. (N. Braz.) well-dressed person. ‖ adj. ready: 1. prompt, prepared, willing, inclined, disposed. 2. quick, swift, unhesitating, expeditious. 3. available, handy. 4. (pop.) pennyless, stonebroke.
~ **para impressão** ready for printing. **estar** ~ **com** to be through with, have finished. **estou** ~ **a confessar** I am free to confess. **ele sabia sua lição e estava** ~ **com as respostas** he knew his lesson and was forward with his answers. **estou** ~ **para ir** I am prepared to go. **estar** ~ **para** to await, be prepared to do s. th.

pronto-socorro s. m. (pl. **prontos-socorros**) ambulance station, first-aid clinic.
prontuário s. m. 1. promptuary: a) repository, storehouse. b) prompt-book, enchiridion, handbook. 2. (Braz.) register of a person's antecedents at the police.
prônubo adj. nuptial.
anel ~ wedding ring, marriage ring.
pronúcleo s. m. pronucleus, primitive nucleus.
pronúncia s. f. 1. pronouncing, pronunciation; enunciation, articulation; utterance. 2. sentence or judgement, indictment.
pronunciação s. f. (pl. **-ões**) 1. pronunciation. 2. verdict.
pronunciado adj. 1. pronounced, articulate, distinct, well-marked, sharp. 2. indicted.
pronunciamento s. m. 1. proclamation. 2. pronunciamento, insurrection, rebellion, revolt.
pronunciar v. 1. to pronounce, articulate, utter, speak. 2. to deliver a discourse. 3. to pass sentence, indict, adjudge. 4. to declare, announce, proclaim. 5. ~**-se**: a) to declare o. s., make declarations. b) to revolt.
~**-se contra** to pronounce against. ~ **mal** to mispronounce. ~ **uma sentença** to render judgement.
pronunciável adj. m. + f. (pl. **-áveis**) pronounceable, enunciable, utterable.
pronúncio s. m. substitute of a Papal nuncio.
propagação s. f. (pl. **-ões**) propagation: 1. generation, procreation, breeding. 2. dissemination, spreading, diffusion, divulgation; transmission.
~ **do cristianismo** propagation of Christianity.
propagador s. m. propagator, spreader, diffuser, promoter. ‖ adj. propagatory, propagative.
propaganda s. f. propaganda: any means of propagating doctrines or making known ideas or things; advertising, publicity.
fazer ~ to propagate, advertise. **folhetos de** ~ advertising matter. **seção de** ~ publicity department.
propagandista s. m. + f. propagandist; canvasser.
propagar v. 1. to propagate: a) multiply, reproduce, procreate. b) increase, augment. c) disseminate, scatter, spread, diffuse. 2. ~**-se** to extend, spread, transmit; have offspring.
propagativo adj. propagative, propagatory.
propagem s. f. (pl. **-ens**) (bot.) propago, bulblet.
propágulo s. m. (bot.) propagulum.
propalar v. to blab, let out, divulge, noise, publish, disclose.
propano s. m. (chem.) propane.
propanona s. f. (chem.) propanone; acetone.
proparoxítono s. m. (gram.) proparoxitone, a word with the accent on the antepenultimate syllable. ‖ adj. proparoxítone.
propatia s. f. (med.) symptoms of a disease.
propedêutica s. f. propaedeutics: the preliminary instruction for the study of any art or science.
propedêutico adj. propaedeutic(al).
propelir v. to propel, impel, drive forward.
propendente adj. m. + f. inclined, tending, bent, propensive.
propender v. 1. to be inclined, be not upright. 2. to be propense or in favour of s. th., tend to.
propensão s. f. (pl. **-ões**) 1. propensity, propension. 2. disposition, inclination, tendency, penchant, proneness.
propenso adj. propense, inclined; disposed, willing, minded to, ready; prone. ‖ **-amente** adv. propensely.
propiciação s. f. propitiation, expiation, atonement, reconciliation, satisfaction.

propiciador s. m. propitiator. ‖ adj. propitiating.
propiciar v. to propitiate, appease, render favourable, conciliate, reconcile.
propiciatório (I) s. m. propitiatory, the mercy-seat.
propiciatório (II) adj. propitiatory, conciliatory.
sacrifício ~ peace offering.
propício adj. propitious, promising, auspicious, benevolent, kind, favourable, opportune, expedient.
aguardar um momento mais ~ to wait for a better opportunity.
propilamina s. f. (chem.) propylamin(e).
propileno s. m. (chem.) propylene.
propileu s. m. (archit.) propylaeum, monumental entrance or gateway.
propilo s. m. (chem.) propyl.
propina s. f. 1. propine, gratuity, tip, drink-money. 2. fee, entrance fee, emoluments.
propinação s. f. (pl. -ões) propination: act of drinking to a person's health and offering him the cup.
propinador s. m. person who drinks someone's health and offers him the cup.
propinar v. to propine: 1. pledge in drinking, drink to a person's health, offer to drink. 2. present (esp. a drink money), tip.
propinqüidade s. f. propinquity, proximity, nearness in time or space, kindred.
propínquos s. m. pl. relations, kinsfolk. ‖ adj. propínquo near, neighbouring; approaching, imminent.
proplasma s. m. proplasm, mold; rough sketch.
proplástica s. f. proplastics, the art of making molds.
proplástico adj. proplastic, pertaining to mold making.
própole, própolis s. f. propolis, bee-glue, a resinous substance which bees use as building material.
proponente s. m. + f. proponent, proposer, propounder. ‖ adj. proponent, proposing.
propor v. 1. to propose, suggest, recommend, present, offer (for discussion). 2. to intend, mean, have in view. 3. ~-se to propose o. s., offer o. s., offer one's services.
~ casamento to propose marriage. ~ melhores condições to propose better conditions. o homem propõe e Deus dispõe man proposes but God disposes.
proporção s. f. (pl. -ões) proportion: 1. relation (of one thing to another), ratio, rate. 2. symmetry, harmony. 3. (math.) the equality of relations. 4. dimension, shape, form.
~ contínua continued proportion. ~ inversa inverse proportion. à ~ proportionately, according to, in proportion. em ~ pro rata, in proportion. fora de ~ out of proportion. em justa ~ in due proportion. não está em nenhuma ~ com it bears no proportion to.
proporcionado adj. proportioned, proportional, proportionate; commensurate; harmonic. ‖ -amente adv. proportionately.
bem ~ well-proportioned.
proporcionador s. m. one who proportions. ‖ adj. proportioning.
proporcional adj. m. + f. (pl. -ais) proportionate, proportional. ‖ ~mente adv. proportionally.
proporcionalidade s. f. proportionateness, proportionality, adequacy, ratability.
proporcionar v. 1. to proportion, proportionate, adjust, form symetrically. 2. to present, provide, offer, afford, give. 3. ~-se to offer or present itself.
~ a despesa com as suas rendas to proportion one's expenditure to one's revenue. se se ~ ocasião if occasion offers itself. isto me proporciona grande satisfação it affords me great satisfaction. isto lhe proporcionará um feriado this will give you a holiday.

proporcionável adj. m. + f. (pl. -áveis) proportionable.
proposição s. f. (pl. -ões) proposition: 1. proposal. 2. statement, assertion; thesis. 3. (gram.) clause. 4. (math.) problem.
propositado adj. m., proposital m. + f. (pl. -ais) purposed, willful, deliberate. ‖ -amente adv. willfully, purposively.
propósito s. m. 1. purpose, design, intention, aim, object. 2. matter, topic. 3. fitness, conveniency.
a ~ by the way. a que ~? for what purpose? com o ~ to the effect. de ~ purposely, on purpose, aforethought. falar a ~ to speak to the purpose. fora de ~ out of reason, ill-timed. sem ~ aimless, objectless. vir a ~ de to serve one's turn.
proposta s. f. 1. proposal, offer, suggestion, bid. 2. proposition, motion.
~ de casamento offer of marriage. isto sim, que é ~! now you are talking! fazer uma ~ to make an offer, overture.
proposto s. m. 1. representative, locum tenens. 2. thing proposed. ‖ adj. proposed, offered.
propriedade s. f. 1. propriety, fitness, appropriateness, accuracy, justness. 2. quality, peculiarity, character. 3. propensity, tendency, inclination. 4. real estate, possession, property, wealth, riches, acres, belonging; domain; ownership.
~ agrícola cultivada pelo dono home farm. ~ alugada tenancy. ~ coletiva common ground. ~ literária copyright. ~ a título precário estate at sufferance. direitos de ~ property rights. falar com ~ to speak with propriety. grandes ~s broad acres. pôr em leilão a ~ de alguém to sell someone up. privar da ~ to unstate. pequena ~ small holding.
proprietário s. m. proprietor, owner, holder, possessor. ‖ adj. proprietary.
~ de armazém warehouseman. ~ de minas de carvão coal owner, coal master. ~ de navio ship owner. ~ de siderurgia iron master. ~ de terras land owner, landlord.
próprio s. m. 1. property, peculiar quality, characteristic; propriety. 2. messenger, express. ‖ adj. proper: 1. peculiar. 2. private, own, belonging to one. 3. fit, suitable, appropriate, becoming. 4. correct, right, just, exact, literal. 5. opportune. 6. self, personal. 7. like, resembling. ‖ propriamente adv. properly.
o ~ ar que respirei the very air I breathed. ~ de pertaining to. a -a pessoa I, the number one. ~ para publicação fit for publication. a -a verdade truth itself. casa -a a house of one's own. é isto da sua -a produção? is this your own growth? firmado de ~ punho under one's hand and seal. incendiaram-lhe a -a casa they burnt his house about his ears. minhas -as palavras my exact words. não ter nada de ~ to have nothing. nome ~ proper name, proper noun. uma palavra na sua -a significação a word in its proper signification. por si ~ of his own initiative. repórter ~ staff reporter. não foi propriamente agradável it was not exactly pleasant. a si ~ to oneself.
proptoma s. m., proptose f. (path.) proptosis, prolapse, protrusion.
propugnáculo s. m. 1. bulwark, rampart, fortified place. 2. (fig.) support.
propugnador s. m. propugner, defender, vindicator. ‖ adj. defending, vindicating.
propugnar v. to propugn, defend, vindicate, fight for.
propulsão s. f. (pl. -ões) propulsion, a driving forward. ~ a jacto jet.
propulsar v. 1. to drive, impel, propel. 2. to keep away, repel.

propulsor s. m. propeller, propellant, pusher. ‖ adj. (also **propulsivo**) propulsive, propulsory, propelling, driving.
eixo ~ propelling shaft. **tubo do eixo** ~ propeller tube.
prorrogação s. f. (pl. -ões) prorogation, putting off, adjournment, postponement, deferment.
~ **do contrato** renewal of the contract. ~ **do parlamento** adjournment of Parliament.
prorrogado adj. deferred, postponed.
prorrogar v. to prorogue, prorogate, put off, adjourn, extend, postpone.
prorrogativo adj. prorogative.
prorrogável adj. m. + f. (pl. -áveis) that may be prorogued; postponable.
prorromper v. to break out, burst.
~ **em lágrimas** to burst into tears.
prosa s. f. 1. prose. 2. rodomontade, jaw, swagger. 3. talk, prate, chatter. 4. courtship. 5. m. boastful or loquacious person. ‖ adj. (Braz.) loquacious, talkative.
prosador s. m. prosaist, proser, prose writer.
prosaico adj. prosaic(al), vapid, dull, tedious, commonplace, bread-and-butter, matter-of-fact.
prosaísmo s. m. prosaism, prosaicness.
prosaísta s. m. + f. prosaist, prose writer.
prosápia s. f. 1. progeny, ancestry, generation, race. 2. pride, haughtiness, arrogance, vainglory, conceit.
prosar v. 1. to prose, write or compose in prose, prosify. 2. (Braz.) to chat, coze.
proscênio s. m. 1. proscenium, part of the theater before the stage (plate P 2). 2. stage.
proscrever v. to proscribe: 1. banish, ban, outlaw, exile. 2. forbid, interdict, prohibit.
proscrição s. f. (pl. -ões) 1. proscription, outlawry, interdiction, banishment. 2. condemnation.
proscrito s. m. an exile, outlaw. ‖ adj. proscribed exiled, outlawed.
proscritor s. m. proscriber. ‖ adj. proscriptive.
proseador s. m. (Braz.) talker, chatterer, babbler, gossip. ‖ adj. talkative.
prosear v. to talk, chat, prattle, chin.
proselitismo s. m. proselytism, conversion to a new opinion, system or party.
prosélito s. m. proselyte, convert.
prosencéfalo s. m. (zool.) prosencephalon.
prosênquima s. m. (bot.) prosenchyma.
prosificar v. to prosify, write in prose.
prosista s. m. + f. 1. prose writer, proser. 2. chatterer, loquacious person. ‖ adj. talkative, loquacious.
prosódia s. f. prosody.
prosódico adj. prosodic(al), relating to the rules of prosody.
prosonomásia s. f. prosonomasia, a kind of pun.
prosopalgia s. f. (path.) prosopalgia, facial neuralgia.
prosopálgico adj. (path.) prosopalgic.
prosopografia s. f. prosopography.
prosopopéia s. f. 1. (rhet.) prosopopeia. 2. bombastic discourse. 3. (N. Braz.) vainglory, conceit.
prospecção s. f. (pl. -ões) search for a layer or mine of ore.
prosperado adj. that has prospered.
prosperador s. m. person who causes prosperity. ‖ adj. prospering.
prosperar v. to prosper: thrive, flourish, develop; be or become successful, improve, succeed.
o comércio está prosperando commerce is prospering.
prosperidade s. f. prosperity, success, welfare, fortune; happiness.

próspero adj. 1. prosperous, successful, flourishing. 2. favourable, propitious; fortunate. ‖ **prosperamente** adv. prosperously.
um ~ **ano novo!** a prosperous new year!
prospetivo adj. prospective. ‖ **-amente** adv. prospectively.
prospeto s. m. 1. prospectus: circular announcing plans, schemes; printed advertisement. 2. prospect: a) outlook, exposure, view, aspect. b) anticipation. c) possible or probable result, reason or ground of expectation.
prospetor s. m. prospector.
prossecução, prosseguição s. f. (pl. -ões) prosecution, pursuit; continuation; execution.
prosseguidor s. m. prosecutor; pursuer. ‖ adj. prosecuting.
prosseguimento s. m. pursuit, continuation, following, prosecution.
prosseguir v. to prosecute, follow, continue, proceed, take ahead, go on, carry on, pursue.
próstata s. f. (anat.) prostate, the prostate gland.
prostatalgia s. f. (med.) prostatodynia.
prostatectomia s. f. (surg.) protastectomy.
prostático adj. (anat.) prostatic, of or pertaining to the prostate.
prostatite s. f. (med.) prostatitis, inflammation of the prostate.
prostatotomia s. f. (surg.) prostatotomy.
prosternação s. f. (pl. -ões), **prosternamento** m. prostration.
prosternar v. to prostrate: 1. humiliate, humble, reduce to submission. 2. ~-se to throw o. s. to the ground in humble respect or reverence.
próstese s. f. prosthesis: 1. (gram.) the addition of letters or of a prefix. 2. (surg.) a supplying with an artificial part (hand, toot).
prostibular adj. m. + f. of or pertaining to a brothel.
prostibulário s. m. person who frequents brothels; libertine.
prostíbulo s. m. brothel, bawdyhouse.
prostilo s. m. (archit.) prostyle.
prostituição s. f. (pl. -ões) prostitution.
prostituidor s. m. prostituter. ‖ adj. prostituting.
prostituir(-se) v. 1. to prostitute. 2. (fig.) to corrupt, devote to bad use; debase o. s.
prostituta s. f. prostitute, courtesan, whore, strumpet.
prostração s. f. (pl. -ões), **prostramento** m. 1. prostration; exhaustion, debility. 2. collapse, breakdown.
prostrar v. to prostrate: 1. throw down. 2. humble, humiliate. 3. weaken, debilitate, exhaust. 4. ~-se throw o. s. to the ground in humble respect. ~-se aos pés de alguém to throw o. s. to a person's feet.
protagonista s. m. + f. protagonist; leading person; figurant.
protandria s. f. (bot.) prontandry.
protândrico adj. (bot.) protandric.
protanopsia s. f. protanopia: inability to distinguish the red colour.
protargol s. m. (pharm.) protargol.
prótase s. f. protasis: first part of a play or drama.
protático adj. protatic.
prótea s. f. protea: South African shrub.
proteáceas s. f. pl. (bot.) Proteaceae: a family of S. African and Australian dicotyledonous shrubs and trees.
proteção s. f. (pl. -ões) protection: 1. act or fact of protecting. 2. patronage, support; favour; help. 3. defence, guard. 4. security. 5. safeguard. 6. shelter, cover.
sob minha ~ with my support. **para a** ~ **de nossos interesses** to safeguard our interests.

protecionismo s. m. (econ.) protectionism, protective system.
protecionista s. m. + f. (econ.) protectionist, adherent of protectionism. ‖ adj. protectionist.
protegedor s. m. protector. ‖ adj. protecting.
proteger v. to protect: 1. defend. 2. favour, support. 3. guard, shield. 4. safeguard. 5. shelter.
~ **um candidato** to favour a candidate. ~ **contra chuva** to shelter from the rain.
protegido s. m. protegé, favourite. ‖ adj. protected; favoured; sheltered.
protéico (I) adj. protean; multiform.
protéico (II) adj. proteinaceous, proteinic.
proteiforme adj. m. + f. proteiform, protean.
proteína s. f. (biochem.) protein.
proteínico adj. proteinic.
protelação s. f. (pl. -ões) delay, protraction, procrastination, postponement.
protelador s. m. protractor, delayer, procrastinator. ‖ adj. delaying, putting off.
protelar v. to delay, protract, procrastinate, put off, postpone, prolong.
protelatório adj. protractive, dilatory, tardy.
proteólise s. f. (biochem.) proteolysis.
proteolítico adj. (biochem.) proteolytic.
proterânteo adj. (bot.) proterantheous.
proteróglifos s. m. pl. (zool.) Proteroglypha, a suborder of venomous snakes.
protérvia s. f. petulance, pertness, insolence, sauciness.
protervo adj. petulant, insolent, saucy; arrogant, haughty.
prótese s. f. (also **próstese**; gram., surg.) prosthesis.
protestação s. f. 1. protestation, protest. 2. asseveration.
protestador s. m. protester. ‖ adj. protesting.
protestante s. m. + f. 1. (rel.) Protestant. 2. protestant, person who protests. ‖ adj. 1. (rel.) Protestant: of or pertaining to the Protestants. 2. protestant, protesting.
protestantismo s. m. Protestantism.
protestar v. 1. to protest: a) (also com.) make a protest against, object; contradict. b) asseverate, declare solemnly; swear. 2. to profess. 3. to promise.
~ **uma letra** to protest a bill. **o povo protestou contra os impostos** the people protested against the taxes.
protestativo adj. protesting.
protestatório adj. 1. protesting. 2. asseverating; witnessing.
protesto s. m. protest: 1. protestation. 2. remonstrance. 3. disapproval. 4. asseveration, promise, solemn declaration. 5. (jur.) a declaration in a pleading.
~ **de letra** protest of a bill. ~ **por falta de pagamento** protest for nonpayment. **com os ~s de nossa subida admiração** (com. correspondence) with kindest regards.
protético s. m. prosthodontist. ‖ adj. prosthetic.
protetivo adj. protective.
protetor s. m. protector: 1. supporter, promoter, favourer. 2. guard, shield. ‖ adj. protecting: 1. favouring. 2. shielding.
protetora s. f. protectrix, protectress.
protetorado s. m. protectorate: 1. protection (and control) of a weak state by a strong one. 2. the territory so protected. 3. protectorship.
protetoral adj. m. + f. (pl. -ais) protectoral.
protetório adj. protecting; favouring; guarding; sheltering.
proteu s. m. fickle, changeable person.

protista s. m. (biol.) protist.
protistologia s. f. (biol.) protistology.
proto s. m. (S. Braz.) bread of maize and rye.
protoblasto s. m. (biol.) protoblast.
protobrânquios s. m. pl. (zool.) subclass of bivalve molluscs.
protocolar v. to protocolize. ‖ adj. m. + f. pertaining to a protocol.
protocolo s. m. protocol: 1. rule of etiquette. 2. register, record (as of a conference, audience). **registrar em** ~ to make minutes, keep the minutes, depose, record.
protocordados s. m. pl. (zool.) Protochordata, a division of Chordata.
protofílico adj. (chem.) protophilic.
protofilo s. m. the first leaf of a plant.
protófito s. m. one of the Protophytas, plants of the lowest organization.
protogênico adj. (chem.) protogenic.
protógeno s. m. protogenes.
protógino s. m. (petrog.) protogine: a variety of granite.
proto-história s. f. protohistory.
protomártir s. m. (pl. ~es) protomartyr: the first martyr of a cause; in particular St. Stephen.
protomecópteros s. m. pl. (ent.) scorpion flies of the order Mecoptera.
protomedicato s. m. formerly a board of doctors in charge of sanitary inspections.
protomédico s. m. chief physician.
próton s. m. (chem., phys.) proton: nucleous of the atom.
protonauta s. m. first navigator, person who first navigated to a certain region.
protonema s. m. (bot.) protonema.
protonotariado s. m. prothonotaryship.
protonotário s. m. prothonotary: 1. chief notary or chief clerk. 2. (R. C. Church) a member of the Prothonotaries.
protopatia s. f. (med.) protopathy: first symptoms.
protoplasma s. m. protoplasma: a substance that forms the basis of animal and plant life.
protoplasmático, protoplásmico adj. (biol.) protoplasmatic.
protóptero s. m. Protopterus: a genus of dipnoan fishes.
protospôndilos s. m. pl. (ichth.) Protospondyli, Cycloganoidei, a group of ganoid fishes that comprises only the bowfin.
prototérios s. m. pl. (zool.) Prototheria, a subclass of egg-laying mammals: the platypus and the echidna.
protótipo s. m. prototype, archetype, model, pattern.
protóxido s. m. (chem.) protoxide: a compound of oxygen and an element with the lowest proportion of oxygen.
protozoários s. m. pl. (zool.) Protozoa.
protozoologia s. f. protozoology: that branch of zoology dealing with the protozoa.
protraimento s. m. protraction; delay; procrastination, prolongation.
protrair v. to protract, delay, procrastinate, put off, prolong.
protrusão s. f. (pl. -ões) protrusion.
protruso adj. protruded; of or pertaining to protrusion.
protuberância s. f. protuberance, protuberancy, prominence, projection, bulge.
~**s solares** solar streamers.
protuberante adj. m. + f. protuberant, prominent, swelling, bulging, protruding.
protutela s. f. (jur.) protutory, guardianship.

protutor s. m. (jur.) protutor, guardian.
prova s. f. 1. proof: act or fact of proving. 2. experiment, essay, trial. 3. a trying on. 4. rehearsal. 5. examen, examination. 6. test. 7. taste. 8. sample. 9. (math.) check. 10. demonstration. 11. sign, token, mark, indication. 12. evidence. 13. testimony. 14. reason. 15. confirmation. 16. (typogr.) proof sheet. 17. (phot.) copy.
 ~ **de nervos** test of nerves. ~ **escrita** written test, written paper. ~ **oral** oral test. **à** ~ **d'água** waterproof. **à** ~ **de bala** shot-proof. **à** ~ **de bomba** bomb-proof. **à** ~ **de fogo** fire-proof. **a toda** ~ tried, tested, safe. **como** ~ in substantiation of. **como** ~ **de sua lealdade** as a token of his loyalty. **corrigir** ~**s** to read proofs. **dar** ~**s de** to give proofs of. **fazer a** ~ to try, experiment, prove, check. **pôr à** ~ to give a trial of, put to the test. **resistir à** ~ to stand the trial.
provação s. f. (pl. **-ões**) 1. probation: act or fact of proving; trial, proof. 2. probation time. 3. affliction, tribulation, hardship. 4. novitiate.
provado adj. 1. proved; confirmed; demonstrated. 2. examined; tested; tried.
provador s. m. prover: person who proves, examines, tests, demonstrates. ‖ adj. proving.
provadura s. f. 1. sample, taste. 2. trial, test.
provança s. f. = **prova**.
provar v. 1. to prove: a) evince, show, demonstrate. b) try, experiment, essay. c) examine, test. d) check, verify (esp. math.). e) experience, feel, suffer. 2. to taste, sample. 3. to testify. 4. to rehearse. 5. to try on (dress).
 ~ **forças com** to try conclusions with. ~ **sua inocência** to prove one's innocence. ~ **a paciência de alguém** to try a person's patience. ~ **o vinho** to taste the wine.
provará s. m. each one of the items of a bill of indictment.
provável adj. m. + f. (pl. **-áveis**) 1. probable, likely. 2. provable, demonstrable. ‖ **provavelmente** adv. probably.
pouco ~ unlikely. **é mais** ~ **que sim** it is as likely as not.
provecto adj. 1. advanced in years, aged. 2. experienced. 3. well on.
provedor s. m. 1. purveyor. 2. superintendent of a charitable institution.
provedoria s. f. a purveyor's office or district.
proveito s. m. 1. profit, advantage, gain, benefit. 2. progress, improvement.
bom ~**!** 1. may you enjoy it. 2. (iron.) much good may it do you! **fazer, tirar** ~ to make good use of, profit, turn to account. **tirar o maior** ~ **possível** to make the most of.
proveitoso adj. profitable, advantageous, benefic, beneficial; lucrative.
provençal s. m. + f. (pl. **-ais**) Provençal: 1. native or inhabitant of Provence. 2. the Provençal language. ‖ adj. Provençal.
provençalismo s. m. influence of the Provençal literature.
provençalista s. m. + f. an expert in Provençal literature.
proveniência s. f. provenience, origin, source, provenance.
proveniente adj. m. + f. proceeding from, deriving from, originating in.
provento s. m. produce, profit, return, gain, revenue.
prover v. 1. to provide, furnish, supply (**com** with). 2. to give, bestow, grant, confer. 3. to appoint, promote. 4. to look after, care for, attend. 5. ~**-se** to provide o. s. (**de** with).

proverbial adj. m. + f. (pl. **-ais**) proverbial: 1. of or referring to a proverb. 2. known for, notorious. ‖ ~**mente** adv. proverbially.
proverbiar v. to use proverbs.
provérbio s. m. proverb, saying, maxim, adage.
proverbista s. m. + f. person fond of or using too many proverbs.
proveta s. f. test glass, test tube.
 ~ **graduada** (graduated) measuring cylinder, measuring glass (plate F 6).
providência s. f. 1. Providence; God. 2. providence, foresight, prudence. 3. precaution, circumspection. 4. provision, arrangements, preventive measures or steps.
tomar as ~**s necessárias** to take the necessary steps.
providencial adj. m. + f. (pl. **-ais**) providential: 1. of or referring to the Providence. 2. opportune, seasonable, welcome; fortunate, lucky.
providencialismo s. m. providentialism.
providencialista s. m. + f. adherer of providentialism. ‖ adj. adhering to providentialism.
providenciar v. 1. to provide, make arrangements for, take preventive measures. 2. to look after, concern o. s. with. 3. to arrange, prepare. 4. to be provident.
vamos ~ **o pagamento** we shall provide for payment. **providenciarei todo o necessário** I shall take care of all that is necessary.
providente adj. m. + f. provident, prudent, thoughtful, circumspect, far-seeing, far-sighted. ‖ ~**mente** adv. providently.
provido adj. 1. provided or supplied with. 2. provident.
próvido adj. provident.
provigário s. m. provicar: priest in charge of a vicariate.
provimento s. m. 1. provisioning, supply of provisions; equipment. 2. provision, arrangements, preventive measures or steps. 3. nomination, appointment, installation, investiture.
dar ~ (jur.) to grant a petition.
província s. f. province: 1. section, region, district, territory. 2. country, excepting its capital. 3. jurisdiction.
provincial s. m. (pl. **-ais**) provincial: superior of a number of religious houses ‖ adj. m. + f. provincial: of or pertaining to the province.
provincialado, provincialato s. m. (eccl.) dignity or office of a provincial.
provincialismo, provincianismo s. m. provincialism: 1. quality of being provincial. 2. expression or way of speaking typical of a province. 3. provincial manners.
provincianizar-se v. to acquire provincial habits.
provinciano s. m. provincial, person from the province. ‖ adj. provincial, not from the capital.
provindo adj. proceeding, issuing or coming from.
provir v. to proceed, come, issue, arise, result from.
provisão s. f. (pl. **-ões**) provision: 1. supply, store, storage, stock. 2. act or fact of providing. 3. things provided, provisions. 4. governmental instruction or order, writ (as for an installation, investiture and the like).
 ~ **de víveres** supply of provisons. **fazer provisões** to supply o. s. with.
provisional adj. m. + f. (pl. **-ais**) 1. provisional. 2. provisory. 3. interim. ‖ ~**mente** adv. provisionally.
provisionar v. (also **aprovisionar**) to provision.
provisioneiro s. m. (ant.) provisioner, purveyor.
provisor s. m. provisor: 1. (eccl.) purveyor, treasurer of a religious house. 2. (ant.) supplier, provider. ‖ adj. that makes provisions.

provisorado s. m., **provisoria** f. provisorship.
provisório s. m. (Braz.) soldier of an auxiliary and provisory unit. ‖ adj. provisory, provisional, temporary, transitory, interim. ‖ **provisoriamente** adv. provisorily.
provocação s. f. (pl. **-ões**) 1. provocation, provoking, affront. 2. challenge. 3. temptation.
provocador s. m. provoker, a person who provokes. ‖ adj. provoking, provocative.
provocante adj. m. + f. (also **provocador, provocativo, provocatório** m.) provocative; tempting.
provocar v. to provoke: 1. nettle, exasperate, insult, affront, incite, irritate, stir up, instigate. 2. challenge. 3. tempt, allure. 4. cause, promote. 5. move, affect, touch.
~ **uma briga** to kick up a row. ~ **risos** to cause laughter. ~ **sono** to cause sleep.
proxeneta s. m. + f. match-maker, procurer, pimp, intermediary.
proxenético adj. intermediary, of or referring to a match-maker.
proxenetismo s. m. match-making, profession of a procurer.
proximal adj. m. + f. (pl. **-ais**) (anat.) proximal.
proximidade s. f. 1. proximity: a) nearness, contiguity. b) kinship. 2. ~**s** pl. surroundings, vicinity, neighbourhood. 3. little while.
próximo s. m. fellow creature, fellow man. ‖ adj. 1. near, close by, neighbour(ing), adjacent. 2. next. 3. coming, impending, forthcoming.
amor ao ~ charity, altruism. **no dia 10 p. p. (~ passado)** on the 10th. of last month. **no** ~ **ano** in the next year. **no** ~ **futuro** in the near future. **o fim do ano está** ~ the year is coming to its end.
pruca s. f. (Braz., pop.) round wooden seat.
prudência s. f. prudence: 1. circumspection, judiciousness, common sense. 2. caution, discretion. 3. wisdom.
prudencial adj. m. + f. (pl. **-ais**) prudential, discreet, wise. ‖ ~**mente** adv. prudentially.
prudenciar v. 1. to recommend prudence. 2. to be prudent.
prudente adj. m. + f. prudent: 1. discreet, judicious. 2. circumspect, sensible. 3. provident. 4. cautious, careful, thoughtful. 5. wise. ‖ ~**mente** adv. prudently.
pruinoso adj. (bot.) pruinose.
prumada s. f. the vertical (plumb) line.
prumagem s. f. (pl. **-ens**) sounding, plumbing.
prumar v. to sound, plumb, take soundings.
prumo s. m. 1. (archit.) plumb bob (plate A 7). 2. (naut.) plummet, lead, sounding line. 3. cleverness, prudence, common sense, good judgement. 4. saddle (graftage).
a ~ plumb, perpendicular.
pruniforme adj. m. + f. pruniform.
prurido s. m. (also **pruído**) 1. itch, itching. 2. (path.) prurigo, pruritus. 3. (fig.) burning desire, craving; impatience.
pruriente adj. m. + f. itching.
prurigem s. f. (pl. **-ens**) (path., also **prurigo**) prurigo, pruritus: inflammatory disease of the skin.
pruriginoso adj. pruriginous.
prurir v. (also **pruir**) 1. to itch; cause pruritus. 2. to want eagerly. 3. to stimulate. 4. to please, flatter.
prussianismo s. m. Prussianism.
prussianização s. f. (pl. **-ões**) Prussianization.
prussianizar v. to Prussianize.
prussiano s. m. Prussian: native or inhabitant of Prussia. ‖ adj. Prussian.
prussiato s. m. (chem.) prussiate.

prússico adj. prussic (acid).
psamito s. m. (geol.) psammite: any sandstone.
psamófilo adj. (bot.) psammophilous: living in the sand.
psefite s. f. (geol.) psephite.
pselismo s. m. psellism: any defect of speech.
pselafógnatos s. m. pl. (zool.) Pselaphognatha, a subclass of soft-bodied millipeds.
pseudo prefix. pseudo: false, fake.
pseudocarpo s. m. (bot.) pseudocarp.
pseudo-esfera s. f. (pl. **pseudo-esferas**) (geom.) pseudosphere.
pseudomorfo adj. pseudomorphous.
pseudomorfose s. f. pseudomorphosis.
pseudonímia s. f. pseudonymity.
pseudonímico adj. pseudonymic.
pseudônimo s. m. pseudonym: a fictitious or pen name. ‖ adj. pseudonymous.
pseudópode s. m. (zool.) pseudopodium.
pseudoprofeta s. m. false prophet.
pseudoscopia s. f. pseudoscopy.
pseudospermo s. m. (bot.) pseudospermium.
psicagogia s. f. ceremony in which the souls of deceased persons are invoked.
psicagogo s. m. psychagogue: person who invokes the souls of the dead.
psicalgia s. f. (med.) psychalgia, mental distress.
psicálgico adj. (med.) psychalgic.
psicanálise s. f. psychoanalysis: exploration of the unconscious mind, after Freud, in order to heal nervous diseases.
psicanalista s. m. + f. psychoanalyst. ‖ adj. psychoanalytical.
psicastenia s. f. (path.) psychasthenia: neurotic obsessions, phobias.
psicastênico s. m. person suffering from psychasthenia. ‖ adj. psychasthenic.
psichê s. m. dressing table.
psicodinâmico adj. psychodynamic.
psicodinamismo s. m. (philos.) psychodynamics.
psicofísica s. f. psychophysics.
psicofísico adj. psychophysic.
psicofisiologia s. f. psychophysiology.
psicogenia s. f. psychogenesis, creation of the soul.
psicogênico adj. psychogenic.
psicognosia s. f. psychognosis.
psicognóstico adj. psychognostic.
psicografar v. to write through spiritual agency.
psicografia s. f. psychography, writing through spiritual agency.
psicográfico adj. psychographic.
psicógrafo s. m. 1. psychographer: a medium who writes upon the influence of spirits. 2. psychograph: instrument used in psychography.
psicolepsia s. f. psycholepsia.
psicologia s. f. psychology: the science that deals with the human mind, the phenomena of behaviour.
psicológico adj. psychological. ‖ **psicologicamente** adv. psychologically.
psicologismo s. m. (philos.) psychologism.
psicologista s. m. + f. psychologist.
psicólogo s. m. psychologist, person skilled in psychology.
psicomancia s. f. divination by evoking souls.
psicomante s. m. + f. soothsayer who evokes souls for his divination.
psicometria s. f. psychometry: measurement of mental activity.
psicométrico adj. psychometric.
psicômetro s. m. psychometer.
psiconeurose s. f. psychoneurosis.
psiconeurótico adj. psychoneurotic.
psicopata s. m. + f. psychopath: person suffering

from a mental disorder. ‖ adj. psychopathic.
psicopatia s. f. psychopathy, mental disorder.
psicopático adj. psychopathic.
psicopatologia s. f. psychopathology: the study of mental disorders.
psicopatológico adj. psychopathological.
psicose s. f. psychosis: a mental derangement.
psicotécnica s. f. psychotechnology.
psicotecnológico adj. psychotechnological.
psicoterapia s. f. (med.) psychotherapy, psychotherapeutics.
psicoterápico adj. psychotherapic.
psicótico s. m. psychotic, a psychotic person. ‖ adj. psychotic: 1. of or having the nature of a psychosis. 2. having a psychosis.
psicotrópico s. m. (med.) a psychotropic drug. ‖ adj. psychotropic: acting on the mind (of a drug).
psicroestesia s. f. (path.) psychroesthesia: morbid sensation of cold.
psicrometria s. f. psychrometry.
psicrômetro s. m. psychrometer: an instrument for measuring the vapour in the atmosphere.
psila s. f. Psylla, a jumping plant louse.
psilo s. m. a tamer of snakes.
psilomelanita s. f. (min.) psilomelane: a hydrous oxide of manganese.
psique s. f. psyche, the human soul.
psiquialgia s. f. psychalgia, mental distress.
psiquiálgico adj. of or pertaining to psychalgia.
psiquiatra s. m. + f. psychiatrist.
psiquiatria s. f. psychiatry: that part of medical science dealing with mental disorders.
psiquiátrico adj. psychiatric(al).
psíquico adj. psychic: of or pertaining to the soul or mind. ‖ **psiquicamente** adv. psychically.
psiquismo s. m. psychism.
psitacídeo s. m. (ornith.) one of the Psittacidae (parrots). ‖ adj. of or pertaining to the Psittacidae.
psitacismo s. m. psittacism; vain talk, verbosity.
psitacose s. f. (path.) psittacosis, a disease of parrots transmissible to man.
psiu! interj. pst! hush!
psoas s. m. pl. (anat.) psoas: any of the two muscles of the loin.
psoríaco adj. (path.) psoriatic.
psoríase s. f. (path.) psoriasis: a chronic skin disease.
ptármico adj. sternutative, ptarmic, that causes sneezing.
pteridófitos s. m. pl. (bot.) Pteridophyta, a group of flowerless plants: ferns.
pteridografia s. f. (also **pterigrafia**) a description of the Pteridophyta.
pterigóide adj. m. + f., **pterigóideo** m. (anat.) pterygoid, wing-shaped.
ptério, ptérion s. m. (anat.) pterion: juncture of the frontal, parietal and sphenoid bones (skull).
pterocarpo adj. (bot.) pterocarpous.
pterodáctilo, pterodátilo s. m. pterodactyl: one of the extinct flying reptiles. ‖ adj. (zool.) pterodactylous.
pteróforo adj. (ent.) pterophorid.
pteróforos s. m. (ent.) Pterophoridae (moths).
pteróide adj. m. + f., **pteróideo** m. 1. (bot.) fernlike. 2. winglike.
pteroma s. m. (archit.) pteroma: enclosed space as of a portico.
pterópode s. m. (zool.) pteropod, one of the Pteropoda. ‖ adj. m. + f. (zool.) pteropod, having a foot shaped as a winglike lobe or paddle (molluscs).
pterópodes s. m. pl. (zool.) Pteropoda, a division of Tectibranchia (gastropod molluscs).
pterossauro s. m. pterosaur: a fossilized flying reptile.

ptialina s. f. (biochem.) ptyalin: a ferment contained in saliva.
ptialismo s. m. (path.) ptyalism, excessive salivation.
ptilose s. f. (path.) ptilosis: loss of the eyelashes.
ptolemaico adj. Ptolemaic: of or referring to Ptolomy, the geographer and astronomer.
ptomaína s. f. ptomaine: poisenous matter produced by putrefaction.
ptose s. f. (path.) ptosis: prolapse of an organ.
pua s. f. 1. point, prick, prong. 2. point of a spur. 3. point of a drill; bit. 4. brace (for a bit). 5. iron spur for a game-cock. 6. (Braz., sl.) drunkenness.
~ de gaioleiro Archimedean drill (plate F 8).
puã s. f. a (small) crustacean (Callinectes sapidus).
puaço s. m. a goad with a (pointed) spur.
puava adj. m. + f. (Braz.) 1. shy, skittish. 2. unruly, untractable. 3. peevish, cranky.
puba s. f. 1. steeped or macerated cassava. 2. moist and damp grassy ground. 3. coquetry, dandyism. 4. (N. Braz.) stalled ox.
pubar v. to steep cassava in water in order to make it ferment.
puberdade s. f. puberty: period at which sexual maturity is reached.
púbere adj. m. + f. pubescent: reaching puberty, sexual maturity.
pubescência s. f. 1. pubescence, the age of puberty. 2. fine hairy growth, fuzz.
pubescente adj. m. + f. 1. pubescent, reaching maturity. 2. covered with a fine growth of hair; fuzzy.
pubescer s. m. puberty. ‖ v. to reach sexual maturity, attain the age of puberty.
pubiano, púbico adj. pubic: of or pertaining to the pubis.
pubicórneo adj. having the horns covered with hair.
púbis s. m., sg. + pl. (anat.; also **pube**) pubis: the bone forming the anterior part of the~pelvis.
publicação s. f. (pl. -ões) publication: 1. act or fact of publishing. 2. thing published as: a leaflet, book.
as últimas, mais recentes -ões the latest publications.
publicador s. m. publisher. ‖ adj. publishing.
pública-forma s. f. (pl. **públicas-formas**) an authenticated copy (of a document).
publicano s. m. (ancient Rome) publican: collector of tolls.
publicar v. to publish: 1. make known, divulge, spread, disclose. 2. announce, proclaim, declare. 3. bring out books for sale.
acaba de ser publicada uma nova edição da obra a new edition of the book has just been published.
publicidade s. f. publicity: 1. quality of being public. 2. divulgement. 3. advertisement, advertising.
publicista s. m. + f. publicist: 1. a writer on law. 2. a journalist.
publicitário s. m. person who works in the advertising field.
público s. m. 1. public, the people in general. 2. audience, auditorium, hearers, spectators. ‖ adj. public: 1. of or referring to the public. 2. open to all, not private. 3. of or pertaining to the nation or the state.
cargo ~ public office, government appointment. **é de domínio ~** it is common knowledge. **emprego ~** public appointment. **empréstimos ~s** government loans. **em ~** publicly. **promotor ~** public prosecutor. **tornar ~** to make known. **vendido em hasta -a** sold by auction.
publícola s. m. person who loves the people, democrat.

pubo adj. (N. Braz.) 1. fermented. 2. rotten. 3. worn out, tired, fogged.

puçá s. m. 1. (N. Braz.): a) net to catch shrimps. b) tassel of a hammock. 2. a sort of lace. 3. the fruit of the **puçazeiro** (Rauwolfia bahiensis).

puçanga s. f. home-made medicine, household medicine; magical medicine, fetish.

puçanguara s. m. (Braz., Minas) quack, healer.

púcara s. f., **púcaro** m. small pot, cup or mug with ears; drinking cup.

puçazeiro s. m. plant of the family (Rauwolfia bahiensis).

puceiro s. m. a vintager's basket.

pucela s. f. virgin, maid.

pucínia s. f. Pucinia: a genus of fungi.

puço s. m. (N. Braz.) a fishing implement.

pudendo adj. 1. ashamed. 2. shameful. 3. bashful. 4. pudendal.

as partes -as the pudenda.

pudente adj. m. + f. bashful; chaste; modest.

pudera! interj. small wonder! why!

pudibundo adj. 1. bashful, shameful, shamefaced, modest; pudic; chaste. 2. (fig.) rubicund; blushing.

pudicícia s. f. 1. pudicity, chastity, modesty. 2. bashfulness, propriety, shyness.

pudico adj. chaste, modest, bashful, shy. ‖ **pudicamente** adv. bashfully, modestly.

pudim s. m. (pl. **-ins**) 1. (cul.) pudding. 2. (geol., also **pudingue**) pudding stone.

pudor s. m. 1. modesty, chastity. 2. bashfulness, shamefacedness, propriety. 3. shyness.

atentado ao ～ indecent assault. **sem** ～ shameless, unchaste.

puera s. f. (N. Braz., also **ipueira**) 1. pond formed by overflowing rivers. 2. any pool or marshland.

puerícia s. f. childhood; boyhood.

puericultura s. f. child welfare, child care.

pueril adj. m. + f. (pl. **-is**) puerile, childish, foolish, trivial. ‖ ～**mente** adv. childishly.

puerilidade s. f. puerility, childishness, foolishness; futile talk or action, futility.

puerilizar-se v. to behave like a child, become puerile.

puérpera s. f. parturient woman, woman in labour.

puerperal adj. m. + f. (pl. **-ais**) puerperal: of or pertaining to childbirth.

puerpério s. m. (med.) puerperium: the period or state of confinement after labour.

puf! interj. pooh!

pufe s. m. 1. pad or puff of a dress. 2. impudent. 3. pouf.

pufismo s. m. impudent advertising.

púgil s. m. (pl. **-eis**) pugilist, boxer. ‖ adj. m. + f. pugilistic, pertaining to box(ing).

pugilato s. m. 1. boxing, pugilism. 2. serious discussion.

pugilismo s. m. pugilism, boxing, art of boxing.

pugilista s. m. + f. pugilist, boxer; prize-fighter.

pugilo s. m. pinch, quantity that can be taken with two fingers.

pugna s. f. combat, fight, battle, contention, struggle; serious discussion.

pugnacidade s. f. pugnacity, quarrelsome disposition, fighting mood, combativeness.

pugnador adj. pugnacious, combative.

pugnar v. 1. to fight, combat (**por** for; **contra** against). 2. to defend vigorously. 3. to strife, endeavour, struggle. 4. to debate, discuss seriously.

～ **por seus direitos** to fight for one's rights.

pugnaz adj. m. + f. 1. pugnaceous, combative, ready to fight. 2. swaggering. 3. quarrelsome.

puldeira s. f. polishing powder.

puído adj. threadbare.

puir v. 1. to polish. 2. to abrade, wear off.

puíta (I) s. f. a heavy object, a stone or the like, used as an anchor.

puíta (II) s. f. (S. Braz., also **cuíca**) keglike popular musical instrument emitting a grunting sound.

puitar v. (also **poitar, poutar**) to stop, anchor a boat in the middle of the stream.

pujança s. f. 1. puisance, power, might. 2. strength, force, vigour, vitality. 3. exuberance.

pujante adj. m. + f. 1. puissant: strong, powerful, mighty, vigorous, forcible. 2. magnificent. 3. dauntless, daring.

pujar v. 1. to surpass, excel. 2. to conquer, overpower. 3. to exert o. s., struggle for.

pula s. f. (cards) pool.

pulação s. f. (pl. **-ões**) act of jumping.

puladinho s. m. (Braz.) dance of African origin similar to **samba**.

pulado adj. (Braz.) said of the fire scattered by the wind (when land is cleared by burning).

pulador adj. m., **pulante** m. + f. jumping, leaping, hopping.

pula-pula s. m. (pl. **pulas-pulas, pula-pulas**) (Braz., ornith.) a warbler.

pular v. 1. to leap, jump, vault. 2. to bounce, hop. 3. to spring. 4. to pullulate, swarm or abound. 5. to beat, throb (heart). 6. to progress.

～ **a cerca** to vault over the fence. ～ **a corda** to skip rope. ～ **de contente** to leap for joy. ～ **sobre o muro** to clear the wall.

pulcrícomo adj. (poet.) having beautiful hair.

pulcritude s. f. (poet.) pulchritude, beauty, grace.

pulcro adj. (poet.) pulchritudinous, beautiful.

pule s. f. pool, ticket (horse racing).

pulga s. f. (ent.) flea.

andar com a ～ **atrás da orelha** to be uneasy, fear the possibility that something disagreeable may happen. **catar** ～**s** (fig.) to go into details, examine carefully.

pulga-d'água s. f. (pl. **pulgas-d'água**) water flea.

pulgão s. m. (pl. **-ões**) a plant louse.

pulgoso adj. full of fleas, infested with fleas.

pulguedo s. m. 1. a great quantity of fleas. 2. place infested with fleas. 3. (S. Braz.) group of poor tumble-down houses.

pulgueiro s. m. (pop.) blanket.

pulguento adj. full of or infested with fleas.

pulha s. f. 1. jest, joke. 2. fib. 3. trickery. 4. indecency, foul words. 5. m.: a) scoundrel. b) blunderer. ‖ adj. m. + f. 1. despicable, contemptible. 2. indecent. 3. slipshod.

pulhice s. f. 1. low action or word, nasty trick, roguery. 2. miserable way of living. 3. poorness; shabbiness; stinginess.

pulicídeos s. m. pl. (ent.) Pulicidae, the flea family.

pulmão s. m. (pl. **-ões**) 1. (anat.) lung(s), the organ of respiration. 2. (fig.) strong voice.

～ **de aço** iron lung.

pulmoeira s. f. tuberculosis of cattle.

pulmonar adj. m. + f. pulmonary: of or pertaining to the lungs.

pulmonária s. f. (bot.) a lungwort (a lichen, Pulmonaria).

pulmonia, pulmonite s. f. (pop. form of **pneumonia**) pneumonia.

pulmotuberculose s. f. (path.) tuberculosis of the lungs.

pulo s. m. 1. jump, leap, skip, vault; rebound. 2. jerk, start, dash. 3. palpitation. 4. agitation.

aos ～**s** by leaps, by bounds. **dar** ～**s de alegria** to leap for joy. **dar um** ～ to take a leap. **em dois** ～**s** immediately, without delay. **levantar-se num** ～ to jump to one's feet.

pulo-do-nove s. m. (pl. **pulos-do-nove**) (Braz., sl.) a sort of cheating a victim at the gambling table.

pulôver s. m. pullover (plate R 6, 7).

pulpeiro s. m. (S. Braz.) innkeeper; storekeeper.

pulperia s. f. (S. Braz.) a country store or inn.

pulpite s. f. pulpitis: inflammation of the dental pulp.

púlpito s. m. pulpit: 1. stand from which the preacher speaks. 2. preaching, pulpit eloquence.

pulsação s. f. (pl. **-ões**) 1. pulsation: rhythmical vibrating or throbbing, beating. 2. pulse.

pulsar v. 1. to pulsate, beat or throb rhythmically, pulse. 2. to impel. 3. to vibrate. 4. to strike (keys or chords of an instrument).

pulsátil adj. m. + f. (pl. **-eis**) pulsatile; throbbing.

pulsatila s. f. (bot.) pulsatilla: the pasqueflower.

pulsativo adj. pulsative, pulsatory, throbbing rhythmically.

pulsear v. 1. to take the pulse. 2. to apalpate; feel, grope, observe. 3. (S. Braz.) to seize or take hold of resolutely.

pulseira s. f. bracelet, wristband, bangle, wristlet (plate J 3).

pulsímetro s. m. pulsimeter, sphygmograph: instrument for measuring or recording pulsations.

pulso s. m. 1. pulse: rhythmical beating or throbbing of the pulse. 2. wrist. 3. (fig.) strength, vigour. ~ **fraco** weak pulse. ~ **irregular** irregular pulse. ~ **rápido** fast beating pulse. **a** ~ by force. **de** ~ strong, firm, energetic. **tomar o** ~ 1. to take the pulse. 2. (fig.) to grope, observe.

pulsógrafo s. m. pulsimeter.

pultáceo adj. pultaceous, pappy, macerated, softened.

pululância s. f. pullulation, abundant growth, luxuriance; puisance.

pululante adj. m. + f. pullulating, teeming, abounding with, rank.

pulular v. 1. to pullulate: a) produce abundantly. b) grow rankly. c) swarm with. d) sprout or spring up. 2. (fig.) to boil, be ebullient, be agitated.

pulveráceo adj. covered with dust.

pulvéreo adj. dusty, like dust, reduced to dust.

pulverescência s. f. pulverulence.

pulverização s. f. (pl. **-ões**) pulverization. 1. transformation into powder. 2. (fig.) destruction.

pulverizado adj. pulverized, in form of powder.

pulverizador s. m. pulverizer; sprayer. ‖ adj. pulverizing, reducing to dust; spraying.

pulverizar v. 1. to pulverize: a) reduce to powder or dust. b) spray. c) destroy utterly, demolish. 2. ~**se** to be reduced to powder or dust.

pulverizável adj. m. + f. (pl. **-áveis**) pulverizable.

pulveroso adj. powdery, pulverulent.

pulverulência s. f. pulverulence.

pulverulento adj. pulverulent; powdered, covered with dust.

pum! interj. boom, pang.

puma s. m. (zool.) puma (Felis concolor).

puna s. f. 1. cold plateau in the Andes. 2. mountain sickness (of the Andes).

punaré s. m. (N. Braz.) a large reddish rat. ‖ adj. yellowish, tan (horse).

punção s. f. (pl. **-ões**) 1. puncture, prick, perforation. 2. act or fact of puncturing. 3. m.: a) punch, stamp, awl (plate M 6). b) (med.) stippler.

punçar v. (also **puncionar**) 1. to punch. 2. to puncture.

punceta s. f. (mech.) cutting tool.

pun(c)tiforme adj. m. + f. (bot.) pointlike.

pun(c)tura s. f. puncture: hole caused by puncturing.

pundonor s. m. 1. point of honour. 2. sense of honour. 3. self-respect, honour, dignity, decorum.

pundonoroso adj. 1. nice in points of honour. 2. honour-loving; gentlemanly. 3. self-respecting. 4. daring, proud.

punga s. m. 1. (Braz.) poor horse. 2. victim of a pickpocket. 3. thing stolen by a pickpocket. 4. pickpocket. 5. a pickpocket's doings. ‖ adj. m. + f. 1. inferior, of low quality. 2. last (horse-race).

pungente adj. m. + f. pungent: 1. poignant, piercing. 2. painful, bitter. 3. acrid, biting.

pungidor s. m. person who or thing that causes pungency. ‖ adj. pungent.

pungimento s. m. 1. hurting, distress. 2. compunction. 3. stimulus, incitement.

pungir v. 1. to prick, pierce. 2. to hurt. 3. to vex, irritate, torment. 4. to stimulate, incite. 5. to sprout.

pungitivo adj. pungent; piercing.

punguear v. to steal things from people's pockets, pick pockets.

punguista s. m. (also **punga**) pickpocket, pilferer.

punhada s. f. cuff, a blow with the fist.

punhado s. m. 1. handful. 2. a few, small number.

punhal s. m. (pl. **-ais**) 1. dagger, poniard. 2. (fig.) severe offence.

punhalada s. f. 1. stab with a dagger. 2. (fig.) serious offence.

punhete s. m. mitten.

punho s. m. 1. fist. 2. wrist. 3. handle (plates C 13, P 1, S 2). 4. hilt or handle of a sword. 5. handful. 6. a) cuff (of a shirt) (plate R 7). b) (obs.) ruffle. 7. (naut.) clew, tack, throat, peak (of a sail) (plate B 10). ~ **cerrado, fechado** clenched fist. **de próprio** ~ in one's own handwriting. **com a espada em** ~ with the drawn sword.

punibilidade s. f. punishability.

punicáceas s. f. pl. (bot.) Punicaceae, the pomegranate family.

punição s. f. (pl. **-ões**) punishment; penalty, fine.

puníceo adj. reddish, like a pomegranate.

púnico s. m. Punic: the language of Carthage. ‖ adj. Punic: of or pertaining to Carthage.

punidor s. m. punisher. ‖ adj. punishing.

punir (I) v. 1. to punish, inflict a penalty. 2. to reprimand or adopt corrective measures.

punir (II) v. 1. to figth or struggle for. 2. to take up the cudgels for.

punitivo adj. punitive, punishing.

punível adj. m. + f. (pl. **-íveis**) punishable; deserving punishment.

pupa s. f. (zool.) pupa.

pupila s. f. pupil: 1. (anat.) the opening of the iris (plate O). 2. ward, scholar, underage girl in charge of a tutor.

pupilagem s. f. (pl. **-ens**) tutelage; pupilage; wardship.

pupilar (I) adj. m. + f. pupillary: 1. (anat.) of or pertaining to the pupil of the eye. 2. of or referring to a pupil, ward or scholar.

pupilar (II) v. to cry (peacock).

pupilar-se v. to submit as a ward or scholar.

pupilo s. m. 1. ward, pupil, scholar. 2. orphan in charge of a tutor. 3. underaged boy. 4. protegé.

pupíparo s. m. (ent.) the Pupitara: a division of diptera that develop the young as pupae. ‖ adj. pupiparous.

pupunha s. f. the fruit of the **pupunheira**.

pupunheira s. f. a spiny palm tree (Guilielma speciosa).

purê s. m. 1. purée. 2. pap, pulp.

pureza s. f. pureness, purity: 1. quality or state of being pure. 2. cleanness; perfection. 3. innocence, freeness from sin.

purga s. f. 1. purgative, laxative, aperient. 2. (Braz.) a purgative plant.

purgação s. f. (pl. -ões) purgation, purification.

purgador s. m. 1. purger, refiner. 2. (Braz.) workman in charge of purging the sugar in a mill.

purgante s. m. (also **purga** f., **purgativo** m.) purgative, a purging medicine, aperient. ‖ adj. m. + f. purgative, laxative.

purgar v. to purge: 1. clean. 2. purify. 3. refine. 4. clear of guilt, expiate. 5. (med.) cause evacuation.

purgativo s. m. purgative. ‖ adj. purgative.

purgatório s. m. (rel.) purgatory: 1. purification of the souls of the death. 2. any place of temporary suffering.

ter o ~ em vida to have much to suffer.

purgueira s. f. the edible seed of the pine tree.

puri s. m. (Braz.) 1. a variety of cassava. 2. an Indian half-breed.

puridade s. f. 1. purity. 2. (obs.) secret.

à ~ in secret.

purificação s. f. (pl. -ões) purification: 1. cleaning. 2. refining. 3. clearing.

Purificação de Nossa Senhora Purification of the Virgin Mary, Candlemas, on February 2nd.

purificador s. m. 1. purifier, refiner. 2. (eccl.) purificator. 3. finger bowl, finger glass. ‖ adj. (also **purificante** m. + f., **purificativo, purificatório** m.) purifying.

purificar v. 1. to purify: a) clean. b) refine. c) clear. d) free from sin or guilt. 2. **~-se** to become purified; purify o. s.

puriforme adj. m. + f. puriform, like pus.

purina s. f. (chem.) purin(e): a compound related to uric acid.

purismo s. m. purism, rigid purity of language.

purista s. m. + f. purist: person who is very careful about language and style.

puritanismo s. m. 1. Puritanism: the doctrines and practices of the Puritans. 2. (fig.) puritanism: (ostentatious) austerity of principles.

puritano s. m. 1. Puritan: one of the English Protestants of the 16th and 17th centuries. 2. puritan: very austere person, esp. regarding principles and morals. ‖ adj. puritan.

puro adj. 1. pure: 2. clear. 3. unmingled. 4. undefiled, uncorrupted, unspoiled. 5. unmixed, unadulterated. 6. blameless. 7. innocent, chaste. 8. correct, exact (style). 9. genuine. 10. mere, simple. 11. untainted, stainless.

-a bobagem pure nonsense. **-a e simplesmente impossível** just impossible. **à -a força** by sheer force. **água -a** pure water.

púrpura s. f. 1. purple: a) red-blue colour or pigment. b) purple cloth. c) a king's or cardinal's purple robe. d) royal power. e) cardinalate. 2. purpura: a) (med.) a morbid condition of the blood vessels that causes spots on the skin. b) (zool.) a genus of gastropods.

purpurado s. m. (R. C. Church) cardinal. ‖ adj. 1. clad in purple. 2. raised to the cardinalate.

purpurar v. 1. to purple: make or dye purple. 2. to clothe in purple. 3. to raise to the cardinalate.

purpurear, purpurejar v. (also **purpurizar**) 1. to purple, make red. 2. **~-se** to become purple, turn red. 3. to blush.

purpúreo adj. (also **purpurino, púrpuro**) purple; purplish; red).

purpúrico adj. (chem.) purpuric.

purpurina s. f. 1. (chem.) purpurin: a red colouring matter obtained from madder. 2. plant of the family Melastomaceae (order Myrtales).

purrinhém s. m. (pl. -éns) 1. small and very poor house or room. 2. anything poor and miserable.

puruí-grande, puruí-grande-da-mata, puruí-pequeno s. m. (pl. **puruís-grandes, puruís-grandes-da-mata, puruís-pequenos**) plants of the family Rubiaceae.

purulência s. f. purulence, purulency, formation or secretion of pus, suppuration.

purulento adj. purulent, suppurative; full of pus, consisting of pus.

purumã s. m. a palmaceous plant (Pourouma guianensis).

purunga s. f., **purungo** m. (also **parongo**) calabash gourd.

purupaqui s. m. (bot.) a Papilonacea (Crotolaria incana).

pururuca s. f. (Braz.) 1. a young coconut. 2. gravel, coarse sand. 3. = **canjica**. 4. a variety of hard maize. ‖ adj. hard; friable (coconut).

pus s. m. (med.) pus, matter.

formar ~ to suppurate, fester.

pusilânime s. m. + f. fainthearted person, weakling, coward. ‖ adj. pusillanimous, fainthearted, coward.

pusilanimidade s. f. pusillanimity, faintheartedness, cowardice.

pústula s. f. 1. (med.) pustule, pimple. 2. (fig.): a) corruption, vice. b) scoundrel, awfully bad fellow.

pustulado s. m. person affected with pustules. ‖ adj. (also **pustulento**) pustuled.

pustuloso adj. pustular, pustulous, of the nature of a pustule.

puta s. f. (vulg.) whore.

putativo adj. putative, supposititious, supposed.

puteação s. f. (pl. -ões) (S. Braz.) a dressing down with foul words.

puteal s. m. (pl. -ais) well curb.

putear v. (S. Braz.) to scold using foul language.

putirão, putirom, putirum s. m. = **muxirão**.

putredinoso adj. 1. rotten, putrid. 2. corrupt; foul.

putrefação s. f. (pl. -ões) 1. putrefaction, decomposition, putridness, putridity. 2. corruption.

putrefaciente adj. m. + f., **putrefativo** m. (also **putrefatório**) putrefactive, putrefying, causing putrefaction.

putrefato adj. (also **putrefeito**) 1. putrefied, rotten, putrid, decayed. 2. corrupt.

putrefazer v. (also **putrificar**) 1. to putrefy, rot, decompose, decay. 2. to corrupt. 3. **~-se** to become rotten or corrupt.

putrescência s. f. putrescence.

putrescente adj. m. + f. putrescent.

putrescibilidade s. f. putrefactiveness.

putrescível adj. m. + f. (pl. -íveis) putrescible, susceptible of putrefaction.

pútrido adj. 1. putrid, rotten, putrefied, decayed. 2. corrupt. 3. pestilential.

putuca s. m. (N. Braz., pop.) ill-starred fellow.

putumuju s. m. (Braz.) a tree of the family Leguminosae (Centrolobium robustum).

puxa (I) s. m. (Braz.) 1. (S., vulg.) flatterer, lickspittle. 2. (N.) a certain dance.

puxa (II) interj. of surprise: why! now!

~, como eu estou cansado! I am tired I can tell you! **~, que caro!** why! how expensive!

puxá s. m. (Braz.) asthma.

puxação s. f. (pl. -ões) transport of wood in the Amazonian forests.

puxada s. f. 1. draft: a) act or fact of drawing (as loads by an animal). b) act of taking in the net (fishing). 2. long way or journey. 3. pull, go. 4. lean-to (building). 5. first card which a partner plays.

puxadeira s. f. 1. strap, band, string, loop. 2. handle, knob or the like. 3. pulling of a shoe.

puxadinho s. m. dandy, fop, coxcomb. ‖ adj. dandyish, foppish, coxcombical.

puxado (I) s. m. (Braz.) 1. (pop.) asthma. 2. lean-to (building). ‖ adj. 1. elegant, spruce. 2. refined, affected (speech). 3. exquisite (food). 4. high, exorbitant (price). 5. exhaustive (work). 6. pulled, drawn. **foi um dia** ~ it was a tough day. **trabalho muito** ~ hard, difficult work.

puxado (II) s. m. (S. Braz.) a sort of fandango.

puxador s. m. handle, knob, puller (as of a drawer) (plate A 13).

puxadoura s. f. (also **puxadoira**, tech.) dolly.

puxa-encolhe s. m., sg. + pl. (N. Braz.) 1. vexatious indecision, irresoluteness. 2. impertinence.

puxamento s. m. 1. drawing, pulling, hauling. 2. (Braz., pop.) asthma.

puxante adj. m. + f. (also **puxativo** m.) 1. drawing, pulling. 2. piquant, sharp. 3. stimulating.

puxão s. m. (pl. -ões) pull, tug, jerk, yank. **arrancar com um** ~ to yank out. **dar um** ~ to give a wrench.

puxa-puxa s. f. (pl. **puxa-puxas**) a sort of sticky caramel.

puxar v. 1. to pull, draw, haul, drag, tug. 2. to pluck. 3. to attract, incline, dispose, impel, urge. 4. to bring along as a consequence, result in. 5. to resemble, look after. 6. (coll.) to fawn, wheedle.

~ **uma conversa** to strike up a conversation. ~ **o lustre** to wipe sparkling clean. ~ **para si** to attract to o. s. ~ **pela espada** to draw one's sword. ~ **pela língua** to make one speak or blab out secrets. ~ **pela música** to have an inclination for music. ~ **pelas orelhas** to pull a person's ears. ~ **pelo remo** to tug at the oar. ~ **por quantas tem** to do one's best. **os cavalos puxam um carro** the horses draw a cart. **a pústula puxa** the pustule suppurates (maturates).

puxa-saco s. m. sg., **puxa-sacos** sg. + pl. (Braz., coll.) wheedler, cajoler, lickspittle, toady.

puxavante s. m. 1. a farrier's butteris. 2. strongly seasoned food. 3. driving rod of a railway engine. 4. tug, pull, jerk. 5. shove, push. ‖ adj. m. + f. piquant, seasoned, stimulant.

puxavão s. m. (pl. -ões) a violent shove or push.

puxa-verão s. m. (pl. **puxa-verões**) (Braz.) bird of the family Icteridae.

puxa-vista s. m. (pl. **puxa-vistas**) sandwich man, person who carries placards or posters through the streets.

puxe! interj. begone! off with you! get out!

puxeira s. f. (Braz.) coiô, catarrh.

puxo s. m. (med.) 1. tenesmus. 2. labour, travail.

Q

Q, q s. m. sixteenth letter of the Portuguese alphabet. ‖ adj. the sixteenth of an order or class.

quacre s. m. Quaker: member of the Society of Friends.

quacrismo s. m. Quakerism: the practices or beliefs of the Quakers.

quaderna s. f. 1. (her.) quartering. 2. face of a die (or dice) with four spots.

quadernado adj. quaternate: composed of four or arranged in sets of four (leaves, flowers).

quadernal s. m. (pl. **-ais**) (also **cadernal**) pulley block.

quadra s. f. 1. square place, yard or enclosure. 2. card with four spots. 3. quatrain, quartet, stanza of four lines. 4. a series of four. 5. (Braz.) block: distance along a street between two cross streets. 6. (fig.) age, period; time; season; occasion. 7. court: place for playing basketball, tennis, hand--ball or other games. 8. lineal measure of 132 meters. 9. measure of surface equivalent to 17,424 square meters. 10. flag of a flagship.
~ **do ano** season of the year.

quadrado s. m. 1. square: a) (geom.) quadrate, parallelogram with four equal sides and four right angles. b) (math.) squared number. c) (mil.) a body o! soldiers formed into a square figure. 2. (Braz.) square truck for wood transportation. ‖ adj. 1. square, foursquare, quadrate. 2. (Braz., pop.) stupid, dull; ignorant; uncouth, rude.
~ **perfeito** a perfect square. **metro** ~ square meter. **raiz -a** (math.) square root.

quadrador s. m. 1. squarer: person who squares. 2. frame maker. ‖ adj. squaring.

quadradura s. f. = **quadratura.**

quadragenário s. m. quadragenarian: forty years old person. ‖ adj. quadragenarian: forty years old.

quadragésima s. f. 1. period of forty days. 2. (eccl.) Quadragesima: a) the first Sunday of Lent. b) (obs.) = **quaresma.**

quadragesimal adj. m. + f. (pl. **-ais**) quadragesimal, Lenten.

quadragésimo s. m. fortieth. ‖ adj. fortieth.
a -a parte the fortieth part.

quadrangulado adj. m., **quadrangular** m. + f. quadrangular: having four sides and four angles.

quadrângulo s. m. (geom.) quadrangle: polygon with four sides and four angles, tetragon, quadrilateral.

quadrantal adj. m. + f. (pl. **-ais**) (obs.) 1. cubic(al). 2. quadrantal.

quadrante s. m. 1. quadrant: the fourth part of a circle. 2. dial (of a clock).

quadrão s. m. (N. E. Braz.) an octave of sung popular poetry.

quadrar v. to square: 1. quadrate, make square. 2. (math.) multiply a number by itself. 3. (fig.) conform, beseem; agree, harmonize; fit, suit, tally.
isto quadra com o que eu ouvi this is in agreement with what I have heard.

quadrarão s. m. (pl. **-ões**) quadroon: person having one fourth Negro blood. ‖ adj. having one fourth Negro blood.

quadrático adj. quadratic: 1. square. 2. of or pertaining to a square.

quadratim s. m. (pl. **-ins**) (print.) quad(rat).

quadratriz s. f. (geom.) quadratrix.

quadratura s. f. (also **quadradura**) quadrature: 1. (math.) the finding of a square equal in area to a given curved figure. 2. (astr.) position of two heavenly bodies 90° distant from each other. 3. quarter of the moon.

descobrir a ~ **do círculo** to square the circle. **isto significa a** ~ **do círculo** that means squaring the circle.

quadrela s. f. 1. section of a wall. 2. wall (of a building).

quadrelo s. m. (obs.) quarrel: square-headed bolt shot from a crossbow.

quadrialado adj. four-winged.

quadribásico adj. (chem.) quadribasic: said of an acid with four hydrogen atoms.

quadricapsular adj. m. + f. (bot.) quadricapsular: having four capsules.

quadricelular adj. m. + f. (bot.) quadricellular: divided into four cells.

quadricipital adj. m. + f. (pl. **-ais**) (anat.) quadricipital: of or pertaining to the quadriceps.

quadricípite s. m. (anat.) quadriceps: the extensor of the thigh. ‖ adj. m. + f. quadricipital.

quadricolor adj. m. + f. four-coloured: having four different colours.

quadricórneo adj. (zool.) quadricorn(ous): having four antennae or horns.

quadrícula s. f. small square.

quadriculado adj. m., **quadricular** m. + f. checkered, ruled in squares, square-lined.
papel ~ graph paper.

quadricular v. to chequer, checker, divide into small squares, rule into squares, crossline. ‖ adj. = **quadriculado.**

quadrículo s. m. small square.

quadricúspide adj. m. + f. (bot.) quadricuspidal: provided with four sharp points.

quadridentado adj. (zool.) quadridentate.

quadridigitado adj. (zool.) quadridigitate, tetradactylous, four-fingered.

quadrienal adj. m. + f. (pl. **-ais**) quadrennial: 1. of or pertaining to a period of four years. 2. occurring once in four years.

quadriênio s. m. (also **quatriênio**) quadr(i)ennium: a period of four years.

quadrifendido, quadrífido adj. quadrifid.

quadriflóreo adj. (bot.) having four flowers.

quadrifoliado adj. (bot.) quadrifoliolate: having four leaflets (said of a compound leaf).

quadrifólio adj. (bot.) quadrifoliate.

quadriforme adj. m. + f. quadriform: having four different forms.

quadriga s. f. quadriga: 1. chariot drawn by four horses abreast. 2. set of four horses.

quadrigêmeo, quadrigêmino adj. 1. (anat.) quadrigeminal, quadrigeminous. 2. fourfold, quadruple.

quadrigeminado adj. (bot.) quadrigeminate, growing in fours.

quadrigúmeo adj. (bot.) having four edges.

quadrijugado adj. (bot.) quadrijugate.

quadríjugo adj. (poet.) four-in-hand, drawn by four horses.

quadril s. m. (pl. **-is**) 1. hip, haunch (plate C 18). 2. hipbone. 3. rump (of beef).

quadrilateral adj. m. + f. (pl. **-ais**) quadrilateral, four-sided.

quadrilátero s. m. quadrilateral: 1. (geom.) quadrangular figure or area, four-sided polygon. 2. (mil.) space defended by four enclosing fortresses. ‖ adj. four-sided.

quadrilha s. f. 1. gang, band (thieves). 2. squadron (airplanes). 3. pack (hounds). 4. (fig.) crowd. 5. (Braz., pop.) rabble, mob. 6. quadrille: a) square dance. b) any music for such dance. 7. cavalcade, joust. 8. herd of horses.
~ **de aviões** a squadron of airplanes. **uma ~ de ladrões** a gang of thieves. **vamos dançar uma ~?** let us dance a quadrille?

quadrilhado adj. = quadriculado.

quadrilheiro s. m. 1. gangster: member of a gang of thieves. 2. highwayman; bandit.

quadrilobado, quadrilobulado adj. (bot.) quadrilobate: having four lobes or lobules.

quadriloculado adj. m., **quadrilocular** m. + f. (bot.) quadrilocular.

quadrilongo s. m. (geom.) oblong, long rectangle. ‖ adj. parallelogrammic, oblong.

quadrímano adj. (zool.) quadrimanous, four-handed.

quadrimestral adj. m. + f. (pl. **-ais**) 1. concerning a period of four months. 2. happening every fourth month: occurring once in four months.

quadrimestre s. m. a period of four months.

quadrimotor s. m. airplane equipped with four motors. ‖ adj. equipped with four motors.

quadringentenário s. m. quadricentennial: the 400th anniversary of an event or its commemoration.

quadringentésimo s. m. the four hundredth. ‖ adj. four hundredth.

quadrinha s. f. (mus., poet.) popular ditty or verses, ding dong.

quadrinhos s. m. pl. (Braz.) comic strips, classic comics.

quadrinizar v. to adapt a story to a comic strip form.

quadrinômio s. m. (math.) quadrinomial: algebraic expression of four terms.

quadripartição s. f. quadripartition: division into four parts.

quadripartido, quadripartito adj. quadripartite: divided into four parts.

quadripétalo adj. (Braz., bot.) having four petals.

quadrirreme s. f. (hist.) quadrireme: galley with four banks of oars.

quadrissilábico, quadrissílabo adj. (gram.) quadrisyllabic: consisting of four syllables.

quadrivalente adj. m. + f. (chem.) quadrivalent, tetravalent: having a valence of four.

quadrivalve, quadrivalvular adj. m. + f. **quadrivalvulado** m. (bot.) quadrivalve, quadrivalvular.

quadrívio s. m. 1. place or point where four streets meet or cross; cross-roads, cross-way. 2. (Greek hist.) quadrivium, the four sciences: geometry, arithmetic, astronomy and music.

quadro s. m. 1. square, quadrilateral. 2. frame (plates A 11, M 12, V 3). 3. picture frame, mounting. 4. painting, picture, canvas (plate D 4). 5. image, figure, portrait. 6. (bill)board; notice board. 7. card, map, chart. 8. panel. 9. table, schedule. 10. list, rol, roster. 11. summary. 12. (also ~**-negro**) blackboard. 13. (theat.) scene, tableau. 14. (fig.) sight, panorama, view. 15. personnel, crew: staff. 16. (Braz., sport) team. 17. (fig.) crew, gang.
~ **a óleo** oil painting. ~ **de avisos** bulletin board, billboard. ~ **de distribuição** (elect., teleph.) switch-board. ~ (also **painel**) **de medidores** meter board, meter panel (plate E 3). ~ **sinóptico** tabular summary, synoptic chart. ~ **vivo** (theat.) tableau vivant. ~ **vivo** (Fr.) tableau vivant, living picture. **o paciente foi acometido de ~ cerebral** the patient presented a not yet identified brain problem. **exposição de ~s** picture gallery. **nosso ~ de empregados** our office force, our employees, our staff.

quadro-negro s. m. (pl. **quadros-negros**) blackboard.

quadrúmano adj. (zool.) quadrumanous, four-handed.

quadrupedante adj. m. + f. quadrupedal: quadruped, four-footed.

quadrupedar v. (poet.) to go on all four feet.

quadrúpede s. m. 1. (zool.) quadruped: four-footed animal. 2. (fig.) stupid person, brute. ‖ adj. m. + f. quadruped, four-footed.

quadruplicação s. f. (pl. **-ões**) quadruplication.

quadruplicar v. to quadruplicate: quadruple, make fourfold, multiply by four, double twice.

quádruplo s. m. quadruple: number or sum four times as great as another. ‖ adj. quadruple, fourfold.

qual adj. m. + f. (pl. **quais**) which, that which, that one, such as. ‖ pron. which, who, whom, that. ‖ conj. how, as. ‖ interj. what! fiddlesticks!
~ **deles?** which of them? ~ **destes livros você quer?** which of these books do you want? ~ **dos dois?** which of the two? ~ **é a altura daquele monte?** how high is that hill? ~ **é o cão tal é o dono** like master, like dog. ~ **nada!** nonsense! of course not! **a ~ dos nossos teatros você deseja ir?** to which of our theatres do you wish to go? **cada ~ com seu igual** birds of a feather flock together, like with like. **com o ~?** with whom? with which? **de ~ dos quadros você gostou mais?** which of the pictures did you like best? **do ~** of which; of whom. **dos quais todos concordaram** all of whom assented. **é este o motivo pelo ~ nós o fazemos** that is why we do it. **seja ~ for** be it whatever it may. **seja ~ for o lado que você escolher** whichever side you choose. **seja ~ for o resultado** whatsoever the result may be. **tal e ~** just as, just like. **tal ~ você queria** such as you would have it. **todos os quais** all of which.

qualidade s. f. quality: 1. the characteristic of anything; kind, class, qualification (plate Q). 2. property, nature. 3. character, attribute. 4. feature, trait. 5. capacity, condition. 6. rank, standing. 7. degree of excellence. 8. importance, weight. 9. aptitude, suitability.
~**s secundárias** (philos.) secondary qualities. **da melhor ~** of the first waters. **na sua ~ de professor** in his character as master. **na ~ de** in the capacity of. **tecido de boa ~** fabric of good quality.

qualificação s. f. (pl. **-ões**) 1. qualification: a) the act of qualifying. b) the state of being qualified. 2. classification, specification. 3. characterization, designation, denomination.

qualificado adj. 1. qualified, able, competent. 2. appropriate, well-tried. 3. distinct, distinguished, eminent. 4. noble.

qualificador s. m. qualifier: one who or that which qualifies; classifier. ‖ adj. qualifying.

qualificar v. 1. to qualify: a) attribute a quality to. b) classify, class. c) designate, denominate. d) (gram.) express a quality or modify the meaning. e) describe. f) characterize, distinguish. g) consider, regard, repute. 2. to enable. 3. to select, choose (the best). 4. to estimate, appreciate.

qualificativo adj. qualificative, qualifying: serving to qualify or modify.
adjetivo ~ (gram.) qualifying adjective.

qualificável adj. m. + f. (pl. **-áveis**) qualifiable: capable of being qualified, classifiable.

qualitativo adj. qualitative: determining quality.

qualquer adj. m. + f. (pl. **quaisquer**) any (person, thing, or part), some, a, an, every, either, certain. ‖ pron. any (person, thing) one, either, each, everyone.
~ **coisa** anything. ~ **dia** any day. ~ **livro** some book or other. ~ **outro** any one else, any other. ~ **outra coisa** anything else. ~ **pessoa** anybody. ~ **que seja** no matter which. ~ **um** anyone,

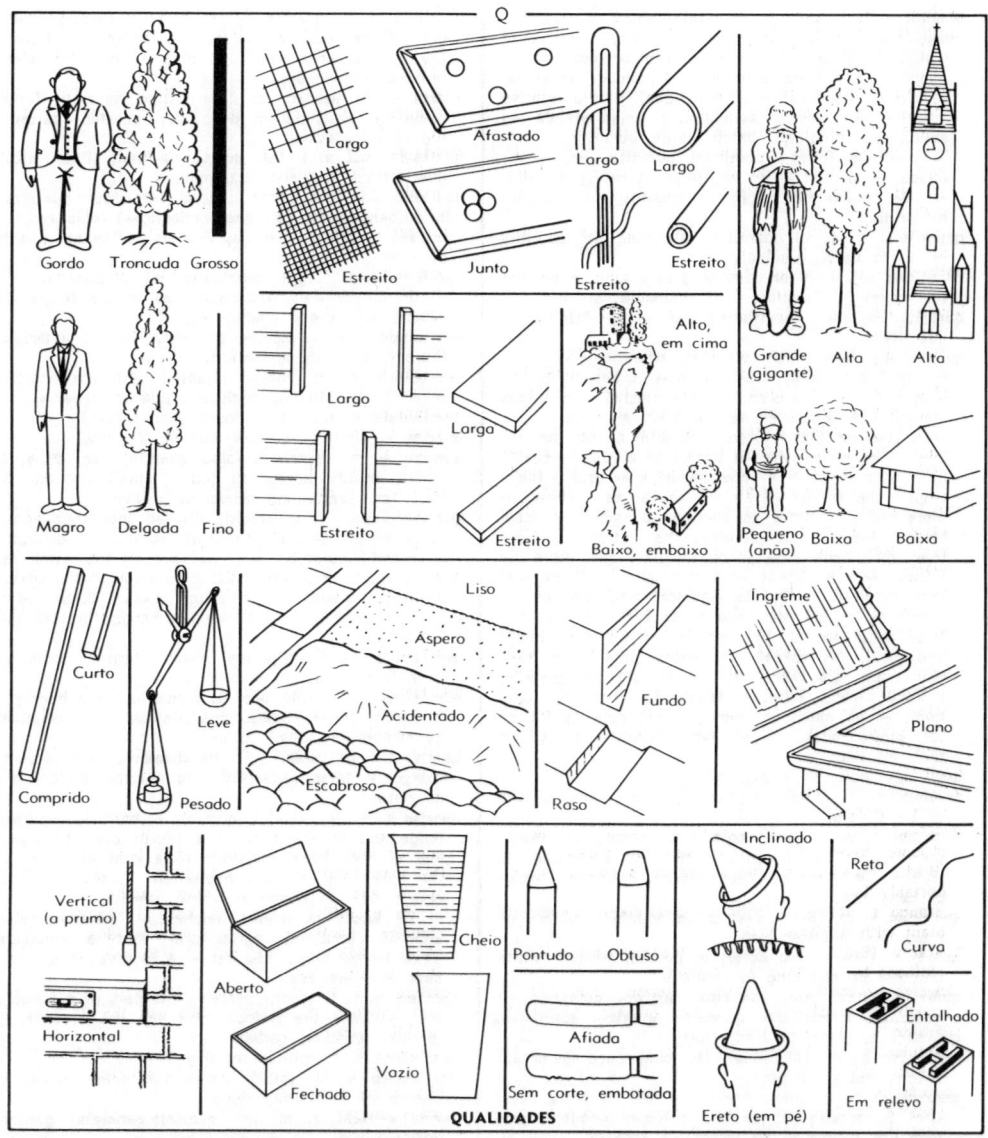

QUALIDADES

Gordo — Troncuda — Grosso — Largo — Afastado — Largo — Largo — Estreito — Estreito — Junto — Estreito — Estreito — Grande (gigante) — Alta — Alta

Magro — Delgada — Fino — Largo — Larga — Estreito — Estreito — Alto, em cima — Baixo, embaixo — Pequeno (anão) — Baixa — Baixa

Curto — Leve — Comprido — Pesado — Liso — Áspero — Acidentado — Escabroso — Raso — Fundo — Íngreme — Plano

Vertical (a prumo) — Horizontal — Aberto — Fechado — Cheio — Vazio — Pontudo — Obtuso — Afiada — Sem corte, embotada — Inclinado — Ereto (em pé) — Reta — Curva — Entalhado — Em relevo

anybody. ~ **um (entre dois) serve** either one will do. ~ **um pode ver isto** anyone can see that. **quaisquer razões que tivéssemos** whatever reason we had. **a ~ momento** at a moment's notice. **a ~ preço** at any price. **acontecerá ~ dia** it will happen some day. **de ~ jeito** somehow or other. **de ~ maneira** by any means, at all. **ela está em ~ parte do jardim** she is about the garden. **ela fez sua cama de ~ jeito** she did her bed anyhow. **ela nunca acha tempo para ~ descanso** she never has any rest. **em ~ caso** at all events. **em ~ dos dois grupos** in either group. **em ~ lugar** at any place, anywhere. **em ~ ocasião** some time or other. **em ~ outro lugar** somewhere else. **em ~ tempo** at any time. **toda e ~ pessoa** any person whatever. **utilizável sob ~ condição de tempo** all-weather.

quando adv. when: how soon? at what time? at what (or which) time. ‖ conj. when: 1. at which. 2. at what time. 3. as soon as, as. 4. at the time that, while. 5. at the moment when; in case. 6. if. 7. however, whereas. 8. even if, although. ~ **ela o viu, deu risada** when she saw him she laughed. ~ **irá ele?** when will he go? ~ **menos** at (the) least. ~ **menos se esperava** quite unexpected. ~ **moço** when young. ~ **muito** at the most, at best. **até ~?** till when? **de ~?** from when? **de ~ em ~, de vez em ~** from time to time, once in a while, occasionally. **desde ~?** since when? how long? **ele anda a pé ~ podia ir de carro** he walks when he might ride. **eu escreverei ~ tiver tempo** I shall write when I have time. **o ~ e o porquê** the when and the why.

quantia s. f. 1. amount, sum (of money). 2. quantity.

quantidade s. f. quantity: 1. the property in virtue of which anything may be measured or counted. 2. quantum. 3. amount, sum, deal. 4. number, measure. 5. (pros.) the duration of a syllable. 6. the relative duration of notes or syllables. 7. (also **grande** ~) abundance, boatload, batch, large quantity. ~ **contínua** (phys.) continual quantity. **em** ~ by heaps, in shoals. ~ **de luz** (phys.) quantity of light. ~ **de movimento** (phys.) quantity of motion; momentum.

quantificar v. 1. to quantify: determine the quantity of. 2. to value precisely.

quantioso adj. 1. of or pertaining to a sum or amount (of money). 2. numerous. 3. valuable. 4. rich.

quantitativo adj. quantitative: of or pertaining to quantity.

quanto adj. how much, all that, whatever, as much as; (pl.) how many. ‖ adv. 1. how (great, nice, far, much). 2. as to. ‖ pron. 1. how much(?); (pl.) how many (?). 2. whatever, as much as, all that. ~ **a isso** for that matter. ~ **a mim** as for me, for one. ~ **ao preço** when it comes to costs. ~ **custa?** how much is it? ~ **é?** how much? **a** ~ **está o jogo?** what's the score? ~ **eu sei** as far as I know. ~ **mais cedo**, ~ **antes** as soon as possible. ~ **mais barato, melhor** the cheaper, the better. ~ **mais tem, mais quer** the more he has, the more he wants. ~ **nós rimos!** what we have laughed! ~**s?** how many? **a** ~ **do mês estamos?** what day of the month is it? **ele não sabe a -as anda** he does not know what to do. **por -as tem** (fig.) with might and main. **-as vezes?** how many times? ~**s são?** how many are there? **por** ~ **eu sei** for anything I know. **quem sabe** ~ **tempo** for ever so long. **tanto** ~ as much as. **tanto** ~ **sabemos** as far as we know. **todos** ~**s** all who. **tudo** ~ everything that, all that.

quão adv. how, as. ‖ conj. as.

quapóia s. f. waxflower: an epiphytic tree of the genus Clusia.

quarador s. m. 1. (also **coradouro, coradoiro**) bleachground, bleachyard, place used for bleaching. 2. (Braz., fig.) sunny place which becomes insupportably hot.

quarango s. m. (Braz., also **murta-do-mato**) rubiaceous plant with a bitter bark.

quarar v. (Braz., also **corar**) to bleach: whiten (white clothes) by exposing to sunlight.

quárcico, quarcífero, quarcito, quarço, quarçoso = **quártzico, quartzífero, quartzito, quartzo, quartzoso.**

quarenta s. m. forty. ‖ adj. forty.

quarentão s. m. (pl. **-ões**), (f. **-ona**) quadragenarian: a forty years old person.

quarentena s. f. quarantine: 1. period of forty days, Lent. 2. isolation of persons, ships or goods to prevent the spread of an infectious disease.

quarentenar v. to quarantine: 1. put under quarantine. 2. be in quarantine.

quarentenário s. m. quarantiner: person who quarantines or is quarantined. ‖ adj. 1. of or pertaining to quarantine. 2. quarantining.

quarentona s. f. quadragenarian woman. ‖ adj. f. quadragenarian, forty years old (woman).

quaresma s. f. 1. Lent, Quadragesima: the forty weekdays before Easter. 2. (bot.): a) a Brazilian palm (Coccos flexuosa). b) Brazilian spiderflower. 3. (N. Braz., pop.) m. liar.

quaresmal adj. m. + f. (pl. **-ais**) Lenten, quadragesimal: of or pertaining to Lent.

quaresmar v. to observe Lent.

quaresmeira s. f. (Braz., bot., also **quaresma**) Brazilian spiderflower.

quarta s. f. 1. quarter, fourth part. 2. (Braz.) measure of capacity containing 72 liters. 3. (mus.) the interval of a fourth. 4. jug. 5. short for **quarta-feira:** Wednesday.

quartã s. f. quartan: an intermitting ague or fever occurring every fourth day. ‖ adj. quartan: pertaining to this fever.

quarta-de-final s. f. (pl. **quartas-de-final**) (Braz., ftb.) quarterfinal, a quarterfinal match.

quartado adj. quartered: divided into four quarters.

quarta-doença s. f. (pl. **quartas-doenças**) (also **quarta-moléstia**) Takes' disease, Filatoff's disease, fourth disease.

quarta-feira s. f. (pl. **quartas-feiras**) Wednesday. ~ **de cinzas** Ash Wednesday. **às quartas-feiras** on Wednesday, every Wednesday.

quartaludo adj. 1. having a defect in the quarters (horse). 2. thick and short.

quartanário s. m. person affected with the quartan fever. ‖ adj. affected with the quartan fever.

quartanista s. m. + f. a fourth-year student.

quartar v. (fenc.) to move out of the line.

quartau s. m. (Braz.) 1. (also **quartão**) nag, pony, a small, sturdy horse. 2. (obs.) small cannon. 3. (sl.) very pretty and handsome woman.

quarteado adj. 1. quartered: divided into four equal parts or quarters or into four colours or designs. 2. broad-shouldered and well-proportioned (horse).

quartear v. 1. to quarter: divide into four equal parts. 2. to adorn with four different colours. 3. to dodge by a quarter turn at sticking a banderilla into the bull.

quarteio s. m. (bullfighting) quarter turn at thrusting in a banderilla.

quarteirão s. m. (pl. **-ões**) 1. a quarter of a hundred. 2. block, (city) square, quadrilateral area bounded by streets. 3. (obs.) tithing.

quarteiro s. m. (Braz.) valet de chambre, body servant.

quartejar v. (also **esquartejar**) to quarter: divide into quarters.

quartel s. m. (pl. **-éis**) 1. quarter: a) barrack, caserne, lodgement of soldiers. b) a fourth part. c) (her.) any of four equal divisions of a coat of arms. 2. (by extension) shelter, habitation. 3. (fig.) period, epoch, age. 4. trimester, three months. ~ **de escotilha** (naut.) hatches. ~ **paulista** (also **alqueire paulista**) agricultural surface measure equal to 242 acres. **não dar** ~ **a** to give no quarter. **sem** ~ merciless.

quartela s. f. 1. (zool.) pastern: the part of a horse's foot between the fetlock joint and the coronet. 2. (archit.) bracket, corbel.

quartelada s. f. military mutiny.

quarteleiro s. m. (mil.) noncommissioned officer in charge of a military depot.

quartel-general s. m. (pl. **quartéis-generais**) general headquarters.

quarteto s. m. quartet: 1. quatrain, stanza of four lines. 2. (mus.) composition for four voices or instruments. 3. group of four singers or players who performs quartets. 4. any group of four. ~ **de cordas** string quartet. ~ **de sopro** brass-quartet. ~ **vocal** vocal quartet.

quartil s. m. quartile: aspect of planets when their longitudes differ by 90°. ‖ adj. quartile.

quartilho s. m. 1. measure of capacity equal to 0.6655 liter. 2. pint.

quartinha s. f. (Braz.) jug, pitcher.

quartinho s. m. 1. small room, cubicle. 2. (Braz., pop.) latrine, water closet.

quarto s. m. 1. the fourth part, a quarter. 2. a quarter of an hour. 3. the fourth (person or thing). 4. room (of a house). 5. bedroom. 6. (mil., naut.)

watch. 7. quarter of a hoof (horse). 8. quarter of a quadruped, haunch. 9. (typogr.) quarto. 10. (Braz.) wake (vigil over a corpse). 11. ~s haunch, flank. ‖ adj. fourth.
~ **crescente** crescent: the first quarter of the moon. ~ **de brincar** playroom. ~ **de crianças** nursery room. ~ **de despejo** lumber room. ~ **de dormir** bedroom. ~ **de intervalo** (mus.) quarter tone. ~ **de quilo** quarter of a kilogram. ~ **de solteiro** single room. ~ **dos fundos** back room. ~ **minguante** the wane of moon. ~ **mobiliado** furnished room. ~ **para casal** double room. ~ **para hóspede** guest-chamber, spare room. **este é um ~ confortável** this is a snug room. **formato em ~** (typogr.) in-quarto. **o senhor tem ~s para alugar?** have you apartments to let? **que horas são? um ~ para as duas** what time is it? it is a quarter to two. **às sete horas e um ~** at a quarter past seven. **às sete horas menos um ~** at a quarter to seven.

quarto-e-sala s. m. (pl. **quartos-e-salas**) (Braz.) a two-room apartment consisting of a bedroom and a living room.

quartola s. f. cask, hogshead, small pipe (cask). **uma ~ de vinho** a cask of wine.

quartudo adj. (Braz.) haunchy, big-hipped.

quartzífero adj. (also **quarcífero**) quartziferous: containing quartz.

quartzito s. m. (also **quarcito**) quartzite: rock composed essentialy of quartz.

quartzo s. m. (min., also **quarço**) quartz: hard vitreous mineral consisting of pure silica, the silicon dioxide.

quartzoso adj. (also **quarçoso**) 1. quartzose: composed of quartz. 2. quartzy: of or pertaining to quartz.

quase adv. 1. almost, near(ly), closely, well-night. 2. approximately, about, not quite. 3. within an ace of. 4. scarcely, hardly. 5. next to. 6. quasi, as if. ~ **a mesma coisa** pretty much the same. ~ **do seu tamanho** about your size. ~ **esqueci** I have all but forgotten. ~ **morri de susto** I was frightened to death. ~ **nada** next to nothing, little or nothing. ~ **nunca** hardly ever, almost never. ~ **sempre** nearly always, most of the time. ~ **tão alto** about as high. ~ **teria sido atropelado** he was within an ace of being run over. ~ **uma semana inteira** the inside of a week. **a água subiu ~ à beira do poço** the water rose almost to the top of the well. **é ~ impossível** it is hardly possible. **ele é ~ cego** he is nearly blind. **ele é ~ surdo** he is almost deaf. **estavam ~ todos presentes** nearly all were present. **estou ~ decidido a ir** I have half a mind to go. **são ~ sete horas** it is hard upon seven.

quase-contrato s. m. (pl. **quase-contratos**) (jur.) quasi contract.

quase-delito s. m. (pl. **quase-delitos**) (jur.) quasi delict.

quasimodal adj. m. + f. (pl. **-ais**), **quasimodesco** m. (Braz.) ugly as Quasimodo, personage of Victor Hugo's novel "Notre Dame de Paris"; monstrous.

Quasímodo s. m. 1. Low Sunday. 2. (Braz.) lubber, lout.

quassação s. f. (pl. **-ões**) quassation: the crushing of dry roots and barks, to extract their active principles.

quássia s. f. (bot.) quassia.

quaternado adj. (bot.) quaternate: consisting of four. **folha. -a** quaternate leaf.

quaternário adj. 1. quaternary: a) fourfold, made up of four things. b) Quaternary: designating the geological period following the Tertiary and still continuing. 2. (mus.) quadruple: having four beats. **compasso ~** (mus.) quadruple time.

quaternião s. m. (pharm.) balsam of four ingredients.

quaterno adj. fourfold, quartern: consisting of four (things, elements, etc.).

quati s. m. (Braz.) coati: a tropical racoonlike mammal (genus Nasua).

quatiara s. f. (Braz., zool.) a very venomous pit viper of the family Crotalidae (Bothrops cotiara).

quatorze s. m. (also **catorze**) fourteen. ‖ adj. fourteen.

quatorzeno s. m. (also **décimo quarto**) fourteenth.

quatreiro s. m. (Braz.) cattle thief, a rustler.

quatriduano adj. lasting four days.

quatríduo s. m. period of four days.

quatriênio s. m. (Braz.) (also **quadriênio**) quadr(i)ennium.

quatrilhão, quatrilião s. m. (pl. **-ões**) quadrillion: 1. (Braz. + U.S.A.) a thousand trillions (1 followed by 15 ciphers.) 2. (Engl.) a million trillions (1 followed by 24 ciphers.)

quatrim s. m. (pl. **-ins**) (Port.) 1. former small coin. 2. farthing, trifle, penny.

quatrinca s. f. (cards) four of a kind.

quatro s. m. 1. four. 2. a card or domino with four spots. ‖ adj. four.
aos ~ cantos to the four corners of the earth. **cair de ~** to come a cropper. **ciclo de ~ tempos** (mot.) four-stroke cycle. **os ~ ventos** the cardinal points. **eles tocaram piano a ~ mãos** they played the piano four-handed.

quatro-cantinhos s. m., sg. + pl. puss in the corner, a children's game.

quatrocentista s. m. + f. (hist.) quattrocentist: artist or writer who lived in the 15th century. ‖ adj. quattrocento.

quatrocentos s. m. pl. four hundred. ‖ adj. four hundred.

quatrolho adj. (Braz.) having white eyebrows.

quatro-olhos s. m., sg. + pl. (Braz., pop.) person who wears glasses.

quatro-patacas s. f., sg. + pl. (Braz., bot.) campanilla.

quatro-paus s. m., sg. + pl. 1. the four of clubs. 2. (Braz., pop.) thug, bodyguard.

que adj. (interrogative) what? which? ‖ adv. what, how. ‖ pron. 1. that, which, who, whom, what. 2. (interrogative) what? which? ‖ prep. except, but. ‖ conj. 1. as; for; than. 2. however; that.
~ **aconteceu?** what happened? **de ~ adianta escrever agora?** where is the use of writing now? ~ **belo!** how beautiful! ~ **bobagem!** what a nonsense! ~ **Deus me ajude!** so help me God! ~ **dia é hoje?** what day is today? ~ **diabo você está pensando?** what on earth are you thinking about? ~ **é ~ ele disse?** what did he say? ~ **é ~ há?** what's the matter? ~ **é de João?** where is John? ~ **espécie de livro é?** what kind of book is it? ~ **há com ele?** what is the matter with him? ~ **há de novo?** what's new? ~ **horas são?** what time is it? ~ **livro tem lido?** what book have you read? ~ **lugar bonito!** what a fine place! ~ **mais?** what next? ~ **pena!** what a pity! ~ **tal tomar um chá?** how about having tea? ~ **tolo ele é!** what a fool he is! ~ **vergonha!** what a shame! for shame! ~ **vida!** what a life! **a fim de ~** in order that. **agora ~ chegou o dia** now that the day has come. **aquele ~** he who. **aquilo ~ me concerne** that which concerns me. **assim ~ ela chegar** as soon as she arrives. **bem ~ eu o avisei!** I warned you well enough! **de ~ você está rindo?** what are you laughing at? **de maneira ~** so that. **em ~** wherein. **do ~ than. e não sei o ~ mais** and what not. **este vermelho ~ é a cor mais procurada** this red which is the most demanded colour. **espero ~ sim** I hope so. **eu ~ sou o seu mestre** I who am your master. **houve tempo em ~** there was a time when.

isto sim, ~ é maçã! that's some apple! mais alto ~ ele taller than he. não tenho nada ~ fazer I have nothing to do. onde quer ~ vivam, eles serão felizes they will be happy wherever they live. pelo ~ by which, through which. pela própria razão ~ for the very reason that. por mais ~ faça, nunca o satisfaço whatever I may do, I never satisfy you. qualquer livro ~ any book that. tenho ~ ir I have to go. tudo ~ all that. um empregado ~ eu sei ser honesto an employee who I know is honest.

quê s. m. 1. anything, something. 2. difficulty, obstacle, rub. 3. complication, something wrong. 4. name of the letter Q ‖ interj. of fright and surprise as: why! ~! você por aqui? why! are you here about? compreendi o ~ da coisa I got the hang of it. não há de ~ it's nothing, don't mention it. a ~? what? para ~? what for? por ~? why, for what reason? tem seus ~s it has its drawbacks. um certo ~ a certain something.

queba adj. m. + f. (Braz.) 1. ancient, old. 2. anti-quate(d).

quebra s. f. 1. break(age): a) act of breaking. b) tear, fracture, rupture. c) (electr.) interruption of current. d) interruption, stop(page). e) failure, bank-ruptcy. 2. breach. 3. waste, wastage. 4. hillside. 5. (Braz.) abatement, rebate. 6. m. (Braz., pop., also quebra-quebra): a) shower of blows or strokes. b) brawl, fracas. ‖ adj. (Braz.) 1. bantering; talkative. 2. swaggering. ~ fraudulenta fraudulent bankruptcy. ~ de braço (Braz.) Indian wrestling. ~ de palavra breach of faith. ~ de verso enjambement. dar ~ to go bank-rupt. de ~ in the bargain. sem ~ uninterrupted, complete.

quebra-bunda s. m. (pl. quebra-bundas) (Braz., also mal-de-cadeiras) a parasitic horse disease.

quebra-cabeça s. m. + f. (pl. quebra-cabeças) (pop.) puzzle: 1. difficult problem, poser. 2. enigma, riddle, conundrum. 3. anything complicate and difficult to resolve; (fig.) a nut to crack. 4. jigsaw puzzle.

quebrachal s. m. (pl. -ais) (Braz.) quebracho grove or plantation.

quebracho s. m. (Braz.) quebracho (tree).

quebra-costela s. m. (pl. quebra-costelas) (Braz., fam.) hug: a close embrace.

quebrada s. f. 1. slope, hillside. 2. gully, ravine. 3. (Braz.) bend of a road.

quebra-dedos s. f., sg. + pl. (Braz.) woven lath fence.

quebradeira s. f. 1. = quebra-cabeça. 2. (Braz.) im-pecuniosity, lack of money.

quebradela s. f. act or fact of breaking.

quebradiço adj. fragile, easily broken, frail, delicate, brittle.

quebrado s. m. 1. (math.) fraction. 2. = quebrada: slope. 3. ~s pl. (Braz.) small change (money). ‖ adj. 1. broken, severed. 2. fragmented, in pieces. 3. ruptured, herniated. 4. tired, fatigued, exhausted. 5. decrepit. 6. languid. 7. (Braz.) ruined, bankrupt, broke, very poor, indigent. estou ~ 1. I feel thoroughly knocked up. 2. (Braz.) I am out of funds, I am broken. frase -a (gram.) anacoluthon. verso ~ hemistich.

quebrador s. m. 1. breaker: person who or thing that breaks. 2. Brazil nut gatherer. ‖ adj. breaking.

quebrados s. m. pl. (Braz., pop.) small change.

quebradouro, quebradoiro s. m. (Braz., also zona de arrebentação) surf zone.

quebradura s. f. 1. = quebra. 2. rupture, hernia.

quebra-febre s. f. (pl. quebra-febres) (bot.) lesser centaury (Erythraea centaurium).

quebra-foice s. m. (pl. quebra-foices) (Braz., bot., also mandaravé or quebra-fouce) calliandra.

quebra-freio s. m. (pl. quebra-freios) (Braz.) swagger-ing, valiant person, tough. ‖ adj. 1. wild, rough, savage. 2. skittish. 3. valiant. 4. turbulent.

quebra-galho s. m. (pl. quebra-galhos) 1. trouble-shooter. 2. contrivance, makeshift.

quebra-gelos s. m., sg. + pl. 1. (naut.) icebreaker (plate P 14). 2. device for the removal of ice on an aircraft.

quebra-largado s. m. (pl. quebras-largados) (S. Braz.) = quebra-freio.

quebralhão s. m. (pl. -ões) (S. Braz.) very bad person (or animal). ‖ adj. very bad, evil.

quebra-louças s. m. + f, sg. + pl. (Braz.) desastrous or blatant person; hot-head (also quebra-loiças).

quebra-luz s. m. (pl. quebra-luzes) lamp shade.

quebra-mar s. m. (pl. quebra-mares) breakwater, jetty pier, mole (plate 16).

quebramento s. m. = quebra, quebreira.

quebrança s. f. 1. the breaking of the waves against rocks. 2. (fig.) shock. 3. low tide.

quebra-nozes s. m., sg. + pl. 1. nutcracker: a device for cracking nuts. 2. a certain crowlike bird.

quebrantado adj. 1. broken, debilitated, enfeebled. 2. damaged, harmed.

quebrantamento s. m. 1. breaking, debilitation, enfee-blement. 2. weakness, prostration, depression. 3. infringement, transgression.

quebrantar v. 1. to break. 2. to raze, ruin, destroy. 3. to lower, let down. 4. to debilitate, weaken, enfeeble. 5. to damage, hurt. 6. to conquer, put to rout. 7. to tame, domesticate. 8. to soften, quell, assuage, calm. 9. (fig.) to infringe, transgress, violate. 10. to serve as a lenitive. 11. ~-se: a) to become loose or slack. b) to grow weak. c) to become discouraged. d) to lose vigour. ~ uma lei to infringe a law. ~ sua fé to apostatize. ~ sua palavra (Port.) to break one's word.

quebranto s. m. (also quebrantamento) 1. prostra-tion, weakness, exhaustion. 2. relaxation. 3. be-witching. 4. (pop.) illness supposed to be caused by the influence of an evil eye (esp. upon children). dar ~ to bewitch, look at with the evil eye.

quebra-pedra s. f. (pl. quebra-pedras) 1. plant of the genus Euphorbia (Phyllanthus corcovadensis). 2. euphorbiaceous plant (Euphorbia pilulifera).

quebra-queixo s. m. (pl. quebra-queixos) (Braz.) 1. stogy, cigar of poor quality. 2. jawbreaker, very hard candy, toffy.

quebrar v. (mostly also quebrar-se) 1. to break: a) separate into parts, shatter, smash. b) interrupt, disconnect, disjoin. c) violate, infringe, transgress. d) fail; make or become bankrupt. e) destroy, raze. f) calm down, comb (waves); stop, be dispersed. 2. to weaken, debilitate. 3. to tame, domesticate. 4. to subjugate, conquer, put to rout. 5. to annul, cancel. 6. to incapacitate, disable. 7. (Braz., pop.) to kill. 8. to rupture, part. 9. to breach, fracture, rend. 10. to crack, split, cleave. 11. to protrude (hernia), cause hernia. 12. to bend, turn (street). 13. (Braz., fig.) to beat, sock (face). 14. to stop. ~ a cabeça (fig.) to cudgel one's brains. ~ a fé to break one's faith. ~-se em pedaços to come asunder. ~ a palavra to break one's word. que-brei-lhe a cara I knocked him into a cocked hat. ele quebrou a cabeça (fig.) he raked his brain. ele quebrou a cabeça para resolvê-lo he puzzled his brain over it. ele quebrou o recorde he cut the record. quebrou-se it came to smash.

quebrável adj. m. + f. (pl. -áveis) breakable: capable of being broken.

quebra-ventos s. m., sg. + pl. windbreak (plate F 4).

quebreira s. f. 1. (pop.) prostration, exhaustion, weariness. 2. fatigue. 3. lassitude, languor, weakness. 4. (Braz., also **quebradeira**) lack of money.

quebro s. m. (also **requebro**) 1. inflection, inflexion: change of pitch in the voice; intonation, cadence. 2. flexion or twist with the body. 3. turn, dodge of the body.

quecê, quecé s. m. (N. Braz., also **caxirenguengue**) useless old knife esp. one without a point or handle.

queci-queci s. m. (pl. **queci-quecis**) (Braz., also **quijuba**) conure: a bird of the family Psittacidae (Aratinga solstitialis).

queda s. f. fall: 1. act or result of falling. 2. (fig.): a) decadence, decline, decay. b) ruin, destruction, downfall, collapse. c) discredit, come-down. d) mistake, sin. e) declivity. f) drop, tumble. g) tendency, bent, inclination, aptitude. h) end, finish. i) precipitation. j) plop, plump. k) crack-up, smash. ~ **da produção** decline of production. ~ **de água** waterfall. ~ **de potencial** drop of potential. ~ **de preços** collapse of prices. ~ **desastrosa** nasty fall. ~ **de tensão** drop in voltage. ~ **de cabelo** falling of the hair; (path.) alopecia. **dar uma** ~ to fall. **ele tem** ~ **para a música** he has a bent towards music. **ele sofreu uma** ~ **violenta** he had a bad spill. **isto é uma grande** ~ **para você** that's quite a come-down for you. **uma** ~ **nos preços** a drop in prices. **uma** ~ **de temperatura** a fall of temperature.

queda-de-braço s. f. (Braz.) Indian wrestling.

quedar v. 1. to be quiet. 2. to stay. 3. to restrain o. s. 4. to remain stationed. 5. to remain, to continue. 6. to stop, halt.

quediva s. m. (hist.) khedive: title of the Turkish viceroys of Egypt.

quedo (ê) adj. 1. quiet, still; tranquil. 2. stationary. 3. stopped, motionless. 4. slow, tardy. ~ **e** ~ quietly, slowly. **a pé** ~ at once, without delay.

quefazer s. m. (also **quefazeres** pl.) 1. occupations, job. 2. business, affair. 3. matter. 4. chores, tasks, duties.

quefir s. m. kefir: a species of koumiss produced by fermenting milk.

queijada s. f. cheese-cake.

queijadeira s. f. woman who makes or sells cheese--cakes.

queijadeiro s. m. cheese-cake maker or seller. ‖ adj. of or referring to cheese-cakes.

queijadilho s. m. primrose: plant of the genus Primula.

queijadinha s. f. a coconut sweetmeat.

queijar v. 1. to make cheese. 2. to become cheese.

queijaria s. f. 1. cheese making. 2. dairy, place where cheese is made.

queijeira s. f. 1. = **queijaria**. 2. woman who makes or sells cheese or cheese-cakes. 3. cheese-mold, cheese-plate cover.

queijeiro s. m. 1. cheese maker. 2. cheese-monger: person who deals in or sells cheese. 3. (Braz., pop.) backwoodsman, rustic person.

queijo s. m. cheese: the pressed curd of milk. ~ **duro** (mineiro) hard cheese. ~ **fresco** (mole) soft cheese. ~ **parmesão** Parmesan cheese. ~ **prato** an Edam-like cheese greatly produced in Brazil. ~ **suíço** gruyère. **ele está com a faca e o** ~ **na mão** he has the ball at his feet.

queijoso adj. (also **caseoso**) cheesy; caseous, of, pertaining to or like cheese.

queima s. f. 1. firing, burning: act or process of applying fire to anything; combustion. 2. cremation.

3. (fig.) fire. 4. (Braz., com.) bargain sale. 5. (N. E. Braz.) a marriage without a party. ~ **de fogos** fireworks, a pyrotechnic display. **preço de** ~ (com.) panic price, low price.

queimação s. f. (pl. **-ões**) 1. = **queima**. 2. (fig.): a) impertinence. b) tiresomeness. c) annoyance.

queimada s. f. 1. burn: place where vegetation has been burned away. 2. burned-over land. 3. forest fire. 4. clearance of ground by fire. 5. calcined earth serving as a fertilizer. 6. (fishery) a shoal of sardines. 7. (S. Braz.) a sort of brandy.

queimadeiro s. m. stake: post to which condemned persons were bound to be burned alive.

queimadela s. f. = **queimadura**.

queimado s. m. 1. burnt smell, smell or taste of scorched food. 2. (Braz.) a sort of candy of burned sugar. ‖ adj. 1. burned, burnt; adust. 2. scorched. 3. carbonized. 4. ardent, fiery. 5. hot, warm. 6. frost-bitten. 7. sunburnt, tanned. 8. (Braz.): a) angry, annoyed. b) furious, raging. ~ **pelo sol** sunburned. **cheirar a** ~ to smell of burning.

queimador s. m. burner: person who or thing which burns; incendiary. ‖ adj. burning.

queimador-de-campo s. m. (pl. **queimadores-de-campo**) (S. Braz.) liar.

queimadouro, queimadoiro s. m. burning place.

queimadura s. f. 1. (also **queima**) act of burning. 2. burn: injury on the body caused by fire. 3. plant rust; blight.

queimamento s. m. act of burning.

queimante s. m. (N. Braz., pop.) firearm, gun. ‖ adj. m. + f. burning, hot. 2. piquant.

queimão s. m. (pl. **-ões**) (also **quimão**) kimono. ‖ adj. piquant (red pepper).

queimar v. 1. to burn: a) destroy or damage by fire. b) scorch, toast, parch, singe. c) cremate. d) blaze, flame, set ablaze, aflame. e) set afire. f) bake (bricks, roofing tiles). g) scald. h) ~-**se**: to injure o. s. by fire. 2. to dissipate, waste. 3. to squander (money). 4. to sell out (goods) at low prices, undersell. 5. to destroy morally. 6. to render insensible. 7. (Braz., pop.) to shoot (with a firearm). 8. to be febrile. 9. ~-**se** (Braz.) to be offended; take offence, resent; get angry; become furious. ~-**se pela geada** to freeze, be frostbitten, be nipped by frost. ~ **as pestanas** to work or study till late in the night. ~ **o seu último cartucho** to fire one's last shot. ~-**se pelo sol** to sunburn.

queima-roupa s. f. word used in the adv. locution **à** ~ 1. at close range, point-blank, face to face. 2. suddenly. **deu-lhe um tiro à** ~ he shot him with the gun clapped to his breast.

queimo s. m. acrid or piquant taste, poignancy.

queimar s. m. 1. = **queimo**. 2. intense heat.

queimoso adj. 1. burning, hot. 2. piquant, poignant. 3. warm (weather).

queixa s. f. 1. complaint: a) grievance. b) act of complaining or of expressing a sense of pain. c) formal accusation. 2. offence, resentment, reason for resentment. 3. discontent(ment). 4. (jur.) indictment. 5. lamentation; querulousness. 6. protest, remonstrance, clamo(u)r. ~ **de indenização (por perdas e danos)** (jur.) action for damages. ~ **do peito** (pop.) tuberculosis. **fazer** ~ **de** to complain of. **levantar** ~ **contra alguém** to lodge information against s. o., to sue s.o. **motivo de** ~ grounds for complaint. **ter motivo de** ~ to have reason for complaining about.

queixada s. f. 1. jawbone, mandible, chap, jowl. 2. m. (Braz., zool., also **tacuité**) white-lipped peccary, wild boar.

queixal s. m. (pl. **-ais**) molar tooth. ‖ adj. m. + f. of or pertaining to the chin or jaw.

queixar-se v. 1. to complain: a) grieve. b) express a sense of pain. c) make a formal accusation. d) present a complaint. e) murmur. 2. to groan, moan. 3. to cry, yammer. 4. to be offended, resent, take amiss. 5. to manifest discontent. 6. to lament, wail. 7. to protest, make a protest, remonstrate, clamour. 8. to repine. 9. to reprove, censure. **~-se de alguma coisa** to make a grievance of s. th. **ela queixa-se dele comigo** she complains to me of him. **ela queixou-se junto a ele** she complained to him. **vá ~-se ao bispo!** tell it to Sweeney!

queixeiro adj. said of the wisdom tooth.

queixo s. m. 1. chin, mandible, lower jaw (plates C 12, 18). 2. **~s** pl. the face. **bater o ~** to chatter one's teeth (with cold or fear). **bater os ~s em** (S. Braz.) to reprimand sharply. **derrubar o ~ de** (S. Braz.) to subdue, subjugate. **direito no ~** (box) uppercut. **duro de ~** (Braz.) 1. ´ hard-mouthed (horse). 2. (fig.) self-willed, obstinate. **ele ficou de ~ caído** he dropped his jaw.

queixoso s. m. complainant: 1. complainer, person who complains. 2. person who enters a formal complaint before a magistrate. 3. plaintiff. ‖ adj. 1. complaining, querulous. 2. plaintive, mournful; whining. 3. remonstrant. ‖ **-amente** adv. complainingly. **~ de** complaining of, dissatisfied with.

queixudo adj. big-chinned, big-jawed.

queixume s. m. 1. complaining, complaint. 2. lamentation, whine, wailing. 3. moan, groan; weeping.

queixumeiro s. m. (Braz.) eternal complainer. ‖ adj. (Braz.) 1. maudlin, tearful, weeping. 2. whining; complaining.

quejando adj. such, of the same kind or quality. **e ~s** and the like.

quela s. f. (zool.) chela, pincers.

quelha s. f. 1. flume; trough, chute. 2. narrow way or street.

quelícera s. f. (zool.) chelicera: anterior pair of appendages of the Arachnida.

quelidônia s. f. 1. (bot.) celandine, swallowwort. 2. (petrog.) swallow stone.

quelidônia-menor s. f. (pl. **quelidônias-menores**) (bot.) lesser celandine.

quelífero adj. cheliferous, chelate.

queliforme adj. m. + f. cheliform, pincerlike, chelate.

quelípode s. m. (zool.) cheliped, cheliform leg.

quelônio s. m. (zool.) chelonian: a turtle of the order Chelonia.

quelônios s. m. pl. (zool.) Chelonia, an order of reptiles which includes tortoises and turtles.

quelonite s. f. petrified turtle.

quelonófago s. m. eater of turtles. ‖ adj. feeding on turtles.

quelonografia s. f. description of chelonians (turtles or tortoises).

quelonógrafo s. m. person versed in the study of turtles or tortoises.

quem pron. 1. who; whom; one or anybody who. 2. interrogative: who?, whom? **~ de vocês?** which of you? **~ é?** who is it? **~ está aí?** who goes there? **~ foi?** who was it? **~ me dera ter sucesso!** if only I should succeed! **~ sabe?** who knows? **~ quer que seja** whoever, whosoever. **a ~** to whom. **com ~ você falou?** whom did you speak to? **como ~ diz** as one usually says. **de ~ 1.** whose. 2. of whom, from whom. **de ~ é este livro?** whose book is this? **de ~ mais poderia ser?** whose else might it be? **e sei lá ~ mais** (coll.) and I do not know who all. **falar como ~ é** to speak one's mind freely. **há ~ diga** it is said, reported.

fui eu ~ o disse I said it; it was I who said it. **não estava com ~ eu queria falar** he with whom I wanted to speak was not there. **não há ~** nobody, there's no one who. **os inimigos a ~ um traidor havia mostrado o caminho** the enemies to whom a traitor had shown the path. **não sei ~ possa ajudar-te** I don't know who can help you. **não sei ~ fez isto** I don't know who made this. **não sabem a ~ perguntar** they do not know whom to ask. **por ~ é!** 1. for goodness' sake! for heaven's sake! 2. oh, please, don't mention it! **por ~ perguntou ela?** whom did she inquire for? **seja lá ~ for** whoever it may be. **sua tia, por ~ ele foi educado** his aunt whom he was educated by. **você sabia ~ era?** did you know who that was?

quemose s. f. (med.) chemosis.

quem-te-vestiu s. m., sg. + pl. (Braz.) finch: a bird of the family Fringilidae.

quenga s. f. (N. Braz.) 1. vessel made from a coconut shell. 2. its contents. 3. chicken stew with okra. 4. (sl.) prostitute.

quengada s. f. (Braz.) 1. swindle, fraud, trickery. 2. (N. Braz.): a) stupidity, foolishness. b) (sl.) a group of prostitutes.

quengo s. m. (N. Braz.) 1. vessel made out of a coconut shell. 2. (fig.): a) mind, head. b) talent, intelligence. c) astute person.

quenopodiáceas s. f. pl. (bot.) Chenopodiaceae.

quenopodiáceo adj. (bot.) chenopodiaceous.

quenopódio s. m. chenopod: any plant of the goosefoot family.

quenquém s. f. (Braz.) 1. a sort of ant. 2. m. (ornith.) a blue-headed jay (Cyanotorax cyanopogon).

quentão s. m. (pl. **-ões**) (Braz.) 1. hot (sugar cane) rum with ginger. 2. any hot alcoholic beverage.

quentar s. to warm, heat.

quente s. m. (fig.) bed, hot place. ‖ adj. 1. hot, burning, heated. 2. (very) warm (weather). 3. sultry, torrid. 4. (fig.): a) enthusiastic, animated, ardent, fiery. b) sensual, excited. 5. (Braz., sl.) drunk. **estar muito ~** to broil, be hot. **ferro ~** hot iron. **ele está no ~** (fig.) he is comfortably in his bed. **malhar o ferro enquanto está ~** to strike the iron while it is hot.

quentura s. f. warmth, heat, state of being hot.

quepe s. m. (mil.) kepi: a cap with a flat top.

queque s. m. cake.

quer conj. 1. or. 2. whether or though, notwithstanding. **~ chova ~ faça sol, nós iremos** we shall go rain or shine. **~ ele queira, ~ não** whether he will or not. **~ seja de um modo, ~ seja de outro** in this way or some other. **~ sim, ~ não** whether yes or no. **como ~ que seja** however that may be. **onde ~ que** wherever. **o que ~ que** whatever. **quem ~** whoever.

qüera adj. (S‖ Braz., pop.) 1. valiant, intrepid. 2. fearless, dauntless.

queratina s. f. (chem., zool.) keratin: an albuminous substance forming the principal matter of hair, horns, bills, nails, etc.

querela s. f. 1. (jur.) complaint, indictment, formal accusation, action, lawsuit. 2. discussion, debating. 3. dispute, altercation, controversy. 4. (poet.) mournful song, plaint. **dar ~ contra** to bring an action against.

querelado s. m. (jur.) the accused, defendant: person against whom an action is brought.

querelador s. m., **querelante** m. + f. (jur.) 1. prosecutor. 2. complainant, plaintiff, accuser, demandant. ‖ adj. complaining, accusing.

querelar v. to complain, sue, make a formal accusation.

~ **contra** (jur.) to move an action or lawsuit against, go to law with. **~-se de** to complain of, to lament over, wail, moan.

quereloso adj. 1. querulous, complaining. 2. plaintive, mournful.

querena s. f. 1. (naut.): a) keel; hull, part of a vessel below the waterline. b) draught. 2. (pop.) bearing, course, direction.

virar de ~ to careen, to heave down.

querenagem s. f. (pl. **-ens**) careening.

querenar v. (naut.) to careen: 1. tip or incline a ship on one side in order to repair or calk it. 2. keel over. 3. repair or clean a ship when turned over. ~ **o navio** to careen, heave down the ship.

querença s. f. 1. will, wish, desire. 2. affection, liking, love, fondness. 3. aerie: place where falcons bring up their young. 4. place to which animals have an instinctive addiction.

querenceiro adj. = **querençoso**.

querência s. f. (S. Braz.) 1. favourite grazing of cattle or where it was raised. 2. homestead. 3. native place, dwelling place (of person).

querençoso, querenceiro adj. 1. affectionate, fond, loving. 2. benevolent, affable.

querendão s. m. (pl. **-ões**) (Braz., f. **-one**) 1. animal that adjusts easily to a new place. 2. (by extension) person who makes friends easily. 3. affectionate lover. 4. flirt, flirter. || adj. 1. affectionate, loving, fond. 2. cheerful, joyous.

querente adj. m. + f. desirous of, wanting something.

querê-querê s. m. (pl. **querê-querês**) (Braz., ichth.) a sort of damselfish (Abudefduf marginatus). -

querequexé s. m. (Braz.,) = **reco-reco**.

querer s. m. 1. wish, will, desire, want. 2. affection, liking, love, fondness. 3. intention. || v. 1. to wish (for), want, desire, will. 2. to intend, aspire, mean. 3. to command, enjoin, demand, require. 4. to request, solicit. 5. to crave, long for. 6. to consent, permit, agree. 7. to deserve. 8. to be fond of, to appreciate, have an affection for. 9. **~-se:** a) to like, love one another. b) to admire each other. ~ **a alguém** to love, like s.o. ~ **bem (mal)** to love (hate). ~ **entrar (sair)** to enter (to go out), to want in (out). ~ **o impossível** to cry for the moon. ~ **pegar** to snatch at. **como Deus quiser** as God wills. **como queira** as you like, as you please. **Deus queira!** may it please God to grant it! **Deus quer assim** God wills it. **ela quer que eu vá** she wants me to go. **ela lhe quer bem** she loves him. **não ~ ver nem pintado** 1. to wish someone out of one's sight. 2. to reject or repel with abomination. **não quero vê-lo nem pintado** I can't stand the sight of him. **ele quer passar por poeta** he goes in for being a poet. **ele quer ser historiador** he goes in for a historian. **eu queria estar morto** I wish I were dead. **eu queria que ele fosse** I wish he would go. **eu quero que você o faça** I will have you do it. **eu só queria ver!** I'd just like to see it! **faça como quiser** suit your own convenience, do as you like. **não lhe quero mal por isso** I am not angry with you for that. **não quero isso** I will not have that. **nós o queríamos assim** we willed it to be so. **eu não quisera estar em sua pele** I shouldn't like to be in his skin. **sem ~** unintentionally, involuntarily. **foi sem ~** I did not mean it. **antigamente podíamos fazer tudo como queríamos** formerly we had it all our own way. **quando quiser** at your leisure. **quando um não quer, dois não brigam** it takes two to make a bargain. **queira Deus** please God! **queira fazê-lo, por favor!** be so kind as to do it! **queira entrar** please, come in. **queria estar em casa** I would fain be at home. **quem tudo quer nada tem** to attempt all is to lose

all. **não quer ver?** (won't) will you have a look at it? **eu queria um pouco mais de açúcar** I should like a little more sugar. **.quero que você escreva melhor** I wish you to write better. **que quer você que eu faça?** what will you have me do? **quer-me parecer que** it seems to me that. **o que você quer aqui?** what do you want here? **o que você quer de mim?** what do you want with me? **que quer dizer isso?** what does all this mean? **o que você quer dizer com isso?** what do you mean? **se tudo fosse como você quer** if you had your own way. **vai como nós queremos** we have our will. **o vento sopra para onde quer** the wind blows where it listeth. **você pode ir, se quiser** it is free for you to go. **você quer que ele morra de fome?** would you have him starve? **você quer vir comigo?** would you like to come with me?

querida s. f. 1. darling, dear. 2. sweetheart. || adj. f. of **querido**.

queridinha s. f., **queridinho** m. deary; mavourneen.

querido s. m. 1. darling, dear, beloved person. 2. favourit, pet. 3. sweetheart. || adj. 1. darling, dear, beloved. 2. favourite, esteemed. 3. sweet. ~ **papai (-a mamãe)** (letters) dear father (mother). **meu ~, minha -a** my darling, my pretty. **tornar-se** ~ to endear o. s.

querima, querimônia s. f. (obs.) complaint; discussion.

querite s. f. kerite: a substitute for caoutchouc used as an insulating material.

quermes s. m., sg. + pl. kermes: red dyestuff made out of the dried bodies of female scale insects which live on certain oaks. ~ **mineral** kermes mineral.

quermesse s. f. 1. kermis, kermesse: a) a fair or outdoor festival or merrymaking. b) a rural church festival, rush bearing. 2. charitable bazaar.

quernita s. f. (min.) kernite: hydrous sodium borate; source of borax.

quero-quero s. m. (Braz., ornith.) terutero, teruteru, South American lapwing (Belonopterus cayennensis).

querosenagem s. f. (pl. **-ens**) (Braz.) saturation with kerosene (for agricultural purposes).

querosenar v. (Braz.) to kerosene: saturate or sprinkle with kerosene (for agricultural purposes).

querosene s. m. 1. kerosene: a) oil distilled from petroleum (used in lamps and stoves). b) paraffin oil, coal oil. 2. (Braz.): a) milky-blue diamond. b) (bot.) laurel (Nectandra olaeophora).

quérquera s. f. violent fever and fit of shivering.

quersoneso s. m (obs.) chersonese, a peninsula.

querúbico adj. cherubic(al): of or pertaining to a cherub.

querubim s. m. (pl. **-ins**) cherub: 1. (theol.) one of the second highest order of angels. 2. picture or statue of a beautiful winged child or the winged head of a child.

querubínico adj. cherubic(al): of or pertaining to a cherub.

qüerudo adj. (S. Braz.) 1. valiant, intrepid. 2. fearless, dauntless.

quérulo adj. (poet.) querulous, plaintive, mournful.

quesito s. m. 1. inquiry, query, question. 2. subject or issue for which an opinion is requested. 3. requisite.

questão s. f. (pl. **-ões**) question: 1. interrogation; inquiry, query. 2. subject, matter; thesis, theme, argument. 3. (jur.) point at issue. 4. controversy, debate, dispute, contention. 5. affair. 6. problem. ~ **de honra** affair of honour. ~ **de opinião** a matter of opinion. ~ **de tempo** question of time. ~ **prévia** previous question. **a ~ está em debate** the matter lies at issue. **chegar ao ponto essencial da** ~ to come to the point. **é uma ~ de gosto** it is a matter of taste. **é uma ~ de vida e morte**

it is a case of life and death. **eis a** ~ that's the point. **em** ~ at issue. **ela faz** ~ **de ouvir tudo** she lays great emphasis on being told everything. **entrar em** ~ to come into question, to be taken into consideration. **fazer** ~ **de** to insist on, to attach great importance. **fizemos** ~ **de fazê-lo** we made a point of doing it. **isto é** ~ **de opinião** that's open to question. **o livro em** ~ the book in question. **pôr em** ~ to impeach, put in question. **pôr uma** ~ to ask, put a question. **uma** ~ **de hábito** a matter of habit. **sem** ~ without doubt.

questionador s. m. questioner: person who asks questions. ‖ adj. questioning.

questionar v. to question: 1. call or put in question. 2. debate, dispute, discuss. 3. argue, controvert, object. 4. wrangle.

questionário s. m. questionnaire, questionary: list or series of questions.

questionável adj. m. + f. (pl. **-áveis**) questionable: 1. liable to be called in question, disputable. 2. capable of being questioned.

questiúncula s. f. a little controversy, questions of minor importance.

questor s. m. (Roman hist.) qu(a)estor: a magistrate, judge or treasurer.

questório adj. of or pertaining to a question.

questuário s. m. ambitious or self-seeking person. ‖ adj. ambitious; egoistic, self-seeking.

questuoso adj. lucrative, profitable, advantageous.

questura s. f. (Roman hist.) qu(a)estorship.

queto adj. (fam., also **quieto**) quiet.

quetópode s. m. + f. (zool.) chaetopod. ‖ adj. chaetopodous of or pertaining to the Chaetopoda.

quetua s. m. (Braz., ornith.) tiriba: parrot of the genus Pyrrhura.

quiabeiro s. m. okra: a tall annual herb (Hibiscus esculentus).

quiabento s. m. (Braz., bot.) a sort of cactus (Peireskia zehntneri).

quiabo s. m. okra, gumbo: the pods used in soups and stews.

çuiabo-cheiroso s. m. (pl. **quiabos-cheirosos**) (Braz., bot.) musk mallow.

quiaborana s. f. (Braz.) plant of the genus Malachra.

quiáltera s. f. (mus.) triplet of three notes of equal value executed in the time of only two of them.

quiasma, quiasmo s. m. 1. (gram.) chiasmus. 2. (anat.) chiasma.

quiastro s. m. bandage shaped like an X.

quiba adj. m. + f. strong, robust.

quibandar v. (Braz.) to sift with a sieve (rice, coffee, etc.).

quibando, quibano s. m. (N. Braz.) a sort of sieve for rice, coffee, etc.

quibe s. m. kibbe: an Arab dish, made of deep-fried ground meat and whole wheat flour.

quibebe s. m. pap or purée of pumpkins. ‖ adj. having the consistency of pap of pumpkins.

quibungo s. m. (Braz.) Negro dance.

quiçá adv. 1. perhaps, maybe. 2. who knows? 3. possibly, peradventure, perchance.

quiçaba s. f. (Braz.) earthen jug or pot.

quiçaça s. f. (Braz.) arid soil; cutover land.

quiçama s. f. (Braz.) small wicker hamper.

quiçamã s. m. (Braz.) 1. pap made of manioc starch. 2. variety of sugar cane.

quicê, quicé s. m. (N. Braz.) useless old knife, esp. one without a point or handle.

quício s. m. hinge of a door.

quico s. m. (Braz.) gypsy.

quidam s. m. (Braz.) a nobody, person of no importance.
um ~ quidam: a fellow, certain person, somebody.

qüididade s. f. quiddity: the essence of a thing.

qüididativo adj. quiddidative.

quiescente adj. m. + f. quiescent, resting.

quietação s. f. (pl. **-ões**) 1. tranquil(l)ization. 2. quietude. 3. tranqui(l)lity. 4. stillness, calmness.

quietar v. to quiet: 1. make or cause to be quiet. 2. bring to a state of rest. 3. tranquil(l)ize, calm. 4. pacify, allay.

quietarrão adj. (pl. **-ões**) (f. **-ona**) 1. reserved, silent, of few words. 2. very still and quiet.

quietismo s. m. quietism: a form of mysticism requiring passive meditation on God and divine things, and withdrawal from worldly interests.

quietista s. m. + f. quietist: a practicer of quietism. ‖ adj. quietistic, of or pertaining to quietism.

quieto s. m. (Braz.) rest, tranquil(l)ity; easy life. ‖ adj. quiet: 1. tranquil, serene, calm. 2. restful, easeful. 3. still, motionless. 4. silent. 5. peaceful, pacific. 6. placid, patient. ‖ **-amente** adv. quietly. ‖ ~! interj. be quiet! switch off!
conservar-se ~ to hold or keep one's peace. **ficar** ~ to be quiet, shut up. **fique** ~! be quiet! **ele ficou** ~ he kept quiet. **não pode ficar** ~? can you not be quiet?

quietude s. f. quietude: 1. the state or condition of calm or tranquil(l)ity. 2. repose, rest. 3. peacefulness. 4. serenity, silence.

quigombô, quigombó s. f. (Braz.) okra, gumbo (pods or tree).

quijuba s. m. (Braz., ornith., also **queci-queci**) conure: a parrot (Aratinga solstitialis).

quilaia s. f. (Braz.) soap bark tree (Quilaja saponaria).

quilatação s. f. (pl. **-ões**) assaying: examination or determination of weight.

quilatar v. to assay, value the degree of purity or perfection of gold or gems.

quilate s. m. 1. carat, karat. 2. degree of purity or perfection of gold or gems. 3. (fig.): a) excellence, superiority. b) perfection.
~ **métrico** metric carat. **este relógio é de ouro de 18** ~**s** this is an eighteen carat watch.

quilateira s. f. an instrument for grading gems by size.

quilha s. f. keel: 1. the principal timber of a ship, extending from bow to stern; bottom (plates B 8, 10). 2. hull.
~ **corrediça** (naut.) center-board.

quilhar s. m. ship nail (esp. that used in nailing the floor-timbers). ‖ v. to keel: provide with a keel (ship).

quilíade s. f. chiliad, a thousand.

quiliarco s. m. (Gr. hist.) chiliarch: commander of a thousand men.

quiliare s. m. superficial measure equal to a thousand ares.

quiliarquia s. f. (Gr. hist.) chiliarchia: command over thousand men.

quilífero adj. (physiol.) chyliferous (vessels).

quilificação s. f. (pl. **-ões**) (physiol.) chylification.

quilificar v. to chylify: convert or be converted into chyle.

quilificativo adj. chylific: forming chyle.

quilógono s. m. (geom.) chiliagon: regular polygon of a thousand angles.

quilo (I) s. m. (physiol.) chyle: a milky liquid composed of digested fat and lymph.

quilo (II) s. m. short for **quilograma**.

quilociclo s. m. (radio) kilocycle.

quilógnato s. m. (zool.) diplopod, millipede.

quilograma s. m. kilogram(me): measure of weight equal to a thousand grams.

quilograma-força s. m. (phys.) kilogramme, a unit of force equal to the weight of a kilogramme.

quilogrâmetro s. m. (phys.) kilogrammeter: kilogrammetre: unit of work.

quilohertz s. m. (phys.) kilohertz: a unit of frequency (1,000 hertz).

quilolitro s. m. kiloliter, kilolitre: measure of capacity equal to a thousand liters.

quilombada s. m. (Braz.) common designation for Negro fugitive slaves who took refuge in the **quilombo**.

quilombo s. m. (Braz., hist.) hiding-place of fugitive Negro slaves.

quilometragem s. f. (pl. **-ens**) 1. a distance in kilometers. 2. a measuring in kilometers.

quilometrar v. 1. to express a distance in kilometers. 2. to measure in kilometers.

quilométrico adj. 1. kilometric(al): a) of, pertaining to or expressed in kilometers. b) measuring one kilometer. 2. (fig.) very extensive.

discurso ~ (fam.) long-winded speech.

quilômetro s. m. kilometer, kilometre: measure of length equal to a thousand meters.

quiloplastia s. f. (surg.) chiloplasty: any plastic operation upon the lip.

quiloplástico adj. (surg.) of or pertaining to chiloplasty.

quilópode s. m. 1. chilopod, centipede. 2. ~s pl. Chilopoda.

quilose s. f. chylification.

quiloso adj. chylous: of or pertaining to chyle.

quilovolt s. m. (electr.) kilovolt: one thousand volts.

quilowatt s. m. kilowatt: one thousand watts, a unit of electrical power.

~-hora (electr.) kilowatt-hour.

quilúria, quiluria s. f. (med.) chyluria: presence of chyle in the urine.

quimanga s. f. (N. Braz.) vessel made of a coconut shell for keeping food.

quimão s. m. (pl. **-ões**) kimono: 1. Japanese loose robe fastened with a rash. 2. a woman's loose dressing gown.

quimbanda s. m. 1. Indian witch doctor. 2. (Braz.) voodoo: a) sorcerer. b) rites, magic. 3. any place where voodoo rites are practiced.

quimbandeiro s. m. (Braz.) sorcerer, voodooist.

quimbembe s. m. (N. Braz.) 1. hut; grass shack. 2. ~s pl. amulets, witch charms; pendants, trinkets, gewgaws, fripperies. ‖ adj. ragged, in tatters, poor.

quimbembeques s. m. pl. (N. Braz.) pendants, fripperies, gewgaws; amulets.

quimbombô, quimbombó s. m. (Braz., also **quiabo**) okra.

quimera s. f. 1. (Gr. myth.) Chimera: a fire breathing monster. 2. chimera: a) an absurd mental image. b) fancy, reverie. c) fantastic conceit. 3. (fig.) (day-)dream.

quimérico adj. chimeric(al): 1. like a chimera. 2. imaginary, fanciful, fictitious. 3. visionary, fantastic, unreal. 4. romantic. ‖ **quimericamente** adv. chimerically.

quimerista s. m. + f. fantast, visionary, person who creates chimeras.

quimerizar v. 1. to create chimeras. 2. to imagine, suppose chimerically.

quimiatra s. m. + f. chemiatrist, iatrochemist.

quimiatria s. f. chemiatry, iatrochemistry, chemistry united with medicine.

química s. f. chemistry: science which treats of the composition of matter and its transformations.

~ **aplicada** practical chemistry. ~ **física** physical chemistry. ~ **geral** theoretical chemistry. ~ **industrial** industrial chemistry. ~ **inorgânica** inorganic chemistry. ~ **orgânica** organic chemistry.

químico s. m. chemist: person versed in chemistry. ‖ adj. chemic(al). ‖ **quimicamente** adv. chemically.

quimificação s. f. (pl. **-ões**) chymification: the formation of chyme.

quimificar v. to chymify: turn into chyme.

quimiluminescência s. f. luminous phenomena produced by some chemical reactions.

quimiotaxia s. f. chemotaxis.

quimioterapia s. f. chemotherapy.

quimismo s. m. 1. chemism. 2. chemical abuses.

quimitipia s. f. (printing) chemitype.

quimo s. m. chyme: the pulpy matter into which food is converted by gastric digestion.

quimono s. m. kimono: 1. Japanese loose robe fastened with a rash. 2. a woman's loose dressing--gown.

quimosina s. f. chimosin, rennin, enzyme in the gastric juice that coagulates milk.

quina (I) s. f. 1. corner or edge (as of a table top). 2. five spots (of a card, dice or domino); cinque. 3. a series of five numbers (at lotto). 4. one of the five shields of the Portuguese arms.

quina (II) s. f. (bot.) quina, quinaquina: 1. any of several shrubs or trees with a bitter bark out of which quinine is extracted. 2. cinchona bark, Jesuit's bark. 3. quinine.

quina-branca s. f. (Braz., bot.) (pl. **quinas-brancas**), (also **quina-da-chapada**, pl. **quinas-da-chapada**) copalche.

quina-caribé s. f. (Braz., bot.) (pl. **quinas-caribé**) princewood.

quinado s. m. cinchonized wine. ‖ adj. 1. quinate: a) arranged in five. b) (bot.) arranged in sets of five. 2. cinchonized.

quina-do-campo s. f. (Braz., bot.) (pl. **quinas-do--campo**) copalche.

quinanga s. f. (N. Braz.) wooden bucket to keep food in.

quinar v. 1. to cinchonize, treat with cinchona or quinine. 2. to win at keno or lotto. 3. to cover a row of five numbers (on a keno card).

quinário adj. 1. quinary: a) consisting of or containing five parts or elements. b) divided in a set of five. c) using five as a base (system of notation). 2. (mus.) having five beats (time or measure). 3. (poet.) of five feet (verse).

quinau s. m. 1. correction. 2. corrective, correctional mark (in a school lesson).

dar ~ to correct by word).

quina-vermelha s. f. (bot.) (pl. **quinas-vermelhas**) red bark cinchona (Cinchone succirubra).

quincólogo s. m. the five commandments of the R. C. Church.

quincha s. f. (S. Braz.) 1. thatched roof. 2. straw covering for huts (or carts).

quinchador s. m. (S. Braz.) thatcher.

quinchar v. (S. Braz.) to thatch: cover huts (or carts) with thatch or straw.

quincunce s. m. (also **quincôncio**) quincunx: arrangement of five things (as of trees) in a square with one in the center.

quincuncial adj. (pl. **-ais**) (bot.) quincuncial.

qüindecágono s. m. (geom.) quindecagon: a polygon of fifteen sides and fifteen angles.

qüindênio s. m. a set of fifteen.

quindim s. m. (pl. **-ins**) 1. voluptuous movement of the body. 2. prudery, primness. 3. embellishment. 4. petulant gracefulness. 5. graceful elegance, gentleness; meekness. 6. (pop.) difficulty. 7. (Braz.) a cake made with yolk, sugar and coconut.

quinecu s. m. (Braz.) a variety of rice.

qüingentésimo s. m. five hundredth. ‖ adj. five hundreth.

a -a parte the five hundredth part.

quingombô, quingombó, quingobó s. m. (Braz. = **quiabo**.

quingombô-de-espinho s. m. (Braz., bot.) (pl. **quingombôs-de-espinho**) uniccorn plant, devil's-claw.

quinguengu, quinguingu s. m. (Braz.) 1. overtime work; extra working hours. 2. forced extra work of slaves.

quinhão s. m. (pl. **-ões**) 1. portion, partition, parcel, quota. 2. allotment, apportionment, division. 3. (fig.) fate, destiny.

quinhentão s. m. (pl. **-ões**) (Braz., pop.) 1. five hundred réis (now fifty centavos). 2. five hundred thousand réis (now five hundred cruzeiros).

quinhentismo s. m. style, taste etc. characteristic of the cinquecentists.

quinhentista s. m. + f. cinquecentist: a writer of the 16th century. ‖ adj. of or pertaining to the 16th century.

quinhentos s. m. five hundred. ‖ adj. five hundred. **isso são outros ~ (cruzeiros)** (coll.) that is quite another question.

quinhoar v. to apportion, allot.

quinhoeiro s. m. partner; sharer.

quínico adj. (chem.) chinic. **ácido ~** chinic acid.

quinina s. f. (chem.) quinine: very bitter alkaloid obtained from cinchona barks.

quinínico adj. of or pertaining to quinine.

quinino s. m. quinine salts.

quínio s. m. quinine, not purified.

quinismo s. m. (med.) cinchonism: buzzing in the ears or temporary deafness caused by overdoses of cinchona or quinine.

quino s. m. keno, lotto.

qüinquagenário s. m. quinquagenarian: person of more than fifty and less than sixty years. ‖ adj. quinquagenarian: aged between fifty and sixty years.

qüinquagésima s. f. quinquagesima: a period of fifty days. **domingo da ~** Quinquagesima Sunday, Shrove Sunday.

qüinquagésimo s. m. fiftieth. ‖ adj. fiftieth. **a a- parte** the fiftieth part.

qüinqüeangular adj. m. + f. quinquangular, quinque-angled, having five angles.

qüinqüecapsular adj. m. + f. (bot.) quinquecapsular: having five capsules.

qüinqüecelular adj. m. + f. (bot.) having five cells.

qüinqüedentado adj. (zool.) quinquedentate: having five teeth.

qüinqüefoliado, qüinqüefólio adj. quinquefoliate, having five leaves or leaflets.

qüinqüenal adj. m. + f. (pl. **-ais**) quinquennial: occurring every five years.

qüinqüênio s. m. quinquennium: a period of five years.

qüinqüerreme s. f. (obs.) quinquereme: galley with five banks of oars.

qüinqüevalve adj. m. + f. (bot.) quinquevalve: provided with five valves.

qüinqüevalvular adj. m. + f. quinquevalvular: having five valves.

qüinqüevirado, qüinqüevirato s. m. 1. dignity of a quinquevir. 2. tribunal of quinquevirs.

qüinqüéviro s. m. (Roman hist.) quinquevir: one of five special commissioners.

qüinqüídio s. m. a period of five days.

quinquilharias s. f. pl. 1. children's toys. 2. gewgaws, trinkets, fripperies, baubles. 3. bagatelle, trifle.

quinquilheiro s. m. person who makes or sells baubles.

quinquina s. f. (Braz.) a rubiaceous plant with a bitter bark.

quinta s. f. 1. residence of a large rural property. 2. farm. 3. (mus.) fifth, quint. 4. short for **quinta--feira:** Thursday. **estar nas suas sete ~s** to be completely at ease, to be satisfied with life.

quintã adj. said of the quintan fever.

quinta-coluna s. f. 1. fifth column: a group of persons within a country who secretly aid its enemies. 2. m. + f. (pl. **quinta-colunas**) fifth columnist.

quinta-colunista s. m. + f. (pl. **quinta-colunistas**) fifth columnist.

quinta-essência s. f. (pl. **quinta-essências**) quintessence: 1. the pure essence. 2. the purest part (of anything). 3. refinement.

quinta-feira s. f. (pl. **quintas-feiras**) Thursday. **~ santa, ~ maior** Maundy Thursday. **na manhã de ~** on Thursday morning. **todas as quintas-feiras** every Thursday.

quintal s. m. (pl. **-ais**) 1. small rural property with a residence. 2. (back) yard. 3. quintal: former measure of weight, about 120 pounds. **~ métrico** modern quintal (measure of 100 kilograms, or about 220 pounds).

quintalão s. m. (pl. **-ões**) very large (back) yard.

quintalejo s. m. small (back) yard.

quintanista s. m. + f. a fifth-year student.

quintar v. 1. to divide by five. 2. to take the fifth part.

quinteira s. f. farmeress.

quinteiro s. m. farmer, farm caretaker.

quinteto s. m. 1. quintet(te): a) musical composition arranged for five voices or instruments. b) a group of five singers or players who perform quintets. c) any group or set of five (as of a basketball team). 2. = **quintilha**.

quintil adj. m. + f. (astr.) said of the aspect of two planets when separated by the fifth part of the zodiac.

quintilha s. f. a stanza of five verses.

quintilhão, quintilião s. m. (pl. **-ões**) quintillion: 1. (Braz., U. S. A.) a thousand quadrillions (1 followed by 18 ciphers). 2. (Engl.) a million quadrillions (1 followed by 30 ciphers).

quintilho s. m. (bot.) apple of Peru.

quinto s. m. 1. fifth, quint. 2. the fifth part. 3. barrel. 4. **~s** pl. (pop.) hell. ‖ adj. fifth. **vá para os ~s!** go to hell (and stay there)!

quintuplicação s. f. (pl. **-ões**) quintuplication.

quintuplicado adj. quintuplicate, fivefold.

quintuplicador s. m. person who quintuples. ‖ adj. quintuplicating, quintupling.

quintuplicar v. to quintuple, quintuplicate: 1. multiply by five. 2. become fivefold.

quintuplicável adj. m. + f. (pl. **-áveis**) capable of being quintupled.

quíntuplo s. m. quintuple: a quantity five times as great as another. ‖ adj. quintuple, fivefold.

quinze s. m. 1. fifteen. 2. (also **décimo quinto**) fifteenth. ‖ adj. fifteen; fifteenth. **~ para as três** a quarter to three. **daqui a ~ dias** this day fortnight. **dentro de ~ dias** inside of fifteen days. **férias de ~ dias** a fortnight's holiday. **seis horas e ~ minutos** a quarter past six.

quinzena s. f. 1. a period of fifteen days. 2. fortnight, two weeks. 3. (N. Braz.) rent payed by sugar cane planters to the owner of a sugar-mill and consisting of the fifteenth part of the sugar produced. 4. light double-breasted jacket.

quinzenal adj. m. + f. (pl. **-ais**) biweekly, fortnightly, occurring or appearing once in two weeks. ‖ **~mente** adv. biweekly, fortnightly.

quinzenalista s. m. + f. person who receives his salary every fortnight.

quinzenário s. m. a fortnightly periodical or publication.

quioiô s. m. (Braz., bot.) 1. sweet basil. 2. fever plant.

quiosque s. m., kiosk, news stand, band stand (plate E 13).

quiosqueiro s. m. owner of a kiosk.

quipo s. m. quipu, quipo: an aboriginal Peruvian device consisting of a cord with knotted strings of various colours for recording events, keeping accounts, etc.

qüiproquó s. m. (lat.) quid pro quo: misinterpretation.

quiquiriqui s. m. 1. cock-a-doodle-doo, the cock's crow. 2. person of no importance, a nobody. 3. trifle.

quiragra s. f. (med.) chiragra: gouty affection of the hand.

quirana s. f. (N. Braz.) 1. louse. 2. knot of hair. 3. (Port. Africa) eight yards of any cloth.

quirela, quirera s. f. (Braz.) 1. the coarser part of any pulverized substance. 2. broken corn (to feed chicken with). 3. ~s pl. (fig.) small change (money).

quirerear v. to crash corn grains for chicks.

quiri(m) s. m. (Braz., bot.) the Goeldi cordia.

quirina s. f. (Braz.) a toucan of the genus Ramphastar.

quiriquiri s. m. (Braz., ornith.) a small sparrow hawk.

quiriri s. m. (Braz.) dead of night. ‖ adj. 1. silent, still. 2. desert. 3. solitary.

quiriru s. m. (Braz., ornith.) = piriguá.

quirites s. m. pl. Quirites: the citizens of ancient Rome.

quirografário adj. (jur.) chirographary: written by o. s. and not authenticated.

quirografia s. f. chirography: the art, style and character of handwriting.

quirográfico adj. chirographic(al): of or pertaining to handwriting.

quirógrafo s. m. (jur.) chiropragh: 1. obligation given in one's own handwriting. 2. autograph.

quirologia s. f. dactylology: the use of the finger alphabet (as by deaf-mutes).

quirológico adj. of or pertaining to dactylology.

quiromancia, quiroscopia s. f. chiromancy, palmistry: divination by the marks in the palm of the hand.

quiromante s. m. + f. chiromancer, chiromant, palmist, fortuneteller.

quiromântico adj. chiromantic(al): of or pertaining to chiromancy.

quironomia s. f. chironomy: art of moving one's hands in oratory; gesture.

quironômico adj. relating to chironomy.

quirônomo s. m. practitioner or teacher of chironomy.

quiroplasto s. m. chiroplast: apparatus for facilitating the study of piano playing.

quiropodia s. f. chiropody, pedicure.

quiróptero s. m. (zool.) chiropter: a mammal of the order Chiroptera (a bat).

quisto (I) s. m. (med.) cyst, wen.
~ dermóide dermoid cyst. ~ sebáceo sebaceous cyst. ~ social (fig.) a social taint.

quisto (II) adj. (obs.) well-liked; beloved.

quitação (pl. -ões), quitança s. f. (also quitamento m.) 1. quittance: a) discharge or release (as from debt or obligation). b) repayment. 2. acquittance. 3. receipt.
~ plena e rasa receipt in full.

quitado adj. quit, quits.

quitador s. m. quitter: person who quits. ‖ adj. quitting, releasing, discharging.

quitanda s. f. 1. greengrocery: wares or shop of a greengrocer. 2. small shop. 3. tray of street venders. 4. (pop.) baubles, odds and ends.

quitandar v. to sell fresh vegetables and fruit as a greengrocer or street vender.

quitandê s. m. (Braz.) small green beans, used for soups and delicacies.

quitandeira s. f. (Braz.) 1. female greengrocer or a greengrocer's wife. 2. female street vender. 3. market woman. 4. fishwife; an abusive virago.

quitandeiro s. m. 1. greengrocer: a) retailer of fresh vegetables, fruit, eggs, etc. b) an owner of a greengrocery. 2. street vender, street peddler.

quitão s. m. (pl. ões) chiton: tunic worn by the ancient Greeks.

quitar v. 1. to quit: a) exempt, cease or desist from. b) liberate, free (from obligation). c) relieve, release, acquit (from). d) abandon, forsake. e) stop, discontinue. 2. to pardon, let off. 3. to avoid. 4. to prevent. 5. to spare. 6. to settle or adjust (accounts). 7. ~-se: a) to free o. s. b) to get rid of. c) to get divorced or legally separated (man and wife).
~ alguém de alguma coisa to free s. o. from s. th., to pardon a person for a thing.

quite adj. 1. quit, free (form obligations). 2. settled (accounts). 3. divorced.
estamos ~s (fig.) we have finished with each other. estar ~ to have got one's own back, to be paid up. estou ~ com ele I got square with him.

quitina s. f. chitin: the horny substance that forms the outer covering of crustaceans and some insects.

quitinoso adj. (biochem.) chitinous.

quitute s. m. (Braz.) 1. tasty appetizing dish, dainties; titbit. 2. (fig.) meekness, mildness; kindness, endearment.

quituteiro s. m. (Braz.) person skilled in preparing dainties or titbits.

quixaba s. f. 1. (bot., also quixabeira) a sapotaceous tree (Bumelia sartorum). 2. its fruit.

quixiligangue s. m. (Braz., pop. usually ninharia f.) triffle, bauble.

quixó s. m. (N. Braz.) a sort of trap (for small animals as the cavy).

quixotada, quixotice s. f. quixotry; vain boast; romantic and absurd notions or actions.

quixote s. m. quixote: 1. one who acts quixotically. 2. an ingenuous, romantic individual; a dreamer.

quixotesco adj. quixotic: extravagantly or absurdly romantic; pretentious, affected.

quixotismo s. m. quixotism.: 1. boasting, swaggering. 2. exaggerated chivalry.

quizila s. f. (also quizília) 1. repugnance, aversion, antipathy. 2. annoyance, anger. 3. enmity; disagreement.
fazer ~ a to annoy s. o. ter ~ a alguém to dislike s. o., be angry with s. o. ter ~s com to be at variance with.·

quizilar v. 1. to annoy, bore. 2. to irritate. 3. ~-se to get angry (with), become bored.

quizilento adj. annoying.

quociente s. m. (arith.) quotient: 1. result of a division. 2. the number of times one quantity or number is contained in another.

quorum s. m. quorum: number of persons required at an assembly.

quota s. f. (usually cota) quota, share, proportional part, portion, allotment.

quota-parte s. f. (pl. quotas-partes) share, investment.

quotidiano adj. (more frequently cotidiano) daily.

quotiliquê s. m. 1. person of no importance, nobody. 2. trifle, bauble.

quotização s. f. (pl. -ões) (usually cotização) 1. assessment, sharing, parcelling out. 2. stock exchange quotation.

quotizar v. (usually cotizar) 1. to distribute shares, parcel out, assess. 2. to note the stock exchange quotations.

R

R, r s. m. 1. the seventeenth letter of the Portuguese alphabet. 2. the medieval Roman numeral 80. 3. abbr. of **Réaumur** (thermometric scale); **réu** (defendant); **reprovação** (failure in an examination, rejection).

rã s. f. 1. frog. 2. tailless amphibian of the family Ranidae.

~-das-moitas a tree frog (Hyla raddiana). **~-do- -mar** frogfish. **~-gigante-touro** bullfrog.

rabaça s. f. 1. (bot.) a water parsnip. 2. (fig.) dunce.

rabaçã s. f. (ornith.) Paraguayan eared dove.

rabaçal s. m. (pl. **-ais**) 1. place where water parsnips grow. 2. a variety of a Portuguese cheese. ‖ adj. m. + f. of or referring to this cheese.

rabaçaria s. f. (pop.) 1. vegetables, greens. 2. fruits of inferior quality.

rabaceiro adj. fond of fruits and vegetables.

rabacuada s. f. (Braz.) rabble, populace.

rabada s. f. 1. tail. 2. plait of hair. 3. caudal fin. 4. rump, oxtail. 5. the last ones in a race. ,

rabadão s. m. (pl. **-ões**) herdsman.

rabadela, rabadilha s. f. 1. the tail or rump of animals. 2. a fisher's share in the catch.

rabado adj. tailed, caudate.

rabalva s. f. (ornith.) ern(e).

rabalvo adj. white-tailed.

rabanada s. f. 1. French toast. 2. stroke with the tail. 3. (fig.) blast of wind.

rabanal s. m. (pl. **-ais**) growth of radish.

rabanete s. m. (bot.) radish.

rábano s. m. 1. turnip. 2. the root of this plant. 3. horse-radish.

rábano-rústico s. m. (pl. **rábanos-rústicos**) (bot.) wild or field radish.

rabão s. m. (pl. **-ões**) (f. **rabana**) 1. = **rábano**. 2. (sl.) the devil. ‖ adj. 1. short-tailed. 2. bob-tailed.

rabavento adj. flying or sailing before the wind.

rabaz s. m. thief. ‖ adj. m. + f. rapacious.

rabdóide adj. m. + f., **rabdóideo** m. rhabdoid(al), spindle-shaped, rod-shaped.

rabdologia s. f. rhabdology, art or method of calculating by means of small rods.

rabdológico adj. rhabdological.

rabdomancia s. f. rhabdomancy, divination by rods or wands.

rabdomante s. m. + f. rhabdomancer, dowser.

rabdomântico adj. rhabdomantic.

rabeador adj. wagging, whisking (tail).

rabear v. 1. to wag, whisk (the tail). 2. to move restlessly, fidget. 3. to be restless or uneasy. 4. to wheedle around a person, flatter meanly.

rabeca s. f. 1. fiddle, violin. 2. (billiards) cue rest. 3. (ichth.) a fresh-water fish (Bunocephalus bicolor). 4. m. fiddler, violinist.

rabecada s. f. 1. fiddling, fiddle music. 2. (fig.) reprimand. 3. slander, backbiting.

rabecão s. m. (pl. **-ões**) 1. bass fiddle. 2. double bass. 3. (Braz., pop.) black van for the transportation of corpses.

rabeira s. f. 1. track, trace. 2. awn. 3. chaff. 4. tail of a gown. 5. (coll.) back part of anything.

rabejador s. m. bull catcher, one who holds a bull by the tail. ‖ adj. holding a bull by the tail.

rabejar v. to hold a bull by the tail.

rabela s. f. back part of a plough (from share to handle).

rabelaisiano adj. Rabelaisian, characteristic of Rabelais or his works.

rabelo s. m. 1. plough-tail (plate C 13). 2. handle of a plough.

rabequista s. m. + f. 1. fiddler, violinist. 2. (Braz., pop.) would-be-great, meddlesome person.

rabi s. m. rabbi, Jewish master of religious law. ‖ adj. m. + f. = **rabicó**.

rábia s. f. (med.) hydrofobia, rabies.

rabialvo adj. white-tailed.

rabiar v. 1. to rage, rave. 2. to act violently. 3. to grow impatient. 4. to become enraged.

rabiça s. f. plough-tail, plough handle (plate C 13).

rabiçaca s. f. (N. Braz.) 1. shove, push. 2. stroke with the tail.

rabicão (pl. **-ões**), **rabicano** adj. having threads of white hair in the tail (said of horses).

rabicha s. f. back part of a carriage.

rabicho s. m. 1. pigtail. 2. crupper (of a harness) (plate A 12).). tail. 4. hitch rope of a water-wheel. 5. (Braz.) stay. 6. (Braz., pop.) love, passion.

rábico adj. rabietic.

rabicó adj. tailless, docked.

rabicurto adj. short-tailed.

rábido adj. 1. rabid. 2. raging, furious. 3. wild, fierce.

rabifurcado adj. (zool.) fork-tailed.

rabigo adj. 1. that wags constantly its tail. 2. (fig.) active, diligent. 3. (fig.) restless, fussy.

rabilonga s. f. (ornith.) 1. a kind of blue magpie. 2. (Braz.) a squirrel cuckoo.

rabilongo adj. long-tailed.

rabinado s. m. rabbinate: the position or office of a rabbi.

rabinice s. f. 1. mischief, prank. 2. crossness, sullenness.

rabínico adj. rabbinic(al).

rabinismo s. m. rabbinism.

rabinista s. m. + f. rabbinist.

rabino (I) s. m. rabbi, master and teacher of Jewish religious law.

rabino (II) adj. 1. mischievous, frolicsome. 2. peevish cross.

rabioso adj. 1. rabid. 2. irritated, furious. 3. wild, fierce.

rabiosque, rabioste, rabiote s. m. (pop.) the posterior, behind.

rabipreto adj. (zool.) black-tailed.

rabirruivo adj. (zool.) red-tailed.

rabisca s. f. scrawl, scribbling.

rabiscado adj. scrawly.

rabiscador s. m. 1. scribbler. 2. scrawler. ‖ adj. scrawling.

rabiscar v. 1. to scribble, scrawl. 2. to write hastily or carelessly. 3. to draw doodles. 4. to scrabble, scratch.

rabisco s. m. 1. scribble, scrawl. 2. doodle(s). 3. scratch. 4. curlicue, flourish.

rabisseco adj. unproductive, barren, sterile.

rabisteco, rabistel s. m. (fam.) a child's buttocks.

rabo s. m. 1. tail, brush (plate C 12). 2. tail feathers, tail fin. 3. handle (of certain implements). 4. (fam., pop.) buttocks, bottom, posterior. 5. stern.

~ aparado bobtail. **~-de-andorinha** dovetail, swallowtail (plate C 9). **encher o ~** 1. to fill one's belly, to eat one's fill, to cram. 2. to satiate, surfeit. 3. to become annoyed, fed up, weary. **~ de cavalo** horsetail. **~ de peixe** fishtail. **~ do arado** ploughtail. **dar com o ~ na cerca** to kick the bucket, die. **deitar o ~ do olho** to look out of the corner of the eye, to leer upon. **falando do diabo**

aparece o ~ talk of the devil and he is sure to appear. **ele meteu o ~ entre as pernas** he became afraid. **pegar em ~ de foguete** to take the bull by the horns.

rabo-aberto s. m. (pl. **rabos-abertos**) (ichth.) yellow-tailed snapper.

rabo-de-cameleão s. m. (pl. **rabos-de-cameleão**) (Braz., bot.) 1. ifé. 2. African bowstring hemp.

rabo-de-cão s. m. (pl. **rabos-de-cão**) (bot.) dog's-tail.

rabo-de-galo s. m. (pl. **rabos-de-galo**) 1. mare's tail, cirrus cloud. 2. cocktail (appetizer).

rabo-de-macaco s. m. (pl. **rabos-de-macaco**) (bot.) crested dog's-tail.

rabo-de-palha s. m. (pl. **rabos-de-palha**) (Braz.) 1. blot, blemish. 2. (ornith.) red-billed tropic bird.

rabo-de-raposa s. m. (pl. **rabos-de-raposa**) (bot.) 1. bristly foxtail. 2. green foxtail grass. 3. love-lies-bleeding.

rabo-de-rojão s. m. (pl. **rabos-de-rojão**) (bot.) stinking roger.

rabo-de-saia s. m. (pl. **rabos-de-saia**) (Braz., fam.) woman.

rabo-de-tatu s. m. (pl. **rabos-de-tatu**) 1. riding crop. 2. (bot.) lady-slipper.

rabo-leva s. m., sg. + pl. paper or rag tail (primed on s. o. in fun).

rabona s. f. 1. short jacket. 2. (fam.) dress with a train. 3. dress coat. 4. hoe with a short handle.

rabanar v. 1. to crop an animal's tail. 2. to get ahead of (another horse at a race).

rabo-ruivo s. m. (pl. **rabos-ruivos**) (ornith.) black redstart.

raboso adj. long-tailed.

rabotar v. to plane, smooth.

rabate s. m. jack plane.

rabudo adj. long-tailed, tailed.

vestido ~ gown with a long train.

rabugem s. f. (pl. **-ens**) 1. (vet.) mange. 2. ill temper, crossness. 3. fretfulness.

rabugento adj. 1. (vet.) mangy (said of dogs). 2. morose, sullen. 3. cross, cantankerous. 4. (fig.) impertinent. 5. peevish, fretful. || **-amente** adv. peevishly, morosely, petulantly.

que pessoa -a! what a crank!

rabugice s. f. 1. peevishness, fretfulness. 2. crossness, petulance. 3. impertinence. 4. chicanery.

rabuja s. m. + f. cantankerous or peevish person. || adj. 1. cross, cantankerous. 2. peevish, fretful. 3. impertinent.

rabujado adj. said grumblingly.

rabujar v. 1. to act morosely. 2. to be impertinent. 3. to grumble. 4. to scold continually. 5. to whimper.

rábula s. m. 1. pettifogger, shyster. 2. talkative man, prattler.

rabulão s. m. (pl. **-ões**) 1. shyster, lawmonger. 2. boaster.

rabular v. (also **rabulejar**) 1. to pettifog, shyster. 2. to brag, boast. 3. to act in a petty or tricky manner.

rabularia, rabulice s. f. 1. pettifoggery, chicanery. 2. boast, bragging. 3. empty talk, prattle.

rabulista s. m. + f. trickster, pettifogger. || adj. pettifogging.

rabunar v. to prepare the bark of a cork-tree (for production of stoppers).

raça (I) s. f. 1. race. 2. generation, genealogical group. 3. origin, descent, lineage. 4. tribe, family. 5. stock, breed, strain. 6. mankind. 7. ethnical stock. 8. species, pedigree, ancestry.

a ~ amarela the yellow race. na ~ with might and main. a ~ humana mankind. cavalo de ~ thoroughbred horse. de boa ~ well-bred, high-bred.

de ~ mista half-bred. entre ~s diferentes interracial. não é de pura ~ it is underbred, it is not full-blooded.

raça (II) s. f. a crack in the hoof (horses, cattle).

raça (III) s. f. sunbeam.

raçador s. m. a domestic animal kept for breeding. || adj. breeding, reproductive.

ração s. f. (pl. **-ões**) ration, fixed daily allowance of food served out for man or animal; portion.

~ de reserva emergency ration. ~ dobrada double allowance. ~ para um dia daily allowance.

racemado adj. (bot.) racemose.

racêmico adj. (chem.) racemic.

racemífero adj. (bot.) racemiferous.

racemifloro adj. (bot.) racemiflorous.

racemiforme adj. b. + f. racemiform.

racemo s. m. (bot.) 1. raceme, cluster. 2. a bunch of grapes.

racemoso adj. (bot.) racemose, clustered.

racha s. f. 1. crack, cleft, fissure. 2. splinter, sliver, chip.

rachadeira s. f. cleaver, cleaving tool, grafting knife.

rachado adj. cleft, split, cracked.

rachador s. m. 1. woodcutter. 2. hewer, splitter. || adj. splitting.

rachadura s. f. 1. cleft, fissure, crack. 2. splitting, cleaving.

rachão s. m. (pl. **-ões**) (Braz.) 1. mountain gorge, defile. 2. a woodman's axe.

racha-pé s. m. (pl. **racha-pés**) a popular dance in which much noise is made with the heels of shoes; tap dance.

rachar v. 1. to split, cleave. 2. to splinter, shiver. 3. to chap, rive. 4. to insult, offend. 5. to treat roughly, abuse. 6. (Braz.) to split profits, expenses, etc. 7. to open, hew up. 8. ~-se to chink.

~ a conta to split the bill. ~ um madeiro em dois to cleave a block of wood in two. ou vai ou racha it's sink or swim, Pike's Peak or bust.

racial adj. m. + f. (pl. **-ais**) racial. || ~mente adv. racially.

racimo s. m. (bot.) 1. raceme, cluster. 2. a bunch of grapes.

racinar v. (bookbinding) to marble.

raciocinação s. f. (pl. **-ões**) reasoning, ratiocination.

raciocinador s. m. reasoner, ratiocinator. || adj. reasoning.

raciocinar v. 1. to reason, ratiocinate 2. to think. 3. to consider, deliberate. 4. to argue.

raciocinativo adj. ratiocinative, ratiocinatory, discursive.

raciocínio s. m. 1. ratiocination, reasoning. 2. thought. 3. judgment, reasoning power. 4. argumentation, inductions. 5. logic.

sem ~ irrational.

racionabilidade s. f. rationality, rationalness.

racionado adj. rationed, stinted.

ter a comida -a to be kept on short commons.

racional s. m. (pl. **-ais**) a rational being. || adj. m. + f. 1. rational, endowed with reason. 2. reasonable, sensible. 3. logical. 4. laboursaving, methodic(al). 5. sane. || ~mente adv. rationally.

quantidade ~ (math.) rational quantity.

racionalidade s. f. rationality, reasonableness, reason.

racionalismo s. m. 1. rationalism. 2. adherence to the supremacy of reason. 3. (philos.) doctrine that knowledge is exclusively the product of ratiocination.

racionalista s. m. + f. rationalist. || adj. rationalistic.

racionalização s. f. (pl. **-ões**) rationalization.

racionalizar v. 1. to rationalize, make conformable to reason. 2. to ratiocinate, reason. 3. to interpret by

rational principles. 4. to streamline business procedures or production methods.
racionamento s. m. rationing, ration.
racionar v. 1. to ration. 2. to supply with rations. 3. to divide into rations. 4. to put upon allowance.
racionável adj. m. + f. (pl. **-áveis**) reasonable.
racismo s. m. racism.
racista s. m. + f. racist. ‖ adj. racialistic.
raçoeiro s. m. distributer or receiver of rations.
racontar v. to narrate, relate.
raconto s. m. narration, story, report.
radar s. m. radar.
radiação s. f. (pl. **-ões**) 1. irradiation, emission and diffusion of rays. 2. radiation. 3. radiance, radiancy.
~ cósmica cosmic radiation.
radiado s. m. (zool.) the Radiata: a group of invertebrates. ‖ adj. (bot., zool.) radiate, radiated.
radiador s. m. radiator (plate V 3).
radial adj. m. + f. (pl. **-ais**) radial. ‖ **~mente** adv. radially.
radialista s. m. + f. broadcaster.
radiano s. m. (math.) radian, unit angle.
radiante adj. m. + f. 1. radiant, brilliant. 2. radiate. 3. beautiful. 4. splendid. 5. gleeful, joyous. ‖ **~mente** adv. radiantly.
~ de alegria flushed with joy.
radiar v. 1. to radiate, emit rays. 2. to sparkle, scintillate. 3. to beam. 4. to broadcast, transmit by wireless. 5. to difuse, divulge.
radiário s. m. (zool.) the Radiata.
radiatividade s. f. (chem.) radioactivity.
radiativo adj. radioactive.
radiator s. m. (Braz.) radio actor.
radicação s. f. (pl. **-ões**) radication, rootage, rootedness.
radicado adj. 1. radicated, rooted. 2. (fig.) inveterate.
radical s. m. (pl. **-ais**) radical: 1. (pol.) ultraist, adept of radicalism. 2. (phil.) primitive word, root of a word. 3. (math.) radical expression or sign (√). 4. (chem.) fundamental constituent of a compound. ‖ adj. m. + f. 1. radical: of or pertaining to a root. 2. basic, fundamental. 3. essential. 4. (pol.) leftist. 5. thoroughgoing. ‖ **~mente** adv. radically.
houve uma mudança ~ there was a radical change.
medida ~ radical measure.
radicalismo s. m. radicalism, ultraism.
radicalista s. m. + f. radical, ultraist. ‖ adj. m. + f. radical.
radicando s. m. (math.) radicand.
radicar v. 1. to radicate, take root. 2. to root. 3. to plant deeply and firmly. 4. to settle (down).
radicela s. f. (bot.) radicel, radicle, rootlet.
radiciação s. m. (math.) the process of extracting the root of.
radicícola adj. m. + f. radicicolous, living upon roots.
radicifloro adj. (bot.) radiciflorous.
radiciforme adj. m. + f. radiciform, rootlike.
radicívoro adj. radicivorous.
radícula adj. m. + f. radicicolous.
radicoso adj. radicose, rooty, full of roots.
radícula s. f. (bot.) radicule, radicle, rootlet (plate R 1).
radiculado adj. radicular, having roots, rooty.
radicular adj. m. + f. radicular, of or pertaining to roots.
rádio s. m. 1. (anat.) radius: the shorter of the two forearm or forelimb bones. 2. (chem.) radium: a radioactive, metallic element (Ra). 3. radio transmitter or receiver. 4. radiogram, wireless telegram. 5. radiometer.
~ amador ham(-operator.) **~ portátil** portable radio.
anunciador de ~ radio announcer. **aparelho de ~**

radio set. estação de ~ broadcasting station. **fratura do ~** (med.) fracture of the spoke-bone. **programa de ~** broadcast.
radioatividade s. f. radioactivity.
radioativo adj. radioactive.
tornar ~ (phys.) to (radio)activate.
radioator s. m. radio actor.
radioatriz s. f. radio actress.
radiocomunicação s. f. (pl. **-ões**) radio communication.
radiocondutor s. m. radioconductor.
radiocultura s. f. 1. (phys.) branch of physics which deals with the effects of (high-frequency, colour or ultrasonic) radiations on plant growth. 2. the cultural influence of radiobroadcastings.
radiodermite s. f. (med.) radiodermatitis, dermatitis caused by exposure to radiations.
radiodiagnóstico s. m. (med.) radiodiagnosis.
radiodifundir v. to radiobroadcast.
radiodifusão s. f. (pl. **-ões**) broadcasting.
radiodifusor s. m. broadcasting station, broadcaster. ‖ adj. broadcasting.
radioeletricidade s. f. radioelectricity.
radioemissora s. f. radio broadcasting station.
radioespectro s. m. (astr.) radio spectrum.
radiofarol s. m. (pl. **-óis**) radio beacon.
radiofone s. m. radiophone.
radiofonia s. f. radiophony.
radiofônico adj. radiophonic.
radiofonização s. f. (pl. **-ões**) adaptation of a script for radiobroadcasting.
radiofonizar v. to adapt a script for radiobroadcasting.
radiofreqüência s. f. radio frequency.
radiogoniometria s. f. radiogoniometry, direction finding.
radiogoniômetro s. m. radiogoniometer, direction finder.
radiografar v. 1. to radiograph. 2. to radiotelegraph, radio.
radiografia s. f. radiography, roentgenogram, x-ray photograph or inspection.
radiográfico adj. radiographic(al). ‖ **radiograficamente** adv. radiographically.
radiógrafo s. m. radiographer.
radiograma s. m. radiogram, wireless telegram or message.
radiojornal s. m. radio newscast.
radiola s. f. radiophonograph.
radiolário s. m. (zool.) radiolarian, specimen of the Radiolaria. ‖ adj. radiolarian.
radiologia s. f. radiology, roentgenology, science of radioactive substances and their application.
radiológico adj. radiologic(al).
radiologista s. m. + f. radiologist, roentgenologist.
radiometria s. f. (phys.) radiometry.
radiômetro s. m. 1. (naut.) cross-staff. 2. (phys.) radiometer.
radionovela s. f. (Braz.) radio soap opera.
radiopatrulha s. f. flying squad, radio patrol.
carro de ~ prowl car.
radioperador s. m. radio operator.
radioquimografia s. f. (med.) roentgen-kymography.
radioquimógrafo s. m. (med.) radio-kymograph.
radioquimograma s. m. (med.) radio-kymogram.
radiorreceptor s. m. radio receiver.
radioscopia s. f. radioscopy, fluoroscopy.
radioscópico adj. radioscopic(al).
radioso adj. 1. radiant, brilliant. 2. ecstatic. 3. jubilant, joyful. ‖ **-amente** adv. radiantly.
radiossonda s. f. (meteor.) radiosonde.
radioteatro s. m. radio theater.
radiotécnica s. f. radiotechnology.

radiotelefonia s. f. radiotelephony, radiophony.
radiotelefônico adj. radiotelephonic(al).
radiotelegrafia s. f. radiotelegraphy, wireless telegraphy.
radiotelegráfico adj. radiotelegraphic(al).
radiotelegrafista s. m. + f. radio operator, wireless operator.
radioterapêutico adj. radiotherapeutic(al).
radioterapia s. f. (med.) radiotherapy.
radioterápico adj. radiotherapeutic(al).
radiotransmissor s. m. transmitter.
radiouvinte s. m. + f. radio listener.
radônio s. m. (chem.) radon (Rn), niton.
raer v. 1. to sweep the (warm) furnace of a bakery after heating. 2. to pile up salt (in a salt bed).
rafa s. f. 1. (sl.) hunger. 2. (sl.) poverty, penury. 3. (naut.) full tide.
rafado adj. 1. hungry, starved. 2. shabby, threadbare. 3. poor, indigent.
rafaelesco adj. Raphaelesque, Raphaelic.
rafaelista, rafaelita s. m. Raphaelite, painter of the Raphaelic school.
rafaméia s. f. rabble, mob, riffraff.
rafar v. to waste, wear out, fray.
rafeiro s. m. cattle dog, watch-dog.
raffiné adj. (Fr.) 1. delicate, refined, polished. 2. developed to the utmost degree or extent. 3. highly cultured.
ráfia s. f. raffia: 1. (bot.) the palm. 2. its fiber.
ráfide s. f. (bot.) raphides.
rafigrafia s. f. art or system of writing for the blind, in which the letters are represented by raised dots.
rafigráfico adj. of or referring to Braille or similar systems of printing for the blind.
raflesiácea s. f. any plant of the rafflesia family.
raflesiáceo adj. (bot.) rafflesiaceous.
raglã adj. raglan.
ragóideo adj. aciniform.
ragu s. m. ragout.
raia s. f. 1. line, stroke, streak. 2. line in the palm of the hand. 3. octogonal paper kite. 4. race-course. 5. brand on a horse. 6. limit, boundary, ambit. 7. frontier, border. 8. (ichth.): a) common European skate. b) ray. 9. (sl.) blunder, boner, mistake.
~ **elétrica** (ichth.) electric ray. ~**s de uma arma de fogo** twist (of a gun). **fechar a** ~ (turf sl.) to come in last. **passar as** ~**s de** 1. to go too far. 2. to transgress. **tocar as** ~**s** to reach the limit.
raiado adj. 1. striped, streaked. 2. radiated. 3. veined.
raiano s. m. borderer. ‖ adj. bordering upon.
raia-pintada s. f. (pl. **raias-pintadas**) (ichth.) spotted sting-ray.
raiar v. 1. to break (the day), dawn. 2. to emit rays, radiate. 3. to shine, sparkle, gleam. 4. to come in sight, appear, peep out. 5. to rifle. 6. to stripe, streak. 7. to cover with strokes or lines. 8. to reach extremes. 9. to come nearer.
no ~ **do dia** at dawn.
raigota s. f. 1. rootlet, radicle. 2. hangnail.
raigotoso adj. radicant.
raineta s. f. 1. reinette, queen apple. 2. (zool.) tree toad.
rainha s. f. 1. queen. 2. the principal or first among others. 3. a variety of apples or pears. 4. queen bee (plate A 11).
~ **consorte** queen consort. ~ **do céu** Queen of Heaven. ~ **do mar** (Braz.) Iemanjá, queen of the ocean. ~ **mãe** queen mother. ~ **regente** queen regent. ~ **viúva** queen dowager.

rainha-cláudia s. f. (pl. **rainhas-cláudias**) greengage.
rainha-da-noite s. f. (pl. **rainhas-da-noite**) (bot.) queen of the night.
rainha-do-abismo s. f. (pl. **rainhas-do-abismo**) a gesneriaceous herb (Corytholoma canescens).
rainha-dos-lagos s. f. (pl. **rainhas-dos-lagos**) (bot.) water hyacinth.
rainha-dos-prados s. f. (pl. **rainhas-dos-prados**) meadowsweet, queen of the meadow.
rainha-margarida s. f. (pl. **rainhas-margaridas**) (bot.) China aster.
raio s. m. 1. ray, beam. 2. heat radiation. 3. (geom.) radius (plate A 9). 4. spoke of a wheel (plates B 11, R 2). 5. (fig.) signal, sign, indication. 6. flash of lightning, thunderbolt. 7. fatality, disgrace, misfortune. 8. turbulent person.
~ **de ação** sphere of action. ~ **de sol** sunbeam. ~**s alfa** (phys.) alpha rays. ~**s beta** (phys.) beta rays. ~**s catódicos** (phys.) cathode rays. ~**s cósmicos** cosmic rays. ~**s solares** sunshine. ~**s ultravioleta** ultraviolet rays. ~**s X** X rays, roentgen rays. ~ **visual** field of vision. **colocar** ~**s (numa roda)** to let in spokes. **com a rapidez do** ~ with lightning speed; in a flash. **como um** ~ like a streak. **um** ~ **de esperança** a gleam of hope. **partir como um** ~ to go off like a shot. **sem** ~ rayless.
raiva s. f. 1. rage, fury. 2. (vet.) hydrophobia, rabies. 3. hate. 4. dislike, aversion. 5. madness.
ele está com muita ~ he is angry, his bristles are up. **tenho-lhe** ~ I am cross with you.
raivar, raivecer v. 1. to rage, rave. 2. to be extremely angry or furious. 3. to be mad (dog). 4. to burn with desire or lust after. 5. to threaten, menace.
raivejar v. to become angry, shout angrily.
raivento adj. 1. furious, angry. 2. choleric.
raivoso adj. angry, furious, raging. ‖ **-amente** adv. ragefully.
raiz s. f. (pl. **raízes**) 1. root: a) subterranean part of a plant (plates A 14, R 1). b) the hidden cause of anything, base. c) lower part, bottom (plate A 14). d) origin, source. e) (gram.) elementary notional syllable of a word, primtive. f) (math.) root of a quantity. 2. (med.) radicles of a tumour. 3. original or principal site of a rural property.
~ **aérea** aerial root. ~ **cúbica** cube root. ~ **da cauda** tail head (plate G 1). ~ **da serra** foot of a mountain (range). ~ **de cabelo** bulb of a hair. ~ **de dente** fang. ~ **de gengibre** race-ginger. ~ **mestra** taproot. ~ **quadrada** square root. **arrancar com as raízes** to pluck out, (fig.) to destroy completely. **bens de** ~ landed property. **cheio de raízes** rooty. **lançar raízes** to take root, strike root. **até a** ~ **dos cabelos** up to the ears, to the neck, to the brim. **ter raízes** (fig.) to have taken deep roots. **ter raízes na terra** 1. to have landed property. 2. to come from the country.
raizada, raizama s. f., **raizame** m. rootage, roots of a plant; quantity of roots.
raiz-da-china s. f. (pl. **raízes-da-china**), (bot.) chinaroot.
raiz-de-chá s. f. (pl. **raízes-de-chá**), (bot.) tea palm, palm lily.
raiz-de-frade s. f. (pl. **raízes-de-frade**), (bot.) cahinca root.
raiz-de-lopes s. f. (pl. **raízes-de-lopes**), (bot.) Lopez root, Indian root.
raiz-doce s. f. (pl. **raízes-doces**), (bot.) licorice, liquorice.
raiz-do-sol s. f. (pl. **raízes-do-sol**), (bot.) Dutchman's-pipe, pipe.
raizeiro s. m. herb doctor.
raja s. f. stripe, streak.
rajá s. m. raja, rajah.

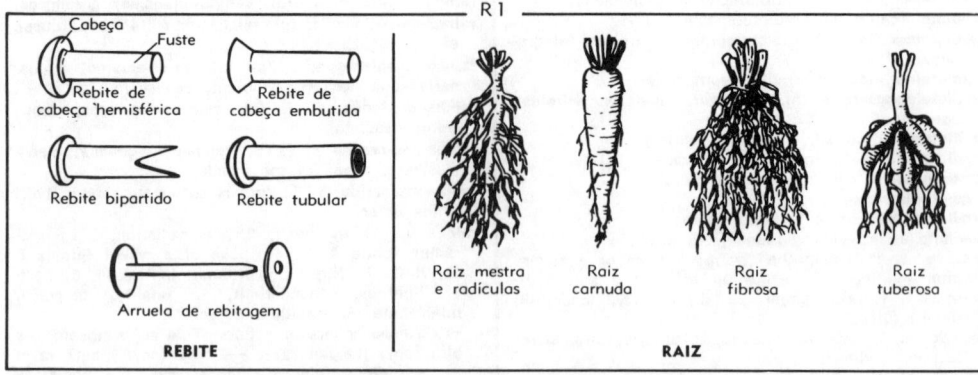

R 1

Cabeça
Fuste

Rebite de cabeça 'hemisférica

Rebite de cabeça embutida

Rebite bipartido

Rebite tubular

Arruela de rebitagem

REBITE

Raiz mestra e radículas

Raiz carnuda

Raiz fibrosa

Raiz tuberosa

RAIZ

rajada s. f. 1. gust of wind, squall, blast. 2. stroke with the tail. 3. (fig.) burst of eloquence. 4. impetuousness. 5. (Braz., mil.) running series of shots. ~ **forte** a heavy squall of wind. ~ **com chuva grosa** a squall of wind accompanied by torrential rain.

rajadão s. m. (Braz.) a mixed breed of cattle.

rajado (I) s. m. rajahship.

rajado (II) adj. striped, streaked, mottled.

rajar v. 1. to stripe, streak. 2. to intermingle. 3. to intersperse.

rajo s. m. part of a pine tree cut off in order to extract turpentine.

rala s. f. 1. (med.) rhonchus. 2. bran, brown flour. **pão de** ~ brown bread.

ralação s. f. (pl. -ões) 1. act of grating. 2. worry, vexation. 3. weariness.

ralador s. m. grater, rasper (plate C 20).

raladura s. f. 1. raspings, scrapings. 2. act of grating.

ralar v. 1. to grate, rasp. 2. to worry, annoy. 3. to chafe, fret. 4. to vex, harass.

isto me rala as tripas it goes against the grain; it is against my liking.

ralé s. f. 1. common people, riffraff, rabble, populace, mob. 2. animals on which raptorial birds usually prey.

raleadura s. f., **raleamento** m. act of thinning out (unripe fruit on trees, foliage) or making less compact.

ralear v. (also **ralentar**) to thin out, make sparse.

raleira s. f. empty spot in a field; glade.

raleiro s. m. (ornith.) water rail.

ralhação s. f. (pl. -ões) scolding, rebuke, chiding.

ralhador s. m. scolder, chider. ‖ adj. scolding.

ralhão s. m. (pl. -ões) (f. -ona) scolder, reprimander.

ralhar v. 1. to scold, rail. 2. to chide. 3. to reprimand, censure. 4. to find fault with. 5. to get angry.

ralho s. m. scolding, chiding, rebuke, reprimand.

ralídeos s. m. pl. (ornith.) Rallidae, the rail family.

ralo s. m. 1. grater, rasper. 2. strainer. 3. sprinkling nozzle. 4. grating. 5. (med.) rhonchus. 6. (zool.) mole cricket. ‖ adj. thin, rare, diluted.

rama s. f. 1. branches, boughs (of a tree). 2. foliage. 3. (weav.) tenter. 4. (typogr.) printer's chase.

lã em ~ raw wool. **pela** ~ superficially. **seda em** ~ raw silk. ~ **da vitória** palm of victory.

ramada s. f. 1. branches, boughs. 2. foliage. 3. trellis, latticework. 4. shelter for ranging cattle. 5. arbour, bower.

ramadã, ramadão s. m. Ramadhan: name of the ninth month of the Moslem year.

ramado adj. branchy, ramate, branched.

ramagem s. f. (pl. -ens) 1. branches, boughs, foliage (plate A 14). 2. (arts) floral or leaf pattern.

ramal s. m. (pl. -ais) 1. strands (of a yarn or rope). 2. railroad branch line. 3. string. 4. telephone extension line. 5. ramification. 6. tassel of a doctor's cap.

ramalhada s. f. 1. boughs, branches. 2. rustling of leaves.

ramalhão s. m. (pl. -ões) (Port., pop.) big branch. ‖ adj. bulky, large in size.

ramalhar v. to rustle, sough.

ramalheira s. f. 1. branches, boughs. 2. (naut.) rowlock strap.

ramalhete s. m. 1. little branch. 2. nosegay, little bunch of flowers, bouquet. 3. cluster. 4. hoarding.

ramalheteira s. f. flower-girl, female florist.

ramalho s. m. 1. big branch. 2. dead bough cut from a tree.

ramalhoso, ramalhudo adj. 1. branchy, full of boughs. 2. (fig.) long-winded, verbose. 3. having long eyelashes.

ramaria s. f. branches, boughs, foliage.

ramear v. to adorn with boughs or branches.

rameira s. f. prostitute.

rameiro s. m. best bidder on a part contract.

ramela s. f. = **remela**.

rameloso adj. blear-eyed, bleary.

ramento s. m. 1. fragment, particle, remnants. 2. (bot.) ramentum.

râmeo adj. growing on branches, rameous.

ramerrão s. m. (pl. -ões) 1. monotonous sound, dull routine, rut. 2. constant use.

rami s. m. ramie (plant and fiber).

ramificação s. f. (pl. -ões) 1. ramification. 2. branching, offshoot. 3. branches of a stem. 4. (fig.) propagation, diffusion.

ramificado adj. 1. ramified, branched. 2. subdivided. 3. forked, furcate.

ramificar v. 1. to divide into branches, ramify. 2. to furcate, subdivide. 3. ~**-se:** a) to branch off. b) (fig.) to propagate, diffuse.

ramifloro adj. (bot.) ramiflorous.

ramiforme adj. m. + f. (bot.) ramiform.

ramilhete s. m. = **ramalhete**.

ramilho s. m. small bough, twig.

raminho s. m. twig (plate A 14).

ramíparo adj. (bot.) ramiparous.

ramnácea s. f. plant of the buckthorn family (Rhamnaceae).

ramnáceo daj. (bot.) rhamnaceous.

ramo s. m. 1. branch, bough. 2. twig, sprig (plate E 8). 3. offshoot. 4. bunch of flowers, nosegay, bou-

quet. 5. division, subdivision, section. 6. ramification. 7. lot of goods bought at an auction. 8.
breadth of a sheet. 9. family branch. 10. (weav.)
passage of the shuttle. 11. branch of business or
profession, interest. 12. tavern bush or emblem.
~ de comércio branch of commerce. **~ de família**
stem (of a family). **~ de negócio** trade, line of
business. **~ de oliveira** olive branch. **~ do rio**
branch of a river. **Domingo de Ramos** Palm Sunday.
isto não é meu ~ this is not within my walk.
ele distinguiu-se em muitos ~s he distinguished
himself in many spheres. **ele nunca vai pôr o pé
em ~ verde** he will never prosper.
ramonadeira s. f. rasp file.
ramosidade s. f. branchiness.
ramoso adj. ramose, ramous, branchy, twiggy.
rampa s. f. 1. ramp, sloping roadway. 2. stage.
rampadouro s. m. sloping ground.
rampante adj. m. + f. (her.) rampant, combatant.
rampear v. to slope.
rampeiro adj. (S. Braz.) low-class, inferior.
ramudo adj. 1. ramose, branchy. 2. dense.
ramúsculo s. m. little branch, twig.
rana s. m. (Braz., sl.) waterfront thief, ship's pilferer.
ranário s. m. froggery, frog farm.
rançado adj. rancid, rank, stale.
rançar, rancescer v. to grow rancid, musty or stale.
ranchada s. f. crowd of people, band, gang.
ranchão s. m. (pl. **-ões**) (Braz.) barrack.
rancharia s. f. (Braz.) group of huts, hut camp.
rancheira s. f. (Braz.) lively folk dance (of Spanish-
-American origin).
rancheiro s. m. 1. messmate, regimental cook. 2.
(Braz.) caretaker of a hut camp.
ranchel s. m. (pl. **-éis**) small mess.
rancheria s. f., **rancherio** m. hut camp.
rancho s. m. 1. group of wanderers or revellers. 2.
fare, ration, chow, grub, food (for seamen, soldiers,
prisoners, etc.). 3. crowd of people. 4. soldiers'
mess. 5. (naut.) crew's quarters. 6. hut, shelter,
lodge, rancho.
~ carnavalesco (Braz.) a Carnival procession.
râncido, râncio adj. rancid, rank, musty.
ranco s. m. branch of a tree.
ranço s. m. 1. rancidity, rancidness. 2. rank smell. 3.
mustiness. 4. (fig.) old things or sayings, rubbish.
‖ adj. rancid, rank.
cheirar a ~ to have a rank smell. **criar ~** to grow
rancid.
rancor s. m. 1. rancour, deep-seated hate. 2. resentment. 3. spite, grudge, ill blood. 4. enmity.
guardar ~ a to have a down on. **sem ~** unresented.
ter ~ contra to bear s. o. a grudge.
rancora s. f. (arch.) altercation, dispute.
rancorar-se v. (arch.) to lodge a complaint.
rancoroso adj. 1. rancorous. 2. resentful, spiteful,
hateful. 3. malicious. ‖ **-amente** adv. rancorously.
rançoso adj. 1. rancid, rusty, rank. 2. stale, musty.
3. (fig.) antiquated, old-fashioned. ‖ **-amente** adv.
ranckly.
toicinho ~ rusty bacon. **tornar ~** to rancify.
randevu s. m. (Fr.) rendez-vous, a brothel.
ranfastídeo s. m. (zool.) specimen of the toucan
family (Ramphastidae). ‖ adj. of or pertaining to
this family.
ranfoteca s. f. (zool.) rhamphotheca.
rangedeira s. f. inner sole, piece of leather put
between the soles.
rangedor adj. m., **rangente** m. + f. creaking, grating.
ranger v. 1. to screak, creak. 2. to grate, grit. 3. to
cause to creak.
ele rangeu os dentes he gnashed his teeth.

rangido s. m. creaking, gnashing, screak.
ouvimos o ~ da porta velha we heard the grating
of the old door.
rangífer, rangífero s. m. (zool.) reindeer, caribou.
rangir v. 1. = **ranger**. 2. to screak, creak. 3. to grate,
grit. 4. to cause to creak.
rango s. m. (Braz., sl.) food; munchies, chow, grub.
ranhar v. to scratch, scrape.
ranheta s. m. + f. impertinent person, curmudgeon.
ranho s. m. snivel, snot, mucus from the nose.
ranhoso adj. snotty, snivelling, snot-nosed.
ranhura s. f. 1. groove (plates A 14, B 4, C 9, E 9).
2. notch rabbet. 3. slot, slit. 4. furrow, trench,
chase.
~ de guia guideway. **~ de um disco** (sound-)track
(record). **fazer ~** to gutter.
ranicultura s. f. frog breeding.
ranídeo s. m. (zool.) specimen of the family Ranidae
(frogs). ‖ adj. ranid.
ranilha s. f. frog of a horse's hoof (plate C 9).
ranino adj. (anat.) ranine.
ranu s. m. plant of the nettle family (Urtica utilis).
ranu-branco s. m. (pl. **ranus-brancos**) (bot.) false
nettle.
rânula s. f. (med.) ranula, small cystic tumour on the
underside of the tongue.
ranunculácea s. f. plant of the family Ranunculaceae.
ranunculáceo adj. (bot.) ranunculaceous.
ranúnculo s. m. (bot.) lesser spearwort, ranunculus,
buttercup, crowfoot.
~ rasteiro creeping buttercup.
ranúnculo-aquático s. m. (pl. **ranúnculos-aquáticos**)
water crowfoot.
ranúnculo-dos-jardins s. m. (pl. **ranúnculos-dos-jar-
dins**) (bot.) Asiatic crowfoot.
ranúnculo-dos-prados s. m. (pl. **ranúnculos-dos-prados**)
(bot.) paigle, meadow crowfoot.
ranzinza adj. m. + f. 1. sullen, sulky. 2. ill-humoured.
3. unruly. 4. impertinent. 5. crabby, crabbed.
ranzinzar v. (Braz.) to be or become sullen, cantankerous or unruly.
rapa s. f. 1. teetotum, small four-sided toy of the top
kind marked with letters on each side, which indicate the player's score. 2. (fam.) glutton.
rapace adj. m. + f. rapacious, ravening.
rapáceo adj. (bot.) resembling a bobtail.
rapacidade s. f. rapacity, rapaciousness, ravenousness.
rapa-cuia s. f. (pl. **rapa-cuias**) (zool.) 1. a snout
beetle. 2. small frog which lives on plants of the
pineapple family, (also called **rapa-coco**).
rapadeira s. f. scraper, rasp, scraping knife.
rapadela s. f. scraping, scratching, rubbing.
rapado adj. 1. scraped, rasped. 2. cropped. 3. clean-
-shaven.
rapador s. m. 1. scraper. 2. (Braz.) completely grazed
or short-cropped pasture. ‖ adj. scraping, rasping.
rapadouro s. m. pasture which has been grazed clean.
rapadura s. f. 1. scraping, scrapings. 2. raspings. 3.
block of raw brown sugar.
rapagão s. m. (pl. **-ões**) strong, healthy lad.
rapalhas s. f. litter of manure which remains in
a stable.
rapante adj. m. + f. (her.) represented in the posture
of scraping the ground.
rapão s. m. (pl. **-ões**) 1. person who gathers litter or
manure. 2. a saltmaker's rake.
rapapé s. m. 1. curtsy, scrape. 2. servile greeting. 3.
flattery, adulation.
fazer ~ to make a leg; scrape a leg.
rapar v. 1. to scrape, scratch. 2. to wear out. 3.
to cut, cut off or short. 4. to rasp, grate. 5. to
cause the death of. 6. to shave close to the skin.
7. to steal, rob. 8. to extort cunningly, cheat. 9.

R 2

RAPOSA

Orelha / Cabeça / Olho / Rabo / Pata / Animal carnívoro

RODA

Bocal / Raio / Pneu / Eixo / Cubo / Válvula / Aro / Roda de bicicleta

ROLAMENTO DE ESFERAS

Esfera / Corrediça interna / Corrediça externa

to paw the ground (horses, dogs, etc.). 10. ~-**se** to shave o. s., cut one's hair.
rapariga s. f. 1. girl, maiden. 2. (pop.) lass, filly.
raparigaça s. f. strong, comely girl.
raparigada s. f. a lot of girls.
raparigota s. f. lass, filly.
raparigueiro s. m. (Braz.) woman chaser. ‖ adj. woman-chasing.
rapa-tábuas s. m., sg. + pl. mediocre carpenter.
rapa-tachos s. m. + f., sg. + pl. gorger, greedy eater, plate licker.
rapateácea s. f. plant of the family Rapateaceae.
rapaz (I) s. m. 1. boy, lad. 2. youth, youngster. 3. young man, fellow, chap. 4. (Braz.) Negro stripling. 5. errand boy, servant. 6. (ornith.) a snipe (Capella undulata).
  ~ **casquilho** knut. ~ **enérgico** a lively, active fellow, (sl.) live wire. ~ **travesso** urchin. **ele é um bom** ~ he is a good sort.
rapaz (II) adj. m. + f. rapacious.
rapazelho, rapazete s. m. litt!e boy, urchin.
rapaziada s. f. 1. a lot of boys, gang of urchins. 2. boyish act or saying, mischievous trick. 3. folly, prank. 4. spree, frolic.
rapazinho s. m. 1. little boy, kid. 2. (Braz., ornith.) spotted sandpiper.
  ~ **de recados** call-boy.
rapazinho-dos-velhos s. m. (pl. **rapazinhos-dos-velhos**) (ornith.) puffbird.
rapazio s. m. 1. group of boys. 2. boys or young men collectively.
rapazola s. m. lad, young man.
rapazote s. m. = **rapazelho.**
rapé s. m. snuff, rappee.
  caixinha de ~ snuff-box.
rapeira s. f. spawning ground.
rapezista s. m. + f. snuff-taker.
rapidez s. f. 1. rapidity. 2. quickness, swiftness. 3. speed, velocity. 4. haste.
  a ~ **das impressões visuais** the fleetingness of visual impressions.
rápido s. m. 1. rapids, chute, swift current. 2. express or special delivery service. 3. express train, fast day train. ‖ adj. 1. rapid, quick, swift. 2. speedy. 3. instantaneous, prompt. 4. active, sharp, brisk. 5. hasty. ‖ **rapidamente** adv. rapidly, speedily, apace, double-quick.
  ~ **como um raio** quick as a lightning. **de tiro** ~ quick-fire (gun). **uma dança** -**a** a giddy dance. **mudança** -**a de tempo** a sudden change in the weather. **uma resposta** -**a** an early reply. **submeter a congelação** -**a** to quick-freeze. **ele aprende rapidamente** he is quick at learning. **eles com-**

preendem rapidamente they are quick of apprehension. **espalha-se rapidamente** it spreads like wildfire.
rapilho s. m. 1. volcanic dust. 2. seaweeds used as manure.
rapina s. f. rapine, robbery, plunder.
  ave de ~ bird of prey.
rapinador s. m. plunderer, robber. ‖ adj. plundering.
rapinagem s. f. (pl. -**ens**) robbery, plunder, pillage.
rapinante s. m. + f. robber, plunderer. ‖ adj. plundering, pillaging, predatory.
rapinar v. 1. to rob, plunder. 2. to take away by force. 3. to commit robbery.
rapineiro s. m. (Braz.) bird of prey. ‖ adj. rapacious, raptorial.
rapioca s. f. (sl.) 1. spree, revel, noisy merrymaking. 2. extravagancy. 3. a rich repast.
rapistro s. m. (bot.) a kind of wild turnip.
rapôncio, raponço s. m. (bot.) 1. rampion. 2. horned rampion.
raposa (ô) s. f. 1. (zool.): a) fox (plate R 2). b) vixen, female fox. 2. fur of a fox. 3. (fig.) sly fellow, cunning or contriving person. 4. (fam.) failure in an examination. 5. (ichth.) thresher.
  caçador de ~ fox-hunter. **cova de** ~ fox hole. ~ **voadora** (zool.) flying fox.
raposada s. f. 1. nap, doze. 2. undisturbed sleep.
raposar v. (Port., fam.) 1. to play truant, shirk lessons. 2. to idle about. 3. to reproof, reprimand. 4. to reject a student (examination).
raposear v. (Braz.) to reject, plough a student in an examination.
raposeira s. f. 1. deep undisturbed sleep. 2. a nap in the mild sun. 3. intoxication, drunkenness. 4. fox hole.
raposeiro s. m. sly or cunning fellow. ‖ adj. sly, artful, cunning.
raposia, raposice s. f. 1. slyness of a fox. 2. artfulness, cunningness. 3. malice, ill will.
raposinhar v. to act in a sly or cunning manner, proceed artfully.
raposinho s. m. 1. fox cub. 2. strong, disagreeable smell (like that of a fox). 3. noxious exhalation.
raposino adj. vixenish, vixenly.
raposo (ô) s. m. 1. (zool.) male fox, dog-fox. 2. sly, cunning fellow.
rapsódia s. f. rhapsody: 1. (hist.) portion of an epic poem (e. g. the Iliad or the Odyssey). 2. literary miscellany. 3. excerpt from a poem. 4. (mus.) improvisation.
rapsódico adj. rhapsodic(al).
rapsodista s. m. + f. rhapsodist.

rapsodo s. m. 1. rhapsode, itinerant bard. 2. (fig.) poet.

rapsodomancia s. f. rhapsodomancy: divination by means of verses.

rapsodomante s. m. + f. rhapsodomancer.

rapsodomântico adj. of or referring to rapsodomancy.

raptado s. m. the victim of a kidnapping. || adj. kidnapped, abducted.

raptar v. 1. to ravish, abduct. 2. to kidnap. 3. to rob, plunder. 4. to grab, snatch away.

rapto (I) s. m. 1. abduction, ravishment. 2. kidnapping. 3. pillage, plunder. 4. rapture, ecstasy.

rapto (II) adj. (poet.) 1. rapid, swift. 2. ecstatic, rapturous.

raptor s. m. abductor, ravisher, kidnapper. || adj. abducting, ravishing, kidnapping.

raque s. f. 1. (anat.) rachis, spinal column. 2. (bot.): a) central axis of an inflorescence. b) the principal petiole of a pinnately compound leaf. 3. (zool.) shaft of a feather.

raqueano adj. rachidean.

raquel s. f. (pl. -éis) (bot.) Guernsey lily or flower.

raqueta s. f. 1. racket, racquet. 2. snow-shoe.

raquialgia s. f. (med.) rachialgia, pain in the spine.

raquianestesia s. f. (med.) spinal anesthesia.

raquidiano adj. rachidian.

raquiocentese s. f. (med.) rachicentesis: puncture into the spinal canal.

ráquis s. f. = raque.

raquítico s. m. rachitic man. || adj. 1. rachitic, rickety. 2. scrubby, stunted.

raquitismo s. m. 1. (med.) rachitis, rickets, inflammation of the spine. 2. (bot.) blight, abortion of seeds. 3. (fig.) feebleness of intellect, weakness of character.

rarear v. 1. to make rare, rarefy. 2. to diminish in density, quantity or number. 3. ~-se to become scarce, rare or thin.

rarefação s. f. (pl. -ões) rarefaction, rarefication, tenuity.

rarefaciente adj. m. + f. rarefactive, rarefying, producing rarefaction.

rarefatível adj. m. + f. (pl. -íveis) rarefiable, capable of being rarefied.

rarefativo adj. rarefactive, rarefying.

rarefato adj. rarefied.

rarefator s. m. rarefactor, rarefactive instrument or device. || adj. rarefactive, rarefying.

rarefazer v. 1. to rarefy; make thin, rare or scarce. 2. to reduce the density of. 3. to dilate, expand. 4. to spread, disperse. 5. ~-se to become rarefied or scarce.

rarefeito adj. rarefied, less dense, tenuous.

rareza s. f. rareness, rarity, scarcity.

raridade s. f. 1. rareness, rarity. 2. infrequency. 3. thinness. 4. uncommonness, unusualness. 5. scarceness, sparseness. 6. singularity, curiosity. 7. extraordinariness, remarkable success.

rarifloro adj. (bot.) rariflorous.

rarípilo adj. having rarely any at all or only a thin coat of hair.

raro adj. rare: 1. unfrequent, sporadic, seldom. 2. thin, not dense. 3. common, unusual. 4. scarce, sparse. 5. singular, unique. 6. subtle, tenuous. 7. extraordinary, exquisite. 8. excellent. 9. small in number or quantity. || -amente adv. rarely, seldom, scarcely, uncommonly.

-as vezes rarely, seldom, few and far between. mato ~ a thin forest. pulso ~ slow pulse. rede -a a net with wide meshes. terra -a (chem.) rare earth.

rás (I) s. m. arras, French tapestry.

rás (II) s. m. ras: title of an Abyssinian prince.

rasa s. f. 1. old dry measure; grain strickle. 2. tariff for manuscripts. 3. rock bottom price. 4. loss of reputation, discredit.

rasadura s. f. act of measuring corn with a strickle.

rasante adj. m. + f. 1. levelling. 2. smoothing, skimming. 3. (fort.) running near or parallel to.

rasão s. m. (pl. -ões) a large strickle (about 20 litres).

rasar v. 1. to measure with a strickle. 2. to level, raze, equalize. 3. to become full. 4. to overflow. 5. to touch lightly, graze. 6. to fill to the brim.

rasca s. f. 1. dragnet, trawl-net. 2. small two-masted fishing boat. 3. (pop.) share in the profit.

rascada s. f. 1. trammel, trawl-net. 2. (fam.) difficulty, vicissitude. 3. predicament, plight, fix. 4. (Port., pop.) swindle, crooked business, rascality.

rascadeira s. f. currycomb.

rascador s. m. rasp, scraper.

rascadura s. f. abrasion, scratch, scratching.

rascância s. f. 1. dryness of wine. 2. tartness, astringency.

rascante s. m. strong, cheap wine. || adj. m. + f. tart, sour, that scratches the throat, sharp to the taste.

rascão s. m. (pl. -ões) 1. vagabond, vagrant, loater. 2. page, manservant. 3. towing-line of a fishing-net. 4. mutton stew.

rascar v. 1. to rasp, grate. 2. to scratch. 3. to splinter, sliver. 4. to pare down, roughhew. 5. to wound, injure. 6. to annoy, disturb. 7. (arch.) to play the lute. 8. to cry, shout, call s. o. in a loud voice.

rascoa s. f. 1. nursemaid, governess. 2. cook, kitchen maid.

rascolnismo s. m. faith and religious principles of a Russian orthodox sect.

rascolnista, rascolnita s. m. + f. disciple of a Russian orthodox sect. || adj. of or referring to this sect.

rascunhar v. 1. to sketch, outline, draw the outline of. 2. to jot down, make rough notes of.

rascunho s. m. 1. first plan, draft, sketch. 2. outline, rough copy. 3. minute, memorandum. 4. rough sketch block.

raseiro adj. 1. flat, shallow. 2. levelled (with a strickle).

rasgadela s. f. rending, tearing, ripping, rent.

rasgado adj. 1. torn, rent. 2. frank, open. 3. unconstrained, unreserved. 4. liberal. 5. lavish, profuse. boca -a large mouth. ele é um homem ~ he is a generous man. sua roupa estava totalmente -a his clothes were torn to shreds.

rasgador s. m. tearer, ripper. || adj. tearing, ripping.

rasgadura s. f. 1. rent, tear. 2. act of rending or tearing. 3. breach. 4. opening, aperture. 5. laceration. 6. gash.

rasgamento s. m. 1. act of rending, tearing or ripping. 2. rent, tear. 3. opening, aperture.

rasga-mortalha s. f. (pl. rasga-mortalhas) (Braz., ornith.) the Paraguayan snipe.

rasgão s. m. (pl. -ões) tear, rent, gash, rip.

rasgar v. 1. to tear, rend. 2. to split, cleave. 3. to lacerate. 4. to wound, hurt. 5. to make a hole in, bore. 6. to open, make an opening. 7. to dissipate, disperse. 8. to touch, move to compunction. 9. to widen, extend. 10. to aggravate, make worse. 11. to plough. 12. to appear, peep. 13. ~-se: a) to manifest itself. b) to become divided or separated. c) to become afflicted or distressed. d) to widen or extend itself.

~ ao meio to tear across. ~ cortesias to be excessively polite. ~ em pedaços to tear to pieces. ~ pelo meio to tear in two. ~ sedas to wear silk ostentatiously, show-off. ela rasgou seu vestido she tore her dress.

rasgo s. m. 1. rip, tear. 2. split, cleft. 3. scratch. 4. dash, verve, spirit. 5. flash of wit or eloquence. 6. generous or noble deed, heroic act. 7. (pop.) self-assurance, ease. 8. expedience, resourcefulness. ~ **de chaveta** key seat. ~**s de eloqüência** bursts of eloquence. **de um** ~ for good, once for all.

raso s. m. 1. plain, flatland, open country. 2. fine, brilliant silk fabric. || adj. 1. even, level. 2. flat, plain. 3. creeping, trailing. 4. common, vulgar, low. 5. (mil.) private, noncommissioned. 6. (Braz.) shallow, not deep (plate Q). **cadeira -a** stool. **campanha -a** flat open country. **corrida -a** flat race. **deixar** ~ to cut very short. **doidice -a** downright madness. **medida -a** strait measure. **soldado** ~ private. **tábua -a** tabula rasa. **tornar tudo** ~ to lay everything flat, to level with the ground. **vagão** ~ platform car.

rasóforo s. m. rhasophore: novice of a monastic order who has not yet received the little habit.

rasoura s. f. 1. strickle, strike. 2. any instrument which serves to level or equalize. 3. rasp, coarse file. 4. burnisher, polisher.

rasourar v. 1. to level with a strickle. 2. to make even, equalize. 3. to put on the same level with.

raspa (I) s. f. shaving, scrapings, filings, chip.

raspa (II) s. f. (Port.) piece of candy.

raspadeira s. f. 1. scraper, scratcher (plates A 7, P 12). 2. rasp. 3. eraser.

raspadela s. f. 1. act of scraping or rasping. 2. erasure. 3. abrasion.

raspado adj. shaven.

raspador s. m. 1. scraper, scratcher, skimmer (plate F 7). 2. eraser, rubber. 3. rasper. 4. raker. || adj. rasping, scraping.

raspadura, raspagem (pl. **-ens**) s. f. 1. scrapings, filings. 2. chipping, splinter. 3. abrasion, erasion. 4. rasure, erasure. 5. rasping.

raspança s. f. 1. scrapings, filings. 2. (Braz.) reprimand, censure.

raspanete s. m. 1. reprimand, censure. 2. scolding. 3. dressing-down.

raspão s. m. (pl. **-ões**) 1. scratch, slight injury on the skin. 2. chafing, gall, sore caused by friction. **a bala tocou-lhe de** ~ the bullet grazed him slightly. **de** ~ obliquely. **ele respondeu de** ~ he answered crossly.

raspar v. 1. to scrape, scratch. 2. to rasp, grate, abrade. 3. to rase, erase. 4. to shave. 5. to destroy. 6. to rub out, wipe off. 7. to touch, wound slightly. 8. ~**-se** to scamper off, escape, run away. **ele escapou raspando** he had a narrow escape.

raspe s. m. 1. a cooper's scraper. 2. (fam.) reprimand, censure.

raspilha s. f. a cooper's scraper, edging tool.

rasqueiro adj. (Braz.) difficult, rare, hard to get.

rasqueta s. f. (naut.) deck scraper.

rasqueteação s. f. (pl. **-ões**) act of currying horses.

rasquetear v. to currycomb.

rasqueteio s. m. act of currying horses or cattle.

rastão s. m. (pl. **-ões**) twig left on the stem of a grape-vine at pruning.

rastaqüera s. m. + f. parvenu, person who has suddenly risen to great wealth; upstart, show-off.

rastaqüerar v. to act like a parvenu, show off.

rastaqüerismo s. m. behaviour of a parvenu, mannerisms of the nouveau riche.

rastear v. to track down, trace, look for something.

rasteira s. f. (pop.) act of tripping a person up, trip. **dar** or **passar uma** ~ **em** 1. to trip a person up. 2. to get the better of. 3. to deceive or delude s. o.

rasteirinha s. f. a low malvaceous herb (Sida procumbens).

rasteiro s. m. (Braz.) bush of the family Polygalaceae (Cryptostomum multicaule). || adj. 1. creeping, crawling. 2. low. 3. humble, modest. 4. abject, contemptible. 5. vulgar, mean. **planta -a** (bot.) creeper.

rastejador s. m. 1. searcher, inquirer. 2. tracer, tracker. 3. creeper. || adj. searching, tracing, trailing.

rastejar v. 1. to trace, track. 2. to follow the track, trace down, pursue. 3. to investigate, inquire into, examine. 4. to calculate approximately, estimate. 5. to drag one's feet, creep, crawl on all four. 6. to show low-mindedness or lack of principles. 7. (fig.) to debase o. s., eat humble pie.

rastejo s. m. 1. tracing, trailing. 2. act of following by the track. 3. (fig.) inquiry, investigation. 4. creeping, crawling.

rastelar v. to hackle, comb, ripple (flax, hemp, etc.)

rastelo (ê) s. m. 1. flax-comb, hackle, ripple. 2. harrow. ~ **para quebrar torrões** clod-crusher.

rastilho s. m. 1. train, line of gunpowder leading to a charge. 2. fuse. 3. (fig.) the alleged or real cause of violent social commotion or agitation (strike, revolution, war).

rasto s. m. 1. track, trace. 2. mark, sign. 3. step, footprint. 4. wake. 5. vestige, spoor. 6. clue. 7. scent. ~ **de pólvora** a train of gunpowder. **andar pelo** ~ **duma moça** to court a girl. **andar de** ~ to creep, crawl. **levar de** ~ to drag along. **seguir pelo** ~ to trace. **sem** ~ trackless. **no seu** ~ on your trail.

rastolho s. m. 1. stubble, stubble field. 2. noise, din, uproar.

rastrear v. 1. to trace, track. 2. to trace down, pursue. 3. to investigate. 4. to calculate approximately. 5. to harrow.

rastrilho s. m. 1. (fort.) portcullis. 2. harrow.

rastro s. m. 1. = **rasto.** 2. (agric.) manure rake. 3. dragnet, trawlnet.

rasura s. f. 1. erasure, rasure. 2. scrapings, filings. 3. place in a text where an erasure was made. 4. grated medicinal herbs or drugs. 5. obliteration.

rasurado adj. 1. that which presents an erasure, a rasure. 2. erased, scratched out, effaced.

rasurar v. 1. to erase, blot out. 2. to scrape, grate. 3. to reduce to filings or chips.

rata s. f. 1. female rat. 2. (sl.) fecund woman. 3. inopportune or improper act. 4. failure, flop, blunder.

ratada s. f. 1. nest of rats. 2. lots of rats. 3. prank, lark, mischief.

ratado adj. infested with rats, eaten by rats.

ratafia s. f. ratafia: any sweet liqueur flavoured with fruit kernels.

ratânia s. f. (Braz.) 1. (bot.) Peruvian or knotty rhatany. 2. the root of this plant used in medicine.

ratânia-do-pará s. f. (pl. **ratânias-do-pará**) (Braz., bot.) Pará or Brazilian rhatany.

ratão s. m. (pl. **-ões**) 1. a large rat. 2. (ichth.) a kind of ray (Miliobatis aquila). 3. (fam.) queer or eccentric fellow. || adj. odd, extravagant, queer, eccentric.

ratão-do-banhado s. m. (pl. **ratões-do-banhado**) (zool.) coypu, nutria.

rataplã, rataplão s. m. rataplan, sound of drumming.

ratar v. to bite or gnaw like a rat.

rataria s. f. lots of rats.

ratazana s. f. 1. female rat. 2. large rat. 3. (zool.) brown or Norway rat. 4. m. + f.: a) queer, funny fellow. b) (Braz., sl.) thief.

rateação s. f. (pl. **-ões**) apportionment, proration, allotment.

rateador s. m. portioner, distributor of proportional shares.

rateamento s. m. apportionment, allotment.

ratear v. 1. to divide proportionally, prorate, average. 2. to portion out, distribute. 3. to assess and give every one his just share.

rateio s. m. 1. apportionment, proportional distribution. 2. proration. 3. allotment, share. 4. (naut.) average.

~ **da transformação de energia** (electr.) power.

rateiro s. m. ratter, ratcatcher. ‖ adj. ratting.

gato (cão) ~ good ratcatching cat (dog).

ratel s. m. (pl. **-éis**) (zool.) ratel.

ratice s. f. 1. amusing act or saying. 2. witty remark, joke. 3. oddity, eccentricity, extravagance.

raticida s. m. rat poison, raticide.

ratificação s. f. (pl. **-ões**) 1. ratification, act of ratifying. 2. confirmation, approbation, sanction. 3. enactment.

ratificado adj. ratified, confirmed, sanctioned.

ratificar v. 1. to ratify. 2. to confirm. 3. to approve or sanction formally. 4. to validate. 5. to corroborate, reaffirm.

ratificável adj. m. + f. (pl. **-áveis**) ratifiable, confirmable, sanctionable.

ratinhar v. 1. to pinch and screw. 2. to be exceedingly parsimonious. 3. to haggle over (prices).

ratinheiro adj. 1. thrifty, parsimonious. 2. haggling, chaffering.

ratinho s. m. 1. small rat or mouse. 2. (fam.) a baby's first tooth. 3. (Port., prov.) moment, instant, short space of time.

ratita s. f. (ornith.) ratite (ostriches, emus, cassowaries, moas).

ratívoro adj. that eats mice or rats.

rato (I) s. m. 1. mouse, rat. 2. (fig.) thief, pilferer. ‖ adj. mouse-coloured.

~ **da Índia** ichneumon. ~ **de biblioteca** bookworm. ~ **de hotel** hotel thief. ~ **gigante** bandicoot. **a bom** ~ **bom gato** tit for tat. ~ **de sacristia** a devotee who lives in churches and sacristies. **estar como o** ~ **no queijo** to feel perfectly well. **muito sabe o** ~ **mas mais o gato** everybody meets with his peer.

rato (II) adj. 1. ratified, confirmed, sanctioned. 2. eccentric, odd, singular, strange.

rato-almiscarado s. m. (pl. **ratos-almiscarados**) muskrat.

rato-branco s. m. (pl. **ratos-brancos**) (S. Braz., pop.) policeman, watchman.

rato-das-searas s. m. (pl. **ratos-das-searas**) harvest mouse.

rato-de-água s. m. (pl. **ratos-de-água**) water rat.

rato-de-espinho s. m. (pl. **ratos-de-espinho**) spiny rat.

rato-doméstico s. m. (pl. **ratos-domésticos**) black rat.

ratoeira s. f. 1. mouse-trap, rat-trap. 2. artifice, trick. 3. snare.

ratona s. f. 1. female rat. 2. large rat. 3. (fig.) eccentric woman. ‖ adj. queer, odd, eccentric, peculiar.

ratoneiro s. m. pilferer, filcher, fingerer, petty thief.

ratonice s. f. pilferage, filching, petty theft.

raucíssono adj. raucous.

ravina s. f. 1. mountain stream. 2. ravine, deep gulch. 3. steep riverbank. 4. arroyo. 5. coulee.

raviôli s. m. Italian ravioli.

raxa s. f. (arch.) coarse cotton fabric.

razão s. f. (pl. **-ões**) 1. reason, reasoning power. 2. good sense, right judgement. 3. justice, right. 4. moral law. 5. cause, motive. 6. argument. 7. proof. 8. knowledge, 9. notice. 10. share, rate. 11. (math.) ratio: relation between two quantities of the same species, proportion. 12. account. 13. m. (com.) ledger book.

~ **de Estado** reason of state. ~ **direta** direct ratio. ~ **natural** common sense. **à** ~ **de** at the rate of. **à** ~ **de dez por cento** at the rate of ten percent. **a** ~ **voltou a imperar** reason resumed her sway. **apresentar -ões** to adduce. **ceder à** ~ to yield to reason. **com toda** ~ with good reason. **com** ~ **ou sem ela** by hook and crook. **ela perdeu a** ~ she lost her reason. **ele tem** ~ he is quite right. **eles tinham boas -ões para acreditar que** they had good reasons to think that. **fortes -ões para fazer** good grounds for doing. **idade da** ~ age of discretion. **lançar no livro** ~ (com.) to carry to the ledger. **não há** ~ **para não dizer a ela** we may well tell her. **nós estávamos sem** ~ we were in the wrong. **pela mesma** ~ for the same reason. **por aquela** ~ for that reason. **por esta** ~ on that account. ~ **social** registered name (comercial or industrial firm). **sem** ~ innocent of reason, reasonless, unfounded, groundless. **tem muita** ~ you are quite right, you have good reason. **você tem** ~ **neste ponto** you are correct in that.

razia s. f. razzia: 1. foray, raid. 2. incursion. 3. plundering, looting. 4. (fig.) destruction. 5. attack.

razoado s. m. 1. plea, defense. 2. speech, discourse. ‖ adj. reasonable, rational. ‖ **-amente** adv. reasonably.

razoamento s. m. 1. reasoning, drawing inferences. 2. argumentation. 3. pleading, defense (of a lawyer).

razoar v. 1. to reason, infer, conclude. 2. to argue. 3. to plead a cause, defend. 4. to discourse.

razoável adj. m. + f. (pl. **-áveis**) 1. reasonable, sensible. 2. rational. 3. sane, sound. 4. moderate, open-minded. 5. tolerant, just. 6. fair, decent. ‖ **razoavelmente** adv. reasonably, rightly, justly.

queixa ~ a reasonable complaint.

ré (I) s. f. (jur.) female defendant or criminal.

ré (II) s. f. stern of a ship.

à ~ (naut.) astern. **marcha à** ~ reverse speed. **para a** ~ toward the stern. **pôr de** ~ to put aside, disregard, spurn.

ré (III) s. m. (mus.) re: the second note of the diatonic scale.

reabastecer v. 1. to supply with fresh provisions. 2. to renew the stocks, replenish. 3. revictual or provision abundantly.

~ **de combustível** to refuel.

reabastecimento s. m. replenishment, restocking, renewal of provisions.

reabertura s. f. reopening.

reabilitação s. f. (pl. **-ões**) 1. rehabilitation. 2. reinstatement. 3. reacquisition of credit or public recognition. 4. justification.

~ **dentária** dental rehabilitation. ~ **motora** motor rehabilitation.

reabilitado adj. rehabilitated, reinstated, justified.

reabilitador s. m. rehabilitator. ‖ adj. rehabilitative.

reabilitar v. 1. to rehabilitate. 2. to reinstate. 3. to re-establish former rights or privileges. 4. to whitewash. 5. to right, justify, clear. 6. to reacquire credit or public esteem. 7. **~-se** to become regenerate.

reabitar v. to re-inhabit.

reabrir v. 1. to reopen, open again. 2. **~-se** to be opened again.

reabsorção s. f. (pl. **-ões**) reabsorption, resorption.

reabsorver v. to reabsorb, resorb, swallow or suck in again.

reação s. f. (pl. **-ões**) 1. reaction. 2. (mech.) resistance. 3. (chem.) chemical transformation or change. 4. (med.) physiological opposition or response. 5. (pol.) countertendency, conservativeness.

~ **ácida** (chem.) acid reaction. ~ **em cadeia** chain reaction. ~ **nuclear** nuclear reaction. ~ **psicológica** psychic response.

reacender v. 1. to light again, relight, rekindle. 2. to activate. 3. to incite, rouse, stir up. 4. to develop. 5. ~-**se** to take hear, cheer up, become encouraged.

reacionário s. m. reactionary, conservative or reactionary. person. ‖ adj. reactionary, opposing liberty and progress.

reacomodar v. to accommodate again, readapt to.

reacusação s. f. (pl. -**ões**) 1. act or effect of accusing again. 2. recrimination, countercharge.

reacusar v. 1. to reaccuse, accuse again. 2. to recriminate, make a countercharge.

readaptação s. f. 1. readaption. 2. (jur.) more compatible investiture in a public office.

readaptar v. 1. to readapt. 2. (jur.) to effect the readaptation of.

readmissão s. f. (pl. -**ões**) readmission, readmittance.

readmitir v. to readmit, admit again.

readormecer v. 1. to fall asleep again. 2. to put to sleep again.

readquirir v. 1. to reacquire. 2. to recover, get back, retrieve. 3. to repurchase, redeem.

reafirmação s. f. (pl. -**ões**) reaffirmation, reassertment.

reafirmar v. to reaffirm, reassert.

reagente s. m. 1. any substance employed to detect the presence of other ones, agent. 2. (chem.) reagent. ‖ adj. m. + f. reactive, reacting.

~ **de ensaio** test reagent. **papel** ~ litmus paper.

reagir v. 1. to react. 2. to answer, respond. 3. to resist. 4. to act in return, counteract. 5. to be opposed, fight against. 6. (mil.) to make counterattacks.

ele não reage he is not responsive. **ele só reage à voz dela** he stirs only to her voice. **não** ~ **a** to be irresponsive to.

reagradecer v. to thank again, renew one's thanks.

reagravação s. f. (pl. -**ões**) 1. new offense. 2. act or circumstance that aggravates again the seriousness of a situation, exacerbation.

reagravar v. 1. to renew an offense. 2. to make worse or aggravate again, exacerbate.

reagrupamento s. m. reassemblage, rally.

reagrupar v. to regroup, reassemble.

reajuntar v. to reassemble, recollect.

reajustamento s. m. readjustment, rearrangement.

reajustar v. 1. to readjust, adjust anew. 2. to rearrange, readapt. 3. (Braz.) to adjust wages or salaries to rising living costs.

reajustável adj. m. + f. (pl. -**áveis**) readjustable.

real (I) s. m. (pl. **reais**) 1. former Portuguese silver coin. 2. former unit of the Portuguese and Brazilian monetary system.

real (II) s. m. (pl. **reais**) 1. camping ground. 2. village, hamlet. 3. rural festivity.

real (III) adj. m. + f. (pl. **reais**) 1. royal, regal. 2. kingly, princely. 3. noble, generous. 4. magnificent, sumptuous. ‖ ~**mente** adv. regally.

ele pertence à família ~ he wears purple.

real (IV) s. m. (pl. **reais**) reality, fact. ‖ adj. 1. real, actual, factual. 2. true, truthful. 3. honest. 4. genuine. 5. certain. ‖ ~**mente** adv. really, actually, truthfully, honestly, indeed.

alegria ~ veritable joy. **como na vida** ~ true to life. **ele fez** ~**mente o que tencionava fazer** he actually did what he intended to do. **era** ~**mente magnífico** it was just marvellous. **estive lá** ~**mente** indeed I was there. **eu o encontrei** ~**mente** I met him as a matter of fact. **foi** ~**mente um problema** it was quite a problem. **número** ~ (math.) real, real number. **potência** ~ (electr.) true power. ~**mente nunca lhe escrevi** it is true I have never

written to her. ~**mente não tenho culpa!** I am sure I can't help it! **valor** ~ economic value.

realçar v. 1. to raise to a higher place. 2. to render conspicuous, enhance. 3. to bring into prominence. 4. to intensify, accentuate, emphasize. 5. to dignify, give distinction to. 6. ~-**se** to rise, ascend, come to prominence, elevate o. s.

as flores ~**am a sua beleza** the flowers underlined her beauty.

realce s. m. 1. distinction. 2. enhancement. 3. high spot. 4. relief. 5. lustre, brilliancy, splendour.

bordar de ~ to trim with embroidery. **dar** ~ **a** to set off, enhance, be a foil to.

realegrar v. 1. to make happy again. 2. ~-**se** to rejoice, become happy again.

realejar v. (Braz.) to repeat over again (like a street organ).

realejo s. m. 1. street organ, barrel organ, hurdy-gurdy. 2. (ornith.) a variety of wren (Leucolepia musica). 3. (Braz.) mouth organ.

tocador de ~ street organ grinder.

realengo adj. 1. royal, regal, kingly. 2. (Port. prov.) disorderly, inordinate. 3. (Braz.) unclaimed, ownerless, public.

realeza (I) s. f. 1. royalty, regality. 2. kingship. 3. (fig.) crown. 4. member of the royal family. 5. (fig.) magnificence, pomp.

realeza (II) s. f. reality, realness, fact.

realgar s. m. (min.) realgar, arsenic monosulfide.

realidade s. f. 1. reality, realness. 2. actuality, fact. 3. truth, verity. 4. (philos.) real, positiveness. 5. substantiality.

as esperanças não corresponderam à ~ facts did not come up to their expectations. **eles tinham de enfrentar a** ~ they had to face hard facts. **na** ~ as a matter of fact, for true, in the concrete.

realimentação s. f. (pl. -**ões**) 1. (electr.) self-excitation. 2. (radio) feedback, regeneration.

realismo (I) s. m. realism: 1. (philos.) doctrine that universals exist independent of intelectual perception. 2. (psych.) doctrine that we have an immediate perception of things external to us. 3. (arts) tendency to represent things in their real forms, fidelity to nature. 4. practical action and/or policy.

realismo (II) s. m. royalism, attachment to the cause of royalty or monarchic government.

realista (I) s. m. + f. realist: adherent of realism. ‖ adj. realistic(al).

ele tem um espírito ~ he has a fact-facing mind.

realista (II) s. m. + f. royalist, supporter of a monarchic government, legitimist. ‖ adj. royalistic(al).

realístico adj. realistic.

realização s. f. (pl. -**ões**) 1. realization. 2. realizing, state of being realized. 3. accomplishment, achievement, attainment. 4. execution, consummation. 5. (com.) turnover, conversion into money (of goods). 6. holding (of a reunion, assembly, etc.) 7. production, fruition.

~ **dos nossos planos** materialization of our plans. ~ **do casamento** consummation of marriage.

realizado adj. realized, accomplished, fulfilled, consummated.

realizador s. m. realizer, accomplisher, executor, producer. ‖ adj. realizing, performing, accomplishing, pushful.

realizar v. 1. to realize. 2. to bring to pass, carry through, put into practice. 3. to fulfil, achieve, accomplish. 4. to consummate. 5. (com.) to transact, convert into cash. 6. to perceive, recognize as fact. 7. ~-**se** to happen, come about, take effect. 8. to produce, create.

a reunião realizou-se em the meeting was held at. **ele conseguiu** ~ **os seus planos** he went through

with his plans. **precisaram** ~ **todo o capital necessário** they had to raise all the necessary money.
realizável adj. m. + f. (pl. -áveis) realizable, achievable, accomplishable, possible.
realugar v. to relet.
reamanhecer v. 1. to awaken again, reawaken. 2. to rejuvenate.
reanexar v. to reannex, reattach, reincorporate.
~**am o país perdido** they reoccupied their lost country.
reanimação s. f. (pl. -ões) reanimation, revivification.
reanimado adj. reanimated, revived, reinvigorated.
reanimador s. m. encourager, reviver. ‖ adj. reanimating, reviving, refreshing, stimulating, encouraging.
reanimar v. 1. to reanimate, restore to life. 2. to revive, revivify. 3. to strengthen, reinvigorate. 4. to refresh. 5. ~**se** to recover hope, courage or energy, respire, rally.
ela reanimou-se she plucked up heart.
reaparecer v. to reappear, appear again.
reaparecimento s. m. reappearance.
reaparelhamento s. m. re-equipment, refitting.
reaparelhar v. to re-equip, refit, prepare for use again.
reaparição s. f. (pl. -ões) reappearance, act or fact of reappearing.
reaplica v. to reapply.
reaprender v. to learn again.
reapresentar v. to present, perform or play again.
reaquecer v. to reheat.
reaquisição s. f. (pl. -ões) reacquisition, repurchase.
reaquistar v. 1. to reacquire, repurchase. 2. to reconquer, recapture.
rearmamento s. m. rearmament, rearming.
rearmar v. to rearm, re-equip with arms.
reascender v. to reascend, rise or ascend again.
reassinar v. to sign again.
reassumir v. 1. to reassume, assume again. 2. to reacquire, repurchase. 3. to retake, recover, resume.
reassumível adj. m. + f. (pl. -íveis) resumable, recoverable.
reassunção s. f. (pl. -ões) reassumption, act of retaking or recovering.
reata s. f. 1. halter rope, hitching rope. 2. ~**s** pl. (naut.) coils of rope, woolding s.
reatado adj. bound or tied again.
reatadura s. f. 1. rebinding, refastening. 2. ~**s** pl. (naut.) wooldings, coils of rope tied round a mast, etc.
reatamento s. m. 1. act or effect of rebinding, reattachment. 2. continuation, re-establishment.
reatância s. f. (electr.) reactance, capacitance, inductance.
reatar v. 1. to rebind, reattach. 2. to reassume, re-establish. 3. to renew, recommence. 4. to take up again, proceed.
~**am os laços de amizade** they renewed their old friendship.
reate s. m. halter rope, hitching rope.
reativar v. to reactivate, revive, reanimate.
reatividade s. f. reactivity, condition of being reactive.
reativo s. m. (chem.) reagent, reactive agent. ‖ adj. reactive.
reato s. m. 1. (jur.) reatus: state or condition of a defendant. 2. (theol.) obligation of active repentance after absolution.
reator s. m. reactor, reagent. ‖ adj. reacting, reactive.
~ **atômico** atomic reactor. ~ **nuclear** nuclear reactor.
reaver v. 1. to have again, get back. 2. to reobtain, recover. 3. to retrieve, recuperate.

reaviar v. 1. to bring again on the right way. 2. to orient, redirect, 3. to guide anew. 4. ~**se:** a) to find one's way again. b) (fig.) to see one's way again.
reavisar v. to advise or warn again.
reaviso s. m. renewed advice or warning.
reavivar v. 1. to revive (memories). 2. to recall, remember well. 3. to renew. 4. to stimulate reminiscences.
eles ~**am aquela velha história** they hashed up that same old story.
rebaçã s. f. (Braz., ornith.) Paraguayan eared dove.
rebaixa s. f. 1. lowering of prices, reduction. 2. abatement, diminution, deduction.
rebaixado adj. 1. lowered, let down again. 2. (fig.) discredited, debased, defamed. 3. despicable, contemptible.
rebaixador s. m. 1. one who lowers (prices), underseller. 2. (carp.) fillister, rabbet plane.
rebaixamento s. m. 1. lowering. 2. reduction. 3. degradation, debasement. 4. depreciation, decrease in value.
rebaixar v. 1. to lower, let down. 2. to reduce the price or value of, cheapen, depreciate. 3. to degrade, demote, debase. 4. to vulgarize. 5. to discredit. 6. to humiliate, humble. 7. (carp.) to plane down, rough-plane. 8. ~**se** to debase o. s., humble o. s.
o concorrente rebaixou os preços the competitor undercut prices. ~**am o fundo do poço** they deepened the well.
rebaixe, rebaixo s. m. 1. lowering, act or result of letting down s. th. 2. reduction, depreciation. 3. degradation, humiliation. 4. depression, hollow place. 5. recess, indentation. 6. (carp.) rabbet, groove. 7. (archit.): a) span of a staircase. b) garret chamber. c) areaway.
rebalçar v. 1. to become boggy or marshy. 2. to stagnate, be or become stagnant. 3. (fig.) to make or become corrupt.
rebanhada s. f. 1. a large flock, big herd. 2. (fig.) multitude, crowd.
rebanhar v. 1. to unite in a herd, form a flock. 2. to gather, collect. 3. to reunite. 4. to agglomerate, crowd together.
rebanhio adj. living in herds or flocks.
rebanho s. m. 1. flock of sheep, herd of cattle. 2. drove, bunch, troop. 3. cattle, livestock. 4. (rel.) congregation. 5. (ornith.) kestrel. 6. rabble, crowd.
rebar v. to fill up a wall with rough stones or rocks.
rebarba s. f. 1. sharp edge, barb. 2. (met.) burr, fin. 3. prong of a jewel mounting. 4. (typogr.) space between two regular lines of print.
rebarbar v. to remove the burr, trim off, deburr, plane.
rebarbativo adj. 1. double-chinned, fat. 2. (fig.) rough, coarse, uncouth. 3. surly, sullen, crabbed, cross. 4. irritating, provoking. 5. disagreeable.
rebate s. m. 1. act or effect of striking again. 2. repelling, act of beating back (enemy). 3. sudden invasion, surprise attack. 4. act or signal of warning, alarm. 5. (fig.) tip, hunch. 6. reminder. 7. terror, fear, fright. 8. (com.) discount, deduction.
dar ~ to give alarm. **sino de** ~ storm bell. **tocar a** ~ to sound the tocsin. ~ **falso** false alarm.
rebatedor s. m. (com.) discounter, bill broker, exchange broker. ‖ adj. 1. striking or beating again. 2. alarming. 3. discounting.
rebater v. 1. to strike again. 2. to repel, beat back (enemy). 3. to parry a blow. 4. to refute, disprove. 5. to restrain, curb, hold in check. 6. to fight (disease). 7. (com.) to discount. 8. to criticize,

censure. 9. to clinch (a nail). 10. (sports) to return, kick back. 11. to bend (hammering).

~ **uma acusação** to refute a charge. ~ **força com força** to repel force by force. **ele rebateu seu detrator** he silenced his maligner. ~ **uma dor** to assuage a pain.

rebatida s. f. 1. repellence. 2. act of driving back (enemy). 3. (sport) rally, undercut. 4. refutation, disproof.

rebatido adj. 1. repelled, beaten back. 2. much beaten, trampled or pressed down. 3. clinched (nail). 4. (com.) discounted. 5. refuted, disproved.

rebatimento s. m. 1. striking, beating again. 2. driving away, pushing back, repulsion. 3. (com.) discount, deduction. 4. (mat.) axonometric projection. 5. reverberation.

rebatinha s. f. 1. children's toy, plaything. 2. any thing much sought after.

às ~**s** provoking rivalry. **andar às** ~**s** to compete with, strive for. **vender à** ~ to sell to the highest bidder.

rebatismo s. m. (rel.) rebaptization, rebaptizing.

rebatizador s. m. (rel.) rebaptizer. ‖ adj. rebaptizing.

rebatizar v. to rebaptize, rechristen.

rebato s. m. 1. threshold, doorsill. 2. stairstep.

rebeca s. f. (Braz., pop.) = **rabeca**.

rebeijar v. to kiss again.

rebel s. m. (pl. -**éis**) rebel. ‖ adj. m. + f. rebel, contumacious.

rebelado s. m. rebel, mutineer.

rebelador adj. rebellious, insurgent, defiant.

rebelão adj. (pl. -**ões**) 1. unmanageable, restive (horse). 2. obstinate, headstrong. 3. unruly. 4. refractory.

rebelar v. 1. to stir up to rebellion, cause to revolt. 2. to rebel, revolt (against). 3. ~-**se**: a) to stand up against, rise against. b) (fig.) to oppose, resist.

eles se ~**am contra os seus opressores** they arose against their oppressors.

rebelde s. m. + f. 1. rebel, insurgent, mutineer. 2. deserter. ‖ adj. m. + f. 1. rebel, insurgent, revolutionary. 2. unsubmissive, disobedient. 3. unruly, defiant. 4. (med.) refractory. ‖ ~**mente** adv. rebelliously, disobediently, refractorily.

ele sofreu duma tosse ~ he suffered from an obstinate cough.

rebeldia s. f. 1. rebellion, insurrection, revolt. 2. rebelliousness. 3. (fig.) opposition, resistance. 4. (med.) refractoriness. 5. defiance, disloyalty. 6. obstinacy, stubbornness.

rebelião s. f. (pl. -**ões**) 1. rebellion, revolt. 2. insurrection, mutiny. 3. disobedience, insubordination. 4. (fig.) opposition, resistance.

rebelionar v. to stir up to rebellion, cause to revolt.

rebeloso adj. rebellious, insurgent, unsubmissive, defiant.

rebém (I) s. m. (pl. -**éns**) whip, lash.

rebém (II) adv. (obs.) very well, splendid.

rebencaço s. m., **rebencada** f. a flick with a whip.

rebenque s. m. (Braz.) quirt, horsewhip.

rebenqueado adj. (S. Braz.) 1. beaten, whipped, flogged. 2. tired, worn out.

rebenqueador s. m. (S. Braz.) 1. flogger, whipper. 2. one who punishes frequently. 3. (fam.) seductive or fascinating quality of a person which causes a lover's undoing.

rebenquear v. (S. Braz.) 1. to whip, flog. 2. (fig.) to mistreat, hurt (esp. a lover's feelings).

rebentação s. f. (pl. -**ões**) 1. act of bursting, breaking open. 2. pounding of waves, surf.

rebentão s. m. (pl. -**ões**) 1. shoot, offshoot, sprout. 2. (fig.) progeny, offspring. 3. scrub vegetation. 4. (Port.) steep street or way.

rebentãozal s. m. (pl. -**ais**) (S. Braz.) tract of land covered with scrubs and brushes.

rebentar v. 1. to burst, split open. 2. to blow up, explode. 3. to thrust forward. 4. to roar, resound. 5. to outburst. 6. to break lose. 7. to fall into pieces, crack, split. 8. to irrupt, emanate. 9. to begin to blossom. 10. to appear suddenly, become manifest. 11. to shoot, sprout. 12. to be dominated (by violent feelings). 13. to tire out, drive to death (a horse).

~ **a chorar** to burst into tears. ~ **de gordo** to become very fat. ~ **de riso** to burst out laughing. ~ **em blasfêmias** to burst out in curses. **a guerra rebentou** war broke out. **rebentou em chamas** it flared into flames.

rebentina, rebentinha s. f. (fam.) 1. rage, anger. 2. fit of rage, outburst of fury. 3. passion.

rebento s. m. 1. shoot, sprout. 2. (bot.) ratoon, sapling. 3. (fig.) offspring. 4. (fig.) product. 5. burgeon, bud.

rebentona s. f. (S. Braz.) 1. important pending business. 2. political row or unrest. 3. riot, tumult, mutiny.

rebicar v. to make up, rouge the face.

rebique s. m. 1. make-up, rouge. 2. excessive affectation of style. 3. extravagant finery, affected elegance.

rebitador s. m. riveter, riveting machine.

rebitagem s. f. (pl. -**ens**), **rebitamento** m. riveting (plate R 1).

rebitar v. 1. to rivet. 2. to clinch (bolts, nails). 3. to fasten with rivets or nails.

rebite s. m. 1. rivet (plate R 1). 2. clinch.

~ **de cabeça escareada** flush rivet. ~ **explosivo** explosive rivet.

rebo (ê) s. m. (pl. **rebos**) gravel, rough stone, grit.

reboante adj. m. + f. resounding, re-echoing, reverberating.

reboar v. to resound, re-echo, reverberate.

rebobinadeira s. f. (papermaking) winding frame, winder.

rebobinar v. to rewind, re-coil, reel again.

rebocado adj. 1. plastered, coated. 2. towed (like a trailer).

rebocador s. m. 1. tug, towboat (plate P 16). 2. (N. Braz.) touter who tries to employ workmen as rubber tappers and gatherers. 3. plasterer. ‖ adj. 1. towing. 2. plastering.

rebocadura s. f. 1. act of towing, towage. 2. plastering, roughcast.

rebocar v. 1. to plaster, coat with stucco. 2. to tow, take in tow.

reboco (ô) s. m. (pl. **rebocos**) 1. plaster, roughcast, parget. 2. plasterwork.

reboço s. m. (Braz.) new coat of plaster.

rebojar v. (Braz.) 1. to bulge, swell out. 2. to swirl, eddy. 3. to drive together (cattle), herd.

rebojo (ô) s. m. (pl. **rebojos**) (Braz.) 1. whirlwind. 2. eddy, whirlpool. 3. foam or froth of swiftly moving water. 4. southwest wind.

rebolada s. f. (Braz.) 1. field set with one type of native plants only. 2. group of trees or shrubs in an open field. 3. thicket, dense underbrush.

rebolado s. m. swinging movement of the hips, swaying or waddling motion.

perder o ~ 1. to become confused, mixed up. 2. to become upset, disconcerted. 3. (col.) to put one's nose out of joint.

rebolão s. m. (pl. -**ões**) 1. braggart, boaster. 2. (Braz.) a kind of tick. ‖ adj. boasting, bragging.

rebolar v. 1. to roll, tumble. 2. to shake the hips, waddle. 3. to shimmy. 4. to twirl around, revolve rapidly. 5. ~-se to swagger, wiggle, shake one's body. 6. to wallow, welter.

rebolaria s. f. 1. bragging, swaggering, boasting. 2. excessive and tawdry finery, affected elegance.

rebolcar v. 1. to let roll, tumble. 2. to revolve rapidly, twirl. 3. to fling, throw, hurl. 4. to welter, wallow, slosh (animals). 5. ~-se to shake one's body, walk with a rolling gait.

reboldrosa s. f. = **rebordosa**.

rebolear v. 1. to swing, twirl and fling like a lasso. 2. to sway, swagger. 3. ~-se to swing one's hips, walk with mincing steps, walk with a rolling gait.

reboleira s. f. 1. the thickest part of a wood, camp or field. 2. (Braz.) clump of trees in an open camp, coppice. 3. dirt which falls from a grindstone, forming muddy residues in the grindstone box.

reboleiro (I) s. m. 1. great cattle bell. 2. = **reboleira** 1, 2.

reboleiro (II) adj. (Braz.) 1. homing (cattle), living and grazing near the farmhouse and stables. 2. said of a shifty steer.

reboliço adj. 1. resembling a grindstone. 2. revolving, turning around itself.

rebolir v. 1. to swagger, shake one's body. 2. to walk rapidly, hurry. 3. to revolve, spin, rotate. 4. to stir up, grow agitated. 5. to sway, waggle. 6. to swing the hips, shake one's body.

rebolo s. m. 1. grindstone, whetstone, abrasive weel. 2. (pop.) cylinder. 3. (plant path.) measles of the olive tree.

~ **de esmeril** emery-wheel.

rebolqueada s. f. (S. Braz.) act of weltering or wallowing.

rebolquear-se v. (S. Braz.) to welter, wallow.

reboludo adj. 1. plump, bulky. 2. roundish, rounded. 3. rotund.

rebombar v. 1. to boom, resound. 2. to re-echo.

rebombeação s. f. (pl. **-ões**) (Braz., sl.) weakness, bad state of health.

rebôo s. m. 1. resonance, act of resounding. 2. reverberation, re-echo. 3. (phys.) reflexion of sound.

reboque s. m. 1. act of towing, towage. 2. trailer, vehicle hauled by another (plate B 15). 3. tow-rope. 4. towed barge. 5. (fig.) act or fact of having somebody in tow, subordinate. 6. (Braz.) prostitute, streetwalker. 7. plaster, rough-cast.

~ **aéreo** aerotowing. **taxa de** ~ towage. **usaram um** ~ **de aço** they used a steel dragline.

reboquear v. to tow, take in tow.

rebora s. f. (obs.) 1. legal age for marriage. 2. ratification (of contracts).

rebordagem s. f. (pl. **-ens**) 1. damage caused by a ship's collision. 2. indemnity for such a damage.

rebordão adj. (pl. **-ões**) wild, sylvan (said of plants used for living or quickset hedges).

castanheiro ~ wild chestnut tree.

rebordar v. 1. to embroider elaborately. 2. to flange, bevel. 3. to smooth the edges of plate-glass. 4. to embroider again.

rebordo (ô) s. m. turned edge, brim, fold.

rebordosa s. f. 1. censure, reprimand, reproof. 2. severe illness, disease. 3. difficult situation, dilemma, serious predicament. 4. relapse, severe recurrence of an illness.

reborquiada s. f. (S. Braz.) cattle rope, lariat.

rebotado adj. blunt, not sharp, dull.

rebotalho s. m. 1. trash, rubbish, junk. 2. refuse, dregs, leavings. 3. trifles. 4. crumbs, morsel, scrap. 5. scum, dross, outcasting.

rebotar v. 1. to make blunt or dull. 2. to take the edge off. 3. to grow tired or weary, be bored

with. 4. to discourage, dishearten. 5. to repel, drive back, beat.

~ **o inimigo** to throw the enemy back.

rebote s. m. 1. large wooden jack plane. 2. (Braz., sport) second rebound (of a ball or football).

reboto adj. 1. blunt, dull. 2. rude, uncouth. 3. stupid, ignorant.

rebraço s. m. (ant.) part of the armour which covered the arm from the elbow to the shoulder.

rebradar v. to roar again, yell.

rebramar, rebramir v. 1. to resound, reverberate. 2. to roar, bellow, low. 3. to shout, vociferate. 4. (fig.) to grow angry, flare up.

rebrilhante adj. m. + f. radiant, refulgent, shining again, splendiferous.

rebrilhar v. 1. to shine again. 2. to glitter or sparkle intensely. 3. to radiate, be very bright, be resplendent.

rebrotar v. to sprout again, produce new shoots.

rebuçado s. m. 1. piece of candy wrapped in paper, lollipop. 2. (fig.) anything said or done with perfection. 3. a disguised person. ‖ aɑj. concealed, disguised, muffled up, dissembled.

rebuçar v. 1. to hide, conceal. 2. to muffle up, veil, cloak. 3. to disguise, dissemble, dissimulate. 4. ~-se to keep in hiding, disguise o. s., dissemble, feign.

rebuço s. m. 1. collar of a gown. 2. coat lapel. 3. hood, cowl, large collar of a cloak. 4. (fig.) disguise, mask. 5. (fig.) insincerity.

ele respondeu sem ~**s** he answered blankly. **dizer a verdade sem** ~**s** to tell the naked truth. **trabalharam de** ~ they toiled secretly.

rebuliçar v. (Braz.) to be on the move, make haste, bustle, be very active.

rebuliço s. m. 1. clamour, noise, uproar. 2. tumult, hubbub. 3. fuss, excitement, fluster. 4. confusion, disorder, medley. 5. welter, rumpus, turmoil.

em ~ upside down. **fazer** ~ to rampage. **pôr em** ~ to set in an uproar.

rebulir v. 1. to stir, move again. 2. to compose, put together. 3. to correct, amend, retouch. 4. to improve. 5. to go up and down, walk from side to side. 6. to stir up, rouse.

rébus s. m. rebus.

rebusca s. f. 1. act of searching for. 2. research, searching again. 3. gleaning. 4. inquiry.

rebuscado adj. 1. searched for, looked after. 2. (fig.) highly refined, highly cultured, accomplished. 3. desired.

ela faz distinções demasiadamente -as she splits hairs. **ele é muito** ~ he is really recherché.

rebuscar v. 1. to search again. 2. to search thoroughly. 3. to dress with excessive elegance, spruce up. 4. to refine, perfect. 5. to glean. 6. to ransack, rummage. 7. (Braz.) ~-se to land a favourable deal, succed in, fix things well for o. s. 8. to sponge, mooch.

rebusco s. m. 1. new or repeated search. 2. research. 3. gleaning. 4. looking for leftover grapes in a vineyard after the crop has been brought in.

rebusnar v. (arch.) to bray.

rebusque s. m. (S. Braz.) 1. favourable settlement, arrangement. 2. deal, bargain.

recacau s. m. (Braz.) disorder, confusion, nubbub, racket, uproar.

recachar v. 1. to shrug one's shoulders (proudly or contemptuously). 2. to set a trap in retaliation.

recacho s. m. 1. haughtiness, pride. 2. elegance. 3. affected posture or attitude, airs, affected manner. 4. harshness, severity. 5. airing of one's views, free expression of one's feelings.

recadeiro s. m. errand-boy, messenger. ‖ adj. of or referring to errands and messages, relative to messengers.

recadista s. m. + f. person who goes on errands.

recado (I) s. m. 1. verbal communication, word. 2. information, message. 3. errand, commission. 4. scoldings, reprimand. 5. ~s pl. greetings, compliments, regards.

dai-lhe meus ~s remember me to him. **dar um** ~ to send word. **deixar** ~ to leave word. **ele mandou** ~ he sent word. **levar** ~ (fam.) to be reprimanded. **moço de** ~ errand-boy, messenger, runner. ~ **tolo** a fool's errand.

recado (II) s. m. 1. caution, prudence. 2. circumspection.

a bom ~ safe, free or out of danger.

recados s. m. pl. (S. Braz.) complete saddle with its trimmings.

recaída s. f. (also **recaimento** m.) 1. act or effect of falling back. 2. recurrence. 3. (med.) relapse, recidivation, setback.

o paciente teve uma ~ **séria** the patient has had a serious relapse.

recaidiço adj. relapsing, subject to recidivation, recidivous.

recair v. 1. to fall again, fall back. 2. to return to a previous state, backslide. 3. to relapse into. 4. to befall, occur, happen again. 5. to revert.

o acento recai sobre a última sílaba the accent falls on the last syllable. **a tarefa recaiu sobre ele** the task fell on him.

recalcado adj. 1. depressed, trodden down. 2. beaten down, rammed. 3. concentrated, massed. 4. restrained. 5. (Braz.): a) tired out (due to excessive body weight). b) slow to work, lazy.

recalcador s. m. winepress. ‖ adj. pressing, squeezing, crushing down.

recalcamento s. m. 1. act or fact of pressing down. 2. repression, suppression. 3. settling (of a building). 4. (psych.) exclusion of undesirable impulses from consciousness.

recalcar v. 1. to step on, tread on. 2. to press down, crush down, trample. 3. to compress, condense, squeeze together. 4. to insist, reiterate. 5. to curb, restrain, check, subdue. 6. (Braz.) to sprain, dislocate (joint, limb).

recalcitração (pl. **-ões**), **recalcitrância** s. f. 1. recalcitrance, recalcitration. 2. reluctance. 3. stubbornness, obstinacy.

recalcitrante s. m. + f. recalcitrant, stubborn or obstinate person. ‖ adj. recalcitrant, reluctant, renitent, stubborn, refractory.

recalcitrar v. 1. to recalcitrate. 2. to resist, refuse obedience 3. to manifest stubborn opposition. 4. to insist on, persist in. 5. to retort, talk back rudely. 6. to be or become obstinate. 7. to revolt against. 8. to kick backwards.

recalcular v. to recalculate, recount.

recálculo s. m. recalculation, second account.

recaldear v. to weld again, weld firmly together.

recalescência s. f. (met.) recalescence.

recalmão s. m. (pl. **-ões**) (naut.) lull between great storms.

recalque s. m. 1. act or fact of pressing down. 2. repression, suppression. 3. settling of a foundation (wall, building). 4. (psych.) exclusion of undesirable impulses from conscious mind. 5. stuffing, cramming.

bomba de ~ pressure pump.

recamado adj. embroidered.

roupas -as de ouro garments worked with gold. **o céu** ~ **de estrelas** the star-paved sky.

recamador s. m. embroiderer.

recamadura s. f. embroidery, adornment, ornament.

recamar v. 1. to embroider, trim with embroidery. 2. to adorn, decorate. 3. to embroider with raised stitches. 4. to cover, overlay. 5. ~**-se** to line or cover. 6. to fill.

recâmara s. f. 1. wardrobe, closet. 2. dressing room. 3. retreat, place of retirement. 4. household utensils. 5. alcove. 6. gun breech (of firearms).

recambiar v. 1. (com.) to return an unaccepted or unpaid bill of exchange. 2. to rechange, change again. 3. to send back. 4. to exchange, interchange. 5. to give back, devolve, pass on. 6. (Braz.) to make a full turn with the body.

recâmbio s. m. 1. act or fact of returning. 2. (com.) re-exchange, redraft. 3. (com.) returning of a bill of exchange. 4. (com.) expense incurred when returning an unaccepted or unpaid bill, protest charges.

conta de ~ return invoice. **letra de** ~ return bill.

recambó s. m. (cards) duration of a rubber.

recamo s. m. 1. raised embroidery, relief stitch embroidery. 2. ornament, decoration. 3. (fig.) adornment, ornate.

recantação s. f. (pl. **-ões**) 1. act of singing again. 2. emphatic singing. 3. recantation, retraction.

recantar v. 1. to sing again. 2. to sing emphatically. 3. to retract, recant. 4. to revoke, recall.

recanto s. m. 1. recess, nook, corner. 2. hiding place, place of concealment. 3. cubbyhole, den. 4. retreat.

~ **do nosso coração** (fig.) the innermost secrets of our heart.

recapacitar v. 1. to persuade or convince again. 2. to call to mind.

recapado adj. (Braz.) recapped (tires).

recapar v. to recap, retread (tires).

recapear v. to cover with a new layer of asphalt.

recapitulação s. f. (pl. **-ões**) 1. recapitulation. 2. act of synthesizing, summary. 3. repetition, review.

curso de ~ refresher course.

recapitulante adj. m. + f. recapitulative, recapitulatory.

recapitular v. 1. to recapitulate. 2. to synthesize, summarize, sum up. 3. to repeat, review, enumerate again.

recapitulativo adj. recapitulative, recapitulatory.

receptor s. m. receptor, one who catches again.

recapturar v. to recapture, capture again, retake.

recarbonização s. f. (pl. **-ões**) recarbonization, recarburization.

recarbonizar v. to recarbonize, recarburize.

recarga s. f. 1. fresh load, reload. 2. reshipment. 3. (bullfight) second charge of a bull.

recargar v. (bullfight) 1. to check the attack of the bull. 2. to repeat the attack, recharge.

recarregar v. to reload, recharge, load excessively.

recasar v. to remarry, marry a second time.

recatado adj. 1. modest, moderate. 2. discreet. 3. reserved, restrained. 4. prudent, cautious, circumspect. 5. coy. ‖ **-amente** adv. modestly, discreetly, cautiously, coyly.

recatar v. 1. to keep in safety, hide secretly. 2. to guard, safeguard. 3. to shield, protect. 4. to caution, forewarn. 5. ~**-se:** a) to be cautious, prudent or circumspect. b) to hide o. s. c) to be on one's guard. 6. to search again, search thoroughly.

recativar v. to capture again, recapture, catch again.

recativo s. m. subdued or wholly dominated person. ‖ adj. captive, subdued, subjugated, dominated.

recato s. m. 1. modesty, bashfulness. 2. honesty. 3. prudence, caution, circumspection. 4. reservedness. 5. secrecy. 6. retreat, hiding place.

recauchutado — recepagem 1059

com ~ cautiously, warily. no ~ do futuro in the womb of the future. tudo está a bom ~ all is safe.

recauchutado adj. recapped (tires).
pneu ~ retread.

recauchutar v. to recap, retread (tires).

recavação s. f. (pl. -ões) wash, washing (erosion by running water).

recavar v. 1. to dig again, dig many times. 2. to insist in, persist on. 3. to extract from (by digging), excavate, unearth.

recavém s. m. (pl. -éns) 1. the rear end of a cart bed. 2. (S. Braz., fig.) hind part of the body, behind.

receado adj. feared, dreaded, causing apprehension.

recear v. 1. to fear, dread. 2. to be afraid of 3. to apprehend. 4. to distrust, doubt. 5. ~-se to stand in fear of, be apprehensive.

ele receia endividar-se he fears making debts. **receio que...** I am afraid that... **receio que estejamos atrasados** I am afraid we shall be late. **receio uma dificuldade** I apprehend a difficulty.

recebedor s. m. 1. receiver. 2. recipient. 3. tax-collector, gatherer. ‖ adj. receiving, gathering, collecting.

recebedoria s. f. 1. office of tax-collector, excise office. 2. treasury. 3. collectorship. 4. custom office.

receber v. 1. to accept, take, get. 2. to cash in, take in, collect (money, debts). 3. to admit, harbour, shelter. 4. to greet, welcome. 5. to receive. 6. to give lodging to, take in as guest. 7. to receive communication. 8. to take advantage of, avail o. s. of. 9. to accept as husband or wife, marry. 10. to obtain, attain. 11. to achieve, succeed. 12. to endure. 13. to take possession of. 14. to support, bear, put up with. 15. to give receptions, entertain. ~ **a comunhão** (rel.) to commune. ~ **avaria** to suffer damage. ~ **com alegria** to welcome warmly. ~ **com braços abertos** to receive with open arms. ~ **hóspedes** to receive guests. ~ **informações sobre** to get wind of. ~ **ordens de marcha** to receive march orders. **recebeu a carta?** have you got the letter? **recebi-o em recompensa** I got it for a reward. **recebi hoje sua carta** your letter reached me to-day. **recebi mais do que esperava** I got more than I bargained for. **recebeu o dinheiro à vista** he got cash at sight. **recebeu o diploma da universidade** he graduated from university. **recebi uma boa educação** I received a good education. **ainda não recebi notícias dele** I have not yet heard from him. **ela recebe muita visita** she sees much company. **ele foi bem recebido** he met with a good reception. **ele foi recebido na estação** he was met at the station. **ele não o recebeu!** he shut the door upon him! **ele recebeu uma bofetada** he got his face slapped. **eles recebem muitos amigos** they entertain a great deal. **tem de recebê-lo como marido** you have to accept him as a husband.

recebimento s. m. 1. act or fact of receiving. 2. (arch.) apartment, room, hall, parlour. 3. receivership. 4. reception. 5. receipt. 6. admission. 7. acceptance. 8. marriage, wedding.

acusamos o ~ **de sua carta** we acknowledge receipt of your letter. **dia do** ~ wedding day. **logo após o** ~ **(da correspondência)** upon entry (of the mail). **o** ~ **diário chega a** the daily takings amount to.

recebível adj. m. + f. (pl. -íveis) receivable, acceptable, collectable.

receio s. m. 1. fear, dread, terror. 2. apprehension. 3. apprehensiveness, fearfulness. 4. uncertainty, doubt, misgiving(s). 5. distrust.

ela abriga um ~ **infundado** she harbours a groundless fear. **ele avançou com grande** ~ he pushed

forward with great trepidation. **ele está em constante** ~ **pela sua vida** he goes in constant fear of his life. **sem** ~ fearless. **ele tem** ~ **de o fazer** he fights shy of doing it.

receita s. f. 1. income, revenue, proceeds. 2. taking(s), receipt(s). 3. budget. 4. (med.) recipe, formula, prescription. 5. food. 6. (fig.) counsel, advice. ~ **bruta** gross earnings. ~ **do Estado** state revenue. **aviar uma** ~ to put up a prescription. **livro de** ~**s de cozinha** cookbook. ~ **pública** public revenue.

receitante adj. m. + f. prescribing, formulating advice.

receitar v. 1. (med.) to prescribe (a remedy), make out a prescription. 2. to advise, counsel.

receitário s. m. (pharm.) 1. an apothecary's file of prescriptions. 2. pharmacopoeia. 3. prescription book.

receituário s. m. (pharm.) 1. pharmacopoeia. 2. prescription book.

recém- adv. newly, recently, lately.

recém-casado adj. (pl. **recém-casados**) newly married or wed.

recém-chegado s. m. (pl. **recém-chegados**) newcomer. ‖ adj. newly arrived, newcomer, fresh.

recém-convertido adj. (pl. **recém-convertidos**) newly converted.

recém-falecido s. m. (pl. **recém-falecidos**) recently deceased person. ‖ adj. recently deceased.

recém-feito adj. (pl. **recém-feitos**) recently made or done, fresh.

recém-nado s. m. (pl. **recém-nados**), **recém-nascido** (pl. **recém-nascidos**) a new-born baby. ‖ adj. new-born.

recenar v. to gild or silver again.

recendência s. f. 1. fragrance, perfume. 2. strong scent. 3. agreeable odour.

recendente adj. m. + f. fragrant, odorous, redolent, sweet-smelling.

recender v. 1. to smell sweetly, be odoriferous. 2. to exhale a strong aroma. 3. to give forth an agreeable scent.

recendor s. m. fragrance, perfume, strong pleasant aroma.

recensão s. f. (pl. -ões) 1. census. 2. survey, verification. 3. enumeration, counting. 4. comparing of a published text with the original manuscript, proof-reading.

recenseado s. m. registered voter, person included in a census. ‖ adj. registered, polled, included in a census.

recenseador s. m. census taker, pollster, registrar. ‖ adj. registering, polling.

recenseamento s. m. 1. census. 2. survey, verification. 3. official enumeration, counting (population, animals, demographic density, etc.).

recensear v. 1. to take a census or poll. 2. to survey, verify. 3. to count, enumerate. 4. (com.) to audit (accounts).

recenseio s. m. act or result of census-taking or polling.

recental s. m. (pl. -ais) sucking lamb, lambkin.

recente adj. m. + f. (abs. sup. -íssimo) 1. recent. 2. modern, new. 3. late, fresh, novel. ‖ ~**mente** adv. recently, newly.

ele trouxe uma nova -íssima he brought a red-hot news.

recentidade s. f. recentness, recency.

receoso adj. 1. afraid, fearful. 2. anxious, apprehensive. 3. distrustful, suspicious. 4. uneasy. 5. timid. ‖ -**amente** adv. fearfully, apprehensively, anxiously, distrustfully.

recepagem s. f. (pl. -ens) lopping of plants close to the ground.

recepção s. f. (pl. -ões) 1. reception. 2. act or fact of receiving. 3. admittance. 4. receipt. 5. welcome.

~ **amigável,** ~ **cordial** warm welcome. ~ **de mercadorias** receipt of goods. ~ **social** party. **era uma** ~ **muito concorrida** it was a real crush. **sala de** ~ drawing room.

recepcionar v. to receive guests, entertain, throw a party.

recepcionista s. m. + f. (Braz.) receptionist, reception clerk, deskman.

recepisse s. m. (L.) receipt, voucher.

receptação s. f. (pl. -ões) receiving of stolen goods.

receptacular adj. m. + f. (bot.) receptacular.

receptáculo s. m. 1. receptacle, container. 2. vessel. 3. place of refuge, retreat, shelter. 4. reservoir, pool. 5. torus: part of the axis of a flower which bears the floral leaves.

as grandes cidades são o ~ **de todos os vícios** great cities are the sink of all vices.

receptador s. m. receiver of stolen goods, (sl.) fence. ‖ adj. receiving, concealing (stolen goods).

receptar v. to receive, conceal (stolen goods).

receptibilidade s. f. receptibility, receptiveness.

receptível adj. m. + f. (pl. -íveis) receptible, receptive.

receptividade s. f. 1. receptivity, receptiveness. 2. penetrativeness. 3. open-mindedness.

receptivo adj. receptive, receptible, susceptive, open-minded. ‖ -**amente** adv. receptively, susceptively.

receptor s. m. receiver: 1. cashier, treasurer. 2. receiver, receptor (of stolen goods), accessory. 3. (telegr., teleph.) receiving instrument (plate M 9). 4. (radio) wireless receiving set.

~ **de alta fidelidade** hi-fi (high-fidelity) receiver. ~ **de telefone** earpiece. ~ **de televisão** televisor.

recessivo adj. recessive, subordinate.

recesso s. m. 1. recess, corner. 2. alcove, niche. 3. retreat, hiding place. 4. retirement.

rechã s. f. (also **rechano, rechão** m.) tableland, plateau, gully.

rechaçar v. 1. to repel, repulse. 2. to throw back, fight off. 3. to resist, oppose. 4. to drive back, beat back. 5. (fig.) to contradict, refute.

~**am o golpe** they fended off the blow.

rechaço s. m. 1. repulsion. 2. a striking back. 3. driving or pushing back. 4. rebound, recoil. 5. (fig.) resistance, opposition. 6. old dance and dance melody.

recheado s. m. stuffing. ‖ adj. stuffed, filled, crammed, full, replete. ‖ -**amente** adv. fully, plentifully.

ele tem uma bolsa -a he has a fat purse.

recheadura s. f. 1. act of stuffing or filling. 2. stuffing, filling.

rechear v. 1. to stuff, fill with seasoning. 2. to cram, make full. 3. to make abundant, enrich. 4. ~-**se** to fill one's pockets.

~ **um frango** to stuff a pullet. ~-**se de conhecimentos** to cram one's head full.

rechega s. f. act of tapping pine trees for resin.

rechegar v. 1. to tap pine trees for resin. 2. (saltmaking) to stir up the brine.

rechego s. m. a hunter's blind, shooting box.

recheio s. m. 1. stuffing, farcing. 2. act of stuffing. 3. filling. 4. dressing.

~ **de uma casa** furniture of a house.

rechiar v. 1. to sizzle. 2. to make a hissing sound. 3. to creak.

rechinante adj. m. + f. hissing, creaking, whizzing, squeaky.

rechinar v. to creak, hiss, whiz, frizzle.

rechino s. m. creaking, hissing, whizzing.

rechonchudo adj. thickset, round, rotund, stumpy, crummy.

reciário s. m. (Roman hist.) gladiator, retiary.

recibo s. m. written receipt, acquittance, voucher.

~ **aduaneiro** docket. ~ **de depósito** warrant. **dar o** ~ to hand over the quittance. **entregar contra** ~ to hand out on receipt. **passar** ~ to write out a receipt.

reciclagem s. f. (Braz.) pedagogical updating: refresher course.

reciclar v. to do the pedagogical, cultural, etc., updating.

recidiva s. f. 1. return, reappearance. 2. (med.) relapse, reincidence.

recidivar v. to return, relapse, suffer a setback.

recidivo adj. relapsing, recidivous.

recife s. m. reef, skerry, key.

~ **de coral** coral reef. **cheio de** ~**s** reefy.

recifense s. m. + f. (Braz.) native or inhabitant of Recife. ‖ adj. of, pertaining to or relative to the city of Recife.

recifoso adj. full of reefs, reefy.

recingir v. to gird or encircle again.

recinto s. m. 1. enclosure, enclosed space. 2. verge, precinct, limited area. 3. dooryard. 4. sanctuary. ~ **de tênis** tennis court.

récipe s. m. recipe, medical prescription.

recipiendário s. m. recipiendary, accepted candidate, new member-elect. ‖ adj. of or referring to a recipiendary.

recipiente s. m. 1. recipient, receiver. 2. vessel, receptacle, balloon, container (plate V 2). 3. (mech.) recipient of an air pump. ‖ adj. m. + f. recipient.

~ **de armazenagem** storage bin. ~ **de barro** terrine. ~ **de pó** dust-holder (plate A 6).

reciprocação s. f. (pl. -ões) reciprocation, reciprocity. ~ **de direitos e deveres** equivalence of rights and duties.

reciprocar v. 1. to reciprocate, make reciprocal. 2. to act interchangeable. 3. to make a return for something done or given. 4. to compensate. 5. to exchange, interchange. 6. to alternate. 7. ~-**se** to correspond to each other, act alternately.

reciprocidade s. f. reciprocity, reciprocalness, reciprocality, mutuality.

recíproco s. m. 1. (gram.) reciprocal verb. 2. (math.) reciprocal proportion. ‖ adj. 1. reciprocal, reciprocative. 2. mutual. 3. interchangeable. 4. alternate. 5. subject to exchange or permutation. ‖ **reciprocamente** adv. reciprocally, mutually, alternatively, in return, vice versa.

não ~ unreciprocated. **nossa antipatia era -a** our dislike was reciprocal.

récita s. f. theatrical performance, recital, declamation.

recitação s. f. (pl. -ões) 1. recitation, recital. 2. declamation.

recitado s. m. recitation, recitative. ‖ adj. 1. recited, repeated by heart. 2. declamatory, recitative. 3. rehearsed.

recitador s. m. reciter, recitalist, declaimer.

recital s. m. (pl. -ais) recital, concert, theatrical or musical performance of one artist.

recitante s. m. + f. reciter, recitalist. ‖ adj. reciting, performing a solo.

recitar v. 1. to recite, declaim. 2. to read with a clear loud voice. 3. to narrate, relate. 4. to rehearse. 5. to perform a recitative.

fi-lo ~ **as lições** I heard him his lessons. ~ **cantando** to intonate.

recitativo s. m. 1. recitative. 2. declamatory passage of an opera or concert. 3. melodramatic performance. ‖ adj. recitative.

reclamação s. f. (pl. -ões) 1. reclamation. 2. complaint. 3. demand. 4. claim. 5. protest, objection. ~ nova redemand.

reclamado adj. reclaiming, reclaimed, protesting. não ~ unreclaimed, unclaimed.

reclamador s. m. reclaimer, reclaimant, protester. ‖ adj. reclaiming.

reclamante s. m. + f. reclaimer, reclaimant, protester. ‖ adj. claiming, demanding, protesting.

reclamar v. 1. to oppose o. s. to. 2. to object, impugn. 3. to protest, complain about. 4. to require, request. 5. to attract birds with a birdcall. 6. to invoke, implore. 7. to vindicate. ~ sem direito a devolução to arrogate the devolution.

reclamável adj. m. + f. (pl. -áveis) claimable, demandable, redemandable, reclaimable.

reclamista s. m. + f. (Braz.) propagandist.

reclamo, reclame s. m. 1. propaganda. 2. advertisement. 3. birdcall, decoy-whistle or bird. 4. allurement, enticement. 5. act of attracting attention. 6. (newsprint) catchword, direction word. 7. propagandistic activity of a firm.

reclassificar v. to reclassify (a public officer) for salary purposes.

reclinação s. f. (pl. -ões) leaning back, reclination, reclining.

reclinado adj. 1. turned or curved down or backwards. 2. reclinate, reclining, recumbent. 3. (bot.) reclined. ‖ -amente adv. reclinatedly, recumbently.

reclinar v. 1. to lean back, recline. 2. to fold, bend back. 3. to recurve, curve downwards. 4. to lie down. 5. to lean against. 6. ~-se: a) to rest, repose. b) to bow down.
ele reclinou-se na cadeira he sat back in his chair.

reclinatório s. m. any object fit to lean upon; pillow, cushion, headrest.

reclinável adj. m. + f. reclinable.

recluir v. to confine, shut up, seclude.

reclusão s. f. (pl. -ões) 1. reclusion, recluseness. 2. recess. 3. seclusion, confinement. 4. cell, prison. 5. restraint.

recluso s. m. recluse, hermit, monk; prisoner. ‖ adj. recluse, solitary, secluded, cloistered.

recobramento s. m. recovery, recuperation (of something lost).

recobrar v. 1. to acquire again, reacquire. 2. to recover, regain, recuperate. 3. to retrieve, retake. 4. ~-se: a) to be restored to health, rally. b) to free o. s. from (illness, difficulties, etc.), escape from. c) to be encouraged, cheer up.
~ as forças to gather strength. ~ a saúde to pick up. ~ os sentidos to recover one's senses. não recobrado unrecovered.

recobrável adj. m. + f. (pl. -áveis) recoverable, retrievable.

recobrimento s. m. (geol.) deposition of older rock formations on younger layers.

recobrir v. 1. to cover again, recover. 2. to cover well. 3. ~-se to cover o. s. again.

recobro (ô) s. m. 1. act or fact of covering again. 2. recuperation, regaining, retrieving. 3. rally, recovery.

recocto adj. 1. cooked over again. 2. overboiled, overdone.

recognição s. f. (pl. -ões) recognition, perception of identity, acknowledgement.

recognitivo adj. recognitory, fit for investigation or identification.

recoitar v. to anneal (metals).

recoleta s. f. 1. nun of the order of St. Francis. 2. monastery of Recollects. 3. (fig.) austere mode of life.

recoleto s. m. 1. Franciscan monk. 2. person who leads an ascetic life. ‖ adj. 1. of or referring to the order of St. Francis. 2. (fig.) austere, ascetic, solitary.

recolha s. f. 1. act of gathering or sheltering. 2. stable. 3. garage.

recolhedor s. m. 1. gatherer, collector. 2. (Braz.) cowboy who rounds up cattle and horses, driving them to the corral .

recolher v. 1. to guard, safeguard, preserve. 2. to take care of, take into custody. 3. to shelter, harbour. 4. to harvest, bring in a crop. 5. to collect, cash in. 6. to receive, accept. 7. to reunite, assemble. 8. to attain, obtain (as recompense). 9. to entertain, exercise hospitality. 10. to compile, amass (information, etc.). 11. to gather, pick up. 12. to shrink, shrivel. 13. to withdraw from circulation. 14. to make shorter. 15. to bear in mind, remember. 16. to lead or drive back. 17. to return home (native place or land). 18. to conceal, hide. 19. to compress, constrict. 20. to tie or shut up. 21. ~-se: a) to seek refuge, take shelter. b) to retire, go to bed, (coll.) tumble in. c) to lie down, rest. d) to retreat, withdraw from social life. e) to meditate. f) to treat o. s. for (skin eruption, rash, etc.). g) to economize, save.
~ ao canil to kennel. ~ as mercadorias to remove the merchandise. ~ as tropas espalhadas to rally the dispersed soldiers. ~ as velas to furl the sails. ~ o ar puro to breathe the pure air. ~ o trigo no celeiro to get in the corn. ~ o peixe na rede to catch fish in a net. ~ um livro to withdraw a book from circulation. ~-se à vida privada to retire to private life. ~-se a desoras to keep late hours. ~-se cedo to go to bed in good time. ~-se em si mesmo to compose o. s., reflect upon one's life. toque de ~ (mil.) retreat.

recolhida s. f. 1. retirement, retreat. 2. withdrawal. 3. recluse, lay sister. 4. (Braz.) driving in the cattle from the pasture.

recolhido adj. 1. retired. 2. solitary, secluded. 3. withdrawn. 4. reserved. 5. meditating, dwelling in thought.

recolhimento s. m. 1. act or fact of retiring, retirement. 2. shelter, home, refuge. 3. barn, garage. 4. privacy, secrecy. 5. contemplation, meditation. 6. intensive life. 7. house for recluses, asylum. 8. (ethn.) couvade.
~ dos frutos bringing in of the crop. ~ das tropas retreat of soldiers.

recolho s. m. 1. act or fact of gathering, collection. 2. retirement. 3. strong heavy breath. 4. spouting of a whale.

recolocar v. to put back, restore.
~-am o quadro they replaced the painting.

recolonização s. f. (pl. -ões) recolonization, re-establishment of a colony, resettlement.

recolonizar v. to recolonize, re-establish a colony, resettle.

recolorir v. to dye or paint again.

recombinação s. f. (pl. -ões) recombination, new combination, (biol.) cross over.

recombinar v. to recombine, recompose, rearrange.

recomeçado adj. recommenced, renewed, resumed, continued.

recomeçar v. 1. to recommence, begin again. 2. to renew. 3. (com.) reopen. 4. to resume, continue.

recomeçável adj. m. + f. (pl. -áveis) capable of being recommenced, resumable, renewable.

recomeço (ê) s. m. 1. act of beginning again, recommencement. 2. restart. 3. reopening (school, business enterprise, etc.).

recomendação s. f. (pl. **-ões**) 1. act of recommending. 2. recommendation, commendation. 3. recommendableness, commendable qualities. 4. advice, suggestion, counsel. 5. warning. 6. **-ões** pl. greetings, compliments, regards.
   carta de ~ letter of recommendation, letter of introduction. **com -ões do Sr. N.** with Mr. N's compliments. **dê minhas -ões à sua senhora** give my kindest regards to your wife. **ele lhe fez uma** ~ **acerca de** he cautioned him against.

recomendado s. m. recommendee, one who is recommended. ‖ adj. recommended.

recomendador s. m. recommender, one who recommends.

recomendar v. 1. to recommend. 2. to commend, praise. 3. to counsel, give advice, suggest. 4. to prefer, favour. 5. to order, charge, entrust with. 6. to remind s. o. to. 7. ~**-se**: a) to present one's compliments, send greetings or regards. b) to be or become recommendable; recommend o. s.
   este lugar se recomenda pelo ar puro this place commends itself by its good air. **feito que se recomenda** a commendatory act. ~ **calorosamente** to boost. ~ **com insistência** to urge. **-ram-me que procurasse o senhor** I was referred to you. **-ei-lhe especialmente** I gave him strict injunction.

recomendatório, recomendativo adj. recommendatory, advisory, serving to recommend or to attract favourable attention.

recomendável adj. (pl. **-áveis**) recommendable, advisable, commendable. ‖ **recomendavelmente** adv. recommendably, advisably.
   não ~ uncommendable. **pouco** ~ unworthy.

recomissionar v. to commission again, recommission.

recompensa, recompensação s. f. (pl. **-ões**) 1. act or fact of rewarding. 2. recompense, reward. 3. prize, premium. 4. compensation, pay, remuneration, gratification. 5. award, meed, requital.
   não há ~ **sem esforço** no cross, no crown. **sem** ~ rewardless. **uma** ~ **justa** a worthy reward.

recompensado adj. recompensed, rewarded, compensated, requited.
   ele foi mal ~ he got small thanks. **mal** ~ ill requited.

recompensador s. m. rewarder, recompenser, indemnifier. ‖ adj. rewarding, requiting, compensatory.

recompensar v. 1. to retribute, give an equivalent for. 2. to reward, recompense. 3. to premiate. 4. to compensate, pay, fee, remunerate. 5. to indemnify, repair; 6. to punish. 7. to requite, gratify. 8. to award, crown.
   ~ **a bondade com ingratidão** to repay kindness with ingratitude.

recompensável adj. m. + f. pl. **-áveis**) 1. worthy of recompense, deserving reward. 2. awardable, rewardable, requitable, remunerable.

recompilação s. f. (pl. **-ões**) recompilation, new compilation.

recompilador s. m. recompiler, recollector. ‖ adj. recompiling.

recompilar v. to compile or collect again, recompile.

recompor v. 1. to recompose, compose again. 2. to give a new form to, renew. 3. to reset, reframe. 4. to set in order again, reorganize. 5. to re-establish, restore. 6. to reconcile, harmonize. 7. ~**-se**: a) to be recomposed. b) to become reconciled with. c) (chem.) to form a new compound.

recomposição s. f. (pl. **-ões**) 1. recomposition, rearrangement. 2. reconciliation. 3. (pol.) recomposi-

tion of the cabinet (ministers or governmental advisers).

recomposto adj. recomposed, rearranged, reset.

recomprar v. to repurchase, to buy again.

recôncavo s. m. 1. deep cave, grotto, hollow. 2. fold. 3. den, lair. 4. environs (of a city). 5. (Braz.) name of an exceptionally fertile region on the coast of the state of Bahia.

reconcentração s. f. (pl. **-ões**) act or effect of reconcentrating, reconcentration.

reconcentrado adj. 1. reconcentrated, thoroughly concentrated. 2. very private, intimate. 3. meditative, contemplative. 4. (chem.) strongly concentrated or acid.

reconcentrar v. 1. to concentrate again, reconcentrate. 2. to bring or direct to a common center, reunite. 3. to harbour deep in one's heart (feelings, sentiments). 4. to converge upon a common center. 5. ~**-se**: a) to gather into one body. b) to lead a solitary life. c) to ponder, meditate.

reconciliação s. f. (pl. **-ões**) 1. reconciliation, reconcilement. 2. restoration of friendship. 3. atonement. 4. (rel.) repetition of the confession (out of devotion). 5. reconsecration of a profaned church or temple.
   dia da ~ day of atonement.

reconciliado s. m. (eccl., rel.) reconcilee. ‖ adj. reconciled, acquitted.

reconciliador s. m. reconciler, conciliator. ‖ adj. reconciling, reconciliatory.

reconciliar v. 1. to reconcile, conciliate. 2. to establish peace (among, between), appease. 3. to restore friendship. 4. to attain the grace of God. 5. to reach an agreement. 6. ~**-se** to ingratiate or reconcile o. s., become reconciled with.
   ~**am as opiniões antagônicas** they patched up their differences. **ele reconciliou-se com ela** he made peace with her.

reconciliatório adj. reconciliatory, conciliatory, reconciling.

reconciliável adj. m. + f. (pl. **-áveis**) reconcilable, capable of reconciliation.

recondicionar v. to recondition, overhaul.

recôndito s. m. 1. corner, recess. 2. hiding place. ‖ adj. 1. hidden, concealed. 2. recondite. 3. abstruse. 4. unknown. 5. obscure.
   os ~**s do coração humano** the secret recesses of the human heart.

reconditório s. m. hiding place, retreat, refuge.

recondução s. f. (pl. **-ões**) 1. act of leading back or reconducting. 2. devolution, return. 3. renewing, continuation, prorogation. 4. re-election, renomination.

reconduzir v. 1. to lead back, reconduct. 2. to devolve, return. 3. to renew, continue, prorogate. 4. to re-elect, renominate. 5. to reconvey, send again.

reconfessar v. to confess again.

reconfortante s. m. (med.) restorative, tonic. ‖ adj. m. + f. comforting, restorative, reinvigorating, refreshing, stimulant.

reconfortar v. 1. to recomfort. 2. to refresh. 3. to strengthen, reinvigorate. 4. to ease, soothe, relieve. 5. to stimulate. 6. console. 7. ~**-se** to grow healthy or strong again, recover one's forces.

reconforto (ô) s. m. reinvigoration, comfort, new strength, uplifting.

recongraçar v. = **reconciliar.**

reconhecedor s. m. 1. acknowledger, recognizer. 2. (mil.) runner. ‖ adj. acknowledging, recognizing, appreciative.

reconhecença s. f. (arch.) 1. = **reconhecimento.** 2. (eccl.) tribute paid to the bishop or the chapter.

3. (Braz.) landmark or lighthouse on the coast for guiding navigation.

reconhecer v. 1. to recognize, know again. 2. to acknowledge, admit. 3. to verify, ascertain. 4. to understand, comprehend. 5. to make sure, find out. 6. (mil.) to reconnoitre. 7. to observe, take a view of. 8. to explore, examine. 9. to declare, assert, affirm. 10. to be grateful, express thanks. 11. to asseverate. 12. to accept as legal or correct, accredit. 13. to know, feel. 14. to avow, avouch. 15. to adopt. 16. to consider good, veracious or legitime. 17. to esteem, distinguish. 18. **~-se** to make a confession, own, declare o. s.
~ a legalidade da exigência to acknowledge the legality of the claim. **~ o erro** to see one's mistake. **~ pela voz** to tell by the voice. **~ por filho** to acknowledge one's parenthood. **~ sua culpa** to confess one's fault. **reconhece você esta assinatura?** do you acknowledge this signature? **reconheço estar sob a influência dele** I confess myself to be under his influence. **reconheço que é verdade** I acknowledge it to be true. **ele reconheceu-se culpado** he declared himself guilty. **eu o ~ia em qualquer lugar** I should know him anywhere. **não ~** to disown, repudiate.

reconhecido adj. 1. thankful, grateful. 2. recognized. 3. admitted, acknowledged. 4. avowed. || **-amente** adv. 1. trankfully, gratefully. 2. admittedly, avowedly. 3. confessedly.
~ das suas obrigações conscious of one's duties. **ele foi ~ competente** he was found competent. **estou-lhe muito ~** I am much obliged to you. **não ~** undiscerned, unowned, unrecognized.

reconhecimento s. m. 1. recognition, cognizance. 2. acknowledgement, admission. 3. gratitude, thankfulness. 4. recompense, reward, compensation. 5. reconnoitring, reconnaissance. 6. declaration, affirmation. 7. adoption. 8. confession. 9. concession, allowance. 10. atonement.
~ aéreo air reconnaissance. **~ de dívida** I. O. U. = I owe you. **em ~ a** in recognition of. **manifestar o seu ~** to testify one's gratitude. **sinal de ~** distinctive mark, (med.) diagnostic symptom.

reconhecível adj. m. + f. (pl. **-íveis**) 1. recognizable, cognizable. 2. acknowledgeable, confirmable. 3. knowable, distinguishable, easy to recognize.

reconquista s. f. reconquest, reconquering, aim of conquest.

reconquistar v. 1. to reconquer, conquer again. 2. to recapture, regain. 3. to recover, retake by force. 4. to rewin.

reconsagrar v. to reconsecrate, consecrate again, dedicate again.

reconsertar v. to repair again, remend.

reconsideração s. f. (pl. **-ões**) 1. reconsideration, re-considering. 2. reflexion. 3. second consideration, new deliberation. 4. change of mind. 5. reponderation.

reconsiderar v. 1. to reconsider, consider again. 2. to give a second thought, think over again. 3. to redeliberate, change one's mind. 4. to ponder, meditate. 5. to disavow, unsay.
ele reconsiderou o negócio he gave the business a second thought.

reconsolidar v. to reconsolidate, consolidate again, make firm again.

reconstituição s. f. (pl. **-ões**) reconstitution, recomposition, reform.

reconstituinte s. m. (med.) reconstituent, restorative, tonic. || adj. m. + f. 1. reconstituent, restoring. 2. rebuilding. 3. recomposing. 4. (med.) restorative, tonic.

reconstituir v. 1. to reconstitute, constitute again. 2. to recompose. 3. to rebuild, re-establish. 4. to strengthen, invigorate.

reconstrução s. f. (pl. **-ões**) 1. reconstruction, rebuilding. 2. reform. 3. reorganization. 4. something reconstructed.

reconstruído adj. reconstructed, rebuilt, reformed.

reconstruir v. 1. to reconstruct, rebuild. 2. to reorganize. 3. to reform. 4. to restore.

reconstrutor s. m. reconstructor, rebuilder, restorator.

recontado adj. 1. recounted, recalculated. 2. retold, related.

recontamento s. m. 1. act of recounting, recalculation. 2. repeated narration or report. 3. detailed account.

recontar v. 1. to count again, recount. 2. to calculate anew. 3. to retell, relate again, report anew. 4. to retail.

recontente adj. m. + f. very content, highly pleased or satisfied.

reconto (I) s. m. iron fitting at the butt of a lance.

reconto (II) s. m. 1. recount, recalculation. 2. retelling, repeated narration. 3. (Port., prov.) public calling up, summons.

recontro s. m. 1. encounter, skirmish, brush. 2. combat, battle. 3. conflict, clash. 4. chance meeting.

reconvalescença s. f. reconvalescence, recovery, restoration.

reconvalescente s. m. + f. reconvalescent person. || adj. reconvalescent.

reconvalescer v. 1. to recover from illness, regain one's strength. 2. to get better. 3. to be restored (to health).

reconvenção s. f. (pl. **-ões**) 1. reconvention. 2. (jur.) countercharge, counteraction, countersuit. 3. (fig.) recrimination.

reconvindo adj. (jur.) countercharging, recriminating.

reconvir v. 1. to counterclaim, countercharge. 2. to file a countersuit. 3. to recriminate, charge back on an accuser. 4. to get back, recover.

recopilação s. f. (pl. **-ões**) 1. compilation. 2. summary, abstract. 3. abridgment. 4. recapitulation.

recopilador s. m. compiler, summarizer, abridger, collector. || adj. compiling, summarizing, collecting.

recopilar v. 1. to compile, collect, gather. 2. to abridge, make an abstract of. 3. to recapitulate. 4. to sum up, summarize, epitomize.

recordação s. f. (pl. **-ões**) 1. remembrance, recollection, recordation. 2. memory, power or faculty of recalling. 3. reminiscence. 4. memento, token, souvenir.

recordador s. m. recorder, reminder, one who re-members or reminds. || adj. recalling, remembering, reminding.

recordar v. 1. to remember, recall. 2. to recollect. 3. to bear in mind, call to mind. 4. to be similar to. 5. to commemorate, indulge in reminiscences. 6. to relive, reproduce (in our mind.)
~am a lição they learned the lesson by heart. **não me recordo mais do seu nome** his name escapes me.

recordativo, recordatório adj. reminding, reminiscent, recordatory.

recorde s. m. record (in sports), special prowess, feat, accomplishment.
foi um ~ mundial it was an all-time record. **quebrar o ~** to break or beat the record.

recordista s. m. + f. record holder, record breaker, champion. || adj. record-holding .

recordo (ô) s. m. remembrance, recollection, recordation, reminiscence.

reco-reco s. m. (Braz.) musical instrument made of a piece of bamboo with notches cut into it and over which a rod is rubbed to produce a rhythmical sound.

recorrência s. f. recurrence, act or fact of occurring again.

recorrente s. m. + f. (jur.) appellant. ‖ adj. recurring.

recorrer v. 1. to run over, go through again. 2. to search, scrutinize. 3. to investigate, inquire into. 4. to evoke, call forth. 5. (typogr.) to overrun a page. 6. to ask for help, request protection. 7. to apply, resort to. 8. (jur.) to appeal to. ~ **a** to fall back upon, resort to, have recourse to. **eles ~am ao povo** they appealed to the country. **recorremos a nossas reservas** we trenched upon our reserves. **ele recorreu da sentença** he lodged an appeal. ~ **o texto** to go over the text.

recorrido s. m. (jur.) appellee.

recorrível adj. m. + f. (pl. **-íveis**) appealable, subject to or admitting appeal.

recortada s. f. (Braz.) a kind of fandango and dance tune.

recortado s. m. (Braz.) country-dance and music. ‖ adj. indented, denticulate, crenate, jagged, escalloped.

tijolo ~ queen closer.

recortador s. m. cutter, pinker. ‖ adj. cutting, clipping, pinking.

recortar v. 1. to cut out, trim, clip. 2. to slash, slice. 3. to carve, chisel. 4. to indent, scallop. 5. to cut figures (into paper). 6. to place at intervals, intersperse, interpose. 7. to outline, appear (resembling recut paper figures). 8. to cut again.

recorte s. m. 1. act or fact of cutting out. 2. indentation, indenture. 3. carving. 4. newspaper clipping, press cutting. 5. cut cloth or paperwork. 6. pruning. 7. a bullfighter's feint.

recortilha s. f. punch, cutter, jagging iron.

recoser v. to resew, sew over again.

recosta s. f. (Braz.) slope, hill or mountain-side, declivity.

recostar v. 1. to recline, lean back. 2. to incline, bend. 3. to lean against. 4. to prop up, rest on.

recosto (ô) s. m. 1. resting place, retreat. 2. lounge, sofa, couch. 3. (Braz.) mountain slope, hillside.

recova, recovagem (pl. **-ens**) s. f. 1. payload and business of muleteers. 2. carrier, forwarding business, transporter. 3. transport, conveyance. 4. transport charges.

récova s. m. = **récua**.

recovar v. 1. to transport, convey (baggage or other goods). 2. to work as a muleteer.

recoveira s. f. 1. female mule driver, female muleteer. 2. fisherman's yoke (to transport on the shoulder a pole with two baskets).

recoveiro s. m. 1. carrier, transporter. 2. muleteer, mule driver.

recovo (ô) s. m. 1. act of reclining or leaning back. 2. act of leaning on one's elbows.

recozedor s. m. annealer. ‖ adj. annealing.

recozer v. 1. to cook again. 2. to boil or bake again. 3. to overcook, cook too much, overdo. 4. to anneal, temper.

recozido adj. cooked or boiled again, overcooked, overdone, annealed.

recozimento s. m. 1. cooking, boiling. 2. overcooking, overboiling. 3. (met.) annealing.

recrava s. f. groove cut in the stonework of a doorway to hold the wooden door-frame or the door-hinges.

recravar v. to nail again, nail much.

recreação s. f. (pl. **-ões**) 1. recreation. 2. amusement, distraction. 3. sport. 4. pastime. 5. enjoyment, relaxation.

recreador s. m. person who takes things easy or looks for amusement. ‖ adj. amusing, pleasant, sportive, relaxing.

recrear v. 1. to recreate. 2. to rest, relax. 3. to entertain, divert. 4. to play, make fun, make merry. 5. **~-se:** a) to feel pleasure or satisfaction. b) to amuse o. s. c) to have a good time, take recreation.

recreativo adj. 1. recreative, refreshing. 2. amusing, exhilarating, diverting. 3. sportive. ‖ **-amente** adv. recreatively.

recreatório adj. m., **recreável** m. + f. (pl. **-áveis**) recreative, recreational.

recreio s. m. 1. recreation. 2. relaxation, refreshment. 3. diversion, distraction, entertainment. 4. summer-house, playground. 5. interval, school recess time. 6. game, play, sport. **hora de** ~ playtime. **parque de** ~ pleasure ground. **viagem de** ~ pleasure trip.

recrementício adj. (med.) recrementitious, recremental.

recremento s. m. (med.) recrement, recrementitious secretion, dross.

recrescência s. f. growth, excrescence, new growth.

recrescente adj. m. + f. that grows again, recrescent.

recrescer v. 1. to grow again. 2. to increase, augment. 3. to sprout out, shoot up again. 4. to become more intense. 5. to happen, befall. 6. to be left over, rest, be more than enough.

recrescido adj. that grew again.

recrescimento s. m. 1. regrowth, new growth. 2. increase, augmentation. 3. intensification. 4. happening, occurrence. 5. surplus, rest, leftover. 6. excess, redundancy.

recrestar v. 1. to burn or scorch again. 2. to dry up, parch.

recria s. f. 1. new or late rearing, breeding, hatching. 2. aftergrowth, offshoots, new generation (of animals).

recriação s. f. (pl. **-ões**) 1. act of creating again. 2. raising or breeding anew. 3. to increase the stock of animals on a farm. 4. new creation or invention.

recriar v. 1. to create again. 2. to raise, breed or bring up again. 3. to restock the farmyard. 4. to reproduce, invent anew.

recriminação s. f. (pl. **-ões**) 1. act or fact of recriminating. 2. countercharge, recrimination. 3. exprobration.

recriminador s. m. recriminator. ‖ adj. recriminating, recriminatory.

recriminar v. 1. to recriminate, make a countercharge or accusation. 2. to reproach, censure, reprimand.

recriminatório adj. recriminatory, recriminative, recriminating.

recristalização s. f. (chem.) recrystallization.

recru adj. very raw, badly annealed.

recrudescência s. f. 1. recrudescence. 2. renewed or intensified activity. 3. intensification. 4. (med.) aggravation (after a remission).

recrudescente adj. m. + f. 1. recrudescent. 2. renewed or intensified (activity). 3. intensifying. 4. (med.) aggravating.

recrudescer v. 1. to recrudesce. 2. to renew or intensify (activity). 3. (med.) to aggravate, break out again, change for the worse. 4. to increase, augment.

recrudescimento s. m. 1. recrudescence, recrudescency. 2. intensification. 3. (med.) fresh outbreak (of an illness), relapse, aggravation. 4. increase, augmentation.

recruta s. m. 1. (mil.) recruit, newly enlisted soldier or sailor, rookie. 2. novice, beginner. 3. new member (of a school, club, society). 4. f.: a) group of draftees or conscripts (of a certain year). b) military training of new recruits. c) (Braz.) troop of agricultural labourers, field hands. d) (S. Braz.) herd of cattle (belonging to one farm). e) (S. Braz.) dispersed cattle, straying cattle.
recrutado adj. conscript, drafted, recruited.
recrutador s. m. 1. recruiter, enlistment officer. 2. (S. Braz.) cowboy who gathers and drives home stray cattle.
recrutamento s. m. 1. (mil.) recruitment, recruiting, recruital. 2. enlistment, conscription. 3. canvassing, procuring, solicitating (new adepts or members). 4. (S. Braz.) herding of cattle, looking for stray animals, round up.
recrutar v. 1. (mil.) to recruit. 2. to enlist, conscribe, draft. 3. to canvass, procure, enlist (new adepts, members, etc.). 4. to levy, collect troops for service. 5. (S. Braz.) to herd or gather cattle, look for stray animals.
~am os rapazes à força para o exército they pressed the boys into the army.
recruzamento s. m. (biol.) backcross, act of crossing a hybrid with one of its parents.
recruzar v. to recross, cross again, cross repeatedly.
recruzetado adj. having at the end of each crossarm a small cross.
recua s. f. recoil, rebound, kick (of firearms).
récua s. f. 1. a train of pack animals. 2. herd of pack animals, herd of mules. 3. load transported by these animals. 4. (depr.) gang, band, mob.
recuada s. f., **recuamento** m. = recuo.
recuadeira s. f. breeching (harness).
recuado adj. 1. at the tail end of a field, an area. 2. backwards. 3. distant, far off. 4. old, remote.
recuanço s. m. backspin of a billiard ball.
recuar v. 1. to put, pull or draw back. 2. to regress, retrace one's steps. 3. to walk back, move backward, retreat. 4. to lose ground, give way. 5. to hesitate, waver. 6. to be slow or tardy, be late. 7. to draw back, recoil, flinch. 8. to try to withdraw from a compromise. 9. to reconsider, desist, give up (idea, intention, trip). 10. to harbour reactionary ideas, be conservative. 11. to disavow, recant, repudiate (ideas formerly expressed). 12. to retrograde, recede. 13. to cause to retrograde, drive back, move backwards, oblige s. o. to walk back. 14. to shy, shrink from.
~ uma peça (chess) to retreat. ~ um carro da garagem to back a car out of the garage. ~am diante de they shrank from. ~am ignominiosamente they turned their tails. ~am para a antiga linha de defesa they fell back to their old line of defense. esta arma de fogo recua muito this firearm has a haevy kick. fazer ~ um cavalo to back a horse. ir -ando to go slowly back, lose ground.
recúbito s. m. recumbency, recumbent position or attitude, reclining.
recuidar v. 1. to consider, think over with care. 2. to ponder, revolve in mind. 3. to take everything into account, deliberate, think over thoroughly.
recultivar v. to recultivate, cultivate again.
recumbente adj. m. + f. recumbent, reclining, leaning against.
recumbir v. to be in a recumbent position, recline, lean back, rest upon.
recunhamento s. m. recoinage, remintage.
recunhar v. to recoin, coin anew, mint or stamp again.
recuo s. m. 1. act or fact of moving backwards, retrocession. 2. recoiling, recoil. 3. recession. 4.

kick (of firearms). 5. retreat, retirement. 6. (mech.) return movement, backing. 7. revulsion. 8. setback. 9. (swimming) backstroke.
~ das ondas undertow.
recuperação s. f. 1. recuperation, recovery. 2. reconquest. 3. reclamation, salvage. 4. retrieval, regaining.
recuperado adj. recuperated, recovered, reclaimed, redeemed.
recuperador s. m. recuperator, recoverer, rescuer, redeemer. ‖ adj. recuperative, recuperatory, recuperating.
recuperar v. 1. to recuperate, recover. 2. to recoup. 3. to re-acquire, repurchase. 4. to retake, retrieve. 5. to reobtain, regain. 6. to reclaim, redeem. 7. to recover (from illness, fatigue), gain new strength. 8. to recapture, win back. 9. to require indemnity or reimbursement.
~ a saúde to get well. ~ o juízo to settle down. ~ o tempo perdido to make up for lost time. ele conseguiu ~ o terreno perdido (sport) he managed to fetch up the lost ground. ela recuperou as forças she picked up her strength.
recuperativo adj. recuperative, tending to recovery, restorative.
recuperável adj. m. + f. (pl. -áveis) 1. recuperable, recoverable. 2. reclaimable. 3. reobtainable, retrievable. 4. that may be recaptured or won back.
recorrência s. f. (med.) recurrence, periodical or frequent returning.
recorrente adj. m. + f. recurrent, returning, running back.
recurso s. m. 1. act and fact of running back or running again. 2. (jur.) appeal, recourse (to a superior court). 3. reclamation, claim, complaint. 4. petition, application for help. 5. aid, help, assistance. 6. means, funds, resources, money. 7. remedy, medicine. 8. ~s pl. riches, wealth, possessions. 9. refuge, shelter, haven.
~ da maré reflux of the tide; ebb. ~s humanos human resources. em último ~ in the last resort. ele dispõe de poucos ~s he has little to depend upon. ela está sem ~s she is resourceless. não se preocupe, ele tem os ~s dont't worry your head off, he has the pocketbook. um homem de grandes ~s a man of considerable means. ~ extraordinário extraordinary recourse (to a superior court).
recurva s. f. (Braz.) contortion, twisting.
recurvação s. f. (pl. -ões) recurvation, recurvature.
recurvado adj. 1. recurvate. 2. curved, bent. 3. twisted, contorted. 4. arched. 5. bowed down, bent over.
recurvar v. 1. to curve again, recurve. 2. to curve back, bend over, bow back, crook. 3. to twist, contort. 4. to form into an arch. 5. ~-se to bow, stoop, be inclined.
recurvo adj. 1. recurved, crooked. 2. bent backwards. 3. recurvate. 4. twisted, contorted. 5. bowed down, bent over.
recusa, recusação (pl. -ões) s. f. 1. act or fact of refusing. 2. denial, refusal. 3. rejection, declination, non-acceptance. 4. non-compliance, non--cooperation. 5. rebuff, repulse. 6. (jur.) challenge.
~ de admissão non-admission. ~ de aceite refusal of acceptance. ~ de uma demanda dismissal. ele me deu uma ~ peremptória he gave me a flat refusal. em caso de ~ in case of a refusal. receber uma ~ to be refused.
recusado adj. refused, rejected, not accepted, snubbed.
recusador s. m. 1. refuser, denier. 2. (jur.) challenger. ‖ adj. refusing.
recusante adj. m. + f. refusing, rejecting, recusant.

recusar v. 1. to refuse, deny. 2. to reject, not to accept, decline. 3. to oppose, act against. 4. to deny, not admit. 5. to prohibit, forbid. 6. ~-se to refuse obedience, resist, rebel against. ~ um pretendente to refuse a suitor. ~ uma oferta to refuse an offer. ~am aprovação ao projeto they disapproved the project. ~am-lhe a porta they denied him admission. ~am o candidato they reprobated the candidate. ~am o jurado they objected against the juror. ele recusa he says nay. eu me ~ia a fazê-lo I should scorn to do it.

recusativo adj. refusing, negative, rejective.

recusável adj. m. + f. (pl. -áveis) refusable, rejectable, exceptionable, deserving refusal. ‖ **recusavelmente** adv refusably, exceptionably.

recuso s. m. 1. refusal, denial. 2. (Port. prov.) complaint, accusation. 3. expedient.

redação s. f. (pl. -ões) 1. act or fact of composing a script. 2. redaction. 3. style or manner of writing. 4. editorship. 5. editorial staff. 6. home office, building of the editorial staff of a newspaper, editorial room.

redada s. f. 1. act of casting a fishing-net. 2. draught, haul, catch (of fish). 3. (Braz.) brood, nestful of fledglings.

redar (I) v. to give again, give back, regive.

redar (II) v. to cast a fishing-net, catch in a net.

redargüente adj. m. + f. retorting, refuting, recriminating.

redargüição s. f. (pl. -ões) 1. retort, retortion, quick sharp reply. 2. rejoinder, rebuttal. 3. refutation. 4. recrimination.

redargüidor s. m. retorter, recriminator. ‖ adj. retorting, recriminating.

redargüir v. 1. to retort, give a quick sharp reply. 2. to rejoin, rebut. 3. to refute, return an argument. 4. to recriminate.

redator s. m. 1. editor, newspaper editor, redactor. 2. writer, journalist. 3. ~es pl. editorial staff. ~ chefe editor in chief. ~ da parte financeira (newspaper) city editor. ~ substituto subeditor.

redatora s. f. editress.

rede (ê) s. f. 1. fabric wrought or woven into meshes (plate B 11). 2. net, fishing net (plate P 9). 3. hair net. 4. wire gauze, wire netting. 5. water, gas or sewerage system. 6. electric distribution system. 7. (anat.) nervous system. 8. trap, snare. 9. (Braz.) hammock. 10. (S. Braz.) herd of homing cattle which includes a certain number of stray animals. ~ de apanhar pássaros fowling net, clapnet. ~ de arrasto trawlnet, trawl, dragnet. ~ de esgotos sewerage system. ~ de proteção guard net. ~ de radiodifusão radio transmission network. ~ ferroviária railway network. ~ pequena de pesca seine, landing net, casting net. ~ rodoviária highway system. ~ telefônica, telegráfica telephone, telegraphic network. armar uma ~ to lay a snare or trap. cair na ~ to fall into the trap, em forma de ~ retiary. lançar a ~ to net.

rédea s. f. 1. reins, bridle (plate A 12). 2. (fig.) direction, control. 3. (fig.) rule, command, governance. ~ de bridão snaffle rein (plate C 12). ~ do freio curb rein (plate C 12). à ~ solta at full speed, at full gallop. bancar na ~ to stop a galloping horse suddenly. dar ~s à imaginação to give reins to one's imagination. deitar a mão às ~s to stop a horse. largar a ~ to loosen the reins. a mão que segura as ~s bridle-hand. ter as ~s do governo to hold the reins of the government. voltar as ~s to give back the reins (of an undertaking).

redeclarar v. to declare again, reaffirm.

redecretar v. to decree again, re-enact.

rede-foie s. f. (pl. **redes-foie**) funnel-shaped net, hoop net.

redeiro s. m. 1. net knitter, netmaker. 2. small fishing net.

redemocratizar v. to redemocratize.

redemoinhado adj. whirling, put into or passing through a whirlpool.

redemoinhador adj. 1. whirling, twirling. 2. restless, unquiet (said of cattle).

redemoinho s. m. 1. whirl, swirl. 2. eddy, vortex. 3. whirlwind. o ~ do tempo the whirligig of time.

redenção s. f. (pl. -ões) 1. redemption. 2. redeeming. 3. ransom. 4. (rel.) salvation, deliverance, atonement. ~ de Cristo the Cross.

redengar-se v. (Braz., sl.) to break again, melt, liquefy, get out of joint, fall to pieces.

redenho s. m. 1. (anat.) the great omentum. 2. shrimp net. 3. special net for gathering floating seaweed.

redente s. m. 1. (fort.) redan. 2. step like increase of the superstructure of a wall built on sloping ground.

redentor s. m. 1. redeemer, saviour. 2. (rel.) the Redeemer, Jesus Christ. ‖ adj. redeeming, leading to salvation, redemptive, saving.

redentorista s. m. + f. Redemptorist.

rede-pé s. f. net to fish in shallow waters.

redescender, redescer v. to redescend, descend again.

redescobrimento s. m. rediscovery, discovering anew.

redescobrir v. to rediscover, reveal again, unearth again.

redescontar v. to rediscount, deduct again.

redesconto s. m. 1. rediscount. 2. act of rediscounting. 3. rediscounted bill.

redestilar v. to redistil, distil again or anew.

redibição s. f. (pl. -ões) (jur.) redhibition: the act of annulling a sale and devolution of the article to the seller on account of a material defect.

redibir v. (jur.) 1. to avoid or annul a sale (purchase) on account of a material defect. 2. to resell goods to the original seller.

redibitório adj. (jur.) redhibitory.

redigir v. 1. to write, write down. 2. to express one's thoughts in writing. 3. to compose. 4. to redact, pen, draught. 5. to edit a newspaper or write professionally for a periodical.

redil s. m. 1. corral. 2. sheep-pen or fold. 3. cot(e), coop for small domestic animals. 4. (fig.) flock, congregation.

redimir v. 1. to redeem, regain. 2. to ransom. 3. to buy off, exempt. 4. to atone for. 5. to repurchase, reacquire. 6. to liberate, free, save. 7. ~-se to redeem o. s., extricate o. s. from. ~ um penhor to take out of pawn.

redimível adj. m. + f. (pl. -íveis) redeemable, retrievable, that can and should be redeemed.

redingote s. m. redingote, riding coat, frock coat.

redinha s. f. small net, shrimp net.

redintegrar v. 1. to redintegrate. 2. to restore to integrity, renovate. 3. to renew. 4. to reinstate.

redissolver v. to redissolve, dissolve again.

redistribuir v. to redistribute, distribute again, recast.

redito adj. said again, said many times, repeated.

rédito s. m. 1. act of returning. 2. profit, gain. 3. advantage. 4. income, proceeds. 5. product, result. 6. interest.

rediviva s. f. rose of Jericho, resurrection plant.

redivivo adj. redivivus, resuscitated, revived, renewed, (fig.) reborn.

redizer v. 1. to say again. 2. to say many times, repeat. 3. to tell again, retell (what other people told us). 4. to relate, narrate over again.

redobrado adj. 1. reduplicate. 2. folded again. 3. redoubled, intensified.

redobramento s. m. 1. redoubling, reduplication. 2. increase, augmentation. 3. (med.) periodic aggravation of a disease.

redobrar v. 1. to redouble, reduplicate. 2. to quadruple. 3. to augment, increase considerably. 4. to repeat. 5. to peal (the bells) over again. 6. to intensify. 7. to twitter, chirp. 8. (med.) to become severer (illness, attack).

redobre s. m. 1. (mus.) trill. 2. warbling, chirping. 3. double-dealing, duplicity, falsity. 4. crookedness, swindling, deceit, piece of roguery.

redobro (ô) s. m. 1. twice the double. 2. quadruple. 3. redoubling, reduplication. 4. increase, augmentation.

redolente adj. m. + f. 1. (poet.) fragrant. 2. redolent, aromatic.

redoma s. f. glass shade, vial, bell jar.

redomão s. m. (pl. -ões) (S. Braz.) 1. a half broken horse. 2. wild horse that is being tamed. ‖ adj. squeezing, pressing (said of new clothes, shoes, etc.).

redomoneação s. f. (pl. -ões) (S. Braz.) act or process of taming a horse.

redomonear v. (S. Braz.) to tame, break in (horses).

redonda s. f. (Braz., ftb.) soccer ball.

redondeado adj. rounded, rotund.

redondear v. to make round, round off, become round.

redondel s. m. (pl. -éis) 1. circular arena, bull rign. 2. a kind of havelock.

redondela s. f. small wheel, ring, washer.

redondeza s. f. 1. round, roundness, rondure. 2. rotundness, chubbiness. 3. surroundings, environs. 4. suburbs.

redondil adj. m. + f. (pl. -is) round, spherical, circular.

redondilha s. f. (poet.) roundel, rondel.

redondo adj. 1. round, circular (plate F 5). 2. globular, spherical. 3. cylindrical. 4. curved. 5. (fig.) fat, stout, rotund, chubby. 6. outspoken. ‖ -amente adv. roundly, chubbily.

com velas -as (naut.) square-rigged. **digo-lhe -amente** I tell you flat. **ele calculava em números ~s** he reckoned with round figures. **ele caiu de ~** he fell down flat. **recusaram -amente** they refused flatly. **vela -a** (naut.) square sail.

redopiar v. to twirl, swirl, twirl, spin.

redopio s. m. twirling, swirling, twisting, spinning.

redor (l) s. m. 1. circle, circuit. 2. contour, outline. 3. environs, surroundings. 4. suburb.

ao ~, de ~, em ~ round, all round, all about, around, about. **as crianças ficaram em ~ de seu pai doente** all the children were about their sick father. **ele olha em ~** he looks about him. **os campos ao ~ de Cambridge** the fields about Cambridge.

redor (ô) (II) s. m. workman in a saltern.

redouça s. f. (Braz.) a child's swing.

redourar v. 1. to regild, gild again. 2. to illuminate brightly.

redra s. f. (agric.) second dressing of vines.

redrar v. (agric.) to dig around vines a second time, to weed a second time (in a vineyard).

redução s. f. (pl. -ões) 1. reduction, reducing. 2. abbreviation, summary. 3. diminution, abatement. 4. subduing, bringing under subjection. 5. (com.) deduction, cut, cutting (prices). 6. act of bringing back to the original place. 7. (surg.) setting of bones or joints.

~ de despesas retrenchment of expenses. **~ de medidas estrangeiras** conversion of foreign measures. **~ de salário** cut in pay. **~ de velocidade** slowing down, speed reduction. **concordaram com uma ~ de preços** they agreed on a price cut.

reducente adj. m. + f. reducing, tending to reduce, reductive.

redundância s. f. 1. redundance, redundancy. 2. pleonasm. 3. superfluity, excess (esp. use of more words than needed).

redundante adj. m. + f. 1. redundant. 2. pleonastic. 3. superfluous, excessive. 4. abounding, exuberant. ‖ ~mente adv. redundantly.

redundar v. 1. to overflow, run over. 2. to be redundant or profuse. 3. to originate from, derive, result from. 4. to redound to. 5. to come to pass, happen. 6. to change into.

redundou em vantagem para ele it redounded to his advantage.

reduplicação s. f. (pl. -ōse) 1. reduplication, redoubling. 2. repetition. 3. increase, augmentation. 4. repetition of a syllable or a letter of a word. 5. (rhet.) repetition of certain keywords of a discourse (in order to stress their importance).

reduplicar v. 1. to reduplicate, double again. 2. to repeat. 3. to increase, augment. 4. to multiply. 5. to repeat a syllable or word, reiterate.

reduplicativo s. m. (gram.) reduplicative word, word which indicates repetition. ‖ adj. reduplicative, reiterative, double.

redutibilidade s. f. reducibility, quality of being reducible.

redutível adj. m. + f. (pl. -íveis) 1. reducible, that may be reduced. 2. (arith.) divisible (said of a fraction).

redutivo adj. reductive, reducible, reductional.

reduto s. m. 1. (fort.) redoubt, outwork, temporary fortification. 2. (fig.) key. 3. (Braz.) swelling ground (free from inundations).

redutor s. m. 1. (mech.) reducer, reducing device. 2. reducent, reducing agent. ‖ adj. reducing, reductive.

redúvio s. m. (zool.) assassin bug.

reduzido adj. reduced, diminished, cut, bated.

~ à pobreza reduced to poverty.

reduzir v. 1. to reduce: a) decrease. b) restrict, compress. c) bring down, lower. d) subdue, bring to subjection. e) concentrate, compress, reduce to a greater density. f) set (bones). 9) simplify (fractions). h) abridge, sum up. i) belittle, minify. j) diminish. k) compel, oblige. l) transform, change, convert. m) lessen, weaken. n) (chem.) bring to a metallic state. o) deoxydize. p) combine with or subject to hydrogen. 2. to separate, disaggregate. 3. to bring back to. 4. to mitigate, soothe, allay, soften. 5. ~-se: a) to limit or confine o. s. to. b) to amount, come to. c) to arrive at an inferior position, be reduced to. d) to be converted or transformed. e) to become softened. f) to shrink, contract itself.

~ a carvão to carbonize. **~ a cinzas** to reduce to ashes. **~ a fome** to famish. **~ a marcha** to shift into a lower gear. **~ a nada** to reduce to nothing. **~ a breves palavras** to sum up. **~ às suas partes integrantes** to resolve. **~ a pedaços** to grind to pieces. **~ a pó** to grind down to powder, triturate. **~ à pobreza** to reduce to poverty. **~ a polpa** to pulpify. **~ a população** to depopulate. **~ proporcionalmente** to scale down. **~ a sonoridade** to tone dawn. **~ a temperatura** to attemper. **~ a um tipo inferior** to degrade. **~ a voltagem** to lower down the voltage. **a casa ficou reduzida a pó** the house crumbled into dust. **precisamos reduzi-lo** we must reduce it in compass. **todo seu discurso se**

reduz nisto all his discourse comes to this. **seu salário foi reduzido** his salary was pared down.

reduzível adj. m. + f. (pl. **--íveis**) reducible, compressible, diminishable.

reedição s. f. (pl. **-ões**) re-edition, new edition, reprint, reissue.

reedificação s. f. (pl. **-ões**) re-edification, rebuilding, reconstruction.

reedificado adj. re-edified, rebuilt, reconstructed.

reedificador s. m. rebuilder. || adj. rebuilding, reconstructing.

reedificar v. 1. to rebuild, re-edify. 2. to reconstruct. 3. to build or construct again. 4. to reform. 5. to re-establish.

reeditar v. to re-edit, republish, publish again, reprint, reissue.

reeducação s. f. (pl. **-ões**) re-education, rehabilitation through education.

reeducador s. m. re-educator, rehabilitator.

reeducar v. 1. to re-educate, educate again. 2. to complete or perfect the education of. 3. to rehabilitate through education.

reeleger v. to chose or elect again, re-elect.

reelegível adj. m. + f. (pl. **-íveis**) re-eligible, capable of being elected again, susceptible to re-election.

reeleição s. f. (pl. **-ões**) re-election, act of electing again.

reeleito s. m. a re-elected person. || adj. re-elected, elected again.

reembarcar v. to re-embark, embark again, reship, transship.

reembarque s. m. re-embarkation, reshipment, transshipment.

reembolsado adj. reimbursed, refunded, repaid.

reembolsar v. 1. to reimburse. 2. to pay back, repay. 3. to indemnify. 4. to be in possession of (an outstanding amount), be refunded for.

reembolsável adj. m. + f. (pl. **-áveis**) reimbursable, repayable, refundable.

reembolso (ô) s. m. reimbursement, repayment, refund, recoupment.

~ **postal** direct mail order.

reemenda s. f. 1. new emendation, second correction. 2. remending, repatching. 3. emending over again.

reemendar v. to emend again, recorrect, correct over again.

reemergência s. f. re-emergence, re-emergency.

reemergir v. to re-emerge, emerge again.

reempossar v. to give again possession to, reinstall in office.

reempregar v. to re-employ, use again.

reemprego (ê) s. m. renewed employment, repeated use.

reencadernar v. to rebind a book.

reencapar v. to put a new cover on (a book).

reencarnação s. f. (pl. **-ões**) reincarnation.

reencarnar v. to reincarnate, incarnate again.

reencenar v. to restage, to play or perform again.

reencher v. to refill, fill up again.

reenchimento s. m. refilling, refill.

reencontrar v. to meet or find again.

reencontro s. m. a new or second meeting.

reendossar v. to reendorse.

reendosso s. m. reendorsement.

reengajamento s. m. re-engagement, re-employment.

reengajar-se v. to engage o.s. again, re-employ o.s.

reenlaçar v. to refasten, tie, join or bind again.

reenlace s. m. refastening, binding again.

reentrada s. f. re-entrance, return, comeback.

reentrância s. f. 1. re-entrance, re-entering. 2. re-entering angle or curve. 3. bay, recess.

reentrante adj. m. + f. re-entrant, forming a recess.

reentrar v. 1. to re-enter, enter again. 2. to go home, go to bed.

reenviar v. 1. to send again, redispatch. 2. to remit. 3. to return, send back again. 4. to rechange, change again.

reenvidar v. 1. to raise again one's stakes. 2. to redouble one's efforts. 3. to reply in kind.

reenvio s. m. act of sending back, return, reshipping, redispatching.

reerguer v. 1. to re-erect, reconstruct. 2. to raise again. 3. to elevate or exalt again.

reescrever v. to rewrite, write a second time.

reespumas s. f. pl. (Braz.) sugar made of the scum of the first cooking.

reestabelecer v. to re-establish, restore, establish anew.

reestruturar v. to restructure.

reexpedição s. f. act of reshipping, transshipment, new dispatching.

reexpedir v. 1. to reship, transship. 2. to dispatch again, re-export. 3. to send off again (what one has received), redirect.

reexportação s. f. (pl. **-ões**) re-exportation, re-export, exportation of imported goods, transshipment.

reexportador s. m. re-exporter, forwarding agent of a free port.

reexportar v. to re-export, reship, transship, export again imported goods.

reextraditar v. to reextradite.

refalar v. to speak again, talk anew.

refalsado adj. 1. unsincere, false. 2. disloyal. 3. deceitful, tricky, fraudulent. 4. feigned, deceptive, hypocritical.

refalsamento s. m. falsehood, disloyalty, deceit, fraud, hypocrisy.

refalsear v. 1. to betray, be disloyal to. 2. to deceive, delude. 3. to double-cross, cheat. 4. to mislead, mystify.

refazedor s. m. remaker, repairer. || adj. remaking, repairing; mending over again, refitting.

refazer v. 1. to make once more, make over again. 2. to reform, remodel. 3. to reorganize, recompose. 4. to repair, mend again. 5. to correct. 6. to renew. 7. to re-establish, recover, refresh, reinvigorate. 8. to indemnify, compensate. 9. to feed, nourish. 10. to supply, furnish. 11. ~**-se**: a) to recover one's forces, rally, gather strength. b) to supply or furnish o. s. with new provisions.

~ **o exército** to raise new troops. ~ **o vestido** to remodel the gown. ~**-se da fadiga** to gather strength, repose.

refazimento s. m. 1. remaking, remodeling. 2. re-establishment, recovery. 3. repair, remending. 4. compensation, indemnification.

refece adj. m. + f. 1. base, vile. 2. miserable, wretched. 3. mean, infamous. 4. low, inferior. 5. common, ordinary. 6. easy. 7. cheap, dirt-cheap.

refecer v. to cool, grow cool or lukewarm.

refectivo, refectório s. m. tonic, restorative (medicine). || adj. restorative.

refega s. f. 1. skirmish, fray, brush. 2. whirlwind, gust of wind.

refegado adj. pleated, folded, tucked.

refegar v. 1. to pleat, fold. 2. to wrinkle, crease, furrow. 3. to crumple.

refego (ê) s. m. 1. fold, pleat. 2. tuck. 3. crease. 4. wrinkle.

fazer um ~ **num vestido** to take out a tuck from a dress.

refeição s. f. (pl. **-ões**) 1. meal, repast. 2. repose. 3. (fig.) table.

~ **alegre** racket. ~ **comercial** table d'hôte. ~ **de assobio** snack, (Braz.) lunch, coffee, bread and butter. ~ **ligeira** refreshment, bite. **fazer uma** ~ to have a meal. **ter -ões fartas** to keep a good table. **uma** ~ **reforçada** a square meal. **uma** ~ **régia** food fit for a king.

refeito adj. 1. restored, recovered. 2. mended, repaired. 3. fat, thickset, plump.

refeitoreiro s. m. caretaker or master of a refectory (of a monastery, boarding school, etc.).

refeitório s. m. refectory, dining-hall, mess hall, commons.

refém s. m. (pl. **-éns**) 1. hostage. 2. open city or fortified place held by the enemy as a pledge. 3. ransom, amount paid for the release of a prisoner. 4. security, pledge.

refender v 1.. to split anew, cleave, slit or splinter again. 2. to splinter. 3. to slash, cut. 4. to beat, strike. 5. to carve, chisel, make relief work.

refendimento s. m. 1. act or effect of splitting, cleaving or splintering. 2. (arts) alto relievo, high relief.

referência s. f. 1. act of referring. 2. reference, indication. 3. allusion, hint. 4. mention, notice. 5. remark, citation. 6. respect, regard. 7. concern. 8. ~s pl. references, written statement(s) of a candidate's qualifications.

com ~ **a** regarding to, with reference to. **ela tem boas** ~s she has good qualifications. **fazer** ~ **a** to make reference to, allude to. ~ **de nível** a reference point on a terrain. ~s **de apresentação** credentials.

referenda s. f. act or effect of countersigning, countersignature.

referendar v. 1. to countersign, sign in addition to (an other signature). 2. to authenticate, attest. 3. to accept responsibility as to the enactment and execution of a decree.

referendário s. m. referendary, minister or chief clerk who countersigns.

referente adj. m. + f. 1. referring to, relating to. 2. relative, regarding. 3. referential. 4. concerning, respecting.

referido adj. 1. above-mentioned, aforesaid. 2. reported. 3. cited, quoted.

referimento s. m. 1. act of referring, reference. 2. allusion, hint. 3. remark, observation. 4. report. 5. narration, tale. 6. assignment, task consignment.

referir v. 1. to refer. 2. to narrate, tell, relate. 3. to report. 4. to allude, hint. 5. to cite, mention. 6. to ascribe to, assign, attribute to, consign. 7. to concern, have reference to. 8. to apply to, respect. 9. ~-**se** to be relative to.

a quem se referia o homem? whom had the man in mind? **as palavras se referem à sua obra** his words have a bearing on his work. **isto não se refere a você** this does not apply to you. **não se refere a** it is extraneous to. **posso** ~-**me a você?** may I use your name? **ele referiu-se ao assunto** he touched the topic.

refermentação s. f. (pl. **-ões**) refermentation.

refermentar v. to referment, ferment again.

refervente adj. m. + f. boiling, bubbling again, boiling excessively.

referver v. 1. to reboil, boil again, boil a lot. 2. to ferment. 3. to incite, stimulate, animate. 4. to become inflamed, get excited. 5. to intensify. 6. to effervesce. 7. to flare up, become heated. 8. to become tumultuous, cause a tumult.

refervido adj. reboiled, boiled again, spoiled by repeated boiling.

refestelar-se v. 1. to loll, lollop. 2. to recline, lean back. 3. to relax, repose. 4. to stretch out, lie down. 5. to revel, make merry. 6. to divert o. s.

refestelo (ê) s. m. 1. merrymaking, frolic. 2. festivity, ball, party. 3. satisfaction. 4. easy, comfortable position.

refez adj. m. + f. 1. base, vile, mean. 2. easy, simple, cheap.

ela o fez de ~ she did it easily.

refiar v. 1. to respin, spin again. 2. to divide in strands or sheets.

refil s. m. (Braz.) refill.

refilador adj. obstinate, stubborn, rebellious.

refilão s. m. (pl. **-ões**) recalcitrant, rebellious person, backbiter. ‖ adj. refractory, stubborn, rebellious, backbiting.

de ~ (Braz.) slightly, superficially.

refilar v. 1. to bite back, retort. 2. to attack, assault. 3. to react, counteract, counter. 4. to recalcitrate.

refilhar v. 1. to put forth new shoots, sprout again. 2. to multiply, spread, scatter, diffuse.

refilho s. m. new shoots or sprouts, offshoot.

refiltrar v. to refilter, filter again.

refinação s. f. (pl. **-ões**) 1. act or process of refining or purifying. 2. refining, refinery. 3. building and apparatus for refining, refining plant. 4. refinement, subtlety. 5. sugar refinery.

refinado adj. 1. purified, pure. 2. refined, subtle. 3. polished, cultured. 4. downright, thorough. 5. shrewd, clever. 6. nice, polite, fine. ‖ **-amente** adv. refinedly.

açúcar ~ refined sugar. **gosto** ~ refined taste. **febre -a** acute fever. **malícia -a** refined malice. **não** ~ uncultured, unkempt, crude. **seu modo nada tem de** ~ his manners are far from being refined. **um malandro** ~ a precious scoundrel.

refinador s. m. 1. refiner. 2. purifier. 3. (fig.) chastener, reformer. ‖ adj. refining, purifying.

refinadura s. f. 1. refining, refinery. 2. refinement, culture.

refinamento s. m. 1. refining, refinery. 2. refinement, culture, refinedness. 3. niceness, polish, polishedness. 4. excess, exaggeration. 5. gentlemanly or ladylike bearing.

refinanciar v. to refinance.

refinar v. 1. to refine, purify. 2. to civilize, cultivate. 3. to make stronger, intensify. 4. to improve, better, perfect. 5. to free from deleterious matter, eliminate impurities, filter, strain, percolate. 6. to make more conspicuous. 7. ~-**se** a) to become pure, purer or more refined. b) to improve or perfect o. s. c) to grow more cultivated.

~ **duas vezes** to refine twice.

refinaria s. f. refinery, sugar refinery, skimming plant. ~ **de petróleo** oil refinery.

refincar v. 1. to thrust or drive in with force (nails, stakes, etc.). 2. to fasten anew, clinch again.

reflada s. f. 1. blow with a rifle butt. 2. rifle shot.

reflar v. (Braz.) to beat or drive away with the rifle butt.

refle s. m. 1. rifle, short shotgun or musket. 2. (Braz.) short saber, bayonet (as used by policemen).

refletido adj. 1. prudent, cautious. 2. sensible, thoughtful, thinking. 3. deliberate. 4. considerate, judicious. 5. reflected. ‖ **-amente** adv. 1. reflectively, thoughtfully. 2. reflectedly.

refletidor s. m. reflector, headlight, searchlight. ‖ adj. reflecting.

refletir v. 1. to reflect. 2. to turn, throw or fall back. 3. to deflect, divert. 4. to give back an image, mirror. 5. to reveal, disclose. 6. to reproduce. 7. to rebound, spring back. 8. to resound, re-echo. 9. to consider carefully, ponder, meditate, contemplate. 10. to coincide with. 11. ~-**se**: a) to be shown, reproduced or mirrored. b) to become manifest.

ele agiu sem ~ he acted thoughtlessly. **ele refletiu sobre o problema** he pondered over the problem. **~am bem todo o negócio** they chewed well the whole business. **sem ~ on first thoughts. seu rosto refletiu claramente grande surpresa** surprise was written large on her face.

refletivo adj. 1. reflective, pondering. 2. pensive, thoughtful. 3. serious, sober. 4. deliberative.

refletor s. m. reflector, searchlight, headlight (plates B 11, E 5). || adj. reflecting.

reflexão s. f. (pl. **-ões**) 1. reflection, reflexion. 2. reflex. 3. contemplation, meditation. 4. reverberation of light. 5. consideration. 6. prudence, caution. 7. retort, reply.
~ **tardia** afterwit, afterthought. **ângulo de** ~ angle of reflection. **fazer** ~: 1. to mirror. 2. to ponder. **perdido em -ões** lost in thoughts in a brown study.

reflexibilidade s. f. reflexibility, reflectiveness.

reflexionar v. 1. to ponder, meditate. 2. to object, argue. 3. to reflect, think. 4. to consider, cogitate.

reflexível adj. m. + f. (pl. **-íveis**) reflexible.

reflexivo adj. 1. reflexive, reflective. 2. (gram.) referring back to the subject. || **-amente** adv. reflexively, reflectively.
pronome (verbo) ~ (gram.) reflexive pronoun (verb).

reflexo s. m. 1. reflex, reflection. 2. reflected light or image, sheen. 3. imitation. 4. indirect influence. 5. (physiol.) involuntary reaction, reflex action. || adj. 1. reflected. 2. deflected. 3. indirect, intermediate. 4. (gram.) reflexive.
~ **rotuliano** (med.) knee reflex. **ação de** ~ reflex action.

reflorescência s. f. reflorescence, blossoming anew.

reflorescente adj. m. + f. reflorescent, reflowering.

reflorescer v. 1. to blossom again, reflourish, reflower. 2. (fig.) to recover, reinvigorate, rejuvenate. 3. to revive, reanimate.

reflorescido adj. reflourished, blooming again.

reflorescimento s. m. act or fact of reflowering, reflorescence, second flowering.

reflorestador s. m. person who promotes reforestation, planter of new forests. || adj. reforesting, replanting (of forests).

reflorestamento s. m. reforestation, reforestment.

reflorestar v. to reforest, forest anew, reafforest, renew forest cover.

reflorido adj. reflourished, blooming anew, covered with new blossoms.

reflorir v. 1. to flower or blossom again, reflourish. 2. (fig.) to recover strength, reinvigorate, rejuvenate. 3. to revive.

refluência s. f. refluence, reflux, flowing back.

refluente adj. m. + f. refluent, flowing back, ebbing.

refluir v. 1. to flow back, reflow. 2. to recede, retrocede (flood). 3. to return, go back to the starting point. 4. to run, flow or overflow, flood. 5. to regurgitate.

réfluo adj. refluent, flowing back, ebbing.

refluxo s. m. 1. act of flowing back, reflow. 2. refluence, refluency. 3. ebb, ebbing. 4. recess, retrocession.
fluxo e ~ flow and ebb, high tide and ebbing.

refocilamento s. m. 1. refreshment, refreshing. 2. restoration of strength, recovery. 3. reanimation, revival. 4. recreation, pleasure.

refocilante adj. m. + f. refreshing, strengthening, recreative.

refocilar v. 1. to refresh, revive. 2. to strengthen, fortify. 3. to restore, reanimate. 4. to recreate. 5. **~-se** to revel, make merry, seek diversion, enjoy o. s.

refogado s. m. butter sauce, meat gravy, any dish fried with butter, onions or herbs.

refogar v. 1. to fry with butter or oil, onions, parsley or other herbs. 2. to stew, boil slowly, simmer.

refolego s. m. (N. Braz.) needlework.

refolgar v. to repose, rest, take things easy.

refolgo (ô) s. m. 1. rest, repose. 2. recreation. 3. relief, ease, comfort.

refolhado adj. 1. wrapped in leaves, covered with leaves. 2. pleated, folded, tucked. 3. (fig.) hidden, disguised. 4. deceitful, sly.

refolhamento s. m. 1. pleat, tuck. 2. fold. 3. disguise, dissimulation.

refolhar v. 1. to wrap in folds or leaves. 2. to disguise, dissemble. 3. to cover up, conceal, hide.

refolho (ô) s. m. 1. ruffle, pleat, plait, fold. 2. (fig.) dissimulation, dissembling, disguise.

refolhudo adj. 1. pleated, plaited, folded. 2. ramose, having dense foliage.

reforçado adj. 1. reinforced, strengthened. 2. strong, vigorous. 3. robust, stocky, brawny.

reforçador s. m. 1. an explosive that, in a chain, detonates the rupturing charge. 2. a booster rocket. || adj. that reinforces, strengthens.

reforçar v. 1. to give additional force to. 2. to reinforce, strengthen. 3. to intensify. 4. to amplify. 5. to reinvigorate, restore, reanimate. 6. **~-se:** a) to become stronger. b) to acquire more strength or vigour. c) to rely on force or support. 7. (mil.) to supply additional troops or reinforcement.

reforçativo adj. tending to fortify or strengthen, reinvigorative.

reforço (ô) s. m. 1. reinforcement, reinforcing (plate V 5). 2. supply of additional forces, new assistance. 3. succour, relief, help. 4. backing. 5. enforcement. 6. recruiting, recruitment. 7. brace (plates E 6, C 11).
~ **de fole** bellows backing, reinforcement.

reforma s. f. 1. reform, reformation. 2. new form, modification. 3. (rel.) Reformation: important religious movement of the 16th century, Protestantism. 4. amendment, correction.
~ **agrária** agrarian reform.

reformação s. f. (pl. **-ões**) reform, reforming, reformation, correction.

reformado s. m. 1. pensioner, retired officer. 2. Protestant. || adj. 1. reformed, retired. 2. converted (to Protestantism).

reformador s. m. reformer, redresser, remodeller. || adj. reformative, reformational.

reformar v. 1. to reform. 2. to give a new or better form, improve. 3. to remodel, make over. 4. to reconstruct, rebuild. 5. to reorganize, renovate. 6. to correct, mend. 7. to repair, rectify. 8. to re-establish, restore. 9. to suppress. 10. to better, amend. 11. to remould, reshape. 12. to renew. 13. **~-se:** a) to revictual o. s. b) to regenerate o. s., mend one's ways. c) to gather new strength. d) to be pensioned off, obtain permission to retire from active service. e) to put through a reform. f) to return to the original form.
~ **uma sentença** to amend or change a judgment. **o governo reformou-o no posto de capitão** the government put him on the retired list as a captain.

reformativo adj. reforming, reformative, reformatory.

reformatório s. m. house of correction, reformatory, protectory. || adj. reformatory, reformative.

reformável adj. m. + f. (pl. **-áveis**) reformable, renewable.

reformista s. m. + f. reformer, reformist. || adj. referring to reform.

reformular v. to reformulate, formulate again.

refornecer v. to resupply, furnish again.

refração s. f. (pl. **-ões**) 1. (phys.) refraction, deflection. 2. (med.) aberration.
~ **dupla** (opt.) double refraction.
refrangência s. f. refraction, refractivity, refractiveness.
refrangente adj. m. + f. refracting, refractive.
refranger v. 1. to refract. 2. ~**-se** to be refracted, be reflected.
refrangibilidade s. f. refrangibility, refrangibleness.
refrangível adj. m. + f. (pl. **-íveis**) refrangible, capable of being refracted.
refranzear v. (arch.) to crack jokes, jest, banter.
refrão s. m. (pl. ~**s** and **-ões**) 1. refrain. 2. adage, saying. 3. proverb. 4. burden of a song.
refratar v. 1. to refract, deflect. 2. ~**-se** to be reflected or deflected.
refratário s. m. 1. refractory or intractable person. 2. (mil.) deserter. ‖ adj. 1. refractory. 2. intractable, unmanageable. 3. unruly, pervicacious. 4. unsubmissive, disobedient. 5. stubborn. 6. restive. 7. fractious. 8. (med.) immune.
~ **ao fogo** refractory. **tijolo** ~ firebrick.
refrativo adj. refractive, refracting, deflective, refringent.
refrato adj. refracted, subject to refraction.
refratômetro s. m. (phys.) refractometer.
refrator adj. refractive, serving or tending to refract.
refreado adj. 1. curbed, restrained. 2. moderate.
refreador s. m. refrainer, coercer, restrainer. ‖ adj. refraining.
refreadouro s. m. 1. (arch.) brake. 2. (fig.) self-restraint, moral.
refreamento s. m. 1. restraint. 2. restraining, refraining. 3. moderation. 4. constraint, curbing, rein.
refrear v. 1. to refrain, restrain. 2. to coerce, repress. 3. to curb, check. 4. to subdue, hold in. 5. to bridle, rein in. 6. to moderate. 7. to conquer. 8. ~**-se:** a) to restrain o. s. b) to abstain from. c) to be moderate.
~ **a língua** to curb one's tongue. ~ **os apetites** to repress one's passions. **tenho de refreá-los** I must keep them in check. **vamos refreá-los** we shall hold them in.
refreável adj. m. + f. (pl. **-áveis**) restrainable.
refrega s. f. 1. fight, combat. 2. fray, skirmish. 3. dispute, quarrel. 4. re-encounter. 5. (Braz.) storm, tempest (of short duration).
refregar v. to fight, quarrel, dispute, brawl.
refreio s. m. 1. act of checking, curbing or holding in. 2. bridle, rein(s), bit. 3. restraint.
refrém s. m. (pl. **-éns**) = **refrão.**
refrescado adj. refreshed, reanimated, revived, comforted.
refrescamento s. m. act or effect of refreshing, comforting, refreshment.
refrescante adj. m. + f. refreshing, cooling, crisp, comforting.
refrescar v. 1. to refresh, freshen. 2. to make cool, refrigerate. 3. to reanimate, revive, reinvigorate. 4. to relieve, soothe, mitigate. 5. to drop, decrease (temperature), become cooler. 6. ~**-se:** a) to refresh o. s. b) to renew one's forces or energy. c) to become again livelier. d) to take a refreshment, quench one's thirst. e) to calm down.
~ **a memória** to remember. **o vento está refrescando** the wind freshens.
refresco (ê) s. m. 1. refreshment. 2. comfort, ease, rest. 3. cooling draught, drink. 4. refrigeration. 5. relief, succour. 6. (sl.) a beating, spanking.
refrigeração s. f. (pl. **-ões**) 1. act or effect of cooling. 2. refrigeration, freezing. 3. cooling, chilling. 4. alleviation.

refrigerador s. m. refrigerator, freezer, cooler, ice chest, spray-cooler. ‖ adj. refrigerating, cooling, chilling.
refrigerante s. m. refreshment, refresher, cooling (soft) drink. ‖ adj. m. + f. refrigerant, cooling, refreshing, refrigeratory.
refrigerar v. 1. to refresh, cool. 2. to make fresh or cooler. 3. to protect from the heat. 4. to comfort, relieve. 5. to allay, mitigate, soothe. 6. ~**-se:** a) to enjoy the fresh air, refresh o. s. b) to feel eased or comforted.
refrigerativo s. m. refrigerant, refreshment, refresher. ‖ adj. refreshing, refrigerative, refrigeratory, cooling.
refrigeratório adj. refrigeratory, refrigerant, refrigerative, cooling.
vaso ~ cooling vessel, cooler.
refrigério s. m. 1. refrigeration, freezing. 2. well-being produced by coolness. 3. refreshment, refrigerant. 4. relief, comfort.
refringência s. f. 1. (opt.) refringency, refringence. 2. (phys.) refractivity.
refringente adj. m. + f. (phys.) refringent, refractive, deflecting.
refrondescente adj. m. + f. growing green or verdant again.
refrulho s. m. (Braz.) murmur, rustle, whispering.
refugado adj. 1. disregarded, spurned. 2. refused, rejected. 3. castoff, thrown out.
refugador s. m. 1. rejecter, refuser. 2. (S. Braz.) renitent stray cattle (that refuses to come back to the corral). ‖ adj. 1. rejecting, refusing. 2. (S. Braz.) said of renitent stray cattle.
refugar v. 1. to reject, refuse to accept. 2. to throw aside, cast off. 3. to despise, scorn, disdain. 4. to discard. 5. (S. Braz.) to refuse to return to the corral (stray cattle).
refugiado s. m. refugee, fugitive, displaced person. ‖ adj. fugitive.
refugiar-se v. 1. to take refuge, seek shelter. 2. to withdraw from one's native country, emigrate. 3. to hide o. s. 4. to look for protection.
a raposa refugiou-se na cova the fox took to the earth.
refúgio s. m. 1. refuge. 2. shelter, asylum. 3. sanctuary, haven, harbour. 4. (fig.) anchor, port, protection. 5. retreat.
refugir v. 1. to fly again, flee anew. 2. to flow back, reflow. 3. to recede, retrocede. 4. to try to escape, run away. 5. to slip away, shun, shirk. 6. to avoid, free o. s., get free from.
refugo s. m. 1. refuse, rejection. 2. garbage, sweepings, tailings. 3. rejection, outcasting, outscouring. 4. waste, scrap, rubbish. 5. dross, dreg. 6. chaff, dirt. 7. spoilage.
refulgência s. f. refulgence, refulgency, radiance, splendour.
refulgente adj. m. + f. 1. refulgent, fulgent. 2. radiant, brilliant. 3. relucent, shining, resplendent. 4. flashy. ‖ ~**mente** adv. refulgently.
refulgir v. 1. to shine resplendently. 2. to shine, glitter, sparkle. 3. (fig.) to distinguish o. s., come to prominence.
refundar v. to dig deeper, deepen, make deeper.
refundição s. f. (pl. **-ões**) recast, recasting, remelting, new cast.
refundir v. 1. to cast again. 2. to recast, refound. 3. to remelt. 4. to pour (liquids) from one vessel into another. 5. to remodel, reform, correct. 6. to rejoin, reconnect, amass. 7. ~**-se:** a) to melt away, dissolve. b) to disappear. c) to change into, convert into, be transformed.

refusar v. 1. to refuse, deny. 2. to reject, decline. 3. to oppose.

refutação s. f. (pl. **-ões**) 1. refutation, refute. 2. disproof, disproval. 3. confutation. 4. rebuttal.

refutador s. m. refuter, disprover. ‖ adj. refuting, rebutting.

refutar v. 1. to refute. 2. to deny the truth of, belie. 3. to contradict, disprove. 4. to rebut, confute. 5. not to accept, reject, impugn. 6. to oppose, object, contest. 7. to annul, cancel, abrogate.

refutatório adj. refutatory, refutative, disproving.

refutável adj. m. + f. (pl. **-áveis**) 1. refutable, refutative. 2. rebuttable, answerable. 3. disprovable. 4. vanquishable. ‖ **refutavelmente** adv. refutably, answerably.

rega s. f. 1. irrigation, watering. 2. affusion. 3. (pop.) rain.

rega-bofe s. m. (pl. **rega-bofes**) 1. festivity, feast. 2. revelery, merrymaking. 3. pleasure, amusement. 4. racket, spree.

regaçar v. to tuck up, turn or gather up.

regaço s. m. 1. lap. 2. (fig.) bosom, bowels. 3. shelter, retreat.

regada s. f. 1. farm, farmyard. 2. irrigated field.

regadeira s. f. 1. heavy shower. 2. torrent, freshet. 3. irrigation ditch. 4. drain, gutter.

regadia s. f. 1. watering, irrigation. 2. watered land.

regadio s. m. 1. act of watering. 2. irrigation, watering. ‖ adj. watered, irrigated.

campo de ~ irrigated field.

regador s. m. watering can or pot, sprinkler, waterer (plate J 2). ‖ adj. watering, sprinkling.

regadura s. f. 1. watering, irrigation. 2. sprinkling. 3. affusion. 4. (pop.) rain.

regalado adj. 1. delicate, dainty. 2. rich, sumptuous. 3. agreeable, pleasant. 4. delicious, relishing. 5. pampered, coddled. ‖ **-amente** adv. delicately, deliciously, abundantly.

ele é um homem ~ he is an epicure. **eles têm uma mesa** -a they keep a very good table. **levaram uma vida** -a they led a rich life, they lived in luxury.

regalador s. m. host, entertainer, feaster. ‖ adj. delightful, pleasant, pleasing, charming, enchanting.

regalão s. m. (pl. **-ões**) (f. **-ona**) 1. reveller, feaster. 2. epicure, gastronom, glutton. ‖ adj. 1. revelling, feasting. 2. dainty, epicurean. 3. gluttonous, immoderate, intemperate.

regalar v. 1. to regale, entertain, feast. 2. to please, delight, gratify. 3. to divert, amuse. 4. to coddle, pamper. 5. to drink to, toast. 6. to present a gift to. 7. to have a good time. 8. ~-se: a) to keep a good table, fare well, luxuriate. b) to feel great pleasure in, rejoice in. c) to take care of o. s., make much of o. s.

regalamo-nos com um pouco de vinho we treated ourselves to some wine. ~**am o grande artista** they feasted the great artist.

regalardoar v. to reward or recompense again, repay twice the value.

regalengo adj. regal, royal.

regalia s. f. 1. regal rights or privileges. 2. prerogative, special or exclusive right(s). 3. freedom, liberties.

~**s reais**, regalia, sovereignty. ~ **de sangue** royal kinship.

regalismo s. m. regalism: doctrine of royal supremacy.

regalista s. m. + f. regalist, upholder of royal sovereignty.

regalo s. m. 1. regalement. 2. pleasure, delight. 3. dainty gift, gift, donation. 4. leisure, tranquil life. 5. wristlet, muff (plate R 6). 6. regale, treat, sumptuous repast. 7. dainty, delicacy.

é um ~ it is wonderful. ~ **dos olhos** delightful sight.

regalona s. f. 1. a kind of olive tree. 2. (Port., prov.) a variety of plum-tree. 3. idle luxurious woman. 4. f. of **regalão**.

regalório s. m. feasting, high jinks, spree, revelry.

reganhar v. 1. to regain, win back. 2. to reacquire, repurchase. 3. to recuperate, recover, rehave.

regar v. 1. to water, irrigate. 2. to sprinkle. 3. to wash, bathe. 4. to moisten, make wet. 5. to take a drink (liquor) to the meal, wash down with a drink (food). 6. to inundate, flood.

ela o regou com água she slopped it with water.

regata s. f. (sport) regatta, boat race.

~ **de veleiros** sailing match.

regatão s. m. (pl. **-ões**) 1. huckster, retail dealer. 2. (Braz.) Amazonian river trader. ‖ adj. haggling, dickering.

regatar v. 1. to peddle, hawk. 2. to sell at retail, regrate.

regateador s. m. haggler, bargainer. ‖ adj. haggling, bargaining.

regatear v. 1. to haggle over the price, bargain. 2. to drive a hard bargain. 3. to depreciate, undervalue. 4. to give unwillingly or parsimoniously. 5. to discuss rudely, dicker hard.

~**am por centavos** they drove a hard deal.

regateio s. m. haggling, bargaining, wrangling.

regateira s. f. 1. huckstress, itinerant (female) trader. 2. shrew, quarrelsome rude woman, wicked tongue. 3. fishwife or market woman.

regateiro s. m. 1. huckster, itinerant vendor. 2. haggler, bargainer, cheapener. ‖ adj. (Braz.) vainglorious, conceited.

regateirona s. f. extremely quarrelsome woman (used as a superlative of **regateira**).

regatia s. f. life, behaviour or trade of a huckster or huckstress.

regato s. m. brooklet, creek, rivulet, streamlet, rill.

regedor s. m. 1. administrator. 2. jurat. 3. chairman of the board of parish counsellors. ‖ adj. governing, directing, administrating.

~ **da justiça** chief justice, president of the supreme court.

regedoria s. f. office, authority and jurisdiction of a **regedor**.

regeira s. f. 1. supporting beam (which props up a ship at launching). 2. (S. Braz.) leather strap fastened to the ear of draught oxen (in order to guide the animals).

regelação s. f. (pl. **-ões**) (phys.) phenomenon of recongelation of broken lumps of ice.

regelado adj. congealed, frozen, extremely cold.

regelador adj. freezing, chilling.

regelante adj. m. + f. freezing, chilling, tending to freeze.

regelar v. 1. to freeze, congeal. 2. to chill. 3. ~-se to become frozen.

regélido adj. extremely cold, deeply frozen.

regelo (ê) s. m. 1. refreezing. 2. glazed frost, white frost. 3. (fig.) insensibility, indifference, coldness.

regência s. f. 1. regency. 2. office, authority and jurisdiction of a ruler. 3. reigning, governing. 4. government, administration. 5. (gram.) regimen, government: syntactical relation between words.

regencial adj. m. + f. (pl. **-ais**) of, referring to or relative to regency.

regeneração s. f. (pl. **-ões**) 1. regeneration. 2. renovation, reform. 3. reclamation. 4. amendment. 5. (electr.) feedback. 6. conversion.

regenerado adj. regenerate, renewed, reformed, (fig.) spiritually reborn.

regenerador s. m. regenerator: 1. renewer, reformer. 2. (mech.) recuperator. ‖ adj. regenerative, regeneratory.
~ do vapor de escape (mech.) dead steam recuperator.
regenerando adj. regenerating, tending to regenerate, bound to spiritual recreation.
regenerante adj. m. + f. regenerating, tending to regenerate.
regenerar v. 1. to regenerate. 2. to reproduce, build up again what has been destroyed. 3. to restore, renew. 4. to reorganize. 5. to improve, better. 6. to amend, correct. 7. **~-se:** a) to gather new strength, revive. b) to mend one's ways. c) to rehabilitate ̇o. s.
regenerativo adj. regenerative, prone to regenerate.
regenerável adj. m. + f. (pl. **-áveis**) regenerable, regenerative, amendable.
regentar v. (arch.) = **reger.**
regente s. m. + f. 1. regent, governor, ruler. 2. (mus.) maestro, conductor. 3. leader. ‖ adj. regent, ruling, governing.
reger v. 1. to govern, rule, reign. 2. to manage, administer. 3. to direct, guide. 4. (mus.) to conduct. 5. to teach, lecture. 6. to occupy the chairmanship of a faculty. 7. to be sovereign or regent. 8. **~-se:** a) to act according to rules or principles, follow strict rules. b) to behave, accomodate o. s.
regerar v. to generate again, regenerate.
régia s. f. a king's palace, manor-house, castle.
região s. f. (pl. **-ões**) 1. large tract of land, area. 2. country, province. 3. region, zone, section. 4. realm. 5. (anat.) part, division (of the body). 6. (mil.) military district. 7. conservation.
~ de caça hunt. **~ de alta pressão** (meteor.) high-pressure area. **~ florestal** woodland. **~ fronteiriça** borderland. **~ lombar** lumbar region (plate C 18). **~ montanhosa** highland. **~ militar** military region. **~ natural** natural region. **grande ~** each one of the great regions into which Brazil is divided. **~ púbica** pubic region. **~ tropical** tropics. **~ umbilical** (anat.) umbilical region. **-ões árticas** artic regions. **da ~** regionary.
regicida s. m. + f. regicide: killer or murderer of a king or queen.
regicídio s. m. regicide: killing or murdering of a king or queen.
regicidismo, regicismo s. m. doctrine maintaining the elimination of royal sovereignty and monarchic government.
regime s. m. (also **regímen** pl. **regimens, regímenes**) 1. regime, regimen. 2. mode or principles of ruling, political system. 3. (med.) rational use of food, diet. 4. (gram.) syntactical relation between words. 5. rate of flow or discharge (liquids, river systems, etc.). 6. disciplinary rules. 7. administration, management. 8. methods or processes of cultivation, rational exploitation of landed property.
~ de comunhão de bens (jur.) matrimonial joint ownership of property. **~ de seperação de bens** (jur.) separate ownership of property of married people. **~ presidencial** (pol.) presidential regime.
regimental adj. m. + f. (pl. **-ais**) regimental, of or referring to regimentation.
regimentar v. to regulate, bring under control. ‖ adj. m. + f. regimental, regulating, regulatory.
regimento s. m. 1. act or effect of governing. 2. government, administration. 3. guide rule, direction. 4. regime, form of government. 5. (mil.) regiment, body of soldiers, troops. 6. (fig.) a lot of people, crowd. 7. discipline, order. 8. (med.) regimen, diet. **ele tem um ~ de filhos** he has a lot of children.

~ interno internal rules (as of a club), statutes, bylaws.
régio adj. 1. royal, regal. 2. kinglĭke, kingly. 3. (fig.) splendid, magnificent. ‖ **regiamente** adv. regally, royally.
água -a (chem.) aqua regia. **carta -a** royal charter.
regional adj. m. + f. (pl. **-ais**) 1. regional, sectional, local. 2. (med.) endemical.
regionalismo s. m. 1. regionalism. 2. provincialism, provinciality. 3. localism. 4. idiomatic language or expression. 5. (arts) regional character of literary and other works of art.
regionalista s. m. + f. regionalist, provincialist. ‖ adj. regionalistic.
regirar v. 1. to let gyrate, revolve. 2. to spin, twirl, whirl. 3. to rotate, turn round its axis. 4. to veer round (wind).
regiro s. m. 1. gyration, rotation. 2. circumlocution, periphrase.
registração, registação s. f. (pl. **-ões**) registration, registering.
registrado, registado s. m. 1. registered letter or package. 2. registrant. ‖ adj. registered, recorded. **marca -a** trade-mark, proprietary name. **não ~** unrecorded.
registrador, registador s. m. 1. registrar, registrary. 2. registrant. 3. recorder, filer. 4. (mech.) recording device. ‖ adj. recording.
registrar, registar v. 1. to register, enregister. 2. to book, list. 3. to write down, inscribe. 4. to record. 5. to preserve the memory of, tell or write the history of. 6. to manifest, declare, state. 7. to insure (against). 8. to enlist, enrol, matriculate. 9. (S. Braz.) to register the livestock, separating it from other cattle. 10. (com.) to control, check up.
~ por importância superior ao valor real to overregister. **~ seu nome** to send in one's name. **~ um nascimento** to give notice of a birth. **~ uma carta** to register a letter. **~ uma marca comercial** to register a trade-mark. **ele registrou toda a história** he chronicled all the events. **eles ~am a velocidade do carro** they clocked the car.
registrável, registável adj. m. + f. (pl. **-áveis**) registrable, recordable, enterable.
registro, registo s. m. 1. register, record. 2. registry, registration office. 3. registration, enrol(l)ment, entry. 4. file, list, entry-book, ledger. 5. protocol. 6. stop knob, flute stop, register (of musical instruments). 7. timbre (of voices or instruments). 8. post insurance. 9. small picture of a saint. 10. stopcock, stop valve, tap, pet cock (plates E 3, R 8). 11. regulator (watch, clock). 12. (mus.) gamut of higher voices of a musical scale. 13. (mech.) gauge, damper, slide valve (plate C 5). 15. catalogue, index. 16. (S. Braz.): a) separation of ranging cattle (with regard to ownership). b) cattle roundup.
~ civil registry office. **~ de avaliações** rate-book. **~ de compras** book of commissions, purchase book. **~ de documentos** registration of documents. **~ de gaveta** (mech.) slide valve. **~ de partida dobrada** cross-entry. **~ de nomes e endereços** directory. **~ de títulos** bill-book. **~ de tropas** muster-roll. **~ eleitoral** pollbook. **~ genealógico de cavalos** studbook. **ficha de ~** entry form. **remeter sob ~** to dispatch registered. **tocar todos os ~s** to let no stone unturned, set all wheels going.
rego (ê) s. m. 1. channel, duct. 2. gutter, drain (plate C 11). 3. furrow. 4. trench, irrigation ditch. 5. parting of the hair. 6. rut, wheel track.
de ~ em ~ furrow by furrow. **pisar fora do ~** (Braz.) to proceed badly, neglect one's duty.

RÉGUA DE CÁLCULO E DISCO DE CÁLCULO

regô s. m. (Braz.) scarf worn by Negro women on the head.

regoado adj. furrowed, rutted, grooved.

regoar v. to furrow, plough, make ruts.

regolfo s. m. 1. turbine. 2. backwater, backwash. 3. countercurrent, crosscurrent. 4. accumulation of water and rise of the water-level (caused by dams, pillars of bridges, etc.).

regorjeado adj. similar to a trill, warbled.

regorjear v. to warble very much, trill, utter trilling sounds.

regorjeio s. m. act of warbling or trilling, warble, trill.

regougante adj. m. + f. 1. groaning, moaning. 2. grumbling, mumbling. 3. croaking, uttering hoarse cries.

regougar v. 1. to groan, moan. 2. to grumble, gripe, mumble. 3. to croak, utter hoarse cries, yelp.

regougo s. m. 1. howl, yelp, yawp. 2. any deep hoarse sound or cry.

regozijado adj. cheerful, merry, gay, rejoicing.

regozijador s. m. one who rejoices or causes merriness, merrymaker. ‖ adj. joyful, cheerful, exhilarating.

regozijar v. 1. to rejoice, cheer. 2. to cause merriment or pleasure. 3. to delight, please, gladden. 4. ~-se to take delight in, be gladdened by, be satisfied or pleased with, jubilate.

regozijo s. m. 1. great pleasure or joy. 2. mirth, glee. 3. deep satisfaction, gladness. 4. expression of joy, rejoicing. 5. feast, festivity. 6. revelry, spree. 7. jubilation, exultation.

regra s. f. 1. ruler, metal or wood strip used for measuring. 2. rulings on paper, ruled paper. 3. norm, standard. 4. rule, principle, maxim. 5. law, decree. 6. statutes of some religious orders. 7. pattern, model. 8. common practice, custom. 9. guide, guideposts. 10. care. 11. order. 12. (med.): a) regimen, diet. b) ~s pl. menstruation. 13. canon. ~ convencional conventionality. ~ de companhia ou de sociedade rule of society. ~ de falsa posição (arith.) rule of false position. ~ de proceder injunction. ~ de três (arith.) rule of three, rule of proportion, golden rule. ~ fixa formula. em ~ as a rule. estabelecer uma ~ to lay down a rule. estar com as ~s to discharge the menses. a exceção confirma a ~ the exception proves the rule. não há ~ sem exceção there is no rule without exception. por via de ~ usually, according to custom. tornar-se ~ to become the rule. uma ~ fixa a hard and fast rule.

regras-de-fé s. f. pl. (rel.) laws of faith: ecclesiastical laws, canon laws.

regrado adj. 1. sensible, reasonable. 2. moderate, temperate. 3. ruled (said of paper). 4. regular, orderly.

regra-inteira s. f. (pl. **regras-inteiras**), (Braz., pop.) viola with twelve strings (accompanying instrument for singers).

regrante adj. m. + f. 1. regulated. 2. observant, observing (any religious law or precept).

regrar v. 1. to rule, draw lines (on paper). 2. to regulate, set in order. 3. to moderate. 4. to guide, direct. 5. to subject to certain rules or precepts.

6. to make uniform. 7. ~-se: a) to guide o. s. by. b) to regulate one's life. c) to regenerate o. s., remodel one's life. d) to moderate o. s.

regra-três s. m. (Braz.) 1. (ftb.) each of the two players who, in official soccer games, remain on the reserve bench. 2. a substitute.

regraxar v. to apply paint so fine in texture as to remain transparent.

regraxo s. m. method and process of application of fine, translucent paint.

regredir v. to retrograde, recede, withdraw.

regressão s. f. (pl. -ões) 1. regression, regressing. 2. retrocession, retrogression. 3. throwback. 4. return. 5. (mech.) return movement. 6. (rhet.) repetition of words in inverted order and a different meaning. 7. (phon.) return to a previous etymologic form.

regressar v. 1. to return, go back. 2. to come back, return home. 3. to send back, cause to return.

regressista s. m. (Braz., hist.) regressionist: political faction, favouring the re-establishment of the monarchy (under Pedro I). ‖ adj. of or referring to this monarchistic movement.

regressivo adj. 1. regressive, retrogressive. 2. reactive. 3. (phon.) regressive assimilation of a letter (under the influence of the following one).

regresso s. m. 1. return, returning. 2. going or coming back. 3. reversion, regress. 4. throwback. 5. (jur.) appeal, remedy, legal means to recover a right or obtain redress. **por ocasião de seu** ~ on his return. **sem** ~ irrevocable.

regreta s. f. (typogr.) reglet, small ruler.

regrista s. m. + f. (depr.) 1. precisionist, pedant. 2. braggart, boaster. ‖ adj. 1. pedantic, formalistic. 2. vainglorious, boastful, braggart. 3. chattering, garrulous.

régua s. f. ruler, rule, straight edge (plates A 7, P 12). ~ **de cálculo** slide rule (plate R 3). ~ **de compositor** composing rule. ~ **de paralelas** parallel ruler. ~ **de plaina** fence of a plane. ~ **graduada** scale.

régua-tê s. f. T-square.

regueira s. f., **regueiro** m. 1. rivulet, creek, small stream. 2. irrigation or drainage ditch. 3. (Braz.) furrow along the backbone.

reguengo s. m. crown land, land belonging to the king, royal domain. ‖ adj. regal, royal, kingly.

reguinga s. m. + f. contradicter, objector, contester.

reguingar v. 1. to object, remonstrate. 2. to reply sharply, retort. 3. to contest. 4. to kick back, recalcitrate.

regulação s. f. (pl. -ões) 1. regulation, regulating. 2. rule, principle. 3. adjustment, rectification. 4. control. 5. arrangement, settlement. **roda** ~ **do avanço** (mech.) feed wheel.

regulado adj. regulated, regular, ruled, ordered, fixed.

regulador s. m. 1. regulator: a) (mech.) governor, corrector, any regulating device (plates B 13, C 13, E 3, M 12, 3). b) pendulum (of a clock), balance wheel (of a watch). ‖ adj. regulating, regulative, regulatory. ~ **ajustável** adjustable regulator. ~ **centrífugo** flyball governor. ~ **de ar do carburador** choke. ~

de emergência emergency governor. ~ **de pressão** throttle. ~ **de tensão** potential regulator. ~ **para iluminação** dimmer. ~ **térmico** thermostat. ~ **rápido** high-speed regulator.

regulagem s. f. (Braz.) regulation, adjustment of machines, motors, etc.

regulamentação s. f. (pl. **-ões**) 1. regulation, act of regulating. 2. publication of rules, bylaws or statutes. 3. adjustment, settlement.

regulamentar (I) adj. m. + f. of, referring to or relative to regulation(s), regulative, regulatory.

regulamentar (II) v. 1. to regulate, bring under control. 2. to arrange, settle, order. 3. to subject to order or regulations.

regulamentário adj. regulative, regulatory.

regulamento s. m. 1. regulation, rule. 2. ordinance, statute, bylaw. 3. resolution, determination. 4. precept, principle. 5. law, decree, edict. 6. official interpretation of laws and principles or their execution.

~ **de trânsito** rules of the road.

regular (I) s. m. 1. regular occurrence. 2. regular soldier or member of a religious order. 3. habitual customer or frequenter. || adj. m. + f. 1. regular, constant, conformable to rule. 2. legal, lawful. 3. natural, normal. 4. well-proportioned, symmetrical. 5. dutiful, correct, obedient to law and order. 6. punctual. 7. middling, neither good nor bad. 8. uniform, consonant. 9. even. 10. fair, clean, respectable. || ~**mente** adv. regularly.

apareceu um número ~ there appeared quite a few. **ele leva uma vida** ~ he leads an orderly life.

regular (II) v. 1. to regulate. 2. to subject to rules or laws. 3. to direct, guide. 4. to determine, decide. 5. to regularize, make uniform or regular. 6. to adjust, rectify, set right, bring in order. 7. to repress, restrain, restrict. 8. to correct, calibrate, modulate. 9. to conform to, agree with. 10. to serve as a rule or guidepost. 11. to correspond, work correctly or satisfactorily. 12. to amount approximately to, estimate at about. 13. ~**-se** to guide o. s. by.

~ **a sua vida pelos ditames da razão** to rule one's life by the dictates of reason. ~ **um assunto** to settle an affair. ~**am a temperatura do forno** they attempered the oven. **ela não regula bem** she has got a twist in her character, she's wrong in the garret.

regularidade s. f. 1. regularity. 2. regulation. 3. punctuality, steadiness. 4. order, method, orderliness. 5. harmony. 6. uniformness, equality. 7. strictness, correctness. 8. strict observance (of rules, laws).

regularização s. f. (pl. **-ões**) regularization, act of regularizing.

regularizador s. m. regulator, evener, regulating device. || adj. regulating, regulative, regulatory.

regularizar v. 1. to regularize, regulate. 2. to make steady or uniform. 3. to rectify, set right, bring in order. 4. to methodize. 5. ~**-se** to regulate itself, function accurately, operate well.

regularizarei o negócio I'll square things. **vamos** ~ **a situação** we'll straighten out this situation.

regulável adj. m. + f. (pl. **-áveis**) regulable, regulatory, adjustable.

regulete s. m. flat wooden moulding used to separate panels; fillet, reglet, listel, bracket.

régulo s. m. 1. kinglet, native ruler. 2. (chem.) regulus. 3. (astr.) Regulus: star in the constellation Leo.

regurgitação s. f. (pl. **-ões**) regurgitation, backward flow, a casting up.

regurgitar v. 1. to regurgitate. 2. to overflow, run over. 3. to pour, rush or surge back. 4. to vomit. 5. to be replete or overfull.

rei s. m. 1. king, monarch, sovereign. 2. (fig.) magnate, tycoon. 3. (cards) playing card picturing a king (plate B 5). 4. (chess) king (plate X).

dia de Reis Epiphany. **sem** ~ **nem roque** aimlessly, at random.

reicua s. f. a kind of file used to sharpen combs.

rei-das-codornizes s. m. (pl. **reis-das-codornizes**), (Braz., ornith.) landrail, corn crake.

reide s. m. 1. raid, foray, rapid attack, predatory incursion. 2. long excursion, journey. 3. pleasure trip, sportly feat.

reídeos s. m. pl. (ornith.) Rheidae: a family of ratite birds of S. America.

reiforme s. m. ratite, bird of the order Ratitae.

reigada s. f. hollow along the buttock or the rump of certain animals.

reima s. f. 1. olive juice. 2. (med.) rheum. 3. bad temper.

reimão s. m. (pl. **-ões**) 1. animal without regular dwelling place. 2. (zool.) black panther.

reimoso adj. 1. rheumy. 2. bad for the blood. 3. irritated, ill-tempered. 4. quarrelsome, pugnacious.

reimplantar v. to reimplant.

reimpressão s. f. (pl. **-ões**) 1. reprint, reprinting. 2. new impression. 3. new edition, new publication, reissue.

~ **clandestina** surreptitious publication.

reimpressor s. m. reprinter, publisher or editor who reprints. || adj. reprinting.

reimprimir v. to reprint, republish, make a new impression or edition.

reinação s. f. (pl. **-ões**) 1. merrymaking, high jinks. 2. carousal, revelry. 3. (Braz.) naughtiness, mischievous trick.

reinaço s. m. (pop.) rut, oestrus.

reinadio s. m. merrymaking, revelry, spree.

reinado s. m. 1. reign. 2. duration and jurisdiction of a sovereign. 3. supremacy, predominancy, predominance.

durante o ~ **de** in (or under) the reign of...

reinador adj. naughty, mischievous, wanton.

você é um menino ~**!** you are a naughty boy.

reinante s. m. + f. 1. ruler. 2. king, queen. 3. regent. || adj. 1. ruling, reigning, governing. 2. predominant, prevailing.

reinar v. 1. to reign, rule, govern. 2. to be enthroned, be king, queen or regent of. 3. to dominate, control. 4. to predominate, prevail. 5. to be in force, be usual or customary. 6. to spread, rage (custom, epidemic, etc.). 7. to become famous or notable. 8. to carry out, bring to pass. 9. (pop.) to play, carouse, revel. 10. to amuse o. s., fool around. 11. (Braz.) to be naughty, play mischievous tricks. 12. (Port., prov.) to become irritated, enraged.

reincidência s. f. 1. reincidence, reincidency. 2. relapse, recidivation. 3. obstinacy, pertinacy. 4. backsliding, wilfulness.

reincidente adj. m. + f. 1. recidivistic, recidivous. 2. relapsing, backsliding.

reincidir v. 1. to relapse, fall back (into vice, crime, bad habit, etc.). 2. to repeat once again. 3. to be recidivous. 4. to be self-willed, be obstinate.

reincitar v. to reincite, rouse, instigate again.

reincorporação s. f. (pl. **-ões**) reincorporation.

reincorporar v. to reincorporate, unite, blend or merge again.

reinfecção s. f. (pl. **-ões**) reinfection, additional infection.

reinflamar v. 1. to reinflame, set alight again. 2. to rouse, incite again. 3. to become inflamed or incensed.

reinfundir v. to reinstil, infuse, inculcate again.

reingressar v. to reenter.

reiniciar v. to begin or initiate again, recommence, restart.

reinícola s. m. expert in national legislation. ‖ adj. m. + f. of, referring to or relative to the realm.

reino s. m. 1. kingdom, monarchy. 2. realm, domain, dominion, empire. 3. (natural hist.) one of the divisions in which all objects, plants, and animals are classified. 4. group of beings with common traits and qualities.
~ **animal** animal kingdom. ~ **das fadas** fairy land. o ~ **de Deus** the kingdom of God. **par do** ~ peer of the kingdom. **Reino Unido da Grã-Bretanha** United Kingdom of Great Britain. **um** ~ **por um cavalo!** a kingdom for a horse! (Shakespeare).

reinol adj. (pl. **-óis**) born in a kingdom, of or referring to a realm.

reinquirir v. to cross-examine, interrogate anew.

reinscrever v. to reinscribe, sign up again, inscribe anew.

reinstalação s. f. (pl. **-ões**) reinstallation, reinstal(l)-ment.

reinstalar v. 1. to reinstall, install again. 2. to reinstate. 3. to re-establish, restore.

reinstituição s. f. (pl. **-ões**) reinstitution, re-establishment.

reinstituir v. to reinstitute, found or establish again.

reintegração s. f. (pl. **-ões**) 1. reintegration. 2. restoration. 3. repeated or renewed integration. 4. reposition, reinstatement.
a ~ **realizou-se no paço municipal** the repossession took place in the city hall.

reintegrador s. m. reintegrator, restorator, restorer. ‖ adj. reintegrating.

reintegrar v. 1. to reintegrate, restore. 2. to renew. 3. to reinstate, reinstall, place again in a (former) position. 4. ~-se to settle or establish o. s. again, become reintegrated.

reintegro s. m. 1. reintegration, restoration. 2. lottery premium equal to the ticket price.

reintroduzir v. to reintroduce, introduce again or anew.

reinvestir v. to reinvest.

reinvidar v. 1. to raise once more (a bet). 2. to reply, retort, answer sharply. 3. to avenge o. s., get even, recoup one's losses. 4. to countercharge, pay back in the same coin.

reira s. f. 1. (med.): a) pain in the kidneys. b) diarrhea. 2. ~s pl.: a) buttock, lower back. b) kidneys.

reisado s. m. 1. celebration of Epiphany. 2. popular dramatic dance (usually performed on January 6th, day of the Magi).

reiteração s. f. (pl. **-ões**) reiteration, repetition, renewal.

reiterado adj. reiterated, repeated. ‖ **-amente** adv. repeatedly, reiteratedly.

reiterar v. 1. to reiterate, repeat. 2. to say over again. 3. to renew. 4. to reaffirm, ingeminate.

reiterativo adj. reiterative, repeated, reiterating.

reiterável adj. m. + f. (pl. **-áveis**) reiterable, apt to be repeated.

reitor s. m. 1. rector, head of a university or college. 2. headmaster, principal. 3. (eccl.) pastor, minister, prior.
~ **de universidade** president of a university. ~ **de uma faculdade** dean. **ele foi feito** ~ **do seminário** he was elected provost of the seminary.

reitora s. f. headmistress.

reitorado s. m. 1. rectorship, rectorate. 2. dignity and authority of a rector. 3. duration of the rectorship.

retoral adj. m. + f. (pl. **-ais**) rectorial, of or pertaining to a rector or a rectorate.

reitoria s. f. 1. rectorship, rectory. 2. office or authority of a rector. 3. duration of a rectorship.

reiúna s. f. 1. flintlock, old-fashioned shotgun. 2. (Braz.) shoe with rubber sides. ‖ adj. f. of or referring to such a flintlock.

reiunada s. f. (Braz.) a lot of stray horses, group of horses belonging to the government.

reiunar v. (Braz.) to cut the ears (of cattle, horses) in order to mark the animals as public property.

reiúno s. m. (Braz.) 1. state-owned or ownerless cattle. 2. ugly or worn out horse. ‖ adj. supplied by the government (said with regard to a soldier's uniform and outfit).

reivindicação s. f. (pl. **-ões**) 1. act of claiming, reclamation. 2. claim, demand (for rights, compensation or return of property). 3. (jur.) revindication, revendication. 4. counterclaim.

reivindicador s. m. claimant, claimer. ‖ adj. claiming, demanding.

reivindicante adj. m. + f. claiming, demanding, revindicative.

reivindicar v. 1. to revindicate. 2. (jur.) to vindicate, assert one's legal right. 3. to recover, regain. 4. to reclaim, demand.
~am **a herança** they laid claim to the inheritance.

reivindicativo adj. revindicative, concerning revindication or demands.

reivindicável adj. m. + f. (pl. **-áveis**) claimable, subject to revindication.

reixa s. f. 1. small board or plank. 2. bars, window grate, grating. 3. window blind, Venetian blinds. 4. quarrel, brawl, strife. 5. (pop.) anger, hate.

reixador s. m. (pop.) quarrelsome person.

reixar v. (Braz.) to quarrel, wrangle, altercate, dispute.

reizete, reizinho s. m. (depr.) kinglet, native ruler.

rejeição s. f. (pl. **-ões**) 1. rejection, refusal. 2. exclusion. 3. repulse, repudiation. 4. denial.

rejeitado adj. 1. castoff, castaway. 2. rejected. 3. unsuccessful.

rejeitar v. 1. to reject. 2. to cast or throw away. 3. to refuse, decline to accept. 4. to repudiate, repulse, reprobate. 5. to spurn, scorn. 6. to discard, condemn. 7. to disallow, disown. 8. to vomit. 9. to disapprove, repel. 10. to negate, oppose. 11. to throw, fling. 12. to keep away.
a proposta foi rejeitada the proposal fell to the ground. **ela rejeitou sua proposta de casamento** she rejected his proposal of marriage, (U. S. A., coll.) she sent him to the shower. ~am **as cartas** (gambling) they discarded the hand. ~am **delicadamente o convite** they declined the invitation. ~am **o plano** they laid aside the plan.

rejeitável adj. m. + f. (pl. **-áveis**) rejectable, that may or should be rejected or refused.

rejeito s. m. 1. (arch.) javelin. 2. the part of the foreleg between the knee and the shoulder. 3. (Braz.) act of rejection.

rejubilação s. f. (pl. **-ões**) rejoicing, jubilation, exultation, delight.

rejubilante adj. m. + f. rejoicing, rejubilant.

rejubilar v. 1. to cause great joy, bring happiness to. 2. to jubilate, exult, rejoice. 3. to feel great pleasure or satisfaction. 4. to be very glad. 5. to make merry.

rejúbilo s. m. rejoicing, joyfulness, exultation, delight.

rejubiloso adj. joyful, glad, rejoicing, jubilant.

rejuntado adj. articulate, jointed, segmented.

rejuntamento s. m. (Braz., archit.) 1. act or process of flushing, pointing. 2. tuck pointing: fillet of building cement (used to cover the joints in brickwork) (plate A 7).

rejuntar v. 1. (Braz., archit.) to articulate, joint. 2. to flush. 3. to seal the joints.

rejurar v. to swear again, repeat an oath.

rejuvenescente s. m. + f. rejuvenator. ‖ adj. rejuvenescent.

rejuvenescer v. 1. to rejuvenate, rejuvenize, make young again. 2. to renew, renovate. 3. to appear to be young or younger. 4. ~-se to become youthful again.

rejuvenescimento s. m. rejuvenescence, rejuvenation, regeneration.

rela s. f. 1. (zool.) tree toad. 2. bird trap.

relação s. f. (pl. -ões) 1. act of reporting. 2. description, report. 3. narrative, recital. 4. roll, list, register. 5. resemblance, analogy. 6. connection, relationship. 7. comparison. 8. court of appeal. 9. (mus.) interval. 10. (arith.) ratio, rate. 11. affinity. 12. communication, correspondence. 13. regard, respect. 14. -ões pl.: a) familiarity, intimacy. b) acquaintance. c) kinship, kindred.
~ alfabética index. ~ amigável come-hither. -ões amistosas amity. -ões comerciais business connections. -ões de produção production relations. -ões espirituais communion. -ões exteriores foreign affairs. ~ familiar kinship. ~ mútua interrelation. -ões pessoais commerce (with). -ões públicas public relations. -ões sexuais sexual intercourse. sem ~ relationless. ter boas (más) -ões com to be on good (bad) terms with. com ~ a with regard to. cortar as -ões com to sever one's connection with. cortei as -ões com ele I cut connection with him. ele tem boas -ões he is well connected. ele tem boas -ões com he is on good footing with. ele rompeu todas as -ões comigo he broke off all communication with me. em ~ a respecting, in respect to. em ~ a isto in this connection. em ~ com taken with. estabelecimento de -ões amigáveis rapprochement. estar em boas -ões to be on friendly footing. estar em -ões amigáveis com to be on friendly terms with. estamos de -ões cortadas we are not on speaking terms. eu mantinha -ões com ele I kept company with him. há uma ~ íntima entre estas duas ciências there is a close alliance between these two sciences. lembrei-lhe nossas -ões de parentesco I called cousins with him. manter -ões amorosas com to be entangled with. más -ões estragam boas maneiras evil communications corrupt good manners. nós não mantemos -ões we do not visit. não tenho ~ com ele I have no commerce with him. não tenho -ões com I have no communication with.

relacionado adj. related, connected, conversant, having relations with.
bem ~ well-disposed, affined. ~ mutuamente interrelated.

relacional adj. m. + f. (pl. -ais) relational, of or pertaining to kinship.

relacionamento s. m. relationship, connection.

relacionar v. 1. to relate, tell, report. 2. to include in a list, inscribe, register. 3. to expound, explain. 4. to procure connections, try to enter into relationship with. 5. to enrol, catalogue. 6. to confront, compare. 7. to make acquainted, establish relations or analogies. 8. ~-se: a) to link, connect, join, unite. b) to connect, associate. c) to bring into relationship with. d) to have reference to. e) to become acquainted with; enter into connexion with.

relacrar v. to reseal with wax.

relamber v. 1. to lick again, relick. 2. ~-se to lick again one's lips.

relambório s. m. laziness, indolence, idleness. ‖ adj. 1. uninteresting, dull, tedious. 2. lazy, idle.

relampadear v. = relampaguear.

relâmpago s. m. 1. lightning, flash of lightning. thunderbolt. 2. brilliancy, effulgence, brightness. 3. sudden luminous appearance. 4. (fig.) any quick and transient occurrence. 5. sheet-lightning.
como um ~ like a house on fire. ~ de calor summer lightning.

relampagueante adj. m. + f. (also relampeante, relampejante, relampear) flashing (like a thunderbolt), glittering, sparkling.

relampaguear, relampejar v. (also relampadear) 1. to lighten. 2. to glitter, sparkle. 3. to appear like a flash of lightning. 4. to execute or quick and transient occurrence. 5. sheet-lightning.

relançar v. to cast a quick glance upon, glance at.

relance s. m. 1. glance, glimpse. 2. (bullfighting) the second unexpected encounter of the torero with the charging bull.
de ~ 1. by chance. 2. at a glance. ganhar de ~ to win at the first throw. olhamos a casa de ~ we took a peep at the house. perceber de ~ to catch a glimpse at. num ~ at one view.

relancear s. m. glance, glimpse, quick look. ‖ v. to glance at, cast a furtive look at.

relapsão s. f. (pl. -ões) relapse, sliding back, reincidence, recurrence.

relapsia s. f. relapse, recurrence, backsliding into crime, vice or error.

relapso s. m. relapser, recidivist, backslider. ‖ adj. 1. relapsing, backsliding. 2. recidivous. 3. obstinate, refractory, contumacious.

relar v. 1. to grate, scrape. 2. (Braz.) to touch lightly. 3. (Port., prov.) to croak.

relasso adj. slack, lax, sloppy, slipshod.

relatar v. 1. to mention, discuss casually. 2. to tell, narrate. 3. to refer to. 4. to expound, explain. 5. to describe. 6. to report.

relatividade s. f. 1. relativity, relativeness. 2. conditionality. 3. (phys.) theory of relativity.

relativismo s. m. relativism, relativity of knowledge.

relativo adj. 1. relative, relating to. 2. concerning, referring, respecting. 3. pertinent, relevant. 4. fortuitous, accidental. 5. comparative. 6. proportional. 7. (gram.) referring to an antecedent word, sentence or clause. ‖ -amente adv. relatively.
é ~ a it is pertinent to. isto não é ~ a this is irrelative to. número ~ relative number. umidade -a relative humidity.

relato s. m. 1. report, account. 2. representation. 3. narration, description.

relator s. m. reporter, relator, narrator.

relatório s. m. 1. written report. 2. account, relation. 3. information. 4. statement, official neturns. 5. protocol, minute.
~ de visita feita ao cliente (com.) call report.

relax s. m. (Engl.) relax.

relaxação s. f. (pl. -ões) 1. relaxation. 2. loosening, unbending. 3. slackness. 4. negligence, carelessness, remissness.

relaxado s. m. slouch, slacker; negligent, sloven or dissolute person. ‖ adj. 1. loose, slack. 2. relaxed. 3. careless, remiss, negligent. 4. sloven, slouchy. 5. slipshod. 6. demoralized, dissolute. 7. requesting compulsory collection (of overdue debts). ‖ -amente adv. relaxedly, negligently, frowzily.

relaxador s. m. slouch; negligent, sloven or dissolute person. ‖ adj. relaxing, slackening, slouchy.

relaxamento s. m. 1. slackness, looseness. 2. negligence, carelessness, remissness. 3. demoralization. 4. slovenliness.

relaxante adj. m. + f. relaxing, slackening, relaxant.

relaxar v. 1. to relax. 2. to slacken, loosen. 3. to reduce tension or force. 4. to permit the non-observance of law and order. 5. to tolerate, pardon, absolve (from sin or fault). 6. to moderate, abate, ease. 7. to make less severe or rigorous. 8. to corrupt, pervert. 9. to weaken, make lax. 10. to request the judicial collection (of overdue taxes or contributions). 11. ~-se: a) to become weakened, enfeeble. b) to grow lazy, lax or negligent. c) to become demoralized or dissolute.
~ o ventre to loosen the belly. ~ os cuidados to unbend one's cares, grow lax or remiss.

relaxe s. m. 1. act of relaxing, loosening or tolerating. 2. (jur.) compulsory collection of overdue taxes. 3. negligence.

relaxidão s. f. (pl. -ões) 1. relaxation. 2. loosening, unbending. 3. slackness. 4. negligence, remissness.

relaxo s. m. (Braz.) 1. discourse in rhymes. 2. boastful or witty saying, pun. || adj. relaxed, slack, loose, negligent.

relé s. m. 1. (electr.) relay. 2. f. = ralé.
~ de retardamento (electr.) delay relay.

release s. m. (Engl.) news release.

relegação s. f. (pl. -ões) relegation, banishment, exile.

relegar v. 1. to relegate. 2. to exile, banish. 3. to remove, dismiss. 4. to expatriate. 5. to despise, disdain. 6. ~-se to withdraw, bury o. s. in a colony or a secluded place.

releixar v. (Braz.) = relaxar.

releixo (I) s. m. 1. path or side trail along a wall or ditch. 2. berm, berme. 3. overhang or drainage of a wall. 4. uncultivated ground alongside a wall. 5. sharp edge (of a knife, scythe, etc.).

releixo (II) s. m. (Port., prov.) negligence, carelessness, disregard.

releixo (III) adj. (N. Braz., pop.) 1. slack, negligent, careless. 2. shameless.

relembrança s. f. remembrance, recollection, reminiscence.

relembrar v. 1. to remember again. 2. to put in mind, call to mind, recollect. 3. to reminisce, indulge in memories.

relembrável adj. m. + f. (pl. -áveis) rememorable, worthy of being remembered.

relentado adj. 1. exposed to open air. 2. wet, damp.

relentar v. 1. to moisten, make damp. 2. to form dew. 3. to bedew, cover with mist. 4. ~-se: a) to become dewy or moist. b) to grow cool. c) to refresh o. s.

relento s. m. 1. dampness of the night. 2. dew, moisture. 3. slackness or looseness produced by the damp night air.
dormir ao ~ to sleep in the open air. passar a noite ao ~ to camp out.

reler v. to reread, read again, read repeatedly.

reles adj. m. + f., sg. + pl. 1. contemptible, despicable. 2. shabby, poor. 3. very vulgar, common. 4. worthless. 5. feeble.

relevado adj. 1. salient, raised. 2. projecting, jutting out. 3. superior. 4. pardoned, absolved, exempted.

relevador s. m. pardoner, absolver. || adj. pardoning, absolving, indulgent.

relevamento s. m. 1. act or effect of pardoning. 2. pardon, indulgence. 3. exemption. 4. release, relief, ease. 5. excuse, apology.

relevância s. f. 1. prominence, weightiness. 2. importance, significance. 3. consequence, consequentiality.

relevante s. m. matter of consequence, any important or indispensable requirement. || adj. m. + f. 1. important, of consequence. 2. weightly, considerable. 3. indispensable.

relevar v. 1. to render conspicuous, bring into prominence. 2. to permit, allow. 3. to exempt. 4. to excuse, pardon, forgive. 5. to release, discharge. 6. to be important, be of consequence. 7. to be necessary or indispensable. 8. to emboss. 9. ~-se to become notable or eminent, distinguish o. s.

relevável adj. m. + f. (pl. -áveis) pardonable, excusable.

relevo (ê) s. m. 1. relievo, relief (plates E 9, J 2, Q). 2. embossed work. 3. salience, projection. 4. (fig.) distinction, eminence. 5. importance, consequence. 6. brightness, vividness.
alto ~ high relief. baixo ~ low relief. de ~ outstanding. em ~ raised. isso dá-lhe ~ it acts as a foil to her. meio ~ half relief. ornar com ~s to emboss. ~ tipográfico thermography.

relha s. f. 1. ploughshare, cutter of the plough (plate C 13). 2. rim of a wheel.

relhaço s. m., relhada f. blow with a whip.

relhador s. m. a long whip.

relhar v. to lash, flog, beat with a whip.

relheira s. f. 1. rut, furrow, track worn by a wheel. 2. (Port., prov.) blow.

relheiro s. m. 1. rut, furrow, track worn by a wheel. 2. ~ pl. (N. Braz.) countercurrent or whirlpool near the coast.

relho (I) adj. very old, ancient, antiquated.

relho (ê) (II) s. m. rawhide or cowhide whip.

relhota s. f., relhote m. small coulter of a ploughshare.

relicário s. m. 1. reliquary, shrine or depository for relics, tabernacle. 2. feretory.
colocar num ~ to enshrine.

relicitação s. f. (pl. -ões) new licitation, new public sale or auction.

relicitar v. to expose for sale at an auction for a second time.

religar v. to retie, bind again, rebind thoroughly.

religião s. f. (pl. -ões) 1. religion. 2. religiousness, piety. 3. religious doctrine(s), cult. 4. duty, obligation. 5. religious order. 6. faith, belief. 7. belief in God. 8. church, congregation.
~ de Malta order of the knights of Malta. ele falou sobre a ~ católica he spoke about Catholicism. sem ~ ungodly.

religionário s. m. sectarian, Protestant, reformist, dissenter.

religiosa s. f. nun, votaress.
casa de ~s nunnery, convent.

religiosidade s. f. 1. religiosity, religiousness. 2. religious conscience. 3. piety, devotion. 4. religious disposition or tendency.

religioso s. m. 1. member of a monastic order, monk. 2. religious person. || adj. 1. religious. 2. pious, devout. 3. scrupulous, strict. 4. spiritual, godly. 5. sacred. || -amente adv. devoutly, religiously, devotionally, (fig.) punctually.
casa -a monastery, convent. de convicção -a pious-minded, heaven-minded. vida -a religious or monastic life.

relimar v. 1. to file again. 2. to polish. 3. to improve, perfect.

relinchão adj. (pl. -ões) (S. Braz.) 1. gay, cheerful, joyous, merry, frolicsome. 2. neighing.

relinchar v. to neigh, whinny.

relincho s. m. neigh, whinny.

relíquia s. f. 1. relic. 2. venerated object. 3. anything precious or rare. 4. ~s pl. relics: a) remains of

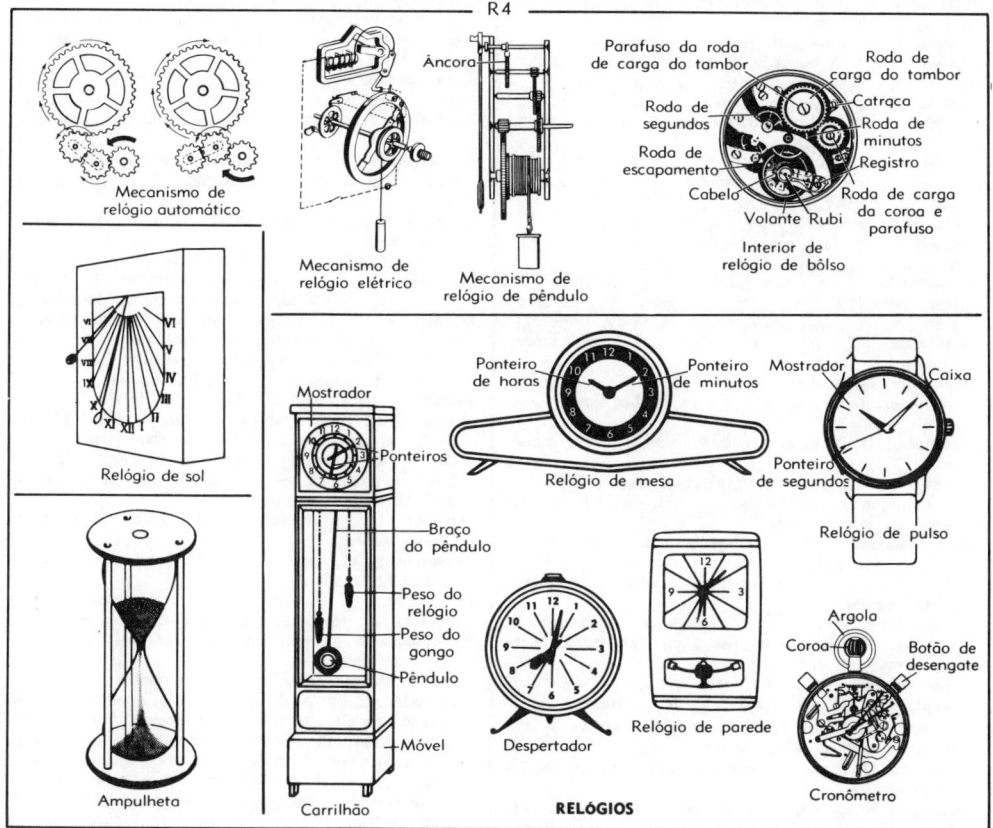

R 4

Mecanismo de relógio automático

Mecanismo de relógio elétrico

Âncora

Mecanismo de relógio de pêndulo

Parafuso da roda de carga do tambor
Roda de carga do tambor
Roda de segundos
Catraca
Roda de minutos
Roda de escapamento
Registro
Cabela
Roda de carga da coroa e parafuso
Volante Rubi
Interior de relógio de bôlso

Relógio de sol

Mostrador

Ponteiros

Braço do pêndulo

Peso do relógio

Peso do gongo

Pêndulo

Móvel

Ampulheta

Carrilhão

Ponteiro de horas
Ponteiro de minutos
Mostrador
Caixa

Relógio de mesa
Ponteiro de segundos

Despertador

Relógio de parede

Relógio de pulso

Argola
Coroa
Botão de desengate

Cronômetro

RELÓGIOS

the bodies or clothes of saints. b) antiquities. 5. ruin. 6. (fig.) memento, souvenir.
~s **humanas** relics of primitive peoples.

reliquiário s. m. reliquary, shrine.

relógio s. m. 1. watch, clock (plates A 4, E 2, R 4). 2. timepiece. 3. (Braz.) meter (instrument for measuring electricity, gas, water, etc.).
~ **calendário** calender watch. ~ **de ponto** time clock. ~ **de precisão** chronometer. ~ **de pulso** a wristwatch. ~ **de quartzo** quartz watch. ~ **de repetição** a repeater. ~ **de sol** sundial (plate R 4). ~ **de torre** tower clock. **acertar um** ~ to set a clock or watch. **o** ~ **está adiantado (atrasado)** the clock is fast (slow). **mão de** ~ hand of a clock, watch hand. **precisamos dar corda ao** ~ we have to wind up the clock or watch.

relógio-pulseira s. m. (pl. **relógios-pulseiras**) wrist watch.

relojo s. m. (arch., pop.) watch, clock.

relojoaria s. f. the art of watchmaking. 2. a watchmaker's shop. 3. the works of a timepiece. 4. watch manufactory.

relojoeiro s. m. watchmaker, clockmaker.

relotear v. to redivide lots (land).

reloucado adj. stark mad, insane.

relumbrar v. 1. to shine brightly. 2. to sparkle, glitter. 3. to radiate light, glow.

relutação s. f. (pl. **-ões**) act of resisting or struggling against, opposition.

relutância s. f. 1. resistance, opposition. 2. fighting spirit. 3. aversion, repugnancy. 4. reluctance, reluctancy. 5. insistence, stubbornness.

relutante adj. m. + f. reluctant, unwilling, loath, averse. ‖ ~**mente** adv. reluctantly, unwillingly, aversely.

relutar v. 1. to fight again. 2. to struggle against, strive. 3. to resist, offer strong opposition. 4. to feel reluctance or repugnance, to reluct.

relutividade s. f. (electr.) reluctivity.

reluzente adj. m. + f. 1. brilliant, very bright. 2. sparkling, glittering. 3. shining. 4. refulgent, radiant.

reluzir v. 1. to shine brightly. 2. to sparkle, glitter. 3. to glimmer, glow, gleam. 4. to manifest itself vividly. 5. to flash.
nem tudo que reluz é ouro not all that glitters is gold.

relva s. f. 1. grass. 2. turf, sward. 3. sod. 4. lawn, meadow.

relvado s. m. grassplot, lawn, turf.

relva-dos-caminhos s. f. (pl. **relvas-dos-caminhos**) 1. rough meadow grass. 2. low spear grass, annual blue grass.

relvão s. m. (pl. **-ões**) meadow, grassland, pasture. ‖ adj. feeding on grass, grazing, browsing.

relvão-da-abissínia s. m. (pl. **relvões-da-abissínia**) (bot.) teff.

relvar v. 1. to cut grass, mow. 2. to be overgrown with grass.

relva-turca s. f. (pl. **relvas-turcas**) (bot.) mossy saxifrage, lady's-cushion.

relvedo s. m. grassplot, lawn, turf, meadow.

relvejar v. 1. to cover with grass, let grow grass. 2. to be covered with grass, be turfed.

relvoso adj. grassy, lawny, turfy.

remada s. f. 1. stroke with the oar. 2. act of rowing. 3. (pop.) pull, drink.

remado adj. 1. equipped with oars. 2. driven by oars.

remador s.. m. 1. rower, oarsman, oar. 2. boatman, paddler, sculler. ‖ adj. rowing, paddling.

ele é um bom ~ he pulls a good oar.

remadura s. f. (act of) rowing, row.

remanchado adj. tardy, slow, lingering.

remanchador (I) s. m. edging or crimping tool.

remanchador (II) s. m. loiterer, lagger, tardy or sluggish person. ‖ adj. slow, sluggish, tardy, lingering.

remanchão adj. (pl. **-ões**) slow, sluggish, tardy, lingering.

remanchar, remanchear (I) v. 1. to delay, put off. 2. to linger, loiter, tarry. 3. ~-se to be slow, tardy or sluggish.

remanchar (II) v. to clinch, bead, flange (sheet metal work).

remancho s. m. 1. slowness, sluggishness. 2. laziness. 3. negligence, remissness. 4. rest, repose, leisure (esp. an idler's rest).

remanejamento s. f. 1. reorganization. 2. recomposition. 3. rewriting.

remanejar v. 1. to reorganize. 2. to recompense. 3. to rewrite.

remanescente s. m. + f. 1. remainder, residue(s). 2. remnant. 3. rest. 4. surplus. ‖ adj. remaining, resting, remanent, leftover.

remanescer v. 1. to be left over, be more than enough. 2. to rest, remain. 3. to survive.

remangar v. 1. to tuck up one's sleeves. 2. to threaten with a raised arm.

remaniscar v. (Braz.) to make a rash and unexpected movement.

remanisco s. m. (Braz.) rash, unexpected movement. ‖ adj. agile, swift.

remansado adj. 1. peaceful. 2. calm, still. 3. slow. 4. lazy, slack.

remansar-se v. to stand still, stop running or flowing.

remansear v. 1. to stand still, stop flowing. 2. to become stagnant. 3. to grow slow or sluggish. 4. to be calm or quiet.

remanso s. m. 1. immobility, stoppage. 2. calmness, stillness. 3. tranquility, quietude. 4. stagnant water. 5. (Braz.) countercurrent near the riverside, backwater, backwash. 6. ease, rest, repose. 7. tardiness, sluggishness. 8. (N. Braz.) widening of the river-bed (usually below rapids).

remansoso adj. 1. peaceful. 2. calm, still, quiet. 3. slow. 4. lazy, slack.

remar v. 1. to row, oar. 2. to paddle, canoe. 3. to pull or ply the oars. 4. to swim. 5. to flutter, hover about (insects). 6. (fig.) to fight, struggle. ~ à ré to row backwards. ~ arrancado to pull hard with the oars. ~ com dois remos to scull. ~ com um só remo to wriggle. ~ contra a maré to row or swim against the tide. ~ com toda força to lay to the oars. ~ longo to row with long strokes. ~ prato to row with flat oars. ~ suavemente to paddle. cessar de ~ to rest on one's oars. perícia de ~ oarsmanship.

remarcação s. f. (pl. **-ões**) 1. renewed marking, relabelling. 2. (com.) price reduction.

remarcar v. 1. to re-mark, give a new designation to. 2. to relabel, tag again. 3. (com.) to reduce the price, cut.

rema-rema s. m. (Braz.) toy car that moves as impelled with motions similar to those of oarsmen.

remascar v. 1. to chew again. 2. to ruminate. 3. (fig.) to meditate, ponder.

remastigação s. f. (pl. **-ões**) remastication, chewing again, rumination.

remastigar v. to remasticate, chew the cud, ruminate, chew well.

rematação s. f. (pl. **-ões**) 1. offering, bidding. 2. outbidding. 3. sale at an auction. 4. (jur.) adjudication.

rematado adj. complete, consummate, perfect, downright, utter.

ele é um tolo ~ he is a precious fool.

rematador s. m. 1. finisher, perfecter. 2. highest bidder (at an auction). ‖ adj. finishing, completing.

rematar v. 1. to finish, conclude. 2. to achieve, accomplish. 3. to complete, terminate. 4. to crown, decorate, adorn. 5. to sell at auction. 6. to close. 7. ~-se to come to an end, be finished.

remate s. m. 1. end, conclusion. 2. finish, finishing. 3. (archit.) finial, capital, closer. 4. (fig.) highest point, apogee. 5. crowning ornament, adornment. **dar** ~ **a** to bring to an end, proceed with the finishing touches. ~ **de coluna em forma de almofada** cushion capital.

remedar v. 1. to imitate, mimic. 2. to mock. 3. to impersonate.

remedeio s. m. (pop.) 1. remedy, curative. 2. help, expedient, resource.

remediado adj. 1. well off, in comfortable circumstances. 2. remedied. 3. repaired, mended.

remediador s. m. improver, repairer, help. ‖ adj. improving, attenuating.

remediar v. 1. to give or apply remedies. 2. to cure, remedy. 3. to relieve, attenuate, palliate. 4. to amend, repair, rectify. 5. to check, stop, thwart. 6. to supply the most indispensable wants. 7. to hinder, hamper. 8. to forewarn. 9. ~-se: a) to meet one's own expenses. b) to put up with (second rate or makeshift substitutes). c) to overcome difficulties, extricate o. s. 10. to heal, cure. 11. to attemper, redress.

~ **abusos** to thwart abuse or fallacy. **aquilo não se pode** ~ that cannot be helped. **mais vale prevenir do que** ~ prevention is better than cure. **o que não se pode** ~ **tem-se de tolerar** what can't be cured must be endured.

remediável adj. m. + f. (pl. **-áveis**) remediable, curable, that can be helped, mended or repaired.

remedição s. f. (pl. **-ões**) measuring again.

remédio s. m. 1. remedy, medicament, medicine. 2. curative, cure. 3. relief. 4. resource, expedient, shift. 5. help, assistance.

~ **de venda autorizada** officinal medicament. ~ **para todos os males** cure-all. **não ter nem um para** ~ to have absolutely none at all. **não haver** ~ to be unavoidable, uncurable or indispensable. **para isto não há** ~ that is not to be remedied. **para tudo há** ~ **a não ser para a morte** there is a cure for everything but death. **sem** ~ irredeemable.

remedir v. to measure once again.

remedo (ê) s. m. imitation, copy, mockery, mimicry.

remeirada s. f. (Braz.) group of rowers, crowd of oarsmen.

remeiro s. m. rower, oarsman, paddler, sculler. ‖ adj. 1. easy to be rowed. 2. (fig.) rapid, swift.

remela s. f. 1. gummy secretion from the eyes. 2. (med.) running of the eyes, blear-eyedness. 3. (Braz.) pulp of grated green coconuts.

remelado adj. blear-eyed, bleary.

remelão adj. (pl. **-ões**) (f. **-ona**) 1. soft and honeylike (said of burnt sugar). 2. = **remeloso**.

remelar v. 1. to become blear-eyed. 2. to make burned sugar.

remelexo s. m. (N. Braz.) 1. swaying, waggling. 2. rambling, valuptuous movement. 3. lively folk dance.

remelgado adj. (pop.) suffering from an abnormal eversion of the eyelid.

remeloso, remeleiro, remelento adj. blear-eyed, bleary.

remembrança s. f. remembrance, recollection, memory.

remembrar v. to remember again, bring to one's mind, have a recollection.

rememoração s. f. (pl. -ões) 1. act or effect of remembering. 2. remembrance, recollection. 3. reminiscence.

rememorar v. 1. to remember, recollect. 2. to recall, remind. 3. to reminisce.

rememorativo adj. rememorative, reminding, reminiscent.

rememorável adj. m. + f. (pl. -áveis) rememberable, memorable, retraceable.

remêmoro adj. (poet.) memorable, unforgettable, reminiscent.

remendado adj. 1. patched, mended. 2. spotted, speckled. 3. stained.

que pode ser ~ patchable.

remendagem s. f. (pl. -ens) act of patching, mending or darning.

remendão s. m. (pl. -ões) (f. -ona) 1. patcher, mender, cobbler, botcher, darner, tinker, piecer. 2. bungler, clumsy or negligent workman. ‖ adj. patching, mending, bungling.

ele é um alfaiate ~ he is a botcher. **ele é apenas um ~** he is nothing but a tinker.

remendar v. 1. to patch, mend (plate P 15). 2. to repair. 3. to stitch up, darn. 4. to botch, tap, cobble. 5. to piece up, fudge. 6. to vamp.

remendeira s. f. darning woman, woman who repairs clothes.

remendeiro s. m. + adj. = **remendão**.

remendo s. m. 1. patch, botch. 2. piece of cloth for mending. 3. mending, patching, darning. 4. spotted hide (of cattle).

remendona s. f. 1. darning woman, woman who repairs clothes. 2. clumsy or unskilled woman.

remenicar v. 1. to reply, retort. 2. to object. 3. to reply in kind, backbite.

remense s. m. + f. native or inhabitant of Reims (France). ‖ adj. of, pertaining to or relative to Reims.

remerecedor adj. meritorious, deserving thanks, well-deserving.

remerecer v. to deserve (thanks or honours) in a high degree, be worthy of highest praise or appreciation.

remergulhar v. to resubmerge, submerge again.

remessa s. f. 1. remittance, remitting. 2. transmittal, shipment. 3. money or sum remitted. 4. parcel, letter. 5. delivery, forwarding. 6. consignment. 7. act of throwing or flinging.

remessão s. m. (pl. -ões) 1. throw, act of hurling or flinging. 2. missile, projectile. 3. any device for hurling missiles.

remessar v. to throw, hurl, fling.

remesso (ê) s. m. 1. act of throwing, hurling; cast. 2. missile, javelin.

remetente s. m. + f. 1. remitter, shipper. 2. forwarder, sender. 3. consigner. 4. addresser. ‖ adj. remitting, sending.

remeter v. 1. to remit, send. 2. to forward, ship, expedite. 3. to deliver, send off. 4. to mail, post. 5. to put off, defer, postpone. 6. to recommend. 7. to submit, yield. 8. to expose. 9. to hand over, entrust with. 10. **~-se**: a) to devote o. s. to.

b) to trust in, rely on. c) to be about to do, be in favour of doing. d) to refer to, allude to. 11. to attack, assail.

~-me-ei a tudo que vos parecer mais conveniente I'll stand to whatsoever you will consider fit. **~am a questão ao silêncio** they passed over the subject in silence. **~am o assunto a ele para julgá-lo** they referred the business to him for judgement. **~am o dinheiro sob registro** they sent the money by registered mail.

remetida s. f., **remetimento** m. 1. attack, assault. 2. charge, onset. 3. thrust.

remexedor adj. 1. stirring, mixing. 2. disturbing.

remexer v. 1. to stir or mix again. 2. to stir up thoroughly, mix over again. 3. to move, shake. 4. to rummage, jumble. 5. to agitate, disturb. 6. to put in disorder, turn upside down. 7. **~-se** to become animated, lively; busy o. s., bestir o. s.

~am a terra de um canteiro they raked the ground of one garden bed. **remexemos tudo** we left no stone unturned. **~am agitadamente** they fluttered around excitedly.

remexido adj. (fam.) 1. stirred up again. 2. restless, unquiet. 3. frolicsome, cheerful. 4. boisterous, turbulent.

remição s. f. (pl. -ões) 1. redemption, redeeming. 2. ransom. 3. deliverance. 4. retrieval. 5. quittance.

remido adj. redeemed, freed, liberated.

remidor s. m. redeemer, deliverer, liberator, ransomer. ‖ adj. redeeming, delivering, liberating.

rêmige (I) s. m. pen-feather, flag-feather, pinion.

rêmige (II) adj. m. + f. rowing, paddling, sculling.

remígio s. m. 1. pen-feather, flag feather, pinion, (ornith.) remex. 2. flight of birds. 3. flapping of the wings.

remigração s. f. (pl. -ões) 1. remigration. 2. return to the original place, repatriation. 3. new migration.

remigrado adj. remigrated, having migrated again or home.

remigrar v. 1. to remigrate. 2. to migrate again. 3. to return to one's original place. 4. to repatriate or become repatriated.

reminar-se v. 1. to revolt against, rebel, rise against. 2. to refuse obedience.

reminhol s. m. (pl. -óis) large copper spoon (used in sugar making).

reminiscência s. f. 1. reminiscence, reminiscency. 2. recollection, remembrance. 3. memory.

remípede s. m. a remiped animal. ‖ adj. m. + f. remiped, having feet like oars.

remir v. 1. to redeem. 2. repurchase, reacquire, retrieve. 3. to free, set at liberty. 4. to rescue, save, free from captivity. 5. to indemnify, make amends to. 6. to expiate, atone for. 7. to pay off, pay back, buy off (mortgage, ransom, etc.). 8. **~-se** to rehabilitate, redeem or regenerate o. s.

~ o penhor to recover a pawn. **~ o vexame** to rid o. s. of a trouble. **~ uma fortaleza** to relieve a fortress.

remirar v. 1. to look again, gaze anew. 2. to observe with great attention. 3. to look at o. s. in a mirror.

remissa s. f. 1. stake(s) (at gambling). 2. adjournment, postponement. 3. reserve, reticence, self-restraint.

remissão s. f. (pl. -ões) 1. remission, act of remitting. 2. forgiveness, pardon. 3. absolution. 4. mitigation, moderation. 5. discouragement, dejection. 6. respite. 7. remittance.

remissível adj. m. + f. (pl. -íveis) 1. remissible, that may be remitted or forgiven. 2. absolvable. 3. pardonable, excusable.

remissivo adj. 1. remissive, forgiving. 2. abating, subsiding. 3. allusive, hinting.

remisso adj. 1. remiss, lax, negligent. 2. indolent, lazy. 3. careless, thoughtless. 4. slow, tardy. 5. slack, limp.

remissor, remissório adj. remissive, remissory, tending to remit, redemptive.

remitarso adj. (zool.) having remiform feet.

remitência s. f. 1. remission. 2. (med.) temporary interruption or diminution of pathological symptoms.

remitente adj. m. + f. remittent, remitting, temporarily abating.

remitir v. 1. to remit. 2. to forgive, pardon, condone. 3. to absolve. 4. to excuse, consider pardoned. 5. to give a receipt, acknowledge payment of. 6. to abate, slacken, diminish. 7. to restitute, give back. 8. to grow less intense, to moderate. 9. (med.) to be remitting, abate or moderate temporarily. 10. ~-se to become less intense, mitigate, ease.

remível adj. m. + f. (pl. -íveis) redeemable, redemptible, releasable.

remo s. m. 1. oar, paddle (plates B 8, 9). 2. (fig.) rowing.

~ **comprido** sweep. ~ **de duas pás** double-bladed paddle (plate B 9). **armar os** ~**s** to ship oars. **desarmar os** ~**s** to unship oars. **desprovido de** ~**s** oarless. **guarnecido de** ~ oared. **impelir com** ~**s** to paddle. **pá do** ~ palm.

remoagem s. f. 1. regrinding, remilling. 2. reground grain; grist.

remoalho s. m. cud.

remoçado adj. rejuvenated, reinvigorated, regenerated, renewed.

remoçador s. m. rejuvenator. ‖ adj. rejuvenating, rejuvenescent.

remoção s. f. (pl. -ões) 1. removal, remotion. 2. transfer. 3. ablation. 4. withdrawal. 5. deposal.

remoçar v. 1. to make fresh or young again. 2. to rejuvenate, rejuvenesce. 3. to regenerate. 4. to renew, renovate. 5. ~-se to become young again, grow robust, grow strong again.

remoçativo adj. rejuvenating, rejuvenescent.

remodelação s. f. (pl. -ões) 1. act of remodelling, remodelment. 2. recast. 3. transformation, modification.

remodelador s. m. remodel(l)er, reformer. ‖ adj. remodel(l)ing, reforming.

remodelagem s. f. (pl. -ens), **remodelamento** m. act of remodelling, remodelment.

remodelar v. 1. to model again, remodel. 2. to recast. 3. to reform. 4. to modify considerably, alter, change.

remoedura s. f. rumination, chewing of the cud.

remoela s. f. 1. spite, mark of contempt. 2. taunt. 3. malice.

remoer v. 1. to grind again, grind slowly and thoroughly. 2. to chew the cud, ruminate. 3. to importune, annoy, disturb. 4. ~-se: a) to be worried about, saddened by. b) to grow furious or angry.

remoído s. m. (Braz.) wheat middlings, bran.

remoinhada s. f. act of moving in circles, rotation, gyration.

remoinhar v. 1. to go or flow in circles. 2. to spin, whirl, eddy. 3. to revolve, rotate, gyrate. 4. to let spin or rotate.

remoinho s. m. 1. whirlpool, eddy. 2. act or effect of whirling. 3. rotation, gyration. 4. whirlwind, whirlblast. 5. spiral-formed tuft of hair.

remoinhoso adj. whirling, swirling, turning around swiftly.

remolada s. f. remolade, piquant sauce or salad dressing.

remolar s. m. oar-maker, oar manufacturer.

remolhado adj. steeped, wet, soaked again.

remolhar v. 1. to soak, steep. 2. to wet again. 3. to soften by immersion. 4. to lay into water for steeping.

remolho (ô) s. m. (pl. **remolhos**) 1. soaking, steeping. 2. act of wetting again. 3. (fam.) any illness which requests bed rest.

pôr de ~ **um negócio** to wait till a matter is ripe.

remondagem s. f. (pl. -ens) act of reweeding.

remondar v. to weed again.

remonta s. f. 1. supply of fresh horses for the cavalry. 2. remount, fresh horse. 3. horses and cattle for the army. 4. military purchasers of horses and cattle. 5. (pop.) repair, reform.

remontado adj. 1. very high, lofty. 2. (fig.) sublime. 3. distant, remote.

remontagem s. f. (pl. -ens) reconstitution, reassemblage.

remontar v. 1. to ascend, go up. 2. to lift up, raise. 3. to exalt. 4. to supply fresh horses (army), provide with remounts. 5. to repair, mend, patch. 6. to cause to take refuge in the mountains. 7. to put on finishing touches. 8. to go back, return to the original source or cause. 9. ~-se: a) to mount. b) to rise or soar very high. c) to grow very proud. d) to speak about long forgotten or dead persons.

~ **a uma fonte** to remount to a source. ~ **à origem** to retrace one's steps.

remonte s. m. 1. act of remounting, mounting. 2. ascension. 3. repair, mending, patching (esp. shoes). 4. shoe leather used for mending.

remoque s. m. 1. witty remark. 2. taunt, reproach. 3. sarcastic words, scoff, gibe. 4. allusion, insinuation.

remoqueador s. m. person who makes witty or sarcastic remarks, taunter, giber. ‖ adj. taunting, gibing.

remoquear v. 1. to offend with witty or sarcastic remarks. 2. to taunt, scoff, jeer at. 3. to gibe, flout 4. to tease.

remora s. f. 1. adjournment, postponement. 2. delay, putting off. 3. (fig.) obstacle, hindrance.

rêmora s. f. (ichth.) remora, sucking fish.

remorado adj. 1. delayed, retarded. 2. put off. 3. lagging, lingering, slow. 4. hindered.

remorar v. (arch.) 1. to delay, retard. 2. to slow down. 3. to tarry, linger, lag.

remordaz adj. m. + f. 1. very mordant, biting. 2. sarcastic, caustic.

remorder v. 1. to bite again, sting. 2. to bite repeatedly. 3. to slander, backbite, speak ill of a person. 4. to torture, torment. 5. to afflict, grieve. 6. to muse, brood over. 7. to dwell on a subject, hash over. 8. ~-se: a) to feel the sting of remorse. b) to become enraged or furious.

remordimento s. m. 1. act or effect of biting again. 2. remorse, repentance.

remoroso adj. delaying, hindering, lagging behind.

remorso s. m. 1. remorse, repentance. 2. stings of conscience, regret. 3. compunction. 4. self-reproach.

ele tem ~**s** his conscience pricks him, he feels the twinges of conscience. **ele voltou impelido pelos** ~**s** he came back conscience-stricken. **sem** ~**s** remorseless.

remoto adj. 1. distant, remote. 2. out of the way, far-off. 3. long ago, ancient. 4. vague. 5. removed. ‖ **-amente** adv. remotely.

até o canto mais ~ to the uttermost corner. **ele está muito** ~ **de fazer isto** he is very far from doing this. **num passado muito** ~ far back in the past. **tempos** ~**s** auld lang syne.

removedor s. m. (Braz.) remover of spots, paint, varnish, etc.

remover v. 1. to move again. 2. to change from one place to another, remove. 3. to transfer. 4. to drive or push away. 5. to dismiss, discharge. 6. to displace, put out of the way. 7. to free o. s. from. 8. to shake, stir. 9. to frustrate, baffle. 10. to avoid, shun, dodge. 11. to carry, bring away. 12. to induce. 13. to withdraw. 14. to eloign. 15. to brush, sweep. 16. to dissolve, wash, obliterate. ~ **de um lugar para outro** to transplant. ~ **de sua resolução** to divert s. o. from his purpose. ~ **do cargo** to discharge, unseat. ~ **as manchas** to clean, remove stains. ~ **as dificuldades** to remove the obstacles.

removimento s. m. 1. act of removing. 2. removal. 3. displacement, discharge.

removível adj. m. + f. (pl. -íveis) removable, that may be removed.

remudar v. to change again, displace or remove once more.

remugir v. 1. to moo again, moo repeatedly. 2. to bellow, roar. 3. to call down a curse upon, proffer imprecations.

remuneração s. f. (pl. -ões) 1. act or effect of rewarding. 2. remuneration, recompense. 3. premium, price. 4. gratification. 5. salary, wages. 6. fee, payment. ~ **por trabalhos extraordinários** overwages.

remunerado adj. salaried, paid, rewarded.

remunerador s. m. remunerator, recompenser, rewarder. ‖ adj. remunerating, rewarding.

remunerar v. 1. to remunerate. 2. to recompense, reward. 3. to satisfy. 4. to salary, fee, pay. 5. to gratify.

remunerativo, remuneratório adj. 1. remunerative, remunerary. 2. affording payment or reward. 3. profitable. 4. defrayable.

remunerável adj. m. + f. (pl. -áveis) remunerable, rewardable.

remuneroso adj. 1. remunerative, remuneratory. 2. generous. 3. rewarding.

remurmurar v. to murmur again, murmur repeatedly.

remurmúrio s. m. act and effect of murmuring again, remurmuring.

rena s. f. (zool.) reindeer.

renal adj. m. + f. (pl. -ais) renal, relating to the kidneys.

renano adj. of, referring to or relative to the Rhine or the Rhineland.

renão adv. nay, not at all, on no condition.

renascença s. f. 1. renascence, rebirth, renascency. 2. renewal, revival. 3. (cap.) Renaissance. ‖ adj. m. + f. of, referring to or relative to the Renaissance.

renascente adj. m. + f. 1. renascent. 2. growing or springing up anew. 3. reappearing. 4. reproduced, renewed.

renascentista s. m. + f. Renaissance man, adept or scholar of the Renaissance. ‖ adj. m. + f. Renaissant.

renascer v. 1. to born again. 2. to grow or sprout again. 3. to revive, resuscitate. 4. to be reproduced, reappear. 5. to begin a new life or activity. 6. to give a new impulse to. 7. to regenerate o. s.

renascido adj. newborn, reborn.

renascimento s. m. 1. renascence. 2. revival. 3. renewal. 4. rebirth, resuscitation. 5. regeneration.

renavegar v. to navigate again, return to the starting point.

renda (I) s. f. 1. lace (plate R 6). 2. lacework, delicate openwork fabric made of linen, silk or cotton.

~ **de agulha** point-lace. ~ **de bilros** bobbin-lace, bone-lace. ~ **de Bruxelas** Brussels lace. ~ **de filó** cotton lace. ~ **de tear** machine woven or net lace.

renda (II) s. f. 1. rent. 2. amount of a rent. 3. revenue, income. 4. proceeds, accrual. 5. gains. 6. (fig.) result. **consta que ele tem uma** ~ **mensal de cem libras** he is said to be worth hundred pounds a month. **gastar as suas** ~**s adiantadas** to eat the calf in the cow's belly. **pagar a** ~ to pay the rent. **pelo décuplo da** ~ **anual** at a ten year's purchase. ~ **anual** annuity, yearly income. ~ **nacional** national revenue. ~ **per capita** per capita income. ~ **proveniente de capital** unearned income. ~**s públicas** public revenue. ~ **vitalícia** life-annuity, life interest. **viver das suas** ~**s** to live upon one's revenues.

rendabilidade s. f. profitability, lucrativeness.

rendado s. m. lacework, lace-trimmings. ‖ adj. lace-trimmed.

rendão s. m. coarse lace.

rendar (I) v. to decorate with lace or lacework, furnish with lace.

rendar (II) v. 1. to pay rent. 2. to give or accept on lease. 3. to let.

rendaria s. f. 1. art of lace making. 2. lace industry, laceworks.

rendedouro adj. 1. profitable, lucrative. 2. productive.

rendeira (I) s. f. 1. female lacemaker, lace embroiderer. 2. (ornith.) bearded manakin.

rendeira (II) s. f. 1. (female) tenant, lessee of a rural property. 2. woman who leases or lets a rural property. 3. wife of a tenant farmer.

rendeiro (I) s. m. lacemaker, lace manufacturer, lace-seller.

rendeiro (II) s. m. 1. tenant farmer, renter, lessee. 2. lessor, man who leases, farms out or lets out rural properties. 3. rent collector, receiver of rents.

rendengue s. m. (N. Braz.) 1. part of the body between the waistline and the groins. 2. small bell, hand bell.

render v. 1. to subject, subjugate, subdue. 2. to conquer, vanquish. 3. to oblige to surrender. 4. to occupy the place of, relieve. 5. to move, affect, fill with emotion. 6. to produce as profit, pay, produce income. 7. to be the cause of. 8. to oblige to give up. 9. to produce, yield. 10. to weaken, make feeble. 11. to render, give, lend. 12. to be useful or profitable, offer advantages. 13. to crack, rend, split. 14. to suffer from a rupture. 15. to lay down arms, give up. 16. to lag, delay, need a long time for termination. 17. ~**-se:** a) to cease to resist, subject o. s. to, give o. s. up. b) to comply with, yield to any demand. c) to be tired, prostrate. ~ **a alma** to give up the spirit, die. ~ **graças** to return thanks. ~ **homenagem** to pay homage. ~ **honra** to do honours. ~ **uma sentinela** to relieve a sentry. ~**am-se incondicionalmente** they surrendered unconditionally. **ela rendeu-se** she surrendered, yielded. **fazer** ~ **o negócio** to draw advantage from a business. **não lhe rendeu nada** it did not pay him a penny. **os exércitos** ~**am-se diante...** the armies went down before... **os seus bens rendem-lhe mil libras cada ano** his estate yields him thousand pounds a year.

rendez-vous s. m. (Fr.) = randevu.

rendição s. f. (pl. -ões) 1. surrender, a giving (o. s.) up. 2. (arch.) ransom, price paid for the redemption from captivity. 3. capitulation, fall. 4. spell, relief of one person by another.

rendido adj. 1. split, rent. 2. submissive, compliant, obedient. 3. (fig.) contemplative, meditative. 4. (med.) ruptured, hernial.

rendidura s. f. 1. split or crack in the woodwork of a ship. 2. (pop.) hernia, rupture.

rendilha s. f. fine lace, very narrow lace, lace edging, tracery.

rendilhado adj. 1. ornamented with fine lace, lacy. 2. provided with tracery. 3. (fig.) resembling lacework.

rendilhar v. 1. to adorn with lacework. 2. to ornament with designs resembling lacework. 3. to trim.

rendimento s. m. 1. revenue, income. 2. return(s), profit, yield. 3. crop, fruitage. 4. product, fruit. 5. surrender. 6. submission, compliance. 7. interest. 8. output. 9. luxation, dislocation of bones. 10. efficiency (machines, work, etc.). 11. ~s pl. respectful compliments.
apresentar maior ~ no trabalho to outwork. homem que vive de ~s man of independent means. ~ anual bruto yearly gross income. ~ efetivo effective power. ~ líquido net proceeds, net profit, clear profit. ~ real actual efficiency. ~s públicos revenue. teste de ~ efficiency test.

rendoso adj. 1. profitable, lucrative. 2. fruitful, productive. 3. remunerative, yielding. ‖ -amente adv. profitably, lucratively, productively.
este negócio é muito ~ this business pays well.

renegação s. f. (pl. -ões) act or fact of renegading, renegation, denial.

renegada s. f. omber: a card game.

renegado s. m. 1. renegade. 2. apostate. 3. (fam.) turn-coat. 4. (pop.) wicked or knavish fellow. 5. (mil.) deserter. ‖ adj. apostate, faithless, recreant.

renegador s. m. 1. renegade, apostate. 2. (arch.) one who curses or swears, blasphemer. ‖ adj. faithless, treacherous, recreant, renegading.

renegar v. 1. to deny, disown. 2. to abjure, renounce, forswear. 3. to curse, swear, blaspheme. 4. to hate, detest. 5. to betray, double-cross. 6. to refute, disprove. 7. to repel, reject. 8. to despise, disdain, scorn. 9. to change sides, rat, abandon (political party, religious group, etc.). 10. to become a renegade. 11. to dispense with, give up.
muitos ~am a nossa fé many fell from our faith.

renete s. m. butteris, drawknife.

renga s. f. (pop.) rank, row, file.

rengalho s. m. (pop.) 1. fabric appropriate for embroideries. 2. netting without any embroidery.

rengo (I), **rengue** s. m. gauze, transparent cotton muslin used for lacework.

rengo (II) s. m. lameness (of horses). ‖ adj. lame.

rengo (III) s. m. (Port. prov.) grass.

rengue s. m. rank, row, file.

renguear s. (S. Braz.) to become lame, limp.

rengueira s. f. (S. Braz.) lameness, limping.

renhideiro s. m. (Braz.) pit for cockfights.

renhido adj. 1. hotly disputed. 2. cruel, bloody. 3. hard-fought. 4. warmly debated. 5. fierce, implacable.
uma peleja -a a desperate fight.

renhimento s. m. act or effect of fighting, disputing or quarreling.

renhir v. 1. to dispute, debate. 2. to argue. 3. to contest, oppose. 4. to wrangle, quarrel. 5. to fight stubbornly or fiercely.

reniforme adj. reniform, kidney-shaped (plate F 5).

rênio s. m. (chem.) rhenium (symbol Re).

renitência s. f. 1. stubbornness, obstinacy. 2. resistance, opposition. 3. renitence, renitency. 4. reluctance.

renitente adj. 1. renitent. 2. stubborn, obstinate. 3. reluctant. 4. refractory, resistant, recalcitrant. 5. tough.

renitir v. 1. to resist, withstand. 2. to oppose. 3. to be obstinate, persist in. 4. to be refractory, obdurate or stubborn.

renomado adj. renowned, reputed, famous.

renome s. m. 1. repute, reputation. 2. fame, glory. 3. prestige, renown. 4. credit, standing.
de ~ well-known. sem ~ renownless.

renova s. f. 1. shoot, sprout, offshoot. 3. (fig.) descendants, offspring.

renovação s. f. (pl. -ões) renovation, renewing, revival, resurrection.

renovador s. m. renovator, renewer, reformer. ‖ adj. adj. renovating.

renovamento s. m. renovation, renewal, resuscitation.

renovar v. 1. to renovate, renew. 2. to give the appearance of newness or freshness. 3. to furbish, freshen. 4. to ameliorate, improve. 5. to substitute an old thing for a new one, to replace. 6. to recommence, begin again, repeat. 7. to repair, reform, make again. 8. to revive, restore, resuscitate. 9. to give new brilliancy or luster. 10. to give new force or vigour. 11. to sprout, put forth new shoots. 12. to follow or succeed each other. 13. ~-se: a) to rejuvenate or regenerate o. s. b) to grow strong again. c) to reappear, appear again. d) to be repeated.
~ a memória to renew the memory, call to the mind. ~ um pedido to repeat an order.

renovo (ô) s. m. 1. sprout, offshoot. 2. scion, twig. 3. offspring. 4. (Port., prov.) vegetable garden. 5. ~s pl. agricultural products. 6. outgrowth.

renque s. m. + f. 1. rank, row. 2. alignment. 3. disposition, arrangement.

renrém s. m. (pl. -éns) (N. Braz.) constant or continued quarrel.

rentabilidade s. f. rentability.

rentar v. 1. to affront, insult. 2. to court, flirt. 3. to make love to. 4. to provoke. 5. to pass close to. 6. to taunt, defy.

rente (I) adj. m. + f. 1. close by, near. 2. close-cut. 3. flush, flat. ‖ adj. closely, even with, on a level with.
cortar ~ to cut close. ~ ao chão close to the ground. ~ da terra 1. even with the ground. 2. (bot.) acaulous, having no stalk or stem.

rente (II) adj. m. + f. 1. ready, willing. 2. assiduous.

renteador s. m. suitor, wooer, admirer, follower. ‖ adj. philandering.

rentear v. 1. to cut off, cut very short. 2. to pass close by. 3. to flirt, make love, philander.

rentura s. f. markmanship.

renuente adj. m. + f. renouncing, negative, shaking the head (in order to indicate a negative answer).

renuído s. m. rejecting or negative movement with the head. ‖ adj. rejecting, negative.

renuir v. to renounce, reject, refuse.

renúncia s. f. 1. renunciation, renouncement. 2. rejection. 3. resignation, desistance. 4. self-denial, self-renunciation, sacrifice. 5. disclaiming, abjuration. 6. relinquishment. 7. (jur.) quitclaim, waiver.

renunciação s. f. (pl. -ões) renouncement, renunciation.

renunciador s. m. renouncer, abdicator, relinquisher. ‖ adj. renouncing.

renunciamento s. m. act or result of renouncing, renunciation.

renunciante s. m. + f. renouncer. 2. abdicator. 3. relinquisher, disclaimer. ‖ adj. renouncing, disclaiming.

renunciar v. 1. to renounce, resign. 2. to reject, repel. 3. to refuse, revoke. 4. to desist, leave voluntarily (position, office, etc.), abandon. 5. to abdicate. 6. to disown, disclaim. 7. (cards) to revoke, not follow suit. 8. to abnegate, abjure. 9. to relinquish, forego, waive.
~ a to divest o. s. of. ~ ao jogo to throw up the

game. ~ **ao mundo** to forsake the pleasures of this world. ~ **à própria vontade** to practise self--denial. ~ **a um direito sob juramento** to abjure one's claim. **ele renunciou a todos os prazeres** he renounced all joys. **o rei renunciou ao trono** the king abdicated his throne. **os ministros ~am** the ministers have resigned.

renunciativo adj. renunciative, renunciatory.

renunciatório s. m. (jur.) transferee, acquirer of waived rights.

renunciável adj. m. + f. (pl. **-áveis**) that may be renounced, renunciable.

renutação s. f. (pl. **-ões**) negative or repulsive movement with the head.

renutrir v. 1. to nourish again. 2. to give new nourishment. 3. to eat, nourish o. s. again.

renzilha s. f. (pop.) quarrel, brawl, riot.

reocupação s. f. (pl. **-ões**) reoccupation.

reocupar v. 1. to reoccupy, occupy again. 2. to reconquer.

reóforo s. m. (electr.) rheophore.

reômetro s. m. (electr.) rheometer, galvanometer.

reordenação s. f. (pl. **-ões**) reordination, act of ordaining again.

reordenar v. 1. to reordain, ordain anew. 2. to put again in order, rearrange. 3. to confer new orders to.

reorganização s. f. (pl. **-ões**) reorganization, reform, rearrangement.

reorganizador s. m. reorganizer, reformer. ‖ adj. reorganizing.

reorganizar v. 1. to reorganize, organize anew. 2. to improve, better, ameliorate. 3. to reform, rearrange.

reoscópio s. m. (electr.) rheoscope, galvanoscope.

reostato, reóstato s. m. (electr.) rheostat, resistor for regulating currents.

reótomo s. m. (electr.) rheotome, interruptor.

reotropismo s. m. (bot.) rheotropism, tropism in which the stimulating factor is a fluid (esp. water).

repa s. f. (pop.) thin or baldish hair.

repagar v. 1. to repay, pay again, pay back. 2. to pay well.

repaginação s. f. (typogr.) repagination, repaging.

repaginar v. (typogr.) to repaginate, repage.

repandirrostro adj. (zool.) repandorostrate.

repanhar v. 1. to crease, wrinkle. 2. to snatch away, pick up.

reparação s. f. (pl. **-ões**) 1. reparation. 2. repair, repairing. 3. reform, refitting. 4. indemnity, indemnification. 5. satisfaction. 6. expiation, atonement. 7. redress, restitution, compensation. 8. amends.

pagar -ões to make amends. **-ões de guerra** reparations for war damages. ~ **total de navios** overhauling of ships.

reparadeira s. f. inquisitive or prying woman.

reparado adj. repaired, mended, fixed up, redressed.

reparador s. .m 1. repairer, restorer. 2. observer. 3. redresser. 4. recoverer. 5. reformer. ‖ adj. repairing, reparative, reparatory.

reparar v. 1. to repair, mend. 2. to make (over) again. 3. to restore, re-establish. 4. to retouch, finish, make perfect. 5. to improve, ameliorate. 6. to remedy. 7. to correct. 8. to make amends for. 9. to indemnify. 10. to take notice, see, observe, concentrate the attention on. 11. to be prudent, look around carefully. 12. ~**-se:** a) to take shelter, seek refuge. b) to request or obtain compensation for (losses, damages, etc.). 13. to renovate, renew. 14. to expiate, atone for.

não ~ to oversee, not to be attentive. **ninguém reparou em** nobody took notice of. ~ **o dano** to repair a damage, indemnify s. o.

tempo perdido não se repara time lost cannot be regained.

reparatório adj. reparative, repairing, reparatory, restoring.

reparável adj. m. + f. (pl. **-áveis**) reparable, retrievable, noticeable.

reparecer v. to reappear.

reparo s. m. 1. repair, repairing. 2. restoration. 3. observation, notice. 4. critic, censure. 5. shield, protection, defense. 6. watchfulness. 7. entrenchment. 8. gun carriage. 9. advertence. 10. objection, disapproval. 11. remark.

repartição s. f. (pl. **-ões**) 1. partition, partitionment. 2. department, administrative or governmental office. 3. secretariat. 4. division, distribution. 5. branch, section.

~ **pública** governmental department.

repartideira s. f. 1. copper pan used in sugar mills. 2. woman who divides, distributes or shares.

repartido adj. 1. parted, divided. 2. (Braz.) doubtful, uncertain, hesitating.

repartidor s. m. 1. divider, sharer, distributor. 2. (math.) divisor. ‖ adj. dividing, sharing, distributing.

~ **de avarias** (com.) average adjuster.

repartimento s. m. 1. division or subdivision of a building. 2. partition. 3. compartment. 4. division, separation. 5. section, department. 6. confluence of several rivers forming a common channel.

repartir v. 1. to separate, slice, split. 2. to distribute, allot, dole out. 3. to partition. 4. to share. 5. to apply, employ, use. 6. ~**-se:** a) to be divided. b) to branch off, furcate. c) to spread. d) to dedicate one's attention to several subjects. 7. (math.) to divide.

eles ~am meio por meio they went fifty-fifty. ~**am entre si a quantia em discussão** they split the difference.

repartitivo adj. distributive, separative, subject or tending to division.

repartível adj. m. + f. (pl. **-íveis**) distributable, separable, dividable.

repassada s. f. (S. Braz.) every attempt to mount a wild horse in order to break it in.

repassado adj. 1. full. 2. steeped, soaked. 3. impregnated, saturated. 4. having the form of a sling or noose.

repassador s. m. (S. Braz.) horse tamer.

repassar v. 1. to pass again, repass. 2. to drench, soak. 3. to read over again, examine again. 4. to recall, remember. 5. to impregnate, saturate in. 6. to penetrate. 7. (Braz.) to mount again a wild horse (in order to break it in). 8. to ooze, percolate, exude. 9. to fill. 10. to spill, pour out. 11. to let soak or steep. 12. ~**-se:** a) to be drenched, soaked or imbibed. b) to be or become strongly affected, imbued with. 13. to review (troops, etc.). 14. to rehearse.

repasse, repasso s. m. (Braz.) 1. every new attempt to mount a wild horse in order to break it in. 2. the last part of the cotton crop. 3. act of culling or gleaning coffee beans after harvest (as prophylactic measure against the coffee borer).

repastar v. 1. to lead again to pasture. 2. to feed, nourish. 3. to feast, regale with food and drink. 4. to fare well, eat a substantial meal. 5. ~**-se** to enjoy o. s., be delighted, regale o. s. with good food.

repasto s. m. 1. a lot of food. 2. repast. 3. increase of cattle food or pasture. 4. banquet, feast.

repatanar-se v. to linger, loll, recline o. s. lazely, stretch out.

repatriação s. f. (pl. **-ões**) repatriation, remigration.

repatriado s. m. returning emigrant. ‖ adj. repatriate.

repatriador s. m. one who foments the repatriation (of emigrants). ‖ adj. repatriating.

repatriamento s. m. repatriation, act or process of repatriating.

repatriar v. 1. to repatriate, send back to the country of origin. 2. to remigrate, return home to one's own country.

repechar v. (S. Braz.) 1. to ascend, climb (a mountain, stairs, etc.). 2. to rise slightly, form an insignificant elevation (ground).

repecho s. m. (S. Braz.) 1. sloping street or way. 2. acclivity, hillside. 3. irregular ground.

repedir v. to ask again, ask insistently, request once more.

repelão s. m. (pl. -ões) 1. pull, push. 2. violent thrust, shock. 3. attack, sudden charge, assault.

repelar v. 1. to pull, push, pull by the hair. 2. to dishevel one's own hair.

repelência s. f. 1. repellence, repellency. 2. repugnance. 3. disgust, repulsion. 4. forbiddingness.

repelente adj. m. + f. 1. repellent, repugnant. 2. repulsive, disgusting. 3. foul, nasty. 4. shocking, forbidding. ‖ ~mente adv. repellently.

repelido s. m. 1. violent push, shock. 2. rough treatment, rudeness. ‖ adj. 1. repelled, repulsed. 2. expulsed, expelled, ousted. 3. not accepted, not admitted.

repelir v. 1. to repel, repulse. 2. to drive, beat or force back. 3. to expulse, expel. 4. not to admit, refuse entrance, admission or approximation. 5. to reject, spurn. 6. to avoid, shun. 7. to feel aversion. 8. to be incompatible with. 9. to defend. 10 to retort, repudiate. 11. ~-se to repel one another. ~ o inimigo to fence off the enemy.

repelo (ê) s. m. 1. violence. 2. pull, push. 3. attack.

repenicado s. m. 1. act of chiming or pealing. 2. chime, pealing sound.

repenicar v. 1. to chime, peal. 2. to percuss metallic objects. 3. to ring, toll (bells). 4. to produce shrill, strident sounds.

repenique s. m. 1. act of chiming or pealing. 2. chiming or pealing sound.

repensar v. to rethink, ponder, reconsider.

repente s. m. 1. suddenness, impulsive, hasty or thoughtless act or utterance. 2. outburst, sudden fit.
de ~ all at once, with a rush, suddenly.

repentino adj. 1. sudden, abrupt, instantaneous. 2. unexpected, unforeseen. 3. rapid, snappy. 4. acute. ‖ -amente adv. suddenly, abruptly, unexpectedly.
ataque ~ raid. ela -amente virou-se para mim she flashed round upon me. ele apareceu -amente he appeared out of the clear sky. ele partiu -amente he departed unexpectedly. morte -a sudden death.

repentista s. m. + f. improvisator, extemporary speaker. ‖ adj. improvising, extemporary.

repercussão s. f. (pl. -ões) 1. repercussion. 2. reverberation, echo. 3. rebound, recoil, reflection. 4. replication. 5. effect.

repercussivo adj. repercussive, repellent, reverberating.

repercutente adj. m. + f. reflecting, rebounding. resounding.

repercutir v. 1. to reverberate, re-echo. 2. to rebound, recoil. 3. to produce sounds. 4. to give a new direction to, deflect, reflect. 5. to throw back. 6. to report. 7. ~-se: a) to be or become reflected. b) to have an indirect influence upon, have repercussions.
sua fama repercutia pela cidade inteira the town rang with his fame.

repergunta s. f. 1. act of questioning again. 2. (jur.) cross-examination.

reperguntar v. to interrogate again, put new questions, cross-examine.

repertório s. m. 1. repertory. 2. list, index. 3. catalogue. 4. compilation, collection. 5. notebook. 6. program, repertoire. 7. (fig.) expert, person well versed or competent in any subject.

repes s. m., sg. + pl. rep, repp.

repesador s. m. weight controller. ‖ adj. weighing again, controlling the weight.

repesar v. 1. to weigh again. 2. control the weight, verify the weight of. 3. to examine carefully.

repeso (ê) (I) s. m. (pl. **repesos**) 1. act of weighing again. 2. weight control office.

repeso (ê) (II) adj. repentant, penitent, repenting.

repeteco s. m. (Braz., sl.) repetition, act of repeating.

repentenar-se v. 1. to linger, loll. 2. to lean back lazily.

repetência s. f. 1. repetition, repeating. 2. (med.) reflux (of humours).

repetente s. m. + f. (education) repeater, student who frequents a class a second time. ‖ adj. repeating.

repetição s. f. (pl. -ões) 1. repetition, act of repeating. 2. (rhet.) repetition of the same word, reiteration. 3. recurrence, reappearance. 4. reduplication. 5. rehearsal. 6. (mus.) echo. 7. copy. 8. recapitulation, coaching. 9. m. repeating firearm.
relógio de ~ repeating clock, repeater.

repetido adj. 1. repeated, repetitional. 2. iterative, reiterant. 3. renewed. 4. frequent. 5. reiterated. ‖ -amente adv. repeatedly, frequently, renewedly, once and again.
eu lhe disse repetidas vezes I told him ever so often.

repetidor s. m. coach, rehearser, repeater. ‖ adj. repeating, repetitional.

repetir v. 1. to repeat. 2. to say over again, rehash. 3. to catch again, recur (illness). 4. to spread, become known. 5. to reflect. 6. (education) to frequent a course a second time. 7. to do over again. 8. to redouble, reduplicate. 9. to rehearse. 10. to reappear. 11. to tell, report again. 12. ~-se to happen again.
~ o ataque to return to the charge. ~ enfadosamente to harp always on the same string. ~am toda a história they thrashed the whole thing over.

repicador s. m. ringer, chimer. ‖ adj. chiming.

repicagem s. f. (pl. -ens). 1. rising of bells. 2. transplantation.

repica-ponto s. m. excellence, perfection.

repicar v. 1. to pierce or prick again. 2. to transplant. 3. to chime, peal, ring. 4. to mince, chop. 5. to toll solemnly (bells).

repimpado adj. 1. crammed (with food), well-fed. 2. lolling, leaning back lazily. 3. comfortably seated.

repimpar v. 1. to stuff one's belly, cram. 2. to satiate, satisfy. 3. ~-se: a) to linger, loll, lean back lazily. b) to get one's fill. c) to feast, indulge in.

repinchar v. to splash, bespatter.

repintar v. 1. to repaint, paint again. 2. to copy, reproduce. 3. to make lively, give new life to. 4. to portray, paint a picture of. 5. to make a blurred inverted copy of new print (on the preceding page).

repique s. m. 1. tolling or pealing of bells. 2. clashing of two billiard balls. 3. alarm, tocsin. 4. festive chiming.

repiquetar v. to control or rectify the position of stakes (of a boundary).

repiquete (ê) s. m. 1. steep sideway or street. 2. variable winds. 3. repeated pealing of bells. 4. (Braz.)

relapse, setback. 5. (N. Braz.) severe drought. 6. (Braz., Amazonas) swell of rising water (caused by heavy rainfall in the region of the headwaters).

repisa s. f. act or effect of treading again.

vinho de ~ wine of the last pressing.

repisado adj. well-trodden, well-worn, (fig.) rehashed.

repisar v. 1. to tread over again, retread. 2. to trample, crush. 3. to press. 4. to repeat over and over again, reiterate. 5. to insist on, talk insistently. 6. to hash over, harp on.

~ **uma velha história** to dish up an old story.

repisativo adj. repetitious, tediously repeating.

replanta s. f. 1. planting or replanting of empty spots in fields or forests, reforestation of clearings. 2. (Braz.) tree planted in substitution of one cut down.

replantação s. f. (pl. -ões) **replantio** m. replantation, planting again, replanting.

replantar v. to replant, plant again or anew.

repleção s. f. (pl. -ões) 1. repletion, fullness. 2. plenum. 3. surfeit.

repleno (I) s. m. filled and levelled ground, embankment.

repleno (II) adj. very full, replete, filled up.

repletar v. to make very full, fill to capacity.

repleto adj. 1. replete. 2. very full, filled up. 3. crammed, stuffed. 4. congested, crowded. 5. satisfied, sated. 6. well-provided.

as ruas estavam -as de gente the streets were choke-full of people. **tocaram numa casa -a** (theat.) they played for a packed house.

réplica, replicação (pl. -ões) s. f. 1. response, reply. 2. repartee, rebuttal. 3. rejoinder, replication. 4. (arts) replica, facsimile, very close copy. 5. (mus.) repeat. 6. (jur.) objection, counterplea.

ele apresentou sua ~ he introduced his affirmative defence. **sem** ~ without reply. **sua** ~ **foi mordaz** her comeback was sarcastic.

replicador s. m. replier, respondent, replicant. ‖ adj. replying.

replicar v. 1. to answer, reply. 2. to rejoin, rebut. 3. to respond, repartee. 4. to refute, object. 5. to recriminate, retort.

replicativo adj. (bot.) replicate, folded back upon itself.

repolegar, repolgar v. 1. to fold, double. 2. to decorate with an ornamental moulding.

repolego (ê) s. m. (pl. **repolegos**) 1. ornamental fillet or moulding. 2. fillet of dough which forms the border of a pie.

repolga s. f. a kind of mushroom raised on chestnut trees.

repolhal s. m. (pl. -ais) cabbage field, cabbage plantation.

repolhar v. to grow to a round head, to cabbage, have the form of a cabbage.

repolho (ô) s. m. cabbage, common or drum-head cabbage.

~ **chinês** (bot.) Chinese cabbage. ~ **crespo** borecole, kail. ~ **roxo** Scotch kale, red cabbage. **salada de** ~ **cru** coleslaw.

repolhudo adj. 1. cabbage-headed. 2. grown to a round head. 3. (fig.) plump, rotund, round, fat.

alface -a cabbage lettuce.

repoltrear-se v. 1. to linger, dally. 2. to lean back lazily. 3. to sit down comfortably. 4. to stretch out, recline in an easy chair.

reponta s. f. 1. formation of a new point, reappearance of a point. 2. (fenc.) ripost(e), quick return thrust. 3. (Braz.) beginning of the flood-tide. 4. (Braz.) flood.

repontão s. m. (pl. -ões) strongheaded or recalcitrant person, grumbler. ‖ adj. recalcitrant, cross, cranky.

repontar v. 1. to reappear, come up again. 2. to dawn, grow light. 3. to attack. 4. to turn back. 5. to retort, give a sharp reply, to recalcitrate. 6. to show up, come into view. 7. to reply rudely or grumblingly. 8. to cause to flow back, flow in (tide). 9. (Braz.) to drive cattle (in a certain direction).

ao ~ **da madrugada** at day-break.

reponte s. m. (Braz.) act of driving away, act of driving cattle.

repontuar v. to punctuate again.

repor v. 1. to replace, put back again. 2. to restitute, refund. 3. to restore to the original state or condition. 4. ~**-se**: a) to replace o. s. b) to restore one's health. 5. to re-establish. 6. to make good.

reportação s. f. (pl. -ões) 1. act or effect of turning back or withdrawing. 2. moderation, modesty.

reportado adj. moderate, modest, temperate, right, correct, patient.

reportagem s. f. (pl. -ens) 1. newspaper report. 2. act of writing newsprint. 3. reporters collectively, class of reporters. 4. interview, report, statement, feature, sport news.

~ **cinematográfica** screen record. ~ **de rádio** sound story. ~ **elogiosa** (about artists, etc.) write-up.

reportamento s. m. 1. moderation, modesty. 2. act or method of news reporting. 3. statement or remark with regard to a certain event.

reportar v. 1. to turn back, withdraw. 2. to transport. 3. to turn round, revolve. 4. to attribute, impute, consider as cause of. 5. to moderate. 6. ~**-se**: a) to moderate o. s. b) to allude to, mention.

~**-se a** to refer o. s. to. ~**-se de um trecho a outro** to make cross-references.

repórter s. m. + f. (pl. **repórteres**) reporter, journalist, news writer.

~ **cinematográfico** screen reporter. ~ **do teatro da guerra** war correspondent. ~ **esportivo** sports caster. ~ **medíocre** ink slinger. ~ **próprio** (of a newspaper) staff reporter.

reposição s. f. (pl. -ões) replacement, restitution, re-establisment, restoration.

~ **de um osso deslocado** reposition.

repositório s. m. 1. repository. 2. chest of drawers. 3. depository, store. 4. compilation. ‖ adj. of or referring to a repository.

reposta s. f. 1. stake at omber (cards). 2. answer, reply.

repostada s. f. rude, sharp or uncourteous reply.

repostar v. to reply rudely, give a sharp, coarse or uncivil answer.

repostaria s. f. 1. pastry kitchen, room in a rich household where sweets and liqueurs are made. 2. domestic personnel. 3. kitchen utensils.

reposteiro s. m. 1. drape, drapery, hangings, door curtain. 2. groom of the royal household who had to take care of the portieres. 3. chamberlain, yeoman of the royal wardrobe and stores. 4. royal treasurer. 5. footman, butler.

repotrear-se v. to linger, lounge, lean back lazily (in a chair).

repousar v. 1. to rest, repose. 2. to calm, quiet. 3. to appease, ease. 4. to be resting, sleep, slumber. 5. to take things easy, relax. 6. to linger, lounge. 7. to stare, look fixedly into the air. 8. not to work, be inactive. 9. to be or remain in a certain place or position. 10. to relieve from pain. 11. to be buried, be committed to the grave, be dead.

repouso s. m. 1. rest, repose: a) tranquillity, calmness. b) ease, peace of mind. c) inactivity. 2. sleep, slumber (plate P 18). 3. (arch., naut.) anchorage, berth.

repovoar v. 1. to people again or anew, repopulate. 2. to restock.

repreendedor s. m. reprehender, reproacher, rebuker, expostulator. ‖ adj. reprehending, carping, fault-finding.

repreender v. 1. to reprehend, reprimand. 2. to reproach, censure. 3. to upbraid, vituperate, bawl out. 4. to admonish, expostulate. 5. to chide, reprove, rebuke.

~ **alguém severamente** to reprimand s. o. severely, U. S. A., sl.) to rap a person's knuckles, haul s. o. over the coals. ~**am-na por** they took her to task for, they read her a lecture. ~**am o menino muitas vezes** they found often fault with the boy. **ele o repreendeu paternalmente** he admonished him in a fatherly manner, he talked to him like a Dutch uncle. **repreenda-o severamente!** reprimand him severely!, (sl.) give him a wigging!

repreensão s. f. (pl. -ões) 1. reprehension, reprimand. 2. reproach, censure. 3. upbraiding, chiding, scolding. 4. rebuke, blame. 5. expostulation, exprobration. 6. reproof. 7. admonition.

~ **pública** denunciation, impeachment. ~ **conjugal** curtain lecture.

repreensível adj. m. + f. (pl. -íveis) reprehensible, censurable, objectionable, rebuk(e)able, reprovable. ‖ **repreensivelmente** adv. reprehensibly.

repreensivo adj. reprehensive, admonitory, rebukeful, faultfinding, remonstrative. ‖ **-amente** adv. reprehensively, exceptionally.

repreensor s. m. reprehender, blamer, reprover, expostulator, censurer. ‖ adj. reprehensive, faultfinding.

repregar v. 1. to nail again, fasten well with nails. 2. to decorate with studs. 3. to rivet.

reprego s. m. 1. act of nailing again. 2. act of fastening well with nails. 3. ornamental studding with nails.

represa (ê) s. f. dam, dike. 2. sluice, flood-gate, weir. 3. catchment, reservoir. 4. artificial lake formed by dammed up water. 5. (fig.) accumulation. 6. repair of a wall. 7. a recaptured ship. 8. (archit.) bracket, small pedestal, stand. 9. pent-up feelings.

represado adj. 1. repressed, dammed up. 2. restrained, stopped, kept back. 3. stagnant, not flowing. 4. suspended.

represador s. m. 1. reprisalist, one who takes (s. th.) back by force. 2. one who or thing that dams up. ‖ adj. damming up, restraining, keeping back, stopping.

represadura s. f. act of restraining, keeping back or damming up.

represália s. f. 1. reprisal, retaliation. 2. revenge. 3. sanction.

como ~ as a retaliative measure. **em** ~ **de** in reprisal for. **exercer** ~**s** to make reprisals on.

represamento s. m. act or process of restraining, keeping back or damming up.

represar v. 1. to dam up, dike. 2. to stop, pen up, embank. 3. to restrain, repress. 4. to hinder, hamper. 5. to confine in prison. 6. to suffocate, choke. 7. to reprise, recover forcibly.

~ **as lágrimas** to forbear weeping. ~ **os sentimentos** to pen up one's feelings. ~**am o navio** they recaptured the ship.

representação s. f. (pl. -ões) 1. representation: a) act of representing. b) exhibition, depiction, figuration. c) presentation. d) picture, image, statue. e) performance, acting, interpretation. f) personation. g) agency. h) representatives collectively. i) display,

outward show. 2. remonstrance, expostulation. 3. expenses incurred by representation.

~ **comunal** vestry. ~ **em perspectiva linear** representation in linear perspective. ~ **gráfica** graph. ~ **pictórica** portrayal.

representado adj. represented, substituted, depicted.

representador s. m. representer, actor, player, impersonator. ‖ adj. representing, acting, impersonating.

representante s. m. + f. 1. representative. 2. player, actor, impersonator. 3. minister, ambassador, delegate. 4. attorney, deputy. 5. agent. 6. commissary. 7. substitute, proxy. 8. exponent. ‖ adj. representing, representative.

ele será meu ~ he will be my proxy. **ela é uma boa** ~ she is a good actress. ~ **autorizado** procurator.

representar v. 1. to be the image of, bring before the mind, show. 2. to personate, impersonate. 3. to represent. 4. to make known. 5. to play, perform, act. 6. to exhibit. 7. to serve as minister, ambassador, deputy, etc. 8. to substitute, replace. 9. to act as attorney or proxy. 10. to typify, signify. 11. to be similar to, resemble. 12. to reproduce, image, portray, paint. 13. to describe, depict, delineate. 14. to make a display of (one's rank or position). 15. to act as, fulfil a function. 16. to be representative, act as agent. 17. to lodge a claim, protest or remonstrance. 18. ~**-se:** a) to imagine, call to one's mind. b) to offer itself, come to mind. c) to serve as a symbol.

~ **exageradamente** to overplay. ~ **insatisfatoriamente** (theat.) to underact. ~ **mal um papel** (theat.) to flunk, do a fluff. ~ **um papel com sucesso** to support a character. **ele representa um partido** he sits for constituency. **fui representado por ele** I was represented by him. **um filme com Tyron representando o papel principal** a film featuring Tyron.

representativo adj. representative, exhibitive, figurative, ambassadorial.

representável adj. m. + f. (pl. -áveis) representable, capable of being represented, representative, actable, acting.

representear v. to make each other a present, give a gift in return.

represo (ê) adj. 1. restrained, repressed. 2. rearrested, caught again. 3. dammed up, kept back.

repressão s. f. (pl. -ões) 1. repression, suppression. 2. check, constraint, restraint. 3. coercion. 4. moderation.

repressivo adj. repressive, tending to repress. ‖ **-amente** adv. repressively.

repressor s. m. represser, coercer. ‖ adj. repressing.

repressório adj. repressive, tending to restrain or repress.

reprimenda s. f. 1. reprimand, reprehension. 2. disapproval. 3. severe admonishment. 4. correction. 5. expostulation, remonstrance.

reprimido adj. 1. repressed, restrained. 2. contained. 3. oppressed.

reprimir v. 1. to curb, check. 2. to stop. 3. to repress, restrain. 4. to moderate. 5. to dam up, keep down. 6. to conceal, hide, not to show. 7. to subdue, subject. 8. to violate, force, coerce. 9. to delay, postpone. 10. to trouble, annoy. 11. ~**-se** to refrain from, control or moderate o. s.

reprimi meu desapontamento I choked down my disappointment. ~ **as lágrimas** to forbear weeping. **ele tinha de** ~ **os seus sentimentos** he had to crush down his feelings.

reprimível adj. m. + f. (pl. -íveis) repressible, restrainable, coercible.

reprincipiar v. to begin again, recommence.

reprise s. f. (Fr.) (theat.) repeated performance, rerun.
réprobo s. m. reprobate, castaway, outcast. ‖ adj. reprobate, castaway.
reprochar v. 1. to reproach, rebuke. 2. to censure. 3. to upbraid, scold. 4. to tell s. o. to his face, speak one's mind.
reproche s. m. reproach, upbraiding, censure.
reprodução s. f. (pl. -ões) 1. reproduction. 2. copy, replica, replication. 3. propagation, procreation. 4. repetition, duplicate. 5. transcript, transcription. ~ **assexuada** asexual reproduction, monogenesis. ~ **sexuada** sexual reproduction. ~ **de uma obra-prima** reproduction of a masterpiece.
reprodutibilidade s. f. reproducibility, reproductiveness.
reprodutível adj. m. + f. (pl. -íveis) reproducible, capable of being reproduced.
reprodutivo adj. reproductive, tending to reproduce.
reprodutor s. m. 1. reproducer. 2. procreator. 3. any domestic animal kept for breeding, studhorse, bull, he-goat, ram. ‖ adj. reproductive, progenitive.
reprodutriz s. f. any female animal kept for breeding purposes, brood-mare, brood-sow, ewe. ‖ adj. reproductive, progenitive.
reproduzir v. 1. to reproduce. 2. to produce again or anew, present or introduce again. 3. to recommence, begin again, repeat. 4. to transcribe, copy. 5. to multiply, propagate. 6. to imitate, portray. 7. to render, represent, perform again. 8. ~-**se** to self-perpetuate through generations, be repeated, multiply.
reproduzível adj. m. + f. (pl. -íveis) reproducible.
reprofundar v. 1. to make deeper, deepen. 2. to submerge, immerse. 3. to sink.
reprografia s. f. reprography: facsimile reproduction of graphic matter.
reprometer v. to promise again, promise repeatedly.
repromissão s. f. (pl. -ões) 1. renewed or repeated promise. 2. mutual or reciprocal promise.
reprovação s. f. (pl. -ões) 1. act of reproving, reproof. 2. censure, reproach, rebuke. 3. damnableness, disapprobation. 4. disdain, contempt. 5. rejection, failure. 6. reproval, disapproval. 7. (exam.) reprobation.
ela me olhou com ~ she looked at me with reproach. **ele a observou com** ~ he looked at her reprovingly. **incorri na sua** ~ I incurred his condemnation. ~ **em exame** (fam.) pluck, plough, flunk.
reprovado s. m. person who failed at an examination. (sl.) flunk. ‖ adj. 1. reproved. 2. damned, condemned. 3. rejected, refused. 4. reprobate. 5. (exam.) flunked, unapproved.
ela foi -a no exame she failed in her examination. **ele foi** ~ he fell through, he took a plough, he was plucked.
reprovador s. m. reprover. ‖ adj. reprobative, reprobatory.
reprovar (I) v. 1. to disapprove, reprove. 2. to censure, upbraid, rebuke. 3. to reject, turn down. 4. to admonish. 5. to condemn. 6. to vote against. 7. (exam.) to reprobate, deny approval.
~**am o seu modo de agir** they censured his manner of proceeding. **a câmara reprovou o projeto** the House turned down, voted against the project.
reprovar (II) v. to prove, try or taste again, prove repeatedly.
reprovativo adj. reprobative, reprobatory.
reprovável adj. m. + f. (pl. -áveis) reprovable, rebuk(e)able, unapproving, condemnable, exceptionable.
repruir, reprurir v. 1. to cause pruritus. 2. to inflame. 3. to itch again, suffer from prurigo. 4. (fig.) to become excited.

reptação s. f. (pl. -ões) challenge, defiance, provocation.
reptador s. m. challenger, defier, provoker. ‖ adj. challenging.
reptante (I) s. m. + f. challenger, provoker. ‖ adj. challenging.
reptante (II) s. m. + f. crawling or creeping animal, reptil. ‖ adj. crawling, creeping, reptilian.
reptar (I) v. 1. to challenge, defy. 2. to provoke, irritate. 3. to oppose.
reptar (II) v. to crawl, creep, trail along the ground.
reptil, réptil s. m. (pl. -reptis, répteis) 1. (zool.) reptile. 2. (pop.) crawler, creeper. 3. (fig.) mean or contemptible person. 4. (zool.) the class of Reptilia. ‖ adj. m. + f. (pl. reptis, répteis) 1. crawling, creeping. 2. (zool.) of or referring to the reptiles, reptilian. 3. (fig.) contemptible.
que devora reptis reptilivorous.
repto s. m. challenge, provocation, open defiance.
república s. f. 1. republic, government elected by the people. 2. commonweal, commonwealth. 3. (fam.) loosely organized society, disordered group. 4. group of students living together and splitting expenses. 5. their common dwelling place.
~ **popular** (pol.) People's Republic.
republicanismo s. m. republicanism: principles of republican government.
republicanização s. f. (pl. -ões) republicanization.
republicanizar v. 1. to republicanize, make republican. 2. to transform into a republic. 3. to adapt o. s. to republican principles.
republicano s. m. republican. ‖ adj. republican.
republicar v. to republish, publish again, re-edit.
republicida s. m. + f. 1. destroyer of a republic. 2. antirepublican.
republicídio s. m. destruction of a republic.
república s. m. 1. public-spirited man. 2. supporter of republican principles, republican. ‖ adj. republican, public-spirited.
republiqueta s. f. (depr.) a very small or insignificant republic.
repudiação s. f. (pl. -ões) repudiation.
repudiante s. m. + f. repudiator, disclaimer. ‖ adj. repudiating.
repudiar v. 1. to repudiate. 2. to divorce. 3. to disown, disavow, disclaim. 4. to renounce. 5. to abjure, forswear. 6. to reject, repel. 7. to abandon, forsake, desert.
repudiável adj. m. + f. (pl. -áveis) repudiable, admitting repudiation.
repúdio s. m. 1. act or effect of repudiating. 2. repudiation. 3. disclaiming. 4. abjuration. 5. denial.
repugnância s. f. 1. repugnance, repugnancy. 2. aversion, averseness, antipathy. 3. distaste, dislike, disgust. 4. reluctance, unwillingness. 5. distastefulness, abhorrence. 6. repulsion. 7. scruples.
ele sentiu ~ **pelo álcool** he loathed alcohol. **ele sentiu certa** ~ he felt a particular abomination. **ter** ~ **de** to be disgusted with. **trabalharam com** ~ they worked reluctantly.
repugnante adj. m. + f. 1. repugnant, repellent. 2. repulsive, disgusting. 3. shocking, unsavoury. 4. loathsome, abhorrent. 5. reluctant. 6. forbidding, shameful. 7. contrary to reason. ‖ ~**mente** adv. repugnantly, loathingly.
as suas maneiras são ~**s** his manners are repellent.
repugnar v. 1. to repugn. 2. to react, fight against. 3. to reject, repel. 4. to dislike, loathe. 5. to refuse to accept. 6. to be reluctant to. 7. to cause aversion, provoke antipathy. 8. to feel repugnance. 9. to be contrary or against. 10. to be incompatible with. 11. to oppose, resist.

o absurdo repugna à razão the absurd is contrary to reason; the absurd stands against reason.

repulsa, repulsão s. f. (pl. **-as, -ões**) 1. repulse, repulsion. 2. repellence. 3. refusal, rebuff. 4. propulsation. 5. opposition.

repulsar v. 1. to repulse. 2. to repel. 3. to drive away, beat back. 4. to rebuff, snub. 5. to refuse. 6. to reject.

repulsivo adj. 1. repulsive, repugnant, repelent. 2. ugly, vile, odious. 3. revolting, forbidding. 4. unpalatable, unsavoury. ‖ **-amente** adv. repulsively, offensively, unpalatably.

repulso s. m. repulse, repulsion. ‖ adj. repulsed, rejected, beaten back.

repulsor adj. repulsive, repellent.

repululação s. f. (pl. **-ões**) repullulation, act or fact of sprouting again.

repulular v. 1. to repullulate, sprout again. 2. to bud or sprout abundantly. 3. to be born again. 4. to multiply, increase.

repulverizar v. to pulverize again.

repurgação s. f. (pl. **-ões**) repurgation, new cleansing.

repurgar v. to repurge, cleanse or purify again.

repurificação s. f. (pl. **-ões**) repurification, purification of the highest degree.

repurificar v. to repurify, purify again, purify thoroughly.

reputação s. f. (pl. **-ões**) 1. reputation, repute. 2. fame, renown. 3. character, standing, name. 4. credit, creditability. 5. note, honour. 6. authority. **a boa** ~ soundness of character. **ele tem uma má** ~ he is ill-famed. **homem de** ~ a man of note, a man of renown. **uma mancha na sua** ~ a blot on his escutcheon.

reputado adj. reputed, renowned, putative.

reputar v. 1. to repute. 2. to deem, consider, 3. to regard, reckon. 4. to attribute a good name to, give a good credit to. 5. to evaluate, value at. 6. ~-**se** to consider o. s. as, rate o. s.

repuxada s. f. (Port., prov.) reprehension, rebuke, reproach, censure.

repuxão s. m. 1. act of driving or pulling back. 2. a hard pull.

repuxar v. 1. to pull violently. 2. to pull, jerk or draw back. 3. to stretch tightly, draw tightly. 4. to refine. 5. to spout, spurt, gush out. 6. to prop, shore up.

tubo repuxado sem costuras solid-drawn tube.

repuxo s. m. 1. fountain, water works, waterspout. 2. talus, slope given to the rampart of a wall. 3. buttress. 4. prop, stay, support. 5. recess. 6. the act of drawing (back). 7. recoil (of a gun). 8. (Braz.) excessive or hard work. **ele não agüenta o** ~ (fam.) he does not stand the strain.

requebém s. m. (pl. **-éns**) the back part of an oxcart.

requebrado adj. 1. languishing, lingering. 2. amorous, enamoured. 3. affected, prim. 4. (bot.) refracted.

requebrador s. m. 1. admirer, sweetheart, wooer. 2. waddler. ‖ adj. wooing, philandering, waddling.

requebrar v. 1. to walk in a languishing manner. 2. to court, woo, make love. 3. to use melodious, tender or amorous expressions. 4. to waddle, walk with a swaying motion.

requebro (ê) s. m. (pl. **requebros**) 1. languishing or voluptuous movement. 2. tender or amorous language. 3. warbling of the voice. 4. (mus.) trill. 5. dalliance, fondling.

requeijão s. m. (pl. **-ões**) cheesecurds, cottage cheese, curd.

requeima s. f. (Braz.) 1. act of burning or scorching (unbroken land). 2. parchedness, extreme dryness.

requeimação s. f. (pl. **-ões**) scorching, burning, parchedness, dryness.

requeimado adj. 1. completely burned. 2. parched, dry, scorched. 3. toasted, tanned. 4. aching, bruised. 5. hurt, sore, offended. 6. (Braz.) dark-spotted (hide of cattle).

requeimar v. 1. to burn thoroughly. 2. to tan, make brown (by exposure to sun or fire). 3. to parch, scorch. 4. to toast. 5. to have a sharp, pungent or tart flavour. 6. ~-**se:** a) to be resentful of, feel keenly about. b) to feel hurt or offended.

requeime s. m. 1. poignance, poignancy. 2. piquant flavour. 3. acridity.

requentado adj. 1. heated or warmed again (food). 2. (fig.) hashed over again, repeatedly discussed.

requentão s. m. (pl. **-ões**) (Braz.) coffee with brandy or cognac.

requentar v. 1. to heat or warm up again (food). 2. to suffer from the prolonged action of heat. 3. to taste of smoke or spoiled spices.

requeredor s. m. 1. petitioner, applicant. 2. procurator. 3. plaintiff. ‖ adj. petitioning, requesting.

requerente s. m. + f. 1. petitioner. 2. solicitant, applicant. 3. procurator. ‖ adj. petitioning, requesting, demanding.

reque-reque s. m. = **reco-reco.**

requerer v. 1. to request, ask or apply for. 2. to petition, appeal to. 3. to exact, demand. 4. to solicit, claim. 5. to need, require. 6. to merit, deserve. 7. to request the presence or help of. 8. to court, woo. 9. to order, summon. 10. to formulate a petition or application for. 11. ~-**se** to be in want of, be necessary, be required. **aquilo requer muito cuidado** it wants great care. **ele requereu uma patente** he filed a patent application. **requer-se muita atenção** a lot of attention is requested. ~ **desquite** to apply for separation or divorce.

requerido adj. requested, demanded, required, petitioned, requisite.

requerimento s. m. 1. formal petition. 2. solicitation, application. 3. demand, request. 4. requirement, requisition. 5. postulation. **ele dirigiu um** ~ **a** he put a petition to.

requerível adj. m. + f. (pl. **-íveis**) requirable, demandable.

requesta s. f. 1. solicitation, petition. 2. courtship. 3. challenge. 4. strife, quarrel, dispute.

requestador s. m. 1. suitor, wooer. 2. petitioner, applicant. ‖ adj. wooing, courting.

requestar v. 1. to solicit, request. 2. to court, woo. 3. to pretend. 4. to strive for, vie for (or with).

requesto s. m. 1. request, demand. 2. solicitation, petition. 3. quarrel.

réquiem s. m. Requiem, requiem: 1. a Mass for the dead. 2. musical setting for this mass.

requieto adj. very quiet, still, silent.

requietude s. f. quietude, calmness, silence.

requife s. m. trimming, lace for trimming or binding.

requinta s. f. 1. high-pitched clarinet. 2. viola or guitar with high-pitched strings. 3. m. musician playing these instruments.

requintado adj. 1. developed to the utmost degree or extent. 2. perfected, practised or exercised. 3. delicate, refined, polished. 4. highly cultured. 5. consummated, accomplished. 6. affected. **maneiras -as** politeness of manners. **gosto** ~ refined taste, cultivated taste.

requintar v. 1. to bring to the highest degree of perfection. 2. to refine, purify. 3. to make exquisite or very elegant. 4. to sublimate. 5. to perfect, make excellent. 6. to behave in a refined manner.

7. ~-se: a) to show affectation, act in an affected manner. b) to perfect o. s.

requinte s. m. 1. refinement, refinedness. 2. quintessence. 3. affectation. 4. elevation or perfection to the highest degree. 5. excessive scheming, cold-bloodedness.

requintista s. m. + f. musician who plays a high-pitched clarinet or guitar.

requisição s. f. (pl. -ões) 1. requisition. 2. solicitation. 3. requirement, demand, request. 4. exaction.

requisitar v. 1. to requisition. 2. to require, request. 3. to make a demand, solicit. 4. to claim rightfully. 5. to commandeer, press to military service. 6. to embargo.

requisito s. m. 1. requisite. 2. requirement. 3. qualification. 4. condition, indispensable quality, postulate. 5. legal requirement. ~ indispensável prerequisite. ~s teatrais stage properties.

requisitório s. m. requisitory: the prosecutor's formal demand for the punishment of the accused person. ‖ adj. requisitory.

rês s. f. 1. cattle for slaughter. 2. any quadruped bred for meat production. 3. livestock, cattle. ~ assada barbecue. ~ de gado ovino ovine.

rés adj. m. + f. close, level, even with. ‖ adv. at the base, close to, at the bottom.

resbalosa s. f. (S. Braz., sl.) knife.

resbordo s. m. (naut.) port.

rescaldado adj. 1. very hot or warm. 2. experienced, tried, tested. 3. disillusioned, disappointed.

rescaldamento s. m. act or process of rescalding, overheating.

rescaldar v. 1. to scald again. 2. to overheat.

rescaldeiro s. m. chafing-dish, chafer, warming-pan.

rescaldo s. m. 1. reflected heat from a furnace. 2. hot embers or cinders. 3. act of watering the smouldering ashes after a conflagration. 4. (fig.) remains. 5. rain of volcanic ashes. 6. chafing-dish, chafer, warming-pan.

rescindimento s. m. abrogation, annulment, rescission.

rescindir v. 1. to break, sever. 2. to dissolve, rescind. 3. to annul, cancel, abrogate. 4. to repeal. 5. to break off, cut off, make void. 6. to invalidate, render of no value. ele rescindiu o contrato he got off the contract.

rescindível adj. m. + f. (pl. -íveis) rescissible, rescindable, annullable, repealable.

rescisão (I) s. f. (pl. -ões) 1. rescission, abrogation. 2. annulment. 3. repeal. 4. cancellation. 5. interruption, break, suspension. prazo de ~ period of notice.

rescisão (II) s. f. (pl. -ões) (jur.) revocation, annulling, rescission.

rescisório adj. rescissory, revoking, annulling.

rescrever v. to rescribe, write again, write back.

rescrição s. f. (pl. -ões) written money order; cheque.

rescrito s. m. rescript: 1. (eccl.) official written answer of the Pope concerning theological questions. 2. official or authoritative reply. 3. act of rewriting. ‖ adj. rewritten, rescript. ~ de revisão de processo (jur.) writ of error.

rés-do-chão s. m. downstairs, ground floor.

resedá s. m., **reseda** f. 1. (bot.) reseda, mignonette. 2. flower of this plant. 3. perfume made from this flower.

resedá-amarelo s. m. (pl. resedás-amarelos) (bot.) Brazil thryallis.

resedácea s. f. a plant of the family Resedaceae.

resedáceo adj. (bot.) resedaceous.

resedal s. m. (pl. -ais) 1. plot of resedas, ground planted with resedas. 2. (bot.) henna (Lawsonia inermis).

resenha s. f. 1. review, reviewal. 2. detailed description or report. 3. summary, abridgement, digest. 4. counting, enumeration. 5. inventory, list. ele apresentou uma ~ dos acontecimentos he submitted an abstract of the events.

resenhar v. 1. to write a detailed report. 2. to make a list or inventory of. 3. to enumerate, recount. 4. to specify.

resenho s. m. 1. examination of the characteristic qualities of a horse (in order to distinguish it from others). 2. mark, distinguishing sign (usually on the left leg of a horse).

reserva s. f. 1. act of reserving. 2. reservation, reservedness. 3. restriction, restraint. 4. store, stock. 5. reserve fund, nest egg, reserve. 6. shyness, coyness. 7. unapproachableness, reticence. 8. privacy. 9. (mil.) reserve troops, reservists. 10. discretion, discreetness. 11. substitute. 12. offishness, stand-offishness, distance. 13. margin. 14. dissimulation. 15. caution, circumspection. 16. extra supply, iron ration. 17. (N. Braz.) a fenced pasture. 18. continence.
~ de passagens booking of tickets. ~ florestal forestal reserve (plate F 4). ~ monetária cash-reserve. ~ natural natural reservation; State or National Park. âncora de ~ spare anchor. ele falou com ~ he spoke reservedly. ele o comprou sob ~ he bought it on approval. ele tem sempre algum dinheiro de ~ he always has some money in store. eles dão sem ~ they give freely. esta soma é de ~ this sum is tied up. fundo de ~ reserve fund. meter de ~ to reserve, store. ração de ~ iron ration. sem ~ without reserve. ter em ~ to have in reserve. uma peça de ~ a spare part.

reservação s. f. (pl. -ões) reservation, act of reserving, limitation.

reservado s. m. private booth, compartment, box (in a restaurant, theatre, etc.). ‖ adj. 1. reserved. 2. private, particular. 3. secret, secretive, confidential. 4. cautious, circumspect. 5. aloof, reticent. 6. unapproachable, undemonstrative, uncommunicative. 7. resentful, spiteful, vindictive. 8. cold, stiff, unbending. 9. unsociable, stand-offish. 10. chaste, self-contained. ‖ -amente adv. reservedly, unsociably, unapproachably, aloofly, tête-à-tête, secretively.
~ de imprensa press box. lugar ~ reserved seat. não ~ unreserved. território ~ reservation.

reservador s. m. reserver, preserver. ‖ adj. reserving.

reservar v. 1. to reserve, set apart. 2. to retain, keep. 3. to put away, store up. 4. to make a secret of. 5. to save, set by. 6. to withhold. 7. to use sparingly. 8. to let alone, destine for. 9. to defend, preserve. 10. ~-se: a) to be reserved. b) to safeguard, set aside for.
~ para um fim determinado to appropriate. ~ um lugar to book a place. esta casa de campo foi reservada para o filho mais moço this country house has been set apart for the youngest son. reservei para mim a próxima dança com ela I made sure of her for the next dance. reservamo-nos o direito de we reserve ourselves the right to. reservamos nossas energias we reserved our energies.

reservativo adj. reservative, reserving, saving.

reservatório s. m. 1. reservoir, tank (plates C 11, T 2). 2. deposit, store. 3. vessel, receiver. ‖ adj. reservatory, reservative.
~ de água water tank (plate T 2). ~ de ar air vessel. ~ de óleo oil chamber, oil sump.

reservista s. m. reservist, reserve, member of the military reserves.

reservo (ê) s. m. (pl. **reservos**) 1. (N. Braz.) big, well-kept pasture around the manor of sugar plantations. 2. = **reserva.**

resfolegado adj. quiet, calm, untroubled.

resfolegadouro s. m. air vent, breathing hole.

resfolegar, resfolgar v. 1. to breathe. 2. to pant, puff, gasp for breath. 3. to relax, repose, respite. 4. to spout, spurt. 5. to expel, eject. 6. to wheeze, puff. 7. (pop.) snort.

o trem partiu resfolegando the train puffed out of the station.

resfôlego, resfolgo s. m. 1. respiration, breathing. 2. exhalation. 3. panting, gasp. 4. (pop.) snort.

resfriadeira s. f. 1. cooling place, coolhouse (in sugar mills). 2. (N. Braz.) earthen pitcher (used to keep the water cool).

resfriado s. m. (med.) cold, catarrh. ‖ adj. 1. cold, chilly. 2. chilled, iced, frozen. 3. suffering from a cold. 4. roupy, hoarse.

ele está ~ he has a cold. **no mínimo peguei um ~!** if I haven't caught a cold!

resfriador s. m. cooling vessel, cooler, refrigerator. ‖ adj. cooling.

resfriadouro s. m. 1. cooling place. 2. cooler, refrigerator.

resfriamento s. m. 1. act or process of cooling. 2. cooling. 3. (med.) cold, chill, catarrh. 4. watering place for cattle.

resfriar v. 1. to cool again. 2. to (make) cool, freeze. 3. to grow cold, become chilly. 4. (med.) to catch a cold. 5. to discourage, dishearten. 6. to reduce ardour or enthusiasm. 7. to diminish, lessen (activity, interest, etc.). 8. to abate, relent. 9. to grow lukewarm.

~ por meio de água to water-cool.

resgatador s. m. ransomer, redeemer, releaser. ‖ adj. ransoming, redeeming, releasing, rescuing.

resgatar v. 1. to ransom. 2. to free from captivity. 3. to redeem, release, rescue. 4. to buy off. 5. to pay off. 6. to atone, purge. 7. to emancipate. 8. to accomplish, fulfill. 9. to recover. 10. **~-se:** a) to redeem o. s. b) to free o. s. from captivity.

não resgatado unredeemed. **~am o anel** they took the ring out of pawn. **~am a letra de câmbio** they discharged the bill of exchange.

resgatável adj. m. + f. (pl. **-áveis**) ransomable, redeemable, retrievable.

resgate s. m. 1. ransom. 2. redemption, deliverance. 3. liberation, discharge. 4. quittance. 5. price paid for the liberation of a prisoner.

~ de estadia (naut.) dispatch money. **sem ~** ransomless.

resguardado adj. cautious, circumspect, shielded, protected, covered.

resguardar v. 1. to guard, protect. 2. to defend. 3. to shelter, shield. 4. to save. 5. to wrap up warmly, protect against the cold. 6. to observe, look at, watch. 7. to accomplish, fulfill. 8. **~-se:** a) to defend or protect o. s. b) to safeguard o. s. against.

resguardo s. m. 1. protection. 2. guard, watch. 3. shield, shelter, guard (plate R 8). 4. diet. 5. care, caution, circumspection. 6. prudence. 7. decency, seemliness, propriety. 8. defense. 9. secret, secrecy. 10. vigilance, watchfulness.

dar ~ a to protect somebody from. **ter de ~** to have in store.

residência s. f. 1. residence, residency. 2. dwelling, home, abode. 3. place, seat. 4. address. 5. railroad division. 6. domicile.

~ paroquial rectory. **~ temporária** lodge. **~ permanente** permanent abode. **ter ~ fixa** to be stationary.

residencial s. m. + f. (pl. **-iais**) residential, residentiary.

bairro ~ residential quarters.

residente s. m. + f. resident, diplomatic agent. ‖ adj. m. + f. resident, residential, residentiary.

residir v. 1. to reside. 2. to live, dwell. 3. to inhabit, stay. 4. to domicile, settle.

residual adj. m. + f. (pl. **-uais**) 1. residual, residuary. 2. remaining, left over. 3. remanent.

residuário adj. residuary, of the nature of a residuary.

resíduo s. m. 1. residue. 2. remainder, rest, remnant. 3. (chem.) radical. 4. refuse, rubbish, waste. 5. pickings, tailings. 6. lees, grounds, dreg. 7. ashes. 8. residuum, leavings. 9. **~s** pl. atavistic tendencies in modern thought.

~s de combustão residue of combustion. **~ insolúvel** insoluble residue.

resignação s. f. (pl. **-ões**) 1. resignation, resignment. 2. voluntary renunciation, abnegation. 3. endurance, patience. 4. relinquishment. 5. forbearance, longanimity.

~ à vontade de Deus full submission to God's will. **carregaram a cruz com ~** they bore their cross philosophically.

resignado adj. resigned, acquiescent, uncomplaining, submissive. ‖ **-amente** adv. resignedly, patiently, uncomplainingly.

resignante s. m. + f. resigner, surrenderer, abdicator. ‖ adj. resigning, abdicating, renouncing.

resignar v. 1. to resign. 2. to give up, surrender. 3. to abdicate. 4. to renounce, withdraw from. 5. **~-se** to be resigned, resign or adjust o. s. to.

resignatário s. m. resigner. ‖ adj. resigning, renouncing.

resignável adj. m. + f. (pl. **-áveis**) that may be resigned.

resilição s. f. (pl. **-ões**) 1. resiliation. 2. rescission, annulment. 3. cancelling. 4. abrogation.

a ~ de um contrato rescission of a contract.

resiliência s. f. resiliency, resilience, elasticity.

resiliente adj. m. + f. resilient, rebounding, elastic.

resilir v. to rescind, annul, cancel, make void, invalidate.

resina s. f. resin, rosin, gum: organic substance secreted by pines, firs and similar trees.

~ aromática balm, balsam. **~ de copaíba** copaiba. **~ fóssil** fossil resin. **~ sintética** resinoid.

resinado adj. resinous, resinaceous.

resinagem s. f. (pl. **-ens**) 1. extraction of resin. 2. application of resin. 3. treatment with resin. 4. resinification.

resina-goma s. f. (pl. **resinas-goma**) gum resin.

resinar v. 1. to extract resin. 2. to resin, apply resin, coat with resin. 3. to treat with resin. 4. to mix with resin.

resinento adj. resinous, resiny, resinaceous.

resinificar v. 1. to resinify. 2. to convert into or treat with resin. 3. to give a resinous or gummy appearance to.

resiniforme adj. m. + f. resiniform, resinoid.

resinóide adj. m. + f. resinoid, resinlike.

resinoso adj. resinous, resiny, rosiny.

resipiscência s. f. 1. resipiscence, resipiscency. 2. repentance. 3. contrition. 4. change of heart, reformation.

resistência s. f. 1. resistance, act or effect of resisting. 2. opposition. 3. obstacle, hindrance. 4. reaction. 5. moment(um) of inertia. 6. stubbornness, renitence, recalcitrance. 7. strength, solidity, solidness. 8. force, strength. 9. toughness. 10. staying power, stamina, endurance. 11. fortitude. 12. (med.) tolerance. 13. electrical resistance. 14. defensive fight, defense. 15. (phys.) nonconductibility.

~ ao avanço drag. ~ ao frio tolerance for cold. ~ à pressão strength of compression. ~ à ruptura strength of rupture, breaking strain. ~ à tração tensile strength. ~ elétrica true (or ohmic) resistance. ~ física hardness. ~ passiva passive resistance. ~ política secreta underground resistance. bobina de ~ resistance coil. capacidade de ~ staying power. falta de ~ nonresistance. opuseram--nos ~ we were resisted. prova de ~ strength testing. sem ~ unresisted, unopposed.
resistente adj. m. + f. 1. resistant. 2. hardy, strong, tough. 3. firm, stable. 4. solid. 5. stubborn. 6. staminal. 7. (med.) tolerant. 8. obstinate, refractory. || ~mente adv. resistantly, tolerantly.
~ às intempéries weatherproof. ~ para serviços pesados for hard wear. não ~ non-resistant. tornar ~ às intempéries to weatherproof.
resistibilidade s. f. resistlbility, power of resistance.
resistir v. 1. to resist, withstand. 2. not to yield or give in. 3. to oppose. 4. to defend, offer resistance, ward off, face. 5. not to succumb, hold out, stand fast. 6. to subsist. 7. to endure, last. 8. to conserve, preserve.
~ abertamente to defy. ~ à prova to stand the test, stand fire. ~ à supremacia to bear up against odds. ~ à tempestade to weather the storm. ~ até o fim to die in the last ditch. ele resiste à tentação he is superior to temptation. os muros ~am ao impacto the walls stood the shock.
resistível adj. m. + f. (pl. -íveis) resistible, faceable.
resistividade s. f. resistivity, capacity for resistance.
resistor s. m. (electr.) resistor.
reslumbrar v. to shine through.
resma s. f. ream: 20 quires or 500 sheets of paper.
resmelengar v. (N. Braz.) to appear, show o. s.
resmelengo s. m. (N. Braz.) grumbler. || adj. grumbling, grouchy, cantankerous.
resmuda s. f. (pop.) modification, change, inverted order.
resmungão s. m. (pl. -ões) (f. resmungona) grumbler, grouch, cantankerous person. || adj. grumbling, cantankerous.
resmungar, resmonear v. 1. to mutter, mumble. 2. to grumble. 3. to murmur. 4. to growl, nag. 5. to croak, grouse, grunt.
~ contra to cry against. sem ~ ungrudging.
resmungo s. m. 1. mutter, mumble. 2. gripe, nagging. 3. grumble, grouch.
reso s. m. (zool.) rhesus, rhesus monkey.
resolubilidade s. f. resolubility, resolubleness, resolvability.
resolução s. f. (pl. -ões) 1. resolution. 2. deliberation, decision. 3. purpose, will, determinateness. 4. intention, determination, decision. 5. boldness, courage. 6. conclusion, solution, resolve. 7. transformation. 8. loosening of the bowels. 9. (med.) dissolving.
tomar uma ~ to make up one's mind.
resolutivo s. m. 1. (med.) resolutive. 2. resolvent. || adj. resolutive, dissolvent, resolvent.
resoluto adj. 1. resolute. 2. courageous, dauntless. 3. decided, resolved, determined. 4. unwavering, unhesitating, unswerving. 5. purposeful, firm, intent on. 6. stubborn, unyielding. || -amente adv. 1. resolutely, resolvedly. 2. determinedly, decidedly. 3. courageously, pluckily. 4. stubbornly.
ele avançou -amente he advanced resolutely, went through thick and thin.
resolutório adj. resolutory, explanatory, serving to resolve.
resolúvel adj. m. + f. (pl. -úveis) resoluble, resolvable.
resolvente s. m. 1. (med.) resolvent. 2. solvent. || adj. m. + f. resolvent.

resolver v. 1. to resolve. 2. to decide, solve. 3. to conclude, determine. 4. to liquidate, settle. 5. to dissolve, undo. 6. to separate, decompose. 7. to explain, clear up. 8. to transform. 9. to reduce to. 10. to determine. 11. ~-se: a) to be reduced to, be divided into (composite elements). b) to come to a conclusion. c) to be ready to. d) to dissolve gradually and imperceptibly. e) to consist of, be constituted of. f) to change into, transform into.
~ um problema to solve a problem. ~ uma dificuldade to solve or settle a difficulty. ele hesitava mas eu consegui resolvê-lo he hesitated but I happened to induce him to a decision. ele resolveu o caso he settled the affair, cut the knot. eles ~am tudo they got things done. os perigos hão de ~-se the dangers will certainly disappear. tentaram ~ o negócio they tackled the job.
resolvido adj. 1. resolved, settled. 2. decided, determined. 3. resolute, firm, bent on, set. 4. solved.
estou ~ a ir I am determined to go.
resolvível adj. m. + f. (pl. -íveis) resolvable, solvable.
respaldar (I) s. m. back of a chair.
respaldar (II) v. 1. to smooth down, polish. 2. to make flat or level. 3. to repair a torn sheet of paper.
respaldo s. m. 1. act of smoothing down. 2. back of a chair. 3. backrest of a carriage seat. 4. the candles and the crucifix of an altar. 5. sore caused by the saddle (on the back of horses).
respançadura s. f., respançamento m. 1. erasing, erasure. 2. scraping, rasping.
respançar v. to erase, rub out, scrape off.
respe s. m. (Braz., fam.) censure, reproach, upbraiding.
respectivo, respetivo adj. 1. respective, relating to. 2. concerning. 3. particular, individual. 4. own, peculiar. || -amente adv. respectively, particularly, relatively.
respeitabilidade s. f. respectability, respectableness, dignity, reputability, reputableness, venerability.
respeitado adj. respected, considered, worthy, esteemed.
respeitador s. m. respecter. || adj. respecting, worshipful, respectful.
respeitante adj. m. + f. respective, concerning, referring to, relating to.
respeitar v. 1. to respect, esteem. 2. to treat respectfully. 3. to honour, venerate. 4. to be afraid of, fear, dread. 5. to consider, regard, hold in esteem. 6. to comply with, fulfill. 7. to heed, mind, take care of. 8. to preserve, guard, shield (from evil, damage, etc.). 9. to refer to, have relation to. 10. ~-se: a) to be respected, command respect. b) to respect o. s. 11. to spare.
~ alguém profundamente to hold s. o. in awe. ~emos o contrato we'll honour the contract. ele não respeita nada he stops at nothing. respeitamos sua arte we paid tribute to his art. respeite seu melindre spare her blushes.
respeitável adj. m. + f. (pl. -áveis) 1. respectable, deserving respect. 2. venerable, estimable. 3. worthy, reputable. 4. formidable, imposing. 5. important. 6. decent, proper. 7. creditable. 8. worshipful. || respeitavelmente adv. respectably, reputably, venerably.
respeito s. m. 1. respect, regard, esteem. 2. consideration, considerateness. 3. reverence, veneration. 4. fear, dread. 5. submission, deference. 6. point of view, aspect. 7. honour, worship. 8. importance. 9. bearing, relation. 10. ~s pl. compliments.
a ~ de regarding, in point of, concerning, anent to. a esse ~ nada há a dizer in this respect there is nothing to be said. a nenhum ~ in no respect at

all. **a que ~?** what for? **a todos os ~s** in all aspects, in every respect. **com ~ àquela informação** to touching that information. **com o devido ~** with all due respect, with due subjection to. **com ~ ao tópico** with an eye to this topic. **dizer ~ a** to concern. **em qualquer ~** upon all accounts. **falta de ~** disrespect, impoliteness. **merecedor de ~** awe-commanding, awful. **não ter ~ por** to pay no attention to. **o devido ~** the due respect. **por meu ~** on my account. **por ~ a** in duty to, out of respect for. **que diz ~** as regards, regarding. **que impõe ~** awe-commanding, awe-inspiring. **sua atitude com ~ à guerra** your attitude towards war.

respeitoso adj. 1. respectful, deferential. 2. dutiful, submissive. 3. reverential. ‖ **-amente** adv. respectfully, dutifully, regardfully.

respiga s. f. 1. (act of) gleaning. 2. (carp.) mortise.

respigadeira s. f. 1. gleaning woman. 2. (carp.) mortising machine. ‖ adj. f. gleaning, picking up, gathering.

respigador s. m. gleaner (plate C 16). ‖ adj. gleaning, picking up.

respigadura s. f. act of gleaning, gathering, picking up.

respigão s. m. (pl. **-ões**) hangnail.

respigar v. 1. to glean, pick up ears of corn (left on the field after the harvest). 2. to gather leftover spikes of grain. 3. (fig.) to gather or collect at random. 4. to collect, compile.

respingador s. m. recalcitrant or obstinate person, stubborn fellow. ‖ adj. obstinate, recalcitrant, stubborn.

respingão s. m. (pl. **-ões**) (f. **-ona**) stubbornly rebellious or obstinate person. ‖ adj. obstinate, rebellious, recalcitrant.

respingar (I) v. 1. to sprinkle, spray (with water). 2. to sparkle, scintillate. 3. to crackle.

respingar (II) v. 1. to oppose, resist. 2. to recalcitrate 3. to grumble, find fault with. 4. to answer reluctantly or grumblingly. 5. to kick back, react violently.

respingo s. m. 1. aspersion, spatter. 2. sparkling. 3. crackling. 4. a kicking back. 5. opposition, resistance.

respirabilidade s. f. respirability, breathableness.

respiração s. f. (pl. **-ões**) 1. (physiol.) respiration, act or effect or breathing. 2. breath. 3. one inspiration and expiration.

~ ofegante wheeze. **~ profunda** fetching of breath, fetch. **falta de ~** shortness of breath. **suspensão da ~** (med.) apnea.

respirador s. m. respirator, inspirator. ‖ adj. breathing.

respiradouro s. m. air-hole, vent, breather, air-drain.

respiramento s. m. act and process of breathing, respiration.

respirar v. 1. to breathe. 2. to inhale and exhale, respire. 3. (fig.) to be, live. 4. to appear, manifest itself. 5. to rest, repose. 6. to have a breathing spell, respite. 7. to blow. 8. to absorb and expel (air). 9. to disclose, reveal. 10. to manifest one's wishes. 11. to feed or live on.

~ de alívio to take a breath. **ele pôde ~ novamente** he got his second wind. **ele respirou profundamente** he fetched a deep breath. **meu serviço não me deixa ~** my business gives me no breathing time. **naquela casa tudo respira alegria** in that home everything breathes joy. **sem ~** (fig.) incessantly.

respiratório adj. respiratory.

doença das vias -as respiratory disease.

respirável adj. m. + f. (pl. **-áveis**) respirable, breathable.

respiro s. m. 1. respiration, act of breathing, breath. 2. (fig.) rest, breathing spell. 3. respite (granted for payment of a debt). 4. air-hole, vent, air-drain.

resplandecência s. f. resplendence, resplendency, brilliance, flamboyancy.

resplandecente adj. m. + f. 1. resplendent. 2. bright, shining, brilliant. 3. refulgent, fulgent. 4. lucid, sheeny, relucent. 5. flaring, blazing. 6. effulgent, lustrous. ‖ **~mente** adv. resplendently.

resplandecer, resplendecer, resplender v. 1. to shine, glitter, sparkle. 2. to emblaze, flare resplendently. 3. to manifest itself with brilliancy. 4. to distinguish o. s., become notable. 5. to reflect the brilliancy or splendour of, reflect lustrously.

resplendência s. f. resplendence, resplendency, brilliance, splendour.

resplendente adj. m. + f. 1. resplendent. 2. bright, shining, brilliant.

resplêndido adj. very splendid, resplendent, dazzlingly bright.

resplendor s. m. 1. resplendence, resplendency. 2. splendour. 3. brightness, brilliancy. 4. effulgence, radiance, fulgor. 5. aureole, halo. 6. glory, nimbus. 7. fame, renown.

o sol apareceu com ~ the sun appeared resplendently.

resplendoroso adj. splendorous, magnificent, glorious.

respondão s. m. (pl. **-ões**) (f. **-ona**) 1. backbiter. 2. one who gives rude or insolent answers. 3. bully, coarse or churlish fellow. ‖ adj. rude, impolite, churlish, backbiting, snappish, soucy.

respondedor s. m. 1. answerer, replier. 2. = **respondão**. ‖ adj. 1. answering, replying. 2. rude, impolite. 3. snappish.

respondência s. f. 1. respondence, respondency. 2. correspondence, communication. 3. connections, contacts, social relations.

respondente s. m. + f. (jur.) respondent, defendant. ‖ adj. respondent.

responder v. 1. to respond, reply, answer. 2. to communicate, write in answer to. 3. to give an answer, answer back, answer in a churlish or uncivil manner. 4. to react, act in response to. 5. to retort, object. 6. to correspond. 7. to be equivalent. 8. to be in harmony with. 9. to face, come face to face. 10. to be opposed, contrary to. 11. to be agreeable to. 12. **~-se** to correspond with. 13. to be responsible for, answer for.

~ por to account for, vouch for. **é favor ~ pela volta do correio aéreo** please, reply by return of air mail. **ele respondeu com insolência** he answered back. **ele responde pela segurança dela** he is responsible for her security. **ele respondeu ao meu olhar** he stared back at me. **não me responda mal!** don't bandy words with me. **não responda!** do not answer back, don't answer! **responde ao louco segundo sua loucura** answer a fool according to his folly.

respondido adj. answered, replied, returned, settled.

respondível adj. m. + f. (pl. **-íveis**) answerable, accountable, liable.

responsabilidade s. f. 1. responsibility, responsibleness. 2. duty, trust. 3. answerableness, accountability. 4. charge, liability, burden.

ele declinou a ~ he refuted any liability. **ele tem grande ~** he bears heavy responsibility. **ele tem uma posição de ~** he has a post of consequence. **lançar a ~ sobre o vizinho** to put the blame at the neighbour's door. **não assumo a ~ por ele** I wash my hands of him. **~ moral** responsibility, moral duty.

responsabilizar v. 1. to make or consider responsible. 2. to impute or ascribe responsibility to. 3. to blame, brand as. 4. to become responsible for, be answerable for, vouch for.

eu me responsabilizo pela sua honestidade I warrant him honest. **não podemos responsabilizá-lo pelo prejuízo** we cannot make him liable for the damage.

responsar v. 1. (eccl.): a) to pray responsories. b) to say or sing in reply (to the priest's prayer). 2. to speak evil of, backbite. 3. to murmur. 4. to ask for or request s. th.

responsável s. m. + f. (pl. **-áveis**) responsible person, leader, manager, voucher. ‖ adj. responsible, answerable, accountable, liable, chargeable. ‖ **responsavelmente** adv. responsibly, answerably.

ele é o ~ do jornal he is the chief editor of the paper. **ele é ~ por** he is liable for. **ele foi considerado ~** he got the blame. **ser ~ por** to be answerable for.

responsivo adj. 1. that includes an answer. 2. responsive, responsory. 3. answerable. 4. answering, replying.

eles são mutuamente ~s they are corresponsive.

responso s. m. 1. (eccl.): a) antiphon, antiphony. b) response, responsory. 2. (fam.) upbraiding, scolding. 3. (pop.) murmuring.

responsório s. m. (eccl.) responsory, many responses.

resposta s. f. 1. response, rejoinder. 2. answer, reply. 3. replication, repartee. 4. solution, conclusion. 5. (fenc.) riposte. 6. tirecracker, skyrocket.

~ ao pé da letra retort, literal answer. **~ engenhosa** repartee. **~ decisiva** final answer. **~ favorável** favourable reply. **~ malcriada** backchat, back talk. **~ negativa** refusal. **em ~ a sua carta de** in answer to your letter of. **sempre de ~ pronta** always ready with an answer. **ter a ~ na ponta da língua** to be quick on the draw. **uma criança não deve dar ~s** a child must not answer again.

respostada s. f. sharp or rude answer, severe reply, retort.

resquício s. m. 1. residue, remainder, rest. 2. vestige, trace, mark. 3. small fragments, tiny bits. 4. chink, crack. 5. leftovers.

ressaber v. 1. to know perfectly well. 2. to taste strongly of, have a strong flavour of. 3. to have a typical flavour which reminds us of. 4. to be aware of, have knowledge of.

ressabiado adj. 1. suspicious, distrustful. 2. timid, frightened, kittish. 3. sensitive, touchy, resentful.

ressabiar v. 1. to have a bad taste. 2. to become a bad taste. 3. to take offense, resent. 4. to be annoyed, feel keenly about.

ressabido adj. 1. well-known. 2. well-educated, erudite, learned. 3. very skilful, very clever, well-experienced.

ressábio s. m. 1. rancidity, unpleasant taste. 2. aftertaste. 3. vestige, trace, indicia. 4. resentment.

ressaca s. f. 1. surf, undertow (plate C 19). 2. flux and reflux. 3. small bay or harbour formed by the flux of the tide. 4. breakers. 5. (Braz.) hang-over, aftereffect of a spree. 6. disgust, displeasure.

hoje ele está com ~ today he is crapulent.

ressacado (I) s. m. drawee of a new bill of exchange or a return draft.

ressacado (II) adj. (Braz.) having a hang-over.

ressacar v. 1. to redraw, draw a new bill of exchange. 2. **~-se** to suffer from the aftereffect of a drunken carousal.

ressaco s. m. (Braz.) glade, clearing.

ressaibo s. m. 1. bad taste, rancidity. 2. after-taste. 3. (fig.) vestige, trace. 4. resentment, grudge. 5. unruliness (of beasts).

ressaio s. m. wide place in front of a house, public square.

ressair v. 1. to go out again. 2. to jut out, project, protrude. 3. to become bulky. 4. to distinguish o. s.

ressalgada s. f. (S. Braz.) a heap of salted meat ready for drying.

ressaltado adj. jutting out, salient.

ressaltar v. 1. to stick out, stand out. 2. to protrude, project. 3. to give prominence to, make noteworthy. 4. to rebound, spring back or again. 5. to distinguish o. s., become notable or famous. 6. to underscore. 7. to shine. 8. to show, appear. 9. to emphasize, point out.

ressalte s. m. 1. salience, projection. 2. jutting out, standing out. 3. prominence. 4. relief.

ressaltear v. 1. to reassault, assault again. 2. to bound or leap again, rebound. 3. to spring back repeatedly.

ressalto s. m. 1. jutting out, standing out. 2. resilience, resiliency. 3. salience, projection, shoulder (plates S 3, T 5). 4. bounce, rebound. 5. prominence, importance. 6. relief. 7. (tech.) tappet, cam.

ressalva s. f. 1. certificate of exemption from military service. 2. proviso, reservation. 3. exception. 4. (jur.) defeasance. 5. safety clause, safe-conduct, warrant of security. 6. special clause (of a contract). 7. errata note.

ressalvar v. 1. to make an exception, except. 2. to warrant safety or exemption. 3. to take exception from, grant a special reservation or proviso. 4. to caution, forewarn. 5. to safeguard, protect, hold free from danger or damage. 6. to correct, make errata notes. 7. to exempt, free, liberate. 8. **~-se** to offer apologies, excuse o. s.

ressaque (I) s. m. (com.) redraft, second draft or copy, return draft.

ressaque (II) s. m. (Port., prov.) = **ressaca.**

ressarcido adj. compensated, indemnified, repaired.

ressarcimento s. m. 1. act or effect of compensating. 2. indemnification. 3. compensation, indemnity. 4. amends. 5. reparation.

ressarcir v. 1. to indemnify, reimburse. 2. to compensate. 3. to make amends for, make good. 4. to repair, make again, renew.

ressaudar v. 1. to resalute, return a salutation. 2. to greet again. 3. to greet one another.

ressecado adj. dry, parched, baked.

resseção, ressecção s. f. (pl. **-ões**) (surg.) resection. **sujeitar à ~** (surg.) to undergo a resection.

ressecar (I) v. (surg.) to cut or pare away, resect.

ressecar (II) v. 1. to dry again, dry up. 2. to exsiccate, dry thoroughly. 3. to subject to a process of evaporation. 4. **~-se** to become very dry or concentrated, parch.

resseco (ê) adj. very dry, parched.

ressegar v. to mow again, reap again.

ressegurar v. 1. to reinsure, insure again. 2. to reassure.

resseguro s. m. 1. reinsurance. 2. reassurance. ‖ adj. reinsured.

resselar v. to seal again, put a second seal on, reseal.

ressemeadura s. f. act or process of sowing a second time.

ressemear v. to resow, sow a second time, sow again.

ressentido adj. 1. resentful. 2. hurt, offended. 3. easily offended. 4. (pop.) slightly rotted, beginning to decay (said of fruits).

ressentimento s. m. 1. resentment. 2. umbrage, offense. 3. animosity, ranco(u)r. 4. pique, dudgeon.

com ~ resentingly. **ele não conserva qualquer ~** he does not bear any grudge. **sem ~** unresented.

ressentir v. 1. to feel again, feel anew. 2. to resent, feel keenly about. 3. to take offense, be resentful of. 4. to warn, caution. 5. to take notice, perceive

6. to become excited or angry. 7. to feel the effect of, suffer under the consequences of. 8. ~-se: a) to regard o.s. offended. b) to show one's resentment. c) to be aware of an insult.
ela ressentiu-se com ele she took a pique against him. **ela ressentiu-se de** she took umbrage at. **ele ressente-se muito disso** he takes it very much to heart, he harbours a grudge for it.
ressequido adj. 1. parched, dried up. 2. withered, shrivelled.
ele tem lábios ~s he has parched lips.
ressequir v. 1. to dry up, desiccate. 2. to wither, shrivel. 3. to become dry.
resserenar v. 1. to make very quiet. 2. to become calm again. 3. to tranquilize, render serene or peaceful. 4. ~-se to grow calm, quiet down, subside.
ressereno adj. very serene, extremely calm or quiet, quieted, stilled.
resservir v. to serve again, serve repeatedly.
ressicação s. f. (pl. -ões) extreme dryness, desiccation.
ressicar v. 1. to dry up. 2. to dry again. 3. to become exceedingly dry or concentrated. 4. to wither, shrivel.
ressoador s. m. resonator, device for giving resonance. ‖ adj. resounding.
ressoante adj. m. + f. 1. resonant, resounding. 2. vibrant. 3. ringing, clangorous. ‖ ~mente adv. resoundingly, resonantly.
ele tem uma voz ~ he has a throaty voice.
ressoar v. 1. to tune, intone. 2. to resound, reverberate. 3. (fig.) to play, sing. 4. to echo, re-echo. 5. to ring, peal, clang. 6. to sound again. 7. to resonate, vibrate.
as montanhas ~am the mountains rang again. **o barulho ainda ressoa nos meus ouvidos** my ears still ring with the clamour. **os sinos ~am ominosamente** the bells knelled ominously. **o trovão ressoou mais alto que as nossas vozes** the thunder outroared our voices.
ressobrar v. 1. to be left over again. 2. to superabound, abound excessively. 3. to be over and above.
ressoca s. f. (Braz.) the second cutting and harvesting of sugar-cane.
ressolana s. f. scorching sunshine, noonday heat, excessive heat.
ressoldar v. to resolder, reweld, weld again.
ressolhador adj. (S. Braz.) breathing hoarsely, wheezing (said of cattle and horses).
ressolhar v. 1. to suffer from the eyes in consequence of an excessive exposure to strong sunlight. 2. to wheeze, breathe with an audible piping or whistling (cattle, horses).
ressolto adj. dissolved, disintegrated, decomposed, liquidated.
ressonadela s. f. 1. act of resounding. 2. snoring. 3. resounding, chiming. 4. sleep, slumber.
ressonador s. m. 1. resounder, resonator. 2. snorter. ‖ adj. resounding.
ressonância s. f. resonance: 1. act of resounding. 2. quality of being resonant. 3. resounding, echo. 4. (phys.) phenomenon of intensification and enrichment of sound which occurs when the frequencies of the applied force and of the vibrating body are identical. 5. vibration, reflection of sonorous waves.
ressonante adj. m. + f. resonant, resounding, consonant. ‖ ~mente adv. resonantly.
ressonar v. 1. to resound. 2. to re-echo, reverberate. 3. to ring, peal, chime. 4. to snore, breathe heavily. 5. (fig.) to sleep.
ressono s. m. long and deep sleep.

ressoprar v. to blow again.
ressorção s. f. (pl. -ões) 1. resorption, reabsorption, transpiration. 3. (med.) resudation.
ressorver v. to absorb again, resorb, reabsorb.
ressuar v. to sweat abundantly.
ressudação s. f. (pl. -ões) 1. distillation. 2. perspiration, transpiration. 3. (med.) resudation.
ressudar v. 1. to distil(l). 2. to perspire, transpire, sweat. 3. to perspire or sweat again. 4. to exude. 5. to percolate.
ressulcar v. to plough or furrow again, groove again.
ressumar, ressumbrar v. 1. to drip, trickle, ooze through. 2. to pour out, shed. 3. to distil. 4. to reveal, show, manifest. 5. to let see, make evident. 6. to perspire, transpire. 7. to percolate. 8. to become clear or evident.
ressunção s. f. (pl. -ões) 1. act or effect of reassuming. 2. resumption. 3. reintegration, restoration. 4. new display or exposition.
ressupinação s. f. (pl. -ões) (bot.) resupination, inverted position.
ressupinado adj. (bot.) resupinate, inverted in position.
ressupinar v. to lie on the back with the face turned upwards, take a resupine position.
ressupino adj. 1. turned upwards. 2. lying on the back with the face turned upward. 3. (bot.) resupinate, inverted in position. 4. inclined backwards. 5. reversed, inverted.
ressurgente adj. m. + f. resurgent, rising again, reviving.
ressurgido adj. resuscitated, revived, renewed, resurrected.
ressurgimento s. m. resuscitation, resurgence, renascence.
ressurgir v. 1. to emerge again. 2. to resurge, rise again. 3. to be resurrected. 4. to come to life again, revive, resuscitate. 5. to reappear, manifest itself again.
ressurreição s. f. (pl. -ões) 1. act of re-emerging. 2. resurrection, resuscitation. 3. (fam.) extraordinary and unexpected cure. 4. (fig.) renovation, renewal. 5. (eccl.) Resurrection, feast of Resurrection. 6. resurgence, rising.
ressurreicionista s. m. + f. resurrectionist.
ressurtir v. 1. to jump into the air, leap, bounce up. 2. to stand or get up impetuously. 3. to appear, emerge, manifest itself.
ressuscitação s. f. (pl. -ões) 1. resuscitation, resurrection. 2. reappearance.
ressuscitado s. m. resuscitated or revived person. ‖ adj. resuscitated.
ressuscitador s. m. resuscitator, one who brings to life again, reviver. ‖ adj. resuscitating, reviving, renewing, resuscitative.
ressuscitar v. 1. to cause to arise or reappear. 2. to bring to life again, raise from the dead. 3. to revive, reanimate. 4. to renew, renovate. 5. to reproduce, make over again. 6. to resuscitate, resurrect, resurge. 7. (fam.) to escape from a great danger.
~ a memória de grandes homens to revive the memory of great men. **~ dos mortos** to rise from the dead.
resuscitável adj. m. + f. (pl. -áveis) resuscitable.
restabelecer v. 1. to establish again, re-establish. 2. to return, replace, bring back to the original state or condition. 3. to restore, revive. 4. to renew, renovate. 5. to repair, reconstruct, rebuild, reform. 6. to create, call into existence. 7. ~-se to recover one's health, be restored to health. 8. to retrieve, redress. 9. to reinstate, reinact.
~ o equilíbrio to redress the balance. **~-se de uma doença** to convalesce, recover from an illness.

R5

RESTAURANTE

Labels in image: Toldo, Torneira de cerveja, Porta giratória, Bar, Garçonete, Hóspedes no terraço, Cozinheiro-chefe, Garção de bar, Vestiário, Guardadora de roupa, Gancho, Janela de serviço, Cabide, Mensageira, Cozinheira, Bar, Balcão do bar, Cadeira de bar, Garção, Copos, Porteiro, Hóspede, Pratos, Bandeja, Canudo, Carrinho de chá, Cardápio, Garção-chefe, Sofá, Cálice, Cinzeiro, Copo alto, Lista de vinhos, Bilha, Cadeira, Pratinho, Pires, Mesa, Bufete

ela está completamente restabelecida she is perfectly well again. ele já se restabeleceu? is he about again? ele restabeleceu-se he got round again. ele restabeleceu-se depressa he made a quick recovery. eles ~am a ordem they established order.

restabelecido adj. re-established, restored to health, recovered.

ele não está ~ he is unrecovered.

restabelecimento s. m. 1. the act of re-establishing. 2. re-establishment, recovery. 3. healing. 4. resurrection, revival, restoration. 5. restitution, reinstatement. 6. resettlement.

resta-boi s. m. (pl. resta-bois) (bot.) restharrow, cammock, horse's breath.

restagnação s. f. (pl. -ões) stagnation, restagnation, new stoppage of flow.

restampa s. f. reimpression, second or new impression or engraving.

restampar v. to reimpress, reimprint, stamp again.

restante s. m. 1. rest, remainder. 2. residue. ‖ adj. m. + f. remaining, remanent, residuary, residual.

ele pagou o ~ he made up the full sum.

restar v. 1. to rest, remain. 2. to be left over. 3. to survive, remain existent, outlive. 4. to remain to be done, be failing or missing. 5. to be extant or restant. 6. to want, be short of. 7. to owe the balance.

restam-lhe apenas poucos dias de vida but a few days of life are left to him.

restauração s. f. (pl. -ões) 1. act of restoring or state of being restored. 2. restoration, restoring. 3. re-establishment, resettlement. 4. repair, reparation. 5. restitution, repossession. 6. national resurrection, reacquisition of national independence. 7. reinstatement of a dynasty. 8. recovery, replacement.

conseguirám a ~ de todos os bens they achieved the restauration of all their possessions.

restaurado adj. restored, re-established, repaired, recovered.

restaurador s. m. restorer, re-establisher, liberator. ‖ adj. restoring, refreshing, reviving.

restaurante s. m. 1. restaurant, public eating house (plate R 5). 2. (pop.) chophouse, grubbery. 3. café. ‖ adj. m. + f. restoring, restorative.

restaurar v. 1. to recuperate, recover. 2. to recapture, regain. 3. to retrieve. 4. to repair, renovate. 5. to freshen, furbish. 6. to regenerate, restore, revive. 7. to begin again. 8. to resettle. 9. ~se to restore or refresh o. s., be restored to health. 10. to give new lustre to.

restaurativo adj. 1. restoring, restorative. 2. (med.) analeptic.

restaurável adj. m. + f. (pl. -áveis) restorable, retrievable, that can be recovered or re-established.

reste s. m. 1. (billiards) cue rest, cue bridge. 2. lance-rest (on the breastplate of the armour). 3. (Port., prov.) dishcloth.

restelar v. (also rastelar) to comb (flax, hemp, etc.) with a hackle.

restelo (ê) s. m. hackle, flax-comb.

resteva s. f. 1. stubble, stubble field. 2. stowage, method and process of stowing. 3. a ship's hold.

réstia s. f. 1. rope braided from reeds or sedge grass. 2. beams of light.

~ de cebolas ou alhos a string of onions or garlic.

restiforme adj. m. + f. ropelike.

restilação s. f. (pl. -ões) redistillation, new distillation.

restilada s. f. (Braz.) residual fluid formed during the distillation of brandy.

restilar v. to redistil, distil again or anew.

restilo s. m. 1. act or process of redistillation. 2. faints. 3. (Braz.) brandy, any distilled alcoholic drink.

restinga s. f. 1. sandbank, shoal. 2. salt marsh. 3. reef, shelf. 4. long spit of land running into the sea. 5. small tract of wood bordering a river or the seashore. 6. (Braz.) strip of wood separating or bordering pastures. 7. lagoon.

restingal s. m. (pl. -ais) 1. tract of land dotted with many lagoons. 2. a lot of coppices bordering rivers or the seashore.

restingão s. m. (pl. -ões) (S. Braz.) road bordered by forests.

restingueiro s. m. (Braz.) rustic, yokel, backwoodsman.

restinguir v. to extinguish again, suppress, destroy.

restionácea s. f. 1. plant of the family Restionaceae. 2. (pl.) Restionaceae.

restionáceo adj. (bot.) restionaceous.

restituição s. f. (pl. **-ões**) 1. restitution. 2. restoration, returning. 3. reconveyance, redeliverance, devolution. 4. reintegration, remise. 5. rehabilitation.
exigiram plena ~ they requested full compensation.
restituído adj. returned, restored.
restituidor s. m. restorer, restitutor, one who makes restitutions. ‖ adj. restituting, restoring, returning.
restituir v. 1. to restitute. 2. to restore, return. 3. to reconvey, redeliver. 4. to replace, substitute. 5. to refund, give back. 6. to re-establish. 7. to indemnify. 8. to recover, retrieve. 9. ~**-se**: a) to become reintegrated. b) to come to the former state, come back again. c) to provide o. s. with (what was missing). d) to reinstate o. s. in (former position, power, etc.).
ele restituiu o livro he returned the book, he gave the book back. ~ **à vida** to restore to life. **eles têm de** ~ **a quantia** they have to pay back the sum.
restituitório adj. restitutory, restitutive.
restituível adj. m. + f. (pl. **-íveis**) repayable, returnable, refundable.
resto s. m. 1. rest. 2. (math.) remainder. 3. remnant, remain. 4. (chem.) residue. 5. vestige, trace. 6. surplus. 7. end, end product. 8. leftover. 9. scrap. 10. (com.) balance. 11. ~**s** pl.: a) ruins. b) mortal remains. 12. (billiards) cue rest.
de ~ as for the rest, besides. ~**s mortais** mortal remains.
restolhada s. f. 1. a lot of stubbles, many stubbles. 2. rustling or creaking noise. 3. uproar, clamour, bustle.
restolhal s. m. (pl. **-ais**) stubble field, harvest field (plate C 16).
restolhar v. 1. to make a rustling or creaking noise (as of walking on a stubble field). 2. to gather stubbles or straws. 3. to glean. 4. to stir up a racket, make noise. 5. to cull, pick out.
restolho (ô) s. m. 1. stubbles. 2. stubble field, harvest field. 3. eddish, rowen, aftermath. 4. (Braz.) residues, remainder, rest(s).
restribar v. 1. to resist, withstand. 2. not to give up or yield. 3. to oppose firmly. 4. to set one's foot firmly against. 5. ~**-se**: a) to be firm in the saddle. b) to brace o. s. up. c) to rely upon, lean upon.
restrição s. f. (pl. **-ões**) 1. act of restricting. 2. restriction, limitation. 3. restraint, restraining.
~ **da liberdade** curtailment of liberty. ~ **mental** mental reservation. **sem** ~ without reservation, unconditional.
restringência s. f. restringency, astringency.
restringente s. m. (med.) astringent, styptic. ‖ adj. m. + f. restringent, astringent, deterrent, binding, styptic.
restringir v. 1. to restrict, restringe. 2. to straiten, narrow. 3. to restrain, subdue. 4. to squeeze, constrict. 5. to shorten, diminish. 6. to confine, limit. 7. to reduce. 8. to check, bridle. 9. ~**-se**: a) to limit or confine o. s. or itself. b) to refrain from.
restringível adj. m. + f. (pl. **-íveis**) restrainable, limitable.
restritiva s. f. (gram.) restrictive clause or word.
restritivo adj. 1. restrictive, limited. 2. astringent. 3. restraining. 4. select, classified. 5. provincial. ‖ **-amente** adv. restrictively, restrainedly, limitatively.
restrito adj. 1. restricted, limited. 2. strait, narrow. 3. privative. 4. exclusive. ‖ **-amente** adv. restrictedly, limitatively, exclusively, privatively.
eles vivem em circunstâncias -as they live in straitened circumstances.
restrugir v. 1. to resound, resound repeatedly. 2. to reverberate, re-echo. 3. to let resound or reverberate.

restucar v. 1. to plaster again. 2. to plaster well. 3. to fill cracks and chinks with plaster.
resulta s. f. result, effect, consequence.
resultado s. m. 1. result. 2. consequence, effect. 3. deliberation. 4. issue, outcome, upshot. 5. end, ultimate. 6. product. 7. crop, harvest. 8. (fig.) progeny, offspring.
~ **aproximado** approximate result; approximation. ~ **da multiplicação** (math.) product. **dar** ~ pan out well. **falta de** ~ unfruitfulness. **meus esforços não deram** ~ my efforts were thwarted. **muito barulho para pouco** ~ much cry and little wool. **não deu** ~ it came to nothing. **o** ~ **coroa a obra** all's well that ends well. **sem** ~ resultless, unfruitful, issueless. **seu plano não dá** ~ your plan does not work.
resultância s. f. result, resultant.
resultante s. f. 1. (mech.) resultant, resultant force. 2. line that indicates the direction of the resultant force. ‖ adj. m. + f. resultant, attendant, consequential.
resultar v. 1. to result. 2. to proceed, spring or arise from. 3. to be the consequence or effect of. 4. to derive from, ensue, follow. 5. to originate, arise from. 6. to emanate, flow forth. 7. to change into, become. 8. to be the result, sum, product or quotient. 9. to follow, come after.
~ **em fracasso** to result in a failure. ~ **em nada** to go up like smoke. **a medida resultou em benefício dele** the measure turned out to his advantage. **que resultou disso?** what was the end of it? **resulta disso** it follows from this.
resumido adj. 1. resumed. 2. abridged. 3. condensed, concise. 4. short, brief. ‖ **-amente** adv. 1. concisely, succinctly. 2. shortly, briefly. 3. in an abridged manner. 4. curtly, laconically.
resumidor s. m. abbreviator, abridger, recapitulator. ‖ adj. abridging, summarizing, condensing, abbreviating.
resumir v. 1. to abbreviate, abridge. 2. to make a summary or abstract of. 3. to represent symbolically. 4. to epitomize, excerpt. 5. to compact, compress, condense. 6. to recapitulate. 7. to extract. 8. to cut, curtail, brief. 9. to reduce, synthetize, diminish. 10. ~**-se** to be summed up, abridged or condensed.
ele resumiu a história he made a cut in the story. **para** ~ **em poucas palavras** to cut a long story short. **todo o negócio ficou resumido a nada** the whole business was reduced to nothing.
resumo s. m. 1. abridgement, abbreviation. 2. resume, abstract, summary. 3. synopsis, excerpt, extract. 4. recapitulation, summing up. 5. compilation. 6. outlines. 7. (jur.) docket.
ele fez um ~ **dos fatos** he made a brief of the facts. **em** ~ **tratava-se de** in short it came to.
resvaladeiro s. m. a steep or slippery place.
resvaladiço, resvaladio s. m. 1. a steep or slippery place. 2. dangerous slope. ‖ adj. 1. slippery, lubricous. 2. steep. 3. (fig.) dangerous.
resvaladouro s. m. 1. a slippery place. 2. declivity, steep slope. 3. cliff, precipice. 4. action or fact that endangers the dignity or the good fame. 5. danger, peril.
resvaladura s. f. 1. act or effect of slipping. 2. skidding, slipping. 3. skid trace, track made by slipping or skidding.
resvalamento s. m. gliding, slipping.
resvalar v. 1. to let slip or fall. 2. to slide, glide. 3. to slip, slither, skid. 4. to cast, throw, hurl. 5. to cause to fall. 6. to fall down. 7. to skate. 8. to escape from, flee, fly. 9. to stumble, trip. 10.

to begin to err, go wrong, commit a fault. 11. to bring upon o. s., become liable to.
ele resvalou pesadamente he had a heavy fall.
resvalo s. m. 1. act of slipping or sliding. 2. steep or slippery place. 3. slope, declivity.
resvés adv. 1. close, even with. 2. at the bottom, near the base. 3. exactly, justly.
reta s. f. 1. straight line. 2. straight trace or stroke. 3. straight stretch of a road. 4. (sport, horse racing) home stretch.
~ **final** final stretch, home stretch. **em linha** ~ as the crow flies.
retábulo s. m. (eccl.) 1. retable, altar piece. 2. decorated panel.
retaco, retacado adj. (S. Braz.) stout, thickset, stubby.
retaguarda s. f. 1. rearguard, rear of an army. 2. back, tail-end.
atacar o inimigo pela ~ to attack the enemy in the rear. **ele está na** ~ he is among the stragglers. **fecharam a** ~ they brought up the rear.
retal adj. m. + f. (pl. -ais) rectal, of or pertaining to the rectum.
retalhação s. f. (pl. -ões) act of cutting or shredding to pieces.
retalhado adj. 1. cut up, cut into pieces. 2. chopped, shredded. 3. slashed, stabbed. 4. divided. 5. (S. Braz.) sterilized (horses).
retalhador s. m. 1. cutter, shredder. 2. retailer, retail seller. ‖ adj. cutting, shredding, retailing.
retalhadura s. f. act of cutting or shredding into small pieces.
retalhar v. 1. to cut into small pieces. 2. to shred. 3. to cut grooves into, cut up or out. 4. to chop, chine. 5. to stab, slash. 6. to wound. 7. to rend, tear asunder. 8. to fractionate. 9. to divide. 10. to hurt, offend, injure. 11. to sell at retail. 12. to sterilize (horses).
um profundo desgosto retalhou o seu coração a deep sorrow pierced his heart.
retalheiro s. m. retailer, retail dealer. ‖ adj. retailing.
retalhista s. m. + f. retailer, retail dealer, small trader. ‖ adj. 1. retailing. 2. of or referring to the retail trade.
retalho s. m. 1. morsel, little piece. 2. shred, snip. 3. cuttings, parings, scissorings. 4. end. 5. remnant. 6. retail. 7. scrap, slice. 8. fraction.
a ~ by bits, at retail. **mercador de** ~**s** retailer, shopkeeper. **ser** ~ **da mesma peça** to be birds of a feather, two of a kind.
retaliação s. f. (pl. -ões) 1. retaliation. 2. reprisal, requital.
retaliado adj. retaliated, retributed, revenged.
retaliar v. 1. to retaliate. 2. to reply in kind, strike back. 3. to take revenge. 4. to make reprisals. 5. to return like for like, make requital.
retama s. f. (bot.) 1. woadwaxen. 2. retem.
retambana s. f. (pop.) upbraiding, scolding, bawling.
retame s. m. molasses, treacle. ‖ adj. reacquiring a viscid consistency (said of sugar molasses or honey).
retanchar v. 1. to substitute an old twig of a vine for a new one. 2. to set a new shoot or spring. 3. to clip a shoot close to the ground.
retanchoa s. f. planting of new vines, pruning of new shoots.
retangular adj. m. + f. rectangular, right-angled, square.
retangularidade s. f. rectangularity, squareness, rectangularness.
retângulo s. m. rectangle, square, right-angled parallelogram. ‖ adj. rectangular, right-angled.

retardação s. f. (pl. -ões) 1. retardation. 2. retarding, lagging. 3. delay, slowdown. 4. postponement, adjournment.
retardado adj. 1. retarded, delayed, postponed. 2. stunted, blunt-witted. ‖ **-amente** adv. delayingly, retardedly, slowly.
retardador s. m. delayer, retarder. ‖ adj. delaying, retarding.
retardamento s. m. 1. retardation, retarding, retardment. 2. lagging, dilatoriness. 3. delay, slowdown. 4. postponement, adjournment.
retardão s. m. (pl. -ões) 1. slow, phlegmatic or lazy person, lazybones. 2. restive horse. ‖ adj. 1. slow, sluggish. 2. lazy, slothful. 3. phlegmatic. 4. obstinate, restive.
retardar v. 1. to retard. 2. to delay, slow down. 3. to hinder, impede, obstruct. 4. to slow down, slacken. 5. to postpone, put off. 6. to linger, lag. 7. to protract, prolong. 8. to temporize. 9. to defer. 10. ~-**se**: a) to be or come late. b) to walk slowly. c) to be long in.
de novo ~**am a resposta** again they were putting off the answer.
retardatário s. m. 1. latecomer. 2. laggard, straggler. 3. dilatory payer. ‖ adj. 1. tardy, slow. 2. lagging, retardatory. 3. in arrear, dilatory.
retardativo adj. 1. retardative, retardatory. 2. delaying. 3. hindering.
retarde s. m. (Braz.) 1. delay. 2. retarding, retardation. 3. hindrance. 4. backwardness. 5. tardiness. 6. dilatoriness.
retardio adj. 1. tardy, late. 2. slow, sluggish, laggard. 3. dilatory.
retardo s. m. 1. retard, retardation. 2. delay, lag. 3. slowdown. 4. (mus.) prolongation of one sound of a chord (which forms the basic sound of the next chord).
retectomia s. f. (surg.) proctotomy.
retelhado adj. re-tiled, newly covered with tiles.
retelhadura s. f. re-tiling, roofing, repair of the roofing of a house.
retelhar v. 1. to roof again, re-tile. 2. to repair the tiling of a house. 3. to tile again or anew.
retém s. m. (pl. -éns) 1. act or effect of retaining. 2. retention. 3. rest. 4. stock, store, reserve. 5. depot, storehouse. 6. guard of a prison.
retemperação s. f. (pl. -ões) 1. retempering. 2. purification. 3. strengthening.
retemperar v. 1. to retemper, temper again. 2. to give new force, strength or hardness to. 3. to fortify, strengthen. 4. to improve, better, ameliorate. 5. to purify.
retenção s. f. (pl. -ões) 1. retention, retaining. 2. restraint, suppression. 3. delay, deferment. 4. reserve. 5. detention, retainment. 6. (med.) abnormal retaining of a secretion which is to be expelled. 7. retentiveness.
~ **de um projeto de lei** pocket-veto. ~ **particular** close arrest.
retentiva s. f. 1. retentiveness, retentive memory. 2. prudence, circumspection, caution.
retentivo adj. retentive, tending to retain, having a good memory.
ele tem uma memória -a he has a tenacious memory. **falta-lhe a faculdade -a** he lacks retentiveness. **não** ~ irretentive.
retentor s. m. (f. **retentriz**) retainer, keeper, retentor, one who has retentive capacity. ‖ adj. retaining, retentive.
reter v. 1. to keep, retain. 2. not to let escape, hold back. 3. to guard, safeguard. 4. to detain, restrain. 5. to confine, imprison. 6. to remember, keep in mind. 7. to learn by heart, memorize. 8. to im-

mobilize, withhold, suppress. 9. to hinder, bind, tie up. 10. to conserve, preserve. 11. ~-se: a) to stop, halt. b) to refrain from, abstain from. c) not to advance, hold o. s. back.
ele reteve a respiração he caught his breath. **eles retiveram o projeto** they pocketed the project. **que é que nos retém?** what hinders us to proceed? **retiveram a mercadoria** they bonded the merchandise. **retiveram o negócio** they bottled the business up.
retesado adj. taut, stiff, tight, tense, rigid.
retesar v. 1. to stretch, make tense, strain. 2. to stiffen, tighten. 3. ~-se to become stiff or taut, become hard.
~ a vela (naut.) to flatten the sail.
reteso (ê) adj. stiff, taut, tense, rigid.
reticência s. f. 1. reticence. 2. reserve in speech and manner. 3. reservedness, secretiveness. 4. (gram.) omission points, ellipsis.
reticenciar v. 1. to place constraints, reserves on. 2. to express o. s. reticently, incompletely.
reticente adj. m. + f. 1. reticent. 2. reserved. 3. uncommunicative, silent. 4. close-tongued, close-mouthed.
rético s. m. 1. native or inhabitant of Rhaetia, Rhaetian. 2. Rhaeto-Romanic: Romance dialects spoken in southeastern Switzerland. ‖ adj. Rhaetian, Rhaeto-Romanic.
reticórneo adj. (zool.) having straight tentacles.
retícula s. f. 1. a small net. 2. reticle. 3. reticule.
reticulação s. f. (pl. -ões) reticulation, network.
reticulado, adj. m., **reticular** m. + f. 1. netlike, meshy, netted. 2. cancellate, cancellated. 3. reticular, reticulate, retiform.
retículo s. m. 1. a small net, mesh. 2. network, reticulation. 3. reticle, reticule. 4. (bot.) fibrous network that lines the petiole of a leaf. 5. (zool.) reticulum: the second stomach of the ruminants. 6. (phot.) reticulation: network of fine points or corrugations produced intentionally (in order to give a picture a hazy character), screen. 7. cross wires.
retidão s. f. (pl. -ões) 1. rightness, righteousness. 2. rectitude, honesty. 3. integrity, equity, straightforwardness. 4. justice, fair play. 5. virtue, principle, propriety. 6. accuracy, correctitude.
a ~ do seu caráter the probity of his character. **não houve dúvida quanto a sua ~** there was no doubt about his incorruptness.
retido adj. restrained, refrained, curbed, pent-up.
~ pelo mau tempo weather-bound, storm-bound.
retífica s. f. (Braz., pop.) a shop which rectifies, adjusts motors.
retificação s. f. (pl. -ões) 1. rectification. 2. rectifying. 3. emendation, correction. 4. adjustment. 5. redress. 6. (chem.) purification, redistillation.
~ da freqüência das ondas (radio) modulation of wave length. **~ de superfícies planas** face grinding.
retificado adj. 1. rectified. 2. corrected, set right. 3. adjusted, regulated. 4. (chem.) redistilled, purified.
retificador s. m. 1. rectifier. 2. adjuster, corrector. 3. emendator. 4. (radio) detector. 5. (tech.) dressing-tool. ‖ adj. rectifying, rectificative, rectificatory.
~ a selênio (tech.) selenium rectifier. **máquina ~a** (tech.) grinder.
retificar v. 1. to rectify. 2. to arrange in a straight line, straighten. 3. to correct, amend. 4. (chem.) to redistil, purify, refine. 5. (geom.) to determine the length of a curve (or portion of it). 6. to redress, right. 7. to adjust. 8. ~-se: a) to regenerate o. s. b) to mend one's ways, correct o. s.
retificativo adj. rectificative, serving to rectify, rectificatory.

retificável adj. m. + f. (pl. -áveis) rectifiable, capable of being rectified, emendable.
retifloro adj. (bot.) rectiflorous.
retiforme adj. m. + f. 1. retiform, netlike, reticulate(d). 2. (bot.) rotate. 3. straight, right.
retígrado adj. rectigrade, that moves in a straight line.
retilíneo adj. rectilineal, rectilinear, right-lined.
retilinidade s. f. rectilinearity, rectilinearness.
retina s. f. (anat.) retina: the sensitive membrane of the eye (plate O).
retináculo s. m. (anat., bot., zool.) retinaculum.
retinérveo adj. 1. retinerved, having reticular or netlike nervures. 2. (bot.) reticulately nerved, net-veined.
retingir v. 1. to redye, dye again. 2. to dye thoroughly.
retiniano, retínico adj. retinal, retinian.
retininte adj. m. + f. ringing, jingling, tinkling, that resounds.
retinir v. 1. to jingle, tinkle. 2. to echo, resound, reverberate. 3. to produce a loud or sharp sound. 4. to create a deep impression upon. 5. to let resound or re-echo. 6. to clank, clink.
~am os seus ouvidos his ears tinkled.
retinite s. f. (med.) retinitis, inflammation of the retina.
retintim s. m. (pl. -ins) 1. a jingling, tinkling. 2. clank, jingle, clang. 3. the sound of brass instruments.
retinto adj. 1. redyed, coloured again. 2. dark-coloured.
retípede adj. m. + f. (zool.) having on the soles a reticulated epidermis.
retiração s. f. (pl. -ões) 1. retreat, act of retiring. 2. withdrawal. 3. evacuation, departure. 4. (typogr.) printing of the backside of a sheet.
retirada s. f. 1. act of retiring or withdrawing. 2. retreat, withdrawal, countermarch. 3. retirement. 4. evacuation. 5. departure. 6. clearage, removal. 7. (N. Braz.) migration of drought victims.
bater em ~ to yield the palm, retreat, take to flight. **tocar a ~** to sound a retreat. **~ estratégica** (mil.) strategic retreat, withdrawal.
retirado adj. 1. retired. 2. solitary, secluded. 3. reclusive, remote. 4. lone, lonesome. 5. private. 6. sequestered. 7. secret. 8. shy. ‖ -amente adv. solitarily, reclusively.
eles vivem uma vida -a they live a retired life. **isto é um lugar ~** that's a lonely place. **não ~** unclaimed.
retiramento s. m. retirement, solitude, retreat.
retirante s. m. + f. 1. migrant from the drought region of northeastern Brazil. 2. (bot.) a starbur (Acanthospermum hispidum). ‖ adj. retiring, retreating.
retirar v. 1. to draw back, withdraw. 2. to take away, remove. 3. to retract, recant, disavow. 4. to deprive of, sequester. 5. to obtain, get. 6. to save, preserve from. 7. to receive, make a profit from. 8. ~-se: a) to depart, leave, go away. b) to retreat, abandon. c) to evacuate, vacate. d) to retire, go to bed. e) to give up, back out, take to flight. f) to seek privacy, withdraw from social life. g) to give up (business). 9. to annul, cancel. 10. to free, liberate.
~ as ofensas to retract the insults. **~ o direito de** 1. to annul the right to. 2. to deprive of the right to. **ele retirou-se furtivamente** he slunk away. **ele retirou-se ao seu quarto** he confined himself to his room. **ele retirou seu amigo da prisão** he bailed his friend out of prison. **ele retirou a sua promessa** he went back on his promise. **~am-se depressa**

they ducked away, they jerked away. **retirei-me de tudo** I withdrew within myself.

retireiro s. m. (Braz.) herdsman.

retiro s. m. 1. solitary place, solitude, seclusion. 2. retreat, retiredness. 3. reclusion, recluseness. 4. nest, nook, den. 5. privacy, privateness. 6. haunt. 7. exile. 8. cloister. 9. (Braz.) winter pasture. 10. (Braz.) hut or shelter in the midst of a plantation. 11. (N. Braz.) rude hut of rubber collectors. **cada ano ele faz um ~ espiritual** every year he goes into retreat. **o ~ das tropas** the withdrawal of the troops.

retirrostro adj. (zool.) rectirostral, having a straight beak.

retite s. f. (med.) inflammation of the rectum.

retitude s. f. righteousness, rectitude, honesty.

reto (I) s. m. 1. (arch.) challenge, defiance: 2. **~s** pl. (Braz.) gabbling, prattling, empty talk. **deixe de ~s!** stop the silly prattling!

reto (II) s. m. (anat.) rectum, terminal part of the intestine. ‖ adj. 1. straight (plate Q). 2. right, direct. 3. even, plain. 4. without curve or bend. 5. vertical. 6. impartial, equitable, just. 7. righteous. 8. upright, upstanding, erect. ‖ **-amente** adv. equitably, rightfully, straightly, honestly. **ângulo ~** right angle. **bem ~** straight as an arrow. **ele é um homem muito ~** he is a straight fellow. **seguiram a sua razão -a** they followed their sound reason.

retocado adj. retouched, refurbished, finished.

retocador s. m. 1. retoucher, finisher. 2. a goldsmith's file. ‖ adj. retouching, finishing.

retocadouro s. m. (phot., typogr.) retouching frame.

retocar v. 1. to retouch, touch up again. 2. to finish, complete. 3. to improve, ameliorate. 4. to correct, emend. 5. to deburr, burr. 6. to put the last hand to, give finishing touches to.

retomada s. f. retaking, recapturing, recovering.

retomar v. 1. to retake, take again. 2. to recover, retrieve. 3. to resume. 4. to get back, recapture.

retombo s. m. (Braz.) verification or reconstitution of the boundaries of an agricultural property.

retoque s. m. 1. retouching, finishing touch(es). 2. correction, emendation. 3. polish, finish. **ele deu os últimos ~s** he gave the finishing touches to.

retor s. m. rhetor: teacher or master of rhetoric.

retorcedeira s. f. twisting machine.

retorcedura s. f. twisting, winding, twirling, twist.

retorcer v. 1. to twist again, retwist. 2. to wrench, writhe. 3. to rewind. 4. to wreathe, wriggle. 5. **~-se:** a) to squirm, twist about. b) to contort o. s. c) to dodge, use a subterfuge, practice mean shifts. **~-se como uma enguia** to wriggle like an eel. **~ tudo** to use tortuous ways.

retorcida s. f. (Braz.) 1. turn of the road, curve. 2. variety of fandango.

retorcido adj. 1. twisted, turned around. 2. winding. 3. writhing. 4. kinky, knurly. 5. (fig.) cunning, shrewd. ‖ **-amente** adv. twistedly, windingly, writhingly, wryly.

retórica s. f. 1. rhetoric, art of expressive speech. 2. eloquence. 3. persuasive power. 4. oratory. 5. flowery or bombastic style. **ele usou muitas figuras de ~** he used many figures or speech.

retoricar v. 1. to speak or write rhetorically. 2. to rhetoricate, rhetorize.

retórico s. m. 1. rhetor, teacher or master of rhetoric. 2. writer of a treatise on rhetoric. 3. rhetorician, orator. 4. speaker who uses an ornate or inflated style. ‖ adj. 1. rhetorical, of or relative to rhetoric.

2. elocutionary, declamatory. ‖ **-amente** adv. rhetorically.

retornamento s. m., **retornança** f. (arch.) 1. act or effect of returning. 2. return, going or coming back. 3. exchange, barter.

retornar v. 1. to return. 2. to go or come back. 3. to give or bring back. 4. to refund, compensate. 5. to turn, turn again.

retorno (ô) s. m. 1. return, regress. 2. going back, coming back. 3. exchange of goods, barter. 4. recurrence, recurrency. 5. gift presented in return. 6. reward. **carga de ~** home freight. **~ do carro** (typewriter) backspacer. **eterno ~** eternal return: 1. the doctrine of the periodic recurrence of events. 2. (rel.) doctrine of the transmigration of souls. **viagem de ~** return journey, homeward trip.

retorquir, retorqüir v. 1. to reply. 2. to rejoin, retort. 3. to talk back, rebut. 4. to object (to), oppose. 5. to contrapose. 6. to refute, contradict, disprove. 7. to carry on an argument, argue.

retorsão s. f. (pl. -ões) 1. act or effect of twisting. 2. retortion, turning, bending. 3. replication. 4. sharp reply, rebuttal. 5. redress, reparation (of a wrong).

retorta s. f. 1. (chem.) retort. 2. the curved part of the crozier.

retorto adj. curved, bent, twisted.

retoscopia s. f. (med.) proctoscopy: inspection of the rectum.

retoscópico adj. (med.) proctoscopic(al).

retoscópio s. m. (med.) proctoscope, instrument for inspecting the rectum.

retostar v. to toast again, toast too much.

retouça s. f. 1. balance, balancing. 2. a child's swing.

retoucar v. 1. to dress the hair again. 2. to don, put on (the head).

retouçar (I) v. 1. to balance, swing. 2. to frisk about. 3. to frolic, romp. 4. to roll or tumble in the grass. 5. to wallow, flounder.

retouçar (II) v. (Port., prov.) to graze, browse.

retouço s. m. 1. leap, jump, hop. 2. romping. 3. frolic, frisking.

retovado adj. (S. Braz.) 1. covered or coated with leather. 2. (fig.) artful, cunning. 3. deceptive, false.

retovamento s. m. (S. Braz.) leather lining, leather covering.

retovar v. (S. Braz.) to cover, coat or line with leather.

retovo (ô) s. m. (S. Braz.) 1. leather covering, leather lining. 2. hide of a dead calf or foal.

retração s. f. (pl. -ões) 1. retraction, retracting. 2. withdrawing, withholdment. 3. recoil. 4. (concrete) shrinkage.

retraçar v. 1. to retrace. 2. to trace over again. 3. to reduce to shreds.

retraço s. m. 1. chopped straw, chaff. 2. remains of straw mixed into the fodder. 3. rubbish, trash, residues.

retradução s. f. (pl. -ões) retranslation, new translation.

retradutor s. m. retranslator. ‖ adj. retranslating.

retraduzir v. to retranslate, translate anew.

retraído adj. 1. withdrawn, retracted. 2. retired, retiring. 3. shy, restrained, reserved. 4. offish, close-mouthed. 5. unsociable, undemonstrative, uncompanionable. 6. self-contained. ‖ **retraidamente** adv. reservedly, offishly, unsociably, retractedly.

retraimento s. m. 1. retraction, act or process of retracting. 2. retreat, solitude. 3. retirement, withdrawal. 4. contraction. 5. reservedness, stand-offishness. 6. seclusion, privacy. 7. reduction of volume, shrinking.

retrair v. 1. to draw back, withdraw. 2. to retract. 3. to contract, shrink. 4. to hold back. 5. to retire. 6. to restrain, withhold. 7. to hide, conceal. 8. to flinch, wince. 9. not to show, suppress. 10. to hinder. 11. to liberate, free. 12. to save. 13. ~-se: a) to give ground, recede. b) to isolate o. s., withdraw from the world. c) to depart, leave. d) to hide one's thoughts, keep secret. e) to become reserved.
ela retraiu-se she effaced herself, she drew in her horns. **ela retraiu-se do mundo** she forsook the world. **não se retraia de todo o mundo** don't shut yourself away from everybody. **você não pode ~ a promessa** you can't go back on your promise.
retramar v. to plot or contrive again.
retranca s. f. 1. breeching, breeching body, crupper (plate A 12). 2. (naut.) boom (plate B 10). 3. (naut.) any part of the wooden structure which supports a ship in launching. 4. (fam.) thrift, frugality.
ele vive numa ~ terrível he lives in a terrible pinch. **fazer a ~ de** (typogr.) to break up, distribute (a form).
retrança s. f. dense crown of a tree.
retrançar v. to rebraid, braid again.
retranscrever v. to retranscribe, transcribe again or anew.
retranscrição s. f. (pl. -ões) retranscription.
retransferir v. to retransfer, transfer again, reconvey.
retransir v. 1. to transgress, trespass. 2. to penetrate. 3. to try to make out the inmost thoughts. 4. to affect, fill up.
retransmissão s. f. (pl. -ões) 1. retransmission, new transmission. 2. reconveyance. 3. (radio) rebroadcast.
retransmitir v. 1. to retransmit, transmit again. 2. (radio) to rebroadcast.
retratação s. f. (pl. -ões) 1. retractation. 2. retraction, recantation. 3. revocation, recall, disclaimer. 4. palinode. 5. confession or acknowledgement of an error.
retratado adj. 1. painted, portrayed. 2. drawn, featured. 3. photographed, depicted. 4. mirrored, reflected. 5. well delineated (in word or writing).
retratador (I) s. m. 1. portraitist. 2. photographer. 3. depicter, recanter. || adj. depicting, portraying, photographing, recanting.
retratador (II) s. m. retractor, revoker, person who disavows or repudiates. || adj. retracting, disavowing, repudiating.
retratar (I) v. 1. to portray, paint. 2. to draw, picture. 3. to photograph. 4. to reproduce the image of, represent exactly. 5. to feature, depict, delineate. 6. to show, make manifest. 7. to describe in words or writing. 8. ~-se: a) to be portrayed. b) to be mirrored or reflected. c) to show o. s., appear.
a alegria retratou-se no seu rosto joy unfolded itself in her face. **no filho retratou-se de novo o pai** the son became his father's spitting image.
retratar (II) v. 1. to retract, recant. 2. to unsay. 3. to draw or pull back, withdraw. 4. to treat again or anew. 5. to disavow. 6. to confess one's error or evil action.
ele tem de ~-se he has to eat the leek. **~ um juramento** to unswear. **~ uma afirmação** to revoke an assertion.
retratável adj. m. + f. (pl. -áveis) 1. retractable. 2. portrayable.
retrátil, retráctil adj. m. + f. (pl. -eis) 1. retractile, retractible, retractable. 2. causing or producing retraction. 3. retractive.
retratilidade s. f. 1. retractility. 2. retractiveness.

retratista s. m. + f. 1. portraitist, portrait painter. 2. photographer.
retrativo adj. retractive, retractible, serving to retract.
retrato s. m. 1. image, likeness. 2. picture, portrait. 3. reproduction, representation. 4. photograph. 5. double, second self, person who looks like another one. 6. character, characteristic appearance, resemblance. 7. description. 8. model. 9. effigy.
ela é o ~ fiel de sua mãe she is the very picture of her mother. **ele fez um ~ de meio corpo** he made a half-length portrait. **o ~ é muito natural** the picture is her (his) very self. **~ falado** composite picture.
retravar v. 1. to bind or tie again. 2. to begin again, recommence. 3. to block or brake again.
retre s. m. 1. officer of the lansquenets. 2. hired bodyguard, henchman.
retrecheiro s. m. lazy, slow or stupid fellow. || adj. lazy, sluggish, stupid.
retremer v. to tremble again, tremble repeatedly.
retreta s. f. 1. evening roll call, tattoo. 2. a queen's chambermaid. 3. closet, toilet, privy. 4. (Braz.) outdoor concert of a band.
tocar a ~ (mil.) to sound the retreat.
retrete s. f. 1. latrine. 2. m. water closet, lavatory, privy.
retretista s. m. + f. soldier or musician who sounds the retreat. || adj. beating or sounding the tattoo.
retribuição s. f. (pl. -ões) 1. retribution, recompense. 2. remuneration, payment, reimbursement. 3. compensation. 4. reward, premium. 5. wage, pay. 6. gratitude, thankfulness. 7. requital.
retribuído adj. retributed, rewarded, requited.
não ~ unrequited. **que pode ser ~** renderable.
retribuidor s. m. retributor, rewarder, recompenser. || adj. retributing, retributive, rewarding.
retribuir v. 1. to retribute. 2. to recompense, reward. 3. to compensate, repay. 4. to give something in return, reciprocate. 5. to award a prize to, give a premium to. 6. to requite.
~ uma visita to return a visit.
retribuível adj. m. + f. (pl. -íveis) rewardable, returnable, requitable.
retrilhar v. to tread again, retread.
retrincado adj. 1. secretive, sly. 2. cunning, artful. 3. malicious.
retrincar v. 1. to crunch again, crush again with one's teeth. 2. to lock or block again. 3. to give a bad sense to, interpret maliciously. 4. to misconstrue, misunderstand. 5. to murmur. 6. to gnash one's teeth.
retriz s. f. rectrix, one of the tail feathers of a bird.
retro s. m. first page of several leaves. || adv. behind, back of, backward, rearward. || interj. away!, be gone!
retro- pref. meaning behind, backward, retrograde.
retroação s. f. (pl. -ões) 1. retroaction. 2. reciprocal action. 3. retroactive operation or effect. 4. reaction.
retroagir v. 1. to retroact. 2. to act backward, act in return or opposition to. 3. to react. 4. to act reciprocally. 5. to remodel, change what already has been done.
retroalimentação s. f. (electronics, med.) feedback.
retroar v. 1. to resound, boom or thunder again. 2. to boom or thunder repeatedly and lastingly. 3. to re-echo, reverberate.
retroatividade s. f. retroactivity.
retroativo adj. 1. retroactive. 2. affecting what is past. 3. operating backward. 4. retrospective. || -amente adv. retroactively.
retrocarga s. f. act of loading a fire-arm at the breech.

retrocedência s. f. retrocedence, retrocession.
retrocedente s. m. retrocedent element or cause, retrocessive agent. ‖ adj. m. + f. retrocedent, retroceding, retrograde.
retroceder v. 1. to retrocede. 2. to cede or grant back. 3. to go or step back. 4. to recede, retire. 5. to go badly, decay, decline. 6. to retrograde, retrogress. 7. to desist.
retrocedimento s. m. 1. act or process of retroceding. 2. retrocession, retrogression. 3. recession.
retrocessão s. f. (pl. **-ões**) 1. retrocession, receding. 2. (jur.) cession of a right that has been acquired by assignment. 3. retrogression. 4. (med.) metastasis.
retrocessivo adj. retrocessive, retograde, tending to retrocede, producing retrocession.
retrocesso s. m. 1. retrocession, retroceding. 2. retrogression, regression. 3. retreat, withdrawal, a going back. 4. delay, retardation. 5. retrogradation. 6. (typewriter) backspacer (plate M 2). 7. (mech.) backset, backward travel.
~ de arma de fogo recoil, kick (firearm).
retrocontagem s. f. countdown.
retroflexão s. f. (pl. **-ões**) 1. act of reflexing, state of being retroflexed. 2. (med.) retroflexion, retroflection.
retroflexo adj. retroflex, bent backward, reflexed.
retrogradação s. f. (pl. **-ões**) 1. retrogradation, retrogression. 2. act of going back, return to a primitive state. 3. (astr.) antecedence.
retrogradante adj. m. + f. retrograding, retrogradatory.
retrogradar v. 1. to retrograde, retrogress. 2. to go backward, recede. 3. to decline from better to worse, degenerate. 4. to go back to an earlier or primitive state. 5. to proceed in opposition to progress, be reactionary. 6. to turn back, reverse. 7. to cause to recede.
retrógrado s. m. 1. retrograde. 2. reactionary. ‖ adj. retrograde, backward, retral, reactionary.
retrogressão s. f. (pl. **-ões**) retrogression, retrogradation, backward movement, degeneration.
retropropulsão s. f. (astronautics) retrofire.
retropulsão s. f. 1. (med.) retropulsion. 2. repelling, pushing back.
retrorso adj. 1. (bot.) retrorse, postrorse. 2. bent backward or downward.
retrós s. m. (pl. **retroses**) twisted sewing silk, spun silk, thrown silk.
retrosaria s. f. 1. a lot of twisted sewing silk. 2. a silk merchant's business, silk thread manufacturer. 3. notions shop.
retroseiro s. m. silk merchant, silk dealer, silk embroiderer.
retrospecção, retrospeção s. f. (pl. **-ões**) 1. retrospection. 2. act of looking back on the past, retrospect. 3. reference to s. th. prior.
retrospectivo, retrospetivo adj. retrospective, directed backward, contemplative of the past, retroactive. ‖ **-amente** adv. retrospectively, with reference to the past, retroactively.
retrospecto, retrospeto s. m. 1. retrospection, retrospect. 2. observation or contemplation of the past. 3. review of the past, reminiscence.
retrosseguir v. 1. to retrocede, recede. 2. to retrograde, retrogress.
retrotrair v. 1. to make retroactive. 2. to act or effect backward. 3. to withdraw off, hold back. 4. to recede, retrocede. 5. to retreat, give ground, retrace one's steps.
retrovenda s. f. restricted sale, sale with the proviso of redemption or annulment of contract.
retrovender v. to sell with the proviso of redemption or annulment of contract.

retrovendição s. f. (pl. **-ões**) restricted sale, sale with the proviso of redemption or annulment of contract.
retroversão s. f. (pl. **-ões**) 1. translation back into the original language, retranslation. 2. retroversion, backward displacement. 3. (med.) retroflexion of an organ.
retroverso adj. retroverse, turned backward.
retroverter v. 1. to retrovert, revert. 2. to turn back. 3. to make retroactive. 4. to retract. 5. to retranslate, translate into the original language.
retrovertido adj. retroverse, turned backward, reverted.
retrovisor s. m. rear view mirror.
retrucar v. 1. to reply, answer. 2. to retort, talk back. 3. (cards) to raise the bet.
retruque s. m. 1. act or effect of answering. 2. retort, talking back. 3. rejoinder, reply. 4. (billiards) rebound. 5. retaliation. 6. (cards) raising of the bet.
retumbância s. f. 1. resounding, reverberation. 2. re-echo. 3. responsive sound, reflection of sound. 4. repercussion, resonance.
retumbante adj. m. + f. 1. resounding, sounding. 2. resonant, repercussive, reverberating. 3. rumbling, rolling. ‖ **~mente** adv. resoundingly, resonantly, rumblingly.
retumbar v. 1. to resound, reverberate. 2. to echo, re-echo. 3. to rumble, make a rolling sound.
retumbo s. m. 1. resound, reverberation. 2. re-echo. 3. repercussion, resonance, percussion.
retundir v. 1. to repress, suppress. 2. to moderate, restrain, keep within bounds. 3. to hold back, curb.
returno s. m. (Braz., sports) return match, return play, revanche.
retuso adj. (bot.) retuse, having the apex rounded or obtuse.
réu s. m. 1. defendant, respondent. 2. culprit, delinquent. 3. criminal, convict. 4. forfeiter. 5. approver. ‖ adj. guilty, accused, criminal.
reuchliniano s. m. a follower of Reuchlin (Johann Reuchlin, German humanist and philologue 1455--1522) or Reuchlinism. ‖ adj. Reuchlinian, of or referring to Reuchlin.
reuma s. f. (med.) rheum, catarrh; (pop.) running of the nose.
reumametria s. f. science and/or method of measuring the speed of flowing liquids.
reumamétrico adj. of, referring to or relative to the measuring of the speed of flowing liquids.
reumâmetro s. m. instrument for determining the speed of flowing liquids.
reumatalgia s. f. (med.) rheumatalgia, rheumatic pain.
reumatálgico adj. rheumatalgic.
reumático s. m. rheumatic, one affected with rheumatism. ‖ adj. rheumatic.
reumatismal adj. m. + f. (pl. **-ais**) rheumatismal, rheumatic.
reumatismo s. m. (med.) rheumatism, rheumatic fever, arthritis.
~ articular agudo (path.) acute articular rheumatism.
reumatóide adj. m. + f. rheumatoid(al), resembling rheumatism, afflicted with rheumatism.
reumatologia s. f. rheumatology.
reumoso adj. rheumy, rheumic, affected with rheum.
reunião s. f. (pl. **-ões**) 1. reunion. 2. act of reuniting. 3. meeting, meet. 4. gathering, party. 5. rally, conference, convention. 6. combination, combine. 7. assemblage, assembly. 8. convocation. 9. sitting, seance. 10. turn-out. 11. council, consistory.
~ amigável social gathering, (U. S. A.) sociable. **~ de belezas** galaxy of beauties. **~ de cúpula** top-level meeting. **~ festiva de noite** dress-up occasion. **~ ministerial** cabinet council. **~ plenária do parla-**

mento the High Court of Parliament. ~ **secreta (religiosa)** conventicle. ~ **só de homens** stag party. **fui a uma** ~ I went to a gathering. **marcar uma** ~ to call a meeting. **o presidente dissolveu a** ~ the president broke up the meeting, left the chair.

reunir v. 1. to reunite. 2. to unite again or anew. 3. to assemble, congregate, meet. 4. to form a group, rally. 5. to harmonize, reconcile. 6. to sew, stitch together. 7. to reannex. 8. to fit together, rejoin. 9. to restore the unity of. 10. ~-**se:** a) to come together with, join. b) to meet, flock together, come together, rally. c) to appear in person, show up, attend. 11. to concentrate, accumulate. 12. to amass, heap up. 13. to incorporate. 14. (mil.) to muster.

ela reuniu em si todas as boas qualidades she embodied all good qualities. **ele reuniu a família** he brought his family together. **eles se ~am em sindicato** they formed a syndicate.

reurbanizar v. to reurbanize.

revacinação s. f. (pl. -**ões**) revaccination, second vaccination.

revacinar v. to revaccinate, vaccinate a second time.

revalidação s. f. (pl. -**ões**) revalidation, restoration of validity, reconfirmation, renewed validity.

revalidador s. m. one who revalidates. ‖ adj. revalidating.

revalidar v. 1. to revalidate. 2. to restore validity, validate again. 3. to give more legal force to. 4. to renew. 5. to confirm. 6. to legitimate anew.

revalorização s. f. (pl. -**ões**) revalorization, restoration of value.

revalorizar v. to revalorize, restore the value of, give new value to.

revanche s. f. (Fr.) revenge, retaliation, getting even with.

revedor (I) s. m. reviewer, reviser, censor, examiner. ‖ adj. revising, reviewing, censoring.

revedor (II) s. m. (N. Braz.) well, spring with its pool.

reveillon s. m. (Fr.) New Year's eve party.

revel s. m. + f. 1. rebel, rebeller. 2. rebellious or insubordinate person. 3. (jur.) delinquent who fails to appear in court when summoned, defaulter. ‖ adj. 1. rebellious, insubordinate. 2. defaultant, defaulting. 3. (fig.) negligent.

revelação s. f. (pl. -**ões**) 1. act or effect of revealing. 2. revelation, revealment. 3. discovery, disclosure. 4. divine inspiration. 5. divine disclosure or manifestation, religious feeling. 6. development. 7. emanation. 8. betrayal, indiscretion. 9. exposure. 10. fact or person revealed.

revelado adj. revealed, disclosed, manifest. **não** ~ untold.

revelador s. m. 1. revealer, discloser. 2. (phot.) developer. 3. (chem.) test, reagent. ‖ adj. 1. revealing, disclosing. 2. (phot.) developing. 3. (chem.) testing by reagent.

revelar (I) v. 1. to unveil, unmask. 2. to reveal, disclose. 3. to divulge, uncloak, unfold. 4. to make manifest, display, lay bare. 5. to expose, betray. 6. to detect, discover. 7. to disinter, unearth. 8. to indicate, show. 9. to make known or manifest through divine inspiration. 10. (phot.) to develop. 11. to tell, utter. 12. ~-**se:** a) to become manifest, manifest itself. b) to bare one's heart, disclose o. s. c) to make o. s. known.

~ **insuficientemente** (phot.) to underdevelop. ~ **os seus planos** to show one's cards. ~ **por tempo demasiadamente longo** (phot.) to overdevelop. **ela revelou o seu caráter verdadeiro** she betrayed her true character. **ele revelou covardia** he showed the

white feather. **ele revelou o segredo** he disclosed the secret. (fam.) he let the cat out of the bag.

revelar (II) v. 1. to be rebellious or insubordinate. 2. to default, fail to appear in court (when summoned).

revelável adj. m. + f. (pl. -**áveis**) 1. revealable. 2. (phot.) developable.

revelho s. m. very old person. ‖ adj. very old, macrobian.

revelhusco adj. 1. somewhat old, elderly. 2. hard-grained. 3. middle-aged.

revelia s. f. 1. non-appearance, default. 2. (jur.) non-suit.

à ~ in absence, without knowledge (of the defendant). **ele foi sentenciado à** ~ he was sentenced in default. **eles deixaram correr o negócio à** ~ they neglected the business completely.

revelim s. m. (pl. -**ins**) (fort) ravelin, demilune.

revelir v. 1. (med.) to draw off or away bodily humours. 2. to sweat, transpire. 3. to let blood, phlebotomize.

revência s. f. (N. Braz.) part of a valley which lies immediately under a river barrage.

revenda s. f. resale, second sale.

revendão s. m. (pl. -**ões**) (f. -**ona**) hawker, huckster, peddler. ‖ adj. reselling, hawking, peddling.

revendedor s. m. 1. hawker, huckster. 2. peddler. 3. reseller. 4. middleman. ‖ adj. reselling, hawking, peddling.

revender v. to resale, sell again, sell at retail.

revendição s. f. (pl. -**ões**) 1. act of reselling. 2. resale, second sale.

revendilhão s. m. (pl. -**ões**) (f. -**ona**) 1. hawker, huckster. 2. pedlar, peddler. 3. retailer. ‖ adj. reselling, hawking, peddling.

revendível adj. m. + f. (pl. -**íveis**) resalable, that may be sold again.

revenerar v. 1. to venerate. 2. to revere profoundly. 3. to show respect.

rever (I) v. 1. to see again, see a second time. 2. to review, observe with special attention, stare at. 3. to examine carefully, consider critically. 4. to correct, revise, proofread. 5. to amend. 6. ~-**se:** a) to see o. s. again (as in children or members of the family). b) to observe o. s. carefully, look at o. s. in a mirror. c) to be pleased, take pleasure in.

eles precisavam ~ **as contas** they had to examine the accounts.

rever (II) v. 1. to transude, transpire. 2. to show, demonstrate. 3. to reveal, divulge, make public.

reverberação s. f. (pl. -**ões**) reverberation, repercussion.

reverberante adj. m. + f. reverberating, reflecting (heat, light, etc.), reverberant.

reverberar v. 1. to reverberate. 2. to reflect, flash back. 3. to make brilliant or resplendent. 4. to shine, sparkle.

reverberatório adj. reverberatory, acting by reverberation.

reverbério s. m. (pop.) upbraiding, severe reprehension.

reverbero s. m. 1. act or effect of reverberating. 2. reverberation. 3. reflection. 4. reverberator. 5. street light or lamp. 6. reflector. 7. splendour, brilliancy.

forno de ~ reverberatory furnace, reverberatory.

reverdecer v. 1. to make green again. 2. to cover with greenery, break out again, sprout anew. 3. to invigorate, fortify. 4. to make new again. 5. to bring to the mind, remember. 6. to become green again. 7. to fortify or invigorate o. s. 8. to become young or youthful again, rejuvenate, rejuvenesce.

reverdecimento s. m. verdancy, act of becoming green again.

reverdejar v. to become green again, make or become very green.

reverência s. f. 1. reverence. 2. deference, profound respect. 3. veneration. 4. honours, homage, courtesy. 5. admiration, adoration. 6. fear, awe. 7. bow, bowing, obeisance. 8. Reverence, your Reverence: respectful form of addressing a clergyman. 9. curts(e)y.

reverenciado adj. reverenced, respected, honoured, obeisant.

reverenciador s. m. reverencer, reverer, worshipper. ‖ adj. reverencing, revering, worshipping.

reverencial adj. m. + f. (pl. -ais) reverential.

reverenciar v. 1. to treat with reverence. 2. to respect, honour, reverence. 3. to venerate, adorate. 4. to fear, stand in awe of.

reverencioso adj. 1. reverential, respectful. 2. ceremonious, formal. 3. polite. ‖ -amente adv. reverentially, ceremoniously.

reverendas s. f. pl. (eccl.) dimissory letters.

reverendíssima s. f. Your (His) Reverence: respectful form of addressing ecclesiastics.

reverendíssimo s. m. Right Reverend, Most Reverend, respectful form of addressing ecclesiastic dignitaries. ‖ adj. most reverend.

reverendo s. m. Reverend, a priest. ‖ adj. reverend, worthy of reverence or veneration, awful, respectful.

reverente adj. m. + f. reverent, reverential, respectful. ‖ ~-mente adv. reverentially, respectfully, devoutly.

reverificação s. f. (pl. -ões) reverification, act of checking or verifying again.

reverificador s. m. rechecker, customs officer who recontrols the work done by the inspectors. ‖ adj. rechecking, recontrol(l)ing.

reverificar v. 1. to verify again, recheck. 2. to control, compare, collate. 3. to revise, re-examine.

reversal adj. m. + f. (pl. -ais) (jur.) 1. revertive, revertible. 2. confirmatory (with regard to a given promise).

cartas -ais letters in which certain concessions are granted in exchange for a counterproposal.

reversão s. f. (pl. -ões) 1. reversion, act of reversing. 2. reversal. 3. return, comeback. 4. (jur.) escheatage. 5. devolution.

reversar v. 1. to vomit, throw up. 2. to return.

reversibilidade s. f. reversibility.

reversível adj. m. + f. (pl. -íveis) 1. reversible, capable of being reversed. 2. revertible, returnable. 3. (phys.) capable of reversing a reaction. 4. (jur.) reverting (said of property that has to revert to the original owner).

reversivo adj. reversive, reversible, revertible. ‖ -amente adv. reversively, reversibly.

reverso s. m. 1. backside, reverse. 2. opposite, contrariness. 3. verso. 4. dorsum. ‖ adj. 1. reverse, reversing. 2. opposite, contrary. 3. adverse. 4. perverse, depraved. 5. turned around, twisted.

revertátur s. m. (typogr.) revision: turn type sign.

reverter v. 1. to return, go back. 2. to revert, retrograde. 3. to invert. 4. to recoil. 5. to restore, restitute. 6. to turn to the contrary. 7. to redound, result in. 8. to change into.

a propriedade reverte de direito ao herdeiro legítimo the estate vests in the heir at law.

revertério s. m. (Braz., pop.) a turn for the worse.

revertível adj. m. + f. (pl. -íveis) revertible.

revés s. m. (pl. **reveses**) 1. reverse. 2. backside, opposite side. 3. stroke with the back of the hand. 4. the opposite, contrary. 5. setback, throwback. 6. disappointment. 7. check. 8. vicissitude, misfortune.

9. disaster. 10. unsuccessfulness, failure. 11. defeat.

ao ~ a) inside out, on the reverse. b) on the contrary. **ele sofreu um** ~ he met with a reverse. ~ **da fortuna** bad luck, turn of the die, a down. **sofreram um** ~ they suffered an eclipse.

revessa s. f. 1. countercurrent. 2. backwater, eddy. 3. sea current which changes its direction. 4. valley of the roof (plate T 5).

revessado adj. mutual, by turns. ‖ -amente adv. alternatively, by turns.

revessar v. 1. to reverse. 2. to turn inside out or upside down. 3. to do by turns.

revesso (ê) adj. 1. reversed. 2. turned backward or the contrary way. 3. (fig.) twisted, turned.

revestido adj. covered, coated, faced.

revestidura s. f. act or process of coating or covering.

revestimento s. m. 1. revetment, revetting. 2. covering, lining, coating, facing (plate L 1). 3. overlay, sheathing (plate F 5). 4. (tech.) jacket, bushing. ~ **com parquetes** parquetry. ~ **de penas** feathering. ~ **de tábuas** boarding. **sem** ~ coatless.

revestir v. 1. to revest, vest again. 2. to clothe or dress again. 3. to dress up, dress formally or showily. 4. to cover, coat, line. 5. (fort.) to revet. 6. to close, hide. 7. to pass o. s. off as, impose fraudulently. 8. to overlay, sheath. 9. to face, reline. 10. to encase, enwrap. 11. to invest, endow. 12. to give the aspect of. 13. ~-**se**: a) to vest o. s., dress up for. b) to arm or outfit o. s. c) to give the appearance of, take on airs. d) to resemble. e) to imitate, copy. 14. to jacket, case.

~-**am-se de paciência** they armed themselves with patience. ~ **com couro** to cover with leather. ~ **com metal** to braze. ~ **de tábuas** to clapboard, weatherboard. ~ **de pedras** to stone. ~ **de tijolos** to stean, (stein), brick. ~ **uma parede com papel pintado** to wallpaper, decorate. **revestiu-se de grande brilho** it took a brilliant course (festivity).

revezado adj. alternate, by turns. ‖ -amente adv. alternatively.

revezador s. m. substitute, proxy. ‖ adj. alternative, alterning, rotative.

revezamento s. m. 1. alternation. 2. rotation. 3. relief, relay. 4. reciprocal alternation, alternative.

revezar v. 1. to substitute alternatively, alternate. 2. to rotate. 3. to relieve, relay. 4. to take turns, do alternately.

revezo (ê) s. m. reserve pasture where the cattle is held during the replantation of the principal pasture.

revibrar v. to vibrate again.

reviçar v. to grow or flourish again.

revidar v. 1. to reply in kind, retort. 2. to correspond, requite. 3. to retribute. 4. to take revenge for an offense with another one. 5. (fenc.) to ripost(e). 6. to contradict. 7. to object to.

revide s. m. 1. retaliation. 2. reprisal, requital. 3. (cards) raising of a bet.

revigorante adj. m. + f. reinvigorating, strengthening.

revigorar v. 1. to give new strength or vigour to. 2. to reanimate, revive, revigorate. 3. ~-**se** to grow strong again, refortify o. s., gather new strength.

revimento s. m. 1. transpiration. 2. sweating, perspiration. 3. percolation. 4. sweating of a moist wall.

revinda s. f. 1. act of coming again. 2. return, returning. 3. regress.

revindita s. f. 1. revenge in retaliation. 2. second revenge. 3. redress, satisfaction. 4. requital.

revingar v. 1. to revenge again, take revenge a second time. 2. to retaliate, retribute, requite.

revir (I) v. to return, come home again, regress.

revir (II) v. to transpire, sweat, exude.

revira s. f. (N. Braz.) Negro dance and its music.

revirado s. m. (Braz.) 1. dish made of corn or manioc meal mixed with beans and meat or fish. 2. provisions (esp. for a journey). 3. gang of rowdies.
reviramento s. m. 1. act or effect of turning completely. 2. reversal, eversion. 3. sudden change (of opinions, ideas, etc.).
revirão s. m. (pl. **-ões**) welt of a shoe.
revirar v. 1. to turn, turn over again. 2. to turn inside out or upside down. 3. to twist, wrench. 4. to change, modify, alter. 5. to return, regress. 6. to evert, overset, upturn. 7. **~-se:** a) to turn around again. b) to persue, persecute. c) to revolt against.
reviravolta s. f. 1. complete reversal of position. 2. turn, overturn, reverse. 3. about-face. 4. ebb. 5. pirouette. 6. rotation, spin. 7. (Braz., pop.) return, a coming or going back.
houve uma ~ completa da opinião pública there was a complete veering round of public opinion.
revirete s. m. 1. sharp, witty or piquant remark. 2. retort, comeback.
revisão s. f. (pl. **-ões**) 1. revision, revisal. 2. revise, act of revising, review. 3. reading, proofreading. 4. re-examination, resurvey. 5. careful analysis of a law, lawsuit or decree with a view to its reform, rectification or annulment. 6. recension, overhaul, overhauling.
revisar v. 1. to visa again, give a second visa to. 2. to revise, review. 3. to read again, look over again. 4. to recense, overhaul. 5. to proofread, correct, re-edit. 6. to re-examine, resurvey.
ele revisa provas tipográficas he corrects proof.
revisionismo s. m. revisionism, advocacy of revision (constitution, laws, etc.).
revisionista s. m. + f. revisionist, one who favours revisionism. ‖ adj. revisionist, favouring revisionism.
revisitar v. to visit again, revisit.
revisível adj. m. + f. (pl. **-íveis**) reviewable, capable of being seen.
revisor s. m. 1. reviewer, reviser. 2. proofreader, reader. 3. corrector. 4. comptroller. 5. examiner, censor. 6. ticket inspector.
ele é ~ contábil juramentado he is a chartered accountant. **~ de provas** correctór of the press.
revisório adj. revisional, revisory, revisionary.
revista s. f. 1. act of revising, looking over again. 2. review, revisal. 3. survey, inspection. 4. muster, parade. 5. recension. 6. investigation, search, rummage. 7. (theat.) revue, muiscal comedy. 8. periodical, magazine. 9. publication, journal. 10. digest. 11. bulletin. 12. overhauling.
~ ilustrada pictorial. **~ publicada bimensalmente** bimonthly. **as tropas passaram em ~** the troops passed in review, the troops paraded. **eles procederam à ~ da casa** they set about a search of the house.
revistado adj. 1. revised, reviewed. 2. examined, searched. 3. inspected. 4. ransacked. 5. passed in review.
revistador s. m. 1. reviser, reviewer. 2. (mil.) inspecting officer. 3. examiner, investigator. ‖ adj. revising, passing in review.
revistar v. 1. to review, view again. 2. to examine, revise. 3. (mil.) to hold a review, inspect the troops. 4. to ransack, rummage. 5. to search, investigate. 6. to proceed with a legal search.
revisteca s. f. an insignificant or worthless magazine.
revisteiro s. m. revuist, writer of revues.
revisto adj. 1. revised, reviewed. 2. examined, inspected. 3. corrected. 4. checked. 5. amended.
revitalização s. f. (pl. **-ões**) revitalization, revitalizing.

revitalizar v. to revitalize, animate or revive again.
revivente adj. m. + f. 1. reviving, revivified. 2. reanimating.
reviver v. 1. to revive, revivify. 2. to return to consciousness. 3. to wake. 4. to renew. 5. to resuscitate, reanimate. 6. to grow strong again. 7. to reappear, manifest itself again. 8. to remind, cause to remember. 9. to freshen, refresh. 10. to take into use again.
revivescência s. f. 1. reviviscence, reviviscency. 2. revival, reanimation. 3. renewal, restoration.
revivescente adj. m. + f. revivescent, tending to revive, causing revival. ‖ **~mente** adv. reviviscently, revivably.
revivescer v. 1. to revive, revivify. 2. to return to consciousness, wake. 3. to renew, renovate. 4. to resuscitate, reanimate. 5. to reinvigorate, grow strong again. 6. to reappear. 7. to cause to remember. 8. to freshen, refresh. 9. to take into use again.
revivescimento s. m. 1. reviviscence, reviviscency. 2. revival, reanimation. 3. renewal, restoration.
revivescível adj. m. + f. (pl. **-íveis**) reviviscible, capable of reviving.
revivificação s. f. (pl. **-ões**) 1. revivification, revivifying. 2. revival, reanimation. 3. restoration. 4. (chem.): a) reduction, recovery of a metallic state. b) reactivation.
revivificante adj. m. + f. reviving. ‖ **~mente** adv. revivingly.
revivificar v. 1. to revivify. 2. to reinvigorate, reanimate. 3. to revive, freshen. 4. (theol.) to give new spiritual life to. 5. (chem.): a) to reduce, bring to a metallic state. b) to reactivate.
revivo adj. 1. reviving, revived. 2. resuscitated. 3. lively.
revoada s. f. 1. act of flying again or flying back. 2. flight (of birds), flock. 3. (fig.) opportunity, fitting occasion.
revoar v. 1. to fly again, fly back. 2. to soar, fly aloft. 3. to hover in the upper air. 4. to flutter, flit about. 5. to be or become agitated, grow uneasy.
revocação s. f. (pl. **-ões**) 1. revocation, act of revoking. 2. recall, recallment. 3. evocation. 4. repeal, annulment. 5. restitution.
revocar v. 1. to revoke, revocate. 2. to recall, call back. 3. to call again. 4. to request the return. 5. to evoke, evocate. 6. to cancel, annul. 7. to withdraw. 8. to refund, replace, give back.
revocatório adj. revocatory, tending to revoke.
revocável adj. m. + f. (pl. **-áveis**) revocable, recallable, retractable. ‖ **-avelmente** adv. revocably.
revogabilidade s. f. revocability, revocableness, defeasibility.
revogação s. f. (pl. **-ões**) 1. revocation, revokement. 2. (jur.) reversal, repeal. 3. cancellation, annulment. 4. recall, disaffirmation. 5. countermand. 6. (jur.) defeasance.
~ de doação ou legado (jur.) ademption.
revogado adj. revoked, cancelled, repealed, extinct. **não ~** unrepealed.
revogador s. m. revoker, reverser, canceller. ‖ adj. revoking.
revogante adj. m. + f. revoking, revocative.
revogar v. 1. to revoke, revocate. 2. to annul, cancel, rescind. 3. to unmake, undo, give up. 4. to repeal, recall, reverse. 5. to abolish. 6. to countermand, unwill, disaffirm.
~ uma doação to adeem a donation. **~am a terceira cláusula do contrato** they deprived of effect the third clause of the contract. **~am a sentença** they quashed the sentence.

revogatória s. f. revocatory act or document.
revogatório adj. revocatory, rescissory, revoking, re-calling.
revogável adj. m. + f. (pl. **-áveis**) 1. revocable, repealable. 2. reversible, retractable. 3. cancellable. 4. defeasible.
revolcar v. 1. to tumble. 2. to roll over, roll and toss about. 3. to rotate, spin around. 4. to throw, hurl, fling.
revolta s. f. 1. revolt, rebellion. 2. insurrection, insurgence, subversion. 3. mutiny, riot. 4. uprising, rising. 5. disorder. 6. (fig.) resentment, indignation. 7. revulsion, aversion. 8. (agric.) second crosswise tillage (of land).
em ~ up in arms.
revoltado s. m. rebel, revolter, insurgent. ‖ adj. revolted, revolting, insurgent, rebellious, seditious, subversive.
ele estava ~ com he cried shame upon.
revoltador s. m. rebel, revolter. ‖ adj. revolting, rebellious.
revoltante adj. m. + f. 1. revolting. 2. disgusting, shocking. 3. ungodly. 4. gruesome, frightful. 5. repulsive. 6. nauseating.
revoltão s. m. (pl. **-ões**) disorganized or inordinate movement.
revoltar v. 1. to revolt, rebel. 2. to raise up against, turn against. 3. to be disgusted, shocked or grossly offended. 4. to oppose, repel. 5. to disgust, resent. 6. to come back again, return. 7. to feel repugnance or aversion for. 8. to cause repugnance or indignation. 9. **~-se:** a) to riot, mutiny, rise on (or against). b) to be or become revolted. c) to feel indignation.
isso me revoltou it stirred my blood.
revoltear v. 1. to turn around repeatedly. 2. to wallow, roll about, welter. 3. to rotate, revolve. 4. to dance in a swinging or swaying manner. 5. **~-se** to twirl around.
revolto (ô) adj. 1. excited, agitated. 2. recurved, bent back or down. 3. turbulent, boisterous. 4. furious, angry. 5. disheveled, tousled. 6. violent, rough. 7. billowy (sea). 8. twisted.
cabelo ~ unkempt hair. **mar ~** a boisterous sea. **tempo ~** dark, cloudy weather. **terra -a** freshly ploughed ground. **tudo está ~** everything is topsy-turvy.
revoltoso s. m. rebel, insurgent, revolter. ‖ adj. revolted, turbulent.
revolução s. f. (pl. **-ões**) 1. revolution: a) act or effect or turning around. b) rotation, progressive circular motion. c) insurrection, rebellion. d) gyration, spinning movement. e) complete orbit of a celestial body. f) the time taken in completing the orbit. g) (sociol.) any radical change of fundamental principles or institutions. h) change, alteration. i) fundamental change of political organization. 2. natural transformation of the terrestrial crust. 3. moral perturbation, indignation. 4. revulsion, repugnance.
~ industrial industrial revolution.
revolucionado adj. revolutionized, overthrown, completely changed.
revolucionamento s. m. 1. revolution, revolt. 2. instigation to revolt. 3. revolutionizing. 4. fundamental transformation or change.
revolucionar v. 1. to revolutionize. 2. to incite, instigate (to revolution). 3. to stir up, turn over. 4. to render revolutionary. 5. to transform, change fundamentally. 6. to upset, disturb. 7. to provoke a tumult, cause commotion. 8. **~-se** to become revolted.

revolucionário s. m. 1. revolutionary, revolutionist, revolutioner. 2. revolutionizer. 3. progressionist, evolutionist. 4. inventor. 5. innovator, renewer, pioneer. ‖ adj. 1. revolutionary, subversive. 2. progressive. ‖ **-ariamente** adv. revolutionarily.
revolucionarismo s. m. revolutionism, revolutionary doctrines or principles.
revoluteante adj. m. + f. turning round, whirling, spinning around.
revolutear s. m. act of revolving, spinning around or flitting about. ‖ v. 1. to turn around, revolve. 2. to spin, whirl, wheel around. 3. to flit about, flutter.
revoluto adj. 1. revolved. 2. turned upside down and inside out. 3. stirred up, agitated. 4. (bot.) revolute, rolled backward or downward.
revolutoso adj. (bot.) revolute, rolled backward or downward.
revolvedor s. m. 1. revolving person or agent. 2. agitator, rouser. ‖ adj. revolving, upsetting, agitating, inciting.
revolver v. 1. to revolve. 2. to turn round, turn over again. 3. to turn over in one's mind, meditate. 4. to rummage, ransack, move round, tumble over. 5. to roll, rotate. 6. to excite, rouse, stir up. 7. to mix, mingle, blend. 8. to investigate, examine carefully. 9. to dig, excavate. 10. to circle, circumvolve. 11. to pass in review. 12. to irritate, upset. 13. to mutiny, revolt. 14. to disorder, disturb. 15. **~-se:** a) to welter, wallow. b) to trundle, move about in an inordinate manner. c) to spin, twirl. d) to busy or bestir o. s.
ele revolveu a terra he ploughed the ground. **ele revolveu tudo de baixo para cima** he turned everything topsy-turvy. **~ céu e terra** to move heaven and earth. **revolveu-se o mar** the sea grew rough.
revólver s. m. (pl. **revólveres**) 1. revolver, gun, (sl.) rod. 2. revolving nosepiece of a microscope (plate M 9).
ele tinha um ~ de seis tiros he had a six-shooter. **~ de pintura** spray pistol, spray gun (plate P 12).
revolvido adj. revolved, stirred, wrought-up, disturbed, agitated.
revolvimento s. m. revolution, revolving, revolvency.
revôo s. m. 1. act of flying again. 2. flying to and fro. 3. (Braz., cockfighting) the first attack of the gamecocks.
révora s. f. age of puberty, legal age for marrying.
revulsão s. f. (pl. **-ões**) (med.) revulsion, counterirritation.
revulsar v. (med.) to apply revulsion, cause revulsion, treat with revulsive remedies or agents, counterirritate.
revulsivo s. m. (med.) revulsive, revulsive remedy or agent, derivative. ‖ adj. (med.) revulsive, revulsionary, derivative.
revulsor s. m. (med.) chemical or mechanical irritant, revulsor.
revulsório adj. revulsionary, revulsive.
rexenxão s. m. (ornith.) a kind of blackbird (Scaphidurus niger).
reza s. f. prayer, praying, oration, rogation, supplication.
rezada s. f. common prayer for the dead.
rezado adj. 1. prayed, said in prayer. 2. told in secrecy, confidential. 3. much commented, much talked about.
rezador s. m. 1. praying man, devotee. 2. (Braz.) quack, faith-healer. ‖ adj. praying.
rezão s. m. (pl. **-ões**) (f. **rezona**) 1. (arch., pop. = **razão**). 2. (Port., prov.) religious person who is given to prolonged prayers.

rezar v. 1. to pray, say one's prayers. 2. to supplicate. 3. to read in the book of prayers, read the divine service. 4. to mention, say, tell. 5. to mutter, murmur. 6. to grumble. 7. to make a supplication to God or the Saints. 8. to ask earnestly for, call for. 9. to treat, deal with, entreat.

~ **o rosário** to tell one's beads. **as cartas rezam que** the letters purport that. **ela reza** she says her prayers. **o livro reza aqui** the book says here.

rezaria s. f. many prayers, continued praying.
rezina s. m. + f. pighead, stubborn, pigheaded or cantankerous person. ‖ adj. stubborn, pigheaded, cantankerous.
rezinga s. f. 1. grumble, gripe. 2. quarrel, altercation. 3. recalcitrance, stubbornness. 4. controversy.
rezingão s. m. (pl. **-ões**) (f. **rezingona**) grumbler, grouch, growler. ‖ adj. grumbling, growling, grouchy.
rezingar v. 1. to grumble, gripe. 2. to quarrel, squabble, altercate. 3. to recalcitrate, show stubbornness. 4. to dispute, contend for.
rezingueiro s. m. grumbler, grouch, growler. ‖ adj. grumbling, grouchy.
ria s. f. 1. estuary, mouth of a river. 2. river branch. 3. **~s** pl. ria.
riachão s. m. (pl. **-ões**) river, stream.
riacho s. m. rivulet, streamlet, brook, creek, bourn(e).
riamba s. f. (Braz., bot.) hemp, marijuana.
riba s. f. 1. high river bank. 2. steep slope, cliff. 3. (pop.) top, summit. 4. (Braz.) coffee-hulling machine.
de ~ from above, yonder, over and above.
ribada s. f. steep shore line, high river bank.
ribaldaria, ribaldia s. f. ribaldry, ribald act or saying.
ribaldo s. m. 1. rascal, scoundrel. 2. ribald. ‖ adj. ribald, ribaldish.
ribalta s. f. (theat.) row of footlights, limelight, floats (plate P 2).
ribamar s. m. 1. seashore. 2. high bank of a river or seashore. 3. land bordering a river, shoreland.
ribança s. f. (arch.) steep river bank.
ribanceira s. f. 1. steep bank of a river. 2. ravine. 3. cliff, steep slope. 4. bank, brae. 5. brink, border line.
ribeira s. f. 1. tract of land on a waterside. 2. bank, shore. 3. watering, irrigation. 4. riverine country. 5. high bank of a river. 6. rivulet, streamlet, brook. 7. (N. Braz.) riverine pasture or grazing of several farms.
ribeirada s. f. 1. strong and fast-running watercourse. 2. torrent, rapid stream. 3. gush, great volume of liquid (water, blood, etc.) gushing forth, outpouring.
ribeirão s. m. (pl. **-ões**) 1. (Braz.) ground suitable for diamond mining or washing. 2. large river, stream.
ribeirar v. (N. Braz.) to brand the cattle (before driving it to the common riverine grazing).
ribeirinha s. f. 1. rivulet, streamlet. 2. creek, brook. 3. **~s** pl. wading birds (collectively).
ribeirinho s. m. 1. riverain, one who lives near a river. 2. messenger, porter. 3. sand or rubble carrier. ‖ adj. 1. riverine, waterside. 2. riparian, riverain. 3. marginal.
ribeiro s. m. 1. rivulet, streamlet. 2. brook, creek. 3. (archit.) valley of a roof. ‖ adj. designative a certain kind of wheat.
ribete s. m. 1. hem, border. 2. seam. 3. welt. 4. brook, creek.
riboflavina s. f. (biochem.) riboflavin, vitamin B-2, lactoflavin.
ribombância s. f. booming, thundering, resounding.
ribombante adj. m. + f. booming, thundering, resounding.

ribombar v. 1. to boom, resound. 2. to thunder. 3. to echo, re-echo. 4. to rumble, make a heavy rolling sound. 5. to rattle. 6. to peal.
ribombo s. m. 1. thundering, clap of thunder. 2. roaring, rolling (sound). 3. boom, rumble. 4. peal. 5. resounding.
riça (I) s. f. (hatmaking) hair which falls from the felt when passing through the carding-machine.
riça (II) adj. f. frizzed, fuzzy (said of chicken feathers).
ricaço s. m. (pop.) rich person, moneybag, moneygrubber, nabob.
rica-dona s. f. (pl. **ricas-donas**) wife, daughter or heiress of a rich man.
ricanho s. m. rich but stingy fellow, miser. ‖ adj. niggardly, stingy, avaricious.
riçar v. 1. to make frizzly or curly. 2. to curl, become curled. 3. to bristle, stand on end. 4. to ruffle, dishevel.
ricercar s. m., **ricercata** f. ricercare, ricercata: a polyphonic choral composition on a sacred text, fugue.
richarte s. m. (sl.) little fat man. ‖ adj. stout, thickset, fat.
ricino s. m. castor-oil plant, ricinus.
rico s. m. a wealthy person, well-to-do. ‖ adj. 1. rich, wealthy. 2. abundant, plentyful. 3. fertile, productive. 4. precious, costly, valuable. 5. magnificent, splendid, superb. 6. (fig.): a) beautiful. b) happy, fortunate. 7. prosperous, substantial. ‖ **-amente** adv. richly, wealthily, splendidly, prosperously.
as classes -as the well-to-do, wealthy people. **avarento ~ não tem parentes nem amigos** the rich miser has neither kinsfolk nor friends. **casar com moça -a** to marry a fortune. **ele se faz de ~** he pretends to be rich. **ele é muito ~** he is very affluent. **eles são novos ~s** they are upstarts. **homem ~** magnate. **o distrito é ~ em gado** the district is well stocked with cattle. **são podres de ~** they are rolling in money. **ser ~ em** to abound (in, with).
rimas -as (lit., Fr.) rimes riches, rich rhymes.
riço s. m. 1. pad with tapering ends for the hairdo, (U. S. A., coll.) rat. 2. woolen fabric with a curly velvety surface. ‖ adj. curly, frizzed.
ricochete s. m. 1. rebound, bound, bouncing. 2. ricochet. 3. repercussion. 4. retrocession. 5. consequence, effect. 6. (fam.) scoff, taunt. 7. jest, mockery, railery.
ricochetear v. (also **ricochetar**) to ricochet, rebound, fly back, bounce back.
rico-homem s. m. (pl. **ricos-homens**) grandee, nobleman.
ricota s. f. ricotta (a cottage cheese).
ricto s. m. 1. rictus, gape of a mouth or muzzle. 2. grimace, contraction of the mouth (when laughing, etc.). 3. wrinkle, pucker.
ridência s. f. joy, cheerfulness, mirth.
ridente adj. m. + f. 1. smiling. 2. gay, cheerful, merry. 3. content, satisfied. 4. (fig.) luxuriant, thriving.
ridicularia s. f. 1. ridiculous act or saying. 2. jest. 3. trifle, bauble. 4. derisiveness, frivolousness. 5. ridiculosity.
ridicularização s. f. (pl. **-ões**) act or practice of exciting laughter, satire.
ridicularizador s. m. ridiculer, jester. ‖ adj. ridiculing, ridiculous, jesting.
ridicularizar v. 1. to ridicule, poke fun at. 2. to joke, jest. 3. to scoff, jeer, deride. 4. to make ridiculous. 5. to mock, taunt. 6. to travesty, burlesque.
eles ~am-me they made game of me. **não ridicula-**

rizem este homem don't poke fun at that man. ~-am-no they laughed him to scorn
ridículo s. m. 1. ridiculous act or saying. 2. ridiculousness, ridiculosity. 3. ridiculous person. ‖ adj. 1. ridiculous. 2. comic, laughable. 3. absurd, preposterous. 4. queer, foolish. 5. extravagant, frivolous. 6. burlesque. 7. farcial, farcical. ‖ **ridiculamente** adv. ridiculously, absurdly, foolishly, farcically.
ela o expôs ao ~ she held him up to ridicule. **fazer figura -a** to make an exhibition of oneself. **fazer-se** ~ to make a fool of o.s. **não se torne** ~ **em público** don't make an exhibition of yourself. **trataram-no de** ~ they made him the laughingstock.
rididico s. m. (ornith.) yellow-fronted woodpecker.
rieira s. f. furrow, rut.
riel s. m. riel: Cambodian currency.
rifa (I) s. f. raffle.
rifa (II) s. f. steep road, craggy path, steep slope.
rifada s. f. sequence of cards of the same suit.
rifador s. m. raffler. ‖ adj. raffling.
rifão s. m. (pl. -ões) proverb, adage, maxim, popular saying.
rifar v. 1. to raffle, dispose off by means of a raffle. 2. to cast or draw lots. 3. (sl.) to steal, rob. 4. pilfer, filch, swipe. 5. to whinny, neigh.
rifenho s. m. native or inhabitant of Er Rif (the coastal region of Morocco). ‖ adj. Riffian.
rifle s. m. rifle, carbine.
rigidez s. f. 1. rigidity, stiffness. 2. severity, strictness. 3. inflexibility. 4. austerity. 5. asperity, harshness. 6. formality.
~ **cadavérica** rigor mortis.
rígido adj. 1. rigid. 2. not pliant, not flexible. 3. stiff, unbending. 4. severe, strict. 5. precise, accurate. 6. austere. 7. stern, hard. 8. rough. 9. dour. 10. rigorous. ‖ **rigidamente** adv. rigidly, severely, sternly, dourly, formally.
demasiado ~ overrigid. **ele é um homem de caráter** ~ he is a man of unyielding character. **uma regra -a e inalterável** a hard and fast rule.
rigodão s. m. rigodoon: a lively dance and its music.
rigor s. m. 1. rigidity, rigidness. 2. hardness, harshness. 3. force, energy. 4. severity, strictness, sternness. 5. rudeness, roughness. 6. punctuality. 7. rigour, rigorousness. 8. austerity, austereness. 9. inclemency, asperity (of weather, climate, etc.). 10. insensibility, insensibleness. 11. (bot.) polygony (Polygonum orientale). 12. acerbity, asperity.
em traje de ~ in full rig; in formal dress. **com** ~ rigorously. **no** ~ **do inverno** in the dead of winter, in the deep of winter. **o** ~ **da lei** the rigour of the law. **trataram-no com** ~ they used him severely.
rigorismo s. m. 1. rigorism, rigourism. 2. rigidity in principle. 3. strictness, severity. 4. exactness, preciseness.
~ **de princípios** doctrinarianism.
rigorista s. m. + f. rigourist, precisian. ‖ adj. rigouristic, precisian.
rigorosidade s. f. 1. rigorousness. 2. sternness, strictness. 3. severity, harshness. 4. austerity, austereness.
rigoroso adj. 1. rigorous. 2. inflexible, unbending. 3. rigid, stiff. 4. inhuman. 5. demanding, exacting. 6. precise, accurate. 7. severe, stern, strict. 8. inclement. 9. rude, rough, rugged. 10. scrupulous, punctilious. ‖ **-amente** adv. rigorously, sternly, strictly, inclemently.
ele tem de ser observado -amente he must be watched closely. **eles agiram -amente** they conformed strictly to rules.
rijeza s. f. hardness, rigidness, stiffness, rigidity, tightness.

rijo s. m. the principal or most essential part of. ‖ adj. 1. rigid, stiff. 2. inflexible, unyielding, unbending. 3. hard, harsh. 4. solid, firm. 5. vigorous. 6. unfeeling. 7. tough, wiry. ‖ **-amente** adv. rigidly, stiffly, tightly, unyieldingly.
ele é um pouco ~ he is somewhat toughish.
rijoso adj. very rigid, unyielding, tight or tough.
rijume s. m. (Braz., pop.) regime, regimen.
ril s. m. reel: a lively dance and dance music.
rilhador s. m. gnawer, chewer, nibbler. ‖ adj. gnawing, chewing, nibbling.
rilhadura s. f. gnawing, nibbling, chewing.
rilhar v. 1. to gnaw, nibble. 2. to chew. 3. to munch, crunch. 4. to grind the teeth. 5. to grate.
rilheira s. f. a goldsmith's crucible.
rim s. m. (pl. rins) 1. (anat.) kidney. 2. pl. the inferior part of the lumbar region. 3. (archit.) spandrel.
região em redor do ~ adrenal region. ~ **flutuante** (med.) floating kidney.
rima s. f. 1. rhyme, repetition of the same sound at the end of two or more verses. 2. stack, heap, pile. 3. fissure, cleft. 4. chink, crack. 5. ~s pl. verses.
~ **feminina** feminine rhyme. ~ **infantil** nursery rhyme. ~s **consoantes** perfect rhymes. ~s **toantes** assonance. ~s **cruzadas** alternate rhymes.
rimado adj. rhymed, versified, jingly.
rimador s. m. rhymer, rhymester, versifier. ‖ adj. rhyming.
rimar v. 1. to rhyme, make rhymes or verses. 2. to form a rhyme. 3. to turn into verses, versify. 4. to conform, harmonize. 5. (fig.) to go well together, suit each other. 6. to be proper, fitting or decent. 7. to befit, behoove.
rimário s. m. a group of rhymes, poetry, book of verses.
rimático adj. of, referring to or relative to rhymes and verses.
rimbombar v. to thunder, boom, resound.
rimbombo s. m. thundering, clap of thunder, roaring, rumble, boom.
rim-de-boi s. m. (pl. rins-de-boi) (bot.) Brazilian cotton.
rimoso adj. rimose, full of fissures, cracked.
rímula s. f. (arch.) small crack or chink, fissure, crevice.
rinalgia s. f. (med.) rhinalgia, pain in the nose.
rinálgico adj. (med.) rhinalgic.
rinçagem s. f. hair rinse.
rincão s. m. (pl. -ões) 1. hidden corner, secluded place. 2. sylvan retreat. 3. place of retirement, nook. 4. (archit.) valley of a roof. 5. groove, stria, threadlike channel. 6. (carp.) grooving plane. 7. (S. Braz.) coppice, clump of trees.
rinchada s. f. 1. (sl.) horse laughter, roars of laughter. 2. neighing.
rinchão (I) s. m. (pl. -ões) 1. (bot.): a) hedge mustard. b) false valerian. 2. (ornith.) green woodpecker, popinjay.
rinchão (II) adj. (pl. -ões) (f. rinchona) neighing, neighing a lot.
rinchar s. m. neighing, whinnying. ‖ v. 1. to neigh, whinny. 2. to creak. 3. to grind the teeth.
rinchavelhada s. f. (hum.) loud laughter, horse-laugh, peal or burst of laughter.
rincho s. m. whinny, neigh, cry of a horse.
rincobdela s. f. (zool.) specimen of the Rhynchobdellida (an order of leeches).
rincocéfalo s. m. (zool.) rhynchocephalian.
rincóforo s. m. (zool.) specimen of the Rhyncophora (group of snout beetles). ‖ adj. rhynchophoran, rhynchophorous.

rinconar v. 1. to pen up cattle. 2. to drive the cattle to the camp. 3. (S. Braz.) to encamp, camp.

rinconista s. m. + f. 1. camper. 2. herdsman.

ringir v. 1. to gnaw, chew. 2. to grind or gnash the teeth. 3. to creak, squeak.

ringue s. m. (sport) ring, prize ring, arena of a circus.

rinha s. f. (Braz.) 1. cockpit, a pit for cockfights. 2. (pop.) quarrel, bout, fight. 3. cockfight, cock-fighting.

rinhadeiro, rinhedeiro s. m. (Braz.) pit for cockfights, cockpit.

rinhão s. m. (pl. -ões) 1. (arch., pop.) kidney. 2. (arch., fig.) fatty tissue, fat.

rinhar v. 1. (Braz.) to fight (as cocks), let cocks fight. 2. (S. Braz.) to quarrel, fight.

rinite s. f. (med.) rhinitis, inflammation of the nose.

rinoceronte s. m. (Braz.) rhinoceros.

rinocerôntico adj. (zool.) rhinocerial, rhinocerotic.

rinofaringite s. f. (med.) rhinopharingitis.

rinofima s. f. (med.) rhinophyma, acne of the nasal region.

rinofonia s. f. (med.) nasal or twangy voice.

rinologia s. f. (med.) rhinology: medical science treating of the nose.

rinológico adj. (med.) rhinologic(al).

rinologista s. m. + f. rhinologist.

rinoplastia s. f. (med.) rhinoplasty, plastic surgery of the nose.

rinoplástico adj. (med.) rhinoplastic.

rinoptia s. f. (med.) esotropia, strabismus in which the eye turns inward towards the nose.

rinorrafia s. f. (med.) suture of the borders of a nasal ulcer.

rinorragia s. f. (med.) rhinorrhagia, nosebleed.

rinorrágico adj. (med.) rhinorrhagic(al).

rinorréia s. f. (med.) rhinorrhea, excessive mucous secretion from the nose.

rinorréico adj. (med.) rhinorrheal.

rinoscleroma s. m. (med.) rhinoscleroma, sinusitis.

rinoscopia s. f. (med.) rhinoscopy, examination of the nasal cavity.

rinoscópio s. m. (med.) rhinoscope, instrument for examining the nose.

rinostegnose s. f. (med.) obstruction of the nasal passages.

rinque s. m. a roller-skating rink.

rio s. m. 1. river, stream. 2. water, watercourse. 3. torrent. 4. (fig.) great quantity.
~ **abaixo** down the river, downstream. ~ **acima** up the river. ~ **tapado** river whose mouth is completely closed up (by sands, or flat beaches). **ele ganha ~s de dinheiro** he makes pots of money. **peixe do** ~ fresh-water fish. **vau de** ~ river crossing, ford. **o** ~ **da unidade nacional** the national unity, (São Francisco) river.

rio-grandense-do-norte s. m. + f. (pl. **rio-grandenses--do-norte**) native or inhabitant of Rio Grande do Norte (Braz.). ‖ adj. of, pertaining to or relative to this state.

rio-grandense-do-sul s. m. + f. (pl. **rio-grandenses-do--sul**) native or inhabitant of Rio Grande do Sul (Braz.). ‖ adj. of, pertaining to or relative to this state.

riólito s. m. (petrog.) rhyolite, granitic lava.

rio-platense s. m. + f. (pl. **rio-platenses**) native or inhabitant of the River Plate region (Argentine). ‖ adj. of, pertaining to or referring to this region.

ripa (I) s. f. the act of hackling (flax, linen, etc.).

ripa (II) s. f. 1. narrow and long strip of wood. 2. lath, batten (plates C 4, 11, T 5). 3. shingle, chip. 4. clap-board.

meter a ~ **em** to give a good thrashing; (fig.) criticize.

ripa (III) s. f. high riverbank, river bluff, steep slope.

ripada s. f. 1. stroke with a lath. 2. thrashing, whipping, beating. 3. (fig.) upbraiding, scolding. 4. (Braz., pop.) drop of brandy.

ripado s. m. 1. lath-work, lattice-work. 2. plant house made of laths. 3. grating, railing, fence made of laths.

ripador s. m. a ripple (for flax, hemp, etc.).

ripadura, ripagem s. f., **ripamento** m. rippling or hackling of flax.

ripal adj. m. + f. (pl. -ais) fixing, fastening (strips of laths or shingles).

ripançar v. to ripple or hackle (as flax).

ripanço s. m. 1. flax ripple, hackle. 2. garden rake, harrow. 3. couch, sofa. 4. leisure, repose. 5. laziness. 6. indolent person. 7. (pop.) book containing the divine service of the Holy Week.

ripar (I) v. 1. to nail battens or laths on. 2. to lath, board. 3. to fence in. 4. to produce lath strips or latticework. 5. (Braz.) to thrash, beat. 6. (fig.) to criticize, censure.

ripar (II) v. 1. to comb linen or flax. 2. to hackle, ripple. 3. to clear the ground from stones with a harrow or rake. 4. to strip a branch of its fruit with one gliding movement of the nearly closed hand. 5. (Braz.) to shear a horse's mane.

ripária s. f. (bot.) American vine.

ripeira s. f. lath, batten, shingle.

ripeiro (I) s. m. (bot.) lichen of the family Lecideadaceae (Eschweilera polyantha).

ripeiro (II) adj. (Braz.) suitable for ripping into strips of wood.

ripiado adj. full of rough stones and rubble.

ripícola adj. m. + f. riparian, riverain.

ripídio s. m. (bot.) rhipidium.

ripidólito s. m. (min.) ripidolite.

ripina s. f. (Braz., ornith.) the double-toothed hawk.

ripio s. m. 1. rubble, pieces of rough stone, stone chips. 2. pebbles, gravel. 3. (fig.) expletive word, word used to fill up a sentence or to complete a poetic measure.

riposta s. f. (fenc.) ripost(e), thrust after a parry.

ripostar v. 1. (fenc.) to ripost(e), make a return thrust after a parry. 2. (fig.) to reply quickly, retort, rebut.

ripuários s. m. pl. (hist.) Ripuarian peoples, peoples who established themselves in the 4th century on both banks of the Rhine.

riqueza s. f. 1. wealth, riches. 2. wealthiness, richness. 3. abundance, affluence. 4. resources, substance. 5. fertility. 6. money, fortune. 7. wealthy people (collectively). 8. bonanza, cornucopia. 9. treasure. 10. property.
a ~ **tem os seus deveres** property has its duties.

rir v. 1. to laugh. 2. to smile, smirk. 3. to deride, mock. 4. to joke, jest. 5. to be gay, appear cheerful. 6. to peal with laughter, burst out laughing. 7. to sneer, snicker.
~ **a bandeiras despregadas** to shriek with laughter, split one's sides laughing, roar with laughter. ~ **à custa de outro** to laugh at someone's expense. ~ **alto** to cachinnate. ~ **ao sol** to laugh foolishly. ~ **às gargalhadas** to cackle, guffaw. ~ **à socapa** to chuckle, laugh into one's sleeve, chortle. ~ **à vontade** to laugh away. ~ **com riso amarelo** to laugh on the wrong side of the mouth. ~ **da desgraça alheia** to delight in mischief. ~ **manso** to titter. ~ **para as paredes** to laugh like a fool. ~**-se de** to laugh at. **ele faz a gente** ~ he keeps one in stitches. **fazer** ~ to amuse. **fazer** ~ **à sua custa**

to make o. s. a laughingstock. **ri melhor quem ri por último** he laughs best who laughs last.

risada s. f. loud laughter, peal of laughter.

risão adj. (pl. **-ões**) fond of laughing, risible, given to laughing.

risca s. f. 1. act or effect of scratching. 2. stroke dash. 3. stripe, streak. 4. part, parting (of the hair) (plates C 18, P 8). 5. line, ray. 6. (sport, play) aim, end, taw. 7. furrow.
à ~ precisely, exactly, literally. **fazer** ~ to cause disorder, provoke quarrel, oppose o. s. to. ~ **de união** hyphen. **~s da palma da mão** lines of the hand. ~ **de dois fios** (typogr.) the equal sign.

riscado s. m. striped linen or cotton fabric. ‖ adj. striped, streaked.
ele entende do ~ he knows the subject perfectly well, is competent, (coll.) has a dab at it. ~ **em linhas cruzadas** crisscrossed.

riscador s. m. scriber, tracer, scratch awl. ‖ adj. scribing, scratching.

riscadura s. f., **riscamento** m. 1. act or effect of scratching. 2. stripe, streak. 3. erasure. 4. striping.

riscar v. 1. to scratch out, rub out. 2. to expunge, delete. 3. to blot out. 4. to cross or strike out. 5. to line, trace, mark with lines. 6. to expel, cut off from membership. 7. to erase. 8. to eliminate from. 9. to scribe, scratch. 10. to stripe, streak, striate. 11. to cancel, obliterate. 12. to lose someone's friendship, be excluded from. 13. to engage in conflict with, quarrel with. 14. to provoke. 15. to delineate, outline. 16. to draw up, plan. 17. to try a knife before cutting or stabbing.
~ **da lista** to strike off the rolls. ~ **em cruz** to cross. ~ **da memória** to erase from the memory. **ele riscou a linha** he ran his pen through the line. **esta palavra precisa ser riscada** this word will have to go.

risco (I) s. m. 1. scratch. 2. stroke, dash. 3. stripe, streak. 4. outline, delineation. 5. trace, mark. 6. sketch, rough draft. 7. (sl.) stab with a knife. 8. stroke of a pen.

risco (II) s. m. 1. danger, peril. 2. venture, hazard. 3. unsafeness, perilousness, dangerousness. 4. chance, risk. 5. stake.
assumir um ~ to take a risk. **a todos os** ~ at all hazards, at all events. **com** ~ **de sua vida** at the peril of his life. **correr um** ~ to run a risk. **dar dinheiro a** ~ to venture one's money. **por seu** ~ at your peril. **por sua conta e** ~ for your account and risk.

riscoso adj. risky, dangerous.

risibilidade s. f. risibility, laughableness, risibleness.

risível s. m. (pl. **-íveis**) laughing stock. ‖ adj. 1. risible, laughable. 2. droll, ridicule. ‖ **-ivelmente** adv. risibly.

riso s. m. 1. laughter, laughing. 2. glee, joy. 3. smile. 4. derision, sneer. 5. laughingstock, ridiculous thing. 6. cheerfulness, mirth, merriment.
~ **alto** horse-laugh. ~ **à socapa** chortle. **perdido de** ~ dying with laughter, bursting with laughter. **ataque de** ~ a fit of laughter. **com** ~ laughingly. **forçar um** ~ **amarelo** to force a halfhearted smile. **morrer de** ~ to laugh o. s. to death, to split one's sides with laughter.

risonho adj. 1. smiling, cheerful. 2. riant, laughing. 3. exhilarated, frolicsome. 4. pleasant, agreeable. 5. satisfied. ‖ **-amente** adv. cheerfully, laughingly, pleasantly.
estar com a cara -a to be on the broad grin. **semblante** ~ cheerful look or countenance.

risório s. m. 1. (anat.) risorius. 2. (pop.) laughing muscle. ‖ adj. of, pertaining to or relative to this muscle.

risota s. f. 1. laughter, laughing. 2. mocking laugh, sneer. 3. joyfulness, merriment. 4. fun.

risote s. m. + f. 1. mocker, scoffer. 2. sarcastic person. 3. blasphemer. ‖ adj. scoffing, mocking, jeering, derisive.

risoto s. m. risotto, rice cooked with cheese, meat and gravy.

rispidez, rispideza s. f. 1. harshness, roughness. 2. severity. 3. sternness. 4. burliness, crustiness. 5. gruffness, crabbedness.

ríspido adj. 1. harsh, rough. 2. severe, stern. 3. intractable, unmanageable. 4. gruff, churlish, crabbed. ‖ **rispidamente** adv. harshly, roughly, sharply, rebukingly.
ele mandou-o embora em tom ~ he told him sharply to go.

rissole s. m. (Fr.) rissole: a small roll of minced meat or fish mixed with bread crumbs, eggs, etc., enclosed in a thin pastry and fried.

riste s. m. lance rest.
de dedo em ~ with a warning finger. **de lança no** ~ with the lance in the rest (ready to attack).

riteira s. f. plant of the family Malpighiaceae (Burdachia primatocarpa).

ritidoma s. m. rhytidome, thick and gnarled bark of old trees.

ritmado adj. rhythmic(al), cadenced, recurrent.

ritmar v. 1. to mark with rhythm, give rhythm to. 2. to subject to a certain rhythm. 3. to cadence.

rítmica s. f. 1. rhythmics: science or theory of rhythm. 2. the part of musical theory which studies the influence of rhythm on melodious expression.

rítmico adj. rhythmic(al), cadenced, measured, accentual. ‖ **ritmicamente** adv. rhythmically, measuredly.

ritmista s. m. + f. (Braz.) 1. percussionist. 2. the person who, in samba schools, beats the time of the **batucada**.

ritmo s. m. 1. rhythm, flow of cadence. 2. cadence, meter. 3. (mus.) beat. 4. tempo, time. 5. pitch, rate.
acompanhar o ~ to keep time. **continuar em** ~ **lento** to jog along. **regulação do** ~ timing. ~ **poético** poetical cadence or metre. **sem** ~ rhythmless. **em** ~ **de Brasília** (Braz.) hastily, in double-quick time.

ritmopéia s. f. rhythmopoeia, rhythmic art or method.

rito s. m. 1. ceremony or the complete regulation of ceremonies of a religion. 2. rite, ritual act. 3. cult, sect. 4. observance. 5. any formal and ceremonial act.

riton s. m. (hist.) rhyton, drinking vessel formed like the head of an animal or woman.

ritornelo s. m. (mus.) ritornello, prelude, interlude.

ritual s. m. (pl. **-ais**) 1. (rel.) book containing ceremonial rules of a church. 2. ceremonial, form of conducting a religious service. 3. code of ceremonies. 4. ritual, rife. 5. service, ordinance. 6. liturgy. ‖ adj. m. + f. ritual, formulary, liturgic(al).

ritualismo s. m. ritualism: 1. science and study of rituals or liturgies. 2. strict observance of, or special fondness for ritualistic forms. 3. ceremonialism.

ritualista s. m. + f. ritualist: 1. one skilled in rituals. 2. one who advocates ritualism. 3. ceremonialist. ‖ adj. ritualistic.

rival s. m. + f. (pl. **rivais**) 1. rival. 2. antagonist, opponent. 3. concurrent, competitor. 4. emulator. ‖ adj. rival, emulous.
sem ~ without rival, unrival(l)ed, paramount.

rivalidade s. f. 1. rivalry, rivalship. 2. antagonism, opposition. 3. concurrence, competition. 4. emulation. 5. (fig.) jealousy, envy.

rivalizar v. 1. to rival. 2. to compete. 3. to strive to equal or excel. 4. to dispute. 5. to emulate. 6. to vie with. 7. to oppose. 8. to be in rivalry. 9. to be jealous of, envy. 10. to act as a rival, enter into competition. 11. to be or become equal, match. **eles se rivalizam** they vie with each other.

rivalizável adj. m. + f. (pl. **-áveis**) that can be rivalled, capable of rivalry, matchable.

rivícola adj. m. + f. (bot.) riparian, riparial.

rixa s. f. 1. quarrel, dispute. 2. wrangle. 3. brawl, row, fracas. 4. disorder. 5. fight, feud. 6. discord, disagreement.
~s velhas old sores.

rixador s. m. 1. quarrelsome pugnacious person. 2. ruffian, brawler, rowdy. 3. disputer. ‖ adj. quarrelsome, pugnacious, rowdy.

rixar v. 1. to quarrel, wrangle. 2. to brawl, altercate. 3. to be quarrelsome, provoke dispute or disorder.

rixento adj. quarrelsome, pugnacious, disorderly, cantankerous.

rixoso adj. 1. quarrelsome. 2. pugnacious. 3. given to brawls or fights. 4. fractious, unruly. 5. cross, cantankerous. 6. rowdyish.

rizadura s. f. (naut.) 1. (act o*í*) reefing. 2. reefing rope.

rizagra s. f. special forceps for extracting tooth stumps.

rizanto adj. (bot.) rhizanthous, producing flowers directly from the root.

rizar v. (naut.) to reef, reduce a sail by taking in a part of it.

rizes s. m. pl. (naut.) reefs, reef points, lanyard.
meter a vela nos ~ to take up a part of the sail.

rizicultor s. m. rice grower, rice planter.

rizicultura s. f. rice-growing, rice-planting.

rizina s. f. (bot.) 1. Rhizina: a genus of fungi. 2. rhizine, rhizoid.

rizoblasto s. m. (bot.) rhizoblast, germ with only one rootlet.

rizocárpico adj. (bot.) rhizocarpic, rhizocarpous.

rizofagia s. f. rhizophagy, habit of feeding on roots.

rizófago adj. rhizophagous, feeding on roots.

rizofilo s. m. plant whose leaves produce roots. ‖ adj. producing roots (said of the leaves of certain plants).

rizófilo adj. (bot.) rhizophilous, living on roots, radicicolous.

rizoforácea s. f. 1. plant of the family Rhizophoraceae. 2. Rhizophoraceae: a family of trees and shrubs (order Myrtales).

rizoforáceo adj. (bot.) rhizophoraceous.

rizografia s. f. (bot.) rhizography: description of roots.

rizográfico adj. (bot.) rhizographic(al).

rizóide s. m. (bot.) rhizoid, rootlike filaments (in ferns and mosses).

rizoma s. m. (bot.) rhizoma, rhizome, rootstalk, rootstock.

rizomatoso adj. (bot.) rhizomatous.

rizomélico adj. (anat.) rhizomelic, pertaining to the roots of the extremities.

rizomorfo adj. (bot.) rhizomorphous, rhizomorphic, rootlike.

rizópode s. m. (zool.) 1. rhizopod. 2. **~s** pl. Rhizopoda: a division of Protozoa. ‖ adj. m. + f. rhizopod, rhizopodous.

rizóstomo adj. (zool.) rhizostomatous, rhizostomous.

rizotaxia s. f. rhizotaxy, arrangement or disposition of the roots of a plant.

rizotomia s. f. (surg.) rhizotomy.

rizotônico adj. (gram.) stressed on the first or root syllable.

roaz s. m. (zool.) harbour porpoise. ‖ adj. 1. gnawing. 2. carping. 3. destructive. 4. ravenous.

roaz-de-bandeira s. m. (pl. **roazes-de-bandeira**) (zool.) killer whale.

robalete s. m. 1. (naut.) bilge keel. 2. (zool.) small robalo, snook.

robalo s. m. (ichth.) robalo, snook.

robalo-de-areia s. m. (pl. **robalos-de-areia**) (ichth.) ten-pounder.

robe s. m. (Fr.) dressing gown.

robissão s. m. (pl. **-ões**) (Braz.) frock-coat.

roble s. m. oak tree, oakwood, white oak, roble.

robledo s. m. oak grove, oak thicket.

robô s. m. robot: 1. an automaton. 2. a person who acts and works mechanically, without thinking.

roboração s. f. (pl. **-ões**) roboration, strengthening, confirmation.

roborante adj. m. + f. roborant, strengthening, confirmatory.

roborar v. (also **roborizar**) 1. to increase the force of, strengthen. 2. to corroborate, roborate. 3. to confirm, ratify. 4. to invigorate.

roborativo adj. corroborative, roborative, confirmatory.

roboredo s. m. oak grove, oak thicket.

robustecedor adj. fortifying, strengthening, confirmatory.

robustecer v. 1. to make strong or robust. 2. to strengthen, fortify. 3. to harden, consolidate. 4. to roborate, corroborate. 5. to confirm, consolidate. 6. to enlarge, aggrandize. 7. **~-se:** a) to become strong or robust. b) to steel o. s. c) to exalt or enhance o. s.

robustez, robusteza, robustidão s. f. 1. robustness, burliness. 2. force, vigour. 3. hardiness, endurance. 4. lustiness.

robusto adj. 1. robust, burly. 2. strong, vigorous. 3. courageous. 4. solid, sound. 5. sturdy, tough, hardy. 6. stout. 7. powerful. 8. (coll.) lusty, strapping. 9. rugged, rough.
ele é um homem ~ he is a husky man.

roca s. f. 1. distaff, spinning-wheel. 2. (naut.) wooden pieces used to strengthen a (broken) mast. 3. ancient trimming of the sleeves. 4. wooden pedestal for the pictures of Saints. 5. rocks, broken stones.

roça s. f. 1. tract of newly cleared land. 2. act of clearing the ground. 3. open brush country. 4. corn or manioc field. 5. clearing, clearance. 6. rural regions, as opposed to a city or town.

rocada s. f. 1. the portion of flax or linen a distaff can hold. 2. a blow with a distaff.

roçada s. f. 1. cutting, burning and clearing of undergrowth. 2. cleared land, ground ready for planting.

roçadela s. f. act of cutting, burning and clearing the ground.

rocado s. m. heap of big rocks. ‖ adj. rocky, full of rocks.

roçado s. m. 1. cleared ground, field. 2. clearing, glade. 3. (Braz.) manioc field or corn field.

roçador s. m. one who clears land; weeder, planter, cultivator, farmer.

roçadoura s. f. scythe.

roçadura s. f. 1. act of clearing the land. 2. weeding. 3. abrasion, rubbing. 4. light touch.

roçagante adj. m. + f. 1. trailing, training. 2. rustling (like silk).

roçagar v. 1. to trail, train, drag along. 2. to make a rustling sound (as silken garments). 3. to touch slightly.

roçagem s. f. (pl. **-ens**) act or process of clearing the ground.

rocal s. m. (pl. **-ais**) string of beads or pearls. ‖ adj. m. + f. hard as rock.

rocalha s. f. 1. a lot of beads or pearls. 2. string of beads.

rocambole s. m. (Braz.) 1. a kind of fandango and accompanying music. 2. roly-poly (pastry) (plate D 3).

rocambolesco adj. 1. entangled, complicated. 2. full of unexpected incidents. 3. rash, precipitate.

roçamento s. m. act or process of clearing the land.

rocar v. (chess) to castle (plate X).

roçar v. 1. to clear the land of underwood (for planting). 2. to graze, touch lightly. 3. to cut down, fell. 4. to abrase, rub. 5. to scratch, fray. 6. to drag along, train. 7. ~-se: a) to glide, skid. b) to rub o. s. against.

rocaz adj. m. + f. growing or living on rocks.

rocedão s. m. (pl. -ões) twine, shoemaker's thread.

rocega s. f. (naut.) 1. act of dredging the bottom for lost objects (anchors, anchor-ropes, etc.). 2. a dragrope or cable.

rocegar v. to drag or sweep the bottom (of a river or harbour) for lost objects (anchors, cables, etc.).

roceira s. f. (Braz.) popular name of a number of pernicious leaf-cutting ants.

roceiro s. m. 1. planter, farmer. 2. one who clears the ground for planting; farmhand, clearer, weeder. 3. rustic, backwoodsman. ‖ adj. 1. of or pertaining to newly cleared land. 2. said of domestic animals which invade customarily new plantations when pasturing.

roceiro-planta s. m. (pl. **roceiros-plantas**) (Braz., ornith.) the striped cuckoo.

rocha s. f. 1. mass of compact hard stone, solid mineral matter. 2. large boulders, rock(s). 3. mineral(s). 4. (fig.) anything unchangeable or unshakable as rocks.
~ **calcária** limestone. ~ **errática** erratic rock. ~ **ígnea** igneous rock. ~ **siliciosa** burr-stone. ~ **vulcânica** vulcanic rock. **cristal de** ~ rock crystal. **ele é firme como uma** ~ he is as firm as rock. ~ **magmática** magmatic rock. ~ **sedimentar** sedimentary rock.

rochaz adj. m. + f. (pl. ~es) growing or living on rocks.

rochedo s. m. 1. steep, rugged rock, crag. 2. rock, stone. 3. cliff, bluff. 4. reef. 5. (anat.) petrous bone.

rochina s. f. (Braz.) a variety of manioc.

rochoso adj. 1. full of rocks, rocky. 2. stony. 3. cragged, clifflike.

rociada s. f. dewfall, formation of dew, dew.

rociar v. 1. to cover with dew. 2. to bedew, besprinkle. 3. to spread about like dew. 4. to become dewy.

rocim s. m. (pl. -ins) a small and weak horse, nag, jade.

rocinal adj. m. + f. (pl. -ais) of or relative to a nag.

rocinante s. m. a small and weak horse, nag, jade.

rocinar v. (S. Braz.) to make very docile, break in (horses) for the harness.

rocinha s. f. 1. little farm in the country, ranch. 2. small clearing. 3. house on the outskirts of a town surrounded by a garden. 4. country seat or mansion.

rocio (I) s. m. dew, mist, drizzle.

rocio (II) s. m. (Braz.) worn-out field used as pasture.

rócio s. m. (Braz., pop.) pride, vanity, self-conceit.

rocioso adj. dewy, misty, moist with dew.

rock-and-roll s. m. (Engl.) rock'n'roll.

rocló s. m. old-fashioned overcoat, roquelaure.

roço (I) s. m. (N. Braz., pop.) dew, dewfall, mist.

roço (ô) (II) s. m. 1. cutting of stones (in a quarry). 2. groove made in a block of stone (to split it up).

rococó s. m. 1. rococo, rococo style. 2. excessive or extravagant ornamentation. 3. old or old-fashioned things. ‖ adj. rococo: 1. of or pertaining to rococo in style. 2. florid, ornamented with flourishes. 3. old-fashioned. 4. of bad taste.

roda s. f. 1. wheel, circle (plates C 13, 15, R 2, 4, V 3). 2. (naut.) stempost or sternpost of a ship. 3. circumference, circuit. 4. turn-box (in the wall of a convent, asylum, etc.). 5. gyration, circular or spiral movement. 6. distribution (of s. th.) to surrounding persons. 7. respectless treatment. 8. round slice of a fruit. 9. passage of time. 10. social group, circle of friends, clique, round. 11. class, social rank. 12. a foundling hospital, asylum. 13. (hist.) instrument of torture, rack. 14. the outspread tail of a peacock. 15. (mech.) sheave. 16. (anat.) kneecap.
~ **d'água** water-wheel. ~ **de azenha** mill-wheel. ~ **de carro** cart-wheel. ~ **de coroa** crown wheel. ~ **de direção** circle guide; guide wheel. ~ **de engrenagem** rock-wheel. ~ **de moldes** (typogr.) mould disk, ratchet wheel, dog wheel (plate F 8). ~ **dentada** rack-wheel, gear-wheel, sprocket (plate B 11). ~ **de oleiro** potter's wheel. ~ **de regulagem do avanço** feed wheel. ~ **de reserva** stepney, step wheel. ~ **de rosca-sem-fim** worm wheel. ~ **de vento** fan wheel. ~ **diretriz** guide wheel (plate B 11). ~ **do leme** (naut.) steering-wheel (plate L 2). ~ **familiar de amigos** coterie. ~ **hidráulica de tomada por cima** overshot water-wheel. ~ **intermediária** idle wheel, idler. ~ **livre** freewheel. ~ **motriz** driving-wheel (plate B 11). ~ **pequena** truckle. ~ **traseira** rear wheel (plate M 12). **andar à** ~ to go in circles. **as crianças formaram uma** ~ the children formed into a ring. **de duas** ~**s** two-wheeled. **ele sofreu o suplício da** ~ he was broken upon the wheel. **eles fizeram a** ~ **à moça** they courted the girl. **sempre estou com a cabeça à** ~ I am always feeling giddy. **untar as** ~**s**: 1. to grease the wheels. 2. (fig.) to bribe s. o. **brincar de** ~ to play ring-a-ring o'roses; to join hands and dance and sing in a circle.

rodada s. f. 1. a complete turn of a wheel. 2. (Braz.) cold reception, act of rejecting or ousting somebody. 3. each round of drinks served to a group of friends. 4. (sport) each group of matches in a championship. 5. (S. Braz.) a falling headforemost (horse, or from a horse).

roda-de-pau s. f. (pl. **rodas-de-pau**) (Braz., pop.) thrashing, beating.

rodado s. m. 1. wheels of a cart or carriage. 2. width or roundness of a skirt. 3. rut, track (of wheels). ‖ adj. 1. wheeled, equipped with wheels. 2. elapsed, passed by (time). 3. (N. Braz.) spotted, dappled (horse).

rodador adj. stumbling or falling frequently (said of certain horses).

rodagem s. f. (pl. -ens) 1. a set of wheels. 2. gear or wheelwork of a machine. 3. wheel factory.

roda-gigante s. f. (pl. **rodas-gigantes**) (Braz.) Ferris wheel.

rodamento s. m. = **redemoinho**.

rodamontada s. f. rodomontade, vain boasting, swaggering.

rodante s. m. yoke of a water pump (driven by horses or oxen). ‖ adj. m. + f. rolling, (fig.) current, in style.

rodapé s. m. 1. (archit.) skirting board, baseboard, foot panel (plate D 4). valance, drapery covering the sides of a bed. 3. a serial publication at the bottom of a newspaper page. 4. wood panel covering the latticework of balconies.

roda-pisa s. f. (pl. **roda-pisas**) 1. hem of a skirt. 2. (archit.) washboard, skirting board.

rodaque s. m. (arch.) old-fashioned waistcoat.

rodar (I) v. 1. to roll. 2. to turn round, twirl. 3. to gyrate, rotate, revolve. 4. to move in circles, circle. 5. to torture on the wheel. 6. to float or navigate with the current. 7. to tumble, fall down. 8. to drive a car, travel in a car. 9. to meet with failure, have bad luck.

rodar (II) v. to rake up, work with the rake.

roda-viva s. f. (pl. **rodas-vivas**) 1. incessant movement, fuss. 2. commotion, confusion. 3. uneasiness, unrest.

rodeado adj. surrounded, encircled, encompassed.

rodeador s. m. (N. Braz.) place for the roundup of cattle.

rodeamento s. m. act or effect of encircling or surrounding.

rodear s. m. act of surrounding, encircling, roundup. ‖ v. 1. to surround, encircle. 2. to move around in circle, encompass, circle. 3. to rotate, gyrate, spin. 4. to engird, belt. 5. to detour. 6. to ensphere, ring in. 7. to keep (someone) company, live together with, have intimacy with. 8. **~-se:** a) to be accompanied. b) to surround o. s. with. c) to summon, send for. 9. to environ, hover round.

rodeio s. m. 1. act or effect of surrounding or encircling. 2. circumlocution, periphrasis. 3. subterfuge, pretext. 4. evasion, deviousness. 5. detour 6. circumambulation, circumvolution. 7. (Braz.) roundup of cattle, rodeo.

com ~s indirectly, in a roundabout way. **ele usou de ~s** he beat about the bush, he made a long rigmarole. **ele lhe perguntou sem ~s** he asked him point blank. **ele falou sem ~s** he used plain language. **sem ~s** without ifs or ans, fair and square. **parar ~** (S. Braz.) to round up cattle.

rodeira s. f. 1. nun or woman in charge of the turn-box in a foundling asylum. 2. track, rut (plate C 8). 3. carriageway. 4. (Braz.) wheels of a cart or carriage.

rodeiro s. m. 1. axle of a cart or carriage. 2. axletree, axle shaft, axis. 3. a pair of wheels on the same axle. ‖ adj. of, pertaining to or relative to wheels.

rodela s. f. 1. a small wheel or ring. 2. roundel, small circular shield. 3. (anat.) kneecap, kneepan. 4. (Braz.) boasting.

ele conta ~s he tells us tales.

rodeleiro s. m. buckler, soldier armed with a shield. ‖ adj. shielded.

rodelo s. m. a shoe patch, patchwork.

rodeta s. f. small wheel.

rodete s. m. 1. spool, reel. 2. bobbin on which silk or yarn is wound.

rodício s. m. spiked iron ball at the end of a scourge.

rodilha s. f. 1. scrub cloth, dishclout. 2. mop, swab. 3. rolled and twisted cloth pad (put under burdens carried on the head). 4. (fig.) worthless or despicable person. 5. (Port., prov.) knee.

rodilhão s. m. (pl. **-ões**) 1. large scrub cloth or dishclout. 2. small wheel of a cart or barrow. 3. sheave of a water-wheel.

rodilhar v. to wind around, twist, curl.

rodilho s. m. 1. scrub cloth, dishclout. 2. mop, swab. 3. rolled and twisted cloth pad (put under burdens carried on the head). 4. rag. 5. unprincipled or despicable person.

rodilhudo adj. (S. Braz.) having circular swellings on the fetlock joints and knees (said of horses).

rodinha s. f. 1. small wheel. 2. (Braz.) pinwheel (fireworks).

ródio (I) s. m. (chem.) rhodium (symbol: Rh).

ródio (II) s. m. Rhodian: native or inhabitant of Rhodes. ‖ adj. Rhodian.

rodízio s. m. 1. waterwheel. 2. shift, relay work, scheduling of work. 3. turn, rotation. 4. caster (wheel). 5. shady deal, sharp practices.

eles trabalham em ~ they work in turns.

rodo (ô) (I) s. m. (pl. **rodos**) rake (without teeth), wooden scraper, squeegee.

a ~ abundantly, plentifully.

rodo (ô) (II) s. m. (pl. **rodos**) knee.

rodocrosita s. f. (min.) rhodochrosite.

rododendro s. m. (bot.) rhododendron.

rodoferroviário adj. rail-motor.

rodogástreo adj. having a rose-coloured belly (insects).

rodografia s. f. description of roses, treatise on roses.

rodográfico adj. of, pertaining to or relative to a treatise on roses.

rodolego s. m. (N. Braz.) popular name of several kinds of ticks.

rodoleira s. f. (Braz., ichth.) caribe.

rodolita s. f. (min.) rhodolite.

rodologia s. f. (bot.) science and study of roses.

rodológico adj. of or relative to the scientific study of roses.

rodomoça s. f. (Braz.) a bus stewardess.

rodonita s. f. (min.) rhodonite.

rodopelo s. m. feathery tuft or fringe or hair (on the skin of animals).

rodopinte adj. m. + f. swirling, eddying, vortical.

rodopiar v. 1. to whirl about, twirl. 2. to hover round. 3. to turn round. 4. to circle, revolve, spin, rotate. 5. to go or move in circles.

nós rodopiamos dentro da sala we whirl round the room.

rodopio s. m. 1. whirl, whirling. 2. turning round, circumvolution. 3. rotation, spinning, gyration. 4. feathery tuft or twist of hair.

andar em ~s to move or turn round in narrow circles.

rodopsina s. f. erythropsin, visual purple, rhodopsin.

rodóptero adj. having rose-coloured wings (insects).

rodospermo adj. (bot.) having rose-coloured seed grains, rhodospermous.

rodóstomo adj. (zool.) rhodostomous, having a rose--coloured mouth.

rodouça s. f. = **rodilha**.

rodovalho s. m. (ichth.) turbot.

rodovia s. f. highway, (U. S. A.) thruway.

~ de duas pistas dual-carriage-way.

rodoviária s. f. (Braz.) bus station.

rodoviário adj. (Braz.) of, pertaining to or relative to a highway.

polícia -a highway police.

rede -a highway network or system.

rodura s. f. 1. act or process of raking together. 2. act of heaping up. 3. heap, pile. 4. a rakeful.

roedeira s. f. (N. Braz.) 1. epizootic disease of the cattle (which manifests itself at the base of the horns). 2. (pop.) jealousy, envy.

roedeiro s. m. a device used in falconry.

roedor s. m. 1. (zool.) rodent(s). 2. (pop.) drunkard. ‖ adj. 1. rodent, gnawing, biting. 2. corroding.

preocupações ~as griping worries.

roedura s. f. 1. act of gnawing. 2. nibbling, corroding. 3. sore caused by constant friction. 4. corrosion.

roel s. m. (pl. **roéis**) washer, flat iron ring.

roentgen s. m. roentgen: international unit of X radiation.

roentgendiagnóstico s. m. (med.) roentgenodiagnostics, art of diagnosing by means of X-rays.

roentgenfotografia s. f. roentgenography, X-ray photography.

roentgenologia s. f. roentgenology, radiology.
roentgenologista s. m. + f. roentgenologist.
roentgenterapia s. f. roentgenotherapy.
roer v. 1. to gnaw, nibble. 2. to bite, chew. 3. to corrode. 4. to erode. 5. to consume, wear down, use up. 6. to torment, afflict. 7. to hurt, offend. 8. to fret. 9. to destroy. 10. to throw away. 11. to screw down. 12. to meditate, ponder. 13. to mutter, grumble, backbite. 14. to talk ill of, slander. 15. (Braz.): a) to get drunk. b) to be jealous.
~ **as unhas** to bite one's fingernails; (fig.) worry or fret about. ~ **um osso** to pick a bone. **este negócio é duro de** ~ it is a hard job to settle this business. ~ **a corda** to fail one's promise.
rofo s. m. wrinkle, scratch, mark. ‖ adj. 1. wrinkled. 2. unpolished, rough. 3. dull, dim.
rogação s. f. (pl. **-ões**) 1. rogation. 2. petition, request. 3. supplication. 4. entreaty. 5. (Roman hist.) proposal of a law or decree presented to the people for ratification. 6. **-ões** pl. public prayers, litanies.
semana das -ões Rogation-week (week before Whitsunday).
rogado adj. prayed for, supplicated, entreated, requested.
não ~ unprompted, unsolicited.
rogador s. m. 1. supplicant. 2. intercessor. 3. mediator, arbitrator. ‖ adj. supplicant, entreating, interceding.
rogal adj. m. + f. (pl. **-ais**) of, pertaining to or relative to a funeral pyre.
rogar v. 1. to implore, supplicate. 2. to solicit, request. 3. to beg, pray for. 4. to beseech, entreat. 5. to plead, appeal, impetrate. 6. to woo.
ele faz-se ~ he seeks to be entreated, plays hard to get. ~ **pragas** to curse, imprecate.
rogativa s. f. prayer, supplication, entreaty, request, petition.
rogativo adj. supplicating, entreating, pleading, requesting. ‖ **-amente** adv. supplicatorily, entreatingly.
rogatória s. f. 1. rogative, supplication. 2. request, entreaty. 3. rogatory exclamation, sentence or discourse. 4. (jur.) certiorari.
rogatório adj. 1. rogatory. 2. supplicatory, supplicant. 3. precatory.
rogo (ô) s. m. 1. act or effect of asking for. 2. prayer, supplication. 3. entreaty. 4. petition, pleading, plea. 5. request, appeal. 6. apology.
a ~ **de** or **a seu** ~ at his request, at the request of. **carta de** ~ commendatory letter.
roído adj. 1. gnawed, corroded, worm-eaten. 2. (N. Braz., pop.) drunk.
~ **pelas traças** moth-eaten.
rojador s. m. crawler, creeper. ‖ adj. crawling, creeping, trailing.
rojão s. m. (pl. **-ões**) 1. act or effect of dragging along. 2. sound produced by dragging. 3. (pop.) drawn out chord (on the guitar). 4. rocket. 5. forced march. 6. exhaustive continuous work. 7. the hoofbeat of a galloping horse. 8. the course of an illness. 9. diapason. 10. mode of procedure, conduct. 11. noise produced by a sky-rocket. 12. (bullfighting) banderilla. 13. crackling, crisp toasted pork fat. 14. (bot.) a marifold (Tagetes minuta).
rojar v. 1. to drag along the ground, trail. 2. to draw or haul slowly. 3. to fling, hurl, throw. 4. to crawl, creep. 5. to clear land (for planting). 6. ~-**se**: a) to drag o. s. along. b) to walk with a heavy and unsteady step, walk with difficulty.
rojo (ô) (I) s. m. (pl. **rojos**) 1. act of dragging along, trailing the ground. 2. the sound produced by dragging.
andar de ~ to creep, crawl. **de** ~ trailing, creeping.
rojo (ô) (II) s. m. (pl. **rojos**) (Port., prov.) 1. blood-red or deep-red colour. 2. incandescence.

rol s. m. (pl. **róis**) 1. roll, list. 2. register, registry. 3. file, roster. 4. scroll. 5. (jur.) docket.
a ~ detailed. **pôr no** ~ to insert in a roll, register. ~ **das despesas** bill of expenses. ~ **dos soldados** muster roll.
rola (ô) s. f. (ornith.) 1. turtle dove. 2. common name of several small doves and pigeons.
rola-azul s. f. (pl. **rolas-azuis**) (Braz., ornith.) a variety of ground dove (Claravis pretiosa).
rola-bosta s. m. (pl. **rola-bostas**) common name of several scarabaeid beetles, tumblebug.
rola-cabocla s. f. (pl. **rolas-caboclas**) (Braz., ornith.) a variety of dove (Columbigallina talpacoti).
rolado adj. 1. enrolled, rolled (up). 2. rolling.
mar ~ rolling sea, choppy sea.
rolador s. m. 1. trolley. 2. roll, roller. 3. cylinder. ‖ adj. 1. rolling. 2. cooing.
rolagem s. f. (pl. **-ens**) (agric.) clod roller, heavy roll used to break earth clumps and clods.
rola-grande s. f. (pl. **rolas-grandes**) (Braz., ornith.) = **rola-cabocla**.
rolamento s. m. 1. act of rolling. 2. rolling (of a ship or of the sea). 3. welter. 4. (mech.) bearing.
~ **aquecido** (railway sl.) hotbox, overheated journal-box. ~ **de esferas** ball bearing (plate R 2). ~ **de rolos** roller bearing.
rolandiano adj. (anat.) Rolandic, of or relative to the Rolandic fissure (central sulcus).
rolante adj. m. + f. rolling, rotating, revolving.
fogo ~ (mil.) running fire. **o material** ~ **da ferrovia** the rolling stock of the railway.
rolão s. m. (pl. **-ões**) 1. pollard, bran, grit. 2. heavy wooden roller. 3. rod or bar placed under a heavy load (in order to roll it along). 4. (naut.) roller, a series of long heavy waves. 5. (N. Braz.) a grey dove appreciated as a game bird. 6. (Braz., folklore) an imaginary monstrous creature.
rola-pequena s. f. (pl. **rolas-pequenas**) (Braz., ornith.) ground dove.
rolar (I) v. 1. to roll, move by rolling along. 2. to cause to revolve. 3. to move in circles. 4. to set in motion, cause to go ahead. 5. to tumble, fall over. 6. to trundle, troll. 7. to welter. 8. to cut into logs (a tree). 9. to run on wheels. 10. to spin, whirl. 11. ~-**se**: a) to roll or move ahead. b) to sway, move with a rolling gait. c) to rise (waves), become rough (sea). 12. to resound.
~ **em terra por força própria** (aeron.) to taxi (on the airfield). ~**am na lama** they wallowed in the mire. **ela rolou os olhos** she goggled her eyes. **fizeram-no** ~ **morro abaixo** they sent him rolling down the hill. ~ **de rir** to roll with laughter.
rolar (II) v. 1. to coo (like doves). 2. (fig.) to utter kind words or endearments.
roldana s. f. (mech.) pulley, sheave, runner, block (plates A 10, E 2, G 5).
~ **de contato de bonde** tramway trolley. ~ **de guia** guide pulley. ~ **de um cadernal** cogwheel.
roldão s. m. (pl. **-ões**) 1. confusion, disorder. 2. precipitation, rashness, haste.
de ~ pell-mell, in confusion, precipitately.
roleira s. f. candlestick.
roleiro s. m. 1. act of rolling. 2. (Port., prov.) stack of wheat. ‖ adj. rolling, rotating, revolving.
mar ~ rolling or choppy sea. **navio** ~ rolling or tossing ship.
roleta s. f. roulette: 1. a gambling game. 2. the roulette wheel.
roleta-paulista s. f. (pl. **roletas-paulistas**) (Braz.) a test of daringness: crossing deliberately a street at full speed, during red light.
roleta-russa s. f. (pl. **roletas-russas**) Russian roulette.

rolete s. m. 1. roller, smal wheel. 2. caster. 3. a .hatter's roller. 4. plaited roll of hair. 5. the part of a stem of sugar-cane that lies between two nodes (or joints). 6. a piece of peeled sugar-cane. ~ **esticador** tightener. ~ **arrastado de excêntrico** cam follower roll. ~ **de contato** contact roller.

rolha (ô) s. f. 1. cork, stopper (plate G 2). 2. (sl.) scoundrel, rascal. 3. sly or cunning person. 4. silence imposed by force. 5. plug. **tirar a** ~ to uncork; (fig., fam.) to talk too much.

rolhado adj. corked, plugged up.

rolhador s. m. corking machine or instrument.

rolhadura, rolhagem s. f. (pl. ~**s, -ens**) act of corking bottles.

rolhar v. to cork bottles, stopper, close with a stopple.

rolheiro s. m. 1. corkmaker, cork manufacturer. 2. torrent, violent stream. 3. sheaf of wheat or rye. || adj. of or relative to cork production.

rolho (ô) adj. (pop.) fat, plump, chubby.

roliço adj. 1. round, roundish. 2. roly-poly, chubby. 3. plump, stout. 4. rotund. || **-amente** adv. roundishly, fatly.

rolim s. m. (pl. **-ins**) (ichth.) sunfish.

rolinha s. f. 1. (ornith.) common name of several doves (Columbia picui and related species). 2. (N. Braz.) a popular dance and accompanying melody. 3. (ornith.) talpacoti.

rolista s. m. (Braz., sl.) rowdy, ruffian, brawler. || adj. m. + f. disorderly, rowdy.

rolo (ô) s. m. 1. cylinder. 2. road roller, steam roller. 3. spiked heavy roller (used to roughen up the ground). 4. taper, wax candle. 5. package, bundle, roll (of paper, etc.). 6. roller, heavy waves. 7. whirlpool, eddy. 8. roll of hair, curl. 9. (typogr.) inking-roller, inker. 10. (fig.) multitude, agglomeration (of people). 11. (Braz.) brawl, row, riot. 12. mix-up, confusion. 13. male turtle-dove. 14. coil, wad. 15. painter's roller (plate P 12). ~ **de filmes** (phot.) film cartridge. ~ **de notas bancárias** bank roll. ~ **de papel de imprensa** web (of a printing press). ~ **de passar tinta** inking-roller, inker. ~ **para massas** rolling pin, paste roller (plates C 20, D 3). ~ **dador** (typogr.) inking roller, inker. ~ **tomador** (typogr.) ductor, ductor roller, drop roller.

rolotê s. m. (Fr., dressmaking) rouleau, a rolled trimming for a woman's dress.

Roma s. f. Rome. ~ **não se fez num dia** Rome was not built in a day.

romã s. f. 1. (bot.) pomegranate. 2. (naut.) the bulkiest part of a mast. 3. (ant.) a Roman woman.

romagem s. f. (pl. **-ens**) 1. pilgrimage, peregrination. 2. (fig.) instructive or recreational journey.

romaico s. m. Romaic: the modern Greek language. || adj. Romaic: of or pertaining to modern Greece an its language.

romana s. f. Roman balance, steelyard.

romança s. f. 1. ballad, epic or romantic song. 2. (mus.) ballade.

romançada s. f. (depr.) a lot of novels.

romançaria s. f. many romances or novels, romances or novels collectively.

romance s. m. 1. romance, novel. 2. fiction. 3. tale, fable, story. 4. Romance languages: any language developed from the vulgar Latin. 5. plot of intrigues. 6. incident, episode. 7. romantic love affair. || adj. m. + f. of, pertaining to or relative to Romance languages. ~ **barato** shilling shocker. ~ **baseado na realidade** key novel. ~ **criminal** thriller, detective story, penny dreadful, (sl.) whodunit. **um belo** ~ a nice work of fiction.

romanceação s. f. (pl. **-ões**) act of writing in form of a romance or novel.

romanceado adj. 1. written or told in form of a romance. 2. fanciful.

romancear v. 1. to tell or write down in form of a romance. 2. to romance. 3. to translate into or express in vernacular language. 4. to Romanize. 5. to invent stories, write novels or romances. 6. to exaggerate. 7. to indulge in fantastic stories, tell fibs.

romanceiro s. m. 1. collection of romances or novels. 2. collection of poems and popular songs (which make up the poetic literature of a nation). || adj. romantic, sentimental.

romanche s. m. Romansh, Romansch: the Rhaeto--Romanic dialects spoken in southeastern Switzerland.

romancismo s. m. 1. romanticism. 2. romantic character or style. 3. romantic tales, descriptions or fiction.

romancista s. m. + f. romancist, writer of romances, novelist.

romaneio s. m. (com.) packing or shipping list.

romanesco s. m. 1. romantic character. 2. Romanesque style in literature. 3. expression of boundless imagination in literature without consideration of reality. || adj. 1. Romanesque. 2. romantic, imaginary, fictitious. 3. dreamy, chimerical. 4. ardent, passionate.

romani s. m. Rom(m)any, Romanes: the language of the gypsies.

românico s. m. 1. Romance languages collectively. 2. Romance style in architecture. || adj. Romance, Romanic.

romanista s. m. + f. Romanist: 1. scholar of Roman law and institutions. 2. specialist of Romance languages and philology.

romanização s. f. (pl. **-ões**) Romanization, Romanizing.

romanizar v. to Romanize: 1. make Roman, give a Roman aspect to. 2. adapt to the spirit of Romance languages. 3. subject to Roman influence. 4. imitate Roman customs, speech and mannerisms.

romanizável adj. m. + f. (pl. **-áveis**) capable of being Romanized.

romano s. m. 1. Roman, native or citizen of Rome. 2. Latin: language of the ancient Romans. 3. Romanic. || adj. 1. of, pertaining to or referring to Rome (Italy). 2. Latin, Romance (languages). 3. Romanic, Romanish, Roman.

romano-bizantino adj. (pl. **romano-bizantinos**) Romano-Byzantine.

romanticismo s. m. romanticism, romantism.

romântico s. m. romantic, romantic writer or poet. || adj. 1. romantic. 2. dreamy, chimerical. 3. poetic, sentimental. 4. fantastic, fictitious, imaginary. 5. (arts) of or relative to romanticism.

romantismo s. m. 1. (arts) romanticism, romantism. 2. romantic or romanesque character. 3. romantic sentiment.

romantizar v. 1. to romanticize, give a romantic form or character to. 2. to tell in form of a romance. 3. to fancy, imagine. 4. ~**-se**: a) to put on romantic airs. b) to conceive the plot of a romance, write a romance.

romão s. m. 1. (arch.) Roman, native or inhabitant of Rome. 2. (arts, archit.) Byzantine style. || adj. Romano-Byzantine, Byzantine.

romãozinho s. m. (Braz., pop.) devil, fiend, Old Nick.

romaria s. f. 1. pilgrimage, peregrination. 2. procession. 3. reunion of devout people to celebrate a religious feast. 4. festival. 5. (fig.) a group of excursionists. 6. multitude.

romãzeira s. f. (bot.) pomegranate tree.

romãzeiral s. m. (pl. -ais) a grove of pomegranate trees.

rômbico adj. 1. rhombic(al), rhombus-shaped. 2. (cryst.) orthorhombic.

rombifoliado adj. (bot.) rhombifoliate, having rhombiform leaves.

rombifólio s. m. (bot.) rhomboid leaf.

rombiforme adj. m. + f. rhombiform, rhombic, rhomboid.

rombo (I) s. m. 1. forced entry, act of breaking into. 2. hole, gap, orifice. 3. (fig.) embezzlement. 4. rift, split. 5. leak.

rombo (II) s. m. 1. (geom.) rhomb, rhombus. 2. diamond, lozenge. ‖ adj. 1. flat, blunt. 2. (fig.) dull, stupid. 3. pointless.

romboédrico adj. 1. rhombohedral, rhombohedric. 2. (cryst.) derivable from a rhombohedron.

romboedro s. m. rhombohedron: six-sided prism whose faces are parallelograms.

romboidal s. m. (pl. -ais) (anat.) rhomboideus (muscle). ‖ adj. m. + f. rhomboid.

rombóide s. m. (geom.) rhomboid, parallelogram with oblique angles whose adjacent sides are unequal.

rombospermo adj. (bot.) having rhomboidal seed grains.

rombudo adj. 1. very blunt. 2. badly clipped or pared. 3. not sharp, pointless. 4. (fig.) stupid, dull. 5. rude.

romeira s. f. 1. female pilgrim, woman who accompanies a peregrination or procession. 2. large embroidered collar worn by female pilgrims, embroidered cape. 3. pomegranate tree.

romeiral s. m. (pl. -ais) a grove of pomegranate trees.

romeiro s. m. 1. pilgrim, peregrinator. 2. propugnator of great ideals or conceptions. 3. (Port., prov.) rosemary bush. 4. pilot fish.

romeliota s. m. + f. Rumelian, native or inhabitant of Rumelia (name of the former Turkish possessions on the Balkan peninsula). ‖ adj. Rumelian.

romenho s. m. dialect spoken by Portuguese gypsies.

romeno s. m. Rumanian, Romanian: 1. native or inhabitant of Rumania. 2. the language of Rumania. ‖ adj. Rumanian, Romanian.

Romeu s. m. Romeo: 1. (lit.) the hero of Shakespear's tragedy "Romeo and Juliet". 2. (fig.) a lover.

rominhol s. m. (pl. -óis) copper cup mounted on a long stick used in sugar making.

rompante s. m. 1. fury, rage, violent anger. 2. impetuosity, vehemence. 3. haughtiness, arrogance. 4. (archit.) springer of an arch. ‖ adj. m. + f. arrogant, haughty, proud.

rompão s. m. (pl. -ões) 1. calk of a horseshoe. 2. (Port., prov.): a) impetuosity, vehemence. b) fury, violent anger.

rompedeira s. f. a blacksmith's chisel, punch.

rompedor s. m. 1. destroyer, breaker. 2. one who wears out his clothes very soon. ‖ adj. breaking, destroying, disruptive.

rompedura s. f. 1. rupture, disruption. 2. rent, tear. 3. breach. 4. fracture. 5. (surg.) hernia.

rompe-gibão s. m. (pl. rompe-gibões) (bot.) chupon, bumelia.

rompente adj. m. + f. 1. breaking, bursting through. 2. attacking. 3. haughty, arrogant. 4. (her.) rampant.

leão ~ rampant lion.

romper s. m. 1. breaking, break. 2. rupture. 3. breach. 4. beginning, commencement, onset. 5. split. ‖ v. 1. to break, break up. 2. to split asunder. 3. to destroy. 4. to tear, rend. 5. to tear into pieces, dilacerate. 6. to shatter, smash. 7. to break open,

in or through. 8. to begin, commence. 9. to interrupt. 10. to violate, infringe. 11. to defeat, beat, rout. 12. to disperse, put to flight. 13. to conquer, vanquish. 14. to penetrate. 15. to reveal, disclose. 16. to throw o. s. against, oppose, fight. 17. to attack, assault. 18. to appear, emerge, show up. 19. to come forth, originate. 20. to irrupt, burst forth. 21. to become known. 22. to spurt, gush out. 23. to sever, separate, disrupt. 24. to cut (relations with). 25. to disconnect. 26. to rift, rip, rupture. 27. to shoot, fire. 28. to break the ground, till the soil. 29. to react. 30. to act, pass over or run along with impetuosity. 31. to sprout, bud, burgeon. 32. ~-se: a) to break up, burst. b) to rip apart, tear asunder. c) to wear out, become spoiled or damaged.

~ a fita da chegada (sports) to breast the tape. ~ as hostilidades to fall in with the enemy. ~ em choro, ~ em pranto to burst into tears. ~ o namoro to jilt a lover. ~ o silêncio to interrupt the silence, begin to speak. ~ um segredo to reveal a secret. ~ um caminho to open a road, (fig.) pave the way for. ~ uma lança pelo amigo to defend a friend. rompeu pelas linhas inimigas he broke through the enemy lines. rompi as relações com ele I broke off relations with him, I have done with him, (coll.) I sent him to Coventry. rompi em gargalhadas I broke into laughter. o namorado rompeu com ela her lover chucked her over. a corda rompeu-se pelo esforço the rope split under the strain. ao ~ do dia at daybreak, at dawn, at the peep of the day. ele rompeu com os vizinhos he broke (fell out) with his neighbours. o anel rompeu-se the ring snapped.

rompe-saias s. f., sg. + pl. plant of the family Compositae (Helminthia echioides).

rompida s. f. (S. Braz.) start at horse racing.

rompimento s. m. 1. act of breaking, disruption. 2. rupture. 3. split, burst, smash. 4. severance. 5. breach. 6. interruption. 7. start, beginning, onset.

houve um ~ entre eles there was a rupture between them. no ~ da guerra at the outbreak of war. o ~ de relações diplomáticas the rupture of diplomatic relations. ~ de contrato breach of covenant.

ronca s. f. 1. snoring, snore. 2. grapnel, grappling hook. 3. the drones of a bagpipe. 4. (fig.) bravado, boastful threat. 5. foghorn. 6. roaring. 7. (Braz., pop.) upbraiding, censure.

meter a ~ em 1. to slander, backbite. 2. to bring into ill repute. 3. to criticize sharply.

roncada s. f. 1. act of snoring. 2. (Port., coll.) a nap.

roncadeira s. f. (N. Braz., mus.) a kind of kettledrum used to produce a rhytmical scratching or rasping sound.

roncador s. m. 1. snorer. 2. boaster, braggart. 3. (ichth.): a) hogfish. b) pigfoot. c) grunt, grunter. 3. (Braz., pop.) waterfall, cataract. ‖ adj. 1. snoring. 2. roaring, groaning. 3. boastful, braggart.

roncadura s. f. 1. snore, snoring. 2. crash, sound produced by the explosion of a bladder. 3. roaring. 4. grunting. 5. rasping or scratching sound.

roncante adj. m. + f. snoring, roaring, grunting, groaning.

roncar v. 1. to snore, breathe with a rasping sound. 2. to roar. 3. to boom, resound. 4. to rumble, drone. 5. to snort. 6. to groan. 7. to boast, brag. 8. to threaten. 9. to cry like a buck in heat.

ele ronca no sono he snores, (coll.) drives his pigs to market.

roncaria s. f. 1. act of snoring. 2. rasping sound of a heavy or short breath. 3. hoarseness. 4. bravado, boasting, bragging. 5. the hollow sound of wind instruments.

ronçaria s. f. 1. slowness, slackness. 2. laziness, indolence. 3. negligence, carelessness. 4. neglect. 5. loafing.

roncear v. 1. to move slowly. 2. to dawdle, loiter, lounge about. 3. to dally, loaf, waste time. 4. (naut.) to sail slowly.

ronceirismo s. m. 1. slowness, tardiness. 2. slackness. 3. dullness, indolence. 4. laziness. 5. negligence. 6. any system opposed to progress, reactionary system or principles.

ronceiro adj. 1. slow, slow-moving, sluggish. 2. slack, tardy, dilatory. 3. dull, indolent. 4. lazy, slothful. 5. negligent. 6. reactionary.

roncha s. f. (N. Braz.) reddish mark on the skin caused by an insect sting.

ronchar v. (N. Braz.) to suffer from insect stings, be bitten by insects.

roncice s. f. 1. habitual or intentional slowness, sluggishness or negligence. 2. laziness. 3. dullness, indolence.

ronco s. m. 1. snore, snoring. 2. roaring. 3. grunting. 4. snarl, snarling, growl. 5. snort, grunt. 6. purring. 7. hollow rasping sound. 8. (med.) rhonchus, severe hoarseness. 9. bravado, boast, brag. || adj. hoarse, raucous.

roncolho adj. badly gelded or castrated.

roncor s. m. (N. Braz.) 1. snore, snoring. 2. harsh rasping sound. 3. hoarseness, raucousness. 4. rhonchus, difficult breath. 5. wheeze, wheezing sound.
o ~ da morte the rattles of death.

ronda s. f. 1. round, inspection (of sentinels or pickets). 2. patrol, prowl, rounds. 3. watch, beat. 4. round dance. 5. roundup (of cattle, criminals, etc.). 6. a game of chance.
andar de ~ to walk the rounds. eles fizeram a ~ they went their round. usaram um carro de ~ the used a prowl-car.

rondador s. m., **rondante** m. + f. 1. patrolman, patroller, watchman, prowler. 2. (N. Braz.) stick, used to twist together and hold firmly the strings of a package, harness, packsaddle, etc. || adj. patrolling, inspecting, prowling.

rondão s. m. (pl. -ões) 1. confusion, disorder. 2. precipitation. 3. (Braz., zool.) the barber bug (transmitter of the Chagas disease).

rondar, rondear v. 1. to walk the rounds, round. 2. to watch, be on the lookout. 3. to patrol, prowl. 4. to walk around. 5. to shift, veer around (wind). 6. to inspect. 7. (pop.) to hang around.
o vento ronda para o sul the wind is backing to the south.

rondel s. m. (pl. -éis) (poet.) rondel, roundel.

rondó s. m. 1. (poet.) rondeau. 2. (mus.) rondo.

rongó s. f. (Braz., pop.) prostitute.

ronha s. f. 1. (vet.) scabies, mange. 2. (pop.) craftiness, cunning. 3. demoralization, depravity.

ronhento, ronhoso adj. 1. (vet.) scabby, mangy. 2. (fig.) sly, cunning

ronquear v. to clean tunnies, prepare and pickle tunnies.

ronqueira s. f. 1. rasping sound of heavy breathing. 2. hoarseness, raucousness. 3. wheeze. 4. pulmonary disease of cattle. 5. roar. 6. (Braz.) iron tube filled with gunpowder and mounted on a wooden stick (used as pyrotechnical bomb).

ronquejador s. m. snorer, roarer. || adj. snoring, roaring.

ronquejante adj. m. + f. snoring, roaring.

ronquejar v. 1. to snore. 2. to wheeze, snort. 3. to roar. 4. to rumble, groan.

ronquenho adj. hoarse, raucous, wheezy, husky.

ronquidão s. f., **ronquido** m. (pl. -ões, ~s) 1. wheeze, wheezing (of horses). 2. hoarseness, raucousness. 3. snore, snoring. 4. snorting.

ronrom s. m. purr, purring (as of a cat).

ronronante adj. m. + f. purring, humming, whirring.

ronronar v. 1. to purr, 2. to hum, buzz. 3. to whir.

ropálico adj. rhopalic (verses, poems).

ropalócero s. m. insect belonging to the division of the Rhopalocera (butterflies). || adj. rhopaloceral, rhopalocerous.

roque s. m. 1. (chess) rook, castle. 2. (chess) castling. 3. (ornith.) a petrel.

roquefort s. m. (Fr.) Roquefort cheese.

roqueira s. f. 1. (mil.) ancient stone mortar. 2. blunderbuss. 3. (Braz.) = **ronqueira**. 4. small mortar.

roqueirada s. f. a series of mortar shots, a mortar shot.

roqueiro (I) s. m. distaff maker, manufacturer of spinning-wheels. || adj. of or relative to spinning-wheels and their production.

roqueiro (II) adj. 1. full of rocks, rocky. 2. consisting of rocks. 3. built on rocks. 4. rocklike.
castelo ~ a castle built on rocks.

roque-roque s. m. 1. act of gnawing, nibbling. 2. the sound produced by gnawing.

roquete s. m. 1. (eccl.) surplice, an outer vestment of white linen worn over the cassock; rochet (plate P 5). 2. ratchet, brace, drill. 3. (her.) chevron.

ror s. m. 1. a great quantity. 2. abundance. 2. lots, heaps, piles. 4. multitude.

rorante adj. m. + f. (poet.) dewy, moist with dew, roric.

rorar v. (Braz., poet.) 1. to bedew, cover or moist with dew. 2. to become wet with dew.

rorejante adj. m. + f. (poet.) dewy, roric, moist with dew.

rorejar v. (poet.) 1. to bedew, dew, moisten with dew. 2. spray, besprinkle. 3. to spatter, spurt forth in drops. 4. to bubble up, gush out. 5. to perspire, exude.

rórido adj. (poet.) dewy, roscid, moisted by dew.

rorídula s. f. Roridula: a genus of insectivorous shrubs.

roridulácea s. f. plant of the family Roridulaceae (Byblidaceae).

roriduláceo adj. (bot.) roridulaceous, byblidaceous.

rorífero adj. (poet.) roriferous, dewy, generating dew.

rorífluo adj. (poet.) rorifluent, flowing with dew.

ró-ró s. m. burr of a whirling top (or peg).

rorqual s. m. (pl. -ais) (zool.) rorqual, finner, piked whale.

rosa s. f. 1. rose, any plant or flower of the genus Rosa. 2. rosy cheeks. 3. (fig.) beautiful young woman. 4. a die used by bookbinders for stamping gold letters, gilding tool, pallet. 5. (archit.) rose window, rosette. 6. (mus.) the soundhole of string instruments. 7. any rose-coloured spot on the skin. || adj. m. + f. rosy, rose-coloured.
~ branca (bot.) blush rose. ~ brava, ~ canina (bot.) dog-rose. ~ damascena (bot.) damask rose. eles vivem num mar de ~s they live in the seventh heaven of delight, they are supremely happy. não há ~ sem espinhos no rose without a thorn. num mar de ~s on a bed of roses.

rosa-almiscarada s. f. (pl. **rosas-almiscaradas**) (bot.) abelmosk, abelmusk.

rosa-amarela s. f. (pl. **rosas-amarelas**) yellow rose, Austrian brier, sweet brier, eglantine.

rosaça s. f. 1. rosette, architectural ornament resembling a rose. 2. (archit.) rose window.

rosácea (I) s. f. (archit.) 1. rosette. 2. rose window. 3. escutcheon plate. ~ **de cinco cúspides** (archit.) cinquefoil.

rosácea (II) s. f. 1. plant of the rose family (Rosaceae). 2. **rosáceas** pl. the Rosaceae, the rose family. 3. rosacean, rose.

rosáceo adj. 1. (bot.) rosaceous, rosacean. 2. rose, rosy, rose-coloured. 3. rose-shaped.

rosa-choque, rosa-shocking s. m., sg. + pl. shocking pink (colour). ‖ adj. m. + f., sg. + pl. of or relating to shocking pink.

rosa-cruz s. m. 1. Rosicrucianism: an esoteric secret society founded in the 15th century: their principles, ritual and customs. 2. Rosicrucian: adherent of Rosicrucianism.

rosa-da-china s. f. (pl. **rosas-da-china**) China rose, Bengal rose.

rosa-da-turquia s. f. (pl. **rosas-da-turquia**) Jerusalém thorn.

rosa-de-agulha s. f. (pl. **rosas-de-agulha**) (naut.) compass rose.

rosa-de-cão s. f. (pl. **rosas-de-cão**) dog-rose.

rosa-de-cem-folhas s. f. (pl. **rosas-de-cem-folhas**) cabbage rose.

rosa-de-gueldres s. f. (pl. **rosas-de-gueldres**) guelder--rose, snowball, pincushion, bush cranberry.

rosa-de-jericó s. f. (pl. **rosas-de-jericó**) rose of Jericho, resurrection plant.

rosa-de-musgo s. f. (pl. **rosas-de-musgo**) moss rose.

rosa-de-são-francisco s. f. (pl. **rosas-de-são-francisco**) cotton rose, confederate rose.

rosa-de-vênus s. f. (pl. **rosas-de-vênus**) queen's lily.

rosado adj. 1. rose-coloured, rosy. 2. roseate, rosaceous. 3. damask. 4. florid, flush. 5. ruddy. **ela tem uma tez -a** she has a florid complexion. **mel** ~ honey of roses. **óleo** ~ rose-oil.

rosa-do-céu s. f. (pl. **rosas-do-céu**) rose of heaven.

rosa-dos-ventos s. f. (pl. **rosas-dos-ventos**) mariner's compass card.

rosa-do-ultramar s. f. (pl. **rosas-do-ultramar**) hollyhock.

rosal s. m. (pl. **-ais**) 1. rosary, rosetum. 2. rose garden, rose bed.

rosalgar s. m. (min.) realgar, arsenic monosulphide.

rosalgarino adj. of or referring to realgar, realgarine.

rosália s. f. (bot.) mountain rose (Antigonum leptopus).

rosalvo adj. pink, pinkish.

rosa-pálida s. f. (pl. **rosas-pálidas**) carnation.

rosar v. 1. to render rose-coloured. 2. to redden, make red. 3. to blush. 4. to become rose-coloured or pink. 5. **~-se** (fig.) to be or become ashamed.

rosário s. m. 1. (rel.) Rosary: a series of prayers said while meditating on a religious mystery. 2. rosary: chaplet, a string of beads used in counting prayers. 3. (mining) kibble-chain. **rezar o** ~ to tell over the rosary.

rosário-bravo s. m. (pl. **rosários-bravos**) (bot.) Indian oak.

rosário-de-jambu s. m. (pl. **rosários-de-jambu**) (bot.) eugenia.

rosa-rubra s. f. (pl. **rosas-rubras**) red rose, French rose.

rosa-shocking s. m., sg. + pl. = **rosa-choque.**

rosassolis s. m., sg. + pl. rosa solis (liqueur).

rosbife s. m. roast-beef.

rosca (ô) s. f. 1. thread, screw thread. 2. a spiral line or trace on any object. 3. a twisted or ring-shaped loaf of bread or cake. 4. coils or ringlets of a snake. 5. (zool.) cutworm. 6. (pop.) drunkenness, drunken spree. 7. (bot.) screw tree. 8. twist, torsion. 9. m. + f. a crafty, cunning or fickle person, treacherous person.

~ **diferencial** differential screw. ~ **macha** external thread, male screw. ~ **para tubos** pipe thread. ~ **sem fim** 1. spindle, perpetual screw, worm (plate P 4). 2. (auto) steering screw. ~ **torcida** (cozida em gordura) cruller. ~ **transportadora** conveyor screw or worm. **compasso de** ~ screw compasses. **cortar ~s** to cut screws, cut a thread. **fazer** ~ to thread. **filete de** ~ screw thread.

roscado adj. threaded, having a screw thread. **tampa -a** threaded cock.

roscar v. 1. to cut a thread or screw thread. 2. to screw down or together, screw.

róscido adj. (poet.) dewy, roscid, moisted by dew.

roscioso adj. dewy, roscid, roric, covered with dew.

rosear v. 1. to put forth rose-buds. 2. to develop as a rose. 3. to render rose-coloured. 4. to become rose-coloured or pink.

roseira s. f. 1. rosebush, rosier. 2. rose, rose-bud. 3. any plant of the family Rosaceae. ~ **brava** sweet brier. ~ **canina** dog-rose. ~ **francesa** French rose.

roseiral s. m. (pl. **-ais**) 1. rosary, rosetum. 2. rose garden, rose bed. 3. plantation of roses.

roseirista s. m. + f. 1. grower of roses. 2. fancier of roses.

roselha s. f. (bot.) a rockrose.

roselita s. f. (min.) roselite: a rose-coloured arsenate of calcium, cobalt, and manganese.

róseo adj. 1. of or relative to a rose or roses. 2. rosy, rose, rose-coloured. 3. resembling a rose. 4. fragrant. 5. ruddy. 6. blushing.

roséola s. f. (med.) roseola, rose rash, rubella.

roseta s. f. 1. a little rose. 2. rowel of a spur. 3. spiked iron ball at the end of a scourge. 4. rosette. 5. rose-shaped ornament or embroidery. 6. rosetted button or badge worn in the buttonhole as the insignia of a decoration. 7. red or reddish spot on the skin. 8. (bot.) cockspur.

roseta-de-pernambuco s. f. (pl. **rosetas-de-pernambuco**) plant of the cactus family (Rhypsalis sarmentosa).

rosetão s. m. (pl. **-ões**) (archit.) ornament resembling a large rose.

rosete adj. m. + f. light pink, pinkish.

rosetear v. to rowel, spur with a rowel.

roseteiro s. m. (S. Braz.) 1. an overgrazed pasture where only a few dry stalks of grass are left. 2. the proprietor of such a pasture. ‖ adj. overgrazed, worn out, poor (said of pastures).

rosicler s. m. 1. (min.) ruby silver ore, pyrargyrite. 2. rose or pink hue. 3. string (of pearls). ‖ adj. m. + f. light rose, pink.

rosiflor adj. m. + f. having rose or pink flowers.

rosigastro adj. (zool.) having a rose-coloured belly.

rosilho adj. sorrel, red-yellow (horse).

rosinha s. f. a little rose.

rosita s. f. (min.) aluminum silicate (with a rosy hue).

rosmaninhal s. m. (pl. **-ais**) a grove of rosemary bushes, garden planted with rosemary or French lavender bushes.

rosmaninho s. m. (bot.) 1. rosemary. 2. French lavender. 3. bushmint. 4. the aromatic flowers of these plants.

rosmaninho-bravo s. m. (pl. **rosmaninhos-bravos**) (bot.) marsh tea.

rosnadela, rosnadura s. f. 1. snarl, snarling. 2. growl. 3. grumbling, muttering.

rosnador s. m. grumbler, mutterer. ‖ adj. snarling, grumbling, growling.

rosnar s. m. snarl, snarling, growl. ‖ v. 1. to mutter, murmur. 2. to grumble, rumble. 3. to snarl, growl. 4. to maunder.

rosnento adj. (N. Braz.) snarling, growling, snarling much.

rosquear v. 1. = **roscar**. 2. (Port., prov.): a) to fall down (forming slings or rolling away). b) to punish, beat.

rosquilha s. f., **rosquilho** m. a ring-shaped cooky, ring-shaped small loaf, dough-nut.

rosquinha s. f. (zool.) 1. mollusc of the family Trochidae (Neomphalius viridulus). 2. = **rosquilha** (plate D 3).

rossiniano adj. of, resembling or relative to Rossini's (Italian composer and musician) art and music.

rossinismo s. m. (mus.) Rossini's interpretation and school of music.

rossio s. m. 1. plaza, public square. 2. big open market place. 3. large tract of cleared land in front of a farmhouse.

rostear v. (S. Braz.) 1. to face, look straight at. 2. to meet face to face. 3. to dare, brave. 4. to fell or cut down a tree so that it falls in the direction of the woodcutters.

rostelo s. m. rostellum: 1. (zool.) beak-shaped prolongation of the head. 2. (bot.) small projection beneath the retinacula (in orchids).

rostir v. 1. (sl.) to mistreat, mishandle. 2. to hit in the face. 3. to masticate, chew. 4. (Braz.) to rub, scratch, scrape.

rosto s. m. 1. face, front part of the head (plate C 18). 2. visage. 3. mien, physiognomy. 4. countenance, attitude. 5. front, fore part. 6. frontispiece. 7. head (of a coin, etc.). ~ **a** ~ face to face, vis-à-vis. ~ **da medalha** face of the medal. ~ **visto de perfil** half face. ~ **gravado** (typogr.) frontispiece. **em** ~ **da cidade** facing the town. **fazer** ~ **a:** 1. to face, be in front of. 2. to oppose, resist. **lançar no** ~ to throw into the face; (fig.) to upbraid severely. **trazer o coração no** ~ to be kind-hearted or open-hearted.

rostolho s. m. escutcheon of a keyhole.

rostrado adj. 1. shaped like a beak or spur. 2. beaked, rostral, rostrate(d).

rostral adj. m. + f. (pl. **-ais**) 1. rostral. 2. rostriform. 3. of, pertaining to or relative to the frontispiece (of a book). 4. beak-shaped or spur-shaped (said of the prow of a ship). 5. decorated with beak-shaped forms.

rostricórneo adj. (zool.) rostricorneous.

rostriforme adj. m. + f. rostriform, beaked.

rostrilho s. m. (bot.) little rostrum, little spur.

rostro s. m. 1. a bird's beak. 2. beak-shaped or spur-shaped figure-head on a ship's prow. 3. (bot.) spurlike prolongation of the corolla. 4. rostrum, platform, tribune (for orators). 5. proboscis of insects. 6. face.

rota (I) s. f. 1. fight, contest, bout. 2. rout, defeat. 3. direction, route, course. 4. circular route, round, circuit. 5. track. 6. way, walk. 7. Sacred Roman Rota: supreme ecclesiastical court of appeal. ~ **aérea** air route, airway, air-line. ~ **marítima** sea-route, sea-way. **de** ~ **batida, em** ~ **batida** in headlong flight. **navio na** ~ **para a China, Índia** Chinaman, Indiaman.

rota (II) s. f. 1. (bot.) rattan, rotang. 2. fibre of the rattan palm. 3. a thin walking stick (made from the stems of this palm).

rota (III) s. f. an ancient lutelike string instrument.

rotação s. f. (pl. **-ões**) 1. rotation, act of rotating. 2. gyration. 3. spin, twist, twirling. 4. circumvolution, circuit, round. 5. rolling. 6. alternative sequence of acts or facts, recurrence. 7. (agric.) crop rotation. ~ **à esquerda** anti-clockwise rotation. ~ **básica** base speed. ~ **de culturas** rotation of crops. **núme-**

ro de -ões por minuto number of revolutions per minute (abr. r.p.m.) ~ **da Terra** the rotation of the earth.

rotáceo adj. 1. wheel-shaped, rotiform. 2. (bot.) rotate. 3. (zool.) trochal.

rotacismo s. m. rhotacism, misuse or mispronunciation of the letter "r", substitution of some other sound for that of "r".

rotacista adj. m. + f. rhotacistic.

rotador s. m. 1. (anat.) rotator, muscle which rotates a limp. 2. (zool.) rotifer, specimen of the Rotifera. 3. ~**es** pl. (zool.) the class of Rotifera. || adj. rotating, gyrating, rotatory.

rotante adj. m. + f. rotating, gyrating, rotatory.

rotar v. 1. to go or move in circles. 2. to rotate, revolve. 3. to circumvolve, circulate.

rotariano s. m. Rotarian, member of the Rotary Club. || adj. Rotarian.

rotativa s. f. (print.) rotary press, rotary printing press.

rotatividade s. f. 1. rotativity, rotation. 2. crop rotation. **alta** ~ high rotation.

rotativismo s. m. rotativism, rotation in office or government.

rotativo adj. rotative, rotational, rotary, rotatory, revolving.

rotatório s. m. (zool.) rotifer, specimen of the Rotifera. || adj. 1. rotating, revolving. 2. rolling. 3. rotative, rotatory, rotational. 4. vertiginous.

rotear (I) v. 1. to clear the ground for planting. 2. to bring land under cultivation. 3. to cultivate, plant.

rotear (II) v. 1. to steer a ship, navigate. 2. to sail, journey on a ship. 3. to become seasick.

rotear (III) v. to cane chairs, make rattan seats and backs (for chairs).

rotearia s. f. act of clearing land for cultivation.

roteiro (I) s. m. 1. itinerary, route (of a journey). 2. road-book, logbook, guide-book. 3. pilot instructions, sailing directions. 4. (fig.) norm, rule, regulation. 5. syllabus.

roteiro (II) s. m. rattan-work or wicker-work maker.

rotejar-se v. 1. to become known, spread abroad. 2. to disclose, divulge. 3. to be known, be accepted (as fact). 4. to pretend to be.

rotenona s. f. (chem.) rothenone.

rotífero s. m. (zool.) rotifer, specimen of the Rotifera. || adj. rotiferal, rotiferous, wheeled.

rotiforme adj. m. + f. 1. (zool.) rotiform. 2. (bot.) rotate. 3. wheel-shaped.

rotim s. m. (pl. **-ins**) 1. (bot.) rattan palm. 2. rattan, cane.

rotina s. f. 1. routine. 2. regular or customary course of (business, occupation, amusement, etc.). 3. rote, custom, practice. 4. uneventfulness. 5. rut, groove. **a** ~ **cotidiana** the daily routine, the daily run. **cair na** ~ to fall into the old groove. ~ **burocrática** red-tape.

rotineira s. f. routine, custom, usual practice.

rotineiro s. m. 1. routinist. 2. automaton. 3. (depr.) Jack in office, hack. || adj. 1. routine, routinish. 2. habitual, customary. 3. uneventful. 4. groovy.

roto (ô) s. m. ragged or shabby fellow, ragamuffin. || adj. 1. ragged, tattered. 2. shabby, ratty. 3. torn. 4. broken. ~ **de mãos** open-handed, lavish.

rotofoto s. f. (typogr.) photocomposer, photocomposing machine.

rotogravura s. f. (print.) rotogravure.

rotoimpressão s. f. (typogr.) web-fed rotary printing process.

rotor s. m. (mech., electr.) rotor, impeller, armature (plate T 6).

rótula s. f. 1. grating, lattice-work, trellis. 2. (anat.) knee-cap, patella, rotula. 3. (anat., of horses) stifle-bone.

rotulação s. f. (pl. -ões) act of affixing a label, labelling.

rotulado adj. 1. labelled. 2. (fig.) marked, designated. 3. resembling a rotula. 4. (bot.) cancellate(d).

rotulagem s. f. (pl. -ens) act or process of labelling.

rotular (I) adj. m. + f. rotular, rotulian, of or relative to the patella.

rotular (II) v. 1. to label, affix a label. 2. to mark, designate. 3. to ticket, docket, tag. 4. to serve as a label.

rotuliano adj. rotulian, rotular.

rótulo s. m. 1. label (plate C 4). 2. mark, lettering. 3. ticket, docket. 4. inscription, heading, title. 5. brief description. 6. lattice-work in front of a peephole or window.
~ **gomado** sticker. **sem** ~ unlabelled.

rotunda s. f. 1. (archit.) rotunda, round building. 2. circular place.

rotundicolo adj. (zool.) rotundicollum, having a round collar or neck.

rotundidade s. f. 1. rotundity, roundness. 2. (fig.) plumpness, obesity.

rotundifólio adj. (bot.) rotundifolious, rotundifoliate.

rotundiventre adj. m. + f. (zool.) rotundiventral.

rotundo adj. 1. rotund. 2. round, roundish. 3. plump, chubby. 4. obese, fat.

rotura s. f. 1. rupture. 2. breach. 3. rent, crack. 4. fracture.

roubado adj. robbed, stolen, despoiled, ravaged.

roubador s. m. robber, thief. ‖ adj. robbing, ravaging.

roubalheira s. f. (coll.) 1. important, audacious or shocking robbery. 2. exorbitant price or charge. 3. spoliation or embezzlement of public funds.

roubar v. 1. to rob, take away by force. 2. to plunder, steal, burglarize, rifle. 3. to deprive of, strip of. 4. to hold up. 5. to spoil, ravage, ransack. 6. to rustle (cattle). 7. to lift, swipe, filch. 8. to rape. 9. to liberate, save. 10. to commit a robbery, act thievishly. 11. ~-**se**: a) to avoid, shirk from. b) to steal away from, escape. c) to take to flight. 12. to pick, pinch.
~**am-no de mim** they took it from me. ~ **no jogo** to rook. ~ **objetos roubados** (sl.) to swag. ~ **pesca ou caça** to poach. ~ **um beijo** to steal a kiss.

roubo s. m. 1. act or effect of robbing. 2. robbery, theft. 3. stolen goods, loot, booty. 4. rape. 5. (fam.) excessive price or fee charged for a merchandise or service. 6. spoliation, embezzlement.

rouco adj. hoarse, raucous, harsh, husky. ‖ -**amente** adv. hoarsely.

roufenhar v. 1. to nasalize, speak with a nasal twang. 2. to speak with a hoarse or husky voice. 3. to have a raucous or croaky voice.

roufenho adj. 1. nasal, twangy (sound, voice). 2. hoarse, raucous, husky.

round s. m. (Engl., boxing) round.

roupa s. f. 1. clothes, clothing, vesture, wearing apparel, wear (plate R 6). 2. dress, garment, garb, attire. 3. costume, habit. 4. body-clothing. 5. things, duds.
~ **branca** body linen. ~ **de baixo** underwear, undergarments, underclothes, smalls. ~ **de bebê** babies' wear (plate R 6). ~ **de cama** bedclothes, bedding, bed linen (plates C 7, D 4). ~ **de gala** dress clothes. ~ **de malha** tricot, knitwear. ~ **de mesa** table-linen. ~ **de ver a Deus** (Braz.) one's Sunday best. ~ **ensaboada** washing in soak (plate L 3). ~ **feita** ready-made clothes. ~ **interior** underwear. ~ **lavada** washing. ~ **para crianças** children's clothes, children's wear (plate R 6). ~ **para lavar** laundry, wash. ~ **para praia** beach suit (plate R 6). ~**s de banho** bathing costumes (plate B 3). ~**s para homens**, ~**s para cavalheiros** men's wear, gentlemen's wear (plate R 7). ~ **para senhoras** ladies' wear (plate R 6). ~ **suja** soiled or dirty linen. ~ **suja se lava em casa** wash your dirty linen at home. ~ **usada** worn clothes, (coll.) hand-me-down. **ele tirou a** ~ he took off his clothes. **ele trocou de** ~ he changed his clothes. **ele vestiu um terno de** ~ he wore a complete (three-pieced) suit. **em** ~ **caseira** in a house dress. **está na** ~! it is in the wash!. **estenda a** ~! hang up the wash. **etiqueta de** ~ tab. **vestido com** ~ **leve** thinly clad.

roupa-de-franceses s. f. (pl. **roupas-de-franceses**) common property, everybody's affair.

roupagem s. f. (pl. -ens) 1. underwear and clothes collectively. 2. garments, vesture. 3. artistic reproduction of clothes. 4. (fig.) outwardness, external appearance, superficiality. 5. bauble, gewgaw, trifle.

roupão s. m. (pl. -ões) 1. dressing gown. 2. (also ~ **de banho** bathing gown, bathing wrap, bathing coat (plate R 7). 3. house coat. 4. robe, wrapper.

roupar v. 1. to dress, clothe. 2. to provide with clothing. 3. to drape, arrange drapery.

rouparia s. f. 1. a lot or heap of clothes. 2. underwear and clothes collectively. 3. clothes shop, clothing establishment, warehouse for ready-made clothes. 4. wardrobe, clothes closet.

roupa-velha s. f. (pl. **roupas-velhas**) (Braz.) 1. stew made from rests of meat and meal. 2. Brazilian dish made from minced meat or jerked beef mixed with beans, manioc or flour.

roupavelheiro s. m. old clothes dealer, junkman, ragman.

roupeira s. f. 1. woman who takes care of the linen (in a household). 2. (female) keeper of the wardrobe.

roupeiro (I) s. m. 1. wardrobe, clothes closet. 2. keeper of the wardrobe or linen.

roupeiro (II) s. m. (Port., prov.) cheese maker.

roupeta s. f. 1. cassock, dalmatic, tunic. 2. m. (depr.) parson, cleric.

roupido adj. 1. clothed, dressed. 2. well-supplied with clothes.

roupinha s. f. 1. dim. of **roupa**. 2. bodice, short and tightly fitting jacket.

roupiquinha s. f. (Braz.) simple and modest garments.

rouquejado adj. hoarse, husky, croaky.

rouquejante adj. m. + f. croaky, hoarse.

rouquejar v. 1. to utter hoarse or husky sounds. 2. to suffer from hoarseness. 3. to croak, caw. 4. to bellow. 5. to roar, howl.

rouquenho adj. 1. somewhat hoarse. 2. nasal, twangy. 3. husky, raucous.

rouquice, rouquidão s. f. (pl. ~**s**, -ões) (also rouqueira). 1. hoarseness, huskiness. 2. raucousness, raucity. 3. (vet.) roup.

rouquido s. m. 1. harsh or hoarse sound caused by a whistling breath. 2. laboured or noisy breathing. 3. raucousness, huskiness.

rouxinol s. m. (pl. -óis) 1. (ornith.) nightingale. 2. (port.) philomel. 3. (fig.) a very good singer. 4. (ornith.) Brazilian wren.

rouxinol-da-muralha s. m. (pl. **rouxinóis-da-muralha**) (ornith.) redstart, starfinch.

roxear v. 1. to purple, make or dye purple. 2. to become purple.

Alças
Alça
Avental
Pregas
Renda
Combinação
Vestido
Combinação de calça e corpinho
Penteador
Casaco
Cinto
Camisola
Pijama
Sombrinha
Bolsa
Chapéu
Boina
Luvas
Meias
Escarpim
Sapato aberto
Chinelo

Gola
Blusa
Lapela
Manga
Cinto
Casaco
Saia
Saia e blusa
Tailleur
Cachecol
Véu
Casaco
Vestido
Cauda
Conjunto (vestido e casaco)
Vestido de baile
Óculos de sol
Pulôver
Calça esporte
Peúga
Sapatos de esporte
Traje de esporte
Roupa de praia

Boina
Casaquinho de peles
Gola de pele
Regalo
Casaco de peles
Casaco de inverno
Botas
Capa de chuva
Saia-calça
Vestido caseiro
Guarda-pó

ROUPAS PARA SENHORAS

Suspensórios
Camisa
Blusa esporte
Boné
Sobretudo
Calça
Calça rancheira
Bainha
Peúga
Calças
Peúga
Sapato atado com cordões
Sapato apresilhado
Sandália
Meia curta

ROUPA PARA CRIANÇAS

Jaqueta de malha
Touca
Meias curtas
Alça
Bordado
Bôlso
Botão
Aventalzinho
Fralda
Babador
Sapatinho de lã
Camisa
Camiseta
Roupa de dormir

ROUPA PARA BEBÊS

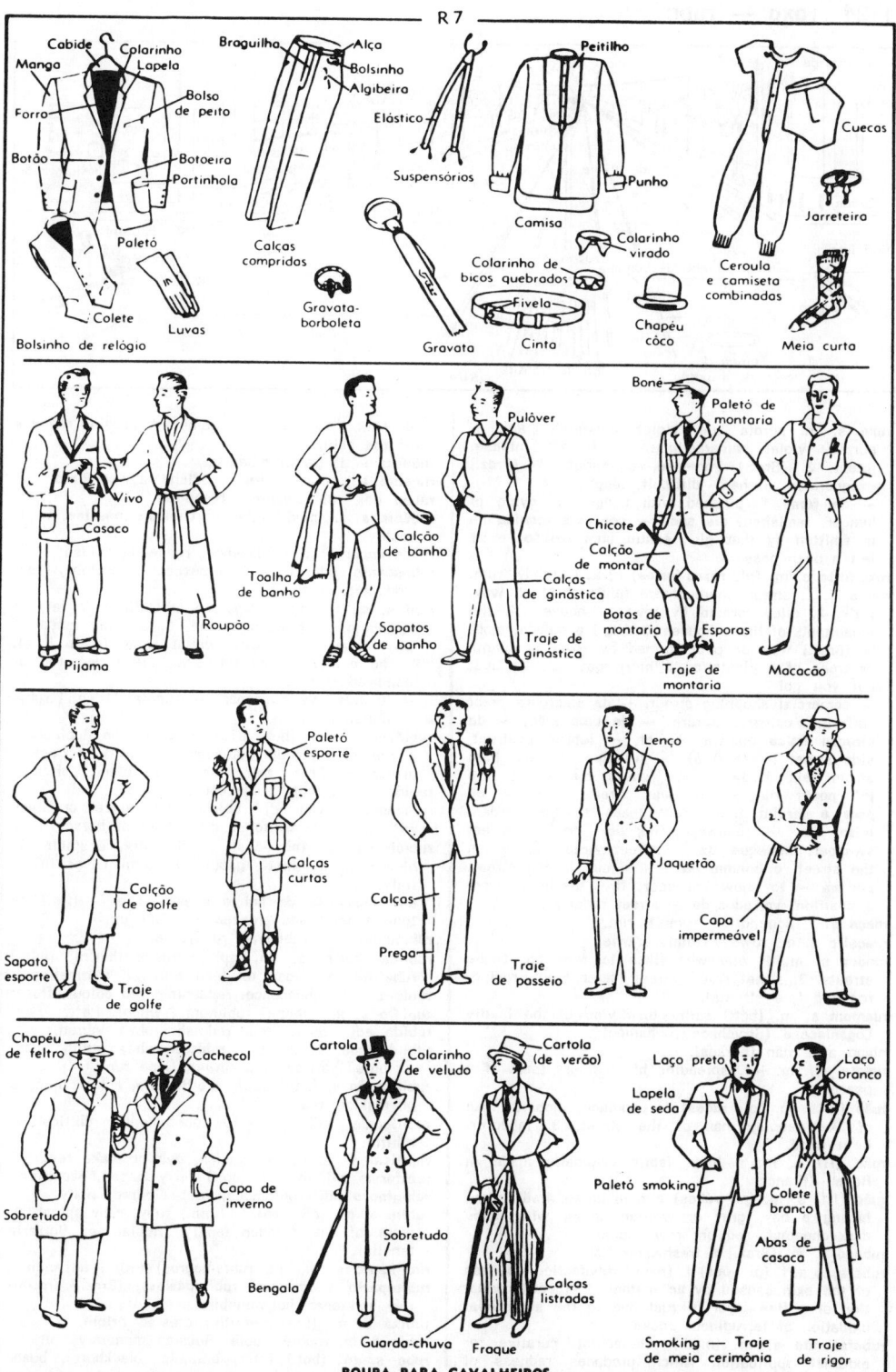

ROUPA PARA CAVALHEIROS

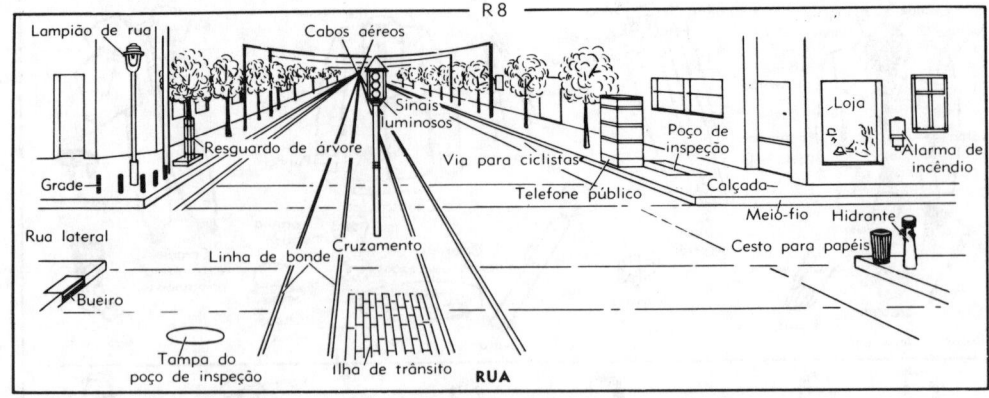

R 8

Lampião de rua — Cabos aéreos — Sinais luminosos — Loja — Poço de inspeção — Alarma de incêndio — Resguardo de árvore — Via para ciclistas — Calçada — Grade — Telefone público — Meió-fio — Hidrante — Rua lateral — Linha de bonde — Cruzamento — Cesto para papéis — Bueiro — Tampa do poço de inspeção — Ilha de trânsito — **RUA**

roxo s. m. purple hue, violet, amaranth. ‖ adj. 1. purple, violet, amaranthine. 2. (Braz.) intense, intent. 3. (Braz.) immense, enormous. 4. (Braz.) exaggerated. 5. hard, difficult, tough.
~ **de fome** 1. pinched with hunger. 2. dying of hunger, famished. **ele anda ~ por esta menina** he is smitten by that girl. **sentiu uma paixão -a** he felt a deep passion.

roxo-forte s. m. (pl. **roxos-fortes**) (Braz.) brandy, rum.

rua s. f. 1. street, thoroughfare (plate R 8). 2. way, walk. 3. alley formed by rows of houses. 4. the inhabitants of those houses. 5. (fig.) populace, mob. 6. (Braz.) way or path formed by rows of plants or trees of a plantation. ‖ interj. get out! be off!, out you go!
~ **comercial** shopping street. ~ **da amargura** great suffering, calvary; torture. ~ **de uma mão**, ~ **de direção única** one-way street. ~ **lateral** bystreet, side street (plate R 8). ~ **principal** avenue, high street. **ela é da** ~ she walks the street. **ele foi posto na** ~ he was fired. **esta** ~ **dá para o jardim** this street leads to the garden. **leito da** ~ roadway. **limpador de** ~ street sweeper. **moleque da** ~ street Arab. **na** ~ on the street. **o homem da** ~ the man in the street. **pôr na** ~ to show the door, fire, discharge from a position. **varredor de** ~ street orderly.

ruaça s. f. commotion, tumult, riot.

ruaceiro s. m. rowdy, rioter, brawler.

ruador s. m. 1. one who likes to rove about the streets. 2. street raker, street loafer. ‖ adj. roving, roaming (the streets).

ruamom s. m. (bot.) sarmentose vine of the family Loganiaceae (Strychnos rouhamon).

ruano adj. roan (horses).

ruante adj. m. + f. spreading his feathers (said of a peacock).

ruão (I) s. m. (pl. **ruões**) 1. populace, mob. 2. man of the people, man of the street. 3. labourer, farm hand.

ruão (II) s. m. a linen fabric originally made in Rouen (France).

ruão (III) s. m. (pl. **ruões**) a roan horse. ‖ adj. roan, having a bay, gray or whitish colour with some dark chestnut, red or brown spots.

rubago s. m. (Braz.) a freshwater fish.

rubefação s. f. (pl. **-ões**) 1. (med.) rubefaction, redness of the skin caused by an irritant. 2. (geol.) formation of a fine layer of rust due to the superficial oxidation of ferruginous rocks.

rubefaciente s. m. (med.) rubefacient, curative for external application which produces redness of

the skin. ‖ adj. m. + f. rubefacient, causing redness (of the skin).

rubelita s. f. (min.) rubellite.

rubente adj. m. + f. red, reddish, ruby-coloured.

rúbeo adj. ruby-coloured, blood-red.

rubéola s. f. (med.) rubeola, German measles, rose--rash.

rubescência s. f. rubescence, reddening, flush.

rubescente adj. m. + f. rubescent, becoming red, reddening, flushing.

rubi s. m. 1. (min.) ruby, red crystallized variety of corundum. 2. precious stone. 3. a thing made of ruby, jewel of a watch, pallet stone (plate R 4). 4. the colour of the ruby. 5. (poet.) deep-red or blood-red colour.
~ **do Brasil** yellow topaz. ~ **oriental** Oriental ruby. ~ **sintético** boule.

rubiácea s. f. 1. (bot.) a specimen of the Rubiaceae. 2. **rubiáceas** pl. the Rubiaceae: a family of tropical plants. 3. (Braz., coll.) the coffee plant, coffee.

rubiáceo adj. (bot.) rubiaceous.

rubicano, rubicão adj. rubican: bay, sorrel or black with flecks of white or gray (said of horses).

rubicão s. m. (pl. **-ões**) 1. difficulty, obstacle. 2. hindrance. 3. (hist., geogr.) Rubicon (river in N. Italy).
ele encheu-se de ânimo e passou o ~ (fig.) he took a heart and crossed the Rubicon.

rubicundo adj. rubicund, ruddy, red.

rubi-da-sibéria s. m. (pl. **rubis-da-sibéria**) (min.) rubellite, pale-rose to deep ruby-red tourmaline.

rubidez s. f. rubescence, reddening, red colour, flush.

rubídio s. m. (chem.) rubidium (symbol: Rb).

rúbido adj. (poet.) red, reddish, ruby-coloured.

rubi-do-cabo s. m. (pl. **rubis-do-cabo**) (min.) ruby--coloured variety of a garnet, Cape ruby.

rubificação s. f. (pl. **-ões**) rubification, act or process of making red.

rubificante adj. m. + f. rubefacient, rubificative, rubific.

rubificar v. to rubify, redden, dye or make red.

rubiforme adj. m. + f. (bot.) berry-shaped, bacciform.

rubiginoso adj. rubiginous, rust-coloured, rusty.

rubim s. m. (pl. **-ins**) 1. (min.) ruby, ruby spinel. 2. plant of the madder family (Rubiaceae: Borreria tenella).

rubi-negro s. m. (pl. **rubis-negros**) (min.) almandine.

rubitopázio s. m. (pl. **rubitopázios**), (Braz., ornith.) ruby-and-topaz hummingbird.

rubixá s. m. (Braz., ornith.) crested oriole.

rublo s. m. rouble, ruble, Russian monetary unit.

rubo s. m. (bot.) brier, bramble, blackberry, bush.

rubor s. m. 1. state or quality of being red. 2. redness. 3. red or ruby hue. 4. shame, modesty. 5. bashfulness. 6. blush.

ruborescer v. 1. to become red. 2. to make red, redden, rubify. 3. to flush, blush. 4. (fig.) to feel shame, become ashamed.

ruborização s. f. (pl. -ões) act or fact of reddening, blushing.

ruborizar v. 1. to make red, redden, rubify. 2. to become red. 3. to flush, blush. 4. (fig.) to feel ashamed.

rubrica s. f. 1. vermillion, red ochre, red chalk. 2. rubric, heading. 3. note, mark, sign. 4. caption. 5. check, countersign. 6. sign manual, special instructions, directions (to actors). 7. abbreviation of a signature, initials.

rubricado adj. rubricated, checked, countersigned.

rubricador s. m. rubricator, one who rubricates. ‖adj. rubricating.

rubricar v. 1. to rubricate. 2. to countersign, sign. 3. to initial. 4. to check. 5. to arrange in a rubric. 6. to rubrify.

rubricista s. m. + f. rubrician, rubricist.

rubricolo adj. (zool.) having a ruby-coloured neck.

rubricórneo adj. (zool.) having red or ruby-coloured feelers.

rubrigástreo, rubrigastro adj. (zool.) having a red belly.

rubrípede adj. m. + f. (zool.) having red feet.

rubrirrostro adj. (zool.) ruby-rostrate, having a red beak.

rubro adj. 1. ruby-red, blood-red, rouge. 2. vermilion, coral. 3. aglow, rubious. 4. rubicund, ruddy. 5. blush, flush.

~ **de cólera** flushed with anger. **surgiu pela neblina o disco ~ do sol** there emerged from the fog the fiery red disk of the sun.

ruçar v. 1. to make grey or whitish. 2. to become grey. 3. to age, grow old, become older. 4. to fade.

ruçar-se v. (pop.) 1. to smile with satisfaction. 2. to show o. s. cheerful and happy (in expectation of a reward, gift, etc.).

rucilho adj. having a white, red and black fell (said of a horse).

ruço s. m. (Braz.) a dense, heavy fog. ‖ adj. 1. grey, whitish. 2. faded, lusterless. 3. (pop.) light brown or sandy hair.

rude adj. m. + f. 1. rude, crude. 2. uncultivated, uneducated. 3. uncivil, ill-mannered, indelicate, unpolished. 4. ungentle, ungracious, unkind. 5. provincial, peasantlike, boorish. 6. rough, rugged, harsh, raw. 7. short, abrupt. 8. brute, brutish. 9. clumsy. 10. vulgar. ‖ ~**mente** adv. rudely, curtly, brusquely.

ela foi ~ she was off hand. **eles usam linguagem ~** they use strong language.

rudez, rudeza s. f. 1. rudeness, crudity, crudeness. 2. unmannerliness, roughness, ungraciousness. 3. ruggedness, asperity. 4. curtness, abruptness. 5. coarseness, churlishness. 6. ignorance.

rudimentar adj. m. + f. 1. rudimental, rudimentary. 2. primitive. 3. primordial. 4. elementary. 5. barbaric. ‖ ~**mente** adv. rudimentally, rudimentarily. **noções ~es** elements.

rudimento s. m. 1. rudiment, underlying principle. 2. element, grounds. 3. beginning, commencement. 4. first step, basic principle. 5. notion, A.B.C., general knowledge. 6. (biol.) undeveloped state of an organ, organ just beginning to develop.

~**s das ciências naturais** A.B.C. of science.

rudo adj. rude, crude, rough, coarse, boorish.

rueiro adj. 1. of, pertaining to or relative to streets. 2. fond of being in the streets.

ruela (I) s. f. bystreet, little street, alley, lane.

ruela (II) s. f. iron ring, washer.

rufador s. m. drummer. ‖ adj. drumming.

rufar v. 1. to beat the drum. 2. to drum, tattoo. 3. to call together with the sound of drums. 4. to produce a drumming sound. 5. to furnish with folds or pleats. 6. to give the form of pleats, fold into pleats. 7. to frill.

rufianesco adj. ruffianish, ruffianly.

rufião s. m. (pl. **rufiões**) (f. **rufiona**) 1. ruffian. 2. hooligan, bully, rowdy, thug. 3. (pop.) bully, fancy man. 4. pander, pimp. 5. (S. Braz.) a studhorse. 6. philanderer.

rufiar v. 1. to lead the life of a ruffian. 2. to be licentious or brutal. 3. to play the pander. 4. (S. Braz.) to look for breeding animals.

ruficarpo adj. (bot.) ruficarpous.

ruficórneo adj. (zool.) having red feelers, ruficornate.

rufigástreo adj. (zool.) having a red belly, red-bellied.

rufinérveo adj. (zool.) rufinerval, having red nerves.

rúfio s. m. ruffian, hooligan, rowdy.

rufipalpo adj. (zool.) rufipalpate, having a red palpus.

rufista s. m. + f. drummer.

rufitarso adj. (zool.) rufitarsal.

rufla s. f. 1. act of ruffling, rustling or fluttering. 2. a rustling sound (as produced by leaves, the swish of silk, etc.).

ruflante adj. m. + f. rustling, swishing (sound).

ruflar v. 1. to move about producing a rustling sound. 2. to rustle, rush, swish. 3. to ruffle. 4. to quiver, flutter, flit about. 5. to cause to tremble.

rufo (I) s. m. drumbeat, tattoo. 2. rolling of the drum, any sound resembling a tattoo, ruff. 3. ruffle, trill, ruche.

rufo (II) s. m. coarse file, rasp.

rufo (III) adj. (poet.) auburn, reddish-yellow, red.

ruga s. f. 1. wrinkle, small crease of the skin. 2. corrugation. 3. cockle, pucker. 4. fold, furrow. 5. plica, rivel. 6. (geol.) small bend or flexure in a formation of rocks.

sem ~ wrinkleless, unwrinkled.

rugado adj. rutted, wrinkled, furrowed.

rugar v. 1. to wrinkle, crease. 2. to furrow. 3. to fold.

rúgbi s. m. Rugby, Rugby football, rugger.

ruge s. m. rouge: reddish cosmetic for colouring the cheeks.

ruge-ruge s. m. (pl. **ruge-ruges, ruges-ruges**) 1. rustling or swishing sound. 2. rushing, murmuring. 3. creaking or squeaking noise. 4. (Braz.) noise, clamour. 5. (Braz.) hubbub, tumult, confusion, disorder.

rugido s. m. 1. bellow. 2. roar of a lion. 3. growl, growling. 4. a hollow sound.

rugidor s. m. roarer. ‖ adj. roaring.

rugiente adj. m. + f. bellowing, roaring.

rugir v. 1. bellowing. 2. roaring, roar (as of a lion). 3. growl, growling. 4. thunder. ‖ v. 1. to roar, howl. 2. to bellow. 3. to make a rustling or swishing sound. 4. to rumble, rustle. 5. to murmur. 6. to resound. 7. to growl. 8. to make a rubbing or scraping noise. 9. to yell, shout, cry out, vociferate. 10. to thunder.

rugitar v. 1. to make noise. 2. to roar, howl. 3. to bellow. 4. to rumble, rustle. 5. to yell, shout, vociferate. 6. to murmur.

rugosidade s. f. rugosity, quality of being rugous.

rugoso adj. 1. rugose, rugous. 2. wrinkled, creasy. 3. full of wrinkles. 4. dry, shrivelled, wizened. 5.

scraggy, furrowy. 6. (bot.) bullate. 7. rugged, rough.

ruibarbo s. m. (bot.) rhubarb, (U. S. A.) pieplant.

ruibarbo-de-china s. m. (pl. **ruibarbos-da-china**) (bot.) Chinese rhubarb.

ruidar v. to make noise.

ruído s. m. 1. noise, din. 2. hubbub, racket. 3. clamour, uproar. 4. rustling, rustle. 5. loudness. 6. tumult, row. 7. clattering, clatter. 8. (fig.) rumour, hearsay. 9. (fig.) fame, renown. 10. (fig.) ostentation, pomp.

~ **cósmico** (astr.) cosmic noise, galactic noise. ~ **de água corrente** babbling, gurgling. ~ **de motor** knocking of a motor. ~ **de passos** tread. **um** ~ **surdo** a baffled noise. ~ **do reator** (nucl. eng.) reactor noise. ~ **na comunicação** (radio) interference; distortion of sound. ~ **térmico** (electronics) thermal noise.

ruidoso adj. 1. noisy, boisterous. 2. uproarious, tumultuous. 3. loud. 4. (fig.) sensational, causing a stir. 5. pompous, showy, ostentatious. 6. blatant, rackety. || **-amente** adv. noisily, boisterously, blatantly, tumultuously.

ruim adj. (pl. **ruins**) 1. bad, ill. 2. unsavoury, awful. 3. wretched, miserable. 4. vile, rotten, wicked. 5. rascally, ill-natured. 6. useless, worthless. 7. (Braz., pop.) gangrenous (said of a wound). 8. atrocious, cruel. 9. poor, inferior.

agiram de maneira ~ they acted badly. **a um** ~, ~ **e meio** set a thief to catch a thief. **ele é um homem muito** ~ he is a fearful man. **eles passaram um tempo** ~ they had thin times. **o tempo era muito** ~ the weather was terrible.

ruína s. f. 1. ruin, wreck. 2. downfall, collapse. 3. destruction, deterioration. 4. shipwreck. 5. havoc, loss. 6. ruins. 7. relics. 8. debris. 9. ruination, devastation, fatality.

a causa de sua ~ **foi...** his undoing was... **cair em** ~**s** to fall into ruins. **causar a própria** ~ to cut one's own throat. **ele estava cavando a sua própria** ~ he was digging his own grave. **foi tudo para a** ~ everything went to wreck and ruin. **levaram-no à** ~ they brought him to ruin. **na iminência da** ~ **completa** on one's last legs. **uma** ~ **daquilo que ele era** a wreck of his former self.

ruinação s. f. (pl. **-ões**) ruination, act of ruining.

ruinaria s. f. a lot of ruins, several tumble-down buildings.

ruindade s. f. 1. badness, wickedness. 2. unholiness. 3. baseness, vileness. 4. depravity. 5. evil deed or action. 6. malice, malignity. 7. infamy.

ruinoso adj. 1. ruinous. 2. causing or tending to cause ruin. 3. destructive, pernicious. 4. ruined, dilapidated. 5. wasteful. 6. ramshackle, tumble-down. 7. (fig.) menacing, perilous, risky. || **-amente** adv. ruinously, perniciously.

estado ~ unrepair. **gastos** ~**s** wasteful expenditures.

ruinzeira s. f. (Braz., pop.) 1. indisposition. 2. premonitory symptons of a coming illness. 3. poor state of health.

ruir v. 1. to tumble down (or in), collapse. 2. to fall into ruins. 3. to crumble away, crash.

ruiva s. f. 1. (bot.) madderwort. 2. (ornith.) song thrush, mavis, throstle. 3. woman with auburn or red hair. 4. morning or sunset glow, red morning or evening sky. 5. (min.) rutile.

ruivacento adj. reddish, somewhat auburn or red.

ruiva-da-índia s. f. (pl. **ruivas-da-índia**) (bot.) Indian madder.

ruiva-dos-tintureiros s. f. (pl. **ruivas-dos-tintureiros**) (bot.) madder.

ruividão s. f. (pl. **-ões**) auburn, red-yellow.

ruivo s. m. 1. auburn or red-haired man. 2. (ichth.) red gurnard, red crooner. 3. (bot.) a three-awn grass. || adj. 1. rufous, reddish-yellow, auburn, russet. 2. red-haired.

rulo s. m. cooing.

rum s. m. rum, liquor prepared by fermenting molasses.

ruma (I) s. f. pile, stack, heap.

ruma (II) interj. gee-ho!, gee up! (an oxcart driver's shout).

rumar v. 1. to steer to, head for. 2. to set a course. 3. to ply. 4. to go or travel to.

~ **para a costa** (naut.) to run in with the land. ~ **para o norte** to head north, to north. ~**am para a casa** they went home.

rumba s. f. rumba, a lively Negro dance.

rumbeador adj. (Braz.) able to find one's way in the woods.

rume (I) s. m. (zool.) rumen, paunch, first stomach of the ruminants.

rume (II) s. m. + f. Rumelian, native or inhabitant of Rumelia. || adj. Rumelian.

rúmen s. m. (pl. **rumens, rúmenes**) rumen, paunch.

ruminação s. f. (pl. **-ões**) 1. rumination, chewing of the cud. 2. (fig.) reflection, meditation. 3. (fig.) pondering, consideration.

ruminador s. m. ruminant. || adj. ruminating.

ruminadouro s. m. (zool.) rumen, paunch.

ruminante s. m. (zool.) 1. ruminant, ruminator, ruminant animal. 2. ~**s** pl. Ruminantia: division of the mammals. || adj. m. + f. ruminant, ruminating, chewing the cud.

ruminar v. 1. to ruminate, chew the cud. 2. to consider, ponder. 3. to muse. 4. to reflect, meditate.

rumo s. m. 1. each one of the compass bearings. 2. (naut.) rhumb, bearing. 3. route, course. 4. setting, set. 5. (fig.) manner of proceeding. 6. direction.

~ **ao exterior** outward-bound. ~ **corrigido para compensar o abatimento** (naut.) course corrected for leeway. **andaram** ~ **à cidade** they walked in the direction of the town. **eles se foram** ~ **a** they left, headed for... **desfechar o** ~ (naut.) 1. to head in a certain direction. 2. to set a course. **mudar o** ~ **de um navio** to put about a ship, to tack. **mudaram o** ~ (fig.) they flew off at a tangent. **qual é o seu** ~? (naut.) how is her head? **sem** ~ adrift, afloat. **tomar outro** ~ to go off on a new tack.

rumor s. m. 1. rumour, rumor. 2. indistinct noise, din. 3. murmur, whisper, whispering. 4. report, tidings. 5. hearsay, talk, grapevine. 6. rumble. 7. fame, renown.

há ~**es** there are whispers. **houve certos** ~**es** something was in the air. **ouvimos o** ~ **das vozes** we heard the rumbling of voices.

rumorejante adj. m. + f. murmuring, rustling, soughing.

rumorejar v. 1. to rustle, buzz. 2. to murmur, whisper, rumble. 3. to spread a rumour. 4. to be common talk, be in the air. 5. to tell in secret, confide in.

rumorejo s. m. 1. rustle, rustling. 2. buzz, murmur of voices. 3. whispering, rumbling. 4. rumour, hearsay. 5. gossip. 6. ripple, sough.

rumoroso adj. 1. noisy, loud. 2. blatant, clamorous. 3. sensational, causing a stir. 4. controversial, polemical.

runa (I) s. f. the sap of pine trees.

runa (II) s. f. (hist.) rune(s), character of the runic alphabet.

rúnico adj. runic(al), of or pertaining to a rune.

runologia s. f. runology, science of runes.

rupequeiro s. m. (Braz., ornith.) tiriba.

rupestre adj. m. + f. 1. growing on rocks. 2. engraved upon rocks. 3. rupestrian, rupestral.

rupia (I) s. f. (med.) rupia.

rupia (II) s. f. rupee: an East Indian silver coin.

rupícola adj. m. + f. (bot., zool.) rupicolous, living on or among rocks.

rúptil adj. m. + f. (pl. rúpteis) 1. breakable, easily broken. 2. brittle, fragile. 3. (bot.) ruptile, dehiscing irregularly.

ruptilidade s. f. 1. frangibility. 2. brittleness. 3. dehiscence.

ruptório s. m. (surg.) cauterizing iron.

ruptura s. f. 1. act or effect of breaking, breakage. 2. disruption, rupture. 3. breach. 4. fracture, break. 5. rent, rip, crack. 6. (med.) hernia. 7. disunion. 8. interruption. 9. abruption. 10. sunderance, severance. 11. parting.
~ das linhas inimigas (mil.) break-through. ~ de pneumático blowout. ~ de tubulação pipe burst.

rural adj. m. + f. (pl. rurais) 1. rural, of or pertaining to the country. 2. rustic. 3. agricultural. 4. sylvan. 5. bucolic.

ruralismo s. m. 1. ruralism, ruralness. 2. rural character or life. 3. (pop.) predominance of rural matters in the economic life of a country. 4. (arts) representation of rural scenes.

ruralista s. m. + f. ruralist, artist who reproduces rural scenes.

ruralizar v. 1. to ruralize, rusticate. 2. to give a rural appearance to. 3. to become rural. 4. to adapt to rural life.

rurícola adj. living in the country, agricultural.

rurígena s. m. + f. person born in the country, native of the country. ‖ adj. rurigenous.

rurografia s. f. treatise on fields and their agricultural utilization, rurigraphy.

rurográfico adj. rurigraphic.

rurógrafo s. m. rurigrapher, specialist of rurigraphy.

rusga s. f. 1. noise, clamour, din. 2. disorder, confusion. 3. brawl, row. 4. quarrel, squabble. 5. disagreement, dissension. 6. divergence of opinion. 7. tiff, miff. 8. razzia, raid (of the police).

rusgar v. 1. to quarrel, squabble. 2. to make a noise, kick up a row. 3. to raid (the hide-out of criminals).

rusguento adj. 1. quarrelsome. 2. given to brawls. 3. noisy, uproarious. 4. grumbling, grumpy. 5. dissatisfied, discontented with. 6. cantankerous, implicating.

rush s. m. (Engl.) rush: 1. a great affluence of vehicles, heavy traffic, in one direction. 2. an eager movement of many people, as in the gold rush. 3. (sports) the final and forceful attempt of an entrant to beat his competitors.

rusma s. f. a depilatory (used in the Orient).

russélia s. f. Russelia: a genus of shrubs.

Rússia s. f. Russia.

russianas s. f. pl. (N. Braz.) a pair of boots (said to be made of Russian leather).

russiano s. m. 1. Russian: native or inhabitant of Russia. 2. ~s pl. the Slavic peoples who live in European Russia (collectively). ‖ adj. Russian.

russificação s. f. (pl. -ões) Russification.

russificar v. 1. to Russify, render Russian, Russianize. 2. to convert to Russian ideals, customs and practices.

russilhonas s. f. pl. (S. Braz.) riding-boots or top-boots.

russo s. m. 1. native or inhabitant of Russia. 2. the predominant language of Russia. ‖ adj. Russian: of or pertaining to Russia, its inhabitants and language.

russófilo s. m. Russophile. ‖ adj. Russophile.

russófobo s. m. Russophobe. ‖ adj. Russophobiac.

ruste s. m. (Braz., sl.) one who cheats his accomplices at the distribution of the booty.

rusticar v. to rusticate: 1. ruralize, reside or live in the country. 2. adapt o. s. to rural life. 3. till the land, cultivate. 4. (archit.) roughhew, chisel.

rusticidade s. f. 1. rusticity, rusticalness. 2. rustic manners. 3. roughness, cloddishness. 4. boorishness. 5. ignorance.

rústico s. m. 1. peasant, farmer. 2. ploughman, rustic. 3. yokel, boor, hillbilly. ‖ adj. 1. rustic, rural. 2. countryfied. 3. bucolic, homely, sylvan. 4. rough. 5. boorish, loutish. ‖ rusticamente adv. rustically, boorishly, coarsely.

rustidor s. m. (Braz., sl.) hiding place, hide-out.

rustir v. (Braz., sl.) to deceive, dupe, cheat.

rusto s. m. (Braz., sl.) deceit, swindle, cheating at the distribution of the loot.

rutabaga s. f. (bot.) rutabaga, Swedish turnip, navew.

rutácea s. f. a plant of the family Rutaceae.

rutáceo adj. (bot.) rutaceous.

rutênico s. m. Ruthenian: 1. native or inhabitant of Ruthenia. 2. the Ruthenian language. ‖ adj. Ruthenian.

rutênio s. m. (chem.) ruthenium (symbol Ru).

ruteno s. m. Ruthenian, Ruthene. ‖ adj. Ruthenian.

rutilação s. f. (pl. -ões) 1. brilliancy, intense brightness. 2. splendour. 3. resplendence, refulgence.

rutilância s. f. brilliancy, resplendence, splendour, refulgence.

rutilante adj. m. + f. 1. rutilant. 2. bright, brilliant. 3. shining, glittering. 4. resplendent, refulgent. 5. flashy.

rutilar v. 1. to rutilate. 2. to shine, glitter, gleam. 3. to be resplendent. 4. to flash, sparkle. 5. to make extremely bright or brilliant. 6. to blaze, flame, glow.

rutílio, rutilo s. m. (min.) rutile.

rutilo s. m. the act of shining, glittering, brilliancy.

rútilo adj. rutilant, brilliant, resplendent, flashy.

rutina s. f. (chem., pharm.) rutin.

rútulo s. m. member of the Rutuli (ancient inhabitants of Latium). ‖ adj. of or relative to this people.

ruvinhoso adj. 1. rusty. 2. worm-eaten. 3. (fig.) ill-humoured, cantankerous. 4. petulant, whimsical.

S

S, s s. m. 1. eighteenth letter of the Portuguese alphabet. 2. S-shaped object or curve. 3. abbr. of: a) **São, Santo, Santa** St., Saint. b) **Sua** Your, His, Her as in **S. A. Sua Alteza** Your (His, Her) Highness. **S. E. Sua Eminência** Your (His) Eminency; **S. S. Sua Senhoria** or **Sua Santidade** Your (His) Lordship, Your (His) Holyness. c) **Sociedade** as in S/A **Sociedade Anônima** joint-stock company. d) **sul** south.

sã adj. fem. flexion of **são**: healthy.

sabá s. m. 1. Sabbath: day of rest and worship among the Jews and some Christians. 2. supposed midnight reunion of witches and demons.

sabadeador s. m. 1. Sabbatarian, Sabbath-keeper. ‖ adj. Sabbatarian.

sabadear v. (also **sabatizar**) to Sabbatize, keep the Sabbath.

sábado s. m. 1. Saturday, the seventh day of the week. 2. (Jewish) Sabbath.
~ **gordo** the Saturday preceding the Sunday of carnival. ~ **de aleluia**, ~ **santo** Holy Saturday, the Saturday before Easter.

sabagante s. m. (N. Braz., pop.) individual, person.

sabão (I) s. m. (pl. **-ões**) 1. soap, washing soap (plate L 3) (toilet soap is **sabonete**). 2. (fig.) reprimand, scolding.
~ **de barba** shaving soap. ~ **de coco** coconut soap. ~ **em pó** soap powder (plate L 3). **passar um ~ a alguém** to chide a person; call a person on the carpet.

sabão (II) s. m. (pl. **-ões**) (hum.) extraordinarily wise man.

sabão-de-soldado s. m. (pl. **sabões-de-soldado**) (Braz.) (also **saboeiro, melão-de-soldado** pl. **melões-de-soldado**) plant of the family Sapindaceae; soapberry.

sabarense s. m. + f. (Braz.) native of Sabará (Minas Gerais). ‖ adj. of or referring to Sabará.

sabático adj. sabbatical, Sabbatical.

sabatina s. f. 1. weekly repetition or review of lessons. 2. schoolwork or examination (usually on Saturdays). 3. examination. 4. (fig.) discussion. 5. Saturday prayer.

sabatinar v. 1. to recapitulate, review. 2. to discuss in detail and captiously.

sabatineiro adj. 1. of or referring to schoolwork or examinations. 2. of or referring to a (round-table) discussion.

sabatino adj. 1. sabbatical. 2. = **sabático**.
ano ~ (rel., hist.) Sabbatical year.

sabatismo s. m. Sabbatarianism.

sabatizar v. to Sabbatize.

sabável adj. m. + f. (pl. **-áveis**) (Braz.) tasteful, savoury.

sabedor s. m. learned or knowing person, savant, sage. ‖ adj. 1. acquainted with, aware of. 2. learned, knowing.

sabedoria s. f. 1. wisdom, knowledge, learning, erudition. 2. sagacity, prudence, discretion.

sabeísmo s. m. 1. Sabaism: star worship. 2. Sabianism: an Asian gnostic sect.

sabeísta, sabeíta s. m. + f. Sabaist: star worshipper.

sabelianismo s. m. (rel. hist.) Sabellianism.

sabeliano s. m. (rel. hist.) Sabellian.

sabença s. f. (pop.) knowledge, learning, science.

saber (I) v. 1. to know: be aware or cognizant of, have information about. 2. to recognize, identify, be able to distinguish from. 3. to be learned, have practical knowledge of, be skilled in, be intelli-

gent, understand. 4. to be acquainted with; to recognize as true. 5. ~ **a** to taste of, smack like. ~ **bem** to please, gratify. ~ **de cor (e salteado)** to know by heart, know perfectly well. ~ **por ouvir dizer** to know by hearsay. **a** ~ namely; that means. **ao que sabemos** as far as we know. **dar a** ~ to make known. **eu sei o que estou dizendo** I know what I am talking about. **fiquei sabendo disto** I came to know about. **fique sabendo de uma vez para sempre que você está errado** and know once and for all that you are wrong. **já se sabe que não é verdade** it is understood it is not true. **lá sei eu!** I'll be blessed if I know. **não que eu saiba** not that I should know of. **não** ~ **a quantas anda** to be in a mess. **não** ~ **o que fazer** to be at one's wit's end, be at a loss. **quem sabe ele vem hoje** maybe he will be coming today. **vir a** ~ to come to know. **você sabe falar inglês?** can you speak English?, do you speak English?

saber (II) s. m. 1. knowledge, learning, erudition wisdom. 2. scholarship, instruction. 3. acquirements

saberecar v. (Braz.) 1. to toast, to roast brown; scorch, singe. 2. to thrash, beat.

saberente s. m. + f. (N. Braz.) wiseacre. ‖ adj. clever.

saberete s. m. (Braz., pop., also **saberente**) 1. superficial knowledge, smattering. 2. m. + f. wiseacre, busybody. ‖ adj. m. + f. meddlesome.

sabeu s. m. (f. **sabéia**) Sabaean: native of Saba (bib. Sheba).

sabiá s. m. (Braz., ornith.) song-thrush.

sabiacica s. m. (Braz.) (also **araçuaiava**) a species of parrot.

sabiá-da-mata s. m. (pl. **sabiás-da-mata**) (Braz., ornith.) a thrush (Turdus fumigatus).

sabiá-do-campo s. m. (pl. **sabiás-do-campo**) (Braz., ornith.) the Brazilian mockingbird.

sabiá-piranga s. m. (pl. **sabiás-pirangas**) (also **sabiá-laranjeira, sabiá-verdadeiro**) (Braz., ornith.) the rufous bellied thrush.

sabichão s. m. (pl. **-ões**) (f. **sabichã, sabichona**) 1. wiseacre. 2. wise or learned person. ‖ adj. clever, learned, erudite.

sabichar v. to try to know; to inquire here and there, nose about.

sabichona s. f. (also **sabichã**) 1. very erudite woman. 2. bluestocking. 3. pedantic lady.

sabichoso adj. ill-used (learning, knowledge).

sabidas s. f. pl. word used in the adv. loc. **às** ~ openly, clearly, not hidden.

sabido adj. 1. known. 2. wise, intelligent, learned. 3. smart, shrewd, cunning. 4. skilful. ‖ **-amente** adv. 1. clearly, evidently. 2. cleverly.
é ~ it is understood. **ele é muito** ~ he is a smart fellow. **um homem** ~ a wise man, a downy old bird.

sabina s. f. (bot.) savin.

sabinada s. f. (Braz., hist.) revolution in Bahia during the regency.

sabino (I) s. m. Sabine. ‖ adj. Sabine.

sabino (II) adj. roan (horse).

sábio s. m. learned man, wise man, scholar, scientist. ‖ adj. (abs. sup. **sapientíssimo**) wise, learned, scholarly, erudite, judicious. ‖ **sabiamente** adv. wisely.
os ~**s** the learned world, the scientists.

sabitu s. m. (Braz.) = **saúva**.

sabível adj. m. + f. (pl. **-íveis**) knowable.

sable s. m. (her.) sable, black.

saboaria s. f. 1. soap-house, soap shop. 2. soap--works, soap factory.

saboeira s. f. 1. woman who sells soap. 2. (bot.) soapberry.

saboeiro s. m. 1. soapmaker, person who makes or sells soap. 2. = **saboneteira**.

saboiano s. m. Savoyard: native of Savoy. ‖ adj. Savoyard: of or referring to Savoy.

sabonete s. m. 1. toilet soap. 2. reprimand.

saboneteira s. f. (also **saboeiro** m., **saboneira** f.) soap dish, soap bowl, soap holder.

sabor s. m. 1. savour, taste, flavour, relish. 2. power to affect the taste; zest. 3. (fig.) quality, nature, character. 4. whim, caprice.

ao ~ **das ondas** at the mercy of the waves. **comida sem** ~ tasteless food.

saborear v. 1. to relish, savour. 2. to taste. 3. to smack or suggest the presence of. 4. to flavour, add flavour to. 5. ~**-se** (fig.) to enjoy (o. s.), take pleasure in, delight.

saboroso adj. (also **saborido**) 1. savoury, tasty, relishing, appetizing, palatable, luscious, delicious. 2. agreeable, pleasant, delightful. ‖ **-amente** adv. tastily; pleasantly.

saborra s. f. (med.) = **saburra**.

sabotagem s. f. (pl. **-ens**) sabotage, intentional damage as caused by strikers or underground movements; passive resistance.

sabotar v. to sabotage; wreck, damage; sap, undermine; offer passive resistance.

sabraço s. m. (Braz.) stroke with a sabre.

sabre s. m. (also **terçado**) sabre: cavalry sword.

sabucar v. (Braz.) to flatter, cajole, fawn on.

sabugado adj. (Braz.) 1. flogged. 2. weak, beat, worn down.

sabugal s. m. (pl. **-ais**) ground on which elderberry trees grow, a growth of elders.

sabugar v. (N. Braz.) to flog, spank.

sabugo s. m. 1. slough: the spungy substance in the horns of oxen. 2. pith. 3. (anat.) root of the fingernail. 4. root of the tail. 5. (bot.) elder. 6. pith of the elder. 7. corncob.

sabugueiro s. m. (Braz., bot.) elder (tree or bush).

sabugueiro-d'água s. m. (pl. **sabugueiros-d'água**) the European cranberry bush.

sabujar v. to fawn on, to act servilely, flatter, cajole.

sabujice s. f. fawning, cringing, wheedling.

sabujo s. m. 1. bloodhound (plate C 3). 2. trackhound, beagle, hunting dog. 3. (fig.) cringer, fawner, toady, lickspittle, heeler.

sabuloso adj. sandy, sabulous, gravelly, gritty.

saburra s. f. (med.) 1. saburra, granular sedimentary deposit in the stomach. 2. fur, coating of the tongue.

língua ~ furred tongue.

saburrar v. (naut.) to ballast.

saburrento, saburroso adj. furred, coated, full of fur.

saca s. f. 1. bag, large sack. 2. surf, swell of the sea. 3. wild cat of Madagascar. 4. (obs.) exportation.

saca-balas s. m., sg. + pl. (surg.) forceps, bullet--drawer, ball-extractor.

saca-bocado s. m. (pl. **saca-bocados**) punch; punching machine, punch chisel.

saca-bucha s. m. (pl. **saca-buchas**) 1. (mil.) wad-hook. 2. (fig.) trick (to get something).

sacabuxa s. f. (mus.) 1. sackbut. 2. former name for a trombone.

sacaca s. f. (N. Braz.) sorcery.

sacada s. f. 1. (archit.) balcony, bay, jutty, terrace; bay window, balcony window. 2. sackful, bagful. 3. jogging or jolting (of a horse). 4. (com.) exportation; export duty.

sacadela s. f. 1. pull; jerk; yank; tug. 2. the act of pulling up the fishing-line.

sacado s. m. 1. (jur. + com.) drawee, person on whom a draft or bill is drawn. 2. (N. Braz.) lake formed through the swelling of a river.

sacador s. m. 1. (jur. + com.) drawer of a bill of exchange. 2. (Port.) gatherer, collector or receiver of public revenues. ‖ adj. (com.) drawing.

saca-filaça s. f. (pl. **saca-filaças**) (mil.) wire-riddle, wad-hook.

sacaí s. m. (also **sacanga** f.) (Braz.) dry brush-wood or branches of trees, kindlings.

sacalão s. m. (pl. **-ões**) 1. jerk, pull. 2. sudden pull of the reins.

saca-molas s. m., sg. + pl. 1. dental forceps. 2. (fig.) a bad dentist, tooth-puller.

sacana s. m. (sl.) 1. filthy fellow, rascal. 2. pederast. 3. mocker.

saca-nabo s. m. (pl. **saca-nabos**) (naut.) piston rod of a ship's pump.

sacanagem s. f. (pl. **-ens**) (Braz. sl.) 1. filthy behaviour, dirtiness; unfairness. 2. derision, raillery, mockery.

sacanear v. (Braz.) 1. to behave in a filthy, dirty or rascally manner. 2. to irritate, annoy, pester.

sacanga s. f. = **sacaí**.

sacão s. m. (pl. **-ões**) jolt, jerk, jump, plunge (of a horse).

sacar v. 1. to draw out, tear out, pull out, extract, drag, haul. 2. (obs.) to export. 3. to derive, gain, profit. 4. (com.) to draw against.

~ **a curto prazo** (com.) to draw at short date. ~ **a espada** to draw the sword. ~ **a descoberto** (com.) to overdraw. ~ **dinheiro sobre o navio e carga** to borrow on bottomry, on the ship's security.

sacarato s. m. (chem.) saccharate.

sacaria s. f. a quantity of sacks.

saçaricar v. to wriggle, squirm (in dancing).

sacarídeo s. m. (chem.) glucide, any of a class of carbohydrates (glycoses and glycosides). ‖ adj. (chem.) similar to sugar.

sacarífero adj. sacchariferous, saccharic.

sacarificação s. f. saccharification.

sacarificar v. to saccharify, convert into sugar.

sacarificável adj. m. + f. (pl. **-áveis**) saccharificable.

sacarímetro s. m. saccharimeter: polarimeter for measuring the amount of sugar in a solution.

sacarina s. f. saccharin: a very sweet, white crystalline substance made from coal tar.

sacarino adj. 1. saccharine: a) of sugar, of the nature of sugar. b) containing sugar. c) (sickishly) sweet. 2. feeding on sugar.

sacarívoro adj. feeding on sugar.

sacaróide adj. m. + f. saccharoid, crystalline, granular.

saca-rolhas s. m., sg. + pl. 1. corkscrew. 2. (bot.) a screw tree.

sacarologia s. f. a treatise on sugar.

sacarose s. f. saccharose, sucrose, cane or beet sugar.

sacaroso adj. saccharous.

saca-trapo s. m. (pl. **saca-trapos**) 1. (mil.) wad-hook; worm; cleaning rod. 2. (fig., pop.) very stout person; pot-belly. 3. (fig.) craftiness, artfulness.

sacaveno s. m. native or inhabitant of Sacavém (Portugal). ‖ adj. from Sacavém.

saceliforme adj. m. + f. (bot.) sacciform, saclike.

sacelo s. m. 1. sacellum: small temple; sanctuary. 2. capsular monospermous fruit (with one seed only).

sacerdócio s. m. 1. priesthood. 2. priestly function or office. 3. honourable mission or profession.

sacerdotal adj. m. + f. (pl. **-ais**) sacerdotal, priestly.

sacerdotalismo s. m. sacerdotalism; clericalism, theocracy.
sacerdote s. m. 1. priest, clergyman, cleric, ecclesiastic. 2. priestlike person on account of his function or spirit.
sacerdotisa s. f. priestess: female priest of non--Christian religions.
sacha s. f. 1. hoe. 2. act of hoeing; weeding.
sachador s. m. raker, weeder, hoer. ‖ adj. raking, hoeing, weeding.
sachadura s. f. weeding, raking, hoeing.
sachar v. to hoe, weed, clear the ground of weeds, rake.
sachê s. m. sachet.
sacho s. m. weeding hoe; spud.
sachola s. f. small hoe (plate E 4).
sacholada s. f. blow or hit with a hoe.
sacholar v. to hoe, uproot or dig with a hoe.
saci s. m. (Braz.) 1. (pop.) folkloric figure of a little one-legged Negro, also called **saci-pererê**. 2. (ornith.) the striped cuckoo.
saciado adj. satiated, sated, satisfied.
saciar v. 1. to satiate, sate, gratify, satisfy to the full. 2. to cloy, glut, eat one's fill.
~ a sede to quench one's thirst. **~ a fome** to appease one's hunger.
saciável adj. m. + f. (pl. **-áveis**) satiable.
saciedade s. f. satiety: 1. satiation. 2. (fig.) loathsomeness, wearisomeness.
saci-pererê s. m. (pl. **sacis-pererê**) (Braz., pop.) = **saci**.
saco (I) s. m. 1. sack, bag; sac (plates C 16, P 1). 2. sackful. 3. sackcloth. 4. (Braz.) bay. 5. small travelling bag. 6. (coll.) fat person. 7. (vulg.) scrotum purse.
~ de papel paper bag. **comprar nabos em ~** to buy a pig in a poke. **despejar o ~** to say all, make a clean breast. **estar de ~ cheio** to have had enough, to be fed up, to have had it. **meter a viola no ~** to hold one's tongue. **~ de água quente** hot water bottle. **~ de café** a small paper or cotton bag used for straining coffee; coffee strainer. **~ de dormir** sleeping bag. **~ de pancada** a person who is beaten a lot, anvil, poor wretch.
saco (II) s. m. (obs.) sacking, plundering, pillaging.
sacófaro s. m. (obs.) 1. penitent who wore a sack. 2. valise. 3. purse. 4. pouch.
sacola s. f. wallet, knapsack.
sacolejar v. 1. to shake (a liquid), agitate. 2. to move, touch, impress.
sacolejo s. m. shaking (liquid).
saco-roto s. m. (pl. **sacos-rotos**) (fam.) blabber.
sacra s. f. (R. C. Church) canon of the mass.
sacramentado s. m. person who has administered or received a sacrament. ‖ adj. said of such a person.
sacramental adj. m. + f. (pl. **-ais**) 1. sacramental. 2. consuetudinary, customary.
sacramentar v. 1. to administer or receive the sacrament. 2. to administer the extreme unction. 3. to transubstantiate.
sacramentário s. m. Sacramentarian (Calvinist).
sacramento s. m. sacrament: 1. solemn religious ceremony. 2. **Sacramento** Sacrament: the Eucharist; the consecrated Host. 3. an oath. 4. **~s** pl. the last sacraments, as extreme unction.
Santíssimo Sacramento the blessed consecrated Host. **~ dos enfermos** extreme unction; sacrament of the infirm.
sacrário s. m. 1. (R. C. Church) tabernacle. 2. sacrarium; sanctuary; shrine. 3. (fig.) refuge.
sacratíssimo adj. abs. sup. of **sagrado** most sacred, most holy.
sacrificador s. m. sacrificer. ‖ adj. sacrificing.
sacrifical adj. m. + f. (pl. **-ais**) sacrificial.

sacrificante s. 1. m. + f. sacrificer. 2. m. the priest who says mass. ‖ adj. m. + f. sacrificing.
sacrificar v. to sacrifice: 1. offer (as to God). 2. immolate. 3. give up in behalf of something. 4. sell at a loss. 5. relinquish, resign. 6. **~-se**: a) to devote o. s. to. b) to sacrifice o. s. for.
sacrificativo adj. sacrificeable.
sacrificatório adj. sacrificatory.
sacrifício s. m. sacrifice: 1. offering (as to God); thing offered. 2. immolation. 3. abnegation, self--denial. 4. (fig.) loss.
o Santo Sacrifício (R. C. Church) Mass.
sacrículo s. m. acolyte.
sacrilégio s. m. sacrilege; profanation; irreverence; desecration; violation of sacred things.
sacrílego adj. sacrilegious, guilty of sacrilege, irreverent.
homem ~ sacrilegist.
sacripanta, sacripante s. m. + f. person of ill character, rascal, scoundrel, villain. ‖ adj. villainous.
sacrista s. m. sexton, sacristan (pop. form of **sacristão**).
sacristã s. f. 1. vestry-nun. 2. laywoman who keeps the vestry. 3. a sacristan's wife.
sacristania s. f. office and/or dwelling of a sacristan or vestry-nun.
sacristão s. m. (pl. **-ães**) sacristan, sexton; church--clerk, vestry-keeper.
bens de ~ cantando vêm, cantando vão lightly won lightly gone.
sacristia s. f. sacristy; vestry-room.
sacro s. m. (anat.) sacrum; a composite bone at the lower part of the spine. ‖ adj. 1. holy, sacred; (fig.) venerable. 2. (anat.) sacral.
o ~ colégio (R. C. Church) the College of Cardinals. **música -a** sacred music. **osso ~** sacrum.
sacrossanto adj. sacrosanct, sacred, holy.
sacubaré s. m. (Braz.) a species of orchid.
sacudida, sacudidura s. f. 1. shake, shaking, toss(ing); jolt. 2. a shaking off of the dust.
sacudidela s. f. 1. light shock. 2. shaking; jolt. 3. agitation.
sacudido adj. 1. shaken. 2. jerked; jolting. 3. quick, agile. 4. unrestrained, unhampered. 5. expeditious. 6. (Braz.) slender, elegant, handsome. 7. strong, rude, tough, courageous. 8. skilful, expert, versed.
sacudidor s. m. shaker. ‖ shaking.
sacudidura s. f., **sacudimento** m. (also **sacudida**) shaking; jolt; jerk; shock.
sacudir v. to shake: 1. shake off. 2. move, tremble, rock, quiver, quake, vibrate. 3. toss, jerk, jolt, jar. 4. shock, disturb, agitate; rouse, stir up, enliven. 5. weaken or make less convincing, firm or stable. 6. shake hands. 7. **~-se** shake o. s.
~ a cabeça to shake one's head. **~ a cauda** (dog) to wag the tail, fawn. **~ o jugo** to shake off the yoke. **~ levemente** to joggle. **~ o pó a alguém** to cudgel one, give a person a sound beating. **~ o pó dos sapatos** to shake the dust off one's feet.
sacular adj. m. + f. saccular.
saculiforme adj. m. + f. sacciform, saclike.
sáculo s. m. saccule: 1. (bot.) small sac. 2. (anat.) sacculus: the saccule of the ear.
sacupema s. f. (Braz., also **sapopema**) surface roots which grow up the trunk; prop root.
sacurê s. m. (Braz.) disease of the tapioca plant.
sádico s. m. sadist. ‖ adj. sadistic.
sadio adj. healthy, healthful, sound, wholesome. ‖ **-amente** adv. soundly, wholesomely.
juízo ~ soundness of judgement.
sadismo s. m. sadism.
sadista s. m. + f. sadist. ‖ adj. sadistic.

saduceísmo s. m. (rel.) Sadduceeism.
saduceu s. m. (f. **-éia**) (rel.) Sadducee.
safa interj. clear the way! be gone! good heavens!
safadagem, safadeza, safadice s. f. (Braz.) knavishness, baseness, rascality; trickishness; shamelessness.
safadinho adj. (N. Braz., fam.) funny (used mostly for children).
safadismo s. m. (Braz., also **safadagem**) knavishness; trickishness; base demeanour.
safado s. m. 1. trickster. 2. (also ironic.) rogue. ‖ adj. 1. worn out, threadbare. 2. (pop.) shameless. 3. (Braz.) immoral; pornographic. 4. (N. Braz., ironic.) roguish. 5. upset, irritated, cross.
safanão s. m. (pl. **-ões**) flounce; fling; push, thrust; yank; jerk.
safar v. 1. to wear out. 2. (naut.) to unload, clear, disembarrass. 3. to steal, pilfer, take away. 4. **~-se**: a) to escape, run away, take to the heels, tail away, sneak away (off), hedge. b) to get rid of, get free from.
sáfara s. f. 1. stony desert. 2. high and steep rock or cliff.
safardana s. m. rascal, scoundrel; contemptible good-for-nothing fellow; mean, low person.
safári s. m. safari.
safaria adj. designative of a sort of pomegranate.
sáfaro adj. 1. rude, rustical, unpolished. 2. sterile, barren, waste, wild, unproductive. 3. distant, faraway, remote.
  falcão ~ wild hawk.
safarrascada s. f. (Braz., sl.) obstacle; difficulty; mess.
safena s. f. (anat.) saphena: principal vein of the leg.
sáfico adj. Sapphic.
  verso ~ Sapphic verse.
safio s. m. (ichth.) a sort of conger (sea eel).
sáfio adj. 1. rude, unpolished. 2. distrustful. 3. = **sáfaro.**
safira s. f. sapphire: 1. blue-coloured precious stone. 2. blue.
safirina s. f. (min.) sapphirine.
safismo s. m. (med.) Sapphism, Lesbianism.
safo adj. 1. worn out, much used. 2. escaped, runaway. 3. disembarrassed, cleared, freed. 4. (put) afloat.
safões s. m. pl. sheepskin trousers used by shepherds.
safra (I) s. f. 1. anvil. 2. (fig.) a slave of his work.
safra (II) s. f. 1. crop, harvest. 2. harvest time.
safrão s. m. (pl. **-ões**) (naut.) wooden afterpiece of the rudder.
safreiro s. m. (Braz.) auxiliary farm hand during harvest time.
safrejar v. 1. to run a sugar mill. 2. to produce (sugar mill).
saga s. f. 1. saga, medieval tale of Icelandic or Norwegian heroes. 2. witch. 3. (ant.) the rear guard of an army.
sagacidade s. f. sagacity: 1. perspicacity; sound judgment, mental acuteness. 2. shrewdness; cunningness.
sagão s. m. less used form of **saguão.**
sagaz adj. m. + f. 1. sagacious: a) wise in a keen practical way. b) astute, sharp-witted. c) perspicacious, intelligent. d) apprehensive. e) shrewd. f) clever, keen, smart. g) (fig.) eagle-eyed, farsighted. 2. (Braz., pop.) quick (riding horse). ‖ **~mente** adv. sagaciously.
  cavalo ~ clever horse. **comentário ~** a sagacious comment.
saginar v. to feed; fatten.
sagitado adj. sagittate; arrow-shaped (plate F 5).

sagital adj. m. + f. (pl. **-ais**) sagittal: 1. = **sagitado.** 2. (anat.) referring to the suture between the parietal and the skull.
sagitária s. f. arrowhead: 1. the head of an arrow. 2. (bot.) Sagittaria.
Sagitário s. m. (astr.) Sagittarius: 1. a southern constellation. 2. the ninth sign of the Zodiac, the Archer. ‖ **sagitário** adj. armed with bow and arrow.
sagitífero adj. (poet.) sagittiferous, bearing arrows.
sagitifoliado adj. (bot.) sagittiform, shaped like an arrow (leaves).
sagração s. f. consecration; anointment.
sagrado s. m. 1. sacred thing or place. 2. respectfulness. ‖ adj. (abs. sup. **sacratíssimo**) sacred, holy, hallowed, consecrated, sanctified; taboo. ‖ **-amente** adv. blessedly, sacredly.
  Sagrado Coração de Jesus Sacred Heart of Jesus. **Sagrada Família** Holy Family. **Escritura Sagrada** Holy Writ.
sagrar v. to consecrate: 1. make holy; sanctify, hollow. 2. dedicate or devote.
  ~ uma igreja to dedicate a church.
sagu s. m. sago: starch prepared from the pith of the sago palm (**sagüeiro**) used for culinary purposes.
saguá s. m. (Braz.) a certain salt-water fish.
saguão s. m. (pl. **-ões**) (less used form: **xaguão**) 1. porch. 2. entrance-hall, vestibule, foyer, lobby. 3. inner yard or court; atrium.
saguaritá s. m. (Braz., also **muçarete**) mollusc of the family Purpuridae.
saguate s. m. (†) present, gift.
sagüeiro s. m. (bot.) sago palm, sago tree.
sagüi s. m. (Braz., zool., also **sagüim**) tamarin, marmoset, sapajou, sagoin: one of the small S. American prehensile-tailed monkeys (often kept as pet).
sagüi-caratinga s. m. (pl. **sagüis-caratinga**) (Braz., zool.) white-headed sagoin.
sagüiguaçu s. m. (Braz., zool.) masked sagoin.
sagüipiranga s. m. (Braz., zool., also **mico-leão-vermelho**) silky tamarin.
sagüi-preto s. m. (pl. **sagüis-pretos**) (Braz., zool.) negro tamarin.
sagum s. m. variety of sago.
saí (I) s. m. 1. (zool.) capuchin (monkey). 2. (Braz., ornith.) honey creeper.
saí (II) s. m. (also **bonzo**) Buddhist priest.
saia s. f. 1. skirt: 1. piece of women's garment (plate R 6). 2. (tech.) casing (plate L 1).
  ~ da chaminé (naut.) funnel casing. **~ da vela** (naut.) bonnet. **~ de baixo** petticoat, underskirt.
  agarrado às ~s da mãe tied to his mother's apron strings. **pôr ~ em** to frock.
saia-balão s. f. (pl. **saias-balão**) crinoline, hoop-skirt.
saia-calça s. f. culotte(s).
saial s. m. (pl. **-ais**) formerly a garment of a coarse darkish cloth, for men and women.
saião (I) s. m. (pl. **-ões**) (ant.) hangman, executioner.
saião (II) s. m. (pl. **-ões**) (bot.) houseleek, sengreen.
saibo s. m. 1. taste, flavour. 2. bad taste.
  com ~ tangy.
saibramento s. m. act of covering with coarse sand or gravel.
saibrão s. m. (pl. **-ões**) sandy or clayey soil (good for planting sugar-cane).
saibrar v. 1. to cover with gravel, or coarse sand. 2. to prepare the soil for planting vines, etc.
saibro s. m. gross sand, gravel.
saibroso adj. gravelly; sandy.
saicanga s. f. (Braz.) a carnivorous fresh-water fish.
saída s. f. 1. outlet, means of exit, loophole, issue. 2. going out, parting; depart; voyage out. 3. sale, ready market. 4. exportation. 5. egress, exit, way

out (plate E 13). 6. retiring, retirement. 7. (sport): a) start. b) (ftb.) kickoff.
~ de água water escape. ~ de banho, ~ de praia beach wrap, garment, robe. ~ de emergência emergency exit. ~ para descarga vomitory. ~ precipitada outrush. achar uma ~ (fig.) to unthread. direito de entrada e ~ duty of entry and exportation. o livro não tem ~ the book is a poor seller. sem ~ ventless, blind. ter boa ~ to meet a ready market. ter boas ~s to give always rapid and witty answers. um beco sem ~ a blind alley.

saído adj. 1. gone out. 2. salient, sticking out. 3. (Braz., pop.) disembarrassed, forward, bold; meddlesome.

saidor s. m. (S. Braz.) starting place at a horse-race. ‖ adj. leaving, departing.

saieta s. f. 1. serge. 2. (Braz.) a fermented coconut drink.

saiga s. f. (zool.) saiga, an antelope.

saijé s. m. (also saipé, ichth.) a species of dorado.

saimel s. m. (pl. -éis) (archit.) springer; first stone of a capital that begins to form the curve of an arch.

saimento s. m. 1. funeral; funeral procession. 2. (Braz.) boldness, impudence; meddlesomeness; bad manners.

sainete s. m. 1. bait, given as reward to a hawk. 2. (fig.) redress, amends; restoration. 3. taste, flavour. 4. jest, humour. 5. short comedy or farce.

saino s. m. (Braz., pop., also zaino) 1. dark-brown or black horse. 2. (fig.) villain, good-for-nothing, rascal. ‖ adj. dark-brown (horse).

saio s. m. (ant.) sort of loose upper coat.

saiote s. m. petticoat.

saipé s. m. (Braz., ichth., also saijé) a species of dorado.

sair v. 1. to go, come or step out. 2. to leave, quit, retire; withdraw. 3. (fig.) to go beyond limits, exceed. 4. to emerge. 5. to issue from. 6. to come into being. 7. to be accomplished. 8. to be published (book). 9. to be established (law). 10. to sell (well). 11. to jut or stick out.
~ a alguém to take after s. o. ~ às carreiras to rush out, bang out. ~ a jacto to jet. ~ a nado to swim out. ~ ao ar livre to take the air. ~ às pressas to hurry out, bolt. ~ à semelhança de to take after. ~ bem (mal) to turn (or fall) out well (badly). ~ caro to cost much. ~ com honra ou ~ bem to come off honourably. ~ com ímpeto to erupt. ~ como vencedor to run out a winner. ~ da cadeia to get out of prison. ~ da infância to come out of infancy, be past childhood. ~ da moda to go out of fashion. ~ de carro to go for a drive. ~ das dívidas to get out of dept. ~ de fininho to sneak out, to steal away, go on tiptoe. ~ do embaraço to get out of trouble. ~ de viagem to go on a journey. ~ do alinhamento to outstand. ~ do caminho to stand aside. ~ do ovo to hatch. ~ do propósito to step out of one's subject. ~ em batalha to take the field. ~ em busca de to go after. ~ em fluxo to gush. ~ fora de si to lose one's head. ~ fora dos eixos to go beyond the bounds. ~ fora dos limites da razão to swerve from reason. ~ fora do seu caminho to get out of one's way. ~ ileso to get out unhurt. ~ o rio da madre to overflow the banks (river), to swell. ~ precipitadamente to rush out. ~ na surdina to leave, depart quickly; to vamose. ao ~ do sol at sunrise. a rolha não quer ~ the cork won't come out. as manchas não querem ~ the stains won't come out. ele acaba de ~ he has just gone out. fazer ~ to get, drive, squeeze or put out. vai ~ bem parecido the likeness will come out well.

ele saiu agora he has just gone out. não sai disso (fig.) it remains at that point, there is no go. não saio disto I stick to that. saia o que ~ whatever happens or falls out. saiu a sentença contra ele it has gone against him. saiu certo o que ele disse his words have come true. ~-se bem to succeed. ~-se mal to come off badly. ~-se brilhantemente to come off with flying colours. ele saiu da companhia he left the company.

saíra s. f. (Braz.) bird of the family Tanagridae, a species of blackbird.

sairara s. m. (Braz., zool., also saitauá) a species of monkey.

saivá s. m. (Braz.) underwood, brushwood.

saixê s. m. (Braz., zool.) = saí.

sajica adj. m. + f. (N. Braz.) strong; robust.

saju s. m. (Braz., zool.) a species of monkey of the family Cebidae.

sal s. m. (pl. sais) salt: 1. sodium chloride. 2. (fig.) wit, piquancy, smartness.
~ amargo ou ~ de Epsom sodium sulphate or Epsom salts. ~ amoníaco sal ammoniac; ammonium chloride. ~ de cozinha common salt, sodium chloride. ~-gema rock-salt. ~ marinho sea-salt, bay-salt. ~ mineral mineral salt. ~ para cheirar smelling salt, hartshorn. ~ refinado table salt. ele não vale o ~ que come he is not worth his salt. pedra de ~ a lump of salt. sem ~ saltless. pôr o ~ na moleira to make one lose one's patience.

sala (I) s. f. large room; saloon; hall.
~ de audiências judgement hall. ~ de aula classroom. ~ de baile ball-room. ~ de café coffee-room. ~ das caldeiras ou fornalhas stoke-hold. ~ da câmara municipal guild-hall. ~ de armas armory, gun room. ~ de controle (radio) control room. ~ de espetáculos theatre, auditorium. ~ de espera waiting-room; antechamber; vestibule (plate E 13). ~ de esportes gymnasium. ~ de estar living-room; parlour. ~ de fumar smoking-room. ~ de jantar dining-room. ~ de jogo card-room. ~ de operação operating-room; surgery. ~ de recepção reception-room. ~ de reunião meeting-hall. ~ de sessões assembly-room. ~ de trabalho workroom. ~ de tribunal courtroom. ~ dos milagres church room where ex-votos are stored and put on display. fazer ~ a to entertain guests.

sala (II) s. f. (ant.) metal tray.

salabórdia s. f. tastelessness; insipid talk.

salácia, salacidade s. f. lewdness; lechery.

salada s. f. 1. salad: a dish of vegetables, fruits, meat or fish with dressing, served cold. 2. (fig.) mess, confusion.
~ de alface lettuce salad. ~ de frutas fruit salad. óleo para ~ salad-oil. tempero para ~ salad-dressing.

saladeira s. f. salad dish or salad bowl.

saladeirista s. m. (S. Braz.) owner of a dried meat industry.

saladeiro s. m. (S. Braz.) establishment where dried meat is produced; dried meat industry.

sala-e-quarto s. m. (Braz.) two-room apartment: a living room and a bedroom.

salafrário s. m. (pop.) scoundrel, blackguard, bounder.

salamaleque s. m. 1. salaam: Turkish salutation. 2. (fig., pop.) exaggerated bow, affected salutation.

salamandra s. f. 1. (zool.) salamander. 2. a mythical lizard, supposed to live in fire. 3. m. (fig.): a) anyone who can stand great heat. b) (Braz.) a fire-fighter in the oil industry.
~-aquática swift (lizard). ~-negra Alpine salamander. ~-terrestre fire salamander.

salamanquense s. m. + f. (Spain; also **salamanquino, salamanticense, salamântico**) native of Salamanca. ‖ adj. of or referring to Salamanca.

salamanta s. f. (Braz.) name given to some snakes as the boa.

salame s. m. salami: a kind of highly seasoned uncooked (Italian) sausage.

salamim s. m. old kind of dry measure.

salaminho s. m. a variety of salami.

salão (I) s. m. (pl. **-ões**) 1. great hall. 2. saloon; ball-rom. 3. salon: picture gallery. 4. Salon: annual exhibition of pictures. 5. (Braz.) barbershop. ~ **de baile** dance-hall; ball-room. ~ **de barbeiro** barbershop. ~ **de beleza** beauty parlour. ~ **de chá** tea-room. ~ **de café** coffee-shop. ~ **de festas** assembly room; banqueting room. ~ **de sinuca** poolroom. **o** ~ **de 1949** the Salon of 1949.

salão (II) s. m. 1. loamy or clayey soil; clay-ground. 2. a sort of petrified clay on the bottom of rivers or of the sea. 3. stony impermeable layer or ground.

salariado s. m. individual who works for a salary, wage earner.

salariar v. to allow a salary or wages; take in pay.

salário s. m. 1. salary, wages, pay(ment), income. 2. (fig.) reward.

~-**base,** ~ **profissional** base salary, base pay, base wage. ~-**família** family allowance; allowance for dependents. ~ **insignificante** pittance. ~ **mínimo** living wage. ~ **por hora** wages per hour. **décimo terceiro** ~ thirteenth salary: extra remuneration, equivalent to a month's salary, to be paid by December. **um** ~ **de fome** a mere pittance; starvation wage.

salaz adj. m. + f. (abs. sup. **salacíssimo**) salacious, lustful, luxuriant.

saldar v. 1. to balance an account, close or settle an account. 2. to liquidate, have done with. 3. to sell at a cheap price in order to clear out. ~ **contas** to settle accounts (also fig.).

saldo s. m. 1. (com.) balance, overbalance. 2. remainder, remnants, surplus, rest. 3. (fig.) revenge. ‖ adj. quit, even, settled.

~ **a pagar** balance due; arrears. ~ **devedor** balance due. ~ **médio** bank balance. ~ **negativo** debit balance. ~ **positivo** credit balance. **qual é o** ~ **da minha conta?** what's the balance of my account?

saleiro s. m. 1. salter, salt-man: salt-maker or salt-merchant. 2. salt-cellar (plate M 1). 3. salt-box, salt-store. 4. salt-lick. 5. (S. Braz.) salinous soil. 6. new branch of horn (antler). ‖ adj. salt, of or referring to salt.

salema s. f. (ichth.) porkfish.

salepo s. m. 1. (bot.) a species of orchid. 2. salep, nutritive substance extracted from the tubers of some orchids.

salernitano s. m. native of Salerno (Italy). ‖ adj. of or referring to Salerno.

salésia s. f. (rel.) Salesian Sister: nun of the Order of the Visitation of Our Lady.

salesiano s. m. (rel.) Salesian: member of the order of the Salesians. ‖ adj. Salesian: of or referring to the Salesian order.

saleta s. f. small hall, sitting-room, waiting-room.

salga s. f. (also **salgação, salgadura**) salting, curing; pickling.

salgação s. f. 1. salting. 2. witchcraft, sorcery.

salgadeira s. f. 1. place or box where meat, fish, etc. are salted. 2. (bot.) salt-bush.

salgadinhos s. m. pl. (Braz.) small salty appetizers.

salgado s. m. almost unproductive seashore soil. ‖ adj. 1. salt, salted, salty, pickled, brackish. 2.

(fig.) witty, piquant; a bit improper. 3. (fig.) very dear, costly; (too) expensive. ‖ **-amente** adv. in a salty way.

água-a salt water, **observação -a** salty remark. **preço** ~ very high price.

salgador s. m. salter, person who salts. ‖ adj. referring to a salter.

salgadura s. f. salting, curing.

~ **do bacalhau** dunning.

salgalhada s. f. (pop.) confusion, mess, farrago, hodgepodge, medley.

salgar v. 1. to salt, to season with salt. 2. to pickle, kipper, cure, corn. 3. to throw salt on the threshold (witchcraft).

~ **uma conta** to salt a bill.

sal-gema s. m. rock-salt, mineral salt, sodium chloride.

salgo adj. (Braz.) wall-eyed (horse).

salgueiral s. m. (pl. **-ais**) growth or standing of willows.

salgueirinha s. f. (bot.) purple loosestrife.

salgueiro s. m. (bot.) willow, river mangrove. ~ **chorão** weeping willow. ~ **francês** osier. ~ **preto** black willow.

salicácea s. f. (bot.) specimen of the Salicaceae, the willow family.

salicáceo adj. (bot.) salicaceous.

salicícola adj. m. + f. living on willow trees.

salicifoliado adj. (bot.) salicaceous, willowy (leaf).

salicilato s. m. (chem.) salicylate.

salicílico adj. salicylic.

ácido ~ salicylic acid.

saliciloso adj. salicylous.

ácido ~ salicylous (or saliculous) acid.

salicinácea s. f. plant of the willow family.

salicíneo adj. salicaceous, willowy, referring or similar to a willow tree.

salicívoro adj. feeding on leaves and flowers of the willow tree.

sálico adj. Salic: referring to the Salian Franks or the Salic law.

Lei -a Salic law.

salícola adj. m. + f. saliferous, saliniferous: containing salt or producing salt.

salicultura s. f. salt-works; salt production.

saliência s. f. salience, prominence, overhang, relief (plate M 11).

salientar v. 1. to point out, accentuate, stress, emphasize. 2. to jut out; emboss. 3. ~-**se:** a) to stick up, stand out. b) to become conspicuous. c) to distinguish o. s.

ele salienta este fato he lays stress upon that fact.

saliente adj. m. + f. salient, that projects outwardly, prominent, jutting out, outstanding.

salífero adj. saliferous: producing or containing salt.

salificação s. f. (chem.) salification.

salificar v. (chem.) to salify.

salificável adj. m. + f. (pl. **-áveis**) salifiable.

salimancia s. f. fortune-telling, by ways of spreading salt on a table and reading the design.

salimante s. m. + f. person who performes **salimancia**.

salimântico adj. referring to **salimancia**.

salina s. f. saline, saltern, salt-works, salt-mine, salt-pit.

salinação, salinagem s. f. (chem.) salification: process by which salt is made to crystallize.

salinar v. to crystallize (salt).

salinável adj. m. + f. (pl. **-áveis**) salifiable.

salineiro s. m. 1. salter: person who manufactures or deals in salt. 2. worker of the salt industry. ‖ adj. saliniferous, referring to salines.

salinidade s. f. saltishness, saltiness, salinity.

salino adj. 1. saline, salinous, salt. 2. born at the seaside.
fonte -a brine spring.
salinômetro s. m. salinometer.
sálio s. m. Salian: 1. (Rom. hist.) one of the Salii, priests of Mars. 2. (hist.) a Salian Frank of the lower Rhine. ‖ adj. Salian: referring to the Roman priests or to the Salian Franks.
salitração s. f. (chem.) nitrification.
salitrado adj. containing saltpetre.
salitrar v. to nitrify: 1. oxidize to nitrates or nitrites. 2. impregnate with nitrates (soil, etc.).
salitraria s. f. refinery for nitre (factory).
salitre s. m. 1. (chem.) saltpetre, nitrate, nitre. 2. a fertilizer, of sodium nitrate or potassium nitrate.
salitreira s. f. saltpetre-mine.
salitreiro s. m. saltpetre-man, saltpetre-maker. ‖ adj. producing saltpetre.
salitrização s. f. nitrification.
salitrizar v. to nitrify, impregnate with or convert into saltpetre.
salitroso adj. nitrous, impregnated with nitre.
saliva s. f. spittle, saliva, dribble.
salivação s. f. salivation.
salival adj. m. + f. (pl. **-ais**) salival, salivary.
salivante adj. m. + f. salivant, salivating.
salivar v. 1. to salivate, eject saliva, drivel. 2. to spit. ‖ adj. m. + f. salivary.
glândulas ~**es** salivary glands.
salivoso adj. salivous, salivary.
salmanticense s. m. + f., **salmantino** m. native of Salamanca (Spain). ‖ adj. of or referring to Salamanca.
salmão s. m. (pl. **-ões**) salmon 1. a fish very appreciated for food and game: 2. light yellowish-pink (colour).
~ **novo** botcher; parr. ~**-rei** blueback salmon. ~ **salgado e defumado** kipper. ~**-truta** sea-trout. **escada para** ~ salmon-ladder.
salmear v. 1. to sing, read or recite psalms. 2. to speak, recite or write monotonously. 3. to sing sadly or monotonously.
sálmico adj. psalmodical.
salmilhado adj. (Braz.) mottled, dappled (white and yellow).
salmista s. m. + f. 1. psalmodist, psalmist: a composer of psalms. 2. m. (rel.) the Psalmist (David).
salmo s. m. psalm: sacred song or poem, an anthem.
livro de ~**s** a book containing psalms, psalter.
salmodia s. f. 1. psalmody: art, act or practice of singing psalms. 2. monotony in reciting, reading or writing.
salmodiar v. to psalmodize: to sing or write psalms; chant (monotonously).
salmoeiro s. m. container for brine.
salmonado adj. (zool.) reddish, like the meat of a salmon.
salmonejo s. m. (ichth., also **salmarino, salmonete**) salmonet, surmullet. ‖ adj. salmonoid: similar to the salmon.
salmonídeo s. m. (ichth.) a specimen of the family Salmonidae (salmons, trouts). ‖ adj. salmonoid, salmonlike.
salmoura s. f. 1. brine, pickle. 2. (fig.) reproof, wigging, sound thrashing.
em ~ in pickle, in salt. **pôr de** ~ to cure. **tratar com** ~ to brine.
salmourar v. 1. to pickle, season with brine. 2. (fig.) to ill-treat, thrash, beat.
~ **alguém** to give a fellow a sound spanking.
salobre adj. m. + f. (also **salobro** m.) briny, brackish, salty.
água -a brackish water. **homem** ~ tiresome man

saloiada s. f. (depr.) a lot of yokels or rustics; villagers.
saloiice s. f. rudeness, clumsiness, coarseness, boorishness.
saloio s. m. 1. countryman who lives around Lisbon. 2. villager; rustic person, yokel, boor, lumpkin, lout, clod-hopper. ‖ adj. rustic; rude, clumsy, loutish, boorish, yokelish.
salomônico adj. Solomonic.
saloneiro s. m. (Braz.) steward, waiter (of a ship).
saloquinina s. f. (chem.) phenil salicylate of quinine.
salossantol s. m. (chem.) a product of the dissolution of salol in an essence of sandal.
salpa s. f. (zool.) salpa: any of the transparent oceanic tunicates.
salpicado adj. 1. sprinkled with salt. 2. bedewed, (be)sprinkled. 3. spotted, speckled, spattered.
~ **de estrelas** studded with stars.
salpicador s. m. 1. salter, one who sprinkles s. th. with salt. 2. spotter. ‖ adj. 1. salting. 2. besprinkling. 3. dotting, speckling.
salpicadura s. f. speck, spot, spatter, splash, sprinkle.
salpica-lamas s. m., sg. + pl. (Braz.) office-boy (of a notary's office).
salpicão s. m. (pl. **-ões**) 1. sausage of pickled loin of pork or smoked ham. 2. a kind of pork-pie.
salpicar v. (also **salpintar**) 1. to corn, powder with salt. 2. to besprinkle. 3. to splash, spatter, dash. 4. to freak, fleck, mottle, dot, speckle. 5. (fig.) to spot, blemish, defame.
~ **com lama ou pintas** to daggle.
salpico s. m. 1. sprinkle, splash. 2. speck, spot, dot, drop of anything dashed. 3. (fig.): a) smart, biting jest. b) blemish, slander.
salpimenta s. f. mixture of salt and pepper. ‖ adj. m. + f. ash-coloured, speckled, grey and white.
salpimentar v. 1. to season with salt and pepper. 2. (fig.) to quiz, scoff, ill-treat.
salpingite s. f. (med.) salpingitis.
salpintar v. (Braz.) = **salpicar**.
salpresar v. to season slightly with salt; to corn or to powder with salt.
salpreso adj. (pl. **salpresos**) corned or powdered with salt; salted; salty.
salsa s. f. 1. (bot.) garden parsley. 2. sharp sauce, relish.
salsa-americana s. f. (pl. **salsas-americanas**) (bot., also **salsaparrilha**) sarsaparilla; sarsa.
salsa-brava s. f. (pl. **salsas-bravas**) (bot.) mountain parsley.
salsada s. f. (pop.) intricate affair; confusion, mess, muddle, imbroglio.
salsa-da-praia s. f. (pl. **salsas-da-praia**) (bot.) morning glory.
salsa-da-rocha s. f. (pl. **salsas-da-rocha**) (bot.) stone parsley.
salsa-leitosa s. f. (pl. **salsas-leitosas**) (bot.) water hemlock.
salsão s. m. (bot.) celery.
salsaparrilha s. f. (bot., also **salsa-americana**) sarsaparilla.
salsa-selvagem s. f. (pl. **salsas-selvagens**) (bot.) fool's parsley.
salseira s. f. sauce-boat; saucer.
salseirada s. f. shower of rain, downpour.
salseiro s. m. 1. shower of rain, downpour. 2. (Braz.) conflict, disorder, discord, brawl, row, quarrel.
salsicha s. f. sausage, Vienna sausage, Frankfurter, (U. S. A., sl.) hot dog.
salsichão s m large-sized sausage.
salsicharia s. f. 1. sausage factory. 2. a pork-butcher's shop.

salsicheiro s. m. person who makes or sells sausages, pork-butcher.

salsinha s. f. 1. dim. of salsa: garden parsley. 2. (pop.) foolish, ignorant or effeminate man; milksop, sissy.

salso adj. (poet.) salt, salted (sea).

salsugem s. f. 1. saliness; salt mud (of a saltern). 2. saltiness. 3. impetigo, a disease of the skin.

salsuginoso adj. salsuginous; brackish.

salta-atrás s. m. + f., sg. + pl. (N. Braz.) name given in the XVIII century to the offspring of mamelukes and Negro women.

salta-caminho s. m. (pl. salta-caminhos) (Braz., ornith.) = tico-tico.

salta-caroço s. m. (pl. salta-caroços) a species of peach whose stone does not stick to the fruit.

saltada s. f. 1. jump, bound, leap. 2. attack, assault. 3. a ranging about to rob and kill. 4. padding or robbing on the highway. 5. domiciliary visit for inspection. 6. short visit or call.

saltado adj. 1. leaped, jumped. 2. jutting, projecting.

saltador s. m. 1. leaper, jumper, vaulter. 2. (zool.) grasshopper. ‖ adj. leaping, jumping, saltant.

saltadouro s. m. (also saltadoiro) special net to catch mullets.

salta-martim s. m. (pl. salta-martins) (Braz.) a species of snapping glow-worm.

saltante adj. m. + f. 1. leaping, jumping; dancing. 2. (her.) salient, in a leaping posture, saltant (animal on a coat of arms).

saltão s. m. (pl. -ões) 1. animal or person who jumps much or hastily. 2. (pop.) grasshopper; spring--beetle; skipper. ‖ adj. leaping; jumpy; that springs much or hastily.

saltão-da-praia s. m. (pl. saltões-da-praia) beach flea, sand hopper.

salta-pocinhas s. m., sg. + pl. (pop.) affected person, with a mincing and effeminate gait.

saltar v. 1. to leap, jump, bound, bounce, spring, dance. 2. to jump to one's feet. 3. to alight, get down. 4. to leap over, skip, pass over. 5. to attack, assault. 6. to move suddenly and quickly. 7. to change direction, shift (wind). 8. to shoot, bud, sprout.

~ a corda to skip the rope. ~ aos olhos or à vista to strike the eye, be obvious. ~ a parede to jump over the wall. ~ da cama to jump out of bed. ~ de alegria to jump for joy. ~ de pára--quedas to parachute; (mil. sl.) to bail out. ~ de um assunto a outro to digress from the matter. ~ do ônibus to alight from the bus. ~ dos trilhos to jump the track or rails. ~ em terra to land, disembark. ~ fora 1. to get loose, snap off, come off. 2. to leap out. ~ mais que outrem to outleap. ~ no inimigo to fall upon the enemy. ~ para fora to spring forth, jump out, leap out. ~ para trás to start or spring back. ~ por to leap over, clear. ~ por cima or por sobre to overleap, overjump. ~ sobre to leap upon. ~ uma linha to miss a line. fazer ~ aos ares to blow up, explode.

saltaram-lhe as lágrimas aos olhos tears started from her eyes.

salta-regra s. m. (pl. salta-regras) bevel(-square); square.

saltarelo s. m. 1. a leaper, jumper. 2. saltarello, a popular Venetian dance. ‖ adj. fond of jumping, leaping or dancing.

saltaricar, saltarilhar, saltarinhar v. to hop, trip; go by little jumps or skips.

saltatriz s. f. female ballet dancer; leaping girl or girl fond of leaping. ‖ adj. f. jumping, leaping, dancing.

salteada s. f. (also salteamento m.) 1. big leap. 2. assault, attack.

salteado adj. 1. attacked, assaulted, robbed. 2. following in an irregular succession, alternated, interpolated.

saber de cor e ~ to know by heart, to have at one's finger-tips.

salteador s. m. highwayman, brigant, bandit, footpad. ‖ adj. assaulting.

salteamento s. m. = salteada.

saltear v. 1. to assault by surprise; attack in order to rob or kill. 2. to rob on the highway. 3. to take by assault, by surprise or unprepared. 4. to sack. 5. to lead a burglar's or robber's life. 6. to skip (pages in a book).

salteira s. f. (Braz.) 1. heel-lift. 2. small spur (military use).

salteiro s. m. heel-maker, person who makes wooden heels for shoes.

saltério s. m. 1. psalter, Book of Psalms. 2. psaltery, an ancient musical instrument played by plucking the strings. 3. (vet., also folhoso) psalterium, the third stomach of a ruminant, the manyplies.

saltígrado adj. (zool.) saltigrade.

saltimbanco s. m. 1. mountebank, juggler; acrobat. 2. charlatan; quack.

saltinho s. m. dim. of salto: little leap.

saltitante adj. m. + f. 1. saltatory. 2. hopping, tripping. 3. skipping.

saltitar v. 1. to trip constantly. 2. to show inconstancy; to digress.

salto s. m. 1. leap, bound, hop, jump, vault (plate C 12). 2. (fig.) flight of the imagination; digression. 3. assault, robbery. 4. waterfall, cataract. 5. shoe heel (plate B 16). 6. omission.

~ com impulso flying jump. ~ com vara pole vault. ~ de altura high jump. ~ de anjo swan dive. ~ de borracha rubber heel. ~ de bota ou sapato heel of a boot or shoe. ~ de distância, de comprimento, de extensão long jump, broad jump. ~ de vento (naut.) shift of wind. ~ mortal somersault, back flip. ~ ornamental fancy diving. ~ parado standing jump. ~ para fora outleap. ~ de pára-quedas parachute jump. ~ triplo hop, step and jump. aos ~s leaping. colocar ~s em sapatos to heel a pair of shoes. dar um ~ to take a leap. de um ~ at a jump. ir ou vir num ~ to go or come quickly. um ~ no escuro a leap in the dark.

saltos-furtados s. m. pl. (N. Braz.) artfulness, shrewdness; whim.

salubre (I) s. m. carding equipment in a spinning--mill.

salubre (II) adj. m. + f. (abs. sup. salubérrimo) salutary, salubrious, wholesome, healthful.

ar ~ salubrious air. ferida ~ slight wound that is easily cured.

salubridade s. f. salubrity, salubriousness, wholesomeness, healthfulness.

salubrificar v. to make healthy; improve; to render sanitary; to cleanse.

saludador s. m. quack, charmer, conjurer, charlatan.

saludar v. to quack, to treat as a quack, charm with words, to conjure, spell.

salutar adj. m. + f. 1. salutary, wholesome, healthful; profitable, beneficial. 2. (fig.) moralizing, edifying.

conselhos ~es salutary advice.

salutífero adj. (poet.) 1. salutary, wholesome. 2. (fig.) useful, beneficial, favourable.

salva s. f. 1. (bot.) sage, salvia. 2. volley, discharge, salute with guns, rockets, fireworks, etc. 3. salver, tray.

uma ~ de artilharia a volley of gun-fire. ~ de gargalhadas burst of laughter. ~ estrepitosa de palmas peals of applause. uma ~ de palmas ou aplausos a round of applause. ~ real a 21 gun salute. dar uma ~ to volley.

salvação s. f. (pl. -ões) salvation: 1. salvage, rescue from danger; preservation; means of keeping from destruction, ill or hurt. 2. redemption, deliverance. 3. salutation, greeting.
Exército da Salvação Salvation Army.

salvádego s. m. salvage (money payed in reward for saving a ship or its goods).

salva-do-brasil s. f. (pl. salvas-do-brasil) (bot.) the cardinal salvia.

salva-do-campo s. f. (pl. salvas-do-campo) (bot.) a bushmint.

salvador s. m. 1. saviour, deliverer, redeemer. 2. Salvador Jesus Christ, the Saviour. ‖ adj. saving.

salvadorácea s. f. (bot.) a dicotyledonous plant of the family Salvadoraceae.

salvadoráceo adj. (bot.) salvadoraceous.

salvadorenho s. m. Salvadorian: native or inhabitant of El Salvador. ‖ adj. Salvadorian: referring to El Salvador.

salvados s. m. pl. salvage, salvaged goods; the remains of a wreckage or fire, remnants, saved property.

salvagem s. (pl. -ens) 1. f. ancient piece of artillery. 2. m. + f. (also selvagem) savage, barbarian. 3. m. salvage rights. ‖ adj. m. + f. (ant., pop.) savage.

salvaguarda s. f. 1. safeguard. 2. safe-conduct. 3. guaranty, security. 4. protection. 5. precaution.

salvaguardar v. 1. to safeguard, protect. 2. to defend, shield. 3. to preserve. 4. to guarantee, warrant.

salvamento s. m. 1. salvation (the act of saving). 2. salvage, rescue, deliverance. 3. preservation. 4. safety.
~ de navio salvage of a ship. despesas de ~ salvage money. trabalhos de ~ salvage operation.

salvar v. 1. to save: a) rescue, deliver, free. b) protect, defend, screen, preserve. c) redeem. 2. to excuse, justify. 3. to jump or skip over, leap. 4. to salute; volley. 5. ~-se to seek safety, take refuge or shelter; save o. s., flee, make one's escape.
~ alguém do afogamento to fish somebody up. ~ a honra to vindicate one's honour. ~ as aparências to save appearance, to save one's face. salve-se quem puder! each one for himself! ele salvou minha vida he saved my life. para ~-lhe a vida to save his life.

salvarana s. f. a Braz. tree that yields good timber.

salvatela s. f. (anat.) salvatella, a vein on the dorsum of the little finger and hand. ‖ adj. indicative of the salvatella.

salvatério s. m. 1. salvation. 2. excuse. 3. means of escape, loophole.

salvatoriano s. m. Salvadorian, native or inhabitant of San Salvador. ‖ adj. Salvadorian, of or referring to San Salvador.

salvável adj. m. + f. (pl. -áveis) savable, that may be saved, redeemable.

salva-vidas s. m., sg. + pl. 1. life-saver (plate P 17). 2. safety buoy, lifebuoy, life-belt.
barco ~ life-boat (plate P 17).

salve! interj. hail!
Deus vos ~! God save you!

salve-rainha s. f. (pl. salve-rainhas) Hail Mary; Ave Maria: a prayer to the Virgin Mary.

salveta s. f. 1. (bot.) garden sage. 2. salver, tray.

salvina s. f. (N. Braz., bot.) a bushmint (Hyptis recurvata Pohl).

salvínia s. f. (bot.) salvinia, a genus of water ferns.

salviniácea s. f. a plant of the family. Salviniaceae.

salviniáceo adj. (bot.) salviniaceous.

salvo adj. 1. safe, unhurt. 2. secure. 3. sheltered. 4. sound. 5. unmolested. ‖ prep. save, except, unless, but.
~ aviso contrário unless otherwise advised. ~ erro ou omissão (abbr. S.E.O.) errors and omissions excepted. ~ força maior except in case of an inevitable accident. a ~ in safety. a ~ de safe from. a seu ~ unmolested. o doente está ~ the patient is out of danger. pôr-se a ~ to save one's bacon; run for one's life. são e ~ safe and sound.

salvo-conduto s. m. (pl. salvos-condutos, salvo-condutos) 1. safe-conduct, pass, passport. 2. (fig.) security, privilege.

samambaia s. f. (Braz., bot.) 1. a fern or any of various polypodies. 2. (N.) a Bromelia.

samambaiaçu s. f. (Braz., bot., also xaxim) a tree fern.

samambaial s. m. (pl. -ais) (Braz.) place rich with samambaias.

samangar v. (N. Braz.) to be lazy, idle.

samango s. m. (N. Braz., also maltrapilho) lazy-bones.

samanguaiá s. m. (Braz.) a clam (shellfish).

samão s. m. (pl. -ões) (Braz., also signo-saimão) amulet, talisman.

sâmara s. f. (bot.) samara.

samário s. m. (chem.) samarium, a rare-earth metal.

samaritano s. m. 1. Samaritan: native or inhabitant of Samaria, Palestine. 2. samaritana f. a nurse. ‖ adj. Samaritan, of or referring to Samaria.
um bom ~ a good Samaritan.

samorra s. f. 1. ancient coat or frock of sheepskin fur. 2. (depr.) priest.

samarreiro s. m. dealer in sheepskins.

samaúma, samaumeira s. f. (Braz., bot., also sumaúma, sumaumeira) the kapok ceiba.

samauqui s. m. (Braz.) = sambaqui.

samba s. m. 1. samba, the most popular Brazilian dance of African origin. 2. (pop.) = cachaça.
~ de breque a samba originated in Rio de Janeiro, in which the singer stops abruptly in order to fit in a few spoken phrases, of a humoristic nature.
~-enredo a samba sung during the Carnival samba school parades.

sambacaetá s. m. (Braz., bot., also alfazema-de-caboclo) a hyssop.

sambador s. m. (Braz., also sambista, sambeiro) samba dancer. ‖ adj. said of a samba dancer.

sambaíba s. m. (Braz.) a pumpwood.

sambamba s. f. (Braz.) = charque.

sambambaia s. f. (Braz.) = samambaia.

sambambaial s. m. (Braz.) = samambaial.

sambango s. m. (Braz., pop.) simpleton; idiotic, silly person; fool. ‖ adj. foolish, silly, conceited.

sambango s. m. (Braz.) weak person.

sambaqui s. m. (Braz., archaeol.) (also cernambi, casqueiro, sarnambi, samanqui) prehistoric deposits of shells, kitchen refuse and skeletons found on the coast or at river sides near the Brazilian coast.

sambaquieiro s. m. (Braz., archaeol.) explorer of a sambaqui.

sambar v. (Braz.) 1. to dance the samba. 2. to dance.

sambarca s. f. 1. breast band of a harness. 2. beam nailed to the door of a distrained house. 3. (obs.) breastband of a woman.

sambarco s. m. (ant.) old shoe; slipper.

sambaré s. m. (Braz.) = samburá.

samba-roda s. m. (S. Braz.) a form of the fandango.

sambeiro s. m. (Braz.) = **sambista.**

sambenitar v. (hist.) to dress a person with a sanbenito.

sambenito s. m. (hist.) sanbenito (Span. San Benito) a kind of yellow-green linen garment worn by persons condemned by the Inquisition.

sambernardo s. m. Saint Bernard dog.

sambexuga s. f. (ant.) = **sanguessuga.**

sambiquira s. f. (S. Braz.) uropygium of a fowl.

sambista s. m. + f. (Braz.) a samba composer or dancer. ‖ adj. said of a samba composer or dancer.

sambladura s. f. a joining, mortise, rabbet.

samblar v. to do joiner's work; mortise, to tenon, splice.

sambocar v. (N. Braz.) to extract, draw.

sambongo s. m. (N. Braz.) a sweet made of coconut raspings.

sambuca s. f. (mus.) sambuca, trigon.

sambudo adj. (N. Braz.) big-bellied.

samburá s. m. (Braz.) a kind of round wicker fish-basket.

pescar para o seu ~ to mind one's own affairs.

samessuga s. f. (Port. prov.) = **sanguessuga.**

sâmio s. m. 1. Samian, native or inhabitant of Samos, Greek isle. 2. red or black pottery made from Samian earth. ‖ adj. Samian: of or referring to Samos.

samnita s. m. + f. Samnite, one of an ancient Italian people. ‖ adj. Samnite, of or referring to the Samnites.

samo s. m. sap-wood, alburnum.

samoiedo s. m. Samoyed, member of a race of Siberian Mongols. ‖ adj. (also **samoiédico**) of or referring to the Samoyeds.

samorim s. m. zamorin, title of the Hindu sovereign of Calicut.

samouco s. m. 1. incrustation of stones. 2. (bot.) a sort of tamarisk.

samovar s. m. samovar, Russian tea-urn.

sampar v. (S. Braz.) to cast, throw.

samurai s. m. samurai, member of the Japanese military cast.

saná s. f. (Braz.) common name of various species of water birds.

sanã-de-samambaia s. m. (pl. **sanãs-de-samambaia**) (Braz., ornith.) (also **acauã**) the white-throated rail (Porzana albicollis).

sananduva s. f. (S. Braz.) = **corticeira.**

sanar v. 1. to cure, heal. 2. (fig.) to make amends for; to compose.

sanativo adj. sanative, sanatory.

sanatório s. m. 1. sanatorium, health resort. 2. sanitarium. 3. convalescent home.

sanável adj. m. + f. (pl. **-áveis**) sanable, curable, healable.

sanca s. f. (archit.) ogee, cove.

sancadilha s. f. 1. trip, stumble. 2. wedge.

lançar ~ 1. to step upon a person's heel. 2. (also fig.) to trip a person.

sanção s. f. (pl. **-ões**) sanction: 1. decree. 2. approbation. 3. confirmation. 4. ratification. 5. penalty or reward.

~ **pragmática** pragmatic sanction.

sancarrão s. m. (pl. **-ões**) augm. of **sanco.** ‖ adj. 1. ugly. 2. ignorant.

sancionado adj. 1. sanctioned. 2. (fig.) confirmed, approved.

sancionador s. m. ratifier, sanctioner. ‖ adj. sanctioning; confirmatory; ratifying.

sancionar v. to sanction, give or lend sanction; confirm, approbate, approve, validate; ratify; support.

sanco s. m. 1. shank, a bird's leg from the claw to the thigh. 2. (fig.) thin leg.

sandália s. f. sandal (a form of shoe) (plates B 16, R 6).

sândalo s. m. sandal, sandalwood (tree and perfume).

sândalo-bastardo s. m. (pl. **sândalos-bastardos**) bastard sandalwood.

sândalo-branco s. m. (pl. **sândalos-brancos**) white sandalwood.

sândalo-vermelho s. m. (pl. **sândalos-vermelhos**) red sandalwood.

sandáraca s. f. 1. sandarac resin. 2. (min.) red arsenic.

sandejar v. (also **ensandecer**) to act foolishly.

sandeu s. m. a fool or madman. ‖ adj. foolish, silly, nonsensical.

sandia s., f. of **sandeu:** foolish woman. ‖ adj. foolish.

sandice s. f. folly, sottishness, stupidity, nonsense.

sandim s. m. (bot.) the Italian buckthorn.

sandio adj. foolish, sottish, stupid, nonsensical.

sanduíche s. m. sandwich.

~ **americano** (Braz.) a ham and fried egg sandwich. ~ **de queijo** cheese sandwich.

saneador s. m. 1. improver, meliorator. 2. sanitationist. ‖ adj. 1. improving. 2. meliorative. 3. sanitary; curing.

saneamento s. m. 1. sanitation. 2. improvement, melioration. 3. cultivation, clearance. 4. repair, reparation. 5. reconciliation.

sanear v. 1. to sanitate, make wholesome or habitable. 2. to improve, meliorate. 3. to repair. 4. to excuse, allay. 5. ~-**se** to grow better.

~-**se com alguém** to make one's peace with a person.

saneável adj. m. + f. (pl. **-áveis**) that can be improved, meliorated, rendered sanitary.

sanedrim s. m. (Jewish hist., also **sinedrim**) Sanhedrin: highest tribunal of the Jews.

sanefa s. f. 1. valance, pelmet. 2. (carp.) traverse, crosspiece, cleat.

~ **de cortina** pelmet (plate D 4).

sanfenal s. m. (pl. **-ais**) (Braz.) place abounding in sainfoin.

sanfeno s. m. (bot.) sainfoin, fenugreek.

sanfona s. f. 1. accordion. 2. hurdy-gurdy. 3. folding chamber, bellows of a camera, etc. (plate F 3). 4. (coll.) crib (of students).

sanfonado adj. (Braz.) pleated or folded like an accordion.

sanfoneiro s. m. 1. an accordionist. 2. a hurdy-gurdy player.

sanfonina s. f. 1. dim. of **sanfona**, small accordion. 2. concertina. 3. unmelodious, poor song. 4. m. + f. accordionist.

sanfoninar v. 1. to play the accordion. 2. to play badly any instrument. 3. (fig.): a) to importune, worry. b) to repeat over and again.

sanga s. f. (S. Braz.) 1. entrance into the fishing net or trap. 2. deep erosive gully. 3. rivulet, small stream. 4. secondary rice products.

sangado adj. (S. Braz.) 1. caught in the net (fish). 2. (fig.) rachitic, stunted.

sangalho s. m. ancient measure equal to fine quarts or selamins.

sangangu s. m. (N. Braz., pop.) 1. disorder, riot, tumult. 2. intrigue, tittle-tattle.

sangra s. f. dark liquid pressed out of olives.

sangradeira s. f. tool used for rubber latex extraction.

sangrado adj. 1. bloody. 2. wounded. 3. (fig.) exhausted.

sangrador s. m. bleeder, blood-letter. ‖ adj. that bleeds.

sangradouro s. m. (Braz., also **sangrador**) 1. (tech.) bleeder valve. 2. taphole (of a blast furnace) (plate A 6). 3. water furrow, drainage ditch. 4. (N. Braz.) throat or canyon (outlet of high waters).

sangradura s. f. blood-letting, bleeding, tapping.

sangrar v. 1. to let blood; to bleed; to open a vein. 2. to cut trenches, carry off water to drain. 3. (fig.): a) to hurt, consume, exhaust. b) to fleece; (sl.) soak a person. c) to approach for money. 4. to tap (as a rubber tree). 5. to drop, fall in drops. 6. ~-se to bleed, to let or lose blood. **com as mãos a** ~ with bleeding hands.

sangrento adj. 1. sanguinolent, sanguinary, bloody. ‖ **-amente** adv. bloodily.

sangria s. f. 1. bleeding; letting of blood; bloodshed. 2. negus, a drink of vine, water and sugar. 3. extorsion.
~ **desatada** (Braz.) something that needs immediate attention. ~ **nasal** nosebleed. **dar uma** ~ **a alguém** to fleece a person, to drain a person's purse.

sangue s. m. 1. blood. 2. family, lineage, race. 3. (fig.) life; temper; disposition.
~ **arterial** arterial blood. ~ **azul** blue blood. ~ **coagulado** cruor, gore, clotted blood. ~ **das uvas** wine. ~ **de Cristo** the blood of Christ: wine. ~ **real** royal blood. ~, **suor e lágrimas** blood, sweat and tears. ~ **puro** thoroughbred, clean-bred. ~ **venoso** venous blood. ~ **vital** life-blood. **banco de** ~ blood bank. **banhado em** ~ bathed in blood. **a** ~ **frio** cold-blooded. **charco de** ~ pool of blood. **dar** ~ to give blood. **derramar** ~ to spill blood. **de** ~ **quente** hot-tempered. **estancar o** ~ to stop the blood. **estar a fogo e** ~ **com alguém** to be at deadly enmity with a person. **esvair-se em** ~ to bleed to death. **exame de** ~ blood test. **fazer ferver o** ~ to make one's blood boil. **gelar o** ~ **nas veias** to freeze one's blood. **intoxicação do** ~ blood poisoning. **meio-**~ half-blood. **não lhe ficou gota de** ~ **no corpo** he was deadly pale with terror. **sem** ~ bloodless. **ser feito de carne e** ~ (fig.) to be subject to err. **ter** ~ **de barata** to be meek, spiritless. **tinto em** ~ bloody, begored.

sangue-de-boi s. m. (pl. **sangues-de-boi**) (Braz., ornith.) the vermilion flycatcher.

sangue-de-drago, sangue-de-dragão s. m. (pl. **sangues-de-drago, sangues-de-dragão**) (bot.) dragon's blood: a resinous substance.

sangue-de-tatu adj. f., sg. + pl. (Braz.) said of a type of red soil appropriate for coffee growing.

sangueira s. f. 1. stream of blood; pool of blood; abundant loss of blood. 2. battle, slaughter.

sangue-novo s. m. (pl. **sangues-novos**) (Braz.) 1. popular designation for certain cutaneous eruptions. 2. (in an enterprise) young personnel (in counterposition to the older ones).

sanguento adj. (also **sangrento**) 1. bloody; blood-bespotted, stained with blood; sanguifluous. 2. sanguinary, bloody-minded.

sanguessuga s. f. 1. leech, bloodsucking worm. 2. (fig.) one who drains another person's purse.

sanguífero adj. (poet.) sanguiferous: conveying blood.

sanguificação s. f. (pl. **-ões**) (med.) sanguification.

sanguificar v. to sanguify: to produce blood.

sanguificativo adj. sanguifacient.

sanguífico adj. sanguific, sanguifying.

sanguina s. f. sanguine: 1. (min.) sanguine-stone, haematite. 2. red crayon. 3. drawing in red crayon.

sanguinária s. f. 1. (bot.) the prostrate knotweed. 2. red clay.

sanguinário adj. sanguinary, cruel, bloody, blood-thirsty, bloody-minded.

sanguínea s. f. 1. (bot.) knot-grass. 2. (also **sanguinária**) red clay.

sanguíneo s. m. a full-blooded or red(-faced) person. ‖ adj. 1. sanguine; sanguineous, full of blood. 2. blood-coloured.
pessoa -a sanguine person. **vasos** ~s blood vessels.

sanguinhar v. (S. Braz.) to slip or skip in the mud.

sanguinheiro s. m. (bot.) the glossy buckthorn.

sanguinho (I) s. m. 1. (eccl.) purificatory, a small towel used to wipe the chalice.

sanguinho (II) s. m. (bot.) dogwood, dogberry-tree.

sanguinho (III) adj. sanguine, full of blood.

sangüinidade s. f. consanguinity.

sanguino s. m. red(dish) colour. ‖ adj. (also **sangüíneo**) sanguine, sanguineous.

sanguinolência s. f. bloodshedding, carnage, cruelty.

sanguinolento, sanguinoso, adj. sanguinolent, sanguinary, bloody, barbarous.

sanguissedento adj. (poet.) bloodthirsty; ruthless.

sanha s. f. wrath, fury, rage, anger, ire.

sanhá s. m. (N. Braz., ornith.) name of various tanagers.

sanhaço s. m. (Braz., ornith., also **sanhaçu**) any tanager, especially of the genus Thraupis.

sanhaço-de-fogo s. m. (pl. **sanhaços-de-fogo**) (Braz., ornith., also **canário-do-mato**) the saira tanager.

sanhaço-pardo s. m. (pl. **sanhaços-pardos**) (Braz., ornith., also **bico-de-veludo**) a brown capped tanager.

sanharão s. m. (pl. **-ões**) (Braz., also **sanharó, torce-cabelo**) one of the various small stingless bees.

sanhoso adj. 1. angry, furious. 2. fierce. 3. ill-tempered; peevish, wrathful.

sanhudo adj. 1. (also **sanhoso**) grim; irascible. 2. (fig.) terrible; awful. ‖ **sonhudamente** adv. angrily, wrathfully, grimly.

sanícula s. f. (bot.) sanicle.

sanícula-dos-montes s. f. (pl. **sanículas-dos-montes**) (bot.) the meadow saxifrage.

sanidade s. f. 1. sanity. 2. health conditions. 3. sanitation. 4. hygiene. 5. salubrity.

sânie s. f. (med.) salues, ichor.

sanificador s. m. person who sanifies; improver. ‖ adj. sanitary; improving.

sanificar v. to sanify, sanitate, make healthful or sanitary; clear (slums); improve.

sanioso adj. (med.) sanious.

sanitário adj. sanitary; medical. ‖ **sanitariamente** adv. sanitarily.
água -a sanitary water. **comissão -a** sanitary commission. **cordão** ~ sanitary cordon.

sanitarista s. m. + f. sanitarian, sanitarist, sanitationist; hygienist.

sanja s. f. 1. gutter or drain in the fields; ditch. 2. gully, drain sewer.

sanjar v. 1. to make gutters, drains or gullies. 2. to drain fields.

sanquitar v. to knead.

sansadurninho s. m. (vulg.) hypocrite; dissembler; knave. ‖ adj. hypocritical; dissembling; knavish.

sansão s. m. 1. (tech.) a kind of crane. 2. strong man.

sanscrítico adj. Sanskritic.

sanscritismo s. m. study of the Sanskrit; doctrines derived from such study.

sanscritista s. m. + f. Sanskritist, person versed in the Sanskritic languages.

sânscrito s. m. Sanskrit, the ancient Aryan language of the Hindus. ‖ adj. Sanskrit, Sanskritic.

sansimonismo s. m. Saint-Simonian: political system of the French socialist Saint-Simon.

sansimonista s. m. + f. Saint-Simonist, Saint-Simonite, an adherent of Saint-Simon, French socialist. ‖

adj. Saint-Simonian: of or referring to the Saint--Simonism.

santa s. f. 1. (f. of **santo**) saint, canonized woman. 2. (fig.) saintly person; good, innocent, virtuous woman. 3. image of a saint woman.

santa-cruz s. f. (pl. **santas-cruzes**) (Braz.) small chapel or cross on the roadside, erected, usually, in memory of someone who died there.

santa-fé s. f. Brazilian grass used for thatching.

santafezal s. m. (pl. **-ais**) (Braz.) place abounding in **santa-fé** grass.

santaláceas s. f. pl. (bot.) the family Santalaceae to which the sandalwoods belong.

santaláceo adj. (bot.) santalaceous.

santa-luzia s. f. (pl. **santas-luzias**) (Braz.) 1. (fam.) ferule, palmer. 2. a moraceous tree.

santa-maria s. f. (pl. **santas-marias**) (bot.) 1. campanilla. 2. yellow bell.

sant'ana s. f. (Braz., pop.) the month of July; the month of Saint Anne.

santantoninho s. m., **santantoninho-onde-te-porei** sg. + pl. a petted or pampered person; apple of the eye; touch-me-not.

santantônio s. m. (Braz.) pommel of a saddle.

santareno s. m. native or inhabitant of Santarém, Portugal. ‖ adj. of or referring to Santarém.

santarrão s. m. (pl. **-ões**) (also **santão**) 1. augm. of **santo**. 2. bigot; pious fraud; prudish person; hypocrite. ‖ adj. sanctimonious, hypocritical; prudish.

santa-vitória s. f. (pl. **santas-vitórias**) (N. Braz., fam.) ferule.

santeiro s. m. person who makes or sells images of saints. ‖ adj. sanctimonious, bigoted, fanatic, superstitiously devoted.

santelmo s. m. St. Elmo's fire, corposant.

santiagueiro, **santiaguês** (pl. **-eses**) (f. **-esa**) s. m. native or inhabitant of Santiago. ‖ adj. of or referring to Santiago.

santiâmen, **santiamém** s. m. moment, instant. **em um ~** (fam.) in a trice, in an instant.

santico s. m. (pop.) jewel with the image of a saint.

santidade s. f. 1. holiness, sanctity. 2. the pope's title.
Sua Santidade His Holiness (the pope).

santificação s. f. (pl. **-ões**) sanctification, sanctifying.

santificado adj. sanctified; blessed, sacred, hallowed. **dia ~** religious feast day, Saint's Day.

santificador s. m. sanctifier. ‖ adj. sanctifying.

santificante adj. m. + f. sanctifying.

santificar v. to sanctify, hallow; make holy; glorify, moralize. **~ o dia do domingo** to keep holy the Sunday.

santificável adj. m. + f. (pl. **-áveis**) sanctifiable, that can be sanctified.

santigar, **santiguar** v. 1. to bless, to hallow. 2. to consecrate. 3. to make the sign of the cross.

santilão s. m. (pl. **-ões**) (pop.) hypocrite, bigot.

santimônia s. f. sanctimony, sanctimoniousness, hypocrisy.

santimonial adj. m. + f. (pl. **-ais**) sanctimonious; hypocritic, bigoted.

santinho s. m. 1. dim. of **santo**. 2. little printed image of a saint. 3. sanctimonious person. **~ de pau oco** fraud, person who is not as good as he looks.

Santíssimo s. m. the Sacrament, the holy Eucharist, the blessed, consecrated Host. ‖ **santíssimo** adj. (abs. sup. of **santo**) most holy. **o ~** the holy Eucharist.

santista s. m. + f. (Braz.) native or inhabitant of Santos (a city in the State of São Paulo). ‖ adj. of or referring to Santos.

santo s. m. 1. saint. 2. (fig.) a very virtuous good person. ‖ adj. saint, saintly, holy, sacred, pure. ‖ **-amente** adv. holily.
~s de casa não fazem milagres no one is a prophet in his own country. **~ Deus!** good heavens! **o ~ Gral** the Holy Grail. **~ óleo** (eccl.) chrism, holy oil. **~ padroeiro** patron saint. **~ sacrifício** the sacrifice of the Mass. **~ sepulcro** Holy Sepulcher. **-a ceia** Last Supper. **-a Sé** Apostolic See. **a cada ~ o seu candelabro** honour to whom honour is due. **cidade -a** Holy City. **corpo ~** corposant, St. Elmo's fire. **despir um ~ para vestir outro** to rob Peter to pay Paul. **dia de todos os ~s** All Saints' Day. **dia ~** holiday. **o Espírito Santo** the Holy Ghost, Holy Spirit. **ficar com o ~ e a esmola** to kill two birds with one stone. **fazer cara de ~** to pull a sanctimonious face. **fazer perder a paciência a um ~** to try the patience of a saint. **fazer-se de ~** to play the saint. **o ~ ofício** the Holy Office, Inquisition. **quinta-feira -a** Holy Thursday. **o Santo Padre** the Pope, Pontiff. **semana -a** Holy Week. **ser o ~ do dia** to be the man in vogue. **todo ~ dia** the whole blessed day. **Todos os Santos** All Saints. **ter ~ forte** 1. to be immune to witchcraft and sorcery. 2. to be well backed or patronized; have God on one's side.

santo-e-senha s. m. (pl. **santo-e-senhas**) watchword; catchword; password.

santola s. f. (also **centola**) partan, spider-crab.

santolina s. f. (bot.) santolina, lavender-cotton, cotton-weed.

santolinha s. f. dim. of **santola**, hairy-crab, lady-crab.

santonina s. f. (bot.) santonica, sea wormwood: a vermifuge plant.

santoral s. m. (pl. **-ais**) 1. hagiology: book containing the lives of saints. 2. book of sermons or panegyrics. 3. psalter.

santuário s. m. sanctuary: 1. a holy place. 2. a church, shrine, temple, holy of holies. 3. asylum; refuge. 4. (fig.) one's innermost; heart, soul.

sanzala s. f. (Braz., pop.) = **senzala**.

são (I) abr. of **santo** always used when the saint's name starts with a consonant **São Paulo, São Pedro** in opposition to **Santo Antônio**.

são (II) s. m. (pl. **sãos**) 1. healthy man. 2. healthy or sound part. 3. soundness; perfect condition. ‖ adj. (f. **sã**) 1. sound, wholesome. 2. healthy, healthful, sane, vigorous, robust. 3. undamaged, safe, secure. 4. correct, reliable. 5. judicious. 6. thorough. **~ conselho** prudent advice. **~ de espírito** sane, of sound mind. **sã doutrina** a sound doctrine. **~ e salvo** safe and sound. **alimento ~** wholesome food. **homem de juízo ~** a judicious man. **juízo ~** sound judgement. **ser ~ como um perro** to be as sound as a bell.

são-gonçalo s. m. (pl. **são-gonçalos**) (Braz.) person who presents another's marriage proposal.

são-joanense s. m. + f. (pl. **são-joanenses**) (Braz.) native or inhabitant of São João del-Rei (a city in the State of Minas Gerais). ‖ adj. of or referring to São João del-Rei.

são-joanesco, **são joanino** adj. (pl. **são-joanescos, são--joaninos**) (Braz.) of or referring to Saint John. **festa são-joanesca** St. John's festivity.

são-pauleiro s. m. (pl. **são-pauleiros**) (N. Braz.) the migrant laborer who comes from Bahia to work on farms in São Paulo.

são-salavá s. m. (pl. **são-salavás**) (Braz., folklore) a spirit of the woods of indigenous origin.

são-tomé s. f. (pl. **são-tomés**) (Braz.) a kind of banana plant from the island of São Tomé, Africa.

são-tomense s. m. + f. (pl. **são-tomenses**) native or inhabitant of the island of São Tomé, Africa. ‖ adj. of or referring to São Tomé.

sapa s. f. 1. spade, shovel. 2. (mil.) sap, the act of sapping. 3. (Port. prov.) short woman. 4. (fig.) insidious undermining or subversion.

trabalho de ~ underhand work.

sapador s. m. 1. (mil.) sapper. 2. pioneer. 3. (fig.) underminer.

sapal s. m. (pl. **-ais**) 1. moor, marsh. 2. place full of toads.

sapão s. m. (pl. **-ões**) 1. augm. of **sapo** big toad. 2. (bot., also **pau-brasil**) sapa wood.

sapar v. 1. to sap: a) undermine. b) approach by mines, trenches. c) render unstable by wearing away the foundation. d) (fig.) to subvert or destroy insidiously. 2. to work with a spade.

saparia s. f. 1. a lot of frogs or toads; frogs or toads as a whole. 2. (Braz., fam.) gang, boys.

vamos sair, ~ get out of here, kids.

sapata s. f. 1. low shoe, slipper; laced boot. 2. (naut.) dead block, deadeye. 3. (archit.) overspan, console bracket. 4. leather pad on the keys of musical instruments.

~ **do freio** (mot.) brake shoe. **levar com a** ~ to be driven away.

sapatada s. f. 1. blow with a shoe. 2. blow with the paw.

sapatão s. m. (pl. **-ões**) 1. augm. of **sapato,** a large shoe; clodhopper; wooden shoe. 2. (Braz.) name formerly given to the Portuguese living in São Paulo.

sapataria s. f. 1. shoe shop, shoe store. 2. shoemaking, trade of a shoemaker. 3. factory where shoes are made.

sapateada s. f. 1. stamping or trampling with the feet. 2. (S. Braz.) ancient regional dance.

sapateado s. m. 1. = **sapatada.** 2. tap-dance, patter, popular dance at which time is beaten noisily with the heels.

~ **com tamancos** clog-dance.

sapateador s. m. tap-dancer. ‖ adj. pattering, beating (heels).

sapatear v. 1. to tap-dance, clog; to dance beating the heels. 2. to beat time with the foot.

sapateio s. m. tap-dancing.

sapateira s. f. 1. a shoemaker's wife. 2. a woman who makes or sells shoes. 3. shoe closet. 4. a plant of the family Melastomaceae.

sapateiro s. m. 1. shoemaker, bootmaker, cobbler. 2. shoe-seller. 3. (Braz.) fisher who never catches a fish. 4. botcher, bungler.

~ **remendão** cobbler, (sl.) job-cobbler.

sapateta s. f. 1. simple slipper. 2. clatter of shoe heels or sabots.

sapatilha s. f. 1. leather pad on the keys of musical instruments. 2. a hatmaker's tool.

sapatilho s. m. (naut.) thimbles, bull's eyes.

sapatinho s. m. 1. dim. of **sapato,** small shoe, baby's bootee, child's shoe (plates B 16, R 6). 2. (bot.) a slipper-flower.

sapatinho-do-diabo s. m. (pl. **sapatinhos-do-diabo**) (Braz., bot.) a masturtium.

sapato s. m. shoe (plates B 16, R 6, 7).

~ **com fivela** buckshoe. ~ **de baile** dancing shoe, pumps. ~**s de banho** bathing-shoes (plates B 3, R 7). ~ **de defunto** doubtful promise. ~ **de malhão** a shoe made of raw leather. ~ **de pau** wooden shoe, sabot. ~**s de pelica** kid shoes. ~ **de salto alto** high-heeled shoe. ~ **de salto baixo** low-heeled shoe. ~**s de tênis** sneakers. ~ **ferrado** hobnailed

shoe. **andar com** ~**s de feltro** to move very secretly and carefully. **andar com pedras no** ~ to be very suspicious or diffident. **calçar os** ~**s** to put on one's shoes. **com** ~**s gastos** down at the heels. **cordão de** ~**s** shoe-lace. **dar um lustro aos** ~**s** to put a good shine on the shoes. **descalçar os** ~**s** to take off one's shoes. **é ali que aperta o** ~ that's where the shoe pinches. **esperar por** ~**s de defunto** to entertain vain hopes. **o maior tamanho em** ~**s** the biggest size in shoes. **orelha de** ~ tab.

sapatorra s. f. (also **sapatorro** m.) clumsy shoe, bargelike shoe.

sapatranca s. f. (also **sapatrancas** pl.) = **sapatorra.**

sapel interj. shoo! away with you! scram!

sapé s. m. (Braz.) 1. satintail or sape grass, much used for thatching. 2. (N. Braz.) basket.

sapear v. (Braz.) to look on; to kibitz.

sapeca (I) s. f. Chinese coin, with an orifice in the centre.

sapeca (II) s. f. flirt, coquette. ‖ adj. flirtatious.

sapeca (III) s. f. 1. singeing. 2. beating, thrashing. 3. bungling.

sapecação s. f. (Braz.) singeing, process of scorching mate leaves.

sapecado s. m. (S. Braz.) animal with reddish hair. ‖ adj. reddish-haired (animal).

sapecadouro s. m. (Braz.) drying place for mate leaves.

sapecar (I) v. (Braz.) 1. to parch, dry, singe (as tea). 2. (pop.) to thrash; beat slightly. 3. to do imperfectly, bungle. 4. to deal a blow.

sapecar (II) v. (Braz.) (fig.) 1. to flirt. 2. to amuse o. s. 3. to loaf, idle.

sapequeiro s. m. (N. Braz.) soil recently burned.

sapequismo s. m. (Braz., fam.) coquetry, fondness of flirting.

sapezal s. m. (pl. **-ais**) (Braz., also **sapezeiro**) 1. place abounding with sape grass. 2. sterile ground.

sápia s. f. fir: 1. the tree. 2. the wood.

sapicuá s. m. (Braz.) 1. travelling bag or sack, a kit. 2. cylinder of bamboo or a piece of horn to keep diamonds in.

sápido adj. sapid, savoury, palatable.

sapieira s. f. (Braz., pop.) sape grass and dry vegetation on sterile soil.

sapiência s. f. sapience, wisdom, scholarship.

vossa ~ (ironical address) your sapiency.

sapiencial adj. m. + f. (pl. **-ais**) sapiential.

sapiente adj. m. + f. sapient, wise. ‖ ~**mente** adv. wisely.

sapindácea s. f. plant of the soapberry family (Sapindaceae).

sapindáceo adj. (bot.) sapindaceous.

sapinho s. m. 1. dim. of **sapo,** little toad. 2. = **sapinhos.**

sapinhos s. m. pl. 1. (med.) aphthae, thrush, little white patches in the mouth of babies. 2. a morbid affection on a horse's tongue.

sapiranga s. f. (Braz., med.) blepharitis: inflammation of the eyelids.

sapirangui s. m. (Braz., bot.) one of the Gramineae.

sapiroca s. f. (S. Braz.) blepharitis with loss of the eyelashes. ‖ adj. (eyes and eyelids) 1. red and swollen. 2. having no eyelashes. 3. white-eyed (horses).

sapitica s. m. (Braz., ornith., also **saí**) species of honey creeper or sugarbird.

sapituca s. f. (Braz., pop.) 1. bewilderment, stunning. 2. intoxication, drunkenness.

sapo s. m. 1. toad. 2. (Braz., pop.) kibitzer. 3. (S. Braz.) disguised inspector.

~ **da terra** (fig.) greedy-guts. **dizer** ~**s e saramantingas contra alguém** to speak very evil of a person. **pedra de** ~ toadstone. **ser inimigos como o** ~ **com a rã** to be in great enmity one with another.

sapo-concho s. m. (pl. **sapos-conchos**) fresh-water tortoise.

sapo-cururu s. m. (pl. **sapos-cururu, sapos-cururus**) the agua-toad, the most common toad of Brasil.

sapo-do-mar s. m. (pl. **sapos-do-mar**) (Braz., ichth. also **baiacu**) a puffer, globefish.

saponáceo adj. saponaceous; that can be used as soap.

saponário adj. (pharm.) saponary.

saponificação s. f. (pl. **-ões**) (chem.) saponification.

saponificar v. to saponify: convert into soap.

saponificável adj. m. + f. (pl. **-áveis**) saponificable.

saponiforme adj. m. + f. saponiform, soaplike.

saponina s. f. (chem.) saponin.

sapopema, sapopemba s. f. (Braz.) large prop root which grows along with the trunk.

saporema s. m. (Braz.) plant disease characterized by abnormal suberization, mostly of the tapioca plant.

saporífero, saporífico adj. saporific, saporous: having flavour or giving flavour to.

sapota s. f. (Braz., bot.) the sapote, marmalade-tree and fruit.

sapotáceas s. f. pl. Sapotaceae, the sapodilla family.

sapotáceo adj. (bot.) sapotaceous.

sapotaia s. f. (Braz., bot.) the dog caper, bottle cod.

sapoti s. m. (Braz.) sapodilla: an edible fruit.

sapotizeiro s. m. (Braz., bot.) sapodilla: a large evergreen tree.

saprema s. f. (Braz.) fulcrum: the fixed point on which a bar of a lever rests or about which it turns.

sapremar v. (Braz.) to lift weights by means of a lever and a fulcrum.

saprófago s. m. saprophagan: a lamellicorn beetle living on decomposed vegetable matter. ‖ adj. saprophagous.

saprófilo adj. saprophyte, saprophilous.

saprófito s. m. saprophyte: a vegetable organism that grows on decaying organic matter.

sapu s. m. (Braz., also **sapujuba**) a Brazilian conirostral bird.

sapuá s. m. (Braz.) small cultivated ground.

sapucaia, sapucaieira s. f. (Braz., bot.) sapucaya, any large tree of the genus Lecythis.

sapucainha s. f. (Braz., also **canudo-de-pito**) a tree whose nuts yield an oil used in the treatment of leprosy.

sapucaio s. m. (N. Braz., pop.) devil.

sapucairana s. f. (Braz.) a tree of the family Lecythidaceae.

sapupira-da-mata s. f. (pl. **sapupiras-da-mata**) (bot., also **sapupira-do-campo**) the Brazilian alcornoco.

saputá s. m. (Braz.) a tree of the family Caryocaraceae.

saquarema s. m. (Braz., hist.) nickname of the conservative party or its members during the monarchy.

saque (I) s. m. 1. bank draft, bill, the act of drawing a bill of exchange. 2. (sport) service, serve.
~ **a curto prazo** short-dated bill. ~ **a longo prazo** long-dated bill. ~ **à vista** bill or draft at sight. ~ **bem acolhido** honoured draft. ~ **de favor** (com.) kite. ~ **de letra** (com.) drawing. ~ **mal acolhido** dishonoured draft. ~ **a descoberto** an overdraft.

saque (II) s. m. (also **saqueio**) sack, pillage, plunder, robbery.

saquê s. m. sake: a Japanese alcoholic beverage of fermented rice.

saqueador s. m. plunderer, pillager; devastator. ‖ adj. plundering, pillaging.

saquear v. 1. to sack, plunder, pillage; to devastate, to spoil.

saqueio s. m. = **saque** II.

saquete s. m. small sac or bag.

saquilhão s. m. (pl. **-ões**) branch in the mouldboard of the plough to enlarge the furrow.

saquim s. m. (also **sequim**, pl. **-ins**) kosher butcher's knife.

saquinho s. m. 1. dim. of **saco**, small sac. 2. (mil.) cartridge, cartouch.
~ **de papel** paper bag, paper sac.

saquitel s. m. (pl. **-éis**) = **saquete**.

sarã s. m. (Braz.) = **sarandi**.

sarabanda s. f. 1. saraband: a Spanish dance of the XVI century. 2. (fam.) reprimand, reprehension. 3. tumult, riot, agitation.
passar uma ~ to give a wigging to.

sarabandear v. 1. to dance the saraband. 2. to dance.

sarabatana s. f. 1. Indian blowgun, a trunk to shoot with. 2. a sort of speaking trumpet, megaphone. 3. horn.

sarabiana s. f. (Braz.) fish of the family Cichlidae.

sarabulhento adj. (also **sarabulhoso**) 1. rugged, rough. 2. (pop.) pimpled, blotchy.

sarabulho s. m. 1. roughness or flaw on the surface of china or earthenware. 2. blister, pimple.

saraça s. m. + f. fine cotton fabric.

saracoteador s. m. rambler, stroller. ‖ adj. 1. rambling, strolling. 2. wriggling (as the hips when dancing).

saracotear v. 1. to gad, ramble, range. 2. to straggle about without any settled purpose. 3. to rock, wriggle, move the hips in dancing. 4. to flirt.

saracoteio s. m. (also **saracote, saracoteamento**) 1. the act of rambling. 2. the wriggling and rocking movements of the hips in dancing.

saracura s. f. (Braz.) 1. (bot.) a trumpet-creeper. 2. (ornith.) the wood rails, shore-birds.

saracura-da-canarana s. f. (pl. **saracuras-da-canarana**) (zool., also **frango-d'água-azul**) the purple gallinule.

saracura-da-praia s. f. (pl. **saracuras-da-praia**) (zool.) a Spix's wood rail.

saracura-do-norte s. f. (pl. **saracuras-do-norte**) (Braz., bot.) a water primrose.

sarado adj. 1. healed, cured. 2. (sl.) brave, courageous. 3. clever, shrewd. 4. gluttonous.

saragoça s. f. brown, woollen cloth first manufactured at Saragossa, Spain.

saragoçano s. m. native or inhabitant of Saragossa, Spain. ‖ adj. of or referring to Saragossa.

saraiva s. f. 1. hail; hailstone. 2. (fig.) hail of things coming down with swiftness or violence.

saraivada s. f. 1. hail, hailstorm. 2. (fig.) discharge, volley. 3. (fig.) shower of questions.

saraivar v. 1. to hail. 2. to destroy or ruin by hail. 3. (fig.) to fall as hail.

saraizal s. m. (Braz.) trees growing on beaches, subject to submerging up to the branches during the rainy season.

saramago s. m. (bot.) wild rape, wild radish.

saramátulo s. m. shoot of a stag.

saramba s. f. (Braz.) a sort of fandango dance.

sarambé s. m. (S. Braz., pop.) fool, simpleton, ass.

sarambelada s. f. (Braz.) 1. foolery. 2. nonsense, silliness.

sarambeque s. m. a very gay Negro dance, popular in the XVII and XVIII centuries.

saramoco s. m. (S. Braz.) bad crop.

sarampão s. m. (med.) attack of measles.

sarampelo s. m. (med.) rubella, German measles.

sarampento s. m. (Braz.) person affected with measles. ‖ adj. measled, measly.

sarampo s. m. (med.) measles, an infectious disease indicated by a papular rash.

saranda s. m. (Braz.) loafer, vagabond. ‖ adj. loafing, rambling, idle.

sarandagem s. f. (pl. **-ens**) (Braz.) vagabondage, vagrancy.

sarandalhas s. f. pl. (also **sarandalhos**) 1. chaff. 2. leavings, remains. 3. (fig.) mob, rabble.

sarandear v. (S. Braz.) 1. = **sarabandear**. 2. = **saracotear**. 3. to capriole (horse).

sarandi s. m. (Braz.) 1. waste, sterile ground. 2. small rocky island.

saranga, sarango adj. (Braz., pop.) foolish, silly; conceited.

sarangravaia s. f. (Braz.) stunted bushwood; thornbush.

sarapanel s. m. (pl. **-éis**) (archit.) elliptic arch; baskethandle arch.

sarapantão adj. (pl. **-ões**) (pop.) = **sarapintado**.

sarapantar v. (pop.) 1. to frighten, startle; to stun, stupefy. 2. **~-se** to be frightened, stupefied.

sarapatel s. m. (pl. **-éis**) 1. haggis, a dish of the boiled blood and viscera of hogs. 2. (fig.) medley, hodgepodge.

sarapieira s. f. (Braz.) nonsense, silliness; absurdity.

sarapilheira s. f. (also **serapilheira**) sarp-cloth, sarplier.

sarapintado adj. (pop., also **sarapantão**) 1. freckled, spotted; mottled, piebald. 2. vary-coloured, pied.

sarapintar v. 1. to spot, speckle. 2. to dot, mottle, freckle. 3. to paint vary-coloured.

sarapó s. m. (N. Braz.) 1. (ichth.) carapo. 2. (also **beiju**) a coconut or tapioca cake.

sarapueira s. f. (Braz., also **manta**) a layer of fallen leaves in the woods.

saraquá s. m. (S. Braz.) a sort of wooden hoe for corn planting.

sarar v. to heal: 1. restore to health. 2. cure. 3. correct, repair, mend. 4. grow or become sound, recover health.

~ uma ferida to heal a wound.

sarará s. m. + f. (Braz.) 1. nickname given to the Brazilian half-breed of the Amazon area. 2. mongrel with reddish curly hair, albino. ‖ adj. designating such a type of person.

sararaca s. f. (Braz., Amazon) arrow the Indians use to catch fish.

sarassará s. m., (Braz.) = **sarará**.

sarau s. m. 1. soirée: an evening reunion or party (private, in the theatre, or club). 2. evening concert.

~ beneficente benefit-night.

sarça s. f. (bot., also **azinheiro** m.) bramble, blackberry vine. 2. bramble patch, bramble hedge. 3. thorn, bush; brier, briar; grove.

sarçal s. m. (pl. **-ais**) place abounding with brambles, brier patch, bramble hedge.

sarcasmo s. m. sarcasm: 1. a bitter, taunting, ironical or wounding remark. 2. bitter irony; gibe, taunt.

sarcástico adj. sarcastic, taunting, ironical. ‖ **sarcasticamente** adv. sarcastically.

observação -a a cutting remark.

sarcocárpio s. m. (bot.) sarcocarp.

sarcocele s. f. (path.) sarcocele: fleshy enlargement of the testicle.

sarcocola s. f. sarcocolla, sarcocol, a gum-resin.

sarcocoleira s. f. Sarcocolla: a plant from which the sarcocolla resin is obtained.

sarcoderma s. m. (bot.) sarcoderm: an intermediate fleshy layer of some seeds.

sarcódico adj. (biol.) sarcodic.

sarcódio s. m. (biol.) sarcode, animal protoplasm.

sarcofagídeos s. m. pl. (ent.) Sarcophagidae: the flesh flies, a family of dipterous insects.

sarcófago s. m. 1. sarcophagus, stone-coffin. 2. cenotaph. ‖ adj. sarcophagous, sarcophagal: 1. feeding on flesh. 2. like a sarcophagus.

sarcofilo s. m. (bot.) the fleshy part of a leaf.

sarcóideo adj. (biol.) sarcoid, resembling flesh.

sarcolema s. m. (anat., also **miolema**) sarcolemma: the tubular membrane sheathing muscular tissue.

sarcólito s. m. (min.) sarcolite.

sarcologia s. f. (anat.) sarcology, treatise on the soft parts of the body.

sarcológico adj. sarcological.

sarcoma s. m. (path.) sarcoma: a malignant tumour.

sarcomatoso adj. (path.) sarcomatous.

sarcônfalo s. m. (path.) sarcomphalum.

sarçoso adj. bushy; brambled.

sarcótico adj. (med.) sarcotic, producing flesh.

sarda (I) s. f. (ichth.) a sort of small mackerel.

sarda (II) s. f. (more used **~s** pl.) freckle, speckle.

~s no rosto freckles, speckles in the face.

sardanapalesco adj. effeminate; glutton; licentious.

sardanisca, sardanita s. f. (Braz.) 1. a wall lizard. 2. (pop.) affected, prudish woman.

sardento adj. (also **sardo**) freckled, freckly.

sardinha s. f. 1. (ichth.) sardine, pilchard (Sardina pilchardus). 2. (sl.) razor.

~ de conserva tinned sardines. **como ~ em canastra** packed like sardines. **não vale uma ~** it's worth nothing. **tirar a ~** (Braz.) to strike playfully, with the indicator and middle finger, someone's buttocks. **tirar a ~ com a mão do gato** to seek one's advantage on another's expense.

sardinheira s. f. 1. woman who sells sardines. 2. sardine-fishing. 3. a net or boat used to catch sardines.

sardinheiro s. m. 1. sardine-seller. 2. sardine-fisher. 3. (min.) = **sárdio**. ‖ adj. relating to sardines.

sárdio s. m. (min.) sard, sarde or sardone, a variety of carnelian stone, brown in colour.

sardo s. m. Sardinian: native or inhabitant of the island of Sardinia, Italy. ‖ adj. 1. Sardinian: of or referring to Sardinia. 2. = **sardento**.

sardônia s. f. 1. = **sardônica**. 2. (bot.) crowfoot (Ranunculus sceleratus).

sardônica s. f. (min., also **sardônia**) sardonyx: Sardian stone, dark orange or orange-red in colour.

sardônico (I) adj. referring to the sardonyx.

sardônico (II) adj. sardonic, sardonian: 1. affected, insincere. 2. sneering, malignant, bitterly ironical. ‖ **-amente** adv. sardonically.

sardoso adj. = **sardento**.

sargaça s. f. (bot.) rock-rose.

sargaço s. m. (bot.) sargasso, sargassum, gulf-weed, seaweed.

mar de ~ Sargasso sea.

sargentear v. 1. to do the duty of a sergeant, to take the command. 2. to weary, fatigue. 3. to boss about.

sargento (I) s. m. sergeant, serjeant.

~ instrutor drill sergeant. **~-quartel-mestre** quartermaster sergeant. **~-mor** sergeant-major. **~-porta-bandeira** colour sergeant. **primeiro-~** sergeant-major, top-sergeant.

sargento (II) s. m. carpenter's clamp, bench-screw, turn-buckle.

sargo s. m. (ichth.) sargus, sea bream.

sári s. m. (India) sari.

sariema s. f. (Braz., zool., also **seriema**) the crested seriema.

sarigüê s. m., **sarigüéia** f. (zool., also **gambá**) a marsupium mammal, the opossum.

sarilhar v. 1. to reel thread or yarn. 2. to pile arms. 3. to pace up and down. 4. to misbehave. 5. to fidget.

sarilho s. m. 1. reel, windle, winder. 2. draw-beam. 3. the gear of a water wheel. 4. gun rack, rack of arms in the form of a pyramid. 5. turn round the horizontal bar. 6. (pop.) confusion, agitation, disorder. 7. (fig.) fool, idiot.
~ **de armas** a pile of arms. **andar num** ~ to be always in motion. **fazer um** ~ to raise a fuss. **meter-se em** ~**s** to get into a mess. **que** ~**!** here is a pretty kettle of fish!
saripoca s. m. (Braz., ornith., also **araçaripoca**) toucanet.
sarja s. f. serge: twilled woollen or silk fabric.
sarjação s. f. (pl. **-ões**) (also **sarja, sarjadura**) scarifying, scarification, slight incision, cupping.
sarjadeira s. f. (Braz., med.) scarificator.
sarjador s. m. (med.) 1. scarifier. 2. scarificator. ‖ adj. scarifying.
sarjar v. 1. (med.) to scarify; cup. 2. to twill (fabric).
~ **a alguém** (pop.) to screw s. o.
sarjel s. m. (pl. **-éis**) (also **sarjão**) coarse woollen fabric.
sarjeta (I) s. f. 1. gutter (plate E 11). 2. drain.
tirar alguém da ~ to pick s. o. up in the gutter.
sarjeta (II) s. f. thin or narrow serge.
sarmentício adj. (bot.) sarmentose, sarmentous.
sarmentífero adj. bearing runners, bearing sarmentum.
sarmento s. m. (bot.) 1. sarmentum; cut off twig or branch of a vine. 2. layer, shoot, scion.
sarmentoso adj. (bot., also **sarmentício**) sarmentose, sarmentous.
sarna s. f. 1. itch, prurigo, mange, scabies: a contagious skin disease. 2. disease of the olive-tree. 3. (pop.) a very tiresome person.
~ **castelhana** shanker. **procurar** ~ **para se coçar** to ask for trouble. **ser uma** ~ 1. to be a glutton; greedy. 2. to be a pest, a bore, tiresome, irksome.
sarnambi s. m. (Braz.) = **sambaqui**.
sarnento s. m. 1. scabious person. 2. (Braz., pop.) devil. ‖ adj. (also **sarnoso**) 1. itchy, scabious, pruriginous. 2. rancid, rank, evil-smelling.
saroba s. f. (Braz., ornith., also **sarova, pucaçu**) the southern rufous pigeon.
sarobá s. m. (Braz.) land covered by a low rated second growth.
sarópode s. m. + f. (zool.) having hairy paws.
saros s. m. (astr.) saros.
sarpar v. (naut., also **zarpar**) to weigh anchor.
sarrabalho s. m. (S. Braz.) country dance, a kind of fandango.
sarrabulhada s. f. 1. great amounts of **sarrabulho**. 2. haggis, hodgepodge. 3. (fig.): a) filthiness, piggishness. b) confusion, uproar, tumult, noise.
sarrabulho s. m. 1. curdled blood of a hog. 2. a stew made thereof. 3. a dish made of pork. 4. (fig.) uproar, tumult, noise.
sarraceniácea s. f. a member of the Sarraceniaceae, a family of dicotyledonous plants.
saraceniáceo adj. (bot.) sarraceniaceous.
sarraceno s. m. Saracen, Moor, Arab; an Arab or Moslem at the times of the Crusades. ‖ adj. Saracenic, Saracenical, Arab.
sarrafaçal s. m. (pl. **-ais**) (pop.) bungler, botcher, dabbler.
sarrafaçar v. 1. = **sarjar**. 2. to botch, bungle.
sarrafada s. f. a blow with a lath; a beating, thrashing.
sarrafão s. m. (pl. **-ões**) a strong lath.
sarrafar v. 1. to cut into thick laths. 2. to do badly, botch.
sarrafascada s. f. (N. Braz., pop.) brawl.
sarrafo (I) s. m. lath, slat (plate T 6).
sarrafo (II) s. m. money-changer, cambist in Portuguese India.
sarrafusca s. f. (pop.) uproar, tumult, noise, disorder.

sarrão s. m. (pl. **-ões**) (also **surrão**) sac or bag of leather used for the transport of cereals to the mill.
sarrento adj. 1. tartarous. 2. (med., also **saburroso**) furred.
sarrido s. m. difficulty in breathing, shortness of breath, asthma.
sarro s. m. 1. argol, tartar. 2. fur, crust. 3. furring formed on the tongue. 4. nicotine deposits within a pipe. 5. any of various catfishes. 6. amusing or funny person (or thing).
tirar um ~ (Braz.) 1. to seek voluptuous contact, especially in crowded places (movies, theater, etc.). 2. to make fun of s. o., mock.
sarta s. f. 1. shrouds of a ship. 2. string.
saru adj. m. + f. (Braz., Amazon) 1. insane. 2. quiet, with no sign of fish (lake).
saruê s. m. (N. Braz.) 1. (also **gambá**) opossum. 2. ear of corn bearing few corns. ‖ adj. m. + f. = **albino.**
sassafrás s. m. (Braz., bot.) sassafras: a tree with an aromatic bark.
satã s. m. (also **diabo**) Satan, devil, Lucifer.
satanás s. m. (pl. **-ases**) Satan, the archfiend, the devil.
satânico s. m. (Braz., pop.) devil. ‖ adj. satanic, satanical. ‖ **-amente** adv. satanically, diabolically.
satanismo s. m. satanism, satanicalness, a diabolical disposition, doctrine or conduct.
satanista s. m. + f. satanist.
satélite s. m. 1. satellite: a) (astr.) a secondary planet revolving round a primary one. b) an obsequious follower, dependant. c) a state dominated by a stronger neighbour. d) a space missile. 2. a paid evildoer, henchman. 3. close friend. 4. a certain mineral which indicates the presence of diamonds.
países ~**s** satellite nations. ~ **artificial** satellite: a man-made object put into orbit. **cidade** ~ satellite town.
sátira s. f. satire, lampoon, sarcasm, verse or prose in which wickedness or folly of persons are held up to ridicule.
satirião s. m. (pl. **-ões**) (bot.) satyrium, stander grass.
satiríase s. f. (med.) satyriasis.
satírico s. m. satirist: one who writes or employs satire. ‖ adj. satiric, satirical, libellous, cutting, ironical, mordaceous. ‖ **satiricamente** adv. satirically.
estilo ~ satiric style. **poema** ~ a satirical poem. **poeta** ~ satirist, lampooner. **versos** ~**s** lampoon.
satirista s. m. + f. (also **satírico** m.) satirist: one who writes or employs satire.
satirizar v. 1. to satirize, lampoon. 2. to write satires on. 3. to criticize with satire.
sátiro s. m. satyr: 1. an ancient sylvan deity represented with the legs of a goat and living in the forest. 2. (fig.) a lecherous man. 3. (zool.) a butterfly of the family Agapetidae.
satisdação s. f. (pl. **-ões**) (ancient jur.) bail, security, surety.
satisdar v. (obs.) to bail, to put in bail, to stand bail, give or stand security.
satisfação s. f. (pl. **-ões**) satisfaction: 1. pleasure, pride. 2. gratification, contentment. 3. payment of a debt, fulfilment of an obligation. 4. reparation, compensation, amends, explanation. 5. (teol.) atonement, performance of penance.
com ~ **de** to the satisfaction of. **dá-me muita** ~ it affords me great pleasure. **dar** ~ **a uma queixa** to settle a complaint. **dar -ões** to explain, excuse. **dar uma** ~ to offer an apology. **é uma** ~ **saber que...** it is a satisfaction to know that... **exprimir a sua** ~ to express one's delight. **foi uma grande** ~ **para mim** it was most pleasing for me. **pedir**

uma ~ to demand satisfaction. ter ~ em to find satisfaction in.

satisfatório adj. 1. satisfactory: giving satisfaction, satisfying, sufficient, adequate, agreeable, meeting all needs or desires. 2. making amends, compensating. 3. (teol.) atoning. ‖ **satisfatoriamente** adv. satisfactorily.

satisfazer v. to satisfy: 1. supply or gratify to the full, content, please. 2. fulfil, comply with, discharge, perform. 3. satiate, surfeit. 4. pay or discharge a debt. 5. be sufficient for, meet the desires. 6. free from doubt, convince, give satisfaction, persuade. 7. make amends, compensate. 8. (teol.) atone.
~ **a fome** to appease the hunger. ~ **aos argumentos** to answer the objection. ~ **as exigências** to fulfil the requirements. ~ **a sua obrigação** to discharge a duty or obligation. ~ **inteiramente** to satisfy fully. ~ **os seus compromissos** to comply with one's engagements. ~**-se com pouco** to cut and contrive. ~ **uma dívida** to meet a debt. ~ **uma reclamação** to discharge a claim. ~ **um apetite** to satisfy a craving. ~ **um desejo** to satisfy a wish. ~ **um pedido** to comply with a request. **isto não me satisfaz** this does not satisfy me. **nada o satisfaz** nothing satisfies him.

satisfeito adj. satisfied: 1. content, happy, pleased, cheerful, comfortable. 2. satiate, satiated. 3. fulfilled, met.
~ **com o bom resultado** pleased with the good result. ~ **com o procedimento de** satisfied with the conduct of. ~ **consigo** self-complacent. ~ **de si** complacent. **ainda não está** ~? are you not pleased yet? **bem** ~ well-pleased. **dar-se por** ~ to pronounce o. s. satisfied. **ele ainda não está** ~ (fig.) he sticks out his chin for more. **ele não vai** ~ he goes away discontented. **estou** ~ **com** I am pleased with. **mostrar-se** ~ to show satisfaction. **muito** ~ delighted, well-content.

sativo adj. (bot.) sative: sown or planted.

sátrapa s. m. satrap: 1. a governor of a province under the ancient Persians. 2. a governor of a dependency, often a tyrant. 3. despotic person.

satrapear v. 1. to live like a satrap; live in great splendour, tyrannize, oppress. 2. (fig.) to play the fine gentleman.

satrapia s. f. satrapy: province or authority of a satrap.

saturabilidade s. f. (chem.) saturability.

saturação s. f. (pl. -ões) (chem.) saturation: the state of being saturate.
ponto de ~ saturation point.

saturado adj. saturated: 1. soaked or impregnated thoroughly. 2. intense, deep; full. 3. (chem.) combined with the greatest possible amount of another substance. 4. (fig.) sick, tired.
ele está ~ **de poesias** his mind is steeped in poetry. **solução** -**a** satured solution. **vapor** ~ saturated steam.

saturador s. m. (chem.) saturator, a substance that neutralizes acidity or alkalinity. ‖ adj. saturating.

saturante adj. m. + f. 1. (chem.) saturant, saturating. 2. (fig.) tedious, tiresome.

saturar v. (chem.) to saturate: 1. soak or impregnate thoroughly. 2. (chem.) cause a substance to combine with the greatest possible amount of another substance. 3. fill or charge so that it will hold no more. 4. satiate.
~ **demais** to oversaturate.

saturável adj. m. + f. (pl. -áveis) (chem.) saturable.

saturnal s. f. (pl. -ais) 1. saturnalia: orgy, period of unrestrained revelry and license, debauchery. 2. Saturnalia: ancient Roman festival in honour of Saturn. ‖ adj. m. + f. Saturnalian: referring to the god Saturn or the feasts in his honour.
festas -ais Saturnalia: the feasts of Saturn.

saturnino (I) adj. Saturnian, Saturnine: born under the sign of Saturn, having a melancholic, silent or gloomy temperament.

saturnino (II) adj. saturnine, referring to lead and its compounds.

saturnismo s. m. (med.) saturnism, plumbism, lead-poisoning.

saturno (I) s. m. 1. **Saturno** Saturn: one of the major planets of the solar system. 2. the weather. 3. sweltry hot weather.

saturno (II) s. m. (chem.) lead.

saturno (III) adj. saturnalian, orgiastic, revelling.

sauá s. m. (Braz., ichth., also **saá**) a marmoset.

saúba s. f. (Braz.) = **saúva**.

saubal s. m. (Braz.) = **sauval**.

saúco s. m. the coffin of a horse's hoof.

saudação s. f. (pl. -ões) salutation: 1. the act of saluting. 2. greeting, welcome. 3. a salute.
~ **amável** welcome. ~ **angélica** angelical salute. **com minhas -ões** with my compliments. **palavras de** ~ words of welcome. **responder a uma** ~ to regreet.

saudade s. f. 1. longing, yearning, ardent wish or desire. 2. homesickness, nostalgia. 3. (bot.) scabious, columbine. 4. (Braz.) a seamen's song. 5. (S. Braz.) compliments, affectionate greetings to absent persons.
estou cada vez com mais ~ **de você** I miss you more and more every day. **matar ou desafogar** ~**s** to visit or see again a person or place one likes very much. **meu coração tem** ~ **de** my heart aches for. **morro de** ~ **de vê-lo** I die with impatience to see him. **tenho muita** ~ **dele** I miss him very much. **ter** ~ **da sua terra ou pátria** to be homesick, to have a longing or hankering for one's home or country.

saudador s. m. saluter, person who salutes. ‖ adj. saluting, salutational.

saudante adj. m. + f. saluting, salutatory.

saudar v. to salute: 1. greet with a gesture or words of welcome, respect or recognition. 2. meet with kind words, a bow, a kiss, a volley. 3. hail, honour by raising the hand to the head, by firing guns or dipping flags. 4. perform a salute.
~ **com vivas** to cheer. ~ **dando salva** to volley. ~ **respeitosamente** to reverence. ~**-se** to salute one another. **saudaram-nos por ocasião de sua chegada** they greeted us on their arrival.

saudável adj. m. + f. (pl. -áveis) sound, healthy, wholesome, salutary, salubrious, beneficial, sanitary. ‖ **saudavelmente** adv. soundly, salutarily, healthily.
clima ~ a healthy climate. **criança** ~ healthy child. **ele leva uma vida** ~ he leads a healthy life. **um lugar** ~ a healthy place.

saúde s. f. 1. health. 2. healthiness, healthfulness, soundness, wholesomeness. 3. vigour. ‖ **saúde!** interj. cheerio! your health!
~ **de corpo e espírito** health of body and mind. ~ **pública** public health. **apesar do seu precário estado de** ~ in spite of his ill-health. **a** ~ **é um bem precioso** good health is a great asset. **à sua** ~! your health! here's to you! **beber à** ~ **de alguém** to drink a person's health, to toast a person. **casa de** ~ infirmary, hospital. **cheio de** ~ bouncing. **estar de boa** ~ to be in good health. **por falta de** ~ owing to poor health. **ter a** ~ **abalada** to be in failing health. **ter pouca** ~ to suffer from ill-health. **ultimamente a sua** ~ **era precária** latterly he had been in failing health. **vendendo** ~ bursting with health. **você está vendendo** ~ you look the picture of health.

saudosismo s. m. a longing or yearning for bygone days.

saudosista s. m. + f. eulogizer of the past "our time". ‖ adj. eulogizing the past days.

saudoso adj. 1. longing, yearning, ardent. 2. heartfelt, nostalgic, regretful. 3. late, departed. ‖ **-amente** adv. longingly, ardently.

~ **da pátria** homesick. **olhos** ~**s** languishing eyes.

sauí s. m. (zool.) 1. (Braz.) = **sagüi**. 2. a small caterpillar.

sauiá s. m. (Braz., zool.) a spring rat.

sauim s. m. (pl. **-ins**) (Braz., zool.) = **sagüi**.

saúna s. f. (Braz., ichth., also **azeiteira**) a small white equipment appropriate for such a bath. 3. (fig.) a very hot place. 4. (Braz. sl.) a closed place where various people smoke pot.

saúna s. f. (Braz., ichth, also **azeiteira**) a small white mullet.

sauni s. m. (Braz., ornith.) the white-breasted nun bird.

saurá s. m. (Braz., ornith., also **papa-açaí**) the red chatterer.

sáurio s. m. (zool.) saurian, an order of reptiles including lizards, crocodiles and the extinct Sauria. ‖ adj. saurian.

saurófago adj. (zool.) saurophagous: feeding on lizards and other reptiles.

saurografia s. f. saurography: book dealing with saurians.

saurográfico adj. referring to saurography.

saurógrafo s. m. person who writes about saurians.

saurologia s. f. the part of zoology dealing with saurian reptiles.

saurológico adj. referring to the study of saurian reptiles.

saurólogo s. m. person specialized in the study of saurians.

sautor s. m. a figure formed by two slanting pieces like an X resembling the St. Andrew's cross.

saúva s. f. (Braz., ent., also **saúba**) sauba ant, a leaf-cutting ant living in subterranean colonies.

sauval s. m. (pl. **-ais**) (Braz., also **saubal, sauveiro**) the subterranean nest of the sauba ants.

savacu s. m. (Braz.) the black-crowned night heron.

savacu-de-coroa s. m. (pl. **savacus-de-coroa**) (Braz., ornith.) the Guianan yellow-crowned night heron.

savana s. f. savanna, savannah, prairie.

savate s. f. savate: a kind of French fight, by ways of kicks.

saveiro s. m. 1. long and narrow fishing boat. 2. (also **saveirista**) fisher who uses such a boat or one of its crew.

savelha s. f. (ichth.) little shad; menhaden.

savitu s. m. (S. Braz.) a male sauba ant.

savoir-faire s. m. (Fr.) savoir-faire: capacity for appropriate action; tact.

savoir-vivre s. m. (Fr.) savoir-vivre: good breeding; good manners.

saxão s. m. (pl. **-ões**) Saxon: 1. individual of the Saxons, a Germanic people. 2. its language. ‖ adj. Saxon: of or referring to the Saxons or their language.

saxátil adj. m. + f. (pl. **-eis**) (also **saxícola**) saxatile, saxicoline: that is or lives among the rocks and stones; pertaining to rocks.

sáxeo adj. stony.

saxífraga s. f. (bot.) saxifrage, a rock plant. ‖ adj. saxifragous.

saxífraga-branca s. f. (pl. **saxífragas-brancas**) (bot.) the meadow saxifrage.

saxifragácea s. f. (bot.) specimen of the Saxifragaceae.

saxifragáceo adj. saxifragaceous: referring or similar to the saxifrage.

saxífrago adj. saxifragous: breaking or destroying stone or calculi.

saxofone s. m. (mus., also **saxofono**) saxophone, wind instrument of brass used as a substitute for the clarinet.

saxofonista s. m. + f. saxophonist.

saxônio s. m. Saxon: natural or inhabitant of Saxony, Germany. ‖ adj. Saxon; of or referring to Saxony.

saxoso adj. stony, full of stones, abounding with stones.

saxotrompa s. f. (mus.) saxhorn, althorn.

sazão s. f. (pl. **-ões**) season: 1. one of the four divisions of the year. 2. (fig.) proper time, opportunity. **em** ~ at the proper time. **sem** ~, **fora da** ~ out of season.

sazonado adj. seasoned: 1. brought to maturity, ripe, mellow. 2. (fig.) experienced, competent.

não ~ unripened, unseasoned. **tempo** ~ convenient time.

sazonamento s. m. seasoning, ripening.

sazonar v. to season: 1. ripen, bring to maturity, mellow; grow ripe; become fully developed. 2. (fig.): a) temper. b) become experienced.

sazonável adj. m. + f. (pl. **-áveis**) 1. seasonable: a) suitable to the season. b) coming at the right or proper time. 2. productive, capable of yielding.

se (I) refl. pers. pron. himself, herself, itself, oneself, yourself, yourselves, themselves, each other, one another.

diz-~ they say. **nunca** ~ **deve levar a faca à boca** you should never take your knife to your mouth. **que** ~ **pode fazer?** what can one do? **por todas estas razões deduz-**~ **que** from all these reasons it follows that.

se (II) conj. if, whether, provided, in case that, supposing.

~ **ao menos** if only. ~ **bem que** even though. ~ **eu fora rei** if I were king. ~ **não** if not. ~ **não fosse o seu auxílio** except for your help. ~ **eu ao menos pudesse** if I only could. ~ **é que...** if at all... ~ **você me ama, fique quieto** if you love me, be quiet. **avise-nos** ~ **você vem ou fica** let us know whether you come or stay. **como** ~ as if. **ele se comporta como** ~ **não o estivesse vendo** he acts as though he did not see it. **não sabemos** ~ we do not know if. **não sei** ~ **ele está em casa** I don't know whether he is at home. **oh,** ~ **eu soubesse seu nome!** oh, that I knew her name!

sé s. f. 1. see; cathedral; minster; the principal church in a diocese.

a Santa Sé the Papal See, the Holy See.

seara s. f. 1. cornfield, field sown with corn. 2. tilled land. 3. harvest. 4. (fig.) association, party. ~ **de trigo** wheat-field.

seareiro s. m. 1. tiller, husbandman, sower; 2. owner of a small farm; poor farmer.

seba s. f. alga, sea-wrack used as manure, especially for vine yards.

sebaça s. f. (N. Braz.) armed assault, robbery.

sebáceo adj. 1. sebaceous, fallowy, fatty. 2. dirty, greasy.

sebastianismo s. m. (Port. hist.) Sebastianism: the party or the convictions of the Sebastianists.

sebastianista s. m. + f. Sebastianist: 1. (Port. hist.) believer in the return of king Dom Sebastian from Africa. 2. (Braz. hist.) pejorative designation for the monarchists after the republic was proclaimed.

sebastião s. m. 1. (ichth.) a kind of shark. 2. (pop.) fool, idiot.

sebe s. f. quickset, hedge; fence (plates A 4, V 4). ~ **viva** quickset hedge. **cercar com** ~ to fence, inclose with a hedge.

sebeiro s. m. person who prepares and sells tallow.

sebentice s. f. dirtiness, greasiness, filthiness (esp. of the garments).

sebento s. m. dirty fellow. ‖ adj. 1. tallowy, greasy. 2. dirty, filthy, unclean.

sebereba s. f. (N. Braz., also **chibé, jacuba**) refreshment, drink of manioc flour with water and sometimes seasoned with rum.

sebinho s. m. 1. dim. of **sebo**. 2. (Braz., ornith.) honey creeper.

sebipira s. f. (Braz., bot., also **sapupira**) common name of the locust tree and the Guianan ormosia.

sebipira-falsa s. f. (pl. **sebipiras-falsas**) (Braz.) a tree of the family Leguminosae.

sebista s. m. + f. (Braz.) owner of a secondhand bookstore.

sebite s. m. (Braz., pop.) 1. bold turbulent fellow. 2. (N. Braz., ornith.) = **sebito**. ‖ adj. m. + f. 1. bold, forward. 2. restless. 3. meddlesome.

sebito s. m. (N. Braz., ornith, also **caga-sebinho**) the hangnest tody-tyrant.

sebo s. m. 1. tallow, suet, grease, fat. 2. (Braz.) secondhand bookstore. 3. flirt. ‖ **~l** si. interj. to express disappointment or irritation.

metido a ~ said of a person who puts on airs, strikes poses, is vainglorious, pompous, pretentious. **pôr ~ nas canelas** 1. to take to one's heels, take flight, run for one's life, scoot, skedaddle. 2. to beat a retreat, withdraw, turn tail. **vela de ~** tallow-candle.

seborréia s. f. (med.) seborrhoea.

seborréico adj. (med.) seborrhoeic.

seboso adj. 1. tallowish, tallowy, suety, fatty. 2. (Braz.) dirty, filthy, unclean.

sebruno adj. (Braz.) grayish (horse).

seca (I) s. f. a drying, wiping, putting out to dry.

seca (II) s. f. (pop.) 1. wearisomeness, tediousness, irksomeness, difficulties. 2. dull and tedious conversation, endless talk. 3. ado. 4. m. a) tattler, prattler, babbler. b) bore. **sem regras nem ~s** without much ado.

seca (ê) s. f. 1. dryness, drought, aridity, aridness, torridity. 2. (N. Braz.): a) = **tuberculose**. b) (pop.) long severe winter. ‖ **-amente** adv. 1. dryly, aridly. 2. (fig.) dryly, coldly, roughly.

secação s. f. (pl. **-ões**) drying; airing; desiccation; putting out to dry.

secador s. m. 1. dryer, desiccator. 2. (Braz.) coffee-grain dryer. ‖ adj. drying.

~ de cabelo hair dryer. **~ monolúcido** (papermaking) a large drying drum for one-side coated paper.

secadouro s. m. (also **secadoiro**) drying house, drying place.

secagem s. f. (pl. **-ens**) the act of drying.

secante (I) s. m. (paint) desiccative drug, drier. ‖ adj. m. + f. drying, desiccative.

secante (II) s. m. + f. (fig.) troublesome fellow, bore. ‖ adj. boring, tedious, troublesome.

secante (III) s. f. (geom.) secant. ‖ adj. m. + f. secant, cutting.

seção, secção s. f. (pl. **-ões**) section: 1. separation. 2. part cut off, partion. 3. division, slice. 4. partition; department, branch. 5. component part (plate P 9). 6. (biol.) subdivision of a group. 7. part of a writing, chapter. 8. cross-section.

~ cônica conic section. **~ de propaganda** publicity department. **~ pessoal** personnel department. **~ plenária** plenum. **~ transversal** cross-section. **~ vertical** profile.

secar (I) v. to dry: 1. dry up, get or become dry, free of moisture: desiccate. 2. evaporate. 3. drain. 4. wipe. 5. fade, wither, droop, pine, languish. 6. parch. 7. (fig.) waste away, fall off, consume. 8. **~-se:** a) to dry, become dry. b) to be parched. c) to

wither. d) to dry up. e) to fade, pine, waste away. **~ ao fogo** to dry against the fire. **~ ao sol** to sun-dry. **~ arenque ou salmão** to kipper. **~ a roupa ao sol** to dry the clothes in the sun. **~ em estufa** or **em forno** to oven-dry. **fazer ~** to blight, nip. **o poço secou** the well is dry. **o sol secou o trigo** the sun has parched the wheat.

secar (II) v. (pop.) to tire, weary.

secarrão adj. (pl. **-ões**) very dry.

secativo s. m. siccative drug. ‖ adj. siccative, exsiccative.

secessão s. f. secession, separation.

secesso s. m. retirement, retreat, solitude.

sécia s. f. 1. a self-conceited and dandyish woman, coquette. 2. a gown for women. 3. fancy, whim, humour. 4. defect, fault. 5. (bot.) China aster.

sécio s. m. 1. self-conceited person, a beau, dandy. 2. rambler, stroller. ‖ adj. 1. presumptuous, arrogant. 2. dandyish. 3. rambling, strolling.

secional, seccional adj. m. + f. (pl. **-ais**) sectional. ‖ **-mente** adv. departmental.

secionar, seccionar v. to part: 1. cut into sections. 2. divide.

seco (ê) s. m. (pl. **secos**) 1. (N. Braz.) shoal, sandbank. 2. pl. dry foods, dry provisions (in opposition to **molhados** liquids). ‖ adj. dry: 1. devoid of moisture. 2. barren, arid. 3. rough, coarse. 4. faded, withered. 5. thirsty, droughty. 6. (fig.) lifeless, uninteresting, dull, frigid, cold; uncommunicative, taciturn. 7. (pop.) consumed, wasted, exhausted, empty. 8. (Braz., fam.) desirous, eager.

~ ao sol sun-dried. **~ como uma palha** as dry as a bone. **secos e molhados** groceries, grocery. **a dinheiro ~** wages given to a servant without boarding. **ama-seca** dry nurse. **batalha seca** sham fight. **dar em ~ com a moeda** to ruin o. s. **doca seca** dry dock. **em ~** aground, dry. **engolir em ~** to swallow (one's emotion). **ficar em ~** (fig.) to be at a stand. **homem ~** prosy fellow. **o navio deu em ~** the ship sanded. **pão ~** unbuttered bread. **recepção seca** cold reception. **riso ~** forced smile. **tempo ~** dry weather. **terreno ~** thirsty soil. **tosse seca** dry cough.

secreção s. f. (pl. **-ões**) (physiol.) secretion: 1. act or effect of secreting. 2. matter secreted by a gland or other organ. 3. (geol.) lode, mineral vein filling fissures in rocks.

secreta s. f. 1. (eccl.) silent prayer. 2. (pop.) = **latrina**. 3. m. secret police agent.

secretar v. (med., less used form of **segregar**) 1. to secrete. 2. **~-se** to be secreted.

secretaria s. f. 1. secretaryship, clerkship. 2. office, chancery, bureau, secretariat. 3. ministry.

secretária s. f. 1. woman secretary. 2. woman confidant. 3. writing-desk.

secretariado s. m. secretariat(e): 1. the office. 2. the secretaries, clerkship.

secretariar v. to be a secretary, to do the work of a secretary.

secretário s. m. 1. secretary. 2. confidant. 3. minister of state. 4. writing-desk. 5. (zool.) secretary-bird.

~ de embaixada secretary of legation. **~ de Estado** secretary of state. **~ de paróquia** vestry clerk. **~ municipal** town clerk. **~ particular** private secretary.

secretário-geral s. m. (pl. **secretários-gerais**) general secretary.

secreto s. m. secret; secrecy. ‖ adj. 1. secret, private. 2. hidden, concealed, occult, mysterious. 3. unknown, undivulged. 4. retired. ‖ **-amente** adv. secretly.

gaveta secreta secret drawer. **homem** ~ reserved or discreet man. **o mais** ~ the innermost. **porta -a** jib-door. **quarto** ~ secret room. **serviço** ~ secret service. **tratado** ~ secret treaty. **reuniram-se -amente** they sat conclave.

secretor s. m. secretor. || adj. secretory.

secretório adj. secretory, secretive.

sectário s. m. 1. sectarian. 2. partisan, partyist, adherent. 3. proselyte, convert. || adj. sectarian, denominational.

sectarismo s. m. 1. sectarianism. 2. partisanship.

séctil adj. m. + f. (pl. **-eis**) sectile, cuttable.

sector s. m. = **setor**.

sectura s. f. (pharm.) a cutting into small pieces.

secular s. m. 1. layman, laic. 2. secular clergyman, priest belonging to no regular order. || adj. m. + f. 1. lay, secular, temporal; profane. 2. archaic. 3. occurring during or lasting a century, an age or a very long period of time; happening from century to century. || **~mente** adv. secularly, temporally.

braço ~ laity, temporal power. **clero** ~ secular clergy.

secularidade s. f. secularity: state of being secular.

secularização s. f. (pl. **-ões**) secularization.

secularizar v. to secularize, make secular, convert from spiritual appropriation to secular use.

século s. m. (also **centúria** f.) 1. century: a period of hundred years. 2. (fig.) age; generation; time; world. 3. secular life.

~ de ouro golden age; (fig.) happy times. **de ~ em ~** from age to age. **durante muitos ~s** for ages. **há um ~ que não o vejo** I have not seen him for ages. **o nosso ~** our age or century, our days. **o ~ das luzes** the 19 th century. **por todos os ~s** or **pelos ~s dos ~s** for ever and ever, to all eternity.

secundar v. 1. to second, assist, sustain, help, aid, serve. 2. to encore, repeat.

~ os esforços de to second the efforts of.

secundário adj. secondary, subordinate, minor; non essential. || **secundariamente** adv. secondarily, collaterally.

acentuação -a secondary accent. **artilharia -a** secondary artillery. **as coisas -as** the inessentials. **educação -a** secondary education. **efeito** ~ side-effect, after-effect. **enrolamento** ~ (electr.) secondary winding. **escola -a** secondary school. **importância -a** secondary importance. **pilha -a** secondary cell.

secundarista s. m. + f. (Braz.) high school student, secondary school student.

secundina s. f. secundine: 1. (bot.) the membrane surrounding the nucleous. 2. **~s** pl. the placenta and other parts connected with the foetus, the after-birth.

secundogênito s. m. second son. || adj. second-born.

secura s. f. 1. dryness, lack of moisture, want of rain; thirst. 2. (fig.) coldness, unconcern, indifference. 3. (Braz., pop.) ardent desire, sexual longing.

secure s. f. (also **segure**) 1. (Roman hist.) axe of the fasces. 2. a big axe.

securiforme adj. m. + f. securiform, axe-shaped.

securígero adj. securigerous.

seda (ê) s. f. 1. silk: fine, soft thread spun by silk-worms. 2. (bot.) bristles, seta. 3. (Braz.) a kind, affable person. 4. (ironic.) a sensitive person. 5. **~s** pl.: a) the silky hair of some animals. b) (pop.) garments made of silk.

~ bruta tussore. **~ crua** tussore silk, raw silk, floss. **~ lavrada** figured silk. **~ ondeada** watered silk. **~ vegetal** New Zealand flax. **artigos de ~** silk goods. **bicho-da-~** silkworm. **criação da ~** sericulture, culture or breeding of silkworms. **papel de** ~ tissue-paper. **vestido de** ~ silk dress.

sedã s. m. the sedan automobile.

sedação s. f. allaying, mitigation.

sedaço s. m. bolting-cloth.

sedal adj. m. + f. (pl. **-ais**) (anat.) anal.

sedalha s. f. (also **sedela**) snell, horse-hair fishing line.

sedalina s. f. a kind of fabrik imitating silk.

sedar (I) v. to calm, alleviate, appease, moderate, assuage, mitigate.

sedar (II) v. to hatchel, hackle, comb flax.

sedativo s. m. (med.) sedative, calmative, depressant. || adj. sedative.

sede s. f. 1. seat, headquarters, ground, an established place or center. 2. bishop's see, see.

~ de associação comercial commercial trade-hall. **~ de comarca** seat of the court of a district. **~ de distrito** seat of a Justice of the Peace. **~ de governo** seat of a government. **~ de município** seat of a municipality. **~ social** head-office. **~ de um clube** club-house.

sede (ê) s. f. 1. thirst, thirstiness, dryness. 2. (pop.) urge for revenge. 3. (fig.) greediness, impatience; craving, strong desire.

apagar ou matar a ~ to quench one's thirst. **estar com ~** to be thirsty. **ter ~** to thirst.

sedear v. to polish with silk (in the goldsmith's trade).

sedeca s. f. (N. Braz., pop.) diarrhea.

sedeiro s. m. hackle, hatchel, flax-comb, hemp-comb.

sedela s. f. (also **sedalha**) fishing-line.

trincar a ~ to frustrate or deceive the hopes.

sedenho s. m. 1. (surg. + vet.) seton, fontanel. 2. (also **sedém**) (Braz.) horse-hair, mane. 3. (also **sedém**) (N. Braz., pop.) seat, hind part, buttocks.

abrir um ~ (surg. + vet.) to rowel.

sedentariedade s. f. sedentariness.

sedentário s. m. person who lives a sedentary life. || adj. sedentary: 1. that requires sitting. 2. stationary, attached to one place. || **sedentariamente** adv. sedentarily.

profissão -a sedentary profession.

sedento adj. (also **sedente** m. + f., in this form, poet.) thirsty: 1. feeling thirst, athirst. 2. (fig.) eager, desirous.

~ de amor desirous for love, (sl.) on for one's greens. **~ de prazer** pleasure-seeking.

sede-sede s. m. (pl. **sede-sedes**) (N. Braz.) = **saci**.

sedeúdo adj. like silk, silky; hairy.

sediado adj. headquartered.

sedição s. f. (pl. **-ões**) sedition, rebellion, revolt, mutiny, tumult, riot.

sedicioso s. m. rioter. || adj. seditious, factious, mutinous, insurgent, rebellious; tumultuous. || **-amente** adv. seditiously, mutinously.

sedígero adj. that produces silk.

sedimentação s. f. 1. 1. (also geol.) sedimentation. 2. subsidence.

sedimentar (I) adj. m. + f. sedimentary, mothery.

sedimentar (II) v. to form sediment.

sedimentário adj. sedimentary.

sedimento s. m. sediment, settlings, lees, dregs, deposit.

sedimentoso adj. sedimentary, dreggy, full of lees.

sedonho s. m. a disease of hogs characterized by the growth of bristles in the throat.

sedoso adj. silken, silky, like silk; hairy, shaggy.

sedução s. f. (pl. **-ões**) seduction, seducement, temptation, allurement; alluringness, charm, witchery.

sédulo adj. sedulous, diligent, active; solicitous.

sedutor s. m. seducer, misleader, enticer; corrupter. || adj. seducing, seductive, alluring, charming; attractive; fascinating, enchanting. || **~mente** adv. seductively.

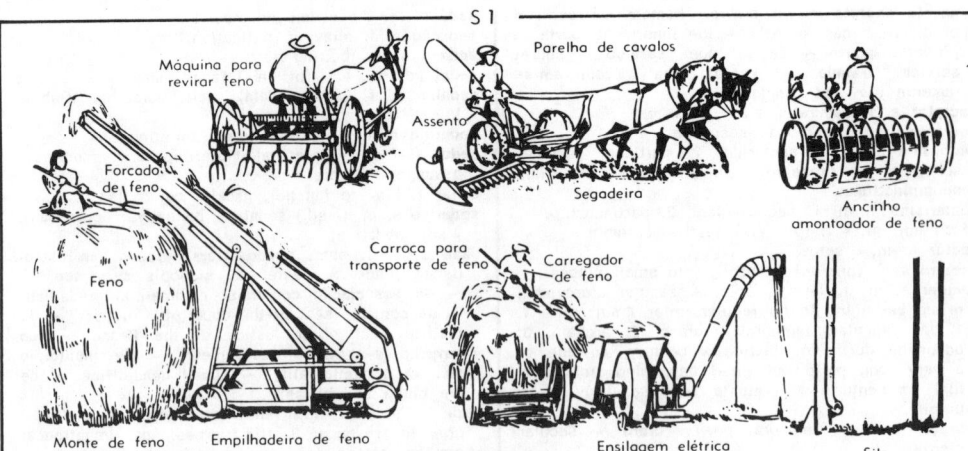

S 1

Máquina para revirar feno

Parelha de cavalos

Assento

Forcado de feno

Segadeira

Ancinho amontoador de feno

Feno

Carroça para transporte de feno

Carregador de feno

Monte de feno   Empilhadeira de feno

Ensilagem elétrica

Silo

SEGA DE FENO

seduzimento s. m. seduction, seducement.

seduzir v. to seduce: 1. tempt, mislead, lead astray, corrupt, deprave, cause to surrender chastity. 2. to allure, lure, charm, bewitch. 3. to deceive, betray. **ele foi seduzido a beber** he was tempted to drink.

seduzível adj. m. + f. (pl. **-íveis**) seducible.

sega s. f. (also **segada, segadura**) 1. harvest, reaping-time. 2. the act of reaping or mowing.
~ **de feno** haymaking (plate S 1).

sega (ê) s. f. co(u)lter, the cutter of a plough (plate C 13).

segadeira s. f. 1. mower, mowing-machine, harvester, machine for harvesting, reaper (plates C 16, S 1). 2. lawn-mower. 3. scythe.

segador s. m. mower, reaper, harvester, harvestman, sickleman. ‖ adj. harvesting, reaping.
~**a mecânica** reaping machine.

segadouro adj. (also **segadoiro**) harvesting; fit to be mowed, ready to be harvested, ripe.
foice segadoura scythe.

segadura s. f. = **sega**.

segão s. m. (pl. **-ões**) coulter, ploughshare.

segar v. 1. to mow, crop, harvest, cut, reap. 2. (fig.) to mow down.

sege s. f. 1. chaise, curricle, tilbury. 2. coach, carriage.

segeiro s. m. 1. person who made chaises. 2. coach-maker.

segetal adj. m. + f. (pl. **-ais**) of or pertaining to a cornfield.

segmentação s. f. segmentation.
~ **do ovo** (biol.) cleavage, segmentation.

segmentar (I) adj. m. + f. (also **segmentário** m.) segmental, segmentary.

segmentar (II) v. to segment, divide into segments.

segmento s. m. segment: 1. a section, division, a portion cut or marked off as separable. 2. (geom.) a part cut off from a figure by a line or plane (plate A 9).

segnícia, segnície s. f. indolence, sloth, negligence.

segredar v. 1. to tell in secret, to confide. 2. to whisper, murmur, speak in a low voice.

segredeiro adj. 1. telling secrets, confiding. 2. whispering.

segredista s. m. + f. 1. whisperer. 2. talebearer; mystery-monger. 3. person who keeps secrets.

segredo (ê) s. m. (pl. **segredos**) 1. secret: a) something (to be) kept back or concealed; mystery. b) secrecy;

secretiveness. c) privacy; confidence; whisper. d) recess, secret place, room or drawer. 2. safe code. ~ **de Estado** state secret. ~ **do êxito** secret of success. ~ **inviolável** inviolable secret. ~ **muito importante** top secret. ~ **político** political secret. ~ **profissional** professional secret. **segredos da natureza** secrets of nature. **agir ou manter em** ~ to hugger-mugger. **confiamos-lhe o** ~ we let him into the secret. **conheço o** ~ I am in the secret. **deitar algum** ~ **à rua** to let out some secret. **ele denunciou o** ~ he gave away the game. **em** ~ in secret, in secrecy. **fechadura de** ~ puzzle-lock. **guardamos** ~ we kept it secret. **guardar um** ~ to keep a secret. **não se pode guardar** ~ **disto** there can be no secrecy about it. **preciso descobrir o** ~ **disto** I must get behind this. **revelar um** ~ to betray a secret. **sabe guardar** ~? can you keep a secret?

segregação s. f. (pl. **-ões**) segregation, separation, seclusion; secretion.
~ **racial** racial segregation, discrimination, apartheid.

segregar v. 1. to segregate, separate, seclude, isolate. 2. to secrete.
ela segredou-se she secluded herself.

segregatício adj. referring to segregation.

segregativo adj. 1. segregative. 2. (gram.) partitive.

seguida s. f. (also **seguimento** m.) 1. following, pursuing. 2. continuation. ‖ ~**mente** adv. without interruption, consecutively; afterwards.
em ~ after that, directly afterwards, right away.

seguidilha s. f. 1. seguidilla, a popular Spanish dance and the music therefore. 2. a sequence in the poker game.

seguidilheiro s. m. person who dances the seguidilla.

seguidinho adv. (S. Braz., pop.) frequently, commonly.

seguido adj. 1. followed, continued, continuous, immediate, without interruption. 2. connected, coherent.
dias ~**s** days on end. **não pode dizer duas palavras** ~**as** he cannot say two words together.

seguidor s. m. follower, adherent; sectarian; partisan. ‖ adj. adherent; following; satellite.

seguilhote s. m. (Braz.) six months old whale-calf still unweaned.

seguimento s. m. 1. following, pursuance, pursuing. 2. continuation, sequence; prosecution. 3. compliance. **em** ~ in pursuance. **ter** ~ to proceed.

seguinte s. m. 1. the next, the following. 2. ~s pl. sequentes. ‖ adj. m. + f. next, following, sequential, ensuing, sequent, subsequent. **aconteceu o** ~ this is what happened. **o capítulo** ~ the next chapter. **no dia** ~ the following day. **os itens foram os** ~**s** the heads were as follows.

seguir v. to follow: 1. go or come after. 2. pursue, chase. 3. watch, observe, spy, keep the mind or attention fixed on. 4. walk along, go along. 5. accompany; shadow. 6. proceed, go on, continue. 7. attend (a course). 8. adhere to, be sectarian of, side with. 9. imitate, copy. 10. act according to, observe, obey to, be guided by. 11. understand, grasp the meaning of. 12. engage in, practise as a profession. 13. ~-**se** result of, result. ~ **alguém** to follow s. o. ~ **alguém nos calcanhares** to follow at the heels of s. o., (sl.) tail after s. o. ~ **as instruções** to follow the instructions. ~ **as pisadas de** to follow in the footsteps of. ~ **as pegadas de** to dog. ~ **a sua opinião** to go one's own way. ~ **avante** (naut.) to go forward. ~ **de perto** to follow on the heel of s. o. ~ **depressa** to hurry on. ~ **diretamente** to follow right ahead. ~ **disfarçadamente** to shadow, keep under surveillance. ~ **insistentemente** to dog. ~ **o bom caminho** to take the right path. ~ **caminho** to be on the way. ~ **o exemplo** to take example by. ~ **o inimigo** to pursue the enemy. ~ **os conselhos da mãe** to heed mother's advice. ~ **o seu caminho** to continue on one's way. ~ **o rasto, a pista de** to dog. ~ **para o norte** to proceed north. ~ **pelo primeiro trem** to leave by the first train. ~ **por mau caminho** to be on the wrong tack. ~ **um programa** to follow a plan. ~ **viagem** to pursue one's journey. **a** ~ following, next. **segue-se que** the result is that, it follows that. **siga o meu conselho** follow my advice. **eles seguem-no** they follow after him. **ele seguiu-me** he stepped into my shoes. **ele seguiu a carreira de professor** he took up teaching. **quem segue?** who is next? **que segue?** what next?

segunda s. f. 1. second proof sheet. 2. (mus) second. 3. short for **segunda-feira**.

segunda-feira s. f. (pl. **segundas-feiras**) Monday. **a reunião está marcada para** ~ the meeting is scheduled on Monday.

segundanista s. m. + f. second-year student.

segundar v. 1. to repeat, do over again. 2. (fig.) to second, assist, aid, support. ~ **matrimônio** to marry again.

segundeiro adj. secondary. **moinho** ~ mill that grinds only secondary cereals, as maize.

segundo (I) s. m. second: 1. the next after the first in rank, importance, etc. 2. sixtieth part of a minute of time or angular measure. 3. a person who attends or assists a boxer or a duelist. 4. (S. Braz.) a reliable assistant or second man. ‖ adj. second: 1. next, immediately following the first in time or place. 2. secondary. 3. (fig.) similar, alike. ‖ adv. (also -**amente**) secondly, in the second place. -**a classe** second class. **causa** ~ second or second-ary cause. **chegar em** ~ **lugar** to come off second best. **comprar em** -**a mão** to buy second-hand. **de** -**a classe** second rate. **ela tem papel de** -**a ordem** she plays a minor part, the second fiddle. **em** ~ **lugar** secondly. **pão de** -**a** brown bread. **tornou-se a sua** -**a natureza** it has become second nature to him.

segundo (II) prep. according to, in conformity to, pursuant to. ~ **as ordens de** according to the orders of. ~ **meu conhecimento** to my knowledge. ~ **os nossos**

cálculos according to our calculations. ~ **o nosso uso** in conformity with our custom. ~ **sargento** second sergeant. ~ **tenente** second lieutenant.

segundo-cadete s. m. (pl. **segundos-cadetes**) second cadet.

segundogênito s. m. second son. ‖ adj. second-born.

segura s. f. hoop-knife, a cooper's adze.

seguração s. f. (pl. -**ões**) 1. (also **seguro**) insurance. 2. (also **segurança**) safety, security.

segurado s. m. insured person, policyholder. ‖ adj. insured, assured.

segurador s. m. insurer, assurer, underwriter. ‖ adj. insuring.

seguradora s. f. (Braz.) insurance company.

segurança s. f. security: 1. state of being or feeling secure. 2. certainty, assurance, sureness, confidence, surety, insurance. 3. safety, safeguard, freedom from danger or risk. 4. a pledge, guarantee, bail, warranty. **alfinete de** ~ safety pin. **cabo de** ~ emergency cable. **cofre de** ~ strong box. **com** ~ reliably, assuredly. **corrente de** ~ safety chain. **cortina de** ~ (theat.) safety curtain. **ele está em** ~ **absoluta** he is quite secure. **em** ~ in safety. **fecho de** ~ safety catch. **fósforo de** ~ safety match. **freio de** ~ emergency brake. **para** ~ for safety's sake. **válvula de** ~ safety valve.

segurar v. 1. to secure, make safe or secure; guard, shield, protect, support, assist, aid. 2. to prevent from fall or ruin, to firm, fasten, bind, pin, brace, hold, clamp or cling. 3. to catch, grasp, hold fast. 4. to contain, hold. 5. to insure, assure, guarantee, warrant. ~ **a vida** to insure one's life. **segura bem!** hold tight! ~ **com alfinetes** to pin up. ~ **com força** to hold firmly. ~ **contra acidentes** to insure against accidents. ~ **firmemente** to cinch. ~ **na mão** to hold in one's hand. ~ **o lápis** to hold the pencil. ~-**se** to hold fast, steady oneself. **segure-se!** hold on! ~ **a vela** (fig.) to play gooseberry. **ele não se deixa** ~ there is no holding him. **o meu chapéu não se segura** my hat won't stay on.

segurável adj. m. + f. (pl. -**áveis**) insurable, assurable.

segure s. f. (also **secure**) 1. (Roman hist.) axe of the fasces. 2. a big axe.

segurelha s. f. (bot.) savory.

segureza, seguridade s. f. = **segurança**.

seguro s. m. 1. insurance, assurance. 2. security, secureness, certainty. 3. guarantee, bail. 4. protection, support, shelter. ‖ adj. 1. secure, safe, free from danger or apprehension. 2. firm, steady, unshakable. 3. reliable, trustworthy; doubtless, sure, certain, infallible. 4. imprisoned. ‖ -**amente** adv. safely. ~ **a prazo fixo** terminable insurance. ~ **contra acidentes** accident-insurance. ~ **de vida** assurance; life insurance. ~ **em grupo** group insurance; salary deduction insurance. **o** ~ **morreu de velho!** be always on the safe side! prevention is better than cure! **absolutamente** ~ cock sure. **apólice de** ~ insurance policy. **companhia de** ~**s** insurance company. **ele é** ~ he is tight-fisted, stingy. **ele está** ~ **de si** he feels sure of himself. **estar** ~ to be on the safe side; to feel confident. **estar** ~ **de alguém** to be sure of somebody. **uma obra** -**a** a solid building. **pode estar** ~ **disto** you may be sure of that, can gamble on that. **pôr em lugar** ~ to reposit.

seiada s. f. a series of deep recesses in a mountain.

seibo s. m. (Braz.) a coral tree (family Leguminosae, Erythrina falcata).

seio s. m. 1. breast: the front part of the human body where the mammal glands are located;

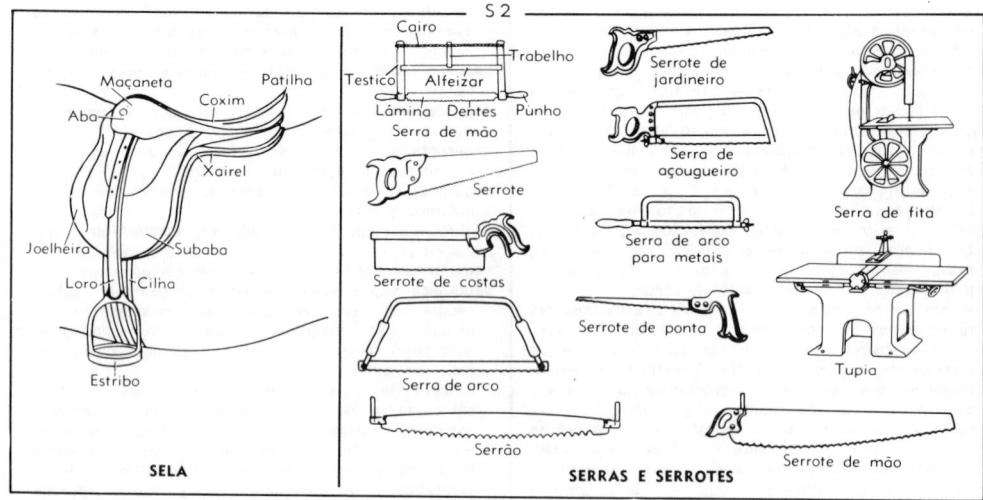

S 2

SELA

Maçaneta · Coxim · Patilha · Aba · Xairel · Joelheira · Subaba · Loro · Cilha · Estribo

Cairo · Trabelho · Testico · Alfeizar · Lâmina · Dentes · Punho · Serra de mão · Serrote · Serrote de costas · Serra de arco · Serrão

Serrote de jardineiro · Serra de açougueiro · Serra de arco para metais · Serrote de ponta · Serra de fita · Tupia · Serrote de mão

SERRAS E SERROTES

bosom; a woman's breast. 2. sinuosity, bend, curve. 3. gulf, bay, sinus. 4. (naut.) bight, the loop of a rope. 5. (fig.): a) source of nourishment. b) heart, pith, core, innermost; soul. c) secrecy, recess, privacy.
~ **basilar** (anat.) basilar sinus. **bico de** ~ teat. **no ~ da família** within one's family. **no ~ da Igreja** within the pale of the Church. **no ~ de** among, in the midst of. **ser do ~ de alguém** to be somebody's bosom friend.
seira s. f. wicker or esparto basket, frail.
seis s. m. 1. (the number) six. 2. card or dice bearing the six. ‖ adj. six, sixth.
corpo ~ (typogr.) nonpareil. **de ~ rodas** six-wheeled.
seiscentismo s. m. style, taste and school of the 17th century.
seiscentista s. m. + f. a writer of the seventeenth century. ‖ adj. referring to the 17th century.
seiscentos s. m. pl. six hundred.
seisdobro s. m. sextuple.
seita s. f. sect: 1. a doctrine or system separated from the general opinion. 2. group of people following such a system. 3. a party, a faction. 4. a denomination.
seiúda adj. (Braz.) bosomy.
seiva s. f. 1. sap, juice of a plant. 2. lushness. 3. (fig.) blood; vigour, energy.
a ~ da mocidade the sap of youth. **sem ~** juiceless; sapless, insipid.
seival s. m. (pl. **-ais**) (S. Braz.) 1. place abounding with coralbeans. 2. an extensive grassy marsh. 3. marshy place.
seivo s. m. (Braz.) a large open field.
seivoso adj. (bot.) sappy, juicy, succulent; vigorous.
seixas s. f. (bookbinding) each of the margins of a book cover (brochure) that is slightly larger than the book body.
seixada s. f. a hit with a stone or pebble, a stone-throw.
seixal s. m. (pl. **-ais**) place full of pebbles.
seixeiro s. m. (N. Braz., pop.) swindler.
seixo s. m. 1. pebble, flint, flint-stone. 2. (N. Braz., pop.) swindle.
seixoso adj. pebbly, pebbled, flinty, full of pebbles.
seja conj. + interj. be it.
~ **assim ou** ~ **assado** be it this way or the other.

sela s. f. saddle (plate S 2).
~ **para damas** pillion. ~ **túrcica** (anat.) sella turcica. **arção de** ~ pommel of a saddle.
selada s. f. narrow pass between hills, strait, saddle (plate M 11).
selado (I) s. m. 1. the waistline curve. 2. the curved inner side of the foot. 3. (Braz., geogr.) saddle, saddle back. ‖ adj. 1. saddled. 2. (N. Braz., geogr.) saddle-backed.
selado (II) adj. stamped; sealed.
assinado e ~ under hand and seal. **envelope** ~ stamped envelope. **papel** ~ stamped sheet of paper.
selador s. m. 1. saddler. 2. sealer; person who puts stamps on. ‖ adj. 1. saddling. 2. sealing.
seladouro s. m. (also **seladoiro**) 1. part of a horse's back where the saddle is placed. 2. (fig.) the waistline of a garment.
seladura s. f. the act of saddling.
selagem s. f. (pl. **-ens**) a sealing or providing with a stamp.
selaginelácea s. f. (bot.) one of the Selaginellaceae.
selagináceo adj. (bot.) selaginellaceous.
selagote s. m. (Braz.) rustic saddle much used in the country.
seláquio s. m. (ichth.) selachian. ‖ adj. (also **cartilaginoso**) selachian.
selar (I) v. 1. to saddle. 2. (Braz.) to cede, yield.
selar (II) v. 1. to stamp, affix a stamp to. 2. to rubber-stamp. 3. to seal, apply a signet on. 4. (fig.) to ratify, certify or make binding. 5. (fig.) to finish, destroy, extinguish. 6. to close tightly, shut.
~ **papel** to stamp or seal paper. ~ **uma carta** to put a stamp on a letter.
selaria s. f. saddlery.
seleção s. f. (pl. **-ões**) 1. selection: a) the act of selecting. b) choice, excerption, assortment. c) (biol.) process of sorting out animals or vegetal organisms suitable for survival. 2. team of selected players.
~ **canarinho** (Braz., ftb.) the Brazilian team (the gold yellow of the players' shirts reminds the color of canaries). ~ **manual** hand sorting. ~ **natural** natural selection. **-ões para um campeonato** selections for a match.

selecionado s. m. (also **seleção** f.) team of selected players, choosen team. ‖ adj. eclectic(al).
selecionador s. m. selector. ‖ adj. selecting, eclectic(al).
selecionar v. to select, sort, pick, choose, elect. ~ **cuidadosamente** to pick and choose.
seleiro s. m. saddler, harness maker. ‖ adj. 1. good at riding, firm in the saddle. 2. a horse already used to the saddle.
seleniado adj. (chem.) selenitic, selenitical.
selênico adj. 1. referring to the moon and its movements. 2. (chem.) selenic, selenious. **ácido** ~ selenic acid.
selenífero adj. seleniferous.
selênio s. m. (chem.) selenium: a non-metallic element.
selenita s. selenite: 1. m. hypothetical inhabitant of the moon. 2. f. (min.) old denomination for gypsum.
selenitoso adj. selenious, selenitic.
selenocêntrico adj. (astr.) selenocentric.
selenografia s. f. selenography: a description of the moon.
selenográfico adj. selenographic, selenographical.
selenógrafo s. m. selenographer.
selenóstato s. m. instrument for observing the movements of the moon.
selenotopografia s. f. topography of the moon.
selenotopográfico adj. referring to the topography of the moon.
seleta s. f. 1. anthology, chosen literary passages, florilegium. 2. a species of juicy, aromatic pear. 3. variety of orange.
seletar v. (also **selecionar**) to select, sort, choose.
seletividade s. f. selectivity (also radio).
seletivo adj. selective. ‖ **-amente** adv. selectively.
seleto adj. 1. select, selected, choice, picked. 2. different, exquisite; excellent, distinct.
seletor s. m. selector.
self-indução s. f. (pl. **self-induções**) (electr.) self-induction.
selha s. f. piggin: a low wooden vessel.
selim (I) s. m. (pl. **-ins**) saddle of a bicycle (plates B 11, M 12).
selim (II) s. m. (Goa) a bunch of coconuts.
selo (ê) s. m. (pl. **selos**) 1. seal, cachet. 2. postage stamp. 3. label. 4. stamp, signet. 5. taken, signal, guarantee.
~ **branco** embossed seal or stamp. ~ **da alfândega** custom's seal. ~ **de franquia** post mark. ~ **de recibo** receipt stamp. ~ **fiscal** revenue stamp. ~ **postal** postage stamp (plate C 10). **álbum para selos postais** stamp album. **coleção de selos** stamp collection. **imposto de** ~ stamp-duty. **inutilizar um** ~ to cancel a stamp. **passar uma coisa sem** ~ (fig.) to believe a thing without examination. **pôr o** ~ **a um negócio** to conclude an affair.
selo-de-salomão s. m. (pl. **selos-de-salomão**) (bot.) Solomon's seal.
selva s. f. 1. jungle, land covered with forest or dense, matted vegetation. 2. (fig.) a heap or lot of mingled things.
selvagem s. m. + f. (pl. **-ens**) 1. a savage; a member of a savage tribe; barbarian. 2. coarse, rough fellow. ‖ adj. 1. savage, wild, from the jungle; not tamed or domesticated. 2. uncivilized, savage, barbaric, uncultivated. 3. rude, brutal, cruel, intractable, barbarous, ferocious.
animais -ens wild beasts. **aves -ens** wild fowl. **costumes -ens** savage customs. **raças -ens** savage races.
selvageria s. f. (also **selvajaria**) savagery, savageness, wildness, fierceness, brutality, savagedom, savagism.

selvagíneo, selvagino adj. 1. wild, savage, ferocious. 2. referring to the wild beasts.
selvático adj. (also **silvático**) savage, wild, of the jungle. ‖ **selvaticamente** adv. savagely.
selvoso adj. woody, characterized by jungles.
sem prep. 1. without, lacking, wanting, sine. 2. free from, less.
~ **abrir mão dos interesses** without prejudice to one's interests. ~ **acento** stressless. ~ **álcool** non-alcoholic. ~ **barba** clean-shaven, beardless. ~ **casa** homeless. ~ **causa** causeless. ~ **cerimônia** without regard for. ~ **contar** excluding. ~ **cuidados** free from care. ~ **demora** without delay. ~ **derramamento de sangue** without shedding of blood. ~ **dificuldade** easily. ~ **culpa** innocent, clear. ~ **dinheiro** out of money. ~ **dinheiro, ~ casa ou ~ amigos** without money, home or friends. ~ **dote** fortuneless. ~ **dúvida** without doubt. ~ **efeito** without effect. ~ **esforço** strainless. ~ **falta** without fail. ~ **fé** faithless. ~ **fim** without end, endless. ~ **garantia** without any guarantee. ~ **hesitação** unhesitatingly. ~ **igual** unequalled. ~ **livro** without a book. ~ **mais discussão** without further discussion. ~ **mais nem menos** without further ado. ~ **medo** fearless. ~ **número** without number, innumerably. ~ **que eu lá vá** without my going there. ~ **o auxílio de ninguém** with no one to help. ~ **parar** on and on. ~ **pensar** unthinkingly. ~ **perda de tempo** without loss of time. ~ **piedade** inexorably. ~ **receio** unhesitatingly. ~ **responsabilidade** without responsibility. ~ **rumo** at random. ~ **sal** without salt, insipid. ~ **saúde não há felicidade** without health happiness is impossible. ~ **solda** weldless. ~ **sorte** out of luck. ~ **trabalho** out of work. ~ **tom nem som** without rhyme or reason. ~ **uma lágrima sequer** with never a tear. ~ **valor** of no worth. ~ **vegetação** herbless. ~ **ver** without seeing. **coisas** ~ **importância** mere nothings. **é melhor você ficar** ~ **isso** you are better without. **estou** ~ **dinheiro** I am short of cash. **eu o farei** ~ **ele** I shall do it without him. **ficamos** ~ **jantar** we went without our supper. **andar** ~ **bengala** to walk without a stick. **passar** ~ to do without. **todos** ~ **exceção** all without exception.
semafórico s. m. person who operates semaphores. ‖ adj. semaphoric(al).
semáforo s. m. semaphore, signal post (plate V 4).
semana s. f. week: 1. period of seven days from Sunday to Saturday inclusively. 2. a period of seven consecutive days. 3. the six working days.
~**s a fio** weeks running. ~ **da Paixão** Passion-week. ~ **das têmporas** Ember week. ~ **dos nove dias** a week that will never come to pass. ~**s e** ~**s** week in week out. ~ **furada** a broken week. ~ **inglesa** a five-day week. ~ **Santa** Holy Week, Passion Week. **uma** ~ **sim uma** ~ **não** every other week. **antes do fim da** ~ before the week is out. **a próxima** ~ next week. **a** ~ **passada** last week. **a** ~ **seguinte** the following week. **à** ~ by the week. **a** ~ **que vem** the coming week. **daqui a uma** ~ a week from today. **de duas em duas** ~**s** every two weeks. **de hoje a uma** ~ today week. **dentro de uma** ~ within the next week. **duas vezes por** ~ twice a week. **durante a** ~ in the week. **faz uma** ~ a week ago. **fim de** ~ week end. **não a vejo há** ~**s** I have not seen you for weeks. **na** ~ **que vem** next week. **que dia da** ~**?** at what day of the week? **para a** ~ **dos nove dias** when two Sundays come together. **só daqui a muitas** ~**s** weeks ahead. **todas as** ~**s** every week. **uma** ~ **de viagem** a week's journey.
semanal adj. m. + f. (pl. **-ais**) weekly, hebdomadal. ‖ ~**mente** adv. weekly, by the week.

periódico ~ weekly paper. **publicação** ~ weekly publication.

semanário s. m. weekly (publication). ‖ adj. (also **semanal**) weekly, hebdomadary.

semancol s. m. (Braz., hum.) perceptibility of being boresome.

semântica s. f. (phil., also **semasiologia, sematologia, semiologia**) semantics, semasiology, the study of the meaning of words as distinct from their derivation.

semântico adj. semantic(al), referring to signification or meaning (in language).

semasiologia, sematologia s. f. 1. semasiology, sematology, (spiritualism) semantics. 2. science of the signs of spirits.

semblante s. m. 1. face, visage. 2. physiognomy, aspect, countenance, mien, look, appearance.

~ **alegre** gay air. ~ **caído** fallen looks. **bom** ~ healthful countenance. **fazer** ~ to feign, to dissemble.

sem-cerimônia s. f. (pl. **sem-cerimônias**) 1. unceremoniousness, informality, offhandedness. 2. rudeness, roughness, abrupt manners.

sêmea s. f. bran. 2. bread of bran, grey-bread.

semeação s. f. (pl. **-ões**) sowing.

semeada s. f. 1. sown land or field. 2. seed time. 3. seeding.

semeador s. m. 1. sower. 2. sowing machine. ‖ adj. sowing, that sows.

semeadouro s. m. (also **semeadoiro**) ground convenient for sowing. ‖ adj. good or fit for sowing.

semeadura s. f. 1. sowing, seeding, setting. 2. seed that is to be sown.

semear v. 1. to sow, seed, plant, scatter seed for growth. 2. (fig.) to set thick, cover all over. 3. to strew, spread, dessiminate, propagate.

~ **a mão** to broadcast, sow by scattering with the hand. ~ **aveia** to sow oats. ~ **discórdias** to seed the seeds of dissension, to spread or propagate enmity. ~ **trigo** to sow wheat. ~ **um terreno** to sow a field. **o campo é semeado de rosas** the field is strewed with roses. **o céu está semeado de estrelas** the sky is seeded with stars. ~**am vento e colheram tempestade** they sowed the wind and reaped the storm.

semeável adj. m. + f. (pl. **-áveis**) fit or prepared for sowing.

semelhança s. f. (also **similitude**) likeness, resemblance, analogy, similarity, similitude, conformity. ~ **com** likeness to. **à ~ de** in the likeness of. **ter** ~ **com** to bear resemblance to.

semelhante s. m. fellow creature. ‖ adj. m. + f. analogous, like, resembling, alike, similar, in parallel with. ‖ ~**mente** adv. likely, similarly.

cada qual ama o seu ~ like will to like. **coisa** ~ **a compaixão** such a thing as pity. **ele não fez** ~ **coisa** he did no such thing.

semelhar(-se) v. 1. to resemble, be similar to, look like, have the appearance of. 2. to remind. 3. to compare, confront.

semelhável adj. m. + f. (pl. **-áveis**) that can be resembled to.

sêmen s. m. (pl. **semens, sêmenes**) 1. seed. 2. semen, sperm, seminal matter.

sêmen-contra s. f. (pl. **semens-contra**) 1. (pharm.) semen-contra, santonica. 2. (bot.) Levant wormseed (Artemisia cina).

semental adj. m. + f. (pl. **-ais**) 1. belonging to seed. 2. that is a good reproducer.

cavalo ~ stallion. **trigo** ~ wheat for sowing.

sementão s. m. (pl. **-ões**) (also **porta-sementes**) plant grown for seeds; seed tree.

sementar v. 1. = **semear**. 2. (Braz.) to supply seeds to; supply sugar-cane cuttings to.

semente s. f. seed: 1. seed-corn for sowing; sperm; semen. 2. (fig.) origin, source.

~ **das pérolas** seed-pearl. ~ **de Alexandria** wormseed. **lançar a** ~ **de** to sow the seeds of. **ficar para** ~ 1. to be reserved for breeding. 2. to live forever.

sementeira s. f. 1. sowing (the seed). 2. time of sowing any grain, seedtime. 3. seed. 4. seed plot, seed field. 5. (fig.) origin. 6. scattering.

sementeiro s. m. 1. seedbag, seed-cloth, seed-basket. 2. sower, seeder. ‖ adj. seeding, sowing.

semestral adj. m. + f. (pl. **-ais**) (also **semestre**) half--yearly, semi-annual, bi-annual, occurring every six months. ‖ ~**mente** adv. bi-annually.

semestralidade s. f. semestral allowance; semestral payment.

semestre s. m. semester, six consecutive months, half-year. ‖ adj. m. + f. semestral.

sem-fim (I) s. m. (pl. **sem-fins**) 1. indeterminate number or quantity. 2. undefined, unlimited space.

sem-fim (II) s. m. (pl. **sem-fins**) (Braz.) = **saci**.

semi-analfabeto s. m. (pl. **semi-analfabetos**) a semi-literate person. ‖ adj. semiliterate.

semi-ânime adj. m. + f. 1. half-dead. 2. exanimate, lifeless.

semi-anual adj. m. + f. semi-annual, semestral.

semi-anular adj. m. + f. semi-annular.

semibárbaro adj. semi-barbarous.

semibreve s. f. (mus.) semibreve (plate N 1).

semicapro s. m. (myth.) a being, half goat and half man as the fauns and satyrs. ‖ adj. referring to the fauns, satyrs, etc.

semicerrar v. to half-close, close partially.

semichas s. f. pl. over-measure of liquids and cereals, excess.

semicilíndrico adj. semi-cylindric(al).

semicircular adj. m. + f. (also **semicírculo**) semicircular, half-round, semi-circled, referring to the semicircle.

semicírculo s. m. semicircle: 1. a half circle. 2. mathematical instrument for measuring angles. ‖ adj. semicircular.

semicolcheia s. f. (mus.) semiquaver (plate N 1).

semicondutor s. m. (phys.) semiconductor.

semiconsoante s. f. (gram.) semi-consonant, vowel employed as consonant in a crescent diphthong.

semicúpio s. m. semicupium, hip bath.

semidéia s. f. = **semideusa**.

semideiro s. m. path; short cut.

semideus s. m. 1. demigod. 2. the offspring of a god and a goddess or of a goddess and a human being. 3. divinized hero, benefactor.

semideusa s. f. (also **semidéia**) demigoddess: 1. fabulous woman having qualities superior to a human being but inferior to a goddess. 2. divinized heroine.

semidiáfano adj. semi-diaphanous.

semidiâmetro s. m. semidiameter.

semidisco s. m. semidisk.

semiditongo s. m. a crescent diphthong.

semidítono s. m. (mus.) semiditone, semiditono, demiditone.

semidivindade s. f. semidivinity: 1. character or quality of a demigod. 2. a demigod or a demigoddess.

semidivino adj. semidivine.

semidobrado adj. semidouble.

semidouto s. m. a half-learned person. ‖ adj. half--learned, superficially learned.

semidúplex adj. m. + f. (pl. **semidúplices**) semiduplex, semidouble.

semifendido adj. semisegmented, half-split.
semiflósculo s. m. (bot.) semifloscule, semifloret.
semifluido adj. semifluid.
semifusa s. f. (mus.) hemidemisemiquaver (plate N 1).
semiglobuloso adj. (bot.) semiglobular.
semi-internato s. m. (pl. semi-internatos) 1. state of being semi-internal. 2. day-boarding school.
semi-interno adj. (pl. semi-internos) day-boarding.
semilunar s. m. (anat.) semilunar bone. ‖ adj. m. + f. semilunar, semilunary.
semilunático adj. half-lunatic.
semilúnio s. m. semilunation, half-moon.
semimorto adj. 1. half-dead. 2. torpid, benumbed. 3. (fig.) tired out, exhausted.
seminação s. f. (pl. -ões) 1. (bot.) semination. 2. (med.) coitus.
seminal adj. m. + f. (pl. -ais) seminal: 1. referring to seed. 2. (fig.) productive.
seminário s. m. seminary: 1. seed plot. 2. (fig.) center of creation or production. 3. training school for priesthood. ‖ adj. seminal, spermatic.
seminarista s. m. seminarist; boarding student at a seminary.
seminarístico adj. seminarian.
seminífero adj. 1. seminific(al). 2. (bot.) seminiferous.
condutos ~s seminiferous ducts.
semínima s. f. (mus.) crotchet, quarter-note (plate N 1).
semino s. m. each of the floats sustaining a certain kind of fishing-net.
seminu adj. half-naked.
semínula s. f. (also semínulo m.) 1. seminule: little grain of seed. 2. (bot.) spore.
seminulífero adj. seminuliferous.
semi-oficial adj. m. + f. (pl. -ais) semi-official.
semiografia s. f. semiography, semeiography: representation by signs, notation.
semiográfico adj. semiographical.
semiologia s. f. (also semiótica) semiology, semeiology: 1. (med.) symptomatology: the branch of medicine dealing with symptoms. 2. (phil.) semantics, semasiology, the science of the meanings of words.
semiológico adj. semiological, semiotical, symptomatic.
semiótica s. f. (also semiologia) 1. semiotics, semeiotics. 2. art of military signalling.
semiparente adj. m. + f. kindred, related by affinity.
semipedal adj. m. + f. (pl. -ais) semipedal.
semipleno adj. 1. half-full. 2. (fig.) incomplete.
semiprova s. f. semi-proof, half-proof, incomplete proof.
semipútrido adj. semirotten, half-putrid.
semi-racional adj. m. + f. (pl. semi-racionais) half-witted, very silly, stupid.
semi-roto adj. (pl. semi-rotos) semiragged, half-broken.
semi-sábio adj. (pl. semi-sábios) half-learned.
semi-selvagem adj. m. + f. (pl. semi-selvagens) 1. semisavage, semiwild. 2. brutal; very rude.
sêmita s. f. = senda.
semita s. m. + f. Semite: 1. one of the Semitic group or language, which comprehend the Hebrews, Assyrians, Aramaeans, Phoenicians and Arabs. 2. Jew. ‖ adj. Semitic; Jewish.
semítico adj. Semitic: of or referring to the Semites, Jewish.
semitismo s. m. Semitism.
semitom s. m. (pl. -ons) semitone, demitone, half-note.
semitransparente adj. m. + f. semi-transparent.
semitropical adj. m. + f. semitropical.
semiústo adj. half-burnt, singed, scorched.

semíviro s. m. half-man, demi-man, eunuch.
semivivo adj. half-dead, half-alive.
semivogal s. f. (pl. -ais) (gram.) semi-vowel.
sem-nome adj. m. + f., sg. + pl. 1. anonymous, nameless. 2. (Braz.) not qualifiable.
sem-número s. m. (pl. sem-números) numberless, innumerable quantity, immense number.
um ~ de homens numberless men.
semodagem s. f. (N. Braz.) unmannerliness; noise, uproar, prank, mischievous trick.
sêmola, semolina s. f. semolina, semola, grits.
semostração s. f. (pl. -ões) (Braz.) vanity, futility, tendency to show off, make a display of wealth, intelligence, money, etc.
semostradeira s. f. (Braz.) girl who likes to show off. ‖ adj. given to ostentation.
semoto adj. distant, retired.
semovente s. m. + f. self-moving, self-walking creatures.
bens -s livestock.
sem-par adj. m. + f., sg. + pl. unequalled, matchless, peerless, having no equal.
sempiterno adj. sempiternal: eternal, everlasting, perpetual.
sempre s. m. the ages; all past and future time. ‖ adv.: 1. always, ever. 2. constantly, incessantly. 3. however, yet, nevertheless. 4. really, in fact, actually. 5. forever, aye, forevermore, ad infinitum. ~ é certo que... it's true after all that... ~ que whenever; provided that. ~ o receava I feared it all along. a ~ crescente pobreza the ever increasing poverty. como ~ as always, as usual. de ~ as always. história de ~ same old story. nem ~ not always. para ~ for aye, for ever, for ever and a day, for a month of Sundays, everlastingly. para todo o ~ for ever and ever. quase ~ nearly always. uma queixa que ~ se repete an ever recurrent complaint.
sempre-lustrosa s. f. (pl. sempre-lustrosas) .(Braz.) Brazil bougainvillea (B. spectabilis).
sempre-noiva s. f. (pl. sempre-noivas) (also sanguinária) knotgrass, pink weed.
sempre-viva s. f. (pl. sempre-vivas) sempervivum, evergreen, houseleek.
sem-pulo s. m. (pl. sem-pulos) (Braz., ftb.) kick given when both the player and the ball are in mid-air.
sem-razão s. f. (pl. sem-razões) 1. unfounded act or opinion, unreason. 2. wrong, injustice.
sem-sal adj. m. + f., sg. + pl. 1. insipid, dull, not salted. 2. (fig.) spiritless, witless.
sem-segundo adj. unique, matchless, unequalled.
sem-termo s. m. + f., sg. + pl. endless time. ‖ adj. endless, unending, ceaseless.
sem-vergonha s. m. + f., sg. + pl. (Braz.) shameless, impudent person. ‖ adj. shameless, blushless, unabashed, unashamed.
sem-vergonhez, sem-vergonheza, sem-vergonhice s. f., sem-vergonhismo m. (pl. sem-vergonhezes, sem-vergonhezas, sem-vergonhices, sem-vergonhismos) (Braz.) shamelessness, boldness, unashamed behaviour.
sena (I) s. f. six: 1. card or dice having six pips or points. 2. ~s pl. a piece of domino bearing the double-six.
sena (II) s. f. (bot., also sene) senna; any of various species of Cassia.
senáculo s. m. seat of the senatus, the ancient Roman senate.
senado s. m. senate: 1. the state council of the ancient Romans. 2. guildhall. 3. the upper legislative house in various bicameral parliaments. 4. senate house.

senador s. m. senator: 1. a member of a senate. 2. (S. Braz., fig.) a very old horse.

senal adj. m. + f. (pl. **-ais**) designating a very small, uncut diamond.

senão s. m. fault, defect. ‖ adv. except, save, else, otherwise. ‖ conj. but, if not, unless, saving, else, or, except, either, without. ‖ prep. except, but.
~ **quando** suddenly, then. ~ **que** but also, rather, on the contrary. ~ **também** but also. **ele nada faz** ~ **jogar** he does nothing but play.

senário adj. senary, consisting of six.

senatoria s. f. (Braz.) senatorship.

senatorial adj. m. + f. (also **senatório** m.) senatorial, senatorian. ‖ **~mente** adv. senatorially.

senatriz s. f. senator's wife.

senatus-consulto s. m. (pl. **senatus-consultos**) senatus consultum, a decree of the Roman senate.

senciente adj. m. + f. sentient, having sensation.

sencilha s. f. (S. Braz.) money given as a loan to card players by a kibitzer.

sencilheiro s. m. (S. Braz.) 1. creditor. 2. money--lender, in particular one who lends to card players.

senda s. f. 1. narrow road, footpath, path (plate C 8). 2. (fig.) routine, habit.
~ **para cavalheiros** bridle-path (plate C 8).

sendeiro s. m. 1. rip: a) hack, jade, old wicked horse or ass. b) (vulg.) a good-for-nothing, sponger. 2. (Braz.) small but robust pack animal. ‖ adj. 1. old and wicked (horse). 2. (vulg.) good-for-nothing, parasitic. 3. small and robust (packhorse). 4. (N. Braz., pop.) big.

sendos adj. m. pl. (also **sengos, senhos**) designating two same objects belonging to two persons, carrying each one his own.
eles traziam ~ **livros** both brought each his book.

sene s. m. (bot., also **sena** II) senna: any of various species of Cassia.

senecionídeo adj. (bot.) referring or similar to the groundsel.

senectude s. f. agedness, old age, oldness; decrepitude, senility.

sene-do-campo s. f. (pl. **senes-do-campo**) (Braz., bot.) common name for the Cassia cathartica.

senegalês s. m. (pl. **-eses**) (f. **-esa**) Senegalese: natural or inhabitant of the Senegal, Africa. ‖ adj. Senegalese: of or referring to the Senegal.

senegalesco adj. Senegalese.

senembi, senembu s. m. (Braz., also **senimbu**) the common iguana.

senescal s. m. (pl. **-ais**) (hist.) seneschal: medieval steward or major-domo in royal houses who often had the power of a judge.

senescalia s. f. seneschalship.

senga s. f. (S. Braz.) 1. scraps, leavings. 2. bran. 3. oyster and shellfish shells.

sengar v. (Braz.) to sift, riddle, screen.

sengo adj. (ant.) 1. intelligent, witty, smart. 2. serious, grave, judicious. 3. (Port. prov.) sly.

sengos adj. m. pl. = **sendos**.

senha s. f. 1. signal, sign, wink, password. 2. receipt, voucher. 3. ticket which garantees the admission or readmission in an assembly or a theatre.
~ **de teatro** counter ticket.

senhor s. m. 1. owner, proprietor, possessor, seignior, master. 2. sir, mister (abbr. Mr.). 3. (Braz.) lord. 4. used before a common noun gives the idea of something excellent, perfect. 5. master and proprietor of a sugar plantation complex. ‖ adj. lordly, distinguished. ‖ pron. you.
~**? sir?** ~ **da hoste** commander in chief. ~ **de engenho** sugar-mill owner. ~ **de morgado** tenant in fee tail. **cada um é** ~ **em sua casa** a man's

house is his castle. **caro** ~ dear sir. **como disse o** ~**? sir? Deus Nosso Senhor** the Lord God. **estar** ~ **da situação** to be master of the situation. **fazer de** ~ to lord it. **fazer-se de** ~ to make o. s. master. **ficar** ~ **do campo** to remain master of the field, to carry the day. **ficar** ~ **do fogo** to get the fire under. **meus** ~**es** gentlemen. **não,** ~ no, sir. **no ano de Nosso Senhor** in the year of Our Lord. **Nosso Senhor Jesus Cristo** Our Lord Jesus Christ. **o dia do Senhor** the Lord's day. **o Senhor** the Lord, God. **o** ~ **tem passado bem?** have you been well? **prezado** ~ dear sir. **ruim** ~ **cria ruim servidor** like master like man. **ser o** ~ **da casa** to have the run of the place. .**ser** ~ **de** to be the master of. **sim,** ~ yes, sir. **sou** ~ **de mim mesmo** I am my own master. **tomar o Senhor** to receive Holy Communion.

senhora s. f. 1. mistress (abbr., Mrs.), lady, landlady. 2. wife, housewife. ‖ pron. you.
~ **congressista** congresswoman. **altar de Nossa Senhora** Lady-altar. **a** ~ **Castro está em casa?** is Mrs. Castro in? **capela dedicada a Nossa Senhora** Lady-chapel. **dia de Nossa Senhora** Lady--Day. **ela estava inteiramente** ~ **de si** she was perfectly mistress of herself. **minhas** ~**s e meus senhores** ladies and gentlemen. **Nossa Senhora** Our Lady, the blessed Virgin Mary. **uma perfeita** ~ a perfect lady.

senhoraça s. f. (pop.) woman of humble origin who tries to seem a lady, wearing luxurious and smart dresses.

senhoraço s. m. 1. man who tries to appear to be of much importance. 2. a bigwig.

senhoreador s. m. master, dominator. ‖ adj. ruling; domineering.

senhorear v. 1. to conquer, domineer, master, govern, subject. 2. to exercise dominion, control, bridle. 3. (also ~**-se**) to take possession of, appropriate.

senhoria s. f. 1. lordship, ladyship. 2. seigniory. 3. landlord, landlady: proprietor of a house, to whom rent is paid.
~ **de Veneza** the seigniory or republic of Venice. **Vossa Senhoria** Your Lordship; Your Honour.

senhoriagem s. f. seigniorage, royalty: 1. tribute paid to a seigniory. 2. percentage paid to the Crown for the coining of new coins. 3. difference between the intrinsic and nominal value of the coin.

senhorial adj. m. + f. (pl. **-ais**) seignioral, manorial, belonging to the lord of a manor.

senhoril adj. m. + f. (pl. **-is**) 1. lordly, manorial. 2. lordlike, ladylike, grave, elegant, majestic.

senhorinha s. f. (Braz., also **senhorita**) miss, unmarried girl.

senhorio s. m. 1. seigniory, lordship. 2. power, dominion, demain. 3. landlord, owner or proprietor of a house.
pagar a renda ao ~ to pay the rent to the landlord. **terra de** ~ lordship.

senhorita s. f. 1. small lady, woman of small size. 2. (Braz., also **senhorinha**) miss, unmarried girl.

senhor-velho s. m. (pl. **senhores-velhos**) (Braz.) the former owner of a slave.

senhos s. m. pl. = **sendos**.

sênica s. f. popular designation for arsenic.

senil adj. m. + f. (pl. **-is**) senile, old, infirm, worn--out; referring to old age.

senilidade s. f. senility, old age; intellectual weakness due to the age.

sênior s. m. (pl. **seniores**) (antonym of junior) senior, older: 1. one older than another. 2. person older in rank or service. 3. sportsman, holder of first prizes. ‖ adj. m. + f. senior, older, elder: 1. to denote the elder of two persons with the same name. 2. older, superior.

seno s. m. (math.) sine: the straight line drawn from one extremity of an arc of a circle perpendicular to the diameter passing through the other extremity.
~ **de um ângulo** sine of an angle: the ratio of such a line to the radius of the arc subtending an angle.

senóide s. f. (mat., also **sinosóide**) sine wave representing the variations of the sine.

senoniano s. m. Senonian: natural or inhabitant of Sens, France. ‖ adj. Senonian: 1. of or referring to Sens. 2. (geol.) a division of the upper Cretaceous in France and Belgium.

sensabor s. m. + f. 1. tastelessness, insipidity. 2. insipid, tasteless person. ‖ adj. insipid, having no taste.

sensaborão s. m. (pl. **-ões**) (f. **-ona**) platitudinarian, a dull person. ‖ adj. platitudinous, dull, uninteresting.

sensaboria s. f. 1. vapidness, tastelessness, insipidity. 2. (fam.) a disagreeable incident.

sensação s. f. (pl. **-ões**) 1. sensation: a) physical feeling, impression, mental perception. b) exciting event. c) thrilling experience, furore. 2. (fig.) sensibility, moral shock.
~ **de aborrecimento** a feeling of weariness. ~ **de horror** creeps. ~ **de sede** sensation of thirst. **causou** ~ it made furore. **tenho uma** ~ **esquisita** I feel queer. **ter** ~ **de calor** to have a sensation of heat. **uma forte** ~ a thrilling experience. **uma** ~ **agradável** a pleasant sensation.

sensacional adj. m. + f. (pl. **-ais**) sensational, remarkable, thrilling, epochmaking, earth-shaking.

sensacionalista adj. sensationalistic.

sensacionismo s. m. sensationalism, ballyhoo.

sensatez s. f. judiciousness, sensibleness, sobermindedness, wisdom, discreetness, prudence.

sensato adj. judicious, sensible, rational, considerate, soberminded, reasonable, discreet, prudent. ‖ **-amente** adv. wisely, with sense.
não seria ~ **se você assim procedesse** it would not be wise of you to do so. **observação -a** a sensible remark. **um homem** ~ a sensible man.

sensibilidade s. f. sensibility: a) faculty of feeling. b) sentimentalism, sensitiveness. c) susceptibility, touchiness. 2. (some instruments) sensitivity, precision.
ferir a ~ **de alguém** to hurt someone's feelings.

sensibilizador adj. (also **sensibilizante** m. + f.) 1. sensitizing. 2. moving, affecting.

sensibilizar v. 1. to sensitize, penetrate. 2. to touch, move. 3. **~-se** to be touched, moved.
as palavras sensibilizaram-me profundamente the words moved me profoundly.

sensificar v. 1. to sensitize. 2. to bring to sensibility or to life.

sensitiva s. f. 1. (also **dormideira, malícia**) a sensitive plant (Mimosa pudica). 2. touchy person.

sensitivo adj. sensitive, sensory, sentient. ‖ **-amente** adv. sensitively, sentiently.

sensível adj. m. + f. (pl. **-íveis**) (also **sensivo** m.) sensible: 1. sentient, sensitive, impressionable. 2. perceptible, appreciable. 3. judicious, reasonable. 4. (fig.) compassionate, finely strung, tender, nice, sad. 5. (mus.) sensitive. ‖ **sensivelmente** adv. sensibly; grievingly, grievously.
~ **à luz** sensitive to light. ~ **baixa de preços** a substantial price reduction. **demasiadamente** ~ overstrung. **este é o ponto** ~ that is the sore spot.

ser ~ to be sensitive. **ter a pele** ~ to be thin-skinned.

senso s. m. sense: 1. sound judgement, sagacity, keenness, wisdom. 2. reasoning, understanding, appreciation. 3. meaning, signification. 4. seriousness, gravity, circumspection. 5. direction, course.
~ **comum** common sense. ~ **de honra** sense of honour. ~ **de humor** sense of humour. ~ **de responsabilidade** sense of responsibility. ~ **estético** aesthetic feeling. ~ **íntimo** inner conscience. ~ **moral** moral sense. ~ **prático** practical good sense, (U. S. A., coll.) horse-sense. **bom** ~ good sense. **dotado de bom** ~ level-headed. **é questão puramente de bom** ~ it's purely a matter of common sense. **não há** ~ **em suas palavras** his words are empty of sense.

sensor s. m. sensor: common designation for devices such as radars and sonars.

sensorial adj. m. + f. (pl. **-ais**) sensorial, sensory.

sensório s. m. (anat.) sensorium: the seat of sensation. ‖ adj. sensorial, sensuous.

sensual s. m. (pl. **-ais**) sensualist. ‖ adj. m. + f. sensual, sensuous, luxurious, voluptuous, libidinous, lustful, fleshy, lewd, lubricous. ‖ **~mente** adv. sensually, erotically.

sensualidade s. f. sensuality, sensualness, voluptuousness, fleshliness.

sensualismo s. m. 1. (philos.) sensualism. 2. sensuality.

sensualista s. m. + f. sensualist, epicure. ‖ adj. sensualistic, voluptuary.

sensualizar v. to sensualize, animalize.

sentada s. f. (S. Braz.) sudden stop by a horse at gallop.

sentador adj. 1. seating, taking a seat. 2. (S. Braz.) having the habit of sudden stops (horse and fig. person).

sentar v. 1. to seat, place. 2. to fix, settle. 3. (S. Braz.) to stop suddenly a horse at gallop. 4. **~-se** to sit down, take a seat.
~ **praça** to enlist, enrol, enter. **~-se à mesa** to sit down at table. **~-se ao lado de** to sit down by. **ela sentou-se à nossa mesa** she sat down at our table. **é melhor ~-se à sombra** you had better sit in the shade. **estar sentado na cama** to be up in bed. **ficar sentado** to keep one's seat. **mandar** ~ to tell to sit down. **não te sentes muito tempo ao sol** don't sit too long in the sun. **por favor, sente-se** please, take a seat, please, be seated. **se estás fatigado sentemo-nos** if you are tired let us sit down. **tornar a** ~ to reseat.

sentença s. f. sentence: 1. a series of words that express a complete thought. 2. proverb, maxim, saying containing moral instructions. 3. a judicial decision, verdict. 4. decision, judgement, opinion. 5. divine judgement.
~ **absolutória** acquittal. ~ **arbitral** award, arbitration. ~ **definitiva** final sentence or judgment. ~ **de morte** death-warrant. ~ **favorável** favourable verdict. ~ **judicial** condemnation. **~s proverbiais** winged words. **cada cabeça, cada** ~ everyone to his own taste. **cumprir uma** ~ to serve a sentence. **dar uma** ~ to pass sentence or judgment.

sentenciação s. f. sentence method: process of teaching to read sentence by sentence.

sentenciado s. m. convict, condemned. ‖ adj. judged, sentenced, condemned.

sentenciador s. m. sentencer, judge. ‖ adj. that pronounces sentence.

sentenciar v. 1. to pass or pronounce sentence upon. 2. to take a decision. 3. to judge, convict, doom. 4. to give an opinion.
~ **à revelia de alguém** to default. **ele foi sentenciado como assassino** he was sentenced a mur-

derer. **o júri sentenciou em assassínio** the jury returned a verdict of murder.

sentencioso adj. 1. of the form of, or containing a sentence. 2. sententious: a) saying much in few words. b) pithy, concise. 3. pompous in tone. ‖ **-amente** adv. sententiously.

sentido s. m. 1. each of the five senses. 2. feeling, appreciation. 3. good sense, judgment. 4. signification, orientation, direction, acceptation, precaution, attention. 5. sense: one of two opposite directions, negative or positive. 6. (phys.) direction (positive or negative). 7. ~s pl.: a) sensuality. b) intellectual faculties. ‖ adj. 1. sensible. 2. sorry, grieved. 3. sad, moaning. 4. hurt, scandalized. ‖ **-amente** adv. grievously, resentfully. ‖ ~! interj. attention! ~ **de força** direction of force. ~ **do olfato** sense of smell. ~ **do ouvido** sense of hearing. ~ **do tato** sense of touch. ~ **figurado** figurative sense. ~ **literal** literal sense. ~ **próprio** proper sense. ~ **restrito** strict sense. ~ **tátil** tactile sense. ~ **vulgar** common meaning. **compreender o** ~ to catch the sense. **em posição de** ~ standing in attention. **em** ~ **contrário** in the opposite direction. **em** ~ **oposto a** against. **em todos os** ~s from every angle. **estar** ~ to repent. **ficar** ~ **por** to be hurt by. **não tem** ~ it doesn't make sense. ~ **horário** clockwise. **sexto** ~ sixth sense. **no mesmo** ~ to the same effect. **no** ~ **exato** strictly speaking. **no verdadeiro** ~ **da palavra** in the true sense of the word. **num** ~ in a way. **órgão de** ~ sense organ. **os cinco** ~s the five senses. **o sexto** ~ the sixth sense. **perder os** ~s to swoon. **recuperar os** ~ to recover one's senses. **sem** ~s unconscious. **sem** ~ purposeless; null. **ter duplo** ~ to have a double meaning. **tomar** ~ to pay attention.

sentimental adj. m. + f. (pl. **-ais**) 1. sentimental, emotional, impressionable, tender-hearted, romantic. 2. mawkish. ‖ ~**mente** adv. sentimentally, effusively.

novela ~ sentimental novel. **pessoa** ~ sentimental person. **um caso** ~ a love affair.

sentimentalidade s. f. sentimentality.

sentimentalismo s. m. sentimentalism: 1. sentimentality, emotionalism. 2. litterary or artistic style in which sentimentalism is predominating.

sentimentalista s. m. + f. sentimentalist. ‖ adj. sentimentalist.

sentimentalizar v. to sentimentalize, become sentimental.

sentimento s. m. sentiment: 1. feeling. 2. sensibility, emotion. 3. comprehension, perception. 4. sorrow, regretfulness, repentance. 5. passion. 6. presentiment, apprehension. 7. pl. sensibilities, good nature. 8. condolences.

~ **de culpa** guilty feelings. ~ **de piedade** the sense of pity. ~ **de solidariedade** fellow-feeling. ~s **nobres** noble sentiments. ~s **patéticos** pathetics. ~ **patriótico** patriotic sentiment. ~ **religioso** devotion. **apelar para o** ~ to appeal to sentiment. **com profundo** ~ **meu** to my great sorrow. **maus** ~s ill feelings. **o** ~ **geral** the general feeling. **o** ~ **trágico da vida** the tragic sense of life. **sem** ~ stony; stepmotherly.

sentina s. f. 1. bilge, the sink of a ship. 2. latrine. 3. dirty place. 4. vicious person.

sentinela s. f. 1. sentry: a) sentinel. b) watchman, guard. 2. (Braz., bot.) a paspalum grass.

~ **avançada** outsentry. ~ **perdida** forlorn hope. **de** ~ on sentry-go. **estar de** ~ to watch, stand sentinel. **fazer quarto de** ~ to stand sentinel over. **render uma** ~ to relieve guard.

sentir s. m. 1. sentiment, feeling. 2. opinion. ‖ v. 1. to feel, distinguish by the senses. 2. to experience.

3. to perceive, be sensible of. 4. to have a presentiment, know. 5. to regret, grudge, be sorry, grieve. 6. to suffer, be impressed with. 7. to be moved or affected. 8. to opine, think, judge. 9. to resent, take offence. 10. ~-**se:** a) to feel, feel o. s.; be self-conscious. b) to resent.

~-**se à altura de** to feel up to. ~-**se à vontade com alguém** to feel at home with someone. ~-**se bem** to feel well. ~-**se chocado** to be shocked. ~-**se com coragem** to feel courageous. ~ **desgosto** to be grieved. ~-**se doente** to feel ill, feel run down. ~ **dores agudas** to feel sharp pains. ~-**se feliz** to feel happy. ~ **fome** to be hungry. ~-**se fora do seu elemento** to feel like a fish out of water. ~ **inclinação para** to feel inclined to. ~ **mágoa** to be grieved. ~ **profundamente** to lay to heart. ~-**se só** to feel lonely. **como se sente?** how do you feel? **eu sinto ter de ouvir** I am concerned to hear. **eu sinto ter que dizer** I am sorry to say. **fazer** ~ to inspire. **ficar sentido por** to be hurt at. **fizeram** ~ **o seu descontentamento** they gave utterance to their discontent. **não me sinto bem** I do not find myself very well. **vou** ~ **muito a sua falta** I shall miss you no end.

senzala s. f. (Braz.) slave house or quarter.

sépala s. f. (bot.) sepal.

sepalóide adj. m. + f. (bot.) sepaloid.

separação s. f. (pl. **-ões**) separation, separateness: 1. dissociation, dissolution, division, sequestration, secession, disaggregation. 2. partition, division, screen. 3. distance, remoteness. 4. divorce, dissolution of matrimony.

~ **de bens** legal separation of estate. ~ **de corpos** legal separation, judicial separation (of a married couple). ~ **judicial** judicial separation.

separado adj. separate: 1. disconnected, severed, disunited, disengaged, dissociated, considered apart. 2. distinct, individual, different. ‖ **-amente** adv. separately.

cada livro -amente each book separately. **em** ~ separately. **viver** ~ **de** to live in separation from.

separador s. m. 1. separator, parter, sorter. 2. (electr.) barrier. 3. milk-skimmer. ‖ adj. separating, parting.

separar v. to separate: 1. disunite, disconnect, sever. 2. devide, part, put asunder, set or keep apart. 3. part, disconnect, withdraw. 4. disperse, scatter. 5. dissolve, disintegrate, decompose. 6. divorce, turn away from, leave. 7. ~-**se:** a) to disaggregate, disintegrate. b) to part with, leave, go from.

~ **com força** to tear asunder. ~-**se de** to part with. ~-**se de alguém** to leave somebody. ~-**se judicialmente** to divorce. **ela teve de** ~-**se dele** she had to part with him. **ele separou-se de** he cut himself loose from. **eles** ~**am-se** they parted company. **eles** ~**am-se como amigos** they parted friends. **mundos os separam** they are worlds asunder.

separata s. f. separatum, off-print.

separatismo s. m. separatism.

separatista s. m. + f. separatist. ‖ adj. separatist, referring to separatism.

separativo adj. separative, separatory.

separatório s. m. (chem.) separatory. ‖ adj. separatory, separative.

separável adj. m. + f. (pl. **-áveis**) separable, partible.

sépia s. f. sepia: dark brown substance of cuttle-fish, much used in painting.

sepícola adj. m. + f. sepicolous.

sepsia s. f. (med.) sepsis, putrefaction.

septeto s. m. (mus., also **séptuor**) septet(te): musical composition for seven voices or seven instruments.

septicemia s. f. (med.) septic(a)emia, sepsis: blood poisoning.

septicêmico adj. septicemic.

septicida adj. m. + f. (bot.) septicidal: the dehiscence of a fruit in which the pod splits.

séptico adj. (med.) septic, septical, not aseptic.

septífero adj. (bot.) septiferous: bearing septa.

septifoliolado adj. (bot.) seven-foliolated.

septiforme adj. m. + f. 1. septiform: shaped like a septum. 2. seven-formed: presenting seven forms.

septífrago adj. (bot.) septifragal.

septo s. m. (biol., also **dissepimento**) septum: a partition between two cavities.
~ **de desvio** deflector. ~ **nasal** nasal septum. ~ **transverso** septum transversum.

septômetro s. m. instrument used to sample and analyze the quantity of organic matter contained in the air.

séptuor s. m. (mus.) = **septeto.**

sepulcral adj. m. + f. (pl. **-ais**) sepulchral: 1. charnel, funeral. 2. (fig.) dark, gloomy, extremely pale. ‖ ~**mente** adv. sepulchrally.
lousa ~ tombstone. **silêncio** ~ peace of the grave.

sepulcrário s. m. burying-ground, burial-place, burial--ground, burying-place, churchyard, cemetery.

sepulcro s. m. 1. sepulchre, grave, tomb. 2. (fig.) a place where many people die. 3. that which hides like a tomb.
o Santo Sepulcro the Holy Grave.

sepultador s. m. grave-maker, grave-digger, sexton. ‖ adj. that buries.

sepultamento s. m. 1. the act of burying s.o. sepulture, burial, entombment. 2. (fig.) the act of secluding o. s. or retiring from the world.

sepultante adj. m. + f. that buries.

sepultar v. to bury: 1. inter, inhumate, sepulchre. 2. hide, keep, guard, conceal. 3. to submerge, immerge, sink. 4. entomb. 5. ~**-se** to seclude o. s.; retire from the world.
~**-se no deboche** to sink in debauchery. ~**-se vivo** to bury o. s. in solitude.

sepulto adj. buried.

sepultura s. f. (also **sepulcro, túmulo** m.) 1. sepulture, grave, tomb, sepulchre. 2. (fig.) death. 3. place where many people die.
dar ~ to bury. **estar com um pé na** ~ to have one foot in the grave. **levar à** ~ to cause death.

sepultureiro s. m. (also **coveiro**) grave-maker, grave--digger, sexton.

séquano s. m. individual of the Sequani, an old Gallic race, which lived at the left border of the Saône, France. ‖ adj. of or referring to the Sequani.

sequaz s. m. follower; sectator; partisan. ‖ adj. m. + f. sequacious; following, adherent, partisan.
~ **de alguém** a follower of s. o.

sequeiro s. m. 1. waste: plot of barren land. 2. place for drying clothes, pottery, etc. 3. (N. Braz.) shallow river, full of stones. ‖ adj. unirrigated, arid, barren.

seqüela s. f. 1. sequel, consequence, result. 2. act of following, succeeding. 3. sequence of things. 4. band, gang, pack.

seqüência s. f. 1. sequence: continuation, continuity, progression, succession, series. 2. a connected series as in books, cards, music, cinema, etc.
~ **das estações** the sequence of the seasons. ~ **de cinco cartas** (cards) quint. ~ **de idéias** train of thoughts. ~ **dos fatos** the sequence of the facts. ~ **máxima** (cards) ace-high straight.

seqüente adj. m. + f. sequent, sequential, following. ‖ ~**mente** adv. in the sequel.

sequer adv. at least, so much as, even.
nem ~ not even, without so much as. **nem** ~ **um** never so much as one.

seqüestração s. f. (pl. **-ões**) sequestration.

seqüestrado s. m. 1. the victim of a kidnapping. 2. the victim of a sequestration. ‖ adj. 1. kidnapped. 2. sequestered.

seqüestrador s. m. 1. sequestrator. 2. kidnapper. ‖ adj. sequestering.

seqüestrar v. to sequester: 1. (jur.) sequestrate. 2. set apart, seclude, isolate, separate. 3. confiscate, appropriate, seize.

seqüestrável adj. m. + f. (pl. **-áveis**) sequestrable, attachable.

seqüestro s. m. 1. sequestration: a) the holding of property until legal claims are satisfied. b) seclusion, isolation, separation. c) confiscation, seizure. d) (path.) sequestrum. 2. sequestrator. 3. sequestered object.
fazer ~ to sequester.

sequiar v. (S. Braz.) to talk, discuss.

sequidão s. f. (pl. **-ões**) 1. dryness. 2. (fig.) dullness, roughness. 3. frigidity, indifference.
falar com ~ to speak roughly.

sequilho s. m. cracknell: a simple dry cake or biscuit.

sequioso adj. 1. thirsty, desirous to drink. 2. dry, arid, barren. 3. (fig.) desirous, eager, avid. ‖ **-amente** adv. 1. thirstily. 2. (fig.) desirously, eagerly.

sequista s. m. + f. (Braz.) a boring person. ‖ adj. boring, tiresome, dull.

séqüito, séquito s. m. 1. suite, train, attendance, entourage, retinue. 2. escort, following. 3. (fig.) friendship, sympathy, popularity.

sequóia s. f. (bot.) sequoia: a gigantic Californian conifer.

ser s. m. (pl. **seres**) 1. being, creature. 2. existence, life. 3. nature, substance, constitution. 4. reality, truth. ‖ v. to be: 1. exist. 2. have existence in fact, physical or mental. 3. become. 4. happen. 5. belong. 6. be made of, consist. 7. cost. 8. be used for, serve as. 9. concern.
~ **alguém** to be somebody. ~ **bastante** to be enough. ~ **breve** to be brief. ~ **capaz** to be able. ~ **cauteloso** to be cautious, take care. ~ **competente** to be competent. ~ **contra** to be against. ~ **credor** to have credit. ~ **curioso, perguntador** to poke and pry. ~ **da mesma opinião** to be of the same opinion. ~ **amigo de alguém** to be a friend to one, to side with a person. ~ **de pouco valor** to be of little value. ~ **doente** to be sick. ~ **esperto** to be clever. ~ **fonte de preocupações** to lie at one's heart. ~ **humano** 1. s. human being. 2. v. to be human. ~ **impossível** to be impossible. ~ **maior e vacinado** to be one's own master; to act as one pleases. ~ **nada** to be nothing. ~ **natural de** to be a native of. ~ **necessário** to be necessary. ~ **um obstáculo** to lie in the way. ~ **o mesmo** to be the same. ~ **ou não** ~ to be or not to be. ~ **preferível** to be preferable. ~ **responsável** to lie on the head of. ~ **sem querer** to happen accidentally. ~ **senhor de si** to be master of o. s. ~ **um homem liquidado** to be a broken man. ~ **útil** to be useful. ~ **vivo** 1. s. being. 2. v. to be quick. **ainda que fosse** even if it were so. **a não** ~ **assim** but for this. **a não** ~ **que** save that. **antes fosse** I would that it had been. **assim seja** amen, I hope so. **como é ele?** what is he like? **como se fosse possível** as if it were possible. **é** yes, that is right. **é boa!** that's a good one! **é isso mesmo** that's just it. **ele é contra mim** he goes against me. **é minha vez** it's my turn. **é que...** it's just that... **era sobre o fim da semana** it was

towards the end of the week. **era no outono** it was in autumn. **era uma vez um rei** once upon a time there was a king. **foi ele que** it was he who. **fosse eu, se eu fosse** were I. **fosse de quem fosse** whose ever it might be. **fosse qual fosse** whichever, whoever it might be. **isso é com ele** that is his affair. **isto é** that is. **não é?** isn't it so? aren't you? **o ferro é duro** iron is hard. **o que é feito dele?** what is become of him? **o que será?** what can the matter be? **o Ser supremo** the supreme Being. **quem me dera que isso fosse verdade** I would that it were true. **quem me dera ser rico** if only I were rich. **quem me dera ser jovem outra vez** I wish I were young again. **quanto é isto?** how much is this? **são cerejas** it is cherries. **se assim for** if that be the case. **seja assim** be it so. **seja como for** be it as it may. **sendo que** seeing that. **será bom** it will be good. **seria melhor não** it would be better not to. **será que?** I wonder if? **sou eu** it's I, it's me.

seráfico adj. 1. seraphic(al). 2. (fig.) beatific(al), devout. ‖ **seraficamente** adv. seraphically, in a seraphical manner.
~ **amor** seraphic love.

serafim s. m. (pl. **-ins**) seraph.

serafina s. f. 1. a woollen cloth. 2. (N. Braz.) church organ.

seral adj. (ecology) seral.

serão s. m. (pl. **-ões**) 1. work done in the evening, overtime. 2. evening, night's rendezvous. 3. evening-party; soirée.

serapieira s. f. (Braz.) = **sarapieira**.

serapilheira s. f. (also **sarapilheira**) 1. sarpler, sackcloth, burlaps. 2. (Braz.) poor and creeping undergrowth.

sereia s. f. siren: 1. mermaid: mythological being half woman half fish. 2. an enticing woman; woman with a melodious voice. 3. a device for sounding signals, hooter. 4. an apparatus producing musical tones. 5. (zool.) mud-eel.
~ **de nevoeiro** foghorn.

sereíba s. f. (Braz., bot.) Indian fig.

sereibuna s. f. (Braz.) a wild mangrove.

serelepe s. m. (Braz.) 1. (also **caxinguelê**) a kind of ground squirrel. 2. (fig.) a smart, sharp and lively person. ‖ adj. m. + f. lively, clever, tricky.

serena s. f. 1. a kind of slow churn. 2. a troubadour song.

serenada s. f. 1. = **serenata**. 2. (S. Braz.) drizzle. 3. serene dew.

serenagem s. f. act of serening, calming.

serenar v. to serene: 1. cheer, make cheerful, calm, pacify. 2. grow quiet, calm down. 3. drizzle, mist. 4. clear up, grow fair. 5. (N. Braz.) stay (something) in the damp night air. 6. dance, shake the body. 7. observe from the outside the festivities going on inside a house. 8. **~-se** to become serene, tranquil; to calm.
~ **os ânimos** to quiet animosities. **pôr a ~** to put out all night in the dew.

serenata s. f. serenade: 1. (also **seresta**) open-air evening concert. 2. a simple and melodious air, sung or played to or in honour of s. o. under his (or her) window.
cantar uma ~ to serenade (a lady). **fazer uma ~** to give a serenade.

serenatista s. m. + f. (Braz.) serenader.

serenidade s. f. serenity, sereneness, tranquility, peacefulness, calmness.
~ **de ânimo** serenity, calmness of mind. **conservar a ~** to keep one's head. **perder a ~** to lose self-control, go off the deep end.

sereníssimo adj. 1. abs. superl. of **sereno** = most serene. 2. Serene Highness: a title of honour and royalty.

sereno (I) s. m. 1. serene, dew, mist. 2. (Braz.) drizzle, a slow rain. 3. crowd gathered to observe from the outside a party going on inside a house. 4. open air. ‖ adj. serene: 1. cheerful, quiet, placid, tranquil. 2. pure. 3. undisturbed. 4. clear, fair, unclouded. ‖ **-amente** adv. serenely.
~ **como um lago** as smooth as a millpond. **as águas -as do Atlântico** the serene waters of the Atlantic. **dormir ao ~** to sleep in the open air. **gota -a** (med.) drop serene. **noite -a** still evening. **no ~** in the open air. **uma vida -a** a quiet life.

sereno (II) s. m. a kind of night-watchman, in Spain.

seres s. m. pl. Seres: name for the inhabitants of ancient China.

seresma s. f. 1. a weak or useless and indolent woman. 2. (also **coruja**) old and ugly woman. 3. anything repulsive or nauseous. 4. m. scarecrow: a good-for-nothing.

seresta s. f. (Braz., also **serenata**) serenade.

seresteiro s. m. (also **serenatista** m. + f.) serenader.

sergipano s. m., **sergipense** m. + f. natural or inhabitant of the state of Sergipe, Brazil. ‖ adj. of or referring to Sergipe.

seriação s. f. seriation: 1. the act of seriating. 2. disposition of things in series. 3. classification.

seriado adj. seriate. ‖ **-amente** adv. seriately.

serial adj. m. + f. (pl. **-ais**) serial: 1. referring to series. 2. ordered in series.

seriar v. to seriate: 1. arrange in series. 2. make the classification of. 3. order.

seriário adj. serially: 1. referring to a series. 2. done by series.

seribeiro s. m. (N. Braz.) fisherman.

seribolo s. m. (N. Braz., pop.) uproar; confusion; noise; tumult.

seríceo adj. (poet.) silky, silklike, sericeous.

sericícola s. m. + f. (ci)culturist: person engaged in the breeding of silkworms or the production of raw silk. ‖ adj. seri(ci)cultural.

sericicultor s. m. (also **sericícola**) seri(ci)culturist.

sericicultura s. f. seri(ci)culture: the breeding of silkworms and the production of raw silk.

sericígeno adj. silk-producing.

sérico (I) adj. silken.

sérico (II) adj. of or referring to serum.

sericóia, sericora s. f. (Braz., zool.) a wood rail (Aramides cajanea cajanea).

sericori s. f. (Braz., zool.) a small wood rail.

sericultor s. m. = **sericicultor**.

sericultura s. f. = **sericicultura**.

seridó s. m. (Braz.) 1. a cotton growing zone in Paraíba and Rio Grande do Norte. 2. a certain kind of cotton growing there.

série s. f. series: 1. a number, set or continued succession of homogenous things. 2. sequence, row, set. 3. succession, continuation. 4. (math., chem., geol.) succession, group.
produção em ~ larg scale or mass production. **fora de ~** out of the ordinary; unusual, exceptional. ~ **contínua** continuum. ~ **descontínua** broken series. ~ **sucessiva** chain. **dar uma ~ de conferências** to give a course of lectures. **ela passou por toda ~ de sentimentos** she ran through the whole gamut of feelings. **ligação em ~** (electr.) series connection, tandem connection. **motor ligado em ~** series-connected engine. **produção em ~** mass production. **uma ~ de acontecimentos** a train of events. **uma ~ de colunas** a series of columns.

seriedade — serra 1159

uma ~ de desastres a succession of disasters.
uma ~ de mentiras a web of lies.
seriedade s. f. seriousness: 1. quality of being earnest. 2. gravity, sobriety, solemnity. 3. integrity.
seriema s. f. (Braz., ornith.) the crested cariama (Cariama cristata).
serifa s. f. (typogr.) serif.
serigaria s. f. (also sirgaria II) manufacturing place of the silkman.
serigola s. f. (Braz.) s. an iron or leather ring in a bull's nose, by which it is bridled. 2. (N. Braz.) throatlatch of a horse.
serigote s. m. (S. Braz.) a type of harness saddle.
serigrafar v. (typogr.) to print or reproduce by means of serigraphy.
serigrafia s. f. (typogr.) 1. serigraphy: the art of making serigraphs. 2. serigraph: a color print made by the silkscreen process.
serigueiro s. m. silkman, lace maker.
seriguilha s. f. rough woolen cloth, without pile.
seringa s. f. 1. syringe, squirt. 2. (pop.) quarrelsome person. 3. (Braz.) rubber latex.
~ hipodérmica hypodermic syringe.
seringação s. f. (also seringadela) syringing, squirting.
seringada s. f. 1. jet from a syringe. 2. syringing.
seringador s. m. (S. Braz., sl.) a boring person. || adj. troublesome, irksome, boring.
seringal s. m. (pl. -ais) (Braz.) 1. place abounding with rubber trees. 2. (N. Braz.) a property or plantation usually at riversides.
seringalista s. m. (N. Braz.) proprietor of a rubber plantation, usually called patrão = boss.
seringar v. to syringe, squirt: 1. inject, drive the fluid of a syringe into. 2. sluice, spray with the fluid of the syringe. 3. (pop.) bore, importune.
seringarana s. f. (Braz., bot.) sapium.
seringatório s. m. injection, medicine made to be injected by a syringe. || adj. referring to a syringe.
seringueira s. f. (Braz.) rubber-tree of the family Euphorbiaceae (Hevea brasiliensis).
seringueira-barriguda s. f. (pl. seringueiras-barrigudas) (Braz.) plant of the family Euphorbiaceae (Hevea spruceana).
seringueira-branca s. f. (pl. seringueiras-brancas) (Braz.) tree of the family Euphorbiaceae (Hevea randiana).
seringueira-chicote s. f. (pl. seringueiras-chicote) (Braz.) tree of the family Euphorbiaceae (Hevea benthamiana).
seringueira-itaúba s. f. (pl. seringueiras-itaúba) (Braz.) tree of the family Euphorbiaceae (Hevea lutea).
seringueira-vermelha s. f. (pl. seringueiras-vermelhas) (Braz.) tree of the family Euphorbiaceae (Hevea guianensis).
seringueiro s. m. (N. Braz.) rubber latex extractor, rubber gatherer.
sério s. m. gravity, seriousness, prudence. || adj. 1. serious, severe, grave, earnest. 2. reliable, trustworthy. 3. decent, modest. || seriamente adv. 1. seriously. 2. really.
demasiado ~ overearnest. eles tomam seu plano muito a ~ they are very serious about their plan. é ~ it's no joke. está ~? are you serious? estou absolutamente ~ I am quite serious. estou bem ~ I am in bitter earnest. isto é um passo ~ this is a serious step. não falas a ~ quando dizes... you don't mean to tell me that... procurei ficar ~ I tried to keep a straight face. ter uma conversa a ~ to have a serious talk. um caso ~ a serious matter. tomar a ~ to take to heart.
sermão s. m. (pl. -ões) 1. discourse, sermon, preach. 2. (fig.) severe lecture, reprimand. 3. tedious discourse.

~ da Montanha the Sermon on the Mount. pregar um ~ to give a lecture.
sermonário s. m. 1. book or collection of sermons. 2. sermonizer.
sernambiguara s. m. (Braz., ichth., also tambó) the round pompano.
seroada s. f. 1. overtime night work. 2. long evening. fazer ~ to sit up to work.
seroar v. 1. to work in the evening. 2. to be together in the evening.
serôdio adj. 1. late, tardy. 2. backward (unseasoned). 3. (bot.) serotinous.
serologia s. f. (path.) serology.
serosa s. f. (med.) serosa.
serossanguíneo adj. (pl. serossanguíneos) sero-sanguinolent: composed of serosity and blood.
serosidade s. f. (med.) serosity: 1. the state. 2. the fluid.
seroso adj. serous, like whey.
seroterapia s. f. (med., also soroterapia) serotherapy.
seroterápico adj. (med., also soroterápico) serotherapic.
serpe s. f. 1. (poet.) serpent. 2. old piece of ordnance. 3. (archit.) ornamental serpentiform line.
~ do mosquete cock of a match-lock musket.
serpeante adj. m. + f. (also serpejante, serpentante, serpenteante) winding, meandering, creeping, twisting, bending.
serpear v. (also serpejar, serpentar, serpentear) 1. to serpentine, go winding about, crawl, wind, meander. 2. twine, squirm, wriggle.
serpentão s. m. (pl. -ões) serpent: an old-fashioned wooden bass wind-instrument.
serpentária s. f. (bot., also serpentina) serpentaria, snakeroot, used for medicinal purposes.
serpentário s. m. 1. Serpentário (astr.) Serpentarius, Ophiuchus: a northern constellation. 2. (ornith.) serpent eater, secretary-bird. 3. (Braz.) serpentarium.
serpente s. f. serpent: 1. (zool.) snake. 2. (pop.) a hag, an ugly woman. 3. malevolent, treacherous person.
encantador de ~s snake charmer.
serpentear v. 1. = serpear. 2. to coil.
o rio serpenteava pelo vale the river wound its way through the valley.
serpentífero adj. (poet.) serpentiferous: that produces serpents.
serpentiforme adj. m. + f. serpentiform, serpentine, snaky.
serpentina s. f. 1. branched candlestick, cane with three triangularly disposed candles at the top of it, used on the Saturday of the Holy Week. 2. (chem.) worm. 3. serpentin, carnival paper ribbon. 4. serpentine: a) (bot.) Virginia snakeroot. b) (mil.) culverin, saker. c) (min.) a fibrous rock spotted like a snake-skin.
~ de refrigeração cooling worm. ~ de tubos coil.
serpentino adj. 1. serpentine, serpentile: of or belonging to a serpent. 2. serpentiform. 3. containing serpentine veins as serpentine marble.
língua -a ill tongue. pedra -a serpentine stone.
serpiginoso adj. (med.) serpiginous: said of certain skin diseases.
serpilho s. m. (bot.) = serpão.
serra s. f. 1. saw (plate S 2). 2. (fig.) mountain ridge, mountain range (plate M 11). 3. mountain. 4. a stack of straw or corn. 5. (ichth.) bonito (Sarda sarda). 6. (S. Braz.) narrow strip accompanying the sides of a river.
~ braçal whipsaw. ~ cilíndrica crown-saw. ~ circular circular or buzz saw (plate A 7). ~ de arco bow-saw (plate S 2). ~ de arco para metais hacksaw (plate S 2). ~ de cadeia chain-saw. ~ de fita

bandsaw, ribbon saw. ~ **de mão** buck saw, bow saw (plates M 4, S 2). ~ **de podar** pruning saw (plate J 2). ~ **de vaivém** gigsaw. ~ **elétrica** electric saw. ~ **grande para toras** board saw. ~ **mecânica** mechanical saw. ~ **tico-tico** fret saw. **cortar em pedaços com a** ~ to saw up. **ir à** ~ (fig.) to get huffed. **recortar com** ~ to saw out. **subir a** ~ (fig.) to become angry. **travadeira de** ~ saw-set.

serra-abaixo s. f. (Braz.) 1. name of the meridional part of the State of Rio de Janeiro. 2. the coastal area lying between the ocean and the Serra do Mar.

serra-acima s. f. (Braz.) the northern part of the State of Rio de Janeiro.

serra-boca s. m. (pl. **serra-bocas**) (N. Braz.) name of a certain tow-line.

serrabulho s. m. = **sarrabulho**.

serração, serradela s. f. (act of) sawing.

serradela s. f. (bot.) serradella, bird's foot.

serradiço adj. sawed and squared (timber).

serrado adj. 1. sawed, sawn. 2. that has the toothed appearance of a saw; serrated.

serrador s. m. 1. sawyer, sawer. 2. big hand-saw for straw. 3. (Braz., ornith., also **serra-serra**) the blue-black grassquit. ‖ adj. sawing.

serradura s. f. 1. (act of) sawing. 2. (also **serragem**) sawing, sawdust.

serra-feia s. f. (pl. **serras-feias**) (Braz., ichth.) a species of caribe.

serra-garoupa s. f. (pl. **serras-garoupa**) (ichth.) a species of grouper.

serragem s. f. (pl. -**ens**) 1. (Braz.) scobs, sawdust. 2. (act of) sawing.

serralha s. f. (bot.) sonchus, sowthistle.

serralhar v. 1. to cut, carve, file, smooth, polish like a locksmith or metal worker. 2. to work as a locksmith. 3. to be as noisy as a locksmith.

serralharia s. f. workshop of a locksmith or metal worker.

serralheiro s. m. locksmith; metal worker.

serralho s. m. seraglio: 1. ancient palace of the Turkish sultan. 2. harem. 3. women living in the harem. 4. (fig.) brothel.

serrana s. f. 1. mountaineer: woman living in the mountains. 2. rustic and simple woman. 3. (S. Braz.) country dance, a kind of fandango.

serrania s. f. 1. mountain ridge, cordillera. 2. (fig.) turbulent sea.

serranice s. f. manner and customs of the mountaineers.

serranilha s. f. bucolic song of the ancient Portuguese troubadours.

serrano s. m. 1. mountaineer, highlander. 2. countryman. ‖ adj. 1. mountainous. 2. living in the mountains, rustic.

serrão s. m. 1. = **serrano**. 2. two-handled cross-cut saw (plate S 2).

serra-osso s. m. (pl. **serra-ossos**) (N. Braz., pop.) 1. hoedown, cheap public dance. 2. family dance, improvised dance.

serra-pau s. m. (pl. **serra-paus**) (Braz.) any of various wood beetles.

serrar v. 1. to saw. 2. (Braz., sl.) to catch, lay hold of.
~ **de cima** to be on top, call the tune. ~ **em pranchas** to plank. ~ **madeira** to saw timber. **cavalete para** ~ **madeira** sawing-horse.

serraria (I) s. f. 1. sawframe, sawyer's frame. 2. lumber-mill, saw-mill.

serraria (II) s. f. mountain range: a series of mountain ridges.

serra-serra s. m. (pl. **serra-serras**) (Braz., ornith., also **alfaiate, tisiu**) the blue-black grassquit.

serrátil adj. m. + f. (pl. -**eis**) serratile, serrate, serriform, saw-shaped.
corpo ~ solid having five superficies, three of which are parallelograms and the other two are equal and parallel triangles.

serrazina s. f. 1. importunity, pesterousness. 2. m. + f. pesterer, nagger. ‖ adj. m. + f. nagging, pestering.

serrazinar v. to pester, importune, nag.

serreado adj. serrate, serrated, serriform (plate F 5).

serrear v. to serrate, give the form of a saw, notch, cut saw-toothed.

sérreo adj. sawlike, serriform, serrate.

serreta s. f. 1. little hilock. 2. small saw. 3. (N. Braz.) a part of the whaler.

serridênteo adj. (zool.) serratodentate.

serril adj. m. + f. (pl. -**is**) 1. unpolished, rude, rough, rustic. 2. mountainous. 3. (fig.) untamed, unbroken, wild. 4 = **sérreo**.

serrilha s. f. 1. serration, milling, a sawlike edge. 2. a serriform ornament. 3. serrated edge of the coin. 4. spiked curb, a part of a bridle. 5. Spanish silver coin.

serrilhado adj. serrulate(d), serrate, milled (plate F 5).

serrilhador s. m. a coin milling-machine.

serrilhar v. 1. to serrate, rim, mill. 2. to bridle a bolting horse by alternate pulls of the reins.

serrim s. m. 1. serradella. 2 (Port.) sawdust.

serrinho s. m. (S. Braz.) = **serradura** 2.

serrino adj. (also **serrátil**) serrate, saw-shaped.

serrípede adj. m. + f. (zool.) serriped, having serrated feet.

serrirrosto adj. (ornith.) serrirostrate: having a serrated bill.

serro s. m. (pl. **serros**) mountain ridge.

serrota s. f. (Braz., also **serrote**) hand-saw.

serrotado adj. 1. hand-saw cut. 2. badly sawn. 3. (Braz.) trimmed with fine lace imitating a saw.

serrotagem s. f. (act of) hand-sawing.

serrotar v. 1. to cut with a hand-saw. 2. to saw badly or irregularly.

serrote s. m. 1. hand-saw (plates F 2, M 4, S 2). 2. hillock or small mountain ridge.
~ **de arco** frame or bow saw. ~ **de ponta** pad or compass saw (plates F 2, S 2). ~ **de samblar** tenon saw (plate F 2). ~ **para metal** hack saw (plate F 1).

sertã s. f. (also **sartã**) frying-pan.

sertanejo s. m. inlander, dweller of the back-country. ‖ adj. 1. of or from the back-country or wilderness. 2. that lives in the back-country. 3. rude, rough, sylvan.

sertania s. f. (Braz.) the interior, the backwoods.

sertanista s. m. (Braz.) 1. (also **bandeirante**) member of an armed band of early explorers in Brazil. 2. m. + f. person knowing or travelling the interior, the hinterland of the country.

sertanizar v. to run through the interior of the backwoods.

sertão s. m. (pl. -**ões**) 1. interior, midland part, heart of the country, hinterland, back-country, wilderness. 2. forest in the heart of the country or remote from the sea, (U. S. A.) backwoods. 3. (N. Braz.) arid and remote interior.
cidades do ~ inland towns.

seruaia s. f. (Braz., also **marimari**) a plant of the family Leguminosae.

sérum s. m. 1. serum. 2. whey.

serutinga s. f. (Braz., bot., also **serubuna**) a species of mangrove.

serva s. f. 1. servant, attendant, servant-maid. 2. woman slave.

servente s. 1. m. + f. servant, attendant, helper. 2. m. servant, handy man, jobber, underworker, understrapper. ‖ adj. serving, attendant.
~ **de pedreiro** hodman, hod-carrier (plate A 7).
serventia s. f. 1. usefulness. 2. use, service, utility. 3. servitude, slavery. 4. (archit.) passage, inlet, entrance. 5. service executed temporarily or in another's name. 6. servants work.
aquilo é de grande gasto e de nenhuma ~ that is very chargeable, and of no use at all. **não ter** ~ **nenhuma** to be good for nothing, of no service. **ter muita** ~ to be very serviceable.
serventuário s. m. deputy or substitute, one who executes an office.
serviçal s. m. + f. (pl. **-ais**) servant, one who earns a living by serving, underling. ‖ adj. 1. relating to servants or slaves. 2. serviceable, ready to serve one, officious, friendly. 3. useful, advantageous. ‖ ~**mente** adv. serviceably, obligingly.
serviçalismo s. m. serviceableness.
serviço s. m. service: 1. occupation of a servant. 2. act, fact or means of serving. 3. duty required. 4. employment, job, work. 5. performance of official or professional duties. 6. good offices. 7. a religious rite, divine service. 8. military duty. 9. a set of dishes. 10. advantage, help, benefit.
~ **aéreo** air service. ~ **civil** civil service. ~ **corrente** routine duties. ~ **de campanha** field-duty. ~ **de correio** postal service. ~ **de mesa** dinner service. ~ **de prata** a set of silverware. ~ **de vésperas** vesper. ~ **diário** daily service. ~ **doméstico** housework. ~ **externo** outside service. ~ **funerário** undertaking. ~ **militar** military service. ~ **de saúde** quarantine service. ~ **malfeito** patchery. ~ **obrigatório** compulsory service. ~ **ocasional** char, odd job. ~ **pesado** heavy service. ~ **público** public service. ~ **religioso** divine service. ~ **salariado** work for wages. ~ **secreto** secret service. ~ **telefônico** telephone service. **apto para o** ~ fit for service. **a** ~ **de** at the service of. **dedicado ao** ~ on the job. **deixar o** ~ to give up, or leave the service. **estão a** ~ they are in waiting. **estão fora do** ~ they are out of service. **estar de** ~ to be on duty. **em** ~ in work. **em** ~ **ativo, emprego definitivo** in ordinary. **folha de** ~**s** service record. **mau** ~ bad job. **não brincar em** ~ not to let the grass grow under one's feet; to mind one's business. **oficial a** ~ officer in waiting. **o navio foi posto em** ~ the ship was put into commission. **o** ~ **está incluído?** is attendance included? **posto de** ~ (for cars) service station. **o Sr. prestou-me um grande** ~ you have rendered me a great service. **processo do** ~ working order. **que lindo** ~! what a fine job! **roupa de** ~ service-dress. **tempo de** ~ time, term of service.
servidão s. f. (pl. **-ões**) servitude: 1. slavery, vassalage, bondage. 2. service. 3. (jur.) easement, compulsory service. 4. public right of free passage over a ground of private property. 5. obligation.
servidiço adj. old, worn out.
servido adj. 1. served. 2. worn out, used.
como Deus é ~ **as** God wills. **está** ~ **almoçar conosco?** will you join us for lunch? **está** ~? are you served?, (fig.) may I offer you part of my lunch, repast, etc.? **o primeiro que chega é o melhor** ~ first come, first served. **o senhor é** ~? does it please you, sir? **se Deus for** ~ if it shall please God.
servidor s. m. servant: 1. server, attender, domestic. 2. official. ‖ adj. 1. attendant, serving. 2. punctual. 3. obsequious.
~ **de damas** beau, fop. ~**es do Estado** civil servants. ~ **público** public servant; civil servant.

serviente adj. m. + f. servient.
servil adj. m. + f. (pl. **-is**) 1. servile, obsequious, sequacious, slavish. 2. vile, obscene, disgraceful. ‖ ~**mente** adv. servilely, slavishly.
indivíduo ~ servile individual, minion.
servilha s. f. 1. a sort of boat for the catching of sardines. 2. a sort of light shoes of fine leather used in processions.
servilheiro s. m. fisher of sardines.
servilheta s. f. servant-maid, housemaid.
servilismo s. m. servility, servileness, obsequiousness, slavishness.
sérvio s. m. Serb, Serbian; natural or inhabitant of Serbia, Europe. ‖ adj. Serb, Serbian: of or referring to Serbia.
servir v. to serve: 1. labor as a servant. 2. perform the duties of a position. 3. wait, attend on. 4. benefit, help, assist. 5. be useful, serviceable. 6. spend time doing something. 7. furnish, supply. 8. render military service. 9. obey and worship God. 10. treat, act toward. 11. suit, be satisfactory, suitable. 12. suffice, avail. 13. put the ball into play at tennis. 14. ~**-se** a) to make use of. b) to help o. s. (at table). c) to avail o. s. of.
~ **a bola** to serve the ball, give service. ~ **a Deus** to serve or worship God. ~ **à mesa** to serve up a meal. ~ **à pátria** to serve one's country. ~ **ativamente no exército** to be in active service. ~ **café em copos** to serve coffee in glasses. ~ **de** to serve as. ~ **de criado** to be in service, be a servant. ~ **de guia** to guide. ~ **de lição** to serve as a lesson. ~ **de norma** to serve as guidance. ~ **de testemunha** to be an evidence, to come in as a witness. ~ **no exército** to serve in the army. ~ **o chá** to pour out tea. ~ **os amigos** to serve one's friends. ~ **para** 1. to serve for. 2. to lend itself or o. s. to. ~**-se da ocasião** to improve the opportunity, seize the opportunity. ~**-se de** to employ, make use of, avail o. s. of. ~**-se mal de uma coisa** to make an ill use of a thing. ~ **um freguês** to attend a customer. ~ **um ofício** to execute an office. ~ **vinho a** to serve wine. ~ **voluntariamente** to volunteer. **aquele serve** that one will do. **aquilo não me servia de nada** that has availed me nothing. **as crianças serviam-se de fruta** the children helped themselves to some fruit. **em que posso servi-lo?** what can I do for you? **estes sapatos não me servem** these shoes don't fit me. **ir** ~ to go out to service. **isso não serve** it won't do. **isto não serve para nada** this serves no purpose. **isto pode** ~**-lhe** this may be of some use to you. **isto serve bem** this answers very well. **já não me sirvo dele** I am not using it any more. **para que serve?** what is good for? **posso** ~**-me do telefone?** may I use your telephone? **permita-me que o sirva** allow me to serve you. **qualquer coisa serve** anything will do. **sirva-se** help yourself. **sirva-se de mais** please, have some more. **serve!** that will do! **serve da mesma maneira** it will do just as well. **terei prazer em servi-lo** I'll be glad to serve you.
servível adj. m. + f. (pl. **-eis**) serviceable.
servo s. m. 1. servant. 2. slave, drudge, vassal. 3. (hist.) serf, villain: a feudal labourer attached to an estate. ‖ adj. 1. in bondage. 2. in service.
~ **do senhor** your servant, sir.
sésamo s. m. 1. (bot.) sesame: Indian plant with oily seeds. 2. (fig.) a key to a mystery.
abre-te, ~ open, sesame.
sesamóideo adj. sesamoid: 1. (anat.) sesamoidal, designating small bones developed in tendons. 2. shaped like a sesame-seed.
sesgo adj. 1. sloping, oblique. 2. twisted.

sesma (ê) s. f. (also sesmo) 1. (ant.) sixth of any-thing. 2. old measure, about 8½ in.

sesmar *v. (ant.) to portion, divide lands by ses-marias.

sesmaria s. f. 1. allotment: plot of uncultivated land assigned to settlers by the Portuguese kings. 2. (Braz.) old agrarian measure, today still used in the South.

sesmeiro s. m. 1. (ant.) distributor of sesmarias. 2. allottee to whom was given a sesmaria.

sesmo (ê) s. m. (pl. sesmos) 1. uncultivated land divided for distribution. 2. (ant.) limit, partition. 3. = sesma.

sesquiáltera s. f. 1. (mus.) sesquialtera: an interval with the ratio of 3 to 2, a perfect fifth. 2. (math.) sesquialter ratio: denoting a ratio of 1½ to 1.

sesquicentenário s. m. (Braz.) sesquicentennial: the anniversary or celebration of an event that occurred 150 years before. ‖ adj. sesquicentennial.

sesquipedal adj. m. + f. (pl. -ais) sesquipedalian: 1. sesquipedal, measuring a foot and a half. 2. (hum.) excessively long (words or verses).

sessão (I) s. f. (pl. -ões) 1. session: a) sitting. b) assembly. c) the space for which an assembly sits. 2. (Braz.) each of the successive shows every day in a cinema or theatre.

abriu-se a ~ the chair is taken. em ~ secreta in secret session, (jur.) in camera. encerrar a ~, le-vantar a ~ to close the meeting. estar em ~ to be in session, to sit.

sessão (II) s. f. (Port.) earth-humidity.

sessar v. (Braz.) 1. to sift. 2. to winnow with a sieve.

sessenta s. m. sixty, threescore.

sessentão s. m. (pl. -ões) (f. -ona) sexagenarian. ‖ adj. sexagenarian.

séssil adj. m. + f. (pl. -eis) (bot.) sessile: attached by the base, having no stalk or peduncle (plate F 5).

sessilifloro adj. (bot.) sessile-flowered.

sessilifoliado adj. (bot.) sessile-leaved.

sesso (ê) s. m. (vulg.) buttocks, posteriors.

sesta s. f. siesta: 1. nap taken after lunch. 2. time of the afternoon's nap. 3. the hottest time of the day.

dormir a ~ to take a siesta or a nap after lunch.

escrever ~ por balhesta to be very much mistaken.

sesteada s. f. (S. Braz.) 1. act of taking the siesta. 2. place used by travellers and cattle drovers for the siesta.

sestear v. 1. to take an after lunch nap. 2. to shelter o. s. or the cattle from the heat of the day.

sesteiro s. m. (ant.) 1. measure of capacity of about 9 or 12 Imperial gallons. 2. weight of about 23 ounces.

sestércio s. m. sesterce, sestertius, a small Roman coin.

sestrar v. (Braz., sl.) to make passes in a corporal fight, called capoeira.

sestro s. m. 1. destiny, fate, fortune. 2. fault, bad custom, vice. 3. bad advice or counsel. ‖ adj. 1. left. 2. (fig.) sinister. 3. bad, dishonest.

~ agouro bad omen. deu-lhe o ~ de ir a Roma the fancy took him to go to Rome. tomar ~s to take odd decisions.

sestroso adj. 1. unruly, ill-natured, refractory. 2. ca-pricious, whimsical. 3. head-strong or jadish (horse). 4. (Braz., sl.) given to capoeiragem a typical Bra-zilian corporal fight.

set s. m. (Engl.) set: a group of three games in tennis.

seta s. f. 1. arrow, dart. 2. pointer, hand of a clock. 3. (bot.) arrowhead. 4. (astr.) Arrow, Sagitta: a constellation. 5. (Braz.) = estilingue.

~ de direção 1. arrow (of direction), guide-post. 2. (mot.) indicator arm, directional light (plate

V 3). ~ indicadora indication arrow. atirar com ~ to shoot arrows. ferido com ~ shot or wounded with an arrow.

setáceo adj. setaceous, bristly.

setada s. f. 1. hit or wound of an arrow. 2. arrowshot.

seta-de-amor s. f. (pl. setas-de-amor) a rutile crystal in hyaline quartz.

sete s. m. 1. the number seven. 2. card or dice bearing seven. ‖ adj. seven; seventh.

~ de copas seven of hearts (plate B 5). ~ de Setembro Brazilian Independence Day. a guerra dos ~ anos the Seven Years' War. as ~ maravilhas do mundo the seven wonders of the world. botas de ~ léguas seven league boots. os ~ pecados capi-tais the seven deadly sins. pintaram o ~ there were wild goings-on.

setear v. to wound with an arrow, dart.

sete-barbas s. m., sg. + pl. (Braz.) leather-fish.

sete-casacas s. m., sg. + pl. (Braz.) 1. plant of the family Leguminosae. 2. plant of the family Myr-taceae.

sete-cascos s. m., sg. + pl. (Braz.) plant of the family Monimiaceae.

setecentismo s. m. style, taste and school of the writers of the XVIII century.

setecentista s. m. + f. writer of the XVIII century. ‖ adj. referring to the XVIII century or to its writers.

setecentos adj. seven hundred.

sete-cores s. m., sg. + pl. (Braz., ornith.) the green-headed tanager.

sete-couros s. m., sg. + pl. (N. Braz.) a kind of tu-mour growing under the heels.

sete-e-meio s. m. (pl. sete-e-meios) a card game, similar to blackjack.

sete-em-porta s. m., sg. + pl. (S. Braz.) a card game with twenty one or more packs of cards.

sete-em-rama s. m., sg + pl. (bot.) tormentilla, cin-quefoil.

sete-estrelo s. m. (pop., astr.) the Pleiad, a constel-lation.

seteira s. f. embrasure, loophole, crenelle.

seteiro s. m. archer, bowman. ‖ adj. arrow shooting.

setembrizada s. f. (Braz.) military sedition in Per-nambuco in 1831.

setembro s. m. September, ninth month of the year.

setemesinho adj. born in the seventh month of preg-nancy (child).

setêmplice adj. m. + f. (poet.) sevenfold, septuple.

setena (I) s. f. (also setilha) strophe with seven verses.

setena (II) adj. f. septan: recurring on the seventh day (fever).

setenado adj. (bot.) septenate, heptaphylous, seven--leaved.

setenal adj. m. + f. (pl. -ais) septennial.

setenário s. m. septenary: 1. period of seven days or years. 2. a religious feast lasting seven days. ‖ adj. septenary, containing or having the value of seven.

setenato s. m. political power lasting seven years.

setênfluo adj. (poet.) running from seven fountains.

setenial adj. m. + f. (pl. -ais) septennial: lasting seven years.

setênio s. m. septennium: a period of seven years.

seteno s. m. the seventh day, the crisis day of certain diseases.

setenta adj. seventy, threescore and ten.

a casa dos ~ the seventies.

setentrião s. m. septentrion: 1. north. 2. North Pole. 3. north wind.

setentrional s. m. + f. (pl. -ais) a northern person. ‖ adj. northern, septentrional, from the north or from the North Pole.

setenvirado s. m. septemvirate: 1. office or rank of a septemvir. 2. assembly or tribunal of septemvirs.

setenviral adj. m. + f. (pl. **-ais**) of or referring to the septemvirs.

setênviro s. m. septemvir: one of the seven Roman priests or judges forming a festivities committee to supervise the feasts, celebrated in honor of the gods, or after public games.

sete-portas s. f., sg. + pl. (Braz., also **jataí**) a small black and yellow stingless bee.

sete-sangrias s. f., sg. + pl. (Braz.) sweetleaf, a medicinal plant.

sete-virtudes s. f., sg. + pl. (Braz., pop.) = **cachaça**.

setia s. f. mill-race, mill-leat, flume, chute, gutter.

setial s. m. (pl. **-ais**) 1. adorned pew. 2. footstool. 3. natural mound that can be used as a bench.

seticlávio s. m. group of the seven musical clefs.

seticole adj. m. + f. (poet.) having seven hills.

seticolor adj. m. + f. having seven colours.

seticorde adj. m. + f. having seven chords.

seticórneo adj. (zool.) having setiform or bristly antennae.

setífero adj. 1. setiferous. 2. setigerous, producing silk.

setiforme adj. m. + f. setiform, bristly.

setígero adj. 1. setiferous. 2. (bot.) setigerous.

setilha s. f. = **setena** (I).

setilhão, setilião s. m. (pl. **-ões**) septillion; in Brazil and Portugal the eighth power of one thousand.

sétima s. f. 1. (mus.) seventh, septime. 2. a run of seven cards all of one suit.

setimino s. m. septet.

sétimo s. m. seventh part. ‖ adj. seventh.

setingentésimo s. m. seven-hundredth part. ‖ adj. seven-hundredth.

setissílabo s. m. septisyllable: a verse of seven syllables. ‖ adj. septisyllabic: having seven syllables.

setíssono adj. having seven sounds.

setívoco adj. (poet.) having seven voices.

setor, sector s. m. sector: 1. a section of a fortification with an officer in charge. 2. astronomical instrument consisting of an arc of 20° to 30° and of an eyeglass. 3. (geom.) part of a circle included between two radii and an arc (plate A 9). 4. (math.) a rule consisting of two linked arms marked with sines, tangents, etc. 5. (Braz.) a branch of activity or a field of action.

setoura s. f. large scythe for mowing grass or wheat.

setrossos s. m. pl. linchpins, axlepins, forelocks in the axletrees of gun-carriages.

setuagenário s. m. septuagenarian. ‖ adj. septuagenary.

Setuagésima s. f. Septuagesima Sunday.

setuagésimo s. m. seventieth part. ‖ adj. seventieth.

setubalense s. m. + f. a native or inhabitant of Setúbal, Portugal. ‖ adj. (also **setubalão** m.) of or referring to Setúbal.

setuplicar v. 1. to septuple. 2. to multiply by seven. 3. (also **~-se**) to become seven times bigger.

sétuplo s. m. septuple. ‖ adj. septuple, sevenfold.

seu (I) s. m. that which is yours, his, hers, theirs. ‖ adj. (f. **sua**) his, her, your, their, thereof. ‖ pron. his, his own, hers, her own, yours, your own, theirs, their own.

ele levará a sua idéia avante he will insist upon his idea. **este livro é ~** this book is yours. **fazer das suas** to play foolish tricks. **ficar na sua** to stick to his point. **isso é ~?** is this yours? **o erro é ~** the error is yours. **os ~s** his relations, his people. **ter de ~** to be well-off. **um dos ~s amigos** a friend of hers.

seu (II) (pop.) a colloquial reduced form of **senhor**. **~ Paulo** Mr. Paulo.

seu-vizinho s. m. (pl. **seus-vizinhos**) (fam.) the ring finger.

seva (I) s. f. (Braz.) act of grating manioc roots.

seva (II) s. f. (Braz.) horizontal liana or rope for the drying of tobacco leaves.

sevadeira s. f. (Braz.) 1. wheel or machine for the grating of manioc roots. 2. woman who grates manioc roots.

sevador s. m. (Braz.) = **sevadeira**.

sevandija s. f. 1. vermin, parasite. 2. m. + f. (fig.) cringer, lickspittle, toady, sycophant, parasite.

sevandijar-se v. to cringe, lick someone's shoes, toady, fawn.

sevar v. (Braz.) to grate manioc roots.

severidade s. f. 1. severity, rigorousness. 2. rigidity, inflexibility of character.

severizar v. to turn severe.

severo adj. severe: 1. austere, grave, rigorous, harsh. 2. strict in dicipline, accurate, exact. 3. bitter, painful, distressing. 4. unadorned, simple but elegant. ‖ **-amente** adv. severely.

bancar o pai ~ (coll.) to do the heavy father. **criticar -amente alguém** to criticize s. o. severely. **tornar menos ~** to relent. **tratar -amente** to deal harshly. **um pai ~** a strict parent.

seviciador s. m. person who ill-treats. ‖ adj. who ill-treats.

seviciar v. to ill-treat, maltreat.

sevícias s. f. pl. (also **sevícia**) 1. ill-treatment, maltreatment. 2. inhumanity, beastly cruelty.

dar divórcio por ~ (jur.) to divorce for ill-treatment.

sevilhana s. f. 1. a big folding-knife with a curved blade. 2. (also **redondil**) a variety of olive. 3. popular song of Seville, Spain.

sevilhano s. m. (also **hispalense** m. + f.) Sevillian: native or inhabitant of Seville, Spain. ‖ adj. Sevillian: of or referring to Seville.

sevo adj. cruel, inhuman, severe, ferocious.

sexagenário s. m. (also **sessentão**) sexagenarian. ‖ adj. sexagenary. sexagesimal, sexagenarian.

divisão -a division into sixty parts.

sexagésima s. f. sexagesima: 1. the sixtieth part of a whole. 2. Sexagesima Sunday; the second Sunday before Lent.

sexagesimal adj. m. + f. (pl. **-ais**) sexagesimal, sixtieth.

sexagésimo s. m. the sixtieth part. ‖ adj. sixtieth, sexagesimal.

sexangular adj. m. + f. (also **sexangulado, sexângulo** m.) sexangular, sexangled, hexangular, hexagonal.

sex-appeal s. m. (Engl.) sex appeal: sex attraction.

sexcelular adj. m. + f. (bot.) sexlocular: having six cells.

sexcentésimo s. m. six hundredth part. ‖ adj. six hundredth.

sexdigital adj. m. + f. (pl. **-ais**) sexdigital, hexadactylous: having six toes or fingers (said of a limb).

sexdigitário s. m. sexdigitate (individual). ‖ adj. sexdigitate.

sexenal adj. m. + f. (pl. **-ais**) sexennial: 1. happening every six years. 2. occurring once in six years. 3. lasting six years.

sexênio s. m. sexennian: a period of six years.

sexífero adj. having sex.

sexo s. m. sex: 1. special conformation which distinguishes male and female. 2. the quality of being male or female. 3. (Braz.) the genitals.

~ feminino female sex. **~ forte** the stronger sex. **~ fraco** the weaker sex. **~ masculino** masculine sex. **ambos os ~s** man and woman. **belo ~** fair sex. **o ~ devoto** nuns collectively. **sem distinção de ~ ou idade** without distinction of sex or age:

o segundo ~ the second sex: women. **o terceiro** ~ the third sex: homosexuals.

sexologia s. f. sexology: the science dealing with human sexual behaviour.

sexta (I) s. f. (mus.) sixth (interval).

sexta (II) s. f. the third of the four parts of the day for the ancient Romans.

sexta (III) s. f. sext: one of the Canonical hours.

sexta-feira s. f. (pl. **sextas-feiras**) Friday; the sixth day of the week.

~ **Santa** Good Friday.

sextanista s. m. + f. a sixth-year student.

sextante s. m. sextant: 1. mathematical instrument for measuring angles. 2. the sixth part of a circle or an arc of 60°. 3. (astr.) a small northern constellation.

sextavado adj. sixangled, sexangular, hexagonal.

sextavar v. to cut six-sided.

sexteto s. m. (mus.) sextet, sextette.

sextil adj. m. + f. (pl. **-is**) (astr.) sextile: denoting the aspect of two planets when the angular distance between them is of 60°.

sextilha s. f. sextain: a stanza containing six verses.

sextilhão, sextilião adj. (pl. **-ões**) sextillion: in Brazil and Portugal the seventh power of one thousand.

sextina s. f. sestina: a poem consisting of six sextains and one tercet.

sexto s. m. sixth part. ‖ adj. sixth.

~ **centenário** sexcentenary. **no** ~ **ano** in the sixth year. **o** ~ **dia da semana** the sixth day of the week.

sêxtulo s. m. (pharm.) sextula: 1. weight of four scruples. 2. the sixth part of one ounce.

sêxtuor s. m. (mus.) sextet.

sêxtuplo s. m. (also **seisdobro**) sextuple. ‖ adj. sextuple, sixfold, six times.

sexual adj. m. + f. (pl. **-ais**) sexual: 1. of or referring to sex. 2. having sex. 3. what characterizes the sex. 4. (biol.) gamic. ‖ ~**mente** adv. sexually, sexy.

relações -ais sexual intercourse.

sexualidade s. f. sexuality.

sexualismo s. m. sexualism.

sexy adj. m. + f. sexy: exciting or intended to excite sexual desire.

sezão s. f. (pl. **-ões**) intermittent fever, malaria, paludism (more used in the plural).

sezeno s. m. (obs.) a kind of cloth of sixteen hundred threads of warp.

sezonático adj. malaria producing, malarial, infected with or affected by malaria.

shakespeariano adj. Shakespearean: of or referring to Shakespeare.

shopping center s. m. (Engl.) shopping center, shopping plaza.

short s. m. (Engl.) 1. shorts. 2. a short film.

show s. m. (Engl.) show: a presentation of entertainment.

si (I) s. m. (mus.) si, B, seventh note of the diatonic scale.

~ **bemol** B flat. ~ **maior** B major. ~ **menor** B minor. ~ **natural** B natural. ~ **sustenido** B sharp.

si (II) pron. himself, herself, itself, oneself, yourself, yourselves, themselves.

~ **mesma** herself, itself. ~ **mesmo** oneself, himself, itself. **dar por** ~ to regain one's senses. **dar sinal de** ~ to show signs of life. **de** ~ **mesmo** by himself. **ela não está à altura de** ~ **mesma** she is not quite herself. **ela olhou em volta de** ~ **she** looked around her. **ele voltou a** ~ he came to himself. **em** ~ **mesmo** in itself. **fora de** ~ besides himself, out of his wits. **para** ~ to himself. **por** ~ **só** of his own accord. **ser senhor de** ~ to be one's own man, depend upon nobody. **ter confiança em** ~ **próprio** to have self-confidence. **tomar sobre** ~ **um negócio**

to take upon one a business. **tornar em** ~ to come to one's self again. **uma ação que em** ~ **é indiferente** an action indifferent in itself.

si (III) adv. (ant.) yes.

siá s. f. (Braz.) = **sinhá**.

siagonagra s. f. (med.) articular rheumatism of the inferior maxilla.

sialagogo s. m. (med.) sialogogue: a medicine causing salivation. ‖ adj. salivant.

sialismo s. m., **sialorréia** f. (med.) salivation, sialorrhea: excessive flow of saliva.

siamês s. m. (pl. **-eses**) Siamese: native or inhabitant of Siam, Indochina. ‖ adj. Siamese: of or referring to Siam.

sianinha s. f. a lace edging in a zig-zag pattern.

siar v. to close (the wings) for a quicker descent.

siba s. f. (zool.) cuttle-fish: a mollusc of which the sepia ink is extracted.

sibarismo s. m. sybaritism.

sibarita s. m. + f. sybarite: voluptuary and effeminate person. ‖ adj. sybaritic(al).

sibarítico adj. sybaritic(al).

sibaritismo s. m. sybaritism.

siberiano s. m. Siberian: native or inhabitant of Siberia, Russia. ‖ adj. Siberian: of or referring to Siberia.

sibila s. f. sibyl: 1. a prophetess in ancient times. 2. (fam.) witch, old hag.

sibilação s. f. 1. sibilation, sibilance, hissing. 2. (med.) a sibilant rale in the respiratory organs.

sibilante adj. m. + f. sibilant, hissing, whistling. ‖ ~**mente** adv. whizzingly.

sibilar v. 1. to sibilate, hiss, whistle, zip. 2. to imitate the hissing of a serpent.

sibilino adj. sibylline: 1. relating to a sibyl. 2. (fig.) mysterious, enigmatic.

sibilo s. m. 1. sibilation, whistle, zip, whish. 2. imitation of the hissing of a serpent.

sibipira s. f. (Braz., bot.) = **sicupira**.

sibipiruna s. f. (Braz.) a tree of the family Leguminosae.

sica s. f. a dagger of the ancient Romans.

sicambro s. m. Sicambrian. individual of the Sicambry, an ancient Germanic race. ‖ adj. Sicambrian, of or referring to this race.

sicário s. m. 1. sicarian: a payed assassin. 2. criminal, malefactor.

sicatividade s. f. siccative quality.

sicativo s. m. siccative: a cicatrizant medicine. ‖ adj. siccative, drying.

siciliana s. f. (mus.) siciliana: a kind of Sicilian dance.

siciliano s. m. (also **sículo**) Sicilian: native or inhabitant of Sicily, Italy. ‖ adj. Sicilian: of or referring to Sicily.

sicite s. f. wine made of figs, used by the ancient.

siclo s. m. shekel: Jewish silver coin.

sico s. m. (also **bicho-de-pé**) the chigoe.

sicófago s. m. that lives on figs. ‖ adj. living on figs.

sicofanta s. m. + f. sycophant, slanderer, scoundrel, lickspittle.

sicofantismo s. m. sycophantism: character of a sycophant.

sicomancia s. f. sycomancy: divination by means of writing the question on a fig leaf.

sicomante s. m. + f. person performing sycomancy.

sicomântico adj. referring to the **sicomancia**.

sicômoro s. m. (bot.) sycamore: the false platan.

sicônio s. m. (bot.) syconium: a special infructescense, as in the figs.

sicose s. f. (med., also **mentagra**) sycosis: a pustular eruption on the scalp or bearded part of the face.

sicótico adj. referring to the sycosis.
sicrano s. m. such a one, Mr. so-and-so, indeterminate person.
sicupira s. f. (also sucupira) (Braz.) two trees of the family Leguminosae (Ormosia coccinea and Ormosia coarctata).
sicuri s. m. (N. Braz., ichth.) a kind of shark.
sideração s. f. (pl. -ões) sideration: 1. astrological influence upon life or health. 2. horoscope. 3. fulmination. 4. sudden destruction.
sideral adj. m. + f. (pl. -ais) (poet. also sidéreo) sideral, sidereal, astral, starry.
siderar v. 1. to fulminate. 2. to stupefy, astound, amaze.
sidérico adj. 1. = sideral. 2. ferric, ferrous, ferruginous.
siderismo s. m. siderism: star worship.
siderita (I) s. f. (bot.) sideritis, iron-wort, ground-pine.
siderita (II) s. f. (min.) siderite: sparry iron, rhombohedral iron-ore consisting of ferrous carbonate.
siderogáster adj. m. + f. (zool.) having a ferruginous abdomen.
siderografia s. f. siderography: the art of engraving on steel.
siderográfico s. f. siderographic(al).
siderógrafo s. m. siderographist.
siderolítico adj. designative of a special formation of the inferior Oligocene in the Jura region, in which the granulated iron minerals abound.
sideromancia s. f. sideromancy: supposed divination by means of throwing straws on red-hot iron and observing the burning and the smoke.
sideromante s. m. + f. sideromant.
sideromântico adj. sideromantic.
sideroscópio s. m. sideroscope: instrument for detecting the influence of magnets upon bodies.
siderose s. f. 1. (min.) siderite: sparry iron-ore. 2. (med.) siderosis: deposition of iron in an organ.
sideróstato s. m. siderostat, astronomical instrument for measuring star light.
siderotecnia s. f. siderotechny: metallurgy of iron.
siderotécnico adj. belonging to the metallurgy of iron.
siderurgia s. f. 1. siderurgy: metallurgy of iron. 2. ironworks.
proprietário de ~ iron master.
siderúrgico adj. (also siderotécnico) siderurgic(al): belonging to the metallurgy of iron.
sidônio s. m. Sidonian: native or inhabitant of Sidon, ancient Phoenicia. ‖ adj. Sidonian: of or referring to Sidon.
sidra s. f. cider, apple-wine.
siemens s. m. (electr.) mho: the unit of electrical conductance.
sienito s. m. (min.) syenite: a granular igneous rock.
sifão s. m. (pl. -ões) siphon, syphon: 1. a curved tube having two unequal branches used for conveying liquids over the edge of a vessel through the force of atmospheric pressure. 2. siphon-trap, S-trap (plate E 3). 3. siphon-bottle. 4. (zool.) a suctorial organ.
sifilicômio s. m. a hospital or dispensary for the treatment of syphilis.
sifilide s. f. (med.) syphilide: syphilitic manifestation on the skin or mucous membranes.
sífilis s. f. (med.) syphilis, lues: an infectious venereal disease produced by a micro-organism.
sifilítico s. m. (med.) syphilitic, luetic. ‖ adj. syphilitic, syphilous, luetic.
sifilização s. f. syphilization.
sifilizar v. to syphilize.
sifilografia s. f. (also sifiligrafia) (med.) syphilography.
sifilográfico adj. (also sifiligráfico) (med.) syphilographic(al).

sifilógrafo s. m. (also sifilígrafo) (med.) a specialist in syphilography.
sifiloma s. m. (med.) syphiloma: a syphilitic tumour.
sifonápteros s. m. pl. (zool.) Siphonaptera: an order of bloodsucking insects (the fleas).
sifonóforo s. m. (zool.) a siphonophore.
sifonóide adj. m. + f. siphoniform, siphon-shaped.
sifonóstomo s. m. siphonostome: a siphonostomatous fish. ‖ adj. (zool.) siphonostomatous: having a siphoniform mouth.
sigilação s. f. (pl. -ões) the act of sealing.
sigilar (I) adj. m. + f. sigillary.
sigilar (II) v. to sigillate, seal, stamp.
sigilária s. f. sigillaria: a fossil plant.
sigilismo s. m. religious schism manifested in Portugal, in the XVIII century, and whose great error was the violation of the secrecy of the confessional.
sigilista s. m. + f. a sectarian of the sigilismo.
sigilo s. m. 1. seal, signet, sigil, secret. 2. (ant.) stamp.
~ da confissão secrecy due to confession. deve ser observado ~ absoluto strict secrecy must be observed.
sigilografia s. f. sigillography: the study of stamps.
sigla s. f. 1. abbreviature. 2. old medal or monument. 3. monogram.
sigma s. m. sigma: letter of the Greek alphabet.
sigmático adj. sigmatic.
sigmatismo s. m. sigmatism.
sigmóide adj. m. + f. sigmoid(al).
sigmoidite s. f. (med.) sigmoiditis: inflammation of a part of the colon.
signa s. f. (also sina) flag, banner, standard.
signatário s. m. signatory, undersigned, signer. ‖ adj. signatory.
potência -a signatory power.
significação s. f. (pl. -ões), significado m. signification, significance, meaning, sense.
~ secundária secondary meaning. ~ subentendida sub-audition. falta de ~ unmeaningness.
significador s. m. signifier: one who signifies. ‖ adj. signifying, significative, expressive.
significante adj. m. + f. significant, significative, senseful.
significar v. 1. to signify, mean, denote. 2. to imply, hint. 3. to participate, tell, express, show.
isto não significa muito it does not amount to much. o que acha que significa este desenho? what does the drawing suggest to you? que significa isto? what is the meaning of this?
significativo adj. significative, significant, expressive. ‖ -amente adv. significantly.
isto é bem ~ that is saying a great deal. olhares ~s telltale looks.
signo s. m. sign: 1. (astr.) one of the twelve divisions of the Zodiac. 2. (astr.) constellation corresponding to each one of the twelve signs of the Zodiac. 3. (mus.) a note.
signo-salomão s. m. pl. signos-salomão) (also signo-de-salomão, signo-saimão, signo-salmão) Solomon's seal: 1. a talisman or amulet in the shape of a six-pointed star. 2. (bot.) lily of the mountain, white root.
sílaba s. f. syllable.
dividir em ~s to syllabify.
silabação s. f. syllabication, syllabification.
silabada s. f. mistake in the pronunciation or in the accent of a word.
silabar v. to syllable, syllabicate, syllabize, spell.
silabário s. m. syllabary: first reading-book.
silábico adj. syllabic. ‖ silabicamente adv. syllabically.

silabismo s. m. syllabism.
sílabo s. m. (R. C. Church) syllabus: summary of propositions condemned as erroneous by the pope.
silagem s. f. (also **ensilagem**) (pl. -ens) ensilage: 1. process of preserving fodder in a silo. 2. silage: the fodder thus preserved.
silenciador s. m. silencer: 1. a device for deadening the sound of a gun. 2. a muffler for an internal combustion engine. ‖ adj. silencing.
silenciar v. to silence: 1. reduce to silence, hush. 2. omit. 3. be silent, keep silent, not to speak.
silenciário s. m. 1. (hist.) silentiary: a dignitary at the Byzantine court (who had to maintain silence and order). 2. (eccl.) member of certain religious orders who are obliged to absolute silence.
silêncio s. m. silence: 1. silentness, stillness. 2. calm, quiet. 3. noiselessness. 4. voicelessness. 5. uncommunicativeness. 6. dumbness. 7. (fig.) secrecy. 8. hush. 9. muteness. ‖ interj. silence!, mum!, whist! **~!, cale-se!** silence!, hold your tongue! **~ de morte** dead silence. **o ~ da noite** the dead time of the night. **o ~ vale ouro** silence is golden. **passar em ~** to pass over in silence. **pôr ~** to command silence. **romper o ~** to break silence.
silencioso s. m. 1. a taciturn person. 2. (mot.) silencer, muffler. 3. any silencing device. ‖ adj. silent: 1. speechless. 2. still, quiet. 3. noiseless, soundless. 4. dumb, mute. 5. uncommunicative, tacit. 6. voiceless, mousy, mum. ‖ -amente adv. silently.
silente adj. m. + f. (poet.) silent.
silepse s. f. 1. (gram.) syllepsis. 2. (rhet.) use of a word in metaphorical and literal sense at the same time. 3. (philos.) reflex knowledge, thought directed back upon the mind by introspection.
siléptico adj. sylleptic(al). ‖ **silepticamente** adv. sylleptically.
silesiano s. m. Silesian: native or inhabitant of Silesia (Germany). ‖ adj. Silesian: of, pertaining to or relative to Silesia.
sílex s. m. (min.) silex, silica, flint.
~ córneo (petrog.) chert, whin.
sílfide s. f. 1. (myth.) sylph, sylphid. 2. (fig., poet.) a delicate, graceful woman. 3. (poet.) a fleeting image.
silfídico adj. sylph-like, sylphidine, sylphish.
silfo s. m. (myth.) sylph, gnome, hobgoblin, elf.
silha s. f. 1. a square stone on which beehives are placed. 2. a row of beehives. 3. (obs.) chair.
silhal s. m. (pl. -ais) 1. one or several rows of beehives. 2. a great number of beehives. 3. a place where groups of beehives are kept, apiary.
silhão s. m. (pl. -ões) 1. (fort.) sillon: defensive work in the middle of a wide ditch around a castle or fortress. 2. side-saddle. 3. augm. of **silha.**
silhar s. m. 1. (archit.) ashlar, ashler. 2. a square stone used for facing. 3. bottom stone of a beehive.
silharia s. f. mason's work, construction in which square stones are employed for building or facing.
silhueta s. f. 1. silhouette, profile, outline (of a face or figure). 2. sky-line. 3. umbrage.
silhuetagem s. f. (phot.) subduing or even effacing the background of a photograph for accentuating the face.
sílica s. f. (min.) silica, silex, silicon dioxide.
silicato s. m. (chem.) silicate.
~ de alumínio aluminium silicate. **~ de magnésio** magnesium silicate. **~ de sódio** sodium silicate.
silícico adj. (chem.) silicic, siliceous.
silicícola adj. m. + f. silicicolous: growing in siliceous soil (plants).
silicífero adj. siliciferous, producing silica.

silicificação, silificação s. f. silicification.
silicificar, silificar v. to silicify, silicize.
silício s. m. (chem.) silicium, silicon (symbol Si).
silicioso adj. siliceous, flinty.
silicose s. f. (med.) silicosis: occupational lung disease caused by the inhalation of stone dust.
sililuia s. f. (pop.) halleluia.
silimanita s. f. (min.) fibrolite, aluminium silicate.
silindra s. f. a herb of the family Saxifragaceae (Philadelphus coronarius).
síliqua s. f. (bot.) silique.
siliqüiforme adj. m. + f. (bot.) siliquiform.
siliquoso adj. (bot.) siliquous, siliquose.
silo s. m. silo, pit for corn, garner (plate S 1).
~ de trigo granary. **~ para armazenagem de cereais** silo, grain elevator: building for storing grains.
silogeu s. m. (Braz.) a meeting place for literary and/or scientific associations.
silogismo s. m. (logic, logistic) syllogism.
silogístico adj. (logic) syllogistic(al).
silogizar v. to syllogize, deduce by means of a syllogism, employ syllogisms.
siluriano s. m. (geol.) Silurian: the Silurian period or system. ‖ adj. Silurian.
silurídeo s. m. (ichth.) a silurid, a catfish of the family Siluridae. ‖ adj. silurid.
siluro (I) s. m. (ichth.) sheatfish.
siluro (II) s. m. Siluridan: a member of a pre-Celtic race which formerly inhabited the southern parts of Britain.
silva s. f. 1. (bot.) blackberry, bramble. 2. (poet.) poetical composition in which a verse of ten metrical feet is followed by a six-foot blank verse. 3. a literary or scientific miscellany. 4. girdle made of wire, worn on the skin as a penance. 5. (mil.) gold lace, silver lace, galloon on the cuff or collar of a uniform. 6. an elongated blotch close about the nostrils of a horse.
silvado s. m. (also **silvedo**) 1. a blackberry thicket, bramble thicket. 2. a hedge made of blackberry bushes or brambles.
silva-macha s. f. (pl. **silvas-machas**) (bot.) dog-rose.
silvano s. m. 1. (Roman myth.) sylvan deity, sylvan spirit. 2. forest people, rustic. 3. yokel, boor. ‖ adj. sylvan.
silvão s. m. (pl. -ões) (bot.) dog-rose, dog briar.
silvar v. 1. to whistle, blow a whistle. 2. to sibilate, hiss. 3. to breathe in, inhale. 4. to pipe, whiz(z).
silvático adj. wild, savage.
silveira s. f. 1. (bot.) blackberry, bramble. 2. a blackberry thicket. 3. briar patch. 4. (Braz.) a dish made of chopped meat.
silvestre adj. m. + f. 1. silvan, sylvan, sylvestral. 2. savage, wild. 3. barren. 4. woodsy. 5. dwelling or living in the woods. 6. unsown.
silviano adj. (anat.) of, pertaining to or relative to the Sylvian suture.
silvícola s. m. + f. savage, barbarian, aborigine. ‖ adj. living in the woods, silvicolous.
silvicultor s. m. 1. silviculturist. 2. forester.
silvicultura s. f. 1. silviculture, sylviculture. 2. cultivation of forest trees. 3. forestation.
silvo s. m. 1. whistle, whistling. 2. hiss, whizz. 3. a shrill sound. 4. a hissing or rattling sound produced by serpents. 5. swish. 6. ping.
silvoso adj. 1. full of brambles or briars. 2. enclosed by brambles or other bushes, hedged in.
sim s. m. 1. act of expressing consent, acquiescence, approval. 2. an affirmative reply. 3. a yes; yea. ‖ adv. 1. yes; yea, aye. 2. all right. 3. absolutely. 4. exactly. ‖ interj. naturally!, of course!, rather! **~, senhor (senhora)!** yes, Sir (Madam)! **creio que ~** I believe so. **ele deu o ~** he said yes, he con-

sented. **ele não disse nem** ~, **nem não** he said neither yes nor no. **pelo** ~, **pelo não** in view of the doubt. **penso que** ~ I think so. **sem dúvida penso que** ~ I should think so. **um dia** ~, **um dia não** every other day.

simão s. m. (pl. **-ões**) 1. (pop., sl.) monkey, ape. 2. (fishermen's sl.) a strong cold southwind.

simaruba s. f. Simarouba; a genus of tropical trees of the family Simaroubaceae.

simarubáceas s. f. pl. Simaroubaceae: a family of tropical trees or shrubs.

simarubáceo adj. (bot.) simaroubaceous.

simbaíba s. f. a plant of the family Caryophyllaceae (Dadiva Iixa).

simbionte s. m. (biol.) symbiont, symbion.

simbiose s. f. (biol.) 1. symbiosis: association of heterogeneous organisms dependent on each other for existence. 2. parasitism. 3. (ant.) common life.

simbiota s. m. (biol.) symbiote, symbiont.

simbiótico adj. (biol.) symbiotic(al). || **simbioticamente** adv. symbiotically.

simbléfaro s. m. (med., surg.) symblepharon.

simbólica s. f. 1: symbolic: a) (theol.) the symbolic manifestations of a certain creed or religion. b) symbology: the science of symbols. 2. symbolicalness.

simbólico adj. 1. symbolic(al). 2. allegoric(al), figurative, emblematical. 3. (theol.) of or relative to the symbolical manifestations of religious faith. 4. typic(al). 5. hieroglyphic. || **simbolicamente** adv. symbolically, emblematically, figuratively.

simbolismo s. m. symbolism: 1. representation by means of symbols. 2. (poet.) allegoric poetry (at the end of the XIX century). 3. (arts) artistic allegorization of nature or life. 4. (theol.) symbolics.

simbolista s. m. + f. symbolist: 1. one who uses symbols. 2. one skilled in the interpretation of symbols. 3. follower of symbolism. || adj. symbolist, symbolistic(al).

simbolístico adj. symbolistic(al).

simbolização s. f. (pl. **-ões**) symbolization, typification, representation.

simbolizado adj. symbolized, figured.

simbolizador s. m. symbolizer, symbolist. || adj. symbolizing.

simbolizar v. 1. to symbolize, symbol. 2. to represent by symbols. 3. to typify, type. 4. to emblematize. 5. to figure, represent. 6. to denote. 7. to speak or write symbolically. 8. to summarize, epitomize. 9. to image.

símbolo s. m. 1. symbol. 2. token, sign (plate X). 3. figure, image. 4. mark, note. 5. emblem, badge. 6. (rel.) visible sign of a sacrament, symbolism of a creed. 7. (shorthand) sigla. 8. (numismatics) coiner's mark, mint mark. 9. (psych.) the manifestation of an unconscious thought or desire. 10. standard. 11. slogan.

a cruz, ~ **da religião cristã** the cross, symbol of the Christian religion. **um coração como** ~ **de amor** a heart as a type of love. **usar** ~**s** to symbolize, represent by symbols.

simbologia, simbolologia s. f. symbology.

simbológico, simbolológico adj. symbological.

simetria s. f. 1. symmetry. 2. harmoniousness, harmony. 3. proportion. 4. regularity.

~ **bilateral** (geom.) bilateral symmetry.

simétrico adj. 1. symmetric(al). 2. harmonious. 3. formal. || **simetricamente** adv. symmetrically.

simetrizar v. to symmetrize, make symmetrical, have symmetry.

simianismo s. m. 1. (philos.) a philosophical doctrine which maintains that the human race descends from apes. 2. monkeyshines, mimicry.

simiano adj. apish, monkeyish.

simiesco adj. 1. simian, apelike. 2. apish, monkeyish. 3. simian, simial. || **-amente** adv. apishly.

símil adj. m. + f. (pl. **símeis**; abs. sup. **similimo**) (poet.) similar, like, analogous.

similar s. m. a similar, a similar person or object. || adj. m. + f. 1. homogeneous. 2. similar, having a general likeness, alike. 3. uniform. 4. approximate. 5. semblable, semblant. 6. akin.

ele não encontra ~ he doesn't find his parallel.

similaridade s. f. 1. similarity. 2. likeness, resemblance. 3. kinship. 4. parallelism, correspondence. 5. alliance.

falta de ~ inconformity.

simile s. m. 1. simile. 2. a similar. 3. analogy. 4. comparison of similar things. || adj. m. + f. similar.

similifloro adj. (bot.) having all flowers alike.

similitude s. f. 1. similitude. 2. similarity, resemblance. 3. likeness, semblance. 4. approach. 5. analogy.

similitudinário adj. similitudinary.

símio s. m. simian, monkey, ape. || adj. simian, simioid, simious, apish, monkeyish.

~ **antropóide** anthropoid, anthropoid ape.

simira s. f. (bot.) plant of the family Rubiaceae (Psichotria simira).

simongoiá s. m. (zool.) a mollusc of the family Mactridae (Mesodesma mactroides).

simonia s. f. simony, barratry, illegal traffic with church property, preferments or benefices, illegal sale of holy things.

simoníaco s. m. simoniac: one who committed the crime of simony. || adj. simoniacal, simonious.

simonte s. m. snuff made of the best leaf. || adj. designating snuff of the best quality.

simpatia s. f. 1. sympathy. 2. affinity, relationship between human beings, organisms or living matter. 3. congeniality, compatibility. 4. appeal, winsomeness. 5. affection, liking (for), fancy (for). 6. appreciation, admiration. 7. attachment. 8. feeling, fellow-feeling.

causar ~ to arouse the liking or appreciation of, appeal to. **chorei de** ~ I wept for company. **com** ~ sympathetically. **ele não goza de** ~ **com seus colegas** he has no appeal for his colleagues. **gozar da** ~ **de seus amigos** to be in favour with one's friends. **sentir** ~ **por** to have an affection for. **tenho** ~ **por ela** I feel sympathy for her. **ter** ~ to sympathize.

simpático adj. 1. sympathetic(al). 2. winsome, appealing. 3. engaging, attractive, charming. 4. warm-hearted. 5. (biol.) autonomous. || **simpaticamente** adv. sympathetically.

nervo ~ (anat., med.) sympathetic nerve.

simpatista s. m. + f. sympathist: believer in sympathism.

simpatizante s. m. + f. 1. sympathizer. 2. follower, supporter, adherent. 3. friend. || adj. sympathetic(al), sympathizing, kindly inclined towards.

~ **dum partido político** sympathizer of a political party, camp-follower, fellow-traveller.

simpatizar v. 1. to sympathize, feel an affection for. 2. to take a liking to. 3. to feel inclined towards.

~ **com** to feel with, commiserate, condole.

simpetálico adj. (bot.) sympetalous.

simpétalo adj. (bot.) gamopetalous.

simplacheirão s. m. (pl. **-ões**) simpleton, fool, dolt. || adj. very simple, foolish, stupid.

simplão s. m. (pl. **-ões**) (student's sl.) formerly a school grade or ranking corresponding to: fair or satisfactory.

simpléctico, simplético s. m. (anat., zool.) symplectic: the symplectic bone. || adj. symplectic.

simples (I) s. m. + f., sg. + pl. (also pl. **símplices**) 1. a simpleton, an ignorant person. 2. a humble, modest or unassuming person. ‖ adj. 1. simple: a) uncompounded, uncombined. b) unadorned, plain. c) (fig.) easy to be understood, facile, uncomplicated. d) evident, clear. e) natural, unaffected, inartificial. f) ordinary, vulgar. g) ingenuous, naive, innocent. h) unsophisticated, simple-hearted. i) unpretending. j) ignorant, stupid, silly. k) unartful, artless. l) (bot.) without branches or subdivisions; having a single carpel (plate F 5). 2. single. 3. unmixed, pure. 4. exclusive. 5. unique, singular. 6. (gram.) conjugated without auxiliary verb. 7. (chem.) elementary. 8. frank, open. ‖ ~**mente** adv. 1. simply, plainly. 2. artlessly, unaffectedly. 3. chastely. **de efeito** ~ (tech.) single-acting. **ele agiu em virtude duma** ~ **suspeita** he acted on a bare suspicion. **fratura** ~ (med.) simple fracture. **fração** ~ (math.) simple fraction. **foi** ~**mente maravilhoso** it was nothing short of marvellous. **juros** ~ simple interest. **meu lenço sumiu** ~**mente** my handkerchief has clean gone. **nó** ~ slip-knot. **o calor foi** ~**mente horrível** the heat was something frightful. **vestidinho** ~ a wispish dress.

simples (II) s. m. pl. (archit.) centre mould for the construction of an arch.

simplesmente s. m. formerly a school grade or ranking corresponding to: fair or satisfactory. ‖ adv. simply.

simpleza s. f. simplicity.

símplice adj. m. + f. = **simples** (I).

símplices s. m. pl. 1. (pharm.) simples, medicinal plants. 2. (pharm.) each of the ingredients which make up a remedy. 3. the component parts of inks or paints. 4. the constituent elements of any body.

simplicidade s. f. 1. simplicity. 2. naturalness. 3. naïveness, innocence, ingenuousness. 4. facility. 5. chastity, chasteness. 6. artlessness, unaffectedness. 7. silliness. 8. plainness of thought, expression or style. 9. simple-mindedness. 10. singleness. 11. sincerity. 12. unsophisticatedness, unsophistication. 13. homeliness. 14. credulity. 15. rudeness. 16. modesty, humbleness. 17. purity.

simplicíssimo adj. abs. sup. of **simples** very simple.

simplicista s. m. + f. 1. a herb doctor. 2. person skilled in simples and their application. 3. one who writes a treatise on medicinal herbs.

simplificação s. f. (pl. -**ões**) simplification, facilitation.

simplificado adj. simplified.

simplificador s. m. simplifier: one who or that which simplifies. ‖ adj. simplifying.

simplificar v. 1. to simplify, make simple or simpler. 2. to facilitate, make easier or less complex. 3. to clarify. 4. to elucidate, explain. 5. (math.) to reduce a fraction to its lowest terms. 6. (Braz.) to apply the mark "fair" or "satisfactory" to a pupil's schoolwork.

simplismo s. m. 1. simplism. 2. faulty reasoning (which does not take into consideration all the elements necessary for the solution). 3. oversimplification.

simplista s. m. + f. simplicist, simplist: one who practises simplism. ‖ adj. simplicistic(al).

simploce s. f. (rhet.) symploce.

simplório s. m. 1. simpleton. 2. silly or stupid fellow. 3. dullard. 4. greenhorn. 5. dupe. 6. nincompoop. ‖ adj. simple-minded, silly, stupid, half-witted, zany.

simpósio s. m. 1. symposium. 2. banquet, feast.

simptose s. f. (path.) 1. symptosis. 2. weakness, debility. 3. thinness, leanness.

sim-senhor s. m. (pl. **sim-senhores**) a bird of the family Cotingidae (Lipaugus vociferans).

simulação s. f. (pl. -**ões**) 1. simulation. 2. act of simulating, pretense. 3. disguise, masquerade. 4. elusiveness. 5. sham, feint. 6. camouflage. 7. affectation.

simulacro s. m. 1. simulacrum. 2. an image, effigy. 3. imitation. 4. appearance, semblance. 5. make-believe. 6. imperfect reproduction or copy. 7. sham. 8. dummy. 9. a spectre, spook. 10. mimicry.

simulado adj. 1. simulate. 2. sham, mock. 3. false. 4. assumed, affected. 5. feigned. 6. indirect. 7. artful. ‖ -**amente** adv. artfully, feignedly, affectedly. **combate** ~ sham fight. **janela -a** false window.

simulador s. m. 1. simulator. 2. imitator, faker. 3. pretender. 4. palterer, swindler. 5. camouflager. 6. make-believer. ‖ adj. simulating.

simular v. 1. to simulate. 2. to feign, dissemble. 3. to palter. 4. to sham. 5. to camouflage. 6. to imitate. 7. to counterfeit. 8. to assume, pretend, affect. 9. to act, personate. 10. to profess. **ela simulou inocência** she assumed innocence. **ela simulou surpresa** she affected surprise. **ele simulou doença** he pretended illness, (naut. sl.) he swung the lead. ~**am arrependimento** they professed remorse. ~ **um ataque** (mil.) to feint.

simulatório adj. simulatory.

simulcadência s. f. (rhet.) termination of a sentence or phrase with words of the same cadence.

simulcadente adj. m. + f. (rhet.) having the same cadence.

simulídeos s. m. pl. (ent.) Simuliidae: the blackfly family.

simultaneidade s. f. 1. simultaneity, simultaneousness. 2. synchronism. 3. coincidence.

simultâneo adj. 1. simultaneous, happening at the same time. 2. synchronous, synchronistic(al). 3. concurrent, concomitant. 4. coinstantaneous, coincidental. ‖ **simultaneamente** adv. simultaneously, concomitantly, all at once, together.

simum s. m. (pl. -**ns**) simoom: a dusty hot desert wind (N. Africa).

sina s. f. 1. ensign, flag, banner. 2. (fam.) lot, fate, fortune. 3. portion, share. 4. destiny.

sinagelástico adj. (zool.) living in groups or flocks.

sinagoga s. f. 1. synagogue, Jewish temple. 2. Jewish congregation, assembly of Hebraic worshippers. 3. (pop.) noise, uproar, clamour. 4. (pop.) disorder, tumult. 5. (sl.) head.

sinal s. m. (pl. -**ais**) 1. signal. 2. sign. 3. mark, indication. 4. signature. 5. (railways) semaphore, signal (plate E 12). 6. outward manifestation. 7. evidence, vestige. 8. gesture. 9. mole on the skin. 10. beauty spot. 11. birthmark. 12. (com.) earnest money. 13. omen, portent, presage. 14. badge. 15. seal. 16. symptom. 17. wonder, miracle. 18. (naut.) waft, signal of distress. 19. cipher. 20. summons. 21. note, notice. 22. scar. 23. stigma. 24. denotement, denotation. 25. prognostication. 26. print, impress, impression. 27. trace.
~ **de advertência** warning, beacon. ~ **de corneta** tucket. ~ **de crescendo** (mus.) swell. ~ **de exame ou de controle** check. ~ **de intercalação** caret. ~ **de intervalo** time signal. ~ **de manobra** (railway) marshalling signal (plate E 12). ~ **de partida** start signal, (naut.) Blue Peter (flag). ~ **de perigo** danger-signal, warning, alarm, (naut.) red flag, waft. ~ **de referência** (typogr.) dagger, double dagger. ~ **de respeito** tribute of respect. ~ **de tráfego** traffic sign (plate E 14). ~ **luminoso de trânsito**, ~ **semafórico** traffic light, blinker, (U. S. A., coll.) flash (plate R 8). ~ **milagroso** wonder-sign. ~ **por conta** retaining fee. ~ **telefônico** call.

cabina de controle de -ais (railway) signal-box. **cavalete de -ais** (railway) signal gantry. **dar ~ de partida** (sports) to drop the flag. **deram ~ de alarma** they sounded the alarm. **ele deu o ~** (sports) he called time. **ele fez o ~-da-cruz** he made the sign of the cross. **em ~ de** in token of. **fazer ~ com a mão** to beckon, wave. **fazer o ~-da-cruz sobre** to cross, bless. **tomaram-no por mau ~** they looked upon it as a bad sign.

sinalagmático adj. (jur.) of, pertaining to or relative to a bilateral contract.

sinalar v. 1. to signalize. 2. to mark, set a mark on. 3. to designate. 4. to choose as a type or standard. 5. to mention, point out. 6. **~-se** to become manifest.

sinal-da-cruz s. m. (pl. **sinais-da-cruz**) act of crossing o. s.

sinalefa s. f. 1. (gram.) synaloepha, synalepha: the blending of two vowels into one, the contraction of syllables. 2. (bookbinding) gilding tool, pallet.

sinaleiro s. m. 1. signalman, flagman, signaller. 2. traffic policeman. 3. (railway) semaphorist. **corpo de ~s** signal corps.

sinalização s. f. (pl. **-ões**) 1. act or result of signalizing. 2. traffic signs or signals. 3. system and principles of signalling. **aparelho de ~** signalling device. **fio de ~** signalling wire. **poste de ~** signal post.

sinalizar v. 1. to work as signalman or semaphorist. 2. to signal, signalize. 3. to telegraph. 4. to mark. 5. to equip with signs or signals.

sinantéreo adj. (bot.) synantherous.

sinantia s. f. synanthy: abnormal coalescence of separate flowers.

sinantocarpado adj. (bot.) synanthocarpous.

sinápico adj. (chem.) sinapic, sinapine.

sinapismo s. m. (med.) mustard plaster, sinapism.

sinapizar v. to sinapize, flavour with mustard.

sinartrose s. f. (anat.) synarthrosis.

sina-sina s. f. (pl. **sina-sinas**) a tree of the family Leguminosae (Parkinsonia aculeta).

sincarpado adj. (bot.) syncarpous.

sincárpio s. m. (bot.) syncarp.

sinceiral s. m. (pl. **-ais**) a plantation of willows.

sinceiro s. m. (bot.) willow.

sincelo s. m. icicle.

sinceridade s. f. 1. sincerity, sincereness. 2. frankness, openness, open-heartedness. 3. fairness of character. 4. simplicity, simple-mindedness. 5. cordiality, heartiness. 6. true-heartedness. 7. faith, faithfulness. 8. seriousness, integrity. 9. candour. 10. purity. 11. unaffectedness, unfeignedness. 12. single-mindedness. 13. whole-heartedness.

sincero adj. 1. sincere. 2. frank, open, free-spoken. 3. honest, true, truthful. 4. simple, guileless, unfeigned, unaffected. 5. explicit, direct. 6. cordial, hearty, heartfelt. 7. devout, faithful. 8. candid. 9. serious, righteous. 10. single-minded. 11. plain, plain-spoken, outspoken. 12. amicable, friendly. ‖ **-amente** adv. 1. sincerely. 2. frankly, freely. 3. fairly. 4. honestly, faithfully. 5. artlessly, unaffectedly, ingenuously. 6. seriously, earnestly. **necessito de seu conselho ~** I want your candid advice.

sincipital adj. m. + f. (pl. **-ais**) (anat.) sincipital: of, to or relative to the sinciput.

sincipúcio s. m. (anat.) sinciput.

sinclinal adj. m. + f. (pl. **-ais**) (geol.) synclinal.

sínclise s. f. (gram.) the intercalation of a pronoun in a word (e. g. **referir-se-á**).

sinclítica s. f. (gram.) the word intercalated in another one.

sinclítico adj. (gram.) of or relative to or designating an interpolated pronoun.

sinclitismo s. m. (gram.) 1. the intercalation of a word in another one. 2. the grammatical rules which govern the intercalation of pronouns in other words.

sincondrose s. f. (anat.) synchondrosis.

sincondrotomia s. f. (med., surg.) synchondrotomy, symphyseotomy.

sincondrotômico adj. (med.) synchondrotomic(al).

síncopa s. f. (mus.) syncopation, syncope.

sincopado adj. (mus.) syncopated.

sincopal adj. m. + f. (pl. **-ais**) syncopal, syncopic.

sincopar v. (gram., mus.) to syncopate, syncopize.

síncope s. f. syncope: 1. (med.) temporary loss of consciousness, fainting fit, swooning. 2. (gram.) the elision of one or more letters from the middle of a word. 3. (mus.) musical syncopation.

sincotilédone adj. m. + f. (bot.) syncotyledonous.

sincotiledôneo adj. (bot.) syncotyledonous: having the cotyledons united.

sincraniano adj. (anat., zool.) syncraniate.

sincrético adj. syncretic(al), syncretistic(al), ecletic.

sincretismo s. m. syncretism: the blending of antagonistic religious or philosophical systems into one, ecletism.

sincretista s. m. + f. syncretic, syncretist, promoter or defender of syncretism. ‖ adj. syncretistic(al).

síncrise s. f. 1. syncrisis. 2. opposition, contrariness. 3. antithesis. 4. the formation of a diphthong by reunion of two vowels. 5. (chem.) coagulation of heterogenous mixtures (liquids).

sincrítico adj. 1. of, pertaining to or relative to syncrisis. 2. (med.) astringent.

sincronia s. f. (also phon.) synchrony.

sincrônico adj. 1. synchronous, synchronistic(al). 2. simultaneous, concurrent in time. 3. contemporaneous. ‖ **-amente** adv. synchronously, synchronistically.

sincronismo s. m. 1. synchronism. 2. mutual relationship of synchronous events. 3. simultaneousness. 4. concurrence of events or facts.

sincronista s. m. + f. synchronizer. ‖ adj. synchronizing.

sincronização s. f. (pl. **-ões**) synchronization.

sincronizado adj. synchronized, synchronous. **engate ~** (tech.) sliding engagement.

sincronizador s. m. (tech.) synchronizer: synchronizing device (plate M 3).

sincronizar v. 1. to synchronize. 2. to describe, relate or expound synchronously. 3. to coordinate actions which happen at the same time. 4. (motion pictures) to adjust with utmost precision the simultaneous reproduction of sound and image.

síncrono adj. synchronous, synchronistic(al).

sindactilismo, sindatilismo s. m. (med., zool.) syndactilism.

sindáctilo, sindátilo adj. (med., zool.) syndactil(e).

sindectomia s. f. (med., surg.) syndectomy, peritomy.

sindérese s. f. 1. synderesis, synteresis. 2. natural ability to distinguish correctly between right and wrong. 3. discretion, circumspection. 4. common sense.

sindesmografia s. f. (anat.) syndesmography: a treatise on the anatomy of ligaments.

sindesmográfico adj. (anat.) syndesmographic(al).

sindesmologia s. f. (anat.) syndesmology, the anatomy of ligaments.

sindesmológico adj. (anat.) syndesmologic(al).

sindesmose s. f. (anat.) syndesmosis.

sindesmotomia s. f. (surg.) syndesmotomy.

sindesmotômico adj. (surg.) syndesmotomic(al).

sindicação s. f. (pl. **-ões**) 1. syndication: act or result of syndicating. 2. investigation, inquiry. 3. controlling, checking. 4. organization of a syndicate.

sindical adj. m. + f. (pl. **-ais**) syndical.

sindicalismo s. m. 1. syndicalism. 2. unionism. 3. doctrine and principles of the organization of syndicates. 4. defense of syndicalism.

sindicalista s. m. + f. supporter or defender of syndicalism, syndicalist. ‖ adj. syndicalistic(al).

sindicalização s. f. (pl. **-ões**) syndicalization.

sindicalizar v. 1. to syndicalize, syndicate. 2. to unionize. 3. to bring under the control of a syndicate.

sindicância s. f. 1. syndication. 2. investigation, inquiry. 3. inquest. 4. probe.

sindicante s. m. + f. 1. syndic, syndicateer. 2. chief magistrate or arbitrator. 3. public investigator. 4. special representative or trustee of a business corporation. 5. patron, advocate. ‖ adj. investigating, probing, inquiring, syndicalizing.

sindicar v. 1. to investigate, inquire into. 2. to make an examination of, subject to control. 3. to try to obtain informations (requested by a superior authority). 4. to organize into a syndicate or trade union.

sindicatado s. m. a member of a trade or labour union.

sindicato s. m. 1. syndicate. 2. an association of financiers (united for the execution of a special business project). 3. trust, cartel. 4. labour union, trade union. 5. (depr.) unfair or fraudulent business transaction. 6. dignity, office and authority of a syndic.

sindicatório s. m. syndicator, syndicateer. ‖ adj. of, pertaining to or relative to a syndicate.

síndico s. m. 1. syndic. 2. chief magistrate or attorney. 3. corporation lawyer, special representative or trustee of a business corporation. 4. patron, advocate. 5. solicitor, lawyer, proctor.

~ **de massa falida** (com., jur.) receiver, trustee or assignee in bankruptcy.

síndroma, síndrome s. m. (med., path.) syndrome: the combination of symptons in a certain disease.

sinecura s. f. sinecure, a profitable "soft" job or position.

sinecurismo s. m. sinecurism, possession of sinecures, governmental system based on sinecurists.

sinecurista s. m. + f. sinecurist: one who holds a sinecure.

sinédoque s. f. (rhet.) synecdoche: a figure of speech in which a part is used for the whole and vice versa.

sinedrim, sinédrio s. m. (pl. **-ins**, **-ios**) (hist.) Sanhedrin: the great council or tribunal of the Jews, consisting of an equal number of priests, scribes and elders.

sineira s. f. bell-gable, bell loft of a tower.

sineiro s. m. 1. bell-ringer, toller, sexton. 2. bell manufacturer, bell-founder. ‖ adj. equipped with bells (tower, steeple).

sinema s. f. (bot.) synema.

sinemático adj. (bot.) 1. of, pertaining to or relative to stamens. 2. staminate. 3. staminiferous.

sinequia s. f. (med.) synechia.

sinérese s. f. (gram.) synaeresis, syneresis.

sinergia s. f. (med.) synergy, synergism.

sinérgico adj. (med.) synergic, synergistic(al).

sinérgides s. f. pl. (bot.) synergidae.

sinergismo s. m. 1. (med.) synergism, synergy. 2. (theol.) synergism: a doctrine which maintains that the salvation of man can only be the result of human willingness and divine grace.

sinergista s. m. + f. synergist: one who holds the theological doctrine of synergism. ‖ adj. synergistic(al).

sínese s. f. (gram.) synesis.

sinestesia s. f. 1. (physiol.) synaesthesia, synesthesia. 2. (psych.) photism, phonism.

sineta s. f. a small bell, call bell, hand bell.

sineta s. f. Synetha: a genus of coleopterous insects.

sinetar v. to mark with a seal or stamp.

sinete s. m. 1. seal. 2. print, impress. 3. stamp, mark. 4. signet, sigil.

anel de ~ signet ring.

sínfise s. f. (anat., med., zool.) symphysis.

sinfisiário, sinfisiano, sinfísio adj. (anat., med., zool.) of, pertaining to or relative to symphysis.

sinfisiotomia s. f. (med., surg.) symphyseotomy.

sinfisiotômico adj. (med., surg.) symphyseotomic(al).

sínfito s. m. (bot.) comfrey (Symphytium officinalis).

sinfonia s. f. 1. symphony: a musical composition for a full band of instruments. 2. a harmony of sounds. 3. a symphony concert. 4. a symphony orchestra. 5. interval embracing eight diatonic degrees. 6. orchestral introduction or termination to a vocal composition or opera.

~ **de câmara** chamber music.

sinfônico adj. (mus.) symphonic(al), symphonious. ‖ **-amente** adv. symphonically.

sinfonista s. m. + f. symphonist: 1. a member of a symphony orchestra. 2. composer of symphonies. ‖ adj. of, pertaining to or relative to symphonies and symphonists.

sinfonizar v. (mus.) to compose symphonies, harmonize.

singamia s. f. (biol., bot.) syngamy.

singeleira s. f. a fishing net with fine meshes (for small fishes).

singeleza, singelez s. f. 1. singleness. 2. simplicity, simpleness. 3. chastity. 4. ingenuousness, artlessness. 5. naturalness. 6. sincerity.

singelo adj. 1. plain, simple. 2. sincere, unfeigned. 3. artless, unpretending. 4. chaste. 5. single. 6. inoffensive. 7. innocent, ingenuous. 8. unrhetorical. 9. not doubled. ‖ **-amente** adv. unpretentiously, unpretendingly.

singênese s. f. 1. (philos.) a doctrine which maintains the simultaneous creation of all living beings and matter. 2. (biol.) syngenesis.

singenesista s. m. + f. adherent or defender of the doctrine of simultaneous creation. ‖ adj. of or relative to simultaneous creation.

singradura s. f. (naut.) 1. a day's sail or run. 2. sailing course. 3. the distance travelled in one day.

singráfico adj. syngraphical.

síngrafo s. m. (jur.) syngraph: deed signed by all the parties concerned.

singrante adj. m. + f. (naut.) ready to sail.

singrar v. 1. to sail. 2. to make sail for. 3. to navigate.

~ **os mares** (poet.) to cross the seas.

singular s. m. (gram.) singular, the singular number. ‖ adj. m. + f. 1. individual. 2. belonging or interesting one person only. 3. single. 4. one, only one, unique. 5. singular, extraordinary. 6. particular. 7. remarkable. 8. odd, peculiar, quaint. 9. unusual, strange.

um acontecimento ~ a unique event; an event as one in a thousand.

singularidade s. f. 1. singularity, singularness. 2. particularity, uniqueness. 3. remarkableness, extraordinariness. 4. rareness. 5. oddity, oddness, queerness. 6. whimsy, whimsicalness. 7. extravagance.

S 3

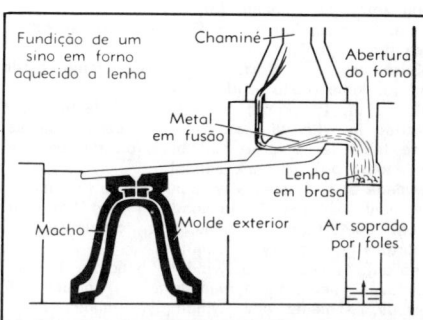

Fundição de um sino em forno aquecido a lenha — Chaminé — Abertura do forno — Metal em fusão — Lenha em brasa — Macho — Molde exterior — Ar soprado por foles

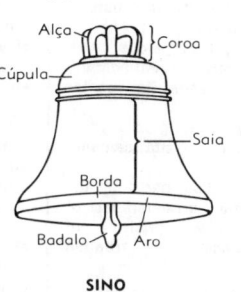

Alça — Coroa — Cúpula — Saia — Borda — Badalo — Aro

SINO

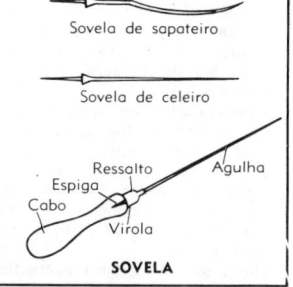

Sovela de sapateiro — Sovela de celeiro — Ressalto — Agulha — Espiga — Cabo — Virola

SOVELA

singularizar v. 1. to singularize, make singular. 2. to distinguish from others, single out. 3. to individuate, particularize. 4. to confer privileges on. 5. to specify, itemize. 6. to except, exclude from. 7. ~-**se** to distinguish o. s.

singulto s. m. (poet.) sob, sobbing, hiccup.

singultoso adj. (poet.) sobbing.

sinhá s. f. (Braz.) corruption of the word **senhora** = Mistress (used formerly by Negro slaves).

sinhá-moça s. f. (pl. **sinhás-moças** or **sinhá-moças**) corruption of the words **mocinha** and **senhorita** = little miss, missy.

sinhaninha s. f. 1. a lace edging in a zigzag pattern. 2. white rum.

sinhazinha s. f. (Braz.) little miss, an affectionate form of address used formerly by Negro slaves for the master's daughter.

sinhô s. m. (Braz.) corruption of the word **senhor** = Mister, Master (used formerly by Negro slaves).

sinhô-moço s. m. (pl. **sinhôs-moços** or **sinhô-moços**) (Braz.) a Negro corruption of the word **senhor** used formerly by slaves for their Master's son(s).

sínico adj. 1. of, pertaining to or typical of China. 2. of, pertaining to or relative to those groups of Chinese living in Portuguese territories.

sinimbu s. m. (zool.) iguana.

sinistra s. f. the left hand.

sinistrado s. m. victim of an accident or losses. ‖ adj. injured by an accident, damaged, lost.

sinistrar v. to suffer an accident, loss or damage (esp. insured property).

sinistrismo s. m. left-handedness.

sinistro s. m. 1. accident, casualty. 2. disaster, calamity. 3. catastrophe, cataclysm. 4. ruin. 5. damage, loss. ‖ adj. 1. left, on the left. 2. sinister, ominous. 3. sinistrous, dismal. 4. fateful, fatal. 5. evil, wrong. 6. doleful, dire. ‖ -**amente** adv. sinisterly, sinistrously, ominously, fatally.

sinistrogiro adj. sinistrogyrate, inclined toward the left, moving to the left.

sinistrorso adj. (bot.) sinistrorse.

sino (I) s. m. 1. bell (plate S 3). 2. any bell-shaped object or instrument. 3. diving bell. ~ **de alarma** alarm bell. ~ **de mergulhador** diving bell, airlock. ~ **de rebate** storm bell. ~ **de recolher** the curfew bell. ~ **para bruma** fog-bell. **ter ou tomar a forma de** ~ to be or become bell-shaped.

sino (II) s. m. gulf, bay.

sínoco adj. (med.) synochal, synochous. **febre -a** synocha: an inflammatory continued fever.

sinodal adj. m. + f. (pl. -**ais**) synodal; of, pertaining to or typical of a synod, synodic, synodical. ‖ ~**mente** adv. synodically, synodally.

sinodático adj. occurring in a synod.

sinódico s. m. (eccl.) 1. a collection of synodical decrees or resolutions. 2. synodicon.

sínodo s. m. (eccl.) synod: ecclesiastical council, a meeting of several adjoining presbyteries.

sinologia s. f. sinology: systematic study of the Chinese, their culture and language.

sinológico adj. sinologic(al).

sinólogo s. m. sinologue, sinologist, sinologer. ‖ adj. sinologistical.

sinonímia s. f. 1. synonymity: quality ar state of being synonymous. 2. synonymy. 3. the study of synonyms. 4. the use of synonyms.

sinonímica s. f. the study of synonyms and their correct use.

sinonímico adj. synonymic(al), synonymous. ‖ **sinonimicamente** adv. synonymically, synonymously.

sinonimista s. m. + f. synonymist: student or scholar of synonyms, compiler of synonyms. ‖ adj. dealing with, treating of synonyms.

sinonimizar v. 1. to make synonymous. 2. to form synonyms.

sinônimo s. m. synonym: word of the same meaning or nearly the same implication as another. ‖ adj. synonymous, synonymic.
dar ~**s** to synonymize. **estudo de** ~**s** synonymy. **exprimir por** ~**s** to express by means of synonyms. **palavra** -**a** synonymic word, synonym.

sinople, sinopla s. m. sinople: 1. (her.) vert, green (of escutcheons). 2. (min.) ferruginous quartz.

sinopse s. f. 1. synopsis. 2. analysis. 3. summary, abridgement, conspectus. 4. abstract.
~ **de um livro** blurb.

sinóptico, sinótico adj. 1. synoptic(al). 2. characterized by synopsis. 3. abridged, resumed, abbreviated. ‖ **sinopticamente, sinoticamente** adv. synoptically.

sinoptizar v. 1. to synoptize, make a synopsis of. 2. to resume, abridge, abbreviate.

sino-salomão, sino-samão s. m. (pl. **sinos-salomão, sinos-samão**) (also **sino-saimão, sino-salmão,** pl. **sinos-saimão, sinos-salmão**) Solomon's seal, Solomon's star.

sinosteografia s. f. (anat.) synosteography: study and description of the articulations.

sinosteologia s. f. (anat., med.) synosteology, arthrology.

sinosteose s. f. (anat.) synosteosis: fusion of two or more separate bones.

sinosteotomia s. f. (med., surg.) synosteotomy: surgery of articulations.

sinótico adj. synoptic(al).

sinóvia s. f. (anat.) synovia, synovial fluid.

sinovial adj. m. + f. (pl. -**ais**) synovial, secreting synovia. ‖ ~**mente** adv. synovially.

sinovite s. f. (med.) synovitis: inflammation of a synovial membrane.

sínquise s. f. (gram.) 1. synchysis: confusion of words in a sentence. 2. inversion of the natural order of words. 3. (rhet.) hyperbaton.

sinsépalo adj. (bot.) synsepalous, gamosepalous.

sintagma s. m. syntagma: a treatise methodically divided in chapters, groups or classes (for easier reference).

sintático adj. syntactic(al): of or pertaining to syntax, according to the rules of syntax. ‖ **sintaticamente** adv. syntactically.

sintaxe s. f. (gram.) syntax: 1. that part of the grammar which teaches the due arrangement of words in sentences. 2. the correct position of words and clauses in a sentence. 3. a treatise on syntax.

sintáxico adj. (gram.) syntactic(al).

sintecar v. (Braz.) to varnish (floor).

sinteco s. m. (trademark) a transparent, durable, floor varnish.

síntese s. f. synthesis: 1. composition, a putting together of two or more things. 2. generalization. 3. the process of reasoning from general principles or facts to complex effects or systems. 4. (chem.) the uniting of elements into a compound. 5. scientific or literary survey. 6. (math.) solution of a mathematical proposition by simple deduction from known theorems. 7. intellectual structure and organization of a system.

sintético adj. 1. synthetic(al). 2. made or organized by logical synthesis. 3. compositive. 4. accumulated. 5. resumed, abridged, abbreviated. 6. artificial. ‖ **sinteticamente** synthetically, artificially.

resina -a synthetic resin.

sintetismo s. m. (med., surg.) all the steps necessary to set a fracture and to keep it reduced.

sintetizador s. m. synthesist, synthetist, synthesizer.

sintetizar v. 1. to synthesize, synthetize. 2. to constitute by synthesis. 3. to make a synthesis of. 4. to abridge, epitomize. 5. to resume, sum up.

sintoma s. m. 1. symptom. 2. indication, sign, token. 3. (fig.) clue, trace. 4. (fig.) omen, augury.

sintomático adj. symptomatic(al).

sintomatismo s. m. (med.) 1. symptomatics, symptomatology. 2. symptomatic medicine. 3. a school of medicine which restricts its activity to the fighting of the symptoms of an illness.

sintomatista s. m. + f. upholder or defender of symptomatic medicine. ‖ adj. of, pertaining to or typical of symptomatic medicine.

sintomatologia s. f. (med.) symptomatology, semiotics.

sintomatológico adj. symptomatologic(al).

sintomatologista s. m. + f. symptomatologist: student or scholar of symptomatology. ‖ adj. versed in symptomatology.

sintomia s. f. 1. (rhet.) brevity, conciseness. 2. first rough outline, sketch, rough draft.

sintonia s. f. 1. syntony. 2. (radio) tuning in, syntonization. 3. (psych.) responsive disposition.

alcance de ~ (radio) tuning range. **agudez de** ~ (radio) tuning sharpness.

sintonina s. f. (biochem.) syntonin.

sintonização s. f. (pl. -ões) 1. act or process of syntonizing. 2. syntonization: tuning of a radio, tuning-in.

sintonizado adj. (radio) syntonized, tuned in, syntonic. **circuito** ~ (radio) tuned circuit.

sintonizador s. m. (electronics) tuner.

sintonizar v. 1. to syntonize. 2. (radio) to tune in, pick up (a certain wave length).

eu sintonizo Londres I listen in to London.

sintrão s. m. (pl. **sintrãos**) (also **sintrense** m. + f.) native or inhabitant of Sintra (Port.). ‖ adj. of, pertaining to or relative to Sintra.

sinuado adj. (bot.) sinuate (plate F 5).

sinuca s. f. corruption of the English word "snooker". **mesa de** ~ pool table.

sinueleiro adj. (S. Braz.) designating tame cattle used to domesticate wild herds.

sinuelo s. m. (S. Braz.) 1. a flock of tame cattle corralled in with wild animals in order to domesticate them. 2. a large bell hung on the neck of the leading bull or pack animal.

sinuosidade s. f. 1. sinuosity, sinuousness. 2. sinuous movement, winding. 3. flexuosity. 4. (fig.) tergiversation, subterfuge. 5. undulation, circumvolution. 6. tortuosity, tortility. 7. squirm.

sinuoso adj. 1. sinuous. 2. winding, bending. 3. (bot.) sinuate. 4. serpentine, meandrine. 5. tortuous. 6. flexuous. ‖ **-amente** adv. windingly, sinuously.

sinusite s. f. (med.) sinusitis: inflammation of the sinus.

sinusoidal adj. m. + f. (pl. **-ais**) (match., phys.) sinusoidal, sine-shaped.

sinusóide s. f. (math.) sinusoid.

sionismo s. m. 1. Zionism, Zion movement. 2. the study of Jewish history and culture esp. with regard to their cultural and religious center Jerusalem.

sionista s. m. + f. Zionist. ‖ adj. Zionistic.

sipaio, sipai s. m. (India) Hindu soldier disciplined and trained in accordance with European standards by British officers; sepoy.

siparuna s. f. a tropical shrub of the family Monimiaceae — the boldo family (Siparuna guianensis).

sipaúba s. f. a shrub of the family Combretaceae (Combretum ascendens).

sipe s. f. (ethn.) clan, kinsfolk, the fundamental unit of tribal society.

sipia s. f. (N. Braz.) white rum.

sipilho s. m. (naut.) the useless end of a hawser.

sipipira s. f. (bot.) = **sicupira**.

sipoúba s. f. a tree of the family Leguminosae (Parkia discolor).

siracusano s. m. Syracusian, Syracusan: native or inhabitant of Syracuse (Sicily, Italy). ‖ adj. Syracusian.

sirage s. m. sesame oil.

sire s. m. sire, sir.

sirena (I) s. f. (myth.) ‾ siren, mermaid.

sirena (II) s. f. siren(e), syren, electrical siren.

sirênico adj. (poet.) sirenic(al), fascinating.

sirenídeo, sirênio s. m. (zool.) 1. sirenian, one of the Sirenia. 2. ~s pl. Sirenia: an order of large aquatic mammals including the sea-cows, manatees and other groups.

sirga s. f. (naut.) 1. tow. 2. tow-line, towing-rope, tow-rope. 3. drag-rope. 4. cablet.

sirgagem s. f. (pl. **-ens**) towing, towage, trackage.

sirgar v. 1. to tow, take in tow. 2. to drag a boat by a long line, haul along. 3. to track, warp.

sirgaria (I) s. f. a rope and hawser factory, rope spinnery.

sirgaria (II) s. f. silk spinning mill.

sirgideira s. f. (naut.) cordage of a vessel, tackle.

sirgo s. m. 1. (entom.) silkworm. 2. smooth woollen fabric.

sirgueiro s. m. silk spinner, silk thrower.

sirguilha s. f. a coarse woollen fabric.

siri s. m. (Braz., zool.) common name of several species of crustaceans of the family Portunidae: a crab.

siríaco s. m. the language of the Syrians, Aramaic. ‖ adj. Syrian, Syriac.

siríase s. f. (med.) siriasis, sunstroke.

siricaia s. f. (Braz.) a dish made with milk, sugar and eggs.

sirigaita s. f. 1. (ornith.) a wren. 2. (coll.) a lively, high-spirited woman. 3. a frolicsome, artful woman, flirting girl.

sirigaitar v. (coll.) to behave coquettishly.

sirigóia s. m. (Braz.) a saltwater crab of the family Portunidae (Cronius ruber).

siringe s. f. (anat., zool.) syrinx.

siringodendro s. m. syringodendron: a fossilized plant of the Cretaceous period.

siringomielia s. f. (med.) syringomyelia: a degenerative disease of the spinal cord.

siringotomia s. f. (med., surg.) syringotomy.

sírio (I) s. f. (astr.) Sirius, Dog-Star, Canicula.

sírio (II) s. m. Syrian: native or inhabitant of Syria (Asia Minor). ‖ adj. Syrian.

sírio (III) s. m. (Braz.) a bag used for the transport of manioc flour.

siriri (I) s. m. (Braz., ornith.) walking tyrant.

siriri (II) s. m. (Braz., zool.) an edible mussel of the family Mytilidae (Mytilus alagoensis).

siriri (III) s. m. (Braz.) a male termite.

siririca (I) s. f. (Braz.) a kind of fishhook.

siririca (II) adj. m. + f. (Braz., pop.) 1. crazy, rattle-brained. 2. foolish. 3. ill-bred, rude, vulgar.

siriritinga s. f. (Braz., ornith.) the solitary flycatcher (Myiodynastes solitarius).

siriruia s. f. (Braz.) a swarm of flying ants.

sirito s. m. (N. Braz.) ornamental trimmings or lacework on feminine undergarments.

siriú s. f. (Braz.) a bird of the family Momotinae (Baryphthengus ruficapillus).

siriúba s. f. (bot.) black mangrove, mangle.

siriubal s. m. (pl. **-ais**) mangrove forest, mangrove thicket.

sirizada s. f. (Braz.) a crab delicacy.

siroco s. m. sirocco.

siroposo adj. syrupy.

sirtes s. m. + f. pl. 1. reef, shoal. 2. sandbank. 3. quicksand. 4. (fig.) dangers, peril, risks.

sirvente s. f. 1. a critical or satyrical poetry. 2. minstrel song, song of praise.

sirventesca s. f. minstrel song.

sisa s. f. 1. (jur.) a conveyance tax (on transfer of real estate "inter vivos"). 2. (obs.) purchase and sales tax. 3. (fig.) fraudulent deduction or discount.

sisal s. m. (bot.) 1. sisal, sisal-hemp (Agava sisalana). 2. henequen (Agava rigida).

fibra de ~ sisal-grass, sisal-hemp.

sisar v. 1. to collect conveyance tax. 2. to impose conveyance tax. 3. to shortchange, give less than the correct value. 4. to pad an expense account. 5. to take away, deprive of. 6. to subtract fraudulently. 7. to reduce, diminish. 8. to pay conveyance tax in excess to real value.

sismal adj. m. + f. (pl. **-ais**) seismal, seismic, indication of the direction of an earthquake.

sísmico adj. 1. seismic, seismal. 2. of the nature of or caused by an earthquake. 3. cataclysmal, cataclysmic.

abalo ~ earthquake.

sismo s. m. seismism: scientific designation of an earthquake, earthquake phenomena.

sismografia s. f. seismography: description of earthquakes, the art of registering earthquakes.

sismógrafo s. m. (phys.) seismograph: an apparatus which registers earthquakes, their duration and intensity; seismometer.

sismologia s. f. seismology.

sismológico adj. seismologic(al).

sismométrico adj. seismometric(al).

sismômetro s. m. seismometer.

siso s. m. 1. judgment. 2. criterion. 3. common sense. 4. circumspection, prudence.

de ~ seriously, in earnest. **dente do** ~ wisdom tooth. **ele não tem** ~ he has not a grain of sense.

sissarcose s. f. (anat.) syssarcosis.

sistáltico adj. systolic, systaltic.

sistema s. m. 1. system. 2. aggregation of different parts. 3. the essential thesis of a doctrine; theory. 4. assemblage of similar parts. 5. fundamental social and political principles of government. 6. arrangement, combination, composition. 7. the complex rules and laws which govern certain phenomena. 8. plan, scheme, organization. 9. mode, means, method. 10. a connected body of principles in science. 11. habit, usage, practice. 12. a regular method or order. 13. (natural sciences) a method of scientific classification based on a small number of distinctive qualities. 14. (geol.) a group of strata, reunion of different geological strata. 15. (physiol.) apparatus. 16. frame, form, structure.

~ **azóico** (geol.) azoic system. ~ **binário** (math.) binary system. ~ **cambriano** (geol.) Cambrian system. ~ **de centralização pública** centralism. ~ **decimal** (math.) decimal system. ~ **de elevação a contrapesos** (theat.) counter-weight flying system (plate P 2). ~ **de lubrificação** greasing system. ~ **de ventilação** exhaust system. ~ **duodenário** duodenary system. ~ **governamental** political system. ~ **isométrico** (cryst.) isometrical system. ~ **nervoso da vida vegetativa** (anat., physiol.) autonomic nervous system. ~ **planetário** planetary system. ~ **nervoso** nervous system. ~ **quadrático** (cryst.) tetragonal system. ~ **solar** solar system. ~ **temperado** (mus.) temperament. ~ **territorial** territorialism. **eles agiram por** ~ they acted on a preconceived idea, they acted on principle.

sistemática s. f. 1. systematics, taxonomy. 2. art, method and process of classification.

sistemático adj. 1. systematic(al). 2. forming a system. 3. in accordance with a system. 4. methodic(al). 5. (med., scient.) systemic, organic. 6. formal. 7. orderly, regular. 8. through. ‖ **sistematicamente** adv. systematically, methodically, systemically, regularly.

sistematização s. f. (pl. **-ões**) 1. systematization, systemization. 2. adjustment (to a system). 3. classification.

sistematizador s. m. systematizer, systemizer. ‖ adj. systemizing, systematizing.

sistematizar v. 1. to systemize, systematize. 2. to bring into a system. 3. to arrange methodically, classify, codify. 4. to digest.

sistematologia s. f. systematology, systematics.

sistematológico adj. systematologic(al), systematic(al).

sistematologista s. m. + f. systematologist; systematist.

sistilo s. m. (archit.) systile; intercolumnation of two different diameters.

sistina s. f. the Sistine Chapel: the Pope's private chapel in the Vatican. ‖ adj. of, pertaining to or relative to the Sistine Chapel.

sistino adj. of or relative to any Pope named Sixtus.

sistolar adj. m. + f. (physiol.) systolic.

sístole s. f. 1. (med., physiol.) systole: contraction of the heart. 2. (gram.) the shifting of the tonic accent of a word to the preceding syllable.

sistólico adj. systolic.

sistro s. m. (hist., mus.) sistrum: a kind of cithern used by Egyptians in the worship of Isis.

sisudez, sisudeza s. f. 1. circumspection, prudence. 2. wisdom. 3. judiciousness. 4. seriousness, gravity. 5. deportment, personal bearing. 6. common sense.

sisudo s. m. a serious, prudent man, a sober fellow. ‖ adj. 1. judicious, discerning. 2. wise, sensible.

3. serious, grave. 4. poised. 5. hard-headed. 6. prudent.

sita s. f. (ornith.) Sitta: a genus of nuthatches.

sitarrão s. m. (pl. -ões) (N. Braz.) a big ranch or farm.

sitiado s. m. a besieged person or place. ‖ adj. 1. surrounded by enemy forces. 2. beleaguered, besieged.

sitiador s. m. besieger. ‖ adj. besieging.

sitiano s. m. (N. Braz.) countryman, one who lives on a ranch or farm in the hinterland, backwoodsman.

sitiante (I) s. m. + f. besieger, beleaguerer. ‖ adj. besieging, beleaguering.

sitiante (II) s. m. + f. 1. owner of a ranch or farm. 2. countryman, countrywoman.

sitiar v. 1. to lay siege to. 2. to besiege, siege, beleaguer. 3. to beset, begird. 4. (mil.) to invest, surround with an army. 5. (fig.) to importune.

sitibundo adj. (poet.) thirsty, eager, avid.

sitieiro s. m. rancher, farmer, countryman.

sítio (I) s. m. 1. place, local, locality. 2. ground, soil. 3. site, the scene of a noteworthy or historical event. 4. (Braz.) farm, ranch, country seat, estate. 5. any place in the hinterland. 6. share-cropping.

sítio (II) s. m. 1. siege, beleaguerment. 2. investment.

em estado de ~ in a state of siege. levantar o ~ to raise a siege. o governo decretou o estado de ~ the government enacted martial law.

sitioca s. f. (Braz.) a small farm or ranch.

sitiofobia s. f. (med.) sitiophobia, sitophobia.

sitiologia s. f. sitiology, sitology: a treatise on food and alimentation.

sitiológico adj. sitiological.

sitiólogo s. m. one versed in sitiology, sitiologuer.

sitiomania s. f. (med.) sitiomania: a morbid craving for food.

sitiotoxismo s. m. (med.) sitotoxism, food poisoning.

sito (I) s. m. 1. mould, mildew. 2. mustiness.

sito (II) adj. situated, located.

sitófago adj. sitophagous, wheat-eating.

situação s. f. 1. situation: a) act of situating, emplacement. b) position, posture. c) location, place, lay. d) economical or political state of affairs. e) circumstances, condition, business conditions. f) employment. 2. state, station. 3. (theat.) climax of a play. 4. predicament, plight; difficulty. 5. (Braz.) small farm, ranch.

~ aflitiva harrowing plight. ~ comercial business outlook. ~ confusa confused situation, (fig.) troubled waters. ~ crítica emergency, difficulty, (coll.) edge, corner. ~ desvantajosa unfavourableness, tight spot. ~ financeira financial position. ~ oposta opposition. a ~ é crítica the situation is serious. ele está em boa ~ he is at a fine pass, he is well off. ele está em má ~ he is in a fix, he is at low ebb, in a sad plight, in a hole (or tight corner). ele está numa ~ muito infeliz he is very unfortunately situated. em ~ difícil in straightened circumstances. estavam em ~ idêntica they were in the same situation, they rowed in the same boat. minha ~ financeira está ruim my finances are low. eu não estava em ~ de... I was not in a position to... na ~ atual in existing circumstances. se estivesse na minha ~ if you were in my situation, (fig.) if you were in my shoes.

situacionismo s. m. (Braz.) the predominant political party, the governing political group.

situacionista s. m. + f. a member or supporter of the governing political group or party. ‖ adj. of, pertaining to or characteristic of the party in power.

situado adj. situated, located, placed, circumstanced. ~ além do limite outlying. ~ ao norte do rio Tâmisa cispontine (of the Thames). ficar ~ to be located. onde está -a a vila? where is the village situated?

situante s. m. (N. Braz.) rancher, farmer, countryman.

situar v. 1. to place, put in place. 2. to situate, locate. 3. to position. 4. to establish. 5. to mark, point out, assign a place to. 6. to locate geographically. 7. ~-se to place o. s., find a job.

sítula s. f. situla, a wide open wooden vase or pail.

sizetese s. f. (rhet.) a figure of speech which establishes a basis for argumentation.

sizígia s. f., **sizígio** m. (astr.) syzygy.

sketch s. m. sketch.

slogan s. m. slogan.

smoking s. m. (Engl.) tuxedo, dinner-jacket, dinner-suit (plate R 7).

só adj. m. + f. 1. without company, alone. 2. unique, single, sole. 3. lone, lonely. 4. by himself (herself). 5. solitary, secluded. 6. unassisted, helpless. ‖ **só, somente** adv. only, solely, merely, solitarily, barely, uniquely, not other than, just.

de um assento ~ single-seated. de uma ~ mão 1. single-handed. 2. with only one coat of paint. de um olho ~ single-eyed. ela estava completamente ~ neste mundo she was all alone in this world. ela viveu ~ she lived unbefriended. ele leva não ~ a sua esposa mas também sua irmã he takes not only his wife but also his sister. isto se entende por si ~! this is self-evident. não somente,... mas também... not only,... but also... nós estávamos ~s we were alone. nós seremos somente três we shall be only three. o livro é ~ bobagem the book is so much nonsense. somente ontem only yesterday. uma desgraça nunca vem ~ a misfortune never comes alone. uma palavra somente! but one word!

soaberto adj. half-open, ajar.

soabrir v. to open partly, set ajar.

soada s. f. 1. tone, sound. 2. intonation of a song. 3. noise, din. 4. report, rumour. 5. rumbling, murmur.

soadeiro adj. notable, famous.

soado adj. 1. sounded, struck (as a bell). 2. sounding, ringing. 3. famous, notable. 4. reported, rumoured.

soagem s. f. (pl. -ens) bluewed, viper's bugloss, echium.

soalha s. f. (mus.) each one of the loose metal disks or plates of a tambourine.

soalhado s. m. flooring, wooden planks for flooring, floor.

soalhar (I) v. 1. to shake the tambourine. 2. to strike the metallic disks of a tambourine. 3. to jingle.

soalhar (II) v. 1. to plank a floor with boards. 2. to cover with a floor or flooring.

soalheira s. f. 1. the hottest time of the day. 2. sunniness, intense sunshine. 3. exposition to the sun. 4. calmness, calm.

soalheiro s. m. 1. a sunny spot, place in the sun. 2. reunion of idle scandalmongers (usually older people who like to sit in the sun). ‖ adj. 1. exposed to the sun. 2. sunny, sun-drenched.

soalho (I) s. m. 1. floor, flooring (plate D 4). 2. ground. 3. wooden floor.

soalho (II) s. m. = **soalheiro**.

soante adj. m. + f. 1. sounding, ringing. 2. vibrant. 3. resonant. 4. sonorous.

soão s. m. (pl. -ões) east or north-east wind.

soar v. to sound: 1. produce a sound. 2. indicate or proclaim by a sound. 3. clang, ding, jingle. 4. strike (a bell), ring. 5. tune. 6. toll, peal, chime. 7. be spread or rumoured. 8. resound. 9. sing,

chant, carol. 10. strike the nour. 11. (fig.) celebrate, commemorate. 12. praise.
isto soa bem that sounds fine, it rings true. ~ **lugubremente (sinos)** knell. ~ **novamente** to resound. ~ **com som agudo** to tang. **o bem soa, o mal voa** good news is rumoured but bad news flies.
sob prep. sub, under, below, beneath (plate P 18).
~ **juramento** under oath. ~ **o olhar de todos** with every one looking. ~ **palavra de honra** bound by one's word of honour. ~ **pena de morte** under pain of death. ~ **qualquer condição** under any circumstance, at all. ~ **sua supervisão** under his care. **aqueles que estão** ~ **as suas ordens** those who are under him.
soba s. m. West African tribal chief.
sobado s. m. (Africa) territory under the authority of a **soba**.
sobalçar v. 1. to raise up, elevate. 2. to lift. 3. to exalt.
sobarbada (I) s. f. curb of hempen rope.
sobarbada (II) s. f. a chuck under the chin.
sobeira s. f. a second row of tiles under the eaves of a house.
sobejado adj. 1. in excess, more than enough. 2. leftover. 3. overabounding.
sobejar v. 1. to overabound, superabound. 2. to be in excess (of necessity), be more than enough. 3. to be superfluous. 4. to be left (over), remain. 5. to make up for, renew supplies.
sobejidão s. f. (pl. **-ões**) 1. superabundance, redundancy. 2. excess, superfluity. 3. power, vigour. 4. immensity.
sobejo s. m. 1. leftover food, leavings. 2. refuse, riffraff. 3. candle-end. 4. rest. 5. excess. ‖ adj. 1. excessive, too much. 2. overabundant. 3. enormous, immense. 4. numberless, innumerable. ‖ **-amente** adv. excessively, overabundantly, enormously, innumerably.
soberana s. f. 1. a female sovereign, sovereigness. 2. queen, imperatrix. 3. mistress. 4. woman who, among others, occupies a position of leadership.
soberania s. f. 1. sovereignty. 2. office, dignity and authority of a sovereign. 3. supreme power, domination, reign. 4. moral supremacy. 5. domain, dominion. 6. masterdom, masterhood. 7. paramountcy.
soberanizar v. 1. to elevate to the position of a sovereign. 2. to sovereignize, make a sovereign of. 3. to exalt, praise, laud.
soberano s. m. 1. sovereign. 2. imperator, monarch, king. 3. ruler, potentate. 4. prince, lord. 5. pound sterling. ‖ adj. sovereign, supreme, paramount, absolute, magnificent. ‖ **-amente** adv. sovereign, supremely, paramountly, supremely.
~ **absoluto** despot, autocrat.
soberba s. f. 1. pride, haughtiness. 2. presumption, arrogance. 3. height, eminence. 4. uppishness.
soberbaço s. m. an overbearing person, a ridiculously vain individual. ‖ adj. excessively proud or arrogant, haughty, vain, vainglorious.
soberbão s. m. (pl. **-ões**) an overbearing or vainglorious fellow. ‖ adj. uppish, haughty, arrogant, excessively vain.
soberbete s. m. person who shows a slight inclination to haughtiness or arrogance. ‖ adj. somewhat proud or haughty.
soberbia s. f. 1. pride. 2. haughtiness, loftiness. 3. excessive arrogance.
soberbo s. m. 1. a proud person. 2. an overbearing or vainglorious individual. ‖ adj. 1. superb. 2. proud, prideful, proudhearted. 3. haughty, arrogant. 4. vainglorious. 5. domineering. 6. splendid, sumptuous. 7. grandiose, grand. 8. sublime. 9. magnifi-

cent. 10. high, lofty. 11. imperious, lordly. ‖ **-amente** adv. superbly, elatedly, loftily.
soberboso adj. (pop.) superb, splendid, magnificent.
sobernal s. m. (pl. **-ais**) 1. excessive physical or intellectual work. 2. overwork, overstrain. 3. overfatigue, great weariness, exhaustion.
sobestar v. 1. to be under, be below. 2. to be inferior in position. 3. to be inferior to.
sobgrave adj. m. + f. (mus.) under the grave.
sobiador s. m. a bird of the family Cotingidae (Tijuca atra).
sobnegar v. (rarely used) 1. to hide, conceal. 2. to withhold (illegally). 3. to defraud.
sobole s. m. 1. (bot.) soboles, sucker, stolon. 2. shoot, sprout. 3. (fig.) offspring, progeny.
soboró adj. m. + f. (Braz.) empty, hollow (fruit kernel).
soborralhadouro s. m. oven-broom.
soborralhar v. to bake under the embers.
soborralho s. m. 1. the heat maintained by hot embers. 2. hot ashes, hot cinders. ‖ adj. baked under the embers.
sobpé s. m. foot, root, base.
sobpor v. 1. to put under, place below. 2. to underrate, underestimate. 3. to disregard, disdain.
sobra s. f. 1. surplus, overplus. 2. overmeasure, overmuch. 3. excess, abundance. 4. remnant, remainder. 5. residue. 6. fag end. 7. **~s** pl. leftover, rests, remains.
de ~ superabundantly, more than enough, exceedingly. **ficar de** ~ to be left over, be left alone. **não tenho um minuto de** ~ I have not a minute to spare. **temos tempo de** ~ we have time and to spare. **tempo de** ~ plenty of time.
sobraçar v. 1. to put under the arm. 2. to carry under the arm. 3. to grasp, seize, secure. 4. to help, assist a person. 5. to hold in one's arms. 6. to embrace. 7. **~-se** to walk arm in arm with.
sobradar v. 1. to construct a house of two or more stories. 2. to plank a floor with boards.
sobrado (I) s. m. 1. a house of two (or more) stories. 2. upper story of a house. 3. wooden floor. 4. mansion of a large plantation owner.
sobrado (II) adj. 1. abundant. 2. excessive. 3. rich, affluent, wealthy. 4. leftover.
sobral s. m. (pl. **-ais**) a cork oak grove, a cork oak plantation.
sobrançaria s. f. (also **sobranceria**) 1. pride. 2. haughtiness, superciliousness. 3. arrogance. 4. disdain, contempt. 5. frown, scowl.
sobrancear v. 1. to be arrogant or act arrogantly. 2. to treat haughtily. 3. to exceed, surpass. 4. to excel, outdo, be superior to. 5. to superpose, lay over or above.
sobranceiro adj. 1. superior, higher. 2. dominant, predominant. 3. prominent, distinguished. 4. with a high hand, high and mighty. 5. proud. 6. arrogant, haughty. 7. mettlesome. 8. supercilious. ‖ **~, -amente** adv. with pride, arrogantly, superciliously, from a high or elevated position, superiorly. **estar** ~ to tower (over).
sobrancelha s. f. brow, eyebrow (plate O).
ela tem ~s pretas she is black-browed.
sobrancelhudo adj. having big or bushy eyebrows.
sobrar v. 1. to overabound, superabound, be in excess of, be more than enough. 2. to be superfluous. 3. to remain, rest. 4. to run over, overflow. 5. to overmeasure. 6. to exceed, be superior.
ela estava sobrando (coll.) she was the fifth wheel. **não me sobrou tempo para fazê-lo** I found no time to do it. **não sobrou nada** there was nothing left.

sobras s. f. pl. 1. scrap, garbage. 2. offal. 3. oddments. 4. pickings. 5. trimmings. 6. surplus, overplus.

sobrasil s. m. (Braz.) a tree of the family Rubiaceae (Rustia formosa).

sobre (I) s. m. (naut.) topsail, skysail, the highest sails of a ship. ‖ prep. 1. about, above, across, at. 2. besides. 3. concerning. 4. hereabout, hereupon. 5. immediately. 6. in addition to. 7. in consequence of. 8. more than, over, over and above. 9. on, upon (plate P 18). 10. super, supra. 11. to, towards. 12. up. **~ isto** hereon, hereupon. **~ o que ela está falando?** what is she talking about? **a opinião dele ~ o assunto** his opinion about this topic. **de nove vezes ~ dez** nine times out of ten. **ele tomou ~ si a tarefa** he took this assignment upon himself. **eles falaram ~ o negócio** they spoke about their business. **pisar ~** to tread on. **sacar ~** (com.) to draw on. **saltar ~** to overspring. **ter autoridade ~** to have authority over.

sobre (II) s. m. (pop.) uropygium.

sobreabundar v. to superabound, be excessively abundant.

sobreaguado adj. under water, inundated, waterlogged, flooded.

sobreagudo adj. very sharp or pointed.

sobrealcunha s. f. a second nickname.

sobreanca s. f. saddlecloth.

sobreano s. m. (S. Braz.) a yearling calf, heifer.

sobreapelido s. m. a second surname or nickname.

sobrearco s. m. lintel.

sobreaviso s. m. 1. precaution, previous care. 2. forethought. 3. prudence, circumspection. 4. prevention. ‖ adj. warned, cautioned, prudent. **estar de ~** to be on the alert.

sobreaxilar adj. m. + f. (bot.) supra-axillary, suprafoliaceous.

sobrebico s. m. the upper part of a beak (of a hawk).

sobrecabecear v. (bookbinding) to sew or glue a headband to a book.

sobrecana s. f. splint: exostosis on the upper part of the cannon bone of a horse.

sobrecanja s. f. (sl.) a frock coat.

sobrecapa s. f. 1. overcoat, raglan. 2. (of books) dust-cover, dust-jacket, wrapper (plate L 4). **pôr ~ no livro** to jacket a book.

sobrecarga s. f. 1. overburden, overload. 2. surcingle. 3. extra load which upsets the equilibrium of the cargo. 4. surcharge, overcharge. 5. postmark, mail cancel. 6. overweight. 7. m. (naut.) supercargo.

sobrecarregado adj. overloaded, surcharged, supercharged. **~ de serviço** up to the eyes in work. **não ~** unencumbered.

sobrecarregar v. 1. to overload, overburden. 2. to overlade, overfreight. 3. to surcharge, overcharge. 4. to increase excessively. 5. to encumber. 6. to vex, harass. 7. to oppress. 8. to saddle. 9. to overtax. 10. to overtask. 11. to supercharge. **~ um terreno de edificações** to overbuild a lot.

sobrecarta s. f. 1. envelope, cover. 2. a second letter. 3. confirmatory letter. 4. address (of a letter).

sobrecasaca s. f. a frock coat, redingote.

sobreceleste, sobrecelestial adj. m. + f. (pl. ~s, -iais) supercelestial, divine.

sobrecenho s. m. sullen look, scowl, frown.

sobrecéu s. m. canopy, tester.

sobrechegar v. = **sobrevir**.

sobrecheio adj. 1. overfull, very full, overfilled. 2. heaped up. 3. filled to repletion.

sobreclaustra s. f. **sobreclaustro** m. upper cloister.

sobrecoberta s. f. second covering.

sobrecomposto adj. (bot.) double compound (said of leaves).

sobrecomum adj. m. + f. (pl. -uns) (gram.) having the same form for both genders (**dentista, artista**, etc.).

sobrecopa s. f. cover, lid.

sobrecoser v. to oversew, sew over a seam.

sobrecostilhar s. m. (Braz.) a slab of beef from the ribs.

sobrecostura s. f. oversewing, sewing a second time.

sobrecoxa s. f. (Braz., pop.) real thigh (fowls).

sobrecu s. m. (pop.) uropygium.

sobrecurva s. f. (vet.) curb, windgall.

sobredental adj. m. + f. (pl. -ais) (anat.) supradental.

sobredente s. m. 1. a tooth sitting on the top of another one. 2. false tooth. 3. snag tooth.

sobredito adj. 1. above or before-mentioned. 2. already mentioned. 3. forenamed.

sobredivino adj. superdivine, more than divine.

sobredourado s. m. gelded work, gilded ornament. ‖ adj. gilded, overgilded.

sobredourar v. 1. to overgild, gild a second time. 2. to illuminate (the peaks) with golden sunrays. 3. (fig.): a) to entreat, plead. b) to enlarge, aggrandize. c) to portray in lively (but deceptive) colours. d) to win more distinction or splendour.

sobreeminência s. f. supereminence, supreme eminence, magnificence.

sobreeminente adj. m. + f. supereminent, very elevated, lofty, magnificent, sumptuous.

sobreerguer v. 1. to raise (s. th.) higher than another object. 2. to become superior or higher than...

sobreestadia s. f. (naut.) demurrage of a vessel.

sobreestar v. = **sobrestar**.

sobreexaltação s. f. superexaltation.

sobreexaltar v. 1. to exalt excessively. 2. to superexalt.

sobreexcedente adj. m. + f. exceeding, surpassing.

sobreexceder v. 1. to exceed considerably, superexceed. 2. to surpass, surmount, excel. 3. to go beyond, overstep the limits. 4. to get the better of, have an advantage over. 5. to outdo, outstrip.

sobreexcelência s. f. superexcellence, superexcellency.

sobreexcelente adj. m. + f. superexcellent, sublime, supreme.

sobreexcitação s. f. (pl. -ões) 1. act or result of extreme or excessive excitation. 2. superexcitation. 3. great nervous excitation and the disturbance caused by it.

sobreexcitar v. 1. to superexcite. 2. to excite extremely or excessively. 3. to rouse, stir up or impress considerably. 4. to incite. 5. to stimulate, animate. 6. to influence, instigate.

sobreface s. f. 1. (fort.) the space between the outward angle of a bulwark and the lengthened flank. 2. surface.

sobrefoliáceo adj. (bot.) suprafoliaceous.

sobregata s. f. (naut.) 1. mizzen topgallant sail. 2. the yeard and yardarm of the mizzen topgallant sail.

sobregatinha s. f. (naut.) 1. mizzen royal sail. 2. the yard and yardarm which supports this sail.

sobregávea s. f. (naut.) topsail.

sobregoverno s. m. supreme government, supreme power.

sobre-humano adj. (pl. sobre-humanos) 1. superhuman, preterhuman. 2. beyond human power or strength. 3. supernatural. 4. (fig.) sublime.

sobreira s. f. (bot.) a cork oak.

sobreiral s. m. (pl. -ais) a cork oak grove, cork oak plantation.

sobreiro s. m. 1. cork oak, cork tree. 2. Hispania oak. 3. bastard cork tree. 4. saman, rain tree.

sobrejacente adj. m. + f. 1. superjacent. 2. lying on or upon, overlying. 3. (geol.) designating vulcanic rocks (which are overlying granitic strata).

sobrejoanete s. m. (naut.) 1. main royal sail. 2. mizzen royal sail.

sobrejoanetinho s. m. (naut.) each one of the skysails.

sobrelanço s. m. 1. superior bid. 2. outbidding. 3. a bid followed by another (or higher) one.

sobrelátego s. m. cinches of a saddle.

sobreleito s. m. (archit.) roughcast of a wall.

sobrelevante adj. m. + f. surmounting, overtopping, surpassing.

sobrelevar v. 1. to be higher than. 2. to surmount, rise above. 3. to get the better of, surpass. 4. to make higher. 5. to dominate, predominate. 6. to conquer, defeat. 7. to raise, elevate. 8. to suffer, endure. 9. ~-se to distinguish o. s., become prominent or conspicuous.

sobreliminar s. m. (constr.) transom of a drawbridge.

sobreloja s. f. 1. entresol. 2. intermediate story of a building. 3. mezzanine.

sobrelotação s. f. (pl. -ões) 1. quantity which surpasses the normal loading capacity of a vessel or vehicle. 2. overburden, overload. 3. surcharge.

sobremachinho s. m. fleshy excrescence caused by an inflammation of the fetlock joint of horses.

sobremaneira adv. 1. excessively, extremely. 2. much, greatly. 3. extraordinarily.

sobremanhã s. f. dawn, break of day, morning.

sobremão s. m. splint on a foreleg of a horse.
  de ~ (fig.) earnestly, diligently, with perfection, abundantly, leisurely.

sobremaravilhar v. 1. to amaze or astonish considerably. 2. to dazzle. 3. to startle, terrify. 4. to be or become surprised, wonder, marvel beyond measure.

sobremarcha s. f. (tech.) overdrive.

sobremesa s. f. 1. dessert, a course of fruit or pastry served after the meal. 2. sweet(s). 3. coffee. 4. toppings.

sobremodo adv. 1. excessively, extremely. 2. much, greatly. 3. extraordinarily.

sobremunhoneiras s. f. pl. (mil.) trunnion band, trunnion bracer (of a cannon).

sobrenadante adj. m. + f. floating, swimming, afloat, supernatant.

sobrenadar v. 1. to swim on the surface. 2. to float. 3. to drift along. 4. to be buoyed up on the surface of a liquid.

sobrenatural s. m. (pl. -ais) 1. the supernatural, a supernatural influence, being or power. 2. miracle. 3. the other world. ‖ adj. m. + f. 1. supernatural. 2. supranatural, preternatural. 3. superhuman. 4. unearthly, weird. 5. transcendental, divine. 6. beyond nature, otherworldly. 7. psychic. 8. miraculous. 9. extraordinary.

sobrenaturalidade s. f. 1. supernaturalness, supernaturalism. 2. unearthliness. 3. weirdness. 4. transcendentality.

sobrenervo s. m. (vet.) a tumour developed from a nerve.

sobrenome s. m. 1. surname. 2. family name. 3. patronymic, cognomen.

sobrenomear v. 1. to surname. 2. to nickname.

sobrenumerável adj. m. + f. (pl. -áveis) innumerable, countless.

sobreolhar v. 1. to look haughtily or arrogantly. 2. to look with contempt. 3. to look down upon. 4. to give s. o. the cold shoulder.

sobreolho (ô) s. m. 1. precaution, previous care. 2. prudence, forethought. 3. attention.

sobreosso s. m. (vet.) ringbone, splint.

sobrepaga s. f. 1. overpay, additional pay. 2. extra pay. 3. gratification, gratuity, reward.

sobrepairar v. to hang or hover over.

sobrepartilha s. f. (jur.) reapportionment of an estate.

sopreparto s. m. (med., vet.) 1. all the phenomena which manifest themselves after parturition. 2. afterbirth. 3. the period of time from childbirth until full recovery. ‖ adv. after parturition.

sobrepasso s. m. (Braz.) 1. (ftb.) a goalkeeper's infringement (fourth step with ball in hands). 2. (basketball) walking.

sobrepé s. m. (vet.) a bony excrescence on the crown of the hoof (of horses, mules etc.).

sobrepeliz s. f. (pl. -es) (eccl.) surplice, cotta.

sobrepensado adj. 1. thoughtful, mindful. 2. considered, reflected, deliberated. ‖ adv. 1. thoughtfully. 2. well deliberated. 3. aforethought, with premeditation. 4. intentionally, deliberatedly.

sobrepensar v. 1. to think over carefully. 2. to reflect, ponder. 3. to deliberate. 4. to turn over in one's mind. 5. to meditate.

sobrepesar v. 1. to weigh heavily upon one's heart. 2. to grieve, make sad. 3. to think over carefully, ponder. 4. to be very cumbersome or annoying.

sobrepeso (ê) s. m. (pl. **sobrepesos**) 1. surcharge, additional charge. 2. overweight. 3. counterweight.

sobrepor v. 1. to put on or upon. 2. to lean against. 3. to juxtapose. 4. to superpose. 5. to add to, increase. 6. to superimpose. 7. to join, connect. 8. to overlay, lap, overlap. 9. (fig.) to hold in high esteem, appreciate highly. 10. to set before. 11. to imbricate.

sobreporta s. f. transom of the door.

sobreposição s. f. (pl. -ões) 1. act or result of superposing. 2. superposition. 3. imbrication, overlapping. 4. juxtaposition, placing side by side. 5. superimposition. 6. increase, addition.

sobreposse adv. 1. excessively, extremely. 2. too much. 3. unwilling, involuntary.

sobreposto s. m. an ornate vestment worn over the garments. ‖ adj. superimposed, superincumbent, imbricate.

sobrepovoar v. to overpopulate, further the population of.

sobrepratear v. 1. to silver. 2. to electroplate with silver, coat with silver. 3. to lay out with silver plates.

sobrepujamento s. m., **sobrepujança** s. f. 1. act or result of surpassing. 2. outclassing, outstripping. 3. domination. 4. victory, conquest.

sobrepujante adj. m. + f. surpassing, exceeding, excelling.

sobrepujar v. 1. to tower above, surmount. 2. to raise above. 3. to surpass, overreach, overstep. 4. to overcome, get the better of, triumph over. 5. to outstrip, exceed in physical prowess. 6. to be or become superior to. 7. to dominate, predominate. 8. to be victorious, conquer. 9. to excel, outdo, outmaster. 10. to outbid. 11. to lick.
  ~ dificuldades to surmount difficulties. **~ em número** to predominate, outnumber.

sobrequilha s. f. (naut.) keelson.

sobre-restar v. 1. to remain, be left over (after others). 2. to survive, remain existent. 3. to stay on. 4. to rest.

sobre-rodela s. f. (pl. **sobre-rodelas**) a soft tumour on the knee(s) of horses.

sobre-rolda s. m. + f. (pl. **sobre-roldas**) (mil., police) counterround, inspector of a policeman's beat, roundsman.

sobre-roldar v. to check the sentinels or guards, inspect the policemen on duty.

sobre-ronda s. (pl. **sobre-rondas**) 1. f. supervision and control of sentinels, guardsmen or policemen. 2.

m. + f. officer in charge to lead the counterrounds, police inspector, roundsman.

sobre-rondar v. 1. to lead the counterround(s). 2. to check on sentinels or guards. 3. to observe, pay attention to, watch. 4. to examine, control.

sobre-rosado adj. (pl. **sobre-rosados)** pinkish.

sobre-saia s. f. (pl. **sobre-saias)** overskirt.

sobre-saturação s. f. (pl. **sobre-saturações)** supersaturation.

sobre-saturar v. to supersaturate, saturate excessively.

sobrescrever v. 1. to superscribe. 2. to write on or upon, write on the outside or cover. 3. to address a letter.

sobrescritar v. 1. to prepare the envelope or label of. 2. to write the address (of a letter). 3. to address. 4. to destine, direct to.

sobrescrito s. m. 1. envelope, cover. 2. address, destination (of a letter or parcel). 3. directions. 4. superscription.

sobre-semear v. 1. to sow over, sow a second time, resow. 2. to sow superficially.

sobre-ser v. = **sobrestar.**

sobre-sinal s. m. (pl. **sobre-sinais)** 1. an emblem, badge or insignia worn on the clothes. 2. an outward sign.

sobre-solar v. to put a second sole or new soles on shoes.

sobre-soleira s. f. (pl. **sobre-soleiras)** lintel.

sobresperar v. 1. to wait a lot of time. 2. to set *one's hopes in, hope for.

sobressair v. 1. to be salient, be projecting, jut out. 2. to project above, stand out. 3. to underscore, underline, point out. 4. to catch one's eye, attract attention. 5. to (seem to) increase in size, loom up. 6. to become visible. 7. to excel, surpass, eclipse. 8. to stick up. 9. ~-**se** to distinguish o. s., be or become prominent. 10. to be conspicuous. **ele sobressai da multidão** he is pre-eminent.

sobressalente s. m. + adj. m. + f. = **sobresselente.**

sobressaltar v. 1. to take by assault, assail, attack. 2. to take by surprise, take unawares. 3. to surprise, amaze. 4. to frighten, terrify. 5. to scare, shock. 6. to jump over, go beyond, to transpose. 7. to omit, skip. 8. ~-**se** to become frightened, take alarm.

sobressaltear v. 1. to take by assault, assail, attack. 2. to take by surprise, take unawares. 3. to attack treacherously. 4. to jump over, skip over. 5. to scare, shock. 6. ~-**se** to take alarm, become frightened.

sobressalto s. m. 1. an unforeseen event, sudden surprise. 2. alarm. 3. start. 4. dread, fright, fear. 5. moral or physical disturbance, inquietude, uneasiness.
acordar de ~ to start out of one's sleep. **de** ~ by surprise, unawares. **levantar-se com** ~ to rise suddenly from one's seat, start up.

sobressarar v. 1. to heal superficially. 2. to improve temporarily. 3. to palliate a disease.

sobresselente s. m. (also **sobressalente)** 1. surplus, overplus. 2. rest, remainder. 3. spare part, duplicate part. || adj. m. + f. 1. projecting, jutting out, salient. 2. surplus, overplus. 3. supernumerary. 4. spare, held in reserve.
peças ~**s** spare parts. **roda** ~ spare tyre, spare tire.

sobrestante s. m. 1. superintendent. 2. overseer. 3. watchman, guard. || adj. m. + f. 1. discontinuing, interrupted. 2. ceasing. 3. overlooking. 4. lofty, towering.

sobrestar v. (also **sobreestar)** 1. not to continue, not to carry on; to discontinue. 2. to halt, come to a standstill, stop, give up. 3. to cease. 4. to abstain from, refrain from. 5. to be towering over or

imminent. 6. to suspend, interrupt, debar temporarily from. 7. to delay, retard, slow down.

sobrestimar v. 1. to overestimate, overvalue. 2. to appreciate a lot. 3. to overrate, overreckon, overcount. 4. to overassess. 5. to outbid.

sobre-substancial adj. m. + f. (pl. **-ais)** supersubstantial, more than substantial, very or exceedingly substantial.

sobretarde s. f. 1. the late afternoon, end of the afternoon. 2. dusk, nightfall. || adv. at dusk or nightfall, in the early evening.

sobretaxa s. f. 1. surtax, supercharge, surcharge. 2. additional charge. 3. excess fare.
~ **postal** excess postage.

sobretaxar v. 1. to surtax, surcharge. 2. to pay additional freight charges, pay excess postage.

sobretecer v. to overweave, overweb, interweave.

sobretelma s. f. excessive wilfulness or obstinacy. || adv. in an exceedingly obstinate manner, with pertinacy.

sobreterrestre adj. m. + f. 1. superterrestrial, superterranean. 2. terrestrial, wordly.

sobretoalha s. f. a veil or towel laid over another one for protection.

sobretudo (I) s. m. 1. overcoat, coat. 2. top-coat, surcoat, great-coat (plates R 6, 7). 3. overalls.

sobretudo (II) adv. 1. over all, above all. 2. chiefly, mainly. 3. principally, essentially. 4. especially.

sobrevença s. f. 1. surprise, surprisal. 2. event, occurrence. 3. unexpected arrival.

sobrevento (I) s. m. a gust of wind, squall.

sobrevento (II) s. m. 1. an unforeseen occurrence, sudden event. 2. a troublesome affair, mess, trouble.

sobreveste s. f. upper garment, upper-coat, overcoat.

sobrevestir v. 1. to put on one garment over another. 2. to clothe, cover with. 3. to overlay, coat, face.

sobrevigiar v. 1. to superintend, supervise. 2. to check, control. 3. to watch over.

sobrevindo s. m. 1. person who arrives unexpectedly. 2. the sudden or unexpected arrival. || adj. happening, occurring, arriving (unexpectedly).

sobrevir v. (also **sobrechegar)** 1. to befall, come to pass. 2. to happen, occur (as a consequence of or after a previous event). 3. to come upon (suddenly or unexpectedly). 4. to supervene, bechance. 5. to descend on̨ (upon). 6. to happen in the meanwhile or unawares, turn up.
ele sobreveio ao cair da noite he dropped in at night-fall. **se lhe sobreviesse uma desgraça...** if some mischance should befall him, if he should como to some mischance... **sobreveio-lhes a morte** death overtook them. **sobreveio-nos a noite** night overtook us.

sobrevirtude s. f. a veil that nuns wear over their cowl.

sobrevivência s. f. survival.

sobrevivente s. m. + f. survivor, outliver, overliver. || adj. surviving, outliving, extant, perennial.

sobreviver v. 1. to survive, outlive, overlive. 2. to outlast, remain, continue to exist. 3. to live longer than. 4. to escape from accident or death. 5. to resist, oppose.

sobrevivo s. m. survivor, outliver. || adj. outliving, surviving.

sobrevoar v. to fly over.

sobrevôo s. m. overflying: a flying over.

sobriedade s. f. 1. sobriety. 2. abstemiousness, temperance. 3. gravity, seriousness. 4. frugality, frugalness. 5. (fig.) moderation.
falta de ~ insobriety.

sobrinha s. f. niece: a brother's or sister's daughter.

sobrinho (I) s. m. nephew: a brother's or sister's son.

sobrinho (II) s. m. (naut.) each one of the skysails.

sobrinha-neta s. f. (pl. **sobrinha-netas**) grand-niece.

sobrinho-neto s. m. (pl. **sobrinho-netos**) grand-nephew.

sóbrio adj. 1. sober. 2. temperate, abstinent, abstemious.' 3. grave, serious. 4. austere, stern. 5. canny. 6. steady. 7. frugal, economical. 8. simple, artless. ‖ **sobriamente** adv. 1. sober, soberly. 2. temperately. 3. cannily. 4. frugally. 5. moderately.

sobro s. m. 1. cork oak. 2. the wood of this tree.

sob-roda s. f. (pl. **sob-rodas**) stones, bumps or holes in the road.

sobrolho s. m. 1. eyebrow, brow. 2. precaution, caution. 3. prudence, forethought. 4. attention.

sobrosso s. m. 1. an irksome or annoying thing or matter. 2. embarrassment, difficulty. 3. impediment. 4. fear, fright, dread.

soca s. f. 1. popular designation of the rhizoma or underground stem of a plant. 2. the second harvest of sugar cane, rice or tobacco. 3. (Port., prov.) a wooden shoe. 4. a tuft of grass.

socado s. m. (Braz.) a short saddle with high bow and cantle (as used by horse tamers). ‖ adj. 1. pounded, battered. 2. restored, remade. 3. hit. 4. smashed, crushed, trodden down or upon. 5. intrusive. 6. hidden, concealed. 7. thickset, stout.

socador (I) adj. hard trotting (said of horses).

socador (II) s. m. beetle, pestle, stamper.

socadura s. f. 1. act or process of pounding. 2. tamping, battering. 3. mashing.

socairo (I) s. m. 1. (naut.) line, thin rope. 2. a leather strap or a piece of cord used as a brake on vehicles.

socairo (II) s. m. 1. cave at the foot of a mountain. 2. den, lair. 3. shelter. 4. foot of a mountain.

socalcar v. 1. to press well. 2. to tread on, trample on. 3. to crush under foot. 4. to mash, smash.

socalco s. m. 1. a level, narrow stretch of land, terrace. 2. a narrow ledge on the slope of a mountain.

socancra s. m. + f. 1. an artful, willy or cunning person. 2. a miser. ‖ adj. 1. artful, wily, cunning. 2. deceitful. 3. avaricious, mean. **à ~** secretly, on the sly.

socapa s. f. 1. disguise. 2. ruse, cunning. 3. pretence. **à ~** furtively, secretly, under disguise, under false pretence, underhandedly. **ele estava. se divertindo à ~** he laughed in his sleeve.

socar (I) v. 1. to strike with the fist. 2. to beat, thrash. 3. to bruise, hurt. 4. to smash, crush, mash. 5. to pound, tamp. 6. to knead. 7. to ram down the ‘charge of a gun. 8. to pummel, punch. 9. to batter (earth, gravel, stones). 10. to stamp, bray in a mortar. 11. **~-se:** a) to come to blows, thrash each other. b) to hide o. s., take refuge. c) to isolate o. s. d) to cram or gorge o. s., overfeed. 12. to trot, run in a trot (horses, mules). 13. to box.

socar (II) v. (Braz.) to sprout again after the first harvest (sugar cane).

socar (III) v. to put on sandals or wooden shoes.

socarrão s. m. (pl. **-ões**) (f. **socarrona**) old cunning scoundrel.

socava s. f. cave, underground cave or den.

socavado s. m. the clearing away of debris and trash. ‖ adj. excavated, undermined.

socavão s. m. (pl. **-ões**) 1. a large cave, cavern. 2. hiding place, hideout. 3. subterranean passage or gallery. 4. lair, den. 5. shelter. 6. secluded place.

socavar v. 1. to excavate. 2. to undermine. 3. to dig up, mine.

sochantrado s. m. office, work and dignity of a subchanter or assistant choir leader.

sochantre s. m. assistant choir leader, subchanter.

sochantrear v. to act as assistant choir leader or subchanter.

sochão s. m. (pl. **-ões**) (Port. prov.) a cave or cavern excavated in the mountainside.

sociabilidade s. f. 1. sociability, sociableness. 2. companionableness, companionability. 3. communicativeness. 4. associability. 5. neighbourliness, conviviality. 6. conversableness. 7. behaviour and mannerisms of one who lives in society. 8. sociality.

sociabilizar v. 1. to make sociable or companionable. 2. to unite in a friendly group, form a society.

social adj. m. + f. (pl. **-ais**) 1. social, social-minded. 2. of, pertaining to or characteristic of society. 3. sociable, companionable, convivial. 4. friendly, amicable. 5. aggregative. 6. gregarious. ‖ **~mente** adv. socially.

assistência ~ social assistance. **crédito ~** social credit. **deveres sociais** social duties. **ordem ~** social order. **razão ~** registered name by which a commercial or industrial firm is known.

social-democrata s. m. + f. (pl. **social-democratas**) social democrat, member of the Social Democratic Party.

socialismo s. m. socialism: politico-economical theory or system which plans governmental ownership and administration of all means of production and substitution of competition by free co-operation.

socialista s. m. + f. socialist: a member of a socialist party, collectivist. ‖ adj. socialistic, collectivistic.

socialização s. f. 1. act or process of socializing. 2. socialization. 3. (sociology) promotion and development of mutual understanding, collective feeling and co-operative spirit. 4. complete absorption of an individual in a group.

socializar v. 1. to socialize. 2. to render social. 3. to unite in a society, communize. 4. to subject to the rules of an association. 5. to render socialistic. 6. **~-se** to become social.

sociável adj. m. + f. (pl. **-áveis**) 1. social, social--minded. 2. sociable, companionable. 3. associable, clubable. 4. civilized, urban, courteous. 5. neighbourly. 6. conversational, communicative. ‖ **sociavelmente** adv. companionably, sociably, communicatively.

ele é muito ~ he is a good mingler, he sees much company. **ele não é ~** he is not a conversationalist.

sociedade s. f. 1. society. 2. companionship, friendly intercourse. 3. a group of gregarious animals. 4. social body, association. 5. guild, institute. 6. any co-operative social organism with common activi-ites, duties and interests. 7. (com.) corporation, company, consortium. 8. partnership, copartnership. 9. high society, fashionable set, connection. 10. community, life in community. 11. club. 12. organization. 13. college.

~ anônima incorporated company, joint-stock company, stock company. **~ beneficente** benefit society. **~ construtora** building society. **~ de crédito** loan--society. **~ religiosa** or **fraternal** religious order. **a alta ~** high life, people of fashion, rank and fashion. **camada inferior da ~** the lower classes of society, the masses. **contrário à ~** unsocial, anti-social. **dama da alta ~** society lady. **ela foi introduzida à ~ no último dezembro** she came out last December. **ela pertence à ~?** does she belong to society? **ele foi excluído da ~** he was expelled from society, (coll.) he was sent to Coventry. **ele freqüenta a melhor ~** he moves in the best circles. **ele vive longe da ~** he leads a secluded life. **escória da ~** waifs and strays of society. **mexericos da alta ~** society gossip. **nas rodas mais altas da ~** in the highest walks of society.

societário s. m. 1. member of a society. 2. associate, companion. 3. partner, copartner. ‖ adj. 1. societary, societarian. 2. designating an animal of social habits. 3. of or belonging to a society.

sócio s. m. 1. member of society. 2. associate, partner, copartner. 3. shareholder, sharer. 4. fellow, comrade, companion. 5. joint owner, consociate. 6. working partner. 7. consort. 8. accomplice, accessory. 9. allottee. ‖ adj. associate(d). **~ ativo** working partner, acting partner. **~ capitalista** dormant partner. **~ de clube** club-man. **~ comanditário** dormant partner, silent partner, sleeping partner. **~ passivo** dormant partner. **~ principal** senior partner. **~ responsável** (com.) contributory. **direitos e obrigações de ~** associateship. **prover de ~** to partner.

sociocracia s. f. (Braz.) sociocracy.

sociocrata s. m. + f. sociocrat: upholder or defender of sociocracy. ‖ adj. sociocratic(al).

sócio-cultural adj. sociocultural.

sócio-econômico adj. socioeconomic.

sócio-gerente s. m. (com.) managing partner.

sociologia s. f. sociology: 1. objective study of social conditions and development. 2. science which treats of the origin, nature and evolution of society. 3. the study of social institutions and their organization. **~ econômica** economic sociology. **~ vegetal** (bot.) phytosociology.

sociológico adj. sociologic(al).

sociólogo s. m. sociologist: scholar of sociology.

soco s. m. 1. (hist.) a kind of sandal worn by Greek actors. 2. a shoe with a wooden sole; patten, clog. 3. (fig.) farce. 4. (fig.) matter of little or no importance. 5. (archit.) socle or square basis under a pedestal. 6. footstool. 7. apparent foundation of a wall. 8. market.

soco (ô) (I) s. m. 1. a blow with the fist or hand. 2. blow, punch. 3. sock, paste, plug. 4. fistycuff. 5. facer. 6. indentation, dent, notch. **dar um ~ em alguém** to strike out for s.o.

soco (ô) (II) interj. (Braz.) fie!, what a shame!, don't say so!, what a surprise!

socó s. m. (Braz.) common name of several species of wading birds of the family Ardeidae; a heron.

socó-boi s. m. (pl. **socós-boi**) (Braz., ornith.) tiger bittern.

soçobrado adj. upturned, capsized, foundered, stranded, wrecked.

soçobrar v. 1. to turn upside down, turn end over end. 2. to subvert, overthrow. 3. to sink, founder. 4. (naut.) to keel over, capsize. 5. to go under, be shipwrecked. 6. **~-se**: a) to get lost, come to ruin. b) to lose o. s. c) to become upset or perturbed. d) to lose courage, to despair.

soçobro (ô) s. m. (pl. **soçobros**) (also **soçobra** f.) 1. complete submersion. 2. shipwreck, wreck, foundering, sinking. 3. capsizing. 4. disaster, loss, damage. 5. discouragement.

socó-estudante s. m. (pl. **socós-estudante**) (Braz.) = **socozinho**.

socoí, socó-mirim s. m. (pl. **socó-mirins**) (ornith.) green heron.

socoró s. m. 1. a plant of the family Rutaceae (Sohnregia excelsa). 2. a solanaceous plant (Solandra grandiflora).

socorrer v. 1. to succour, defend, protect, aid, help, assist. 2. to relieve. 3. to alleviate, mitigate. 4. to redress, rescue. 5. to administer. 6. **~-se**: a) to look for help or assistance. b) to avail o. s. of, make use of, resort. c) to ask for help; to request support or help. **~ alguém** to give aid to. **ele a socorreu** he came to her rescue. **eles ~am as vítimas** they aided the

victims. **não ~am os vizinhos** they failed to assist their neighbours.

socorrido adj. succoured, helped, relieved, supplied. **não ~** unrelieved.

socorrimento s. m. act of helping, assistance, aid, rescue.

socorrista s. m. + f. (Braz.) 1. professionally qualified first aid person. 2. member of a first aid organization.

socorro s. m. 1. succour, relief. 2. aid, help, assistance. 3. redress. 4. protection. ‖ interj. help! **ambulatório de pronto ~** first aid station. **ele correu em ~ de** he ran to the aid of. **ir de ~ to** to come to some one's aid. **primeiros ~s** first aid. **requisitaram um carro de ~** they demanded an ambulance car. **vir em ~ de** to come to the rescue of.

socovão s. m. (pl. **-ões**) 1. a deep cave or cellar under a house. 2. subterranean cave or gallery. 3. hiding place.

socó-vermelho s. m. (pl. **socós-vermelhos**) (Braz., ornith.) red heron (Ardea erythromela).

socozinho s. m. (Braz.) a wading bird of the family Ardeidae (Butorides striata).

socrático adj. Socratic(al).

soda (I) s. f. 1. (chem.) sodium hydroxide, soda, caustic soda. 2. crystallized sodium carbonate. 3. soda-water. **~ extraída de algas** kelp. **~ limonada** lemon squash. **~ cáustica** caustic soda.

soda (II) s. f. (bot.) saltwort (Salsola kali).

sodalício s. m. sodality, fellowship, fraternity.

sódico adj. (chem.) sodic.

sódio s. m. (chem.) sodium (symbol Na), natron. **aluminato de ~** sodium aluminate. **bicarbonato de ~** sodium bicarbonate, efferverscent powder. **carbonato de ~** sodium carbonate. **fosfato de ~** sodium phosphate. **silicato de ~** sodium silicate. **sulfato de ~** sodium sulphate. **sulfito de ~** sodium sulphite.

sodomia s. f. sodomy, pederasty, bestiality.

sodômico adj. sodomitical, of or relative to sodomy.

sodomita s. m. + f. sodomite, pederast.

sodomítico adj. sodomitical.

sodomismo s. m. sodomitism, sodomy.

sodomizar v. to practise sodomy.

soeiras s. f. pl. customs, habits, usage.

soer v. 1. to accustom, habituate. 2. to be accustomed to, do usually. 3. to be inured to.

soerguer v. 1. to raise slightly, raise a little. 2. to lift, elevate. 3. **~-se** to raise o. s. with difficulty. 4. to be uplifted or raised.

soez adj. m. + f. (pl. **~es**) base, low, vile, worthless.

sofá s. m. 1. sofa, couch (plate R 5). 2. day-bed, Persian bed. 3. divan. 4. settee, davenport (plate C 2).

sofá-cama s. m. (pl. **sofás-camas**) sofa-bed, day-bed, davenport.

sofá-de-arrasto, sofá-rasteiro s. m. (pl. **sofás-de-arrasto, sofás-rasteiros**) (N. Braz., pop.) a mat of roughly woven straw or rushes.

sofisma s. m. 1. sophism: an argument intended to deceive. 2. sophistry, philosophism. 3. fallacy, fallaciousness. 4. quibble, quodlibet.

sofismar v. 1. to sophisticate. 2. to act or talk in a sophisticated manner. 3. to evade, dodge. 4. to deceive slyly with sophism. 5. to cavil. 6. to employ sophism, reason sophisticatedly.

sofista s. m. + f. 1. sophist. 2. casuist. 3. quodlibetarian, quibbler. 4. captious or fallacious reasoner.

sofistaria s. f. 1. sophistry. 2. sophistical argument or speech. 3. sophistic fallacies collectively.

sofística s. f. 1. sophistic, that part of logic which studies the Sophists, sophistic reasoning and its refutation. 2. the art, method and principles of a sophist. 3. the art of sophistic reasoning, sophistry.

sofisticação s. f. (pl. **-ões**) 1. sophistication. 2. sophistry, sophistical misrepresentation. 3. act or result of sophistical reasoning. 4. a quibble.

sofisticado adj. 1. sophisticated. 2. falsified, adulterated. 3. not natural, artificial. 4. affected, unnatural.

sofisticar v. 1. to sophisticate. 2. to act or talk in a sophisticated manner. 3. to falsify, adulterate. 4. to treat with subtlety. 5. to employ sophism, use sophistry.

sofisticaria s. f. 1. sophistry, sophistical reasoning. 2. sophism, sophistical argument, quibble.

sofístico adj. 1. sophistic(al), sophisticated. 2. casuistic(al). 3. misleading, deceptive. 4. fallacious. 5. quodlibetical. 6. caviling. || **sofisticamente** adv. sophistically, casuistically, fallaciously.

sofito s. m. (archit.) soffit.

soflagrante s. m. (Braz., pop.) instant, right moment. **no** ~ just in the right moment, immediately.

sofomania s. f. (psych.) sophomania: morbid wish to show great erudition or wisdom.

sofomaníaco s. m. (psych.) sophomaniac; one who suffers from sophomania. || adj. sophomaniac(al).

sofômano s. m. 1. (psych.) sophomaniac. 2. sham philosopher, prig, wiseacre. || adj. 1. sophomaniac(al). 2. conceited, priggish, feigning erudition.

sofralda s. f. (Braz.) foot of a mountain.

sofraldar v. 1. to tuck in or up (shirttail, coat). 2. (fig.) to raise s. th. a little bit (in order to find out what is under it). 3. to lift, uplift, elevate.

sofrê s. m. (Braz., ornith.) an oriole (Xanthornus jacamai).

sofreada, sofreadura s. f. 1. act or result of checking or curbing. 2. check restraint. 3. repression, suppression. 4. (fig.) reproach, censure.

sofreamento s. m. 1. restraint, repression, checking. 2. curbing in, bridling.

sofrear v. 1. to bridle, curb. 2. to check, refrain, restrain. 3. to repress, hold back, hold in check. 4. to correct, rectify. 5. ~**-se** to contain o. s., refrain from.

sofredor s. m. sufferer, endurer. || adj. suffering, tolerating.

sôfrego adj. 1. voracious, greedy. 2. avid, eager, grasping. 3. impatient, restless. 4. ambitious. || **-amente** adv. greedily, avidly, impatiently.

sofreguidão s. f. 1. greediness, voraciousness. 2. avidity, graspingness. 3. gluttony. 4. impatience, restlessness. 5. ambition. 6. covetousness.

sofrenaço s. m. **sofrenada** f., **sofrenão** m. a strong pull on the reins (to stop horses).

sofrenar v. to hold in the reins, bridle (horses), bring to a standstill.

sofrer v. to suffer: 1. bear, endure. 2. experience, sustain. 3. stand, undergo. 4. put up with, support. 5. tolerate. 6. admit, permit, allow. 7. ache, smart, feel pain. 8. experience damages or losses. 9. forbear with patience.
~ **colapso** to break down, collapse. ~ **de ansiedade** to be anxious, apprehensive. ~ **de calor** to swelter. ~ **dores ou torturas intensas** to agonize. ~ **erosão** to undergo erosion, erode. ~ **fome** to starve. ~ **mentalmente** to suffer mental pains, smart, writhe. ~ **pena** to expiate. ~ **prejuízos** to sustain loss(es). ~ **privações** to want, suffer from want. ~ **uma derrota pesada** to sustain a crushing defeat. **as plantas** ~**am com a geada** the plants were touched with frost. **deixar alguém** ~ **as consequências de seus erros** to let s. o. take the consequences of his faults, stew in his own juice. **ele sofre continuamente de asma** he is a martyr

to asthma, he is a sufferer from asthma. **ele sofre de gota** he suffers from gout. **ele sofre do coração** he has heart trouble, he has a heart condition. **ele sofre pelo seu crime** he suffers for his crime. **ele sofreu muito** he went through much. **ele sofreu um ferimento grave** he sustained a bad injury. **fazer** ~ to torment, torture. **sofrendo de pesar** stricken with grief. **sofrendo dos mesmos defeitos** affected by the same faults, (coll.) tared with the same brush. **terá que** ~ **por isso!** you shall smart for it!

sofreu s. m. (N. Braz., ornith.) = **sofrê**.

sofrido adj. suffered, endured, patiently forborne.

sofrimento s. m. 1. suffering, sufferance. 2. pain, agony. 3. torment. 4. trouble, hardship. 5. endurance. 6. anguish, sorrow, trial, tribulation.
~ **de fome** starvation. ~ **de tântalo** tantalization.

sofrível adj. m. + f. (pl. **-íveis**) 1. sufferable, endurable. 2. supportable. 3. nearly sufficient, middling. 4. reasonable. 5. passable, tolerable. 6. so-so, quite good. 7. decent. || **sofrivelmente** adv. 1. sufferably, endurably. 2. sufficiently. 3. passably. 4. decently.

soga s. f. 1. a rope twisted from esparta grass or rushes, hemp rope. 2. leather thong. or strap.

sogabano s. m. a Moslem Negro priest (who takes care of small groups of Moslem Negroes living in Brazil).

sogaço s. m. 1. a blow with a hemp rope. 3. good and strong esparta or hemp fibers.

sogar v. to shackle with a hemp rope.

sogra s. f. 1. monther-in-law. 2. a rolled cloth pad (placed under an object carried on the head).

sograr v. (Braz., sl.) to live at an inlaw's expense.

sogro s. m. father-in-law.

sogros s. m. pl. parents-in-law.

soguá, soguaguá s. m. (Braz.) a freshwater fish (Prochilodus vimboides).

sogueiro s. m. a small enclosed pasture, corral.

soidão s. f. (poet.) solitude.

soído s. m. sound, tone.

soim s. m. (pl. **-ins**) (Braz.) popular designation of several kinds of saki monkeys.

soirée s. f. (Fr.) soirée: an evening party or gathering.

soiteira s. f. whip lash, whip.

soja s. m. (bot.) soybean, soja, soy.

soligar v. 1. to subject (by sheer force). 2. to dominate. 3. to hold back, check. 4. to stand, put up with, endure.

sol (I) s. m. (pl. **sóis**) 1. (astr.) sun, luminary center of the solar system. 2. sunlight, sunshine. 3. (poet.) Titan, Phoebus. 4. (her.) a circle with twelve rays on an escutcheon. 5. (phys.) sol: a stabilized colloidal solution. 6. a fish of the family Tetraodontidae (Tetrodon mola). 7. (fig.) day, brightness, brilliance, splendour.
ao ~ in the sun. **de** ~ **a** ~ from sun to sun. **de tez tostada pelo** ~ tanned. **o lado exposto ao** ~ the sunny side. **o nascer do** ~ the sunrise. **o pôr-do-**~ the sunset. **o** ~ **estava alto** the sun was riding high. **o** ~ **pica** the sun scorches. **pôr ao** ~ to expose to the sunrays. **queimado pelo** ~ sunburnt, sun-tanned. **relógio de** ~ sun-dial. **ressecado pelo** ~ sun-baked, sun-dried. **sem** ~ sunless. **ver o** ~ **quadrado** (Braz., pop.) to be in jail.

sol (II) s. m. (mus.): the fifth tone of any diatonic scale.

sola s. f. 1. sole-leather. 2. the sole of a shoe (plates B 16, C 14). 3. sole of a foot, tread. 4. shaft of a cart or harrow. 5. a sweetmeat made with cassava flour and sugar.

~ **dupla de calçado** clump. ~ **externa** outsole. **de** ~ **e vira** well prepared for anything. **meia** ~ half sole. **pôr** ~ **dupla** to clump. **entrar de** ~ (Braz., ftb.) to faultily dispute the ball.
solado s. m. the sole of a shoe, sole-leather. ‖ adj. soled, new-soled (shoes).
solador s. m. cobbler, soler.
solais s. m., sg. + pl. the part of a mountain ridge or top where the downslope begins.
solama s. f. 1. scorching sunshine, burning sun. 2. excessive heat, swelter.
solanáceas s. m. pl. (bot.) Solanaceae: the nightshade or potato family.
solanáceo adj. (bot.) solanaceous.
solancar v. 1. to work with dedication at a wearisome job. 2. to drudge, work hard, toil at a difficult task.
solandre s. m. (vet.) spavin.
solanina s. f. (chem.) solanine.
solano s. m. Solanum: a genus of herbs and shrubs of the nightshade family.
solante (I) s. m. + f. (Braz.) partner at a card game (solo).
solante (II) s. m. sun hat.
solão (I) s. m. sandy or clayey soil.
solão (II) s. m. 1. scorching sunshine, burning sun. 2. excessive heat, swelter.
solapa s. f. 1. a cave the entrance of which is hidden or nearly closed by boulders. 2. sap, undermining. 3. (fig.) ruse, trick, artifice. 4. disguise. **à** ~ secretly, under disguise, furtively, under false pretence, underhandedly.
solapado adj. 1. excavated, hollowed out. 2. undermined. 3. recondite, hidden, secret. 4. disguised. 5. clandestine.
solapador s. m. sapper, excavator. ‖ adj. undermining.
solapamento s. m. 1. a cave the entrance of which is hidden. 2. sap, undermining. 3. washout.
solapão s. m. (pl. **-ões**) a large cavity formed by erosion, washout.
solapar v. 1. to hollow out, excavate. 2. to form a cave or cavity in. 3. to undermine; mine, sap. 4. to upset, overturn. 5. to raze, ruin, destroy. 6. to hide, conceal. 7. to disguise, dissemble. 8. ~-se to hide o. s., take refuge to.
solapo s. m. a cavity formed in the banks of a river.
solar (I) s. m. manor-house, manor-place, manor, mansion.
solar (II) s. m. sol: Peruvian monetary unit.
solar (III) adj. m. + f. solar: of, pertaining to or relative to a sun or solar system. **mancha** ~ sunspot. **plexo** ~ (anat.) solar plexus. **raios** ~**es** solar rays. **sistema** ~ solar system.
solar (IV) adj. m. + f. of, pertaining to or relative to the sole of a shoe.
solar (V) v. to sole a shoe, put new soles on shoes, to tap.
solar (VI) v. 1. (cards) to play solo, win at solo. 2. (mus.) to perform, play or sing alone (without accompaniment).
solarengo s. m. lord of a manor-house. ‖ adj. manorial.
solário s. m. 1. solarium, sun porch. 2. terrace, roof terrace. 3. sun-dial.
salarização s. f. (phot.) solarization (overexposure).
solau s. m. (Braz.) a steep, muddy side street.
solavancar v. to jolt, jostle, bump, bounce.
solavanco s. m. 1. jolt, jerk. 2. bump. 3. jog trot, joggle.
a carreta caminha aos ~**s** the cart jolts along.
solaz s. m. 1. distraction, absent-mindedness. 2. relaxation, consolation. ‖ adj. m. + f. consoling, solacing.
solcris s. m. eclipse of the sun.

solda (I) s. f. 1. solder: metallic alloy used to join metallic surfaces. 2. soldering, welding. 3. a soldered joint, weld.
~ **autógena** autogenous welding, gas torch welding. ~ **elétrica** electric welding. ~ **forte** brazing. **sem** ~ weldless.
solda (II) s. f. (bot.) 1. wild madder. 2. infant's-breath. 3. white bedstraw.
soldada s. f. 1. wages, a day labourer's or soldier's pay. 2. salary. 3. (fig.) reward, premium.
soldadeiro s. m. employee, wage earner. ‖ adj. wage earning.
soldadesca s. f. 1. troops, a body of soldiers. 2. military classes, soldiers collectively. 3. soldiery. 4. a band of mercenary or undisciplined soldiers.
soldadesco adj. soldierly, soldierlike.
soldado (I) s. m. 1. soldier. 2. private, enlisted man. 3. swordsman, warfarer, man-at-arms. 4. any military man. 5. (fig.): a) backer. b) champion. 6. (ornith.) an oriole (Icterus tibilais). 7. (ichth.) a freshwater fish (Cataphractus calichtys). 8. ~**s** pl. troops, arrayal, array.
~ **da infantaria** infantryman, foot soldier. ~ **de acampamento** camper. ~ **de cavalaria** cavalryman. **Soldado Desconhecido** Unknown Soldier, Unknown Warrior. ~ **do corpo de guarda** guardsman. ~ **do exército territorial** territorial. ~ **experimentado** old soldier or warrior, battleworn soldier. ~ **pára-quedista** paratrooper. ~ **raso** private, common soldier, buck private. **os** ~**s rasos** rank and file. **brincar de** ~ to play at soldiers. **indigno de um** ~ unsoldierlike. ~ **recruta** recruit, newly enlisted soldier.
soldado (II) adj. 1. soldered, welded. 2. united, connected, joined, attached. 3. glued.
soldador s. m. welder, jointer. ‖ adj. soldering, welding.
soldadura s. f. 1. act or process of soldering. 2. soldering, welding. 3. weld, soldering seam. **sem** ~ weldless.
soldagem s. f. (pl. **-ens**) soldering, welding, forge welding.
~ **a topo** butt weld. ~ **elétrica** electric welding. ~ **enviesada** scarf welding.
soldanela s. f. 1. Soldanella: a genus of alpine herbs (family: Primulaceae). 2. soldanel. 3. sea bell, sea bindweed.
soldar v. 1. to solder, weld. 2. to join, unite, connect. 3. to tinker. 4. to fasten, fix. 5. ~-**se**: a) to become united. b) to become glued together. c) to heal, become closed (a wound).
~ **canto com canto,** ~ **a topo** to butt-weld. ~ **com latão** to braze. **arame para** ~ welding rod. **ferro de** ~ soldering bolt, soldering iron. **forno de** ~ welding furnace.
soldável adj. m. + f. (pl. **-áveis**) weldable.
soldo (ô) s. m. (pl. **soldos**) 1. salary of military officers. 2. soldier's pay. 3. sou: a French copper coin (the twentieth part of a franc).
soldra s. f. (vet.) stifle joint.
solecismo s. m. 1. solecism. 2. ungrammatical use of a word in a sentence, incorrectness of language. 3. violation of syntax. 4. absurdity. 5. mistake, error. 6. guilt.
solecista s. m. + f. solecist: one who commits solecisms. ‖ adj. solecistic(al).
solecizar v. 1. to solecize. 2. to commit solecisms. 3. to use solecisms.
soledade s. f. 1. solitude, isolation. 2. a remote or solitary place. 3. seclusion, retirement. 4. loneliness, solitariness. 5. mental depression or deep melancholy caused by loneliness.
sol-e-dó s. m. (pl. **sol-e-dós**) (pop.) 1. any trivial popular music. 2. a simple monotonous tune. 3. a

mediocre music band or orchestra. 4. vulgar music. 5. a guitar and viola concert.
soleira (I) s. f. 1. sill, door-sill. 2. door-stone. 3. threshold (plate P 16). 4. carriage step, footboard. 5. metal plate under the draw-bar connection of a carriage. 6. chain or strap of a spur.
soleira (II) s. f. 1. the hottest time of the day. 2. sunniness. 3. sunburning. 4. excessive warmth, heat, swelter. 5. exposition to the sun. 6. calmness, calm.
solene adj. m. + f. 1. solemn. 2. celebrated every year with public festivities. 3. pompous, magnificent. 4. portentous, ominous. 5. grave, serious. 6. sumptuous, splendid. 7. sober, somber. 8. formal, conventional. 9. majestic, grand. ‖ ~**mente** adv. 1. solemnly. 2. magnificently. 3. portentously. 4. sumptuously. 5. emphatically.
a inauguração ~ **do novo edifício** the solemn consecration of the new building. **ato** ~ **governamental** state occasion. **ele falou** ~**mente** he spoke in grave accents. **missa** ~ high mass. **um juramento** ~ a solemn oath.
solenidade s. f. 1. solemnity. 2. solemn act or ceremony. 3. solemnization. 4. celebration, festiveness, festivity. 5. (fam., coll.) emphasis: impressiveness of speech or manners. 6. (coll.) arrogance, haughtiness.
solenização s. f. (pl. -ões) 1. act or process of solemnizing. 2. solemnization. 3. celebration, commemoration. 4. exaltation, dignification.
solenizador s. m. solemnizer. ‖ adj. solemnizing, celebrating.
solenizar v. 1. to solemnize. 2. to celebrate or commemorate with solemnity. 3. to make solemn, give a solemn aspect to.
solenoglifo s. m. 1. solenoglyph: a solenoglyphic snake. 2. ~s pl. Solenoglypha: a group of snakes with two tubular erectile fangs.
solenóide s. m. (electr.) solenoid: a tubular coil of wire used for the production of a magnetic field. ~ **do duplicador** (electr.) duplicator solenoid.
solércia s. f. 1. quickness of wit. 2. shrewdness, cunning. 3. sharpness, smartness. 4. ruse, stratagem, trick.
solerte s. m. + f. 1. a sagacious, shrewd or cunning person. 2. crook, rascal. ‖ adj. 1. sagacious, intelligent. 2. cunning, shrewd. 3. solert, skillful. 4. industrious, diligent. 5. crooked, fraudulent.
soles s. m., sg. + pl. a swingle-tree for two or more yokes of oxen.
soleta s. f. 1. a thin sole or inner sole for shoes. 2. small sole.
soletração s. f. (pl. -ões) act or result of spelling. **erro de** ~ misspelling.
soletrador s. m. speller: one who spells. ‖ adj. spelling.
soletrar v. 1. to spell. 2. to read carefully, pronouncing letter by letter. 3. to read badly. 4. (fig.) to understand, comprehend, decipher, perceive, discern, guess. ~ **mal** to misspell.
solevantar, solevar v. 1. to raise a little from the ground, lift slightly. 2. to erect or raise with difficulty. 3. ~**-se** to get up gradually, just a little bit or with difficulty, raise o. s., arise.
solfa s. f. (mus.) 1. sol-fa. 2. music notes, written music. 3. the art of sol-faing. 4. solmization.
solfado adj. (of paper) ruled over the whole page.
solfar (I) v. 1. to repair the worn-out pages of a book. 2. to increase the margin of a page (of a sheet or book). 3. to paste guards or ornamental borders on a page.
solfar (II) v. (mus.) to sol-fa.
solfatara s. f. (geol.) solfatara.
solfatárico adj. (geol.) solfataric(al).

solfejar v. (mus.) to sol-fa, solmizate, sing or read the notes of a piece of music.
solfejo s. m. (mus.) 1. sol-fa, solfeggio. 2. solmization. 3. to practise sol-faing. 4. ~s pl. musical exercise book of solfeggios.
solferino s. m. solferino red, fuchsine.
solfista s. m. + f. (mus.) 1. sol-faist. 2. (pop.) musician, composer or professional performer.
solha (ô) s. f. 1. flounder, flatfish (Pleuronectes flexus). 2. fluke, sole (Solea solea).
solha-reis s. f. (pl. **solhas-reis**) (ichth.) sturgeon.
solhar (I) adj. (anat.) peroneal.
solhar (II) v. to lay a wood floor, plank the floor, lay a parquet flooring.
solheira s. f. a special net for flounder and sturgeon fishing.
solho (ô) s. m. (pl. **solhos**) wooden floor, parquet, parquetry.
solia s. f. 1. (formerly) a woollen fabric. 2. a garment made from this material.
solicitação s. f. (pl. -ões) 1. solicitation. 2. request. 3. appeal, entreaty. 4. postulation. 5. call(ing). 6. incitement. 7. suit. ~ **de trunfo** (cards) a call for trumps.
solicitado adj. 1. solicited. 2. requested. **não** ~ unsolicited, unsought, undesired.
solicitador s. m. (jur.) 1. solicitor. 2. legal adviser, proctor. 3. suitor: one who sues or prosecutes. ‖ adj. requesting, soliciting, solicitant. ~ **acadêmico** (Braz., jur.) academic solicitor.
solicitante s. m. + f. solicitant. ‖ adj. solicitant.
solicitar v. 1. to solicit. 2. to seek, search for, look for. 3. to endeavour to obtain. 4. to ask, beg, petition. 5. to request. 6. to appeal. 7. to apply for. 8. to entreat. 9. to court, woo. 10. to act as solicitor or proctor. 11. to induce to, incite. 12. to attract. 13. to make petitions, appeal to legal authorities. 14. ~**-se:** a) to become worried. b) to care for. 15. to invite, bid.
~ **com insistência** to urge. ~ **a mal** to try to induce to evil. ~ **por** to appeal for. ~ **um negócio** to attend to or manage a business. ~ **votos** to canvass.
solicitável adj. m. + f. (pl. -áveis) that may be solicited, requestable, appealable.
solícito adj. 1. careful, thoughtful. 2. diligent, industrious. 3. active. 4. solicitous. 5. eager, full of zest. 6. attentive, mindful. 7. obliging. 8. restless, anxious.
solicitude s. f. 1. solicitude. 2. carefulness, thoughtfulness. 3. diligence, industry, assiduity. 4. forwardness. 5. solicitousness. 6. anxiousness, concern, anxiety.
solidago s. m. (bot.) golden rod.
solidão s. f. (pl. -ões) 1. solitude. 2. solitariness, loneliness, lonesomeness. 3. a solitary or lonely place. 4. isolation, seclusion. 5. privacy, retiredness. 6. exile. 7. wilderness, desert. ~ **a dois** shared solitude (of a couple).
solidar v. 1. to make solid, solidify. 2. to confirm, corroborate. 3. to strengthen.
solidariedade s. f. 1. solidarity. 2. community of interests. 3. interdependence. 4. solidary rights of creditors with regard to one debtor. 5. joint liability. 6. fellowship, comradeship, friendship.
solidário adj. 1. solidary. 2. mutual, reciprocal. 3. common, joint. 4. harmonious, corresponding. 5. jointly liable. ‖ **solidariamente** adv. solidarily. **letra -a** (com.) promissory note. **responsabilidade -a** joint responsibility, unlimited responsibility.
solidarizar v. 1. to make or render solidary, solidarize, unite. 2. ~**-se:** a) to be or declare o. s. solidary. b) to act in common interests.

solidéu s. m. 1. calotte, plain skullcap, cap. 2. (eccl.) zucchetto.
~ **cardinalício** (eccl.) a cardinal's red zucchetto.
solidez s. f. 1. solidity, solidness. 2. resistance, firmness. 3. durability, durableness, lastingness. 4. security, reliance. 5. compactness, massiveness. 6. hardness. 7. consistence. 8. soundness. 9. validity. 10. concreteness.
sem ~ unsoundly.
solidificação s. f. (pl. -ões) 1. solidification. 2. setting, set. 3. concretion. 4. consolidation, stabilization.
solidificado adj. 1. solidified, solid. 2. set. 3. hard. 4. compact. 5. consolidate(d).
solidificador s. m. 1. solidifier. 2. consolidator. 3. solidifying agent. || adj. solidifying, consolidating.
solidificar v. 1. to solidify, render solid. 2. to coagulate; congeal, concrete, cake. 3. to set, settle. 4. to fix. 5. to consolidate. 6. to make robust, strengthen. 7. ~-se to become solid, grow hard.
sólido s. m. 1. a solid, any solid body or substance. 2. (geom.) body. || adj. 1. solid. 2. consistent, compact. 3. lasting, durable. 4. entire, whole, sound. 5. upright. 6. massive, massy. 7. hard, rocky. 8. firm. 9. stout, stocky. 10. strong. 11. steady. 12. substantial. 13. real, true. 14. robust, vigorous. 15. (fig.) indisputable, incontestable. 16. (phys.) three-dimensional. 17. dependable. || **solidamente** adv. 1. solidly. 2. concretely. 3. stably, durably. 4. compactly. 5. strongly.
argumentos ~**s** well-founded arguments, sledgehammer arguments. **ele é um homem de convicções -as** he is a man of firm convictions. **não** ~ unsolid, unsound, unsubstantial. **uma refeição -a** a substantial meal.
solidônia s. f. a shrub of the family Nyctaginaceae (Boerhavia paniculata).
solífugo adj. (poet.) 1. shunning the sunlight. 2. fond of dawn or twilight. 3. nocturnal, nightly.
soliloquiar v. to soliloquize, talk to o. s.
solilóquio s. m. soliloquy, monologue.
solimão s. m. (pl. -ões) a corrosive sublimate, bichloride of mercury; (pop.) any poisonous drink.
solina s. f. (pop.) scorching sunshine, excessive heat.
solinhadeira s. f. a quarryman's hammer.
solinhar v. to plane wood or cut stone along a marked line.
solinho s. m. act of hewing wood or stone.
sólio s. m. 1. a royal seat, throne. 2. (eccl.) a papal or episcopal chair (on a dais with a canopy). 3. (fig.) royal authority and power.
solípede s. m. + f. (zool.) soliped. || adj. soliped, solipedous, solipedal.
solipsismo s. m. (philos.) solipsism; philosophical doctrine which asserts the absolute subjectivity of existence and reality.
solista s. m. + f. soloist: 1. a musical performer who plays or sings a solo in a concert. 2. one who flies solo in an airplane.
solitária s. f. 1. (zool.) tapeworm, taenia (Taenia solium). 2. a necklace (resembling somewhat the rings of a tapeworm). 3. (Braz.) a cell for solitary confinement.
solitário s. m. 1. solitarian, a solitary man. 2. hermit, eremite. 3. monk, cenobite. 4. solitaire, a jewel set with a single diamond or other precious gem. 5. a small flower vase with a long and narrow neck. || adj. 1. solitary: a) living alone, lone. b) lonely, forlorn. c) secluded, unfrequented. d) unsociable, uncouth. e) desert, wild, desolate. f) retired, reclusive. 2. windowed. 3. cloistral. 4. secret. || **solitariamente** adv. solitarily, lonely, reclusively.
ele leva uma vida -a he leads a solitary life. **ele**

tem hábitos de ~ he has solitary habits. **vôo** ~ solitary flight, solo flight.
solito adj. (pop.) alone, all alone.
sólito adj. 1. used, accustomed. 2. usual, habitual.
solitude s. f. (poet.) 1. solitude. 2. solitariness. 3. loneliness. 4. a secluded, lonely place.
solmização s. f. (pl. -ões) (mus.) solmization.
solo (I) s. m. 1. soil, the upper layer of earth. 2. firm land, ground. 3. earth, clod. 4. floor, story of a building.
a importância da conservação do ~ the importance of top-soil conservation. **remoção da camada superior do** ~ top-soil removal, top-soiling. **acima do** ~ overground. ~ **duro** hardpan.
solo (II) s. m. solo: 1. a piece of music written for or executed by one singer, player or performer. 2. a game of cards (a variety of whist). 3. the first solo flight of a new pilot.
solo-asfalto s. m. (pl. **solos-asfaltos**) soil-cement.
solovox s. m. (mus.) electronic instrument provided with a small keyboard.
sol-posto s. m. (pl. **sóis-postos**) sunset, the time of sunset.
sol-quadrado s. m. (pl. **sóis-quadrados**) (Braz., pop.) jail.
solsticial adj. m. + f. (pl. -**ais**) solstitial.
solstício s. m. solstice, solstitial point.
~ **de inverno** winter solstice. ~ **de verão** summer solstice.
solta (ô) s. f. 1. act or result of freeing, unfastening. 2. a shackle for horses and cattle. 3 (fig. + obs.) prison. 4. (Braz.) a pasture where cattle is kept for fattening.
à ~ freely, without shackles, in liberty.
soltada s. f. act of setting free a pack of hounds.
soltado adj. loose, let loose, released.
soltador s. m. releaser, liberator. || adj. releasing, liberating.
soltar v. 1. to unfasten, untie, unbind. 2. to loosen, loose. 3. to let go, let loose. 4. unhitch, unhook. 5. to unleash, unlace. 6. to free, set free. 7. to unchain, unlink. 8. to release, dismiss, discharge. 9. (naut.) to unfurl (sails, flags). 10. to slacken, slack. 11. to unpen, uncage. 12. to disengage. 13. to exonerate from obligations. 14. to hurl, throw, let fly. 15. to let out a secret, vent, let slip a word. 16. to start on one's way. 17. to take one's hands off, abandon. 18. to ease, ease off. 19. to unscrew, unfix. 20. to sluice. 21. ~-se: a) to get loose, come undone. b) to be separated from. c) to run freely.
~ **a língua** to let loose one's tongue. ~ **a rédea a alguém** to give one his fling. ~ **as rédeas** to give the reins, yield the hand. ~ **a voz** to give voice. ~ **da cadeia** to release from prison, enfranchise. ~ **o cabelo** to dishevel. ~ **os cães** to uncouple the dogs. ~ **piada** to wisecrack. ~ **uma questão** to solve, clear up a question. ~-**se em injúrias contra alguém** to break out in invectives against s. o. ~ **uma gargalhada** to break out into a fit of laughter. ~ **um grito** to give a cry. ~ **um papagaio** to fly a kite. ~ **vapor** to let off steam.
solteira s. f. 1. single woman, spinster, bachelor girl, maid(en). 2. a marine fish of the family Carangidae (Scombroises occidentalis). || adj. f. 1. single, unmarried (woman). 2. without offspring.
solteirão s. m. (pl. -ões) (f. **solteirona**) 1. a middle-aged or elderly single man. 2. confirmed bachelor.
solteirismo s. m. 1. bachelorhood, bachelordom, bachelorship. 2. wifelessness. 3. celibacy, celibate.
solteiro s. m. single man, bachelor, celibate. || adj. 1. single, unmarried, unwed(ded). 2. wifeless, mateless. 3. (of a week) without holiday or fastday.

solteirona s. f. middle-aged single woman, old maid, spinster.
próprio de ~ old maidish.
solto (ô) adj. 1. free, unattached. 2. unbound, untied; independent. 3. unfastened, unfixed. 4. released, liberated. 5. slack. 6. loose. 7. dissolute, licentious. 8. without definite home harbour or landing place (ship). 9. unrhymed (verses).
língua -a a loose tongue. **palavras -as** licentious talk. **vento** ~ a heavy storm. **verso** ~ blank verse, blank rhyme. **vida -a** loose manners, licentious life.
soltura s. f. 1. act or effect of liberating. 2. freeing, liberation. 3. release, delivery from prison, discharge. 4. acquittal. 5. impertinence, insolence. 6. licentiousness, dissoluteness. 7. solution; interpretation, explanation.
~ **do ventre** loose bowels, diarrhea.
solubilidade s. f. (phys., chem.) solubility, solubleness.
solubilizar v. to solubilize, make soluble.
soluçado adj. interrupted by sobs.
soluçante adj. m. + f. sobbing, weeping, hiccupy.
solução s. f. (pl. **-ões**) 1. solution: a) act or result of solving (problem). b) conclusion. c) answer, explanation, elucidation, denouement. d) interruption. e) key. f) the overcoming of difficulties. g) general solution of an algebraic equation or result of a mathematical problem. h) (chem.) mixture with a solvent. 2. (com.) payment.
este negócio está aguardando ~ this business is pendent, this is pending matter. **não há** ~ there is no known answer, there is no solution, it is insoluble. **sem** ~ unsolved, (fig.) keyless. ~ **de continuidade** solution of continuity. ~ **de um problema** resolution of a problem. ~ **ideal** the best solution.
soluçar s. m. 1. sob, sobbing. 2. hiccup, hiccough. ‖ v. 1. to sob. 2. to speak with sobs. 3. to whimper, whine. 4. to hiccup, hiccough. 5. to rustle, rush, roar (wind or waves). 6. to get agitated, become excited. 7. to roar, howl.
solucionar v. 1. to give a solution, find a solution for. 2. to resolve, decide. 3. to work out a solution (for a problem, difficulty).
soluço s. m. 1. sob, sobbing. 2. hiccup, hiccough. 3. whimpering, whining, convulsive weeping. 4. (naut.) tossing or heaving of a ship. 5. din, clamour.
soluçoso adj. sobbing, sobby, uttered with sobs.
solutivo adj. 1. dissolvable, dissoluble. 2. solvent. 3. laxative.
soluto s. m. 1. (phys., chem.) solute, a dissolved substance. 2. solution. ‖ adj. 1. loose, free. 2. unbound, untied. 3. dissolved, liquified.
solúvel adj. m. + f. (pl. **-úveis**) 1. dissolvable, dissoluble. 2. soluble. 3. resolvable.
não ~ insoluble, indissoluble, insolvable. **substancias -úveis** solutes, solvable substances.
solvabilidade s. f. 1. solvability. 2. solubility. 3. (com.) solvency, commercial responsibility, responsibleness.
solvável adj. m. + f. (pl. **-áveis**) 1. solvable. 2. soluble, dissolvable. 3. resolvable, explainable. 4. (com.) solvent, responsible, capable of meeting one's debts.
solvência s. f. (com.) solvency, solvability.
a sua ~ **é fora de dúvida** (com.) his ability to pay is out of question.
solvente s. m. 1. solvent, solvent agent, remover. 2. ~**s** pl. (chem.) extractive substances. ‖ adj. m. + f. 1. solvent. 2. dissolving, soluble, dissolvable. 3. resolvent, solvable. 4. (com.) capable to pay, responsible.
solver v. 1. to solve. 2. to explain, resolve. 3. to puzzle out, clear up (mystery, problem, difficulty).

4. to pay, settle a debt. 5. to relieve, release from. 6. to separate, disintegrate. 7. to untie, unfasten. 8. to dissolve. 9. to become free (from debts, obligations) clear, settle balances.
solvibilidade s. f. (com.) solvency.
solvível adj. m. + f. (pl. **-íveis**) (com.) solvent, solvable, able to pay one's debts, active.
som s. m. (pl. **sons**) 1. sound. 2. vocal or musical sound, tone, voice. 3. tonality. 4. sounding. 5. noise, din. 6. (fig.) manner, behaviour.
~ **agudo** shrill sound. ~ **baixo** deep tone, bourdon. ~ **grave** drone. ~ **gutural** guttural, guttural sound. ~ **indistinto** blur. ~ **metálico** twang, twangle, clash. ~ **rijo** clangour. ~ **surdo** dead sound, thump. **à prova de** ~ sound-proof. **ao** ~ **de...** to the sound of..., (fig.) according to. **dizer em alto e bom** ~ to say in a clear and loud voice, speak distinctly. **falar sem tom nem** ~ to speak without rhyme nor reason. **mudança de** ~ soundshift.
soma (I) s. f. 1. sum, result of an addition. 2. total, total amount. 3. addition, summation. 4. totality, quantity. 5. count. 6. number. 7. a great portion. 8. a whole, aggregate. 9. (fig.) substance.
~ **total** sum total. **em** ~ in all, all in all, all told. **ele a vendeu pela** ~ **de...** he sold it for the total amount of...
soma (II) s. m. (anat., zool.) soma: 1. the complete structure of a living body. 2. the physical organism (in opposition to the mind and Psyche).
soma (III) s. f. (bot.) soma (Sarcostemma acidum).
soma (IV) s. m. (Angola, West Africa) designation of a tribal chief.
somali s. m. + f. Somal, Somali: 1. a native or inhabitant of Somaliland. 2. the language spoken by the Somalis. ‖ adj. of, pertaining to or relative to this country, its people and language.
somar v. 1. to sum, sum up, add up. 2. to count, calculate by adding. 3. to total, totalize. 4. to result, have as a sum. 5. to amount to. 6. to summarize, condense. 7. to recapitulate. 8. to gather, accumulate.
ela somou as suas impressões she put two and two together. **máquina de** ~ adding machine, adder, totalizer.
somático adj. (med.) somatic(al), physical, corporeal: of, pertaining to or affecting the body. ‖ **somaticamente** adv. somatically.
somatologia s. f. somatology.
somatológico adj. somatological.
somatório s. m. 1. sum, sum total. 2. total amount, total. 3. (fig.) totality. ‖ adj. of or referring to a sum.
sombra s. f. 1. shadow, shade. 2. darkness. 3. night. 4. blot, blemish. 5. the dark parts of a picture or drawing. 6. shadiness. 7. (astr.) umbra. 8. cloud, fog. 9. dusk. 10. hachure. 11. spectre, spiritual appearance, phantom. 12. trace, track, vestige. 13. rudimentary notions of any art or science. 14. protection, shelter. 15. seclusion, loneliness. 16. mystery. 17. lamp-shade.
~ **e água fresca** (Braz., pop.) a happy-go-lucky life, dolce far niente, pleasant idleness. **à** ~ in the shade, (pop.) in prison. **à** ~ **de sua proteção** under his (her) protection. **a** ~ **levantou-se** the cloud lifted. **as** ~**s da noite** the shades of night. **boa** ~ a good sign, a good omen. **de má** ~ unwillingly. **ela ficou reduzida a uma** ~ she was the mere ghost of herself. **ele é agora apenas a** ~ **de uma** ~ he is now but the shadow of a shade. **fazer** ~ **a** to stand in some one's light, eclipse s. one's merit. **nenhuma** ~ **de prova** not a shred of evidence. **nem por** ~**s** not in the least. **sem** ~ shadowless, shadeless, unshaded, unshadowed. **sem** ~ **de**

dúvida without the slightest doubt. **ter medo de sua própria** ~ to be afraid of one's own shadow. **um homem de boa (má)** ~ a kindly (evil) looking man.

sombral s. m. (pl. **-ais**) a shady place.

sombrar v. to shade: protect from sunlight (or light).

sombreação s. f. (pl. **-ões**) adumbration.

sombreado s. m. the shading of a picture or drawing. ‖ adj. shaded, shadowed, overshadowed, bosky, bowery.

não ~ unshaded, unshadowed. ~ **de gravura** tint.

sombreamento s. m. (arts) hatching.

sombrear v. 1. to shade, shadow. 2. to screen from light or heat. 3. to obscure, darken. 4. to maculate, stain, soil. 5. (arts) to paint with graduations of light or colour. 6. (fig.) to grieve. 7. to overshade. 8. to adumbrate.

sombreireiro s. m. 1. a manufacturer of sombreros, hatter, sombrero-maker. 2. sombrero vendor.

sombreiro s. m. sombrero, a broad-brimmed straw or felt hat.

sombrejar v. 1. to shadow, shade. 2. to protect from light. 3. ~**-se** to protect o. s. from the sun's rays.

sombrela s. f. a bell-shaped earthen vessel used to protect young plants from the weather.

sombrinha s. f. 1. parasol, sunshade (plates G 4, R 6). 2. ~**s** pl. galanty show, phantasmagoria.

sombrio s. m. 1. a shady place. 2. umbrageousness. 3. (ornith.) the yellow pipit (Anthus lutescens). ‖ adj. 1. shady, shadowy. 2. producing shadow. 3. protected from light. 4. obscure, umbrageous. 5. dark, dim, dusky. 6. sad, downcast, gloomy, sullen. 7. frowning, moody. 8. dismal, dreary. 9. somber, sober. 10. cloudy, clouded. 11. severe, rigorous, very strict. 12. despotic. 13. murky, misty, nebulous. 14. morose, dour. 15. funereal, sepulchral. 16. grave. ‖ **-amente** adv. shadily, obscurely, somberly, etc.

sombroso adj. 1. shady, shadowy. 2. dark, umbrageous. 3. gloomy. 4. sombrous. 5. producing shadow(s).

someiro s. m. 1. wind-chest of an organ. 2. lintel of a door or window. 3. (archit.) impost of an arch.

somenos adj. m. + f., sg. + pl. 1. inferior, of inferior quality. 2. of little worth, paltry. 3. of less value than. 4. ordinary, common, vulgar. 5. disreputable. **de** ~ insignificant, unimportant. **isto é uma questão de** ~ this is a trifling matter.

somiticar v. to act in a mean or miserly way, be avaricious, greedy or stingy.

somiticaria s. f. 1. avarice. 2. greed, avidity. 3. stinginess, niggardliness. 4. meanness.

somítico s. m. 1. miser, skinflint. 2. niggard, a meanly close-fisted person. ‖ adj. avaricious, greedy, covetous, stingy, mean, miserly.

somitiquice s. f. 1. avarice. 2. avaricious act. 3. greediness, avidity. 4. covetousness. 5. sordid parsimony.

sonador adj. designating the sound produced by a galloping horse, galloping.

sonambular v. to somnambulate. walk when asleep.

sonambúlico adj. somnambulistic, somnambulic. ‖ **sonambulicamente** adv. somnambulistically.

sonambulismo s. m. (med.) somnambulism, sleep--walking, night-walking.

sonâmbulo s. m. somnambulist, sleepwalker, night--walker, noctambulist. ‖ adj. somnambulistic, noctambulous.

sonância s. f. 1. sonance, sonancy. 2. sound, tone. 3. music. 4. tune, melody.

sonante adj. m. + f. 1. sonant, sounding. 2. toned, intonated, tonic. 3. ringing, vibrant. 4. voiceful, vocal (with).

sonar s. m. (naut.) sonar.

sonata (I) s. f. (mus.) sonata.

sonata (II) s. f. a nap, forty winks.

sonatina s. f. (mus.) sonatina, short sonata.

sonda s. f. 1. deep-sea lead, sounding lead. 2. (med., surg.) probe, style, catheter, searcher. 3. lead-line, sounding line. 4. oil derrick. 5. plumb line, plummet. 6. (fig.) search, investigation. 7. means of investigation. 8. depth, deepness, profundity. 9. depth gauge, sea gauge.

sondá s. f. (Braz.) a long coarse line used for angling.

sondador s. m. 1. sounder. 2. delver. 3. fathomer. 4. probe. ‖ adj. sounding, probing, delving.

sondagem s. f. (pl. **-ens**) 1. sounding. 2. perforation, drilling (made in order to study the geological structure of the soil). 3. exploration. 4. plumbing. 5. (meteor.) the act or process of measuring the atmospheric conditions at various heights. 6. (med., surg.) probing. 7. act of sounding out s. o.

sondar v. 1. to sound: a) find out the depth of waters. b) search, delve into; to fathom; throw out a feeler; to evaluate, appraise; to investigate, explore; to query. 2. (med., surg.) to probe. 3. (sl.) to die.

sondareza s. f. sounding line.

sondável adj. m. + f. (pl. **-áveis**) soundable, fathomable.

soneca s. f. 1. somnolence, sleepiness, drowsiness. 2. a short sleep, nap, doze, snooze, slumber.

sonega s. f. unlawful concealment, misappropriation.

sonegação s. f. (pl. **-ões**) 1. illegal withholdment. 2. unlawful concealment. 3. defraudation, defraudment. 4. misapplication, misappropriation. 5. theft.

sonegador s. m. withholder, defrauder. ‖ adj. concealing, withholding, defrauding.

sonegados s. m. pl. objects or values unlawfully withheld or concealed, defrauded taxes.

sonegamento s. m. act or method of unlawful withholdment, defraudation, misappropriation.

sonegar v. 1. to withhold or conceal unlawfully. 2. to misapply, misappropriate. 3. to defraud, cheat. 4. to steal, filch, deprive of secretly. 5. not to pay (taxes, debts, etc.). 6. to shirk from, shun, dodge (an unpleasant task or duty).

soneira s. f. 1. sleepiness, somnolence. 2. drowsiness. 3. inertness, lethargy.

sonetar, sonetear v. 1. to write sonnets. 2. to give the form of a sonnet to.

sonetilho s. m. a sonnet of short verses.

sonetista s. m. + f. sonnetist, composer of sonnets. ‖ adj. sonneting, sonnetizing, sonneteering.

soneto (ê) s. m. sonnet, a short poem.

songamonga s. m. + f. a cunning or artful person, trickster.

sonhador s. m. 1. visionary. 2. dreamer, day-dreamer. 3. dozer. 4. star-gazer. ‖ adj. dreamy, dreaming, moony.

sonhar v. 1. to dream. 2. to day-dream, think idly. 3. to imagine, fancy. 4. to have a fixed idea. **deixa de** ~**!** come back to earth!

sonhim s. m. (pl. **-ins**) (zool.) a saki monkey.

sonho s. m. 1. dream: a) a series of involuntary images passing through the mind in sleep. b) utopia. c) fiction, fancy. d) vision. e) day-dream, wish-thinking. f) phantasy, a fleeting thing or image. g) an ardent wish. 2. friedcake, cruller. **ela comprou um** ~ **de um vestido** she bought a beauty of a dress. **realizaram-se todos os seus** ~**s** all her dreams came alive. **nem por um** ~ by no means. ~ **dourado** golden dream.

sonial adj. m. + f. (pl. **-ais**) of, pertaining to or relative to dreams; dreamy, visionary, dreamlike.

sônico adj. sonic, concerning sound, phonic.

sonido s. m. 1. sound, tone. 2. noise, din, racket. 3. murmur, rumbling. 4. rumour.

o ~ das árvores no vento the rustling of the trees in the wind.

sonífero s. m. soporific, soporiferous drug or draught, opiate. ‖ adj. soporific, soporiferous, soniferous.

soníloquo s. m. a person who talks when asleep. ‖ adj. talking while asleep, somniloquous.

sono s. m. 1. sleep, slumber. 2. rest, repose. 3. sleepiness, drowsiness. 4. state of being asleep. 5. (fig.) inertia, inertness. 6. dullness of mind, indolence. 7. laziness.

~ **agitado** dog-sleep. ~ **da morte** dead sleep. ~ **leve** catnap, doze, dog-sleep, slumber. ~ **profundo**, ~ **pesado** sound or deep sleep. ~ **perturbado** broken sleep. **doença do** ~ (med.) sleeping-sickness. **estar com** ~ to be sleepy, be drowsy. **dormir a** ~ **solto** to sleep soundly, sleep like a log. **dormir d'um** ~ to sleep through the night without awaking. **não perca o** ~ **por causa disto** don't lose any sleep over it. **pegar no** ~ to fall asleep. **sem** ~ sleepless, unsleeping. **ter** ~ **pesado** to be a heavy sleeper. **tirar do** ~ to awake(n), arouse. **tonto de** ~ sleep-drunk.

sonolência s. f. 1. somnolence, somnolency. 2. sleepiness, drowsiness, doziness. 3. dormancy. 4. imperfect or light sleep, slumber. 5. (fig.) torpor, sluggishness.

sonolento adj. 1. somnolent. 2. sleepy, inclined to sleep. 3. drowsy, slumberous. 4. somniferous, soporific. 5. inert, torpid, sluggish. ‖ **-amente** adv. somnolently, drowsily, dozily, sluggishly.

sonometria s. f. (phys.) sonometry, audiometry.

sonométrico adj. (phys.) sonometric(al), audiometric(al).

sonômetro s. m. (phys.) sonometer, audiometer.

sonoridade s. f. 1. sonority, sonorousness. 2. quality of producing sound(s). 3. loudness, volume; richness, fullness (of sound).

sonorização s. f. (pl. -ões) act, process or result of making sonorous.

sonorizar v. 1. to render sonorous. 2. to sound, resound. 3. to produce sounds.

sonoro adj. 1. sonorous. 2. producing sound. 3. resonant. 4. loud, full; rich, deep (in sound). 5. voiced, voiceful. 6. harmonious. 7. vibrant. ‖ **-amente** adv. sonorously, harmoniously, sonorantly.

filme ~ vocal film, talking film, sound-film. **onda -a** sound wave.

sonoroso adj. 1. sonorous. 2. full sounding, resonant, resounding. 3. melodious, harmonious.

sonoteca s. f. (neologism) sound-effects library.

sonoterapia s. f. (med.) sleep therapy; induced sleep.

sonsa, sonsice s. f. 1. slyness, artfulness, cunning. 2. feigned sagacity. 3. dissimulation.

pela ~, **pela sonsice** on the sly, secretly.

sonsinho adj. 1. crooked. 2. sly, crafty, scheming. 3. sharp, clever, smart.

sonso adj. 1. sly, artful, cunning. 2. clever, smart, crafty. 3. furtive, secretive. 4. crooked, deceptive.

sonsonete s. m. a derisive inflection of voice which indicates irony.

sopa s. f. 1. soup. 2. sop, broth. 3. bread soaked in broth. 4. any well drenched or soaked matter. 5. an easy task or affair, pushover, cinch. 6. (Braz., geol.) strata of solidified gravel. 7. (N. Braz.) a small bus.

~ **de aveia** gruel. ~ **de tartaruga** turtle soup. **ela não é** ~ she's a tough customer. **como** ~ **souplike. dar** ~ (sl.) easy to be stolen; (coll.) easy to be conquered (woman). **isto caiu como** ~ **no mel** this happened just at the right moment, that came in very handy. **isto é** ~ that's a cinch. **voltei feito** ~ I came home soaked to the skin.

sopapear v. to slap, strike, cuff, buffet.

sopapo s. m. 1. blow with the fist. 2. slap, wipe. 3. hit, rap, knock. 4. drubbing, thrashing.

sopé s. m. 1. the base or foot of a mountain (plate M 11). 2. foothill, knoll, mound. 3. bottom, the lowest part (of a mountain, hill, wall).

no ~ **da colina** at the foot of the hill.

sopeador s. m. represser, suppressor, one who checks, curbs in or humiliates. ‖ adj. repressive, checking, humiliating.

sopeamento s. m. 1. act or result of repression. 2. act of putting the foot on or trampling down. 3. subjection, subjugation. 4. restraint, check. 5. humiliation.

sopear v. 1. to trample down, crush under foot, tread on. 2. to hamper, hinder, encumber. 3. to repress, restrain. 4. subject, subjugate. 5. to humiliate.

sopeira s. f. tureen, soup tureen (plate M 1).

sopeiro s. m. 1. person fond of soup. 2. (coll.) a sponger, parasite. ‖ adj. 1. of or pertaining to soup. 2. fond of soup. 3. (coll.) living upon others, parasitic.

sopesar v. 1. to lift a weight with the hand in order to estimate its weight. 2. to bear the weight of. 3. to counterweigh, balance. 4. to keep balance, hold the equilibrium. 5. to distribute methodically and parsimoniously.

sopeso (ê) s. m. 1. act of estimating the weight of a thing by lifting it with the hand. 2. equilibration, counterbalancing.

sopetarra s. f. (fam.) 1. snack, bite, fat morsel. 2. a rich soup.

sopetear v. 1. to soak, steep. 2. to sop, dunk. 3. to savour, relish. 4. to enjoy.

sopiar v. to baptize at home.

sopista s. m. + f. person fond of soup.

sopitado adj. 1. sleepy, drowsy. 2. asleep. 3. lazy, sluggish. 4. effeminate, prissy.

sopitar v. 1. to lull to sleep. 2. to calm, tranquillize. 3. to soothe. 4. to break down, to weaken, enfeeble. 5. to make effeminate, become effeminate. 6. to fill with (new) hopes, stimulate. 7. to dominate, conquer.

sopito adj. 1. sleepy, drowsy. 2. asleep. 3. lazy, sluggish. 4. effeminate, prissy.

sopontadura s. f. 1. underscoring (with little points). 2. (proofreading) mark indicating the restoration of words that had been crossed out.

sopontar v. 1. to underscore, mark, underline (with little points). 2. (proofreading) to restore what had been crossed out (with litle points under the word(s) to be kept).

sopor s. m. 1. sleepiness, drowsiness. 2. somnolence, somnolency. 3. torpor, apathy. 4. stupor, lethargy.

soporado adj. 1. sleepy, drowsy. 2. somnolent. 3. torpid, apathetic(al). 4. soporiferous.

soporativo s. m. 1. (pharm.) soporific, soporiferous drug or medicament. 2. (fig.) dull or tiresome matter. ‖ adj. 1. soporific, soporiferous, somniferous. 2. narcotic. 3. (fig.) dull, irksome, annoying.

soporífero s. m. (pharm.) soporific, soporiferous drug or medicament, opiate. ‖ adj. 1. soporific, soporiferous. 2. sleepy, drowsy, slumberous. 3. narcotic, hypnotic.

soporífico s. m. (pharm.) soporific, opiate. ‖ adj. soporiferous, soporific, somniferous.

soporizar v. 1. to lull to sleep. 2. to calm, tranquillize. 3. to soothe. 4. to break down, enfeeble, weaken. 5. to stimulate. 6. to dominate.

soporoso adj. 1. sleepy, drowsy. 2. somnolent, torpid. 3. soporiferous, soporific, soporose.

soportal s. m. (pl. **-ais**) 1. the lower part of a portal. 2. sill, door-sill. 3. door-stone. 4. threshold. 5. atrium. 6. hall, vestibule. 7. courtyard.

soprado adj. blown.

soprador s. m. 1. blower. 2. breather, whiffer. ‖ adj. blowing.

sopranista s. m. (mus.) sopranist, treble singer.

soprano s. m. + f. (mus.) 1. soprano, the highest voice of a woman or a boy. 2. soprano singer (man or woman). 3. descant, treble.
coloratura, ~ **que canta coloratura** coloratura soprano.

soprar v. 1. to blow (on, up). 2. to produce a current of air. 3. to whiffle, puff. 4. to fan. 5. to waft. 6. to inflate with air. 7. to be or put out of breath. 8. to whisper or breathe s. th. into a person's ear. 9. to suggest, hint at (slyly or secretly). 10. to prompt. 11. (chess, checkers) to remove or eliminate a piece. 12. to inspire.
~ **em rajadas** to whiffle. ~ **sobre** to overblow. **a fortuna lhe soprou** he had a mighty windfall. **ela soprou a vela** she blew out the candle. **ele soprou a gaita** he blew on the mouth organ. **ele soprou-lhe o segredo** he revealed him the secret. **o vento sopra do norte** the wind sets from the north.

sopresar v. 1. to seize as prey, capture. 2. to take by storm.

soprilho s. m. a very fine and transparent variety of silk.

sopro (ô) s. m. (pl. **sopros**) 1. puff of air, whiff. 2. exhalation. 3. blowing, blast. 4. breath, breathing. 5. afflation. 6. breeze, puff of wind. 7. (fig.): a) influence. b) instigation, incitement. c) insinuation, hint. d) denunciation, delation.
~ **anfórico** (med.) pneuma. ~ **cardíaco** (med.) cardiac murmur, heart murmur. ~ **de vento** waft. ~ **vital** (med.) pneuma. **instrumento de** ~ (mus.) wind instrument. **música de** ~ music of brass instruments, music of a brass band. **num** ~ in a moment, in a trice. **podem derrubá-lo num** ~ they could blow him down with a blast.

soque s. m. 1. blow, cuff, hit. 2. smack. 3. crushing, pounding.

soquear v. 1. to strike with the fist. 2. to hit, give a blow. 3. to crush, pound. 4. to knead.

soqueira (I) s. f. 1. the rootstock of rice plants or sugar-cane after cutting. 2. a sugar-cane plantation which produces a rich aftermath. ⸜

soqueira (II) s. f. knuckles, knuckle-duster.

soqueixado adj. joined, connected or bound under the jaw (chin).

soqueixar v. to join, connect or bind under the jaw (chin).

soqueixo s. m. 1. ligature or bandage which passes under the chin. 2. towel or neckcloth knotted under the chin.

soquete (I) s. m. 1. (mil.) ramrod, rod used for driving home the charge of a gun. 2. rammer, tamper, beetle. 3. sock, light blow, tap. 4. socket, lamp socket (plate M 5). 5. (Braz., pop.) stew. 6. (Braz., pop.) a badly cooked meal. 7. a half-length stocking.

soquete (II) s. m. socket wrench.

soquetear v. 1. (mil.) to ram the charge into a gun. 2. to give a light blow to, sock. 3. to tamp, pound.

soqueteiro s. m. 1. a loafer who does occasionally odd jobs. 2. sponger, parasite.

sor (I) s. m. abbr. form of **senhor**: mister.

sor (II) s. f. abbr. form of **soror**: sister, lay sister.

sorar v. 1. to convert into whey. 2. to transform into serum.

Sorbona s. f. Sorbonne; the University of Paris.

sorbônico adj. Sorbonic(al), of, pertaining to or relative to the Sorbonne.

sorbonista s. m. + f. Sorbonist: 1. a student at the Sorbonne. 2. a doctor of the Sorbonne.

sorda s. f. a beef soup thickened with manioc flour and scrambled eggs.

sordícia, sordície s. f. (also **sordidez, sordideza**) 1. sordidness, paltriness. 2. filthiness, dirtiness. 3. squalidness, squalidity, squalor. 4. nastiness, sluttishness. 5. indignity, outrage. 6. base avarice. 7. depravity, vileness.

sórdido adj. 1. dirty, filthy. 2. sordid, vile, base. 3. nasty, disgusting. 4. squalid, repulsive, repellent. 5. torpid, inert, apathetic. 6. indecent, obscene. 7. excessively or meanly avaricious. 8. foul. 9. sluttish. 10. shameful. ‖ **sordidamente** adv. sordidly, nastily, miserably, paltrily.

sorete s. m. (S. Braz.) hardened fecal matter.

sorgo s. m. (bot.) 1. sorghum. 2. guinea corn, broomcorn. 3. Indian millet, African millet. 4. durra.

sorgo-de-alepo s. m. (pl. **sorgos-de-alepo**) (bot.) Johnson grass.

sorgo-doce s. m. (pl. **sorgos-doces**) (bot.) sorgo, sugar sorghum, sweet sorghum.

sorgo-de-vassoura s. m. (pl. **sorgos-de-vassoura**) (bot.) broomcorn.

soriano s. m. Sorian, native or inhabitant of Soria (Spain). ‖ adj. Sorian.

sorites s. m., sg. + pl. (logics) sorites.

sorítico adj. (logics) soritic(al).

sorna (ô) s. f. 1. indolence, sluggishness. 2. laziness, slothfulness. 3. sleepiness, drowsiness. 4. nap, doze, snooze. 5. m. + f. lazy, indolent or irksome person, impertinent or rude individual. ‖ adj. m. + f. 1. inert, torpid. 2. indolent, sluggish. 3. lazy. 4. irksome, annoying, impertinent.

sornar (I) v. 1. to be indolent or lazy. 2. to act in a sluggish or negligent manner. 3. to dawdle, day-dream.

sornar (II) v. (Port., prov.) to snore.

sorneiro s. m. lazybones, indolent or negligent fellow, dawdler. ‖ adj. lazy, sluggish, indolent, dawdling.

soro s. m. (bot.) sorus.

soro (ô) s. m. (pl. **soros**) 1. serum; the thin transparent part of the blood which remains after coagulation. 2. the whey of milk. 3. any serous fluid.

soroca s. f. 1. the lair of a wildcat or puma. 2. landslide, washout. 3. cave-in.

sorocabano s. m. native or inhabitant of Sorocaba (São Paulo, Braz.). ‖ adj. of, pertaining to or relative to this town.

sorocabuçu s. m. (Braz.) a landslide of considerable proportions.

sorodiagnóstico s. m. (path.) serum diagnosis, the art or process of recognizing a disease based on symptomatic alterations of the blood serum.

sorologia s. f. (med.) serology.

sorológico adj. (med.) serologic(al), imunologic(al).

sorologista s. m. + f. serologist.

soronga adj. m. + f. foolish, silly, stupid, simple-minded.

sorongo s. m. (Braz.) a Negro dance of African origin. ‖ adj. foolish, silly, stupid.

soror s. f. (pl. **sorores**) a title given to nuns; sister, lay sister.

soronal adj. m. + f. (pl. **-ais**) of, pertaining to or relating to a nun; sororal, sisterly.

sororato s. m. (anthr.) a form of matrimony (among aboriginal peoples) in which one of the wife's sisters partakes in the conjugal life.

sororicida s. m. + f. sororicide: one who murders his (her) sister.

sororicídio s. m. sororicide: the murder of a sister.

sorório adj. sororal, sisterly.

sororó s. m. (Braz., sl.) 1. fight, brawl. 2. disorder, confusion. 3. riot.

sororoca s. f. 1. (Braz.) death rattle, death struggle. 2. (Braz., ichth.) Spanish mackerel. 3. (N. Braz., zool.) jaguar.

sororocar v. to breathe heavily and with a gurgling sound (as dying people do).

sorose s. f. (bot.) sorosis: a compound fleshy fruit (like that of the pineapple, strawberry, mulberry).

soroso adj. 1. of or pertaining to a serum. 2. serous. 3. having or producing a serous fluid. 4. wheyey.

soroterapia s. f. (med.) serum therapy.

soroterápico adj. (med.) of, pertaining to or characteristic of serum therapy.

sorrabar v. 1. to go behind s. o., follow. 2. (fig.) to flatter, fawn upon.

sorrate s. m. artifice, cunning, shrewdness.

de ~ in a sly manner, cunningly, secretly.

sorrateiro adj. 1. cunning, shrewd, astute. 2. tricky, crafty. 3. sneaky, stealthy. 4. underhand. ‖ **-amente** adv. cunningly, slyly, stealthily, furtively.

entrar -amente para roubar to go on the sneak.

sorrelfa s. f. 1. slyness, artfulness, cunning. 2. disguise used to deceive or cheat: ruse, trick. 3. m. + f. an artful, tricky or avaricious person. ‖ adj. m. + f. 1. sly, cunning. 2. deceptive, tricky. 3. avaricious.

à ~ furtively, secretly, under disguise, under false pretence, underhandedly.

sorrelfo adj. 1. secretive; on the sly. 2. covert, under disguise. 3. artfull, cunning. 4. furtive, secretive. 5. deceptive, crooked. 6. covetous, avaricious.

sorridente adj. m. + f. 1. smiling. 2. radiant, beaming. 3. grinning. 4. cheerful, gay. 5. genial. ‖ ~**mente** adv. cheerfully, smilingly, beamingly.

sorrir v. 1. to smile, laugh gently. 2. to beam (at), look with joy. 3. to express pleasure, happiness or joy. 4. to fill (s. o.) with hope. 5. to show o. s. complaisant or affable. 6. to express a slight contempt, fleer. 7. to deride, jeer. 8. to grin.

~ **de desprezo** to smile disdainfully. ~ **maliciosamente** to sneer at. ~**-se amorosamente** to look or smile amorously. ~**-se loucamente** to split one's sides with laughing. **ela sorriu para mim** she gave me a smile.

sorriso s. m. 1. smile. 2. act of smiling. 3. gentle laugh. .4. a look of pleasure or kindness. 5. grin, grinning. 6. manifestation of sympathy or irony.

cumprimentar com um ~ to greet with a smile. **concordar com um** ~ to smile approval. **ela deu-me um** ~ she smiled at me. **ele respondeu com um** ~ **amarelo** he answered with a sickly smile. **espantar as preocupações com um** ~ to smile away the cares.

sorro s. m. (Braz.) 1. sly fox, rascal, cunning or treacherous fellow. 2. male fox. ‖ adj. sly, cunning, treacherous.

sorte s. f. 1. destiny, fate. 2. fortune, chance, luck. 3. doom. 4. lot, kismet, hap. 5. hazard, risk. 6. success, successfulness. 7. share, allotment. 8. (mil.) enrolment for military or naval service decided by lot. 9. lottery ticket or slip. 10. manner, mode. 11. happiness. 12. lucky strike, hit. 13. portion.

~ **das armas** contingencies of war. ~ **de loteria** prize in a lottery, hitter. ~ **grande** ticket drawing the highest lottery prize. ~ **no jogo** good run at play. **à má** ~, **envidar forte** if you have bad luck try hard to make up! **arrisque a** ~**!** try your luck!, take your chance! **a** ~ **está contra ele** the chances are against him. **a** ~ **muda** the tide turns. **boa** ~**!** good luck! **de boa** ~ in luck. **deitar** ~**s** to cast lots. **de má** ~ out of luck. **ele deixou correr a** ~ he left everything to fate. **ele está**

sem ~ he is unlucky, (coll.) he is down upon his luck. **ele não tem** ~ **no jogo** he is unlucky at cards. **ele sempre tem** ~ he is always lucky, has always the kick on his side. **ele tirou a** ~ **grande!** he drew the first prize, brought home the bacon! **falta de** ~ inauspiciousness. **ganhar a** ~ to win the toss. **isto me coube por** ~ it fell to my lot. **lançar** ~**s** to cast lots. **má** ~ bad luck, ill fortune, rough luck, a hard line. **muita** ~ a great piece of luck. **pouca** ~ bad luck. **por** ~ luckily, incidentally, fortuitously. **sem** ~ luckless, unfortunate, star-crossed. **tentar a** ~ to try one's fortune, try one's luck. **ter má** ~ to be unlucky, (coll.) be down on one's luck. **ter** ~ to be lucky, fare well. **toda** ~ **de coisas** all kinds of things. **trabalharam de tal** ~ **que** they worked in such a manner that... **trazer má** ~ **a** to bring misfortune upon s. o. **virou-se a** ~ luck turned around.

sorteado s. m. (Braz., mil.) draftee, conscript (chosen by lot). ‖ adj. 1. (mil.) drafted, conscript. 2. selected, chosen. 3. varied, variegated. 4. sorted, assorted.

sorteador s. m. 1. sorter, classifier. 2. caster of lots, diviner. ‖ adj. 1. sorting. 2. casting lots.

sorteamento s. m. 1. sortition: act of casting lots. 2. allotment. 3. assortment. 4. balloting.

sortear v. 1. to choose or pick out by lot. 2. to divide or apportion by lot. 3. to raffle, dispose of by lot or lottery. 4. to cast lots, draw lots. 5. to assort, classify. 6. to vary, variegate. 7. to portion, mete out.

sorteio s. m. 1. sortition, act or result of casting lots. 2. allotment. 3. raffle, lottery. 4. assortment.

sortida s. f. (mil.) sortie, sally, outfall.

sortido s. m. assortment. ‖ adj. assorted, sorted.

não ~ unassorted, unsized.

sortilégio s. m. 1. sortilege. 2. witchcraft, sorcery, witchery. 3. machination, collusion.

sortílego s. m. sortileger, fortuneteller, soothsayer. ‖ adj. witching.

sortimento s. m. 1. act or result of sorting out, classification. 2. assortment. 3. supply, stock (of any kind of goods). 4. a group formed by assortment. 5. medley. 6. variety. 7. choice.

sortir v. 1. to supply, furnish, provide. 2. to variegate, vary. 3. to blend, mix, compound. 4. to purchase. 5. to stock, put in stock. 6. to sort, assort. 7. to fall to by lot. 8. ~**-se** to renew one's stocks, buy new provisions.

sortudo adj. (Braz., sl.) lucky fellow, lucky dog.

soruma s. f. (East Africa, bot.) hemp.

sorumbático adj. 1. somber, shady, shadowy. 2. sad, glum, dejected. 3. sullen, moody, dour. ‖ **sorumbaticamente** adv. somberly, dejectedly, dourly.

sorumbatismo s. m. 1. melancholy, gloominess. 2. sorrow, sadness. 3. moodiness, depression.

sorva (ô) s. f. the fruit of the service or rowan tree, sorb.

sorvado adj. 1. half rotten (fruit). 2. over-ripe (fruit). 3. enfeebled, weakened.

sorval adj. (pl. -ais) soft, mellow, over-ripe.

sorvalhada s. f. a great heap of fruit (of different size or quality) strewn on the ground.

sorvar v. 1. to begin to rot, rot, decay (fruits). 2. to be weakened, enfeebled. 3. to make soft (fruits). 4. to show sign of fermentation (fruits).

sorvedouro s. m. 1. whirlpool, vortex, eddy. 2. maelstrom. 3. gulf. 4. abyss. 5. yawn, chasm.

sorvedura s. f. draught, swallow, gulp.

sorveira s. f. 1. service tree, rowan tree, sorb. 2. couma, sorva, cow tree.

sorver v. 1. to sip, suck. 2. to lap up. 3. to absorb, aspirate, draw in by suction. 4. to drink little by little. 5. to swallow. 6. to engulf, sink, submerge. 7. (fig.) to destroy, annihilate.

ele sorveu a injúria he swallowed the offence.

sorvete s. m. 1. ice: any frozen dessert. 2. sherbet, frappé. 3. fruit ice, hokey-pokey. **~ cremoso** ice-cream. **~ de frutas** tutti-frutti. **~ de suco de fruta com água e açúcar** water ice. **vendedor de ~** ice-cream vendor, iceman.

sorveteira s. f. ice-cream freezer, freezer.

sorveteiro s. m. ice-cream vendor, ice-cream peddler, iceman.

sorveteria s. f. 1. ice-cream shop. 2. freezer.

sorvo (ô) s. m. (pl. **sorvos**) 1. sipping, small draught. 2. swallow. 3. pull.

sós used in the adverbial locution **a ~:** all by oneself, quite alone, tête-à-tête.

sósia s. m. any person who resembles closely another one; double, second self, counterpart.

soslaio s. m. obliquity; state of being oblique. **ao ~** slantingly. **com um olhar de ~** out of the tail of one's eye. **de ~** askew, askance, askant, aslant, obliquely, leeringly.

sossega s. f. 1. a calming down or comforting. 2. rest, repose. 3. ease, quiet, calm.

sossegado adj. 1. quiet, calm. 2. tranquil, still, easeful. 3. reposeful, restful. 4. sleepy, drowsy. 5. uneventful. ‖ **-amente** adv. 1. calmly, quietly. 2. tranquilly. 3. reposefully, restfully. **estar ~** to rest quietly. **natureza -a** reposefulness.

sossegador s. m. 1. soother, calmer. 2. tranquillizer. 3. mitigator. ‖ adj. soothing, calming.

sossegar v. 1. to calm, quiet. 2. to tranquillize, soothe. 3. to put to rest. 4. to appease, pacify. 5. to rest, repose. 6. to become calm or quiet, calm down.

sossego (ê) s. m. (pl. **sossegos**) 1. act or effect of calming down. 2. tranquility, calmness, calm. 3. dispassion. 4. quiet, peace, peacefulness. 5. ease, rest, repose. 6. requiem. 7. reposedness, restfulness. 8. equanimity. **com ~** quietly. **falta de ~** inquietude. **~ de espírito** balance of mind, peace of mind.

sosso adj. stone (used without cement) for the construction of a wall.

sota s. f. 1. (cards) queen. 2. rest, respite. 3. repose, leisure. 4. (naut.) lull, calm. 5. **~s** pl. the first pair of horses in a carriage drawn by four, six or more horses. 6. postillion, outrider. 7. a subaltern. **dar ~ e ás** to outwit s. o.

sotádico adj. (Greek hist.) Sotadic: of, pertaining to or characteristic of the Greek poet Sotades.

sota-embaixador s. m. (pl. **sota-embaixadores**) vice--ambassador.

sotaina (I) s. f. 1. cassock. 2. (pop.) a clergyman, priest.

sotaina (II) s. f. (Port., prov.) a thrashing, spanking.

sótão s. m. (pl. **-ões**) 1. attic, garret, room on the top storey of a house (just under the roof). 2. loft, cockloft. 3. sollar. **ele tem macaquinhos no ~** he has bats in his belfry, he has a maggot in his brain.

sota-piloto s. m. (pl. **sota-pilotos**) (naut.) second pilot.

sotaque s. m. 1. foreign accent, foreign mode of pronunciation, brogue. **ele tem um ~ francês** he has a French accent.

sotaquear v. 1. to jibe, scoff. 2. to taunt. 3. to talk with an accent.

sotaventado adj. (naut.) alee.

sotaventear v. (naut.) 1. to fall to leeward, turn to leeward. 2. to sail under the lee. 3. to make leeway.

sotavento s. m. (naut.) leeside (of a ship), lee, leeward. **a ~** (naut.) under the lee of, under the wind, lee, leeward, alee. **para ~** leeward, off.

sota-voga s. m. (pl. **sota-vogas**) (rowing) the oarsman next to the stroke.

sotéia s. f. roof terrace, flat roof, open gallery, platform.

soterração s. f. (pl. **-ões**) act or result of burying or covering with earth.

soterrado adj. covered with earth, buried in the earth.

soterramento s. m. 1. act of putting under the earth or of filling with earth. 2. (obs.) burial, interment, sepulture.

soterrâneo s. m. + adj. = **subterrâneo.**

soterrar v. 1. to bury, put into the earth. 2. to cover with earth. 3. (obs.) to give rise to fear, frighten, terrify. 4. **~-se** (fig.) to bury o. s.

soto-almirante s. m. (pl. **soto-almirantes**) rear admiral, vice-admiral.

soto-capitão s. m. (pl. **soto-capitães**) (naut.) the second in command on a ship, first mate.

soto-mestre s. m. (pl. **soto-mestres**) a boatswain's assistent, vice-master of a merchant vessel.

soto-ministro s. m. (pl. **soto-ministros**) steward of a monastery.

sotopor v. 1. to put beneath, place under or below. 2. to omit, leave out. 3. to postpone, leave behind. 4. to shelve, disregard. 5. to pretermit, neglect.

sotoposto adj. placed beneath.

sotrancão adj. (pl. **-ões**) (f. **-ona, -oa**) 1. disguised, dissembled. 2. indolent, sluggish. 3. wily, artful, cunning.

sotrancar v. 1. to forestall, hinder. 2. to surround, encircle, embrace. 3. to monopolize. 4. to attain, achieve.

sotreta s. m. + f. 1. a base or vile person. 2. good--for-nothing. 3. worthless fellow or thing. ‖ adj. 1. vile, base, mean. 2. worthless, having no value or dignity.

soturnidade, soturnez, soturnice s. f. 1. saturninity. 2. taciturnity. 3. sullenness, moroseness. 4. sadness.

soturno adj. 1. saturnine. 2. somber, gloomy, glum. 3. sullen, morose. 4. dejected, depressed. 5. lugubrious, mournful. 6. silent, quiet.

souto s. m. 1. a plantation of chestnut trees. 2. (Braz.) a grove of wild Brazil-nut trees. 3. coppice, copse.

sova s. f. 1. beating, thrashing. 2. caning, basting. 3. drubbing, trimming, licking. 4. whipping. 5. (Braz., coll.) daily use.

sovaco s. m. 1. (anat.) axilla. 2. armhole, armpit. 3. dress-preserver.

sovado adj. 1. crumpled, wrinkled. 2. trampled, down--trodden. 3. crushed, ground. 4. beaten, struck, hit. 5. tired.

sovadura s. f. kneading.

sovaqueira s. f. 1. (Braz.) armhole, armpit. 2. perspiration from the armpit. 3. the odour of that perspiration. 4. (vet.) a cinch gall.

sovaquinho s. m. 1. dim. form of **sovaco.** 2. perspiration odour from the armpit. ‖ adj. of, pertaining to or characteristical of this odour.

sovar v. 1. to knead, work the dough. 2. to batter. 3. to drub, thrash, beat. 4. to tread on, trample on, press (grapes). 5. to grind, crush into small fragments. 6. to wear or use a lot. 7. to curry, dress hides.

sovela s. f. 1. bradawl, awl (plate S 3). 2. pricker, broach. 3. prod. 4. stiletto. 5. (ent.) yellow fever mosquito. 6. (ornith.) avoset. **à ~** prancing, rearing up, frightened, on edge.

sovelada s. f. 1. a thrust or stab with an awl. 2. a hole made with an awl.

sovelão s. m. (pl. **-ões**) a large awl.

sovelar v. 1. to pierce or perforate with an awl. 2. (fig.) to pierce, penetrate. 3. (N. Braz., pop.) to needle, nag.

soveleiro s. m. 1. awl maker, manufacturer of awls. 2. awlseller.

soveral s. m. (pl. **-ais**) = **sobral**.

sovereiro s. m. = **sobreiro**.

soverter v. 1. (obs.) to subvert, corrupt. 2. (Braz.) to bury.

sovéu s. m. (Braz.) a coarse lasso, lariat.

sovi s. m. (ornith.) 1. a tinamou (Tinamus sevi). 2. a bird of the family Falconidae (Ictinea plumbea).

soviete s. m. soviet, governing council of workmen, peasants and soldiers (in Russia).

soviético adj. 1. soviet, sovietic. 2. Russian.

a **Rússia Soviética** Soviet Russia. **União Soviética** Soviet Union.

sovietismo s. m. sovietism, communism, Bolshevism.

sovietista s. m. + f. sovietist, follower or defender of communism, Bolshevist. ‖ adj. sovietic(al), soviet, communistic(al), Bolshevistic(al).

sovina s. f. 1. a wooden peg or pin. 2. (carp.) dovetail, swallowtail. 3. taper file, close file. 4. m. + f. miser, skinflint, niggard. ‖ adj. m. + f. 1. avaricious, hard-fisted. 2. parsimonious. 3. niggardly, costive. 4. churlish, sordid.

sovinada s. f. 1. thrust or stab with the awl (or any other piercing instrument). 2. a witty or spicy saying, bon mot, piquant remark.

sovinar v. 1. to perforate with an awl or any other piercing instrument. 2. (fig.) to offend, aggrieve, hurt the feelings. 3. to molest, annoy, pester.

sovinice s. f. (also **sovinaria**) 1. avariciousness. 2. covetousness, greediness. 3. parsimony, parsimoniousness. 4. shabbiness, cheese-paring, stinginess. 5. churlishness.

sozinho adj. 1. quite alone, alone. 2. single, single-handed. 3. solo, sole. 4. unaided, unassisted. 5. unique. ‖ adv. all alone, single-handedly, solely, uniquely.

ela **não pode fazer isso -a** she cannot do that by herself. **ela vive -a** she lives quite alone, she lives all by herself. **ele está ~ no mundo** he stands alone in this world. **ele o fez ~** he did it by himself. **precisamos fazer tudo ~s** we have to do everything without assistance. **quero falar-lhe ~** I should like a private talk with you.

speaker s. m. speaker, radio announcer.

spinozismo s. m. (philos.) Spinozism; a form of pantheism taught by Benedict Spinoza (17th century).

spinozista s. m. + f. Spinozist, follower or adherent of Spinozism. ‖ adj. Spinozistic(al).

status-quo s. m. (L.) status quo.

sua possessive adj. and pron., the f. of **seu**: 1. adj. his, her, its, your, their. 2. pron. his, hers, its, yours, theirs.

aquelas **são ~s casas** those houses are his (hers, yours, theirs). eles **salvaram a ~ vida** they saved their life. **faremos a ~ vontade** we shall comply with your wishes. **minha amiga e ~** my friend and yours. **sou inteiramente de ~ opinião** there I am entirely with you. **uma de ~s amigas** one of your (his, her, their) friends.

suã s. f. 1. the lower part of a loin of pork. 2. rachis, spinal column of an animal.

suaçuapara s. m. (Braz.) a white-spotted variety of deer, fallow deer (Odocoileus suacuapara).

suaçupita s. m. (Braz.) a variety of red deer, brocket (Mazama americana).

suaçupucu s. m. (Braz.) a ruminant of the family Cervidae (Blastocerus dichotomus).

suaçutinga s. m. (Braz.) a variety of deer, brocket (Mazama simplicicornis).

suadeira s. f. (also **bastos** m. pl.) the padded parts of a saddle or packsaddle.

suadela s. f. 1. act of sweating. 2. transpiration, perspiration.

suado adj. 1. sweaty, perspiring. 2. wet with sweat, covered with sweat. 3. (fig.) fatiguing, difficult, hard won, demanding a strenous effort. ‖ **-amente** adv. sweatily, perspiringly, fatiguingly.

suador s. m. 1. sweater, one who sweats profusely (human beings as well as animals). 2. sudorific. ‖ adj. 1. sweating, perspiring. 2. sudorific.

suadouro s. m. 1. act or result of sweating, perspiration. 2. sudorific, diaphoretic. 3. act of washing pots and pans in warm water. 4. that part of a horse's back where the saddle lies. 5. a woollen saddle-cloth. 6. sweater.

suante adj. m. + f. sweating, perspiring.

suão s. m. a hot south wind, simoom, simoon. ‖ adj. south, blowing from the south.

suar (I) v. 1. to sweat, perspire. 2. to transpire, exhale. 3. to exude, drip, trickle. 4. to spill, pour, shed. 5. to sprout, shoot forth. 6. to swelter. 7. to work hard, labour, toil. 8. (pop.) to distill. 9. to achieve or obtain by hard work.

ele **suava em bica** he ran with sweat.

suar (II) s. m. (bot.) butternut tree.

suarabácti s. m. (gram., phon.) anaptyxis: a variety of epenthesis in which a vowel is inserted into a group of consonants, e. g. **pneu** becomes **peneu**.

suarabáctico adj. (gram., phon.) anaptyctic(al).

suarda s. f. 1. wool oil, yolk. 2. a greasy sediment which remains in the fulling mill after fulling. 3. a clod of dirt or stain in the wool to be carded.

suarento adj. 1. sweaty, perspiring. 2. covered with sweat. 3. moist with sweat. 4. (fig.) laborious, difficult.

suástica s. f. swastica, fylfot.

suave adj. m. + f. 1. suave: a) agreeable, pleasing, pleasant. b) bland, mild, mellow, gentle. c) kind, affable, sweet. d) delicate. e) mellifluent. f) lenient. 2. (mus.) pianissimo, piano. 3. soft, smooth. 4. flossy, sleeky. 5. euphonical, euphonious. 6. easy. 7. (pop.) cheap, purchasable at a low price. ‖ **~mente** adv. suavely, softly, gently.

com olhos ~s soft-eyed. **seus modos ~s conquistaram todos os corações** her sweet manners won every heart.

suavidade s. f. 1. suaveness: a) quality of being suave. b) mildness; gentleness. c) sweetness, meekness. d) mellifluence, blandness. e) leniency. 2. grace, graciousness. 3. amenity. 4. tranquility of soul, peacefulness. 5. divine grace.

suaviloqüência s. f. suaviloquence: sweetness and gentleness of expression, suavity of speech.

suaviloqüente adj. m. + f. (also **suavíloquo**) suaviloquent.

suavização s. f. act or result of making suave or gentle, extenuation, mitigation, relenting.

suavizado adj. mitigated, softened, eased, made gentle.

não **~** unmitigated, unredeemed.

suavizador adj. mitigating, relaxative, soothing.

suavizante adj. m. + f. soothing, palliative, moderating.

suavizar v. 1. to render suave. 2. to soothe, alleviate. 3. to soften, milden. 4. to mitigate, allay. 5. to mollify, dulcify. 6. to subdue. 7. to extenuate, ease off.

as **árvores ~am sua queda** the trees broke his fall.

suba s. f. (S. Braz., pop.) increase of prices, raising of price, dearth.
subaéreo adj. subaerial.
subafluente s. m. subaffluent.
subagudo adj. (med., path.) subacute.
subalado adj. (natural history) having winglike appendices.
subalar adj. m. + f. subalary: under the wings.
subalimentação s. f. subalimentation, undernourishment.
subalimentado adj. undernourished, underfed, half-starved.
subalimentar v. 1. to undernourish, underfeed. 2. to provide with too little food.
subalpino adj. subalpine.
subalternação s. f. (pl. **-ões**) 1. subalternation: a) act of rendering subaltern. b) quality or state of being subaltern. 2. subordination.
subalternado adj. (obs.) subaltern, subordinate(d), secondary, inferior.
subalternar v. 1. to render subaltern, subordinate. 2. to put in an inferior place, rank below. 3. to subdue, subject to. 4. ~-se to alternate, take turns.
subalternidade s. f. 1. quality of being subaltern. 2. subalternity. 3. inferiority, subordination. 4. dependency.
subalternizar v. 1. to make subaltern, subordinate. 2. to put in an inferior place, rank below. 3. ~-se: a) to become subaltern or inferior to. b) to subordinate o. s. c) to debase o. s.
subalterno s. m. 1. subaltern. 2. subordinate: person holding an inferior place or rank. 3. secondary, inferior. 4. (mil.) a commissioned officer below the rank of captain. 5. (fam., coll.) underling. ‖ adj. 1. subaltern, subordinate. 2. inferior, secondary. 3. petty. 4. (mil.) non-commissioned.
subalugar v. to sublet, underlet.
subaluguel, subaluguer s. m. (pl. **-éis, -eres**) subrenting, subletting.
subáptero adj. (zool.) subapterous: resembling somewhat apterous insects, brachypterous.
subaquático adj. subaquatic, submarine, underwater.
subáqueo adj. subaquatic, submarine.
subarbústeo adj. (bot.) 1. subshrubby: of, pertaining to or characteristic of undershrubs. 2. designating plants the branches of which dry up every year.
subarbustivo adj. (bot.) undershrubby, subshrubby, shrubby or woody at the base.
subarbusto s. m. (bot.) subshrub, undershrub, low woody plant ranking between a herb and a tree.
subarqueado adj. somewhat arched or curved.
subarrendamento s. m. 1. act or result of subletting. 2. subtenancy, underletting, undertenancy.
subarrendar v. 1. to sublet, let to a third person. 2. to sublease, underlet, underlease.
subarrendatário s. m. sublessor, sublessee, underletter, underlessee. ‖ adj. subleasing.
subastação, subasta s. f. (pl. **-ões**, ~s) (jur.) forced auction, legal auction.
subatômico adj. (phys.) subatomic.
subaxilar adj. m. + f. subaxilary. 1. under the axilla. 2. (bot.) under the axil formed by the branch of a plant with the stem.
sub-bibliotecário s. m. (pl. ~s) assistant librarian.
sub-boreal adj. m. + f. (pl. **sub-boreais**) (meteor.) subboreal, very cold.
subcampanulado adj. (bot.) subcampanulate.
subcapilar adj. m. + f. subcapillary.
subcarbonato s. m. (chem.) subcarbonate.
subcaudal adj. m. + f. (pl. **-ais**) (zool.) subcaudal. beneath the tail, on the ventral side of the tail.
subcarga s. f. (artillery) undercharge.

subchefe s. m. 1. subchief, subordinate chief. 2. assistant director, vice-director.
subciência s. f. subdivision of a science.
subcilíndrico adj. (bot.) subcylindrical.
subcinerício adj. 1. subcinereous, subcineritious. 2. lying under the ashes. 3. baked under the ashes. 4. of, typical of or relative to ashes.
subcircunscrição s. f. (pl. **-ões**) subcircumscription.
subclasse s. f. subdivision of a class, subclass, subdivision.
subclavicular adj. m. + f., **subclávio** m. (anat.) subclavian, subclavicular, subclavial.
subcloreto s. m. (chem.) subchloride.
subcomissão s. f. (pl. **-ões**) subcommission, subcommittee.
subcomissário s. m. subcommissioner.
subconjuntival adj. m. + f. (pl. **-ais**) (anat.) subconjúnctival: situated under the conjunctiva.
subconsciência s. f. 1. semiconsciousness: obscure or dimmed conscience. 2. (psych.) subconsciousness.
subconsciente s. m. 1. the unconscious. 2. unconsciousness. 3. (psych.) the subconscious, unconsciousness. ‖ adj. m. + f. subconscious: dormant in the unconscious.
subconsumo s. m. (econ.) underconsumption.
subcontrário adj. 1. (logics) subcontrary: designating propositions which somewhat contradict each other. 2. contrary in an inferior degree.
subcordiforme adj. m. + f. (bot.) nearly heart-shaped.
subcorrente s. f. 1. undercurrent. 2. submarine current.
subcostal adj. m. + f. (pl. **-ais**) (anat.) subcostal: situated under or below the ribs.
subcutâneo adj. subcutaneous: situated under the skin. ‖ **subcutaneamente** adv. subcutaneously.
subdecano s. m. subdean: substitute or assistant of a dean.
subdécuplo adj. subdecuple: containing part of ten.
subdelegação s. f. (pl. **-ões**) subdelegation: 1. act or process of subdelegating. 2. office, dignity and authority of a subdelegate. 3. succursal, branch office, branch store.
subdelegado s. m. 1. subdelegate: assistant or substitute of a delegate. 2. inspector, checker, controller. ‖ adj. subdelegate, subdelegated.
subdelegante adj. m. + f. subdelegating.
subdelegar v. 1. to subdelegate. 2. to transmit an office or authority to a substitute or delegate. 3. to transmit by delegation.
subdelegável adj. m. + f. (pl. **-áveis**) that may be subdelegated.
subdelírio s. m. (path.) subdelirium.
subdesenvolvido adj. undergrown, underdeveloped.
subdesenvolvimento s. m. underdevelopment.
subdiaconato s. m. (eccl.) subdeaconry, subdeaconship, office, dignity and authority of a deacon.
subdiaconisa s. f. (eccl.) subdeaconess: female subdeacon, wife of a subdeacon.
subdiácono s. m. (eccl.) subdeacon.
subdialeto s. m. subdialect: branch or subdivision of a dialect, brogue.
subdireção s. f. (pl. **-ões**) 1. office, dignity and authority of a subdirector. 2. assistant or deputy directorship.
subdiretor s. m. subdirector: assistant or substitute of a director, deputy director.
subdividir v. 1. to subdivide. 2. to divide again, divide a second time. 3. to separate into smaller parts.
subdivisão s. f. (pl. **-ões**) 1. subdivision. 2. new or second division. 3. a part or thing made by subdivision. 4. suballocation. 5. separation of a whole into parts.

~ **de família** subfamily, tribe. ~ **de terrenos em pequenos lotes** subdivision of real estate into small building lots.
subdivisionário adj. subdivisional, subdivisive.
subdivisível adj. m. + f. (pl. -íveis) subdivisible.
subdominante s. f. (mus.) subdominant.
subduplo adj. subduple, subdouble, subduplicate.
subelemento s. m. secondary element.
subemenda s. f. subamendment, subemendation.
subemprazamento s. m. 1. subrenting, subletting. 2. (feudal law) subinfeudation.
subemprazar v. 1. to sublease, subrent, sublet. 2. (feudal law) to subinfeudate.
subempreitada s. f. subcontract.
subempreitar v. to subcontract the partial or total execution of a job.
subenfiteuse s. f. (jur.) subinfeudation, subemphyteusis, emphyteutic sublease of (agricultural) land.
subenfiteuta s. m. + f. subemphyteuta, subinfeudatory.
subenfiteuticar v. 1. to subinfeud, subinfeudate, sublease emphyteutic land. 2. to hold emphyteutic land(s) as subtenant.
subenfitêutico adj. subemphyteutic(al).
subentender v. 1. to perceive or interpret correctly an implication. 2. to infer the meaning of. 3. to suppose, presume. 4. to admit intellectually.
subentendido s. m. 1. any thing or matter which is fairly to be understood though not expressed. 2. implicitness. 3. idea or meaning tacitly comprised, implication. ‖ adj. 1. implied, implicit. 2. latent. 3. plainly to be understood though not expressed. **isto é** ~ this must not be discussed, that is understood.
subepígrafe s. f. subepigraph.
súber s. m. (bot.) suber: cork tissue.
suberina s. f. (chem.) suberine.
suberização s. f. (bot.) suberization: the formation of cork tissue on the cork tree.
suberizar v. (bot.) to suberize.
suberoso adj. (bot.) suberous, suberose.
subescapular adj. m. + f. (anat.) subscapular: of, pertaining to or beneath the scapula.
subespécie s. f. subspecies: subdivision of a species.
subespinhal adj. m. + f. (pl. -ais), (anat.) subspinous: situated beneath the spinal column.
subestimar v. (Braz.) 1. to underestimate, misestimate. 2. to minimize. 3. to underrate, undervalue. **ele subestima o trabalho do seu colega** he sets too low an estimate upon his colleague's work. **nunca subestime a força duma mulher** don't ever underrate the power of a woman.
subestrutura s. f. 1. substructure, understructure. 2. groundwork. 3. (archit.) foundation.
subexposição s. f. (phot.) underexposure.
subface s. f. the inferior part of the head of an insect.
subfamília s. f. (bot., zool.) subfamily: subdivision of a family.
subfaturar v. to underbill.
subfoliáceo adj. (bot.) subfoliaceous: resembling a leaf.
subfretar v. 1. to charter again. 2. to sublet a ship by charter. 3. to subcontract the transport of goods.
subgenérico adj. (biol., bot., zool.) subgeneric(al): of or pertaining to a subgenus.
subgênero s. m. (biol., bot., zool.) subgenus: subdivision of a genus.
subglabro adj. (bot.) subglabrous: nearly glabrous.
subglobuloso adj. subglobulous, subglobulose: nearly globulous, subglobular.
subgrave adj. (mus.) contrabass.

subgrupo s. m. sub-group.
subida s. f. 1. ascension, ascent. 2. raise, rise, rising. 3. acclivity. 4. slope, upgrade, upward slope. 5. climb, climbing, clambering. 6. uprise, uprising. ~ **de posto** advancement. ~ **de preços** rise in prices. ~ **difícil** difficult clamber. **de grande** ~, **grande queda** hasty climbers have sudden falls. **durante a** ~ **da maré** at flood tide, at the rising of the tide.
subideira s. f. (ornith.) tree creeper (Dendrocolaptes platirostris).
subido adj. 1. high, lofty. 2. raised, elevated. 3. sublime, exalted. 4. excessive. 5. dear, expensive. 6. excellent, consummate. 7. pompous.
subimento s. m. 1. raise, rise. 2. elevation, ascent. 3. augmentation, increase. 4. excess, overplus.
subinflamação s. f. (pl. -ões), (med.) subinflammation: mild inflammation.
subinflamatório adj. (med.) subinflammatory.
subinte adj. m. + f. ascending, climbing, rising, increasing.
subinspetor s. m. subinspector.
subintendência s. f. 1. subintendancy. 2. office, dignity and authority of a subintendant. 3. district committed to the charge of a subintendant.
subintendente s. m. subintendant: assistant or substitute of an intendant.
subir v. 1. to ascend, rise, go up. 2. to mount up, climb up to anything, scale. 3. to elevate, raise. 4. to fly upwards, soar. 5. to grow higher. 6. to advance, rise in position or rank. 7. to clamber, shin up. 8. to increase, augment. 9. to exalt, enhance, heighten. 10. to pass from a grave to a high sound. 11. to mount (horse, wagon, vehicle). 12. to lift, transport to a higher place. 13. to flood, overflow, flow upwards (tide), inundate. 14. to graduate. 15. to get up, stand up. 16. ~-**se** to go up; rise.
~ **a bordo do avião** to board the airplane. ~ **a escada** to climb the stairs. ~ **ao ar** to rise into the air, soar. ~ **ao púlpito** to mount the pulpit. ~ **ao trono** to mount the throne. ~ **com dificuldade** to clamber up. ~ **de posição** to rise in rank. ~ **de preço** to grow more expensive. ~ **e descer** to ascend and descend. ~ **para o trem** to board the train. ~ **uma grande fortuna** to raise one's fortune, accumulate a great fortune. ~ **a um cavalo** to mount a horse. ~ **um pico** to climb a peak. ~ **verticalmente** to rise vertically. **a maré está subindo** the flood (tide) is rising, it is at the flood. **ela vinha subindo a rua** she came up the street. **ele subiu no conceito de seus amigos** he rose in his friends' esteem. **ele subiu o rio** he sailed up the river. **os preços** ~**am** prices have risen. **o vinho sobe-lhe à cabeça** the wine flies easily into his head. **todos os preços sobem rapidamente** all prices shoot up.
subitaneidade s. f. suddenness, abruptness, hastiness.
subitâneo adj. subitaneous, sudden, abrupt, unexpected, hasty. ‖ **subitaneamente** adv. suddenly, unexpectedly, hastily.
súbitas s. f. pl. hurry, haste — used in the adverbial locution: **a** ~ suddenly, hastily.
súbito s. m. 1. a sudden or unexpected occurrence. 2. surprise. 3. sally, spurt. 4. sudden fit. ‖ adj. 1. sudden, abrupt. 2. unexpected, surprising. 3. swift. 4. all at once. 5. instantaneous. 6. precipitous, precipitate. ‖ ~ and **subitamente** adv. sudden, unexpectedly, all at once, instantaneously.
aparecer subitamente to pop up. **entrar subitamente** to pop in. **de** ~ suddenly, abruptly.
subjacente adj. m. + f. subjacent, underlying.

subjeção s. f. (pl. **-ões**) (rhet.) subjection: a figure of speech in which the speaker formulates a question presupposing or implying an adequate reply.

subjetivação s. f. (pl. **-ões**) 1. act or result of subjectivizing. 2. subjectiveness, subjectivity.

subjetivar v. 1. to subjectivize, render subjective. 2. to consider subjective. 3. to ascribe exclusively to a subject.

subjetividade s. f. 1. subjectiveness, subjectivity. 2. subjective quality or character.

subjetivismo s. m. subjectivism: 1. philosophical doctrine which maintains the subjectivity i. e. the relativity of knowledge. 2. (arts) the expression of subjective feeling or thinking in arts, literature and music.

subjetivo s. m. that which is subjective. || adj. subjective: 1. of or pertaining to a subject. 2. (gram.) used as a subject (nominative: occurring in the subject case. 3. reflecting personal prejudices or limitations. 4. characteristic of an individual. || **-amente** adv. subjectively.

subjugação s. f. (pl. **-ões**) subjugation: 1. act of subjugating. 2. state of being subjugated, subduedness. 3. conquest.

subjugado adj. 1. subjugated, dominated. 2. tame. 3. conquered.

subjugador s. m. subjugator, vanquisher, conqueror, subduer. || adj. subjugating, vanquishing.

subjugante adj. m. + f. subjugating, dominating.

subjugar v. 1. to subjugate, conquer by force. 2. to dominate (intellectually or morally). 3. to compel to submit. 4. to subdue, subject, subordinate. 5. to influence deeply. 6. to conquer, vanquish. 7. to overpower, overwhelm. 8. to bow, break, yoke, enslave. 9. to tame. 10. to suppress, repress. 11. to quell. 12. **~-se** to refrain from, dominate o. s. **a revolta foi subjugada no início** the revolt was quelled in the beginning. **ser subjugado** to come (pass) under the yoke. **~am os seus inimigos** they brought their enemies under subjection.

subjunção s. f. (pl. **-ões**) subjunction, subjoining; act of joining s. th. immediately after an other.

subjuntiva s. f. (gram., phon.) 1. postposition: the second vowel of a diphthong. 2. vanish.

subjuntivo s. m. (gram.) subjunctive mood, subjunctive. || adj. subjunctive, subordinated.

sublacustre adj. m. + f. sublacustrine; under the waters of a lake.

sublenhoso adj. (bot.) having a stem which is woody at the basis and herbaceous at the top.

sublevação s. f. (pl. **-ões**) 1. sublevation, uprising. 2. revolt, rebellion. 3. uplift, upheaval, upthrow. 4. disturbance, agitation. 5. faction.

sublevador s. m. rebel, revolter, mutineer. || adj. 1. lifting, raising. 2. inciting, arousing.

sublevar v. 1. to sublevate: lift, raise. 2. to heave up. 3. to incite, arouse to action, spur on. 4. to rebel, revolt. 5. **~-se** to take up arms, revolt against.

sublimação s. f. (pl. **-ões**) sublimation: 1. act or process of sublimating. 2. state of being sublimed. 3. (psych.) the transformation of primitive impulses into positive actions of a superior order. 4. (phys.) the direct passage from the solid to the gaseous state or vice versa.

sublimado s. m. sublimate: a substance produced by sublimation. || adj. sublimate, sublimated: 1. (chem.) produced by sublimation. 2. elevated, lifted up, raised. 3. exalted, refined. 4. aggrandized.

sublimar v. 1. to sublime: a) make sublime. b) exalt, glorify. c) (chem.) sublimate: cause to sublime. d) (phys.) pass directly from the solid to the gaseous state and vice versa. e) purify by sublimation. f) elevate in rank or honours. 2. to raise,

lift up (to greater height or perfection). 3. (fig.) to etherealize. 4. **~-se** to become sublime, distinguished or exalted.

sublimatório s. m. (chem.) sublimatory: a vessel used for chemical sublimations. || adj. sublimational, sublimatory.

sublimável adj. m. + f. (pl. **-áveis**) sublimable.

sublime s. m. sublime: that is sublime, acme, the highest degree of perfection. || adj. m. + f. 1. sublime: a) high, lofty, elevated. b) majestic, grand, grandiose. c) splendid, glorious. d) unearthly, divine, supernal. e) exalted. f) supremely perfect, excellent. 2. powerful. 3. charming. || **~mente** adv. sublimely.

sublimidade s. f. 1. sublimity, sublimeness. 2. loftiness, great height. 3. perfection, excellence. 4. exaltedness. 5. transcendence, transcendency. 6. ideal. 7. eminence.

subliminal adj. m. + f. (pl. **-ais**) subliminal.

sublinear adj. m. + f. sublinear; written under the line, interlinear.

sublingual adj. m. + f. (pl. **-ais**) (anat.) sublingual; situated under the tongue.

sublinha s. f. underscore, underline; a line drawn under a word.

sublinhar v. 1. to underline, underscore; draw a line under a word or sentence. 2. to point out, indicate. 3. to stress, emphasize. 4. to make conspicuous.

subliterato s. m. a mediocre or overpretentious man of letters, penny-a-liner.

subliteratura s. f. mediocre or trashy literature.

sublobulado adj. (bot.) sublobulate; completely or nearly divided into lobules.

sublocação s. f. (pl. **-ões**) 1. act of subletting. 2. sublease, underletting. 3. subtenancy.

sublocador s. m. underletter, subletter, sublessor.

sublocar v. 1. to underlet, sublet. 2. to underlease, sublease. 3. to relet.

sublocatário s. m. 1. subtenant, sublessee. 2. underlessee, undertenant. 3. roomer.

sublunar adj. m. + f. sublunary.

subluxação s. f. (pl. **-ões**) (med.) subluxation.

submarino s. m. (also **submarinho**) (naut.) a submarine (boat), sub, U-boat. || adj. submarine, undersea, living under the surface of the sea.

submaxilar adj. m. + f. (anat.) submaxillary, inframaxillary; pertaining to or situated beneath the lower jaw.

submental adj. m. + f. (pl. **-ais**) (anat.) submental; situated beneath the chin.

submergir v. 1. to inundate, overflow. 2. to cover with water, flood, deluge. 3. to submerge, submerse. 4. to sink, dive, plunge. 5. to drown. 6. to swallow. 7. to absorb, engulf. 8. to overwhelm. 9. to destroy. 10. **~-se** to become completely submerged. 11. to sink, go under, founder.

submergível adj. m. + f. (pl. **-íveis**) capable of being submerged, submergible, sinkable.

submersão s. f. (pl. **-ões**) 1. submergence, submersion. 2. inundation, deluge, flood. 3. drowning. 4. indent in a horse's hoof (caused by a blow or kick).

submersível s. m. (pl. **-íveis**) submarine boat, submarine, submergible. || adj. m. + f. 1. submergible, submersible. 2. (bot.) submerged, submersed.

submerso adj. 1. submerged, submersed. 2. underwater. 3. sunken. 4. (bot.) submersed, submarine. **cidade -a** submersed city. **proa -a** (naut.) sunken forecastle. **recife ~** sunken rock.

submeter v. 1. to submit: render an object of, expose to. 2. subject, subdue. 3. to subjugate, dominate. 4. to conquer. 5. to subordinate. 6. to commit, compel. 7. to lay under, exhibit (for examination or approval). 8. **~-se** to submit: a)

surrender, subject o. s. b) yield, resign, truckle. c) bend, bow. 9. to become tame.
~ **à apreciação de** to submit (s. th.) for appreciation to. ~ **à aprovação** to submit for approval. ~ **a uma prova** to prove. ~ **a tensão excessiva** to overstrain. ~ **à votação** to put to the vote. ~**-se a um tratamento** to submit to a treatment. ~**-se a uma operação** to undergo an operation. ~**-se à vontade de Deus** to resign to the will of God.
submetimento s. m. submission, subjection.
submetralhadora s. f. submachine-gun.
subministração s. f. (pl. **-ões**) subministration.
subministrador s. m. subministrator. ‖ aaj. subministrating.
subministrar v. 1. to subministrate, subminister. 2. to supply, furnish, provide with. 3. to administer.
submissão s. f. (pl. **-ões**) 1. submission, submissiveness. 2. subjection, subordination. 3. vassalage. 4. humility. 5. compliance, conformity. 6. resignation. 7. obedience. 8. duty, dutifulness. 9. acquiescence. 10. (fig.) yoke.
com ~ submissively, dutifully, humbly.
submisso adj. submissive: 1. obedient, dutiful. 2. inferior, subordinate. 3. compliant, conformable. 4. humble, docile. 5. uncomplaining, unresisting, yielding. 6. broken, tamed. 7. acquiescent. ‖ **-amente** adv. submissively, yieldingly, acquiescently, reverentially.
com voz -a with a low voice.
submúltiplo s. m. (arith.) submultiple; an aliquote part of a number, divisor, factor, coefficient.
submundo s. m. underworld: the criminal members of society; people living by vice or crime; the world of organized crime.
subnasal adj. m. + f. (pl. **-ais**) subnasal, situated under the nose.
subnitrato s. m. (chem.) subnitrate.
subnormal s. f. (pl. **-ais**) (geom.) subnormal; part of the axis of a curve which lies between the ordinate and the' normal. ‖ adj. m. + f. subnormal, below normal.
subnutrição s. f. underfeeding, undernourishment, malnutrition.
subnutrido adj. underfed, undernourished.
subnutrir v. to underfeed, undernourish.
suboccipital adj. m. + f. (pl. **-ais**) suboccipital.
subocular adj. m. + f. subocular, suborbital, situated below the eye.
suboficial s. m. (mil.) noncommissioned officer, corporal sergeant, (naut.) petty officer.
suborbicular adj. m. + f. (anat.) suborbital.
suborbitário adj. (anat.) suborbital.
subordem s. f. (pl. **-ens**) suborder: subdivision of an order, category of classification (also biol., bot., zool.).
subordinação s. f. (pl. **-ões**) 1. subordination: a) act or result of subordinating. b) inferiority of rank or dignity. c) obedience, subjection. d) subservience. 2. (gram.) interdependence of words or phrases, subordinate clause. 3. (philos.) subsumption.
subordinada s. f. (gram.) subordinate clause.
subordinado s. m. 1. subordinate: a) inferior, underling. b) servant, servitor. 2. dependant, dependent. ‖ adj. subordinate: 1. dependant, secondary. 2. inferior. 3. subaltern. 4. subsidiary. 5. accessory. 6. petty. ‖ **-amente** adv. subordinately.
a Igreja foi -a ao Estado the church was harnessed to the wheels of the state. **suas ações estavam -as à sua ambição** ambition underlay all his actions. **frase -a** (gram.) subordinate clause.
subordinador s. m. 1. one who enforces subordination.

2. one who subordinates or classifies. ‖ adj. subordinating.
subordinante adj. m. + f. subordinating, subordinative.
subordinar v. 1. to subordinate: a) subject, subdue. b) place in an order or rank below s. th. or s. o. else. c) bring under the control of a higher principle. d) consider of less value. e) attribute secondary rank or importance. 2. ~**-se**: a) to submit to, subject o. s. to. b) to contain o. s., refrain from.
subordinativo adj. subordinative.
subornação s. f. (pl. **-ões**), **subornamento** m. = **suborno**.
subornado adj. suborned, bribed, venal, corrupt.
subornador s. m. suborner: briber, corrupter, corruptor. ‖ adj. subornative.
subornar v. 1. to suborn, subornate: corrupt, bribe, buy, (coll.) grease, palm. 2. to attract by deceit. 3. to mislead to an unlawful action.
ele tentou suborná-lo he tried to suborn him, (fam.) he tried to oil his palm. ~ **um policial** to bribe a policeman, (U. S. A., sl.) to fix a cop.
subornável adj. m. + f. (pl. **-áveis**) bribable: open to bribery, venal, corruptible.
suborno (ô) s. m. subornation: 1. act or result of suborning. 2. (jur.) embracery. 3. bribery, corruption.
subparágrafo s. m. subparagraph; subdivision of a paragraph.
subpericárdio adj. (anat.) subpericardial: situated beneath the pericardium.
subperitoneal adj. m. + f. (pl. **-eais**) (anat.) subperitoneal.
subperpendicular adj. m. + f. (math.) subperpendicular, subnormal.
subpolar adj. m. + f. 1. (astr.) subpolo: under the visible pole (said of the position of a star). 2. subpolar.
subpor v. to put under, place beneath or below.
subprefeito s. m. 1. subprefect. 2. assistant mayor.
subprefeitura s. f. 1. subprefecture. 2. office, dignity and scope of authority of an assistant mayor. 3. administrative subdistrict of a municipality.
subprocurador s. m. (Braz.) subprocurator.
sub-raça s. f. subrace, subbreed.
subproduto s. m. subproduct, byproduct, derivate.
subraji s. f. (Braz., bot.) plant of the buckthorn family (Cyanotus speciosa).
sub-reino s. m. (pl. **sub-reinos**) (biol.) phylum, phyla.
sub-reitor s. m. (pl. **sub-reitores**) subrector.
sub-repção s. f. (pl. **sub-repções**) 1. (jur.) subreption, unlawful concealment or misrepresentation of facts. 2. favour obtained by fraudulent means.
sub-reptício adj. (pl. **sub-reptícios**) subreptitious. surreptitious. ‖ **sub-repticiamente** adv. subreptitiously.
sub-rogação s. f. (pl. **sub-rogações**) (jur.) subrogation, judicial substitution or transference of rights, succession.
sub-rogado adj. (pl. **sub-rogados**) subrogated, surrogate.
sub-rogador s. m. (pl. **sub-rogadores**) subrogator, surrogate. ‖ adj. subrogating.
sub-rogante adj. m. + f. (pl. **sub-rogantes**) subrogating, subrogatory.
sub-rogar v. 1. to subrogate, surrogate: a) put in the place of another, substitute. b) act as substitute. 2. to transfer rights or duties to.
sub-rogatório adj. (pl. **sub-rogatórios**) subrogatory.
sub-rostrado adj. (pl. **sub-rostrados**) (natural hist.) subrostrate; resembling a small beak.
subscrever v. to subscribe: 1. underwrite, undersign. 2. sign, endorse. 3. accept, approve, sanction (system, opinion, principles, etc.). 4. assent, consent. 5. adjust o. s. to, resign o. s. to 6. assume

an obligation, contribute to. 7. subscribe to a newspaper or magazine. 8. acquiesce, agree.

subscrição s. f. (pl. -ões) subscription: 1. act or result of subscribing. 2. consent, agreement. 3. donation, donative. 4. contribution. 5. amount of money subscribed.
~ **pública de ações** public subscription of shares. **renovar uma** ~ to renew a subscription. **por meio de** ~ by subscription.

subscritar v. 1. to put one's signature on (letter, document). 2. = **subscrever**.

subscrito adj. subscript.

subscritor s. m. subscriber, signer. ‖ adj. subscribing.

subseção, subsecção s. f. (pl. -ões) subsection, subdivision.

subsecivo adj. subsecive, subsicive: 1. cut away, separated as overmuch. 2. left-over, remaining over. 3. secondary, accessory.

subsecretariado s. m. undersecretaryship: office, dignity and authority of an undersecretary.

subsecretário s. m. undersecretary.

subsecutivo adj. (more used **consecutivo**) subsecutive, consecutive, successive.

subseguir v. 1. to follow after. 2. to be, go or come after. 3. to come later. 4. ~-se to follow immediately after.

subsentido s. m. 1. secondary meaning. 2. subordinate notion. 3. hidden intention or meaning.

subseqüência s. f. 1. subsequence: quality of being subsequent. 2. sequence, following after, continuance.

subseqüente adj. m. + f. 1. subsequent: a) sequent, ensuing. b) posterior. c) immediate. d) following after. e) further, later. 2. secondary. ‖ ~mente adv. subsequently, secondarily, afterward(s).
~ **ao casamento** postmarital. ~ **ao nascimento** postnatal. **acontecimento** ~ after-event. **endossante** ~ subsequent endorser (of a bill).

subserviência s. f. 1. subservience, subserviency: a) amenability, obsequiousness. b) servility. 2. flattery.

subserviente adj. m. + f. subservient: 1. serving to s. o. 2. obsequious. 3. servile. 4. wheedling, adulatory, crawling. 5. truckling. ‖ ~mente adv. subserviently, obsequiously.

subséssil adj. m. + f. (pl. -eis) (bot.) subsessile.

subsidiado s. m. one who receives a subsidy. ‖ adj. subsidized.

subsidiar v. to subsidize: 1. give a subsidy to. 2. assist, help, aid.

subsidiário adj. 1. subsidiary: a) relating to subsidy. b) aiding by a subsidy, supplementary, auxiliary. c) strengthening, fortifying. 2. collateral. ‖ **subsidiariamente** adv. subsidiarily.

subsídio s. m. 1. subsidy: a) aid, assistance, help. b) grant, allowance. c) subvention. d) amount contributed to a worthy public or social cause. e) bounty. 2. (Braz.) fees of legislators (senators, deputies).
~ **concedido por dia** per diem allowance. ~ **de campanha** (mil.) field-allowance. ~ **para crianças** children's allowance.

subsinuoso adj. subsinuous; somewhat sinuous.

subsistência s. f. 1. subsistence: a) state or quality of being subsistent. b) sustenance. c) support. d) maintenance, breadwinning. 2. stability, persistence.

subsistente adj. m. + f. subsistent, subsisting.

subsistir v. to subsist: 1. exist, continue to live. 2. survive. 3. persist, endure, remain. 4. keep in form or force. 5. provide one's livelihood.

subsolo s. m. 1. subsoil: a) substrate, substratum. b) underground. 2. basement, basement floor, ground floor.

água do ~ subsoil water. **camada dura do** ~ pan, hardpan. **no** ~ underground.

subsônico adj. subsonic.

substabelecer v. 1. to put one thing in the place of another. 2. to substitute, appoint as substitute. 3. to replace. 4. to transfer to another person (rights, duties, obligations). 5. to subrogate.

substabelecimento s. m. substitution, subrogation.

substância s. f. substance: 1. material, matter. 2. essence. 3. essential constituents of any material. 4. amount, body. 5. the nutritive elements of food. 6. pith, gist. 7. solidity, firmness. 8. force, vigour. 9. (chem.) body of a chemical element, compound or mixture. 10. alimentation. 11. stuff. 12. wealth, riches, property.
comer alimentos que têm ~ to eat nourishing food. **em** ~ in substance, in short, without particulars.

substanciado adj. resumed, concentrated, sinthesized.

substancial s. m. (pl. -ais) 1. the essential, essentiality, essentialness. 2. substance. 3. the most important part of (a matter, business, discourse etc.). ‖ adj. m. + f. 1. of or relating to substance, material. 2. real, essential. 3. nourishing, nutritive. 4. fundamental. 5. meaty. 6. tangible, bodily. 7. abundant, hearty. 8. forceful. 9. instructive. 10. important.
tomaram uma refeição ~ they took a hearty meal.

substancialidade s. f. substantiality: quality or state of being substantial.

substancialismo s. m. (philos.) substantialism (opposed to idealism).

substancialista s. m. + f. (philos.) substantialist. ‖ adj. substantialistic.

substancializar v. 1. to substantialize: make substantial, convert into substance. 2. to consider as substance.

substanciar v. 1. (med.) to prescribe or give nutritive food to. 2. to nourish, feed. 3. to fortify, strengthen. 4. (fig.) to substantiate, corroborate. 5. to make robust.

substancioso adj. substantial: 1. rich in substance. 2. strengthening, invigorating. 3. forceful. 4. hearty 5. nourishing, nutritive.

substantificar v. (philos.) substantify, substantialize: render concrete.

substantivação s. f. (gram.) act of changing into a substantive or noun.

substantivado adj. substantivized, substantized; converted into or considered as a noun.

substantival adj. m. + f. (pl. -ais) (gram.) substantival.

substantivar v. to substantivize, substantize: 1. convert into a substantive or noun. 2. give the character of a noun to. 3. use as a noun.

substantivo s. m. (gram.) substantive, noun. ‖ adj. substantive: 1. (gram.) designating a person or thing. 2. self-subsistent, independent. 3. designating dyes which do not require the application of a mordant. 4. expressing existence. ‖ **-amente** adv. substantively, substantially.
~ **abstrato** abstract noun. ~ **coletivo**, ~ **comum** common noun. ~ **concreto** concrete noun. ~ **próprio** proper noun. ~ **verbal** verbal noun. **verbo** ~ substantive verb.

substatório adj. checking, stopping, (jur.) injunctive. **mandado** ~ (jur.) injunction, reprieve.

substituição s. f. (pl. -ões) substitution: 1. act or result of substituting. 2. replacement. 3. designation of a heir in case of his refusal to accept the inheritance. 4. change. 5. supersedence, supersession. 6. shift, relay, spell, relief.

substituído s. m. person who has been substituted by another. ‖ adj. substituted, replaced, renewed.

substituinte s. m. ╪ f. substitute, deputy, proxy, person who replaces another. ‖ adj. substituting, substitutional, substitutionary.

substituir v. 1. to substitute: a) put (a person or thing) into the place of another. b) replace, take the place of, compensate for. c) do duty for, act as substitute. d) change, displace. e) relay, relieve. f) supplant, supersede. g) succeed to. 2. ~-se to take the place of, be put in the place of. ~ um ator ou atriz (theat.) to double for an actor. ele foi substituído por um homem de mais idade he has been replaced by an older man. ele substituiu as batatas pelo milho he replaced the potatoes by the corn. ele substituiu o seu colega he relieved his colleague.

substituível adj. m. + f. (pl. -íveis) replaceable, substitutable.

substitutivo s. m. 1. substitution, replacement. 2. emendation. 3. alteration of a law text. ‖ adj. substitutive.

substituto s. m. substitute: 1. successor, proxy. 2. replacer, stopgap. 3. representative, deputy. 4. succedaneum, surrogate. 5. makeshift. ‖ adj. substituting, substitute. ~ de ator understudy. atuar como ~ to stand proxy.

substrato s. m. substratum, substrate.

substrução s. f. (pl. -ões) 1. substructure, understructure. 2. groundwork. 3. foundation.

substrutura s. f. 1. substructure. 2. undercarriage.

subsultar v. (poet.) to bounce, jump up repeatedly.

subtangente s. f. (geom., math.) subtangent.

subtendente s. f. (geom.) chord of an arch. ‖ adj. subtendent.

subtender v. 1. to extend under. 2. (geom.) to subtend.

subtenente s. m. (mil.) sublieutenant, warrant officer.

subtensa s. f. (geom.) subtense; chord of an arch.

subterfúgio s. m. subterfuge: 1. excuse, shift. 2. text, blind, plea. 3. evasion, dodge, ruse, feint, elusion. usar de ~ to tergiversate.

subterfugir v. 1. to make use of subterfuges. 2. to escape, dodge. 3. to shun, shirk. 4. to flee, run away.

subterrâneo s. m. (also **soterrâneo**) 1. a subterranean place, cave, cavern. 2. basement. ‖ adj. (also **soterrâneo, subtérreo**) subterranean, underground, subterraneous. no andar subtérreo downstairs.

subtil adj. m. + f., **subtileza, subtilidade, subtilização** s. f., **subtilizar** v. = sutil, sutileza, sutilidade, sutilização, sutilizar.

subtipo s. m. (natural hist.) subtype, secondary type.

subtítulo s. m. sub-title, sub-heading (plate L 4.)

subtônica s. f. (mus.) subtonic.

subtração s. f. (pl. -ões) subtraction: 1. act or process of subtracting. 2. (jur.) unlawful withholding of rights. 3. defalcation. 4. (math.) diminution, deduction.

subtraendo s. m. (math.) subtrahend.

subtrair v. 1. to take away stealthily or fraudulently. 2. to steal, defalcate. 3. to withdraw, retract. 4. to let disappear. 5. (math.) to subtract. 6. to deduct, diminish. 7. to dodge, shun. 8. to let escape. 9. to filch. 10. ~-se to fly from, get away from, escape.

subtrativo s. m. (math.) subtrahend; amount to be subtracted. ‖ adj. subtractive.

subtribo s. m. (natural hist.) subtribe.

subtropical adj. subtropical.

subulado adj. (natural hist.) subulate: awl-shaped, tapering.

subumano adj. 1. subhuman. 2. inhumane.

suburbano adj. 1. suburban, suburbial. 2. uptown. 3. outskirt. 4. inhabiting the suburbs.

subúrbio s. m. 1. suburb. 2. ~s pl. outskirts, environs, confines.

suburgo s. m. (Braz., pop.) a quiet leisurely hamlet.

subvenção s. f. (pl. -ões) subvention, subsidy: 1. pecuniary help, grant. 2. assistance, support. 3. baunty.

subvencionado adj. subventioned, subventionary.

subvencionador s. m. subventioning person or agency. ‖ adj. subventioning, subventionary.

subvencional adj. m. + f. (pl. -ais) subventionary.

subvencionar v. to subventionize: 1. subsidize. 2. assist, aid, help.

subverbete s. m. subentry.

subversão s. f. (pl. -ões) 1. subversion: a) act or process of subverting. b) overthrow. 2. revolt, rebellion. 3. insubordination.

subversivo adj. 1. subversive. 2. revolutionary.

subversor s. m. subverter. ‖ adj. subverting.

subvertedor s. m. subverter ‖ adj. subverting.

subverter v. 1. to subvert: a) overturn, overthrow. b) destroy, ruin. c) knock down. d) confuse, disturb, trouble. e) disorganize, disarrange. f) pervert, corrupt. 2. to cause the foundering of, let sink. 3. to revolutionize, rouse to revolt. 4. ~-se: a) to drown, submerge, sink. b) to ruin o.s., go broke. c) to suffer complete destruction.

sucará s. m. (Braz., bot.) a shrub of the daisy family (Chuquiragua spinescens).

sucata s. f. scrap(s), scrap iron, junk iron.

sucção, sução s. f. (pl. -ões) suction, suck, aspiration. tubo de ~ suction-pipe, suction tube.

sucedâneo s. m. 1. succedaneum: remedy used as a substitute. 2. substitute, thing used in place of another, ersatz. ‖ adj. succedaneous, substitute, artificial.

suceder v. 1. to succeed: a) follow after, come next, to ensue. b) happen, occur, come to pass, eventuate. c) befall, betide. d) act as a substitute, be successor of. e) inherit from. 2. ~-se: a) to come next. b) to happen or arrive consecutively. ~ freqüentemente to occur frequently. ele sucede seu pai he succeeds to his father. nada de grave sucedeu nothing serious happened. suceda o que ~ whatever may come to pass, come what may, at any rate. sucede que it happens that. tornar a ~ to recur, occur repeatedly.

sucedido s. m. an occurrence, incident, event, happening. ‖ adj. 1. having occurred, happened. 2. successful. bem-~ 1. successful, resultful. 2. blessed. ele foi bem-~ nos seus negócios his business prospered. ele será bem-~ he will not fail to succeed. eles foram mal ~s they were unsuccessful, they were unfortunate.

sucedimento s. m. 1. succession: act or result of succeeding. 2. happening, occurrence, event.

sucessão s. f. (pl. -ões) succession: 1. act or result of succeeding. 2. sequence, series, continuation, continuity. 3. progression. 4. train. 5. inheritance, heritage. 6. (fig.) lineage, descent. 7. (fig.) characteristic qualities transmitted to the descendants. ~ abintestada (jur.) distribution of the personal estate of an intestate. ~ ao trono succession to the throne. direito de ~ right of inheritance or succession. em ~ rápida in quick succession. guerra de ~ (U.S.A.) war of succession.

sucessível adj. m. + f. (pl. -íveis) 1. entitled to inherit by succession. 2. capable of succession.

sucessivo adj. 1. succeeding. 2. successive: a) successional, consecutive, sequential. b) progressive. ‖ -amente adv. successively, successionally.

sucesso s. m. 1. outcome, consequence, result. 2. occurrence, event, fact. 3. conclusion. 4. (coll., fam.) childbirth. 5. success. 6. triumph. lucky strike. 7. eclat, sensation, hit.
a festa foi um ~ the party was a success. **bom** ~ success, successfulness, god luck. **com** ~ with success, (coll., student sl.) swimmingly. **ele tem** ~ **em tudo** he succeeds in everything. **encadeamento de** ~**s** a streak of good luck. **eu lhe desejo todo o** ~**l** I wish you well. **fazer** ~ to do good, to do well. **não ter** ~ to fail, come to grief. **o plano foi um** ~ **completo** the scheme fully succeeded. **ter grande** ~ to score a hit. **ter** ~ to succeed, (coll.) to thrive, arrive.

sucessor s. m. successor: 1. aftercomer. 2. heir. 3. one who occupies a place, position or office which another has left. ‖ adj. succeeding, following.

sucessorial adj. m. + f. (pl. **-ais**) successional, successive.

sucessório adj. successional, successive.

súcia s. f. 1. gang, mob, rabble (rowdies or thieves). 2. spree, revelry.

suciar v. 1. to be one of a mob, belong to a gang. 2. to bum around, loiter, loaf.

suciata s. f. 1. a crowd of disorderly people or criminals. 2. mob, gang. 3. revelry, spree, binge.

sucino s. m. (min.) yellow amber.

sucinto adj. 1. succinct: a) brief, short, concise. b) terse. 2. abbreviated. ‖ **-amente** adv. succinctly.

súcio s. m. 1. mobster, mobsman. 2. good-for-nothing, vagabond, loafer, lazy lounger. 3. scoundrel, rascal. 4. bungler, dauber.

suco s. m. 1. juice, sap. 2. (fig.) essence. 3. (pop.) blood. 4. (Braz., fam.) a very agreeable, good, beautiful or attractive thing, stunner.
~ **de limão** lemon juice. ~ **de frutas** fruit juice. ~ **de uva** grape juice, stum. ~ **gástrico** gastric juice. **perder ou tirar** ~ (pop.) to bleed. **veja que** ~**!** look there, what a beauty!

suctorial adj. m. + f. (zool.) suctorial: adapted for suction.

sucuabo s. m. (Braz.) a fishing-line protected against fishbites.

suçuaia s. f. (Braz., bot.) 1. woolly elephant's foot. 2. tobacco weed. 3. devil's grandmother.

suçuapara s. m. (Braz.) a big variety of deer.

suçuarana s. f. (Braz.) 1. (zool.) a) cougar, puma. b) panther. c) mountain lion. 2. (pop., fig.) an ill-tempered woman.

súcubo s. m. (Braz., folklore) succubus: a demon assuming female form (supposed to cause nightmares). ‖ adj. 1. of, pertaining to or relative to a succubus. 2. placed beneath.

suculência s. f. 1. succulence, juiciness, abundance of juices. 2. sappiness.

suculento adj. (also **sucoso**) 1. succulent, juicy. 2. sappy. 3. pulpy, pappy. 4. rich. 5. lush, ripe. 6. substantial. 7. fat. ‖ **-amente** adv. suculently, pulpily, lushly.

sucumbido adj. 1. succumbed, defeated. 2. dejected, depressed, downhearted.

sucumbir v. to succumb: 1. yield, submit. 2. sink down under the weight of. 3. go under. 4. perish. 5. not to resist. 6. lose heart, despair. 7. die, stop to exist. 8. be defeated, be overcome. 9. be suppressed or abolished.
~ **debaixo de uma carga** to sink beneath a burden. **ele sucumbiu ao inimigo** he succumbed to his foe. **o leão sucumbiu ao tiro de sua espingarda** the lion fell to his rifle.

sucupira s. m. = **sicupira**.

sucuri s. 1. f. (also **sucuriju, sucuriú, sucuruju, su-**

sucujuba) (zool.) anaconda. 2. m. (N. Braz., ichth.) a kind of shark.

sucursal s. f. (pl. **-ais**) 1. branch, branch office. 2. branch establishment. 3. chain store. ‖ adj. m. + f. succursal.

sucuru s. m. puffbird.

sucussão s. f. (pl. **-ões**) succussion.

sucutuba adj. m. + f. succulent, juicy.

sucuuba s. f. a tree of the dogbane family (Plumeria attenuata).

sucuubarana s. f. a tree of the family Malpighiaceae (Pterandrium arama).

sudação s. f. (pl. **-ões**) (med.) 1. sudation. 2. sweat, sweating. 3. perspiration.

sudâmina s. f. (med.) sudamina, sudamen, (pop.) prickly heat.

sudanês s. m. (pl. **-eses**) (f. **-esa**; pl. **-esas**) Sudanese: 1. native or inhabitant of the Sudan. 2. the language spoken by the Sudanese people. ‖ adj. Sudanese.

sudário s. m. 1. sudarium: a) sweat cloth. b) handkerchief. c) (eccl.) the holy handkerchief. 2. cerement, cerecloth. 3. (fig.) display of reprehensible things.
~ **axilar** dress-shield.

súdito, súbdito s. m. 1. subject, liege. 2. vassal. ‖ adj. subject, subordinated, subjected, inferior.

sudoestada s. f. a strong south-west wind, souther.

sudoeste s. m. 1. south-west. 2. southwestern direction. 3. southwester: a southwestern wind. ‖ adj. m. + f. south-west, southwestern.
ao ~ southwestern, southwestward. **de** ~ southwesterly: from the south-west. **em direção para** ~ southwesterly, southwestward. **em direção para sudoeste** south-southwestward.

sudorese s. f. (med.) diaphoresis: profuse perspiration.

sudorífero, sudorífico s. m. (also **sudatório**) 1. (med.) sudorific, sudatory, diaphoretic: a sweat producing agent or medicine. 2. sweater. ‖ adj. sudoriferous, sudorific, sudatory, diaphoretic, perspirative.

sudoríparo adj. sudoriparous: provoking or producing sweat, sudoriferous, perspiratory.
glândula **-a** sweat gland.

sueca s. f. 1. (cards) quadrille: a game of cards played by four players with fourty cards. 2. a lively square-dance, rapid quadrille. 3. the music for this dance.

sueco s. m. 1. Swede: native or inhabitant of Sweden. 2. Swedish, Swedish language. ‖ adj. Swedish.

suede s. m. suede, tanned leather with a napped surface.

suedine s. f. suede, or such imitating cloth.

sueira s. f. (Braz.) hard work, drudgery.

sueltista s. m. + f. (also **topaquista**) leader writer.

suelto s. m. (also **tópico**) leaderette.

suestada s. f. a strong south-east wind, southeaster.

sueste s. m. (also **sudeste**) 1. south-east. 2. southeastward direction. 3. southeaster: a south-east wind. 4. sou'wester: a heavy seaman's hat of oiled cloth or canvas. ‖ adj. m. + f. south-east, southeastern.
ao ~, **em direção para** ~ southeasterly, southeastward. **de** ~ southeasterly: from the south-east.

suéter s. m. sweater, jersey.

sueto s. m. 1. school holiday. 2. rest, repose, leisure. 3. (obs.) usual habit, custom.

suficiência s. f. sufficiency: 1. quality or state of being sufficient. 2. adequaçy, adequateness. 3. ability, capacity. 4. fill.

suficiente s. m. 1. enough, sufficiency. 2. a mark on school work corresponding to: fair, satisfactory.

‖ adj. m. + f. sufficient: 1. adequate. 2. enough, satisfying. 3. competent. 4. (mark on schoolwork) fair, satisfactory. 5. capable, able. ‖ ~mente adv. sufficiently, adequately, satisfyingly, enough, well. **ele comeu ~mente** he ate to the fill. **isto é ~ para mim** that is sufficient for me. **mais do que ~** enough and to spare. **ter uma renda ~** to be comfortably off.

sufismo s. m. (philos., rel.) Sufism: a school of Mohammedan mysticism.

sufista s. m. + f. Sufist: follower or defender of Sufism. ‖ adj. m. + f. Sufistic.

sufixal adj. m. + f. (pl. -ais) suffixal: of or pertaining to a suffix.

sufixar v. to suffix: 1. add a suffix to the end of a word. 2. postfix. 3. append.

sufixo s. m. (gram.) suffix, postfix affix: 1. suffixed letter or syllable. 2. ending of a word.

suflê s. m. (cul.) soufflé.

sufocação s. f. (pl. -ões) 1. suffocation: a) act of suffocating. b) effect of being suffocated. c) choke, strangulation. 2. sultriness, oppressiveness.

sufocado adj. 1. suffocated. 2. smothered.

sufocador s. m. choker. ‖ adj. suffocating, choking.

sufocamento s. m. asphyxiation.

sufocante adj. m. + f. 1. suffocating, suffocative: a) choking, choky. b) close, stifling. 2. sultry, oppressive, sweltering. 3. fusty. ‖ ~mente adv. oppressively, chokingly.

sufocar v. 1. to suffocate: a) cause suffocation in. b) choke, stifle. c) smother. d) jugulate, strangle, strangulate. e) drown. f) throttle, repress. g) asphyxiate. h) extinguish. 2. to suppress, subdue, quench, overcome. 3. to debilitate.

~am a revolta rapidamente they quenched the revolt rapidly. **~ o alento** to discourage, dishearten.

sufocativo adj. 1. suffocative, suffocating. 2. suitable for repressions.

sufragâneo s. m. 1. suffragan. 2. (eccl.) suffragan bishop. 3. (eccl.) suffragan diocese. ‖ adj. suffragan, suffraganal.

sufragar v. 1. to suffragate, suffrage. 2. to approve or support by suffrage. 3. to favour, side with. 4. to pray for the soul of. 5. to give alms for the salvation (of a person's soul). 6. to supplicate, entreat.

sufrágio s. m. suffrage. 1. vote, voting, voice. 2. approval, assent. 3. prayer, almsgiving or any other act of piety for the salvation of a person's soul.

~ para mulheres female suffrage, women's suffrage. **~ universal** universal suffrage. **~ proporcional** proportional representation (voting).

sufragista s. m. + f. 1. suffragist: supporter, follower of universal suffrage. 2. voter. 3. f. woman suffragist; suffragette; militant female advocate of woman suffrage. ‖ adj. suffragial, suffragistic(al), suffragatory.

sufumigação s. f. (pl. -ões) (also sufumígio m.) 1. suffumigation: act or process of fumigating from below. 2. (med.) application of smoke or vapour in a therapeutic treatment. 3. purification of the atmosphere by combustion of odorific substances.

sufumigar v. 1. to suffumigate, fumigate from below, apply suffumigation to. 2. to purify the air by fumigation.

sufusão s. f. (pl. -ões) (med.) suffusion.

sugação s. f. (pl. -ões) act of sucking.

sugador s. m. 1. sucker, one who sucks. 2. (zool.) proboscis, suctorial organ. 3. (tech.) sucking port, suction pipe. ‖ adj. sucking, suctorial, suction.

sugadouro s. m. 1. (zool.) proboscis, suctorial organ. 2. (tech.) sucking port.

sugar v. 1. to suck: a) draw in or take up by suction. b) extract. c) absorb. 2. to embezzle, take away fraudulently. 3. to extort.

sugerir v. 1. to suggest: a) insinuate, infuse, instill, inspire. b) prompt, propose. c) hint, point, intimate. d) tip. e) remember, imply. f) recommend. g) advance, promote, further, foster. 2. to proportion, furnish.

ele sugeriu uma modificação dos planos he proposed a change of the layout. **permite-me ~ um passeio** may I suggest a walk? **sugeri-lhe esta possibilidade** I suggested this possibility to him. **sugeri-lhes que partissem** I suggested that they might leave. **sugerimos-lhe que cantasse** we proposed him to sing.

sugerível adj. m. + f. (pl. -eis) suggestible.

sugestão s. f. (pl. -ões) suggestion. 1. act or effect of suggesting. 2. insinuation, intimation. 3. cue, hint. 4. pointer, tip. 5. proposal. 6. presentment. 7. hypnotic suggestion.

dominar por meio da ~ to hypnotize. **ele me deu uma ~** he gave me a cue. **minha ~ foi aceita** my proposal was accepted. **pela ~ do meu amigo** at the suggestion of my friend.

sugestionar v. 1. to suggestion: influence by suggestion. 2. to inspire, stimulate. 3. to suggest.

sugestionável adj. m. + f. (pl. -eis) suggestible: easily influenced by suggestions.

sugestivo adj. 1. suggestive, suggestible. 2. significant. 3. adumbrative. ‖ -amente suggestively.

sugesto s. m. (Roman hist.) suggestum: raised platform (for public orators), pulpit.

sugilação s. f. (pl. -ões) 1. suggillation: a) act or result of suggillating. b) (med.) an ecchymosis. 2. a scorbutic blotch on the skin. 3. cadaverous lividness.

sugilar v. to suggillate: 1. hurt, bruise. 2. cause an ecchimosis in. 3. (fig.) defame, malign. 4. (fig.) vituperate, vilify.

suia s. f. (ornith.) a kind of parrot.

suíça s. f., **suíças** s. f. pl. side whiskers, whiskers.

suicida s. m. + f. suicide: one who attempts or committed suicide. ‖ adj. suicidal, characteristic of suicide, having served as an instrument for suicide.

suicidar-se v. 1. to suicide, commit suicide, lay hands upon o. s. 2. (fig.) to destroy one's own existence, ruin o. s.

suicídio s. m. suicide: 1. self-murder. 2. self-destruction. 3. (fig.) ruin or unhappiness caused by one's own faults.

suíço s. m. Swiss: native or inhabitant of Switzerland. ‖ adj. Swiss, Helvetian.

suídeo s. m. (zool.) 1. animal of the swine family. 2. ~s pl. Suidae: a family consisting of wild and domestic swine.

suiná, suinara, suindá, suindara s. f. (Braz., ornith.) the common barn owl (Stryx flammea perlata).

suíno s. m. swine, pig, a hog. ‖ adj. swinish.

suinocultor s. m. pig breeder, hog raiser.

suinocultura s. f. pig breeding, raising.

suiriri s. m. (ornith.) 1. walking tyrant. 2. yellow--browed tyrant. 3. kingbird.

suíte s. f. 1. (mus.) suite: a) a musical composition in a series of themes. b) sequence, series. c) retinue. 2. m. used in the slang expression: **dar o ~** to get away, escape, scram.

sujar v. 1. to make dirty, dirty. 2. to stain, spot, tarnish, maculate. 3. to blot, blemish, blotch. 4. to befoul, begrime, besmear. 5. to soil, mess up. 6. (sl.) to demoralize, corrupt. 7. to refute, contradict. 8. to defecate. 9. to contaminate. 10. to smut, smudge, bedraggle. 11. to defile, pollute, sully. 12. ~-se: a) to besmear or spatter o. s. b) to become dirty. c) ot commit infamous acts. d) to maculate or taint one's honour. e) to evacuate involuntarily. ~ com baba to beslaver. ~ com tinta to blot with ink. ~ no lodo to draggle. ~ o bom nome de alguém to sully a person's fair name.

sujeição s. f. (pl. -ões) 1. subjection: a) act of subjecting or subduing. b) submission, subordination. 2. domination. 3. dependence. 4. allegiance. 5. bondage, serfage. 6. discipline. 7. liability. 8. resignation.

sujeira s. f. 1. dirt, filth, grime. 2. filthiness, swinishness. 3. squalidness, squalidity, dinginess. 4. slovenliness. 5. sweeps, sweepings. 6. slosh, muck. 7. soil. 8. uncleanness. 9. mess. 10. foul play.

sujeita s. f. a nondescript woman or woman whose name one will not mention.

sujeitador s. m. subduer, subjugator. ‖ adj. subjecting, subduing.

sujeitar v. 1. to subject: a) submit, subjugate, subdue, subordinate. b) lay under, down, obligate. c) constrain, coerce. d) make dependent. 2. to dominate. 3. ~-se: a) to submit, yield, acquiesce. b) to surrender. c) to conform to, bow, obey. ~ à disciplina to discipline. ~ a sofrimento ou provação to try, penalize. ~ pelo temor to overawe. vou sujeitá-lo à sua decisão I'll submit it to your decision, I'll put it to you.

sujeito s. m. 1. subject: a) citizen, liege, vassal. b) topic, subject matter. c) (gram.) that word or wordgroup of a proposition of which s. th. is predicated. d) (philos.) that part of a proposition, theme or discourse of which a quality or relation may be affirmed. 2. individual, nondescript man, a man whose name we will not mention. 3. (Braz., pop.) slave. 4. (pop.) fellow, chap, guy, blighter, bloke, beggar. ‖ adj. subject: 1. subordinate. 2. dependent. 3. liable, exposed to. 4. obedient, subdued. 5. dominated. ~ a fiscalização subject to fiscal control. ~ a imposto liable to duty. ~ a sanção penal liable to be punished. ~ à-toa bummer, waster. ~ arrogante arrogant fellow, jackanapes. ~ esfarrapado tatterdemalion. ~ formidável a devil of a fellow, (sl.) corker, wacker. ~ inútil ou mau a useless or bad fellow, (sl.) bad egg. ele é um ~ bruto he is a rough customer. ele está ~ à asma he is subject to asthma. estar ~ a to be subject, liable, exposed to. ficar ~ a penalidade to incur a penalty. todos estamos ~s a errar we are all liable to make mistakes. um ~ azarado an unlucky fellow, (sl.) a lame duck. um bom ~ a good fellow, (hum.) a good old skin. um ~ esquisito a queer fellow, (coll.) an odd stick.

sujidade s. f. 1. dirtiness, filthiness. 2. griminess. 3. slovenliness, sluttisheness. 4. excrement, excreta. 5. trash, refuse, rubbish.

sujigola s. f. curb strap of a riding bridle.

sujo s. m. 1. (pop.) the devil. 2. second growth on cleared land. ‖ adj. 1. dirty, filthy. 2. greasy. 3. soiled. 4. nasty, foul, smutty. 5. swinish, piggish, hoggish. 6. unclean, messy. 7. sordid, sloven, sloppy. 8. squalid. 9. indecent, indecorous. 10. corrupt. 11. dishonest, crooked. 12. discredited, untrustworthy. ‖ -amente adv. filthily, piggishly, dirtily.

sul s. m. 1. south. 2. southward direction. 3. a south wind. ‖ adj. m. + f. south, southern. a janela dá para o ~ the window faces south. ao ~ south, southward. ao ~ de Londres to the south of London. vento sul south wind.

sula s. f. (bot.) sulla, sulla clover, French honeysuckle (Hedysarum coronarium).

sul-americano adj. South American.

sulão s. m. (also sulvento) (N. Braz.) a southwind.

sulaque s. m. (tech.) slide valve of a steam engine.

sulaventear v. (also sotaventar) (naut.) to sail to the leeward, make leeway.

sulavento s. m. (also sotavento) (naut.) lee, leeward direction. a ~ leeward.

sulcado adj. 1. sulcate: a) ploughed, furrowed, rutted. b) grooved. c) wrinkled. 2. rimose, rimous.

sulcar v. 1. to sulcate: a) furrow, plough up, ridge. b) groove, channel, rut. c) trench. d) wrinkle. 2. to traverse, cross (the sea).

sulco s. m. furrow: 1. trench made by a plough. 2. groove, channel, rut. 3. wrinkle. 4. wake of a vessel, dead water. 5. track. ~ jugular jugular groove (plate C 12).

sulfa s. f. sulfa (short for sulfanilamide).

sulfanilamida s. f. (chem., pharm.) sulfanilamide, sulphanilamide.

sulfatagem s. f. (pl. -ens) 1. application of cupric or ferrous sulphates. 2. treatment of plants with copper vitriol.

sulfatar v. 1. to treat with cupric or ferrous sulphate. 2. to besprinkle with copper vitriol (vines).

sulfatização s. f. (chem.) sulphatization.

sulfatizar v. (chem.) to sulphatize, sulphate: convert into sulphate.

sulfato s. m. (chem.) sulphate. ~ ácido bisulfate, bisulphate. ~ de ácido plaster, plaster of Paris. ~ de chumbo sulphate of lead. ~ de cobre bluestone. ~ de magnésio sulphate of magnesia. ~ de potássio sulphate of potash. ~ de sódio sodium sulphate. ~ de zinco zinc sulphate. ~ ferroso ferrous sulphate, copperas. ~ mercúrico mercuric sulphate.

sulfeto s. m. (chem.) sulphide. ~ de bário barium sulphide. ~ de cálcio calcium sulphide. ~ de cobre natural copper glance. ~ de hidrogênio sulphide of hydrogen. ~ de mercúrio (min.) cinnabar. ~ de potássio potassium sulphide. ~ de sódio sodium sulphide. ~ de zinco zinc sulphide.

sulfídrico adj. (chem.) hydrosulphuric.

sulfito s. m. (chem.) sulphite. ~ de sódio sodium sulphite.

súlfur s. m. (pl. súlfures) (chem.) sulphur.

sulfuração s. f. (chem.) sulphuration.

sulfurado adj. (chem.) sulphurated, sulphurized, treated or impregnated with sulphur.

sulfurar v. to sulphurate, sulphurize: 1. mix or combine with sulphur. 2. treat with sulphur.

sulfúreo adj. sulphureous, sulphury.

sulfureto (ê) s. m. (also sulfeto) (chem.) sulphid(e).

sulfúrico adj. (chem.) sulphuric,

sulfurino adj. sulphur-coloured.

sulfuroso adj. (chem.) sulphurous, sulphureous. fonte -a sulphur spring.

sulídeos s. m. pl. (ornith.) Sulidae.

sulimão s. m. (pop.) corrosive sublimate.

sulipa s. f. (N. Braz.) (railway) sleeper.

sulista s. m. + f. (Braz., also suleiro, sulino) southerner: native or inhabitant of the southern part of Brazil. ‖ adj. southern.

sul-rio-grandense s. m. + f. (pl. sul-rio-grandenses) native or inhabitant or Rio Grande do Sul (federal state in the south of Brazil). ‖ adj. of, pertaining to or characteristic of Rio Grande do Sul and its inhabitants.

sultana s. f. 1. sultana, sultaness: a) a sultan's wife. b) a sultan's mistress who bore him a son. c) title of the sultan's daughters. 2. (ornith.) the sultana bird. 3. (bot.) plant of the daisy family (Centaurea americana).

sultanado, sultanato s. m. sultanship, sultanate.

sultão s. m. (pl. **-ões**) 1. sultan: a) ruler, sovereign (of the Turks). b) title of some Mohammedan princes. c) (fig.) autocrat, absolute ruler, powerful prince. 2. (fig., pop.) a man who has many love affairs.

sultão-dos-matos s. m. (pl. **sultões-dos-matos**) (Braz.) sylvan spirit of the Brazilian folklore.

sulvento s. m. (also **sulão**) southwind.

suma (I) s. f. 1. sum, sum total. 2. summa, synthesis. 3. substance. 4. summary. 5. epitome, abstract. **em ~** all told, when all is said, in short, when all comes to all.

suma (II) s. f. (also **cipó-suma**) (bot.) a South American climbing plant of the violet family (Anchieta salutaris).

sumaca (I) s. f. a small two-master.

sumaca (II) s. f. (N. Braz.) jerked beer.

sumagrar v. to dye, or tan with sumac.

sumagre s. m. (also **açumagre**) sumac, sumach: a) the plant. b) the tanning material.

sumagre-da-virgínia s. m. (pl. **sumagres-da-virgínia**) (bot.) 1. staghorn sumach. 2. vinegar tree.

sumagreiro s. m. dyer's helper who prepares sumac or dye-wood for the bath.

sumagre-venenoso s. m. (pl. **sumagres-venenosos**) (bot.) 1. poison ivy. 2. markweed. 3. climath.

sumanta s. f. (S. Braz.) = **surra**.

sumaré s. m. (bot.) an orchid (Cyctopodium punctatum)

sumaré-de-pedras s. m. (pl. **sumarés-de-pedras**) (bot.) an orchid (Cyctopodium Andersonni).

sumarento adj. (also **sumoso**) 1. juicy, succulent. 2. lush. 3. sappy.

sumariante s. m. (jur.) judge who presides the formal indictment. ‖ adj. m. + f. of, pertaining to or relative to a formal arraignment.

sumariar v. 1. to summarize. 2. to synthesize. 3. to abstract. 4. to abbreviate. 5. to sum up.

sumário s. m. summary, resumé: 1. digest, abbreviation, docket. 2. abstract, brief, precis, synopsis. 3. extract. ‖ adj. summary: 1. concide, succint. 2. condensed. 3. short, brief. 4. simple. 5. made without delay or formality. ‖ **sumariamente** adv. summarily, concisely, briefly, neck and crop. **~ de uma obra** argument. **o ~ da acusação** (jur.) the substance of the accusation. **processo ~** (jur.) summary jurisdiction.

sumaúma, sumaumeira s. f. (Braz., bot.) kapok tree, ceiba tree, god tree, silk cotton tree (Ceiba petandra).

sumbaré s. m. (S. Braz., pop.) flirtation, love affair.

sumé s. m. (Braz.) a legendary figure revered by South American aborigines.

sumetume s. m. (N. Braz.) 1. escape hole in the burrow of a capybara. 2. mouth of a cave or underground gallery.

sumiço s. m. (also **sumição, sumidura** f.) 1. disappearance, vanishing. 2. wrong way or track. 3. escape, flight.

sumidade s. f. 1. highness, eminence, prominence. 2. celebrity. 3. summit, top, apex. 4. a very high-standing or distinguished personality.

sumidiço adj. evanescent: that easily disappears.

sumido adj. 1. hidden, concealed: that scarcely can be seen. 2. evanished, disappeared. 3. faint, weak. 4. nearly inaudible. 5. far, distant. 6. lean, thin. 7. hollow, sunken.

sumidouro s. m. 1. sink, drain. 2. escape hole. 3. gutter, sewer.

sumilher s. m. (Port.) steward of the royal household.

sumir v. 1. to let disappear. 2. to disappear, vanish. 3. to lose. 4. to submerge, sink. 5. to hide, conceal. 6. to drown. 7. to spend, waste, squander. 8. to extinguish, quench. 9. to destroy. 10. to recede. 11. to tail away, pack o. s., scram. 12. to eliminate. 13. **~-se**: a) to sink, drown. b) to hide o. s. c) to go out (e. g. light or fire). d) to get lost. e) to take to flight, get away. 14. to delete, plot out. **ele sumiu-se com o roubo** he walked off with the plunder. **suma-se!** get out of here!, scram!

sumista s. m. + f. summist: writer of summas or synthesis.

sumo (I) s. m. (also **suco**) 1. juice, sap. 2. lushness.

sumo (II) adj. 1. very high, lofty. 2. superior. 3. supreme, extreme, most excellent. 4. maximum. ‖ **-amente** adv. very highly, extremely, supremely. **~ pontífice** pontifex maximus, the pope. **~ sacerdote** high priest. **ao ~** in the highest degree. **ele está -amente revoltado** he is extremely indignant.

sumo-da-cana s. m. (pl. **sumos-da-cana**) (Braz., pop.) sugar-cane brandy, white rum, booze.

sumpção, sunção s. f. (pl. **-ões**) 1. swallow: act or result of swallowing. 2. sumption, consumption.

sumpes s. m., sg. + pl. (S. Braz.) a popular festivity with dancing, shindig, spree, revelry.

sumpto, sunto s. m. 1. expense, expenditure. 2. outlay. 3. cost, price. 4. charge.

súmula s. f. summula: 1. epitome, abridgement, docket, a short summary. 2. compendium.

sumulista s. m. + f. summulist: author of a summula, compiler, resumer, abridger, summist.

suna s. f. (rel.) Sunna(h): 1. a collection of religious rules and traditions handed down from Mohammed. 2. the orthodox principles of Mohammedan faith.

sundo s. m. 1. (anat., zool.) anus. 2. (anat.) pudendum: the external sexual organs of the female.

sunfa s. f. (S. Braz.) = **surra**.

sunga s. f. (Braz., — in some regions: s. m.) 1. a kind of panties for children. 2. swim trunks.

sungar v. (Braz.) 1. to hitch up (trousers, skirt). 2. to lift up, raise up (any drooping object). 3. to hold back (with difficulties) the discharge of nasal mucus, snuffle.

sunita s. m. + f. (rel.) Sunnite: member of the largest and most orthodox Mohammedan sect.

suntuário, sumptuário adj. sumptuary.

suntuosidade, sumptuosidade s. f. sumptuosity: 1. magnificence, luxuriousness. 2. costliness, luxe. 3. princeliness, nobleness, splendidness, pompousness.

suntuoso, sumptuoso adj. sumptuous: 1. magnificent, luxurious. 2. costly, expensive. 3. noble, splendid. 4. (fig.) rich, proud. 5. superb. 6. pontifical. 7. palatial. ‖ **-amente** adv. sumptuously, luxuriously, pontifically. **uma construção -a** a proud building.

sununga s. f. (Braz.) a manioc field planted in summer.

suor s. m. 1. sweat: a) perspiration, transpiration. b) act of sweating. c) dew. 2. (fig.) hard work, drudgery. 3. (fig.) the result of hard work, fatigue. **cheio de ~** sweaty. **com ~** sweatily. **com o ~ do meu rosto** by the sweat of my brow. **manchado com ~** sweatstained. **ter ~es de frio** to break out in a cold sweat.

suor-de-alambique s. m. (pl. **suores-de-alambique**) (Braz., pop.) sugar-cane brandy, white rum, booze.

supedâneo s. m. 1. footstool. 2. footrest, footboard (of a bench). 3. pedestal, stand. 4. (fig.) basis, foundation.

supeditar v. 1. to furnish, provide, supply. 2. to administer, apply.

super- pref. super- signifying over, above, beyond, higher, superior, excess.

superabundância s. f. 1. superabundance: a) excessive amount or quantity, overflow, superfluity. b) redundance. c) exuberance, exuberancy, rampancy. d) plethora. e) oversupply. 2. overgrowth. ~ **de elementos comprovantes** galores of corroborating proof. **a ~ de trigo no mercado** the oversupply of wheat on the market. **com ~** overflowingly.

superabundante adj. m. + f. superabundant: 1. superabounding. 2. overflowing, overfull. 3. redundant. 4. lavish, copious. 5. exuberant, luxurious. 6. excessive. ‖ **~mente** adv. 1. superabundantly. 2. lavishy. 3. excessively.

superabundar v. to superabound: 1. overabound, exist abundantly or in excessive quantities. 2. be overfull, overflow. 3. be more than enough, be in excess. 4. be full. 5. spill over.

superado adj. 1. defeated, overcome. 2. removed, displaced. 3. passé, obsolete.

superalimentação s. f. 1. superalimentation, cramming, overfeeding. 2. supercharging.

superalimentado adj. (tech.) supercharged.

superalimentar v. 1. to overfeed: cram, stuff, fill excessively with food. 2. (mech.) to supercharge (a motor).

superante adj. m. + f. 1. surpassing. 2. advantageous. 3. excelling, excellent.

superaquecedor s. m. (tech.) superheater.

superaquecido adj. (tech.) superheated, overheated.

superaquecer v. 1. to superheat, overheat. 2. **~-se** to become excessively hot. **~ o ferro** to burn the iron. **~ o vapor** to superheat steam.

superaquecimento s. m. act or result of overheating, superheating.

superar v. 1. to conquer, vanquish. 2. to defeat, overcome. 3. to dominate. 4. to subjugate, subdue. 5. to destroy. 6. to surmount, surpass, outmatch. 7. to reach the top of, top. 8. to paragon. 9. to outdo, outrange. 10. to excell, outclass. 11. to outdare. **~ as expectativas** to top expectations. **~ em importância** to surpass in importance, precede. **~ tudo** to crown all. **ela não me supera** she is not superior to me. **ele foi superado pelo seu rival** he was thrown into the shade by his rival. **ele te supera de longe** he is more than a match to you. **superamo-lo com facilidade** we bested him easily.

superável adj. m. + f. (pl. **-áveis**) surpassable, surmountable, that can be overcome.

superávit s. m. (com.) superavit, surplus, excess supply.

supercalandra s. f. papermaking supercalender, superrolling machine.

supercampeão s. m. (Braz.) grand champion.

superciliar adj. m. + f. (anat.) superciliary.

supercílio s. m. (poet.) eyebrow.

supercilioso adj. 1. having thick eyebrows. 2. superciliary. 3. supercilious, arrogant. 4. severe, austere, strict.

supercivilizado adj. supercivilized.

supercompressão s. f. pl. **-ões**) (tech.) supercompression.

supercompressor s. m. (tech.) supercharger.

superdimensionado adj. oversized.

superdominante s. f. (mus.) superdominant.

superdotado s. m. (Braz.) genious. ‖ adj. highly gifted, endowed, talented.

superelevação s. f. superelevation, bank, cant (road, railway).

supereminência s. f. 1. supereminence, supereminency. 2. extraordinary elevation. 3. pre-eminence.

supereminente adj. m. + f. supereminent, pre-eminent.

superestimar v. (Braz.) to overestimate, overrate. **ele superestima as honrarias** he thinks too highly of the honours, he overvalues the honours.

superestrutura s. f. superstructure: 1. (railway) permanent way. 2. (pol.) the ideological, religious, philosophical and political principles of a social class.

superexaltado adj. very exalted, overexcited.

superexcitar v. = **sobreexcitar**.

superexcitável adj. m. + f. (pl. **-áveis**) overexcitable.

superfecundação s. f. (pl. **-ões**) (physiol.) superfecundation: fertilization of more than one ovum.

superfetação s. f. (pl. **-ões**), (med.) superfetation: 1. secund conception before the birth of the first. 2. (fig.) excrescence, useless appendage.

superficial adj. m. + f. (pl. **-ais**) superficial: 1. being on or pertaining to the surface. 2. not deep or profound. 3. not penetrating. 4. understanding only what is obvious or apparent. 5. external, outside. 6. shallow. 7. frivolous, flippant, flimsy. 8. cursory, discursive. 9. trifling. 10. dilettantish, amateurish. 11. shallow-brained, bird-witted. 12. slight, sloppy. 13. formal. 14. skin-deep, lip-deep. ‖ **~mente** adv. superficially, slightly, cursorily, perfunctorily. **água ~** surface-water. **saber ~** smattering. **tensão ~** (phys.) surface tension.

superficialidade s. f. 1. superficiality. 2. shallowness. 3. cursoriness. 4. flashiness.

superficialismo s. m. superficialism, superficiality.

superfície s. f. surface: 1. superficies. 2. outside, exterior. 3. (geom.) face, plane. 4. side. **~ curva** curved surface. **~ da terra** surface of the earth. **~ de deslize** running surface (plate E 9). **~ de revolução** surface of revolution. **~ plana** plane surface. **mineração na ~** strip mining.

superfino adj. superfine, very fine, overfine, of the best quality.

superfluidade s. f. superfluity, superfluousness.

supérfluo s. m. superfluity, surplus, excess, unnecessary. ‖ adj. superfluous, unnecessary, useless. ‖ **superfluamente** adv. superfluously.

super-homem s. m. (pl. **super-homens**) superman.

superintendência s. f. superintendency: 1. office of a superintendent. 2. superintendence, supervision.

superintendente s. m. + f. superintendent. ‖ adj. superintendent.

superintender v. to superintend, oversee, supervise, direct, manage, inspect.

superior s. m. superior: 1. person superior to s. o. 2. head of a monastery. ‖ adj. (also **súpero**) superior: 1. higher, upper, loftier. 2. of a higher grade or position. 3. of better quality, excellent. 4. greater. **~ a suas possibilidades** beyond his possibilities. **as camadas ~es** the upper classes. **de um plano ~** from a higher level. **de ~ qualidade** of superior quality. **escola ~** secondary school; high school. **por ordens ~es** by authority. **rendas 100% ~es às do ano passado** receipts 100% up on those of the last year.

superiora s. f. superior, Mother Superior; prioress.

superiorato s. m. office or dignity of a superior.

superioridade s. f. superiority.

superlativador s. m. person who employs excessively the superlative. ‖ adj. marked by excessive use of the superlative.

superlativar v. to put into the superlative.

superlativo s. m. (gram.) superlative. ‖ adj. 1. superlative. 2. of the highest degree.

superlotar v. to overcrowd, fill excessively, to overload. **os trens estavam superlotados** the trains were overcrowded.

supermercado s. m. supermarket.

superno adj. (also **supernal** m. + f., pl. **-ais**) 1. supernal. 2. (fig.) excellent.

superoxidação s. f. (chem.) superoxygenation.

superpopulação s. f. excessive population.

superpor v. to superpose.

superposição s. f. (pl. **-ões**) superposition.

superpotência s. f. superpower; an extremely powerful nation.

superpovoado adj. overpopulated.

superpovoamento s. m. overpopulation.

superprodução s. f. overproduction.

super-quadra s. f. (Braz.) a residential area of 200 m by 200 m with apartment houses, play-grounds, gardens and schools.

super-realismo s. m. (pl. **super-realismos**) surrealism.

super-realista s. m. + f. (pl. **super-realistas**) surrealist. ‖ adj. surrealistic.

supersaturação s. f. (pl. **-ões**) supersaturation.

supersaturar v. to supersaturate.

supersecreção s. f. (pl. **-ões**) excessive secretion.

supersensível adj. m. + f. (pl. **-íveis**) supersensible.

supersônico adj. (phys.) supersonic.

superstição s. f. (pl. **-ões**) superstition.

supersticiosidade s. f. superstitiousness.

supersticioso s. m. superstitious person. ‖ adj. superstitious. ‖ **-amente** adv. superstitiously.

supérstite adj. surviving.

supersubstancial adj. m. + f. (pl. **-ais**) excessively substantial.

superumeral s. m. (pl. **-ais**) superhumeral.

supervacâneo, supervácuo adj. supervacaneous, superfluous, useless, void.

superveniência s. f. supervenience.

superveniente adj. m. + f. supervenient.

supervisionar v. to supervise.

supervivência s. f. (also **sobrevivência**) survival.

supervivente s. m. + f. (also **sobrevivente**) survivor. ‖ adj. surviving.

supetão s. m. word used in the expression: **de ~** suddenly, unexpectedly.

supimpa adj. m. + f. (Braz., coll.) spanking, fine, swell.

supinação s. f. (pl. **-ões**) (physiol.) supination.

supinador s. m. (anat.) supinator. ‖ adj. referring to the supinators.

supino adj. supine: 1. lying on the back with the face upwards. 2. turned up. 3. (fig.) excessive.

suplantação s. f. 1. supplantation, supplanting, act or fact of superseding. 2. treading, tramping.

suplantador s. m. 1. supplanter. 2. treader, tramper. ‖ adj. 1. supplanting. 2. treading, tramping.

suplantar v. to supplant, supersede, replace, take the place, to oust. 2. to tread, tramp (grapes).

suplementar adj. m. + f. (also **suplementário** m.) supplemental, additional. ‖ **~mente** adv. supplementarily.

suplemento s. m. supplement: 1. addendum, appendix. 2. (math.) the angle that added to another one makes 180º.

suplente s. m. + f. substitute, proxy, person who takes the place of another. ‖ adj. substitutional.

supletivo, supletório adj. suppletive.

súplica, suplicação s. f. supplication: humble petition or prayer.

suplicado s. m. (jur.) accused.

suplicante s. m. + f. 1. supplicant, petitioner. 2. suitor. 3. (Braz., coll.) John Doe. ‖ adj. supplicant, entreating, suppliant.

suplicar v. to supplicate: 1. beg humbly, entreat, implore, beseech. 2. pray. 3. plead.

suplicatório adj. supplicatory.

súplice adj. m. + f. suppliant, supplicant, supplicating, beseeching.

suplicado s. m. executed criminal. ‖ adj. 1. tortured. 2. executed.

supliciar v. 1. to torture; hurt; molest. 2. to execute. put to death.

suplício s. m. 1. corporal punishment. 2. torture. 3. capital punishment, death. 4. (fig.) torment, pain.

supor v. to suppose, assume, presume, think, imagine, believe.

suponho que é tempo de irmos I suppose it is time to go. **suponho que está errado** I guess it is wrong.

suportar v. to support: 1. suffer, endure; stand, tolerate; show forbearance. 2. bear the weight of, hold up.

eu não suporto este calor I cannot stand this heat. **eu não suporto este sujeito** I cannot bear, endure that fellow.

suportável adj. m. + f. (pl. **-áveis**) supportable, tolerable, bearable.

suporte s. m. 1. support, stay, prop (plates B 4, 9, C 15). 2. (tech.) bearer, holder, rest, bracket, leg (plates B 11, C 15, G 5).

~ da mola spring bracket. **~ de lâmpada** bulb holder. **~ estribo** (mot.) step hanger.

suposição s. f. (pl. **-ões**) supposition, conjecture, presumption, surmise; assumption.

é apenas uma ~ it is nothing more than a supposition.

suposticio, supositivo adj. 1. supposititious; supposed. 2. fictitious; sham, false.

supositório s. m. (med.) suppository.

suposto s. m. supposition, presumption. ‖ adj. supposed, presumed, assumed, hypothetic(al).

~ que supposing that, even if. **~ que isto fosse verdade** granting this to be true.

supra-axilar adj. (pl. **supra-axilares**) (bot.) supra-axillary.

supracaudal adj. m. + f. (pl. **-ais**) (zool.) supracaudal.

supracitado, supradito adj. above-metioned, mentioned before.

supraclavicular adj. m. + f. (pl. **-ais**) (anat.) supraclavicular.

supramundano adj. supramundane.

supranasal adj. m. + f. (pl. **-ais**) (anat., zool.) supranasal.

supranatural adj. m. + f. (pl. **-ais**) supranatural.

supranaturalismo s. m. supranaturalism.

supranaturalista s. m. + f. supranaturalist. ‖ adj. supranaturalistic.

supranumerado adj. numbered above.

supranumerário s. m. supernumerary. ‖ adj. supernumerary.

supra-realismo s. m. (pl. **supra-realismos**) surrealism.

supra-realista s. m. + f. (pl. **supra-realistas**) surrealist. ‖ adj. surrealistic.

supra-renal adj. m. + f. (pl. **supra-renais**) (anat.) suprarenal.

supra-sensível adj. m. + f. (pl. **supra-sensíveis**) supersensible.

supra-sumo s. m. (pl. **supra-sumos**) top, utmost, highest, ideal, acme.

supraterrâneo adj. of or referring to the surface of the earth; that is on the surface of the earth.

supratorácico adj. (anat.) suprathoracic.

supremacia s. f. supremacy, supremity, sovereignty, supreme authority or power, domination, preponderance.

supremo s. m. (coll.) Supreme Court. ‖ adj. (also **súpero**) supreme, highest; utmost, predominant.

o chefe ~ da nação the president of the country.

supressão s. f. (pl. **-ões**) suppression: extinction, annihilation, cancellation, omission.

supressivo, supressor, supressório adj. suppressive.

supridor s. m. 1. supplier, furnisher. 2. completer, substituter, compensater. 3. helper, aider. ‖ adj. supplying, furnishing.

suprimento s. m. 1. supply. 2. subsidy; loan. 3. suppliance; supplyment. 4. assistance; aid.

suprimido adj. suppressed: 1. abolished, cancel(l)ed, omitted. 2. concealed.

suprimir v. to suppress: 1. abolish, cancel, omit, eliminate, extinguish. 2. hide, conceal, hold back; not to mention, silence.

suprir v. 1. to supply, furnish. 2. to complete. 3. to substitute, compensate (for). 4. to make up for. 5. to fill in or out. 6. to help, aid.
este livro supriu uma falta this book filled a gap.

suprível adj. m. + f. (pl. **-íveis**) 1. suppliable. 2. replaceable.

supuração s. f. (pl. **-ões**) suppuration.

supurado adj. (also **supurante** m. + f.) suppurating, purulent.

supurar v. to suppurate, fester, ulcer, produce pus.

supurativo s. m. (pharm.) suppurative. ‖ adj. (also **supuratório**) suppurative.

suputação s. f. (pl. **-ões**) calculation.

suputar v. to calculate, compute.

sura (I) s. f. (also **panturrilha**) calf of the leg.

sura (II) s. f. fermented palm juice.

surdear v. to feign to be deaf.

surdez s. f. deafness, lack of hearing.

surdimutismo s. m. deaf-mutism.

surdina s. f. (mus.) mute, sordine.
à ~, na ~ secretly, on the sly, stealthy.

surdinar v. to cause a babbling, purling sound; to rustle.

surdir v. 1. to rise, emerge, surge, appear. 2. to gush, well, issue. 3. to go ahead (as in a boat). 4. to result from.

surdista s. m. + f. lifeboatman.

surdo s. m. deaf person. ‖ adj. 1. deaf: a) unable to hear. b) insensible; heedless; unattentive; not inclined to listen or hear. 2. (phon.) voiceless. 3. muffled (sound). 4. secret. 5. dull (colours).
~ como uma porta stone-deaf. **ensurdecer um ~** to make an awful loud noise. **fazer-se ~** not to listen, not to care for.

surdo-mudez s. f. (pl. **surdo-mudezes**) deaf-mutism.

surdo-mudo s. m. (pl. **surdos-mudos**) deaf-mute. ‖ adj. deaf-mute, deaf-and-dumb.

surfe s. m. surfing: the sport of riding the surf.

surfista s. m. + f. (Braz.) one who practices surfing.

surgida s. f. (N. Braz.) the reappearance of a harpooned whale.

surgidouro s. m. (naut., also **surgidoiro**) anchoring place, anchorage, roadstead.

surgir v. 1. to arise, come to sight, appear, emerge; to arouse. 2. to come to the surface. 3. to well, issue, gush. 4. (naut.) to enter a port; to anchor. 5. to result from, be a consequence of.
fazer ~ dúvidas to cause to arise doubts. **surgiu uma dúvida** a doubt arose.

suri adj. (Braz.) sleeveless.

surmenage s. f. (Fr.) fatigue, overwork, strain.

suro adj. (Braz.) tailless.

surpreendente adj. m. + f. surprising, astonishing, amazing; remarkable, admirable, wonderful. ‖ **~mente** adv. surprisingly.

surpreender v. (also **supresar**) to surprise: 1. take unawares in the act, attack without warning, take aback. 2. astonish, amaze, startle, astound. 3. **~-se** to be astonished, be taken by surprise.
ele foi surpreendido 1. he was caught red-handed, in the act. 2. he was caught napping. **eles foram surpreendidos pela noite** they were overtaken by the night.

surpresa (ê) s. f. surprise: 1. surprisal. 2. cause of surprise. 3. state of being surprised. 4. astonishment, amazement. 5. attack without warning.
o resultado não representa ~ alguma the result represents no surprise at all. **por grande ~ minha** to my great surprise. **que ~ vê-lo** what a surprise to see you here. **tirar o caráter de ~ a** to kill the surprise of a thing.

surpreso (ê) adj. 1. surprised. 2. astounded, amazed. 3. startled, perplexed.
fiquei bastante ~ I was very much surprised.

surra s. f. thrashing, spanking, beating, flogging, whipping.
deram-lhe uma boa ~ he got a sound spanking; they took the sawdust out of him.

surrado (I) adj. 1. worn, worn out, worse for the use. 2. tanned, curried. 3. beaten.

surrado (II) adj. filthy, dirty.

surrador s. m. 1. currier, tanner. 2. beater, flogger. ‖ adj. 1. currying, tanning. 2. beating, flogging.

surramento s. m. 1. currying, tanning. 2. beating, flogging.

surrão s. m. (pl. **-ões**) 1. a shepherd's bag or poke. 2. a dirty fellow. 3. dirty clothes, worn out clothes.
arrastar ~ to brag, boast.

surrar v. 1. to curry, tan, dress leather. 2. to beat, flog, spank, hide. 3. **~-se** to become worse for the use (clothes), become threadbare.

surrealismo s. m. surrealism.

surrealista s. m. + f. surrealist. ‖ adj. surrealistic.

surriada s. f. 1. volley: simultaneous discharge of guns. 2. foam of breaking waves. 3. (coll.) jeer, derision, scoff, taunt.
fazer ~ to hoot, hiss.

surriba s. f. (agric.) a scarifying.

surribar v. (agric.) to scarify: dig the earth around a tree.

surripiar, surripilhar, surrupiar v. to purloin, steal, pilfer, filch; to cheat, trick out of.

surro s. m. 1. dirt, dirtiness, filth, filthiness. 2. rubbish, waste, debris, trash.

surtida s. f. (mil.) 1. sortie, sally. 2. sally-port. 3. charge, onslaught.

surtir v. to occasion, give rise to, result in, have or come as a consequence.
surtiu efeito it worked, had the desired result.

surto s. m. 1. soaring. 2. outbreak. 3. (com.) boom. 4. impetus, impulse, dash. ‖ adj. anchored.
um ~ epidêmico an outbreak of epidemics.

surtum s. m. (pl. **-uns**) vest (formerly used).

suru adj. m. + f. tailless.

suruanã s. f. a marine turtle.

suruba s. f. (Braz.) 1. a big walking stick, cane. 2. shameful love-making. ‖ adj. m. + f. good, excellent; strong.

surubada s. f. a blow with the **suruba** (walking stick).

surubi, surubim s. m. fish of the family Siluridae.

surucar v. to collapse, come down.

surucuá s. m. trogon; bird of the family Trogonidae.

surucucu s. f. a venomous Brazilian snake (Lachesis mutus).

surucucurana s. f. (Braz.) one of the aglyphous snakes.

suruje s. m. (Braz.) termite mound.

surunganga s. m. hooligan, rowdy, roughneck. ‖ adj. daring, courageous.

surungo s. m. (S. Braz.) shilling-hop, skip.

sururina s. f. (Braz., ornith.) a tinamon.

sururu s. m. (Braz.) 1. an edible mollusc. 2. (coll.) shindy, fracas, brawl, scuffle. 3. plant of the family Tiliaceae.

sururuca s. f. a coarse sieve.

sururucar v. to sift, pass through a sieve.

sus interj. go on! courage!

suscetibilidade s. f. susceptibility, susceptibleness; touchiness.

suscetibilizar v. 1. to hurt (feelings), offend, grieve. 2. ~-se to feel hurt, offended.

suscetível s. m. (pl. -íveis) sensitive or touchy person. || adj. 1. susceptible, susceptive. 2. sensitive. 3. touchy, easily hurt.

suscitação s. f. (pl. -ões) suscitation, arousal, instigation, stimulation; suggestion.

suscitador s. m. person who suscitates; rouser. ||adj. rousing.

suscitar v. 1. to suscitate, rouse, excite. 2. to cause, give rise to, occasion, engender, create. 3. to suggest.

isto suscita dúvidas this gives rise to doubts. **suscitou uma onda de protestos** it raised a storm of protest.

suscitável adj. m. + f. (pl. -áveis) that may give rise to; suggestive of.

suserania s. f. suzerainty.

suserano s. m. suzerain. || adj. suzerain.

suspeição s. f. (pl. -ões) suspicion; distrust.

suspeita s. f. suspicion, distrust, diffidence, doubt. **acima de toda** ~ above all suspicion. **causar ~s** to arouse suspicion. **lançar ~s sobre** to cast suspicion on. **eu tenho minhas ~s a respeito dele** I have my doubts about him.

suspeitador s. m. suspecter. || adj. suspecting.

suspeitar v. to suspect: 1. distrust. 2. have doubts about. 3. be suspicious. 4. suppose, imagine, conjecture. **quem ~ia isto?** who would ever suspect it?

suspeito adj. suspect: 1. suspected. 2. suspicious. 3. doubtful, questionable. 4. untrustworthy. 5. (fam.) fishy. **tornar-se** ~ 1. to fall under suspicion. 2. (jur.) to inculpate o. s.

suspeitoso adj. doubtful, questionable. || -amente adv. doubtfully.

suspender v. to suspend: 1. hang, hang up. 2. hoist. 3. supersede, put off, delay, postpone. 4. interrupt. 5. cease, stop (esp. temporarily). 6. keep in suspense, keep at bay. 7. deprive of an office; dismiss temporarily. ~ **o trabalho** to strike, to down tools. ~ **o fogo** to stop firing. ~ **uma ação jurídica** to stay an action. ~ **uma seção** to adjourn a meeting.

suspensão s. f. (pl. -ões) 1. act of suspending, suspension. 2. (tech. mot.) device for suspending. 3. a hanging up. 4. interruption. 5. cessation, stoppage. 6. postponement, deferment. 7. temporary dismissal. 8. (mus.) a holding of a tone or set of tones. ~ **Cardan ou cardânica** Cardan's suspension.

suspense s. m. suspense: a moment of great tension.

suspensivo adj. suspensive.

suspenso adj. suspended: 1. hanging. 2. interrupted. 3. stopped. 4. in abeyance, debarred. **estar em** ~ to be undecided, in suspense. **deixar em** ~ to leave in abeyance. **ele foi** ~ **por três dias** he was suspended for three days.

suspensório s. m. 1. (med.) suspensory. 2. trace stay (harness strap). 3. ~s pl. suspenders, braces; shoulder straps (plates R 6, 7). || adj. suspensory.

suspicaz adj. m. + f. 1. suspected. 2. suspicious, distrustful, doubting.

suspirado adj. greatly desired or longed for, hankered after.

suspirador s. m. sigher, person who suspires (frequently). || adj. sighing.

suspirar v. 1. to sigh; suspire. 2. to want earnestly, wish very much, long for, hanker after, pine for.

3. to say sadly; lament, grieve. 4. to blow gently.

suspiro s. m. 1. sigh; suspiration; breath. 2. a longing for. 3. vent (barrel, cask). 4. a sweet of the white of an egg and sugar (plate D 3). 5. (bot.) scabious. **até o meu último** ~ to my last breath or gasp. **dar o último** ~ to breathe one's last.

suspiroso adj. 1. sighing. 2. mournful; lamenting.

sussurrante adj. m + f. 1. rustling. 2. whispering, murmuring. 3. lisping. 4. purling, rippling. 5. humming.

sussurrar v. 1. to rustle. 2. to whisper, murmur. 3. to lisp. 4. to purl, ripple. 5. to hum, buzz.

sussurro s. m. 1. rustle. 2. whisper, whispering, murmur. 3. lisp, lisping sound. 4. purl, purling. 5. hum, buzz.

sustança, sustância s. f. 1. (pop.) = **substância**. 2. (Braz., pop.) vigour, strength.

sustar v. 1. to stop, halt, stay, arrest, bring to a standstill; suspend. 2. ~-se to come to a stop.

sustatório adj. that causes a stop.

sustenido s. m. (mus.) sharp (plate N 1).

sustentação s. m. (pl. -ões) sustentation; sustenance, maintenance; subsistence.

sustentáculo s. m. 1. support. 2. stay, prop. 3. (fig.) supporter.

sustentador s. m. supporter, sustainer. || adj. (also **sustentante** m. + f.) supporting, sustaining.

sustentar v. 1. to sustain: a) support. b) bear the weight of; hold up, keep up, prop. c) supply the sustenance for; maintain, pay the costs, provide for. d) patronize, favour; uphold, defend, back. e) suffer. 2. to assert, affirm, maintain. 3. to strengthen, fortify. 4. ~-se: a) to resist, defend o. s. b) to keep on the same level, maintain o.s., live on. ~ **uma conversação** to keep up a conversation. ~ **uma família** to keep up a family. ~ **uma opinião** to hold up an opinion. ~ **a sua palavra** to stick to one's word. ~-se **de ar** to live on air, to starve. ~ **o peso dos negócios** to bear the weight of business.

sustentável adj. m. + f. (pl. -áveis) maintainable. supportable, sustainable.

sustento s. m. maintenance: 1. support. 2. sustenance, food, nourishment.

suster v. 1. to support, prop. 2. to sustain. 3. to meet, face. 4. to resist. 5. to check, restrain, moderate. 6. to stop, bring to a halt. 7. ~-se: a) to keep o. s. up. b) to refrain o. s.

sustimento s. m. support; sustainment.

sustinente adj. m. + f. supporting, sustaining.

susto s. m. fright, shock, alarm, appalment; scare; fear. **pregar um** ~ to scare, frighten, to give a person a start. **ele escapou com o** ~ he was more frightened than hurt. **levei um tremendo** ~ I was awfully frightened, I was terror-stricken.

su-sudoeste s. m. south-southwest. || adj. south-southwest.

su-sueste s. m. south-southeast. || adj. south-southeast.

suta s. f. 1. level, level square (plate F 2). 2. (N. Braz.) group of persons who call on their neighbour late in the night to help him do his (farm) work.

sutache s. f. braid.

sutambaque s. m. frock-coat, Prince Albert coat.

sutar v. to join or adjust by means of a level.

sutiã s. m. brassière, bra.

sutil s. m. (pl. -is) (also **subtil**) = **sutileza**. || adj. m. + f. subtile: 1. subtle. 2. tenuous, rarefied. 3. perspicaceous. 4. wily, crafty, insidious. 5. delicate, very fine.

sútil adj. m. + f. (pl. **súteis**) sewed, stitched.

sutileza s. f. (also **subtileza, sutilidade, subtilidade**) subtileness, subtility, subtleness, subtlety.

sutilização s. f. (pl. -ões) (also **subtilização**) subtilization.

sutilizar v. (also **subtilizar**) to subtilize: 1. make subtle. 2. make or introduce fine distinctions. 3. refine; rarefy.

sutinga s. f. (Braz.) a variety of cassava.

sutra s. m. (India) sutra.

sutura s. f. suture: 1. act of sewing. 2. seam. 3. (anat.) seamlike juncture of two parts, esp. bones (skull) (plate C 17). 4. (surg.) the sewing of a wound or the sewn part.

sutural adj. m. + f. (pl. -ais) sutural.

suturar v. to suture: join or unite by a suture or by sewing.

suxar v. to loosen, slacken; release; widen.

suxo adj. slackened, loose, slack.

swap s. m. (econ.) swap, an exchange, a trade.

T

T, t s. m. the nineteenth letter of the Portuguese alphabet. ‖ adj. nineteenth of an order or class. ‖ **t** abbr. of **tonelada** (ton); **t**. abbr. of **termo** (term), **tomo** (tome, volume).

tá interj. stop!, hold!, forbear!

taba s. f. (Braz.) 1. Indian village or settlement. 2. sort of game played in the south.

tabacada s. f. (Braz.) slap, box on the ear, blow.

tabacal s. m. (pl. **-ais**) tobacco plantation, tobacco field. ‖ adj. m. + f. belonging to tobacco.

tabacaria s. f. tobacco shop, tobacconist's shop, cigar store.

tabaco s. m. tobacco.
~ **para fumar** smoking tobacco. ~ **em folha** leaf tobacco. ~ **em rolo** pigtail tobacco. **bolsa de** ~ tobacco-pouch. **levar para o seu** ~ (fig.) to be taught a lesson.

tabaco-bom s. m. (pl. **tabacos-bons**) (Braz., ornith.) one of the goatsuckers.

tabagismo s. m. (med.) tobaccoism: abuse of smoking and its effect on health.

tabaiacu s. m. (N. Braz.) long underwater reef.

tabanídeo s. m. (usually **mutuca** f.) horsefly.

tabaque s. m. (Braz.) drum of a hollow log, made and used by the Indians and Negroes.

tabaquear v. 1. to smoke tobacco. 2. to snuff, take a snuff.

tabaqueira s. f. 1. snuffbox. 2. tobacco-pouch. 3. (fig.) nostrils.

tabaqueiro s. m. 1. tobacconist, dealer in tobacco. 2. person who uses tobacco or snuff. ‖ adj. 1. relating to tobacco. 2. said of a person who uses tobacco.

tabaquista s. m. + f. snuffer or smoker; person who uses tobacco.

tabardilha s. f. small tabard.

tabardilho s. m. (path.) petechial fever.

tabardo s. m. tabard: short loose overcoat or cloak worn by heralds.

tabaréu s. m. 1. rookie: unexperienced soldier. 2. (fig.) greenhorn; botcher; bungler; booby.

tabaroa s. f. (Braz.) country woman.

tabatinga s. f. sedimentary variety of clay used in pottery.

tabatingal s. m. (pl. **-ais**) place where **tabatinga** is found.

tabe s. f. (path.) tabes: 1. locomotive ataxia. 2. (obs.) chronic emaciation.

tabefe s. m. 1. whey. 2. eggnog: milk beaten with sugar and eggs. 3. (pop.) box on the ear, slap, blow, cuff, buffet.

tabela s. f. 1. table (of contents, etc.), chart. 2. list, catalogue, schedule, appendix, index, roster. 3. cushion of a billiard table. 4. (fig.) allusion, remark.
~ **de juros** interest table. ~ **de preços** price list. **chegar à** ~ to arrive on time. **por** ~ indirectly. **repreensão por** ~ an indirect rebuke. **vender à** ~ to sell at fixed price(s).

tabelado adj. controlled (price), with a fixed price.

tabelamento s. m. control of prices.

tabelar v. 1. to put on the (standard) price list. 2. to control, restrain, regulate (prices). 3. to sell according to the price list. ‖ adj. m. + f. belonging to a table, list or appendix.

tabelião s. m. (pl. **-ães**) (f. **tabelioa**) notary, notary public.

tabeliar v. to exercise the functions of a notary.

tabelinha s. f. (Braz., ftb.) a quick, repeated exchange of the ball.

tabelioa s. f. a notary's wife. ‖ adj. f. 1. bad, unintelligible (handwriting). 2. routine (expression).
letra ~ scrawl, careless handwriting.

tabelionado, tabelionato s. m. office of a notary.

taberna s. f. tavern, pot-house, inn, public house.

tabernáculo s. m. tabernacle: 1. (eccl.) container of the consecrated elements of the Eucharist. 2. Jewish temple. 3. temporary dwelling, tent. 4. place of worship for a large audience.

tabernal adj. m. + f. (pl. **-ais**) 1. relating to a public house. 2. dirty, filthy, unclean. ‖ ~**mente** adv. dirtily, uncleanly.

tabernário s. m. innkeeper. ‖ adj. tavern, of or referring to an inn or tavern.

taberneiro s. m. innkeeper, taverner, tapster.

tabescente adj. m. + f. tabescent, wasting away. ‖ ~**mente** adv. tabescently.

tabético adj. tabetic.

tabi s. m. tabby, taffeta.

tabica s. f. 1. wedge. 2. (naut.) sideplank around the deck, plank of the gunwale. 3. (Braz., bot.) withe. 4. switch. 5. (Braz., fig.) lean person.

tabicada s. f. (Braz.) blow with a switch.

tabicar v. 1. to split or separate with a wedge, cleave, rive. 2. to insert a partition wall.

tábido adj. 1. rotten, foul. 2. corrupt, depraved. 3. tabid.

tabífico adj. producing rottenness, corrupting.

tabijara s. m. (Braz.) brave person, daredevil.

tabique s. m. 1. thin (wooden) partition, wall. 2. (bot.) septum.

tabizar v. to tabby, give a wavy or watered appearance to.

tabla s. f. sheet metal, metal plate; lamina.

tablada s. f. (S. Braz.) 1. cattle market. 2. place where salt meat is prepared.

tablado s. m. 1. stage: a) raised floor of a theatre. b) raised platform, scaffold. 2. boxing ring.

tablatura s. f. (mus.) tablature.

tablete s. m. (Braz.) tablet, bar, slab.

tablilha s. f. 1. billiard table cushion. 2. (fig.) indirect way or method.
~ **de forrar** planks used in the ceiling of a ship.

tablóide s. m. (newspaper) tabloid. ‖ adj. m. + f. (Braz.) lozenge-shaped.

tabo s. m. a sort of Asiatic or African craft.

taboca s. f. (Braz.) 1. (also **taquara**) bamboo. 2. name of an ant. 3. segment of bamboo filled with powder for fireworks. 4. small shop, store. 5. (fig.) disappointment, deception. 6. fraud, deceit, cheat. 7. refusal, rejection.
passar ~ (Braz., sl.) to disengage o. s.

taboca-gigante s. f. (pl. **tabocas-gigantes**) (Braz.) large bamboo used in housebuilding, for light masts, ladders and as raw material for paper mills, etc.

tabocal s. m. (pl. **-ais**) (Braz.) thicket of bamboos, place where bamboos grow.

taboeira s. f. (Braz.) a stunted, degenerated plant.

taboqueador s. m. swindler, cheat, impostor. ‖ adj. fraudulent, deceitful.

taboquear v. to deceive, defraud, delude; bluff; break one's word.

taboqueiro s. m. (N. Braz.) owner of a small store. ‖ adj. 1. excessively dear. 2. fraudulent, usurious. ‖ -**amente** adv. usuriously.

tabu (I) s. m. taboo, tabu: (rel.) system of setting persons or things apart as sacred or cursed. ‖ adj. m. + f. taboo, tabu: 1. set apart as sacred. 2. prohibited, forbidden.

declarar um objeto como ~ to put a tabu upon a subject.

tabu (II) s. m. (Braz.) badly cleaned sugar (spoilt in the processing).

tabu (III) s. m. (Braz., bot., also **tabua** f.) cattail.

tábua s. f. 1. board: a) deal, plank (plate A 8). b) chart, map; list, table. c) notice board (plate E 13). d) table of a game. 2. each side of a horse's or other animal's neck. 3. (fig.) a rejection of a marriage proposal.

~ de barquilha (naut.) logboard. **~ de bater carne** chopping board (plate C 20). **~s de forro** sheathing planks. **~ de lavar roupa** scrubbing board (plate L 3). **~s logarítmicas** logarithmic tables. **~ de mármore** marble slab. **~ de mesa** table top, leaf of a table. **~ de passar roupa** ironing board. **~ rasa** (fig.) blank canvas. **~ de salvação** (fig.) last resource. **dar ~ a** (Braz.) to deceive, disappoint, jilt. **fazer ~ rasa** (fig.) to make a clean sweep of. **levar ~** to come off badly, be defeated, get the mitten. **na ~ da venta** to someone's face, right in front of.

tabuada s. f. 1. multiplication table. 2. elementary notions of arithmethic. 3. table of logarithms. 4. (coll.) index, register, roster, series.

tabuado s. m. 1. wooden floor, planking. 2. fence, pile, or partition of boards.

tabual s. m. (pl. **-ais**) cattail plantation.

tabuão s. m. (pl. **-ões**) 1. large or heavy board or plank. 2. small wooden bridge.

tabuinha s. f. 1. slat, small or thin board, lath. 2. (pl.) Venetian blind, wooden shutter.

tabujajá s. m. (Braz.) heron: a long-necked wading bird.

tábula s. f. (also **távola**) 1. man (of games like draughts). 2. (obs.) gaming table.

tabulado s. m. 1. wooden floor, planking. 2. wooden paling or fence. 3. improvised platform or stage. 4. wooden partition.

tabulador s. m. tabulator: space bar of a typewriter.

tabulão s. m. (pl. **-ões**) worktable of a goldsmith or jeweler.

tabular adj. m. + f. tabular: 1. flat like a table. 2. computed from tables. 3. arranged in columns. ‖ **~mente** adv. tabularly.

tabulário adj. illustrated with xylographs.

tabuleiro s. m. 1. chessboard, checkerboard. 2. flower bed. 3. salt pan. 4. salver, tray. 5. stair landing. 6. tin to bake cakes on. 7. roadway across a bridge (plate P 14). 8. (Braz.) barren tableland. 9. (N. Braz.): a) turtle nest. b) sandbank in a river. **~ de xadrez** chessboard. **~ do jogo de damas** draughtboard.

tabuleta s. f. 1. signboard, facia (plate V 5). 2. brass-plate. 3. name-plate (plate E 11). 4. (Braz.) small board put on a lamb's muzzle to prevent it from sucking.

tabulista s. m. + f. person who makes up astronomic or geographic tables, lists, etc.

taburno s. m. 1. footstool. 2. stairstep. 3. sepulchral cover plate.

taca (I) s. f. 1. belt, leather strap. 2. flail.

meter a ~ em to slander, backbite, calumniate.

taca (II) s. f. (Braz.) blow, knock.

taca (III) s. f. (bot.) arrowroot (of the genus Maranta).

taça s. f. cup: 1. pot, pewter, goblet, vessel. 2. trophy. 3. glass, drinking vessel with a stem and foot (plate C 14).

tacaca s. f. (Braz.) importunate human body odour.

tacacá s. m. (N. Braz.) dish prepared of tapioca, tucupi (manioc-juice and pepper), garlic and shrimps.

tacacazeiro s. m. (Braz.) tropical tree of the genus Sterculia.

tacada s. f. 1. blow, stroke or hit with a stick or cue. 2. winning or gaining of a large sum or pool. 3. (fig.) severe shock. 4. touch (for money, gift, or loan).

de uma ~ all at once, at one go. **~ em falso** failure; miscue.

tacanhear v. to act niggardly or meanly; be narrow-minded.

tacanhice s. f. (also **tacanharia, tacanhez, tacanheza**) 1. narrow-mindedness, illiberality. 2. niggardliness. 3. smallness, narrowness. 4. stupidity.

tacanho adj. 1. short, not tall. 2. avaricious, niggard, stingy, shabby. 3. stupid, narrow-minded. ‖ **-amente** adv. niggardly, etc.

tacaniça s. f. 1. eaves, gutter. 2. (archit.) hip rafter.

tacão s. m. (pl. **-ões**) 1. heel of a boot or shoe. 2. stamping with the feet (theatre). ‖ adj. miserly, narrow-minded, stubborn.

tacape s. m. (Braz., hist.) club, cudgel for human sacrifices among the Indians.

tacar v. (Braz.) 1. to flourish, brandish. 2. to strike, hit, beat, buffet, slap.

tacaré s. m. (Braz., bot.) a sort of manioc, cassava.

taceira s. f. showcase, glass box of a goldsmith or jeweler.

tacelo s. m. (sculp.) any part of a statue or its model.

tacha (I) s. f. 1. tack: sharp, flat-headed nail, shoe stud (plates B 16, P 15). 2. (fig.) blemish, blot, disgrace, fault, defect.

~ de vidraceiro panel pin (plate P 15). **pôr ~ em** to find fault with.

tacha (II) s. f. (Braz.) large boiler used in sugar mills.

tachá s. m. (Braz., ornith.) crested screamer.

tachã s. f. (ornith.) a great, white-shouldered tanager.

tachada s. f. potful, full boiler.

tachador s. m. censor, faultfinder, reproacher. ‖ adj. faultfinding, reproachful.

tachão (I) s. m. (pl. **-ões**) 1. (large) blot, spot. 2. (fig.) blemish, fault, disgrace.

tachão (II) s. m. (pl. **-ões**) large, flat-headed nail, clout nail, tack, stud (plate P 15).

tachar v. 1. to tax, censure, criticize. 2. (fig.) to brand, stigmatize. 3. to spot, stain, sully. 4. (pop.) to get drunk(en).

tachear v. to tack, fasten or stud with tacks, stitch together.

tacheiro s. m. (N. Braz.) worker, helper in a sugar mill.

tachim s. m. (pl. **-ins**) leather case to keep a luxuriously bound book.

tachinho s. m. small tack.

tachismo s. m. (paint.) tachism.

tacho s. m. 1. bowl, pan, pot, boiler (broad, shallow vessel of metal or earthenware). 2. ancient Portuguese measure of 25 litres. 3. (Braz., pop.) inferior piano or watch. 4. (N. Braz.) red-haired, carroty or sandy person.

tachonar v. 1. to fasten with tacks. 2. to adorn with brass studs. 3. to spot, speckle. 4. to enamel, polish.

taci s. m. (N. Braz. also **tabaiacu**) long underwater reef.

taciba s. f. (Braz.) a variety of ant.

tacibura s. f. (N. Braz.) name of an Amazonian ant.

tácito adj. tacit: 1. silent, reserved, dumb. 2. implied, implicit, understood. ‖ **tacitamente** adv. tacitly.

taciturnidade s. f. taciturnity, reticence, reserve, misanthropy, dumbness.

taciturno adj. taciturn, reserved, dumb, moody, reticent, uncommunicative, close-mouthed. ‖ **-amente** adv. taciturnly, etc.

taco (I) s. m. 1. billiard cue, golf club, hockey stick, cricket or polo mallet. 2. handle. 3. wooden plug. 4. dowel. 5. parquet block. 6. (fig.) a squat man. 7. (S. Braz., fig.) clever, knowing or dexterous person. 8. audacious fellow, daredevil.

taco (II) s. m. (N. Braz.) 1. mouthful, a bit of anything. 2. (Port., prov.) slight repast in the afternoon.

tacógrafo s. m. tachograph.

tacomaré s. m. (Braz.) a variety of sugar cane.

tacometria s. f. tachometry.

tacômetro s. m. tachometer; speedometer: instrument to measure or indicate speed.

táctil, tactilidade, tacto, etc. = **tátil, tatilidade, tato,** etc.

taculté s. m. (Braz., zool., also **queixada**) wild boar, white-lipped peccary.

tacuru (I) s. m. (also **tacuri**) anthill (sometimes mounting up to 7 ft.).

tacuru (II) s. m. (Braz., also **tacurua, tacuruba** f.) trivet of stones to support cooking vessels.

taçuru s. m. (Braz., ent., also **bicho-de-pé**) chigoe.

tacuruzal s. m. (pl. **-ais**) (S. Braz.) area overspread with anthills.

tael s. m. (pl. **taéis**) tael: a Chinese silver monetary unit.

tafetá s. m. taffeta, glossy silk.

tafiá s. m. (also **cachaça** f.) tafia: a kind of rum distilled from sugar-cane.

tafofobia s. f. taphephobia, fear of being buried alive.

tafona s. f. (S. Braz., also **atafona**) hand mill, quern; water mill.

tafoneiro s. m. (S. Braz.) owner of a mill. ‖ adj. 1. working at a mill (said of an ox). 2. (fig.) only half-domesticated (horse).

taful s. m. (pl. **-uis**) 1. gambler, gamester, person given to gambling. 2. dandy, fop, coxcomb, person with affected manners. ‖ adj. m. + f. coxcombical, dandyish, foppish, affected, prim.

tafulão s. m. (pl. **-ões**) (Braz.) masher, Don Juan, seducer.

tafular v. to live dandyishly, play the dud.

tafularia s. f. 1. dandyism, foppishness. 2. group of dandies, gamblers or frivolous persons.

tafuleira s. f. (S. Braz.) attractive,, charming, seductive girl.

tafulhar v. (also **atafulhar**) 1. to cram, stuff, push, eat greedily, gorge. 2. to fill excessively.

tafulho s. m. 1. cork, plug, stopper. 2. cramming, stuffing, filling.

tafulice s. f. 1. dandyism, foppishness. 2. group of dandies.

tafulo s. m. (S. Braz., pop.) sweetheart, darling, suiter, beau, boy friend. ‖ adj. foppish, dandyish.

tafulona s. f. (S. Braz.) charming, attractive, seductive girl.

tagal adj. m. + f. (pl. **-ais**) Filipine, Philippine.

tagalo s. m. Filipino.

tagantaço s. m. (Braz., also **tagantada**) stroke, lash or cut with a whip.

tagantar v. to lash, whip, flog, switch, scourge.

tagante s. m. ancient whip, scourge, thong.

taganteador s. m. scourger, flogger. ‖ adj. whipping, flogging, scourging.

tagantear v. (also **tagantar**) to whip, lash, scourge, flog.

tagarela s. 1. m. + f. chatterer, chatterbox, clatterer, cackler, prattler, jabberer, rattler, rattlehead, blab-ber, babbler; gossip. 2. f. hubbub, uproar, brawl, clamour, tumult, noisy quarrel, riot. 3. f. (Braz.) speed regulator of the millstones. ‖ adj. m. + f. garrulous, gabbling, prattling, talkative, loquacious.

tagarelar v. 1. to chatter, clatter, prattle, jabber, babble, gabble, rattle, gossip. 2. to tattle, tell or reveal indiscreetly, disclose.

tagarelice s. f. 1. talkativeness, garrulity, loquacity, long tongue, jabber, gabbling, rattle. 2. blab, indiscretion, tattle. 3. gossip.

tagarote s. m. 1. (ornith.) hobby. 2. poor man who lives on alms or from charity; pauper, parasite.

tagaté s. m. (Braz.) caress, pat, expression of affection.

tagetes s. m. pl. (bot.) tagetes: French marigold.

tágico adj. (poet.) belonging to the Tagus (river in Portugal).

tágide s. f. (poet.) nymph of the Tagus (river in Portugal).

taguá s. m. (Braz., bot., also **tauá**) ivory palm.

taguicati s. m. (N. Braz., zool., also **queixada**) a white-lipped peccary.

taiá s. m. (Braz., bot., also **taioba, taiova** f.; **jarro, pé-de-bezerro** m.) taro; elephant's ear (arum family).

taiaçu s. m. 1. (Braz.) tiger bittern: a wading bird. 2. (Braz.) mammal of the genus Suidae, swine family; a peccary.

taiaçuíra s. m. (Braz., ornith.) ground cuckoo.

taiá-jararaca s. m. (pl. **taiás-jararaca**) (Braz.) plant of the arum (Araceae) family.

taieira s. f. (N. Braz.) mulattoes' festival on Epiphany.

taifa s. f. (naut., obs.) 1. number of marines grouped for combat on the forecastle or quarter-deck. 2. (Braz.) the stewards on board a ship; stewards collectively.

taifeiro s. m. (naut., obs.) 1. one of the unit of marines grouped for combat on the forecastle or quarter-deck. 2. steward, cabin boy.

taiga s. f. taiga: sparse type of forest in Northern Russia and Siberia.

tailleur s. m. (Fr.) tailor-made lady's suit (dress of two parts) (plate R 6).

taimado adj. 1. malicious. 2. catty, foxy. 3. spiteful, mean. ‖ **-amente** adv. maliciously.

taimbé s. m. (Braz., also **itaimbé**) pointed and steep hill or mountain; cliff, crag, precipice.

tainha s. f. (ichth.) mullet, esp. the Brazilian mullet.

tainheira s. f. (Braz.) 1. net for mullet fishing. 2. canoe supplied with a mullet net.

tainhota s. f. (Braz.) a fish of the family Exocoetidae (Cypsilurus heterurus).

taioba s. f. 1. (Braz., bot., also **taiá, taiova** f.; **jarro, pé-de-bezerro, talo, tarro** m.) taro, elephant's ear (arum family). 2. (Braz., Rio de Janeiro, fig.) second-class streetcar. 3. (N. Braz.) buttock, rump.

taiobal s. m. (pl. **-ais**) (Braz.) taro field.

taioca s. f. 1. (Braz., ent.) red-brown ant. 2. m. + f. (Braz.) person of Negro and Indian offspring.

taipa s. f. partition; wall of mud, lath-and-plaster wall; stucco.

casa de ~ loam hut, mud hut. **~ de pilão** partition made of pounded gravel and pebble-stones.

taipal s. m. (pl. **-ais**) (also **taipão**) 1. plaster wall, mud wall, wall of clay mortar. 2. wooden mold for concrete constructions. 3. shutters (of a shop). 4. screen. 5. lattice. 6. side walls of a truck or cart.

taipar v. 1. to make a mud wall. 2. to partition, enclose with mud walls; to clay or loam a wall. 3. to pug..

taipeira s. f. (Braz.) a sort of stingless bee.

taipeiro s. m. 1. person who makes mud walls. 2. (N. Braz.) plate full of a variety of food.

taita s. m. (S. Braz.) braggart, boaster, bully, ruffian, swagger. ‖ adj. swaggering, boastful, bragging.

taitiano s. m. Tahitian: 1. habitant of Tahiti. 2. language spoken in Tahiti. ‖ adj. Tahitian.

taititu s. m. 1. (Braz., zool.) collared peccary. 2. roller of a manioc mill.

taiuiá s. m. (Braz.) plant of the pumpkin and squash species.

tajá s. m. (N. Braz., bot.) caladium.

tajã s. m. Moorish saber with a short and large blade.

tajacica s. f. (N. Braz., also **amoré** m.) a certain freshwater fish.

tajaçu s. m. (Braz., ornith., also **taiaçu, caititu**) tiger bittern.

tajaçuíra s. f. (Braz., ornith., also **mãe-de-porco**) a ground cuckoo.

tajupá s. m. (Braz., also **tajupar, tijupá**) 1. Indian hut. 2. shack covered with straw. 3. (N. Braz.) tent cloth to cover a canoe, awning of a canoe.

tajurá s. m. (Braz., bot., also **tinhorão**) caladium.

tai s. m. + f. (pl. **tais**) 1. a certain person, one. 2. (Braz., sl.) important person, big shot. ‖ adj. such, like, resembling, similar, of that kind. ‖ adv. so, · thus, accordingly, consequently. ‖ pron. this, that.

~ **como** as. ~ **e** ~ **coisa** a certain thing. ~ **pai** ~ **filho** like father, like son. ~ **senhor** ~ **criado** like master, like man. ~ **qual eu havia dito** exactly as I had told you. **de** ~ **maneira** in such a way, of such a kind. **em** ~ **caso** in that case. **nunca ouvi** ~ **coisa** I never heard of such a thing. **fulano de** ~ John Doe. **um** ~ **João** a certain John. **a** ~ **ponto** to such a degree or extent. **que** ~**?** what do you think of it? **que** ~ **um cigarro?** (sl.) how about a cigarette? **que** ~ **se jantarmos agora?** suppose we had supper now? **é** ~ **e qual** it is exactly the same.

tala (I) s. f. 1. trenching, furrowing, tilling, ditching. 2. devastation, destruction, ravaging.

tala (II) s. f. 1. clamp, splice, splint. 2. (Braz.) whip, leather strap. 3. (mech.) fishplate (plate V 4). 4. lath. 5. (S. Braz.) branch of the queen palm; switch made of the leaf of a queen palm. 6. ~**s** (pl.) difficulties, troubles, dilemma.

ganhar na ~ (S. Braz.) to win with great effort (horse). **eu me vi em** ~**s** I was in a dilemma; I had difficulties.

talabartaria s. f. (S. Braz., also **talabarteria**) saddlery, workshop of a saddler, harnessry.

talabarte s. m. baldric: belt for a horn, sword or banner; shoulder belt.

talabarteiro s. m. (S. Braz.) saddler, harness maker, beltmaker.

talaço s. m. (S. Braz.) blow, stroke with a whip or switch, switching, flogging.

talado s. m. a jeweler's or goldsmith's boring tool. ‖ adj. devastated, destroyed, demolished.

talador s. m. 1. person who makes trenches, ditches; tiller. 2. devastator, destroyer, ravager, destructor. ‖ adj. 1. trenching, tilling. 2. devastating, destructing, ravaging.

talagada s. f. (Braz.) swig, deep draught of an alcoholic drink.

talagarça s. f. (also **telagarça**) canvas for embroidery or tapestry.

talambor s. m. secret lock.

talamento s. m. trenching, ditching, tilling.

talâmico adj. (bot.) thalamic: of or referring to the thalamus.

tálamo s. m. 1. thalamus: a) (anat.) subdivision of the diencephalon. b) (bot.) receptacle, torus. 2. nuptial bed; double bed. 3. (fig.) nuptials, wedding, marriage.

talante s. m. 1. will, choice, wish, desire. 2. diligence. **a seu belo** ~ according to his own sweet will.

talão (I) s. m. (pl. **-ões**) 1. heel (foot and shoe). 2. buttress of a horse's hoof (plate C 9). 3. (archit.) ogee: a sort of molding. 4. sprig of vine left over at pruning. 5. bead of a tire. 6. coupon stub, counterfoil, voucher of a check or receipt. ~ **de cheques** checkbook. ~ **de identidade** identity tag. ~ **de pedidos** order book. ~ **de justificação** (typogr.) justification bar or block.

talão (II) s. m. (pl. **-ões**) = **telão**.

talar (I) s. m. (myth.) talaria: winged sandals of Hermes or Mercury. ‖ adj. m. + f. reaching to the heels.

hábito ~ a priest's or friar's gown.

talar (II) v. 1. to trench, surround with or cut trenches. 2. to till, plough. 3. to devastate, destroy, ravage, lay waste.

talassa s. m. name of Portuguese monarchists or reactionists.

talassia s. f. seasickness.

talássico adj. thalassic: of or pertaining to the sea.

talassiófito s. m. thalassiophyte: marine algae.

talassocracia s. f. thalassocracy: mastery at sea, sea power.

talassocrata s. m. + f. thalassocrat: person interested in oceanography.

talassofobia s. f. thalassophobia: morbid fear or fright of the sea.

talassófobo s. m. one who is morbidly afraid of the sea.

talassografia s. f. thalassography, oceanography.

talassográfico adj. thalassographic, oceanographic.

talassômetro s. m. thalassometer: a tide gauge.

talaveira s. m. 1. (Braz., obs.) burlesque name of a palace servant. 2. (S. Braz.) nickname for a person who cannot ride on horseback.

talaveirada s. f. (S. Braz.) 1. a piece of bad horsemanship. 2. (depr.) a group of unskilled horsemen.

tálcico adj. talcous, talcose.

talcito s. m. (petrog.) talc chist.

talco s. m. 1. talc; talcum. 2. French chalk. 3. tinsel, showy thing of little value. ~ **em pó** talcum powder.

talcoso adj. talcose, talcous.

taleiga s. f. 1. small sack or bag, wallet, knapsack. 2. former measure for solid and liquid merchandise.

taleigada s. f. 1. unit of one **taleiga**. 2. a bagful.

taleigo s. m. 1. narrow long bag. 2. budget.

taleira s. f. brace, clamp, bracket.

talentaço s. m. (coll.) one of great talents, highly talented person.

talentão s. m. (pl. **-ões**) 1. highly talented person. 2. talent, ability, accomplishment, endowment. 3. talent: ancient weight and money.

talento s. m. 1. (fig.) talent, ability, aptitude, accomplishment, endowment, dowry, faculty, ingeniousness, ingenuity. 2. (pop.): a) muscularity, vigour, force. b) boldness, daring, courage. ~ **artístico** artistry. **ter** ~ **para a música** to have a turn for music. **ele tem** ~ **inato para o jornalismo** he has an outspoken sense for journalism. **uma menina de** ~ a girl of many accomplishments.

talentoso adj. talented, able, gifted, smart, clever, of parts. **um homem** ~ a man of talent(s).

táler s. m. (pl. **táleres**) thaler: a former German silver monetary unit.

talha (I) s. f. 1. cut, cutting, score, tally. 2. engraving with a chisel or graver; carved work, carving. 3. (obs.) a species of tribute, levy, tax. 4. (tech.)

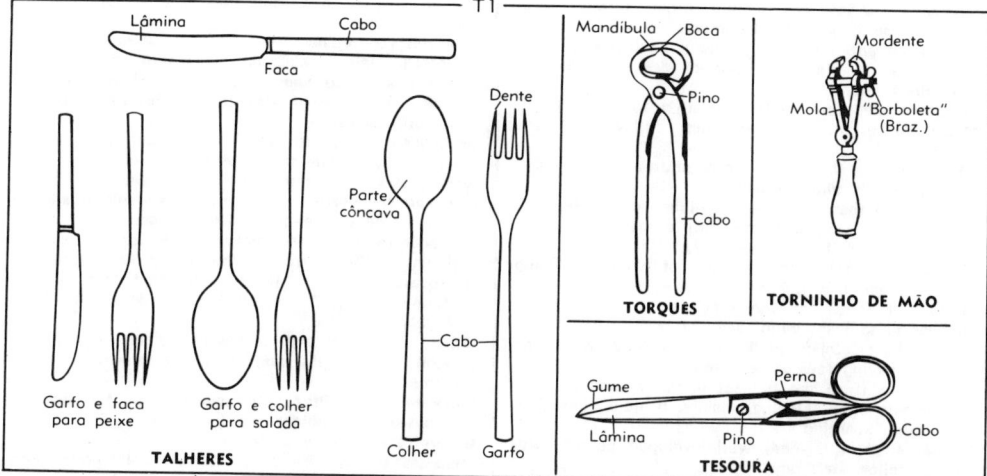

T 1

TALHERES

Lâmina   Cabo
Faca

Dente

Parte côncava

Cabo

Cabo

Garfo e faca para peixe

Garfo e colher para salada

Colher   Garfo

Mandíbula   Boca
Pino

Cabo

TORQUÊS

Mordente

Mola   "Borboleta" (Braz.)

TORNINHO DE MÃO

Gume   Perna
Cabo
Lâmina   Pino

TESOURA

tackle, block and tackle, pulley block, pulley, whip and derry (plates A 7, 8, G 5). 5. (med., also **cistomia**) lithotomy: incision into the bladder to remove stones. 6. deal at cards. 7. (naut.) burton, jiggers.

talha (II) s. f. 1. large earthen vessel. 2. sheet metal vessel for oil. 3. (fig.) portions of salt of a salt bed.

talhada s. f. 1. slice, cutting, chop, piece. 2. (coll.) reprimand, reproof, scolding. 3. sweets prepared of raw brown sugar and manioc meal.

talhadão s. m. (pl. -ões) 1. (Braz.) cleft on the earth's surface. 2. entrance to a grot(to), cave. 3. river-bed enclosed by steep walls.

talhadeira s. f. 1. chisel, firmer chisel, driver, driving chisel, splitter (plates F 1, 2, M 6). 2. cleaver, chopping knife.

talhadia s. f. 1. lopping (of trees). 2. a stand of chopped trees.

talhadiço adj. (Braz.) said of trees or underbrush which can be chopped or cut down.

talhado s. m. (Braz.) 1. precipice, cliff, crag, rocky overhang, slope. 2. a stretch of river between high rocky walls. ‖ adj. 1. cut. 2. carved. 3. engraved. 4. sliced. 5. chopped. 6. fashioned or fit for, proper (also fig.). 7. sour (milk).

talhador s. m. 1. cutter, chopper. 2. cleaver: a) butcher. b) knife. 3. chopping board or block. 4. plate to carve meat on. ‖ adj. 1. cutting, slicing, chopping, carving. 2. engraving.

talhadura s. f. (also **talhamento** m.) 1. cutting, cleaving, chopping, craving. 2. engraving, chiseling.

talha-frio s. m. (pl. **talha-frios**) engraving tool, chisel for woodwork, cold chisel.

talha-mar s. m. (pl. **talha-mares**) 1. (naut.) cutwater, stem, forefoot. 2. (archit.) starling. 3. (Braz., ornith.) black skimmer.

talhante adj. m. + f. cutting, cleaving, sharp.

talhão (I) s. m. (pl. -ões) 1. large planting field, stripe of land. 2. tray, board. 3. (N. Braz.) piece of a carved whale.

talhão (II) s. m. (pl. -ões) (Port. prov.) large earthen waterpot.

talhar v. 1. to cut, cut off, cut out, slice, slash. 2. to crave, hew, crimp, hack, chap, cleave. 3. to hackle, shape, whittle. 4. to engrave. 5. to chase. 6. to sculpture, chisel. 7. to work, fashion. 8. to

share, apportion, distribute. 9. to adjust, prepare, adapt. 10. to plow (sea). 11. to deal (cards). 12. **~-se:** a) to split, crack, cleave. b) to curdle, coagulate, become spoiled.

~ um molde to cut out a pattern. **~ pedras** to hew stones.

talharia s. f. large number of **talhas** or **talhos**.

talharim s. m. (pl. -ins) vermicelli, flat, narrow noodle.

talharola s. f. a cutting tool used in velvet weaving.

talhe s. m. cut, fashion, style, figure, form, shape, build, make; stature, size.

talher s. m. 1. set of knife, fork and spoon (plate T 1). 2. **~es** pl. cutlery, table ware. 3. cover (at table). 4. (fig.) each of the places at table. 5. cruet-stand.

jantar para 20 ~es supper for 20 guests. **pôr mais um ~** to lay one more cover (place at table).

talhinha s. f. (naut.) small block-and-pulley.

talho s. m. (also **talhamento**) 1. cut, cutting, chopping (meat in a butchery). 2. butchery, a butcher's shop. 3. a butcher's chopping block. 4. lapping, pruning (trees). 5. stroke with a sword or knife. 6. narrow long field. 7. rectangular pools or compartments of a salt marsh (salina). 8. shape, form. **bom ~ de letra** good handwriting. **vir a ~ de foice** to come at the right time or to the purpose.

tália s. f. plant of tropical America (arrowroot family).

talião s. m. talion, retaliation.

lei de ~ law of retaliation.

tálico adj. thallic, thallous.

talictro s. m. (bot., also **talitro**) meadow rue, fen rue, maidenhair rue.

talim s. m. (pl. -ins) baldric: sword-belt, horn-belt, shoulder-belt.

talinga s. f. (naut.) 1. cable, rope, anchor rope. 2. clinch.

talingadura s. f. (naut.) clinch, clinching.

talingar v. (naut.) to clinch, bend (cable).

tálio s. m. (chem.) thallium (metallic element used in alloys and glassmaking).

talionar v. to retaliate; apply the law of retaliation.

talionato s. m. talion, law of retaliation.

talipe s. m. taliped, clubfoot.

talípede s. m. + f. taliped: person who has one foot or both feet deformed.

talisca s. f. 1. cleft, crack, chink, crevice (of a rock). 2. (carp.) chip, splinter, sliver; spline.

talismã s. m. talisman, amulet, fetish, fetich, charm magic figure, periapt, phylactery.

talismânico adj. talismanic, magic, phylacteric.

talmude s. m. Talmud: book of Jewish civil and religious law.

talmúdico adj. Talmudic(al): relating to the Talmud.

talmudista s. m. + f. Talmudist: follower of the Talmud.

talo s. m. 1. (bot.): a) stalk, petiole, bind, stem. b) thallus. 2. shaft, shank.

~ flexível (bot.) bine. ~ de milho corn stalk.

talocha s. f. (also esparavel m.) a mason's mortar-board, trowel, float (plate A 7).

talófito s. m. tallophyte, a class of plants including fungi, algae and lichens.

talona s. f. (bot.) Java devil pepper.

talonear v. to lash, whip, scourge.

taloso adj. 1. stalky, stalklike. 2. stalked, with long stalks; having few or no leaves.

taluda s. f. (fig.) the highest prize of lottery.

taludamento s. m. sloping, making a slope, beveling, inclining, scarping.

taludão s. m. (pl. -ões). well-developed person, vigorous fellow, tall boy.

taludar v. to slope, bevel, render inclined, scarp, give a slant to.

talude s. m. 1. talus, inclination, acclivity, slope, slant, ramp, ascent, shelving. 2. agger.

taludo adj. 1. stalky, grown-up, caulescent. 2. well-developed, vigorous, lanky, tall, stout, corpulent, strong.

talvegue s. m. sinuous line of a valley, line of the lowest part of a valley.

talvez adv. perhaps, maybe, perchance, peradventure, by chance, possibly, eventually; (obs.) mayhap.

tamacarica s. f. (naut.) tent roof on deck, deck-awning.

tamanca s. f. 1. wooden shoe, low wooden sabot, clog, patten. 2. (Braz.) brake shoe (of a cart).

pôr-se nas suas ~s to be obstinate, stubborn, to oppose. trepar-se nas ~s (Braz., coll.) to get angry.

tamancada s. f. a blow or kick with a wooden shoe.

tamancão s. m. (pl. -ões) (Braz., bot.) cork tree.

tamancar v. (Braz., also atamancar) to botch, patch, make hastily or badly.

tamancaria s. f. workshop where wooden shoes are made or shop where they are sold.

tamanco s. m. 1. sabot, shoe with a wooden sole, patten, clog (plate C 14). 2. (N. Braz.) footboard or foothold on a raft. 3. (Braz.) sort of (wooden) axle bearing of an oxcart. 4. brake shoe (of a cart).

tamancudo adj. (Braz.) common, vulgar, coarse.

tamanduá (I) s. m. (zool., also avaro, papa-formiga) tamandua, tamanoir: an anteater, ant bear.

tamanduá (II) s. m. (Braz.) 1. difficult moral problem. 2. big lie.

tamanduá-açu s. m. (pl. tamanduás-açus) (Braz., zool., also tamanduá-bandeira pl. tamanduás-bandeira; tamanduá-cavalo pl. tamanduás-cavalo) great anteater, ant bear.

tamanduaí s. m. (Braz., zool., also tamanduá-mirim, colete, jaleco, meleta, mixila) little two-toed ant bear.

tamanhão s. m. (pl. -ões) (f. tamanhona) tall and strong person. || adj. big, tall, strong, stout, large.

tamanhinho adj. very small, little, tiny, minute.

ficar ~ de alguma coisa to become afraid of something.

tamanho s. m. 1. size, bulk, proportion, scale, volume, extent, dimension, gauge. 2. tallness, amplitude, bigness, ampleness, voluminousness. || adj. so

great, large, big; so remarkable, distinguished, eminent.

~ desproporcionado oversize. ~ natural life-size; (paint.) plain scale. de ~ médio middle-sized. uma pessoa do seu ~ a person of your inches. qual é o ~? what size is it? ultrapassar em ~ to outmeasure.

tamanquear v. 1. to walk in wooden shoes; wear sabots. 2. to clatter or rattle with clogs.

tamanqueira s. f. (Braz., bot.) cork tree.

tamanqueira-de-leite s. f. (pl. tamanqueiras-de-leite) (Braz.) tree of the genus Apocynaceae.

tamanqueiro s. m. 1. maker or seller of wooden shoes. 2. (Braz.) tree of the family Verbenaceae.

tamaquaré s. m. 1. (Braz.) hardwood tree of the .genus Caraipa. 2. medicinal oil made of the resin of this tree.

tâmara s. f. date: fruit of the date palm.

tamaral s. m. (pl. -ais) stand or growth of date palms.

tamarana s. f. (Braz., also cuidaru m.) flat wooden club used by Indians.

tamareira s. f. date palm.

tamarga, tamargueira s. f. (bot.) 1. tamarisk, salt cedar. 2. tamarisk gall.

tamargal s. m. (pl. -ais) (also tramagal) tamarisk field or growth.

tamari s. m. (Braz.) tamarin, marmorset: a little monkey of tropical America.

tamariácea s. f. one of the tamarisk plants.

tamaricáceo adj. (bot.) belonging to the tamarisk family.

tamarindal s. m. (pl. -ais) growth or stand of tamarinds.

tamarindo s. m. (bot., also tamarindeiro m., tamarineira f.; tamarineiro, tamarinheiro, jubaí m.) tamarind: 1. the tree. 2. its fruit.

tamariz s. m. (bot., also tamargueira f.) African tamarisk.

tamaru s. m. (Braz., zool.) squilla, mantis shrimp.

tamarutaca s. f. (Braz., zool., also tambarutaca, tamburutaca, lagosta-gafanhoto, mãe-de-camarão) large squilla, mantis shrimp (or prawn).

tamati s. m. (Braz., zool.) heart shell, cockle.

tamatiá s. m. (Braz., ornith.) boatbill (genus Cancroma).

tamatião s. m. (Braz.) a puffbird.

tamba s. f. (Braz.) fermented Indian drink prepared of boiled tapioca and diluted with water.

tambá s. m. (Braz., zool.) bivalvular shell or conch.

tambaca s. f. (also tambaque) tombac: alloy of gold and silver, copper and zinc, etc.

tambaíba s. f. (Braz.) wild tree with yellow and black striped wood, used in joinery.

tambaque (I) s. m. (also tambaca) tombac.

tambaque (II) s. m. (N. Braz.) inferior metal, counterfeit gold.

tambarutaca s. f. (Braz., zool., also tamarutaca) large squilla, mantis crab, shrimp.

tambataruga s. f. (also espinho-de-vintém m.) prickly tree of the ash family.

tambatajá s. m. (Braz., bot.) caladium.

tambeira s. f. (S. Braz., zool.) tame heifer. || adj. f. 1. docile, tame. 2. domesticated. 3. gentle.

tambeirada s. f. (S. Braz.) group of tame and young cattle.

tambeiro s. m. (Braz.) 1. stable. 2. tame cattle. 3. colt of a leading mare.

também adv. also, so, beside, besides, too, item, likewise, then, thereto, therewith, therewithal, either, yet, further, moreover.

~ há os seguintes then there are the following. ~ não neither. senão ~ but also. eles ~ vêm they are coming too. **está com fome? eu** ~ are you hungry? So am I. **se ele não vai, ela** ~ **não irá** if he does not go she will not go either.

tambetá s. m. (Braz.) Indian ceramic vase.

tâmbi s. m. 1. Angolese funeral ceremony. 2. (ichth.) a species of the minnows.

tambica s. f. leaden sinker of a fishing net.

tambo (I) s. m. 1. bridal bed, nuptial bed. 2. (fig.) nuptials, wedding, marriage.

tambo (II) s. m. (Braz.) 1. country house. 2. shed, cattle barn. 3. (S.) dairy farm.

tambó s. m. (Braz., ichth.) round pompano.

tamboeira s. f. (N. Braz., also **tamboera**) 1. stunted manioc root. 2. underdeveloped sugar cane. 3. sudden thunder-shower.

tambona s. f. (S. Braz.) a certain coffeepot.

tambor s. m. 1. drum: a) (mus.) tambour, tom-tom (Hindu's drum); drummer. b) a metal barrel for a liquid, as oil. c) (anat.) eardrum, the tympanum of the ear. d) (archit.) tambour, cylindrical stone used in the construction of columns. 2. (mech.) cylinder (as of a lock). 2. spool, reel. ~ **basco** tambourine. ~ **de cabo** cable drum. ~ **de coluna** (archit.) tambour. ~ **de freio** brake drum (plate M 12). ~ **de relógio** barrel of a watch; ratch. ~ **de roda de propulsão** paddle box. ~ **rotativo** tumbling barrel. ~ **de provas** (typogr.) proof press.

tamborete s. m. 1. tabouret, footstool, low stool. 2. (naut.) reinforcement planks.

tamboril (I) s. m. (pl. -is) (also **tamborim**) tambourine, tabor.

tamboril (II) s. m. (pl. -is) (Braz., also **peixe-sapo**) frog-fish, angler, a kind of ray.

tamborilada s. f. drum beat.

tamborilar v. 1. to drum, tom-tom. 2. to pelt, patter, hurtle. 3. (fig.) to drum up. 4. to annoy with discords; repeat over and over.

tamborileiro s. m. 1. tambourine player. 2. drummer. || adj. 1. playing the tambourine. 2. drumming.

tamborilete s. m. small tambour or drum; street drum.

tamborim s. m. (pl. -ins) (also **tamboril**) tambourine, tambour, timbrel (plate B 4).

tambor-mor s. m. (pl. **tambores-mores**) drum major.

tambu s. m. (Braz.) 1. samba drum. 2. a wood beetle.

tamburi s. m. (Braz.) an earpod tree.

tamburipará s. m. (Braz., also **tamburupará, tangurupará**) a nun bird.

tamburutaca s. f. (zool., also **tamarutaca**) squilla, mantis shrimp (or prawn). hrimp.

tamearama s. f. (Braz.) climbing plant of the species Euphorbia.

tamiça s. f. thin cord of esparto.

tamiceiro s. m. maker or seller of esparto cords. || adj. referring to an esparto cordmaker or seller.

tâmil s. m. (also **tâmul**) tamil: Dravidian language spoken in Sri Lanka and South India.

tamina s. f. (Braz., his.) 1. the daily food ration of a slave. 2. bowl or vessel for this daily ration. 3. water allowance per capita from public fountains during the dry season. **por** ~ little by little, gradually.

tamis s. m. tamis: 1. silk sieve, strainer of cloth. 2. English woollen cloth.

tamisação s. f. (pl. -ões) sieving, straining, sifting.

tamisar v. 1. to sieve, strain, sift; bolt. 2. to purify, cleanse.

tamo s. m. black bryony (medicinal plant).

tamoeiro s. m. 1. pole or shaft of an oxcart. 2. leatherstrap to fasten the yoke to the shaft of the oxcart.

tamoio s. m. (Braz.) one of the Tamoio Indians. || adj. of or belonging to the Tamoio tribe.

tampa s. f. 1. cover(ing), lid (plates C 4, 20, E 10, L 3, M 1, P 10, 19, R 8). 2. cork, stopple, stopper (of a bottle). 3. (Braz., sl.) cap, hat. 4. (tech.) cap (plates C 11, L 1, M 13). 5. top (table). ~ **de panela** potlid. ~ **traseira de carroça** tailboard. ~ **com rosca** screw cap. **sem** ~ lidless.

tampado adj. 1. lidded, covered. 2. stopped, closed. 3. dense, thick. **comer** ~ (N. Braz., pop.) to be in difficulties, be in hot water, be in a fix.

tampão s. m. (pl. -ões) 1. large cover or lid. 2. tampion, bung, spile. 3. dowel, plug. 4. (surg.) compress, tampon. 5. manhole cover.

tampar v. 1. to cover with or as with a lid, shut, top. 2. to cork, stopple, stopper (a bottle). 3. to bung. 4. to plug, spile. 5. (tech.) to cap.

tampinha s. f. 1. (Braz.) popular game played by children with bottle caps. 2. (coll.) m. + f. dumpy person, hop-o'-my-thumb.

tampo (I) s. m. 1. barrel top. 2. (mus.) resounding boards (of a stringed instrument). 3. seat cover of a toilet.

tampo (II) s. m. hide of a perished ox or cow. ~ **harmônico** belly (of a violin) (plate V 5).

tamponamento s. m. 1. plugging, spiling, doweling. 2. (surg.) tamponment.

tamponar v. to plug, bung, shut up, stopper.

tampouco adv. either, neither. **ele não leu o livro, nem eu** ~ he has not read the book, nor have I either.

tanaceto s. m. (also **tanásia**) tansy: perennial herb with aromatic leaves.

tanado adj. tan-coloured, tanned, chestnut-coloured.

tanagrídeo s. m. American bird of the genus Tanagra.

tanajuba s. f. (Braz., also **guarajuba**) 1. tree of the genus Peltogyne. 2. (ornith.) one of the parakeets.

tanajura s. f. (Braz., ent.) a female sauba ant.

tanásia s. f. (bot., also **tanaceto**) tansy.

tanato s. m. (chem.) tannate.

tanatofobia s. f. thanatophobia: morbid fear of death.

tanatologia s. f. thanatology: scientific study of death.

tanchagem s. f. (pl. -ens) (bot.) waybread, plaintain, roadweed.

tanchagem-aquática s. f. (pl. **tanchagens-aquáticas**) water plaintain.

tanchão s. m. (pl. -ões) (bot., also **chantão**) 1. vine cutting or stake, vine prop. 2. prop of a vine, palisade. 3. slip, young plant, layer.

tanchar v. 1. to plant sticks or cuttings, set twigs or layers. 2. to drive in poles or stakes.

tanchim s. m. (pl. -ins) (Braz.) pocket knife, penknife.

tandem s. m. (pl. -ens) tandem: bicycle with seats for two persons (plate B 11). **andar de** ~ to drive tandem.

tanduju s. m. (Braz.) fish of the stargazer family.

tanga (I) s. f. 1. breechcloth, loincloth. 2. (N. Braz.) fringes of a hammock. **ficar de** ~ (Braz., pop.) to have nothing whatsoever left over, be completely run down, be absolutely broke. **ficar de** ~, **pote e esteira** to live in extreme poverty.

tanga (II) s. f. ancient Portuguese coin in the East Indies.

tangapema s. m. (Braz.) Indian club.

tangar (I) v. to cover with a loincloth.

tangar (II) v. to dance the tango.

tangará s. m. (Braz., also **atangará**) tanager; bird of the family Pipridae.

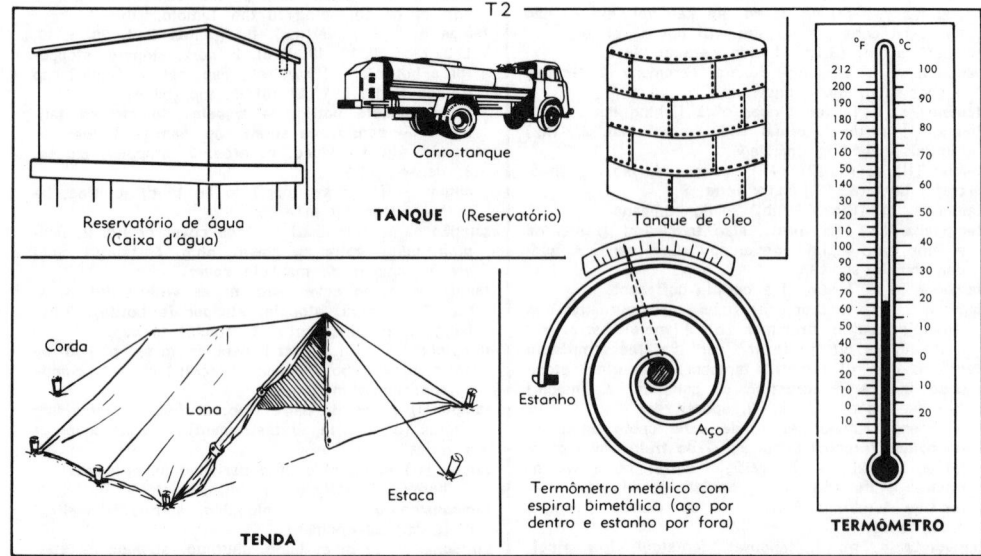

T 2

Reservatório de água
(Caixa d'água)

TANQUE (Reservatório)

Carro-tanque

Tanque de óleo

Corda

Lona

Estaca

TENDA

Estanho

Aço

Termômetro metálico com
espiral bimetálica (aço por
dentro e estanho por fora)

TERMÔMETRO

°F   °C

---

tangedor s. m. 1. player of (a stringed) instrument. 2. muleteer. ‖ adj. (mus.) playing.

tangedouras, tangedoiras s. f. pl. (also **tangedouros, tangedoiros** m.) supports or feet of a blacksmith's bellows.

tange-fole s. m. (pl. **tange-foles**) 1. person in charge of the bellows in a blacksmith's shop, bellows blower. 2. person who stimulates another to speak more than he should.

tangência s. f. tangency: 1. state of being tangent. 2. (geom.) point of contact of two lines or two surfaces.

tangencial adj. m. + f. (pl. **-ais**) tangential.

tangenciar v. to touch, be tangent to, contact, graze.

tangente s. f. 1. tangent: (geom.) straight line which touches a curve or curved surface without crossing it (plate A 9). 2. (fig.) last resort, escape, loophole. 3. (Braz.) straight stretch (of a railway or road) after a curve. ‖ adj. m. + f. tangent, touching.

~ **trigonométrica** ratio of the sine to the cosine of an arc. **escapar pela tangente** to have a narrow escape, (school) to scrape through.

tanger v. 1. to play a musical instrument, pluck a stringed instrument. 2. to sound, ring, toll (bells). 3. to drive (cattle). 4. to blow a blacksmith's bellows. 5. (fig.) to relate to, concern, refer to. 6. to touch slightly.

~ **a mesma corda** to harp, repeat always the same thing. ~ **de casa** to drive out from home.

tangerina s. f. (bot., also **bergamota, vergamota, laranja-cravo, mexerica, mexeriqueira, mandarina, mimosa, laranja-mimosa**) tangerine, mandarin, mandarin orange.

tangerineira s. f. mandarin orange tree, tangerine tree.

tangerino s. m. (also **tingitano**) Tangerine: native or inhabitant of Tangier. ‖ adj. 1. Tangerine: of or relating to Tangier. 2. (N. Braz.) cattle drover on foot or horseback.

tange-tange s. m. (pl. **tanges-tanges**) (Braz., bot.) a species of lupine.

tange-viola s. m. (pl. **tange-violas**) (Braz., ent., also **toca-viola**) cerambycid beetle.

tangibilidade s. f. tangibleness, tangibility.

tangível adj. m. + f. (pl. **-íveis**) 1. tangible. 2. palpable, tactile. 3. impressionable, perceptible, sensible. 4. corporeal. ‖ **tangivelmente** adv. tangibly.

tanglomanglo s. m. (Braz., also **tangolomango**) 1. evil spell or deed, sorcery, witchcraft. 2. persistent bad luck. 3. sickness caused by sorcery.

tango s. m. tango (South American dance for couples).

tanguista s. m. + f. tango dancer.

tangurupará s. m. (Braz., also **tamburupará**) nun bird.

taniça s. f. (N. Braz.) 1. pigtail tobacco, twisted tobacco. 2. one of the grating laths around tobacco rolls.

tânico adj. (chem.) tannic, containing tan.

ácido ~ tannic acid.

tanino s. m. (chem.) tannin.

taninoso adj. tanniferous, containing tannin.

tanjão s. m. (pl. **-ões**) (f. **tanjona**) loafer, sluggard, lazybones, indolent person.

tanoa s. f. coopery, cooperage: 1. a cooper's work, barrelmaking. 2. a cooper's workshop.

tanoar v. to cooper, make barrels, casks.

tanoaria s. f. (also **tonelaria**) cooperage: 1. workshop of a cooper. 2. a cooper's work.

tanoeiro s. m. 1. cooper, hooper, barrelmaker, tubber. 2. (Braz., zool.) one of the tree toads.

tanque (I) s. m. 1. tank, reservoir, cistern (plate T 2). 2. lochan, flash, basin, pool, pond. 3. washtub, vat. 4. (N. Braz.) dam, weir.

~ **de água** water tank, cistern, reservoir. ~ **de gasolina** fuel tank (plates M 12, V 3). ~ **de óleo** oil tank (plates M 12, T 2). ~ **de peixes** fish pond. **encher o** ~ to fill up the tank. **carro** ~ tank car. **navio** ~ tank steamer. ~ **misturador** (papermaking) mixer. **encher o** ~ (U. S. A., mot.) to gas up.

tanque (II) s. m. (mil.) tank.

tanso s. m. simpleton, fool, sluggard. ‖ adj. foolish, dumb, goofy, sluggish. ‖ **-amente** adv. dumbly.

tantã (I) s. m. tom-tom: a native drum of India or Africa; gong.

tantã (II) adj. m. + f. (Braz.) weak-minded, daft, imbecile, silly, senile, touched.

ele é meio ~ he is a little touched.

tantálico adj. 1. (chem.) tantalic, relating to or derived from tantalum. 2. (myth.) tantalizing (referring to Tantalus, son of Zeus).

tantalita s. f. (min.) tantalite.

tantalização s. f. (pl. **-ões**) tantalization.

tantalizar v. to tantalize, cause tortures like those of Tantalus; to tease arousing unrealizable desires.

tântalo (I) s. m. (chem.) tantalum: metal used for electric lamp filaments.

Tântalo (II) s. m. (myth.) Tantalus: son of Zeus.

o suplício de ~ the tortures of Tantalus.

tantanguê s. m. (Braz.) children's hide-and-seek game.

tantas-folhas s. f. pl. (Braz.) 1. tripe. 2. (zool.) omasum, manyplies, the third stomach of a ruminant.

tantinho s. m. a little bit.

tanto s. m. an indeterminable quantity; amount, sum, extent, range. ‖ adj. as much, so much; as many, so many; so large, so great. ‖ adv. 1. to such a degree, number or extent. 2. in such a way, thus. ~ **como** as much as. ~ **elas como nós estávamos no teatro** both they and we were in the theatre. ~ **faz que** it is not important whether. ~ **faz como** ~ **fez** it is much the same. ~ **mais** the more so. ~ **melhor** all the better, so much the better. ~ **mais que** all the more since. ~ **pior** so much the worse. ~ **quanto** in so far as, all of, in as much as. ~ **mais quanto** particularly as. ~ **quanto possível** as much as possible. **-a sorte** such good luck. **-as e -as vezes** often and often, oft and oft. **algum** ~ rather. **às -as** finally, suddenly. **cento e ~s** hundred and odd. **gostaria** ~ **de andar a pé como de bonde** I would as soon walk as go by tram. **está um** ~ **frio** it is rather cold. **não** ~ **assim** not exactly that. **não é para** ~ it is not so bad. **não grite** ~ do not shout like that. **para mim** ~ **faz** it is all one to me. **para** ~ therefore. **ela tem exatamente** ~ **quanto a sua irmã** she has every bit as much as her sister. **ele sofreu** ~ **as dores** he suffered such pain. **um** ~ something. **uns ~s** a few. **valem** ~ **quanto ouro** they are worth their weight in gold.

tão adv. so, such, that, as, so much. ~ **bem** as well. ~ **certo como estou vivo** as sure as I live. **~... como... as... as.** ~ **facilmente** that easily. ~ **grande é meu desejo** such is my wish. ~ **longe** that far. ~ **logo ele chegou, começamos a jantar** no sooner did he come than we began the supper. ~ **pouco** so little. ~ **velho** that old, so old. **não** ~ **bonito** not so pretty. **esta lâmpada é** ~ **boa como aquela** this lamp is as good as that. ~ **logo** as soon as. ~ **prudente como valente** as prudent as courageous.

taoca s. f. 1. (Braz., ornith.) an antbird (Formicarius analis). 2. (N. Braz., ent.) army ant.

taoísmo s. m. Taoism: Chinese religion based on Laotze's dogma.

taoísta s. m. + f. Taoist.

taoístico adj. Taoistic.

tão-só, tão-somente adv. only, merely, simply.

tapa (I) s. f. 1. side wall of a hoof. 2. tampion of a gun. 3. (Braz., also m.): a) slap, rap, flap, cuff. b) clincher, statement or argument that settles a problem; answer that imposes silence. 4. (Braz.) blindfold for an unruly mule or horse to facilitate its harnessing.

tapa (II) s. f. (Braz., also **linguado-lixa**) a tonguefish.

tapa-boca s. m. (pl. **tapa-bocas**) 1. slap on the mouth to impose silence. 2. woollen shawl or muffler.

tapacu s. m. (N. Braz., ornith.) a species of the parakeets.

tapada s. f. 1. fenced terrain, enclosure. 2. hunting ground, preserve, deer park.

tapado s. m. (S. Braz.) winter coat for ladies. ‖ adj. 1. hidden, covered. 2. plugged, tamponed, corked.

3. closed, stopped. 4. (fig.) stupid, dull, slow-witted. 5. drawn out, protractive.

ele é muito ~ he is thick in the head. **com os olhos ~s** blindfold.

tapador s. m. 1. cover(ing), lid. 2. cork, stopple, stopper. 3. tampion, plug.

tapadouro s. m. axle end of a coach.

tapadura s. f. (also **tapamento, tapume** m.) 1. hedge, fence, hedgerow, enclosure or the like. 2. act of covering, stopping, plugging, tamponing.

tapagem s. f. (pl. **-ens**) 1. wooden trap to catch fish in a river. 2. simple earthen dam or barrier to catch fish. 3. fish weir. 4. screen, fence, enclosure. 5. excrement.

tapalúna s. f. (Braz., also **tapalúno** m.) an Amazonian hardwood tree.

tapamento s. m. 1. act or fact of covering, stopping, plugging, tamponing. 2. hedge, hedgerow, fence, enclosure, screen.

tapa-misérias s. m., sg. + pl. overcoat to cover shabby clothes.

tapanhaúna s. m. + f. (hist.) African Negro in Brazil.

tapa-nuca s. f. (pl. **tapa-nucas**) sunshade attached to a headgear for protection of the nape.

tapa-olhos s. m., sg. + pl. (also **tapa-olho**) slap on the eyes, hit in the eyes.

tapar v. 1. to close, plug, fill up, stuff up, tamp. 2. to stop, dam. 3. to shut up, block, choke, hinder, obstruct. 4. to cover. 5. to disguise, hide. 6. to hedge, fence in, enclose, shut off. 7. to blindfold. 8. ~**-se**: a) to hold one's mouth. b) to silence for fear.

~ **a boca a alguém** to have a person shut up, to silence s. o. ~ **um buraco** 1. to stop up, obstruct a hole. 2. (fig.) to pay a debt. ~ **os olhos** to blindfold; dazzle. ~ **os ouvidos** to stop one's ears.

tapa-sol s. m. (pl. **tapa-sóis**) Venetian blind.

tapeação s. f. (pl. **-ões**) (Braz.) swindle, cheat, trickery, humbug, hoax, fake, bogus, counterfeit, sham.

tapeador s. m. swindler, cheat, humbugger, faker, duper, tricker, counterfeiter. ‖ adj. cheating, deceitful, tricking, faking, duping.

tapear (I) v. 1. to slap, strike, bob, rap, tap. 2. (S. Braz.) to ride a horse guiding it by slaps with the open hand.

tapear (II) v. to deceive, fake, trick, humbug, fool, dupe; disguise, feign, dissemble.

tapeçar v. to carpet, cover with carpets.

tapeçaria s. f. 1. drapery, carpets, tapestry, hangings, curtains, cushions, arras. 2. upholstery, a draper's shop, trim shop. 3. grassplot, lawn, flowery meadow.

tapeceiro s. m. 1. maker or seller of carpets, curtains, hangings, tapestries. 2. upholsterer.

tapejara s. m. (Braz., also **baqueano, vaqueano**) 1. guide, scout. 2. person who knows thoroughly a certain region. 3. harbour pilot. 4. experienced person, expert. ‖ adj. (S. Braz.) courageous, bold.

tapera s. f. (Braz.) 1. abandoned countryseat, village or manor. 2. decayed, ruined house. 3. bad and ugly place. 4. fallow land. ‖ adj. m. + f. 1. lacking one eye or both eyes. 2. crazy, foolish, flighty.

taperebá s. m. (Braz., also **cajá**) tree of the cashew family.

taperebazinho s. m. (Braz., bot.) croton.

taperu s. m. (N. Braz., zool., also **tapicuru, tapuru**) bot(t): the larva of the botfly that infects horses.

tapetar v. to carpet, cover with carpets or tapestry.

tapete (ê) s. m. 1. carpet, stair-carpet, tapis, tapestry, floor-cloth, matting, rug, bedside rug (plate D 4). 2. (fig.) grassplot, lawn; ground full of flowers, carpet of flowers.

tapiaçu s. m. (Braz., also **tapiçuá**) one of the stingless bees.

tapiara (I) s. f. (Braz., ichth.) a species of mullet.

tapiara (II) s. m. (Braz.) scamp, rascal, rogue, knave.

tapiculm s. m. (pl. -ins) (Braz., ent.) conical nest of termites.

tapicuri s. m. (Braz.) manioc wine.

tapicuru s. m. (Braz., ornith.) white-faced glossy ibis.

tapieira s. f. (Braz.) one of the stingless bees.

tapigo s. m. 1. hedge, fence. 2. (mil.) barricade, paling.

tapinha s. f. 1. slap, flap, pat. 2. (Braz., pop.) diaper.

tapioca s. f. 1. tapioca: nutritive preparation of cassava starch. 2. confection of tapioca with layers of grated coconut. 3. paper-kite.

tapiocuí s. m. (S. Braz.) Indian designation for cassava starch.

tapir s. m. (Braz., zool., also **anta** f.) tapir.

tapirá-caiena s. m. (pl. **tapirás-caiena**) (Braz., bot., also **canafístula** f.) golden shower senna.

tapiragem s. f. (Braz., ethn.) an Indian process of artificially changing the colour of the feathers of live birds.

tapiranga s. f. bird of the tanager family.

tapiretê s. m. (Braz., zool.) small tapir.

tapiri s. m. (N. Braz.) round hut, shack, cabin, cottage, thatched cottage.

tapiriba s. f. (Braz.) yellow fruit like a plum that grows on the **cajazeiro**.

tapiti s. m. (Braz., zool.) tapeti: rodent of the family Leporidae.

tapiucaba s. m. (Braz.) a species of wasp.

tapiz s. m. (obs.) tapis, carpet, tapestry, floorcloth.

tapizar v. 1. to carpet, cover with carpets, adorn with curtains or hangings. 2. ~-se to become covered with flowers or grass (ground).

tapona s. f. blow, stroke, hit, box.

tápsia s. f. thapsia: medicinal plant.

tapucaja s. f. (Braz., ornith.) wood ibis.

tapuia s. m. + f., **tapuio** m. (Braz.) 1. former Tupian designation for any other tribe or any strangers considered hostile. 2. name of any savage Indian. 3. (N.) dark-complexioned Indian mestizo with straight black hair.

tapuirana s. f. (Braz.) special fabric to make hammocks from.

tapuísa s. m. (Braz.) hunting box; improvised hut or hovel built by hunters or explorers; shelter, refuge.

tapulhar v. 1. to stop up, plug. 2. to obstruct, jam.

tapulho s. m. plug, stopple, stopper, tampion, cork.

tapume s. m. 1. hedge, hedgerow, fence. 2. enclosure, boarding, fence made of planks (plate A 7). 3. paling, palisade. 4. screen, partition.

taquara s. f. (Braz.) 1. one of the varieties of small bamboos. 2. (ornith.) motmot.

taquara-do-reino s. f. (pl. **taquaras-do-reino**) (Braz., bot.) giant reed.

taquaral s. m. (pl. -ais) (Braz., bot.) 1. bamboo growth, bamboo thicket. 2. canebrake.

taquari s. m. (Braz.) 1. plant of the grass family. 2. pipestem. 3. bamboo pipe. || adj. small-caliber (shotgun).

taquariço adj. (Braz.) thin, lean, meagre; slender as a hop-pole.

taquari-do-mato s. m. (pl. **taquaris-do-mato**) (Braz.) a basket grass.

taquaruçu s. m. (bot., also **taboca-gigante** f.) a variety of very strong and high bamboos.

taquear v. 1. to overlay with wooden flooring blocks. 2. to parquet.

taqueira (I) s. f. rack for billiard cues.

taqueira (II) s. f. (Braz., bot.) a variety of flat and small pumpkins.

taqueiro s. m. parquet layer, parquetry maker.

taqueometria s. f. tachymetry.

taqueométrico adj. tachymetric.

taqueômetro s. m. tachymeter: surveying instrument, theodolite.

taquicardia s. f. (med.) tachycardia: palpitation of the heart.

taquifagia s. f. (med.) tachyphagia: the devouring of food.

taquigrafar v. (also **estenografar**) to write shorthand, stenograph.

taquigrafia s. f. (also **estenografia**) tachygraphy, stenography, shorthand.

taquigráfico adj. (also **estenográfico**) tachygraphical, tachygraphic, stenographic. || **taquigraficamente** adv. tachygraphically.

taquígrafo s. m. (also **estenógrafo**) tachygrapher, stenographer.

taquímetro s. m. 1. tachymeter. 2. speedometer.

taquipnéia s. f. (path.) tachypnoea, tachypnea: abnormally fast respiration.

taquiri s. m. (Braz., ornith.) designation for young herons.

tara (I) s. f. 1. tare: a) deduction of the weight of boxes, wrappings, containers, etc. from the gross weight of goods. b) the weight of those wrappings or containers. c) counterweight used in double weighing. 2. defect, fault, flaw; moral or physical (hereditary) deficiency or imperfection; degeneration.

tara (II) s. f. 1. former silver coin of India. 2. Siamese silver weight.

tara (III) s. f. (Braz.) bird of the ibis family.

tarado s. m. abnormal, degenerate person propensive to (sexual) crime. || adj. 1. tared. 2. moronic, debauched, perverted, degenerated, immoral.

taraíra s. f. = **traíra**.

taralhão s. m. (pl. -ões) 1. (ornith.) bee-bird, flycatcher. 2. meddler, busybody.

taralhar v. (Braz.) to peep, twitter, chirp, titter.

tarambola s. f. (ornith.) golden plover, stonechat.

tarambola-coleirada s. f. (pl. **tarambolas-coleiradas**) (ornith.) ring plover.

tarambote s. m. (pop.) 1. instrumental and vocal concert. 2. ancient popular song.

taramela s. f. 1. wooden latch to fasten a door or window. 2. mill clapper. 3. (fig.) gabbler, talker, chatterbox, babbler, gossiper. 4. twaddle, idle talk.

taramelagem s. f. (pl. -ens) (Braz.) talkativeness, loquacity, gossip, glibness.

taramelar, taramelear v. to gabble, prattle, babble, chat, jabber.

tarampabo s. m. a species of palm tree.

tarampantão s. m. (pl. -ões) beat of the drum.

tarangalho s. m. (ichth.) halfbeak.

tarantela s. f. tarantella: Neapolitan music and dance.

tarantismo s. m. (med.) tarantism: sickness caused by the tarantula's bite, arousing an uncontrollable desire to dance.

tarântula s. f. tarantula: large poisonous spider.

tarar v. to tare: determine or indicate the tare of.

tarara s. f. (agric.) winnowing machine, fan.

tarará s. m. (Braz.) onomatopoeic word suggesting the sound of a trumpet.

tararaca s. f. (S. Braz.) a sylvan mouse. || adj. m. + f. (S. Braz.) clumsy, awkward, foolish, crazy.

tararucu s. m. (Braz., also **fedegoso**) plant of the family Leguminosae.

tarasca s. f. 1. ugly and bad woman. 2. old sword. 3. monster. 4. (Braz., ornith.) tree creeper.

tarasco s. m. coarse, rude, severe person. ‖ adj. coarse, rude, raw, severe.

taratufo s. m. (Braz., bot.) tubercle.

taraxaco s. m. (bot.) dandelion, lion's tooth, taraxacum.

tarca s. f. (S. Braz.) tally.

tardada s. f. 1. act or fact of being late. 2. delay, retardation, slowness, lagging.

tardador s. m. delayer, loiterer, dawdler, tarrier, deferrer. ‖ adj. 1. slow. 2. delaying, dilatory, tardy. 3. sluggish, lingering. 4. behindhand. ‖ ~amente adv. slowly.

tardamento s. m., **tardança** f. 1. slowness. 2. delay, retardation. 3. tardiness, lateness, procrastination.

tardar v. 1. to delay, tarry, lag, procrastinate, wait, postpone. 2. to loiter, dawdle, linger, hang, drag. 3. to be late.

o mais ~ at the longest. sem ~ without delay. não ~ em fazer to do rightaway.

tarde s. f. afternoon, evening, vesper. ‖ adv. tardily, late.

~ demais overlate. cedo ou ~ earlier or later. a ~ do dia anterior overnight. à ~ far in the day. antes ~ do que nunca better late than never. até ~ far, till late. boa- ~ good afternoon. cada quarta-feira à ~ every Wednesday afternoon. de ~ afternoon. fazer-se ~ to grow late. hoje à ~ this afternoon. mais ~ later, later on, afterwards, afterward. já vai ~ it is high time (to be gone). vir ~ to come at a late hour.

tardeza s. f. tardiness, lateness, delay, retardation.

tardígrado s. m. (zool.) tardigrade: one of the Tardigrada. ‖ adj. tardigrade, moving slowly.

tardinha s. f. late afternoon, beginning of the evening.

tardinheiro s. m. slow, sluggard, dawdler, lazybones, phlegmatic person. ‖ adj. 1. lazy. 2. phlegmatic, slow, tardy, dilatory, indolent, sluggish. ‖ -amente adv. slowly.

tardio adj. 1. lazy, slow, phlegmatic, dilatory, lag. 2. late, inopportune, inconvenient, untimely. ‖ -amente adv. 1. slowly. 2. lately.

tardo, tardonho adj. 1. slow, lazy, indolent, phlegmatic, tardy, sluggish, dull. 2. clumsy, awkward. ‖ -amente adv. slowly, clumsily.

tardoz s. f. the unhewn inner side of a stone; the rough side of a wall.

tarear (I) v. to thrash, drub, beat, cudgel.

tarear (II) v. 1. to tare. 2. (Port., prov.) to equilibrate, balance. 3. (Braz.) to equilibrate (a load) on an animal's back.

tarecada s. f. 1. foolishness, silliness. 2. rumble, noise, bustle. 3. lumber, rubbish, litter.

tarecagem, tarecama s. f. (S. Braz.) lumber, rubbish, litter (unnecessary or disused household articles that cram the rooms).

tareco s. m. 1. fool, silly. 2. naughty or mischievous person. 3. unnecessary or worthless (household) articles; lumber, rubbish, junk. 4. (Braz.) a sort of biscuit.

tarefa s. f. 1. task: a) quantity of work to be done. b) duty. c) assignment. d) job, function. e) undertaking. 2. earthenware vessel for the oil in an olive press. 3. (Braz.) ancient land measure.

~ diária journey work. ~ difícil hard task. ~ de restabelecer a ordem the work of restoring order. incumbir alguém de uma ~ to set someone a task. você tem ~ árdua à sua frente you have a hard task in wait for you.

tarefeiro s. m. 1. pieceworker, jobman, jobber. 2. contractor, entrepreneur, undertaker.

tarega s. m. 1. secondhand dealer, junkman. 2. scrap iron.

taregicagem s. f. (pl. -ens) trade of a secondhand dealer, purchase and sale of old worthless things; a junkman's occupation.

tareia (I) s. f. (Port.) drubbing, thrashing, flogging. dar uma ~ to give a sound spanking.

tareia (II) s. f. (Port., prov.) 1. task, chore, agricultural labour. 2. work, labour.

tarelar v. to chatter, clatter, prattle, jabber, babble, gossip.

tarelice s. f. talkativeness, loquacity, gabbling, gossip.

tarelo s. m. impertinent talker, gossip, babbler.

targana s. f. (ichth., also **tainha**) a species of mullet.

tari s. m. liquor prepared of fermented palm juice.

tarifa s. f. 1. tariff. 2. custom tariff, duty. 3. table of charges or rates.

tarifação s. f. 1. fixation of tariff. 2. clearance.

tarifar v. to tariff, fix a tariff upon.

tarima s. f. estrade or dais, platform under a canopy.

tarimba s. f. 1. a soldier's wooden bedstead, bunk, cot. 2. (fig.) military life.

ele tem ~ (S. Braz.) he is a man of experience.

tarimbado adj. (Braz.) experienced, versed in, well-practiced.

tarimbar v. to serve in the army, be a soldier.

tarimbeiro s. m. 1. common soldier, trooper. 2. officer risen from the rank of a common soldier. ‖ adj. coarse, rough, common, rude, impolite.

tariota s. m. (Braz., ichth., also **tralhoto**) four-eyes.

tarja s. f. 1. painted or ornamented border for an inscription or emblem. 2. mourning border, mourning edge. 3. targe: an ancient round shield.

tarjado adj. 1. bordered with an ornamental design. 2. black-bordered, mourning-edged.

~ de preto provided with a mourning border.

tarjar v. to border, surround with an ornamental (or black) border or edge.

tarjeta s. f. narrow border, edge, ornamental or mourning stripe.

tarlatana s. f. tarlatan, fine muslin.

taro s. m. taro: tropical plant of the arum family.

tarolo s. m. small piece of firewood.

taroque s. m. (Braz., also **cornimboque**) a sort of tobacco box made of a bull's horn.

tarouco adj. 1. stupid, silly, idiotic, foolish, dense, stolid. 2. daft, deranged. 3. amnestic, forgetful due to old age.

tarouquice s. f. silliness, stupidity, boorishness, imbecility.

tarpão s. m. (pl. -ões) tarpon, silverfish, silverking.

tarrabufado s. m. bombastic empty talk, idle chatter.

tarraçada s. f. 1. large quantity of drink. 2. a bowlful.

tarraco s. m. a squat(ty) person. ‖ adj. short and fat, squat.

tarraço s. m. large milk pail.

tarrada (I) s. f. pailful, quantity of liquid contained in a pail.

tarrada (II) s. f. (India) light speedy canoe.

tarrafa s. f. 1. fishing net, casting net, sweep net. 2. old, ragged coat. 3. (N. Braz.) a kind of lace.

tarrafar v. to fish with a casting net or sweep net.

tarrafear v. 1. to fish with a casting net. 2. to pull an ox by his tail to make him fall down.

tárraga s. f. ancient Spanish dance.

tarraxa s. f. 1. screw or twist of a screw. 2. thread. 3. wedge. 4. peg, dowel, plug. 5. screw cutter, screw die, screw cutting die (plate F 1).

tarraxar v. to screw, fasten with or as with a screw, rivet.

tarraxo s. m. = tarraxa 1, 2, 3, 4.

tarro (I) s. m. 1. milk pail. 2. (S. Braz., bot., also **taioba** f.) taro, elephant's ear.

tarro (II) s. m. (Port., prov.) tartar, scale.

tarsalgia s. f. (med.) tarsalgy: neuralgia of the foot.

tarsiano adj. (anat., zool.) tarsal, tarsoid.

tarso s. m. 1. (anat.): a) ancle, ankle. b) the tarsal plate of the eyelid. 2. (zool.): a) tarsometatarsus, shank. b) the terminal segment in the leg of an insect.

tartago s. m. (bot.) caper spurge.

tartamelar, tartamelear v. (also **tartamudear**) to stammer, stutter, falter.

tartamelo s. m. (also **tartamudo**) stammerer, stutterer. ‖ adj. stammering, stuttering, faltering.

tartamudez s. f. stammering, stuttering, faltering.

tartana s. f. tartan(e): small Mediterranean vessel.

tartaranha s. f. 1. fishing boat used on the Tagus river. 2. drag net, trawl.

tartaranhão s. m. (pl. **-ões**) common name of some birds of prey.

tartaranhão-azulado s. m. (pl. **tartaranhões-azulados**) (ornith.) hen harrier, hen harrow.

tartarato s. m. (chem.) tartrate.

tartarear v. 1. to stammer, stutter, falter. 2. to speak an unintelligible language (children). 3. to gibber. 4. to prattle, gabble, gossip.

tartáreo adj. (poet.) Tartarean: referring to the Tartarus (hell).

tartárico adj. 1. (chem.) tartaric, tartareous, containing or belonging to tartar. 2. Tartarian: of or pertaining to Tartary.
ácido ~ tartaric acid.

tartarizar v. (chem.) to tartarize: mix with tartar (of wine).

tártaro (I) s. m. 1. (poet.) Tartarus (hell, Hades). 2. tartar of wine, of teeth or of a boiler; scale.
formação de ~ tartarization.

tártaro (II) s. m. stammerer, stutterer, falterer.

tártaro (III) s. m. Tartar, Tatar: native of Tartary (Asia). ‖ adj. Tartarian, of or pertaining to Tartary.

tartaroso adj. tartaric, containing or referring to tartar or scale.

tartaruga s. f. 1. (zool.) turtle, tortoise. 2. (fig.) scarecrow, old and ugly person.
~ fluvial hiccatee. **~ grega** Greek tortoise. **~ palustre** diamond-back terrapin. **carapaça de ~** tortoise shell, carapace.

tartaruga-de-pente s. f. (pl. **tartarugas-de-pente**) hawksbill turtle.

tartaruga-do-amazonas s. f. (pl. **tartarugas-do-amazonas**) (Braz., zool.) a species of freshwater tortoise.

tartufcar v. to dissemble, feign, disguise.

tartufice s. f. Tartuffism, hypocrisy, disguisement, dissimulation.

tartufo s. m. tartuffe, hypocrite, dissembler.

tartufista adj. m. + f. tartuffish.

tarubá s. f. (N. Braz.) fermented beverage containing tapioca.

taruca, taruga s. f. (zool.) vicuña (S. American ruminant).

tarugar v. to dowel, peg, fasten with dowels, joggle.

tarugo s. m. 1. wooden pin, peg, slug, joggle. 2. dowel (plate C 9). 3. squat(ty) person. 4. (Braz., pop.) magnate, tycoon.

tarumã s. m. (Braz., also **tarumã-de-espinho, tarumã--tuirã**) a verbenaceous tree (genus Vitex).

tasca (I) s. f. 1. swingling, beating, scutching, dressing (flax, hemp, etc.). 2. (Braz., pop.) beating, whipping, thrashing.

tasca (II) s. f. (also **tasco** m.) low taphouse, tavern, public-house, inn, pothouse.

tascadeira s. f. woman who beats, dresses or scutches flax.

tascante s. m. taverner, innkeeper. ‖ adj. m. + f. swingling, beating, scutching, dressing (flax or hemp).

tascar v. 1. to swingle, beat, scutch, dress (flax). 2. to bite. 3. to chew, champ. 4. to crunch. 5. to gnaw, nibble. 6. to give to another a bite or bit of something one is eating or enjoying. 7. (Braz., pop.) to beat, whip, thrash.
~ o freio to bite the bit.

tasco s. m. scutch, tow, hurds (as of flax).

Tasmânia s. f. 1. (geogr.) Tasmania. 2. (bot.) Tasmanian myrtle.

tasmaniano s. m. Tasmanian: native or inhabitant of Tasmania. ‖ adj. Tasmanian: of or pertaining to Tasmania.

tasna, tasneira s. f. (bot.) tansy ragwort, ragweed, cankerweed.

tasneirinha s. f. (bot.) groundsel, birdseed.

tasqueiro s. m. taverner, innkeeper, publican.

tasquinha s. f. scutch, swingle, flax brake.

tasquinhar v. 1. to swingle, beat, scutch, dress. 2. to nibble, pick, eat in little bits, eat daintily. 3. to slander, backbite.

tassalho s. m. a large slice, cut, piece, chunck, lump.

tasto s. m. (mus.) fret (plates B 4, G 2).

tataíra s. f. (Braz., ent., also **caga-fogo** m.) firefly.

tatajiba, tatajuba s. f. (Braz.) a fustic tree.

tatajuba-de-espinho s. f. (pl. **tatajubas-de-espinho**) (Braz., bot.) old fustic, dyer's mulberry.

tatalar s. m. (Braz.) whir as of a wing stroke. ‖ v. 1. to rattle, clack, clatter. 2. to whir, flutter.

tatamba s. m. + f. (Braz.) 1. stammerer, stutterer, tongue-tied person. 2. shy, timid person; fool, booby.

tatapiririca s. f. (Braz., also **pau-pombo** m.) hardwood tree of the cashew family.

tataporas s. f. pl. (med., also **cataporas**) chicken-pox.

tataraneto s. m. (also **tetraneto**) great-great-great--grandson.

tataranha s. m. + f. timid, shy, bashful person. ‖ adj. timid, shy, bashful; diffident. ‖ **~mente** adv. timidly.

tataranhar v. 1. to stammer, stutter, falter. 2. to be embarrassed, become disconcerted. 3. to grope. 4. to be irresolute.

tataranho s. m. stammerer, stutterer, falterer. ‖ adj. stammering, stuttering, faltering.

tataravô s. m. great-great-great-grandfather.

tátaro s. m. stammerer, stutterer, falterer. ‖ adj. stammering, stuttering, faltering.

tate interj. look out! steady! mind! ‖ adv. thus it happened.

tateamento s. m. grope: act of groping.

tateante adj. m. + f. 1. fumbling, groping. 2. touching. 3. (fig.) sounding, probing.

tatear v. 1. to fumble, grope, grabble. 2. to touch, feel, poke. 3. to sound, probe. 4. to grope one's way.

tateável adj. m. + f. (pl. **-áveis**) 1. touchable. 2. (fig.) that may be sounded or probed.

tatera s. f. (Braz., ornith.) larger swallow-wing.

tatibitate s. m. + f. 1. stammerer, stutterer. 2. timid, shy or bashful person. 3. fool, simpleton. ‖ adj. 1. stammering, stuttering, faltering. 2. timid, shy, bashful. 3. foolish, silly.

tática s. f. tactics: 1. (mil.) ability to dispose troops, land, air or naval forces for combat. 2. (fig.) method of procedure; policy.

tático s. m. tactician. ‖ adj. tactical. ‖ **taticamente** adv. tactically.

tátil, táctil adj. m. + f. (pl. **-eis**) tactile: 1. of or pertaining to the sense of touch. 2. touchable.

tatilidade, tactilidade s. f. 1. tactility, tangibility. 2. taction.

tato, tacto (I) s. m. 1. touch, feeling, tactile sense. 2. tact: a) sensibility, fineness of feeling, adroitness, discretion. b) diplomacy, prudence. ~ **suave** featheriness. **falta de** ~ gaucherie, tactlessness. **frio ao** ~ cold to the touch. **macio ao** ~ soft to the touch.

tato (II) s. m. (Braz. and Port., prov.) stammerer, stutterer, falterer. ‖ adj. stammering, stuttering.

tatu s. m. 1. (zool.) armadillo. 2. (Braz.) a variety of domestic swine. 3. (N. Braz.) a shelter against rain covered with palm leaves. 4. ~s pl. (Braz., fig.) brothers without a sister or sisters without a brother.

tatuagem s. f. (pl. **-ens**) 1. tattooage, tattooing. 2. tattoo; tattoo mark or figure.

tatuaíva s. m. (Braz., zool., also **tatupeba**) poyou.

tatuapara s. m. (Braz., zool., also **tatu-bola**) three-banded armadillo, apar.

tatuar v. to tattoo, to mark with tattoos.

tatu-bola s. m. (pl. **tatus-bola**) (Braz., zool.) apar: the three-banded armadillo (Tolypeutes tricinctus).

tatu-canastra s. m. (pl. **tatus-canastra**) (also **tatuaçu**) giant armadillo.

tatu-de-rabo-mole s. m. (pl. **tatus-de-rabo-mole**) tatouay.

tatuetê, tatu-galinha s. m. (pl. **tatus-galinha**), **tatu-verdadeiro** m. (pl. **tatus-verdadeiros**) peba.

tatu-peludo s. m. (pl. **tatus-peludos**) poyou.

tatuquira s. m. (Braz.) sand-fly of the genus Phlebotomus.

tatura, tactura s. f. touching, feeling.

taturana s. f. 1. (Braz., also **lagarta-de-fogo**) a species of caterpillar. 2. a species of wasp. 3. (Braz., fig.) albino.

tatuzinho s. m. (Braz.) 1. (zool.) a small armadillo. 2. wood louse.

tau s. m. tau cross, the Greek letter T (emblem used on the habits of the canons of St. Anthony).

tauá s. m. (Braz.) native word for: 1. alluvial clay or argil containing iron peroxide. 2. yellow ink made of this argil and used in pottery. 3. ivory palm.

tauaçu s. m. anchor stone of rafts used by sea-fishermen in northeastern Brazil.

tauari s. m. (Braz.) 1. (bot.) Colombian mahogany. 2. (bot.) couratari. 3. (N.) hut covered with straw. 4. sheets of couratari bark used as cigarrette covers by the natives.

tauatinga s. f. = **tabatinga**.

tauísmo s. m. Taoism: religion based on Lao-tze's doctrines.

tauísta s. m. + f. Taoist, follower of the Taoistic religion. ‖ adj. Taoistic, of or relating to Taoism.

taulipangue s. m. (Braz.) Indian of the Taulipangue tribe. ‖ adj. of or referring to the Taulipangues.

taumaturgia s. f. thaumaturgy, magic, conjuring.

taumatúrgico adj. thaumaturgic(al), magical.

taumaturgo s. m. thaumaturge, magician; conjurer.

tauoca s. f. (Braz., ornith. also **pinto-do-mato** m.) ant thrush.

taura s. m. (S. Braz.) bold fellow, daredevil; bully. ‖ adj. courageous, bold.

táureo, taurino adj. (poet.) taurine: bullish, oxlike.

tauricéfalo adj. (also **taurocéfalo**) bull-headed.

tauricórneo adj. having horns like a bull.

taurífero adj. abounding in or raising bulls.

tauriforme adj. m. + f. tauriform; like a bull.

tauro s. m. Taurus: one of the zodiacal constellations.

tauromaquia s. f. tauromachy: bullfighting.

tauromáquico adj. tauromachian: of or relating to bullfighting.

tautocronismo s. m. tautochronism: simultaneousness.

tautócrono adj. tautochronous, synchronous.

tautofonia s. f. tautophony: repetition of the same sound.

tautofônico adj. tautophonical, repeating the same sound.

tautograma s. f. poem in which all words begin with the same letter.

tautologia s. f. tautology: repetition of the same thing in different expressions.

tautológico adj. tautologous, tautologic(al). ‖ **tautologicamente** adv. tautologically.

tautomeria s. f. (chem.) tautomerism.

tautometria s. f. tautometry, monotony.

tautossilábico adj. tautosyllabic.

tautossilabismo s. m. tautosyllabism: repetition of the same syllable in one word (for inst.: motmot).

tauxia s. f. damascene, damascening, inlay, marquetry.

tauxiar v. 1. to damascene, inlay. 2. to blush, redden.

tava s. f. (S. Braz.) 1. hock (of cattle, horses). 2. a Gaucho game (to fling the hock in the air and try to land it flat).

tavanês adj. (pl. **-eses**) (f. **-esa**, pl. **-esas**) 1. unquiet. 2. active, busy, diligent. 3. turbulent. 4. rash, rattlebrained, heedless, careless, thoughtless.

tavão s. m. (pl. **-ões**) gadfly, horsefly, oxfly, cleg.

taverna s. f. tavern, inn, pothouse, winehouse, public-house, taphouse; jerry-shop, saloon.

taverneiro s. m. taverner, innkeeper, tapster.

tavoca s. f. growth of shrubs along a beach or river bank.

távola s. f. = **tábula**.

tavolagem s. f. 1. gambling house, gaming house. 2. gambling, addiction to gambling.

tavolatura s. f. (mus.) tablature.

taxa s. f. 1. impost, contribution, duty, scot, toll, excise, assessment, tribute, costums, average. 2. rate, tax, fixed price, tariff. 3. surcharge. ~ **adicional** supertax. ~ **de atracação** pierage. ~ **de desconto bancário** bank rate, discount rate. ~ **de juros** rate of interests. ~ **de matrícula** entrance fee, enrolment fee. ~ **de pavimentação** pavage. ~ **portuária** harbour-dues. ~ **suplementar** extra tax. ~ **de trânsito** transit-duty.

taxação s. f. (pl. **-ões**) taxation, appraisement, rating, price-fixing, taxing, assessment, valuation.

taxácea s. f. plant of the family Taxaceae.

taxáceo adj. (bot.) taxaceous: of or referring to the family Taxaceae.

taxador s. m. taxer, rater, rate fixer, appraiser, valuer, appreciator, assessor.

taxar v. 1. to rate, fix a value or a price, regulate. 2. to tax, impose a tax on, value, estimate, assess, tariff. 3. to consider, censure, blame. 4. to limit, restrain, restrict.

taxativo adj. 1. valuational, rating, taxing. 2. limiting, limitative. 3. restricted. ‖ **-amente** adv. 1. valuationally. 2. restrictedly.

taxável adj. m. + f. (pl. **-áveis**) ratable, chargeable, leviable, assessable. ‖ **taxavelmente** adv. ratably.

taxe s. f. (med.) taxis.

táxi s. m. cab, taxicab, taxi. ~ **aéreo** taxiplane. **andar de** ~ to taxi. **chamar um** ~ to call a cab. **ponto (de estacionamento) de** ~s taxi rank.

taxi s. f. (Braz.) 1. ant tree. 2. (N. Braz.) ant living in the leafstalks of the ant tree.

taxícola adj. m. + f. living as a parasite on a yew.

taxidermia s. f. taxidermy: art of preparing the skins of animals and stuffing and mounting them in a lifelike manner.

taxidérmico adj. taxidermic, taxidermal. ‖ **taxidermicamente** adv. taxidermally.

taxidermista s. m. + f. taxidermist.

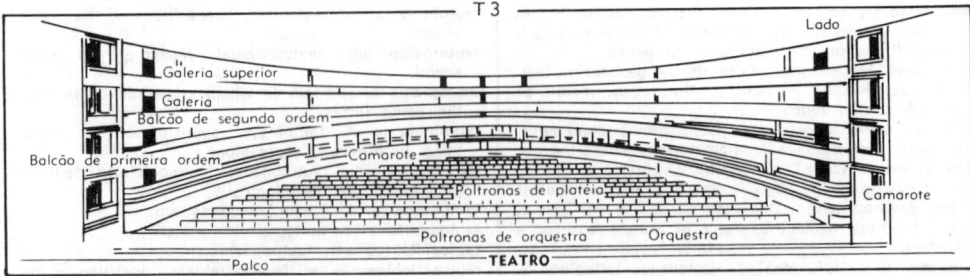

T 3

TEATRO

taxiforme adj. m. + f. (bot.) yewlike.

taxi-girl s. f. (Engl.) taxi dancer.

taxímetro s. m. 1. taxicab. 2. taximeter, automatic fare indicator.

taxina s. f. taxin: a resin extracted from yew leaves.

taxiologia s. f. (also taxologia) taxonomy: the science of classification.

taxionomia s. f. taxinomy: law and principles of scientific classification, especially in botany and zoology.

taxionômico adj. taxonomic(al), classificatory.

taxi-preto s. m. (pl. taxis-pretos) (bot.) long John.

taxira s. f. (Braz.) a species of ant.

taxizal s. m. (pl. -ais) (Braz.) a stand or growth of yews.

taxo s. m. (bot.) yew.

taxologia s. f. taxology, taxonomy: science of classification.

taxológico adj. taxologic(al), taxonomic(al).

taxólogo s. m. taxologist, taxonomer.

taylorismo s. m. Taylorism: scientific industrial management after F. W. Taylor.

tcheco s. m. Czech, native or inhabitant of Bohemia; by extension: of Czechoslovakia. ‖ adj. Czechish, Czechic.

tcheco-eslovaco s. m. (pl. techo-eslovacos) Czecho-slovakian: native or inhabitant of Czechoslovakia. ‖ adj. Czechoslovakian: of or pertaining to Czecho-slovakia.

te pron. you, to you.

peço-te I ask you, I pray you. não te deixes enganar don't let you be taken in. eu te vi I saw you. eu te dei isto I gave it to you.

té prep. apheresis of até: till, until.

tê s. m. the letter T.

régua ~ T square. ferro ~ tee iron, tee bar.

teácea s. f. any plant of the tea family.

teáceo adj. theaceous: 1. (bot.) of or belonging to the tea plants. 2. relating to the beverage.

teada s. f. 1. a piece of linen. 2. white goods; canvas.

teagem s. f. tissue: 1. texture, web, network, fabric, canvas. 2. (biol.) cellular texture.

teantropia s. f. theantropism, a treatise on theantropy.

teantropista s. m. + f. (also teantropo m.) theantropist.

tear s. m. 1. a weaver's loom. 2. a bookbinder's sewing machine. 3. clockwork; wheelwork, mechanism (of a watch).

teatinar v. to roam, ramble, rove, stray, stroll.

teatino s. m. 1. (rel.) Theatine: member of the order founded by Caraffa. 2. (Braz.) stray horse or ox. 3. (fig.) stranger, foreigner. ‖ adj. 1. stray. 2. strange, foreign.

teatrada s. f. theatricals.

teatral adj. m. + f. (pl. -ais) theatrical: 1. relating to the theater. 2. pompous, ostentatious, pretentious, showy, garish, gaudy.

teatralidade s. f. theatricalism, theatricality, staginess.

teatralismo s. m. (Braz.) theatricalism.

teatrista s. m. + f. playgoer, person who goes often to the theater. ‖ adj. playgoing.

teatro s. m. 1. theater, theatre, playhouse, stage (plate T 3). 2. dramatic art. 3. dramatic works as a whole. 4. (fig.) scene.
~ de guerra seat of war, theater of war. ~ lírico lyrical theater. ~ de marionetes puppet show. ~ de variedades vaudeville. no ~ at the play. peça de ~ play, drama.

teatrólogo s. m. playwright, dramatist.

teatro-revista s. m. (pl. teatros-revista) (Braz.) variety show, vaudeville show.

tebaida s. f. (fig.) 1. refuge, retirement. 2. solitude, isolation. 3. wilderness, desert, waste.

tebano s. m. Theban: native or inhabitant of Thebes (city in ancient Greece). ‖ adj. Theban, Thebaic.

tebas s. m., sg. + pl. (S. Braz., pop.) 1. big shot, important person. 2. courageous man, tough, bully. ‖ adj. 1. big, important. 2. courageous, bold.

teca (I) s. f. 1. teak (East Indian tree). 2. (Braz.) a tree of the genus Leguminosae.

teca (II) s. f. theca: spore case, capsule.

tecar v. to hit one marble against another (in games).

tecedeira s. f. female weaver, weaveress.

tecedor s. m. 1. weaver, cloth weaver, webster; knitter. 2. (fig.) plotter, intriguer, conspirator, schemer. ‖ adj. 1. weaving; knitting. 2. plotting, intriguing, conspirating.

tecedura s. f. 1. texture, web, tissue. 2. plot, intrigue, scheme, conspiration.

tecelagem s. f. (pl. -ens) 1. a weaver's work, weaving. 2. a weaver's trade; textile industry.

tecelão s. m. (pl. -ões) (f. teceloa) weaver, cloth-weaver, webster, twiner.

tecer v. 1. to weave, web, tissue. 2. to twist, spin, wreathe, make a network. 3. to interlace, entwine. 4. to write, compose; prepare. 5. to wriggle. 6. to intrigue, plot, scheme, contrive. 7. ~-se to become entangled, interwoven.
~ hinos de louvor to praise highly. ~ os seus comentários to comment on. ~ um discurso to frame a discourse. ~ uma negociação to start a negotiation.

tecido s. m. 1. tissue, woven fabric, texture, cloth, textile; web, woof, weft, twist. 2. ~s pl. textiles, woven fabrics. ‖ adj. 1. woven. 2. (fig.) designed, schemed, plotted.
~ adiposo (anat.) adipose (fatty) tissue. ~ celular (anat.) tissue, tela. ~ de crina haircloth. ~ estampado print, cotton print. ~ de jérsei jersey. ~ de malha tricot. ~ de prata silver tissue.

tecla s. f. 1. key (organ, piano, typewriter) (plate P 10). 2. (fig.) sensitive string, weak point.
bater sempre a mesma ~ (fig.) to harp always on the same string, repeat the same thing over and over. não toque esta ~ do not harp that string, do not mention that.

teclado s. m. keyboard: 1. keys, fingerboard, clavier, ivories (piano) (plate P 10). 2. the arrangement of the keys of a typewriter.

teclar v. (Braz.) to tap (typewriter); to strike (keys).

tecleador s. m. keyboarder.

tecnécio s. m. (chem.) technetium.

técnica s. f. 1. technic, technique, know-how. 2. practice, exercise, workmanship, skill.

técnico s. m. 1. technicist, technician. 2. expert. || adj. technical. || **tecnicamente** adv. technically. **ciência -a** technical science. **detalhes ~s** technicalities. **escola -a** school of technology, technical college. **habilidade -a** technical skill. **termo ~** technical term.

tecnicolor s. m. Technicolor. || adj. Technicolored.

tecnocracia s. f. technocracy.

tecnocrata s. m. + f. technocrat.

tecnografia s. f. technography.

tecnográfico adj. technographic(al). || **tecnografica- mente** adv. technographically.

tecnologia s. f. technology: 1. science of industry. 2. technical terms and/or their explication.

tecnológico adj. technologic(al). || **tecnologicamente** adv. technologically.

tecnólogo s. m. technologist.

tecó s. m. (N. Braz.) cacoethes: mania; bad habit or custom. || adv. as usually.

tecóforos s. m. pl. (zool.) Thecophora, a suborder of Testudinata: turtles and tortoises.

teco-teco s. m. (pl. **teco-tecos**) single-motored airplane.

tecto, teto s. m. roof, ceiling.

tectônica, tetônica s. f. tectonics: 1. the art of constructing buildings. 2. the part of geology relating to the structure of the earth's crust.

tectônico, tetônico adj. tectonic.

tectriz, tetriz s. f. (ornith.) tectrice: tail feather or wing feather.

tecum s. m. (pl. **-uns**) fiber of the leaves of a Brazilian palm used to weave hammocks.

te-déum s. m. (pl. **te-déuns**) Te Deum (Catholic hymn).

tédio s. m. 1. tedium, tediousness, wearisomeness, irksomeness. 2. boredom. 3. disgust; loathsomeness.

tedioso adj. tedious, wearisome, weariful, irksome. 2. tiresome, exhaustible, uninteresting. 3. stupid, dull, boring. || **-amente** adv. tediously, wearisomely.

tefe-tefe s. m. (pl. **tefe-tefes**) 1. throb of the heart, palpitation, panting. 2. (Braz., sl.) motorcar. || adv. nimbly.

tefromancia s. f. tephromancy: divination based on the examination of sacrificial ashes.

tefromântico adj. of or referring to tephromancy.

tegão s. m. (pl. **-ões**) mill hopper, grain hopper.

tegui s. m. (Braz., ornith. also **tovacá** f.) a species of ant thrush.

tégula s. f. (ornith.) tegula.

tegumentar adj. m. + f. tegumental, tegumentary.

tegumento s. m. (anat., bot., zool.) tegument, integument: 1. coat, coating. 2. epidermis. 3. testa of a seed. 4. calix and corolla of a flower.

teia (I) s. f. 1. texture, tissue, web; woof, cloth, woven fabric, textile. 2. plot, intrigue, scheme, conspiration. 3. railing, grating. 4. choir screen, chancel. 5. phantom, chimera.
~ de aranha spiderweb, cobweb.

teia (II) s. f. (poet.) torch, flambeau.

teiforme adj. m. + f. tealike; infused, made like tea.

teiga s. f. 1. a sort of (wicker)basket. 2. former measure of corn.

teima s. f. obstinacy, obstinateness, forwardness, wilfulness, stubbornness, dourness, pertinence.

teimar v. to insist, persist, persevere; be obstinate, stubborn.
ele teima em havê-lo visto he insists on having seen it.

teimosa s. f. (N. Braz., pop.) firewater, rum, liquor.

teimosia, teimosice s. f. wilfulness, obstinacy, stubbornness, pertinacity, headiness, bullheadedness, persistance.

teimoso s. m. 1. crank; obstinate, wilful person. 2. (Braz.) tumbler (toy). || adj. insistent, obstinate, wilful, stubborn, bullheaded, pigheaded, dour, forward. || **-amente** adv. obstinately.

teína s. f. (chem.) theine.

teiró s. m. + f. 1. obstinacy, wilfulness, stubbornness. 2. implication, quarrel, squabble. 3. (S. Braz.) doubt, suspicion, distrust, misgiving.

teiru s. m. (Braz.) sort of fife or flute of the Indians.

teísmo s. m. theism: 1. belief in God as the creator of the universe. 2. sickness caused by the abuse of tea.

teísta s. m. + f. theist, follower of theism. || adj. theistical.

teiú s. m. (Braz.) 1. (zool.) teju, a species of lizard. 2. plant of the family Euphorbiaceae (Jatropho opipera).

teixe s. m. ancient golden trinket.

teixo s. m. (bot.) yew.

tejadilho s. m. 1. roof or covering of a vehicle. 2. lean-to roof, pentroof; canopy.

tejoila s. f. one of the bones of a horse's hoof.

teju, tejuaçu s. m, (zool.) teju, a species of lizard.

tela s. f. 1. web, woven fabric, texture, tissue, network. 2. (paint.) canvas; painting, picture. 3. screen of a cinema (plate E 5). 4. wire netting. **vir à ~** to come under discussion. **~ engomada** buckram. **~ de televisão** telescreen.

telagarça s. f. = **talagarça**.

telamão s. m. (pl. **-ões**) (archit., also **télamon**, pl. **~s**) telemon: male figure serving to support entablatures, cornices, etc.

telangiectasia s. f. (med.) telangiectasis.

telão s. m. (pl. **-ões**) (also **talão**) advertising drop screen in front of cinema screens or theater stages.

telar v. (N. Braz.) to put wire gauzes or wire screens on the doors or windows to keep out the mosquitoes.

teleator s. m. (Braz.) TV actor.

telecinésia s. f. telekinesis.

telecomando, telecontrole s. m. remote control.

telecomunicação s. f. telecommunication.

teledinâmico adj. telodynamic.

teleférico s. m. telpher. || adj. telpher.

teleferismo s. m. telpherage.

telefonar v. to call, phone, telephone, ring up.
~ a alguém to give someone a call. **~ para alguém** to ring up someone. **telefonaram-lhe** there was a call for you. **estar telefonando** to be on the wire.

telefone s. m. telephone (plate E 3).
~ automático automatic telephone, dial telephone (plate T 4). **~ público** public call box, pay phone (plates E 13, R 8, T 4). **no ~** on or over the telephone. **por ~** telephonically.

telefonema s. m. (also **telefonada** f.) call, telephone call.
~ interurbano trunk call.

telefonia s. f. telephony.

telefônico adj. telephonic.
aparelho ~ telephone receiver. **cabina -a** telephone booth, telephone box. **chamado ~** telephone call. **estação -a** telephone exchange. **ligação -a** telephone connection. **lista -a** telephone directory.

T 4

Telefone público
Estante
Lista telefônica
Porta
Cabina da telefone público
Posto de telefone

Gancho
Fone
Disco
Abertura para colocar a moeda
Instruções
Concha de devolução
Telefone público

TELEFONE

Bocal transmissor
Fone
Gancho
Receptor
Fio flexível
Disco
Batente
Caixa, base
Telefone automático

telefonista s. m. + f. 1. telephonist. 2. telephone operator.
telefoto s. m. telephoto.
telefotografia s. f. 1. telephotography. 2. telegraph.
telefotográfico adj. telephotographic. ‖ **telefotograficamente** adv. telephotographically.
telega s. f. telega: Russian four-wheeled cart.
telegonia s. f. (biol.) telegony.
telegrafar v. to telegraph, cable, wire; signal.
telegrafia s. f. telegraphy.
~ **sem fio** wireless telegraphy.
telegráfico adj. 1. telegraphic, wired, cabled. 2. (fig.) scanty, resumed (style). ‖ **telegraficamente** adv. telegraphically.
aparelho ~ tape-machine. **código** ~ telegraph code. **estação** -a telegraph office. **estilo** ~ telegraphese. **poste** ~ telegraph pole.
telegrafista s. m. + f. telegrapher, telegraphist.
telégrafo s. m. 1. telegraph, wire; ticker. 2. telegraph office.
~ **portátil** field telegraph. ~ **sem fio** wireless telegraph.
telegrama s. m. telegram, cable, wire.
formulário para ~ telegraph form. **mensageiro para** ~**s** telegraph boy. **por** ~ by telegram, by cable.
teleinterruptor s. m. remote control switch.
telejornal s. m. (Braz.) TV newscast, telecast news.
telemetria s. f. telemetry.
telemétrico adj. telemetric(al). ‖ **telemetricamente** adv. telemetrically.
telêmetro s. m. telemeter, range-finder (plates F 6, M 3).
telenovela s. f. (Braz.) TV soap opera.
teleobjetiva s. f. (phot.) telephoto lens.
teleologia s. f. teleology.
teleológico adj. teleologic(al). ‖ **teleologicamente** adv. teleologically.
teleósteo s. m. (zool.) teleost, osseous fish. ‖ adj. teleostean: of or pertaining to the (sub)class Teleostei.
telepatia s. f. telepathy, thought-transference; thought-reading.
telepático adj. telepathic. ‖ **telepaticamente** adv. telepathically.
telescopia s. f. telescopy.
telescópico adj. telescopic. ‖ **telescopicamente** adv. telescopically.
telescópio s. m. telescope, spy-glass (small telescope) (plate B 13).
~ **binocular** binocular. ~ **fotográfico** phototelescope.

telésia s. f. (min.) telesia; white sapphire.
telespectador s. m. (Braz.) TV watcher, televiewer. ‖ adj. (Braz.) TV watching, televiewing.
teleteatro s. m. (Braz.) teleplay, a play written for or shown on TV.
teletipista s. m. + f. teletypist, teletype.
teletipo s. m. teletype.
teletransmissão s. f. (pl. -ões) transmission of television.
teletransmissor s. m. transmitter of television.
teletransmissora s. f. television station.
televisão s. f. television, video.
locutor de ~ telecaster. **programa de** ~ telecast. **tela de receptor de** ~ telescreen.
televisar v. to televise.
televisionado adj. televised.
televisor s. m. television receiver.
televisora s. f. television station, telestation.
telex s. m. (tech.) telex, a teletypewriter.
telexar v. (tech.) to telex, send a message through a teletypewriter.
telha s. f. 1. (roofing) tile (plate T 5). 2. whim, fancy, caprice, mania, crotchet.
~ **de beiral** drip (tile). ~ **de cumeeira** ridge tile, hip tile (plate T 5). ~ **holandesa** pan tile (plate T 5). ~ **de vidro** glass tile. **ter uma** ~ **de menos** to have a tile loose, be crackbrained.
telhado s. m. 1. roof; tiling (plate T 5). 2. wire tack. 3. (sl.) mania, infatuation, craze.
~ **de chapa galvanizada ondulada** galvanized corrugated iron roof (plate T 5). ~ **de vidro** (fig.) evil reputation, bad fame. ~ **de duas águas** gable roof, saddle roof (plate T 5). ~ **de quatro águas** hip roof. ~ **de três águas** hip and valley roof (plate T 5). ~ **de colmo** thatched roof, straw roof (plate T 5). ~ **de tábuas** boarded roof (plate T 5).
telhador s. m. 1. tiler, roofer; slater. 2. cover of a earthen vessel.
telhadura s. f. 1. roofing, roof covering, tiling (plate T 5). 2. tileworks, tilery; place where tiles are made.
~ **de ardósia** slating, slate roofing (plate T 5). ~ **plana** plain tiling (plate T 5).
telhal s. m. (pl. -ais) tile kiln.
telhão s. m. (pl. -ões) large tile; pressed tile.
telhar v. to tile, roof, cover a roof with tiles.
telha-vã s. f. (pl. telhas-vãs) 1. roof without boarding; room without ceiling. 2. tile laid without mortar.
telheira s. f. tileworks, tilery, tile factory.
telheiro s. m. 1. tilemaker, tiler. 2. shed covered with tiles, Dutch barn, penthouse, outhouse, hovel (plate A 4).

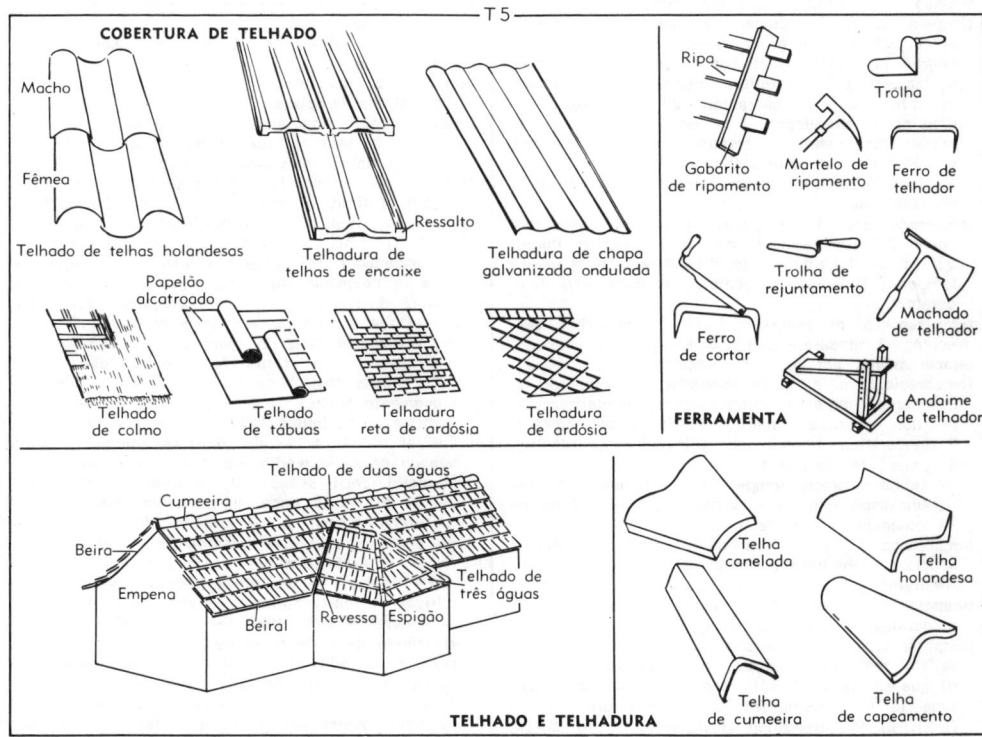

COBERTURA DE TELHADO

Macho

Fêmea

Telhado de telhas holandesas

Papelão alcatroado

Telhadura de telhas de encaixe

Ressalto

Telhadura de chapa galvanizada ondulada

Telhado de colmo

Telhado de tábuas

Telhadura reta de ardósia

Telhadura de ardósia

Ripa

Trolha

Gabárito de ripamento

Martelo de ripamento

Ferro de telhador

Trolha de rejuntamento

Ferro de cortar

Machado de telhador

Andaime de telhador

FERRAMENTA

Telhado de duas águas

Cumeeira

Beira

Empena

Beiral

Revessa

Espigão

Telhado de três águas

Telha canelada

Telha holandesa

Telha de cumeeira

Telha de capeamento

TELHADO E TELHADURA

---

telhice s. f. (pop.) mania, craze, whim, odd notion.
telho s. m. 1. earthen lid or cover. 2. tile bat, shard.
telhudo adj. (pop.) crackbrained, eccentric, crazy. ‖ **-amente** adv. eccentrically.
telilha s. f. thin web or screen; gauze.
telite s. f. (med.) thelitis.
teliz s. f. saddle-cloth, caparison.
telófase s. f. (biol.) telophase.
telso s. m. (zool.) telson.
telúrico adj. telluric: 1. (chem.) relating to tellurium. 2. tellural, of or pertaining to the earth.
telúrio s. m. (chem.) tellurium.
telurismo s. m. tellurism: the natural forces of the earth and their influence on customs and habits of men.
tema s. m. theme: 1. topic. 2. subject, thesis, argument. 3. exercise. 4. text. 5. radical syllable or word root. 6. (mus.) motive.
  ~ de discussão topic of discussion. **~ de uma fuga** (mus.) proposition. **~ de um livro** subject-matter.
temário s. m. (Braz.) programme or list of items of a congress or conference.
temático adj. thematic. ‖ **tematicamente** adv. thematically.
temba s. m. (Braz., pop.) devil.
tembé, tembê s. m. (Braz.) precipice, cliff; brink.
tembequara s. m. + f. (Braz.) name given to Indians who pierce their lips.
tembetá s. m. (Braz.) Tupian name for a labret (but not the **botoque**).
temblar v. (mus.) to tune, put in tune.
temente adj. m. + f. fearful, anxious. ‖ **~-mente** adv. anxiously.

  ~ a Deus God-fearing, religious, pious, godly, devout.
temer v. 1. to fear, (coll.) funk. 2. to doubt, apprehend, dread. 3. to reverence, respect, venerate. 4. **~-se (de)** to fear, be afraid, stand in fear (of).
  temendo que... for fear of...
temerário adj. temerarious: 1. rash, foolhardy, hardy, reckless, headstrong, hot-blooded, inconsiderate. 2. daring, bold, overbold, presumptuous. 3. risky, venturous, adventurous. ‖ **temerariamente** adv. temerariously, etc.
temeridade s. f. temerity: 1. rashness, recklessness, precipitation, random, hardiness, foolhardiness. 2. boldness, overboldness, daring, audaciousness. 3. riskness, venturousness.
temero adj. (N. Braz., also **temível**) fearful, dreadful.
temeroso adj. 1. fearful, dreadful, timorous, terrible, dire, appalling. 2. frightened, afraid, alarmed.
temibilidade s. f. terribleness, dreadfulness, frightfulness.
temido (I) adj. 1. appalling, frightening, terrifying; feared, dreaded. 2. (fig.) bold, courageous. ‖ **-amente** adv. appallingly, etc.
temido (II) adj. 1. fearful, anxious, timorous. 2. timid, diffident. ‖ **-amente** adv. fearfully, etc.
temível adj. m. + f. (pl. **-íveis**) 1. appalling, dreadful, terrific, terrible, direful. 2. (fig.) formidable. ‖ **temivelmente** adv. dreadfully, terrifically.
temor s. m. 1. dread, fear. 2. anxiety, apprehension, timorousness. 3. reverence, awe, devotion. 4. (fig.) fright, terror, horror. 5. care, carefulness; zeal. 6. timidity.
  por ~ a Deus for fear of God.

tempão s. m. (Braz., pop.) long time.

têmpera s. f. 1. temper: a) seasoning, flavour, spice. b) hardening of steel, attemperment. c) degree of temper, state of hardness (of metals). d) temperament, mentality, mettle, disposition, cast of mind; nature, character. 2. temperature. 3. painting in distemper. 4. wedge or coin used in certain instruments. 5. treatment a falcon or hawk received the day before the hunting. ~ **superficial** (tech.) face-hardening. **de velha** ~ old-fashioned.

temperado adj. 1. tempered, seasoned, flavoured, spicy. 2. temperate: a) moderate, mild (climate); agreeable. b) hardened, toughened (steel). c) (mus.) tempered (interval or scale). ‖ **-amente** adv. temperately.

temperador s. m. temperer. ‖ adj. 1. tempering, seasoning. 2. moderating. 3. hardening.

temperamental adj. m. + f. temperamental.

temperamento s. m. (also **tempérie** f.) 1. temper: a) seasoning, spice. b) temperament, mentality, disposition, character, nature, spirit, mood, humour. 2. moderation, temperance, self-restraint, frugality. 3. (mus.) temperament. ~ **calmo** a placid temper. **de** ~ **fogoso** hot tempered. **disposição do** ~ attitude of mind. **falta de** ~ tameness, lifelessness.

temperança s. f. temperance, moderation; frugality; sobriety, soberness, abstinence, self-control, self--restraint.

temperante adj. m. + f. 1. tempering, seasoning. 2. moderating. 3. soothing, mitigating.

temperar v. 1. to temper: a) season, flavour, spice, relish, zest. b) moderate, calm, soften, mitigate. c) quench, harden, chill, anneal (metal). d) (mus.) tune to a temperament. 2. to mix properly. 3. (fig.): a) to strengthen, invigorate. b) to check, repress. c) appease, harmonize, conciliate. 4. ~**-se** to keep moderation, abstain, restrain, refrain.

temperatura s. f. (also **tempérie**) 1. temperature: a) degree of heat according to a scale. b) degree of heat of a human body, fever. 2. (fig.) situation. **elevação de** ~ rise in temperature. **como está a** ~? (fig.) how are things? **medir ou ver a** ~ to take the temperature. **tabela de** ~ temperature--chart. **ter** ~ to have a temperature (fever).

tempereiro s. m. 1. iron used by weavers to prevent the cloth from shrinking. 2. any of the four wooden crosspieces of a noria.

temperilha s. f. (fig.) calmative, sedative.

temperilho s. m. 1. way of driving a team, manner of holding the reins. 2. poor seasoning. 3. (vet.) tasty excipient.

tempero s. m. 1. seasoning, spice, condiment, zest, sauce. 2. dressing of food. 3. taste, savour, flavour, relish. 4. (fig.) way, means, way out. 5. palliative, lenitive.

tempestade s. f. tempest: 1. storm, rainstorm, thunderstorm. 2. (fig.) commotion, trouble, tumult. ~ **de areia** dust storm. ~ **num copo de água** a storm in a teacup. ~ **de aplausos** round after round of applause. **após a** ~ **vem a bonança** after a storm comes a calm. **ele levantou uma** ~ he brought a storm about his ears. **preso pela** ~ stormbound.

tempestear v. 1. to tempest, agitate. 2. to rage, make a hell of a noise; to bluster. 3. to persecute, harass, pester.

tempestivo adj. in time, well-timed, seasonable, opportune, suitable.

tempestuar v. to rage, rave, become furious, get angry.

tempestuosidade s. f. storminess, tempestuousness.

tempestuoso adj. tempestuous: 1. stormy, flawy, puffy, blowy, windy, squally, gusty. 2. rough, wild, furious, rude, blustering, boisterous. ‖ **-amente** adv. tempestuously.

templário s. m. Templar: member of the order of the Knights Templars.

templo s. m. 1. temple: a) public edifice for religious service. b) seat of Freemasons' meetings. c) order of the Knights Templars. 2. church.

tempo s. m. 1. time: a) duration, period, spell, while, length of time. b) epoch, era. c) opportunity, turn. d) season, tide, hour. e) (mus.) tempo, tempi, movement. f) leisure. 2. weather. 3. (gram.) tense. ~ **ameaçador (de chuva)** threatening weather. **o** ~ **está chegando** the time draws on. ~ **chuvoso** wet or duck's weather. ~ **de colheita** harvest. **um** ~ **curto** a short time. ~**s desfavoráveis** bad times. ~ **é dinheiro** time is money. ~ **e espaço** time and space. ~ **e eternidade** time and eternity. ~ **de explosão** (tech.) combustion stroke. ~ **de funcionamento** (tech.) time of operation. ~ **de guerra** wartime. ~ **integral** full time. ~ **imemorial** time out of mind. **é** ~ **de laranjas** oranges are in season now. ~ **médio** meantime. ~ **morto (pouco negócio)** dead season. **o** ~ **mostrará** time will show. **do** ~ **da onça** old-time. **em** ~**s passados** in olden times. **o** ~ **passou** time is up. ~ **de paz** peacetime. ~ **péssimo** abominable weather. **o** ~ **está péssimo hoje** the weather is atrocious to-day. ~ **de posse** tenure. **nos** ~**s primitivos** in early times. ~ **ruim** time of trouble. ~ **sideral** sideral time. ~ **solar** solar time. ~ **suficiente para ele estar aqui** time enough he were here. **o** ~ **todo** all that time. ~**s vindouros** aftertimes. **o** ~ **de** · **vôo** the time of flight. **a** ~ betimes, (U. S. A.) forehanded. **ainda em** ~ just in time. **avisar em** ~ to give fair warning. **por causa do** ~ under stress of weather. **cada coisa em seu** ~ everything in its season. **com o** ~ in the long run. **com o** ~ **vencido** time-expired. **como são os** ~**s atualmente** as times go. **desabar o** ~ (Braz., pop.) to rain pitchforks. **desde aquele** ~ thence. **desde aquele** ~ **em diante** thenceforth. **em seu devido** ~ in due course. **durante certo** ~ for a certain time. **economizando** ~ timesaving. **em** ~ on terms, in time, well-timed, timeful (good). **encontrar bom** ~ (naut.) to make good weather. **vai fechar o** ~ (fig.) there is trouble ahead. **fora de** ~ out of time. **ganhar** ~ to gain time. **gastar** ~ to waste time. **já não há mais** ~ there is no more time. **mais algum** ~ some time longer. **por mais** ~ by the length of time. **matar** ~ to kill time. **no meio** ~ between times, in the meantime. **ao mesmo** ~ at the same time. **há muito** ~ long since, early. **muito** ~ **atrás** for a long time past. **por muito** ~ for long. **nossos** ~**s** these times of ours. **passar o** ~ to quiddle. **passar do** ~ to overtime. **passar o** ~ **sonhando** to drowse away the time. **passei um** ~ **formidável** I had the time of my life. **perda de** ~ broken time. **perder** ~ to idle. **não perder o seu** ~ to make the most of one's time. **se o** ~ **permitir** weather permitting. **há pouco** ~ of late, latterly. **primeiro (segundo)** ~ (ftb.) first (second) half-time. **previsão do** ~ weather forecast. **em qualquer** ~ at any time. **há quanto** ~ **você já está aqui?** how long have you been here? **desde os** ~**s remotos** from time immemorial, time out of memory. **em seu** ~ in its proper time. **em um só** ~ at one time, simultaneously. **superar no** ~ to outspan. **tanto** ~ **como** as long as, as much time as. **de** ~ **em** ~ at intervals, from time to time. **no** ~ **dos**

Afonsinhos in days long past. **no ~ em que se amarrava cachorro com lingüiça** in better times. **dar ~ ao ~** to wait and see, take or bide one's time. **ele toma seu ~** he takes his good old time. **trabalho que toma ~** work of time. **tudo em seu ~** all in good time, there is a time for everything. **em velhos ~s** in times of old, old-time.

tempo-quente s. m. (pl. **tempos-quentes**) (Braz.) 1. disorder, tumult, row; violent discussion. 2. (Braz., folklore) **saci**: little one-legged Negro phantom.

temporada s. f. 1. period. 2. stay, space of time. 3. season. **~ lírica** theatrical season, opera season. **~ morta** dead season. **~ na praia** vacation at the beach, time at the beach. **passamos uma ~ agradável** we had a good time.

temporal (I) s. m. (pl. -ais) 1. temporal power. 2. tempest, rainstorm, hailstorm, gust, flaw, shower. 3. (fig.) commotion. ‖ adj. m. + f. 1. temporary, secular. 2. mundane, wordly. 3. temporal, transient. ‖ **~mente** adv. temporally.

temporal (II) s. m. (anat.) the temporal region of the head; temporal bone (plate C 17). ‖ adj. m. + f. temporal, of the temples.

temporalidade s. f. 1. temporality, temporalness, temporariness. 2. provisionalness, provisionality. 3. **~s** (pl.) temporalities of the Church.

temporalizar v. to make temporal, secularize.

temporaneidade s. f. temporariness, transientness, transitoriness.

temporão adj. rareripe, early ripe, ratheripe; rath, hasting; premature, early, extemporaneous.

temporário adj. 1. temporary, fleeting, transient. 2. provisory, provisional, makeshift. ‖ **temporariamente** adv. temporarily, ad interim.

têmporas s. f. pl. 1. (anat.) temples. 2. ember days, ember-tide.

temporização s. f. (pl. -ões) (also **temporizamento** m.) temporization, procrastination, lingering, postponement.

temporizador s. m. temporizer, delayer, procrastinator, loiterer, lingerer. ‖ adj. temporizing, proscrastinating, lingering. ‖ **~amente** adv. temporizingly.

temporizar v. to temporize: 1. procrastinate, delay, linger, dawdle, saunter, lag. 2. gain time, wait for better opportunities. 3. acquiesce, accede, assent, yield.

tempo-será s. m. (Braz.) hide-and-seek (children's game).

tem-tem s. m. (pl. **tem-tens**) 1. toddling, a baby's walking. 2. a species of bird of the tanager family.

tem-tenzinho s. m. (pl. **tem-tenzinhos**) (Braz., ornith.) a species of falcon.

temulência s. f. (also med.) temulency: intoxication, inebriation, drunkenness.

temulento adj. temulent, intoxicating, intoxicated, drunk, inebriate. ‖ -amente adv. temulently.

tenacidade s. f. 1. tenacity, tenaciousness, adhesion, toughness. 2. (fig.) obstinacy, sturdiness, doggedness, stubbornness, pertinacity. 3. avarice, covetousness, greed, avidity.

tenalha s. f. (fort.) tenaille.

tenalhão s. m. (pl. -ões) (fort.) tenaillon.

tênar s. m. (pl. **~es**) (anat.) thenar: palm (of the hand).

tenaz (I) s. f. tongs, forceps, pliers, pincers (especially those of a blacksmith) (plate L 1).

tenaz (II) adj. m. + f. 1. tenacious: a) adherent, glutinous, viscous, stick, close, firm, tough. b) (fig.) stubborn, dogged, persistant, obstinate, head-

strong, dour. 2. avaricious, greedy. ‖ **~mente** adv. tenaciously.

tenca s. f. (ichth.) tench.

tença s. f. 1. pension, periodical allowance, annuity. 2. (obs.) possessing, maintenance.

tenção s. f. (pl. -ões) 1. intention, purpose, plan, aim, design, end; resolution. 2. (jur.) judgement, a judge's opinion. 3. (her.) emblem, device, motto. 4. (mus.) ancient ballad. 5. play on words, pun.

tencionar v. 1. to intend, plan, purpose, mean, contemplate, design. 2. (jur.) to judge, pass sentence, decide in a law court. **tenciono ir lá** I mean to go there. **ele não tencionava fazer mal** he thought no harm. **o lugar que você tenciona** the place you mean.

tencionário s. m. pensioner, one who receives a pension.

tenda s. f. 1. awning, tent, canvas (plates P 17, T 2). 2. stand, stall (market), pavillion. 3. small shop. 4. a) a pedlar's or hawker's wares. b) the box he carries his wares in or his pack of wares. 5. the boiler department of a sugar-mill. 6. (N. Braz.) set of cups for gathering caoutchouc. **~ de oxigênio** (med.) oxygen tent. **armar ~s** to pitch tents.

tendal (I) s. m. (pl. -ais) place where sheep are shorn.

tendal (II) s. m. 1. deck awning. 3. place in sugar-mills where the moulds are put to cool.

tendal (III) s. m. (S. Braz.) 1. place where meat and fish are hung to dry. 2. clothes rope, clothes line.

tendão s. m. (pl. -ões) (anat.) tendon, sinew. **~ de Aquiles** Achilles' tendon. **~ da perna** hamstring.

tendedeira s. f. board for the unbaked loaves (bakery).

tendeiro s. m. 1. chandler; hawker; shopkeeper. 2. (pop.) devil.

tendência s. f. tendency: 1. inclination, bent, fail, bias. 2. propensity, proneness, proclivity, disposition, predisposition. 3. penchant. 4. vocation, calling. 5. aptitude, conduciveness. 6. trend, drift. 7. direction, current, undercurrent; gravitation. **~ da conjuntura** business trend. **~ geral** tenor, the general run of things. **~ à gulodice** belly worship. **~ da opinião moderna** current of modern opinion. **~ da opinião pública** set of public opinion. **~ à perfeição** perfectiveness. **análise de ~** trend analysis. **ele possui ~ para exagerar** he shows a disposition to exaggerate. **ter uma ~ para** to have a tendency to.

tendencioso adj. tendentious, partial, biassed, (fig.) coloured. ‖ -amente adv. tendentiously. **jornal ~** paper with a marked tendency, tendentious paper. **notícias -as** tendentious news. **livro ~** purpose book.

tendente (I) s. m. plant of the mallow family.

tendente (II) adj. m. + f. 1. tending, prone, driving, apt. 2. vocational.

tendepá s. m. (Braz., also **rixa**) quarrel, brawl, squabble.

tender v. 1. to incline, lean, verge. 2. to tend, dispose, predispose. 3. to set, trend. 4. to gravitate, direct, run, conduce, drive. 5. to spread, stretch out, unfold, straighten (as sails). 6. to mould bread. 7. **~-se** to extend, reach. **~ para** to tend towards. **~ para o mesmo ponto** to converge. **isto tende a ser esquecido facilmente** this is apt to be forgotten.

tênder s. m. (pl. **tênderes**) tender (of a locomotive). **locomotiva sem ~** tank engine (railway).

tendilha s. f. small tender.

tendilhão s. m. (pl. -ões) camp tent.

tendinha s. f. (Braz.) small tent; small cheap shop.
tendinoso adj. tendinous, tendonous, relating to the tendon, sinewy. ‖ **-amente** adv. tendinously.
tendola s. f. shabby tent.
Tênebra s. f. (eccl.) Tenebrae.
tenebrário s. m. (eccl.) a chandelier used in the Tenebrae.
tenebricosidade s. f. (obs.) tenebrosity, darkness, obscurity.
tenebricoso adj. (obs.) tenebrous, dark, obscure, deranged (mind). ‖ **-amente** adv. tenebrously.
tenebrosidade s. f. 1. tenebrosity, darkness, obscurity, gloom. 2. terribleness, horror, frightfulness. 3. disturbance, excitement, agitation.
tenebroso adj. 1. tenebrous, dark, obscure, gloomy, dim, sad, swarthy. 2. terrible, horrible, frightful. 3. worried, disturbed, troubled, agitated.
tenedura s. f. (S. Braz.) excrement of wild animals.
tenência s. f. 1. lieutenancy: rank or commission of a lieutenant. 2. habitation of a lieutenant. 3. (fig.) vigor, firmness, solidity, prudence, foresight. 4. (S. Braz.) manners, customs, habits.
   tomar ~ de (Braz.) to give heed to, to observe, examine carefully.
tenente s. m. 1. (mil.) lieutenant. 2. deputy, representative, substitute.
tenente-coronel s. m. (pl. **tenentes-coronéis**) (mil.) lieutenant-colonel.
tenesmo s. m. (med.) tenesmus.
tenesmódico adj. (Med.) tenesmic. ‖ **tenesmodicamente** adv. tenesmically.
tengo-tengo adv. (N. Braz., pop.) slowly, slowly and easily.
tênia s. f. (zool.) taenia, tapeworm.
teníase s. f. (med.) taeniasis.
tenífugo adj. (med.) taeniacidal, expelling or destroying tapeworms.
tenióide adj. m. + f. (zool.) taenioid.
teníóptero adj. (zool.) taeniate: striped (wings or fins).
teniossomo adj. (zool.) taeniosomous.
tênis s. m., sg. + pl. tennis, lawn tennis.
   ~ de mesa table tennis, ping-pong. **bola de ~** tennis ball. **quadra de ~** tennis court. **raqueta de ~** tennis racket.
tenista s. m. + f. tennis player.
tenoísmo s. m. obedience of the Japanese to their emperor.
tenor s. m. (mus.) tenor: 1. the highest male voice. 2. tenorist.
tenotomia s. f. (surg.) tenotomy, cutting of a tendon.
tenro adj. tender: 1. young, weak, immature. 2. mild, soft. 3. sensible, affectionate, delicate. 4. mellowy, pappy. ‖ **-amente** adv. tenderly.
   carne -a tender meat.
ternura s. f. tenderness: 1. weakness, 2. softness, mildness. 3. sensibility, love, affection.
tensão s. f. (pl. **-ões**) 1. tension, tenseness, tensity. 2. stretch, strain, stress.
   ~ arterial arterial pressure. **~ nos bornes** terminal voltage. **~ superficial** surface strain. **alta ~** (electr.) high tension. **bobina de ~** pressure coil. **sem ~** unstrained. **sob ~** tensioned.
tense s. f. (obs., mus.) ballad sung by two troubadours.
tensiômetro s. m. (mech.) tensiometer.
tensivo adj. tensive, tensional. ‖ **-amente** adv. tensively.
tenso adj. 1. tense, tight, taut, strained. 2. (fig.) intense. ‖ **-amente** adj. tensely.
tensor s. m. 1. (anat., math.) tensor. 2. (mech.) adjusting rod; turn buckle. ‖ adj. tensive.

tenta s. f. 1. (surg.) probe. 2. a sort of mock fight with heifers.
tentação s. f. (pl. **-ões**) (also **tentamento** m.) temptation: enticement, allurement; seduction, bait.
tentaculado adj. tentaculate(d), tentacled.
tentacular adj. m. + f. tentacular.
tentaculífero adj. (zool.) tentaculiferous, pertaining to the Tentaculifera.
tentaculiforme adj. m. + f. tentaculiform.
tentáculo s. m. 1. (zool.) tentacle (polyp); feeler (as of insects); horn (as of a snail). 2. (fig.) means to achieve one's purpose.
tentado adj. tempted, incited, seduced; attracted.
tentador s. m. 1. tempter, seducer, allurer. 2. (fig.) devil. ‖ tempting, inciting, seductive, enticing, alluring; attractive. ‖ **~amente** adv. seductively.
tentame, tentâmen s. m. (pl. **tentamens, tentâmenes**) attempt, endeavour, effort.
tentar v. 1. to try, assay, test, experiment. 2. to attempt, endeavour, undertake, risk, venture; seek, solicit. 3. to tempt, entice, fascinate, seduce, allure, bait, decoy, dangle.
   ~ convencer alguém to try to convince s. o., argue with s. o. **~ a Deus** to tempt God. **~ um disfarce** to attempt a disguise. **~ fazer alguma coisa** to try one's hand at. **~ fortuna** to seek one's fortune. **~ a sorte** to run one's fortune. **~ contra a vida de alguém** to attempt upon a man's life. **a oportunidade me tentou** the occasion tempted me.
tentativa s. f. (also **tentamento** m.) 1. trial, assay, experiment. 2. attempt, essay, endeavour, effort. 3. bid, offer. 4. temptation.
   ~ de assassínio attempt at murder. **~ e erro** trial and error. **farei uma ~** I'll have a go at it.
tentativo adj. tentative, trial, experimental. ‖ **-amente** adv. tentatively.
tenteador s. f. 1. essayer; prober, examiner. 2. bungler, groper, fumbler. ‖ adj. 1. essaying; examining, probing. 2. fumbling, groping.
tentear (I) v. 1. (surg.) to probe. 2. to search, explore, examine. 3. to test, try, attempt. 4. to fumble, grope, sound, sift; grope one's way.
tentear (II) v. 1. to count with counters, calculate, compute. 2. to take care of, entertain. 3. to score, keep scores.
tenteio s. m. 1. probing, groping, searching. 2. calculating. 3. (S. Braz.) manner of holding the reins.
tenterê s. m. (N. Braz., zool.) a species of alligator.
tentilhão s. m. (ornith.) 1. siskin, a song-bird. 2. chaffinch, aberdevine.
tentilhão-grande-dos-pomares s. m. (pl. **tentilhões-grandes-dos-pomares**) (ornith.) greater titmouse, ox-eye.
tentilhão-montês s. f. (pl. **tentilhões-monteses**) (ornith.) brambling.
tento (I) s. m. 1. care, attention, caution, circumspection, good sense, prudence. 2. (paint.) maulstick, mahlstick (plate P 12). 3. (fig.) calculation, computation, reckoning. 4. (sl.) slap, strike, blow.
   dar ~ to be careful about. **sem ~** careless. **tomar ~** to pay attention.
tento (II) s. m. 1. (Braz., ftb.) goal. 2. score, point (in games). 3. counter, mark.
   marcamos dois ~s we scored two goals (ftb.).
tento (III) s. m. (S. Braz.) leather thong or lash (especially for farm uses).
tento-da-carolina s. m. (pl. **tentos-da-carolina**) (bot.) bad tree, Barbados pride, coralwood (Adenanthera pavonina).
tento-pequeno s. m. (pl. **tentos-pequenos**) (bot.) Indian licorice.

tentório s. m. (mil.) tent, field shed.
tênue adj. m. + f. tenuous: 1. fine, subtil, fragile, thin, slender; easy. 2. small, little, minute. 3. weak, feeble, faint. 4. insignificant, trifling, petty. 5. aethereal, airy, rarefied. ‖ ~mente adv. tenuously.
tenuidade s. f. tenuousness, tenuity: 1. subtlety, slenderness, thinness. 2. smallness, minuteness. 3. weakness, frailness. 4. insignificance.
tenuifloro adj. tenuiflorous, having small flowers or blossoms.
tenuifoliado adj. (bot.) tenuifolious.
tenuípede adj. m. + f. (zool.) tenuipede.
tenuirrostro adj. (zool.) tenuirostral.
tenuta s. f. (mus.) note with a tenuto mark.
tenuto adv. (mus.) tenuto.
teobromina s. f. (chem.) theobromine.
teocal s. m. (pl. -ais) (archaeol.) teocalli.
teocracia s. f. theocracy: government by a sacerdotal class.
teocrata s. m. + f. theocrat.
teocrático adj. theocratic, theocratical. ‖ **teocraticamente** adv. theocratically.
teocratizar v. to give a theocratic form to.
teodicéia s. f. theodicy.
teodolito s. m. theodolite: surveying instrument used for measuring angles.
teofonia s. f. theophany.
teofrastácea s. f. any shrub or tree of the family Theophrastaceae.
teogonia s. f. theogony.
teogônico adj. theogonic.
teologastro s. m. theologaster.
teologia s. f. 1. theology: science of religious beliefs; study of God and his relation to man. 2. religious system or doctrine. 3. theological works as a whole.
teológico adj. theological. ‖ **teologicamente** adv. theologically.
teologismo s. m. misuse of the theological doctrines; theologism.
teologizar v. to theologize: reason, discourse about theology.
teólogo s. m. theologian, theologician: 1. person skilled in theology. 2. student of or writer on theology.
teomancia s. f. theomancy: supposedly inspired divination.
teomania s. f. theomania: madness which makes the person believe to be God or to be inspired by Him.
teomaníaco s. m. person suffering from theomania. ‖ adj. theomaniac.
teomântico adj. theomantic: relating to theomancy.
teor s. m. 1. wording, text. 2. tenor: a) meaning, purport. b) (fig.) manner, way, mode, style. 3. (chem.) contents, proportion.
~ **alcoólico** alcohol contents. **do mesmo** ~ of the same tenor. **do seguinte** ~ to the following effect.
teorema s. m. (math.) theorem, proposition.
teorético adj. theoretic(al), abstract. ‖ **teoreticamente** adv. theoretically.
teoria (I) s. f. (also **teórica**) theory: 1. abstract knowledge based on speculation. 2. ism, doctrine, system of principles. 3. notion, concept; view, idea, hypothesis, assumption. 4. utopia, visionary or impractical system.
na ~ in the abstract. **na** ~ **é fácil, mas na prática?** very good in theory, but will it work?
teoria (II) s. f. 1. (Greek hist.) a delegation for games, to consult an oracle, or to offer sacrifices, etc. 2. persons moving in procession.
teórico s. m. 1. theoretician, doctrinaire. 2. (fig.) utopia. ‖ adj. theorical, speculative, abstract, doctrinaire. ‖ **teoricamente** adv. theoretically.

teorista s. m. + f. theorist.
teorizar v. to theorize, speculate; methodize.
teose s. f. deification.
teosinto s. m. (bot.) teosinte.
teosofia s. f. theosophy: 1. the philosophy. 2. the religious system founded in the U. S. A. in 1875.
teosófico adj. theosophic(al). ‖ **teosoficamente** adv. theosophically.
teosofismo s. m. theosophism.
teosofista s. m. + f. (also **teósofo** m.) theosophist.
tepe s. m. turret in the form of a wedge (to line a bastion).
tepidez s. f. tepidity, tepidness: 1. lukewarmness. 2. (fig.) half-heartedness, flabbiness.
tépido adj. (also **tepente** m. + f.) tepid: 1. lukewarm, slightly warm. 2. half-hearted, flabby, limp. ‖ **tepidamente** adv. tepidly.
tequila s. f. tequila: a Mexican liquor.
ter v. 1. to have, possess, own. 2. to hold, keep, occupy, retain, carry, contain. 3. to get, obtain, arrive to, receive. 4. to bear, beget, give birth to. 5. to judge, think, believe, consider. 6. ~**-se** a) hold or consider o. s., account or maintain o. s. b) to hold out, keep (one's position). ~ **amizade com** to be friends with. ~ **ares de** to look like. ~ **aversão a** to dislike. ~ **boa aceitação** to be well received, meet with approval, sell well. ~ **boa fama** to be well-spoken of. ~ **frio** to be (feel) cold. ~ **bom êxito** to succeed. ~ **bom nome** to enjoy a great reputation. ~ **cara de** to look like. ~ **com** to have to do with. ~ **confiança em** to confide in. ~ **comunicação** to communicate. ~ **em conta** to rate, consider. ~ **coragem** to dare. ~ **as costas quentes** to be supported by someone. ~ **cuidado** to be careful, take care, watch. ~ **direito a** to deserve, have a right to. ~ **dívidas ou obrigações** to owe. ~ **dúvida** to be in doubt, be uncertain. ~ **fé** to trust. ~ **inclinação para** to give to something, have an inclination towards. ~ **jeito** 1. to look like. 2. to be skilled, skilful. ~ **lugar** 1. to admit. 2. to happen. ~ **a mania de** to have a mania for, (coll.) be crazy about. ~ **mão** to deal (cards). ~ **medo de** to stand in fear of. ~ **em mente** to conceive, have in mind, bear in mind. ~ **muito que fazer** to have much to do. ~ **necessidade** to need. ~ **obrigação** to be obliged, must. ~ **pena de** to be sorry about or for. ~ **por** to consider, deem, judge. ~ **prazer em** to enjoy. ~ **pressa** to be in haste. ~ **pretensão sobre** to claim. ~ **relações com** 1. to be related to, regard. 2. to keep company, consort, take up with. ~ **a palavra de alguém** to have someone's word. ~ **que ir** to be obliged to go. ~ **sangue-frio** to be cold-blooded, cool as a cucumber. ~ **saudade de** to long for. ~ **sede** to be thirsty. ~ **sorte** to be lucky, succeed. ~ **tato** to be tactful. ~ **temor de** to stand in awe of. ~ **tendência para** to incline to. ~ **toda a certeza** 1. to be quite certain. 2. to be dead sure. ~ **uma telha de mais ou menos** to have a screw loose. ~ **em vista** to have in view. ~ **vontade de** to want, wish. ~**-se bem a cavalo** to sit well on horseback. ~**-se em pé** to stand, stand up. **tenha a bondade de me dizer** be so kind (as) to tell me. **tenha chegado** he will have arrived. **teremos chuva** we shall have rain. **eu tinha dúvidas a respeito** I entertained doubts as to. **teremos de esperar** we shall have to wait. **é tido como fracasso** it is written down a failure. **tem graça!** how nice! **eles têm esta mercadoria em estoque** they carry a stock of these goods. **tive notícias dele** I heard from him. **tenha paciência!** 1. be patient! 2. keep your bristles down! 3. take it easy! 4. wait and see! **tenho raiva dele** I am angry with him, (coll.) have it in for him. **você**

tem razão you are right. você não tem razão you are wrong. tenho-me por feliz I account myself happy. tenho de reunir os fatos I must get the facts together. ele teve sucesso he succeeded. eu poderia ter vindo I could have come. a criança teve um dente the child has cut a tooth. o livro teve muitas edições the book went into many editions. não ~ o que dizer to have nothing to say. não tem importância it does not matter. não temos nada com isso we have nothing to do with that. não tivemos nada que fazer we had too much time on our hands. não ~ nenhuma orientação to have nothing to go upon. não tem perigo don't you worry! não tem de que se queixar there is no reason for complaint. não ~ de seu to have nothing. quantos anos ela tem? how old is she? o que é que você tem? what ails you? o que deve ser feito? what is going to be done? que tem isso? what is the matter? ser tido em boa conta to be in great esteem, be esteemed.

teraíra s. m. (N. Braz., zool.) a small lizard.

terapeuta s. m. + f. therapeutist. 2. therapist.

terapêutica s. f. (also terapia) 1. therapeutics, art of healing. 2. therapy, treatment of diseases.
~ ocupacional (med.) occupational therapy.

terapêutico adj. therapeutic(al), curative, remedial. ‖ -amente adv. therapeutically.
ginástica -a hygienic gymnastics.

terapia s. f. therapy.

teratia s. f. (biol.) teratosis, monstrosity.

teratogenia s. f. (biol.) teratogeny: formation of monsters.

teratogênico adj. (biol.) teratogenic, teratoid. ‖ -amente adv. teratogenically.

teratologia s. f. (biol.) teratology, study of monsters and malformations.

teratológico adj. (biol.) teratological. ‖ teratologicamente adv. teratologically.

teratologista s. m. + f., teratólogo m. (biol.) teratologist.

teratoma s. f. (med.) teratoma, teratoid tumour.

teratopagia s. f. condition or state of Siamese twins.

teratoscopia s. f. divination based on the observation of events supposed to be miraculous.

térbio s. m. (chem.) terbium.

terça (ê) (I) s. f. 1. the third part. 2. tierce: a) (eccl.) office of the third hour. b) sequence of three cards (piquet). c) (mus.) third. 3. (archit.) purlin, purline. 4. (N. Braz.) a certain liquid measure.

terça (ê) (II) s. f. aphaeresis of terça-feira Tuesday.

terçã s. f. (med.) tertian fever or ague (which recurs every third day).

terçado s. m. 1. short, broad sword. 2. (Braz.) a large knife; machete.

terçador s. m. intercessor; mediator. ‖ adj. interceding, mediative.

terça-feira s. f. (pl. terças-feiras) Tuesday.
~ gorda Shrove Tuesday.

terção s. m. (pl. -ões) shoot of vine left by the pruner.

terçar v. 1. to mix three things (ingredients). 2. to divide into three parts. 3. to cross swords, intercede, fight for. 4. to set something athwart, diagonally.
~ a capa to throw the coat over the shoulders.
~ armas to cross swords.

terceira s. f. 1. = terça. 2. mediatrix. 3. procuress. 4. (mus.) third, tierce.

terceiranista s. m. + f. third year student, upper-class student.

terceiro s. m. 1. third of an order or series (also persons). 2. third part. 3. mediator, intercessor. 4.

pimp, procurer. 5. member of the third order of St. Francis. ‖ adj. third. ‖ -amente adv. thirdly.
-a categoria third rate. -a classe third-class. -a via third copy (letter or document). em ~ lugar thirdly, in the third place. jornal de -a categoria trumpery paper. seguro contra ~s third party insurance. viajar em -a (motoring) to go in top-gear.

tercenário s. m. 1. person who receives the third part of an inheritance. 2. prebendary who gets the third part of the benefits of a prebend.

tercetar v. (obs.) to compose tercets.

terceto s. m. (mus.) 1. trio: composition for three voices or instruments or its performance. 2. tercet, triplet: metrical unit of three verses.

tércia s. f. (eccl., also terça) office of the third hour.

terciário adj. tertiary: 1. of the third degree, rank or formation. 2. (geol.) pertaining to the Tertiary. ‖ terciariamente adv. tertiarily.

tércio-décimo adj. (pl. tércio-décimos) thirteenth.

tercionário s. m. (med.) person suffering from tertian fever. ‖ adj. affected with a tertian fever.

terciopelo s. m. a variety of velvet.

terço (ê) s. m. (pl. terços) 1. third part of anything. 2. chaplet, string of beads (third part of the rosary). 3. (mil.) regiment. 4. middle part of a ship. 5. (S. Braz.) leather strip or bag.
rezar o ~ to tell one's beads.

terçó s. m. the youngest child in a family, nestling.

terçol s. m. (pl. -óis) (med.) sty(e), eyesore.

terebintáceo adj. terebinthine, of or similar to turpentine.

terebinteno s. m. (chem.) terebenthene, pinene.

terebintina s. f. 1. turpentine. 2. (Braz., pop.) fire-water, rum.

terebintinar v. prepare or mix with turpentine.

terebinto s. m. (bot.) terebinth.

térebra s. m. (zool.) terebra.

terebrante adj. m. + f. 1. perforating, boring, drilling. 2. piercing (pain). ‖ -mente adv. piercingly.

terebrar v. to terebrate, bore with a gimlet, pierce, perforate, drill; penetrate.

terecaí s. m. (Braz., zool.) a species of turtle.

teredo s. m. (ent.) teredo, shipworm, pileworm, borer.

teremembé s. m. + f. (Braz.) Indian of the Teremembé tribe. ‖ adj. of or relating to the Teremembés.

teremim s. m. (pl. ins) theremin: electromagnetic musical instrument invented by the Russian Theremin.

terém-terém s. m. (pl. terém-teréns) (Braz., ornith.) terutero, teruteru.

tereno s. m. (Braz., ornith., also gaturamo-rei) a Euphonia.

teréns s. m. pl. (N. Braz.) furniture and household utensils.

terereca s. m. + f. (Braz.) gossip, braggart, big talker. ‖ adj. talkative, gossipy; unsteady, inconstant.

teres s. m. pl. possessions, riches, means, property.

tereterê s. m. (N. Braz.) clayey soil, muddy ground.

tereticaude adj. m. + f. (zool.) tereticaudate.

teretifoliado adj. (bot.) teretifolious.

teretiforme adj. m. + f. teretiform.

teretirrostro adj. (zool.) teretirostrate.

teréu-teréu s. m. (pl. teréu-teréus) (Braz., ornith., also quero-quero) a species of lapwing.

tergal adj. m. + f. (pl. -ais) (zool.) tergal, tergant, dorsal.

tergeminado adj. (bot.) tergeminate. ‖ -amente adv. tergeminately.

tergêmino adj. trifid; threefold. ‖ -amente adv. threefoldly.

tergito s. m. (zool.) tergite: the dorsal plate of a segment of an arthropod.

tergiversação s. f. (pl. **-ões**) tergiversation, prevarication, vacillation; subterfuge.

tergiversador s. m. tergiversator, prevaricator, shuffler. ‖ adj. (also **tergiversante** m. + f.) tergiversating, shuffling.

tergiversar v. to tergiversate, prevaricate, shuffle; quibble, wriggle, flinch, shift.

tergo s. m. (zool.) tergum, tergite, back.

teriacal adj. m. + f. (pl. **-ais**) theriacal: relating to theriac(a).

teriaga s. f. theriac(a): 1. antidote against poison or a poisonous animal's bite. 2. household medicine. 3. treacle: a sort of syrup.

teringoá s. f. (Braz., ent.) a species of sylvan bee.

termal adj. m. + f. (pl. **-ais**) thermal. ‖ **~mente** thermally.

termântico adj. exciting, stimulating; warming.

termas s. f. pl. thermae: 1. thermal baths. 2. hot springs, thermal springs. 3. public baths in ancient Rome.

termelétrica s. f. thermoelectric.

termeletricidade s. f. thermoelectricity: electricity produced by heat.

termelétrico adj. thermoelectric. ‖ **termeletricamente** adv. thermoelectrically.

termestesia s. f. thermestesia: sensitiveness to heat.

termia s. f. (phys.) thermal unit.

termiatria s. f. therapeutics by means of thermal baths.

térmico adj. thermic: 1. relating to thermal springs or baths. 2. relating to heat. ‖ **termicamente** adv. thermically.

garrafa **-a** vacuum bottle. **refinação de metais por processos ~s** thermal refining. **unidade -a** 1. heat unit. 2. thermal unit. **valor ~** thermal power.

termidor s. m. (hist.) Thermidor: eleventh month of the first French republic.

termidoriano s. m. (hist.) Thermidorian. ‖ adj. Thermidorian: relating to the occurrences on 9 Thermidor, 1794.

terminação s. f. (pl. **-ões**) 1. termination, end, finish. 2. expiration, conclusion. 3. extremity, final part. 4. ending (of a word), inflection, suffix.
~ falsa enjambment.

terminal s. m. (pl. **-ais**) (electr.) terminal (plate C 9). ‖ adj. m. + f. 1. terminal, terminating. 2. limiting, limitative. ‖ **~mente** adv. terminally.

estação **~** terminal station.

terminante adj. m. + f. terminative, conclusive, ending; categorical, decisive, definite. ‖ **~mente** adv. terminatively, utterly.

terminar v. 1. to terminate, bring to an end, end, finish, close, conclude, complete. 2. to expire. 3. (fig.) to settle. 4. to limit, bound, set boundaries, restrict.
~ com to end up by, to abut. **~ em** (gram.) to end in. **~ por** to terminate by. **não se lastima o que bem termina** all's well that ends well.

terminativo adj. terminative, terminational. ‖ **-amente** adv. terminatively.

término s. m. terminus: 1. terminal. 2. termination, ending, conclusion. 3. limit, boundary, landmark.

terminologia s. f. terminology: terms peculiar to a certain branch of business or science, nomenclature.

terminológico adj. terminological. ‖ **terminologicamente** terminologically.

térmita, térmite s. f. (ent.) termite, white ant.

termo s. m. Thermos bottle, vacuum bottle.

termo (ê) s. m. 1. term: a) limit, limitation. b) boundary, landmark. c) time limit, span, period, spell, duration. d) (jur.) tenor, text, stipulation. e) word, vocable, expression. f) (logics) word or group of words of a syllogism. g) (math.) member of a

fraction, proportion, etc. 2. termination, end, finish, ending, expiration. 3. surroundings, neighbourhood (of a city). 4. **~s** manners, ways, behaviour, deportment, conduct. 5. (Braz.) death rattle.
~ médio average, median, ordinary. **~ náutico** sea-term. **~ técnico** technical term. **com bons ~s** kindly, obligingly. **com maus ~s** roughly, unkindly. **dar ~s** to set bounds, put an end, stop. **dar ~ a alguém** to give a person time. **em ~s** within limits; in due form, in order. **meio ~** moderation, medium. **pôr ~ a** to put an end to, to make an end, stop. **em que ~s está o negócio?** how is business? how are things running?

termobarômetro s. m. (phys.) thermo-barometer.

termocautério s. m. thermo-cautery.

termodinâmica s. f. (phys.) thermodynamics, branch of physics dealing with the relation between heat and mechanical work.

termodinâmico adj. thermodynamic. ‖ **termodinamicamente** adv. thermodynamically.

termoeletricidade s. f. (phys.) thermoelectricity, electricity produced by heat.

termoelétrico adj. (phys.) thermoelectrical. ‖ **termoeletricamente** thermoelectrically.

termoestesia s. f. (phys.) = termestesia.

termofilia s. f. thermophily.

termogênese s. f. (biol.) thermogenesis, production of heat (in the human body and in animals).

termógrafo s. m. thermograph.

termografia s. f. thermography.

termologia s. f. branch of physics dealing with heat.

termológico adj. (phys.) thermological. ‖ **termologicamente** adv. thermologically.

termomagnético adj. thermomagnetic. ‖ **termomagneticamente** adv. thermomagnetically.

termomagnetismo s. m. (phys.) thermomagnetism, magnetism produced by heat.

termometria s. f. (phys.) thermometry, heat measuring.

termométrico adj. thermometric. ‖ **termometricamente** adv. thermometrically.

termômetro s. m. thermometer: 1. instrument to measure temperature (plate T 9). 2. (fig.) indicator of conditions, qualities, standings.

termomultiplicador s. m. (phys.) thermopile, thermoelectric battery.

termonuclear adj. m. + f. thermonuclear.

termopenetração s. f. (pl. **-ões**) (med.) diathermy.

termoplástico adj. (phys.) thermoplastic. ‖ **termoplasticamente** adv. thermoplastically.

termoquímica s. f. (phys., chem.) thermochemistry.

termoscopia s. f. (phys.) thermoscopy, measure of heat.

termoscópico adj. thermoscopic. ‖ **termoscopicamente** adv. thermoscopically.

termoscópio s. m. (phys.) thermoscope, instrument for indicating differences of temperature.

termossifão s. f. (pl. **-ões**) (phys.) thermosiphon.

termostático adj. (phys.) thermostatic. ‖ **termostaticamente** adv. thermostatically.

termóstato s. m. thermostate, instrument that regulates temperature.

termotaxia s. f. (biol.) thermotaxis, reaction to heat (organism).

termoterapia s. f. (med.) thermotherapy: treatment by heat.

termotipia s. f. (phys.) thermotype.

ternado adj. (bot.) ternate, arranged in groups of three. ‖ **-amente** adv. ternately.

ternário adj. ternary, ternal, consisting of three. ‖ **ternariamente** adv. ternally.

tempo **~** (mus.) triple proportion.

terneirada, terneiragem s. f.. (S. Braz.) herd of calves.

terneiro s. m. (Braz.) calf.

terno (I) s. m. 1. ternary, triplet, trio; a group of three, threesome, triad, tierce. 2. card. or die with three spots. 3. a men's suit consisting of three pieces. 4. (S. Braz.) team of three pairs of oxen. 5. (fig.) group, band.

terno (II) adj. tender, endearing, gentle, delicate, mild; loving, amorous, touching. || **-amente** adv. tenderly.

ternura s. f. tenderness, windness, sensitiveness, gentleness, attention; dearness, love, affection.

tero-tero s. m. (pl. **tero-teros**) (Braz., ornith., also **quero-quero**) a species of lapwing.

terpina s. f. (chem.) terpene, terpin.

terra s. f. 1. earth, world, globe. 2. land, ground, soil, clod; shore, coast. 3. moulding clay; dust, dirt; loam, mud, mire. 4. native land, birthplace, country, motherland, nation. 5. domains, territories. 6. landed property, estate.
~ **alcalina** (chem.) alkaline earth. ~ **arada** ploughed field (plate A 4). ~ **arável** arable land, plough land (plate A 4). ~ **argilosa** clay, clay bottom. ~**s estrangeiras**, ~ **alheia** foreign land, outland. ~**s extensas** broad acres. ~ **lavada** swampland. ~ **firme** terra firma: a) land not covered by water. b) mainland. ~ **inculta** waste (land). ~ **de infusórios** infusorial earth. ~ **maravilhosa** wonderland. ~ **natal** native land, birthplace, motherland. ~ **de ninguém** no man's land. **terra pastural** pastoral land. ~ **de planta** forming ground. **Terra da Promissão** Promised Land. ~ **roxa** (Braz.) rich red soil for coffee planting. ~ **safada** (S. Braz.) exhausted land, impoverished land. **Terra Santa** Holy Land, Palestine. ~ **de Siena** sienna. ~ **de sombra** umber. ~ **vegetal** humus. ~ **virgem** virgin land. **avistar** ~ (naut.) to make land. **chapa de** ~ (tech.) earth plate. **cheio de** ~ (Braz., pop.) luxurious, rich. **debaixo da** ~ under the sod, underground. **de** ~ **em** ~ from one country to another. **descer à** ~ to land, go on land, go ashore. **deitar** ~ **nos olhos de alguém** to throw dust in a person's eyes. **em direção à** ~ ashore, earthward(s). **um filho da** ~ a son of the soil. **fio (de)** ~ (radio) ground wire. **forças de** ~ (mil.) land forces. **largar** ~ **para favas,** **meter** ~ **em meio** (Braz., pop.) to escape, run away, take to one's heels. **minha** ~ **é o Brasil** I was born in Brazil. **na** ~ aboveground, on the earth, under the sun. **preso à** ~ earth-bound. **proprietário de** ~**s** territorial owner. **saltar em** ~ to land, come ashore. **viajar por** ~ to travel by land.

terra-a-terra adj. m. + f., sg. + pl. pedestrian, trivial, common, popular, dull.

terraço s. m. (also, but less used **terrado**) terrace: 1. roof terrace, platform, flat roof. 2. (geol.) raised shore line.

terracota s. f. terracotta: 1. reddish-brown pottery. 2. object made of this material.

terral s. m. (pl. **-ais**) **terralão** (pl. **-ões**) land wind, land breeze. || adj. m. + f. blowing from the land.

terramicina s. f. (pharm.) terramycin.

terramoto s. m. (less used form of **terremoto**) earthquake, tremor of the earth.

terra-nova s. m. + f. (pl. **terra-novas** and **terras-novas**) Newfoundland (dog).

terrantês s. m. (pl. **-eses**) a species of green grape. || adj. native, natural.

terrão s. m. (pl. **-ões**) (also **torrão**) clod, lump of soil.

terraplenagem s. f. (pl. **-ens**) earthwork, embankment, levelling of the ground.

terraplenar v. to embank, fill with earth, level, make even (ground).

terrapleno s. m. 1. rampart, embankment. 2. (fort.) terreplein. 3. levelled ground. 4. terrace, platform.

terráqueo adj. terraqueous: consisting of land and water.

terreal adj. m. + f. (pl. **-ais**) (also **terrenal**) terrestrial, pertaining to the earth, earthy; mundane, worldly. || ~**mente** adv. terrestrially.

terreiro (I) s. m. 1. yard. 2. courtyard, public place, square. 3. terrace, roof terrace. 4. (Braz.) place where fetichism is practised.
tirar a ~ to provoke, challenge.

terreiro (II) adj. (also **térreo**) 1. earthy. 2. terreous. 3. even, on ground level.

terremoto s. m. earthquake.

terrenho adj. terrestrial: 1. of or pertaining to the earth. 2. mundane, worldly.

terreno s. m. 1. terrain, ground, soil, glebe, land; site, groundplot. 2. (geol.) formation. 3. (fig.) branch of activities, matter, subject. || adj. terrestrial, worldly, mundane, earthy, terrene. || **-amente** adv. terrestrially.
~ **acidentado** uneven land. ~ **arborizado** woodland. ~ **aurífero** gold field. ~ **para construção** ground plot, building site. ~ **cultivado** plantation, tilled land. ~ **pantanoso** moorland. ~ **terciário** (geol.) Tertiary formation. ~ **úmido** weeping ground. ~ **undante** undulating ground. **ceder** ~ to give way. **ganhar** ~ to gain ground. **perder** ~ to lose ground. **ele pisa em** ~ **perigoso** he skates over thin ice. **preparar** ~ to break land. **sondar** ~ to feel one's way.

terrento adj. earthy, earth-coloured; dim, lusterless.

térreo adj. 1. earthy, terrestrial. 2. even with the ground, low. || **terreamente** adv. earthly; downstairs. **andar** ~ ground floor. **casa -a** a one-story house.

terrestre adj. m. + f. terrestrial, earthbound, earthy, mundane, worldly.
globo ~ terrestrial globe. **magnetismo** ~ terrestrial magnetism.

terréu s. m. waste land, fallow land.

terribilidade s. f. terribleness, fearfulness, awfulness, tremendousness, dreadfulness.

terriço s. m. (agric.) humus, decomposed vegetal or animal matter.

terrícola s. m. + f. animal that lives in/on the earth. || adj. terricolous, living in/on the earth.

terrier s. m. terrier (dog) (plate C 3).

terrificante adj. m. + f. (also **terrífico** m.) terrific, terrifying, frightful, horrifying. || ~**mente** adv. terrifically.

terrificar v. 1. to terrify, horrify, frighten, appal. 2. to startle, alarm, scare, intimidate.

terrígeno adj. terrigenous, earthborn, from the earth.

terrina s. f. tureen, vessel from which soup is served.

terriola s. f. hamlet, small village, settlement, cluster of country houses.

terríssono adj. frightening (noise, sound).

territorial adj. m. + f. (pl. **-ais**) territorial, pertaining to a territory. || ~**mente** adv. territorially.
limite ~ territorial boundary. **propriedade** ~ landed interest.

territorialidade s. f. territoriality: territorial rights, status or quality.

território s. m. territory, land, country, dominion; region, area, district; circumscription.

terrível adj. m. + f. (pl. **-íveis**) 1. terrific, terrible, awful, awesome, horrible, frightful, dreadful, fearsome, dire, shocking, grim, grisly, hideous. 2. formidable, extraordinary. || **terrivelmente** adv. terribly.

terrívomo adj. expelling or vomiting earth.

terroada s. f. (also **torroada**) a number of clods; blow with a clod.

terror s. m. 1. terror, horror, awe, fright, fear, dread, consternation, panic, dismay. 2. (hist.) Terror: period of the French revolution.

terrorismo s. m. terrorism; government of terror.

terrorista s. m. + f. 1. terrorist, (U. S. A., sl.) weatherman. 2. (fig.) pessimist. ‖ adj. terroristic. **regime** ~ reign of terror.

terrorizar v. (also **aterrorizar**) to terrorize, frighten, terrify; alarm.

terroso adj. = **terrento**.

terrulento adj. 1. earthen, earth-coloured, dull. 2. (fig.) bile, base, worthless, despicable.

terso adj. 1. clear, neat, concise. 2. polished, bright, brilliant, smooth. 3. (fig.) correct, exact, accurate. 4. vernacular, native.

tersol s. m. (pl. **-óis**) (eccl.) a priest's napkin or towel used during the mass at the lavabo.

tertúlia s. f. family party, meeting, social gathering; literary assembly.

tesão s. m. (pl. **-ões**) 1. tension, strained condition. 2. stiffness, rigidity, rigour, toughness, severity.

tesar v. (also **entesar**) to toughen, stiffen, stretch, make taut.

tese s. f. thesis: 1. proposition. 2. subject for a composition. 3. dissertation. 4. hypothesis. 5. discussion of a thesis.
em ~ generally speaking.

teso (ê) (I) s. m. (pl. **tesos**) 1. steep hill, steep. 2. hilltop. 3. (Braz.) a raised ground not reached by the flood.

teso (ê) (II) adj. (pl. **tesos**) (f. **tesa**, pl. **tesas**) 1. tense, taut, tight, stretched, drawn, tough. 2. stiff, inflexible, inelastic, rigid; starched. 3. hard, solid, firm. 4. strong, vigorous; impetuous, violent, vehement. 5. (S. Braz., sl.) broke, ruined, penniless. 6. steep.

tesoura s. f. (also **tesoira**) 1. scissors, a pair of scissors, shears (plates A 5, T 1). 2. cross reins of a pair of draught animals. 3. (fig.) backbiter, slanderer. 4. (archit.) truss, woodwork of a roof. 5. (ornith.) a flycatcher. 6. (zool.) a crab of the family Ocypodidae. ~ **de alavanca** (tech.) alligator shears. ~ **de caranguejo** claw (as of a lobster). ~ **de podar** pruning shears (plate J 2). ~ **de unhas** nail scissors.

tesourada s. f. (also **tesoirada**) 1. cut or stroke with the scissors. 2. cutting or biting remark, slander, calumny.

tesoura-do-campo s. f. (pl. **tesouras-do-campo**) (ornith.) yetapa.

tesourão s. m. (pl. **-ões**) (mech., also **tesoirão**) 1. large scissors; shearing anvil. 2. (ornith.) swallow-tailed kite.

tesourar v. (also **tesoirar**) 1. to scissor, cut with scissors; shear. 2. to backbite, slander, calumniate.

tesouraria s. f. (also **tesoiraria**) 1. treasury, treasure house. 2. exchequer. 3. treasureship, a treasurer's office. 4. burse, bursey.

tesoureiro s. m. (also **tesoireiro**) 1. treasurer. 2. chamberlain (of a city).
~ **da universidade** bursar.

tesourinha s. f. (also **tesoirinha**) 1. small scissors. 2. tendril, clasper. 3. (Braz., ornith.) a species of chatterer.

tesouro s. m. (also **tesoiro**) 1. treasure, riches, wealth, chest, purse, hoard. 2. treasury, exchequer, public purse. 3. (fig.) person or thing of great value. ~ **de conhecimentos** stock of knowledge. **a menina é um** ~ the girl is a treasure. **fazer** ~**s** to hoard riches. **meu** ~**!** my treasure!

tessálico adj. Thessalian.

tessálio, téssalo s. m. Thessalian: native or inhabitant of Thessaly (district in ancient Greece). ‖ adj. Thessalian: of or pertaining to Thessaly.

tessalonicense s. m. + f. Thessalonian: inhabitant or native of Thessalonica (ancient name of Salonika — Greece). ‖ adj. Thessalonian: of or pertaining to Thessalonica.

tesselário s. m. 1. mosaicist. 2. person skilled in mosaic decorations. 3. dice maker.

téssera s. f. (Roman hist.) tessera: 1. tablet used to transmit a commander's order. 2. a sort of ivory die. 3. (rel.) objects like dice serving as sign or token among the first Christians.

tesserário s. m. (hist.) messenger (bearer of a tessera) among the Roman armies.

tessitura s. f. 1. (mus.) tessitura, compass, range of a voice or instrument. 2. (fig.) contexture, structure.

testa s. f. 1. forehead, brow (plates C 12, 18). 2. (bot.) testa, epistern. 3. front: a) (mil.) van, head. b) (fig.) front, forepart, face, head, nose (plate P 13).
~ **de esquadra** (naut.) leading vessel, capital ship. ~ **de ferro** (fig.) dummy, figurehead, man of straw. **comer com a** ~ (N. Braz., fig.) to want or long for eagerly. **estar à** ~ **de** to be at the head of. **pôr-se à** ~ **de** to place o.s. at the head of.

testaça s. f. (pop.) large forehead, a high brow.

testáceo adj. 1. testacian, testacious: of shells, having a shell. 2. brick red.

testaçudo adj. headstrong, self-willed, obstinate, stubborn. ‖ **-amente** adv. stubbornly, headstrongly.

testada s. f. 1. stretch of a street or road facing a house. 2. butt, sudden blow with the head. 3. (Braz.) nonsense, foolishness, blunder.
varrer a ~ to decline responsability, declare o. s. innocent.

testa-de-ferro s. m. (pl. **testas-de-ferro**) figurehead, man of straw, front, dummy.

testador s. m. (also **testante** m. + f.) 1. testator, person who makes a will, bequeather. 2. ~**a** f. testatrix. ‖ adj. testate: having made a will.

testamental adj. m. + f. (pl. **-ais**) testamental, testamentary. ‖ ~**mente** adj. testamentally.

testamentaria s. f. 1. executorship. 2. the execution of a will. 3. administration of a legacy.

testamentário s. m. heir by will, legatee. ‖ adj. testamentarious, testamentary.

testamenteiro s. m. executor of a will. ‖ adj. making testaments.

testamento s. m. will, testament.
~ **autêntico** authentic testament. ~ **místico** sealed will. ~ **nuncupativo** nuncupative will. ~ **hológrafo** holographic will. **abertura de um** ~ reading of a will. **deserdar por** ~ to disinherit by will. **fazer o seu** ~ to make one's will. **o Novo Testamento** (bib.) The New Testament. **o Velho Testamento** (bib.) the Old Testament.

testar (I) v. 1. to make a will, bequeath, legate, devise. 2. to testify, affirm, declare, give evidence, witness.

testar (II) v. (Port., prov.) to stiffen, stretch, make taut.

testavilhar v. (S. Braz.) 1. to stumble, trip; slip, slide. 2. (fig.) to vacillate, sway, waver, oscillate; become neglectful, disregard.

teste (I) s. m. 1. test, examination, research, trial. 2. list of questions for testing.

teste (II) s. f. (obs.) witness.

testectomia s. f. (surg.) castration, gelding.

testeira s. f. 1. front, forepart. 2. frontage. 3. frontpiece, front, browband of a harness (plates A 12, C 12). 4. headband, white cloth that covers a nun's forehead. 5. head of a table or box. 6. gable (end).

testemunha s. f. 1. witness, evidence. 2. testimony; attestation; proof. 3. ~**s** landmarks.

~ **auricular** earwitness, auricular witness. ~ **de defesa** witness of defence. ~ **falsa** false witness. **Testemunhas de Jeová** (rel.) Jehovah's Witnesses. ~ **de vista** eyewitness. **banco das** ~**s** witness-box.

testemunhador s. m. witness. ‖ adj. bearing or giving evidence, witness; testifying, witnessing.

testemunhal adj. m. + f. (pl. **-ais**) testimonial.

testemunhar v. 1. to witness, bear witness, testify, give evidence, attest, confirm. 2. to serve as witness. 3. to prove, depose, evince, show. 4. to see, notice, watch. ~ **confiança** to show confidence.

testemunhável adj. m. + f. (pl. **-áveis**) 1. testimonial; evidential, confirmatory, corroborative. 2. credible, believable, trustworthy.

testemunho s. m. 1. testimony, proof, evidence, witness. 2. attest, attestation, report, testimonial certificate. 3. (geol.) hillocks left by erosion. **dar** ~ to bear witness. **em** ~ **de que** in witness whereof.

testico s. m. any of the sidepieces of a bow saw (plate S 2).

testicular adj. m. + f. (anat.) testicular, testiculate.

testículo s. m. (anat.) testicle: male sex gland, spermary.

testículo-de-cão s. m. (pl. **testículos-de-cão**) (bot.) male orchis (Orchis mascula), an orchid.

testificação s. f. (pl. **-ões**) 1. testification, testation, evidence, witness, attestation. 2. testifying.

testificador s. m., **testificante** m. + f. testificator, testifier, witness. ‖ adj. testifying.

testificar v. 1. to testify, bear witness, give evidence. 2. to certify, attest, declare. 3. to affirm, prove, depone.

testilha s. f. quarrel, brawl, dispute, discord, altercation, contention, strife, conflict.

testilhar v. to quarrel, brawl, dispute, altercate, contend, strive, wrangle.

testilho s. m. top of a box.

testo (I) adj. 1. firm, steady, determined, resolute. 2. unflinching, inflexible, stubborn. 3. serious, earnest. ‖ **-amente** adv. firmly.

testo (II) s. m. (N. Braz., pop.) blow, box, stroke.

testo (ê) s. m. 1. cover, lid, potlid. 2. skull, cranium of an ox. 3. sooty encrustment of a pot. 4. any of the side pieces of a handsaw (also **testico**). 5. (coll.) brains, wits.

testudinídeo s. m. (zool.) one of the Testudinidae, a family of turtles.

testudo adj. 1. large-headed. 2. (fig.) butt-headed, obstinate, stubborn, headstrong. ‖ **-amente** adv. stubbornly.

tesura s. f. 1. stiffness, firmness, tautness; rigidity, inflexibility. 2. vanity, conceit, self-esteem, pride, arrogance.

teta s. m. theta: the eighth letter of the Greek alphabet.

teta (ê) s. f. teat, tit, nipple; udder dug.

tetania s. f. (med.) tetany.

tetânico adj. (med.) tetanic. ‖ **-amente** adv. tetanically.

tetaniforme adj. m. + f. (med.) tetanuslike.

tetanizar v. to tetanize.

tétano s. m. (med.) tetanus; lockjaw, trismus.

tetas s. m. pl. milksop, unmanly fellow, weakling.

tête-à-tête s. m. (Fr.) tête-à-tête: a private conversation between two persons.

tetéia s. f. 1. charm, trinket; trifle. 2. (Braz.): a) toy, nice thing. b) beloved person.

tetérrimo adj. 1. most terrible, hideous, atrocious, abominable, dreadful. 2. very dark (as clouds).

teteté adj. m. + f. (Braz.) relapsing, backsliding, backfalling. ‖ adv. frequently.

tetéu s. m. (Braz., ornith., also **quero-quero**) a species of lapwing.

tetéu-de-savana s. m. (pl. **tetéus-de-savana**) (Braz.) a wading bird.

tetim s. m. (pl. **-ins**) a sort of cement made of brick powder, lime and oil.

tetipoteira s. f. (bot.) a species of grape.

teto s. m. (also **tecto**) 1. ceiling, roof (plates A 1, B 15, D 4). 2. (by extension) shelter, cover, refuge. 3. (pop.) good sense, judgement. 4. (fig.) limit (prices, raisings). ~ **absoluto** (aeron.) absolute ceiling. **preço** ~ top price. **sem** ~ without a roof over one's head. **sociedade** ~ holding company.

tetrabrânquio adj. (zool.) tetrabranchiate.

tetracampeão s. m. four-time champion. ‖ adj. of or relating to four-time championship.

tetrácero adj. (zool.) having four antennae or feelers.

tetraciclo adj. (bot.) tetracyclic: having four cycles or whorls.

tetracloreto s. m. (chem.) tetrachloride.

tetracolo, **tetracólon** (Greek and Latin prosody) tetracolon.

tetracordo s. m. (mus.) tetrachord: 1. ancient lyre with four strings. 2. scale of four tones forming half an octave.

tetradáctilo, **tetradátilo** adj. (zool.) tetradactyl: having four digits.

tetraédrico adj. (geom.) tetrahedral.

tetraedro s. m. (geom.) tetrahedron: solid bounded by four plane faces.

tetraexaedro s. m. tetrahexahedron: solid bounded by twenty-four faces.

tetrafilo adj. (bot.) tetraphyllous: having four leaves.

tetrágino adj. (bot.) tetragynous: having four pistils.

tetragonal adj. m. + f. (pl. **-ais**) (geom.) tetragonal. **sistema** ~ tetragonal system.

tetragônico adj. tetragonal, four-sided.

tetrágono s. m. (geom.) tetragon: a plane figure having four angles.

tetragrama s. m. tetragram: a word of four letters. ‖ adj. four-lettered.

tetralogia s. f. tetralogy: 1. four dramatic works of the ancient Greek theatre: three tragedies and a satyric piece. 2. (mus.) a series of four operas.

tetrâmero s. m. a beetle of the order Coleoptera. ‖ adj. tetrameral, tetramerous: divided into four parts.

tetrâmetro s. m. tetrameter: Greek or Latin verse consisting of four feet, galliambic.

tetrandro adj. (bot.) tetrandrous: having four stamens.

tetraneto s. m. great-great-grandson.

tetrapétalo adj. (bot.) tetrapetalous: having four petals.

tetrápode adj. m. + f. (zool.) tetrapod: having four feet or members.

tetráptero adj. (zool., bot.) tetrapterous: having four wings or appendages like wings.

tetrarca s. m. tetrarch: governor of the fourth part of an ancient Roman province.

tetrarquia s. f. tetrarchy: 1. district governed by a tetrarch; a tetrarch's office. 2. subdivision of an ancient Greek phalanx.

tetrarritmo adj. tetrarhythmical: having four rhythms.

tetraspermo adj. (bot.) tetraspermous: having four seeds.

tetrassépalo adj. (bot.) tetrasepalous: having four sepals (calix leaves).

tetrassílabo adj. (gram.) tetrasyllabic: having four syllables.

tetrástico s. m. tetrastich: a poem of four lines or verses. ‖ adj. tetrastichal: having four lines.

tetrastilo s. m. (archit.) tetrastyle: a building, etc. with four pillars. ‖ adj. tetrastylous: having four pillars.

tetravalente adj. m. + f. tetravalent: having a valence of four.

tetravô s. m. great-great-great-grandfather.

tetravó s. f. great-great-great-grandmother.

tetricidade s. f. 1. austerity, sternness, gruesomeness. 2. sadness, gloominess, sorrowfulness.

tétrico adj. 1. sad. 2. gloomy, mournful, sorrowful. 3. macabre, funereal, gruesome, awful, horrible. ‖ **tetricamente** adv. sadly, awfully.

tetro adj. 1. black, dark, gloomy, dim, dusky, somber. 2. horrible, terrible, frightful, dreadful. ‖ **-amente** adv. darkly, horribly.

tetrodo s. m. (electr.) tetrode.

tetudo adj. having a large breast.

teu (f. **tua**) 1. poss. adj. your: thy. 2. poss. pron. yours; thine.

os ~s your relatives, your family, your people. **é meu? não, é teu!** is it mine? no, it is yours!

téu s. m. (Braz., ornith., also **tovaca** f.) an ant thrush.

teúba s. f. (Braz.) a small yellow bee.

têucrio s. m. (also **carvalhinha** f.) plant of the speedwell family.

teúdo adj. kept, maintained.

teurgia s. f. theurgy, miracle; sorcery, magic.

teúrgico adj. theurgic(al), magic, miraculous.

teurgista s. m. + f. theurgist, magician, sorcerer, wizard.

teutão s. m. (pl. **-ões**) Teuton: member of an ancient German tribe. ‖ adj. Teutonic: of or relating to the Teutons.

téu-téu s. m. (pl. **téu-téus**) (ornith., also **quero-quero**) a species of lapwing.

teuto adj. Teutonic, German.

teuto-brasileiro s. m. (pl. **teuto-brasileiros**) Brazilian of German descent.

teutônico adj. Teutonic; German.

ordem -a Teutonic Order.

tevê s. f. TV.

têxtil adj. m. + f. (pl. **-eis**) textile, woven.

indústria ~ textile industry, cloth manufacture.

fibra de celulose para uso ~ textile pulp.

texto s. m. text: 1. the very words of an author. 2. the printed words of a book etc. 3. theme of a sermon based on a verse or passage of the Bible. **~ falso** pseudograph. **~ original** original text. **~ revisto** revised text.

textual adj. m. + f. (pl. **-ais**) textual, literal, verbal. ‖ **~mente** adv. textually.

textuário s. m. textuary, text-book.

textura s. f. 1. texture, fabric, weft. 2. structure, arrangement of parts in a whole. 3. grain.

texugo s. m. 1. (zool.) badger, brock. 2. (pop.) corpulent or well-fed person.

tez s. f. complexion, colour of the skin; cutis, epidermis.

~ rosada rosy complexion. **de ~ clara** fair-complexioned.

ti pron. (after prepositions) you, yourself; (poet.) thee. **a ti, de ti, para ti** to you, from you, for you.

tia s. f. 1. aunt. 2. (pop.) old maid. 3. (sl.) procuress.

~-avó great aunt. **ficar para ~, ficar no caritó** to remain unmarried.

tíade s. f. bacchante.

tiambo s. m. (Braz., bot.) sugar-cane.

tiamina s. f. (biochem.) thiamin(e), vitamin B 1.

tianha s. f. 1. (Braz., pop.) stubbornness, obstinacy; bad manners; 2. fury, rage, madness.

tiaporanga s. f. (pop.) drunkenness.

tiara s. f. 1. the Pope's diadem or triple crown. 2. (fig.) papal dignity.

tiã-tiã s. m. (pl. **tiã-tiãs**) (Braz., ornith.) a seedeater.

tiba s. f. (Braz.) place where persons are gathered or where many things are accumulated. ‖ adj. m. + f. 1. full, replete. 2. large, big, great, important. ‖ **~mente** adv. largely.

tibe interj. (N. Braz.) expression of repulse or contempt.

tibetano s. m. Tibetan, inhabitant or native of Tibet. ‖ adj. Tibetan: of or relating to Tibet.

tíbia s. f. (anat.) 1. tibia, shinbone. 2. fife, flute, a shepherd's flute.

tibial adj. m. + f. (pl. **-ais**) (anat.) tibial.

tibiez, tibieza s. f. lukewarmness, indolence, slackness, halfheartedness, indifference, remissness.

tíbio adj. 1. tepid. 2. (fig.) lukewarm, indolent, indifferent, slothful, sluggish. ‖ **tibiamente** adv. tepidly.

tibira s. f. (N. Braz.) 1. cow that yields but little milk. 2. (Braz.) an unskilled milker.

tiborna s. f. 1. hot bread soaked in oil. 2. (fig.) mixture, medley. 3. poor wine. 4. (bot.) a species of frangipani. 5. residue of distillation.

tibornice s. f. (pop.) medley, hodgepodge.

tibuna s. m. (Braz., also **boca-de-barro**) a stingless bee.

tibungar v. (N. Braz.) to dive, plunge; sink, submerge.

tibungo s. m. thud, thumping; sound caused by a plunge into the water. ‖ interj. (N. Braz.) plop! plump! splash!

ticaca s. f. (Braz., pop., also **gambá** m.) 1. opossum. 2. worthless thing, trash.

tição s. m. (pl. **-ões**) 1. firebrand, brand, piece of burned wood, ember. 2. very tawny, dark person; (fig.) devil.

~ apagado (N. Braz., pop.) a Negro dressed in black. **~ do inferno** makebate; dirty person.

tico s. m. 1. a bit, bite, morsel, a little. 2. tic, twitch.

~ nervoso nervous tic.

tiçoada s. f. stroke or blow with a firebrand.

tiçoeiro s. m. poker: metal rod to stir the fire (plate L 1).

tiçonado adj. singed, burned, scorched; having black spots.

ticonha s. f. (Braz., ichth.) a species of ray.

tico-tico s. m. (pl. **tico-ticos**) 1. (Braz., ornith.) crown sparrow. 2. (fig.): a) a little thing or person, triple. b) elementary school.

serra ~ fret saw, scroll saw.

tico-tico-do-biri s. m. (pl. **tico-ticos-do-biri**) (ornith., also **cachimbó**) a spinetail.

ticuanga s. f. (N. Braz.) manioc cake made with coconut, chestnut and sugar.

ticuca s. f. (ornith., also **quicuca**) an owl.

ticum s. m. (pl. **-uns**) (Braz., also **tucum**) a palm tree.

ticuna s. f. (Braz., also **curare** m.) curare, curari: poison for fish extracted from a vine.

ticura s. f. (Braz., ent. also **tucura**) a species of grasshopper.

tido p. p. of **ter** 1. had, owned. 2. reputed, considered. **é ~ como bom** it is supposed to be good.

tié s. m. (Braz.) bird of the tanager family.

tietê, tietei s. m. (Braz., ornith.) a tanager.

tietinga s. m. (Braz., ornith.) magpie; shrike.

tifa s. f. (bot.) flag, cattail.

tifácea s. f. plant of the family Typhaceae.

tifáceo adj. (bot.) typhaceous: of or relating to the Typhaceae.

tífico adj. (med.) typhous, typhoid: relating to typhus or the typhoid fever.

tiflite s. f. (med.) typhlitis: inflammation of the caecum.

tiflografia s. f. Braille (system of printing for blind persons).

tiflógrafo s. m. instrument to print Braille characters.

tiflologia s. f. typhlology: science of instruction for blind persons.

tiflológico adj. typhlologic(al), relating to typhlology.

tiflólogo s. m. typhlologist.

tiflopídeos s. m. pl. (zool.) Typhlopidae, the blind snake family.

tifo s. m. (med. also **tifo abdominal**) typhoid fever.

~ **exantemático** typhus. ~ **icteróide** (also **febre amarela**) yellow fever.

tifóide adj. m. + f., **tifóideo** m. (med.) typhoid.

tifoso s. m. (med.) person suffering from typhus. ‖ adj. typhous.

tigela s. f. 1. bowl; cup, drinking vessel; porringer, dish (plates B 7, V 2). 2. a sort of clay saucer. 3. cup used for caoutchouc gathering. 4. (Braz.) measure equivalent to one litre.

de meia-~ mediocre, ordinary. **quebrar a** ~ (N. Braz.) to dress, wear or use something for the first time.

tigelada s. f. 1. a bowlful, kettleful. 2. a variety of pudding.

tigrado adj. spotted like a tiger, leopard or jaguar; tigerlike.

gato ~ tabby cat.

tigre s. m. 1. (zool.) tiger; f. tigress. 2. (fig.) cruel, ferocious or brutal person. 3. (ent.) tiger beetle. 4. (hist.) barrel for gathering feces. 5. (sl.) medical student of the first year; student who repeats a year more than once. ‖ adj. m. + f. tigerlike, spotted like a tiger, leopard or jaguar.

tigresa s. f. (Braz., zool.) tigress.

tigrino adj. tigrine, tigerish; bloodthirsty as a tiger. **-amente** adv. tigrinely.

tigüera, tiguera s. f. (Braz., agric.) harvested maize field; stubble field.

cair na ~ (S. Braz.) to disappear, be lost.

tijoleira s. f. 1. tile fragments for pavements, brickbat. 2. large brick.

tijoleiro s. m. brickmaker; bricklayer.

tijolo s. m. 1. brick (plate A 7). 2. a goldsmith's boring tool. 3. brick of candy or sweet. 4. (Braz., sl.) flirtation, flirting.

~ **assentado de comprido** stretcher (plate 7). ~ **de fecho** closer, king closer (bigger than half a brick) (plate A 7). ~ **furado** air brick. ~ **de Holanda** Dutch glazed tile. ~ **de paramento** facing brick, face brick. ~ **refratário** firebrick. ~ **travado** header. ~ **de turfa** peat brick. ~ **vitrificado** clinker. **construído de** ~**s** bricken, brick-built. **fazer** ~ (Braz., sl.) to flirt.

tijuca s. m. (Braz., ornith.) a whistler.

tijucada s. f., **tijucal** m. (pl. **-ais**) (Braz., also **tujucada**) morass, bog, swamp, slough.

tijuco s. m. morass, slough, mud, mire, ooze, bog, marsh, swamp.

fazer ~ to resort, go frequently to.

tijupá, tijupaba, tijupar s. m. (Braz., also **tajupá**) 1. Indian hut. 2. straw-roofed shack or hut. 3. (N. Braz.) awning of a canoe.

til s. m. (pl. **tis**) tilde, tittle: diacritical mark indicating nasalization: **não, pães**.

tilar, tildar v. to tilde, put a tilde on.

tilbureiro s. m. driver or owner of a tilbury.

tílburi s. m. tilbury, cab, a sort of gig.

tilha s. f. a ship's deck.

tilhado adj. (naut.) decked.

tília s. f. (bot.) linden, lime, tell.

~ **americana** basswood. ~ **prateada** silver lime.

tiliácea s. f. any tree of the family Tiliaceae.

tiliáceo adj. (bot.) tiliaceous: relating to the family Tiliaceae.

tilintar v. to tinkle, jingle, chink, ting.

tiloma s. m. (med.) corn, callus.

tilose s. f. (med.) 1. callus. 2. tylosis.

timaço s. m. (Braz., pop.) great team.

timalo s. m. (ichth.) Thymallus: a genus of fishes to which belong the graylings.

timão (I) s. m. (pl. **-ões**) 1. pole (of a coach). 2. beam (of a plough). 3. (naut.) tiller, rudder, helm. 4. thill, shaft. 5. (fig.) control, direction, command.

timão (II) s. m. (pl. **-ões**) (Braz.) a long nightgown.

timbale s. m. 1. kettledrum, timbal, tymbal. 2. atabal.

timbaleiro s. m. kettledrummer.

timbó s. m. 1. (Braz., bot.) timbo (Paullinia pinnata): a woody vine (the bark contains a poison to kill fish). 2. (Braz., pop.) softness, sluggishness, torpor, numbness (of the limbs).

timbó-boticário s. m. (pl. **timbós-boticários**) (Braz., bot.) a lancepod.

timbó-de-caiena s. m. (pl. **timbós-de-caiena**) (Braz., bot.) Surinam poison.

timbó-do-rio-de-janeiro s. m. (pl. **timbós-do-rio-de--janeiro**) (Braz., bot., also **canapu**) ground cherry.

timboína s. f. (chem.) timboin.

timbó-japonês s. m. (pl. **timbós-japoneses**) (Braz., bot.) derris.

timborana s. m. (Braz.) lancepod tree.

timboúva s. m. (Braz.) a timber tree.

timbragem s. f. (pl. **-ens**) stamping, marking with a crest or emblem.

timbrar v. 1. to mark with an emblem, crest or coat of arms; stamp. 2. to attribute, qualify, class. 3. to call, name. 4. to pride o. s. on, boast.

papel timbrado commercial paper.

timbre (I) s. m. 1. (her.) ensign, emblem, seal, crest, coat of arms. 2. (by extension) mark, stamp. 3. (fig.) point of honour; whim; height, top.

timbre (II) s. m. (mus.) 1. timbre, colour, expression, tone. 2. timbral: ancient musical instrument similar to the tambourine.

timbroso adj. 1. careful, meticulous. 2. having timbre. **-amente** adv. meticulously.

timbu s. m. (Braz., zool.) opossum.

timbuar v. (Braz., pop., med.) to relapse.

time s. m. (sports) team.

timeleácea s. f. (bot.) any species of the family Thymeleaceae.

timeleáceo adj. thymeleaceous: relating to the family Thymeleaceae.

timiatecnia s. f. the art of making perfumes.

tímico adj. (anat.) thymic: relating to the thymus gland.

timidez s. f. timidity, timidness, timorousness, shyness, diffidence. coyness; faint-heartedness, fearfulness, bashfulness.

tímido adj. timid, shy, coy, bashful, diffident; faint, faint-hearted, fearful, fearsome. ‖ **timidamente** adv. timidly.

timo s. m. 1. (anat.) thymus. 2. (bot.) thyme.

timocracia s. f. timocracy: government of the wealthy class.

timocrático adj. timocratic. ‖ **timocraticamente** adv. timocratically.

timol s. m. (chem.) thymol.

timoneira s. f. (naut.) porthole (rudder).

timoneiro s. m. 1. steersman, helmsman, timoneer, coxswain. 2. leader, pilot, guide, director.

timorato adj. 1. timorous, timid, half-hearted. 2. conscientious, scrupulous. ‖ **-amente** adv. timorously.

timpanal adj. (pl. **-ais**) tympanic: relating to the tympanum (middle ear).

timpanilho s. m. tympan (of a printing press).

timpanismo s. m. (path.) tympanism, tympanites: distension of the abdomen.

timpanite s. m. tympanitis.

timpanítico adj. (med.) tympanitic, relating to tympanites.

timpanizar v. (med.) to cause tympanites; affect with tympanites.

tímpano s. m. 1. a rotative cylinder that raises water from a reservoir or stream. 2. (archit.) tympanum spandrel, door panel. 3. kettledrum. 4. tympan of a printing press. 5. (anat.) tympanum, middle ear, eardrum.

timucu s. m. (Braz., ichth.) a needlefish.

tina s. f. tub, wooden vessel, butt, trough, vat, keeve. ~ **para lavar ouro** sluice box. ~ **para lavar roupa** washtub, dolly tub (plate L 3). ~ **para tomar banho** bathing tub.

tinada s. f. a tubful, a vatful.

tinalha s. f. vintage tub.

tincal s. m. (min.; also **tincar**) tincal, tinkal, crude borax.

tincaleira s. f. a goldsmith's tincal box.

tinção s. f. (pl. **-ões**) dye, tincture, tinge of colour, tint.

tineira s. f. (ent.) moth.

tineleiro s. m. 1. keeper of a dining-room for servants. 2. one who eats in a dining-room for servants.

tinelo s. m. dining-room for servants.

tineta s. f. (pop.) mania, whim, fancy, odd notion, caprice, freak, conception.

tinga s. f. (Braz., ichth.) 1. a sea fish. 2. a species of freshwater tortoise.

tingidor s. m. dyer. ‖ adj. dyeing, tinging.

tingidura s. f. (also **tintura**) dye, tincture, tinge of colour, tint.

tingir v. 1. to dye, tint, tinge, tincture; colour, imbue, stain, engrain, impregnate. 2. ~-**se** to blush. ~ **um fato (terno)** to dye a suit. ~ **de verde** to (dye) green. ~ **de vermelho** to encrimson.

tingitano s. m. Tangerine, native or inhabitant of Tangier. ‖ adj. Tangerine: of or relating to Tangier.

tingível adj. m. + f. (pl. **-íveis**) tingible, colourable.

tinguaciba s. f. (Braz., bot.) prickle ash.

tinguaçu s. m. (Braz., ornith.) a species of cuckoo.

tinguaíto s. m. (petrog.) tinguaite.

tingui s. m. (Braz., bot.) a sort of liana used to poison fish.

tingui-de-peixe s. m. (pl. **tinguis-de-peixe**) (Braz., bot.) jacquinia (used to poison fish).

tinguijada s. f. (N. Braz.) fishing with tingui.

tinguijar v. 1. to throw tingui into a river to poison fish. 2. to be poisoned by tingui.

tinha (I) s. f. 1. (med.) tinea, ringworm, scab, scurf. 2. defect, imperfection. ~ **favosa** (med.) favus. ~ **dos pés** athlete's foot.

tinha (II) s. f. (also **tina**) tub, vessel, butt, vat.

tinhanha s. f. (also **troca**) barter, exchange.

tinhorão s. m. (pl. **-ões**) (Braz., bot.) caladium.

tinhoso s. m. 1. person suffering from tinea. 2. (pop.) devil. ‖ adj. 1. scurfy, scabby, suffering from tinea. 2. nauseating, repugnant, disgusting. ‖ **-amente** adv. scurfily.

tinideira, tinidora s. f. (Braz.) great straits, difficulties, dilemma; want of money. ‖ adj. f. of **tinidor**.

tinido s. m. tinkling, jingling, clinking, tingling; ding-dong (bell), ringing sound.

tinidor s. m. object that tinkles. ‖ adj. (also **tininte** m. + f.) tinkling, ringing, jingling.

tinir v. 1. to clink, clank, ding, tinkle, jingle, ring, chink, tingle; clatter. 2. to buzz in the ears. 3. to tremble (with fright or cold). 4. to feel very hungry. **estar a** ~ to be penniless.

tino (I) s. m. 1. judgment, discernment, good sense, intelligence. 2. prudence, diplomacy. 3. tact, sensibility, adroitness, discretion. 4. tactile sense, feeling. **dar** ~ to take notice. **perder o** ~ to lose one's self-command. **sem** ~ foolishly.

tino (II) s. m. = **tina**.

tinote (I) s. m. (pop.) the brains.

tinote (II) s. m. small tub, vat, butt, vessel.

tinta s. f. 1. dye, tincture, colour, paint, ink. 2. shade, nuance, tone, hue of a colour. 3. variety of grapes. ~ **de aquarela** water-colour. ~ **brilhante** glossy ink. ~ **da China, nanquim** China ink. ~ **frescal** wet paint! ~ **de impressor** printer's ink. ~ **indelével** indelible ink. ~ **invisível ou simpática** invisible ink, sympathetic ink. ~ **mate** mat ink, nongloss ink. ~ **a óleo** oil colour, oil-paint. ~ **seca** dry paint. **borrão de** ~ ink blot. **caixa de** ~s paint box. **frasco de** ~ ink bottle. **lápis** ~ ink pencil. **meia-**~ half tone. **rolo de passar** ~ inking roller. **tomar muita** ~ to become too familiar.

tinteiro s. m. 1. inkpot, inkwell, inkstand, inkholder (plate E 2). 2. (Braz.) magnetite powder. **deixar alguma coisa no** ~ to omit a thing on writing (also on purpose). **ficar no** ~ to be left unwritten, be forgotten.

tintim s. m. used in the adverbial locution: ~ **por** ~ minutely, point for point, in full detail, particularly. **contar** ~ **por** ~ to detail, give full account. **explicar** ~ **por** ~ to give chapter and verse.

tintinabular v. (Braz.) to tintinnabulate, ring bells, jingle plates.

tintinábulo s. m. tintinnabulum: 1. small bell. 2. tinkling.

tintinar v. = **tilintar**.

tinto adj. 1. dyed, tinged, coloured; stained; red (wine or grapes). 2. (fig.) dirty, soiled, spotted.

tintorial adj. m. + f. (pl. **-ais**) tinctorial, pertaining to colour or dyes, colouring.

tintura s. f. 1. dyeing. 2. dye, colour, tint, hue, stain. 3. (pharm.) tincture. 4. (fig.) smattering, superficial knowledge.

tinturaria s. f. 1. dyeing, dye works, a dyer's office; dyehouse. 2. cleaning, a cleaner's work, cleaning establishment.

tintureira s. f. 1. female dyer, proprietress of a dye-house. 2. (ichth.) a sort of shark. 3. (Braz.) tree whose seedpods are used for dyeing.

tintureiro s. m. 1. dyer, cleaner, owner of a dye-house. 2. (bot.) a variety of red grapes. 3. (pop.) (also **viúva-alegre** f.) Black Maria (police car).

tintureiro-das-pedras s. m. (pl. **tintureiros-das-pedras**) (Braz., zool.) a species of mollusc.

tio s. m. uncle. ~ **Cosme** (S. Braz.) old Negro. ~ **Sam** Uncle Sam, an American, person from the United States.

tioálcool s. m. (chem.) thioalcohol.

tio-avô s. m. (pl. **tios-avós** or **tios-avôs**) great-uncle granduncle.

tioca s. f. (Braz.) a large black ant.

tiocianato s. m. (chem.) thiocyanate.

tioéter s. m. (chem.) thioether.

tiofeno s. m. (chem.) thyophene.

tiofenol s. m. (chem.) thiophenol.

tiom-tiom s. m. (pl. **tiom-tions**) (Braz., ornith.) one of the goatsuckers.

tiônico adj. (chem.) thionic: containing sulphur.

tionina s. f. (chem.) thionine, Lauth's violet.

tiopirina s. f. (chem.) thiopyrine.

tiorba s. f. (mus.) theorbo: a sort of lute used in the 16th and 17th centuries.

tiorega s. f. (N. Braz., pop.) difficulty; rub.

tiorga s. f. (S. Braz., pop.) drunkenness.

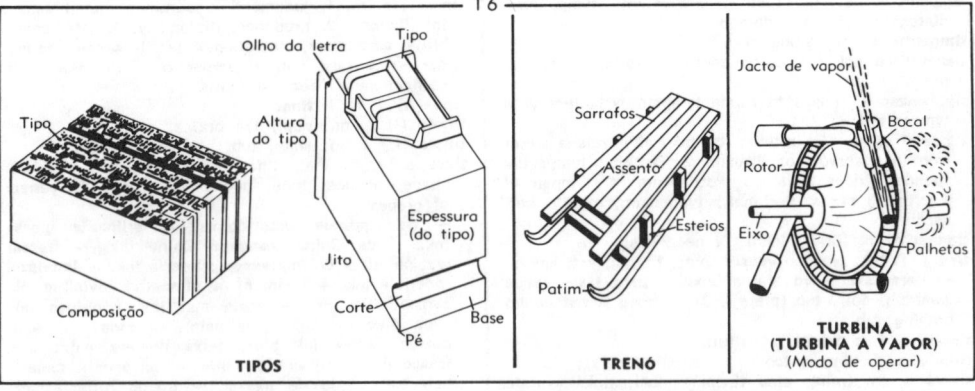

TIPOS   TRENÓ   TURBINA
(TURBINA A VAPOR)
(Modo de operar)

tiossulfato s. m. (chem.) thiosulphate.
tiossulfúrico adj. (chem.) thiosulphuric.
tipa s. f. 1. hussy, wench, strumpet. 2. plant of the family Leguminosae.
tipacoema s. f. (N. Braz.) low tide in the morning.
tipão s. m. (Braz., fam.) 1. a strange, curious type; an eccentric person. 2. a good looking, attractive person.
tipi s. m. (Braz., bot.) guinea-hen weed.
típico adj. typic(al), characteristical, representative, symbolic, emblemic. ‖ **tipicamente** adv. typically.
tipió s. m. (Braz., ornith.) a small finch.
tipisca s. f. lake formed by an overflow of the Amazonas river and its affluents.
tipiti s. m. (Braz.) 1. (bot.) jacitara palm. 2. tipiti: a cylinder of the jacitara palm used to express poisonous cassava juice. 3. (pop.) difficulties, embarrassment.
tiple s. m. + f. (mus.) treble, soprano.
tipo s. m. 1. type (for printing), letter, stamp (plates M 2, T 6). 2. pattern, fashion, norm, example, nature. 3. kind, sort, variety, group, class. 4. prototype. 5. (pop.) fellow, guy, chap. 6. excentric person, extravagant man.
~ **cheio** (typogr.) extrabold. ~ **gótico** black letter. ~ **grosso** (typogr.) blackface. os ~s **humanos** the human types. ~ **de navio** class of ship. ~ **negrito** (typogr.) boldface, bold type. ~ **meio negrito** (typogr.) clarendon. ~ **padrão**, ~ **padronizado** standard type. ~ **perfeito** personification. ~ **redondo** (typogr.) Roman type (plate L 4). ~ **sanguíneo** (med.) sanguine temperament. um ~ **taciturno** a close customer. **fundição de** ~s type foundry. **um carro de novo** ~ a car of a new pattern. **ele é o** ~ **do marinheiro** he is the very type of a seaman. **que** ~ **esquisito** what a specimen, what a queer fellow.
tipocromia s. f. colour printing.
tipofsete s. m. (typogr.) dry offset printing, letterset.
tipografar v. to print.
tipografia s. f. typography: 1. art of printing. 2. printing plant.
tipográfico adj. typographical. ‖ **tipograficamente** adv. typographically.
prova ~a proof sheet. **revisor de provas -as** proof reader.
tipógrafo s. m. typographer, setter, compositor, typesetter, printer.
tipóia (I) s. f. 1. hammock, a sort of palanquin. 2. cab, carriage. 3. (Braz.) shelter of foliage.
tipóia (II) s. f. 1. arm sling. 2. small travelling hammock; an old hammock.
tipóia (III) s. f. wench, strumpet.

tipólita s. f. typolite, fossil.
tipologia s. f. typology: interpretation of types.
tipológico adj. typologic(al), relating to typology.
tipometria s. f. (typogr.) typometry.
tiptologia s. f. typtology: spiritistic practices.
tiptólogo s. m. typtologist.
tipu s. m., **tipuana** f. (Braz.) tipu tree.
tiquara s. f. (N. Braz.) refreshing drink, mixture of manioc flour with sugar and water.
tique s. m. 1. tic, twitch, bad habit. 2. (med.) spasmodic contraction of the face. 3. a bit, a little morsel of something.
~ **nervoso** nervous tic. **nem** ~ **nem taque** nothing.
tique-taque s. m. (pl. **tique-taques**) 1. tick-tack (sound made by a ticking clock or watch). 2. pitapat (sound of the beating heart).
tíquete s. m. ticket, pass.
tique-tique s. m. (pl. **tique-tiques**) tick, tick-tack.
tiquinho s. m. iota, pinch, dash.
tiquira s. f. (N. Braz.) alcoholic drink made of manioc; manioc brandy.
tira s. f. 1. band, ribbon. 2. strip, stripe, strap. 3. tab, flap, screed. 4. m. (Braz., sl.) policeman, police detective.
~ **de couro** thong. ~ **de pano** strip of cloth. ~ **de papel** paper strip. **fazer** ~s to tear into straps. **quebrar a** ~ to die.
tira-bragal s. m. (pl. **tira-bragais**) 1. (med.) padded belt to support a hernia. 2. truss, part of a horse's harness.
tiração s. f. (N. Braz.) felling of wood, logging.
tira-cisma s. f. (pl. **tira-cismas**) 1. heavy pocket-knife in the blade of which are engraved the words: **tira-cisma**. 2. a weapon or whip to intimidate eventual aggressors.
tiracolo s. m. shoulder belt, baldric, bandoleer belt. **a** ~ crosswise: over one shoulder and under the other.
tirada s. f. 1. act or fact of drawing, pulling, removing. 2. exportation of goods. 3. long walk, long stretch of road. 4. long space of time. 5. tirade, rant: long speech or declamation.
de uma ~ at one stretch, at one draft, in one go.
tiradeira s. f. (Braz.) 1. leather belt or chain that ties two pairs of oxen of a cart together when they move one pair behind the other. 2. fishing-rod with several hooks. 3. (N. Braz.) woman who husks cocoa-beans. 4. (Braz.) traces, leather straps for beasts of draught in a sugar mill.
tiradela s. f. drawing, pulling, taking away.
tirador s. m. 1. (typogr., also ~ **de provas**) proof puller (person). 2. (naut.) tackle, fall. 3. (N. Braz.) person who husks cocoa-beans. 4. (N. Braz.) miner.

~ **de provas** (typogr.) 1. proof puller (person). 2. proof press (machine).

tirador-de-cipó s. m. (pl. **tiradores-de-cipó**) (Braz., pop.) runaway Negro.

tiradoura s. f. beam of a cart or plough.

tira-dúvidas s. m., sg. + pl. person who removes doubts, who resolves or settles a question.

tira-fundo s. m. (pl. **tira-fundos**) 1. auger. 2. screw to fasten the rail-chairs to the sleeper.

tiragem s. f. (pl. **-ens**) 1. drawing, pulling, hauling. 2. circulation, issue: printing, edition. 3. drawing of metal. 4. draft, draught of a chimney. 5. collection of letters (post office).

~ **forçada** forced draft. ~ **de provas** pulling of proofs. ~ **à sorte** drawing of lots.

tira-gosto s. m. (pl. **tira-gostos**) (Braz.) a salty titbit (along with a drink).

tira-linhas s. m., sg. + pl. 1. drawing pen, ruling pen, bow-pen, tracer (plate D 2). 2. rule to draw lines.

tira-manchas s. m., sg. + pl. cleaner (preparation).

tira-manha s. m. (pl. **tira-manhas**) (Braz.) a small beetle.

tirambóia s. f. (Braz., ent. also **jaquiranabóia**) a lantern fly.

tiramento s. m. (also **tiradura** f.) 1. act or fact of taking, drawing, pulling. 2. (obs.) collecting of taxes or revenues.

tirana (I) s. f. tyranness, shrewish wife, termagant, scold; (fig.) Xantippe.

tirana (II) s. f. 1. (Braz.) a sort of fandango (dance for two persons). 2. hoe.

tiranete s. m. petty tyrant, tyrannous person.

tirania s. f. 1. tyranny, despotism, oppressiveness, oppression; absolutism, autocracy. 2. (coll.) ingratitude.

tiranicida s. m. + f. tyrannicide, one who kills a tyrant.

tiranicídio s. m. tyrannicide, killing of a tyrant.

tirânico adj. tyrannical, tyrannous, despotic, oppresive, imperious, domineering; arbitrary; cruel, barbarous, harsh. ‖ **-amente** adv. tyrannically.

tiranizador s. m. tyrant. ‖ adj. tyrannical, despotic, oppresive, arbitrary.

tiranizar v. to tyrannize, despotize, domineer, oppress, rule despotically.

tirano s. m. tyrant, despot, oppressor, autocrat, usurpator, bully. ‖ adj. tyrannical, despotic, oppressive; harsh, cruel, barbarous. ‖ **-amente** adv. tyrannically.

tira-nódoas s. m., sg. + pl. spot remover, stain cleaner.

tirante s. m. 1. trace for beasts of draught (plate A 12). 2. (archit.) architrave, trussed beam. 3. driving rod, connecting rod of a steam engine. 4. (mach.) coupling rod. ‖ adj. m. + f. drawing, inclining to, showing a propensity to. ‖ prep. save, except.

~ **a azul** blueish, bluish. ~ **de ligação** (tech.) coupling rod.

tirão (I) s. m. (pl. **-ões**) 1. pull, haul, tug, jerk. 2. long walk.

tirão (II) s. m. (pl. **-ões**) apprentice.

tira-olhos s. m., sg. + pl. 1. (ent.) dragonfly.

tirapé s. m. a shoemaker's stirrup.

tira-prosa s. m. (pl. **tira-prosas**) (Braz., coll.) ruffian, rowdy, bully.

tirar v. 1. to draw, pull, drag (as a weapon). 2. to take off or away, remove. 3. to extract. 4. to deprive. 5. to exclude, extinguish, suppress. 6. to print, make copies. 7. to take out, get out, set free, take away. 8. to steal. 9. to deduct, subtract, diminish. 10. to shoot.

~ **a afeição** to disaffect. ~ **água de um barco**

to bail out water from a boat. ~ **do algarismo anterior** (math.) to borrow. ~ **uma amostra** to sample. ~ **o ânimo ou a coragem** to discourage. ~ **o brilho** to blot. ~ **da cadeia sob fiança** to bail out (from prison). ~ **do caminho** to clear out of the way. ~ **a carga** to discharge. ~ **a casca** to peel, shell, husk. ~ **o chapéu** to cap, take off the hat. ~ **de cima** to take down. ~ **o cinto** to unbelt. ~ **uma conclusão dos fatos** to put two and two together. ~ **as conseqüências** to draw inferences. ~ **uma conta** to draw up an account. ~ **as cordas** to unstring. ~ **um dente** to have a tooth extracted. ~ **de dentro** to take out. ~ **desforra** to avenge o. s. ~ **as dificuldades** to remove the difficulties. ~ **um diploma** to take a diploma. ~ **da doca** (naut.) to undock. ~ **um documento de licença** to take out a licence. ~ **todas as dúvidas** to remove all doubts. ~ **de uma embarcação** to disembark. ~**-se do embaraço** to get out of troubles. ~ **a falta** to pardon an absence from school. ~ **uma fatura** to make out an invoice. ~ **férias** to vacation, take a vacation. ~ **um fiapo com** to flirt with. ~ **fora** to fetch out. ~ **por força** to rape, wrench, wrest, writhe. ~ **uma fotografia** to take a photograph. ~ **informações** to make inquiries. ~ **licença** to get a licence. ~ **a limpo** to make a clean copy. ~ **lucro** to profit. ~ **do seu lugar** to displace. ~ **manchas** to wash clean. ~ **da mente, da memória** to let go, forget. ~ **medida** to measure, take a measurement. ~ **a mesa** to clear (the table). ~ **a metade** to halve. ~ **um molde** to draw a pattern. ~ **a nata do leite** to skim the cream off. ~ **a um para pagar o outro** to rob Peter to pay Paul. ~ **os ossos** to bone. ~ **partido de** to exploit. ~ **as penas** to deplume. ~ **a prova** (math.) to check up a calculation, throw off. ~ **provas tipográficas** to pull galley proofs. ~ **proveito** to benefit, capitalize. ~ **a roupa** to undress. ~ **o saldo** to strike a balance. ~ **a sardinha com a mão do gato** to use someone as a cat's paw. ~ **à sorte** to draw lots, to try one's fortune. ~ **a sorte grande** to win the great (lottery) prize. ~ **o valor** to depreciate. ~ **o vento das velas de um barco** (naut.) to blanket. ~ **a verde** to incline to green. ~ **violentamente** to rash. **ajude-o a** ~ **o casaco** help him off with his coat. **não tire o corpo** don't flinch! **ele tirou-lhe o dinheiro com sua lábia** he coaxed her out of her money. **ele tirou-se da lama e caiu no atoleiro** he went farther and fared worse. **o menino foi tirado da escola** the boy was withdrawn from the school. **foi tirado das minhas mãos** it was taken off my hands. **a peça pode ser tirada** the piece takes out. **tiraram-lhe a prosa** they took him down a peg. **tenho de** ~ **satisfação** I have a crow to pick with him. **sem** ~ **nem pôr** exactly, without exaggeration, for all the world like. **tirar-lhe-ei o vício de contar vantagem** I'll teach him to tell tales.

tira-teimas s. m., sg. + pl. 1. a decisive argument, final word. 2. (by extension) a dictionary.

tira-testa s. m. (pl. **tira-testas**) headstall of a bridle.

tiravira s. m. 1. parbuckle, a double sling. 2. galliwasp, lizard fish.

tirázio s. m. loud report (as of a firearm).

tireóide s. f. (anat.) thyroid: 1. the gland. 2. the cartilage. ‖ adj. m. + f. thyroid: 1. of or relating to the thyroid gland or cartilage. 2. shield-shaped.

tireóideo adj. (anat.) thyroid(al).

tireoidite s. f. (med.) thyroiditis: inflammation of the thyroid gland.

tirete s. m. (gram.) hyphen.

tiriba, tiribaí s. m. (Braz., ornith.; also **tiriva**) tiriba, a parrot of the genus Pyrrhura.

tiriba-pequeno s. m. (pl. **tiribas-pequenos**) (Braz., ornith.) a white-eared parrot.

tirintintim s. m. imitation of the sound of a trumpet.

tírio s. m. Tyrian: native or inhabitant of Tyre (town of Phoenicia). ǁ adj. Tyrian: 1. of or pertaining to Tyre. 2. purple, scarlet.

tiriri s. m. (Braz., ornith.) (also **suiriri**) a species of tyrant.

tiririca s. f. 1. (Braz.) plant of the sedge family. 2. (Braz.) a sort of rapids in the Pará river obstructing navigation. 3. m. (sl.) pickpocket, pilferer, scoundrel. ǁ adj. m. + f. (Braz., pop.) irate, infuriated, mad, angry.

tirirical s. m. (pl. -ais) (Braz.) ground covered with sedge.

tiritana s. f. 1. a coarse dress of flannelette, worn by countrywomen. 2. (bot.) pellitory.

tiritante adj. m. + f. shivering, shaking, trembling (with cold).

tiritar v. to shiver, quiver, shake, tremble (with cold).

tiriúma adj. m. + f. (Braz.) unaccompanied, alone, lonely.

tiro s. m. 1. shot, pop, shooting, firing; discharge of a firearm. 2. report (of a gun). 3. charge of a gun. 4. throw (as of a lasso or bolas). 5. target range, shooting gallery. 6. allusion, hint, a cutting remark. 7. impetuosity. 8. trace (of a beast of draught). 9. a team of such beasts. 10. act of drawing a cart by animals. 11. distance to be run by a race horse. 12. (Braz., sl. also **tirázio**) assault, robbery, holdup.
~ **ao alvo** target practice. ~ **de alvorada** morning watch gun. ~ **de canhão** cannon shot, gunfire. ~ **de carabina** rifle shot. ~ **cego**, ~ **perdido** random shot. ~ **a esmo** shot at rovers. ~ **de espingarda** musket shot. ~ **falhado** misfire. ~ **de guerra** (Braz.) military training school. ~ **de misericórdia** coup de grâce. **de** ~ **rápido** quick-fire. ~ **de recolher** night watch gun. ~ **de revólver** revolver shot. ~ **de seis cavalos** a team of six horses. **achar-se ao alcance de** ~ **de canhão** to be within cannon shot. **ângulo de** ~ (ballistics) elevation. **dar um** ~ **na praça** (Braz., sl.) to proclaim a fraudulent bankruptcy. **levar um** ~ to be shot; be hurt by a firearm. **linha de** ~ line of sight. **trocar** ~s to exchange shots.

tiro (II) s. m. (poet.) purple.

tirocínio s. m. 1. apprenticeship, tyrocinium, pupilage. 2. military training (to gain promotion).

tiro-de-guerra s. m. (pl. **tiros-de-guerra**) (Braz.) military training centre.

tirolês s. m. (pl. -eses) (f. -esa) Tyrolese: native or inhabitant of Tyrol. ǁ adj. Tyrolese: of or pertaining to Tyrol.

tirolesa s. f. Tyrolienne: a Tyrolese peasant dance and song.

tirólita s. f. (min.) tyrolite.

tiromancia s. f. divination by making use of cheese.

tironeada s. f. (S. Braz.) a pull with the reins in order to spur a horse.

tironear v. (S. Braz.) to pull the reins of a horse in order to spur it.

tirosina s. f. (biochem.) tyrosine: a crystalline amino acid.

tirotear v. to fire, volley, shoot.

tiroteio s. m. 1. firing, shooting, volley, musketry. 2. (fig.) rapid to and fro of words in a discussion.

tirrênio, tirreno adj. Tyrrhenian, Etruscan.

tirsígero adj. (poet.) bearing a thyrsus.

tirso s. m. thyrsus: 1. Bacchus' spear adorned with ivy and vine leaves and a fir cone at the top. 2. thyrse: inflorescence of a pyramidal form.

tisana s. f. (med.) ptisan, tisane.

tisanóptero s. m. (ent.) thrips.

tisanuro s. m. (ent.) bristletail.

tisco s. m. (Braz., fam.) jot, mite, sliver, bit.

tísica s. f. (med.) phthisis, hectic fever, consumption, tuberculosis (of the lungs).
~ **galopante** galloping consumption. ~ **pulmonar** pulmonary tuberculosis.

tísico adj. consumptive, hectic, phthisical.

tisiologia s. f. (med.) phthisiology.

tisiológico adj. (med.) phthisical.

tisiologista, tisiólogo s. m. (med.) phthisiologist.

tisna s. f. (also **tisnadura**) lampblack, printer's ink, blackening.

tisnado s. m. (Braz., pop.) devil. ǁ adj. darkish, dusky; sunburnt, swarthy.

tisnar v. 1. to blacken, smut, soot, besmear, sully. 2. ~-se to become scorched, sunburnt.

tisne s. m. 1. soot, smudge, smear. 2. lampblack. 3. black spot.

titã s. m. 1. (myth.) Titan. 2. (fig.) a person of superhuman strength and intellect, a superman. 3. a large crane.

titânico adj. titanic, titanesque, gigantic, colossal, herculeous, huge, immense. ǁ **-amente** adv. titanically.

titanífero adj. (chem.) titaniferous, containing titanium.

titânio s. m. (chem.) titanium.

titanita s. f. (min.) titanite, sphene.

titara s. f. (Braz., bot.) jacitara palm.

titela s. f. 1. breast of a chicken, fowl, etc. 2. (fig.) the best part of a thing.

titeragem s. f. (pl. -ens) puppetry.

títere s. m. 1. puppet, marionette. 2. (fig.) jumping Jack, dandy, pawn, mountebank.

titerear v. 1. to wirepull (marionettes), perform a puppet show. 2. to act like a puppet.

titereiro, titeriteiro s. m. puppeteer, puppet-player, puppetman, wirepuller. ǁ adj. 1. referring to puppetry, puppet-playing. 2. puppetlike.

titeri s. m. (Braz., ornith.) firewood gatherer.

titia s. f. auntie.
ela ficou para ~ she is on the shelf.

titica s. f. 1. (Braz.) birds' excrement. 2. (fig.) worthless thing or unworthy person.

titicar v. (Braz.) to nudge, jab, poke, dig.

titilação s. f. (pl. -ões), **titilamento** m. tittilation, tickle.

titilante adj. m. + f. tickling, thrilling.

titilar (I) adj. m. + f. (anat.) said of the armpit veins.

titilar (II) v. to titillate, tickle.

titímalo s. m. a plant of the spurge family.

titinga s. f. (N. Braz.) freckles, spots.

titio s. m. (Braz., children) uncle.

titônia s. f. (poet.) daybreak, sunrise.

titubeação s. f. (pl. -ões) (path.) titubancy, titubation (constant change of position caused by nervousness).

titubeante adj. m. + f. 1. staggering, tottering, unsteady. 2. hesitating, faltering. 3. vacillating, flinching. ǁ ~**mente** adv. staggeringly.

titubear (rarely used **titubar**) v. 1. to stagger, totter, wabble, dodder, toddle. 2. to falter, hesitate, waver. 3. to vacillate, doubt. 4. to tergiversate.
sem ~ without hesitation.

titulado adj. titled, having a title.

titular (I) s. m. + f. 1. noble person. 2. m. title-holder; cabinet member. ǁ adj. titular, honorary, nominal.

titular (II) v. 1. to title, entitle, give a title, call. 2. to register a title. 3. to titrate.

tituleira s. f. (typogr.) headletter machine.

tituleiro s. m. (typogr.) headliner, the operator of a headletter machine.

título s. m. title: 1. designation of a literary production (plate L 4). 2. heading. 3. caption. 4. name, denomination. 5. top line. 6. label, inscription, lettering. 7. voucher, bond, deep, policy, note. 8. subdivision of a document, treatise, etc. 9. motivation, reason, claim (of rights). 10. pretext, pretence. **a ~ de** in the quality of, on pretence of. **a ~ de experiência** by way of trial. **a ~ honorífico** honorary. **~ de anuidade** annuity bond. **~ de dívida** bond. **~ de página ou coluna** cross heading. **~ privilegiado** privileged claim. **~ de renda** stock certificate. **falso ~** (typogr.) bastard title, half title (plate L 4). **portador de ~** titleholder. **sem ~** titleless.

tiú s. m. (Braz.) plant of the spurge family.

tiúba s. f. (N. Braz., pop.) rum, firewater.

tiupá s. m. (Braz.) = **tijupá**.

tiziu s. m. (Braz., ornith.) a passerine bird of the family Fringillidae (Volatinia jacarina L.).

tlim s. m. (pl. **tlins**) tinkle: imitation of the sound made by coins or by a small bell.

tlintar v. = **tilintar**.

tmese s. f. (gram.) tmesis.

toa s. f. (naut.) tow, towline, towrope, warp. **à ~** 1. worthless. 2. at random, without purpose, anyhow, carelessly. 3. in vain. **falar à ~** to speak at random. **ficar à ~** to hang about. **levar um navio à ~** to tow a ship.

toada s. f. 1. tune, air, melody. 2. sound, noise. 3. rumour, report, hearsay. 4. style, fashion, manner. **mudar de ~** to play or sing another tune. **numa ~** (Braz., pop.) without interruption, endlessly.

toadeira s. f. (N. Braz.) a whale which dives after having been harpooned.

toadilha s. f. little melody or tune.

toalete s. toilet: 1. f. the act of dressing o. s. (bathing, dressing, hair arranging, make-up, etc.). 2. m. a woman's gala dress. 3. m. a women's toilet room.

toalha s. f. towel cloth. **~ de água** sheet of water. **~ de altar** altar cloth. **~ de banho** bath towel (plates B 3, R 7). **~ felpuda** fluffy towel. **~ de mesa** tablecloth (plate M 8). **~ rolante** roller towel. **~ de rosto** face towel (plate B 3). **~ sem-fim** jack towel. **pôr a ~** to lay the cloth.

toalheiro s. m. towel horse, towel rack.

toalhete s. m. 1. small towel. 2. (obs.) napkin.

toalhinha s. f. 1. little towel. 2. a nun's veil or towel.

toante adj. m. + f. sounding, consonant, rhyming.

toar v. 1. to sound, resound. 2. to thunder, boom, roar. 3. to lease, agree, fit, suit. 4. to harmonize or be in tune with.

toba s. m. (Braz., ornith.) common booby.

tobatinga s. f. (Braz.) = **tabatinga**.

tobeiro s. m. (N. Braz., sl.) pederast, sodomite.

tobiano (I) adj. relating to the Brazilian author Tobias Barreto.

tobiano (II) adj. (S. Braz.) white-spotted (horse).

tobó s. m. (Braz., sl.) a large diamond (among prospectors).

tobogã s. m. toboggan (sled and slope).

toca s. f. 1. burrow, den, lurking hole, lair, kennel. 2. (fig.) mean habitation, abode, lodge. **~ de coelho** rabbit burrow. **~ de raposa** fox-earth. **fazer ~s** to burrow, make burrows.

tocada s. f. tryout (race horse), test.

tocadela s. f. (also **tocadura**) 1. touch, act of touching or feeling, a slight contact. 2. (fam.) toccata.

tocadilho s. m. game similar to backgammon.

toca-discos s. m., sg. + pl. (mus.) record player; grammophone pick-up. **~ automático** automatical record player.

tocado adj. (S. Braz., pop.) tipsy, jolly, screwy. ‖ **-amente** adv. tipsily.

tocador s. m. 1. player (of an instrument), ringer (of bells). 2. (Braz.) muleteer, driver of mules, cattle drover. ‖ adj. (mus.) 1. playing. 2. driving (cattle).

toca-fita s. m. (pl. **toca-fitas**) (Braz.) tape recorder.

tócai s. m. Tokay: a Hungarian wine.

tocaia s. f. (S. Braz.) ambush, trap, blind.

tocaiar v. to ambush, lurk, entrap, lie in wait.

tocaio s. m. (S. Braz., also **xará**) namesake. ‖ adj. having the same name.

tocajé s. m. (Braz., bot.) a species of roupala.

toca-lápis s. m., sg. + pl. the leg of a compass carrying the pencil.

tocamento s. m. = **toque** (I) 1., 2., 3., 4.

tocandira s. f. (Braz., zool.) tucandera.

tocante adj. m. + f. 1. touching, moving, feeling, affecting, pathetic. 2. concerning, pertaining. ‖ **~mente** adv. movingly. **no ~** a regarding to, as to, concerning.

toca-pinos s. m., sg. + pl. drive punch.

tocar (I) v. 1. to touch, feel, contact, brush, strike, graze. 2. to abut, be contiguous to, limit; reach. 3. to play (an instrument), perform, sound, toot. 4. to ring (bells), clang, chink. 5. to concern, regard, respect, refer. 6. to impress, inspire, affect, move. 7. (Braz.) to drive out or away; to call (at port). 8. **~-se** to contact. **~ a** to refer to. **~ o céu com o dedo** to be most happy. **~ os copos** to touch glasses. **~ na corda sensível de alguém**, **~ na ferida** to touch one's soft spot. **~ no assunto** to touch upon the matter. **~ a corneta ou clarim** to bugle, trumpet. **~ uma jiga** (mus.) to jig. **~ ao de leve** to slide over, skim over. **~ mal um instrumento** to thrum. **~ à missa** to ring for mass. **~ de ouvido** (mus.) to play by ear, pick out. **~ para fora** to drive, whip out of. **~ para trás** to drive or whip back. **~ de perto** to strike closely. **~ rabeca** to play a fiddle, tweedle. **~ viola sem corda** to talk idly. **toque!** get along, drive on! **a casa dele toca com a minha** his house is next to mine. **~ a quatro mãos** to play a duet. **~ as raias do descuido** to trench upon carelessness. **os extremos se tocam** extremes touch. **isto não me toca** that's not my alley; that doesn't concern me. **não toque!** hands off!. **o navio tocou no Rio de Janeiro** the ship called at Rio de Janeiro. **pelo tocar** by the feel. **pelo que me toca** as far as I am concerned. **ser tocado da cidade** to be run out of town.

tocar (II) s. m. (Braz.) sickness of cattle caused by lack of salt.

tocari s. m. (bot.) Brazil nut.

tocarola s. f. 1. handshake. 2. dissonant musical performance. **dar uma ~** to shake hands.

tocata s. f. 1. musical performance. 2. (mus.): a) toccata. b) serenade. c) piece of instrumental music. d) composition which enables the player to exhibit his mastery.

toca-viola s. m. (pl. **toca-violas**) (Braz., also **tange-viola**) cerambycid beetle.

tocha s. f. 1. large candle, firebrand, torch, flambeau; lampad. 2. (Braz.) tree stump, tree without a top. **acender uma ~** (Braz., mil. sl.) to leave the military quarter for a day or night without permission.

tocheira s. f., **tocheiro** m. candleholder, torch holder.

toco s. m. (pl. **tocos**) 1. stub, stump, butt (as of a a tree, cigarette, torch, pencil, etc.). 2. a sort of club, stick. 3. (Braz., sl.) portion or share of a booty, plunder or theft. ‖ adj. (S. Braz.) resolute. ~ de amarrar besta (N. Braz., pop.) stumpy. bater os tocos (Braz., pop.) to depart, go away.

toco-duro s. m. (pl. tocos-duros) a two-wheel cart without springs.

tocografia s. f. (med.) description of childbirth.

tocologia s. f. tocology, tokology, science of obstetrics, midwifery.

tocológico adj. (surg.) obstetric(al).

tocólogo s. m. obstetrician.

toda (ô) adj. f. of todo.

toda (I) s. f. (also todeiro m.) tody: bird of the genus Todus, robin.

toda (II) s. f. Toda: a Dravidian language.

todavia conj. but, yet, still, however, nevertheless, though. ‖ adv. notwithstanding.

todo s. m. 1. the whole, entirety, entireness, completeness, totality, aggregate. 2. union, mass. 3. generality. 4. ~s pl. each and every, one and all, every one, all people. ‖ adj. 1. all, whole, complete, entire. 2. every, any.
  toda a América all America, the whole America. ~s a baldear! all change! toda a cidade all the town. toda a sua energia his whole energy. ~s os dias every day. toda espécie de every kind of, all kinds of. toda a família all the family, the whole family. toda a gente everybody. ~ homem quer ser feliz every man wants to be happy. ~s juntos bodily, one and all. ~s os meios all means. ~ o mundo all the world. ~s nós all of us. ~s os países the whole of the countries. todas as suas palavras his every word. toda a pressa all speed. ~s e qualquer one and all. ~s quantos all those who, as many as. ~s os quinze dias every fortnight. ~s os riscos all risks. Todos os Santos (dia) All Saints' Day. toda vestida de verde dressed all in green. todas as vezes as often as, every time that. ~s de uma vez all at once, all at the same time. ao ~ altogether, all in all, all told, at the most, as much as possible. como um ~ as a whole. em ~ caso in any case, at all events. convite a ~s general invitation. com ~ o meu coração with all my heart. a ~ custo anyway, at any price. o dia ~ all the day. ter ~s os direitos be fully entitled. em toda a extensão at full length. com toda a força de voz at the top of the voice. a ~ galope at full gallop. ela estava toda humilde she was clothed with humility. de ~ jeito at all events. o motivo ~ the why and wherefore. durante a noite toda the whole night through. em ~ o país all over the country, throughout the country. em toda parte all about, far and near. seguro contra ~s os riscos all-in insurance. moça para ~s os serviços maid of all works. com toda a sinceridade with all my heart. por ~ o tempo all along. a toda velocidade at full speed, at full pelt. durante toda a vida all through one's life. à vista de ~s in the eyes of all, in the public eye. ler a carta toda to read the letter through.

Todo-poderoso s. m. The Almighty. ‖ todo-poderoso adj. (pl. todo-poderosos) almighty, omnipotent.

toé s. m. (Braz., bot. also maricaua) shrub of the nightshade family (Datura insignis).

toeira s. f. the second and penultimate string of a guitar.
  estar nas ~s (Braz., pop.) to be in a fog, in a mess.

toesa s. f. 1. fathom: ancient measure of six feet. 2. (pop.) a large foot.

tofo s. m. (med.) tophus: a calcareous concretion in the body.

toga s. f. toga: 1. (ant.) loose garment worn by Roman citizens. 2. gown, garb, robe (of a magistrate). 3. (fig.) magistracy.

togado s. m. judge; magistrate. ‖ adj. 1. wearing a toga, gowned. 2. magisterial.

toicinho s. m. lard, pork fat, bacon (plate A 2). ~ defumado bacon. fatia de ~ a slice of bacon.

toirada s. f., toirear v., toireiro, toiro s. m. = tourada, tourar, toureiro, touro.

tojal s. m. (pl. -ais) ground covered with gorse, place full of whin.

tojeiro s. m. person who gathers furze or gorse.

tojo s. m. (bot.) furze, gorse, whin.

tojo-molar s. m. (pl. tojos-molares) (bot.) dwarf whin.

tojoso adj. (bot.) gorsy, furzy.

tola (I) s. f. (vulg.) 1. head, brains. 2. intelligence, judgement, good sense.

tola (II) s. f. a sort of wooden pincers used by a combmaker.

tola (ô) (III) s. + adj., f. of tolo.

tolano s. m. (chem.) tolan(e), white crystalline hydrocarbon.

tolaz s. m. + f. fool, stupid fellow, simpleton. ‖ adj. very foolish, silly.

tolda (I) s. f. 1. awning. 2. quarter-deck. 3. maize granary, corncrib.

tolda (II) s. f. 1. act or fact of covering with an awning. 2. clouding of the wine.

toldador adj. overcasting, clouding, overshadowing.

toldar v. 1. to cover with an awning, hang or spread an awning over. 2. to darken, cloud, obscure, blur, dim, gloom. 3. to overcast, overlay, overcloud, overshadow. 4. ~-se to get tipsy, become foolish; become spoiled.

toldo (ô) s. m. 1. awning, tilt; sun blind (of a shop), canopy (plate R 5). 2. (S. Braz.) settlement of half-civilized Indians.

toledana s. f. Toledo: a sword blade manufactured in the Spanish town of Toledo.

toledano s. m. Toledan, native or inhabitant of Toledo. ‖ adj. Toledan: of or relating to Toledo.

toleima s. f. foolishness, conceitedness, folly, silliness, vanity.

toleirão s. m. (pl. -ões) (f. -ona) fool, imbecil, simpleton, booby. ‖ adj. foolish, silly, stupid, weak-minded.

tolejar v. to speak or act foolishly.

tolerabilidade s. f. tolerability, tolerableness, sufferableness, supportableness, endurability.

tolerada s. f. registered prostitute.

tolerância s. f. tolerance: 1. endurance, sufferance. 2. broad-mindedness. 3. toleration, indulgence. 4. allowance for error.

tolerante adj. m. + f. tolerant: 1. enduring, indulgent. 2. forbearing. 3. broad-minded, wide. ‖ ~mente adv. tolerantly.

tolerantismo s. m. toleration: the doctrine of tolerance.

tolerar v. 1. to tolerate, endure, bear, forbear, suffer, support, indulge. 2. to stand, abide. 3. to permit, admit, allow.
  ela não tolera críticas she is impatient of reproof. não o tolero I cannot bear him, (coll.) I can't stick him. não se toleram there's no love lost between them. não toleramos isto sem protesto we won't tolerate it without protesting, (coll.) we won't take it lying down. não tolero o jeito dele I just cannot stand his manners.

tolerável adj. m. + f. (pl. -áveis) tolerable: 1. endurable, bearable, sufferable, supportable. 2. passable, admissible. 3. satisfactory. ‖ toleravelmente adv. tolerably.

tolete s. m. 1. (naut.) thole, thole pin. 2. (Braz.) pointed stick with which Indians catch alligators. 3. (wooden) roller. 4. tobacco roll.

toleteira s. f. (naut.) oarlock, rowlock: a support for an oar (plate B 9).

tolher v. 1. to hinder, check, obstruct, impede, hamper. 2. to embarrass, debar, prevent, restrain, oppose. 3. to palsy, paralyse, stop. 4. to disable, cripple, lame. 5. ~-se to become crippled, disabled or paralysed.
~ os movimentos de alguém to hinder someone's movements. ~-se de medo to get frozen with fear. ~-se de frio to grow stiff with cold. ele tolhe meu caminho he is in my way.

tolhido adj. 1. paralysed, palsied, disabled, lame, crippled; paralytic. 2. benumbed, numb. 3. checked, hindered.

tolhimento s. m. (also **tolheita** f.) obstacle, hindrance, benumbedness, impediment, obstruction; disability, lameness, palsy.

tolice s. f. 1. foolishness, folly, silliness, conceitedness, vanity. 2. stupidity, fatuity. 3. nonsense, fudge, humbug, rot. 4. fiddle-faddle, trifle, blunder. ~ incrível screaming nonsense. dizer ~s to talk nonsense, (sl.) to talk rot. ele só pensa em ~s he minds nothing but trifles. que ~! what nonsense! (sl.) what rot!

tolina s. f. sponging, cheating of a fool.

tolinar v. to sponge, dupe, cheat a fool.

tolineiro s. m. sponger, cheat, sharper, smell-feast.

tolo s. m. fool, simpleton, idiot, stupid fellow, jackdaw, gudgeon pinhead; (sl.) zany, gawk. ‖ adj. 1. foolish, crazy, daft, ignorant, loony, silly, simple, conceited, half-witted, witless. 2. stupid, fatuous, soft brained.
fazer alguém de ~ to pull one's leg. fui ~ bastante para consentir I was fool enough to consent. um grupo de ~s a set of fools. não se faça de ~ don't make a fool of yourself. não há ~ como ~ velho no fool like an old one. não seja ~ be your age.

tolontro s. m. a swelling, boil, bump, tumour, truftle.

tolu s. m. tolu balsam.

tolueno s. m. (chem.) toluene, a hydrocarbon.

tom s. m. tone: 1. tension, inflection (of tissue). 2. (mus.): a) sound, pitch of the voice. b) key. 3. intonation, accent. 4. dye, tinge, shade, touch, nuance, tune, temper. 5. mode, note, mental or moral attitude, tenor, drift.
~ azulado a touch of blue. ~ básico ground colour. ~ cardíaco heart sound. ~ dogmático dogmaticalness. ~ fundamental (mus.) keynote. ~ maior major tone or key. ~ menor minor tone or key. dar ~ to tone, lead the choir. o ~ do discurso the tone of the speech. meio ~ undertone. mudar de ~ to change one's note. não me fale nesse ~ don't speak to me in that tone. sem ~ nem som without rhyme or reason. num ~ zangado in an angry tone.

toma (I) s. f. act of taking.

toma (II) interj. there! take it! (also scornfully).

tomada s. f. 1. taking, seizure, attack, capture, conquest; fall. 2. (electr.): a) plug. b) plug socket, socket, jack, contact box (plates D 4, M 5). 3. water reservoir.
~ de ar air intake. ~ de parede (electr.) wall socket. ~ de posição taking of a stand. ~ de posse a taking over. ~ postiça (electr.) contact box.

tomadia s. f. 1. taking, seizure, capture, catch. 2. capture of contraband or smuggled goods; booty.

tomadiço adj. peevish, fretful, choleric, soon angry, easily excitable. ‖ -amente adv. peevishly.

tomador s. m. the taker of a loan, borrower.

tomados s. m. pl. (pop.) folds, tuck. ‖ adj. sg. **tomado** 1. taken, seized, caught. 2. (fig.) tipsy; crazy.
~ de ciúmes jealous. ~ de medo seized with fear, frightened, afraid. ~ de pânico panic-stricken. ~ do vinho drunk.

tomadura s. f. gall, hurt, sore (on a horse's back).

tomar v. to take: 1. seize, catch, capture; lay hold of, grasp; conquer; take possession of. 2. gather, collect; receive, get, gain, win. 3. eat, drink. 4. take away, steal, deprive of. 5. imitate, copy. 6. assume, accept, admit, consider.
~ um advogado to engage a lawyer. ~ de assalto to take by assault, take by storm. ~ assento em to take one's seat (as in Congress). ~ uma bebida to have a drink. ~ boa nota to take due note. ~ à boa parte to take in the right way. ~ o bonde em movimento to jump a tram. ~ a seu cargo to undertake. ~ as coisas às avessas to take things wrong. ~ muita confiança to take liberties. ~ conhecimento de to take notice of. ~ conselho to hold counsel. ~ em consideração to take into consideration, bethink, consult, consider, allow. ~ conta to take on, look after, see after, attend to, assume, keep, administer. ~ em conta to take into account. ~ conta de si to care for o. s. ~ de cor to learn by heart. ~ coragem to take courage. ~ um costume to fall into a habit. ~ cuidado to be careful, watch out. ~ uma decisão to reach a decision. ~ a dianteira to outstrip, outpace, overrun. ~ emprestado to borrow. ~ como esposa to take for a wife, to wive. ~ exemplo to take warning. ~ fogo 1. to catch fire. 2. (fig.) to get into a passion. ~ fôlego to catch one's breath. ~ forças to gather strength. ~ o freio nos dentes (fig.) 1. to run away. 2. to resist, oppose. ~ gosto to delight. ~ ilegalmente, sem direito to arrogate. ~ informações to make inquiries. ~ férias to vacation. ~ uma garrafa to crack a bottle. ~ a iniciativa to take the lead (in doing). ~ seu lanche to have one's breakfast. ~ a liberdade to take the liberty. ~ o lugar 1. to occupy (a place, seat). 2. to displace. ~ a mal to take amiss. ~ medidas to take steps. ~ muito tempo to take too much time. ~ por modelo 1. to take as a model. 2. (fig.) to copy. ~ nota to take account of, annotate, jot down. ~ a oportunidade to take a chance. ~ ordens to take holy orders, be ordained. ~ a palavra to take the floor (as in Congress). ~ parte to take part. ~ o partido de to take the side of. ~ pé to feel one's legs, touch ground. ~ a peito to take to heart. ~ por to take for. ~ posição to take one's stand. ~ posse de to occupy, annex. ~ precauções to take precautions. ~ providências to take steps, measures. ~ o pulso to feel the pulse. ~ seu rumo próprio to strike out a line of one's own. ~ satisfação to demand satisfaction. ~-se de to be overcome by. ~ sentido (mil.) to stand at attention. ~ (algo) a sério to take something seriously. ~ de surpresa to take by surprise. ~ por testemunha to call as witness. ~ vôo to take wing. ~ vulto to grow in volume. não ~ conhecimento to overlook, disregard. estou tomando conta desta casa I am in charge of this house. ele toma conta do negócio todo he runs the whole show. ele foi tomado de dores na perna a pain took him in the leg. ele tomou a si o encargo he took it up himself. tomei-o pelo seu irmão I mistook you four your brother. tomou-nos a noite the night overtook us. tomas-me por parvo? do you take me for a fool? foram tomadas todas as providências all arrange-

ments have been made. **ele tomou o resto** he finished off the dish. **ele tomou rumo certo** he steered a straight course. **isto toma todo meu tempo** it takes up all my time. **ele tomou um trago** he took a drink, (coll.) wetted his whistle. **por quem me toma?** what do you take me for? **temos de ~ outro trem** we must change trains. **toma lá, dá cá** give-and-take. **tomo as coisas como são** I take the bad with the good. **tomará parte nisto?** will you have a share in it? **vale mais um toma que dois te darei** a bird in the hand is worth two in the bush.

tomara interj. (Braz.) God grant! let us hope for the best!
~ que não I hope not. **~ eu que assim fosse!** would it were so! **~ ter-me ido embora** I wish I had gone away.

tomara-que-caia s. m., sg. + pl. (Braz., sl.) strapless dress or blouse. ‖ adj. m. + f., sg. + pl. strapless.

tomatada s. f. tomato juice, tomato pulp.

tomate s. m. (bot.) tomato: 1. plant. 2. fruit; love apple.

tomate-do-amazonas s. m. (pl. **tomates-do-amazonas**) Amazon tomato.

tomate-de-sodoma s. m. (pl. **tomates-de-sodoma**) (bot.) apple of Sodom, Sodom apple.

tomateira s. f., **tomateiro** m. 1. patch of a shoe. 2. tomato plant.

tomba (I) s. f. 1. vamp. 2. leather back of a book with the title and the author's name.

tomba (II) s. f. (also **espelina**) plant of the cucumber family.

tombada s. f. (S. Braz., also **vertente**) watershed.

tombadilho s. m. (naut.) poop, poop deck, quarter--deck.
~ de passeio promenade deck. **~ superior** hurricane deck. **subir ao ~** to go on deck.

tombador (I) s. m. 1. stumbler, person who stumbles, tumbles or falls. 2. (N. Braz.) worker in a sugar--mill. ‖ adj. tumbling, stumbling, falling down, toppling.

tombador (II) s. m. (Braz.) tableland, plateau with a steep slope toward a river.

tomba-las-águas s. m., sg. + pl. (N. Braz., also **tromba-las-águas**) place where two tides meat in a channel with two openings to the sea.

tombamento s. m. act of falling, stumbling, tumbling, toppling.

tombão s. m. (N. Braz.) rough sea.

tombar (I) v. 1. to tumble, stumble, topple; throw or fall down, plump. 2. to overthrow, upset, overturn, tilt, tip. 3. to reel, stagger. 4. (N. Braz., pop.) to change the course or way (on a trip).
tombe isto topple this down. **fazer ~ to purl,** overturn. **os que tombaram na guerra** the fallen (during the war). **o vaso tombou** the vase went over.

tombar (II) v. to register lands, make an inventory of lands.

tombo (I) s. m. 1. tumble, fall, plumper, cropper. 2. turnover, upset. 3. a high waterfall. 4. (pop.) capacity, nature, temperament of a person.
~ de dados throw of dice. **andar aos ~s** to stumble or stagger along. **dar o ~ em alguém** (Braz., pop.) to prejudice someone, let a person down. **dar, levar um ~** to tumble, fall down.

tombo (II) s. m. land-office; collection or register of charters and grants of land.

tômbola s. f. 1. lotto, bingo. 2. tombola, a sort of lottery (esp. at a bazaar).

tombolar v. 1. to win at lotto. 2. to win a tombola prize.

tomé s. m. (Braz., sport. sl.) sudden discontinuation of play by one of the players.
dar o ~ to abandon the game.

tome-juízo s. m. (pl. **tome-juízos**) (Braz., sl.) firewater, rum.

tomento s. m. 1. tow, hurds, hards, scutch, oakum, refuse (of flax, hemp, etc.). 2. (bot.) tomentum: dense covering of woolly hairs.

tomentoso adj. (bot.) tomentose: densely covered with woolly hairs.

tomilhal s. m. (pl. **-ais**) ground covered with thyme.

tomilho s. m. (bot., also **timo**) thyme, pungent and aromatic herb used for seasoning.

tomíparo adj. (biol.) said of plants or animals which reproduce by division.

tomismo s. m. Thomism: philosophical and theological doctrine of Thomas Aquinas.

tomista s. m. + f. Thomist: follower of Thomism. ‖ adj. Thomist(ic): of or relating to Thomism.

tomístico adj. Thomistic: relating to Thomas Aquinas and his doctrine.

tomo s. m. 1. tome, volume, part of a large work (bound separately); book. 2. (fig.) value, importance, worth.
razões que têm ~ weighty reasons.

tomografia s. f. (med.) tomography: a diagnostic technique using X-rays.

tomotocia s. f. (surg.) Caesarean section or operation.

tona (I) s. f. 1. (bot.) pellicle, bast, inner bark (of a tree); skin, rind, peel, epicarp. 2. surface.
à ~ up. **manter-se à ~ da água** to keep afloat (also fig.). **vir à ~** to come to the surface.

tona (II) s. f. (Braz.) a partridgelike bird.

tona (III) s. f. river-craft in Goa.

tonadilha s. f. a rustic song; little melody.

tonal adj. m. + f. (pl. **-ais**) tonal: of or relating to a tone or tonality. ‖ **~amente** adv. tonally.

tonalidade s. f. tonality: 1. (mus.): a) character of tone. b) system of tones. c) key. 2. (paint.): a) scheme of a picture. b) tint, shade; colouring.
~ azul blue tone or tint, blueness. **controle de ~** tone control (of a radio set).

tonalito s. m. (petrog.) tonalite, a quartz-diorite rock.

tonalização s. f. (pl. **-ões**) (mus., paint.) art of giving a tone to.

tonalizar v. (mus., paint.) to give a tone to.

tonante adj. m. + f. thundering, thunderous, deafening; very loud. ‖ **~mente** adv. most loudly.

tonar v. to thunder.

tondinho s. m. 1. (archit.) tondino; torus, tore, respond. 2. (anat.) tarsus, ancle, ankle.

tonel s. m. (pl. **-éis**) 1. tun, vat, tub, large cask, barrel. 2. (fig.) drunkard, boozer, sot. 3. (obs.) ton.

tonelada s. f. ton (weight of 1,000 kg).
~ métrica metric ton. **~ de registro** register ton.

tonelagem s. f. (pl. **-ens**) tonnage: 1. capacity of a ship. 2. burden, lastage, cargo, load, ballast, shipping.
~ bruta gross tonnage. **~ de registro** register tonnage.

tonelaria s. f. (also **tonoaria**) cooperage.

tôni s. m. clown, buffon.

tônica s. f. tonic: 1. (mus.) the fundamental note of a key; key-note. 2. (gram.) accented, stressed syllable of a word; tonic vowel.

tonicidade s. f. tonicity: 1. the state of being tonic. 2. flexibility of muscle fibers.

tônico s. m. (med.) tonic: corroborative, an invigorating medicine. ‖ adj. tonic: 1. invigorating, bracing, strengthening, roborant, restorative. 2. (mus.) of or pertaining to a key-note, fundamental. 3. (gram.) accentual, voiced, stressed. 4. predominant. ‖ **-amente** adv. tonically.

~ **nervino** nervine. **acento** ~ tonic accent, primary accent.

tonificante adj. m. + f. tonic: animating, invigorating, strengthening. ‖ ~**mente** adv. tonically.

tonificar v. to invigorate, strengthen, animate, refresh, brace; tone up.

tonilho s. m. 1. tune, air. 2. song, little melody.

toninha s. f. 1. (ichth.) a young tunny. 2. (zool.) harbour porpoise.

tonismo s. m. (med.) tetanics, lockjaw.

tonite s. f. tonite: an explosive consisting of gun-cotton and nitrate.

tonitruante adj. m. + f., **tonítruo, tonitruoso** m. thundering, thunderous.

tono s. m. 1. (mus.) tone; aria, song. 2. attitude. 3. (physiol.) tonus, muscular tonus. 4. sense, feeling.

tonógrafo s. m. (physiol.) tonograph.

tonometria s. f. tonometry, measuring of tension or pressure.

tonômetro s. m. tonometer, instrument for measuring tension or pressure (blood, vapour, steam, etc.).

tonoplasto s. m. (biol.) tonoplast.

tonsila s. f. (anat.) tonsil.

tonsilar adj. m. + f. tonsil(l)ar.

tonsilite s. f. (med.) tonsillitis: inflammation of the tonsils.

tonsura s. f. tonsure: 1. custom or rite of shaving the crown (of a priest). 2. the shaven crown of a priest.

tonsurado s. m. a priest. ‖ adj. tonsured, shaved.

tonsurar v. to tonsure, make a tonsure on; shave the head of a priest.

tonta s. f. foolish woman.

tontear v. 1. to act foolishly, to fool; stupefy, trifle. 2. to talk nonsense.

tonteira, tontice s. f. foolery, foolishness, nonsense; dizziness; dotage.

tontina s. f. tontine, annuity.

tonto s. m. fool, simpleton, imbecil, dolt; puzzlehead, dotard. ‖ adj. 1. giddy, dizzy, flighty, swimming; mazy, barmy. 2. foolish, tipsy, crazy, silly; puzzle-headed. 3. stupid, dull, dense, idiotic. ‖ **-amente** adv. giddily, foolishly.

tontonguê s. m. (Braz.) children's hide-and-seek game.

tontura s. f. giddiness, dizziness, swimming (in the head) vertigo, disturbance.

topa s. f. teetotum (of children).

topada s. f. stumbling, tumbling, trip, tripping, false step.

topador s. m. (Braz., sl.) 1. Jack of all trades, a handy man. 2. daredevil, person who accepts any challenge. ‖ adj. 1. stumbling, tumbling, tripping. 2. handy, skilful, clever. 3. accepting any kind of business. 4. valient, forward.

topar v. 1. to meet, encounter, come across; find. 2. (Braz., sl.) to agree, consent (bet, game, enterprise). 3. to run or strike against; collide. 4. to stumble, tumble, trip. 5. (Braz.) to goad an ox, wound an ox with the goad.

~ **uma brincadeira** to take a joke. ~ **com** to hit upon; meet with. ~ **com alguém** to come across s. o., (coll.) come flush on one. ~ **a parada** to accept a challenge. **eu topo aquilo** I agree. **topei-o na praia** I met him on the beach.

toparca s. m. toparch.

toparquia s. f. toparchy.

topatinga s. m. (Braz., hist.) nick-name of the Dutch during the invasion period.

topa-tudo s. m., sg. + pl. (Braz., sl.) person engaged in all sorts of business; Jack-of-all-trades; person who accepts any challenge, bet or the like.

topázio s. m. topaz: semiprecious stone (usually of yellow colour).

~ **falso** false topaz (a sort of yellow quartz). ~ **oriental** yellow sapphire.

tope s. m. 1. clash, striking; collision. 2. top, summit. 3. (naut.) masthead. 4. cockade, rosette, knot. 5. embarrassment, impediment, obstacle, hindrance.

topetada s. f. 1. butt with the head. 2. blow with a club or heavy hammer.

topetar v. 1. to butt with the head; bump one's head against. 2. to touch the top or the highest point; top. 3. to mount, ascend.

~ **com as estrelas** to reach to the stars.

topete (ê) s. m. 1. toupee, topknot, crest, forelock; tuft of feathers or hair, panache (plate C 12). 2. (Braz.) impudence, insolence, cheekiness, sauciness. **abaixar o** ~ to bring or come dom a peg or two.

topeteira s. f. = **festeira.**

topetudo adj. 1. wearing a toupee. 2. (Braz.) said of a horse with a long mane. 3. impudent, shameless.

topiaria s. f. topiary, art of cutting trees and shrubs into ornamental forms.

topiário s. m. topiarist: gardener skilled in cutting trees and shrubs into ornamental forms.

tópica s. f. the science of topical remedies.

tópico s. m. 1. topic: a) subject, theme; heading, matter, text. b) argument; literary composition or conversation. c) topical remedy. 2. (Braz., journal) leader: an editorial article, leading article. 3. ~**s** pl. commonplaces. ‖ adj. topical: 1. of or pertaining to a place. 2. relating to a heading or subject. 3. (journal) referring to the topics of the day. 4. (med.) of local application. ‖ **topicamente** adv. topically.

topinambo s. m. (bot.) Jerusalem artichoke.

topiquista s. m. + f. (Braz., journal) author of editorial articles or leading articles.

topo s. m. (obs.) impact, shock, clash, collision.

topo s. m. 1. summit, top, peak, acme, highest point. 2. upper part. 3. end, extremity, edge.

de ~ suddenly, all of a sudden.

topofobia s. f. topophobia: morbid fear of certain places.

topófobo s. m. person suffering from topophobia.

topografia s. f. topography: 1. detailed description of a place. 2. the art to design local features on maps, etc. 3. (anat.) description of the anatomy of particular parts of the human body.

topográfico adj. topographical. ‖ **topograficamente** adv. topographically.

topógrafo s. m. topographer.

topologia s. f. topology: 1. study of a place (esp. relating to its history). 2. (math.) a branch of superior geometry (analysis situs).

topológico adj. topological.

toponímia s. f. toponymy: linguistic and historical studies of place names.

toponímico adj. toponymic(al).

topônimo s. m. toponym: place name.

toporama s. m. panorama of a certain place.

toque (ô) s. m. 1. touch, contact; taction, feeling. 2. (mil.) call, recall, toot. 3. (mus.) playing, striking, chime, sounding; blast. 4. handclasp, handshake. 5. vestige, sign, trace. 6. retouching. 7. artistic touch. 8. bouquet, distinctive aroma (of wine). 9. aid, inspiration. 10. rotten spot (of a fruit). 11. test, assay, trial, proof, standard.

~ **de alvorada** (mil.) reveille, rouse. ~ **de buzina de caça** call of the hunter's horn. ~ **de campainha** ring (of a bell). ~ **de clarim ou corneta** blast, bugle call, tuck. ~ **a finados** death-bell. ~ **da graça** aid, inspiration by God. ~ **de pincel** touch, stroke (brush). ~ **de reunião** (mil.) assembly, tattoo. ~ **de retirada** retire signal. ~ **de silêncio** taps, lights out, last post. ~ **de sinos** clangour (of bells), ding-dong. ~ **de tambor** drumbeat. **ao mais leve** ~ at the slightest touch. **pedra de** ~ touch-stone.

toque (II) s. m. oriental name for carbuncle (red precious stone).

toque (III) s. m. toque: a lady's hat.

toque-emboque s. m. croquet (a game).

toqueiro s. m. a rubber-gatherer who works on an output basis.

toque-toque s. m. (pl. **toque-toques**) (Braz.) quickstep.

tora (I) s. f. 1. (mil., sl.) share or portion of meat. 2. portion, share. 3. (Braz., sl.) nap, short sleep, doze. 4. log, timber, trunk of a tree.

tora (II) s. f. Torah (Law of Moses).

tora (III) s. f. (Braz., bot.) coffeeweed.

torácico adj. thoracic.

toracocentese s. f. (surg.) thoracocentesis.

toracolombar adj. m. + f. (anat.) thoracolumbar.

toracometria s. f. thoracometry: measurement of the thorax.

toracoplastia s. f. (surg.) thoracoplasty: plastic surgery of the thorax.

toracoscopia s. f. thoracoscopy: diagnostic examination of the chest.

torado adj. 1. cut into logs. 2. bobtailed.

toral s. m. (pl. **-ais**) the strongest part of a spear or lance.

toranja s. f. (bot.) grapefruit.

torar v. 1. to cut into stumps or logs. 2. (N. Braz., pop.) to cut (saw) into pieces. 3. (S. Braz., pop.) to go away, depart.

tórax s. m., sg. + pl. (anat.) thorax, chest, breast.

torbenita s. f. torbenite, uranite.

torça s. f. 1. lintel. 2. an oblong squared stone.

torçado s. m. lintel of a door.

torçal s. m. (pl. **-ais**) 1. silk cord; twisted silk. 2. (Braz.) halter (rope and headstall).

torçalado adj. decked with twisted silk.

torção s. f. (pl. **-ões**) 1. torsion, turn, intorsion. 2. twisting, squirming, wriggling.

torcaz adj. m. + f. (ornith.) said of a species of pigeon.

torce-cabelo s. m. (pl. **torce-cabelos**) (ent.) stingless bee of the genus Melipona.

torcedela s. f. (also **torcedura**) twist, twisting, wrench.

torcedor s. m. 1. twister, wringer, throwster; spindle; twisting machine. 2. (fig.) rooter, person who cheers or applauds. || adj. 1. twisting, wriggling, squirming. 2. cheering, applauding, inciting.

torcedura s. f. 1. twist, act of twisting; wrench, winding. 2. turn, sprain, wring. 3. distortion, subterfuge, evasion.

torcer v. 1. to twist, turn, wring, wrench, bend, twine; curl, screw. 2. to distort, contort, sprain, crick, dislocate. 3. to pervert, misinterpret, alter the meaning. 4. to root, pull for; entice, cheer. 5. **~-se** to writhe, squirm, grow crooked, wriggle. ~ **a boca** to make a wry face. ~ **o caminho** to take a different way, deviate. ~ **fio** to twist thread. ~ **as mãos em desespero** to wring one's hands in despair. ~ **o nariz** to turn up one's nose, sniff at. ~ **a orelha e não deitar sangue** to repent, see one's mistake. ~ **os seus pauzinhos** to pull strings, wirepull. ~ **o pé** to strain the foot or ankle. ~ **o pescoço da galinha** to wring the hen's neck; kill by twisting the neck. **~-se de riso** to be convulsed by laughter. ~ **roupa** to wring clothes (wring water out from washing). ~ **seda** to twist silk. ~ **o sentido das leis** to twist or force the sense of a text (law). ~ **a verdade** to stretch truth. **antes quebrar que** ~ rather break than yield. **é**

aí que a porca torce o rabo that's where the shoe pinches. **não dar o braço a** ~ to refuse to admit anything.

torcicolo s. m. 1. winding, roundabout way. 2. subterfuge, evasion. 3. (fig.) ambiguity. 4. (med.) torticollis, stiff neck, crick in the neck. 5. (ornith.) wryneck.

torcida s. f. 1. wick. 2. (Braz.): a) act of rooting and cheering (in a game). b) group of rooters or cheerers.

torcido adj. tortuous, twisted, wrested, wreathed; crooked; sinuous, sinuate, curved; oblique. **coluna -a** a wreathed column.

torcilhão s. m. (pl. **-ões**) (surg.) pl. gripes, intestinal colic.

torcimento s. m. = **torcedura**.

torço s. m. 1. = **torcedura**. 2. (N. Braz.) a shawl wound around the head like a turban.

torcular (I) adj. m. + f. of the shape of a small (printing) press or small (metal) polisher.

torcular (II) v. to smooth, polish (with or as with a **tórculo**).

tórculo s. m. 1. small printing press. 2. apparatus for polishing metals or crystals.

tordilhada s. f. (S. Braz.) a lot or quantity of dapple--gray horses.

tordilho adj. dapple, dapple-gray, dapple-grey (horse).

tordo s. m. 1. (ornith.) thrush. 2. a species of Mediterranean fish.

tordo-americano s. m. (pl. **tordos-americanos**) (ornith.) cat-bird.

tordo-branco s. m. (pl. **tordos-brancos**) (ornith.) mavis, redwing.

tordo-canoro s. m. (pl. **tordos-canoros**) (ornith.) song--thrush.

tordo-visgueiro s. m. (pl. **tordos-visgueiros**) (ornith.) missel-thrush.

tordo-zornal s. m. (pl. **tordos-zornais**) (ornith.) fieldfare.

torém (I) s. m. (pl. **-éns**) (Braz., bot.) trumpetwood, snakewood.

torém (II) s. m. (pl. **-éns**) a bamboo flute.

torena s. m. (S. Braz.) notable, person of distinction; courageous person. || adj. notable, distinguished, courageous.

torênia s. f. torenia (a genus of tropical herbs).

toreumatografia s. f. toreumatography: description of ancient basso-rilievos.

toreumatógrafo s. m. expert in toreumatography.

toreuta s. m. person who sculptures toreutics.

torêutica s. f. toreutics: carved or embossed work, esp. in metal.

torga s. f., **torgo** m. (bot., also **urze**) heather, common heath, briar.

tori s. m. torii: gateway of a Shinto temple.

torilo s. m. (bot.) bract, leaf from the axil of which a floral axis arises.

torínio, tório s. m. (chem.) thorium, a radioactive element.

torita s. f. (min.) thorite; thorium silicate.

tormenta s. f. 1. violent storm, tempest. 2. (fig.) vexation, turbulence, trouble, disturbance; agitation.

tormentilha s. f. (bot.) tormentil.

tormento s. m. 1. torment, worriment, affliction, distress, anguish. 2. torture, pain, martyrdom. 3. agony, mortification, suffering.

tormentório adj. stormy, tempestuous, turbulent.

tormentoso adj. 1. tempestuous, boisterous, stormy, turbulent, violent. 2. (fig.) vexatious, worrisome, embarrassing, troublesome, tormenting. || **-amente** adv. tormentingly.

torna s. f. 1. compensation; restitution. 2. return, rendition, requital. 3. earnest-money.

tornada (I) s. f. 1. returning. 2. (poet.) final strophe of a sestina (consisting of three verses).

tornada (II) s. f. rest of the contents of a cask spilt when the tap is removed.

tornadiço adj. deserting, apostate, renegade, faithless; changeable, fickle.

tornado s. m. tornado: tropical thunderstorm.

tornadura s. f. tool to bend barrel hoops or wickers; machine to make hoops.

torna-fio s. m. (pl. **torna-fios**) a combmaker's tool.

tornar v. 1. to return; go, turn or come back or again. 2. to give back, send back, repay. 3. to reply, answer, retort. 4. to translate, transform. 5. to render, change, convert. 6. **~-se** to become, get, grow into, turn into.
~ acessível to open up. **~ alegre** to animate. **~ amargo** to bitter. **~ apresentável** to link into shape. **~ atrás** to turn back. **~ banal** to commonplace. **~ a bater** to strike again. **~-se cinzento** to grizzle. **~ confuso** to complicate, perplex, embarrass. **~ conhecido** to make or become known, blaze. **~ contente** to content. **~ digno** to dignify. **~ a empregar capital** to reinvest money. **~ a falar de um assunto** to come back to a subject. **~ a fazer** to do again, make again. **~ fora de moda** to outmode. **~ a filmar** (cinema) to retake. **~ gelatinoso** to jelly. **~-se granulado** to granulate. **~-se hábito** to grow into a habit. **~ impudente** to brazen. **~ impossível** to render impossible. **~-se inapto** to disqualify, disable. **~ inerte** to stagnate. **~ nulo** to nullify, render void. **~ pálido** to turn pale. **~-se um peso para alguém** to lie hard or heavy on. **~-se polposo** to pulp. **~-se preto** to blacken, darken. **~-se mais profundo** to deepen. **~-se público** to leak out. **~(-se) ridículo** to turn into ridicule. **~ a si** to regain consciousness. a melancolia tornou-se sua segunda natureza his melancholy grew upon him. o tempo passa e não torna time passes away never to return. tudo se torna fácil quando se quer where there's a will, there's a way. ele tornou-se pálido e corado, alternadamente his colour came and went. ele tornou-se um rapaz diligente he has turned out a diligent boy.

tornassol s. m. (pl. **-óis**) (bot.) sunflower, heliotrope. **papel de ~** litmus paper.

torna-viagem s. f. (pl. **torna-viagens**) 1. return voyage, return from a sea voyage. 2. refuse, leavings.

torneado adj. 1. turned, well-turned, roundish, rolling. 2. (fig.) well chosen (words).

torneador s. m. 1. turner. 2. tool of a gunsmith. 3. a wheelwright's workbench. ‖ adj. turning (on the lathe).

torneamento s. m. turning.
~ de madeira wood turning.

tornear (I) v. 1. to turn; turn round; turn on a lathe. 2. to shape, mold; polish. 3. to surround, encompass.

tornear (II) v. to joust, tilt; take part in a tournament.

tornearia s. f. 1. a turner's work or office. 2. a turner's workshop, turnery.

torneável adj. m. + f. (pl. **-áveis**) turnable.

torneio (I) s. m. 1. act or fact of turning, shaping on a lathe. 2. refinement of a phrase. 3. flexible elegance of forms.

torneio (II) s. m. 1. tournament, joust, tourney, tilt. 2. (fig.) discussion, polemics.

torneira s. f. 1. tap, faucet, cock (plates B 3, C 20, D 1, E 3, P 19). 2. plug, spile, spigot, register.
~ com parafuso de pressão screw-down cock (plate E 3). **~ de cerveja** beer tap (plate R 5). **~ de derivação** twig tap (plate E 13). **~ de fechamento**

stopcock (plate E 13). **~ de fundo** (naut.) sea cock. **~ de gás** gas tap (plate F 3). **~ de prova** test cock. **fechar a ~** to turn off the tap.

torneiro s. m. turner, person who works on a lathe.

torneja s. f. axle-pin, linch-pin.

tornejar v. 1. to turn a corner. 2. to curve, bend, make round. 3. to meander (river). 4. to surround, encompass.

tornel s. m. (pl. **-éis**) 1. swivel. 2. each of the handles of a bow saw.

tornilheiro s. m. (mil.) deserter. ‖ adj. deserting, abandoning the service without (permission) leave.

tornilho s. m. 1. (mil., obs.) a sort of punishment. 2. (fig.) a risky move; pinch.

torninho s. m. 1. small vice (plates F 1, P 4). 2. small lathe.

torniquete s. m. 1. turnstile; wicket. 2. (surg.) torniquet: instrument for compressing an artery. 3. small vice. 4. (hist.) rack, instrument of torture. 5. drudgery; embarrassment, difficulty; pinch.

torno (ô) s. m. (pl. **tornos**) 1. lathe. 2. vice. 3. faucet, spigot; tap. 4. wooden peg, pin. 5. a round; turn around.
~ de bancada 1. bench lathe, turn bench. 2. (also **torninho**) vice, vise (plates F 1, P 4). **~ de faces** face lathe. **~ de fiar** spinning wheel. **~ de fiar lã** throstle, machine for spinning wool. **~ de mão** vice. **~ mecânico** power lathe. **~ de oleiro** potter's wheel. **~ a pedal** foot lathe. **~ revólver** capstan lathe. **~ de repuxar** mandril. **em ~** around, about, all around. **olhar em ~ de si** to look about.

tornozeleira s. f. (Braz.) an ankle pad.

tornozelo s. m. (anat.) tarsus, ancle, ankle; anklebone (plates C 18).

toro (I) s. m. 1. trunk or stump (of a tree), log. 2. (trunk) of a body; torso. 3. heath, heather. 4. (archit.) torus (lowest molding of the base of a column). 5. (math.) torus.

toro (II) s. m. (poet.) bridal bed, nuptial bed.

toro (III) s. m. (bot.) = **torilo**.

toró (I) s. m. (Braz.) 1. (zool.) spiny rat. 2. (N. Braz.) bird of the genus Tinamus. 3. a small trumpet or bugle of the Indians.

toró (II) s. m. heavy downpour, rainstorm.

toró (III) adj. m. + f. (Braz.) said of a person who has a finger or a digital bone missing.

torocana s. f. (Braz.) drum made out of a log, with which Indians give informations (signals) to their neighbours.

torom-torom s. m. (pl. **torom-torons**) (Braz., ornith.) ant king.

toronja s. f. (bot., also **toranja**) grapefruit.

toropixi s. m. (Braz.) umbrella bird.

tororó s. m. (Braz., sl.) idle talk, gabble. ‖ adj. m. + f. (Braz.) 1. short, thickset. 2. cut short, trimmed, clipped.

tororoma s. f. (N. Braz.) noisy and impetuous watercourse.

toroso adj. torose, torous; pulpy, fleshy, corpulent.

torpe (I) adj. m. + f. 1. base, vile, dirty, shameful, unworthy. 2. obscene, indecent. 3. dishonest, scurrilous. ‖ **~mente** adv. basely.

torpe (II) adj. m. + f. 1. torpid, apathetic. 2. timid, bashful. ‖ **~mente** adv. torpidly.

torpecer v. (also **entorpecer**) 1. to make torpid, benumb, stupefy, deaden. 2. to grow torpid or benumbed.

torpedear v. (also **torpedar**) 1. to torpedo, attack with a torpedo. 2. to destroy (as with torpedoes). 3. (fig.) to wreak, shatter, ruin.

torpedeamento s. m. (also **torpedagem** f., pl. **-ens**) torpedoing, destroying by torpedoes.

torpedeiro s. m. (mil.) torpedo-boat.

torpedo s. m. torpedo: a dirigible self propelling submarine projectile.
~ **aéreo** aerial torpedo. **lança** ~s torpedo tube. **peixe** ~ (ichth.) crampfish, electric ray.

torpente adj. m. + f. torpid, numb, benumbed. || ~**mente** adv. torpidly, numbly.

torpeza, torpidade s. f. (also **torpitude**) 1. turpitude, baseness, depravity, vileness, dirtiness, paltriness, meanness. 2. nastiness, filthiness, indecency, lewdness.

tórpido adj. torpid, numb, benumbed; apathetic, dull.

torpor s. m. torpor, torpidity, numbness, dormancy; lethargy, apathy; daze.

torque s. m. (mech.) torque.

torquês s. f. (pl. **-eses**) pincers, a pair of pincers; gripping tool (plates F 1, M 4, T 1).

torra s. f. 1. act of toasting or roasting. 2. (Braz., min.) carbonado of inferior quality.

torração s. f. 1. act of toasting. 2. (Braz., coll.) sale at any price; selling off at a loss, fire sale.

torrada s. f. toast: sliced bread, browned before a fire.
~ **com manteiga** buttered toast. ~ **com queijo derretido** rarebit. **sobre** ~ on toast.

torradeira s. f. toaster.

torrado s. m. (N. Braz.) popular dance, a sort of samba. || adj. 1. toasted, roasted, crisp, crispy. 2. parched, dried, browned. 3. scorched, torrid. || **-amente** adv. crisply.
~ **pelo sol** sunburnt. **bolacha -a** crisp biscuit.

torrador s. m. toaster, roaster.
~ **de café** coffee roaster.

torrão s. m. (pl. **-ões**) 1. clod, lump or mass of soil, turf or clay. 2. glebe, terrain, tract of land. 3. (fig.) cob, clump, lump, bat. 4. (N. Braz., by extension) sandy clay, clay shoal. 5. ~**s** pl. farmland.
~ **de açúcar** sugar-loaf. ~ **natal** native land.

torrar v. 1. to toast, roast, brown, grill, crisp. 2. to parch, dry, scorch. 3. (Braz., fig.) to sell off at a loss.

torre s. f. 1. tower, steeple. 2. pylon. 3. fortress. 4. (chess) castle, rook (plate X).
~ **d'água** water tower. ~ **albarrã**, ~ **de observação** watch tower. ~ **de Babel** tower of Babel. ~ **de borbulhamento** (oil) bubble tower. ~ **de comando** submarine conning tower. ~ **de igreja** steeple. ~ **de mensagem** donjon, keep. ~ **de relógio** clock tower. ~ **de sinos** campanile, bell tower, belfry. ~ **de tiro** gun turret. **alto como uma** ~ as tall as a poplar tree.

torreado adj. 1. towered, turreted. 2. tower-shaped.

torreame s. m. (N. Braz.) castlelike, towering clouds.

torreante adj. m. + f. towering, towerlike. || ~**mente** adv. toweringly.

torreão s. m. (pl. **-ões**) 1. turret, small tower, pavilion (at an angle of a larger building).
~ **de defesa** bartizan.

torrear v. (also **torrejar**) 1. to surround or adorn with towers or turrets. 2. to tower, be lofty.

torrefação s. f. (pl. **-ões**) torrefaction, torrefying, roasting, toasting.

torrefato, torrefeito adj. torrefied, toasted, roasted, scorched, browned.

torrefator s. m. roaster, toaster. || adj. roasting, toasting.

torrefazer v. to torrify, roast, toast, scorch, parch.

torreira s. f. 1. violent heat of the sun; solar heat, noonday heat. 2. high noon.

torrencial adj. m. + f. (pl. **-ais**) torrential, pouring, like a torrent. || ~**mente** adv. torrentially.
chove ~**mente** it is pouring with rain. **a chuva cai** ~**mente** the rain comes down in sheets.

torrente s. f. 1. torrent, downpour, flow, stream, flood, cataract, gush. 2. multitude, plenty, abundance.
~ **de lágrimas** a flood of tears. ~ **de luz** a flood of light. ~ **de palavras** a stream of words, spate of talk.

torrentoso adj. torrent, rushing, rapid. || **-amente** adv. torrentially.

torresmo s. m. 1. crackling (browned rasher of lard), scrap. 2. (S. Braz., fig.) fat child, roly-poly child, fatty.

tórrido adj. torrid, very hot, burning.
zona -a torrid zone.

torrificar v. = **torrefazer.**

torrija s. f. toast soaked in wine and covered with eggs and sugar.

torrinha s. f. 1. turret. 2. (aeron.) astrodome. 3. (theat.) peanut gallery.

torrinheiro s. m. (theat.) person who habitually takes the peanut gallery.

torroada s. f. 1. large quantity of clods. 2. blow with a clod. 3. (Braz.) stretch of (high)land full of well-yielding rubber trees. 4. (N. Braz.) crack or fissure in a dried up swampy ground.

torso (I) s. m. torso: trunk of a body or statue.

torso (II) s. m. (obs.) spiral column. || adj. twisted, crooked, bent.

torta s. f. 1. tart, pie, patty (plate D 3). 2. cake, oil cake (residue used for fertilizing and feed).
~ **de maçã** apple pie. ~ **de algodão** cotton cake, oil cake.

torteira s. f. patty pan, baking pan.

tortelos s. m. cross-eyed person. || adj. cross-eyed, strabismic(al).

tortinha s. f. tartlet.

torto s. m. (obs.) injury, harm, grievance, unjustness, wrong. || adj. 1. twisted, crooked, bent, curved, oblique, tortuous, winding. 2. deformed, distorted. 3. wrong, unfair, deceitful, unjust, awry, dishonest. 4. one-eyed, squint-eyed, cross-eyed. || **-amente** adv. tortuously.
~ **das pernas** bandy-legged. **a** ~ **e a direito** (fig.) left and right, blindly. **a** ~ **ou a direito** right or wrong, by hook or by crook. **boca -a** splaymouth, wrymouth. **olhar de** ~ **em través** to look askew upon, squint. **pau que** ~ **nasce, nunca ou tarde se endireita** as the twig is bent, so grows the tree; what is bred in the bone, will come out in the flesh.

tortor s. m. (naut.) Spanish windlass.

tortual, tortureiral s. m. (pl. **-ais**) lever of a (wine) press.

tortulho s. m. 1. (bot.) young mushroom. 2. bundle of cleaned an dried guts (for sale). 3. (fig.) stubby or squat person.

tortuosidade s. f. 1. tortuosity, tortuousness, sinuosity, tortility, wryness. 2. twist, turn.

tortuoso adj. 1. tortuous, crooked, curved, sinuous, bent, winding; distortional. 2. untrue, false, disloyal, injust. || **-amente** adv. tortuously.

tortura s. f. 1. torture. 2. pain, anguish, torment, agony. 3. (fig.) grief, heartbreak, sorrow, lament.

torturado s. m. the victim of a torture. || adj. tortured.

torturador s. m. torturer. || adj. torturing.

torturante adj. m. + f. tormenting, torturing, grievous, painful; afflictive, distressing. || ~**mente** adv. torturingly.

torturar v. 1. to torture, rack, torment. 2. to distress, afflict, grieve, bother, worry. 3. ~**-se** to grieve, fry, fret.

tórulo s. m. (bot.) torulus, small torus.

toruloso adj. (bot.) torulose, torulous.

torunguenga s. m. (S. Braz.) 1. fearless person. 2. expert in the use of arms. 3. m. + f. skilful player of a guitar, a mouth organ or an accordeon. ‖ adj. fearless, brave, valiant, courageous, intrepid. ‖ ~mente adv. fearlessly.

torvação s. f. (pl. -ões) (also **torvamento** m.) 1. perturbation, disorder, confusion, disturbance. 2. (fig.) trouble, apprehension, restlessness. 3. tiff, quarrel. 4. moodiness.

torvado adj. perturbed, disturbed, upset, confused.

torvar v. 1. to perturb, disturb, upset, agitate, disquiet. 2. ~-se to get irritated, become sullen or moody.

torvelinhante adj. m. + f. (Braz.) whirling, reeling, turning round. ‖ ~mente adv. whirlingly.

torvelinhar v. to whirl, eddy, gyrate, twirl, swirl.

torvelinho, torvelino s. m. 1. whirl, eddy, vortex, gyration. 2. whirlwind, whirlpool, swirl.

andar num ~ to be in a whirl.

torvo s. m. atrociousness, frightfulness, terribleness. ‖ adj. (pl. **torvos**) (f. **torva**, pl. **torvas**) 1. grim, stern, merciless. 2. moody, frowning. 3. frightful, dreaful, terrific. ‖ **-amente** adv. grimly.

com olhos torvos with a grim look.

tosa (I) s. f. shear, shearing (sheep).

tosa (II) s. f. 1. beating, cudgelling, thrashing, drubbing. 2. (fig.) reproof, reprehension, rebuke, reprimand.

tosador s. m. 1. shearer, one who shears, fleecer, (obs.) sherman. 2. clothworker. 3. cudgeller. ‖ adj. 1. shearing, fleecing. 2. beating, cudgelling, thrashing, drubbing.

tosadura s. f. act of shearing; (sheep) shearing.

tosão s. m. (pl. -ões) 1. fleece (of a sheep). 2. net used to catch trouts. 3. a Spanish order of knighthood (the Golden Fleece).

tosar (I) v. 1. to shear, fleece, clip, scutch. 2. to browse, crop. 3. (fig.) to nibble, gnaw. 4. to graze a pasture.

tosar (II) v. to beat, thrash, cudgel, drub.

toscanejar v. to doze, nod, slumber, drowse, snooze, nap.

toscano (I) s. m. Tuscan: native or inhabitant of Tuscany (district in central Italy). ‖ adj. Tuscan: 1. relating to Tuscany. 2. (archit.) pertaining to the Tuscan order (ancient Roman classical style).

toscano (II) adj. (Braz.) big-nosed.

toscar v. (sl. to see, perceive, notice, understand.

tosco (ô) adj. (pl. **toscos**) (f. **tosca**, pl. **toscas**) 1. rough, uncouth, rude, unpolished, coarse. 2. unwrought, unformed, primitive. 3. clumsy, awkard, inept, gauche. ‖ **-amente** adv. roughly.

tosquia s. f. 1. shearing, clipping. 2. shearing time. 3. (fig.) harsh critique, sharp dressing-down.

tosquiadela s. f. 1. clipping, slight shearing. 2. (fig.) reprimand, rebuke.

tosquiado adj. 1. sheared, clipped, polled. 2. close-cropped.

não ~ unpolled.

tosquiador s. m. shearer, fleecer, clipper. ‖ adj. shearing, fleecing, clipping, cropping.

tosquiar v. 1. to shear, clip, fleece, crop, poll. 2. (fig.) to shave a person, despoil, rob, fleece, strip.

ir buscar lã e vir tosquiado to go for wool and return shorn.

tosse s. f. cough, coughing, tussis.

~ **de cachorro** hacking cough. ~ **comprida** whooping cough. ~ **convulsa** pertussis. ~ **seca** dry cough. **uma** ~ **sufocante** a racking cough.

tossegoso adj. coughing, troubled with a cough.

tossidela s. f. (pop.) coughing, cough, hack.

tossido s. m. a coughing in order to call attention, to give a signal or to manifest an opinion.

tossir v. 1. to cough, hack. 2. to be troubled with a cough.

tosta s. f. toast, slice of browned bread.

tostadela s. f. toasting, light roasting.

tostado adj. 1. toasted, browned. 2. sunburnt; brunet.

tostadura s. f. toasting, roasting; scorching, parching.

tostão s. m. (pl. -ões) Brazilian nickel coin of 100 **réis**, now 10 **centavos**.

sem ~ penniless. **não vale um** ~ it is not worth a toss.

tostar v. 1. to toast, roast, parch, scorch, embrown, singe; tan. 2. ~-se to become scorched, brown, be parched.

toste (I) s. m. 1. toast: a drinking to a person's health. 2. buttered toast.

toste (II) s. m. (obs.) bench of galley slaves.

toste (III) adj. m. + f. rapid, speedy. ‖ adj. rapidly, immediately, presently.

total s. m. (pl. -ais) total, totality, whole, sum. amount, entire, full, integral. ‖ adj. m. + f. total, whole, entire, integral, complete, full, plenary, absolute, utter, universal. ‖ ~mente adv. totally. **eclipse** ~ total eclipse. **no** ~ in the gross, in the aggregate. **perda** ~ total loss. **ruína** ~ utter ruin.

totalidade s. f. 1. totality, entirety, universality; utterness, wholeness, plenitude. 2. the whole sum, quantity or number.

à ~ in all. **a** ~ **de seu sucesso** the utterness of his results. **a quase** ~ almost all.

totalitário adj. totalitarian.

totalitarismo s. m. totalitarianism: government controlled by a political group which does not permit the existence of other political parties.

totalitarista s. m. + f. totalitarian: adherent of totalitarianism. ‖ adj. totalitarian, of or pertaining to totalitarianism.

totalização s. f. (pl. -ões) totalization.

totalizador s. m. totalizator, totalizer, parimutuel.

totalizar v. to totalize.

totem, tóteme s. m. (pl. -ens, -emes) totem: animal or other natural object taken as a clan emblem by certain native tribes.

totêmico adj. totemic.

totemismo s. m. totemism: belief in totems.

totipalmas s. f. pl. a genus of animals which have the toes united by a web.

totó s. m. (pop.) little dog.

touca s. f. 1. toque: a lady's small brimless hat; bonnet, cap (plate R 6). 2. a nun's coif.

~ **de banho** bathing cap (plate B 3).

toucado s. m. hairdressing, coiffure, headdress, hairdo. ‖ adj. coiffured; wearing a toque.

toucador s. m. 1. hairdresser, coiffeur. 2. dressing table, vanity table, toilet table. 3. dressing room, toilet room. 4. toilet set, toilet service, vanity.

toucar v. 1. to dress the hair, coif. 2. to adorn, embellish. 3. to wear a toque. 4. ~-se to dress one's hair.

touceira s. f. (also **toiceira**) 1. big shoot of a tree. 2. clump of roots. 3. stub or stump of a tree.

toucinho s. m. (also **toicinho**) lard, bacon.

toupeira s. f. 1. (zool.) mole, mould, warp, talpa. 2. (fig.) person with small blinking eyes; nearsighted person. 3. (pop.) half-witted man, booby, mug. 4. old slattern or slut.

toupeirinha s. f. (ent.) mole cricket.

tourada s. f. (also **toirada**) 1. bullfight, bullfighting. 2. drove of bulls.

toural s. m. (pl. -ais) (also **toiral**) 1. cattle market. 2. place where rabbits feed (and where the hunter waits for them).

toureação s. f. (pl. -ões) (S. Braz., also **toireação**) bullfighting.

tourear v. (also **toirear**) 1. to fight bulls, goad bulls. 2. to harass, worry, annoy, pester. 3. (S. Braz.) to flirt.

toureio s. m. (also **toireio**) bullfighting.

toureiro s. m. (also **toireiro**) toreador, bullfighter, torero, matador. ‖ adj. bullfighting.

tourejão s. m. (pl. **-ões**) (also **toirejão**) axle pin.

touril s. m. (pl. **-is**) ox stall, place where the bulls are kept until they enter the arena.

tourinha s. f. (also **toirinha**) a sham bullfight with docile heifers.

tournée s. f. (Fr.) tour.

touro s. m. (also **toiro**) 1. bull. 2. (fig.) a strong man. 3. (astr.) Taurus. 4. **~s** pl. bullfigh(ing). **~ bravo** wild bull. **~ de capa** a bull ready for castration. **~ gordo** stocker. **~ novo** steer. **lançar a capa ao ~** to quit all a man has to save himself. **pegar o ~ pelos chifres** to take the bull by the horns. **ver-se nos chifres do ~** to be in great danger.

tourunguenga s. m. + f. = **torunguenga**.

touruno adj. (S. Braz.) said of a bull improperly castrated.

touta s. f. (pop., also **toita**) head, occiput, (hinder part of the head).

touteador s. m. (also **toiteador**) chatterer, fool, simpleton, silly person. ‖ adj. foolish, silly, simple.

toutear v. (also **toitear**) to talk idly, act foolishly, play the fool.

toutiçada s. f. (also **toitiçada**) blow on the hindhead or the occiput.

toutiço s. m. (also **toitiço**) 1. hindhead, occiput. 2. nape; head.

toutinegra s. f. (ornith.) blackcap.

tovaca s. f. (ornith.) an ant thrush.

tovacuçu s. f. (Braz., ornith.) antking.

toxemia s. f. (med.; also **toxiquemia**) toxemia, toxaemia, blood poisoning.

toxicar v. (also **intoxicar**) to poison.

toxicidade s. f. 1. toxicity, poisonousness, banefulness. 2. quantity of poison necessary to kill an animal in proportion to its weight.

tóxico s. m. toxin, poison, toxic drug. ‖ adj. toxicant; narcotic. ‖ **-amente** adv. poisonously.

toxicóforo adj. yielding poison.

toxicografia s. f. a treatise or description of toxins.

toxicográfico adj. said of a treatise on toxins.

toxicologia s. f. toxicology: science which treats of poisons.

toxicológico adj. toxicological.

toxicólogo s. m. toxicologist.

toxicomania s. f. toxicomania, drug addiction.

toxicômano s. m. person suffering from toxicomania, drug addict.

toxidez s. f. toxicity.

toxima s. f. 1. toxin(e). 2. antitoxin(e).

toxiquêmico adj. toxemic, toxaemic.

toxofilo adj. (bot.) having leaves shaped like arrowheads.

toxóide s. m. (med.) antitoxin.

toxoplasmose s. f. (path.) toxoplasmosis.

trabal adj. (pl. **-ais**) appropriate for nailing girders. **prego ~** clasp nail.

trabalhadeira s. f. diligent or hard-working woman. ‖ adj. f. 1. industrious, diligent, laborious. 2. hard-working.

trabalhado adj. worked, wrought, elaborate, laboured; well-made.

trabalhador s. m. 1. worker, workman. 2. toiler; person who works hard. 3. (S. Braz.) stud-ass. ‖ adj. laborious, diligent, industrious, hard-working, sedulous, busy, plodding. **~ em aço** steelworker. **~ agrícola** farm hand. **ser muito ~** to work like a horse.

trabalhão s. m. hard work, tiring work, drudgery, enormous job; (sl.) a hell of a work or task.

trabalhar v. 1. to work, labour, toil, exert o. s. 2. to drudge. 3. to make efforts, strive, perform, struggle. 4. to run, function, operate, move. 5. to act (on the stage). 6. to realize, accomplish, execute. 7. to manipulate, shape, mold, form. 8. to trouble, worry, harass, tire, fatigue. **~ com agulha** to needle, work with the needle. **~ alternadamente** to work by turns. **~ arduamente** to drudge, work doggedly. **~ para o bispo** to work without reward, have a thankless task, work for a dead horse. **~ aos bocados** to work only by snatches. **~ em conjunto** to work together, to team. **~ como construtor** to build. **~ por conta própria** to work for o. s. **~ contra** to counterwork, work against. **~ demais** to overplay, overtoil. **~ demoradamente em alguma coisa** to work a long time at s. th., hammer something. **~ de dia** to work in the daytime. **~ duramente ou com grande energia** to work hard, like a horse. **~ por empreitada** to work by contract. **~ como escrevente** to clerk. **~ excessivamente** to overlabour. **~ numa fazenda** to work upon a farm, ranch. **~ de graça** to work for nothing. **~ sem interrupção** to work without intermission. **~ muito** to fag. **~ de noite** to work at night. **~ pesadamente** to travail. **~ sem proveito, em vão** to work in vain, plough the sands. **~ em rodízio** to take turns at work. **~ do raiar ao pôr-do-sol** to work from sunrise to sunset. **~ por salário inferior** to undercut. **~ a terra** to till the ground. **~ por todas as vias** to toil and moil. **~ com zelo** to fettle, work with care. **comer sem ~** to eat the bread of idleness. **fazer ~** to start, set going. **fingir que trabalha** to give eyeservice, pretend to work. **ele já trabalha no teatro há vinte anos** he has been on the stage for twenty years.

trabalheira s. f. 1. hard work, toil, drudgery. 2. bustle, effort.

trabalhismo s. m. labourism: principle to secure the economic rights of the working classes.

trabalhista s. m. labourite: member of a labour party. ‖ adj. m. + f. of or pertaining to the working classes or labour parties.

trabalho s. m. 1. work, labour, task, toil; doing, ado. 2. effort, exertion, struggle. 3. job, employment, service, occupation; duty. 4. business, trade. 5. performance, achievement, result (of work), production, piece of work. 6. **~s** pl. proceedings, enterprise, undertaking. **~ adicional** extra work. **~ de agulha** needlework. **~ árduo** moil, travail. **~ artístico** art work. **~ avulso** odd job. **~ braçal, ~ manual** manual work, handiwork. **~ caseiro** homework. **~ em contrário** counterwork. **~ de crochê** crochet. **~ diário** daily task, trivial round. **~ por dia** daywork, journey work. **~ doméstico** homework, housewifery, chore. **~ embutido** inlaid work. **~ de empreitada** taskwork. **~ enfadonho** wearisome work, drudgery, (coll.) donkey-work. **~ de equipe** teamwork. **~ de escravo** slave labour. **~ de escritório** clerical work. **~ excessivo** overwork. **~ fácil** easy work, (mil.) bobby's job. **~ feito e pago por peças** piecework. **~s forçados** forced labour. **~ por hora** timework. **~ inquietante** anxious work. **~ intelectual** brainwork. **~ malfeito** botchery. **~ mal remunerado** poorly paid work. **~ mental** headwork. **~ em mina** mining, work in a mine. **~ de ocasião** odd job, chore. **~ penoso** drudgery, fatigue, collar work. **~ perdido** waste of time. **~ em relevo** chasing work. **~ de rotina**

routine work, donkey-work. ~ **de sapa** spadework, underhand work. ~ **sujo** dirty work. ~ **em xadrez** checker work. ~ **bem começado é caminho meio andado** work well begun is half done. ~ **comum**, ~ **de nenhum** too many cooks spoil the broth. **bom** ~! good work! **com muito** ~ with much difficulty. **companheiro de** ~ fellow worker, (pop.) mate. **dá muito** ~ it takes a lot of doing. **dar-se ao** ~ to bother. **eu me dei ao** ~ **de** I endeavoured to, I put myself out of the way to. **dia do** ~ Labour Day. **é** ~ **demais** it is too much trouble. **fazer bom** ~ to do good work. **forçar seu caminho com duro** ~ to work round. **meter-se em** ~**s** to get into trouble. **não há atalho sem** ~ there's no short cut to success. **não se dê ao** ~ save yourself the trouble. **não vale o** ~ **que dá** it is not worth the trouble, not worth the candle. **pôr o** ~ **em dia** to catch up with one's work. **sem** ~ breadless, out of job, out of work. **sem** ~ **nada se alcança** no pains, no gains. **sobrecarregar de** ~ to overtask. **subir à custa de** ~ to work one's way up. **voltar à vida de** ~ to return to the plough.

trabalhoso adj. 1. hard, toilful, toilsome, arduous, difficult. 2. painful, fatiguing, tiring, troublesome. ‖ **-amente** adv. hardly.

trabécula s. f. 1. a small (wooden) beam. 2. (anat.) trabecula.

trabelho s. m. 1. toggle, tightener, tightening lever of a frame saw (plates S 2). 2. chessman.
sem trelho nem ~ having neither head nor tail; confusedly, without order. **colocar** ~ to toggle.

trabucada s. f. 1. shot with a trebuchet, noise made by a trebuchet. 2. (by extension) noise; rattle, roar, rumble.

trabucador s. m. 1. person who works hard for his living. 2. (S. Braz., pop.) diligent, industrious man. ‖ adj. hard-working, laborious, industrious, diligent.

trabucar v. 1. to attack with a trebuchet. 2. to cause to sink (ships). 3. to work hard. 4. to work noisily. 5. to agitate, rouse, stir up.
quem não trabuca não manduca no work no pay.

trabuco s. m. 1. trebuchet, trebucket (Middle Ages) a sort of engine used to cast stones against the enemies; catapult, ballista. 2. a sort of blunderbuss. 3. (Braz., pop.) big cigar, esp. one of poor quality.

trabuqueiro s. m. highwayman armed with a blunderbuss.

trabuquete s. m. a small trebuchet, catapult or blunderbuss.

trabuzana s. f. (pop.) 1. tempest, storm. 2. disease, sickness; surfeit. 3. drunkenness. 4. (Braz., pop.) row, riot, disorder, mutiny. 5. m. rowdy, bully, ruffian.

traça (I) s. f. 1. clothes moth, codling moth, silverfish, bookworm. 2. (fig.) any destructive agent that causes a gradual wasting away. 3. tedious person, bore.

traça (II) s. f. 1. tracing, first sketch, draft. 2. plan, scheme. 3. (fig.) cunning, craft, trick. 4. aspect, appearance, look.

traçado s. m. trace, tracing, plan, drawing, design. ‖ adj. drawn, traced, sketchy, delineated, designed. **-amente** adv. tracedly.

traçador s. m. 1. designer, tracer, liner, sketcher, draftsman, draughtsman. 2. crosscut saw (plate F 2). ‖ adj. tracing, designing, drawing.

tracajá s. m. (N. Braz.) a species of fresh-water turtle.

tracalhaz s. m. (pop.; also **tracanaz**) a big slice, portion or lump; hunk, hunch.

tracambista s. m. + f. (Braz.) scoundrel, scamp, scalawag.

traçamento s. m. sketch, drawing, design, outline, delineation.

traçanga s. f. (Braz., ent.) carpenter ant.

tração s. f. (pl. **-ões**) traction, tension, pull, pulling. ~ **dinâmica** (tech.) dynamic thrust. ~ **elétrica** electric traction (plate M 10). **animal de** ~ draft animal. **força de** ~ tensile stress. **prova de ruptura por** ~ tensile test. **resistência à** ~ tensile strength.

traçar (I) v. 1. to trace, draw, delineate, outline, work out, sketch, draught, draft. 2. to plan, map, graph, chart. 3. to project, scheme. 4. to rule, line. 5. to scribe, inscribe, frame. 6. to describe.
~ **uma linha** to draw, extend a line. ~ **uma sublinha** to underscore, underline. ~ **a lápis** to pencil. ~ **o perfil** to draw the profile.

traçar (II) v. 1. to gnaw, eat, destroy (moths). 2. to cut up, cut into pieces. 3. (fig.) to grieve, worry, trouble.

tracejado adj. hatched, marked with little lines.
linha -a broken line (plate L 1).

tracejar v. 1. to trace, sketch, draw, outline, draw lines. 2. to hatch, mark with little lines. 3. to plan, project, scheme.

tracista s. m. + f. 1. tracer, designer, draughtsman. 2. plotter, schemer. ‖ adj. tracing, drawing, sketching.

traço s. m. 1. trace, line, streak, dash. 2. stroke of a pen, pencil or brush. 3. trait, feature, aspect, character, touch. 4. trail, track; vestige, sign, indication; footprint, footstep, mark. 5. (archit.) proportion of ingredients for concrete. 6. point of intersection of two lines. 7. (N. Braz., pop.) draught of a drink.
~ **característico** peculiarity. ~**s de família** family features. ~ **final** (mus.) double bar. ~ **de ligação** (mus.) bind. ~ **de referência** reference mark. ~ **de união** hyphen. **desenho a** ~ line-drawing. **um bom** ~ **(de caráter)** a fine touch (character). **nem um** ~ not a tittle, not a shred. **nenhum** ~ **de perigo** no trace of danger. **sem** ~ traceless. **sem um** ~ **de malícia** without a grain of malice. **ter** ~**s de** to be tinged with.

tracoma s. m. (med.) trachoma: a chronic disease of the eye characterized by inflammatory granulations.

tracomatoso s. m. (med.) person suffering from trachoma. ‖ adj. trachomatous.

tracuá s. f. (Braz.) 1. (ent.) a species of ant. 2. medicinal plant of the arum family.

tradar, tradear v. to bore with an auger (esp. extracting oil of the copal tree).

tradescância s. f. (bot.) a spiderwort.

tradição s. f. (pl. **-ões**) tradition: 1. unwritten transmission of beliefs, costumes, etc., from generation to generation. 2. the knowledge of such transmission. 3. (fig.) remembrance, memory. 4. **-ões** pl. folklore.

tradicional adj. m. + f. (pl. **-ais**) traditional, of or pertaining to tradition, habitual. ‖ ~**mente** adv. traditionally.

tradicionalismo s. m. traditionalism: 1. acceptance of tradition. 2. belief based upon tradition.

tradicionalista s. m. + f. traditionalist: 1. adherent to traditionalism. 2. expert in traditions. ‖ adj. traditionalistic.

tradicionário s. m. traditionist: person versed in traditions or adherent to traditionalism. ‖ adj. traditionary.

trado s. m. 1. bolt auger, drill, boring-tool; broach, piercer (plate F 8). 2. (also **verruma** f.) gimlet (plate F 8). 3. borehole.

tradução s. f. (pl. **-ões**) translation: 1. act of translating. 2. translated work, version.

~ **literal** literal translation. ~ **livre** free translation. **fazer -ões** to do translations, translate. **a ~ está bem feita** the translation is well-done.

tradutor s. m. translator: person who translates a text from one language into another; interpreter. ‖ adj. translating.

~ **juramentado** sworn translator.

traduzir v. 1. to translate: put, turn or render from one language into another. 2. to express, interpret. 3. to manifest itself, appear.

~ **para o francês** to translate, put or turn into French. ~ **mal** to mistranslate. ~ **novamente** to retranslate. **ele traduziu-o rapidamente para o inglês** he hastily threw it into English. **é fácil para ~ it** translates well.

traduzível adj. m. + f. (pl. **-íveis**) translatable.

trafegar v. (also **trafeguear**) 1. to transit, pass through. 2. to traffic, negotiate, trade; buy and sell. 3. to work hard, labour, toil.

tráfego s. m. 1. traffic, trade, business, commerce. 2. transit, transportation, transport. 3. transport department (as of a company or railway). 4. trouble, drudgery, toil and moil.

~ **aéreo** air traffic. ~ **de passageiros** passenger traffic. ~ **aéreo de passageiros** air passenger service. ~ **de automóveis** motor traffic. ~ **de curta distância** short-distance traffic. ~ **engarrafado** traffic jam. ~ **ferroviário** traffic by railway. ~ **marítimo** sea traffic. ~ **preferencial** traffic with the right of way. **aberto ao ~ público** open to public traffic. **afluência de ~** pressure of traffic. **linha de ~** line of communication. **sinal de ~** traffic sign.

traficância s. f. 1. trade, business, commerce. 2. (pop.) roguery, rascality, waggery, swindling, knavery, graft, shifting.

traficante s. m. + f. 1. trafficker, trader, dealer. 2. (pop.) swindler, rascal, rogue, knave, crook. ‖ adj. m. + f. roguish, knavish, dishonest, fraudulent, deceitful. ‖ **~mente** adv. roguishly.

traficar v. 1. to traffic, trade, negotiate, deal, barter. 2. to deal fraudulently, swindle, trick, cheat.

tráfico s. m. 1. traffic, trade, business, commerce. 2. (pop.) underhanded deal, shady business.

~ **das brancas** white slave traffic. ~ **ilícito de narcóticos** drug traffic.

tragacanto s. m. tragacanth: 1. plant that yields gum (milk vetch). 2. (pharm.) gum obtained from the plants of the genus Astragalus.

goma de ~ gum tragacanth.

tragada s. f. 1. draft, draught, pull, swig, a long draft (cigarette or drink). 2. (Braz.) act of devouring, swallowing, engulfing.

tragadeiro s. m. (also **tragadouro**) 1. gullet, gulf, gorge, precipice. 2. (pop.) throat, esophagus.

tragador s. m. devourer, swallower; glutton, gormandizer. ‖ adj. devouring, swallowing, engulfing.

tragadouro s. m. (also **tragadoiro**) gulf, abyss; whirlpool, vortex, eddy.

tragamento s. m. swallowing, engulfing, devouring.

traga-mouros s. m., sg. + pl. (also **traga-moiros**) rude fellow, bully, browbeater; ruffian, blusterer; boor.

tragar v. 1. to devour, swallow, engulf, absorb. 2. to gulp down, drink in large drafts, to gorge, pouch. 3. to put up with, hold out, bear, endure. 4. to inhale tabacco smoke. 5. to swallow, believe (unhesitatingly).

ele foi tragado pelas ondas he was swallowed up by the waves. **não posso tragá-lo** I cannot stand him.

tragédia s. f. tragedy: 1. drama, story with an unhappy theme, buskin. 2. art to compose or act a drama. 3. sad event, disaster, calamity, tragic fate.

~ **sangrenta** fatal tragedy. **parar em ~** to end mournfully.

trágica s. f. tragedienne, actress of a tragedy.

trágico s. m. tragedian: 1. actor of a tragedy. 2. writer of a tragedy. ‖ adj. tragic, mournful, shocking, sad, terrible, fatal, disastrous, dreadful. ‖ **tragicamente** adv. tragically.

ele perdeu a vida tragicamente he lost his life tragically.

tragicomédia s. f. tragicomedy, a drama with tragic and comic events.

tragicômico adj. tragicomic(al).

trago (I) s. m. 1. draught, draft, gulp, swallow, pull, swig. 2. hardship, tribulation, misfortune, bad event.

~ **de bebida** whet, draught, sip. ~ **de despedida** grace cup. **de um só ~** at one draught or gulp. **tomar um ~ da garrafa** to take a pull at the bottle. **tomar um ~ a mais** to have one over the eight. **vamos tomar um ~** let us take a drink, have a wet, let us wet the whistle.

trago (II), **trágus** s. m. (anat.) tragus: part of the inner ear.

tragueado adj. S. Braz.) half-drunk.

traguear v. (S. Braz.) to gulp down, pouch, gorge.

traguinho s. m. (coll.) pony, sip, tot (of whisky or the like).

traição s. f. (pl. **-ões**) (Braz., pop. also **traidoria**) 1. treason, treachery, betrayal; perfidy, perfidiousness, falseness, faithlessness, disloyalty. 2. noisy raising of a farmer by his neighbour who comes to help him and who arrives in the midst of the night with his farm hands.

crime de alta ~ high treason. **matar à ~** to kill by treachery.

traiçoeiro adj. treacherous, treasonable, perfidious, traitorous; disloyal, false, unreliable. ‖ **-amente** adv. treasonably, treacherously.

traidor s. m. traitor, betrayer, renegade, turncoat. ‖ adj. traitorous, perfidious, treacherous; disloyal, false, deceitful, treasonable.

trailer s. m. (Engl.) trailer: a cart, wagon, or van for hauling furniture, etc. 2. a closed vehicle designed to be pulled by an automobile, generally used for camping. 3. a short film containing scenes from a feature picture to be shown.

traimento s. m. less used form of **traição**.

traineira s. f. 1. trawlboat, trawler. 2. (Braz.) net for catching sardines.

trair v. 1. to betray, be false, double-cross; reveal, disclose; peach, impeach, indict; blab. 2. **~-se** to betray o. s., give o. s. away.

~ **sua pátria** to become a traitor to one's country. ~ **um segredo** to disclose a secret.

traíra s. f. (Braz.) a species of voracious freshwater fish.

pegar ~ (N. Braz., fig.) to nod, doze, drowse, nap.

trairambóia s. f. (Braz., ichth.) lepdosiren.

trairão s. m. (pl. **-ões**) one of the large-sized **traíras**, a voracious freshwater fish.

trajar v. 1. to wear, put on, dress, vesture, costume. 2. **~-se** to dress o. s.

~ **bem** to dress well. ~ **de luto** to wear mourning. ~ **de branco** to wear white clothes.

traje s. m. (also **trajo**) 1. dress, cloth(es), garb, apparel, attire, attirement, vestment, clothing, array. 2. costume; robe, suit, habit. 3. **~s** pl. accoutrements, accouterments, regalia.

~ **de banho** bathing suit. ~ **de cerimônia, etiqueta ou gala** full dress, formal dress. ~ **de corte** court dress. ~ **de esporte** sport clothes (plate R 6). ~ **domingueiro** Sunday best. ~ **a fantasia** fancy dress.

~ **de golfe** golf suit (plate R 7). ~**s menores** pl. underclothes. ~ **de montaria** riding habit, riding suit (plate R 7). ~ **ordinário** everyday dress. ~ **de passeio** street clothes (plate R 7). ~ **de rigor** evening dress, evening attire, dress suit (plate R 7). ~ **de viúva** widow's weeds.
trajeto s. m. 1. stretch, length, distance. 2. crossing, passage, course, way.
ele falou durante o ~ todo he kept talking the whole way.
trajetória s. f. 1. trajectory: the course of a projectile or a heavenly body. 2. (fig.) way, manner.
tralha s. f. (also **tralho** m.) 1. small fishing net. 2. mesh or knot of a fishing net. 3. (naut.) bolt-rope. 4. (Braz.) luggage, baggage. 5. old household articles, rubbish.
~ **de esteira** (naut.) foot-rope. ~ **de gurutil** (naut.) head rope. ~ **de testa** (naut.) leech rope. **toda a ~** luggage and kit, bag and baggage; the whole plunder.
tralhada s. f. (Braz.) (old) household articles.
tralhar v. 1. to cast a small fishing net. 2. (naut.) to marl the sail to the boltrope.
tralhoada s. f. 1. jumble, mixture, medley, farrago. 2. confusion, disorder.
tralhoto s. m. (Braz., ichth., also **tariota**) four-eyes.
trama (I) s. f. 1. woof, weft, texture, web. 2. plot, scheme, conspiracy, complot, cabal, intrigue (also of a drama). 3. (Braz.) rocket, illicit business, crooked deal. 4. (S. Braz.) roof frame.
urdir uma ~ to contrive a plot.
trama (II) s. f. (obs.) pest, pestilence; sickness; ailment.
tramador s. m. 1. weaver. 2. plotter, intriguer, contriver, conspirator. ‖ adj. 1. weaving. 2. intriguing, conspiratorial, contriving.
tramaga s. f., **tramagal** m., **tramagueira** f. = **tamarga**, **tamargal**, **tamargueira**.
tramanzola s. m. + f. (S. Braz.) young lazy person, softy.
tramar v. 1. to weave, woof. 2. to complot, cabal, scheme, plot, intrigue, contrive, frame; manoeuvre, devise. 3. ~**-se** to conspire.
bem tramado fine spun. **ele trama algo** he has a design, he is driving at something.
tramazeira s. f. (bot.) mountain ash, rowan tree.
tramba-las-águas s. m., sg. + pl. = **tomba-las-águas.**
trambalear, trambalhar v. (S. Braz.) to stagger, tumble, stumble, totter, reel.
trambecar v. to stagger, totter, shake like a drunk person.
trambelho s. m. = **trabelho.**
trambicar v. (Braz., sl.) to trick, cheat, hoax, bluff.
trambique s. m. (Braz., sl.) trickery, diddle, hoax, bluff.
trambiqueiro s. m. (Braz., sl.) a trickster, hoaxer, cheater, diddler. ‖ adj. tricky, cheating, humbugging.
trambolhada s. f. a lot of things tied together; bunch.
trambolhão s. m. (pl. **-ões**) 1. fall, tumble, a tumbling down. 2. (pop.) jolt, butt, jerk. 3. (fig.) failure, fiasco, piece of bad luck.
trambalhar v. 1. to stagger, tumble down, topple, fall down. 2. (pop.) to jabber, stammer, stutter, falter.
trambolho s. m. 1. clog, weight fastened to an animal's leg to hinder its motion. 2. (fig.) encumbrance, hindrance, impediment, burden. 3. bunch (of keys, etc.). 4. (pop.) heavy person.
tramela s. f. = **taramela.**

tramelo s. m. (zool.) little mouse.
tramista s. m. crook, slicker, rascal, swindler.
trâmite s. m. 1. path, course, way. 2. ~**s** pl. means, ways or channels, (official) formalities, procedure.
tramóia s. f. chicane, trick, intrigue; swindle.
são ~s dele these are his practices.
tramoeiro s. m. (Braz.) plotter, intrigant, swindler, rascal, cheater, defrauder.
tramolhada s. f. slough, marsh, fen, morass.
tramontana s. f. 1. tramontana: north wind. 2. tramontane: polestar, North Star. 3. course, direction, orientation.
perder a ~ to be at a loss, be at one's wits end; lose one's bearings.
tramontar s. m. setting of the sun beyond the mountains. ‖ v. to set (the sun).
trampa (I) s. f. (vulg.) rubbish, rot.
trampa (II) s. f. 1. (obs.) defraudation, swindle, cheat, deceit. 2. intrigue. 3. (S. Braz.) a hunter's trap or snare.
trampão (pl. **-ões**) (obs.) = **trampolineiro.**
trampear v. to cheat, swindle, cozen, trick, take in.
trampesco s. m. (N. Braz. + Port., prov.) clout, cuff, blow.
trampolim s. m. (pl. **-ins**) springboard, leaping board, jumping board (plates B 3, G 3).
~ **para mergulhar** diving board.
trampolina, trampolinada, trampolinagem, trampolinice s. f. 1. cheating, knavery, trickery. 2. swindle, defraudation, trick, cheat.
trampolinar v. to swindle, cheat, trick, fraud, cozen, overreach, take in, dupe, deceive.
trampolineiro s. m. swindler, crook, cheater, rascal, trickster. ‖ adj. swindling, cheating, deceitful.
tramposear v. (S. Braz.) 1. to meddle. 2. to trick, cheat, deceive, dupe, cozen.
tramposo (I) adj. (vulg.) nauseating, disgusting; filthy, dirty, swinish.
tramposo (II) adj. meddlesome, impertinent; crooked, shifty, deceitful.
trâmuel s. m. 1. tramway. 2. tramway-line. 3. district--railway.
tranar v. 1. to swim across, cross a water by swimming. 2. to cut, slit.
tranca s. f. 1. bar, crossbar, transverse locking bar. 2. (by extension) hindrance, obstacle, obstruction, check. 3. breastband of a harness. 4. (fig.) large trace or line. 5. (vulg.) person of bad manners, rowdy. ‖ adj. low, mean, stingy, shabby.
trança s. f. 1. tress, braid, plait, pigtail (plate P 8). 2. galloon or strip (embroidery). 3. (Braz.) plot, scheme, intrigue. 4. (N. Braz., pop.) conflict, row.
trancação s. m. (S. Braz.) coryza, cold in the head.
trancada s. f. 1. stroke or blow with a bar, cudgelling. 2. weir, stockade across a river.
trançadeira s. f. ribbon for the hair; fillet.
trancado adj. barred, bolted, fastened with bars, locked up, fast, shut.
a porta está -a the door is fast, is shut.
trançado s. m. 1. tress, plait, braid, pigtail. 3. ribbon for the hair, fillet. 3. plaitwork.
trançador s. m. (S. Braz.) 1. plaiter (of leather or a horse's mane). 2. intriguer, intrigant, plotter, conspirator. ‖ adj. tressing, plaiting, braiding.
trancafiar v. (Braz., pop., also **trincafiar**) to put under lock and key, incarcerate, imprison, arrest.
trancamento s. m. barring, bolting, securing with bars.
trancão s. s. (pl. **-ões**) (Braz.) 1. push, jostle, collision, clash, bump, jolt. 2. (ftb.) charge.
trancar v. 1. to bar, fasten, secure with bars, to bolt, latch, lock, shut up. 2. to arrest, imprison, incarcerate, put under lock and key. 3. to cancel,

make null and void. 4. to finish, bring to an end. 5. (Braz., ftb.) to charge, jostle, push. 6. ~-**se** to close or shut o. s. up.

~ **a porta depois que o ladrão entrou** after death the doctor.

trançar v. 1. to tress, plait, braid, twist, interlace, entwine, wreathe; weave. 2. (Braz., pop.) to walk about. 3. to crisscross (when dancing the fandango).

trancaria s. f. large quantity of bars or logs.

tranca-ruas s. m., sg. + pl. bully, rowdy, rough, ruffian.

tranca-trilhos s. m., sg. + pl. barrier or gate at a railway crossing.

trancelim s. m. (pl. **-ins**) 1. a thin braid, bobbin, gold braid. 2. thin gold chain.

trancha s. f. a tinsmith's edging tool.

trancinha s. f. 1. small plait. 2. narrow braid, bobbin; galloon or string (used in embroidery). 3. (Braz.) plot, scheme, intrigue, conspiration. 4. m. + f. intriguer, plotter. ‖ adj. intriguing, designing.

tranco s. m. 1. collision, jolt, push, jog, bump, jerk, jounce, jostle. 2. (S. Braz.) trot.

aos ~**s e barrancos** by fits and starts; over hedge and ditch. **por** ~**s e barrancos** through foul and fair.

trancucho, trancudo adj. (S. Braz.) tipsy, slightly drunk.

trangalhadanças s. m. + f., sg. + pl. tall and clumsy person, gawk, lout.

trangla s. f. stair-rod for a carpet.

trangola s. m. (sl.) tall and lean person, lamp-post.

tranqueado adj. (N. Braz.) curbed, checked (horse).

tranquear v. (Braz.) 1. to trot (horse). 2. (N.) to curb, refrain, check (horse). 3. to clog, obstruct, bar.

tranqueira s. f. 1. stockade, palisade, fence. 2. trench, barrier, gate. 3. brush, branches, half-burned trees.

tranqueiro s. m. any of the supporting parts of a sawing jack.

tranqueta s. f. latch, bolt, catch, pawl (of a door or window) (plate C 11).

tranquia s. f. barrier, bar.

tranquibernar v. to cheat, trick, fraud, trap.

tranquiberneiro s. m. tricker, trickster, swindler, cheat, deceiver, impostor. ‖ adj. swindling, cheating, deceiving.

tranquibérnia, tranquibernice s. f. trick, cheat, swindle, fraud, trap, deception.

tranqüilidade s. f. 1. tranquility, peace, quiet, serenity, stillness, calm, placidity. 2. silence, rest, repose, ease.

tranqüilizador s. m. tranquilizer. ‖ adj. tranquilizing, reassuring, lulling. ‖ ~**amente** adv. reassuringly.

é ~ **saber** it is a satisfaction to know.

tranqüilizar v. 1. to tranquilize, quiet, appease, still, reassure, calm, allay; pacify, set at ease. 2. ~-**se** to become quiet, tranquil.

~ **o espírito** to set one's mind at ease. **tranqüilizaram-se os ânimos** the excited feelings calmed down.

tranqüilo adj. tranquil, calm, peaceful, easy, quiet, undisturbed, serene; still, placid, sedate. ‖ **-amente** adv. quietly.

águas **-as** still waters. **deixe-me** ~ leave me alone. **fique** ~**!** take it easy, calm down! **viver -amente** to live at ease. **ter o espírito** ~ to preserve a tranquil mind.

tranquito s. m. (Braz.) a good pacer (horse).

transa s. f. (Braz., sl.) 1. understanding, connection, bond. 2. pact, agreement, alliance. 3. machination, scheme, plot. 4. a love affair.

transação s. f. (pl. **-ões**) 1. transaction, dealing, business, deal; operation, proceeding, negotiation, affair. 2. m. (Braz., sl.) crook, rascal, sharper.

-ões comerciais business. **-ões locais** local business. **-ões recíprocas** mutual dealings.

transacionar v. to transact, deal, negotiate, do or carry on business.

~ **com** to trade with. ~ **com bancos** to bank.

transalpino adj. transalpine, beyond the Alps.

transamazônico adj. transamazonic.

transandino adj. trans-Andean: 1. situated on the other side of the Andes. 2. crossing the Andes.

transar v. (Braz., sl.) 1. to see eye to eye, understand one another. 2. to lay heads together, scheme, collude, machinate. 3. to have a love affair (with).

transatlântico s. m. transatlantic steamer. ‖ adj. transatlantic: 1. located across the Atlantic Ocean. 2. crossing the Atlantic Ocean.

transato adj. (also **transacto**) past, previous, former, anterior, bygone.

transator s. m. (also **transactor**) transactor, businessman, dealer. ‖ adj. transacting, dealing, negotiating.

transbordamento s. m. (also **trasbordamento**) overflow, overflowing, inundation.

transbordante adj. m. + f. overflowing, overfull, brimful.

um coração ~ a full heart.

transbordar v. (also **trasbordar**) 1. to overflow, overspread, spill over; run over; slop, overbrim, swell over. 2. to turn over. 3. to inundate, flood, overswell, gush, stream.

transbordo (ô) s. m. (pl. **transbordos**) (also **trasbordo**) 1. overflow, overflowing. 2. tran(s)shipment, transfer, change.

~ **de passageiros** tran(s)shipment of passengers.

transcaspiano adj. trans-Caspian: 1. crossing the Caspian Sea. 2. beyond the Caspian Sea.

transcendência s. f. transcendence, transcendency.

transcendental adj. m. + f. (pl. **-ais**) transcendental: 1. characteristic of transcendentalism. 2. supernatural, metaphysical, abstract.

transcendentalismo s. m. transcendentalism: 1. transcendental thought and language. 2. doctrine of the German philosopher Kant. 3. (philos.) doctrines of Emerson and others in the U.S.A.

transcendentalista s. m. + f. transcendentalist: adherent to transcendentalism. ‖ adj. transcendental.

transcendentalizar v. 1. to become transcendental. 2. to give transcendental features to.

transcendente adj. m. + f. transcendent: 1. exceeding ordinary limits, superior, extraordinary. 2. important, far-reaching. 2. supernatural.

transcender v. to transcend: 1. overtop, overpass, excel, exceed, surmount, be above. 2. (geom.) surpass. 3. be superior, rise above.

transcoação s. f. (pl. **-ões**) filtration, percolation.

transcoar v. 1. to strain, filter, distill. 2. to filtrate, percolate. 3. to transpire, exhale, transude, ooze.

transcontinental adj. m. + f. (pl. **-ais**) transcontinental: 1. crossing a continent. 2. beyond a continent.

transcorrer v. to elapse, go by, pass (time), glide away.

hoje transcorre o aniversário de sua filha today is his daughter's birthday.

transcrever v. 1. to transcribe: write a copy of, copy. 2. to transfer, translate.

transcrição s. f. (pl. **-ões**) transcription: 1. transcribing, copying. 2. copy, transcript.

transcrito s. m. transcript: 1. copy. 2. transfer, translation. ‖ adj. transcribed, copied.

transcritor s. m. transcriber. ‖ adj. transcribing, copying.

transculturação s. f. transculturation.

transcurar v. 1. to neglect, disregard, ignore. 2. to forget, overlook.

transcurral s. m. (pl. -ais) (Braz.) pen, a small enclosure aside of a larger one to keep in animals which are to be branded.

transcursão s. f. course, lapse or passage (of time).

transcursar v. to pass away, go beyond; elapse, glide away (as time).

transcurso s. m. course, passage of time.
~ da vida course of life.

transdanubiano adj. trans-Danubian. 1. crossing the Danube. 2. beyond the Danube.

transe s. m. 1. anguish, trouble, distress, difficulty, danger; crisis, predicament. 2. death, demise.
~ da morte pangs of death. a todo o ~ at all hazards; at all costs; by any means.

transecular adj. m. + f. through ages and centuries.

transepto s. m. (archit.) transept: the shorter part of a cruciform church.

transeunte s. m. + f. transient, passer-by. ‖ adj. transient, transitory, passing; ephemeral, short-lived.

transfazer v. = transformar.

transferência s. f. transference: 1. transfer, removal, change. 2. conveyance. 3. demise.
~ de bens ou direitos cession. ~ de crédito transfer of credit. ~ para outra instância remittal. certificado de ~ transfer deed. registro de ~ transfer-book. pedir ~ to ask to be transferred.

transferidor s. m. 1. transferrer. 2. (math.) protractor: instrument for measuring angles.

transferir v. 1. to transfer. 2. to remove, convey, transport. 3. to transmit, communicate. 4. to put off, postpone, defer, adjourn. 5. to pass, assign, cede, grant. 6. ~-se to move away.
fui transferido I got my remove.

transferível adj. m. + f. (pl. -íveis) transferable; demisable, conveyable; that may be deferred.

transfiguração s. f. (pl. -ões) 1. transfiguration, transformation, change in appearance. 2. Transfiguration of Jesus: a) change in the appearance on the mountain. b) its festival commemoration on August 6th.

transfigurado s. m. transformation, change, modification, alteration. ‖ adj. transfigured, changed, altered, transformed.

transfigurador s. m. one who transfigures. ‖ adj. transfiguring, transforming, changing, altering.

transfigurar v. to transfigure, transform, alter, change, convert, transmute, modify.

transfixação s. f. (pl. -ões) transfixion, a piercing through.

transfixão s. f. (pl. -ões) (med.) transfixion: process of amputation.

transfixar v. to transfix, pierce through, impale.

transformação s. f. (pl. -ões) transformation, alteration, version, modification, permutation, transfiguration, metamorphosis.

transformador s. m. transformer: 1. person who transforms, changes. 2. (electr.) apparatus for transforming a current. ‖ adj. transforming, modifying, altering, changing.
(electr.) ~ aumentador step-up transformer. ~ redutor step-down transformer. ~ de corrente current transformer. ~ de voltagem voltage transformer.

transformante adj. m. + f. transforming, modifying, altering, changing.

transformar v. 1. to transform, alter, change, modify, vary; transfigure, convert, transmute, metamorphose. 2. ~-se to be transformed, undergo a change, change into.
~ água em vinho to turn water into wine. ~ em dinheiro to turn s. th. into money. ~ promessas em atos to translate promises into actions. ~ um

vestido to alter a dress. o príncipe transformou-se em rã the prince changed into a frog.

transformativo adj. transformative.

transformável adj. m. + f. (pl. -áveis) transformable.

transformismo s. m. transformism: development of a species from another by various transformations.

transformista s. m. + f. 1. (biol.) transformist. 2. (Braz.) quick-change artist.

transfretano adj. 1. beyond the strait of Gibraltar. 2. ultramarine, overseas.

trânsfuga s. m. + f. 1. deserter, runaway; turncoat, ratter. 2. apostate, renegade.

transfugir v. to desert, rat, abandon.

transfundir v. 1. to transfuse, convey, transfer, pour (into another vessel). 2. diffuse, spread, scatter. 3. infiltrate, inoculate. 4. ~-se to alter, change, undergo a change.

transfusão s. f. (pl. -ões) transfusion, transfusing.
~ de sangue (med.) blood transfusion.

transgredir v. 1. to transgress, infringe, violate, infract, offend, break (law). 2. to overpass, go beyond, exceed, trespass.
~ a lei to break the law. ~ um regulamento to trespass against a rule.

transgressão s. f. (pl. -ões) transgression: 1. infringement, violation, offense, sin, trespass. 2. (geol.) invasion of land by sea water.
~ da lei infringement of the law.

transgressivo adj. transgressive, lawbreaking.

transgressor s. m. transgressor, lawbreaker, violator, infringer, offender, trespasser. ‖ adj. transgressive, lawbreaking. ‖ ~amente adv. transgressively.
~ da paz peacebreaker. os ~es serão punidos pela lei trespassers will be prosecuted.

transiberiano s. m. Trans-Siberian Railway. ‖ adj. Trans-Siberian: 1. crossing Siberia. 2. beyond Siberia.

transição s. f. (pl. -ões) transition: 1. transience, transiency. 2. passage, shift, change.
~ repentina sudden transition, leap. período de ~ period of transition.

transido adj. numb, benumbed, chilled.
~ de frio benumbed with cold. ~ de medo shivering with fright.

transigência s. f. 1. compromise, agreement, compliance, acquiescence. 2. indulgence, tolerance, gentleness, endurance.

transigente s. m. + f. acquiescent person. ‖ adj. condescending, compliant, submissive, yielding, meek, acquiescent.

transigir v. to compromise, condescend, acquiesce, agree, compound, come to terms, yield, temporize.

transigível adj. m. + f. (pl. -íveis) acquiescent, conformable. ‖ transigivelmente adv. acquiescently.

transilvano s. m. Transylvanian: native or inhabitant of Transylvania. ‖ adj. Transylvanian: of or belonging to Transylvania.

transir v. 1. to pass through; penetrate. 2. ~-se to chill, be numbed or paralyzed, tremble (with cold or fear).
~ de frio to be numbed with cold. ~ de medo to shake in one's shoes.

transistor s. m. (electronics) transistor.

transistorizado adj. (electronics) transistorized.

transistorizar v. (electronics) to transistorize: to equip with transistors.

transitador adj. travelling or passing through.

transitar v. 1. to transit, pass, go or pass through. 2. to change, alter, modify (state or condition). 3. to travel, journey. 4. to be promoted, be moved up (as a pupil).
~ à classe superior to move up to the next class (pupil). o país transitou de monarquia a república the country changed from a monarchy to a republic.

1254 transitável — transpirável

transitável adj. m. + f. (pl. **-áveis**) passable, usable, practicable.
a estrada já é ~ the road is already passable. **estrada** ~ passable road.
transitar v. (gram.) to give a transitive form to.
transitivo adj. 1. transitional. 2. (gram.) transitive: governing an object.
verbo ~ transitive verb.
transitivo-predicativo (pl. **transitivo-predicativos**) adj. (gram.) factitive.
transitivo-relativo adj. (pl. **transitivo-relativos**) (gram.) transitive-relative: governing a direct and an indirect object.
trânsito s. m. 1. transit, passage, conveyance. 2. traffic, flow of vehicles, etc. 3. crowd of people. 4. (fig.) change, transition, death. 5. (Braz., topogr.) transit theodolite.
~ **ferroviário** train service. ~ **intenso** heavy traffic. **direitos de** ~ transit duties. **mercadorias em** ~ transit goods. **regular o** ~ to control the traffic.
transitoriedade s. f. transitoriness.
transitório adj. 1. transitory, passing, transient, fleeting, ephemeral, fugacious; momentary, brief, temporary, short-lived. 2. mortal. || **transitoriamente** adv. transitorily.
transjordânico adj. Transjordanian: of or pertaining to Transjordan (former name of Jordan).
translação s. f. (pl. **-ões**) 1. transfer, remove. 2. metaphor (figure of speech). 3. (mech.) motion of a body. 4. translation.
transladação s. f. = **trasladação, traslado**.
translato adj. (also **translatício**) 1. removed, transferred. 2. (gram.) metaphorical; figurative. 3. postponed.
transliteração s. f. (pl. **-ões**) transliteration.
transliterar v. to transliterate: represent a letter of one language by the corresponding one of another language.
translucidez s. f. translucency, semi-transparency, pellucidity.
translúcido adj. 1. translucent, semitransparent. 2. pellucid, limpid, diaphanous, clear, transparent. || **translucidamente** adv. translucently.
translumbrar v. to dazzle.
transluzente adj. m. + f. translucent, transparent, limpid, clear, diaphanous.
transluzimento s. m. transparency, diaphaneity.
transluzir v. 1. to be translucent, shine, glow, glisten or glimmer through, transiluminate. 2. to come to light, become known, appear. 3. to be obvious. 4. ~**-se** to reveal or reflect.
transmarino adj. ultramarine, overseas, beyond the sea.
transmeável adj. m. + f. (pl. **-áveis**) 1. permeable. 2. (med.) that may pass through the pores.
transmigração s. f. (pl. **-ões**) transmigration, metempsychosis: passing (of the soul) from one body to another.
transmigrador s. m., **transmigrante** m. + f. transmigrant, transmigrator. || adj. transmigratory.
transmigrar v. 1. to transmigrate: pass from one place to another, move away, change. 2. to pass into another body (soul).
transmigratório adj. transmigratory, passing from one place or condition to another.
transmissão s. f. (pl. **-ões**) transmission, transmittal: 1. act or process of transmitting. 2. communication, conduction, transposition. 3. (mech.) gears.
~ **de calor** conduction of heat. ~ **por engrenagem** transmission by gearing. ~ **hidráulica** fluid drive. ~ **de pensamento** transmission of thought. ~ **radiofônica** radio broadcasting. ~ **de telegramas** translation of telegrams. **engrenagem de** ~ transmission

gear wheel. **título de** ~ assignment, transfer of a title.
transmissibilidade s. f. transmissibility, possibility of being transmitted.
transmissível adj. m. + f. (pl. **-íveis**) 1. transmissible, transmittable. 2. communicable. 3. assignable.
transmissivo adj. transmissive, transferable.
transmissor s. m. 1. (teleph.) transmitter (plate T 4). 2. telegraph key. || adj. transmitting, transmissive.
~ **de ondas curtas** short-wave transmitter. ~ **rádio-telefônico** radio-telephonic transmitter. **estação transmissora** wireless station.
transmitir v. to transmit: 1. transfer, send, deliver, forward. 2. pass on, hand over, convey, bequeath. 3. communicate, tell, impart. 4. conduct, traject. 5. broadcast.
~ **uma ordem** to send on an order. ~ **por rádio** to broadcast. ~ **pelo telefone** to transmit by phone. ~ **pela tradição** to hand down by tradition. **foi-nos transmitido** it has come down to us. **ele transmitiu-me o seu resfriado** he has given me his cold.
transmodulação s. f. (pl. **-ões**) cross modulation.
transmontano adj. transmontane, transmontane, ultramontane: situated beyond the mountains.
transmontar v. 1. to cross or pass over the mountains. 2. to surpass, go beyond, exceed, overstep, excel. 3. to sink below the horizon, disappear or set (sun).
transmudação s. f. (pl. **-ões**) **transmudamento** m. (also **transmutação** f.) transmutation: 1. alteration, change, fluctuation. 2. conversion, transformation.
transmudar v. to transmute: 1. alter, change. 2. convert, transform. 3. ~**-se** change into.
transmutabilidade s. f. transmutability, transmutableness.
transmutativo adj. transmutative.
transmutável adj. m. + f. (pl. **-áveis**) transmutable. || **transmutavelmente** adv. transmutably.
transnadar v. (also **tranar**) to swin across, cross a river by swimming.
transnominação s. f. (pl. **-ões**) metonymy.
transobjetivo adj. (gram.) factitive.
transoceânico adj. transoceanic: 1. crossing the ocean. 2. overseas, ultramarine, beyond the ocean.
transordinário adj. extraordinary, uncommon: beyond the ordinary.
transpadano adj. transpadane, situated beyond the Po (Italian river).
transparecer v. 1. to appear or shine through. 2. to become visible, be evident. 3. ~**-se** to reveal itself, become manifest.
deixar ~ to imply, hint, insinuate.
transparência s. f. transparency, transparence, pellucidness, pellucidity, diaphaneity, limpidity.
transparentar v. 1. to make transparent. 2. transilluminate, enlighten. 3. to become transparent or visible. 4. to be evident.
transparente s. m. transparence. || adj. m. + f. 1. transparent, translucent. 2. limpid, lucid, clear, pellucid, gauzy, diaphanous. 3. evident, obvious, patent, manifest, distinct. || ~**-mente** adv. transparently, evidently.
transpassar v. 1. to pass over, go beyond. 2. to overstep, exceed, excel. 3. to transgress, trespass, 4. to pierce through. 5. to postpone, transfer. 6. to copy, transcribe. 7. to translate.
transpiração s. f. (pl. **-ões**) transpiration, perspiration, transudation, exhalation; sweating; exudation.
transpirar v. 1. to transpire, sweat, exude, perspire, exhale. 2. to become known or public, leak out, be evident.
o segredo transpirou the secret leaked out.
transpirável adj. m. + f. (pl. **-áveis**) transpirable.

transplantação s. f. (pl. -ões) (also transplante m.) transplantation.

transplantador s. m. 1. transplanter, gardener. 2. any planting tool. ‖ adj. transplanting.

transplantar v. 1. to transplant. 2. to translocate, move. 3. to transmigrate. 4. to transfer, change into, translate.

transplantatório adj. transplantable.

transplante s. m. transplant, transplantation.

transplatino adj. beyond the River Plate (Argentine).

transpor v. 1. to transpose, transport, transfer, interchange. 2. to cross over, traverse, pass. 3. to pass over or beyond. 4. to leap or jump over, vault. 5. to overrun. 6. to misplace. 7. (mus.) to put into a different key.
~ um obstáculo to hurdle an obstacle. o cavalo transpôs a cerca the horse vaulted the fence.

transportação s. f. (pl. -ões) transportation, transport, conveyance, removal.

transportador s. m. transporter, trucker; conveyer, mover.
~ de carga dumper.

transportamento s. m. 1. transportation. 2. transport, ecstasy, rapture, exaltation, trance.

transportar v. 1. to transport, carry, convey; bear; tote, haul. 2. to entrance, enrapture, ravish, charm. 3. (mus.) to transpose. 4. to communicate, transmit, transfer. 5. to pass, change. 6. ~-se to be transported (passion).
~ em barco to boat, lighter. ~ mercadorias to carry goods, trade. ~ passageiros e bagagem to carry passengers and luggage. ~ por via aérea to airlift, wing. a ~ to be carried forward, carry over (in bookkeeping).

transportável adj. m. + f. (pl. -áveis) transportable, portable, conveyable.

transporte s. m. 1. transport, transportation, conveyance; conduction, carriage, waftage; vehicle. 2. troopship, trooper, vessel to transport soldiers and military supplies. 3. carrying over, sum carried over (in bookkeeping). 4. exstasy, rapture, ravishment. 5. (mus.) transposal. 6. (geol.) transportation.
~ aéreo air service. ~ auxiliar (min.) secondary haulage. ~ em caminhão ou vagão truckage. ~ fluvial ou marítimo water carriage. ~ de mercadorias goods traffic. ~ pago carriage paid. ~ rodoviário land carriage. despesas de ~ transport charges, charges of conveyance. instalação para o ~ de sacos sack handling plant. meios de ~ means of conveyance.

transposição s. f. (pl. -ões) transposition, transposal, conversion, metathesis.

tarnspositivo adj. transpositional, transpositive.

transposto adj. transposed, transferred; overcome, passed, surpassed.

tarnsrenano adj. beyond the Rhine (river in Germany).

transtagano adj. beyond the Tagus (river in Portugal).

transtornado adj. disturbed, perturbed, upset, confused, perplexed, overturned.

transtornar v. 1. to overturn, turn turtle. 2. to disorder, discompose, throw into disorder, unsettle. 3. to disturb, perturb, upset, derange, perplex, confuse, trouble, agitate. 4. to change, alter; adulterate. 5. ~-se to become perturbed or irritated, upset.

transtorno (ô) s. m. (pl. transtornos) upset, disappointment, perturbation, confusion, trouble, derangement; adversity, misfortune; incovenience, moil.

transtravado adj. having the right hind foot and the forefeet white (horse).

transtrocar v. 1. to invert, change, reverse, alter. 2. to confuse, confound.

transubstanciação s. f. (pl. -ões) transubstantiation, transubstantiating, transformation (esp. of bread and wine into the body and the blood of Christ).

transubstancial adj. m. + f. (pl. -ais) transubstantial.

transubstanciar v. 1. to transubstantiate, change into another substance, transform, transmute. 2. ~-se to change into.

transudação s. f. (pl. -ões) transudation, transpiration, perspiration; sweating, exhalation.

transudar v. 1. to transude, transpire, sweat, perspire, exude. 2. to filtrate, ooze, percolate.

transudato s. m. (physiol.) transudate.

transumanar v. to transhumanize, make humane, humanize; civilize.

transumância s. f. transhumance: seasonal changing of pasturage (cattle).

transumante adj. said of the cattle that periodically changes grazing grounds.

transumar v. to change the grazing grounds (cattle).

transunto s. m. 1. transcript, copy, duplicate. 2. image, (obs.) counterpart, replex. 3. example, model.

transvaliana s. f. (N. Braz.) a sort of firecracker.

transvaliano s. m. Transvaalian: native or inhabitant of Transvaal (S. Africa). ‖ adj. Transvaalian: of or relating to Transvaal.

transvasar v. to transfuse, pour out into another vessel, decant.

transvazar v. 1. to decant, spill. 2. to empty, shed, pour out.

transverberar v. 1. to reflect. 2. to shine, shine through, be translucent. 3. to manifest itself.

transversal s. f. (pl. -ais) 1. (geom.) transversal, transversal line. 2. a line of collateral relatives. 3. m. (anat.) transversum, transverse muscle. ‖ adj. m. + f. transverse, transversal, thwart, oblique, cross. ‖ ~-mente adv. obliquely, transversally, broadways, broadwise.
eixo ~ transverse axis. seção ~ crosscut, cross-section.

transversalidade s. f. transversality.

transverso s. m. (anat.) transversum, transverse muscle. ‖ adj. 1. transverse, crosswise, overthwart. 2. oblique.

transverter v. 1. to overturn, overthrow. 2. to upset. 3. to transform, change. 4. to convert, translate. 5. ~-se to change into.

transvestir v. (Braz.) 1. to transvest, disguise. 2. to mask, hide. 3. to metamorphose, transmute.

transviar v. 1. to wander, err. 2. to deviate, lead astray, misguide. 3. to embezzle. 4. to corrupt, debase, taint, pervert. 5. ~-se to stray, go astray; get lost.

transvio s. m. 1. act or fact of going or leading astray. 2. deviation.

transvoar v. to cross flying, fly across.

tranvia s. f. tramway, suburban railway; streetcar.

trapa (I) s. f. 1. trap, pitfall, snare. 2. lifting cable.

Trapa (II) s. f. the Trappist order (founded in La Trappe, France).

trapaça, trapaçaria s. f. 1. fraud, knavery, deceit, trick, cheat, swindle, fiddle. 2. foul dealing, hanky-panky, jugglery, humbuggery, sculduddery.

trapacear v. to cheat, swindle, deceive, gyp, trick, dupe, hoax, cozen, overreach.

trapaceiro s. m. (also trapacento, trapaçador) trickster, swindler, crook, cheater, juggler, humbugger, cozener, impostor, deceiver, sharper. ‖ adj. deceitful, fraudulent, swindling, tricky. ‖ -amente adv. deceitfully, fraudulently.

trapagem s. f. (pl. -ens) (also trapalhada, traparia) rag pile, lot of rags.

trapalhada s. f. 1. confusion, disorder, jumble, hodgepodge, topsy-turvy. 2. entanglement, com-

plication, mess, imbroglio, misunderstanding. 3. trickery, swindle, fraud, cheating.
que ~! what a mess!
trapalhado adj. half-curdled (milk).
trapalhão (I) s. m. (pl. **-ões**) (f. **-ona**) 1. dabbler, fumbler, bungler, blunderer. 2. rag, tatter. 3. ragamuffin. ‖ adj. 1. clumsy, awkward, blundering, unskilful. 2. ragged, shabby.
trapalhão (II) s. m. trickster, swindler, crook, cheater, juggler, deceiver. ‖ adj. deceitful, cheating, fraudulent, tricky.
trapalhice (I) s. f. rags, tatters, tattered clothes.
trapalhice (II) s. f. swindle, trick, cheat, fraud, knavery, deceit.
trapel interj. crack!
trapear v. to flap (sails), clap, clash.
trapeira s. f. 1. trap, pitfall, snare. 2. (archit.) lucarne, garret window, dormer window, skylight (plate J 1). 3. garret, attic, gablet, dormer. 4. (S. Braz., pop.) confusion, hodgepodge, disorder, jumble. 5. female ragpicker.
trapeiro s. m. 1. ragman. 2. (Braz.) ragpicker, rag gatherer.
trapejar v. to flap, clap, clash, crack, snap.
trape-zape s. m. (pl. **trape-zapes**) clashing of swords (during a fight).
trapeziforme adj. m. + f. trapeziform (formed like a trapezium), trapezoidal.
trapézio s. m. 1. trapezium: a) geometrical figure of four sides, trapeze. b) (anat.) trapezoid: a wristbone. 2. trapeze (used by acrobats).
trapezista s. m. + f. trapezist (acrobat).
trapezoedro s. m. trapezohedron: a solid of trapezoidal faces.
trapezoidal adj. m. + f. (pl. **-ais**) trapezoid(al).
trapezóide s. m. 1. (anat.) trapezoid (wristbone). 2. (geom.) trapezium. ‖ adj. m. + f. trapezoid(al).
trapiarana s. f. (Braz.) plant of the violet family.
trapiche s. m. 1. warehouse of a quay or near a waterfront. 2. (N. Braz.) sugar mill propelled by animal traction.
trapicheiro s. m. proprietor or manager of a **trapiche**.
trapincola adj. m. + f. (Braz., pop.) swindling, cheating, deceitful.
trapista s. m. + f. Trappist: monk or nun of the Cistercian order of La Trappe. ‖ adj. Trappist: of or relating to the order of La Trappe.
trapizonga s. f. (Braz., pop.) 1. medley, rigmarole; confusion, disorder. 2. junk, lumber, lot of worthless household articles.
trapo s. m. 1. rag, tatter, shred, frazzle. 2. sediment or ground of certain liquids. 3. bush of the staff tree family. 4. **~s** pl. old clothes, shreds, slop clothes. **boneca de ~s** rag doll. **língua de ~s** stammering (a baby's talk). **sacola de ~s** rag bag. **a todo o ~** (S. Braz., pop.) at full tilt, headlong. **não ter um ~ para se cobrir** not to have a rag to one's back.
trapoeraba s. f. (Braz., bot.) a spiderwort.
trapoerabana s. f. (Braz., bot.) French-weed.
trápola s. f. trap, pitfall, snare, gin.
trapuz s. m. plump: sound of a falling object. ‖ interj. plop! plump!
traque s. m. (Braz.) firecracker.
traqueal adj. m. + f. (pl. **-ais**) tracheal.
traqueano adj. trachean, tracheate.
traquear v. (also **traquejar**) to pursue, chase, hunt, track, harass.
traquéia s. f. 1. (anat.) trachea, windpipe. 2. (bot.) tracheia, tracheid.
traquéia-artéria s. f. (pl. **traquéias-artéria**) trachea of the human body.
traquejado adj. 1. persecuted, harassed, chased, pursued. 2. (Braz.) skilled, experienced.

traquejar v. 1. to persecute, pursue, chase, harass, track. 2. to beat (woods). 3. to become skilled or experienced. 4. (Braz., sl., mil.) reprimand, disapprove of.
traquejo s. m. practice, experience, skill, ability, proficiency.
traqueliano adj. (anat.) referring to the trachelium.
traquelismo s. m. (med.) trachelism: spasmodic contraction of the muscles of the neck.
traqueocele s. f. (med.) tracheocele: tumour of the trachea.
traqueorragia s. f. (med.) tracheorrhage: discharge of blood from the trachea.
traqueorrágico adj. (med.) relating to tracheorrhagia.
traqueostenose s. f. (med.) tracheostenosis: contraction of the trachea.
traqueotomia s. f. (surg.) tracheotomy: operation for opening the trachea through the neck.
traqueotômico adj. relating to tracheotomy.
traquete s. m. (naut.) foresail.
mastro do ~ foremast.
traquinada s. f. 1. clamour, blare, stir, bustle. 2. frisk, gambol, frolic, escapade (children), mischief, naughtiness. 3. plot, scheme, intrigue.
traquinar v. to frolic, frisk, prank, wanton; be restless, mischievous, naughty.
traquinas s. m. + f., sg. + pl. (also **traquina** m. + f., **traquino** m.) prankster, frolicker, frisker, naughty or mischievous child or adult. ‖ adj. mischievous, naughty; troublesome, restless, frisky, impish, wild, prankish, fidgety.
traquinice s. f. prank, frolic, frisk, gambol, escapade; mischief.
traquitana s. f. (also **traquitana**) 1. four-wheel carriage for two persons. 2. (pop.) rattletrap.
traquitanda s. f. (Braz.) a pole of an apparatus for raising water to which a horse is tied.
traquítico adj. (petrog.) trachytic.
traquito s. m. (petrog.) trachyte: a light-coloured volcanic rock consisting mainly of feldspar.
trás (I) prep. + adv. behind, after, back.
andar para ~ to walk backwards, retrocede. **de ~** from behind. **de ~ para diante** backward, reverse. **de frente para ~** from front to rear. **deixar muito para ~** to leave far behind. **para ~** back, backward(s), behind. **ir para ~** to go backwards, blench. **mover-se para ~** to back up. **olhar para ~** to glance backwards, look back. **por ~ de** behind.
trás (II) interj. bang!
trasanteontem adv. (also **transantontem**) three days ago.
trasbordamento s. m. (also **transbordamento**) overflow, overflowing.
rocha de ~ (geol.) effusive rock.
trasbordante adj. m. + f. (also **transbordante**) over flowing, running over, brimful, too full.
trasbordar v., **trasbordo** s. m. = **transbordar, transbordo**.
traseira s. f. 1. rear, hinder part. 2. rear guard.
traseiro s. m. (pop.) the behind, bum, posterior, sit-me-down. ‖ adj. back, hind, hindmost, posterior, rear, rearward.
eixo ~ rear axle. **janela -a** rearview window (of a car). **lanterna ou luz -a** taillight. **o mais ~** the sternmost. **pára-lama ~** rear fender. **parte -a** stern, back. **pata -a** hindhand. **porta -a** back-door. **tampa -a de carroça** tailboard.
trasfega, trasfegadura s. f. (also **trasfego** m.) decantation, a pouring into another vessel, drawing off, racking.
trasfegador s. m. person who pours something (wine) from one vessel into another. ‖ adj. pouring out, drawing off, decanting.

trasfegar v. 1. to pour out, draw off, rack, decant (wine). 2. to deal, trade, be active, lively, busy.

trasflor s. m. embossed golden ornament on enamel.

trasfogueiro s. m. backlog, firedog, andiron.

trasfoliar v. to copy (a drawing, etc.) tracing on a transparent paper.

trasgo s. m. 1. hobgoblin, elf, fairy, sprite, pixy; bugbear, ghost. 2. mischievous person.

trasguear v. = traquinar.

trasladação s. f. (pl. -ões) 1. translation, transcription, copy. 2. removal, transfer.

trasladador s. m. 1. translator, transcriber, copier. 2. remover. ‖ adj. removing, transcribing.

trasladar v. 1. to transfer. 2. to remove; transport. 3. to transcribe, copy; translate. 4. to exemplify, paraphrase. 5. to postpone, defer. 6. ~-se to change over to.

traslado s. m. 1. transfer, removal. 2. transcript, transcription, copy, duplicate; translation. 3. paraphrase. 4. image, reflex; (obs.) counterpart. 5. example, model.

traslar s. m. the backside of a hearth or fireplace.

trasmontano adj., **transmontar** v. = transmontano, transmontar.

trasorelho s. m. (med.) parotitis: inflammation of the parotid glands; mumps.

traspassação s. f. (pl. -ões), **traspassamento** m. 1. passing over. 2. crossing over. 3. act or fact of piercing through. 4. transgression. 5. transcription. 6. transference. 7. removal.

traspassar v. 1. to pass or cross òver, go beyond. 2. to overstep; exceed, excel. 3. to transgress, trespass. 4. to pierce through; (fig.) hurt, wound. 5. to postpone, defer. 6. to copy, transcribe, translate. 7. to transmit, transfer; cede; sell. 8. ~-se to faint, die.

traspasse s. m. 1. transfer; assignment, sublease, making over. 2. decease, death.

traspasso s. m. 1. transfer. 2. infringement. 3. great pain or grief. 4. delay, postponement, deferment.

traspés s. m. pl. staggering, stumbling, lurch.

traspilar s. m. pillar or column behind another.

trastalhão s. m. (pl. -ões) (f. -ona) (pop., also **trastejão**) scamp, rascal, archknave, rogue.

trastaria s. f. (S. Braz.) lumber, shoddy, dross.

traste s. m. 1. piece of furniture; household utensil. 2. old household article; lumber; shoddy. 3. (Braz.) rascal, rogue, knave, scamp, worthless fellow, good-for-nothing.

trastejar (I) v. 1. to deal in secondhand goods. 2. (Braz.) to provide with furniture. 3. to manage or supervise a household. 4. to trifle about. 5. to play the scamp.

trastejar (II) v. (Braz.) 1. to play out of tune. 2. (fig.) to stammer, falter. 3. to vacillate, hesitate. 4. to break rank; behave improperly.

trasto s. m. string of a bass viola.

trasvasar v. = transvasar.

trasvisto adj. 1. seen from the side. 2. askance. 3. frowned upon.

tratada s. f. (also **tratantada**) rascality, roguery, knavery.

tratadista s. m. + f. author of a scientific treatise.

tratado s. m. 1. treaty, agreement, pact, convention, accord, concordat. 2. treatise about sciences, arts, etc.; dissertation.

~ **de comércio** commercial treaty. ~ **sobre leis** a book on laws. ~ **sobre medicamentos** dispensatory (book). ~ **de paz** treaty of peace.

tratador s. m. 1. negotiator. 2. caretaker. 3. cattle feeder, horseherd. ‖ adj. taking care of.

tratamento s. m. 1. treatment, treating, handling, usage. 2. attendance. 3. reception, welcome. 4.

application of remedies, cure, medical treatment. 5. daily ration, diet. 6. address, honorary title, title of degree or graduation.

~ **consecutivo** aftertreatment. ~ **cruel** raw deal, hard treatment. ~ **cuidadoso** tender care. ~ **de cavalos** grooming of horses (plate C 12). ~ **por injeções** injection treatment. ~ **malvado** ill treat, ill turn. ~ **médico** medical attendance. ~ **prévio** preliminary treatment. **ele dá-lhe o** ~ **de senador** he gives him the title of a Senator. **fazer um** ~ to take a cure. **sob** ~ under cure. **submeter-se a um** ~ to undergo a cure.

tratantada, tratantice s. f. swindle, rascality, roguery, knavery.

tratante s. m. + f. (also **tratista**) 1. rascal, crook, scoundrel, knave, rogue. 2. (obs.) dealer, businessman. ‖ adj. crooked, rascally, roguish, knavish.

tratar v. 1. to treat. 2. to deal with. 3. to handle. 4. (med.) to attend, cure, dress, care for; prescribe. 5. to consider, regard. 6. to transact, negotiate, settle, entertain, undertake, manage, arrange. 7. to discuss, discourse, concern. 8. (chem.) to process. 9. to entitle, title. 10. ~-se to take care of o. s.

~ **alguém como um cachorro** to treat s. o. like dirt. ~ **alguém friamente** to give the cold shoulder to s. o. ~ **de alguma coisa** to be about s. th. ~ **por alto** to deal with superficially. ~ **com aspereza** to treat brusquely. ~ **do assunto** to get down to business. ~ **de cavalos** to groom. ~ **sem cerimônia, com familiaridade** to treat familiarly. ~ **com** to deal with. ~ **como sendo indigno de atenção** to laugh out of court. ~ **de cima para baixo** to talk down to. ~ **com diplomacia** to treat diplomatically. ~ **com estima** to treat with regard, make much of. ~ **de fazer** to take o. s. to doing. ~ **com o máximo desprezo** to laugh to scorn. ~ **do mesmo modo** to do like for like. ~ **com mimo** to tiddle. ~ **de negócios** to attend to business. ~ **de um paciente** to nurse a patient, treat a patient. ~ **com muito respeito** to pay great attention. ~ **da roupa** to see the clothes. ~-se **bem** to keep a good table. **de que se trata?** what is the matter? what is it about? **já está tudo tratado** it's all settled. **o médico tratou da minha gastrite** the doctor treated me for gastritis. **o livro trata de História** the book is concerned with history. **não se trata disso** that is not the question. **ter outras coisas mais importantes a** ~ to have to attend to other, more important matters; have other fish to fry. **trata-se de um caso sério** a serious matter is at stake. **tratou de arranjar outra moradia** he went about looking for another dwelling. **você precisa** ~ **da sua vida** 1. you must care for yourself, make the ends mend. 2. you must mind your own business.

tratável adj. m. + f. (pl. -áveis) 1. tractable, treatable, manageable. 2. easy, facile. 3. docile, tame, compliant.

tratear v. 1. to mistreat, torture, rack. 2. to afflict, torment, worry.

trato (I) s. m. 1. treating, treatment, dealing, handling, usage. 2. caring for, therapy. 3. agreement, contract. 4. daily ration, food, board, fare, table. 5. behaviour. 6. address, title. 7. manner of life; culture. 8. ~s pl. rack, torture.

mau ~ rough usage, mistreatment. **dar** ~s **à bola** (pop.) to cudgel one's brains. **pessoa de fino** ~ person of refined manners. **ser de ruim** ~ to be hard to deal with.

trato (II) s. m. 1. tract (of land), terrain. 2. lapse of time, interval, pause. 3. versicle prayed in a Requiem (mass).

trator s. m. tractor (plate C 16).
~ **agrícola** farm tractor. ~ **de esteiras** or **lagartas** crawler tractor, caterpillar tractor.
tratório adj. tractional, tractive, serving to draw.
traumático adj. traumatic.
traumatismo s. m. (med., also **trauma**) traumatism, trauma.
traumatologia s. f. (med.) traumatology: medical branch dealing with traumatism.
traumatólogo s. m. (med.) traumatologist.
trauta s. f. spoor, trail, track (of an animal to be hunted).
trautear v. 1. to hum, trill, sing, flute. 2. (pop.): a) to reprimand. b) to pester, nag, incommode, inconvenience.
trava s. f. 1. restraint, act of restraining, drawing back, check. 2. bolt, key bolt. 3. fetter, shackle, clog, hobble, tether (for an animal). 4. beam. 5. (port.) setting (of a saw).
travação s. f. (archit. + tech.) 1. bracing, joining, clamping. 2. connection, union, junction. 3. link, joint. 4. restraint. 5. (tech.) locking. 6. saw-setting.
trava-contas s. m., sg. + pl. dispute, controversy, difference, altercation (esp. about settlement of accounts).
travada s. f. (Braz.) the act of braking (a vehicle in motion).
travadeira s. f. (also **travadoura**) 1. saw set, tool for setting a saw. 2. (archit.) bondstone.
travados s. m. pl. travadoes: storms on the coast of Guinea. ‖ adj. **travado** 1. connected, joined, linked, locked (together). 2. intimate, close. 3. restrained, tongue-tied. 4. braced, checked, stayed. 5. hobbled (horse). 6. furious, exasperated (fight).
travador s. m. 1. person who joins, restrains, hampers, etc. 2. saw set: tool for setting a saw. ‖ adj. 1. joining, linking. 2. restraining, hampering.
travadoura s. f. (also **travadoira**) 1. saw set (tool). 2. (archit.) bondstone.
travadouro s. m. (also **travadoiro**) pastern: part of a horse's leg between the fetlock and the coffin joint.
travagem s. f. (pl. -**ens**) 1. (Braz., vet.) hypertrophy of a horse's gum (causing loss of teeth). 2. braking.
traval adj. m. + f. (pl. -**ais**) pertaining to a beam or girder.
travamento s. m. = **travação**.
travanca s. f. 1. obstacle, impediment, hindrance. 2. stumbling-block; shackle, clog.
travão s. m. (pl. -**ões**) 1. shackle, manacle, clog, fetter for animals. 2. brake, check (esp. for wheels). ~ **as quatro rodas** four-wheel brake. ~ **automático** self-acting brake. ~ **elétrico** electric brake. **alavanca do** ~ brake lever.
travar v. 1. (tech.) to join, connect, brace, unite. 2. to restrain, impede, hamper. 3. to brake: apply a brake to. 4. to fetter, shackle, clog. 5. to lock, bar. 6. to keep down, moderate, check. 7. to set the teeth of a saw. 8. to embitter; taste bitterly, taste acrid or sour. 9. ~-**se** to be joined or linked, attached.
~ **amizade** to become friendly, contract friendship. ~ **automaticamente** to brake automatically. ~ **batalha** to engage in battle. ~ **combate** to join combat. ~ **conhecimento ou relações com** to come to know, get acquainted with, establish relations with, pick up with. ~ **conversa com alguém** to engage a person in a conversation. ~ **espadas** to cross swords. ~ **o passo** to drag one's feet. ~ **com peia** to hopple. ~-**se de razões** to cross words, discuss. **eu travei o carro** I stopped the car. ~ **a serra** to set the teeth of a saw.

trave s. f. (also **trava**) 1. wooden beam, bar, crossbar (plate P 6). 2. (archit.) girder, stringer, transom.
travejamento s. m. framing, framework of beams or girders; timberwork.
travejar v. (archit.) to lay the beams, provide the beams; frame; timber.
travento adj. acrid, sharp, tart, harsh (to the taste). ‖ -**amente** adv. acridly.
travertino s. m. (min.) travertine: crystalline calcium carbonate formed by spring waters.
través s. m. slant, bias, diagonal, traverse; obliquity. **de** ~ across, crosswise, athwart, aslant. ~ **de fortuna** misfortune. **olhar de** ~ to look down one's nose, look askew, squint.
travessa s. f. 1. (archit.) beam, bar, crossbar, lintel, girder, transom, traverse, batten, rail (plates A 8, 13, B 2, C 11, E 6, J 1, P 10). 2. (railway) sleeper, tie. 3. lane, by-lane, bystreet, alley, crossroad. 4. connecting passageway. 5. platter, dish for serving meat. 6. bar pin, side comb (for the hair).
~ **de elo** stud of a chain (plate C 4). ~ **em cruz** diagonal stay. ~ (or **viga**) **horizontal** (gym.) balancing bar (plate P 6). ~ **para queijo** cheese plate. **porta** ~ side door. **por portas** ~**s** in secret.
travessão (I) s. m. (pl. -**ões**) 1. dash. 2. (mus.) bar to separate the compasses; division.
travessão (II) s. m. (pl. -**ões**) 1. large beam. 2. beam of a balance. 3. (N. Braz.) a sectioned reef across a river.
~ **de andaime** putlog (plate A 8).
travessão (III) s. m. (pl. -**ões**) contrary wind, cross-wind. ‖ adj. cross, contrary.
travessão (IV) adj. (pl. -**ões**) athwart, oblique, transverse.
travessar v. (also **atravessar**) to traverse, cross over.
travessear v. to be naughty, misbehave, fidget.
travesseiro s. m. (Port. **travesseira** f.) 1. pillow, bolster, cushion (plates C 7, D 4). 2. pillow-case, pillow-slip.
consultar o ~ to take counsel of one's pillow, sleep over something.
travessia s. f. 1. crossing, passage. 2. cross-wind, contrary wind. 3. (Braz.) forestalling the sale of (goods). 4. long open road.
~ **sobre o rio** crossing of the river. ~ **das ruas** crossing over the streets. **má** ~ rough passage.
travesso adj. transverse, athwart, crossed.
travesso adj. 1. gamesome, frisky, frolic, wild. 2. mischievous, naughty; turbulent, restless, prankish, impish, noisy. ‖ -**amente** adv. mischievously.
travessura s. f. 1. prank, gambol, frisk, practical joke. 2. trick; knavery, roguishness; mischief.
travesti s. m. 1. disguise (apparel). 2. (by extension) any disguise.
travicha s. f. (Braz.) = **travadoura**.
travinca s. f. 1. small beam. 2. pin, bolt.
travo, travor s. m. 1. bitterness, tartness, sourness, acridness. 2. (after-)taste. 3. unpleasant impression.
travoela s. f. a small auger or broach.
travoso adj. = **travento**.
trazedor s. m. bringer, carrier, bearer, messenger. ‖ adj. bringing, carrying, bearing.
trazer v. 1. to bring. 2. to fetch. 3. to carry. 4. to introduce. 5. to bear. 6. to convey, conduct, lead, drive, transport. 7. to wear, don, put on, have on. 8. to gain, receive, inherit, bequeath. 9. to cause, occasion, effect, produce. 10. ~-**se** to dress o. s.
~ **à baila** to introduce, mention, bring up for discussion. ~ **benefício** to bring in profit. ~ **boas notícias** to bear good tidings. ~ **na boca** to mention frequently. ~ **o braço ao peito** to carry one's arm in a sling. ~ **consigo** 1. to have about one. 2. to entail, involve. ~ **às costas** to carry

upon one's back. ~ **à lembrança, memória** to call to mind. ~ **em mente** to bear in mind. ~ **nas palmas das mãos** to esteem, value. ~ **no pensamento** to have on one's mind. ~ **para cima da mesa** to bring out a matter for discussion. ~ **para dentro** to fetch in. ~ **à tona** to bring to the surface, (fig.) bring out (from concealment). **esse cão sabe apanhar e** ~ that hound can fetch and carry. **glória traz inveja** fame causes envy. **traga-me os meus sapatos** bring me my shoes. **que vento o trouxe aqui?** what wind blew you hither?

trazida s. f., **trazimento** m. carrying, bearing, bringing, fetching, conveying.

trebelhar v. 1. to move a chessman; play at chess. 2. (obs.) to play; rejoice.

trebelho s. m. 1. dance. 2. folly, joke. 3. = **trabelho**.

treboçu s. m. (Braz.) bulky person or animal.

trecentésimo s. m. the three hundredth part. ‖ adj. three hundredth.

trecentista s. m. + f. author or painter of the 12th century.

trecheio adj. overfull, abundant, plentiful. ‖ **-amente** adv. abundantly.

trecho s. m. 1. period, space of time. 2. space, stretch, distance, section. 3. (mus.) interval. 4. (mus. + lit.) passage. 5. chapter, extract, part.

a ~**s** at intervals, now and then. **a breve** ~ shortly after, soon. ~ **por** ~ gradually.

treco s. m. (Braz., sl.) a small, relatively insignificant thing; stuff, trash, junk, rubbish.

tredécimo adj. = **trezeno**.

tredo adj. disloyal, treacherous, false. ‖ **-amente** adv. treacherously.

tréfego adj. 1. turbulent, restless, unquiet. 2. mischievous, naughty. 3. sly, cheating, crafty, deceitful. ‖ **-amente** adv. turbulently.

trefilação s. f. (pl. **-ões**) wire drawing.

trefilador s. m. wiredrawer.

trefilar v. to wiredraw.

trégua s. f. 1. armistice, truce. 2. rest, pause, respite; calm, tranquility.

treição s. f. (pl. **-ões**) (Braz., obs., pop.) = **traição**.

treina s. f. 1. animal on which a hawk or falcon were fed to train them on that kind of prey. 2. (fig.) food, meal, repast.

treinado adj. (also **trenado**) trained, drilled (for chase, race or sport).

treinador s. m. (also **trenador**) trainer, coach, games master.

~ **de cavalos** horsebreaker.

treinagem s. f., **treinamento** m. training, coaching, exercise, drill.

treinar v. (also **trenar**) 1. to train, drill, coach; break in (horses). 2. to exercise, school, practise, instruct.

~ **cavalos de corrida** to train race horses. ~**-se para uma corrida** to train for a race. ~ **alguém na natação** to teach s. o. swimming.

treino s. m. (also **treno**) training, coaching, drill(ing); exercise, practice; preparation.

treita s. f. 1. vestige, footstep, trace, track, mark. 2. norm, rule; example.

treitento adj. cunning, smart; tricky, shifty, crafty. ‖ **-amente** adv. smartly.

treito adj. prone to, accustomed to.

trejeitador s. m. 1. grimacer, mocker; juggler. 2. (obs.) a sort of cake. ‖ adj. making faces, grimacing.

trejeitar v. to grimace, make faces.

trejeiteiro s. m. grimacer; mocker; juggler.

trejeito s. m. 1. grimace, wry face, caper, antic. 2. sleight-of-hand, juggle.

trejurar v. 1. to swear three times. 2. to swear often or frequently.

trela s. f. 1. leash, strap (for dogs). 2. (pop.) talk, chat, gossip. 3. (fig.) licence, liberty, leave. 4. (Braz.) prank, gambol.

dar ~ **a** (Braz.) 1. to encourage another to flirt; to take to a person. 2. (fig.) to give the rains.

treladar v. (obs.) = **trasladar**.

trelência s. f. (Braz.) gossiping, tattling; encouragement to familiarities.

trelente s. m. + f. 1. prattler, gossip. 2. meddler. 3. troublemaker.

treler v. 1. to gossip, tattle, prattle. 2. to meddle, intrude, interfere. 3. to encourage to familiarities. 4. not to know what one is doing or talking. 5. (Braz., pop.) to have doubts, distrust. 6. to become weak-minded.

trelho s. m. churn-staff (for making butter).

sem ~ **nem trabelho** without rhyme or reason.

treliça s. f. (Braz.) latticework, frame-work, truss-frame, trestlework.

ponte com armação em ~ lattice bridge. **viga em** ~ lattice girder.

treloso adj. (Braz.) 1. mischievous, naughty, impish. 2. troublesome, impertinent. ‖ **-amente** adv. mischievously.

trem s. m. (pl. **trens**) 1. (Braz.) train (railway). 2. retinue, suite; (sl.) hangers-on. 3. furniture of a house. 4. kitchenware. 5. luggage, bags. 6. carriage, coach. 7. (S. Braz.) worthless fellow. 8. **trens** pl. (Braz.) goods and chattels.

~ **de aterrissagem** landing gear. ~ **cargueiro** freight train. ~ **expresso** express train. ~ **interurbano** interurban train. **o** ~ **descarrilhou** the train ran off the rails. **ir de** ~ to train. **tomar um** ~ to take a train.

trema s. m. (gram.) diaeresis, dieresis: a mark put over a vowel to indicate that it is pronounced separately from the following one.

tremado adj. (gram.) diaeretic, dieretic.

tremandrácea s. f. (bot.) a species of the dicotyledons.

tremar (I) v. to mark with a diaeresis.

tremar (II) v. to unravel, separate the threads of, unweave.

tremate s. m. (Braz.) plant of the daisy family (genus Compositae).

trematódeo s. m. (zool.) trematode, flatworm, fluke.

tremebundo adj. 1. trembling, tremulous, quaking. 2. dreadful, fearful, tremendous.

tremecém adj. m. + f. (pl. **-éns**) lasting three months.

tremedal s. m. (pl. **-ais**) 1. marsh, swamp, morass, bog. 2. (N. Braz.) extensive floating vegetation on rivers. 3. (fig.) moral degradation.

tremedeira s. f. 1. trembling, quaking. 2. shivering fit. 3. agony, pangs of death. 4. malaria.

tremedor s. m. trembler, person who shivers. ‖ adj. trembling, quaking, shivering.

tremelear v. 1. to quiver, quake, shiver. 2. to be perplexed. 3. to stammer, falter.

tremelica s. m. + f. fainthearted person; poltroon. ‖ adj. fainthearted, weak, coward, timid, scary. ‖ ~**mente** adv. faintheartedly.

tremelicante adj. m. + f. (also **tremelicoso** m.) tremulous, trembling, shivering.

tremelicar v. to tremble, quaver, quiver, quake, shiver, shake.

tremelique s. m. shiver, tremble, shake.

tremeluzente adj. m. + f. flickering, shimmery, blinking, twinkling, sparkling.

tremeluzir v. to sparkle, twinkle, flicker, flare, twiddle.

tremembé s. m. (Braz.) swampland, quagmire, river lowlands.

tremendo adj. 1. tremendous, terrifying. 2. awful, dreadful, frightful, terrible, horrible, fearful. 3.

extraordinary, formidable. 4. immense, enormous, huge. ‖ **-amente** adv. tremendously.

um susto ~ a tremendous fright. **uma tarefa -a** an enormous task, a hell of a job. **uma -a asneira** a tremendous blunder, (sl.) a howler. **uma -a derrota** an awful defeat.

tremente adj. m. + f. trembling, trembly, quivering, shivering, quaking, shaky.

tremer v. 1. to tremble, quake, dither, shake, quiver, quaver. 2. to throb, palpitate. 3. to shiver, shudder. 4. to vibrate, oscillate. 5. to fear, dread.
~ **de** to quiver with. ~ **de cólera** to tremble with rage. ~ **no corpo todo** to shiver all over. ~ **e estremecer** to shake and quake. ~ **de medo** to be seized with fear. ~ **em pensar** to tremble to think, shudder at the thought. ~ **como varas verdes** to tremble like a leaf, shake in one's shoes. **sua mão tremia pela idade** his hand shook from age.

treme-treme s. m. (pl. **treme-tremes**; also **tremes-tremes**) (Braz.) 1. electric eel. 2. (bot.) quaking grass, dodder grass.

tremês adj. m. + f. (pl. **-eses**), **tremesinho** m. = **tremecém**.

tremido s. m. tremor, quiver, quake, trembling, shiver. ‖ adj. (pop.) 1. doubtful, dubious. 2. risky, shaky. ‖ **-amente** 1. doubtfully. 2. (agric.) overripe.

letra -a a shaky handwriting.

tremifusa s. f. (mus.) demisemiquaver, thirty-second note.

trêmito s. m. (Braz.) 1. quivering. 2. thrill. 3. noise, din, clamour. 4. excitement, rage.

tremó s. m. 1. pier: the solid part of a wall between windows. 2. pier glass, large mirror (plate M 14).

tremoçada s. f. large quantity of lupines.

tremoçal s. m. (pl. **-ais**) lupine plantation.

tremoçar v. (Port., prov.) to scatter lupine seeds.

tremoceiro s. m. 1. (bot.) lupine. 2. salesman of lupine seeds.

tremoço (ô) s. m. (pl. **tremoços**) lupine (plant and seed).

tremoço-amarelo s. m. (pl. **tremoços-amarelos**) (bot.) yellow lupine.

tremoço-azul s. m. (pl. **tremoços-azuis**) (bot.) bluebonnet.

tremoço-branco s. m. (pl. **tremoços-brancos**) (bot.) white lupine.

tremolita s. f. (min.) tremolite: a variety of amphibole, a silicate of calcium and magnesium.

tremonha s. f. hopper of a mill.

tremonhado s. m. receptacle into which the meal falls coming from the millstones.

tremor s. m. 1. tremor, shake, thrill, quiver. 2. palpitation, throb, dither, shudder, shiver, quaking.
~ **dos artistas** stage fright. ~ **de terra** earthquake.

trempe s. f. 1. trivet, tripod. 2. raft of three logs (instead of five). 3. (pop.) trio: group of three persons. 4. set of three stones for putting a pot on.

tremulação s. f. (pl. **-ões**) 1. tremble, trembling. 2. flicker, shivering, fluttering. 3. waving.

tremulante adj. m. + f. waving, fluttering, shaking.

tremular v. 1. to tremble, quaver, quiver. 2. to wave, flutter, swing. 3. to flicker, twinkle, glimmer, shimmer. 4. to vascillate, hesitate, waver. 5. to quaver, trill.

tremulina s. f. glimmer, shimmer, glister, sparkle, twinkle.

trêmulo s. m. 1. (mus.) tremolo. 2. ~s pl. ornamental flowers made of precious stones. ‖ adj. 1. tremulous, trembling, shaky, vibrant. 2. timid, fearful, hesitant. 3. sparkling.

tremura s. f. 1. tremor, tremble, trembling. 2. ~s pl. fright, anguish; troubles.

trena s. f. 1. hair ribbon. 2. tape, tapeline. 3. tape measure.

trenado adj., **trenador** s. m., **trenar** v. = **treinado, treinador, treinar**.

trenheira s. f. (Braz., pop.) lot of goods and chattels; household stuff; a part of a person's things.

treno (I) s. m. lament, elegy, threnode, dirge.

treno (II) s. m. = **treino**.

trenó s. m. sled, sledge, sleigh, toboggan; coaster (plate T 6).
~ **duplo** bobsleigh.

trenodia s. f. monody, threnody: a funeral song.

trepa (I) s. f. (pop.) 1. beating, thrashing, cudgelling. 2. reprimand, scolding, wigging.

trepa (II) s. f. (obs.) ruffles or flounce of a dress.

trepação s. f. (pl. **-ões**) 1. slander, columny, defamation. 2. jeering, railery.

trepada s. f. 1. climb, ascent. 2. slope, acclivity, declivity.

trepadeira s. f. 1. creeper: a) (bot.) creeping or climbing plant; hedge bindweed, rambler. b) (ornith.) spider-catcher, nut-hatch; any of various creeping birds. 2. slanderer, backbiter. ‖ adj. 1. creeping, climbing. 2. maligning, slanderous, evil speaking.

trepador s. m. 1. creeper. 2. scansorial bird. 3. calumniator, slanderer, backbiter. ‖ adj. 1. creeping, climbing. 2. slanderous, calumniatory.

trepa-moleque s. m. (pl. **trepa-moleques**) 1. (Braz., obs.) a double-doored cupboard. 2. high comb. 3. (ornith.) wood ibis. 4. (ent.) rove beetle.

trepanação s. f. (pl. **-ões**) (surg.) trepanning, trepanation.

trepanar v. (surg.) to trepan, trephine, perforate the skull with a trephine.

trépano s. m. (surg.) trepan, trephine (instrument to perforate the skull, sort of saw).

trepar v. 1. (also bot. and zool.) to creep, climb. 2. to ascend, mount, scale, clamber. 3. to rise, become important. 4. to calumniate, malign, slander, backbite.
~ **na alma de alguém** to dress down a person, give a sound wigging to. ~ **numa árvore** to climb up a tree. ~ **como um macaco** to climb like a monkey.

trepidação s. f. (pl. **-ões**) 1. trepidation, vibration, trembling. 2. agitation, perturbation, fear, alarm. 3. slight earthquake.

trepidante adj. m. + f. tremulous, shaking; afraid. ‖ ~**mente** adv. tremulously.

trepidar v. 1. to tremble, shake, oscillate, vibrate, quake. 2. to agitate, perturb. 3. to hesitate, vacillate.
sem ~ unhesitatingly. **ele respondeu sem** ~ he answered point-blank.

trepidez s. f. 1. tremor, trembling. 2. fright, anguish.

trépido adj. 1. tremulous, trembling. 2. frightened, afraid. 3. waving, fluttering.

tréplica s. f. (also **contra-réplica**) rejoinder, rebutter, answer.

treplicar v. to rejoin, rebut, answer.

treponema s. f., **treponemo** m. (bact.) one of the spirochaetas.

três s. m. 1. (the number) three. 2. trey (cards, dice, etc.). 3. (mus.) treble. ‖ adj. three.
~ **em um** triune. ~ **por cento** three per cent. ~ **quartos** three-quarters. ~ **vezes** three times, thrice. ~ **vezes mais** three times as much, threefold. **às duas por** ~ two out of three times. **composto de** ~ **cores** trichromatic. **de** ~ **andares** three-storied. **dois é bom,** ~ **é demais** two is company, three is a crowd. **em** ~ by threes. **jogo em** ~ three-handed. **navio de** ~ **cobertas**

three-decker. **navio de** ~ **mastros** three-master. **os** ~ all three of them. **receptor de** ~ **válvulas** three--valve receiver. **a regra de** ~ the rule of three.

tresandar v. 1. to cause to go back, turn back. 2. to stink, have a bad smell. 3. to disturb, upset.

trescalante adj. m. + f. having a strong smell.

trescalar v. to smell strongly; emit a strong odour; penetrate (odour or smell).

tresdobrado adj. triplicate, treble, triple, threefold.

tresdobradura s. f. tripling, trebling, triplication.

tresdobrar v. to triple, triplicate, treble, render three-fold.

tresdobre s. m. triple. || adj. m. + f. triple, treble, threefold, triplex, triplicate.

tresdobro (ô) s. m. (pl. **tresdobros**) triple.

três-estrelinhas s. f. pl. (***) three asterisks (put under an anonym writing or for replacing actual names of persons or places).

tresfolegar v. to pant, gasp, puff, breathe hard.

tresgastar v. to spend too much, lavish, squander, dissipate; waste.

três-irmãos s. m., sg. + pl. a plant of the soapberry family.

tresler v. 1. to read backwards. 2. to dote, grow heedless by too much reading.

tresloucado s. m. madman, lunatic, crazy person. || adj. crazy, mad, deranged, insane, cracked, foolish. || **-amente** crazily.

tresloucar v. to madden, craze; to become insane, mad, or crazy.

tresmalhado adj. strayed, escaped, fugitive; runaway; lost, off course, gone astray.

tresmalhar v. 1. to let drop a stich (at knitting). 2. to suffer to escape, let go, lose. 3. ~**-se** to run away, escape, stray, scatter, disband, disappear.

tresmalho (I) s. m. straying, escaping, disappearing.

tresmalho (II) s. m. 1. trammel, a sort of fish net. 2. disappearance.

três-marias s. f. pl. 1. (astr.) Orion's belt. 2. (bot.) bougainvillea.

tresnoitar v. 1. to keep from sleeping, keep awake. 2. to pass a sleepless night, to pass waking.

treso adj. (obs.) disloyal, treacherous, false. || **-amente** adv. disloyally.

trespano s. m. ticking, tick.

trespassar v., **trespasse** s. m. = traspassar, traspasse.

três-por-dois s. m., sg. + pl. (Braz., ent.) a species of vespid.

três-portas s. f., sg. + pl. (ent.) a small stingless bee.

três-potes s. m., sg. + pl. (Braz., bot.) a species of a trumpet creeper.

tresquiáltera s. f. (mus.) triplet: three notes played in the time of only two of them.

tressuar v. to sweat, perspire or transpire very much.

trestampar v. to play the fool, dote, talk childishly.

tresvariado adj. 1. raving, wild, delirious. 2. doting. 3. irrational.

tresvariar v. 1. to rave. 2. to act foolishly. 3. to dote. 4. to talk idly.

tresvario s. m. raving, madness, delirium; dotage, mental disturbance.

tresvoltear v. to take three or more turns; turn around.

treta s. f. 1. dexterity, deftness, quickness. 2. stratagem, feint, contrivance, false attack, craft, device; dodge. 3. ~**s** pl.: a) prattle, smooth talk. b) nonsense.

tretear v. (Braz.) to feign, sham; deceive; contrive; dodge.

treteiro s. m. dodger, rascal, crook, scalawag. || adj. crooked, rascally.

trevas s. f. pl. 1. darkness, obscurity, gloom, mirkiness, murkiness; night. 2. ignorance, want of

knowledge, inexperience. 3. matins of the last days in the Holy Week; Tenebrae. **ao cair das** ~**s** at nightfall. **quarta-feira de** ~ Wednesday of the Holy Week.

trevo s. m. (bot.) clover, shamrock, wood sorrel.

trevo-aquático s. m. (pl. **trevos-aquáticos**) (bot.) buck bean.

trevo-azul s. m. (pl. **trevos-azuis**) (bot.) blue melilot.

trevo-branco s. m. (pl. **trevos-brancos**) (bot.) white clover, Dutch clover.

trevo-cervino s. m. (pl. **trevos-cervinos**) (bot.) hemp agrimony.

trevo-do-egito s. m. (pl. **trevos-do-egito**) (bot.) bersin clover.

trevo-encarnado s. m. (pl. **trevos-encarnados**) (bot.) crimson clover.

trevo-híbrido s. m. (pl. **trevos-híbridos**) (bot.) alsike.

trevo-de-quatro-folhas s. m. (pl. **trevos-de-quatro-folhas**) (bot.) four-leafed clover.

trevoso adj. = tenebroso.

treza s. m. thirteen. || adj. thirteenth.

treze-de-maio s. m., sg. + pl. (Braz.) nickname sometimes given to the Negroes.

trezena s. f. 1. a group or set of thirteen. 2. a period of thirteen days. 3. a sort of prayers during thirteen days before a Saint's Day.

trezeno adj. thirteenth.

trezentos adj. pl. three hundred.

triacanto adj. (bot.) having three spines.

tríada, tríade s. f. triad: 1. trinity. 2. (mus.) chord of three tones or notes, common chord.

triadelfo adj. (bot.) triadelphous: having the stamens in three bundles.

triaga s. f. (also **teriaga**) theriac.

triagem s. f. 1. selection, choice. 2. sorting, separating.

triagueiro s. m. person who prepares the theriac.

trialado adj. having three wings.

triândria s. f. (bot.) triandria: group of flowers with three stamens.

triândrico, triândrio, triandro adj. (bot.) triandrian, triandrous.

triangulação s. f. (pl. **-ões**) 1. triangulation, division into triangles. 2. surveying by dividing into triangles.

triangulado adj. divided into triangles.

triangulador s. m. (Braz.) triangulator: person who surveys or operates by triangulation.

triangular (I) adj. m. + f. triangular: 1. relating to a triangle. 2. three-cornered, three-angled, trigonal, trigonous, triquetrous; deltaic. || ~**mente** adv. triangularly.

triangular (II) v. to triangulate, divide into triangles.

triangularidade s. f. triangularity.

triângulo s. m. triangle: 1. geometrical triangular figure, trigon. 2. triangle-formed musical instrument. 3. name of a constellation of the Northern Hemisphere. 4. a sort of square. ~ **acutângulo** acute-angled triangle. ~ **curvilíneo** curvilinear triangle. ~ **eqüilátero** equilateral triangle. ~ **escaleno** scalene triangle. ~ **esférico** spherical triangle. ~ **isósceles** isosceles triangle. ~ **oxígono** oxygon. ~ **plano** plane triangle. ~ **reto** orthogon.

triarquia s. f. 1. triarchy: government by three persons, triumvirate. 2. country divided into three governmental sections.

trias s. m. Trias: geological formation.

triásico adj. (geol.) Triassic.

triaxífero adj. (bot.) triaxal, triaxial: having three axes.

tríbade s. f. tribade, Lesbian.

tribadismo s. m. tribadism, Lesbianism.

tribal adj. m. + f. (pl. **-ais**) (also **tribul**) tribal: belonging to a tribe. ‖ ~**mente** adv. tribally.

tribo s. f. tribe: 1. race, folk. 2. clan, family, rod. 3. (ancient hist.) cast, class. ~ **de selvagens** tribe of savages. **chefe da** ~ head of the tribe. **membro de uma tribo** tribesman. **sistema de** ~**s** tribalism.

triboeletricidade s. f. triboelectricity: electricity resulting from friction.

tribofar v. (Braz.) to cheat at horse racing; to cheat in any game.

tribofe s. m. (Braz.) 1. cheating at horse racing; cheating in any game. 2. flirtation.

tribofeiro s. m. (Braz.) individual who cheats at races or in some game.

triboluminescência s. f. triboluminescence.

tribometria s. f. tribometry.

tribométrico adj. tribometric(al).

tribômetro s. m. tribometer, an apparatus for measuring friction.

tríbraco s. m. (pros.) tribrach: metrical foot of three short syllables.

tribracteado adj. (bot.) tribracteate.

tribracteolado adj. (bot.) tribracteolate: furnished with three bractlets.

tribufu adj. (pop., also **trubufu**) poorly or badly dressed.

tribulação s. f. (pl. **-ões**) 1. tribulation, grief, trouble, affliction, distress. 2. adversity, adverseness.

tríbulo s. m. (bot.) land caltrop.

tríbulo-aquático s. m. (pl. **tríbulos-aquáticos**) (bot.) water chestnut.

tribuna s. f. 1. tribune, rostrum, stand, platform (for a speaker); pulpit, gallery. 2. (fig.) eloquence, oratory. ~ **da imprensa** reporters' gallery. **subir à** ~ to mount the rostrum.

tribunado, tribunato s. m. 1. tribunate, tribuneship. 2. period of a tribuneship.

tribunal s. m. (pl. **-ais**) tribunal: 1. judgement seat, bench for judges. 2. court of justice, forum, bar. 3. council, law, judgement, jurisdiction. ~ **de apelação** Court of Appeal. ~ **arbitral** Court of Arbitration. ~ **de contas** Audit Office, Court of Audit. ~ **do distrito** District Court. ~ **itinerante** Circuit Court. ~ **de justiça** Law Court. ~ **de pequenos delitos ou de polícia** Police Court. ~ **de primeira instância** Country Court. ~ **superior, supremo** High Court of Judicature. ~ **superior da Marinha** admiralty. **levar perante um** ~ to put into court. **ministro do supremo** ~ Lord Chief Justice.

tribunício adj. tribunicial, tribunician.

tribuno s. m. tribune: 1. (Rom. Hist.) a sort of magistrate. 2. (fig.) defender of popular rights; demagogue.

tributação s. f. (pl. **-ões**) taxation, assessment, contribution.

tributado adj. taxed, assessed, paid in tribute. **não** ~ untaxed.

tributal adj. m. + f. (pl. **-ais**) concerning tributes.

tributar v. 1. to lay a tribute on, impose a tax on, tax, assess. 2. to pay tribute. 3. to dedicate, render homage. 4. to become tributary; contribute.

tributário s. m. tributary: 1. contributor, tax-payer. 2. stream that flows into a larger stream, confluent. ‖ adj. 1. tributary, contributary, contributing. 2. confluent. ‖ **tributariamente** adv. tributarily. **capacidade -a** taxable capacity.

tributável adj. m. + f. (pl. **-áveis**) taxable, ratable, tollable; tributary.

tributo s. m. 1. tribute, contribution, duty, toll, due. 2. tax, impost. 3. dedication, homage, mark of respect, esteem.

~ **de admiração** mark of esteem. ~ **de vassalos** vassalage. **pagar** ~ **à natureza** to pay tribute to nature: die.

tribuzana s. = **trabuzana.**

trica s. f. 1. chicane, quibble. 2. cheat, fraud. 3. intrigue, plot. 4. futility, trifle.

tricampeão s. m. a three-time champion (club, athlete, etc.). ‖ adj. three-time champion.

tricana s. f. 1. coarse woollen fabric. 2. a petticoat made of this fabric. 3. countrywoman of Portugal.

tricapsular adj. m. + f. (bot.) tricapsular: having three capsules.

tricéfalo s. m. a three-headed being. ‖ adj. tricephalous, three-headed.

tricelular adj. m. + f. three-celled.

tricenal adj. m. + f. (pl. **-ais**) tricennial: lasting thirty years.

tricentenário s. m. tercentenary, tricentenary; three-hundredth anniversary. ‖ adj. tricentenary, tercentenary, tercentennial.

triciclo s. m. tricycle, velocipede; tricar.

tricípite s. m. (anat.) triceps: the three-headed extensor muscle at the back of the upper arm. ‖ adj. m. + f. triceps: three-headed.

triclínico adj. (cryst.) triclinic: having three axes inclined at oblique angles.

triclínio s. m. (ant.) triclinium: Roman dining room with three couches around a table.

tricô s. m. tricot: 1. knitting. 2. stockinet, jersey. **agulha de** ~ knitting needle.

tricociste s. f. (zool.) trichocyst.

tricoglossia s. f. (med.) trichoglossia: hairy appearance due to the hypertrophy of the papillae.

tricóide adj. m. + f. trichoid, hairlike, capillary.

tricologia s. f. trichology: treatise on hair and skin.

tricolor adj. m. + f. tricolour, tricoloured, having three colours.

tricoma s. m. (path.) trichome: a disease of the hair.

tricórdio s. m. (mus.) trichord: instrument with three strings.

tricorne adj. m. + f. tricorn, three-horned.

tricórnio s. m. tricorn, tricorne, three-cornered hat.

tricotar, tricotear v. to knit.

tricotiledôneo adj. (bot.) tricotyledonous: having three cotyledons (first group of leaves raising from a seed).

tricotomia s. f. (bot.) trichotomy: threefold division.

tricotômico adj. trichotomous.

tricótomo adj. divided into (sets of) three.

tricroísmo s. m. trichroism: property of exhibiting three different colours.

tricromia s. f. three-colour process (of printing).

tricrômico adj. trichromic.

tricúspide adj. m. + f. tricuspid: having three cusps or points.

tridáctilo, tridátilo adj. (zool.) tridactil(ous): having three fingers or toes.

tridentado adj. tridentate: having three dents or prongs.

tridente s. m. 1. trident: a) the scepter of Neptune. b) (fig.) naval supremacy. 2. weapon with three prongs. 3. (fig.) the sea. ‖ adj. m. + f. tridental, tridentate: having three dents or prongs.

tridênteo adj. concerning the trident.

tridentífero, tridentígero adj. (poet.) bearing a trident.

tridentino s. m. Tridentine: native or inhabitant of Trent (Italy). ‖ adj. Tridentine: of or pertaining to Trent.

tridi s. m. (ornith., also **macuquinho**) the sharp-tailed creeper.

tridimensional adj. m. + f. (pl. **-ais**) tridimensional: of three dimensions, cubic.

tridimita s. f. (min.) tridymite: vitreous form of silica.

triduano adj. triduan, lasting three days.

tríduo s. m. triduo, triduum: 1. a period of three days. 2. three days service of prayers.

triécico adj. trioecius: having male, female and hermaphrodite flowers on three different plants of the same species.

triedro s. m. (geom.) 1. a trihedral angle. 2. trihedron. || adj. trihedral, having three faces.

trienado s. m. (also **triênio**) triennial: period of three years.

trienal adj. m. + f. (pl. -**ais**) triennial: 1. lasting three years. 2. bearing fruit once in three years. || ~**mente** adv. triennially.

triênio s. m. 1. triennial: a period of three years. 2. administration of an office during three years.

triental s. f. Trientalis: the family of the primrose.

triestino s. m. Triestine: native of inhabitant of Trieste (Italy). || adj. Triestine: of or pertaining to Trieste.

trifacial adj. (anat., also **trigêmeo**) trifacial, trigeminal (said of a nerve of the face).

trifásico adj. (electr.) three-phase.
 corrente -a three-phase current. **motor** ~ three- -phase motor.

trifauce adj. m. + f. (poet.) having three jaws.

trífido adj. (zool., bot., also **trigêmino**) trifid: having three folds or lobes; three-cleft; trigeminal.

trifilo adj. (bot.) triphyllous.

trifloro adj. (poet.) triflorous, trifloral.

trifoliado adj. (bot.) trifoliate, trifoliated, trefoil (plate F 5).

trifólio s. m. 1. (bot.) trifolium, trefoil, clover, sham- rock. 2. (archit.) trefoil.

trifoliose s. f. trifoliosis: poisoning (of horses) caused by alsike.

trifório s. m. triforium: a gallery above the arches of a church.

triforme adj. m. + f. triform, triformed.

trifurcação s. f. (pl. -**ões**) trifurcation: division into three (branches or forks).

trifurcar v. to trifurcate: divide into three (branches or forks).

triga (I) s. f. (also **trigança**) haste, speed, urgency.

triga (II) s. f. carriage with three horses.

trigal s. m. (pl. -**ais**) wheat field, cornfield (plate C 16).

trigamia s. f. trigamy: crime of having three hus- bands (or wives) simultaneously.

trigamilha s. f. bread made of wheat and corn meal. || adj. said of a mixture of wheat and corn meal.

trígamo s. m. 1. trigamist: person married to three wives at the same time. 2. person who has married three times.

trigar-se v. to hurry up, make haste.

trigêmeo s. m. triplet, trilling, each of three children born at the same birth. || adj. 1. relating to triplets. 2. trifacial.

trigeminada s. f. a window with six openings.

trigêmino adj. trifid, triple, trigeminal, having three folds or lobes.

trigênea s. f. a family of anonaceous plants.

trigésimo s. m. thirtieth part. || adj. thirtieth.

triginia s. f. trigynia: an order of plants with three pistils.

triginico, trígino adj. (bot.) trigynous: having three pistils.

trigla s. f. trigla: a family of fishes: Triglidae.

tríglifo s. m. triglyph: 1. (archit.) ornament on a frieze of Doric style. 2. (min.) a sort of crystal.

triglota s. m. + f. person who speaks three lan- guages. || adj. 1. triglot: speaking three languages. 2. trilingual: written in three languages.

trigo s. m. wheat (corn): 1. the plant. 2. the seed (used for breadstuff). || adj. wheaten.
 ~ **moído** grist. **ceifar o** ~ to cut the corn. **farinha de** ~ wheat flour. **separar o joio do** ~ to separate the tares from the wheat.

trigo-cachudo s. m. (pl. **trigos-cachudos**) (bot.) leghorn straw, poulard wheat.

trigo-candial s. m. (pl. **trigos-candiais**) (bot.) one- -grained wheat, St. Peter's corn.

trigo-de-milagre s. m. (pl. **trigos-de-milagre**) (bot.) mummy wheat.

trigo-durázio s. m. (pl. **trigos-durázios**) (bot.) durum wheat.

trigo-mouro s. m. (pl. **trigos-mouros**) (bot.) French wheat or buckwheat.

trigonal adj. m. + f. (pl. -**ais**) trigonal, triangular.

trígono s. m. 1. (astr.) trigon: aspect of planets 120 degrees apart. 2. a genus of mollusca. || adj. trigo- nous, trigonal. || **trigonamente** adv. trigonously.

trigonocéfalo s. m. trigonocephalous being. || adj. trigonocephalous: having a triangular head.

trigonocórneo adj. (ent.) said of an insect with triangular antennae.

trigonometria s. f. trigonometry: the part of ma- thematics relating to triangles.

trigonométrico adj. trigonometric(al).

trigoso adj. hasty, speedy, quickly; hurried; impa- tient. || -**amente** adv. hastily.

trigrama s. m. trigram, trigraph: 1. a word of three letters. 2. a vowel or diphtong represented by three letters.

trigueirão s. m. (pl. -**ões**) (ornith.) corn bunting.

trigueiro s. m. brunet. || adj. wheat-coloured, brunet, brown, swarthy.

triguenho adj. 1. pertaining to or like wheat. 2. = **trigueiro**.

triguera s. f. (bot.) the nightshade or potato family.

triguilho s. m. chaff (of wheat).

trijugado adj. (bot.) trijugate, trijugous: having three pairs of leaflets.

trilar v. to trill, quaver, warble.

trilateral adj. m. + f. (pl. -**ais**) (geom.) trilateral: having three sides.

trilátero s. m. trilateral figure, triangle. || adj. tri- lateral.

trilema s. m. trilemma.

trilha, trilhada s. f. 1. trace, track, runway, trail footstep; footpath, way (plate G 5). 2. thrashing (grain). 3. (fig.) example. 4. (Port., prov.) beating, cudgelling.
 ~ **sonora** sound-track.

trilhado adj. 1. thrashed, beaten. 2. trodden. 3. well-known, common, well-worn.
 caminho ~ beaten track.

trilhador s. m. 1. thrasher, thresher. 2. thrashing- -machine. || adj. thrashing, threshing.

trilhadura s. f., **trilhamento** m. 1. thrashing, thresh- ing. 2. trail.

trilhão s. m. (pl. -**ões**) (also **trilião**) trillion (corre- sponds to an English billion).

trilhar v. 1. to thrash, thresh, flail, beat. 2. to tread out, press down, trample; crush, bruise. 3. to tread, follow (a road). 4. to wander, tramp.

trilheira s. f. (Braz.) footpath through a forest.

trilho s. m. 1. thrasher, harrow, flail. 2. churn-staff. 3. trail, track, guideway, rail (plate B 9). 4. rou- tine practice, use. 5. (Braz.) rail (of a tramway or railway) (plates B 15, E 12, 13, V 4).
 ~ **dentado** cograil. ~ **de guia** guide rail. ~ **de roda** tread of a wheel.

trílice (I) s. m. (bot.) genus of the family Triliaceae.

trílice (II) adj. m. + f. consisting of three threads.

trilíngüe s. m. + f., adj. m. + f. = **triglota**.

triliteral adj. m. + f. (pl. **-ais**), **trilítero** m. triliteral: consisting of three letters.

trílito s. m. trilith, triliton: prehistoric stone monument.

trilo s. m. (mus.) trill, quaver, warble.

trilobado adj. trilobate, trilobal, trilobated, trilobed: having three lobes.

trilobite s. m. (zool.) trilobite: a species of prehistoric marine arthropods.

trilocular adj. m. + f. (bot.) trilocular: three-celled.

trilogia s. f. trilogy: 1. a series of three dramas. 2. (by extension) any series of three literary or musical compositions. 3. triad.

trilógico adj. relating to a trilogy.

trilongo s. m. (poet.) Greek or Latin verse of three long syllables.

trimaculado adj. trimacular.

trimembre adj. m. + f. trimembral.

trimensal adj. m. + f. (pl. **-ais**) trimensual; trimestrial.

trímero s. m. (chem.) trimer. ‖ adj. trimerous: divided into three parts.

trimestral adj. m. + f. (pl. **-ais**) trimestrial; trimensual: 1. lasting three months. 2. once in three months. 3. every three months, threemonthly. ‖ **~mente** adv. trimestrially.

sessões -ais quarter sessions.

trimestralidade s. f. (Braz.) sum paid from three to three months, trimestrial payment.

trimestre s. m. 1. period of three months; quarter of a year. 2. quarterly payment. ‖ adj. m. + f. trimestrial.

trimétrico adj. trimeter, trimetric(al): consisting of three measures. ‖ **trimetricamente** adv. trimetrically.

trímetro s. m. trimeter: a verse of three measures having two feet each.

trimorfia s. f., **trimorfismo** m. trimorphism: property of crystallizing in three different forms.

trimorfo adj. (cryst.) trimorphic, trimorphous.

trimotor s. m. trimotor: aeroplane with three motors. ‖ adj. having three motors.

trimúrti s. f. (India) Trimurti: trinity of three faces of nature (creative, conservative and destructive).

trinado s. m. trill, shake, quaver, chirp, rolling, warble.

~ do rouxinol the warbling of the nightingale.

trinar v. to trill, shake, quaver, chirp, roll, warble.

trinca (I) s. f. trine: 1. set of three analogous things; three cards of the same value. 2., gang (of boys).

trinca (II) s. f. 1. (Braz.) scratch, crack, chink, split. 2. (Port. prov.) a bite, mouthful, nibble.

trinca-cevada s. f. (pl. **trincas-cevadas**) a sort of popular game.

trincada s. f. 1. scratching, cracking. 2. mouthful, nibble, bite.

trincado adj. 1. scratched, split, cracked. 2. bitten off. 3. (fig.) sly, malicious, foxy.

trincadura s. f. chink, crack, split.

trinca-espinhas s. m., sg. + pl. (pop.) bean pole.

trinca-ferro s. m. (pl. **trinca-ferros**) (Braz., ornith.) grand tanager (Saltator maximus).

trincafiar v. (also **trancafiar**) 1. to sew with a shoemaker's thread. 2. (naut.) to lash. 3. (fig.) to incarcerate, imprison, put under lock and key.

trincafio s. m. 1. a shoemaker's thread, string. 2. (naut.) lash. 3. (fig.) subtility, craftiness, skill. 4. hemp for tightening a nut of a screw.

trincal s. m. = **tincal.**

trinca-nozes s. m., sg. + pl. (Braz., ornith.) red crossbill.

trincar v. 1. to crush, bite, crunch, munch. 2. to nibble, chew. 3. to snap, crack. 4. (naut.) to lash the guns. 5. (N. Braz.) to tingle, jingle. 6. **~-se** to rage, despair; get angry.

trincha s. f. 1. adz(e), specially of a carpenter; chisel. 2. shavings (mostly of wood). 3. nail puller. 4. (paint.) broad brush (plate E 8, P 12). 5. (Braz., vulg.) any tool to break open a door.

trinchador s. m. carver, chiseler. ‖ adj. carving, chiseling.

trinchante s. m. + f. 1. carver, trencher. 2. m. carving knife, trencher (plate M 1). 3. carving table. ‖ adj. carving, trenching.

trinchão s. m. (pl. **-ões**) 1. carver. 2. a sort of carving knife. 3. (obs.) large slice, hunch.

trinchar v. to trench, carve, cut up (meat).

trincheira s. f. 1. trench, rifle pit. 2. parapet, barrier, ditch. 3. (Braz.) shelter, screen, fence, partition of boards or planks.

trincheiro s. m. step, foothold in a trenchwall.

trinchete s. m. paring knife, a shoemaker's knife.

trincho s. m. 1. trencher; dish or board for carving on. 2. way of carving. 3. board on which cheese in moulds is put. 4. (fig.) way out, knack, loophole; way to get over a difficulty.

trinco s. m. 1. door latch, small spring lock, spring bolt, latch bolt (plate F 1). 2. snap with the fingers; click.

~ automático door spring. **chave de ~** latch key.

trincolejar v. = **tilintar.**

trincolhos-brincolhos s. m. pl. a child's toy.

trindade s. f. 1. Trinity: a) union of God Father, Son and the Holy Ghost; Three in One, triunity. b) Trinity Sunday. c) name of a religious order. d) triad, trine. 2. **~s** pl. Angelus, Angelus bell.

tocar às ~s to toll the Angelus.

trinervado, trinérveo adj. (bot.) trinervate, three-nerved.

trineta s. f. great-great-granddaughter.

trineto s. m. great-great-grandson.

trinfar s. m. chirp, twitter. ‖ v. to chirp, twitter.

trinitário s. m. monk of the Trinitarian Order. ‖ adj. belonging to the Trinitarian Order.

trinitrofenol s. m. (chem.) trinitrophenol, picric acid.

trinitrotuoleno s. m. (chem.) trinitrotuolene.

trino (I) s. m. (also **trinado**) trill, shake, quaver, warble.

trino (II) s. m. Trinitarian (monk). ‖ adj. 1. Trinitarian. 2. triune, trine, ternal.

trinogeto s. m. the genus Solanaceae (nightshade and potato family).

trinômine adj. m. + f. (poet.) having three names.

trinômio s. m. trinominal: 1. (bot.) trinominal scientific name. 2. (math.) expression of three terms with the sign plus or minus or both.

trinque s. m. 1. peg or rack for a coat, coat hanger. 2. (Braz., fig.) spruceness, elegance, polish of dress, neatness.

andar ou estar no ~ to be well-dressed, fashionable. **novo do ~** spick and span new.

trinta s. m. 1. thirty. 2. thirties.

a casa dos ~ the thirties. **ele já passou os ~** he is over thirty; out of the thirty. **uns ~** about thirty, some thirty.

trinta-e-um s. m. thirty-one: designation of a card game.

bater o ~ (fig.) to kick the bucket, to die.

trintanário s. m. lackey, footman, hired servant.

trintão s. m. (pl. **-ões**) person of thirty years, person in his (or her) thirties. ‖ adj. thirtyish: thirty years old.

trintar v. to be thirty years old; reach thirty years of age.

trinta-réis s. m., sg. + pl. (Braz., ornith.) royal tern, white-headed tern.

trintário s. m. trental: 1. a series of thirty masses for a deceased person. 2. a month's mind, commemoration service on the thirthieth day after a person's death.

trintena s. f. 1. group of thirty persons; 2. set of thirty things. 3. thirtieth.

trintenário s. m. person of thirty years. ‖ adj. thirtyish.

trintídio s. m. 1. period of thirty days. 2. a month's mind.

trio s. m. trio: 1. triplet, a set of three. 2. (mus.): a) composition for three voices or instruments. b) second part of a minuet, scherzo or march.

trióico adj. trioecious: having male, female and hermaphrodite flowers on three different plants. ‖ **trioicamente** adv. trioeciously.

tríodo s. m. (radio) vacuum tube with three electrodes.

triolé s. m. triolet: a stanza of eight lines with a special rhyme.

trional s. m. (med.) trional: a hypnotic drug.

triovulado adj. (bot.) having three ovules.

tripa s. f. 1. intestine, gut, tripe. 2. ~s pl. entrails, bowls, guts.

~ **gaiteira** (N. Braz., pop.) large intestine. ~s da **verga grande** (naut.) the main gears. **fazer das** ~s **coração** to put on a bold face, set a good face on a bad business; pluck up courage. **à** ~ **forra** opulently. **viver à** ~ **forra** to live on the fat of the land, in clover.

tripa-de-galinha s. f. (pl. **tripas-de-galinha**) (Braz., bot.) wart herb, rosewood.

tripagem, tripalhada s. f. tripery, entrails, guts.

tripanossomíase s. f. (med.) trypanosomiasis: disease caused by infection with trypanosomes.

tripanossomo s. m. trypanosome: a parasitic protozoan infecting the blood of animal and man.

triparia s. f. tripeshop, place where tripes are sold.

tripartição s. f. (pl. **-ões**) tripartition: division into three parts.

tripartido adj. tripartite, three partite. ‖ **-amente** adv. tripartitely.

tripartir v. 1. to divide into three parts. 2. ~**-se** to become divided into three parts.

tripartível adj. m. + f. (pl. **-íveis**) divisable into three parts.

tripé s. m. 1. tripod, trivet; spider, a three-legged support (plate F 6). 2. three-legged stool.

tripeça s. f. 1. three-legged stool (plate C 2). (fig.) a shoemaker's job. 3. (sl.) meeting of three conspirators.

tripeiro s. m. 1. tripe-seller, tripemonger, tripeman. 2. (Port.) nickname of a native of Oporto.

tripétalo adj. (bot.) tripetalous: having three petals.

tripetrepe adv. step by step, with slow steps; quietly, gently.

tripleto s. m. (phys.) triplet.

triplex, tríplex s. m., sg. + pl. (Braz.) a triplex apartment. ‖ adj. m. + f., sg. + pl. triplex.

triplicação s. f. (pl. **-ões**) triplication, triplicating, triplicature.

triplicado adj. tripled, triplicate, triple; threefold, treble.

triplicar v. to triplicate, triple, treble, multiply by three, three-ply.

triplicata s. f. third copy.

triplicidade s. f. triplicity.

triplinervado, triplinérveo adj. (bot.) trinervate, trinerve, trinerved, three-nerved.

triplo s. m. (also **triple**) triple, triplicate, treble, triplex, (also **tríplice** m. + f.). ‖ adj. triple, triplex, treble, trinal, triplicate; three-ply, threefold.

o ~ **de** triple as many as. **máquina de expansão -a triple** expansion engine.

triplóptero adj. (zool.) having tripartite wings or fins.

tripó s. m. three-legged stool with a (triangular) leather seat.

trípoda, trípode s. f. tripod: 1. (Greek hist.) a three-footed stool on which a priestess (of Delphi) used to sit, giving her oracles. 2. ancient three-legged vase. 3. trivet.

tripófago adj. (zool.) feeding on insects and worms.

trípole s. m. 1. tripoli, infusorial earth, siliceous deposit. 2. rottenstone.

tripolino, tripolitano s. m. Tripolitan: native or inhabitant of Tripoli (N. África). ‖ adj. Tripolitan: of or belonging to Tripoli.

tripsina s. f. (biochem.) trypsin: a ferment contained in the pancreatic juice.

tríptico s. m. triptych: 1. picture on three panels. 2. a writing tablet with three leaves.

triptona s. f. (med.) tryptone: peptone formed during digestion.

tripudiante s. m. + f. rejoicer; person who leaps for joy. ‖ adj. tripudiant: dancing or leaping for joy.

tripudiar v. 1. to tripudiate, dance for joy, rejoice, exult. 2. to live in debauchery or wantonness. 3. ~**-se** to mire, bog down.

tripúdio s. m. 1. tripudiation, dancing for joy, great rejoycing. 2. libertism, debauchery.

tripulação s. f. (pl. **-ões**) crew; the crew of a ship; personnel.

~ **do avião** flight crew. **com** ~ **reduzida** undermanned. **toda** ~ (naut.) all hands.

tripulante s. m. + f. member of the crew, seaman, sailor. ‖ adj. pertaining to the crew.

tripular v. to man [a ship, airplane], furnish with men.

~ **insuficientemente** to underman.

triquestroques s. m. pl. (pop.) pun, play on words; inversion of the order of words.

triquete s. m. used only in the expression: **a cada** ~ everywhere; at every step, ever and ever.

triquetraque (I) s. m. a sort of firework.

triquetraque (II) s. m. tric-trac, tricktrack, backgammon.

triquetraz s. m. (also **traquinas**) mischievous or naughty child; meddler.

tríquetro s. m. triskelion. ‖ adj. triquetrous, triangular.

triquíase s. f. (med.) trichiasis: affection of the eyelashes.

triquina s. f. trichina: a parasitic nematode worm which infects the intestine or muscles of pigs.

triquinado, triquinoso adj. trichinous.

triquinose s. f. (med.) trichinosis: disease caused by trichinae.

triquismo s. m. (surg.) filiform fracture.

trirradiado adj. triradiate: having three rays.

trirramoso adj. having three branches.

trirregno s. m. 1. triarchy. 2. the Pope's tiara.

trirreme s. f. trireme: a galley with three banks of oars.

trirretângulo adj. trirectangular, having three rectangles.

tris interj. imitative sound of cracking glass.

triságio s. m. (eccl.) Trisagion: a hymn wherein the word "Sanctus" is repeated three times.

trisanual adj. m. + f. (pl. **-ais**) triennal: 1. lasting three years. 2. once in three years. 3. every third year, from three to three years.

trisarquia s. f. triarchy: government of three rulers.

trisavó s. f. great-great-grandmother.

trisavô s. m. great-great-grandfather.

trisca s. f. ill will, rancour.

triscado adj. (Braz., pop.) drunk.

triscar v. 1. to quarrel, dispute, disagree, brawl. 2. (Braz.) to graze, touch slightly.

tríscele s. m. triskelion: an emblem composed of three branches radiating from a center.

trismegisto adj. trismegistic, three times great. (in mythology) said of Hermes and Tot.

trismo s. m. (med.) trismus, lockjaw: spasm of the muscles of mastication.

trispermo adj. (bot.) trispermous, three-seeded.

trisqueira s. f. (Braz., ichth.) name of a shark.

trissacramental adj. m. + f. (pl. -ais) trisacramental.

trissar s. m. chirp, twitter. ‖ v. to chirp, twitter.

trissecar v. (math.) to trisect, divide into three equal parts.

trissecção, trisseção s. f. (pl. -ões) trisection: division into three equal parts.

trissector, trissetor s. m. (math.) trisector: instrument for dividing angles into three equal parts. ‖ adj. trisecting: dividing into three equal parts.

trissépalo adj. (bot.) trisepalous: having three sepals.

trissilábico adj. trisyllabic(al): having three syllables. ‖ **trissilabicamente** adv. trisyllabically.

trisso s. m. chirp of the swallow.

trissulco adj. trisulcate, trifid, three-cleft.

tristaminífero adj. (bot.) tristaminate: having three stamens.

triste s. m. + f. 1. a sad or unhappy person. 2. m. poem of Argentine gaúchos. ‖ adj. 1. sad, dreary, sorrowful, mournful. 2. unhappy, wretched, joyless. 3. melancholic, sullen, dejected, elegiac, depressed, miserable, heavy, cloudy, lugubrious, sombre, dark. 4. lamentable, bad, pitiful. ‖ ~mente adv. sadly. estar ~ to feel sad. fazer um papel ~ to cut a sorry figure.

triste-pia s. m., sg. + pl. (Braz., ornith.) bobolink, reedbird.

triste-vida s. f. (pl. **tristes-vidas**) (Braz., ornith.) tyrant flycatcher.

tristeza s. f. (also, less used **tristura**) 1. sorrow, sadness, grief, affliction, unhappiness, wretchedness. 2. melancholy, joylessness, dejection, dolour, cheerlessness, depression. 3. mournfulness, murkiness, dumps, moodiness. ~s não pagam dívidas no use crying over spilt milk; care killed the cat. entregar-se à ~ to give o. s. up to sorrow. seria uma grande ~ it would be a great distress.

trístico adj. (biol.) tristichous: arranged in three vertical rows.

tristimania s. f. chronic melancholy.

tristonho adj. 1. unhappy, depressed, dejected, wretched. 2. frightful, terrible. ‖ -amente unhappily.

tritão s. m. (pl. -ões) 1. (myth.) Triton: semigod of the sea. 2. (zool.) triton: a) eft, newt of the genus Triturus. b) large shell of the genus Triton.

triteísmo s. m. tritheism: doctrine that Father, Son and Holy Spirit are three distinct Gods.

triteísta s. m. + f. tritheist: adherent or follower of the tritheistic doctrine. ‖ adj. tritheistic(al), relating to tritheism.

triternado adj. (bot.) triternate: thrice ternate, three times subdivided into three leaflets.

tritíceo adj. 1. relating to wheat. 2. like wheat.

triticultor s. m. wheatgrower.

triticultura s. f. wheat growing.

tritongo s. m. (gram.) triphthong: combination of three vowels forming one sound.

tritoniano adj. (geol.) fossiliferous (formation).

trítono s. m. (mus.) tritone: a dissonant interval of three tones.

tritopina s. f. (chem.) tritopine.

trituberculado adj. (biol.) tritubercular, having three tubercles.

tritura, trituração s. f. (pl. -ões), **trituramento** m. trituration: 1. triturating, crunching, champ. 2. grinding.

triturar v. 1. to triturate, pulverize, powder, mill, grind, thrash. 2. to bruise, afflict, hurt, offend; torment; grieve.

triturável adj. m. + f. (pl. -áveis) triturable.

triunfador s. m. triumpher, vanquisher, conqueror. ‖ adj. triumphant: 1. successful, victorious. 2. exulting, rejoicing.

triunfal adj. m. + f. (pl. -ais) triumphal.

triunfante adj. m. + f. triumphant, victorious, exultant, successful, glorious.

triunfar v. 1. to triumph: a) win, conquer, be successful, prevail over, gain a victory. b) celebrate victory. c) exult. 2. ~-se to glory in, pride o. s. on, boast. nós triunfamos we won the day, the field.

triunfo s. m. 1. triumph: a) victory, conquest, success. b) jubilation, ovation. 2. a sort of card game. 3. central adornment of a table at a banquet.

triunvirado s. m. (also **triunvirato**) 1. triumvirate. 2. (by extension) government by a group of three.

triunviral adj. m. + f. (pl. -ais) triumviral.

triúnviro s. m. (Roman hist.) triumvir: 1. magistrate executing public administration together with two others. 2. member of a triumvirate.

trivalência s. f. (chem.) trivalence: a valence of three.

trivalente adj. m. + f. (chem.) trivalent: having a valence of three.

trivial s. m. (pl. -ais) (Braz.) everyday dishes, plain cooking, bread-and-butter. ‖ adj. m. + f. trivial: 1. common, commonplace, trite, hackneyed, stale, prosaic, inexceptional. 2. trifling, petty, banal, small, futile, unimportant, flat, flimsy. ‖ ~mente adv. trivially.

trivialidade s. f. 1. trivialism, triviality, trivialness, triteness, commonplaceness, unimportance. 2. flimsiness, platitude, pettiness, banality.

trívio s. m. 1. trivium: (Middle Ages) the three subjects of liberal arts: grammar, logic and rhetoric. 2. crossroads.

trivoli s. m. (N. Braz.) merry-go-round.

triz (I) s. m. 1. trice, toucher. 2. instant, moment. por um ~ within an ace of, as near as a toucher, on the point of. por um ~ ele teria sido atropelado he was within an ace of being run over. escapar por um ~ to escape by the skin of one's teeth, escape by a hair's breadth.

triz (II) s. f. (med., pop., also **icterícia**) jaundice, yellows.

troada s. f. loud noise, roar, rumbling; thunder.

troante adj. m. + f. roaring, rumbling, thundering.

troar s. m. thunder. ‖ v. to thunder: rumble, roar, boom, peal; bark (gun).

troca s. f. 1. change, mutation, permutation, conversion. 2. exchange, interchange, barter, truck, commerce; trade, swap. ~ de cartas exchange of letters. ~ de idéias exchange of views, consultation, conversation, counsel. em ~ in return, in exchange. ~ por ~ measure for measure.

troça (I) s. f. 1. spree, revelry, joke, jest. 2. banter, mockery, derision, persiflage. expor à ~ to hold a person up to ridicule. fazer ~ de to make fun of, poke fun at; hoot, tout.

troça (II) s. f. (naut.) parrel, truss, hawser. tralha da ~ (naut.) parrel tackle.

trocadilhar v. 1. to make puns; 2. to quibble. 3. to tell anecdotes.

trocadilhista s. m. + f. 1. punster. 2. quibbler.

trocadilho s. m. 1. pun. 2. quibble, play on words. 3. equivoke. 4. ambiguity. 5. anecdote.

trocado s. m. 1. ancient popular dance. 2. change (money). 3. ~s pl.: a) puns; quibbles; anecdotes. b) embroidering.

trocador s. m. + f. exchanger. ‖ adj. exchanging.

trocaico s. m. (pros.) trochaic: measure of verse consisting of a trochee (foot of two syllables). ‖ adj. trochaic.

trocal s. f. (pl. -ais) (ornith.) a species of pigeon.

trocano s. m. (Braz., also **torocana**) Indian drum made out of a log.

trocanter s. m. (anat.) trochanter: bony process on the upper part of the femur.

troca-pernas s. m., sg. + pl. (Braz., pop.) vagabond, vagrant, loafer, tramp.

trocar v. 1. to change, turn, alter, replace, commute, permute, substitute. 2. to change by mistake, confound, confuse. 3. to exchange, interchange, convert, bank. 4. to barter, trade, truck. 5. ~-se to exchange, alter.
~ **cartas** to correspond, communicate by letters. ~ **dinheiro** to change money (into smaller units). ~ **dinheiro brasileiro por dinheiro inglês** to exchange Brazilian money for English money. ~ **idéias** to exchange views, confer, counsel. ~ **a lâmpada** to replace the (old) lamp (for a new one). ~ **lugares** to change places. ~ **nomes** to confuse names. ~ **palavras** to chop, equivocate. ~ **pernas** (pop.) to walk, tramp. ~ **prisioneiros de guerra** to exchange prisoners of war. ~ **de roupa** to change clothes, re-dress. ~ **a vontade** to change one's mind. **vou me** ~ I am going to change (clothes).

troçar v. to scoff, jeer, mock, guy, joke, ridicule, laugh at, jest.
troçamos dele we made game of him, (coll.) had him on.

trocarte s. m. (surg.) trocar, trochar: a stylet for draining an internal part of fluid.

troca-tintas s. m., sg. + pl. 1. dauber, bad painter. 2. (by extension) botcher, bungler.

trocável adj. m. + f. (pl. -áveis) exchangeable, replaceable, commutative, convertible.

trocaz adj. m. + f. = **torcaz.**

trochada s. f. 1. blow with a cudgel; stroke, knock. 2. (Port. prov.) slap in the face.

trochado s. m. fancy needlework in silk or tissue.

trochar v. to rifle, groove the barrel of a gun.

trocho s. m. cudgel, rough stick.

trociscação s. f. (pl. -ões) (pharm.) 1. fragmentation, pulverization. 2. preparation of troches.

trociscar v. 1. (pharm.) to fragmentate, pulverize. 2. to make troches.

trocisco (I) s. m. (pharm.) troche: pastil, a medicine tablet.

trocisco (II) s. m. 1. any little thing (mostly old and useless). 2. fragment, broken piece.

trocista s. m. + f. mocker, scoffer, derider, joker, wag. ‖ adj. joking, scoffing, mocking.

tróclea s. f. (anat.) trochlea: a pulley-like part of the humerus articulating with the ulna.

troclear adj. m. + f. (anat.) trochlear, trochleate.

troco (ô) s. m. 1. small change, small coin. 2. change (money). 3. (fig.) pert answer, quick repartee.
a ~ **de** at the price of, in exchange for. **dar o** ~ (sl.) to pay back in the same coin, give tit for tat. **não tenho** ~ **para lhe dar** I cannot give you change.

troço s. m. (Braz.) 1. thing, object. 2. lumber, old household utensils; rubbish. 3. (sl.) influential person, big shot.

troço (ô) s. m. 1. cudgel, rough stick. 2. trunk, stump of a tree. 3. fragment, broken piece. 4. body of soldiers; lot of people. 5. (naut.) junks.

trococéfalo adj. (zool.) roundheaded.

trocóideo adj. (anat.) trochoid, pivotal, rotating on a longitudinal axis.

troféu s. m. 1. trophy. 2. emblem, ensign. 3. (fig.) victory, triumph. 4. booty. 5. (Braz., sl.) thingumbob, thingumabob.

trófico adj. (phys.) trophic; pertaining to nutrition.

trófide s. f. (bot.) the genus Artecarpus (breadfruit family).

trofoneurose s. f. (med.) trophesy: nervous disturbance in nutrition.

trofosperma s. m. (bot.) trophosperm, ovules.

trofotropismo s. f. (bot.) trophotropism.

trogalho s. m. small lace or ribbon.

troglodita s. m. + f. troglodyte: cave-man, cave-dweller. ‖ adj. troglodytic(al), dwelling in caves, living in caves.

tróia (I) s. f. ancient game: a simulated combat on horseback.

tróia (II) s. f. (Braz.) large fishing-net.

troiar v. (Braz.) to fish with a large net.

tróica s. f. troika: large Russian sled drawn by three horses.

trolado adj. (Braz.) drunk.

trole s. m. (Braz.) 1. railroad handcar; small four-wheeled car on a railroad. 2. cart used on farms and in small towns. 3. trolley, trolly.

trolha s. f. (Port. prov.) a funnel-shaped tube used for sausage making.

trolha (ô) s. f. 1. trowel, brick trowel, laying trowel (plates A 7, T 5). 2. (Braz.) plastering trowel, panel, mortarboard (plate A 7). 3. unskilled mason, bricklayer. 4. ragamuffin, tatterdemalion, ragged fellow.
~ **de rejuntamento** jointer (plate A 7). ~ **de retoque** pointing trowel (plate A 7).

trolha (ô) (II) s. f. (pop.) blow, slap.

trolho (I) s. m. an ancient measure of capacity.

trolho (II) s. m. (pop.) a squat person.

trolista s. m. (Braz.) individual who moves a railroad handcar.

trololó s. m. (Braz.) light music.

trom s. m. sound of a gun; sound of the thunder.

tromba s. f. 1. trunk (of an elephant or tapir), snout of a pig. 2. proboscis. 3. (sl.) mug, face. 4. waterspout. 5. (Braz.) isolated hill.
~ **de água** waterspout. ~ **da chaminé** the shaft of a chimney. **fazer** ~s to look sullen, to pout.

trombada s. f. impact, clashing, collision.

trombadinha s. m. (Braz., pop., sl.) a violent pickpocket, mostly a youngster, sometimes acting in groups.

tromba-de-elefante s. f. (pl. **trombas-de-elefante**) (bot.) a species of agave.

trombar v. (Braz.) 1. to collide, crash. 2. to pull an ugly face, look sullen.

trombeta (I) s. f. 1. (mus.) trumpet, tuba, horn, clarion, bugle. 2. (fig.) talebearer, newsmonger. 3. a poisonous weed of the nightshade family. 4. m. trumpeter, one who sounds a trumpet.
~ **bastarda** (mus.) coaching horn. ~ **da fama** fame, reputation. ~ **falante**, ~ **marinha** megaphone.

trombeta (II) s. f. 1. (ichth.) flutemouth. 2. (Braz.) muzzle for a horse.

trombeta-azul s. f. (pl. **trombetas-azuis**) (bot.) common morning-glory.

trombeta-do-juízo-final s. f. (pl. **trombetas-do-juízo-final**) (bot.) pompous datura.

trombeta-grande s. f. (pl. **trombetas-grandes**) (bot.) angel's trumpet.

trombetear v. 1. to trumpet: a) sound a trumpet, puff. b) emit a trumpetlike (shrill) tone. 2. to proclaim, announce, ballyhoo.

trombeteiro s. m. 1. trumpeter: a) a person who trumpets, a trumpet player. b) a genus of long--necked and long-tailed S. American birds. 2. (ent.) a species of mosquito.

trombetinha s. f. a small trumpet; ear-trumpet.

trombo s. m. (med.) thrombus: a coagulum of blood.

trombombó s. m. (Braz.) method of fishing mullets (by fastening straw mats to the boat sides).

trombone s. m. trombone: 1. the instrument. 2. the trombonist.

trombone-de-pistões s. m. (pl. **trombones-de-pistões**) (mus.) trumpet with pistons; French horn.

trombose s. f. (med.) thrombosis: formation of a thrombus.

trombudo adj. 1. having a trunk or snout. 2. (fig.) frowning, sullen, rude, crabbed, grouchy.

trompa s. f. 1. trumpet, horn, trump, bugle. 2. (S. Braz.) muzzle for a horse.

~ **de caça** hunting horn (plate C 17). ~ **de Eustáquio** (anat.) syrinx, Eustachian tube (connecting the middle ear with the nasopharynx). ~ **de Falópio** (anat.) Fallopian tube: oviduct. ~ **do juízo final** last trump, last trumpet. ~ **de pistões** French horn.

trompaço s. m., **trompada** f., **trompázio** m. (Braz.) blow, bump (especially as with the trunk or snout).

trompar, trompear v. (Braz.) to bump, collide, clash.

trompeta s. m. (S. Braz.) 1. good-for-nothing. 2. kill--joy, wet blanket, spoilsport.

trompetada s. f. disheartenment.

trompista s. m. + f. trumpet maker.

trom-trom s. m. (pl. **trom-trons**) (Braz., ornith.) ant king.

trona s. f. (min.) trona: a combination of normal and acid sodium carbonate.

tronante adj. m. + f. thundering, rumbling, roaring.

tronar (I) v. to thunder, rumble, roar, boom.

tronar (II) v. 1. to throne, occupy a throne. 2. to domineer, rule, command.

tronchar v. 1. to cut short, curtail, chop off. 2. to mutilate.

troncho s. m. 1. stump. 2. stalk of a cabbage; part of a fallen tree; stub. ‖ adj. 1. curtailed, cut short, chopped off. 2. mutilated. 3. (Braz.) crooked, bent, twisted.

tronchuda s. f. a variety of cabbage.

tronchudo adj. 1. thick-stalked. 2. (fig.) stout, stocky.

tronco (I) s. m. 1. trunk: a) stem of a tree (plate A 14). b) body, torso (plate C 18). c) barrel (trunk of an animal) (plate C 12). d) main body. 2. (hist.) stock, stake (for punishment). 3. trave, frame (for cattle or horses). 4. mast (of a ship). 5. stem, pedigree, lineage, race. 6. (geom.) frustum. 7. (N. Braz.) a drunken spree.

~ **de amarrar onça** (N. Braz., pop.) squat person. ~ **de pirâmide** (geom.) frustum of a pyramid. **de** ~ **alto** long-stemmed. **o barco bateu contra um** ~ the boat struck a tree trunk.

tronco (II) adj. truncated, cut off, mutilated.

troncudo adj. (Braz.) sturdy, strong, muscular, vigorous (plate Q).

tronear, tronejar = tronar (II).

troneira s. f. embrasure in a wall to fire through; parapet for a gun.

troneto s. m. a small throne (esp. for the Eucharist).

trono (I) s. m. throne: 1. a royal seat, dais. 2. royal power, dignity, sovereignty. 3. ~**s** pl. (theol.) the third rank of angels.

elevar ao ~ to raise to the throne. **herdeira do** ~ **crown princess. sem** ~ throneless. **subir ao** ~ to ascend the throne, become king.

trono (II) s. m. roaring, rumbling, thundering; thunder.

tronqueira, tronqueirada s. f. (Braz.) 1. gatepost. 2. (S.) bank of a river with fallen trees covered with parasites and lianas. 3. (N.) trunks in a river-bed difficulting navigation.

tronqueiro s. m. (obs.) jailor, jailer, gaoler.

troostita s. f. (min.) troostite.

tropa s. f. 1. troop, band, host; number of people. 2. ~**s** pl. troops, army, soldiers, soldiery, garrison, effectives, array, military forces. 3. (Braz.) caravan of pack animals. 4. (S. Braz.) a herd of cattle on their way to the slaughterhouse.

~**s aéreas** flying corps. ~**s de barro**, ~**s de cachimbo** (N. Braz., pop.) civil troops. ~**s de guarda** lifeguards. ~**s de linha** regular army. ~**s de pára-quedistas** parachute troops. ~**s de reserva** reserve troops, reserves, subsidiaries. **em** ~**s** by troops. **estar com a** ~ to be on commando. **levantar** ~ to recruit, levy. **revista de** ~**s** parade.

tropacocaína s. f. (pharm.) tropacocaine.

tropa-fandanga s. f. (pl. **tropas-fandangas**) mob, rabble, crowd.

tropeada s. f. trampling, stamping with the feet.

tropear (I) v. 1. to trample, clatter. 2. to make a tumult, a confusion.

tropear (II) v. to work as muleteer.

tropeão (I) s. m. (pl. -**ões**) (also **tropeçamento**) stumbling, stumble, slip, trip, false step.

aos -ões by fits and starts.

tropeão (II) adj. (pl. -**ões**) floundering (habitually, esp. a horse).

tropeçar v. 1. to stumble, tumble over, slip, flounder, struggle, trip, reel. 2. to hesitate, falter, be perplexed. 3. to blunder, err, commit a fault.

~ **com dificuldades** to meet with difficulties.

tropeço (ê) (I) s. m. (pl. **tropeços**) 1. stumble, trip; false step. 2. stumbling block, obstacle, impediment, hitch, balk, baulk, rub.

andar aos tropeços to jounce along.

tropeço (ê) (II) s. m. (pl. **tropeços**) (Port., prov.) blunder, mistake, oversight, error.

tropeçudo adj. that stumbles frequently.

trôpego adj. 1. moving with difficulty; torpid, hobbling. 2. shaky, unsteady, tottery.

tropeirada s. f. drivers of pack animals, muleteers.

tropeiro s. m. (Braz.) 1. driver of pack animals, muleteer. 2. (S.) cattle dealer. 3. (zool.) gray screaming pika.

tropel s. m. (pl. -**éis**) 1. uproar, tumult, confusion. 2. trampling, stamping of feet, shuffle, trotting. 3. throng, crowd, mob, rabble; flock, multitude. 4. clatter or tramping of hoofs.

de ~ confusedly, tumultuously. **em** ~ pell-mell, in a huddle. **entrar de** ~ to enter helter-skelter. **um** ~ **de perguntas** a rush of questions.

tropelia s. f. 1. disorder, tumult, uproar, confusion. 2. prank, mischief, trouble, stir. 3. vexation. 4. oppression, ill-treatment. 5. (fig.) misfortune, prejudice, damage.

~**s da fortuna** the vicissitudes of fortune. **causar** ~**s** to cause a tumult, raise a storm.

tropeolácea s. f. (bot.) the genus Tropaeolaceae.

tropeoláceo adj. (bot.) tropaeolaceous: relating to the nasturtium family.

tropicada s. f. (S. Braz.) stumble, trip, flounder, slip.

tropical adj. m. + f. (pl. -**ais**) tropical: 1. pertaining to the tropics. 2. (fig.) very hot, burning hot, sultry. ‖ ~**mente** adv. tropically.

calor ~ tropical heat. **doença** ~ disease of the tropics. **frenesim** ~ tropical frenzy. **fruta** ~ tropical fruit. **planta** ~ tropical plant.

tropicalismo s. m. tropicalism.

tropicalista s. m. + f. specialist in tropical subjects, especially an expert in tropical diseases.

tropicão s. m. (pl. **-ões**) stumbling, stumble, slip, false step; floundering, struggling.

tropicar v. to stumble continuously.

trópico s. m. 1. tropic: a circle of the celestic sphere parallel to the equator. 2. (geogr.) tropics: the tropical regions. 3. a tropic bird. ‖ adj. tropic: relating to the tropics, tropical.
~ **do Câncer** tropic of Cancer. ~ **do Capricórnio** tropic of Capricorn.

tropilha s. f. (Braz.) 1. (S.) a drove of horses that follows a leading mare. 2. (N.) a band of roisterers or vagabonds.

tropismo s. m. (biol.) tropism: direction of growth due to an external stimulus (light, etc.).

tropo s. m. (gram.) trope: use of a word in a figurative sense; figure of speech.

tropologia s. f. tropology: 1. method of using figuratives in writing and speech. 2. treatise on tropes.

tropológico adj. tropological. ‖ **tropologicamente** adv. tropologically.

troponômico adj. relating to the change which an object suffers due to time and place.

tropopausa s. f. (meteor.) tropopause, boundary between the troposphere and the stratosphere.

troposfera s. f. (meteor.) troposphere, the atmosphere surrounding the earth.

troquel s. m. (pl. **-éis**) a die for coining or striking medals.

troqueu s. m. (pros.) troches: a foot of a long and a short syllable.

troquilídio s. m. (ornith.) trochilus, hummingbird.

tróquilo s. m. (archit.) trochilus, scotia, an annular molding.

trotador s. m. trotter, trotting horse. ‖ adj. trotting.

trotão s. m. (pl. **-ões**) (f. **trotona**) trotter, trotting horse.

trotar v. (also **trotear**) 1. to trot, lope. 2. to ride a horse at trot, make a horse trot. 3. (Braz.) to haze; jeer, deride, mock.

trote s. m. 1. trot (plate C 12). 2. lope, jog. 3. (Braz.) hazing, banter, derision, mockery. 4. (by extension) banter by telephone disguising one's voice.
~ **brando** dog-trot. ~ **escolar** hazing (school). ~ **largo** canter. ~ **lerdo, meio** ~ jog-trot. ~ **travado** jerky pace. **a** ~ trotting, in a trot, in haste, hastily. **andar sempre a** ~ to be kept on the trot. **dar** ~ to haze. **em** ~ at full trot. **exibir um cavalo em** ~ to trot out. **sair em** ~ to trot away. **viver num** ~ **de peludo** to be on the trot all day.

troteada s. f. (S. Braz.) 1. trotting, trot. 2. walk at a trot.

troteador s. m. (Braz.) hazer, hooter, person who banters another one.

troteiro s. m. 1. trotter, trotting horse. 2. (obs.) curier, postil(l)ion.

trottoir s. m. (Fr.) 1. sidewalk, footpath. 2. sidewalk prostitution.
fazer ~ to play the hooker on sidewalks.

trouxa s. f. (also **troixa**) 1. bundle of clothes, truss, pack(age), fardel. 2. m. + f. sucker, booby, fool, cully, dupe, gull, gudgeon. ‖ adj. foolish, fatuous, simple, stupid.
arrumar a sua ~ to pack one's traps, get going. **bancar o** ~ to play the giddy goat. **sempre com a** ~ **nas costas** always on the move.

trouxe-mouxe s. m. used in the expressions: **a** ~ at random, in disorder, higgledy-piggledy. **fazer as coisas a** ~ to do things anyhow, without care.

trouxinha s. f. (Braz., sl.) a small pack(age) of pot.

trova s. f. ballad; popular song or tune.

trovador s. m. (also **troveiro**) 1. troubadour; bard; minstrel. 2. (by extension) poet, rhymer.

trovadoresco adj. like a troubadour; of or pertaining to a troubadour.

trovão (I) s. m. (pl. **-ões**) thunder, roaring, grumble, rumble.
detonação de ~ thunderclap, peal of thunder. **muito** ~ **é sinal de pouca chuva** a barking dog seldom bites. **o ribombar do** ~ the roaring of the thunder. **voz de** ~ thundering voice.

trovão (II) s. m. (obs.) trovador.

trovar v. to compose or sing ballads, make rhymes; versify.

trovejante adj. m. + f. thundering, thunderous, roaring, rumbling.

trovejar s. m. thunder, rumble. ‖ v. (also **trovoar**) 1. to thunder, roar, grumble; lighten, flash, fulminate; storm. 2. to cry, shout, clamour; raise a storm, make a hell of a noise.

trovejo s. m. (Braz.) dispute, quarrel, squabble.

troviscada s. f. amount of spurge flax thrown into a river to stun and catch fish.

troviscado adj. (S. Braz., pop.) intoxicated, a little drunk, tipsy.

troviscal s. m. (pl. **-ais**) (bot.) a growth of spurge flax or spurge-laurels.

troviscar v. 1. (pop.) to thunder slightly. 2. (S. Braz.) to get half-drunk. 3. to beat with a stick.

trovisco (I) s. m. (bot.) spurge flax, spurge-laurel.

trovisco (II) s. m. (S. Braz.) blow with a stick.

trovisco-macho s. m. (pl. **troviscos-machos**) (bot.) a species of spurge.

trovisqueira s. f. (bot.) spurge flax.

trovista s. m. troubadour, minstrel, bard.

trovoada s. f. 1. thunderstorm. 2. (fig.) hubbub, tumult; quarrel, squabble. 3. (ornith.) an ant catcher.

trovoso adj. roaring, rumbling, thundering, thunderous.

troz-troz s. m., sg. + pl. (N. Braz.) rainstorm, downpour, shower.

truaca s. f. (N. Braz., pop., also **bebedeira**) binge, drollery, spree.

truanaz s. m. (also **truão**) buffoon, jester, clown.

truanear v. to play the clown, jest, act as a buffoon.

truanesco adj. funny, droll, clownish.

truania, truanice s. f. drollery, buffoonery, clownishness.

trubufu adj. (Braz., pop.) ragged, shaggy, tattered and torn.

trucada s. f. 1. bluff, act or fact of bluffing. 2. misstatement.

trucar v. to stake, wager at a game of cards.
~ **de falso** 1. to bluff, vie (at cards). 2. to boast, brag.

trucidação s. f. (pl. **-ões**) murder, decapitation, a cutting of the throat.

trucidar v. 1. to murder, kill. 2. to savage, slaughter. 3. to decapitate.

trucilar s. m. the song of a throstle or thrush.

truco s. m. (S. Braz.; also **truque**) a certain game of cards.

truculência s. f. truculence, truculentness, truculency, harshness, fierceness, savageness; cruelty, ferocity.

truculento adj. truculent, cruel, savage, ferocious, fierce, harsh. ‖ **-amente** adv. truculently.

trufa s. f. (bot., also **túbera**) truffle: a subterranian fungus.

trufar v. (cul.) 1. to stuff with truffles. 2. (obs.) to jeer, deride, scoff, mock.

trufeira s. f. place where truffles grow.

trufeiro s. m. truffler, person who sells or grows truffles. ‖ adj. relating to truffles.

trugimão, turgimão s. m. (pl. **-ões**) dragoman: an interpreter (Near East and Iran).

truirapeva s. m. one of the Brazilian lizards.

truísmo s. m. truism: self-evident truth.

trumbuca s. f. a certain wild bee.

truncado adj. fragmented, incomplete; mutilated; truncate(d).

palavras -as garbled words.

truncar v. 1. to truncate, cut off, lop. 2. shorten, lessen, curtail, mutilate (as a text).

truncária s. f. (bot.) the genus Melastoma.

truncha s. f. (Braz., sl.) 1. crowbar. 2. Old Nick, the devil.

trunfa s. f. 1. a sort of turban. 2. (obs.) headdress used by women. 3. unkempt hair, mop of hair; disorderly mane.

trunfada (I) s. f. ruff (at cards); a lot of trumps.

trunfada (II) s. f. (N. Braz.) oar rest of a raft.

trunfar v. 1. to trump, ruff. 2. (S. Braz.) to strike at or beat, to cudgel. 3. to be important, influential, have a say.

trunfo s. m. 1. a certain game of cards. 2. prevailing suit of cards. 3. trump card (joker). 4. (fig.) important person, big shot, bigwig.

cortar com o ~ to take with a trump. **jogar ~** to lead off a trump. **manter um ~ na reserva** to have an ace in the hole. **pedir ~** to call for trump. **ter todos os ~s na mão** to hold all the trump cards.

truque s. m. 1. a long billiard table; one of the various manners to play billiards. 2. a certain game at cards. 3. (pop.) trick, artifice, wile, dodge; deceit, fake, shift. 4. truck of a railroad car; bogie.

~ de mágico sleight-of-hand trick. **conhecer todos os ~s** to know all the tricks.

truqueiro s. m. (S. Braz.) billiard player.

truste s. m. trust: a combination of firms holding a monopoly.

truta s. f. 1. trout, a fresh-water fish similar to the salmon. 2. (Braz., sl.) shady business, an underhanded deal.

~ pequena troutlet, troutling. **não se pescam ~s a bragas enxutas** no gains without pains.

truta-arco-íris s. f. (pl. **trutas-arco-íris**) (ichth.) rainbow trout.

truta-comum s. f. (pl. **trutas-comuns**) (ichth.) brown trout, river, trout.

truta-salmoneja s. f. (pl. **trutas-salmonejas**) (ichth.) kelt, sea trout.

trutífero adj. trouty.

truz s. m. blow, slap, knock, rap. ‖ interj. crash!

de ~ excellent, first-rate, astonishing, superb, capital, topping, splendid.

tsé-tsé s. f. (pl. **tsé-tsés**) tsetse fly (that causes the sleeping-sickness).

tu s. m. the addressing as thee. ‖ pers. pron. you, thou, thee.

~ és you are, thou art. **~ mesmo** you yourself, thyself. **e ~?** and you? and what about you? **tratar por ~** to thou, thee.

tua (f. of **teu**) poss. pron. your, thy; thine, yours.

~ casa your house. **a casa é ~ ?** is the house yours?

tuaiá s. m. (N. Braz.) 1. faraway forest of rubber trees. 2. (by extension) any remote region.

tuaiuçu s. m. (Braz., bot., also **utuapoca** f.) a muskwood.

tuba (I) s. f. 1. tuba, bass horn. 2. (fig.) poetical style. 3. m. person who plays a tuba.

tuba (II) s. f. (Braz., also **tibá**) place where many persons or things are aggregated.

tubáceo adj. tubular.

tubagem s. f. (pl. **-ens**) 1. set of tubes or pipes. 2. laying of tubes or pipes.

tubaiaia s. f. (Braz., ornith.) a species of heron.

tubarão s. m. (pl. **-ões**) 1. (ichth.) shark, thresher, dogfish. 2. (fig.) big-time-operator, profiteer. 3. (N. Braz.) extremely high mountain range.

tubário adj. (anat.) relating to the Eustachian or Fallopian tube.

tubeira s. f. nozzle, spout of a tube.

túbera s. f. (bot., also **trufa**) truffle; swine bread.

tuberáceo adj. relating or similar to a truffle.

tuberculado adj. m., **tubercular** m. + f. tuberculate, tuberculated, tubercular: having tubercles.

tuberculífero adj. tuberculated: having or producing tubercles.

tuberculiforme adj. m. + f. like a tubercle.

tuberculina s. f. tuberculin(e): a sterile liquid used in the diagnosis and treatment of tuberculosis.

teste de ~ tuberculine test.

tuberculinizar v. to inject tuberculine, make the tuberculine test.

tuberculização s. f. (pl. **-ões**) tuberculization.

tuberculizar v. 1. to tuberculize: infect with tubercles or tuberculosis, become tuberculous. 2. to cause tuberculosis.

tubérculo s. m. tubercle: 1. (bot.) a nodule on the root of a plant, small tuber. 2. (anat.) small granular nodule formed in an organ. 3. (path.) small granular nodule caused by the bacillus of Koch.

tuberculose s. f. (med.) tuberculosis: infectious disease caused by the tubercle bacillus.

~ intestinal intestinal tuberculosis. **~ óssea** tuberculosis of bones. **~ pulmonar** pulmonary tuberculosis, phthisis; consumption, white plague.

tuberculoso s. m. person suffering from tuberculosis. ‖ adj. tuberculous: 1. (med.) affected by tuberculosis, tabetic, consumptive. 2. (bot.) tubercular.

tuberiforme, tuberóide adj. m. + f. tuberiform, having the form of a tube.

tuberosa s. f. (bot., also **angélica**) tuberose.

tuberosidade s. f. (anat., biol.) tuberosity, tuberousness.

tuberoso adj. tuberous, tuberose.

tubi s. m. (Braz., also **toba, tubim**) a wild bee.

tubiba s. f. (Braz.) a small stingless bee.

tubífero adj. tubiferous.

tubifloro adj. (bot.) having a tubular corolla.

tubiforme adj. m. + f. tubiform, tubulose, tubulous, tubulate, having the form of a tube.

tubixaba s. m. (Braz., also **morubixaba**) tribal chief.

tubo s. m. tube: 1. pipe, channel; chute (plates A 6, B 4, E 3, 10). 2. (anat.) duct, aqueduct. 3. cylindrical metal container for tooth-paste, etc. (plate P 12).

~ acotovelado (tech.) swan-neck. **~ de admissão** intake tube, inlet manifold. **~ de água** water conduit, water pipe, water main. **~ de ajustamento** pipe fitting. **~ de alimentação** feed pipe. **~ de ar** air pipe (plate V 1). **~ de borracha** hose, rubber tube, rubber pipe (plate A 6). **~ de cachimbo** pipe-stem (plate F 7). **~ de caldeira** boiler flue. **~ capilar** capillary. **~ de chaminé** chimney pot. **~ curvo** bent tube, bent pipe. **~ de descida** down pipe. **~ de descarga** waste pipe, outlet pipe, drain tube, discharger, flushing pipe, exhaust (plates B 3, D 1, E 10). **~ de distribuição** distributing pipe. **~ de ensaio** proof tube, test tube. **~ de escape** exhaust tube, exhaust manifold. **~ de esgoto** waste drainage pipe. **~ fluorescente** fluorescent tube. **~ de gás** gas pipe (plate F 3). **~ inconsútil** seamless tube. **~ de injeção** injection pipe. **~ lança-torpedo** torpedo tube. **~ de lubrificação** oil pipe. **~ mestre, ~ principal** main tube, main pipe (plate M 9). **~ mestre de gás** gas main (plate E 3). **~ de nível** level gauge, water gauge. ~ **de órgão** organ pipe. ~ **pequeno** tubule. ~ **porta-vento** blast pipe (plate C 16). ~ **de redução** reducer, reducing pipe (plate C 1). ~ **de saída** jet. ~ **soldador** blow pipe. ~ **de subida** stand pipe (plate A 6). ~ **em T** tee (tube). ~ **telescópio variável** draw tube. ~ **de vácuo** vacuum tube. ~ **de vapor** steam pipe (plate V 1). ~ **de ventilação** ventilation pipe (plate P 19). ~ **de vidro** glass tube. **braçadeira para** ~s pipe clip. **chave de** ~s pipe wrench. **junção de** ~s pipe coupling. **rosca para** ~s pipe thread.

tubulação s. f. (pl. **-ões**) tubulation, piping, tubing. **ruptura de** ~ pipe burst.

tubulado adj. (also **tubiforme** m. + f.) tubulate, tubulated.

tubuladura s. f. tubulure, piping, tubing.

tubular adj. m. + f. tubular.

tubulária s. f. (zool.) a genus of anthozoan polyps.

tubulífero adj. tubuliferous.

tubulifloro adj. (bot.) tubuliflorous: having all the flowers with tubular corollas.

tubuliforme adj. m. + f. tubuliform: having the form of a small tube.

túbulo s. m. tubule, a small tube.

tubuloso adj. tubulous, tubiform.

tubulura s. f. (chem.) tubulure: a short tubular opening.

tubuna s. f. (Braz., vet.) saddle gall.

tucanaçu s. m. (Braz., ornith.) toco toucan.

tucaninho s. m. (Braz., ornith., also **araçari-banana**) the yellow aracari.

tucano (I) s. m. 1. toucan: bird of the genus Ramphastidae. 2. (astr.) Toucan: austral constellation.

tucano (II) s. m. (Braz.) Indian of the Tucano tribe. ‖ adj. of or pertaining to this tribe.

tucano-de-bico-preto s. f. (pl. **tucanos-de-bico-preto**) (Braz., ornith.) ariel toucan.

tucano-de-peito-branco s. m. (pl. **tucanos-de-peito-branco**) (Braz., ornith.) white-breasted toucan.

tucano-grande s. m. (pl. **tucanos-grandes**) (Braz., ornith., also **tucanaçu**) toco toucan.

tucho s. m. (mach.) tappet.

tuco s. m. (S. Braz.) section man, worker in charge of the maintenance of a railroad (section).

tuco-tuco s. m. (pl. **tuco-tucos**) (S. Braz., zool.) a small burrowing rodent.

tucujá s. m. (Braz.) a plant of the dogbane family.

tucum s. m. (pl. **-uns**) (Braz., also **ticum, tucunzeiro**) a certain palm tree.

tucumã s. f. (Braz.) 1. tucuma, a palm tree. 2. (zool.) a semiaquatic fresh-water turtle. ‖ adj. f. said of the red-stalked manioc.

tucunaré s. m. (Braz.) 1. fresh-water fish of the genus Cichlydae. 2. (bot.) climber of the genus Leguminosae.

tucupi s. m. a seasoning prepared of pepper and manioc juice.

tucura s. f. (Braz.) 1. (ent.) a species of grasshopper. 2. (N.) repeated kisses, endearment. **fazer** ~s to kiss repeatedly, over and again.

tucuri s. m. (S. Braz., ent., also **tacuru**) chigoe.

tucuruva s. f. abandoned termitary.

tucuxi s. m. (Braz., zool.) a species of porpoise.

tudel s. m. (pl. **-éis**) (mus.) a metal tube in certain instruments.

tudesco s. m. German, Teuton. ‖ adj. German, Teutonic.

tudo s. m. everything, stock and block, all, the whole. ‖ pron. everything, all, anything.
~ **asneira** all nonsense. ~ **bem considerado** all in all. ~ **compreendido** in full. ~ **foi feito** all has been done. ~ **incluído** all-in. ~ **isto está muito bem, mas...** that is all very well, but... ~ **isso não**

me importa it's all the same to me. ~ **junto** all together. ~ **menos** anything but, all but. ~ **a mesma coisa** one and the same. ~ **ou nada** I'll win the horse or lose the saddle; neck or nothing. ~ **quanto, o que** whatever. ~ **que há de bom** everything good there is. ~ **de uma vez** holus-bolus. **além de** ~ over all. **antes de** ~ first of all; before all else. **com** ~ **isso** however; in spite of. **ele tem** ~ **na mão** he holds all the things. **e** ~ **mais** and all the rest of it. **eu fiz** ~ I left no stone unturned. **faça** ~ **o que quiser** do whatever you like. **isso diz** ~ that speaks volumes. **isto é** ~! **basta!** that's all! **jogar** ~ to play for the tout, or for all. **nem por** ~ **deste mundo** not for ever so much. **nem** ~ **que reluz é ouro** all is not gold that glitters. **sobre** ~ above all.

tufa s. m. (Braz., pop.) ruffian, bully, braggart, rude fellow, boor.

tufão s. m. (pl. **-ões**) hurricane, typhoon, tornado, windstorm, storm, whirlwind; gale.

tufar v. 1. to form into tufts; to swell, be puffed up, flare out. 2. ~-**se** to become puffed up.

tufo (I) s. m. 1. tuft (of hairs, feathers, grass); bunch, cluster. 2. ruffle, flock, bush, aigrette, top. 3. (tech.) plug, pintle.

tufo (II) s. m. (geol.) tuff (calc-tuff); tufa.

tufoso adj. tufted, puffed out, puffy, swollen, flocculent.

tugir v. to mutter, whisper; stir, budge.
não ~ **nem mugir** not to say a word; hold one's tongue; shut up.

tugue s. m. 1. thug: member of an Indian sect, a former fraternity of assassins. 2. (pop.) bloodthirsty man.

tugúrio s. m. 1. hut, shack, howel, cottage, cabin. 2. (by extension) hideout, refuge.

tuí s. m. (Braz., ornith., also **tuim**) lovebird.

tuia s. f. (bot.) arborvitae.

tuição s. f. (jur.) defense.

tuidara s. f. (ornith., also **coruja**) owl.

tuijuva s. f. a fustic tree.

tuim s. m. (Braz., ornith.) lovebird (Forpus passerinus vividus).

tuíra (I) s. f. (Braz., bot.) an iridaceous plant used as a purging medicine.

tuíra (II) adj. m. + f. (N. Braz.) ashen; dirty, faded.

tuiroca s. f. (N. Braz.) catching of fish by poisoning (stunning) them when they take shelter under river banks.

tuíste s. m. twist (dance).

tuitivo adj. defensive, protective.

tuiuiú s. m. (Braz., ornith., also **cabeça-de-pedra**) the wood ibis.

tuiupara s. m. (Braz.) bird or the stork family.

tuiúva s. f. (Braz., also **tuiuba**) a stingless bee.

tujucada s. f. **tujucal, tujuco** m. = **tijucada, tijucal, tijuco**.

tule s. m. tulle, fine net of silk or cotton for veils and dresses.

tulha s. f. 1. receptacle for olives in oil mills. 2. granary, barn, cornfloor, pit. 3. (by extension) cornloft. 4. (Braz.) place, ground or floor for drying fruit.

túlio s. m. (chem.) thulium.

tulipa s. f. 1. (bot.) tulip. 2. name of certain shells.

tulipa-da-áfrica s. f. (pl. **tulipas-da-áfrica**) tulip tree, bell flambeau tree.

tumba (I) s. f. 1. tomb, grave, repository; bier. 2. tombstone. 3. a bookbinder's bolster for gilding book covers.
o que o berço dá a ~ **o leva** once a use and ever a custom, what is bred in the bone will come out in the flesh.

tumba (II) s. m. + f. unlucky person (especially at gambling); ill-starred fellow.

tumbal adj. m. + f. (pl. -ais) (also tumbeiro) relating to a tomb or grave.

tumbança s. f. (N. Braz.) dish made out of caju (nuts and juice) and sugar.

tumbeiro (I) s. m. coffin-bearer.

tumbeiro (II) s. m. (S. Braz.) loafer, sponger, parasite, vagabond, vagrant. || adj. funny, truant, vagrant.

tumbice s. f. bad luck (especially at gambling), unluckiness.

tumefação s. f. (pl. -ões) (med.) tumefaction: swelling, tumour.

tumefaciente adj. m. + f. tumefacient, swelling.

tumefacto, tumefato adj. tumefied, swollen.

tumefazer, tumeficar v. to tumefy: swell or become swelled.

tumeficante adj. m. + f. tumefying, tumefacient, swelling.

tumente adj. m. + f. swollen.

tumescência s. f. (also intumescência) tumescence: slight swelling.

tumescente adj. m. + f. (also intumescente) slightly tumid.

tumescer v. (also intumescer) to intumesce, swell up.

tumidez s. f. tumidity, tumidness.

túmido adj. 1. tumid, turgid, swollen, inflated, bloated. 2. (fig.) arrogant, haughty, uppish.

tumor s. m. (med.) tumour, tumor, tumidity, boil, wen. ~ benigno benign tumour. ~ branco tuberculosis. ~ encistado talpa. ~ maligno malignant tumour, cancerous tumour. ~ sebáceo steatoma, sebaceous cyst.

tumoroso adj. tumorous; tumid, swollen.

tumular (I) adj. m. + f. tumular(y). pedra ~ tombstone.

tumular (II) v. to bury, entomb.

tumulário adj. tumulary.

túmulo s. m. 1. tomb, grave, sepulcher, sepulchral monument, repository, vault, resting-place, tumulus; mound, barrow. 2. (fig.) death. fiel até ao ~ faithful till death. sem ~ tombless.

tumulto s. m. 1. tumult, uproar, turbulence, outburst, commotion, disturbance, clamour; ruckus, hubbub, riot, confusion, shindy, broil. 2. agitation of mind, disorder, distemper. provocar ~ to cause a tumult, (sl.) kick up a shindy.

tumultuar v. 1. to tumultuate, cause or stir up a tumult, to mob, excite, agitate. 2. to become tumultuous.

tumultuário, tumultuoso adj. tumultuary, tumultuous, turbulent, disorderly, uproarious, boisterous, mobbish, violent, confused, agitated. || tumultuariamente, tumultuosamente adv. tumultuously.

tuna (I) s. f. (bot.) a species of cactus.

tuna (II) s. f. 1. idle life, vagrancy, vagabondage. 2. troupe of musical students. andar à ~ to lead the life of a vagrant, idle about the town.

tunador s. m. vagrant, vagabond, loafer, tramp. || adj. vagrant, vagabond, nomadic, erratic.

tunal s. m. (pl. -ais) (bot.) nopal.

tunante s. m. 1. vagrant, vagabond, idler, drifter, a lazy fellow. 2. one of the musical students of a troupe. || adj. m. + f. idling, vagabond, vagrant, drifting, erratic, truant.

tunar v. to idle, drift, loaf, ramble, tramp.

tuncum s. m. (Braz., sl.) cash, money.

tunda s. f. 1. thrashing, drubbing, whopping, beating. 2. bitter criticism.

tundá s. m. (Braz.) 1. a wide dress with several underskirts. 2. (sl.) buttocks. 3. swelling on the back.

tundar v. to beat, thrash, cudgel soundly.

tundra s. f. tundra: level treeless plains in Russia and Canada.

túnel s. m. (pl. túneis) tunnel, underground passage. ~ de vento wind tunnel. atravessar um ~ to pass through a tunnel.

tunesino s. m. Tunesian: native or inhabitant of Tunis or Tunisia (N. Africa). || adj. Tunisian: of or pertaining to Tunis or Tunisia.

tunga s. f. (Braz., ent. also bicho-de-pé m.) chigoe, chigger.

tungada s. f. (Braz.) blow, stroke, knock; shock, collision, clash.

tungador s. m. (Braz.) stubborn fellow, obstinate person. || adj. insistent, obstinate, willful, stubborn, bullheaded.

tungar v. (Braz.) 1. to insist, persist, persevere, be obstinate or stubborn. 2. to beat, thrash, spank; hit, knock. 3. to trick, cheat, deceive, dupe. 4. (coll.) to dunk, dip (as bread into milk).

tungstato s. m. (chem.) tungstate, salt of tungstic acid.

tungstênio s. m. (chem.) tungsten; wolfram; metallic element of the chromium family.

túngstico adj. (chem.) tungstic.

tungue s. m. tung tree, tung oil tree.

tunguear v. (Braz.) to rest, repose; lie; sleep.

tunguete s. m. (Braz., sl.) any dishonest game.

tungurupará s. m. (Braz., ornith.) a nunbird.

túnica s. f. 1. tunic: loose garment worn by ancient Romans. 2. (eccl.) dalmatic, tunicle. 3. (anat.) mantle, tunica, enveloping membrane. 4. (bot.) integument, covering husk.

tunicado s. m. (zool.) tunicate: subphylum, marine chordate.

tunicela s. f., tuniquete m. 1. a small tunic. 2. (eccl.) dalmatic, tunicle (plate P 5).

tuno s. m., adj. = tunante.

tuntunqué s. m. (Braz., pop.) ruffian, bully, braggart.

tupá, tupã s. m. (Braz.) Tupian name for thunder.

tupé s. m. (N. Braz.) a sort of mat used either for drying (small) farm products on it or as an awning for boats.

tupi s. m. + f. (Braz.) 1. Indian of the Tupi tribe. 2. language spoken by the Tupis who live near the Amazon river (also called língua franca). 3. any of the various Tupian tribes. || adj. Tupian: of or relating to the Tupis.

tupia s. f. 1. profiling machine for wood; shaper. 2. jack; weight lifter, lifting tool.

tupiçaba s. f. (Braz., bot., also tupixaba) sweet broomwort.

túpico adj. (Braz.) Tupian.

tupina s. f. (Braz.) daredevil. || adj. decided, resolute, tenacious; fearless.

tupinambá s. m. (Braz.) 1. m. + f. Indian of the group of Tupinamba tribes. 2. (fig.) boss. || adj. of or pertaining to the Tupinambas.

tupinambo, tupinambor s. m. (Braz., bot.) artichoke, Jerusalem artichoke.

tupixá s. m., tupixaba f. (Braz., bot.) sweet broomwort.

tupurapo s. m. (Braz.) plant of the gentian family: tachia.

turaniano s. m. Turanian: 1. member of the Ural--Altaic stock. 2. the Ural-Altaic group of languages.

turba s. f. 1. crowd, rout, mob, rabble. 2. people, multitude. 3. chorus, group of singers.

turbação s. f. (pl. -ões) (also turbamento m.) disorder, disturbance, perturbation; confusion, trouble.

turbador s. m. disturber, perturbator, troublemaker. || adj. disturbing, perturbating, troublesome.

turbamulta s. f. turbulent people, mob, rout, rabble.

turbante s. m. turban: 1. a headdress worn by Moslems and men of the Levant. 2. a woman's headdress similar to a turban.

turbar v. 1. to darken, dim; become overcast. 2. to trouble, disturb, agitate, perturb, disorder, confuse, upset, roil, ruffle, vex. 3. to muddle. 4. ~-se to grow cloudy; get troubled.

turbativo adj. disturbing, troublesome, perturbative. ‖ -amente adv. disturbingly.

turbelário s. m. (zool.) 1. turbellarian, planarian, flatworm. 2. ~s pl. Turbellaria.

túrbido adj. 1. turbid, cloudy. 2. disturbed, confused. 3. muddy.

turbilhão s. m. (pl. -ões) 1. vortex, whirlpool; swirl, eddy, maelstrom, abyss. 2. tornado, whirlwind. 3. (fig.) tumult, uproar, confusion, agitation.
ter a cabeça num ~ to be giddy, have one's thoughts in a whirl.

turbilhonar v. to whirl, spin, eddy, swirl, twirl.

turbina s. f. (tech.) turbine.
~ **de água** water turbine. ~ **de ar comprimido** compressed air turbine. ~ **de gás** gas turbine. ~ **hidráulica** hydraulic turbine. ~ **de marcha a ré** (naut.) reversing turbine. ~ **a vapor** steam turbine (plate T 6). **conduto para** ~ **hidráulica** penstock.

turbinação s. f. (pl. -ões) (Braz., also **turbinagem**, pl. -ens) turbination, turbinage.

turbinado adj. turbinate: 1. (anat., zool.) turbinal. 2. (bot.) shaped like an inverted cone. 3. (zool.) rolled in a spiral as certain shells.

turbiniforme adj. m. + f. turbiniform, turbinoid.

turbinoso adj. turbinal, whirling, spinning.

turbito s. m. (bot.) turpeth, Indian jalap.

turbito-mineral s. m. (chem.) turpeth mineral.

turbo-acionado adj. (pl. **turbo-acionados**) turbo-driven.

turbo-alternador s. m. (pl. **turbo-alternadores**) turbo-alternator.

turbo-bomba s. f. (pl. **turbo-bombas**) turbopump.

turbo-compressor s. m. (pl. **turbo-compressores**) turbocompressor, turbosupercharger.

turbo-dínamo s. m. (pl. **turbo-dínamos**) turbodynamo.

turboélice s. m. (aeron.) turboprop (engine and plane).

turbo-gerador s. m. (pl. **turbo-geradores**) turbogenerator.

turbojacto s. m. (pl. **turbojactos**) (aeron.) turbojet.

turbopropulsor s. m. (pl. **turbopropulsores**) turbo-propeller engine, turboprop.

turborreator s. m. (pl. **turborreatores**) turbojet.

turbulência s. f. turbulence, agitation, bluster, rowdyism, boisterousness; uproar, tumult, disorder, disturbance.

turbulento s. m. a turbulent person. ‖ adj. turbulent, troublesome, inquiet, factious, agitated, boisterous; rowdy, riotous, mutinous, mobbish, wild. ‖ -amente adv. turbulently.

turcalhada s. f. (depr.) multitude of Turks.

túrcica s. f. (anat.) sella turcica.

turco s. m. 1. Turk, native or inhabitant of Turkey. 2. the Turkish language. 3. (naut.) davit, cathead. 4. (Braz.) name given to all the people of the Middle East (Syrians, Ottomans, etc.). ‖ adj. Turkish.
~ **da prestação** (Braz.) hawker (of small goods). **banho** ~ Turkish bath. **tapete** ~ Turkey carpet.

turcomano s. m. Turkoman: 1. one of the Turkish or Tartar nomads. 2. their language.

turdídeo adj. turdoid, similar to a thrush, thrushlike.

tureba s. m. (N. Braz., pop., also **valentão**) braggart, ruffian, rude fellow.

turfa s. f. turf, peat, semicarbonized plant residues used for fuel.

turfe s. m. the turf: 1. race-course. 2. horse racing.

turfeira s. f. turf, peatery, peat-bog, peat-moss.

turfista s. m. + f. (Braz.) turfite: person devoted to or living by horse racing.

turfoso adj. turfy, peaty.

turgência s. f. turgidity.

turgescência s. f. turgescence, turgidity, swelling, puffiness.

turgescente adj. m. + f. turgescent, turgid, swelling, inflated, tumefacient.

turgescer(-se) v. to become turgid, swell, tumefy.

turgidez s. f. turgidity, turgescence, swelling.

túrgido adj. m. (also **turgente** m. + f.) 1. turgid, swollen, inflated. 2. vainly pompous, plethoric. ‖ **turgidamente** adv. turgidly.

turgimão s. m. (pl. -ões) (also **trugimão**) dragoman (interpreter in the Near East and Iran).

turião s. m. (pl. -ões) (bot.) turion, shoot (as asparagus); sucker, runner.

turibular v. 1. to incense, cense, thurify, burn. 2. (fig.) to flatter, blandish, wheedle, cajole, beguile, charm.

turibulário s. m. 1. censer, thurifer, acolyte. 2. (fig.) cajoler, blandisher, flatterer.

turíbulo s. m. turible, censer.

turícremo adj. (poet.) used for burning incense.

turiferar v. to incense, cense, thurify.

turiferário s. m. thurifer: person who carries the censer in religious solemnities.

turífero adj. thuriferous.

turificação s. f. (pl. -ões) thurification, burning of incense.

turificador s. m. person who burns incense, perfumes. ‖ adj. (also **turificante** m. + f.) incensing, perfuming, producing frankincense.

turificar v. to incense, burn incense, perfume with incense.

turíngia s. f. (bot.) a variety of oranges.

turíngio adj. from Thuringia (Germ.).

turino (I) adj. relating to incense.

turino (II) adj. Frisian, of Friesland.

turiri s. f. (Braz., ornith., also **sururina**) pileated tinamon.

turismo s. m. touring, tourism, travelling for pleasure or recreation.

turista s. m. + f. tourist, excursionist, tripper.

turístico adj. tourist, sightseeing.

turma (I) s. f. 1. (Ancient Rome) a troop of cavalry. 2. squadron. 3. group, division (school or class). 4. gang, squad, shift, crew, team. 5. batch, lot; band. 6. (Braz.) people, folks.
~ **de dia** day shift. ~ **de trabalho** outfit. ~ **de revezamento** relay team.

turma (II) s. f. ancient Siamese coin.

turmalina s. f. tourmaline: mineral of various colours.
~ **comum** schorl, common black tourmaline. ~ **de magnésio** brown tourmaline.

turmeiro s. m. (Braz.) one of a road shift.

túrnepo s. m. (bot.) a variety of turnip.

túrnepo-amarelo s. m. (pl. **túrnepos-amarelos**) (bot.) bird rape.

túrnepo-branco s. m. (pl. **túrnepos-brancos**) (bot.) common white turnip.

turno s. m. 1. turn. 2. shift, spell. 3. team. 4. division, group. 5. (Braz.) bout, round, a period of play, inning. 6. period at school, hour.
fazer alguma coisa por ~ to take turns about. **por** ~s by rotation, by turns, by spells, one after another. **ele, por seu** ~ he for his part or turn.

turpilóquio s. m. 1. dirty expression, indecent talk. 2. an obscene discourse.

turquesa s. f. (min.) turquoise: a semiprecious stone.

turquesado adj. turquoise-coloured.

turqui adj. m. + f. deep-blue.
azul ~ sky-coloured.

turra s. f. 1. butt, push or knock with the head. 2. stubborn dispute; bickering, altercation. 3. (Braz.) obstinate person, stubborn fellow.

andar às ~s com alguém to be on bad terms with someone, be at sixes and sevens with.

turrão s. m. (pl. **-ões**) (pop.) 1. blockhead, stubborn person. 2. clod, hard lump of soil.

turrar v. 1. to strike, knock or butt with the head. 2. to be obstinate, persist, bicker, wrangle.

turriculado adj. (zool.) turreted (shells).

turriforme adj. m. + f. tower-shaped.

turrífrago adj. (poet.) that destroys and overturns towers.

turrígero adj. (poet.) castled.

turrista s. m. + f. stubborn or headstrong person.

turturinar v. (poet.) 1. to coo. 2. to groan.

turturino adj. relating to a turtledove.

turucué s. m. (Braz., ornith., also **curutié**) a tree creeper.

turumbamba s. m. (sl.) brawl, dispute, riot, quarrel.

turuna s. m. (Braz., pop.) daredevil, rowdy. ‖ adj. strong, powerful, important.

turundundum s. m. (pl. **-uns**) (Braz., pop.) riot, row, fracas, brawl.

tururi s. m. (bot.) Brazil nut.

tururié s. m. (Braz., ornith., also **curutié**) a tree creeper.

tururim s. m. (pl. **-ins**) (Braz., ornith.) a small tinamon.

turvação s. f. (pl. **-ões**), **turvamento** m. 1. perturbation, disturbance, anxiety, uneasiness. 2. overcasting (weather). 3. clouding (wine).

turvar v. 1. to darken, dim, dazzle, obscure, cloud. 2. to muddy. 3. to trouble, disturb, confuse, upset. 4. **~-se:** a) to become turbid. b) to grow cloudy. c) to grow sullen.

turvejar v. to become turbid.

turvo s. m. disturbance, disorder. ‖ adj. 1. muddy, dreggish, feculent. 2. cloudy, overcast. 3. darkish, dim. 4. troublesome. 5. confused, agitated, disturbed.

de olhos ~s blear-eyed. **água -a** muddy water.

pescar em águas -as to fish in troubled waters.

tussilagem s. f. (pl. **-ens**) (bot.) coltsfoot, foalfoot.

tussol s. m. medication used against whooping cough.

tussor s. m. tussah silk.

tuta-e-meia s. f. (pop.) a bit, trifle, almost nothing.

comprar por ~ to buy for a song.

tutano s. m. 1. (anat.) marrow, medulla. 2. (fig.) essence, substance.

tutear v. to thou, thee.

tutela s. f. tutelage; chaperonage, guardianship, tutorship, tutorage; protection; ward, custody.

sob a ~ de in ward to, under the custody of.

tutelado s. m. tutored person. ‖ adj. protected, tutored, subject to a guardian.

tutelar (I) adj. tutelar(y), protective, defensive.

tutelar (II) v. to tutor, protect, defend, patronize.

tutia s. f. (chem.) tutty: crude zinc oxide.

tutor s. m. 1. tutor, curator, preceptor, guardian, protector. 2. stake or support for a plant or young tree.

~ de menores guardian.

tutorar v. = **tutelar** (II).

tutoria s. f. tutorship, guardianship, tutelage.

tutriz s. f. tutrix.

tutu (I) s. m. (Braz.) bugbear, bogey, ogre; big shot.

tutu (II) s. m. a dish prepared of beans, bacon and manioc meal.

tutumumbuca s. m. (Braz., pop., also **manda-chuva**) big shot, important person.

tuvira s. f. (Braz., ichth.) fresh-water eel.

tuxaua s. m. (Braz.) 1. chief of a tribe. 2. (by extension) political leader.

tuzina s. f. (S. Braz.) beating, cudgelling.

tweed s. m. (Engl.) tweed.

tzar, tzaréviche, s. m., **tzarevna, tzarina** f., **tzarismo** m. = **czar, czaréviche, czarevna, czarina, czarismo.**

tzigano s. m. gypsy. ‖ adj. gypsy.

U

U, u s. m. 1. the twentieth letter of the Portuguese alphabet. 2. the twentieth of an order or class.
U (chem.) symbol for uranium.
uacá s. m. (Braz., also guapebeira f.) plant of the family Quiinaceae (Quiina decastyla).
uaçacu s. m. (Braz.) Attalea palm tree.
uacanga s. f. plant of the family Palmaceae.
uacapu s. m. (Braz., also acapu) tree of the family Papilionaceae, furnishing partridgewood.
uacarau s. m. (Braz., ornith., also bacurau) common name of several birds of the family Caprimulgideae.
uacari s. m. (Braz., zool.) ouakari: any of several South American monkeys of the genus Cacajao.
uai interj. (Braz.) oh!, exclamation of surprise.
uaicima s. f. (Braz., bot., also guaxima) Caesar weed.
uaiúa s. f. (Braz., Amazon) stagnancy of (river) waters.
uamiri(m) s. m. (Braz.) small arrow for a blow-pipe.
uapé, uapê s. m. (Braz., bot.) = vitória-régia.
uapuçá s. m. (zool.) orabassu.
uariquina s. f. (Braz., bot.) variety of red pepper.
uarirama s. f. (Braz.) bird of the family Alcedinidae.
uaru s. m. (Braz.) fresh-water fish of the family Cichlidae.
uatapu s. m. (Braz.) horn which is supposed to attract fish (Indians of the Pará region).
uauá s. m. (Braz., also pirilampo) glow-worm.
uauaçu s. m. (bot.) babassu.
ubá s. f. (Braz.) 1. Indian dugout, pirogue. 2. (also candiubá, canabrava) herbaceous plant of the family Annonaceae.
ubaia s. f. (Braz., bot.) = uvaia.
ubarana, uborana s. f. (Braz., ichth.) 1. ladyfish. 2. ten-pounder.
ubatã s. m. (Braz., bot., also aderno) zorro.
ubeba s. f. (Braz., ichth.) cabezon.
uberdade s. f. 1. abundance, opulence, copiousness, plenty. 2. fertility, fruitfulness, rich growth.
úbere s. m. (also ubre) udder, dug. ‖ adj. m. + f. (also ubertoso) abundant, fruitful, fertile, uberous.
ubérrimo obs. sup. of úbere: most fertile or abundant.
ubi s. m. (Braz., also ubim) name of several palm trees.
ubicação s. f. (pl. -ões) ubiety.
ubijara s. f. (Braz., zool.) slow-worm or blind-worm.
ubiqüidade s. f. (also ubiquação) ubiquity, omnipresence.
ubiqüitário s. m. (eccl.) ubiquitarian. ‖ adj. omnipresent.
ubíquo adj. ubiquitous, ubiquitary, omnipresent.
ubuçu s. m. (Braz., also buçu) a species of palm tree.
uca s. f. (Braz., sl., also cachaça) brandy.
ele está na ~ he is drunk.
uçá s. m. (Braz., zool.) a species of crab (Ucides cordatus).
ucasse s. m. (hist.) ukase: 1. an edict or decree of the Czar. 2. decree of any absolutistic government.
ucha s. f. 1. provision chest, provision chamber. 2. pantry, larder.
ficar à ~ to go out empty-handed.
uchão s. m. (pl. -ões) butler, steward.
ucharia s. f. 1. pantry, store-room, larder. 2. store--house. 3. granary. 4. (fig.) lucrative thing, job, etc.
ucraniano s. m. Ukrainian: native or inhabitant of the Ukraine. ‖ adj. Ukrainian.
udométrico adj. pluviometric, udometric.
udômetro s. m. udometer, pluviometer, rain-gauge.

udu s. m. (Braz., also juruva f.) motmot.
ué, uê interj. (Braz.) well! exclamation denoting surprise or fright.
ufa interj. expressing admiration, irony or fatigue, whew!
à ~ 1. abundantly, copiously. 2. at another's expense.
ufanar v. 1. to render proud. 2. to flatter. 3. ~-se: a) to boast, be proud of, extol(l). b) to be satisfied or pleased. c) to give o. s. airs.
isto me ufana I am happy about it.
ufania s. f. 1. boasting. 2. vainglory, conceit. 3. presumption, arrogance.
ufano adj. (also ufanoso) 1. vain, conceited. 2. vainglorious, boasting, proud, overweening. 3. pleased with o. s. 4. valiant. 5. gallant. 6. elegant, showy.
estar ufano de (com) alguma coisa to be proud of s. th., (coll.) to be puffed up with s. th.
ufanoso adj. conceited, arrogant.
ui interj. ugh! expression of disgust, surprise, or aversion.
uiai interj. (Braz., pop., also uai) exclamation of surprise.
uiara s. f. (Braz., also iara) = mãe-d'água.
uiofobia s. f. pathological aversion to one's own children.
uirapiana s. f. (Braz., ornith.) jacamar.
uirapuru s. m. (Braz.) songbird of the family Pipridae, supposed to bring good luck to its owner.
uísque s. m. whisk(e)y.
uisqueria s. f. (S. Braz.) a whisky bar.
uíste s. m. (cards) whist.
uivada s. f. (Braz.) acute and long howl.
uivador s. m. howler. ‖ adj. (also uivante m. + f.) howling.
uivar s. m. = uivo. ‖ v. 1. to howl, yowl. 2. to yell, yelp. 2. to rage. 4. to bawl, cry. 5. to cry in pain. 6. to roar.
o vento uiva através da porta the wind whistles and howls through the door.
uivo s. m. 1. howl. 2. (fig.) yell(ing), yelp, bawl(ing).
ulano s. m. (Germ., mil.) uhlan, lancer.
úlcera s. f. 1. (path.) ulceration, open sore. 2. disease destroying the woody tissue of trees.
~ gástrica gastric ulcer. ~ duodenal duodenal ulcer.
ulceração s. f. (pl. -ões) (path.) ulceration, fester.
ulcerado adj. ulcerous, ulcerated.
ulcerar(-se) v. 1. to ulcerate, suppurate, fester, rankle. 2. (fig.) to afflict. 3. to torture, torment. 4. to hurt. 5. to corrupt.
ulcerativo adj. ulcerative, ulcerous.
ulceroso adj. ulcerous.
ulemá s. m. ulema: doctor of sacred law and interpreter of the Koran.
uliginário adj. (bot.) uliginose: growing in muddy places.
uliginoso adj. 1. marshy, swampy, oozy. 2. muddy, miry. 3. = uliginário.
ulissiponense s. m. + f. native or inhabitant of Lisbon. ‖ adj. of or referring to a native or inhabitant of Lisbon.
ulite s. f. (med.) gingivitis.
ulmáceo adj. (bot.) 1. elmlike. 2. ulmaceous: pertaining to the family Ulmaceae. 3. similar to an elm.
ulmária s. f. (bot., also barba-de-bode) goat's-beard, meadowsweet (Filipendula ulmaria).
ulmeiro, ulmo s. m. (bot., also olmeiro, olmo) elm.

ulna s. f. (anat.) ulna: 1. the inner bone of the forearm. 2. a corresponding bone in the foreleg of an animal.

ulnal adj. m. + f. (pl. **-ais**) (also **ulnário**) ulnar.

ulo s. m. (Braz.) 1. groan, lament. 2. cry of agony.

ulótrico s. m. (anthr., also **ulótrique**) specimen of the Ulotrichi: in Huxley's classification, the races with woolly or crispy hair. ‖ adj. ulotrichous.

ulterior adj. m. + f. 1. ulterior, situated beyond, or on the farther side, posterior. 2. later. 3. further, remoter. 4. subsequent. ‖ ~**mente** adv. ulteriorly, afterward(s).

ulterioridade s. f. quality of **ulterior**, remoteness.

ultimação s. f. (pl. **-ões**) 1. termination, finishing. 2. perfection, completion, finishing touch. 3. (com.) closing, conclusion.

ultimado adj. 1. concluded, finished, complete(d), ended. 2. closed (business).

ultimar v. 1. to terminate, finish, end, come to an end. 2. to put an end to. 3. (com.) to close. 4. to conclude, complete, integrate.

últimas s. f. pl. 1. final throes, last moments. 2. decisive cast (of dice). 3. extreme poverty, utter misery. 4. rudest crossness. 5. highest degree. **ele está nas** ~ it is all up with him. **dizer as** ~ **a alguém** to throw s. o. the worst vulgarities in his face. ~ **condições** ultimatum.

ultimato s. m. 1. ultimatum: a final proposal or statement of conditions. 2. designation of the last molecules to which a body can be reduced. 3. the ultimate, final objective or end, also something fundamental.

último s. m. last: in rank, order or quality; farthest. ‖ adj. 1. last. 2. ultimate, latter, late(st), most recent, preceding. 3. lowest. 4. utmost, extreme. 5. decisive. 6. final, finishing. 7. hindmost, rearward. 8. downmost. ‖ **ultimamente** adv. lastly, lately, latterly, finally, recently, of late. **-a demão** finish. **-a esperança** forlorn hope. **-a formal** (mil.) as you were! a **-a vez** the last time. a **-a palavra** the last word. **até a -a gota** to the uttermost drop. a **-a vontade** the last will and testament, the dying wish. o ~ the last of all, aftermost, endmost. **lutaram até o** ~ **cartucho** they fought to the bitter end. o ~ **da fila** the last in the row. **no** ~ **momento** at the last moment, at the eleventh hour. o ~ **prazo final** respite. o **Último dos Moicanos** the Last of Mohicans. **nos** ~**s anos** of late years. ~ **suspiro** parting breath. **dar o** ~ **suspiro** to breathe one's last, gasp out one's life. **ele foi o** ~ **de todos** he was the very last.

ultra-humano adj. (pl. **ultra-humanos**) preterhuman.

ultrajador s. m. 1. reviler, slanderer. 2. insulter, affronter. 3. injurer. ‖ adj. (also **ultrajante, ultrajoso**) 1. reviling, slanderous. 2. insulting, injurious, offensive. 3. outrageous.

ultrajar v. 1. to revile, slander. 2. to insult, affront, offend. 3. to injure, outrage. 4. to violate.

ultraje s. m. 1. affront, offence, insult. 2. defamation. calumny. 3. revile(ment). 4. outrage.

ultramar s. m. 1. overseas territory, possession or colony. 2. ultramarine: blue pigment prepared by powdering lapis lazuli. **ir para** ~ to go overseas.

ultramarino adj. (also **transmarino, transoceânico**) 1. oversea(s). 2. foreign. 3. ultramarine, transmarine, transoceanic. **domínios** ~**s** oversea dominions.

ultramicroscópico adj. ultramicroscopic.

ultramicroscópio s. m. ultramicroscope.

ultramoderno adj. ultramodern.

ultramontanismo s. m. ultramontanism.

ultramontano (I) s. m. + adj. = **transmontano.**

ultramontano (II) s. m. (rel.) ultramontanist. ‖ adj. ultramontane.

ultrapassado adj. overshot.

ultrapassar v. 1. to surpass, exceed. 2. to pass over or beyond. 3. to exceed the limits. 4. to leave behind, fetch over, overtake. 5. to get ahead of. 6. to cap, trump, transcend. 7. to outreach, outstrip. 8. to transgress. **as suas idéias ultrapassam a nossa época** his ideas are ahead of our time. **isto ultrapassa os seus deveres** it is in excess of his duty. **isto está ultrapassando os limites** it knocks the bottom out of the cask, it beats all.

ultra-som s. m. (pl. **ultra-sons**) supersonic sound waves.

ultravermelho adj. ultrared.

ultravioleta adj. m. + f., sg. + pl. ultraviolet. **raios** ~ ultraviolet rays.

ultravírus s. m., sg. + pl. (bact.) ultravirus: ultramicroscopic or filtrable virus.

ultriz, ultrice s. f. (poet.) vindictive woman. ‖ adj. vindictive.

ululação s. f. (also **ululo**) 1. ululation, howling. 2. mournful bawling. 3. roaring, moaning (wind). 4. screaming, yelling, crying.

ululador s. m. howler, bawler, yeller, crier. ‖ adj. (also **ululante**) ululant, crying, howling, yelling. **o óbvio ululante** the highly obvious.

ulular s. m. = **ululação.** ‖ v. 1. to ululate, howl (dog). 2. to cry out, bawl. 3. to vociferate. 4. to shriek, scream, yell. 5. to roar, moan (wind).

ulva s. f. kind of seaweed.

um s. m. (pl. **uns**) (f. **uma**) one: 1. cardinal number. 2. single person or thing. ‖ adj. 1. one. 2. indivisible. 3. single. 4. certain. ‖ indefinite article a, an. ‖ indefinite pron. one: 1. some person or thing. 2. any person or thing. ~ **certo,** ~ **tal** one (a certain). ~ **dia sim,** ~ **dia não** (~ **sim,** ~ **não**) every other day. ~ **e outro** both, either. ~ **pelo outro** for each other. ~ **pouco** something. ~ **por** ~ one by one. **uns, umas** some. **ele não possui o gênio de** ~ **Napoleão** he has not at all the genius of a Napoleon. **nem** ~**, nem outro** neither of them. **ora** ~**, ora outro** by turns. **uns dizem que sim, outros que não** some say so, others say no. **vou falar com** ~ **de cada vez** I shall talk to one at a time. **de uma e outra parte** on both sides. **era uma vez** (fairy tales) once upon a time. **uma dos diabos** a damned mess. **é uma das suas** that is quite him (her). **à uma** simultaneously. **ele tomou umas e outras** (sl.) he had a couple of drinks. **ele deu uma de gostosão** (Braz., sl.) he acted the lady-killer.

umbanda s. m. = **quimbanda.**

umbaru s. m. (Braz., bot., also **cânhamo-brasileiro**) brown Indian hemp, ambary.

umbaúba s. f. (Braz.) trumpet tree, snakewood.

umbela s. f. 1. (also **guarda-chuva** m.) umbrella, sunshade. 2. small and round pallium. 3. canopy. 4. (bot.) umbrellalike inflorescence, umbel.

umbelado adj. umbellarꞧ umbellate(d).

umbelífera s. f. (bot.) specimen of the Umbelliferae.

umbelífero adj. (bot.) umbelliferous, umbellate(d).

umbeliforme adj. m. + f. (bot.) umbellar.

umbigada s. f. push with the navel or the belly. (esp. in an Indians' dance). 2. the umbilical region.

umbigo s. m. (anat.) navel, umbilicus (plate C 18).

umbigo-de-vênus s. m. (pl. **umbigos-de-vênus**) (bot.) navelwort, wall pennywort, wall penny grass.

umbigueira s. f. (Braz.) umbilical affection of calves.

umbilicado adj. umbilicate(d): like a navel.

umbilical adj. m. + f. (pl. **-ais**) umbilical: of or pertaining to the navel.
cordão ~ (anat.) navel-string, umbilical cord.
umbraculífero adj. (bot.) umbraculiferous, umbraculiform: umbrella-shaped.
umbráculo s. m. (bot.) umbraculum: umbrella-shaped appendage, as the capitulum of the sporophore in some liverworts.
umbral s. m. (pl. **-ais**) (also **ombreira de porta** f.) doorjamb, doorpost, threshold.
umbrático adj. 1. umbrageous. 2. obscure. 3. imaginary, phantastic.
umbrátil adj. m. + f. (pl. **-eis**) 1. umbrageous. 2. phantastic(al). 3. allegoric(al).
umbrela s. f. (also **umbela**) umbrella.
umbria s. f. 1. (poet.) umbrageous place. 2. the shadowy or northern part of a mountain.
úmbrico s. m. 1. the Umbrian dialect. ‖ adj. Umbrian.
umbrícola adj. m. + f. living in the shade.
umbrífero adj. (poet.) umbrageous, umbriferous.
umbrina s. f. (ichth.) omber, ombre, ombra.
úmbrio, umbro s. m. (also **úmbrico**) 1. native or inhabitant of Umbria. 2. the Umbrian dialect. ‖ adj. Umbrian.
umbro s. m. 1. deerhound, staghound. 2. = **úmbrico**.
umbroso adj. 1. umbrageous, shady. 2. obscure. 3. dark. 4. bushy, leafy, shadowy.
umburana s. f. (Braz., bot.) umburana.
umbuzeiro s. m. (Braz.) umbra tree.
ume s. m. (also **alume**) alum.
pedra-~ alum stone, alunite.
umectação s. f. (pl. **-ões**) humectation: wetting or moistening; moistness.
umectante adj. m. + f. (also **umectativo**) humectant, moist(ening).
umectar v. 1. (med.) to moisten. 2. to dilute, dissolve.
umedecer v. 1. to humidify, moisten, humefy, dampen, wet slightly. 2. ~-**se** to get slightly wet. 3. to dip. ~ **com orvalho** to dew.
umedecido adj. wettish.
umedecimento s. m. 1. moistening, wetting, wetness. 2. dampness, moistness, humectation.
umente adj. m. + f. (poet.) moist.
umeral, umerário adj. (anat., zool.) humeral: of or pertaining to the humerus.
úmero s. m. (anat.) humerus: the bone of the upper arm, from the shoulder to the elbow.
umidade s. f. humidity, moistness, damp(ness), slight wetness, dank(ness), wateriness.
umidificar v. to humidify, moisturize.
úmido adj. 1. moist, humid, dank, damp, slightly wet. 2. aqueous. 3. weeping, dewy. 4. watery. ‖ **umidamente** adv. dankly, wetly.
terreno ~ boggy ground, weeping. **tempo** ~ moist or rainy weather. **esta sala é -a** this room is damp (cold).
unanimar v. to agree, attain unanimity, make unanimous.
unânime adj. m. + f. 1. unanimous, agreed, of like mind. 2. consentient, proceeding from mutual accord. ‖ ~**mente** adv. unanimously.
votaram ~**mente contra a nova lei** they went solid against the new law.
unanimidade s. f. 1. unanimity, unanimousness, unity, harmony. 2. consensus.
por ~ without a dissentient vote, by general agreement.
unanimismo s. m. unanimism: philosophical doctrine of the French writer Jules Romains.
unanimista s. m. + f. (philos.) unanimist. ‖ adj. unanimistic.
unau s. m. (zool.) unau: an Amazon sloth.

unção s. f. (pl. **unções**) 1. unction, inunction. 2. anointment, anointing. 3. (fig.) piety, compassion. 4. appeasing or persuasive way of speaking.
úncia s. f. (also **polegada**) inch.
uncial adj. m. + f. (pl. **-ais**) uncial (said of a type of letters used before the 10th century).
unciforme s. m. (anat.) unciform (bone). ‖ adj. m. + f. uncinate, unciform, hook-shaped.
uncinado adj. 1. uncinate. 2. with claw(s); hooked.
uncirrostro s. m. one of the hook-billed wading birds. ‖ adj. hook-billed.
undação s. f. (pl. **-ões**) 1. river-course. 2. inundation, flood.
undante adj. m. + f. (also **ondulante**) 1. undulating, wavy. 2. conveying much water.
undécimo s. m. the eleventh part. ‖ adj. eleventh.
na -a hora at the eleventh hour, only just in time.
undécuplo s. m. quantity eleven times superior to another. ‖ adj. elevenfold.
undícola s. m. + f. water animal or plant. ‖ adj. living in the water.
undífero adj. 1. wavy, waved, undulant. 2. containing waters.
undiflavo adj. (poet.) having golden-coloured waves.
undifluo adj. fluctuating, moving in waves.
undíssono adj. roaring (like waves).
undívago adj. floating, drifting.
undoso adj. (also **ondeante** m. + f.) 1. wavy. 2. undulating, waving.
ungido s. m. anointed person. ‖ adj. 1. anointed (also with holy oils as the extreme unction). 2. consecrated (with holy oils).
ungir v. 1. to anoint, oil: a) besmear with oil or an unguent. b) consecrate with holy oils. 2. to administer the extreme unction. 3. to purify. 4. to invest. 5. ~-**se** to correct, improve oneself, get better.
úngüe, úngüis s. m. (anat.) the small and thin lachrymal bone.
ungueal adj. m. + f. (pl. **-ais**) (anat.) ungual: pertaining to, resembling or bearing a nail, claw or hoof.
ungüentáceo, ungüentário adj. (pharm.) unguentary.
ungüento s. m. unguent, balm, salve, ointment, unction, liniment.
ungüiculado adj. 1. unguiculate(d): (bot.) ending like a nail (petal). 2. (zool.) unguiculate: pertaining to the Unguiculata.
ungüífero adj. having nails or claws.
ungüiforme adj. m. + f. clawlike, nail-shaped.
ungüinoso adj. unguinous, unctuous, oily.
ungulado s. m. (zool.) ungulate: any hoofed quadruped; one of the Ungulata. ‖ adj. ungulate: of or pertaining to the Ungulata.
unha s. f. 1. nail (of fingers and toes). 2. claw, talon. 3. (zool.) operculum of various shells. 4. claw (of a crab). 5. toe (of a hoof) (plate C 9). 6. recurved or pointed part (tool). 7. callosity on the back of beasts. 8. (tech.) fang, claw (plate M 5).
~ **de âncora** fluke (of an anchor), bill(hook) (plate A 6). ~ **de pé** toenail. ~ **do dedo** fingernail. ~ **encravada** ingrowing nail. ~**s de fome** niggard, miser, close-fisted person. **à** ~ **with bare hands. defender-se com** ~**s e dentes** to fight tooth and nails. **enterrar a** ~ (pop.) to sell for a high price. **fazer as** ~**s** 1. to pare, clip or cut the nails. 2. to have one's nails cut. 3. to have one's nails manicured. **pegar o touro à** ~ to take the bull by the horns. **ser carne e** ~ **com alguém** to be like hand and glove.
unhaca s. m. + f. 1. (hum. also **avaro** m.) miser. 2. intimate or bosom friend.
unhada s. f. (also **unhaço** m.) 1. a nail scratch. 2. claw: wound caused by clawing.
unha-de-cavalo s. f. (pl. **unhas-de-cavalo**) (bot.) coltsfoot, foal-foot.

unha-de-fome s. m. + f., sg. + pl. (also **unhas-de-fome**) miser, niggard.

unha-de-gato s. f. (pl. **unhas-de-gato**) 1. (bot.) cat's-claw. 2. (Braz.) rake (tool).

unhamento s. m. 1. clawing, scratching. 2. layer (of vines).

unhão s. m. (pl. **-ões**) (naut.) splice.

unhar v. 1. to scratch, claw, tear (with the nails). 2. to cast anchor. 3. (hort.) to layer. 4. (Braz., sl.) to steal.

unheiro s. m. hangnail, agnail, whitlow, felon: inflammation or sore under or around the nail.

união s. f. (pl. **-ões**) 1. union: a) marriage, match. b) confederation, confederacy, league, alliance, pact, association. c) political party. d) **União** the Union. e) junction, juncture, adhesion. f) contact, connection. g) concord, combination, harmony. h) (mech. also **junção de** ~) union coupling (for pipes), joint. i) coalition, coalescence, fusion. j) unity, unification. 2. copulation of animals. 3. (mech.) screw cap, screw joint.
a ~ **faz a força** union is strength. ~ **de rosca** screw joint. **traço de** ~ (gram.) hyphen.

uniarticulado adj. (zool.) uniarticulate.

uniaxial adj. m. + f. (pl. **-ais**) uniax(i)al: having only one axis.

unicapsular adj. m. + f. (bot.) unicapsular: having only one capsule.

unicelular adj. m. + f. (bot.) unicellular.

unicidade s. f. unicity, oneness, uniqueness.

único s. m. unique: a unique specimen, thing, circumstance or person. ‖ adj. 1. unique: a) single, alone, sole, only, one, one and only. b) unequal(l)ed. c) peculiar. 2. exclusive, singular. 3. exceptional, rare. 4. incomparable, unmatched, unparallel(l)ed. ‖ **unicamente** adv. only, solely, all, uniquely.
o ~ **caso desta natureza** the only such case. **caso** ~ solitary instance. **filho** ~ single child. **finalidade** -a single purpose. **preço** ~ single price. **você não é o** ~ **que o admira** you are not alone in your admiration of him. **a** -a **maneira** the only way. **o** ~ **no gênero** the only one of its kind. **a** -a **e verdadeira fé** the only true faith. **prato** ~ one dish meal. **rua de mão** -a oneway street.

unicolor adj. m. + f. unicolour(ed), concolorous; self-coloured, solid-coloured, or whole-coloured.

unicorne s. m. 1. unicorn. 2. (ornith.) screamer. ‖ adj. m. + f. unicornous, one-horned.

unicórnio s. m. 1. a kind of rhinoceros (Rhinoceros unicornis). 2. = **unicorne**. 3. the horn of a rhinoceros.

unicúspide adj. m. + f. unicuspid, single-pointed.

unidade s. f. unity: a) the number one. b) oneness, singleness. c) totality. d) uniformity, accord. e) harmony, concord. 2. union. 3. monad. 4. unit. 5. body of soldiers. 6. (naut., mil.) tactical unit.
~ **de medidas** unit of measure. **as três** ~s **que regem o drama** the dramatic unities. ~ **monetária** monetary unit. ~ **de posse** (jur.) unity of possession. ~ **militar** corps. **duas** ~s dyad. ~ **naval** (naut.) task force.

unido adj. 1. united: joined, joint, combined, allied, conjoint. 2. tied. 3. contacted. 4. connected. 5. (in)corporate. 6. wedded. ‖ **-amente** adv. unitedly.
Estados Unidos da América United States of America. **eles foram** ~s **pelos laços matrimoniais** they were joined in marriage. **estar** ~ to stand together.

unificação s. f. (pl. **-ões**) unification, unity.

unificador s. m. unifier. ‖ adj. unifying.

unificar v. 1. to unify: make or form into one. 2. to standardize. 3. to gather, adapt or subject to

one purpose only. 4. ~-**se**: a) to join, unite, incorporate. b) to concentrate.

unifoliado, unifólio adj. (bot.) unifoliate: having only one leaf.

uniforme s. m. uniform, regimentals. ‖ adj. m. + f. 1. uniform. 2. identic(al), same, equal. 3. regular. 4. constant, immutable, unchanging, equable, unvaried. 5. steady. 6. even. ‖ ~**mente** adv. uniformly.

uniformidade s. f. 1. uniformity, uniformness. 2. monotony. 3. constancy. 4. coherence. 5. (fig.) conformity. 6. evenness. 7. equality. 8. steadiness.

uniformização s. f. (pl. **-ões**) uniformization.

uniformizado adj. 1. made uniform. 2. uniformed.

uniformizador s. m. person who uniformizes. ‖ adj. that uniformizes.

uniformizar v. (also **uniformar**) to uniformize: 1. make uniform. 2. provide with a uniform. 3. unify.

unigênito s. m. only-begotten, single child. ‖ adj. only-begotten.
o **Unigênito Jesus Christ**.

unijugado adj. (bot.) unijugate: having only one pair.

unilabiado adj. (bot.) unilabiate: having only one lip or liplike part.

unilateral adj. m. + f. (pl. **-ais**) unilateral: 1. one-sided, pertaining to or occurring on one side only. 2. (jur.) affecting one side, party or person only. ‖ ~**mente** adv. unilaterally.

unilateralidade s. f. one-sidedness, unilateral nature or quality.

unilíngüe adj. m. + f. unilingual: composed in or using one language only.

unilobado, unilobulado adj. unilobed, unilobate: having one lobe only.

unímano adj. one-handed: having one hand.

uninervado adj. (bot.) having only one vein or nerve as a leaf of a pine tree.

uninominal adj. m. + f. (pl. **-ais**) uninominal: 1. consisting of, or pertaining to a single name or term. 2. containing but one name.

unionismo s. m. unionism.

unionista s. m. + f. unionist. ‖ adj. unionist(ic).

uniparidade s. f. act or fact of giving birth to only one young at a time.

uníparo adj. (zool.) uniparous: 1. said of a female that gives birth to only one young at a time. 2. (bot.) producing but one axis at each branching.

unipedal adj. m. + f. (pl. **-ais**) uniped: having only one foot or leg.

unipessoal adj. m. + f. (pl. **-ais**) unipersonal: 1. existing in one person. 2. (gram.) used only in one person.

unipétalo adj. (bot.) unipetalous.

unipolaridade s. f. unipolarity.

unir v. 1. to unite, join, connect, adjoin. 2. to unify. 3. to fasten, attach. 4. to combine, consolidate. 5. to link. 6. to bind, tie. 7. to associate, incorporate, affiliate. 8. to conciliate, reconcile. 9. to gather, bring together. 10. to reunite. 11. to join in marriage. 12. ~-**se**: a) to adhere. b) to join, consociate, ally, colligate, unite, associate oneself with. c) (mil.) to effect a junction. d) to confederate. 13. to fuse.
~-**se para** to unite to. ~-**se num assunto** to unite in s. th. **eles** ~**am-se em casamento** they were joined in marriage. ~-**se a um partido** to join a party. **o canal une os dois mares** the channel joins the two seas. ~-**se** (rivers) to meet. ~-**se para o mesmo fim** to combine for one purpose. ~ **duas famílias pelo casamento** to unite two families by marriage. **as linhas parecem** ~-**se** the lines seem to converge.

unirrefringente adj. m. + f. (phys.) unrefracting.

unissex adj. m. + f. unisex.

unissexuado adj. unissexual m. + f. (pl. -ais) unisexual: 1. (bot.) diclinous. 2. (zool.) not hermaphrodite.

unissonância s. f. 1. unisonance. 2. concordance. 3. (mus.) harmony, melody. 4. monotony.

uníssono s. m. (mus.) unison. ‖ adj. (also unissonante m. + f.) unisonant, unisonous.
em ~ in unison.

unitário s. m. 1. (rel.) Unitarian: person who maintains that God exists as only one being. 2. unitarist. ‖ adj. unitarian, unitary.

unitarismo s. m. Unitarianism: a unitary theory or system.

unitivo adj. unitive: characterized by, or tending to produce union.

univalência s. f. univalence.

univalente adj. m. + f. univalent, monovalent.

univalve adj. m. + f. (bot., zool.) univalve(d).

univalvular adj. m. + f. univalvular.

universal s. m. (pl. -ais) universal: 1. one who or that which is universal. 2. (philos.) universal proposition. 3. (philos.) universal concept. ‖ adj. m. + f. universal: 1. of or pertaining to the universe. 2. unlimited. 3. all-embracing. 4. general, ecumenic(al), common, public. ‖ ~mente adv. universally, ecumenically.

universalidade s. f. universality, totality.

universalismo s. m. universalism.

universalização s. f. (pl. -ões) universalization.

universalizar v. 1. to universalize, make universal. 2. to generalize.

universidade s. f. university: 1. institution of learning. 2. the members of a university collectively. 3. college, school. 4. academy.
ele abandonou a ~ he went down from the university. ele freqüenta a ~ he is at the university.

universitário s. m. professor or student of a university. ‖ adj. universitarian: of or pertaining to a university, academic(al).

universo s. m. 1. universe: a) this world, the world of human experience, mankind. b) (astr.) the entire celestial cosmos, space. c) nature. d) the whole creation. 2. the solar system. 3. the society. 4. (fig.) a whole. ‖ adj. universal.

univocidade s. f. univocity: univocal quality or character.

unívoco adj. univocal: 1. having one meaning only. 2. of the same nature. 3. unisonous, uniform, unanimous.

uno adj. one, sole, only one, single.

unóculo s. m. one-eyed person. ‖ adj. uniocular: having only one eye.

untadela s. f. slight anointment, greasing.

untador s. m. greaser, anointer, dauber (plate D 3). ‖ adj. greasing.

untar v. 1. to anoint, daub. 2. to grease. 3. to (be)smear. 4. to rub in. 5. to salve. 6. to oil.
~ as mãos a alguém (fig.) to grease (bribe) a person.

unto s. m. 1. (hog's-)lard. 2. animal fat. 3. oil. 4. greasing. 5. grease. 6. pomade, unguent.

untuosidade s. f. 1. unctuosity, unctuousness, greasiness. 2. slipperiness. 3. fatness.

untuoso adj. 1. unctuous, greasy. 2. lubricated. 3. slippery. 4. (fig.) amorous, loving, sweet, mellifluous, suave. 5. smooth, bland.

untura s. f. 1. (also untadura, unto m.) greasing, grease. 2. unguent, (an)ointment, salve. 3. pomade. 4. (fig.) superficiality.

upa s. f. 1. jerk, leap, skip, frisk. 2. capriole (horse). ‖ interj. 1. hop!, jump!, go!, quick! 2. interj. of surprise: oh!
~! levanta-te! up with you!

upanichade s. m. Upanishad (Vedic literature).

upar v. to capriole (horse).

uquirana s. f. (Braz.) Surinam cabbage tree.

ura s. f. (Braz., ent.) larva of a botfly.

úraco s. m. (anat.) urachus.

uracrasia s. f. incontinence of urine.

uraliano adj. Uralian.

uralita s. f. (min.) uralite.

uralitização s. f. uralitization.

uralo-altaico adj. (pl. uralo-altaicos) Ural-Altaic: 1. of or pertaining to the Urals and the Altai. 2. designating a great linguistic family, the Ural-Altaic languages.

urânico adj. uranic, containing uranium.

uraninita s. f. (min.) uraninite.

urânio s. m. (chem.) uranium.

uranismo s. m. uranism: homosexuality among males.

uranista s. m. + f. uranist.

uranita s. f. (min.) uranite.

Urano s. m. (astr.) Uranus.

uranografia s. f. uranography.

uranográfico adj. uranographic(al).

uranógrafo s. m. (also astrônomo) uranographer, astronomer, uranographist.

uranologia s. f. uranology.

uranometria s. f. uranometry.

uranômetro s. m. uranometer.

uranoscopia s. f. uranoscopy, astrology.

uranoscópico adj. uranoscopic, astrologic(al).

uranoso adj. uranous.

urapará s. m. (Braz.) Indians' bow.

urari s. m. (Braz., bot.) curare.

urato s. m. (chem.) urate: salt of uric acid.

uraúna s. f. (bot.) Brazilian rosewood, palisander.

urbanidade s. f. urbanity, urbaneness: 1. politeness, polishedness, suavity, elegance. 2. civility. 3. courtesy, courtliness.

urbanismo s. m. city or town planning.

urbanista s. m. + f. urbanist: specialist in city or town planning. ‖ adj. urbanistic.

urbanístico adj. urbanistic: referring to city or town planning.

urbanita s. m. + f. urbanite: city dweller, townsman. ‖ adj. urban.

urbanização s. f. (pl. -ões) urbanization.

urbanizar v. 1. to urbanize: a) render urban. b) polish. 2. to civilize, refine.

urbano adj. 1. urban: belonging to a city or town, civic, townish, civil. 2. urbane: a) refined, polished, polite. b) courteous. c) civilized.

urbe s. f. city.

urca s. f. (naut.) hooker: Dutch or Irish vessel with two masts. ‖ adj. m. + f. (N. Braz.) great.

urceolado adj. m., urceolar m. + f. urceolate, urceolar: urn-shaped.

urceolífero adj. (bot.) having urceolus.

urcéolo s. m. (bot.) urceolus: an urn-shaped organ or part.

urco s. m. Frisian horse; fire horse. ‖ adj. (Braz.) huge and beautiful (horse).

urdideira s. f. 1. weaver, woman warper. 2. warp (frame).

urdidor s. m. 1. warper, weaver. 2. warp (beam). 3. artificer. 4. (fig.) intriguer.

urdidura s. f., urdimento, urdume m. 1. warp(ing). 2. (fig.) intrigue, plot. 3. chain.

urdir v. 1. to warp, weave. 2. to (com)plot. 3. to form threads into a web. 4. (fig.) to intrigue. 5. to machinate, contrive.

uredíneo s. m. (bot.) specimen of the Uredinales, an order of parasitic fungi, known as rusts, or rust fungi, from the rustlike spots or pustules they produce on various leaves and stems. ‖ adj. (bot.)

uredineous: of the nature of a uredo, belonging to the order Uredinales.

uredo s. m. 1. (bot.) uredo. 2. itch(ing), nettle-rash.

uréia s. f. (chem.) urea.

uréico adj. ureal.

uremia s. f. (med.) ur(a)emia.

urêmico adj. (med.) ur(a)emic.

urência s. f. heat, glow, ardour, burning.

urente adj. m. + f. hot, glowing, ardent, burning.

ureômetro s. m. ureometer: instrument showing the amount of urea in the urine.

ureter s. m. (anat.) ureter: duct from the kidneys to the bladder.

uretérico adj. ureteral, ureteric.

ureterite s. f. (med.) ureteritis: inflammation of the ureter.

urético adj. urinary, diuretic.

uretra s. f. (anat.) urethra.

uretral adj. m. + f. (pl. **-ais**) urethral.

uretrite s. f. (med.) urethritis: inflammation of the urethra.

uretroscopia s. f. (med.) urethroscopy: examination of the urethra by means of an urethroscope.

uretroscópio s. m. urethroscope.

uretrotomia s. f. (surg.) urethrotomy.

urgebão, urgevão s. m. (bot.) vervain.

urgência s. f. 1. urgency: a) quality or state of being urgent. b) need, exigence, exigency. 2. press(ure), rapidity, speed, haste. 3. quickness. 4. expedition, instancy.

com extrema ~ with utmost expedition.

urgente adj. m. + f. 1. urgent: exigent, urging, pressing, in priority. 2. essential. 3. impending, imminent, immediate, instant. 4. imperative. ‖ **~mente** adv. urgently.

mensagem ~ priority message. **-íssimo** (abs. sup.) with dispatch.

urgir v. 1. to urge: a) be urgent, press. b) drive, impel, push forward (with effort), crowd. c) excite. d) intensify. e) instigate. 2. to claim. 3. to be necessary.

o tempo urge time presses.

uricemia s. f. (med.) uric(a)emia.

úrico adj. (chem.) uric.

ácido ~ uric acid.

urina s. f. urine.

urinação s. f. (pl. **-ões**) urination.

urinar v. to urinate: 1. make water, pass water. 2. piss. 3. (children) piddle.

urinário adj. urinary.

urinífero adj. uriniferous: having urine.

uriníparo adj. uriniparous: conducting urine.

urinol s. m. (pl. **-óis**) urinal, urinary: 1. vessel for holding urine. 2. building or enclosure for urinating purposes. 3. (sl.) jerry, chamber-pot.

urinoso adj. urinous.

urlunduba s. f. (Braz., bot.) urunday (Astronium urundeuva).

urna s. f. 1. urn: a) vessel used for holding liquids; for preservating the ashes of the dead; for holding lots to be drawn. b) (bot.) (in mosses) the theca or capsule. 2. ballot-box. 3. coffin.

pôr em ~ to inurn. **~ funerária** funerary urn, coffin, tomb.

urnário s. m. 1. table on which the Romans placed the urns (of water). 2. (bot.) urn, theca. ‖ adj. urnal, urn-shaped.

uro s. m. (zool.) urus, aurochs.

urobilina s. f. (biochem.) urobilin.

urobilinogênio s. m. (biochem.) urobilinogen: colourless chromogen found in urine.

urocele s. f. (med.) urocele: swelling of the scrotum due to extravasation of urine into it.

urocroma s. f. (biol.) urochrome.

urodelo s. m. (zool.) urodelan: specimen of the Urodela. ‖ adj. urodele, caudate.

urodiálise s. f. (med.) urodialysis.

urólito s. m. (med.) urolith.

urologia s. f. urology: medical science relating to urine or urinary organs.

urológico adj. urologic(al).

urologista s. m. + f. urologist.

uropigial adj. m. + f. (pl. **-ais**) uropygial.

uropígio s. m. 1. (zool.) uropygium, rump. 2. (fig.) parson's nose.

uroscopia s. f. (med.) uroscopy.

uroscópico adj. (med.) uroscopic.

urrar v. to roar: 1. bellow, yell. 2. bawl, howl.

urro s. m. 1. roar, bellow. 2. bawl, yell, howl. 3. scream.

ursa s. f. she-bear.

Ursa-Maior s. f. (astr.) Great Bear, Ursa Major.

Ursa-Menor s. f. (astr.) Little Bear, Ursa Minor, Cynosure.

ursada s. f. (Braz.) treason, perfidy, disloyalty (specially of friends).

ursídeo s. m. (zool.) specimen of the Ursidae. ‖ adj. = ursino.

ursinho s. m. toy bear, teddy-bear.

ursino adj. ursine: of, pertaining to or like a bear or the bear family.

urso s. m. 1. bear: a) (zool.) any carnivorous animal of the family Ursidae. b) gruff or surly person. 2. excellent or distinguished student. 3. disloyal friend. 4. (fable) bruin. ‖ adj. 1. bear(like). 2. rough, rude, uncouth. 3. disloyal (friend).

~-pardo grizzly bear. **amigo ~** disloyal friend. **fazer figura de ~** to cut a poor figure.

urso-branco s. m. (pl. **ursos-brancos**) (zool.) (white) polar bear.

urso-do-mar s. m. (pl. **ursos-do-mar**) (zool.) fur seal.

urso-escuro s. m. (pl. **ursos-escuros**) (zool.) brown bear.

ursulina s. f. Ursuline: one of an order of nuns founded by St. Ursula.

urticação s. f. (pl. **-ões**) urtication.

urticáceas s. f. pl. (bot.) Urticaceae.

urticáceo adj. urticaceous.

urticante adj. m. + f. urticant, acrid.

urticária s. f. (med.) urticaria, hives, nettle-rash, uredo.

urtiga s. f. (bot.) Urtica: 1. small nettle. 2. artillery plant. 3. stinging-nettle.

urtiga-amarela s. f. (pl. **urtigas-amarelas**) (bot.) yellow archangel.

urtiga-brava s. f. (pl. **urtigas-bravas**) (bot.) chichicaste.

urtiga-de-mamão s. f. (pl. **urtigas-de-mamão**) (bot.) spurge nettle, tread-softly.

urtiga-do-mar s. f. (pl. **urtigas-do-mar**) (bot.) sea-nettle.

urtigal s. m. (pl. **-ais**) place full of nettles.

urtiga-morta s. f. (pl. **urtigas-mortas**) (bot.) white archangel, white dead nettle.

urtigão s. m. (pl. **-ões**) (bot., also **urtiga-maior** f.) common nettle, great nettle, scratchbush.

urtigar (also **urticar**) v. 1. to urticate: sting or flog with nettles. 2. to thrash, flog.

urtiga-vermelha s. f. (pl. **urtigas-vermelhas**) (bot.) chichicaste.

uru s. m. (ornith.) a crested partridge.

urubamba s. f. (Braz., bot.) jacitara palm.

urubu s. m. (Braz., ornith.) black vulture.

urubu-caçador s. m. (pl. **urubus-caçadores**) (Braz., ornith.) turkey-buzzard, turkey-vulture.

urubu-rei s. m. (pl. **urubus-rei**) (ornith.) king vulture.

urubuzar v. (Braz.) to cast the evil eye on, to jinx.

urucaca s. f. (Braz.) a plain woman, hag.

urucu s. m. (Braz., bot.) annatto.

urucubaca s. f. (Braz., also **caiporismo** m.) persistent misfortune, bad luck.

dar ~ em to come upon bad times, to strike with misfortune, to suffer ill luck.

urucueiro, urucuuba, urucuzeiro s. m. (Braz.) achiote, annatto tree (Bixa orellana).

urucurana s. f. (Braz., bot.) urucu-rana.

uruguaio s. m. Uruguayan. ‖ adj. Uruguayan.

urumbeba, urumbeva s. m. inlander, backsettler.

urundeúva s. f. (bot.) urunday.

urupê s. m. (Braz., bot.) purging agaric, white agaric.

urupema s. f. (Braz.) a kind of sieve of vegetal fibre used in the kitchen.

urupuca s. f. (Braz.) 1. = **arapuca**: snare, trap (specially to catch birds). 2. small wooden cage placed around young coffee plants.

urutu s. m. (Braz., zool.) urutu, a viper.

urutueira s. f. (Braz.) name of a wild bee.

urzal s. m. (pl. **-ais**) heath(er) (wood or plantation), fell.

urze s. f. (bot.) heath(er), ling.

urze-branca s. f. (pl. **urzes-brancas**) (bot.) tree heath, brier.

urze-das-camarinhas s. f. (pl. **urzes-das-camarinhas**) (bot.) Portugal crakeberry.

urze-das-vassouras s. f. (pl. **urzes-das-vassouras**) (bot.) broom heath, bell heather.

urze-de-cheiro s. f. (pl. **urzes-de-cheiro**) (bot.) breath--of-heaven.

urzela s. f. (bot.) Angola weed, canary moss, archil.

usado adj. 1. usual, common. 2. used (up), spent. 3. worn-out, threadbare. 4. old. 5. secondhand. 6. accustomed.

livros muito ~s well thumbed books. **esta palavra é -a muitas vezes no plural** this word often takes the plural. **as calças estão muito -as** the trousers are much the worse for use. **para ser ~ só em grandes ocasiões** for best wear. **roupa -a** worn clothes, seedy clothes.

usagre s. m. (med.) impetigo: skin disease characterized by the formation of pustules.

usança s. f. usage, usance: 1. use, employment. 2. custom, habitual use.

usar v. 1. to use: a) employ. b) accustom, habituate. c) make use of, utilize. d) apply. e) spend. 2. to wear, dress. 3. to be accustomed. 4. to deteriorate, waste. 5. to hackney, fray. 6. **~-se** to be in fashion, be in use.

~ como pretexto to ·lay hold of or on, allege. **~ luvas** to wear gloves. **para ~ no verão** for summer wear. **modo de ~** direction for use. **ele usa a calça até furá-la** he wears the trousers into holes. **que tamanho (de sapato) você usa?** what size (of shoes) do you take? **ele não usa escova de dentes** he is guiltless of a toothbrush. **não usamos isso** we have no use for it. **você pode usá-lo** you can put it to use. **usei-o para uma viagem** I used it for a journey.

usável adj. m. + f. (pl. **-áveis**) us(e)able, wearable.

useiro adj. accustomed (to do something), used, usual, customary, wonted.

~ e vezeiro all the go. **ser ~ e vezeiro** to be used to, to be given to doing the same thing repeatedly.

usina s. f. work(shop), works, (manu)factory, mill, plant, establishment.

~ de aço steel-works. **~ de açúcar** sugar factory or refinery. **~ (elétrica)** electric light and power station,

power plant. **~ de gás** gas-works. **~ hidráulica** hydraulic power plant, waterworks. **~ hidrelétrica** hydro-electric power station.

usinado adj. machine-made.

usineiro s. m. (Braz.) owner, proprietor of a sugar factory. ‖ adj. of or pertaining to a factory, mill, refinery, etc.

úsnea s. f. (bot.) Usnea: a genus of lichens.

uso s. m. 1. use: a) method or way of using. b) employ(ment). c) application, service. d) utilization. e) function, utility. f) custom, habit(ude), usage, usance, wont. g) form, style. h) praxis, procedure. 2. action. 3. fashion, wear(ing). 4. practice, performance.

~ geral common usage. **~ popular** folk-custom. **bom ~ diário** good for everyday wear. **ele fez ~ deste livro** he made use of this book. **fazer mau ~** to misuse. **fizeram bom ~ de** they made good use of. **fora de ~** out of use. **mau ~** misemployment. **não ficou melhor com o ~, está gasto** it is the worse for wear. **para ~ externo** (pharm.) for outward application. **para ~ na cidade** for town wear. **para ~ nas escolas** for use in schools. **posso fazer ~ de seu nome?** may I make use of your name?

ustão s. f. (pl. **-ões**) 1. burning, combustion. 2. conflagration. 3. cauterization.

ustório adj. burning, facilitating the combustion.

ustulação s. f. (pl. **-ões**) ustulation.

ustular v. 1. to ustulate. 2. (met.) to roast. 3. to singe, burn.

usual adj. m. + f. (pl. **-ais**) 1. usual: a) in common use, normal, used. b) habitual, accustomed, customary, frequent. c) regular, commonplace, everyday, ordinary, general. d) familiar. 2. typical. ‖ **~mente** adv. usually, habitually, typically, as a rule, generally.

usuário s. m. (jur.) usuary; usufructuary. ‖ adj. 1. usufructuary. 2. for own use. 3. (Braz., hist.) said of a slave who worked for one and belonged to another master.

usucapião s. m. (jur.) usucapion, udal, prescription.

usucapiente s. m. + f. (jur.) usucapient. ‖ adj. usucapionary.

usucapir v. 1. (jur.) to usucapt. 2. to predominate.

usucapto adj. (jur.) usucaptable.

usufruir, usufrutuar v. to usufruct.

usufruto s. m. usufruct, fruition, enjoyment.

usufrutuário s. m. usufructuary, life-renter, possessor. ‖ adj. usufructuary, beneficial.

usura s. f. 1. usury, interest, usuriousness. 2. avarice, ambition, shabbiness, niggardliness. 3. abrasion.

emprestaram com ~ they lent at usury.

usurar v. to practice usury.

usurário, usureiro s. m. 1. usurer. 2. (pop.) (money) jobber. 3. niggard, miser. ‖ adj. usurious.

usurpação s. f. (pl. **-ões**) 1. usurpation, encroachment. 2. inroad. 3. arrogation.

usurpador s. m. 1. usurper, encroacher. 2. intruder. ‖ adj. 1. usurping. 2. intruding.

usurpar v. 1. to usurp, encroach. 2. to arrogate. 3. to assume (without right).

ela não deve ~ a autoridade she must not assume the authority.

utar v. to winnow, fan.

utensílio s. m. utensil: 1. instrument (esp. of domestic use). 2. tool. 3. implement. 4. ware. 5. **~s** pl. things.

~s de cozinha kitchen utensils, hollow ware, kitchenware (plates C 20, D 3).

uterino adj. uterine: of or pertaining to the uterus or womb.

furor ~ nymphomania. **irmãos** ~**s** uterine brothers (born from the same mother, but from different fathers).

uterite s. f. (path.) uteritis.

útero s. m. (anat.) uterus, womb, matrix.

uteromania s. f. (path.) uteromania, nymphomania.

uteroscopia s. f. (med.) uteroscopy.

útil s. m. (pl. **úteis**) 1. utility: that which is useful. ‖ adj. m. + f. 1. useful, practical, constructive. 2. beneficial, profitable, advantageous, serviceable. 3. expedient, convenient. 4. ordinary. 5. helpful. ‖ **utilmente** adv. usefully.

dias úteis workdays. **posso ser** ~? can I be of any service? **procurei ser** ~ I made myself useful. **juntar o** ~ **ao agradável** to join profit to pleasure.

utilidade s. f. 1. utility, use(fulness). 2. convenience, advantage, expedience. 3. value, profitability, profitableness. 4. helpfulness. 5. ~**s** pl. useful things, factors, implements, utensils.

isto me é de grande utilidade this is very useful to me. **sem** ~ useless.

utilitário s. m. utilitarian. ‖ adj. utilitarian, practical, matter-of-fact, useful.

utilitarismo s. m. utilitarianism.

utilitarista s. m. + f. utilitarian. ‖ adj. utilitarian.

utilização s. f. (pl. **-ões**) utilization: act of utilizing, application.

utilizar v. 1. to utilize: a) make useful. b) profit. c) make use of, apply. 2. to (make) gain(s). 3. to use, put to use. 4. to take advantage of, turn to account.

utilizável adj. m. + f. (pl. **-áveis**) utilizable, usable, applicable.

Utopia s. f. 1. Utopia: book by Sir Thomas More, describing an ideal commonwealth. 2. chimera, dream, fancy.

país de ~ fool's paradise.

utópico adj. 1. Utopian: of, pertaining to or resembling Utopia. 2. chimeric(al), visionary, fantastic, unreal, fanciful.

utopismo s. m. utopianism.

utopista s. m. + f. utopian(ist), visionary. ‖ adj. = **utópico.**

utraquista s. m. (rel.) utraquist, calixtin.

utricular, utriculiforme adj. m. + f. 1. utricular: of or pertaining to a utricle. 2. utriculiform: like a utricle.

utriculária s. f. (bot.) bladderwort, popweed.

utrículo s. m. 1. small bag. 2. utricle: a) cell of an animal or plant. b) (anat.) saclike cavity, esp. one in the labyrinth of the inner ear.

utriculoso adj. utricular: having utricles.

utriforme adj. m. + f. utriform: having the form of a leather bottle or wineskin.

uva s. f. 1. grape: a berry constituting the fruit of the vine. 2. (Braz., sl.) cutie: attractive woman or girl.

um cacho de ~**s** a bunch of grapes (plate B 1). **bago de** ~ grape. **semente de** ~ grapestone. **ser uma** ~ (fig.) to be a peach (a sexy woman).

uva-brava s. f. (pl. **uvas-bravas**) (bot.) sorrel vine.

uvaça s. f. a lot of grapes.

uvada s. f. grape jam, uvate.

uva-de-cão s. f. (pl. **uvas-de-cão**) (bot.) bitter-sweet, dulcamara.

uva-de-urso s. f. (pl. **uvas-de-urso**) (bot.) bearberry.

uva-espim s. f. (pl. **uvas-espim**) (bot.) barberry, pepperidge (Berberis vulgaris).

uvaia, uvaieira s. f. (Braz., bot.) uvalha.

uval s. m. (pl. **-ais**) (pop.) piles, hemorrhoids. ‖ adj. m. + f. grapy, resembling grapes.

uva-passa s. f. (pl. **uvas-passas**) raisin; plum.

uvário adj. having small berries like grapes.

uva-ursina s. f. (pl. **uvas-ursinas**) (bot.) bearberry.

úvea s. f. (anat.) uvea: the inner coloured layer of the iris.

uveíte s. f. (path.) uveitis: inflammation of the uvea.

úvula s. f. (anat.) uvula, plectrum.

uvular adj. m. + f. (anat.) uvular: of or pertaining to the uvula.

uvulária s. f. (bot.) double-tongue.

uvulite s. f. (path.) uvulitis: inflammation of the uvula.

uxoricida s. m. uxoricide: a wife-murderer.

uxoricídio s. m. uxoricide: wife-murder.

uxório adj. uxorious: of or pertaining to a wife.

uzífur(o) s. m. cinnabar: a native mercuric sulphide, vermilion.

V

V, v s. m. the twenty-first letter of the Portuguese alphabet. || abbr. of: **vosso, vossa, vide.**
V. A. = **Vossa Alteza** Your Excellency. **V. S.** = **Vossa Senhoria** you (esp. in letters).
vá interj. scat! be gone! (U. S. A., sl.) scram!
vaca s. f. 1. cow; (U. S. A., sl.) bossy. 2. its meat, beef. 3. (fig.) source (of revenues, advantages). 4. pool: a joint subscription of minor amounts as for a wager or for beneficial purposes (among colleagues). 5. (vulg.) strumpet, prostitute. 6. (Braz.): a) sluggard. b) a hundred cruzeiros bank note.
voltar à ~ fria (fig.) to pick up the thread, return to the point or subject of talk. **carne de ~** beef.
vacada s. f. 1. a herd of cows. 2. a stampede of cows.
vacagem s. f. (pl. **-ens**) a quantity or herd of cows.
vacal adj. (pl. **-ais**) (Braz.) low, indecent.
vaca-leiteira s. f. (pl. **vacas-leiteiras**) (S. E. Braz.) 1. a milkman's truck. 2. a bosomy, big-breasted woman.
vaca-marinha s. f. (pl. **vacas-marinhas)** sea cow, manatee.
vacância s. f. (also **vacatura**) 1. vacancy. 2. time during which a post is vacant. 3. avoidance.
vacante adj. m. + f. 1. vacant, free, empty. 2. (jur.) in abeyance.
vacar v. 1. to vacate. 2. to be free, vacant. 3. to be on vacation, to be on holiday. 4. to be at leisure. 5. to dedicate, apply o. s. to.
vacaria s. f. 1. a herd of cows. 2. cattle. 3. cowshed or stable. 4. cow farm, grange.
vacaril adj. (pl. **-is**) (Port.) of or referring to cows or cattle.
vacilação s. f. (pl. **-ões**) 1. vacillation, hesitation, falter(ing), waver. 2. irresolution. 3. oscillation, vibration. 4. perplexity.
vacilante adj. m. + f. (also **vacilatório**) 1. vacillating, hesitating, wavering, shilly-shally, faltering. 2. irresolute. 3. oscillating, fluctuating. 4. perplex. 5. unsteady. || **~mente** adv. vacillatingly, waveringly, irresolutely, unsteadily.
vacilar v. 1. to vacillate, hesitate, waver, be irresolute, shilly-shally, falter, tergiversate. 2. to oscillate, fluctuate, vibrate. 3. to perplex, shock. 4. to be unsteady. 5. to reel, stagger, totter. 6. to weaken, lose strength.
sem ~ unwavering(ly). **que não vacila** unfaltering.
vacina s. f. 1. vaccine, cowpox. 2. bacterial vaccine.
~ anti-rábica antirabic vaccine. **~ antivariólica** vaccine against smallpox.
vacinação s. f. (pl. **-ões**) vaccination, inoculation.
lanceta para ~ vaccine-point.
vacinador s. m. vaccinator. || adj. vaccinating.
vacinal adj. m. + f. (pl. **-ais**) vaccine, vaccinal.
vacinar v. to vaccinate, inoculate with vaccine.
vacínico adj. vaccine, vaccinal.
vacinogenia s. f. vaccinogeny.
vacinogênico adj. vaccinogenous.
vacinoterapia s. f. vaccine therapy.
vacuidade s. f. 1. vacuity, vacuousness, emptiness, hollowness. 2. inanity. 3. (fig.) vanity.
vacum s. m. cattle, oxen. || adj. bovine, of or referring to cattle.
gado ~ cattle, oxen.
vácuo s. m. 1. vacuum, hollow (plate B 4). 2. gap, void, vacuity, vacancy. || adj. vacuous, empty, void.
~ imperfeito partial or poor vacuum. **tubo de ~** (electr.) vacuum tube.

vacuolar adj. m. + f. vacuolar, vacuolate.
vacúolo s. m. (biol.) vacuole.
vadeabilidade s. f. fordableness.
vadeação s. f. (pl. **-ões**) wading, fording.
vadeador s. m. wader.
vadear v. to wade through, ford.
vade-mécum s. m. (pl. **vade-mécuns**) vade mecum, manual, handbook.
vadeoso adj. fordy, having many fords.
vadiação s. f. (pl. **-ões**) (also **vadiagem, vadiice**) vagrancy, idleness, vagabondage, loafing.
eles levam uma vida de ~ they indulge in idleness, they lead an idle life.
vadiar v. 1. to idle, laze, loaf, lounge. 2. to vagabond, truant. 3. to hang about, drone. 4. (fam., sl.) to mike, mooch.
vadio s. m. 1. idler, vagrant, lounger, lazy-bones, loafer; (sl.) lounge-lizard; (U. S. A.) poke. 2. vagabond, truant, tramp, tramper. || adj. 1. vagrant, idle. 2. vagabond, truant. 3. sluggish, lazy.
vadoso adj. fordable.
vaga (I) s. f. 1. (large) wave, billow. 2. swell, surge.
~ batida cross swell. **~ comprida e forte** long heavy swell.
vaga (II) s. f. 1. vacancy. 2. leisure. 3. **~s** pl., vacant situations.
ele precisa preencher a ~ he must fill the vacancy. **não há ~s** no vacancy.
vagabundagem s. f. (pl. **-ens**) 1. vagabondage, vagrancy, roving, dawdle. 2. the vagabonds (pl.).
vagabundear v. 1. to vagabond. 2. to laze, idle. 3. to truant. 4. to rove, loiter. 5. to tramp, mooch.
vagabundo s. m. 1. vagabond, vagrant, runagate. 2. lazybones, idler. 3. runabout, roamer, rover, tramp(er). 4. rogue, rascallion, knave. 5. ragamuffin, sad dog. || adj. 1. vagabond, vagrant. 2. idle. 3. roving, rambling, erratic. 4. inferior, of low quality. 5. common, low. 6. worthless, poor.
vagação s. f. = **vacância.**
vágado s. m. giddiness, dizziness, vertigo, fainting fit.
vagagem s. f. (pl. **-ens**) (sl.) vagrancy, idleness, vagabondage.
vagalhão s. m. (pl. **-ões**) billow, breaker, comber, surge, sea.
formar -ões to billow.
vaga-lume s. m. (pl. **vaga-lumes**) 1. (also **pirilampo**) glowworm, lightning bug, firefly. 2. (Braz., cinema) usher, attendant.
vagamundear v. 1. to vagabond. 2. to idle, loaf, take it easy. 3. to bum, mooch. 4. to rove, roam.
vagamundo s. m. vagabond, tramp, beachcomber.
vagância s. f. vacancy.
vagante adj. m. + f. 1. vacant, free. 2. vagrant.
vagão s. m. (pl. **-ões**) waggon, railway car, railway carriage (plates E 13, V 1).
~ raso platform car, flatcar, bogie. **~ restaurante** dining car. **~ salão** parlour car, Pullman car. **~ para gado** cattle car. **~ correio** postal car. **~ de carga** freight car. **~ de carga fechado** van.
vagar (I) s. m. 1. leisure(liness), idleness. 2. free time, spare time. 3. lack of occupation, disengagement. 4. laziness. 5. slowness, lentor. 6. opportunity. || v. to vacate, be or become vacant, empty, unoccupied.
com ~ at leisure. **ter ~** to be at leisure.
vagar (II) v. 1. to rove, ramble, wander, roam, run about. 2. to spread, be scattered. 3. to float on the waves. 4. to idle.

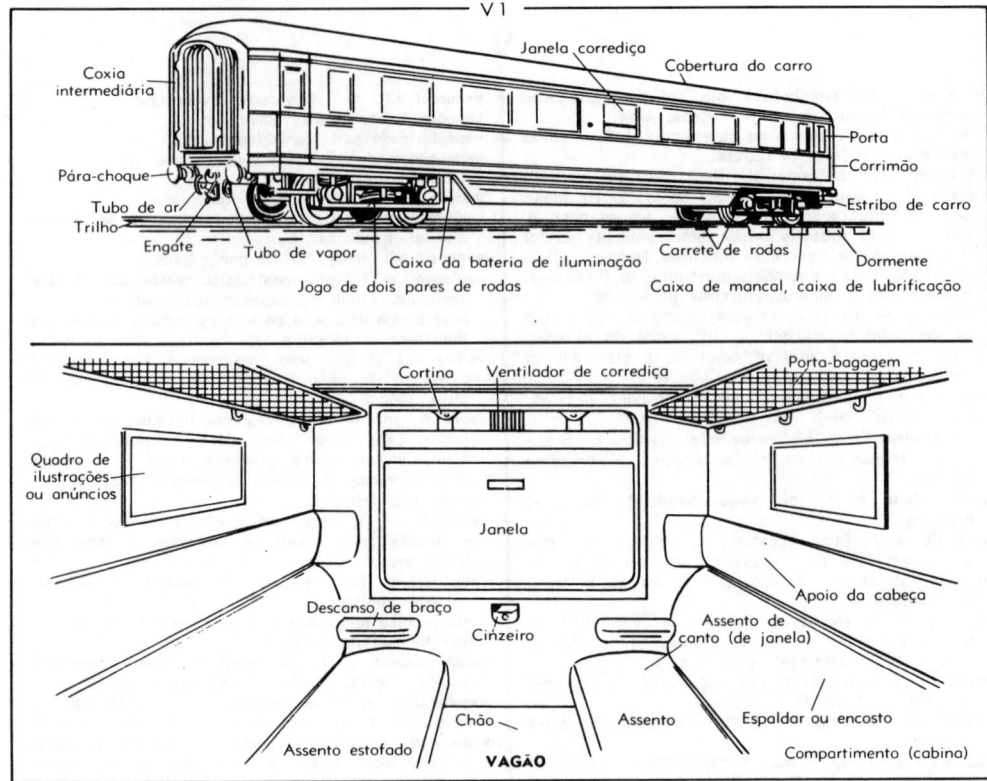

Coxia intermediária — Janela corrediça — Cobertura do carro — Porta — Corrimão — Pára-choque — Tubo de ar — Trilho — Engate — Tubo de vapor — Caixa da bateria de iluminação — Jogo de dois pares de rodas — Carrete de rodas — Caixa de mancal, caixa de lubrificação — Estribo de carro — Dormente

Cortina — Ventilador de corrediça — Porta-bagagem — Quadro de ilustrações ou anúncios — Janela — Descanso de braço — Cinzeiro — Apoio da cabeça — Assento de canto (de janela) — Chão — Assento — Espaldar ou encosto — Assento estofado — **VAGÃO** — Compartimento (cabina)

vagareza s. f. slowness, tardiness, sluggishness.

vagaroso adj. (also **vagarento**) 1. slow, tardy, sluggish. 2. dull, stagnant, snail-paced. 3. easy, easygoing. 4. languid, leisurely. 5. (mus.) adagio, andante. 6. lax. 7. hesitating. 8. embarrassed. ‖ -**amente** adv. slowly, easily, leisurely.
deram um passeio ~ they went for a crawl.

vagatura s. m. vacancy.

vagem s. f. (pl. -**ens**) 1. French bean, kidney bean, haricot bean, snap bean. 2. husk, shuck, pod.

vagido s. m. 1. a newborn child's crying. 2. wailing, moan, groan.

vagina s. f. (anat., bot.) vagina.

vaginal adj. m. + f. (pl. -**ais**) (anat., bot.) vaginal.

vaginiforme adj. m. + f. shaped like a vagina.

vaginismo s. m. (med.) vaginismus.

vagínula s. f. (bot.) vaginula.

vaginulado adj. (bot.) vaginulate.

vagir s. m. = **vagido**. ‖ v. 1. to cry (babies). 2. to groan, moan. 3. to lament.

vago s. m. 1. vagueness. 2. indecision. 3. confusion. ‖ adj. 1. vacant, vacuous, open, free, unfilled, empty. 2. uncertain, roundabout, dubious, ambiguous, equivocal, vague. 3. vagrant, rambling. 4. dim, faint, blurry. ‖ -**amente** adv. vacantly, dubiously, dimly, etc.
horas vagas free hours, spare time. **uma casa vaga** an uninhabited house. **o nervo** ~ (anat.) vagus. **lugar** ~ vacancy.

vagonete s. m. 1. wagonette, trolley, tilting cart. 2. (railway) truck, lorry. 3. (mining) truck, dog (plate M 10).

vagueação s. f. (pl. -**ões**) 1. wandering, errantry, roving, rambling, itineracy, gad. 2. vagabondage, vagrancy. 3. idleness. 4. reverie, daydream. 5. floating (on the waves).

vaguear v. (also **vaguejar**) 1. to walk or wander about, perambulate, rove, ramble, err, prowl. 2. to tramp, nomadize. 3. to idle, loiter, loaf. 4. to daydream. 5. to be inconstant, fickle. 6. to float, fluctuate.

vagueiro s. m. piece of barren land.

vagueza s. f. 1. vagueness. 2. (painting) lightness of colours, tenuousness.

vaia s. f. 1. hoot(ing). 2. scoff, derision. 3. mockery.
levar ~ to be hissed at.

vaiar v. to catcall, hoot, hiss at, boo.

vaidade s. f. 1. vanity, vainness, pride, conceitedness, vaingloriousness, flatulence, airs. 2. emptiness, hollowness. 3. futility.

vaidoso adj. 1. vain, conceited, proud, flatulent. 2. presumptuous, puffed up, haughty, vainglorious, peacockish. 3. foppish, coquettish. ‖ -**amente** adv. vainly, conceitedly, presumptuously, etc.

vai-não-vai s. m., sg. + pl. shilly-shally, irresolution, vacillation.

vaivém s. m. (pl. **vaivéns**) 1. teeter, seesaw, rocking motion. 2. fluctuation, sway. 3. vicissitude, ups and downs. 4. coming and going.
porta ~ swinging door. **fazer movimento de** ~ to seesaw. **os vaivéns da sorte** the ups and downs of life.

vala s. f. 1. trench, ditch, drain, dike, trough. 2. (also ~ **comum**) common grave. 3. (Braz.) periodically dried bed of a river.

~ **cabocla** (Braz.) boundary trench. **abrir** ~s to cut trenches.

valada s. f. large or long trench, ditch.

valadio adj. 1. said of a piece of land cut by trenches. 2. said of a roof with loose tiles.

valado s. m. 1. ditch-and-hedge surrounding a rural property. 2. rural property surrounded with a ditch--and-hedge. 3. mound around a rural property.

valador s. m. worker who makes ditches.

valagem s. f. (pl. -ens) earthwork, rampart, ditch.

valão s. m. (pl. -ões) Walloon. ‖ adj. Wallonian.

valáquio s. m. Wallach, Wallachian. ‖ adj. Wallachian.

valar v. 1. to provide or surround with ditches. 2. to open gutters or drains. 3. to wall in, fence in. 4. to fortify, defend. 5. to surround, encircle. ‖ adj. m. + f. of or pertaining to a ditch, drain.

valdeiro adj. vagrant, vagabond, roguish.

valdevinos s. m., sg. + pl. 1. idler, loiterer, wastrel. 2. rogue, scamp. 3. rascal, cheat. 4. poor wretch.

vale (I) s. m. 1. valley, vale, dale. 2. plain. 3. dean, dell, coomb. 4. strath.

~ **de lágrimas** slough of despond. **por montes e** ~s over hill and dale. **ir para o** ~ **dos lençóis** to go to bed.

vale (II) s. m. 1. (com.) credit note, bill, bond, chit, draw, voucher. 2. IOU = I owe you (acknowledgment of debt).

~ **postal** money order (M. O.), postal order (plate C 10). **pagar** ~ (Braz.) to make a drawback; become afraid; (fig.) break down.

valedio adj. valid, current.

valedor s. m. supporter, protector, defender. ‖ adj. 1. helping, assisting, protecting. 2. worth.

valedouro, valedoiro adj. valid, lawful.

valeira s. f. (also **valeta**) 1. small ditch or drain. 2. dingle, wooded valley.

valeiro s. m. (Braz.) ditcher: person who makes demarcation ditches.

valência (I) s. f. (chem.) valence, valency.

valência (II) s. f. (Braz., op.) 1. worth, value, merit. 2. usefulness, serviceability, handiness.

valenciana s. f. Valenciennes: fine French lace.

valenciano s. m. Valencian. ‖ adj. Valencian.

valencina s. f. Valencian fabric.

valentão s. m. (pl. -ões) bully, rowdy, hector, ruffian, braggart, swashbuckler, daredevil. ‖ adj. ruffian, bragging.

bancar o ~ to swagger.

valente s. m. courageous, intrepid, valiant person, daredevil, darer. ‖ adj. m. + f. 1. valiant, courageous, intrepid, bold, daring, brave, stouthearted, gallant. 2. energetic, strong, tough, strenuous. ‖ ~**mente** adv. valiantly, etc.

valentia s. f. 1. valiantness, valour. 2. prowess, achievement, feat, bravery. 3. energy, power, strength, force, stalwartness. 4. capability, ability.

valentona s. f. valiant woman. ‖ adj. f. valiant.

à ~ by force, violently.

valer v. 1. to value, be worth. 2. to be valuable. 3. to cost. 4. to deserve. 5. to protect, help, assist. 6. to mean, signify. 7. to be valid, have force or power. 8. to be useful, serviceable. 9. ~**-se (de)** to avail o. s. of, to have recourse to, take refuge with.

vale a pena it is worth it, it is worth while; it pays its way. **vale o preço** it is worth its price. **vale-lhe dez xelins** it is worth ten shillings to him. **vale quanto pesa** it is as good as it looks. **valeu-se dos amigos para compilar o livro** he laid his friends under contribution to compile the book. **valha-me Deus!** so help me God! **valha-te a breca!** go to hell (and stay there)! **fazer** ~ **os seus direitos** to stake a claim. **isto ou coisa que o valha** this or something

like it. **mais vale um pássaro na mão do que dois voando** a bird in the hand is worth two in the bush. **não vale nada!** it isn't worth a farthing! **não valeu a pena para ele** it has not paid his way. **não vale um caracol** it is not worth a rush. **ele não vale nada** he is not worth a fig. **não vale o que come** he is not worth his salt. **o cavalo não vale a sua ração** the horse eats his head off. **sua sentença vale muito** his judgement carries great weight. **quanto vale?** how much is it worth? **a saúde vale mais do que a riqueza** health is above wealth. **tanto vale!** it's about the same! **ela chorou a** ~ she cried her fill. **ele valeu-se de influências superiores** he hitched her waggon to a star. **este bilhete vale para duas pessoas** this ticket admits two. **tempo a** ~ tons of time. **um dólar vale quatro xelins** one dollar exchanges for four shillings. ~ **quanto pesa** to be worth its (his, her) weight in gold.

valerianato s. m. (chem.) valerianate.

valeriânico adj. (chem.) valeric.

valeta s. f. ditch, drain, channel, kennel, gutter (plate C 8).

valete s. m. (cards) knave, jack, bower (plate B 5).

valetudinário s. m. valetudinarian. ‖ adj. valetudinary, sickish.

vale-tudo s. m. 1. all-in-wrestling, catch-as-catch-can, no holds barred. 2. situation in which all is fair.

valhacouto s. m. 1. shelter, refuge. 2. asylum. 3. protection.

valia s. f. 1. worth, value. 2. price. 3. favour, merit. 4. worthiness.

validação s. f. (pl. -ões) validation; acknowledgement.

validade s. f. validity, legality, force, authenticity, vigo(u)r.

validar v. to validate, legalize, authenticate, acknowledge.

validez s. f. 1. validity; legal force. 2. soundness, robustness, good health.

valido s. m. favourite, minion.

válido adj. 1. valid, legal, binding. 2. sound, healthy. 3. (jur.) available. 4. effective. ‖ **validamente** adv. validly, etc.

ser aceito como ~ to pass current. **não** ~ invalid, bad. **por quanto tempo é** ~ **este bilhete?** for how long is this ticket available?

valimento s. m. 1. worth, value. 2. esteem, respect. 3. favour, protection. 4. support. 5. influence, importance. 6. merit, service.

valioso adj. 1. valuable, worthy, precious, costly, rich. 2. valid. 3. important. 4. merited, meritorious. ‖ **-amente** adv. valuably, etc.

valisa, valise s. f. valise, gripsack, portmanteau, small suitcase.

valo (I) s. m. 1. intrenchment. 2. (hist.) lists. 3. trench. 4. overhang, slope.

valo (II) s. m. trawl-net.

valor s. m. 1. valo(u)r, value, worth. 2. courage, braveness, gallantry, intrepidity. 3. effort. 4. force, mettle, feck. 5. merit(ousness). 6. virtue. 7. price, amount. 8. (mus.) duration. 9. fitness, efficacy, efficiency. 10. currency, rate, exchange.

~ **de publicidade** advertising value. ~ **específico,** ~ **ouro** gold point. ~ **máximo** peak value. ~ **nominal** nominal value. ~ **nutritivo** food value. ~ **segurável** insurable value. ~ **térmico** thermal power. ~**es estrangeiros** foreign exchange. ~**es imóveis** real estate. ~**es móveis** personal estate, movables. **acima (abaixo) do** ~ above (below) the value. **carta com** ~ **declarado** money letter. **aparentar mais que o** ~ **real** a penny plain and twopence coloured. **dei muito** ~ **a isto** I set great store by it. **ela não dá** ~ **ao que tem** she does not appreciate what she has. **isto dá valor a suas palavras** that adds weight to his words. **um homem de grande** ~ a man of great worth. **não dou** ~ **algum a isto** I attach no value at all to it, (coll.) I give a darn for it. **de pouco** ~ halfpenny, of little worth, base. **sem** ~ null and void, useless, refuse, unvalued, vain, hollow, bad, riffraff, nought. **ter** ~ to be valuable, to stand good.

valorar v. to appraise, value, assay, set a value on.

valorização s. f. (pl. **-ões**) 1. valorization. 2. valuation. 3. appreciation.

valorizador adj. valorizing.

valorizar v. 1. to valorize. 2. to value. 3. to appraise, appreciate. 4. to prize. 5. to increase the value of.

valorosidade s. f. valorousness.

valoroso adj. 1. valorous, worthy. 2. valiant, manly, courageous. 3. strong, powerful. 4. active, diligent, industrious. ‖ **-amente** adv. valorously, etc.

valquíria s. f. (myth.) valkyrie.

valsa s. f. waltz (music and dance).

valsador s. m. waltzer.

valsar v. to waltz, dance the waltz.

valsista s. m. + f. waltzer. ‖ adj. waltzing.

valva s. f. (bot. + zool.) valve.

valváceo adj. valvate.

valvar adj. m. + f. (pl. **-ais**) valvelike, valvar.

válvula s. f. 1. valve (plates B 11, 14, M 13, P 11, R 2). 2. sluice, gate.
~ **de admissão** inlet valve. ~ **de alimentação** feed valve. ~ **de borboleta** disk valve. ~ **de descarga** outlet valve, spill valve. ~ **de escape** escape valve, exhaust valve. ~ **de esfera** ball valve. ~ **de recalque** discharge valve. ~ **de segurança** safety valve (plate C 5). **em forma de** ~ valvular. **provido de** ~**s** valved. **sem** ~**s** valveless.

valvular adj. m. + f. valvular, valval.

vamos interj. up! come! go! buck up! hurry up!

vamos-embora s. m., sg. + pl. (Braz.) bee of the genus Melipona.

vampírico adj. vampiric.

vampirismo s. m. vampirism.

vampiro s. m. vampire: 1. a bloodsucking ghost. 2. (fig.) a bloodsucker. 3. a woman who debases her lover. 4. an actress who plays such parts. 5. spectre bat, great vampire, false vampire.

vanádio s. m. (chem.) vanadium (symbol V).

vandálico adj. Vandalic, vandalic.

vandalismo s. m. Vandalism.

vândalo s. m. 1. Vandal. 2. destroyer of works of art. ‖ adj. vandalic.

vanecer = **desvanecer**.

vanglória s. f. vainglory, vaunting, boasting, showing-off, vanity.

vangloriar v. 1. to puff up, praise, flatter. 2. ~**-se** to boast (of), brag, pride, egotize, rodomontade, swagger, buck.
ela se vangloria de... she prides herself upon... **ele se vangloria de sua fortuna** he piques himself on his money. **ele vangloriou-se daquilo** he made it his vaunt, he made vaunt of it.

vanglorioso adj. vainglorious, conceited, proud, boastful.

vanguarda s. f. vanguard, advance guard, van, forefront, front, head.
ele está na ~ he stands in the forefront. **na** ~ in the first flight.

vanguardeiro s. m. (fig.) pioneer. ‖ adj. foremost.

vanguejar v. 1. to slip. 2. to vacillate.

vanilina s. f. vanillin.

vaniloquência s. f. 1. talkativeness. 2. vain talk.

vanilóquio s. m. prittle-prattle, vain talk.

vaníloquo, vaniloqüente adj. 1. given to vain talk. 2. bragging.

vantagem s. f. (pl. **-ens**) 1. advantage. 2. boot. 3. profit, gain, margin, catch; (sl.) bulge. 4. convenience, interest. 5. pro. 6. (fig.) capital. 7. forehand. 8. (sport) bisque.
~ **concedida** handicap, odds given at play. **vantagens pessoais** loaves and fishes. **as vantagens e desvantagens** the ins and outs. **as vantagens são seis contra dois** the odds are six to two. **ter pequena** ~ **sobre** to have the edge on. **conseguir** ~ **sobre alguém** to gain an advantage over, (coll.) to get the jump on, to steal a march upon s. o. **levar** ~ **sobre** to have the advantage of. **ele leva** ~ **sobre seu rival** he gains upon his rival. **ele não leva** ~ **comigo** he cuts no ice with me. **qual é a** ~ **disto?** what is the good of that? **temos uma** ~ **de seis pontos** we are up six points. **contar -ens** to brag, talk big, blow one's trumpet.

vantajoso adj. 1. advantageous, favourable, profitable, gainful. 2. fruitful, purposive. 3. (sl.) plummy. 4. worth-while. ‖ **-amente** adv. advantageously.
é um negócio ~ it's a bargain. **isto me é** ~ it stands me in good stead.

vão s. m. (pl. ~**s**) 1. empty space, void, vacuum. 2. interstice. 3. interspace. 4. (archit.) span, bay (plate A 12). 5. (aeron.) bay. 6. niche, break. 7. (Braz.): a) barren plains. b) valley. 8. narrow, pass. ‖ adj. 1. vain, void, futile, useless, fruitless. 2. empty. 3. false, unfounded. 4. vaporous, frivolous, fronthy. 5. vainglorious.
~ **da parede** wall channel. ~ **de elevador** well. ~ **de escada** space under the staircase. ~ **de janela** window opening, window recess. ~ **de porta** door opening. **em** ~ in vain, purposelessly, to no end, to no effect, without avail. **foi tudo em** ~ it was all in vain. **invocar em** ~ to take in vain (the name of God).

vápido adj. vapid, insipid, dull.

vapor s. m. 1. vapour, steam, fume. 2. steamship, ship, steamer (plates P 16, 17). 3. (N. Braz.) train. 4. halitus, exhalation. 5. reek. 6. ~**es** pl. intoxication.
~ **de alta pressão** high-pressure steam. ~ **de rodas** paddle steamer, side-wheeler. ~ **de escape** exhaust steam. ~ **saturado** saturated vapour. ~ **vivo** live steam. **aquecimento a** ~ steam heating. **barcaça a** ~ steam launch. **caldeira de** ~ steam boiler. **máquina a** ~ steam engine. **navegação a** ~ steam navigation. **produzir** ~ to get up steam. **soltar** ~ to let off steam. **a todo** ~ at full steam.

vaporação s. f. (pl. **-ões**) evaporation.

vaporar v. 1. to evaporate, turn into vapor. 2. to steam.

vaporável adj. m. + f. (pl. **-áveis**) evaporable.

vaporífero adj. vaporiferous, vaporific.

vaporização s. f. (pl. **-ões**) vaporization.

vaporizador s. m. vaporizer, pulverizer. ‖ adj. vaporizing.

vaporizar v. 1. to vaporize, evaporate. 2. to pulverize.

vaporosidade s. f. vaporousness.

vaporoso adj. 1. vaporous, vapourish, vaporiferous. 2. very light or thin. 3. airlike, airy. 4. incomprehensible. 5. vain. 6. (fig.) fantastic. ‖ **-amente** adv. vaporously.

vapular v. to whip, flog.

vaqueanar v. (Braz.) to work as a guide or helmsman.

vaqueano s. m. (Braz.) 1. guide, one who knows a region thoroughly. 2. helmsman. 3. expert.

vaqueira s. f. cowgirl.

vaqueirada s. f. group of cowboys.

vaqueiragem s. f. (pl. **-ens**) work or profession of a cowboy.

vaqueirar v. to work as a cowboy.

vaqueiro s. m. 1. vaquero, herdsman, cowkeeper, wrangler, neatherd. 2. cowboy, cowpuncher, drover. ‖ adj. of or pertaining to cattle.

vaquejada s. f. rodeo: roundup of cattle.

vaquejador s. m. (Braz.) path that leads to the roundup.

vaquejar v. (N. Braz.) to pursue, press hard.

vaquejo s. m. (N. Braz.) pursuit, torment.

vaqueta s. f. 1. thin leather (for lining). 2. rib (of an umbrella).

vaquilhona s. f. (N. Braz.) young cow, heifer.

vaquinha s. f. (dim. of **vaca**) young cow, heifer.

fazer uma ~ to pass the hat, take up a collection.

vara (I) s. f. 1. stick, rod, switch, staff, pole, stave, cane (plate G 4). 2. a magistrate's ensign, warder. 3. judgeship, jurisdiction. 4. measure of about 1.10 m., ell. 5. gauge, measure. 6. punishment. 7. herd of pigs. 8. tall and skinny person. 9. beam (timber). 10. wand.

~ **de calibrar** gauging rod. ~ **para cortina** tringle, dowel. ~ **enviscada** lime twig. ~ **mágica** wishing rod, divining rod. ~ **de passadeira** carpet rod. ~ **de pescar** fishing rod (plate P 9). ~ **para saltos** jumping rod. ~s **fixas** (gym.) scaling poles (plate P 6). ter uma ~ **de condão** to have extraordinary abilities. **tremer como** ~s **verdes** to tremble like an aspen leaf. **passar pelas** ~s to run the gauntlet. **salto a vara** (athl.) pole jump, pole vaulting.

vara (II) s. f. (India) typhoon.

varação s. f. (pl. -ões) 1. (naut.) beaching. 2. (Braz.) land transport of a watercraft around falls.

varada s. f. stroke with a rod, blow with a switch.

varador s. m. gauger (of casks, etc.).

varadouro s. m. 1. shallow, where ships are run upon for repair. 2. (fig.) place for rest and talk. 3. (Braz.): a) improvised waterway to avoid falls. b) channel between a lake and a river.

varal s. m. (pl. -ais) 1. shaft or pole of a carriage or sedan-chair, thill. 2. clothes-line. 3. poles to dry fishing-nets on.

~ **do arado** plough beam.

varanda s. f. 1. veranda, balcony. 2. (U. S. A.) piazza, porch. 3. terrace. 4. railing (of a balcony or the like). 5. toothed wheel of an oil press.

varandado s. m. (N. Braz.) a sort of penthouse around rural buildings.

varandim s. m. (pl. -ins) 1. narrow balcony or varanda. 2. platform. 3. low window railing.

varão s. m. (pl. -ões) 1. man, male. 2. worthy, respectable man, knight. 3. rung, rod. 4. rail. ‖ adj. masculine.

varapau s. m. 1. stick, staff, pole, hop-pole. 2. m. + f. (fig.) tall person, skinny fellow.

varar v. 1. to beat with a stick. 2. to run aground, run on a shallow; beach a ship. 3. to stick, pierce, trespass. 4. to go beyond. 5. to cross (river). 6. to expell, throw out. 7. to frighten, shock. 8. to amaze. 9. to disappoint. 10. to fall short. 11. to break out. 12. to penetrate into.

vareador s. m. punter.

vareagem s. f. (pl. -ens) 1. measurement by **varas**. 2. punting.

varear v. 1. to measure by **varas**. 2. to punt (boat).

varedo s. m. rafters that sustain the lathwork of a roof.

vareio s. m. (S. Braz.) 1. raving delirium. 2. shock, fright. 3. spanking. 4. severe lecture.

vareiro s. m. (Braz.) punter (boat).

vareja (I) s. f. (also **varejamento** m., **varejadura** f.) 1. beating. 2. fustigation. 3. trouble. 4. search, searching. 5. storming (see **varejar**).

vareja (II) s. f. (ent.) meat fly.

varejador s. m. 1. beater. 2. fustigator. 3. searcher, ransacker. ‖ adj. 1. beating. 2. fustigating. 3. searching. 4. storming.

varejante s. m. (Braz.) retail dealer.

varejão s. m. (pl. -ões) 1. large staff, pole or rod. 2. barge-pole.

varejar v. 1. to beat with a stick or pole (a tree). 2. to spank. 3. to measure by **varas**. 4. to attack, harass, fustigate. 5. to trouble, annoy. 6. to search, ransack; (sl.) to pull. 7. to throw out or away. 8. to shoot, batter. 9. to blow hard.

varejeira s. f. (ent.) blowfly, nitter.

varejista s. m. + f. retail dealer, retailer. ‖ adj. retail.

varejo s. m. 1. search (for stolen goods or contraband). 2. severe reprimand. 3. retail (sales); shopkeeping.

a ~ at or by retail. **vender** a ~ to retail.

vareque s. m. (bot.) wrack.

vareta s. f. 1. small rod or cane (plate E 6). 2. ramrod, rammer. 3. leg of a compass.

~ **de guarda-chuva** rib, stretcher (of an umbrella) (plate G 4). ~ **de bomba** bucket rod. ~ **de pintar** guiding stick (of a painter).

varga s. f. 1. swampy lowland. 2. trap, sort of fishing net.

varge, várgea s. f. = **várzea**.

vargedo s. m. 1. plain. 2. cultivated extensive valley. 3. lowland on riversides.

vargem s. f. = **várzea**.

varginha s. f. dim. of **vargem**.

vargueiro s. m. person who makes fishtraps (**vargas**).

vária s. f. (Braz.) a newspaper's small commentary; paragraph.

variabilidade s. f. 1. variability, variableness. 2. alterability, uncertainty. 3. inconstancy, unsteadiness, fickleness.

variação s. f. (pl. -ões) 1. change, alteration, modification, diversification. 2. fluctuation. 3. (mus.) variation.

~ **de velocidade** fluctuation in speed. ~ **da agulha** variation of the compass.

variado adj. 1. varied, various, miscellaneous. 2. different, diverse. 3. inconstant, fickle. 4. inconsiderate, frivolous. 5. delirious. 6. many-coloured, variegated, checkered. 7. assorted, multifarious. ‖ **-amente** adv. variedly, variously.

variante s. f. 1. variant (also gram.). 2. version, reading. 3. variation. 4. difference. 5. branch-line (railway). 6. deviation. ‖ adj. m. + f. variant.

variar v. 1. to vary (also mus.). 2. to change, alter, modify. 3. to diversify, differ. 4. to alternate. 5. to shade, variegate, chequer. 6. to deviate. 7. to be different. 8. to inflect. 9. to rave, be or go mad, be delirious, talk nonsense.

~ **o passo da hélice** (aeron.) to feather the airscrew.

variável adj. m. + f. (pl. -áveis) 1. variable, changeable, various, variant. 2. inconstant, unsteady, changeful. 3. unfixed, uncertain. 4. fickle, shuttlecock, desultory. 5. choppy, chopping. 6. unequal. 7. fluctuating. ‖ **variavelmente** adv. changeably, etc.

varicela s. f. (med.) chicken pox, varicella (more usually **catapora**).

varicocele s. f. (med.) varicocele.

varicosidade s. f. (med.) varicosity.

varicoso adj. (med.) varicose.

variedade s. f. variety: 1. diversity, diverseness, variousness, miscellaneousness. 2. inconstancy. 3. (bot., zool.) species, subspecies. 4. vaudeville.

muitas ~s **de frutas** various kinds of fruits.

variegação s. f. (pl. -ões) variegation, diversity of colours.

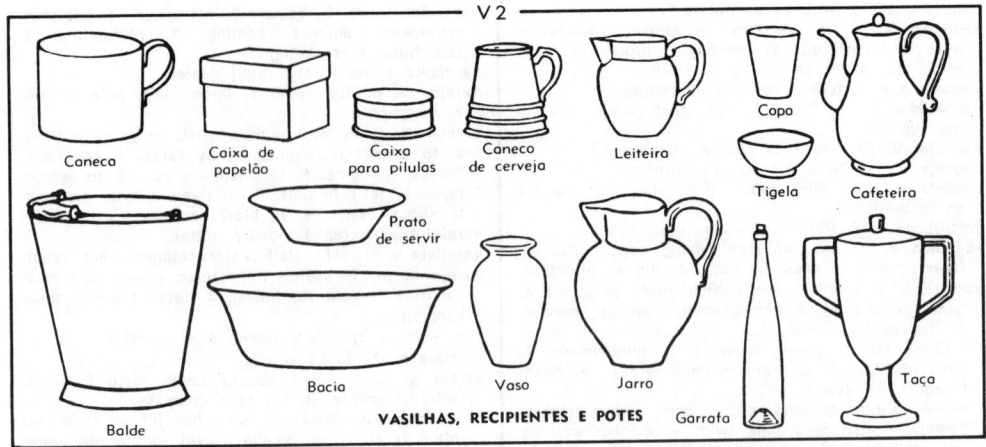

V 2

Caneca · Caixa de papelão · Caixa para pílulas · Caneco de cerveja · Leiteira · Copa · Tigela · Cafeteira · Prato de servir · Bacia · Vaso · Jarro · Taça · Balde · VASILHAS, RECIPIENTES E POTES · Garrafa

variegado adj. variegated: 1. varying, various, varied, diversified, miscellaneous. 2. multicoloured, vari-coloured, colourful, pied. 3. dapple, motley. ‖ **-mente** adv. variegatedly.

variegar v. to variegate: 1. give different colours to. 2. shade, grade colours. 3. diversify, change, vary.

varina s. f. (Port.) fishwife.

varinha s. f. (dim. of **vara**) rod, wand, switch.
~ **de condão** divining rod, dowsing rod.

varino s. m. narrow and long boat.

vário adj. 1. various. 2. variegated, multicoloured. 3. different, diverse, diversified. 4. hesitating. 5. inconstant. 6. fickle. 7. ~**s** pl. some, sundry, several, many. 8. perplex. 9. restless. 10. contradictory.

varíola s. f. (med.) variola, smallpox.

variolar adj. m. + f. (med.) variolar.

variólico adj. (med.) variolic.

variolóide s. f. (med.) varioloid, mild form of small-pox.

varioloso s. m. person affected by variola. ‖ adj. variolous.

variômetro s. m. variometer.

variz s. f. (med.) varix.

varjão s. m. (pl. **-ões**) extensive plain (see **várzea**).

varjota s. f. small plain (see **várzea**).

varloas s. f. pl. (naut.) releasing ropes or tackles.

varoa s. f. 1. virago. 2. heroine.

varola s. f. = **vareta**.

varonia s. f. 1. manliness, masculinity. 2. male line.

varonil adj. (pl. **-is**) 1. manly, manlike, manful, male, viril. 2. strong. 3. heroic. ‖ adv. manly.

varonilidade s. f. virility, manliness, manhood.

varrão (pl. **-ões**), **varrasco** s. m. boar.

varredeira s. f. (naut.) the lower studding sail.

varredela s. f. sweep(ing).

varredor s. m. sweep(er), person who sweeps. ‖ adj. sweeping.
~ **de rua** street orderly, sweeper, scavenger.

varredoura s. f. (also **varredoira**) 1. drag-net, sweep--net. 2. destruction, havoc, slaughter. ‖ adj. said of a certain drag-net.

varredouro s. m. (also **varredoiro**) oven broom, oven mop (plate P 1).

varredura s. f. 1. sweep(ing). 2. rubbish, garbage, dust. 3. food scraps. 4. remnants. 5. winnowing.

varrer v. 1. to sweep, broom, besom. 2. to clean. 3. to turn out. 4. to disperse. 5. to put to flight, drive along. 6. to exhaust. 7. to empty, pour out. 8. to eat up. 9. to clear up. 10. to destroy, lay

in ruins, extinguish. 11. to drag. 12. to lose credit. 13. to disappear. 14. to forget.
~ **à baia** to rake. ~ **para baixo** to sweep down. **as ondas varrem a praia** the waves sweep the beach. **a tempestade varre tudo diante de si** the storm sweeps everything before it.

varrição s. f. (pl. **-ões**) sweep(ing).

varrido s. m. 1. sweep(ing). 2. sweepings. ‖ adj. 1. swept, cleaned. 2. (fig.) crazy, mad.
ele é um doido ~ he is stark mad.

varsoviana s. f. Varsovienne.

varudo adj. long and straight-stemmed.

várzea s. f. 1. cultivated plain; lea. 2. (Braz.) low and flat land alongside a watercourse; holm.

varzino adj. of or pertaining to a **várzea**.

vasa s. f. 1. slime and mud deposits of a river or the sea. 2. mud, mire. 3. (fig.) moral degradation. 4. mob, rabble, riffraff. 5. trough of an oilpress.

vasca s. f. 1. convulsions. 2. pangs of death, rattle, stertor. 3. nausea, sickly feeling.
nas ~**s da morte** (to be) in pangs of death, (to lie) in death-bed.

vascolejador s. m. shaker: person who shakes a liquid. ‖ adj. 1. shaking. 2. revolving, stirring. 3. disquieting.

vascolejamento s. m. 1. shaking (liquid). 2. agitation.

vascolejar v. 1. to shake (liquids). 2. to stir up, disquiet, perturb, agitate.

vasconcear v. 1. to speak **vasconço** (a Basque dialect). 2. to gibber, talk nonsense. 3. to joke, jest. 4. to express dubiously.

vasconço s. m. 1. Basque (dialect). 2. gibberish.

vascongado s. m. Biscayan, Basque. ‖ adj. Biscayan, Basque.

vascoso adj. convulsive, having nausea.

vascular adj. m. + f. (anat., bot.) vascular.

vascularidade s. f. vascularity.

vascularização s. f. (pl. **-ões**) vascularization.

vascularizado adj. vascularized.

vascular v. 1. to sweep, clean. 2. to search, ransack, comb, fossick, ferret about.

vasculho s. m. (also **basculho**) broom or brush on a long stick (to clean walls and ceilings).
~ **de forno** oven broom.

vaselina s. f. vaseline.

vasento adj. (also **vasoso**) muddy, miry.

vasilha s. f. 1. vessel, receptacle for liquids, can, pail, basin, etc. (plate V 2). 2. barrel, cask. 3. (obs.) ship.

vasilhame s. m. a lot of vessels or casks.
vaso s. m. 1. vase, flowerpot. 2. vessel: a) receptacle, urn, bowl, pot, jar (palte V 2). b) ship. 3. chamberpot, pan of a closet bowl (plate P 19). 4. (anat.) vein, artery. 5. (astr.) Urn. 6. (obs.) black fabric (for mourning).
~ **aéreo** (bot.) air vessel. ~ **de flores** flower vase. ~ **de guerra** man-of-war, capital ship. ~ **linfático** (anat.) cistern. ~ **de rio** river bed. ~ **sagrado** patina. ~ **sangüíneo** blood vessel.
vasomotor (also **vasimotor**) s. m. (anat.) vasomotor.
vasoso adj. = **vasento**.
vasquear v. (Braz.) 1. to become scarce. 2. to feel sick, nauseated.
vasqueiro adj. (Braz.) 1. nauseating. 2. scarce, not abundant. 3. rare. 4. difficult. 5. squint-eyed.
tempo ~ hard times.
vasquejar v. 1. to feel sick, have nauseas, be in convulsions. 2. to tremble, flicker. 3. to agonize. 4. to vacillate.
vasquim s. m. (pl. **-ins**) (Braz.) bodice.
vasquinha s. f. (obs.) 1. dress with many pleats around the waist. 2. bodice.
vassalagem s. f. (pl. **-ens**) 1. vassalage: a) state of being a vassal. b) tribune of a vassal. c) fealty. d) servitude. 2. a number of vassals.
vassalar v. to render tribute as a vassal.
vassalo s. m. vassal, feudatory, liege, subject, dependant. ‖ adj. vassal, feudatory.
vassoura s. f. (also **vassoira**) 1. broom, besom, sweeping-brush (plates E 8, 11). 2. (Braz., sl.) man with many love affairs. 3. m. apprentice in an office. 4. inferior employee.
~ **mecânica** dirt scraper. **cabo de** ~ broomstick.
vassourada s. f. (also **vassoirada**) 1. blow with a broom(stick). 2. sweep(ing). 3. sweepings.
vassoura-do-campo s. f. (pl. **vassouras-do-campo**) (bot.) switch sorel.
vassourar v. (also **vassoirar**) to sweep, broom.
vassoureiro s. m. (also **vassoireiro**) broommaker, broom seller.
vassourinha s. f. (also **vassoirinha**) 1. wisp, whisk, whisk broom. 2. a children's game. 3. name of a Portuguese song. 4. (bot.) broomweed.
vassouro s. m. (also **vassoiro**) oven broom.
vastidão s. f. (pl. **-ões**) 1. vastness, wideness, ampleness, amplitude, immenseness, hugeness. 2. momentousness.
vasto adj. vast: 1. great, colossal, huge. 2. ample, wide, extensive. 3. far-flung. 4. (fig.) great, important, prodigious. ‖ **-amente** adv. vastly.
vatapá s. m. Brazilian dish (made of manioc flour, oil, pepper, fish, meat).
vate s. m. 1. soothsayer, prophet. 2. poet.
vaticana s. f. the Vatican library.
Vaticano s. m. Vatican: 1. the pope's seat. 2. the papal authority. ‖ adj. Vatican.
vaticinador s. m. diviner, vaticinator, foreseer, foreteller, foreboder, prophet. ‖ adj. vaticinal, prophetic(al).
vaticinante adj. m. + f. vaticinal.
vaticinar v. to vaticinate, foretell, prophesy, predict, divine, prognosticate, presage, augur.
vaticínio s. m. (also **vaticinação** f.) vaticination, foretelling, prediction, divining, prognostication, prophecy.
vatídico adj. vaticinal, oracular.
vau s. m. 1. ford, crossing, passage. 2. shallow, shoal, sandbank. 3. reef. 4. chance, occasion. 5. (naut.) beam.
~ **de orelha** (Braz.) river crossing where a horse must swim. ~ **de cauda** (Braz.) river crossing

where a horse can wade. ~ **de convés** (naut.) deck beam. **passar a** ~ to ford or cross a river.
vaudeville s. m. (Fr.) vaudeville, variety.
vavassalo s. m. a vassal's vassal.
vavavá s. m. (Braz.) 1. din, noise, uproar, hubbub, agitation. 2. bustle, hushing, running.
vaza s. f. 1. cards played in one round, book. 2. carved work.
vaza-barris s. m., sg. + pl. 1. reefy coast causing many shipwrecks. 2. (fig.) place of hidden riches. 3. (coll.) ruin.
vazador s. m. 1. goldsmith. 2. bit, boring tool, punch. 3. melter, founder; carver (see **vazar**). ‖ adj. boring; melting; carving (see **vazar**).
~ **para correias** belt punch.
vazadouro s. m. (also **vazadoiro**) 1. refuse pit. 2. sewer.
vazamento s. m. (also **vazadura** f.) 1. leak, leakage, leakiness, seepage. 2. melting, founding. 3. emptying, spilling. 4. flow, discharge (river). 5. carving.
vazante s. f. 1. ebb tide, low water. 2. (Braz.) bottoms, holm, lowland at the margin of a river. ‖ adj. m. + f. receding.
índice da ~ low-water mark. **início da** ~ the beginning of the ebb.
vazanteiro s. m. (N. Braz.) holm farmer or inhabitant of the lowlands of river margins.
vazão s. f. (pl. **-ões**) 1. sewage. 2. flowing out, outflow. 3. flow, discharge (river). 4. emptying. 5. vent. 6. sales. 7. conclusion (business, sales). 8. outlet.
ele achou um meio para dar ~ **à sua má índole** he found an outlet for his bad temper.
vazar v. 1. to empty. 2. to spill. 3. to pour out. 4. to drain. 5. to leak, ooze. 6. to flow into, discharge, run (river). 7. to tear out (eye). 8. to carve. 9. to hollow out, excavate. 10. to drink. 11. to found, melt, cast. 12. to conquer. 13. to recess, decrease, ebb. 14. to be transparent.
o tanque está vazando the tank is leaking.
vazia s. f. (pop.) hip, haunch.
vaziador adj. said of a horse that evacuates too much.
vaziamento s. m. = **esvaziamento**.
vaziar v. 1. = **esvaziar**. 2. evacuate too much (horse).
vazio s. m. 1. emptiness, vacuum, vacuity. 2. blank. 3. vanity. 4. deficiency. 5. (anat.) flank, side. 6. ~**s** pl. haunch (horse). ‖ adj. 1. empty (plate Q). 2. unoccupied, vacant, vacuous. 3. void, vain, futile, silly, inane. 4. uninhabited, deserted. 5. blank. 6. meaningless. ‖ **-amente** adv. emptily.
corre em ~ (tech.) it runs free. **teatro** ~ a thin house. **ele olhou o** ~ he stared into the space.
vaziúdo adj. (Braz.) lean, shaky (horse).
veação s. f. (pl. **-ões**) 1. hunting of wild animals. 2. game, venison.
veada s. f. hind (female of the red deer).
veadeiro s. m. 1. deerhound, buckhound. 2. deer hunter.
veado s. m. 1. hart, stag, male deer, red deer. 2. (Braz. vulg.) homosexual, pansy.
~ **de dois anos** brocket, pricket. ~ **de quatro anos** staggart. ~ **gordo** hart of grease. ~ **com armação de dez pontas** hart of ten. **bancar** ~ **to** run away.
veador s. m. (obs.) hunter, huntsman.
vearia s. f. house to keep the venison.
vectação s. f. (pl. **-ões**) act or fact of riding (on a vehicle).
vector s. m. (geom.) vector (plate A 9). ‖ adj. vectorial.
veda s. f. 1. (hunt.) close season. 2. prohibition.
Veda s. m. (rel.) Veda.

vedação s. f. (pl. -ões) 1. prohibition. 2. impediment, hindrance. 3. stoppage. 4. closing. 5. barrier. 6. shutting off, blocking. 7. enclosure, fence. 8. packing, gasket, şeal(ing).

vedado adj. 1. forbidden, prohibited. 2. walled in, fenced in.

vedar v. 1. to impede. 2. to hinder, hamper. 3. to prohibit, forbid, interdict, proscribe. 4. to stop, bar. 5. to close, shut, stunch. 6. to enclose, fence in. 7. to seal. ~ **com pregão** to decry. ~ **um rombo** to stop a leak.

vedável adj. m. + f. (pl. -áveis) that can be impeded, prohibited, stopped, etc.

vedeta s. f. 1. (mil., naut.) vedette. 2. advanced guard. 3. mounted sentinel. 4. (theat., cin.) star.

vedeta-da-praia s. f. (pl. **vedetas-da-praia**) (ornith.) sanderling.

vedete s. f. (theat., cin., TV) star (woman).

vedetismo s. m. stardom, celebrity.

védico adj. (rel.) Vedaic.

vedismo s. m. (rel.) Vedaism.

vedo s. m. 1. fence, enclosure. 2. (bot.) pipal.

vedóia s. m. (N. Braz.) cheat, swindler, sharper, impostor, rogue.

vedor s. m. 1. overseer, inspector, controller, fiscal. 2. intendant. 3. person who searches for springs.

vedoria s. f. office or function of an inspector or overseer.

veeiro s. m. (Braz.) vein of ore.

veemência s. f. 1. vehemence, vehemency. 2. passion, ardour, fervour. 3. eagerness, violence, impetuosity. 4. vivacity. 5. keenness.

veemente adj. m. + f. 1. vehement. 2. impetuous, violent. 3. enthusiastic, fervorous, passionate. 4. irritable. 5. boisterous. 6. vigorous. || ~**mente** adv. vehemently.

vegetabilidade s. f. vegetability.

vegetação s. f. (pl. -ões) vegetation: 1. plant life; plants. 2. (med.) exuberance, morbid outgrow. 3. growth. ~ **rasteira** underbrush. **cobrir de** ~ to overgrow.

vegetal s. m. (pl. -ais) plant, vegetal, vegetable. || adj. m. + f. vegetal, vegetable. **reino** ~ vegetable kingdom. **gordura** ~ vegetable fat. **vida** ~ botany.

vegetalidade s. f. vegetality.

vegetalina s. f. antidote to snake poison.

vegetalizar v. 1. to shape like a vegetal. 2. to take the form of a plant.

vegetante adj. m. + f. vegetating.

vegetar v. to vegetate: 1. grow as plants, lead a passive life; drift along. 2. produce vegetation. 3. (med.) produce outgrowths.

vegetarianismo s. m. vegetarianism.

vegetariano s. m. vegetarian. || adj. vegetarian. **regime** ~ vegetable diet.

vegetarista s. m. + f. vegetarian who admits milk, butter, eggs, etc.

vegetativo adj. vegetative: 1. fertile, productive. 2. plantlike, plantal. 3. (biol.) autonomous.

vegetável adj. m. + f. (pl. -áveis) vegetable, vegetative.

végeto adj. vigorous, strong.

vegetoanimal adj. m. + f. (pl. -ais) vegeto-animal.

veia s. f. 1. vein: a) blood vessel. b) grain (of wood); streak, wave, cloud (of marble). c) (min.) fissure in a rock, bed of mineral, lode, thread. d) underground water. e) tendency, vocation, gift, streak. f) (bot.) fibre forming the framework of a leaf. g) disposition, humo(u)r. 2. (fig.) core, main point.

~ **de poeta** poetical vein. ~ **jugular** (anat.) jugular vein. **sua** ~ **secou** his humour has dried up. **ele tem** ~ **artística** he is of an artistic vein. **não estou de** ~ **para brincar** I am in no mood for joking. **com** ~**s** veined. **sem** ~**s** veinless.

veia-artéria s. f. pulmonary vein.

veiculador adj. transporting, transmitting.

veicular (I) adj. m. + f. vehicular.

veicular (II) v. 1. to transport in a vehicle. 2. to introduce. 3. to transmit, propagate, diffuse.

veículo s. m. vehicle: 1. means of transport, conveyance. 2. means of transmission or promotion; medium. 3. (pharm.) excipient. ~ **a motor** motor vehicle (plate V 3). **servir de** ~ to act as transmitter.

veieira s. f. (Braz.) beehive.

veiga s. f. holm, bottoms, plain.

veio s. m. 1. (min., geol.) vein, lode, thread, streak, seam. 2. brook, rivulet. 3. (mech.) shaft, spindle, arbor, axle. 4. (fig.) main point, essence. 5. cloud (of marble). 6. (Braz.) crank. ~ **mineral** dike. ~ **metálico** reef. ~ **de carvão** coal seam. **com** ~**s** grainy.

veirado adj. (her.) vairy.

veiro s. m. vair: 1. ~**s** pl. costly furs. 2. their heraldic representation.

veiúdo adj. said of a hound that sometimes hunts well sometimes not.

veja! interj. look! come! lo! see!

vela (I) s. f. 1. (naut.) sail, convas, sheet (plate B 10). 2. (fig.) ship. 3. vane of a windmill. ~ **ao torço** lugsail. ~ **de capa** storm sail. ~ **de carangueja** trysail. ~ **de estai** staysail. ~ **de joanete** topgallant, topsail. ~ **latina** storm jib. ~ **mestra** main sail (plate B 10). **abaixar as** ~**s** to strike sails. **à** ~ under sail. **a toda** ~ under (full) sail. **diminuir as** ~**s** to take in sail. **fazer-se à** ~ to set sail, depart. **levantar a** ~ to go under sail. **sem** ~**s** under bare poles.

vela (II) s. f. 1. candle. 2. candle power. 3. light. 4. (med.) bougie. 5. wake, watch, vigil. ~ **de cera** bougie, taper. ~ **de estearina** composite candle, stearic candle. ~ **de ignição** sparking plug, spark plug (plate M 13). ~ **de sebo** tallow candle. **estar com a** ~ **na mão** to be dying.

velacho s. m. 1. (naut.) fore-topsail. 2. (Braz.) nickname.

vela-da-pureza s. f. (pl. **velas-da-pureza**) (bot.) Spanish dagger.

velado adj. 1. veiled. 2. covered, hidden, concealed. 3. wakeful (night).

velador s. m. 1. wooden candlestick. 2. watcher. || adj. watchful, watching.

veladura s. f. 1. watch, veiling. 2. wakefulness. 3. (paint.) glazing.

velame(n) s. m. 1. the whole set of sails of a ship. 2. (fig.) disguise, mask, veil. ~ **do pára-quedas** (aeron.) canopy.

velame-branco s. m. (pl. **velames-brancos**) (bot.) flannelflower.

velamento s. m. 1. veiling. 2. (fig.) concealing, hiding. 3. blurring.

velar (I) v. 1. to veil. 2. to conceal, hide. 3. to keep secret. 4. to darken, cloud, shadow; overcast. 5. to overpaint.

velar (II) v. 1. to wake: a) watch, guard. b) be or keep awake. c) keep watch or vigil. d) sit up with a (sick) person. 2. to keep burning (lamp). 3. ~**-se** to stand upon one's guard. 4. to be greatly interested in. 5. to protect, give support, patronize, back.

velar s. f. (gram.) velar. || adj. m. + f. velar.

V 3

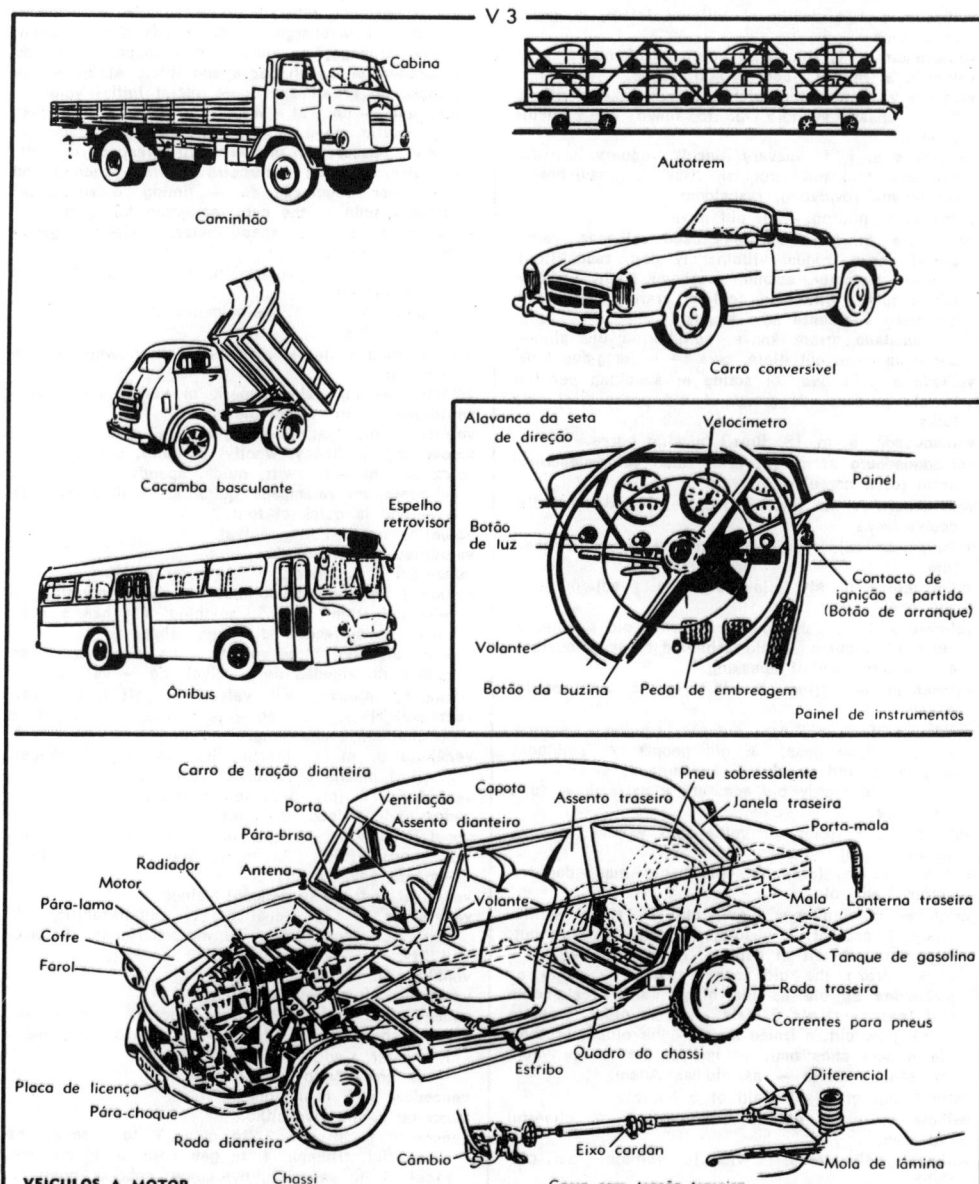

Cabina

Caminhão

Autotrem

Carro conversível

Caçamba basculante

Espelho retrovisor

Ônibus

Alavanca da seta de direção

Velocímetro

Painel

Botão de luz

Contacto de ignição e partida (Botão de arranque)

Volante

Botão da buzina — Pedal de embreagem

Painel de instrumentos

Carro de tração dianteira

Porta
Ventilação
Capota
Assento traseiro
Pneu sobressalente
Janela traseira

Pára-brisa
Assento dianteiro
Porta-mala

Radiador
Antena
Motor
Pára-lama
Volante
Mala
Lanterna traseira
Cofre
Tanque de gasolina
Farol
Roda traseira
Correntes para pneus

Placa de licença
Estribo
Quadro do chassi
Diferencial
Pára-choque

Roda dianteira
Câmbio
Eixo cardan
Mola de lâmina

VEÍCULOS A MOTOR
Chassi
Carro com tração traseira

velário s. m. (hist.) velarium.
velarização s. f. (pl. -ões) (gram.) velarization.
velarizar v. (gram.) to velarize.
velatura s. f. an overpainting.
velear v. to equip or provide with sails.
veleidade s. f. 1. velleity, fancy, caprice, whim, faint wish, slight desire, freak. 2. fickleness, inconstancy. 3. utopia.
veleira s. f. outdoor maid of a sister's convent.
veleiro (I) s. m. 1. sailing ship, sailing vessel, sailer, windjammer (plate P 16). 2. sailmaker. ‖ adj. fast--sailing; fast.

veleiro (II) s. m. condlemaker.
veleiro (III) s. m. outdoor servant of a monastery.
velejar v. to sail; navigate.
~ **novamente** to resail. ~ **melhor** to outsail.
velenho s. m. (bot.) henbane.
veleta s. f. weathercock: 1. weather vane. 2. fickle person, chameleon.
velha s. f. 1. old woman; crone. 2. (fam.) mother. 3. (pop.) death.
coisas do arco-da-velha things to write home about.
contos de ~ old woman's tales.
velhacaço s. m. villain, rogue, scoundrel.

velhacada s. f. 1. devilment, villainy, infamy. 2. group of villains.

velhacagem s. f. (pl. **-ens**) villainy, infamy.

velhacão s. m. (pl. **-ões**) villain, rogue.

velhacar v. 1. to act roguishly, behave like a villain. 2. to cheat, swindle. 3. to leave one's debts unpaid.

velhacaria s. f. 1. knavery, deceit, roguery, artifice, foxiness, foul play, roguish trick. 2. knavishness, ruffianism, rowdyism, rascaldom.

velhaças s. m., sg. + pl. old man.

velhaco s. m. (also but less used **velhacaz, velhacório**) knave, rogue, villain, sly dog, rascal(lion), sharper, swindler, scamp, vagabond. || adj. 1. knavish, roguish, villainous, foxlike, crafty, trickish. 2. dissolute. || **-amente** adv. knavishly.

~ **rematado** arrant knave, hard-boiled old sinner. **ser mais** ~ to outvillain. **cara de** ~ hang-dog look.

velhada s. f. 1. way of acting or speaking peculiar to old persons. 2. group of old persons. 3. old folks.

velhaqueador s. m. (S. Braz.) bucking horse.

velhaqueadouro s. m. (S. Braz., also **velhaqueadoiro**) groin (of a horse).

velhaquear v. to cheat, deceive, fraud, swindle, double-cross.

velhaquesco adj. 1. roguish, knavish, foxy. 2. libertine.

velhaquete s. m. sly fellow, slyboots. || adj. m. + f. sly, foxy.

velharia s. f. 1. behaviour peculiar to old people. 2. old stuff, rubbish. 3. old-fashioned habit or custom. 4. obsolete way of speaking.

velhantado adj. (less used form of **avelhantado**) oldish, old.

velhice s. f. 1. old age, oldness, agedness, elderliness. 2. hoar(iness). 3. old people. 4. sulkiness peculiar to old people. 5. anecdotage.

~ **vigorosa** sturdy old age. **até a extrema** ~ to a great age.

velhinha s. f. (dim. of **velha**) old woman, granny, gammer. || adj. f. old.

velhinho s. m. (dim. of **velho**) old man, dad(dy), gaffer. || adj. old.

velho s. m. old man. || adj. old: 1. aged, senile, hoary. 2. ancient. 3. obsolete, archaic. 4. worn out. 5. antiquated, out of date. 6. often practised.

o ~ (Braz.) the old man (father). ~ **como as pirâmides** as old as the hills. **Velho Testamento** Old Testament. **ele é mais** ~ he is older. **fazer-se** ~ to grow old. **o irmão mais** ~ the eldest brother. **ele é seis anos mais** ~ que eu he is six years my senior. **muito** ~ as old as Adam.

velhori adj. gray(ish) (said of a horse).

velhote s. m. 1. elderly man, oldster. 2. cheerful old man.

velhusco, velhustro s. m. (fam.) = **velhote**. || adj. old-(ish).

velicação s. f. (pl. **-ões**) pinching.

velicar v. to pinch.

velicativo adj. 1. pinching. 2. pungent.

velífero adj. (poet.) carrying sails.

velilho s. m. 1. a sort of gauze. 2. transparent veil.

velino s. m. vellum: paper resembling parchment.

velívago adj. that sails, that is propelled by sails.

velívolo adj. that sails quickly.

velo s. m. 1. fleece, clip. 2. carded wool. 3. hide or wool of cattle.

~ **de ouro** the Golden Fleece.

veloce adj. m. + f. = **veloz**.

velocidade s. f. velocity, speed(iness), fastness, swiftness, quickness, celerity.

~ **ascensional** rate of climb. ~ **de escoamento** velocity of discharge. ~ **de picada** diving speed. ~ **de propagação** velocity of propagation. ~ **do obturador** (phot.) shutter speed (plate M 3). ~ **em relação ao ar** air speed. ~ **inicial** initial velocity. **com uma** ~ **de...** at a velocity of... **em** ~ **espantosa** at a terrific speed, at full tear. **grande** ~ posthaste, tantivy. **passar com grande** ~ to sweep by or past. **primeira, segunda e terceira** ~ first, second and third gear. **regulação de** ~ timing. **o automóvel corria a toda** ~ the car was going top gear.

velocímetro s. m. speedometer; velocity gauge (plates B 15, V 3).

velocino s. m. 1. sheepskin, fell. 2. (myth.) the Golden Fleece.

velocípede s. m. 1. velocipede. 2. bicycle. || adj. quick, nimble.

velocipedista s. m. + f. cyclist; person who rides a velocipede.

velocíssimo adj. (abs. superl. of **veloz**) very swift.

velódromo s. m. velodrome.

velório s. m. deathwatch, lyke-wake.

veloso adj. 1. fleecy, woolly. 2. hairy, shaggy.

veloz adj. m. + f. swift, quick, speedy, fast, flying.

~ **como um relâmpago** quick as a lightning. **ela é** ~ she is quick of foot.

veludilho s. m. cotton velvet.

veludíneo adj. velvetlike.

veludinha s. f. velvetlike fabric for padding.

veludo s. m. (dim. **veludinho**) 1. velvet, velveting. 2. velure; fustian; sag. 3. anything that has a soft, velvetlike surface. || adj. hairy, shaggy.

~ **de algodão** cotton velvet. ~ **de lã** velour. ~ **de seda e de algodão** terry velvet. **de** ~ velvet.

veludoso, velutíneo adj. velvetlike, soft like velvet.

vem-cá-siriri s. m., sg. + pl. (Braz.) name of a popular dance and song.

venábulo s. m. 1. javelin, hunting spear, assegai. 2. (fig.) means of defence; resource.

venação s. f. (pl. **-ões**) venery, hunting.

venado adj. veined, that has veins.

venal (I) adj. m. + f. (pl. **-ais**) venal: 1. purchasable. 2. corrupt(ible). 3. mercenary. 4. prostitute. || ~**mente** adv. venally.

venal (II) adj. (also **venoso**) veined.

venalidade s. f. venality: 1. purchasability. 2. corruption, corruptness. 3. mercenariness. 4. bribability.

venalizar v. to corrupt, bribe.

venatório adj. venatic(al).

vencedor s. m. 1. conqueror, victor, conquistador, vanquisher, queller, defeater. 2. winner, champion. 3. master. || adj. victor, victorious.

~ **de um prêmio** prize winner.

vencedora s. f. championess.

vencelho s. m. = **vencilho**.

vencer v. 1. to win. 2. to gain. 3. to succeed, be successful, triumph. 4. to get, earn. 5. to surpass, excel. 6. to vanquish, overcome, subdue, quell. 7. to restrain, repress. 8. to master, overpower, surmount. 9. to resist, withstand. 10. to persuade. 11. to cover a distance. 12. to expire, fall due. 13. (sl.) to lick, whack. 14. to overcrowd, overplay, tide over.

~ **dificuldades** to overcome difficulties, to wangle, win through. ~ **ou morrer** to do or die. ~**am** they made their way. **vencemos** we won the day. **vencemos nossos inimigos** we triumphed over our enemies. ~ **a resistência** to wear down the resistance. ~ **de longe** to drub. ~ **no jogo** to outplay. ~ **em número de votos** to outvote. **vence-se o pagamento** the payment becomes due. ~**am de** (or **por**) **três a um** (football) they won three to one. **pagamentos a** ~

payments due. **o aluguel vence no dia primeiro** the rent is up on the first. **precisamos tentar ~** we must try to succeed. **ela venceu a crise** she turned the corner. **nossos amigos vencem a demanda** our friends carry the cause. **ele venceu-o lutando** he wresfled him down. **ele venceu-o facilmente** he took it in his stride.

vencibilidade s. f. vincibility.

vencida s. f. = **vencimento**.
levar de ~ to get the better of.

vencido s. m. loser, underdog. || adj. 1. vanquished, overcome, subdued, conquered. 2. beaten. 3. (sl.) washed up. 4. (com.) due, payable.
~ há muito tempo long past due. **ainda não ~** 1. (com.) undue. 2. unsubdued. **dar-se por ~** to throw up the sponge. **ter ~ as maiores dificuldades** to be out of the wood. **título ~** a past due bill.

vencilho s. f. (also **vencelho**) 1. a sort of straw rope. 2. osier or the like used to bind sheaves.

vencimento s. m. 1. conquest, overcoming. 2. triumph. 3. expiration, maturity, matureness. 4. appointment, salary, earnings.
~ do prazo expiration of the term. **dia de ~** date or day of maturity. **no ~** when due. **no ~ de** on the expiration of. **pagável no ~** payable when due. **não dar ~ a** not to answer to, not to provide for.

vencível adj. m. + f. (pl. **-íveis**) 1. conquerable, superable, vencible. 2. (com.) that becomes due.
letra ~ em trinta dias bill payable in thirty days.

venda s. f. 1. sale, selling. 2. grocery, grog-shop. 3. bandage over the eyes, blindfold (also fig.).
~ a prazo sales on instalment. **~ a varejo** retail. **~ à vista** cash down sales. **~ especial a preços reduzidos** bargain sale. **~ com antecedência** advance booking. **~ em leilão** sale by auction. **~ por atacado** wholesale. **~ pública** public sale. **~s obtidas** turnover. **~s rápidas** quick returns. **à ~** for sale. **à ~ em** to be had at. **comissão sobre as ~s** sales commission. **condições de ~** terms of sale. **de má ~** unsalable. **direito exclusivo de ~** exclusive sales rights. **imposto sobre as ~s** sales tax. **preço de ~** sales price. **secção de ~s** sales department. **ter boa ~** to meet with good sales.

vendado adj. veiled, blindfold.

vendagem s. f. (pl. **-ens**) 1. = **venda**. 2. sales comission. 3. blindfolding.

vendar v. 1. to blindfold, veil, hood. 2. (fig.) to prevent from seeing, confuse, obscure.
~ os olhos to hoodwink.

vendaval s. m. (pl. **-ais**) windstorm, storm, gale.

vendável adj. m. + f. (pl. **-áveis**) 1. sal(e)able, vendible. 2. negotiable, marketable, merchantable.

vendedeira s. f. saleswoman, female street vendor.

vendedor s. m. 1. salesman, seller, vendor. 2. agent. 3. monger. 4. bargainor. 5. shop assistant.
~ ambulante chapman, tranter, huckster(er). **~ de cereais ou sementes** corn chandler. **~ de leite** dairyman. **~ de pássaros, cães e outros animais** fancier. **~ de tintas** colourman.

vendedora s. f. 1. saleswoman, saleslady. 2. lady-clerk, shop-girl, shop assistant. 3. bargainor.
~ de leite dairymaid, dairywoman.

vendedouro s. m. (obs., also **vendedoiro**) market place. || adj. saleable.

vendeiro s. m. 1. innkeeper. 2. grocer.

vendelhão s. m. (pl. **-ões**) (Braz.) 1. = **vendeiro**. 2. huckster(er).

vendemiário s. m. Vendémiaire: first month of the calendar of the French Revolution.

vender v. to sell: 1. vend, dispose of. 2. make sales, deal in. 3. be sold. 4. betray.
~ a crédito to trust. **~ a prazo** to sell on instalments. **~ a preço de banana** to knock down for a song. **~ a preço mais elevado, mais caro** to oversell, outsell. **~ à vista** to sell cash. **~ cara a sua vida** to sell one's life dearly. **~ com redução, ~ a preço inferior** to undersell, to cut under. **~ em leilão** to outcry, auction. **~ no varejo** to retail. **~ pelas ruas** to cadge, hawk. **~ por atacado** to wholesale. **~ por qualquer preço** to force off. **vende-se** (advertisement) to be sold, for sale. **vende-se bem** it sells well. **vende-se como pão quente** it sells like hot cake. **oferecê-lo-ei para ~** I'll put it up for sale. **tornar a ~** to resell.

vendeta s. f. vendetta, blood feud, blood revenge.

vendibilidade s. f. vendibility, saleability.

vendição s. f. (pl. **-ões**) (rare) sale.

vendido s. m. person who sold himself, cheat, traitor. || adj. 1. sold. 2. bribed. 3. betrayed. 4. ill at ease, surprised, disappointed.
achar-se ~ to be betrayed or cheated. **estar, sentir-se ~** to feel uncomfortable, ill at ease. **o carro tem de ser ~** the car must go.

vendilhão s. m. (pl. **-ões**) (f. **-ona**) hucksterer, hawker, peddler.

vendista s. m. + f. shopkeeper, innkeeper.

vendível adj. (pl. **-íveis**) saleable, vendible, marketable.

venefício s. m. empoisoning.

venéfico adj. 1. venefical, poisonous. 2. malefic, harmful.

venenífero adj. veneniferous.

veneníparo adj. that segregates poison.

veneno s. m. 1. poison, venom, bane. 2. toxine, toxicant. 3. virus, virulence. 4. (fig.): a) anything dangerous, corruptive or deadly. b) malignity, rancour. c) malignant, spiteful person. 5. (vet.) a sort of carbuncle.
~ para ratos ratsbane. **deitar ~** (fig.) to spit poison. **dente de ~** poison fang. **sem ~** venomless. **temo o ~ de sua pena** I fear the virulency of his pen.

venenosidade s. f. poisonousness, venomousness.

venenoso adj. 1. poisonous, poison, venomous, toxic(ant), nocuous, baneful, virulent. 2. (fig.): a) deleterious, viparine, snaky. b) malignant, spiteful. c) pestilent. || **-amente** adv. poisonously, etc.
cobra -a poisonous snake. **uma língua -a** (fig.) a venomous tongue.

venera s. f. 1. scallop shell. 2. token of a military order. 3. condecoration.

venerabilidade s. f. venerability, venerableness.

venerabundo adj. reverent, worshipful.

veneração s. f. (pl. **-ões**) 1. veneration, worship, adoration, cult. 2. reverence, respect. 3. dread. 4. hero worship.

venerado adj. 1. venerated, adored, worshipped. 2. reverenced, respected, esteemed.

venerador s. m. worshipper, adorer, venerator, reverencer. || adj. worshipful.

venerar v. 1. to venerate, worship, adore. 2. to revere, respect greatly, regard.

venerável s. m. master of a Freemasons' lodge. || adj. m. + f. (pl. **-áveis**) (also **venerando** m.) 1. venerable, worthy of veneration, worshipful, revered. 2. respectable. 3. sacred. 4. antique, ancient. || **veneravelmente** adv. venerably.

venéreo s. m. (pop.) syphilis. || adj. 1. vener(e)al. 2. sensual, erotic.
doença -a venereal disease.

venereologia s. f. (med.) venereology.

venereologista s. m. + f. (med.) venereologist.

vênero adj. of or pertaining to Venus.

veneta s. f. 1. fit of madness, frenzy. 2. whim(sy), fancy, freak, caprice, humour; crinkum-crankum. **deu-lhe na ~ de ir embora** he got it in his head to leave.

veneziana s. f. Venetian blind, sun blind, shutter, jalousie, shade.

veneziano s. m. Venetian: native or inhabitant of Venetia. ‖ adj. Venetian.

venezolano, venezuelano s. m. Venezuelan: native or inhabitan of Venezuela. ‖ adj. Venezuelan.

vênia s. f. 1. permission, leave. 2. pardon. 3. bow, reverence.

veniaga s. f. 1. merchandise, commodity. 2. trickery, cheat, fraud.

veniagar v. 1. to trade, do business. 2. do deal fraudulently, swindle.

venial adj. m. + f. (pl. -ais) venial, slight, trifling (esp. of sins). ‖ ~mente adv. venially.

venialidade s. f. veniality, venialness.

venida s. f. 1. sudden attack. 2. investigation. 3. (fencing) blow, pass.

venifluo adj. that flows in the veins.

venoso adj. 1. veined, veiny. 2. of or pertaining to veins.

venta s. f. 1. nostril. 2. ~s pl. nose. 3. (fig.) face. 4. person with a stub nose. **acender as ~s** (N. Braz.) to sense danger (horse or dog). **atirar uma recusa nas ~s de alguém** to throw a refusal into a person's face. **dar a ~** (Braz.) to tire, exhaust. **de cabelinho na ~** cross as two sticks. **ficar de ~s inchadas** (Braz.) to pout, be vexed. **dizer tudo o que vem às ~s** (fam.) to speak freely, open up, bare one's mind. **esfregar nas ~s de** to rub a th. in a person's teeth.

ventana s. f. (obs.) 1. window. 2. pockets of a billiard table. 3. fan. 4. steeple window. 5. (Braz.) rowdy, rough. 6. malicious horse.

ventanear v. 1. to air, ventilate, fan. 2. to shake, agitate.

ventaneira s. f. 1. = ventania. 2. (bellows) clack valve. **saber onde ter as ~s** to know what's what.

ventanejar v. 1. to blow, wind. 2. (pop.) to fart.

ventania s. f. windstorm, blow, gale, flaw, wind.

ventanilha s. f. pocket of a billiard table.

ventanista s. m. (Braz., sl.) thief who enters through the window.

ventar v. 1. to blow, wind, breathe, bluster. 2. to fart. 3. to be favourable. 4. to manifest, evidence suddenly.

ventarola s. f. fan.

venteira s. f. a calf's muzzle (to prevent it from sucking).

ventena s. f. 1. = ventana. 2. (pop.) harlot, prostitute.

ventígeno adj. that produces wind.

ventilabro s. m. winnowing machine.

ventilação s. f. (pl. -ões) 1. ventilation, airing, aeration (plate V 3). 2. (fig.) discussion, debate. **falta de ~** closeness.

ventilador s. m. ventilator, aerator, fan (plates M 3, V 1). ‖ adj. ventilating. **~ centrífugo** fan blower.

ventilar v. to ventilate: 1. air, expose to air, aerate. 2. blow. 3. fan. 4. vent. 5. agitate. 6. winnow. 7. discuss, debate.

ventilativo adj. ventilative.

ventinho s. m. (dim. of vento) draught of air, breathing, gentle breeze, cat's-paw.

vento s. m. 1. wind: a) air, draught of air, drift. b) flatulence. c) scent (also fig.). d) vanity e) influence. 2. flaw in a casting. 3. (fig.) something quick.

~s alísios trade-winds. **~ contrário** head wind, contrary wind; noser. **~ de popa** tail wind. **~ duro** (Braz.) steady wind. **~s equinociais** equinoctials. **~ favorável** fair wind. **~ intenso, forte,** gale, buster. **~ lateral** cross wind. **~ norte** Boreas. **~ sul** Notus, Auster. **~ variável** (naut.) variable. **à mercê do ~** adrift. **açoitado pelo ~** tempest-tossed, tempest-beaten. **levado pelo ~** before the wind, wind-blown; gone with the wind. **o barco ficou ao sabor do ~** the boat drove with the weather. **(velejar) contra o ~** (to sail) in the wind's eyes. **a favor do vento** on the wind. **retido por ~s contrários** wind-bound (naut.). **sem ~** 1. windless. 2. breathless. **ter ~ de bombordo** to be on the port tack. **o ~ amainou** the wind is down. **está soprando um ~ forte** the wind is very high. **rápido como o ~** on the wings of the wind. **espalhado por todos os ~s** thrown to the winds. **moinho de ~** windmill. **pelos quatro ~s** in all directions. **bons ~s o levem!** how good that he left! **ir de ~ em popa** 1. to sail under a fair wind. 2. (fig.) to prosper. **ver donde sopra o ~** to see which way the cat jumps. **eles sabem de onde o ~ sopra** they know where the wind hits. **ele vira a casaca de acordo com o ~** he sings and dances in all weather. **nós falamos ao ~** we spoke to the wind. **beber os ~s por** to be quite enthusiastic about. **aos quatro ~s** to the four winds, in all directions. **ver de que lado sopra o ~** to see how the wind blows.

ventoinha s. f. 1. weathercock, vane. 2. blower, fan. 3. (fig.) fickle person.

ventor s. m. dog that has a good scent; bloodhound.

ventosa s. f. 1. (med.) cupping glass, cup. 2. (zool.) sucker.

ventosidade s. f. 1. windiness. 2. flatus, flatulence, 3. exhalation.

ventoso s. m. Ventose: sixth month of the French Revolutionary calendar. ‖ adj. 1. windy, stormy, airy, blowy. 2. flatulent. 3. (fig.) futile, vain, arrogant.

vento-virado s. m. (Braz. pop.) 1. colic. 2. constipation.

ventral adj. m. + f. (pl. -ais) ventral.

ventre s. f. 1. venter, womb, belly, abdomen (plate G 1). 2. (fig.) core. **prisão de ~** constipation.

ventrícola adj. fond of good eating.

ventricular adj. m. + f. ventricular.

ventrículo s. m. (anat.) ventricle. **~ do coração ou do cérebro** ventricle of the heart or the brain.

ventrilavado adj. white-bellied (horse).

ventrilho s. m. bellyband (of a harness) (plate A 12).

ventriloquia s. f. ventriloquism.

ventriloquismo s. m. ventriloquism.

ventriloquista s. m. + f. ventriloquist.

ventríloquo s. m. ventriloquist, polyphonist. ‖ adj. ventriloquial, ventriloquistic.

ventripotente adj. m. + f. 1. strong-stomached. 2. fond of much good eating.

ventrudo adj. 1. potbellied, big-bellied. 2. fat, obese.

ventura s. f. 1. (good or bad) luck, fate, fortune, lot. 2. venture, jeopardy, hazard, risk, chance. 3. happiness, blessedness, felicity. **as ~s da vida** the perhapses of life. **à ~** at haphazard. **por~** perhaps.

venturo adj. future, coming.

venturoso adj. 1. lucky, fortunate, happy, felicitous. 2. hazardous.

vênula s. f. small vein.

venulado adj. that has small veins.

Vênus s. f. Venus: 1. Roman goddess. 2. beautiful woman. 3. planet. 4. (alchemy) copper.

Venusino s. m. Horace, the Roman poet. ‖ **venusino** adj. 1. Horatian. 2. Venusian.

venustidade s. f. beauty, gracefulness.

venusto adj. beautiful, graceful.

ver v. 1. to see, behold, regard, sight, descry, eye. 2. to watch, look at, scrutinize. 3. to witness. 4. to notice, observe. 5. to perceive. 6. to discern, understand. 7. to examine, find out. 8. to ponder, think. 9. to conclude. 10. to consider. 11. to reckon. 12. to imagine, conceive. 13. to foresee. 14. to be careful about, take care. 15. to visit, travel over. 16. to meet, pay a visit, call on (a person). 17. to recognize. 18. to attend, visit (doctor).
~ **a olho nu** to see with the naked eye. ~ **as coisas como são** to see things as they are. ~ **longe** (fig.) to see far. ~ **para crer** seeing is believing. ~ **por acaso** to see accidentally, oversee. ~-**se num aperto** to be in a tight spot. ~-**se obrigado** to see oneself compelled to. **deixe-me** ~! let me see! **agora estou vendo, agora compreendo** now I see. **ela está vendo coisas** she sees things. **está vendo!** there now! **ele faz que não vê** he shuts his eyes to. **fazer** ~ **a** to advert. **eu preciso fazê-lo** ~ **a verdade** I must open his eyes to the truth. **ela vê tudo, é atenta** she has her eyes about her. **eu vejo o assunto sob o mesmo prisma que ele** I see eye to eye with him on the question. **eu o vi pela primeira vez** I set my eyes on him for the first time. **gosto de vê-lo longe** he is my pet abomination. **isto é o que eu queria** ~ I'd watch it! **a meu** ~ in my estimation, as I take it, to my reckoning. **não tenho nada a** ~ **com isto** my hand is out, I have no truck with it. **não o vejo há anos** I have not seen him for years. **não o vi mais** I saw the last of him. **nunca chego a vê-lo** I never catch sight of him. **não posso vê-lo!** I hate the very sight of him. **o que os olhos não vêem o coração não sente** what the eyes do not see, the heart does not grieve over. **quem te viu e quem te vê!** you have been doing nicely! **vale a pena** ~ **isto** this is worth seeing. **vamos** ~! we shall see! **veja isto** attend to this. **veja lá!** be careful! **veja lá de não perdê-lo!** see you do not lose it! **vejo que é impossível** I find it impossible.

veracidade s. f. veracity, veraciousness, truthfulness, truth, verity, veritableness.
ela é a ~ **em pessoa** she is the soul of truthfulness.

vera-efígie s. f. (pl. **veras-efígies**) facsimile.

veranal adj. m. + f. (pl. **-ais**) summer(l)y.

veranear v. 1. to summer, estivate, rusticate. 2. to go to or be at a summer resort.

veraneio s. m. 1. (also **estação de** ~) summer resort. 2. act of spending the summer at a resort, at the seaside, the country.

veranista s. m. + f. holidayer, summerite, vacationer.

veranito s. m. light or short summer.

verão s. m. summer.
~ **de São Martinho** Indian summer. **casa de** ~ summerhouse. **férias de** ~ summer holidays. **hora de** ~ summertime. **na força do** ~ at the height of summer.

veras s. f. pl. realities, truths.
com todas as ~ truthfully, sincerely.

verascópio s. m. verascope: stereoscopic camera.

veratrina s. f. (pharm.) veratrine.

veratro s. m. (bot.) white hellebore.

veraz adj. m. + f. veracious, veritable, truthful.

verba s. f. 1. clause, item of a document. 2. available sum or amount. 3. budget. 4. commentary, note.

~ **para desemprego** dole. ~ **para imprevistos** contingency (amount). **votação de** ~ token vote.

verbal adj. m. + f. (pl. **-ais**) verbal: 1. (gram.) of or pertaining to a verb. 2. oral, not written, parol(e). ‖ ~**mente** adv. verbally, by word of mouth. **combinação** ~ verbal arrangement. **flexão** ~ (gram.) verbal inflexion.

verbalismo s. m. verbalism.

verbalista s. m. + f. verbalist. ‖ adj. following the style of the verbalists.

verbalização s. f. (pl. **-ões**) verbalization.

verbalizador s. m. verbalizer.

verbalizar v. to verbalize.

verbasco s. m. (bot.) verbascum, great mullein, Aaron's beard.

verbena s. f. (bot.) vervain, verbena.

verbenáceo adj. (bot.) verbenaceous.

verberação s. f. (pl. **-ões**) 1. flagellation, whipping, lashing. 2. fustigation. 3. reproof, censure, castigation.

verberador adj. m., **verberante** m. + f. 1. flagellant, beating. 2. punitive. 3. reprobative, reproachful.

verberão s. m. (bot.) vervain.

verberar v. 1. to flagellate, whip, flog. 2. to fustigate, punish. 3. to baste. 4. to censure, reprove. 5. to reproach. 6. to reverberate.

verberativo adj. verberative.

verbete s. m. 1. note, notice, jotting, annotation. 2. (Braz.) entry of a dictionary.

verbiagem s. f. (pl. **-ens**) verbiage, verbosity, wordiness.

verbo s. m. 1. (gram.) verb. 2. word, expression. 3. **o Verbo**: Jesus Christ, the Word.
~ **auxiliar** auxiliary verb. ~ **reflexivo** reflexive verb. ~ **transobjetivo** factitive verb. **rasgar o** ~ (Braz.) to deliver a speech.

verborragia s. f. (also **verborréia**) verbiage, wordiness, verbosity.

verborrágico, verborréico adj. verbose, wordy, prolix.

verbosidade s. f. 1. verbosity, verbalism, verbiage, verboseness. 2. talkativeness, loquaciousness. 3. burst of eloquence. 4. windiness.

verboso adj. 1. verbose, wordy. 2. talkative, loquacious, garrulous. 3. fluent. 4. prolix, diffuse, prolegomenous. 5. windy. ‖ **-amente** adv. verbosely, wordily.

verçudo adj. 1. leafy. 2. hairy, hirsute. 3. cross, sullen.

verdacho s. m. green paint. ‖ adj. greenish.

verdade s. f. 1. truth, true, verity, veracity. 2. correctness, exactness, justness. 3. faith, sincerity, fidelity. 4. fact, reality.
~! of a verity! ~ **evidente, nua** home truth. ~ **nua e crua** unvarnished truth, plain facts. ~ **é que...** the truth is that... **é** ~**!** very true! **é** ~**?** is it that so? **é a** ~**?** is that a fact? **é** ~ **então?** is it true then? **a** ~ **virá à tona** murder will out. **na** ~**!** indeed! faith! **em** ~**!** in all verity! **as** ~**s eternas** the eternal verities. **tomar como** ~ to take something as gospel. **mas será** ~**?** but quaere is it true? **para dizer a** ~ **as** a matter of fact, in truth. **para dizer a** ~**, não o admitirei** in fact, I won't put up with it. **dizer a** ~ to speak true. **duvido que seja a** ~ I doubt the truth of it. **não há nada de** ~ **nisto** there is no truth in it. **dizer as** ~**s a alguém** to tell s. o. home truths. **cair na** ~ to see, comprehend. **ser a** ~ **em pessoa** to be the personification of truth.

verdadeiro s. m. true, truth. ‖ adj. 1. true, truthful, veracious, veridical. 2. real, actual, virtual. 3. exact, certain. 4. sincere, reliable, honest. 5. genuine. ‖ **-amente** adv. truthfully, really, etc.

é um ~ absurdo it is a perfect nonsense. **um amigo ~** a true friend, a veritable friend. **ele mostrou seu ~ caráter** (fig.) he showed the cloven hoof. **ele é um ~ diabo** he is a devil incarnate. **tenho uma -a biblioteca** I've got a whole library. **mostrou-se ser ~** it proved (to be) true.

verdasca s. f. switch, rod, twig.

verdascada s. f. blow with a switch.

verdascar v. to beat with a switch.

verdasco s. m. sort of very sour wine.

verde s. m. 1. green colour. 2. green fodder. 3. (Braz.): a) rainy season. b) mate (beverage). c) first growth of the pastures after the yearly fires. ‖ adj. green: 1. coloured like grass, emerald. 2. verdant, verdurous. 3. immature, unripe. 4. (fig.) young, inexperienced, crude, tender, callow. 5. fresh, raw (meat). 6. flourishing. 7. vigorous.
~s anos da mocidade salad days. **~ como a grama** grass green. **de cor ~** greenly. **o ~ das plantas** verdancy, verdure. **com olhos ~s** green-eyed. **plantar o ~ para colher o maduro** (fig.) to beat about the bush. **estão ~s!** (fig.) sour grapes! **caldo ~** cabbage soup.

verdeal s. m. (pl. **-ais**) 1. beadle of the university of Coimbra. ‖ adj. m. + f. greenish.

verdear v. (Braz.) 1. to green (esp. of pastures). 2. to feed a horse on green fodder, let it graze on the pasture. 3. to drink mate.

verde-bexiga s. f. (pl. **verdes-bexiga**) dark-green colour, containing cows' gall.

verdecer v. 1. to green, make or become green. 2. = **verdear.**

verde-gaio s. m. (pl. **verdes-gaio**) name of a popular music and dance. ‖ adj. m. + f., sg. + pl. pale-green.

verdeio s. m. (also **verdejo**) 1. green fodder for a horse. 2. viridescence.

verdejante adj. m. + f. verdant, green(ing), virid, verdurous. ‖ **~mente** adv. verdantly.

verdejar v. (also **verdecer**) to green, be or become green.

verdelha s. f. (ornith.) yellow hammer.

verdelhão s. m. (pl. **-ões**) (ornith.) green linnet.

verde-mar s. m. (pl. **verdes-mar**) aquamarine, sea green. ‖ adj. m. + f., sg. + pl. green-blue.

verde-montanha s. m. (pl. **verdes-montanha**) dark-green. ‖ adj. m. + f., sg. + pl. dark-green.

verdezelha s. f. (bot.) bindweed.

verdete s. m. 1. (chem.) verdigris. 2. a kind of grape.

verdisseco adj. half dry, almost dry.

verdizela s. f. switch of a snare for birds.

verdoengo, verdolengo adj. not quite ripe.

verdor s. m. 1. verdure, verdancy, verdurousness, viridity. 2. (fig.) inexperience, rawness. 3. exuberance of vegetation, vigour.

verdoso adj. (also **esverdeado, verdejante**) 1. greenish, greeny. 2. not quite ripe. 3. verdant, verdurous.

verdugo s. m. 1. executioner, hangman, Jack Ketch, death's man. 2. (railway) flange. 3. (fig.) driver, tormentor, harrower, inhuman person. 4. small pointed knife. 5. (obs.) edgeless sword. 6. (naut.) channel of a ship.

verdura s. f. 1. greens, vegetable, garden-stuff, verdure; (U. S. A.) truck. 2. greenness: a) viridity, verdancy. b) (fig.) inexperience, youth, rawness.
as ~s da mocidade the wild oaths of youth.

verdureiro s. m. (S. Braz., also **verduleiro**) greengrocer.

vereação s. f. (pl. **-ões**) 1. town council. 2. office or dignity of a member of a town council; aldermanship. 3. period of such an office.

vereador s. m. town councillor, city father, alderman, assemblyman.

vereamento s. m., **vereança** f. aldermanship, aldermanry.

verear v. to act as an alderman.

verecúndia s. (obs.) shame.

verecundo adj. (obs.) shameful.

vereda s. f. 1. path, footpath, byway, bypath, short-cut (plates C 8, F 4). 2. (Braz.): a) swampy plains between hills and rivers. b) bottoms, holm. 3. direction, way. 4. occasion, moment.
de ~ right away.

veredeiro s. m. (Braz.) very dedicated farmer.

veredicto s. m. verdict: 1. judgement of a jury, finding, assize. 2. judgement, opinion.

verga s. f. 1. stick, switch, twig. 2. lath. 3. metal rod or bar. 4. (naut.) yard; crossjack, spar. 5. (archit.) drip moulding; linel. 6. furrow cut by a plough.
~ da mezena mizen yard. **~ redonda** square sail yard. **~ do joanete grande** main-topgallant yard.

vergada s. f. (bot.) bryony.

vergal s. m. (pl. **-ais**) trace (harness).

vergalhada s. f. 1. lash, stroke with a whip. 2. roguery, knavery, villainy.

vergalhão s. m. (pl. **-ões**) 1. square iron bar. 2. (naut.) boom, square bar.

vergalhar v. to whip, lash, flog, cowhide.

vergalho s. m. 1. horsewhip, cowhide, scourge, bull's pizzle. 2. (pop.) scoundrel, rogue, knave.

vergame s. m. the yards of a ship.

vergamota s. f. (S. Braz.) tangerine.

vergão s. m. (pl. **-ões**) 1. w(h)eal, wale, streak of a blow, stripe, welt. 2. augmentative form of **verga.**

vergar v. 1. to bend, bow, curve. 2. to fold, double. 3. to give ground, sag. 4. to humble, abate, abase, submit. 5. to pity, move, touch. 6. to accustom, get accustomed to.
a mesa vergou-se sob o peso the table groaned under the weight.

vergasta s. f. 1. switch, rod, cane, twig. 2. (fig.) scourge, flagellum. 3. whip, lash. 4. flogging.

vergastar v. 1. to whip, flog, lash, switch, cane, weal. 2. (fig.) to fustigate, harass, beat.

vergável adj. m. + f. (pl. **-áveis**) flexible.

vergel s. m. (pl. **-éis**) garden, orchard.

vergonha s. f. 1. shame. 2. ashamedness, sense of shame. 3. bashfulness. 4. blush(ing). 5. timidity, shyness, decorum. 6. dishonour, disgrace. 7. genitals. **sem ~** brassy, shameless. **que ~!** what a shame! **fie! oof! faugh!** for shame! **não tem ~?** are you not ashamed? **ter ~ de** to be ashamed of. **ser a ~ de** to be a disgrace to. **ser a ~ da família** to be the black sheep of the family. **querer esconder-se de ~** to sink into the earth. **corar de ~, rubro de ~** to blush, suffused with blushes. **perder a ~** to lose all shame. **ele trouxe ~ sobre todos eles** he brought shame on them all. **é uma pouca ~** it's a shame. **não ter ~ na cara** to have no self-respect; to feel no shame.

vergonheira s. f. lot of vexations; great shame.

vergonhosa s. f. (bot.) sensitive plant.

vergonhoso adj. 1. shameful, opprobrious. 2. modest, timid, bashful. 3. unworthy, foul, low, base. 4. reproachful, infamous. 5. disreputable, disgraceful. 6. indecent, obscene. ‖ **-amente** adv. shamefully, etc.
é ~ it is shameful. **partes -as** privy parts, genitals.

vergôntea s. f. 1. sprig, shoot, sprout, scion, layer, runner, side slip. 2. (naut.) spar. 3. (fig.) offspring, issue.

vergonteado adj. spriglike.

vergontear v. to shoot forth, sprout.

vergueiro s. m. 1. switch, rod. 2. wooden handle of some tools. 3. (naut.) pendant (rudder); jack-stay.

vergueta s. f. (her.) perpendicular divisionary bar.

veridicidade s. f. veraciousness, veracity, truthfulness.

verídico adj. 1. veracious, veridical, true, truthful. 2. real, just. 3. faithful.

verificação s. f. (pl. -ões) verification, examination, control(ment), check, proof, test, inquiry.
~ das contas check account.

verificador s. m. 1. verifier, examiner, controller. 2. customs officer. ‖ adj. controlling, checking.

verificar v. to verify, examine, find out, check, control, test.
~ os votos to canvass. ~ uma conta to check an account. ~ um caso to go into a matter. **verificou-se que foi bem-sucedido** it was found to succeed. **ele verificou se a porta estava fechada** he made sure that the door was locked.

verificativo adj. verificative.

verificável adj. m. + f. (pl. -áveis) verifiable, controllable, checkable.

verismo s. m. verism.

verista s. m. + f. verist. ‖ adj. veristic.

verme s. m. 1. worm, grub, vermin, dew-worm, larva. 2. (fig.) inward torment.
~ da consciência worm of conscience. ~ **filiforme** threadworm. ~ **intestinal** helminth. **até um ~ reage quando é pisado** even a worm will turn. **sem ~** wormless.

vermelhaço adj. 1. rather red, reddish. 2. rosy.

vermelhão s. m. (pl. -ões) 1. vermilion, cinnabar. 2. rose (colour). 3. colour, ruddy complexion. 4. (poet.) vermeil. 5. redness.

vermelh(e)ar v. (also **vermelhejar**) 1. to be red(dish). 2. to flush.

vermelhecer v. to become red.

vermelhidão s. f. (pl. -ões) 1. red, redness, reddishness. 2. flush(ing), blush, erubescence.

vermelhinha s. f. (also **jogo-da-vermelhinha**) sort of card game.

vermelho s. m. 1. red, rubric. 2. cinnabar. 3. sort of varnish. 4. (fig.) communist. ‖ adj. red, ruddy, rubious, scarlet, crimson, rubicund.
~ **amarelado** salmon, bisque. ~ **cereja** cherry. ~ **como um peru** red as a turkey-cock. ~ **de cobre** copper. ~ **escuro** coral, garnet. ~ **vivo** blood red. **de rosto** ~ blowzy, blowzed. **ele estava** ~ **de raiva** he glowed indignation. **de** (or **com**) **cor -a** redly. **pintar de** ~ to red(den).

vermelho-henrique s. m. (pl. **vermelhos-henrique**) (Braz., ichth.) lane snapper.

vermicida s. m. vermicide, vermifuge. ‖ adj. vermifuge.

vermiculado adj. (also **vermiculoso**) vermiculate(d) (design).

vermicular adj. m. + f. vermicular, wormlike.

vermiculária s. f. (bot.) stone crop.

vermículo s. m. vermicule.

vermiculura s. f. (archit.) vermiculation.

vermiforme adj. m. + f. vermiform, wormlike, worm-shaped, lumbriciform.
apêndice ~ vermiform appendix.

vermífugo s. m. vermifuge, helminthic. ‖ adj. vermifugal, anthelmintic.

vérmina s. m. 1. vermin. 2. (fig.) any undermining agent.

verminação s. f. (pl. -ões) vermination.

verminado adj. 1. vermiculated, verminous. 2. (fig.) undermined, destroyed, consumed.

verminar v. 1. to grow or breed vermin. 2. to become debased, corrupt.

vermineira s. f. breeding place of vermin (as birds' food).

verminose s. f. (med.) verminosis.

verminoso adj. verminous, caused by vermin.

vermívoro adj. vermivorous, feeding on worms.

vermizela s. f. a vermin harmful to some roots.

vermute s. m. vermouth.

vernação s. f. (pl. -ões) (bot.) 1. vernation. 2. foliation.

vernaculidade s. f., **vernaculismo** m. vernacularity, purity, vernacularism.

vernaculista s. m. + f. vernaculist.

vernaculização s. f. (pl. -ões) vernacularization.

vernaculizar v. to vernacularize.

vernáculo s. m. vernacular, mother tongue. ‖ adj. vernacular: 1. native, regional, national. 2. genuine, pure.
em ~ in the vernacular.

vernal adj. m. + f. (pl. -ais) vernal: 1. occurring in the spring. 2. (fig.) springlike. ‖ ~**mente** adv. vernally.
ponto ~ vernal equinox.

vernalização s. f. (pl. -ões) (bot.) vernalization.

vernante adj. m. + f. vernal.

vernissage s. m. (Fr., paint.) vernissage, varnishing day.

verniz s. m. 1. varnish. 2. lake, gum-lac, shellac. 3. gloss, polish. 4. (fig.) superficial politeness of manners, outside show.

vernizagem s. f. copper coating before engraving.

verno adj. = **vernal.**

vero adj. true, veracious.

veronês s. m. Veronese. ‖ adj. Veronese.

verônica s. f. (eccl.) veronica. 2. woman who carries the veronica in a procession. 3. (bot.) speedwell, veronica.

verossímil adj. m. + f. (pl. -eis) (also **verossimilhante**) probable, likely, verisimilar.
é assaz ~ it is likely enough.

verossimilhança, **verossimilitude** s. f. verisimilitude, likelihood, probability.

verrina s. f. 1. each of Cicero's discourses against Verres. 2. violent (public) accusation. 3. harsh criticism.

verrineiro s. m. harsh critic. ‖ adj. criticizing, accusatory.

verrinista s. m. + f. and adj. (Braz.) = **verrineiro.**

verrucal adj. m. + f. (pl. -ais) of or pertaining to warts.

verrucária s. f. (bot.) wartwort.

verrucífero adj. (also **verrucoso, verrugoso, verruguento**) warty, full of warts, verrucose.

verruciforme adj. m. + f. wartlike.

verruga s. f. wart, verruca, mole.

verruma s. f. borer, bit, gimlet, drill, bolt auger, wimble (plates F 8, M 4).

verrumão s. m. (pl. -ões) (augmentative form of **verruma**) large-sized borer.

verrumar v. 1. to bore, drill, wimble, perforate. 2. to prick, goad. 3. to afflict, torment, torture. 4. to ponder, think over, meditate, muse.

versa s. f. (corn)field laid down by rain or storm.

versado adj. 1. versed, skilled, experienced, proficient in, well-informed, expert. 2. read, well-read. 3. studied, learned.
~ **nos clássicos** classical. **sou** ~ **no assunto** I am at home in this subject. **ele está bem** ~ **em matemática** he is up in mathematics. **ele é** ~ **na matéria** he is up on it.

versal s. m. (pl. -ais) capital letter. ‖ adj. m. + f. capital, initial (letter).

versalete s. m. (typogr.) small capital.

versalhada s. f. (deprec.) 1. a lot of poems, poetry. 2. bad poetry.

versão s. f. (pl. **-ões**) 1. version: a) translation. b) view, explanation, possibility. c) change of direction, turn. 2. rumour. 3. revolution of a celestial body.
~ **cinematográfica** film version. **ele me deu a sua** ~ **do incidente** he gave me his version of the incident.

versar (I) v. 1. to turn. 2. to examine. 3. to practise, exercise. 4. to study. 5. to deal with, treat of. 6. to consist. 7. to ponder. 8. to decant. 9. to be reported.
o discurso versou sobre política the discourse ran upon politics. **a dificuldade versa nisto** there is the difficulty.

versar (II) v. to versify.

versaria s. f. = **versalhada**.

versátil adj. m. + f. (pl. **-eis**) versatile: 1. changeable, inconstant, fickle. 2. having many aptitudes, all-round.

versatilidade s. f. versatility, manysidedness.

versejador s. m. versifier, rimer, metrician, poetaster.

versejadura s. f. versifying, riming.

versejar v. 1. to versify, rime, verse. 2. (deprec.) to make bad poetry.

verseto s. m. 1. verset: a) verse, as from the Bible or Koran. b) (mus.) short interlude or prelude. 2. (print.) versicle.

versicolor adj. versicolo(u)r, variegated.

versículo s. m. 1. verse of the Bible. 2. versicle. 3. verset.

versidade s. f. (North. Braz.) variety, quality.

versífero adj. that rhymes.

versificação s. f. (pl. **-ões**) versification, metrical version.

versificador s. m. versifier, poetaster. || adj. that versifies.

versificar v. = **versejar**.

versífico adj. of or pertaining to verse.

versista s. m. + f. versifier. || adj. that versifies.

verso (I) s. m. 1. verse, rime, rhyme. 2. stich, stave. 3. poetry. 4. poem. 5. versification. 6. (N. Braz.) broad hint.
~ **anapéstico** anapest. ~ **leonino** leonine verse. ~**s ruins** doggerel. ~ **trocaico** trochaic. **em** ~ in verse.

verso (II) s. m. 1. back, reverse, verso. 2. overleaf. 3. tail (coin).
vide ~ turn over. **no** ~ overleaf.

versudo adj. leafy.

versuto adj. crafty, cunning, shrewd.

vértebra s. f. (anat.) vertebra, spondyl(e).

vertebrado s. m. vertebrate. || adj. (also **vertebroso**) vertebrate.
animal ~ vertebrate animal.

vertebral adj. m. + f. (pl. **-ais**) vertebral.
coluna ~ vertebral column.

vertedor s.m. 1. jug. 2. translator. || adj. outpouring.

vertedouro s. m. (also **vertedoiro**) 1. (naut.) scoop. 2. spillway.

vertedura s. f. 1. outflow. 2. overmeasure, overflow.

vertente s. f. 1. slope, declivity, versant, downhill, downgrade. 2. (geol.) hogback. 3. one of the sides of a roof. || adj. m. + f. outpouring, overflowing.

verter v. 1. to flow, run, gush, pour, spout. 2. to spill. 3. to shed. 4. to overflow. 5. to diffuse. 6. to translate. 7. to urinate. 8. to rise (river). 9. to flow into (river). 10. to leak, ooze.
~**am muito sangue** 1. they shed much blood. 2. they suffered much. ~ **lágrimas** to weep. ~ **para o português** to translate into Portuguese.

vertical s. f. (pl. **-ais**) vertical: a vertical line. || adj. m. + f. 1. vertical, perpendicular, plumb, upright

(plate Q). 2. above the head. || ~**mente** adv. vertically.

verticalidade s. f. verticality, verticalness, plumbness.

vértice s. m. vertex: 1. top, height, apex, summit (plate A 11). 2. top of the head. 3. point opposite to the base of a triangle; point in which the sides of an angle meet (plate A 9).
~ **de uma curva** cusp.

verticidade s. f. verticity.

verticilado adj. (bot.) verticilate, whorled.

verticilo s. m. (bot.) verticil, cycle, whorl.

vertigem s. f. (pl. **-ens**) 1. vertigo, giddiness, dizziness, maziness. 2. faint, swoon. 3. madness, ecstasy. 4. (fig.) sudden temptation.

vertiginoso adj. 1. vertiginous, causing giddiness or vertigo. 2. very quick. 3. perturbing, infatuating.
|| **-amente** adv. vertiginously.

verve s. f. verve, bounce.

vesânia s. f. mental insanity.

vesânico adj. of or pertaining to mental insanity.

vesano adj. 1. insane, mad. 2. frentic, delirious.

vesco adj. edible, eatable, esculent.

vesgo s. m. squinter, squint-eyed person. || adj. squint(-eyed), squinting, strabismal.
ele é ~ he has a cast in his eye, he has a squint; (fam.) he looks two ways to find a Sunday. **olhar** ~ to look awry.

vesguear v. 1. to squint: a) be cross-eyed. b) look askance. 2. (fig.) to see badly.

vesgueiro adj. squint(-eyed).

vesguice s. f. squint-eyedness.

vesicação s. f. (pl. **-ões**) (med.) vesication.

vesical adj. m. + f. (pl. **-ais**) (anat.) vesical.

vesicante s. m. (med., also **vesicatório**) vesicant, vesicatory. || adj. m. + f. vesicant, vesicatory.

vesicar v. to vesicate, blister.

vesícula s. f. vesicle: 1. bladder, blister, bubble, bleb. 2. (biol.) cyst, ampulla. 3. (ichth.) air bladder.
~ **biliar** gall bladder.

vesicular, vesiculoso adj. vesicular, bladdery, bullate.

vespa s. f. 1. wasp. 2. (fig.) crosspatch.
semelhante a ~ wasplike, waspy.

vespão s. m. (pl. **-ões**) (ent.) hornet.

vespeiro s. m. wasps' nest, vespiary (also fig.).
ele mexeu num ~ he brought a hornets' nest about his ears.

Vésper s. m. 1. Vesper: the evening star. 2. (fig.) the West, Occident.

véspera s. f. 1. afternoon, evening. 2. eve: evening, day or period before some event; brink. 3. vespers: evening prayers, evening song.
~ **de Ano-Novo, noite de São Silvestre** New Year's Eve. ~ **de Natal** Christmas Eve. ~ **de Todos os Santos** Halloween. ~ **do dia de Reis** Twelfth Night. **na** ~ **de** on the eve of. **estar em** ~**s de** to be on the brink of. **não se morre na** ~ nobody dies before his hour.

vesperal s. m. (pl. **-ais**) 1. vesperal (book). 2. (Braz.) afternoon entertainment; matinée; prom. || adj. m. + f. 1. vesper(tine), vespertian. 2. afternoon, evening.

Véspero s. m. = **Vésper**.

vespertino s. m. evening paper. || adj. 1. vesper(tine), of or pertaining to the evening. 2. (astr.) acronical.

vessada s. f. fertile valley.

vessadela s. f. deep ploughing.

vessadouro s. m. (also **vessadoiro**) 1. = **vessadela**. 2. right to plough a land.

vessar v. to plough deeply.

vestal s. f. (pl. **-ais**) vestal: 1. (Roman hist.) virgin consecrated to Vesta. 2. pure or virginal woman. || adj. m. + f. vestal, virginal, chaste, pure.

veste s. f. (also **vestuário** m., **véstia**, **vestidura** f.) vest, vestment, vesture, apparel, garment, clothes (plates R 6, 7).

vestfaliano s. m. Westphalian. ‖ adj. Westphalian.

véstia s. f. loose jacket, sometimes of leather, as used by North Brazilian cowboys.

vestiaria s. f. 1. vestiary, vestry, robing room. 2. clothes, clothings, garments.

vestiário s. m. (also **vestuário**) 1. dressing room. 2. cloakroom. 3. cloakroom attendant. 4. = **vestiaria**. 5. boudoir.

vestibular adj. m. + f. vestibular.

vestíbulo s. m. 1. vestibule (also anat.). 2. entry, entrance hall, lobby. 3. passage, passageway. 4. porch. 5. foyer. 6. atrium. 7. yard.

vestido s. m. dress, frock, garment, a lady's gown, vesture (plate R 6).
~ **da manhã** morning frock. ~ **de baile** evening frock, evening dress (plate R 6). ~ **de noiva** bridal gown, bridal dress. ~ **lavável** washable frock, (coll.) tub frock. ~ **para passeio** walking dress. ~ **para a tarde** tea gown. **cortar o** ~ **conforme o pano** to cut one's coat according to one's cloth.

vestidura s. f. 1. = **veste**. 2. ceremony of investment of a priest or nun.

vestígio s. m. vestige: 1. footprint, trail. 2. clue, mark, trace, sign, evidence. 3. remnant, remains. **sem** ~ clueless, trackless, traceless. **o quarto inteiro apresentava** ~**s de sua presença** vestiges of her presence were all over the room.

vestimenta s. f. 1. = **veste(s)**. 2. clerical vestments, church attire (plate P 5). 3. array(al).

vestioso adj. vestmental, vestiary.

vestir s. m. act or fact of clothing, dressing. ‖ v. 1. to dress, clothe, garb, (en)robe; put on, slip on. 2. to accoutre, equip. 3. to array, attire, apparel, rig up. 4. to vest, invest (with). 5. to endue, indue. 6. to wear. 7. to tailor for. 8. to cover, line. 9. to disguise. 10. to protect, shelter. 11. to adorn, embellish. 12. ~**-se** to dress o. s.
~ **bem** to dress well. ~ **a capa** to put on the coat. ~ **costume** to costume. ~ **(roupas de) luto** to put on mourning, to lay out. ~ **mal** to dress badly. ~ **apressadamente** to throw on. ~**-se bem** to dress well, (coll.) buck, dink. ~**-se garridamente** to dizen. ~**-se de luto** to go into mourning. ~**-se de novo** to redress. **ele vestiu o seu casaco** he drew on his coat. **ela se vestiu** she dressed herself. **ela se veste muito bem** she dresses very well. **ela foi para** ~**-se** she went to array herself, she clothes herself. **que devo** ~? what shall I use, wear? **bem vestido** well-tailored, braw, well-groomed, well turned out. **vestido de preto** black. **vestido de verde** clad in green.

vestuário s. m. 1. clothes, clothing, apparel, attire, array, raiment, garment. 2. tog(gery). 3. covering. ~ **e alimentação** clothing and board, (coll.) back and belly. ~ **berrante** finery. **peças de** ~ body clothes.

vesuvianita s. f. (min.) vesuvianite.

vetar s. to veto, refuse, interpose.

veteranice s. f. quality of being a veteran.

veterano s. m. 1. veteran (also mil.). 2. (coll.) vet, old-timer. 3. high school students of advanced courses. 4. expert. ‖ adj. veteran (also mil.).
~ **de guerra** (coll.) war-horse.

veterinária s. f. veterinary medicin.

veterinário s. m. veterinary, veterinarian, horse doctor, farrier; (coll.) vet. ‖ adj. veterinary; (coll.) vet.

vetiver s. m. (bot.) vetiver.

veto s. m. veto, interdiction, negative.

vetor s. m. = **vector**.

vetustez s. f. oldness; vetusty.

vetusto adj. 1. old. 2. ancient, archaic, antique. 3. vetust.

véu s. m. 1. veil(ing), covering, curtain (plates A 11, R 6). 2. film. 3. fall (of women's hats). 4. wimple (of nuns). 5. (fig.) pretext, disguise, pretense. 6. shadow, sorrow, grief.
~ **palatino** (anat.) soft palate. **coloquemos um** ~ **sobre a cena** (fig.) let us drop a veil over the scene. **levantar o** ~ to lift the curtain. **rasgar o** ~ to speak plainly, openly. **sem** ~ veilless. **sob o véu da noite** under the curtain of night. **tomar o** ~ to take the veil.

vevuia s. f. (Braz. ornith.) partridge dove.

vexação s. f. (pl. **-ões**) vexation, molestation, torment, pique, annoyance.

vexado adj. 1. vexed, annoyed. 2. (N. Braz.) hasty, hurried.

vexador s. m. vexer, harasser. ‖ adj. vexatious.

vexame s. m. 1. vexation, annoyance. 2. grievance, worriment. 3. shame. 4. abuse, offense, insult. 5. (N. Braz.) haste. 6. (path.): a) palpitation of the heart. b) cardiac asthma.

vexante adj. m. + f. vexatious.

vexar v. 1. to vexate: a) molest, annoy. b) torment, afflict, harass, worry. c) (sl.) buffalo, horse rub, rot. 2. to humiliate, ashame, discompose. 3. to insult, offend. 4. (Braz.) to speed up.

vexativo, vexatório adj. 1. vexatious, annoying, nasty. 2. mischievous, mischief-making. 3. humiliatory, shameful. ‖ **vexatoriamente** adv. vexatiously.

vexilar adj. m. + f. (bot.) vexillary.

vexilário s. m. (hist.) vexillary: standard-bearer.

vexilo s. m. (hist., bot.) vexillum: banner.

vez s. f. (pl. **vezes**) 1. time, turn, bout. 2. occasion, opportunity. 3. (cards) hand.
algumas vezes several times. **aquela** ~ at that time. **às vezes** sometimes, at times. **de quem é a** ~? who is up? who goes? **desta** ~ for this time, for the nonce. **de** ~ **em quando** every now and then, now and again, now and then, by spells, once in a while, off and on, ever and anon, on occasion, occasional. **de uma** ~ at a time, at one dash, at a stress. **de uma** ~ **para sempre** once for all, for good and all. **duas vezes** twice, bis. **duas vezes maior** twice as large. **em** ~ **de** for, in lieu of, else, instead. **é minha** ~ **de pedir uma rodada** it's my shout this time. **é minha** ~ it's my turn. **era uma** ~ once upon a time. **espere a sua** ~ await your turn. **fazer as vezes de alguém** to represent, substitute a person. **mais uma** ~ anew, once again, once more, yet again, over again. **muitas vezes** again and again, times out of number, many times, often. **na maior parte das vezes** usually, more often than not. **pela primeira** ~ for the first time. **raras vezes** infrequently. **tantas e tantas vezes** oft and oft. **três vezes três são nove** three times three are nine. **uma** ~ **na vida** once in life, in a blue moon. **uma** ~ **que isto é assim...** once this is so... **ele apareceu pela última** ~ **em cena** he took his last curtain.

vezar v. to accustom, get accustomed to.

vezeira s. f. 1. herd of swine. 2. herd that takes turns with another on the pasture.

vezeiro s. m. 1. = **vezeira**. 2. owner of a herd of swine. ‖ adj. 1. habituated, accustomed, used to. 2. relapsing.

vezo (ê) s. m. 1. habit, custom, use, usage. 2. vice.

via s. f. 1. way: a) path, street, road. b) direction, route. c) means, channel, line. d) mode, manner, fashion. 2. (anat.) duct. 3. original (**primeira** ~) or copy (**segunda** ~) of a document. 4. railroad. 5. gauge of a railroad. ‖ prep. via, by, by way of.

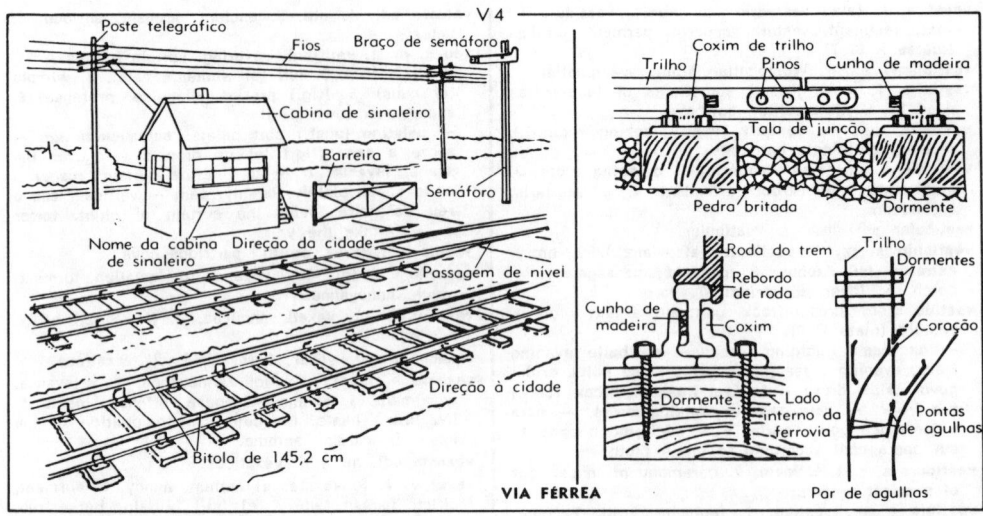

VIA FÉRREA

~ **de uma só mão, direção única** one-way street. ~ **dupla** double track. ~ **férrea** railway, railroad (plate V 4). ~ **para ciclistas** cycle track (plate R 8). ~ **permanente** permanent way, roadbed. ~ **preferencial** arterial highway. ~ **principal** trunk road, through street, artery. ~ **pública** thoroughfare. **chegar às** ~**s de fato** to come to grips. **estar em** ~**s de** to be about to. **por** ~ **de regra** usually. **por** ~ **férrea, marítima, aérea** by railroad, by sea, by airmail. **por** ~ **terrestre** overland. **ele seguiu para Roma** ~ **Paris** he went via Paris to Rome. **por** ~ **das dúvidas** just in case, to make sure, to play safe.

viabilidade s. f. practicability, viability, workability.

viação s. f. (pl. **-ões**) 1. traffic, long-distance trafic. 2. road system, street net. 3. means of transport.

viador s. m. 1. traveller. 2. passenger. 3. (hist.) chamberlain of the queen.

viaduto s. m. viaduct, overpass.

viagear v. (S. Braz.) to work as a commercial traveller.

viageiro s. m. 1. traveller. 2. rover, wanderer. ‖ adj. travelling, of or pertaining to travel.

viagem s. f. (pl. **-ens**) 1. travel, voyage, journey. 2. expedition. 3. cruise. 4. ride. 5. flight. 6. wander(-ing). 7. tour, sally, trip, excursion.

~ **ao estrangeiro** foreign tour. ~ **através da Espanha** tour of Spain. ~ **de ida e de volta** round trip, double journey, voyage out and home. ~ **de núpcias** wedding trip. ~ **de recreio** joy ride. ~ **de volta, regresso** voyage home, return voyage. ~ **inaugural (de um navio)** virgin cruise. **boa** ~**! feliz** ~**!** have a nice trip! a pleasant journey to you! **descrição de -ens** book of travels. **em** ~ **para** bound to; on the journey, on track; out of town. **narração de** ~ traveller's tale. **sair de** ~ to start. **uma** ~ **de três dias, trinta milhas** a three days', thirty miles' journey.

viajado adj. travelled.

viajante s. m. + f. 1. traveller; voyage(u)r; wanderer (plate E 13). 2. passenger. 3. peregrinator. ‖ adj. travelling, wandering, itinerant.

~ **comercial** (Brit.) commercial. **vendedor** ~ commercial traveller.

viajar v. 1. to travel, voyage, journey, tour. 2. to wander. 3. to sally. 4. to cruise. 5. to ride.

~ **clandestinamente** to hop the freight, ride the blind. ~ **com bilhete mensal** to commute. ~ **de bonde** to tram. ~ **de lugar em lugar** to travel about. ~ **de primeira classe no trem** to travel first-class by rail. ~ **de trem** to go by train, to rail(way). ~ **em balsa ou jangada** to raft. ~ **para fazer discursos políticos** to stump the country. ~ **pedindo carona** (U. S. A.) to hitchhike. ~ **por via aérea** to travel by air; to plane, hop. **viajamos pelo Brasil** we toured Brazil. **ele viajou (este pedaço) de trem** he trained it. **ele viaja muito** he gets about.

viajor s. m. = **viageiro**.

Via-láctea s. f. (astr.) Milky Way.

vianda s. f. 1. viand, victuals, food. 2. meat. 3. fowl (meat).

viandante s. m. + f. 1. traveller, voyager. 2. wanderer, rover, wayfarer. ‖ adj. wayfaring.

viandar v. to travel, roam, wander, peregrinate.

viandeiro s. m. 1. = **viandante**. 2. person fond of food, glutton, gourmand.

viário adj. relating to means and ways of transport. **sistema** ~ transport system.

via-sacra s. f. (pl. **vias-sacras**) stations of the cross. **fazer a** ~ 1. to pray at the fourteen pictures of the cross. 2. to go to church during the Holy Week. 3. (fig.) to see all friends for help.

viático s. m. viaticum: 1. provision of travelling money or food. 2. (eccl.) the Communion given to sick.

viatura s. f. vehicle, means of transport.

viável adj. m. + f. (pl. **-áveis**) 1. practicable (way). 2. doable, possible. 3. viable, strong.

víbora s. f. viper: 1. adder. 2. (fig.) malignant person.

vibordo s. m. (naut.) gunwale, gunnel.

vibração s. f. (pl. **-ões**) 1. vibration: a) vibrancy. b) oscillation, trepidation, tremor, shaking. 2. (phys.) undulation, wave. 3. (mus.) tremolo. 4. pulse, pulsation. 5. (phonet.) trill. 6. (fig.) thrill.

vibrador s. m. 1. vibrator. 2. (elect.) trembler. 3. sounder, buzzer.

vibrante adj. m. + f. 1. vibrant, vibrating. 2. flickering.

vibrar v. 1. to vibrate. 2. to oscillate, tremulate. 3. to shake. 4. to flicker, flutter. 5. to swing. 6. to pulse, pulsate, throb. 7. to tremble. 8. to quiver. 9. to sound. 10. to trill. 11. to touch (mus. strings).

12. to move (feelings). 13. to shock. 14. to brandish. ~ **golpes** to lay on, beat.

vibratilidade s. f. vibratility.

vibratório adj. vibratile, vibratory.

vibrisas s. f. pl. (anat., zool.) vibrissas.

viburno s. m. (bot.) viburnum (sheeperry, black haw).

viçar v. 1. = vicejar. 2. (fig.) to develop(e), augment, spread. 3. (North, Braz.): a) to conceive (animal). b) to rut. 4. (Braz.) to have the vice of eating earth.

vicarial adj. m. + f. (pl. -ais) vicariate, vicarious, vicarial.

vicariato s. m. 1. vicarage, vicariate, vicarship. 2. duration of a vicariate. 3. residence of a vicar. 4. replacement in any function.

vicário adj. vicarious.

vice- pref. vice-

vice-almirantado s. m. (pl. **vice-almirantados**) vice--admirality.

vice-almirante s. m. (pl. **vice-almirantes**) vice-admiral.

vice-chanceler s. m. (pl. **vice-chanceleres**) vice-chancellor.

vice-cônsul s. m. (pl. **vice-cônsules**) vice-consul.

vice-consulado s. m. (pl. **vice-consulados**) 1. vice--consulate. 2. vice-consulship.

vice-governador s. m. (pl. **vice-governadores**) vice--governor, lieutenant governor, deputy governor.

vicejante adj. m. + f. thriving, luxuriant, exuberant.

vicejar v. 1. to thrive, flourish, bloom. 2. to grow luxuriantly, exuberantly. 3. (also fig.) to exuberant.

vicejo s. m. exuberance, exuberancy, rankness.

vicenal (pl. -ais), **vicenário** adj. vicennial.

vicênio s. m. period of twenty years.

vicentino s. m. native or inhabitant of São Vicente. ‖ adj. of or pertaining to São Vicente.

vice-presidência s. f. (pl. **vice-presidências**) vice-presidentship, vice-presidency.

vice-presidente s. m. + f. (pl. **vice-presidentes**) vice--president.

vice-real adj. (pl. **vice-reais**) viceroyal, viceregal.

vice-regência s. f. (pl. **vice-regências**) vice-regency.

vice-rei s. m. (pl. **vice-reis**) viceroy.

vice-reinado s. m. (pl. **vice-reinados**) viceroyalty.

vice-reitor s. m. (pl. **vice-reitores**) prorector.

vice-reitorado s. m. (pl. **vice-reitorados**) prorectorate.

vice-secretário s. m. (pl. **vice-secretários**) undersecretary.

vice-versa adv. locution vice versa, contrariwise, conversely.

vichi s. f. 1. Vichy water. 2. variety of cotton fabric.

viciação s. f. (also **viciamento** m.) 1. vitiation. 2. corruption. 3. invalidation.

viciado s. m. addict, fiend. ‖ adj. 1. vitiated, vicious. 2. addicted. 3. foul. 4. perverted, corrupted. 5. contaminated. 6. invalidated. ‖ -amente adv. viciously. ~ **em entorpecentes** drug addict. **ele está ~ na bebida** he indulges in drinking, he is a slave to drink. **não ~** unvitiated.

viciador s. m. 1. vitiator. 2. perverter, corrupter. 3. falsifier. ‖ adj. 1. vitiating. 2. corruptive. 3. adulterant.

viciar v. 1. to vitiate: a) contaminate, infect. b) corrupt, deprave, spoil, pervert. 2. to adulterate, falsify. 3. to seduce. 4. ~-se to addict, indulge.

vicinal adj. m. + f. (pl. -ais) vicinal, neighbouring.

vicinalidade s. f. vicinity.

vício s. m. 1. vice: a) viciousness, bad habit. b) demoralization. c) immorality, lewdness, depraviousness, abandonment. d) addiction, indulgence. e) fault, imperfection, defect. f) physical deformity, taint. 2. (N. Braz.) vice of eating earth. ~ **da bebida** drinking habit. **dado a um ~** addicted.

viciosidade s. f. 1. viciousness, depravity. 2. defectiveness, faultiness.

vicioso adj. vicious: 1. defective, faulty. 2. corrupt. 3. immoral, abandoned, depraved. 4. wicked. ‖ -amente adv. viciously. **o círculo ~** the vicious circle.

vicissitude s. f. vicissitude: 1. change of fortune. 2. alternation, fluxion. 3. alteration. **as ~s da vida** the ups and downs of life.

vicissitudinário adj. vicissitudinarious.

viço s. m. 1. rankness, luxuriance, lushness, exuberance. 2. vigour, energy, flushness. 3. fire, ardor (of a rested animal). 4. excessive fondness, 5. greenness, verdure. **as rosas estavam em pleno ~** the roses were in full flush. **sem ~** withered.

viçoso adj. 1. rank, luxuriant, lush, exuberant. 2. blooming, flourishing. 3. fresh, vernal. 4. youthful, crisp. ‖ -amente adv. rankly, luxuriantly.

vicunha s. f. 1. (zool.) vicunha. 2. its wool.

vida s. f. 1. life: a) existence, being. b) lifetime; (fig.) days. c) way or course of life, conduct, manner; (coll.) swim. d) hereafter, future life. e) animation, zest, vivacity, liveliness. f) spirit. g) vitality, vigour. h) biography. 2. origin. 3. subsistence, support. ~ **circense** circus life, canvas. ~ **conjugal** wedlock. ~ **de vagabundo** roving life. ~ **doméstica** family life. ~ **errante** errantry. ~ **futura** future life. ~ **militar** warfare, camp. ~ **miserável, pobre** vegetation, low life. ~ **rica** high life. ~ **rústica** country life. **aproveitei minha ~** I have had my time. **assim é a ~** that's life, such is life, life is like that. **barco salva-vidas** life-boat. **cair na ~** to become a prostitute. **com ~** alive, living. **cuidar, tratar da própria ~** to stick to one's last; mind one's own business. **dar a ~ por alguma coisa** to give one's life for something. **dar ~ a (uma reunião)** to animate (a party). **de ~ curta** short-lived. **de ~ longa** long-lived. **em ~** in lifetime. **em perigo de ~** in danger of life. **enquanto há ~ há esperança** while there's life there's hope. **entre a ~ e a morte** between life and death. **falta de ~** inanimateness. **ganhar a ~** to earn one's livelihood. **levar boa ~** to lead an easy life. **levar ~ de cachorro** to lead a sad, a dog's life, a wretched life. **luta pela ~** struggle for existence, for life. **meio de ~** livelihood. **nunca na ~** (U. S. A.) (coll.) not by a long shot. **nunca na minha ~** never in my life. **para salvar a ~** for one's life, for dear life. **para toda a ~** for life. **para toda a ~ e mais seis meses** for ever and a day. **passar desta para outra melhor** to pass away, go to one's last resting place. **perder a ~** to lose one's life. **recobrar a ~** to come to life, recover conscience. **seguro de ~** life assurance, life insurance. **sem ~** lifeless, inanimate, spiritless, insentient. **tirar a ~ a alguém** to kill a person. **uma questão de ~ e de morte** a matter of life or death. **vencer na ~** to get on in life. **vender caro a ~** to sell one's life dear.

vidama s. m. (hist.) vidame.

vidamia s. f. (hist.) dignity of a vidame.

vidão s. m. (also **vidoca** f.) opulent, easygoing life.

vidar (I) s. m. (obs.) tool to manufacture teeth of combs.

vidar (II) v. to plant vines.

vide s. f. 1. layer of vine. 2. grapevine.

vide-branca s. f. (pl. **vides-brancas**) (bot.) traveller's joy.

videira s. f. (bot.) vine, grape, grapevine.

videiro s. m. person who cares but for his own interest, individualist.

vidência s. f. clairvoyance.

vidente s. m. + f. 1. clairvoyant, visionary, seer(ess), prophet. 2. person who sees (not blind). 3. clever person. ‖ adj. clairvoyant.

vidoeiro s. m. (bot.) birch.
feito com casca de ~ birchback.

vidonho s. m. vine layer with a piece of the stock.

vidraça s. f. 1. windowpane, window glass. 2. window casement.
desprovido de ~s paneless.

vidraçaria s. f. 1. a glazier's shop, glaziery. 2. a lot of windowpanes. 2. glassworks.

vidraceiro s. m. 1. glazier. 2. manufacturer of window-panes.
massa de ~ putty.

vidracista s. m. + f. glass stainer, annealer.

vidraço s. m. glasslike stone.

vidrado s. m. glazing (for earthenware). ‖ adj. 1. glazed. 2. glassy, vitreous. 3. dull, dim, lusterless.

vidragem s. f. (pl. -ens) glazing: act of coating with a glaze.

vidral s. m. = **vitral.**

vidralhada s. f. a lot of glass.

vidrar v. 1. to glaze, coat with a glazing, varnish. 2. to make or become dim or dull. 3. to make or become glass. 3. to lose one's heart, fall in love.

vidraria s. f. 1. glassworks. 2. a glazier's shop. 3. glass-ware trade. 4. the art of making glass. 5. a lot of glass.

vidreiro s. m. glassmaker, blower; person who works in the glass industry. ‖ adj. glass, pertaining to glass.
indústria -a glass industry.

vidrento adj. (also **vidroso**) 1. glassy: a) like glass. b) dull. c) vitreous. 2. (fig.) irritable, peevish, touchy.

vidrilho s. m. glass bead or trinket.

vidrino adj. 1. glass. 2. glassy, vitreous.

vidro s. m. 1. glass. 2. bottle, flask, phial, vial. 3. sheet or pane of glass. 4. (auto) window glass. 5. (fig.): a) something brittle. b) touchy person.
~ **colorido** stained glass. ~ **de cristal** crystal (glass). ~ **de chumbo** lead glass, flint glass, strass. ~ **de inspeção** inspection glass (plate M 5). ~ **de relógio** clock glass, watch glass, crystal. ~ **despolido** ground glass. ~ **fosco** frosted glass; (phot.) focusing screen. ~ **inquebrável** safety glass. ~ **lapidado** cut glass. ~ **leitoso** bone glass. ~ **óptico** crown glass. ~ **plano** sheet glass. ~ **solúvel** water glass. ~ **ustório** burning glass. **lã de** ~ glass wool.

vidual adj. m. + f. of or pertaining to widowhood.

viegas s. m., sg. + pl. (N. Braz., pop.) anus.

vieira s. f. 1. (zool.) scallop. 2. (her.) scallop shell.

vieirense adj. m. + f. referring to Antônio Vieira, Portuguese classicist.

vieiro s. m. (metallic) vein.

viela s. f. 1. lane, alley, narrow, pass. 2. each of the four iron pieces of a mill wheel.

vienense s. m. + f., **vienês** m. Viennese: native or inhabitant of Vienna. ‖ adj. Viennese.

viés s. m. 1. obliquity; sloping. 2. piece of cloth cut obliquely.
ao ~ slopingly. **de** ~ askance, asquint, awry.

viga s. f. beam, girder, summer, transom, traverse, joist, rafter, ba(u)lk, (square) timber; breastsummer, bressummer (plate A 7).
~ **de armação** (archit.) binder. ~ **de sustentação** binding beam, bearer. ~ **mestra** bearer, beam, crossbeam girder (plate P 14). ~ **retangular** box girder. ~ **U** channel iron. **guarnecer com** ~ to rafter.

vigamento s. m. framework, framing, timbering; beams, rafters.

vigar v. to frame, timber, rafter.

vigararia, vigairaria s. f. vicarage, vicariate.

vigária s. f. nun who substitutes her superior.

vigarice s. f. a bilking, swindle, hoax, confidence trick, skin game.

vigário s. m. 1. vicar, parson. 2. vicegerent, substitute. 3. (Braz.) slyboots; rogue.
Vigário de Cristo Vicar of Christ. ~ **geral** vicar-general. **conto-do-**~ swindle, fraud, cheat, confidence trick. **cair no conto-do-**~ to be cheated.

vigarismo s. m. = **vigarice.**

vigarista s. m. confidence man, bilker, kite.

vigência s. f. legality, force, validity.

vigente adj. m. + f. 1. valid, effective, in force, in vigour, effectual. 2. actual, present, established.

viger v. to be valid, in vigour, in force.

vigésimo s. m. twentieth. ‖ adj. twentieth, vigesimal.

vigia s. f. 1. watch: a) act or fact of watching. b) alertness, vigil, lookout, watchfulness. c) sleeplessness, wake. d) spell. e) m. watch, watchman, guard. f) m. ward. g) m. sentinel, sentry. h) m. observer, spy. 2. vedette. 3. sentry box, watch box. 4. peephole. 5. (naut.) dormer window, porthole, light port; bird's nest.

vigiador s. m. watcher, person who watches. ‖ adj. watching, watchful.

vigiante adj. = **vigilante.**

vigiar v. to watch: 1. observe; guard. 2. keep guard over, take care of, oversee. 3. be on the lookout, be vigilant, be on one's guard. 4. be or remain awake. 5. keep vigil. 6. lie in wait. 7. sentinel. 8. mind, look to.
ela vigiou o seu filho doente she sat out with her sick child. **mantenha-o em observação, vigie-o!** keep a watch of him! **longe de confiar nele, vigio-lhe todos os passos** far from trusting him, I watch him every step.

vigieiro s. m. 1. field guard. 2. quantity of cattle.

vigil adj. m. + f. (pl. **vigeis**) watchful, vigilant, awake.

vigilância s. f. 1. vigilance: a) guard, alertness. b) caution, precaution, care. c) outlook, lookout. d) watch, watchfulness. e) ward. f) wakefulness. 2. diligence.
~ **contínua** watch and ward. **estar sob** ~ **policial** to be on ticket of leave. **estar de** ~ to keep watch and ward. **burlando a** ~ **de seu guarda, o rapaz fugiu** overreaching the watchfulness of his guard, the boy escaped.

vigilante s. m. vigilante, invigilator, watcher. ‖ adj. m. + f. vigilant: 1. careful, heedful, attentive, observant. 2. circumspect. 3. alert, open-eyed. 4. watchful, observant. 5. awake, wakeful. ‖ ~**mente** adv. vigilantly.

vigilar v. = **vigiar.**

vigilenga s. f. (N. Braz.) almost round fishing-boat.

vigilengo s. m. (N. Braz.) fisher using a **vigilenga.**

vigília s. f. 1. vigil: a) night-watch. b) wake, wakefulness. c) eve. d) watch, watchfulness. e) care. 2. lucubration. 3. insomnia.

vigor s. m. vigo(u)r: 1. force, strength, power. 2. robustness. 3. energy. 4. efficiency. 5. emphasis. 6. validity, legality. 7. (sl.) feck, pep, zip, mettle.
em ~ in force, available, alive. **entrar em** ~ to come into operation, into force, become absolute. **entrou em** ~ it took effect. **estar em** ~ to be in force. **tornar a pôr em** ~ to re-enact, revigorate.

vigorante adj. m. + f. 1. alive, in force. 2. invigorating.

vigorar v. (also **vigorizar**) 1. to invigorate, strengthen. 2. to be in force, rule, hold.

vigorite s. f. vigorite (explosive).

vigoroso adj. vigorous: 1. robust, sturdy, tough, sinewy. 2. active, alive. 3. powerful, forceful. 4. firm, energetic(al). 5. mighty.

vigota s. f., **vigote** m. (also **sarrafão** m.) small beam.

vil s. m. + f. (pl. **vis**) vile, base person; wretch, worm. ‖ adj. vile: 1. cheap, worthless. 2. low(ly), inferior, mean, base, foul. 3. commonplace. 4. narrow-minded. 5. shabby, avaricious. 6. despicable, villainous, wicked. 7. wretched, contemptible. 8. unclean, dirty, sordid. ‖ ~**mente** adv. vilely.

vila s. f. 1. small town, borough. 2. villa.
dar **às de vila-diogo** to make away, beat a retreat, to show a clean pair of heels.

vilanagem s. f. (pl. **-ens**) 1. = **vilania**. 2. a lot of villains.

vilanaz s. m. (also **vilanaço**) villain, rogue. ‖ adj. villainous.

vilancete, vilhancete s. m. pastoral poetry.

vilania s. f. 1. villainy. 2. depravity, wretchedness. 3. avarice, avariciousness. 4. low-mindedness.

vilão s. m. (pl. **-ões**) (f. **-oa**) 1. villain, rogue, scoundrel, blackguard. 2. niggard, miser. 3. wretch. 4. countryman, peasant. 5. plebeian. 6. former Portuguese dance. ‖ adj. 1. villainous. 2. village. 3. plebeian. 4. dirty, sordid.

vilegiatura s. f. 1. summer resort. 2. time spent at a summer resort. 3. visit to a summer resort.

vilegiaturar v. to pass time at a summer resort.

vilela, vileta s. f. townlet.

vileza s. f. 1. vileness, villainousness, villainy. 2. lowness, meanness, baseness. 3. avariciousness. 4. wickedness, despicableness. 5. dirtiness, sordidness. 6. foulness, filth.

vilhanesca s. f. pastoral poetry.

vilífero adj. (zool.) villiform.

vilificar v. to vilify.

vilipendiador s. m. vilifier; slanderer, vilipender. ‖ adj. vilipendious.

vilipendiar v. to vilipend, vilify, slander.

vilipêndio s. m. 1. slander, vilification. 2. contempt, despite.

vilipendioso adj. vilipendious.

vilória s. f., **vilório** m. (deprec.) townlet, village.

vilosidade s. f. 1. villosity, hirsuteness. 2. villus.

viloso adj. villous, hirsute, hairy.

vilota s. f. = **vilela**.

vilta s. f. offense, insult, affront.

vimaranense s. m. + f. native or inhabitant of Guimarães (Portugal). ‖ adj. of or pertaining to Guimarães.

vimbunde s. m. (Braz., pop.) slave.

vime s. m. 1. osier, willow, vimen. 2. wattle, withe, wicker.
artigos de ~ basketry, basketwork. **cadeira de** ~ wicker chair. **de** ~ wattle, withy.

vimeiro s. m. (bot.) osier, willow.
~ **novo** withy.

vimieiro s. m. a plot of willow.

vimíneo, viminoso, vimoso adj. wicker.

vináceo adj. 1. vinaceous, winelike. 2. made of wine. 3. mixed with wine.

vinagrar v. (also **avinagrar**) 1. to temper with vinegar. 2. to sour. 3. to make or get angry.

vinagre s. m. 1. vinegar. 2. (fig.): a) something sour. b) peevish, cross person.

vinagreira s. f. 1. vinegar cruet. 2. (bot.) vinegar plant.

vinagreiro s. m. vinegar man, vinegar seller, vinegar maker.

vinagreza s. f. (Braz.) avarice, meanness.

vinagrista s. m. (Braz., hist.) follower of Francisco Vinagre.

vinário adj. winy, vinous.

vincada s. f. crease, plait, fold, wrinkle.

vincado adj. wrinkled, wrinkly, creased.

vincapervinca s. f. periwinkle.

vincar v. 1. to crease, fold, plait. 2. to wrinkle, ruck. 3. to furrow, groove.

vincelho s. m. = **vencilho**.

vincendo adj. falling due (debt).

vincetóxico s. m. (bot.) tame poison.

vincilho s. m. = **vencilho**.

vincituro adj. that will win.

vinco s. m. 1. crease, plait, fold, press. 2. wrinkle, ruck, rumple. 3. groove, furrow. 4. wale, weal. 5. small brass ring. 6. earring. 7. quantity of olives milled at a time.

vinculado adj. 1. entailed. 2. bound, linked. 3. inalienable.

vinculador s. m. 1. entail(ment); entailer. 2. link. ‖ adj. entailing.

vincular v. 1. to entail. 2. to bond. 3. to link. 4. to annex, take, fix the possession. 5. to attach, fasten, bind, tie. 6. to obligate, subject, oblige. 7. to perpetuate.

vinculativo, vinculatório adj. binding, linking.

vínculo s. m. 1. entail, entailment, entailed interest. 2. bond, link. 3. fastening, binding. 4. knot.
~**s matrimoniais** wedlock. **livrar-se de seus** ~**s** to shake off one's chains.

vinda s. f. 1. coming, arrival. 2. forthcoming. 3. return.
dar as boas-~**s a alguém** to welcome a person. **qual é a razão de sua** ~? what is the strength of his coming? **na** ~ on the way here.

vindicação s. f. (pl. **-ões**) vindication, (legal) claim, demand.

vindicador s. m. vindicator. ‖ adj. vindicative.

vindicar v. to vindicate: 1. claim, lay claim, assert a right. 2. justify, maintain. 3. defend. 4. avenge, punish. 5. recover. 6. deraign.

vindicativo adj. 1. vindicative, vindicating, vindicatory. 2. protective. 3. punitive.

vindiço adj. adventitious, foreign.

vindima s. f. (also **vindimadura**) 1. vintage: season or act of gathering grapes. 2. the grapes gathered. 3. (fig.) gain, earnings, acquisition.

vindimado adj. 1. harvested, gathered (grapes). 2. (fig.): a) worn-out. b) dead, killed.

vindimador s. m. (also **vindimadeiro**) vintager, grape gatherer. ‖ adj. of or pertaining to vintage.

vindimar v. 1. to gather grapes. 2. (fig.): a) to harvest, reap. b) to destroy, finish. c) to kill, murder.

vindimo adj. 1. of or pertaining to vintage. 2. autumnal.

vindita s. f. 1. punishment. 2. vengeance, revenge, reprisal.

vindo adj. 1. arrived, come. 2. proceeding from.

vindouro s. m. (also **vindoiro**) (Braz., pop.) newcomer, foreigner. ‖ adj. coming, future, towardly, forthcoming.
em anos ~**s** in after-years. **em dias** ~**s** in days to come. **os séculos** ~**s** after-ages. **os tempos** ~**s** after-times.

víneo adj. (poet.) = **vináceo**.

vingador s. m. 1. avenger, revenger. 2. revenge. ‖ adj. vindictive, retaliatory, avenging. ‖ ~**amente** adv. avengingly.

vingança s. f. 1. vengeance, revenge(ment), avengement. 2. retaliation, retribution, requital. 3. punishment.
desejo de ~ revenge. **por** ~ in revenge; revengeful.

vingar v. 1. to avenge, revenge. 2. to retaliate, retribute. 3. to punish. 4. to attain, reach, succeed. 5. to obtain. 6. to grow, develop(e), come to ripeness. 7. to prosper. 8. to indemnize, compensate. 9. ~-se: a) to take revenge. b) to declare o. s. satisfied.

vinguei-me I took revenge. **ela se vingou dele** she took it out of him. **ele vingou-se em seu inimigo** he took vengeance on his foe. **planta que não vinga** uncultivable plant.

vingativo adj. vindictive, revengeful, vindicatory, retaliatory. ‖ **-amente** adv. vindictively.

ele não é ~ he bears no enmity.

vinha s. f. 1. (bot.) vine. 2. vineyard. 3. (fig.) source of gain. 4. bargain.

vinhaça s. f. 1. great quantity of wine. 2. poor wine. 3. drunkenness.

vinháceo adj. vinous.

vinhaço s. m. husks of grapes, grape leavings in the wine press.

vinhadeiro s. m. = **vinheiro**.

vinhaga s. f., **vinhego** m. = **vinhedo**.

vinhal s. m. (pl. **-ais**) 1. vineyard. 2. variety of grapes.

vinhão s. m. 1. good or heady wine. 2. variety of grapes. 3. any strong wine added to a product of inferior quality.`

vinhataria s. f. 1. vinegrowing, viticulture. 2. wine production.

vinhateiro s. m. 1. vineyardist, vinedresser. 2. winegrower. ‖ adj. 1. viticultural. 2. winegrowing.

vinhático s. m. (bot.) Brazilian mahogany.

vinhedo s. m. extensive vinery, vineyard.

vinheiro s. m. 1. vineyardist. 2. guard of a vineyard.

vinheta s. f. 1. vignette. 2. printer's flower, headpiece, tailpiece.

vinhete s. m. light wine.

vinhetista s. m. + f. vignetist.

vinho s. m. wine: 1. fermented juice of grapes or some other fruits. 2. drunkenness.

~ **branco** white wine. ~ **branco do Reno** hock. ~ **de frutas** verjuice. ~ **de maçã** cider. ~ **de mesa** table or dinner wine. ~ **doce** sweet wine. ~ **do Porto** port. ~ **do Reno** Rhenish, Rhine wine. ~ **seco** dry wine. ~ **tinto** red wine; claret. ~ **verde** green wine. **adega de** ~ wine cellar, vault. **barril de** ~ wine cask. **casa de** ~**s** wine shop.**copo de** ~ glass of wine. **copo para** ~ wine glass. **cor de** ~ wine-coloured. **provador de** ~ winetaster. **ser de outra pipa** to be something better (of persons).

vinhoca s. f. poor wine.

vinhoneira s. f. (N. Braz.) = **vioneira**.

vinhoso adj. 1. vinaceous. 2. winy.

vinhote s. m. (pop.) drunkard; boozer.

vínico adj. vinic.

vinícola adj. wine-growing.

estabelecimento ~ winery.

vinicultor s. m. viniculturist, winegrower.

vinicultura s. f. viniculture, viticulture.

vinífero adj. viniferous.

vinificação s. f. (pl. **-ões**) 1. vinification. 2. wine making.

vinificador s. m. vinifacteur: apparatus for wine making.

vinificar v. to convert into wine.

vinolência s. f. drunkenness, inebriation, intoxication.

vinolento adj. 1. drunken, intoxicated. 2. given to drinking, dipsomaniac.

vinosidade s. f. vinosity: vinous quality.

vinoso adj. 1. vinous, winy. 2. wine-coloured.

vinte s. m. twenty. ‖ adj. twenty.

~ **vezes** twenty times, twentyfold. **dar no** ~ to hit the mark, hit the nail on the head. **ela está na casa dos** ~ she is in her twenties. **ño dia** ~ on the twentieth.

vinte-e-um s. m., sg. + pl. (Braz., cards) blackjack.

vintém s. m. (pl. **-éns**) 1. former Brazilian and Portuguese coin. 2. (fig.) money; savings.

eu estou sem um ~ I have no penny, I am broke.

eu não daria um ~ **por aquilo** I should not value it a brass farthing. **jogar a** ~ to play for pennies.

ventena s. f. 1. score, group of twenty. 2. the twentieth part.

vinteno adj. said of a cloth with 2,000 warps.

vinte-pés s. f., sg. + pl. stilt-palm.

viola s. f. 1. (mus.) viol, viola, violin. 2. (bot.) viola.

meter a ~ **no saco** to shut one's mouth, hold one's tongue.

violabilidade s. f. violability.

violação s. f. (pl. **-ões**) 1. violation: a) infringement, infraction. b) transgression, trespass. c) profanation. d) rape, ravishment. 2. offense. 3. break into privacy, breach.

~ **da paz** peacebreaking. ~ **de contrato ou acordo** violation of agreement. **sem** ~ inviolately.

violácea s. f. (bot.) violaceae.

violáceo adj. 1. violaceous: a) (bot.) of the violet family. b) violet (colour). 2. of, pertaining to or like a violet.

violado adj. broken, violated.

violador s. m. violator, transgressor, peacebreaker, ravisher. ‖ adj. violative, profanatory, ravishing.

violal s. m. (pl. **-ais**) field of violets.

violão s. m. (pl. **-ões**) guitar.

violar v. 1. to violate: a) infract, infringe. b) transgress, trespass. c) ravish, rape. d) profane. e) defile, sully. 2. to force. 3. to offend, wrong. 4. to break into a person's privacy, reveal, disclose.

~ **a santidade de** to desecrate. ~ **a virgindade de** to deflour. ~**am-na** they did violence to her.

violatório adj. violative.

violável adj. m. + f. (pl. **-eis**) violable. ‖ **violavelmente** adv. violably.

violeiro s. m. 1. person who makes or sells viols. 2. (Braz.) violist. 3. (ornith.) three-toed jacamar.

violência s. f. violence: 1. vehemence, eagerness. 2. impetuosity, tumultuousness, turbulence. 3. roughness, brutality, irascibility. 4. fierceness, ferocity, rage. 5. violation. 6. profanation. 7. force.

com ~, **à força** at the point of the sword. **abster-se de** ~ to contain o. s.

violentado adj. 1. violated. 2. forced, constrained.

violentador s. m. violator. ‖ adj. violative.

violentar v. 1. to violate. 2. to force. 3. to coerce, constrain. 4. to compel. 5. to break (promise). 6. to break in, force open. 7. to change, alter (wording, meaning).

violento adj. 1. violent. 2. powerful, intense. 3. vehement, passionate. 4. impetuous, tumultuous. 5. irascible. 6. brutal, rude. 7. fierce, wild, ferocious. ‖ **-amente** adv. violently, hammer and tongues.

ele ameaçou violentamente he threatened violently, (U. S. A., coll.) he came the ugly. **morte violenta** violent death. **ser** ~ to act with a high hand.

violeta s. f. 1. violet: a) (bot.) flower of the genus Viola, sweet violet. b) its colour. 2. (mus., obs.) viola. ‖ adj. violet.

violeta-tricolor s. f. (pl. **violetas-tricolores**) (bot.) heartsease, wild pansy.

violeteira s. f. (Braz., bot.) golden dewdrop.`

violinista s. m. + f. violinist, player on the violin, fiddler.

violino s. m. violin: 1. fiddle, viol (plate V 5). 2. violin player, esp. one of an orchestra.

concerto de ~ violin concerto. **tocar** ~ to play violin, play on the fiddle. **tocar o primeiro** ~ to play the first violin.

violoncelista s. m. + f. cellist, violoncellist.

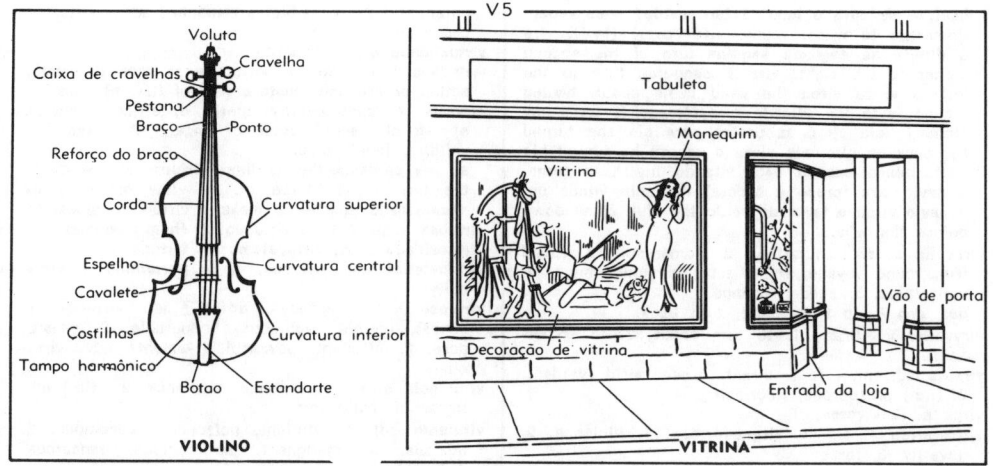

VIOLINO

Voluta
Caixa de cravelhas
Cravelha
Pestana
Braço
Ponto
Reforço do braço
Corda
Curvatura superior
Espelho
Curvatura central
Cavalete
Costilhas
Curvatura inferior
Tampo harmônico
Botao
Estandarte

VITRINA

V 5
Tabuleta
Manequim
Vitrina
Vão de porta
Decoração de vitrina
Entrada da loja

violoncelo s. m. 1. violoncello, cello. 2. violoncellist. 3. (mus.) register.

violonista s. m. + f. guitarist.

vioneira s. f. (Braz.) rope with several harpoons, for fishing.

vipéreo, viperino adj. 1. viperine, viperous, viperish. 2. venomous. 3. (fig.) malignant, wicked, perverse. ‖ **vipereamente, viperinamente** adv. viperishly.

vir v. 1. to come. 2. to arrive. 3. to reach. 4. to amount to. 5. to approach, approximate. 6. to go, walk. 7. to return. 8. to issue from, come from, result. 9. to descend from. 10. to rise, appear. 11. to grow, flourish. 12. to occur. 13. to happen, come about, take place. ~ **abaixo** to tumble down, come down, collapse. ~ **à luz** to become known. ~ **ao mundo** to be born. ~ **a propósito** to suit one's purpose. ~ **a ser** to grow, become. ~ **a si** to recover consciousness. ~ **às mãos** to come to grips. ~ **às mãos de** to fall into the hands of. ~ **atrasado** to be late. ~ **depois** to follow, succeed. ~ **diretamente de** to come clean from. **veio à luz** it came to light. **veio-me à idéia** it came to me. **veio-me a idéia de** the idea crossed my mind. **veio-me à mente** it has come into my head. **venha!** come on! **venha comigo!** come along! **venha já, neste instante!** come here this minute! **venha o que vier** come what may. **venho buscar os livros** I come for the books. **vim pela praia** I came along the beach. **virão dias melhores** better days will come. **como você veio a saber isto?** how came you to know that? **diga-lhe que torne a** ~ tell him to come again. **ele veio à frente** he came to the fore. **ele veio para Londres** he came up to London. **ele vem de família antiga** he comes of an old family. **eu virei** I shall come. **eu viria se** I would come if. **isso não vem ao caso** this has nothing to do with it. **isto vem de acreditar em conversa** this comes from listening to tales. **isto vem a propósito** it fits the occasion. **mandar** ~ to send for, ask for. **nós viemos do campo** we came up from the country. **o que vem agora?** what comes next? **o que vem a ser isto?** and what is this supposed to be? **procure** ~ try and come. **você vem comigo?** are you coming my way?

vira s. f. 1. welt (of a shoe). 2. a popular music and dance. 3. (obs.) very sharp dart.

vira-bosta s. m. (pl. **vira-bostas**) (ent.) tumblebug.

virabrequim s. m. (pl. **-ins**) (mot.) crankshaft (plate M 13).

viração s. f. (pl. **-ões**) 1. breeze, fresh wind, gale. 2. summer fog. 3. act or fact of turning a turtle on its back. 4. laying place of turtles. 5. (Braz.) extra job, extra earnings.

vira-casaca s. m. + f. (pl. **vira-casacas**) turncoat, weathercock, floater.

viracento s. m. apostrophe.

virada s. f. 1. (Braz.): a) turning. b) upset. 2. (sport) turning point (for the better) in a competition.

viradela s. f. act or fact of turning.

viradinho s. m. (Braz.) (also **virado**) dish of beans, flour, eggs and grieves.

virado s. m. (Braz.) = **viradinho**. ‖ adj. 1. overturned, capsized, upside down. 2. (Braz.) playful, jocose, frolicsome.

virador s. m. 1. cable, cablet. 2. (naut.) tow cable. 3. a bookbinder's guilding iron. 4. (railway): a) triangular line to turn the engine. b) turntable.

viragem s. f. (pl. **-ens**) 1. turning (of a motorcar). 2. (phot.) toning bath.

virago s. f. 1. virago. 2. m. cable.

vira-lata s. m. (pl. **vira-latas**) (Braz.) 1. tyke, tike, pooch. 2. (fig.) waif, vagabond.

viramento s. m. act or fact of turning.

vira-mundo s. m. (pl. **vira-mundos**) (Braz., hist.) heavy fetters for slaves.

vira-pedras s. m., sg. + pl. (ornith.) ruddy turnstone.

virar v. 1. to turn: a) reverse, invert. b) change (mind, sides). c) shift. d) transform. e) direct, point. f) rotate, revolve, spin. g) become. h) put the inside out. i) bend. 2. to return. 3. to capsize; keel over. 4. to upset; overthrow. 5. to spill; empty, cant, tip. 6. to fold. 7. **~-se**: a) (Braz.) to do extra work, have an additional job. b) to wheel. **viramos o paletó às avessas** we turned the coat inside out. ~ **a chave** to turn the key. ~ **as coisas de pernas para o ar** to turn things upside down. ~ **as costas para alguém** to turn the back upon s. o. ~ **de borco** to dump. ~ **de querena** to careen. ~ **em roda** (naut.) to boxhaul. ~ **o feno** to toss the hay. ~ **o navio contra o vento** (naut.) to heave to. ~ **as páginas** to leaf. ~ **para cima** to upturn. ~ **para a esquerda** to turn to the left, haw. ~ **para fora** to turn out. ~ **por 180°** to half-face. ~ **a proa para o vento** (naut.) to haul upon the wind. **~-se a favor do vento** (naut.) to veer and haul. ~-se para o lado to turn aside. ~-se repentinamente to wheel round. vire! over! (leaf). vire à direita na segunda esquina turn at the second corner to the right. vire à esquerda turn to the left. o vento virou the wind came about, hauled around. está me virando o estômago it turns my stomach. ela virou as costas para ele she turned her back on him. ele virou a casaca he turned his coat. minha cabeça está virando my head turns. o navio vira (preso à âncora) the ship winds up. o navio virou a favor do vento the ship came down before the wind.

viravolta s. f. 1. turn(ing). 2. somersault. 3. round trip, round voyage, round tour; a going round. 4. vicissitude. 5. sudden change.
dar uma ~ to face about, turn back.

viravoltar v. (Braz.) 1. to turn about. 2. to somersault.

virente adj. m. + f. 1. virent, green, virid, verdant. 2. (fig.) prosperous, flourishing.

virga s. f. = verga.

virga-férrea s. f. (pl. **virgas-férreas**) 1. violence. 2. severity. 3. force.

virgem s. f. (pl. **-ens**) 1. virgin. 2. maid(en), lass, girl. 3. **Virgem:** a) the Virgin (Mary). b) (astr.) Virgo. 4. girl especially dressed to accompany a procession. 5. m. (Braz.) a virginal person. 6. vestal. ǁ adj. virgin: 1. virginal, chaste, maidenly. 2. innocent, pure. 3. fresh. 4. initial, first. 5. untouched, unspoilt. 6. vestal.
a Virgem Maria the Virgin, Virgin Mary. cal ~, cal viva quicklime. cera ~ virgin wax. mata ~ native forest, virgin forest. terra ~ virgin land.

virgiliano adj. Virgilian.

virginal s. m. (pl. **-ais**) (mus.) virginal. ǁ adj. m. + f. virginal.

virgindade s. f. virginity, virginhood.

virgíneo adj. virginal.

virgínia s. f. Virginia (tobacco).

virginiano s. m. Virginian. ǁ adj. Virginian.

virgo s. m. 1. (astr.) Virgo. 2. (pop.) a woman's virginity.

vírgula s. f. (gram.) comma.

virgulação s. f. (pl. **-ões**) (gram.) 1. setting of commas. 2. punctuation, punctuating.

virgular v. (gram.) to insert commas, punctuate.

virgulta s. f. twig, rod, willow.

viridante adj. m. + f. verdant.

víride adj. m. + f. green.

viridente adj. m. + f. verdant, viridescent.

viril s. m. (pl. **-is**) a sort of ampulla. ǁ adj. m. + f. virile: 1. masculine, manlike. 2. yeomanly, vigorous. 3. energetic, diligent. ǁ ~mente adv. virilely.
idade ~ manhood.

virilha s. f. (anat.) groin (plate C 18).

virilidade s. f. virility: 1. manliness, manhood, masculinity. 2. vigour, energy.

virilismo s. m. (med.) virilism.

virilizar v. to strenghten, invigorate, fortify.

viripotente adj. m. + f. 1. nubile, marriageable. 2. strong, robust. 3. manly.

virola s. f. 1. fer(r)ule (plates E 8, S 3). 2. (Braz.) feed guide in a sugar cane press. 3. sort of rubber whip or rubber club.

viroso adj. 1. virous, poisoneous. 2. noxious, harmful. 3. nauseating, repulsive.

virotada s. f. arrow wound (of a virote).

virotão s. m. (pl. **-ões**) augmentative form of virote.

virote s. m. 1. short arrow. 2. cross guard of a sword.

virtual adj. m. + f. (pl. **-ais**) 1. virtual: a) in essence, but not in effect; practical. b) actual, real. c)

potential. 2. possible. ǁ ~mente adv. virtually, practically.

virtualidade s. f. virtuality.

virtude s. f. 1. virtue: a) virtuousness, morality, moral action or practice, austere way of life. b) chastity, purity. c) good quality, merit. d) efficacy, power. e) ~s pl. (eccl.) order of angels. 2. reason. 3. validity, legal force.
as ~s cardeais the cardinal virtues. em ~ de in the face of, in force of, in view of. fazer da necessidade uma ~ to make a virtue of necessity.

virtuose s. m. + f. 1. virtuoso. 2. (hum.) bungler.

virtuosidade s. f., **virtuosismo** m. virtuosity.

virtuosístico adj. virtuous, of or pertaining to virtuosity.

virtuoso s. m. virtuoso, artist. ǁ adj. virtuous: 1. honest, upright, righteous, honourable. 2. chaste, pure. 3. efficient, powerful. ǁ **-amente** adv. virtuously.

virulência s. f. 1. virulence, virulency. 2. (fig.) malignance, malignancy.

virulento adj. 1. virulent, poisonous, venomous. 2. noxious. 3. malignant, acrimonious, rancorous. ǁ **-amente** adv. virulently.

vírus s. m. virus: 1. bacteria, infecting agents, contagion. 2. venom, poison. 3. something that corrupts, corruptive influence.

visada s. f. act or fact of aiming, marking.

visado adj. visaed.

visagem s. f. (pl. **-ens**) 1. visage, countenance, face. 2. excessive gesturing to impress with, showing off.

visão s. f. (pl. **-ões**) vision: 1. (eye)sight, seeing. 2. (fig.) eye. 3. aspect, view. 4. foresight. 5. illusion, chimera, dream, phantasy. 6. apparition, spectre, ghost.

visar v. 1. to aim at, drive at, seek. 2. to take aim, to sight. 3. to direct, tend. 4. to look at. 5. to visa.

vis-à-vis s. m. + f. vis-à-vis. ǁ adj. vis-à-vis.

víscera s. f. 1. (anat.) viscera; inwards, entrails, gut. (usually in pl.). 2. (fig.) core.

visceral adj. m. + f. (pl. **-ais**) (also **visceroso**) visceral.

visco s. m. 1. birdlime. 2. (bot.) mistletoe. 3. (fig.) bait, enticement, allurement.

viscondado s. m. 1. viscounty, viscountcy. 2. viscountship.

visconde s. m. viscount.

viscondessa s. f. viscountess.

viscose s. f. (chem.) viscose.

viscosidade s. f. (also **viscidez**) viscosity, viscousness, lentor, stickiness, clogginess.

viscosímetro s. m. viscosimeter.

viscoso adj. (also **visguento**) viscous, sticky, viscid, limy, jammy, clammy. ǁ **-amente** adv. viscously, etc.

viseira s. f. 1. visor, vizor, face guard, beaver (of a helmet). 2. protection. 3. disguise. 4. view, aspect. 5. frown.
de ~ erguida proudly: holding one's head high or the nose in the air.

visibilidade s. f. 1. visibility. 2. eyeshot. 3. observableness, perceptibility.

visigodo s. m. Visigoth. ǁ adj. (also **visigótico**) Visigothic.

visionar v. 1. to vision, have visions. 2. to imagine, think of, dream. 3. to see.

visionário s. m. visionary: 1. castle-builder, phantast, utopian, idealist. 2. person who has visions. ǁ adj. visionary: 1. visional, phantastic, utopic, doctrinaire, 2. notional, imaginary. 3. dreamy.

visita s. f. 1. visit: a) visiting. b) visitation. c) inspection, survey. d) search(ing). 2. visitant, visitor,

caller. 3. (hist.) tribut in specie. 4. ~s pl. regards, compliments.
~ **aduaneira** examination. ~ **breve** call, flying visit. ~ **domiciliária** domiciliary visit. ~ **obrigatória** duty call. ~ **pessoal para promoção de vendas** canvass. **cartão de** ~ visiting card. **deixar seu cartão de** ~ to leave one's card. **dia de** ~ (hospital) visiting day. **fazer uma** ~ to pay a visit; make a call; look in upon. **multas** ~s many visitors. **nova** ~ revisitation. **pagar uma** ~ to pay a call. **receber** ~s to receive company. **eu tive** ~s I have had visitors. ~ **da cegonha** a visit from the stork, the birth of a child. **fazer uma** ~ **de médico** to call on, look in, drop in.
visitação s. f. (pl. -ões) 1. visitation, visiting. 2. sight-seeing. 3. (rel.) Visitation. 4. (obs.) regards.
visitador s. m. 1. visitor, visitant, caller. 2. inspector. || adj. 1. visiting. 2. inspecting.
Visitandina s. f. (rel.) Visitandine.
visitante s. m. + f. 1. visitant, visitor, caller. 2. company. 3. sight-seer. || adj. visitant, visiting.
~ **não convidado** gate-crasher. **livro dos** ~ visitors' book.
visitar v. 1. to visit: a) call on, see, pay a visit, go on visitation. b) examine, inspect, survey. c) inflict, punish. 2. to attend (doctor). 3. to appear (spirit).
visitamos a galeria we paid a visit to the gallery. ~ **casualmente** to drop in. ~ **a clientela** to canvass. ~ **inopinadamente** to fall in upon. ~ **novamente** to revisit. **eu a visitei** I paid her a visit. **nós nos visitamos** we are on visiting terms. **permite-me visitá-lo?** may I call at your house? **ele nos visitará um dia desses** he will look round one of these days.
visitável adj. m. + f. (pl. -áveis) visitable.
visiva s. f. sight, vision, power of seeing.
visível adj. m. + f. (pl. -íveis) visible: a) perceptible, discernible. b) manifest, plain, clear. c) apparent. 2. public; notorious. 3. at home. 4. outward, external. || **visivelmente** adv. visibly.
bem ~ plain to the view. **não é** ~ it does not show. **a sabedoria de Cristo é** ~ **em suas obras** the wisdom of Christ is apparent in his works.
visivo adj. 1. = **visível**. 2. = **visual**.
vislumbrar v. 1. to catch a glimpse, discern indistinctly, descry. 2. to shimmer, glimmer. 3. to conjecture, surmise. 4. to have a notion; guess. 5. to be similar; remind. 6. to appear, show up.
vislumbre s. m. 1. shimmer, glimmer. 2. glimpse, momentary view. 3. idea, notion. 4. conjecture. 5. trace. 6. likeness.
viso s. m. 1. aspect, appearance, sight. 2. shimmer, glimmer. 3. notion, guess. 4. symptom, sign, trace. 5. small quantity. 6. peak of a mountain. 7. hillock.
visonha s. f. horrible apparition.
visor s. m. 1. (phot.) view finder (plate M 3). 2. (mil.) sight. 3. sighthole, spy-hole.
víspora s. f. lotto.
visporar v. (Braz.) to fill the numbers of a lotto card (also **quinar**).
vista s. f. 1. sight: a) eyesight, vision. b) act or fact of seeing. c) glimpse, blink. d) what is seen: view, aspect, picture, scenery, panorama. e) way of seeing a thing or question, judgement. 2. the eye(s). 3. visor (helmet). 4. outlook, vista, prospect. 5. purpose, intention, plan.
~ **aérea** aerial view; bird's eye view. ~ **curta** shortsightedness. ~ **de cima** plant view. ~ **de frente** full face. ~ **de perto** close-up. ~ **geral** 1. survey. 2. bird's-eye view. ~ **para o oeste** western aspect. **à** ~ 1. in specie. 2. (com.) in mash, at sight. 3. in view. **negócio à** ~ spot transaction. **vender à** ~ to sell for current payment,

sell for cash. **pagamento à** ~ spot cash. **bem à** ~ under one's nose. **está à** ~ it is in view, visible, plain. **até à** ~**!** so long! **dar na** ~ to strike the eye. **não dá na** ~ **a quem não olha** a horse galloping by won't see it. **de** ~ **fraca** weak-eyed, weak-sighted. **de** ~ from sight. **eu o conheço de** ~ I know him by sight. **de** ~ **penetrante** lynx-eyed, keen-sighted. **o espetáculo deleita a** ~ the sight relieves the eyes. **em** ~ **de** for; in consideration of; with an eye to. **em** ~ **disto** on the strength of it. **em** ~ **de sua idade avançada** seeing her age. **ele tem em** ~ **um plano secreto** he has a card up his sleeve. **ter em** ~ to have in one's eyes; to have in one's mind. **fazer** ~ **grossa** to shut one's eyes to. **os campos se prolongam a perder de** ~ the fields stretch as far as the horizon. **perder de** ~ to lose sight of. **ponto de** ~ point of view. **à primeira** ~ at first view, at the first glance. **isto é mais sério do que parece à primeira** ~ there is more in it than strikes the eye. **eu compreendo isto à primeira** ~ I can see that with half an eye. **ela toca à primeira** ~ she plays from sight. **ter boa** ~ to have good sight. **seu quarto tem** ~ **para o mar** his room faces the sea. **longe da** ~ **longe do coração** out of sight out of mind. **fazer** ~ **grossa a** to shut the eyes to, look the other way, overlook.
visto s. m. visé, visa. || adj. 1. accepted, acknowledged. 2. seen. 3. known. 4. examined.
~ **de cima** bird's-eye. ~ **que** respecting; for; in as much as; for as much. ~ **sob este aspecto** regarded in this light. **não** ~ unseen, unwitnessed. **pôr o** ~, **dar o** ~ to put a visa on. **ser pessoa mal-vista** to be disliked, frowned upon. **está** ~ it is obvious, plain.
vistoria s. f. 1. inspection, survey(ing), visit(ation). 2. search, rummage.
~ **domiciliar** domiciliary visit.
vistoriar v. 1. to inspect, examine. 2. to rummage, search. 3. to review.
vistoso adj. 1. showy, sightly, good-looking, stately, attractive. 2. becoming, beautiful. 3. dressy, flash(y). 4. ostentatious. 5. gallant, handsome. || -**amente** adv. showily.
uma moça -a a tight lass.
visual (also **visório**) adj. m. + f. (pl. -ais) visual. || ~**mente** adv. visually.
aculdade ~ visual acuity. **ângulo** ~ visual angle. **campo** ~ visual field. **memória** ~ photographic memory.
visualidade s. f. 1. visuality. 2. vision, utopia, mirage.
visualização s. f. (pl. -ões) visualization.
visualizar v. to visualize.
vitáceo adj. (bot.) vitaceous: of the grape (Vitaceae) family.
vital adj. m. + f. (pl. -ais) 1. vital: a) of or pertaining to life. b) organic. c) important, essential. 2. strengthening, invigorating. || ~**mente** adv. vitally. **partes vitais** vital parts. **questão** ~ vital question.
vitalicidade s. f. lifetime.
vitalício adj. for life, lifelong, lifetime.
vitalidade s. f. vitality: 1. vital force, vital power. 2. vigo(u)r.
vitalina s. f. (N. Braz.) spinster.
vitalismo s. m. (biol.) vitalism.
vitalização s. f. (pl. -ões) vitalization.
vitalizador s. m. vitalizer.
vitalizante adj. vitalizing, invigorating.
vitalizar v. to vitalize: 1. give life to. 2. impart vigour. 3. (fig.) (re)animate.
vitamina s. vitamin(e).
~ B, aneurin. ~ C ascorbic acid.

vitando, vitatório adj. (obs.) 1. that is to be avoided. 2. abominable.

vitascópio s. m. vitascope.

vitela s. f. 1. heifer. 2. calf: a) young of a cow. b) leather made from its skin. 3. veal.

vitelífero adj. yolky, vitelline.

vitelina s. f. 1. (biochem.) vitellin. 2. vitelline membrane.

vitelino adj. vitelline: 1. of or referring to the yolk of an egg. 2. yellow (like the yolk of an egg).

vitelo s. m. 1. male calf, young bull. 2. vitellus.

vitícola s. m. + f., **viticultor** m. viticulturist, vine--dresser, grape grower, vineyardist. ‖ adj. viticultural.

viticultura s. f. viticulture, viniculture.

vitífero adj. 1. of or pertaining to vines. 2. viticultural. 3. covered with vines.

vitiligem s. f. (pl. **-ens**), **vitiligo** m. (path.) vitiligo.

vítima s. f. victim: 1. slain, hurt or sacrified person. 2. person suffering a disaster, a loss. 3. sacrifice, esp. offered to some deity. 4. (fig.) prey, sport.
tornamo-nos ~ **de** we fell a prey to. **ele foi** ~ **de seu credor** he fell a sacrifice to his creditor.

vitimar v. to victimize: 1. sacrifice. 2. kill, slay, injure. 3. cause losses or damages. 4. cheat.

vitimário s. m. (hist.) victimarius, victimizer. ‖ m. + f. of or pertaining to victims.

vitivinícola adj. winegrowing.

vitivinicultor s. m. winegrower.

vitória s. f. 1. victory. 2. triumph, conquest. 3. (fig.) advantage, success, palm. 4. victoria: four-wheeled carriage.
~ **fácil** walkover, walkaway. ~ **ou morte** stand or fall. **conseguir a** ~ to win the day. **obtiveram a** ~ **the day** the day was theirs. **não cantes a** ~ **antes do tempo** don't halloo until you are out of the wood.

vitorianismo s. m. Victorianism.

vitoriano s. m. (hist.) Victorian. ‖ adj. Victorian.

vitoriar v. to shout to, cheer, applaud, acclaim, shout victory.

vitória-régia s. f. (pl. **vitórias-régias**) (bot.) victoria regia.

vitorioso adj. 1. victorious, triumphant. 2. winning, successful. ‖ **-amente** adv. victoriously.
o exército ~ the victorious army. **sair** ~ to come off with flying colours.

vitral s. m. (pl. **-ais**) stained glass window.

vitre s. m. sort of canvas.

vítreo adj. 1. vitreous, vitric, glassy. 2. transparent, hyaline.
humour ~ (med.) hyaloid body.

vitrescibilidade s. f. vitrescibility.

vitrescível adj. m. + f. (pl. **-íveis**) vitrescible, vitrescent.

vitrice s. f. victoress. ‖ adj. f. victorious.

vitrificação s. f. (pl. **-ões**) vitrification, vitrifaction.

vitrificar v. to vitrify: change into glass or become vitreous.

vitrificável adj. m. + f. (pl. **-áveis**) vitrifiable, vitrescible.

vitrina s. f. display window, shopwindow, store window (plates A 2, E 13, V 5).

vitriolado adj. vitriolated.

vitriólico adj. vitriolic; sulfuric.

vitriolização s. f. (pl. **-ões**) vitriolization.

vitriolizar v. to vitriolize.

vitríolo s. m. (chem.) vitriol.
~ **azul** blue vitriol. ~ **branco** white vitriol. ~ **de chumbo** anglesite.

vitrola s. f. victrola, phonograph, gramophone.

vitualhas s. f. pl. victuals, provisions.

vituperação s. f. (pl. **-ões**) vituperation: 1. severe reproach, censure. 2. decry, slander, insult.

vituperador s. m. vituperator, insulter, slanderer.

vituperar v. to vituperate: 1. reproach, censure severely. 2. decry, slander, insult.

vituperável adj. m. + f. (pl. **-áveis**) vituperable.

vitupério s. m. 1. vituperation. 2. infamy, opprobrium, disgrace, shame.

vituperioso adj. vituperative.

viúva s. f. 1. widow, relict. 2. (ornith.) waterchat, widow bird.
~ **alegre** (Braz. sl.) patrol wagon. ~ **dotada** dowager.

viuvar v. (also **enviuvar**) 1. to become a widow or widower. 2. to bereave of husband or wife.

viuvez s. f. 1. widowhood, wifelessness. 2. (fig.): a) solitude, loneliness. b) privation, destitution.

viuvinha s. f. (dim. of **viúva**) 1. widow. 2. sort of dance.

viúvo s. m. widower. ‖ adj. 1. widowed, wifeless. 2. (fig.) destitute, wanting.

viva s. m. viva. ‖ interj. 1. viva! 2. your health! 3. cheerio! hooray!
~ **o rei!** long live the king! ~ **a liberdade!** liberty for ever! **deram três** ~s they gave three cheers.

vivacidade, viveza s. f. 1. vivacity, vivaciousness. 2. liveliness, sprightliness. 3. alacrity. 4. spiritedness.

vivaldino s. m. (pop.) 1. an individual who is lively, alert, quick. 2. a great rascal, rogue.

vivandeira s. f. sutler, canteen woman.

vivandeiro s. m. sutler, canteen man, camp follower.

vivaracho adj. (S. Braz.) 1. vivacious. 2. shrewd, clever, knowing.

vivaz adj. 1. vivacious, lively, sprightly. 2. spirited. 3. bright. 4. (bot.) perennial, long-lived.
a menina é muito ~ the girl is all alive.

vivedor adj. 1. solicitous, diligent. 2. (N. Braz.) money-making.

vivedouro adj. (also **vivedoiro**) 1. viable, capable of living. 2. long-lived. 3. long-lasting.

viveiro s. m. 1. nursery, hotbed. 2. vivarium, run. 3. aquarium; fishpond. 4. great quantity.
~ **de aves** aviary. ~ **de coelhos** coop, warren. ~ **de faisões** pheasantry. ~ **de peixes e tartarugas** crawl. ~ **de plantas** arboretum.

vivência s. f. 1. life, existence, being. 2. experience of life, grasp on life. 3. what has been lived, experienced.

vivenciar v. to live, grasp, experience fully.

vivenda s. f. 1. dwelling, dwelling-place. 2. home, abode. 3. subsistence, livelihood. 4. behaviour.

vivente s. m. + f. liver, breather, mortal, man, human being. ‖ adj. alive, breathing, living.
nenhum ~ no one living.

viver s. m. life. ‖ v. to live: 1. be alive, exist, be, breathe. 2. endure, last. 3. subsist. 4. depend for subsistence upon. 5. enjoy life. 6. reside, dwell. 7. live together. 8. pass or spend a certain kind of life. 9. be nourished, feed.
~ **alegre e despreocupadamente** to live away. ~ **além de suas possibilidades** to live beyond one's means. ~ **amigado** to live tally. ~ **ao deus-dará** to live from hand to mouth. ~ **como cão e gato** to live like cat and dog. ~ **de** to subsist upon. ~ **de verduras** to live on vegetables. ~ **dissolutamente** to live dissolutely, (coll.) womanize. ~ **em chiqueiro** to sty. ~ **em hordas ou bandos** to horde. ~ **modestamente** to crack a crust, vegetate, lead a hard life. ~ **num céu aberto** to feel in heaven. ~ **só** to live alone. **ela vive da costura** she lives by sewing. **o seu pai ainda vive?** is your father still alive? **cansado de** ~ life-weary. **como você consegue** ~ **com tão pouco?** how can you exist on so little? **ele sabe** ~ **com o pouco que ganha** he makes a sufficiency of his income. **ele vive do que ganha no momento**

he lives by his wits. **temos de ~ nesta cova** we have to exist in this hole. **com este papel vive ou morre a peça** this role holds the stage. **ter que ~ to** have one's living. **quem ~ verá** time will show. **o império viveu um período de maior sucesso** the Empire saw a period of greatest success.

víveres s. m. pl. food, provisions, victuals, foodstuff. **~ deterioráveis** perishables.

vividez s. f. vividness.

vivido adj. 1. that has lived a long time. 2. experienced in life.

vívido adj. 1. vivid, lively. 2. brilliant, bright. 3. intense, acute. 4. (fig.) excitant, ardent.

vivificação s. f. vivification, enlivenment.

vivificador s. m. vivifier. ‖ adj. vivifying, vivificative.

vivificante adj. m. + f. vivifying, enlivening, life-giving.

vivificar v. 1. to vivify, vivificate, enliven. 2. to animate, encourage. 3. (fig.) to keep boiling. 4. to vitalize.

vivificativo adj. vivificative.

vivífico adj. vivifying, animating, vitalizing.

viviparidade s. f. viviparity, viviparousness.

viviparo s. m. viviparous animal. ‖ adj. (bot. + zool.) viviparous.

vivisse(c)ção s. f. (pl. **-ões**) vivisection.

vivisse(c)cionista s. m. + f. vivisectionist, vivisector.

vivissectar v. to vivisect.

vivo s. m. 1. living creature. 2. (fig.) core. 3. (tail.) piping (plate R 7). 4. (vet.) vives. ‖ adj. 1. alive, living, breathing. 2. lively, vivacious, brisk. 3. spirited, smart, witted. 4. racy, keen, eager. 5. quick, ready, prompt, alert. 6. irritable, vehement. 7. ardent, intense, persistent. 8. sharp (edge). 9. fresh. 10. gay. 11. bright, high-coloured, rich, colourful. ‖ **vivamente** adv. lively, etc. **os ~s e os mortos** the quick and the dead. **à viva força** by main force. **à viva voz** orally, by word of mouth, viva voce. **água viva** spring water. **cal ~** quicklime. **carne viva** the quick, sensitive, living flesh. **criança viva** a lively child. **mais morto que ~** more dead than alive. **rocha viva** living rock. **sebe viva** quickset hedge. **programa ao ~** (Braz.) live program, show.

vivório s. m. shouts of applause, cheers.

vívula s. f. (vet.) vives.

vizindário s. m. (Braz.) all the neighbours, vicinage.

vizinhada s. f. (Braz.) vicinage, neighbouring families.

vizinhança s. f. 1. neighbourhood: a) all the neighbours, vicinage. b) proximity, nearness, vicinity. c) environs, surroundings. d) immediacy, contiguity, contiguousness. 2. (fig.) likeness, analogy. **fazer boa ~** to be friends with one's neighbours. **na ~** in the neighbourhood.

vizinhar v. to neighbour: 1. be or live near. 2. adjoin, border, be contiguous. 3. draw near, approach.

vizinho s. m. 1. neighbour. 2. tenant, lodger, inhabitant. ‖ adj. 1. neighbour(ing), vicinal, bordering, contiguous, adjacent. 2. near, proximate, surrounding. 3. close (relative). 4. analogous, alike. **impróprio de bom ~** unneighbourly.

vizir s. m. vizier, officer, official in some Mohammedan countries.

vizirado, vizirato s. m. vizierate.

voador s. m. 1. flyer, flier, person or thing that flies. 2. trapeze acrobat. ‖ adj. 1. flying, volant. 2. (fig.) swift, quick. **disco ~** flying saucer. **peixe ~** flying fish.

voadouros s. m. pl. (also **voadoiros**) 1. wing feathers, remiges. 2. (fig.) ways of acting to force one's career.

voadura s. f. flying, flight.

voagem s. f. (pl. **-ens**) chaff.

voante adj. m. + f. 1. flying, volant. 2. (fig.) transient, fleeting. 3. quick, swift.

voar v. to fly: 1. wing. 2. travel through the air. 3. soar, mount, rise in the air. 4. run, make haste, hurry. 5. slip away, pass quickly (time). 6. run away, flee. 7. shun. 8. disappear, vanish rapidly. 9. spread rapidly (rumour). 10. explode, blow up. **~ a baixa altura** (aeron.) to hedge-hop. **~ baixinho** (Braz., fig.) to be down. **~ às cegas** (aeron.) to fly by instruments. **~ em cima de alguém** 1. to fall or set upon a person. 2. to court insistently. **~ em vôo rasteiro** (aeron.) to buzz. **~ melhor ou mais longe que** to overfly. **fazer ~ pelos ares** to blast. **a pedra voou pelos ares** the stone travelled the air.

voborde s. m. (naut.) railing.

vocabular adj. m. + f. of or pertaining to a vocable.

vocabulário s. m. vocabulary: 1. dictionary, wordbook. 2. words peculiar to one field of knowledge.

vocabularista, vocabulista s. m. + f. author of a vocabulary.

vocábulo s. m. vocable, word, term, name.

vocação s. f. (pl. **-ões**) 1. vocation, call(ing), inclination, talent, vein, endowment. 2. (Braz.) proper soil for a tree.

vocacionado adj. gifted, talented, endowed, born for.

vocacional adj. m. + f. (pl. **-ais**) vocational. ‖ **~mente** adv. vocationally.

vocal adj. m. + f. (pl. **-ais**) 1. vocal. 2. oral, in speech. ‖ **~mente** adv. vocally. **cordas vocais** (anat.) vocal chords. **música ~ vocal** music.

vocálico adj. vocalic, vowel. **mutação -a** vowel mutation.

vocalise s. m. (mus.) vocalization.

vocalismo s. m. (gram.) vocalism.

vocalista s. m. + f. vocalist, singer.

vocalização s. f. (pl. **-ões**) vocalization.

vocalizador s. m. vocalizer. ‖ adj. vocalizing.

vocalizar v. 1. (mus.) to vocalize. 2. to vowelize. 3. (phon.) to voice.

vocalizo s. m. (mus.) vocalization.

vocativo s. m. (gram.) vocative. ‖ adj. vocative.

você pron. you; thou. **~ e os seus** you and yours. **isto é lá com ~** that is up to you; that is your chicken. **está em ~** it rests with you. **se não fosse por ~** were it not for you.

vociferação s. f. (pl. **-ões**) vociferation, clamour, bawling.

vociferador s. m. vociferant, yeller. ‖ adj. (also **vociferante** m. + f.) vociferant, vociferous, clamorous.

vociferar v. to vociferate, clamour, yell, bawl, cry, swear, inveigh, thunder forth, bellow.

voçoroca s. f. (Braz.) a falling in, collapse caused by undermining waters.

vodca s. f. vodka.

vodu s. m. voodoo (magic).

voejar v. to flutter, flap, flicker.

voejo s. m. fluttering, flapping, flicker.

voga s. f. 1. vogue: a) mode, style. b) repute. c) popularity. d) fashion, rage. 2. m. stroke-oar. 3. stroke of the oar, row, pulling. **em ~** in season. **estar em ~** to have a good run. **modinha muito em ~** hit song. **a ~ arrancada** at full power. **a ~ surda** rowing noiselessly, with muffled oars.

vogal s. f. (pl. **-ais**) 1. (gram.) vowel, vocal, vocal sound. 2. m. + f. voter. ‖ adj. m. + f. vocal, voiced, intonated. **~ fechada** closed vowel.

vogante adj. m. + f. 1. navigating, sailing, rowing. 2. floating, drifting. 3. prevailing, in vogue, in fashion.

vogar v. 1. to be propelled by oars. 2. to row. 3. to navigate, voyage. 4. to float, drift, glide. 5. to be in vogue, in fashion. 6. to be about (rumour). 7. to prevail.

voivoda s. m. voivode, vaivode.

volante s. m. 1. gauze. 2. shuttlecock. 3. badminton. 4. arrow. 5. (mec.): a) flywheel (plate M 1). b) belt. c) fly. 6. (mot.) steering wheel (plate V 3). 7. lackey, footman. 8. racing motorist. 9. commercial advertising pamphlet, flyer, flier. ‖ adj. m. + f. 1. volant, flying. 2. floating, drifting. 3. fickle, unsteady. 4. movable, portable. 5. errant. 6. transitory.
~ **de relógio** balance wheel. **folha** ~ pamphlet. **no** ~ **at the wheel. pelotão** ~ flying squad.

volantim, volatim s. m. (pl. **-ins**) 1. funambulist, ropedancer, wiredancer, acrobat. 2. messenger, errand boy; (obs.) lackey, footman.

volapuque s. m. Volapuk: artificial language.

volata s. f. 1. (mus.) volata. 2. (Braz.) haste.

volataria s. f. 1. falconry, hawking. 2. birds chased or killed.

volateante adj. m. + f. fluttering, flapping.

volatear v. to flutter, flap, flicker.

volátil s. m. (pl. **-eis**) 1. winged animal, animal that flies. 2. bird. ‖ adj. m. + f. volatile: 1. flying, volant. 2. fugacious, fugitive. 3. fickle, changeable. 4. that vaporizes or evaporates rapidly.
sal ~ volatile salt.

volatilidade s. f. volatility.

volatilização s. f. volatilization.

volatilizante adj. m. + f. volatilizing.

volatilizar v. to volatilize, evaporate.

volatório adj. for flying.

volfrâmio s. m. (chem.) wolfram, tungsten.

volição s. f. (pl. **-ões**) volition: act or fact of willing; decision, choice.

volitante adj. m. + f. 1. volitant, flying. 2. fluttering, flapping.

volitar v. to volitate, flap, flutter.

volitivo adj. volitional, volitive.

volível adj. m. + f. (pl. **-íveis**) willable, that may be wished, depending on the will.

volt s. m. (electr.) volt: unit of electromotive force.

volta s. f. 1. return, regress(ion). 2. recurrency. 3. change: a) alteration. b) surplus of money. 4. replacement. 5 turn(ing), revolution, gyre, rotation, slue, turnabout. 6. vicissitude, defeat. 7. reply. 8. repercussion. 9. circuit. 10. detour, roundabout way, deviation. 11. wind(ing). 12. bend, bent, curve. 13. (Braz.) meander, sinuosity, double. 14. errand.
~ **à posição anterior** comeback. ~ **à selvajaria** a lapse into savage ways. ~ **de fiel** (naut.) clove hitch. **a** ~ **do século** the turn of the century. ~ **em espiral** volution. ~ **e meia falava nisto** he talked about it more often than not. ~ **pela cidade** tour of the town. ~ **rápida, súbita** jink, whirl, quirk. **bilhete de ida e** ~ return ticket. **cortei uma** ~ **com aquilo** that kept me busy, I can tell you. **dar uma** ~ 1. to tour. 2. to go for a trot, take a walk, a round, a stroll. **demos uma** ~ **completa** we have come full circle. **demos uma** ~ we took a turn. **de** ~ back, returned. **de** ~ **aos inícios** back to the beginnings. **no caminho de** ~ home-bound. **efetuar uma** ~ (mil.) to swing into line. **em** ~ **(de)** round about. **estar às** ~**s com a polícia** to be in hot water with the police. **estarei de** ~ **logo** I shall be back soon. **fazer meia-**~ to face about, to about--face. **meia-**~ (mil.) evolution, right about turn. **meia-**~ **volver!** (mil.) about face! **meia-**~ **à es-**

querda! left about! **meia-**~ **à direita!** right about! **numa** ~ **de mão** rapidly. **pagar de** ~ to pay back. **por** ~ **do correio** in course of post, by return post. **por** ~ **das 5 h** at about 5 o'clock. **viagem de** ~ home-journey.

volta-face s. f. (pl. **volta-faces**) retractation.

voltagem s. f. (pl. **-ens**) voltage: electromotive force expressed in volts; tension.
~ **nominal** rating. **excesso de** ~ overvoltage.

voltaico adj. voltaic.
corrente -a voltaic current. **eletricidade** -a voltaic electricity. **solda ao arco** ~ electrical arc welding.

voltaísmo s. m. voltaism.

voltâmetro s. m. voltameter.

voltar v. 1. to return: a) come back, go back, regress. b) recur. c) devolve, give back. d) reply, answer. e) appeal. 2. to turn. 3. to begin anew, recommence. 4. to retrace. 5. to change direction. 6. to cause a change of mind. 7. (naut.) to veer; to wear ship. 8. to revert. 9. to put the inside out, or upside down, reverse. 10. to fold. 11. to revolve: a) whirl, rotate. b) search. 12. to direct, point. 13. to apply.
~ **à baila** to be brought up again for discussion. ~ **as costas a** to turn one's back to. ~ **a cabeça a alguém** to make a person crazy. **voltou-me à memória** it came back to me. **ela voltou a si** she came to herself. **ele voltou logo a si** he came round soon. ~ **à vaca-fria** to return to the point, subject. ~ **atrás** to double; to climb down. **ele agora não pode** ~ **para trás** he cannot go back now. **voltarei** I shall call again. **voltarei num instante** I'll be back in a minute. **voltaremos ao ar às 5 h** (radio) we are on the air at five. **volte!** come back! ~**-se para** to face.

voltarete s. m. ombre: old card game.

voltário adj. fickle.

volte s. m. turning up of the first card when playing ombre.

volteada s. f. 1. (Braz.) roundup of cattle. 2. trap, ambush. 3. walk, tour, trip. 4. voyage.
cair na ~ (animal) to be caught in the roundup.

volteador s. m. 1. ropedancer, funambulist. 2. vaulter. 3. (Braz.) cowboy (engaged to keep the herd together). ‖ adj. that keeps going or circling around.

volteadura s. f., **volteio** m. 1. turning, rotating. 2. flutter(ing). 3. vaulting. 4. ropedancing.

voltear v. (also **voltejar**) 1. to go or turn about. 2. to cause to turn about. 3. to circle about. 4. to whirl, rotate. 5. to round, detour. 6. to make the circuit of. 7. to rummage, stir. 8. to vault. 9. to flutter. 10. to dance on the rope.

volteiro adj. 1. that goes or turns about. 2. fickle, changeable, instable. 3. (obs.) pugnatious, rowdy, turbulent.

voltímetro, voltômetro s. m. (elect.) voltmeter.

voltívolo adj. 1. unstable, inconstant. 2. fickle.

volubilidade s. f. 1. volubility. 2. fickleness. 3. versatileness. 4. changeableness. 5. light-mindedness.

volumão s. m. (pl. **-ões**) large volume.

volumar v. = avolumar. ‖ adj. m. + f. (geom.) volumetric.

volume s. m. volume: 1. capacity, content, cubage. 2. extent. 3. size. 4. mass, bulk. 5. book, tome. 6. pack, packet, bundle. 7. roll, scroll. 8. intensity of sound.
~ **de descarga** (tech.) discharge, delivery. ~ **da voz** compass of the voice. **a todo** ~ (radio) at full volume. **em três** ~**s** three-volumed.

volumétrico adj. volumetric(al). ‖ **volumetricamente** adv. volumetrically.
análise -a volumetric analysis.

volúmetro s. m. volumeter.

voluminoso, volumoso adj. 1. voluminous: a) bulky, large, ample, big. b) filling many books. c) going to a great length. 2. intense, loud (voice, sound).

voluntariado s. m. volunteers collectively.

voluntariedade s. f. 1. voluntariness. 2. spontaneousness. 3. capriciousness. 4. whimsicality.

voluntário s. m. 1. volunteer (also mil.). 2. improver. ‖ adj. voluntary: 1. volunteer. 2. spontaneous. 3. free, gratuitous. 4. willful, headstrong. ‖ **voluntariamente** adv. voluntarily.

voluntariosidade s. f. willfulness, whimsicality, capriciousness.

voluntarioso adj. willful, whimsical, capricious, obstinate.

voluntarismo s. m. (philos.) voluntarism.

volúpia, volu(p)tuosidade s. f. 1. voluptuousness, sensuality, luxuriousness. 2. (fig.) great pleasure.

volu(p)tuário adj. 1. voluptuous, sensual. 2. fond of feasting, frolicsome.

volu(p)tuoso adj. 1. voluptuous, sensual, luxurious. 2. libertine. 3. fond of feasting, given to pleasures; epicurean. 4. arousing sensuality. ‖ **-amente** adv. sensually, voluptuously.

voluta s. f. 1. (archit.) volute, scroll, helix (plate V 5). 2. (zool.) volute. 3. (mus.) scroll.

volutear s. m. rotation, revolution. ‖ v. to turn, rotate, circle.

volúvel adj. m. + f. (pl. **-eis**) 1. voluble. 2. fickle, fluky, shifty. 3. inconstant, changeable. 4. flighty, flyaway. 5. volatile. 6. (bot.) climbing. ‖ **voluvelmente** adv. volubly.

volva s. f. (bot.) volva.

volváceo, volvado adj. (bot.) volvate.

volver s. m. act or fact of turning, etc. ‖ v. 1. to turn, direct. 2. to revolve, rotate, spin. 3. to roll, roll round. 4. to agitate. 5. to transform, change. 6. to return: a) come back. b) give back. 7. to reply, answer, retort. 8. to pass, elapse (time).

~ para o passado to retrospect. **~ pelo mesmo caminho** to retrace. **à direita, ~!** (mil.) right face! **à esquerda, ~!** (mil.) left face!

volvo s. m. (path.; pop., also **nó-nas-tripas**) volvulus.

vólvulo s. m. one of the rings of a curled snake.

vômer s. m. (anat.) vomer: partition bone between the nostrils.

vomeriano adj. (anat.) vomerine.

vômica s. f. (path.) vomica: cavity in the lung with suppuration.

noz ~ vomica.

vomitado s. m. vomit: that which is vomited.

vomitador s. m. person who vomits. ‖ adj. vomiting.

vomitar v. 1. to vomit, spew; (coll.) to cat. 2. to sully with vomit. 3. to eject, throw out or up, discharge, belch forth. 4. to regurgitate, disgorge. **fazer esforços para ~** to keck, retch. **ele vomitou** he was sick. **isto faz ~** that is sickening.

vomitivo s. m. vomitive. ‖ adj. vomitive.

vômito s. m. (also **vomição** f.) 1. vomit, spew, puke, sickness. 2. that which is vomited.

~-negro (path.) vomito negro (yellow fever). **ter ânsias de ~** to feel sick.

vomitório s. m. vomitive, vomitory, emetic. ‖ adj. vomitive, vomitory.

vontade s. f. 1. will. 2. volition. 3. wish, desire, craving. 4. mind, intention, purpose. 5. resolution, determination. 6. fancy, caprice, whim. 7. spontaneity. 8. pleasure. 9. (fig.) appetite; hunger, thirst. 10. inclination, disposition.

~ forte strong will. **à ~** 1. comfy, at large, at will, easygoing, at pleasure, as heart could wish. 2. (mil.) stand easy! 3. arbitrary. **à sua ~** at your convenience, at your discretion. **boa ~** alacrity, good will. **com boa ~** in good part. **de boa ~** nothing loath, with good grace, agreeable. **chorar à ~** to have a good cry. **contra a minha ~** against my will. **escolha à sua ~** take your choice. **estar à ~** to feel comfortable. **esteja à ~** make yourself at home, take your ease. **estou com ~ de dar um passeio** I am in a mood for a walk. **não estou com ~ disto** (fig.) I have no stomach for it. **estou com ~ de aceitar** I am almost tempted to accept. **fazer a ~ de uma criança** to humour a child. **fazer sentir-se à ~** to put a person at his ease. **preciso fazer-lhe a ~** I must do as he wishes. **faça-lhe a ~** give him his wish. **fiz prevalecer minha ~ junto a ele.** I worked my will on him. **seja feita a Tua ~** Thy will be done. **força de ~** will power. **de livre e espontânea ~** of one's own free will. **por livre ~** of one's own motion. **má ~** grudge, ill will, unwillingness, incompliance, unreadiness. **de má ~** unwilling, reluctantly, grudgingly, with a bad grace, incompliant. **pôr-se à ~** to relax. **sem ~** unwilling. **aqui eu me sinto à ~** I feel at my ease here. **servir-se à ~** to help o. s. **ele tem a sua ~** he has his wish. **tenho ~ de dar um passeio** I feel like taking a walk. **ter ~ de** to itch for, to feel like. **ter a sua ~** to have one's way. **tínhamos muita ~ de ficar** we had a good mind to stay. **sua última ~** his last wish, his dying wish. **inteiramente de acordo com a sua ~** at his own sweet will. **onde há uma ~ há um meio** where there is a will there is a way.

vôo s. m. 1. flight: a) act or fact of flying, fly, volitation. b) distance flown. c) soaring (also fig.). 2. quick movement through the air or on the ground. 3. ecstasy, ravishment.

~ acrobático aerobatics. **~ cego** instrument flying, blind flying. **~ da imaginação** flight of fancy. **~ do tempo** flight of time. **~ planado** volplane. **~ rápido (das aves)** flush. **de ~ rápido** swift of flight, swift-winged. **levantar o vôo** 1. (aeron.) to take the air, to take off. 2. (birds) to take wings. **no ~** in the fly.

voracidade s. f. 1. voraciousness, voracity. 2. greed, wolfishness, edacity. 3. ravenousness. 4. gluttony. 5. piggishness.

voragem s. f. (pl. **-ens**) 1. vortex, whirlpool, eddy (also fig.). 2. abyss, yawn, chasm, gulf.

voraginoso adj. 1. full of vortexes, voraginous, gulfy. 2. (fig.) all-devouring.

voraz adj. voracious: 1. rapacious, wolfish. 2. avid, insatiable. 3. greedy, gluttonous, edacious, hoggish. 4. destructive. 5. ambitious. ‖ **~mente** adv. voraciously.

apetite ~ voracious appetite.

vórtice s. m. 1. vortex, whirlpool, eddy. 2. hurricane, tempest, storm. 3. abyss, chasm.

vorticoso adj. vorticose, vortical, whirling.

vos pron. pers. you, to you (direct or indirect object). **em verdade eu ~ digo** (bib.) verily I say unto you.

vós pron. pers. you; (arch.) ye.

vosear v. to address with **vós**.

vosmecê pron. pers. (Braz.) contraction of **vossemecê**.

vossemecê pron. pers. 1. contraction of **Vossa Mercê** you, used by simple (country) people. 2. (Braz., obs.) children's form of addressing their parents and grandparents.

vosso, vossa pron. poss. your, yours. **Vossa Eminência** Your Eminency. **os ~s** your family, folks or relatives.

votação s. f. (pl. **-ões**) voting, poll(ing), election. **~ experimental** (pol.) straw vote. **~ levantando a mão** (pol.) show of hands. **~ (pró ou contra) levan-**

tando-se ou ficando sentado voting by rising or sitting. ~ secreta ballot. admitir por ~ to vote in. decidir por ~ to decide by vote. encabeçar a ~ to be at the head of the poll. fraude na ~ ballot-box stuffing. levar à ~ to put it to the vote.

votado adj. voted; approved or agreed to by voting.

votante s. m. + f. voter, elector, vote. ‖ adj. voting.

votar v. 1. to vote, give a vote, express by vote, to ballot, decide pro or against, to elect, poll. 2. to promise, vow, consecrate, destinate, devote, pledge. 3. to sacrifice.
~ contra to pip, blackball. ~ pró ou contra to call forth the yeas and nays. direito de ~ voting-right. pessoa que não vota nonvoter.

votivo adj. votive, given by a vow.
missa -a votive mass. caráter ~ votiveness.

voto s. m. 1. vote: a) promise, vow. b) ardent wish or desire. c) election. d) ballot, voice. e) expression or decision obtained by vote. f) wish or opinion expressed by vote. g) right to vote, suffrage. h) prayer. 2. oath. 3. offering.
~ afirmativo placet, aye. ~ de censura vote of censure. ~ de confiança vote of confidence. ~ contrário blackball. ~ decisivo, de qualidade casting voice, casting vote. ~s favoráveis the ayes. ~ negativo no. ~ pró e contra the ayes and noes. ~ secreto secret vote, ballot. aceito com 23 ~s contra 11 agreed to by 23 votes to 11. com os melhores ~s with all good wishes. com os melhores ~s para as festas with the best compliments for the season. dar o seu ~ a to give one's voice for. deram o seu ~ they cast their votes. derrotar por ~s to vote down. eliminar por meio de ~ to vote away. fazer um ~ to swear an oath. fazer ~s to profess. ela fez os ~s she took the vows. a maioria dos ~s é a favor the yeas have it. ~ de Minerva casting vote, casting voice.

vovente s. m. + f. vower. ‖ adj. votive.

vovô s. m. (Braz., children's language) grandpa(pa).

vovó s. f. (Braz., children's language) grandma(ma), granny, gran.

voz s. f. 1. voice: a) sound uttered by man and animals. b) faculty of speaking. c) ability to sing. d) cry, call. e) vote. f) suffrage, right to speak. g) (gram.) relation of the subject to the action. h) rumour. 2. tone, accent. 3. word or phrase. 4. loud complaint, clamour. 5. order given in a loud voice. 6. wording of a music.
~ ativa (gram.) active voice. ~ da consciência the voice of conscience, the inner voice. ~ baixa undertone. ~ corrente common report, cry. ~ de falsete head voice. ~ metálica a throat of brass. ~ passiva (gram.) passive voice. ~ do povo the popular cry, the common voice. ao alcance da ~ within cry, within hail. ela está com excelente ~ she is in splendid voice. ele não está com boa ~ he is not in voice. com ~ clara clear-voiced. dar ~ de prisão to arrest. de uma só ~ with one voice. de viva ~ spoken, orally, verbally. em ~ alta aloud. em ~ baixa in a low voice, soft-spoken, in a whisper. falar em ~ macia to coo. levantar a ~ to lift up one's voice; to shout, yell. mais ~es do que nozes much ado about nothing. ter ~ ativa to have the say, run the show.

vozeador s. m. crier, brawler, squaller.

vozear s. m. 1. bawl. 2. cry, outcry. ‖ v. 1. to speak in a loud voice. 2. to bawl, shout, yell, cry, halloo. 3. to clamour, brawl.

vozearia s. f. (also vozeada, vozeria f.; vozeamento m.) 1. bawl(ing), shouting, yelling, crying. 2. clamour(ing), vociferation, jabber. 3. racket, fracas.

vozeirão s. m. (pl. -ões) 1. strong voice. 2. strong-voiced person.

vozeiro s. m. 1. talker, babbler; (sl.) yap. 2 = vozeirão. ‖ adj. talkative, loquacious, blabby.

vozerio s. m. act or fact of bawling; vociferousness.

vu s. m. (Braz.) twinkle, instant.
num ~ in a twinkle.

vulcanicidade s. f. volcanicity, volcanism.

vulcânico adj. volcanic: 1. of or referring to a volcano, produced by a volcano. 2. composed of volcanos. 3. (fig.) like a volcano, violent, intense, impetuous.
pó ~ ash(es).

vulcanismo s. m. 1. volcanism. 2. (fig.) disastrous outbreak, eruption.

vulcanista s. m. volcanist, volcanologist.

vulcanite s. f. 1. vulcanite. 2. ebonite.

vulcanização s. f. (pl. -ões) vulcanization.

vulcanizador s. m. vulcanizer.

vulcanizar v. 1. to vulcanize. 2. to volcanize, calcine. 3. (fig.) to inflame, arouse enthusiasm. 4. ~-se (fig.) to get excited, enthoused.

vulcanologia s. f. (geol.) volcanology.

vulcanologista s. m. volcanologist.

vulcão s. m. (pl. -ões, ~s) 1. volcano (plate M 11). 2. (fig.): a) impetuous person. b) eminent danger.
~ ativo, inativo e extinto active, dormant and extinct volcano. boca de ~ crater.

vulfenita s. f. (min.) wulfenite.

vulgacho s. m. (also ralé) populace, mob, rabble.

vulgar s. m. 1. that which is vulgar. 2. the vernacular. ‖ v. = divulgar. ‖ adj. m. + f. vulgar: 1. general, popular, plebeian. 2. common, commonplace, banal, trivial, everyday, penny-a-line. 3. low, flat, coarse. ‖ ~mente adv. vulgarly.

vulgaridade s. f. 1. vulgarity, vulgarism: a) commonness. b) banality, triviality. c) coarseness, grossness. d) low-mindedness, flatness. 2. vulgar person.

vulgarismo s. m. vulgarism, vulgarity.

vulgarização s. f. (pl. -ões) vulgarization.

vulgarizador s. m. vulgarizer. ‖ adj. vulgarizing.

vulgarizar v. 1. to vulgarize, make vulgar or common. 2. to divulge, make known or public, propagate. 3. to debauch, debase, degrade.

vulgata s. f. Vulgate: Latin version of the Scriptures.

vulgívago adj. degrading, debasing.

vulgo s. m. 1. the vulgar, the people, the masses. 2. the mob, rabble. ‖ adv. vulgarly, ordinarily, commonly.

vulgocracia s. f. 1. dominance of the popular classes. 2. democracy.

vulnerabilidade s. f. vulnerability.

vulneração s. f. (pl. -ões) act or fact of hurting, wounding or offending.

vulneral adj. m. + f. (pl. -ais) (also vulnerário m.) vulnerary, for healing wounds.

vulnerante adj. m. + f. (also vulnerativo m.) 1. hurting, wounding. 2. offending.

vulnerar v. 1. to hurt, wound. 2. to offend.

vulnerária s. f. (bot.) woundwort, kidney vetch.

vulnerário adj. vulnerary.

vulnerável adj. m. + f. (pl. -áveis) 1. vulnerable, that can be hurt or wounded. 2. susceptible of attack or offense. 3. impeachable. 4. weak. ‖ vulneravelmente adv. vulnerably.
o ponto ~ the weak point.

vulnífico adj. vulnific, wounding.

vulpino adj. 1. vulpine, foxy, foxlike. 2. shrewd, crafty, cunning. 3. treacherous.

vulto s. m. 1. face, countenance. 2. body, figure. 3. aspect, image; form, shadow. 4. size, bulk, amount. 5. importance, consequence. 6. important person, big shot. 7. ponderation.

de ~ important. **tomar** ~ to increase, take shape, become important. **um grande** ~ **da história** a famous figure in history.
vultoso adj. voluminous, bulky.
vultuosidade s. f. (path.) congestion of the face.
vultoso adj. (path.) attacked by congestion of the face.
vulturino adj. vulturine, vulturous, of or referring to a vulture.
vulva s. f. (anat.) vulva.
vulvar adj. (also **vulvário**; anat.) vulvar.

vulvária s. f. (bot.) stinking goosefoot.
vulvite s. f. (med.) vulvitis.
vulvuterino adj. vulvouterine.
vunje adj. m. + f. (Braz.) sly, cunning.
vunvum s. m. (Braz.) barber bug (the Chagas' disease transmitter).
vunzar v. (Braz., pop.) to rummage.
vurmo s. m. pus.
vurmoso adj. containing pus, purulent.
vuvu s. m. (Braz.) row, quarrel; hubbub, rumpus.

W

W, w s. m. letter used in Portugal and Brazil only in internationally known symbols and abbreviations and in foreign words adopted by the Portuguese language.
W abbr. of **watt internacional** international watt.
W 1. (chem.) symbol for **volfrâmio** tungsten (wolfram). 2. (geogr.) symbol for **oeste** West.
w abbr. of **watt** the unit of electrical power.

wagnerianismo s. m. Wagnerianism: the dramatical and musical theories of Richard Wagner, German composer.
wagneriano s. m. Wagnerian: one who adopts the theories of Richard Wagner. ‖ adj. Wagnerian: of or pertaining to Wagner or Wagnerianism.
wattímetro s. m. wattmeter.

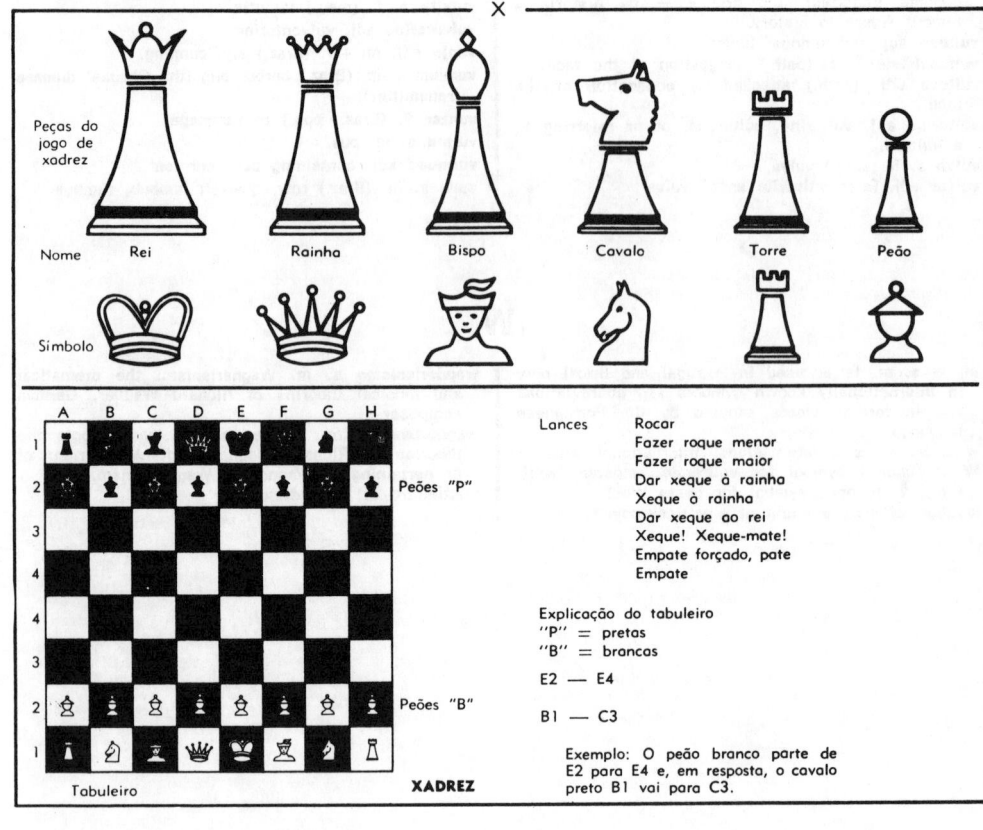

Peças do jogo de xadrez

Nome: Rei, Rainha, Bispo, Cavalo, Torre, Peão

Símbolo

A B C D E F G H		

Tabuleiro   **XADREZ**

Peões "P"

Peões "B"

Lances   Rocar
Fazer roque menor
Fazer roque maior
Dar xeque à rainha
Xeque à rainha
Dar xeque ao rei
Xeque! Xeque-mate!
Empate forçado, pate
Empate

Explicação do tabuleiro
"P" = pretas
"B" = brancas

E2 — E4

B1 — C3

Exemplo: O peão branco parte de E2 para E4 e, em resposta, o cavalo preto B1 vai para C3.

X

X, x s. m. 1. the twenty-second letter of the Portuguese alphabet. 2. Roman numeral for ten. 3. (math.) the first unknown quantity. 4. (chem.) symbol for xenon. 5. minimal amount. ‖ adj. concerning the X-rays.

xá s. m. Shah: title of the ruler of Iran.

xaboque s. m. (Braz., pop.) 1. piece, slice, bite. 2. hunk, chunk, portion.

xabraque s. m. shabrack: a saddlecloth often of goatskin, used by European light cavalry.

xabregano s. m. a Franciscan of a monastery in Xabregas.

xácara s. f. bollad, ditty, romance (in verse).

xacoco s. m. insipid. ‖ adj. insipid, flat, dull.

xadrez s. m. 1. chess: game for two persons with sixteen pieces each on a board divided into sixty-four alternated squares in black and white (plate X). 2. chessboard. 3. check, chequered pattern or fabric. 4. railing. 5. mosaic. 6. (Braz., pop.) prison, hoosegow, jail. 7. (naut.) grating.

xadrezado adj. chequered; checky.

xadrezar v. to checker, chequer: mark with small squares like a chessboard.

xadrezista s. m. + f. (also **enxadrista**) chesser, chessist, chess player.

xaguão s. m. (also **saguão**) back yard, hall.

xaia s. f. (bot.) Indian madder.

xalá, xajá s. f. (ornith.) crested screamer.

xairel s. m. (pl. **xairéis**) saddlecloth, horsecloth (plate S 2).

xale s. m. 1. shawl, Afghan. 2. plaid.
~ **de Tonquim** shawl pattern.

xalmas s. f. pl. rack: frame fitted to a wagon to carry bulky loads.

xamanismo s. m. (rel.) shamanism.

xamanista s. m. + f. shamanist. ‖ adj. shamanist(ic).

xambregado adj. (N. Braz., pop. also **embriagado**) drunk.

xampu s. m. shampoo.

xanteína s. f. (chem.) xanthein: yellow insoluble colouring matter extracted from yellow flowers.

xantelasma s. m. (med.) shanthoma.

xântico adj. xanthic: 1. pertaining to or tending toward the yellow colour. 2. (chem.) of or pertaining to xanthine.

xantina s. f. (chem.) xanthin(e): microcrystalline compound found in blood, urine, the liver, and in the juices of certain plants.

xântio s. m. (bot.) xanthium, cocklebur.

xantita s. f. (min.) yellowish variety of vesuvianite.

xanto s. m. a yellow precious stone.

xantocarpo adj. (bot.) xanthocarpus.

xantogênico adj. (med.) relating to the virus of the yellow fever.

xantoma s. m. xanthoma: a skin disease.

xantopsia s. f. xanthopsia.

xantose s. f. (biol., med.) xanthosis.

xantóxilo adj. (bot.) xanthoxylin.

xantungue s. m. Shantung (variety of pongee).

xara s. f. 1. wooden arrow hardened in fire. 2. (bot.) rock-rose.

xará s. m. + f. 1. (Braz., pop. also **xarapa, xarapim, xera, xero**) namesake, homonym. 2. m. country-dance.

xarda s. f. czardas: a Magyar dance in 2/4 or 4/4 measure starting very slowly and ending in a rapid whirl.

xarelete, xerelete s. m. (Braz., ichth.) jurel, runner.

xareta s. f. a fishing-net.

xaréu s. m. (Braz.) 1. (ichth.) cavalla. 2. horsecloth. 3. (pop.) intense cold (low temperature).

xaroco s. m. siroco: a hot wind from N. Africa blowing across S. Europe.

xaropada s. f. 1. cough medicine, sirup, syrup. 2. tiresome thing; rub. 3. (Braz., pop.) prosy, boresome talk.

xaropar v. to treat with sirup.

xarope s. m. 1. (pharm.): a) sirup, syrup. b) ptisan. 2. home-made remedy. 3. (Braz., pop.) purgative medicine. 4. (Braz., pop.) a tiresome thing.

o espetáculo foi um verdadeiro ~ the show was a wash-out. **~ para tosse** cough sirup.

xaroposo adj. 1. syrupy. 2. sticky. 3. (Braz., pop.) tiresome.

xarroco s. m. fishes of the genus Lophius.

xavante s. m. + f. Chavante: Indian of the tribe of Chavantes. ‖ adj. of or referring to the Chavantes.

xaveco s. m. 1. (naut.) xebec. 2. crazy ship. 3. old worthless boat. 4. old worthless thing. 5. a nobody.

xavier adj. m. + f. (Braz., sl.) 1. ashamed, downcast. 2. insipid, dull, flat.

xaxim s. m. (Braz., bot.) 1. the trunk of certain tree ferns (family Cyatheaceae), used in floriculture (as plant pots). 2. any of these plants.

xelim s. m. (pl. **-ns**) shilling (British silver coin and money 1 £ = 20/-, 1 s. = 12 pence).

xelma s. f. (also **xalmas**) rack: spreading framework.

xenartros s. m. pl. (zool.) xenarthra.

xendengue adj. m. + f. (N. Braz.) 1. thin, lean. 2. futile, useless. 3. vain.

xenelasia s. f. (Gr. hist.) banishment of foreigners.

xênio s. m. (Gr. hist.) xenium: present for a guest or stranger.

xenofilia s. f. xenophilism.

xenófilo s. m. xenophile person. ‖ adj. xenophile.

xenofobia s. f. xenophobia.

xenófobo s. m. xenophobe, jingoist.

xenogamia s. f. (bot.) xenogamy.

xenomania s. f. xenomania: a mania for foreign customs, institutions, manners, fashions, etc.

xenomórfico adj. (min.) xenomorphic.

xenônio s. m. (chem.) xenon.

xepa s. f. (Braz., naut.) meal, food, chow.

xepeiro s. m. 1. soldier who lives in quarters. 2. poor devil, beggar; person who does odd jobs.

xeque (I) s. m. 1. (chess) check (plate X). 2. political crisis. 3. (parliament) opposition of majority.

dar um ~ to give check. **pôr em ~** to keep in check, curb.

xeque (II) s. m. sheik(h): the head of a Bedouin family, clan, or tribe.

xeque-mate s. m. (pl. **xeques-mate**) (chess also **xaque-mate**) mate, checkmate: the winning movement

when one king is in check and cannot escape from that position (plate X).

xeque-xeque s. m. (Braz., bot.) balloon vine, heartpea.

xerasia s. f. (med.) xerasia: a disease of the hair.

xerém s. m. (Braz.) 1. thick corn flour. 2. popular dance of Ceará.

xerengue s. m. (Braz.) old worthless knife.

xereta (ê) s. m. + f. (Braz.) 1. interferer. 2. intriguer. 3. telltale. 4. gossip. 5. disturber. 6. busibody. 7. (sl.) Jack Sauce.

esse ~ está dando cabo da nossa paciência this meddler is getting on our nerves.

xeretar, xeretear v. (Braz.) 1. to interfere. 2. to flatter, fawn, coax.

xerez s. m. 1. sherry: strong wine made in Spain. 2. variety of black grape.

xerga s. f. 1. coarse woollen cloth. 2. (Braz.) kind of pallet placed under the packsaddle of the beast.

xerife (I) s. m. sherif, shereef: 1. the chief magistrate of Mecca. 2. a descendant of Mohammed.

xerife (II) s. m. sheriff: the chief executive officer of a county or shire charged with the keeping of the peace, the execution of writs, sentences, etc.

xerofagia s. f. (rel.) xerophagy: the Christian rule of fasting.

xerófago s. m. one who professes xerophagy.

xerófilo adj. (bot.) xerophilous: adapted to live in hot, dry climates.

xerófita s. f. (bot.) xerophyte.

xerófito adj. (bot.) xerophitic: indicative of desert plants.

xeroftalmia s. f. (med.) xerophthalmia.

xerografia s. f. xerography: the division of geography treating of the dry parts of the terrestrial globe.

xerotribia s. f. (med.) xerotripsis.

xérox s. m. xerox.

xerografia s. f. xerography.

xerocar v. to xerox.

xerva s. f. sort of flax.

xetrar v. (Braz., pop.) to have a disappointment.

xeura s. f. (naut.) moulding, scantling, gauge.

xexéu s. m. (Braz.) 1. (also **bodum**) rank smell, rancidity. 2. (ornith., also **japim**) cacique.

xi interj. pish!

xiba s. f. (Braz.) a sung dance; the samba.

xibaro s. m. (Braz.) mulatto.

xibimba s. m. + f. (S. Braz., pop.) fat person.

xibio s. m. (Braz.) small diamond for diamond pencils.

xicaca s. f. (Braz.) basket.

xícara s. f. cup, bowl (plate M 8).

~ grande regular cup. **~ pequena** demitasse. **~ e pires** cup and saucer. **uma ~ de chá** a cup of tea. **meia ~ de leite** half a cup of milk. **por favor, ponha só meia ~ de café** please, don't pour me more than half a cup of coffee.

xicarada s. f. cupful: quantity a cup holds.

xícara-e-pires s. f. (pl. **xícaras-e-pires**) (bot.) cup-and-saucer, Canterbury bell.

xié s. m. (Braz., zool.) a crablike crustacean.

xifofilo adj. (bot.) xiphophyllus.

xifóide(o) adj. (anat.) xiphoid: like a sword, ensiform.

xifoidiano adj. (anat.) xiphoidal, xiphoid.

xifopagia s. f. characteristic of the xiphopagus.

xifópagos s. m. pl. xiphopagus: a monster consisting of twins united at the epigastrium, as the Siamese twins. ‖ adj. xiphopagic, xiphopagous.

xila s. m. filth, dirt.

xilarmônico s. m. (mus., also **xilofone, xilofono**) xylophone: instrument consisting of a graduated series of wooden bars, vibrating when struck or rubbed.

xilema s. m. (bot.) xylem.

xilônio, xileno s. m. (chem.) xylene.

xilindró s. m. (Braz., sl.) jail, gaol, prison, hoosegow.

xilite s. f. (chem.) xylitol: a pentahydroxy alcohol, obtained as a sirupy liquid by reduction of xylose.

xilo s. m. cotton plant.

xilocarpo s. m. (bot.) xylocarp: a hardy woody fruit. ‖ adj. xylocarpous.

xilócopo adj. (zool., also **xilótomo**) xylotomous: said of the insects capable of boring or cutting wood.

xilófago s. m. (zool.) Xylophaga.

xilófilo adj. (zool.) xylophilous: living on wood.

xilofone s. m. (mus.) xylophone.

xiloglifia s. f. xyloglyphy: artistic wood carving.

xiloglifico adj. of or relating to xyloglyphy.

xilóglifo s. m. person who is skilled in xyloglyphy.

xilografia s. f. xylography: wood-engraving, wood-cutting.

xilográfico adj. xylographic(al).

xilógrafo s. m. xylographer, wood carver, wood-engraver, wood-cutter.

xilogravura s. f. xylograph: 1. engraving on wood. 2. xylographic print.

xilóide adj. m. + f. xyloid: 1. resembling wood. 2. woody: of the nature of wood. 3. ligneous.

xiloidina s. f. xyloidin(e): a high explosive produced by the action of nitric acid on starch or wood fibre.

xilolatria s. f. worship of wooden idols.

xilologia s. f. xylology: a treatise on or of the natural history of woods.

xilológico adj. of or relating to xylology.

xilólogo s. m. one who is versed in xylology.

xilomancia s. f. xylomancy: divination by means of pieces of wood.

xilomante s. m. + f. practiser of xylomancy.

xilomântico adj. of or referring to xylomancy.

xilótomo adj. (zool.) xylotomous.

ximango s. m. (ornith., also **caracaraí**) caracara, chimango.

ximbaúva s. f. (Braz., bot.) a species of acacia.

ximbé, ximbeva adj. m. + f. 1. said of the dog which has an undershot jaw, like a bulldog. 2. snub-nosed: said of a person who has a short and flat nose.

ximbica s. f. (Braz., pop.) a certain card game.

ximbo s. m. (S. Braz.) 1. stray horse. 2. vagabond.

ximbute s. m. (Braz., pop.) short and potbellied person.

xingação (pl. -ões), **xingadela** s. f., **xingamento** m. (Braz.) chiding, scolding; abuse, revilement.

xingar v. (Braz.) 1. to chide, scold, rail. 2. to abuse, revile, inveigh (against). 3. to offend (with abusive language). 4. to call names. 5. to swear. 6. to clapperclaw.

na raiva, ele xingou-o de tudo quanto foi nome angry, he called him all sorts of names.

xingaraviz s. m. (Braz.) 1. meddler, interferer. 2. busybody.

xingatório adj. (Braz.) scolding, abusing, insulting; wounding.

xingo s. m. (Braz.) abusive language, swearword.

xintó, xintoísmo s. m. Shinto(ism).

xintoísta s. m. + f. Shintoist. ‖ adj. Shintoist(ic).

xinxilha s. m. (obs., pop.) a nobody.

xinxim s. m. (N. Braz.) ragout of chicken with salt, onion, garlic, oil, shrimps and pips of pumpkin.

xiquexique s. m. (Braz., bot.) 1. yellow lupine. 2. a kind of cactus (Pilocereus Gouneliei).

xiridáceas s. f. pl. (bot.) Xyridaceae.

xiridáceo adj. (bot.) xyridaceous.

xirimbambada s. f. (Braz., pop.) brawl, fight, riot, tumult.

xiririca s. f. (Braz., pop.) rapid, riffle.

xis s. m., sg. + pl. ex, exes (letter).

xisto s. m. 1. (petrog.) schist. 2. xystus: a) a long and open portico for athletic exercises. b) a garden walk, garden terrace.

~ argiloso shale.

xistóide adj. m. + f. schistoid: resembling schist.

xistosidade s. f. (petrog.) schistosity, foliation.

xistoso adj. schistose, schistous: of the nature or structure of schist.

xixarro s. m. (ichth.) 1. cigarfish, mackerel scad. 2. saurel.

xixi s. m. (Braz., pop.) 1. = **xixixi**. 2. urination, urine, piss.

fazer ~ (children) to piddle, to make water.

xixica s. f. (Braz., pop., also **gorjeta**) tip, gratuity.

xixixi s. m. (Braz., also **apaga-pó, garoa**) drizzling rain.

xô interj. shool

xodó s. m. (Braz., pop.) 1. (also **namoro**) flirtation. 2. girl friend, sweetheart. 3. boy friend.

xofrango s. m. (ornith.) young osprey.

xucrice s. f., **xucrismo** m. (Braz., sl.) roughness, rudeness; dullness, stupidity.

xucro adj. (Braz.) 1. untamed, wild (animal); unbroken (horse). 2. stupid, foolish; rude.

ser ~ to be slow in the uptake.

xué, xuê s. m. (Braz., zool.) a kind of toad of the genus Bufo.

xumbregar v. (N. Braz., sl.) to importune, pester.

xurdir v. to drudge, toil, moil.

xuri s. m. (Braz., ornith., also **avestruz**) ostrich.

xurumbambo s. m. (Braz., pop.) lumber, junk, rubbish.

Y

Y, y s. m. letter used in Portugal and Brazil only in internationally known symbols and abbreviations.

Y (chem.) symbol for yttrium.

y (math.) the second unknown quantity.

yd abbr. of **yard**.

Z

Z, z s. m. 1. the twenty-third and last letter of the Portuguese alphabet. 2. (math.) the third unknown quantity.

zabaneira s. f. hussy, jade, wench, impudent or shameless woman (or girl), woman of doubtful character.

zabumba s. m. 1. bass drum. 2. (hum.) top hat. 3. (Braz., bot.) thorn apple, Jimson weed.

zabumbar v. 1. to beat a bass drum. 2. to beat, knock, strike. 3. to stun, make giddy. 4. (fig.) to divulge, spread (news).

zaburro s. m. (bot., also **acaburro**) maize, Indian corn, Guinea corn. ‖ adj. of or indicative of a variety of Indian corn.

zafimeiro adj. 1. clever, smart, brisk. 2. knavish, rascally. 3. crafty, cunning.

zaga s. f. 1. assagai: South African tree of the dogwood family from whose wood the spears called assagai were once made. 2. (ftb.) backfield, full back position.

zagaia s. f. (also **azagaia**) assagai, assegai.

zagaiar v. (also **azagaiar**) to assagai.

zagal s. m. (pl. **-ais**) shepherd, herdsman.

zagala s. f. shepherdess.

zagalejo, zagaleto s. m. young shepherd.

zagalote s. m. a small lead bullet, buckshot.

zagorrino, zagorro s. m. knave, rogue. ‖ adj. knavish, rascally.

zagucho adj. sharp, spirited, alive.

zagueiro s. m. (ftb.) (full)back: player stationed at the back of the team.

~ **direito (esquerdo)** (ftb.) right (left) back.

zagunchada s. f. 1. spear thrust, dart thrust. 2. blame, reprimand. 3. mockery. 4. cutting remark.

zagunchar v. 1. to dart, shoot or send forth suddenly; spear. 2. to tease. 3. to blame, reprove, taunt.

zaguncho s. m. dart, javelin, (light) spear.

zaibo adj. 1. awry, crooked. 2. squint-eyed, cross-eyed. 3. knock-kneed.

zaino adj. 1. zain: a) dark-brown (horse). b) having a uniform dark colour, without white spots (horse). 2. (fig.) knavish, treacherous, false, perfidious.

zambaio s. m. (also **estrábico**) squint, squint-eyed person. ‖ adj. squinting, cross-eyed.

zambê s. m. (Braz., also **coco**) coconut.

zambo s. m. (Braz.) zambo, sambo: person of mixed Indian and Negro blood. ‖ adj. 1. said of persons who have Indian and Negro blood. 2. (sl.) fool, simpleton.

zamboa s. f. (Braz., bot.) a kind of cider.

zamboada s. f. (Braz.) underbrush, thicket.

zamboeira s. f. a kind of lemon.

zamboque s. m. (Braz.) a sort of bee.

zamborrada s. f. 1. a heavy shower, rainfall, downpour. 2. (fig.) a great deal.

zambro adj. (also **zambeta**) bandy-legged, bow-legged, baker-legged, baker-kneed.

zambujal s. m. (pl. **-ais**) (also **azambujal**) plantation of olea.

zambujeiro, zambujo s. m. (bot., also **azambujeiro, azambujo**) olea(ster): the wild variety of the olive.

zâmia s. f. (bot.) zamia.

zampar v. 1. to eat greedily, quickly and with avidity. 2. to devour, cram. 3. to pack up, stuff (with straw).

zanaga s. m. + f. (also **zambaio**) squint-eyed person. ‖ adj. squinting, cross-eyed; one-eyed.

zanga s. f. 1. aversion, indignation, hatred, crossness. 2. dislike, antipathy. 3. anger, rage. 4. bad luck. 5. importunity. 6. (Braz.) disarrangement. 7. miff, tiff.

ter uma ~ to have a tiff (with).

zangado adj. 1. indignated, exasperated, disgusted, angry, infuriate, irascible. 2. piqued, miffy, vexed. 3. annoyed, inflamed. 4. out of temper, sullen. 5. fractious.

estou ~ **com ele** I am vexed with him. **ele fica** ~ **por...** he feels bad about... **por que é que você está** ~? why are you angry? what is eating you?

zangador s. m. annoyer, wounder, pesterer. ‖ adj. annoying, making angry.

zangalete s. m. silk or cotton cloth.

zangalhão, zangalho s. m. = **zangaralhão**.

zângano s. m. 1. (fig.) parasite, hanger-on. 2. sponger. 3. deceitful jobber. 4. (fig.) fool, jester. 5. pettifogger, hedge-lawyer.

zangão s. m. (pl. **-ãos, -ões**) (also **zângão**) 1. drone: a) humble-bee, male honeybee (plate A 11). b) idler, loafer; sponger. 2. exploiter. 3. = **zângano**. 4. vexery. 5. (Braz.) salesman; forwarding agent; canvasser.

zangar (I) v. 1. to annoy, make angry, set someone's nerves on edge. 2. to molest, worry, torment. 3. to bring out of temper. 4. ~**-se**; a) to become angry, irritated, incensed, enraged, get into a temper. b) to be or become exasperated. c) to be angry; to fret, miff.

ela zangou-se comigo she got angry with me.

zangar (II) v. (Port.) to cross over, pass over (jumping).

zangaralhão s. m. (pl. **-ões**) (f. **-ona**) tall, ill-favoured fellow.

zangarelha s. f., **zangarelho** s. m. casting net, sweep net, sweep-seine, dragnet.

zangarilhar v. to go up and down, move to and fro.

zangarilho s. m. a person who goes up and down frequently.

zangarrear v. to strum (guitar), thum, twang.

zangarreio s. m. strum: act or sound of strumming.

zanguizarra s. f. 1. uproar, row, hubbub. 2. agitation, tumult. 3. strum (of a guitar). 4. noise of strumming.

zanguizarrear v. 1. to strum. 2. to sound stridently.

zangurriana s. f. 1. monotonous ditty or song. 2. hum. 3. (pop., also **zangurrina**) drunkenness.

zanho adj. (Braz., pop.) dissembled, feigned, hypocritical, false, sly.

zanolho s. m. (also **estrábico, zarolho**) squint-eyed person. ‖ adj. squint-eyed, cross-eyed.

zântio s. m. (bot.) spiny clotbur.

zanzador adj. wandering, perambulatory.

zanzar v. (Braz., also **vaguear**) 1. to rove, ramble, wander, loiter. 2. to roam, perambulate, walk up and down.

não fique zanzando pelas ruas! don't loiter about in the streets!

zanzibarita s. m. + f. Zanzibari: a native of Zanzibar. ‖ adj. of or pertaining to Zanzibar.

zanzo s. m. (Braz., bot.) queensland hemp.

zão-zão s. m. (also **zumzum**) 1. buzzing, hum. 2. rumour.

zape s. m. (also **pancada**) blow, knock, slap. ‖ interj. slibber!, smack!, bang!

zápete s. m. (cards) 1. game also called **truque**. 2. the four of clubs in this game.

zapoteca s. m. + f. 1. Zapotec: one of the Zapotecan Indians (Oaxaca, Mexico). 2. their language. ‖ adj. Zapotecan: of or pertaining to these Indians.
zapupe s. m. (bot.) zapupe.
zarabatana s. f. blowpipe, blowtube, blowgun, pea- -shooter, bean-shooter, puttyblower.
zaraga s. f. (Braz.) a kind of cretonne.
zaragalhada s. f. 1. = **zaragata**. 2. rabble, mob, populace.
zaragata s. f. 1. disorder, tumult, uproar, riot, row. 2. confusion, muddle. 3. noise, outcry, din, hubbub. 4. bustle, turmoil.
zaragateiro s. m. 1. rioter. 2. bustler. 3. muddler. ‖ adj. 1. tumultuous, uproarious, riotous. 2. noisy, rowdy. 3. confusional, turbulent.
zaragatoa s. f. 1. swab: a bit of sponge, cloth or absorbent cotton to apply medicaments (esp. in the nostrils and throat). 2. medicine applied by means of a swab.
zaragatoa-menor s. f. (pl. **zaragatoas-menores**) (bot.) fleawort.
zarandalha s. f. (obs.) trifle, bauble, gewgaw, thing of no value.
zaranza s. m. + f. 1. scatterbrain, reckless person; potterer. 2. plant of the family Gramineae. ‖ adj. 1. scatterbrained, disturbed. 2. foolish. 3. drunk.
zaranzar v. 1. (also **vaguear**) to loiter. 2. to walk awkwardly, lounge. 3. to fuss, potter.
zarapelho s. m. (Port.) devil.
zarcão s. m. (min.) minium, red lead, the colour vermelion.
zarco adj. 1. light blue-eyed. 2. said of horses with a white speck or circle around the eyes.
zarelha s. f. an indiscreet or meddlesome woman, busybody.
zarelhar v. 1. to meddle with, interfere. 2. to intrigue, involve. 3. to romp, play pranks or tricks. 4. to play the fool.
zarelho s. m. 1. meddlesome person, busybody, mischief-maker. 2. mischievous or naughty child. 3. scatterbrain.
zargo adj. (Braz.) said of a horse having one or both eyes white.
zargunchada, zargunchar, zarguncho = **zagunchada, zagunchar, zaguncho.**
zarolho adj. (also **caolho, zanolho**) 1. squint-eyed, cross-eyed. 2. one-eyed, blind of one eye. 3. said of the maize beginning to ripen.
zarpar v. 1. (also **sarpar**) to weigh anchor, sail (away). 2. (Braz., also **fugir**) to escape, run away. 3. to leave for (a trip). 4. to start.
o navio zarpou às 10 horas the ship weighed anchor at ten o'clock. **ele zarpou da cidade** he ran away from town.
zarro s. m. 1. (naut.) headline. 2. (ornith.) white-eyed duck. ‖ adj. 1. (also **embriagado**) drunk. 2. (Braz.) desirous, eager for. 3. troublesome, uncomfortable, annoying. 4. complicated, irksome.
estar ~ por alguma coisa to be eager for s. th.
zarza s. f. (Braz., bot.) sarsaparilla.
zarzuela s. f. zarzuela: a Spanish variety of operetta, vaudeville or comic opera.
zás(-trás) interj. bang(-off)!, slish!, slash!, wump!, thwick-thwack!, crack!, pop!
~, quebrou-se o ovo! crack, went the egg! **isto para quebrar foi zás-trás!** it broke in a twinkling.
zavar v. to bite furiously.
zê s. m. zed, zee.
Zé s. m. short for **José.**
zebo s. m. (zool., also **gebo**) an Indian ox.
zebra (ê) s. f. 1. (zool.) zebra. 2. (fig.) stupid person. 3. (Braz., coll.) striped uniform used by prisoners.

4. (Braz., sports lottery) an unexpected, unpredicted result.
a loteria esportiva deu ~ the lottery did not turn out as expected (a favorite team).
zebrado s. m. a thing striped like a zebra. ‖ adj. zebrine, zebralike: having stripes like zebras.
zebral adj. m. + f. (pl. **-ais**) (also **zebrário, zebrino**) zebrine, zebral.
zebrar v. to stripe (like a zebra).
zebrino adj. zebrine.
zebróide s. m. 1. (zool.) zebrula, zebrule: a cross (-breed) between a male zebra and a female horse. 2. stupid or incompetent person, fool. ‖ adj. m. + f. 1. zebroid: like or pertaining to a zebra. 2. fool, stupid.
zebruno adj. (Braz.) said of semidark horse.
zebu s. m. (zool.) zebu: the humped Indian ox or cow.
zebu(z)eiro s. m. (Braz.) person who deals in or breds zebus.
Zeca s. m. Joe.
zé-da-véstia s. m. (pl. **zés-da-véstia**) (pop. also **João- -ninguém**) nobody, cipher.
zé-dos-anzóis s. m. (pl. **zés-dos-anzóis**) (pop.) 1. Mr. So-and-So, such-and-such a man. 2. (also **João- -ninguém**) nobody.
zefir s. m. zephyr cloth, kind of cotton fabric.
zéfiro s. m. zephyr: 1. the West wind. 2. any soft, gentle breeze.
zelação s. f. (pl. **-ões**) 1. (also **estrela-cadente**) shooting star, bolide. 2. = **exalação.**
zelador s. m. 1. janitor, watcher, caretaker, keeper, overseer, inspector. 2. conservator, custodian. ‖ adj. (also **zelante**) watching.
zeladora s. f. janitress.
zelandês s. m. (pl. **-eses**) (f. **-esa**; pl. **-esas**) Zeeland- er: native or inhabitant of Zeeland (in the Nether- lands). ‖ adj. of or relative to Zeeland.
zelar v. 1. to watch over, keep an observant eye on. 2. to administer, manage, oversee. 3. to treat carefully. 4. to care, feel interested. 5. to take an interest in. 6. to be jealous.
~ pelos seus interesses to know on which side one's bread is buttered. **~ pelos seus negócios** to attend to one's business. **~ pela ordem** to see that everything is (put) right.
zelo (ê) s. m. (pl. **zelos**) 1. zeal(ousness), watchful- ness, care. 2. devotion, affection, dedication. 3. interest. 4. fervency, earnestness, ardour, fervour. 5. forwardness, solicitude. 6. pl. jealousy, jealous- ness. 7. diligence, assiduity.
o ~ dos Apóstolos the devotion of the Apostles. **ter zelos** to be jealous.
zeloso adj. 1. zealous, acting with zeal, careful. 2. diligent, assiduous. 3. watchful. 4. dedicated, devoted. 5. affectionate, ardent, fervent. 6. solici- tous, forward. 7. jealous. ‖ **-amente** adv. zealously, carefully, earnestly.
zelote adj. m. + f. feigning to be jealous or zealous.
zelotipia s. f. (obs.) zelotypia, zelotypie: 1. jealousy. 2. a morbid zeal or zealousness.
zenda, zende s. m. Zend: the translation and explana- tion of the Zoroastrian Avesta. ‖ adj. m. + f. Zendic.
Zenda-avesta s. m. Zend-Avesta: a collection of the sacred scriptures of the Parsis or Zoroastrians.
zenital adj. m. + f. (pl. **-ais**) zenithal: of or pertain- ing to the zenith.
zênite s. m. zenith: 1. the point in the heavens directly overhead, the upper pole of the horizon. 2. the highest point, culmination, top, apex, summit, vertex.

zeófago adj. feeding on maize.

zeólita s. f. (min.) zeolite.

zepelim s. m. (pl. **-ins**) Zep(pelin), zeppelin: any rigid airship of the type first constructed by the Count von Zeppelin.

zé-pereira s. m. (pl. **zé-pereiras**) (Braz.) 1. a carnivalesque rhythm. 2. player of this rhythm.

zé-povinho, zé-povo s. m. (pl. **zé-povinhos, zé-povos**) (Braz., also **ralé**) the people, populace, pleb, rabble.

zé-prequeté s. m. (pl. **zés-prequeté**) (Braz., pop., also **joão-ninguém**) a nobody, cipher, an insignificant person.

zero s. m. zero: 1. a cipher, the O-shaped algarism. 2. nothing. 3. the point on a scale from which positive or negative quantities are reckoned. 4. in the Celsius and Reaumur thermometers it is at the point at which water congeals. 5. nobody, insignificant person. 6. (sl.) ought. 7. null, nought, nil. **acima (abaixo) de** ~ above (below) zero. **às** ~ **horas** at the zero hour. **no ponto** ~ down at zero. **ele é um** ~ **na sociedade** he is a nobody in society. **ficar reduzido a** ~ 1. to become utterly destitute, be hard up. 2. to fall to the ground, come to nothing. ~ **a** ~ love all.

zero-quilômetro s. m., sg. + pl. brand-new car. ‖ adj. m. + f., sg. + pl. brand-new (car, apparatus, machine).

zesto s. m. zest: orange or lemon peel (used as flavouring for liquors, etc.).

zeta s. m. zeta: the sixth letter of the Greek alphabet.

zetacismo s. m. zetacism.

zetética s. f. (math., philos.) zetetic: search, investigation, as in algebra, to determine an unknown quantity.

zetético adj. zetetic.

zeugma s. m. (Gram.) zeugma: figure in which a verb or adjective governs or modifies two nouns, to only one of which it is logically applicable.

zeugmático adj. zeugmatic.

zeunerita s. f. (min., also **uranita**) zeunerite.

zibelina s. f. zibel(l)ine: 1. (zool.) sable. 2. a kind of soft woollen fabric with long silky hairs on the right side. ‖ adj. zibel(l)ine: of or pertaining to sables.

zibeta s. m. (zool.) zibet(h).

zigodá(c)tilo adj. zygodactyl(ic), zygodactylous, zygodactyle, yoke-toed: having the toes arranged in pairs.

zigofilácea s. f. (bot.) specimen of the Zygophyllaceae.

zigofiláceo adj. (bot.) zygophyllaceous.

zigoma s. m. (anat.) zygoma: zygomatic bone or cheek-bone, malar bone (plate C 17).

zigomático adj. (anat. + zool., also **zigômato**) zygomatic, jugal: of, or pertaining to the zygoma (malar bone).

zigospório s. m. (bot.) zygospore.

zigoto s. m. (biol.) zygote.

ziguezague s. m. 1. zigzag, line with sharp turns or angles. 2. sinuosity, bend, winding. 3. stiff neck. 4. swaggering, a zigzagged way of going. **mover-se em** ~ to move zigzag. **metro em** ~ foot-rule.

ziguezagueante adj. m. + f. zigzagging, zigzagged, zigzaggy.

ziguezaguear v. 1. to zigzag. 2. to make in a zigzag fashion. 3. (naut.) to back and fill. 4. to meander, reel about.

ziguezigue s. m. 1. a children's toy. 2. (ent.) cicade. 3. (fig.) mischievous child. 4. (Braz., ent.) dragonfly.

ziguizira s. f. (Braz., sl.) any disease one cannot or does not want to name.

zímase s. f. (also **zimeose**) 1. zymase, enzyme. 2. vine-disease.

zimbório s. m. (archit.) dome, cupola, lantern, canopy.

zimbrada s. f. 1. lashing or flogging. 2. (naut.) rolling, rocking.

zimbral s. m. (pl. **-ais**) place where juniper grows.

zimbrar v. 1. to lash, flog, switch, beat. 2. to balance, rock, pitch (chip). 3. to refine the sound of a drum.

zimbro (I) s. m. (bot.) common juniper.

zimbro (II) s. m. dew.

zimeose s. f. vine-disease (that causes the vine to engross).

zímico adj. (chem.) zymic, zymotic: of or pertaining to fermentation.

zimogenia s. f. zymogenesis: chemical fermentation.

zimogênico adj. zymogenic: 1. producing fermentation. 2. of or pertaining to zymogen.

zimogênio s. m. (biol.) zymogen.

zimologia s. f. zymology: treatise on fermentation.

zimológico adj. zymological: of or referring to fermentation.

zimoscópio s. m. (biochem.) zymoscope: instrument for measuring the power of fermentation.

zimose s. f. (chem.) zymosis: fermentation.

zimotecnia s. f. zymotechnics: art of inducing and applying fermentation for technical uses.

zimotécnico adj. zymotechnic(al).

zimótico adj. zymotic: of, pertainning to or caused by fermentation.

zina (I) s. f. 1. apogee, apex, acme, culmination. 2. top, pitch. 3. the last degree of intensity. 4. fury, rage.

zina (II) s. f. (bot., also **zínia**) zinnia.

zinabre s. m. (also **azinhavre**) verdigris: the green rust of brass or copper.

zincado adj. zincified.

zincagem s. f. (chem.) zincification, zincifying, galvanization.

zincar v. (chem.) to zinc(ify), galvanize, cover or coat with zinc.

zincato s. m. (chem.) zincate.

zíncico adj. (chem.) zinc(ic), zinky, zincous, zincoid.

zinco s. m. 1. (chem.) zinc: a bluish white metal. 2. galvanized metal sheet (for coverings). 3. (Braz.): a) large knife, sabre. b) (sl.) money. c) nickel coin. **sulfato de** ~ zinc sulphate. **branco de** ~ zinc white. **placa de** ~ zinc plate. **óxido de** ~ zinc oxide.

zincografar v. to zincograph: print by zincography.

zincografia s. f. zincography: the art or process of providing zinc plates with a printing surface.

zincográfico adj. zincographic(al).

zincógrafo s. m. zincographer.

zincogravura s. f. 1. zincograph(y): print from a zinc plate. 2. zincography.

zinga s. f. (Braz.) pole or oar to propel a boat or raft.

zingador s. m. (Braz.) poler: one who poles a boat, esp. a punt.

zingamocho s. m. 1. weathercock, weather vane. 2. pinnacle, summit, top.

zingar v. 1. to scull (a boat). 2. to pole: to impel or push by pole, as a punt or boat.

zingarear v. 1. to wander, roam, rove. 2. to gypsy: to live or roam like a gypsy.

zíngaro s. m. zíngaro, zingano: a gypsy.

zingiberáceo adj. zingiberaceous.

zingração s. f. (pl. **-ões**) 1. jesting, mockery, derision. 2. contempt, disdain. 3. trickery.

zingrar v. 1. to jest, scoff, mock, deride. 2. to trick, dupe. 3. to disdain. 4. to attach no importance to.

zinho s. m. (Braz., sl.) guy, fellow, chap. ‖ suf. designative of diminution. **João, Joãozinho** John, Johnny.

zínia s. f. zinnia (plant of the aster family).

zinideira s. f. a sort of bull-roarer.

zinir v. (also **zunir**) to whiz, hum.

zinzilular s. m. twitter, chirp (of swallows). ‖ v. to twitter, chirp.

zip, zíper s. m. zipper.

zircão s. m., **zirconita** f. (min.) zircon.

zircônio s. m. (chem.) zirconium.

zirro s. m. (ornith.) swift.

zizânia s. f. (also **cizânia**) 1. (bot.) zizania. 2. (fig.) disharmony, discord. 3. (pop.) brawl, row, strife.

ziziar v. 1. to chirr, chirp, stridulate. 2. to whistle, whiz(z). 3. to shrill.

zoada s. f. (also **zunido, zumbido**) whiz(zing), hum, buzz.

zoantários s. m. pl. (zool.) Zoantharia.

zoante adj. m. + f. whizzing, humming. 2. (phon.) voiced.

zoantropia s. f. zoanthropy: insanity in which the patient believes to be one of the lower animals.

zoantropo s. m. person attacked by zoanthropy.

zoar v. 1. (also **zunir**) to whiz, hum, buzz. 2. to howl, roar (wind).

zodiacal adj. m. + f. (pl. **-ais**) zodiacal: of or pertaining to the zodiac.

zodíaco s. m. (astr.) zodiac: zone of the ecliptic, which the sun traverses during a year.

os signos do ~ the signs of the zodiac.

zoécia s. f. (zool.) zooecium: cell or tube enclosing the feeding zooids of the Bryozoa.

zoeira s. f. 1. (also **zoada**) whiz(zing), hum. 2. (Braz., sl.) disorder, tumult, quarrel, noise.

zoilo s. m. zoilean critic, a man like Zoilus, bitter, envious in his critic.

zoina s. f. (Port., sl.) prostitute, harlot, harebrained woman. ‖ adj. m. + f. stunned, dizzy, giddy.

zoísmo s. m. zoism.

zombador s. m. (also **zombeirão, zombeteiro**) 1. scoffer, jester, jeerer. 2. mocker, sneerer, scorner 3. derider, ridiculer, flouter. ‖ adj. 1. scoffing, jesting, jeering. 2. scornful, mocking. 3. taunting. 4. sportful.

zombar v. 1. to mock, scoff, jeer, sneer, flout. 2. to banter. 3. to joke, jest, sport. 4. to make jokes. 5. to make fun of. 6. to deceive, disappoint. 7. to ridicule, deride.

~ de to poke fun at. ~ de alguém to make game (or a jest) of someone. eles zombaram dele they made a mock of him, they made sport of him. eles zombaram dele a ponto de desconcertá-lo they sneered him out of countenance.

zombaria s. f. 1. mockery, sneer, jeer. 2. raillery, derision. 3. flout, sarcasm, ridicule. 4. joking, sport, jesting, jape.

zombeirão s. m. (pl. **-ões**) (also **zombador;** f. **zombeirona**) mocker. ‖ adj. (also **zombador**) mocking.

zombetear v. (also **zombar**) to mock.

zombeteiro s. m. (also **zombador**) mocker. ‖ adj. (also **zombador**) mocking. ‖ **-amente** adv. mockingly.

zona s. f. 1. zone: a) area, girdle, belt, stripe. b) section of a city, region, country(side). c) any of the five great divisions of the earth's surface bounded by imaginary lines parallel to the equator. d) (med.) shingles, herpes zoster. 2. (Braz., sl.) red-light district. 3. climate.

~ franca free zone. ~ frígida frigid zone. ~ temperada temperate zone. ~ tórrida torrid zone. ~ proibida prohibited zone. ~ de silêncio silent area or zone. ~ interurbana (teleph.) trunk zone. ~ urbana (teleph.) local area.

zonado adj. m. zoned: marked with coloured and concentric bands.

zonal adj. m. + f. (pl. **-ais**) zonal.

zona-zoster s. f. (pl. **zonas-zosteres**) (med.) herpes zoster, shingles, zona.

zonchadura s. f. pumping.

zonchar v. to pump.

zoncho s. m. (tech.) pump handle, pump lever.

zonzar, zonzear v. (Braz.) to stun, be stunned, make dizzy, make giddy.

zonzeira s. f. (Braz., also **tonteira** f., **atordoamento** m.) dizziness, giddiness.

zonzo adj. (Braz., also **tonto, atordoado**) dizzy, giddy, stunned.

ele ficou ~ com o movimento (do tráfego) he got dizzy from the intense traffic.

zoobia s. f. (natural history) bios: 1. animal and plant life. 2. organic nature.

zoóbio adj. entozoic, entozoan.

zoobiologia s. f. the science of animal life.

zoocorografia s. f. description of animals of a particular region.

zoófago s. m. zoophagan. ‖ adj. zoophagous, carnivorous.

zoofilia s. f. zoophilia, zoophily.

zoófilo s. m. zoophilist. ‖ adj. zoophilous: 1. (bot.) said of the plants pollinized by animals. 2. zoophilic: loving animals.

zoofitário adj. zoophytoid.

zoofítico adj. zoophytic(al).

zoófito s. m. zoophyte: animal resembling plants such as corals and sponges.

zoofobia s. f. zoophobia: morbid fear of animals.

zoófobo s. m. person who has a morbid fear of animals.

zoofórico adj. (archit.) zoophoric.

zoóforo s. m. (archit.) zoophorus: a continuous frieze carved in relief with figures of men and animals.

zoogenia s. f. zoogeny, zoogony, viviparism: generation of animals and the formation of their organs.

zoogênico adj. zoogenic: of or referring to zoogeny.

zoogeografia s. f. zoogeography, the faunal zoology: the study of the geographical distribution of animals.

zoogeográfico adj. zoogeographic(al): of or pertaining to zoogeography.

zoogeógrafo s. m. zoogeographer: zoologist versed in zoogeography.

zooglẽia s. f. (bact.) zoogloea: a colony of bacteria forming a jellylike mass held together by a mucinous substance.

zoografar v. to describe or depict animals, their form and habits.

zoografia s. f. zoography, descriptive zoology: description or depiction of animals.

zoográfico adj. zoographic(al): of or pertaining to zoography.

zoógrafo s. m. zoographer, zoographist.

zooiatra c. m. + f. veterinarian, horse doctor.

zooiatria s. f. veterinary medicine.

zooiátrico adj. veterinary: of or pertaining to veterinary medicine.

zoóide adj. m. + f. zooidal: resembling animals.

zoólatra s. m. + f. zoolater: worship(p)er of animals.

zoolatria s. f. zootheism, zoolatry: worship of animals.

zoolátrico adj. zootheistic: of or pertaining to zootheism.

zoólite s. m. (also **zoomorfite**) zoolite, zoolith: a fossil animal.

zoolítico adj. zoolit(h)ic: of or pertaining to zoolites.

zoologia s. f. zoology: the science treating of animals.

zoológico adj. zoologic(al): of or referring to zoology. **jardim** ~ zoological garden, zoo.

zoologista s. m. + f., **zoógico** m. zoologist: one skilled in zoology.

zoomagnético adj. zoomagnetic: relative to zoomagnetism.

zoomancia s. f. zoomancy: the art of divination by examination of animals.

zoomania s. f. excessive love for animals.

zoomante s. m. + f. person who practises zoomancy.

zoomântico adj. zoomantic: of or pertaining to zoomancy.

zoometria s. f. zoometry.

zoomorfismo s. m. zoomorphism: representation of gods under the form of animals.

zoonitado adj. said of the articulate animals.

zoonito s. m. zoonite: one of the segments of which the body of an articulate or vertebrate animal is composed.

zoonomia s. f. the laws of animal life collectively considered.

zoonosologia, zoopatologia s. f. zoopathology: the study of the diseases of animals.

zoonosológico, zoopatológico adj. zoopathological.

zooparasito s. m. (zool.) zooparasite: any parasitic animal.

zooquímica s. f. zoochemistry.

zooscopia s. f. scientific (also microscopic) examination of animals.

zoosperma s. m. (biol.) zoosperm.

zootaxia s. f. zootaxy: the classification of animals.

zootáxico adj. zootaxic(al), referring to the classification of animals.

zootecnia s. f. 1. zootechny: breeding and domestication of animals. 2. (obs.) the art of stuffing animals.

zootécnico adj. zootechnic: of or relating to zootechny.

zooterapêutica, zooterapia s. f. zootherapy: veterinary medicine.

zootomia s. f. zootomy: the dissection or anatomy of animals.

zootômico adj. zootomic(al): of or pertaining to the anatomy of animals.

zootomista s. m. + f. zootomist: person versed in zootomy.

zopeiro adj. 1. lame, crippled. 2. doddering, tottery. 3. (fig.) timid, shy. 4. inactive, lazy, sluggard.

zopo s. m. 1. lame person. 2. totterer. 3. (fig.) shy person. 4. lazybones. || adj. = **zopeiro**.

zorate, zorato s. m. lunatic, crazy person. || adj. mad, crazy, lunatic(al), insane.

zorilha s. f. (zool.) zoril, Cape polecat.

zornão adj. (pl. -ões) 1. braying (ass.). 2. (fig.) fond of women.

zornar v. (Port.) to bray.

zorô s. m. (Braz.) dish made of shrimps and okras.

zoroástico adj. Zoroastrian: of or pertaining to Zoroastrianism.

zoroastrismo s. m. (also **masdeísmo**) Zoroastri(ani)sm: the ancient Persian religion of the Magi.

zorra (I) s. f. 1. (heavy) lorry, dray, truck. 2. sled, trundle. 3. very slow person or thing. 4. trawl-net for catching crabs or shrimps.

zorra (II) s. f. an old fox.

zorragar v. (also **azorragar**) to scourge, whip, flagellate.

zorrague s. m. (also **azorrague**) whip, scourge.

zorreiro s. m. (also **zorrão**) sluggish person, lazybones. || adj. 1. slow, slack, sluggish, indolent. 2. said of a short-stalked corn.

zorrilho s. m. (Braz., zool.) swunk, zorril(la).

zorro s. m. 1. (zool.) zorro: a fox. 2. (Port.) bastard: an illegitimate child, foundling. 3. (Braz.) lazybones, knave. 4. an old servant. || adj. 1. cunning. 2. slack, slow.

andar de ~ to crawl, go on all fours.

zoster s. m. zoster: 1. girdle. 2. (med.) shingles, herpes zoster.

zostera s. f. Zostera, eelgrass: a genus of marine plants.

zote s. m. + f. simpleton, imbecile, idiot, fool. || adj. silly, foolish, idiotic(al).

zotismo s. m. silliness, foolishness, stupidity, obtuseness.

zoupeiro s. m. (also **zopo**) 1. lame person. 2. totterer. 3. lazybones. 4. shy person. || adj. (also **zopeiro**) 1. lame, crippled. 2. tottery. 3. (fig.) timid, shy. 4. lazy, inactive.

zo(u)vineira s. f. gossip, gossiping woman.

zo(u)vineiro s. m. intriguer, mischief-maker. || adj. gossipy, intriguing.

zuarte s. m. blue nankeen: cotton cloth originally brought from China.

zuavo s. m. Zouave: soldier of an Algerian infantry corps in the French service.

zuca s. 1. m. + f. simpleton, silly person. 2. f. drunkenness.

zuco adj. 1. simple, silly. 2. drunk(en).

zuído s. m. (Port.) humming, buzzing in the ears.

zuidouro s. m. (Port.) hum, continuous murmuring sound.

zuir v. (also **zunir, zumbir**) to whiz, hum, buzz.

zulo, zulu s. m. + f. Zulu: 1. native of Zululand. 2. the Zulu language. || adj. Zulu: of or pertaining to the Zulus or their language.

zumba interj. bang!

zumbaia s. f. 1. exaggerate courtesy, profound reverence. 2. salaam: oriental salutation.

zumbaiar v. 1. to make an exaggerate courtesy. 2. to flatter, adulate. 3. to pay court to.

zumbar v. 1. (also **zumbir, zunir**) to whiz, hum. 2. to make a very loud noise. 3. (Port.) to thrash, beat, strike.

zumbido s. m. 1. hum, buzz, whiz(z). 2. tingle, whir. 3. drone; zing.

zumbidor adj. (also **zunidor**) humming, buzzing.

zumbir v. to hum: 1. buzz, whir, whiz. 2. drone, murmur. 3. zing, zoom.

zumbo s. m. confused sound, buzzing noise, buzz, drone.

zumbrir-se v. to curve, bow down; humiliate o. s.

zunga s. m. (Braz., pop., also **bicho-de-pé**) chigo(e).

zunido, zunimento s. m. 1. whiz(z), whir, buzz, hum. 2. tingle. 3. hiss(ing). 4. zing, drone.

zunidor adj. (also **zumbidor**) humming, buzzing.

pião ~ humming-top.

zunir v. (also **zinir, zumbir**) 1. to whiz(z), whir, drone, buzz. 2. to hum. 3. to tingle. 4. to hiss, whistle (through the air). 5. to zing, zoom.

o vento zune através da porta the wind whistles (howls) through the door.

zunzum s. m. (pl. -ns) 1. (also **zumbido**) hum(ming), buzz(ing). 2. (also **zunzunzum**): a) rumour, report. b) intrigue, tittle-tattle.

zunzunar v. 1. to whiz, hum. 2. to drone. 3. to be rumoured, be in the air.

zupa interj. whang.

zupar v. 1. to beat with a sledge hammer. 2. to beat, thrash.

zura(co) s. m. (S. Braz., pop., also **usurário**) niggard, miser. || adj. stingy, miserly, avaricious.

zurbada s. f. 1. stroke, knock. 2. blow. 3. push, impelling. 4. shower, downpour.

zureta s. m. + f. (Braz.) 1. insane, lunatic person. 2. upset person. ‖ adj. 1. insane. 2. upset.

zurrada s. f. = zurro.

zurrador s. m. brayer. ‖ adj. braying.

zurrapa s. f. slop, inferior wine.

zurrar v. 1. to bray, heehaw. 2. (Braz., fig.) to work hard. 3. to talk nonsense.

zurraria s. f. the braying of many asses.

zurre interj. scram, off with you.

zurro s. m. 1. bray(ing), heehaw: the harsh cry of an ass. 2. rattle: an instrument with which a rattling sound is made.

zuruó adj. m. + f. (Braz.) foolish, mad, stunned.

zurupar v. (Braz., sl.) to steal, lift, pilfer, swipe.

zurzidela s. f. lashing, thrashing, whipping.

zurzir v. 1. to lash, flog, switch. 2. to hurt, maltreat. 3. to beat, thrash (cruelly). 4. to scold severely.

FREQUENTLY USED PORTUGUESE ABBREVIATIONS

Abreviaturas freqüentemente usadas em português

A

A ampère ‖ (chem.) argônio.
a are(s).
(a) assinado.
A. autor (of books, etc.; pl. **AA.**).
a. arroba(s) (also **arr.**).
Ab. Abade (also **Ab.ᵉ**).
ABL Academia Brasileira de Letras.
abr. abril.
AC Estado do Acre.
Ac (chem.) actínio.
a. C., A. C. antes de Cristo.
A/C ao(s) cuidado(s).
ACB Aero Clube do Brasil. ‖ Automóvel Clube do Brasil.
ACM Associação Cristã de Moços.
A. D. anno Domini (no ano do Senhor).
A. F. audiofreqüência ‖ alta fidelidade.
af.ᵒ afeiçoado, afetuoso.
Ag (chem.) prata (argentum).
ag. agosto.
Al (chem.) alumínio.
AL Estado de Alagoas.
Al. alameda.
alm. almirante.
alq. alqueire(s).
alv. alvará.
Am (chem.) amerício.
AM Estado do Amazonas.
A. M. ave-maria.
am.ᵒ amigo.
AP Território do Amapá.
ap. aprovado.
ap., apart. apartamento.
Arco. arcebispo (or **Arc.ᵒ**).
As (chem.) arsênio, arsênico.
asp. aspirante.
At (chem.) astatínio.
A. T. alta tensão.
atm. atmosfera.
Au (chem.) ouro (aurum).
aux. auxiliar.
av. aviação ‖ aviador.
Av. avenida.
A. V. alta voltagem.

B

B (chem.) boro.
b (phys.) bária, microbar.
B. Beato, Beata.
b. braça(s).
BA Estado da Bahia.
Ba (chem.) bário.
BB Banco do Brasil.
Be (chem.) berílio.
Bel. Bacharel (also **B.ᵉˡ**).
B. F. boas-festas.
Bi (chem.) bismuto.
bibl. bibliografia ‖ bibliográfico ‖ biblioteca.

BIRD Banco Internacional de Reconstrução e Desenvolvimento.
BIT Bureau Internacional do Trabalho.
Bk (chem.) berquélio.
bm. baixa-mar.
B. M. V. Beata Maria Virgem.
BN Biblioteca Nacional.
BR Brasil, (Engl.) Brazil.
Br (chem.) bromo.
br. brochado(s), brochura(s).
brig. brigadeiro.
B. V. barlavento.

C

C (chem.) carbônio, carbono. ‖ coulomb.
c. canto(s) (of a poem) ‖ (theat.) cena ‖ cento.
c/ com ‖ (com.) conta.
c. a. corrente alternada.
Ca (chem.) cálcio.
ca (measure) centiare(s).
CA Caixa de Amortização.
cal caloria, caloria-grama.
c.-alm. contra-almirante.
cap. capitão ‖ capítulo (pl. **caps.**).
cap. frag. capitão-de-fragata.
cap. m. g. capitão-de-mar-e-guerra.
cap.-ten. capitão-tenente.
card. cardeal.
cat. catálogo.
cav. cavalaria.
CBD Confederação Brasileira de Desportos
CB Corpo de Bombeiros.
c/c (com.) conta-corrente.
Cd (chem.) cádmio.
CE Estado do Ceará.
Ce (chem.) cério.
C. E. E. Comissão Econômica para a Europa.
cel. coronel (also . c.ᵉˡ).
cent. (currency) centavo(s).
Cf (chem.) califórnio.
CFN Corpo de Fuzileiros Navais.
CFP Conselho Federal de Petróleo.
cg centigrama.
cgr centigrado.
CGS (phys.) centímetro, grama e segundo (centimeter-gram-second).
chancel. chancelaria.
Cia. companhia (com., mil.) (also **C.ᶦᵃ**).
CIC Conselho de Imigração e Colonização. ‖ Cartão de Identificação do Contribuinte.
CIF, cif. custo, seguro e frete.
CIS Comissão de Imposto Sindical.
cit. citação ‖ citado(s), citada(s).
CJI Comissão Jurídica Internacional.
Cl (chem.) cloro.
cl centilitro(s).
Cl. clérigo.

C. M. Casa da Moeda.
Cm (chem.) cúrio.
cm centímetro(s).
cm² centímetro(s) quadrado(s).
cm³ centímetro(s) cúbico(s).
cm/s centímetro(s) por segundo.
CNAEE Conselho Nacional de Águas e Energia Elétrica.
CNBA Comissão Nacional de Belas-Artes.
CND Conselho Nacional de Desportos.
CNLD Comissão Nacional do Livro Didático.
CNP Comissão Nacional do Petróleo.
Co (chem.) cobalto.
COAP Comissão de Abastecimento e Preços.
cód. códice (pl. **códs.**).
Cód. Código.
COFAP Comissão Federal de Abastecimento e Preços.
col. coluna (pl. **cols.**).
Col. Colégio (also **Col.ᵒ**).
com. comandante ‖ comendador.
COMAP Comissão Municipal de Abastecimento e Preços.
côn. cônego.
cons. conselheiro (also **cons.ᵒ**).
cop. copiado.
cor. coroa(s) (currency).
côv. côvado.
CPOR Centro de Preparação dos Oficiais da Reserva.
Cr (chem.) cromo.
Cr$ (Brazilian currency) cruzeiro(s).
cr.ᵃ criada.
cr.ᵒ criado.
Cs (chem.) césio.
Cu (chem.) cobre (cuprum).
cump.ᵗᵒ cumprimento.
c. v. cavalo-vapor.
Cx, cx caixa.

D

d dina.
d/ (com.) dias.
D. (com.) deve ‖ digno ‖ Dom ‖ Dona ‖ (theat.) direita.
D. A. (theat.) direita alta.
dag decagrama(s).
dal decalitro(s).
dam decâmetro(s).
dam² decâmetro(s) quadrado(s).
DASP Departamento Administrativo do Serviço Público.
dast decastéreo(s).
D. B. (theat.) direita baixa.
d. C., D. C. depois de Cristo.
DCT Departamento de Correios e Telégrafos.
DCTM Delegacia de Costumes, Tóxicos e Mistificações.
DD. digníssimo.

DE Diretoria do Ensino.
DEC Departamento de Ensino Comercial.
dec. decreto.
DEF Departamento de Educação Física.
DEI Departamento de Ensino Industrial.
DEIC Departamento Estadual de Investigações Criminais.
DER Departamento de Estradas de Rodagem.
DES Departamento de Ensino Superior.
desc. desconto.
desp. despesa.
DETRAN Departamento Estadual de Trânsito.
dez. dezembro (also **dez.º**).
DF Distrito Federal.
dg decigrama(s).
dgr decigrado(s).
DI Departamento de Intendência ‖ Departamento de Investigação. ‖ Divisão de Infantaria.
dic. dicionário.
DIN Departamento de Imprensa Nacional.
dipl. diploma.
diss. (gram.) dissilábico, dissílabo.
dist. (school) distinto.
dit. (gram.) ditongo.
div. divisão, divisões.
díz. dízimo(s).
dl decilitro(s).
dm decímetro(s).
dm² decímetro(s) quadrado(s).
dm³ decímetro(s) cúbico(s).
DNE Departamento Nacional de Educação.
DNEF Departamento Nacional de Estradas de Ferro.
DNER Departamento Nacional de Estradas de Rodagem.
DNT Departamento Nacional do Trabalho.
doc. documento (pl. **docs.**).
DOPS Departamento de Ordem Política e Social.
DP Delegacia de Polícia.
Dr. Doutor (pl. **Drs.**).
Dra. Doutora (also **Dr.ª**; pl. **Dr.ªˢ**).
DRF Delegacia de Roubos e Falsificações.
dr.º (com.) dinheiro.
DSP Departamento de Segurança Pública.
DSS Diretoria do Serviço da Saúde.
DST Departamento do Serviço de Trânsito.
DV Departamento de Vigilância.
d/v (com.) dias de vista.
Dy (chem.) disprósio (dysprosium).
dz. dúzia(s).

E

E. editor (pl. **EE.**). ‖ (theat.) esquerda ‖ este.
E (chem.) einstênio.
E. A. (theat.) esquerda alta.
E. B. (theat.) esquerda baixa ‖ estibordo.
E. C. era cristã.
écl. écloga(s).
ecles. eclesiástico.
ed. edição.
E. D. espera deferimento.
EFCB Estrada de Ferro Central do Brasil.
e. g. por exemplo (exempli gratia).
eletr. eletricista.
E. M. estado-maior ‖ em mão.
Ema. Eminência (also **Em.ª**).
emb. embalagem.
Emmo. Eminentíssimo (also **Em.ᵐᵒ**).
emol. emolumentos.
E. M. P. em mão própria.
EN Escola Normal ‖ Escola Naval.
enc. encadernado(s).
End. tel. endereço telegráfico.
E. N. E. és-nordeste.
enf. enfermeiro.
eng. engenharia.
eng.º engenheiro.
Enol. Enologia.
Entom. Entomologia.
epíst. epístola(s).
Er (chem.) érbio.
E. R. espera resposta.
E. R. M. espera receber mercê.
ES Estado do Espírito Santo.
esc. escudo(s) (currency).
Esc. Escola.
E. S. E. és-sudeste.
est. estância(s) (of a poem) ‖ estante(s) ‖ estrofe(s).
Est. estrada.
etc. et cetera.
étn. étnico.
Eu (chem.) európio.
E. U. A. Estados Unidos da América.
E. U. B. Estados Unidos do Brasil.
E. U. V. Estados Unidos de Venezuela.
ex. exemplar(es) ‖ exemplo(s).
Excia. Excelência (also **Ex.ª**).
Exma. Excelentíssima (also **Ex.ᵐᵃ**).
Exmo. Excelentíssimo (also **Ex.ᵐᵒ**).
expr. expressão.

F

F (chem.) flúor.
F. (theat.) frente, ou fundo ‖ fulano.
f. (gram.) feminino ‖ forma ‖ (mus.) forte.
f., fl., fol. folha (pl. **fls., fols.**).
FAB Força Aérea Brasileira.
Fac. Faculdade.
farm. farmacêutico ‖ farmácia.
fasc. fascículo(s).
Fe (chem.) ferro.
fev. fevereiro (also **fev.º**).
FCD Faculdade Católica de Direito.
FEB Força Expedicionária Brasileira.
ff. (mus.) fortíssimo.
FIFA Federação Internacional de Futebol Associação.
fig. figura ‖ figuradamente.
Fm (chem.) férmio.
FMA Federação Metropolitana de Atletismo.
FMB Federação Metropolitana de Basquetebol.
FMF Federação Metropolitana de Futebol.
FMI Fundo Monetário Internacional.
FMN Federação Metropolitana de Natação.
FMV Federação Metropolitana de Volibol.
FN Território de Fernando de Noronha.
FND Faculdade Nacional de Direito.
FNF Faculdade Nacional de Filosofia.
FNM Faculdade Nacional de Medicina.
FNO Faculdade Nacional de Odontologia.
F.º (com.) filho.
fog. fogueiro, foguista.
folh. folheto.
fot. fotógrafo.
FPF Federação Paulista de Futebol.
fr. franco(s) (currency).
Fr. Frei.
fs. fac-símile(s).

G

g grama(s).
Ga (chem.) gálio.
gav. gaveta.
GB Guanabara.
G. C. Guarda Civil.
Gd (chem.) gadolínio.
g.ᵈᵉ grande.
Ge (chem.) germânio.
gen. general.
Geod. Geodésia.
gloss. glossário(s).
Glót. Glótica.
g. m. guarda-marinha.
GMT Greenwich Mean Time (horário médio de Greenwich).
GO Estado de Goiás.
G. P. gloria Patri (glória ao Pai).
G/P ganhos e perdas.
gr. (peso) grão(s) ‖ grátis ‖ grego.
gr., g. grau(s).
gr., grs. grosa(s).
Grafol. Grafologia.

H

H (chem.) hidrogênio ‖ (electr.) henry.
h hora(s).
H. (com.) haver (also **H.ᵉʳ**).
ha hectare(s).
hab. habitantes.
h. c. honoris causa.
He (chem.) hélio.
hebr. hebraico.
herd.º herdeiro.
Hf (chem.) háfnio.
Hg (chem.) mercúrio (hydrargyrum).
hg hectograma(s).
Hidrogr. Hidrografia.

Hist. História.
Histol. Histologia.
hl hectolitro(s).
hm hectômetro(s).
hm² hectômetro(s) quadrado(s).
Ho (chem.) hólmio.
hol. holandês.
hon. honorário.
Hortic. Horticultura.
H. P. cavalo-vapor (horse-power).
hw hectowatt(s).
hW hectowatt internacional.

I

I (chem.) iodo.
IAPB Instituto de Aposentadoria e Pensões dos Bancários.
IAPC Instituto de Aposentadoria e Pensões dos Comerciários.
IAPEE Instituto de Aposentadoria e Pensões dos Empregados da Estiva.
IAPI Instituto de Aposentadoria e Pensões dos Industriários.
IAPM Instituto de Aposentadoria e Pensões dos Marítimos.
IAPTC Instituto de Aposentadoria e Pensões dos Empregados em Transportes de Cargas.
ib. ibidem (no mesmo lugar).
IBA Instituto Brasileiro de Aeronáutica. ‖ Instituto de Biologia Animal.
IBC Instituto Brasileiro do Café.
IBGE Instituto Brasileiro de Geografia e Estatística.
id. idem (o mesmo).
I. H. S. Iesus, hominum salvator (Jesus, salvador dos homens).
Ilma. Ilustríssima (also **II.ᵐᵃ**).
Ilmo. Ilustríssimo (also **II.ᵐᵒ**).
Imac.ᵃ Imaculada.
IML Instituto Médico Legal.
In (chem.) índio.
IN Imprensa Nacional.
INAMPS Instituto Nacional de Assistência Médica e Previdência Social.
índ. índice.
inf. infantaria ‖ infante ‖ (gram.) infinitivo, infinito ‖ infixo.
I. N. R. I. Iesus Nazarenus Rex Iudaeorum (Jesus Nazareno, Rei dos Judeus).
Io (chem.) íon.
IPASE Instituto de Pensões e Aposentadoria dos Servidores do Estado.
Ir (chem.) irídio.
isl. islandês.
it., ital. italiano.

J

jan. janeiro (also **jan.ᵒ**).
jap. japonês.
J. C. Jesus Cristo.
JCB Jóquei Clube Brasileiro.

JEC Juventude Estudantil Católica.
JIC Juventude Independente Católica.
JOC Juventude Operária Católica.
J.ʳ Júnior (also **Jr.**).
JUC Juventude Universitária Católica.
jul. julho.
jun. junho.
Jur. Jurisprudência.

K

K (chem.) potássio (kalium).
kc quilociclo(s).
kg quilograma(s).
kl quilolitro(s).
km quilômetro(s).
km² quilômetro(s) quadrado(s).
km³ quilômetro(s) cúbico(s).
K. O. knock out (fora de combate).
Kr. (chem.) criptônio (krypton).
kV quilovolt(s).
kW quilowatt(s).
kWh quilowatt-hora(s).

L

l litro(s).
£ libra(s) (currency).
l. (com.) lançado ‖ (com.) letra(s) ‖ linha(s) ‖ (address) loja(s).
l. livro (also **l.ᵒ** or **liv.**).
L. largo.
La (chem.) lantânio.
LAO Liceu de Artes e Ofícios.
lat. latim ‖ latino ‖ latitude.
lat. vulg. latim vulgar.
lb libra(s) (weight).
LBA Legião Brasileira de Assistência.
lég. légua (pl. **légs.**).
Li (chem.) lítio.
Lit. Literatura.
Liturg. Liturgia.
log. logaritmo.
long. longitude.
lr. lira(s) (currency).
Ls.ᵃ Lisboa.
Ltda. Limitada (also **Lt.ᵈᵃ**).
Lu (chem.) lutécio.

M

m metro(s) ‖ minuto(s) (also **min**).
m² metro(s) quadrado(s).
m³ metro(s) cúbico(s).
m/ (com.) meu(s), minha(s).
m. mês, meses ‖ masculino.
MA Estado do Maranhão.
mA miliampère(s).
m.ᵃ mesma ‖ minha.
MA Ministério da Agricultura.
MAe Ministério da Aeronáutica.
m/a (com.) meu aceite.
maj. major.

mal. marechal.
mam miriâmetro(s).
MAM Museu de Arte Moderna.
maq. maquinista.
Matem. Matemática.
Mb megabária(s).
Mc megaciclo(s).
m/c minha carta ‖ minha conta.
m.ᶜᵒ março.
m/d (com.) meses de data.
M. D. muito digno.
M.ᵃ Madre.
ME Ministério do Exército.
MEC Ministério da Educação e Cultura.
mecân. Mecânica.
méd. médico.
méd. vet. médico veterinário.
Metal. Metalurgia.
Métr. Métrica.
MF Ministério da Fazenda.
MG Estado de Minas Gerais. ‖ Ministério da Guerra.
Mg (chem.) magnésio ‖ Miriagrama(s).
mg miligrama(s).
mgr miligrado(s).
MI Ministério do Interior.
mi milha(s) marítima(s) internacional(-ais).
MIC Ministério da Indústria e Comércio.
mil. milha(s) ‖ miliciano.
Miner. Mineralogia.
mit. mitológico.
Mit. Mitologia.
MJ Ministério da Justiça.
ml mililitro(s).
m/l (com.) minha letra.
Ml mirialitro(s).
MM. meritíssimo.
mm milímetro(s).
mm² milímetro(s) quadrado(s).
mm³ milímetro(s) cúbico(s).
Mm miriâmetro(s).
MM Ministério da Marinha.
MME Ministério de Minas e Energia.
Mn (chem.) manganês.
Mo (chem.) molibdênio.
m.ᵒ mesmo ‖ maio.
m/o (com.) minha ordem.
MOBRAL Movimento Brasileiro de Alfabetização.
mod. moderno.
Mons. Monsenhor.
m.ᵒʳ morador.
m/p (com.) meses de prazo.
MRE Ministério das Relações Exteriores.
ms. manuscrito (pl. **mss.**).
m.ˢ mais.
MS Estado de Mato Grosso do Sul. ‖ Ministério da Saúde.
MT Estado de Mato Grosso. ‖ Ministério do Trabalho.
m.ᵗᵃ muita.
m.ᵗᵒ muito.
muit.ᵐᵒ muitíssimo.
Mv (chem.) mendelévio.
mV milivolt(s).
MVOP Ministério da Viação e Obras Públicas.

N

N (chem.) nitrogênio.
n/ nossa ‖ nosso.
n. nome.
N. norte.
Na (chem.) sódio (natrium).
N. B. nota bene (note bem).
Nb (chem.) nióbio.
n/c nossa carta ‖ nossa casa ‖ (com.) nossa conta.
n/ch (com.) nosso cheque.
Nd (chem.) neodínio.
N. da R. nota da redação.
N. do A. nota do autor.
N. do E. nota do editor.
N. do T. nota do tradutor.
Ne (chem.) neônio ou néon.
N. E. nordeste.
Nl (chem.) níquel.
n/l (com.) nossa letra.
N. N. Não nominado, anônimo.
N. N. E. nor-nordeste.
N. N. O. nor-noroeste (also N. N. W.).
n.º número.
n/o (com.) nossa ordem.
No (chem.) nobélio.
N. O. Noroeste (also N. W.).
N. Obs. nihil obstat.
nor. norueguês.
nov. novembro (also nov.º).
n. p. nome próprio.
n/s (com.) nosso saque.
N. S. Nosso Senhor.
N. Sª Nossa Senhora.
N. S. J. C. Nosso Senhor Jesus Cristo.
N. T. (bib.) Novo Testamento.

O

O (chem.) oxigênio.
• grau.
O: oeste.
o/ (com.) ordem.
OAA Organização da Alimentação e da Agricultura.
OAB Ordem dos Advogados do Brasil.
OACI Organização da Aviação Civil Internacional.
ob. obra(s).
ob. cit. obra(s) citada(s).
obed. obediente.
obr.º obrigado.
obr.mo obrigadíssimo.
obs. observação.
of. oferece(m) (also Of.).
OIT Organização Internacional do Trabalho.
OMM Organização Mundial de Meteorologia.
OMS Organização Mundial de Saúde.
O. N. O. oés-noroeste.
ONU Organização das Nações Unidas.
Ornit. Ornitologia.
Os (chem.) ósmio.

O. S. O. oés-sudoeste.
OTAN Organização do Tratado do Atlântico Norte.
out. outubro (also out.º).
Oz onça (ancient weight).

P

P (chem.) fósforo (phosphorus).
P. praça ‖ Padre (also P.º).
p. (com.) por ‖ (com.) próximo ‖ palmo (measure; pl. ps.).
PA Estado do Pará.
Pa (chem.) protoactínio.
pág. página (also p.; pl. págs. or pp.).
pal. palavra(s).
Paleogr. Paleografia.
Paleont. Paleontologia.
Paro. Pároco (also Par.º).
part. apass. partícula apassivadora.
part. explet. partícula expletiva.
Patol. Patologia.
PB Estado da Paraíba.
Pb (chem.) chumbo (plumbum).
P. B. peso bruto.
pc. pacote(s).
p/c (com.) por conta.
pç peça(s).
Pd (chem.) paládio.
P. D. pede deferimento.
PDS Partido Democrático Social.
PE Estado de Pernambuco.
P. E. Polícia Especial.
P. E. F. por especial favor.
P. E. O. por especial obséquio.
p. ex. por exemplo.
p. f. próximo futuro.
P. F. por favor.
pg. pago ‖ pagou.
PI Estado do Piauí.
P. J. pede justiça.
P. L. peso líquido.
Pm (chem.) prometeu.
PM Polícia Militar ‖ Prefeitura Municipal.
PMDB Partido do Movimento Democrático Brasileiro.
P. M. E. por mercê especial.
P. M. O. por muito obséquio.
p. m. o. m. pouco mais ou menos.
P. M. P. por mão própria.
P. N. pai-nosso.
Po (chem.) polônio.
Poét. Poética.
pol. polegada(s).
p. p. por procuração ‖ próximo passado.
PR Estado do Paraná ‖ Presidência da República ‖ Príncipe Real.
Pr. (chem.) praseodímio.
pret. prefeito ‖ prefixo.
pres. presidente.
P. R. J. pede recebimento e justiça.
probl. problema(s).
proc. processo ‖ procuração ‖ procurador.
prof. professor (pl. profs.).
prof.ª professora.
pros. prosódia.

prov. provedor ‖ provisão ‖ provisório.
p. s. puro-sangue (horse).
P. S. post scriptum.
Pt (chem.) platina.
PT Partido dos Trabalhadores.
PTB Partido Trabalhista Brasileiro.
PTN Partido Trabalhista Nacional.
Pu (chem.) plutônio.
PUC Pontifícia Universidade Católica.

Q

q. quintal, quintais (weight).
q. b. quantidade bastante (in medical prescriptions).
q.do quando.
Q. G. quartel-general.
ql. quilate(s).
q. s. quantum satis.
q.ta quanta.
q.to quanto.
quart. quarteirão.
q. v. quod vide ‖ queira ver ‖ queira voltar.

R

R. Rei ‖ reprovado (school: not promoted) ‖ réu ‖ rua.
Ra (chem.) rádio.
R.ª Rainha.
rad. radical ‖ radiograma.
RAA Regimento de Artilharia Antiaérea.
R. A. E. Repartição de Águas e Esgotos.
RB Território do Rio Branco.
RC Regimento de Cavalaria.
Re (chem.) rênio.
rec. receita.
rec.º (com.) recebido.
red. redução.
ref. reformado.
reg. regimento ‖ regular.
reg.º registro ‖ registrado ‖ regulamento.
Rem.te remetente (also Remet.).
rep. reprovado (school: not promoted).
Rep. Repartição.
res. (mil.) reserva.
Rev. Reverendo (also Rev.do) ‖ Revista.
Revmo. Reverendíssimo (also Rev.mo).
RFA República Federal da Alemanha.
RFB República Federativa do Brasil.
Rh (chem.) ródio (rhodium).
RI Regimento de Infantaria.
RJ Estado do Rio de Janeiro.
RM Região Militar.
RN Estado do Rio Grande do Norte.
Rn (chem.) radônio.
RO Estado de Rondônia.
RP Rádio-Patrulha.
RR Território de Roraima.
RS Estado do Rio Grande do Sul.
Ru (chem.) rutênio.